The STRONGEST STRONG'S

EXHAUSTIVE CONCORDANCE OF THE BIBLE

Larger Print Edition

About the Authors

Dr. James Strong (LL.D., S.T.D.) devoted 35 years of his life to the creation of his concordance. *Strong's Exhaustive Concordance of the Bible* was first published in the 1890s and has been acclaimed an indispensable reference work of Bible students and scholars ever since. Dr. Strong was professor of exegetical theology at Drew Theological Seminary from 1868 to 1893.

John R. Kohlenberger III is a specialist in the application of computers to Bible-related reference projects. He has taught at Multnomah School of Bible and Western Seminary in Portland and has produced *The NIV Interlinear Hebrew-English Old Testament*, the *Zondervan NIV Exhaustive Concordance*, and *The NRSV Concordance, Unabridged.*

James A. Swanson is a specialist in applying database management to biblical studies and has degrees in theology and ministry. He has taught at Multnomah Bible College and is coeditor with John R. Kohlenberger III on several Old and New Testament language concordances. He is also author of the ground-breaking *Dictionary of Biblical Languages With Semantic Domains: Hebrew and Aramaic.*

The

STRONGEST STRONG'S

EXHAUSTIVE CONCORDANCE OF THE BIBLE

Larger Print Edition

JAMES STRONG, LL.D., S.T.D.

FULLY REVISED AND CORRECTED BY
John R. Kohlenberger III *and* James A. Swanson

ZONDERVAN®
GRAND RAPIDS, MICHIGAN 49530 USA

ZONDERVAN.COM/
AUTHORTRACKER

We want to hear from you. Please send your comments about this book to us in care of zreview@zondervan.com. Thank you.

ZONDERVAN®

The Strongest Strong's Exhaustive Concordance of the Bible Larger Print Edition

Requests for information should be addressed to:

Zondervan, *Grand Rapids, Michigan 49530*

ISBN-10: 0-310-24697-0 (larger print)
ISBN-13: 978-0-310-24697-8 (larger print)

Printed in China

06 07 08 09 • 20 19 18 17 16 15 14 13 12 11 10 9 8 7 6 5 4

The STRONGEST STRONG'S

EXHAUSTIVE CONCORDANCE OF THE BIBLE

Larger Print Edition

JAMES STRONG, LL.D., S.T.D.

FULLY REVISED AND CORRECTED BY
John R. Kohlenberger III *and* James A. Swanson

ZONDERVAN®
GRAND RAPIDS, MICHIGAN 49530 USA

ZONDERVAN.COM/
AUTHORTRACKER

We want to hear from you. Please send your comments about this book to us in care of zreview@zondervan.com. Thank you.

ZONDERVAN®

The Strongest Strong's Exhaustive Concordance of the Bible Larger Print Edition

Requests for information should be addressed to:

Zondervan, *Grand Rapids, Michigan 49530*

ISBN-10: 0-310-24697-0 (larger print)
ISBN-13: 978-0-310-24697-8 (larger print)

Printed in China

06 07 08 09 • 20 19 18 17 16 15 14 13 12 11 10 9 8 7 6 5 4

CONTENTS

DEDICATION

This concordance is dedicated to the memory of

Dr. James Strong

1822–1894

PREFACE

A BRIEF HISTORY OF THE STRONGEST STRONG'S EXHAUSTIVE CONCORDANCE PROJECT

The King James Version was published in 1611. Its first multilingual concordance, Robert Young's *Analytical Concordance to the Bible*, appeared 268 years later. It took forty years of manual labor. In 1894, James Strong's *Exhaustive Concordance to the Bible* joined Young's. It too involved nearly three decades of labor. The Revised Standard Version was completed in 1952, and its first multilingual concordance was issued in 1988: *Eerdmans' Analytical Concordance to the Revised Standard Version*, edited by Richard E. Whitaker. The New American Standard was published in 1971. *The New American Standard Exhaustive Concordance of the Bible* (Holman) appeared in 1981, a project that involved more than ten years and seventy contributors under the general editorship of Robert L. Thomas. Between 1979 and 1999, a team of scholars and computer analysts produced ten concordances to the New International Version. The data developed over a twenty-year period for The NIV Concordance Project form the foundation for *The Strongest Strong's Exhaustive Concordance.*

Within two years of its inception in October of 1979, and just three years after the release of the New International Version itself, The NIV Concordance Project created *The NIV Complete Concordance* (Zondervan, 1981, retitled *The New International Bible Concordance* in 1999). The following year, 1982, saw the release of *The NIV Handy Concordance*, which is also printed in millions of NIV Bibles as the NIV "Mini" or "Standard" Concordance. (Anglicized editions of these two *Concordances* were prepared and published by Hodder and Stoughton in 1983 and 1985, respectively.) A further abridgment, known in-house as the NIV "Micro" Concordance, was also made in 1982 and is published only in NIV Bibles.

Work on *The NIV Exhaustive Concordance* began in 1983, pairing editors Edward W. Goodrick and John R. Kohlenberger III with computer analysts Dennis B. Thomas and Barbara Perz. Proofreaders James Swanson and Donald Potts put in so many hours on the project that they were named associate editors. The analysts developed software that would assist the editors to manually interrelate or "match up" the NIV to the Hebrew, Aramaic, and Greek originals. The primary focus of this "match-up" process was on the identification of the lexical or root form of each Hebrew, Aramaic, and Greek word and on the description of the interrelation of each word of the original with each word of the NIV. The "match-up" process and its several levels of proofreading took six years—from 1983 through 1989.

The database that resulted from this process contains nearly 900,000 lines, each of which has five fields of data. Thus, the database contains nearly 4,500,000 items of information that required at least ten million editorial decisions. This database, dubbed the "Portland Index" after its place of origin, can be read in either the order of the NIV or the order of the original languages. Since its completion in 1990, it has been featured in all of Zondervan's Bible software. Following Ed Goodrick's untimely passing in 1992, Kohlenberger and Swanson continued refining the Portland Index and used it to produce several other multilingual concordances, including *The Exhaustive Concordance to the Greek New Testament* (Zondervan, 1995), *The Greek-English Concordance to the New Testament* (Zondervan, 1997), *The Hebrew-English Concordance to the Old Testament* (Zondervan, 1998), and the second edition of *The NIV Exhaustive Concordance*, with expanded and enhanced dictionary-indexes (Zondervan, 1999).

Work on *The Strongest Strong's Exhaustive Concordance* began in 1998. Working from a public-domain database of the 1894 edition of Strong's Concordance provided by Scott Musser, computer analyst Ed van der Maas developed a program to compare and merge the contents of the Portland Index with Strong's analysis. Jim Swanson spent a year working through the resulting files verse-by-verse to resolve conflicts between the two analyses of the Bible. Meanwhile, working with June Gunden and her colleagues at Peachtree Editorial and Proofreading, John Kohlenberger developed the first electronic edition of the Cambridge Paragraph Bible of 1873, the best modern edition of the King James Version. John applied this KJV database to Jim's analyzed files and spent a year enhancing and correcting the Strong's edition of the Portland Index and converting the enhanced dictionary-indexes of *The NIV Exhaustive Concordance* into the order of Strong's numbering system.

As a result, *The Strongest Strong's Exhaustive Concordance* is the most thoroughly analyzed and most accurate concordance ever produced for the King James Version.

ACKNOWLEDGMENTS

The Strongest Strong's Exhaustive Concordance was conceived of and championed by Jack Kuhatschek, Executive Editor at Zondervan. It truly would not have been done without his involvement. Stan Gundry, Vice President and Editor-in-Chief at Zondervan, was always there to make decisions and to provide encouragement and support. Senior Editor Verlyn D. Verbrugge worked through all the proofs with his insightful attention to detail.

Scott Musser provided the original public-domain database that served as the starting point of the project. Ed van der Maas developed the programming to merge the NIV data of the Portland Index with the KJV data from Strong. Tim Hare of Telios Systems wrote the programming that created the main concordance and the KJV indexes for the dictionaries. Brent Knopf wrote the programming to convert the related words indexes from G/K numbers to Strong numbers.

June Gunden and her colleagues at Peachtree Editorial and Proofreading did an excellent job of reading the Cambridge Paragraph Bible of 1873 against the KJV text used to produce *The Strongest Strong's Exhaustive Concordance*. Special thanks to Dr. Donald Brake of Multnomah Biblical Seminary for loaning us his personal copy of this rare Bible.

As always, we must thank our families for their patience, encouragement, and support. John Kohlenberger thanks his wife, Carolyn, and children, Sarah and Joshua. Jim Swanson thanks his wife, Sandi, and children, Jonathan, David, and Natanya.

INTRODUCTION

Dr. James Strong (1822–1894) was professor of exegetical theology at Drew Theological Seminary from 1868 to 1893. During his quarter century at Drew, his most important publication was considered to be the massive 10-volume *Cyclopaedia of Biblical, Theological, and Ecclesiastical Literature* (1867–1881), coedited with John McClintock. But today few would doubt his most important publication to be *The Exhaustive Concordance to the Bible*, still a best-seller more than a century after its initial publication in 1894.

The Exhaustive Concordance remains a monument to Strong's brilliant design and excellent editing, especially considering that all of its hundreds of thousands of contexts and thousands of dictionary entries were researched, collated, and typeset by hand without the benefit of computers! But with advances in biblical scholarship and the assistance of computer technology, even Strong's *Concordance* can be significantly improved. This introduction will first explain the nature of Bible concordances, then list the unique features of Strong's *Concordance*, and then detail the new and improved features of *The Strongest Strong's Exhaustive Concordance: Larger Print Edition.*

Bible Concordances in General

A concordance is an index to a book. It is usually arranged in alphabetical order and shows the location of each word in the book. In addition, it often supplies several words of the context in which each word is found.

There are two kinds of Bible concordances for the nonspecialist: those that deal only with the English text of the Bible version on which they are based, and those that also deal with the Hebrew, Aramaic, and Greek texts from which the Bible version was translated.

Examples of English-only concordances are *Cruden's Complete Concordance* for the King James Version and the *NIV Complete Concordance*. The best-known examples of multilingual concordances are Young's *Analytical Concordance* and Strong's *Exhaustive Concordance*, both based on the King James Version (KJV).

An *analytical* concordance is organized in English alphabetical order and shows a complete index of all the different words of a given translation (with the exception of the most common articles, conjunctions, prepositions, and pronouns, such as *a, and, to,* and *he*). Each entry is subdivided according to the Hebrew, Aramaic, or Greek words that underlie the English. Each reference in these subdivisions is listed with a brief context. The analytical concordance also contains index-lexicons of biblical language vocabulary, showing the various English words that translate them.

An *exhaustive* concordance by definition should contain every reference to every word of the Bible version on which it is based. An exhaustive concordance is organized in English alphabetical order, indexes every word of the Bible, and lists every single biblical reference in which that word appears. For all but the most common words (which are indexed by reference only), a context is also given with each reference.

Strong's *Exhaustive Concordance* in Particular

Strong's *Concordance* went beyond the mere listing of words and references to give "exhaustive" a whole new meaning in biblical reference books.

In Strong's *Concordance* the relationship of the English to the original languages is indicated by a numbering system that was originally devised for his *Concordance.* Strong made a list of the Hebrew and "Chaldee" (Aramaic) words used in the Old Testament and of the Greek words used in the New. To each word he assigned a number, indicating its alphabetical order. This number appears at the end of most context lines to indicate the word the English translates. By consulting the dictionaries in the back of Strong's *Concordance*, the user can match numbers in order to identify the biblical word, to see its "root" definition, and to find its range of translation in the KJV.

Improvements in *The Strongest Strong's*

An exhaustive word index to the KJV and a simple guide to the relation of the English Bible to the original languages, Strong's *Concordance* has remained unsurpassed for more than a century. However, advances in biblical scholarship and computer technology, as well as shortcomings in Strong's methodology, have made a new edition desirable and even necessary. Earlier "new" or "expanded" editions of Strong did little other than minor corrections or resetting the original in new type or adding features not intrinsic to the concordance. The *Strongest Strong's Exhaustive Concordance* rebuilt the original from the ground up. Using a gentle pun based on his name, we seek to honor and improve on the strengths of Strong's innovative excellence.

First, we started with the best modern edition of the KJV: the Cambridge Paragraph Bible of 1873, edited by F. H. A. Scrivener. Dr. Scrivener was commissioned by Cambridge University Press to create a standardized edition of the KJV to eliminate all of the errors and inconsistencies that had crept into the text in two and a half centuries of printing. Dr. Scrivener spent seven years comparing at least fifteen early editions and all the important editions of the eighteenth and nineteenth centuries in order to conform all matters of italicizing, punctuation and spelling to the exacting standards of the late nineteenth century, while following closely the principles evident in the first editions of 1611. To this standard *The Strongest Strong's* conforms meticulously.

Second, our contexts reflect the KJV text more accurately. As just mentioned, they follow the spelling and punctuation of the 1873 edition with computer-verified accuracy. But beyond that, we also include all the italics of the 1873 edition. The KJV translators used italic type to show English words that were supplied in translation, but did not directly translate a word in the original Hebrew, Aramaic, or Greek. Because Strong's *Concordance* shows the relationship between the original languages and the English, it is extremely significant to show these italicized words and phrases. In the 1873 edition of the KJV, 34,712 words are italicized, but only *The Strongest Strong's* shows italics in the contexts.

Third, our contexts reflect the relationship of the original languages and the English far more exhaustively than the original edition. Since most of Strong's contexts index a single word with a single number, the user gets the wrong impression that the KJV is a word-for-word, one-to-one translation. But the translators often translated single words with phrases, phrases with single words, and phrases with idiomatic phrases. *The Strongest Strong's* uses bold type and multiple Strong numbers to indicate tens of thousands of multi-word translation not indexed in any other edition.

Fourth, Strong's dictionaries are flawed by a methodology of the nineteenth century that has come to be called the "root fallacy." He assumed that biblical words could be defined by the sum of their parts. But just as we do not think that a *pineapple* is an apple that grows on a pine tree or that a *butterfly* is a fly that likes butter, so we should not use this methodology to define biblical words as was so common in the nineteenth and even the twentieth centuries. Our dictionaries are based on the latest dictionaries, lexicons, and word study books, reflecting great advances in biblical scholarship.

Fifth, the indexes in Strong's dictionaries do not list KJV words by their exact spelling, often making it more difficult to find the exact concordance entries. Our indexes are generated from the same database that generated the concordance, so the indexed words are spelled exactly as in the KJV. And, as an added feature, each word has a statistic indicating the number of times it translates any Hebrew, Aramaic, or Greek word in the KJV. No other edition of Strong's has these features.

Sixth, as one would expect with such an enormous work done over so many years and involving so many people, there are errors in Strong's concordance and dictionaries. For example, under the heading RED, the references in Acts 7:36 and Hebrews 11:29 have the number *2281* at the end of the context lines; however, this is the number for the Greek word for "sea," not "red." Even the "new" and "corrected" editions repeat this error. *The Strongest Strong's* goes farther than any other edition in correcting the generally excellent work of the original editor.

Seventh, *The Strongest Strong's Exhaustive Concordance: Larger Print Edition*, takes all the advanced scholarship of the original *Strongest Strong's* but presents them in a significantly larger and easier-to-read type. No other large-print concordance has more contexts or more up-to-date information.

FEATURES OF THE STRONGEST STRONG'S EXHAUSTIVE CONCORDANCE

The Strongest Strong's is divided into three major sections: (1) the Main Concordance, (2) the Index of Articles, Conjunctions, Particles, Prepositions, and Pronouns, and (3) the Biblical Language Dictionary-Indexes.

THE MAIN CONCORDANCE

Below is a typical entry from the Main Concordance:

AARON (319) [AARON'S, AARONITES]
Ex 4:14 and he said, Is not **A** the Levite thy brother? 175
4:27 the LORD said to **A**, "Go into the wilderness 175

The heading consists of:
(1) the indexed word (AARON);
(2) the frequency count in parentheses (319);
(3) the list of related words (AARON'S, AARONITES).

The context lines consist of:
(1) the book-chapter-verse reference;
(2) the context for the indexed word;
(3) the number key to the Dictionary-Index.

HEADINGS

There are three kinds of headings: (1) KJV word headings, (2) KJV Index references, and (3) "See" references.

KJV Word Headings

The 1873 Edition of the KJV contains 790,915 total words (in the 66 canonical books), with a unique vocabulary of 12,858. *The Strongest Strong's* is an exhaustive alphabetic index to every word of the KJV.

The simplest heading is composed of the KJV word and its frequency count, for example:

ABBA (3)

The frequency count lists the total number of times the word appears in the KJV, which is also the number of contexts listed in the concordance. *The Strongest Strong's* is the first exhaustive KJV concordance to provide this information.

The headings show the indexed words exactly as they are spelled in the KJV. In a few instances a word occurs both as a compound word and as a hyphenated word, as in the case of "Beth-lehem," the OT spelling, and "Bethlehem," the NT spelling. For these words, both forms appear in the heading and the contexts are all organized under that heading:

BETHLEHEM, BETH-LEHEM (39)

If the English word occurs in other forms or spellings, these words appear in square brackets following the frequency count:

ABASE (4) [ABASED, ABASING]

ABASED (4) [ABASE]

ABASING (1) [ABASE]

Rather than listing all related words after each indexed word, the editors chose one indexed word to act as the "group heading." All related words are listed after the group heading, and each of the related word headings points back to the group heading. In the example above, ABASE serves as the group heading for ABASED and ABASING.

The headings also group together words that share common elements. For example:

HEART (830) [BROKEN-HEARTED, FAINTHEARTED, HARDHEARTED, HEART'S, HEARTED, HEARTS, MERRYHEARTED, STOUTHEARTED, TENDERHEARTED]

In addition to studying related words, these lists also allow *The Strongest Strong's* to be used with any edition of the KJV. Most of the differences among the countless settings and printings of the KJV are found in italics, punctuation, and spelling. Italics and punctuation do not affect a concordance, but spelling certainly does. Use the related words lists to find all forms and spelling variations of any word. For example, the past tense of "fetch" is not only spelled "fetched," but also "fet" and "fetcht." In the 1873 edition of the KJV (as in the 1611 edition), "more" is also spelled "moe" and "mo."

KJV Index References

Four hundred twenty-four words occur a total of 531,417 times—two-thirds the bulk of the KJV! These words are exhaustively indexed in their own section: the Index of Articles, Conjunctions, Particles, Pronouns, Etc. (see page xiii). These words are also represented by headings in the Main Concordance, with a message referring to this special index:

A (8718) [AN] See Index

"See" References

The King James or Authorized Version has been the dominant English Bible translation from the early seventeenth century to the latter half of the twentieth century. Because of this, the KJV has had profound impact on the language of the Church. Similarly in the last half of the twentieth century, new Bible translations and biblical reference books began to impact the language of the Church. *The Strongest Strong's* includes nearly 1,100 "see" references to 1,500 proper names and key words that are spelled differently in modern versions from the KJV:

CAESAR; CAESAR'S See CESAR; CESAR'S

HOLY SPIRIT See also HOLY GHOST

SINFUL NATURE See CARNAL; FLESH

CONTEXT LINES

Concordances are word indexes. At the very least, they index the book, chapter, and verse in which these words are located. Most concordances also show each word within a brief phrase or clause: a context. This gives the user a better idea of the use of the word and helps to locate a specific verse that contains that word.

The purpose of context lines in a concordance is merely to help the reader recognize or find a specific verse in the Bible. For word study—or any kind of Bible study—the context offered by a concordance is rarely enough to go on. Nevertheless, sometimes a short sentence or a whole verse fits on one line, as in the case of John 11:35: "Jesus wept." Under the heading PRAISE, *The Strongest Strong's* was able to present almost the entirety of Psalm 150 on thirteen consecutive lines!

Taken by themselves, context lines can and do misrepresent the teaching of Scripture by omitting key words. "There is no God" is a context taken straight from Psalm 14:1. Of course the Bible does not teach this; it is what "the fool hath said in his heart"! Similarly, a context for Leviticus 24:16 might read "the LORD, shall be put to death" while the text actually says "he that is born in the land, when he blasphemeth the name of the LORD, shall be put to death."

Great care has been taken by the editors, programmers, and proofreaders of *The Strongest Strong's* to create contexts that are informative and accurate. But the reader should always check word contexts by looking them up in the KJV itself. "The Wicked Bible," a KJV edition of 1631, accidentally omitted the word "not" from the seventh commandment, for which the printers were fined 300 pounds sterling! Though there are no such fines for misleading contexts, the editors are still deeply concerned that *The Strongest Strong's* be used discerningly.

Bible Translating and Concordance Making

Traduttore traditore, "the translator is a traitor," is an ancient proverb oft quoted in books about Bible translations. To a degree this proverb is true, for no translation can perfectly bring over all the meaning and nuances of one language into another. Because no two languages share identical grammar and an identical range of word meanings, not even the best-intentioned word-for-word translation can claim to perfectly represent the original.

If the translator is a traitor, the concordance maker must be a partner in crime. For no multilingual concordance can perfectly represent both the English and biblical language texts it indexes. It can perfectly represent the vocabulary of the English text, for it needs only to list the location of each of its words. In this respect a concordance is either absolutely right or absolutely wrong. But when a concordance attempts to display the relationship between the English text and the biblical languages, it falls heir to the same difficulties that face the Bible translator.

Much of Bible translation involves one-to-one relationships. More often than not, אֱלֹהִים (Strong number 430) is translated "God," Ἰησοῦς (*2424*) is "Jesus," and ἀγαπάω (*25*) is "love." This part of translating and concordance making is easy.

Often, however, more than one word is needed in English to render a word in the originals. For example, the Greek word τεκνίον (*5040*) is "little child" or "little children" twelve times in the KJV. Conversely, one English word can translate several words from the originals. The simple preposition "before" translates two Hebrew words (3807.1+6440) 958 times.

Sometimes, because of differences in idiom, it takes several English words to translate two or more words from the original languages. This is called "dynamic equivalence" or "functional equivalence." For example, the famous KJV expletive "God forbid!" translates one word in Hebrew and two words in Greek—neither of which has either "God" or "forbid" as part of its "literal" meaning! Nevertheless, "God forbid!" is the *functional* equivalent of the Greek and Hebrew phrases.

Multilingual concordances of the past, following the lead of the original Strong's *Concordance*, have tended to display the relationship between English and the original languages as if it were almost always one-to-one. Scan a few columns of Strong's *Concordance*, and you see context after context presenting one indexed word followed by one number. Over the years, this has lent support to the misconception that the KJV is an absolutely "literal," word-for-word translation. However, the original preface to the KJV stated, "We have not tied our selves to an uniformity of phrasing, or to an identity of words, as some peradventure would wish that we had done."

The Strongest Strong's, by means of two different typefaces in the context line and a greatly enhanced use of Strong's numbering system, shows more fully than any previous KJV concordance the interrelation of the English text and the biblical languages.

Context Lines: Word-for-Word Translation

The simplest context line presents four items of information. First, the location of the indexed word by book, chapter, and verse. Second, the context line. Third, within the context line, the indexed word is abbreviated by its first letter and is *usually* in bold type. Fourth, a number at the right margin indicates the Hebrew, Aramaic, or Greek word the indexed word translates. For example, under the heading AARON on page 1:

Ex	4:14	and he said, Is not **A** the Levite thy brother?	175
	4:27	the LORD said to **A,** "Go into the wilderness	175

Note that the book abbreviation is not repeated in the second reference. Book abbreviations are repeated at the top of the first column of each page (see pages 2 and 3). A complete list of KJV book abbreviations appears at the beginning of the Main Concordance.

The numbering system indicates which biblical language is translated. Hebrew and Aramaic words are represented by numbers in normal "roman" type, from 1 through 8674. Greek word numbers are in italics, from *1* through *5624*.

After compiling his original word list, Strong added two Hebrew words and two Greek words. To keep them in order he added an apostrophe or prime symbol to the preceding number. So when you see 1699' and 6211' at the end of OT contexts, be sure to match the number *and* the symbol in the Hebrew-Aramaic dictionary-index. Though added to the Greek numbering system, Strong did not use words *2312'* and *2526'* in the concordance.

Strong also did not include the Hebrew and Aramaic articles, conjunctions, prepositions, and pronouns that attach to words as prefixes and suffixes, though he regularly refers to these terms in his dictionaries. Because of the far more exhaustive analysis of *The Strongest Strong's*, we added these fifty forms to Strong's list. But since we did not want to change his numbering system, we added decimals to his numbers. The first two additions involve the first letter of the Hebrew and Aramaic alphabet, so the first entries in the Hebrew-Aramaic dictionary-index are now 0.1 and 0.2.

Because *The Strongest Strong's* shows the italics of the KJV in its contexts, if an indexed word is italicized in the KJV, it is bold and italic in the context. For example, in Mark 5:24 *Jesus* is italicized: the KJV translators supplied the name for clarity, though it was not in the Greek. Appropriately, the context in *The Strongest Strong's* is:

5:24 And ***J*** went with him; and much people NIG

Note the abbreviation "NIG" instead of a number at the end of the context line. This indicates the word *Jesus* is "Not in Greek." The abbreviation "NIH" (Not in Hebrew [Aramaic]) is used in the OT.

Context Lines: Multiple-Word Translation

One English Word—Multiple Original Words. When the indexed word translates more than one word from the original, this is indicated by an appropriate number of Strong numbers at the end of the line. This is especially true of numbers. "Twelve," for example, always translates a combination of two Hebrew or Aramaic words in the OT, though it is one-to-one in the NT:

Nu	1:44	the princes of Israel, being **t** men:	6240+8147
Mk	3:14	And he ordained **t**, that they should be with	*1427*

The original Strong's usually shows multiple numbers for such numerals (though some "new" editions do not), but rarely shows multiple numbers for the more than 14,000 times that KJV translators used this multi-word translation technique.

Multiple-word Translation. As mentioned above, the Greek word τεκνίον (*5040*) is translated "little child" or "little children" twelve times in the KJV. If you were to look up the word "little" in any edition of Strong's and look at the context for 1 John 2:1, you would find the word abbreviated by its first letter with the number *5040* at the end of the line. However, if you looked up the word "children" you would find the same thing:

1Jo 2: 1 My *l* children, these things write *5040*

1Jo 2: 1 My little *c*, these things write I *5040*

In these examples, it would appear that the Greek word number *5040* meant only "little" or "children," depending on which entry you looked up first. Nothing in the context line would inform you that Greek word *5040* actually means "little children."

The Strongest Strong's has solved the problem of indicating such multiple-word translations by putting *all* the words in bold type. Here is the same example of 1 John 2:1, under the headings "little" and "children":

1Jn 2: 1 My **l children**, these *things* write I unto *5040*

1Jn 2: 1 My **little c**, these *things* write I unto you, *5040*

If more than one English word is used to render several words from the original, the typefaces and the Strong numbers show all the words involved in this multiple-word translation. Such is the case of "with child" in Matthew 1:18, as indexed under CHILD:

Mt 1: 18 **with c** of the Holy Ghost. *1064+1722+2192*

The use of multiple Strong numbers and bold type, first introduced in *The NIV Exhaustive Concordance*, show at a glance all the words involved in more than 44,000 instances of multiple-word translation in English and in more than 14,000 instances of multiple-word translation of the original languages. For these conventions alone, *The Strongest Strong's* is truly the most exhaustive concordance to the KJV.

Context Lines: "Substitution" Translation

Bible translators often substitute nouns for pronouns and pronouns for nouns for clarity. For example, Matthew 9:10 reads "as Jesus sat at meat in the house, behold, . . ." "Jesus" here translates Greek word *846*, which is not the proper name Ἰησοῦς (*2424*), but the pronoun αὐτός, "he." Such "substitutionary" translations are common and acceptable in Bible translations, but other concordances treat them as if they were one-to-one translations.

The Strongest Strong's indicates substitutionary translation by attaching a raised "S" to the bolded letter:

Mt 9: 10 as **J**S sat at meat in the house, behold, *846*

The KJV is not unique in using substitutionary translation. *The Strongest Strong's* is unique in displaying it.

Context Lines: "Not in Hebrew" and "Not in Greek"

Because modern English and ancient Hebrew, Aramaic, and Greek do not have identical rules of grammar and style, translators must often add words for the sake of clarity. For example, Mark 16:9 begins, "Now when Jesus was risen early. . . ." Other editions of Strong have no number at the end of this context line under the entry JESUS because there is no Greek word for "Jesus" in this verse; it was supplied by the translators to give a subject to the verb.

The Strongest Strong's indicates KJV words that are not in the originals by using the code NIH, "Not In Hebrew," for both the Hebrew and Aramaic of the Old Testament and NIG, "Not In Greek," for the New. Under the heading ABRAHAM, we find, for example:

Ge 21: 33 ***A*** planted a grove in Beer-sheba, and NIH

Ac 7: 8 and so ***A*** begat Isaac, and circumcised him NIG

As in the case of Mark 16:9, these proper names were supplied for clarity, for the benefit of the reader.

Context Lines: Shaded Background

Because most editions of the KJV produced today have the words of Jesus in red letter, all contexts that contain words of Jesus are highlighted with a shaded background.

THE INDEX OF ARTICLES, CONJUNCTIONS, PREPOSITIONS, PRONOUNS, ETC.

In order to keep *The Strongest Strong's Exhaustive Concordance: Larger Print Edition* reasonable in size and price, there are fewer words in the Main Concordance and more words in the Index than in the regular edition of *The Strongest Strong's.* However, the larger print edition has more contexts and more significant words in its Main Concordance than any other larger print edition.

The Main Concordance indexes 259,698 references to 12,435 KJV words. The Index of Articles, Conjunctions, Prepositions, Pronouns, Etc. indexes 531,417 references to 424 KJV words. The format of the Index of Articles, Etc. is very simple. Each of the 424 words has its own heading, followed by a frequency count. For example:

A (8718)

The 424 words of this section are indexed without contexts, since providing contexts would be of little benefit to the reader and would more than double the size of *The Strongest Strong's*! Book, chapter, and verse references appear in biblical order. Each book is set in bold print for easy location.

One word in the Index of Articles, Etc. has a selection of contexts in the Main Concordance. The word "will" is exhaustively indexed in the Index of Articles, Etc. But the 200 cases where "will" directly translates a Greek or Hebrew word also appear with contexts in the Main Concordance. This includes all references to "the will of God."

THE BIBLICAL LANGUAGE DICTIONARY-INDEXES

At the end of each context line in the Main Concordance is a code or a Strong number, describing the relationship of the KJV to the original languages. Two Biblical Language Dictionary-Indexes list all of the words that are found in the Hebrew, Aramaic, and Greek texts from which the KJV was translated. These lists are in the alphabetical order of each of the languages, which is also the order of the Strong numbering system.

Note that in keeping with some reference works of the nineteenth century, Strong merged Hebrew and Aramaic (or "Chaldee") into one list. All major reference works of the twentieth century treat these as two separate languages. Further, he also alphabetized the letters שׂ and שׁ as though they were the same character, though again all major reference works since have treated them as distinct. In order to preserve Strong's numbering system, *The Strongest Strong's* retained his sorting conventions.

The Dictionary-Indexes to *The Strongest Strong's* have three features not found in the indexes or dictionaries of any other KJV concordance. First, for all but sixteen highly frequent words, *The Strongest Strong's* lists all the KJV words and phrases that translate each word of the original, showing multiple-word translation and substitution translation. Second, *The Strongest Strong's* sorts the KJV word indexes according to their frequency and provides the exact number of times these words and phrases are used in the KJV. Third, the KJV words and phrases indexed are in their exact textual spelling, so the user can locate its heading in the Main Concordance without any further cross-referencing.

The entry for Greek word *25* can serve as an example for most features of both Dictionary-Indexes:

> ***26*** **ἀγάπη**, ***agapē***, n. GK: *27* [→ *25*]. love, in the NT usually the active love of God for his Son and his people, and the active love his people are to have for God, each other, and even enemies; love feast, the common meal shared by Christians in connection with church meetings:– love [85], charity [27], charitably (*+2596*) [1], dear [1], feasts of charity [1], love's [1]

The entry begins with the Strong number, in bold type for easy location. Next is the lexical form or dictionary form of the Greek word, followed by its transliteration (in bold italics), the part of speech (abbreviated), the Goodrick/Kohlenberger number, and related words (listed by Strong number in square brackets, see below for more on related words).

The transliteration follows the system used in Zondervan's *New International Dictionary of New Testament Theology* and *New International Dictionary of Old Testament Theology and Exegesis.* A complete transliteration and pronunication guide, as well as a list of abbreviations, appears before each index.

The Goodrick/Kohlenberger or G/K numbering system was developed for *The NIV Exhaustive Concordance.* Since it takes into account thousands of words and word forms not in Strong's system, the G/K numbering system is widely used in modern reference books. For those who wish to consult these more up-to-date and thorough resources, the G/K number (or numbers) is included for every entry in both Dictionary-Indexes.

The six heading elements are concluded by a period. Following the period is an essential definition for the word as it is used in the NT. These definitions can be as brief as one or two words. In the case of hundreds of theologically and culturally significant words, like ἀγάπη, the definition functions as a concise expository dictionary. In the case of a proper name, like "Bethlehem," the definition will include the possible meaning of the name in the originals: "*house of bread;* poss. *temple [house] of Lakhmu.*"

The definition ends with a colon and a dash (:–). Following this symbol is a list of all the ways in which the word is translated in the KJV, in descending order of frequency. If two words (or phrases) have the same frequency, they are listed in alphabetical order. Following the KJV word is its frequency count, in square brackets. Word *3588* (the article ὁ), which occurs almost 20,000 times in the NT, and fifteen highly-frequent Hebrew words are not indexed exhaustively, but their most frequent KJV equivalents are listed. These sixteen entries end with an asterisk (*).

One-to-one translations are indicated by one KJV word, as in the case of the first and last KJV words in the example above. Multiple-word translations are indicated in two ways: by multiple KJV words and/or multiple Strong numbers. The next-to-the-last word, "feasts of charity [1]," indicates a multiple-word KJV translation. If you look up "charity" and "feasts" in the Main Concordance, you will find the following contexts under Jude 1:12:

Jude 1:12 These are spots in your **feasts of c** when they *26*

Jude 1:12 These are spots in your **f of charity** when *26*

Under both headings, the phrase "feasts of charity" is shown to be the definition of Greek word *26*. (Multiple-word translation is described above on pages xii-xiii.)

When a KJV word or phrase translates more than one word of the original, the Strong number of the additional word (or words) precedes the frequency count in parentheses. This is seen in entry *26* in "charitably (*+2596*) [1]."

"Substitution" translation (see above, page xiii) is noted with a raised "s," as in the Main Concordance. The example on page xiii cited a substitute translation of word *846* by the word "Jesus" in Mt 9:10. The corresponding index in the entry for word *846* is "Jesus^S [1]."

Related Words

One popular element of Strong's original dictionaries has been intentionally omitted in *The Strongest Strong's.* Following the majority of nineteenth century scholarship, Strong attempted to explain the meaning of each word by referring to its alleged "root" meaning. Though popularized in many other dated reference books like Vine's *Expository Dictionary of New Testament Words,* this practice has been largely abandoned by modern scholars, who often label it the "root fallacy."

In his original entry on Hebrew word 3563, Strong explains:

> *koce* . . . [is] from an unused root mean. to *hold* together; a *cup* (as a container), often fig. a *lot* (as if a potion); also some unclean bird, prob. an *owl* (perh.from the cup-like cavity of its eye)

In his attempt to relate the "unused root meaning" to both "cup" and "owl," he stretches for an explanation that would apply to almost any animal with an eyeball, since all eyeballs are set in cup-like cavities!

Modern scholars understand that word 3563 is actually two completely different words, one meaning "cup" and the other "owl." Though spelled identically in Hebrew, in other related ancient languages they have different spellings. This is seen in the KJV word "cleave," which means both "stick together" (Ge 2:24) and "cut apart" (Zec 14:4). Though spelled the same in the KJV, in Old English the two meanings had separate spellings: *clifan* and *cleofan* respectively. One should not attempt to relate the meanings of these separate words, just as Strong should not have in thousands of cases.

Instead of attempting such speculative analysis and perpetuating the root fallacy, the Dictionary-Indexes of *The Strongest Strong's* list all biblical words that are related by common elements. The arrow symbol (→) points to a word or a list of words that share common elements with the word in the entry. These related words lists are provided to allow the user to do more thorough word studies. These studies, however, should be done carefully with more attention paid to contextual definitions than fanciful etymologies.

Dictionary Definition versus KJV Translation

The original dictionaries in Strong's *Concordance* often give a single "root" definition for each word. This is often misunderstood as the *only* definition or the "literal" meaning of the word and can be misused to criticize other valid translations of the word—even in the KJV itself! The entry for ποιέω (*4160*) lists 76 different KJV words and phrases that translate this common word, yet Strong's original dictionary simply defines this word as "to *make* or *do*." Either the KJV translators were wrong in 96% of their definitions or there is more to the meaning of ποιέω than "to *make* or *do*"!

The KJV translations that follow the definition are listed in order from most used to least used. They represent careful choices the KJV translators made to render each word accurately and understandably in its context. But they also represent the translators' express principle not to tie themselves to "a uniformity of phrasing or identity of words." The KJV translations list is a good indicator of the range of a word's meaning in seventeenth-century English, as the dictionary definition is a good summary of meaning in modern English. Use these resources together, not in opposition.

For further and more detailed word studies, there are a wide variety of resources available that are keyed to Strong's numbering system.

On a basic level, there is the popular but dated *Expository Dictionary of Biblical Words* (Nelson), indexed to Strong numbers. More up-to-date and superior in methodology and OT word studies is Zondervan's *New International Encyclopedia of Bible Words*, edited by Larry Richards and indexed to G/K numbers.

On an intermediate level, there is *The NIV Theological Dictionary of New Testament Words* (Zondervan), edited by Verlyn D. Verbrugge from the four-volume *New International Dictionary of New Testament Theology* (Zondervan), edited by Colin Brown. This excellent tool gives important information for the most theologically significant words of the NT. It is keyed to G/K numbers, but also has indexes to convert G/K to Strong and Strong to G/K. For the OT, *The Theological Wordbook of the Old Testament* (Moody) uses its own numbering system, but does have a key to Strong numbers.

On an advanced level the four-volume *New International Dictionary of New Testament Theology* (Zondervan), edited by Colin Brown, and the five-volume *New International Dictionary of Old Testament Theology and Exegesis*, edited by Willem VanGemeren, are outstanding resources for deeper research. Both have English indexes and indexes to Greek and Hebrew words spelled in the same transliteration system used in *The Strongest Strong's*. The *NIDOTTE* is also keyed to G/K numbers and has an index to Strong's numbers.

Less conservative, but excellent in scholarship, are the three-volume *Theological Lexicon of the New Testament* (Hendrickson) by Ceslas Spicq and the *Theological Lexicon of the Old Testament* (Hendrickson) edited by Jenni and Westermann. Both of these sets are keyed to Strong's numbers and to a variety of more advanced resources for students of biblical languages.

IN CONCLUSION

To Ralph Waldo Emerson, "A foolish consistency is the hobgoblin of little minds." To the editors of the *The Strongest Strong's Exhaustive Concordance*, there is no such thing as a foolish consistency in a biblical reference book. Every effort has been made by the editors, programmers, and proofreaders to make the *The Strongest Strong's* consistent and error-free. Strong's and Young's *Concordances* have each been through more than two dozen revisions, and we realize that our work has not been perfect either.

If you find anything that appears to be an error, write to The KJV Concordance Project, c/o Zondervan, 5300 Patterson Avenue, S.E., Grand Rapids, MI 49530.

THE STRONGEST STRONG'S EXHAUSTIVE CONCORDANCE

LARGER PRINT EDITION

FEATURES OF THE MAIN CONCORDANCE

KJV WORD HEADING
The indexed word as spelled in the KJV (see the introduction, pages x, xi).

FREQUENCY COUNT
Total number of occurrences in the KJV (see the introduction, page xi).

RELATED WORD LIST
Other spellings and related words in the KJV (see the introduction, page xi).

ACCEPT (25) [ACCEPTABLE, ACCEPTABLY, ACCEPTANCE, ACCEPTATION, ACCEPTED]

Ex 22:11 the owner of it shall **a** *thereof,* and he shall 3947

STRONG NUMBER
Refers to the biblical-language dictionary-indexes; one- to four-digit normal "roman" type is Hebrew or Aramaic; *italic* is Greek (see the introduction, pages xii–xiv).

ITALIC TYPEFACE
Indicates words that are italicized in the KJV (see the introduction, pages x, xii).

INDEXED WORD
Abbreviated by its first letter, usually in **bold** type.

BIBLICAL REFERENCE
See the abbreviations table below.

ADDITIONAL STRONG NUMBER(S)
Indicates more than one Hebrew, Aramaic, or Greek word is represented by the KJV translation (see the introduction, pages xii, xiii).

Ge 32:20 peradventure he will **a** of me. 5375+6440

BOLD TYPEFACE
In addition to the indexed word, indicates multiple-word translation (introduction, pages xii, xiii).

Eph 1: 6 wherein he hath **made** us **a** in the beloved: *5487*

NIG OR NIH
"Not in Greek" and "Not in Hebrew/ Aramaic" indicates the indexed word was supplied for clarity in translation (see the introduction, pages xii, xiii).

Ge 41:25 God hath shewed Pharaoh what he is **a** to NIH

SHADED BACKGROUND
Contexts containing the words of Jesus, printed in red letter in most editions of the KJV, are highlighted with a shaded background (see the introduction, page xiii).

Lk 4:24 No prophet is **a** in his own country. *1884*

A (8718) [AN] See Index

KJV INDEX REFERENCES
Refers to an index of highly frequent words (see the introduction, page xi).

"SEE" REFERENCES
Cross-references key words from various edtions of the KJV and from modern translations and reference books to KJV vocabulary (see the introduction, page xi).

ABYSS See BOTTOMLESS

ACHBOR See ACBOR

ABBREVIATIONS FOR THE BOOKS OF THE BIBLE

Ge	Genesis	1Ch	1 Chronicles	La	Lamentations	Hag	Haggai	Eph	Ephesians	2Pe	2 Peter
Ex	Exodus	2Ch	2 Chronicles	Eze	Ezekiel	Zec	Zechariah	Php	Philippians	1Jn	1 John
Lev	Leviticus	Ezr	Ezra	Da	Daniel	Mal	Malachi	Col	Colossians	2Jn	2 John
Nu	Numbers	Ne	Nehemiah	Hos	Hosea	Mt	Matthew	1Th	1 Thessalonians	3Jn	3 John
Dt	Deuteronomy	Est	Esther	Joel	Joel	Mk	Mark	2Th	2 Thessalonians	Jude	Jude
Jos	Joshua	Job	Job	Am	Amos	Lk	Luke	1Ti	1 Timothy	Rev	Revelation
Jdg	Judges	Ps	Psalms	Ob	Obadiah	Jn	John	2Ti	2 Timothy		
Ru	Ruth	Pr	Proverbs	Jnh	Jonah	Ac	Acts	Tit	Titus		
1Sa	1 Samuel	Ecc	Ecclesiastes	Mic	Micah	Ro	Romans	Phm	Philemon		
2Sa	2 Samuel	SS	Song of Solomon	Na	Nahum	1Co	1 Corinthians	Heb	Hebrews		
1Ki	1 Kings	Isa	Isaiah	Hab	Habakkuk	2Co	2 Corinthians	Jas	James		
2Ki	2 Kings	Jer	Jeremiah	Zep	Zephaniah	Gal	Galatians	1Pe	1 Peter		

Other Abbreviations

S.	Epistle subscript
T	Psalm title

THE STRONGEST STRONG'S EXHAUSTIVE CONCORDANCE

A

A (8718) [AN] See Index

AARON (319) [AARON'S, AARONITES]

Ex 4:14	and he said, Is not A the Levite thy brother?	175
4:27	the LORD said to A, Go into the wilderness	175
4:28	Moses told A all the words of the LORD	175
4:29	Moses and A went and gathered together all	175
4:30	A spake all the words which the LORD had	175
5: 1	afterward Moses and A went in, and	175
5: 4	Wherefore do ye, Moses and A, let	175
5:20	they met Moses and A, who stood in	175
6:13	the LORD spake unto Moses and unto A,	175
6:20	to wife; and she bare him A and Moses:	175
6:23	A took him Elisheba, daughter of	175
6:26	*These are* that A and Moses, to whom	175
6:27	from Egypt: *these are* that Moses and A.	175
7: 1	and A thy brother shall be thy prophet.	175
7: 2	and A thy brother shall speak unto Pharaoh,	175
7: 6	and A did as the LORD commanded them,	175
7: 7	A fourscore and three years old, when they	175
7: 8	the LORD spake unto Moses and unto A,	175
7: 9	then thou shalt say unto A, Take thy rod, and	175
7:10	And Moses and A went in unto Pharaoh, and	175
7:10	and A cast down his rod before Pharaoh, and	175
7:19	Say unto A, Take thy rod, and stretch out	175
7:20	Moses and A did so, as the LORD	175
8: 5	the LORD spake unto Moses, Say unto A,	175
8: 6	A stretched out his hand over the waters of	175
8: 8	Pharaoh called for Moses and A, and said,	175
8:12	Moses and A went out from Pharaoh: and	175
8:16	Say unto A, Stretch out thy rod, and	175
8:17	for A stretched out his hand with his rod,	175
8:25	Pharaoh called for Moses and for A, and	175
9: 8	the LORD said unto Moses and unto A,	175
9:27	called for Moses and A, and said unto them,	175
10: 3	Moses and A came in unto Pharaoh, and	175
10: 8	and A were brought again unto Pharaoh:	175
10:16	Pharaoh called for Moses and A in haste;	175
11:10	and A did all these wonders before Pharaoh:	175
12: 1	unto Moses and A in the land of Egypt,	175
12:28	the LORD had commanded Moses and A,	175
12:31	And he called for Moses and A by night, and	175
12:43	the LORD said unto Moses and A, This *is*	175
12:50	as the LORD commanded Moses and A, so	175
15:20	the sister of A, took a timbrel in her hand;	175
16: 2	against Moses and A in the wilderness:	175
16: 6	and A said unto all the children of Israel,	175
16: 9	Moses spake unto A, Say unto all	175
16:10	as A spake unto the whole congregation of	175
16:33	Moses said unto A, Take a pot, and put an	175
16:34	so A laid it up before the Testimony, to be	175
17:10	A, and Hur went up *to* the top of the hill.	175
17:12	A and Hur stayed up his hands, the one on	175
18:12	A came, and all the elders of Israel, to eat	175
19:24	thou shalt come up, thou, and A with thee:	175
24: 1	thou, and A, Nadab, and Abihu, and	175
24: 9	A, Nadab, and Abihu, and seventy of	175
24:14	behold, A and Hur *are* with you: if any man	175
27:21	A and his sons shall order it from evening to	175
28: 1	take thou unto thee A thy brother, and his	175
28: 1	*even* A, Nadab and Abihu, Eleazar and	175
28: 2	thou shalt make holy garments for A thy	175
28: 4	they shall make holy garments for A thy	175
28:12	A shall bear their names before the LORD	175
28:29	A shall bear the names of the children of	175
28:30	A shall bear the judgment of the children of	175
28:35	it shall be upon A to minister: and his sound	175
28:38	that A may bear the iniquity of the holy	175
28:41	And thou shalt put them upon A thy brother,	175
28:43	they shall be upon A, and upon his sons,	175
29: 4	A and his sons thou shalt bring unto the door	175
29: 5	put upon A the coat, and the robe of	175
29: 9	A and his sons, and put the bonnets on them:	175
29: 9	and thou shalt consecrate A and his sons.	175
29:10	A and his sons shall put their hands upon	175
29:15	A and his sons shall put their hands upon	175
29:19	A and his sons shall put their hands upon	175
29:20	put *it* upon the tip of the *right* ear of A, and	175
29:21	sprinkle *it* upon A, and upon his garments,	175
29:24	And thou shalt put all in the hands of A, and	175
29:27	*even* of *that* which *is* for A, and of *that*	175
29:29	the holy garments of A shall be his sons'	175
29:32	A and his sons shall eat the flesh of the ram,	175
29:35	thus shalt thou do unto A, and to his sons,	175
29:44	I will sanctify also both A and his sons,	175
30: 7	A shall burn thereon sweet incense every	175
30: 8	when A lighteth the lamps at even, he shall	175
30:10	A shall make an atonement upon the horns	175
30:19	For A and his sons shall wash their hands	175
30:30	thou shalt anoint A and his sons, and	175
31:10	the holy garments for A the priest, and	175
32: 1	people gathered themselves together unto A,	175
32: 2	A said unto them, Break off the golden	175
32: 3	*were* in their ears, and brought *them* unto A.	175
32: 5	when A saw *it,* he built an altar before it;	175
32: 5	A made proclamation, and said, To morrow	175
32:21	Moses said unto A, What did this people	175
32:22	A said, Let not the anger of my lord wax hot:	175
32:25	(for A had made them naked unto *their*	175
32:35	because they made the calf, which A made.	175
34:30	when A and all the children of Israel saw	175
34:31	A and all the rulers of the congregation	175
35:19	*place,* the holy garments for A the priest,	175
38:21	by the hand of Ithamar, son to A the priest.	175
39: 1	and made the holy garments for A;	175
39:27	coats *of* fine linen *of* woven work for A,	175

Ex	39:41	and the holy garments for **A** the priest,	175
	40:12	thou shalt bring **A** and his sons unto the door	175
	40:13	thou shalt put upon **A** the holy garments,	175
	40:31	Moses and **A** and his sons washed their	175
Lev	1: 7	the sons of **A** the priest shall put fire upon	175
	3:13	the sons of **A** shall sprinkle the blood thereof	175
	6: 9	Command **A** and his sons, saying, This *is*	175
	6:14	the sons of **A** shall offer it before	175
	6:16	the remainder thereof shall **A** and his sons	175
	6:18	All the males among the children of **A** shall	175
	6:20	This *is* the offering of **A** and of his sons,	175
	6:25	Speak unto **A** and to his sons, saying, This *is*	175
	7:10	and dry, shall all the sons of **A** have,	175
	7:33	He among the sons of **A**, that offereth	175
	7:34	have given them unto **A** the priest and	175
	7:35	This *is the portion* of the anointing of **A**, and	175
	8: 2	Take **A** and his sons with him, and	175
	8: 6	Moses brought **A** and his sons, and	175
	8:14	**A** and his sons laid their hands upon	175
	8:18	**A** and his sons laid their hands upon	175
	8:22	**A** and his sons laid their hands upon	175
	8:30	sprinkled *it* upon **A**, *and* upon his garments,	175
	8:30	sanctified **A**, *and* his garments, and his sons,	175
	8:31	Moses said unto **A** and to his sons, Boil	175
	8:31	**A** and his sons shall eat it.	175
	8:36	So **A** and his sons did all things which	175
	9: 1	*that* Moses called **A** and his sons, and	175
	9: 2	he said unto **A**, Take thee a young calf for a	175
	9: 7	Moses said unto **A**, Go unto the altar, and	175
	9: 8	**A** therefore went unto the altar, and slew	175
	9: 9	the sons of **A** brought the blood unto him:	175
	9:21	the right shoulder **A** waved *for* a wave	175
	9:22	**A** lift up his hand towards the people, and	175
	9:23	**A** went into the tabernacle of	175
	10: 1	Nadab and Abihu, the sons of **A**, took either	175
	10: 3	Moses said unto **A**, This *is it* that	175
	10: 3	I will be glorified. And **A** held his peace.	175
	10: 4	the sons of Uzziel the uncle of **A**, and	175
	10: 6	Moses said unto **A**, and unto Eleazar and	175
	10: 8	And the LORD spake unto **A**, saying,	175
	10:12	Moses spake unto **A**, and unto Eleazar and	175
	10:16	Ithamar the sons of **A** which were left *alive,*	175
	10:19	**A** said unto Moses, Behold, *this* day have	175
	11: 1	And the LORD spake unto Moses and to **A**,	175
	13: 1	the LORD spake unto Moses and **A**,	175
	13: 2	then he shall be brought unto **A** the priest, or	175
	14:33	the LORD spake unto Moses and unto **A**,	175
	15: 1	And the LORD spake unto Moses and to **A**,	175
	16: 1	Moses after the death of the two sons of **A**,	175
	16: 2	said unto Moses, Speak unto **A** thy brother,	175
	16: 3	Thus shall **A** come into the holy *place:* with	175
	16: 6	**A** shall offer *his* bullock of the sin offering,	175
	16: 8	**A** shall cast lots upon the two goats; one lot	175
	16: 9	**A** shall bring the goat upon which	175
	16:11	**A** shall bring the bullock of the sin offering,	175
	16:21	**A** shall lay both his hands upon the head of	175
	16:23	**A** shall come into the tabernacle of	175
	17: 2	Speak unto **A**, and unto his sons, and unto all	175
	21: 1	Speak unto the priests the sons of **A**, and	175
	21:17	Speak unto **A**, saying, Whosoever *he be* of	175
	21:21	hath a blemish, of the seed of **A** the priest,	175
	21:24	Moses told *it* unto **A**, and to his sons, and	175
	22: 2	Speak unto **A** and to his sons, that they	175
	22: 4	What man soever of the seed of **A** *is* a leper,	175
	22:18	Speak unto **A**, and to his sons, and unto all	175
	24: 3	shall **A** order it from the evening unto	175
Nu	1: 3	and **A** shall number them by their armies.	175
	1:17	**A** took these men which are expressed by	175
	1:44	which Moses and **A** numbered, and	175
	2: 1	the LORD spake unto Moses and unto **A**,	175
	3: 1	These also *are* the generations of **A** and	175
	3: 2	these *are* the names of the sons of **A**;	175
	3: 3	These *are* the names of the sons of **A**,	175
	3: 4	priest's office in the sight of **A** their father.	175
	3: 6	and present them before **A** the priest,	175
	3: 9	thou shalt give the Levites unto **A** and to his	175
	3:10	thou shalt appoint **A** and his sons, and	175
	3:32	Eleazar the son of **A** the priest *shall be* chief	175
	3:38	*shall be* Moses, and **A** and his sons,	175
	3:39	**A** numbered at the commandment of	175
	3:48	is *to be* redeemed, unto **A** and to his sons.	175
	3:51	money of them that were redeemed unto **A**	175
	4: 1	the LORD spake unto Moses and unto **A**,	175
	4: 5	**A** shall come, and his sons, and they shall	175
	4:15	when **A** and his sons have made an end of	175
	4:16	*to* the office of Eleazar the son of **A**	175
	4:17	the LORD spake unto Moses and unto **A**,	175
	4:19	they approach unto the most holy *things:* **A**	175
	4:27	At the appointment of **A** and his sons shall	175
	4:28	the hand of Ithamar the son of **A** the priest.	175
	4:33	under the hand of Ithamar the son of **A**	175
	4:34	Moses and **A** and the chief of	175
	4:37	**A** did number according to	175
	4:41	**A** did number according to	175
	4:45	**A** numbered according to the word of	175
	4:46	whom Moses and **A** and the chief of Israel	175
	6:23	Speak unto **A** and unto his sons, saying,	175
	7: 8	under the hand of Ithamar the son of **A**	175
	8: 2	Speak unto **A**, and say unto him, When thou	175
	8: 3	**A** did so; he lighted the lamps thereof over	175
	8:11	**A** shall offer the Levites before the LORD	175
	8:13	And thou shalt set the Levites before **A**, and	175
	8:19	I have given the Levites *as* a gift to **A** and	175
	8:20	**A**, and all the congregation of the children of	175
	8:21	**A** offered them *as* an offering before	175
	8:21	**A** made an atonement for them to cleanse	175
	8:22	the tabernacle of the congregation before **A**,	175
	9: 6	before Moses and before **A** on that day:	175
	10: 8	the sons of **A**, the priests, shall blow with	175
	12: 1	and **A** spake against Moses because	175
	12: 4	unto Moses, and unto **A**, and unto Miriam,	175
	12: 5	of the tabernacle, and called **A** and Miriam:	175
	12:10	**A** looked upon Miriam, and behold, *she was*	175
	12:11	**A** said unto Moses, Alas, my lord, I beseech	175
	13:26	to **A**, and to all the congregation of	175
	14: 2	murmured against Moses and against **A**:	175
	14: 5	**A** fell on their faces before all the assembly	175
	14:26	the LORD spake unto Moses and unto **A**,	175
	15:33	sticks brought him unto Moses and **A**,	175
	16: 3	together against Moses and against **A**,	175
	16:11	and what *is* **A**, that ye murmur against him?	175
	16:16	thou, and they, and **A**, to morrow:	175
	16:17	thou also, and **A**, each *of you* his censer.	175
	16:18	of the congregation with Moses and **A**.	175
	16:20	the LORD spake unto Moses and unto **A**,	175
	16:37	Speak unto Eleazar the son of **A** the priest,	175
	16:40	no stranger, which *is* not of the seed of **A**,	175
	16:41	murmured against Moses and against **A**,	175
	16:42	was gathered against Moses and against **A**,	175
	16:43	**A** came before the tabernacle of	175
	16:46	Moses said unto **A**, Take a censer, and	175
	16:47	**A** took as Moses commanded, and ran into	175
	16:50	**A** returned unto Moses unto the door of	175
	17: 6	and the rod of **A** *was* among their rods.	175
	17: 8	the rod of **A** for the house of Levi was	175
	18: 1	the LORD said unto **A**, Thou and thy sons	175
	18: 8	the LORD spake unto **A**, Behold, I also	175
	18:20	the LORD spake unto **A**, Thou shalt have	175
	18:28	the LORD'S heave offering to **A** the priest.	175
	19: 1	the LORD spake unto Moses and unto **A**,	175
	20: 2	together against Moses and against **A**.	175
	20: 6	**A** went from the presence of the assembly	175
	20: 8	**A** thy brother, and speak ye unto the rock	175
	20:10	**A** gathered the congregation together before	175
	20:12	the LORD spake unto Moses and **A**,	175
	20:23	spake unto Moses and **A** in mount Hor,	175
	20:24	**A** shall be gathered unto his people: for he	175
	20:25	Take **A** and Eleazar his son, and bring them	175
	20:26	strip **A** of his garments, and put them upon	175
	20:26	and **A** shall be gathered *unto his people,* and	175
	20:28	Moses stripped **A** of his garments, and	175
	20:28	and **A** died there in the top of the mount:	175
	20:29	when all the congregation saw that **A** was	175
	20:29	they mourned for **A** thirty days, *even* all	175
	25: 7	the son of Eleazar, the son of **A** the priest,	175
	25:11	the son of Eleazar, the son of **A** the priest,	175
	26: 1	and unto Eleazar the son of **A** the priest,	175
	26: 9	and against **A** in the company of Korah,	175
	26:59	and she bare unto Amram **A** and Moses, and	175
	26:60	unto **A** was born Nadab, and Abihu, Eleazar,	175
	26:64	whom Moses and **A** the priest numbered,	175
	27:13	thy people, as **A** thy brother was gathered.	175
	33: 1	their armies under the hand of Moses and **A**.	175
	33:38	**A** the priest went up into mount Hor at	175
	33:39	**A** *was* an hundred and twenty and	175
Dt	9:20	the LORD was very angry with **A** to have	175
	9:20	and I prayed for **A** also the same time.	175
	10: 6	there **A** died, and there he was buried;	175

Dt 32:50 as A thy brother died in mount Hor, and 175
Jos 21: 4 the children of A the priest, *which were* of 175
21:10 Which the children of A, *being* of 175
21:13 Thus they gave to the children of A 175
21:19 All the cities of the children of A, the priests, 175
24: 5 I sent Moses also and A, and I plagued 175
24:33 Eleazar the son of A died; and they buried 175
Jdg 20:28 the son of Eleazar, the son of A, 175
1Sa 12: 6 *It is* the LORD that advanced Moses and A, 175
12: 8 then the LORD sent Moses and A, 175
1Ch 6: 3 of Amram; A, and Moses, and Miriam. 175
6: 3 The sons also of A; Nadab, and Abihu, 175
6:49 A and his sons offered upon the altar of 175
6:50 And these *are* the sons of A; Eleazar his son, 175
6:54 of the sons of A, of the families of 175
6:57 to the sons of A they gave the cities of 175
15: 4 And David assembled the children of A, and 175
23:13 The sons of Amram; A and Moses: and 175
23:13 A was separated, that he should sanctify 175
23:28 A for the service of the house of 175
23:32 the charge of the sons of A their brethren, 175
24: 1 Now *these are* the divisions of the sons of A. 175
24: 1 The sons of A; Nadab, and Abihu, Eleazar, 175
24:19 to their manner, under A their father, 175
24:31 sons of A in the presence of David the king, 175
2Ch 13: 9 the sons of A, and the Levites, and 175
13:10 *are* the sons of A, and the Levites *wait* upon 175
26:18 the LORD, but to the priests the sons of A, 175
29:21 he commanded the priests the sons of A to 175
31:19 Also of the sons of A the priests, *which were* 175
35:14 the priests the sons of A *were busied* in 175
35:14 and for the priests the sons of A. 175
Ezr 7: 5 son of Eleazar, the son of A the chief priest: 175
Ne 10:38 the priest the son of A shall be with 175
12:47 sanctified *them* unto the children of A. 175
Ps 77:20 like a flock by the hand of Moses and A. 175
99: 6 Moses and A among his priests, and 175
105:26 his servant; *and* A whom he had chosen. 175
106:16 in the camp, *and* A the saint of the LORD. 175
115:10 O house of A, trust in the LORD: he *is* their 175
115:12 house of Israel; he will bless the house of A. 175
118: 3 Let the house of A now say, that his mercy 175
135:19 of Israel: bless the LORD, O house of A: 175
Mic 6: 4 I sent before thee Moses, A, and Miriam. 175
Lk 1: 5 and his wife *was* of the daughters of A, and *2*
Ac 7:40 Saying unto A, Make us gods to go before us: *2*
Heb 5: 4 but he that is called of God, as *was* A. *2*
7:11 and not be called after the order of A? *2*

AARON'S (31) [AARON]
Ex 6:25 Eleazar A son took him *one* of the daughters 175
7:12 but A rod swallowed up their rods. 175
28: 1 and Abihu, Eleazar and Ithamar, A sons. 175
28: 3 that they may make A garments to 175
28:30 they shall be upon A heart, when he goeth in 175
28:38 it shall be upon A forehead, that Aaron may 175
28:40 for A sons thou shalt make coats, and 175
29:26 thou shalt take the breast of the ram of A 175
29:28 it shall be A and his sons' by a 175+3807.1
Lev 1: 5 and the priests, A sons, shall bring the blood, 175
1: 8 the priests, A sons, shall lay the parts, 175
1:11 the priests, A sons, shall sprinkle his blood 175
2: 2 he shall bring it to A sons the priests: and 175
2: 3 of the meat offering *shall be* A 175+3807.1
2:10 left of the meat offering *shall be* A 175+3807.1
3: 2 A sons the priests shall sprinkle the blood 175
3: 5 A sons shall burn it on the altar upon 175
3: 8 A sons shall sprinkle the blood thereof round 175
7:31 but the breast shall be A and his sons'. 175
8:12 he poured of the anointing oil upon A head, 175
8:13 Moses brought A sons, and put coats upon 175
8:23 put *it* upon the tip of A right ear, and 175
8:24 he brought A sons, and Moses put of 175
8:27 he put all upon A hands, and upon his sons' 175
9:12 A sons presented unto him the blood, 175
9:18 A sons presented unto him the blood, 175
24: 9 it shall be A and his sons'; and 175+3807.1
Nu 17: 3 thou shalt write A name upon the rod of 175
17:10 Bring A rod again before the Testimony, 175
Ps 133: 2 that ran down upon the beard, *even* A beard: 175
Heb 9: 4 and A rod that budded, and the tables of *2*

AARONITES (2) [AARON]
1Ch 12:27 Jehoiada *was* the leader of the A, and 175
27:17 the son of Kemuel: of the A, Zadok: 175

ABADDON (1)
Rev 9:11 *pit,* whose name in the Hebrew tongue *is* A, *3*

ABAGTHA (1)
Est 1:10 Harbona, Bigtha, and A, Zethar, and Carcas, 5

ABANA (1)
2Ki 5:12 *Are* not A and Pharpar, rivers of Damascus, 71

ABARIM (4) [IJE-ABARIM]
Nu 27:12 Get thee up into this mount A, and see 5682
33:47 pitched in the mountains of A, before 5682
33:48 they departed from the mountains of A, 5682
Dt 32:49 Get thee up into this mountain A, 5682

ABASE (4) [ABASED, ABASING]
Job 40:11 behold every one *that is* proud, and a him. 8213
Isa 31: 4 nor a himself for the noise of them: 6031
Eze 21:26 *him that is* low, and a *him that is* high. 8213
Da 4:37 and those that walk in pride he *is* able to a. 8214

ABASED (4) [ABASE]
Mt 23:12 whosoever shall exalt himself shall be a; *5013*
Lk 14:11 For whosoever exalteth himself shall be a; *5013*
18:14 every one that exalteth himself shall be a; *5013*
Php 4:12 I know both *how* to be a, and I know *how* *5013*

ABASING (1) [ABASE]
2Co 11: 7 Have I committed an offence in a myself *5013*

ABATED (6)
Ge 8: 3 and fifty days the waters were a. 2637
8: 8 to see if the waters were a from off the face 7043
8:11 Noah knew that the waters were a from off 7043
Lev 27:18 and it shall be a from thy estimation. 1639
Dt 34: 7 his eye was not dim, nor his natural force a. 5127
Jdg 8: 3 their anger was a toward him, when he had 7503

ABBA (3)
Mk 14:36 And he said, A, Father, all *things are* possible *5*
Ro 8:15 Spirit of adoption, whereby we cry, A, Father. *5*
Gal 4: 6 of his Son into your hearts, crying, A, Father. *5*

ABDA (2)
1Ki 4: 6 Adoniram the son of A *was* over 5653
Ne 11:17 A the son of Shammua, the son of Galal, 5653

ABDEEL (1)
Jer 36:26 Shelemiah the son of A, to take Baruch 5655

ABDI (3)
1Ch 6:44 of Kishi, the son of A, the son of Malluch, 5660
2Ch 29:12 Kish the son of A, and Azariah the son of 5660
Ezr 10:26 and Jehiel, and A, and Jeremoth, and Eliah. 5660

ABDIEL (1)
1Ch 5:15 Ahi the son of A, the son of Guni, chief of 5661

ABDON (8)
Jos 21:30 with her suburbs, A with her suburbs, 5658
Jdg 12:13 after him A the son of Hillel, a Pirathonite, 5658
12:15 A the son of Hillel the Pirathonite died, 5658
1Ch 6:74 with her suburbs, and A with her suburbs, 5658
8:23 And A, and Zichri, and Hanan, 5658
8:30 his firstborn son A, and Zur, and Kish, and 5658
9:36 his firstborn son A, then Zur, and Kish, 5658
2Ch 34:20 A the son of Micah, and Shaphan 5658

ABED-NEGO (15) [AZARIAH]
Da 1: 7 of Meshach; and to Azariah, of A. 5664
2:49 and he set Shadrach, Meshach, and A, 5665
3:12 of Babylon, Shadrach, Meshach, and A; 5665
3:13 to bring Shadrach, Meshach, and A. 5665
3:14 *Is it* true, O Shadrach, Meshach, and A, 5665
3:16 and A, answered and said to the king, 5665
3:19 against Shadrach, Meshach, and A: 5665
3:20 A, *and* to cast *them* into the burning fiery 5665
3:22 that took up Shadrach, Meshach, and A. 5665
3:23 three men, Shadrach, Meshach, and A, 5665
3:26 spake, and said, Shadrach, Meshach, and A, 5665
3:26 *hither.* Then Shadrach, Meshach, and A, 5665
3:28 Meshach, and A, who hath sent his angel, 5665
3:29 Meshach, and A, shall be cut in pieces, and 5665
3:30 Meshach, and A, in the province of 5665

A

ABEL (16) [ABEL-BETH-MAACHAH]
Ge 4: 2 she again bare his brother **A**. And Abel was 1893
4: 2 **A** was a keeper of sheep, but Cain was a 1893
4: 4 **A**, he also brought of the firstlings of his 1893
4: 4 the LORD had respect unto **A** and to his 1893
4: 8 Cain talked with **A** his brother: and it came 1893
4: 8 that Cain rose up against **A** his brother, and 1893
4: 9 said unto Cain, Where *is* **A** thy brother? 1893
4:25 appointed me another seed instead of **A**, 1893
1Sa 6:18 even unto the great *stone of* **A**, 59
2Sa 20:14 he went through all the tribes of Israel unto **A**, 59
20:15 and besieged him in **A** of Beth-maachah, 59
20:18 They shall surely ask *counsel* at **A**: 59
Mt 23:35 from the blood of righteous **A** unto the blood of 6
Lk 11:51 From the blood of **A** unto the blood of 6
Heb 11: 4 By faith **A** offered unto God a more excellent 6
12:24 that speaketh better *things* than *that of* **A**. 6

ABEL-BETH-MAACHAH (2) [BETH-MAACHAH]
1Ki 15:20 and Dan, and **A**, and all Cinneroth, 59
2Ki 15:29 **A**, and Janoah, and Kedesh, and Hazor, and 59

ABEL-MAIM (1)
2Ch 16: 4 and **A**, and all the store cities of Naphtali. 66

ABEL-MEHOLAH (3)
Jdg 7:22 *and* to the border of **A**, unto Tabbath. 65
1Ki 4:12 beneath Jezreel, from Beth-shean to **A**, 65
19:16 Elisha the son of Shaphat of **A** shalt thou 65

ABEL-MIZRAIM (1) [MIZRAIM]
Ge 50:11 wherefore the name of it was called **A**, 67

ABEL-SHITTIM (1) [SHITTIM]
Nu 33:49 from Beth-jesimoth *even* unto **A** in the plains 63

ABEZ (1)
Jos 19:20 And Rabbith, and Kishion, and **A**, 77

ABHOR (19) [ABHORRED, ABHORREST, ABHORRETH, ABHORRING]
Lev 26:11 amongst you: and my soul shall not **a** you. 1602
26:15 or if your soul **a** my judgments, so that *ye* 1602
26:30 of your idols, and my soul shall **a** you. 1602
26:44 neither will I **a** them, to destroy them 1602
Dt 7:26 detest it, and thou shalt **utterly a** it; 8581+8581
23: 7 Thou shalt not **a** an Edomite; for he *is* thy 8581
23: 7 thou shalt not **a** an Egyptian; because 8581
1Sa 27:12 **made** his people Israel **utterly to a** 887+887
Job 9:31 the ditch, and mine own clothes shall **a** me. 8581
30:10 They **a** me, they flee far from me, and 8581
42: 6 Wherefore I **a** *myself,* and repent in dust 3988
Ps 5: 6 the LORD will **a** the bloody and 8581
119:163 I hate and **a** lying: *but* thy law do I love. 8581
Pr 24:24 shall the people curse, nations shall **a** him: 2194
Jer 14:21 Do not **a** *us,* for thy name's sake, do not 5006
Am 5:10 and they **a** him that speaketh uprightly. 8581
6: 8 I **a** the excellency of Jacob, and hate his 8374
Mic 3: 9 that **a** judgment, and pervert all equity. 8581
Ro 12: 9 **A** *that which is* evil; cleave to *that which is* *655*

ABHORRED (16) [ABHOR]
Ex 5:21 you have **made** our savour **to be a** in 887
Lev 20:23 all these *things,* and therefore I **a** them. 6973
26:43 and because their soul **a** my statutes. 1602
Dt 32:19 when the LORD saw *it,* he **a** *them,* 5006
1Sa 2:17 for men **a** the offering of the LORD. 5006
2Sa 16:21 all Israel shall hear that thou art **a** of thy 887
1Ki 11:25 mischief that Hadad *did:* and he **a** Israel, 6973
Job 19:19 All my inward friends **a** me: and 8581
Ps 22:24 For he hath not despised nor **a** the affliction 8262
78:59 *this,* he was wroth, and greatly **a** Israel: 3988
89:38 thou hast cast off and **a**, thou hast been 3988
106:40 insomuch that he **a** his own inheritance. 8581
Pr 22:14 he that is **a** of the LORD shall fall therein. 2194
La 2: 7 cast off his altar, he hath **a** his sanctuary, 5010
Eze 16:25 hast **made** thy beauty **to be a**, and 8581
Zec 11: 8 soul lothed them, and their soul also **a** me. 973

ABHORREST (2) [ABHOR]
Isa 7:16 the land that thou **a** shall be forsaken of 6973
Ro 2:22 thou that **a** idols, dost thou commit *948*

ABHORRETH (5) [ABHOR]
Job 33:20 So that his life **a** bread, and his soul dainty 2092
Ps 10: 3 blesseth the covetous, *whom* the LORD **a**. 5006
36: 4 in a way *that is* not good; he **a** not evil. 3988
107:18 Their soul **a** all *manner of* meat; and 8581
Isa 49: 7 to him whom the nation **a**, to a servant of 8581

ABHORRING (1) [ABHOR]
Isa 66:24 and they shall be an **a** unto all flesh. 1860

ABI (1)
2Ki 18: 2 His mother's name also *was* **A**, the daughter 21

ABIA (4)
1Ch 3:10 **A** his son, Asa his son, Jehoshaphat his son, 29
Mt 1: 7 and Roboam begat **A**; and Abia begat Asa; *7*
1: 7 and Roboam begat Abia; and **A** begat Asa; *7*
Lk 1: 5 priest named Zacharias, of the course of **A**: *7*

ABIAH (4)
1Sa 8: 2 was Joel; and the name of his second, **A**: 29
1Ch 2:24 **A** Hezron's wife bare him Ashur the father of 29
6:28 sons of Samuel; the firstborn Vashni, and **A**. 29
7: 8 Jerimoth, and **A**, and Anathoth, and Alameth. 29

ABIALBON (1)
2Sa 23:31 **A** the Arbathite, Azmaveth the Barhumite, 45

ABIASAPH (1)
Ex 6:24 the sons of Korah; Assir, and Elkanah, and **A**: 23

ABIATHAR (30) [ABIATHAR'S]
1Sa 22:20 named **A**, escaped, and fled after David. 54
22:21 **A** shewed David that Saul had slain 54
22:22 David said unto **A**, I knew *it* that day, when 54
23: 6 when **A** the son of Ahimelech fled to David *to* 54
23: 9 he said to **A** the priest, Bring hither the ephod. 54
30: 7 David said to **A** the priest, Ahimelech's son, 54
30: 7 And **A** brought thither the ephod to David. 54
2Sa 8:17 and Ahimelech the son of **A**, *were* the priests; 54
15:24 **A** went up, until all the people had done 54
15:27 Ahimaaz thy son, and Jonathan the son of **A**. 54
15:29 **A** carried the ark of God again *to* Jerusalem: 54
15:35 not there with thee Zadok and **A** the priests? 54
15:35 thou shalt tell *it* to Zadok and **A** the priests. 54
17:15 said Hushai unto Zadok and to **A** the priests, 54
19:11 king David sent to Zadok and to **A** the priests, 54
20:25 *was* scribe: and Zadok and **A** *were* the priests: 54
1Ki 1: 7 Joab the son of Zeruiah, and with **A** the priest: 54
1:19 **A** the priest, and Joab the captain of the host: 54
1:25 and the captains of the host, and **A** the priest; 54
1:42 behold, Jonathan the son of **A** the priest came: 54
2:22 for **A** the priest, and for Joab the son of 54
2:26 unto **A** the priest said the king, Get thee *to* 54
2:27 So Solomon thrust out **A** from being priest 54
2:35 the priest did the king put in the room of **A**. 54
4: 4 the host: and Zadok and **A** *were* the priests: 54
1Ch 15:11 And David called for Zadok and **A** the priests, 54
18:16 and Abimelech the son of **A**, *were* the priests; 54
24: 6 Ahimelech the son of **A**, and *before* the chief 54
27:34 *was* Jehoiada the son of Benaiah, and **A**: 54
Mk 2:26 house of God in the days of **A** the high priest, *8*

ABIATHAR'S (1) [ABIATHAR]
2Sa 15:36 Zadok's *son,* and Jonathan **A** *son;* and 54+3807.1

ABIB (6)
Ex 13: 4 *This* day came ye out in the month **A**. 24
23:15 in the time appointed of the month **A**; 24
34:18 commanded thee, in the time of the month **A**: 24
34:18 for in the month **A** thou camest out from 24
Dt 16: 1 Observe the month of **A**, and keep 24
16: 1 for in the month of **A** the LORD thy God 24

ABIDA (1) [ABIDAH]
1Ch 1:33 and Epher, and Henoch, and **A**, and Eldaah. 28

ABIDAH (1) [ABIDA]
Ge 25: 4 and Epher, and Hanoch, and **A**, and Eldaah. 28

ABIDAN (5)
Nu 1:11 Of Benjamin; **A** the son of Gideoni. 27
2:22 the captain of the sons of Benjamin *shall be* **A** 27
7:60 On the ninth day **A** the son of Gideoni, 27
7:65 this *was* the offering of **A** the son of Gideoni. 27
10:24 of Benjamin *was* **A** the son of Gideoni. 27

ABIDE (81) [ABIDETH, ABIDING, ABODE, ABODEST]

Ge 19: 2 Nay; but we will a in the street **all night**. 3885
22: 5 his young men, A you here with the ass; 3427
24:55 Let the damsel a with us *a few* days, at 3427
29:19 should give her to another man: a with me. 3427
44:33 let thy servant a instead of the lad a 3427
Ex 16:29 a ye every man in his place, let no man go 3427
Lev 8:35 Therefore shall ye a *at* the door of 3427
19:13 not a with thee **all night** until the morning. 3885
Nu 22: 5 of the earth, and they a over against me: 3427
31:19 do ye a without the camp seven days: 2583
31:23 Every thing that may a the fire, 935+871.1
35:25 he shall a in it unto the death of the high 3427
Dt 3:19 shall a in your cities which I have given 3427
Jos 18: 5 Judah shall a in their coast on the south, 5975
18: 5 the house of Joseph shall a in their coasts 5975
Ru 2: 8 from hence, but a here **fast** by my maidens: 1692
1Sa 1:22 before the LORD, and there a for ever. 3427
5: 7 The ark of the God of Israel shall not a 3427
19: 2 and a in a secret place, and hide thyself: 3427
22: 5 Gad said unto David, A not in the hold; 3427
22:23 A thou with me, fear not: for he that 3427
30:21 whom they had **made** also **to** a at the brook 3427
2Sa 11:11 The ark, and Israel, and Judah, a in tents; 3427
15:19 return to thy place, and a with the king: 3427
16:18 choose, his will I be, and with him will I a. 3427
1Ki 8:13 a settled place for thee to a **in** for ever. 3427
2Ch 25:19 a now at home; why shouldest thou meddle 3427
32:10 ye trust, that ye a in the siege in Jerusalem? 3427
Job 24:13 the ways thereof, nor a in the paths thereof. 3427
38:40 *their* dens, *and* a in the covert to lie in wait? 3427
39: 9 be willing to serve thee, or a by thy crib? 3885
Ps 15: 1 LORD, who shall a in thy tabernacle? 1481
61: 4 I will a in thy tabernacle for ever: I will 1481
61: 7 He shall a before God for ever: O prepare 3427
91: 1 shall a under the shadow of the Almighty. 3885
Pr 7:11 and stubborn; her feet a not in her house: 7931
19:23 *he that hath it* shall a satisfied; he shall not 3885
Ecc 8:15 for that shall a **with** him of his labour 3867
Jer 10:10 the nations shall not be **able to** a his 3557
42:10 If ye will still a in this land, then will I 3427
49:18 saith the LORD, no man shall a there, 3427
49:33 there shall no man a there, nor *any* son of 3427
50:40 *so* shall no man a there, neither shall any 3427
Hos 3: 3 unto her, Thou shalt a for me many days; 3427
3: 4 For the children of Israel shall a many days 3427
11: 6 the sword shall a on his cities, and 2342
Joel 2:11 *is* great and very terrible; and who can a it? 3557
Mic 5: 4 of the LORD his God; and they shall a: 3427
Na 1: 6 who can a in the fierceness of his anger? 6965
Mal 3: 2 who *may* a the day of his coming? and 3557
Mt 10:11 in it is worthy; and there a till ye go thence. 3306
Mk 6:10 there a till ye depart from that place. 3306
Lk 9: 4 ye enter into, there a, and thence depart. 3306
19: 5 for to day I must a at thy house. 3306
24:29 they constrained him, saying, A with us: 3306
Jn 12:46 believeth on me should not a in darkness. 3306
14:16 that he may a with you for ever; 3306
15: 4 A in me, and I in you. As the branch cannot 3306
15: 4 bear fruit of itself, except it a in the vine; 3306
15: 4 no more can ye, except ye a in me. 3306
15: 6 If a man a not in me, he is cast forth as a 3306
15: 7 If ye a in me, and my words abide in you, 3306
15: 7 If ye abide in me, and my words a in you, 3306
15:10 my commandments, ye shall a in my love; 3306
15:10 Father's commandments, and a in his love. 3306
Ac 15:34 Notwithstanding it pleased Silas to a there *1961*
16:15 and a *there*. And she constrained us. 3306
20:23 saying that bonds and afflictions a me. 3306
27:31 to the soldiers, Except these a in the ship, 3306
1Co 3:14 If any *man's* work a which he hath built 3306
7: 8 It is good for them if they a even as I. 3306
7:20 Let every man a in the same calling 3306
7:24 wherein he is called, therein a with God. 3306
7:40 But she is happier if she so a, after my 3306
16: 6 And it may be that I will a, yea, and *3887*
Php 1:24 Nevertheless to a in the flesh *is* more *1961*
1:25 I know that I shall a and continue with you 3306
1Ti 1: 3 As I besought thee to a *still* at Ephesus, *4357*
1Jn 2:24 Let *that* therefore a in you, which ye have 3306
2:27 as it hath taught you, ye shall a in him. 3306
2:28 And now, little children, a in him; that, 3306

ABIDETH (30) [ABIDE]

Nu 31:23 all that a not the fire ye shall make go 935+871.1
2Sa 16: 3 unto the king, Behold, he a at Jerusalem: 3427
Job 39:28 She dwelleth and a on the rock, upon 3885
Ps 49:12 Nevertheless man *being* in honour a not: 3885
55:19 and afflict them, even he that a of old. 3427
119:90 thou hast established the earth, and it a. 5975
125: 1 *which* cannot be removed, *but* a for ever. 3427
Pr 15:31 The ear that heareth the reproof of life a 3885
Ecc 1: 4 generation cometh: but the earth a for ever. 5975
Jer 21: 9 He that a in this city shall die by the sword, 3427
Jn 3:36 not see life; but the wrath of God a on him. 3306
8:35 And the servant a not in the house for ever: 3306
8:35 in the house for ever: *but* the son a ever. 3306
12:24 fall into the ground and die, it a alone: 3306
12:34 We have heard out of the law that Christ a 3306
15: 5 He that a in me, and I in him, the same 3306
1Co 13:13 And now a faith, hope, charity, these three; 3306
2Ti 2:13 If we believe not, *yet* he a faithful: 3306
Heb 7: 3 unto the Son of God; a a priest continually. 3306
1Pe 1:23 word of God, which liveth and a for ever. 3306
1Jn 2: 6 He that saith *he* a in him ought himself also 3306
2:10 He that loveth his brother a in the light, and 3306
2:14 and the word of God a in you, and ye have 3306
2:17 but he that doeth the will of God a for ever. 3306
2:27 which ye have received of him a in you, 3306
3: 6 Whosoever a in him sinneth not: 3306
3:14 He that loveth not *his* brother a in death. 3306
3:24 And hereby we know that he a in us, by 3306
2Jn 1: 9 and a not in the doctrine of Christ, hath not 3306
1: 9 He that a in the doctrine of Christ, he hath 3306

ABIDING (9) [ABIDE]

Nu 24: 2 he saw Israel a *in his tents* according to 7931
Jdg 16: 9 lying in wait, a with her in the chamber. 3427
16:12 *there were* liers in wait a in the chamber. 3427
1Sa 26:19 for they have driven me out *this* day from a 5596
1Ch 29:15 earth *are* as a shadow, and *there is* none a. 4723
Lk 2: 8 **in** the same **country** shepherds a in the field, *63*
Jn 5:38 And ye have not his word a in you: 3306
Ac 16:12 and we were in that city a certain days. *1304*
1Jn 3:15 that no murderer hath eternal life a in him. 3306

ABIEL (3)

1Sa 9: 1 the son of A, the son of Zeror, the son of 22
14:51 and Ner the father of Abner *was* the son of A. 22
1Ch 11:32 of the brooks of Gaash, A the Arbathite, 22

ABIEZER, ABI-EZER (7) [ABI-EZRITE, ABI-EZRITES]

Jos 17: 2 for the children of A, and for the children of 44
Jdg 6:34 blew a trumpet; and A was gathered after him. 44
8: 2 of Ephraim better than the vintage of A? 44
2Sa 23:27 A the Anethothite, Mebunnai the Hushathite, 44
1Ch 7:18 bare Ishod, and A, and Mahalah. 44
11:28 son of Ikkesh the Tekoite, A the Antothite, 44
27:12 The ninth *captain* for the ninth month *was* A 44

ABI-EZRITE (1) [ABI-EZER]

Jdg 6:11 in Ophrah, that *pertained* unto Joash the A: 33

ABI-EZRITES (2) [ABI-EZER]

Jdg 6:24 unto this day it *is* yet in Ophrah of the A. 33
8:32 of Joash his father, in Ophrah of the A. 33

ABIGAIL (17)

1Sa 25: 3 man *was* Nabal; and the name of his wife A: 26
25:14 one of the young men told A, Nabal's wife, 26
25:18 A made haste, and took two hundred loaves, 26
25:23 when A saw David, she hasted, and 26
25:32 David said to A, Blessed *be* the LORD God 26
25:36 A came to Nabal; and behold, he held a feast 26
25:39 David sent and communed with A, to take her 26
25:40 when the servants of David were come to A to 26
25:42 And A hasted, and rose, and rode upon an ass, 26
27: 3 and A the Carmelitess, Nabal's wife. 26
30: 5 and A the wife of Nabal the Carmelite. 26
2Sa 2: 2 and A Nabal's wife the Carmelite. 26
3: 3 Chileab, of A the wife of Nabal the Carmelite; 26
17:25 that went in to A the daughter of Nahash, 26
1Ch 2:16 Whose sisters *were* Zeruiah, and A. And 26
2:17 A bare Amasa: and the father of Amasa *was* 26
3: 1 the second Daniel, of A the Carmelitess: 26

ABIHAIL (6)
Nu 3:35 families of Merari *was* Zuriel the son of **A**: 32
1Ch 2:29 And the name of the wife of Abishur *was* **A**, 32
5:14 These *are* the children of **A** the son of Huri, 32
2Ch 11:18 *and* **A** the daughter of Eliab the son of Jesse; 32
Est 2:15 the daughter of **A** the uncle of Mordecai, 32
9:29 the daughter of **A**, and Mordecai the Jew, 32

ABIHU (12)
Ex 6:23 bare him Nadab, and **A**, Eleazar, and Ithamar. 30
24: 1 and **A**, and seventy of the elders of Israel; 30
24: 9 and **A**, and seventy of the elders of Israel: 30
28: 1 Nadab and **A**, Eleazar and Ithamar, 30
Lev 10: 1 Nadab and **A**, the sons of Aaron, took either 30
Nu 3: 2 the firstborn, and **A**, Eleazar, and Ithamar. 30
3: 4 Nadab and **A** died before the LORD, 30
26:60 was born Nadab, and **A**, Eleazar, and Ithamar. 30
26:61 Nadab and **A** died, when they offered strange 30
1Ch 6: 3 Nadab, and **A**, Eleazar, and Ithamar. 30
24: 1 Nadab, and **A**, Eleazar, and Ithamar. 30
24: 2 But Nadab and **A** died before their father, and 30

ABIHUD (1)
1Ch 8: 3 sons of Bela were, Addar, and Gera, and **A**, 31

ABIJAH (20) [ABIJAM]
1Ki 14: 1 At that time **A** the son of Jeroboam fell sick. 29
1Ch 24:10 The seventh to Hakkoz, the eighth to **A**, 29
2Ch 11:20 which bare him **A**, and Attai, and Ziza, and 29
11:22 Rehoboam made **A** the son of Maachah 29
12:16 of David: and **A** his son reigned in his stead. 29
13: 1 king Jeroboam *began* **A** to reign over Judah. 29
13: 2 And there was war between **A** and Jeroboam. 29
13: 3 **A** set the battle in array with an army of 29
13: 4 **A** stood up upon mount Zemaraim, which *is* 29
13:15 and all Israel before **A** and Judah. 29
13:17 **A** and his people slew them *with* a great 29
13:19 **A** pursued after Jeroboam, and took cities 29
13:20 recover strength again in the days of **A**: 29
13:21 **A** waxed mighty, and married fourteen wives, 29
13:22 the rest of the acts of **A**, and his ways, and 29
14: 1 So **A** slept with his fathers, and they buried 29
29: 1 his mother's name *was* **A**, the daughter of 29
Ne 10: 7 Meshullam, **A**, Mijamin, 29
12: 4 Iddo, Ginnetho, **A**, 29
12:17 Of **A**, Zichri; of Miniamin, of Moadiah, Piltai; 29

ABIJAM (5) [ABIJAH]
1Ki 14:31 And **A** his son reigned in his stead. 38
15: 1 the son of Nebat reigned **A** over Judah. 38
15: 7 Now the rest of the acts of **A**, and all that he 38
15: 7 And there was war between **A** and Jeroboam. 38
15: 8 **A** slept with his fathers; and they buried him 38

ABILENE (1)
Lk 3: 1 of Trachonitis, and Lysanias the tetrarch of **A**, 9

ABILITY (7) [ABLE]
Lev 27: 8 according to his **a** that vowed shall 3027+5381
Ezr 2:69 They gave after their **a** unto the treasure of 3581
Ne 5: 8 We after our **a** have redeemed our brethren 1767
Da 1: 4 such as *had* **a** in them to stand in the king's 3581
Mt 25:15 to every man according to his several **a**; *1411*
Ac 11:29 the disciples, every man according to his **a**, *2141*
1Pe 4:11 *let him do it* as of the **a** which God giveth: *2479*

ABIMAEL (2)
Ge 10:28 And Obal, and **A**, and Sheba, 39
1Ch 1:22 And Ebal, and **A**, and Sheba, 39

ABIMELECH (65) [ABIMELECH'S]
Ge 20: 2 and **A** king of Gerar sent, and took Sarah. 40
20: 3 But God came to **A** in a dream by night, and 40
20: 4 **A** had not come near her: and he said, Lord, 40
20: 8 Therefore **A** rose early in the morning, and 40
20: 9 Then **A** called Abraham, and said unto him, 40
20:10 And **A** said unto Abraham, What sawest thou, 40
20:14 **A** took sheep, and oxen, and menservants, 40
20:15 And **A** said, Behold, my land *is* before thee: 40
20:17 God healed **A**, and his wife, and 40
20:18 closed up all the wombs of the house of **A**, 40
21:22 that **A** and Phichol the chief captain of his 40
21:25 Abraham reproved **A** because of a well of 40
21:26 **A** said, I wot not who hath done this thing: 40
21:27 took sheep and oxen, and gave *them* unto **A**; 40
21:29 **A** said unto Abraham, What *mean* these seven 40
21:32 **A** rose up, and Phichol the chief captain of his 40
26: 1 Isaac went unto **A** king of the Philistims unto 40
26: 8 that **A** king of the Philistims looked out at a 40
26: 9 **A** called Isaac, and said, Behold, of a surety 40
26:10 **A** said, What *is* this thou hast done unto us? 40
26:11 **A** charged all *his* people, saying, He that 40
26:16 **A** said unto Isaac, Go from us; for thou art 40
26:26 **A** went to him from Gerar, and Ahuzzath *one* 40
Jdg 8:31 also bare him a son, whose name he called **A**. 40
9: 1 **A** the son of Jerubbaal went to Shechem unto 40
9: 3 their hearts inclined to follow **A**; for they said, 40
9: 4 wherewith **A** hired vain and light persons, 40
9: 6 house of Millo, and went, and made **A** king, 40
9:16 in that ye have made **A** king, and if ye have 40
9:18 upon one stone, and have made **A**, 40
9:19 *then* rejoice ye in **A**, and let him also rejoice 40
9:20 let fire come out from **A**, and devour the men 40
9:20 and from the house of Millo, and devour **A**. 40
9:21 and dwelt there, for fear of **A** his brother. 40
9:22 When **A** had reigned three years over Israel, 40
9:23 God sent an evil spirit between **A** and the men 40
9:23 men of Shechem dealt treacherously with **A**: 40
9:24 and their blood be laid upon **A** their brother, 40
9:25 along *that* way by them: and it was told **A**. 40
9:27 their god, and did eat and drink, and cursed **A**. 40
9:28 Who *is* **A**, and who *is* Shechem, that we 40
9:29 were under my hand; then would I remove **A**. 40
9:29 he said to **A**, Increase thine army, and 40
9:31 he sent messengers unto **A** privily, saying, 40
9:34 **A** rose up, and all the people that *were* with 40
9:35 **A** rose up, and the people that *were* with him, 40
9:38 thy mouth, wherewith thou saidst, Who *is* **A**, 40
9:39 the men of Shechem, and fought with **A**. 40
9:40 **A** chased him, and he fled before him, and 40
9:41 **A** dwelt at Arumah: and Zebul thrust out Gaal 40
9:42 went out *into* the field; and they told **A**. 40
9:44 And **A**, and the company that *was* with him, 40
9:45 And **A** fought against the city all that day; and 40
9:47 it was told **A**, that all the men of the tower of 40
9:48 And **A** gat him up *to* mount Zalmon, he and 40
9:48 **A** took an axe in his hand, and cut down a 40
9:49 and followed **A**, and put *them* to the hold, and 40
9:50 went **A** to Thebez, and encamped against 40
9:52 **A** came unto the tower, and fought against it, 40
9:55 when the men of Israel saw that **A** was dead, 40
9:56 Thus God rendered the wickedness of **A**, 40
10: 1 after **A** there arose to defend Israel Tola 40
2Sa 11:21 Who smote **A** the son of Jerubbesheth? did 40
1Ch 18:16 and **A** the son of Abiathar, *were* the priests; 40
Ps 34: T when he changed his behaviour before **A**; 40

ABIMELECH'S (2) [ABIMELECH]
Ge 21:25 which **A** servants had violently taken away. 40
Jdg 9:53 cast a piece of a millstone upon **A** head, 40

ABINADAB (13)
1Sa 7: 1 and brought it into the house of **A** in the hill, 41
16: 8 Jesse called **A**, and made him pass before 41
17:13 and next unto him **A**, and the third Shammah. 41
31: 2 and **A**, and Malchishua, Saul's sons. 41
2Sa 6: 3 brought it out of the house of **A** that *was* in 41
6: 3 Uzzah and Ahio, the sons of **A**, drave the new 41
6: 4 they brought it out of the house of **A** which 41
1Ki 4:11 The son of **A**, *in* all the region of Dor; 41
1Ch 2:13 and **A** the second, and Shimma the third, 41
8:33 and Malchishua, and **A**, and Eshbaal. 41
9:39 and Malchishua, and **A**, and Eshbaal. 41
10: 2 and **A**, and Malchishua, the sons of Saul. 41
13: 7 of God in a new cart out of the house of **A**: 41

ABINOAM (4)
Jdg 4: 6 called Barak the son of **A** out of 42
4:12 they shewed Sisera that Barak the son of **A** 42
5: 1 and Barak the son of **A** on that day, 42
5:12 and lead thy captivity captive, thou son of **A**. 42

ABIRAM (11)
Nu 16: 1 the son of Levi, and Dathan and **A**, the sons 48
16:12 Moses sent to call Dathan and **A**, the sons of 48
16:24 about the tabernacle of Korah, Dathan, and **A**. 48
16:25 Moses rose up and went unto Dathan and **A**; 48
16:27 of Korah, Dathan, and **A**, on every side: 48
16:27 Dathan and **A** came out, and stood *in* the door 48

Nu 26: 9 sons of Eliab; Nemuel, and Dathan, and **A**. 48
26: 9 This *is that* Dathan and **A**, *which were* famous 48
Dt 11: 6 what he did unto Dathan and **A**, the sons of 48
1Ki 16:34 he laid the foundation thereof in **A** his 48
Ps 106:17 up Dathan, and covered the company of **A**. 48

ABISHAG (5)
1Ki 1: 3 found **A** a Shunammite, and brought her to 49
1:15 **A** the Shunammite ministered unto the king. 49
2:17 that he give me **A** the Shunammite to wife. 49
2:21 Let **A** the Shunammite be given to Adonijah 49
2:22 why dost thou ask **A** the Shunammite for 49

ABISHAI (25)
1Sa 26: 6 and to **A** the son of Zeruiah, brother to Joab, 52
26: 6 And **A** said, I will go down with thee. 52
26: 7 So David and **A** came to the people by night: 52
26: 8 said **A** to David, God hath delivered thine 52
26: 9 David said to **A**, Destroy him not: for who 52
2Sa 2:18 of Zeruiah there, Joab, and **A**, and Asahel: 52
2:24 Joab also and **A** pursued after Abner: and 52
3:30 So Joab and **A** his brother slew Abner, 52
10:10 he delivered into the hand of **A** his brother, 52
10:14 *then* fled they *also* before **A**, and entered *into* 52
16: 9 Then said **A** the son of Zeruiah unto the king, 52
16:11 And David said to **A**, and to all his servants, 52
18: 2 a third part under the hand of **A** the son of 52
18: 5 the king commanded Joab and **A** and Ittai, 52
18:12 hearing the king charged thee and **A** and Ittai, 52
19:21 But **A** the son of Zeruiah answered and said, 52
20: 6 David said to **A**, Now shall Sheba the son of 52
20:10 **A** his brother pursued after Sheba the son of 52
21:17 But **A** the son of Zeruiah succoured him, and 52
23:18 **A**, the brother of Joab, the son of Zeruiah, 52
1Ch 2:16 of Zeruiah; **A**, and Joab, and Asahel, three. 52
11:20 **A** the brother of Joab, he was chief of 52
18:12 Moreover **A** the son of Zeruiah slew of 52
19:11 he delivered unto the hand of **A** his brother, 52
19:15 they likewise fled before **A** his brother, and 52

ABISHALOM (2)
1Ki 15: 2 name *was* Maachah, the daughter of **A**. 53
15:10 name *was* Maachah, the daughter of **A**. 53

ABISHUA (5)
1Ch 6: 4 Eleazar begat Phinehas, Phinehas begat **A**, 50
6: 5 And **A** begat Bukki, and Bukki begat Uzzi, 50
6:50 Eleazar his son, Phinehas his son, **A** his son, 50
8: 4 And **A**, and Naaman, and Ahoah, 50
Ezr 7: 5 The son of **A**, the son of Phinehas, the son of 50

ABISHUR (2)
1Ch 2:28 And the sons of Shammai; Nadab, and **A**. 51
2:29 And the name of the wife of **A** *was* Abihail, 51

ABITAL (2)
2Sa 3: 4 and the fifth, Shephatiah the son of **A**; 37
1Ch 3: 3 The fifth, Shephatiah of **A**: the sixth, 37

ABITUB (1)
1Ch 8:11 And of Hushim he begat **A**, and Elpaal. 36

ABIUD (2)
Mt 1:13 And Zorobabel begat **A**; and Abiud begat *10*
1:13 and **A** begat Eliakim; and Eliakim begat Azor; *10*

ABJECTS (1)
Ps 35:15 *yea,* the **a** gathered themselves together 5222

ABLE (160) [ABILITY]
Ge 13: 6 the land was not **a to bear** them, that they 5375
15: 5 tell the stars, if thou be **a** to number them: 3201
33:14 and the children be **a to endure**, 7272+3807.1
Ex 10: 5 that *one* cannot be **a** to see the earth: 3201
18:18 thou art not **a** to perform it thyself alone. 3201
18:21 shalt provide out of all the people **a** men, 2428
18:23 *so,* then thou shalt be **a** to endure, 3201
18:25 Moses chose **a** men out of all Israel, and 2428
40:35 Moses was not **a** to enter into the tent of 3201
Lev 5: 7 if he be not **a to bring** a lamb, then he shall 1767
5:11 if he be not **a to bring** two 3027+5381
12: 8 if she be not **a to bring** a 1767+3027+4672
14:22 such as he is **a to get**; 3027+5381
14:31 *Even* such as he is **a to get**, the one 3027+5381
14:32 whose **hand is** not **a to get** *that* 3027+5381
25:26 be **a** to redeem it; 1767+3027+5381+3509.1
25:28 if he be not **a** to restore *it* to 1767+3027+4672
25:49 or if he be **a**, he may redeem himself. 3027+5381
Nu 1: 3 all that *are a to* go forth *to* war in Israel: NIH
1:20 upward, all that *were a to* go forth *to* war; NIH
1:22 upward, all that *were a to* go forth *to* war; NIH
1:24 upward, all that *were a to* go forth *to* war; NIH
1:26 upward, all that *were a to* go forth *to* war; NIH
1:28 upward, all that *were a to* go forth *to* war; NIH
1:30 upward, all that *were a to* go forth *to* war; NIH
1:32 upward, all that *were a to* go forth *to* war; NIH
1:34 upward, all that *were a to* go forth *to* war; NIH
1:36 upward, all that *were a to* go forth *to* war; NIH
1:38 upward, all that *were a to* go forth *to* war; NIH
1:40 upward, all that *were a to* go forth *to* war; NIH
1:42 upward, all that *were a to* go forth *to* war; NIH
1:45 all that *were a to* go forth *to* war in Israel; NIH
11:14 I am not **a** to bear all this people alone, 3201
13:30 for we are **well a to overcome** it. 3201+3201
13:31 We be not **a** to go up against the people; 3201
14:16 Because the LORD was not **a** to bring this 3201
22:11 peradventure I shall be **a** to overcome 3201
22:37 am I not **a** indeed to promote thee to 3201
26: 2 all that *are a to* go *to* war in Israel. NIH
Dt 1: 9 I am not **a** to bear you myself alone: 3201
7:24 there shall no man *be a to* stand before thee, NIH
9:28 Because the LORD was not **a** to bring 3201
11:25 There shall no man *be a to* stand before NIH
14:24 for thee, so that thou art not **a** to carry it; 3201
16:17 Every man *shall give* as he is **a**, 3027+4979
Jos 1: 5 There shall not any man *be a to* stand before NIH
14:12 I shall *be a to* drive them out, as the LORD NIH
23: 9 no man hath *been a to* stand before you unto NIH
Jdg 8: 3 what was I **a** to do in comparison of you? 3201
1Sa 6:20 Who is **a** to stand before this holy LORD 3201
17: 9 If he be **a** to fight with me, and to kill me, 3201
17:33 Thou art not **a** to go against this Philistine 3201
1Ki 3: 9 for who is **a** to judge this thy *so* great a 3201
9:21 whom the children of Israel also were not **a** 3201
2Ki 3:21 they gathered all that *were a to* put on NIH
18:23 if thou be **a** on thy part to set riders upon 3201
18:29 for he shall not be **a** to deliver you out of 3201
1Ch 5:18 men *a to* bear buckler and sword, and NIH
9:13 **very a** men *for* the work of the service of 2428
26: 8 **a** men for strength for the service, 2428
29:14 that we should be **a** to offer *so* 3581
2Ch 2: 6 who is **a** to build him a house, 3581+6113
7: 7 was not **a** to receive the burnt offerings, 3201
20: 6 so that none **is a to withstand** thee? 3320+5973
20:37 that they were not **a** to go to Tarshish. 6113
25: 5 thousand choice *men, a to* go forth *to* war, NIH
25: 9 The LORD **is a** to give thee much more 3426
32:13 **any ways a** to deliver their lands out 3201+3201
32:14 that your God should be **a** to deliver you 3201
32:15 kingdom was **a** to deliver his people out of 3201
Ezr 10:13 and *we are* not **a** to stand without, 3581
Ne 4:10 so that we are not **a** to build the wall. 3201
Job 41:10 him up: who then is **a** to stand before me? NIH
Ps 18:38 I have wounded them that they were not **a** 3201
21:11 *which* they are not **a** *to perform.* 3201
36:12 are cast down, and shall not be **a** to rise. 3201
40:12 that I am not **a** to look *up;* they are moe 3201
Pr 27: 4 but who is **a to stand** before envy? 5975
Ecc 8:17 to know *it,* yet shall he not be **a** to find *it.* 3201
Isa 36: 8 if thou be **a** on thy part to set riders upon 3201
36:14 for he shall not be **a** to deliver you. 3201
47:11 upon thee; thou shalt not be **a** to put it off: 3201
47:12 if so be thou shalt be **a** to profit, if so 3201
Jer 10:10 the nations shall not be **a to abide** his 3557
11:11 which they shall not be **a** to escape; 3201
49:10 and he shall not be **a** to hide himself: 3201
La 1:14 *from whom* I am not **a** to rise up. 3201
Eze 7:19 their gold shall not be **a** to deliver them in 3201
33:12 neither shall the righteous be **a** to live for 3201
46: 5 for the lambs **as** he shall be **a** to give, 3027
46:11 to the lambs **as** he is **a** to give, and a hin of 3027
Da 2:26 Art thou **a** to make known unto me 3546
3:17 our God whom we serve *is* **a** to deliver us 3202
4:18 **a** to make known unto me 3202
4:18 thou *art* **a**; for the spirit of the holy gods *is* 3546
4:37 those that walk in pride he *is* **a** to abase. 3202
6:20 **a** to deliver thee from the lions? 3202
Am 7:10 the land is not **a** to bear all his words. 3201
Zep 1:18 Neither their silver nor their gold shall be **a** 3201

A

Mt	3: 9	that God is a of these stones to raise up	1410
	9:28	Believe ye that I am a to do this?	1410
	10:28	kill the body, but are not a to kill the soul:	1410
	10:28	rather fear him which is a to destroy both	1410
	19:12	He that is a to receive *it,* let him receive *it.*	1410
	20:22	Are ye a to drink *of* the cup that I shall	1410
	20:22	*with?* They say unto him, We are a.	1410
	22:46	And no *man* was a to answer him a word,	1410
	26:61	I am a to destroy the temple of God, and	1410
Mk	4:33	word unto them, as they were a to hear *it.*	1410
Lk	1:20	thou shalt be dumb, and not a to speak,	1410
	3: 8	That God is a of these stones to raise up	1410
	12:26	then be not a *to do that thing which is* least,	1410
	13:24	will seek to enter in, and shall not be a.	2480
	14:29	is not a to finish *it,* all that behold *it* begin	2480
	14:30	man began to build, and was not a to finish.	2480
	14:31	consulteth whether he be a with ten	1415
	21:15	which all your adversaries shall not be a to	1410
Jn	10:29	no *man* is a to pluck *them* out of my	1410
	21: 6	now they were not a to draw it for	2480
Ac	6:10	And they were not a to resist the wisdom	2480
	15:10	which neither our fathers nor we were a to	2480
	20:32	which is a to build *you* up, and to give you	1410
	25: 5	said he, which among you are a, go down	1415
Ro	4:21	he had promised, he was a also to perform.	1415
	8:39	shall be a to separate us from the love of	1410
	11:23	for God is a to graff them in again.	1415
	14: 4	holden up: for God is a to make him stand.	1415
	15:14	a also to admonish one another.	1410
1Co	3: 2	for hitherto ye were not a *to bear it,* neither	1410
	3: 2	not able *to bear it,* neither yet now are ye a.	1410
	6: 5	not one that shall be a to judge between his	1410
	10:13	you to be tempted above that you are a;	1410
	10:13	way to escape, that ye may be a to bear *it.*	1410
2Co	1: 4	that we may be a to comfort them which	1410
	3: 6	Who also hath made us a ministers of	2427
	9: 8	And God *is* a to make all grace abound	1415
Eph	3:18	May be a to comprehend with all saints	1840
	3:20	Now unto him that is a to do exceeding	1410
	6:11	that ye may be a to stand against the wiles	1410
	6:13	that ye may be a to withstand in the evil	1410
	6:16	wherewith ye shall be a to quench all	1410
Php	3:21	according to the working whereby he is a	1410
2Ti	1:12	I am persuaded that he is a to keep that	1415
	2: 2	who shall be a to teach others also.	2425
	3: 7	never a to come to the knowledge of	1410
	3:15	which are a to make thee wise unto	1410
Tit	1: 9	that he may be a by sound doctrine both to	1415
Heb	2:18	he is a to succour them that are tempted.	1410
	5: 7	tears unto him that was a to save him from	1410
	7:25	Wherefore he is a also to save them to	1410
	11:19	Accounting that God *was* a to raise *him* up,	1415
Jas	1:21	which is a to save your souls.	1410
	3: 2	*and* a also to bridle the whole body.	1415
	4:12	who is a to save and to destroy:	1410
2Pe	1:15	a after my decease to have these *things*	4160
Jude	1:24	Now unto him that is a to keep you from	1410
Rev	5: 3	under the earth, was a to open the book,	1410
	6:17	wrath is come; and who shall be a to stand?	1410
	13: 4	the beast? who is a to make war with him?	1410
	15: 8	and no *man* was a to enter into the temple,	1410

ABNER (62) [ABNER'S]

1Sa	14:50	and the name of the captain of his host *was* A,	74
	14:51	and Ner the father of A *was* the son of Abiel.	74
	17:55	he said unto A, the captain of the host, Abner,	74
	17:55	he said unto Abner, the captain of the host, A,	74
	17:55	A said, *As* thy soul liveth, O king, I cannot	74
	17:57	A took him, and brought him before Saul with	74
	20:25	A sat by Saul's side, and David's place was	74
	26: 5	and A the son of Ner, the captain of his host:	74
	26: 7	but A and the people lay round about him.	74
	26:14	to A the son of Ner, saying, Answerest thou	74
	26:14	son of Ner, saying, Answerest thou not, A?	74
	26:14	A answered and said, Who *art* thou *that* criest	74
	26:15	David said to A, *Art* not thou a *valiant* man?	74
2Sa	2: 8	But A the son of Ner, captain of Saul's host,	74
	2:12	A the son of Ner, and the servants of	74
	2:14	A said to Joab, Let the young men now arise,	74
	2:17	A was beaten, and the men of Israel, before	74
	2:19	Asahel pursued after A; and in going he	74
	2:19	right hand nor to the left from following A.	74
	2:20	A looked behind him, and said, *Art* thou	74
	2:21	A said to him, Turn thee aside to thy right	74
	2:22	A said again to Asahel, Turn thee aside from	74
	2:23	wherefore A with the hinder end of the spear	74
	2:24	Joab also and Abishai pursued after A: and	74
	2:25	gathered themselves together after A,	74
	2:26	A called to Joab, and said, Shall the sword	74
	2:29	A and his men walked all that night through	74
	2:30	Joab returned from following A: and when he	74
	3: 6	that A made himself strong for the house of	74
	3: 7	*Ish-bosheth* said to A, Wherefore hast thou	74
	3: 8	was A very wroth for the words of	74
	3: 9	So do God to A, and more also, except, as	74
	3:11	he could not answer A a word again, because	74
	3:12	A sent messengers to David on his behalf,	74
	3:16	said A unto him, Go, return. And he returned.	74
	3:17	A had communication with the elders of	74
	3:19	A also spake in the ears of Benjamin: and	74
	3:19	A went also to speak in the ears of David in	74
	3:20	So A came to David *to* Hebron, and	74
	3:20	David made A and the men that *were* with	74
	3:21	A said unto David, I will arise and go, and	74
	3:21	David sent A away; and he went in peace.	74
	3:22	A *was* not with David in Hebron; for he had	74
	3:23	A the son of Ner came to the king, and	74
	3:24	behold, A came unto thee; why *is* it *that* thou	74
	3:25	Thou knowest A the son of Ner, that he came	74
	3:26	out from David, he sent messengers after A,	74
	3:27	when A was returned *to* Hebron, Joab took	74
	3:28	for ever from the blood of A the son of Ner:	74
	3:30	So Joab and Abishai his brother slew A,	74
	3:31	gird you with sackcloth, and mourn before A.	74
	3:32	they buried A in Hebron: and the king lift up	74
	3:32	lift up his voice, and wept at the grave of A;	74
	3:33	the king lamented over A, and said, Died	74
	3:33	over Abner, and said, Died A as a fool dieth?	74
	3:37	it was not of the king to slay A the son of Ner.	74
	4: 1	when Saul's son heard that A was dead in	74
	4:12	and buried *it* in the sepulchre of A in Hebron.	74
1Ki	2: 5	unto A the son of Ner, and unto Amasa	74
	2:32	not knowing *thereof, to wit,* A the son of Ner,	74
1Ch	26:28	A the son of Ner, and Joab the son of Zeruiah,	74
	27:21	of Benjamin, Jaasiel the son of A:	74

ABNER'S (1) [ABNER]

2Sa	2:31	of A men, *so that* three hundred and	74

ABOARD (1)

Ac	21: 2	unto Phenicia, we went a, and set forth.	1910

ABODE (69) [ABIDE]

Ge	29:14	And he a with him the space of a month.	3427
	49:24	his bow a in strength, and the arms of his	3427
Ex	24:16	the glory of the LORD a upon mount	7931
	40:35	because the cloud a thereon, and the glory	7931
Nu	9:17	in the place where the cloud a, there	7931
	9:18	as long as the cloud a upon the tabernacle	7931
	9:20	of the LORD they a in their tents,	2583
	9:21	when the cloud a from even unto	1961
	9:22	the children of Israel a in their tents, and	2583
	11:35	*unto* Hazeroth; and a at Hazeroth.	1961
	20: 1	the people a in Kadesh; and Miriam died	3427
	22: 8	and the princes of Moab a with Balaam.	3427
	25: 1	Israel a in Shittim, and the people begun to	3427
Dt	1:46	So ye a in Kadesh many days,	3427
	1:46	according unto the days that ye a *there.*	3427
	3:29	So we a in the valley over against	3427
	9: 9	I a in the mount forty days and forty nights,	3427
Jos	2:22	unto the mountain, and a there three days,	3427
	5: 8	that they a in their places in the camp,	3427
	8: 9	a between Beth-el and Ai, on the west side	3427
Jdg	5:17	Gilead a beyond Jordan: and why did Dan	7931
	5:17	on the sea shore, and a in his breaches.	7931
	11:17	would not consent: and Israel a in Kadesh.	3427
	19: 4	retained him; and he a with him three days:	3427
	20:47	and a in the rock Rimmon four months.	3427
	21: 2	a there till even before God, and lift up	3427
1Sa	1:23	So the woman a, and gave her son suck	3427
	7: 2	to pass, while the ark a in Kirjath-jearim,	3427
	13:16	with them, a in Gibeah of Benjamin:	3427
	22: 6	(now Saul a in Gibeah under a tree in	3427
	23:14	David a in the wilderness in strong holds,	3427
	23:18	David a in the wood, and Jonathan went to	3427
	23:25	a rock, and a in the wilderness of Maon.	3427
	25:13	and two hundred a by the stuff.	3427
	26: 3	David a in the wilderness, and he saw that	3427

1Sa 30:10 for two hundred a *behind,* which were so 5975
2Sa 1: 1 and David had a two days in Ziklag; 3427
11:12 So Uriah a in Jerusalem that day, and 3427
15: 8 For thy servant vowed a vow while I a at 3427
1Ki 17:19 where he a, and laid him upon his own bed. 3427
2Ki 19:27 I know thy a, and thy going out, and 3427
Ezr 8:15 and there a we in tents three days: 2583
8:32 came *to* Jerusalem, and a there three days. 3427
Isa 37:28 I know thy a, and thy going out, and thy 3427
Jer 38:28 So Jeremiah a in the court of the prison 3427
Mt 17:22 And while they a in Galilee, Jesus said unto *390*
Lk 1:56 And Mary a with her about three months, *3306*
8:27 neither a in *any* house, but in the tombs. *3306*
21:37 a in the mount that is called *the mount* of *835*
Jn 1:32 from heaven like a dove, and it a upon him. *3306*
1:39 where he dwelt, and a with him that day: *3306*
4:40 tarry with them: and he a there two days. *3306*
7: 9 these *words* unto them, he a *still* in Galilee. *3306*
8:44 and a not in the truth, because there is no *2476*
10:40 John at first baptized; and there he a. *3306*
11: 6 he a two days *still* in the *same* place where *3306*
14:23 come unto him, and make *our* a with him. *3438*
Ac 1:13 where a both Peter, and James, and John, *2650*
12:19 down from Judea to Cesarea, and *there* a. *1304*
14: 3 a they speaking boldly in the Lord, *1304*
14:28 And there they a long time with *1304*
17:14 but Silas and Timotheus a there still. *5278*
18: 3 same craft, he a with them, and wrought: *3306*
20: 3 And *there* a three months: and when *4160*
20: 6 Troas in five days; where we a seven days. *1304*
21: 7 the brethren, and a with them one day. *3306*
21: 8 was *one* of the seven; and a with him. *3306*
Gal 1:18 to see Peter, and a with him fifteen days. *1961*
2Ti 4:20 Erastus a at Corinth: but Trophimus have I *3306*

ABODEST (1) [ABIDE]
Jdg 5:16 Why a thou among the sheepfolds, to hear 3427

ABOLISH (1) [ABOLISHED]
Isa 2:18 And the idols he shall utterly a. 2498

ABOLISHED (5) [ABOLISH]
Isa 51: 6 and my righteousness shall not be a. 2865
Eze 6: 6 be cut down, and your works may be a. 4229
2Co 3:13 stedfastly look to the end of that which is a: *2673*
Eph 2:15 Having a in his flesh the enmity, *even* *2673*
2Ti 1:10 who hath a death, and hath brought life and *2673*

ABOMINABLE (23) [ABOMINATION]
Lev 7:21 or any a unclean *thing,* and eat of the flesh 8263
11:43 Ye shall not make yourselves a with any 8262
18:30 that *ye* commit not *any one* of *these* a 8441
19: 7 if it be eaten at all on the third day, it *is* a; 6292
20:25 ye shall not make your souls a by beast, 8262
Dt 14: 3 Thou shalt not eat any a *thing.* 8441
1Ch 21: 6 for the king's word was a to Joab. 8581
2Ch 15: 8 put away the a idols out of all the land of 8251
Job 15:16 How much more a and filthy *is* man, 8581
Ps 14: 1 They are corrupt, they have done a works, 8581
53: 1 Corrupt are they, and have done a iniquity: 8581
Isa 14:19 thou art cast out of thy grave like an a 8581
65: 4 and broth of a *things is in* their vessels; 6292
Jer 16:18 carcases of their detestable and a things. 8441
44: 4 Oh, do not this a thing that I hate. 8441
Eze 4:14 neither came there a flesh into my mouth. 6292
8:10 a beasts, and all the idols of the house of 8263
16:52 that thou hast committed more a than they: 8581
Mic 6:10 the wicked, and the scant measure *that is* a? 2194
Na 3: 6 I will cast a filth upon thee, and make thee 8251
Tit 1:16 but in works they deny *him,* being a, and *947*
1Pe 4: 3 revellings, banquetings, and a idolatries: *111*
Rev 21: 8 and the a, and murderers, and *948*

ABOMINABLY (1) [ABOMINATION]
1Ki 21:26 he did very a in following idols, 8581

ABOMINATION (76) [ABOMINABLE, ABOMINABLY, ABOMINATIONS]
Ge 43:32 for that *is* an a unto the Egyptians. 8441
46:34 for every shepherd *is* an a unto 8441
Ex 8:26 for we shall sacrifice the a of the Egyptians 8441
8:26 shall we sacrifice the a of the Egyptians 8441
Lev 7:18 it shall be an a, and the soul that eateth of it 6292
11:10 *is* in the waters, they *shall be* an a unto you: 8263
11:11 They shall be even an a unto you: ye shall 8263
11:11 but you shall have their carcases in a. 8262
11:12 in the waters, that *shall be* an a unto you. 8263
11:13 these *are they which* ye shall have in a 8262
11:13 they shall not be eaten, they *are* an a: 8263
11:20 going upon *all* four, *shall be* an a unto you. 8263
11:23 have four feet, *shall be* an a unto you. 8263
11:41 that creepeth upon the earth *shall be* an a; 8263
11:42 them ye shall not eat; for they *are* an a. 8263
18:22 with mankind, as with womankind: it *is* a. 8441
20:13 both of them have committed an a: 8441
Dt 7:25 for it *is* an a to the LORD thy God. 8441
7:26 Neither shalt thou bring an a into thine 8441
12:31 for every a to the LORD, which he hateth, 8441
13:14 *that* such a is wrought among you; 8441
17: 1 for that *is* an a unto the LORD thy God. 8441
17: 4 *that* such a is wrought in Israel: 8441
18:12 For all that do these *things are* an a unto 8441
22: 5 that do so *are* a unto the LORD thy God. 8441
23:18 for even both these *are* a unto the LORD 8441
24: 4 is defiled; for that *is* a before the LORD: 8441
25:16 *are* an a unto the LORD thy God. 8441
27:15 or molten image, an a unto the LORD, 8441
1Sa 13: 4 *that* Israel also was had in a with 887
1Ki 11: 5 and after Milcom the a of the Ammonites. 8251
11: 7 the a of Moab, in the hill that *is* before 8251
11: 7 the a of the children of Ammon. 8251
2Ki 23:13 for Ashtoreth the a of the Zidonians, 8251
23:13 and for Chemosh the a of the Moabites, and 8251
23:13 for Milcom the a of the children of 8441
Ps 88: 8 thou hast made me an a unto them: 8441
Pr 3:32 For the froward *is* a to the LORD: but 8441
6:16 LORD hate: yea, seven *are* an a unto him: 8441
8: 7 and wickedness *is* an a to my lips. 8441
11: 1 A false balance *is* a to the LORD: but 8441
11:20 *They that are* of a froward heart *are* a unto 8441
12:22 Lying lips *are* a to the LORD: but 8441
13:19 but *it is* a to fools to depart from evil. 8441
15: 8 The sacrifice of the wicked *is* an a to 8441
15: 9 The way of the wicked *is* an a unto 8441
15:26 The thoughts of the wicked *are* an a to 8441
16: 5 Every one *that is* proud in heart *is* an a to 8441
16:12 *It is* an a to kings to commit wickedness: 8441
17:15 even they both *are* a to the LORD. 8441
20:10 both of them *are* alike a to the LORD. 8441
20:23 Divers weights *are* an a unto the LORD; 8441
21:27 The sacrifice of the wicked *is* a: how much 8441
24: 9 *is* sin: and the scorner *is* an a to men. 8441
28: 9 hearing the law, even his prayer *shall be* a. 8441
29:27 An unjust man is an a to the just: and 8441
29:27 *he that is* upright in the way *is* a to 8441
Isa 1:13 incense *is* an a unto me; the new moons 8441
41:24 of nought: an a *is he that* chooseth you. 8441
44:19 and shall I make the residue thereof an a? 8441
66:17 swine's flesh, and the a, and the mouse, 8263
Jer 2: 7 my land, and made mine heritage an a. 8441
6:15 they ashamed when they had committed a? 8441
8:12 they ashamed when they had committed a? 8441
32:35 that *they* should do this a, to cause Judah to 8441
Eze 16:50 were haughty, and committed a before me: 8441
18:12 up his eyes to the idols, hath committed a, 8441
22:11 one hath committed a with his neighbour's 8441
33:26 ye work a, and ye defile every one his 8441
Da 11:31 they shall place the a that maketh desolate. 8251
12:11 the a that maketh desolate set up, 8251
Mal 2:11 an a is committed in Israel and 8441
Mt 24:15 therefore shall see the a of desolation, *946*
Mk 13:14 But when ye shall see the a of desolation, *946*
Lk 16:15 amongst men is a in the sight of God. *946*
Rev 21:27 neither *whatsoever* worketh a, or *maketh* a *946*

ABOMINATIONS (76) [ABOMINATION]
Lev 18:26 and shall not commit any of these a; 8441
18:27 (For all these a have the men of the land 8441
18:29 For whosoever shall commit any of these a, 8441
Dt 18: 9 thou shalt not learn to do after the a of 8441
18:12 of these a the LORD thy God doth drive 8441
20:18 they teach you not to do after all their a, 8441
29:17 ye have seen their a, and their idols, wood 8251
32:16 *gods,* with a provoked they him to anger. 8441
1Ki 14:24 they did according to all the a of 8441
2Ki 16: 3 the fire, according to the a of the heathen, 8441
21: 2 after the a of the heathen, whom 8441
21:11 Manasseh king of Judah hath done these a, 8441

2Ki 23:24 all the **a** that were spied in the land of 8251
2Ch 28: 3 burnt his children in the fire after the **a** of 8441
33: 2 the LORD, like unto the **a** of the heathen, 8441
34:33 Josiah took away all the **a** out of all 8441
36: 8 his **a** which he did, and that which was 8441
36:14 transgressed very much after all the **a** of 8441
Ezr 9: 1 *doing* according to their **a**, *even* of 8441
9:11 of the people of the lands, with their **a**, 8441
9:14 join in affinity with the people of these **a**? 8441
Pr 26:25 him not: for *there are* seven **a** in his heart. 8441
Isa 66: 3 and their soul delighteth in their **a**. 8251
Jer 4: 1 if thou wilt put away thine **a** out of my 8251
7:10 say, We are delivered to do all these **a**? 8441
7:30 they have set their **a** in the house which is 8251
13:27 *and* thine **a** on the hills in the fields. 8251
32:34 they set their **a** in the house, which is called 8251
44:22 because of the **a** which ye have committed; 8441
Eze 5: 9 do any more the like, because of all thine **a**. 8441
5:11 with all thine **a**, therefore will I also 8441
6: 9 which they have committed in all their **a**. 8441
6:11 Alas for all the evil **a** of the house of Israel: 8441
7: 3 and will recompense upon thee all thine **a**. 8441
7: 4 and thine **a** shall be in the midst of thee: 8441
7: 8 and will recompense thee for all thine **a**. 8441
7: 9 and thine **a** *that* are in the midst of thee; 8441
7:20 they made the images of their **a** *and* of their 8441
8: 6 *even* the great **a** that the house of Israel 8441
8: 6 thee yet again, *and* thou shalt see greater **a**. 8441
8: 9 and behold the wicked **a** that they do here. 8441
8:13 *and* thou shalt see greater **a** that they do. 8441
8:15 *and* thou shalt see greater **a** than these. 8441
8:17 commit the **a** which they commit here? 8441
9: 4 that cry for all the **a** that be done in 8441
11:18 and all the **a** thereof from thence. 8441
11:21 heart of their detestable things and their **a**, 8441
12:16 that they may declare all their **a** among 8441
14: 6 and turn away your faces from all your **a**. 8441
16: 2 of man, cause Jerusalem to know her **a**, 8441
16:22 in all thine **a** and thy whoredoms thou hast 8441
16:36 with all the idols of thy **a**, and by the blood 8441
16:43 not commit *this* lewdness above all thine **a**. 8441
16:47 after their ways, nor done after their **a**: 8441
16:51 thou hast multiplied thine **a** more than they, 8441
16:51 hast justified thy sisters in all thine **a** which 8441
16:58 Thou hast borne thy lewdness and thine **a**, 8441
18:13 he hath done all these **a**; he shall surely die; 8441
18:24 doeth according to all the **a** that the wicked 8441
20: 4 cause them to know the **a** of their fathers: 8441
20: 7 Cast ye away every man the **a** of his eyes, 8251
20: 8 they did not every man cast away the **a** of 8251
20:30 and commit ye whoredom after their **a**? 8251
22: 2 yea, thou shalt shew her all her **a**. 8441
23:36 yea, declare unto them their **a**; 8441
33:29 of all their **a** which they have committed. 8441
36:31 own sight for your iniquities and for your **a**. 8441
43: 8 name by their **a** that they have committed: 8441
44: 6 of Israel, let it suffice you of all your **a**, 8441
44: 7 broken my covenant because of all your **a**. 8441
44:13 and their **a** which they have committed. 8441
Da 9:27 for the overspreading of **a** he *shall* make *it* 8251
Hos 9:10 and *their* **a** were according as they loved. 8251
Zec 9: 7 and his **a** from between his teeth: 8251
Rev 17: 4 having a golden cup in her hand full of **a** and 946
17: 5 THE MOTHER OF HARLOTS AND **A** OF 946

ABOUND (19) [ABOUNDED, ABOUNDETH, ABOUNDING, ABUNDANCE, ABUNDANT, ABUNDANTLY]
Pr 28:20 A faithful man shall **a** with blessings: but 7227
Mt 24:12 And because iniquity shall **a**, the love of 4129
Ro 5:20 the law entered, that the offence might **a**. 4121
5:20 sin abounded, grace did **much more a**: 5248
6: 1 Shall we continue in sin, that grace may **a**? 4121
15:13 peace in believing, that ye may **a** in hope, 4052
2Co 1: 5 For as the sufferings of Christ **a** in us, so 4052
8: 7 as ye **a** in every *thing, in* faith, and 4052
8: 7 love to us, *see* that ye **a** in this grace also. 4052
9: 8 And God *is* able to **make** all grace **a** 4052
9: 8 in all *things,* may **a** to every good work: 4052
Php 1: 9 that your love may **a** yet more and more in 4052
4:12 *how* to be abased, and I know *how* to **a**: 4052
4:12 to be hungry, both to **a** and to suffer need. 4052
4:17 I desire fruit that *may* **a** to your account. 4121
4:18 But I have all, and **a**: I am full, 4052
1Th 3:12 and **a** in love one towards another, 4052
4: 1 *so* ye would **a** more *and more.* 4052
2Pe 1: 8 For if these *things* be in you, and **a**, 4121

ABOUNDED (5) [ABOUND]
Ro 3: 7 For if the truth of God hath *more* **a** through 4052
5:15 one man, Jesus Christ, hath **a** unto many. 4052
5:20 But where sin **a**, grace did much more 4121
2Co 8: 2 their deep poverty **a** unto the riches of their 4052
Eph 1: 8 Wherein he hath **a** toward us in all wisdom 4052

ABOUNDETH (3) [ABOUND]
Pr 29:22 and a furious man **a** in transgression. 7227
2Co 1: 5 in us, so our consolation also **a** by Christ. 4052
2Th 1: 3 every one of you all towards each other **a**; 4121

ABOUNDING (3) [ABOUND]
Pr 8:24 when *there were* no fountains **a** with water. 3513
1Co 15:58 always **a** in the work of the Lord, 4052
Col 2: 7 been taught, **a** therein with thanksgiving. 4052

ABOUT (632) See Index

ABOVE (223) See Index

ABRAHAM (231) [ABRAHAM'S, ABRAM, ABRAM'S]
Ge 17: 5 be called Abram, but thy name shall be **A**; 85
17: 9 God said unto **A**, Thou shalt keep my 85
17:15 And God said unto **A**, *As for* Sarai thy wife, 85
17:17 Then **A** fell upon his face, and laughed, and 85
17:18 **A** said unto God, O that Ishmael might live 85
17:22 talking with him, and God went up from **A**. 85
17:23 **A** took Ishmael his son, and all that were born 85
17:24 **A** *was* ninety years old and nine, when he was 85
17:26 In the selfsame day was **A** circumcised, and 85
18: 6 And **A** hastened into the tent unto Sarah, and 85
18: 7 **A** ran unto the herd, and fetcht a calf tender 85
18:11 Now **A** and Sarah *were* old *and* well stricken 85
18:13 the LORD said unto **A**, Wherefore did Sarah 85
18:16 **A** went with them to bring them on the way. 85
18:17 Shall I hide from **A** *that thing* which I do; 85
18:18 Seeing that **A** shall surely become a great and 85
18:19 that the LORD may bring upon **A** that which 85
18:22 but **A** stood yet before the LORD. 85
18:23 **A** drew near, and said, Wilt thou also destroy 85
18:27 **A** answered and said, Behold now, I have 85
18:33 as soon as he had left communing with **A**: 85
18:33 with Abraham: and **A** returned unto his place. 85
19:27 **A** gat up early in the morning to the place 85
19:29 that God remembered **A**, and sent Lot out of 85
20: 1 **A** journeyed from thence toward the south 85
20: 2 **A** said of Sarah his wife, She *is* my sister: 85
20: 9 Then Abimelech called **A**, and said unto him, 85
20:10 Abimelech said unto **A**, What sawest thou, 85
20:11 **A** said, Because I thought, Surely the fear of 85
20:14 gave *them* unto **A**, and restored him Sarah his 85
20:17 So **A** prayed unto God: and God healed 85
21: 2 and bare **A** a son in his old age, 85
21: 3 **A** called the name of his son that was born 85
21: 4 **A** circumcised his son Isaac being eight days 85
21: 5 **A** *was* an hundred years old, when his son 85
21: 7 And she said, Who would have said unto **A**, 85
21: 8 **A** made a great feast the *same* day that Isaac 85
21: 9 which she had born unto **A**, mocking. 85
21:10 Wherefore she said unto **A**, Cast out this 85
21:12 God said unto **A**, Let it not be grievous in thy 85
21:14 **A** rose up early in the morning, and 85
21:22 the chief captain of his host spake unto **A**, 85
21:24 And **A** said, I will swear. 85
21:25 **A** reproved Abimelech because of a well of 85
21:27 **A** took sheep and oxen, and gave *them* unto 85
21:28 **A** set seven ewe lambs of the flock by 85
21:29 Abimelech said unto **A**, What *mean* these 85
21:33 *A* planted a grove in Beer-sheba, and NIH
21:34 **A** sojourned in the Philistines' land many 85
22: 1 that God did tempt **A**, and said unto him, 85
22: 1 did tempt Abraham, and said unto him, **A**: 85
22: 3 **A** rose up early in the morning, and 85
22: 4 Then on the third day **A** lift up his eyes, and 85
22: 5 **A** said unto his young men, Abide you here 85
22: 6 **A** took the wood of the burnt offering, and 85
22: 7 And Isaac spake unto **A** his father, and said, 85
22: 8 **A** said, My son, God will provide himself a 85
22: 9 **A** built an altar there, and laid the wood in 85
22:10 **A** stretched forth his hand, and took the knife 85
22:11 him out of heaven, and said, **A**, Abraham: 85

Ge	22:11	him out of heaven, and said, Abraham, **A**:	85
	22:13	**A** lifted up his eyes, and looked, and	85
	22:13	**A** went and took the ram, and offered him up	85
	22:14	**A** called the name of that place Jehovah-jireh:	85
	22:15	the angel of the LORD called unto **A** out of	85
	22:19	So **A** returned unto his young men, and	85
	22:19	to Beer-sheba; and **A** dwelt at Beer-sheba.	85
	22:20	that it was told **A**, saying, Behold, Milcah,	85
	23: 2	**A** came to mourn for Sarah, and to weep for	85
	23: 3	**A** stood up from before his dead, and	85
	23: 5	the children of Heth answered **A**, saying unto	85
	23: 7	**A** stood up, and bowed himself to the people	85
	23:10	Ephron the Hittite answered **A** in the audience	85
	23:12	**A** bowed down himself before the people of	85
	23:14	And Ephron answered **A**, saying unto him,	85
	23:16	**A** hearkened unto Ephron; and	85
	23:16	**A** weighed to Ephron the silver, which he had	85
	23:18	Unto **A** for a possession in the presence of	85
	23:19	**A** buried Sarah his wife in the cave of	85
	23:20	were made sure unto **A** for a possession of a	85
	24: 1	And **A** was old, *and* well stricken in age: and	85
	24: 1	and the LORD had blessed **A** in all things.	85
	24: 2	**A** said unto his eldest servant of his house that	85
	24: 6	**A** said unto him, Beware thou that thou bring	85
	24: 9	the servant put his hand under the thigh of **A**	85
	24:12	O LORD God of my master **A**, I pray thee,	85
	24:12	and shew kindness unto my master **A**.	85
	24:27	Blessed *be* the LORD God of my master **A**,	85
	24:42	and said, O LORD God of my master **A**,	85
	24:48	and blessed the LORD God of my master **A**,	85
	25: 1	again **A** took a wife, and her name *was*	85
	25: 5	And **A** gave all that he had unto Isaac.	85
	25: 6	which **A** had, Abraham gave gifts, and	85
	25: 6	**A** gave gifts, and sent them away from Isaac	85
	25: 8	**A** gave up the ghost, and died in a good old	85
	25:10	The field which **A** purchased of the sons of	85
	25:10	there was **A** buried, and Sarah his wife.	85
	25:11	it came to pass after the death of **A**, that God	85
	25:12	the Egyptian, Sarah's handmaid, bare unto **A**:	85
	25:19	of Isaac, Abraham's son: **A** begat Isaac:	85
	26: 1	the first famine that was in the days of **A**.	85
	26: 3	I will perform the oath which I sware unto **A**	85
	26: 5	Because that **A** obeyed my voice, and kept my	85
	26:15	had digged in the days of **A** his father,	85
	26:18	which they had digged in the days of **A** his	85
	26:18	had stopped them after the death of **A**:	85
	26:24	and said, I *am* the God of **A** thy father:	85
	28: 4	And give thee the blessing of **A**, to thee, and	85
	28: 4	thou art a stranger, which God gave unto **A**.	85
	28:13	I *am* the LORD God of **A** thy father, and	85
	31:42	the God of **A**, and the fear of Isaac, had been	85
	31:53	The God of **A**, and the God of Nahor, the God	85
	32: 9	O God of my father **A**, and God of my father	85
	35:12	the land which I gave **A** and Isaac, to thee I	85
	35:27	*is* Hebron, where **A** and Isaac sojourned.	85
	48:15	before whom my fathers **A** and Isaac did	85
	48:16	and the name of my fathers **A** and Isaac;	85
	49:30	which **A** bought with the field of Ephron	85
	49:31	There they buried **A** and Sarah his wife;	85
	50:13	which **A** bought with the field for a	85
	50:24	this land unto the land which he sware to **A**,	85
Ex	2:24	God remembered his covenant with **A**,	85
	3: 6	the God of **A**, the God of Isaac, and the God	85
	3:15	the God of **A**, the God of Isaac, and the God	85
	3:16	the God of **A**, of Isaac, and of Jacob,	85
	4: 5	the God of **A**, the God of Isaac, and the God	85
	6: 3	I appeared unto **A**, unto Isaac, and unto Jacob,	85
	6: 8	the which I did swear to give it to **A**,	85
	32:13	Remember **A**, Isaac, and Israel, thy servants,	85
	33: 1	unto the land which I sware unto **A**, to Isaac,	85
Lev	26:42	also my covenant with **A** will I remember;	85
Nu	32:11	shall see the land which I sware unto **A**,	85
Dt	1: 8	**A**, Isaac, and Jacob, to give unto them and	85
	6:10	to **A**, to Isaac, and to Jacob, to give thee great	85
	9: 5	sware unto thy fathers, **A**, Isaac, and Jacob.	85
	9:27	Remember thy servants, **A**, Isaac, and Jacob;	85
	29:13	unto thy fathers, to **A**, to Isaac, and to Jacob.	85
	30:20	to **A**, to Isaac, and to Jacob, to give them.	85
	34: 4	This *is* the land which I sware unto **A**,	85
Jos	24: 2	the father of **A**, and the father of Nachor:	85
	24: 3	I took your father **A** from the *other* side of	85
1Ki	18:36	said, LORD God of **A**, Isaac, and of Israel,	85
2Ki	13:23	because of his covenant with **A**, Isaac, and	85
1Ch	1:27	Abram; the same *is* **A**.	85
	1:28	The sons of **A**; Isaac, and Ishmael.	85
	1:34	**A** begat Isaac. The sons of Isaac; Esau and	85
	16:16	*Even of the covenant* which he made with **A**,	85
	29:18	O LORD God of **A**, Isaac, and of Israel,	85
2Ch	20: 7	gavest it to the seed of **A** thy friend for ever?	85
	30: 6	turn again unto the LORD God of **A**, Isaac,	85
Ne	9: 7	the Chaldees, and gavest him the name of **A**;	85
Ps	47: 9	*even* the people of the God of **A**:	85
	105: 6	O ye seed of **A** his servant, ye children of	85
	105: 9	Which *covenant* he made with **A**, and his oath	85
	105:42	his holy promise, *and* **A** his servant.	85
Isa	29:22	who redeemed **A**, concerning the house of	85
	41: 8	whom I have chosen, the seed of **A** my friend.	85
	51: 2	Look unto **A** your father, and unto Sarah *that*	85
	63:16	though **A** be ignorant of us, and	85
Jer	33:26	*any* of his seed *to be* rulers over the seed of **A**,	85
Eze	33:24	saying, **A** was one, and he inherited the land:	85
Mic	7:20	the truth to Jacob, *and* the mercy to **A**,	85
Mt	1: 1	Jesus Christ, the son of David, the son of **A**.	*11*
	1: 2	**A** begat Isaac; and Isaac begat Jacob; and	*11*
	1:17	So all the generations from **A** to David *are*	*11*
	3: 9	within yourselves, We have **A** to *our* father:	*11*
	3: 9	of these stones to raise up children unto **A**.	*11*
	8:11	and shall sit down with **A**, and Isaac, and	*11*
	22:32	I am the God of **A**, and the God of Isaac, and	*11*
Mk	12:26	I *am* the God of **A**, and the God of Isaac, and	*11*
Lk	1:55	to our fathers), to **A**, and to his seed for ever.	*11*
	1:73	The oath which he sware to our father **A**,	*11*
	3: 8	within yourselves, We have **A** to *our* father:	*11*
	3: 8	of these stones to raise up children unto **A**.	*11*
	3:34	was *the son* of Isaac, which was *the son* of **A**,	*11*
	13:16	ought not this *woman,* being a daughter of **A**,	*11*
	13:28	when ye shall see **A**, and Isaac, and Jacob,	*11*
	16:23	and seeth **A** afar off, and Lazarus in his	*11*
	16:24	And he cried and said, Father **A**, have mercy	*11*
	16:25	But **A** said, Son, remember that thou in thy	*11*
	16:29	**A** saith unto him, They have Moses and	*11*
	16:30	And he said, Nay, father **A**: but if one went	*11*
	19: 9	this house, forsomuch as he also is a son of **A**.	*11*
	20:37	when he calleth the Lord the God of **A**, and	*11*
Jn	8:39	and said unto him, **A** is our father.	*11*
	8:39	ye would do the works of **A**.	*11*
	8:40	which I have heard of God: this did not **A**.	*11*
	8:52	**A** is dead, and the prophets; and thou sayest,	*11*
	8:53	Art thou greater than our father **A**, which is	*11*
	8:56	Your father **A** rejoiced to see my day: and	*11*
	8:57	not yet fifty years old, and hast thou seen **A**?	*11*
	8:58	verily, I say unto you, Before **A** was, I am.	*11*
Ac	3:13	The God of **A**, and of Isaac, and of Jacob,	*11*
	3:25	God made with our fathers, saying unto **A**,	*11*
	7: 2	The God of glory appeared unto our father **A**,	*11*
	7: 8	and so *A* begat Isaac, and circumcised him	NIG
	7:16	laid in the sepulchre that **A** bought for a sum	*11*
	7:17	which God had sworn to **A**, the people grew	*11*
	7:32	the God of **A**, and the God of Isaac, and	*11*
	13:26	children of the stock of **A**, and	*11*
Ro	4: 1	What shall we say then that **A** our father,	*11*
	4: 2	For if **A** were justified by works, he hath	*11*
	4: 3	**A** believed God, and it was counted unto him	*11*
	4: 9	for we say that faith was reckoned to **A** for	*11*
	4:12	walk in the steps of *that* faith of our father **A**,	*11*
	4:13	*was* not to **A**, or to his seed, through the law,	*11*
	4:16	but to that also which is of the faith of **A**;	*11*
	9: 7	Neither, because they are the seed of **A**,	*11*
	11: 1	of the seed of **A**, *of* the tribe of Benjamin.	*11*
2Co	11:22	so *am* I. Are they the seed of **A**? so *am* I.	*11*
Gal	3: 6	Even as **A** believed God, and it was accounted	*11*
	3: 7	are of faith, the same are the children of **A**.	*11*
	3: 8	preached before the gospel unto **A**, *saying,* In	*11*
	3: 9	which be of faith are blessed with faithful **A**.	*11*
	3:14	That the blessing of **A** might come on	*11*
	3:16	Now to **A** and his seed were the promises	*11*
	3:18	of promise: but God gave *it* to **A** by promise.	*11*
	4:22	For it is written, that **A** had two sons, the one	*11*
Heb	2:16	*of* angels; but he took on *him* the seed of **A**.	*11*
	6:13	For when God made promise to **A**, because	*11*
	7: 1	who met **A** returning from the slaughter of	*11*
	7: 2	To whom also **A** gave a tenth *part* of all;	*11*
	7: 4	the patriarch **A** gave the tenth of the spoils.	*11*
	7: 5	though they come out of the loins of **A**:	*11*
	7: 6	is not counted from them received tithes of **A**,	*11*
	7: 9	who receiveth tithes, payed tithes in **A**.	*11*
	11: 8	By faith **A**, when he was called to go out into	*11*
	11:17	By faith **A**, when he was tried, offered up	*11*

Jas 2:21 Was not A our father justified by works, *11*
2:23 A believed God, and it was imputed unto him *11*
1Pe 3: 6 *Even* as Sara obeyed A, calling him lord: *11*

ABRAHAM'S (19) [ABRAHAM]

Ge 17:23 every male among the men of A house; 85
20:18 house of Abimelech, because of Sarah A wife. 85
21:11 the thing was very grievous in A sight 85
22:23 eight Milcah did bear to Nahor, A brother. 85
24:15 son of Milcah, the wife of Nahor, A brother, 85
24:34 And he said, I *am* A servant. 85
24:52 that, when A servant heard their words, 85
24:59 and her nurse, and A servant, and his men. 85
25: 7 these *are* the days of the years of A life which 85
25:12 A son, whom Hagar the Egyptian, 85
25:19 And these *are* the generations of Isaac, A son: 85
26:24 and multiply thy seed for my servant A sake. 85
28: 9 had Mahalath the daughter of Ishmael A son, 85
1Ch 1:32 Now the sons of Keturah, A concubine: 85
Lk 16:22 and was carried by the angels into A bosom: *11*
Jn 8:33 We be A seed, and were never in bondage to *11*
8:37 I know that ye are A seed; but ye seek to kill *11*
8:39 Jesus saith unto them, If ye were A children, *11*
Gal 3:29 then are ye A seed, and heirs according to *11*

ABRAM (54) [ABRAHAM]

Ge 11:26 and begat A, Nahor, and Haran. 87
11:27 Terah begat A, Nahor, and Haran; and 87
11:29 A and Nahor took them wives: the name of 87
11:31 Terah took A his son, and Lot the son of 87
12: 1 Now the LORD had said unto A, Get thee 87
12: 4 So A departed, as the LORD had spoken 87
12: 4 A *was* seventy and five years old when he 87
12: 5 A took Sarai his wife, and Lot his brother's 87
12: 6 A passed through the land unto the place of 87
12: 7 And the LORD appeared unto A, and said, 87
12: 9 A journeyed, going on still toward the south. 87
12:10 and A went down into Egypt to sojourn there; 87
12:14 to pass, that, when A was come into Egypt, 87
12:16 he entreated A well for her sake: and he had 87
12:18 Pharaoh called A, and said, What *is* this *that* 87
13: 1 And A went up out of Egypt, he, and his wife, 87
13: 2 A *was* very rich in cattle, in silver, and 87
13: 4 there A called on the name of the LORD. 87
13: 5 which went with A, had flocks, and herds, and 87
13: 8 A said unto Lot, Let there be no strife, I pray 87
13:12 A dwelled in the land of Canaan, and 87
13:14 the LORD said unto A, after that Lot was 87
13:18 A removed his tent, and came and dwelt in 87
14:13 one that had escaped, and told A the Hebrew; 87
14:13 of Aner: and these *were* confederate with A. 87
14:14 when A heard that his brother was taken 87
14:19 and said, Blessed *be* A of the most high God, 87
14:21 the king of Sodom said unto A, Give me 87
14:22 A said to the king of Sodom, I have lift up 87
14:23 lest thou shouldest say, I have made A rich: 87
15: 1 word of the LORD came unto A in a vision, 87
15: 1 unto Abram in a vision, saying, Fear not, A: 87
15: 2 A said, Lord GOD, what wilt thou give me, 87
15: 3 A said, Behold, to me thou hast given no 87
15:11 down upon the carcases, A drove them away. 87
15:12 was going down, a deep sleep fell upon A; 87
15:13 he said unto A, Know of a surety that thy seed 87
15:18 day the LORD made a covenant with A, 87
16: 2 Sarai said unto A, Behold now, the LORD 87
16: 2 And A hearkened to the voice of Sarai. 87
16: 3 after A had dwelt ten years in the land of 87
16: 3 and gave her to her husband A to be his wife. 87
16: 5 Sarai said unto A, My wrong *be* upon thee: 87
16: 6 A said unto Sarai, Behold, thy maid *is* in thy 87
16:15 Hagar bare A a son: and Abram called his 87
16:15 A called his son's name, which Hagar bare, 87
16:16 A *was* fourscore and six years old, 87
16:16 six years old, when Hagar bare Ishmael to A. 87
17: 1 when A was ninety years old and nine, 87
17: 1 the LORD appeared to A, and said unto him, 87
17: 3 A fell on his face: and God talked with him, 87
17: 5 Neither shall thy name any more be called A, 87
1Ch 1:27 A; the same *is* Abraham. 87
Ne 9: 7 who didst choose A, and broughtest him forth 87

ABRAM'S (7) [ABRAHAM]

Ge 11:29 the name of A wife *was* Sarai; and the name 87
11:31 and Sarai his daughter in law, his son A wife; 87
12:17 with great plagues because of Sarai A wife. 87
13: 7 there was a strife between the herdmen of A 87
14:12 they took Lot, A brother's son, who dwelt in 87
16: 1 Now Sarai A wife bare him no *children:* and 87
16: 3 Sarai A wife took Hagar her maid 87

ABROAD (80)

Ge 10:18 the families of the Canaanites **spread a.** 6327
11: 4 lest we be **scattered a** upon the face of 6327
11: 8 So the LORD **scattered** them **a** from 6327
11: 9 from thence did the LORD **scatter** them **a** 6327
15: 5 he brought him forth **a**, and said, 2351+1886.5
19:17 they had brought them forth **a**, 2351+1886.5
28:14 thou shalt **spread a** to the west, and to 6555
Ex 5:12 So the people were **scattered a** throughout 6327
9:29 I will **spread a** my hands unto the LORD; 6566
9:33 **spread a** his hands unto the LORD: 6566
12:46 of the flesh **a** out of the house; 2351+1886.5
21:19 walk **a** upon his staff, then 2351+871.1+1886.1
40:19 he **spread a** the tent over the tabernacle, 6566
Lev 13: 7 if the scab **spread much a** in 6581+6581
13:12 if a leprosy **break out a** in the skin, 6524+6524
13:22 if it **spread much a** in the skin, then 6581+6581
13:27 *and* if it be **spread much a** in 6581+6581
14: 8 and shall **tarry a** out of his tent seven days. 3427
18: 9 *whether she be* born at home, or born **a**, 2351
Nu 11:32 they **spread** *them* **all a** for 7849+7849
Dt 23:10 shall he go **a** out of the camp, 2351+4480
23:12 the camp, whither thou shalt go forth **a**: 2351
23:13 it shall be, when thou wilt ease thyself **a**, 2351
24:11 Thou shalt stand **a**, and the man to whom 2351
24:11 bring out the pledge **a** unto thee. 2351+1886.5
32:11 **spreadeth a** her wings, taketh them, 6566
Jdg 12: 9 *whom* he sent **a**, and took in thirty 2351+1886.5
12: 9 took in thirty daughters from **a** for his sons. 2351
1Sa 9:26 both of them, he and Samuel, **a**. 2351+1886.5
30:16 behold *they were* **spread a** upon all 5203
2Sa 22:43 mire of the street, *and* did **spread** them **a**. 7554
1Ki 2:42 walkest *a* any whither, that thou shalt surely NIH
2Ki 4: 3 **a** of all thy neighbours, 2351+4480+1886.1
1Ch 13: 2 us send **a** unto our brethren **every where**, 6555
14:13 again **spread** themselves **a** in the valley. 6584
2Ch 26: 8 his name **spread a** even to the entering in 1980
26:15 his name spread **far a**; 4480+5704+7350+3807.1
29:16 the Levites took *it*, to carry *it* out **a** 2351+1886.5
31: 5 as soon as the commandment **came a**, 6555
Ne 1: 8 I will **scatter** you **a** among the nations: 6327
Est 1:17 For *this* deed of the queen shall **come a** 3318
3: 8 There is a certain people **scattered a** and 6340
Job 4:11 and the stout lion's whelps are **scattered a.** 6504
15:23 He **wandereth a** for bread, *saying*, Where 5074
40:11 **Cast a** the rage of thy wrath: and 6327
Ps 41: 6 he goeth **a**, he telleth *it*. 2351+1886.1+3807.1
77:17 sent out a sound: thine arrows also **went a.** 1980
Pr 5:16 Let thy fountains be dispersed **a**, 2351+1886.5
Isa 24: 1 and **scattereth a** the inhabitants thereof. 6327
28:25 doth he not **cast a** the fitches, and 6327
44:24 that **spreadeth a** the earth by myself; 7554
Jer 6:11 I *will* pour *it* out upon the children **a**, and 2351
La 1:20 **a** the sword bereaveth, at home *there* 2351+4480
Eze 34:21 scattered them **a**; 413+2351+1886.1+1886.5
Zec 1:17 through prosperity shall yet be **spread a**; 6327
2: 6 for I have **spread** you **a** as the four winds 6566
Mt 9:26 And the fame hereof **went a** into all that *1831*
9:31 **spread a** his **fame** in all that country. *1310*
9:36 they fainted, and were **scattered a**, *4496*
12:30 he that gathereth not with me **scattereth a.** *4650*
26:31 the sheep of the flock shall be **scattered a.** *1287*
Mk 1:28 And immediately his fame **spread a** *1831*
1:45 publish *it* much, and to **blaze a** the matter, *1310*
4:22 kept secret, but that it should come **a.** *1519+5318*
6:14 heard *of him;* (for his name was **spread a**:) *5318*
Lk 1:65 all these sayings were **noised a** throughout *1255*
2:17 **made known a** the saying which was told *1232*
5:15 *much* the more **went** there a fame **a** of him: *1330*
8:17 that shall not be known and come **a.** *1519+5318*
Jn 11:52 the children of God that were **scattered a.** *1287*
21:23 Then **went** this saying **a** among *1831*
Ac 2: 6 Now when this **was noised a**, *1096+3588+5456*
8: 1 they were all **scattered a** throughout *1289*
8: 4 Therefore they that were **scattered a** went *1289*
11:19 Now they which were **scattered a** upon *1289*
Ro 5: 5 the love of God is **shed a** in our hearts by *1632*
16:19 For your obedience is **come a** unto all *men*. I *864*

2Co 9: 9 (As it is written, He hath **dispersed a**; 4650
1Th 1: 8 place your faith to God-ward is **spread a**; 1831
Jas 1: 1 tribes which are **scattered a**, 1290+1722+3588

ABRONAH See EBRONAH

ABSALOM (104) [ABSALOM'S]

2Sa 3: 3 A the son of Maacah the daughter of Talmai 53
13: 1 that A the son of David had a fair sister, 53
13:20 A her brother said unto her, Hath Amnon thy 53
13:22 A spake unto his brother Amnon neither good 53
13:22 for A hated Amnon, because he had forced his 53
13:23 that A had sheepshearers in Baal-hazor, 53
13:23 and A invited all the king's sons. 53
13:24 A came to the king, and said, Behold now, 53
13:25 the king said to A, Nay, my son, let us not all 53
13:26 said A, If not, I pray thee, let my brother 53
13:27 A pressed him, that he let Amnon and all 53
13:28 Now A had commanded his servants, saying, 53
13:29 the servants of A did unto Amnon as Absalom 53
13:29 the servants of Absalom did unto Amnon as A 53
13:30 A hath slain all the king's sons, and there is 53
13:32 for by the appointment of A *this* hath been 53
13:34 A fled. And the young man that kept 53
13:37 A fled, and went to Talmai, the son of 53
13:38 So A fled, and went to Geshur, and was there 53
13:39 *soul of* king David longed to go forth unto A: 53
14: 1 perceived that the king's heart *was* toward A. 53
14:21 go therefore, bring the young man A again. 53
14:23 went to Geshur, and brought A *to* Jerusalem. 53
14:24 So A returned to his own house, and saw not 53
14:25 to be so much praised as A for his beauty: 53
14:27 unto A there were born three sons, and 53
14:28 So A dwelt two full years in Jerusalem, and 53
14:29 Therefore A sent for Joab, to have sent him to 53
14:31 came to A unto *his* house, and said unto him, 53
14:32 A answered Joab, Behold, I sent unto thee, 53
14:33 when he had called for A, he came to 53
14:33 ground before the king: and the king kissed A. 53
15: 1 that A prepared him chariots and horses, and 53
15: 2 A rose up early, and stood beside the way of 53
15: 2 A called unto him, and said, Of what city *art* 53
15: 3 A said unto him, See, thy matters *are* good 53
15: 4 A said moreover, Oh that I were made judge 53
15: 6 on this manner did A to all Israel that came to 53
15: 6 so A stole the hearts of the men of Israel. 53
15: 7 that A said unto the king, I pray thee, let me 53
15:10 A sent spies throughout all the tribes of Israel, 53
15:10 then ye shall say, A reigneth in Hebron. 53
15:11 with A went two hundred men out of 53
15:12 A sent *for* Ahithophel the Gilonite, 53
15:12 for the people increased continually with A. 53
15:13 The hearts of the men of Israel are after A. 53
15:14 us flee; for we shall not *else* escape from A: 53
15:31 Ahithophel *is* among the conspirators with A. 53
15:34 and say unto A, I will be thy servant, O king; 53
15:37 *into* the city, and A came *into* Jerusalem. 53
16: 8 the kingdom into the hand of A thy son: 53
16:15 And A, and all the people the men of Israel, 53
16:16 the Archite, David's friend, was come unto A, 53
16:16 that Hushai said unto A, God save the king, 53
16:17 A said to Hushai, *Is* this thy kindness to thy 53
16:18 Hushai said unto A, Nay; but whom 53
16:20 said A to Ahithophel, Give counsel among 53
16:21 Ahithophel said unto A, Go in unto thy 53
16:22 So they spread A a tent upon the top of 53
16:22 A went in unto his father's concubines in 53
16:23 of Ahithophel both with David and with A. 53
17: 1 Moreover Ahithophel said unto A, Let me 53
17: 4 the saying pleased A well, and all the elders 53
17: 5 said A, Call now Hushai the Archite also, 53
17: 6 when Hushai was come to A, Absalom spake 53
17: 6 come to Absalom, A spake unto him, saying, 53
17: 7 Hushai said unto A, The counsel that 53
17: 9 is a slaughter among the people that follow A. 53
17:14 A and all the men of Israel said, The counsel 53
17:14 that the LORD might bring evil upon A. 53
17:15 Thus and thus did Ahithophel counsel A and 53
17:18 Nevertheless a lad saw them, and told A: but 53
17:24 A passed over Jordan, he and all the men of 53
17:25 A made Amasa captain of the host instead of 53
17:26 So Israel and A pitched *in* the land of Gilead. 53
18: 5 for my sake with the young man, *even* with A. 53
18: 5 gave all the captains charge concerning A. 53
18: 9 A met the servants of David. And Absalom 53
18: 9 A rode upon a mule, and the mule went under 53
18:10 and said, Behold, I saw A hanged in an oak. 53
18:12 Beware *that* none *touch* the young man A. 53
18:14 and thrust them through the heart of A, 53
18:15 Joab's armour compassed about and smote A, 53
18:17 they took A, and cast him into a great pit in 53
18:18 Now A in his lifetime had taken and reared up 53
18:29 And the king said, *Is* the young man A safe? 53
18:32 said unto Cushi, *Is* the young man A safe? 53
18:33 as he went, thus he said, O my son A, my son, 53
18:33 O my son Absalom, my son, my son A: 53
18:33 God I had died for thee, O A, my son, my son. 53
19: 1 the king weepeth and mourneth for A. 53
19: 4 O my son A, O Absalom, my son, my son. 53
19: 4 O my son Absalom, O A, my son, my son. 53
19: 6 that if A had lived, and all we had died *this* 53
19: 9 and now he is fled out of the land for A. 53
19:10 A, whom we anointed over us, is dead in 53
20: 6 the son of Bichri do us more harm than *did* A: 53
1Ki 1: 6 goodly *man;* and *his mother* bare him after A. 53
2: 7 to me when I fled because of A thy brother. 53
2:28 after Adonijah, though he turned not after A. 53
1Ch 3: 2 A the son of Maachah the daughter of Talmai 53
2Ch 11:20 after her he took Maachah the daughter of A; 53
11:21 Rehoboam loved Maachah the daughter of A 53
Ps 3: T Psalm of David, when he fled from A his son. 53

ABSALOM'S (5) [ABSALOM]

2Sa 13: 4 unto him, I love Tamar, my brother A sister. 53
13:20 So Tamar remained desolate *in* her brother A 53
14:30 it on fire. And A servants set the field on fire. 53
17:20 when A servants came to the woman to 53
18:18 and it is called unto this day, A place. 53

ABSENCE (2) [ABSENT]

Lk 22: 6 him unto them **in the a of** the multitude. 817
Php 2:12 presence only, but now much more in my **a**, 666

ABSENT (11) [ABSENCE]

Ge 31:49 and thee, when we are **a** one from another. 5641
1Co 5: 3 I verily, as **a** in body, but present in spirit, 548
2Co 5: 6 home in the body, we are **a** from the Lord: 1553
5: 8 and willing rather to be **a** from the body, 1553
5: 9 we labour, that, whether present or **a**, 1553
10: 1 among you, but being **a** am bold toward you: 548
10:11 as we are in word by letters when we are **a**, 548
13: 2 being **a** now I write to them which 548
13:10 Therefore I write these *things* being **a**, 548
Php 1:27 whether I come and see you, or *else* be **a**, 548
Col 2: 5 For though I be **a** in the flesh, yet am I with 548

ABSTAIN (6) [ABSTINENCE]

Ac 15:20 that *they* **a** from pollutions of idols, and 568
15:29 That *ye* **a from** meats offered to idols, and 568
1Th 4: 3 that ye should **a** from fornication: 568
5:22 **A** from all appearance of evil. 568
1Ti 4: 3 to marry, *and commanding* to **a from** meats, 568
1Pe 2:11 and pilgrims, **a from** fleshly lusts, 568

ABSTINENCE (1) [ABSTAIN]

Ac 27:21 But after long **a** Paul stood *forth* in the midst 776

ABUNDANCE (68) [ABOUND]

Dt 28:47 gladness of heart, for the **a** of all *things;* 7230
33:19 for they shall suck *of* the **a** of the seas, and 8228
1Sa 1:16 for out of the **a** of my complaint and 7230
2Sa 12:30 brought forth the spoil of the city in great **a**. 7235
1Ki 1:19 slain oxen and fat cattle and sheep in **a**, 7230
1:25 slain oxen and fat cattle and sheep in **a**, 7230
10:10 there came no more such **a** of 7230+3807.1
10:27 sycomore trees that *are* in the vale, for **a**. 7230
18:41 and drink; for *there is* a sound of **a** of rain. 1995
1Ch 22: 3 David prepared iron in **a** for the nails for 7230
22: 3 the joinings; and brass in **a** without weight; 7230
22: 4 Also cedar trees in **a**: for 369+4557
22:14 and iron without weight; for it is in **a**: 7230
22:15 *there are* workmen with thee in **a**, 7230
29: 2 *of* precious stones, and marble stones in **a**. 7230
29:21 and sacrifices in **a** for all Israel: 7230
2Ch 1:15 the sycomore trees that *are* in the vale for **a**. 7230
2: 9 Even to prepare me timber in **a**: for 7230
4:18 Solomon made all these vessels in great **a**: 7230
9: 1 and gold in **a**, and precious stones: 7230
9: 9 spices great **a**, and precious stones: 7230+3807.1

2Ch 9:27 trees that *are* in the low plains in **a**. 7230
11:23 he gave them victual in **a**. And he desired 7230
14:15 carried away sheep and camels in **a**, and 7230
15: 9 for they fell to him out of Israel in **a**, 7230
17: 5 and he had riches and honour in **a**. 7230
18: 1 Jehoshaphat had riches and honour in **a**, 7230
18: 2 Ahab killed sheep and oxen for him in **a**, 7230
20:25 they found among them in **a** both riches 7230
24:11 did day by day, and gathered money in **a**. 7230
29:35 also the burnt offerings *were* in **a**, with 7230
31: 5 the children of Israel **brought in a** 7235
32: 5 of David, and made darts and shields in **a**. 7230
32:29 and possessions of flocks and herds in **a**: 7230
Ne 9:25 and oliveyards, and fruit trees **in a**: 7230+3807.1
Est 1: 7 royal wine **in a**, according to the state of 7227
Job 22:11 canst not see; and **a** of waters cover thee. 8229
36:31 judgeth he the people; he giveth meat in **a**. 4342
38:34 the clouds, that **a** of waters may cover thee? 8229
Ps 37:11 shall delight themselves in the **a** of peace. 7230
52: 7 trusted in the **a** of his riches, *and* 7230
72: 7 **a** of peace so long as the moon endureth. 7230
105:30 Their land **brought forth** frogs in **a**, in 8317
Ecc 5:10 nor he that loveth **a** *with* increase: 1995
5:12 the **a** of the rich will not suffer him to 7647
Isa 7:22 for the **a** of milk *that they* shall give he 7230
15: 7 Therefore the **a** they have gotten, and 3502
47: 9 *and* for the great **a** of thine enchantments. 6109
60: 5 the **a** of the sea shall be converted unto 1995
66:11 and be delighted with the **a** of her glory. 2123
Jer 33: 6 will reveal unto them the **a** of peace and 6283
Eze 16:49 **a** of idleness was in her and in her 7962
26:10 By reason of the **a** of his horses their dust 8229
Zec 14:14 gold, and silver, and apparel, in great **a**. 7230
Mt 12:34 speak good *things?* for out of the **a** of *4051*
13:12 shall be given, and he shall **have** *more* **a**: *4052*
25:29 hath shall be given, and he shall **have a**: *4052*
Mk 12:44 For all *they* did cast in of their **a**; *4052*
Lk 6:45 for of the **a** of the heart his mouth speaketh. *4051*
12:15 for a man's life consisteth not in the **a** of *4052*
21: 4 For all these have of their **a** cast in unto *4052*
Ro 5:17 much more they which receive **a** of grace *4050*
2Co 8: 2 How that in a great trial of affliction the **a** *4050*
8:14 *that* now at *this* time your **a** *may be a* *4051*
8:14 that their **a** also may be *a supply* for your *4051*
8:20 that no *man* should blame us in this **a** which *100*
12: 7 measure through the **a** of the revelations, *5236*
Rev 18: 3 waxed rich through the **a** of her delicacies. *1411*

ABUNDANT (13) [ABOUND]
Ex 34: 6 longsuffering, and **a** in goodness and truth, 7227
Isa 56:12 shall be as this day, *and* much more **a**. 3499
Jer 51:13 **a** in treasures, thine end is come, *and* 7227
1Co 12:23 upon these we bestow **more a** honour; *4055*
12:23 our uncomely *parts* have **more a** *4055*
12:24 having given **more a** honour to that *part* *4055*
2Co 4:15 that the **a** grace might through *4121*
7:15 And his inward affection is **more a** toward *4056*
9:12 is **a** also by many thanksgivings unto God; *4052*
11:23 in labours **more a**, in stripes above *4056*
Php 1:26 That your rejoicing may be *more* **a** in Jesus *4052*
1Ti 1:14 And the grace of our Lord was **exceeding a** *5250*
1Pe 1: 3 which according to his **a** mercy hath *4183*

ABUNDANTLY (32) [ABOUND]
Ge 1:20 Let the waters **bring forth a** 8317+8318
1:21 which the waters **brought forth a**, 8317
8:17 that they may **breed a** in the earth, and 8317
9: 7 **bring forth a** in the earth, and 8317
Ex 1: 7 **increased a**, and multiplied, and 8317
8: 3 the river shall **bring forth** frogs **a**, 8317
Nu 20:11 the water came out **a**, and the congregation 7227
1Ch 12:40 and oil, and oxen, and sheep **a**: 7230+3807.1
22: 5 David prepared **a** before his death. 7230+3807.1
22: 8 Thou hast shed blood **a**, and 7230+3807.1
2Ch 31: 5 and the tithe of all *things* brought they in **a**. 7230
Job 12: 6 into whose hand God bringeth *a*. NIH
36:28 the clouds do drop *and* distil upon man **a**. 7227
Ps 36: 8 They shall be **a satisfied** with the fatness of 7301
65:10 *Thou* **waterest** the ridges thereof **a**: 7301
132:15 I will **a bless** her provision: I will 1288+1288
145: 7 They shall **a utter** the memory of thy great 5042
SS 5: 1 O friends; drink, yea, **drink a**, O beloved. 7937
Isa 15: 3 every one shall howl, weeping **a**. 3381
35: 2 It shall **blossom a** and rejoice even 6524+6524
55: 7 and to our God, for he will **a** pardon. 7235
Jn 10:10 and that they might have *it more* **a**. *4053*
1Co 15:10 but I laboured **more a than** they all: *4054*
2Co 1:12 in the world, and **more a** to you-wards. *4056*
2: 4 the love which I have **more a** unto you. *4056*
10:15 by you according to our rule **a**, *1519+4050*
12:15 though the **more a** I love you, the less I be *4056*
Eph 3:20 do exceeding **a** above all that we ask *1537+4053*
1Th 2:17 endeavoured the **more a** to see your face *4056*
Tit 3: 6 Which he shed on us **a** through Jesus Christ *4146*
Heb 6:17 willing **more a** to shew unto the heirs of *4054*
2Pe 1:11 an entrance shall be ministered unto you **a** *4146*

ABUSE (3) [ABUSED, ABUSERS, ABUSING]
1Sa 31: 4 and thrust me through, and **a** me. 5953
1Ch 10: 4 lest these uncircumcised come and **a** me. 5953
1Co 9:18 that *I* **a** not my power in the gospel. *2710*

ABUSED (1) [ABUSE]
Jdg 19:25 and **a** her all the night until the morning: 5953

ABUSERS (1) [ABUSE]
1Co 6: 9 nor **a** of themselves **with mankind,** *733*

ABUSING (1) [ABUSE]
1Co 7:31 as not **a** *it:* for the fashion of this world *2710*

ABYSS See BOTTOMLESS

ACBOR See ACHBOR

ACCAD (1)
Ge 10:10 Erech, and **A**, and Calneh, in the land of 390

ACCEPT (25) [ACCEPTABLE, ACCEPTABLY, ACCEPTANCE, ACCEPTATION, ACCEPTED, ACCEPTEST, ACCEPTETH, ACCEPTING]
Ge 32:20 peradventure he will **a** of me. 5375+6440
Ex 22:11 the owner of it shall **a** *thereof,* and he shall 3947
Lev 26:41 then **a** of the punishment of their iniquity: 7521
26:43 they shall **a** of the punishment of their 7521
Dt 33:11 his substance, and **a** the work of his hands: 7521
1Sa 26:19 thee up against me, let him **a** an offering: 7306
2Sa 24:23 unto the king, The LORD thy God **a** thee. 7521
Job 13: 8 Will ye **a** his person? will ye contend for 5375
13:10 reprove you, if ye do secretly **a** persons. 5375
32:21 Let me not, I pray you, **a** *any* man's person, 5375
42: 8 for him will I **a**: lest *I* deal with you 5375+6440
Ps 20: 3 all thy offerings, and **a** thy burnt sacrifice. 1878
82: 2 and **a** the persons of the wicked? 5375
119:108 **A**, I beseech thee, the freewill offerings of 7521
Pr 18: 5 *It is* not good to **a** the person of the wicked, 5375
Jer 14:10 therefore the LORD doth not **a** them; 7521
14:12 and an oblation, I will not **a** them: 7521
Eze 20:40 there will I **a** them, and there will I require 7521
20:41 I will **a** you with *your* sweet savour, when I 7521
43:27 and I will **a** you, saith the Lord GOD. 7521
Am 5:22 I will not **a** *them:* neither will I regard 7521
Mal 1: 8 he be pleased with thee, or **a** thy person? 5375
1:10 neither will I **a** an offering at your hand. 7521
1:13 should I **a** this of your hand? saith 7521
Ac 24: 3 We **a** *it* always, and in all places, most noble *588*

ACCEPTABLE (23) [ACCEPT]
Lev 22:20 ye not offer: for it shall not be **a** for you. 7522
Dt 33:24 let him be **a** to his brethren, and let him dip 7521
Ps 19:14 be **a** in thy sight, O LORD, 7522+3807.1
69:13 *is* unto thee, O LORD, *in* an **a** time: 7522
Pr 10:32 The lips of the righteous know what is **a**: 7522
21: 3 judgment *is* more **a** to the LORD than 977
Ecc 12:10 The Preacher sought to find out **a** words: 2656
Isa 49: 8 In an **a** time have I heard thee, and in a day 7522
58: 5 call this a fast, and an **a** day to the LORD? 7522
61: 2 To proclaim the **a** year of the LORD, and 7522
Jer 6:20 your burnt offerings *are* not **a**, nor your 7522
Da 4:27 let my counsel be **a** unto thee, and break off 8232
Lk 4:19 To preach the **a** year of the Lord. *1184*
Ro 12: 1 holy, **a** unto God, *which is* your reasonable *2101*
12: 2 *that* good, and **a**, and perfect, will of God. *2101*
14:18 in these *things* serveth Christ *is* **a** to God, *2101*
15:16 the offering up of the Gentiles might be **a**, *2144*
Eph 5:10 Proving what is **a** unto the Lord. *2101*
Php 4:18 a sacrifice **a**, well pleasing to God. *1184*
1Ti 2: 3 and **a** in the sight of God our Saviour; *587*
5: 4 for that is good and **a** before God. *587*

1Pe 2: 5 a to God by Jesus Christ. 2144
2:20 *it,* ye take it patiently, this *is* a with God. 5485

ACCEPTABLY (1) [ACCEPT]
Heb 12:28 whereby we may serve God a with 2102

ACCEPTANCE (1) [ACCEPT]
Isa 60: 7 they shall come up with a on mine altar, 7522

ACCEPTATION (2) [ACCEPT]
1Ti 1:15 *This is* a faithful saying, and worthy of all a, 594
4: 9 *This is* a faithful saying and worthy of all a. 594

ACCEPTED (29) [ACCEPT]
Ge 4: 7 If thou doest well, *shalt thou* not be a? and 7613
19:21 I have a thee concerning this thing, 5375+6440
Ex 28:38 that they may be a before the LORD. 7522
Lev 1: 4 it shall be a for him to make atonement for 7521
7:18 it shall not be a, neither shall it be imputed 7521
10:19 should it have been a in the sight of 3190
19: 7 third day, it *is* abominable; it shall not be a. 7521
22:21 or sheep, it shall be perfect to be a; 7522
22:23 but for a vow it shall not be a. 7521
22:25 *be* in them: they shall not be a for you. 7521
22:27 thenceforth it shall be a for an offering 7521
23:11 sheaf before the LORD, to be a for you: 7522
1Sa 18: 5 he was a in the sight of all the people, and 3190
25:35 to thy voice, and have a thy person. 5375
Est 10: 3 and a of the multitude of his brethren, 7521
Job 42: 9 the LORD also a Job. 5375+6440
Isa 56: 7 their sacrifices *shall be* a upon mine altar; 7522
Jer 37:20 I pray thee, be a before thee, 5307
42: 2 our supplication be a before thee, and 5307
Lk 4:24 No prophet is a in his own country. 1184
Ac 10:35 and worketh righteousness, is a with him. 1184
Ro 15:31 I have for Jerusalem may be a of the saints; 2144
2Co 5: 9 or absent, we may be a of him. 2101
6: 2 I have heard thee in a time a, and in the day 1184
6: 2 behold, now *is* the a time; behold, now *is* 2144
8:12 *it is* a according to that a man hath, *and* 2144
8:17 For indeed he a the exhortation; but 1209
11: 4 or another gospel, which ye have not a, 1209
Eph 1: 6 wherein he hath **made** us a in the beloved: 5487

ACCEPTEST (1) [ACCEPT]
Lk 20:21 neither a thou the person *of any,* but 2983

ACCEPTETH (4) [ACCEPT]
Job 34:19 *How much less to him* that a not 5375
Ecc 9: 7 a merry heart; for God now a thy works. 7521
Hos 8:13 and eat *it; but* the LORD a them not; 7521
Gal 2: 6 God a no man's person:) for they who 2983

ACCEPTING (1) [ACCEPT]
Heb 11:35 and others were tortured, not a deliverance; 4327

ACCESS (3)
Ro 5: 2 By whom also we have a by faith into this 4318
Eph 2:18 For through him we both have a by one 4318
3:12 and a with confidence by the faith of him. 4318

ACCESSORIES See FURNITURE

ACCHO (1)
Jdg 1:31 did Asher drive out the inhabitants of A, 5910

ACCIDENTALLY See UNAWARES

ACCO See ACCHO

ACCOMPANIED (4) [ACCOMPANY]
Ac 10:23 and certain brethren from Joppa a him. 4905
11:12 Moreover these six brethren a me, 2064+4862
20: 4 And there a him into Asia Sopater of 4902
20:38 no more. And they a him unto the ship. 4311

ACCOMPANY (1) [ACCOMPANIED, ACCOMPANYING]
Heb 6: 9 and *things* that a salvation, though we thus 2192

ACCOMPANYING (1) [ACCOMPANY]
2Sa 6: 4 which *was* at Gibeah, a the ark of God: 5973

ACCOMPLISH (13) [ACCOMPLISHED, ACCOMPLISHING, ACCOMPLISHMENT]
Lev 22:21 offerings unto the LORD to a *his* vow, 6381
1Ki 5: 9 receive *them:* and thou shalt a my desire, 6213
Job 14: 6 till he shall a, as a hireling, his day. 7521
Ps 64: 6 out iniquities; they a a diligent search: 8552
Isa 55:11 it shall a that which I please, and it shall 6213
Jer 44:25 ye will **surely** a your vows, and 6965+6965
Eze 6:12 thus will I a my fury upon them. 3615
7: 8 upon thee, and a mine anger upon thee: 3615
13:15 Thus will I a my wrath upon the wall, and 3615
20: 8 to a my anger against them in the midst of 3615
20:21 to a my anger against them in 3615
Da 9: 2 that *he* would a seventy years in 4390
Lk 9:31 spake of his decease which he should a at 4137

ACCOMPLISHED (26) [ACCOMPLISH]
2Ch 36:22 by the mouth of Jeremiah might be a, 3615
Est 2:12 so were the days of their purifications a, 4390
Job 15:32 It shall be a before his time, and his branch 4390
Pr 13:19 The desire a is sweet to the soul: but *it is* 1961
Isa 40: 2 cry unto her, that her warfare is a, that her 4390
Jer 25:12 come to pass, when seventy years are a, 4390
25:34 and of your dispersions are a. 4390
29:10 That after seventy years be a at Babylon I 4390
39:16 and they shall be *a* in that day before thee. NIH
La 4:11 The LORD hath a his fury; he hath poured 3615
4:22 The punishment of thine iniquity is a, 8552
Eze 4: 6 when thou hast a them, lie again on thy 3615
5:13 Thus shall mine anger be a, and I will 3615
5:13 in my zeal, when I have a my fury in them. 3615
Da 11:36 and shall prosper till the indignation be a: 3615
12: 7 when *he* shall have a to scatter the power of 3615
Lk 1:23 soon as the days of his ministration were a, 4130
2: 6 the days were a that she should be 4130
2:21 And when eight days were a for 4130
2:22 according to the law of Moses were a, 4130
12:50 and how am I straitened till it be a! 5055
18:31 concerning the Son of man shall be a. 5055
22:37 that this that is written must yet be a in me, 5055
Jn 19:28 Jesus knowing that all *things* were now a, 5055
Ac 21: 5 And when we had a *those* days, 1822
1Pe 5: 9 knowing that the same afflictions are a in 2005

ACCOMPLISHING (1) [ACCOMPLISH]
Heb 9: 6 the first tabernacle, a the service *of God.* 2005

ACCOMPLISHMENT (1) [ACCOMPLISH]
Ac 21:26 to signify the a of the days of purification, 1604

ACCORD (16) [ACCORDING, ACCORDINGLY]
Lev 25: 5 **That which groweth of it own** a of thy 5599
Jos 9: 2 with Joshua and with Israel, *with* one a. 6310
Ac 1:14 These all continued **with one** a in prayer 3661
2: 1 they were all **with one** a in one place. 3661
2:46 continuing daily **with one** a in the temple, 3661
4:24 they lift up their voice to God **with one** a, 3661
5:12 they were all **with one** a in Solomon's 3661
7:57 their ears, and ran upon him **with one** a, 3661
8: 6 And the people **with one** a gave heed unto 3661
12:10 the city; which opened to them **of his own** a: 844
12:20 but they came **with one** a to him, and, 3661
15:25 good unto us, being assembled **with one** a, 3661
18:12 the Jews made insurrection **with one** a 3661
19:29 they rushed **with one** a into the theatre. 3661
2Co 8:17 **of his own** a he went unto you. 830
Php 2: 2 the same love, *being* of **one** a, of one mind. 4861

ACCORDING (793) [ACCORD] See Index

ACCORDINGLY (1) [ACCORD]
Isa 59:18 a he will repay, fury to his 5921+3509.1

ACCOUNT (17) [ACCOUNTED, ACCOUNTING, ACCOUNTS]
2Ki 12: 4 *the* a, the money that every man is set at, NIH
1Ch 27:24 neither was the number put in the a of 4557
2Ch 26:11 according to the number of their a by 6486
Job 33:13 for he **giveth** not a of any of his matters. 6030
Ps 144: 3 the son of man, that thou **makest** a of him? 2803
Ecc 7:27 *counting* one by one, to find out the a: 2808
Mt 12:36 they shall give a thereof in the day of 3056
18:23 which would take a of his servants. 3056
Lk 16: 2 give an a of thy stewardship; for thou 3056
Ac 19:40 we may give an a of this concourse. 3056
Ro 14:12 every one of us shall give a of himself to 3056
1Co 4: 1 Let a man so a of us, as of the ministers of 3049
Php 4:17 but I desire fruit that *may* abound to your a. 3056
Phm 1:18 or oweth *thee* ought, **put** that **on** mine a; 1677
Heb 13:17 as they that must give a, that they may do it 3056
1Pe 4: 5 Who shall give a to him that is ready to 3056

2Pe 3:15 And **a** *that* the longsuffering of our Lord *is* 2233

ACCOUNTED (12) [ACCOUNT]
Dt 2:11 Which also were **a** giants, as the Anakims; 2803
2:20 (That also was **a** a land of giants: 2803
1Ki 10:21 it was nothing **a** of in the days of Solomon. 2803
2Ch 9:20 it was *not* any thing **a** of in the days of 2803
Ps 22:30 it shall be **a** to the Lord for a generation. 5608
Isa 2:22 in his nostrils: for wherein is he *to be* **a** of? 2803
Mk 10:42 Ye know that they which are **a** to rule over *1380*
Lk 20:35 But they which shall be **a worthy** to obtain *2661*
21:36 that ye may be **a worthy** to escape all these *2661*
22:24 which of them should be **a** the greatest. *1380*
Ro 8:36 we are **a** as sheep for the slaughter. *3049*
Gal 3: 6 and it was **a** to him for righteousness. *3049*

ACCOUNTING (1) [ACCOUNT]
Heb 11:19 **A** that God *was* able to raise *him* up, *3049*

ACCOUNTS (1) [ACCOUNT]
Da 6: 2 that the princes might give **a** unto them, 2942

ACCURSED (20) [CURSE]
Dt 21:23 (for he that is hanged *is* **a** of God;) that thy 7045
Jos 6:17 the city shall be **a**, *even* it, and all that *are* 2764
6:18 any wise keep *yourselves* from the **a thing**, 2764
6:18 lest ye **make** *yourselves* **a**, when ye take of 2763
6:18 when ye take of the **a thing**, and make 2764
7: 1 Israel committed a trespass in the **a thing**: 2764
7: 1 of the tribe of Judah, took of the **a thing**: 2764
7:11 for they have even taken of the **a thing**, and 2764
7:12 before their enemies, because they were **a**: 2764
7:12 except ye destroy the **a** from amongst you. 2764
7:13 *There is* an **a thing** in the midst of thee, 2764
7:13 until ye take away the **a thing** from among 2764
7:15 *that* he that is taken with the **a thing** shall 2764
22:20 of Zerah commit a trespass in the **a thing**, 2764
1Ch 2: 7 of Israel, who transgressed in the **thing a**. 2764
Isa 65:20 *being* an hundred years old shall be **a**. 7043
Ro 9: 3 For I could wish that myself were **a** from *331*
1Co 12: 3 by the Spirit of God calleth Jesus **a**: *331*
Gal 1: 8 we have preached unto you, let him be **a**. *331*
1: 9 you than that ye have received, let him be **a**. *331*

ACCUSATION (10) [ACCUSE]
Ezr 4: 6 wrote they *unto him* an **a** against 7855
Mt 27:37 And set up over his head his **a** written, *156*
Mk 15:26 And the superscription of his **a** was written *156*
Lk 6: 7 that they might find an **a against** him. *2724*
19: 8 **taken** any *thing* from any *man* **by false a**, *4811*
Jn 18:29 said, What **a** bring you against this man? *2724*
Ac 25:18 brought none **a** of *such things* as I supposed: *156*
1Ti 5:19 Against an elder receive not an **a**, but *2724*
2Pe 2:11 bring not railing **a** against them before *2920*
Jude 1: 9 durst not bring against *him* a railing **a**, but *2920*

ACCUSE (16) [ACCUSATION, ACCUSED, ACCUSER, ACCUSERS, ACCUSETH, ACCUSING]
Pr 30:10 **A** not a servant unto his master, lest he 3960
Mt 12:10 on the sabbath days? that they might **a** him. *2723*
Mk 3: 2 on the sabbath day; that they might **a** him. *2723*
Lk 3:14 violence to no man, neither **a** *any* **falsely**; *4811*
11:54 out of his mouth, that they might **a** him. *2723*
23: 2 And they began to **a** him, saying, We found *2723*
23:14 *touching those things* whereof ye **a** him: *2723*
Jn 5:45 Do not think that I will **a** you to the Father: *2723*
8: 6 that they might have to **a** him. *2723*
Ac 24: 2 *forth,* Tertullus began to **a** *him,* saying, *2723*
24: 8 of all these *things,* whereof we **a** him. *2723*
24:13 prove *the things* whereof they now **a** me. *2723*
25: 5 are able, go down with *me,* and **a** this man, *2723*
25:11 be none *of these things* whereof these **a** me, *2723*
28:19 not that I had ought to **a** my nation of. *2723*
1Pe 3:16 they may be ashamed that **falsely a** your *1908*

ACCUSED (14) [ACCUSE]
Da 3: 8 Chaldeans came near, and **a** the Jews. 399+7170
6:24 they brought those men which had **a** 399+7170
Mt 27:12 And when he was **a** of the chief priests and *2723*
Mk 15: 3 And the chief priests **a** him of many *things:* *2723*
Lk 16: 1 the same was **a** unto him that he had wasted *1225*
23:10 and scribes stood and vehemently **a** him. *2723*
Ac 22:30 certainty wherefore he was **a** of the Jews, *2723*
23:28 known the cause wherefore they **a** him, *1458*
23:29 Whom I perceived to be **a** of questions of *1458*
25:16 before that he which is **a** have the accusers *2723*
26: 2 all *the things* whereof I am **a** of the Jews: *1458*
26: 7 king Agrippa, I am **a** of the Jews. *1458*
Tit 1: 6 having faithful children not **a** of riot *1722+2724*
Rev 12:10 which **a** them before our God day and *2723*

ACCUSER (1) [ACCUSE]
Rev 12:10 for the **a** of our brethren is cast down, *2725*

ACCUSERS (8) [ACCUSE]
Jn 8:10 unto her, Woman, where are those thine **a**? *2725*
Ac 23:30 gave commandment to *his* **a** also to say *2725*
23:35 said he, when thine **a** are also come. *2725*
24: 8 Commanding his **a** to come unto thee: *2725*
25:16 before that he which is accused have the **a** *2725*
25:18 Against whom when the **a** stood *up,* they *2725*
2Ti 3: 3 trucebreakers, **false a**, incontinent, fierce, *1228*
Tit 2: 3 not **false a**, not given to much wine, *1228*

ACCUSETH (1) [ACCUSE]
Jn 5:45 there is *one* that **a** you, *even* Moses, *2723*

ACCUSING (1) [ACCUSE]
Ro 2:15 and *their* thoughts the mean while **a** or *2723*

ACCUSTOMED (1) [CUSTOM]
Jer 13:23 may ye also do good, that are **a to** do evil. 3928

ACELDAMA (1)
Ac 1:19 **A**, that is to say, The field of blood. *184*

ACHAIA (11)
Ac 18:12 And when Gallio was the deputy of **A**, *882*
18:27 And when he was disposed to pass into **A**, *882*
19:21 he had passed through Macedonia and **A**, *882*
Ro 15:26 **A** to make a certain contribution for the poor *882*
16: 5 who is the firstfruits of **A** unto Christ. *882*
1Co 16:15 that it is the firstfruits of **A**, and *that* they *882*
2Co 1: 1 with all the saints which are in all **A**: *882*
9: 2 of Macedonia, that **A** was ready a year ago; *882*
11:10 stop me of this boasting in the regions of **A**. *882*
1Th 1: 7 to all that believe in Macedonia and **A**. *882*
1: 8 of the Lord not only in Macedonia and **A**, *882*

ACHAICUS (2)
1Co 16:17 coming of Stephanas and Fortunatus and **A**: *883*
16: S and Fortunatus, and **A**, and Timotheus. *883*

ACHAN (6) [ACHAR]
Jos 7: 1 for **A**, the son of Carmi, the son of Zabdi, 5912
7:18 **A**, the son of Carmi, the son of Zabdi, 5912
7:19 Joshua said unto **A**, My son, give, I pray 5912
7:20 **A** answered Joshua, and said, Indeed I have 5912
7:24 took **A** the son of Zerah, and the silver, and 5912
22:20 Did not **A** the son of Zerah commit a 5912

ACHAR (1) [ACHAN]
1Ch 2: 7 **A**, the troubler of Israel, who transgressed 5917

ACHAZ (2) [AHAZ]
Mt 1: 9 and Joatham begat **A**; and Achaz begat *881*
1: 9 Joatham begat Achaz; and **A** begat Ezekias; *881*

ACHBOR (7)
Ge 36:38 Baal-hanan the son of **A** reigned in his 5907
36:39 Baal-hanan the son of **A** died, and 5907
2Ki 22:12 **A** the son of Michaiah, and Shaphan 5907
22:14 Ahikam, and **A**, and Shaphan, and Asahiah, 5907
1Ch 1:49 Baal-hanan the son of **A** reigned in his 5907
Jer 26:22 *namely,* Elnathan the son of **A**, and 5907
36:12 Elnathan the son of **A**, and Gemariah 5907

ACHIM (2)
Mt 1:14 and Sadoc begat **A**; and Achim begat Eliud; *885*
1:14 and Sadoc begat Achim; and **A** begat Eliud; *885*

ACHISH (21)
1Sa 21:10 fear of Saul, and went to **A** the king of Gath. 397
21:11 the servants of **A** said unto him, *Is* not this 397
21:12 and was sore afraid of **A** the king of Gath. 397
21:14 said **A** unto his servants, Lo, you see 397
27: 2 six hundred men that *were* with him unto **A**, 397
27: 3 David dwelt with **A** at Gath, he and his men, 397
27: 5 David said unto **A**, If I have now found 397
27: 6 **A** gave him Ziklag that day: wherefore 397
27: 9 the apparel, and returned, and came to **A**. 397

1Sa 27:10 **A** said, Whither have ye made a road to day? 397
27:12 **A** believed David, saying, He hath made his 397
28: 1 **A** said unto David, Know thou assuredly, 397
28: 2 David said to **A**, Surely thou shalt know 397
28: 2 **A** said to David, Therefore will I make thee 397
29: 2 his men passed on in the rereward with **A**. 397
29: 3 What *do* these Hebrews *here?* And **A** said 397
29: 6 **A** called David, and said unto him, Surely, 397
29: 8 David said unto **A**, But what have I done? 397
29: 9 **A** answered and said to David, I know that 397
1Ki 2:39 away unto **A** son of Maachah king of Gath. 397
2:40 and went to Gath to **A** to seek his servants: 397

ACHMETHA (1)
Ezr 6: 2 there was found at **A**, in the palace that *is* in 307

ACHOR (5)
Jos 7:24 and they brought them *unto* the valley of **A**. 5911
7:26 was called, The valley of **A**, unto this day. 5911
15: 7 went up toward Debir from the valley of **A**, 5911
Isa 65:10 the valley of **A** a place for the herds to lie 5911
Hos 2:15 and the valley of **A** for a door of hope: 5911

ACHSAH (5)
Jos 15:16 to him will I give **A** my daughter to wife. 5915
15:17 and he gave him **A** his daughter to wife. 5915
Jdg 1:12 to him will I give **A** my daughter to wife. 5915
1:13 and he gave him **A** his daughter to wife. 5915
1Ch 2:49 of Gibea: and the daughter of Caleb *was* **A**. 5915

ACHSHAPH (3)
Jos 11: 1 to the king of Shimron, and to the king of **A**, 407
12:20 of Shimron-meron, one; the king of **A**, one; 407
19:25 was Helkath, and Hali, and Beten, and **A**, 407

ACHZIB (4)
Jos 15:44 Keilah, and **A**, and Mareshah; nine cities 392
19:29 thereof are at the sea from the coast to **A**: 392
Jdg 1:31 nor of Ahlab, nor of **A**, nor of Helbah, nor of 392
Mic 1:14 the houses of **A** *shall be* a lie to the kings of 392

ACKNOWLEDGE (16) [ACKNOWLEDGED, ACKNOWLEDGEMENT, ACKNOWLEDGETH, ACKNOWLEDGING]
Dt 21:17 he shall **a** the son of the hated *for* 5234
33: 9 neither did he **a** his brethren, nor knew his 5234
Ps 51: 3 For I **a** my transgressions: and my sin *is* 3045
Pr 3: 6 In all thy ways **a** him, and he shall direct 3045
Isa 33:13 and ye *that are* near, **a** my might. 3045
61: 9 all that see them shall **a** them, that they *are* 5234
63:16 be ignorant of us, and Israel **a** us not: 5234
Jer 3:13 Only **a** thine iniquity, that thou hast 3045
14:20 We **a**, O LORD, our wickedness, *and* 3045
24: 5 will I **a** them that are carried away captive 5234
Da 11:39 whom he shall **a** *and* increase *with* glory: 5234
Hos 5:15 till they **a** their **offence**, and seek my face: 816
1Co 14:37 let him **a** that *the things* that I write unto *1921*
16:18 therefore **a** ye *them that are* such. *1921*
2Co 1:13 *things* unto you, than what you read or **a**; *1921*
1:13 and I trust you shall **a** even to the end; *1921*

ACKNOWLEDGED (3) [ACKNOWLEDGE]
Ge 38:26 Judah **a** *them*, and said, She hath been more 5234
Ps 32: 5 I **a** my sin unto thee, and mine iniquity 3045
2Co 1:14 As also you have **a** us in part, that we are *1921*

ACKNOWLEDGEMENT (1) [ACKNOWLEDGE]
Col 2: 2 to the **a** of the mystery of God and of *1922*

ACKNOWLEDGETH (1) [ACKNOWLEDGE]
1Jn 2:23 *but he that* **a** *the Son hath the* [Father] [also.] NIG

ACKNOWLEDGING (3) [ACKNOWLEDGE]
2Ti 2:25 give them repentance to the **a** of the truth; *1922*
Tit 1: 1 the **a** of the truth which is after godliness, *1922*
Phm 1: 6 **a** of every good *thing* which is in you in *1922*

ACQUAINT (1) [ACQUAINTANCE, ACQUAINTED, ACQUAINTING]
Job 22:21 **A** now thyself with him, and be at peace: 5532

ACQUAINTANCE (11) [ACQUAINT]
2Ki 12: 5 priests take *it* to them, every man of his **a**: 4378
12: 7 therefore receive no *more* money of your **a**, 4378
Job 19:13 and mine **a** are verily estranged from me. 3045
42:11 all *they that had been of* his **a** before, and 3045
Ps 31:11 my neighbours, and a fear to mine **a**: 3045
55:13 a man mine equal, my guide, and mine **a**. 3045
88: 8 Thou hast put away mine **a** far from me; 3045
88:18 put far from me, *and* mine **a** *into* darkness. 3045
Lk 2:44 sought him among *their* kinsfolk and **a**. *1110*
23:49 And all his **a**, and the women that followed *1110*
Ac 24:23 that *he* should forbid none of his **a** to *2398*

ACQUAINTED (2) [ACQUAINT]
Ps 139: 3 my lying down, and art **a** *with* all my ways. 5532
Isa 53: 3 of men; a man of sorrows, and **a with** grief: 3045

ACQUAINTING (1) [ACQUAINT]
Ecc 2: 3 unto wine, (yet **a** mine heart with wisdom) 5090

ACQUIT (2)
Job 10:14 and thou wilt not **a** me from mine iniquity. 5352
Na 1: 3 will not **at all a** *the wicked:* 5352+5352

ACRE (1) [ACRES]
1Sa 14:14 within as it were a half **a** of land, 4618

ACRES (1) [ACRE]
Isa 5:10 ten **a** of vineyard shall yield one bath, and 6776

ACSAH See ACHSA; ACHSAH

ACSHAPH See ACHSHAPH

ACT (4) [ACTIONS, ACTIVITY, ACTS]
Isa 28:21 and bring to pass his **a**, his strange act. 5656
28:21 and bring to pass his act, his strange **a**. 5656
59: 6 and the **a** of violence *is* in their hands. 6467
Jn 8: 4 was taken in adultery, **in the very a**. *1888*

ACTIONS (1) [ACT]
1Sa 2: 3 of knowledge, and by him **a** are weighed. 5949

ACTIVITY (1) [ACT]
Ge 47: 6 if thou knowest *any* man of **a** amongst 2428

ACTS (66) [ACT]
Dt 11: 3 his miracles, and his **a**, which he did in 4639
11: 7 your eyes have seen all the great **a** of 4639
Jdg 5:11 rehearse the **righteous a** of the LORD, 6666
5:11 *even* the **righteous a** *towards* 6666
1Sa 12: 7 of all the **righteous a** of the LORD, 6666
2Sa 23:20 of Kabzeel, who had **done** many **a**, 6467
1Ki 10: 6 that I heard in mine own land of thy **a** 1697
11:41 the rest of the **a** of Solomon, and all that he 1697
11:41 *are* they not written in the book of the **a** of 1697
14:19 the rest of the **a** of Jeroboam, how he 1697
14:29 Now the rest of the **a** of Rehoboam, and 1697
15: 7 Now the rest of the **a** of Abijam, and 1697
15:23 The rest of all the **a** of Asa, and all his 1697
15:31 Now the rest of the **a** of Nadab, and all that 1697
16: 5 Now the rest of the **a** of Baasha, and 1697
16:14 Now the rest of the **a** of Elah, and all that 1697
16:20 Now the rest of the **a** of Zimri, and 1697
16:27 Now the rest of the **a** of Omri which he did, 1697
22:39 Now the rest of the **a** of Ahab, and all that 1697
22:45 Now the rest of the **a** of Jehoshaphat, and 1697
2Ki 1:18 Now the rest of the **a** of Ahaziah which he 1697
8:23 the rest of the **a** of Joram, and all that he 1697
10:34 Now the rest of the **a** of Jehu, and all that 1697
12:19 the rest of the **a** of Joash, and all that he 1697
13: 8 Now the rest of the **a** of Jehoahaz, and 1697
13:12 the rest of the **a** of Joash, and all that he 1697
14:15 Now the rest of the **a** of Jehoash which he 1697
14:18 the rest of the **a** of Amaziah, *are* they not 1697
14:28 Now the rest of the **a** of Jeroboam, and 1697
15: 6 the rest of the **a** of Azariah, and all that he 1697
15:11 the rest of the **a** of Zachariah, behold, 1697
15:15 the rest of the **a** of Shallum, and 1697
15:21 the rest of the **a** of Menahem, and all that 1697
15:26 the rest of the **a** of Pekahiah, and all that he 1697
15:31 the rest of the **a** of Pekah, and all that he 1697
15:36 Now the rest of the **a** of Jotham, and all that 1697
16:19 Now the rest of the **a** of Ahaz which he did, 1697
20:20 the rest of the **a** of Hezekiah, and all his 1697
21:17 Now the rest of the **a** of Manasseh, and 1697
21:25 Now the rest of the **a** of Amon which he 1697
23:19 did to them according to all the **a** that he 4639
23:28 Now the rest of the **a** of Josiah, and all that 1697
24: 5 Now the rest of the **a** of Jehoiakim, and 1697

1Ch 11:22 man of Kabzeel, who had **done** many **a**; 6467
29:29 Now the **a** of David the king, first and last, 1697
2Ch 9: 5 which I heard in mine own land of thine **a**, 1697
9:29 Now the rest of the **a** of Solomon, first and 1697
12:15 Now the **a** of Rehoboam, first and last, *are* 1697
13:22 the rest of the **a** of Abijah, and his ways, 1697
16:11 behold, the **a** of Asa, first and last, lo, 1697
20:34 Now the rest of the **a** of Jehoshaphat, first 1697
25:26 Now the rest of the **a** of Amaziah, first and 1697
26:22 Now the rest of the **a** of Uzziah, first and 1697
27: 7 Now the rest of the **a** of Jotham, and all his 1697
28:26 Now the rest of his **a** and of all his ways, 1697
32:32 Now the rest of the **a** of Hezekiah, and 1697
33:18 Now the rest of the **a** of Manasseh, and 1697
35:26 Now the rest of the **a** of Josiah, and 1697
36: 8 Now the rest of the **a** of Jehoiakim, and 1697
Est 10: 2 all the **a** of his power and of his might, and 4639
Ps 103: 7 his **a** unto the children of Israel. 5949
106: 2 Who can utter the **mighty a** of 1369
145: 4 to another, and shall declare thy **mighty a**. 1369
145: 6 shall speak of the might of thy **terrible a**: 3372
145:12 known to the sons of men his **mighty a**, 1369
150: 2 Praise him for his **mighty a**: praise him 1369

ACTS OF RIGHTEOUSNESS See ALMS

ACZIB See ACHZIB

ADADAH (1)
Jos 15:22 And Kinah, and Dimonah, and **A**, 5735

ADAH (8)
Ge 4:19 the name of the one *was* **A**, and the name of 5711
4:20 **A** bare Jabal: he was the father of such as 5711
4:23 his wives, **A** and Zillah, Hear my voice; 5711
36: 2 **A** the daughter of Elon the Hittite, and 5711
36: 4 **A** bare to Esau Eliphaz; and 5711
36:10 Eliphaz the son of **A** the wife of Esau, 5711
36:12 these *were* the sons of **A** Esau's wife. 5711
36:16 the land of Edom; these *were* the sons of **A**. 5711

ADAIAH (9)
2Ki 22: 1 *was* Jedidah, the daughter of **A** of Boscath. 5718
1Ch 6:41 son of Ethni, the son of Zerah, the son of **A**, 5718
8:21 **A**, and Beraiah, and Shimrath, the sons of 5718
9:12 **A** the son of Jeroham, the son of Pashur, 5718
2Ch 23: 1 Maaseiah the son of **A**, and Elishaphat 5718
Ezr 10:29 and **A**, Jashub, and Sheal, and Ramoth. 5718
10:39 And Shelemiah, and Nathan, and **A**, 5718
Ne 11: 5 of Hazaiah, the son of **A**, the son of Joiarib, 5718
11:12 **A** the son of Jeroham, the son of Pelaliah, 5718

ADALIA (1)
Est 9: 8 And Poratha, and **A**, and Aridatha, 118

ADAM (30) [ADAM'S]
Ge 2:19 brought *them* unto **A** to see what he would 120
2:19 whatsoever **A** called every living creature, 120
2:20 **A** gave names to all cattle, and to the fowl of 120
2:20 for **A** there was not found a help meet for 120
2:21 God caused a deep sleep to fall upon **A**, 120
2:23 **A** said, This *is* now bone of my bones, and 120
3: 8 **A** and his wife hid themselves from 120
3: 9 the LORD God called unto **A**, and 120
3:17 unto **A** he said, Because thou hast hearkened 120
3:20 **A** called his wife's name Eve; because 120
3:21 Unto **A** also and to his wife did the LORD 120
4: 1 **A** knew Eve his wife; and she conceived, 120
4:25 **A** knew his wife again; and she bare a son, 120
5: 1 This *is* the book of the generations of **A**. 120
5: 2 blessed them, and called their name **A**, in 120
5: 3 And **A** lived an hundred and thirty years, and 120
5: 4 the days of **A** after he had begotten Seth 120
5: 5 all the days that **A** lived were nine hundred 120
Dt 32: 8 when he separated the sons of **A**, 120
Jos 3:16 from the city **A**, that *is* beside Zaretan: 121
1Ch 1: 1 **A**, Sheth, Enosh, 121
Job 31:33 If I covered my transgressions as **A**, by 120
Lk 3:38 which was *the son* of **A**, which was *the son* of *76*
Ro 5:14 Nevertheless death reigned from **A** to Moses, *76*
1Co 15:22 For as in **A** all die, even so in Christ shall all *76*
15:45 The first man **A** was made a living soul; *76*
15:45 the last **A** *was made* a quickening spirit. *76*
1Ti 2:13 For **A** was first formed, then Eve. *76*
2:14 And **A** was not deceived, but the woman *76*
Jude 1:14 And Enoch also, the seventh from **A**, *76*

ADAM'S (1) [ADAM]
Ro 5:14 sinned after the similitude of **A** transgression, *76*

ADAMAH (1)
Jos 19:36 And **A**, and Ramah, and Hazor, 128

ADAMANT (2)
Eze 3: 9 As an **a** harder than flint have I made thy 8068
Zec 7:12 Yea, they made their hearts *as* an **a stone**, 8068

ADAMI (1)
Jos 19:33 and **A**, Nekeb, and Jabneel, unto Lakum; 129

ADAR (10)
Jos 15: 3 went up to **A**, and fetched a compass to 146
Ezr 6:15 finished on the third day of the month **A**, 144
Est 3: 7 *to* the twelfth *month,* that *is,* the month **A**. 143
3:13 which *is* the month **A**, and *to take* the spoil 143
8:12 of the twelfth month, which *is* the month **A**. 143
9: 1 in the twelfth month, that *is,* the month **A**, 143
9:15 on the fourteenth day also of the month **A**, 143
9:17 On the thirteenth day of the month **A**; and 143
9:19 made the fourteenth day of the month **A** *a* 143
9:21 keep the fourteenth day of the month **A**, 143

ADBEEL (2)
Ge 25:13 Nebajoth; and Kedar, and **A**, and Mibsam, 110
1Ch 1:29 Nebajoth; then Kedar, and **A**, and Mibsam, 110

ADD (33) [ADDED, ADDETH, ADDITION, ADDITIONS]
Ge 30:24 The LORD shall **a** to me another son. 3254
Lev 5:16 holy *thing,* and shall **a** the fifth *part* thereto, 3254
6: 5 shall **a** the fifth *part* more thereto, *and* 3254
27:13 he shall **a** a fifth *part* thereof unto thy 3254
27:15 he shall **a** the fifth *part* of the money of thy 3254
27:19 he shall **a** the fifth *part* of the money of thy 3254
27:27 and shall **a** a fifth *part* of it thereto: 3254
27:31 he shall **a** thereto the fifth *part* thereof. 3254
Nu 5: 7 **a** unto it the fifth *part* thereof, and give *it* 3254
35: 6 to them ye shall **a** forty and two cities. 5414
Dt 4: 2 Ye shall not **a** unto the word which I 3254
12:32 thou shalt not **a** thereto, nor diminish from 3254
19: 9 shalt thou **a** three cities moe for thee, 3254
29:19 of mine heart, to **a** drunkenness *to* thirst: 5595
2Sa 24: 3 Now the LORD thy God **a** unto 3254
1Ki 12:11 with a heavy yoke, I will **a** to your yoke: 3254
12:14 your yoke heavy, and I will **a** to your yoke: 3254
2Ki 20: 6 I will **a** unto thy days fifteen years; and 3254
1Ch 22:14 have I prepared; and thou mayest **a** thereto. 3254
2Ch 10:14 made your yoke heavy, but I will **a** thereto: 3254
28:13 *already,* ye intend to **a** *more* to our sins 3254
Ps 69:27 **A** iniquity unto their iniquity: and let them 5414
Pr 3: 2 long life, and peace, shall they **a** to thee. 3254
30: 6 **A** thou not unto his words, lest he reprove 3254
Isa 29: 1 **a** ye year to year; let them kill sacrifices. 5595
30: 1 not of my Spirit, that *they* may **a** sin to sin: 5595
38: 5 behold, I will **a** unto thy days fifteen years. 3254
Mt 6:27 Which of you by taking thought can **a** one *4369*
Lk 12:25 which of you with taking thought can **a** *4369*
Php 1:16 supposing to **a** affliction to my bonds: *2018*
2Pe 1: 5 giving all diligence, **a** to your faith virtue; *2023*
Rev 22:18 If any *man* shall **a** unto these *things,* God *2007*
22:18 **a** unto him the plagues that are written in *2007*

ADDAN (1)
Ezr 2:59 Tel-harsa, Cherub, **A**, *and* Immer: 135

ADDAR (1) [HAZAR-ADDAR]
1Ch 8: 3 sons of Bela were, **A**, and Gera, and Abihud, 146

ADDED (16) [ADD]
Dt 5:22 he **a** no **more**. And he wrote them in two 3254
1Sa 12:19 for we have **a** unto all our sins *this* evil, 3254
Jer 36:32 there were **a** besides unto them many like 3254
45: 3 for the LORD hath **a** grief to my sorrow; 3254
Da 4:36 and excellent majesty was **a** unto me. 3255
Mt 6:33 and all these *things* shall be **a** unto you. *4369*
Lk 3:20 **A** yet this above all, that he shut up John in *4369*
12:31 and all these *things* shall be **a** unto you. *4369*
19:11 And as they heard these *things,* he **a** and *4369*
Ac 2:41 the same day there were **a** *unto them* about *4369*
2:47 And the Lord **a** to the church daily such as *4369*
5:14 And believers were the more **a** to the Lord, *4369*

Ac 11:24 and much people was **a** unto the Lord. *4369*
Gal 2: 6 *somewhat* in conference **a** nothing to me: *4323*
3:15 no *man* disannulleth, or **a** thereto. *1928*
3:19 It was **a** because of transgressions, till *4369*

ADDER (4) [ADDER'S]
Ge 49:17 an **a** in the path, that biteth the horse heels, 8207
Ps 58: 4 *they are* like the deaf **a** *that* stoppeth her 6620
91:13 Thou shalt tread upon the lion and **a**: 6620
Pr 23:32 biteth like a serpent, and stingeth like an **a**. 6848

ADDER'S (1) [ADDER]
Ps 140: 3 like a serpent; **a** poison *is* under their lips. 5919

ADDETH (3) [ADD]
Job 34:37 For he **a** rebellion unto his sin, he clappeth 3254
Pr 10:22 it maketh rich, and he **a** no sorrow with it. 3254
16:23 his mouth, and **a** learning to his lips. 3254

ADDI (1)
Lk 3:28 which was *the son* of **A**, which was *the son* of *78*

ADDICTED (1)
1Co 16:15 *that* they have **a** themselves to the ministry *5021*

ADDITION (1) [ADD]
1Ki 7:30 undersetters molten, at the side of every **a**. 3914

ADDITIONS (2) [ADD]
1Ki 7:29 and oxen *were certain* **a** made of thin work. 3914
7:36 proportion of every one, and **a** round about. 3914

ADDON (1)
Ne 7:61 Tel-haresha, Cherub, **A**, and Immer: 114

ADER (1)
1Ch 8:15 And Zebadiah, and Arad, and **A**, 5738

ADIEL (3)
1Ch 4:36 Asaiah, and **A**, and Jesimiel, and Benaiah, 5717
9:12 Maasiai the son of **A**, the son of Jahzerah, 5717
27:25 treasures *was* Azmaveth the son of **A**: 5717

ADIN (4)
Ezr 2:15 The children of **A**, four hundred fifty and 5720
8: 6 Of the sons also of **A**; Ebed the son of 5720
Ne 7:20 The children of **A**, six hundred fifty and 5720
10:16 Adonijah, Bigvai, **A**, 5720

ADINA (1)
1Ch 11:42 **A** the son of Shiza the Reubenite, a captain 5721

ADINO (1)
2Sa 23: 8 the captains; the same *was* **A** the Eznite: 5722

ADITHAIM (1)
Jos 15:36 and **A**, and Gederah, and Gederothaim; 5723

ADJURE (5) [ADJURED]
1Ki 22:16 How many times shall I **a** thee that thou tell 7650
2Ch 18:15 How many times shall I **a** thee that thou say 7650
Mt 26:63 said unto him, I **a** thee by the living God, *1844*
Mk 5: 7 I **a** thee by God, that thou torment me not. *3726*
Ac 19:13 We **a** you by Jesus whom Paul preacheth. *3726*

ADJURED (2) [ADJURE]
Jos 6:26 Joshua **a** *them* at that time, saying, 7650
1Sa 14:24 for Saul had **a** the people, saying, Cursed *be* 422

ADLAI (1)
1Ch 27:29 in the valleys *was* Shaphat the son of **A**: 5724

ADMAH (5)
Ge 10:19 Gomorrah, and **A**, and Zeboim, even unto 126
14: 2 Shinab king of **A**, and Shemeber king of 126
14: 8 the king of **A**, and the king of Zeboiim, and 126
Dt 29:23 of Sodom, and Gomorrah, **A**, and Zeboim, 126
Hos 11: 8 how shall I make thee as **A**? *how* shall I set 126

ADMATHA (1)
Est 1:14 Shethar, **A**, Tarshish, Meres, Marsena, *and* 133

ADMINISTERED (2) [ADMINISTRATION]
2Co 8:19 which is **a** by us to the glory of the same *1247*
8:20 us in this abundance which is **a** by us: *1247*

ADMINISTRATION (1) [ADMINISTERED, ADMINISTRATIONS]
2Co 9:12 For the **a** of this service not only supplieth *1248*

ADMINISTRATIONS (1) [ADMINISTRATION]
1Co 12: 5 And there are differences of **a**, but the same *1248*

ADMIRATION (2) [ADMIRED]
Jude 1:16 *words,* having *men's* persons in **a** *2296+4383*
Rev 17: 6 when I saw her, I wondered *with* great **a**. *2295*

ADMIRED (1) [ADMIRATION]
2Th 1:10 and to be **a** in all them that believe (because *2296*

ADMONISH (3) [ADMONISHED, ADMONISHING, ADMONITION]
Ro 15:14 all knowledge, able also to **a** one another. *3560*
1Th 5:12 and are over you in the Lord, and **a** you; *3560*
2Th 3:15 not as an enemy, but **a** *him* as a brother. *3560*

ADMONISHED (5) [ADMONISH]
Ecc 4:13 and foolish king, who will no more be **a**. 2094
12:12 further, by these, my son, be **a**: of making 2094
Jer 42:19 know certainly that I have **a** you *this* day. 5749
Ac 27: 9 the fast was now already past, Paul **a** *them,* *3867*
Heb 8: 5 **a** of God when he was about to make *5537*

ADMONISHING (1) [ADMONISH]
Col 3:16 and **a** one another in psalms and hymns and *3560*

ADMONITION (3) [ADMONISH]
1Co 10:11 and they are written for our **a**, upon whom *3559*
Eph 6: 4 them up in the nurture and **a** of the Lord. *3559*
Tit 3:10 *is* a heretick after the first and second **a**, *3559*

ADNA (2)
Ezr 10:30 **A**, and Chelal, Benaiah, Maaseiah, 5733
Ne 12:15 Of Harim, **A**; of Meraioth, Helkai; 5733

ADNAH (2)
1Ch 12:20 **A**, and Jozabad, and Jediael, and Michael, 5734
2Ch 17:14 **A** the chief, and with him mighty *men* of 5734

ADO (1)
Mk 5:39 unto them, Why make ye *this* **a**, and weep? *2350*

ADONI-BEZEK (3)
Jdg 1: 5 they found **A** in Bezek: and they fought 137
1: 6 **A** fled; and they pursued after him, and 137
1: 7 **A** said, Threescore and ten kings, 137

ADONIJAH (26)
2Sa 3: 4 the fourth, **A** the son of Haggith; and 138
1Ki 1: 5 **A** the son of Haggith exalted himself, 138
1: 7 the priest: and they following **A** helped *him.* 138
1: 8 which *belonged* to David, were not with **A**. 138
1: 9 **A** slew sheep and oxen and fat cattle by 138
1:11 Hast thou not heard that **A** the son of 138
1:13 sit upon my throne? why then doth **A** reign? 138
1:18 now behold, **A** reigneth; and now, my lord 138
1:24 **A** shall reign after me, and he shall sit upon 138
1:25 drink before him, and say, God save king **A**. 138
1:41 **A** and all the guests that *were* with him 138
1:42 **A** said *unto him,* Come in; for thou *art* a 138
1:43 Jonathan answered and said to **A**, Verily our 138
1:49 all the guests that *were* with **A** were afraid, 138
1:50 **A** feared because of Solomon, and arose, 138
1:51 Behold, **A** feareth king Solomon: 138
2:13 **A** the son of Haggith came to Bath-sheba 138
2:19 unto king Solomon, to speak unto him for **A**. 138
2:21 Let Abishag the Shunammite be given to **A** 138
2:22 thou ask Abishag the Shunammite for **A**? 138
2:23 if **A** have not spoken this word against his 138
2:24 he promised, **A** shall be put to death *this* day. 138
2:28 for Joab had turned after **A**, though he turned 138
1Ch 3: 2 of Geshur: the fourth, **A** the son of Haggith: 138
2Ch 17: 8 **A**, and Tobijah, and Tob-adonijah, Levites; 138
Ne 10:16 **A**, Bigvai, Adin, 138

ADONIKAM (3)
Ezr 2:13 The children of **A**, six hundred sixty and six. 140
8:13 of the last sons of **A**, whose names *are* these, 140
Ne 7:18 The children of **A**, six hundred threescore 140

ADONIRAM (2)
1Ki 4: 6 and **A** the son of Abda *was* over the tribute. 141

1Ki 5:14 months at home: and A was over the levy. 141

ADONI-ZEDEK (2)
Jos 10: 1 when A king of Jerusalem had heard how 139
10: 3 Wherefore A king of Jerusalem sent unto 139

ADOPTION (5)
Ro 8:15 but ye have received the Spirit of a, 5206
8:23 waiting for the a, to wit, the redemption of 5206
9: 4 to whom pertaineth the a, and the glory, 5206
Gal 4: 5 that we might receive the a of sons. 5206
Eph 1: 5 a of children by Jesus Christ to himself, 5206

ADORAIM (1)
2Ch 11: 9 And A, and Lachish, and Azekah, 115

ADORAM (2)
2Sa 20:24 A was over the tribute: and Jehoshaphat 151
1Ki 12:18 king Rehoboam sent A, who was over 151

ADORN (2) [ADORNED, ADORNETH, ADORNING]
1Ti 2: 9 that women a themselves in modest 2885
Tit 2:10 that they may a the doctrine of God our 2885

ADORNED (4) [ADORN]
Jer 31: 4 thou shalt again be a with thy tabrets, and 5710
Lk 21: 5 how it was a with goodly stones and gifts, 2885
1Pe 3: 5 who trusted in God, a themselves, being in 2885
Rev 21: 2 prepared as a bride a for her husband. 2885

ADORNETH (1) [ADORN]
Isa 61:10 and as a bride a herself with her jewels. 5710

ADORNING (2) [ADORN]
1Pe 3: 3 Whose a let it not be that outward adorning 2889
3: 3 Whose adorning let it not be that outward a NIG

ADRAMMELECH (3)
2Ki 17:31 Sepharvites burnt their children in fire to A 152
19:37 that A and Sharezer his sons smote him with 152
Isa 37:38 that A and Sharezer his sons smote him with 152

ADRAMYTTIUM (1)
Ac 27: 2 And entering into a ship of A, we launched, 98

ADRIA (1)
Ac 27:27 as we were driven up and down in A, 99

ADRIATIC See ADRIA

ADRIEL (2)
1Sa 18:19 that she was given unto A the Meholathite 5741
2Sa 21: 8 whom she brought up for A the son of 5741

ADULLAM (8) [ADULLAMITE]
Jos 12:15 king of Libnah, one; the king of A, one; 5725
15:35 Jarmuth, and A, Socoh, and Azekah, 5725
1Sa 22: 1 departed thence, and escaped to the cave A: 5725
2Sa 23:13 in the harvest time unto the cave of A: 5725
1Ch 11:15 to the rock to David, into the cave of A; 5725
2Ch 11: 7 And Beth-zur, and Shoco, and A, 5725
Ne 11:30 Zanoah, A, and in their villages, at Lachish, 5725
Mic 1:15 he shall come unto A the glory of Israel. 5725

ADULLAMITE (3) [ADULLAM]
Ge 38: 1 turned in to a certain A, whose name was 5726
38:12 to Timnath, he and his friend Hirah the A. 5726
38:20 sent the kid by the hand of his friend the A, 5726

ADULTERER (3) [ADULTERY]
Lev 20:10 the a and the adulteress shall surely be put 5003
Job 24:15 The eye also of the a waiteth for 5003
Isa 57: 3 the seed of the a and the whore. 5003

ADULTERERS (9) [ADULTERY]
Ps 50:18 with him, and hast been partaker with a. 5003
Jer 9: 2 for they be all a, an assembly of 5003
23:10 For the land is full of a; for because 5003
Hos 7: 4 They are all a, as an oven heated by 5003
Mal 3: 5 against the a, and against false swearers, 5003
Lk 18:11 unjust, a, or even as this publican. 3432
1Co 6: 9 nor idolaters, nor a, nor effeminate, 3432
Heb 13: 4 but whoremongers and a God will judge. 3432
Jas 4: 4 Ye a and adulteresses, know ye not that 3432

ADULTERESS (5) [ADULTERY]
Lev 20:10 and the a shall surely be put to death. 5003
Pr 6:26 and the a will hunt for the precious life. 376+802
Hos 3: 1 a woman beloved of her friend, yet an a, 5003
Ro 7: 3 to another man, she shall be called an a: 3428
7: 3 so that she is no a, though she be married to 3428

ADULTERESSES (3) [ADULTERY]
Eze 23:45 they shall judge them after the manner of a, 5003
23:45 because they are a, and blood is in their 5003
Jas 4: 4 Ye adulterers and a, know ye not that 3428

ADULTERIES (5) [ADULTERY]
Jer 13:27 I have seen thine a, and thy neighings, 5004
Eze 23:43 said I unto her that was old in a, Will they 5004
Hos 2: 2 and her a from between her breasts; 5005
Mt 15:19 murders, a, fornications, thefts, 3430
Mk 7:21 evil thoughts, a, fornications, murders, 3430

ADULTEROUS (4) [ADULTERY]
Pr 30:20 Such is the way of an a woman; she eateth, 5003
Mt 12:39 and a generation seeketh after a sign; 3428
16: 4 and a generation seeketh after a sign; 3428
Mk 8:38 and of my words in this a and 3428

ADULTERY (40) [ADULTERER, ADULTERERS, ADULTERESS, ADULTERESSES, ADULTERIES, ADULTEROUS]
Ex 20:14 Thou shalt not commit a. 5003
Lev 20:10 the man that committeth a with another 5003
20:10 even he that committeth a with his 5003
Dt 5:18 Neither shalt thou commit a. 5003
Pr 6:32 But whoso committeth a with a woman 5003
Jer 3: 8 Israel committed a I had put her away, 5003
3: 9 committed a with stones and with stocks. 5003
5: 7 they then committed a, and 5003
7: 9 commit a, and swear falsely, and 5003
23:14 they commit a, and walk in lies: 5003
29:23 have committed a with their neighbours' 5003
Eze 16:32 But as a wife that committeth a, 5003
23:37 That they have committed a, and blood is 5003
23:37 with their idols have they committed a, 5003
Hos 4: 2 killing, and stealing, and committing a, 5003
4:13 and your spouses shall commit a. 5003
4:14 nor your spouses when they commit a: 5003
Mt 5:27 them of old time, Thou shalt not commit a: 3431
5:28 committed a with her already in his heart. 3431
5:32 of fornication, causeth her to commit a: 3429
5:32 marry her that is divorced committeth a. 3429
19: 9 and shall marry another, committeth a: 3429
19: 9 her which is put away doth commit a. 3429
19:18 Thou shalt not commit a, Thou shalt not 3431
Mk 10:11 marry another, committeth a against her. 3429
10:12 be married to another, she committeth a. 3429
10:19 Do not commit a, Do not kill, Do not steal, 3431
Lk 16:18 and marrieth another, committeth a: 3431
16:18 put away from her husband committeth a. 3431
18:20 Do not commit a, Do not kill, Do not steal, 3431
Jn 8: 3 brought unto him a woman taken in a; 3430
8: 4 Master, this woman was taken in a, in 3431
Ro 2:22 that sayest a man should not commit a, 3431
2:22 not commit adultery, dost thou commit a? 3431
13: 9 For this, Thou shalt not commit a, 3431
Gal 5:19 which are these; A, fornication, 3430
Jas 2:11 Do not commit a, said also, Do not kill. 3431
2:11 Now if thou commit no a, yet if thou kill, 3431
2Pe 2:14 Having eyes full of a and that cannot cease 3428
Rev 2:22 them that commit a with her into great 3431

ADUMMIM (2)
Jos 15: 7 that is before the going up to A, 131
18:17 which is over against the going up of A, and 131

ADVANCED (4)
1Sa 12: 6 It is the LORD that a Moses and Aaron, 6213
Est 3: 1 a him, and set his seat above all the princes 5375
5:11 how he had a him above the princes and 5375
10: 2 of Mordecai, whereunto the king a him, 1431

ADVANTAGE (4) [ADVANTAGED, ADVANTAGETH]
Job 35: 3 For thou saidst, What a will it be unto thee? 5532
Ro 3: 1 What a then hath the Jew? or what profit is 4053
2Co 2:11 Lest Satan should get an a of us: for we are 4122
Jude 1:16 men's persons in admiration because of a. 5622

ADVANTAGED (1) [ADVANTAGE]
Lk 9:25 For what is a man a, if he gain the whole 5623

ADVANTAGETH (1) [ADVANTAGE]
1Co 15:32 what a it me, if the dead rise not? 3786

ADVENTURE (2) [ADVENTURED]
Dt 28:56 which would not a to set the sole of her 5254
Ac 19:31 desiring *him* that *he* would not a himself 1325

ADVENTURED (1) [ADVENTURE]
Jdg 9:17 a his life far, and delivered you out of 7993

ADVERSARIES (36) [ADVERSARY]
Ex 23:22 and an adversary unto thine a. 6887
Dt 32:27 lest their a should behave themselves 6862
32:43 will render vengeance to his a, and will be 6862
Jos 5:13 said unto him, *Art* thou for us, or for our a? 6862
1Sa 2:10 The a of the LORD shall be broken to 7378
2Sa 19:22 that ye should *this* day be a unto me? 7854
Ezr 4: 1 Now *when* the a of Judah and 6862
Ne 4:11 our a said, They shall not know, 6862
Ps 38:20 also that render evil for good are mine a; 7853
69:19 my dishonour: mine a *are* all before thee. 6887
71:13 *and* consumed that are a to my soul; 7853
81:14 and turned my hand against their a. 6862
89:42 Thou hast set up the right hand of his a; 6862
109: 4 For my love they are my a: but I *give* 7853
109:20 *Let* this *be* the reward of mine a from 7853
109:29 Let mine a be clothed with shame, and 7853
Isa 1:24 I will ease me of mine a, and avenge me of 6862
9:11 Therefore the LORD shall set up the a of 6862
11:13 and the a of Judah shall be cut off: 6887
59:18 accordingly he will repay, fury to his a, 6862
63:18 our a have trodden down thy sanctuary. 6862
64: 2 to boil, to make thy name known to thine a, 6862
Jer 30:16 all thine a, every one of them, shall go into 6862
46:10 that *he* may avenge him of his a: 6862
50: 7 their a said, We offend not, because they 6862
La 1: 5 Her a are the chief, her enemies prosper; 6862
1: 7 the a saw her, *and* did mock at her 6862
1:17 *that* his a *should be* round about him: 6862
2:17 he hath set up the horn of thine a. 6862
Mic 5: 9 Thine hand shall be lift up upon thine a, 6862
Na 1: 2 the LORD will take vengeance on his a, 6862
Lk 13:17 And when he had said these *things,* all his a 480
21:15 which all your a shall not be able to gainsay 480
1Co 16: 9 is opened unto me, and *there are* many a. 480
Php 1:28 And in nothing terrified by *your* a: which is 480
Heb 10:27 fiery indignation, which shall devour the a. 5227

ADVERSARY (22) [ADVERSARIES]
Ex 23:22 and an a unto thine adversaries. 6696
Nu 22:22 stood in the way for an a against him. 7854
1Sa 1: 6 her a also provoked her sore, for to make 6869
29: 4 to battle, lest in the battle he be an a to us: 7854
1Ki 5: 4 *so that there is* neither a nor evil occurrent. 7854
11:14 the LORD stirred up an a unto Solomon, 7854
11:23 God stirred him up *another* a, Rezon 7854
11:25 he was an a to Israel all the days of 7854
Est 7: 6 a and enemy *is* this wicked Haman. 376+6862
Job 31:35 and *that* mine a had written a book. 376+7379
Ps 74:10 O God, how long shall the a reproach? 6862
Isa 50: 8 *is* mine a? let him come near to me. 1167+4941
La 1:10 The a hath spread out his hand upon all her 6862
2: 4 *he* stood *with* his right hand as an a, and 6862
4:12 would not have believed that the a and 6862
Am 3:11 An a *there shall be* even round about 6862
Mt 5:25 Agree with thine a quickly, whiles thou art 476
5:25 lest at any time the a deliver thee to 476
Lk 12:58 When thou goest with thine a to 476
18: 3 unto him, saying, Avenge me of mine a. 476
1Ti 5:14 give none occasion to the a to speak 480
1Pe 5: 8 because your a the devil, as a roaring lion, 476

ADVERSITIES (2) [ADVERSITY]
1Sa 10:19 who himself saved you out of all your a 7451
Ps 31: 7 my trouble; thou hast known my soul in a; 6869

ADVERSITY (10) [ADVERSITIES]
2Sa 4: 9 who hath redeemed my soul out of all a, 6869
2Ch 15: 6 of city: for God did vex them with all a. 6869
Ps 10: 6 not be moved: for *I shall* never *be* in a. 7451
35:15 in mine a they rejoiced, and 6761
94:13 mayest give him rest from the days of a, 7451
Pr 17:17 at all times, and a brother is born for a. 6869
24:10 *If* thou faint in the day of a, thy strength *is* 6869
Ecc 7:14 be joyful, but in the day of a consider: 7451
Isa 30:20 *though* the Lord give you the bread of a, 6862
Heb 13: 3 bound with *them; and* them which suffer a, 2558

ADVERTISE (2)
Nu 24:14 I will a thee what this people shall do to thy 3289
Ru 4: 4 I thought to a thee, saying, Buy *it* 241+1540

ADVICE (9) [ADVISE]
Jdg 19:30 of it, take a, and speak *your minds.* 5779
20: 7 of Israel; give here your a and counsel. 1697
1Sa 25:33 blessed *be* thy a, and blessed *be* thou, 2940
2Sa 19:43 that our a should not be first had in 1697
2Ch 10: 9 What a give ye that we may return answer 3289
10:14 answered them after the a of the young 6098
25:17 Amaziah king of Judah took a, and sent to 3289
Pr 20:18 by counsel: and with good a make war. 8458
2Co 8:10 And herein I give *my* a: for this is 1106

ADVISE (3) [ADVICE, ADVISED, ADVISEMENT]
2Sa 24:13 now a, and see what answer I shall return 3045
1Ki 12: 6 How do you a that *I* may answer this 3289
1Ch 21:12 a thyself what word I shall bring again to 7200

ADVISED (2) [ADVISE]
Pr 13:10 but with the well a *is* wisdom. 3289
Ac 27:12 the more part a to depart thence also, 1012+5087

ADVISEMENT (1) [ADVISE]
1Ch 12:19 for the lords of the Philistines upon a sent 6098

ADVOCATE (1)
1Jn 2: 1 any *man* sin, we have an a with the Father, 3875

AENEAS (2)
Ac 9:33 And there he found a certain man named A, 132
9:34 And Peter said unto him, A, Jesus Christ 132

AENON (1)
Jn 3:23 And John also was baptizing in A near to 137

AFAR (51) [FAR] See Index

AFFAIRS (8)
1Ch 26:32 matter pertaining to God, and a of the king. 1697
Ps 112: 5 lendeth: he will guide his a with discretion. 1697
Da 2:49 over the a of the province of Babylon: 5673
3:12 set over the a of the province of Babylon, 5673
Eph 6:21 But that ye also may know my a, *and* 2596+3588
6:22 that ye might know our a, and *that* he 3588+4012
Php 1:27 or *else* be absent, I may hear of your a, 4012
2Ti 2: 4 entangleth himself with the a of *this* life; 4230

AFFECT (2) [AFFECTED, AFFECTETH]
Gal 4:17 They zealously a you, *but* not well; yea, 2206
4:17 would exclude you, that you might a them. 2206

AFFECTED (2) [AFFECT]
Ac 14: 2 made their minds evil a against 2559
Gal 4:18 But *it is* good to be zealously a always in a 2206

AFFECTETH (1) [AFFECT]
La 3:51 Mine eye a mine heart because of all 5953

AFFECTION (6) [AFFECTIONATELY, AFFECTIONED, AFFECTIONS]
1Ch 29: 3 I have set my a to the house of my God, 7521
Ro 1:31 without natural a, implacable, unmerciful: 794
2Co 7:15 And his inward a is more abundant toward 4698
Col 3: 2 Set your a on *things* above, not on *things* 5426
3: 5 fornication, uncleanness, inordinate a, 3806
2Ti 3: 3 Without natural a, trucebreakers, 794

AFFECTIONATELY (1) [AFFECTION]
1Th 2: 8 So being a desirous of you, we were 2442

AFFECTIONED (1) [AFFECTION]
Ro 12:10 *Be* kindly a one to another with brotherly 5387

AFFECTIONS (2) [AFFECTION]
Ro 1:26 this cause God gave them up unto vile a: 3806
Gal 5:24 Christ's have crucified the flesh with the a 3804

AFFINITY (3)
1Ki 3: 1 Solomon made a with Pharaoh king of 2859
2Ch 18: 1 in abundance, and joined a with Ahab. 2859
Ezr 9:14 join in a with the people of these 2859

A

AFFIRM (3) [AFFIRMED]
Ro 3: 8 and as some a that we say,) 5346
1Ti 1: 7 neither what they say, nor whereof they a. 1226
Tit 3: 8 these *things* I will that thou a **constantly**, 1226

AFFIRMED (3) [AFFIRM]
Lk 22:59 of one hour after another **confidently** a, 1340
Ac 12:15 But she **constantly** a that it was *even* so. 1340
25:19 *which was* dead, whom Paul a to be alive. 5335

AFFLICT (36) [AFFLICTED, AFFLICTEST, AFFLICTION, AFFLICTIONS]
Ge 15:13 and they shall a them four hundred years; 6031
31:50 If thou shalt a my daughters, or if thou 6031
Ex 1:11 taskmasters to a them with their burdens. 6031
22:22 Ye shall not a any widow, or 6031
22:23 If thou a them **in any wise**, and they 6031+6031
Lev 16:29 ye shall a your souls, and do no work *at all,* 6031
16:31 ye shall a your souls, *by* a statute for ever. 6031
23:27 ye shall a your souls, and offer an offering 6031
23:32 a sabbath of rest, and ye shall a your souls: 6031
Nu 24:24 shall a Asshur, and shall afflict Eber, and 6031
24:24 shall a Eber, and he also shall perish for 6031
29: 7 and ye shall a your souls: 6031
30:13 and every binding oath to a the soul, 6031
Jdg 16: 5 that we may bind him to a him: 6031
16: 6 wherewith thou mightest be bound to a 6031
16:19 she began to a him, and his strength went 6031
2Sa 7:10 neither shall the children of wickedness a 6031
1Ki 11:39 I will for this a the seed of David, but 6031
2Ch 6:26 turn from their sin, when thou dost a them; 6031
Ezr 8:21 that *we* might a ourselves before our God, 6031
Job 37:23 and *in* plenty of justice: he will not a. 6031
Ps 44: 2 *how* thou didst a the people, and cast them 7489
55:19 God shall hear, and a them, even he that 6031
89:22 upon him; nor the son of wickedness a him. 6031
94: 5 thy people, O LORD, and a thine heritage. 6031
143:12 and destroy all them that a my soul: 6887
Isa 9: 1 afterward did **more grievously** a *her by* 3513
51:23 I will put it into the hand of them that a 3013
58: 5 a day for a man to a his soul? *is it* to bow 6031
64:12 thou hold thy peace, and a us very sore? 6031
Jer 31:28 to throw down, and to destroy, and to a; 7489
La 3:33 For he doth not a willingly nor grieve 6031
Am 5:12 they a the just, they take a bribe, and 6887
6:14 they shall a you from the entering in of 3905
Na 1:12 I have afflicted thee, I will a thee no more. 6031
Zep 3:19 at that time I *will* undo all that a thee: 6031

AFFLICTED (55) [AFFLICT]
Ex 1:12 the more they a them, the more they 6031
Lev 23:29 For whatsoever soul *it be* that shall not be a 6031
Nu 11:11 Wherefore hast thou a thy servant? 7489
Dt 26: 6 and a us, and laid upon us hard bondage: 6031
Ru 1:21 against me, and the Almighty hath a me? 7489
2Sa 22:28 the a people thou wilt save: but thine eyes 6041
1Ki 2:26 thou hast been a in all where*in* my father 6031
2:26 afflicted in all where*in* my father was a. 6031
2Ki 17:20 a them, and delivered them into the hand of 6031
Job 6:14 To him that is a pity *should be shewed* 4523
30:11 Because he hath loosed my cord, and a me, 6031
34:28 unto him, and he heareth the cry of the a. 6041
Ps 18:27 For thou wilt save the a people; but 6041
22:24 nor abhorred the affliction of the a; 6041
25:16 mercy upon me; for I *am* desolate and a. 6041
82: 3 fatherless: do justice to the a and needy. 6041
88: 7 and thou hast a *me with* all thy waves. 6031
88:15 I *am* a and ready to die from *my* youth *up:* 6041
90:15 to the days *wherein* thou hast a us, 6031
102: T A Prayer of the a, when he is 6041
107:17 because of their iniquities, are a. 6031
116:10 therefore have I spoken: I was greatly a: 6031
119:67 Before I was a I went astray: but now have 6031
119:71 *It is* good for me that I have been a; that I 6031
119:75 and *that* thou *in* faithfulness hast a me. 6031
119:107 I am a very much: quicken me, O LORD, 6031
129: 1 Many a time have they a me from my 6887
129: 2 Many a time have they a me from my 6887
140:12 LORD will maintain the cause of the a, 6041
Pr 15:15 All the days of the a *are* evil: but *he that is* 6041
22:22 he *is* poor: neither oppress the a in the gate: 6041
26:28 A lying tongue hateth *those that are* a by it; 1790
31: 5 pervert the judgment of any of the a. 1121+6040
Isa 9: 1 when at the first he **lightly** a the land of 7043
49:13 his people, and will have mercy upon his a. 6041
51:21 thou a, and drunken, but not with wine: 6041
53: 4 esteem him stricken, smitten of God, and a. 6031
53: 7 He was oppressed, and he was a, yet he 6031
54:11 O thou a, tossed with tempest, *and* 6041
58: 3 *wherefore* have we a our soul, and 6031
58:10 soul to the hungry, and satisfy the a soul; 6031
60:14 The sons also of them that a thee shall 6031
63: 9 In all their affliction he was a, and 6862
La 1: 4 her virgins *are* a, and she *is* in bitterness. 3013
1: 5 for the LORD hath a her for the multitude 3013
1:12 wherewith the LORD hath a *me* in the day 3013
Mic 4: 6 her that is driven out, and *her* that I have a; 7489
Na 1:12 Though I have a thee, I will afflict thee no 6031
Zep 3:12 I will also leave in the midst of thee an a 6041
Mt 24: 9 Then shall they deliver you up to be a, and *2347*
2Co 1: 6 And whether we be a, *it is* for your *2346*
1Ti 5:10 the saints' feet, if she have relieved the a, *2346*
Heb 11:37 being destitute, a, tormented; *2346*
Jas 4: 9 Be a, and mourn, and weep: let your *5003*
5:13 Is any among you a? let him pray. Is any *2553*

AFFLICTEST (1) [AFFLICT]
1Ki 8:35 and turn from their sin, when thou a them: 6031

AFFLICTION (75) [AFFLICT]
Ge 16:11 because the LORD hath heard thy a. 6040
29:32 Surely the LORD hath looked upon my a; 6040
31:42 God hath seen mine a and the labour of my 6040
41:52 caused me to be fruitful in the land of my a. 6040
Ex 3: 7 I have surely seen the a of my people 6040
3:17 I will bring you up out of the a of Egypt 6040
4:31 that he had looked upon their a, then 6040
Dt 16: 3 bread therewith, *even* the bread of a; 6040
26: 7 looked on our a, and our labour, and 6040
1Sa 1:11 if thou wilt indeed look on the a of thine 6040
2Sa 16:12 be that the LORD will look on mine a, 5771
1Ki 22:27 feed him with bread of a and with water of 3906
22:27 with bread of affliction and with water of a, 3906
2Ki 14:26 For the LORD saw the a of Israel, *that it* 6040
2Ch 18:26 feed him with bread of a and with water of 3906
18:26 with bread of affliction and with water of a, 3906
20: 9 cry unto thee in our a, then thou wilt hear 6869
33:12 when he was in a, he besought the LORD 6887
Ne 1: 3 captivity there in the province *are* in great a 7451
9: 9 didst see the a of our fathers in Egypt, and 6040
Job 5: 6 Although a cometh not forth of the dust, 205
10:15 of confusion; therefore see thou mine a; 6040
30:16 the days of a have taken hold upon me. 6040
30:27 and rested not: the days of a prevented me. 6040
36: 8 in fetters, *and* be holden in cords of a; 6040
36:15 He delivereth the poor in his a, and 6040
36:21 for this hast thou chosen rather than a. 6040
Ps 22:24 For he hath not despised nor abhorred the a 6039
25:18 Look upon mine a and my pain; and 6040
44:24 *and* forgettest our a and our oppression? 6040
66:11 us into the net; thou laidst a upon our loins. 4157
88: 9 Mine eye mourneth by reason of a: 6040
106:44 Nevertheless he regarded their a, when he 6862
107:10 of death, *being* bound in a and iron; 6040
107:39 low through oppression, a, and sorrow. 7451
107:41 Yet setteth he the poor on high from a, and 6040
119:50 This *is* my comfort in my a: for thy word 6040
119:92 I should then have perished in mine a. 6040
119:153 Consider mine a, and deliver me: for I do 6040
Isa 30:20 the bread of adversity, and the water of a, 3906
48:10 I have chosen thee in the furnace of a. 6040
63: 9 In all their a he was afflicted, and the angel 6869
Jer 4:15 and publisheth a from mount Ephraim. 205
15:11 in the time of evil, and in the time of a. 6869
16:19 my fortress, and my refuge in the day of a, 6869
30:15 Why criest thou for thine a? thy sorrow *is* 7667
48:16 *is* near to come, and his a hasteth fast. 7451
La 1: 3 Judah is gone into captivity because of a, 6040
1: 7 Jerusalem remembered in the days of her a 6040
1: 9 O LORD, behold my a: for the enemy 6040
3: 1 I *am* the man *that* hath seen a by the rod of 6040
3:19 Remembering mine a and my misery, 6040
Hos 5:15 my face: in their a they will seek me early. 6862
Am 6: 6 but they are not grieved for the a of Joseph. 7667
Ob 1:13 thou shouldest not have looked on their a in 7451
Jnh 2: 2 I cried by reason of mine a unto 6869
Na 1: 9 a shall not rise up the second time. 6869
Hab 3: 7 I saw the tents of Cushan in a: *and* 205

Zec 1:15 and they helped forward the a. 7451
8:10 that went out or came in because of the a: 6862
10:11 he shall pass through the sea *with* a, and 6869
Mk 4:17 when a or persecution ariseth for *2347*
13:19 For *in* those days shall be a, such as was *2347*
Ac 7:11 the land of Egypt and Canaan, and great a: *2347*
7:34 I have seen the a of my people which is in *2561*
2Co 2: 4 For out of much a and anguish of heart I *2347*
4:17 For our light a, which is but for a moment, *2347*
8: 2 How that in a great trial of a the abundance *2347*
Php 1:16 supposing to add a to my bonds: *2347*
4:14 that ye did communicate with my a. *2347*
1Th 1: 6 having received the word in much a, *2347*
3: 7 we were comforted over you in all our a *2347*
Heb 11:25 Choosing rather to **suffer a with** the people *4778*
Jas 1:27 visit the fatherless and widows in their a, *2347*
5:10 for an example of **suffering a**, and *2552*

AFFLICTIONS (13) [AFFLICT]
Ps 34:19 Many *are* the a of the righteous: but 7451
132: 1 LORD, remember David, *and* all his a: 6031
Ac 7:10 And delivered him out of all his a, and *2347*
20:23 saying that bonds and a abide me. *2347*
2Co 6: 4 in a, in necessities, in distresses, *2347*
Col 1:24 fill up that which is behind of the a of *2347*
1Th 3: 3 That no *man* should be moved by these a: *2347*
2Ti 1: 8 be thou **partaker of** the a of the gospel *4777*
3:11 Persecutions, a, which came unto me at *3804*
4: 5 But watch thou in all *things,* **endure a**, *2553*
Heb 10:32 ye endured a great fight of a; *3804*
10:33 a gazingstock both by reproaches and a; *2347*
1Pe 5: 9 knowing that the same a are accomplished *3804*

AFFORDING (1)
Ps 144:13 garners *may be* full, a all manner of store: 6329

AFFRIGHT (1) [AFFRIGHTED]
2Ch 32:18 on the wall, to a them, and to trouble them; 3372

AFFRIGHTED (9) [AFFRIGHT]
Dt 7:21 Thou shalt not be a at them: for the LORD 6206
Job 18:20 as they that went before were a. 270+8178
39:22 He mocketh at fear, and is not a; 2865
Isa 21: 4 My heart panted, fearfulness a me: 1204
Jer 51:32 burnt with fire, and the men of war are a. 926
Mk 16: 5 in a long white garment; and they were a. *1568*
16: 6 And he saith unto them, Be not a: Ye seek *1568*
Lk 24:37 But they were terrified and a, and *1719*
Rev 11:13 and the remnant were a, and gave glory to *1719*

AFOOT (2) [FOOT]
Mk 6:33 and ran a thither out of all cities, and *3979*
Ac 20:13 had he appointed, minding himself to **go a**. *3978*

AFORE (7) [AFOREHAND, AFORETIME]
2Ki 20: 4 a Isaiah was gone out *into* the middle court, 3808
Ps 129: 6 which withereth a it groweth up: 6927
Isa 18: 5 For a the harvest, when the bud is 6440+3807.1
Eze 33:22 was upon me in the evening, a 6440+3807.1
Ro 1: 2 (Which he had **promised** a by his prophets *4279*
9:23 which he had a **prepared** unto glory, *4282*
Eph 3: 3 the mystery; (as I **wrote** a in few *words,* *4270*

AFOREHAND (1) [AFORE]
Mk 14: 8 she is **come a** to anoint my body to *4301*

AFORETIME (7) [AFORE]
Ne 13: 5 where a they laid the meat 6440+3807.1
Job 17: 6 the people; and a I was *as* a tabret. 6440+3807.1
Isa 52: 4 My people went down a 7223+871.1+1886.1
Jer 30:20 Their children also shall be as a, and 6924
Da 6:10 before his God, as he did a. 1836+4481+6928
Jn 9:13 They brought to the Pharisees him that a *4218*
Ro 15: 4 For whatsoever *things* were **written** a were *4270*

AFRAID (193) [FEAR]
Ge 3:10 and I was a, because I *was* naked; 3372
18:15 saying, I laughed not; for she was a. 3372
20: 8 in their ears: and the men were sore a. 3372
28:17 he was a, and said, How dreadful *is* this 3372
31:31 and said to Laban, Because I was a: 3372
32: 7 Jacob was greatly a and distressed: and 3372
42:28 their heart failed *them,* and they were a, 2729
42:35 saw the bundles of money, they were a. 3372
43:18 the men were a, because they were brought 3372
Ex 3: 6 hid his face; for he was a to look upon God. 3372
14:10 marched after them; and they were sore a: 3372
15:14 The people shall hear, *and* be a: 7264
34:30 and they were a to come nigh him. 3372
Lev 26: 6 shall lie down, and none shall **make** *you* a: 2729
Nu 12: 8 were ye not a to speak against my servant 3372
22: 3 Moab was sore a of the people, because 1481
Dt 1:17 you shall not be a of the face of man; 1481
1:29 unto you, Dread not, neither be a of them. 3372
2: 4 dwell in Seir; and they shall be a of you: 3372
5: 5 for ye were a by reason of the fire, and 3372
7:18 Thou shalt not be a of them: *but* shalt well 3372
7:19 do unto all the people of whom thou *art* a. 3373
9:19 For I was a of the anger and 3025
18:22 thou shalt not be a of him. 1481
20: 1 a people more than thou, be not a of them: 3372
28:10 of the LORD; and they shall be a of thee. 3372
28:60 diseases of Egypt, which thou wast a of; 3025
31: 6 a good courage, fear not, nor be a of them: 6206
Jos 1: 9 be not a, neither be thou dismayed: 6206
9:24 we were sore a of our lives because of you, 3372
11: 6 said unto Joshua, Be not a because of them: 3372
Jdg 7: 3 saying, Whosoever *is* fearful and a, let him 2730
Ru 3: 8 that the man was a, and turned himself: 2729
1Sa 4: 7 the Philistines were a, for they said, God is 3372
7: 7 heard *it,* they were a of the Philistines. 3372
17:11 they were dismayed, and greatly a. 3372
17:24 the man, fled from him, and were sore a. 3372
18:12 Saul was a of David, because the LORD 3372
18:15 himself very wisely, he was a of him. 1481
18:29 Saul was yet the more a of David; and 3372
21: 1 Ahimelech was a at the meeting of David, 2729
21:12 and was sore a of Achish the king of Gath. 3372
23: 3 unto him, Behold, we *be* a here in Judah: 3373
28: 5 he was a, and his heart greatly trembled. 3372
28:13 the king said unto her, Be not a: for what 3372
28:20 was sore a, because of the words of 3372
31: 4 armourbearer would not; for he was sore a: 3372
2Sa 1:14 How wast thou not a to stretch forth thine 3372
6: 9 David was a of the LORD that day, 3372
14:15 *it is* because the people have **made** me a: 3372
17: 2 and weak handed, and will **make** him a: 2729
22: 5 the floods of ungodly men **made** me a; 1204
22:46 and they shall be a out of their close places. 2296
1Ki 1:49 the guests that *were* with Adonijah were a, 2729
2Ki 1:15 be not a of him. And he arose, and 3372
10: 4 they were exceedingly a, and said, Behold, 3372
19: 6 Be not a of the words which thou hast 3372
25:26 *to* Egypt: for they were a of the Chaldees. 3372
1Ch 10: 4 armourbearer would not; for he was sore a. 3372
13:12 David was a of God that day, saying, 3372
21:30 for he was a because of the sword of 1204
2Ch 20:15 Be not a nor dismayed by reason of this 3372
32: 7 be not a nor dismayed for the king of 3372
Ne 2: 2 but sorrow of heart. Then I was very sore a, 3372
4:14 the rest of the people, Be not ye a of them: 3372
6: 9 For they all **made** us a, saying, Their hands 3372
6:13 that I should be a, and do so, and sin, and 3372
Est 7: 6 Haman was a before the king and 1204
Job 3:25 and *that* which I was a of is come unto me. 3025
5:21 neither shalt thou be a of destruction when 3372
5:22 neither shalt thou be a of the beasts of 3372
6:21 ye see *my* casting down, and are a. 3372
9:28 I am a of all my sorrows, I know that thou 3025
11:19 shalt lie down, and none shall **make** *thee* a; 2729
13:11 Shall not his excellency **make** you a? 1204
13:21 from me: and let not thy dread **make** me a. 1204
15:24 Trouble and anguish shall **make** him a; 1204
18:11 Terrors shall **make** him a on every side, 1204
19:29 Be ye a of the sword: for wrath *bringeth* 1481
21: 6 Even when I remember I am a, and 926
23:15 when I consider, I am a of him. 6342
32: 6 wherefore I was a, and durst not shew you 2119
33: 7 Behold, my terror shall not **make** thee a, 1204
39:20 Canst thou **make** him a as a grasshopper? 7493
41:25 he raiseth up *himself,* the mighty are a: 1481
Ps 3: 6 I will not be a of ten thousands of people, 3372
18: 4 and the floods of ungodly men **made** me a. 1204
18:45 and be a out of their close places. 2727
27: 1 strength of my life; of whom shall I be a? 6342
49:16 Be not thou a when one is made rich, 3372
56: 3 *What* time I am a, I will trust in thee. 3372
56:11 I will not be a what man can do unto me. 3372
65: 8 in the uttermost parts are a at thy tokens: 3372

A

Ps 77:16 O God, the waters saw thee; they were **a**: 2342
83:15 and **make** them **a** with thy storm. 926
91: 5 Thou shalt not be **a** for the terror by night; 3372
112: 7 He shall not be **a** of evil tidings: his heart is 3372
112: 8 His heart *is* established, he shall not be **a**, 3372
119:120 fear of thee; and I am **a** of thy judgments. 3372
Pr 3:24 When thou liest down, thou shalt not be **a**: 6342
3:25 Be not **a** of sudden fear, neither of 3372
31:21 She is not **a** of the snow for her household: 3372
Ecc 12: 5 Also *when* they shall be **a** of *that which is* 3372
Isa 8:12 neither fear ye their fear, nor be **a**. 6206
10:24 dwellest in Zion, be not **a** of the Assyrian: 3372
10:29 Ramah is **a**; Gibeah of Saul is fled. 2729
12: 2 *is* my salvation; I will trust, and not be **a**: 6342
13: 8 they shall be **a**: pangs and sorrows shall take 926
17: 2 lie down, and none shall **make** *them* **a**. 2729
19:16 it shall be **a** and fear because of the shaking 2729
19:17 mention thereof shall be **a** in himself, 6342
20: 5 they shall be **a** and ashamed of Ethiopia 2865
31: 4 he will not be **a** of their voice, nor abase 2865
31: 9 his princes shall be **a** of the ensign, 2865
33:14 The sinners in Zion are **a**; fearfulness hath 6342
37: 6 Be not **a** of the words that thou hast heard, 3372
40: 9 lift *it* up, be not **a**; say unto the cities of 3372
41: 5 the ends of the earth were **a**, drew near, and 2729
44: 8 Fear ye not, neither be **a**: have not I told 7297
51: 7 of men, neither be ye **a** of their revilings. 2865
51:12 that thou shouldest be **a** of a man *that* shall 3372
57:11 of whom hast thou been **a** or feared, 1672
Jer 1: 8 Be not **a** of their faces: for I *am* with thee to 3372
2:12 O ye heavens, at this, and be **horribly a**, 8175
10: 5 Be not **a** of them; for they cannot do evil, 3372
26:21 when Urijah heard *it*, he was **a**, and fled, 3372
30:10 and be quiet, and none shall **make** *him* **a**. 2729
36:16 they were **a** both one and other, and 6342
36:24 Yet they were not **a**, nor rent their 6342
38:19 I am **a** of the Jews that are fallen to 1672
39:17 the hand of the men of whom thou *art* **a**. 3016
41:18 for they were **a** of them, because 3372
42:11 Be not **a** of the king of Babylon, of whom 3372
42:11 of the king of Babylon, of whom ye *are* **a**; 3373
42:11 be not **a** of him, saith the LORD: 3372
42:16 the famine, whereof ye were **a**, shall follow 1672
46:27 and at ease, and none shall **make** *him* **a**. 2729
Eze 2: 6 thou, son of man, be not **a** of them, 3372
2: 6 neither be **a** of their words, though briers 3372
2: 6 be not **a** of their words, nor be dismayed at 3372
27:35 their kings shall be **sore a**, they shall 8175+8178
30: 9 in ships to **make** the careless Ethiopians **a**, 2729
32:10 and their kings shall be horribly **a** for thee, 8175
34:28 dwell safely, and none shall **make** *them* **a**. 2729
39:26 safely in their land, and none **made** *them* **a**. 2729
Da 4: 5 I saw a dream which **made** me **a**, and 1763
8:17 he came, I was **a**, and fell upon my face: 1204
Joel 2:22 Be not **a**, ye beasts of the field: for 3372
Am 3: 6 blown in the city, and the people not be **a**? 2729
Jnh 1: 5 the mariners were **a**, and cried every man 3372
1:10 were the men **exceedingly a**, 1419+3372+3374
Mic 4: 4 his fig tree; and none shall **make** *them* **a**: 2729
7:17 they shall be **a** of the LORD our God, and 6342
Na 2:11 the lion's whelp, and none **made** *them* **a**? 2729
Hab 2:17 *which* **made** them **a**, because of men's 2865
3: 2 I have heard thy speech, *and* was **a**: 3372
Zep 3:13 and lie down, and none shall **make** *them* **a**. 2729
Mal 2: 5 he feared me, and was **a** before my name. 2865
Mt 2:22 of his father Herod, he was **a** to go thither: *5399*
14:27 saying, Be of good cheer; it is I, be not **a**. *5399*
14:30 he saw the wind boysterous, he was **a**; *5399*
17: 6 *it*, they fell on their face, and were sore **a**. *5399*
17: 7 touched them, and said, Arise, and be not **a**. *5399*
25:25 And I was **a**, and went and hid thy talent in *5399*
28:10 Then said Jesus unto them, Be not **a**: go tell *5399*
Mk 5:15 and in his right mind: and they were **a**. *5399*
5:36 of the synagogue, Be not **a**, only believe. *5399*
6:50 Be of good cheer: it is I; be not **a**. *5399*
9: 6 wist not what to say; for they were **sore a**. *1630*
9:32 not *that* saying, and were **a** to ask him. *5399*
10:32 and as they followed, they were **a**. *5399*
16: 8 they any *thing* to any *man*; for they were **a**. *5399*
Lk 2: 9 about them: and they were sore **a**. *5399+5401*
8:25 And they being **a** wondered, saying one to *5399*
8:35 and in his right mind: and they were **a**. *5399*
12: 4 Be not **a** of them that kill the body, and *5399*
24: 5 And as they were **a**, and bowed down *their* *1719*
Jn 6:19 nigh unto the ship: and they were **a**. *5399*
6:20 But he saith unto them, It is I; be not **a**. *5399*
14:27 your heart be troubled, neither let it be **a**. *1168*
19: 8 heard that saying, he was the more **a**; *5399*
Ac 9:26 but they were all **a** of him, and believed not *5399*
10: 4 he was **a**, and said, What is it, Lord? *1719*
18: 9 Be not **a**, but speak, and hold not thy peace: *5399*
22: 9 with me saw indeed the light, and were **a**; *1719*
22:29 and the chief captain also was **a**, after he *5399*
Ro 13: 3 Wilt thou then not be **a** of the power? *5399*
13: 4 But if thou do *that which is* evil, be **a**; *5399*
Gal 4:11 I am **a** of you, lest I have bestowed upon *5399*
Heb 11:23 they were not **a** of the king's *5399*
1Pe 3: 6 do well, and are not **a** *with* any amazement. *5399*
3:14 happy *are ye*: and be not **a** of their terror, *5399*
2Pe 2:10 they are not **a** to speak evil of dignities. *5141*

AFRESH (1) [FRESH]
Heb 6: 6 they **crucify** to themselves the Son of God **a**, *388*

AFTER (1180) [AFTERWARD, AFTERWARDS, HEREAFTER] See Index

AFTERNOON (1)
Jdg 19: 8 they tarried until **a**, and 3117+5186+1886.1

AFTERWARD (64) [AFTER] See Index

AFTERWARDS (15) [AFTER] See Index

AGABUS (2)
Ac 11:28 And there stood up one of them named **A**, and *13*
21:10 down from Judea a certain prophet, named **A**. *13*

AGAG (8) [AGAGITE]
Nu 24: 7 his king shall be higher than **A**, and 90
1Sa 15: 8 he took **A** the king of the Amalekites alive, 90
15: 9 Saul and the people spared **A**, and the best of 90
15:20 and have brought **A** the king of Amalek, and 90
15:32 Bring you hither to me **A** the king of 90
15:32 **A** came unto him delicately. And Agag said, 90
15:32 **A** said, Surely the bitterness of death is past. 90
15:33 Samuel hewed **A** in pieces before the LORD 90

AGAGITE (5) [AGAG]
Est 3: 1 Haman the son of Hammedatha the **A**, 91
3:10 it unto Haman the son of Hammedatha the **A**, 91
8: 3 to put away the mischief of Haman the **A**, 91
8: 5 by Haman the son of Hammedatha the **A**, 91
9:24 the **A**, the enemy of all the Jews, 91

AGAIN (672) See Index

AGAINST (1667) See Index

AGAR (2) [HAGAR]
Gal 4:24 which gendereth to bondage, which is **A**. *28*
4:25 For *this* **A** is mount Sinai in Arabia, and *28*

AGATE (3) [AGATES]
Ex 28:19 third row a ligure, an **a**, and an amethyst. 7618
39:12 third row, a ligure, an **a**, and an amethyst. 7618
Eze 27:16 and fine linen, and coral, and **a**. 3539

AGATES (1) [AGATE]
Isa 54:12 I will make thy windows *of* **a**, and thy gates 3539

AGE (42) [AGED, AGES]
Ge 15:15 thou shalt be buried in a good **old a**. 7872
18:11 and Sarah *were* old *and* well stricken in **a**; 3117
21: 2 and bare Abraham a son in his **old a**, 2208
21: 7 for I have born *him* a son in his **old a**. 2208
24: 1 Abraham was old, *and* well stricken in **a**: 3117
25: 8 died in a good **old a**, an old man, and 7872
37: 3 because he *was* the son of his **old a**: 2208
44:20 and a child of *his* **old a**, a little one; 2208
47:28 **whole a** of Jacob was an 2416+3117+8141
48:10 Now the eyes of Israel were dim for **a**, *so* 2207
Nu 8:25 from the **a** of fifty years they shall cease 1121
Jos 23: 1 that Joshua waxed old *and* stricken in **a**. 3117
23: 2 said unto them, I am old *and* stricken in **a**: 3117
Jdg 8:32 the son of Joash died in a good **old a**, 7872
Ru 4:15 of *thy* life, and a nourisher of thine **old a**: 7872
1Sa 2:33 thine house shall die **in the flower of** their **a**. 376
1Ki 14: 4 for his eyes were set by reason of his **a**. 7869
15:23 Nevertheless in the time of his **old a** he was 2209
1Ch 23: 3 Now the Levites were numbered from the **a** 1121

1Ch 23:24 from the **a** of twenty years and upward. 1121
29:28 he died in a good **old a**, full of days, riches, 7872
2Ch 36:17 old man, or **him that stooped for a**: 3486
Job 5:26 Thou shalt come to *thy* grave in a **full a**, 3624
8: 8 of the former **a**, and prepare *thyself* to 1755
11:17 *thine* **a** shall be clearer than the noonday; 2465
30: 2 profit me, in whom **old a** was perished? 3624
Ps 39: 5 and mine **a** *is* as nothing before thee: 2465
71: 9 Cast me not off in the time of **old a**; 2209
92:14 They shall still bring forth fruit in **old a**; 7872
Isa 38:12 Mine **a** is departed, and is removed from 1755
46: 4 *even* to *your* **old a** I *am* he; and *even* to 2209
Zec 8: 4 man with his staff in his hand for very **a**. 3117
Mk 5:42 for she was *of the a* of twelve years. NIG
Lk 1:36 she hath also conceived a son in her **old a**: *1094*
2:36 of Aser: she was of a great **a**, *1722+2250+4260*
3:23 himself began *to be* about thirty **years of a**, *2094*
8:42 about twelve **years of a**, and she lay a *2094*
Jn 9:21 he is of **a**; ask him: he shall speak for *2244*
9:23 Therefore said his parents, He is of **a**; *2244*
1Co 7:36 if she **pass the flower of** *her* **a**, *1510+5230*
Heb 5:14 meat belongeth to *them that are* of **full a**, *5046*
11:11 of a child when *she* was past **a**, *2244+2540*

AGED (9) [AGE]
2Sa 19:32 Now Barzillai was a very **a man**, 2204
Job 12:20 and taketh *away* the understanding of the **a**. 2205
15:10 *are* both the grayheaded and **very a men**, 3453
29: 8 and the **a** arose, *and* stood *up*. 3453
32: 9 neither do the **a** understand judgment. 2205
Jer 6:11 be taken, the **a** with *him that is* full of days. 2205
Tit 2: 2 That the **a men** be sober, grave, temperate, *4246*
2: 3 The **a women** likewise, *that they be* in *4247*
Phm 1: 9 *thee*, being such a one as Paul the **a**, *4246*

AGEE (1)
2Sa 23:11 after him *was* Shammah the son of **A** 89

AGES (4) [AGE]
Eph 2: 7 That in the **a** to come he might shew *165*
3: 5 Which in other **a** was not made known unto *1074*
3:21 the church by Christ Jesus throughout all **a**, *1074*
Col 1:26 the mystery which hath been hid from **a** *165*

AGO (13)
1Sa 9:20 for thine asses that were lost three days **a**, 3117
2Ki 19:25 Hast thou not heard **long a** 4480+7350+3807.1
Ezr 5:11 that was builded these many years **a**, 4481+6928
Isa 22:11 unto him that fashioned it **long a**. 4480+7350
37:26 Hast thou not heard **long a**, 4480+7350+3807.1
Mt 11:21 Sidon they would have repented **long a** in *3819*
Mk 9:21 How **long** is it **a** since this came unto him? *5550*
Lk 10:13 they had a **great while a** repented, sitting in *3819*
Ac 10:30 Four days **a** I was fasting until this hour; *575*
15: 7 know how that **a good while a** *575+744+2250*
2Co 8:10 to do, but also to be forward **a year a**. *575+4070*
9: 2 that Achaia was ready **a year a**; *575+4070*
12: 2 a man in Christ above fourteen years **a**, NIG

AGONE (1)
1Sa 30:13 left me, because three days **a** I fell sick. NIH

AGONY (1)
Lk 22:44 And being in an **a** he prayed more earnestly: *74*

AGREE (7) [AGREED, AGREEMENT, AGREETH]
Mt 5:25 **A with** thine adversary quickly, *2132*
18:19 That if two of you shall **a** on earth as *4856*
20:13 didst not thou **a with** me for a penny? *4856*
Mk 14:59 so did their witness **a together**. *1510+2470*
Ac 15:15 And to this **a** the words of the prophets; *4856*
1Jn 5: 8 and the blood: and *these* three **a** in one. *1510*
Rev 17:17 to fulfil his will, and to **a**, *1106+1520+4160*

AGREED (8) [AGREE]
Am 3: 3 Can two walk together, except they be **a**? 3259
Mt 20: 2 And when he had **a** with the labourers for a *4856*
Mk 14:56 but *their* witness **a** not **together**. *1510+2470*
Jn 9:22 for the Jews had **a** already, that if any *man* *4934*
Ac 5: 9 How *is it* that ye have **a together** to tempt *4856*
5:40 And to him they **a**: and when they had *3982*
23:20 The Jews have **a** to desire thee that thou *4934*
28:25 And when they **a not** among *800+1510*

AGREEMENT (6) [AGREE]
2Ki 18:31 Make *an a* with me *by* a present, and NIH
Isa 28:15 with death, and with hell are we at **a**; 2374
28:18 and your **a** with hell shall not stand; 2380
36:16 Make *an a* with me *by* a present, and NIH
Da 11: 6 come to the king of the north to make an **a**: 4339
2Co 6:16 And what **a** hath the temple of God with *4783*

AGREETH (2) [AGREE]
Mk 14:70 art a Galilean, and thy speech **a** *thereto*. *3662*
Lk 5:36 the piece that was *taken* out of the new **a** *4856*

AGRIPPA (12)
Ac 25:13 And after certain days king **A** and *67*
25:22 Then **A** said unto Festus, I would also hear *67*
25:23 when **A** was come, and Bernice, with great *67*
25:24 King **A**, and all men which are here present *67*
25:26 and specially before thee, O king **A**, that, *67*
26: 1 Then **A** said unto Paul, Thou art permitted to *67*
26: 2 king **A**, because I shall answer for myself this *67*
26: 7 For which hope's sake, king **A**, I am accused *67*
26:19 Whereupon, O king **A**, I was not disobedient *67*
26:27 King **A**, believest thou the prophets? I know *67*
26:28 Then **A** said unto Paul, Almost thou *67*
26:32 Then said **A** unto Festus, This man might *67*

AGROUND (1) [GROUND]
Ac 27:41 where two seas met, they **ran** the ship **a**; *2027*

AGUE (1)
Lev 26:16 consumption, and the **burning a**, that shall 6920

AGUR (1)
Pr 30: 1 The words of **A** the son of Jakeh, *even* 94

AH (18) [AHA] See Index

AHA (10) [AH, HA] See Index

AHAB (92) [AHAB'S]
1Ki 16:28 and **A** his son reigned in his stead. 256
16:29 eighth year of Asa king of Judah *began* **A** 256
16:29 **A** the son of Omri reigned over Israel in 256
16:30 **A** the son of Omri did evil in the sight of 256
16:33 **A** made a grove; and Ahab did more to 256
16:33 **A** did more to provoke the LORD God of 256
17: 1 said unto **A**, *As* the LORD God of Israel 256
18: 1 third year, saying, Go, shew thyself unto **A**; 256
18: 2 Elijah went to shew himself unto **A**. 256
18: 3 **A** called Obadiah, which *was* the governor 256
18: 5 **A** said unto Obadiah, Go into the land, 256
18: 6 **A** went one way by himself, and 256
18: 9 deliver thy servant into the hand of **A**, 256
18:12 *so* when I come and tell **A**, and he cannot 256
18:16 So Obadiah went to meet **A**, and told him: 256
18:16 and told him: and **A** went to meet Elijah. 256
18:17 it came to pass, when **A** saw Elijah, 256
18:17 when Ahab saw Elijah, that **A** said unto him, 256
18:20 So **A** sent unto all the children of Israel, and 256
18:41 And Elijah said unto **A**, Get thee up, eat and 256
18:42 So **A** went up to eat and to drink. And Elijah 256
18:44 he said, Go up, say unto **A**, Prepare *thy* 256
18:45 great rain. And **A** rode, and went to Jezreel. 256
18:46 and ran before **A** to the entrance of Jezreel. 256
19: 1 **A** told Jezebel all that Elijah had done, and 256
20: 2 he sent messengers to **A** king of Israel into 256
20:13 there came a prophet unto **A** king of Israel, 256
20:14 **A** said, By whom? And he said, Thus saith 256
20:34 *said* **A**, I will send thee away with *this* NIH
21: 1 hard by the palace of **A** king of Samaria. 256
21: 2 **A** spake unto Naboth, saying, Give me thy 256
21: 3 Naboth said to **A**, The LORD forbid it me, 256
21: 4 **A** came into his house heavy and displeased 256
21:15 and was dead, that Jezebel said to **A**, Arise, 256
21:16 to pass, when **A** heard that Naboth was dead, 256
21:16 that **A** rose up to go down to the vineyard of 256
21:18 Arise, go down to meet **A** king of Israel, 256
21:20 **A** said to Elijah, Hast thou found me, 256
21:21 will cut off from **A** *him that* pisseth against 256
21:24 Him that dieth of **A** in the city the dogs shall 256
21:25 (But there was none like unto **A**, which did 256
21:27 it came to pass, when **A** heard those words, 256
21:29 Seest thou how **A** humbleth himself before 256
22:20 Who shall persuade **A**, that he may go up 256
22:39 Now the rest of the acts of **A**, and all that he 256

A

1Ki 22:40 So A slept with his fathers; and Ahaziah his 256
22:41 Judah in the fourth year of A king of Israel. 256
22:49 said Ahaziah the son of A unto Jehoshaphat, 256
22:51 Ahaziah the son of A *began* to reign over 256
2Ki 1: 1 rebelled against Israel after the death of A. 256
3: 1 Now Jehoram the son of A *began* to reign 256
3: 5 it came to pass, when A was dead, that 256
8:16 in the fifth year of Joram the son of A king 256
8:18 of the kings of Israel, as did the house of A: 256
8:18 for the daughter of A was his wife: and 256
8:25 In the twelfth year of Joram the son of A 256
8:27 And he walked in the way of the house of A, 256
8:27 sight of the LORD, as *did* the house of A: 256
8:27 for he *was* the son in law of the house of A. 256
8:28 he went with Joram the son of A to the war 256
8:29 down to see Joram the son of A in Jezreel, 256
9: 7 thou shalt smite the house of A thy master, 256
9: 8 For the whole house of A shall perish: and 256
9: 8 I will cut off from A *him that* pisseth against 256
9: 9 I will make the house of A like the house of 256
9:25 and thou rode together after A his father, 256
9:29 in the eleventh year of Joram the son of A 256
10: 1 A had seventy sons in Samaria. And Jehu 256
10:10 LORD spake concerning the house of A: 256
10:11 that remained of the house of A in Jezreel, 256
10:17 he slew all that remained unto A in Samaria, 256
10:18 and said unto them, A served Baal a little; 256
10:30 hast done unto the house of A according to 256
21: 3 and made a grove, as did A king of Israel; 256
21:13 and the plummet of the house of A: 256
2Ch 18: 1 in abundance, and joined affinity with A. 256
18: 2 after *certain* years he went down to A to 256
18: 2 A killed sheep and oxen for him in 256
18: 3 A king of Israel said unto Jehoshaphat king 256
18:19 Who shall entice A king of Israel, that he 256
21: 6 kings of Israel, like as did the house of A: 256
21: 6 for he had the daughter of A to wife: and 256
21:13 like to the whoredoms of the house of A, and 256
22: 3 also walked in the ways of the house of A: 256
22: 4 the sight of the LORD, like the house of A: 256
22: 5 went with Jehoram the son of A king of 256
22: 6 down to see Jehoram the son of A at Jezreel, 256
22: 7 had anointed to cut off the house of A. 256
22: 8 executing judgment upon the house of A, 256
Jer 29:21 of A the son of Kolaiah, and of Zedekiah, 256
29:22 LORD make thee like Zedekiah and like A, 256
Mic 6:16 all the works of the house of A, and ye walk 256

AHAB'S (2) [AHAB]
1Ki 21: 8 So she wrote letters in A name, and 256
2Ki 10: 1 to them that brought up A *children*, saying, 256

AHARAH (1)
1Ch 8: 1 Ashbel the second, and A the third, 315

AHARHEL (1)
1Ch 4: 8 and the families of A the son of Harum. 316

AHASAI (1)
Ne 11:13 the son of A, the son of Meshillemoth, 273

AHASBAI (1)
2Sa 23:34 Eliphelet the son of A, the son of 308

AHASUERUS (30) [AHASUERUS']
Ezr 4: 6 in the reign of A, in the beginning of his 325
Est 1: 1 Now it came to pass in the days of A, (this *is* 325
1: 1 (this *is* A which reigned, from India even 325
1: 2 when the king A sat on the throne of his 325
1: 9 *in* the royal house which *belonged* to king A. 325
1:10 that served in the presence of A the king, 325
1:15 of the king A by the chamberlains? 325
1:16 that *are* in all the provinces of the king A. 325
1:17 The king A commanded Vashti the queen to 325
1:19 That Vashti come no *more* before king A; 325
2: 1 when the wrath of king A was appeased, 325
2:12 maid's turn was come to go in to king A, 325
2:16 So Esther was taken unto king A into his 325
2:21 and sought to lay hand on the king A. 325
3: 1 After these things did king A promote 325
3: 6 *were* throughout the whole kingdom of A, 325
3: 7 in the twelfth year of king A, they cast Pur, 325
3: 8 Haman said unto king A, There is a certain 325
3:12 in the name of king A was it written, and 325
6: 2 who sought to lay hand on the king A. 325
7: 5 the king A answered and said unto Esther 325
8: 1 On that day did the king A give the house of 325
8: 7 the king A said unto Esther the queen and 325
8:12 Upon one day in all the provinces of king A, 325
9: 2 throughout all the provinces of the king A, 325
9:20 that *were* in all the provinces of the king A, 325
9:30 and seven provinces of the kingdom of A, 325
10: 1 the king A laid a tribute upon the land, and 325
10: 3 For Mordecai the Jew *was* next unto king A, 325
Da 9: 1 In the first year of Darius the son of A, 325

AHASUERUS' (1) [AHASUERUS]
Est 8:10 he wrote in the king A name, and sealed *it* 325

AHAVA (3)
Ezr 8:15 them together to the river that runneth to A; 163
8:21 Then I proclaimed a fast there, at the river A, 163
8:31 we departed from the river of A on 163

AHAZ (42) [ACHAZ]
2Ki 15:38 his father: and A his son reigned in his stead. 271
16: 1 A the son of Jotham king of Judah *began* to 271
16: 2 Twenty years old *was* A when he *began* to 271
16: 5 they besieged A, but could not overcome 271
16: 7 So A sent messengers to Tiglath-pileser king 271
16: 8 A took the silver and gold that was found *in* 271
16:10 king A went *to* Damascus to meet 271
16:10 king A sent to Urijah the priest the fashion 271
16:11 to all that king A had sent from Damascus: 271
16:11 Urijah the priest made *it* against king A 271
16:15 king A commanded Urijah the priest, saying, 271
16:16 according to all that king A commanded. 271
16:17 And king A cut off the borders of the bases, 271
16:19 Now the rest of the acts of A which he did, 271
16:20 A slept with his fathers, and was buried with 271
17: 1 In the twelfth year of A king of Judah *began* 271
18: 1 *that* Hezekiah the son of A king of Judah 271
20:11 by which it had gone down in the dial of A. 271
23:12 *were* on the top of the upper chamber of A, 271
1Ch 3:13 A his son, Hezekiah his son, Manasseh his 271
8:35 *were*, Pithon, and Melech, and Tarea, and A. 271
8:36 A begat Jehoadah; and Jehoadah begat 271
9:41 and Melech, and Tahrea, *and A*. NIH
9:42 A begat Jarah; and Jarah begat Alemeth, 271
2Ch 27: 9 of David: and A his son reigned in his stead. 271
28: 1 A *was* twenty years old when he *began* to 271
28:16 At that time did king A send unto the kings 271
28:19 Judah low because of A king of Israel; 271
28:21 For A took away a portion *out* of the house 271
28:22 more against the LORD: this *is that* king A. 271
28:24 A gathered together the vessels of the house 271
28:27 A slept with his fathers, and they buried him 271
29:19 which king A in his reign did cast away in 271
Isa 1: 1 Jotham, A, *and* Hezekiah, kings of Judah. 271
7: 1 it came to pass in the days of A the son of 271
7: 3 Go forth now to meet A, thou, and 271
7:10 Moreover the LORD spake again unto A, 271
7:12 A said, I will not ask, neither will I tempt 271
14:28 In the year that king A died was this burden. 271
38: 8 which is gone down in the sun dial of A, 271
Hos 1: 1 Jotham, A, *and* Hezekiah, kings of Judah, 271
Mic 1: 1 A, *and* Hezekiah, kings of Judah, which he 271

AHAZIAH (37)
1Ki 22:40 and A his son reigned in his stead. 274
22:49 said A the son of Ahab unto Jehoshaphat, 274
22:51 A the son of Ahab *began* to reign over Israel 274
2Ki 1: 2 A fell down through a lattice in his upper 274
1:18 Now the rest of the acts of A which he did, 274
8:24 of David: and A his son reigned in his stead. 274
8:25 A the son of Jehoram king of Judah *begin* to 274
8:26 twenty years old *was* A when he *began* to 274
8:29 A the son of Jehoram king of Judah went 274
9:16 A king of Judah was come down to see 274
9:21 king of Israel and A king of Judah went out, 274
9:23 fled, and said to A, *There is* treachery, 274
9:23 and said to Ahaziah, *There is* treachery, O A. 274
9:27 when A the king of Judah saw *this*, he fled 274
9:29 son of Ahab *began* A to reign over Judah. 274
10:13 Jehu met with the brethren of A king of 274
10:13 they answered, We *are* the brethren of A; 274
11: 1 when Athaliah the mother of A saw that her 274
11: 2 the daughter of king Joram, sister of A, 274
11: 2 took Joash the son of A, and stale him from 274

2Ki	12:18	Jehoram, and **A**, his fathers, kings of Judah,	274
	13: 1	twentieth year of Joash the son of **A** king of	274
	14:13	the son of Jehoash the son of **A**,	274
1Ch	3:11	Joram his son, **A** his son, Joash his son,	274
2Ch	20:35	of Judah join himself with **A** king of Israel,	274
	20:37	Because thou hast joined thyself with **A**,	274
	22: 1	the inhabitants of Jerusalem made **A** his	274
	22: 1	So **A** the son of Jehoram king of Judah	274
	22: 2	two years old *was* **A** when he *began* to reign,	274
	22: 7	the destruction of **A** was of God by coming	274
	22: 8	the sons of the brethren of **A**, that ministered	274
	22: 8	that ministered to **A**, he slew them,	274
	22: 9	he sought **A**: and they caught him, (for he	274
	22: 9	So the house of **A** had no power to keep still	274
	22:10	when Athaliah the mother of **A** saw that her	274
	22:11	took Joash the son of **A**, and stole him from	274
	22:11	the priest, (for she was the sister of **A**,)	274

AHBAN (1)

1Ch 2:29 *was* Abihail, and she bare him **A**, and Molid. 257

AHER (1)

1Ch 7:12 children of Ir, *and* Hushim, the sons of **A**. 313

AHI (2)

| 1Ch | 5:15 | **A** the son of Abdiel, the son of Guni, | 277 |
| | 7:34 | **A**, and Rohgah, Jehubbah, and Aram. | 277 |

AHIAH (4)

1Sa	14: 3	And **A**, the son of Ahitub, Ichabod's brother,	281
	14:18	Saul said unto **A**, Bring hither the ark of	281
1Ki	4: 3	Elihoreph and **A**, the sons of Shisha, scribes;	281
1Ch	8: 7	Naaman, and **A**, and Gera, he removed them,	281

AHIAM (2)

| 2Sa | 23:33 | **A** the son of Sharar the Hararite, | 279 |
| 1Ch | 11:35 | **A** the son of Sacar the Hararite, Eliphal | 279 |

AHIAN (1)

1Ch 7:19 **A**, and Shechem, and Likhi, and Aniam. 291

AHIEZER (6)

Nu	1:12	Of Dan; **A** the son of Ammishaddai.	295
	2:25	the captain of the children of Dan *shall be* **A**	295
	7:66	On the tenth day **A** the son of Ammishaddai,	295
	7:71	this *was* the offering of **A** the son of	295
	10:25	over his host *was* **A** the son of	295
1Ch	12: 3	The chief *was* **A**, then Joash, the sons of	295

AHIHUD (2)

| Nu | 34:27 | the children of Asher, **A** the son of Shelomi. | 282 |
| 1Ch | 8: 7 | he removed them, and begat Uzza, and **A**. | 284 |

AHIJAH (20)

1Ki	11:29	that the prophet **A** the Shilonite found him in	281
	11:30	**A** caught the new garment that *was* on him,	281
	12:15	which the LORD spake by **A** the Shilonite	281
	14: 2	behold, there *is* **A** the prophet, which told	281
	14: 4	went *to* Shiloh, and came *to* the house of **A**.	281
	14: 4	**A** could not see; for his eyes were set by	281
	14: 5	the LORD said unto **A**, Behold, the wife of	281
	14: 6	*so*, when **A** heard the sound of her feet,	281
	14:18	which he spake by the hand of his servant **A**	281
	15:27	Baasha the son of **A**, of the house of	281
	15:29	which he spake by his servant **A**	281
	15:33	son of **A** to reign over all Israel in Tirzah,	281
	21:22	like the house of Baasha the son of **A**, for	281
2Ki	9: 9	and like the house of Baasha the son of **A**:	281
1Ch	2:25	and Bunah, and Oren, and Ozem, *and* **A**.	281
	11:36	Hepher the Mecherathite, **A** the Pelonite,	281
	26:20	**A** *was* over the treasures of the house of	281
2Ch	9:29	in the prophecy of **A** the Shilonite, and in	281
	10:15	which he spake by the hand of **A**	281
Ne	10:26	And **A**, Hanan, Anan,	281

AHIKAM (20)

2Ki	22:12	**A** the son of Shaphan, and Achbor the son of	296
	22:14	**A**, and Achbor, and Shaphan, and Asahiah,	296
	25:22	over them he made Gedaliah the son of **A**,	296
2Ch	34:20	**A** the son of Shaphan, and Abdon the son of	296
Jer	26:24	Nevertheless the hand of **A** the son of	296
	39:14	committed him unto Gedaliah the son of **A**	296
	40: 5	to Gedaliah the son of **A** the son of Shaphan,	296
	40: 6	went Jeremiah unto Gedaliah the son of **A** to	296
	40: 7	Gedaliah the son of **A** governor in the land,	296

	40: 9	Gedaliah the son of **A** the son of Shaphan	296
	40:11	Gedaliah the son of **A** the son of Shaphan;	296
	40:14	Gedaliah the son of **A** believed them not.	296
	40:16	Gedaliah the son of **A** said unto Johanan	296
	41: 1	came unto Gedaliah the son of **A** to Mizpah;	296
	41: 2	smote Gedaliah the son of **A** the son of	296
	41: 6	unto them, Come to Gedaliah the son of **A**.	296
	41:10	had committed to Gedaliah the son of **A**:	296
	41:16	after *that* he had slain Gedaliah the son of **A**,	296
	41:18	Nethaniah had slain Gedaliah the son of **A**,	296
	43: 6	Gedaliah the son of **A** the son of Shaphan,	296

AHILUD (5)

2Sa	8:16	and Jehoshaphat the son of **A** *was* recorder;	286
	20:24	and Jehoshaphat the son of **A** *was* recorder:	286
1Ki	4: 3	Jehoshaphat the son of **A**, the recorder.	286
	4:12	Baana the son of **A**; *to him pertained*	286
1Ch	18:15	and Jehoshaphat the son of **A**, recorder.	286

AHIMAAZ (15)

1Sa	14:50	wife *was* Ahinoam, the daughter of **A**:	290
2Sa	15:27	**A** thy son, and Jonathan the son of Abiathar.	290
	15:36	**A** Zadok's *son*, and Jonathan Abiathar's *son*;	290
	17:17	Now Jonathan and **A** stayed by En-rogel;	290
	17:20	they said, Where *is* **A** and Jonathan?	290
	18:19	said **A** the son of Zadok, Let me now run,	290
	18:22	said **A** the son of Zadok yet again to Joab,	290
	18:23	**A** ran *by* the way of the plain, and	290
	18:27	*is* like the running of **A** the son of Zadok.	290
	18:28	**A** called, and said unto the king, All is well.	290
	18:29	**A** answered, When Joab sent the king's	290
1Ki	4:15	**A** *was* in Naphtali; he also took Basmath	290
1Ch	6: 8	Ahitub begat Zadok, and Zadok begat **A**,	290
	6: 9	**A** begat Azariah, and Azariah begat	290
	6:53	Zadok his son, **A** his son.	290

AHIMAN (4)

Nu	13:22	where **A**, Sheshai, and Talmai, the children	289
Jos	15:14	Sheshai, and **A**, and Talmai, the children of	289
Jdg	1:10	and they slew Sheshai, and **A**, and Talmai.	289
1Ch	9:17	and Talmon, and **A**, and their brethren.	289

AHIMELECH (16) [AHIMELECH'S]

1Sa	21: 1	Then came David to Nob to **A** the priest: and	288
	21: 1	**A** was afraid at the meeting of David, and	288
	21: 2	David said unto the priest, The king hath	288
	21: 8	David said unto **A**, And is there not here	288
	22: 9	Jesse coming to Nob, to **A** the son of Ahitub:	288
	22:11	the king sent to call **A** the priest, the son of	288
	22:14	**A** answered the king, and said, And who *is*	288
	22:16	**A**, thou, and all thy father's house.	288
	22:20	And one of the sons of **A** the son of Ahitub,	288
	23: 6	when Abiathar the son of **A** fled to David *to*	288
	26: 6	answered David and said to **A** the Hittite,	288
2Sa	8:17	and **A** the son of Abiathar, *were* the priests;	288
1Ch	24: 3	of Eleazar, and **A** of the sons of Ithamar,	288
	24: 6	**A** the son of Abiathar, and *before* the chief	288
	24:31	**A**, and the chief of the fathers of the priests	288
Ps	52: T	unto him, David is come to the house of **A**.	288

AHIMELECH'S (1) [AHIMELECH]

1Sa 30: 7 **A** son, I pray thee, bring me hither 288

AHIMOTH (1)

1Ch 6:25 And the sons of Elkanah; Amasai, and **A**. 287

AHINADAB (1)

1Ki 4:14 **A** the son of Iddo *had* Mahanaim: 292

AHINOAM (7)

1Sa	14:50	the name of Saul's wife *was* **A**, the daughter	293
	25:43	David also took **A** of Jezreel; and they were	293
	27: 3	**A** the Jezreelitess, and Abigail	293
	30: 5	**A** the Jezreelitess, and Abigail the wife of	293
2Sa	2: 2	**A** the Jezreelitess, and Abigail Nabal's wife	293
	3: 2	firstborn *was* Amnon, of **A** the Jezreelitess;	293
1Ch	3: 1	the firstborn Amnon, of **A** the Jezreelitess;	293

AHIO (6)

2Sa	6: 3	Uzzah and **A**, the sons of Abinadab,	283
	6: 4	the ark of God: and **A** went before the ark.	283
1Ch	8:14	And **A**, Shashak, and Jeremoth,	283
	8:31	And Gedor, and **A**, and Zacher.	283
	9:37	and **A**, and Zechariah, and Mikloth.	283
	13: 7	of Abinadab: and Uzza and **A** drave the cart.	283

AHIRA (5)
Nu 1:15 Of Naphtali; **A** the son of Enan. 299
2:29 of Naphtali *shall be* **A** the son of Enan. 299
7:78 On the twelfth day **A** the son of Enan, 299
7:83 this *was* the offering of **A** the son of Enan. 299
10:27 children of Naphtali *was* **A** the son of Enan. 299

AHIRAM (1) [AHIRAMITES]
Nu 26:38 of **A**, the family of the Ahiramites: 297

AHIRAMITES (1) [AHIRAM]
Nu 26:38 of Ahiram, the family of the **A**: 298

AHISAMACH (3)
Ex 31: 6 the son of **A**, of the tribe of Dan: 294
35:34 *both* he, and Aholiab, the son of **A**, of 294
38:23 son of **A**, of the tribe of Dan, an engraver, 294

AHISHAHAR (1)
1Ch 7:10 and Zethan, and Tharshish, and **A**. 300

AHISHAR (1)
1Ki 4: 6 **A** *was* over the household: and 301

AHITHOPHEL (20)
2Sa 15:12 Absalom sent *for* **A** the Gilonite, 302
15:31 **A** *is* among the conspirators with Absalom. 302
15:31 turn the counsel of **A** into foolishness. 302
15:34 mayest thou for me defeat the counsel of **A**. 302
16:15 came *to* Jerusalem, and **A** with him. 302
16:20 said Absalom to **A**, Give counsel among you 302
16:21 **A** said unto Absalom, Go in unto thy father's 302
16:23 the counsel of **A**, which he counselled in 302
16:23 so *was* all the counsel of **A** both with David 302
17: 1 Moreover **A** said unto Absalom, Let me now 302
17: 6 **A** hath spoken after this manner: 302
17: 7 The counsel that **A** hath given *is* not good at 302
17:14 the Archite *is* better than the counsel of **A**. 302
17:14 appointed to defeat the good counsel of **A**, 302
17:15 Thus and thus did **A** counsel Absalom and 302
17:21 for thus hath **A** counselled against you. 302
17:23 when **A** saw that his counsel was not 302
23:34 Eliam the son of **A** the Gilonite, 302
1Ch 27:33 **A** *was* the king's counseller: and Hushai 302
27:34 after **A** *was* Jehoiada the son of Benaiah, 302

AHITUB (15)
1Sa 14: 3 And Ahiah, the son of **A**, Ichabod's brother, 285
22: 9 coming to Nob, to Ahimelech the son of **A**: 285
22:11 the son of **A**, and all his father's house, 285
22:12 Saul said, Hear now, thou son of **A**. And he 285
22:20 one of the sons of Ahimelech the son of **A**, 285
2Sa 8:17 Zadok the son of **A**, and Ahimelech the son 285
1Ch 6: 7 begat Amariah, and Amariah begat **A**, 285
6: 8 **A** begat Zadok, and Zadok begat Ahimaaz, 285
6:11 begat Amariah, and Amariah begat **A**, 285
6:12 **A** begat Zadok, and Zadok begat Shallum, 285
6:52 his son, Amariah his son, **A** his son, 285
9:11 of Zadok, the son of Meraioth, the son of **A**, 285
18:16 Zadok the son of **A**, and Abimelech the son 285
Ezr 7: 2 of Shallum, the son of Zadok, the son of **A**, 285
Ne 11:11 of Zadok, the son of Meraioth, the son of **A**, 285

AHLAB (1)
Jdg 1:31 nor of **A**, nor of Achzib, nor of Helbah, 303

AHLAI (2)
1Ch 2:31 Sheshan. And the children of Sheshan; **A**. 304
11:41 Uriah the Hittite, Zabad the son of **A**, 304

AHOAH (1)
1Ch 8: 4 And Abishua, and Naaman, and **A**, 265

AHOHITE (5)
2Sa 23: 9 *was* Eleazar the son of Dodo the **A**, 266+1121
23:28 Zalmon the **A**, Maharai the Netophathite, 266
1Ch 11:12 the **A**, who *was one* of the three mighties. 266
11:29 Sibbecai the Hushathite, Ilai the **A**, 266
27: 4 course of the second month *was* Dodai an **A**, 266

AHOLAH (5)
Eze 23: 4 the names of them *were* **A** the elder, and 170
23: 4 Samaria *is* **A**, and Jerusalem Aholibah. 170
23: 5 And **A** played the harlot when she was mine; 170
23:36 of man, wilt thou judge **A** and Aholibah? 170
23:44 so went they in unto **A** and unto Aholibah, 170

AHOLIAB (5)
Ex 31: 6 I, behold, I have given with him **A**, the son 171
35:34 *both* he, and **A**, the son of Ahisamach, of 171
36: 1 wrought Bezaleel and **A**, and every wise 171
36: 2 Moses called Bezaleel and **A**, and every 171
38:23 with him *was* **A**, son of Ahisamach, of 171

AHOLIBAH (6)
Eze 23: 4 *were* Aholah the elder, and **A** her sister: 172
23: 4 Samaria *is* Aholah, and Jerusalem **A**. 172
23:11 when her sister **A** saw *this,* she was more 172
23:22 Therefore, O **A**, thus saith the Lord GOD; 172
23:36 Son of man, wilt thou judge Aholah and **A**? 172
23:44 so went they in unto Aholah and unto **A**, 172

AHOLIBAMAH (8)
Ge 36: 2 **A** the daughter of Anah the daughter of 173
36: 5 **A** bare Jeush, and Jaalam, and Korah: 173
36:14 these were the sons of **A**, the daughter of 173
36:18 these *are* the sons of **A** Esau's wife; 173
36:18 these *were* the dukes *that came* of **A** 173
36:25 Dishon, and **A** the daughter of Anah. 173
36:41 Duke **A**, duke Elah, duke Pinon, 173
1Ch 1:52 Duke **A**, duke Elah, duke Pinon, 173

AHUMAI (1)
1Ch 4: 2 begat Jahath; and Jahath begat **A**, and Lahad. 267

AHUZAM (1)
1Ch 4: 6 Naarah bare him **A**, and Hepher, and 275

AHUZZAM See AHUZAM

AHUZZATH (1)
Ge 26:26 **A** *one* of his friends, and Phichol the chief 276

AHZAI See AHASAI

AI (36) [HAI]
Jos 7: 2 Joshua sent men from Jericho *to* **A**, 5857
7: 2 And the men went up and viewed **A**. 5857
7: 3 or three thousand men go up and smite **A**; 5857
7: 4 and they fled before the men of **A**. 5857
7: 5 the men of **A** smote of them about thirty 5857
8: 1 of war with thee, and arise, go up *to* **A**: 5857
8: 1 I have given into thy hand the king of **A**, 5857
8: 2 thou shalt do to **A** and her king as thou 5857
8: 3 all the people of war, to go up *against* **A**: 5857
8: 9 abode between Beth-el and **A**, on the west 5857
8: 9 and Ai, on the west side of **A**: 5857
8:10 the elders of Israel, before the people *to* **A**. 5857
8:11 the city, and pitched on the north side of **A**: 5857
8:11 *there was* a valley between them and **A**. 5857
8:12 to lie in ambush between Beth-el and **A**, 5857
8:14 when the king of **A** saw *it,* that they hasted 5857
8:16 all the people that *were* in **A** were called 5857
8:17 there was not a man left in **A** or Beth-el, 5857
8:18 out the spear that *is* in thy hand toward **A**; 5857
8:20 when the men of **A** looked behind them, 5857
8:21 they turned again, and slew the men of **A**. 5857
8:23 the king of **A** they took alive, and 5857
8:24 slaying all the inhabitants of **A** in the field, 5857
8:24 that all the Israelites returned *unto* **A**, and 5857
8:25 twelve thousand, *even* all the men of **A**. 5857
8:26 utterly destroyed all the inhabitants of **A**. 5857
8:28 Joshua burnt **A**, and made it a heap for 5857
8:29 the king of **A** he hanged on a tree until 5857
9: 3 Joshua had done unto Jericho and to **A**, 5857
10: 1 had heard how Joshua had taken **A**, 5857
10: 1 her king, so he had done to **A** and her king; 5857
10: 2 because it *was* greater than **A**, and all 5857
12: 9 the king of **A**, which *is* beside Beth-el, one; 5857
Ezr 2:28 The men of Beth-el and **A**, two hundred 5857
Ne 7:32 The men of Beth-el and **A**, an hundred 5857
Jer 49: 3 Howl, O Heshbon, for **A** is spoiled: cry, 5857

AIAH (6)
Ge 36:24 the children of Zibeon; both **A**, and Anah: 345
2Sa 3: 7 whose name *was* Rizpah, the daughter of **A**: 345
21: 8 the two sons of Rizpah the daughter of **A**, 345
21:10 Rizpah the daughter of **A** took sackcloth, 345
21:11 told David what Rizpah the daughter of **A**, 345
1Ch 1:40 And the sons of Zibeon; **A**, and Anah. 345

AIATH (1)
Isa 10:28 He is come to A, he is passed to Migron; 5857

AIDED (1)
Jdg 9:24 a him in the killing of his 853+2388+3027

AIJA (1)
Ne 11:31 and A, and Beth-el, and in their villages, 5857

AIJALON (8)
Jos 19:42 And Shaalabbin, and A, and Jethlah, 357
21:24 A with her suburbs, Gath-rimmon with her 357
Jdg 1:35 Amorites would dwell in mount Heres in A, 357
12:12 was buried in A in the country of Zebulun. 357
1Sa 14:31 the Philistines that day from Michmash to A: 357
1Ch 6:69 A with her suburbs, and Gath-rimmon with 357
8:13 heads of the fathers of the inhabitants of A, 357
2Ch 11:10 Zorah, and A, and Hebron, which are in 357

AIJELETH (1)
Ps 22: T To the chief Musician upon A Shahar, 365

AILED (1) [AILETH]
Ps 114: 5 What a thee, O thou sea, that thou 3807.1

AILETH (7) [AILED]
Ge 21:17 said unto her, What a thee, Hagar? 4100+3807.1
Jdg 18:23 and said unto Micah, What a thee, 3807.1
18:24 is this that ye say unto me, What a thee? 3807.1
1Sa 11: 5 What a the people that they weep? 3807.1
2Sa 14: 5 the king said unto her, What a thee? 3807.1
2Ki 6:28 the king said unto her, What a thee? 3807.1
Isa 22: 1 What a thee now, that thou art wholly 3807.1

AIN (5)
Nu 34:11 Shepham to Riblah, on the east side of A; 5871
Jos 15:32 and Shilhim, and A, and Rimmon: 5871
19: 7 A, Remmon, and Ether, and Ashan; 5871
21:16 A with her suburbs, and Juttah with her 5871
1Ch 4:32 A, Rimmon, and Tochen, and Ashan, 5871

AIR (39)
Ge 1:26 over the fowl of the a, and over the cattle, 8064
1:28 over the fowl of the a, and over every 8064
1:30 to every fowl of the a, and to every thing 8064
2:19 beast of the field, and every fowl of the a; 8064
2:20 to the fowl of the a, and to every beast of 8064
6: 7 the creeping thing, and the fowls of the a; 8064
7: 3 Of fowls also of the a by sevens, the male 8064
9: 2 upon every fowl of the a, upon all that 8064
Dt 4:17 of any winged fowl that flieth in the a, 8064
28:26 shall be meat unto all fowls of the a, 8064
1Sa 17:44 I will give thy flesh unto the fowls of the a, 8064
17:46 Philistines this day unto the fowls of the a, 8064
2Sa 21:10 suffered neither the birds of the a to rest on 8064
1Ki 14:11 in the field shall the fowls of the a eat: 8064
16: 4 his in the fields shall the fowls of the a eat. 8064
21:24 in the field shall the fowls of the a eat. 8064
Job 12: 7 the fowls of the a, and they shall tell thee: 8064
28:21 and kept close from the fowls of the a. 8064
41:16 that no a can come between them. 7307
Ps 8: 8 The fowl of the a, and the fish of the sea, 8064
Pr 30:19 The way of an eagle in the a; the way of a 8064
Ecc 10:20 for a bird of the a shall carry the voice, and 8064
Mt 6:26 Behold the fowls of the a: for they sow not, 3772
8:20 and the birds of the a have nests; 3772
13:32 so that the birds of the a come and lodge in 3772
Mk 4: 4 and the fowls of the a came and devoured it 3772
4:32 that the fowls of the a may lodge under 3772
Lk 8: 5 and the fowls of the a devoured it. 3772
9:58 have holes, and birds of the a have nests; 3772
13:19 the fowls of the a lodged in the branches of 3772
Ac 10:12 and creeping things, and fowls of the a. 3772
11: 6 and creeping things, and fowls of the a. 3772
22:23 off their clothes, and threw dust into the a, 109
1Co 9:26 so fight I, not as one that beateth the a: 109
14: 9 what is spoken? for ye shall speak into the a. 109
Eph 2: 2 according to the prince of the power of the a, 109
1Th 4:17 them in the clouds, to meet the Lord in the a: 109
Rev 9: 2 the a were darkened by reason of the smoke 109
16:17 seventh angel poured out his vial into the a; 109

AJALON (2)
Jos 10:12 and thou, Moon, in the valley of A. 357
2Ch 28:18 A, and Gederoth, and Shocho with 357

AKAN (1)
Ge 36:27 Ezer are these; Bilhan, and Zaavan, and A. 6130

AKELDAMA See ACELDAMA

AKIM See ACHIM

AKKAD See ACCAD

AKKUB (8)
1Ch 3:24 A, and Johanan, and Dalaiah, and Anani, 6126
9:17 A, and Talmon, and Ahiman, and 6126
Ezr 2:42 the children of A, the children of Hatita, 6126
2:45 the children of Hagabah, the children of A, 6126
Ne 7:45 the children of A, the children of Hatita, 6126
8: 7 Bani, and Sherebiah, Jamin, A, Shabbethai, 6126
11:19 A, Talmon, and their brethren that kept 6126
12:25 Obadiah, Meshullam, Talmon, A, 6126

AKRABBIM (2)
Nu 34: 4 shall turn from the south to the ascent of A, 6137
Jdg 1:36 the Amorites was from the going up to A, 6137

ALABASTER (3)
Mt 26: 7 having an a box of very precious ointment, 211
Mk 14: 3 there came a woman having an a box of 211
Lk 7:37 brought an a box of ointment, 211

ALAMETH (1)
1Ch 7: 8 Jerimoth, and Abiah, and Anathoth, and A. 5964

ALAMMELECH (1)
Jos 19:26 A, and Amad, and Misheal; and reacheth to 487

ALAMOTH (2)
1Ch 15:20 and Benaiah, with psalteries on A; 5961
Ps 46: T for the sons of Korah, A Song upon A. 5961

ALARM (10)
Nu 10: 5 When ye blow an a, then the camps that lie 8643
10: 6 When you blow an a the second time, then 8643
10: 6 they shall blow an a for their journeys. 8643
10: 7 shall blow, but you shall not sound an a. 7321
10: 9 then ye shall blow an a with the trumpets; 7321
2Ch 13:12 his priests with sounding trumpets to cry a 7321
Jer 4:19 the sound of the trumpet, the a of war. 8643
49: 2 that I will cause an a of war to be heard in 8643
Joel 2: 1 and sound an a in my holy mountain: 7321
Zep 1:16 the trumpet and a against the fenced cities, 8643

ALAS (20) See Index

ALBEIT (2)
Eze 13: 7 The LORD saith it; a I have not spoken? 2050.1
Phm 1:19 I will repay it: a I do not say to thee how 2443

ALEMETH (3)
1Ch 6:60 A with her suburbs, and Anathoth with her 5964
8:36 Jehoadah begat A, and Azmaveth, and 5964
9:42 Jarah begat A, and Azmaveth, and Zimri; 5964

ALEXANDER (6)
Mk 15:21 the father of A and Rufus, to bear his cross. 223
Ac 4: 6 and A, and as many as were of the kindred 223
19:33 And they drew A out of the multitude, 223
19:33 And A beckoned with the hand, and 223
1Ti 1:20 Of whom is Hymeneus and A; whom I have 223
2Ti 4:14 A the coppersmith did me much evil: 223

ALEXANDRIA (3) [ALEXANDRIANS]
Ac 18:24 born at A, an eloquent man, and mighty in 221
27: 6 And there the centurion found a ship of A 222
28:11 three months we departed in a ship of A, 222

ALEXANDRIANS (1) [ALEXANDRIA]
Ac 6: 9 and A, and of them of Cilicia and of Asia, 221

ALGUM (3) [ALMUG]
2Ch 2: 8 fir trees, and a trees, out of Lebanon: 418
9:10 brought a trees and precious stones. 418
9:11 the king made of the a trees terraces to 418

ALIAH (1)
1Ch 1:51 duke Timnah, duke A, duke Jetheth, 5933

ALIAN (1)
1Ch 1:40 A, and Manahath, and Ebal, Shephi, and 5935

ALIEN (5) [ALIENATE, ALIENATED, ALIENS]
Ex 18: 3 he said, I have been an **a** in a strange land: 1616
Dt 14:21 may eat it; or thou mayest sell *it* unto an **a**: 5237
Job 19:15 me for a stranger: I am an **a** in their sight. 5237
Ps 69: 8 and an **a** unto my mother's children. 5237
Isa 61: 5 the sons of the **a** *shall be* your plowmen 5236

ALIENATE (1) [ALIEN]
Eze 48:14 nor **a** the firstfruits of the land: 5674

ALIENATED (7) [ALIEN]
Eze 23:17 with them, and her mind was **a** from them. 3363
23:18 my mind was **a** from her, like as my mind 3363
23:18 like as my mind was **a** from her sister. 5361
23:22 from whom thy mind is **a**, and I will bring 5361
23:28 the hand *of them* from whom thy mind is **a**: 5361
Eph 4:18 being **a** from the life of God through *526*
Col 1:21 that were sometime **a** and enemies in *your* *526*

ALIENS (3) [ALIEN]
La 5: 2 is turned to strangers, our houses to **a**. 5237
Eph 2:12 being **a** from the commonwealth of Israel, *526*
Heb 11:34 in fight, turned to flight the armies of the **a**. *245*

ALIKE (11) [LIKE]
Dt 12:22 and the clean shall eat of them **a**. 3162
15:22 and the clean *person shall eat it* **a**, 3162
1Sa 30:24 that tarrieth by the stuff: they shall part **a**. 3162
Job 21:26 They shall lie down **a** in the dust, and 3162
Ps 33:15 He fashioneth their hearts **a**; he considereth 3162
139:12 and the light *are* both **a** *to thee*. 3509.1
Pr 20:10 both of them *are* **a** abomination to 1571
27:15 rainy day and a contentious woman are **a**. 7737
Ecc 9: 2 All *things come* **a** to all: *there is* one 834+3509.1
11: 6 whether they both *shall be* **a** good. 259+3509.1
Ro 14: 5 another esteemeth every day *a*. Let every NIG

ALIVE (88) [LIVE]
Ge 6:19 into the ark, to **keep** *them* **a** with thee; 2421
6:20 *sort* shall come unto thee, to **keep** *them* **a**. 2421
7: 3 to **keep** seed **a** upon the face of all 2421
7:23 Noah only remained *a*, and *they* that *were* NIH
12:12 they will kill me, but they will **save** thee **a**. 2421
43: 7 of our kindred, saying, *Is* your father yet **a**? 2416
43:27 the old man of whom ye spake? *Is* he yet **a**? 2416
43:28 our father *is* in good health, he *is* yet **a**. 2416
45:26 Joseph *is* yet **a**, and he *is* governor over all 2416
45:28 *It is* enough; Joseph my son *is* yet **a**: 2416
46:30 I have seen thy face, because thou *art* yet **a**. 2416
50:20 as *it is* this day, to **save** much people **a**. 2421
Ex 1:17 but **saved** the men children **a**. 2421
1:18 and have **saved** the men children **a**? 2421
1:22 and every daughter ye shall **save** **a**. 2421
4:18 *are* in Egypt, and see whether they be yet **a**. 2416
22: 4 If the theft be certainly found in his hand **a**, 2416
Lev 10:16 the sons of Aaron which were left *a*, saying, NIH
14: 4 for him that is to be cleansed two birds **a** 2416
16:10 shall be presented **a** before the LORD, 2416
26:36 *upon* them that are left *a* of you I will send a NIH
Nu 16:33 went down **a** into the pit, and the earth 2416
21:35 his people, until there was none left him **a**: 8300
22:33 now also I had slain thee, and **saved** her **a**. 2421
31:15 unto them, Have ye **saved** all the women **a**? 2421
31:18 by lying with him, **keep** **a** for yourselves. 2421
Dt 4: 4 your God *are* **a** every one of you *this* day. 2416
5: 3 *even* us, who *are* all of us here **a** *this* day. 2416
6:24 that he might **preserve** us **a**, as *it is at* this 2421
20:16 thou shalt **save** **a** nothing that breatheth: 2421
31:27 behold, while I am yet **a** with you *this* day, 2416
32:39 I kill, and I **make** **a**; I wound, and I heal: 2421
Jos 2:13 *that* ye will **save** **a** my father, and 2421
6:25 Joshua **saved** Rahab the harlot **a**, and her 2421
8:23 the king of Ai they took **a**, and brought him 2416
14:10 the LORD hath **kept** me **a**, as he said, 2421
Jdg 8:19 if ye had **saved** them **a**, I would not slay 2421
21:14 **saved** **a** of the women of Jabesh-gilead: 2421
1Sa 2: 6 The LORD killeth, and **maketh** **a**: 2421
15: 8 he took Agag the king of the Amalekites **a**, 2416
27: 9 **left** neither man nor woman **a**, and 2421
27:11 David **saved** neither man nor woman **a**, 2421
2Sa 8: 2 to death, and *with* one full line to **keep** **a**. 2421
12:18 Behold, while the child was *yet* **a**, 2416
12:21 and weep for the child, *while it was* **a**; 2416
12:22 While the child *was* yet **a**, I fasted and 2416
18:14 while he *was* yet **a** in the midst of the oak. 2416
1Ki 18: 5 find grass to **save** the horses and mules **a**, 2421
20:18 they be come out for peace, take them **a**; 2416
20:18 they be come out for war, take them **a**. 2416
20:32 And he said, *Is* he yet **a**? he *is* my brother. 2416
21:15 for money: for Naboth is not **a**, but dead. 2416
2Ki 5: 7 and said, *Am* I God, to kill and to **make** **a**, 2421
7: 4 if they **save** us **a**, we shall live; and if they 2421
7:12 we shall catch them **a**, and get into the city. 2416
10:14 he said, Take them **a**. And they took them 2416
10:14 they took them **a**, and slew them at the pit 2416
2Ch 25:12 *other* ten thousand *left* **a** did the children of 2416
Ps 22:29 and none can **keep** **a** his own soul. 2421
30: 3 thou hast **kept** me **a**, that I should not go 2421
33:19 from death, and to **keep** them **a** in famine. 2421
41: 2 LORD will preserve him, and **keep** him **a**; 2421
Pr 1:12 Let us swallow them up **a** as the grave; and 2416
Ecc 4: 2 dead more than the living which are yet **a**. 2416
Jer 49:11 fatherless children, I will **preserve** *them* **a**; 2421
Eze 7:13 although they were yet **a**: 2416+871.1+1886.1
13:18 will ye **save** the souls **a** *that come* unto 2421
13:19 and to **save** the souls **a** that should not live, 2421
18:27 is lawful and right, he shall **save** his soul **a**. 2421
Da 5:19 whom he would he **kept** **a**; and whom he 2418
Mt 27:63 while he was yet **a**, After three days I will *2198*
Mk 16:11 when they had heard that he was **a**, and *2198*
Lk 15:24 For this my son was dead, and is **a again**; *326*
15:32 for this thy brother was dead, and is **a again**; *326*
24:23 a vision of angels, which said that he was **a**. *2198*
Ac 1: 3 To whom also he shewed himself **a** after *2198*
9:41 the saints and widows, presented her **a**. *2198*
20:12 And they brought the young man **a**, and *2198*
25:19 *was* dead, whom Paul affirmed to be **a**. *2198*
Ro 6:11 **a** unto God through Jesus Christ our Lord. *2198*
6:13 as *those that are* **a** from the dead, and *2198*
7: 9 For I was **a** without the law once: but *2198*
1Co 15:22 even so in Christ shall all be **made a**. *2227*
1Th 4:15 that we which are **a** *and* remain unto *2198*
4:17 Then we which are **a** *and* remain shall be *2198*
Rev 1:18 and behold, I am **a** for evermore, Amen; *2198*
2: 8 and the last, which was dead, and is **a**; *2198*
19:20 *These* both were cast **a** into a lake of fire *2198*

ALL (5621) See Index

ALLAMMELECH See ALAMMELECH

ALLEGING (1)
Ac 17: 3 Opening and **a**, that Christ must needs have *3908*

ALLEGORY (1)
Gal 4:24 Which *things* are an **a**: for these are the two *238*

ALLELUIA (4)
Rev 19: 1 voice of much people in heaven, saying, **A**; *239*
19: 3 And again they said, **A**. And her smoke rose *239*
19: 4 God that sat on the throne, saying, Amen; **A**. *239*
19: 6 the voice of mighty thunderings, saying, **A**: *239*

ALLIED (1)
Ne 13: 4 the house of our God, *was* **a** unto Tobiah: 7138

ALLON (2)
Jos 19:33 from **A** to Zaanannim, and Adami, Nekeb, 438
1Ch 4:37 the son of **A**, the son of Jedaiah, the son of 438

ALLON BACUTH See ALLON-BACHUTH

ALLON-BACHUTH (1)
Ge 35: 8 an oak: and the name of it was called **A**. 439

ALLOW (3) [ALLOWANCE, ALLOWED, ALLOWETH]
Lk 11:48 Truly ye bear witness that ye **a** the deeds of *4909*
Ac 24:15 which they themselves also **a**, *4327*
Ro 7:15 For *that* which I do I **a** not: for what I *1097*

ALLOWANCE (2) [ALLOW]
2Ki 25:30 his **a** was a continual allowance given him of 737
25:30 his allowance was a continual **a** given him of 737

ALLOWED (1) [ALLOW]
1Th 2: 4 But as we were **a** of God to be put in trust *1381*

ALLOWETH (1) [ALLOW]
Ro 14:22 not himself in *that thing* which he **a**. *1381*

ALLURE (2)
Hos 2:14 I *will* **a** her, and bring her *into* 6601
2Pe 2:18 they **a** through the lusts of the flesh, *1185*

ALMIGHTY (57) [MIGHT]
Ge 17: 1 and said unto him, I *am* the **A** God; 7706
28: 3 God **A** bless thee, and make thee fruitful, 7706
35:11 God said unto him, I *am* God **A**: be fruitful 7706
43:14 God **A** give you mercy before the man, 7706
48: 3 God **A** appeared unto me at Luz in the land 7706
49:25 *by* the **A**, who shall bless thee *with* 7706
Ex 6: 3 by *the name of* God **A**, but *by* my name 7706
Nu 24: 4 which saw the vision of the **A**, falling *into a* 7706
24:16 *which* saw the vision of the **A**, falling *into a* 7706
Ru 1:20 for the **A** hath dealt very bitterly with me. 7706
1:21 against me, and the **A** hath afflicted me? 7706
Job 5:17 despise not thou the chastening of the **A**: 7706
6: 4 For the arrows of the **A** *are* within me, 7706
6:14 but he forsaketh the fear of the **A**. 7706
8: 3 or doth the **A** pervert justice? 7706
8: 5 and make thy supplication to the **A**; 7706
11: 7 canst thou find out the **A** unto perfection? 7706
13: 3 Surely I would speak to the **A**, and I desire 7706
15:25 and strengtheneth himself against the **A**. 7706
21:15 What *is* the **A**, that we should serve him? 7706
21:20 and he shall drink of the wrath of the **A**. 7706
22: 3 *Is it any* pleasure to the **A**, that thou art 7706
22:17 from us: and what can the **A** do for them? 7706
22:23 If thou return to the **A**, thou shalt be built 7706
22:25 the **A** shall be thy defence, and thou shalt 7706
22:26 then shalt thou have thy delight in the **A**, 7706
23:16 my heart soft, and the **A** troubleth me: 7706
24: 1 seeing times are not hidden from the **A**, 7706
27: 2 and the **A**, *who* hath vexed my soul; 7706
27:10 Will he delight himself in the **A**? will he 7706
27:11 *that* which *is* with the **A** will I not conceal. 7706
27:13 *which* they shall receive of the **A**. 7706
29: 5 When the **A** *was* yet with me, *when* my 7706
31: 2 *what* inheritance of the **A** from on high? 7706
31:35 my desire *is, that* the **A** would answer me, 7706
32: 8 the inspiration of the **A** giveth them 7706
33: 4 and the breath of the **A** hath given me life. 7706
34:10 *from* the **A**, *that he should commit* iniquity. 7706
34:12 neither will the **A** pervert judgment. 7706
35:13 not hear vanity, neither will the **A** regard it. 7706
37:23 *Touching* the **A**, we cannot find him out: 7706
40: 2 Shall he that contendeth with the **A** instruct 7706
Ps 68:14 When the **A** scattered kings in it, it was 7706
91: 1 shall abide under the shadow of the **A**. 7706
Isa 13: 6 it shall come as a destruction from the **A**. 7706
Eze 1:24 as the voice of the **A**, the voice of speech, 7706
10: 5 as the voice of the **A** God when he 7706
Joel 1:15 as a destruction from the **A** shall it come. 7706
2Co 6:18 my sons and daughters, saith the Lord **A**. *3841*
Rev 1: 8 which was, and which is to come, the **A**. *3841*
4: 8 saying, Holy, holy, holy, Lord God **A**, *3841*
11:17 O Lord God **A**, which art, and wast, and *3841*
15: 3 and marvellous *are* thy works, Lord God **A**; *3841*
16: 7 Lord God **A**, true and righteous *are* thy *3841*
16:14 to the battle of that great day of God **A**. *3841*
19:15 of the fierceness and wrath of **A** God. *3841*
21:22 for the Lord God **A** and the Lamb are *3841*

ALMODAD (2)
Ge 10:26 Joktan begat **A**, and Sheleph, and 486
1Ch 1:20 Joktan begat **A**, and Sheleph, and 486

ALMON (1)
Jos 21:18 with her suburbs, and **A** with her suburbs; 5960

ALMOND (2) [ALMONDS]
Ecc 12: 5 the **a tree** shall flourish, and 8247
Jer 1:11 And I said, I see a rod of an **a tree**. 8247

ALMON-DIBLATHAIM (2)
Nu 33:46 from Dibon-gad, and encamped in **A**. 5963
33:47 they removed from **A**, and pitched in 5963

ALMONDS (8) [ALMOND]
Ge 43:11 little honey, spices, and myrrh, nuts, and **a**: 8247
Ex 25:33 Three bowls **made like unto a**, *with* a knop 8246
25:33 three bowls **made like a** in the other 8246
25:34 *shall be* four bowls **made like unto a**, 8246
37:19 Three bowls **made after the fashion of a** 8246
37:19 three bowls **made like a** in another branch, 8246
37:20 candlestick *were* four bowls **made like a**, 8246
Nu 17: 8 and bloomed blossoms, and yielded **a**. 8247

ALMOST (11)
Ex 17: 4 shall I do unto this people? they be **a** 4592+5750
Ps 73: 2 *as for* me, my feet were **a** gone; 4592+3509.1
94:17 my soul had **a** dwelt *in* silence. 4592+3509.1
119:87 They had **a** consumed me upon 4592+3509.1
Pr 5:14 I was **a** in all evil in the midst of 4592+3509.1
Ac 13:44 And the next sabbath day came **a** the whole *4975*
19:26 but **a** throughout all Asia, this Paul hath *4975*
21:27 And when the seven days were **a** ended, *3195*
26:28 **A** thou persuadest me to be a *1722+3641*
26:29 that hear me this day, were both **a**, *1722+3641*
Heb 9:22 And **a** all *things* are by the law purged with *4975*

ALMS (13) [ALMSDEEDS]
Mt 6: 1 Take heed that *ye* do not your **a** before *1654*
6: 2 Therefore when thou doest *thine* **a**, do not *1654*
6: 3 But when thou doest **a**, let not thy left hand *1654*
6: 4 That thine **a** may be in secret: and *1654*
Lk 11:41 But rather give **a** *of* such *things* as *you* *1654*
12:33 Sell that ye have, and give **a**; *1654*
Ac 3: 2 to ask **a** of them that entered into *1654*
3: 3 about to go into the temple, asked an **a**. *1654*
3:10 sat for **a** at the Beautiful gate of the temple: *1654*
10: 2 which gave much **a** to the people, and *1654*
10: 4 thine **a** are come up for a memorial before *1654*
10:31 thine **a** are had in remembrance in the sight *1654*
24:17 Now after many years I came to bring **a** to *1654*

ALMSDEEDS (1) [ALMS]
Ac 9:36 full of good works and **a** which she did. *1654*

ALMUG (3) [ALGUM]
1Ki 10:11 brought in from Ophir great plenty of **a** 484
10:12 the king made *of* the **a** trees pillars for 484
10:12 there came no such **a** trees, nor were seen 484

ALOES (5)
Nu 24: 6 as the **trees of lign a** *which* the LORD hath 174
Ps 45: 8 and **a**, *and* cassia, out of the ivory palaces, 174
Pr 7:17 my bed *with* myrrh, **a**, and cinnamon. 174
SS 4:14 myrrh and **a**, with all the chief spices: 174
Jn 19:39 and brought a mixture of myrrh and **a**, *250*

ALONE (108) See Index

ALONG (30) See Index

ALOOF (1)
Ps 38:11 my friends stand **a from** my sore; 4480+5048

ALOTH (1)
1Ki 4:16 the son of Hushai *was* in Asher and in **A**: 1175

ALOUD (19) [LOUD]
Ge 45: 2 he **wept a**: and 1065+5414+6963+871.1
1Ki 18:27 and said, Cry **a**: 1419+6963+871.1
Ezr 3:12 **shouted a** for 6963+7311+8643+871.1+3807.1
Job 19: 7 not heard: I **cry a**, but *there is* no judgment. 7768
Ps 51:14 my tongue shall **sing a** of thy 7442
55:17 and at noon, will I pray, and **cry a**: 1993
59:16 I will **sing a** of thy mercy in the morning: 7442
81: 1 **Sing a** unto God our strength: make a 7442
132:16 and her saints shall **shout a for joy**. 7442+7444
149: 5 in glory: let them **sing a** upon their beds. 7442
Isa 24:14 the LORD, they shall **cry a** from the sea. 6670
54: 1 break forth *into* singing, and **cry a**, 6670
58: 1 Cry **a**, spare not, lift up thy voice 1627+871.1
Da 3: 4 a herald cried **a**, To you it is 2429+871.2
4:14 He cried **a**, and said thus, Hew down 2429+871.2
5: 7 The king cried **a** to bring in 2429+871.2
Hos 5: 8 **cry a** *at* Beth-aven, after thee, O Benjamin. 7321
Mic 4: 9 Now why dost thou **cry out a**? *is* 7321+7452
Mk 15: 8 And the multitude **crying a** began to desire *310*

ALPHA (4)
Rev 1: 8 I am **A** and Omega, the beginning and *1*
1:11 Saying, I am **A** and Omega, the first and *1*
21: 6 I am **A** and Omega, the beginning and the end. *1*
22:13 I am **A** and Omega, the beginning and the end, *1*

ALPHEUS (5)
Mt 10: 3 James the *son* of **A**, and Lebbeus, *256*

Mk	2:14	he saw Levi the *son* of **A** sitting at	256
	3:18	and James the *son* of **A**, and Thaddeus, and	256
Lk	6:15	James the *son* of **A**, and Simon called	256
Ac	1:13	James *the son* of **A**, and Simon Zelotes, and	256

ALREADY (31) [READY]

Ex	1: 5	seventy souls: for Joseph was in Egypt ***a***.	NIH
2Ch	28:13	LORD ***a***, ye intend to add *more* to our sins	NIH
Ne	5: 5	***a***: neither *is it* in our power *to redeem them;*	NIH
Ecc	1:10	it hath been **a** of old time, which was	3528
	2:12	the king? *even* that which hath been **a** done.	3528
	3:15	*that* which *is* to be hath **a** been; and God	3528
	4: 2	Wherefore I praised the dead which are **a**	3528
	6:10	That which hath been is named **a**, and *it is*	3528
Mal	2: 2	yea, I have cursed them **a**, because ye do	NIH
Mt	5:28	committed adultery with her **a** in his heart.	*2235*
	17:12	That Elias is come **a**, and they knew him	*2235*
Mk	15:44	And Pilate marvelled if he were **a** dead:	*2235*
Lk	12:49	the earth; and what will I, if it be **a** kindled?	*2235*
Jn	3:18	but he that believeth not is condemned **a**,	*2235*
	4:35	the fields; for they are white **a** to harvest.	*2235*
	9:22	for the Jews had agreed **a**, that if any *man*	*2235*
	9:27	I have told you **a**, and ye did not hear:	*2235*
	11:17	that he had *lien* in the grave four days **a**.	*2235*
	19:33	and saw that he was dead **a**, they brake not	*2235*
Ac	11:11	**immediately** there were three men **a** come	*1824*
	27: 9	because the fast was **now a** past, Paul	*2235*
1Co	5: 3	but present in spirit, have judged **a**,	*2235*
2Co	12:21	I shall bewail many which have **sinned a**,	*4258*
Php	3:12	Not as though I had **a** attained, either were	*2235*
	3:12	had already attained, either were **a** perfect:	*2235*
	3:16	Nevertheless, whereto we have ***a*** attained,	NIG
2Th	2: 7	For the mystery of iniquity doth **a** work:	*2235*
1Ti	5:15	For some are **a** turned aside after Satan.	*2235*
2Ti	2:18	saying that the resurrection is past **a**;	*2235*
1Jn	4: 3	and *even* now **a** is it in the world.	*2235*
Rev	2:25	But *that* which ye have ***a*** hold fast till I	NIG

ALSO (1768) See Index

ALTAR (378) [ALTARS]

Ge	8:20	Noah builded an **a** unto the LORD; and	4196
	8:20	and offered burnt offerings on the **a**.	4196
	12: 7	there builded he an **a** unto the LORD,	4196
	12: 8	there he builded an **a** unto the LORD, and	4196
	13: 4	Unto the place of the **a**, which he had made	4196
	13:18	and built there an **a** unto the LORD.	4196
	22: 9	Abraham built an **a** there, and laid	4196
	22: 9	and laid him on the **a** upon the wood.	4196
	26:25	he builded an **a** there, and called upon	4196
	33:20	he erected there an **a**, and called it	4196
	35: 1	make there an **a** unto God, that appeared	4196
	35: 3	I will make there an **a** unto God,	4196
	35: 7	he built there an **a**, and called the place	4196
Ex	17:15	Moses built an **a**, and called the name of it	4196
	20:24	An **a** of earth thou shalt make unto me, and	4196
	20:25	if thou wilt make me an **a** of stone,	4196
	20:26	shalt thou go up by steps unto mine **a**,	4196
	21:14	thou shalt take him from mine **a**, that he	4196
	24: 4	builded an **a** under the hill, and	4196
	24: 6	and half of the blood he sprinkled on the **a**.	4196
	27: 1	thou shalt make an **a** *of* shittim wood,	4196
	27: 1	five cubits broad; the **a** shall be foursquare:	4196
	27: 5	thou shalt put it under the compass of the **a**	4196
	27: 5	the net may be even to the midst of the **a**.	4196
	27: 6	thou shalt make staves for the **a**, staves of	4196
	27: 7	staves shall be upon the two sides of the **a**,	4196
	28:43	when they come near unto the **a** to minister	4196
	29:12	put *it* upon the horns of the **a** with thy	4196
	29:12	all the blood beside the bottom of the **a**.	4196
	29:13	*is* upon them, and burn *them* upon the **a**.	4196
	29:16	and sprinkle *it* round about upon the **a**.	4196
	29:18	thou shalt burn the whole ram upon the **a**:	4196
	29:20	sprinkle the blood upon the **a** round about.	4196
	29:21	shalt take of the blood that *is* upon the **a**,	4196
	29:25	burn *them* upon the **a** for a burnt offering,	4196
	29:36	thou shalt cleanse the **a**, when thou hast	4196
	29:37	thou shalt make an atonement for the **a**,	4196
	29:37	sanctify it; and it shall be an **a** most holy:	4196
	29:37	whatsoever toucheth the **a** shall be holy.	4196
	29:38	*is that* which thou shalt offer upon the **a**;	4196
	29:44	tabernacle of the congregation, and the **a**:	4196
	30: 1	thou shalt make an **a** to burn incense upon:	4196
	30:18	tabernacle of the congregation and the **a**,	4196
	30:20	when they come near to the **a** to minister,	4196
	30:27	and his vessels, and the **a** of incense,	4196
	30:28	the **a** of burnt offering with all his vessels,	4196
	31: 8	with all his furniture, and the **a** of incense,	4196
	31: 9	the **a** of burnt offering with all his furniture,	4196
	32: 5	when Aaron saw *it,* he built an **a** before it;	4196
	35:15	the incense **a** and his staves, and	4196
	35:16	The **a** of burnt offering with his brasen	4196
	37:25	he made the incense **a** *of* shittim wood:	4196
	38: 1	he made the **a** of burnt offering *of* shittim	4196
	38: 3	he made all the vessels of the **a**, the pots,	4196
	38: 4	he made for the **a** a brasen grate of network	4196
	38: 7	staves into the rings on the sides of the **a**,	4196
	38: 7	it withal; he made *the a* hollow with boards.	NIH
	38:30	and the brasen **a**, and the brasen grate for it,	4196
	38:30	grate for it, and all the vessels of the **a**,	4196
	39:38	the golden **a**, and the anointing oil, and	4196
	39:39	The brasen **a**, and his grate of brass, his	4196
	40: 5	thou shalt set the **a** of gold for the incense	4196
	40: 6	thou shalt set the **a** of the burnt offering	4196
	40: 7	the tent of the congregation and the **a**,	4196
	40:10	thou shalt anoint the **a** of the burnt offering,	4196
	40:10	and all his vessels, and sanctify the **a**:	4196
	40:10	the altar: and it shall be an **a** most holy.	4196
	40:26	he put the golden **a** in the tent of	4196
	40:29	he put the **a** of burnt offering *by* the door of	4196
	40:30	the tent of the congregation and the **a**,	4196
	40:32	when they came near unto the **a**,	4196
	40:33	court round about the tabernacle and the **a**,	4196
Lev	1: 5	sprinkle the blood round about upon the **a**	4196
	1: 7	of Aaron the priest shall put fire upon the **a**,	4196
	1: 8	that *is* on the fire which *is* upon the **a**:	4196
	1: 9	the priest shall burn all on the **a**, *to be* a	4196
	1:11	he shall kill it on the side of the **a**	4196
	1:11	sprinkle his blood round about upon the **a**.	4196
	1:12	that *is* on the fire which *is* upon the **a**:	4196
	1:13	shall bring *it* all, and burn *it* upon the **a**:	4196
	1:15	the priest shall bring it unto the **a**, and	4196
	1:15	and wring off his head, and burn *it* on the **a**;	4196
	1:15	shall be wrung out at the side of the **a**:	4196
	1:16	cast it beside the **a** on the east part, by	4196
	1:17	the priest shall burn it upon the **a**, upon	4196
	2: 2	shall burn the memorial of it upon the **a**,	4196
	2: 8	unto the priest, he shall bring it unto the **a**.	4196
	2: 9	and shall burn *it* upon the **a**:	4196
	2:12	they shall not be burnt on the **a** for a sweet	4196
	3: 2	sprinkle the blood upon the **a** round about.	4196
	3: 5	Aaron's sons shall burn it on the **a** upon	4196
	3: 8	the blood thereof round about upon the **a**.	4196
	3:11	the priest shall burn it upon the **a**: *it is*	4196
	3:13	the blood thereof upon the **a** round about.	4196
	3:16	the priest shall burn them upon the **a**: *it is*	4196
	4: 7	the **a** of sweet incense before the LORD,	4196
	4: 7	at the bottom of the **a** of the burnt offering,	4196
	4:10	the priest shall burn them upon the **a** of	4196
	4:18	horns of the **a** which *is* before the LORD,	4196
	4:18	at the bottom of the **a** of the burnt offering,	4196
	4:19	all his fat from him, and burn *it* upon the **a**.	4196
	4:25	put *it* upon the horns of the **a** of burnt	4196
	4:25	at the bottom of the **a** of burnt offering.	4196
	4:26	he shall burn all his fat upon the **a**, as	4196
	4:30	put *it* upon the horns of the **a** of burnt	4196
	4:30	all the blood thereof at the bottom of the **a**.	4196
	4:31	the priest shall burn *it* upon the **a** for a	4196
	4:34	put *it* upon the horns of the **a** of burnt	4196
	4:34	all the blood thereof at the bottom of the **a**;	4196
	4:35	the priest shall burn them upon the **a**,	4196
	5: 9	of the sin offering upon the side of the **a**;	4196
	5: 9	shall be wrung out at the bottom of the **a**:	4196
	5:12	a memorial thereof, and burn *it* on the **a**,	4196
	6: 9	of the burning upon the **a** all night unto	4196
	6: 9	and the fire of the **a** shall be burning in it.	4196
	6:10	consumed with the burnt offering on the **a**,	4196
	6:10	and he shall put them besides the **a**.	4196
	6:12	the fire upon the **a** shall be burning in it;	4196
	6:13	The fire shall ever be burning upon the **a**;	4196
	6:14	offer it before the LORD, before the **a**.	4196
	6:15	shall burn *it upon* the **a** *for* a sweet savour,	4196
	7: 2	shall he sprinkle round about upon the **a**.	4196
	7: 5	the priest shall burn them upon the **a** *for* an	4196
	7:31	the priest shall burn the fat upon the **a**: but	4196
	8:11	he sprinkled thereof upon the **a** seven	4196
	8:11	anointed the **a** and all his vessels, both	4196
	8:15	put *it* upon the horns of the **a** round about	4196

Lev	8:15	purified the **a**, and poured the blood at	4196
	8:15	and poured the blood at the bottom of the **a**,	4196
	8:16	their fat, and Moses burned *it* upon the **a**.	4196
	8:19	Moses sprinkled the blood upon the **a**	4196
	8:21	and Moses burnt the whole ram upon the **a**:	4196
	8:24	Moses sprinkled the blood upon the **a**	4196
	8:28	burnt *them* on the **a** upon the burnt	4196
	8:30	of the blood which *was* upon the **a**, and	4196
	9: 7	Go unto the **a**, and offer thy sin offering,	4196
	9: 8	Aaron therefore went unto the **a**, and	4196
	9: 9	put *it* upon the horns of the **a**, and poured	4196
	9: 9	poured out the blood at the bottom of the **a**:	4196
	9:10	of the sin offering, he burnt upon the **a**;	4196
	9:12	which he sprinkled round about upon the **a**.	4196
	9:13	and the head: and he burnt *them* upon the **a**.	4196
	9:14	*them* upon the burnt offering on the **a**.	4196
	9:17	a handful thereof, and burnt *it* upon the **a**,	4196
	9:18	which he sprinkled upon the **a** round about,	4196
	9:20	the breasts, and he burnt the fat upon the **a**:	4196
	9:24	consumed upon the **a** the burnt offering and	4196
	10:12	and eat it without leaven beside the **a**:	4196
	14:20	and the meat offering upon the **a**:	4196
	16:12	of fire from off the **a** before the LORD,	4196
	16:18	he shall go out unto the **a** that *is* before	4196
	16:18	put *it* upon the horns of the **a** round about.	4196
	16:20	and the **a**, he shall bring the live goat:	4196
	16:25	of the sin offering shall he burn upon the **a**.	4196
	16:33	for the **a**, and he shall make an atonement	4196
	17: 6	**a** of the LORD *at* the door of	4196
	17:11	I have given it to you upon the **a** to make	4196
	21:23	nor come nigh unto the **a**, because he hath a	4196
	22:22	fire of them upon the **a** unto the LORD.	4196
Nu	3:26	by the **a** round about, and the cords of it for	4196
	4:11	upon the golden **a** they shall spread a cloth	4196
	4:13	they shall take away the ashes from the **a**,	4196
	4:14	and the basons, all the vessels of the **a**;	4196
	4:26	by the tabernacle and by the **a** round about,	4196
	5:25	before the LORD, and offer it upon the **a**:	4196
	5:26	burn *it* upon the **a**, and afterward shall	4196
	7: 1	both the **a** and all the vessels thereof, and	4196
	7:10	the princes offered *for* dedicating of the **a**	4196
	7:10	princes offered their offering before the **a**.	4196
	7:11	on *his* day, for the dedicating of the **a**.	4196
	7:84	This *was* the dedication of the **a**, in the day	4196
	7:88	This *was* the dedication of the **a**, after *that*	4196
	16:38	them broad plates *for* a covering of the **a**:	4196
	16:39	made broad *plates for* a covering of the **a**:	4196
	16:46	put fire therein from off the **a**, and put on	4196
	18: 3	nigh the vessels of the sanctuary and the **a**,	4196
	18: 5	of the sanctuary, and the charge of the **a**:	4196
	18: 7	your priest's office for every thing of the **a**,	4196
	18:17	thou shalt sprinkle their blood upon the **a**,	4196
	23: 2	Balaam offered on *every* **a** a bullock and	4196
	23: 4	I have offered upon *every* **a** a bullock and	4196
	23:14	and offered a bullock and a ram on *every* **a**.	4196
	23:30	and offered a bullock and a ram on *every* **a**.	4196
Dt	12:27	upon the **a** of the LORD thy God:	4196
	12:27	out upon the **a** of the LORD thy God,	4196
	16:21	near unto the **a** of the LORD thy God,	4196
	26: 4	set it down before the **a** of the LORD thy	4196
	27: 5	there shalt thou build an **a** unto the LORD	4196
	27: 5	unto the LORD thy God, an **a** of stones:	4196
	27: 6	Thou shalt build the **a** of the LORD thy	4196
	33:10	and whole *burnt sacrifice* upon thine **a**.	4196
Jos	8:30	Joshua built an **a** unto the LORD God of	4196
	8:31	an **a** of whole stones, over which no *man*	4196
	9:27	for the **a** of the LORD, *even* unto this day,	4196
	22:10	the half tribe of Manasseh built there an **a**	4196
	22:10	there an altar by Jordan, a great **a** to see to.	4196
	22:11	the half tribe of Manasseh have built an **a**	4196
	22:16	in that ye have builded you an **a**, that ye	4196
	22:19	in building you an **a** beside the altar of	4196
	22:19	in building you an altar beside the **a** of	4196
	22:23	That we have built us an **a** to turn from	4196
	22:26	Let us now prepare to build us an **a**,	4196
	22:28	Behold the pattern of the **a** of the LORD,	4196
	22:29	to build an **a** for burnt offerings, for meat	4196
	22:29	besides the **a** of the LORD our God that *is*	4196
	22:34	the children of Gad called the **a** *Ed*: for it	4196
Jdg	6:24	Gideon built an **a** there unto the LORD,	4196
	6:25	throw down the **a** of Baal that thy father	4196
	6:26	build an **a** unto the LORD thy God upon	4196
	6:28	the **a** of Baal was cast down, and the grove	4196
	6:28	the second bullock was offered upon the **a**	4196
	6:30	because he hath cast down the **a** of Baal,	4196
	6:31	because *one* hath cast down his **a**.	4196
	6:32	because he hath thrown down his **a**.	4196
	13:20	went up toward heaven from off the **a**,	4196
	13:20	the LORD ascended in the flame of the **a**.	4196
	21: 4	built there an **a**, and offered burnt offerings	4196
1Sa	2:28	to offer upon mine **a**, to burn incense,	4196
	2:33	*whom* I shall not cut off from mine **a**,	4196
	7:17	and there he built an **a** unto the LORD.	4196
	14:35	Saul built an **a** unto the LORD: the same	4196
	14:35	the same was the first **a** that he built unto	4196
2Sa	24:18	rear an **a** unto the LORD in	4196
	24:21	of thee, to build an **a** unto the LORD,	4196
	24:25	David built there an **a** unto the LORD,	4196
1Ki	1:50	went, and caught hold on the horns of the **a**.	4196
	1:51	he hath caught hold on the horns of the **a**,	4196
	1:53	and they brought him down from the **a**.	4196
	2:28	and caught hold on the horns of the **a**.	4196
	2:29	of the LORD; and behold, *he is* by the **a**.	4196
	3: 4	offerings did Solomon offer up on that **a**.	4196
	6:20	and *so* covered the **a** *which was of* cedar.	4196
	6:22	also the whole **a** that *was* by the oracle he	4196
	7:48	the **a** of gold, and the table *of* gold,	4196
	8:22	Solomon stood before the **a** of the LORD	4196
	8:31	the oath come before thine **a** in this house:	4196
	8:54	he arose from before the **a** of the LORD,	4196
	8:64	the brasen **a** that *was* before the LORD	4196
	9:25	peace offerings upon the **a** which he built	4196
	9:25	he burnt incense upon **the a** that *was*	2050.2
	12:32	he offered upon the **a** (so did he in Beth-el,)	4196
	12:33	So he offered upon the **a** which he had	4196
	12:33	he offered upon the **a**, and burnt incense.	4196
	13: 1	Jeroboam stood by the **a** to burn incense.	4196
	13: 2	he cried against the **a** in the word of	4196
	13: 2	and said, O **a**, altar, thus saith the LORD;	4196
	13: 2	and said, O altar, **a**, thus saith the LORD;	4196
	13: 3	the **a** *shall be* rent, and the ashes that *are*	4196
	13: 4	which had cried against the **a** in Beth-el,	4196
	13: 4	that he put forth his hand from the **a**,	4196
	13: 5	The **a** also *was* rent, and the ashes poured	4196
	13: 5	and the ashes poured out from the **a**,	4196
	13:32	of the LORD against the **a** in Beth-el,	4196
	16:32	he reared up an **a** for Baal *in* the house of	4196
	18:26	And they leapt upon the **a** which was made.	4196
	18:30	he repaired the **a** of the LORD that was	4196
	18:32	*with* the stones he built an **a** in the name of	4196
	18:32	he made a trench about the **a**, as great as	4196
	18:35	the water ran round about the **a**; and	4196
2Ki	11:11	the temple, *along* by the **a** and the temple.	4196
	12: 9	a hole in the lid of it, and set it beside the **a**,	4196
	16:10	and saw an **a** that *was* at Damascus:	4196
	16:10	to Urijah the priest the fashion of the **a**,	4196
	16:11	Urijah the priest built an **a** according to all	4196
	16:12	come from Damascus, the king saw the **a**:	4196
	16:12	the king approached to the **a**, and	4196
	16:13	blood of his peace offerings, upon the **a**.	4196
	16:14	he brought also the brasen **a**, which *was*	4196
	16:14	from between the **a** and the house of	4196
	16:14	and put it on the north side of the **a**.	4196
	16:15	Upon the great **a** burn the morning burnt	4196
	16:15	the brasen **a** shall be for me to inquire *by*.	4196
	18:22	Ye shall worship before this **a** in	4196
	23: 9	not up to the **a** of the LORD in Jerusalem,	4196
	23:15	Moreover the **a** that *was* at Beth-el, *and*	4196
	23:15	both that **a** and the high place he brake	4196
	23:16	and burnt *them* upon the **a**, and polluted it,	4196
	23:17	that thou hast done against the **a** of Beth-el.	4196
1Ch	6:49	his sons offered upon the **a** of the burnt	4196
	6:49	on the **a** of incense, *and were appointed* for	4196
	16:40	**a** of the burnt offering continually morning	4196
	21:18	set up an **a** unto the LORD in	4196
	21:22	that I may build an **a** therein unto	4196
	21:26	David built there an **a** unto the LORD,	4196
	21:26	heaven by fire upon the **a** of burnt offering.	4196
	21:29	and the **a** of the burnt offering,	4196
	22: 1	this *is* the **a** of the burnt offering for Israel.	4196
	28:18	for the **a** of incense refined gold by weight;	4196
2Ch	1: 5	Moreover the brasen **a**, that Bezaleel	4196
	1: 6	Solomon went up thither to the brasen **a**	4196
	4: 1	Moreover he made an **a** of brass,	4196
	4:19	the golden **a** also, and the tables whereon	4196
	5:12	stood *at* the east *end* of the **a**, and	4196
	6:12	he stood before the **a** of the LORD in	4196
	6:22	the oath come before thine **a** in this house;	4196

A

2Ch 7: 7 the brasen **a** which Solomon had made was 4196
7: 9 for they kept the dedication of the **a** seven 4196
8:12 unto the LORD on the **a** of the LORD, 4196
15: 8 renewed the **a** of the LORD, that *was* 4196
23:10 *along* by the **a** and the temple, by the king 4196
26:16 to burn incense upon the **a** of incense. 4196
26:19 of the LORD, from beside the incense **a**. 4196
29:18 the **a** of burnt offering, with all the vessels 4196
29:19 they *are* before the **a** of the LORD. 4196
29:21 to offer *them* on the **a** of the LORD. 4196
29:22 the blood, and sprinkled *it* on the **a**: 4196
29:22 they sprinkled the blood upon the **a**: 4196
29:22 and they sprinkled the blood upon the **a**. 4196
29:24 reconciliation with their blood upon the **a**, 4196
29:27 to offer the burnt offering upon the **a**. 4196
32:12 Ye shall worship before one **a**, and 4196
33:16 he repaired the **a** of the LORD, and 4196
35:16 to offer burnt offerings upon the **a** of 4196
Ezr 3: 2 and builded the **a** of the God of Israel, 4196
3: 3 they set the **a** upon his bases; for fear *was* 4196
7:17 offer them upon the **a** of the house of your 4056
Ne 10:34 to burn upon the **a** of the LORD our God, 4196
Ps 26: 6 so will I compass thine **a**, O LORD: 4196
43: 4 will I go unto the **a** of God, unto God my 4196
51:19 then shall they offer bullocks upon thine **a**. 4196
118:27 with cords, *even* unto the horns of the **a**. 4196
Isa 6: 6 he had taken with the tongs from off the **a**: 4196
19:19 In that day shall there be an **a** to 4196
27: 9 when he maketh all the stones of the **a** as 4196
36: 7 Ye shall worship before this **a**? 4196
56: 7 sacrifices *shall be* accepted upon mine **a**; 4196
60: 7 shall come up with acceptance on mine **a**, 4196
La 2: 7 The Lord hath cast off his **a**, he hath 4196
Eze 8: 5 northward at the gate of the **a** this image of 4196
8:16 between the porch and the **a**, *were* about 4196
9: 2 they went in, and stood beside the brasen **a**. 4196
40:46 the keepers of the charge of the **a**: 4196
40:47 and the **a** *that was* before the house. 4196
41:22 The **a** *of* wood *was* three cubits high, and 4196
43:13 these *are* the measures of the **a** after 4196
43:13 and this *shall be* the higher place of the **a**. 4196
43:15 So the **a** *shall be* four cubits; and from 2025
43:15 from the **a** and upward *shall be* four horns. 741
43:16 the **a** *shall be* twelve *cubits* long, twelve 741
43:18 These *are* the ordinances of the **a** in the day 4196
43:22 they shall cleanse the **a**, as they did cleanse 4196
43:26 Seven days shall they purge the **a** and 4196
43:27 shall make your burnt offerings upon the **a**, 4196
45:19 upon the four corners of the settle of the **a**, 4196
47: 1 side of the house, at the south *side* of the **a**. 4196
Joel 1:13 howl, ye ministers of the **a**: come, lie all 4196
2:17 weep between the porch and the **a**, and 4196
Am 2: 8 upon clothes laid to pledge by every **a**, 4196
3:14 the horns of the **a** shall be cut off, and 4196
9: 1 I saw the Lord standing upon the **a**: and 4196
Zec 9:15 like bowls, *and* as the corners of the **a**. 4196
14:20 house shall be like the bowls before the **a**. 4196
Mal 1: 7 *Ye* offer polluted bread upon mine **a**; and 4196
1:10 do ye kindle *fire on* mine **a** for nought. 4196
2:13 covering the **a** of the LORD *with* tears, 4196
Mt 5:23 Therefore if thou bring thy gift to the **a**, and *2379*
5:24 Leave there thy gift before the **a**, and *2379*
23:18 And, Whosoever shall swear by the **a**, it is *2379*
23:19 the gift, or the **a** that sanctifieth the gift? *2379*
23:20 Whoso therefore shall swear by the **a**, *2379*
23:35 ye slew between the temple and the **a**. *2379*
Lk 1:11 on the right side of the **a** of incense. *2379*
11:51 which perished between the **a** and *2379*
Ac 17:23 I found an **a** with this inscription, *1041*
1Co 9:13 they which wait at the **a** are partakers with *2379*
9:13 wait at the altar are partakers with the **a**? *2379*
10:18 eat *of* the sacrifices partakers of the **a**? *2379*
Heb 7:13 of which no *man* gave attendance at the **a**. *2379*
13:10 We have an **a**, whereof they have no right *2379*
Jas 2:21 he had offered Isaac his son upon the **a**? *2379*
Rev 6: 9 I saw under the **a** the souls of them that *2379*
8: 3 And another angel came and stood at the **a**, *2379*
8: 3 the golden **a** which was before the throne. *2379*
8: 5 and filled it with fire of the **a**, and cast *it* *2379*
9:13 horns of the golden **a** which is before God, *2379*
11: 1 and the **a**, and them that worship therein. *2379*
14:18 And another angel came out from the **a**, *2379*
16: 7 And I heard another out of the **a** say, *2379*

ALTARS (55) [ALTAR]
Ex 34:13 ye shall destroy their **a**, break their images, 4196
Nu 3:31 the **a**, and the vessels of the sanctuary 4196
23: 1 Build me here seven **a**, and prepare me here 4196
23: 4 I have prepared seven **a**, and I have offered 4196
23:14 and built seven **a**, and offered a bullock and 4196
23:29 Build me here seven **a**, and prepare me here 4196
Dt 7: 5 ye shall destroy their **a**, and break down 4196
12: 3 you shall overthrow their **a**, and break their 4196
Jdg 2: 2 of this land; you shall throw down their **a**: 4196
1Ki 19:10 thrown down thine **a**, and slain thy 4196
19:14 thrown down thine **a**, and slain thy 4196
2Ki 11:18 his **a** and his images brake they in pieces 4196
11:18 slew Mattan the priest of Baal before the **a**. 4196
18:22 and whose **a** Hezekiah hath taken away, 4196
21: 3 he reared up **a** for Baal, and made a grove, 4196
21: 4 he built **a** in the house of the LORD, 4196
21: 5 he built **a** for all the host of heaven in 4196
23:12 the **a** that *were* on the top of the upper 4196
23:12 the **a** which Manasseh had made in the two 4196
23:20 the high places that *were* there upon the **a**, 4196
2Ch 14: 3 For he took away the **a** of the strange *gods*, 4196
23:17 brake his **a** and his images in pieces, and 4196
23:17 slew Mattan the priest of Baal before the **a**. 4196
28:24 he made him **a** in every corner of 4196
30:14 and took away the **a** that *were* in Jerusalem, 4196
30:14 all the **a for incense** took they away, and 6999
31: 1 and the **a** out of all Judah and Benjamin, 4196
32:12 taken away his high places and his **a**, 4196
33: 3 he reared up **a** for Baalim, and 4196
33: 4 Also he built **a** in the house of the LORD, 4196
33: 5 he built **a** for all the host of heaven in 4196
33:15 all the **a** that he had built in the mount of 4196
34: 4 they brake down the **a** of Baalim in his 4196
34: 5 burnt the bones of the priests upon their **a**, 4196
34: 7 when he had broken down the **a** and 4196
Ps 84: 3 *even* thine **a**, O LORD of hosts, my King, 4196
Isa 17: 8 he shall not look to the **a**, the work of his 4196
36: 7 and whose **a** Hezekiah hath taken away, 4196
65: 3 and burneth incense upon **a of brick**; 3843
Jer 11:13 have ye set up **a** to *that* shameful thing, 4196
11:13 *even* **a** to burn incense unto Baal. 4196
17: 1 of their heart, and upon the horns of your **a**; 4196
17: 2 Whilst their children remember their **a** and 4196
Eze 6: 4 your **a** shall be desolate, and your images 4196
6: 5 will scatter your bones round about your **a**. 4196
6: 6 that your **a** may be laid waste and 4196
6:13 be among their idols round about their **a**, 4196
Hos 8:11 Because Ephraim hath made many **a** to sin, 4196
8:11 altars to sin, **a** shall be unto him to sin. 4196
10: 1 of his fruit he hath increased the **a**; 4196
10: 2 he shall break down their **a**, he shall spoil 4196
10: 8 and the thistle shall come up on their **a**; 4196
12:11 their **a** *are* as heaps in the furrows of 4196
Am 3:14 upon him I will also visit the **a** of Beth-el: 4196
Ro 11: 3 thy prophets, and digged down thine **a**; *2379*

AL-TASCHITH (4)
Ps 57: T the chief Musician, **A**, Michtam of David, 516
58: T the chief Musician, **A**, Michtam of David. 516
59: T the chief Musician, **A**, Michtam of David; 516
75: T **A**, A Psalm *or* Song of Asaph. 516

ALTER (4) [ALTERED, ALTERETH]
Lev 27:10 He shall not **a** it, nor change it, a good for a 2498
Ezr 6:11 a decree, that whosoever shall **a** this word, 8133
6:12 that shall put to their hand to **a** *and* 8133
Ps 89:34 nor **a** the thing that is gone out of my lips. 8138

ALTERED (2) [ALTER]
Est 1:19 the Persians and the Medes, that it be not **a**, 5674
Lk 9:29 the fashion of his countenance was **a**, and *2087*

ALTERETH (2) [ALTER]
Da 6: 8 of the Medes and Persians, which **a** not. 5709
6:12 of the Medes and Persians, which **a** not. 5709

ALTHOUGH (16) [THOUGH] See Index

ALTOGETHER (29) [TOGETHER] See Index

ALUSH (2)
Nu 33:13 departed from Dophkah, and encamped in **A**. 442
33:14 they removed from **A**, and encamped at 442

ALVAH (1)
Ge 36:40 duke Timnah, duke A, duke Jetheth, 5933

ALVAN (1)
Ge 36:23 A, and Manahath, and Ebal, Shepho, and 5935

ALWAY (23) [ALWAYS]
Ex 25:30 set upon the table shewbread before me **a**. 8548
Nu 9:16 So it was **a**: the cloud covered it *by day,* 8548
Dt 11: 1 and his commandments **a**. 3117+3605+1886.1
28:33 and crushed **a**: 3117+3605+1886.1
2Sa 9:10 master's son shall eat bread **a** at my table. 8548
1Ki 11:36 **a** before me in Jerusalem, 3117+3605+1886.1
2Ki 8:19 him to give to him **a** 3117+3605+1886.1
Job 7:16 I loathe *it;* I would not live **a**: 5769+3807.1
Ps 9:18 For the needy shall not **a** be 5331+3807.1
119:112 heart to perform thy statutes **a**, 5769+3807.1
Pr 28:14 Happy *is* the man that feareth **a**: but he that 8548
Mt 28:20 and lo, I am with you **a**, *even* 2250+3588+3956
Jn 7: 6 is not yet come: but your time is **a** ready. 3842
Ac 10: 2 alms to the people, and prayed to God **a**. 1275
Ro 11:10 may not see, and bow down their back **a**. 1275
2Co 4:11 For we which live are **a** delivered unto death 104
6:10 As sorrowful, yet **a** rejoicing; as poor, 104
Php 4: 4 Rejoice in the Lord **a**: *and* again I say, 3842
Col 4: 6 Let your speech *be* **a** with grace, 3842
1Th 2:16 they might be saved, to fill up their sins **a**: 3842
2Th 2:13 But we are bound *to* give thanks **a** to God 3842
Tit 1:12 said, The Cretians *are* **a** liars, evil beasts, 104
Heb 3:10 and said, They do **a** err in *their* heart; 104

ALWAYS (62) [ALWAY]
Ge 6: 3 spirit shall not **a** strive with man, 5769+3807.1
Ex 27:20 for the light, to cause the lamp to burn **a**. 8548
28:38 it shall be **a** upon his forehead, that they 8548
Dt 5:29 all my commandments **a**, 3117+3605+1886.1
6:24 our God, for our good **a**, 3117+3605+1886.1
11:12 the eyes of the LORD thy God *are* **a** upon 8548
14:23 fear the LORD thy God **a**. 3117+3605+1886.1
1Ch 16:15 Be ye mindful **a** of his covenant; 5769+3807.1
2Ch 18: 7 prophesied good unto me, but **a** evil: 3117+3605
Job 27:10 will he **a** call upon God? 3605+6256+871.1
32: 9 Great men are not *a* wise: neither do NIH
Ps 10: 5 His ways are **a** grievous; 3605+871.1
16: 8 I have set the LORD **a** before me: because 8548
103: 9 He will not **a** chide: neither will he 5331+3807.1
Pr 5:19 and be thou ravisht **a** with her love. 8548
8:30 rejoicing **a** before him; 3605+6256+871.1
Ecc 9: 8 Let thy garments be **a** white; 3605+6256+871.1
Isa 57:16 for ever, neither will I be **a** wroth: 5331+3807.1
Jer 20:17 and her womb *to be* **a** great *with me.* 5769
Eze 38: 8 of Israel, which have been **a** waste: 8548
Mt 18:10 That in heaven their angels do **a** 1223+3956
26:11 For ye have the poor **a** with you; but me ye 3842
26:11 always with you; but me ye have not **a**. 3842
Mk 5: 5 And **a**, night and day, he was in 1275
14: 7 For ye have the poor with you **a**, and 3842
14: 7 may do them good: but me ye have not **a**. 3842
Lk 18: 1 them *to this end,* that *men* ought **a** to pray, 3842
21:36 ye therefore, and pray **a**, 1722+2540+3956
Jn 8:29 for I do **a** those *things* that please him. 3842
11:42 And I knew that thou hearest me **a**: but 3842
12: 8 For the poor **a** ye have with you; but me ye 3842
12: 8 ye have with you; but me ye have not **a**. 3842
18:20 in the temple, whither the Jews **a** resort; 3842
Ac 2:25 I foresaw the Lord **a** before my face, 1223+3956
7:51 and ears, ye do **a** resist the Holy Ghost: 104
24: 3 We accept *it* **a**, and in all places, 3839
24:16 to have **a** a conscience void of offence 1275
Ro 1: 9 I make mention of you, **a** in my prayers, 3842
1Co 1: 4 I thank my God **a** on your behalf, for 3842
15:58 **a** abounding in the work of the Lord, 3842
2Co 2:14 which **a** causeth us to triumph in Christ, 3842
4:10 **A** bearing about in the body the dying of 3842
5: 6 Therefore *we are* **a** confident, knowing 3842
9: 8 **a** having all sufficiency in all *things,* may 3842
Gal 4:18 But *it is* good to be zealously affected **a** in 3842
Eph 5:20 Giving thanks **a** for all *things* unto God and 3842
6:18 Praying **a** with all prayer and 1722+2540+3956
Php 1: 4 **A** in every prayer of mine for you all 3842
1:20 as **a**, *so* now also Christ shall be magnified 3842
2:12 my beloved, as ye have **a** obeyed, 3842
Col 1: 3 of our Lord Jesus Christ, praying **a** for you, 3842
4:12 **a** labouring fervently for you in prayers, 3842
1Th 1: 2 We give thanks to God **a** for you all, 3842
3: 6 that ye have good remembrance of us **a**, 3842
2Th 1: 3 We are bound to thank God **a** for you, 3842
1:11 Wherefore also we pray **a** for you, that our 3842
3:16 give you peace **a** by all means. 1223+3956
Phm 1: 4 making mention of thee **a** in my prayers, 3842
Heb 9: 6 the priests went **a** into the first tabernacle, 1275
1Pe 3:15 *be* ready **a** to *give* an answer to every *man* 104
2Pe 1:12 **a** in remembrance of these *things,* though ye 104
1:15 to have these *things* **a** in remembrance. 1539

AM (874) [BE] See Index

AMAD (1)
Jos 19:26 Alammelech, and A, and Misheal; and 6008

AMAL (1)
1Ch 7:35 Zophah, and Imna, and Shelesh, and A. 6000

AMALEK (24) [AMALEKITE, AMALEKITES]
Ge 36:12 Esau's son; and she bare to Eliphaz A: 6002
36:16 Duke Korah, duke Gatam, *and* duke A: 6002
Ex 17: 8 came A, and fought with Israel in 6002
17: 9 us out men, and go out, fight with A: 6002
17:10 Moses had said to him, and fought with A: 6002
17:11 when he let down his hand, A prevailed. 6002
17:13 Joshua discomfited A and his people with 6002
17:14 the remembrance of A from under heaven. 6002
17:16 war with A from generation *to* generation. 6002
Nu 24:20 when he looked on A, he took up his 6002
24:20 and said, A *was* the first of the nations; 6002
Dt 25:17 Remember what A did unto thee by 6002
25:19 the remembrance of A from under heaven; 6002
Jdg 3:13 unto him the children of Ammon and A, 6002
5:14 *was there* a root of them against A; 6002
1Sa 15: 2 I remember *that* which A did to Israel, 6002
15: 3 Now go and smite A, and utterly destroy all 6002
15: 5 Saul came to a city of A, and laid wait in 6002
15:20 have brought Agag the king of A, and 6002
28:18 nor executedst his fierce wrath upon A, 6002
2Sa 8:12 of A, and of the spoil of Hadadezer, son of 6002
1Ch 1:36 and Gatam, Kenaz, and Timna, and A. 6002
18:11 and from the Philistines, and from A. 6002
Ps 83: 7 Gebal, and Ammon, and A; the Philistines 6002

AMALEKITE (3) [AMALEK]
1Sa 30:13 young man of Egypt, servant to an A; 376+6003
2Sa 1: 8 *art* thou? And I answered him, I *am* an A. 6003
1:13 I *am* the son of a stranger, an A. 6003

AMALEKITES (24) [AMALEK]
Ge 14: 7 smote all the country of the A, and also 6003
Nu 13:29 The A dwell in the land of the south: and 6002
14:25 (Now the A and the Canaanites dwelt in 6003
14:43 For the A and the Canaanites *are* there 6003
14:45 the A came down, and the Canaanites 6003
Jdg 6: 3 and the A, and the children of the east, 6002
6:33 all the Midianites and the A and 6002
7:12 the Midianites and the A and all 6002
10:12 the A, and the Maonites, did oppress you; 6002
12:15 the land of Ephraim, in the mount of the A. 6003
1Sa 14:48 smote the A, and delivered Israel out of 6002
15: 6 depart, get you down from among the A, 6003
15: 6 So the Kenites departed from among the A. 6002
15: 7 Saul smote the A from Havilah *until* thou 6002
15: 8 he took Agag the king of the A alive, and 6002
15:15 They have brought them from the A: 6003
15:18 Go and utterly destroy the sinners the A, 6002
15:20 and have utterly destroyed the A. 6002
15:32 you hither to me Agag the king of the A. 6002
27: 8 the Geshurites, and the Gezrites, and the A: 6003
30: 1 that the A had invaded the south, and 6003
30:18 David recovered all that the A had carried 6002
2Sa 1: 1 was returned from the slaughter of the A, 6002
1Ch 4:43 they smote the rest of the A that were 6002

AMAM (1)
Jos 15:26 A, and Shema, and Moladah, 538

AMANA (1)
SS 4: 8 look from the top of A, from the top of 549

AMARIAH (16)
1Ch 6: 7 Meraioth begat A, and Amariah begat 568
6: 7 begat Amariah, and A begat Ahitub, 568

A

1Ch 6:11 Azariah begat A, and Amariah begat Ahitub, 568
6:11 Azariah begat Amariah, and A begat Ahitub, 568
6:52 Meraioth his son, A his son, Ahitub his son, 568
23:19 Jeriah the first, A the second, Jahaziel 568
24:23 the sons *of Hebron;* Jeriah *the first,* A 568
2Ch 19:11 A the chief priest *is* over you in all matters 568
31:15 Jeshua, and Shemaiah, A, and Shecaniah, 568
Ezr 7: 3 The son of A, the son of Azariah, the son of 568
10:42 Shallum, A, *and* Joseph. 568
Ne 10: 3 Pashur, A, Malchijah, 568
11: 4 the son of Zechariah, the son of A, the son of 568
12: 2 A, Malluch, Hattush, 568
12:13 Of Ezra, Meshullam; of A, Jehohanan; 568
Zep 1: 1 the son of A, the son of Hizkiah, 568

AMASA (16)

2Sa 17:25 Absalom made A captain of the host 6021
17:25 which A *was* a man's son, whose name *was* 6021
19:13 say ye to A, *Art* thou not *of* my bone, and 6021
20: 4 said the king to A, Assemble me the men of 6021
20: 5 So A went to assemble *the men of* Judah: 6021
20: 8 which *is* in Gibeon, A went before them. 6021
20: 9 Joab said to A, *Art* thou in health, 6021
20: 9 Joab took A by the beard with the right 6021
20:10 A took no heed to the sword that *was* in 6021
20:12 A wallowed in blood in the midst of 6021
20:12 he removed A out of the highway *into* 6021
1Ki 2: 5 unto A the son of Jether, whom he slew, 6021
2:32 the host of Israel, and A the son of Jether, 6021
1Ch 2:17 Abigail bare A: and the father of Amasa 6021
2:17 the father of A *was* Jether the Ishmeelite. 6021
2Ch 28:12 son of Shallum, and A the son of Hadlai, 6021

AMASAI (5)

1Ch 6:25 And the sons of Elkanah; A, and Ahimoth. 6022
6:35 the son of Mahath, the son of A, 6022
12:18 the spirit came upon A, *who was* chief of 6022
15:24 A, and Zechariah, and Benaiah, and 6022
2Ch 29:12 Mahath the son of A, and Joel the son of 6022

AMASHAI (1)

Ne 11:13 A the son of Azareel, the son of Ahasai, 6023

AMASHSAI See AMASHAI

AMASIAH (1)

2Ch 17:16 next him *was* A the son of Zichri, 6007

AMAZED (21) [AMAZEMENT]

Ex 15:15 the dukes of Edom shall be a; the mighty 926
Jdg 20:41 turned *again,* the men of Benjamin were a: 926
Job 32:15 They were a, they answered no more: 2865
Isa 13: 8 they shall be a one at another; their faces 8539
Eze 32:10 I will **make** many people a at thee, and 8074
Mt 12:23 And all the people were a, and said, Is this 1839
19:25 disciples heard *it,* they were exceedingly a, *1605*
Mk 1:27 And they were all a, insomuch that *they* *2284*
2:12 insomuch that *they* were all a, and *1839*
6:51 they were sore a in themselves beyond *1839*
9:15 were **greatly** a, and running to *him* saluted *1568*
10:32 and they were a; and as they followed, *2284*
14:33 and began to be **sore** a, and to be very *1568*
16: 8 for they trembled and were a: *1611*
Lk 2:48 And when they saw him, they were a: and *1605*
4:36 And they were all a, and spake among *2285*
5:26 And they were all a, *1611+2983*
9:43 And they were all a at the mighty power of *1605*
Ac 2: 7 And they were all a and marvelled, *1839*
2:12 And they were all a, and were in doubt, *1839*
9:21 But all that heard *him* were a, and said; *1839*

AMAZEMENT (2) [AMAZED]

Ac 3:10 and a at that which had happened unto him. *1611*
1Pe 3: 6 as ye do well, and are not afraid *with* any a. *4423*

AMAZIAH (40) [OZIAS]

2Ki 12:21 of David: and A his son reigned in his stead. 558
13:12 his might where*with* he fought against A 558
14: 1 reigned A the son of Joash king of Judah. 558
14: 8 A sent messengers to Jehoash, the son of 558
14: 9 Jehoash the king of Israel sent to A king of 558
14:11 A would not hear. Therefore Jehoash king of 558
14:11 A king of Judah looked one another *in* 558
14:13 Jehoash king of Israel took A king of Judah, 558
14:15 and how he fought with A king of Judah, 558
14:17 A the son of Joash king of Judah lived after 558
14:18 the rest of the acts of A, *are* they not written 558
14:21 and made him king instead of his father A. 558
14:23 In the fifteenth year of A the son of Joash 558
15: 1 Azariah son of A king of Judah to reign. 558
15: 3 according to all that his father A had done; 558
1Ch 3:12 A his son, Azariah his son, Jotham his son, 558
4:34 and Jamlech, and Joshah the son of A, 558
6:45 the son of A, the son of Hilkiah, 558
2Ch 24:27 And A his son reigned in his stead. 558
25: 1 A *was* twenty and five years old *when* he 558
25: 5 Moreover A gathered Judah together, and 558
25: 9 A said to the man of God, But what *shall we* 558
25:10 A separated them, to wit, the army that was 558
25:11 A strengthened himself, and led forth his 558
25:13 the soldiers of the army which A sent back, 558
25:14 after that A was come from the slaughter of 558
25:15 anger of the LORD was kindled against A, 558
25:17 A king of Judah took advice, and sent to 558
25:18 Joash king of Israel sent to A king of Judah, 558
25:20 A would not hear; for it *came* of God, that *he* 558
25:21 *both* he and A king of Judah, 558
25:23 Joash the king of Israel took A king of 558
25:25 A the son of Joash king of Judah lived after 558
25:26 Now the rest of the acts of A, first and last, 558
25:27 Now after the time that A did turn away 558
26: 1 made him king in the room of his father A. 558
26: 4 according to all that his father A did. 558
Am 7:10 A *the* priest of Beth-el sent to Jeroboam king 558
7:12 Also A said unto Amos, O thou seer, go, 558
7:14 and said to A, I *was* no prophet, 558

AMBASSADOR (4) [AMBASSADORS, AMBASSAGE]

Pr 13:17 into mischief: but a faithful a *is* health. 6735
Jer 49:14 an a *is* sent unto the heathen, 6735
Ob 1: 1 an a is sent among the heathen, Arise ye, 6735
Eph 6:20 For which I am an a in bonds: that therein I *4243*

AMBASSADORS (8) [AMBASSADOR]

Jos 9: 4 went and **made as if** they had been a, and 6737
2Ch 32:31 Howbeit in *the business of* the a of 3887
35:21 he sent a to him, saying, What have I to do 4397
Isa 18: 2 That sendeth a by the sea, even in vessels 6735
30: 4 were at Zoan, and his a came to Hanes. 4397
33: 7 the a of peace shall weep bitterly. 4397
Eze 17:15 he rebelled against him in sending his a 4397
2Co 5:20 *Now* then we are a for Christ, as though *4243*

AMBASSAGE (1) [AMBASSADOR]

Lk 14:32 he sendeth an a, and desireth conditions of *4242*

AMBER (3)

Eze 1: 4 out of the midst thereof as the colour of a, 2830
1:27 I saw as the colour of a, as the appearance 2830
8: 2 of brightness, as the colour of a. 2830

AMBUSH (7) [AMBUSHES, AMBUSHMENT, AMBUSHMENTS]

Jos 8: 2 lay thee an a for the city behind it. 693
8: 7 ye shall rise up from the a, and seize upon 693
8: 9 they went to **lie in** a, and abode between 3993
8:12 set them to **lie in** a between Beth-el and Ai, 693
8:14 he wist not that *there were* **liers in** a against 693
8:19 the a arose quickly out of their place, and 693
8:21 all Israel saw that the a had taken the city, 693

AMBUSHES (1) [AMBUSH]

Jer 51:12 set up the watchmen, prepare the a: 693

AMBUSHMENT (2) [AMBUSH]

2Ch 13:13 Jeroboam caused an a to come about 3993
13:13 before Judah, and the a *was* behind them. 3993

AMBUSHMENTS (1) [AMBUSH]

2Ch 20:22 the LORD set a against the children of 693

AMEN (78)

Nu 5:22 to rot: And the woman shall say, A, amen. 543
5:22 to rot: And the woman shall say, Amen, a. 543
Dt 27:15 And all the people shall answer and say, A. 543
27:16 his mother. And all the people shall say, A. 543
27:17 And all the people shall say, A. 543
27:18 of the way. And all the people shall say, A. 543
27:19 and widow. And all the people shall say, A. 543
27:20 And all the people shall say, A. 543
27:21 *of* beast. And all the people shall say, A. 543

Dt 27:22 his mother. And all the people shall say, **A**. 543
27:23 in law. And all the people shall say, **A**. 543
27:24 And all the people shall say, **A**. 543
27:25 And all the people shall say, **A**. 543
27:26 to do them. And all the people shall say, **A**. 543
1Ki 1:36 of Jehoiada answered the king, and said, **A**: 543
1Ch 16:36 the people said, **A**, and praised the LORD. 543
Ne 5:13 **A**, and praised the LORD. 543
8: 6 **A**, Amen, with lifting up their hands: 543
8: 6 Amen, **A**, with lifting up their hands: 543
Ps 41:13 and to everlasting. **A**, and Amen. 543
41:13 and to everlasting. Amen, and **A**. 543
72:19 earth be filled *with* his glory; **A**, and Amen. 543
72:19 earth be filled *with* his glory; Amen, and **A**. 543
89:52 *be* the LORD for evermore. **A**, and Amen. 543
89:52 *be* the LORD for evermore. Amen, and **A**. 543
106:48 let all the people say, **A**. Praise ye 543
Jer 28: 6 Even the prophet Jeremiah said, **A**: 543
Mt 6:13 and the power, and the glory, for ever. **A**. *281*
28:20 *even* unto the end of the world. **A**. *281*
Mk 16:20 the word with signs following. **A**. *281*
Lk 24:53 in the temple, praising and blessing God. **A**. *281*
Jn 21:25 contain the books that should be written. **A**. *281*
Ro 1:25 than the Creator, who is blessed for ever. **A**. *281*
9: 5 who is over all, God blessed for ever. **A**. *281*
11:36 *are* all *things:* to whom *be* glory for ever. **A**. *281*
15:33 Now the God of peace *be* with you all. **A**. *281*
16:20 of our Lord Jesus Christ *be* with you. **A**. *281*
16:24 of our Lord Jesus Christ *be* with you all. **A**. *281*
16:27 *be* glory through Jesus Christ for ever. **A**. *281*
1Co 14:16 the unlearned say **A** at thy giving of thanks, *281*
16:24 My love *be* with you all in Christ Jesus. **A**. *281*
2Co 1:20 and in him **A**, unto the glory of God by us. *281*
13:14 of the Holy Ghost, *be* with you all. **A**. *281*
Gal 1: 5 To whom *be* glory for ever and ever. **A**. *281*
6:18 our Lord Jesus Christ *be* with your spirit. **A**. *281*
Eph 3:21 throughout all ages, world without end. **A**. *281*
6:24 love our Lord Jesus Christ in sincerity. **A**. *281*
Php 4:20 our Father *be* glory for ever and ever. **A**. *281*
4:23 of our Lord Jesus Christ *be* with you all. **A**. *281*
Col 4:18 Remember my bonds. Grace *be* with you. **A**. *281*
1Th 5:28 of our Lord Jesus Christ *be* with you. **A**. *281*
2Th 3:18 of our Lord Jesus Christ *be* with you all. **A**. *281*
1Ti 1:17 *be* honour and glory for ever and ever. **A**. *281*
6:16 whom *be* honour and power everlasting. **A**. *281*
6:21 concerning the faith. Grace *be* with thee. **A**. *281*
2Ti 4:18 to whom *be* glory for ever and ever. **A**. *281*
4:22 *be* with thy spirit. Grace *be* with you. **A**. *281*
Tit 3:15 love us in the faith. Grace *be* with you all. **A**. *281*
Phm 1:25 our Lord Jesus Christ *be* with your spirit. **A**. *281*
Heb 13:21 to whom *be* glory for ever and ever. **A**. *281*
13:25 Grace *be* with you all. **A**. *281*
1Pe 4:11 be praise and dominion for ever and ever. **A**. *281*
5:11 *be* glory and dominion for ever and ever. **A**. *281*
5:14 *be* with you all that are in Christ Jesus. **A**. *281*
2Pe 3:18 To him *be* glory both now and for ever. **A**. *281*
1Jn 5:21 keep yourselves from idols. **A**. *281*
2Jn 1:13 The children of thy elect sister greet thee. **A**. *281*
Jude 1:25 dominion and power, both now and ever. **A**. *281*
Rev 1: 6 *be* glory and dominion for ever and ever. **A**. *281*
1: 7 earth shall wail because of him. Even so, **A**. *281*
1:18 and behold, I am alive for evermore, **A**; and *281*
3:14 These *things* saith the **A**, the faithful and *281*
5:14 And the four beasts said, **A**. And the four *281*
7:12 Saying, **A**: Blessing, and glory, and wisdom, *281*
7:12 might, *be* unto our God for ever and ever. **A**. *281*
19: 4 God that sat on the throne, saying, **A**; *281*
22:20 come quickly. **A**. Even so, come, Lord Jesus. *281*
22:21 of our Lord Jesus Christ *be* with you all. **A**. *281*

AMEND (5) [AMENDS]
Jer 7: 3 **A** your ways and your doings, and I will 3190
7: 5 For if you **throughly a** your ways 3190+3190
26:13 Therefore now **a** your ways and 3190
35:15 **a** your doings, and go not after other gods 3190
Jn 4:52 them the hour when he **began to a**. *2192+2866*

AMENDS (1) [AMEND]
Lev 5:16 he shall **make a** for the harm that he hath 7999

AMERCE (1)
Dt 22:19 they shall **a** him in an hundred *shekels* of 6064

AMETHYST (3)
Ex 28:19 the third row a ligure, an agate, and an **a**. 306
39:12 the third row, a ligure, an agate, and an **a**. 306
Rev 21:20 the eleventh, a jacinth; the twelfth, an **a**. *271*

AMI (1)
Ezr 2:57 of Pochereth of Zebaim, the children of **A**. 532

AMIABLE (1)
Ps 84: 1 How **a** *are* thy tabernacles, O LORD of 3039

AMINADAB (3)
Mt 1: 4 And Aram begat **A**; and Aminadab begat *284*
1: 4 and **A** begat Naasson; and Naasson begat *284*
Lk 3:33 Which was *the son* of **A**, which was *the son* *284*

AMISS (4) [MISS]
2Ch 6:37 we have **done a**, and have dealt wickedly; 5753
Da 3:29 which speak **any thing a** against the God 7960
Lk 23:41 our deeds: but this *man* hath done nothing **a**. *824*
Jas 4: 3 Ye ask, and receive not, because ye ask **a**, *2560*

AMITTAI (2)
2Ki 14:25 the son of **A**, the prophet, which *was* of 573
Jnh 1: 1 the LORD came unto Jonah the son of **A**, 573

AMMAH (1) [METHEG-AMMAH]
2Sa 2:24 down when they were come to the hill of **A**, 522

AMMI (1) [LO-AMMI]
Hos 2: 1 Say ye unto your brethren, **A**; 5971+2967.1

AMMIEL (6)
Nu 13:12 Of the tribe of Dan, **A** the son of Gemalli. 5988
2Sa 9: 4 house of Machir, the son of **A**, in Lo-debar. 5988
9: 5 of Machir, the son of **A**, from Lo-debar. 5988
17:27 Machir the son of **A** of Lo-debar, and 5988
1Ch 3: 5 four, of Bath-shua the daughter of **A**: 5988
26: 5 **A** the sixth, Issachar the seventh, 5988

AMMIHUD (10)
Nu 1:10 of Ephraim; Elishama the son of **A**: 5989
2:18 of Ephraim *shall be* Elishama the son of **A**. 5989
7:48 On the seventh day Elishama the son of **A**, 5989
7:53 *was* the offering of Elishama the son of **A**. 5989
10:22 over his host *was* Elishama the son of **A**. 5989
34:20 children of Simeon, Shemuel the son of **A**. 5989
34:28 children of Naphtali, Pedahel the son of **A**. 5989
2Sa 13:37 to Talmai, the son of **A**, king of Geshur. 5989
1Ch 7:26 Laadan his son, **A** his son, Elishama his 5989
9: 4 Uthai the son of **A**, the son of Omri, the son 5989

AMMINADAB (13)
Ex 6:23 daughter of **A**, sister of Naashon, to wife; 5992
Nu 1: 7 Of Judah; Nahshon the son of **A**. 5992
2: 3 Nahshon the son of **A** *shall be* captain of 5992
7:12 the first day was Nahshon the son of **A**, 5992
7:17 *was* the offering of Nahshon the son of **A**. 5992
10:14 over his host *was* Nahshon the son of **A**. 5992
Ru 4:19 And Hezron begat Ram, and Ram begat **A**, 5992
4:20 **A** begat Nahshon, and Nahshon begat 5992
1Ch 2:10 Ram begat **A**; and Amminadab begat 5992
2:10 **A** begat Nahshon, prince of the children of 5992
6:22 **A** his son, Korah his son, Assir his son, 5992
15:10 **A** the chief, and his brethren an hundred 5992
15:11 and Joel, Shemaiah, and Eliel, and **A**, 5992

AMMI-NADIB (1)
SS 6:12 my soul made me *like* the chariots of **A**. 5993

AMMISHADDAI (5)
Nu 1:12 Of Dan; Ahiezer the son of **A**. 5996
2:25 of Dan *shall be* Ahiezer the son of **A**. 5996
7:66 On the tenth day Ahiezer the son of **A**, 5996
7:71 *was* the offering of Ahiezer the son of **A**. 5996
10:25 and over his host *was* Ahiezer the son of **A**. 5996

AMMIZABAD (1)
1Ch 27: 6 the thirty: and *in* his course *was* **A** his son. 5990

AMMON (91) [AMMONITE, AMMONITES, AMMONITESS]
Ge 19:38 the same *is* the father of the children of **A** 5983
Nu 21:24 unto Jabbok, *even* unto the children of **A**: 5983
21:24 for the border of the children of **A** *was* 5983
Dt 2:19 comest nigh over against the children of **A**, 5983

A

Dt	2:19	land of the children of **A** *any* possession;	5983
	2:37	Only unto the land of the children of **A**	5983
	3:11	*is* it not in Rabbath of the children of **A**?	5983
	3:16	*which is* the border of the children of **A**;	5983
Jos	12: 2	*which is* the border of the children of **A**;	5983
	13:10	unto the border of the children of **A**;	5983
	13:25	and half the land of the children of **A**,	5983
Jdg	3:13	And he gathered unto him the children of **A**	5983
	10: 6	the gods of the children of **A**, and the gods	5983
	10: 7	and into the hands of the children of **A**.	5983
	10: 9	Moreover the children of **A** passed over	5983
	10:11	from the children of **A**, and from	5983
	10:17	the children of **A** were gathered together,	5983
	10:18	begin to fight against the children of **A**?	5983
	11: 4	that the children of **A** made war against	5983
	11: 5	that when the children of **A** made war	5983
	11: 6	that we may fight with the children of **A**.	5983
	11: 8	fight against the children of **A**, and be our	5983
	11: 9	again to fight against the children of **A**,	5983
	11:12	unto the king of the children of **A**,	5983
	11:13	the king of the children of **A** answered unto	5983
	11:14	again unto the king of the children of **A**:	5983
	11:15	of Moab, nor the land of the children of **A**:	5983
	11:27	the children of Israel and the children of **A**.	5983
	11:28	Howbeit the king of the children of **A**	5983
	11:29	he passed over *unto* the children of **A**.	5983
	11:30	deliver the children of **A** into mine hands,	5983
	11:31	I return in peace from the children of **A**,	5983
	11:32	the children of **A** to fight against them;	5983
	11:33	Thus the children of **A** were subdued	5983
	11:36	of thine enemies, *even* of the children of **A**.	5983
	12: 1	thou over to fight against the children of **A**,	5983
	12: 2	were at great strife with the children of **A**;	5983
	12: 3	passed over against the children of **A**, and	5983
1Sa	12:12	king of the children of **A** came against you,	5983
	14:47	against the children of **A**, and	5983
2Sa	8:12	of the children of **A**, and of the Philistines,	5983
	10: 1	that the king of the children of **A** died, and	5983
	10: 2	came *into* the land of the children of **A**.	5983
	10: 3	the princes of the children of **A** said unto	5983
	10: 6	when the children of **A** saw that they stank	5983
	10: 6	the children of **A** sent and hired the Syrians	5983
	10: 8	the children of **A** came out, and put	5983
	10:10	put *them* in array against the children of **A**.	5983
	10:11	if the children of **A** be too strong for thee,	5983
	10:14	when the children of **A** saw that the Syrians	5983
	10:14	So Joab returned from the children of **A**,	5983
	10:19	feared to help the children of **A** any more.	5983
	11: 1	they destroyed the children of **A**, and	5983
	12: 9	him with the sword of the children of **A**.	5983
	12:26	fought against Rabbah of the children of **A**,	5983
	12:31	he unto all the cities of the children of **A**.	5983
	17:27	of Nahash of Rabbah of the children of **A**,	5983
1Ki	11: 7	the abomination of the children of **A**.	5983
	11:33	Milcom the god of the children of **A**, and	5983
2Ki	23:13	the abomination of the children of **A**,	5983
	24: 2	bands of the children of **A**, and sent them	5983
1Ch	18:11	from the children of **A**, and from	5983
	19: 1	that Nahash the king of the children of **A**	5983
	19: 2	into the land of the children of **A** to Hanun,	5983
	19: 3	the princes of the children of **A** said to	5983
	19: 6	when the children of **A** saw that they had	5983
	19: 6	the children of **A** sent a thousand talents of	5983
	19: 7	the children of **A** gathered themselves	5983
	19: 9	the children of **A** came out, and put	5983
	19:11	in array against the children of **A**.	5983
	19:12	if the children of **A** be too strong for thee,	5983
	19:15	when the children of **A** saw that the Syrians	5983
	19:19	Syrians help the children of **A** any more.	5983
	20: 1	wasted the country of the children of **A**,	5983
	20: 3	with all the cities of the children of **A**.	5983
2Ch	20: 1	the children of **A**, and with them *other*	5983
	20:10	the children of **A** and Moab and	5983
	20:22	set ambushments against the children of **A**,	5983
	20:23	For the children of **A** and Moab stood up	5983
	27: 5	the children of **A** gave him the same year	5983
	27: 5	So much did the children of **A** pay unto	5983
Ne	13:23	wives of Ashdod, **of A**, *and* of Moab:	5984
Ps	83: 7	Gebal, and **A**, and Amalek; the Philistines	5983
Isa	11:14	and the children of **A** shall obey them.	5983
Jer	9:26	the children of **A**, and Moab, and all *that*	5983
	25:21	Edom, and Moab, and the children of **A**,	5983
	49: 6	again the captivity of the children of **A**,	5983
Da	11:41	Moab, and the chief of the children of **A**.	5983
Am	1:13	three transgressions of the children of **A**,	5983
Zep	2: 8	and the revilings of the children of **A**,	5983
	2: 9	the children of **A** as Gomorrah, *even*	5983

AMMONITE (9) [AMMON]

Dt	23: 3	An **A** or Moabite shall not enter into	5984
1Sa	11: 1	Nahash the **A** came up, and	5984
	11: 2	Nahash the **A** answered them, On this	5984
2Sa	23:37	Zelek the **A**, Naharai the Beerothite,	5984
1Ch	11:39	Zelek the **A**, Naharai the Berothite,	5984
Ne	2:10	and Tobiah the servant, the **A**,	5984
	2:19	the **A**, and Geshem the Arabian,	5984
	4: 3	Now Tobiah the **A** *was* by him, and he said,	5984
	13: 1	that the **A** and the Moabite should not come	5984

AMMONITES (23) [AMMON]

Dt	2:20	and the **A** call them Zamzummims;	5984
1Sa	11:11	and slew the **A** until the heat of the day:	5983
1Ki	11: 1	**A**, Edomites, Zidonians, *and* Hittites;	5984
	11: 5	and after Milcom the abomination of the **A**.	5984
2Ch	20: 1	and with them *other* beside the **A**,	5984
	26: 8	the **A** gave gifts to Uzziah: and his name	5984
	27: 5	fought also with the king of the **A**,	1121+5983
Ezr	9: 1	the Jebusites, the **A**, the Moabites,	5984
Ne	4: 7	and the **A**, and the Ashdodites,	5984
Jer	27: 3	to the king of the **A**, and to the king	1121+5983
	40:11	among the **A**, and in Edom, and	1121+5983
	40:14	**A** hath sent Ishmael the son of	1121+5983
	41:10	and departed to go over to the **A**.	1121+5983
	41:15	with eight men, and went to the **A**.	1121+5983
	49: 1	Concerning the **A**, thus saith	1121+5983
	49: 2	war to be heard in Rabbah of the **A**;	1121+5983
Eze	21:20	may come to Rabbath of the **A**,	1121+5983
	21:28	the Lord GOD concerning the **A**,	1121+5983
	25: 2	set thy face against the **A**,	1121+5983
	25: 3	say unto the **A**, Hear the word of	1121+5983
	25: 5	the **A** a couching place for flocks:	1121+5983
	25:10	Unto the men of the east with the **A**,	1121+5983
	25:10	that the **A** may not be remembered	1121+5983

AMMONITESS (4) [AMMON]

1Ki	14:21	And his mother's name *was* Naamah an **A**.	5984
	14:31	his mother's name *was* Naamah an **A**.	5984
2Ch	12:13	And his mother's name *was* Naamah an **A**.	5984
	24:26	Zabad the son of Shimeath an **A**, and	5984

AMNON (25) [AMNON'S]

2Sa	3: 2	his firstborn was **A**, of Ahinoam	550
	13: 1	and **A** the son of David loved her.	550
	13: 2	**A** was *so* vexed, that he fell sick for his	550
	13: 2	**A** thought it hard for him to do any thing to	550
	13: 3	**A** had a friend, whose name *was* Jonadab,	550
	13: 4	**A** said unto him, I love Tamar, my brother	550
	13: 6	So **A** lay down, and made himself sick: and	550
	13: 6	**A** said unto the king, I pray thee, let Tamar	550
	13: 9	**A** said, Have out all men from me. And they	550
	13:10	**A** said unto Tamar, Bring the meat *into*	550
	13:10	brought *them* into the chamber to **A** her	550
	13:15	**A** hated her exceedingly; so that the hatred	550
	13:15	And **A** said unto her, Arise, be gone.	550
	13:20	unto her, Hath **A** thy brother been with thee?	550
	13:22	Absalom spake unto his brother **A** neither	550
	13:22	for Absalom hated **A**, because he had forced	550
	13:26	I pray thee, let my brother **A** go with us.	550
	13:27	that he let **A** and all the king's sons go with	550
	13:28	and when I say unto you, Smite **A**;	550
	13:29	the servants of Absalom did unto **A** as	550
	13:32	men the king's sons; for **A** only is dead:	550
	13:33	the king's sons are dead: for **A** only is dead.	550
	13:39	for he was comforted concerning **A**,	550
1Ch	3: 1	the firstborn **A**, of Ahinoam the Jezreelitess;	550
	4:20	the sons of Shimon *were*, **A**, and Rinnah,	550

AMNON'S (3) [AMNON]

2Sa	13: 7	Go now *to* thy brother **A** house, and	550
	13: 8	So Tamar went *to* her brother **A** house; and	550
	13:28	Mark ye now when **A** heart is merry with	550

AMOK (2)

Ne	12: 7	Sallu, **A**, Hilkiah, Jedaiah. These *were*	5987
	12:20	Of Sallai, Kallai; of **A**, Eber;	5987

AMON (19)

1Ki	22:26	carry him back unto **A** the governor of	526
2Ki	21:18	of Uzza: and **A** his son reigned in his stead.	526

2Ki 21:19 A *was* twenty and two years old when he 526
21:23 And the servants of A conspired against him, 526
21:24 all them that had conspired against king A; 526
21:25 Now the rest of the acts of A which he did, 526
1Ch 3:14 A his son, Josiah his son. 526
2Ch 18:25 carry him back to A the governor of the city, 526
33:20 and A his son reigned in his stead. 526
33:21 A *was* two and twenty years old when he 526
33:22 for A sacrificed unto all the carved images 526
33:23 but A trespassed more and more. 526
33:25 all them that had conspired against king A; 526
Ne 7:59 of Pochereth Zebaim, the children of A. 526
Jer 1: 2 days of Josiah the son of A king of Judah, 526
25: 3 year of Josiah the son of A king of Judah, 526
Zep 1: 1 in the days of Josiah the son of A, king of 526
Mt 1:10 and Manasses begat A; and Amon begat *300*
1:10 Manasses begat Amon; and A begat Josias; *300*

AMONG (859) [AMONGST] See Index

AMONGST (59) [AMONG] See Index

AMORITE (14) [AMORITES]

Ge 10:16 the Jebusite, and the A, and the Girgashite, 567
14:13 for he dwelt in the plain of Mamre the A, 567
48:22 which I took out of the hand of the A with 567
Ex 33: 2 the A, and the Hittite, and the Perizzite, 567
34:11 I drive out before thee the A, and 567
Nu 32:39 and dispossessed the A which *was* in it. 567
Dt 2:24 I have given into thy hand Sihon the A, 567
Jos 9: 1 the Hittite, and the A, the Canaanite, 567
11: 3 *to* the A, and the Hittite, and the Perizzite, 567
1Ch 1:14 Jebusite also, and the A, and the Girgashite, 567
Eze 16: 3 thy father *was* an A, and thy mother a 567
16:45 mother *was* a Hittite, and your father an A. 567
Am 2: 9 Yet destroyed I the A before them, 567
2:10 the wilderness, to possess the land of the A. 567

AMORITES (73) [AMORITE]

Ge 14: 7 and also the A, that dwelt in Hazezon-tamar. 567
15:16 for the iniquity of the A *is* not yet full. 567
15:21 the A, and the Canaanites, and 567
Ex 3: 8 the A, and the Perizzites, and the Hivites, 567
3:17 the A, and the Perizzites, and the Hivites, 567
13: 5 and the A, and the Hivites, and the Jebusites, 567
23:23 and bring thee in unto the A, and the Hittites, 567
Nu 13:29 and the Hittites, and the Jebusites, and the A, 567
21:13 that cometh out of the coasts of the A: 567
21:13 border of Moab, between Moab and the A. 567
21:21 sent messengers unto Sihon king of the A, 567
21:25 Israel dwelt in all the cities of the A, 567
21:26 *was* the city of Sihon the king of the A, 567
21:29 into captivity unto Sihon king of the A. 567
21:31 Thus Israel dwelt in the land of the A. 567
21:32 and drove out the A that *were* there. 567
21:34 him as thou didst unto Sihon king of the A, 567
22: 2 Zippor saw all that Israel had done to the A. 567
32:33 the kingdom of Sihon king of the A, and 567
Dt 1: 4 After he had slain Sihon the king of the A, 567
1: 7 go *to* the mount of the A, and unto all 567
1:19 saw *by* the way of the mountain of the A, 567
1:20 Ye are come unto the mountain of the A, 567
1:27 to deliver us into the hand of the A, 567
1:44 the A, which dwelt in that mountain, came 567
3: 2 him as thou didst unto Sihon king of the A, 567
3: 8 the A the land that *was* on *this* side Jordan, 567
3: 9 call Sirion; and the A call it Shenir;) 567
4:46 in the land of Sihon king of the A, 567
4:47 of Og king of Bashan, two kings of the A, 567
7: 1 the A, and the Canaanites, and the Perizzites, 567
20:17 and the A, the Canaanites, and the Perizzites, 567
31: 4 kings of the A, and unto the land of them, 567
Jos 2:10 what you did unto the two kings of the A, 567
3:10 the Girgashites, and the A, and the Jebusites. 567
5: 1 it came to pass, when all the kings of the A, 567
7: 7 to deliver us into the hand of the A, 567
9:10 And all that he did to the two kings of the A, 567
10: 5 Therefore the five kings of the A, the king of 567
10: 6 for all the kings of the A that dwell in 567
10:12 up the A before the children of Israel, 567
12: 2 Sihon king of the A, who dwelt in Heshbon, 567
12: 8 the A, and the Canaanites, the Perizzites, 567
13: 4 unto Aphek, to the borders of the A: 567
13:10 all the cities of Sihon king of the A, 567
13:21 all the kingdom of Sihon king of the A, 567
24: 8 I brought you into the land of the A, 567
24:11 the A, and the Perizzites, and the Canaanites, 567
24:12 before you, *even* the two kings of the A; 567
24:15 or the gods of the A, in whose land ye dwell: 567
24:18 even the A which dwelt in the land: 567
Jdg 1:34 the A forced the children of Dan into 567
1:35 the A would dwell in mount Heres in 567
1:36 the coast of the A *was* from the going up to 567
3: 5 A, and Perizzites, and Hivites, and Jebusites: 567
6:10 fear not the gods of the A, in whose land ye 567
10: 8 on the *other* side Jordan in the land of the A, 567
10:11 from the A, from the children of Ammon, 567
11:19 sent messengers unto Sihon king of the A, 567
11:21 so Israel possessed all the land of the A, 567
11:22 they possessed all the coasts of the A, 567
11:23 the A from before his people Israel, 567
1Sa 7:14 there was peace between Israel and the A. 567
2Sa 21: 2 of Israel, but of the remnant of the A; 567
1Ki 4:19 *in* the country of Sihon king of the A, and 567
9:20 *And* all the people that were left of the A, 567
21:26 according to all *things* as did the A, 567
2Ki 21:11 hath done wickedly above all that the A did, 567
2Ch 8: 7 the A, and the Perizzites, and the Hivites, 567
Ezr 9: 1 the Moabites, the Egyptians, and the A. 567
Ne 9: 8 the A, and the Perizzites, and the Jebusites, 567
Ps 135:11 Sihon king of the A, and Og king of Bashan, 567
136:19 Sihon king of the A: for his mercy *endureth* 567

AMOS (8)

Am 1: 1 The words of A, who was among 5986
7: 8 LORD said unto me, A, what seest thou? 5986
7:10 A hath conspired against thee in the midst 5986
7:11 For thus A saith, Jeroboam shall die by 5986
7:12 Also Amaziah said unto A, O thou seer, go, 5986
7:14 answered A, and said to Amaziah, I *was* no 5986
8: 2 he said, A, what seest thou? And I said, 5986
Lk 3:25 which was *the son* of A, which was *the son* *301*

AMOUNTING (1)

2Ch 3: 8 it with fine gold, *a* to six hundred talents. NIH

AMOZ (13)

2Ki 19: 2 to Esai the prophet the son of A. 531
19:20 Isaiah the son of A sent to Hezekiah, saying, 531
20: 1 the prophet Isaiah the son of A came to him, 531
2Ch 26:22 did Isaiah the prophet, the son of A, write. 531
32:20 the prophet Isaiah the son of A, prayed and 531
32:32 the son of A, *and* in the book of the kings of 531
Isa 1: 1 The vision of Isaiah the son of A, which he 531
2: 1 The word that Isaiah the son of A saw 531
13: 1 which Isaiah the son of A did see. 531
20: 2 spake the LORD by Isaiah the son of A, 531
37: 2 unto Isaiah the prophet the son of A. 531
37:21 Then Isaiah the son of A sent unto Hezekiah, 531
38: 1 Isaiah the prophet the son of A came unto 531

AMPHIPOLIS (1)

Ac 17: 1 Now when they had passed through A and *295*

AMPLIAS (1)

Ro 16: 8 Greet A my beloved in the Lord. *291*

AMPLIATUS See AMPLIAS

AMRAM (14) [AMRAM'S, AMRAMITES]

Ex 6:18 A, and Izhar, and Hebron, and Uzziel: 6019
6:20 A took him Jochebed his father's sister to 6019
6:20 the years of the life of A *were* an hundred 6019
Nu 3:19 A, and Izehar, Hebron, and Uzziel. 6019
26:58 of the Korahites. And Kohath begat A. 6019
26:59 she bare unto A Aaron and Moses, and 6019
1Ch 1:41 A, and Eshban, and Ithran, and Cheran. 2566
6: 2 A, Izhar, and Hebron, and Uzziel. 6019
6: 3 the children of A; Aaron, and Moses, and 6019
6:18 the sons of Kohath *were,* A, and Izhar, and 6019
23:12 A, Izhar, Hebron, and Uzziel, four. 6019
23:13 The sons of A; Aaron and Moses: and 6019
24:20 sons of Levi *were these:* Of the sons of A; 6019
Ezr 10:34 Of the sons of Bani; Maadai, A, and Uel, 6019

AMRAM'S (1) [AMRAM]

Nu 26:59 the name of A wife *was* Jochebed, 6019

AMRAMITES (2) [AMRAM]

Nu 3:27 of Kohath *was* the family of the A, and 6020

1Ch 26:23 Of the A, *and* the Izharites, the Hebronites, 6020

AMRAPHEL (2)
Ge 14: 1 it came to pass in the days of A king of 569
14: 9 A king of Shinar, and Arioch king of Ellasar; 569

AMZI (2)
1Ch 6:46 The son of A, the son of Bani, the son of 557
Ne 11:12 the son of Pelaliah, the son of A, the son of 557

AN (1267) [A] See Index

ANAB (2)
Jos 11:21 from A, and from all the mountains of 6024
15:50 And A, and Eshtemoh, and Anim, 6024

ANAH (12)
Ge 36: 2 Aholibamah the daughter of A the daughter 6034
36:14 the daughter of A, daughter of Zibeon, 6034
36:18 *came* of Aholibamah the daughter of A, 6034
36:20 Lotan, and Shobal, and Zibeon, and A, 6034
36:24 the children of Zibeon; both Aiah, and A: 6034
36:24 this *was that* A that found the mules in 6034
36:25 the children of A *were* these; Dishon, and 6034
36:25 Dishon, and Aholibamah the daughter of A. 6034
36:29 duke Shobal, duke Zibeon, duke A, 6034
1Ch 1:38 and A, and Dishon, and Ezer, and Dishan. 6034
1:40 And the sons of Zibeon; Aiah, and A. 6034
1:41 The sons of A; Dishon. And the sons of 6034

ANAHARATH (1)
Jos 19:19 And Hapharaim, and Shion, and A, 588

ANAIAH (2)
Ne 8: 4 A, and Urijah, and Hilkiah, and Maaseiah, 6043
10:22 Pelatiah, Hanan, A, 6043

ANAK (9) [ANAKIMS]
Nu 13:22 Sheshai, and Talmai, the children of A, 6061
13:28 moreover we saw the children of A there. 6061
13:33 the sons of A, *which come* of the giants: 6061
Dt 9: 2 Who can stand before the children of A! 6061
Jos 15:13 *even* the city of Arba the father of A, 6061
15:14 Caleb drove thence the three sons of A, 6061
15:14 and Ahiman, and Talmai, the children of A. 6061
21:11 gave them the city of Arbah the father of A, 6061
Jdg 1:20 and he expelled thence the three sons of A. 6061

ANAKIMS (9) [ANAK]
Dt 1:28 moreover we have seen the sons of the A 6062
2:10 a people great, and many, and tall, as the A; 6062
2:11 also were accounted giants, as the A; 6062
2:21 people great, and many, and tall, as the A; 6062
9: 2 people great and tall, the children of the A, 6062
Jos 11:21 cut off the A from the mountains, 6062
11:22 There was none of the A left in the land of 6062
14:12 for thou heardest in that day how the A 6062
14:15 which *Arba was* a great man among the A. 6062

ANAKITE See ANAKIMS

ANAMIM (2)
Ge 10:13 and A, and Lehabim, and Naphtuhim, 6047
1Ch 1:11 and A, and Lehabim, and Naphtuhim, 6047

ANAMITES See ANAMIM

ANAMMELECH (1)
2Ki 17:31 children in fire to Adrammelech and A, 6048

ANAN (1)
Ne 10:26 And Ahijah, Hanan, A, 6052

ANANI (1)
1Ch 3:24 and Johanan, and Dalaiah, and A, seven. 6054

ANANIAH (2)
Ne 3:23 son of Maaseiah the son of A by his house. 6055
11:32 *And at* Anathoth, Nob, A, 6055

ANANIAS (11)
Ac 5: 1 But a certain man named A, with Sapphira *367*
5: 3 But Peter said, A, why hath Satan filled *367*
5: 5 And A hearing these words fell down, and *367*
9:10 a certain disciple at Damascus, named A; *367*
9:10 and to him said the Lord in a vision, A, *367*
9:12 And hath seen in a vision a man named A *367*
9:13 Then A answered, Lord, I have heard by *367*
9:17 And A went his way, and entered into *367*
22:12 And one A, a devout man according to *367*
23: 2 And the high priest A commanded them that *367*
24: 1 And after five days A the high priest *367*

ANATH (2) [BETH-ANATH]
Jdg 3:31 after him was Shamgar the son of A, 6067
5: 6 In the days of Shamgar the son of A, in 6067

ANATHEMA (1)
1Co 16:22 Lord Jesus Christ, let him be a, Maran-atha. *331*

ANATHOTH (16)
Jos 21:18 A with her suburbs, and Almon with her 6068
1Ki 2:26 Get thee *to* A, unto thine own fields; 6068
1Ch 6:60 with her suburbs, and A with her suburbs. 6068
7: 8 Jerimoth, and Abiah, and A, and Alameth. 6068
Ezr 2:23 The men of A, an hundred twenty and 6068
Ne 7:27 The men of A, an hundred twenty and 6068
10:19 Hariph, A, Nebai, 6068
11:32 *And at* A, Nob, Ananiah, 6068
Isa 10:30 cause *it* to be heard unto Laish, O poor A. 6068
Jer 1: 1 of the priests that *were* in A in the land of 6068
11:21 thus saith the LORD of the men of A, 6068
11:23 for I will bring evil upon the men of A, 6068
29:27 why hast thou not reproved Jeremiah of A, 6069
32: 7 saying, Buy thee my field that *is* in A: 6068
32: 8 Buy my field, I pray thee, that *is* in A, 6068
32: 9 that *was* in A, and weighed him the money, 6068

ANATHOTHITE See ANETHOTHITE; ANETOTHITE

ANCESTORS (1)
Lev 26:45 sakes remember the covenant of their a, 7223

ANCHOR (1) [ANCHORS]
Heb 6:19 Which *hope* we have as an a of the soul, *45*

ANCHORS (3) [ANCHOR]
Ac 27:29 they cast four a out of the stern, and *45*
27:30 they would have cast a out of the foreship, *45*
27:40 And when they had taken up the a, *45*

ANCIENT (26) [ANCIENTS]
Dt 33:15 And for the chief things of the a mountains, 6924
Jdg 5:21 them away, *that* a river, the river Kishon. 6917
2Ki 19:25 *and* of a times that I have formed it? 6924
1Ch 4:22 and Jashubi-lehem. And *these are* a things. 6267
Ezr 3:12 *who were* a men that had seen the first 2205
Job 12:12 With the a *is* wisdom; and *in* length of days 3453
Ps 77: 5 the days of old, the years of a times. 5769
Pr 22:28 Remove not the a landmark, which thy 5769
Isa 3: 2 and the prophet, and the prudent, and the a, 2205
3: 5 shall behave himself proudly against the a, 2205
9:15 The a and honourable, he *is* the head; and 2205
19:11 *am* the son of the wise, the son of a kings? 6924
23: 7 joyous *city,* whose antiquity *is* of a days? 6924
37:26 *and* of a times, that I have formed it? 6924
44: 7 for me, since I appointed the a people? 5769
45:21 who hath declared this from a time? 6924
46:10 from a times *the things* that are not *yet* 6924
47: 6 upon the a hast thou very heavily laid thy 2205
51: 9 awake, as *in* the a days, *in* the generations 6924
Jer 5:15 it *is* a mighty nation, it *is* an a nation, 4480+5769
18:15 to stumble in their ways *from* the a paths, 5769
Eze 9: 6 they began at the a men which *were* before 2205
36: 2 even the a high places are ours in 5769
Da 7: 9 were cast *down,* and the A of days did sit, 6268
7:13 came to the A of days, and they brought 6268
7:22 Until the A of days came, and 6268

ANCIENTS (10) [ANCIENT]
1Sa 24:13 As saith the proverb of the a, 6931
Ps119:100 I understand more than the a, because 2205
Isa 3:14 into judgment with the a of his people, 2205
24:23 in Jerusalem, and before his a gloriously. 2205
Jer 19: 1 *take* of the a of the people, and of 2205
19: 1 of the people, and of the a of the priests; 2205
Eze 7:26 from the priest, and counsel from the a. 2205
8:11 seventy men of the a of the house of Israel, 2205
8:12 hast thou seen what the a of the house of 2205
27: 9 The a of Gebal and the wise *men* thereof 2205

AND (51713) See Index

ANDREW (13)
Mt 4:18 Simon called Peter, and **A** his brother, *406*
10: 2 who is called Peter, and **A** his brother; *406*
Mk 1:16 and **A** his brother casting a net into the sea: *406*
1:29 they entered into the house of Simon and **A**, *406*
3:18 And **A**, and Philip, and Bartholomew, and *406*
13: 3 James and John and **A** asked him privately, *406*
Lk 6:14 and **A** his brother, James and John, Philip *406*
Jn 1:40 and followed him, was **A**, Simon Peter's *406*
1:44 was of Bethsaida, the city of **A** and Peter. *406*
6: 8 One of his disciples, **A**, Simon Peter's *406*
12:22 Philip cometh and telleth **A**: and *406*
12:22 and again **A** and Philip tell Jesus. *406*
Ac 1:13 James, and John, and **A**, Philip, and Thomas, *406*

ANDRONICUS (1)
Ro 16: 7 Salute **A** and Junia, my kinsmen, and *408*

ANEM (1)
1Ch 6:73 with her suburbs, and **A** with her suburbs: 6046

ANER (3)
Ge 14:13 brother of Eshcol, and brother of **A**: 6063
14:24 went with me, **A**, Eshcol, and Mamre; 6063
1Ch 6:70 **A** with her suburbs, and Bileam with her 6063

ANETHOTHITE (1) [ANETOTHITE]
2Sa 23:27 Abiezer the **A**, Mebunnai the Hushathite, 6069

ANETOTHITE (1) [ANETHOTHITE]
1Ch 27:12 for the ninth month *was* Abiezer the **A**, 6069

ANGEL (201) [ANGEL'S, ANGELS, ANGELS', ARCHANGEL]
Ge 16: 7 the **a** of the LORD found her by a 4397
16: 9 the **a** of the LORD said unto her, 4397
16:10 the **a** of the LORD said unto her, I will 4397
16:11 the **a** of the LORD said unto her, Behold, 4397
21:17 the **a** of God called to Hagar out of heaven, 4397
22:11 the **a** of the LORD called unto him out of 4397
22:15 the **a** of the LORD called unto Abraham 4397
24: 7 he shall send his **a** before thee, and 4397
24:40 will send his **a** with thee, and prosper thy 4397
31:11 the **a** of God spake unto me in a dream, 4397
48:16 The **A** which redeemed me from all evil, 4397
Ex 3: 2 the **a** of the LORD appeared unto him in a 4397
14:19 the **a** of God, which went before the camp 4397
23:20 Behold, I send an **A** before thee, to keep 4397
23:23 For mine **A** shall go before thee, and 4397
32:34 behold, mine **A** shall go before thee: 4397
33: 2 I will send an **a** before thee; and I will drive 4397
Nu 20:16 sent an **a**, and hath brought us forth out of 4397
22:22 the **a** of the LORD stood in the way for an 4397
22:23 the ass saw the **a** of the LORD standing in 4397
22:24 the **a** of the LORD stood in a path of 4397
22:25 when the ass saw the **a** of the LORD, she 4397
22:26 the **a** of the LORD went further, and 4397
22:27 when the ass saw the **a** of the LORD, she 4397
22:31 he saw the **a** of the LORD standing in 4397
22:32 the **a** of the LORD said unto him, 4397
22:34 Balaam said unto the **a** of the LORD, 4397
22:35 the **a** of the LORD said unto Balaam, 4397
Jdg 2: 1 an **a** of the LORD came up from Gilgal to 4397
2: 4 when the **a** of the LORD spake these 4397
5:23 Curse ye Meroz, said the **a** of the LORD, 4397
6:11 there came an **a** of the LORD, and 4397
6:12 the **a** of the LORD appeared unto him, 4397
6:20 the **a** of God said unto him, Take the flesh 4397
6:21 the **a** of the LORD put forth the end of 4397
6:21 the unleavened *cakes.* Then the **a** of 4397
6:22 when Gideon perceived that he *was* an **a** of 4397
6:22 I have seen an **a** of the LORD face to face. 4397
13: 3 the **a** of the LORD appeared unto 4397
13: 6 *was* like the countenance of an **a** of God, 4397
13: 9 the **a** of God came again unto the woman as 4397
13:13 the **a** of the LORD said unto Manoah, 4397
13:15 Manoah said unto the **a** of the LORD, 4397
13:16 the **a** of the LORD said unto Manoah, 4397
13:16 For Manoah knew not that he *was* an **a** of 4397
13:17 Manoah said unto the **a** of the LORD, 4397
13:18 the **a** of the LORD said unto him, Why 4397
13:19 *the a* did wondrously; and Manoah and NIH
13:20 that the **a** of the LORD ascended in 4397
13:21 the **a** of the LORD did no more appear to 4397
13:21 Manoah knew that he *was* an **a** of 4397
1Sa 29: 9 thou *art* good in my sight, as an **a** of God: 4397
2Sa 14:17 for as an **a** of God, so *is* my lord the king to 4397
14:20 according to the wisdom of an **a** of God, 4397
19:27 but my lord the king *is* as an **a** of God: 4397
24:16 when the **a** stretched out his hand *upon* 4397
24:16 said to the **a** that destroyed the people, *It is* 4397
24:16 the **a** of the LORD was by 4397
24:17 when he saw the **a** that smote the people, 4397
1Ki 13:18 an **a** spake unto me by the word of 4397
19: 5 an **a** touched him, and said unto him, Arise 4397
19: 7 the **a** of the LORD came again the second 4397
2Ki 1: 3 the **a** of the LORD said to Elijah 4397
1:15 the **a** of the LORD said unto Elijah, 4397
19:35 that the **a** of the LORD went out, and 4397
1Ch 21:12 the **a** of the LORD destroying throughout 4397
21:15 God sent an **a** unto Jerusalem to destroy it: 4397
21:15 said to the **a** that destroyed, *It is* enough, 4397
21:15 the **a** of the LORD stood by 4397
21:16 saw the **a** of the LORD stand between 4397
21:18 the **a** of the LORD commanded Gad to 4397
21:20 Ornan turned back, and saw the **a**; and 4397
21:27 the LORD commanded the **a**; and he put 4397
21:30 of the sword of the **a** of the LORD. 4397
2Ch 32:21 the LORD sent an **a**, which cut off all 4397
Ps 34: 7 The **a** of the LORD encampeth round 4397
35: 5 and let the **a** of the LORD chase *them.* 4397
35: 6 and let the **a** of the LORD persecute them. 4397
Ecc 5: 6 neither say thou before the **a**, that it *was* an 4397
Isa 37:36 the **a** of the LORD went forth, and 4397
63: 9 and the **a** of his presence saved them: 4397
Da 3:28 who hath sent his **a**, and delivered his 4398
6:22 My God hath sent his **a**, and hath shut 4398
Hos 12: 4 he had power over *the* **a**, and prevailed: 4397
Zec 1: 9 And the **a** that talked with me said unto me, 4397
1:11 they answered the **a** of the LORD that 4397
1:12 the **a** of the LORD answered and said, 4397
1:13 the LORD answered the **a** that talked with 4397
1:14 So the **a** that communed with me said unto 4397
1:19 I said unto the **a** that talked with me, 4397
2: 3 the **a** that talked with me went forth, and 4397
2: 3 and another **a** went out to meet him, 4397
3: 1 priest standing before the **a** of the LORD, 4397
3: 3 filthy garments, and stood before the **a**. 4397
3: 5 And the **a** of the LORD stood *by.* 4397
3: 6 the **a** of the LORD protested unto Joshua, 4397
4: 1 the **a** that talked with me came again, and 4397
4: 4 and spake to the **a** that talked with me, 4397
4: 5 the **a** that talked with me answered and 4397
5: 5 the **a** that talked with me went forth, and 4397
5:10 said I to the **a** that talked with me, 4397
6: 4 and said unto the **a** that talked with me, 4397
6: 5 the **a** answered and said unto me, These *are* 4397
12: 8 as the **a** of the LORD before them. 4397
Mt 1:20 *the* **a** of the Lord appeared unto him in a *32*
1:24 sleep did as the **a** of the Lord had bidden him, *32*
2:13 *the* **a** of the Lord appeareth to Joseph in a *32*
2:19 an **a** of the Lord appeareth in a dream to *32*
28: 2 for *the* **a** of the Lord descended from heaven, *32*
28: 5 And the **a** answered and said unto the women, *32*
Lk 1:11 And there appeared unto him an **a** of the Lord *32*
1:13 But the **a** said unto him, Fear not, Zacharias: *32*
1:18 And Zacharias said unto the **a**, Whereby shall *32*
1:19 And the **a** answering said unto him, I am *32*
1:26 And in the sixth month the **a** Gabriel was sent *32*
1:28 And the **a** came in unto her, and said, Hail, *32*
1:30 And the **a** said unto her, Fear not, Mary: *32*
1:34 Then said Mary unto the **a**, How shall this be, *32*
1:35 And the **a** answered and said unto her, *32*
1:38 to thy word. And the **a** departed from her. *32*
2: 9 *the* **a** of the Lord came upon them, and *32*
2:10 And the **a** said unto them, Fear not: *32*
2:13 And suddenly there was with the **a** a *32*
2:21 named of the **a** before he was conceived in *32*
22:43 And there appeared an **a** unto him from *32*
Jn 5: 4 For an **a** went down at a *certain* season into *32*
12:29 it thundered: others said, An **a** spake to him. *32*
Ac 5:19 But *the* **a** of the Lord by night opened *32*
6:15 saw his face as it had been the face of an **a**. *32*
7:30 an **a** of the Lord in a flame of fire in a bush. *32*
7:35 a deliverer by the hand of the **a** which *32*
7:38 the **a** which spake to him in the mount Sina, *32*
8:26 And *the* **a** of the Lord spake unto Philip, *32*
10: 3 an **a** of God coming in to him, and *32*
10: 7 And when the **a** which spake unto Cornelius *32*

A

Ac 10:22 was warned from God by a holy **a** to send for 32
11:13 And he shewed us how he had seen an **a** in his 32
12: 7 *the* **a** of the Lord came upon *him,* and a light 32
12: 8 And the **a** said unto him, Gird thyself, and 32
12: 9 not that it was true which was done by the **a**; 32
12:10 and forthwith the **a** departed from him. 32
12:11 that the Lord hath sent his **a**, and 32
12:15 that it was *even* so. Then said they, It is his **a**. 32
12:23 And immediately *the* **a** of the Lord smote 32
23: 8 there is no resurrection, neither **a** nor spirit: 32
23: 9 but if a spirit or an **a** hath spoken to him, 32
27:23 For there stood by me this night *the* **a** of God, 32
2Co 11:14 for Satan himself is transformed into an **a** of 32
Gal 1: 8 But though we, or an **a** from heaven, 32
4:14 but received me as an **a** of God, *even* as 32
Rev 1: 1 and signified *it* by his **a** unto his servant John: 32
2: 1 Unto the **a** of the church of Ephesus write; 32
2: 8 And unto the **a** of the church in Smyrna write; 32
2:12 And to the **a** of the church in Pergamos write; 32
2:18 And unto the **a** of the church in Thyatira 32
3: 1 And unto the **a** of the church in Sardis write; 32
3: 7 And to the **a** of the church in Philadelphia 32
3:14 And unto the **a** of the church of 32
5: 2 And I saw a strong **a** proclaiming with a loud 32
7: 2 And I saw another **a** ascending from the east, 32
8: 3 And another **a** came and stood at the altar, 32
8: 5 And the **a** took the censer, and filled it with 32
8: 7 The first **a** sounded, and there followed hail NIG
8: 8 And the second **a** sounded, and as *it were* a 32
8:10 And the third **a** sounded, and there fell a great 32
8:12 And the fourth **a** sounded, and the third *part* 32
8:13 heard an **a** flying through the midst of heaven, 32
9: 1 And the fifth **a** sounded, and I saw a star fall 32
9:11 *which is* the **a** of the bottomless *pit,* whose 32
9:13 And the sixth **a** sounded, and I heard a voice 32
9:14 Saying to the sixth **a** which had the trumpet, 32
10: 1 And I saw another mighty **a** come down from 32
10: 5 And the **a** which I saw stand upon the sea and 32
10: 7 But in the days of the voice of the seventh **a**, 32
10: 8 the hand of the **a** which standeth upon the sea 32
10: 9 And I went unto the **a**, and said unto him, 32
11: 1 and the **a** stood, saying, Rise, and measure 32
11:15 And the seventh **a** sounded; and there were 32
14: 6 And I saw another **a** fly in the midst of 32
14: 8 And there followed another **a**, saying, 32
14: 9 And *the* third **a** followed them, saying with a 32
14:15 And another **a** came out of the temple, 32
14:17 And another **a** came out of the temple which 32
14:18 And another **a** came out from the altar, 32
14:19 And the **a** thrust in his sickle into the earth, 32
16: 3 And the second **a** poured out his vial upon 32
16: 4 And the third **a** poured out his vial upon 32
16: 5 And I heard the **a** of the waters say, Thou art 32
16: 8 And the fourth **a** poured out his vial upon 32
16:10 And the fifth **a** poured out his vial upon 32
16:12 And the sixth **a** poured out his vial upon 32
16:17 And the seventh **a** poured out his vial into 32
17: 7 And the **a** said unto me, Wherefore didst thou 32
18: 1 And after these *things* I saw another **a** come 32
18:21 And a mighty **a** took up a stone like a great 32
19:17 And I saw an **a** standing in the sun; and 32
20: 1 And I saw an **a** come down from heaven, 32
21:17 *to* the measure of a man, that is, of *the* **a**. 32
22: 6 the Lord God of the holy prophets sent his **a** 32
22: 8 I fell down to worship before the feet of the **a** 32
22:16 I Jesus have sent mine **a** to testify unto you 32

ANGEL'S (2) [ANGEL]

Rev 8: 4 ascended up before God out of the **a** hand. 32
10:10 And I took the little book out of the **a** hand, 32

ANGELS (93) [ANGEL]

Ge 19: 1 there came two **a** to Sodom at even; and 4397
19:15 the **a** hastened Lot, saying, Arise, take thy 4397
28:12 behold the **a** of God ascending and 4397
32: 1 went on his way, and the **a** of God met him. 4397
Job 4:18 and his **a** he charged with folly: 4397
Ps 8: 5 thou hast made him a little lower than the **a**, 430
68:17 *are* twenty thousand, *even* thousands of **a**: 8136
78:49 trouble, *by* sending evil **a** *among them.* 4397
91:11 For he shall give his **a** charge over thee, 4397
103:20 Bless the LORD, ye his **a**, that excel in 4397
104: 4 Who maketh his **a** spirits; his ministers a 4397
148: 2 Praise ye him, all his **a**: praise ye him, 4397
Mt 4: 6 He shall give his **a** charge concerning thee: 32
4:11 and behold, **a** came and ministered unto him. 32
13:39 the end of the world; and the reapers are *the* **a**. 32
13:41 The Son of man shall send forth his **a**, and 32
13:49 the **a** shall come forth, and sever the wicked 32
16:27 come in the glory of his Father with his **a**: 32
18:10 That in heaven their **a** do always behold 32
22:30 but are as *the* **a** of God in heaven. 32
24:31 And he shall send his **a** with a great sound of 32
24:36 not the **a** of heaven, but my Father only. 32
25:31 and all the holy **a** with him, then shall he sit 32
25:41 prepared for the devil and his **a**: 32
26:53 give me more than twelve legions of **a**? 32
Mk 1:13 wild beasts; and the **a** ministered unto him. 32
8:38 in the glory of his Father with the holy **a**. 32
12:25 but are as *the* **a** which are in heaven. 32
13:27 And then shall he send his **a**, and shall gather 32
13:32 not the **a** which are in heaven, neither the Son, 32
Lk 2:15 as the **a** were gone away from them into 32
4:10 He shall give his **a** charge over thee, to keep 32
9:26 and *in his* Father's, and of the holy **a**. 32
12: 8 Son of man also confess before the **a** of God: 32
12: 9 men shall be denied before the **a** of God. 32
15:10 there is joy in the presence of the **a** of God 32
16:22 was carried by the **a** into Abraham's bosom: 32
20:36 for they are **equal unto** *the* **a**; and are 2465
24:23 saying, that *they* had also seen a vision of **a**, 32
Jn 1:51 and the **a** of God ascending and 32
20:12 And seeth two **a** in white sitting, the one at 32
Ac 7:53 have received the law by the disposition of **a**, 32
Ro 8:38 nor life, nor **a**, nor principalities, nor powers, 32
1Co 4: 9 unto the world, and to **a**, and to men. 32
6: 3 Know ye not that we shall judge **a**? how much 32
11:10 to have power on *her* head because of the **a**. 32
13: 1 I speak with the tongues of men and of **a**, 32
Gal 3:19 *it was* ordained by **a** in the hand of a 32
Col 2:18 in a voluntary humility and worshipping of **a**, 32
2Th 1: 7 be revealed from heaven with his mighty **a**, 32
1Ti 3:16 justified in the Spirit, seen of **a**, preached unto 32
5:21 and the Lord Jesus Christ, and the elect **a**, 32
Heb 1: 4 Being made so much better than the **a**, as he 32
1: 5 For unto which of the **a** said he at any time, 32
1: 6 And let all the **a** of God worship him. 32
1: 7 And of the **a** he saith, Who maketh his angels 32
1: 7 Who maketh his **a** spirits, and his ministers a 32
1:13 But to which of the **a** said he at any time, 32
2: 2 For if the word spoken by **a** was stedfast, and 32
2: 5 For unto *the* **a** hath he not put in subjection 32
2: 7 Thou madest him a little lower than the **a**; 32
2: 9 who was made a little lower than the **a**, 32
2:16 For verily he took not on *him the nature of* **a**; 32
12:22 and to an innumerable company of **a**, 32
13: 2 for thereby some have entertained **a** 32
1Pe 1:12 which *things the* **a** desire to look into. 32
3:22 **a** and authorities and powers being made 32
2Pe 2: 4 For if God spared not the **a** that sinned, but 32
2:11 Whereas **a**, which are greater in power and 32
Jude 1: 6 And the **a** which kept not their first estate, but 32
Rev 1:20 The seven stars are the **a** of the seven 32
3: 5 his name before my Father, and before his **a**. 32
5:11 I heard the voice of many **a** round about 32
7: 1 And after these *things* I saw four **a** standing 32
7: 2 and he cried with a loud voice to the four **a**, 32
7:11 And all the **a** stood round about the throne, 32
8: 2 And I saw the seven **a** which stood before 32
8: 6 And the seven **a** which had the seven 32
8:13 the other voices of the trumpet of the three **a**, 32
9:14 Loose the four **a** which are bound in the great 32
9:15 And the four **a** were loosed, which were 32
12: 7 Michael and his **a** fought against the dragon; 32
12: 7 the dragon; and the dragon fought and his **a**, 32
12: 9 the earth, and his **a** were cast *out* with him. 32
14:10 and brimstone in the presence of the holy **a**, 32
15: 1 seven **a** having the seven last plagues; 32
15: 6 And the seven **a** came out of the temple, 32
15: 7 **a** seven golden vials full of the wrath of God, 32
15: 8 till the seven plagues of the seven **a** were 32
16: 1 voice out of the temple saying to the seven **a**, 32
17: 1 And there came one of the seven **a** which had 32
21: 9 And there came unto me one of the seven **a** 32
21:12 and at the gates twelve **a**, and names written 32

ANGELS' (1) [ANGEL]

Ps 78:25 Man did eat **a** food: he sent them meat to 47

ANGER (234) [ANGERED, ANGRY]

Ge	27:45	Until thy brother's **a** turn away from thee,	639
	30: 2	Jacob's **a** was kindled against Rachel: and	639
	44:18	and let not thine **a** burn against thy servant:	639
	49: 6	for in their **a** they slew a man, and in their	639
	49: 7	Cursed *be* their **a**, for *it was* fierce; and	639
Ex	4:14	the **a** of the LORD was kindled against	639
	11: 8	And he went out from Pharaoh in a great **a**.	639
	32:19	Moses' **a** waxed hot, and he cast the tables	639
	32:22	Let not the **a** of my lord wax hot:	639
Nu	11: 1	the LORD heard *it;* and his **a** was kindled;	639
	11:10	and the **a** of the LORD was kindled greatly;	639
	12: 9	the **a** of the LORD was kindled against	639
	22:22	God's **a** was kindled because he went: and	639
	22:27	Balaam's **a** was kindled, and he smote	639
	24:10	Balak's **a** was kindled against Balaam, and	639
	25: 3	the **a** of the LORD was kindled against	639
	25: 4	that the fierce **a** of the LORD may be	639
	32:10	the LORD'S **a** was kindled the same time,	639
	32:13	the LORD'S **a** was kindled against Israel,	639
	32:14	to augment yet the fierce **a** of the LORD	639
Dt	4:25	the LORD thy God, to **provoke** him **to a**:	3707
	6:15	lest the **a** of the LORD thy God be kindled	639
	7: 4	will the **a** of the LORD be kindled against	639
	9:18	sight of the LORD, to **provoke** him **to a**.	3707
	9:19	For I was afraid of the **a** and hot displeasure,	639
	13:17	may turn from the fierceness of his **a**,	639
	29:20	then the **a** of the LORD and his jealousy	639
	29:23	which the LORD overthrew in his **a**, and	639
	29:24	what *meaneth* the heat of this great **a**?	639
	29:27	the **a** of the LORD was kindled against this	639
	29:28	LORD rooted them out of their land in **a**,	639
	31:17	my **a** shall be kindled against them in that	639
	31:29	to **provoke** him **to a** through the work of	3707
	32:16	with abominations **provoked** they him **to a**.	3707
	32:21	they have **provoked** me **to a** with their	3707
	32:21	I will **provoke** them **to a** with a foolish	3707
	32:22	For a fire is kindled in my **a**, and shall burn	639
Jos	7: 1	the **a** of the LORD was kindled against	639
	7:26	LORD turned from the fierceness of his **a**.	639
	23:16	shall the **a** of the LORD be kindled against	639
Jdg	2:12	unto them, and **provoked** the LORD **to a**.	3707
	2:14	the **a** of the LORD was hot against Israel,	639
	2:20	the **a** of the LORD was hot against Israel;	639
	3: 8	Therefore the **a** of the LORD was hot	639
	6:39	Let not thine **a** be hot against me, and I will	639
	8: 3	their **a** was abated toward him, when he	7307
	9:30	of Gaal the son of Ebed, his **a** was kindled.	639
	10: 7	the **a** of the LORD was hot against Israel,	639
	14:19	his **a** was kindled, and he went up *to* his	639
1Sa	11: 6	those tidings, and his **a** was kindled greatly.	639
	17:28	and Eliab's **a** was kindled against David, and	639
	20:30	Then Saul's **a** was kindled against Jonathan,	639
	20:34	So Jonathan arose from the table in fierce **a**,	639
2Sa	6: 7	the **a** of the LORD was kindled against	639
	12: 5	David's **a** was greatly kindled against	639
	24: 1	again the **a** of the LORD was kindled	639
1Ki	14: 9	to **provoke** me **to a**, and hast cast me	3707
	14:15	their groves, **provoking** the LORD **to a**.	3707
	15:30	**provoked** the LORD God of Israel **to a**.	3707
	16: 2	to sin, to **provoke** me **to a** with their sins;	3707
	16: 7	in **provoking** him **to a** with the work of his	3707
	16:13	**provoking** the LORD God of Israel **to a**	3707
	16:26	to **provoke** the LORD God of Israel **to a**	3707
	16:33	**provoke** the LORD God of Israel **to a**	3707
	21:22	wherewith thou hast **provoked** *me* **to a**,	3707
	22:53	**provoked to a** the LORD God of Israel,	3707
2Ki	13: 3	the **a** of the LORD was kindled against	639
	17:11	wicked things to **provoke** the LORD **to a**:	3707
	17:17	sight of the LORD, to **provoke** him **to a**.	3707
	21: 6	sight of the LORD, to **provoke** *him* **to a**.	3707
	21:15	have **provoked** me **to a**, since the day their	3707
	22:17	that they might **provoke** me **to a** with all	3707
	23:19	had made to **provoke** *the LORD* **to a**,	3707
	23:26	where*with* his **a** was kindled against Judah,	639
	24:20	For through the **a** of the LORD it came to	639
1Ch	13:10	the **a** of the LORD was kindled against	639
2Ch	25:10	to go home *again:* wherefore their **a** was	639
	25:10	and they returned home in great **a**.	639
	25:15	Wherefore the **a** of the LORD was kindled	639
	28:25	**provoked to a** the LORD God of his	3707
	33: 6	sight of the LORD, to **provoke** him **to a**.	3707
	34:25	that *they* might **provoke** me **to a** with all	3707
Ne	4: 5	for they have **provoked** *thee* **to a** before	3707
	9:17	slow to **a**, and of great kindness, and	639
Est	1:12	king very wroth, and his **a** burned in him.	2534
Job	9: 5	know not: which overturneth them in his **a**.	639
	9:13	*If* God will not withdraw his **a**, the proud	639
	18: 4	He teareth himself in his **a**: shall the earth be	639
	21:17	*God* distributeth sorrows in his **a**.	639
	35:15	because *it is* not *so,* he hath visited *in* his **a**;	639
Ps	6: 1	O LORD, rebuke me not in thine **a**,	639
	7: 6	Arise, O LORD, in thine **a**, lift up thyself	639
	21: 9	them as a fiery oven in the time of thine **a**:	6440
	27: 9	*far* from me; put not thy servant away in **a**:	639
	30: 5	For his **a** *endureth but* a moment; in his	639
	37: 8	Cease from **a**, and forsake wrath: fret not	639
	38: 3	soundness in my flesh because of thine **a**;	2195
	56: 7	in *thine* **a** cast down the people, O God.	639
	69:24	and let thy wrathful **a** take hold of them.	639
	74: 1	*why* doth thine **a** smoke against the sheep of	639
	77: 9	hath he in **a** shut up his tender mercies?	639
	78:21	and **a** also came up against Israel;	639
	78:38	many a time turned he his **a** away, and	639
	78:49	He cast upon them the fierceness of his **a**,	639
	78:50	He made a way to his **a**; he spared not their	639
	78:58	For they **provoked** him **to a** with their high	3707
	85: 3	turned *thyself* from the fierceness of thine **a**.	639
	85: 4	and cause thine **a** towards us to cease.	3708
	85: 5	wilt thou draw out thine **a** to all generations?	639
	90: 7	For we are consumed by thine **a**, and by thy	639
	90:11	Who knoweth the power of thine **a**?	639
	103: 8	gracious, slow to **a**, and plenteous in mercy.	639
	103: 9	neither will he keep *his a* for ever.	NIH
	106:29	Thus they **provoked** *him* **to a** with their	3707
	145: 8	slow to **a**, and of great mercy.	639
Pr	15: 1	away wrath: but grievous words stir **up a**.	639
	15:18	but *he that is* slow to **a** appeaseth strife.	639
	16:32	*He that is* slow to **a** *is* better than the mighty;	639
	19:11	The discretion of a man deferreth his **a**; and	639
	20: 2	*whoso* **provoketh** him **to a** sinneth *against*	5674
	21:14	A gift in secret pacifieth **a**: and a reward in	639
	22: 8	reap vanity: and the rod of his **a** shall fail.	5678
	27: 4	Wrath *is* cruel, and **a** *is* outrageous; but	639
Ecc	7: 9	for **a** resteth in the bosom of fools.	3708
Isa	1: 4	**provoked** the Holy One of Israel **unto a**,	5006
	5:25	Therefore is the **a** of the LORD kindled	639
	5:25	For all this his **a** is not turned away, but	639
	7: 4	for the fierce **a** of Rezin with Syria, and	639
	9:12	For all this his **a** is not turned away, but	639
	9:17	For all this his **a** is not turned away, but	639
	9:21	For all this his **a** is not turned away, but	639
	10: 4	For all this his **a** is not turned away, but	639
	10: 5	the rod of mine **a**, and the staff in their hand	639
	10:25	shall cease, and mine **a** in their destruction.	639
	12: 1	thine **a** is turned away, and thou comfortedst	639
	13: 3	have also called my mighty ones for mine **a**,	639
	13: 9	cruel both *with* wrath and fierce **a**, to lay	639
	13:13	of hosts, and in the day of his fierce **a**.	639
	14: 6	he that ruled the nations in **a**, *is* persecuted,	639
	30:27	burning *with* his **a**, and the burden *thereof is*	639
	30:30	with the indignation of *his* **a**, and *with*	639
	42:25	he hath poured upon him the fury of his **a**,	639
	48: 9	For my name's sake will I defer mine **a**, and	639
	63: 3	for I will tread them in mine **a**, and	639
	63: 6	And I will tread down the people in mine **a**,	639
	65: 3	A people that **provoketh** me **to a**	3707
	66:15	to render his **a** with fury, and his rebuke with	639
Jer	2:35	am innocent, surely his **a** shall turn from me.	639
	3: 5	Will he reserve *his a* for ever? will he keep	NIH
	3:12	I will not cause mine **a** to fall upon you:	6440
	3:12	the LORD, *and* I will not keep *a* for ever.	NIH
	4: 8	for the fierce **a** of the LORD is not turned	639
	4:26	presence of the LORD, *and* by his fierce **a**.	639
	7:18	other gods, that *they* may **provoke** me **to a**.	3707
	7:19	Do they **provoke** me **to a**? saith	3707
	7:20	mine **a** and my fury *shall be* poured out upon	639
	8:19	Why have they **provoked** me **to a** with	3707
	10:24	not in thine **a**, lest thou bring me to nothing.	639
	11:17	**provoke** me **to a** in offering incense unto	3707
	12:13	because of the fierce **a** of the LORD.	639
	15:14	for a fire is kindled in mine **a**, *which* shall	639
	17: 4	for ye have kindled a fire in mine **a**,	639
	18:23	deal *thus* with them in the time of thine **a**.	639
	21: 5	even in **a**, and in fury, and in great wrath.	639
	23:20	The **a** of the LORD shall not return,	639
	25: 6	**provoke** me not **to a** with the works of	3707

Jer	25: 7	that *ye* might **provoke** me **to a** with	3707
	25:37	because of the fierce **a** of the LORD.	639
	25:38	of the oppressor, and because of his fierce **a**.	639
	30:24	The fierce **a** of the LORD shall not return,	639
	32:29	unto other gods, to **provoke** me **to a**.	3707
	32:30	**provoked** me **to a** with the work of their	3707
	32:31	hath been to me *as* a **provocation of** mine **a**	639
	32:32	which they have done to **provoke** me **to a**,	3707
	32:37	whither I have driven them in mine **a**, and	639
	33: 5	whom I have slain in mine **a** and in my fury,	639
	36: 7	for great *is* the **a** and the fury that	639
	42:18	As mine **a** and my fury hath been poured	639
	44: 3	they have committed to **provoke** me **to a**,	3707
	44: 6	my fury and mine **a** was poured forth,	639
	49:37	*even* my fierce **a**, saith the LORD;	639
	51:45	his soul from the fierce **a** of the LORD.	639
	52: 3	For through the **a** of the LORD it came to	639
La	1:12	hath afflicted *me* in the day of his fierce **a**.	639
	2: 1	the daughter of Zion with a cloud in his **a**,	639
	2: 1	not his footstool in the day of his **a**!	639
	2: 3	He hath cut off in *his* fierce **a** all the horn of	639
	2: 6	hath despised in the indignation of his **a**	639
	2:21	thou hast slain *them* in the day of thine **a**;	639
	2:22	that in the day of the LORD'S **a** none	639
	3:43	Thou hast covered with **a**, and persecuted us:	639
	3:66	destroy them in **a** from under the heavens of	639
	4:11	he hath poured out his fierce **a**, and	639
	4:16	The **a** of the LORD hath divided them;	6440
Eze	5:13	Thus shall mine **a** be accomplished, and	639
	5:15	when I shall execute judgments in thee in **a**	639
	7: 3	I will send mine **a** upon thee, and will judge	639
	7: 8	and accomplish mine **a** upon thee:	639
	8:17	and have returned to **provoke** me **a**:	3707
	13:13	shall be an overflowing shower in mine **a**,	639
	16:26	thy whoredoms, to **provoke** me **to a**.	3707
	20: 8	to accomplish my **a** against them in	639
	20:21	to accomplish my **a** against them in	639
	22:20	to melt *it;* so will I gather *you* in mine **a** and	639
	25:14	they shall do in Edom according to mine **a**	639
	35:11	I will even do according to thine **a**, and	639
	43: 8	wherefore I have consumed them in mine **a**.	639
Da	9:16	let thine **a** and thy fury be turned away from	639
	11:20	shall be destroyed, neither in **a**, nor in battle.	639
Hos	8: 5	cast *thee* off; mine **a** is kindled against them:	639
	11: 9	I will not execute the fierceness of mine **a**,	639
	12:14	Ephraim **provoked** *him* **to a** most bitterly:	3707
	13:11	I gave thee a king in mine **a**, and took *him*	639
	14: 4	for mine **a** is turned away from him.	639
Joel	2:13	slow to **a**, and of great kindness, and	639
Am	1:11	his **a** did tear perpetually, and he kept his	639
Jnh	3: 9	and repent, and turn away from his fierce **a**,	639
	4: 2	slow to **a**, and of great kindness, and	639
Mic	5:15	I will execute vengeance in **a** and fury upon	639
	7:18	he retaineth not his **a** for ever, because	639
Na	1: 3	The LORD *is* slow to **a**, and great in power,	639
	1: 6	and who can abide in the fierceness of his **a**?	639
Hab	3: 8	*was* thine **a** against the rivers? *was* thy wrath	639
	3:12	thou didst thresh the heathen in **a**.	639
Zep	2: 2	before the fierce **a** of the LORD come upon	639
	2: 2	before the day of the LORD'S **a** come upon	639
	2: 3	ye shall be hid in the day of the LORD'S **a**.	639
	3: 8	them mine indignation, *even* all my fierce **a**:	639
Zec	10: 3	Mine **a** was kindled against the shepherds,	639
Mk	3: 5	he had looked round about on them with **a**,	*3709*
Ro	10:19	*and* by a foolish nation I will **a** you.	*3949*
Eph	4:31	and **a**, and clamour, and evil speaking,	*3709*
Col	3: 8	But now you also put off all *these;* **a**, wrath,	*3709*
	3:21	provoke not your children *to a*, lest they be	NIG

ANGERED (1) [ANGER]

Ps	106:32	They **a** *him* also at the waters of strife, so	7107

ANGLE (2)

Isa	19: 8	all they that cast **a** into the brooks shall	2443
Hab	1:15	They take up all of them with the **a**,	2443

ANGRY (44) [ANGER]

Ge	18:30	he said *unto him,* Oh let not the Lord be **a**,	2734
	18:32	Oh let not the Lord be **a**, and I will speak	2734
	45: 5	be not grieved, nor **a** with yourselves,	2734
Lev	10:16	he was **a** with Eleazar and Ithamar the sons	7107
Dt	1:37	Also the LORD was **a** with me for your	599
	4:21	Furthermore the LORD was **a** with me for	599
	9: 8	that the LORD was **a** with you to have	599
	9:20	the LORD was very **a** with Aaron to have	599
Jdg	18:25	lest **a** fellows run upon thee, and	4751+5315
2Sa	19:42	wherefore then be ye **a** for this matter?	2734
1Ki	8:46	thou be **a** with them, and deliver them to	599
	11: 9	the LORD was **a** with Solomon, because	599
2Ki	17:18	Therefore the LORD was very **a** with	599
2Ch	6:36	thou be **a** with them, and deliver them *over*	599
Ezr	9:14	wouldest thou not be **a** with us till *thou* hadst	599
Ne	5: 6	I was very **a** when I heard their cry and	2734
Ps	2:12	lest he be **a**, and ye perish *from* the way,	599
	7:11	and God is **a** *with the wicked* every day.	2194
	76: 7	may stand in thy sight when once thou art **a**?	639
	79: 5	wilt thou be **a**, for ever? shall thy jealousy	599
	80: 4	how long wilt thou be **a** against the prayer	6225
	85: 5	Wilt thou be **a** with us for ever? wilt thou	599
Pr	14:17	*He that is* soon **a** dealeth foolishly: and	639
	21:19	than with a contentious and an **a** woman.	3708
	22:24	Make no friendship with an **a** man; and	639
	25:23	*doth* an **a** countenance a backbiting tongue.	2194
	29:22	An **a** man stirreth up strife, and a furious	639
Ecc	5: 6	wherefore should God be **a** at thy voice,	7107
	7: 9	Be not hasty in thy spirit to be **a**: for anger	3707
SS	1: 6	my mother's children were **a** with me;	2787
Isa	12: 1	though thou wast **a** with me, thine anger is	599
Eze	16:42	and I will be quiet, and will be no more **a**.	3707
Da	2:12	For this cause the king was **a** and	1149
Jnh	4: 1	Jonah exceedingly, and he was **very a**.	2734
	4: 4	said the LORD, Doest thou well to be **a**?	2734
	4: 9	Doest thou well to be **a** for the gourd?	2734
	4: 9	he said, I do well to be **a**, *even* unto death.	2734
Mt	5:22	That whosoever is **a** with his brother	*3710*
Lk	14:21	of the house being **a** said to his servant,	*3710*
	15:28	And he was **a**, and would not go in:	*3710*
Jn	7:23	are ye **a** at me, because I have made a man	*5520*
Eph	4:26	Be ye **a**, and sin not: let not the sun go	*3710*
Tit	1: 7	not selfwilled, not **soon a**, not given to	*3711*
Rev	11:18	And the nations were **a**, and thy wrath is	*3710*

ANGUISH (17)

Ge	42:21	in that we saw the **a** of his soul, when he	6869
Ex	6: 9	they hearkened not unto Moses for **a** of	7115
Dt	2:25	shall tremble, and be **in a** because of thee.	2342
2Sa	1: 9	for **a** is come upon me, because my life *is*	7661
Job	7:11	I will speak in the **a** of my spirit;	6862
	15:24	Trouble and **a** shall make him afraid;	4691
Ps	119:143	Trouble and **a** have taken hold on me:	4689
Pr	1:27	when distress and **a** cometh upon you:	6695
Isa	8:22	behold trouble and darkness, dimness of **a**;	6695
	30: 6	into the land of trouble and **a**, from whence	6695
Jer	4:31	the **a** as of her that bringeth forth her first	6869
	6:24	**a** hath taken hold of us, *and* pain, as of a	6869
	49:24	fear hath seized on *her:* **a** and sorrows have	6869
	50:43	**a** took hold of him, *and* pangs as of a	6869
Jn	16:21	the child, she remembereth no more the **a**,	*2347*
Ro	2: 9	Tribulation and **a**, upon every soul of man	*4730*
2Co	2: 4	**a** of heart I wrote unto you with many	*4928*

ANIAM (1)

1Ch	7:19	Ahian, and Shechem, and Likhi, and **A**.	593

ANIM (1)

Jos	15:50	And Anab, and Eshtemoh, and **A**,	6044

ANISE (1)

Mt	23:23	for ye pay tithe of mint and **a** and cummin,	*432*

ANKLE (1) [ANKLES]

Ac	3: 7	his feet and **a** bones received strength,	*4974*

ANKLES (1) [ANKLE]

Eze	47: 3	through the waters; the waters *were* to the **a**.	657

ANNA (1)

Lk	2:36	And there was *one* **A**, a prophetess,	*451*

ANNAS (4)

Lk	3: 2	**A** and Caiaphas being the high priests,	*452*
Jn	18:13	And led him away to **A** first; for he was	*452*
	18:24	Now **A** had sent him bound unto Caiaphas	*452*
Ac	4: 6	And **A** the high priest, and Caiaphas, and	*452*

ANOINT (35) [ANOINTED, ANOINTEDST, ANOINTEST, ANOINTING]

Ex	28:41	shalt **a** them, and consecrate them, and	4886
	29: 7	and pour *it* upon his head, and **a** him.	4886

Ex 29:36 for it, and thou shalt **a** it, to sanctify it. 4886
30:26 thou shalt **a** the tabernacle of 4886
30:30 thou shalt **a** Aaron and his sons, and 4886
40: 9 **a** the tabernacle, and all that *is* therein, 4886
40:10 thou shalt **a** the altar of the burnt offering, 4886
40:11 thou shalt **a** the laver and his foot, and 4886
40:13 and **a** him, and sanctify him; 4886
40:15 thou shalt **a** them, as thou didst anoint their 4886
40:15 anoint them, as thou didst **a** their father, 4886
Lev 16:32 whom he shall **a**, and whom he shall 4886
Dt 28:40 but thou shalt not **a** *thyself with* the oil; 5480
Jdg 9: 8 The trees went forth on a time to **a** a king 4886
9:15 If in truth ye **a** me king over you, *then* 4886
Ru 3: 3 **a** thee, and put thy raiment upon thee, and 5480
1Sa 9:16 thou shalt **a** him to be captain over my 4886
15: 1 The LORD sent me to **a** thee to be king 4886
16: 3 thou shalt **a** unto me *him* whom I name 4886
16:12 the LORD said, Arise, **a** him: for this *is* 4886
2Sa 14: 2 **a** not *thyself with* oil, but be as a woman 5480
1Ki 1:34 Nathan the prophet **a** him there king over 4886
19:15 **a** Hazael to be king over Syria: 4886
19:16 Jehu the son of Nimshi shalt thou **a** to be 4886
19:16 shalt thou **a** to be prophet in thy room. 4886
Isa 21: 5 drink: arise, ye princes, *and* **a** the shield. 4886
Da 9:24 and prophecy, and to **a** the most Holy. 4886
10: 3 neither did I **a** myself **at all**, till three 5480+5480
Am 6: 6 and **a** themselves *with* the chief ointments: 4886
Mic 6:15 but thou shalt not **a** *thee with* oil; 5480
Mt 6:17 thou fastest, **a** thine head, and wash thy face; *218*
Mk 14: 8 she is come aforehand to **a** my body to *3462*
16: 1 that they might come and **a** him. *218*
Lk 7:46 Mine head with oil thou didst not **a**: but *218*
Rev 3:18 and **a** thine eyes *with* eyesalve, that thou *1472*

ANOINTED (98) [ANOINT]

Ex 29: 2 with oil, and wafers unleavened **a** with oil: 4886
29:29 to be **a** therein, and to be consecrated in 4888
Lev 2: 4 with oil, or unleavened wafers **a** with oil. 4886
4: 3 If the priest that is **a** do sin according to 4899
4: 5 the priest that is **a** shall take of 4899
4:16 the priest that is **a** shall bring of 4899
6:20 unto the LORD in the day when he is **a**; 4886
6:22 the priest of his sons that is **a** in his stead 4899
7:12 unleavened wafers **a** with oil, and 4886
7:36 in the day that he **a** them, *by* a statute for 4886
8:10 **a** the tabernacle and all that *was* therein, 4886
8:11 **a** the altar and all his vessels, both the laver 4886
8:12 Aaron's head, and **a** him, to sanctify him. 4886
Nu 3: 3 the sons of Aaron, the priests which were **a**, 4886
6:15 wafers of unleavened bread **a** with oil, and 4886
7: 1 had **a** it, and sanctified it, and all 4886
7: 1 and had **a** them, and sanctified them; 4886
7:10 of the altar in the day that it was **a**, 4886
7:84 in the day when it was **a**, by the princes of 4886
7:88 dedication of the altar, after *that* it was **a**. 4886
35:25 high priest, which was **a** with the holy oil. 4886
1Sa 2:10 unto his king, and exalt the horn of his **a**. 4899
2:35 and he shall walk before mine **a** for ever. 4899
10: 1 the LORD hath **a** thee to be captain over 4886
12: 3 me before the LORD, and before his **a**: 4899
12: 5 against you, and his **a** *is* witness this day, 4899
15:17 and the LORD **a** thee king over Israel? 4886
16: 6 said, Surely the LORD'S **a** *is* before him. 4899
16:13 and **a** him in the midst of his brethren; 4886
24: 6 the LORD'S **a**, to stretch forth mine hand 4899
24: 6 seeing he *is* the **a** of the LORD. 4899
24:10 against my lord; for he *is* the LORD'S **a**. 4899
26: 9 forth his hand against the LORD'S **a**, 4899
26:11 forth mine hand against the LORD'S **a**: 4899
26:16 have not kept your master, the LORD'S **a**. 4899
26:23 forth mine hand against the LORD'S **a**. 4899
2Sa 1:14 thine hand to destroy the LORD'S **a**? 4899
1:16 saying, I have slain the LORD'S **a**. 4899
1:21 *as though he had* not *been* **a** with oil. 4899
2: 4 there they **a** David king over the house of 4886
2: 7 also the house of Judah have **a** me king 4886
3:39 And I *am this* day weak, though **a** king; and 4886
5: 3 and they **a** David king over Israel. 4886
5:17 when the Philistines heard that they had **a** 4886
12: 7 I **a** thee king over Israel, and I delivered 4886
12:20 and **a** *himself,* and changed his apparel, and 5480
19:10 Absalom, whom we **a** over us, is dead in 4886
19:21 because he cursed the LORD'S **a**? 4899
22:51 sheweth mercy to his **a**, unto David, and 4899
23: 1 the **a** of the God of Jacob, and the sweet 4899
1Ki 1:39 of oil out of the tabernacle, and **a** Solomon. 4886
1:45 Nathan the prophet have **a** him king in 4886
5: 1 for he had heard that they had **a** him king in 4886
2Ki 9: 3 the LORD, I have **a** thee king over Israel. 4886
9: 6 I have **a** thee king over the people of 4886
9:12 the LORD, I have **a** thee king over Israel. 4886
11:12 they made him king, and **a** him; and 4886
23:30 **a** him, and made him king in his father's 4886
1Ch 11: 3 they **a** David king over Israel, according to 4886
14: 8 when the Philistines heard that David was **a** 4886
16:22 *Saying,* Touch not mine **a**, and do my 4899
29:22 **a** *him* unto the LORD to be the chief 4886
2Ch 6:42 turn not away the face of thine **a**: 4899
22: 7 whom the LORD had **a** to cut off 4886
23:11 Jehoiada and his sons **a** him, and said, 4886
28:15 **a** them, and carried all the feeble of them 5480
Ps 2: 2 the LORD, and against his **a**, *saying,* 4899
18:50 sheweth mercy to his **a**, to David, and to his 4899
20: 6 Now know I that the LORD saveth his **a**; 4899
28: 8 and he *is* the saving strength of his **a**. 4899
45: 7 hath **a** thee *with* the oil of gladness above 4886
84: 9 and look upon the face of thine **a**. 4899
89:20 my servant; with my holy oil have I **a** him: 4886
89:38 thou hast been wroth with thine **a**. 4899
89:51 have reproached the footsteps of thine **a**. 4899
92:10 *of* an unicorn: I shall be **a** with fresh oil. 1101
105:15 *Saying,* Touch not mine **a**, and do my 4899
132:10 sake turn not away the face of thine **a**. 4899
132:17 to bud: I have ordained a lamp for mine **a**. 4899
Isa 45: 1 Thus saith the LORD to his **a**, to Cyrus, 4899
61: 1 the LORD hath **a** me to preach good 4886
La 4:20 the **a** of the LORD, was taken in their pits, 4899
Eze 16: 9 thy blood from thee, and I **a** thee with oil. 5480
28:14 Thou *art* the **a** cherub that covereth; and 4473
Hab 3:13 thy people, *even* for salvation with thine **a**; 4899
Zec 4:14 said he, These *are* the two **a** ones, that stand 3323
Mk 6:13 and **a** with oil many *that were* sick, and *218*
Lk 4:18 he hath **a** me to preach the gospel to *5548*
7:38 his feet, and **a** *them* with the ointment. *218*
7:46 this *woman* hath **a** my feet with ointment. *218*
Jn 9: 6 he **a** the eyes of the blind man with *2025*
9:11 and **a** mine eyes, and said unto me, Go to *2025*
11: 2 (It was *that* Mary which **a** the Lord with *218*
12: 3 and **a** the feet of Jesus, and wiped his feet *218*
Ac 4:27 whom thou hast **a**, both Herod, and *5548*
10:38 How God **a** Jesus of Nazareth with *5548*
2Co 1:21 with you in Christ, and hath **a** us, *is* God; *5548*
Heb 1: 9 hath **a** thee *with* the oil of gladness above *5548*

ANOINTEDST (1) [ANOINT]

Ge 31:13 where thou **a** the pillar, *and* where thou 4886

ANOINTEST (1) [ANOINT]

Ps 23: 5 thou **a** my head with oil; my cup runneth 1878

ANOINTING (28) [ANOINT]

Ex 25: 6 spices for **a** oil, and for sweet incense, 4888
29: 7 shalt thou take the **a** oil, and pour *it* upon 4888
29:21 and of the **a** oil, and sprinkle *it* upon Aaron, 4888
30:25 of the apothecary: it shall be a holy **a** oil. 4888
30:31 This shall be a holy **a** oil unto me 4888
31:11 the **a** oil, and sweet incense for the holy 4888
35: 8 spices for **a** oil, and for the sweet incense, 4888
35:15 the **a** oil, and the sweet incense, and 4888
35:28 and for the **a** oil, and for the sweet incense. 4888
37:29 he made the holy **a** oil, and the pure 4888
39:38 the **a** oil, and the sweet incense, and 4888
40: 9 thou shalt take the **a** oil, and anoint 4888
40:15 for their **a** shall surely be an everlasting 4888
Lev 7:35 This *is the portion* of the **a** of Aaron, and 4888
7:35 of Aaron, and of the **a** of his sons, 4888
8: 2 the **a** oil, and a bullock *for* the sin offering, 4888
8:10 Moses took the **a** oil, and anointed 4888
8:12 he poured of the **a** oil upon Aaron's head, 4888
8:30 Moses took of the **a** oil, and of the blood 4888
10: 7 for the **a** oil of the LORD *is* upon you. 4888
21:10 upon whose head the **a** oil was poured, and 4888
21:12 for the crown of the **a** oil of his God *is* 4888
Nu 4:16 the **a** oil, *and* the oversight of all 4888
18: 8 thee have I given them by reason of the **a**, 4888
Isa 10:27 yoke shall be destroyed because of the **a**. 8081
Jas 5:14 **a** him with oil in the name of the Lord: *218*
1Jn 2:27 But the **a** which ye have received of him *5545*

1Jn 2:27 but as the same a teacheth you of all *things,* 5545

ANON (2)
Mt 13:20 the word, and a with joy receiveth it; 2112
Mk 1:30 sick of a fever, and a they tell him of her. 2112

ANOTHER (448) [ANOTHER'S] See Index

ANOTHER'S (5) [ANOTHER] See Index

ANSWER (131) [ANSWERABLE, ANSWERED, ANSWEREDST, ANSWEREST, ANSWERETH, ANSWERING, ANSWERS] See Index

ANSWERABLE (1) [ANSWER]
Ex 38:18 in the breadth *was* five cubits, a 5980+3807.1

ANSWERED (492) [ANSWER] See Index

ANSWEREDST (2) [ANSWER] See Index

ANSWEREST (6) [ANSWER] See Index

ANSWERETH (13) [ANSWER] See Index

ANSWERING (31) [ANSWER] See Index

ANSWERS (3) [ANSWER] See Index

ANT (1) [ANTS]
Pr 6: 6 Go to the a, thou sluggard; consider her 5244

ANTHOTHIJAH See ANTOTHIJAH

ANTICHRIST (4) [CHRIST]
1Jn 2:18 and as ye have heard that a shall come, 500
2:22 He is a, that denieth the Father and the Son. 500
4: 3 and this is *that spirit* of a, whereof you have 500
2Jn 1: 7 in the flesh. This is a deceiver and an a. 500

ANTICHRISTS (1) [CHRIST]
1Jn 2:18 shall come, even now are there many a; 500

ANTIOCH (19)
Ac 6: 5 and Parmenas, and Nicolas a proselyte of A: 491
11:19 and Cyprus, and A, preaching the word to 490
11:20 Cyrene, which, when they were come to A, 490
11:22 forth Barnabas, that *he* should go as far as A. 490
11:26 he had found him, he brought him unto A. 490
11:26 disciples were called Christians first in A. 490
11:27 days came prophets from Jerusalem unto A. 490
13: 1 Now there were in the church that was at A 490
13:14 they came to A in Pisidia, and went into 490
14:19 And there came thither *certain* Jews from A 490
14:21 *again* to Lystra, and *to* Iconium, and A, 490
14:26 And thence sailed to A, from whence they 490
15:22 men of their own company to A with Paul 490
15:23 the brethren which are of the Gentiles in A 490
15:30 when they were dismissed, they came to A: 490
15:35 Paul also and Barnabas continued in A, 490
18:22 and saluted the church, he went down to A. 490
Gal 2:11 But when Peter was come to A, I withstood 490
2Ti 3:11 afflictions, which came unto me at A, 490

ANTIPAS (1)
Rev 2:13 even in *those* days wherein A *was* my 493

ANTIPATRIS (1)
Ac 23:31 took Paul, and brought *him* by night to A. 494

ANTIQUITY (1)
Isa 23: 7 *Is* this your joyous *city,* whose a *is* of 6927

ANTOTHIJAH (1)
1Ch 8:24 And Hananiah, and Elam, and A, 6070

ANTOTHITE (2)
1Ch 11:28 son of Ikkesh the Tekoite, Abi-ezer the A, 6069
12: 3 and Berachah, and Jehu the A, 6069

ANTS (1) [ANT]
Pr 30:25 The a *are* a people not strong, yet they 5244

ANUB (1)
1Ch 4: 8 Coz begat A, and Zobebah, and the families 6036

ANVIL (1)
Isa 41: 7 *with* the hammer him that smote the a, 6471

ANY (916) [ANYTHING] See Index

ANYTHING (1) [ANY]
1Ch 26:28 whosoever had dedicated *a, it was* under NIH

APACE (3)
2Sa 18:25 And he came a, and drew near. 1980+1980
Ps 68:12 Kings of armies did flee a: and 5074+5074
Jer 46: 5 and are fled a, and look not back: 4498+5127

APART (24) [PART]
Ex 13:12 That thou shalt set a unto the LORD all 5674
Lev 15:19 be blood, she shall be put a seven days: 5079
18:19 as long as she is put a for her uncleanness. 5079
Ps 4: 3 know that the LORD hath set a *him that is* 6395
Eze 22:10 humbled her that was set a for pollution. 5079
Zec 12:12 land shall mourn, every family a; 905+3807.1
12:12 the family of the house of David a, 905+3807.1
12:12 of David apart, and their wives a; 905+3807.1
12:12 the family of the house of Nathan a, 905+3807.1
12:12 of Nathan apart, and their wives a; 905+3807.1
12:13 The family of the house of Levi a, 905+3807.1
12:13 of Levi apart, and their wives a; 905+3807.1
12:13 the family of Shimei a, and 905+3807.1
12:13 of Shimei apart, and their wives a; 905+3807.1
12:14 family a, and their wives apart. 905+3807.1
12:14 family apart, and their wives a. 905+3807.1
Mt 14:13 thence by ship into a desert place a: 2398+2596
14:23 he went up into a mountain a to pray: 2398+2596
17: 1 them up into a high mountain a, 2398+2596
17:19 Then came the disciples to Jesus a, 2398+2596
20:17 the twelve disciples a in the way, 2398+2596
Mk 6:31 Come ye yourselves a into a desert 2398+2596
9: 2 a high mountain a by themselves: 2398+2596
Jas 1:21 Wherefore lay a all filthiness and 659

APELLES (1)
Ro 16:10 Salute A approved in Christ. Salute them 559

APES (2)
1Ki 10:22 and silver, ivory, and a, and peacocks. 6971
2Ch 9:21 and silver, ivory, and a, and peacocks. 6971

APHARSACHITES (2)
Ezr 5: 6 Shethar-boznai, and his companions the A, 671
6: 6 Shethar-boznai, and your companions the A, 671

APHARSATHCHITES (1)
Ezr 4: 9 the Dinaites, the A, the Tarpelites, 671

APHARSITES (1)
Ezr 4: 9 the Tarpelites, the A, the Archevites, 670

APHEK (8)
Jos 12:18 The king of A, one; the king of Lasharon, 663
13: 4 unto A, to the borders of the Amorites: 663
19:30 Ummah also, and A, and Rehob: twenty and 663
1Sa 4: 1 and the Philistines pitched in A. 663
29: 1 gathered together all their armies to A: 663
1Ki 20:26 and went up to A, to fight against Israel. 663
20:30 the rest fled to A, into the city; and *there* a 663
2Ki 13:17 for thou shalt smite the Syrians in A, 663

APHEKAH (1)
Jos 15:53 And Janum, and Beth-tappuah, and A, 664

APHIAH (1)
1Sa 9: 1 son of Bechorath, the son of A, a Benjamite, 647

APHIK (1)
Jdg 1:31 nor of Helbah, nor of A, nor of Rehob: 663

APHRAH See HOUSE OF APHRAH

APHSES (1)
1Ch 24:15 seventeenth to Hezir, the eighteenth to A, 6483

APIECE (8)
Nu 3:47 Thou shalt even take five shekels a 2568+2568
7:86 *of* incense, *weighing* ten *shekels* a, 3709+1886.1
17: 6 every one of their princes gave him a rod a, 259
1Ki 7:15 *of* brass, of eighteen cubits high a: 259+5982
Eze 10:21 Every one had four faces a, and every 702+702
41:24 the doors had two leaves *a,* two turning NIH
Lk 9: 3 neither money; neither have two coats a. 303
Jn 2: 6 the Jews, containing two or three firkins a. 303

APOLLONIA (1)
Ac 17: 1 they had passed through Amphipolis and A, *624*

APOLLOS (10)
Ac 18:24 And a certain Jew named A, born at *625*
19: 1 it came to pass that, while A was at Corinth, *625*
1Co 1:12 and I of A; and I of Cephas; and I of Christ. *625*
3: 4 I am of Paul; and another, I *am* of A; *625*
3: 5 and who *is* A, but ministers by whom ye *625*
3: 6 I have planted, A watered; but God gave *625*
3:22 or A, or Cephas, or the world, or life, or *625*
4: 6 to myself and *to* A for your sakes; *625*
16:12 As touching *our* brother A, I greatly desired *625*
Tit 3:13 the lawyer and A on their journey diligently, *625*

APOLLYON (1)
Rev 9:11 but in the Greek *tongue* hath *his* name A. *623*

APOSTLE (19) [APOSTLES, APOSTLES', APOSTLESHIP]
Ro 1: 1 a servant of Jesus Christ, called *to be* an a, *652*
11:13 inasmuch as I am the a of the Gentiles, *652*
1Co 1: 1 called *to be* an a of Jesus Christ through *652*
9: 1 Am I not an a? am I not free? have I not *652*
9: 2 If I be not an a unto others, yet doubtless I *652*
15: 9 that am not meet to be called an a, because *652*
2Co 1: 1 an a of Jesus Christ by the will of God, and *652*
12:12 Truly the signs of an a were wrought among *652*
Gal 1: 1 Paul, an a, (not of men, neither by man, but *652*
Eph 1: 1 Paul, an a of Jesus Christ by the will of God, *652*
Col 1: 1 an a of Jesus Christ by the will of God, and *652*
1Ti 1: 1 an a of Jesus Christ by the commandment of *652*
2: 7 and an a, (I speak the truth in Christ, *and* *652*
2Ti 1: 1 Paul, an a of Jesus Christ by the will of God, *652*
1:11 and an a, and a teacher of the Gentiles. *652*
Tit 1: 1 a servant of God, and an a of Jesus Christ, *652*
Heb 3: 1 consider the A and High Priest of our *652*
1Pe 1: 1 Peter, an a of Jesus Christ, to the strangers *652*
2Pe 1: 1 a servant and an a of Jesus Christ, *652*

APOSTLES (55) [APOSTLE]
Mt 10: 2 Now the names of the twelve a are these; *652*
Mk 6:30 And the a gathered themselves together unto *652*
Lk 6:13 he chose twelve, whom also he named a; *652*
9:10 And the a, when they were returned, *652*
11:49 I will send them prophets and a, and *some* of *652*
17: 5 And the a said unto the Lord, Increase our *652*
22:14 he sat down, and the twelve a with him. *652*
24:10 which told these *things* unto the a. *652*
Ac 1: 2 unto the A whom he had chosen: *652*
1:26 and he was numbered with the eleven a. *652*
2:37 and said unto Peter and *to* the rest of the a, *652*
2:43 many wonders and signs were done by the a. *652*
4:33 And with great power gave the a witness of *652*
4:36 who by the a was surnamed Barnabas, *652*
5:12 And by the hands of the a were many signs *652*
5:18 And laid their hands on the a, and put them *652*
5:29 and the *other* a answered and said, *652*
5:34 commanded to put the a forth a little space; *652*
5:40 and when they had called the a, and *652*
6: 6 Whom they set before the a: and when they *652*
8: 1 regions of Judea and Samaria, except the a. *652*
8:14 Now when the a which were at Jerusalem *652*
9:27 and brought *him* to the a, and declared unto *652*
11: 1 And the a and brethren that were in Judea *652*
14: 4 part held with the Jews, and part with the a. *652*
14:14 *Which* when the a, Barnabas and Paul, *652*
15: 2 should go up to Jerusalem unto the a and *652*
15: 4 and *of* the a and elders, and they declared all *652*
15: 6 And the a and elders came together for to *652*
15:22 Then pleased it the a and elders, with *652*
15:23 The a and elders and brethren *send* greeting *652*
15:33 let go in peace from the brethren unto the a. *652*
16: 4 that were ordained of the a and elders which *652*
Ro 16: 7 who are of note among the a, *652*
1Co 4: 9 For I think that God hath set forth us the a *652*
9: 5 as well as other a, and *as* the brethren of *652*
12:28 first a, secondarily prophets, *652*
12:29 *Are* all a? *are* all prophets? *are* all teachers? *652*
15: 7 he was seen of James; then of all the a. *652*
15: 9 For I am the least of the a, that am not meet *652*
2Co 11: 5 *I* was not a whit behind the very chiefest a. *652*
11:13 For such *are* **false a**, deceitful workers, *5570*
11:13 transforming themselves into the a of Christ. *652*
12:11 *in* nothing am I behind the very chiefest a, *652*
Gal 1:17 Jerusalem to them which were a before me; *652*
1:19 But other of the a saw I none, save James *652*
Eph 2:20 And are built upon the foundation of the a *652*
3: 5 as it is now revealed unto his holy a and *652*
4:11 And he gave some, a; and some, prophets; *652*
1Th 2: 6 have been burdensome, as *the* a of Christ. *652*
2Pe 3: 2 of the commandment of us the a of the Lord *652*
Jude 1:17 before of the a of our Lord Jesus Christ; *652*
Rev 2: 2 thou hast tried them which say *they* are a, *652*
18:20 *thou* heaven, and ye holy a and prophets; *652*
21:14 in them the names of the twelve a of *652*

APOSTLES' (5) [APOSTLE]
Ac 2:42 And they continued stedfastly in the a *652*
4:35 And laid *them down* at the a feet: and *652*
4:37 brought the money, and laid *it* at the a feet. *652*
5: 2 a certain part, and laid *it* at the a feet. *652*
8:18 on of the a hands the Holy Ghost was given, *652*

APOSTLESHIP (4) [APOSTLE]
Ac 1:25 That *he* may take part of this ministry and a, *651*
Ro 1: 5 By whom we have received grace and a, *651*
1Co 9: 2 for the seal of mine a are ye in the Lord. *651*
Gal 2: 8 in Peter to the a of the circumcision, *651*

APOTHECARIES (1) [APOTHECARY]
Ne 3: 8 repaired Hananiah the son of *one of* the a, 7546

APOTHECARIES' (1) [APOTHECARY]
2Ch 16:14 divers kinds *of spices* prepared by the a art: 4842

APOTHECARY (4) [APOTHECARIES, APOTHECARIES']
Ex 30:25 ointment compound *after* the art of the a: 7543
30:35 a confection *after* the art of the a, 7543
37:29 *according to* the work of the a. 7543
Ecc 10: 1 Dead flies cause the ointment of the a to 7543

APPAIM (2)
1Ch 2:30 the sons of Nadab; Seled, and A: but 649
2:31 the sons of A; Ishi. And the sons of Ishi; 649

APPAREL (28) [APPARELLED]
Jdg 17:10 by the year, and a suit of a, and thy victuals. 899
1Sa 27: 9 and the a, and returned, and came to Achish. 899
2Sa 1:24 who put on ornaments of gold upon your a. 3830
12:20 anointed *himself,* and changed his a, and 8071
14: 2 put on now mourning a, and anoint not 899
1Ki 10: 5 their a, and his cupbearers, and his ascent 4403
2Ch 9: 4 the attendance of his ministers, and their a; 4403
9: 4 his cupbearers also, and their a; and 4403
Ezr 3:10 they set the priests in their a with trumpets, 3847
Est 5: 1 that Esther put on *her* royal *a,* and stood in NIH
6: 8 Let the royal a be brought which the king 3830
6: 9 let *this* a and horse be delivered to the hand 3830
6:10 Make haste, *and* take the a and the horse, 3830
6:11 took Haman the a and the horse, and 3830
8:15 the presence of the king in royal a *of* blue 3830
Isa 3:22 The **changeable suits of** a, and 4254
4: 1 eat our own bread, and wear our own a: 8071
63: 1 this *that is* glorious in his a, travelling in 3830
63: 2 Wherefore *art thou* red in thine a, and 3830
Eze 27:24 and broidered work, and in chests of **rich** a, 1264
Zep 1: 8 and all such as are clothed with strange a. 4403
Zec 14:14 gold, and silver, and a, in great abundance. 899
Ac 1:10 two men stood by them in white a; *2066*
12:21 arrayed in royal a, sat upon his throne, and *2066*
20:33 have coveted no *man's* silver, or gold, or a. *2441*
1Ti 2: 9 that women adorn themselves in modest a, *2689*
Jas 2: 2 in goodly a, and there come in also a poor *2066*
1Pe 3: 3 of wearing of gold, or of putting on of a; *2440*

APPARELLED (2) [APPAREL]
2Sa 13:18 the king's daughters *that were* virgins a. 3847
Lk 7:25 they which are gorgeously a, and *2441*

APPARENTLY (1)
Nu 12: 8 to mouth, even a, and not in dark speeches; 4758

APPEAL (2) [APPEALED]
Ac 25:11 may deliver me unto them. I **a unto** Cesar. *1941*
28:19 *it,* I was constrained to **a unto** Cesar; *1941*

APPEALED (4) [APPEAL]
Ac 25:12 answered, Hast thou **a unto** Cesar? *1941*
25:21 But when Paul had a to be reserved unto *1941*

Ac 25:25 and *that* he himself hath **a to** Augustus, *1941*
26:32 set at liberty, if he had not **a unto** Cesar. *1941*

APPEAR (54) [APPEARANCE, APPEARANCES, APPEARED, APPEARETH, APPEARING]

Ge 1: 9 unto one place, and let the dry *land* **a**: 7200
30:37 **made** the white **a** which *was* in the rods. 4286
Ex 23:15 and none shall **a** before me empty: 7200
23:17 Three times in the year all thy males shall **a** 7200
34:20 and none shall **a** before me empty. 7200
34:23 men children **a** before the Lord GOD, 7200
34:24 when thou shalt go up to **a** before 7200
Lev 9: 4 for to day the LORD will **a** unto you. 7200
9: 6 the glory of the LORD shall **a** unto you. 7200
13:57 if it **a** still in the garment, either in 7200
16: 2 for I will **a** in the cloud upon the mercy 7200
Dt 16:16 Three times in a year shall all thy males **a** 7200
16:16 they shall not **a** before the LORD empty: 7200
31:11 When all Israel is come to **a** before 7200
Jdg 13:21 the angel of the LORD did no more **a** to 7200
1Sa 1:22 that he may **a** before the LORD, and 7200
2:27 Did I **plainly a** unto the house of thy 1540+1540
2Ch 1: 7 In that night did God **a** unto Solomon, and 7200
Ps 42: 2 when shall I come and **a** before God? 7200
90:16 Let thy work **a** unto thy servants, and 7200
102:16 shall build up Zion, he shall **a** in his glory. 7200
SS 2:12 The flowers **a** on the earth; the time of 7200
4: 1 a flock of goats, that **a** from mount Gilead. 1570
6: 5 thy hair *is* as a flock of goats that **a** from 1570
7:12 *whether* the tender grape **a**, *and* 6605
Isa 1:12 When ye come to **a** before me, who hath 7200
66: 5 he *shall* **a** to your joy, and they shall be 7200
Jer 13:26 skirts upon thy face, that thy shame may **a**. 7200
Eze 21:24 so that in all your doings your sins do **a**; 7200
Mt 6:16 that they may **a** unto men to fast. *5316*
6:18 That thou **a** not unto men to fast, but *5316*
23:27 which indeed **a** beautiful outward, but *5316*
23:28 so ye also outwardly **a** righteous unto men, *5316*
24:30 shall **a** the sign of the Son of man in *5316*
Lk 11:44 for ye are as graves which **a not**, and the men *82*
19:11 the kingdom of God should immediately **a**. *398*
Ac 22:30 the chief priests and all their council to **a**, *2064*
26:16 *of those things* in the which I will **a** unto *3700*
Ro 7:13 But sin, that it might **a** sin, working death *5316*
2Co 5:10 For we must all **a** before the judgment seat *5319*
7:12 you in the sight of God might **a** unto you. *5319*
13: 7 not that we should **a** approved, but that ye *5316*
Col 3: 4 shall **a**, then shall ye also appear with him *5319*
3: 4 then shall ye also **a** with him in glory. *5319*
1Ti 4:15 to them; that thy profiting may **a** to all. *5318*
Heb 9:24 now to **a** in the presence of God for us: *1718*
9:28 unto them that look for him shall he **a** *3700*
11: 3 seen were not made of *things* which do **a**. *5316*
1Pe 4:18 where shall the ungodly and the sinner **a**? *5316*
5: 4 And when the chief Shepherd shall **a**, *5319*
1Jn 2:28 that, when he shall **a**, we may have *5319*
3: 2 and it doth not yet **a** what we shall be: *5319*
3: 2 but we know that, when he shall **a**, we shall *5319*
Rev 3:18 *that* the shame of thy nakedness do not **a**; *5319*

APPEARANCE (38) [APPEAR]

Nu 9:15 upon the tabernacle as it were the **a** of fire, 4758
9:16 it *by day*, and the **a** of fire by night. 4758
1Sa 16: 7 for man looketh on the **outward a**, but 5869
Eze 1: 5 this *was* their **a**; they had the likeness of a 4758
1:13 their **a** *was* like burning coals of fire, *and* 4758
1:13 coals of fire, *and* like the **a** of lamps: 4758
1:14 and returned as the **a** of a flash of lightning. 4758
1:16 The **a** of the wheels and their work *was* like 4758
1:16 their **a** and their work *was* as it were a 4758
1:26 of a throne, as the **a** of a sapphire stone: 4758
1:26 likeness as the **a** of a man above upon it. 4758
1:27 as the **a** of fire round about within it, 4758
1:27 from the **a** of his loins even upward, 4758
1:27 from the **a** of his loins even downward, 4758
1:27 I saw as it were the **a** of fire, and it had 4758
1:28 As the **a** of the bow that is in the cloud in 4758
1:28 so *was* the **a** of the brightness round about. 4758
1:28 This *was* the **a** of the likeness of the glory 4758
8: 2 I beheld, and lo, a likeness as the **a** of fire: 4758
8: 2 from the **a** of his loins even downward, 4758
8: 2 as the **a** of brightness, as the colour of 4758
10: 1 as the **a** of the likeness of a throne. 4758
10: 9 the **a** of the wheels *was* as the colour of a 4758
40: 3 whose **a** *was* like the appearance of brass, 4758
40: 3 whose appearance *was* like the **a** of brass, 4758
41:21 the **a** *of the one* as the appearance *of* 4758
41:21 the appearance *of the one* as the **a** *of* 4758
42:11 the way before them *was* like the **a** of 4758
43: 3 *it was* according to the **a** of the vision 4758
Da 8:15 there stood before me as the **a** of a man. 4758
10: 6 his face as the **a** of lightning, and his eyes 4758
10:18 and touched me *one* like the **a** of a man, 4758
Joel 2: 4 The **a** of them *is* as the appearance of 4758
2: 4 The appearance of them *is* as the **a** of 4758
Jn 7:24 Judge not according to the **a**, but *3799*
2Co 5:12 *somewhat* to *answer* them which glory in **a**, *4383*
10: 7 Do ye look on *things* after the **outward a**? *4383*
1Th 5:22 Abstain from all **a** of evil. *1491*

APPEARANCES (2) [APPEAR]

Eze 10:10 *as for* their **a**, they four had one likeness, 4758
10:22 the river of Chebar, their **a** and themselves: 4758

APPEARED (70) [APPEAR]

Ge 12: 7 the LORD **a** unto Abram, and said, 7200
12: 7 an altar unto the LORD, who **a** unto him. 7200
17: 1 the LORD **a** to Abram, and said unto him, 7200
18: 1 the LORD **a** unto him in the plains of 7200
26: 2 the LORD **a** unto him, and said, Go not 7200
26:24 And the LORD **a** unto him the same night, 7200
35: 1 that **a** unto thee when thou fleddest from 7200
35: 7 because there God **a** unto him, when he 1540
35: 9 God **a** unto Jacob again, when he came out 7200
48: 3 God Almighty **a** unto me at Luz in the land 7200
Ex 3: 2 the angel of the LORD **a** unto him in a 7200
3:16 of Isaac, and of Jacob, **a** unto me, saying, 7200
4: 1 will say, The LORD hath not **a** unto thee. 7200
4: 5 and the God of Jacob, hath **a** unto thee. 7200
6: 3 I **a** unto Abraham, unto Isaac, and 7200
14:27 his strength **when** the morning **a**; 6437+3807.1
16:10 the glory of the LORD **a** in the cloud. 7200
Lev 9:23 the glory of the LORD **a** unto all 7200
Nu 14:10 the glory of the LORD **a** in the tabernacle 7200
16:19 the glory of the LORD **a** unto all 7200
16:42 covered it, and the glory of the LORD **a**. 7200
20: 6 and the glory of the LORD **a** unto them. 7200
Dt 31:15 the LORD **a** in the tabernacle in a pillar of 7200
Jdg 6:12 the angel of the LORD **a** unto him, and 7200
13: 3 the angel of the LORD **a** unto the woman, 7200
13:10 unto him, Behold, the man hath **a** unto me, 7200
1Sa 3:21 the LORD **a** again in Shiloh: for 7200
2Sa 22:16 the channels of the sea **a**, the foundations of 7200
1Ki 3: 5 In Gibeon the LORD **a** to Solomon in a 7200
9: 2 That the LORD **a** to Solomon the second 7200
9: 2 as he had **a** unto him at Gibeon. 7200
11: 9 God of Israel, which had **a** unto him twice, 7200
2Ki 2:11 *there* **a** a chariot of fire, and horses of fire, NIH
2Ch 3: 1 where *the LORD* **a** unto David his father, 7200
7:12 the LORD **a** to Solomon by night, and 7200
Ne 4:21 the rising of the morning till the stars **a**. 3318
Jer 31: 3 The LORD hath **a** of old unto me, 7200
Eze 10: 1 **a** over them as it were a sapphire stone, 7200
10: 8 there **a** in the cherubims the form of a 7200
19:11 she **a** in her height with the multitude of her 7200
Da 1:15 at the end of ten days their countenances **a** 7200
8: 1 of king Belshazzar a vision **a** unto me, 7200
8: 1 after that which **a** unto me at the first. 7200
Mt 1:20 *the* angel of the Lord **a** unto him in a *5316*
2: 7 of them diligently what time the star **a**. *5316*
13:26 brought forth fruit, then **a** the tares also. *5316*
17: 3 there **a** unto them Moses and Elias talking *3700*
27:53 went into the holy city, and **a** unto many. *1718*
Mk 9: 4 And there **a** unto them Elias with Moses: *3700*
16: 9 he **a** first to Mary Magdalene, out of whom *5316*
16:12 After that he **a** in another form unto two of *5319*
16:14 Afterward he **a** unto the eleven as they sat *5319*
Lk 1:11 And there **a** unto him an angel of the Lord *3700*
9: 8 And of some, that Elias had **a**; and *5316*
9:31 Who **a** in glory, and spake of his decease *3700*
22:43 And there **a** an angel unto him from *3700*
24:34 Lord is risen indeed, and hath **a** to Simon. *3700*
Ac 2: 3 And there **a** unto them cloven tongues like *3700*
7: 2 The God of glory **a** unto our father *3700*
7:30 there **a** to him in the wilderness of mount *3700*
7:35 a deliverer by the hand of the angel which **a** *3700*
9:17 that **a** unto thee in the way as thou camest, *3700*
16: 9 And a vision **a** to Paul in the night; *3700*

Ac 26:16 for I have a unto thee for this *purpose,* to 3700
27:20 when neither sun nor stars in many days a, 2014
Tit 2:11 that bringeth salvation hath a to all men, 2014
3: 4 and love of God our Saviour toward man a, 2014
Heb 9:26 now once in the end of the world hath he a 5319
Rev 12: 1 And there a a great wonder in heaven; 3700
12: 3 And there a another wonder in heaven; and 3700

APPEARETH (10) [APPEAR]
Lev 13:14 when raw flesh a in him, he shall be 7200
13:43 as the leprosy a in the skin of the flesh; 4758
Dt 2:30 deliver him into thy hand, as *a* this day. NIH
Ps 84: 7 *every one of them* in Zion a before God. 7200
Pr 27:25 The hay a, and the tender grass sheweth 1540
Jer 6: 1 for evil a out of the north, and 8259
Mal 3: 2 who *shall* stand when he a? for he *is* like a 7200
Mt 2:13 *the* angel of the Lord a to Joseph in a 5316
2:19 an angel of the Lord a in a dream to Joseph 5316
Jas 4:14 that a for a little *time,* and then 5316

APPEARING (6) [APPEAR]
1Ti 6:14 until the a of our Lord Jesus Christ: 2015
2Ti 1:10 But is now made manifest by the a of our 2015
4: 1 and the dead at his a and his kingdom; 2015
4: 8 but unto all them also that love his a. 2015
Tit 2:13 and the glorious a of the great God and 2015
1Pe 1: 7 honour and glory at the a of Jesus Christ: 602

APPEASE (1) [APPEASED, APPEASETH]
Ge 32:20 I will a him with the present that 3722+6440

APPEASED (2) [APPEASE]
Est 2: 1 when the wrath of king Ahasuerus was a, 7918
Ac 19:35 And when the townclerk had a the people, 2687

APPEASETH (1) [APPEASE]
Pr 15:18 but *he that is* slow to anger a strife. 8252

APPERTAIN (2) [APPERTAINED, APPERTAINETH]
Nu 16:30 with all that *a* unto them, and they go down NIH
Jer 10: 7 for to thee doth it a: forasmuch as among 2969

APPERTAINED (3) [APPERTAIN]
Nu 16:32 all the men that *a* unto Korah, and all *their* NIH
16:33 They, and all that *a* to them, went down NIH
Ne 2: 8 the gates of the palace which *a* to the house, NIH

APPERTAINETH (1) [APPERTAIN]
Lev 6: 5 *and* give it unto him to whom it a, in NIH

APPETITE (4)
Job 38:39 for the lion? or fill the a of the young lions, 2416
Pr 23: 2 to thy throat, if thou *be* a man **given to a**. 5315
Ecc 6: 7 *is* for his mouth, and yet the a is not filled. 5315
Isa 29: 8 and behold, *he is* faint, and his soul hath a: 8264

APPHIA (1)
Phm 1: 2 And to *our* beloved A, 682

APPII (1)
Ac 28:15 they came to meet us as far as A forum, and 675

APPIUS See APPII

APPLE (8) [APPLES]
Dt 32:10 he kept him as the a of his eye. 380
Ps 17: 8 Keep me as the a of the eye, hide me 380+1323
Pr 7: 2 and live; and my law as the a of thine eye. 380
SS 2: 3 As the **a tree** among the trees of the wood, 8598
8: 5 I raised thee up under the **a tree**: there thy 8598
La 2:18 no rest; let not the a of thine eye cease. 1323
Joel 1:12 the palm tree also, and the **a tree**, 8598
Zec 2: 8 for he that toucheth you toucheth the a of his 892

APPLES (3) [APPLE]
Pr 25:11 A word fitly spoken *is like* a of gold in 8598
SS 2: 5 Stay me with flagons, comfort me with a: 8598
7: 8 of the vine, and the smell of thy nose like a; 8598

APPLIED (3) [APPLY]
Ecc 7:25 I a mine heart to know, and to search, and 5437
8: 9 a my heart unto every work that is done 5414
8:16 When I a mine heart to know wisdom, and 5414

APPLY (4) [APPLIED]
Ps 90:12 that we may a *our* hearts *unto* wisdom. 935
Pr 2: 2 *and* a thine heart to understanding; 5186
22:17 and a thine heart unto my knowledge. 7896
23:12 A thine heart unto instruction, and thine ears 935

APPOINT (41) [APPOINTED, APPOINTETH, APPOINTMENT]
Ge 30:28 he said, A me thy wages, and I will give *it.* 5344
41:34 do *this,* and let him a officers over the land, 6485
Ex 21:13 I will a thee a place whither he shall flee. 7760
30:16 shalt a it for the service of the tabernacle of 5414
Lev 26:16 I will even a over you terror, consumption, 6485
Nu 1:50 thou shalt a the Levites over the tabernacle 6485
3:10 thou shalt a Aaron and his sons, and 6485
4:19 a them every one to his service and to his 7760
4:27 ye shall a unto them in charge all their 6485
35: 6 which ye shall a for the manslayer, that he 5414
35:11 ye shall a you cities to be cities of refuge 7136
Jos 20: 2 **A out** for you cities of refuge, 5414
1Sa 8:11 and a *them* for himself, for his chariots, and 7760
8:12 he will a him captains over thousands, and 7760
2Sa 6:21 to a me ruler over the people of 6680
7:10 Moreover I will a a place for my people 7760
15:15 *to do* whatsoever my lord the king shall a. 977
1Ki 5: 6 servants according to all that thou shalt a: 559
5: 9 *in* flotes unto the place that thou shalt a me, 7971
1Ch 15:16 David spake to the chief of the Levites to a 5975
Ne 7: 3 a watches of the inhabitants of Jerusalem, 5975
Est 2: 3 let the king a officers in all the provinces of 6485
Job 14:13 that thou wouldest a me a set time, and 7896
Isa 26: 1 salvation will *God* a *for* walls and 7896
61: 3 To a unto them that mourn in Zion, to give 7760
Jer 15: 3 I will a over them four kinds, saith 6485
49:19 who *is* a chosen *man, that* I may a over 6485
49:19 who will a me **the time**? and who *is* that 3259
50:44 who *is* a chosen *man, that* I may a over 6485
50:44 who will a me **the time**? and who *is* that 3259
51:27 and Ashchenaz; a a captain against her; 6485
Eze 21:19 Also, thou son of man, a thee two ways, 7760
21:20 A a way, that the sword may come to 7760
21:22 to a captains, to open the mouth in 7760
21:22 to a *battering* rams against the gates, to cast 7760
45: 6 ye shall a the possession of the city five 5414
Hos 1:11 a themselves one head, and they shall come 7760
Mt 24:51 and a *him* his portion with the hypocrites: 5087
Lk 12:46 will a *him* his portion with the unbelievers. 5087
22:29 And I a unto you a kingdom, as my Father 1303
Ac 6: 3 whom we may a over this business. 2525

APPOINTED (126) [APPOINT]
Ge 4:25 *said she,* hath a me another seed instead of 7896
18:14 At the **time a** I will return unto thee, 4150
24:14 *let the same be* she *that* thou hast a for thy 3198
24:44 the LORD hath **a out** for my master's son. 3198
Ex 9: 5 the LORD a a set time, saying, 7760
23:15 in the **time a** of the month Abib; 4150
Nu 9: 2 also keep the passover at his **a season**. 4150
9: 3 at even, ye shall keep it in his **a season**: 4150
9: 7 his **a season** among the children of Israel? 4150
9:13 the offering of the LORD in his **a season**, 4150
Jos 8:14 he and all his people, at a **time a**, before 4150
20: 7 they a Kedesh in Galilee in mount 6942
20: 9 These were the cities a for all the children 4152
Jdg 18:11 six hundred men a *with* weapons of war. 2296
18:16 the six hundred men a *with* their weapons 2296
18:17 men that were a *with* weapons of war. 2296
20:38 Now there was an **a sign** between the men 4150
1Sa 13: 8 according to the set time that Samuel *had a*: NIH
13:11 *that* thou camest not within the days a, and 4150
19:20 Samuel standing *as* a over them, the spirit 5324
20:35 out *into* the field at the **time a** with David, 4150
21: 2 I have a *my* servants to such and such a 3045
25:30 and shall have a thee ruler over Israel; 6680
29: 4 which thou hast a him, and let him not go 6485
2Sa 17:14 For the LORD had a to defeat the good 6680
20: 5 than the set time which he had a him. 3259
24:15 Israel from the morning even to the time a: 4150
1Ki 1:35 I have a him to be ruler over Israel and 6680
11:18 and a him victuals, and gave him land. 559
12:12 as the king had a, saying, Come to me 1696
20:42 hand a man whom I **a to utter destruction**, 2764
2Ki 7:17 the king a the lord on whose hand he 6485
8: 6 So the king a unto her a certain officer, 5414
10:24 Jehu a fourscore men without, and said, 7760
11:18 the priest a officers over the house of 7760
18:14 the king of Assyria a unto Hezekiah king of 7760

1Ch 6:48 Their brethren also the Levites *were* a unto 5414
6:49 *were a* for all the work of the *place* most NIH
9:29 *Some* of them also *were* a to oversee 4487
15:17 So the Levites a Heman the son of Joel; 5975
15:19 *were a* to sound with cymbals of brass; NIH
16: 4 he a *certain* of the Levites to minister 5414
2Ch 8:14 he a, according to the order of David his 5975
20:21 he a singers unto the LORD, and 5975
23:18 Also Jehoiada a the offices of the house of 7760
31: 2 Hezekiah a the courses of the priests and 5975
31: 3 *He a* also the king's portion of his substance NIH
33: 8 of the land which I have a for your fathers; 5975
34:22 *they* that the king *had a,* went to Huldah NIH
Ezr 3: 8 a the Levites from twenty years old and 5975
8:20 the princes had a for the service of 5414
10:14 strange wives in our cities come at a times, 2163
Ne 5:14 Moreover from the time that I was a to be 6680
6: 7 thou hast also a prophets to preach of thee 5975
7: 1 and the singers and the Levites were a, 6485
9:17 in their rebellion a a captain to return to 5414
10:34 of our fathers, at times a year by year, 2163
12:31 a two great *companies of them that gave* 5975
12:44 at that time were some a over the chambers 6485
13:30 a the wards of the priests and the Levites, 5975
13:31 at times a, and for the firstfruits. 2163
Est 1: 8 the king had a to all the officers of his 3245
2:15 the keeper of the women, a. 559
4: 5 whom he had a to attend upon her, and 5975
9:27 and according to their *a* time every year; NIH
9:31 times *a,* according as Mordecai the Jew NIH
Job 7: 1 *Is there* not an **a time** to man upon earth? 6635
7: 3 and wearisome nights are a to me. 4487
14: 5 thou hast a his bounds that he cannot pass; 6213
14:14 *again?* all the days of my **a time** I will wait, 6635
20:29 and the heritage **a unto** him by God. 561
23:14 For he performeth the **thing that is a** for 2706
30:23 *to* death, and *to* the house a for all living. 4150
Ps 44:11 Thou hast given us like sheep a for meat; NIH
78: 5 a a law in Israel, which he commanded our 7760
79:11 preserve thou those that are **a to die;** 1121+8546
81: 3 in the **time a,** on our solemn feast day. 3677
102:20 to loose those that are **a to death;** 1121+8546
104:19 He a the moon for seasons: the sun 6213
Pr 7:20 with him, *and* will come home at the day a. 3677
8:29 when he a the foundations of the earth: 2710
31: 8 of all such as are **a to destruction.** 1121+2475
Isa 1:14 and your a **feasts** my soul hateth: 4150
14:31 and none *shall be* alone in his **a times.** 4151
28:25 and the a barley and the rye *in* their place? 5567
44: 7 order for me, since I a the ancient people? 7760
Jer 5:24 he reserveth unto us the a weeks of 2708
8: 7 stork in the heaven knoweth her **a times;** 4150
33:25 *if* I have not a the ordinances of heaven and 7760
46:17 *but* a noise; he hath passed the **time a.** 4150
47: 7 against the sea shore? there hath he **a it.** 3259
Eze 4: 6 I have a thee each day for a year. 5414
36: 5 which have a my land into their possession 5414
43:21 he shall burn it in the a **place** of the house, 4662
Da 1: 5 the king a them a daily provision of 4487
1:10 who hath a your meat and your drink: 4487
8:19 for at the **time a** the end *shall be.* 4150
10: 1 the thing *was* true, but the **time a** *was* long: 6635
11:27 for yet the end *shall be* at the **time a.** 4150
11:29 At the **time a** he shall return, and 4150
11:35 of the end: because *it is* yet for a **time a.** 4150
Mic 6: 9 hear ye the rod, and who hath **a it.** 3259
Hab 2: 3 For the vision *is* yet for an a **time,** but 4150
Mt 26:19 And the disciples did as Jesus had a them; *4929*
27:10 for the potter's field, as the Lord a me. *4929*
28:16 into a mountain where Jesus had a them. *5021*
Lk 3:13 Exact no more than that which is a you. *1299*
10: 1 After these *things* the Lord a other seventy *322*
22:29 a kingdom, as my Father hath a unto me; *1303*
Ac 1:23 And they a two, Joseph called Barsabas, *2476*
7:44 as he had a, speaking unto Moses, *1299*
17:26 and hath determined the times **before a,** *4384*
17:31 Because he hath a a day, in the which he *2476*
20:13 for so had he a, minding himself to go *1299*
22:10 thee of all *things* which are a for thee to do. *5021*
28:23 And when they had a him a day, *5021*
1Co 4: 9 us the apostles last, as *it were* **a to death:** *1935*
Gal 4: 2 and governors until the **time a** of the father. *4287*
1Th 3: 3 for yourselves know that we are a *2749*
5: 9 For God hath not a us to wrath, but *5087*
2Ti 1:11 Whereunto I am a a preacher, and *5087*
Tit 1: 5 ordain elders in every city, as I had a thee: *1299*
Heb 1: 2 whom he hath a heir of all *things,* by whom *5087*
3: 2 Who was faithful to him that a him, as also *4160*
9:27 And as it is a unto men once to die, but *606*
1Pe 2: 8 whereunto also they were a. *5087*

APPOINTETH (1) [APPOINT]
Da 5:21 and *that* he a over it whomsoever he will. 6966

APPOINTMENT (4) [APPOINT]
Nu 4:27 At the a of Aaron and his sons shall be all 6310
2Sa 13:32 for by the a of Absalom *this* hath been 6310
Ezr 6: 9 according to the a of the priests which *are* 3983
Job 2:11 for they had **made an a** together to come to 3259

APPREHEND (2) [APPREHENDED]
2Co 11:32 *with a garrison,* desirous to a me: *4084*
Php 3:12 I follow *after,* if that I may a *that* for which *2638*

APPREHENDED (3) [APPREHEND]
Ac 12: 4 And when he had a him, he put *him* in *4084*
Php 3:12 *that* for which also I am a of Christ Jesus. *2638*
3:13 Brethren, I count not myself to have a: but *2638*

APPROACH (19) [APPROACHED, APPROACHETH, APPROACHING]
Lev 18: 6 None of you shall a to any that is near of 7126
18:14 thou shalt not a to his wife: 7126
18:19 Also thou shalt not a unto a woman to 7126
20:16 if a woman a unto any beast, and lie down 7126
21:17 let him not a to offer the bread of his God. 7126
21:18 *he be* that hath a blemish, he shall not a: 7126
Nu 4:19 when they a unto the most holy *things:* 5066
Dt 20: 2 that the priest shall a and speak unto 5066
20: 3 you a *this* day unto battle against your 7131
31:14 Behold, thy days a that *thou* must die: 7126
Jos 8: 5 that *are* with me, will a unto the city: 7126
Job 40:19 he that made him can **make** his sword **to a** 5066
Ps 65: 4 **causest to a** *unto thee, that* he may dwell *in* 7126
Jer 30:21 him to draw near, and he shall a unto me: 5066
30:21 for who *is* this that engaged his heart to a 5066
Eze 42:13 where the priests that a unto the LORD 7138
42:14 shall a to *those things* which *are* for 7126
43:19 which a unto me, to minister unto me, 7138
1Ti 6:16 in the light **which no** *man* **can a unto;** *676*

APPROACHED (2) [APPROACH]
2Sa 11:20 Wherefore a ye *so* **nigh** unto the city when 5066
2Ki 16:12 the king a to the altar, and offered thereon. 7126

APPROACHETH (1) [APPROACH]
Lk 12:33 where no thief a, neither moth corrupteth. *1448*

APPROACHING (2) [APPROACH]
Isa 58: 2 of justice; they take delight in **a to** God. 7132
Heb 10:25 and so much the more, as ye see the day a. *1448*

APPROVE (3) [APPROVED, APPROVEST, APPROVETH, APPROVING]
Ps 49:13 yet their posterity a their sayings. Selah. 7521
1Co 16: 3 whomsoever you shall a by *your* letters, *1381*
Php 1:10 That ye may a *things* that are excellent; *1381*

APPROVED (8) [APPROVE]
Ac 2:22 a man a of God among you by miracles and *584*
Ro 14:18 Christ *is* acceptable to God, and a of men. *1384*
16:10 Salute Apelles a in Christ. Salute them *1384*
1Co 11:19 that they *which are* a may be made *1384*
2Co 7:11 In all *things* ye have a yourselves to be *4921*
10:18 For not he that commendeth himself is a, *1384*
13: 7 not that we should appear a, but that ye *1384*
2Ti 2:15 Study to shew thyself a unto God, *1384*

APPROVEST (1) [APPROVE]
Ro 2:18 and a the *things* that are more excellent, *1381*

APPROVETH (1) [APPROVE]
La 3:36 subvert a man in his cause, the Lord a not. 7200

APPROVING (1) [APPROVE]
2Co 6: 4 But in all *things* a ourselves as *4921*

APRONS (2)
Ge 3: 7 fig leaves together, and made themselves a. 2290
Ac 19:12 brought unto the sick handkerchiefs or a, *4612*

APT (4)
2Ki 24:16 all *that were* strong *and* **a** for war, 6213
1Ch 7:40 genealogy of them *that were a* to the war NIH
1Ti 3: 2 given to hospitality, **a to teach**; *1317*
2Ti 2:24 but be gentle unto all *men*, **a to teach**, *1317*

AQUEDUCT See CONDUIT

AQUILA (6)
Ac 18: 2 And found a certain Jew named **A**, born in *207*
18:18 into Syria, and with him Priscilla and **A**: *207*
18:26 whom when **A** and Priscilla had heard, *207*
Ro 16: 3 and **A** my helpers in Christ Jesus: *207*
1Co 16:19 **A** and Priscilla salute you much in the Lord, *207*
2Ti 4:19 Salute Prisca and **A**, and the household of *207*

AR (6)
Nu 21:15 that goeth down to the dwelling of **A**, 6144
21:28 it hath consumed **A** of Moab, *and* the lords 6144
Dt 2: 9 I have given **A** unto the children of Lot *for* 6144
2:18 Thou art to pass over *through* **A**, the coast 6144
2:29 the Moabites which dwell in **A**, did unto 6144
Isa 15: 1 Because in the night **A** of Moab is laid 6144

ARA (1)
1Ch 7:38 of Jether; Jephunneh, and Pispah, and **A**. 690

ARAB (1) [ARABIA, ARABIAN, ARABIANS]
Jos 15:52 **A**, and Dumah, and Eshean, 694

ARABAH (2) [BETH-ARABAH]
Jos 18:18 passed along toward the side over against **A** 6160
18:18 Arabah northward, and went down unto **A**: 6160

ARABIA (8) [ARAB]
1Ki 10:15 *of* all the kings of **A**, and *of* the governors 6153
2Ch 9:14 all the kings of **A** and governors of 6152
Isa 21:13 The burden upon **A**. In the forest in Arabia 6152
21:13 In the forest in **A** shall ye lodge, O ye 6152
Jer 25:24 all the kings of **A**, and all the kings of 6152
Eze 27:21 **A**, and all the princes of Kedar, 6152
Gal 1:17 but I went into **A**, and returned again unto *688*
4:25 For *this* Agar is mount Sinai in **A**, and *688*

ARABIAN (4) [ARAB]
Ne 2:19 the Ammonite, and Geshem the **A**, 6163
6: 1 Geshem the **A**, and the rest of our enemies, 6163
Isa 13:20 neither shall the **A** pitch tent there; 6163
Jer 3: 2 sat for them, as the **A** in the wilderness; 6163

ARABIANS (6) [ARAB]
2Ch 17:11 the **A** brought him flocks, seven thousand 6163
21:16 and of the **A**, that *were* near the Ethiopians: 6163
22: 1 for the band *of men* that came with the **A** to 6163
26: 7 against the **A** that dwelt in Gur-baal, and 6163
Ne 4: 7 the **A**, and the Ammonites, and 6163
Ac 2:11 Cretes and **A**, we do hear them speak in our *690*

ARAD (5)
Nu 21: 1 *when* king **A** the Canaanite, which dwelt *in* 6166
33:40 king **A** the Canaanite, which dwelt in 6166
Jos 12:14 king of Hormah, one; the king of **A**, one; 6166
Jdg 1:16 of Judah, which *lieth* in the south of **A**; 6166
1Ch 8:15 And Zebadiah, and **A**, and Ader, 6166

ARAH (4)
1Ch 7:39 the sons of Ulla; **A**, and Haniel, and Rezia. 733
Ezr 2: 5 The children of **A**, seven hundred seventy 733
Ne 6:18 the son in law of Shechaniah the son of **A**; 733
7:10 The children of **A**, six hundred fifty and two. 733

ARAM (10) [ARAM-NAHARAIM, ARAM-ZOBAH, ARAMITESS, BETH-ARAM, PADAN-ARAM]
Ge 10:22 and Asshur, and Arphaxad, and Lud, and **A**. 758
10:23 the children of **A**; Uz, and Hul, and Gether, 758
22:21 Buz his brother, and Kemuel the father of **A**, 758
Nu 23: 7 the king of Moab hath brought me from **A**, 758
1Ch 1:17 **A**, and Uz, and Hul, and Gether, and 758
2:23 he took Geshur, and **A**, with the towns of 758
7:34 Ahi, and Rohgah, Jehubbah, and **A**. 758
Mt 1: 3 Phares begat Esrom; and Esrom begat **A**; *689*
1: 4 And **A** begat Aminadab; and *689*
Lk 3:33 which was *the son* of **A**, which was *the son* *689*

ARAM MAACAH See SYRIA-MAACHAH

ARAMAIC See SYRIACK

ARAMEAN See ARAMITESS

ARAMEANS See SYRIANS

ARAMITESS (1) [ARAM]
1Ch 7:14 his concubine the **A** bare Machir the father 761

ARAM-NAHARAIM (1) [ARAM]
Ps 60: T when he strove with **A** and 763

ARAM-ZOBAH (1) [ARAM, ZOBAH]
Ps 60: T he strove with Aram-naharaim and with **A**, 760

ARAN (2)
Ge 36:28 The children of Dishan *are* these; Uz, and **A**. 765
1Ch 1:42 *and* Jakan. The sons of Dishan; Uz, and **A**. 765

ARARAT (2)
Ge 8: 4 day of the month, upon the mountains of **A**. 780
Jer 51:27 call together against her the kingdoms of **A**, 780

ARAUNAH (9) [ORNAN]
2Sa 24:16 was by the threshingplace of **A** the Jebusite. 728
24:18 in the threshingfloor of **A** the Jebusite. 728
24:20 **A** looked, and saw the king and his servants 728
24:20 **A** went out, and bowed himself before 728
24:21 **A** said, Wherefore is my lord the king come 728
24:22 **A** said unto David, Let my lord the king take 728
24:23 All *these things* did **A**, *as* a king, give unto 728
24:23 **A** said unto the king, The LORD thy God 728
24:24 the king said unto **A**, Nay; but I will surely 728

ARBA (2) [ARBAH, KIRJATH-ARBA]
Jos 14:15 which *A was* a great man among NIH
15:13 *even* the city of **A** the father of Anak, 704

ARBAH (2) [ARBA]
Ge 35:27 unto the city of **A**, which *is* Hebron, 704
Jos 21:11 they gave them the city of **A** the father of 704

ARBATHITE (2)
2Sa 23:31 Abialbon the **A**, Azmaveth the Barhumite, 6164
1Ch 11:32 Hurai of the brooks of Gaash, Abiel the **A**, 6164

ARBITE (1)
2Sa 23:35 Hezrai the Carmelite, Paarai the **A**, 701

ARCHANGEL (2) [ANGEL]
1Th 4:16 with the voice of the **a**, and with the trump *743*
Jude 1: 9 Yet Michael the **a**, when contending with *743*

ARCHELAUS (1)
Mt 2:22 But when he heard that **A** did reign in Judea *745*

ARCHER (2) [ARCHERS]
Ge 21:20 in the wilderness, and became an **a**. 7199+7235
Jer 51: 3 Against *him that* bendeth let the **a** bend his 1869

ARCHERS (12) [ARCHER]
Ge 49:23 The **a** have sorely grieved him, and 1167+2671
Jdg 5:11 *They that are delivered* from the noise of **a** 2686
1Sa 31: 3 the **a** hit him; 376+3384+7198+871.1+1886.1
31: 3 hit him; and he was sore wounded of the **a**. 3384
1Ch 8:40 **a**, and had many sons, and 1869+7198
10: 3 the **a** hit him, and 4175+7198+871.1+1886.1
10: 3 hit him, and he was wounded of the **a**. 3384
2Ch 35:23 the **a** shot at king Josiah; and the king said 3384
Job 16:13 His **a** compass me round about, he cleaveth 7228
Isa 21:17 the residue of the number of **a**, the mighty 7198
22: 3 are fled together, they are bound by the **a**: 7198
Jer 50:29 Call together the **a** against Babylon: all ye 7228

ARCHES (15)
Eze 40:16 the gate round about, and likewise to the **a**: 361
40:21 the **a** thereof were after the measure of 361
40:22 and their **a**, and their palm trees, 361
40:22 and the **a** thereof *were* before them. 361
40:24 the **a** thereof according to these measures. 361
40:25 in it and in the **a** thereof round about, 361
40:26 up to it, and the **a** thereof *were* before them: 361
40:29 the posts thereof, and the **a** thereof, 361
40:29 in it and in the **a** thereof round about: 361
40:30 the **a** round about *were* five and 361
40:31 the **a** thereof *were* toward the utter court; 361
40:33 and the posts thereof, and the **a** thereof, 361

A

Eze 40:33 and in the **a** thereof round about: 361
40:34 the **a** thereof *were* toward the outward court; 361
40:36 the **a** thereof, and the windows to it round 361

ARCHEVITES (1)
Ezr 4: 9 the Tarpelites, the Apharsites, the **A**, 756

ARCHI (1)
Jos 16: 2 passeth along unto the borders of **A** *to* 757

ARCHIPPUS (2)
Col 4:17 And say to **A**, Take heed to the ministry *751*
Phm 1: 2 and **A** our fellowsoldier, and to the church *751*

ARCHITE (5)
2Sa 15:32 Hushai the **A** *came* to meet him with his coat 757
16:16 to pass, when Hushai the **A**, David's friend, 757
17: 5 Call now Hushai the **A** also, and let us hear 757
17:14 The counsel of Hushai the **A** *is* better than 757
1Ch 27:33 and Hushai the **A** *was* the king's companion: 757

ARCTURUS (2)
Job 9: 9 Which maketh **A**, Orion, and Pleiades, and 5906
38:32 or canst thou guide **A** with his sons? 5906

ARD (3) [ARDITES]
Ge 46:21 and Rosh, Muppim, and Huppim, and **A**. 714
Nu 26:40 the sons of Bela were **A** and Naaman: 714
26:40 *of* **A**, the family of the Ardites: *and* NIH

ARDITES (1) [ARD]
Nu 26:40 *of Ard,* the family of the **A**: *and* of Naaman, 716

ARDON (1)
1Ch 2:18 sons *are* these; Jesher, and Shobab, and **A**. 715

ARE (2946) [BE] See Index

ARELI (2) [ARELITES]
Ge 46:16 Shuni, and Ezbon, Eri, and Arodi, and **A**. 692
Nu 26:17 the Arodites: of **A**, the family of the Arelites. 692

ARELITES (1) [ARELI]
Nu 26:17 of the Arodites: of Areli, the family of the **A**. 692

AREOPAGITE (1) [AREOPAGUS]
Ac 17:34 among the which *was* Dionysius the **A**, and *698*

AREOPAGUS (1) [AREOPAGITE, MARS' HILL]
Ac 17:19 took him, and brought him unto **A**, saying, *697*

ARETAS (1)
2Co 11:32 In Damascus the governor under **A** the king *702*

ARGOB (5)
Dt 3: 4 threescore cities, all the region of **A**, 709
3:13 all the region of **A**, with all Bashan, which 709
3:14 the country of **A** unto the coasts of Geshuri 709
1Ki 4:13 to him *also pertained* the region of **A**, 709
2Ki 15:25 of the king's house, with **A** and Arieh; 709

ARGUING (1) [ARGUMENTS]
Job 6:25 right words! but what doth your **a** reprove? 3198

ARGUMENTS (1) [ARGUING]
Job 23: 4 cause before him, and fill my mouth *with* **a**. 8433

ARIDAI (1)
Est 9: 9 and Arisai, and **A**, and Vajezatha, 742

ARIDATHA (1)
Est 9: 8 And Poratha, and Adalia, and **A**, 743

ARIEH (1)
2Ki 15:25 of the king's house, with Argob and **A**; 745

ARIEL (6)
Ezr 8:16 for **A**, for Shemaiah, and for Elnathan, and 740
Isa 29: 1 Woe to **A**, to Ariel, the city *where* David 740
29: 1 Woe to Ariel, to **A**, the city *where* David 740
29: 2 Yet I will distress **A**, and there shall be 740
29: 2 and sorrow: and it shall be unto me as **A**. 740
29: 7 of all the nations that fight against **A**, 740

ARIGHT (5) [RIGHT]
Ps 50:23 to him that ordereth *his* conversation ***a*** will NIH
78: 8 a generation *that* **set** not their heart **a**, and 3559
Pr 15: 2 The tongue of the wise **useth** knowledge **a**: 3190
23:31 in the cup, *when* it moveth itself **a**. 4339+871.1
Jer 8: 6 and heard, *but* they spake not **a**: 3651

ARIMATHEA (4)
Mt 27:57 there came a rich man of **A**, named Joseph, *707*
Mk 15:43 Joseph of **A**, an honourable counseller, *707*
Lk 23:51 of them;) *he was* of **A**, a city of the Jews: *707*
Jn 19:38 And after this Joseph of **A**, being a disciple *707*

ARIOCH (7)
Ge 14: 1 **A** king of Ellasar, Chedorlaomer king of 746
14: 9 king of Shinar, and **A** king of Ellasar; 746
Da 2:14 wisdom to **A** the captain of the king's guard, 746
2:15 and said to **A** the king's captain, 746
2:15 Then **A** made the thing known to Daniel. 746
2:24 Therefore Daniel went in unto **A**, whom 746
2:25 **A** brought in Daniel before the king in haste, 746

ARISAI (1)
Est 9: 9 and **A**, and Aridai, and Vajezatha, 747

ARISE (149) [RISE]
Ge 13:17 **A**, walk through the land in the length of it 6965
19:15 saying, **A**, take thy wife, and thy two 6965
21:18 **A**, lift up the lad, and hold him in thine 6965
27:19 **a**, I pray thee, sit and eat of my venison, 6965
27:31 Let my father **a**, and eat of his son's 6965
27:43 **a**, flee thou to Laban my brother to Haran; 6965
28: 2 **A**, go to Padan-aram, to the house of 6965
31:13 now **a**, get thee out from this land, 6965
35: 1 **A**, go up to Beth-el, and dwell there: 6965
35: 3 let us **a**, and go up to Beth-el; and I will 6965
41:30 there shall **a** after them seven years of 6965
43: 8 Send the lad with me, and we will **a** and go; 6965
43:13 your brother, and **a**, go again unto the man: 6965
Dt 9:12 the LORD said unto me, **A**, get thee down 6965
10:11 the LORD said unto me, **A**, take thy 6965
13: 1 If there **a** among you a prophet, or 6965
17: 8 If there **a** a matter too hard for thee in NIH
17: 8 shalt thou **a**, and get thee up into the place 6965
Jos 1: 2 now therefore **a**, go over this Jordan, thou, 6965
8: 1 people of war with thee, and **a**, go up *to* Ai: 6965
Jdg 5:12 **a**, Barak, and lead thy captivity captive, 6965
7: 9 unto him, **A**, get thee down unto the host; 6965
7:15 returned into the host of Israel, and said, **A**; 6965
18: 9 they said, **A**, that we may go up against 6965
20:40 when the flame began to **a up** out of 5927
1Sa 9: 3 servants with thee, and **a**, go seek the asses. 6965
16:12 the LORD said, **A**, anoint him: for this *is* 6965
23: 4 And the LORD answered him and said, **A**, 6965
2Sa 2:14 Let the young men now **a**, and play before 6965
2:14 play before us. And Joab said, Let them **a**. 6965
3:21 I will **a** and go, and will gather all Israel 6965
11:20 if so be that the king's wrath **a**, and he say 5927
13:15 And Amnon said unto her, **A**, be gone. 6965
15:14 with him at Jerusalem, **A**, and let us flee; 6965
17: 1 I will **a** and pursue after David *this* night: 6965
17:21 **A**, and pass quickly over the water: 6965
19: 7 Now therefore **a**, go forth, and 6965
22:39 and wounded them, that they could not **a**: 6965
1Ki 3:12 neither after thee shall any **a** like unto thee. 6965
14: 2 **A**, I pray thee, and disguise thyself, 6965
14:12 **A** thou therefore, get thee to thine own 6965
17: 9 **A**, get thee to Zarephath, which *belongeth* 6965
19: 5 touched him, and said unto him, **A** *and* eat. 6965
19: 7 and touched him, and said, **A** *and* eat; 6965
21: 7 **a**, *and* eat bread, and let thine heart be 6965
21:15 and was dead, that Jezebel said to Ahab, **A**, 6965
21:18 **A**, go down to meet Ahab king of Israel, 6965
2Ki 1: 3 **A**, go up to meet the messengers of 6965
8: 1 **A**, and go thou and thine household, and 6965
9: 2 **make** him **a up** from among his brethren, 6965
1Ch 22:16 **A** *therefore*, and be doing, and the LORD 6965
22:19 **a** therefore, and build ye the sanctuary of 6965
2Ch 6:41 Now therefore **a**, O LORD God, into thy 6965
Ezr 10: 4 **A**; for *this* matter *belongeth* unto thee: 6965
Ne 2:20 therefore we his servants will **a** and build: 6965
Est 1:18 Thus *shall there* ***a*** too much contempt and NIH
4:14 deliverance **a** to the Jews from another 5975
Job 7: 4 When shall I **a**, and the night be gone? 6965
25: 3 and upon whom doth not his light **a**? 6965
Ps 3: 7 **A**, O LORD; save me, O my God: 6965
7: 6 **A**, O LORD, in thine anger, lift up thyself 6965

Ps 9:19 **A**, O LORD; let not man prevail: let 6965
10:12 **A**, O LORD; O God, lift up thine hand: 6965
12: 5 the needy, now will I **a**, saith the LORD; 6965
17:13 **A**, O LORD, disappoint him, cast him 6965
44:23 O Lord? **a**, cast *us* not off for ever. 6974
44:26 **A** for our help, and redeem us for thy 6965
68: 1 Let God **a**, let his enemies be scattered: 6965
74:22 **A**, O God, plead thine own cause: 6965
78: 6 *who* should **a** and declare *them* to their 6965
82: 8 **A**, O God, judge the earth: for thou shalt 6965
88:10 shall the dead **a** *and* praise thee? Selah. 6965
89: 9 when the waves thereof **a**, thou stillest 5375
102:13 Thou shalt **a**, *and* have mercy upon Zion: 6965
109:28 when they **a**, let them be ashamed; but 6965
132: 8 **A**, O LORD, into thy rest; thou, and 6965
Pr 6: 9 when wilt thou **a** out of thy sleep? 6965
31:28 Her children **a up**, and call her blessed; 6965
SS 2:13 **A**, my love, my fair one, and come away. 6965
Isa 21: 5 drink: **a**, ye princes, *and* anoint the shield. 6965
23:12 **a**, pass over *to* Chittim; there also shalt 6965
26:19 *together with* my dead body shall they **a**. 6965
31: 2 will **a** against the house of the evildoers, 6965
49: 7 to a servant of rulers, Kings shall see and **a**, 6965
52: 2 the dust; **a**, *and* sit down, O Jerusalem: 6965
60: 1 **A**, shine; for thy light is come, and 6965
60: 2 the LORD shall **a** upon thee, and his glory 2224
Jer 1:17 **a**, and speak unto them all that I command 6965
2:27 their trouble they will say, **A**, and save us. 6965
2:28 let them **a**, if they can save thee in the time 6965
6: 4 war against her; **a**, and let us go up at noon. 6965
6: 5 **A**, and let us go by night, and let us destroy 6965
8: 4 the LORD; Shall they fall, and not **a**? 6965
13: 4 **a**, go to Euphrates, and hide it there in a 6965
13: 6 **A**, go to Euphrates, and take the girdle 6965
18: 2 **A**, and go down *to* the potter's house, and 6965
31: 6 **A** ye, and let us go up *to* Zion unto 6965
46:16 **A**, and let us go again to our own people, 6965
49:28 **A** ye, go up to Kedar, and spoil the men of 6965
49:31 **A**, get you up unto the wealthy nation, 6965
La 2:19 **A**, cry out in the night: in the beginning of 6965
Eze 3:22 he said unto me, **A**, go forth into the plain, 6965
Da 2:39 after thee shall **a** another kingdom inferior 6966
7: 5 said thus unto it, **A**, devour much flesh. 6966
7:17 four kings, *which* shall **a** out of the earth. 6966
7:24 of this kingdom *are* ten kings *that* shall **a**: 6966
Hos 10:14 Therefore shall a tumult **a** among thy 6965
Am 7: 2 *by* whom shall Jacob **a**? for he *is* small. 6965
7: 5 *by* whom shall Jacob **a**? for he *is* small. 6965
Ob 1: 1 **A** ye, and let us rise up against her in battle. 6965
Jnh 1: 2 **A**, go to Nineveh, *that* great city, and 6965
1: 6 **a**, call upon thy God, if so be that God will 6965
3: 2 **A**, go unto Nineveh, *that* great city, and 6965
4: 8 it came to pass, when the sun did **a**, 2224
Mic 2:10 **A** ye, and depart; for this *is* not *your* rest: 6965
4:13 **A** and thresh, O daughter of Zion: for I will 6965
6: 1 **A**, contend thou before the mountains, and 6965
7: 8 when I fall, I shall **a**; when I sit in darkness, 6965
Hab 2:19 to the dumb stone, **A**, it shall teach! 5782
Mal 4: 2 righteousness **a** with healing in his wings; 2224
Mt 2:13 **A**, and take the young child and his mother, *1453*
2:20 **A**, and take the young child and his mother, *1453*
9: 5 be forgiven thee; or to say, **A**, and walk? *1453*
9: 6 **A**, take up thy bed, and go unto thine *1453*
17: 7 and said, **A**, and be not afraid. *1453*
24:24 For there shall **a** false Christs, and *1453*
Mk 2: 9 or to say, **A**, and take up thy bed, and walk? *1453*
2:11 **A**, and take up thy bed, and go thy way into *1453*
5:41 Damsel (I say unto thee) **a**. *1453*
Lk 5:24 **A**, and take up thy couch, and go into thine *1453*
7:14 he said, Young man, I say unto thee, **A**. *1453*
8:54 by the hand, and called, saying, Maid, **a**. *1453*
15:18 I will **a** and go to my father, and will say *450*
17:19 And he said unto him, **A**, go *thy way:* thy *450*
24:38 and why do thoughts **a** in your hearts? *305*
Jn 14:31 *even* so I do. **A**, let us go hence. *1453*
Ac 8:26 **A**, and go toward the south unto the way that *450*
9: 6 **A**, and go into the city, and it shall be told *450*
9:11 **A**, and go into the street which is called *450*
9:34 **a**, and make thy bed. And he arose *450*
9:40 and turning *him* to the body said, Tabitha, **a**. *450*
10:20 **A** therefore, and get *thee* down, and go with *450*
11: 7 I heard a voice saying unto me, **A**, Peter; *450*
12: 7 and raised him up, saying, **A up** quickly. *450*
20:30 Also of your own selves shall men **a**, *450*
22:10 said unto me, **A**, and go into Damascus; *450*
22:16 **a**, and be baptized, and wash away thy sins, *450*
Eph 5:14 and **a** from the dead, and Christ shall give *450*
2Pe 1:19 day dawn, and the day star **a** in your hearts: *393*

ARISETH (11) [RISE]

1Ki 18:44 Behold, there **a** a little cloud out of the sea, 5927
Ps 104:22 The sun **a**, they gather themselves together, 2224
112: 4 Unto the upright there **a** light in 2224
Ecc 1: 5 The sun also **a**, and the sun goeth down, 2224
Isa 2:19 when he **a** to shake terribly the earth. 6965
2:21 when he **a** to shake terribly the earth. 6965
Na 3:17 *but* when the sun **a** they flee away, and 2224
Mt 13:21 or persecution **a** because of the word, *1096*
Mk 4:17 or persecution **a** for the word's sake, *1096*
Jn 7:52 and look: for out of Galilee **a** no prophet. *1453*
Heb 7:15 of Melchisedec there **a** another priest, *450*

ARISING (1) [RISE]

Est 7: 7 the king **a** from the banquet of wine in his 6965

ARISTARCHUS (5)

Ac 19:29 and having caught Gaius and **A**, men of *708*
20: 4 and of the Thessalonians, **A** and Secundus; *708*
27: 2 *one* **A**, a Macedonian of Thessalonica, *708*
Col 4:10 **A** my fellowprisoner saluteth you, and *708*
Phm 1:24 Marcus, **A**, Demas, Lucas, *708*

ARISTOBULUS' (1)

Ro 16:10 Salute them which are of **A** *household*. *711*

ARK (230)

Ge 6:14 Make thee an **a** of gopher wood; 8392
6:14 rooms shalt thou make *in* the **a**, and 8392
6:15 of the **a** *shall be* three hundred cubits, 8392
6:16 A window shalt thou make to the **a**, and 8392
6:16 the door of the **a** shalt thou set in the side 8392
6:18 thou shalt come into the **a**, thou, and 8392
6:19 of every *sort* shalt thou bring into the **a**, 8392
7: 1 Come thou and all thy house into the **a**; 8392
7: 7 into the **a**, because of the waters of 8392
7: 9 went in two and two unto Noah into the **a**, 8392
7:13 wives of his sons with them, into the **a**; 8392
7:15 they went in unto Noah into the **a**, two and 8392
7:17 bare up the **a**, and it was lift up above 8392
7:18 and the **a** went upon the face of the waters. 8392
7:23 and *they* that *were* with him in the **a**. 8392
8: 1 and all the cattle that *was* with him in the **a**: 8392
8: 4 the **a** rested in the seventh month, on 8392
8: 6 that Noah opened the window of the **a** 8392
8: 9 she returned unto him into the **a**, for 8392
8: 9 and pulled her in unto him into the **a**. 8392
8:10 again he sent forth the dove out of the **a**; 8392
8:13 Noah removed the covering of the **a**, and 8392
8:16 Go forth of the **a**, thou, and thy wife, and 8392
8:19 after their kinds, went forth out of the **a**. 8392
9:10 from all that go out of the **a**, to every beast 8392
9:18 that went forth of the **a**, were Shem, and 8392
Ex 2: 3 she took for him an **a** of bulrushes, and 8392
2: 5 when she saw the **a** among the flags, she 8392
25:10 they shall make an **a** of shittim wood: 727
25:14 the staves into the rings by the sides of the **a**, 727
25:14 the ark, that the **a** may be borne with them. 727
25:15 The staves shall be in the rings of the **a**: 727
25:16 thou shalt put into the **a** the Testimony 727
25:21 shalt put the mercy seat above upon the **a**; 727
25:21 in the **a** thou shalt put the Testimony that I 727
25:22 which *are* upon the **a** of the Testimony, 727
26:33 within the vail the **a** of the Testimony: 727
26:34 thou shalt put the mercy seat upon the **a** of 727
30: 6 the vail that *is* by the **a** of the Testimony, 727
30:26 and the **a** of the Testimony, 727
31: 7 the **a** of the Testimony, and the mercy seat 727
35:12 The **a**, and the staves thereof, *with* the mercy 727
37: 1 Bezaleel made the **a** *of* shittim wood: 727
37: 5 the staves into the rings by the sides of the **a**, 727
37: 5 rings by the sides of the ark, to bear the **a**. 727
39:35 The **a** of the Testimony, and the staves 727
40: 3 thou shalt put therein the **a** of the Testimony, 727
40: 3 the Testimony, and cover the **a** with the vail. 727
40: 5 the incense before the **a** of the Testimony, 727
40:20 he took and put the Testimony into the **a**, 727
40:20 set the staves on the **a**, and put the mercy 727
40:20 and put the mercy seat above upon the **a**: 727

Ex	40:21	And he brought the **a** into the tabernacle, and	727
	40:21	and covered the **a** of the Testimony;	727
Lev	16: 2	before the mercy seat, which *is* upon the **a**;	727
Nu	3:31	their charge *shall be* the **a**, and the table,	727
	4: 5	and cover the **a** of Testimony with it:	727
	7:89	seat that *was* upon the **a** of Testimony,	727
	10:33	the **a** of the covenant of the LORD went	727
	10:35	when the **a** set forward, that Moses said,	727
	14:44	nevertheless the **a** of the covenant of	727
Dt	10: 1	into the mount, and make thee an **a** of wood.	727
	10: 2	and thou shalt put them in the **a**.	727
	10: 3	I made an **a** of shittim wood, and hewed two	727
	10: 5	and put the tables in the **a** which I had made;	727
	10: 8	to bear the **a** of the covenant of the LORD,	727
	31: 9	which bare the **a** of the covenant of	727
	31:25	which bare the **a** of the covenant of	727
	31:26	put it in the side of the **a** of the covenant of	727
Jos	3: 3	When ye see the **a** of the covenant of	727
	3: 6	Take up the **a** of the covenant, and pass over	727
	3: 6	And they took up the **a** of the covenant, and	727
	3: 8	the priests that bear the **a** of the covenant,	727
	3:11	Behold, the **a** of the covenant, *even* the Lord	727
	3:13	of the priests that bear the **a** of the LORD,	727
	3:14	the priests bearing the **a** *of* the covenant	727
	3:15	as they that bare the **a** were come unto	727
	3:15	the feet of the priests that bare the **a** were	727
	3:17	the priests that bare the **a** *of* the covenant of	727
	4: 5	Pass over before the **a** of the LORD your	727
	4: 7	before the **a** of the covenant of the LORD;	727
	4: 9	which bare the **a** of the covenant stood:	727
	4:10	For the priests which bare the **a** stood in	727
	4:11	that the **a** of the LORD passed over, and	727
	4:16	Command the priests that bear the **a** of	727
	4:18	when the priests that bare the **a** of	727
	6: 4	seven priests shall bear before the **a** seven	727
	6: 6	Take up the **a** of the covenant, and let seven	727
	6: 6	of rams' horns before the **a** of the LORD.	727
	6: 7	let him that is armed pass on before the **a** of	727
	6: 8	the **a** of the covenant of the LORD	727
	6: 9	the rereward came after the **a**, *the priests*	727
	6:11	So the **a** of the LORD compassed the city,	727
	6:12	and the priests took up the **a** of the LORD.	727
	6:13	the **a** of the LORD went on continually,	727
	6:13	the rereward came after the **a** of the LORD,	727
	7: 6	fell to the earth upon his face before the **a** of	727
	8:33	stood on this side the **a** and on that side	727
	8:33	which bare the **a** of the covenant of	727
Jdg	20:27	(for the **a** of the covenant of God *was* there	727
1Sa	3: 3	where the **a** of God *was,* and Samuel was	727
	4: 3	Let us fetch the **a** of the covenant of	727
	4: 4	that they might bring from thence the **a** of	727
	4: 4	*were* there with the **a** of the covenant of	727
	4: 5	when the **a** of the covenant of the LORD	727
	4: 6	they understood that the **a** of the LORD	727
	4:11	the **a** of God was taken; and the two sons of	727
	4:13	for his heart trembled for the **a** of God.	727
	4:17	are dead, and the **a** of God is taken.	727
	4:18	when he made mention of the **a** of God,	727
	4:19	when she heard the tidings that the **a** of God	727
	4:21	because the **a** of God was taken, and because	727
	4:22	from Israel: for the **a** of God is taken.	727
	5: 1	the Philistines took the **a** of God, and	727
	5: 2	When the Philistines took the **a** of God, they	727
	5: 3	face to the earth before the **a** of the LORD.	727
	5: 4	to the ground before the **a** of the LORD;	727
	5: 7	The **a** of the God of Israel shall not abide	727
	5: 8	What shall we do with the **a** of the God of	727
	5: 8	Let the **a** of the God of Israel be carried	727
	5: 8	they carried the **a** of the God of Israel about	727
	5:10	Therefore they sent the **a** of God *to* Ekron.	727
	5:10	came to pass, as the **a** of God came *to* Ekron,	727
	5:10	They have brought about the **a** of the God of	727
	5:11	Send away the **a** of the God of Israel, and	727
	6: 1	the **a** of the LORD was in the country of	727
	6: 2	What shall we do to the **a** of the LORD?	727
	6: 3	If ye send away the **a** of the God of Israel,	727
	6: 8	take the **a** of the LORD, and lay it upon	727
	6:11	they laid the **a** of the LORD upon the cart,	727
	6:13	and saw the **a**, and rejoiced to see *it.*	727
	6:15	the Levites took down the **a** of the LORD,	727
	6:18	whereon they set down the **a** of the LORD:	727
	6:19	they had looked into the **a** of the LORD,	727
	6:21	The Philistines have brought again the **a** of	727
	7: 1	fetched up the **a** of the LORD, and	727
	7: 1	sanctified Eleazar his son to keep the **a** of	727
	7: 2	to pass, while the **a** abode in Kirjath-jearim,	727
	14:18	said unto Ahiah, Bring hither the **a** of God.	727
	14:18	For the **a** of God was at that time with	727
2Sa	6: 2	to bring up from thence the **a** of God,	727
	6: 3	they set the **a** of God upon a new cart, and	727
	6: 4	*was* at Gibeah, accompanying the **a** of God:	727
	6: 4	the ark of God: and Ahio went before the **a**.	727
	6: 6	Uzzah put forth *his hand* to the **a** of God,	727
	6: 7	*his* error; and there he died by the **a** of God.	727
	6: 9	How shall the **a** of the LORD come to me?	727
	6:10	So David would not remove the **a** of	727
	6:11	the **a** of the LORD continued *in* the house	727
	6:12	unto him, because of the **a** of God.	727
	6:12	brought up the **a** of God from the house of	727
	6:13	that when they that bare the **a** of the LORD	727
	6:15	all the house of Israel brought up the **a** of	727
	6:16	as the **a** of the LORD came *into* the city of	727
	6:17	they brought in the **a** of the LORD, and	727
	7: 2	but the **a** of God dwelleth within curtains.	727
	11:11	The **a**, and Israel, and Judah, abide in tents;	727
	15:24	bearing the **a** of the covenant of God:	727
	15:24	they set down the **a** of God; and	727
	15:25	Carry back the **a** of God *into* the city:	727
	15:29	Abiathar carried the **a** of God again *to*	727
1Ki	2:26	thou barest the **a** of the Lord GOD before	727
	3:15	stood before the **a** of the covenant of	727
	6:19	to set there the **a** of the covenant of	727
	8: 1	that *they* might bring up the **a** of	727
	8: 3	of Israel came, and the priests took up the **a**.	727
	8: 4	they brought up the **a** of the LORD, and	727
	8: 5	*were* with him before the **a**, sacrificing sheep	727
	8: 6	the priests brought in the **a** of the covenant	727
	8: 7	forth *their* two wings over the place of the **a**,	727
	8: 7	the cherubims covered the **a** and the staves	727
	8: 9	*There was* nothing in the **a** save the two	727
	8:21	I have set there a place for the **a**, wherein *is*	727
1Ch	6:31	of the LORD, after that the **a** had rest.	727
	13: 3	let us bring again the **a** of our God to us:	727
	13: 5	to bring the **a** of God from Kirjath-jearim.	727
	13: 6	to bring up thence the **a** of God the LORD,	727
	13: 7	they carried the **a** of God in a new cart out of	727
	13: 9	Uzza put forth his hand to hold the **a**;	727
	13:10	smote him, because he put his hand to the **a**:	727
	13:12	How shall I bring the **a** of God *home* to me?	727
	13:13	So David brought not the **a** *home* to himself	727
	13:14	the **a** of God remained with the family of	727
	15: 1	prepared a place for the **a** of God, and	727
	15: 2	None ought to carry the **a** of God but	727
	15: 2	the LORD chosen to carry the **a** of God,	727
	15: 3	to bring up the **a** of the LORD unto his	727
	15:12	that you may bring up the **a** of the LORD	727
	15:14	bring up the **a** of the LORD God of Israel.	727
	15:15	the children of the Levites bare the **a** of God	727
	15:23	and Elkanah *were* doorkeepers for the **a**.	727
	15:24	did blow with the trumpets before the **a** of	727
	15:24	and Jehiah *were* doorkeepers for the **a**.	727
	15:25	went to bring up the **a** of the covenant of	727
	15:26	when God helped the Levites that bare the **a**	727
	15:27	all the Levites that bare the **a**, and	727
	15:28	Thus all Israel brought up the **a** of	727
	15:29	*as* the **a** of the covenant of the LORD came	727
	16: 1	So they brought the **a** of God, and set it in	727
	16: 4	to minister before the **a** of the LORD,	727
	16: 6	before the **a** of the covenant of God.	727
	16:37	So he left there before the **a** of the covenant	727
	16:37	to minister before the **a** continually,	727
	17: 1	the **a** of the covenant of the LORD	727
	22:19	to bring the **a** of the covenant of the LORD,	727
	28: 2	rest for the **a** of the covenant of the LORD,	727
	28:18	covered the **a** of the covenant of the LORD.	727
2Ch	1: 4	the **a** of God had David brought up from	727
	5: 2	to bring up the **a** of the covenant of	727
	5: 4	of Israel came; and the Levites took up the **a**.	727
	5: 5	they brought up the **a**, and the tabernacle of	727
	5: 6	that were assembled unto him before the **a**,	727
	5: 7	the priests brought in the **a** of the covenant	727
	5: 8	forth *their* wings over the place of the **a**,	727
	5: 8	the cherubims covered the **a** and the staves	727
	5: 9	they drew out the staves *of the **a***, that	NIH
	5: 9	were seen from the **a** before the oracle;	727
	5:10	*There was* nothing in the **a** save the two	727
	6:11	in it have I put the **a**, wherein *is* the covenant	727
	6:41	resting place, thou, and the **a** of thy strength:	727

2Ch 8:11 whereunto the a of the LORD hath come. 727
35: 3 Put the holy a in the house which Solomon 727
Ps 132: 8 into thy rest; thou, and the a of thy strength. 727
Jer 3:16 The a of the covenant of the LORD: 727
Mt 24:38 until the day that Noe entered into the a, *2787*
Lk 17:27 until the day that Noe entered into the a, *2787*
Heb 9: 4 the a of the covenant overlaid round about *2787*
11: 7 prepared an a to the saving of his house; *2787*
1Pe 3:20 while the a was a preparing, wherein few, *2787*
Rev 11:19 there was seen in his temple the a of his *2787*

ARKITE (2)
Ge 10:17 And the Hivite, and the A, and the Sinite, 6208
1Ch 1:15 And the Hivite, and the A, and the Sinite, 6208

ARKITES See ARCHI; ARCHITE

ARM (67) [ARMED, ARMHOLES, ARMIES, ARMOUR, ARMOURBEARER, ARMOURY, ARMS, ARMY]
Ex 6: 6 I will redeem you with a stretched out a, 2220
15:16 by the greatness of thine a they shall be *as* 2220
Nu 31: 3 A some of yourselves unto the war, and 2502
Dt 4:34 by a stretched out a, and by great terrors, 2220
5:15 a mighty hand and by a stretched out a: 2220
7:19 the mighty hand, and the stretched out a, 2220
9:29 mighty power and by thy stretched out a. 2220
11: 2 his mighty hand, and his stretched out a, 2220
26: 8 with an outstretched a, and with great 2220
33:20 teareth the a with the crown of the head. 2220
1Sa 2:31 that I will cut off thine a, and the arm of 2220
2:31 thine arm, and the a of thy father's house, 2220
2Sa 1:10 the bracelet that *was* on his a, and 2220
1Ki 8:42 thy strong hand, and of thy stretched out a;) 2220
2Ki 17:36 with great power and a stretched out a, 2220
2Ch 6:32 thy mighty hand, and thy stretched out a; 2220
32: 8 With him *is* an a of flesh; but with us *is* 2220
Job 26: 2 *how* savest thou the a *that hath* no strength? 2220
31:22 *Then* let mine a fall from *my* shoulder 3802
31:22 and mine a be broken from the bone. 248
35: 9 they cry out by reason of the a of 2220
38:15 and the high a shall be broken. 2220
40: 9 Hast thou an a like God? or, canst thou 2220
Ps 10:15 Break thou the a of the wicked and the evil 2220
44: 3 neither did their own a save them: 2220
44: 3 thine a, and the light of thy countenance, 2220
77:15 Thou hast with *thine* a redeemed thy 2220
89:10 scattered thine enemies with thy strong a. 2220
89:13 Thou hast a mighty a: strong is thy hand, 2220
89:21 mine a also shall strengthen him. 2220
98: 1 and his holy a, hath gotten him the victory. 2220
136:12 a strong hand, and with a stretched out a: 2220
SS 8: 6 upon thine heart, as a seal upon thine a: 2220
Isa 9:20 shall eat every man the flesh of his own a: 2220
17: 5 the corn, and reapeth the ears *with* his a; 2220
30:30 shall shew the lighting down of his a, 2220
33: 2 be thou their a every morning, 2220
40:10 strong *hand,* and his a *shall* rule for him: 2220
40:11 he shall gather the lambs with his a, and 2220
48:14 and his a *shall be on* the Chaldeans. 2220
51: 5 upon me, and on mine a shall they trust. 2220
51: 9 awake, put on strength, O a of the LORD; 2220
52:10 The LORD hath made bare his holy a in 2220
53: 1 to whom is the a of the LORD revealed? 2220
59:16 therefore his a brought salvation unto him; 2220
62: 8 his right hand, and by the a of his strength, 2220
63: 5 mine own a brought salvation unto me; 2220
63:12 the right hand of Moses *with* his glorious a, 2220
Jer 17: 5 maketh flesh his a, and whose heart 2220
21: 5 an outstretched hand and with a strong a, 2220
27: 5 my great power and by my outstretched a, 2220
32:17 by thy great power and stretched out a, 2220
32:21 with a stretched out a, and with great terror; 248
48:25 and his a is broken, saith the LORD. 2220
Eze 4: 7 thine a *shall be* uncovered, and thou shalt 2220
20:33 with a stretched out a, and with fury poured 2220
20:34 with a stretched out a, and with fury poured 2220
30:21 I have broken the a of Pharaoh king of 2220
31:17 *they that were* his a, *that* dwelt under his 2220
Da 11: 6 she shall not retain the power of the a; 2220
11: 6 of the arm; neither shall he stand, nor his a: 2220
Zec 11:17 the sword *shall be* upon his a, and upon his 2220
11:17 his a shall be clean dried up, and his right 2220
Lk 1:51 He hath shewed strength with his a; he hath *1023*
Jn 12:38 to whom hath the a of the Lord been *1023*
Ac 13:17 and with a high a brought he them out of it. *1023*
1Pe 4: 1 a yourselves likewise with the same mind: *3695*

ARMAGEDDON (1)
Rev 16:16 into a place called in the Hebrew tongue A. *717*

ARMED (30) [ARM]
Ge 14:14 he a his trained *servants,* born in his own 7324
Nu 31: 5 of *every* tribe, twelve thousand a for war. 2502
32:17 we ourselves will go ready a before 2502
32:20 if ye will go a before the LORD to war, 2502
32:21 will go all of you a over Jordan before 2502
32:27 every man a for war, before the LORD to 2502
32:29 every man a to battle, before the LORD, 2502
32:30 if they will not pass over with you a, 2502
32:32 We will pass over a before the LORD *into* 2502
Dt 3:18 ye shall pass over a before your brethren 2502
Jos 1:14 ye shall pass before your brethren a, all 2571
4:12 passed over a before the children of Israel, 2571
6: 7 let him that is a pass on before the ark of 2502
6: 9 the a men went before the priests that blew 2502
6:13 the a men went before them; but 2502
Jdg 7:11 outside of the a *men* that *were* in the host. 2571
1Sa 17: 5 his head, and he *was* a with a coat of mail; 3847
17:38 Saul a David with his armour, and he put a 3847
17:38 his head; also he a him with a coat *of mail.* 3847
1Ch 12: 2 *They were* a with bows, and could use both 5401
12:23 of the bands that were ready a to the war, 2502
12:24 and eight hundred, ready a to the war. 2502
2Ch 17:17 with him a *men* with bow and shield two 5401
28:14 So the a men left the captives and the spoil 2502
Job 39:21 He goeth on to meet the a men. 5402
Ps 78: 9 of Ephraim, *being* a, *and* carrying bows, 5401
Pr 6:11 that travelleth, and thy want as an a man. 4043
24:34 that travelleth; and thy want as an a man. 4043
Isa 15: 4 the a soldiers of Moab shall cry out; 2502
Lk 11:21 When a strong *man* a keepeth his palace, *2528*

ARMENIA (2)
2Ki 19:37 they escaped *into* the land of A. 780
Isa 37:38 and they escaped *into* the land of A: 780

ARMHOLES (2) [ARM, HOLE]
Jer 38:12 rags under thine a under the cords. 679+3027
Eze 13:18 to *the women* that sew pillows to all a, 679+3027

ARMIES (43) [ARM]
Ex 6:26 from the land of Egypt according to their a. 6635
7: 4 bring forth mine a, *and* my people 6635
12:17 I brought your a out of the land of Egypt: 6635
12:51 of Israel out of the land of Egypt by their a. 6635
Nu 1: 3 and Aaron shall number them by their a. 6635
2: 3 the camp of Judah pitch throughout their a: 6635
2: 9 and four hundred, throughout their a. 6635
2:10 of the camp of Reuben according to their a: 6635
2:16 four hundred and fifty, throughout their a. 6635
2:18 the camp of Ephraim according to their a: 6635
2:24 and an hundred, throughout their a. 6635
2:25 of Dan *shall be* on the north side by their a: 6635
10:14 the children of Judah according to their a: 6635
10:18 of Reuben set forward according to their a: 6635
10:22 Ephraim set forward according to their a: 6635
10:28 the children of Israel according to their a, 6635
33: 1 Egypt with their a under the hand of Moses 6635
Dt 20: 9 that they shall make captains of the a to 6635
1Sa 17: 1 gathered together their a to battle, 4264
17: 8 he stood and cried unto the a of Israel, and 4634
17:10 I defy the a of Israel this day; 4634
17:23 out of the a of the Philistines, and 4634
17:26 that he should defy the a of the living God? 4634
17:36 seeing he hath defied the a of the living 4634
17:45 the God of the a of Israel, whom thou hast 4634
23: 3 if we come *to* Keilah against the a of 4634
28: 1 that the Philistines gathered their a together 4264
29: 1 gathered together all their a to Aphek: 4264
2Ki 25:23 when all the captains of the a, they and 2428
25:26 and great, and the captains of the a, 2428
1Ch 11:26 Also the valiant *men* of the a *were,* Asahel 2428
2Ch 16: 4 sent the captains of his a against the cities 2428
Job 25: 3 Is there *any* number of his a? and 1416
Ps 44: 9 us to shame; and goest not forth with our a. 6635
60:10 O God, *which* didst not go out with our a? 6635
68:12 Kings of a did flee apace: and she that 6635
SS 6:13 As it were the company of two a. 4264

Isa 34: 2 all nations, and *his* fury upon all their **a**: 6635
Mt 22: 7 and he sent forth his **a**, and destroyed those *4753*
Lk 21:20 ye shall see Jerusalem compassed with **a**, *4760*
Heb 11:34 in fight, turned to flight the **a** of the aliens. *3925*
Rev 19:14 And the **a** which were in heaven followed *4753*
19:19 and the kings of the earth, and their **a**, *4753*

ARMONI (1)
2Sa 21: 8 she bare unto Saul, **A** and Mephibosheth; 764

ARMOUR (24) [ARM]
1Sa 14: 1 said unto the young man that bare his **a**, 3627
14: 6 said to the young man that bare his **a**, 3627
17:38 Saul armed David with his **a**, and he put a 4055
17:39 David girded his sword upon his **a**, and 4055
17:54 it *to* Jerusalem; but he put his **a** in his tent. 3627
31: 9 stripped off his **a**, and sent into the land of 3627
31:10 they put his **a** *in* the house of Ashtaroth: 3627
2Sa 2:21 one of the young men, and take thee his **a**. 2488
18:15 ten young men that bare Joab's **a** 3627
1Ki 10:25 and **a**, and spices, horses, and mules, 5402
22:38 licked up his blood; and they washed his **a**; 2185
2Ki 3:21 all that *were able to* **put on a**, 2290+2296
10: 2 and horses, a fenced city also, and **a**; 5402
20:13 all the house of his **a**, and all that was 3627
1Ch 10: 9 his **a**, and sent into the land of 3627
10:10 they put his **a** *in* the house of their gods, 3627
Isa 22: 8 thou didst look in that day to the **a** of 5402
39: 2 all the house of his **a**, and all that was 3627
Eze 38: 4 all of them clothed with all sorts *of a, even* NIH
Lk 11:22 he taketh *from him* **all** his **a** wherein he *3833*
Ro 13:12 of darkness, and let us put on the **a** of light. *3696*
2Co 6: 7 by the **a** of righteousness on the right hand *3696*
Eph 6:11 Put on the **whole a** of God, that ye may be *3833*
6:13 Wherefore take unto *you* the **whole a** of *3833*

ARMOURBEARER (18) [ARM, BEAR]
Jdg 9:54 hastily unto the young man his **a**, 3627+5375
1Sa 14: 7 his **a** said unto him, Do all that *is* in 3627+5375
14:12 answered Jonathan and his **a**, 3627+5375
14:12 Jonathan said unto his **a**, Come up 3627+5375
14:13 upon his feet, and his **a** after him: 3627+5375
14:13 and his **a** slew after him. 3627+5375
14:14 which Jonathan and his **a** made, was 3627+5375
14:17 and his **a** *were* not *there.* 3627+5375
16:21 him greatly; and he became his **a**. 3627+5375
31: 4 said Saul unto his **a**, Draw thy 3627+5375
31: 4 his **a** would not; for he was sore 3627+5375
31: 5 when his **a** saw that Saul was dead, 3627+5375
31: 6 three sons, and his **a**, and all his men, 3627+5375
2Sa 23:37 **a** to Joab the son of Zeruiah, 3627+5375
1Ch 10: 4 said Saul to his **a**, Draw thy sword, 3627+5375
10: 4 his **a** would not; for he was sore 3627+5375
10: 5 when his **a** saw that Saul was dead, 3627+5375
11:39 the **a** of Joab the son of Zeruiah, 3627+5375

ARMOURY (3) [ARM]
Ne 3:19 going up to the **a** *at* the turning *of the wall.* 5402
SS 4: 4 *is* like the tower of David builded for an **a**, 8530
Jer 50:25 The LORD hath opened his **a**, and 214

ARMS (29) [ARM]
Ge 49:24 the **a** of his hands were made strong by 2220
Dt 33:27 and underneath *are* the everlasting **a**: 2220
Jdg 15:14 the cords that *were* upon his **a** became as 2220
16:12 he brake them from off his **a** like a thread. 2220
2Sa 22:35 so that a bow of steel is broken *by* mine **a**. 2220
2Ki 9:24 smote Jehoram between his **a**, and 2220
Job 22: 9 the **a** of the fatherless have been broken. 2220
Ps 18:34 so that a bow of steel is broken *by* mine **a**. 2220
37:17 For the **a** of the wicked shall be broken: but 2220
Pr 31:17 loins with strength, and strengtheneth her **a**. 2220
Isa 44:12 and worketh it with the strength of his **a**: 2220
49:22 they shall bring thy sons in *their* **a**, and 2684
51: 5 and mine **a** shall judge the people; 2220
Eze 13:20 I will tear them from your **a**, and will let 2220
30:22 will break his **a**, the strong, and that which 2220
30:24 I will strengthen the **a** of the king of 2220
30:24 I will break Pharaoh's **a**, and he shall 2220
30:25 I will strengthen the **a** of the king of 2220
30:25 and the **a** of Pharaoh shall fall down; 2220
Da 2:32 his breast and his **a** of silver, his belly and 1872
10: 6 his **a** and his feet like in colour to polished 2220
11:15 the **a** of the south shall not withstand, 2220
11:22 *with* the **a** of a flood shall they be 2220
11:31 **a** shall stand on his part, and they shall 2220
Hos 7:15 I have bound *and* strengthened their **a**, 2220
11: 3 Ephraim also to go, taking them by their **a**; 2220
Mk 9:36 and when he had **taken** him **in** his **a**, *1723*
10:16 And he **took** them **up in** his **a**, put *his* *1723*
Lk 2:28 Then took he him *up* in his **a**, and *43*

ARMY (82) [ARM]
Ge 26:26 and Phichol the chief captain of his **a**. 6635
Ex 14: 9 of Pharaoh, and his horsemen, and his **a**) 2428
Dt 11: 4 what he did unto the **a** of Egypt, unto their 2428
Jdg 4: 7 the captain of Jabin's **a**, with his chariots 6635
8: 6 that we should give bread unto thine **a**? 6635
9:29 Increase thine **a**, and come out. 6635
1Sa 4: 2 they slew of the **a** in the field about four 4634
4:12 there ran a man of Benjamin out of the **a**, 4634
4:16 I *am* he that came out of the **a**, and I fled to 4634
4:16 of the army, and I fled to day out of the **a**. 4634
17:21 had put *the battle* in array, **a** against army. 4634
17:21 had put *the battle* in array, army against **a**. 4634
17:22 ran *into* the **a**, and came and saluted his 4634
17:48 and ran *toward* the **a** to meet the Philistine. 4634
1Ki 20:19 of the city, and the **a** which followed them. 2428
20:25 number thee an **a**, like the army that thou 2428
20:25 like the **a** that thou hast lost, horse for 2428
2Ki 25: 5 the **a** of the Chaldees pursued after 2428
25: 5 and all his **a** were scattered from him. 2428
25:10 all the **a** of the Chaldees, that *were with* 2428
1Ch 20: 1 *to battle,* Joab led forth the power of the **a**, 6635
27:34 and the general of the king's **a** *was* Joab. 6635
2Ch 13: 3 Abijah set the battle in array with an **a** of 2428
14: 8 Asa had an **a** *of men* that bare targets and 2428
20:21 as *they* went out before the **a**, and to say, 2502
24:24 For the **a** of the Syrians came with a small 2428
25: 7 O king, let not the **a** of Israel go with thee; 6635
25: 9 which I have given to the **a** of Israel? 1416
25:10 the **a** that was come to him out of Ephraim, 1416
25:13 the soldiers of the **a** which Amaziah sent 1416
26:13 under their hand *was* an **a**, three 2428+6635
Ne 2: 9 Now the king had sent captains of the **a** and 2428
4: 2 before his brethren and the **a** of Samaria, 2428
Job 29:25 and sat chief, and dwelt as a king in the **a**, 1416
SS 6: 4 as Jerusalem, terrible as *an a* with banners. NIH
6:10 the sun, *and* terrible as *an a* with banners? NIH
Isa 36: 2 unto king Hezekiah with a great **a**. 2426
43:17 the chariot and horse, the **a** and the power; 2428
Jer 32: 2 the king of Babylon's **a** besieged 2428
34: 1 all his **a**, and all the kingdoms of the earth 2428
34: 7 When the king of Babylon's **a** fought 2428
34:21 into the hand of the king of Babylon's **a**, 2428
35:11 let us go *to* Jerusalem for fear of the **a** of 2428
35:11 and for fear of the **a** of the Syrians: 2428
37: 5 Pharaoh's **a** was come forth out of Egypt: 2428
37: 7 Behold, Pharaoh's **a**, which is come forth 2428
37:10 For though ye had smitten the whole **a** of 2428
37:11 *that* when the **a** of the Chaldeans was 2428
37:11 up from Jerusalem for fear of Pharaoh's **a**, 2428
38: 3 into the hand of the king of Babylon's **a**, 2428
39: 1 of Babylon and all his **a** against Jerusalem, 2428
39: 5 the Chaldeans' **a** pursued after them, and 2428
46: 2 against the **a** of Pharaoh-necho king of 2428
46:22 for they shall march with an **a**, and 2428
52: 4 he and all his **a**, against Jerusalem, and 2428
52: 8 the **a** of the Chaldeans pursued after 2428
52: 8 and all his **a** was scattered from him. 2428
52:14 all the **a** of the Chaldeans, that *were* with 2428
Eze 17:17 Neither shall Pharaoh with *his* mighty **a** 2428
27:10 and of Lud and of Phut were in thine **a**, 2428
27:11 The men of Arvad with thine **a** *were* upon 2428
29:18 his **a** to serve a great service against Tyrus: 2428
29:18 yet had he no wages, nor his **a**, for Tyrus, 2428
29:19 her prey; and it shall be the wages for his **a**. 2428
32:31 and all his **a** slain by the sword, 2428
37:10 up upon their feet, an exceeding great **a**. 2428
38: 4 and all thine **a**, horses and horsemen, 2428
38:15 a great company, and a mighty **a**: 2428
Da 3:20 men that *were* in his **a** to bind Shadrach, 2429
4:35 he doeth according to his will in the **a** of 2429
11: 7 which shall come with an **a**, and shall enter 2428
11:13 come after certain years with a great **a** 2428
11:25 against the king of the south with a great **a**; 2428
11:25 up to battle with a very great and mighty **a**; 2428
11:26 shall destroy him, and his **a** shall overflow: 2428

Joel 2:11 LORD shall utter his voice before his a: 2428
2:20 will remove far off from you the northern *a*, NIH
2:25 my great a which I sent among you. 2428
Zec 9: 8 encamp about mine house because of the a, 4675
Ac 23:27 then came I with an a, and rescued him, *4753*
Rev 9:16 And the number of the a of the horsemen *4753*
19:19 him that sat on the horse, and against his a. *4753*

ARNAN (1)
1Ch 3:21 the sons of A, the sons of Obadiah, 770

ARNON (25)
Nu 21:13 and pitched on the *other* side of A, 769
21:13 for A *is* the border of Moab, between Moab 769
21:14 he did in the Red sea, and *in* the brooks of A, 769
21:24 and possessed his land from A unto Jabbok, 769
21:26 all his land out of his hand, *even* unto A. 769
21:28 *and* the lords of the high places of A. 769
22:36 which *is* in the border of A, which *is* in 769
Dt 2:24 take your journey, and pass over the river A: 769
2:36 which *is* by the brink of the river of A, and 769
3: 8 from the river of A unto mount Hermon; 769
3:12 which *is* by the river A, and half mount 769
3:16 I gave from Gilead even unto the river A, 769
4:48 which *is* by the bank of the river A, 769
Jos 12: 1 from the river A unto mount Hermon, and 769
12: 2 which *is* upon the bank of the river of A, and 769
13: 9 that *is* upon the bank of the river A, and 769
13:16 that *is* on the bank of the river A, and 769
Jdg 11:13 from A even unto Jabbok, and unto Jordan: 769
11:18 pitched on the *other* side of A, but came not 769
11:18 of Moab: for A *was* the border of Moab. 769
11:22 from A even unto Jabbok, and from 769
11:26 all the cities that *be* along by the coasts of A, 769
2Ki 10:33 from Aroer, which *is* by the river A, 769
Isa 16: 2 daughters of Moab shall be *at* the fords of A. 769
Jer 48:20 and cry; tell ye *it* in A, that Moab is spoiled, 769

AROD (1)
Nu 26:17 Of A, the family of the Arodites: of Areli, 720

ARODI (1) [ARODITES]
Ge 46:16 Shuni, and Ezbon, Eri, and A, and Areli. 722

ARODITES (1) [ARODI]
Nu 26:17 Of Arod, the family of the A: of Areli, 722

AROER (16) [AROERITE]
Nu 32:34 of Gad built Dibon, and Ataroth, and A, 6177
Dt 2:36 From A, which *is* by the brink of the river 6177
3:12 from A, which *is* by the river Arnon, and 6177
4:48 From A, which *is* by the bank of the river 6177
Jos 12: 2 who dwelt in Heshbon, *and* ruled from A, 6177
13: 9 From A, that *is* upon the bank of the river 6177
13:16 their coast was from A, that *is* on the bank 6177
13:25 of Ammon, unto A that *is* before Rabbah; 6177
Jdg 11:26 in A and her towns, and in all the cities that 6177
11:33 he smote them from A, even till thou come 6177
1Sa 30:28 to *them* which *were* in A, and to *them* 6177
2Sa 24: 5 they passed over Jordan, and pitched in A, 6177
2Ki 10:33 and the Manassites, from A, 6177
1Ch 5: 8 the son of Joel, who dwelt in A, even unto 6177
Isa 17: 2 The cities of A *are* forsaken: they shall be 6177
Jer 48:19 O inhabitant of A, stand by the way and 6177

AROERITE (1) [AROER]
1Ch 11:44 Shama and Jehiel the sons of Hothan the A, 6200

AROMA See ODOUR; SAVOUR

AROSE (168) [RISE]
Ge 19:15 when the morning a, then the angels 5927
19:33 not when she lay down, nor when she a. 6965
19:35 the younger a, and lay with him; and 6965
19:35 not when she lay down, nor when she a. 6965
24:10 he a, and went to Mesopotamia, unto 6965
24:61 Rebekah a, and her damsels, and they rode 6965
37: 7 and lo, my sheaf a, and also stood upright; 6965
38:19 she a, and went away, and laid by her vail 6965
Ex 1: 8 Now there a up a new king over Egypt, 6965
Dt 34:10 there a not a prophet since in Israel like 6965
Jos 8: 3 So Joshua a, and all the people of war, 6965
8:19 the ambush a quickly out of their place, 6965
18: 8 the men a, and went away: and 6965
24: 9 a and warred against Israel, and sent and 6965
Jdg 2:10 there a another generation after them, 6965
3:20 God unto thee. And he a out of *his* seat. 6965
4: 9 Deborah a, and went with Barak to Kedesh. 6965
5: 7 they ceased in Israel, until that I Deborah a, 6965
5: 7 I Deborah arose, that I a a mother in Israel. 6965
6:28 when the men of the city a early in 7925
8:21 Gideon a, and slew Zebah and Zalmunna, 6965
10: 1 after Abimelech there a to defend Israel 6965
10: 3 after him a Jair, a Gileadite, and 6965
13:11 Manoah a, and went after his wife, and 6965
16: 3 a at midnight, and took the doors of 6965
19: 3 her husband a, and went after her, to speak 6965
19: 5 when they a early in the morning, that he 7925
19: 8 he a early in the morning on the fifth day 7925
20: 8 all the people a as one man, saying, 6965
20:18 the children of Israel a, and went up *to* 6965
Ru 1: 6 she a with her daughters in law, that she 6965
1Sa 3: 6 Samuel a and went to Eli, and said, 6965
3: 8 he a and went to Eli, and said, Here *am* I; 6965
5: 3 when they of Ashdod a early on 7925
5: 4 when they a early on the morrow morning, 7925
9:26 they a early: and it came to pass about 7925
9:26 Saul a, and they went out both of them, 6965
13:15 Samuel a, and gat him up from Gilgal *unto* 6965
17:35 when he a against me, I caught *him* by his 6965
17:48 when the Philistine a, and came and 6965
17:52 the men of Israel and of Judah a, and 6965
18:27 Wherefore David a and went, he and 6965
20:25 Jonathan a, and Abner sat by Saul's side, 6965
20:34 So Jonathan a from the table in fierce 6965
20:41 David a out of *a place* toward the south, 6965
20:42 he a and departed: and Jonathan went *into* 6965
21:10 David a, and fled that day for fear of Saul, 6965
23:13 a and departed out of Keilah, and 6965
23:16 Jonathan Saul's son a, and went to David 6965
23:24 they a, and went to Ziph before Saul: but 6965
24: 4 David a, and cut off the skirt of Saul's robe 6965
25: 1 David a, and went down to the wilderness 6965
25:41 she a, and bowed herself *on her* face to 6965
26: 2 Saul a, and went down to the wilderness of 6965
26: 5 David a, and came to the place where Saul 6965
27: 2 David a, and he passed over with the six 6965
28:23 So he a from the earth, and sat upon 6965
28:25 Then they a up, and went away that night. 6965
31:12 All the valiant men a, and went all night, 6965
2Sa 2:15 there a and went over by number twelve of 6965
6: 2 David a, and went with all the people that 6965
11: 2 that David a from off his bed, and 6965
12:17 the elders of his house a, *and went* to him, 6965
12:20 David a from the earth, and washed, and 6965
13:29 all the king's sons a, and every man gat 6965
13:31 the king a, and tare his garments, and 6965
14:23 So Joab a and went to Geshur, and 6965
14:31 Joab a, and came to Absalom unto *his* 6965
15: 9 Go in peace. So he a, and went to Hebron. 6965
17:22 David a, and all the people that *were* with 6965
17:23 a, and gat him *home* to his house, to his 6965
23:10 He a, and smote the Philistines until his 6965
1Ki 1:50 a, and went, and caught hold on the horns 6965
2:40 Shimei a, and saddled his ass, and went to 6965
8:54 he a from before the altar of the LORD, 6965
11:18 they a out of Midian, and came *to* Paran: 6965
11:40 Jeroboam a, and fled *into* Egypt, 6965
14: 4 a, and went *to* Shiloh, and came *to* 6965
14:17 Jeroboam's wife a, and departed, and 6965
17:10 So he a and went to Zarephath. And when 6965
19: 3 when he saw *that,* he a, and went for his 6965
19: 8 he a, and did eat and drink, and went in 6965
19:21 he a, and went after Elijah, and 6965
2Ki 1:15 he a, and went down with him unto 6965
4:30 not leave thee. And he a, and followed her. 6965
7: 7 Wherefore they a and fled in the twilight, 6965
7:12 the king a in the night, and said unto his 6965
8: 2 the woman a, and did after the saying of 6965
9: 6 he a, and went into the house; and 6965
10:12 he a and departed, and came *to* Samaria. 6965
11: 1 she a and destroyed all the seed royal. 6965
12:20 his servants a, and made a conspiracy, 6965
19:35 when they a early in the morning, behold, 7925
23:25 neither after him a there *any* like him. 6965
25:26 of the armies, a, and came *to* Egypt: 6965
1Ch 10:12 They a, all the valiant men, and took away 6965
20: 4 that there a a war at Gezer with 5975
2Ch 22:10 she a and destroyed all the seed royal of 6965

2Ch 29:12 the Levites **a**, Mahath the son of Amasai, 6965
30:14 they **a** and took away the altars that *were* in 6965
30:27 the priests the Levites **a** and blessed 6965
36:16 until the wrath of the LORD **a** against his 5927
Ezr 9: 5 at the evening sacrifice I **a up** from my 6965
10: 5 **a** Ezra, and made the chief priests, 6965
Ne 2:12 I **a** in the night, I and *some* few men with 6965
Est 8: 4 So Esther **a**, and stood before the king, 6965
Job 1:20 Job **a**, and rent his mantle, and shaved his 6965
19:18 I **a**, and they spake against me. 6965
29: 8 and the aged **a**, *and* stood *up*. 6965
Ps 76: 9 When God **a** to judgment, to save all 6965
Ecc 1: 5 and hasteth to his place where he **a**. 2224
Isa 37:36 when they **a early** in the morning, behold, 7925
Jer 41: 2 **a** Ishmael the son of Nethaniah, and the ten 6965
Eze 3:23 I **a**, and went forth into the plain: and 6965
Da 6:19 the king **a** very early in the morning, and 6966
Jnh 3: 3 So Jonah **a**, and went unto Nineveh, 6965
3: 6 he **a** from his throne, and he laid his robe 6965
Mt 2:14 When he **a**, he took the young child and *1453*
2:21 And he **a**, and took the young child and *1453*
8:15 and she **a**, and ministered unto them. *1453*
8:24 there **a** a great tempest in the sea, *1096*
8:26 Then he **a**, and rebuked the winds and *1453*
9: 7 And he **a**, and departed to his house. *1453*
9: 9 Follow me. And he **a**, and followed him. *450*
9:19 And Jesus **a**, and followed him, and *so* *1453*
9:25 and took her by the hand, and the maid **a**. *1453*
25: 7 Then all those virgins **a**, and trimmed their *1453*
26:62 And the high priest **a**, and said unto him, *450*
27:52 and many bodies of saints which slept **a**, *1453*
Mk 2:12 And immediately he **a**, took up the bed, and *1453*
2:14 Follow me. And he **a** and followed him. *450*
4:37 And there **a** a great storm of wind, and *1096*
4:39 And he **a**, and rebuked the wind, and *1326*
5:42 And straightway the damsel **a**, and walked; *450*
7:24 And from thence he **a**, and went into *450*
9:27 him by the hand, and lifted him up; and he **a**. *450*
14:57 And there **a** certain, and bare false witness *450*
Lk 1:39 And Mary **a** in those days, and went into *450*
4:38 And he **a** out of the synagogue, and *450*
4:39 and immediately she **a** and ministered unto *450*
6: 8 *forth* in the midst. And he **a** and stood *forth*. *450*
6:48 and when the flood **a**, the stream beat *1096*
8:55 her spirit came again, and she **a** straightway: *450*
9:46 Then there **a** a reasoning among them, *1525*
15:14 there **a** a mighty famine in that land; *1096*
15:20 And he **a**, and came to his father. But when *450*
23: 1 And the whole multitude of them **a**, and *450*
24:12 Then **a** Peter, and ran unto the sepulchre; *450*
Jn 3:25 Then there **a** a question between *some* of *1096*
6:18 And the sea **a** by reason of a great wind *1326*
11:29 As soon as she heard *that,* she **a** quickly, *1453*
Ac 5: 6 And the young men **a**, wound him up, and *450*
6: 1 there **a** a murmuring of the Grecians *1096*
6: 9 Then there **a** certain of the synagogue, *450*
7:18 Till another king **a**, which knew not Joseph. *450*
8:27 And he **a** and went: and behold, a man of *450*
9: 8 And Saul **a** from the earth; and when his *1453*
9:18 sight forthwith, and **a**, and was baptized, *450*
9:34 and make thy bed. And he **a** immediately. *450*
9:39 Then Peter **a** and went with them. When he *450*
11:19 **a** about Stephen travelled as far as Phenice, *1096*
19:23 And the same time there **a** no small stir *1096*
23: 7 there **a** a dissension between the Pharisees *1096*
23: 9 And there **a** a great cry: and the scribes *that* *1096*
23: 9 the scribes *that were* of the Pharisees' part **a**, *450*
23:10 And when there **a** a great dissension, *1096*
27:14 But not long after there **a** against it a *906*
Rev 9: 2 and there **a** a smoke out of the pit, as *305*

ARPAD (4) [ARPHAD]

2Ki 18:34 Where *are* the gods of Hamath, and of **A**? 774
19:13 the king of **A**, and the king of the city of 774
Isa 10: 9 *is* not Hamath as **A**? *is* not Samaria as 774
Jer 49:23 Hamath is confounded, and **A**: for they have 774

ARPHAD (2) [ARPAD]

Isa 36:19 Where *are* the gods of Hamath and **A**? 774
37:13 the king of **A**, and the king of the city of 774

ARPHAXAD (10)

Ge 10:22 and Asshur, and **A**, and Lud, and Aram. 775
10:24 And **A** begat Salah; and Salah begat Eber. 775
11:10 and begat **A** two years after the flood: 775
11:11 Shem lived after he begat **A** five hundred 775
11:12 **A** lived five and thirty years, and 775
11:13 **A** lived after he begat Salah four hundred 775
1Ch 1:17 and **A**, and Lud, and Aram, and Uz, and Hul, 775
1:18 And **A** begat Shelah, and Shelah begat Eber. 775
1:24 Shem, **A**, Shelah, 775
Lk 3:36 which was *the son* of **A**, which was *the son* *742*

ARRAY (34) [ARRAYED]

Jdg 20:20 the men of Israel **put** *themselves* **in a** to 6186
20:22 **set** *their* battle again **in a** in the place where 6186
20:22 they **put** *themselves* **in a** the first day. 6186
20:30 **put** *themselves* **in a** against Gibeah, as at 6186
20:33 and **put** *themselves* **in a** at Baal-tamar: 6186
1Sa 4: 2 the Philistines **put** *themselves* **in a** against 6186
17: 2 **set** the battle **in a** against the Philistines. 6186
17: 8 are ye come out to **set** *your* battle **in a**? 6186
17:21 and the Philistines had **put** *the battle* **in a**, 6186
2Sa 10: 8 **put** the battle **in a** *at* the entering in of 6186
10: 9 and **put** *them* **in a** against the Syrians: 6186
10:10 that he might **put** *them* **in a** against 6186
10:17 the Syrians **set** *themselves* **in a** against 6186
1Ki 20:12 Set *yourselves in a*. And they set NIH
20:12 they set *themselves in a* against the city. NIH
1Ch 19: 9 **put** the battle **in a** *before* the gate of 6186
19:10 and **put** *them* **in a** against the Syrians. 6186
19:11 they **set** *themselves* **in a** against 6186
19:17 and **set** *the battle* **in a** against them. 6186
19:17 So when David had **put** the battle **in a** 6186
2Ch 13: 3 Abijah **set** the battle **in a** with an army of 631
13: 3 Jeroboam also **set** the battle **in a** against 6186
14:10 they **set** the battle **in a** in the valley of 6186
Est 6: 9 that they may **a** the man *withal* whom 3847
Job 6: 4 the terrors of God do **set** *themselves* **in a** 6186
40:10 and **a** thyself with glory and beauty. 3847
Isa 22: 7 the horsemen shall **set** themselves **in a** at 7896
Jer 6:23 **set in a** as men for war against thee, 6186
43:12 he shall **a** himself **with** the land of Egypt, 5844
50: 9 they shall **set** *themselves* **in a** against her; 6186
50:14 **Put** *yourselves* **in a** against Babylon round 6186
50:42 *every one* **put in a**, like a man to the battle, 6186
Joel 2: 5 as a strong people **set in** battle **a**. 6186
1Ti 2: 9 broided hair, or gold, or pearls, or costly **a**; *2441*

ARRAYED (11) [ARRAY]

Ge 41:42 **a** him in vestures of fine linen, and put a 3847
2Ch 5:12 and their brethren, *being* **a in** white linen, 3847
28:15 **a** them, and shod them, and gave them to 3847
Est 6:11 **a** Mordecai, and brought him on horseback 3847
Mt 6:29 in all his glory was not **a** like one of these. *4016*
Lk 12:27 *that* Solomon in all his glory was not **a** like *4016*
23:11 mocked *him,* and **a** him **in** a gorgeous robe, *4016*
Ac 12:21 **a in** royal apparel, sat upon his throne, and *1746*
Rev 7:13 What are these which are **a in** white robes? *4016*
17: 4 And the woman was **a in** purple and *4016*
19: 8 granted that she should be **a in** fine linen, *4016*

ARRIVED (2)

Lk 8:26 And they **a** at the country of the Gadarenes, *2668*
Ac 20:15 and the next *day* we **a** at Samos, and tarried *3846*

ARROGANCY (4)

1Sa 2: 3 let *not* **a** come out of your mouth: 6277
Pr 8:13 **a**, and the evil way, and the froward mouth, 1347
Isa 13:11 I will cause the **a** of the proud to cease, and 1347
Jer 48:29 his **a**, and his pride, and the haughtiness of 1347

ARROW (16) [ARROWS]

1Sa 20:36 as the lad ran, he shot an **a** beyond him. 2678
20:37 when the lad was come to the place of the **a** 2678
20:37 the lad, and said, *Is* not the **a** beyond thee? 2678
2Ki 9:24 the **a** went out at his heart, and he sunk 2678
13:17 The **a** of the LORD's deliverance, and 2671
13:17 and the **a** of deliverance from Syria: 2671
19:32 nor shoot an **a** there, nor come before it 2671
Job 41:28 The **a** cannot make him flee: 1121+7198
Ps 11: 2 they make ready their **a** upon the string, 2671
64: 7 God shall shoot at them *with* an **a**; 2671
91: 5 by night; *nor* for the **a** *that* flieth by day; 2671
Pr 25:18 *is* a maul, and a sword, and a sharp **a**. 2671
Isa 37:33 nor shoot an **a** there, nor come before it 2671
Jer 9: 8 Their tongue *is as* an **a** shot out; it speaketh 2671
La 3:12 his bow, and set me as a mark for the **a**. 2671

Zec 9:14 and his **a** shall go forth as the lightning: 2671

ARROWS (41) [ARROW]
Nu 24: 8 and pierce *them* through *with* his **a**. 2671
Dt 32:23 upon them; I will spend mine **a** upon them. 2671
32:42 I will make mine **a** drunk with blood, and 2671
1Sa 20:20 I will shoot three **a** on the side *thereof,* as 2671
20:21 I will send a lad, *saying,* Go, find out the **a**. 2671
20:21 Behold, the **a** *are* on this side of thee, take 2671
20:22 young man, Behold, the **a** *are* beyond thee; 2671
20:36 Run, find out now the **a** which I shoot. 2671
20:38 Jonathan's lad gathered up the **a**, and 2671
2Sa 22:15 he sent out **a**, and scattered them; lightning, 2671
2Ki 13:15 Elisha said unto him, Take bow and **a**. 2671
13:15 arrows. And he took unto him bow and **a**. 2671
13:18 he said, Take the **a**. And he took *them.* And 2671
1Ch 12: 2 *hurling* stones and *shooting* **a** out of a bow, 2671
2Ch 26:15 to shoot **a** and great stones withal. 2671
Job 6: 4 For the **a** of the Almighty *are* within me, 2671
Ps 7:13 he ordaineth his **a** against the persecutors. 2671
18:14 Yea, he sent out his **a**, and scattered them; 2671
21:12 *when* thou shalt make ready *thine a* upon NIH
38: 2 For thine **a** stick fast in me, and thy hand 2671
45: 5 Thine **a** *are* sharp in the heart of the king's 2671
57: 4 whose teeth *are* spears and **a**, and 2671
58: 7 *when* he bendeth *his bow to shoot* his **a**, 2671
64: 3 *and* bend *their bows to shoot* their **a**, 2671
76: 3 There brake he the **a** of the bow, the shield, 7565
77:17 sent out a sound: thine **a** also went abroad. 2687
120: 4 Sharp **a** of the mighty, with coals of 2671
127: 4 As **a** *are* in the hand of a mighty *man;* so 2671
144: 6 shoot out thine **a**, and destroy them. 2671
Pr 26:18 *man* who casteth firebrands, **a**, and death, 2671
Isa 5:28 Whose **a** *are* sharp, and all their bows bent, 2671
7:24 With **a** and with bows shall *men* come 2671
Jer 50: 9 their **a** *shall be* as of a mighty expert *man;* 2671
50:14 that bend the bow, shoot at her, spare no **a**: 2671
51:11 Make bright the **a**: gather the shields: 2671
La 3:13 He hath caused the **a**s of his quiver to enter 1121
Eze 5:16 When I shall send upon them the evil **a** of 2671
21:21 he made *his* **a** bright, he consulted with 2671
39: 3 will cause thine **a** to fall out of thy right 2671
39: 9 the bows and the **a**, and the handstaves, and 2671
Hab 3:11 at the light of thine **a** they went, *and* at 2671

ART (495) [ARTS] See Index

ARTAXERXES (14) [ARTAXERXES']
Ezr 4: 7 in the days of **A** wrote Bishlam, Mithredath, 783
4: 7 of their companions, unto **A** king of Persia; 783
4: 8 against Jerusalem to **A** the king in this sort: 783
4:11 they sent unto him, *even* unto **A** the king: 783
6:14 of Cyrus, and Darius, and **A** king of Persia. 783
7: 1 these things, in the reign of **A** king of Persia, 783
7: 7 in the seventh year of **A** the king. 783
7:11 that the king **A** gave unto Ezra the priest, 783
7:12 **A**, king of kings, unto Ezra the priest, 783
7:21 I, *even* I **A** the king, do make a decree to all 783
8: 1 me from Babylon, in the reign of **A** the king. 783
Ne 2: 1 *in* the twentieth year of **A** the king, *that* wine 783
5:14 unto the two and thirtieth year of **A** the king, 783
13: 6 thirtieth year of **A** king of Babylon came I 783

ARTAXERXES' (1) [ARTAXERXES]
Ezr 4:23 Now when the copy of king **A** letter *was* 783

ARTEMAS (1)
Tit 3:12 When I shall send **A** unto thee, or Tychicus, *734*

ARTEMIS See DIANA

ARTIFICER (2) [ARTIFICERS]
Ge 4:22 an instructor of every **a** in brass and iron: 2794
Isa 3: 3 and the cunning **a**, and the eloquent orator. 2791

ARTIFICERS (2) [ARTIFICER]
1Ch 29: 5 *of* work *to be made* by the hands of **a**. 2796
2Ch 34:11 Even to the **a** and builders gave they *it,* to 2796

ARTILLERY (1)
1Sa 20:40 Jonathan gave his **a** unto his lad, and 3627

ARTS (1) [ART]
Ac 19:19 Many also of them which used **curious a** *4021*

ARUBBOTH See ARUBOTH

ARUBOTH (1)
1Ki 4:10 The son of Hesed, in **A**; to him *pertained* 700

ARUMAH (1)
Jdg 9:41 Abimelech dwelt at **A**: and Zebul thrust out 725

ARVAD (2) [ARVADITE]
Eze 27: 8 of Zidon and **A** were thy mariners: 719
27:11 The men of **A** with thine army *were* upon 719

ARVADITE (2) [ARVAD]
Ge 10:18 the **A**, and the Zemarite, and the Hamathite: 721
1Ch 1:16 the **A**, and the Zemarite, and the Hamathite. 721

ARZA (1)
1Ki 16: 9 drinking *himself* drunk *in* the house of **A** 777

AS (3520) [FORASMUCH, INASMUCH] See Index

ASA (59) [ASA'S]
1Ki 15: 8 of David: and **A** his son reigned in his stead. 609
15: 9 king of Israel reigned **A** over Judah. 609
15:11 **A** did *that* which *was* right in the eyes of 609
15:13 **A** destroyed her idol, and burnt *it* by 609
15:16 there was war between **A** and Baasha king of 609
15:17 *any* to go out or come in to **A** king of Judah. 609
15:18 **A** took all the silver and the gold that were 609
15:18 king **A** sent them to Ben-hadad, the son of 609
15:20 So Ben-hadad hearkened unto king **A**, and 609
15:22 king **A** made a proclamation throughout all 609
15:22 king **A** built with them Geba of Benjamin, 609
15:23 The rest of all the acts of **A**, and all his 609
15:24 **A** slept with his fathers, and was buried with 609
15:25 Israel in the second year of **A** king of Judah, 609
15:28 Even in the third year of **A** king of Judah did 609
15:32 there was war between **A** and Baasha king of 609
15:33 In the third year of **A** king of Judah *began* 609
16: 8 sixth year of **A** king of Judah *began* Elah 609
16:10 and seventh year of **A** king of Judah, 609
16:15 seventh year of **A** king of Judah did Zimri 609
16:23 first year of **A** king of Judah *began* Omri to 609
16:29 eighth year of **A** king of Judah *began* Ahab 609
22:41 Jehoshaphat the son of **A** *began* to reign over 609
22:43 he walked in all the ways of **A** his father; 609
22:46 which remained in the days of his father **A**, 609
1Ch 3:10 Abia his son, **A** his son, Jehoshaphat his son, 609
9:16 Berechiah the son of **A**, the son of Elkanah, 609
2Ch 14: 1 **A** his son reigned in his stead. In his days 609
14: 2 **A** did *that* which *was* good and right in 609
14: 8 And **A** had an army *of men* that bare targets 609
14:10 **A** went out against him, and they set 609
14:11 **A** cried unto the LORD his God, and said, 609
14:12 the LORD smote the Ethiopians before **A**, 609
14:13 **A** and the people that *were* with him pursued 609
15: 2 he went out to meet **A**, and said unto him, 609
15: 2 Hear ye me, **A**, and all Judah and Benjamin; 609
15: 8 when **A** heard these words, and the prophecy 609
15:10 in the fifteenth year of the reign of **A**. 609
15:16 also *concerning* Maachah the mother of **A** 609
15:16 and **A** cut down her idol, and stamped *it,* and 609
15:17 nevertheless the heart of **A** was perfect all 609
15:19 the five and thirtieth year of the reign of **A**. 609
16: 1 thirtieth year of the reign of **A** Baasha king 609
16: 1 none go out or come in to **A** king of Judah. 609
16: 2 **A** brought out silver and gold out of 609
16: 4 And Ben-hadad hearkened unto king **A**, and 609
16: 6 **A** the king took all Judah; and they carried 609
16: 7 at that time Hanani the seer came to **A** king 609
16:10 **A** was wroth with the seer, and put him *in* a 609
16:10 of this *thing.* And **A** oppressed *some* of 609
16:11 behold, the acts of **A**, first and last, lo, 609
16:12 **A** in the thirty and ninth year of his reign 609
16:13 **A** slept with his fathers, and died in the one 609
17: 2 of Ephraim, which **A** his father had taken. 609
20:32 he walked in the way of **A** his father, and 609
21:12 nor in the ways of **A** king of Judah, 609
Jer 41: 9 *was* it which **A** the king had made for fear of 609
Mt 1: 7 and Roboam begat Abia; and Abia begat **A**; *760*
1: 8 And **A** begat Josaphat; and Josaphat begat *760*

ASA'S (1) [ASA]
1Ki 15:14 nevertheless **A** heart was perfect with 609

ASAHEL (18)
2Sa 2:18 of Zeruiah there, Joab, and Abishai, and **A**: 6214

A

2Sa 2:18 and **A** *was as* light of foot as a wild roe. 6214
2:19 **A** pursued after Abner; and in going he 6214
2:20 looked behind him, and said, *Art* thou **A**? 6214
2:21 **A** would not turn aside from following of 6214
2:22 Abner said again to **A**, Turn thee aside 6214
2:23 that as many as came to the place where **A** 6214
2:30 of David's servants nineteen men and **A**. 6214
2:32 they took up **A**, and buried him in 6214
3:27 that he died, for the blood of **A** his brother. 6214
3:30 he had slain their brother **A** at Gibeon in 6214
23:24 **A** the brother of Joab *was* one of the thirty; 6214
1Ch 2:16 of Zeruiah; Abishai, and Joab, and **A**, three. 6214
11:26 Also the valiant *men* of the armies *were,* **A** 6214
27: 7 the fourth month *was* **A** the brother of Joab, 6214
2Ch 17: 8 **A**, and Shemiramoth, and Jehonathan, and 6214
31:13 **A**, and Jerimoth, and Jozabad, and Eliel, 6214
Ezr 10:15 Only Jonathan the son of **A** and 6214

ASAHIAH (2)
2Ki 22:12 and **A** a servant of the king's, saying, 6222
22:14 Ahikam, and Achbor, and Shaphan, and **A**, 6222

ASAIAH (6)
1Ch 4:36 **A**, and Adiel, and Jesimiel, and Benaiah, 6222
6:30 Shimea his son, Haggiah his son, **A** his son. 6222
9: 5 the Shilonites; **A** the firstborn, and his sons. 6222
15: 6 **A** the chief, and his brethren two hundred 6222
15:11 for Uriel, **A**, and Joel, Shemaiah, and Eliel, 6222
2Ch 34:20 and **A** a servant of the king's, saying, 6222

ASAPH (45) [ASAPH'S]
2Ki 18:18 and Joah the son of **A** the recorder. 623
18:37 and Joah the son of **A** the recorder, 623
1Ch 6:39 his brother **A**, who stood on his right hand, 623
6:39 *even* **A** the son of Berachiah, the son of 623
9:15 of Micah, the son of Zichri, the son of **A**; 623
15:17 and of his brethren, **A** the son of Berechiah; 623
15:19 So the singers, Heman, **A**, and Ethan, 623
16: 5 **A** the chief, and next to him Zechariah, Jeiel, 623
16: 5 but **A** made a sound with cymbals; 623
16: 7 to thank the LORD into the hand of **A** 623
16:37 the ark of the covenant of the LORD **A** 623
25: 1 separated to the service of the sons of **A**, 623
25: 2 Of the sons of **A**; Zaccur, and Joseph, and 623
25: 2 the sons of **A** under the hands of Asaph, 623
25: 2 the sons of Asaph under the hands of **A**, 623
25: 6 according to the king's order *to* **A**, Jeduthun, 623
25: 9 Now the first lot came forth for **A** to Joseph: 623
26: 1 the son of Kore, of the sons of **A**. 623
2Ch 5:12 all of them of **A**, of Heman, of Jeduthun, 623
20:14 son of Mattaniah, a Levite of the sons of **A**, 623
29:13 of the sons of **A**; Zechariah, and Mattaniah: 623
29:30 with the words of David, and of **A** the seer. 623
35:15 the singers the sons of **A** *were* in their place, 623
35:15 **A**, and Heman, and Jeduthun the king's seer; 623
Ezr 2:41 the children of **A**, an hundred twenty and 623
3:10 and the Levites the sons of **A** with cymbals, 623
Ne 2: 8 a letter unto **A** the keeper of the king's 623
7:44 the children of **A**, an hundred forty and 623
11:17 son of Micha, the son of Zabdi, the son of **A**, 623
11:22 Of the sons of **A**, the singers *were* over 623
12:35 of Michaiah, the son of Zaccur, the son of **A**: 623
12:46 and **A** of old *there were* chief of the singers, 623
Ps 50: T **A** Psalm of **A**. 623
73: T **A** Psalm of **A**. 623
74: T Maschil of **A**. 623
75: T Al-taschith, **A** Psalm *or* Song of **A**. 623
76: T on Neginoth, **A** Psalm *or* Song of **A**. 623
77: T chief Musician, to Jeduthun, **A** Psalm of **A**. 623
78: T Maschil of **A**. 623
79: T **A** Psalm of **A**. 623
80: T upon Shoshannim-Eduth, **A** Psalm of **A**. 623
81: T chief Musician upon Gittith, *A Psalm* of **A**. 623
82: T **A** Psalm of **A**. 623
83: T **A** Song *or* Psalm of **A**. 623
Isa 36:22 and Joah, the son of **A**, the recorder, 623

ASAPH'S (1) [ASAPH]
Isa 36: 3 the scribe, and Joah, **A** son, the recorder. 623

ASAREEL (1)
1Ch 4:16 of Jehaleleel; Ziph, and Ziphah, Tiria, and **A**. 840

ASAREL See ASAREEL

ASARELAH (1)
1Ch 25: 2 Zaccur, and Joseph, and Nethaniah, and **A**, 841

ASCEND (13) [ASCENDED, ASCENDETH, ASCENDING, ASCENT]
Jos 6: 5 the people shall **a up** every man straight 5927
Ps 24: 3 Who shall **a** into the hill of the LORD? 5927
135: 7 He **causeth** the vapours **to a** from the ends 5927
139: 8 If I **a up** *into* heaven, thou *art* there: if I 5266
Isa 14:13 hast said in thine heart, I will **a** *into* heaven, 5927
14:14 I will **a** above the heights of the clouds; 5927
Jer 10:13 he **causeth** the vapours **to a** from the ends 5927
51:16 he **causeth** the vapours **to a** from the ends 5927
Eze 38: 9 Thou shalt **a** and come like a storm, 5927
Jn 6:62 if ye shall see the Son of man **a up** where he *305*
20:17 I **a** unto my Father, and your Father; *305*
Ro 10: 6 not in thine heart, Who shall **a** into heaven? *305*
Rev 17: 8 and shall **a** out of the bottomless *pit,* and *305*

ASCENDED (19) [ASCEND]
Ex 19:18 the smoke thereof **a** as the smoke of a 5927
Nu 13:22 they **a** by the south, and came unto Hebron; 5927
Jos 8:20 the smoke of the city **a up** to heaven, and 5927
8:21 that the smoke of the city **a**, then 5927
10: 7 So Joshua **a** from Gilgal, he, and all 5927
15: 3 **a up** on the south side unto Kadesh-barnea, 5927
Jdg 13:20 that the angel of the LORD **a** in the flame 5927
20:40 the flame of the city **a up** to heaven. 5927
Ps 68:18 Thou hast **a** on high, thou hast led captivity 5927
Pr 30: 4 Who hath **a up** *into* heaven, or descended? 5927
Jn 3:13 And no *man* hath **a up** to heaven, but he that *305*
20:17 me not; for I am not yet **a** to my Father: *305*
Ac 2:34 For David is not **a** into the heavens: but *305*
25: 1 after three days he **a** from Cesarea to *305*
Eph 4: 8 Wherefore *he* saith, When he **a up** on high, *305*
4: 9 (Now that he **a**, what is it but that he also *305*
4:10 He that descended is the same also that **a up** *305*
Rev 8: 4 **a up** before God out of the angel's hand. *305*
11:12 And they **a up** to heaven in a cloud; and *305*

ASCENDETH (2) [ASCEND]
Rev 11: 7 the beast that **a** out of the bottomless *pit* *305*
14:11 And the smoke of their torment **a up** for ever *305*

ASCENDING (5) [ASCEND]
Ge 28:12 behold the angels of God **a** and 5927
1Sa 28:13 unto Saul, I saw gods **a** out of the earth. 5927
Lk 19:28 he went before, **a up** to Jerusalem. *305*
Jn 1:51 and the angels of God **a** and *305*
Rev 7: 2 And I saw another angel **a** from the east, *305*

ASCENT (4) [ASCEND]
Nu 34: 4 turn from the south to the **a** of Akrabbim, 4608
2Sa 15:30 David went up by the **a** of *mount* Olivet, 4608
1Ki 10: 5 his **a** *by* which he went up *unto* the house 5930
2Ch 9: 4 his **a** *by* which he went up *into* the house of 5944

ASCRIBE (3) [ASCRIBED]
Dt 32: 3 the LORD: **a** ye greatness unto our God. 3051
Job 36: 3 and will **a** righteousness to my Maker. 5414
Ps 68:34 **A** ye strength unto God: his excellency *is* 5414

ASCRIBED (2) [ASCRIBE]
1Sa 18: 8 They have **a** unto David ten thousands, and 5414
18: 8 and to me they have **a** *but* thousands: 5414

ASENATH (3)
Ge 41:45 he gave him to wife **A** the daughter of 621
41:50 which **A** the daughter of Poti-pherah priest 621
46:20 which **A** the daughter of Poti-pherah priest 621

ASER (2) [ASHER]
Lk 2:36 the daughter of Phanuel, of the tribe of **A**: *768*
Rev 7: 6 Of the tribe of **A** *were* sealed twelve *768*

ASH (1)
Isa 44:14 he planteth an **a**, and the rain doth nourish 766

ASHAMED (122) [SHAME]
Ge 2:25 the man and his wife, and were not **a**. 954
Nu 12:14 in her face, should she not be **a** seven days? 3637
Jdg 3:25 And they tarried till *they* were **a**: and behold, 954
2Sa 10: 5 meet them, because the men were greatly **a**: 3637
19: 3 as people being **a** steal away when they flee 3637
2Ki 2:17 when they urged him till *he* was **a**, he said, 954

2Ki 8:11 his countenance stedfastly, until *he* was **a**: 954
1Ch 19: 5 for the men were greatly **a**. And the king 3637
2Ch 30:15 the priests and the Levites were **a**, and 3637
Ezr 8:22 For I was **a** to require of the king a band *of* 954
9: 6 I am **a** and blush to lift up my face to thee, 954
Job 6:20 had hoped; they came thither, and were **a**. 2659
11: 3 thou mockest, shall no man **make** *thee* **a**? 3637
19: 3 you are not **a** *that* you make yourselves 954
Ps 6:10 Let all mine enemies be **a** and sore vexed: 954
6:10 let them return *and* be **a** suddenly. 954
25: 2 let me not be **a**, let not mine enemies 954
25: 3 Yea, let none that wait on thee be **a**: let them 954
25: 3 let them be **a** which transgress without 954
25:20 let me not be **a**; for I put my trust in thee. 954
31: 1 do I put my trust; let me never be **a**: 954
31:17 Let me not be **a**, O LORD; for I have called 954
31:17 let the wicked be **a**, *and* let them be silent in 954
34: 5 were lightened: and their faces were not **a**. 2659
35:26 Let them be **a** and brought to confusion 954
37:19 They shall not be **a** in the evil time: and 954
40:14 Let them be **a** and confounded together that 954
69: 6 O Lord GOD of hosts, be **a** for my sake: 954
70: 2 Let them be **a** and confounded that seek after 954
74:21 O let not the oppressed return **a**: let 3637
86:17 that they which hate me may see *it,* and be **a**: 954
109:28 when they arise, let them be **a**; but let thy 954
119: 6 shall I not be **a**, when I have respect unto all 954
119:46 also before kings, and will not be **a**. 954
119:78 Let the proud be **a**; for they dealt perversely 954
119:80 heart be sound in thy statutes; that I be not **a**. 954
119:116 I may live: and let me not be **a** of my hope. 954
127: 5 they shall not be **a**, but they shall speak with 954
Pr 12: 4 she that **maketh a** *is* as rottenness in his 954
Isa 1:29 For they shall be **a** of the oaks which ye 954
20: 5 be afraid and **a** of Ethiopia their expectation, 954
23: 4 Be thou **a**, O Zidon: for the sea hath spoken, 954
24:23 moon shall be confounded, and the sun **a**, 954
26:11 and be **a** for *their* envy at the people; 954
29:22 the house of Jacob, Jacob shall not now be **a**, 954
30: 5 They were all **a** of a people *that* could not 954
33: 9 Lebanon is **a** *and* hewn down: Sharon is 2659
41:11 that were incensed against thee shall be **a** 954
42:17 turned back, they shall be **greatly a**, 954+1322
44: 9 they see not, nor know; that they may be **a**. 954
44:11 Behold, all his fellows shall be **a**: and 954
44:11 they shall fear, *and* they shall be **a** together. 954
45:16 They shall be **a**, and also confounded, all of 954
45:17 ye shall not be **a** nor confounded world 954
45:24 all that are incensed against him shall be **a**. 954
49:23 for they shall not be **a** that wait for me. 954
50: 7 like a flint, and I know that I shall not be **a**. 954
54: 4 Fear not; for thou shalt not be **a**: neither be 954
65:13 my servants shall rejoice, but ye shall be **a**: 954
66: 5 *shall* appear to your joy, and they shall be **a**. 954
Jer 2:26 As the thief is **a** when he is found, so is 1322
2:26 when he is found, so is the house of Israel **a**; 954
2:36 thou also shalt be **a** of Egypt, as thou wast 954
2:36 ashamed of Egypt, as thou wast **a** of Assyria. 954
3: 3 a whore's forehead, thou refusedst to be **a**. 3637
6:15 Were they **a** when they had committed 954
6:15 nay, they were not **at all a**, neither 954+954
8: 9 The wise *men* are **a**, they are dismayed and 954
8:12 Were they **a** when they had committed 954
8:12 nay, they were not **at all a**, neither 954+954
12:13 and they shall be **a** of your revenues because 954
14: 3 they were **a** and confounded, and 954
14: 4 the plowmen were **a**, they covered their 954
15: 9 she hath been **a** and confounded: and 954
17:13 all that forsake thee shall be **a**, and they that 954
20:11 they shall be greatly **a**: for they shall not 954
22:22 surely then shalt thou be **a** and 954
31:19 I was **a**, yea, even confounded, because I did 954
48:13 Moab shall be **a** of Chemosh, as the house of 954
48:13 as the house of Israel was **a** of Beth-el their 954
50:12 she that bare you shall be **a**: 2659
Eze 16:27 which are **a** of thy lewd way. 3637
16:61 be **a**, when thou shalt receive thy sisters, 3637
32:30 with their terror *they are* **a** of their might; 954
36:32 be **a** and confounded for your own ways, 954
43:10 that they may be **a** of their iniquities: 3637
43:11 if they be **a** of all that they have done, 3637
Hos 4:19 they shall be **a** because of their sacrifices. 954
10: 6 and Israel shall be **a** of his own counsel. 954
Joel 1:11 Be ye **a**, O ye husbandmen; howl, O ye 954
2:26 with you: and my people shall never be **a**. 954
2:27 none else: and my people shall never be **a**. 954
Mic 3: 7 shall the seers be **a**, and the diviners 954
Zep 3:11 In that day shalt thou not be **a** for all thy 954
Zec 9: 5 for her expectation shall be **a**; and the king 3001
13: 4 *that* the prophets shall be **a** every one of his 954
Mk 8:38 Whosoever therefore shall be **a** of me and *1870*
8:38 of him also shall the Son of man be **a**, *1870*
Lk 9:26 For whosoever shall be **a** of me and of my *1870*
9:26 of him shall the Son of man be **a**, *1870*
13:17 said these *things,* all his adversaries were **a**: *2617*
16: 3 the stewardship: I cannot dig; to beg I am **a**. *153*
Ro 1:16 For I am not **a** of the gospel of Christ: for it *1870*
5: 5 And hope **maketh** not **a**; because the love *2617*
6:21 then *in those things* whereof ye are now **a**? *1870*
9:33 whosoever believeth on him shall not be **a**. *2617*
10:11 Whosoever believeth on him shall not be **a**. *2617*
2Co 7:14 boasted any *thing* to him of you, I am not **a**; *2617*
9: 4 should be **a** in this *same* confident boasting. *2617*
10: 8 not for your destruction, I should not be **a**: *153*
Php 1:20 that in nothing I shall be **a**, but *that* with all *153*
2Th 3:14 no company with him, that he may be **a**. *1788*
2Ti 1: 8 therefore **a** of the testimony of our Lord, *1870*
1:12 suffer these *things:* nevertheless I am not **a**: *1870*
1:16 refreshed me, and was not **a** of my chain: *1870*
2:15 a workman that **needeth not to be a**, *422*
Tit 2: 8 that he that is of the contrary *part* may be **a**, *1788*
Heb 2:11 for which cause he is not **a** to call them *1870*
11:16 wherefore God is not **a** to be called their *1870*
1Pe 3:16 they may be **a** that falsely accuse your good *2617*
4:16 *man suffer* as a Christian, let him not be **a**; *153*
1Jn 2:28 and not be **a** before him at his coming. *153*

ASHAN (4)
Jos 15:42 Libnah, and Ether, and **A**, 6228
19: 7 Ain, Remmon, and Ether, and **A**; four cities 6228
1Ch 4:32 Ain, Rimmon, and Tochen, and **A**, 6228
6:59 **A** with her suburbs, and Beth-shemesh with 6228

ASHBEA (1)
1Ch 4:21 that wrought fine linen, of the house of **A**, 791

ASHBEL (3) [ASHBELITES]
Ge 46:21 and **A**, Gera, and Naaman, Ehi, and Rosh, 788
Nu 26:38 of **A**, the family of the Ashbelites: 788
1Ch 8: 1 **A** the second, and Aharah the third, 788

ASHBELITES (1) [ASHBEL]
Nu 26:38 of Ashbel, the family of the **A**: of Ahiram, 789

ASHCHENAZ (2)
1Ch 1: 6 of Gomer; **A**, and Riphath, and Togarmah. 813
Jer 51:27 her the kingdoms of Ararat, Minni, and **A**; 813

ASHDOD (21) [ASHDODITES]
Jos 11:22 only in Gaza, in Gath, and in **A**, 795
15:46 all that *lay* near **A**, with their villages: 795
15:47 **A** *with* her towns and her villages, Gaza *with* 795
1Sa 5: 1 and brought it from Eben-ezer unto **A**. 795
5: 3 when **they of A** arose early on the morrow, 796
5: 5 tread on the threshold of Dagon in **A** unto 795
5: 6 of the LORD was heavy upon **them of A**, 796
5: 6 with emerods, *even* **A** and the coasts thereof. 795
5: 7 when the men of **A** saw that *it was* so, they 795
6:17 for **A** one, for Gaza one, for Askelon one, 795
2Ch 26: 6 the wall of **A**, and built cities about Ashdod, 795
26: 6 built cities about **A**, and among 795
Ne 13:23 also saw I Jews *that* had married wives of **A**, 796
13:24 their children spake half **in the speech of A**, 797
Isa 20: 1 In the year that Tartan came unto **A**, 795
20: 1 sent him,) and fought against **A**, and took it; 795
Jer 25:20 and Ekron, and the remnant of **A**: 795
Am 1: 8 And I will cut off the inhabitant from **A**, and 795
3: 9 Publish in the palaces at **A**, and in 795
Zep 2: 4 they shall drive out **A** at the noon day, 795
Zec 9: 6 a bastard shall dwell in **A**, and I will cut off 795

ASHDODITES (1) [ASHDOD]
Ne 4: 7 the Arabians, and the Ammonites, and the **A**, 796

ASHDOTHITES (1)
Jos 13: 3 the Gazathites, and the **A**, the Eshkalonites, 796

ASHDOTH-PISGAH (3)
Dt 3:17 *even* the salt sea, under **A** eastward. 798

Jos 12: 3 and from the south, under **A**: 798
13:20 And Beth-peor, and **A**, and Beth-jeshimoth, 798

ASHER (43) [ASER, ASHERITES]

Ge 30:13 call me blessed: and she called his name **A**. 836
35:26 of Zilpah, Leah's handmaid; Gad, and **A**: 836
46:17 And the sons of **A**; Jimnah, and Ishuah, and 836
49:20 Out of **A** his bread *shall be* fat, and he shall 836
Ex 1: 4 Dan, and Naphtali, Gad, and **A**. 836
Nu 1:13 Of **A**; Pagiel the son of Ocran. 836
1:40 Of the children of **A**, *by* their generations, 836
1:41 *even* of the tribe of **A**, *were* forty and 836
2:27 that encamp by him *shall be* the tribe of **A**: 836
2:27 the captain of the children of **A** *shall be* 836
7:72 prince of the children of **A**, *offered:* 836
10:26 over the host of the tribe of the children of **A** 836
13:13 Of the tribe of **A**, Sethur the son of Michael. 836
26:44 *Of* the children of **A** after their families: 836
26:46 the name of the daughter of **A** *was* Sarah. 836
26:47 These *are* the families of the sons of **A** 836
34:27 the prince of the tribe of the children of **A**, 836
Dt 27:13 and **A**, and Zebulun, Dan, and Naphtali. 836
33:24 of **A** he said, *Let* Asher *be* blessed with 836
33:24 he said, *Let* **A** *be* blessed with children; 836
Jos 17: 7 the coast of Manasseh was from **A** *to* 836
17:10 and they met together in **A** on the north, and 836
17:11 and in **A** Beth-shean and her towns, 836
19:24 the children of **A** according to their families. 836
19:31 the children of **A** according to their families, 836
19:34 reacheth to **A** on the west side, and to Judah 836
21: 6 out of the tribe of **A**, and out of the tribe of 836
21:30 out of the tribe of **A**, Mishal with her 836
Jdg 1:31 Neither did **A** drive out the inhabitants of 836
5:17 **A** continued on the sea shore, and abode in 836
6:35 he sent messengers unto **A**, and 836
7:23 out of **A**, and out of all Manasseh, and 836
1Ki 4:16 Baanah the son of Hushai *was* in **A** and 836
1Ch 2: 2 Joseph, and Benjamin, Naphtali, Gad, and **A**. 836
6:62 out of the tribe of **A**, and out of the tribe of 836
6:74 out of the tribe of **A**; Mashal with her 836
7:30 The sons of **A**; Imnah, and Isuah, and Ishuai, 836
7:40 All these *were* the children of **A**, heads of 836
12:36 of **A**, such as went forth to battle, expert in 836
2Ch 30:11 Nevertheless divers of **A** and Manasseh and 836
Eze 48: 2 east side unto the west side, a *portion for* **A**. 836
48: 3 by the border of **A**, from the east side even 836
48:34 one gate of Gad, one gate of **A**, one gate of 836

ASHERITES (1) [ASHER]

Jdg 1:32 the **A** dwelt among the Canaanites, 843

ASHES (43)

Ge 18:27 unto the Lord, which *am but* dust and **a**: 665
Ex 9: 8 Take to you handfuls of **a** of the furnace, 6368
9:10 they took **a** of the furnace, and stood before 6368
27: 3 thou shalt make his pans to **receive** his **a**, 1878
Lev 1:16 altar on the east part, by the place of the **a**: 1880
4:12 where the **a** are poured out, and burn him 1880
4:12 where the **a** are poured out shall he be 1880
6:10 take up the **a** which the fire hath consumed 1880
6:11 carry forth the **a** without the camp unto a 1880
Nu 4:13 they shall **take away** the **a** from the altar, 1878
19: 9 a man *that is* clean shall gather up the **a** of 665
19:10 he that gathereth the **a** of the heifer shall 665
19:17 **a** of the burnt *heifer* of purification for sin, 6083
2Sa 13:19 Tamar put **a** on her head, and rent her 665
1Ki 13: 3 the **a** that *are* upon it shall be poured out. 1880
13: 5 and the **a** poured out from the altar, 1880
20:38 and disguised himself with **a** upon his face. 666
20:41 and took the **a** away from his face; 666
2Ki 23: 4 and carried the **a** of them *unto* Beth-el. 6083
Est 4: 1 put on sackcloth with **a**, and went out into 665
4: 3 wailing; *and* many lay in sackcloth and **a**. 665
Job 2: 8 and he sat down among the **a**. 665
13:12 Your remembrances *are* like unto **a**, 665
30:19 the mire, and I am become like dust and **a**. 665
42: 6 I abhor *myself,* and repent in dust and **a**. 665
Ps 102: 9 For I have eaten **a** like bread, and 665
147:16 like wool: he scattereth the hoarfrost like **a**. 665
Isa 44:20 He feedeth on **a**: a deceived heart hath 665
58: 5 and **a** *under him?* wilt thou call this a fast, 665
61: 3 to give unto them beauty for **a**, the oil of joy 665
Jer 6:26 *thee* with sackcloth, and wallow thyself in **a**: 665
25:34 wallow yourselves *in the* **a**, ye principal of NIH
31:40 of the **a**, and all the fields unto the brook of 1880
La 3:16 gravel stones, he hath covered me with **a**. 665
Eze 27:30 they shall wallow themselves in the **a**: 665
28:18 I will bring thee to **a** upon the earth in 665
Da 9: 3 with fasting, and sackcloth, and **a**: 665
Jnh 3: 6 and covered *him* with sackcloth, and sat in **a**. 665
Mal 4: 3 for they shall be **a** under the soles of your 665
Mt 11:21 have repented long ago in sackcloth and **a**. *4700*
Lk 10:13 ago repented, sitting in sackcloth and **a**. *4700*
Heb 9:13 and the **a** of a heifer sprinkling the unclean, *4700*
2Pe 2: 6 **turning** the cities of Sodom and Gomorrha **into a** *5077*

ASHHUR See ASHUR

ASHIMA (1)

2Ki 17:30 and the men of Hamath made **A**, 807

ASHKELON (9) [ASKELON, ESHKALONITES]

Jdg 14:19 he went down *to* **A**, and slew thirty men of 831
Jer 25:20 **A**, and Azzah, and Ekron, and the remnant 831
47: 5 **A** is cut off *with* the remnant of their valley: 831
47: 7 the LORD hath given it a charge against **A**, 831
Am 1: 8 and him that holdeth the sceptre from **A**, and 831
Zep 2: 4 Gaza shall be forsaken, and **A** a desolation: 831
2: 7 in the houses of **A** shall they lie down in 831
Zec 9: 5 **A** shall see *it,* and fear; Gaza also *shall see* 831
9: 5 from Gaza, and **A** shall not be inhabited. 831

ASHKENAZ (1)

Ge 10: 3 of Gomer; **A**, and Riphath, and Togarmah. 813

ASHNAH (2)

Jos 15:33 in the valley, Eshtaol, and Zoreah, and **A**, 823
15:43 And Jiphtah, and **A**, and Nezib, 823

ASHPENAZ (1)

Da 1: 3 the king spake unto **A** the master of his 828

ASHRIEL (1)

1Ch 7:14 The sons of Manasseh; **A**, whom she bare: 844

ASHTAROTH (11) [ASHTORETH]

Jos 9:10 and to Og king of Bashan, which *was* at **A**. 6252
12: 4 of the giants, that dwelt at **A** and at Edrei, 6252
13:12 in Bashan, which reigned in **A** and in Edrei, 6252
13:31 half Gilead, and **A**, and Edrei, cities of 6252
Jdg 2:13 the LORD, and served Baal and **A**. 6252
10: 6 **A**, and the gods of Syria, and the gods of 6252
1Sa 7: 3 the strange gods and **A** from among you, 6252
7: 4 of Israel did put away Baalim and **A**, 6252
12:10 and have served Baalim and **A**: 6252
31:10 they put his armour *in* the house of **A**: and 6253
1Ch 6:71 with her suburbs, and **A** with her suburbs: 6252

ASHTERATHITE (1)

1Ch 11:44 Uzzia the **A**, Shama and Jehiel the sons of 6254

ASHTEROTH KARNAIM (1)

Ge 14: 5 and smote the Rephaims in **A**, 6255

ASHTORETH (3) [ASHTAROTH]

1Ki 11: 5 For Solomon went after **A** the goddess of 6253
11:33 have worshipped **A** the goddess of 6253
2Ki 23:13 for **A** the abomination of the Zidonians, 6253

ASHUR (2) [ASHURITES]

1Ch 2:24 Abiah Hezron's wife bare him **A** the father 806
4: 5 **A** the father of Tekoa had two wives, Helah 806

ASHURBANIPAL See ASNAPPER

ASHURI See ASHURITES

ASHURITES (2) [ASHUR]

2Sa 2: 9 over the **A**, and over Jezreel, and 805
Eze 27: 6 the company of the **A** have made thy 839

ASHVATH (1)

1Ch 7:33 sons of Japhlet; Pasach, and Bimhal, and **A**. 6220

ASIA (21)

Ac 2: 9 in Judea, and Cappadocia, in Pontus, and **A**, *773*
6: 9 and of them of Cilicia and of **A**, *773*
16: 6 of the Holy Ghost to preach the word in **A**, *773*
19:10 that all they which dwelt in **A** heard *773*
19:22 but he himself stayed in **A** for a season. *773*

Ac 19:26 but almost throughout all **A**, this Paul hath *773*
19:27 whom all **A** and the world worshippeth. *773*
19:31 And certain of the **chief of A**, which were *775*
20: 4 And there accompanied him into **A** Sopater *773*
20: 4 and **of A**, Tychicus and Trophimus. *774*
20:16 because he would not spend the time in **A**: *773*
20:18 from the first day that I came into **A**, *773*
21:27 the Jews which were of **A**, when they saw *773*
24:18 Whereupon certain Jews from **A** found me *773*
27: 2 meaning to sail by the coasts of **A**; *773*
1Co 16:19 The churches of **A** salute you. Aquila and *773*
2Co 1: 8 of our trouble which came to us in **A**, *773*
2Ti 1:15 that all they which are in **A** be turned away *773*
1Pe 1: 1 Galatia, Cappadocia, **A**, and Bithynia, *773*
Rev 1: 4 John to the seven churches which are in **A**: *773*
1:11 *it* unto the seven churches which are in **A**; *773*

ASIDE (72) [SIDE] See Index

ASIEL (1)
1Ch 4:35 the son of Seraiah, the son of **A**, 6221

ASK (109) [ASKED, ASKEST, ASKETH, ASKING] See Index

ASKED (119) [ASK] See Index

ASKELON (3) [ASHKELON]
Jdg 1:18 **A** with the coast thereof, and Ekron with 831
1Sa 6:17 for Gaza one, for **A** one, for Gath one, 831
2Sa 1:20 not in Gath, publish *it* not in the streets of **A**; 831

ASKEST (3) [ASK] See Index

ASKETH (11) [ASK] See Index

ASKING (7) [ASK] See Index

ASLEEP (16) [SLEEP]
Jdg 4:21 for he was **fast a**nd weary. So he died. 7290
1Sa 26:12 for they *were* all **a**; because a deep sleep 3463
SS 7: 9 causing the lips of *those that are* **a** to speak. 3463
Jnh 1: 5 of the ship; and he lay, and was **fast a**. 7290
Mt 8:24 was covered with the waves: but he was **a**. *2518*
26:40 and findeth them **a**, and saith unto Peter, *2518*
26:43 And he came and found them **a** again: *2518*
Mk 4:38 in the hinder part of the ship, **a** on a pillow: *2518*
14:40 when he returned, he found them **a** again, *2518*
Lk 8:23 But as they sailed he **fell a**: and there came *879*
Ac 7:60 And when he had said this, he **fell a**. *2837*
1Co 15: 6 unto this present, but some are **fallen a**. *2837*
15:18 Then they also which are **fallen a** in Christ *2837*
1Th 4:13 brethren, concerning them which are **a**, *2837*
4:15 Lord shall not prevent them which are **a**. *2837*
2Pe 3: 4 for since the fathers **fell a**, all *things* *2837*

ASNAH (1)
Ezr 2:50 The children of **A**, the children of Mehunim, 619

ASNAPPAR (1)
Ezr 4:10 whom the great and noble **A** brought over, 620

ASP (1) [ASPS]
Isa 11: 8 child shall play on the hole of the **a**, 6620

ASPATHA (1)
Est 9: 7 And Parshandatha, and Dalphon, and **A**, 630

ASPS (4) [ASP]
Dt 32:33 of dragons, and the cruel venom of **a**. 6620
Job 20:14 is turned, *it is* the gall of **a** within him. 6620
20:16 He shall suck the poison of **a**: the viper's 6620
Ro 3:13 the poison of **a** *is* under their lips: *785*

ASRIEL (2) [ASRIELITES]
Nu 26:31 *of* **A**, the family of the Asrielites: and 844
Jos 17: 2 for the children of **A**, and for the children of 844

ASRIELITES (1) [ASRIEL]
Nu 26:31 *of* Asriel, the family of the **A**: and 845

ASS (86) [ASS'S, ASSES]
Ge 22: 3 saddled his **a**, and took two of his young 2543
22: 5 his young men, Abide you here with the **a**; 2543
42:27 his sack to give his **a** provender in the inn, 2543
44:13 laded every man his **a**, and returned to 2543
49:14 Issachar *is* a strong **a** couching down 2543
Ex 4:20 set them upon an **a**, and he returned to 2543
13:13 every firstling of an **a** thou shalt redeem 2543
20:17 nor his maidservant, nor his ox, nor his **a**, 2543
21:33 not cover it, and an ox or an **a** fall therein; 2543
22: 4 hand alive, whether it be ox, or **a**, or sheep; 2543
22: 9 for **a**, for sheep, for raiment, *or* for any 2543
22:10 If a man deliver unto his neighbour an **a**, or 2543
23: 4 thine enemy's ox or his **a** going astray, 2543
23: 5 If thou see the **a** of him that hateth thee 2543
23:12 that thine ox and thine **a** may rest, and 2543
34:20 the firstling of an **a** thou shalt redeem with 2543
Nu 16:15 I have not taken one **a** from them, 2543
22:21 saddled his **a**, and went with the princes of 860
22:22 Now he was riding upon his **a**, and his two 860
22:23 the **a** saw the angel of the LORD standing 860
22:23 the **a** turned aside out of the way, and 860
22:23 Balaam smote the **a**, to turn her *into* the way. 860
22:25 when the **a** saw the angel of the LORD, 860
22:27 when the **a** saw the angel of the LORD, 860
22:27 was kindled, and he smote the **a** with a staff. 860
22:28 And the LORD opened the mouth of the **a**, 860
22:29 Balaam said unto the **a**, Because thou hast 860
22:30 the **a** said unto Balaam, *Am* not I thine ass, 860
22:30 the ass said unto Balaam, *Am* not I thine **a**, 860
22:32 Wherefore hast thou smitten thine **a** these 860
22:33 the **a** saw me, and turned from me these 860
Dt 5:14 thy maidservant, nor thine ox, nor thine **a**, 2543
5:21 or his **a**, or any *thing* that *is* thy 2543
22: 3 In like manner shalt thou do with his **a**; and 2543
22: 4 Thou shalt not see thy brother's **a** or his ox 2543
22:10 shalt not plow with an ox and an **a** together. 2543
28:31 thine **a** *shall be* violently taken away from 2543
Jos 6:21 and old, and ox, and sheep, and **a**, 2543
15:18 she lighted off *her* **a**; and Caleb said unto 2543
Jdg 1:14 she lighted from off *her* **a**; and Caleb said 2543
6: 4 for Israel, neither sheep, nor ox, nor **a**. 2543
10: 4 had thirty sons that rode on thirty **a colts**, 5895
12:14 that rode on threescore and ten **a colts**: 5895
15:15 he found a new jawbone of an **a**, and 2543
15:16 Samson said, With the jawbone of an **a**, 2543
15:16 with the jaw of an **a** have I slain a thousand 2543
19:28 the man took her *up* upon an **a**, and the man 2543
1Sa 12: 3 or whose **a** have I taken? or whom have I 2543
15: 3 and suckling, ox and sheep, camel and **a**. 2543
16:20 Jesse took an **a** *laden* with bread, and 2543
25:20 it was *so, as* she rode on the **a**, that she 2543
25:23 lighted off the **a**, and fell before David on 2543
25:42 and rose, and rode upon an **a**, 2543
2Sa 17:23 he saddled *his* **a**, and arose, and gat him 2543
19:26 for thy servant said, I will saddle me an **a**, 2543
1Ki 2:40 saddled his **a**, and went to Gath to Achish 2543
13:13 he said unto his sons, Saddle me the **a**. 2543
13:13 So they saddled him the **a**: and he rode 2543
13:23 he had drunk, that he saddled for him the **a**, 2543
13:24 was cast in the way, and the **a** stood by it, 2543
13:27 spake to his sons, saying, Saddle me the **a**. 2543
13:28 the **a** and the lion standing by the carcase: 2543
13:28 had not eaten the carcase, nor torn the **a**. 2543
13:29 and laid it upon the **a**, and brought it back: 2543
2Ki 4:24 she saddled an **a**, and said to her servant, 860
Job 6: 5 Doth the **wild a** bray when he hath grass? 6501
24: 3 They drive away the **a** of the fatherless, 2543
39: 5 Who hath sent out the **wild a** free? or 6501
39: 5 or who hath loosed the bands of the **wild a**? 6171
Pr 26: 3 a bridle for the **a**, and a rod for the fools' 2543
Isa 1: 3 his owner, and the **a** his master's crib: 2543
32:20 forth *thither* the feet of the ox and the **a**. 2543
Jer 2:24 A **wild a** used to the wilderness, 6501
22:19 He shall be buried *with* the burial of an **a**, 2543
Hos 8: 9 up *to* Assyria, a **wild a** alone by himself: 6501
Zec 9: 9 riding upon an **a**, and upon a colt the foal of 2543
9: 9 upon an ass, and upon a colt the foal of an **a**. 860
14:15 of the **a**, and of all the beasts that shall be 2543
Mt 21: 2 and straightway ye shall find an **a** tied, and *3688*
21: 5 and sitting upon an **a**, and a colt the foal of *3688*
21: 5 upon an ass, and a colt the foal of an **a**. *5268*
21: 7 And brought the **a**, and the colt, and put on *3688*
Lk 13:15 sabbath loose his ox or *his* **a** from the stall, *3688*
14: 5 Which of you shall have an **a** or an ox *3688*
Jn 12:14 And Jesus, when he had found a **young a**, *3678*
2Pe 2:16 the dumb **a** speaking with man's voice *5268*

ASS'S (4) [ASS]
Ge 49:11 the vine, and his **a** colt unto the choice vine; 860
2Ki 6:25 until an **a** head was *sold* for fourscore 2543

Job 11:12 though man be born *like* a **wild a** colt. 6501
Jn 12:15 thy King cometh, sitting on an **a** colt. *3688*

ASSAULT (2) [ASSAULTED]
Est 8:11 the people and province that would **a** them, 6696
Ac 14: 5 And when there was an **a** made both of *3730*

ASSAULTED (1) [ASSAULT]
Ac 17: 5 and **a** the house of Jason, and sought to *2186*

ASSAY (1) [ASSAYED, ASSAYING]
Job 4: 2 *If we* **a** to commune with thee, wilt thou be 5254

ASSAYED (4) [ASSAY]
Dt 4:34 Or hath God **a** to go *and* take him a nation 5254
1Sa 17:39 his sword upon his armour, and he **a** to go; 2974
Ac 9:26 he **a** to join himself to the disciples: *3987*
16: 7 come to Mysia, they **a** to go into Bithynia: *3985*

ASSAYING (1) [ASSAY]
Heb 11:29 which the Egyptians **a** to do were drowned. *3984*

ASSEMBLE (20) [ASSEMBLED, ASSEMBLIES, ASSEMBLING, ASSEMBLY]
Nu 10: 3 all the assembly shall **a** themselves to thee 3259
2Sa 20: 4 **A** me the men of Judah *within* three days, 2199
20: 5 So Amasa went to **a** *the men of* Judah: but 2199
Isa 11:12 shall **a** the outcasts of Israel, and 622
45:20 **A** yourselves and come; draw near 6908
48:14 All ye, **a** yourselves, and hear; 6908
Jer 4: 5 **A** yourselves, and let us go into the defenced 622
8:14 **a** yourselves, and let us enter into 622
12: 9 come ye, **a** all the beasts of the field, 622
21: 4 and I will **a** them into the midst of this city. 622
Eze 11:17 **a** you out of the countries where ye have 622
39:17 beast of the field, **A** yourselves, and come; 6908
Da 11:10 and shall **a** a multitude of great forces: 622
Hos 7:14 they **a** themselves for corn and wine, *and* 1481
Joel 2:16 **a** the elders, gather the children, and 6908
3:11 **A** yourselves, and come, all ye heathen, 5789
Am 3: 9 **A** yourselves upon the mountains of 622
Mic 2:12 I will **surely a**, O Jacob, all of thee; 622+622
4: 6 will I **a** her that halteth, and I will gather her 622
Zep 3: 8 that I may **a** the kingdoms, to pour upon 6908

ASSEMBLED (37) [ASSEMBLE]
Ex 38: 8 which **a** *at* the door of the tabernacle of 6633
Nu 1:18 they **a** all the congregation **together** on 6950
Jos 18: 1 the children of Israel **a together** *at* Shiloh, 6950
Jdg 10:17 the children of Israel **a** themselves **together**, 622
1Sa 2:22 how they lay with the women that **a** *at* 6633
14:20 all the people that *were* with him **a** 2199
1Ki 8: 1 Solomon **a** the elders of Israel, and all 6950
8: 2 all the men of Israel **a** themselves unto king 6950
8: 5 of Israel, that were **a** unto him, 3259
12:21 he **a** all the house of Judah, with the tribe of 6950
1Ch 15: 4 David **a** the children of Aaron, and 622
28: 1 David **a** all the princes of Israel, the princes 6950
2Ch 5: 2 Solomon **a** the elders of Israel, and all 6950
5: 3 Wherefore all the men of Israel **a** 6950
5: 6 all the congregation of Israel that were **a** 3259
20:26 on the fourth day they **a** themselves in 6950
30:13 there **a** *at* Jerusalem much people to keep 622
Ezr 9: 4 were **a** unto me every one that trembled at 622
10: 1 there **a** unto him out of Israel a very great 6908
Ne 9: 1 the children of Israel were **a** with fasting, 622
Est 9:18 the Jews that *were* at Shushan **a together** 6950
Ps 48: 4 For lo, the kings were **a**, they passed by 3259
Isa 43: 9 be gathered together, and let the people be **a**: 622
Jer 5: 7 **a** themselves **by troops** *in* the harlots' 1413
Eze 38: 7 all thy company that are **a** unto thee, and 6950
Da 6: 6 princes **a** *together* to the king, 7284
6:11 these men **a**, and found Daniel praying 7284
6:15 these men **a** unto the king, and said unto 7284
Mt 26: 3 Then **a together** the chief priests, and *4863*
26:57 where the scribes and the elders were **a**. *4863*
28:12 And when they were **a** with the elders, and *4863*
Mk 14:53 **with** him were **a** all the chief priests and *4905*
Jn 20:19 the disciples were **a** for fear of the Jews, *4863*
Ac 1: 4 And, being **a together with** them, *4871*
4:31 was shaken where they were **a together**; *4863*
11:26 that a whole year they **a** themselves with *4863*
15:25 good unto us, being **a** with one accord, *1096*

ASSEMBLIES (6) [ASSEMBLE]
Ps 86:14 the **a** of violent *men* have sought after my 5712
Ecc 12:11 and as nails fastened *by* the masters of **a**, 627
Isa 1:13 new moons and sabbaths, the calling of **a**, 4744
4: 5 upon her **a**, a cloud and smoke by day, and 4744
Eze 44:24 keep my laws and my statutes in all mine **a**; 4150
Am 5:21 and I will not smell in your **solemn a**. 6116

ASSEMBLING (2) [ASSEMBLE]
Ex 38: 8 of the looking-glasses of *the women* **a**, 6633
Heb 10:25 Not forsaking the **a** of ourselves **together**, *1997*

ASSEMBLY (49) [ASSEMBLE]
Ge 49: 6 unto their **a**, mine honour, be not thou 6951
Ex 12: 6 the whole **a** of the congregation of Israel 6951
16: 3 to kill this whole **a** with hunger. 6951
Lev 4:13 the thing be hid from the eyes of the **a**, and 6951
8: 4 the **a** was gathered together unto the door 5712
23:36 it *is* a **solemn a**; *and* ye shall do no servile 6116
Nu 8: 9 thou shalt gather the whole **a** of 5712
10: 2 mayest use them for the calling of the **a**, 5712
10: 3 all the **a** shall assemble themselves to thee 5712
14: 5 Aaron fell on their faces before all the **a** of 6951
16: 2 two hundred and fifty princes of the **a**, 5712
20: 6 Aaron went from the presence of the **a** unto 6951
20: 8 gather thou the **a** together, thou, and 5712
29:35 On the eighth day ye shall have a **solemn a**; 6116
Dt 5:22 **a** in the mount out of the midst of the fire, 6951
9:10 of the midst of the fire in the day of the **a**. 6951
10: 4 of the midst of the fire in the day of the **a**: 6951
16: 8 on the seventh day *shall be* a **solemn a** to 6116
18:16 thy God in Horeb in the day of the **a**, 6951
Jdg 20: 2 presented themselves in the **a** of the people 6951
21: 8 to the camp from Jabesh-gilead to the **a**. 6951
1Sa 17:47 all this **a** shall know that the LORD saveth 6951
2Ki 10:20 Jehu said, Proclaim a **solemn a** for Baal. 6116
2Ch 7: 9 in the eighth day they made a **solemn a**: 6116
30:23 the whole **a** took counsel to keep other 6951
Ne 5: 7 And I set a great **a** against them. 6952
8:18 on the eighth day *was* a **solemn a**, 6116
Ps 22:16 the **a** of the wicked have inclosed me: 5712
89: 7 God *is* greatly to be feared in the **a** of 5475
107:32 and praise him in the **a** of the elders. 4186
111: 1 in the **a** of the upright, and *in* 5475
Pr 5:14 evil in the midst of the congregation and **a**. 5712
Jer 6:11 and upon the **a** of young men together: 5475
9: 2 *be* all adulterers, an **a** of treacherous *men*. 6116
15:17 I sat not in the **a** of the mockers, 5475
26:17 and spake to all the **a** of the people, saying, 6951
50: 9 cause to come up against Babylon an **a** of 6951
La 1:15 he hath called an **a** against me to crush my 4150
2: 6 he hath destroyed his **places of** the **a**: 4150
Eze 13: 9 they shall not be in the **a** of my people, 5475
23:24 and wheels, and with an **a** of people, 6951
Joel 1:14 call a **solemn a**, gather the elders *and* 6116
2:15 in Zion, sanctify a fast, call a **solemn a**: 6116
Zep 3:18 *them that are* sorrowful for the **solemn a**, 4150
Ac 19:32 for the **a** was confused; and the more part *1577*
19:39 it shall be determined in a lawful **a**. *1577*
19:41 he had thus spoken, he dismissed the **a**. *1577*
Heb 12:23 To the **general a**, and church of *3831*
Jas 2: 2 For if there come unto your **a** a man with a *4864*

ASSENT (1) [ASSENTED]
2Ch 18:12 *declare* good to the king **with** one **a**; 6310

ASSENTED (1) [ASSENT]
Ac 24: 9 And the Jews also **a**, saying that these *4934*

ASSES (64) [ASS]
Ge 12:16 **he a**, and menservants, and maidservants, 2543
12:16 and maidservants, and **she a**, and camels. 860
24:35 and maidservants, and camels, and **a**. 2543
30:43 and menservants, and camels, and **a**. 2543
32: 5 **a**, flocks, and menservants, and 2543
32:15 and ten bulls, twenty **she a**, and ten foals. 860
34:28 their **a**, and that which *was* in the city, and 2543
36:24 as he fed the **a** of Zibeon his father. 2543
42:26 they laded their **a** with the corn, and 2543
43:18 and take us for bondmen, and our **a**. 2543
43:24 their feet; and he gave their **a** provender. 2543
44: 3 the men were sent away, they and their **a**. 2543
45:23 ten **a** laden with the good things of Egypt, 2543
45:23 and ten **she a** laden with corn and bread and 860

Ge 47:17 and for the cattle of the herds, and for the **a**: 2543
Ex 9: 3 upon the horses, upon the **a**, upon 2543
Nu 31:28 the beeves, and of the **a**, and of the sheep: 2543
31:30 of the beeves, of the **a**, and of the flocks, 2543
31:34 And threescore and one thousand **a**, 2543
31:39 the **a** *were* thirty thousand and 2543
31:45 And thirty thousand **a** and five hundred, 2543
Jos 7:24 his **a**, and his sheep, and his tent, and all 2543
9: 4 took old sacks upon their **a**, and 2543
Jdg 5:10 Speak, ye that ride on white **a**, ye that sit in 860
19: 3 his servant with him, and a couple of **a**: 2543
19:10 *there were* with him two **a** saddled, 2543
19:19 there is both straw and provender for our **a**; 2543
19:21 his house, and gave provender unto the **a**: 2543
1Sa 8:16 and your **a**, and put *them* to his work. 2543
9: 3 the **a** of Kish Saul's father were lost. 860
9: 3 servants with thee, and arise, go seek the **a**. 860
9: 5 lest my father leave *caring* for the **a**, and 860
9:20 as for thine **a** that were lost three days ago, 860
10: 2 The **a** which thou wentest to seek are found: 860
10: 2 lo, thy father hath left the care of the **a**, and 860
10:14 he said, To seek the **a**: and when we saw that 860
10:16 He told us plainly that the **a** were found. 860
22:19 and sucklings, and oxen, and **a**, and sheep, 2543
25:18 hundred cakes *of figs,* and laid *them* on **a**. 2543
27: 9 the **a**, and the camels, and the apparel, and 2543
2Sa 16: 1 with a couple of **a** saddled, and upon them 2543
16: 2 The **a** *be* for the king's household to ride 2543
2Ki 4:22 one of the young men, and one of the **a**, 860
7: 7 left their tents, and their horses, and their **a**, 2543
7:10 and **a** tied, and the tents as they *were.* 2543
1Ch 5:21 *of* **a** two thousand, and *of* men an hundred 2543
12:40 brought bread on **a**, and on camels, and 2543
27:30 over the **a** *was* Jehdeiah the Meronothite: 860
2Ch 28:15 carried all the feeble of them upon **a**, 2543
Ezr 2:67 *their* **a**, six thousand seven hundred and 2543
Ne 7:69 six thousand seven hundred and twenty **a**. 2543
13:15 and bringing in sheaves, and lading **a**; 2543
Job 1: 3 five hundred **she a**, and a very great 860
1:14 and the **a** feeding beside them: 860
24: 5 Behold, *as* **wild a** in the desert, go they 6501
42:12 yoke of oxen, and a thousand **she a**. 860
Ps 104:11 of the field: the **wild a** quench their thirst. 6501
Isa 21: 7 a chariot of **a**, *and* a chariot of camels; 2543
30: 6 their riches upon the shoulders of **young a**, 5895
30:24 the **young a** that ear the ground shall eat 5895
32:14 a joy of **wild a**, a pasture of flocks; 6501
Jer 14: 6 the **wild a** did stand in the high places, 6501
Eze 23:20 whose flesh *is as* the flesh of **a**, and 2543
Da 5:21 and his dwelling *was* with the **wild a**: 6167

ASSHUR (8) [ASSHURIM]
Ge 10:11 Out of that land went forth **A**, and 804
10:22 and **A**, and Arphaxad, and Lud, and Aram. 804
Nu 24:22 until **A** shall carry thee away captive. 804
24:24 and shall afflict **A**, and shall afflict Eber, and 804
1Ch 1:17 **A**, and Arphaxad, and Lud, and Aram, and 804
Eze 27:23 **A**, *and* Chilmad, *were* thy merchants. 804
32:22 **A** *is* there and all her company: his graves 804
Hos 14: 3 **A** shall not save us: we will not ride upon 804

ASSHURIM (1) [ASSHUR]
Ge 25: 3 the sons of Dedan were **A**, and Letushim, 805

ASSHURITES See ASSHURIM

ASSIGNED (3)
Ge 47:22 for the priests had a portion **a** them of 3807.1
Jos 20: 8 they **a** Bezer in the wilderness upon 5414
2Sa 11:16 that he **a** Uriah unto a place where he 5414

ASSIR (5)
Ex 6:24 of Korah; **A**, and Elkanah, and Abiasaph: 617
1Ch 3:17 the sons of Jeconiah; **A**, Salathiel his son, 617
6:22 his son, Korah his son, **A** his son, 617
6:23 his son, and Ebiasaph his son, and **A** his son, 617
6:37 The son of Tahath, the son of **A**, the son of 617

ASSIST (1)
Ro 16: 2 *that* ye **a** her in whatsoever business she *3936*

ASSOCIATE (1)
Isa 8: 9 **A** yourselves, O ye people, and ye shall be 7489

ASSOS (2)
Ac 20:13 we went before to ship, and sailed unto **A**, *789*
20:14 And when he met with us at **A**, we took him *789*

ASSUR (2)
Ezr 4: 2 since the days of Esar-haddon king of **A**, 804
Ps 83: 8 **A** also is joined with them: they have holpen 804

ASSURANCE (7) [ASSURE]
Dt 28:66 and night, and shalt have none **a** of thy life: 539
Isa 32:17 of righteousness quietness and **a** for ever. 983
Ac 17:31 *whereof* he hath given **a** unto all *men,* in *4102*
Col 2: 2 unto all riches of the **full a** of *4136*
1Th 1: 5 and in the Holy Ghost, and in much **a**; *4136*
Heb 6:11 diligence to the **full a** of hope unto the end: *4136*
10:22 Let us draw near with a true heart in **full a** *4136*

ASSURE (1) [ASSURANCE, ASSURED, ASSUREDLY]
1Jn 3:19 the truth, and shall **a** our hearts before him. *3982*

ASSURED (3) [ASSURE]
Lev 27:19 estimation unto it, and it shall be **a** to him. 6965
Jer 14:13 but I will give you **a** peace in this place. 571
2Ti 3:14 which thou hast learned and hast been **a** of, *4104*

ASSUREDLY (9) [ASSURE]
1Sa 28: 1 said unto David, **Know** thou **a**, 3045+3045
1Ki 1:13 **A** Solomon thy son shall reign after me, 3588
1:17 *saying,* **A** Solomon thy son shall reign after 3588
1:30 **A** Solomon thy son shall reign after me, 3588
Jer 32:41 I will plant them in this land **a** with 571+871.1
38:17 If thou wilt **a go forth** unto the king 3318+3318
49:12 to drink of the cup have **a drunken**; 8354+8354
Ac 2:36 Therefore let all the house of Israel know **a**, *806*
16:10 **a gathering** that the Lord had called us for *4822*

ASSWAGE (1) [ASSWAGED]
Job 16: 5 the moving of my lips should **a** *your grief.* 2820

ASSWAGED (2) [ASSWAGE]
Ge 8: 1 to pass over the earth, and the waters **a**; 7918
Job 16: 6 Though I speak, my grief is not **a**: and 2820

ASSYRIA (118) [ASSYRIAN, ASSYRIANS]
Ge 2:14 that *is it* which goeth toward the east of **A**. 804
25:18 *is* before Egypt, as thou goest towards **A**: 804
2Ki 15:19 *And* Pul the king of **A** came against the land: 804
15:20 shekels *of* silver, to give to the king of **A**. 804
15:20 So the king of **A** turned back, and stayed not 804
15:29 of Israel came Tiglath-pileser king of **A**, 804
15:29 of Naphtali, and carried them captive to **A**. 804
16: 7 sent messengers to Tiglath-pileser king of **A**, 804
16: 8 and sent *it for* a present to the king of **A**. 804
16: 9 the king of **A** hearkened unto him: for 804
16: 9 for the king of **A** went up against Damascus, 804
16:10 Damascus to meet Tiglath-pileser king of **A**, 804
16:18 the house of the LORD for the king of **A**. 804
17: 3 him came up Shalmaneser king of **A**; 804
17: 4 the king of **A** found conspiracy in Hoshea: 804
17: 4 brought no present to the king of **A**, as *he* 804
17: 4 therefore the king of **A** shut him up, and 804
17: 5 the king of **A** came up throughout all 804
17: 6 the king of **A** took Samaria, and 804
17: 6 carried Israel away into **A**, and placed them 804
17:23 out of their own land to **A** unto this day. 804
17:24 the king of **A** brought *men* from Babylon, 804
17:26 Wherefore they spake to the king of **A**, 804
17:27 the king of **A** commanded, saying, 804
18: 7 he rebelled against the king of **A**, and 804
18: 9 *that* Shalmaneser king of **A** came up against 804
18:11 the king of **A** did carry away Israel unto 804
18:11 king of Assyria did carry away Israel unto **A**, 804
18:13 **A** come up against all the fenced cities of 804
18:14 Hezekiah king of Judah sent to the king of **A** 804
18:14 the king of **A** appointed unto Hezekiah king 804
18:16 had overlaid, and gave it to the king of **A**. 804
18:17 the king of **A** sent Tartan and Rabsaris and 804
18:19 Thus saith the great king, the king of **A**, 804
18:23 give pledges to my lord the king of **A**, and 804
18:28 the word of the great king, the king of **A**: 804
18:30 be delivered into the hand of the king of **A**. 804
18:31 for thus saith the king of **A**, Make *an* 804
18:33 all his land out of the hand of the king of **A**? 804
19: 4 whom the king of **A** his master hath sent to 804
19: 6 *with* which the servants of the king of **A** 804

A

2Ki 19: 8 found the king of **A** warring against Libnah: 804
19:10 be delivered into the hand of the king of **A**. 804
19:11 thou hast heard what the kings of **A** have 804
19:17 the kings of **A** have destroyed the nations 804
19:20 against Sennacherib king of **A** I have heard. 804
19:32 saith the LORD concerning the king of **A**, 804
19:36 So Sennacherib king of **A** departed, and 804
20: 6 and this city out of the hand of the king of **A**; 804
23:29 against the king of **A** to the river Euphrates: 804
1Ch 5: 6 whom Tilgath-pilneser king of **A** carried 804
5:26 Israel stirred up the spirit of Pul king of **A**, 804
5:26 the spirit of Tilgath-pilneser king of **A**, and 804
2Ch 28:16 Ahaz send unto the kings of **A** to help him. 804
28:20 Tilgath-pilneser king of **A** came unto him, 804
28:21 the princes, and gave *it* unto the king of **A**: 804
30: 6 escaped out of the hand of the kings of **A**. 804
32: 1 *thereof,* Sennacherib king of **A** came, 804
32: 4 Why should the kings of **A** come, and 804
32: 7 be not afraid nor dismayed for the king of **A**, 804
32: 9 After this did Sennacherib king of **A** send 804
32:10 Thus saith Sennacherib king of **A**, 804
32:11 deliver us out of the hand of the king of **A**? 804
32:21 and captains in the camp of the king of **A**. 804
32:22 from the hand of Sennacherib the king of **A**, 804
33:11 the captains of the host of the king of **A**, 804
Ezr 6:22 turned the heart of the king of **A** unto them, 804
Ne 9:32 since the time of the kings of **A** unto this 804
Isa 7:17 departed from Judah; *even* the king of **A**. 804
7:18 and for the bee that *is* in the land of **A**. 804
7:20 by the king of **A**, the head, and the hair of 804
8: 4 shall be taken away before the king of **A**. 804
8: 7 *even* the king of **A**, and all his glory: 804
10:12 the fruit of the stout heart of the king of **A**, 804
11:11 which shall be left from **A**, and from Egypt, 804
11:16 of his people, which shall be left from **A**; 804
19:23 shall there be a highway out of Egypt to **A**, 804
19:23 the Egyptian into **A**, and the Egyptians shall 804
19:24 Israel be the third with Egypt and with **A**, 804
19:25 **A** the work of my hands, and Israel mine 804
20: 1 (when Sargon the king of **A** sent him,) 804
20: 4 So shall the king of **A** lead away 804
20: 6 for help to be delivered from the king of **A**: 804
27:13 which were ready to perish in the land of **A**, 804
36: 1 *that* Sennacherib king of **A** came up against 804
36: 2 the king of **A** sent Rabshakeh from Lachish 804
36: 4 Thus saith the great king, the king of **A**, 804
36: 8 to my master the king of **A**, and I will give 804
36:13 ye the words of the great king, the king of **A**. 804
36:15 be delivered into the hand of the king of **A**. 804
36:16 for thus saith the king of **A**, Make *an* 804
36:18 his land out of the hand of the king of **A**? 804
37: 4 whom the king of **A** his master hath sent to 804
37: 6 where*with* the servants of the king of **A** have 804
37: 8 found the king of **A** warring against Libnah: 804
37:10 not be given into the hand of the king of **A**. 804
37:11 thou hast heard what the kings of **A** have 804
37:18 the kings of **A** have laid waste all 804
37:21 prayed to me against Sennacherib king of **A**: 804
37:33 saith the LORD concerning the king of **A**, 804
37:37 So Sennacherib king of **A** departed, and 804
38: 6 and this city out of the hand of the king of **A**: 804
Jer 2:18 or what hast thou to do in the way of **A**, 804
2:36 of Egypt, as thou wast ashamed of **A**. 804
50:17 first the king of **A** hath devoured him; and 804
50:18 his land, as I have punished the king of **A**. 804
Eze 23: 7 *with* all them *that were* the chosen men of **A**, 804
Hos 7:11 they call *to* Egypt, they go *to* **A**. 804
8: 9 For they are gone up *to* **A**, a wild ass alone 804
9: 3 and they shall eat unclean *things* in **A**. 804
10: 6 It shall be also carried unto **A** *for* a present 804
11:11 of Egypt, and as a dove out of the land of **A**: 804
Mic 5: 6 they shall waste the land of **A** with 804
7:12 day *also* he shall come even to thee from **A**, 804
Na 3:18 Thy shepherds slumber, O king of **A**: 804
Zep 2:13 his hand against the north, and destroy **A**; 804
Zec 10:10 the land of Egypt, and gather them out of **A**; 804
10:11 the pride of **A** shall be brought down, and 804

ASSYRIAN (13) [ASSYRIA]

Isa 10: 5 O **A**, the rod of mine anger, and the staff in 804
10:24 that dwellest in Zion, be not afraid of the **A**: 804
14:25 That *I* will break the **A** in my land, and 804
19:23 the **A** shall come into Egypt, and 804
23:13 *till* the **A** founded it for them that dwell in 804
30:31 of the LORD shall the **A** be beaten down, 804
31: 8 shall the **A** fall with the sword, not of a 804
52: 4 and the **A** oppressed them without cause. 804
Eze 31: 3 the **A** *was* a cedar in Lebanon with fair 804
Hos 5:13 went Ephraim to the **A**, and sent to king 804
11: 5 the **A** shall be his king, because they refused 804
Mic 5: 5 when the **A** shall come into our land: 804
5: 6 thus shall he deliver *us* from the **A**, when he 804

ASSYRIANS (10) [ASSYRIA]

2Ki 19:35 smote in the camp of the **A** an hundred 804
Isa 19:23 and the Egyptians shall serve *with* the **A**. 804
37:36 smote in the camp of the **A** an hundred and 804
La 5: 6 *and to* the **A**, to be satisfied *with* bread. 804
Eze 16:28 hast played the whore also with the **A**, 804+1121
23: 5 on her lovers, on the **A** *her* neighbours, 804
23: 9 into the hand of the **A**, upon whom 804+1121
23:12 She doted upon the **A** *her* neighbours, 804+1121
23:23 Shoa, and Koa, all the **A** with them: 804+1121
Hos 12: 1 and they do make a covenant with the **A**, and 804

ASTAROTH (1)

Dt 1: 4 king of Bashan, which dwelt at **A** in Edrei: 6252

ASTONIED (10) [ASTONISHMENT]

Ezr 9: 3 my head and of my beard, and sat down **a**. 8074
9: 4 and I sat **a** until the evening sacrifice. 8074
Job 17: 8 Upright *men* shall be **a** at this, and 8074
18:20 They that come after *him* shall be **a** at his 8074
Isa 52:14 As many were **a** at thee; his visage *was* so 8074
Jer 14: 9 Why shouldest thou be as a man **a**, as a 1724
Eze 4:17 be **a** one with another, and consume away 8074
Da 3:24 Nebuchadnezzar the king was **a**, and 8429
4:19 was **a** for one hour, and his thoughts 8075
5: 9 *was* changed in him, and his lords *were* **a**. 7672

ASTONISHED (34) [ASTONISHMENT]

Lev 26:32 enemies which dwell therein shall be **a** at it. 8074
1Ki 9: 8 every one that passeth by it shall be **a**, and 8074
Job 21: 5 be **a**, and lay *your* hand upon *your* mouth. 8074
26:11 of heaven tremble and are **a** at his reproof. 8539
Jer 2:12 Be **a**, O ye heavens, at this, and be horribly 8074
4: 9 the priests shall be **a**, and the prophets shall 8074
18:16 every one that passeth thereby shall be **a**, 8074
19: 8 every one that passeth thereby shall be **a** 8074
49:17 every one that goeth by it shall be **a**, and 8074
50:13 every one that goeth by Babylon shall be **a**, 8074
Eze 3:15 remained there **a** among them seven days. 8074
26:16 tremble at every moment, and be **a** at thee. 8074
27:35 All the inhabitants of the isles shall be **a** at 8074
28:19 thee among the people shall be **a** at thee: 8074
Da 8:27 I was **a** at the vision, but none understood 8074
Mt 7:28 the people were **a** at his doctrine: *1605*
13:54 insomuch that they were **a**, and said, *1605*
22:33 heard *this,* they were **a** at his doctrine. *1605*
Mk 1:22 And they were **a** at his doctrine: for he *1605*
5:42 And they were **a** with a great astonishment. *1839*
6: 2 and many hearing *him* were **a**, saying, *1605*
7:37 And were beyond measure **a**, saying, *1605*
10:24 And the disciples were **a** at his words. *2284*
10:26 And they were **a** out of measure, *1605*
11:18 because all the people was **a** at his doctrine. *1605*
Lk 2:47 And all that heard him were **a** at his *1839*
4:32 And they were **a** at his doctrine: for his *1605*
5: 9 For he was **a**, *2285+4023*
8:56 And her parents were **a**: but he charged *1839*
24:22 women *also* of our company **made** us **a**, *1839*
Ac 9: 6 And he trembling and **a** said, Lord, *2284*
10:45 of the circumcision which believed were **a**, *1839*
12:16 opened *the door,* and saw him, they were **a**. *1839*
13:12 being **a** at the doctrine of the Lord. *1605*

ASTONISHMENT (21) [ASTONIED, ASTONISHED]

Dt 28:28 and blindness, and **a** of heart: 8541
28:37 thou shalt become an **a**, a proverb, and a 8047
2Ch 7:21 shall be an **a** to every one that passeth by it; 8074
29: 8 to **a**, and to hissing, as ye see with your 8047
Ps 60: 3 thou hast made us to drink the wine *of* **a**. 8653
Jer 8:21 I hurt; I am black; **a** hath taken hold on me. 8047
25: 9 make them an **a**, and a hissing, and 8047
25:11 whole land shall be a desolation, *and* an **a**; 8047
25:18 a desolation, an **a**, a hissing, and a curse; 8047
29:18 and an **a**, and a hissing, and a reproach, 8047
42:18 and an **a**, and a curse, and a reproach; 8047

Jer 44:12 an **a**, and a curse, and a reproach. 8047
44:22 an **a**, and a curse, without an inhabitant, 8047
51:37 an **a**, and a hissing, without an inhabitant. 8047
51:41 how is Babylon become an **a** among 8047
Eze 4:16 shall drink water by measure, and with **a**: 8078
5:15 an **a** unto the nations that *are* round about 4923
12:19 and drink their water with **a**, 8078
23:33 sorrow, *with* the cup of **a** and desolation, 8047
Zec 12: 4 I will smite every horse with **a**, and 8541
Mk 5:42 And they were astonished with a great **a**. *1611*

ASTRAY (22)
Ex 23: 4 meet thine enemy's ox or his ass **going a**, 8582
Dt 22: 1 not see thy brother's ox or his sheep **go a**, 5080
Ps 58: 3 they **go a** as soon as they be born, speaking 8582
119:67 Before I was afflicted I **went a**: but 7683
119:176 I have **gone a** like a lost sheep; seek thy 8582
Pr 5:23 in the greatness of his folly he shall **go a**. 7686
7:25 decline to her ways, **go** not **a** in her paths. 8582
28:10 Whoso **causeth** the righteous **to go a** in an 7686
Isa 53: 6 All we like sheep have **gone a**; we have 8582
Jer 50: 6 their shepherds have **caused** them **to go a**, 8582
Eze 14:11 That the house of Israel may **go** no more **a** 8582
44:10 away far from me, when Israel **went a**, 8582
44:10 which **went a** away from me after their 8582
44:15 the children of Israel **went a** from me, 8582
48:11 which **went** not **a** when the children of 8582
48:11 astray when the children of Israel **went a**, 8582
48:11 of Israel went astray, as the Levites **went a**. 8582
Mt 18:12 and one of them be **gone a**, doth he not *4105*
18:12 and seeketh that which is **gone a**? *4105*
18:13 of the ninety and nine which **went** not **a**. *4105*
1Pe 2:25 For ye were as sheep **going a**; but are now *4105*
2Pe 2:15 forsaken the right way, and are **gone a**, *4105*

ASTROLOGER (1) [ASTROLOGERS, ASTROLOGIANS]
Da 2:10 things at any magician, or **a**, or Chaldean. 826

ASTROLOGERS (7) [ASTROLOGER]
Isa 47:13 Let now the **a**, the stargazers, 1895+8064
Da 1:20 *and* **a** that *were* in all his realm. 825
2: 2 the **a**, and the sorcerers, and the Chaldeans, 825
4: 7 the **a**, the Chaldeans, and the soothsayers: 826
5: 7 The king cried aloud to bring in the **a**, 826
5:11 **a**, Chaldeans, *and* soothsayers; 826
5:15 now the wise *men*, the **a**, have been brought 826

ASTROLOGIANS (1) [ASTROLOGER]
Da 2:27 hath demanded cannot the wise *men*, the **a**, 826

ASUNDER (21)
Lev 1:17 the wings thereof, *but* shall not **divide** *it* **a**: 914
5: 8 head from his neck, but shall not **divide** *it* **a**: 914
Nu 16:31 that the ground **clave a** that *was* under 1234
2Ki 2:11 and horses of fire, and parted them both **a**; 996
Job 16:12 I was at ease, but he hath **broken** me **a**: 6565
16:13 he **cleaveth** my reins **a**, and doth not spare; 6398
Ps 2: 3 Let us **break** their bands **a**, and cast away 5423
129: 4 he hath **cut a** the cords of the wicked. 7112
Jer 50:23 is the hammer of the whole earth **cut a** 1438
Eze 30:16 No shall be **rent a**, and Noph *shall have* 1234
Hab 3: 6 he beheld, and **drove a** the nations; and 5425
Zec 11:10 I took my staff, *even* Beauty, and **cut** it **a**, 1438
11:14 I **cut a** mine other staff, *even* Bands, that I 1438
Mt 19: 6 hath joined together, let not man **put a**. *5563*
24:51 And shall **cut** him **a**, and appoint *him* his *1371*
Mk 5: 4 and the chains had been **plucked a** by him, *1288*
10: 9 hath joined together, let not man **put a**. *5563*
Ac 1:18 he **burst a** in the midst, and all his bowels *2997*
15:39 sharp *between them,* that they **departed a** *673*
Heb 4:12 piercing even to the **dividing a** of soul and *3311*
11:37 they were **sawn a**, were tempted, *4249*

ASUPPIM (2)
1Ch 26:15 and to his sons the house of **A**. 624
26:17 four a day, and toward **A** two *and* two. 624

ASWAN See SYENE

ASYNCRITUS (1)
Ro 16:14 Salute **A**, Phlegon, Hermas, Patrobas, *799*

AT (1571) See Index

ATAD (2)
Ge 50:10 they came to the threshingfloor of **A**, 329
50:11 saw the mourning in the floor of **A**, they 329

ATARAH (1)
1Ch 2:26 had also another wife, whose name *was* **A**; 5851

ATAROTH (5)
Nu 32: 3 **A**, and Dibon, and Jazer, and Nimrah, and 5852
32:34 of Gad built Dibon, and **A**, and Aroer, 5852
Jos 16: 2 along unto the borders of Archi *to* **A**, 5852
16: 7 it went down from Janohah *to* **A**, and 5852
1Ch 2:54 **A**, the house of Joab, and half of 5852

ATAROTH-ADAR (1) [ATAROTH-ADDAR]
Jos 18:13 the border descended *to* **A**, near the hill that 5853

ATAROTH-ADDAR (1) [ATAROTH-ADAR]
Jos 16: 5 of their inheritance on the east side was **A**, 5853

ATE (3) [EAT]
Ps 106:28 and **a** the sacrifices of the dead. 398
Da 10: 3 I **a** no pleasant bread, neither came flesh nor 398
Rev 10:10 book out of the angel's hand, and **a** it **up**; *2719*

ATER (5)
Ezr 2:16 The children of **A** of Hezekiah, ninety and 333
2:42 the children of **A**, the children of Talmon, 333
Ne 7:21 The children of **A** of Hezekiah, ninety and 333
7:45 the children of **A**, the children of Talmon, 333
10:17 **A**, Hizkijah, Azzur, 333

ATHACH (1)
1Sa 30:30 and to *them* which *were* in **A**, 6269

ATHAIAH (1)
Ne 11: 4 **A** the son of Uzziah, the son of Zechariah, 6265

ATHALIAH (17)
2Ki 8:26 his mother's name *was* **A**, the daughter of 6271
11: 1 when **A** the mother of Ahaziah saw that her 6271
11: 2 in the bedchamber from **A**, so that he was 6271
11: 3 six years. And **A** *did* reign over the land. 6271
11:13 when **A** heard the noise of the guard *and* 6271
11:14 **A** rent her clothes, and cried, Treason, 6271
11:20 they slew **A** with the sword *beside* 6271
1Ch 8:26 And Shamsherai, and Sheharia, and **A**, 6271
2Ch 22: 2 His mother's name also *was* **A** the daughter 6271
22:10 when **A** the mother of Ahaziah saw that her 6271
22:11 hid him from **A**, so that she slew him not. 6271
22:12 God six years: and **A** reigned over the land. 6271
23:12 Now when **A** heard the noise of the people 6271
23:13 **A** rent her clothes, and said, Treason, 6271
23:21 after that they had slain **A** with the sword. 6271
24: 7 For the sons of **A**, *that* wicked woman, 6271
Ezr 8: 7 Jeshaiah the son of **A**, and with him 6271

ATHENIANS (1) [ATHENS]
Ac 17:21 (For all the **A** and strangers which were *117*

ATHENS (7) [ATHENIANS]
Ac 17:15 that conducted Paul brought him unto **A**: *116*
17:16 Now while Paul waited for them at **A**, his *116*
17:22 midst of Mars' hill, and said, *Ye* men **of A**, *117*
18: 1 After these *things* Paul departed from **A**, and *116*
1Th 3: 1 we thought it good to be left at **A** alone; *116*
5: S unto the Thessalonians was written from **A**. *116*
2Th 3: S to the Thessalonians was written from **A**. *116*

ATHIRST (5) [THIRST]
Jdg 15:18 he was sore **a**, and called on the LORD, 6770
Ru 2: 9 when thou art **a**, go unto the vessels, and 6770
Mt 25:44 or **a**, or a stranger, or naked, or sick, or *1372*
Rev 21: 6 I will give unto him that is **a** of the fountain *1372*
22:17 And let him that is **a** come. And whosoever *1372*

ATHLAI (1)
Ezr 10:28 Jehohanan, Hananiah, Zabbai, *and* **A**. 6270

ATONEMENT (81) [ATONEMENTS]
Ex 29:33 eat those *things* wherewith the **a** was **made**, 3722
29:36 every day a bullock *for* a sin offering for **a**: 3725
29:36 when thou hast **made an a** for it, and 3722
29:37 Seven days thou shalt **make an a** for 3722
30:10 Aaron shall **make an a** upon the horns of it 3722
30:10 once in the year shall he **make a** upon it 3722
30:15 the LORD, to **make an a** for your souls. 3722
30:16 thou shalt take the **a** money of the children 3725

Ex 30:16 the LORD, to **make an a** for your souls. 3722
32:30 peradventure I shall **make an a** for your 3722
Lev 1: 4 it shall be accepted for him to **make a** for 3722
4:20 the priest shall **make an a** for them, and 3722
4:26 the priest shall **make an a** for him as 3722
4:31 the priest shall **make an a** for him, and 3722
4:35 the priest shall **make an a** for his sin that 3722
5: 6 the priest shall **make an a** for him 3722
5:10 the priest shall **make an a** for him for his 3722
5:13 the priest shall **make an a** for him as 3722
5:16 the priest shall **make an a** for him with 3722
5:18 the priest shall **make an a** for him 3722
6: 7 the priest shall **make an a** for him before 3722
7: 7 the priest that **maketh a** therewith shall 3722
8:34 commanded to do, to **make an a** for you. 3722
9: 7 **make an a** for thyself, and for the people: 3722
9: 7 of the people, and **make an a** for them; 3722
10:17 to **make a** for them before the LORD? 3722
12: 7 before the LORD, and **make an a** for her; 3722
12: 8 the priest shall **make an a** for her, and 3722
14:18 the priest shall **make an a** for him before 3722
14:19 **make an a** for him that is to be cleansed 3722
14:20 the priest shall **make an a** for him, and 3722
14:21 to **make an a** for him, and one tenth deal of 3722
14:29 to **make an a** for him before the LORD. 3722
14:31 the priest shall **make an a** for him that is to 3722
14:53 open fields, and **make an a** for the house: 3722
15:15 the priest shall **make an a** for him before 3722
15:30 the priest shall **make an a** for her before 3722
16: 6 **make an a** for himself, and for his house. 3722
16:10 to **make an a** with him, *and* to let him go 3722
16:11 shall **make an a** for himself, and for his 3722
16:16 he shall **make an a** for the holy *place,* 3722
16:17 **make an a** in the holy *place,* until he come 3722
16:17 have **made an a** for himself, and for his 3722
16:18 *is* before the LORD, and **make an a** for it; 3722
16:24 **make an a** for himself, and for the people. 3722
16:27 whose blood was brought in to **make a** in 3722
16:30 For on that day shall *the priest* **make an a** 3722
16:32 shall **make** the **a**, and shall put on the linen 3722
16:33 he shall **make an a** for the holy sanctuary, 3722
16:33 he shall **make an a** for the tabernacle of 3722
16:33 he shall **make an a** for the priests, and 3722
16:34 to **make an a** for the children of Israel for 3722
17:11 upon the altar to **make an a** for your souls: 3722
17:11 for it *is* the blood *that* **maketh an a** for 3722
19:22 the priest shall **make an a** for him with 3722
23:27 seventh month *there shall be* a day of **a**: 3725
23:28 for it *is* a day of **a**, to make an atonement 3725
23:28 to **make an a** for you before the LORD 3722
25: 9 in the day of **a** shall ye make the trumpet 3725
Nu 5: 8 beside the ram of the **a**, whereby an 3725
5: 8 whereby an **a** shall be **made** for him. 3722
6:11 a burnt offering, and **make an a** for him, 3722
8:12 the LORD, to **make an a** for the Levites. 3722
8:19 and to **make an a** for the children of Israel: 3722
8:21 Aaron **made an a** for them to cleanse them. 3722
15:25 the priest shall **make an a** for all 3722
15:28 the priest shall **make an a** for the soul that 3722
15:28 before the LORD, to **make an a** for him; 3722
16:46 the congregation, and **make an a** for them: 3722
16:47 on incense, and **made an a** for the people. 3722
25:13 and **made an a** for the children of Israel. 3722
28:22 for a sin offering, to **make an a** for you. 3722
28:30 one kid of the goats, to **make an a** for you. 3722
29: 5 for a sin offering, to **make an a** for you: 3722
29:11 beside the sin offering of **a**, and 3725
31:50 to **make an a** for our souls before 3722
2Sa 21: 3 wherewith shall I **make** the **a**, that ye may 3722
1Ch 6:49 most holy, and to **make an a** for Israel, 3722
2Ch 29:24 upon the altar, to **make an a** for all Israel: 3722
Ne 10:33 for the sin offerings to **make an a** for 3722
Ro 5:11 by whom we have now received the **a**. *2643*

ATONEMENTS (1) [ATONEMENT]
Ex 30:10 year with the blood of the sin offering of **a**: 3725

ATROTH SHOPHAN (1)
Nu 32:35 **A**, and Jaazer, and Jogbehah, 5855

ATTAI (4)
1Ch 2:35 his servant to wife; and she bare him **A**. 6262
2:36 **A** begat Nathan, and Nathan begat Zabad, 6262
12:11 **A** the sixth, Eliel the seventh, 6262
2Ch 11:20 and **A**, and Ziza, and Shelomith. 6262

ATTAIN (6) [ATTAINED]
Ps 139: 6 for me; it is high, I cannot **a unto** it. 3807.1
Pr 1: 5 a man of understanding shall **a** unto wise 7069
Eze 46: 7 lambs according as his hand shall **a unto**, 5381
Hos 8: 5 how long *will it be* ere they **a** to innocency? 3201
Ac 27:12 if by any means they might **a** to Phenice, *2658*
Php 3:11 If by any means I might **a** unto *2658*

ATTAINED (10) [ATTAIN]
Ge 47: 9 have not **a unto** the days of the years of 5381
2Sa 23:19 howbeit he **a** not unto the *first* three. 935
23:23 than the thirty, but he **a** not to the *first* three. 935
1Ch 11:21 howbeit he **a** not to the *first* three. 935
11:25 among the thirty, but **a** not to the *first* three: 935
Ro 9:30 have **a** to righteousness, *2638*
9:31 hath not **a** to the law of righteousness. *5348*
Php 3:12 Not as though I had already **a**, either were *2983*
3:16 Nevertheless, whereto we have *already* **a**, *5348*
1Ti 4: 6 of good doctrine, whereunto thou hast **a**. *3877*

ATTALIA (1)
Ac 14:25 the word in Perga, they went down into **A**: *825*

ATTEND (11) [ATTENDANCE, ATTENDED, ATTENDING, ATTENT, ATTENTIVE, ATTENTIVELY]
Est 4: 5 whom he had appointed to **a upon** her, and 6440
Ps 17: 1 Hear the right, O LORD, **a unto** my cry, 7181
55: 2 **A** unto me, and hear me: I mourn in my 7181
61: 1 Hear my cry, O God; **a** unto my prayer. 7181
86: 6 and **a** to the voice of my supplications. 7181
142: 6 **A** unto my cry; for I am brought very low: 7181
Pr 4: 1 of a father, and **a** to know understanding. 7181
4:20 My son, **a** to my words; incline thine ear 7181
5: 1 **a** unto my wisdom, *and* bow thine ear to 7181
7:24 and **a to** the words of my mouth. 7181
1Co 7:35 that you may **a upon** the Lord without *2145*

ATTENDANCE (4) [ATTEND]
1Ki 10: 5 and the **a** of his ministers, and their apparel, 4612
2Ch 9: 4 and the **a** of his ministers, and their apparel; 4612
1Ti 4:13 Till I come, **give a** to reading, *4337*
Heb 7:13 of which no *man* **gave a at** the altar. *4337*

ATTENDED (3) [ATTEND]
Job 32:12 Yea, I **a** unto you, and behold, *there was* 995
Ps 66:19 *But* verily God hath heard *me;* he hath **a** to 7181
Ac 16:14 that *she* **a unto** the *things* which were *4337*

ATTENDING (1) [ATTEND]
Ro 13: 6 **a continually** upon this very *thing.* *4342*

ATTENT (2) [ATTEND]
2Ch 6:40 *let* thine ears *be* **a** unto the prayer *that is* 7183
7:15 mine ears **a** unto the prayer *that is made* in 7183

ATTENTIVE (5) [ATTEND]
Ne 1: 6 Let thine ear now be **a**, and thine eyes 7183
1:11 let now thine ear be **a** to the prayer of thy 7183
8: 3 the ears of all the people *were a* unto NIH
Ps 130: 2 let thine ears be **a** to the voice of my 7183
Lk 19:48 for all the people were **very a** to hear him. *1582*

ATTENTIVELY (1) [ATTEND]
Job 37: 2 **Hear a** the noise of his voice, and 8085

ATTIRE (3) [ATTIRED]
Pr 7:10 there met him a woman *with* the **a** of a 7897
Jer 2:32 forget her ornaments, *or* a bride her **a**? 7196
Eze 23:15 **exceeding in dyed a** upon their 2871+5628

ATTIRED (1) [ATTIRE]
Lev 16: 4 and with the linen mitre shall he be **a**: 6801

AUDIENCE (12)
Ge 23:10 Abraham in the **a** of the children of Heth, 241
23:13 he spake unto Ephron in the **a** of the people 241
23:16 which he had named in the **a** of the sons of 241
Ex 24: 7 the covenant, and read in the **a** of the people: 241
1Sa 25:24 speak in thine **a**, and hear the words of thine 241
1Ch 28: 8 in the **a** of our God, keep and seek for all 241
Ne 13: 1 in the book of Moses in the **a** of the people; 241
Lk 7: 1 ended all his sayings in the **a** of the people, *189*
20:45 Then **in** the **a** of all the people he said unto *191*
Ac 13:16 Men of Israel, and *ye* that fear God, **give a**. *191*

Ac 15:12 and **gave a** to Barnabas and Paul, *191*
22:22 And they **gave** him **a** unto this word, and *191*

AUGMENT (1)
Nu 32:14 to **a** yet the fierce anger of the LORD 5595

AUGUSTUS (3) [AUGUSTUS']
Lk 2: 1 *that* there went out a decree from Cesar **A**, *828*
Ac 25:21 to be reserved unto the hearing of **A**, *4575*
25:25 and *that* he himself hath appealed to **A**, *4575*

AUGUSTUS' (1) [AUGUSTUS]
Ac 27: 1 *one* named Julius, a centurion of **A** band. *4575*

AUL (2)
Ex 21: 6 master shall bore his ear through with an **a**; 4836
Dt 15:17 thou shalt take an **a**, and thrust *it* through 4836

AUNT (1)
Lev 18:14 not approach to his wife: she *is* thine **a**. 1733

AUSTERE (2)
Lk 19:21 For I feared thee, because thou art an **a** man: *840*
19:22 Thou knewest that I was an **a** man, taking up *840*

AUTHOR (3)
1Co 14:33 For God is not *the* **a** of confusion, but NIG
Heb 5: 9 he became the **a** of eternal salvation unto all *159*
12: 2 Looking unto Jesus the **a** and finisher of *our* *747*

AUTHORITIES (1) [AUTHORITY]
1Pe 3:22 angels and **a** and powers being made *1849*

AUTHORITY (37) [AUTHORITIES]
Est 9:29 and Mordecai the Jew, wrote with all **a**, 8633
Pr 29: 2 When the righteous are **in a**, the people 7235
Mt 7:29 For he taught them as *one* having **a**, and *1849*
8: 9 For I am a man under **a**, having soldiers *1849*
20:25 they *that are* great **exercise a upon** them. *2715*
21:23 By what **a** doest thou these *things?* and *1849*
21:23 these *things?* and who gave thee this **a**? *1849*
21:24 I in like wise will tell you by what **a** I do *1849*
21:27 Neither tell I you by what **a** I do these *1849*
Mk 1:22 for he taught them as *one* that had **a**, and *1849*
1:27 for with **a** commandeth he even the unclean *1849*
10:42 and their great ones **exercise a upon** them. *2715*
11:28 By what **a** doest thou these *things?* and *1849*
11:28 who gave thee this **a** to do these *things?* *1849*
11:29 I will tell you by what **a** I do these *things.* *1849*
11:33 Neither do I tell you by what **a** I do these *1849*
13:34 and gave **a** to his servants, and to every *1849*
Lk 4:36 for with **a** and power he commandeth *1849*
7: 8 For I also am a man set under **a**, *1849*
9: 1 and gave them power and **a** over all devils, *1849*
19:17 in a very little, have thou **a** over ten cities. *1849*
20: 2 by what **a** doest thou these *things?* or *1849*
20: 2 or who is he that gave thee this **a**? *1849*
20: 8 Neither tell I you by what **a** I do these *1849*
20:20 him unto the power and **a** of the governor. *1849*
22:25 they that **exercise a upon** them are called *1850*
Jn 5:27 And hath given him **a** to execute judgment *1849*
Ac 8:27 an eunuch **of great a** under Candace queen *1413*
9:14 And here he hath **a** from the chief priests to *1849*
26:10 having received **a** from the chief priests; *1849*
26:12 Whereupon as I went to Damascus with **a** *1849*
1Co 15:24 have put down all rule and all **a** and power. *1849*
2Co 10: 8 I should boast somewhat more of our **a**, *1849*
1Ti 2: 2 For kings, and *for* all that are in **a**; that we *5247*
2:12 nor to **usurp a over** the man, but to be in *831*
Tit 2:15 and exhort, and rebuke with all **a**. *2003*
Rev 13: 2 him his power, and his seat, and great **a**. *1849*

AVA (1)
2Ki 17:24 from **A**, and from Hamath, and 5755

AVAILETH (4)
Est 5:13 Yet all this **a** me nothing, so long as I see 7737
Gal 5: 6 For in Jesus Christ neither circumcision **a** *2480*
6:15 For in Christ Jesus neither circumcision **a** *2480*
Jas 5:16 fervent prayer of a righteous *man* **a** much. *2480*

AVEN (3) [BETH-AVEN]
Eze 30:17 The young men of **A** and of Phi-beseth shall 205
Hos 10: 8 The high places also of **A**, the sin of Israel, 205
Am 1: 5 cut off the inhabitant from the plain of **A**, 206

AVENGE (17) [VENGEANCE]
Lev 19:18 Thou shalt not **a**, nor bear any grudge 5358
26:25 shall **a the quarrel** of *my* covenant: 5358+5359
Nu 31: 2 **A** the children of Israel of 5358+5360
31: 3 and **a** the LORD of Midian. 5360+5414
Dt 32:43 for he will **a** the blood of his servants, and 5358
1Sa 24:12 and thee, and the LORD **a** me of thee: 5358
2Ki 9: 7 that I may **a** the blood of my servants 5358
Est 8:13 that day to **a** themselves on their enemies. 5358
Isa 1:24 and **a** me of mine enemies: 5358
Jer 46:10 that *he* may **a** him of his adversaries: 5358
Hos 1: 4 I will **a** the blood of Jezreel upon the house 6485
Lk 18: 3 unto him, saying, **A** me of mine adversary. *1556*
18: 5 this widow troubleth me, I will **a** her, *1556*
18: 7 And shall not God **a** his own *1557+3588+4160*
18: 8 I tell you that he will **a** them speedily. *1557*
Ro 12:19 **a** not yourselves, but *rather* give place unto *1556*
Rev 6:10 **a** our blood on them that dwell on *1556*

AVENGED (16) [VENGEANCE]
Ge 4:24 If Cain shall be **a** sevenfold, truly Lamech 5358
Jos 10:13 until the people had **a** themselves upon 5358
Jdg 15: 7 yet will I be **a** of you, and after *that* I will 5358
16:28 that I may be at once **a** of 5358+5359
1Sa 14:24 that I may be **a** on mine enemies. 5358
18:25 to be **a** of the king's enemies. 5358
25:31 or that my lord hath **a** himself: 3467
2Sa 4: 8 the LORD hath **a** my lord the king 5360+5414
18:19 how that the LORD hath **a** him of his 8199
18:31 for the LORD hath **a** thee *this* day of all 8199
Jer 5: 9 shall not my soul be **a** on such a nation as 5358
5:29 shall not my soul be **a** on such a nation as 5358
9: 9 shall not my soul be **a** on such a nation as 5358
Ac 7:24 and **a** him that was oppressed, *1557+4160*
Rev 18:20 for God hath **a** you on her. *2917+2919*
19: 2 hath **a** the blood of his servants at her hand. *1556*

AVENGER (9) [VENGEANCE]
Nu 35:12 be unto you cities for refuge from the **a**; 1350
Dt 19: 6 Lest the **a** of the blood pursue the slayer, 1350
19:12 deliver him into the hand of the **a** of blood, 1350
Jos 20: 3 they shall be your refuge from the **a** of 1350
20: 5 if the **a** of blood pursue after him, then 1350
20: 9 not die by the hand of the **a** of blood, 1350
Ps 8: 2 that *thou* mightest still the enemy and the **a**. 5358
44:16 by reason of the enemy and **a**. 5358
1Th 4: 6 because that the Lord *is* the **a** of all such, *1558*

AVENGETH (2) [VENGEANCE]
2Sa 22:48 *It is* God that **a** me, and that bringeth 5360+5414
Ps 18:47 *It is* God that **a** me, and subdueth 5360+5414

AVENGING (3) [VENGEANCE]
Jdg 5: 2 Praise ye the LORD for the **a** of 6544+6546
1Sa 25:26 *from* **a** thyself with thine own hand, now let 3467
25:33 and *from* **a** myself with mine own hand. 3467

AVERSE (1)
Mic 2: 8 that pass by securely *as men* **a** from war. 7725

AVIM (1) [AVIMS]
Jos 18:23 And **A**, and Parah, and Ophrah, 5761

AVIMS (1) [AVIM]
Dt 2:23 the **A** which dwelt in Hazerim, *even* unto 5761

AVITES (2)
Jos 13: 3 the Gittites, and the Ekronites; also the **A**: 5761
2Ki 17:31 the **A** made Nibhaz and Tartak, and 5761

AVITH (2)
Ge 36:35 his stead: and the name of his city *was* **A**. 5762
1Ch 1:46 his stead: and the name of his city *was* **A**. 5762

AVOID (5) [AVOIDED, AVOIDING, AVOUCHED]
Pr 4:15 **A** it, pass not by it, turn from it, and 6544
Ro 16:17 which ye have learned; and **a** them. *1578*
1Co 7: 2 Nevertheless, to **a** fornication, let every *1223*
2Ti 2:23 But foolish and unlearned questions **a**, *3868*
Tit 3: 9 But **a** foolish questions, and genealogies, *4026*

AVOIDED (1) [AVOID]
1Sa 18:11 *it.* And David **a** out of his presence twice. 5437

A

AVOIDING (2) [AVOID]
2Co 8:20 **A** this, that no *man* should blame us in this *4724*
1Ti 6:20 **a** profane *and* vain babblings, and *1624*

AVOUCHED (2) [AVOID]
Dt 26:17 Thou hast **a** the LORD *this* day to be thy 559
26:18 the LORD hath **a** thee *this* day to be his 559

AVVA See AVA

AVVIM See AVIM

AVVITES See AVIMS; AVITES

AWAIT (1) [WAIT]
Ac 9:24 But their **laying a** was known of Saul. *1917*

AWAKE (42) [WAKE]
Jdg 5:12 **A**, awake, Deborah: awake, awake, utter a 5782
5:12 Awake, **a**, Deborah: awake, awake, utter a 5782
5:12 **a**, awake, utter a song: arise, Barak, and 5782
5:12 awake, **a**, utter a song: arise, Barak, and 5782
Job 8: 6 surely now he would **a** for thee, and 5782
14:12 the heavens *be* no more, they shall not **a**, 6974
Ps 7: 6 **a** for me *to* the judgment *that* thou hast 5782
17:15 be satisfied, when *I* **a**, *with* thy likeness. 6974
35:23 Stir up thyself, and **a** to my judgment, 6974
44:23 **A**, why sleepest thou, O Lord? arise, cast *us* 5782
57: 8 **A up**, my glory; awake, psaltery and harp: 5782
57: 8 Awake up, my glory; **a**, psaltery and harp: 5782
57: 8 and harp: I *myself* will **a** early. 5782
59: 4 without *my* fault: **a** to help me, and behold. 5782
59: 5 the God of Israel, **a** to visit all the heathen: 6974
108: 2 **A**, psaltery and harp: I *myself* will awake 5782
108: 2 and harp: I *myself* will **a** early. 5782
139:18 than the sand: when I **a**, I am still with thee. 6974
Pr 23:35 when shall I **a**? I will seek it yet again. 6974
SS 2: 7 ye stir not up, nor **a** *my* love, till he please. 5782
3: 5 ye stir not up, nor **a** *my* love, till he please. 5782
4:16 **A**, O north wind; and come thou south; 5782
8: 4 stir not up, nor **a** *my* love, until he please. 5782
Isa 26:19 **A** and sing, ye that dwell in dust: for thy 6974
51: 9 **A**, awake, put on strength, O arm of 5782
51: 9 Awake, **a**, put on strength, O arm of 5782
51: 9 **a**, as *in* the ancient days, *in* the generations 5782
51:17 **A**, awake, stand up, O Jerusalem, 5782
51:17 Awake, **a**, stand up, O Jerusalem, 5782
52: 1 **A**, awake; put on thy strength, O Zion; 5782
52: 1 Awake, **a**; put on thy strength, O Zion; 5782
Da 12: 2 that sleep in the dust of the earth shall **a**, 6974
Joel 1: 5 **A**, ye drunkards, and weep; and howl, 6974
Hab 2: 7 **a** that *shall* vex thee, and thou shalt be for 3364
2:19 Woe unto him that saith to the wood, **A**; 6974
Zec 13: 7 **A**, O sword, against my shepherd, and 5782
Mk 4:38 and they **a** him, and say unto him, Master, *1326*
Lk 9:32 and when they were **a**, they saw his glory, *1235*
Jn 11:11 but I go, that I may **a** him **out of sleep**. *1852*
Ro 13:11 that now *it is* high time to **a** out of sleep: *1453*
1Co 15:34 **A** to righteousness, and sin not: for some *1594*
Eph 5:14 **A** thou that sleepest, and arise from *1453*

AWAKED (8) [WAKE]
Ge 28:16 Jacob **a** out of his sleep, and he said, 3364
Jdg 16:14 he **a** out of his sleep, and went away with 3364
1Sa 26:12 and no man saw *it*, nor knew *it*, neither **a**: 6974
1Ki 18:27 *or* peradventure he sleepeth, and must be **a**. 3364
2Ki 4:31 and told him, saying, The child is not **a**. 6974
Ps 3: 5 I laid me down and slept; I **a**; for 6974
78:65 the Lord **a** as one out of sleep, *and* like a 3364
Jer 31:26 Upon this I **a**, and beheld; and my sleep 6974

AWAKEST (2) [WAKE]
Ps 73:20 *so*, O Lord, when *thou* **a**, thou shalt despise 5782
Pr 6:22 and *when* thou **a**, it shall talk *with* thee. 6974

AWAKETH (3) [WAKE]
Ps 73:20 As a dream when *one* **a**; *so*, O Lord, 6974
Isa 29: 8 he eateth; but he **a**, and his soul *is* empty: 6974
29: 8 he **a**, and behold, *he is* faint, and his soul 6974

AWAKING (1) [WAKE]
Ac 16:27 of the prison **a out of** his **sleep**, *1096+1853*

AWARE (3) [WARE]
SS 6:12 Or ever I was **a**, my soul made me *like* 3045
Jer 50:24 also taken, O Babylon, and thou wast not **a**: 3045

Lk 11:44 the men that walk over *them* are not **a** *of* *1492*

AWAY (916) [CASTAWAY] See Index

AWE (3)
Ps 4: 4 **Stand in a**, and sin not: commune with 7264
33: 8 inhabitants of the world **stand in a** of him. 1481
119:161 but my heart **standeth in a** of thy word. 6342

AWOKE (8) [WAKE]
Ge 9:24 Noah **a** from his wine, and knew what his 3364
41: 4 well favoured and fat kine. So Pharaoh **a**. 3364
41: 7 And Pharaoh **a**, and behold, *it was* a dream. 3364
41:21 *still* ill favoured, as at the beginning. So I **a**. 3364
Jdg 16:20 And he **a** out of his sleep, and said, 3364
1Ki 3:15 Solomon **a**; and behold, *it was* a dream. 3364
Mt 8:25 And his disciples came to *him*, and **a** him, *1453*
Lk 8:24 And they came to *him*, and **a** him, saying, *1326*

AXE (11) [AXES]
Dt 19: 5 his hand fetcheth a stroke with the **a** to cut 1631
20:19 trees thereof by forcing an **a** against them: 1631
Jdg 9:48 Abimelech took an **a** in his hand, and 7134
1Sa 13:20 and his coulter, and his **a**, and his mattock. 7134
1Ki 6: 7 that there was neither hammer nor **a** *nor* 1631
2Ki 6: 5 a beam, the **a head** fell into the water: 1270
Isa 10:15 Shall the **a** boast itself against him that 1631
Jer 10: 3 of the hands of the workman, with the **a**. 4621
51:20 Thou *art* my **battle a** *and* weapons of war: 4661
Mt 3:10 And now also the **a** is laid unto the root of *513*
Lk 3: 9 And now also the **a** is laid unto the root of *513*

AXES (7) [AXE]
1Sa 13:21 for the **a**, and to sharpen the goads. 7134
2Sa 12:31 under **a** of iron, and made them pass 4037
1Ch 20: 3 and with harrows of iron, and with **a**. 4050
Ps 74: 5 as he had lifted up **a** upon the thick trees. 7134
74: 6 the carved work thereof at once with **a** 3781
Jer 46:22 come against her with **a**, as hewers of 7134
Eze 26: 9 with his **a** he shall break down thy towers. 2719

AXLETREES (2)
1Ki 7:32 the **a** of the wheels *were* joined to the base: 3027
7:33 their **a**, and their naves, and their felloes, 3027

AZAL (1)
Zec 14: 5 valley of the mountains shall reach unto **A**: 682

AZALIAH (2)
2Ki 22: 3 *that* the king sent Shaphan the son of **A**, 683
2Ch 34: 8 he sent Shaphan the son of **A**, and Maaseiah 683

AZANIAH (1)
Ne 10: 9 both Jeshua the son of **A**, Binnui of the sons 245

AZARAEL (1)
Ne 12:36 Shemaiah, and **A**, Milalai, Gilalai, Maai, 5832

AZAREEL (5)
1Ch 12: 6 Jesiah, and **A**, and Joezer, and Jashobeam, 5832
25:18 The eleventh *to* **A**, *he*, his sons, and 5832
27:22 Of Dan, **A** the son of Jeroham. These *were* 5832
Ezr 10:41 **A**, and Shelemiah, Shemariah, 5832
Ne 11:13 Amashai the son of **A**, the son of Ahasai, 5832

AZAREL See AZARAEL; AZAREEL

AZARIAH (49) [ABED-NEGO, UZZIAH]
1Ki 4: 2 he had; **A** the son of Zadok the priest, 5838
4: 5 **A** the son of Nathan *was* over the officers: 5838
2Ki 14:21 all the people of Judah took **A**, which *was* 5838
15: 1 **A** son of Amaziah king of Judah to reign. 5838
15: 6 the rest of the acts of **A**, and all that he did, 5838
15: 7 So **A** slept with his fathers; and they buried 5838
15: 8 eighth year of **A** king of Judah did 5838
15:17 thirtieth year of **A** king of Judah *began* 5838
15:23 In the fiftieth year of **A** king of Judah 5838
15:27 fiftieth year of **A** king of Judah Pekah 5838
1Ch 2: 8 And the sons of Ethan; **A**. 5838
2:38 And Obed begat Jehu, and Jehu begat **A**, 5838
2:39 **A** begat Helez, and Helez begat Eleasah, 5838
3:12 his son, **A** his son, Jotham his son, 5838
6: 9 Ahimaaz begat **A**, and Azariah begat 5838
6: 9 begat Azariah, and **A** begat Johanan, 5838
6:10 Johanan begat **A**, (he *it is* that executed 5838
6:11 **A** begat Amariah, and Amariah begat 5838

1Ch 6:13 begat Hilkiah, and Hilkiah begat **A**, 5838
6:14 **A** begat Seraiah, and Seraiah begat 5838
6:36 of Elkanah, the son of Joel, the son of **A**, 5838
9:11 **A** the son of Hilkiah, the son of 5838
2Ch 15: 1 the spirit of God came upon **A** the son of 5838
21: 2 **A**, and Jehiel, and Zechariah, and Azariah, 5838
21: 2 and **A**, and Michael, and Shephatiah: 5838
22: 6 **A** the son of Jehoram king of Judah went 5838
23: 1 **A** the son of Jeroham, and Ishmael the son 5838
23: 1 **A** the son of Obed, and Maaseiah the son of 5838
26:17 **A** the priest went in after him, and with him 5838
26:20 **A** the chief priest, and all the priests, 5838
28:12 **A** the son of Johanan, Berechiah the son of 5838
29:12 the son of Amasai, and Joel the son of **A**, 5838
29:12 the son of Abdi, and **A** the son of Jehalelel: 5838
31:10 **A** the chief priest of the house of Zadok 5838
31:13 and **A** the ruler of the house of God. 5838
Ezr 7: 1 of Seraiah, the son of **A**, the son of Hilkiah, 5838
7: 3 the son of **A**, the son of Meraioth, 5838
Ne 3:23 After him repaired **A** the son of Maaseiah 5838
3:24 from the house of **A** unto the turning *of* 5838
7: 7 **A**, Raamiah, Nahamani, Mordecai, Bilshan, 5838
8: 7 Kelita, **A**, Jozabad, Hanan, Pelaiah, and 5838
10: 2 Seraiah, **A**, Jeremiah, 5838
12:33 And **A**, Ezra, and Meshullam, 5838
Jer 43: 2 spake **A** the son of Hoshaiah, and 5838
Da 1: 6 Daniel, Hananiah, Mishael, and **A**: 5838
1: 7 of Meshach; and to **A**, of Abed-nego. 5838
1:11 set over Daniel, Hananiah, Mishael, and **A**, 5838
1:19 like Daniel, Hananiah, Mishael, and **A**: 5838
2:17 Mishael, and **A**, his companions: 5839

AZAZ (1)
1Ch 5: 8 Bela the son of **A**, the son of Shema, 5811

AZAZIAH (3)
1Ch 15:21 and Obed-edom, and Jeiel, and **A**, 5812
27:20 children of Ephraim, Hoshea the son of **A**: 5812
2Ch 31:13 **A**, and Nahath, and Asahel, and Jerimoth, 5812

AZBUK (1)
Ne 3:16 After him repaired Nehemiah the son of **A**, 5802

AZEKAH (7)
Jos 10:10 and smote them to **A**, and unto Makkedah. 5825
10:11 stones from heaven upon them unto **A**, 5825
15:35 Jarmuth, and Adullam, Socoh, and **A**, 5825
1Sa 17: 1 pitched between Shochoh and **A**, 5825
2Ch 11: 9 And Adoraim, and Lachish, and **A**, 5825
Ne 11:30 *at* **A**, and *in* the villages thereof. 5825
Jer 34: 7 were left, against Lachish, and against **A**: 5825

AZEL (6)
1Ch 8:37 *was* his son, Eleasah his son, **A** his son: 682
8:38 And **A** had six sons, whose names *are* these, 682
8:38 and Hanan. All these *were* the sons of **A**. 682
9:43 Rephaiah his son, Eleasah his son, **A** his son. 682
9:44 And **A** had six sons, whose names *are* these, 682
9:44 and Hanan: these *were* the sons of **A**. 682

AZEM (2)
Jos 15:29 Baalah, and Iim, and **A**, 6107
19: 3 And Hazar-shual, and Balah, and **A**, 6107

AZGAD (4)
Ezr 2:12 The children of **A**, a thousand two hundred 5803
8:12 of the sons of **A**; Johanan the son of 5803
Ne 7:17 The children of **A**, two thousand three 5803
10:15 Bunni, **A**, Bebai, 5803

AZIEL (1)
1Ch 15:20 **A**, and Shemiramoth, and Jehiel, and Unni, 5815

AZIZA (1)
Ezr 10:27 and Jeremoth, and Zabad, and **A**. 5819

AZMAVETH (8) [BETH-AZMAVETH]
2Sa 23:31 Abialbon the Arbathite, **A** the Barhumite, 5820
1Ch 8:36 Jehoadah begat Alemeth, and **A**, and Zimri; 5820
9:42 and Jarah begat Alemeth, and **A**, and Zimri; 5820
11:33 **A** the Baharumite, Eliahba the Shaalbonite, 5820
12: 3 Jeziel, and Pelet, the sons of **A**; and 5820
27:25 over the king's treasures *was* **A** the son of 5820
Ezr 2:24 The children of **A**, forty and two. 5820
Ne 12:29 and out of the fields of Geba and **A**: 5820

AZMON (3)
Nu 34: 4 go on *to* Hazar-addar, and pass on to **A**: 6111
34: 5 the border shall fetch a compass from **A** 6111
Jos 15: 4 *From thence* it passed toward **A**, and 6111

AZNOTH-TABOR (1) [TABOR]
Jos 19:34 *then* the coast turneth westward *to* **A**, and 243

AZOR (2)
Mt 1:13 Abiud begat Eliakim; and Eliakim begat **A**; *107*
1:14 And **A** begat Sadoc; and Sadoc begat *107*

AZOTUS (1)
Ac 8:40 But Philip was found at **A**: and *108*

AZRIEL (3)
1Ch 5:24 **A**, and Jeremiah, and Hodaviah, and 5837
27:19 of Naphtali, Jerimoth the son of **A**: 5837
Jer 36:26 Seraiah the son of **A**, and Shelemiah 5837

AZRIKAM (6)
1Ch 3:23 Elioenai, and Hezekiah, and **A**, three. 5840
8:38 **A**, Bocheru, and Ishmael, and Sheariah, 5840
9:14 the son of **A**, the son of Hashabiah, of 5840
9:44 **A**, Bocheru, and Ishmael, and Sheariah, 5840
2Ch 28: 7 **A** the governor of the house, and Elkanah 5840
Ne 11:15 the son of **A**, the son of Hashabiah, the son 5840

AZUBAH (4)
1Ki 22:42 his mother's name *was* **A** the daughter of 5806
1Ch 2:18 son of Hezron begat *children* of **A** *his* wife, 5806
2:19 when **A** was dead, Caleb took unto him 5806
2Ch 20:31 his mother's name *was* **A** the daughter of 5806

AZUR (2)
Jer 28: 1 *that* Hananiah the son of **A** the prophet, 5809
Eze 11: 1 among whom I saw Jaazaniah the son of **A**, 5809

AZZAH (3)
Dt 2:23 *even* unto **A**, the Caphtorims, which came 5804
1Ki 4:24 from Tiphsah even to **A**, over all the kings 5804
Jer 25:20 **A**, and Ekron, and the remnant of Ashdod: 5804

AZZAN (1)
Nu 34:26 children of Issachar, Paltiel the son of **A**. 5821

AZZUR (1)
Ne 10:17 Ater, Hizkijah, **A**, 5809

B

BAAL (63) [BAAL'S, BAAL-BERITH, BAAL-GAD, BAAL-HAMON, BAAL-HANAN, BAAL-HAZOR, BAAL-HERMON, BAAL-MEON, BAAL-PEOR, BAAL-PERAZIM, BAAL-SHALISHA, BAAL-TAMAR, BAAL-ZEBUB, BAAL-ZEPHON, BAALIM, BAMOTH-BAAL, GUR-BAAL, JERUBBAAL, KIRJATH-BAAL, MERIB-BAAL]
Nu 22:41 brought him up *into* the high places of **B**, 1168
Jdg 2:13 the LORD, and served **B** and Ashtaroth. 1168
6:25 throw down the altar of **B** that thy father 1168
6:28 the altar of **B** was cast down, and the grove 1168
6:30 because he hath cast down the altar of **B**, 1168
6:31 that stood against him, Will ye plead for **B**? 1168
6:32 saying, Let **B** plead against him, because 1168
1Ki 16:31 went and served **B**, and worshipped him. 1168
16:32 he reared up an altar for **B** *in* the house of 1168
16:32 up an altar for Baal *in* the house of **B**, 1168
18:19 the prophets of **B** four hundred and fifty, 1168
18:21 if **B**, *then* follow him. And the people 1168
18:25 Elijah said unto the prophets of **B**, 1168
18:26 called on the name of **B** from morning even 1168
18:26 even until noon, saying, O **B**, hear us. 1168
18:40 said unto them, Take the prophets of **B**; 1168
19:18 all the knees which have not bowed unto **B**, 1168
22:53 For he served **B**, and worshipped him, and 1168
2Ki 3: 2 for he put away the image of **B** that his 1168
10:18 and said unto them, Ahab served **B** a little; 1168

2Ki 10:19 therefore call unto me all the prophets of **B**, 1168
10:19 for I have a great sacrifice *to do* to **B**; 1168
10:19 that *he* might destroy the worshippers of **B**. 1168
10:20 Proclaim a solemn assembly for **B**. 1168
10:21 all the worshippers of **B** came, so that there 1168
10:21 they came *into* the house of **B**; and 1168
10:21 the house of **B** was full from one end to 1168
10:22 vestments for all the worshippers of **B**. 1168
10:23 *into* the house of **B**, and said unto 1168
10:23 said unto the worshippers of **B**, Search, and 1168
10:23 the LORD, but the worshippers of **B** only. 1168
10:25 and went to the city of the house of **B**. 1168
10:26 forth the images out of the house of **B**, 1168
10:27 they brake down the image of **B**, and 1168
10:27 brake down the house of **B**, and made it a 1168
10:28 Thus Jehu destroyed **B** out of Israel. 1168
11:18 people of the land went *into* the house of **B**, 1168
11:18 slew Mattan the priest of **B** before 1168
17:16 all the host of heaven, and served **B**. 1168
21: 3 he reared up altars for **B**, and made a grove, 1168
23: 4 all the vessels that were made for **B**, 1168
23: 5 them also that burnt incense unto **B**, to 1168
1Ch 4:33 *were* round about the same cities, unto **B**. 1168
5: 5 Micah his son, Reaia his son, **B** his son, 1168
8:30 and Zur, and Kish, and **B**, and Nadab, 1168
9:36 Zur, and Kish, and **B**, and Ner, and Nadab, 1168
2Ch 23:17 all the people went *to* the house of **B**, and 1168
23:17 slew Mattan the priest of **B** before 1168
Jer 2: 8 the prophets prophesied by **B**, and 1168
7: 9 burn incense unto **B**, and walk after other 1168
11:13 *even* altars to burn incense unto **B**. 1168
11:17 me to anger in offering incense unto **B**. 1168
12:16 as they taught my people to swear by **B**; 1168
19: 5 They have built also the high places of **B**, 1168
19: 5 sons with fire *for* burnt offerings unto **B**, 1168
23:13 they prophesied in **B**, and caused my 1168
23:27 their fathers have forgotten my name for **B**. 1168
32:29 roofs they have offered incense unto **B**, 1168
32:35 they built the high places of **B**, which *are* in 1168
Hos 2: 8 and gold, *which* they prepared for **B**. 1168
13: 1 but when he offended in **B**, he died. 1168
Zep 1: 4 I will cut off the remnant of **B** from this 1168
Ro 11: 4 have not bowed the knee to *the image of* **B**. *896*

BAAL'S (1) [BAAL]
1Ki 18:22 **B** prophets *are* four hundred and fifty men. 1168

BAALAH (5)
Jos 15: 9 the border was drawn *to* **B**, which *is* 1173
15:10 the border compassed from **B** westward 1173
15:11 passed along *to* mount **B**, and went out *unto* 1173
15:29 **B**, and Iim, and Azem, 1173
1Ch 13: 6 David went up, and all Israel, to **B**, *that is,* 1173

BAALATH (3) [BAALATH-BEER]
Jos 19:44 And Eltekeh, and Gibbethon, and **B**, 1191
1Ki 9:18 **B**, and Tadmor in the wilderness, in 1191
2Ch 8: 6 **B**, and all the store cities that Solomon had, 1191

BAALATH-BEER (1) [BAALATH, BEER]
Jos 19: 8 that *were* round about these cities to **B**, 1192

BAAL-BERITH (2) [BAAL, BERITH]
Jdg 8:33 after Baalim, and made **B** their god. 1170
9: 4 ten *pieces* of silver out of the house of **B**, 1170

BAALE OF JUDAH (1) [JUDAH]
2Sa 6: 2 that *were* with him from **B**, 1184

BAAL-GAD (3) [BAAL, GAD]
Jos 11:17 even unto **B** in the valley of Lebanon under 1171
12: 7 from **B** in the valley of Lebanon even unto 1171
13: 5 from **B** under mount Hermon unto 1171

BAAL-HAMON (1) [BAAL]
SS 8:11 Solomon had a vineyard at **B**; he let out 1174

BAAL-HANAN (5) [BAAL, HANAN]
Ge 36:38 **B** the son of Achbor reigned in his stead. 1177
36:39 **B** the son of Achbor died, and 1177
1Ch 1:49 **B** the son of Achbor reigned in his stead. 1177
1:50 when **B** was dead, Hadad reigned in his 1177
27:28 *were* in the low plains *was* **B** the Gederite: 1177

BAAL-HAZOR (1) [BAAL, HAZOR]
2Sa 13:23 that Absalom had sheepshearers in **B**, 1178

BAAL-HERMON (2) [BAAL, HERMON]
Jdg 3: 3 from mount **B** unto the entering in of 1179
1Ch 5:23 they increased from Bashan unto **B** and 1179

BAALI (1)
Hos 2:16 call *me* Ishi; and shalt call me no more **B**. 1180

BAALIM (18) [BAAL]
Jdg 2:11 in the sight of the LORD, and served **B**: 1168
3: 7 their God, and served **B** and the groves. 1168
8:33 went a whoring after **B**, and 1168
10: 6 served **B**, and Ashtaroth, and the gods of 1168
10:10 have forsaken our God, and *also* served **B**. 1168
1Sa 7: 4 the children of Israel did put away **B** and 1168
12:10 and have served **B** and Ashtaroth: 1168
1Ki 18:18 of the LORD, and thou hast followed **B**. 1168
2Ch 17: 3 of his father David, and sought not unto **B**; 1168
24: 7 of the LORD did they bestow upon **B**. 1168
28: 2 and made also molten images for **B**. 1168
33: 3 he reared up altars for **B**, and made groves, 1168
34: 4 they brake down the altars of **B** in his 1168
Jer 2:23 I am not polluted, I have not gone after **B**? 1168
9:14 after **B**, which their fathers taught them: 1168
Hos 2:13 I will visit upon her the days of **B**, 1168
2:17 For I will take away the names of **B** out of 1168
11: 2 they sacrificed unto **B**, and burned incense 1168

BAALIS (1)
Jer 40:14 Dost thou certainly know that **B** the king of 1185

BAAL-MEON (3) [BAAL, BETH-BAAL-MEON, BETH-MEON]
Nu 32:38 Nebo, and **B**, (*their* names being changed,) 1186
1Ch 5: 8 who dwelt in Aroer, even unto Nebo and **B**: 1186
Eze 25: 9 Beth-jeshimoth, **B**, and Kiriathaim, 1186

BAAL-PEOR (6) [BAAL, PEOR]
Nu 25: 3 Israel joined himself unto **B**: and the anger 1187
25: 5 every one his men that were joined unto **B**. 1187
Dt 4: 3 seen what the LORD did because of **B**: 1187
4: 3 for all the men that followed **B**, the LORD 1187
Ps 106:28 They joined themselves also unto **B**, and 1187
Hos 9:10 *but* they went *to* **B**, and 1187

BAAL-PERAZIM (4) [BAAL, PERAZIM]
2Sa 5:20 David came to **B**, and David smote them 1188
5:20 he called the name of that place **B**. 1188
1Ch 14:11 So they came up to **B**; and David smote 1188
14:11 they called the name of that place **B**. 1188

BAALS See BAALIM

BAAL-SHALISHA (1) [BAAL, SHALISHA]
2Ki 4:42 there came a man from **B**, and brought 1190

BAAL-TAMAR (1) [BAAL, TAMAR]
Jdg 20:33 and put *themselves* in array at **B**: 1193

BAAL-ZEBUB (4) [BAAL]
2Ki 1: 2 inquire of **B** the god of Ekron whether I 1176
1: 3 *that* ye go to inquire of **B** the god of Ekron? 1176
1: 6 *that* thou sendest to inquire of **B** the god of 1176
1:16 to inquire of **B** the god of Ekron, 1176

BAAL-ZEPHON (3) [BAAL, ZEPHON]
Ex 14: 2 and the sea, over against **B**: 1189
14: 9 by the sea, beside Pi-hahiroth, before **B**. 1189
Nu 33: 7 again unto Pi-hahiroth, which *is* before **B**: 1189

BAANA (2)
1Ki 4:12 **B** the son of Ahilud; *to him pertained* 1195
Ne 3: 4 unto them repaired Zadok the son of **B**. 1195

BAANAH (10)
2Sa 4: 2 the name of the one *was* **B**, and the name of 1196
4: 5 Rechab and **B**, went, and came about 1196
4: 6 and Rechab and **B** his brother escaped. 1196
4: 9 David answered Rechab and **B** his brother, 1196
23:29 Heleb the son of **B**, a Netophathite, Ittai 1196
1Ki 4:16 **B** the son of Hushai *was* in Asher and 1195
1Ch 11:30 Heled the son of **B** the Netophathite, 1196
Ezr 2: 2 Bilshan, Mizpar, Bigvai, Rehum, **B**. 1196
Ne 7: 7 Bilshan, Mispereth, Bigvai, Nehum, **B**. 1196
10:27 Malluch, Harim, **B**. 1196

BAARA (1)
1Ch 8: 8 them away; Hushim and **B** *were* his wives. 1199

BAASEIAH (1)
1Ch 6:40 The son of Michael, the son of **B**, the son 1202

BAASHA (28)
1Ki 15:16 and **B** king of Israel all their days. 1201
15:17 And **B** king of Israel went up against Judah, 1201
15:19 *and* break thy league with **B** king of Israel, 1201
15:21 when **B** heard *thereof,* that he left off 1201
15:22 timber thereof, where*with* **B** had builded; 1201
15:27 **B** the son of Ahijah, of the house of 1201
15:27 **B** smote him at Gibbethon, 1201
15:28 year of Asa king of Judah did **B** slay him, 1201
15:32 and **B** king of Israel all their days. 1201
15:33 **B** the son of Ahijah to reign over all Israel 1201
16: 1 came to Jehu the son of Hanani against **B**, 1201
16: 3 I will take away the posterity of **B**, and 1201
16: 4 Him that dieth of **B** in the city shall 1201
16: 5 Now the rest of the acts of **B**, and what he 1201
16: 6 So **B** slept with his fathers, and was buried 1201
16: 7 came the word of the LORD against **B**, 1201
16: 8 the son of **B** to reign over Israel in Tirzah, 1201
16:11 his throne, *that* he slew all the house of **B**: 1201
16:12 Thus did Zimri destroy all the house of **B**, 1201
16:12 which he spake against **B** by Jehu 1201
16:13 For all the sins of **B**, and the sins of Elah 1201
21:22 like the house of **B** the son of Ahijah, 1201
2Ki 9: 9 and like the house of **B** the son of Ahijah: 1201
2Ch 16: 1 thirtieth year of the reign of Asa **B** king of 1201
16: 3 go, break thy league with **B** king of Israel, 1201
16: 5 when **B** heard *it,* that he left off building of 1201
16: 6 where*with* **B** was a building; 1201
Jer 41: 9 king had made for fear of **B** king of Israel: 1201

BABBLER (2) [BABBLING]
Ecc 10:11 and a **b** is no better. 1167+3956+1886.1
Ac 17:18 And some said, What will this **b** say? *4691*

BABBLING (1) [BABBLER, BABBLINGS]
Pr 23:29 who hath **b**? who hath wounds without 7879

BABBLINGS (2) [BABBLING]
1Ti 6:20 avoiding profane *and* **vain b**, and *2757*
2Ti 2:16 But shun profane *and* **vain b**: for they will *2757*

BABE (6) [BABES]
Ex 2: 6 behold, the **b** wept. And she had 5288
Lk 1:41 of Mary, the **b** leaped in her womb; *1025*
1:44 the **b** leaped in my womb for joy. *1025*
2:12 Ye shall find *the* **b** wrapped in swaddling *1025*
2:16 and Joseph, and the **b** lying in a manger. *1025*
Heb 5:13 in the word of righteousness: for he is a **b**. *3516*

BABEL (2) [BABYLON]
Ge 10:10 the beginning of his kingdom was **B**, and 894
11: 9 Therefore is the name of it called **B**; because 894

BABES (9) [BABE]
Ps 8: 2 Out of the mouth of **b** and sucklings hast 5768
17:14 leave the rest of their *substance* to their **b**. 5768
Isa 3: 4 *be* their princes, and **b** shall rule over them. 8586
Mt 11:25 and prudent, and hast revealed them unto **b**. *3516*
21:16 Out of the mouth of **b** and sucklings thou *3516*
Lk 10:21 and prudent, and hast revealed them unto **b**: *3516*
Ro 2:20 An instructor of the foolish, a teacher of **b**, *3516*
1Co 3: 1 but as unto carnal, *even* as unto **b** in Christ. *3516*
1Pe 2: 2 As newborn **b**, desire the sincere milk of *1025*

BABOONS See PEACOCKS

BABYLON (286) [BABEL, BABYLON'S, BABYLONIANS, BABYLONISH]
2Ki 17:24 the king of Assyria brought *men* from **B**, 894
17:30 And the men of **B** made Succoth-benoth, and 894
20:12 king of **B**, sent letters and a present unto 894
20:14 are come from a far country, *even* from **B**. 894
20:17 store unto this day, shall be carried unto **B**: 894
20:18 be eunuchs in the palace of the king of **B**. 894
24: 1 In his days Nebuchadnezzar king of **B** came 894
24: 7 for the king of **B** had taken from the river of 894
24:10 king of **B** came up *against* Jerusalem, 894
24:11 Nebuchadnezzar king of **B** came against 894
24:12 the king of Judah went out to the king of **B**, 894
24:12 the king of **B** took him in the eighth year of 894
24:15 he carried away Jehoiachin to **B**, and 894
24:15 he *into* captivity from Jerusalem to **B**. 894
24:16 even them the king of **B** brought captive to 894
24:16 the king of Babylon brought captive to **B**. 894
24:17 the king of **B** made Mattaniah his father's 894
24:20 that Zedekiah rebelled against the king of **B**. 894
25: 1 *that* Nebuchadnezzar king of **B** came, he, 894
25: 6 brought him up to the king of **B** to Riblah; 894
25: 7 with fetters of brass, and carried him *to* **B**. 894
25: 8 year of king Nebuchadnezzar king of **B**, 894
25: 8 a servant of the king of **B**, *unto* Jerusalem: 894
25:11 the fugitives that fell away to the king of **B**, 894
25:13 *in pieces,* and carried the brass of them to **B**. 894
25:20 and brought them to the king of **B** to Riblah: 894
25:21 the king of **B** smote them, and slew them at 894
25:22 whom Nebuchadnezzar king of **B** had left, 894
25:23 heard that the king of **B** had made Gedaliah 894
25:24 dwell in the land, and serve the king of **B**; 894
25:27 of the month, *that* Evil-merodach king of **B**, 894
25:28 throne of the kings that *were* with him in **B**; 894
1Ch 9: 1 *who* were carried away to **B** for their 894
2Ch 32:31 *of* the ambassadors of the princes of **B**, 894
33:11 bound him with fetters, and carried him to **B**. 894
36: 6 him came up Nebuchadnezzar king of **B**, 894
36: 6 and bound him in fetters, to carry him to **B**. 894
36: 7 the vessels of the house of the LORD to **B**, 894
36: 7 to Babylon, and put them in his temple at **B**. 894
36:10 Nebuchadnezzar sent, and brought him to **B**, 894
36:18 and of his princes; all *these* he brought *to* **B**. 894
36:20 from the sword carried he away to **B**; 894
Ezr 1:11 that were brought up from **B** unto Jerusalem. 894
2: 1 whom Nebuchadnezzar the king of **B** had 894
2: 1 king of Babylon had carried away unto **B**, 894
5:12 the hand of Nebuchadnezzar the king of **B**, 895
5:12 and carried the people away into **B**. 895
5:13 in the first year of Cyrus the king of **B** 895
5:14 brought them into the temple of **B**, those did 895
5:14 Cyrus the king take out of the temple of **B**, 895
5:17 which *is* there at **B**, whether it be *so,* that a 895
6: 1 where the treasures were laid up in **B**. 895
6: 5 brought unto **B**, be restored, and 895
7: 6 This Ezra went up from **B**; and he *was* a 894
7: 9 of the first month began he to go up from **B**, 894
7:16 that thou canst find in all the province of **B**, 895
8: 1 of them that went up with me from **B**, 894
Ne 7: 6 whom Nebuchadnezzar the king of **B** had 894
13: 6 thirtieth year of Artaxerxes king of **B** came I 894
Est 2: 6 whom Nebuchadnezzar the king of **B** had 894
Ps 87: 4 of Rahab and **B** to them that know me: 894
137: 1 By the rivers of **B**, there we sat down, yea, 894
137: 8 O daughter of **B**, who art *to be* destroyed; 894
Isa 13: 1 The burden of **B**, which Isaiah the son of 894
13:19 **B**, the glory of kingdoms, the beauty of 894
14: 4 take up this proverb against the king of **B**, 894
14:22 cut off from **B** the name, and remnant, and 894
21: 9 he answered and said, **B** is fallen, is fallen; 894
39: 1 king of **B**, sent letters and a present to 894
39: 3 from a far country unto me, *even* from **B**. 894
39: 6 in store until this day, shall be carried *to* **B**: 894
39: 7 be eunuchs in the palace of the king of **B**. 894
43:14 For your sake I have sent to **B**, and 894
47: 1 and sit in the dust, O virgin daughter of **B**, 894
48:14 he will do his pleasure on **B**, and his arm 894
48:20 Go ye forth of **B**, flee ye from 894
Jer 20: 4 give all Judah into the hand of the king of **B**, 894
20: 4 he shall carry them captive into **B**, and 894
20: 5 and take them, and carry them to **B**. 894
20: 6 thou shalt come *to* **B**, and there thou shalt 894
21: 2 for Nebuchadrezzar king of **B** maketh war 894
21: 4 wherewith ye fight against the king of **B**, and 894
21: 7 into the hand of Nebuchadrezzar king of **B**, 894
21:10 shall be given into the hand of the king of **B**, 894
22:25 into the hand of Nebuchadrezzar king of **B**, 894
24: 1 after that Nebuchadrezzar king of **B** had 894
24: 1 from Jerusalem, and had brought them *to* **B**. 894
25: 1 the first year of Nebuchadrezzar king of **B**; 894
25: 9 Nebuchadrezzar the king of **B**, my servant, 894
25:11 these nations shall serve the king of **B** 894
25:12 *that* I will punish the king of **B**, and that 894
27: 6 the hand of Nebuchadnezzar the king of **B**, 894
27: 8 the same Nebuchadnezzar the king of **B**, 894
27: 8 their neck under the yoke of the king of **B**, 894
27: 9 saying, Ye shall not serve the king of **B**: 894

B

Jer 27:11 their neck under the yoke of the king of **B**, 894
27:12 your necks under the yoke of the king of **B**, 894
27:13 the nation that will not serve the king of **B**? 894
27:14 saying, Ye shall not serve the king of **B**: 894
27:16 *shall* now shortly be brought again from **B**: 894
27:17 not unto them; serve the king of **B**, and live: 894
27:18 king of Judah, and at Jerusalem, go not to **B**. 894
27:20 Which Nebuchadnezzar king of **B** took not, 894
27:20 king of Judah from Jerusalem to **B**, 894
27:22 They shall be carried to **B**, and there shall 894
28: 2 I have broken the yoke of the king of **B**. 894
28: 3 that Nebuchadnezzar king of **B** took away 894
28: 3 away from this place, and carried them *to* **B**: 894
28: 4 of Judah, that went into **B**, saith the LORD: 894
28: 4 for I will break the yoke of the king of **B**. 894
28: 6 carried away captive, from **B** into this place. 894
28:11 **B** from the neck of all nations within 894
28:14 *they* may serve Nebuchadnezzar king of **B**; 894
29: 1 carried away captive from Jerusalem to **B**; 894
29: 3 whom Zedekiah king of Judah sent unto **B** to 894
29: 3 unto Babylon to Nebuchadnezzar king of **B**, 894
29: 4 to be carried away from Jerusalem unto **B**; 894
29:10 years be accomplished at **B** I will visit you, 894
29:15 The LORD hath raised us up prophets in **B**; 894
29:20 whom I have sent from Jerusalem to **B**: 894
29:21 into the hand of Nebuchadrezzar king of **B**; 894
29:22 by all the captivity of Judah which *are* in **B**, 894
29:22 whom the king of **B** roasted in the fire; 894
29:28 For therefore he sent unto us *in* **B**, saying, 894
32: 3 give this city into the hand of the king of **B**, 894
32: 4 be delivered into the hand of the king of **B**, 894
32: 5 he shall lead Zedekiah *to* **B**, and there shall 894
32:28 into the hand of Nebuchadrezzar king of **B**, 894
32:36 into the hand of the king of **B** by the sword, 894
34: 1 when Nebuchadnezzar king of **B**, and all his 894
34: 2 give this city into the hand of the king of **B**, 894
34: 3 eyes shall behold the eyes of the king of **B**, 894
34: 3 thee mouth to mouth, and thou shalt go *to* **B**. 894
35:11 when Nebuchadrezzar king of **B** came up 894
36:29 The king of **B** shall certainly come 894
37: 1 whom Nebuchadrezzar king of **B** made king 894
37:17 be delivered into the hand of the king of **B**. 894
37:19 The king of **B** shall not come against you, 894
38:23 shalt be taken by the hand of the king of **B**: 894
39: 1 came Nebuchadrezzar king of **B** and all his 894
39: 3 And all the princes of the king of **B** came in, 894
39: 3 the residue of the princes of the king of **B**. 894
39: 5 king of **B** to Riblah in the land of Hamath, 894
39: 6 the king of **B** slew the sons of Zedekiah in 894
39: 6 also the king of **B** slew all the nobles of 894
39: 7 bound him with chains to carry him to **B**. 894
39: 9 **B** the remnant of the people that remained in 894
39:11 Now Nebuchadrezzar king of **B** gave charge 894
40: 1 which were carried away captive unto **B**. 894
40: 4 good unto thee to come with me *into* **B**, 894
40: 4 it seem ill unto thee to come with me *into* **B**, 894
40: 5 whom the king of **B** hath made governor 894
40: 7 heard that the king of **B** had made Gedaliah 894
40: 7 that were not carried away captive to **B**; 894
40: 9 dwell in the land and serve the king of **B**, 894
40:11 heard that the king of **B** had left a remnant of 894
41: 2 whom the king of **B** had made governor over 894
41:18 whom the king of **B** made governor in 894
42:11 Be not afraid of the king of **B**, of whom ye 894
43: 3 to death, and carry us away captives *into* **B**. 894
43:10 and take Nebuchadrezzar the king of **B**, 894
44:30 into the hand of Nebuchadrezzar king of **B**, 894
46: 2 which Nebuchadrezzar king of **B** smote in 894
46:13 how Nebuchadrezzar king of **B** should come 894
46:26 into the hand of Nebuchadrezzar king of **B**, 894
49:28 which Nebuchadrezzar king of **B** shall smite, 894
49:30 for Nebuchadrezzar king of **B** hath taken 894
50: 1 The word that the LORD spake against **B** 894
50: 2 say, **B** is taken, Bel is confounded, 894
50: 8 Remove out of the midst of **B**, and go forth 894
50: 9 cause to come up against **B** an assembly of 894
50:13 every one that goeth by **B** shall be 894
50:14 Put *yourselves* in array against **B** round 894
50:16 Cut off the sower from **B**, and him that 894
50:17 last this Nebuchadrezzar king of **B** hath 894
50:18 I *will* punish the king of **B** and his land, 894
50:23 how is **B** become a desolation among 894
50:24 art also taken, O **B**, and thou wast not aware: 894
50:28 that flee and escape out of the land of **B**, 894
50:29 Call together the archers against **B**: all ye 894
50:34 to the land, and disquiet the inhabitants of **B**. 894
50:35 upon the inhabitants of **B**, and upon her 894
50:42 to the battle, against thee, O daughter of **B**. 894
50:43 The king of **B** hath heard the report of them, 894
50:45 of the LORD, that he hath taken against **B**; 894
50:46 At the noise of the taking of **B** the earth is 894
51: 1 I *will* raise up against **B**, and against them 894
51: 2 will send unto **B** fanners, that shall fan her, 894
51: 6 Flee out of the midst of **B**, and deliver every 894
51: 7 **B** *hath been* a golden cup in the LORD'S 894
51: 8 **B** is suddenly fallen and destroyed: howl for 894
51: 9 We would have healed **B**, but she is not 894
51:11 for his device *is* against **B**, to destroy it; 894
51:12 Set up the standard upon the walls of **B**, 894
51:12 which he spake against the inhabitants of **B**. 894
51:24 I will render unto **B** and to all the inhabitants 894
51:29 of the LORD shall be performed against **B**, 894
51:29 to make the land of **B** a desolation without 894
51:30 The mighty *men* of **B** have forborn to fight, 894
51:31 to shew the king of **B** that his city is taken at 894
51:33 The daughter of **B** *is* like a threshingfloor, 894
51:34 Nebuchadrezzar the king of **B** hath devoured 894
51:35 done to me and *to* my flesh *be* upon **B**, 894
51:37 **B** shall become heaps, a dwelling place for 894
51:41 how is **B** become an astonishment among 894
51:42 The sea is come up upon **B**: she is covered 894
51:44 I will punish Bel in **B**, and I will bring forth 894
51:44 more unto him: yea, the wall of **B** shall fall. 894
51:47 do judgment upon the graven images of **B**: 894
51:48 and all that *is* therein, shall sing for **B**: 894
51:49 As **B** *hath caused* the slain of Israel to fall, 894
51:49 so at **B** shall fall the slain of all the earth. 894
51:53 Though **B** should mount up *to* heaven, and 894
51:54 A sound of a cry *cometh* from **B**, and 894
51:55 Because the LORD *hath* spoiled **B**, and 894
51:56 *even* upon **B**, and her mighty *men* are taken, 894
51:58 The broad walls of **B** shall be utterly broken, 894
51:59 Judah *into* **B** in the fourth year of his reign. 894
51:60 a book all the evil that should come upon **B**, 894
51:60 all these words that are written against **B**. 894
51:61 When thou comest *to* **B**, and shalt see, and 894
51:64 Thus shall **B** sink, and shall not rise from 894
52: 3 that Zedekiah rebelled against the king of **B**. 894
52: 4 *that* Nebuchadrezzar king of **B** came, he and 894
52: 9 carried him up unto the king of **B** to Riblah 894
52:10 the king of **B** slew the sons of Zedekiah 894
52:11 the king of **B** bound him in chains, and 894
52:11 carried him to **B**, and put him in prison till 894
52:12 year of Nebuchadrezzar king of **B**, 894
52:12 *which* served the king of **B**, into Jerusalem, 894
52:15 that fell to the king of **B**, and the rest of 894
52:17 and carried all the brass of them to **B**. 894
52:26 and brought them to the king of **B** to Riblah. 894
52:27 the king of **B** smote them, and put them to 894
52:31 *that* Evil-merodach king of **B** in the *first* year 894
52:32 throne of the kings that *were* with him in **B**, 894
52:34 a continual diet given him of the king of **B**, 894
Eze 12:13 I will bring him to **B** *to* the land of 894
17:12 the king of **B** is come *to* Jerusalem, and 894
17:12 princes thereof, and led them with him to **B**; 894
17:16 *even* with him in the midst of **B** he shall die. 894
17:20 I will bring him to **B**, and will plead with 894
19: 9 in chains, and brought him to the king of **B**: 894
21:19 that the sword of the king of **B** may come: 894
21:21 For the king of **B** stood at the parting of 894
24: 2 the king of **B** set himself against Jerusalem 894
26: 7 bring upon Tyrus Nebuchadrezzar king of **B**, 894
29:18 Nebuchadrezzar king of **B** caused his army 894
29:19 of Egypt unto Nebuchadrezzar king of **B**; 894
30:10 by the hand of Nebuchadrezzar king of **B**. 894
30:24 I will strengthen the arms of the king of **B**, 894
30:25 I will strengthen the arms of the king of **B**, 894
30:25 put my sword into the hand of the king of **B**, 894
32:11 The sword of the king of **B** shall come *upon* 894
Da 1: 1 Nebuchadnezzar king of **B** *unto* Jerusalem, 894
2:12 to destroy all the wise *men* of **B**. 895
2:14 was gone forth to slay the wise *men* of **B**: 895
2:18 not perish with the rest of the wise *men* of **B**. 895
2:24 had ordained to destroy the wise *men* of **B**: 895
2:24 unto him; Destroy not the wise *men* of **B**: 895
2:48 him ruler over the whole province of **B**, 895
2:48 of the governors over all the wise *men* of **B**. 895
2:49 over the affairs of the province of **B**: 895

Da 3: 1 up in the plain of Dura, in the province of **B**. 895
3:12 hast set over the affairs of the province of **B**, 895
3:30 and Abed-nego, in the province of **B**. 895
4: 6 to bring in all the wise *men* of **B** before me, 895
4:29 he walked in the palace of the kingdom of **B**. 895
4:30 The king spake, and said, *Is* not this great **B**, 895
5: 7 king spake, and said to the wise *men* of **B**, 895
7: 1 In the first year of Belshazzar king of **B** 895
Mic 4:10 in the field, and thou shalt go *even* to **B**; 894
Zec 2: 7 O Zion, that dwellest *with* the daughter of **B**. 894
6:10 which are come from **B**, and come thou 894
Mt 1:11 about the time they were carried away to **B**: *897*
1:12 And after they were brought to **B**, *897*
1:17 from David until the carrying away into **B** *897*
1:17 from the carrying away into **B** unto Christ *897*
Ac 7:43 and I will carry you away beyond **B**. *897*
1Pe 5:13 The *church that is* at **B**, elected together with *897*
Rev 14: 8 saying, **B** is fallen, is fallen, *that* great city, *897*
16:19 great **B** came in remembrance before God, *897*
17: 5 name written, MYSTERY, **B** THE GREAT, *897*
18: 2 saying, **B** the great is fallen, is fallen, and *897*
18:10 saying, Alas, alas, *that* great city **B**, *897*
18:21 Thus with violence shall *that* great city **B** be *897*

BABYLON'S (8) [BABYLON]
Jer 32: 2 then the king of **B** army besieged Jerusalem: 894
34: 7 When the king of **B** army fought against 894
34:21 into the hand of the king of **B** army, 894
38: 3 be given into the hand of the king of **B** army, 894
38:17 go forth unto the king of **B** princes, 894
38:18 if thou wilt not go forth to the king of **B** 894
38:22 *be* brought forth to the king of **B** princes, 894
39:13 Rab-mag, and all the king of **B** princes; 894

BABYLONIA See BABYLONISH; CHALDEA; CHALDEANS

BABYLONIANS (4) [BABYLON]
Ezr 4: 9 the Apharsites, the Archevites, the **B**, 896
Eze 23:15 *after* the manner of the **B** of Chaldea, 894+1121
23:17 the **B** came to her into the bed of love, 894+1121
23:23 The **B**, and all the Chaldeans, Pekod, 894+1121

BABYLONISH (1) [BABYLON]
Jos 7:21 When I saw among the spoils a goodly **B** 8152

BACA (1)
Ps 84: 6 *Who* passing through the valley of **B** make 1056

BACHRITES (1)
Nu 26:35 of Becher, the family of the **B**: of Tahan, 1076

BACK (155) [BACKBITERS, BACKBITETH, BACKBITING, BACKBITINGS, BACKS, BACKSIDE, BACKSLIDER, BACKSLIDING, BACKSLIDINGS, BACKWARD, CROOKBACKT, HORSEBACK] See Index

BACKBITERS (1) [BACK, BITE]
Ro 1:30 **B**, haters of God, despiteful, proud, *2637*

BACKBITETH (1) [BACK, BITE]
Ps 15: 3 *He that* **b** not with his tongue, nor doeth 7270

BACKBITING (1) [BACK, BITE]
Pr 25:23 so *doth* an angry countenance a **b** tongue. 5643

BACKBITINGS (1) [BACK, BITE]
2Co 12:20 envyings, wraths, strifes, **b**, whisperings, *2636*

BACKS (8) [BACK]
Ex 23:27 I will make all thine enemies **turn** their **b** 6203
Jos 7: 8 when Israel turneth *their* **b** before their 6203
7:12 *but* turned *their* **b** before their enemies, 6203
Jdg 20:42 Therefore they turned *their* **b** before NIH
2Ch 29: 6 of the LORD, and turned *their* **b**. 6203
Ne 9:26 cast thy law behind their **b**, and slew thy 1458
Eze 8:16 *with* their **b** toward the temple of 268
10:12 their **b**, and their hands, and their wings, 1354

BACKSIDE (3) [BACK, SIDE]
Ex 3: 1 he led the flock to the **b** of the desert, and 310
26:12 shall hang over the **b** of the tabernacle. 268
Rev 5: 1 throne a book written within and **on the b**, *3693*

BACKSLIDER (1) [BACK, SLIDE]
Pr 14:14 The **b** in heart shall be filled with his own 5472

BACKSLIDING (12) [BACK, SLIDE]
Jer 3: 6 Hast thou seen *that* which **b** Israel hath 4878
3: 8 when for all the causes whereby **b** Israel 4878
3:11 The **b** Israel hath justified herself more than 4878
3:12 say, Return, thou **b** Israel, saith 4878
3:14 Turn, O **b** children, saith the LORD; for I 7726
3:22 ye **b** children, *and* I will heal your 7726
8: 5 of Jerusalem slidden back *by* a perpetual **b**? 4878
31:22 long wilt thou go about, O thou **b** daughter? 7728
49: 4 thy flowing valley, O **b** daughter? 7728
Hos 4:16 For Israel slideth back as a **b** heifer: 5637
11: 7 my people are bent to **b** from me: 4878
14: 4 I will heal their **b**, I will love them freely: 4878

BACKSLIDINGS (4) [BACK, SLIDE]
Jer 2:19 correct thee, and thy **b** shall reprove thee: 4878
3:22 backsliding children, *and* I will heal your **b**. 4878
5: 6 are many, *and* their **b** are increased. 4878
14: 7 for our **b** are many; we have sinned against 4878

BACKWARD (18) [BACK]
Ge 9:23 went **b**, and covered the nakedness of their 322
9:23 their faces *were* **b**, and they saw not their 322
49:17 the horse heels, so that his rider shall fall **b**. 268
1Sa 4:18 that he fell from off the seat **b** by the side of 322
2Ki 20:10 nay, but let the shadow return **b** ten degrees. 322
20:11 he brought the shadow ten degrees **b**, 322
Job 23: 8 he *is* not *there;* and **b**, but I cannot perceive 268
Ps 40:14 let them be driven **b** and put to shame that 268
70: 2 let them be turned **b**, and put to confusion, 268
Isa 1: 4 of Israel unto anger, they are gone away **b**. 268
28:13 fall **b**, and be broken, and snared, and taken. 268
38: 8 down in the sun dial of Ahaz, ten degrees **b**. 322
44:25 that turneth wise *men* **b**, and maketh their 268
59:14 judgment is turned away **b**, and 268
Jer 7:24 and went **b**, and not forward. 268+3807.1
15: 6 saith the LORD, thou art gone **b**: 268
La 1: 8 yea, she sigheth, and turneth **b**. 268
Jn 18: 6 I am *he*, they went **b**, *1519+3588+3694*

BAD (18) [BADNESS, WORSE, WORST]
Ge 24:50 we cannot speak unto thee **b** or good. 7451
31:24 thou speak not to Jacob either good or **b**. 7451
31:29 thou speak not to Jacob either good or **b**. 7451
Lev 27:10 a good for a **b**, or a bad for a good: 7451
27:10 a good for a bad, or a **b** for a good: 7451
27:12 shall value it, whether it be good or **b**: 7451
27:14 shall estimate it, whether it be good or **b**: 7451
27:33 He shall not search whether it be good or **b**, 7451
Nu 13:19 that they dwell in, whether it *be* good or **b**; 7451
24:13 to do *either* good or **b** of mine own mind; 7451
2Sa 13:22 unto his brother Amnon neither good nor **b**: 7451
14:17 *is* my lord the king to discern good and **b**: 7451
1Ki 3: 9 that *I* may discern between good and **b**: 7451
Ezr 4:12 building the rebellious and the **b** city, and 873
Jer 24: 2 which could not be eaten, they were so **b**. 7455
Mt 13:48 the good into vessels, but cast the **b** away. *4550*
22:10 all as many as they found, both **b** and good: *4190*
2Co 5:10 that he hath done, whether *it be* good or **b**. *2556*

BADE (18) [BID]
Ge 43:17 the man did as Joseph **b**; and the man 559
Ex 16:24 they laid it up till the morning, as Moses **b**: 6680
Nu 14:10 all the congregation **b** stone them with 559
Jos 11: 9 Joshua did unto them as the LORD **b** him: 559
Ru 3: 6 to all that her mother in law **b** her. 6680
1Sa 24:10 *some* **b** *me* kill thee: but *mine eye* spared 559
2Sa 1:18 (Also he **b** *them* teach the children of Judah 559
14:19 he **b** me, and he put all these words in 6680
2Ch 10:12 as the king **b**, saying, Come again to me on 1696
Est 4:15 Esther **b** *them* return Mordecai *this answer:* 559
Mt 16:12 Then understood they how that he **b** *them* *3004*
Lk 14: 9 And he that **b** thee and him come and *2564*
14:10 that when he that **b** thee cometh, he may *2564*
14:12 Then said he also to him that **b** him, *2564*
14:16 man made a great supper, and **b** many: *2564*
Ac 11:12 And the Spirit **b** me go with them, *3004*
18:21 But **b** them **farewell**, saying, I must by all *657*
22:24 **b** that he should be examined by scourging; *3004*

BADEST (1) [BID]
Ge 27:19 I have done according as thou **b** me: 1696

B

BADGERS' (14)
Ex 25: 5 dyed red, and **b** skins, and shittim wood, 8476
26:14 dyed red, and a covering above of **b** skins. 8476
35: 7 dyed red, and **b** skins, and shittim wood, 8476
35:23 skins of rams, and **b** skins, brought *them.* 8476
36:19 and a covering of **b** skins above *that.* 8476
39:34 the covering of **b** skins, and the vail of 8476
Nu 4: 6 shall put thereon the covering of **b** skins, 8476
4: 8 cover the same with a covering of **b** skins, 8476
4:10 thereof within a covering of **b** skins, 8476
4:11 cover it with a covering of **b** skins, and 8476
4:12 cover them with a covering of **b** skins, and 8476
4:14 they shall spread upon it a covering of **b** 8476
4:25 the covering of the **b skins** that *is* above 8476
Eze 16:10 shod thee *with* **b** *skin,* and I girded thee 8476

BADNESS (1) [BAD]
Ge 41:19 I never saw in all the land of Egypt for **b**: 7455

BAG (11) [BAGS]
Dt 25:13 Thou shalt not have in thy **b** divers weights, 3599
1Sa 17:40 put them in a shepherd's **b** which he had, 3627
17:49 David put his hand in *his* **b**, and 3627
Job 14:17 My transgression *is* sealed up in a **b**, and 6872
Pr 7:20 He hath taken a **b** of money with him, 6872
16:11 all the weights of the **b** *are* his work. 3599
Isa 46: 6 They lavish gold out of the **b**, and 3599
Mic 6:11 and with the **b** of deceitful weights? 3599
Hag 1: 6 earneth wages *to put it* into a **b** with holes. 6872
Jn 12: 6 and had the **b**, and bare what was put *1101*
13:29 *of them* thought, because Judas had the **b**, *1101*

BAGGAGE See STUFF

BAGS (3) [BAG]
2Ki 5:23 and bound two talents of silver in two **b**, 2754
12:10 they put up *in* **b**, and told the money that NIH
Lk 12:33 provide yourselves **b** which wax not old, *905*

BAHARUMITE (1)
1Ch 11:33 Azmaveth the **B**, Eliahba the Shaalbonite, 978

BAHURIM (5)
2Sa 3:16 with her along weeping behind her to **B**. 980
16: 5 when king David came to **B**, behold, 980
17:18 came to a man's house in **B**, which had a 980
19:16 which *was* of **B**, hasted and came down with 980
1Ki 2: 8 Shimei the son of Gera, a Benjamite of **B**, 980

BAJITH (1)
Isa 15: 2 He is gone up *to* **B**, and *to* Dibon, the high 1006

BAKBAKKAR (1)
1Ch 9:15 **B**, Heresh, and Galal, and Mattaniah 1230

BAKBUK (2)
Ezr 2:51 The children of **B**, the children of Hakupha, 1227
Ne 7:53 The children of **B**, the children of Hakupha, 1227

BAKBUKIAH (3)
Ne 11:17 **B** the second among his brethren, and 1229
12: 9 Also **B** and Unni, their brethren, *were* over 1229
12:25 Mattaniah, and **B**, Obadiah, Meshullam, 1229

BAKE (9) [BAKED, BAKEMEATS, BAKEN, BAKER, BAKERS, BAKERS', BAKETH]
Ge 19: 3 did **b** unleavened bread, and they did eat. 644
Ex 16:23 **b** *that* which you will bake *to day,* and 644
16:23 bake *that* which you will **b** *to day,* and 644
Lev 24: 5 take fine flour, and **b** twelve cakes thereof: 644
26:26 ten women shall **b** your bread in one oven, 644
1Sa 28:24 and did **b** unleavened bread thereof: 644
2Sa 13: 8 cakes in his sight, and did **b** the cakes. 1310
Eze 4:12 thou shalt **b** it with dung that cometh out of 5746
46:20 where they shall **b** the meat offering; 644

BAKED (4) [BAKE]
Ex 12:39 they **b** unleavened cakes of the dough which 644
Nu 11: 8 and **b** *it* in pans, and made cakes *of* it: 1310
1Ch 23:29 for *that which is* **b** *in* the pan, and for that NIH
Isa 44:19 also I have **b** bread upon the coals thereof; 644

BAKED GOODS See BAKEMEATS

BAKEMEATS (1) [BAKE, MEAT]
Ge 40:17 of all *manner of* **b** for Pharaoh; 644+3978+4639

BAKEN (9) [BAKE]
Lev 2: 4 oblation of a meat offering **b** in the oven, 3989
2: 5 if thy oblation *be* a meat offering ***b*** in a pan, NIH
2: 7 if thy oblation *be* a meat offering ***b*** in NIH
6:17 It shall not be **b** *with* leaven. I have given it 644
6:21 *and when it is* **b**, thou shalt bring it in: 7246
6:21 the **b** pieces of the meat offering shalt thou 8601
7: 9 all the meat offering that is **b** in the oven, 644
23:17 be *of* fine flour; they shall be **b** *with* leaven; 644
1Ki 19: 6 *there was* a cake **b on the coals**, and 7529

BAKER (8) [BAKE]
Ge 40: 1 *his* **b** had offended their lord the king of 644
40: 5 the butler and the **b** of the king of Egypt, 644
40:16 When the chief **b** saw that the interpretation 644
40:20 and of the chief **b** among his servants. 644
40:22 he hanged the chief **b**: as Joseph had 644
41:10 the guard's house, *both* me and the chief **b**: 644
Hos 7: 4 *are* all adulterers, as an oven heated by the **b**, 644
7: 6 their **b** sleepeth all the night; *in* the morning 644

BAKERS (2) [BAKE]
Ge 40: 2 of the butlers, and against the chief of the **b**. 644
1Sa 8:13 and to be cooks, and to be **b**. 644

BAKERS' (1) [BAKE]
Jer 37:21 him daily a piece of bread out of the **b** street, 644

BAKETH (1) [BAKE]
Isa 44:15 yea, he kindleth *it,* and **b** bread; yea, 644

BALAAM (60) [BALAAM'S]
Nu 22: 5 therefore unto **B** the son of Beor to Pethor, 1109
22: 7 they came unto **B**, and spake unto him 1109
22: 8 and the princes of Moab abode with **B**. 1109
22: 9 God came unto **B**, and said, What men *are* 1109
22:10 **B** said unto God, Balak the son of Zippor, 1109
22:12 God said unto **B**, Thou shalt not go with 1109
22:13 **B** rose up in the morning, and said unto 1109
22:14 and said, **B** refuseth to come with us. 1109
22:16 they came to **B**, and said to him, Thus saith 1109
22:18 **B** answered and said unto the servants of 1109
22:20 God came unto **B** at night, and said unto 1109
22:21 **B** rose up in the morning, and saddled his 1109
22:23 **B** smote the ass, to turn her *into* the way. 1109
22:27 of the LORD, she fell down under **B**: 1109
22:28 she said unto **B**, What have I done unto 1109
22:29 **B** said unto the ass, Because thou hast 1109
22:30 And the ass said unto **B**, *Am* not I thine ass, 1109
22:31 Then the LORD opened the eyes of **B**, and 1109
22:34 **B** said unto the angel of the LORD, I have 1109
22:35 the angel of the LORD said unto **B**, 1109
22:35 So **B** went with the princes of Balak. 1109
22:36 when Balak heard that **B** was come, he 1109
22:37 Balak said unto **B**, Did I not earnestly send 1109
22:38 **B** said unto Balak, Lo, I am come unto 1109
22:39 **B** went with Balak, and they came *unto* 1109
22:40 sent to **B**, and to the princes that *were* with 1109
22:41 that Balak took **B**, and brought him up *into* 1109
23: 1 **B** said unto Balak, Build me here seven 1109
23: 2 Balak did as **B** had spoken; and Balak and 1109
23: 2 and **B** offered on *every* altar a bullock and 1109
23: 3 **B** said unto Balak, Stand by thy burnt 1109
23: 4 God met **B**: and he said unto him, I have 1109
23:11 Balak said unto **B**, What hast thou done 1109
23:16 the LORD met **B**, and put a word in his 1109
23:25 Balak said unto **B**, Neither curse them at 1109
23:26 **B** answered and said unto Balak, Told not I 1109
23:27 Balak said unto **B**, Come, I pray thee, I will 1109
23:28 Balak brought **B** *unto* the top of Peor, 1109
23:29 **B** said unto Balak, Build me here seven 1109
23:30 Balak did as **B** had said, and offered a 1109
24: 1 when **B** saw that it pleased the LORD to 1109
24: 2 **B** lift up his eyes, and he saw Israel abiding 1109
24: 3 **B** the son of Beor hath said, and the man 1109
24:10 Balak's anger was kindled against **B**, and 1109
24:10 Balak said unto **B**, I called thee to curse 1109
24:12 **B** said unto Balak, Spake I not also to thy 1109
24:15 **B** the son of Beor hath said, and the man 1109
24:25 **B** rose up, and went and returned to his 1109
31: 8 **B** also the son of Beor they slew with 1109
31:16 children of Israel, through the counsel of **B**, 1109
Dt 23: 4 they hired against thee **B** the son of Beor of 1109
23: 5 thy God would not hearken unto **B**; 1109

Jos 13:22 **B** also the son of Beor, the soothsayer, 1109
24: 9 and called **B** the son of Beor to curse you: 1109
24:10 I would not hearken unto **B**; therefore 1109
Ne 13: 2 and with water, but hired **B** against them, 1109
Mic 6: 5 and what **B** the son of Beor answered him; 1109
2Pe 2:15 following the way of **B** *the son* of Bosor, *903*
Jude 1:11 ran greedily after the error of **B** for reward, *903*
Rev 2:14 hast there them that hold the doctrine of **B**, *903*

BALAAM'S (3) [BALAAM]
Nu 22:25 the wall, and crusht **B** foot against the wall: 1109
22:27 **B** anger was kindled, and he smote the ass 1109
23: 5 the LORD put a word in **B** mouth, and 1109

BALAC (1) [BALAK]
Rev 2:14 who taught **B** to cast a stumblingblock *904*

BALADAN (2)
2Ki 20:12 the son of **B**, king of Babylon, sent letters 1081
Isa 39: 1 the son of **B**, king of Babylon, sent letters 1081

BALAH (1)
Jos 19: 3 And Hazar-shual, and **B**, and Azem, 1088

BALAK (42) [BALAC, BALAK'S]
Nu 22: 2 **B** the son of Zippor saw all that Israel had 1111
22: 4 **B** the son of Zippor *was* king of 1111
22: 7 and spake unto him the words of **B**. 1111
22:10 **B** the son of Zippor, king of Moab, 1111
22:13 said unto the princes of **B**, Get you into 1111
22:14 they went unto **B**, and said, 1111
22:15 **B** sent yet again princes, more, and 1111
22:16 said to him, Thus saith **B** the son of Zippor, 1111
22:18 and said unto the servants of **B**, 1111
22:18 If **B** would give me his house full *of* silver 1111
22:35 So Balaam went with the princes of **B**. 1111
22:36 when **B** heard that Balaam was come, he 1111
22:37 **B** said unto Balaam, Did I not earnestly 1111
22:38 Balaam said unto **B**, Lo, I am come unto 1111
22:39 Balaam went with **B**, and they came *unto* 1111
22:40 **B** offered oxen and sheep, and sent to 1111
22:41 that **B** took Balaam, and brought him up 1111
23: 1 Balaam said unto **B**, Build me here seven 1111
23: 2 **B** did as Balaam had spoken; and Balak 1111
23: 2 **B** and Balaam offered on *every* altar a 1111
23: 3 Balaam said unto **B**, Stand by thy burnt 1111
23: 5 Return unto **B**, and thus thou shalt speak. 1111
23: 7 **B** the king of Moab hath brought me from 1111
23:11 **B** said unto Balaam, What hast thou done 1111
23:13 **B** said unto him, Come, I pray thee, 1111
23:15 he said unto **B**, Stand here by thy burnt 1111
23:16 and said, Go again unto **B**, and say thus. 1111
23:17 **B** said unto him, What hath the LORD 1111
23:18 his parable, and said, Rise up, **B**, and hear; 1111
23:25 **B** said unto Balaam, Neither curse them at 1111
23:26 Balaam answered and said unto **B**, Told not 1111
23:27 **B** said unto Balaam, Come, I pray thee, 1111
23:28 **B** brought Balaam *unto* the top of Peor, 1111
23:29 Balaam said unto **B**, Build me here seven 1111
23:30 **B** did as Balaam had said, and offered a 1111
24:10 **B** said unto Balaam, I called thee to curse 1111
24:12 Balaam said unto **B**, Spake I not also to thy 1111
24:13 If **B** would give me his house full *of* silver 1111
24:25 to his place: and **B** also went his way. 1111
Jos 24: 9 **B** the son of Zippor, king of Moab, arose 1111
Jdg 11:25 now *art* thou any thing better than **B** the son 1111
Mic 6: 5 remember now what **B** king of Moab 1111

BALAK'S (1) [BALAK]
Nu 24:10 **B** anger was kindled against Balaam, and 1111

BALANCE (8) [BALANCES, BALANCINGS]
Job 31: 6 Let me be weighed in an even **b**, that God 3976
Ps 62: 9 to be laid in the **b**, they *are* altogether 3976
Pr 11: 1 A false **b** *is* abomination to the LORD: 3976
16:11 A just weight and **b** *are* the LORD'S: 3976
20:23 unto the LORD; and a false **b** *is* not good. 3976
Isa 40:12 mountains in scales, and the hills in a **b**? 3976
40:15 and are counted as the small dust of the **b**: 3976
46: 6 weigh silver in the **b**, *and* hire a goldsmith; 7070

BALANCES (10) [BALANCE]
Lev 19:36 Just **b**, just weights, a just ephah, and a just 3976
Job 6: 2 my calamity laid in the **b** together! 3976
Jer 32:10 weighed *him* the money in the **b**. 3976
Eze 5: 1 take thee **b** to weigh, and divide *the hair*. 3976
45:10 Ye shall have just **b**, and a just ephah, and 3976
Da 5:27 Thou art weighed in the **b**, and art found 3977
Hos 12: 7 a merchant, the **b** of deceit *are* in his hand: 3976
Am 8: 5 shekel great, and falsifying the **b** by deceit? 3976
Mic 6:11 Shall I count *them* pure with the wicked **b**, 3976
Rev 6: 5 he that sat on him had a **pair of b** in his *2218*

BALANCINGS (1) [BALANCE]
Job 37:16 Dost thou know the **b** of the clouds, 4657

BALD (16) [BALDNESS]
Lev 11:22 the **b locust** after his kind, and the beetle 5556
13:40 whose hair is fallen off his head, he *is* **b**: 7142
13:41 *his head toward* his face, he *is* **forehead b**: 1371
13:42 if there be in the **b head**, or bald forehead, 7146
13:42 or **b forehead**, a white reddish sore; 1372
13:42 it *is* a leprosy sprung up in his **b head**, or 7146
13:42 up in his bald head, or his **b forehead**. 1372
13:43 of the sore *be* white reddish in his **b head**, 7146
13:43 or in his **b forehead**, as the leprosy 1372
2Ki 2:23 and said unto him, Go up, thou **b head**; 7142
2:23 Go up, thou bald head; go up, thou **b head**. 7142
Jer 16: 6 nor **make** themselves **b** for them: 7139
48:37 For every head *shall be* **b**, and every beard 7144
Eze 27:31 **make** themselves **utterly b** for thee, 7139+7139
29:18 every head *was* **made b**, and 7139
Mic 1:16 **Make** thee **b**, and poll thee for thy delicate 7139

BALDNESS (9) [BALD]
Lev 21: 5 They shall not **make b** upon their 7139+7144
Dt 14: 1 nor make *any* **b** between your eyes for 7144
Isa 3:24 instead of well set hair **b**; and instead of a 7144
15: 2 on all their heads *shall be* **b**, *and* 7144
22:12 and to **b**, and to girding with sackcloth: 7144
Jer 47: 5 **B** is come upon Gaza; Ashkelon is cut off 7144
Eze 7:18 upon all faces, and **b** upon all their heads. 7144
Am 8:10 upon all loins, and **b** upon every head; 7144
Mic 1:16 enlarge thy **b** as the eagle; 7144

BALL (1)
Isa 22:18 and toss thee like a **b** into a large country: 1754

BALM (6)
Ge 37:25 camels bearing spicery and **b** and myrrh, 6875
43:11 a little **b**, and a little honey, spices, and 6875
Jer 8:22 *Is there* no **b** in Gilead; *is there* no 6875
46:11 Go up *into* Gilead, and take **b**, O virgin, 6875
51: 8 take **b** for her pain, if so be she may be 6875
Eze 27:17 and Pannag, and honey, and oil, and **b**. 6875

BAMAH (1)
Eze 20:29 the name thereof is called **B** unto this day. 1117

BAMOTH (2) [BAMOTH-BAAL]
Nu 21:19 *to* Nahaliel: and from Nahaliel *to* **B**: 1120
21:20 from **B** *in* the valley, that *is* in the country 1120

BAMOTH-BAAL (1) [BAMOTH, BAAL]
Jos 13:17 Dibon, and **B**, and Beth-baal-meon, 1120

BAND (20) [BANDED, BANDS, HEADBANDS]
Ex 39:23 *with* a **b** round about the hole, *that* it should 8193
1Sa 10:26 there went with him a **b of men**, 2428
1Ki 11:24 unto him, and became captain over a **b**, 1416
2Ki 13:21 they spied a **b** *of men;* and they cast 1416
1Ch 12:18 and made them captains of the **b**. 1416
12:21 they helped David against the **b** *of* 1416
2Ch 22: 1 for the **b** *of men* that came with 1416
Ezr 8:22 to require of the king a **b** *of soldiers* 2428
Job 38: 9 and thick darkness a **swaddling b** for it, 2854
39:10 Canst thou bind the unicorn *with* his **b** in 5688
Da 4:15 even with a **b** of iron and brass, in the tender 613
4:23 even with a **b** of iron and brass, in the tender 613
Mt 27:27 gathered unto him the whole **b** *of soldiers.* *4686*
Mk 15:16 and they call together the whole **b**. *4686*
Jn 18: 3 having received a **b** *of men,* and *4686*
18:12 Then the **b** and the captain and officers of *4686*
Ac 10: 1 a centurion of the **b** called the Italian *band,* *4686*
10: 1 a centurion of the band called the Italian *b*, NIG
21:31 tidings came unto the chief captain of the **b**, *4686*
27: 1 named Julius, a centurion of Augustus' **b**. *4686*

BANDED (1) [BAND]
Ac 23:12 certain of the Jews **b together**, *4160+4963*

B

BANDS (46) [BAND]
Ge 32: 7 and herds, and the camels, into two **b**; 4264
32:10 this Jordan; and now I am become two **b**. 4264
Lev 26:13 I have broken the **b** of your yoke, and 4133
Jdg 15:14 and his **b** loosed from off his hands. 612
2Sa 4: 2 son had two men *that were* captains of **b**: 1416
2Ki 6:23 So the **b** of Syria came no more into 1416
13:20 the **b** of the Moabites invaded the land *at* 1416
23:33 Pharaoh-nechoh **put** him **in b** at Riblah in 631
24: 2 the LORD sent against him **b** of 1416
24: 2 **b** of the Syrians, and bands of 1416
24: 2 **b** of the Moabites, and bands of 1416
24: 2 **b** of the children of Ammon, and sent them 1416
1Ch 7: 4 *were* **b** of soldiers for war, six and 1416
12:23 these *are* the numbers of the **b** that were 7218
2Ch 26:11 of fighting *men,* that went out to war by **b**, 1416
Job 1:17 The Chaldeans made out three **b**, and 7218
38:31 of Pleiades, or loose the **b** of Orion? 4189
39: 5 or who hath loosed the **b** of the wild ass? 4147
Ps 2: 3 Let us break their **b** asunder, and cast away 4147
73: 4 For *there are* no **b** in their death: but 2784
107:14 of death, and brake their **b** in sunder. 4147
119:61 The **b** of the wicked have robbed me: *but* 2256
Pr 30:27 no king, yet go they forth all of them **by b**; 2686
Ecc 7:26 heart *is* snares and nets, *and* her hands *as* **b**: 612
Isa 28:22 ye not mockers, lest your **b** be made strong: 4147
52: 2 loose thyself from the **b** of thy neck, 4147
58: 6 to loose the **b** of wickedness, to undo 2784
Jer 2:20 I have broken thy yoke, *and* burst thy **b**; 4147
Eze 3:25 they shall put **b** upon thee, and shall bind 5688
4: 8 I will lay **b** upon thee, and thou shalt not 5688
12:14 that *are* about him to help him, and all his **b**; 102
17:21 all his fugitives with all his **b** shall fall by 102
34:27 when I have broken the **b** of their yoke, and 4133
38: 6 Gomer, and all his **b**; the house of Togarmah 102
38: 6 *of* the north quarters, and all his **b**: 102
38: 9 and all thy **b**, and many people with thee. 102
38:22 upon his **b**, and upon the many people that 102
39: 4 all thy **b**, and the people that *is* with thee: 102
Hos 11: 4 them with cords of a man, with **b** of love: 5688
Zec 11: 7 I called Beauty, and the other I called **B**; 2254
11:14 I cut asunder mine other staff, *even* **B**, 2254
Lk 8:29 and he brake the **b**, and was driven of *1199*
Ac 16:26 and every one's **b** were loosed. *1199*
22:30 he loosed him from *his* **b**, and *1199*
27:40 and loosed the rudder **b**, and hoised up *2202*
Col 2:19 and **b** having nourishment ministered, *4886*

BANI (15)
2Sa 23:36 the son of Nathan of Zobah, **B** the Gadite, 1137
1Ch 6:46 The son of Amzi, the son of **B**, the son of 1137
9: 4 son of Omri, the son of Imri, the son of **B**, 1137
Ezr 2:10 The children of **B**, six hundred forty and 1137
10:29 of the sons of **B**; Meshullam, Malluch, and 1137
10:34 Of the sons of **B**; Maadai, Amram, and Uel, 1137
10:38 And **B**, and Binnui, Shimei, 1137
Ne 3:17 repaired the Levites, Rehum the son of **B**. 1137
8: 7 **B**, and Sherebiah, Jamin, Akkub, 1137
9: 4 Jeshua, and **B**, Kadmiel, Shebaniah, Bunni, 1137
9: 4 **B**, *and* Chenani, and cried with a loud voice 1137
9: 5 Jeshua and Kadmiel, **B**, Hashabniah, 1137
10:13 Hodijah, **B**, Beninu. 1137
10:14 Parosh, Pahath-moab, Elam, Zatthu, **B**, 1137
11:22 Levites at Jerusalem *was* Uzzi the son of **B**, 1137

BANISHED (2) [BANISHMENT]
2Sa 14:13 the king doth not fetch *home* again his **b**. 5080
14:14 that *his* **b** be not expelled from him. 5080

BANISHMENT (2) [BANISHED]
Ezr 7:26 or to **b**, or to confiscation of goods, or 8332
La 2:14 seen for thee false burdens and **causes of b**. 4065

BANK (14) [BANKS]
Ge 41:17 behold, I stood upon the **b** of the river: 8193
Dt 4:48 which *is* by the **b** of the river Arnon, 8193
Jos 12: 2 which *is* upon the **b** of the river of Arnon, 8193
13: 9 that *is* upon the **b** of the river Arnon, and 8193
13:16 that *is* on the **b** of the river Arnon, and 8193
2Sa 20:15 they cast up a **b** against the city, and 5550
2Ki 2:13 went back, and stood by the **b** of Jordan; 8193
19:32 before it *with* shield, nor cast a **b** against it. 5550
Isa 37:33 it *with* shields, nor cast a **b** against it. 5550
Eze 47: 7 at the **b** of the river *were* very many trees 8193
47:12 by the river upon the **b** thereof, on this side 8193
Da 12: 5 the one on this side of the **b** of the river, 8193
12: 5 the other on that side of the **b** of the river. 8193
Lk 19:23 then gavest not thou my money into the **b**, *5132*

BANKS (5) [BANK]
Jos 3:15 (for Jordan overfloweth all his **b** all 1415
4:18 flowed over all his **b**, as *they did* before. 1415
1Ch 12:15 when it had overflown all his **b**; 1415
Isa 8: 7 over all his channels, and go over all his **b**: 1415
Da 8:16 I heard a man's voice between *the* **b** *of* Ulai, NIH

BANNER (3) [BANNERS]
Ps 60: 4 Thou hast given a **b** to them that fear thee, 5251
SS 2: 4 and his **b** over me *was* love. 1714
Isa 13: 2 Lift ye up a **b** upon the high mountain, 5251

BANNERS (3) [BANNER]
Ps 20: 5 the name of our God we will **set up** *our* **b**: 1713
SS 6: 4 as Jerusalem, terrible as *an army* **with b**. 1713
6:10 as the sun, *and* terrible as *an army* with **b**? 1713

BANQUET (14) [BANQUETING, BANQUETINGS]
Est 5: 4 Haman come *this* day unto the **b** that I have 4960
5: 5 Haman came to the **b** that Esther had 4960
5: 6 the king said unto Esther at the **b** of wine, 4960
5: 8 Haman come to the **b** that I shall prepare 4960
5:12 the king unto the **b** that she had prepared 4960
5:14 go thou in merrily with the king unto the **b**. 4960
6:14 hasted to bring Haman unto the **b** that 4960
7: 1 Haman came to **b** with Esther the queen. 8354
7: 2 Esther on the second day at the **b** of wine, 4960
7: 7 the king arising from the **b** of wine in his 4960
7: 8 garden into the place of the **b** of wine; 4960
Job 41: 6 Shall the companions **make a b** of him? 3739
Da 5:10 and his lords, came into the **b** house: 4961
Am 6: 7 the **b** of them that stretched themselves 4797

BANQUETING (1) [BANQUET]
SS 2: 4 He brought me to the **b** house, and 3196

BANQUETINGS (1) [BANQUET]
1Pe 4: 3 revellings, **b**, and abominable idolatries: *4224*

BAPTISM (22) [BAPTIZE]
Mt 3: 7 the Pharisees and Sadducees come to his **b**, *908*
20:22 to be baptized *with* the **b** that I am baptized *908*
20:23 be baptized *with* the **b** that I am baptized *908*
21:25 The **b** of John, whence was it? from heaven, *908*
Mk 1: 4 preach the **b** of repentance for the remission *908*
10:38 be baptized *with* the **b** that I am baptized *908*
10:39 *with* the **b** that I am baptized *withal* shall ye *908*
11:30 The **b** of John, was *it* from heaven, or *908*
Lk 3: 3 preaching the **b** of repentance for *908*
7:29 being baptized *with* the **b** of John. *908*
12:50 But I have a **b** to be baptized *with;* and *908*
20: 4 The **b** of John, was it from heaven, or *908*
Ac 1:22 Beginning from the **b** of John, unto *that* *908*
10:37 after the **b** which John preached; *908*
13:24 **b** of repentance to all the people of Israel. *908*
18:25 of the Lord, knowing only the **b** of John. *908*
19: 3 ye baptized? And they said, Unto John's **b**. *908*
19: 4 John verily baptized *with* the **b** of *908*
Ro 6: 4 Therefore we are buried with him by **b** into *908*
Eph 4: 5 One Lord, one faith, one **b**, *908*
Col 2:12 Buried with him in **b**, wherein also you are *908*
1Pe 3:21 The like figure whereunto *even* **b** doth also *908*

BAPTISMS (1) [BAPTIZE]
Heb 6: 2 Of the doctrine of **b**, and of laying on of *909*

BAPTIST (14) [BAPTIZE]
Mt 3: 1 In those days came John the **B**, preaching in *910*
11:11 hath not risen a greater than John the **B**: *910*
11:12 And from the days of John the **B** until now *910*
14: 2 said unto his servants, This is John the **B**; *910*
16:14 they said, Some *say that thou art* John the **B**: *910*
17:13 that he spake unto them of John the **B**. *910*
Mk 6:14 That John the **B** was risen from the dead, *907*
6:24 I ask? And she said, The head of John the **B**. *910*
6:25 and by in a charger the head of John the **B**. *910*
8:28 And they answered, John the **B**: but *910*
Lk 7:20 John **B** hath sent us unto thee, saying, *910*
7:28 is not a greater prophet than John the **B**: *910*
7:33 For John the **B** came neither eating bread nor *910*

Lk 9:19 They answering said, John the **B**; but *910*

BAPTIST'S (1) [BAPTIZE]
Mt 14: 8 said, Give me here John **B** head in a charger. *910*

BAPTIZE (9) [BAPTISM, BAPTISMS, BAPTIST, BAPTIST'S, BAPTIZED, BAPTIZEST, BAPTIZETH, BAPTIZING]
Mt 3:11 I indeed **b** you with water unto repentance: *907*
3:11 he shall **b** you with the Holy Ghost, and *907*
Mk 1: 4 John did **b** in the wilderness, and preach *907*
1: 8 but he shall **b** you with the Holy Ghost. *907*
Lk 3:16 unto *them* all, I indeed **b** you with water; *907*
3:16 he shall **b** you with the Holy Ghost and *907*
Jn 1:26 John answered them, saying, I **b** with water: *907*
1:33 but he that sent me to **b** with water, the same *907*
1Co 1:17 For Christ sent me not to **b**, but to preach *907*

BAPTIZED (61) [BAPTIZE]
Mt 3: 6 And were **b** of him in Jordan, *907*
3:13 Galilee to Jordan unto John, to be **b** of him. *907*
3:14 I have need to be **b** of thee, and comest thou *907*
3:16 And Jesus, when he was **b**, went up *907*
20:22 to be **b** *with* the baptism that I am baptized *907*
20:22 to be baptized *with* the baptism that I am **b** *907*
20:23 be **b** *with* the baptism that I am baptized *907*
20:23 be baptized *with* the baptism that I am **b** *907*
Mk 1: 5 and were all **b** of him in the river *of* Jordan, *907*
1: 8 I indeed have **b** you with water: but he shall *907*
1: 9 of Galilee, and was **b** of John in Jordan. *907*
10:38 be **b** *with* the baptism that I am baptized *907*
10:38 be baptized *with* the baptism that I am **b** *907*
10:39 *with* the baptism that I am **b** *withal* shall ye *907*
10:39 that I am baptized *withal* shall ye be **b**: *907*
16:16 He that believeth and is **b** shall be saved; but *907*
Lk 3: 7 the multitude that came forth to be **b** of him, *907*
3:12 Then came also publicans to be **b**, and *907*
3:21 Now when all the people were **b**, it came to *907*
3:21 to pass, *that* Jesus also being **b**, and praying, *907*
7:29 being **b** *with* the baptism of John. *907*
7:30 God against themselves, being not **b** of him. *907*
12:50 But I have a baptism to be **b** *with;* and *907*
Jn 3:22 and there he tarried with them, and **b**. *907*
3:23 water there: and they came, and were **b**. *907*
4: 1 Jesus made and **b** moe disciples than John, *907*
4: 2 (Though Jesus himself **b** not, but *907*
10:40 Jordan into the place where John at first **b**; *907*
Ac 1: 5 For John truly **b** with water; but ye shall be *907*
1: 5 ye shall be **b** with the Holy Ghost not many *907*
2:38 be **b** every one of you in the name of Jesus *907*
2:41 they that gladly received his word were **b**: *907*
8:12 they were **b**, both men and women. *907*
8:13 and when he was **b**, he continued with *907*
8:16 only they were **b** in the name of the Lord *907*
8:36 *here is* water; what doth hinder me to be **b**? *907*
8:38 both Philip and the eunuch; and he **b** him. *907*
9:18 sight forthwith, and arose, and was **b**, *907*
10:47 *man* forbid water, that these should not be **b**, *907*
10:48 And he commanded them to be **b** in *907*
11:16 how that he said, John indeed **b** with water; *907*
11:16 but ye shall be **b** with the Holy Ghost. *907*
16:15 And when she was **b**, and her household, *907*
16:33 and was **b**, he and all his, straightway. *907*
18: 8 Corinthians hearing believed, and were **b**. *907*
19: 3 said unto them, Unto what then were ye **b**? *907*
19: 4 John verily **b** *with* the baptism of *907*
19: 5 When they heard *this,* they were **b** in *907*
22:16 arise, and be **b**, and wash away thy sins, *907*
Ro 6: 3 many of us as were **b** into Jesus Christ were *907*
6: 3 into Jesus Christ were **b** into his death? *907*
1Co 1:13 for you? or were ye **b** in the name of Paul? *907*
1:14 I thank God that I **b** none of you, but Crispus *907*
1:15 Lest any should say that I had **b** in mine own *907*
1:16 And I **b** also the household of Stephanas: *907*
1:16 besides, I know not whether I **b** any other. *907*
10: 2 And were all **b** unto Moses in the cloud and *907*
12:13 For by one Spirit are we all **b** into one body, *907*
15:29 Else what shall they do which are **b** for *907*
15:29 not at all? why are they then **b** for the dead? *907*
Gal 3:27 For as many of you as have been **b** into *907*

BAPTIZEST (1) [BAPTIZE]
Jn 1:25 and said unto him, Why **b** thou then, *907*

BAPTIZETH (2) [BAPTIZE]
Jn 1:33 the same is he which **b** with the Holy Ghost. *907*
3:26 the same **b**, and all *men* come to him. *907*

BAPTIZING (4) [BAPTIZE]
Mt 28:19 **b** them in the name of the Father, and of *907*
Jn 1:28 beyond Jordan, where John was **b**. *907*
1:31 to Israel, therefore am I come **b** with water. *907*
3:23 And John also was **b** in Aenon near to *907*

BAR (7) [BARS]
Ex 26:28 the middle **b** in the midst of the boards 1280
36:33 he made the middle **b** to shoot through 1280
Nu 4:10 of badgers' skins, and shall put *it* upon a **b**. 4132
4:12 badgers' skins, and shall put *them* on a **b**: 4132
Jdg 16: 3 **b** and all, and put *them* upon his shoulders, 1280
Ne 7: 3 **b** *them:* and appoint watches of 270
Am 1: 5 I will break also the **b** of Damascus, and 1280

BARABBAS (11)
Mt 27:16 they had then a notable prisoner, called **B**. *912*
27:17 unto you? **B**, or Jesus which is called Christ? *912*
27:20 the multitude that they should ask **B**, *912*
27:21 will ye *that* I release unto you? They said, **B**. *912*
27:26 Then released he **B** unto them: *912*
Mk 15: 7 And there was *one* named **B**, *which lay* *912*
15:11 that he should rather release **B** unto them. *912*
15:15 released **B** unto them, and delivered Jesus, *912*
Lk 23:18 Away with this *man,* and release unto us **B**: *912*
Jn 18:40 they all again, saying, Not this *man,* but **B**. *912*
18:40 but Barabbas. Now **B** was a robber. *912*

BARACHEL (2)
Job 32: 2 was kindled the wrath of Elihu the son of **B** 1292
32: 6 Elihu the son of **B** the Buzite answered 1292

BARACHIAS (1) [BERECHIAH]
Mt 23:35 Abel unto the blood of Zacharias son of **B**, *914*

BARAK (14)
Jdg 4: 6 called **B** the son of Abinoam out of 1301
4: 8 **B** said unto her, If thou wilt go with me, 1301
4: 9 Deborah arose, and went with **B** to Kedesh. 1301
4:10 **B** called Zebulun and Naphtali to Kedesh; 1301
4:12 they shewed Sisera that **B** the son of 1301
4:14 Deborah said unto **B**, Up; for this *is* the day 1301
4:14 So **B** went down from mount Tabor, and 1301
4:15 with the edge of the sword before **B**; 1301
4:16 **B** pursued after the chariots, and after 1301
4:22 behold, as **B** pursued Sisera, Jael came out 1301
5: 1 and **B** the son of Abinoam on that day, 1301
5:12 arise, **B**, and lead thy captivity captive, 1301
5:15 with Deborah; even Issachar, *and* also **B**: 1301
Heb 11:32 and *of* **B**, and *of* Samson, and *of* Jephthae; *913*

BARAKEL See BARACHEL

BARBARIAN (3) [BARBARIANS, BARBAROUS]
1Co 14:11 I shall be unto him that speaketh a **b**, and *915*
14:11 and he that speaketh *shall be* a **b** unto me. *915*
Col 3:11 **b**, Scythian, bond *nor* free: *915*

BARBARIANS (2) [BARBARIAN]
Ac 28: 4 And when the **b** saw the *venomous* beast *915*
Ro 1:14 I am debtor both to the Greeks, and to the **b**; *915*

BARBAROUS (1) [BARBARIAN]
Ac 28: 2 And the **b people** shewed us no little *915*

BARBED (1)
Job 41: 7 Canst thou fill his skin with **b irons**? or 7905

BARBER'S (1)
Eze 5: 1 take thee a **b** rasor, and cause *it* to pass 1532

BARBS See PRICKS

BARE (186) [BAREFOOT, BAREST, BEAR]
Ge 4: 1 she conceived, and **b** Cain, and said, I have 3205
4: 2 she again **b** his brother Abel. And Abel was 3205
4:17 his wife; and she conceived, and **b** Enoch: 3205
4:20 Adah **b** Jabal: he was the father of such as 3205
4:22 Zillah, she also **b** Tubal-cain, an instructor 3205
4:25 she **b** a son, and called his name Seth: 3205
6: 4 they **b** *children* to them, the same *became* 3205
7:17 **b up** the ark, and it was lift up above 5375

B

Ge 16: 1 Now Sarai Abram's wife **b** him no 3205
16:15 Hagar **b** Abram a son: and Abram called 3205
16:15 his son's name, which Hagar **b**, Ishmael. 3205
16:16 years old, when Hagar **b** Ishmael to Abram. 3205
19:37 the firstborn **b** a son, and called his name 3205
19:38 she also **b** a son, and called his name 3205
20:17 and his maidservants; and they **b** *children.* 3205
21: 2 and **b** Abraham a son in his old age, 3205
21: 3 unto him, whom Sarah **b** to him, Isaac. 3205
22:24 she **b** also Tebah, and Gaham, and 3205
24:24 the son of Milcah, which she **b** unto Nahor. 3205
24:36 Sarah my master's wife **b** a son to my 3205
24:47 Nahor's son, whom Milcah **b** unto him: 3205
25: 2 she **b** him Zimran, and Jokshan, and 3205
25:12 Sarah's handmaid, **b** unto Abraham: 3205
25:26 Isaac *was* threescore years old when she **b** 3205
29:32 **b** a son, and she called his name Reuben: 3205
29:33 she conceived again, and **b** a son; and said, 3205
29:34 she conceived again, and **b** a son; and said, 3205
29:35 she conceived again, and **b** a son: and 3205
30: 1 when Rachel saw that she **b** Jacob no 3205
30: 5 And Bilhah conceived, and **b** Jacob a son. 3205
30: 7 conceived again, and **b** Jacob a second son. 3205
30:10 And Zilpah Leah's maid **b** Jacob a son. 3205
30:12 Zilpah Leah's maid **b** Jacob a second son. 3205
30:17 she conceived, and **b** Jacob the fifth son. 3205
30:19 conceived again, and **b** Jacob the sixth son. 3205
30:21 afterwards she **b** a daughter, and called her 3205
30:23 she conceived, and **b** a son; and said, 3205
31: 8 be thy wages; then all the cattle **b** speckled: 3205
31: 8 be thy hire; then **b** all the cattle ringstraked. 3205
31:39 I **b** the **loss** of it; of my hand didst thou 2398
34: 1 daughter of Leah, which she **b** unto Jacob, 3205
36: 4 Adah **b** to Esau Eliphaz; and 3205
36: 4 to Esau Eliphaz; and Bashemath **b** Reuel; 3205
36: 5 Aholibamah **b** Jeush, and Jaalam, and 3205
36:12 Esau's son; and she **b** to Eliphaz Amalek: 3205
36:14 she **b** to Esau Jeush, and Jaalam, and 3205
38: 3 she conceived, and **b** a son; and he called 3205
38: 4 she conceived again, and **b** a son; and 3205
38: 5 she yet again conceived, and **b** a son; and 3205
38: 5 and he was at Chezib, when she **b** him. 3205
41:50 of Poti-pherah priest of On **b** unto him. 3205
44:27 Ye know that my wife **b** me two *sons:* 3205
46:15 which she **b** unto Jacob in Padan-aram, 3205
46:18 these she **b** unto Jacob, *even* sixteen souls. 3205
46:20 of Poti-pherah priest of On **b** unto him. 3205
46:25 his daughter, and she **b** these unto Jacob: 3205
Ex 2: 2 the woman conceived, and **b** a son: and 3205
2:22 she **b** *him* a son, and he called his name 3205
6:20 to wife; and she **b** him Aaron and Moses: 3205
6:23 she **b** him Nadab, and Abihu, Eleazar, and 3205
6:25 of Putiel to wife; and she **b** him Phinehas: 3205
19: 4 *how* I **b** you on eagles' wings, and 5375
Lev 13:45 his head **b**, and he shall put a covering 6544
13:55 *whether* it *be* **b** **within** or without. 7146
Nu 13:23 and they **b** it between two upon a staff; 5375
26:59 whom *her mother* **b** to Levi in Egypt: 3205
26:59 she **b** unto Amram Aaron and Moses, and 3205
Dt 1:31 seen how that the LORD thy God **b** thee, 5375
31: 9 which **b** the ark of the covenant of 5375
31:25 which **b** the ark of the covenant of 5375
Jos 3:15 as they that **b** the ark were come unto 5375
3:15 the feet of the priests that **b** the ark were 5375
3:17 the priests that **b** the ark *of* the covenant of 5375
4: 9 which **b** the ark of the covenant stood: 5375
4:10 For the priests which **b** the ark stood in 5375
4:18 when the priests that **b** the ark of 5375
8:33 which **b** the ark of the covenant of 5375
Jdg 3:18 he sent away the people that **b** the present. 5375
8:31 she also **b** him a son, whose name he called 3205
11: 2 Gilead's wife **b** him sons; and *his* wife's 3205
13: 2 and his wife *was* barren, and **b** not. 3205
13:24 the woman **b** a son, and called his name 3205
Ru 4:12 of Pharez, whom Tamar **b** unto Judah, 3205
4:13 gave her conception, and she **b** a son. 3205
1Sa 1:20 that she **b** a son, and called his name 3205
2:21 and **b** three sons and two daughters. 3205
14: 1 said unto the young man that **b** his armour, 5375
14: 6 Jonathan said to the young man that **b** his 5375
17:41 the man that **b** the shield *went* before him. 5375
2Sa 6:13 that when they that **b** the ark of the LORD 5375
11:27 and she became his wife, and **b** him a son. 3205
12:15 the child that Uriah's wife **b** unto David, 3205
12:24 she **b** a son, and he called his name 3205
18:15 ten young men that **b** Joab's armour 5375
21: 8 whom she **b** unto Saul, Armoni and 3205
1Ki 1: 6 and *his mother* **b** him after Absalom. 3205
5:15 and ten thousand that **b** burdens, 5375
9:23 which **b** **rule** over the people that wrought 7287
10: 2 *with* camels that **b** spices, and very much 5375
11:20 the sister of Tahpenes **b** him Genubath his 3205
14:28 *that* the guard **b** them, and brought them 5375
2Ki 4:17 **b** a son at that season that Elisha had said 3205
5:23 his servants; and they **b** *them* before him. 5375
1Ch 1:32 she **b** Zimran, and Jokshan, and Medan, 3205
2: 4 Tamar his daughter in law **b** him Pharez 3205
2:17 Abigail **b** Amasa: and the father of Amasa 3205
2:19 took unto him Ephrath, which **b** him Hur. 3205
2:21 threescore years old; and she **b** him Segub. 3205
2:24 Abiah Hezron's wife **b** him Ashur 3205
2:29 and she **b** him Ahban, and Molid. 3205
2:35 his servant to wife; and she **b** him Attai. 3205
2:46 **b** Haran, and Moza, and Gazez: 3205
2:48 Caleb's concubine, **b** Sheber, and Tirhanah. 3205
2:49 She **b** also Shaaph the father of 3205
4: 6 Naarah **b** him Ahuzam, and Hepher, and 3205
4: 9 Because I **b** *him* with sorrow. 3205
4:17 she **b** Miriam, and Shammai, and Ishbah 2029
4:18 his wife Jehudijah **b** Jered the father of 3205
7:14 sons of Manasseh; Ashriel, whom she **b**: 3205
7:14 his concubine the Aramitess **b** Machir 3205
7:16 Maachah the wife of Machir **b** a son, and 3205
7:18 his sister Hammoleketh **b** Ishod, and 3205
7:23 **b** a son, and he called his name Beriah, 3205
12:24 The children of Judah that **b** shield and 5375
15:15 the children of the Levites **b** the ark of God 5375
15:26 when God helped the Levites that **b** the ark 5375
15:27 all the Levites that **b** the ark, and 5375
2Ch 8:10 and fifty, that **b** **rule** over the people. 7287
9: 1 camels that **b** spices, and gold in 5375
11:19 Which **b** him children; Jeush, and 3205
11:20 which **b** him Abijah, and Attai, and Ziza, 3205
14: 8 Asa had an army *of men* that **b** targets and 5375
14: 8 that **b** shields and drew bows, two hundred 5375
Ne 4:17 they that **b** burdens, *with* those that laded, 5375
5:15 *yea,* even their servants **b** **rule** over 7980
Pr 17:25 his father, and bitterness to her that **b** him. 3205
23:25 be glad, and she that **b** thee shall rejoice. 3205
SS 6: 9 she *is* the choice one of her that **b** her. 3205
8: 5 there she brought *thee* forth *that* **b** thee. 3205
Isa 8: 3 and she conceived, and **b** a son. 3205
22: 6 Elam **b** the quiver with chariots of men 5375
32:11 **make** ye **b**, and gird *sackcloth* upon *your* 6209
47: 2 **make** **b** the leg, uncover the thigh, 2834
51: 2 your father, and unto Sarah *that* **b** you: 2342
52:10 The LORD hath **made** **b** his holy arm in 2834
53:12 he **b** the sin of many, and made intercession 5375
63: 9 he **b** them, and carried them all the days of 5190
Jer 13:22 skirts discovered, *and* thy heels **made** **b**. 2554
16: 3 concerning their mothers that **b** them, and 3205
20:14 let not the day wherein my mother **b** me be 3205
22:26 thy mother that **b** thee, into another 3205
49:10 I have **made** Esau **b**, I have uncovered his 2834
50:12 she that **b** you shall be ashamed: 3205
Eze 12: 7 *and* I **b** *it* upon *my* shoulder in their sight. 5375
16: 7 is grown, whereas thou *wast* naked and **b**. 6181
16:22 when thou wast naked and **b**, *and* 6181
16:39 thy fair jewels, and leave thee naked and **b**. 6181
19:11 rods for the sceptres of them that **b** **rule**, 4910
23: 4 were mine, and they **b** sons and daughters. 3205
23:29 and shall leave thee naked and **b**: 6181
23:37 caused their sons, whom they **b** unto me, 3205
Hos 1: 3 which conceived, and **b** him a son. 3205
1: 6 she conceived again, and **b** a daughter. 3205
1: 8 she conceived, and **b** a son. 3205
Joel 1: 7 he hath made it clean **b**, and cast *it* away; 2834
Mt 8:17 took our infirmities, and **b** our sicknesses. *941*
Mk 14:56 For many **b** **false witness** against him, but *5576*
14:57 and **b** **false witness** against him, saying, *5576*
Lk 4:22 And all **b** him **witness**, and wondered at *3140*
7:14 and they that **b** *him* stood still. And he said, *941*
8: 8 and sprang up, and **b** fruit an hundredfold. *4160*
11:27 Blessed *is* the womb that **b** thee, and *941*
23:29 and the wombs that never **b**, and the paps *1080*
Jn 1:15 John **b** **witness** of him, and cried, saying, *3140*
1:32 And John **b** **record**, saying, I saw the Spirit *3140*
1:34 and **b** **record** that this is the Son of God. *3140*

Jn 2: 8 the governor of the feast. And they **b** *it.* *5342*
5:33 unto John, and he **b witness** unto the truth. *3140*
12: 6 had the bag, and **b** what was put *therein.* *941*
12:17 and raised him from the dead, **b record.** *3140*
19:35 And he that saw *it* **b record**, and his record *3140*
Ac 15: 8 which knoweth the hearts, **b** them **witness**, *3140*
1Co 15:37 but **b** grain, it may chance of wheat, or *1131*
1Pe 2:24 Who his own self **b** our sins in his own body *399*
Rev 1: 2 Who **b record** of the word of God, and *3140*
22: 2 which **b** twelve *manner of* fruits, *and* *4160*

BAREFOOT (4) [BARE, FOOT]
2Sa 15:30 and had his head covered, and he went **b**: 3182
Isa 20: 2 And he did so, walking naked and **b**. 3182
20: 3 **b** three years *for* a sign and wonder upon 3182
20: 4 young and old, naked and **b**, 3182

BAREST (3) [BARE]
1Ki 2:26 thou **b** the ark of the Lord God before 5375
Isa 63:19 We are *thine:* thou never **b rule** over them; 4910
Jn 3:26 to whom thou **b witness**, behold, the same *3140*

BARHUMITE (1)
2Sa 23:31 Abialbon the Arbathite, Azmaveth the **B**, 1273

BARIAH (1)
1Ch 3:22 Igeal, and **B**, and Neariah, and Shaphat, six. 1282

BAR-JESUS (1)
Ac 13: 6 a false prophet, a Jew, whose name *was* **B**: *919*

BAR-JONA (1)
Mt 16:17 said unto him, Blessed art thou, Simon **B**: *920*

BARK (1) [BARKED]
Isa 56:10 they *are* all dumb dogs, they cannot **b**; 5024

BARKED (1) [BARK]
Joel 1: 7 hath laid my vine waste, and **b** my fig tree: 7111

BARKOS (2)
Ezr 2:53 The children of **B**, the children of Sisera, 1302
Ne 7:55 The children of **B**, the children of Sisera, 1302

BARLEY (37)
Ex 9:31 the flax and the **b** was smitten: for 8184
9:31 for the **b** *was* in the ear, and the flax *was* 8184
Lev 27:16 a homer of **b** seed *shall be valued* at fifty 8184
Nu 5:15 the tenth *part* of an ephah of **b** meal; 8184
Dt 8: 8 **b**, and vines, and fig trees, and 8184
Jdg 7:13 a cake of **b** bread tumbled into the host of 8184
Ru 1:22 Beth-lehem in the beginning of **b** harvest. 8184
2:17 and it was about an ephah of **b**. 8184
2:23 of Boaz to glean unto the end of **b** harvest 8184
3: 2 he winnoweth **b** to night in 8184
3:15 he measured six *measures* of **b**, and laid *it* 8184
3:17 These six *measures* of **b** gave he me; 8184
2Sa 14:30 field is near mine, and he hath **b** there; 8184
17:28 **b**, and flour, and parched *corn,* and beans, 8184
21: 9 in the first *days,* in the beginning of **b** 8184
1Ki 4:28 **B** also and straw for the horses and 8184
2Ki 4:42 twenty loaves of **b**, and full ears of corn in 8184
7: 1 two measures of **b** for a shekel, in the gate 8184
7:16 two measures of **b** for a shekel, 8184
7:18 Two measures of **b** for a shekel, and 8184
1Ch 11:13 where was a parcel of ground full *of* **b**; 8184
2Ch 2:10 twenty thousand measures of **b**, and 8184
2:15 the wheat, and the **b**, the oil, and the wine, 8184
27: 5 measures of wheat, and ten thousand of **b**. 8184
Job 31:40 instead of wheat, and cockle instead of **b**. 8184
Isa 28:25 the appointed **b** and the rye *in* their place? 8184
Jer 41: 8 and *of* **b**, and *of* oil, and *of* honey. 8184
Eze 4: 9 **b**, and beans, and lentiles, and millet, and 8184
4:12 thou shalt eat it *as* **b** cakes, and thou shalt 8184
13:19 me among my people for handfuls of **b** 8184
45:13 the sixth part of an ephah of a homer of **b**: 8184
Hos 3: 2 *for* a homer of **b**, and a half homer of 8184
3: 2 a homer of barley, and a half homer of **b**: 8184
Joel 1:11 ye vinedressers, for the wheat and for the **b**; 8184
Jn 6: 9 which hath five **b** loaves, and two small *2916*
6:13 with the fragments of the five **b** loaves, *2916*
Rev 6: 6 and three measures of **b** for a penny; *2915*

BARN (4) [BARNFLOOR, BARNS]
Job 39:12 home thy seed, and gather *it into* thy **b**? 1637
Hag 2:19 *Is* the seed yet in the **b**? yea, as yet the vine, 4035
Mt 13:30 burn them: but gather the wheat into my **b**. *596*
Lk 12:24 which neither have storehouse nor **b**; and *596*

BARNABAS (29) [JOSES]
Ac 4:36 who by the apostles was surnamed **B**, *921*
9:27 But **B** took him, and brought *him* to *921*
11:22 and they sent forth **B**, that *he* should go as *921*
11:25 Then departed **B** to Tarsus, for to seek Saul: *921*
11:30 sent it to the elders by the hands of **B** and *921*
12:25 And **B** and Saul returned from Jerusalem, *921*
13: 1 as **B**, and Simeon that was called Niger, and *921*
13: 2 Separate me **B** and Saul for the work *921*
13: 7 who called for **B** and Saul, and desired to *921*
13:43 religious proselytes followed Paul and **B**: *921*
13:46 Then Paul and **B** waxed bold, and said, *921*
13:50 and raised persecution against Paul and **B**, *921*
14:12 And they called **B**, Jupiter; and Paul, *921*
14:14 *Which* when the apostles, **B** and Paul, *921*
14:20 the next day he departed with **B** to Derbe. *921*
15: 2 and **B** had no small dissension and *921*
15: 2 they determined that Paul and **B**, and *921*
15:12 and gave audience to **B** and Paul, *921*
15:22 own company to Antioch with Paul and **B**; *921*
15:25 chosen men unto you with our beloved **B** *921*
15:35 Paul also and **B** continued in Antioch, *921*
15:36 And some days after Paul said unto **B**, Let us *921*
15:37 And **B** determined to take with *them* John, *921*
15:39 and *so* **B** took Mark, and sailed unto Cyprus; *921*
1Co 9: 6 Or I only and **B**, have not we power to *921*
Gal 2: 1 after I went up again to Jerusalem with **B**, *921*
2: 9 to me and **B** the right hands of fellowship; *921*
2:13 insomuch that **B** also was carried away with *921*
Col 4:10 saluteth you, and Marcus, sister's son to **B**, *921*

BARNFLOOR (1) [BARN, FLOOR]
2Ki 6:27 out of the **b**, or out of the winepress? 1637

BARNS (4) [BARN]
Pr 3:10 So shall thy **b** be filled *with* plenty, and 618
Joel 1:17 are laid desolate, the **b** are broken down; 4460
Mt 6:26 neither do they reap, nor gather into **b**; *596*
Lk 12:18 I will pull down my **b**, and build greater; and *596*

BARREL (3) [BARRELS]
1Ki 17:12 a handful of meal in a **b**, and a little oil in a 3537
17:14 The **b** of meal shall not waste, neither shall 3537
17:16 *And* the **b** of meal wasted not, neither did 3537

BARRELS (1) [BARREL]
1Ki 18:33 Fill four **b** *with* water, and pour *it* on 3537

BARREN (23) [BARRENNESS]
Ge 11:30 But Sarai was **b**; she had no child. 6135
25:21 Lord for his wife, because she *was* **b**: 6135
29:31 he opened her womb: but Rachel *was* **b**. 6135
Ex 23:26 cast their young, nor be **b**, in thy land: 6135
Dt 7:14 shall not be male or **female b** among you, 6135
Jdg 13: 2 and his wife *was* **b**, and bare not. 6135
13: 3 Behold now, thou *art* **b**, and bearest not: 6135
1Sa 2: 5 so that the **b** hath born seven; and she that 6135
2Ki 2:19 but the water *is* naught, and the ground **b**. 7921
2:21 be from thence any more death or **b** *land.* 7921
Job 24:21 He evil entreateth the **b** *that* beareth not: 6135
39: 6 and the **b** *land* his dwellings. 4420
Ps 113: 9 He maketh the **b** *woman* to keep house, 6135
Pr 30:16 The grave; and the **b** womb; the earth *that* 6115
SS 4: 2 beareth twins, and none *is* **b** among them. 7909
6: 6 and *there is* not one **b** among them. 7909
Isa 54: 1 Sing, O **b**, thou *that* didst not bear; 6135
Joel 2:20 will drive him into a land **b** and desolate, 6723
Lk 1: 7 because that Elisabeth was **b**, and they both *4723*
1:36 the sixth month with her, who was called **b**. *4723*
23:29 Blessed *are* the **b**, and the wombs that *4723*
Gal 4:27 is written, Rejoice, *thou* **b** that bearest not; *4723*
2Pe 1: 8 they make *you that ye shall* neither *be* **b** nor *692*

BARRENNESS (1) [BARREN]
Ps 107:34 A fruitful land into **b**, for the wickedness of 4420

BARS (38) [BAR]
Ex 26:26 thou shalt make **b** *of* shittim wood; five for 1280
26:27 five **b** for the boards of the other side of 1280
26:27 five **b** for the boards of the side of 1280
26:29 their rings *of* gold *for* places for the **b**: 1280

Ex 26:29 and thou shalt overlay the **b** with gold. 1280
35:11 his **b**, his pillars, and his sockets, 1280
36:31 he made **b** of shittim wood; five for 1280
36:32 five **b** for the boards of the other side of 1280
36:32 five **b** for the boards of the tabernacle for 1280
36:34 their rings *of* gold *to be* places for the **b**, 1280
36:34 for the bars, and overlaid the **b** with gold. 1280
39:33 his **b**, and his pillars, and his sockets, 1280
40:18 put in the **b** thereof, and reared up his 1280
Nu 3:36 the **b** thereof, and the pillars thereof, and 1280
4:31 the **b** thereof, and the pillars thereof, and 1280
Dt 3: 5 *were* fenced *with* high walls, gates, and **b**; 1280
1Sa 23: 7 entering into a town that hath gates and **b**. 1280
1Ki 4:13 great cities *with* walls and brasen **b**: 1280
2Ch 8: 5 fenced cities, *with* walls, gates, and **b**; 1280
14: 7 about *them* walls, and towers, gates, and **b**, 1280
Ne 3: 3 the locks thereof, and the **b** thereof. 1280
3: 6 and the locks thereof, and the **b** thereof. 1280
3:13 the **b** thereof, and a thousand cubits on 1280
3:14 the locks thereof, and the **b** thereof. 1280
3:15 the **b** thereof, and the wall of the pool of 1280
Job 17:16 They shall go down *to* the **b** of the pit, 905
38:10 it my decreed *place,* and set **b** and doors, 1280
40:18 pieces of brass; his bones *are* like **b** of iron. 4300
Ps 107:16 of brass, and cut the **b** of iron in sunder. 1280
147:13 For he hath strengthened the **b** of thy gates; 1280
Pr 18:19 *their* contentions *are* like the **b** of a castle. 1280
Isa 45: 2 of brass, and cut in sunder the **b** of iron: 1280
Jer 49:31 which have neither gates nor **b**, 1280
51:30 burnt her dwelling places; her **b** are broken. 1280
La 2: 9 he hath destroyed and broken her **b**: 1280
Eze 38:11 and having neither **b** nor gates, 1280
Jnh 2: 6 the earth *with* her **b** *was* about me for ever: 1280
Na 3:13 thine enemies: the fire shall devour thy **b**. 1280

BARSABAS (2)
Ac 1:23 And they appointed two, Joseph called **B**, *923*
15:22 *namely,* Judas surnamed **B**, and Silas, *923*

BARSABBAS See BARSABAS

BARTHOLOMEW (4)
Mt 10: 3 Philip, and **B**; Thomas, and Matthew *918*
Mk 3:18 and **B**, and Matthew, and Thomas, and *918*
Lk 6:14 his brother, James and John, Philip and **B**, *918*
Ac 1:13 Philip, and Thomas, **B**, and Matthew, *918*

BARTIMEUS (1)
Mk 10:46 of people, blind **B**, the son of Timeus, *924*

BARUCH (26)
Ne 3:20 After him **B** the son of Zabbai earnestly 1263
10: 6 Daniel, Ginnethon, **B**, 1263
11: 5 Maaseiah the son of **B**, the son of 1263
Jer 32:12 I gave the evidence of the purchase unto **B** 1263
32:13 And I charged **B** before them, saying, 1263
32:16 of the purchase unto **B** the son of Neriah, 1263
36: 4 Jeremiah called **B** the son of Neriah: and 1263
36: 4 **B** wrote from the mouth of Jeremiah all 1263
36: 5 Jeremiah commanded **B**, saying, I *am* shut 1263
36: 8 **B** the son of Neriah did according to all that 1263
36:10 read **B** in the book the words of Jeremiah *in* 1263
36:13 when **B** read the book in the ears of 1263
36:14 the son of Cushi, unto **B**, saying, 1263
36:14 So **B** the son of Neriah took the roll in his 1263
36:15 read it in our ears. So **B** read *it* in their ears. 1263
36:16 afraid both one and other, and said unto **B**, 1263
36:17 they asked **B**, saying, Tell us now, 1263
36:18 **B** answered them, He pronounced all these 1263
36:19 Then said the princes unto **B**, Go, hide thee, 1263
36:26 to take **B** the scribe and Jeremiah 1263
36:27 the words which **B** wrote at the mouth of 1263
36:32 gave it to **B** the scribe, the son of Neriah; 1263
43: 3 **B** the son of Neriah setteth thee on against 1263
43: 6 the prophet, and **B** the son of Neriah. 1263
45: 1 the prophet spake unto **B** the son of Neriah, 1263
45: 2 the God of Israel, unto thee, O **B**; 1263

BARZILLAI (12)
2Sa 17:27 and **B** the Gileadite of Rogelim, 1271
19:31 **B** the Gileadite came down from Rogelim, 1271
19:32 Now **B** was a very aged man, 1271
19:33 the king said unto **B**, Come thou over with 1271
19:34 **B** said unto the king, How long have I to 1271
19:39 the king kissed **B**, and blessed him; 1271
21: 8 up for Adriel the son of **B** the Meholathite: 1271
1Ki 2: 7 shew kindness unto the sons of **B** 1271
Ezr 2:61 the children of Koz, the children of **B**; 1271
2:61 which took a wife of the daughters of **B** 1271
Ne 7:63 the children of Koz, the children of **B**, 1271
7:63 which took *one* of the daughters of **B** 1271

BASE (18) [BASER, BASES, BASEST]
2Sa 6:22 than thus, and will be **b** in mine own sight: 8217
1Ki 7:27 four cubits *was* the length of one **b**, and 4350
7:29 upon the ledges *there was* a **b** above: and 3653
7:30 every **b** had four brasen wheels, and 4350
7:31 thereof *was* round *after* the work of the **b**, 3653
7:32 of the wheels *were* joined to the **b**: 4350
7:34 undersetters to the four corners of one **b**: 4350
7:34 the undersetters *were* of the *very* **b** itself. 4350
7:35 in the top of the **b** *was there* a round 4350
7:35 on the top of the **b** the ledges thereof and 4350
Job 30: 8 of fools, yea, children of **b men**: 1097+8034
Isa 3: 5 and the **b** against the honourable. 7034
Eze 17:14 That the kingdom might be **b**, that *it* might 8217
29:14 and they shall be there a **b** kingdom. 8217
Zec 5:11 and set there upon her own **b**. 4350
Mal 2: 9 and **b** before all the people, 8217
1Co 1:28 And **b** *things* of the world, and *things* which *36*
2Co 10: 1 who in presence *am* **b** among you, but *5011*

BASEMATH See BASHEMATH; BASMATH

BASER (1) [BASE]
Ac 17: 5 unto *them* certain lewd fellows of the **b sort**, *60*

BASES (16) [BASE]
1Ki 7:27 he made ten **b** of brass; four cubits *was* 4350
7:28 the work of the **b** *was on* this *manner:* they 4350
7:37 After this *manner* he made the ten **b**: all of 4350
7:38 *and* upon every one of the ten **b** one laver. 4350
7:39 he put five **b** on the right side of the house, 4350
7:43 And the ten **b**, and ten lavers on the bases; 4350
7:43 And the ten bases, and ten lavers on the **b**; 4350
2Ki 16:17 king Ahaz cut off the borders of the **b**, and 4350
25:13 the **b**, and the brasen sea that *was* in 4350
25:16 the **b** which Solomon had made for 4350
2Ch 4:14 He made also **b** and lavers made he upon 4350
4:14 also bases and lavers made he upon the **b**; 4350
Ezr 3: 3 they set the altar upon his **b**; for fear *was* 4350
Jer 27:19 concerning the **b**, and concerning 4350
52:17 the **b**, and the brasen sea that *was* in 4350
52:20 twelve brasen bulls that *were* under the **b**, 4350

BASEST (2) [BASE]
Eze 29:15 It shall be the **b** of the kingdoms; 8217
Da 4:17 he will, and setteth up over it the **b** of men. 8215

BASHAN (59) [BASHAN-HAVOTH-JAIR]
Nu 21:33 they turned and went up *by* the way of **B**: 1316
21:33 Og the king of **B** went out against them, 1316
32:33 the kingdom of Og king of **B**, the land, 1316
Dt 1: 4 dwelt in Heshbon, and Og the king of **B**, 1316
3: 1 we turned, and went up the way to **B**: and 1316
3: 1 Og the king of **B** came out against us, he 1316
3: 3 Og also, the king of **B**, and all his people: 1316
3: 4 region of Argob, the kingdom of Og in **B**. 1316
3:10 all Gilead, and all **B**, unto Salchah and 1316
3:10 and Edrei, cities of the kingdom of Og in **B**. 1316
3:11 For only Og king of **B** remained of 1316
3:13 the rest of Gilead, and all **B**, *being* 1316
3:13 all the region of Argob, with all **B**, which 1316
4:43 and Golan in **B**, of the Manassites. 1316
4:47 the land of Og king of **B**, two kings of 1316
29: 7 the king of Heshbon, and Og the king of **B**, 1316
32:14 and rams of the breed of **B**, and goats, 1316
33:22 Dan *is* a lion's whelp: he shall leap from **B**. 1316
Jos 9:10 to Og king of **B**, which *was* at Ashtaroth. 1316
12: 4 the coast of Og king of **B**, *which was* of 1316
12: 5 mount Hermon, and in Salcah, and in all **B**, 1316
13:11 all mount Hermon, and all **B** unto Salcah; 1316
13:12 All the kingdom of Og in **B**, which reigned 1316
13:30 their coast was from Mahanaim, all **B**, 1316
13:30 all the kingdom of Og king of **B**, and all 1316
13:30 of Jair, which *are* in **B**, threescore cities: 1316
13:31 and Edrei, cities of the kingdom of Og in **B**, 1316
17: 1 man of war, therefore he had Gilead and **B**. 1316
17: 5 beside the land of Gilead and **B**, 1316
20: 8 Golan in **B** out of the tribe of Manasseh. 1316

Jos 21: 6 out of the half tribe of Manasseh in **B**, 1316
21:27 *they gave* Golan in **B** with her suburbs, 1316
22: 7 Moses had given *possession* in **B**: 1316
1Ki 4:13 which *is* in **B**, threescore great cities *with* 1316
4:19 king of the Amorites, and of Og king of **B**; 1316
2Ki 10:33 *is* by the river Arnon, even Gilead and **B**. 1316
1Ch 5:11 against them, in the land of **B** unto Salchah: 1316
5:12 the next, and Jaanai, and Shaphat in **B**. 1316
5:16 they dwelt in Gilead in **B**, and in her towns, 1316
5:23 they increased from **B** unto Baal-hermon 1316
6:62 out of the tribe of Manasseh in **B**, 1316
6:71 Golan in **B** with her suburbs, and Ashtaroth 1316
Ne 9:22 of Heshbon, and the land of Og king of **B**. 1316
Ps 22:12 strong *bulls* of **B** have beset me round. 1316
68:15 The hill of God *is as* the hill of **B**; a high 1316
68:15 hill of Bashan; a high hill *as* the hill of **B**. 1316
68:22 The Lord said, I will bring again from **B**, 1316
135:11 Og king of **B**, and all the kingdoms of 1316
136:20 Og the king of **B**: for his mercy *endureth* 1316
Isa 2:13 and lifted up, and upon all the oaks of **B**, 1316
33: 9 and **B** and Carmel shake off *their fruits*. 1316
Jer 22:20 lift up thy voice in **B**, and cry from 1316
50:19 he shall feed on Carmel and **B**, and his soul 1316
Eze 27: 6 *Of* the oaks of **B** have they made thine oars; 1316
39:18 of bullocks, all of them fatlings of **B**. 1316
Am 4: 1 Hear this word, ye kine of **B**, that *are* in 1316
Mic 7:14 let them feed *in* **B** and Gilead, as *in* 1316
Na 1: 4 **B** languisheth, and Carmel, and the flower 1316
Zec 11: 2 howl, O ye oaks of **B**; for the forest of 1316

BASHAN-HAVOTH-JAIR (1) [BASHAN, HAVOTH-JAIR, JAIR]
Dt 3:14 after his own name, **B**, unto this day. 1316+2334

BASHEMATH (6)
Ge 26:34 and **B** the daughter of Elon the Hittite: 1315
36: 3 **B** Ishmael's daughter, sister of Nebajoth. 1315
36: 4 bare to Esau Eliphaz; and **B** bare Reuel; 1315
36:10 Reuel the son of **B** the wife of Esau. 1315
36:13 these were the sons of **B** Esau's wife. 1315
36:17 these *are* the sons of **B** Esau's wife. 1315

BASIC PRINCIPLES See RUDIMENTS

BASIN; BASINS See BASON; BASONS; LAVER

BASKET (23) [BASKETS]
Ge 40:17 in the uppermost **b** *there was* of all *manner* 5536
40:17 the birds did eat them out of the **b** upon my 5536
Ex 29: 3 thou shalt put them into one **b**, and 5536
29: 3 bring them in the **b**, with the bullock and 5536
29:23 one wafer out of the **b** of the unleavened 5536
29:32 of the ram, and the bread that *is* in the **b**, 5536
Lev 8: 2 and two rams, and a **b** of unleavened bread; 5536
8:26 out of the **b** of unleavened bread, that *was* 5536
8:31 there eat it with the bread that *is* in the **b** of 5536
Nu 6:15 a **b** of unleavened bread, cakes *of* fine flour 5536
6:17 with the **b** of unleavened bread: 5536
6:19 one unleavened cake out of the **b**, and 5536
Dt 26: 2 shalt put *it* in a **b**, and shalt go unto 2935
26: 4 the priest shall take the **b** out of thine hand, 2935
28: 5 Blessed *shall be* thy **b** and thy store. 2935
28:17 Cursed *shall be* thy **b** and thy store. 2935
Jdg 6:19 the flesh he put in a **b**, and he put the broth 5536
Jer 24: 2 One **b** *had* very good figs, *even* like the figs 1731
24: 2 the other **b** *had* very naughty figs, 1731
Am 8: 1 unto me: and behold, a **b** of summer fruit. 3619
8: 2 I said, A **b** of summer fruit. Then said 3619
Ac 9:25 and let *him* down by the wall in a **b**. *4711*
2Co 11:33 And through a window in a **b** was I let *4553*

BASKETS (15) [BASKET]
Ge 40:16 behold, *I had* three white **b** on my head: 5536
40:18 The three **b** *are* three days: 5536
2Ki 10: 7 put their heads in **b**, and sent him *them* to 1731
Jer 6: 9 thine hand as a grapegatherer into the **b**. 5552
24: 1 two **b** of figs *were* set before the temple of 1736
Mt 14:20 the fragments that remained twelve **b** full. *2894*
15:37 the broken *meat* that was left seven **b** full. *4711*
16: 9 five thousand, and how many **b** ye took up? *2894*
16:10 and how many **b** ye took up? *4711*
Mk 6:43 And they took up twelve **b** full of *2894*
8: 8 up of the broken *meat* that was left seven **b**. *4711*
8:19 how many **b** full of fragments took ye up? *2894*
8:20 how many **b** full of fragments took ye up? *4711*
Lk 9:17 fragments that remained to them twelve **b**. *2894*
Jn 6:13 filled twelve **b** with the fragments of *2894*

BASMATH (1)
1Ki 4:15 he also took **B** the daughter of Solomon to 1315

BASON (5) [BASONS]
Ex 12:22 dip *it* in the blood that *is* in the **b**, and 5592
12:22 side posts with the blood that *is* in the **b**; 5592
1Ch 28:17 *gold* by weight for **every b**; 3713+3713+2050.1
28:17 weight for **every b** of silver: 3713+3713+2050.1
Jn 13: 5 he poureth water into a **b**, and began to *3537*

BASONS (18) [BASON]
Ex 24: 6 Moses took half of the blood, and put *it* in **b**; 101
27: 3 his **b**, and his fleshhooks, and his firepans: 4219
38: 3 the **b**, *and* the fleshhooks, and the firepans: 4219
Nu 4:14 the fleshhooks, and the shovels, and the **b**, 4219
2Sa 17:28 **b**, and earthen vessels, and wheat, and 5592
1Ki 7:40 made the lavers, and the shovels, and the **b**. 4219
7:45 the pots, and the shovels, and the **b**: and 4219
7:50 the **b**, and the spoons, and the censers *of* 4219
2Ki 12:13 snuffers, **b**, trumpets, any vessels of gold, 4219
1Ch 28:17 for the golden **b** *he gave gold* by weight for 3713
2Ch 4: 8 the left. And he made an hundred **b** of gold. 4219
4:11 made the pots, and the shovels, and the **b**. 4219
4:22 the **b**, and the spoons, and the censers, 4219
Ezr 1:10 Thirty **b** of gold, silver basons of a second 3713
1:10 silver **b** of a second sort four hundred and 3713
8:27 Also twenty **b** of gold, of a thousand 3713
Ne 7:70 fifty **b**, five hundred and thirty priests' 4219
Jer 52:19 the **b**, and the firepans, and the bowls, and 5592

BASTARD (2) [BASTARDS]
Dt 23: 2 A **b** shall not enter into the congregation of 4464
Zec 9: 6 a **b** shall dwell in Ashdod, and I will cut off 4464

BASTARDS (1) [BASTARD]
Heb 12: 8 are partakers, then are ye **b**, and not sons. *3541*

BAT (2) [BATS]
Lev 11:19 after her kind, and the lapwing, and the **b**. 5847
Dt 14:18 after her kind, and the lapwing, and the **b**. 5847

BATH (6) [BATHS]
Isa 5:10 ten acres of vineyard shall yield one **b**, and 1324
Eze 45:10 just balances, and a just ephah, and a just **b**. 1324
45:11 and the **b** shall be of one measure, 1324
45:11 that the **b** may contain the tenth part of a 1324
45:14 the ordinance of oil, the **b** *of* oil, 1324
45:14 *ye shall offer* the tenth part of a **b** out of 1324

BATHE (18) [BATHED]
Lev 15: 5 **b** *himself* in water, and be unclean until 7364
15: 6 **b** *himself* in water, and be unclean until 7364
15: 7 **b** *himself* in water, and be unclean until 7364
15: 8 **b** *himself* in water, and be unclean until 7364
15:10 **b** *himself* in water, and be unclean until 7364
15:11 **b** *himself* in water, and be unclean until 7364
15:13 **b** his flesh in running water, and shall be 7364
15:18 they shall *both* **b** *themselves* in water, and 7364
15:21 **b** *himself* in water, and be unclean until 7364
15:22 **b** *himself* in water, and be unclean until 7364
15:27 **b** *himself* in water, and be unclean until 7364
16:26 **b** his flesh in water, and afterward come 7364
16:28 **b** his flesh in water, and afterward he shall 7364
17:15 **b** *himself* in water, and be unclean until 7364
17:16 if he wash *them* not, nor **b** his flesh; then 7364
Nu 19: 7 he shall **b** his flesh in water, and 7364
19: 8 **b** his flesh in water, and shall be unclean 7364
19:19 **b** *himself* in water, and shall be clean at 7364

BATHED (1) [BATHE]
Isa 34: 5 For my sword shall be **b** in heaven: behold, 7301

BATH-RABBIM (1)
SS 7: 4 the *fish*pools in Heshbon, by the gate of **B**: 1337

BATHS (9) [BATH]
1Ki 7:26 of lilies: it contained two thousand **b**. 1324
7:38 one laver contained forty **b**: *and* every laver 1324
2Ch 2:10 twenty thousand **b** of wine, and 1324
2:10 of wine, and twenty thousand **b** of oil. 1324
4: 5 *and* it received and held three thousand **b**. 1324
Ezr 7:22 to an hundred **b** *of* wine, and to an hundred 1325
7:22 to an hundred **b** *of* oil, and salt without 1325

Eze 45:14 out of the cor, *which is* a homer of ten **b**; 1324
45:14 a homer of ten baths; for ten **b** *are* a homer: 1324

BATH-SHEBA (11)
2Sa 11: 3 *one* said, *Is* not this **B**, the daughter of 1339
12:24 David comforted **B** his wife, and went in 1339
1Ki 1:11 Wherefore Nathan spake unto **B** the mother 1339
1:15 **B** went in unto the king into the chamber: 1339
1:16 **B** bowed, and did obeisance unto the king. 1339
1:28 king David answered and said, Call me **B**. 1339
1:31 **B** bowed *with her* face *to* the earth, and 1339
2:13 Adonijah the son of Haggith came to **B** 1339
2:18 **B** said, Well; I will speak for thee unto 1339
2:19 **B** therefore went unto king Solomon, 1339
Ps 51: T came unto him, after he had gone in to **B**. 1339

BATH-SHUA (1)
1Ch 3: 5 four, of **B** the daughter of Ammiel: 1340

BATS (1) [BAT]
Isa 2:20 to worship, to the moles and to the **b**; 5847

BATTERED (1) [BATTERING]
2Sa 20:15 all the people that *were* with Joab **b** 7843

BATTERING (2) [BATTERED]
Eze 4: 2 and set *b* rams against it round about. NIH
21:22 to appoint *b* rams against the gates, to cast a NIH

BATTLE (170) [BATTLEMENT, BATTLEMENTS, BATTLES]
Ge 14: 8 they joined **b** with them in the vale of 4421
Nu 21:33 he, and all his people, to the **b** *at* Edrei. 4421
31:14 which came from the **b**. 4421+6635
31:21 unto the men of war which went to the **b**, 4421
31:27 who went out to **b**, and between all 6635
31:28 of the men of war which went out to **b**: 6635
32:27 before the LORD to **b**, as my lord saith. 4421
32:29 every man armed to **b**, before the LORD, 4421
Dt 2: 9 neither contend with them *in* **b**: 4421
2:24 to possess *it,* and contend with him *in* **b**. 4421
3: 1 he and all his people, to **b** *at* Edrei. 4421
20: 1 When thou goest out to **b** against thine 4421
20: 2 shall be, when ye are come nigh unto the **b**, 4421
20: 3 you approach *this* day unto **b** against your 4421
20: 5 lest he die in the **b**, and another man 4421
20: 6 lest he die in the **b**, and another man eat of 4421
20: 7 lest he die in the **b**, and another man take 4421
29: 7 came out against us unto **b**, and we smote 4421
Jos 4:13 war passed over before the LORD unto **b**, 4421
8:14 men of the city went out against Israel to **b**, 4421
11:19 of Gibeon: all *other* they took in **b**. 4421
11:20 that *they* should come against Israel *in* **b**, 4421
22:33 did not intend to go up against them in **b**, 6635
Jdg 8:13 Gideon the son of Joash returned from **b** 4421
20:14 to go out to **b** against the children of Israel. 4421
20:18 Which of us shall go up first to the **b** 4421
20:20 the men of Israel went out to **b** against 4421
20:22 set *their* **b** again in array in the place where 4421
20:23 Shall I go *up* again to **b** against the children 4421
20:28 Shall I yet again go out to **b** against 4421
20:34 men out of all Israel, and the **b** was sore: 4421
20:39 And when the men of Israel retired in the **b**, 4421
20:39 are smitten down before us, as *in* the first **b**. 4421
20:42 the **b** overtook them; and them which *came* 4421
1Sa 4: 1 Israel went out against the Philistines to **b**, 4421
4: 2 when they joined **b**, Israel was smitten 4421
7:10 the Philistines drew near to **b** against Israel: 4421
13:22 So it came to pass in the day of **b**, that there 4421
14:20 and they came to the **b**: 4421
14:22 they also followed hard after them in the **b**. 4421
14:23 and the **b** passed over *unto* Beth-aven. 4421
17: 1 gathered together their armies to **b**, 4421
17: 2 set the **b** in array against the Philistines. 4421
17: 8 Why are ye come out to set *your* **b** in 4421
17:13 of Jesse went *and* followed Saul to the **b**: 4421
17:13 that went to the **b** *were* Eliab the firstborn, 4421
17:20 forth to the fight, and shouted for the **b**. 4421
17:21 and the Philistines had put *the* **b** in array, NIH
17:28 art come down that *thou* mightest see the **b**. 4421
17:47 for the **b** *is* the LORD'S, and he will give 4421
26:10 or he shall descend into **b**, and perish. 4421
28: 1 that thou shalt go out with me to **b**, thou 4264
29: 4 and let him not go down with us to **b**, 4421
29: 4 lest in the **b** he be an adversary to us: 4421
29: 9 He shall not go up with us to the **b**. 4421
30:24 as his part *is* that goeth down to the **b**, so 4421
31: 3 the **b** went sore against Saul, and 4421
2Sa 1: 4 That the people are fled from the **b**, and 4421
1:25 are the mighty fallen in the midst of the **b**! 4421
2:17 there was a very sore **b** that day; and 4421
3:30 their brother Asahel at Gibeon in the **b**. 4421
10: 8 put the **b** in array *at* the entering in of 4421
10: 9 When Joab saw that the front of the **b** was 4421
10:13 with him, unto the **b** against the Syrians: 4421
11: 1 at the time when kings go forth *to* **b**, that NIH
11:15 ye Uriah in the forefront of the hottest **b**, 4421
11:25 make thy **b** *more* strong against the city, 4421
17:11 and *that* thou go to **b** in thine own person. 7128
18: 6 and the **b** was in the wood of Ephraim; 4421
18: 8 For the **b** was there scattered over the face 4421
19: 3 ashamed steal away when they flee in **b**. 4421
19:10 whom we anointed over us, is dead in **b**. 4421
21:17 Thou shalt go no more out with us to **b**, 4421
21:18 that there was again a **b** with the Philistines 4421
21:19 there was again a **b** in Gob with 4421
21:20 there was yet a **b** in Gath, where was a man 4421
22:40 For thou hast girded me with strength to **b**: 4421
23: 9 *that* were there gathered together to **b**, 4421
1Ki 8:44 If thy people go out to **b** against their 4421
20:14 he said, Who shall order the **b**? And he 4421
20:29 that in the seventh day the **b** was joined: 4421
20:39 servant went out into the midst of the **b**; 4421
22: 4 Wilt thou go with me to **b** *to* 4421
22: 6 Shall I go against Ramoth-gilead to **b**, or 4421
22:15 shall we go against Ramoth-gilead to **b**, or 4421
22:30 I will disguise myself, and enter into the **b**; 4421
22:30 disguised himself, and went into the **b**. 4421
22:35 the **b** increased that day: and the king was 4421
2Ki 3: 7 wilt thou go with me against Moab to **b**? 4421
3:26 when the king of Moab saw that the **b** was 4421
1Ch 5:20 for they cried to God in the **b**, and he was 4421
7:11 *soldiers, fit to* go out *for* war and **b**. 4421
7:40 *and* to **b** *was* twenty and six thousand men. 4421
10: 3 the **b** went sore against Saul, and 4421
11:13 the Philistines were gathered together to **b**, 4421
12: 8 *and* men of war *fit* for the **b**, that could 4421
12:19 came with the Philistines against Saul to **b**: 4421
12:33 Of Zebulun, such as went forth to **b**, 6635
12:36 such as went forth to **b**, expert in war, 6635
12:37 all *manner of* instruments of war for the **b**, 4421
14:15 *that* then thou shalt go out to **b**: 4421
19: 7 together from their cities, and came to **b**. 4421
19: 9 put the **b** in array *before* the gate of 4421
19:10 Now when Joab saw that the **b** was set 4421
19:14 drew nigh before the Syrians unto the **b**; 4421
19:17 and set *the* **b** in array against them. NIH
19:17 So when David had put the **b** in array 4421
20: 1 at the time that kings go out *to* **b**, Joab led NIH
2Ch 13: 3 Abijah set the **b** in array with an army of 4421
13: 3 Jeroboam also set the **b** in array against 4421
13:14 behold, the **b** *was* before and behind: 4421
14:10 they set the **b** in array in the valley of 4421
18: 5 Shall we go to Ramoth-gilead to **b**, or 4421
18:14 shall we go to Ramoth-gilead to **b**, or 4421
18:29 I will disguise myself, and will go to the **b**; 4421
18:29 disguised himself; and they went to the **b**. 4421
18:34 the **b** increased that day: howbeit the king 4421
20: 1 came against Jehoshaphat to **b**. 4421
20:15 for the **b** *is* not yours, but God's. 4421
20:17 Ye shall not need to fight in this *b*: set NIH
25: 8 if thou *wilt* go, do *it,* be strong for the **b**: 4421
25:13 that *they* should not go with him to **b**, fell 4421
Job 15:24 against him, as a king ready to the **b**. 3593
38:23 of trouble, against the day of **b** and war? 7128
39:25 he smelleth the **b** afar off, the thunder of 4421
41: 8 upon him, remember the **b**, do no more. 4421
Ps 18:39 hast girded me *with* strength unto the **b**: 4421
24: 8 and mighty, the LORD mighty *in* **b**. 4421
55:18 in peace from the **b** *that was* against me: 7128
76: 3 the shield, and the sword, and the **b**. 4421
78: 9 carrying bows, turned *back* in the day of **b**. 7128
89:43 and hast not made him to stand in the **b**. 4421
140: 7 thou hast covered my head in the day of **b**. 5402
Pr 21:31 The horse *is* prepared against the day of **b**: 4421
Ecc 9:11 nor the **b** to the strong, neither yet bread to 4421
Isa 9: 5 For every **b** of the warrior *is* with confused 5430
13: 4 of hosts mustereth the host of the **b**. 4421
22: 2 *are* not slain with the sword, nor dead in **b**. 4421
27: 4 set the briers *and* thorns against me in **b**? 4421

Isa 28: 6 for strength to them that turn the **b** to 4421
42:25 the fury of his anger, and the strength of **b**: 4421
Jer 8: 6 his course, as the horse rusheth into the **b**. 4421
18:21 their young men *be* slain by the sword in **b**. 4421
46: 3 the buckler and shield, and draw near to **b**. 4421
49:14 and come against her, and rise up to the **b**. 4421
50:22 A sound of **b** *is* in the land, and of great 4421
50:42 in array, like a man to the **b**, against thee, 4421
51:20 Thou *art* my **b axe** *and* weapons of war: 4661
Eze 7:14 to make all ready; but none goeth to the **b**: 4421
13: 5 to stand in the **b** in the day of the LORD. 4421
Da 11:20 be destroyed, neither in anger, nor in **b**. 4421
11:25 the king of the south shall be stirred up to **b** 4421
Hos 1: 7 nor by sword, nor by **b**, by horses, nor by 4421
2:18 and the sword and the **b** out of the earth, 4421
10: 9 the **b** in Gibeah against the children of 4421
10:14 Shalman spoiled Beth-arbel in the day of **b**: 4421
Joel 2: 5 as a strong people set in **b** array. 4421
Am 1:14 with shouting in the day of **b**, 4421
Ob 1: 1 Arise ye, and let us rise up against her in **b**. 4421
Zec 9:10 and the **b** bow shall be cut off: 4421
10: 3 made them as his goodly horse in the **b**. 4421
10: 4 out of him the nail, out of him the **b** bow, 4421
10: 5 *enemies* in the mire of the streets in the **b**: 4421
14: 2 gather all nations against Jerusalem to **b**; 4421
14: 3 as when he fought in the day of **b**. 7128
1Co 14: 8 who shall prepare himself to the **b**? *4171*
Rev 9: 7 *were* like unto horses prepared unto **b**; *4171*
9: 9 of chariots of many horses running to **b**. *4171*
16:14 to gather them to the **b** of that great day of *4171*
20: 8 and Magog, to gather them together to **b**: *4171*

BATTLEMENT (1) [BATTLE]
Dt 22: 8 then thou shalt make a **b** for thy roof, 4624

BATTLEMENTS (1) [BATTLE]
Jer 5:10 take away her **b**; for they *are* not 5189

BATTLES (6) [BATTLE]
1Sa 8:20 and go out before us, and fight our **b**. 4421
18:17 valiant for me, and fight the LORD'S **b**. 4421
25:28 my lord fighteth the **b** of the LORD, 4421
1Ch 26:27 Out of the spoils won in **b** did they dedicate 4421
2Ch 32: 8 our God to help us, and to fight our **b**. 4421
Isa 30:32 and in **b** of shaking will he fight with it. 4421

BAVAI (1) [BINNUI]
Ne 3:18 their brethren, **B** the son of Henadad, 942

BAY (6)
Jos 15: 2 salt sea, from the **b** that looketh southward: 3956
15: 5 **b** of the sea at the uttermost part of Jordan: 3956
18:19 **b** of the salt sea at the south end of Jordan: 3956
Ps 37:35 and spreading himself like a green **b tree**. 249
Zec 6: 3 in the fourth chariot grisled *and* **b** horses. 554
6: 7 the **b** went forth, and sought to go that *they* 554

BAZLITH (1) [BAZLUTH]
Ne 7:54 The children of **B**, the children of Mehida, 1213

BAZLUTH (1) [BAZLITH]
Ezr 2:52 The children of **B**, the children of Mehida, 1213

BDELLIUM (2)
Ge 2:12 land *is* good: there *is* **b** and the onyx stone. 916
Nu 11: 7 and the colour thereof as the colour of **b**. 916

BE (7012) [AM, ARE, BEEN, BEING, HOWBEIT, IS, WAS, WAST, WERE, WERT, WILL] See Index

BE ESHTARAH See BEESHTERAH

BEACON (1)
Isa 30:17 till ye be left as a **b** upon the top of a 8650

BEALIAH (1)
1Ch 12: 5 **B**, and Shemariah, and Shephatiah 1183

BEALOTH (1)
Jos 15:24 Ziph, and Telem, and **B**, 1175

BEAM (15) [BEAMS]
Jdg 16:14 went away with the pin of the **b**, and 708
1Sa 17: 7 the staff of his spear *was* like a weaver's **b**; 4500
2Sa 21:19 staff of whose spear *was* like a weaver's **b**. 4500
1Ki 7: 6 and the **thick b** *were* before them. 5646
2Ki 6: 2 take thence every man a **b**, and let us make 6982
6: 5 as one was felling a **b**, the axe head fell into 6982
1Ch 11:23 hand *was* a spear like a weaver's **b**; 4500
20: 5 whose spear staff *was* like a weaver's **b**. 4500
Hab 2:11 and the **b** out of the timber shall answer it. 3714
Mt 7: 3 considerest not the **b** that is in thine own *1385*
7: 4 and behold, a **b** *is* in thine own eye? *1385*
7: 5 first cast out the **b** out of thine own eye; *1385*
Lk 6:41 perceivest not the **b** that is in thine own *1385*
6:42 when thou thyself beholdest not the **b** that *1385*
6:42 cast out first the **b** out of thine own eye, *1385*

BEAMS (12) [BEAM]
1Ki 6: 6 that *the* **b** should not be fastened in NIH
6: 9 covered the house with **b** and boards of 1356
6:36 rows of hewed stone, and a row of cedar **b**. 3773
7: 2 cedar pillars, with cedar **b** upon the pillars. 3773
7: 3 *was* covered with cedar above upon the **b**, 6763
7:12 a row of cedar **b**, both for the inner court of 3773
2Ch 3: 7 the **b**, the posts, and the walls thereof, and 6982
Ne 2: 8 that he may give me timber to **make b** for 7136
3: 3 who *also* **laid** the **b** thereof, and set up 7136
3: 6 they **laid** the **b** thereof, and set up the doors 7136
Ps 104: 3 Who **layeth** the **b** of his chambers in 7136
SS 1:17 The **b** of our house *are* cedar, *and* 6982

BEANS (2)
2Sa 17:28 parched *corn*, and **b**, and lentiles, and 6321
Eze 4: 9 **b**, and lentiles, and millet, and fitches, and 6321

BEAR (214) [ARMOURBEARER, BARE, BEARERS, BEAREST, BEARETH, BEARING, BEARS, BIRTH, BIRTHDAY, BIRTHRIGHT, BORN, BORNE, CHILDBEARING, CUPBEARER, CUPBEARERS, FIRSTBORN, HOMEBORN, NEWBORN, STANDARD-BEARER, TALEBEARER]
Ge 4:13 My punishment *is* greater than *I* can **b**. 5375
13: 6 the land was not **able to b** them, that they 5375
16:11 shalt **b** a son, and shalt call his name 3205
17:17 and shall Sarah, that is ninety years old, **b**? 3205
17:19 Sarah thy wife shall **b** thee a son indeed; 3205
17:21 which Sarah shall **b** unto thee at this set 3205
18:13 Shall I of a surety **b** *a child,* which am old? 3205
22:23 these eight Milcah did **b** to Nahor, 3205
30: 3 she shall **b** upon my knees, that I may also 3205
36: 7 they were strangers could not **b** them 5375
43: 9 then let me **b the blame** for ever: 2398
44:32 I shall **b the blame** to my father for ever. 2398
49:15 bowed his shoulder to **b**, and became a 5445
Ex 18:22 and they shall **b** *the burden* with thee. 5375
20:16 Thou shalt not **b** false witness against thy 6030
25:27 be for places of the staves to **b** the table. 5375
27: 7 be upon the two sides of the altar, to **b** it. 5375
28:12 Aaron shall **b** their names before 5375
28:29 Aaron shall **b** the names of the children of 5375
28:30 Aaron shall **b** the judgment of the children 5375
28:38 that Aaron may **b** the iniquity of the holy 5375
28:43 in the holy *place;* that they **b** not iniquity, 5375
30: 4 they shall be for places for the staves to **b** it 5375
37: 5 rings by the sides of the ark, to **b** the ark. 5375
37:14 the places for the staves to **b** the table. 5375
37:15 and overlaid them with gold, to **b** the table. 5375
37:27 to be places for the staves to **b** it withal. 5375
38: 7 rings on the sides of the altar, to **b** it withal; 5375
Lev 5: 1 do not utter *it,* then he shall **b** his iniquity. 5375
5:17 yet is he guilty, and shall **b** his iniquity. 5375
7:18 the soul that eateth of it shall **b** his iniquity. 5375
10:17 *God* hath given it you to **b** the iniquity of 5375
12: 5 if she **b** a maid child, then she shall be 3205
16:22 the goat shall **b** upon him all their iniquities 5375
17:16 bathe his flesh; then he shall **b** his iniquity. 5375
19: 8 Therefore *every one* that eateth it shall **b** 5375
19:18 nor **b any grudge against** the children of 5201
20:17 sister's nakedness; he shall **b** his iniquity. 5375
20:19 his near kin: they shall **b** their iniquity. 5375
20:20 they shall **b** their sin; they shall die 5375
22: 9 lest they **b** sin for it, and die therefore, if 5375
22:16 Or **suffer** them **to b** the iniquity of trespass, 5375
24:15 Whosoever curseth his God shall **b** his sin. 5375
Nu 1:50 they shall **b** the tabernacle, and all 5375
4:15 the sons of Kohath shall come to **b** *it:* but 5375
4:25 they shall **b** the curtains of the tabernacle, 5375
5:31 and this woman shall **b** her iniquity. 5375
7: 9 *that* they should **b** upon *their* shoulders. 5375
9:13 appointed season, that man shall **b** his sin. 5375

B

Nu	11:14	I am not able to **b** all this people alone,	5375
	11:17	they shall **b** the burden of the people with	5375
	11:17	with thee, that thou **b** *it* not thyself alone.	5375
	14:27	How long *shall I* **b** with this evil	NIH
	14:33	**b** your whoredoms, until your carcases be	5375
	14:34	shall ye **b** your iniquities, *even* forty years,	5375
	18: 1	thy father's house with thee shall **b**	5375
	18: 1	thy sons with thee shall **b** the iniquity of	5375
	18:22	of the congregation, lest they **b** sin, and die.	5375
	18:23	and they shall **b** their iniquity:	5375
	18:32	ye shall **b** no sin by reason of it, when ye	5375
	30:15	heard *them;* then he shall **b** her iniquity.	5375
Dt	1: 9	I am not able to **b** you myself alone:	5375
	1:12	How can I myself alone **b** your cumbrance,	5375
	1:31	as a man doth **b** his son, in all the way that	5375
	5:20	Neither shalt thou **b** false witness against	6030
	10: 8	to **b** the ark of the covenant of the LORD,	5375
	28:57	and towards her children which she shall **b**:	3205
Jos	3: 8	thou shalt command the priests that **b**	5375
	3:13	of the priests that **b** the ark of the LORD,	5375
	4:16	Command the priests that **b** the ark of	5375
	6: 4	seven priests shall **b** before the ark seven	5375
	6: 6	let seven priests **b** seven trumpets of rams'	5375
Jdg	13: 3	but thou shalt conceive, and **b** a son.	3205
	13: 5	For lo, thou *shalt* conceive, and **b** a son;	3205
	13: 7	Behold, thou *shalt* conceive, and **b** a son;	3205
Ru	1:12	also to night, and should also **b** sons;	3205
1Sa	17:34	there came a lion and a **b**, and took a lamb	1677
	17:36	Thy servant slew both the lion and the **b**:	1677
	17:37	out of the paw of the **b**, he will deliver me	1677
2Sa	17: 8	as a **b** robbed of her whelps in the field:	1677
	18:19	Let me now run, and **b** the king **tidings**,	1319
	18:20	Thou *shalt* not **b**s tidings this day, but	376
	18:20	but thou shalt **b** **tidings** another day:	1319
	18:20	this day thou shalt **b** no **tidings**, because	1319
1Ki	3:21	it was not my son, which I did **b**.	3205
	21:10	to **b** **witness against** him, saying,	5749
2Ki	18:14	*that* which thou puttest on me will I **b**.	5375
	19:30	take root downward, and **b** fruit upward.	6213
1Ch	5:18	men *able to* **b** buckler and sword, and	5375
2Ch	2: 2	and ten thousand men to **b** burdens,	NIH
Est	1:22	that every man should **b** **rule** in his own	8323
Ps	75: 3	*are* dissolved: I **b** **up** the pillars of it. Selah.	8505
	89:50	*how* I do **b** in my bosom *the reproach of* all	5375
	91:12	They shall **b** thee **up** in *their* hands,	5375
Pr	9:12	but *if* thou scornest, thou alone shalt **b** *it.*	5375
	12:24	The hand of the diligent shall **b** **rule**: but	4910
	17:12	*Let* a **b** robbed of her whelps meet a man,	1677
	18:14	but a wounded spirit who can **b**?	5375
	28:15	*As* a roaring lion, and a ranging **b**; *so is* a	1677
	30:21	and for four *which* it cannot **b**:	5375
Isa	1:14	a trouble unto me; I am weary to **b** *them.*	5375
	7:14	**b** a Son, and shall call his name Immanuel.	3205
	11: 7	the cow and the **b** shall feed; their young	1677
	37:31	take root downward, and **b** fruit upward.	6213
	46: 4	will I carry *you:* I have made, and I will **b**;	5375
	46: 7	They **b** him upon the shoulder, they carry	5375
	52:11	ye clean, that **b** the vessels of the LORD.	5375
	53:11	justify many; for he shall **b** their iniquities.	5445
	54: 1	Sing, O barren, thou *that* didst not **b**;	3205
Jer	5:31	and the priests **b** **rule** by their means;	7287
	10:19	I said, Truly this *is* a grief, and I must **b** it.	5375
	17:21	**b** no burden on the sabbath day,	5375
	17:27	not to **b** a burden, even entering in at	5375
	29: 6	that they may **b** sons and daughters;	3205
	31:19	because I did **b** the reproach of my youth.	5375
	44:22	So that the LORD could no longer **b**,	5375
La	3:10	He *was* unto me *as* a **b** lying in wait, *and*	1677
	3:27	*It is* good for a man that he **b** the yoke in	5375
Eze	4: 4	shalt lie upon it thou shalt **b** their iniquity.	5375
	4: 5	shalt thou **b** the iniquity of the house of	5375
	4: 6	thou shalt **b** the iniquity of the house of	5375
	12: 6	In their sight shalt thou **b** *it* upon *thy*	5375
	12:12	the prince that *is* among them shall **b** upon	5375
	14:10	they shall **b** the punishment of their	5375
	16:52	**b** thine own shame for thy sins that thou	5375
	16:52	be thou confounded also, and **b** thy shame,	5375
	16:54	That thou mayest **b** thine own shame, and	5375
	17: 8	that *it* might **b** fruit, that *it* might be a	5375
	17:23	and **b** fruit, and be a goodly cedar:	6213
	18:19	doth not the son **b** the iniquity of	5375
	18:20	The son shall not **b** the iniquity of	5375
	18:20	neither shall the father **b** the iniquity of	5375
	23:35	therefore **b** thou also thy lewdness and thy	5375
	23:49	and ye shall **b** the sins of your idols:	5375
	32:30	**b** their shame with them that go down to	5375
	34:29	neither **b** the shame of the heathen any	5375
	36: 7	that *are* about you, they shall **b** their shame.	5375
	36:15	neither shalt thou **b** the reproach of	5375
	44:10	their idols; they shall even **b** their iniquity.	5375
	44:12	Lord GOD, and they shall **b** their iniquity.	5375
	44:13	holy *place:* but they shall **b** their shame,	5375
	46:20	that *they* **b** *them* not **out** into the utter	3318
Da	2:39	which shall **b** **rule** over all the earth.	7981
	7: 5	like to a **b**, and it raised up itself on one	1678
Hos	9:16	their root is dried up, they shall **b** no fruit:	6213
	13: 8	I will meet them as a **b** *that is* bereaved of	1677
Am	5:19	man did flee from a lion, and a **b** met him;	1677
	7:10	the land is not able to **b** all his words.	3557
Mic	6:16	ye shall **b** the reproach of my people.	5375
	7: 9	I will **b** the indignation of the LORD,	5375
Zep	1:11	cut down; all they that **b** silver are cut off.	5187
Hag	2:12	If one **b** holy flesh in the skirt of his	5375
Zec	5:10	with me, Whither do these **b** the ephah?	1980
	6:13	he shall **b** the glory, and shall sit and	5375
Mt	3:11	than I, whose shoes I am not worthy to **b**:	*941*
	4: 6	and in *their* hands they shall **b** thee **up**,	*142*
	19:18	not steal, Thou shalt not **b** **false witness**,	*5576*
	27:32	by name: him they compelled to **b** his cross.	*142*
Mk	10:19	Do not **b** **false witness**, Defraud not,	*5576*
	15:21	of Alexander and Rufus, to **b** his cross.	*142*
Lk	1:13	and thy wife Elisabeth shall **b** thee a son,	*1080*
	4:11	And in *their* hands they shall **b** thee **up**,	*142*
	11:48	Truly ye **b** **witness** that ye allow the deeds	*3140*
	13: 9	And if it **b** fruit, *well:* and if not, *then*	*4160*
	14:27	And whosoever doth not **b** his cross, and	*941*
	18: 7	unto him, though he **b** **long** with them?	*3114*
	18:20	Do not steal, Do not **b** **false witness**,	*5576*
	23:26	laid the cross, that *he* might **b** *it* after Jesus.	*5342*
Jn	1: 7	for a witness, to **b** **witness** of the Light,	*3140*
	1: 8	but *was sent* to **b** **witness** of *that* Light.	*3140*
	2: 8	and **b** unto the governor of the feast.	*5342*
	3:28	Ye yourselves **b** me **witness**, that I said, I	*3140*
	5:31	If I **b** **witness** of myself, my witness is not	*3140*
	5:36	the same works that I do, **b** **witness** of me,	*3140*
	8:14	unto them, Though I **b** **record** of myself,	*3140*
	8:18	I am *one* that **b** **witness** of myself, and	*3140*
	10:25	in my Father's name, they **b** **witness** of me.	*3140*
	15: 4	As the branch cannot **b** fruit of itself,	*5342*
	15: 8	is my Father glorified, that ye **b** much fruit;	*5342*
	15:27	And ye also shall **b** **witness**, because	*3140*
	16:12	to say unto you, but ye cannot **b** *them* now.	*941*
	18:23	If I have spoken evil, **b** **witness** of the evil:	*3140*
	18:37	that I should **b** **witness** unto the truth.	*3140*
Ac	9:15	to **b** my name before the Gentiles, and kings,	*941*
	15:10	neither our fathers nor we were able to **b**?	*941*
	18:14	reason would that I should **b** **with** you:	*430*
	22: 5	As also the high priest doth **b** me **witness**,	*3140*
	23:11	so must thou **b** **witness** also at Rome.	*3140*
	27:15	and could not **b** **up into** the wind, we let *her*	*503*
Ro	10: 2	For I **b** them **record** that they have a zeal	*3140*
	13: 9	not steal, Thou shalt not **b** **false witness**,	*5576*
	15: 1	that are strong ought to **b** the infirmities of	*941*
1Co	3: 2	for hitherto ye were not able *to* **b** *it,* neither	NIG
	10:13	way to escape, that ye may be able to **b** *it.*	*5297*
	15:49	we shall also **b** the image of the heavenly.	*5409*
2Co	8: 3	I **b** **record**, *yea,* and beyond *their* power	*3140*
	11: 1	Would *to God* you could **b** **with** me a little	*430*
	11: 1	a little in *my* folly: and indeed **b** **with** me.	*430*
	11: 4	not accepted, ye might well **b** **with** *him.*	*430*
Gal	4:15	for I **b** you **record**, that if *it had been*	*3140*
	5:10	he that troubleth you shall **b** *his* judgment,	*941*
	6: 2	**B** ye one another's burdens, and so fulfil	*941*
	6: 5	For every man shall **b** his own burden.	*941*
	6:17	for I **b** in my body the marks of the Lord	*941*
Col	4:13	For I **b** him **record**, that he hath a great	*3140*
1Ti	5:14	*women* marry, **b** **children**, guide the house,	*5041*
Heb	9:28	So Christ was once offered to **b** the sins of	*399*
Jas	3:12	the fig tree, my brethren, **b** olive berries?	*4160*
1Jn	1: 2	and we have seen *it,* and **b** **witness**, and	*3140*
	5: 7	For there are three that **b** **record** in heaven,	*3140*
	5: 8	And there are three that **b** **witness** in earth,	*3140*
3Jn	1:12	yea, and we also **b** **record**; and ye know	*3140*
Rev	2: 2	how thou canst not **b** *them which are* evil:	*941*
	13: 2	and his feet *were* as *the feet* of a **b**, and	*715*

BEARD (16) [BEARDS]

Lev	13:29	hath a plague upon the head or the **b**;	2206

Lev 13:30 *even* a leprosy upon the head or **b**. 2206
14: 9 off his head and his **b** and his eyebrows, 2206
19:27 neither shalt thou mar the corners of thy **b**. 2206
21: 5 shall they shave off the corner of their **b**, 2206
1Sa 17:35 I caught *him* by his **b**, and smote him, and 2206
21:13 and let his spittle fall down upon his **b**. 2206
2Sa 19:24 nor trimmed his **b**, nor washed his clothes, 8222
20: 9 Joab took Amasa by the **b** with the right 2206
Ezr 9: 3 pluckt off the hair of my head and of my **b**, 2206
Ps 133: 2 that ran down upon the **b**, *even* Aaron's 2206
133: 2 ran down upon the beard, *even* Aaron's **b**: 2206
Isa 7:20 of the feet: and it shall also consume the **b**. 2206
15: 2 *shall be* baldness, *and* every **b** cut off. 2206
Jer 48:37 every head *shall be* bald, and every **b** clipt: 2206
Eze 5: 1 *it* to pass upon thine head and upon thy **b**: 2206

BEARDS (4) [BEARD]
2Sa 10: 4 shaved off the *one* half of their **b**, and 2206
10: 5 Tarry at Jericho until your **b** be grown, and 2206
1Ch 19: 5 Tarry at Jericho until your **b** be grown, and 2206
Jer 41: 5 having their **b** shaven, and their clothes 2206

BEARERS (3) [BEAR]
2Ch 2:18 ten thousand of them *to be* **b of burdens**, 5449
34:13 Also *they were* over the **b of burdens**, and 5449
Ne 4:10 The strength of the **b of burdens** is 5449

BEAREST (5) [BEAR]
Jdg 13: 3 Behold now, thou *art* barren, and **b** not: 3205
Ps 106: 4 with the favour *that thou* **b** unto thy people: NIH
Jn 8:13 said unto him, Thou **b record** of thyself; *3140*
Ro 11:18 thou **b** not the root, but the root thee. *941*
Gal 4:27 it is written, Rejoice, *thou* barren that **b** not; *5088*

BEARETH (26) [BEAR]
Lev 11:25 whosoever **b** *ought* of the carcase of them 5375
11:28 he that **b** the carcase of them shall wash his 5375
11:40 he also that **b** the carcase of it shall wash 5375
15:10 he that **b** *any of* those *things* shall wash his 5375
Nu 11:12 as a nursing father **b** the sucking child, 5375
Dt 25: 6 *that* the firstborn which she **b** shall succeed 3205
29:18 lest there should be among you a root that **b** 6509
29:23 salt, *and* burning, *that* it is not sown, nor **b**, 6779
32:11 taketh them, **b** them on her wings: 5375
Job 16: 8 my leanness rising up in me **b witness** to 6030
24:21 He evil entreateth the barren *that* **b** not: and 3205
Pr 25:18 A man that **b** false witness against his 6030
29: 2 when the wicked **b rule**, the people mourn. 4910
SS 4: 2 whereof every one **b twins**, and none *is* 8382
6: 6 whereof every one **b twins**, and *there is* not 8382
Joel 2:22 for the tree **b** her fruit, the fig tree and 5375
Mt 13:23 and understandeth *it;* which also **b fruit**, *2592*
Jn 5:32 There is another that **b witness** of me; and *3140*
8:18 the Father that sent me **b witness** of me. *3140*
15: 2 Every branch in me that **b** not fruit he *5342*
15: 2 and every *branch* that **b** fruit, he purgeth it, *5342*
Ro 8:16 The Spirit itself **b witness with** our spirit, *4828*
13: 4 be afraid; for he **b** not the sword in vain: *5409*
1Co 13: 7 **B** all *things,* believeth all *things,* hopeth all *4722*
Heb 6: 8 But that which **b** thorns and briers *is* *1627*
1Jn 5: 6 And it is the Spirit that **b witness**, because *3140*

BEARING (22) [BEAR]
Ge 1:29 I have given you every herb **b** seed, 2232
16: 2 the LORD hath restrained me from **b**: 3205
29:35 she called his name Judah; and left **b**. 3205
30: 9 When Leah saw that she had left **b**, she 3205
37:25 from Gilead with their camels **b** spicery 5375
Nu 10:17 of Merari set forward, **b** the tabernacle. 5375
10:21 the Kohathites set forward, **b** the sanctuary: 5375
Jos 3: 3 the priests the Levites **b** it, then ye shall 5375
3:14 the priests **b** the ark *of* the covenant before 5375
6: 8 that the seven priests **b** the seven trumpets 5375
6:13 seven priests **b** seven trumpets of rams' 5375
1Sa 17: 7 *of* iron: and one **b** a shield went before him. 5375
2Sa 15:24 with him, **b** the ark of the covenant of God: 5375
Ps 126: 6 goeth forth and weepeth, **b** precious seed, 5375
Mk 14:13 there shall meet you a man **b** a pitcher of *941*
Lk 22:10 shall a man meet you, **b** a pitcher of water; *941*
Jn 19:17 And he **b** his cross went forth into a place *941*
Ro 2:15 their conscience **also b witness**, and *their* *4828*
9: 1 my conscience **also b** me **witness** in *4828*
2Co 4:10 Always **b about** in the body the dying of *4064*
Heb 2: 4 God **also b** *them* **witness**, both with signs *4901*

13:13 unto him without the camp, **b** his reproach. *5342*

BEARS (2) [BEAR]
2Ki 2:24 there came forth two she **b** out of the wood, 1677
Isa 59:11 We roar all like **b**, and mourn sore like 1677

BEAST (180) [BEAST'S, BEASTS]
Ge 1:24 and **b** of the earth after his kind: 2416
1:25 God made the **b** of the earth after his kind, 2416
1:30 to every **b** of the earth, and to every fowl of 2416
2:19 LORD God formed every **b** of the field, 2416
2:20 fowl of the air, and to every **b** of the field; 2416
3: 1 **b** of the field which the LORD God had 2416
3:14 all cattle, and above every **b** of the field; 2416
6: 7 **b**, and the creeping thing, and the fowls of 929
7: 2 Of every clean **b** thou shalt take to thee by 929
7:14 every **b** after his kind, and all the cattle 2416
7:21 of **b**, and of every creeping thing that 2416
8:19 Every **b**, every creeping thing, and 2416
8:20 took of every clean **b**, and of every clean 929
9: 2 the dread of you shall be upon every **b** of 2416
9: 5 at the hand of every **b** will I require it, and 2416
9:10 and of every **b** of the earth with you; 2416
9:10 go out of the ark, to every **b** of the earth. 2416
34:23 and every **b** of theirs *be* ours? 929
37:20 will say, *Some* evil **b** hath devoured him: 2416
37:33 son's coat; an evil **b** hath devoured him; 2416
Ex 8:17 and it became lice in man, and in **b**; 929
8:18 so there were lice upon man, and upon **b**. 929
9: 9 and upon **b**, throughout all the land of Egypt. 929
9:10 forth *with* blains upon man, and upon **b**. 929
9:19 and **b** which shall be found in the field, 929
9:22 and upon **b**, and upon every herb of the field, 929
9:25 all that *was* in the field, both man and **b**; 929
11: 7 not a dog move his tongue, against man or **b**: 929
12:12 in the land of Egypt, both man and **b**; 929
13: 2 the children of Israel, *both* of man and of **b**: 929
13:12 every firstling that cometh of a **b** which thou 929
13:15 the firstborn of man, and the firstborn of **b**: 929
19:13 whether *it be* **b** or man, it shall not live: 929
21:34 owner of them; and the dead *b* shall be his. NIH
22: 5 shall put in his **b**, and shall feed in another 1165
22:10 or an ox, or a sheep, or any **b**, to keep; 929
22:19 Whosoever lieth with a **b** shall surely be put 929
23:29 and the **b** of the field multiply against thee. 2416
Lev 5: 2 whether *it be* a carcase of an unclean **b**, or a 2416
7:21 or *any* unclean **b**, or any abominable unclean 929
7:24 And the fat of the **b that dieth of itself**, and 5038
7:25 For whosoever eateth the fat of the **b**, 929
7:26 *whether it be* of fowl or of **b**, in any of your 929
11:26 *The carcases* of every **b** which divideth 929
11:39 if any **b**, of which ye may eat, die; he that 929
11:47 between the **b** that may be eaten and 2416
11:47 be eaten and the **b** that may not be eaten. 2416
17:13 which hunteth and catcheth *any* **b** or 2416
18:23 Neither shalt thou lie with any **b** to defile 929
18:23 neither shall any woman stand before a **b** to 929
20:15 if a man lie with a **b**, he shall surely be put to 929
20:15 be put to death: and ye shall slay the **b**. 929
20:16 if a woman approach unto any **b**, and 929
20:16 thou shalt kill the woman and the **b**: 929
20:25 shall not make your souls abominable by **b**, 929
24:18 he that killeth a **b** shall make it good; 929
24:18 a beast shall make it good; **b** for beast. 5315
24:18 a beast shall make it good; beast for **b**. 5315
24:21 he that killeth a **b**, he shall restore it: and 929
25: 7 thy cattle, and for the **b** that *are* in thy land, 2416
27: 9 if *it be* a **b**, whereof *men* bring an offering 929
27:10 and if he shall at all change **b** for beast, then 929
27:10 and if he shall at all change beast for **b**, then 929
27:11 if *it be* any unclean **b**, of which they do not 929
27:11 then he shall present the **b** before the priest: 929
27:27 if *it be* of an unclean **b**, then he shall redeem 929
27:28 *both* of man and **b**, and of the field of his 929
Nu 3:13 all the firstborn in Israel, both man and **b**: 929
8:17 children of Israel *are* mine, *both* man and **b**: 929
31:26 *both* of man and of **b**, thou, and Eleazar 929
31:47 *both* of man and of **b**, and gave them unto 929
Dt 4:17 The likeness of any **b** that *is* on the earth, 929
14: 6 every **b** that parteth the hoof, and 929
27:21 *be* he that lieth with any *manner of* **b**. 929
Jdg 20:48 as the **b**, and all that came to hand: 929
2Ki 14: 9 there passed by a wild **b** that *was* in 2416
2Ch 25:18 there passed by a wild **b** that *was* in 2416

B

Ne	2:12	neither *was there any* **b** with me, save	929
	2:12	beast with me, save the **b** that I rode upon.	929
	2:14	*there was* no place for the **b** *that was* under	929
Job	39:15	or *that* the wild **b** may break them.	2416
Ps	36: 6	O LORD, thou preservest man and **b**.	929
	50:10	For every **b** of the forest *is* mine, *and*	2416
	73:22	*was* I, and ignorant: I was *as* a **b** before thee.	929
	80:13	and the **wild b** of the field doth devour it.	2123
	104:11	They give drink to every **b** of the field:	2416
	135: 8	the firstborn of Egypt, both of man and **b**.	929
	147: 9	He giveth to the **b** his food, *and* to the young	929
Pr	12:10	A righteous *man* regardeth the life of his **b**:	929
Ecc	3:19	that a man hath no preeminence above a **b**:	929
	3:21	the spirit of the **b** that goeth downward to	929
Isa	35: 9	nor *any* ravenous **b** shall go up thereon,	2416
	43:20	The **b** of the field shall honour me,	2416
	46: 1	*they are* a burden to the weary *b*.	NIH
	63:14	As a **b** goeth down into the valley, the Spirit	929
Jer	7:20	upon **b**, and upon the trees of the field, and	929
	9:10	the fowl of the heavens and the **b** are fled;	929
	21: 6	the inhabitants of this city, both man and **b**:	929
	27: 5	the man and the **b** that *are* upon the ground,	929
	31:27	*with* the seed of man, and *with* the seed of **b**.	929
	32:43	ye say, *It is* desolate without man or **b**;	929
	33:10	*shall be* desolate without man and without **b**,	929
	33:10	and without inhabitant, and without **b**,	929
	33:12	*is* desolate without man and without **b**,	929
	36:29	shall cause to cease from thence man and **b**?	929
	50: 3	they shall depart, both man and **b**.	929
	51:62	neither man nor **b**, but that it shall be	929
Eze	14:13	upon it, and will cut off man and **b** from it:	929
	14:17	the land; so that I cut off man and **b** from it:	929
	14:19	it in blood, to cut off from it man and **b**:	929
	14:21	and the noisome **b**, and the pestilence,	2416
	14:21	the pestilence, to cut off from it man and **b**?	929
	25:13	and will cut off man and **b** from it;	929
	29: 8	upon thee, and cut off man and **b** out of thee.	929
	29:11	through it, nor foot of **b** shall pass through it,	929
	34: 8	my flock became meat to every **b** of	2416
	34:28	neither shall the **b** of the land devour them;	2416
	36:11	I will multiply upon you man and **b**; and	929
	39:17	to every **b** of the field,	2416
	44:31	of itself, or torn, whether it be fowl or **b**.	929
Da	7: 5	behold, another **b**, a second, like to a bear,	2423
	7: 6	the **b** had also four heads; and	2423
	7: 7	behold, a fourth **b**, dreadful and terrible,	2423
	7:11	I beheld *even* till the **b** *was* slain, and	2423
	7:19	I would know the truth of the fourth **b**,	2423
	7:23	The fourth **b** shall be the fourth kingdom	2423
Hos	13: 8	them like a lion: the wild **b** shall tear them.	2416
Jnh	3: 7	his nobles, saying, Let neither man nor **b**,	929
	3: 8	But let man and **b** be covered with sackcloth,	929
Mic	1:13	of Lachish, bind the chariot to the **swift b**:	7409
Zep	1: 3	I will consume man and **b**; I will consume	929
Zec	8:10	there was no hire for man, nor any hire for **b**;	929
Lk	10:34	and set him on his own **b**, and brought him	*2934*
Ac	28: 4	saw the *venomous* **b** hang on his hand,	*2342*
	28: 5	And he shook off the **b** into the fire, and	*2342*
Heb	12:20	And if *so much as* a **b** touch the mountain,	*2342*
Rev	4: 7	And the first **b** *was* like a lion, and	*2226*
	4: 7	and the second **b** like a calf, and the third	*2226*
	4: 7	and the third **b** had a face as a man, and	*2226*
	4: 7	and the fourth **b** *was* like a flying eagle.	*2226*
	6: 3	I heard the second **b** say, Come and see.	*2226*
	6: 5	I heard the third **b** say, Come and see.	*2226*
	6: 7	I heard the voice of the fourth **b** say, Come	*2226*
	11: 7	the **b** that ascendeth out of the bottomless	*2342*
	13: 1	and saw a **b** rise up out of the sea,	*2342*
	13: 2	And the **b** which I saw was like unto a	*2342*
	13: 3	and all the world wondered after the **b**.	*2342*
	13: 4	the dragon which gave power unto the **b**:	*2342*
	13: 4	and they worshipped the **b**, saying, Who *is*	*2342*
	13: 4	the beast, saying, Who *is* like unto the **b**?	*2342*
	13:11	And I beheld another **b** coming up out of	*2342*
	13:12	all the power of the first **b** before him,	*2342*
	13:12	which dwell therein to worship the first **b**,	*2342*
	13:14	he had power to do in the sight of the **b**;	*2342*
	13:14	that *they* should make an image to the **b**,	*2342*
	13:15	power to give life unto the image of the **b**,	*2342*
	13:15	that the image of the **b** should both speak,	*2342*
	13:15	the image of the **b** should be killed.	*2342*
	13:17	or the name of the **b**, or the number of his	*2342*
	13:18	understanding count the number of the **b**:	*2342*
	14: 9	If any *man* worship the **b** and his image,	*2342*
	14:11	who worship the **b** and his image, and	*2342*
	15: 2	them that had gotten the victory over the **b**,	*2342*
	16: 2	upon the men which had the mark of the **b**,	*2342*
	16:10	poured out his vial upon the seat of the **b**;	*2342*
	16:13	and out of the mouth of the **b**, and out of	*2342*
	17: 3	saw a woman sit upon a scarlet coloured **b**,	*2342*
	17: 7	and of the **b** that carrieth her, which hath	*2342*
	17: 8	The **b** that thou sawest was, and is not; and	*2342*
	17: 8	when they behold the **b** that was, and is not,	*2342*
	17:11	And the **b** that was, and is not, even he is	*2342*
	17:12	receive power as kings one hour with the **b**.	*2342*
	17:13	give their power and strength unto the **b**.	*2342*
	17:16	the ten horns which thou sawest upon the **b**,	*2342*
	17:17	and give their kingdom unto the **b**,	*2342*
	19:19	And I saw the **b**, and the kings of the earth,	*2342*
	19:20	And the **b** was taken, and with him	*2342*
	19:20	them that had received the mark of the **b**,	*2342*
	20: 4	and which had not worshipped the **b**,	*2342*
	20:10	where the **b** and the false prophet *are*, and	*2342*

BEAST'S (1) [BEAST]

Da	4:16	and let a **b** heart be given unto him;	2423

BEASTS (156) [BEAST]

Ge	7: 2	of **b** that *are* not clean by two, the male and	929
	7: 8	Of clean **b**, and of beasts that *are* not clean,	929
	7: 8	and of **b** that *are* not clean, and of fowls, and	929
	31:39	That which was torn *of b* I brought not unto	NIH
	36: 6	his cattle, and all his **b**, and all his substance,	929
	45:17	lade your **b**, and go, get you unto the land	1165
Ex	11: 5	*is* behind the mill; and all the firstborn of **b**.	929
	22:31	ye eat *any* flesh *that is* torn *of b* in the field;	NIH
	23:11	what they leave the **b** of the field shall eat.	2416
Lev	7:24	the fat of that which is torn *with b*, may be	NIH
	11: 2	These *are* the **b** which ye shall eat among	2416
	11: 2	eat among all the **b** that *are* on the earth.	929
	11: 3	cheweth cud, among the **b**,	929
	11:27	among all *manner of b* that go on *all* four,	2416
	11:46	This *is* the law of the **b**, and of the fowl, and	929
	17:15	that which was torn *with b*, *whether it be*	NIH
	20:25	put difference between clean **b** and unclean,	929
	22: 8	is torn *with b*, he shall not eat to defile	NIH
	26: 6	I will rid evil **b** out of the land, neither shall	2416
	26:22	I will also send wild **b** among you, which	2416
	27:26	Only the firstling of the **b**, which should be	929
Nu	18:15	*whether it be* of men or **b**, shall be thine:	929
	18:15	the firstling of unclean **b** shalt thou redeem.	929
	20: 8	give the congregation and their **b** drink.	1165
	20:11	the congregation drank, and their **b** *also*.	1165
	31:11	and all the prey, *both* of men and of **b**.	929
	31:30	of all *manner of b*, and give them unto	929
	35: 3	and for their goods, and for all their **b**.	2416
Dt	7:22	lest the **b** of the field increase upon thee.	2416
	14: 4	These *are* the **b** which ye shall eat: the ox,	929
	14: 6	*and* cheweth the cud amongst the **b**:	929
	28:26	unto the **b** of the earth, and no man shall fray	929
	32:24	I will also send the teeth of **b** upon them,	929
1Sa	17:44	the fowls of the air, and to the **b** of the field.	929
	17:46	of the air, and to the **wild b** of the earth;	2416
2Sa	21:10	them by day, nor the **b** of the field by night.	2416
1Ki	4:33	he spake also of **b**, and of fowl, and	929
	18: 5	and mules alive, that we leese not all the **b**.	929
2Ki	3:17	*both* ye, and your cattle, and your **b**.	929
2Ch	32:28	stalls for all *manner of* **b**,	929+929+2050.1
Ezr	1: 4	and with gold, and with goods, and with **b**,	929
	1: 6	and with **b**, and with precious things,	929
Job	5:22	neither shalt thou be afraid of the **b** of	2416
	5:23	the **b** of the field shall be at peace with	2416
	12: 7	But ask now the **b**, and they shall teach thee;	929
	18: 3	Wherefore are we counted as **b**, *and*	929
	35:11	Who teacheth us more than the **b** of	929
	37: 8	the **b** go into dens, and remain in their	2416
	40:20	forth food, where all the **b** of the field play.	2416
Ps	8: 7	and oxen, yea, and the **b** of the field;	929
	49:12	abideth not: he is like the **b** *that* perish.	929
	49:20	understandeth not, is like the **b** *that* perish.	929
	50:11	and the **wild b** of the field *are* mine.	2123
	79: 2	the flesh of thy saints unto the **b** of	2416
	104:20	wherein all the **b** of the forest do creep	2416
	104:25	both small and great **b**.	2416
	148:10	**B**, and all cattle; creeping things, and	2416
Pr	9: 2	She hath killed her **b**; she hath mingled her	2874
	30:30	A lion *which is* strongest among **b**, and	929
Ecc	3:18	*they* might see that they themselves are **b**.	929

Ecc	3:19	which befalleth the sons of men befalleth **b**;	929
Isa	1:11	offerings of rams, and the fat of **fed b**;	4806
	13:21	**wild b of the desert** shall lie there; and	6728
	13:22	the **wild b of the islands** shall cry in their	338
	18: 6	of the mountains, and to the **b** of the earth:	929
	18: 6	all the **b** of the earth shall winter upon them.	929
	30: 6	The burden of the **b** of the south: into	929
	34:14	The **wild b of the desert** shall also meet	6728
	34:14	shall also meet with the **wild b of the island**,	338
	40:16	nor the **b** thereof sufficient *for* a burnt	2416
	46: 1	their idols were upon the **b**, and upon	2416
	56: 9	All ye **b** of the field, come to devour,	2416
	56: 9	come to devour, *yea,* all ye **b** in the forest.	2416
	66:20	and upon mules, and upon **swift b**,	3753
Jer	7:33	of the heaven, and for the **b** of the earth;	929
	12: 4	the **b** are consumed, and the birds; because	929
	12: 9	come ye, assemble all the **b** of the field,	2416
	15: 3	and the **b** of the earth, to devour and destroy.	929
	16: 4	fowls of heaven, and for the **b** of the earth.	929
	19: 7	of the heaven, and for the **b** of the earth.	929
	27: 6	the **b** of the field have I given him also to	2416
	28:14	and I have given him the **b** of the field also.	2416
	34:20	of the heaven, and to the **b** of the earth.	929
	50:39	Therefore the **wild b of the desert** with	6728
	50:39	the **wild b of the islands** shall dwell *there,*	338
Eze	5:17	So will I send upon you famine and evil **b**,	2416
	8:10	abominable **b**, and all the idols of the house	929
	14:15	If I cause noisome **b** to pass through	2416
	14:15	no man may pass through because of the **b**:	2416
	29: 5	I have given thee for meat to the **b** of	2416
	31: 6	under his branches did all the **b** of the field	2416
	31:13	all the **b** of the field shall be upon his	2416
	32: 4	I will fill the **b** of the whole earth with thee.	2416
	32:13	I will destroy also all the **b** thereof from	929
	32:13	any more, nor the hoofs of **b** trouble them.	929
	33:27	field will I give to the **b** to be devoured,	2416
	34: 5	they became meat to all the **b** of the field,	2416
	34:25	will cause the evil **b** to cease out of	2416
	38:20	the **b** of the field, and all creeping things	2416
	39: 4	and *to* the **b** of the field to be devoured.	2416
Da	2:38	the **b** of the field and the fowls of	2423
	4:12	the **b** of the field had shadow under it, and	2423
	4:14	let the **b** get away from under it, and	2423
	4:15	*let* his portion *be* with the **b** in the grass of	2423
	4:21	under which the **b** of the field dwelt, and	2423
	4:23	*let* his portion *be* with the **b** of the field,	2423
	4:25	thy dwelling shall be with the **b** of the field,	2423
	4:32	thy dwelling *shall be* with the **b** of the field:	2423
	5:21	his heart was made like the **b**, and	2423
	7: 3	four great **b** came up from the sea,	2423
	7: 7	it *was* diverse from all the **b** that *were*	2423
	7:12	As concerning the rest of the **b**, they had	2423
	7:17	These great **b**, which *are* four, *are* four	2423
	8: 4	so that no **b** might stand before him,	2416
Hos	2:12	and the **b** of the field shall eat them.	2416
	2:18	a covenant for them with the **b** of the field,	2416
	4: 3	with the **b** of the field, and with the fowls	2416
Joel	1:18	How do the **b** groan! the herds of cattle are	929
	1:20	The **b** of the field cry also unto thee: for	929
	2:22	Be not afraid, ye **b** of the field: for	929
Am	5:22	I regard the peace offerings of your **fat b**.	4806
Mic	5: 8	people as a lion among the **b** of the forest,	929
Hab	2:17	the spoil of **b**, *which* made them afraid,	929
Zep	2:14	in the midst of her, all the **b** of the nations:	2416
	2:15	a desolation, a place for **b** to lie down in!	2416
Zec	14:15	and of all the **b** that shall be in these tents,	929
Mk	1:13	and was with the **wild b**; and the angels	*2342*
Ac	7:42	have ye offered to me **slain b** and	*4968*
	10:12	Wherein were all *manner of* **fourfooted b**	*5074*
	10:12	and **wild b**, and creeping things, and	*2342*
	11: 6	and saw **fourfooted b** of the earth, and	*5074*
	11: 6	and **wild b**, and creeping things, and fowls	*2342*
	23:24	And provide *them* **b**, that they may set Paul	*2934*
Ro	1:23	and **fourfooted b**, and creeping things.	*5074*
1Co	15:32	of men I have **fought with b** at Ephesus,	*2341*
	15:39	another flesh of **b**, another of fishes, *and*	*2934*
Tit	1:12	*are* alway liars, evil **b**, slow bellies.	*2342*
Heb	13:11	For the bodies of those **b**, whose blood is	*2226*
Jas	3: 7	For every kind of **b**, and of birds, and	*2342*
2Pe	2:12	But these, as natural brute **b**, made to be	*2226*
Jude	1:10	but what they know naturally, as brute **b**,	*2226*
Rev	4: 6	*were* four **b** full of eyes before and behind.	*2226*
	4: 8	And the four **b** had each of them six wings	*2226*
	4: 9	And when *those* **b** give glory and honour	*2226*
	5: 6	in the midst of the throne and of the four **b**,	*2226*
	5: 8	the four **b** and four *and* twenty elders fell	*2226*
	5:11	about the throne and the **b** and the elders:	*2226*
	5:14	And the four **b** said, Amen. And the four	*2226*
	6: 1	one of the four **b** saying, Come and see.	*2226*
	6: 6	heard a voice in the midst of the four **b** say,	*2226*
	6: 8	and with death, and with the **b** of the earth.	*2342*
	7:11	and *about* the elders and the four **b**, and	*2226*
	14: 3	and before the four **b**, and the elders:	*2226*
	15: 7	And one of the four **b** gave unto the seven	*2226*
	18:13	and **b**, and sheep, and horses, and chariots,	*2934*
	19: 4	twenty elders and the four **b** fell down and	*2226*

BEAT (36) [BEATEN, BEATEST, BEATETH, BEATING]

Ex	30:36	thou shalt **b** *some* of it very small, and	7833
	39: 3	they did **b** the gold into thin plates, and	7554
Nu	11: 8	or **b** *it* in a mortar, and baked *it* in pans, and	1743
Dt	25: 3	**b** him above these *with* many stripes, then	5221
Jdg	8:17	he **b down** the tower of Penuel, and	5422
	9:45	and **b down** the city, and sowed it *with* salt.	5422
	19:22	*and* **b** at the door, and spake to the master	1849
Ru	2:17	until even, and **b out** that she had gleaned:	2251
2Sa	22:43	did I **b** them *as* **small** as the dust of	7833
2Ki	3:25	they **b down** the cities, and *on* every good	2040
	13:25	Three times did Joash **b** him, and	5221
	23:12	did the king **b down**, and brake *them* down	5422
Ps	18:42	did I **b** them **small** as the dust before	7833
	89:23	I will **b down** his foes before his face, and	3807
Pr	23:14	Thou shalt **b** him with the rod, and	5221
Isa	2: 4	they shall **b** their swords into plowshares,	3807
	3:15	mean ye *that* ye **b** my people **to pieces**,	1792
	27:12	*that* the LORD shall **b off** from	2251
	41:15	**b** *them* **small**, and shalt make the hills as	1854
Joel	3:10	**B** your plowshares into swords, and	3807
Jnh	4: 8	the sun **b** upon the head of Jonah, that he	5221
Mic	4: 3	they shall **b** their swords into plowshares,	3807
	4:13	thou shalt **b in pieces** many people: and	1854
Mt	7:25	and the winds blew, and **b upon** that house;	*4363*
	7:27	and the winds blew, and **b upon** that house;	*4350*
	21:35	husbandmen took his servants, and **b** one,	*1194*
Mk	4:37	and the waves **b** into the ship, so that it was	*1911*
	12: 3	and **b** *him,* and sent *him* away empty.	*1194*
Lk	6:48	the stream **b vehemently upon** that house,	*4366*
	6:49	**against** which the stream did **b vehemently**,	*4366*
	12:45	and shall begin to **b** the menservants and	*5180*
	20:10	but the husbandmen **b** him, and sent *him*	*1194*
	20:11	and they **b** him also, and entreated *him*	*1194*
Ac	16:22	their clothes, and commanded to **b** *them.*	*4463*
	18:17	and **b** *him* before the judgment seat.	*5180*
	22:19	**b** in every synagogue them that believed on	*1194*

BEATEN (40) [BEAT]

Ex	5:14	had set over them, were **b**, *and* demanded,	5221
	5:16	behold, thy servants *are* **b**; but the fault *is*	5221
	25:18	*of* **b work** shalt thou make them, in the two	4749
	25:31	*of* **b work** shall the candlestick be made:	4749
	25:36	all it *shall be* one **b work** *of* pure gold.	4749
	27:20	that they bring thee pure oil olive **b** for	3795
	29:40	with the fourth part of a hin of **b** oil;	3795
	37: 7	**b out of one piece** made he them, on	4749
	37:17	*of* **b work** made he the candlestick;	4749
	37:22	all of it *was* one **b work** *of* pure gold.	4749
Lev	2:14	by the fire, *even* corn **b out** of full ears.	1643
	2:16	*part* of the **b corn** thereof, and *part* of	1643
	16:12	and his hands full of sweet incense **b small**,	1851
	24: 2	that they bring unto thee pure oil olive **b** for	3795
Nu	8: 4	this work of the candlestick *was of* **b** gold,	4749
	8: 4	unto the flowers thereof, *was* **b work**:	4749
	28: 5	mingled with the fourth *part* of a hin of **b**	3795
Dt	25: 2	if the wicked *man be* worthy to be **b**,	5221
	25: 2	to be **b** before his face, according to his	5221
Jos	8:15	all Israel *made as if they* were **b** before	5060
2Sa	2:17	Abner was **b**, and the men of Israel, before	5062
1Ki	10:16	made two hundred targets *of* **b** gold:	7820
	10:17	*he made* three hundred shields *of* **b** gold;	7820
2Ch	2:10	twenty thousand measures of **b wheat**, and	4347
	9:15	made two hundred targets *of* **b** gold:	7820
	9:15	six hundred *shekels* of **b** gold went to one	7820
	9:16	three hundred shields *made he of* **b** gold:	7820
	34: 7	had **b** the graven images into powder, and	3807
Pr	23:35	not sick; they have **b** me, *and* I felt *it* not:	1986
Isa	27: 9	altar as chalkstones that are **b in sunder**,	5310
	28:27	the fitches are **b out** with a staff, and	2251
	30:31	the LORD shall the Assyrian be **b down**,	2865

Jer 46: 5 their mighty ones are **b down**, and are fled 3807
Mic 1: 7 graven images thereof shall be **b to pieces**, 3807
Mk 13: 9 and in the synagogues ye shall be **b**: *1194*
Lk 12:47 to his will, shall be **b** with many *stripes*. *1194*
12:48 shall be **b** with few *stripes*. For unto *1194*
Ac 5:40 **b** *them*, they commanded that *they* should *1194*
16:37 They have **b** us openly uncondemned, *1194*
2Co 11:25 Thrice was I **b with rods**, once was I *4463*

BEATEST (2) [BEAT]
Dt 24:20 When thou **b** thine olive tree, thou shalt not 2251
Pr 23:13 for *if* thou **b** him with the rod, he shall not 5221

BEATETH (1) [BEAT]
1Co 9:26 so fight I, not as one that **b** the air: *1194*

BEATING (3) [BEAT]
1Sa 14:16 and they went on **b down** *one another*. 1986
Mk 12: 5 him they killed, and many others; **b** some, *1194*
Ac 21:32 and the soldiers, they left **b** of Paul. *5180*

BEAUTIES (1) [BEAUTY]
Ps 110: 3 in the **b** of holiness from the womb of 1926

BEAUTIFUL (23) [BEAUTY]
Ge 29:17 but Rachel was **b** and well favoured. 3303+8389
Dt 21:11 seest among the captives a **b** woman, 3303+8389
1Sa 16:12 *and* withal of a **b** countenance, and 3303
25: 3 and of a **b** countenance: 3303
2Sa 11: 2 and the woman *was* very **b** to look upon. 2896
Est 2: 7 and the maid *was* fair and **b**; 2896+4758
Ps 48: 2 **B** for situation, the joy of the whole earth, 3303
Ecc 3:11 He hath made every *thing* **b** in his time: 3303
SS 6: 4 Thou *art* **b**, O my love, as Tirzah, 3303
7: 1 How **b** are thy feet with shoes, O prince's 3302
Isa 4: 2 day shall the branch of the LORD be **b** 6643
52: 1 put on thy **b** garments, O Jerusalem, 8597
52: 7 How **b** upon the mountains are the feet of 4998
64:11 Our holy and our **b** house, where our 8597
Jer 13:20 the flock *that* was given thee, thy **b** flock? 8597
48:17 is the strong staff broken, *and* the **b** rod! 8597
Eze 16:12 thine ears, and a **b** crown upon thine head. 8597
16:13 thou wast exceeding **b**, and thou didst 3302
23:42 their hands, and **b** crowns upon their heads. 8597
Mt 23:27 which indeed appear **b** outward, but *5611*
Ac 3: 2 at the gate of the temple which is called **B**, *5611*
3:10 sat for alms at the **B** gate of the temple: *5611*
Ro 10:15 How **b** *are* the feet of them that preach *5611*

BEAUTIFY (3) [BEAUTY]
Ezr 7:27 to **b** the house of the LORD which *is* in 6286
Ps 149: 4 he will **b** the meek with salvation. 6286
Isa 60:13 to **b** the place of my sanctuary; 6286

BEAUTY (49) [BEAUTIES, BEAUTIFUL, BEAUTIFY]
Ex 28: 2 for Aaron thy brother, for glory and for **b**. 8597
28:40 thou make for them, for glory and for **b**. 8597
2Sa 1:19 The **b** of Israel *is* slain upon thy high 6643
14:25 to be so much praised as Absalom for his **b**: 3303
1Ch 16:29 worship the LORD in the **b** of holiness. 1927
2Ch 3: 6 the house with precious stones for **b**: 8597
20:21 that should praise the **b** of holiness, as *they* 1927
Est 1:11 to shew the people and the princes her **b**: 3308
Job 40:10 and array thyself with glory and **b**. 1926
Ps 27: 4 to behold the **b** of the LORD, and 5278
29: 2 worship the LORD in the **b** of holiness. 1927
39:11 thou makest his **b** to consume away like a 2530
45:11 So shall the king greatly desire thy **b**: for he 3308
49:14 their **b** shall consume *in* the grave from 6699
50: 2 Out of Zion, the perfection of **b**, God hath 3308
90:17 let the **b** of the LORD our God be upon 5278
96: 6 strength and **b** *are* in his sanctuary. 8597
96: 9 O worship the LORD in the **b** of holiness: 1927
Pr 6:25 Lust not after her **b** in thine heart; 3308
20:29 and the **b** of old men *is* the gray head. 1926
31:30 Favour *is* deceitful, and **b** *is* vain: *but* 3308
Isa 3:24 of sackcloth; *and* burning instead of **b**. 3308
13:19 the **b** of the Chaldees' excellency, 8597
28: 1 whose glorious **b** *is* a fading flower, 8597
28: 4 the glorious **b**, which *is* on the head of 8597
28: 5 for a diadem of **b**, unto the residue of his 8597
33:17 Thine eyes shall see the king in his **b**: 3308
44:13 of a man, according to the **b** of a man; 8597
53: 2 *there is* no **b** that we should desire him. 4758
61: 3 to give unto them **b** for ashes, the oil of joy 6287
La 1: 6 from the daughter of Zion all her **b** is 1926
2: 1 cast down from heaven *unto* the earth the **b** 8597
2:15 the city that *men* call The perfection of **b**, 3308
Eze 7:20 As for the **b** of his ornament, he set it in 6643
16:14 went forth among the heathen for thy **b**: 3308
16:15 thou didst trust in thine own **b**, and 3308
16:25 hast made thy **b** to be abhorred, and 3308
27: 3 O Tyrus, thou hast said, I *am* of perfect **b**. 3308
27: 4 the seas, thy builders have perfected thy **b**. 3308
27:11 round about; they have made thy **b** perfect. 3308
28: 7 they shall draw their swords against the **b** 3308
28:12 the sum, full *of* wisdom, and perfect in **b**. 3308
28:17 Thine heart was lifted up because of thy **b**, 3308
31: 8 garden of God was like unto him in his **b**. 3308
32:19 Whom dost thou pass **in b**? go down, and 5276
Hos 14: 6 his **b** shall be as the olive tree, and his 1935
Zec 9:17 *is* his goodness, and how great *is* his **b**! 3308
11: 7 the one I called **B**, and the other I called 5278
11:10 I took my staff, *even* **B**, and cut it asunder, 5278

BEBAI (6)
Ezr 2:11 The children of **B**, six hundred twenty and 893
8:11 of the sons of **B**; Zechariah the son of Bebai, 893
8:11 Zechariah the son of **B**, and with him twenty 893
10:28 Of the sons also of **B**; Jehohanan, Hananiah, 893
Ne 7:16 The children of **B**, six hundred twenty and 893
10:15 Bunni, Azgad, **B**, 893

BECAME (106) [BECOME] See Index

BECAMEST (2) [BECOME] See Index

BECAUSE (1209) See Index

BECHER (5)
Ge 46:21 and **B**, and Ashbel, Gera, and Naaman, Ehi, 1071
Nu 26:35 of **B**, the family of the Bachrites: of Tahan, 1071
1Ch 7: 6 Bela, and **B**, and Jediael, three. 1071
7: 8 the sons of **B**; Zemira, and Joash, and 1071
7: 8 and Alameth. All these *are* the sons of **B**. 1071

BECHORATH (1)
1Sa 9: 1 son of Abiel, the son of Zeror, the son of **B**, 1064

BECKONED (6) [BECKONING]
Lk 1:22 for he **b** unto them, and *1269*
5: 7 And they **b** unto *their* partners, which were *2656*
Jn 13:24 Simon Peter therefore **b** to him, that *he* *3506*
Ac 19:33 And Alexander **b** with the hand, and *2678*
21:40 and **b** with the hand unto the people. *2678*
24:10 after that the governor had **b** unto him to *3506*

BECKONING (2) [BECKONED]
Ac 12:17 **b** unto them with the hand to hold their *2678*
13:16 and **b** with *his* hand said, Men of Israel, and *2678*

BECOME (135) [BECAME, BECAMEST, BECOMETH]
See Index

BECOMETH (15) [BECOME]
Ps 93: 5 holiness **b** thine house, O LORD, for ever. 4998
Pr 10: 4 *He* **b** poor that dealeth *with* a slack hand: NIH
17: 7 Excellent speech **b** not a fool: much less do 5000
17:18 **b surety** in the presence of his 6148+6161
Ecc 4:14 also *he that is* born in his kingdom **b** poor. NIH
Mt 3:15 for thus it **b** us to fulfil all righteousness. *4241*
13:22 choke the word, and he **b** unfruitful. *1096*
13:32 and **b** a tree, so that the birds of the air *1096*
Mk 4:19 choke the word, and it **b** unfruitful. *1096*
4:32 and **b** greater than all herbs, and *1096*
Ro 16: 2 as **b** saints, and *that* ye assist her in *516*
Eph 5: 3 be once named amongst you, as **b** saints; *4241*
Php 1:27 Only let your conversation be as it **b** *516*
1Ti 2:10 But (which **b** women professing godliness) *4241*
Tit 2: 3 *that they be* in behaviour **as b holiness**, *2412*

BECORATH See BECHORATH

BED (90) [BED'S, BEDCHAMBER, BEDS,
BEDSTEAD]
Ge 48: 2 strengthened himself, and sat upon the **b**. 4296
49: 4 because thou wentest up to thy father's **b**; 4904
49:33 he gathered up his feet into the **b**, and 4296
Ex 8: 3 upon thy **b**, and into the house of thy 4296
21:18 *his* fist, and he die not, but keepeth *his* **b**: 4904
Lev 15: 4 Every **b**, whereon he lieth that hath 4904

Lev 15: 5 whosoever toucheth his **b** shall wash his 4904
15:21 whosoever toucheth her **b** shall wash his 4904
15:23 if it *be* on *her* **b**, or on *any* thing whereon 4904
15:24 all the **b** whereon he lieth shall be unclean. 4904
15:26 Every **b** whereon she lieth all the days of 4904
15:26 shall be unto her as the **b** of her separation: 4904
1Sa 19:13 laid *it* in the **b**, and put a pillow of goats' 4296
19:15 saying, Bring him up to me in the **b**, that I 4296
19:16 behold *there was* an image in the **b**, 4296
28:23 he arose from the earth, and sat upon the **b**. 4296
2Sa 4: 5 who **lay on a b** at noon. 4904+7901
4: 7 he lay on his **b** in his bedchamber, and 4296
4:11 person in his own house upon his **b**? 4904
11: 2 that David arose from off his **b**, and 4904
11:13 at even he went out to lie on his **b** with 4904
13: 5 Lay *thee* down on thy **b**, and make thyself 4904
1Ki 1:47 And the king bowed himself upon the **b**. 4904
17:19 he abode, and laid him upon his own **b**. 4296
21: 4 he laid him down upon his **b**, and 4296
2Ki 1: 4 Thou shalt not come down from *that* **b** on 4296
1: 6 thou shalt not come down from *that* **b** on 4296
1:16 thou shalt not come down off *that* **b** on 4296
4:10 let us set for him there a **b**, and a table, and 4296
4:21 laid him on the **b** of the man of God, and 4296
4:32 the child was dead, *and* laid upon his **b**. 4296
1Ch 5: 1 but, forasmuch as he defiled his father's **b**, 3326
2Ch 16:14 laid him in the **b** which was filled *with* 4904
24:25 and slew him on his **b**, and he died: 4296
Est 7: 8 Haman was fallen upon the **b** whereon 4296
Job 7:13 When I say, My **b** shall comfort me, 6210
17:13 I have made my **b** in the darkness. 3326
33:15 upon men, in slumberings upon the **b**; 4904
33:19 He is chastened also with pain upon his **b**, 4904
Ps 4: 4 with your own heart upon your **b**, 4904
6: 6 all the night make I my **b** to swim; 4296
36: 4 He deviseth mischief upon his **b**; he setteth 4904
41: 3 The LORD will strengthen him upon the **b** 6210
41: 3 thou wilt make all his **b** in his sickness. 4904
63: 6 When I remember thee upon my **b**, *and* 3326
132: 3 of my house, nor go up into my **b**; 3326+6210
139: 8 if I **make** my **b** in hell, behold, thou *art* 3331
Pr 7:16 I have deckt my **b** *with* coverings of 6210
7:17 I have perfumed my **b** *with* myrrh, aloes, 4904
22:27 why should he take away thy **b** from under 4904
26:14 his hinges, so *doth* the slothful upon his **b**. 4296
SS 1:16 yea, pleasant: also our **b** *is* green. 6210
3: 1 By night on my **b** I sought *him* whom my 4904
3: 7 Behold his **b**, which *is* Solomon's; 4296
5:13 His cheeks *are* as a **b** of spices, *as* sweet 6170
Isa 28:20 For the **b** is shorter than that *a man* can 4702
57: 7 and high mountain hast thou set thy **b**: 4904
57: 8 thou hast enlarged thy **b**, and made thee *a* 4904
57: 8 thou lovedst their **b** where thou sawest *it*. 4904
Eze 23:17 the Babylonians came to her into the **b** of 4904
23:41 satest upon a stately **b**, and a table prepared 4296
32:25 They have set her a **b** in the midst of 4904
Da 2:28 the visions of thy head upon thy **b**, 4903
2:29 thoughts came *into thy mind* upon thy **b**, 4903
4: 5 the thoughts upon my **b** and the visions of 4903
4:10 *were* the visions of mine head in my **b**; 4903
4:13 I saw in the visions of my head upon my **b**, 4903
7: 1 a dream and visions of his head upon his **b**: 4903
Am 3:12 that dwell in Samaria in the corner of a **b**, 4296
Mt 9: 2 him a man sick of the palsy, lying on a **b**: *2825*
9: 6 take up thy **b**, and go unto thine house. *2825*
Mk 2: 4 they let down the **b** wherein the sick of *2895*
2: 9 to say, Arise, and take up thy **b**, and walk? *2895*
2:11 and take up thy **b**, and go thy way into *2895*
2:12 took up the **b**, and went forth before *them* *2895*
4:21 to be put under a bushel, or under a **b**? *2825*
7:30 gone out, and *her* daughter laid upon the **b**. *2825*
Lk 5:18 men brought in a **b** a man which was taken *2825*
8:16 it with a vessel, or putteth *it* under a **b**; *2825*
11: 7 and my children are with me in **b**; *2845*
17:34 that night there shall be two *men* in one **b**; *2825*
Jn 5: 8 unto him, Rise, take up thy **b**, and walk. *2895*
5: 9 and took up his **b**, and walked: *2895*
5:10 it is not lawful for thee to carry *thy* **b**. *2895*
5:11 said unto me, Take up thy **b**, and walk. *2895*
5:12 said unto thee, Take up thy **b**, and walk? *2895*
Ac 9:33 which had kept his **b** eight years, and was *2895*
9:34 arise, and **make** thy **b**. And he arose *4766*
Heb 13: 4 *is* honourable in all, and the **b** undefiled: *2845*
Rev 2:22 I *will* cast her into a **b**, and them that *2825*

BED'S (1) [BED]
Ge 47:31 And Israel bowed himself upon the **b** head. 4296

BEDAD (2)
Ge 36:35 Husham died, and Hadad the son of **B**, 911
1Ch 1:46 Husham was dead, Hadad the son of **B**, 911

BEDAN (2)
1Sa 12:11 **B**, and Jephthah, and Samuel, and 917
1Ch 7:17 the sons of Ulam; **B**. These *were* the sons of 917

BEDCHAMBER (6) [BED, CHAMBER]
Ex 8: 3 into thy **b**, and upon thy bed, and 2315+4904
2Sa 4: 7 he lay on his bed in his **b**, and 2315+4904
2Ki 6:12 the words that thou speakest in thy **b**. 2315+4904
11: 2 in the **b** from Athaliah, so that he 2315+4296
2Ch 22:11 and put him and his nurse in a **b**. 2315+4296
Ecc 10:20 and curse not the rich in thy **b**: 2315+4904

BEDEIAH (1)
Ezr 10:35 Benaiah, **B**, Chelluh, 912

BEDROOM See BEDCHAMBER

BEDS (10) [BED]
2Sa 17:28 Brought **b**, and basons, and earthen vessels, 4904
Est 1: 6 the **b** *were of* gold and silver, upon a 4296
Ps 149: 5 in glory: let them sing aloud upon their **b**. 4904
SS 6: 2 to the **b** of spices, to feed in the gardens, 6170
Isa 57: 2 they shall rest in their **b**, *each one* walking 4904
Hos 7:14 their heart, when they howled upon their **b**: 4904
Am 6: 4 That lie upon **b** of ivory, and 4296
Mic 2: 1 devise iniquity, and work evil upon their **b**! 4904
Mk 6:55 began to carry about in **b** those that were *2895*
Ac 5:15 the streets, and laid *them* on **b** and couches, *2825*

BEDSTEAD (2) [BED]
Dt 3:11 behold, his **b** *was* a bedstead of iron; *is* it 6210
3:11 behold, his bedstead *was* a **b** of iron; *is* it 6210

BEE (1) [BEES]
Isa 7:18 and for the **b** that *is* in the land of Assyria. 1682

BEELIADA (1)
1Ch 14: 7 And Elishama, and **B**, and Eliphalet. 1182

BEELZEBUB (7)
Mt 10:25 they have called the master of the house **B**, *954*
12:24 out devils, but by **B** the prince of the devils. *954*
12:27 And if I by **B** cast out devils, by whom do *954*
Mk 3:22 He hath **B**, and by the prince of the devils *954*
Lk 11:15 He casteth out devils through **B** the chief of *954*
11:18 ye say that I cast out devils through **B**. *954*
11:19 And if I by **B** cast out devils, by whom do *954*

BEEN (331) [BE] See Index

BEER (2) [BAALATH-BEER, BEER-ELIM, BEER-LAHAI-ROI, BEER-SHEBA]
Nu 21:16 from thence *they went* to **B**: that *is* the well 876
Jdg 9:21 and fled, and went to **B**, and dwelt there, 876

BEERA (1)
1Ch 7:37 Shamma, and Shilshah, and Ithran, and **B**. 878

BEERAH (1)
1Ch 5: 6 **B** his son, whom Tilgath-pilneser king of 880

BEER-ELIM (1) [BEER, ELIM]
Isa 15: 8 and the howling thereof *unto* **B**. 879

BEERI (2)
Ge 26:34 to wife Judith the daughter of **B** the Hittite, 882
Hos 1: 1 the son of **B**, in the days of Uzziah, Jotham, 882

BEER-LAHAI-ROI (1) [BEER, LAHAI-ROI, WELL]
Ge 16:14 Wherefore the well was called **B**; behold, 883

BEEROTH (6) [BEEROTHITE, BEEROTHITES]
Dt 10: 6 from **B** of the children of Jaakan *to* Mosera: 881
Jos 9:17 and Chephirah, and **B**, and Kirjath-jearim. 881
18:25 Gibeon, and Ramah, and **B**, 881
2Sa 4: 2 (for **B** also was reckoned to Benjamin: 881
Ezr 2:25 Chephirah, and **B**, seven hundred and forty 881
Ne 7:29 Chephirah, and **B**, seven hundred forty and 881

BEEROTHITE (4) [BEEROTH]
2Sa 4: 2 the sons of Rimmon a **B**, of the children of 886
4: 5 And the sons of Rimmon the **B**, Rechab and 886
4: 9 the sons of Rimmon the **B**, and said unto 886
23:37 Zelek the Ammonite, Naharai the **B**, 886

BEEROTHITES (1) [BEEROTH]
2Sa 4: 3 the **B** fled to Gittaim, and were sojourners 886

BEER-SHEBA (34) [BEER, SHEBA, SHEBAH]
Ge 21:14 and wandered in the wilderness of **B**. 884
21:31 Wherefore he called that place **B**; because 884
21:32 Thus they made a covenant at **B**: then 884
21:33 *Abraham* planted a grove in **B**, and 884
22:19 and they rose up and went together to **B**; 884
22:19 to Beer-sheba; and Abraham dwelt at **B**. 884
26:23 And he went up from thence to **B**. 884
26:33 the name of the city *is* **B** unto this day. 884
28:10 Jacob went out from **B**, and went toward 884
46: 1 came to **B**, and offered sacrifices unto 884
46: 5 Jacob rose up from **B**: and the sons of Israel 884
Jos 15:28 And Hazar-shual, and **B**, and Bizjothjah, 884
19: 2 they had in their inheritance **B**, or Sheba, 884
Jdg 20: 1 from Dan even to **B**, with the land of Gilead, 884
1Sa 3:20 all Israel from Dan even to **B** knew that 884
8: 2 of his second, Abiah: *they were* judges in **B**. 884
2Sa 3:10 and over Judah, from Dan even to **B**. 884
17:11 from Dan even to **B**, as the sand that *is* by 884
24: 2 from Dan even to **B**, and number ye 884
24: 7 went out to the south of Judah, *even to* **B**. 884
24:15 there died of the people from Dan even to **B** 884
1Ki 4:25 and under his fig tree, from Dan even to **B**, 884
19: 3 went for his life, and came *to* **B**, 884
2Ki 12: 1 And his mother's name *was* Zibiah of **B**. 884
23: 8 from Geba to **B**, and brake down the high 884
1Ch 4:28 they dwelt at **B**, and Moladah, and 884
21: 2 Go, number Israel from **B** even to Dan; 884
2Ch 19: 4 he went out again through the people from **B** 884
24: 1 His mother's name also *was* Zibiah of **B**. 884
30: 5 throughout all Israel, from **B** even to Dan, 884
Ne 11:27 and at **B**, and *in* the villages thereof, 884
11:30 they dwelt from **B** unto the valley of 884
Am 5: 5 nor enter *into* Gilgal, and pass not *to* **B**: 884
8:14 O Dan, liveth; and, The manner of **B** liveth; 884

BEES (3) [BEE]
Dt 1:44 as **b** do, and destroyed you in Seir, 1682
Jdg 14: 8 *there was* a swarm of **b** and honey in 1682
Ps 118:12 They compassed me about like **b**; they are 1682

BEESHTERAH (1)
Jos 21:27 and **B** with her suburbs; two cities. 1203

BEETLE (1)
Lev 11:22 the **b** after his kind, and the grasshopper 2728

BEEVES (7)
Lev 22:19 of the **b**, of the sheep, or of the goats. 1241
22:21 or a freewill offering in **b** or sheep, it shall 1241
Nu 31:28 of the **b**, and of the asses, and of the sheep: 1241
31:30 of the **b**, of the asses, and of the flocks, 1241
31:33 And threescore and twelve thousand **b**, 1241
31:38 the **b** *were* thirty and six thousand; of 1241
31:44 And thirty and six thousand **b**, 1241

BEFALL (9) [BEFALLEN, BEFALLETH, BEFELL]
Ge 42: 4 he said, Lest peradventure mischief **b** him. 7122
42:38 if mischief **b** him by the way in the which 7122
44:29 take this also from me, and mischief **b** him, 7136
49: 1 that I may tell you *that* which shall **b** you in 7122
Dt 31:17 and many evils and troubles shall **b** them; 4672
31:29 evil will **b** you in the latter days; because 7122
Ps 91:10 There shall no evil **b** thee, neither shall 413+579
Da 10:14 what shall **b** thy people in the latter days: 7136
Ac 20:22 not knowing the *things* that shall **b** me *4876*

BEFALLEN (7) [BEFALL]
Lev 10:19 the LORD; and such things have **b** me: 7122
Nu 20:14 Thou knowest all the travail that hath **b** us: 4672
Dt 31:21 when many evils and troubles are **b** them, 4672
Jdg 6:13 be with us, why then is all this **b** us? 4672
1Sa 20:26 for he thought, **Something** hath **b** him, 4745
Est 6:13 all his friends every *thing* that had **b** him. 7136
Mt 8:33 **what was b to** the possessed of the devils. *3588*

BEFALLETH (3) [BEFALL]
Ecc 3:19 For that which **b** the sons of men befalleth 4745
3:19 For that which befalleth the sons of men **b** 4745
3:19 befalleth beasts; even one thing **b** them: 4745

BEFELL (5) [BEFALL]
Ge 42:29 and told him all that **b** unto them; 7136
Jos 2:23 of Nun, and told him all *things* that **b** them: 4672
2Sa 19: 7 that **b** thee from thy youth until now. 935+5921
Mk 5:16 And they that saw *it* told them how it **b** to *1096*
Ac 20:19 which **b** me by the lying in wait of *4819*

BEFORE (1799) [BEFOREHAND, BEFORETIME] See Index

BEFOREHAND (5) [BEFORE] See Index

BEFORETIME (11) [BEFORE, TIME]
Dt 2:12 The Horims also dwelt in Seir **b**; 6440+3807.1
Jos 11:10 for Hazor **b** *was* the head of all 6440+3807.1
20: 5 hated him not **b**. 4480+8032+8543
1Sa 9: 9 (**B** in Israel, when a man went to 6440+3807.1
9: 9 for *he that is* now *called* a Prophet was **b** 6440
10:11 knew him **b** saw that behold, 865+4480+8032
2Sa 7:10 afflict them any more, as **b**, 7223+871.1+1886.1
2Ki 13: 5 of Israel dwelt in their tents, as **b**. 8032+8543
Ne 2: 1 Now I had not been **b** sad in his presence. NIH
Isa 41:26 **b**, that we may say, *He is* 4480+6440+3807.1
Ac 8: 9 which **b** in the *same* city used sorcery, and *4391*

BEG (3) [BEGGAR, BEGGARLY, BEGGED, BEGGING]
Ps 109:10 children be continually vagabonds, and **b**: 7592
Pr 20: 4 therefore shall he **b** in harvest, and 7592
Lk 16: 3 I cannot dig; to **b** I am ashamed. *1871*

BEGAN (178) [BEGIN]
Ge 4:26 **b** *men* to call upon the name of 2490
6: 1 when men **b** to multiply on the face of 2490
9:20 Noah **b** *to be* a husbandman, and he planted 2490
10: 8 he **b** to be a mighty *one* in the earth. 2490
41:54 the seven years of dearth **b** to come, 2490
44:12 *and* **b** at the eldest, and left at the youngest: 2490
Dt 1: 5 **b** Moses to declare this law, saying, 2974
Jdg 13:25 the spirit of the LORD **b** to move him at 2490
16:19 she **b** to afflict him, and his strength went 2490
16:22 Howbeit the hair of his head **b** to grow 2490
19:25 when the **day b** to spring, they let her go. 7837
20:31 they **b** to smite of the people, *and* kill, as at 2490
20:39 Benjamin **b** to smite *and* kill of the men of 2490
20:40 when the flame **b** to arise up out of the city 2490
1Sa 3: 2 his eyes **b** *to wax* dim, *that* he could not 2490
2Sa 2:10 years old when he **b** to reign over Israel, NIH
5: 4 David *was* thirty years old when he **b** to NIH
1Ki 6: 1 that he **b** to build the house of the LORD. NIH
14:21 and one years old when he **b** to reign, NIH
15:25 Nadab the son of Jeroboam **b** to reign over NIH
15:33 In the third year of Asa king of Judah **b** NIH
16: 8 sixth year of Asa king of Judah **b** Elah NIH
16:11 it came to pass, when he **b** to reign, as soon NIH
16:23 first year of Asa king of Judah **b** Omri to NIH
16:29 eighth year of Asa king of Judah **b** Ahab NIH
22:41 Jehoshaphat the son of Asa **b** to reign over NIH
22:42 and five years old when he **b** to reign; NIH
22:51 Ahaziah the son of Ahab **b** to reign over NIH
2Ki 3: 1 Now Jehoram the son of Ahab **b** to reign NIH
8:16 son of Jehoshaphat king of Judah **b** to reign. NIH
8:17 two years old was he when he **b** to reign; NIH
8:26 twenty years old *was* Ahaziah when he **b** to NIH
9:29 son of Ahab **b** Ahaziah to reign over Judah. NIH
10:32 In those days the LORD **b** to cut Israel 2490
11:21 Seven years old *was* Jehoash when he **b** to NIH
12: 1 In the seventh year of Jehu Jehoash **b** to NIH
13: 1 of Jehu **b** to reign over Israel in Samaria, NIH
13:10 seventh year of Joash king of Judah **b** NIH
14: 2 and five years old when he **b** to reign, NIH
14:23 Joash king of Israel **b** to reign in Samaria, NIH
15: 1 seventh year of Jeroboam king of Israel **b** NIH
15: 2 Sixteen years old was he when he **b** to NIH
15:13 Shallum the son of Jabesh **b** to reign in NIH
15:17 thirtieth year of Azariah king of Judah **b** NIH
15:23 Menahem **b** to reign over Israel in Samaria, NIH
15:27 Remaliah **b** to reign over Israel in Samaria, NIH
15:32 **b** Jotham the son of Uzziah king of Judah to NIH
15:33 twenty years old was he when he **b** to reign, NIH
15:37 In those days the LORD **b** to send against 2490
16: 1 the son of Jotham king of Judah **b** to reign. NIH

2Ki 16: 2 Twenty years old *was* Ahaz when he ***b*** to NIH
17: 1 In the twelfth year of Ahaz king of Judah ***b*** NIH
18: 1 the son of Ahaz king of Judah ***b*** to reign. NIH
18: 2 five years old was he when he ***b*** to reign; NIH
21: 1 Manasseh *was* twelve years old when he ***b*** NIH
21:19 and two years old when he ***b*** to reign, NIH
22: 1 Josiah *was* eight years old when he ***b*** to NIH
23:31 and three years old when he ***b*** to reign; NIH
23:36 and five year old when he ***b*** to reign; NIH
24: 8 *was* eighteen years old when he ***b*** to reign, NIH
24:18 and one years old when he ***b*** to reign, NIH
25:27 of Babylon, in the year that he ***b*** to reign, NIH
1Ch 1:10 he **b** to be mighty upon the earth. 2490
27:24 Joab the son of Zeruiah **b** to number, but 2490
2Ch 3: 1 Solomon **b** to build the house of 2490
3: 2 he **b** to build in the second *day* of 2490
12:13 and forty years old when he ***b*** to reign, NIH
13: 1 Jeroboam ***b*** Abijah to reign over Judah. NIH
20:22 when they **b** to sing and to praise, 2490
20:31 and five years old when he ***b*** to reign, NIH
21: 5 and two years old when he ***b*** to reign, NIH
21:20 two *years* old was he when he ***b*** to reign, NIH
22: 2 two years old *was* Ahaziah when he ***b*** to NIH
24: 1 Joash *was* seven years old when he ***b*** to NIH
25: 1 and five years old *when* he ***b*** to reign, NIH
26: 3 Sixteen years old *was* Uzziah when he ***b*** to NIH
27: 1 and five years old when he ***b*** to reign, NIH
27: 8 and twenty years old when he ***b*** to reign, NIH
28: 1 Ahaz *was* twenty years old when he ***b*** to NIH
29: 1 Hezekiah ***b*** to reign *when he was* five and NIH
29:17 Now they **b** on the first *day* of the first 2490
29:27 when the burnt offering **b**, the song of 2490
29:27 the song of the LORD **b** *also* with 2490
31: 7 In the third month they **b** to lay 2490
31:10 Since *the people* **b** to bring the offerings 2490
31:21 in every work that he **b** in the service of 2490
33: 1 Manasseh *was* twelve years old when he ***b*** NIH
33:21 and twenty years old when he ***b*** to reign, NIH
34: 1 Josiah *was* eight years old when he ***b*** to NIH
34: 3 he **b** to seek after the God of David his 2490
34: 3 in the twelfth year he **b** to purge Judah and 2490
36: 2 and three years old when he ***b*** to reign, NIH
36: 5 and five years old when he ***b*** to reign, NIH
36: 9 Jehoiachin *was* eight years old when he ***b*** to NIH
36:11 and twenty years old when he ***b*** to reign, NIH
Ezr 3: 6 From the first day of the seventh month **b** 2490
3: 8 **b** Zerubbabel the son of Shealtiel, and 2490
5: 2 **b** to build the house of God which *is* at 8271
7: 9 For upon the first *day* of the first month **b** 3246
Ne 4: 7 *and* that the breaches **b** to be stopped, then 2490
13:19 that when the gates of Jerusalem ***b*** to be NIH
Jer 52: 1 and twenty year old when he ***b*** to reign, NIH
Eze 9: 6 they **b** at the ancient men which *were* 2490
Jnh 3: 4 Jonah **b** to enter into the city a day's 2490
Mt 4:17 From that time Jesus **b** to preach, and to say, *756*
11: 7 Jesus **b** to say unto the multitudes *756*
11:20 Then **b** he to upbraid the cities wherein most *756*
12: 1 and **b** to pluck the ears of corn, and to eat. *756*
16:21 From that time forth **b** Jesus to shew unto his *756*
16:22 and **b** to rebuke him, saying, Be it far from *756*
26:22 and **b** every one of them to say unto him, *756*
26:37 and **b** to be sorrowful and very heavy. *756*
26:74 Then **b** he to curse and to swear, *saying,* I *756*
28: 1 as it **b** to dawn towards the first *day* of NIG
Mk 1:45 and **b** to publish *it* much, and to blaze abroad *756*
2:23 and his disciples **b**, as they went, to pluck *756*
4: 1 And he **b** again to teach by the sea side: and *756*
5:17 And they **b** to pray him to depart out of their *756*
5:20 **b** to publish in Decapolis how great *things* *756*
6: 2 was come, he **b** to teach in the synagogue: *756*
6: 7 and **b** to send them forth by two and two; *756*
6:34 and he **b** to teach them many *things.* *756*
6:55 **b** to carry about in beds those that were sick, *756*
8:11 came forth, and **b** to question with him, *756*
8:31 And he **b** to teach them, that the Son of man *756*
8:32 And Peter took him, and **b** to rebuke him. *756*
10:28 Then Peter **b** to say unto him, Lo, we have *756*
10:32 **b** to tell them what *things* should happen *756*
10:41 And when the ten heard *it,* they **b** to be much *756*
10:47 he **b** to cry out, and say, Jesus, *thou* Son of *756*
11:15 and **b** to cast out them that sold and *756*
12: 1 And he **b** to speak unto them by parables. *756*
13: 5 And Jesus answering them **b** to say, *756*
14:19 And they **b** to be sorrowful, and to say unto *756*
14:33 and **b** to be sore amazed, and to be very *756*
14:65 And some **b** to spit on him, and to cover his *756*
14:69 and **b** to say to them that stood by, This is *756*
14:71 But he **b** to curse and to swear, *saying,* I *756*
15: 8 And the multitude crying aloud **b** to desire *756*
15:18 And **b** to salute him, Hail, King of the Jews. *756*
Lk 1:70 which have been **since** the world **b**:) *575*
3:23 And Jesus himself **b** *to be* about thirty years *756*
4:21 And he **b** to say unto them, This day is this *756*
5: 7 filled both the ships, so that they **b** to sink. NIG
5:21 the scribes and the Pharisees **b** to reason, *756*
7:15 And he that was dead sat up, and **b** to speak. *756*
7:24 he **b** to speak unto the people concerning *756*
7:38 and **b** to wash his feet with tears, and *756*
7:49 And they that sat at meat with *him* **b** to say *756*
9:12 And *when* the day **b** to wear away, then *756*
11:29 he **b** to say, This is an evil generation: *756*
11:53 and the Pharisees **b** to urge *him* vehemently, *756*
12: 1 he **b** to say unto his disciples first *of all,* *756*
14:18 And they all with one *consent* **b** to make *756*
14:30 This man **b** to build, and was not able to *756*
15:14 famine in that land; and he **b** to be in want. *756*
15:24 and is found. And they **b** to be merry. *756*
19:37 the whole multitude of the disciples **b** to *756*
19:45 and **b** to cast out them that sold therein, *756*
20: 9 Then **b** he to speak to the people this *756*
22:23 And they **b** to inquire among themselves, *756*
23: 2 And they **b** to accuse him, saying, We found *756*
Jn 4:52 them the hour when he **b to amend**. *2192+2866*
9:32 **Since** the world **b** was it not heard that any *1537*
13: 5 and **b** to wash the disciples' feet, and to wipe *756*
Ac 1: 1 of all that Jesus **b** both to do and teach, *756*
2: 4 and **b** to speak with other tongues, as *756*
3:21 of all his holy prophets **since** the world **b**. *575*
8:35 and **b** at the same scripture, and *756*
10:37 and **b** from Galilee, after the baptism which *756*
11:15 And as I **b** to speak, the Holy Ghost fell on *756*
18:26 And he **b** to speak boldly in the synagogue: *756*
24: 2 And when he was called *forth,* Tertullus **b** to *756*
27:35 and when he had broken *it,* he **b** to eat. *756*
Ro 16:25 was kept secret **since** the **world b**, *166+5550*
2Ti 1: 9 us in Christ Jesus before the **world b**, *166+5550*
Tit 1: 2 promised before the **world b**; *166+5550*
Heb 2: 3 which at the first **b** to be spoken by *2983*

BEGAT (225) [BEGET]

Ge 4:18 Irad **b** Mehujael: and Mehujael begat 3205
4:18 Mehujael **b** Methusael: and 3205
4:18 begat Methusael: and Methusael **b** Lamech. 3205
5: 3 and **b** *a son* in his own likeness, 3205
5: 4 and he **b** sons and daughters: 3205
5: 6 an hundred and five years, and **b** Enos: 3205
5: 7 Seth lived after he **b** Enos eight hundred 3205
5: 7 seven years, and **b** sons and daughters: 3205
5: 9 And Enos lived ninety years, and **b** Cainan: 3205
5:10 Enos lived after he **b** Cainan eight hundred 3205
5:10 and fifteen years, and **b** sons and daughters: 3205
5:12 lived seventy years, and **b** Mahalaleel: 3205
5:13 Cainan lived after he **b** Mahalaleel eight 3205
5:13 forty years, and **b** sons and daughters: 3205
5:15 lived sixty and five years, and **b** Jared: 3205
5:16 Mahalaleel lived after he **b** Jared eight 3205
5:16 thirty years, and **b** sons and daughters: 3205
5:18 and two years, and he **b** Enoch: 3205
5:19 Jared lived after he **b** Enoch eight hundred 3205
5:19 hundred years, and **b** sons and daughters: 3205
5:21 and five years, and **b** Methuselah: 3205
5:22 Enoch walked with God after he **b** 3205
5:22 hundred years, and **b** sons and daughters: 3205
5:25 and seven years, and **b** Lamech: 3205
5:26 Methuselah lived after he **b** Lamech seven 3205
5:26 and two years, and **b** sons and daughters: 3205
5:28 hundred eighty and two years, and **b** a son: 3205
5:30 Lamech lived after he **b** Noah five hundred 3205
5:30 and five years, and **b** sons and daughters: 3205
5:32 and Noah **b** Shem, Ham, and Japheth. 3205
6:10 Noah **b** three sons, Shem, Ham, and 3205
10: 8 Cush **b** Nimrod: he began to be a mighty 3205
10:13 Mizraim **b** Ludim, and Anamim, and 3205
10:15 Canaan **b** Sidon his firstborn, and Heth, 3205
10:24 Arphaxad **b** Salah; and Salah begat Eber. 3205
10:24 Arphaxad begat Salah; and Salah **b** Eber. 3205
10:26 Joktan **b** Almodad, and Sheleph, and 3205
11:10 and **b** Arphaxad two years after the flood: 3205

B

Ge	11:11	Shem lived after he **b** Arphaxad five	3205
	11:11	hundred years, and **b** sons and daughters.	3205
	11:12	lived five and thirty years, and **b** Salah:	3205
	11:13	Arphaxad lived after he **b** Salah four	3205
	11:13	three years, and **b** sons and daughters.	3205
	11:14	And Salah lived thirty years, and **b** Eber:	3205
	11:15	Salah lived after he **b** Eber four hundred	3205
	11:15	three years, and **b** sons and daughters.	3205
	11:16	lived four and thirty years, and **b** Peleg:	3205
	11:17	Eber lived after he **b** Peleg four hundred	3205
	11:17	thirty years, and **b** sons and daughters.	3205
	11:18	And Peleg lived thirty years, and **b** Reu:	3205
	11:19	Peleg lived after he **b** Reu two hundred	3205
	11:19	nine years, and **b** sons and daughters.	3205
	11:20	lived two and thirty years, and **b** Serug:	3205
	11:21	Reu lived after he **b** Serug two hundred	3205
	11:21	seven years, and **b** sons and daughters.	3205
	11:22	And Serug lived thirty years, and **b** Nahor:	3205
	11:23	Serug lived after he **b** Nahor two hundred	3205
	11:23	hundred years, and **b** sons and daughters.	3205
	11:24	lived nine and twenty years, and **b** Terah:	3205
	11:25	Nahor lived after he **b** Terah an hundred	3205
	11:25	nineteen years, and **b** sons and daughters.	3205
	11:26	and **b** Abram, Nahor, and Haran.	3205
	11:27	Terah **b** Abram, Nahor, and Haran; and	3205
	11:27	and Haran; and Haran **b** Lot.	3205
	22:23	Bethuel **b** Rebekah: these eight Milcah did	3205
	25: 3	Jokshan **b** Sheba, and Dedan. And the sons	3205
	25:19	of Isaac, Abraham's son: Abraham **b** Isaac:	3205
Lev	25:45	*are* with you, which they **b** in your land:	3205
Nu	26:29	Machir **b** Gilead: of Gilead *come*	3205
	26:58	of the Korahites. And Kohath **b** Amram.	3205
Dt	32:18	Of the Rock *that* **b** thee thou art unmindful,	3205
Jdg	11: 1	the son of a harlot: and Gilead **b** Jephthah.	3205
Ru	4:18	generations of Pharez: Pharez **b** Hezron,	3205
	4:19	Hezron **b** Ram, and Ram begat	3205
	4:19	begat Ram, and Ram **b** Amminadab,	3205
	4:20	Amminadab **b** Nahshon, and	3205
	4:20	begat Nahshon, and Nahshon **b** Salmon,	3205
	4:21	And Salmon **b** Boaz, and Boaz begat Obed,	3205
	4:21	And Salmon begat Boaz, and Boaz **b** Obed,	3205
	4:22	And Obed **b** Jesse, and Jesse begat David.	3205
	4:22	And Obed begat Jesse, and Jesse **b** David.	3205
1Ch	1:10	Cush **b** Nimrod: he began to be mighty	3205
	1:11	Mizraim **b** Ludim, and Anamim, and	3205
	1:13	Canaan **b** Zidon his firstborn, and Heth,	3205
	1:18	Arphaxad **b** Shelah, and Shelah begat Eber.	3205
	1:18	Arphaxad begat Shelah, and Shelah **b** Eber.	3205
	1:20	Joktan **b** Almodad, and Sheleph, and	3205
	1:34	Abraham **b** Isaac. The sons of Isaac; Esau	3205
	2:10	Ram **b** Amminadab; and Amminadab begat	3205
	2:10	Amminadab **b** Nahshon, prince of	3205
	2:11	Nahshon **b** Salma, and Salma begat Boaz,	3205
	2:11	Nahshon begat Salma, and Salma **b** Boaz,	3205
	2:12	And Boaz **b** Obed, and Obed begat Jesse,	3205
	2:12	And Boaz begat Obed, and Obed **b** Jesse,	3205
	2:13	Jesse **b** his firstborn Eliab, and	3205
	2:18	Caleb the son of Hezron **b** *children* of	3205
	2:20	And Hur **b** Uri, and Uri begat Bezaleel.	3205
	2:20	And Hur begat Uri, and Uri **b** Bezaleel.	3205
	2:22	Segub **b** Jair, who had three and	3205
	2:36	Attai **b** Nathan, and Nathan begat Zabad,	3205
	2:36	Attai begat Nathan, and Nathan **b** Zabad,	3205
	2:37	Zabad **b** Ephlal, and Ephlal begat Obed,	3205
	2:37	Zabad begat Ephlal, and Ephlal **b** Obed,	3205
	2:38	And Obed **b** Jehu, and Jehu begat Azariah,	3205
	2:38	And Obed begat Jehu, and Jehu **b** Azariah,	3205
	2:39	Azariah **b** Helez, and Helez begat Eleasah,	3205
	2:39	Azariah begat Helez, and Helez **b** Eleasah,	3205
	2:40	Eleasah **b** Sisamai, and Sisamai begat	3205
	2:40	begat Sisamai, and Sisamai **b** Shallum,	3205
	2:41	Shallum **b** Jekamiah, and Jekamiah begat	3205
	2:41	begat Jekamiah, and Jekamiah **b** Elishama.	3205
	2:44	Shema **b** Raham, the father of Jorkoam:	3205
	2:44	father of Jorkoam: and Rekem **b** Shammai.	3205
	2:46	and Moza, and Gazez: and Haran **b** Gazez.	3205
	4: 2	And Reaiah the son of Shobal **b** Jahath; and	3205
	4: 2	and Jahath **b** Ahumai, and Lahad.	3205
	4: 8	Coz **b** Anub, and Zobebah, and the families	3205
	4:11	Chelub the brother of Shuah **b** Mehir,	3205
	4:12	Eshton **b** Beth-rapha, and Paseah, and	3205
	4:14	Meonothai **b** Ophrah: and Seraiah begat	3205
	4:14	Seraiah **b** Joab, the father of the valley of	3205
	6: 4	Eleazar **b** Phinehas, Phinehas begat	3205
	6: 4	begat Phinehas, Phinehas **b** Abishua,	3205
	6: 5	Abishua **b** Bukki, and Bukki begat Uzzi,	3205
	6: 5	Abishua begat Bukki, and Bukki **b** Uzzi,	3205
	6: 6	Uzzi **b** Zerahiah, and Zerahiah begat	3205
	6: 6	begat Zerahiah, and Zerahiah **b** Meraioth,	3205
	6: 7	Meraioth **b** Amariah, and Amariah begat	3205
	6: 7	begat Amariah, and Amariah **b** Ahitub,	3205
	6: 8	Ahitub **b** Zadok, and Zadok begat	3205
	6: 8	begat Zadok, and Zadok **b** Ahimaaz,	3205
	6: 9	Ahimaaz **b** Azariah, and Azariah begat	3205
	6: 9	begat Azariah, and Azariah **b** Johanan,	3205
	6:10	Johanan **b** Azariah, (he *it is* that executed	3205
	6:11	Azariah **b** Amariah, and Amariah begat	3205
	6:11	begat Amariah, and Amariah **b** Ahitub,	3205
	6:12	Ahitub **b** Zadok, and Zadok begat Shallum,	3205
	6:12	Ahitub begat Zadok, and Zadok **b** Shallum,	3205
	6:13	Shallum **b** Hilkiah, and Hilkiah begat	3205
	6:13	begat Hilkiah, and Hilkiah **b** Azariah,	3205
	6:14	Azariah **b** Seraiah, and Seraiah begat	3205
	6:14	begat Seraiah, and Seraiah **b** Jehozadak,	3205
	7:32	Heber **b** Japhlet, and Shomer, and Hotham,	3205
	8: 1	Now Benjamin **b** Bela his firstborn,	3205
	8: 7	he removed them, and **b** Uzza, and Ahihud.	3205
	8: 8	Shaharaim **b** *children* in the country of	3205
	8: 9	he **b** of Hodesh his wife, Jobab, and Zibia,	3205
	8:11	And of Hushim he **b** Abitub, and Elpaal.	3205
	8:32	Mikloth **b** Shimeah. And these also dwelt	3205
	8:33	Ner **b** Kish, and Kish begat Saul, and	3205
	8:33	Kish **b** Saul, and Saul begat Jonathan, and	3205
	8:33	Saul **b** Jonathan, and Malchishua, and	3205
	8:34	*was* Merib-baal; and Merib-baal **b** Micah.	3205
	8:36	Ahaz **b** Jehoadah; and Jehoadah begat	3205
	8:36	Jehoadah **b** Alemeth, and Azmaveth, and	3205
	8:36	and Zimri; and Zimri **b** Moza,	3205
	8:37	Moza **b** Binea: Rapha *was* his son,	3205
	9:38	Mikloth **b** Shimeam. And they also dwelt	3205
	9:39	Ner **b** Kish; and Kish begat Saul; and	3205
	9:39	Kish **b** Saul; and Saul begat Jonathan, and	3205
	9:39	Saul **b** Jonathan, and Malchishua, and	3205
	9:40	*was* Merib-baal: and Merib-baal **b** Micah.	3205
	9:42	Ahaz **b** Jarah; and Jarah begat Alemeth,	3205
	9:42	Jarah **b** Alemeth, and Azmaveth, and	3205
	9:42	and Zimri; and Zimri **b** Moza;	3205
	9:43	Moza **b** Binea; and Rephaiah his son,	3205
	14: 3	and David **b** moe sons and daughters.	3205
2Ch	11:21	**b** twenty and eight sons, and	3205
	13:21	**b** twenty and two sons, and	3205
	24: 3	two wives; and he **b** sons and daughters.	3205
Ne	12:10	Jeshua **b** Joiakim, Joiakim also begat	3205
	12:10	Joiakim also **b** Eliashib, and Eliashib begat	3205
	12:10	also begat Eliashib, and Eliashib **b** Joiada,	NIH
	12:11	Joiada **b** Jonathan, and Jonathan begat	3205
	12:11	begat Jonathan, and Jonathan **b** Jaddua.	3205
Pr	23:22	Hearken unto thy father that **b** thee, and	3205
Jer	16: 3	concerning their fathers that **b** them in this	3205
Da	11: 6	he that **b** her, and he that strengthened her	3205
Zec	13: 3	his mother that **b** him shall say unto him,	3205
	13: 3	his mother that **b** him shall thrust him	3205
Mt	1: 2	Abraham **b** Isaac; and Isaac begat Jacob;	*1080*
	1: 2	and Isaac **b** Jacob; and Jacob begat Judas	*1080*
	1: 2	and Jacob **b** Judas and his brethren;	*1080*
	1: 3	And Judas **b** Phares and Zara of Thamar;	*1080*
	1: 3	and Phares **b** Esrom; and Esrom begat	*1080*
	1: 3	Phares begat Esrom; and Esrom **b** Aram;	*1080*
	1: 4	And Aram **b** Aminadab; and	*1080*
	1: 4	and Aminadab **b** Naasson; and	*1080*
	1: 4	begat Naasson; and Naasson **b** Salmon;	*1080*
	1: 5	And Salmon **b** Booz of Rachab; and	*1080*
	1: 5	and Booz **b** Obed of Ruth; and Obed begat	*1080*
	1: 5	begat Obed of Ruth; and Obed **b** Jesse;	*1080*
	1: 6	And Jesse **b** David the king; and David	*1080*
	1: 6	David the king **b** Solomon of *her that had*	*1080*
	1: 7	And Solomon **b** Roboam; and	*1080*
	1: 7	and Roboam **b** Abia; and Abia begat Asa;	*1080*
	1: 7	and Roboam begat Abia; and Abia **b** Asa;	*1080*
	1: 8	And Asa **b** Josaphat; and Josaphat begat	*1080*
	1: 8	and Josaphat **b** Joram; and Joram begat	*1080*
	1: 8	Josaphat begat Joram; and Joram **b** Ozias;	*1080*
	1: 9	And Ozias **b** Joatham; and Joatham begat	*1080*
	1: 9	and Joatham **b** Achaz; and Achaz begat	*1080*
	1: 9	begat Achaz; and Achaz **b** Ezekias;	*1080*
	1:10	And Ezekias **b** Manasses; and	*1080*
	1:10	and Manasses **b** Amon; and Amon begat	*1080*
	1:10	Manasses begat Amon; and Amon **b** Josias;	*1080*

Mt 1:11 And Josias **b** Jechonias and his brethren, *1080*
1:12 brought to Babylon, Jechonias **b** Salathiel; *1080*
1:12 begat Salathiel; and Salathiel **b** Zorobabel; *1080*
1:13 And Zorobabel **b** Abiud; and Abiud begat *1080*
1:13 and Abiud **b** Eliakim; and Eliakim begat *1080*
1:13 Abiud begat Eliakim; and Eliakim **b** Azor; *1080*
1:14 And Azor **b** Sadoc; and Sadoc begat *1080*
1:14 and Sadoc **b** Achim; and Achim begat *1080*
1:14 Sadoc begat Achim; and Achim **b** Eliud; *1080*
1:15 And Eliud **b** Eleazar; and Eleazar begat *1080*
1:15 and Eleazar **b** Matthan; and Matthan begat *1080*
1:15 begat Matthan; and Matthan **b** Jacob; *1080*
1:16 And Jacob **b** Joseph the husband of Mary, *1080*
Ac 7: 8 and so *Abraham* **b** Isaac, and *1080*
7: 8 and Isaac ***b*** Jacob; and Jacob *begat* NIG
7: 8 and Jacob ***b*** the twelve patriarchs. NIG
7:29 in the land of Madian, where he **b** two sons. *1080*
Jas 1:18 Of his own will **b** he us with the word of *616*
1Jn 5: 1 every one that loveth him that **b** loveth him *1080*

BEGET (10) [BEGAT, BEGETTEST, BEGETTETH, BEGOTTEN, FIRSTBEGOTTEN]
Ge 17:20 twelve princes shall he **b**, and I will make 3205
Dt 4:25 When thou shalt **b** children, and 3205
28:41 Thou shalt **b** sons and daughters, but 3205
2Ki 20:18 which thou shalt **b**, shall they take *away;* 3205
Ecc 6: 3 If a man **b** an hundred *children,* and 3205
Isa 39: 7 which thou shalt **b**, shall they take away; 3205
Jer 29: 6 Take ye wives, and **b** sons and daughters; 3205
Eze 18:10 If he **b** a son *that is* a robber, a shedder of 3205
18:14 Now lo, *if* he **b** a son, that seeth all his 3205
47:22 which shall **b** children among you: 3205

BEGETTEST (2) [BEGET]
Ge 48: 6 which thou **b** after them, shall be thine, *and* 3205
Isa 45:10 him that saith unto *his* father, What **b** thou? 3205

BEGETTETH (3) [BEGET]
Pr 17:21 He that **b** a fool *doeth it* to his sorrow: and 3205
23:24 he that **b** a wise *child* shall have joy of him. 3205
Ecc 5:14 he **b** a son, and *there is* nothing in his hand. 3205

BEGGAR (3) [BEG]
1Sa 2: 8 *and* lifteth up the **b** from the dunghill, to set 34
Lk 16:20 And there was a certain **b** named Lazarus, *4434*
16:22 And it came to pass that the **b** died, and *4434*

BEGGARLY (1) [BEG]
Gal 4: 9 turn ye again to the weak and **b** elements, *4434*

BEGGED (3) [BEG]
Mt 27:58 He went to Pilate, and **b** the body of Jesus. *154*
Lk 23:52 went unto Pilate, and **b** the body of Jesus. *154*
Jn 9: 8 said, Is not this he that sat and **b**? *4319*

BEGGING (3) [BEG]
Ps 37:25 righteous forsaken, nor his seed **b** bread. 1245
Mk 10:46 son of Timeus, sat by the *high*way side **b**. *4319*
Lk 18:35 a certain blind man sat by the way side **b**: *4319*

BEGIN (27) [BEGAN, BEGINNEST, BEGINNING, BEGINNINGS, BEGUN]
Ge 11: 6 all one language; and this they **b** to do: 2490
Dt 2:24 **b** to possess *it,* and contend with him *in* 2490
2:25 This day will I **b** to put the dread of thee 2490
2:31 **b** to possess, that *thou* mayest inherit his 2490
16: 9 **b** to number the seven weeks from *such* 2490
Jos 3: 7 This day will I **b** to magnify thee in 2490
Jdg 10:18 What man *is he* that will **b** to fight against 2490
13: 5 he shall **b** to deliver Israel out of the hand 2490
1Sa 3:12 when I **b**, I will also make an end. 2490
22:15 Did I then **b** to inquire of God for him? 2490
2Ki 8:25 the son of Jehoram king of Judah ***b*** to reign. NIH
Ne 11:17 *was* the principal to **b** the thanksgiving in 8462
Jer 25:29 I **b** to bring evil on the city which is called 2490
Eze 9: 6 whom *is* the mark; and **b** at my sanctuary. 2490
Mt 24:49 And shall **b** to smite *his* fellowservants, and *756*
Lk 3: 8 and **b** not to say within yourselves, *756*
12:45 and shall **b** to beat the menservants and *756*
13:25 and ye **b** to stand without, and to knock at *756*
13:26 Then shall ye **b** to say, We have eaten and *756*
14: 9 thou **b** with shame to take the lowest room. *756*
14:29 is not able to finish *it,* all that behold *it* **b** to *756*
21:28 And when these *things* **b** to come to pass, *756*
23:30 Then shall they **b** to say to the mountains, *756*
2Co 3: 1 Do we **b** again to commend ourselves? or *756*
1Pe 4:17 For the time *is come* that judgment must **b** at *756*
4:17 and if *it* first **b** at us, what *shall* the end *be* NIG
Rev 10: 7 when he shall **b to** sound, the mystery of *3195*

BEGINNEST (1) [BEGIN]
Dt 16: 9 *time as thou* **b** *to put* the sickle to the corn. 2490

BEGINNING (106) [BEGIN]
Ge 1: 1 In the **b** God created the heaven and 7225
10:10 the **b** of his kingdom was Babel, and Erech, 7225
13: 3 the place where his tent had been at the **b**, 8462
41:21 but they *were still* ill favoured, as at the **b**. 8462
49: 3 my might, and the **b** of my strength, 7225
Ex 12: 2 This month *shall be* unto you the **b** of 7218
Dt 11:12 from the **b** of the year even unto the end of 7225
21:17 for he *is* the **b** of his strength; the right of 7225
32:42 from the **b** of revenges upon the enemy. 7218
Jdg 7:19 came unto the outside of the camp *in* the **b** 7218
Ru 1:22 they came *to* Beth-lehem in the **b** of barley 8462
3:10 kindness in the latter end than at the **b**, 7223
2Sa 21: 9 in the first *days,* in the **b** of barley harvest. 8462
21:10 from the **b** of harvest until water dropped 8462
2Ki 17:25 *so* it was at the **b** of their dwelling there, 8462
1Ch 17: 9 waste them any more, as at the **b**, 7223
Ezr 4: 6 reign of Ahasuerus, in the **b** of his reign, 8462
Job 8: 7 Though thy **b** was small, yet thy latter end 7225
42:12 the latter end of Job more than his **b**: 7225
Ps 111:10 The fear of the LORD *is* the **b** of wisdom: 7225
119:160 Thy word *is* true *from* the **b**: and every one 7218
Pr 1: 7 The fear of the LORD *is* the **b** of 7225
8:22 The LORD possessed me *in* the **b** of his 7225
8:23 from the **b**, or ever the earth was. 7218
9:10 The fear of the LORD *is* the **b** of wisdom: 8462
17:14 The **b** of strife *is as* when one letteth out 7225
20:21 inheritance *may be* gotten hastily at the **b**; 7223
Ecc 3:11 that God maketh from the **b** to the end. 7218
7: 8 Better *is* the end of a thing than the **b** 7225
10:13 The **b** of the words of his mouth *is* 8462
Isa 1:26 at the first, and thy counsellors as at the **b**: 8462
18: 2 to a people terrible **from** their **b** hitherto; 4480
18: 7 from a people terrible **from** their **b** hitherto; 4480
40:21 hath it not been told you from the **b**? 7218
41: 4 done *it,* calling the generations from the **b**? 7218
41:26 Who hath declared from the **b**, that we may 7218
46:10 Declaring the end from the **b**, and 7225
48: 3 have declared the former *things* from **the b**; 227
48: 5 I have even from **the b** declared *it* to thee; 227
48: 7 They are created now, and not from **the b**; 227
48:16 I have not spoken in secret from the **b**; 7218
64: 4 For **since the b of the world** *men* 4480+5769
Jer 17:12 A glorious high throne from the **b** *is* 7223
26: 1 In the **b** of the reign of Jehoiakim the son 7225
27: 1 In the **b** of the reign of Jehoiakim the son 7225
28: 1 in the **b** of the reign of Zedekiah king of 7225
49:34 **b** of the reign of Zedekiah king of Judah, 7225
La 2:19 in the **b** of the watches, pour out thine heart 7218
Eze 40: 1 in the **b** of the year, in the tenth *day* of 7218
Da 9:21 whom I had seen in the vision at the **b**, 8462
9:23 At the **b** of thy supplications 8462
Hos 1: 2 The **b** of the word of the LORD by Hosea. 8462
Am 7: 1 he formed grasshoppers in the **b** of 8462
Mic 1:13 she *is* the **b** of the sin to the daughter of 7225
Mt 14:30 and **b** to sink, he cried, saying, Lord, *756*
19: 4 that he which made *them* at the **b** made them *746*
19: 8 your wives: but from the **b** it was not so. *746*
20: 8 them *their* hire, **b** from the last unto the first. *756*
24: 8 All these *are* the **b** of sorrows. *746*
24:21 such as was not since the **b** of the world to *746*
Mk 1: 1 The **b** of the gospel of Jesus Christ, the Son *746*
10: 6 But from the **b** of the creation God made *746*
13:19 such as was not from the **b** of the creation *746*
Lk 1: 2 which from the **b** were eyewitnesses, and *746*
23: 5 all Jewry, **b** from Galilee to this place. *756*
24:27 And **b** at Moses and all the prophets, *756*
24:47 his name among all nations, **b** at Jerusalem. *756*
Jn 1: 1 In the **b** was the Word, and the Word was *746*
1: 2 The same was in the **b** with God. *746*
2:10 Every man **at the b** doth set forth good *4412*
2:11 This **b** of miracles did Jesus in Cana of *746*
6:64 For Jesus knew from the **b** who they were *746*
8: 9 by one, **b** at the eldest, *even* unto the last: *756*
8:25 the same that I said unto you *from* the **b**. *746*
8:44 He was a murderer from the **b**, and *746*

Jn 15:27 because ye have been with me from the **b**. 746
16: 4 And these *things* I said not unto you at the **b**, 746
Ac 1:22 **B** from the baptism of John, unto *that same* 756
11: 4 But Peter *rehearsed the matter* **from the b**, 756
11:15 Holy Ghost fell on them, as on us at the **b**. 746
15:18 are all his works **from** the **b** of the world. 575
26: 5 Which knew me **from** the **b**, if they would 509
Eph 3: 9 which from the **b of the world** hath been hid 165
Php 4:15 know also, that in the **b** of the gospel, 746
Col 1:18 who is the **b**, the firstborn from the dead; 746
2Th 2:13 God hath from the **b** chosen you to salvation 746
Heb 1:10 in the **b** hast laid the foundation of the earth; 746
3:14 if we hold the **b** of *our* confidence stedfast 746
7: 3 having neither **b** of days, nor end of life; 746
2Pe 2:20 the latter *end* is worse with them than the **b**. 4413
3: 4 all *things* continue as *they were* from the **b** 746
1Jn 1: 1 *That* which was from the **b**, which we have 746
2: 7 old commandment which ye had from the **b**. 746
2: 7 is the word which ye have heard from the **b**. 746
2:13 ye have known him that is from the **b**. 746
2:14 ye have known him that is from the **b**. 746
2:24 in you, which ye have heard from the **b**. 746
2:24 If *that* which ye have heard from the **b** shall 746
3: 8 of the devil; for the devil sinneth from the **b**. 746
3:11 this is the message that ye heard from the **b**, 746
2Jn 1: 5 but *that* which we had from the **b**, that we 746
1: 6 That, as ye have heard from the **b**, ye should 746
Rev 1: 8 am Alpha and Omega, the **b** and the ending, 746
3:14 true witness, the **b** of the creation of God; 746
21: 6 I am Alpha and Omega, the **b** and the end. 746
22:13 the **b** and the end, the first and the last. 746

BEGINNINGS (4) [BEGIN]

Nu 10:10 solemn days, and in the **b** of your months, 7218
28:11 in the **b** of your months ye shall offer a 7218
Eze 36:11 and will do better *unto you* than at your **b**: 7221
Mk 13: 8 and troubles: these *are* the **b** of sorrows. 746

BEGOTTEN (24) [BEGET]

Ge 5: 4 the days of Adam after he had **b** Seth were 3205
Lev 18:11 **b** of thy father, she *is* thy sister, thou shalt 4138
Nu 11:12 have I **b** them, that thou shouldest say unto 3205
Dt 23: 8 The children that are **b** of them shall enter 3205
Jdg 8:30 had threescore and ten sons of his body **b**: 3318
Job 38:28 a father? or who hath **b** the drops of dew? 3205
Ps 2: 7 Thou *art* my Son; *this* day have I **b** thee. 3205
Isa 49:21 Who hath **b** me these, seeing I have lost my 3205
Hos 5: 7 for they have **b** strange children: now shall 3205
Jn 1:14 the glory as of the **only b** of the Father,) 3439
1:18 the **only b** Son, which is in the bosom of 3439
3:16 the world, that he gave his **only b** Son, 3439
3:18 in the name of the **only b** Son of God. 3439
Ac 13:33 Thou art my Son, this day have I **b** thee. 1080
1Co 4:15 for in Christ Jesus I have **b** you through 1080
Phm 1:10 whom I have **b** in my bonds: 1080
Heb 1: 5 Thou art my Son, this day have I **b** thee? 1080
5: 5 Thou art my Son, to day have I **b** thee. 1080
11:17 the promises offered up *his* **only b** *son,* 3439
1Pe 1: 3 **b** us **again** unto a lively hope by 313
1Jn 4: 9 that God sent his **only b** Son into the world, 3439
5: 1 that begat loveth him also that is **b** of him. 1080
5:18 but he that is **b** of God keepeth himself, 1080
Rev 1: 5 *and* the **first b** of the dead, and the prince 4416

BEGUILE (2) [BEGUILED, BEGUILING]

Col 2: 4 lest any *man* should **b** you with enticing 3884
2:18 Let no *man* **b** you **of** your **reward** in a 2603

BEGUILED (5) [BEGUILE]

Ge 3:13 The serpent **b** me, and I did eat. 5377
29:25 for Rachel? wherefore then hast thou **b** me? 7411
Nu 25:18 wherewith they have **b** you in the matter of 5230
Jos 9:22 Wherefore have ye **b** us, saying, 7411
2Co 11: 3 as the serpent **b** Eve through his subtilty, so 1818

BEGUILING (1) [BEGUILE]

2Pe 2:14 cannot cease from sin; **b** unstable souls: 1185

BEGUN (13) [BEGIN]

Nu 16:46 gone out from the LORD; the plague is **b**. 2490
16:47 the plague was **b** among the people: 2490
25: 1 the people **b** to commit whoredom with 2490
Dt 2:31 I have **b** to give Sihon and his land before 2490
3:24 thou hast **b** to shew thy servant thy 2490
Est 6:13 before whom thou hast **b** to fall, thou shalt 2490
9:23 the Jews undertook to do as they had **b**, 2490
Mt 18:24 And when he had **b** to reckon, one was 756
2Co 8: 6 that as he had **b**, so he would also finish in 4278
8:10 who have **b before**, not only to do, but 4278
Gal 3: 3 having **b** in the Spirit, are ye now made 1728
Php 1: 6 **b** a good work in you will perform *it* until 1728
1Ti 5:11 for when they have *b to* wax wanton against NIG

BEHALF (13) [BEHAVE, BEHAVED, BEHAVETH, BEHAVIOUR, BEHEADED]

Ex 27:21 **on the b of** the children of Israel. 854+4480
2Sa 3:12 Abner sent messengers to David **on his b**, 8478
2Ch 16: 9 to shew himself strong **in the b of** *them* 5973
Job 36: 2 thee that *I have* yet to speak **on** God's **b**. 3807.1
Da 11:18 a prince for his own **b** shall cause NIH
Ro 16:19 all *men.* I am glad therefore **on** your **b**: 1909
1Co 1: 4 I thank my God always **on** your **b**, for 4012
2Co 1:11 thanks may be given by many **on** our **b**. 5228
5:12 but give you occasion to glory **on** our **b**, 5228
8:24 of your love, and of our boasting **on** your **b**. 5228
9: 3 boasting of you should be in vain in this **b**; 3313
Php 1:29 For unto you it is given **in the b of** Christ, 5228
1Pe 4:16 but let him glorify God on this **b**. 3313

BEHAVE (6) [BEHALF]

Dt 32:27 adversaries should **b** themselves **strangely**, 5234
1Ch 19:13 let us **b** ourselves **valiantly** for our people, 2388
Ps 101: 2 I will **b** myself **wisely** in a perfect way. 7919
Isa 3: 5 the child shall **b** himself **proudly** against 7292
1Co 13: 5 Doth not **b** itself **unseemly**, seeketh not her 807
1Ti 3:15 oughtest to **b** thyself in the house of God, 390

BEHAVED (9) [BEHALF]

1Sa 18: 5 Saul sent him, *and* **b** himself **wisely**: 7919
18:14 David **b** himself **wisely** in all his ways; 7919
18:15 Saul saw that he **b** himself very **wisely**, 7919
18:30 *that* David **b** himself more **wisely** than all 7919
Ps 35:14 I **b** myself as though *he had been* my friend 1980
131: 2 Surely I have **b** and quieted myself, as a 7737
Mic 3: 4 as they have **b** themselves **ill** in their 7489
1Th 2:10 unblameably we **b** ourselves among you 1096
2Th 3: 7 for we **b** not ourselves **disorderly** among 812

BEHAVETH (1) [BEHALF]

1Co 7:36 *he* **b** himself **uncomely** toward his virgin, 807

BEHAVIOUR (4) [BEHALF]

1Sa 21:13 he changed his **b** before them, and 2940
Ps 34: T when he changed his **b** before Abimelech; 2940
1Ti 3: 2 vigilant, sober, of **good b**, given to 2887
Tit 2: 3 *that they be* in **b** as becometh holiness, 2688

BEHEADED (7) [BEHALF]

Dt 21: 6 hands over the heifer that is **b** in the valley: 6202
2Sa 4: 7 **b** him, and took his head, and 5493+7218
Mt 14:10 And he sent, and **b** John in the prison. 607
Mk 6:16 heard *thereof,* he said, It is John, whom I **b**: 607
6:27 and he went and **b** him in the prison, 607
Lk 9: 9 And Herod said, John have I **b**: but who is 607
Rev 20: 4 *I saw* the souls of them that were **b** for 3990

BEHELD (53) [BEHOLD]

Ge 12:14 the Egyptians **b** the woman that she *was* 7200
13:10 up his eyes, and **b** all the plain of Jordan, 7200
19:28 all the land of the plain, and **b**, and lo, 7200
31: 2 And Jacob **b** the countenance of Laban, and 7200
48: 8 Israel **b** Joseph's sons, and said, Who *are* 7200
Nu 21: 9 he **b** the serpent of brass, he lived. 413+5027
23:21 He hath not **b** iniquity in Jacob, 5027
Jdg 16:27 women, that **b** while Samson made sport. 7200
1Sa 26: 5 David **b** the place where Saul lay, and 7200
1Ch 21:15 the LORD **b**, and he repented him of 7200
Job 31:26 If I **b** the sun when it shined, or the moon 7200
Ps119:158 I **b** the transgressors, and was grieved; 7200
142: 4 **b**, but *there was* no man that would know 7200
Pr 7: 7 **b** among the simple ones, I discerned 7200
Ecc 8:17 I **b** all the work of God, that a man cannot 7200
Isa 41:28 For I **b**, and *there was* no man; 7200
Jer 4:23 I **b** the earth, and lo, *it was* without form, 7200
4:24 I **b** the mountains, and lo, they trembled, 7200
4:25 I **b**, and lo, *there was* no man, and all 7200
4:26 I **b**, and lo, the fruitful place *was* a 7200
31:26 Upon this I awaked, and **b**; and my sleep 7200
Eze 1:15 Now as I **b** the living creatures, behold one 7200
8: 2 I **b**, and lo, a likeness as the appearance of 7200

Eze 37: 8 when I **b**, lo, the sinews and the flesh came 7200
Da 7: 4 I **b** till the wings thereof were pluckt, and 2370
7: 6 After this I **b**, and lo another, like a 2370
7: 9 I **b** till the thrones were cast *down,* and 2370
7:11 I **b** then because of the voice of the great 2370
7:11 I **b** *even* till the beast *was* slain, and 2370
7:21 I **b**, and the same horn made war with 2370
Hab 3: 6 he **b**, and drove asunder the nations; and 7200
Mt 19:26 But Jesus **b** *them,* and said unto them, *1689*
Mk 9:15 when they **b** him, were greatly amazed, and *1492*
12:41 **b** how the people cast money into *2334*
15:47 Mary *the mother* of Joses **b** where he was *2334*
Lk 10:18 I **b** Satan as lightning fall from heaven. *2334*
19:41 come near, he **b** the city, and wept over it, *1492*
20:17 And he **b** them, and said, What is this then *1689*
22:56 But a certain maid **b** him as he sat by *1492*
23:55 and **b** the sepulchre, and how his body was *2300*
24:12 he **b** the linen clothes laid by themselves, *991*
Jn 1:14 and dwelt among us, (and we **b** his glory, *2300*
1:42 And when Jesus **b** him, he said, Thou art *1689*
Ac 1: 9 he had spoken these *things,* while they **b**, *991*
17:23 For as I passed by, and **b** your devotions, *333*
Rev 5: 6 And I **b**, and lo, in the midst of the throne *1492*
5:11 And I **b**, and I heard the voice of many *1492*
6: 5 And I **b**, and lo a black horse; and he that *1492*
6:12 And I **b** when he had opened the sixth seal, *1492*
7: 9 After this I **b**, and lo, a great multitude, *1492*
8:13 And I **b**, and heard an angel flying through *1492*
11:12 in a cloud; and their enemies **b** them. *2334*
13:11 And I **b** another beast coming up out of *1492*

BEHEMOTH (1)
Job 40:15 Behold now **b**, which I made with thee; 930

BEHIND (74) See Index

BEHOLD (1326) [BEHELD, BEHOLDEST, BEHOLDETH, BEHOLDING] See Index

BEHOLDEST (4) [BEHOLD]
Ps 10:14 Thou hast seen *it;* for thou **b** mischief and 5027
Mt 7: 3 And why **b** thou the mote that is in thy *991*
Lk 6:41 And why **b** thou the mote that is in thy *991*
6:42 when thou thyself **b** not the beam that is in *991*

BEHOLDETH (4) [BEHOLD]
Job 24:18 he **b** not the way of the vineyards. 6437
41:34 He **b** all high *things:* he *is* a king over all 7200
Ps 33:13 from heaven; he **b** all the sons of men. 7200
Jas 1:24 For he **b** himself, and goeth his way, and *2657*

BEHOLDING (15) [BEHOLD]
Ps 119:37 Turn away mine eyes from **b** vanity; *and* 7200
Pr 15: 3 *are* in every place, **b** the evil and the good. 6822
Ecc 5:11 saving the **b** *of them* with their eyes? 7207
Mt 27:55 And many women were there **b** afar off, *2334*
Mk 10:21 Then Jesus **b** him loved him, and said unto *1689*
Lk 23:35 And the people stood **b**. And the rulers also *2334*
23:48 **b** the *things* which were done, smote their *2334*
23:49 from Galilee, stood afar off, **b** these *things.* *3708*
Ac 4:14 And **b** the man which was healed standing *991*
8:13 **b** *the* miracles and signs *which were* done. *2334*
14: 9 who **stedfastly b** him, and perceiving that he *816*
23: 1 **earnestly b** the council, said, Men *and* *816*
2Co 3:18 with open face **b as in a glass** the glory of *2734*
Col 2: 5 joying and **b** your order, and the stedfastness *991*
Jas 1:23 he is like unto a man **b** his natural face in a *2657*

BEHOVED (2)
Lk 24:46 and thus it **b** Christ to suffer, and to rise *1163*
Heb 2:17 Wherefore in all *things* it **b** him to be made *3784*

BEING (291) [BE] See Index

BEKAH (1)
Ex 38:26 A **b** for every man, *that is,* half a shekel, 1235

BEKER See BACHRITES; BECHER

BEL (3)
Isa 46: 1 **B** boweth down, Nebo stoopeth, their idols 1078
Jer 50: 2 say, Babylon is taken, **B** is confounded, 1078
51:44 I will punish **B** in Babylon, and I will bring 1078

BELA (13) [BELAH, BELAITES]
Ge 14: 2 and the king of **B**, which *is* Zoar. 1106
14: 8 and the king of **B** (the same *is* Zoar); 1106
36:32 **B** the son of Beor reigned in Edom: and 1106
36:33 **B** died, and Jobab the son of Zerah of 1106
Nu 26:38 of **B**, the family of the Belaites: of Ashbel, 1106
26:40 the sons of **B** were Ard and Naaman: 1106
1Ch 1:43 the children of Israel; **B** the son of Beor: 1106
1:44 when **B** was dead, Jobab the son of Zerah 1106
5: 8 **B** the son of Azaz, the son of Shema, 1106
7: 6 **B**, and Becher, and Jediael, three. 1106
7: 7 the sons of **B**; Ezbon, and Uzzi, and Uzziel, 1106
8: 1 Now Benjamin begat **B** his firstborn, 1106
8: 3 the sons of **B** were, Addar, and Gera, and 1106

BELAH (1) [BELA]
Ge 46:21 the sons of Benjamin *were* **B**, and Becher, 1106

BELAITES (1) [BELA]
Nu 26:38 of Bela, the family of the **B**: of Ashbel, 1108

BELCH (1)
Ps 59: 7 Behold, they **b out** with their mouth: 5042

BELIAL (17)
Dt 13:13 *Certain* men, the children of **B**, are gone 1100
Jdg 19:22 the men of the city, certain sons of **B**, 1100
20:13 deliver *us* the men, the children of **B**, 1100
1Sa 1:16 not thine handmaid for a daughter of **B**: 1100
2:12 Now the sons of Eli *were* sons of **B**; 1100
10:27 the children of **B** said, How shall this *man* 1100
25:17 for he *is such* a son of **B**, that *a man* cannot 1100
25:25 I pray thee, regard this man of **B**, 1100
30:22 answered all the wicked men and *men* of **B**, 1100
2Sa 16: 7 thou bloody man, and thou man of **B**: 1100
20: 1 there happened to be there a man of **B**, 1100
23: 6 *the sons of* **B** *shall be* all of them as thorns 1100
1Ki 21:10 set two men, sons of **B**, before him, to bear 1100
21:13 two men, children of **B**, and sat before him: 1100
21:13 the men of **B** witnessed against him, 1100
2Ch 13: 7 the children of **B**, and have strengthened 1100
2Co 6:15 And what concord hath Christ with **B**? or *955*

BELIED (1)
Jer 5:12 They have **b** the LORD, and said, *It is* not 3584

BELIEF (1) [BELIEVE]
2Th 2:13 of the Spirit and **b** of the truth: *4102*

BELIEVE (144) [BELIEF, BELIEVED, BELIEVERS, BELIEVEST, BELIEVETH, BELIEVING, UNBELIEF]
Ex 4: 1 and said, But behold, they will not **b** me, 539
4: 5 That they may **b** that the LORD God of 539
4: 8 it shall come to pass, if they will not **b** thee, 539
4: 8 that they will **b** the voice of the latter sign. 539
4: 9 if they will not **b** also these two signs, 539
19: 9 when I speak with thee, and **b** thee for ever. 539
Nu 14:11 how long will it be ere they **b** me, for all 539
Dt 1:32 Yet in this thing ye did not **b** the LORD 539
2Ki 17:14 that did not **b** in the LORD their God. 539
2Ch 20:20 **B** in the LORD your God, so shall you be 539
20:20 **b** his prophets, so shall ye prosper. 539
32:15 you on this *manner,* neither yet **b** him: 539
Job 9:16 *yet* would I not **b** that he had hearkened unto 539
39:12 Wilt thou **b** him, that he will bring home thy 539
Pr 26:25 When he speaketh fair, **b** him not: for *there* 539
Isa 7: 9 If ye will not **b**, surely ye shall not be 539
43:10 that ye may know and **b** me, and 539
Jer 12: 6 **b** them not, though they speak fair *words* 539
Hab 1: 5 *which* ye will not **b**, though it be told *you.* 539
Mt 9:28 unto them, **B** ye that I am able to do this? *4100*
18: 6 one of these little ones which **b** in me, *4100*
21:25 say unto us, Why did ye not then **b** him? *4100*
21:32 not afterward, that *ye* might **b** him. *4100*
24:23 Lo, here *is* Christ, or there; **b** *it* not. *4100*
24:26 *he is* in the secret chambers; **b** *it* not. *4100*
27:42 down from the cross, and we will **b** him. *4100*
Mk 1:15 God is at hand: repent ye, and **b** the gospel. *4100*
5:36 of the synagogue, Be not afraid, only **b**. *4100*
9:23 Jesus said unto him, If thou canst **b**, *4100*
9:24 cried out, and said with tears, Lord, I **b**; *4100*
9:42 offend one of *these* little ones that **b** in me, *4100*
11:23 shall **b** that *those things* which he saith *4100*
11:24 **b** that ye receive *them,* and ye shall have *4100*
11:31 he will say, Why then did ye not **b** him? *4100*
13:21 here *is* Christ; or lo, *he is* there; **b** *him* not: *4100*
15:32 now from the cross, that we may see and **b**. *4100*

Mk 16:17 And these signs shall follow them that **b**; *4100*
Lk 8:12 lest they should **b** and be saved. *4100*
8:13 which for a while **b**, and in time of *4100*
8:50 **b** only, and she shall be made whole. *4100*
22:67 said unto them, If I tell you, you will not **b**: *4100*
24:25 slow of heart to **b** all that the prophets have *4100*
Jn 1: 7 that all *men* through him might **b**. *4100*
1:12 of God, *even* to them that **b** on his name: *4100*
3:12 I have told you earthly *things,* and ye **b** not, *4100*
3:12 and ye believe not, how shall ye **b**, *4100*
4:21 unto her, Woman, **b** me, the hour cometh, *4100*
4:42 *Now* we **b**, not because of thy saying: *4100*
4:48 ye see signs and wonders, ye will not **b**. *4100*
5:38 for whom he hath sent, him ye **b** not. *4100*
5:44 How can ye **b**, which receive honour one of *4100*
5:47 But if ye **b** not his writings, how shall ye *4100*
5:47 not his writings, how shall ye **b** my words? *4100*
6:29 that ye **b** on *him* whom he hath sent. *4100*
6:30 thou then, that we may see, and **b** thee? *4100*
6:36 That ye also have seen me, and **b** not. *4100*
6:64 But there are some of you that **b** not. *4100*
6:69 And we **b** and are sure that thou art *that* *4100*
7: 5 For neither did his brethren **b** in him. *4100*
7:39 which they that **b** on him should receive: *4100*
8:24 for if ye **b** not that I am *he,* ye shall die in *4100*
8:45 because I tell *you* the truth, ye **b** me not. *4100*
8:46 And if I say the truth, why do ye not **b** me? *4100*
9:18 But the Jews did not **b** concerning him, *4100*
9:35 unto him, Dost thou **b** on the Son of God? *4100*
9:36 Who is he, Lord, that I might **b** on him? *4100*
9:38 And he said, Lord, I **b**. And he worshipped *4100*
10:25 answered them, I told you, and ye **b** not: *4100*
10:26 But ye **b** not, because ye are not of my *4100*
10:37 I do not the works of my Father, **b** me not. *4100*
10:38 But if I do, though ye **b** not me, believe *4100*
10:38 though ye believe not me, **b** the works: *4100*
10:38 that ye may know, and **b**, that the Father *is* *4100*
11:15 that I was not there, to the intent ye may **b**; *4100*
11:27 I **b** that thou art the Christ, the Son of God, *4100*
11:40 I not unto thee, that, if thou wouldest **b**, *4100*
11:42 *it,* that they may **b** that thou hast sent me. *4100*
11:48 let him thus alone, all *men* will **b** on him: *4100*
12:36 While ye have light, **b** in the light, that ye *4100*
12:39 Therefore they could not **b**, because *4100*
12:47 hear my words, and **b** not, I judge him not: *4100*
13:19 it is come to pass, ye may **b** that I am *he.* *4100*
14: 1 ye **b** in God, believe also in me. *4100*
14: 1 ye believe in God, **b** also in me. *4100*
14:11 **B** me that I *am* in the Father, and the Father *4100*
14:11 or else **b** me for the very works' sake. *4100*
14:29 that, when it is come to pass, ye might **b**. *4100*
16: 9 Of sin, because they **b** not on me; *4100*
16:30 by this we **b** that thou camest forth from *4100*
16:31 Jesus answered them, Do ye now **b**? *4100*
17:20 for them also which shall **b** on me through *4100*
17:21 that the world may **b** that thou hast sent me. *4100*
19:35 knoweth that he saith true, that ye might **b**. *4100*
20:25 thrust my hand into his side, I will not **b**. *4100*
20:31 that ye might **b** that Jesus is the Christ, *4100*
Ac 8:37 said, I **b** that Jesus Christ is the Son of God. *4100*
13:39 And by him all that **b** are justified from all *4100*
13:41 a work which you shall in no wise **b**, *4100*
15: 7 should hear the word of the gospel, and **b**. *4100*
15:11 But we **b** that through the grace of the Lord *4100*
16:31 **B** on the Lord Jesus Christ, and thou shalt *4100*
19: 4 that they should **b** on him which should *4100*
21:20 many thousands of Jews there are which **b**; *4100*
21:25 As touching the Gentiles which **b**, we have *4100*
27:25 for I **b** God, that it shall be even as it was *4100*
Ro 3: 3 For what if some did **not b**? shall their *569*
3:22 Christ unto all and upon all them that **b**: *4100*
4:11 he might be the father of all them that **b**, *4100*
4:24 if we **b** on him that raised up Jesus our *4100*
6: 8 we **b** that we shall also live with him: *4100*
10: 9 shalt **b** in thine heart that God hath raised *4100*
10:14 how shall they **b** *in him* of whom they have *4100*
15:31 delivered from them that do **not b** in Judea; *544*
1Co 1:21 of preaching to save them that **b**. *4100*
10:27 If any of them that **b not** bid you *to a feast,* *571*
11:18 be divisions among you; and I partly **b** *it.* *4100*
14:22 not to them that **b**, but to them that believe *4100*
14:22 to them that believe, but to them that **b not**: *571*
14:22 prophesying *serveth* not for them that **b not**, *571*
14:22 that believe not, but for them which **b**. *4100*
2Co 4: 4 hath blinded the minds of them which **b not**, *571*
4:13 I spoken; we also **b**, and therefore speak; *4100*
Gal 3:22 Jesus Christ might be given to them that **b**. *4100*
Eph 1:19 greatness of his power to us-ward who **b**, *4100*
Php 1:29 not only to **b** on him, but also to suffer for *4100*
1Th 1: 7 So that ye were ensamples to all that **b** in *4100*
2:10 we behaved ourselves among you that **b**: *4100*
2:13 effectually worketh also in you that **b**. *4100*
4:14 For if we **b** that Jesus died and rose again, *4100*
2Th 1:10 and to be admired in all them that **b** *4100*
2:11 strong delusion, that they should **b** a lie: *4100*
1Ti 1:16 hereafter **b** on him to life everlasting. *4100*
4: 3 with thanksgiving of them which **b** *4103*
4:10 of all men, specially of those that **b**. *4103*
2Ti 2:13 If we **b not**, *yet* he abideth faithful: *569*
Heb 10:39 but of *them* that **b** to the saving of the soul. *4102*
11: 6 for he that cometh to God must **b** that he is, *4100*
Jas 2:19 dost well: the devils also **b**, and tremble. *4100*
1Pe 1:21 Who by him do **b** in God, that raised him *4100*
2: 7 Unto you therefore which **b** *he is* precious: *4100*
1Jn 3:23 That we should **b** on the name of his Son *4100*
4: 1 **b** not every spirit, but try the spirits *4100*
5:13 These *things* have I written unto you that **b** *4100*
5:13 that ye may **b** on the name of the Son of *4100*

BELIEVED (115) [BELIEVE]

Ge 15: 6 he **b** in the LORD; and he counted it to him 539
45:26 And *Jacob's* heart fainted, for he **b** them not. 539
Ex 4:31 the people **b**: and when they heard that 539
14:31 and **b** the LORD, and his servant Moses. 539
Nu 20:12 and Aaron, Because ye **b** me not, 539
Dt 9:23 and ye **b** him not, nor hearkened to his voice. 539
1Sa 27:12 Achish **b** David, saying, He hath made his 539
1Ki 10: 7 Howbeit I **b** not the words, until I came, and 539
2Ch 9: 6 Howbeit I **b** not their words, until I came, 539
Job 29:24 *If* I laughed on them, they **b** *it* not; and 539
Ps 27:13 *I had fainted,* unless I had **b** to see 539
78:22 Because they **b** not in God, and trusted not 539
78:32 and **b** not for his wondrous works. 539
106:12 Then **b** they his words; they sang his praise. 539
106:24 the pleasant land, they **b** not his word: 539
116:10 I **b**, therefore have I spoken: I was greatly 539
119:66 knowledge: for I have **b** thy commandments. 539
Isa 53: 1 Who hath **b** our report? and to whom is 539
Jer 40:14 But Gedaliah the son of Ahikam **b** them not. 539
La 4:12 would not have **b** that the adversary and 539
Da 6:23 found upon him, because he **b** in his God. 540
Jnh 3: 5 So the people of Nineveh **b** God, and 539
Mt 8:13 and as thou hast **b**, *so* be it done unto thee. *4100*
21:32 the way of righteousness, and ye **b** him not: *4100*
21:32 but the publicans and the harlots **b** him: and *4100*
Mk 16:11 was alive, and had been seen of her, **b not**. *569*
16:13 told *it* unto the residue: neither **b** they them. *4100*
16:14 they **b** not them which had seen him after *4100*
Lk 1: 1 things which are **most surely b** among us, *4135*
1:45 And blessed *is* she that **b**: for there shall be *4100*
20: 5 he will say, Why then **b** ye him not? *4100*
24:11 to them as idle tales, and they **b** them **not**. *569*
24:41 And while they yet **b not** for joy, and *569*
Jn 2:11 forth his glory; and his disciples **b** on him. *4100*
2:22 and they **b** the scripture, and the word *4100*
2:23 in the feast *day,* many **b** in his name, *4100*
3:18 he hath not **b** in the name of the only *4100*
4:39 And many of the Samaritans of that city **b** *4100*
4:41 And many moe **b** because of his own word; *4100*
4:50 And the man **b** the word that Jesus had *4100*
4:53 and himself **b**, and his whole house. *4100*
5:46 For had ye **b** Moses, ye would have *4100*
5:46 ye believed Moses, ye would have **b** me: *4100*
6:64 the beginning who they were that **b** not, *4100*
7:31 And many of the people **b** on him, and said, *4100*
7:48 of the rulers or of the Pharisees **b** on him? *4100*
8:30 As he spake these *words,* many **b** on him. *4100*
8:31 Then said Jesus to those Jews which **b** on *4100*
10:42 And many **b** on him there. *4100*
11:45 seen *the things* which Jesus did, **b** on him. *4100*
12:11 of the Jews went away, and **b** on Jesus. *4100*
12:37 before them, *yet* they **b** not on him: *4100*
12:38 he spake, Lord, who hath **b** our report? *4100*
12:42 among the *chief* rulers also many **b** on him; *4100*
16:27 and have **b** that I came out from God. *4100*
17: 8 and they have **b** that thou didst send me. *4100*
20: 8 first to the sepulchre, and he saw, and **b**. *4100*
20:29 because thou hast seen me, thou hast **b**: *4100*

B

Jn 20:29 *are* they that have not seen, and *yet* have **b**. *4100*
Ac 2:44 And all that **b** were together, *4100*
4: 4 many of them which heard the word **b**; *4100*
4:32 And the multitude of them that **b** were of *4100*
8:12 But when they **b** Philip preaching *4100*
8:13 Then Simon himself **b** also: and when he *4100*
9:26 of him, and **b** not that he was a disciple. *4100*
9:42 all Joppa; and many **b** in the Lord. *4100*
10:45 And they of the circumcision which **b** were *4103*
11:17 unto us, who **b** on the Lord Jesus Christ; *4100*
11:21 and a great number **b**, and turned unto *4100*
13:12 the deputy, when he saw what was done, **b**, *4100*
13:48 as many as were ordained to eternal life **b**. *4100*
14: 1 both of the Jews and *also* of the Greeks **b**. *4100*
14:23 them to the Lord, on whom they **b**. *4100*
15: 5 certain of the sect of the Pharisees which **b**, *4100*
16: 1 certain woman, *which was* a Jewess, and **b**; *4103*
17: 4 And some of them **b**, and consorted with *3982*
17: 5 But the Jews which **b not**, moved with envy, *544*
17:12 Therefore many of them **b**; also of *4100*
17:34 certain men clave unto him, and **b**: *4100*
18: 8 **b** on the Lord with all his house; *4100*
18: 8 and many of the Corinthians hearing **b**, and *4100*
18:27 helped them much which had **b** through *4100*
19: 2 ye received the Holy Ghost since ye **b**? *4100*
19: 9 and **b not**, but spake evil of *that* way before *544*
19:18 And many that **b** came, and confessed, and *4100*
22:19 beat in every synagogue them that **b** on *4100*
27:11 Nevertheless the centurion **b** the master and *3982*
28:24 And some **b** the *things* which were spoken, *3982*
28:24 *things* which were spoken, and some **b not**. *569*
Ro 4: 3 Abraham **b** God, and it was counted unto *4100*
4:17 before *him* whom he **b**, *even* God, *4100*
4:18 Who against hope **b** in hope, that he might *4100*
10:14 they call on *him* in whom they have not **b**? *4100*
10:16 Esaias saith, Lord, who hath **b** our report? *4100*
11:30 For as ye in times past have **not b** God, *544*
11:31 *Even* so have these also now **not b**, *544*
13:11 *is* our salvation nearer than when we **b**. *4100*
1Co 3: 5 *is* Apollos, but ministers by whom ye **b**, *4100*
15: 2 unto you, unless ye have **b** in vain. *4100*
15:11 *it were* I or they, so we preach, and so ye **b**. *4100*
2Co 4:13 is written, I **b**, *and* therefore have I spoken; *4100*
Gal 2:16 even we have **b** in Jesus Christ, *4100*
3: 6 Even as Abraham **b** God, and it was *4100*
Eph 1:13 in whom also after that ye **b**, ye were *4100*
2Th 1:10 (because our testimony among you was **b**) *4100*
2:12 That they all might be damned who **b** not *4100*
1Ti 3:16 **b** on in the world, received up into glory. *4100*
2Ti 1:12 for I know whom I have **b**, and I am *4100*
Tit 3: 8 that they which have **b** in God might be *4100*
Heb 3:18 enter into his rest, but to them that **b not**? *544*
4: 3 For we which have **b** do enter into rest, *4100*
11:31 Rahab perished not with them that **b not**, *544*
Jas 2:23 Abraham **b** God, and it was imputed unto *4100*
1Jn 4:16 and **b** the love that God hath to us. *4100*
Jude 1: 5 afterward destroyed them that **b** not. *4100*

BELIEVERS (2) [BELIEVE]
Ac 5:14 And **b** were the more added to the Lord, *4100*
1Ti 4:12 but be thou an example of the **b**, in word, *4103*

BELIEVEST (8) [BELIEVE]
Lk 1:20 because thou **b** not my words, which shall *4100*
Jn 1:50 I saw thee under the fig tree, **b** thou? *4100*
11:26 believeth in me shall never die. **B** thou this? *4100*
14:10 **B** thou not that I am in the Father, and *4100*
Ac 8:37 If thou **b** with all *thine* heart, *thou* mayest. *4100*
26:27 King Agrippa, **b** thou the prophets? I know *4100*
26:27 thou the prophets? I know that thou **b**. *4100*
Jas 2:19 Thou **b** that there is one God; thou doest *4100*

BELIEVETH (45) [BELIEVE]
Job 15:22 He **b** not that *he* shall return out of darkness, 539
39:24 neither **b** he that *it is* the sound of 539
Pr 14:15 The simple **b** every word: but the prudent 539
Isa 28:16 he that **b** shall not make haste. 539
Mk 9:23 all *things are* possible to him that **b**. *4100*
16:16 He that **b** and is baptized shall be saved; *4100*
16:16 be saved; but he that **b not** shall be damned. *569*
Jn 3:15 That whosoever **b** in him should not perish, *4100*
3:16 that whosoever **b** in him should not perish, *4100*
3:18 He that **b** on him is not condemned: but *4100*
3:18 but he that **b** not is condemned already, *4100*
3:36 He that **b** on the Son hath everlasting life: *4100*
3:36 and he that **b not** the Son shall not see life; *544*
5:24 and **b** on him that sent me, hath everlasting *4100*
6:35 and he that **b** on me shall never thirst. *4100*
6:40 and **b** on him, may have everlasting life: *4100*
6:47 He that **b** on me hath everlasting life. *4100*
7:38 He that **b** on me, as the scripture hath said, *4100*
11:25 he that **b** in me, though he were dead, *4100*
11:26 and **b** in me shall never die. *4100*
12:44 Jesus cried and said, He that **b** on me, *4100*
12:44 **b** not on me, but on him that sent me. *4100*
12:46 that whosoever **b** on me should not abide in *4100*
14:12 verily, I say unto you, He that **b** on me, *4100*
Ac 10:43 that through his name whosoever **b** in him *4100*
Ro 1:16 of God unto salvation to every one that **b**; *4100*
3:26 and the justifier of him which **b** in Jesus. *4102*
4: 5 but **b** on him that justifieth the ungodly, *4100*
9:33 whosoever **b** on him shall not be ashamed. *4100*
10: 4 law for righteousness to every one that **b**. *4100*
10:10 For with the heart *man* **b** unto *4100*
10:11 Whosoever **b** on him shall not be ashamed. *4100*
14: 2 For one **b** that *he* may eat all *things:* *4100*
1Co 7:12 If any brother hath a wife that **b not**, and *571*
7:13 the woman which hath a husband that **b not**, *571*
13: 7 Beareth all *things*, **b** all *things*, hopeth all *4100*
14:24 and there come in one that **b not**, or *571*
2Co 6:15 or what part hath he that **b** with an infidel? *4103*
1Ti 5:16 If any man or **woman that b** have widows, *4103*
1Pe 2: 6 he that **b** on him shall not be confounded. *4100*
1Jn 5: 1 Whosoever **b** that Jesus is the Christ is born *4100*
5: 5 but he that **b** that Jesus is the Son of God? *4100*
5:10 He that **b** on the Son of God hath *4100*
5:10 he that **b** not God hath made him a liar; *4100*
5:10 he **b** not the record that God gave of his *4100*

BELIEVING (8) [BELIEVE]
Mt 21:22 ye shall ask in prayer, **b**, ye shall receive. *4100*
Jn 20:27 *it* into my side: and be not faithless, but **b**. *4103*
20:31 that **b** ye might have life through his name. *4100*
Ac 16:34 and rejoiced, **b** in God with all his house. *4100*
24:14 **b** all *things* which are written in the law *4100*
Ro 15:13 of hope fill you with all joy and peace in **b**, *4100*
1Ti 6: 2 And they that have **b** masters, let them not *4103*
1Pe 1: 8 though now ye see *him* not, yet **b**, *4100*

BELL (4) [BELLS]
Ex 28:34 A golden **b** and a pomegranate, a golden 6472
28:34 a golden **b** and a pomegranate, 6472
39:26 A **b** and a pomegranate, a bell and 6472
39:26 and a pomegranate, a **b** and a pomegranate, 6472

BELLIES (1) [BELLY]
Tit 1:12 Cretians *are* alway liars, evil beasts, slow **b**. *1064*

BELLOW (1) [BELLOWS]
Jer 50:11 fat as the heifer at grass, and **b** as bulls; 6670

BELLOWS (1) [BELLOW]
Jer 6:29 The **b** are burnt, the lead is consumed of 4647

BELLS (4) [BELL]
Ex 28:33 and **b** of gold between them round about: 6472
39:25 they made **b** of pure gold, and put the bells 6472
39:25 put the **b** between the pomegranates upon 6472
Zec 14:20 In that day shall there be upon the **b** of 4698

BELLY (49) [BELLIES]
Ge 3:14 upon thy **b** shalt thou go, and dust shalt 1512
Lev 11:42 Whatsoever goeth upon the **b**, and 1512
Nu 5:21 make thy thigh to rot, and thy **b** to swell; 990
5:22 to make *thy* **b** to swell, and *thy* thigh to rot: 990
5:27 and her **b** shall swell, and her thigh shall rot: 990
25: 8 of Israel, and the woman through her **b**. 6897
Jdg 3:21 from his right thigh, and thrust it into his **b**: 990
3:22 he could not draw the dagger out of his **b**; 990
1Ki 7:20 over against the **b** which *was* by 990
Job 3:11 give up the ghost when I came out of the **b**? 990
15: 2 and fill his **b** *with* the east wind? 990
15:35 forth vanity, and their **b** prepareth deceit. 990
20:15 up again: God shall cast them out of his **b**. 990
20:20 Surely he shall not feel quietness in his **b**, 990
20:23 *When* he is about to fill his **b**, *God* shall cast 990
32:19 Behold, my **b** *is* as wine *which* hath no vent; 990
40:16 and his force *is* in the navel of his **b**. 990
Ps 17:14 whose **b** thou fillest *with* thy hid *treasure:* 990

Ps	22:10	thou *art* my God from my mother's **b**.	990
	31: 9	consumed with grief, *yea,* my soul and my **b**.	990
	44:25	to the dust: our **b** cleaveth unto the earth.	990
Pr	13:25	his soul: but the **b** of the wicked shall want.	990
	18: 8	go down *into* the innermost parts of the **b**.	990
	18:20	A man's **b** shall be satisfied with the fruit of	990
	20:27	searching all the inward parts of the **b**.	990
	20:30	so *do* stripes the inward parts of the **b**.	990
	26:22	go down *into* the innermost parts of the **b**.	990
SS	5:14	his **b** *is as* bright ivory overlaid *with*	4578
	7: 2	thy **b** *is like* a heap of wheat set about with	990
Isa	46: 3	which are borne *by me* from the **b**, which are	990
Jer	1: 5	Before I formed thee in the **b** I knew thee;	990
	51:34	he hath filled his **b** with my delicates,	3770
Eze	3: 3	cause thy **b** to eat, and fill thy bowels with	990
Da	2:32	arms of silver, his **b** and his thighs of brass,	4577
Jnh	1:17	Jonah was in the **b** of the fish three days	4578
	2: 1	the LORD his God out of the fish's **b**,	4578
	2: 2	out of the **b** of hell cried I, *and* thou heardest	990
Hab	3:16	When I heard, my **b** trembled; my lips	990
Mt	12:40	and three nights in the whale's **b**;	*2836*
	15:17	entereth in at the mouth goeth into the **b**,	*2836*
Mk	7:19	it entereth not into his heart, but into the **b**,	*2836*
Lk	15:16	And he would fain have filled his **b** with	*2836*
Jn	7:38	out of his **b** shall flow rivers of living	*2836*
Ro	16:18	not our Lord Jesus Christ, but their own **b**;	*2836*
1Co	6:13	Meats for the **b**, and the belly for meats:	*2836*
	6:13	Meats for the belly, and the **b** for meats:	*2836*
Php	3:19	whose God *is their* **b**, and *whose* glory *is* in	*2836*
Rev	10: 9	and it shall make thy **b** bitter, but it shall be	*2836*
	10:10	as soon as I had eaten it, my **b** was bitter.	*2836*

BELONG (12) [BELONGED, BELONGEST, BELONGETH, BELONGING]

Ge	40: 8	unto them, *Do* not interpretations ***b*** to God?	NIH
Lev	27:24	to whom the possession of the land *did* ***b***.	NIH
Nu	1:50	and over all *things* that **b** to it:	NIH
Dt	29:29	The secret *things* **b** unto the LORD our	NIH
	29:29	*those things* which are revealed **b** unto us	NIH
Ps	47: 9	for the shields of the earth ***b*** unto God: he is	NIH
	68:20	unto GOD the Lord ***b*** the issues from	NIH
Pr	24:23	These *things* also ***b*** to the wise. *It is* not	NIH
Da	9: 9	To the Lord our God ***b*** mercies and	NIH
Mk	9:41	because ye **b** to Christ, verily I say unto	*1510*
Lk	19:42	thy day, the *things* which **b unto** thy peace!	*4314*
1Co	7:32	careth for the *things* that **b** to the Lord,	NIG

BELONGED (11) [BELONG]

Jos	17: 8	Tappuah on the border of Manasseh ***b*** to	NIH
1Sa	21: 7	the chiefest of the herdmen that **b** to Saul.	NIH
1Ki	1: 8	Rei, and the mighty *men* which **b** to David,	NIH
	16:15	which ***b*** to the Philistines.	NIH
2Ki	14:28	and Hamath, *which* ***b*** to Judah, for Israel,	NIH
1Ch	2:23	All these ***b*** *to* the sons of Machir the father	NIH
	13: 6	*that is,* to Kirjath-jearim, which ***b*** to Judah,	NIH
2Ch	26:23	the field of the burial which ***b*** to the kings;	NIH
Est	1: 9	the royal house which ***b*** to king Ahasuerus.	NIH
	2: 9	with **such things as b** to her, and seven	4490
Lk	23: 7	And as soon as he knew that he **b** unto	*1510*

BELONGEST (1) [BELONG]

1Sa	30:13	And David said unto him, To whom ***b*** thou?	NIH

BELONGETH (21) [BELONG]

Nu	8:24	This *is it* that **b** unto the Levites:	NIH
Dt	32:35	To me ***b*** vengeance, and recompence;	NIH
Jdg	19:14	*they were* by Gibeah, which **b** to Benjamin.	NIH
	20: 4	I came into Gibeah that **b** to Benjamin, I	NIH
1Sa	17: 1	which ***b*** to Judah, and pitched between	NIH
	30:14	upon *the coast* which **b** to Judah, and	NIH
1Ki	15:27	at Gibbethon, which ***b*** to the Philistines;	NIH
	17: 9	which **b** to Zidon, and dwell there:	NIH
	19: 3	which **b** to Judah, and left his servant there.	NIH
2Ki	14:11	the face at Beth-shemesh, which ***b*** to Judah.	NIH
2Ch	25:21	at Beth-shemesh, which ***b*** to Judah.	NIH
Ezr	10: 4	Arise; for *this* matter **b** unto thee: we also	NIH
Ps	3: 8	Salvation **b** unto the LORD: thy blessing *is*	NIH
	62:11	have I heard this; that power ***b*** unto God.	NIH
	62:12	Also unto thee, O Lord, ***b*** mercy: for thou	NIH
	94: 1	O LORD God, to whom vengeance **b**;	NIH
	94: 1	O God, to whom vengeance **b**, shew thyself.	NIH
Da	9: 7	righteousness ***b*** unto thee, but unto us	NIH
	9: 8	O Lord, to us ***b*** confusion of face, to our	NIH
Heb	5:14	But strong meat **b** to *them that are* of full	*1510*
	10:30	Vengeance ***b*** unto me, I will recompense,	NIG

BELONGING (5) [BELONG]

Nu	7: 9	the service of the sanctuary **b unto** them	5921
Ru	2: 3	her hap was to light on a part of the field ***b***	NIH
1Sa	6:18	cities of the Philistines ***b*** to the five lords,	NIH
Pr	26:17	*and* meddleth with strife ***b*** not to him,	NIH
Lk	9:10	went aside privately into a desert place **b** to	NIG

BELONGINGS See STUFF

BELOVED (111) [LOVE]

Dt	21:15	one **b**, and another hated, and they have born	157
	21:15	born him children, *both* the **b** and the hated;	157
	21:16	*that* he may not make the son of the **b**	157
	33:12	The **b** of the LORD shall dwell in safety	3039
Ne	13:26	who was **b** of his God, and God made him	157
Ps	60: 5	That thy **b** may be delivered; save *with* thy	3039
	108: 6	That thy **b** may be delivered: save *with* thy	3039
	127: 2	of sorrows: *for* so he giveth his **b** sleep.	3039
Pr	4: 3	tender and only ***b*** in the sight of my mother.	NIH
SS	1:14	My **b** *is* unto me *as* a cluster of camphire in	1730
	1:16	Behold, thou *art* fair, my **b**, yea, pleasant:	1730
	2: 3	of the wood, so *is* my **b** among the sons.	1730
	2: 8	The voice of my **b**! behold, he cometh	1730
	2: 9	My **b** *is* like a roe or a young hart: behold,	1730
	2:10	My **b** spake, and said unto me, Rise up, my	1730
	2:16	My **b** *is* mine, and I *am* his: he feedeth	1730
	2:17	my **b**, and be thou like a roe or a young hart	1730
	4:16	Let my **b** come into his garden, and eat his	1730
	5: 1	drink, yea, drink abundantly, O **b**.	1730
	5: 2	*it is* the voice of my **b** that knocketh *saying,*	1730
	5: 4	My **b** put in his hand by the hole *of*	1730
	5: 5	I rose up to open to my **b**; and my hands	1730
	5: 6	I opened to my **b**; but my beloved had	1730
	5: 6	my **b** had withdrawn himself, *and*	1730
	5: 8	if ye find my **b**, that ye tell him, that I *am*	1730
	5: 9	What *is* thy **b** more than *another* beloved,	1730
	5: 9	What *is* thy beloved more than *another* **b**,	1730
	5: 9	what *is* thy **b** more than *another* beloved,	1730
	5: 9	what *is* thy beloved more than *another* **b**,	1730
	5:10	My **b** *is* white and ruddy, the chiefest	1730
	5:16	This *is* my **b**, and this *is* my friend,	1730
	6: 1	Whither is thy **b** gone, O thou fairest	1730
	6: 1	whither is thy **b** turned aside? that we may	1730
	6: 2	My **b** is gone down into his garden, to	1730
	6: 3	I *am* my beloved's, and my **b** *is* mine:	1730
	7: 9	for my **b**, that goeth *down* sweetly,	1730
	7:11	Come, my **b**, let us go forth *into* the field;	1730
	7:13	old, *which* I have laid up for thee, O my **b**.	1730
	8: 5	from the wilderness, leaning upon her **b**?	1730
	8:14	my **b**, and be thou like to a roe or to a	1730
Isa	5: 1	a song of my **b** touching his vineyard.	1730
Jer	11:15	What hath my **b** to do in mine house,	3039
	12: 7	I have given the **dearly b** of my soul into	3033
Da	9:23	come to shew *thee;* for thou *art* **greatly b**:	2532
	10:11	said unto me, O Daniel, a man **greatly b**,	2532
	10:19	said, O man **greatly b**, fear not: peace *be*	2532
Hos	3: 1	Go yet, love a woman **b** of *her* friend, yet an	157
	9:16	yet will I slay *even* the **b** *fruit* of their	4261
Mt	3:17	saying, This is my **b** Son, in whom I am well	*27*
	12:18	my **b**, in whom my soul is well pleased:	*27*
	17: 5	which said, This is my **b** Son, in whom I am	*27*
Mk	1:11	*saying,* Thou art my **b** Son, in whom I am	*27*
	9: 7	out of the cloud, saying, This is my **b** Son:	*27*
Lk	3:22	from heaven, which said, Thou art my **b** Son;	*27*
	9:35	out of the cloud, saying, This is my **b** Son:	*27*
	20:13	I will send my **b** son: it may be they will	*27*
Ac	15:25	to send chosen men unto you with our **b**	*27*
Ro	1: 7	that be in Rome, **b** of God, called *to be* saints:	*27*
	9:25	my people; and her **b**, which was not beloved.	*25*
	9:25	my people; and her beloved, which was not **b**.	*25*
	11:28	the election, *they are* **b** for the fathers' sakes.	*27*
	12:19	**Dearly b**, avenge not yourselves, but	*27*
	16: 8	Greet Amplias my **b** in the Lord.	*27*
	16: 9	Urban our helper in Christ, and Stachys my **b**.	*27*
	16:12	Salute the **b** Persis, which laboured much in	*27*
1Co	4:14	to shame you, but as my **b** sons I warn *you.*	*27*
	4:17	who is my **b** son, and faithful in the Lord,	*27*
	10:14	Wherefore, my **dearly b**, flee from idolatry.	*27*
	15:58	Therefore, my **b** brethren, be ye stedfast,	*27*
2Co	7: 1	Having therefore these promises, **dearly b**,	*27*
	12:19	but *we do* all *things,* **dearly b**, for your	*27*
Eph	1: 6	wherein he hath made us accepted in the **b**:	*25*

Eph 6:21 a **b** brother and faithful minister in the Lord, *27*
Php 2:12 Wherefore, my **b**, as ye have always obeyed, *27*
4: 1 my brethren **dearly b** and longed for, my joy *27*
4: 1 crown, so stand fast in the Lord, *my* **dearly b**. *27*
Col 3:12 holy and **b**, bowels of mercies, kindness, *25*
4: 7 *who is* a **b** brother, and a faithful minister and *27*
4: 9 With Onesimus, a faithful and **b** brother, *27*
4:14 Luke, the **b** physician, and Demas, greet you. *27*
1Th 1: 4 Knowing, brethren **b**, your election of God. *25*
2Th 2:13 brethren **b** of the Lord, because God hath *25*
1Ti 6: 2 *them* service, because they are faithful and **b**, *27*
2Ti 1: 2 To Timothy, *my* **dearly b** son: Grace, mercy, *27*
Phm 1: 1 unto Philemon *our* **dearly b**, and *27*
1: 2 And to *our* **b** Apphia, *27*
1:16 a brother **b**, specially to me, but how much *27*
Heb 6: 9 But, **b**, we are persuaded better *things* of you, *27*
Jas 1:16 Do not err, my **b** brethren. *27*
1:19 Wherefore, my **b** brethren, let every man be *27*
2: 5 Hearken, my **b** brethren, Hath not God chosen *27*
1Pe 2:11 **Dearly b**, I beseech *you* as strangers and *27*
4:12 **B**, think it not strange concerning the fiery *27*
2Pe 1:17 This is my **b** Son, in whom I am well pleased. *27*
3: 1 This second epistle, **b**, I now write unto you; *27*
3: 8 But, **b**, be not ignorant of this one *thing,* that *27*
3:14 Wherefore, **b**, seeing that ye look for such *27*
3:15 even as our **b** brother Paul also according to *27*
3:17 Ye therefore, **b**, seeing ye know *these things* *27*
1Jn 3: 2 **B**, now are we the sons of God, and it doth *27*
3:21 **B**, if our heart condemn us not, *then* have we *27*
4: 1 **B**, believe not every spirit, but try the spirits *27*
4: 7 **B**, let us love one another: for love is of God; *27*
4:11 **B**, if God so loved us, we ought also to love *27*
3Jn 1: 2 **B**, I wish above all *things* that thou mayest *27*
1: 5 **B**, thou doest faithfully whatsoever thou doest *27*
1:11 **B**, follow not *that which is* evil, but *27*
Jude 1: 3 **B**, when I gave all diligence to write unto you *27*
1:17 But, **b**, remember ye the words which were *27*
1:20 But ye, **b**, building up yourselves on your *27*
Rev 20: 9 the camp of the saints about, and the **b** city: *25*

BELOVED'S (2) [LOVE]

SS 6: 3 I *am* my **b**, and my beloved *is* 1730+3807.1
7:10 I *am* my **b**, and his desire *is* 1730+3807.1

BELOW See DOWNWARD; NETHER; NETHERMOST

BELSHAZZAR (8)

Da 5: 1 **B** the king made a great feast to a thousand 1113
5: 2 **B**, whiles *he* tasted the wine, 1113
5: 9 *was* king **B** greatly troubled, and 1113
5:22 thou his son, O **B**, hast not humbled thine 1113
5:29 commanded **B**, and they clothed Daniel 1113
5:30 In that night *was* **B** the king of 1113
7: 1 In the first year of **B** king of Babylon 1113
8: 1 In the third year of the reign of king **B** a 1112

BELTESHAZZAR (10) [DANIEL]

Da 1: 7 for he gave unto Daniel *the name of* **B**; and 1095
2:26 and said to Daniel, whose name *was* **B**, 1096
4: 8 whose name *was* **B**, according to the name 1096
4: 9 O **B**, master of the magicians, because 1096
4:18 Now thou, O **B**, declare the interpretation 1096
4:19 Daniel, whose name *was* **B**, was astonied 1096
4:19 The king spake, and said, **B**, let not 1096
4:19 **B** answered and said, My lord, the dream 1096
5:12 the same Daniel, whom the king named **B**: 1096
10: 1 unto Daniel, whose name was called **B**; 1095

BEMOAN (5) [BEMOANED, BEMOANING]

Jer 15: 5 or who shall **b** thee? or who shall go aside 5110
16: 5 neither go to lament nor **b** them: 5110
22:10 Weep ye not for the dead, neither **b** him: 5110
48:17 All ye that are about him, **b** him; and all ye 5110
Na 3: 7 who will **b** her? whence shall I seek 5110

BEMOANED (1) [BEMOAN]

Job 42:11 they **b** him, and comforted him over all 5110

BEMOANING (1) [BEMOAN]

Jer 31:18 I have surely heard Ephraim **b** himself *thus;* 5110

BEN (1)

1Ch 15:18 **B**, and Jaaziel, and Shemiramoth, and 1122

BENAIAH (42)

2Sa 8:18 **B** the son of Jehoiada *was over* both 1141
20:23 **B** the son of Jehoiada *was* over 1141
23:20 **B** the son of Jehoiada, the son of a valiant 1141
23:22 These *things* did **B** the son of Jehoiada, 1141
23:30 **B** the Pirathonite, Hiddai of the brooks of 1141
1Ki 1: 8 **B** the son of Jehoiada, and Nathan 1141
1:10 **B**, and the mighty *men,* and Solomon his 1141
1:26 **B** the son of Jehoiada, and thy servant 1141
1:32 the prophet, and **B** the son of Jehoiada. 1141
1:36 **B** the son of Jehoiada answered the king, 1141
1:38 **B** the son of Jehoiada, and the Cherethites, 1141
1:44 **B** the son of Jehoiada, and the Cherethites, 1141
2:25 king Solomon sent by the hand of **B** the son 1141
2:29 Solomon sent **B** the son of Jehoiada, 1141
2:30 **B** came to the tabernacle of the LORD, 1141
2:30 And **B** brought the king word again, saying, 1141
2:34 So **B** the son of Jehoiada went up, and 1141
2:35 the king put **B** the son of Jehoiada in his 1141
2:46 So the king commanded **B** the son of 1141
4: 4 **B** the son of Jehoiada *was* over the host: 1141
1Ch 4:36 and Asaiah, and Adiel, and Jesimiel, and **B**, 1141
11:22 **B** the son of Jehoiada, the son of a valiant 1141
11:24 These *things* did **B** the son of Jehoiada, and 1141
11:31 the children of Benjamin, **B** the Pirathonite, 1141
15:18 **B**, and Maaseiah, and Mattithiah, and 1141
15:20 and Unni, and Eliab, and Maaseiah, and **B**, 1141
15:24 Amasai, and Zechariah, and **B**, and Eliezer, 1141
16: 5 and Eliab, and **B**, and Obed-edom: 1141
16: 6 **B** also and Jahaziel the priests with 1141
18:17 **B** the son of Jehoiada *was* over 1141
27: 5 the third month *was* **B** the son of Jehoiada, 1141
27: 6 This *is that* **B**, *who was* mighty among 1141
27:14 the eleventh month *was* **B** the Pirathonite, 1141
27:34 after Ahithophel *was* Jehoiada the son of **B**, 1141
2Ch 20:14 the son of **B**, the son of Jeiel, the son of 1141
31:13 Eliel, and Ismachiah, and Mahath, and **B**, 1141
Ezr 10:25 and Eleazar, and Malchijah, and **B**. 1141
10:30 Adna, and Chelal, **B**, Maaseiah, Mattaniah, 1141
10:35 **B**, Bedeiah, Chelluh, 1141
10:43 Zabad, Zebina, Jadau, and Joel, **B**. 1141
Eze 11: 1 Pelatiah the son of **B**, princes of the people. 1141
11:13 that Pelatiah the son of **B** died. 1141

BEN-AMMI (1)

Ge 19:38 she also bare a son, and called his name **B**: 1151

BENCHES (1)

Eze 27: 6 of the Ashurites have made thy **b** *of* ivory, 7175

BEND (8) [BENDETH, BENDING, BENT]

Ps 11: 2 For lo, the wicked **b** *their* bow, they make 1869
64: 3 *and* **b** *their bows to shoot* their arrows, 1869
Jer 9: 3 they **b** their tongues *like* their bow *for* lies: 1869
46: 9 and the Lydians, that handle *and* **b** the bow. 1869
50:14 all ye that **b** the bow, shoot at her, spare no 1869
50:29 all ye that **b** the bow, camp against it round 1869
51: 3 Against *him that* bendeth let the archer **b** 1869
Eze 17: 7 this vine did **b** her roots toward him, and 3719

BEN-DEKER See SON OF DEKAR

BENDETH (2) [BEND]

Ps 58: 7 *when* he **b** *his bow to shoot* his arrows, 1869
Jer 51: 3 Against *him that* **b** let the archer bend his 1869

BENDING (1) [BEND]

Isa 60:14 that afflicted thee shall come **b** unto thee; 7817

BENEATH (28) See Index

BENE-BERAK (1)

Jos 19:45 And Jehud, and **B**, and Gath-rimmon, 1139

BENEFACTORS (1)

Lk 22:25 exercise authority upon them are called **b**. *2110*

BENEFICIAL See EXPEDIENT

BENEFIT (5) [BENEFITS]

2Ch 32:25 not again according to the **b** *done* unto him; 1576
Jer 18:10 the good, wherewith I said *I* would **b** them. 3190
2Co 1:15 you before, that you might have a second **b**; *5485*
1Ti 6: 2 are faithful and beloved, partakers of the **b**. *2108*
Phm 1:14 that thy **b** should not be as *it were* of *18*

BENEFITS (3) [BENEFIT]
Ps 68:19 *who* daily loadeth us *with* **b**, *even* the God NIH
103: 2 O my soul, and forget not all his **b**: 1576
116:12 unto the LORD *for* all his **b** towards me? 8408

BENE-JAAKAN (2) [JAAKAN]
Nu 33:31 departed from Moseroth, and pitched in **B**. 1142
33:32 they removed from **B**, and encamped at 1142

BENEVOLENCE (1)
1Co 7: 3 Let the husband render unto the wife due **b**: *2133*

BEN-HADAD (27)
1Ki 15:18 king Asa sent them to **B**, the son of 1130
15:20 So **B** hearkened unto king Asa, and sent 1130
20: 1 **B** the king of Syria gathered all his host 1130
20: 2 the city, and said unto him, Thus saith **B**, 1130
20: 5 said, Thus speaketh **B**, saying, Although I 1130
20: 9 he said unto the messengers of **B**, 1130
20:10 And **B** sent unto him, and said, The gods do 1130
20:12 when *B* heard this message, as he *was* NIH
20:16 **B** *was* drinking *himself* drunk in 1130
20:17 **B** sent out, and they told him, saying, 1130
20:20 **B** the king of Syria escaped on a horse with 1130
20:26 that **B** numbered the Syrians, and went up 1130
20:30 **B** fled, and came into the city, into an inner 1130
20:32 said, Thy servant **B** saith, I pray thee, 1130
20:33 catch *it:* and they said, Thy brother **B**. 1130
20:33 **B** came forth to him; and he caused him to 1130
20:34 *B* said unto him, The cities, which my NIH
2Ki 6:24 that **B** king of Syria gathered all his host, 1130
8: 7 **B** the king of Syria was sick; and it was 1130
8: 9 Thy son **B** king of Syria hath sent me to 1130
13: 3 into the hand of **B** the son of Hazael, 1130
13:24 and **B** his son reigned in his stead. 1130
13:25 the hand of **B** the son of Hazael the cities, 1130
2Ch 16: 2 king's house, and sent to **B** king of Syria, 1130
16: 4 **B** hearkened unto king Asa, and sent 1130
Jer 49:27 and it shall consume the palaces of **B**. 1130
Am 1: 4 which shall devour the palaces of **B**. 1130

BEN-HAIL (1)
2Ch 17: 7 *even* to **B**, and to Obadiah, and 1134

BEN-HANAN (1)
1Ch 4:20 *were,* Amnon, and Rinnah, **B**, and Tilon. 1135

BEN-HESED See SON OF HESED

BENINU (1)
Ne 10:13 Hodijah, Bani, **B**. 1148

BENJAMIN (162) [BEN-ONI, BENJAMIN'S, BENJAMITE, BENJAMITES]
Ge 35:18 name Ben-oni: but his father called him **B**. 1144
35:24 The sons of Rachel; Joseph, and **B**: 1144
42: 4 **B**, Joseph's brother, Jacob sent not with his 1144
42:36 ye will take **B** *away:* all these things are 1144
43:14 may send away your other brother, and **B**. 1144
43:15 took double money in their hand, and **B**; 1144
43:16 when Joseph saw **B** with them, he said to 1144
43:29 saw his brother **B**, his mother's son, and 1144
45:12 eyes see, and the eyes of my brother **B**, 1144
45:14 and wept; and **B** wept upon his neck. 1144
45:22 to **B** he gave three hundred *pieces* of silver, 1144
46:19 sons of Rachel Jacob's wife; Joseph, and **B**. 1144
46:21 the sons of **B** *were* Belah, and Becher, and 1144
49:27 **B** shall ravin *as* a wolf: in the morning he 1144
Ex 1: 3 Issachar, Zebulun, and **B**, 1144
Nu 1:11 Of **B**; Abidan the son of Gideoni. 1144
1:36 Of the children of **B**, *by* their generations, 1144
1:37 *even* of the tribe of **B**, *were* thirty and 1144
2:22 the tribe of **B**: and the captain of the sons of 1144
2:22 the captain of the sons of **B** *shall be* Abidan 1144
7:60 prince of the children of **B**, *offered:* 1144
10:24 of **B** *was* Abidan the son of Gideoni. 1144
13: 9 Of the tribe of **B**, Palti the son of Raphu. 1144
26:38 The sons of **B** after their families: of Bela, 1144
26:41 These *are* the sons of **B** after their families: 1144
34:21 Of the tribe of **B**, Elidad the son of Chislon. 1144
Dt 27:12 and Judah, and Issachar, and Joseph, and **B**: 1144
33:12 *And* of **B** he said, The beloved of 1144
Jos 18:11 the lot of the tribe of the children of **B** 1144
18:20 *was* the inheritance of the children of **B**, 1144
18:21 **B** according to their families were Jericho, 1144
18:28 This *is* the inheritance of the children of **B** 1144
21: 4 and out of the tribe of **B**, thirteen cities. 1144
21:17 out of the tribe of **B**, Gibeon with her 1144
Jdg 1:21 the children of **B** did not drive out 1144
1:21 the Jebusites dwell with the children of **B** 1144
5:14 after thee, **B**, among thy people; out of 1144
10: 9 against **B**, and against the house of 1144
19:14 *were* by Gibeah, which *belongeth* to **B**. 1144
20: 3 (Now the children of **B** heard that 1144
20: 4 I came into Gibeah that *belongeth* to **B**, I 1144
20:10 may do, when they come to Gibeah of **B**, 1144
20:12 of Israel sent men through all the tribe of **B**, 1144
20:13 the children of **B** would not hearken to 1144
20:14 the children of **B** gathered themselves 1144
20:15 the children of **B** were numbered at that 1144
20:17 the men of Israel, beside **B**, were numbered 1144
20:18 first to the battle against the children of **B**? 1144
20:20 men of Israel went out to battle against **B**; 1144
20:21 the children of **B** came forth out of Gibeah, 1144
20:23 battle against the children of **B** my brother? 1144
20:24 against the children of **B** the second day. 1144
20:25 **B** went forth against them out of Gibeah 1144
20:28 battle against the children of **B** my brother, 1144
20:30 against the children of **B** on the third day, 1144
20:31 the children of **B** went out against 1144
20:32 the children of **B** said, They *are* smitten 1144
20:35 the LORD smote **B** before Israel: and 1144
20:36 So the children of **B** saw that they were 1144
20:39 **B** began to smite *and* kill of the men of 1144
20:41 turned *again,* the men of **B** were amazed: 1144
20:44 there fell of **B** eighteen thousand men; all 1144
20:46 So that all which fell that day of **B** were 1144
20:48 Israel turned again upon the children of **B**, 1144
21: 1 any of us give his daughter unto **B** to wife. 1144
21: 6 the children of Israel repented them for **B** 1144
21:13 of **B** that *were* in the rock Rimmon, 1144
21:14 **B** came again at that time; and they gave 1144
21:15 the people repented them for **B**, because 1144
21:16 seeing the women are destroyed out of **B**? 1144
21:17 inheritance for them that be escaped of **B**, 1144
21:18 Cursed *be* he that giveth a wife to **B**. 1144
21:20 they commanded the children of **B**, 1144
21:21 of Shiloh, and go *to* the land of **B**. 1144
21:23 the children of **B** did so, and took *them* 1144
1Sa 4:12 there ran a man of **B** out of the army, and 1144
9: 1 Now there was a man of **B**, whose name 1144
9:16 I will send thee a man out of the land of **B**, 1144
9:21 least of all the families of the tribe of **B**? 1144
10: 2 sepulchre in the border of **B** at Zelzah; 1144
10:20 to come near, the tribe of **B** was taken. 1144
10:21 When he had caused the tribe of **B** to come 1144
13: 2 were with Jonathan in Gibeah of **B**: 1144
13:15 gat him up from Gilgal *unto* Gibeah of **B**. 1144
13:16 present with them, abode in Gibeah of **B**: 1144
14:16 the watchmen of Saul in Gibeah of **B** 1144
2Sa 2: 9 and over **B**, and over all Israel. 1144
2:15 and went over by number twelve of **B**, 1144
2:25 the children of **B** gathered themselves 1144
2:31 the servants of David had smitten of **B**, and 1144
3:19 Abner also spake in the ears of **B**: and 1144
3:19 that seemed *good* to the whole house of **B**. 1144
4: 2 Rimmon a Beerothite, of the children of **B**: 1144
4: 2 (for Beeroth also was reckoned to **B**: 1144
19:17 *there were* a thousand men of **B** with him, 1144
21:14 buried they in the country of **B** in Zelah, 1144
23:29 of Ribai out of Gibeah of the children of **B**, 1144
1Ki 4:18 Shimei the son of Elah, in **B**: 1144
12:21 with the tribe of **B**, an hundred and 1144
12:23 unto all the house of Judah and **B**, and 1144
15:22 king Asa built with them Geba of **B**, and 1144
1Ch 2: 2 Dan, Joseph, and **B**, Naphtali, Gad, and 1144
6:60 out of the tribe of **B**; Geba with her 1144
6:65 out of the tribe of the children of **B**, these 1144
7: 6 *The sons of* **B**; Bela, and Becher, and 1144
7:10 **B**, and Ehud, and Chenaanah, and Zethan, 1144
8: 1 Now **B** begat Bela his firstborn, Ashbel 1144
8:40 and fifty. All these *are* of the sons of **B**. 1144
9: 3 of the children of **B**, and of the children of 1144
9: 7 of the sons of **B**; Sallu the son of 1144
11:31 that pertained to the children of **B**, 1144
12: 2 out of a bow, *even* of Saul's brethren of **B**. 1144
12:16 there came of the children of **B** and 1144
12:29 of the children of **B**, the kindred of Saul, 1144
21: 6 and **B** counted he not among them: 1144

1Ch 27:21 of **B**, Jaasiel the son of Abner: 1144
2Ch 11: 1 *of* the house of Judah and **B** an hundred and 1144
11: 3 and to all Israel in Judah and **B**, saying, 1144
11:10 and Hebron, which *are* in Judah and in **B**, 1144
11:12 having Judah and **B** on his side. 1144
11:23 throughout all the countries of Judah and **B**, 1144
14: 8 out of **B**, that bare shields and drew bows, 1144
15: 2 Hear ye me, Asa, and all Judah and **B**; 1144
15: 8 idols out of all the land of Judah and **B**, 1144
15: 9 he gathered all Judah and **B**, and 1144
17:17 of **B**; Eliada a mighty *man* of valour, and 1144
25: 5 of *their* fathers, throughout all Judah and **B**: 1144
31: 1 and the altars out of all Judah and **B**, 1144
34: 9 remnant of Israel, and of all Judah and **B**; 1144
34:32 **B** to stand *to it.* And the inhabitants of 1144
Ezr 1: 5 up the chief of the fathers of Judah and **B**, 1144
4: 1 **B** heard that the children of the captivity 1144
10: 9 **B** gathered themselves together *unto* 1144
10:32 **B**, Malluch, *and* Shemariah. 1144
Ne 3:23 After him repaired **B** and Hashub over 1144
11: 4 children of Judah, and of the children of **B**. 1144
11: 7 these *are* the sons of **B**; Sallu the son of 1144
11:31 The children also of **B** from Geba *dwelt at* 1144
11:36 Levites *were* divisions *in* Judah, *and* in **B**. 1144
12:34 Judah, and **B**, and Shemaiah, and Jeremiah, 1144
Ps 68:27 There *is* little **B** *with* their ruler, the princes 1144
80: 2 Before Ephraim and **B** and Manasseh stir 1144
Jer 1: 1 that *were* in Anathoth in the land of **B**: 1144
6: 1 O ye children of **B**, gather yourselves to 1144
17:26 from the land of **B**, and from the plain, and 1144
20: 2 the stocks that *were* in the high gate of **B**, 1144
32: 8 in Anathoth, which *is* in the country of **B**: 1144
32:44 and take witnesses in the land of **B**, 1144
33:13 in the land of **B**, and in the places about 1144
37:12 out of Jerusalem to go *into* the land of **B**, 1144
37:13 when he was in the gate of **B**, a captain of 1144
38: 7 the king then sitting in the gate of **B**; 1144
Eze 48:22 the border of Judah and the border of **B**, 1144
48:23 unto the west side, **B** *shall have* a *portion.* 1144
48:24 by the border of **B**, from the east side unto 1144
48:32 of Joseph, one gate of **B**, one gate of Dan. 1144
Hos 5: 8 cry aloud *at* Beth-aven, after thee, O **B**. 1144
Ob 1:19 of Samaria: and **B** *shall possess* Gilead. 1144
Ac 13:21 a man of the tribe of **B**, *by the space of* forty *958*
Ro 11: 1 of the seed of Abraham, *of* the tribe of **B**. *958*
Php 3: 5 of the stock of Israel, of the tribe of **B**, *958*
Rev 7: 8 Of the tribe of **B** *were* sealed twelve *958*

BENJAMIN'S (4) [BENJAMIN]
Ge 43:34 **B** mess was five times so much as any of 1144
44:12 and the cup was found in **B** sack. 1144
45:14 he fell upon his brother **B** neck, and wept; 1144
Zec 14:10 from **B** gate unto the place of the first gate, 1144

BENJAMITE (9) [BENJAMIN]
Jdg 3:15 the son of Gera, a **B**, a man lefthanded: 1145
1Sa 9: 1 the son of Aphiah, a **B**, 376+1121+3227
9:21 Saul answered and said, *Am* not I a **B**, 1145
2Sa 16:11 how much more now *may this* **B** *do it?* let 1145
19:16 a **B**, which *was* of Bahurim, hasted and 1145
20: 1 *was* Sheba, the son of Bichri, a **B**: 376+3227
1Ki 2: 8 Shimei the son of Gera, a **B** of Bahurim, 1145
Est 2: 5 son of Shimei, the son of Kish, a **B**; 376+3227
Ps 7: T concerning the words of Cush the **B**. 1121

BENJAMITES (8) [BENJAMIN]
Jdg 19:16 in Gibeah: but the men of the place *were* **B**. 1145
20:35 the children of Israel destroyed of the **B** 1144
20:36 for the men of Israel gave place to the **B**, 1144
20:40 the **B** looked behind them, and behold, 1144
20:43 *Thus* they inclosed the **B** round about, 1144
1Sa 9: 4 he passed through the land of the **B**, but 3228
22: 7 that stood about him, Hear now, ye **B**; 1145
1Ch 27:12 *was* Abiezer the Anetothite, of the **B**: 1145

BENO (2)
1Ch 24:26 and Mushi: the sons of Jaaziah; **B**. 1121
24:27 **B**, and Shoham, and Zaccur, and Ibri. 1121

BEN-ONI (1) [BENJAMIN]
Ge 35:18 (for she died) that she called his name **B**: 1126

BENT (8) [BEND]
Ps 7:12 he hath **b** his bow, and made it ready. 1869
37:14 and have **b** their bow, to cast down the poor 1869
Isa 5:28 arrows *are* sharp, and all their bows **b**, 1869
21:15 from the **b** bow, and from the grievousness 1869
La 2: 4 He hath **b** his bow like an enemy: *he* stood 1869
3:12 He hath **b** his bow, and set me as a mark 1869
Hos 11: 7 my people are **b** to backsliding from me: 8511
Zec 9:13 When I have **b** Judah for me, filled the bow 1869

BEN-ZOHETH (1)
1Ch 4:20 And the sons of Ishi *were*, Zoheth, and **B**. 1132

BEON (1)
Nu 32: 3 and Elealeh, and Shebam, and Nebo, and **B**, 1194

BEOR (10) [BOSOR]
Ge 36:32 Bela the son of **B** reigned in Edom: and 1160
Nu 22: 5 unto Balaam the son of **B** to Pethor, 1160
24: 3 Balaam the son of **B** hath said, and the man 1160
24:15 Balaam the son of **B** hath said, and the man 1160
31: 8 Balaam also the son of **B** they slew with 1160
Dt 23: 4 they hired against thee Balaam the son of **B** 1160
Jos 13:22 Balaam also the son of **B**, the soothsayer, 1160
24: 9 called Balaam the son of **B** to curse you: 1160
1Ch 1:43 the children of Israel; Bela the son of **B**: 1160
Mic 6: 5 what Balaam the son of **B** answered him; 1160

BERA (1)
Ge 14: 2 *That these* made war with **B** king of 1298

BERACAH See BERACHAH

BERACHAH (3)
1Ch 12: 3 and **B**, and Jehu the Antothite, 1294
2Ch 20:26 assembled themselves in the valley of **B**; 1293
20:26 was called, The valley of **B**, unto *this* day. 1293

BERACHIAH (1)
1Ch 6:39 *even* Asaph the son of **B**, the son of 1296

BERAIAH (1)
1Ch 8:21 Adaiah, and **B**, and Shimrath, the sons of 1256

BEREA (3)
Ac 17:10 sent away Paul and Silas by night unto **B**: *960*
17:13 the word of God was preached of Paul at **B**, *960*
20: 4 accompanied him into Asia Sopater of **B**; *961*

BEREAVE (6) [BEREAVED, BEREAVETH]
Ecc 4: 8 whom do I labour, and **b** my soul of good? 2637
Jer 15: 7 I will **b** *them* **of children**, I will destroy my 7921
Eze 5:17 and evil beasts, and they shall **b** thee; 7921
36:12 shalt no more henceforth **b** them **of men**. 7921
36:14 neither **b** thy nations any more, saith 7921
Hos 9:12 bring up their children, yet will I **b** them, 7921

BEREAVED (6) [BEREAVE]
Ge 42:36 unto them, Me have ye **b of my children**: 7921
43:14 If I be **b of** my **children**, I am bereaved. 7921
43:14 If I be bereaved of my children, I am **b**. 7921
Jer 18:21 let their wives be **b of** their **children**, and 7909
Eze 36:13 devourest up men, and hast **b** thy nations; 7921
Hos 13: 8 meet them as a bear *that is* **b of** her **whelps**, 7909

BEREAVETH (1) [BEREAVE]
La 1:20 abroad the sword **b**, at home *there is* as 7921

BERECHIAH (10) [BARACHIAS]
1Ch 3:20 Ohel, and **B**, and Hasadiah, Jushabhesed, 1296
9:16 and **B** the son of Asa, the son of Elkanah, 1296
15:17 of his brethren, Asaph the son of **B**; and 1296
15:23 **B** and Elkanah *were* doorkeepers for 1296
2Ch 28:12 **B** the son of Meshillemoth, and 1296
Ne 3: 4 them repaired Meshullam the son of **B**, 1296
3:30 After him repaired Meshullam the son of **B** 1296
6:18 the daughter of Meshullam the son of **B**. 1296
Zec 1: 1 the son of **B**, the son of Iddo the prophet, 1296
1: 7 the son of **B**, the son of Iddo the prophet, 1296

BERED (2)
Ge 16:14 behold, *it is* between Kadesh and **B**. 1260
1Ch 7:20 **B** his son, and Tahath his son, and 1260

BEREKIAH See BARACHIAS; BERECHIAH

BERI (1)
1Ch 7:36 Harnepher, and Shual, and **B**, and Imrah, 1275

BERIAH (11) [BERIITES]
Ge 46:17 and Ishui, and **B**, and Serah their sister: 1283
46:17 and the sons of **B**; Heber, and Malchiel. 1283
Nu 26:44 of **B**, the family of the Beriites. 1283
26:45 Of the sons of **B**: of Heber, the family of 1283
1Ch 7:23 he called his name **B**, because it went evil 1283
7:30 and Ishuai, and **B**, and Serah their sister. 1283
7:31 the sons of **B**; Heber, and Malchiel, who *is* 1283
8:13 **B** also, and Shema, who *were* heads of 1283
8:16 and Ispah, and Joha, the sons of **B**; 1283
23:10 *were,* Jahath, Zina, and Jeush, and **B**. 1283
23:11 Jeush and **B** had not many sons; therefore 1283

BERIITES (1) [BERIAH]
Nu 26:44 the Jesuites: of Beriah, the family of the **B**. 1284

BERITES (1)
2Sa 20:14 and *to* Beth-maachah, and all the **B**: 1276

BERITH (1) [BAAL-BERITH]
Jdg 9:46 into a hold of the house of the god **B**. 1286

BERNICE (3)
Ac 25:13 and **B** came unto Cesarea to salute Festus. *959*
25:23 and **B**, with great pomp, and were entered *959*
26:30 and **B**, and they that sat with them: *959*

BERODACH-BALADAN (1) [MERODACH-BALADAN]
2Ki 20:12 At that time **B**, the son of Baladan, king of 1255

BEROTHAH (1)
Eze 47:16 Hamath, **B**, Sibraim, which *is* between 1268

BEROTHAI (1) [BEROTHITE]
2Sa 8: 8 from Betah, and from **B**, cities of 1268

BEROTHITE (1) [BEROTHAI]
1Ch 11:39 Zelek the Ammonite, Naharai the **B**, 1307

BERRIES (2)
Isa 17: 6 three **b** in the top of the uppermost bough, 1620
Jas 3:12 Can the fig tree, my brethren, bear **olive b**? *1636*

BERYL (8)
Ex 28:20 the fourth row a **b**, and an onyx, and 8658
39:13 the fourth row, a **b**, an onyx, and a jasper: 8658
SS 5:14 His hands *are as* gold rings set with the **b**: 8658
Eze 1:16 their work *was* like unto the colour of a **b**: 8658
10: 9 the wheels *was* as the colour of a **b** stone. 8658
28:13 the **b**, the onyx, and the jasper, 8658
Da 10: 6 His body also *was* like the **b**, and his face 8658
Rev 21:20 the eighth, **b**; the ninth, a topaz; the tenth, *969*

BESAI (2)
Ezr 2:49 the children of Paseah, the children of **B**, 1153
Ne 7:52 The children of **B**, the children of Meunim, 1153

BESEECH (67) [BESEECHING, BESOUGHT]
Ex 3:18 now let us go, **we b thee**, three days' 4994
33:18 And he said, **I b thee**, shew me thy glory. 4994
Nu 12:11 Alas, my lord, **I b thee**, lay not the sin upon 4994
12:13 Heal her now, O God, **I b thee**. 4994
14:17 now, **I b thee**, let the power of my Lord be 4994
14:19 Pardon, **I b thee**, the iniquity of this people 4994
1Sa 23:11 God of Israel, **I b thee**, tell thy servant. 4994
2Sa 13:24 **I b thee**, and his servants go with thy 4994
16: 4 I **humbly b** thee *that* I may find grace in 7812
24:10 now, **I b thee**, O LORD, take away 4994
2Ki 19:19 O LORD our God, **I b thee**, 4994
20: 3 **I b thee**, O LORD, remember now how I 577
1Ch 21: 8 now, **I b thee**, do away the iniquity of thy 4994
2Ch 6:40 Now, my God, let, **I b thee**, thine eyes be 4994
Ne 1: 5 said, **I b thee**, O LORD God of heaven, 577
1: 8 Remember, **I b thee**, the word that thou 4994
1:11 O Lord, **I b thee**, let now thine ear be 577
Job 10: 9 Remember, **I b thee**, that thou hast made 4994
42: 4 Hear, **I b thee**, and I will speak: I will 4994
Ps 80:14 Return, **we b thee**, O God *of* hosts: 4994
116: 4 O LORD, I **b** thee, deliver my soul. 577
118:25 Save now, **I b thee**, O LORD: O LORD, 577
118:25 O LORD, **I b thee**, send now prosperity. 577
119:108 Accept, **I b thee**, the freewill offerings of 4994
Isa 38: 3 Remember now, O LORD, **I b thee**, 4994
64: 9 behold, see, **we b thee**, we *are* all thy 4994
Jer 38: 4 **We b thee**, let this man be put to death: 4994
38:20 **I b thee**, the voice of the LORD, which I 4994
42: 2 unto Jeremiah the prophet, Let, **we b thee**, 4994
Da 1:12 Prove thy servants, **I b thee**, ten days; and 4994
9:16 **I b thee**, let thine anger and thy fury be 4994
Am 7: 2 I said, O Lord GOD, forgive, **I b thee**: 4994
7: 5 Then said I, O Lord GOD, cease, **I b thee**: 4994
Jnh 1:14 said, We **b** thee, O LORD, we beseech 577
1:14 We beseech thee, O LORD, **we b thee**, 4994
4: 3 Therefore now, O LORD, take, **I b thee**, 4994
Mal 1: 9 **b** God that he will be gracious unto 2470+6440
Mk 7:32 and they **b** him to put *his* hand upon him. *3870*
Lk 8:28 God most high? I **b** thee, torment me not. *1189*
9:38 saying, Master, I **b** thee, look upon my son: *1189*
Ac 21:39 and, I **b** thee, suffer me to speak unto *1189*
26: 3 wherefore I **b** thee to hear me patiently. *1189*
Ro 12: 1 I **b** you therefore, brethren, by the mercies *3870*
15:30 Now I **b** you, brethren, for the Lord Jesus *3870*
16:17 Now I **b** you, brethren, mark them which *3870*
1Co 1:10 Now I **b** you, brethren, by the name of our *3870*
4:16 Wherefore I **b** you, be ye followers of me. *3870*
16:15 I **b** you, brethren, (ye know the house of *3870*
2Co 2: 8 Wherefore I **b** you that *you* would confirm *3870*
5:20 for Christ, as though God did **b** *you* by us: *3870*
6: 1 *as* workers together *with him,* **b** *you* also *3870*
10: 1 Now I Paul myself **b** you by the meekness *3870*
10: 2 But I **b** *you,* that I may not be bold when I *1189*
Gal 4:12 Brethren, I **b** you, be as I *am;* for I *am* as ye *1189*
Eph 4: 1 **b** you that *ye* walk worthy of the vocation *3870*
Php 4: 2 I **b** Euodias, and beseech Syntyche, *3870*
4: 2 I beseech Euodias, and **b** Syntyche, *3870*
1Th 4: 1 Furthermore then we **b** you, brethren, and *2065*
4:10 but we **b** you, brethren, that *ye* increase *3870*
5:12 And we **b** you, brethren, to know them *2065*
2Th 2: 1 Now we **b** you, brethren, by the coming of *2065*
Phm 1: 9 *Yet* for love's sake I rather **b** *thee,* being *3870*
1:10 I **b** thee for my son Onesimus, whom I *3870*
Heb 13:19 But I **b** *you* the rather to do this, that I may *3870*
13:22 And I **b** you, brethren, suffer the word of *3870*
1Pe 2:11 I **b** *you* as strangers and pilgrims, *3870*
2Jn 1: 5 And now I **b** thee, lady, not as though I *2065*

BESEECHING (3) [BESEECH]
Mt 8: 5 there came unto him a centurion, **b** him, *3870*
Mk 1:40 **b** him, and kneeling down to him, and *3870*
Lk 7: 3 **b** him that he would come and heal his *2065*

BESET (6)
Jdg 19:22 **b** the house **round about,** *and* beat at 5437
20: 5 **b** the house **round about** upon me by 5437
Ps 22:12 strong *bulls* of Bashan have **b** me **round.** 3803
139: 5 Thou hast **b** me behind and before, and 6696
Hos 7: 2 now their own doings have **b** them **about**; 5437
Heb 12: 1 and the sin which doth so **easily b** *us,* and *2139*

BESIDE (95) [BESIDES] See Index

BESIDES (45) [BESIDE] See Index

BESIEGE (11) [BESIEGED, SIEGE]
Dt 20:12 war against thee, then thou shalt **b** it: 5921+6696
20:19 When thou shalt **b** a city a long time, 6696
28:52 he shall **b** thee in all thy gates, until thy 6887
28:52 he shall **b** thee in all thy gates throughout 6887
1Sa 23: 8 go down *to* Keilah, to **b** David and his men. 6696
1Ki 8:37 if their enemy **b** them in the land of their 6887
2Ki 24:11 against the city, and his servants *did* **b** it. 6696
2Ch 6:28 if their enemies **b** them in the cities of their 6887
Isa 21: 2 **b**, O Media; all the sighing thereof have I 6696
Jer 21: 4 which **b** you without the walls, and I will 6696
21: 9 falleth to the Chaldeans that **b** you, he shall 6696

BESIEGED (23) [BESIEGE]
2Sa 11: 1 the children of Ammon, and **b** Rabbah. 6696
20:15 and **b** him in Abel of Beth-maachah, 6696
1Ki 16:17 and all Israel with him, and they **b** Tirzah. 6696
20: 1 he went up and **b** Samaria, and 6696
2Ki 6:24 all his host, and went up, and **b** Samaria. 6696
6:25 behold, they **b** it, until an ass's head was 6696
16: 5 they **b** Ahaz, but could not overcome *him.* 6696
17: 5 went up *to* Samaria, and **b** it three years. 6696
18: 9 Assyria came up against Samaria, and **b** it. 6696
19:24 have I dried up all the rivers of **b** *places.* 4693
24:10 and the city was **b**. 4692+871.1+1886.1
25: 2 the city was **b** unto 935+4692+871.1+1886.1
1Ch 20: 1 of Ammon, and came and **b** Rabbah. 6696

Ecc 9:14 and **b** it, and built great bulwarks against it: 5437
Isa 1: 8 lodge in a garden of cucumbers, as a **b** city. 5341
37:25 I dried up all the rivers of the **b** *places.* 4693
Jer 32: 2 the king of Babylon's army **b** Jerusalem: 6696
37: 5 when the Chaldeans that **b** Jerusalem heard 6696
39: 1 his army against Jerusalem, and they **b** it. 6696
52: 5 So the city was **b** unto 935+4692+871.1+1886.1
Eze 4: 3 it shall be **b**, and thou shalt 4692+871.1+1886.1
6:12 and is **b** shall die by the famine: 5341
Da 1: 1 king of Babylon *unto* Jerusalem, and **b** it. 6696

BESODEIAH (1)
Ne 3: 6 son of Paseah, and Meshullam the son of **B**; 1152

BESOM (1)
Isa 14:23 I will sweep it with the **b** of destruction, 4292

BESOR (3)
1Sa 30: 9 *were* with him, and came to the brook **B**, 1308
30:10 that they could not go over the brook **B**. 1308
30:21 they had made also to abide at the brook **B**: 1308

BESOUGHT (44) [BESEECH]
Ge 42:21 when he **b** us, and we would not hear; 2603
Ex 32:11 Moses **b** the LORD his God, 853+2470+6440
Dt 3:23 I **b** the LORD at that time, saying, 413+2603
2Sa 12:16 David therefore **b** God for the child; and 1245
1Ki 13: 6 the man of God **b** the LORD, and 2470+6440
2Ki 1:13 **b** him, and said unto him, O man of God, 2603
13: 4 Jehoahaz **b** the LORD, and 2470+6440
2Ch 33:12 he **b** the LORD his God, and 853+2470+6440
Ezr 8:23 So we fasted and **b** our God for this: and 1245
Est 8: 3 **b** him with tears to put away the mischief 2603
Jer 26:19 **b** the LORD, and the LORD 853+2470+6440
Mt 8:31 So the devils **b** him, saying, If thou cast us *3870*
8:34 they **b** *him* that he would depart out of their *3870*
14:36 And **b** him that they might only touch *3870*
15:23 And his disciples came and **b** him, saying, *2065*
18:29 and **b** him, saying, Have patience with me, *3870*
Mk 5:10 And he **b** him much that he would not send *3870*
5:12 And all the devils **b** him, saying, Send us *3870*
5:23 And **b** him greatly, saying, My little *3870*
6:56 **b** him that they might touch if it were but *3870*
7:26 she **b** him that he would cast forth the devil *2065*
8:22 man unto him, and **b** him to touch him. *3870*
Lk 4:38 with a great fever; and they **b** him for her. *2065*
5:12 and **b** him, saying, Lord, if thou wilt, *1189*
7: 4 came to Jesus, they **b** him instantly, saying, *3870*
8:31 And they **b** him that he would not *3870*
8:32 they **b** him that he would suffer them to *3870*
8:37 round about **b** him to depart from them; *2065*
8:38 departed **b** him that *he* might be with him: *1189*
8:41 **b** him that *he* would come into his house: *3870*
9:40 And I **b** thy disciples to cast him out; and *1189*
11:37 a certain Pharisee **b** him to dine with him: *2065*
Jn 4:40 they **b** him that *he* would tarry with them: *2065*
4:47 and **b** him that he would come down, and *2065*
19:31 **b** Pilate that their legs might be broken, and *2065*
19:38 **b** Pilate that he might take away the body *2065*
Ac 13:42 the Gentiles **b** that these words might be *3870*
16:15 and her household, she **b** *us,* saying, *3870*
16:39 And they came and **b** them, and *3870*
21:12 that place, **b** him not to go up to Jerusalem. *3870*
25: 2 Jews informed him against Paul, and **b** him, *3870*
27:33 Paul **b** *them* all to take meat, saying, *3870*
2Co 12: 8 For this *thing* I **b** the Lord thrice, that it *3870*
1Ti 1: 3 As I **b** thee to abide *still* at Ephesus, when I *3870*

BEST (25) [GOOD]
Ge 43:11 take of the **b fruits** in the land in your 2173
47: 6 in the **b** of the land make thy father and 4315
47:11 in the **b** of the land, in the land of Rameses, 4315
Ex 22: 5 of the **b** of his own field, and of the best of 4315
22: 5 of the **b** of his own vineyard, shall he make 4315
Nu 18:12 All the **b** of the oil, and all the best of 2459
18:12 and all the **b** of the wine, and of the wheat, 2459
18:29 of all the **b** thereof, *even* the hallowed *part* 2459
18:30 When ye have heaved the **b** thereof from it, 2459
18:32 when ye have heaved from it the **b** of it: 2459
36: 6 marry to whom they **think b**; 2896+5869+871.1
Dt 23:16 where it **liketh** him **b**: 2896+871.1+1886.1
1Sa 8:14 *even* the **b** *of them,* and give *them* to his 2896
15: 9 the **b** of the sheep, and of the oxen, and 4315
15:15 for the people spared the **b** of the sheep and 4315

2Sa 18: 4 unto them, What seemeth you **b** I will do. 3190
1Ki 10:18 of ivory, and overlaid it with the **b** gold. 6338
2Ki 10: 3 Look even out the **b** and meetest of your 2896
Est 2: 9 her maids unto the **b** *place* of the house of 2896
Ps 39: 5 verily every man **at** his **b state** *is* altogether 5324
SS 7: 9 the roof of thy mouth like the **b** wine, 2896
Eze 31:16 the choice and **b** of Lebanon, all that drink 2896
Mic 7: 4 The **b** of them *is* as a brier: the *most* 2896
Lk 15:22 Bring forth the **b** robe, and put *it* on him; *4413*
1Co 12:31 But covet earnestly the **b** gifts: and *2909*

BESTEAD (1)
Isa 8:21 shall pass through it, **hardly b** and hungry: 7185

BESTIR (1)
2Sa 5:24 *that* then thou shalt **b** thyself: 2782

BESTOW (9) [BESTOWED]
Ex 32:29 that he may **b** upon you a blessing *this* day. 5414
Dt 14:26 thou shalt **b** *that* money for whatsoever thy 5414
2Ch 24: 7 of the LORD did they **b** upon Baalim. 6213
Ezr 7:20 which thou shalt have occasion to **b**, 5415
7:20 **b** *it* out of the king's treasure house. 5415
Lk 12:17 I have no room where to **b** my fruits? *4863*
12:18 and there will I **b** all my fruits and *4863*
1Co 12:23 upon these we **b** more abundant honour; *4060*
13: 3 And though I **b** all my goods **to feed** *5595*

BESTOWED (14) [BESTOW]
1Ki 10:26 whom he **b** in the cities for chariots, and 5148
2Ki 5:24 from their hand, and **b** *them* in the house: 6485
12:15 delivered the money to be **b** on workmen: 5414
1Ch 29:25 **b** upon him *such* royal majesty as had not 5414
2Ch 9:25 whom he **b** in the chariot cities, and 3240
Isa 63: 7 according to all that the LORD hath **b on** 1580
63: 7 which he hath **b on** them according to his 1580
Jn 4:38 you to reap *that* whereon ye **b** no **labour**: *2872*
Ro 16: 6 Greet Mary, who **b** much **labour** on us. *2872*
1Co 15:10 his grace which was *b* upon me was not in NIG
2Co 1:11 that for the gift *b* upon us by the means of NIG
8: 1 we do you to wit of the grace of God **b** on *1325*
Gal 4:11 lest I have **b** upon you **labour** in vain. *2872*
1Jn 3: 1 what manner of love the Father hath **b** upon *1325*

BETAH (1)
2Sa 8: 8 from **B**, and from Berothai, cities of 984

BETEN (1)
Jos 19:25 and Hali, and **B**, and Achshaph, 991

BETH BIRI See BETH-BIREI

BETH HAKKEREM See BETH-HACCEREM

BETH HARAM See BETH-ARAM

BETH MAACAH See BETH-MAACHAH

BETH OPHRAH See HOUSE OF APHRAH

BETH PELET See BETH-PALET; BETH-PHELET

BETHABARA (1)
Jn 1:28 These *things* were done in **B** beyond Jordan, *962*

BETH-ANATH (3) [ANATH]
Jos 19:38 Horem, and **B**, and Beth-shemesh; 1043
Jdg 1:33 of Beth-shemesh, nor the inhabitants of **B**; 1043
1:33 and of **B** became tributaries unto them. 1043

BETH-ANOTH (1)
Jos 15:59 Maarath, and **B**, and Eltekon; six cities with 1042

BETHANY (11)
Mt 21:17 he left them, and went out of the city into **B**; *963*
26: 6 Now when Jesus was in **B**, in the house of *963*
Mk 11: 1 unto Bethphage and **B**, at the mount of *963*
11:11 he went out unto **B** with the twelve. *963*
11:12 when they were come from **B**, he was *963*
14: 3 And being in **B** in the house of Simon *963*
Lk 19:29 when he was come nigh to Bethphage and **B**, *963*
24:50 And he led them out as far as to **B**, and *963*
Jn 11: 1 *named* Lazarus, of **B**, the town of Mary and *963*
11:18 Now **B** was nigh unto Jerusalem, *963*
12: 1 six days before the passover came to **B**, *963*

BETH-ARABAH (3) [ARABAH]
Jos 15: 6 and passed along by the north of **B**, 1026
15:61 In the wilderness, **B**, Middin, and Secacah, 1026
18:22 And **B**, and Zemaraim, and Beth-el, 1026

BETH-ARAM (1) [ARAM]
Jos 13:27 **B**, and Beth-nimrah, and Succoth, and 1027

BETH-ARBEL (1)
Hos 10:14 as Shalman spoiled **B** in the day of battle: 1009

BETH-AVEN (7) [AVEN]
Jos 7: 2 which *is* beside **B**, on the east side of 1007
18:12 out thereof were at the wilderness of **B**. 1007
1Sa 13: 5 and pitched in Michmash, eastward from **B**. 1007
14:23 that day: and the battle passed over *unto* **B**. 1007
Hos 4:15 neither go ye up *to* **B**, nor swear, 1007
5: 8 cry aloud *at* **B**, after thee, O Benjamin. 1007
10: 5 shall fear because of the calves of **B**: 1007

BETH-AZMAVETH (1) [AZMAVETH]
Ne 7:28 The men of **B**, forty and two. 1041

BETH-BAAL-MEON (1) [BAAL-MEON]
Jos 13:17 the plain; Dibon, and Bamoth-baal, and **B**, 1010

BETH-BARAH (2)
Jdg 7:24 take before them the waters unto **B** and 1012
7:24 and took the waters unto **B** and Jordan. 1012

BETH-BIREI (1)
1Ch 4:31 and at **B**, and at Shaaraim. 1011

BETH-CAR (1)
1Sa 7:11 and smote them, until *they came* under **B**. 1033

BETH-DAGON (2) [DAGON]
Jos 15:41 **B**, and Naamah, and Makkedah; 1016
19:27 turneth *toward* the sunrising *to* **B**, and 1016

BETH-DIBLATHAIM (1)
Jer 48:22 upon Dibon, and upon Nebo, and upon **B**, 1015

BETH-EL (66) [BETHELITE, EL-BETH-EL, GOD, HOUSE]
Ge 12: 8 thence unto a mountain on the east of **B**, 1008
12: 8 *having* **B** on the west, and Hai on the east: 1008
13: 3 on his journeys from the south even to **B**, 1008
13: 3 been at the beginning, between **B** and Hai; 1008
28:19 he called the name of that place **B**: but 1008
31:13 I *am* the God of **B**, where thou anointedst 1008
35: 1 Arise, go up to **B**, and dwell there: 1008
35: 3 let us arise, and go up to **B**; and I will make 1008
35: 6 that *is*, **B**, he and all the people that *were* 1008
35: 8 she was buried beneath **B** under an oak: 1008
35:15 of the place where God spake with him, **B**. 1008
35:16 they journeyed from **B**; and there was but 1008
Jos 7: 2 on the east side of **B**, and spake unto them, 1008
8: 9 abode between **B** and Ai, on the west side 1008
8:12 set them to lie in ambush between **B** and 1008
8:17 there was not a man left in Ai or **B**, 1008
12: 9 one; the king of Ai, which *is* beside **B**, one; 1008
12:16 king of Makkedah, one; the king of **B**, one; 1008
16: 1 goeth up from Jericho throughout mount **B**, 1008
16: 2 goeth out from **B** to Luz, and passeth along 1008
18:13 to the side of Luz, which *is* **B**, southward; 1008
18:22 And Beth-arabah, and Zemaraim, and **B**, 1008
Jdg 1:22 of Joseph, they also went up *against* **B**: 1008
1:23 the house of Joseph sent to descry **B**. 1008
4: 5 between Ramah and **B** in mount Ephraim: 1008
21:19 *in a place* which *is* on the north side of **B**, 1008
21:19 highway that goeth up from **B** to Shechem, 1008
1Sa 7:16 he went from year to year in circuit *to* **B**, 1008
10: 3 meet thee three men going up to God *to* **B**, 1008
13: 2 with Saul in Michmash and in mount **B**, 1008
30:27 To *them* which *were* in **B**, and to *them* 1008
1Ki 12:29 he set the one in **B**, and the other put he in 1008
12:32 he offered upon the altar (so did he in **B**,) 1008
12:32 he placed in **B** the priests of the high places 1008
12:33 in **B** the fifteenth day of the eighth month, 1008
13: 1 Judah by the word of the LORD unto **B**: 1008
13: 4 which had cried against the altar in **B**, 1008
13:10 returned not by the way that he came to **B**. 1008
13:11 Now there dwelt an old prophet in **B**; and 1008
13:11 that the man of God had done *that* day in **B**: 1008
13:32 word of the LORD against the altar in **B**, 1008
2Ki 2: 2 for the LORD hath sent me to **B**. 1008
2: 2 not leave thee. So they went down *to* **B**. 1008
2: 3 the sons of the prophets that *were at* **B** 1008
2:23 he went up from thence *unto* **B**: and as he 1008
10:29 *to wit*, the golden calves that *were in* **B**, and 1008
17:28 away from Samaria came and dwelt in **B**, 1008
23: 4 and carried the ashes of them *unto* **B**. 1008
23:15 Moreover the altar that *was* at **B**, *and* 1008
23:17 that thou hast done against the altar of **B**. 1008
23:19 to all the acts that he had done in **B**. 1008
1Ch 7:28 habitations *were*, **B** and the towns thereof, 1008
2Ch 13:19 **B** with the towns thereof, and Jeshanah 1008
Ezr 2:28 The men of **B** and Ai, two hundred twenty 1008
Ne 7:32 The men of **B** and Ai, an hundred twenty 1008
11:31 and Aija, and **B**, and *in* their villages, 1008
Jer 48:13 as the house of Israel was ashamed of **B** 1008
Hos 10:15 So shall **B** do unto you because of your 1008
12: 4 he found him *in* **B**, and there he spake with 1008
Am 3:14 upon him I will also visit the altars of **B**: 1008
4: 4 Come *to* **B**, and transgress; *at* Gilgal 1008
5: 5 seek not **B**, nor enter *into* Gilgal, and 1008
5: 5 into captivity, and **B** shall come to nought. 1008
5: 6 and *there be* none to quench *it* in **B**. 1008
7:10 Amaziah *the* priest of **B** sent to Jeroboam 1008
7:13 prophesy not again any more *at* **B**: for it *is* 1008

BETHELITE (1) [BETH-EL]
1Ki 16:34 In his days did Hiel the **B** build Jericho: 1017

BETH-EMEK (1)
Jos 19:27 of Jiphthah-el toward the north side *of* **B**, 1025

BETHER (1)
SS 2:17 or a young hart upon the mountains of **B**. 1335

BETHESDA (1)
Jn 5: 2 which is called in the Hebrew tongue **B**, *964*

BETH-EZEL (1) [EZEL]
Mic 1:11 came not forth *in* the mourning of **B**; 1018

BETH-GADER (1)
1Ch 2:51 of Beth-lehem, Hareph the father of **B**. 1013

BETH-GAMUL (1) [GAMUL]
Jer 48:23 and upon **B**, and upon Beth-meon, 1014

BETH-HACCEREM (2)
Ne 3:14 the son of Rechab, the ruler of part of **B**; 1021
Jer 6: 1 in Tekoa, and set up a sign of fire in **B**: 1021

BETH-HARAN (1) [HARAN]
Nu 32:36 Beth-nimrah, and **B**, fenced cities: and 1028

BETH-HOGLA (1) [BETH-HOGLAH]
Jos 15: 6 the border went up *to* **B**, and passed along 1031

BETH-HOGLAH (2) [BETH-HOGLA]
Jos 18:19 the border passed along to the side of **B** 1031
18:21 and **B**, and the valley of Keziz, 1031

BETH-HORON (14)
Jos 10:10 them *along* the way that goeth up to **B**, 1032
10:11 *and* were in the going down to **B**, 1032
16: 3 unto the coast of **B** the nether, and 1032
16: 5 side was Ataroth-addar, unto **B** the upper; 1032
18:13 that *lieth* on the south side of the nether **B**. 1032
18:14 from the hill that *lieth* before **B** southward; 1032
21:22 with her suburbs, and **B** with her suburbs; 1032
1Sa 13:18 another company turned the way to **B**: and 1032
1Ki 9:17 Solomon built Gezer, and **B** the nether, 1032
1Ch 6:68 with her suburbs, and **B** with her suburbs, 1032
7:24 who built **B** the nether, and the upper, and 1032
2Ch 8: 5 Also he built **B** the upper, and Beth-horon 1032
8: 5 **B** the nether, fenced cities, *with* walls, 1032
25:13 from Samaria even unto **B**, and smote three 1032

BETHINK (2) [THINK]
1Ki 8:47 *Yet* if they shall **b** themselves in 413+3820+7725
2Ch 6:37 *Yet* if they **b** themselves in 413+3824+7725

BETH-JESHIMOTH (3) [BETH-JESIMOTH]
Jos 12: 3 *even* the salt sea on the east, the way to **B**; 1020
13:20 and Ashdoth-pisgah, and **B**, 1020
Eze 25: 9 the country, **B**, Baal-meon, and Kiriathaim, 1020

BETH-JESIMOTH (1) [BETH-JESHIMOTH]
Nu 33:49 from **B** *even* unto Abel-shittim in the plains 1020

BETH-LEBAOTH (1)
Jos 19: 6 **B**, and Sharuhen; thirteen cities and 1034

BETHLEHEM, BETH-LEHEM (39) [BETH-LEHEM-JUDAH, BETH-LEHEMITE, BETHLEHEM]
Ge 35:19 buried in the way to Ephrath, which *is* **B**. 1035
48: 7 there in the way of Ephrath; the same *is* **B**. 1035
Jos 19:15 Nahallal, and Shimron, and Idalah, and **B**: 1035
Jdg 12: 8 And after him Ibzan of **B** judged Israel. 1035
12:10 Then died Ibzan, and was buried at **B**. 1035
Ru 1:19 So they two went until they came *to* **B**. 1035
1:19 it came to pass, when they were come *to* **B**, 1035
1:22 they came *to* **B** in the beginning of barley 1035
2: 4 Boaz came from **B**, and said unto 1035
4:11 worthily in Ephratah, and be famous in **B**: 1035
1Sa 16: 4 which the LORD spake, and came *to* **B**. 1035
17:15 from Saul to feed his father's sheep *at* **B**. 1035
20: 6 *leave* of me that *he* might run *to* **B** his city: 1035
20:28 earnestly asked *leave* of me *to go* to **B**: 1035
2Sa 2:32 the sepulchre of his father, which *was in* **B**. 1035
23:14 garrison of the Philistines *was* then *in* **B**. 1035
23:15 give me drink *of* the water of the well of **B**, 1035
23:16 drew water out of the well of **B**, that *was* by 1035
23:24 of the thirty; Elhanan the son of Dodo *of* **B**, 1035
1Ch 2:51 Salma the father of **B**, Hareph the father of 1035
2:54 **B**, and the Netophathites, Ataroth, 1035
4: 4 the firstborn of Ephratah, the father of **B**. 1035
11:16 and the Philistines' garrison *was* then at **B**. 1035
11:17 give me drink *of* the water of the well of **B**, 1035
11:18 drew water out of the well of **B**, that *was* by 1035
11:26 of Joab, Elhanan the son of Dodo of **B**, 1035
2Ch 11: 6 He built even **B**, and Etam, and Tekoa, 1035
Ezr 2:21 The children of **B**, an hundred twenty and 1035
Ne 7:26 The men of **B** and Netophah, an hundred 1035
Jer 41:17 which *is* by **B**, to go to enter *into* Egypt, 1035
Mic 5: 2 thou, **B** Ephratah, *though thou* be little 1035
Mt 2: 1 Now when Jesus was born in **B** of Judea in *965*
2: 5 And they said unto him, In **B** of Judea: *965*
2: 6 And thou **B**, *in* the land of Juda, art not *965*
2: 8 And he sent them to **B**, and said, Go and *965*
2:16 and slew all the children that were in **B**, and *965*
Lk 2: 4 unto the city of David, which is called **B**; *965*
2:15 Let us now go *even* unto **B**, and see this *965*
Jn 7:42 and out of the town of **B**, where David was? *965*

BETH-LEHEMITE (4) [BETH-LEHEM]
1Sa 16: 1 and go, I will send thee to Jesse the **B**: 1022
16:18 Behold, I have seen a son of Jesse the **B**, 1022
17:58 *I am* the son of thy servant Jesse the **B**. 1022
2Sa 21:19 a **B**, slew *the brother of* Goliath the Gittite, 1022

BETH-LEHEM-JUDAH (10) [BETH-LEHEM, JUDAH]
Jdg 17: 7 there was a young man out of **B** of 1035+3063
17: 8 **B** to sojourn where he could find *a* 1035+3063
17: 9 I *am* a Levite of **B**, and I go to 1035+3063
19: 1 took to him a concubine out of **B**. 1035+3063
19: 2 him unto her father's house to **B**, 1035+3063
19:18 We are passing from **B** toward 1035+3063
19:18 I went to **B**, but I am *now* going *to* 1035+3063
Ru 1: 1 a *certain* man of **B** went to sojourn in 1035+3063
1: 2 and Chilion, Ephrathites of **B**. 1035+3063
1Sa 17:12 *was* the son of that Ephrathite of **B**, 1035+3063

BETH-MAACHAH (2) [ABEL-BETH-MAACHAH]
2Sa 20:14 unto Abel, and *to* **B**, and all the Berites: 1038
20:15 they came and besieged him in Abel of **B**, 1038

BETH-MARCABOTH (2)
Jos 19: 5 And Ziklag, and **B**, and Hazar-susah, 1024
1Ch 4:31 at **B**, and Hazar-susim, and at Beth-birei, 1024

BETH-MEON (1) [BAAL-MEON]
Jer 48:23 and upon Beth-gamul, and upon **B**, 1010

BETH-NIMRAH (2) [NIMRAH]
Nu 32:36 **B**, and Beth-haran, fenced cities: and 1039
Jos 13:27 and **B**, and Succoth, and Zaphon, 1039

BETH-PALET (1) [BETH-PHELET]
Jos 15:27 And Hazar-gaddah, and Heshmon, and **B**, 1046

BETH-PAZZEZ (1)
Jos 19:21 and En-gannim, and En-haddah, and **B**; 1048

BETH-PEOR (4) [PEOR]
Dt 3:29 So we abode in the valley over against **B**. 1047
4:46 side Jordan, in the valley over against **B**, 1047
34: 6 valley in the land of Moab, over against **B**: 1047
Jos 13:20 **B**, and Ashdoth-pisgah, and 1047

BETHPHAGE (3)
Mt 21: 1 and were come to **B**, unto the mount of *967*
Mk 11: 1 unto **B** and Bethany, at the mount of Olives, *967*
Lk 19:29 when he was come nigh to **B** and Bethany, *967*

BETH-PHELET (1) [BETH-PALET]
Ne 11:26 And at Jeshua, and at Moladah, and at **B**, 1046

BETH-RAPHA (1) [RAPHA]
1Ch 4:12 Eshton begat **B**, and Paseah, and Tehinnah 1051

BETH-REHOB (2) [REHOB]
Jdg 18:28 and it was in the valley that *lieth* by **B**. 1050
2Sa 10: 6 of Ammon sent and hired the Syrians of **B**, 1050

BETHSAIDA (7)
Mt 11:21 Woe unto thee, Chorazin, woe unto thee, **B**: *966*
Mk 6:45 and to go to the other side before unto **B**, *966*
8:22 And he cometh to **B**; and they bring a blind *966*
Lk 9:10 a desert place belonging to the city called **B**. *966*
10:13 Woe unto thee, Chorazin, woe unto thee, **B**: *966*
Jn 1:44 Now Philip was of **B**, the city of Andrew *966*
12:21 which was of **B** of Galilee, and desired him, *966*

BETH-SHAN (3) [BETH-SHEAN]
1Sa 31:10 and they fastened his body to the wall of **B**. 1052
31:12 the bodies of his sons from the wall of **B**, 1052
2Sa 21:12 which had stolen them from the street of **B**, 1052

BETH-SHEAN (6) [BETH-SHAN]
Jos 17:11 in Issachar and in Asher **B** and her towns, 1052
17:16 *both they* who *are* of **B** and her towns, and 1052
Jdg 1:27 did Manasseh drive out *the inhabitants of* **B** 1052
1Ki 4:12 *pertained* Taanach and Megiddo, and all **B**, 1052
4:12 beneath Jezreel, from **B** to Abel-meholah, 1052
1Ch 7:29 **B** and her towns, Taanach and her towns, 1052

BETH-SHEMESH (21)
Jos 15:10 went down *to* **B**, and passed on *to* Timnah: 1053
19:22 reacheth to Tabor, and Shahazimah, and **B**; 1053
19:38 Migdal-el, Horem, and Beth-anath, and **B**; 1053
21:16 with her suburbs, *and* **B** with her suburbs; 1053
Jdg 1:33 did Naphtali drive out the inhabitants of **B**, 1053
1:33 nevertheless the inhabitants of **B** and 1053
1Sa 6: 9 goeth up *by* the way of his own coast *to* **B**, 1053
6:12 kine took the straight way to the way of **B**, 1053
6:12 went after them unto the border of **B**. 1053
6:13 *they of* **B** *were* reaping *their* wheat harvest 1053
6:15 the men of **B** offered burnt offerings and 1053
6:19 he smote the men of **B**, because they had 1053
6:20 the men of **B** said, Who is able to stand 1053
1Ki 4: 9 in Shaalbim, and **B**, and Elon-beth-hanan: 1053
2Ki 14:11 Judah looked one another *in* the face at **B**, 1053
14:13 at **B**, and came *to* Jerusalem, and 1053
1Ch 6:59 with her suburbs, and **B** with her suburbs: 1053
2Ch 25:21 *both* he and Amaziah king of Judah, at **B**, 1053
25:23 at **B**, and brought him *to* Jerusalem, and 1053
28:18 and had taken **B**, and Ajalon, and Gederoth, 1053
Jer 43:13 He shall break also the images of **B**, that *is* 1053

BETH-SHEMITE (2) [BETH-SHITTAH]
1Sa 6:14 a **B**, and stood there, where *there was* a 1030
6:18 unto this day in the field of Joshua, the **B**. 1030

BETH-SHITTAH (1) [BETH-SHEMITE]
Jdg 7:22 the host fled to **B** in Zererath, *and* to 1029

BETH-TAPPUAH (1) [TAPPUAH]
Jos 15:53 And Janum, and **B**, and Aphekah, 1054

BETHUEL (10)
Ge 22:22 and Hazo, and Pildash, and Jidlaph, and **B**. 1328
22:23 **B** begat Rebekah: these eight Milcah did 1328
24:15 who was born to **B**, son of Milcah, the wife 1328
24:24 I *am* the daughter of **B** the son of Milcah, 1328
24:47 she said, The daughter of **B**, Nahor's son, 1328

Ge 24:50 Laban and **B** answered and said, The thing 1328
25:20 the daughter of **B** the Syrian of 1328
28: 2 to the house of **B** thy mother's father; 1328
28: 5 son of **B** the Syrian, the brother of 1328
1Ch 4:30 And at **B**, and at Hormah, and at Ziklag, 1328

BETHUL (1)
Jos 19: 4 And Eltolad, and **B**, and Hormah, 1329

BETH-ZUR (4) [ZUR]
Jos 15:58 Halhul, **B**, and Gedor, 1049
1Ch 2:45 *was* Maon: and Maon *was* the father of **B**. 1049
2Ch 11: 7 And **B**, and Shoco, and Adullam, 1049
Ne 3:16 of Azbuk, the ruler of the half part of **B**, 1049

BETIMES (5) [TIME]
Ge 26:31 they **rose up b** in the morning, and 7925
2Ch 36:15 his messengers, **rising up b**, and sending; 7925
Job 8: 5 If thou wouldest **seek** unto God **b**, and 7836
24: 5 they forth to their work; **rising b** for a prey: 7836
Pr 13:24 but he that loveth him chasteneth him **b**. 7836

BETONIM (1)
Jos 13:26 from Heshbon unto Ramath-mizpeh, and **B**; 993

BETRAY (18) [BETRAYED, BETRAYERS, BETRAYEST, BETRAYETH]
1Ch 12:17 if *ye be come* to **b** me to mine enemies, 7411
Mt 24:10 and shall **b** one another, and shall hate one *3860*
26:16 that time he sought opportunity to **b** him. *3860*
26:21 I say unto you, that one of you shall **b** me. *3860*
26:23 with me in the dish, the same shall **b** me. *3860*
26:46 behold, he is at hand that doth **b** me. *3860*
Mk 13:12 Now the brother shall **b** the brother to *3860*
14:10 unto the chief priests, to **b** him unto them. *3860*
14:11 sought how he might conveniently **b** him. *3860*
14:18 One of you which eateth with me shall **b** *3860*
Lk 22: 4 captains, how he might **b** him unto them. *3860*
22: 6 sought opportunity to **b** him unto them in *3860*
Jn 6:64 that believed not, and who should **b** him. *3860*
6:71 for he *it was that* should **b** him, being one *3860*
12: 4 Simon's *son*, which should **b** him, *3860*
13: 2 of Judas Iscariot, Simon's *son*, to **b** him; *3860*
13:11 For he knew who should **b** him; therefore *3860*
13:21 I say unto you, that one of you shall **b** me. *3860*

BETRAYED (19) [BETRAY]
Mt 10: 4 and Judas Iscariot, who also **b** him. *3860*
17:22 The Son of man shall be **b** into the hands of *3860*
20:18 the Son of man shall be **b** unto the chief *3860*
26: 2 and the Son of man is **b** to be crucified. *3860*
26:24 that man by whom the Son of man is **b**: *3860*
26:25 which **b** him, answered and said, Master, is *3860*
26:45 the Son of man is **b** into the hands of *3860*
26:48 Now he that **b** him gave them a sign, *3860*
27: 3 Then Judas, which had **b** him, when he saw *3860*
27: 4 I have sinned in that I have **b** *the* innocent *3860*
Mk 3:19 And Judas Iscariot, which also **b** him. *3860*
14:21 to that man by whom the Son of man is **b**: *3860*
14:41 the Son of man is **b** into the hands of *3860*
14:44 And he that **b** him had given them a token, *3860*
Lk 21:16 And ye shall be **b** both by parents, and *3860*
22:22 but woe unto that man by whom he is **b**. *3860*
Jn 18: 2 Judas also, which **b** him, knew the place: *3860*
18: 5 Judas also, which **b** him, stood with them. *3860*
1Co 11:23 *same* night in which he was **b** took bread: *3860*

BETRAYERS (1) [BETRAY]
Ac 7:52 of whom ye have been now the **b** and *4273*

BETRAYEST (1) [BETRAY]
Lk 22:48 Judas, **b** thou the Son of man with a kiss? *3860*

BETRAYETH (3) [BETRAY]
Mk 14:42 let us go; lo, he that **b** me is at hand. *3860*
Lk 22:21 the hand of him that **b** me *is* with me on *3860*
Jn 21:20 and said, Lord, which is he that **b** thee? *3860*

BETROTH (4) [BETROTHED]
Dt 28:30 Thou shalt **b** a wife, and another man shall 781
Hos 2:19 I will **b** thee unto me for ever; yea, I will 781
2:19 I will **b** thee unto me in righteousness, and 781
2:20 I will even **b** thee unto me in faithfulness: 781

BETROTHED (9) [BETROTH]
Ex 21: 8 who hath **b** her to himself, then shall he let 3259
21: 9 if he have **b** her unto his son, he shall deal 3259
22:16 And if a man entice a maid that is not **b**, and 781
Lev 19:20 **b** to a husband, and not at all redeemed, nor 2778
Dt 20: 7 what man *is there* that hath **b** a wife, and 781
22:23 If a damsel *that is* a virgin be **b** unto a 781
22:25 But if a man find a **b** damsel in the field, and 781
22:27 *and* the **b** damsel cried, and *there was* none 781
22:28 which is not **b**, and lay hold on her, and 781

BETTER (117) [GOOD]
Ge 29:19 Laban said, *It is* **b** that I give her to thee, 2896
Ex 14:12 For *it had been* **b** for us to serve 2896
Nu 14: 3 were it not **b** for us to return into Egypt? 2896
Jdg 8: 2 of Ephraim **b** than the vintage of Abi-ezer? 2896
9: 2 Whether *is* **b** for you, either that all 2896
11:25 now *art* thou **any thing b** than Balak 2896+2896
18:19 *is it* **b** for thee to be a priest unto the house 2896
Ru 4:15 which *is* **b** to thee than seven sons, 2896
1Sa 1: 8 *am* not I **b** to thee than ten sons? 2896
15:22 to obey *is* **b** than sacrifice, *and* to hearken 2896
15:28 to a neighbour of thine, *that is* **b** than thou. 2896
27: 1 *there is* nothing **b** for me than that I should 2896
2Sa 17:14 The counsel of Hushai the Archite *is* **b** than 2896
18: 3 now *it is* **b** that thou succour us out of 2896
1Ki 1:47 God **make** the name of Solomon **b** than thy 3190
2:32 two men more righteous and **b** than he, 2896
19: 4 my life; for I *am* not **b** than my fathers. 2896
21: 2 I will give thee for it a **b** vineyard than it; 2896
2Ki 5:12 **b** than all the waters of Israel? 2896
2Ch 21:13 father's house, *which were* **b** than thyself: 2896
Est 1:19 royal estate unto another *that is* **b** than she. 2896
Ps 37:16 A little that a righteous *man* hath *is* **b** than 2896
63: 3 Because thy lovingkindness *is* **b** than life, 2896
69:31 *This* also shall please the LORD **b than** 4480
84:10 For a day in thy courts *is* **b** than a thousand. 2896
118: 8 *It is* **b** to trust in the LORD than to put 2896
118: 9 *It is* **b** to trust in the LORD than to put 2896
119:72 The law of thy mouth *is* **b** unto me than 2896
Pr 3:14 For the merchandise of it *is* **b** than 2896
8:11 For wisdom *is* **b** than rubies; and all 2896
8:19 My fruit *is* **b** than gold, yea, than fine gold; 2896
12: 9 *is* **b** than he that honoureth himself, and 2896
15:16 **B** *is* little with the fear of the LORD than 2896
15:17 **B** *is* a dinner of herbs where love is, than a 2896
16: 8 **B** *is* a little with righteousness than great 2896
16:16 How much **b** *is it* to get wisdom than gold! 2896
16:19 **B** *it is to be* of an humble spirit with 2896
16:32 *He that is* slow to anger *is* **b** than 2896
17: 1 **B** *is* a dry morsel, and quietness therewith, 2896
19: 1 **B** *is* the poor that walketh in his integrity, 2896
19:22 and a poor *man is* **b** than a liar. 2896
21: 9 *It is* **b** to dwell in a corner of the housetop, 2896
21:19 *It is* **b** to dwell in the wilderness, than with 2896
25: 7 For **b** *it is* that it be said unto thee, 2896
25:24 *It is* **b** to dwell in a corner of the housetop, 2896
27: 5 Open rebuke *is* **b** than secret love. 2896
27:10 *for* **b** *is* a neighbour *that is* near than a 2896
28: 6 **B** *is* the poor that walketh in his 2896
Ecc 2:24 *There is* nothing **b** for a man, *than* that he 2896
3:22 I perceive that *there is* nothing **b**, 2896
4: 3 Yea, **b** *is he* than both they, which hath not 2896
4: 6 **B** *is* a handful *with* quietness, than both 2896
4: 9 Two *are* **b** than one; because they have a 2896
4:13 **B** *is* a poor and a wise child than an old and 2896
5: 5 **B** *is it* that thou shouldest not vow, 2896
6: 3 I say, *that* an untimely birth *is* **b** than he. 2896
6: 9 **B** *is* the sight of the eyes than 2896
6:11 that increase vanity, what *is* man the **b**? 3148
7: 1 A *good* name *is* **b** than precious ointment; 2896
7: 2 *It is* **b** to go to the house of mourning, 2896
7: 3 Sorrow *is* **b** than laughter: for by 2896
7: 3 of the countenance the heart is **made b**. 3190
7: 5 *It is* **b** to hear the rebuke of the wise, 2896
7: 8 **B** *is* the end of a thing than the beginning 2896
7: 8 the patient in spirit *is* **b** than the proud in 2896
7:10 that the former days were **b** than these? 2896
8:15 a man hath no **b** *thing* under the sun, 2896
9: 4 for a living dog *is* **b** than a dead lion. 2896
9:16 said I, Wisdom *is* **b** than strength: 2896
9:18 Wisdom *is* **b** than weapons of war: but 2896
10:11 without enchantment; and a babbler is no **b**. 3504

SS 1: 2 of his mouth: for thy love *is* **b** than wine. 2896
4:10 how much **b** is thy love than wine! and 2895
Isa 56: 5 a name **b** than *of* sons and *of* daughters: 2896
La 4: 9 *They that be* slain with the sword are **b** than 2896
Eze 36:11 will **do b** *unto you* than at your beginnings: 2895
Da 1:20 he found them ten times **b than** all 5921
Hos 2: 7 for then *was it* **b** with me than now. 2896
Am 6: 2 *be they* **b** than these kingdoms? or 2896
Jnh 4: 3 for *it is* **b** for me to die than to live. 2896
4: 8 and said, *It is* **b** for me to die than to live. 2896
Na 3: 8 Art thou **b** than populous No, that was 3190
Mt 6:26 Are ye not much **b than** they? *1308*
12:12 How much then is a man **b than** a sheep? *1308*
18: 6 it were **b** for him that a millstone were *4851*
18: 8 it is **b** for thee to enter into life halt or *2570*
18: 9 it is **b** for thee to enter into life with one *2570*
Mk 9:42 it is **b** for him that a millstone were hanged *2570*
9:43 it is **b** for thee to enter into life maimed, *2570*
9:45 it is **b** for thee to enter halt into life, *2570*
9:47 it is **b** for thee to enter into the kingdom of *2570*
Lk 5:39 desireth new: for he saith, The old is **b**. *5543*
12:24 how much more are ye **b than** the fowls? *1308*
17: 2 It were **b** for him that a millstone were *3081*
Ro 3: 9 are we **b** *than they?* No, in no wise: for we *4284*
1Co 7: 9 for it is **b** to marry than to burn. *2909*
7:38 he that giveth *her* not in marriage doeth **b**. *2908*
8: 8 for neither, if we eat, are we the **b**; neither, *4052*
9:15 for *it were* **b** for me to die, than that *2570+3123*
11:17 that you come together not for the **b**, but *2909*
Php 1:23 and to be with Christ; *which is* far **b**: *2909*
2: 3 *let* each esteem other **b than** themselves. *5242*
Heb 1: 4 Being made so much **b than** the angels, *2909*
6: 9 we are persuaded **b** *things* of you, and *2909*
7: 7 all contradiction the less is blessed of the **b**. *2909*
7:19 the bringing in of a **b** hope *did;* by *2909*
7:22 much was Jesus made a surety of a **b** *2909*
8: 6 by how much also he is the mediator of a **b** *2909*
8: 6 which was established upon **b** promises. *2909*
9:23 the heavenly *things* themselves with **b** *2909*
10:34 in yourselves that *ye* have in heaven a **b** *2909*
11:16 But now they desire a **b** *country,* that is, *2909*
11:35 that they might obtain a **b** resurrection: *2909*
11:40 God having provided some **b** *thing* for us, *2909*
12:24 that speaketh **b** *things* than *that of* Abel. *2909*
1Pe 3:17 For *it is* **b**, if the will of God be so, that *ye* *2909*
2Pe 2:21 For it had been **b** for them not to have *2909*

BETTERED (1) [GOOD]
Mk 5:26 and was nothing **b**, but rather grew worse, *5623*

BETWEEN (232) See Index

BETWIXT (16) See Index

BEULAH (1)
Isa 62: 4 shalt be called Hephzi-bah, and thy land **B**: 1166

BEWAIL (6) [BEWAILED, BEWAILETH]
Lev 10: 6 **b** the burning which the LORD hath 1058
Dt 21:13 **b** her father and her mother a full month: 1058
Jdg 11:37 and **b** my virginity, I and my fellows. 1058+5921
Isa 16: 9 Therefore I will **b** with the weeping of 1058
2Co 12:21 *that* I shall **b** many which have sinned *3996*
Rev 18: 9 with her, shall **b** her, and lament for her, *2799*

BEWAILED (3) [BEWAIL]
Jdg 11:38 and **b** her virginity upon the mountains. 1058
Lk 8:52 And all wept, and **b** her: but he said, *2875*
23:27 of women, which also **b** and lamented him. *2875*

BEWAILETH (1) [BEWAIL]
Jer 4:31 *that* **b** herself, *that* spreadeth her hands, 3306

BEWARE (28)
Ge 24: 6 **B** thou that thou bring not my son thither 8104
Ex 23:21 **B** of him, and obey his voice, provoke him 8104
Dt 6:12 *Then* **b** lest thou forget the LORD, 8104
8:11 **B** that thou forget not the LORD thy God, 8104
15: 9 **B** that there be not a thought in thy wicked 8104
Jdg 13: 4 Now therefore **b**, I pray thee, and drink not 8104
13:13 Of all that I said unto the woman let her **b**. 8104
2Sa 18:12 **B** *that* none *touch* the young man Absalom. 8104
2Ki 6: 9 **B** that *thou* pass not such a place; 8104
Job 36:18 *b* lest he take thee away with *his* stroke: NIH
Pr 19:25 Smite a scorner, and the simple will **b**: and 6191
Isa 36:18 *B* lest Hezekiah persuade you, saying, NIH
Mt 7:15 **B** of false prophets, which come to you in *4337*
10:17 But **b** of men: for they will deliver you up *4337*
16: 6 and **b** of the leaven of the Pharisees and *4337*
16:11 that *ye* should **b** of the leaven of *4337*
16:12 he bade *them* not **b** of the leaven of bread, *4337*
Mk 8:15 **b** of the leaven of the Pharisees, and *of* *991*
12:38 **B** of the scribes, which love to go in long *991*
Lk 12: 1 *of all,* **B** ye of the leaven of the Pharisees, *4337*
12:15 Take heed, and **b** of covetousness: *5442*
20:46 **B** of the scribes, which desire to walk in *4337*
Ac 13:40 **B** therefore, lest that come upon you, *991*
Php 3: 2 **B** of dogs, beware of evil workers, beware of *991*
3: 2 Beware of dogs, **b** of evil workers, *991*
3: 2 beware of evil workers, **b** of the concision. *991*
Col 2: 8 **B** lest any *man* spoil you through philosophy *991*
2Pe 3:17 ye know *these things* before, **b** lest ye also, *5442*

BEWITCHED (3)
Ac 8: 9 and **b** the people of Samaria, giving out that *1839*
8:11 that of long time *he* had **b** them with *1839*
Gal 3: 1 O foolish Galatians, who hath **b** you, *940*

BEWRAY (1) [BEWRAYETH]
Isa 16: 3 hide the outcasts; **b** not him that wandereth. 1540

BEWRAYETH (3) [BEWRAY]
Pr 27:16 ointment of his right hand, *which* **b** *itself.* 7121
29:24 own soul: he heareth cursing, and **b** *it* not. 5046
Mt 26:73 *one* of them; for thy speech **b** thee. *1212+4160*

BEYOND (54) See Index

BEZAI (3)
Ezr 2:17 The children of **B**, three hundred twenty 1209
Ne 7:23 The children of **B**, three hundred twenty 1209
10:18 Hodijah, Hashum, **B**, 1209

BEZALEEL (9)
Ex 31: 2 I have called by name **B** the son of Uri, 1212
35:30 the LORD hath called by name **B** the son 1212
36: 1 wrought **B** and Aholiab, and every wise 1212
36: 2 Moses called **B** and Aholiab, and every 1212
37: 1 **B** made the ark *of* shittim wood: two cubits 1212
38:22 **B** the son of Uri, the son of Hur, of the tribe 1212
1Ch 2:20 And Hur begat Uri, and Uri begat **B**. 1212
2Ch 1: 5 that **B** the son of Uri, the son of Hur, 1212
Ezr 10:30 Mattaniah, **B**, and Binnui, and Manasseh. 1212

BEZALEL See BEZALEEL

BEZEK (3)
Jdg 1: 4 they slew *of* them in **B** ten thousand men. 966
1: 5 they found Adoni-bezek in **B**: and 966
1Sa 11: 8 when he numbered them in **B**, the children 966

BEZER (5)
Dt 4:43 *Namely,* **B** in the wilderness, in the plain 1221
Jos 20: 8 they assigned **B** in the wilderness upon 1221
21:36 **B** with her suburbs, and Jahazah with her 1221
1Ch 6:78 **B** in the wilderness with her suburbs, and 1221
7:37 **B**, and Hod, and Shamma, and Shilshah, 1221

BICHRI (8)
2Sa 20: 1 *was* Sheba, the son of **B**, a Benjamite: 1075
20: 2 *and* followed Sheba the son of **B**: 1075
20: 6 Now shall Sheba the son of **B** do us more 1075
20: 7 to pursue after Sheba the son of **B**. 1075
20:10 brother pursued after Sheba the son of **B**. 1075
20:13 to pursue after Sheba the son of **B**. 1075
20:21 Sheba the son of **B** by name, 1075
20:22 they cut off the head of Sheba the son of **B**, 1075

BICRI See BICHRI

BID (17) [BADE, BADEST, BIDDEN, BIDDETH, BIDDING]
Nu 15:38 **b** them that they make them fringes in 559
Jos 6:10 of your mouth, until the day I **b** you shout; 559
1Sa 9:27 **B** the servant pass on before us, (and 559
2Sa 2:26 ere thou **b** the people return from following 559
2Ki 4:24 slack not *thy* riding for me, except I **b** thee. 559
5:13 *if* the prophet had **b** thee *do some* great 1696
10: 5 and will do all that thou shalt **b** us; 559
Jnh 3: 2 preach unto it the preaching that I **b** thee. 1696
Zep 1: 7 prepared a sacrifice, he hath **b** his guests. 6942
Mt 14:28 be thou, **b** me come unto thee on the water. *2753*

Mt 22: 9 as many as ye shall find, **b** to the marriage. *2564*
23: 3 therefore whatsoever they **b** you observe, *3004*
Lk 9:61 but let me first go **b** them **farewell**, *657*
10:40 **b** her therefore that she help me. *3004*
14:12 lest they also **b** thee **again**, and *479*
1Co 10:27 If any of them that believe not **b** you *to a* *2564*
2Jn 1:10 into *your* house, neither **b** him God speed: *3004*

BIDDEN (14) [BID]
1Sa 9:13 *and* afterwards they eat that be **b**. 7121
9:22 the chiefest place among them that were **b**, 7121
2Sa 16:11 let him curse; for the LORD hath **b** him. 559
Mt 1:24 did as the angel of the Lord had **b** him, *4367*
22: 3 to call them that were **b** to the wedding: *2564*
22: 4 saying, Tell them which are **b**, Behold, *2564*
22: 8 but they which were **b** were not worthy. *2564*
Lk 7:39 Now when the Pharisee which had **b** him *2564*
14: 7 put forth a parable to those which were **b**, *2564*
14: 8 When thou art **b** of any *man* to a wedding, *2564*
14: 8 lest a more honourable *man* than thou be **b** *2564*
14:10 But when thou art **b**, go and sit down in *2564*
14:17 at supper time to say to them that were **b**, *2564*
14:24 That none of those men which were **b** shall *2564*

BIDDETH (1) [BID]
2Jn 1:11 For he that **b** him God speed is partaker of *3004*

BIDDING (1) [BID]
1Sa 22:14 goeth at thy **b**, and *is* honourable in thine 4928

BIDE (1)
Ro 11:23 they also, if they **b** not **still in** unbelief, *1961*

BIDKAR (1)
2Ki 9:25 said *Jehu* to **B** his captain, Take up, *and* 920

BIER (2)
2Sa 3:31 And king David *himself* followed the **b**. 4296
Lk 7:14 And he came and touched the **b**: and *4673*

BIGTHA (1)
Est 1:10 **B**, and Abagtha, Zethar, and Carcas, 903

BIGTHAN (1)
Est 2:21 **B** and Teresh, of those which kept the door, 904

BIGTHANA (1)
Est 6: 2 that Mordecai had told of **B** and Teresh, 904

BIGVAI (6)
Ezr 2: 2 Bilshan, Mizpar, **B**, Rehum, Baanah. 902
2:14 The children of **B**, two thousand fifty and 902
8:14 Of the sons also of **B**; Uthai, and Zabbud, 902
Ne 7: 7 Bilshan, Mispereth, **B**, Nehum, Baanah. 902
7:19 The children of **B**, two thousand threescore 902
10:16 Adonijah, **B**, Adin, 902

BILDAD (5)
Job 2:11 **B** the Shuhite, and Zophar the Naamathite: 1085
8: 1 Then answered **B** the Shuhite, and said, 1085
18: 1 Then answered **B** the Shuhite, and said, 1085
25: 1 Then answered **B** the Shuhite, and said, 1085
42: 9 the Temanite and **B** the Shuhite *and* 1085

BILEAM (1)
1Ch 6:70 with her suburbs, and **B** with her suburbs, 1109

BILGAH (3)
1Ch 24:14 The fifteenth to **B**, the sixteenth to Immer, 1083
Ne 12: 5 Miamin, Maadiah, **B**, 1083
12:18 Of **B**, Shammua; of Shemaiah, Jehonathan; 1083

BILGAI (1)
Ne 10: 8 Maaziah, **B**, Shemaiah: these *were* 1084

BILHAH (11)
Ge 29:29 Laban gave to Rachel his daughter **B** his 1090
30: 3 she said, Behold my maid **B**, go in unto 1090
30: 4 she gave him **B** her handmaid to wife: and 1090
30: 5 And **B** conceived, and bare Jacob a son. 1090
30: 7 **B** Rachel's maid conceived again, and 1090
35:22 and lay with **B** his father's concubine: 1090
35:25 the sons of **B**, Rachel's handmaid; Dan, 1090
37: 2 the lad *was* with the sons of **B**, and with 1090
46:25 These *are* the sons of **B**, which Laban gave 1090
1Ch 4:29 And at **B**, and at Ezem, and at Tolad, 1090
7:13 and Jezer, and Shallum, the sons of **B**. 1090

BILHAN (4)
Ge 36:27 Ezer *are* these; **B**, and Zaavan, and Akan. 1092
1Ch 1:42 The sons of Ezer; **B**, and Zavan, *and* Jakan. 1092
7:10 The sons also of Jediael; **B**: and the sons of 1092
7:10 the sons of **B**; Jeush, and Benjamin, and 1092

BILL (7)
Dt 24: 1 let him write her a **b** of divorcement, and 5612
24: 3 write her a **b** of divorcement, and giveth *it* 5612
Isa 50: 1 Where *is* the **b** of your mother's 5612
Jer 3: 8 put her away, and given her a **b** of divorce; 5612
Mk 10: 4 Moses suffered to write a **b** of divorcement, *975*
Lk 16: 6 Take thy **b**, and sit down quickly, and *1121*
16: 7 unto him, Take thy **b**, and write fourscore. *1121*

BILLOWS (2)
Ps 42: 7 all thy waves and thy **b** are gone over me. 1530
Jnh 2: 3 all thy **b** and thy waves passed over me. 4867

BILSHAN (2)
Ezr 2: 2 **B**, Mizpar, Bigvai, Rehum, Baanah. 1114
Ne 7: 7 Mordecai, **B**, Mispereth, Bigvai, Nehum, 1114

BIMHAL (1)
1Ch 7:33 of Japhlet; Pasach, and **B**, and Ashvath. 1118

BIND (49) [BINDETH, BINDING, BOUND]
Ex 28:28 they shall **b** the breastplate by the rings 7405
39:21 they did **b** the breastplate by his rings unto 7405
Nu 30: 2 or swear an oath to **b** his soul with a bond; 631
30: 3 **b** *herself by* a bond, *being* in her father's 631
Dt 6: 8 thou shalt **b** them for a sign upon thine 7194
11:18 and **b** them for a sign upon your hand, 7194
14:25 **b up** the money in thine hand, and shalt go 6696
Jos 2:18 thou shalt **b** this line of scarlet thread in 7194
Jdg 15:10 To **b** Samson are we come up, 631
15:12 said unto him, We are come down to **b** thee, 631
15:13 we will **b** thee **fast**, and deliver thee 631+631
16: 5 that we may **b** him to afflict him: 631
16: 7 If they **b** me with seven green withs that 631
16:11 If they **b** me **fast** with new ropes that 631+631
Job 31:36 my shoulder, *and* **b** it *as* a crown to me. 6029
38:31 Canst thou **b** the sweet influences of 7194
39:10 Canst thou **b** the unicorn *with* his band in 7194
40:13 dust together; *and* **b** their faces in secret. 2280
41: 5 a bird? or wilt thou **b** him for thy maidens? 7194
Ps 105:22 To **b** his princes at his pleasure; and 631
118:27 **b** the sacrifice with cords, *even* unto 631
149: 8 To **b** their kings with chains, and 631
Pr 3: 3 **b** them about thy neck; write them upon 7194
6:21 **B** them continually upon thine heart, *and* 7194
7: 3 **B** them upon thy fingers, write them upon 7194
Isa 8:16 **B up** the testimony, seal the law among my 6887
49:18 and **b** them *on thee,* as a bride *doth.* 7194
61: 1 he hath sent me to **b up** the broken-hearted, 2280
Jer 51:63 *that* thou shalt **b** a stone to it, and cast it 7194
Eze 3:25 shall **b** thee with them, and thou shalt not go 631
5: 3 a few in number, and **b** them in thy skirts. 6696
24:17 **b** the tire of thine head upon thee, and 2280
30:21 to put a roller to **b** it, to make it strong to 2280
34:16 will **b up** that which was broken, and 2280
Da 3:20 men that *were* in his army to **b** Shadrach, 3729
Hos 6: 1 he hath smitten, and he will **b** us **up**. 2280
10:10 when *they* shall **b** themselves in their two 631
Mic 1:13 of Lachish, **b** the chariot to the swift beast: 7573
Mt 12:29 except he first **b** the strong *man?* and then *1210*
13:30 and **b** them in bundles to burn them: *1210*
16:19 whatsoever thou shalt **b** on earth shall be *1210*
18:18 Whatsoever ye shall **b** on earth shall be *1210*
22:13 **B** him hand and foot, and take him away, *1210*
23: 4 For they **b** heavy burdens and grievous to *1195*
Mk 3:27 except he will first **b** the strong *man;* and *1210*
5: 3 and no *man* could **b** him, no, not with *1210*
Ac 9:14 chief priests to **b** all that call on thy name. *1210*
12: 8 Gird thyself, and **b on** thy sandals. *5265*
21:11 So shall the Jews at Jerusalem **b** the man *1210*

BINDETH (9) [BIND]
Job 5:18 For he maketh sore, and **b up**: 2280
26: 8 He **b up** the waters in his thick clouds; and 6887
28:11 He **b** the floods from overflowing; and 2280
30:18 it **b** me **about** as the collar of my coat. 247
36:13 heap up wrath: they cry not when he **b** them. 631

Ps 129: 7 his hand; nor he that **b sheaves** his bosom. 6014
147: 3 the broken in heart, and **b up** their wounds. 2280
Pr 26: 8 As *he that* **b** a stone in a sling, so *is* he that 6872
Isa 30:26 in the day that the LORD **b up** the breach 2280

BINDING (5) [BIND]
Ge 37: 7 we *were* **b** sheaves in the field, and lo, 481
49:11 **B** his foal unto the vine, and his ass's colt 631
Ex 28:32 it shall have a **b** of woven work round 8193
Nu 30:13 and every **b** oath to afflict the soul, 632
Ac 22: 4 **b** and delivering into prisons both men and *1195*

BINEA (2)
1Ch 8:37 Moza begat **B**: Rapha *was* his son, 1150
9:43 Moza begat **B**; and Rephaiah his son, 1150

BINNUI (7) [BAVAI]
Ezr 8:33 and Noadiah the son of **B**, Levites; 1131
10:30 Mattaniah, Bezaleel, and **B**, and Manasseh. 1131
10:38 And Bani, and **B**, Shimei, 1131
Ne 3:24 After him repaired **B** the son of Henadad 1131
7:15 The children of **B**, six hundred forty and 1131
10: 9 **B** of the sons of Henadad, Kadmiel; 1131
12: 8 Jeshua, **B**, Kadmiel, Sherebiah, Judah, *and* 1131

BIRD (28) [BIRD'S, BIRDS, BIRDS']
Ge 7:14 fowl after his kind, every **b** of every sort. 6833
Lev 14: 6 As for the living **b**, he shall take it, and 6833
14: 6 the living **b** in the blood of the bird *that* 6833
14: 6 the living bird in the blood of the **b** *that* 6833
14: 7 shall let the living **b** loose into the open 6833
14:51 the living **b**, and dip them in the blood of 6833
14:51 dip them in the blood of the slain **b**, 6833
14:52 cleanse the house with the blood of the **b**, 6833
14:52 with the living **b**, and with the cedar wood, 6833
14:53 he shall let go the living **b** out of the city 6833
Job 41: 5 Wilt thou play with him as *with* a **b**? or 6833
Ps 11: 1 to my soul, Flee *as* a **b** *to* your mountain? 6833
124: 7 Our soul is escaped as a **b** out of the snare 6833
Pr 1:17 the net *is* spread in the sight of any **b**. 1167+3671
6: 5 and as a **b** from the hand of the fowler. 6833
7:23 as a **b** hasteth to the snare, and knoweth not 6833
26: 2 As the **b** by wandering, as the swallow by 6833
27: 8 As a **b** that wandereth from her nest, so *is* a 6833
Ecc 10:20 for a **b** of the air shall carry the voice, and 5775
12: 4 he shall rise up at the voice of the **b**, and 6833
Isa 16: 2 *that,* as a wandering **b** cast out of the nest, 5775
46:11 Calling a **ravenous b** from the east, 5861
Jer 12: 9 Mine heritage *is* unto me *as* a speckled **b**, 5861
La 3:52 chased me sore, like a **b**, without cause. 6833
Hos 9:11 their glory shall fly away like a **b**, from 5775
11:11 They shall tremble as a **b** out of Egypt, and 6833
Am 3: 5 Can a **b** fall in a snare upon the earth, 6833
Rev 18: 2 and a cage of every unclean and hateful **b**. *3732*

BIRD'S (1) [BIRD]
Dt 22: 6 If a **b** nest chance to be before thee in 6833

BIRDS (24) [BIRD]
Ge 15:10 against another: but the **b** divided he not. 6833
40:17 the **b** did eat them out of the basket upon 5775
40:19 and the **b** shall eat thy flesh from off thee. 5775
Lev 14: 4 for him that is to be cleansed two **b** alive 6833
14: 5 the priest shall command that one of the **b** 6833
14:49 he shall take to cleanse the house two **b**, 6833
14:50 he shall kill the one of the **b** in an earthen 6833
Dt 14:11 *Of* all clean **b** ye shall eat. 6833
2Sa 21:10 suffered neither the **b** of the air to rest on 5775
Ps 104:17 Where the **b** make their nests: *as for* 6833
Ecc 9:12 and as the **b** that are caught in the snare; 6833
SS 2:12 the time of the singing *of* **b** is come, and NIH
Isa 31: 5 As **b** flying, so will the LORD of hosts 6833
Jer 4:25 and all the **b** of the heavens were fled. 5775
5:27 As a cage *is* full *of* **b**, so *are* their houses 5775
12: 4 the beasts are consumed, and the **b**; 5775
12: 9 the **b** round about *are* against her; 5861
Eze 39: 4 I will give thee unto the ravenous **b** of 6833
Mt 8:20 have holes, and the **b** of the air *have* nests; *4071*
13:32 so that the **b** of the air come and lodge in *4071*
Lk 9:58 have holes, and the **b** of the air *have* nests; *4071*
Ro 1:23 and to **b**, and fourfooted beasts, and *4071*
1Co 15:39 another of fishes, *and* another of **b**. *4421*
Jas 3: 7 and of **b**, and of serpents, and of *things* in *4071*

BIRDS' (1) [BIRD]
Da 4:33 eagles' *feathers,* and his nails like **b** *claws.* 6853

BIRSHA (1)
Ge 14: 2 with **B** king of Gomorrah, Shinab king of 1306

BIRTH (15) [BEAR]
Ex 28:10 rest on the other stone, according to their **b**. 8435
2Ki 19: 3 for the children are come to the **b**, and 4866
Job 3:16 Or as a hidden **untimely b** I had not been; 5309
Ps 58: 8 *like* the **untimely b** of a woman, *that* they 5309
Ecc 6: 3 I say, *that* an **untimely b** *is* better than he. 5309
7: 1 the day of death than the day of one's **b**. 3205
Isa 37: 3 for the children are come to the **b**, and 4866
66: 9 Shall I **bring to the b**, and not cause to 7665
Eze 16: 3 Thy **b** and thy nativity *is* of the land of 4351
Hos 9:11 from the **b**, and from the womb, and 3205
Mt 1:18 Now the **b** of Jesus Christ was on this wise: *1083*
Lk 1:14 gladness; and many shall rejoice at his **b**. *1083*
Jn 9: 1 he saw a man *which was* blind from *his* **b**. *1079*
Gal 4:19 of whom I **travail in b** again until Christ be *5605*
Rev 12: 2 **travailing in b**, and pained to be delivered. *5605*

BIRTHDAY (3) [BEAR, DAY]
Ge 40:20 third day, *which was* Pharaoh's **b**, 3117+3205
Mt 14: 6 But when Herod's **b** was kept, the daughter *1077*
Mk 6:21 that Herod on his **b** made a supper to his *1077*

BIRTHRIGHT (10) [BEAR, RIGHT]
Ge 25:31 And Jacob said, Sell me *this* day thy **b**. 1062
25:32 and what profit shall this **b** do to me? 1062
25:33 sware to him: and he sold his **b** unto Jacob. 1062
25:34 and went his way: thus Esau despised *his* **b**. 1062
27:36 he took away my **b**; and behold, now he 1062
43:33 the firstborn according to his **b**, and 1062
1Ch 5: 1 his **b** was given unto the sons of Joseph 1062
5: 1 genealogy is not to be reckoned after the **b**. 1062
5: 2 the chief ruler; but the **b** *was* Joseph's:) 1062
Heb 12:16 who for one morsel of meat sold his **b**. *4415*

BIRZAITH See BIRZAVITH

BIRZAVITH (1)
1Ch 7:31 and Malchiel, who *is* the father of **B**. 1269

BISHLAM (1)
Ezr 4: 7 in the days of Artaxerxes wrote **B**, 1312

BISHOP (6) [BISHOPRICK, BISHOPS]
1Ti 3: 1 If a man desire the **office of** a **b**, *1984*
3: 2 A **b** then must be blameless, the husband of *1985*
2Ti 4: S ordained the first **b** of the church of *1985*
Tit 1: 7 For a **b** must be blameless, as the steward *1985*
3: S ordained the first **b** of the church of *1985*
1Pe 2:25 unto the Shepherd and **B** of your souls. *1985*

BISHOPRICK (1) [BISHOP]
Ac 1:20 dwell therein: and his **b** let another take. *1984*

BISHOPS (1) [BISHOP]
Php 1: 1 are at Philippi, with the **b** and deacons: *1985*

BIT (3) [BITE, BITS]
Nu 21: 6 among the people, and they **b** the people; 5391
Ps 32: 9 whose mouth must be held in with **b** and 4964
Am 5:19 his hand on the wall, and a serpent **b** him. 5391

BITE (7) [BACKBITERS, BACKBITETH, BACKBITING, BACKBITINGS, BIT, BITETH, BITTEN, HUNGER-BITTEN]
Ecc 10: 8 breaketh a hedge, a serpent shall **b** him. 5391
10:11 Surely the serpent will **b** without 5391
Jer 8:17 and they shall **b** you, saith the LORD. 5391
Am 9: 3 command the serpent, and he shall **b** them: 5391
Mic 3: 5 that **b** with their teeth, and cry, Peace; 5391
Hab 2: 7 Shall they not rise up suddenly that *shall* **b** 5391
Gal 5:15 But if ye **b** and devour one another, *1143*

BITETH (2) [BITE]
Ge 49:17 that **b** the horse heels, so that his rider shall 5391
Pr 23:32 At the last it **b** like a serpent, and 5391

BITHIAH (1)
1Ch 4:18 these *are* the sons of **B** the daughter of 1332

BITHRON (1)
2Sa 2:29 went *through* all **B**, and they came *to* 1338

B

BITHYNIA (2)
Ac 16: 7 come to Mysia, they assayed to go into **B**: *978*
1Pe 1: 1 Galatia, Cappadocia, Asia, and **B**, *978*

BITS (1) [BIT]
Jas 3: 3 Behold, we put **b** in the horses' mouths, *5469*

BITTEN (2) [BITE]
Nu 21: 8 shall come to pass, that every one that is **b**, 5391
21: 9 to pass, that if a serpent had **b** *any* man, 5391

BITTER (38) [BITTERLY, BITTERNESS]
Ge 27:34 he cried with a great and exceeding **b** cry, 4751
Ex 1:14 they **made** their lives **b** with hard bondage, 4843
12: 8 *and* with **b** *herbs* they shall eat it. 4844
15:23 of the waters of Marah, for they *were* **b**: 4751
Nu 5:18 the priest shall have in his hand the **b** water 4751
5:19 be thou free from this **b** water that causeth 4751
5:23 and he shall blot *them* out with the **b** water: 4751
5:24 he shall cause the woman to drink the **b** 4751
5:24 curse shall enter into her, and become **b**. 4751
5:27 become **b**, and her belly shall swell, and 4751
9:11 eat it with unleavened bread and **b** *herbs*. 4844
Dt 32:24 with burning heat, and with **b** destruction: 4815
32:32 *are* grapes of gall, their clusters *are* **b**: 4846
2Ki 14:26 the affliction of Israel, *that it was* very **b**: 4784
Est 4: 1 the city, and cried *with* a loud and a **b** cry; 4751
Job 3:20 that is in misery, and life unto the **b** in soul; 4751
13:26 For thou writest **b** *things* against me, and 4846
23: 2 Even to day *is* my complaint **b**: my stroke 4805
Ps 64: 3 *bows to shoot* their arrows, *even* **b** words: 4751
Pr 5: 4 her end is **b** as wormwood, sharp as a 4751
27: 7 *to* the hungry soul every **b** *thing is* sweet. 4751
Ecc 7:26 I find more **b** than death the woman, 4751
Isa 5:20 that put **b** for sweet, and sweet for bitter! 4751
5:20 that put bitter for sweet, and sweet for **b**! 4751
24: 9 strong drink shall be **b** to them that drink it. 4843
Jer 2:19 and see that *it is* an evil *thing* and **b**, 4751
4:18 because *it is* **b**, because it reacheth unto 4751
6:26 *as* for an only *son*, most **b** lamentation: 8563
31:15 in Ramah, lamentation, *and* **b** weeping; 8563
Eze 27:31 thee with bitterness of heart *and* **b** wailing. 4751
Am 8:10 an only *son*, and the end thereof as a **b** day. 4751
Hab 1: 6 up the Chaldeans, *that* **b** and hasty nation, 4751
Col 3:19 love *your* wives, and be not **b** against them. *4087*
Jas 3:11 forth at the same place sweet *water* and **b**? *4089*
3:14 But if ye have **b** envying and strife in your *4089*
Rev 8:11 of the waters, because they were **made b**. *4087*
10: 9 and it shall **make** thy belly **b**, but it shall be *4087*
10:10 as soon as I had eaten it, my belly was **b**. *4087*

BITTERLY (9) [BITTER]
Jdg 5:23 curse ye **b** the inhabitants thereof; 779
Ru 1:20 for the Almighty hath **dealt** very **b** with 4843
Isa 22: 4 I will weep **b**, labour not to comfort me, 4843
33: 7 the ambassadors of peace shall weep **b**. 4751
Eze 27:30 shall cry **b**, and shall cast up dust upon 4751
Hos 12:14 Ephraim provoked *him* to anger **most b**: 8563
Zep 1:14 the mighty *man* shall cry there **b**. 4751
Mt 26:75 me thrice. And he went out, and wept **b**. *4090*
Lk 22:62 And Peter went out, and wept **b**. *4090*

BITTERN (3)
Isa 14:23 I will also make it a possession for the **b**, 7090
34:11 the cormorant and the **b** shall possess it; 7090
Zep 2:14 the **b** shall lodge in the upper lintels of it; 7090

BITTERNESS (22) [BITTER]
1Sa 1:10 she *was* in **b** of soul, and prayed unto 4751
15:32 Agag said, Surely the **b** of death is past. 4751
2Sa 2:26 knowest thou not that it will be **b** in 4751
Job 7:11 I will complain in the **b** of my soul. 4751
9:18 me to take my breath, but filleth me *with* **b**. 4472
10: 1 I will speak in the **b** of my soul. 4751
21:25 another dieth in the **b** of his soul, and 4751
Pr 14:10 The heart knoweth his own **b**; and 4787
17:25 to his father, and **b** to her that bare him. 4470
Isa 38:15 go softly all my years in the **b** of my soul. 4751
38:17 Behold, for peace I had **great b**: 4751+4843
La 1: 4 her virgins *are* afflicted, and she *is* in **b**. 4843
3:15 He hath filled me with **b**, he hath made me 4844
Eze 3:14 took me away, and I went in **b**, in the heat 4751
21: 6 *thy* loins; and with **b** sigh before their eyes. 4814
27:31 they shall weep for thee with **b** of heart *and* 4751
Zec 12:10 for *his* only *son*, and shall be **in b** for him, 4843
12:10 for him, as one that is **in b** for *his* firstborn. 4843
Ac 8:23 For I perceive that thou art in the gall of **b**, *4088*
Ro 3:14 Whose mouth is full of cursing and **b**: *4088*
Eph 4:31 Let all **b**, and wrath, and anger, and *4088*
Heb 12:15 lest any root of **b** springing up trouble *you*, *4088*

BIZIOTHIAH See BIZJOTHJAH

BIZJOTHJAH (1)
Jos 15:28 And Hazar-shual, and Beer-sheba, and **B**, 964

BIZTHA (1)
Est 1:10 **B**, Harbona, Bigtha, and Abagtha, Zethar, 968

BLACK (18) [BLACKER, BLACKISH, BLACKNESS]
Lev 13:31 the skin, and *that there is* no **b** hair in it; 7838
13:37 and *that* there is **b** hair grown up therein; 7838
1Ki 18:45 that the heaven was **b** *with* clouds and 6937
Est 1: 6 of red, and blue, and white, and **b** marble. 5508
Job 30:30 My skin is **b** upon me, and my bones are 7835
Pr 7: 9 in the evening, in the **b** and dark night: 380
SS 1: 5 I *am* **b**, but comely, O ye daughters of 7838
1: 6 because I *am* **b**, because the sun hath 7840
5:11 his locks *are* bushy, *and* **b** as a raven. 7838
Jer 4:28 earth mourn, and the heavens above be **b**: 6937
8:21 I am **b**; astonishment hath taken hold on 6937
14: 2 they are **b** unto the ground; and the cry of 6937
La 5:10 Our skin was **b** like an oven because of 3648
Zec 6: 2 and in the second chariot **b** horses; 7838
6: 6 The **b** horses which *are* therein go forth 7838
Mt 5:36 thou canst not make one hair white or **b**. *3189*
Rev 6: 5 And I beheld, and lo a **b** horse; and he that *3189*
6:12 and the sun became **b** as sackcloth of hair, *3189*

BLACKER (1) [BLACK]
La 4: 8 Their visage is **b** than a coal; they are not 2821

BLACKISH (1) [BLACK]
Job 6:16 Which are **b** by reason of the ice, *and* 6937

BLACKNESS (6) [BLACK]
Job 3: 5 dwell upon it; let the **b** of the day terrify it. 3650
Isa 50: 3 I clothe the heavens with **b**, and I make 6940
Joel 2: 6 be much pained: all faces shall gather **b**. 6289
Na 2:10 all loins, and the faces of them all gather **b**. 6289
Heb 12:18 burned with fire, nor unto **b**, and darkness, *1105*
Jude 1:13 to whom is reserved the **b** of darkness for *2217*

BLADE (5)
Jdg 3:22 the haft also went in after the **b**; and the fat 3851
3:22 the fat closed upon the **b**, so that he could 3851
Job 31:22 let mine arm fall from *my* **shoulder b**, 7929
Mt 13:26 But when the **b** was sprung up, and *5528*
Mk 4:28 first the **b**, then the ear, after that the full *5528*

BLAINS (2)
Ex 9: 9 shall be a boil breaking forth *with* **b** upon 76
9:10 it became a boil breaking forth *with* **b** upon 76

BLAME (4) [BLAMED, BLAMELESS, UNBLAMEABLE]
Ge 43: 9 then let me **bear the b** for ever: 2398
44:32 I shall **bear the b** to my father for ever. 2398
2Co 8:20 that no *man* should **b** us in this abundance *3469*
Eph 1: 4 be holy and **without b** before him in love: *299*

BLAMED (2) [BLAME]
2Co 6: 3 in any *thing*, that the ministry be not **b**: *3469*
Gal 2:11 him to the face, because he was *to be* **b**. *2607*

BLAMELESS (15) [BLAME]
Ge 44:10 shall be my servant; and ye shall be **b**. 5355
Jos 2:17 We *will be* **b** of this thine oath which thou 5355
Jdg 15: 3 Now shall I be more **b** than the Philistines, 5352
Mt 12: 5 in the temple profane the sabbath, and are **b**? *338*
Lk 1: 6 and ordinances of the Lord **b**. *273*
1Co 1: 8 *that ye may be* **b** in the day of our Lord Jesus *410*
Php 2:15 That ye may be **b** and harmless, the sons of *273*
3: 6 the righteousness which is in the law, **b**. *273*
1Th 5:23 body be preserved **b** unto the coming of our *274*
1Ti 3: 2 A bishop then must be **b**, the husband of one *423*
3:10 use the office of a deacon, being *found* **b**. *410*
5: 7 *things* give in charge, that they may be **b**. *423*
Tit 1: 6 If any be **b**, the husband of one wife, *410*
1: 7 For a bishop must be **b**, as the steward of *410*
2Pe 3:14 found of him in peace, without spot, and **b**. *298*

BLASPHEME (10) [BLASPHEMED, BLASPHEMER, BLASPHEMERS, BLASPHEMEST, BLASPHEMETH, BLASPHEMIES, BLASPHEMING, BLASPHEMOUS, BLASPHEMOUSLY, BLASPHEMY]
2Sa 12:14 **given great occasion** to the enemies of the LORD **to b**, 5006+5006
1Ki 21:10 Thou didst **b** God and the king. 1288
21:13 Naboth did **b** God and the king. 1288
Ps 74:10 shall the enemy **b** thy name for ever? 5006
Mk 3:28 blasphemies wherewith soever they shall **b**: *987*
3:29 But he that shall **b** against the Holy Ghost *987*
Ac 26:11 every synagogue, and compelled *them* to **b**; *987*
1Ti 1:20 unto Satan, that they may learn not to **b**. *987*
Jas 2: 7 Do not they **b** *that* worthy name by *987*
Rev 13: 6 to **b** his name, and his tabernacle, and *987*

BLASPHEMED (16) [BLASPHEME]
Lev 24:11 the Israelitish woman's son **b** the name *of* 5344
2Ki 19: 6 servants of the king of Assyria have **b** me. 1442
19:22 Whom hast thou reproached and **b**? and 1442
Ps 74:18 *that* the foolish people have **b** thy name. 5006
Isa 37: 6 servants of the king of Assyria have **b** me. 1442
37:23 Whom hast thou reproached and **b**? and 1442
52: 5 and my name continually every day *is* **b**. 5006
65: 7 the mountains, and **b** me upon the hills: 2778
Eze 20:27 Yet *in* this your fathers have **b** me, in that 1442
Ac 18: 6 and **b**, he shook *his* raiment, and said unto *987*
Ro 2:24 For the name of God is **b** among the Gentiles *987*
1Ti 6: 1 the name of God and *his* doctrine be not **b**. *987*
Tit 2: 5 that the word of God be not **b**. *987*
Rev 16: 9 and **b** the name of God, which hath power *987*
16:11 And **b** the God of heaven because of their *987*
16:21 and men **b** God because of the plague of *987*

BLASPHEMER (1) [BLASPHEME]
1Ti 1:13 Who was before a **b**, and a persecutor, and *989*

BLASPHEMERS (2) [BLASPHEME]
Ac 19:37 of churches, nor yet **b** of your goddess. *987*
2Ti 3: 2 covetous, boasters, proud, **b**, disobedient to *989*

BLASPHEMEST (1) [BLASPHEME]
Jn 10:36 and sent into the world, Thou **b**; *987*

BLASPHEMETH (5) [BLASPHEME]
Lev 24:16 he that **b** the name of the LORD, he shall 5344
24:16 when he **b** the name *of the LORD,* shall 5344
Ps 44:16 the voice of him that reproacheth and **b**; 1442
Mt 9: 3 scribes said within themselves, This *man* **b**. *987*
Lk 12:10 unto him that **b** against the Holy Ghost it *987*

BLASPHEMIES (6) [BLASPHEME]
Eze 35:12 *that* I have heard all thy **b** which thou hast 5007
Mt 15:19 fornications, thefts, false witness, **b**: *988*
Mk 2: 7 Why doth this *man* thus speak **b**? who can *988*
3:28 **b** wherewith soever they shall blaspheme: *988*
Lk 5:21 saying, Who is this which speaketh **b**? *988*
Rev 13: 5 him a mouth speaking great *things* and **b**; *988*

BLASPHEMING (1) [BLASPHEME]
Ac 13:45 were spoken by Paul, contradicting and **b**. *987*

BLASPHEMOUS (2) [BLASPHEME]
Ac 6:11 We have heard him speak **b** words against *989*
6:13 This man ceaseth not to speak **b** words *989*

BLASPHEMOUSLY (1) [BLASPHEME]
Lk 22:65 And many other *things* **b** spake they against *987*

BLASPHEMY (14) [BLASPHEME]
2Ki 19: 3 *is* a day of trouble, and of rebuke, and **b**: 5007
Isa 37: 3 *is* a day of trouble, and of rebuke, and of **b**: 5007
Mt 12:31 *of* sin and **b** shall be forgiven unto men: *988*
12:31 the **b** against the *Holy* Ghost shall not be *988*
26:65 rent his clothes, saying, He hath **spoken b**; *987*
26:65 behold, now ye have heard his **b**. *988*
Mk 7:22 an evil eye, **b**, pride, foolishness: *988*
14:64 Ye have heard the **b**: what think ye? *988*
Jn 10:33 but for **b**; and because that thou, being a *988*
Col 3: 8 wrath, malice, **b**, filthy communication out *988*
Rev 2: 9 *I know* the **b** of them which say they are *988*
13: 1 and upon his heads the name of **b**. *988*
13: 6 And he opened his mouth in **b** against God, *988*
17: 3 full of names of **b**, having seven heads and *988*

BLAST (8) [BLASTED, BLASTING]
Ex 15: 8 with the **b** of thy nostrils the waters were 7307
Jos 6: 5 *that* when *they* **make a long b** with 4900
2Sa 22:16 at the **b** of the breath of his nostrils. 5397
2Ki 19: 7 I will send a **b** upon him, and he shall hear 7307
Job 4: 9 By the **b** of God they perish, and by 5397
Ps 18:15 at the **b** of the breath of thy nostrils. 5397
Isa 25: 4 when the **b** of the terrible ones *is* as a storm 7307
37: 7 I will send a **b** upon him, and he shall hear 7307

BLASTED (5) [BLAST]
Ge 41: 6 **b** with the east wind sprang up after them. 7710
41:23 withered, thin, *and* **b** with the east wind, 7710
41:27 the seven empty ears **b** with the east wind 7710
2Ki 19:26 and *as* corn **b** before it be grown up. 7711
Isa 37:27 and *as* corn **b** before it be grown up. 7711

BLASTING (5) [BLAST]
Dt 28:22 the sword, and with **b**, and with mildew; 7711
1Ki 8:37 **b**, mildew, locust, *or* if there be caterpillar; 7711
2Ch 6:28 if there be **b**, or mildew, locusts, or 7711
Am 4: 9 I have smitten you with **b** and mildew: 7711
Hag 2:17 I smote you with **b** and with mildew and 7711

BLASTUS (1)
Ac 12:20 having made **B** the king's chamberlain their *986*

BLAZE (1)
Mk 1:45 *it* much, and to **b abroad** the matter, *1310*

BLEATING (1) [BLEATINGS]
1Sa 15:14 then this **b** of the sheep in mine ears, 6963

BLEATINGS (1) [BLEATING]
Jdg 5:16 the sheepfolds, to hear the **b** of the flocks? 8292

BLEMISH (62) [BLEMISHES]
Ex 12: 5 Your lamb shall be **without b**, a male of 8549
29: 1 young bullock, and two rams **without b**, 8549
Lev 1: 3 of the herd, let him offer a male **without b**: 8549
1:10 he shall bring it a male **without b**. 8549
3: 1 he shall offer it **without b** before 8549
3: 6 male or female, he shall offer it **without b**. 8549
4: 3 a young bullock **without b** unto 8549
4:23 a kid of the goats, a male **without b**; 8549
4:28 a kid of the goats, a female **without b**, 8549
4:32 he shall bring it a female **without b**. 8549
5:15 LORD a ram **without b** out of the flocks, 8549
5:18 he shall bring a ram **without b** out of 8549
6: 6 a ram **without b** out of the flock, with thy 8549
9: 2 **without b**, and offer *them* before 8549
9: 3 first year, **without b**, for a burnt offering; 8549
14:10 day he shall take two he lambs **without b**, 8549
14:10 one ewe lamb of the first year **without b**, 8549
21:17 seed in their generations that hath *any* **b**, 3971
21:18 For whatsoever man *he be* that hath a **b**, 3971
21:20 or that hath a **b** in his eye, or be scurvy, or 8400
21:21 No man that hath a **b**, of the seed of Aaron 3971
21:21 he hath a **b**; he shall not come nigh to offer 3971
21:23 nigh unto the altar, because he hath a **b**; 3971
22:19 *offer* at your own will a male **without b**, 8549
22:20 *But* whatsoever hath a **b**, *that* shall ye not 3971
22:21 to be accepted; there shall be no **b** therein. 3971
23:12 **without b** of the first year for a burnt 8549
23:18 seven lambs **without b** of the first year, 8549
24:19 if a man cause a **b** in his neighbour; as he 3971
24:20 as he hath caused a **b** in a man, so shall it 3971
Nu 6:14 one he lamb of the first year **without b** for 8549
6:14 one ewe lamb of the first year **without b** 8549
6:14 and one ram **without b** for peace offerings, 8549
19: 2 wherein *is* no **b**, *and* upon which never 3971
28:19 first year: they shall be unto you **without b**: 8549
28:31 (they shall be unto you **without b**) 8549
29: 2 seven lambs of the first year **without b**: 8549
29: 8 first year; they shall be unto you **without b**: 8549
29:13 of the first year; they shall be **without b**: 8549
29:20 fourteen lambs of the first year **without b**; 8549
29:23 fourteen lambs of the first year **without b**: 8549
29:29 fourteen lambs of the first year **without b**: 8549
29:32 fourteen lambs of the first year **without b**: 8549
29:36 seven lambs of the first year **without b**: 8549
Dt 15:21 if there be *any* **b** therein, *as if it* be lame, 3971
15:21 *as if it be* lame, or blind, *or have* any ill **b**, 3971
17: 1 wherein is **b**, *or* any evil favouredness: 3971

2Sa 14:25 crown of his head there was no **b** in him. 3971
Eze 43:22 of the goats **without b** for a sin offering; 8549
43:23 thou shalt offer a young bullock **without b**, 8549
43:23 and a ram out of the flock **without b**. 8549
43:25 and a ram out of the flock, **without b**. 8549
45:18 thou shalt take a young bullock **without b**, 8549
45:23 seven rams **without b** daily the seven days; 8549
46: 4 sabbath day *shall be* six lambs **without b**, 8549
46: 4 without blemish, and a ram **without b**. 8549
46: 6 *it shall be* a young bullock **without b**, 8549
46: 6 and a ram: they shall be **without b**. 8549
46:13 *of* a lamb of the first year **without b**: 8549
Da 1: 4 Children in whom *was* no **b**, but 3971
Eph 5:27 but that it should be holy and **without b**. *299*
1Pe 1:19 as of a lamb **without b** and without spot: *299*

BLEMISHES (2) [BLEMISH]
Lev 22:25 corruption *is* in them, *and* **b** *be* in them: 3971
2Pe 2:13 Spots *they are* and **b**, sporting themselves *3470*

BLENDED See APOTHECARIES'

BLENDED WINE See LIQUOR

BLESS (127) [BLESSED, BLESSEDNESS, BLESSEST, BLESSETH, BLESSING, BLESSINGS]
Ge 12: 2 and I will **b** thee, and make thy name great; 1288
12: 3 I will **b** them that bless thee, and curse him 1288
12: 3 I will bless them that **b** thee, and curse him 1288
17:16 I will **b** her, and give thee a son also of her: 1288
17:16 I will **b** her, and she shall be *a mother* of 1288
22:17 That in blessing I will **b** thee, and 1288
26: 3 I will be with thee, and will **b** thee; 1288
26:24 will **b** thee, and multiply thy seed for my 1288
27: 4 that my soul may **b** thee before I die. 1288
27: 7 **b** thee before the LORD before my death. 1288
27:10 that he may **b** thee before his death. 1288
27:19 eat of my venison, that thy soul may **b** me. 1288
27:25 my son's venison, that my soul may **b** thee. 1288
27:31 his son's venison, that thy soul may **b** me. 1288
27:34 **B** me, *even* me also, O my father. 1288
27:38 **b** me, *even* me also, O my father. And Esau 1288
28: 3 God Almighty **b** thee, and make thee 1288
32:26 I will not let thee go, except thou **b** me. 1288
48: 9 I pray thee, unto me, and I will **b** them. 1288
48:16 redeemed me from all evil, **b** the lads; 1288
48:20 saying, In thee shall Israel **b**, saying, 1288
49:25 who shall **b** thee *with* blessings of heaven 1288
Ex 12:32 ye have said, and be gone; and **b** me also. 1288
20:24 I will come unto thee, and I will **b** thee. 1288
23:25 and he shall **b** thy bread, and thy water; 1288
Nu 6:23 On this wise ye shall **b** the children of 1288
6:24 The LORD **b** thee, and keep thee: 1288
6:27 the children of Israel; and I will **b** them. 1288
23:20 I have received *commandment* to **b**: 1288
23:25 curse them at all, nor **b** them **at all**. 1288+1288
24: 1 saw that it pleased the LORD to **b** Israel, 1288
Dt 1:11 so many moe as ye *are*, and **b** you, 1288
7:13 love thee, and **b** thee, and multiply thee: 1288
7:13 he will also **b** the fruit of thy womb, and 1288
8:10 thou shalt **b** the LORD thy God for 1288
10: 8 and to **b** in his name, unto this day. 1288
14:29 that the LORD thy God may **b** thee in all 1288
15: 4 for the LORD shall **greatly b** thee 1288+1288
15:10 thy God shall **b** thee in all thy works, 1288
15:18 the LORD thy God shall **b** thee in all that 1288
16:15 the LORD thy God shall **b** thee in all thy 1288
21: 5 and to **b** in the name of the LORD; 1288
23:20 that the LORD thy God may **b** thee in all 1288
24:13 may sleep in his own raiment, and **b** thee: 1288
24:19 that the LORD thy God may **b** thee in all 1288
26:15 **b** thy people Israel, and the land which thou 1288
27:12 shall stand upon mount Gerizzim to **b** 1288
28: 8 he shall **b** thee in the land which 1288
28:12 and to **b** all the work of thine hand: 1288
29:19 that he **b** himself in his heart, saying, I shall 1288
30:16 the LORD thy God shall **b** thee in the land 1288
33:11 **B**, LORD, his substance, and accept 1288
Jos 8:33 that they should **b** the people of Israel. 1288
Jdg 5: 9 among the people. **B** ye the LORD. 1288
Ru 2: 4 they answered him, The LORD **b** thee. 1288
1Sa 9:13 he come, because he doth **b** the sacrifice; 1288
2Sa 6:20 David returned to **b** his household. 1288
7:29 Therefore now let it please thee to **b** 1288
8:10 to **b** him, because he had fought against 1288
21: 3 that ye may **b** the inheritance of 1288
1Ki 1:47 moreover the king's servants came to **b** our 1288
1Ch 4:10 Oh that thou wouldest **b** me **indeed**, 1288+1288
16:43 and David returned to **b** his house. 1288
17:27 let it please thee to **b** the house of thy 1288
23:13 unto him, and to **b** in his name for ever. 1288
29:20 Now **b** the LORD your God. 1288
Ne 9: 5 *and* **b** the LORD your God for ever and 1288
Ps 5:12 For thou, LORD, wilt **b** the righteous; 1288
16: 7 I will **b** the LORD, who hath given me 1288
26:12 in the congregations will I **b** the LORD. 1288
28: 9 Save thy people, and **b** thine inheritance: 1288
29:11 the LORD will **b** his people with peace. 1288
34: 1 I will **b** the LORD at all times: his praise 1288
62: 4 they **b** with their mouth, but they curse 1288
63: 4 Thus will I **b** thee while I live: I will lift up 1288
66: 8 O **b** our God, ye people, and make 1288
67: 1 God be merciful unto us, and **b** us; *and* 1288
67: 6 *and* God, *even* our own God, shall **b** us. 1288
67: 7 God shall **b** us; and all the ends of the earth 1288
68:26 **B** ye God in the congregations, *even* 1288
96: 2 Sing unto the LORD, **b** his name; 1288
100: 4 be thankful unto him, *and* **b** his name. 1288
103: 1 **B** the LORD, O my soul: and all that is 1288
103: 1 and all that is within me, *b* his holy name. NIH
103: 2 **B** the LORD, O my soul, and forget not 1288
103:20 **B** the LORD, ye his angels, that excel in 1288
103:21 **B** ye the LORD, all ye his hosts; 1288
103:22 **B** the LORD, all his works in all places of 1288
103:22 of his dominion: **b** the LORD, O my soul. 1288
104: 1 **B** the LORD, O my soul. O LORD my 1288
104:35 **B** thou the LORD, O my soul. Praise ye 1288
109:28 Let them curse, but **b** thou: when they 1288
115:12 he will **b** *us;* he will bless the house of 1288
115:12 he will bless *us;* he will **b** the house of 1288
115:12 of Israel; he will **b** the house of Aaron. 1288
115:13 He will **b** them that fear the LORD, *both* 1288
115:18 we will **b** the LORD from this time forth 1288
128: 5 The LORD shall **b** thee out of Zion: and 1288
129: 8 we **b** you in the name of the LORD. 1288
132:15 I will **abundantly b** her provision: 1288+1288
134: 1 Behold, **b** ye the LORD, all ye servants of 1288
134: 2 hands *in* the sanctuary, and **b** the LORD. 1288
134: 3 made heaven and earth **b** thee out of Zion. 1288
135:19 **B** the LORD, O house of Israel: bless 1288
135:19 of Israel: **b** the LORD, O house of Aaron: 1288
135:20 **B** the LORD, O house of Levi: ye that 1288
135:20 ye that fear the LORD, **b** the LORD. 1288
145: 1 and I will **b** thy name for ever and ever. 1288
145: 2 Every day will I **b** thee; and I will praise 1288
145:10 O LORD; and thy saints shall **b** thee. 1288
145:21 let all flesh **b** his holy name for ever and 1288
Pr 30:11 their father, and doth not **b** their mother. 1288
Isa 19:25 Whom the LORD of hosts shall **b**, saying, 1288
65:16 earth shall **b** himself in the God of truth; 1288
Jer 4: 2 the nations shall **b** themselves in him, and 1288
31:23 The LORD **b** thee, O habitation of justice, 1288
Hag 2:19 brought forth: from this day will I **b** *you.* 1288
Mt 5:44 Love your enemies, **b** them that curse you, *2127*
Lk 6:28 **B** them that curse you, and pray for them *2127*
Ac 3:26 raised up his Son Jesus, sent him to **b** you, *2127*
Ro 12:14 **B** them which persecute you: bless, and *2127*
12:14 which persecute you: **b**, and curse not. *2127*
1Co 4:12 being reviled, we **b**; being persecuted, *2127*
10:16 The cup of blessing which we **b**, is it not *2127*
14:16 Else when thou shalt **b** with the spirit, *2127*
Heb 6:14 Surely blessing I will **b** thee, and *2127*
Jas 3: 9 Therewith **b** we God, even the Father; and *2127*

BLESSED (302) [BLESS]
Ge 1:22 God **b** them, saying, Be fruitful, and 1288
1:28 God **b** them, and God said unto them, 1288
2: 3 God **b** the seventh day, and sanctified it: 1288
5: 2 **b** them, and called their name Adam, in 1288
9: 1 God **b** Noah and his sons, and said unto 1288
9:26 he said, **B** *be* the LORD God of Shem; 1288
12: 3 in thee shall all families of the earth be **b**. 1288
14:19 he **b** him, and said, Blessed *be* Abram of 1288
14:19 said, **B** *be* Abram of the most high God, 1288
14:20 **b** *be* the most high God, which hath 1288
17:20 I have **b** him, and will make him fruitful, 1288
18:18 all the nations of the earth shall be **b** in 1288
22:18 seed shall all the nations of the earth be **b**; 1288
24: 1 the LORD had **b** Abraham in all things. 1288

B

Ge	24:27	**B** *be* the LORD God of my master	1288
	24:31	he said, Come in, thou **b** of the LORD;	1288
	24:35	the LORD hath **b** my master greatly; and	1288
	24:48	**b** the LORD God of my master Abraham,	1288
	24:60	they **b** Rebekah, and said unto her, Thou *art*	1288
	25:11	of Abraham, that God **b** his son Isaac;	1288
	26: 4	seed shall all the nations of the earth be **b**;	1288
	26:12	an hundredfold: and the LORD **b** him.	1288
	26:29	in peace: thou *art* now the **b** of the LORD.	1288
	27:23	as his brother Esau's hands: so he **b** him.	1288
	27:27	of his raiment, and **b** him, and said, See,	1288
	27:27	smell of a field which the LORD hath **b**:	1288
	27:29	curseth thee, and **b** *be* he that blesseth thee.	1288
	27:33	of all before thou camest, and have **b** him?	1288
	27:33	have blessed him? yea, *and* he shall be **b**.	1288
	27:41	of the blessing wherewith his father **b** him:	1288
	28: 1	**b** him, and charged him, and said unto him,	1288
	28: 6	When Esau saw that Isaac had **b** Jacob, and	1288
	28: 6	that as he **b** him he gave him a charge,	1288
	28:14	seed shall all the families of the earth be **b**.	1288
	30:13	am I, for the daughters will **call** me **b**:	833
	30:27	that the LORD hath **b** me for thy sake.	1288
	30:30	the LORD hath **b** thee since my coming:	1288
	31:55	his sons and his daughters, and **b** them:	1288
	32:29	ask after my name? And he **b** him there.	1288
	35: 9	he came out of Padan-aram, and **b** him.	1288
	39: 5	that the LORD **b** the Egyptian's house for	1288
	47: 7	him before Pharaoh: and Jacob **b** Pharaoh.	1288
	47:10	Jacob **b** Pharaoh, and went out from before	1288
	48: 3	me at Luz in the land of Canaan, and **b** me,	1288
	48:15	he **b** Joseph, and said, God, before whom	1288
	48:20	he **b** them that day, saying, In thee shall	1288
	49:28	their father spake unto them, and **b** them;	1288
	49:28	every one according to his blessing he **b**	1288
Ex	18:10	Jethro said, **B** *be* the LORD, who hath	1288
	20:11	wherefore the LORD **b** the sabbath day,	1288
	39:43	so had they done it: and Moses **b** them.	1288
Lev	9:22	**b** them, and came down from offering of	1288
	9:23	and came out, and **b** the people:	1288
Nu	22: 6	for I wot that *he* whom thou blessest *is* **b**,	1288
	22:12	shalt not curse the people: for they *are* **b**.	1288
	23:11	behold, thou hast **b** *them* **altogether**.	1288+1288
	23:20	and he hath **b**; and I cannot reverse it.	1288
	24: 9	**B** *is* he that blesseth thee, and cursed *is* he	1288
	24:10	thou hast **altogether b** *them* these	1288+1288
Dt	2: 7	For the LORD thy God hath **b** thee in all	1288
	7:14	Thou shalt be **b** above all people:	1288
	12: 7	where*in* the LORD thy God hath **b** thee.	1288
	14:24	when the LORD thy God hath **b** thee:	1288
	15:14	God hath **b** thee thou shalt give unto him.	1288
	16:10	as the LORD thy God hath **b** thee:	1288
	28: 3	**B** *shalt* thou *be* in the city, and blessed *shalt*	1288
	28: 3	in the city, and **b** *shalt* thou *be* in the field.	1288
	28: 4	**B** *shall be* the fruit of thy body, and	1288
	28: 5	**B** *shall be* thy basket and thy store.	1288
	28: 6	**B** *shalt* thou *be* when thou comest in, and	1288
	28: 6	and **b** *shalt* thou *be* when thou goest out.	1288
	33: 1	wherewith Moses the man of God **b**	1288
	33:13	he said, **B** of the LORD *be* his land,	1288
	33:20	of Gad he said, **B** *be* he that enlargeth Gad:	1288
	33:24	he said, *Let* Asher *be* **b** with children;	1288
Jos	14:13	Joshua **b** him, and gave unto Caleb the son	1288
	17:14	forasmuch as the LORD hath **b** me	1288
	22: 6	So Joshua **b** them, and sent them away: and	1288
	22: 7	away also unto their tents, then he **b** them,	1288
	22:33	the children of Israel **b** God, and did not	1288
	24:10	therefore he **b** you **still**:	1288+1288
Jdg	5:24	**B** above women shall Jael the wife of	1288
	5:24	**b** shall she be above women in the tent.	1288
	13:24	and the child grew, and the LORD **b** him.	1288
	17: 2	**B** *be thou* of the LORD, my son.	1288
Ru	2:19	**b** be he that did take knowledge of thee.	1288
	2:20	her daughter in law, **B** *be* he of the LORD,	1288
	3:10	he said, **B** *be* thou of the LORD,	1288
	4:14	women said unto Naomi, **B** *be* the LORD,	1288
1Sa	2:20	Eli **b** Elkanah and his wife, and said,	1288
	15:13	said unto him, **B** *be* thou of the LORD:	1288
	23:21	Saul said, **B** *be* ye of the LORD; for ye	1288
	25:32	to Abigail, **B** *be* the LORD God of Israel,	1288
	25:33	**b** *be* thy advice, and blessed *be* thou,	1288
	25:33	blessed *be* thy advice, and **b** *be* thou,	1288
	25:39	Nabal was dead, he said, **B** *be* the LORD,	1288
	26:25	said to David, **B** *be* thou, my son David:	1288
2Sa	2: 5	said unto them, **B** *be* ye of the LORD,	1288
	6:11	the LORD **b** Obed-edom, and all his	1288
	6:12	The LORD hath **b** the house of	1288
	6:18	he **b** the people in the name of the LORD	1288
	7:29	let the house of thy servant be **b** for ever.	1288
	13:25	howbeit he would not go, but **b** him.	1288
	18:28	and said, **B** *be* the LORD thy God,	1288
	19:39	the king kissed Barzillai, and **b** him;	1288
	22:47	**b** *be* my rock; and exalted be the God of	1288
1Ki	1:48	the king, **B** *be* the LORD God of Israel,	1288
	2:45	king Solomon *shall be* **b**, and the throne of	1288
	5: 7	and said, **B** *be* the LORD *this* day,	1288
	8:14	and **b** all the congregation of Israel:	1288
	8:15	he said, **B** *be* the LORD God of Israel,	1288
	8:55	**b** all the congregation of Israel *with* a loud	1288
	8:56	**B** *be* the LORD, that hath given rest unto	1288
	8:66	they **b** the king, and went unto their tents	1288
	10: 9	**B** be the LORD thy God, which delighted	1288
1Ch	13:14	the LORD **b** the house of Obed-edom,	1288
	16: 2	he **b** the people in the name of the LORD.	1288
	16:36	**B** *be* the LORD God of Israel for ever and	1288
	17:27	O LORD, and *it shall be* **b** for ever.	1288
	26: 5	Peulthai the eighth: for God **b** him.	1288
	29:10	Wherefore David **b** the LORD before all	1288
	29:10	David said, **B** *be* thou, LORD God of	1288
	29:20	all the congregation **b** the LORD God of	1288
2Ch	2:12	**B** *be* the LORD God of Israel, that made	1288
	6: 3	and **b** the whole congregation of Israel:	1288
	6: 4	he said, **B** *be* the LORD God of Israel,	1288
	9: 8	**B** be the LORD thy God, which delighted	1288
	20:26	of Berachah; for there they **b** the LORD:	1288
	30:27	priests the Levites arose and **b** the people:	1288
	31: 8	they **b** the LORD, and his people Israel.	1288
	31:10	for the LORD hath **b** his people; and	1288
Ezr	7:27	**B** *be* the LORD God of our fathers,	1288
Ne	8: 6	Ezra **b** the LORD, the great God. And all	1288
	9: 5	**b** be thy glorious name, which *is* exalted	1288
	11: 2	the people **b** all the men, that willingly	1288
Job	1:10	thou hast **b** the work of his hands, and	1288
	1:21	the LORD hath taken *away;* **b** be	1288
	29:11	When the ear heard *me,* then it **b** me; and	833
	31:20	If his loins have not **b** me, and *if* he were	1288
	42:12	So the LORD **b** the latter end of Job more	1288
Ps	1: 1	**B** *is* the man that walketh not in the counsel	835
	2:12	**b** *are* all they that put their trust in him.	835
	18:46	**b** *be* my rock; and let the God of my	1288
	21: 6	For thou hast made him most **b** for ever:	1293
	28: 6	**B** *be* the LORD, because he hath heard	1288
	31:21	**B** *be* the LORD: for he hath shewed me	1288
	32: 1	**B** *is* he whose transgression *is* forgiven,	835
	32: 2	**B** *is* the man unto whom the LORD	835
	33:12	**B** *is* the nation whose God *is* the LORD;	835
	34: 8	*is* good: **b** *is* the man *that* trusteth in him.	835
	37:22	For such as be **b** of him shall inherit	1288
	37:26	and lendeth; and his seed *is* **b**.	1293
	40: 4	**B** *is that* man that maketh the LORD his	835
	41: 1	**B** *is* he that considereth the poor:	835
	41: 2	him alive; *and* he shall be **b** upon the earth:	833
	41:13	**B** *be* the LORD God of Israel from	1288
	45: 2	thy lips: therefore God hath **b** thee for ever.	1288
	49:18	Though whiles he lived he **b** his soul: and	1288
	65: 4	**B** *is the man whom* thou choosest, and	835
	66:20	**B** *be* God, which hath not turned away my	1288
	68:19	**B** *be* the Lord, *who* daily loadeth us *with*	1288
	68:35	and power unto *his* people. **B** *be* God.	1288
	72:17	*men* shall be **b** in him: all nations shall call	1288
	72:17	blessed in him: all nations shall **call** him **b**.	833
	72:18	**B** *be* the LORD God, the God of Israel,	1288
	72:19	**b** *be* his glorious name for ever: and let	1288
	84: 4	**B** *are* they that dwell in thy house: they will	835
	84: 5	**B** *is* the man whose strength *is* in thee;	835
	84:12	of hosts, **b** *is* the man that trusteth in thee.	835
	89:15	**B** *is* the people that know the joyful sound:	835
	89:52	**B** *be* the LORD for evermore. Amen, and	1288
	94:12	**B** *is* the man whom thou chastenest,	835
	106: 3	**B** *are* they that keep judgment, *and* he that	835
	106:48	**B** *be* the LORD God of Israel from	1288
	112: 1	**B** *is* the man *that* feareth the LORD,	835
	112: 2	the generation of the upright shall be **b**.	1288
	113: 2	**B** be the name of the LORD from this	1288
	115:15	You *are* **b** of the LORD which made	1288
	118:26	**B** *be* he that cometh in the name of	1288
	118:26	we have **b** you out of the house of	1288
	119: 1	**B** *are* the undefiled in the way, who walk in	835
	119: 2	**B** *are* they that keep his testimonies, *and*	835

Ps 119:12 **B** *art* thou, O LORD: teach me thy 1288
124: 6 **B** *be* the LORD, who hath not given us *as* 1288
128: 1 **B** *is* every one that feareth the LORD; 835
128: 4 that thus shall the man be **b** that feareth 1288
135:21 **B** *be* the LORD out of Zion, 1288
144: 1 **B** *be* the LORD my strength, 1288
147:13 he hath **b** thy children within thee. 1288
Pr 5:18 Let thy fountain be **b**: and rejoice with 1288
8:32 for **b** *are they that* keep my ways. 835
8:34 **B** *is* the man that heareth me, watching daily 835
10: 7 The memory of the just *is* **b**: but the name 1293
20: 7 in his integrity: his children *are* **b** after him. 835
20:21 but the end thereof shall not be **b**. 1288
22: 9 He that hath a bountiful eye shall be **b**; 1288
31:28 Her children arise up, and **call** her **b**; 833
Ecc 10:17 **B** *art* thou, O land, when thy king *is* the son 835
SS 6: 9 The daughters saw her, and **b** her; *yea,* 833
Isa 19:25 **B** *be* Egypt my people, and Assyria 1288
30:18 of judgment: **b** *are* all they that wait for him. 835
32:20 **B** *are* ye that sow beside all waters, that send 835
51: 2 him alone, and **b** him, and increased him. 1288
56: 2 **B** *is* the man *that* doeth this, and the son of 835
61: 9 they *are* the seed *which* the LORD hath **b**. 1288
65:23 for they *are* the seed of the **b** of 1288
66: 3 he that burneth incense, *as if* he **b** an idol. 1288
Jer 17: 7 **B** *is* the man that trusteth in the LORD, 1288
20:14 the day wherein my mother bare me be **b**. 1288
Eze 3:12 *saying,* **B** *be* the glory of the LORD from 1288
Da 2:19 Then Daniel **b** the God of heaven. 1289
2:20 **B** be the name of God for ever and ever: 1289
3:28 said, **B** *be* the God of Shadrach, Meshach, 1289
4:34 I **b** the most High, and I praised and 1289
12:12 **B** *is* he that waiteth, and cometh to 835
Zec 11: 5 they that sell them say, **B** *be* the LORD; 1288
Mal 3:12 all nations shall **call** you **b**: for ye shall be a 833
Mt 5: 3 **B** *are* the poor in spirit: for theirs is *3107*
5: 4 **B** *are* they that mourn: for they shall be *3107*
5: 5 **B** *are* the meek: for they shall inherit *3107*
5: 6 **B** *are* they which do hunger and thirst after *3107*
5: 7 **B** *are* the merciful: for they shall obtain *3107*
5: 8 **B** *are* the pure in heart: for they shall see *3107*
5: 9 **B** *are* the peacemakers: for they shall be *3107*
5:10 **B** *are* they which are persecuted for *3107*
5:11 **B** are ye, when *men* shall revile you, and *3107*
11: 6 And **b** is *he,* whosoever shall not be *3107*
13:16 But **b** *are* your eyes, for they see: and *3107*
14:19 he **b**, and brake, and gave the loaves to *his* *2127*
16:17 and said unto him, **B** art thou, *3107*
21: 9 **B** *is* he that cometh in the name of *2127*
23:39 **B** is he that cometh in the name of *2127*
24:46 **B** *is* that servant, whom his lord when he *3107*
25:34 on his right hand, Come, ye **b** of my Father, *2127*
26:26 and **b** *it,* and brake *it,* and gave *it* to *2127*
Mk 6:41 and **b**, and brake the loaves, and gave *them* *2127*
8: 7 and he **b**, and commanded to set them also *2127*
10:16 put *his* hands upon them, and **b** them. *2127*
11: 9 **B** *is* he that cometh in the name of *2127*
11:10 **B** *be* the kingdom of our father David, *2127*
14:22 and **b**, and brake *it,* and gave to them, and *2127*
14:61 Art thou the Christ, the Son of the **B**? *2128*
Lk 1:28 *is* with thee: **b** *art* thou among women. *2127*
1:42 **B** *art* thou among women, and blessed *is* *2127*
1:42 and **b** *is* the fruit of thy womb. *2127*
1:45 And **b** *is* she that believed: for there shall *3107*
1:48 henceforth all generations shall **call** me **b**. *3106*
1:68 **B** *be* the Lord God of Israel; for he hath *2128*
2:28 he him *up* in his arms, and **b** God, and said, *2127*
2:34 And Simeon **b** them, and said unto Mary *2127*
6:20 on his disciples, and said, **B** *be ye* poor: *3107*
6:21 **B** *are ye* that hunger now: for ye shall be *3107*
6:21 **B** *are ye* that weep now: for ye shall laugh. *3107*
6:22 **B** are ye, when men shall hate you, and *3107*
7:23 And **b** is *he,* whosoever shall not be *3107*
9:16 he **b** them, and brake, and gave to *2127*
10:23 **B** *are* the eyes which see *the things* that ye *3107*
11:27 **B** *is* the womb that bare thee, and the paps *3107*
11:28 **b** *are* they that hear the word of God, and *3107*
12:37 **B** *are* those servants, whom the lord when *3107*
12:38 and find *them* so, **b** are those servants. *3107*
12:43 **B** *is* that servant, whom his lord when he *3107*
13:35 **B** *is* he that cometh in the name of *2127*
14:14 And thou shalt be **b**; for they cannot *3107*
14:15 **B** *is he* that shall eat bread in the kingdom *3107*
19:38 **B** *be* the King that cometh in the name of *2127*
23:29 **B** *are* the barren, and the wombs that never *3107*
24:30 and **b** *it,* and brake, and gave to them. *2127*
24:50 and he lift up his hands, and **b** them. *2127*
24:51 And it came to pass, while he **b** them, *2127*
Jn 12:13 **B** *is* the King of Israel that cometh in *2127*
20:29 **b** *are* they that have not seen, and *yet* have *3107*
Ac 3:25 seed shall all the kindreds of the earth be **b**. *1757*
20:35 he said, It is more **b** to give than to receive. *3107*
Ro 1:25 more than the Creator, who is **b** for ever. *2128*
4: 7 *Saying,* **B** *are they* whose iniquities are *3107*
4: 8 **B** *is* the man to whom the Lord will not *3107*
9: 5 *came,* who is over all, God **b** for ever. *2128*
2Co 1: 3 **B** *be* God, even the Father of our Lord *2128*
11:31 which is **b** for evermore, knoweth that I lie *2128*
Gal 3: 8 *saying,* In thee shall all nations be **b**. *1757*
3: 9 they which be of faith are **b** with faithful *2127*
Eph 1: 3 **B** *be* the God and Father of our Lord Jesus *2128*
1: 3 who hath **b** us with all spiritual blessings in *2127*
1Ti 1:11 According to the glorious gospel of the **b** *3107*
6:15 *who is* the **b** and only Potentate, the King *3107*
Tit 2:13 Looking for *that* **b** hope, and the glorious *3107*
Heb 7: 1 from the slaughter of the kings, and **b** him; *2127*
7: 6 and **b** him that had the promises. *2127*
7: 7 And without all contradiction the less is **b** *2127*
11:20 By faith Isaac **b** Jacob and Esau concerning *2127*
11:21 he was a dying, **b** both the sons of Joseph; *2127*
Jas 1:12 **B** *is* the man that endureth temptation: *3107*
1:25 of the work, this *man* shall be **b** in his deed. *3107*
1Pe 1: 3 **B** *be* the God and Father of our Lord Jesus *2128*
Rev 1: 3 **B** *is* he that readeth, and they that hear *3107*
14:13 **B** *are* the dead which die in the Lord from *3107*
16:15 **B** *is* he that watcheth, and keepeth his *3107*
19: 9 **B** *are* they which are called unto *3107*
20: 6 **B** and holy *is* he that hath part in the first *3107*
22: 7 **b** *is* he that keepeth the sayings of *3107*
22:14 **B** *are* they that do his commandments, that *3107*

BLESSEDNESS (3) [BLESS]

Ro 4: 6 Even as David also describeth the **b** of *3108*
4: 9 *Cometh* this **b** then upon the circumcision *3108*
Gal 4:15 Where is then the **b** you spake of? for I *3108*

BLESSEST (3) [BLESS]

Nu 22: 6 for I wot that *he* whom thou **b** *is* blessed, 1288
1Ch 17:27 for thou **b**, O LORD, and *it shall be* 1288
Ps 65:10 with showers: thou **b** the springing thereof. 1288

BLESSETH (8) [BLESS]

Ge 27:29 curseth thee, and blessed *be* he that **b** thee. 1288
Nu 24: 9 Blessed *is* he that **b** thee, and cursed *is* he 1288
Dt 15: 6 For the LORD thy God **b** thee, as he 1288
Ps 10: 3 **b** the covetous, *whom* the LORD 1288
107:38 He **b** them also, so that they are multiplied 1288
Pr 3:33 but he **b** the habitation of the just. 1288
27:14 He that **b** his friend with a loud voice, 1288
Isa 65:16 That he who **b** himself in the earth shall 1288

BLESSING (67) [BLESS]

Ge 12: 2 make thy name great; and thou shalt be a **b**: 1293
22:17 That in **b** I will bless thee, and 1288
27:12 I shall bring a curse upon me, and not a **b**. 1293
27:30 as soon as Isaac had made an end of **b** 1288
27:35 with subtilty, and hath taken away thy **b**. 1293
27:36 and behold, now he hath taken away my **b**. 1293
27:36 he said, Hast thou not reserved a **b** for me? 1293
27:38 his father, Hast thou but one **b**, my father? 1293
27:41 of the **b** wherewith his father blessed him: 1293
28: 4 give thee the **b** of Abraham, to thee, and 1293
33:11 I pray thee, my **b** that is brought to thee; 1293
39: 5 the **b** of the LORD was upon all that he 1293
49:28 every one according to his **b** he blessed 1293
Ex 32:29 that he may bestow upon you a **b** *this* day. 1293
Lev 25:21 I will command my **b** upon you in the sixth 1293
Dt 11:26 I set before you *this* day a **b** and a curse; 1293
11:27 A **b**, if ye obey the commandments of 1293
11:29 that thou shalt put the **b** upon mount 1293
12:15 according to the **b** of the LORD thy God 1293
16:17 according to the **b** of the LORD thy God 1293
23: 5 thy God turned the curse into a **b** unto thee, 1293
28: 8 The LORD shall command the **b** upon 1293
30: 1 the **b** and the curse, which I have set before 1293
30:19 set before you life and death, **b** and cursing: 1293
33: 1 this *is* the **b**, wherewith Moses the man of 1293
33: 7 this *is the* **b** of Judah: and he said, Hear, NIH

Dt 33:16 let *the* **b** come upon the head of Joseph, and NIH
33:23 and full *with* the **b** of the LORD: 1293
Jos 15:19 Who answered, Give me a **b**; for thou hast 1293
Jdg 1:15 she said unto him, Give me a **b**: for thou 1293
1Sa 25:27 now this **b** which thine handmaid hath 1293
2Sa 7:29 with thy **b** let the house of thy servant be 1293
2Ki 5:15 I pray thee, take a **b** of thy servant. 1293
Ne 9: 5 which *is* exalted above all **b** and praise. 1293
13: 2 howbeit our God turned the curse into a **b**. 1293
Job 29:13 The **b** of him that was ready to perish came 1293
Ps 3: 8 thy **b** *is* upon thy people. Selah. 1293
24: 5 He shall receive the **b** from the LORD, 1293
109:17 as he delighted not in **b**, so let it be far from 1293
129: 8 by say, The **b** of the LORD *be* upon you: 1293
133: 3 for there the LORD commanded the **b**, 1293
Pr 10:22 The **b** of the LORD, it maketh rich, and 1293
11:11 By the **b** of the upright the city is exalted: 1293
11:26 **b** *shall be* upon the head of him that selleth 1293
24:25 and a good **b** shall come upon them. 1293
Isa 19:24 *even* a **b** in the midst of the land: 1293
44: 3 thy seed, and my **b** upon thine offspring: 1293
65: 8 and *one* saith, Destroy it not; for a **b** *is* in it: 1293
Eze 34:26 and the places round about my hill a **b**; 1293
34:26 in his season; there shall be showers of **b**. 1293
44:30 that he may cause the **b** to rest in thine 1293
Joel 2:14 and repent, and leave a **b** behind him; 1293
Zec 8:13 so will I save you, and ye shall be a **b**: 1293
Mal 3:10 windows of heaven, and pour you out a **b**, 1293
Lk 24:53 in the temple, praising and **b** God. *2127*
Ro 15:29 I shall come in the fulness of the **b** of *2129*
1Co 10:16 The cup of **b** which we bless, is it not *2129*
Gal 3:14 That the **b** of Abraham might come on *2129*
Heb 6: 7 whom it is dressed, receiveth **b** from God: *2129*
6:14 Surely **b** I will bless thee, and multiplying I *2127*
12:17 when he would have inherited the **b**, he was *2129*
Jas 3:10 Out of the same mouth proceedeth **b** and *2129*
1Pe 3: 9 but contrariwise **b**; knowing that ye are *2127*
3: 9 thereunto called, that ye should inherit a **b**. *2129*
Rev 5:12 and strength, and honour, and glory, and **b**. *2129*
5:13 **B**, and honour, and glory, and power, *2129*
7:12 **B**, and glory, and wisdom, and *2129*

BLESSINGS (12) [BLESS]
Ge 49:25 who shall bless thee *with* **b** of heaven 1293
49:25 **b** of the deep that lieth under, blessings of 1293
49:25 **b** of the breasts, and of the womb: 1293
49:26 The **b** of thy father have prevailed above 1293
49:26 **b** of my progenitors unto the utmost bound 1293
Dt 28: 2 all these **b** shall come on thee, and 1293
Jos 8:34 all the words of the law, the **b** and cursings, 1293
Ps 21: 3 For thou preventest him *with* the **b** of 1293
Pr 10: 6 **B** *are* upon the head of the just: but 1293
28:20 A faithful man shall abound with **b**: but 1293
Mal 2: 2 a curse upon you, and will curse your **b**: 1293
Eph 1: 3 who hath blessed us with all spiritual **b** in *2129*

BLEW (23) [BLOW]
Jos 6: 8 the LORD, and **b** with the trumpets: 8628
6: 9 before the priests that **b** *with* the trumpets, 8628
6:13 on continually, and **b** with the trumpets: 8628
6:16 when the priests **b** with the trumpets, 8628
6:20 So the people shouted when *the priests* **b** 8628
Jdg 3:27 that he **b** a trumpet in the mountain of 8628
6:34 came upon Gideon, and he **b** a trumpet; 8628
7:19 they **b** the trumpets, and brake the pitchers 8628
7:20 the three companies **b** the trumpets, and 8628
7:22 the three hundred **b** the trumpets, and 8628
1Sa 13: 3 the Philistines heard *of it*. And Saul **b** 8628
2Sa 2:28 So Joab **b** a trumpet, and all the people 8628
18:16 Joab **b** the trumpet, and the people returned 8628
20: 1 he **b** a trumpet, and said, We have no part 8628
20:22 he **b** a trumpet, and they retired from 8628
1Ki 1:39 they **b** the trumpet; and all the people said, 8628
2Ki 9:13 and **b** with trumpets, saying, Jehu is king. 8628
11:14 of the land rejoiced, and **b** with trumpets: 8628
Mt 7:25 and the winds **b**, and beat upon that house; *4154*
7:27 and the winds **b**, and beat upon that house; *4154*
Jn 6:18 sea arose by reason of a great wind that **b**. *4154*
Ac 27:13 And when the south wind **b softly**, *5285*
28:13 and after one day the south wind **b**, and *1920*

BLIND (82) [BLINDED, BLINDETH, BLINDFOLDED, BLINDNESS]
Ex 4:11 the dumb, or deaf, or the seeing, or the **b**? 5787
Lev 19:14 nor put a stumblingblock before the **b**, but 5787
21:18 a **b** man, or a lame, or he that hath a flat 5787
22:22 **B**, or broken, or maimed, or having a wen, 5788
Dt 15:21 *if it be* lame, or **b**, *or have* any ill blemish, 5787
16:19 for a gift doth **b** the eyes of the wise, and 5786
27:18 Cursed *be* he that maketh the **b** to wander 5787
28:29 as the **b** gropeth in darkness, and thou shalt 5787
1Sa 12: 3 *any* bribe to **b** mine eyes therewith? 5956
2Sa 5: 6 Except thou take away the **b** and the lame, 5787
5: 8 the Jebusites, and the lame and the **b**, 5787
5: 8 The **b** and the lame shall not come into 5787
Job 29:15 I was eyes to the **b**, and feet *was* I to 5787
Ps 146: 8 The LORD openeth *the eyes of* the **b**: 5787
Isa 29:18 the eyes of the **b** shall see out of obscurity, 5787
35: 5 the eyes of the **b** shall be opened, and 5787
42: 7 To open the **b** eyes, to bring out 5787
42:16 I will bring the **b** by a way *that* they knew 5787
42:18 ye deaf; and look, ye **b**, that *ye* may see. 5787
42:19 Who *is* **b**, but my servant? or deaf, as my 5787
42:19 who *is* **b** as he that is perfect, and blind as 5787
42:19 is perfect, and **b** as the LORD'S servant? 5787
43: 8 Bring forth the **b** people that have eyes, and 5787
56:10 His watchmen *are* **b**: they are all ignorant, 5787
59:10 We grope for the wall like the **b**, and 5787
Jer 31: 8 *and* with them the **b** and the lame, 5787
La 4:14 They have wandered *as* **b** *men* in 5787
Zep 1:17 that they shall walk like **b** *men*, because 5787
Mal 1: 8 if ye offer the **b** for sacrifice, *is it* not evil? 5787
Mt 9:27 two **b men** followed him, crying, and *5185*
9:28 into the house, the **b men** came to him: *5185*
11: 5 The **b** receive their sight, and the lame *5185*
12:22 one possessed with a devil, **b**, and dumb: *5185*
12:22 insomuch that the **b** and dumb both spake *5185*
15:14 they be **b** leaders of the blind. And if *5185*
15:14 they be blind leaders of the **b**. And if *5185*
15:14 And if the **b** lead the blind, both shall fall *5185*
15:14 And if the blind lead the **b**, both shall fall *5185*
15:30 **b**, dumb, maimed, and many others, and *5185*
15:31 the lame to walk, and the **b** to see: *5185*
20:30 two **b men** sitting by the way side, *5185*
21:14 And *the* **b** and *the* lame came to him in *5185*
23:16 Woe unto you, *ye* **b** guides, which say, *5185*
23:17 *Ye* fools and **b**: for whether is greater, *5185*
23:19 *Ye* fools and **b**: for whether *is* greater, *5185*
23:24 *Ye* **b** guides, which strain out a gnat, and *5185*
23:26 *Thou* **b** Pharisee, cleanse first that *which is* *5185*
Mk 8:22 and they bring a **b man** unto him, and *5185*
8:23 And he took the **b man** by the hand, and *5185*
10:46 of people, **b** Bartimeus, the son of Timeus, *5185*
10:49 And they call the **b man**, saying unto him, *5185*
10:51 The **b man** said unto him, Lord, that I *5185*
Lk 4:18 and recovering of sight to the **b**, *5185*
6:39 unto them, Can the **b** lead the blind? *5185*
6:39 unto them, Can the blind lead the **b**? *5185*
7:21 and unto many *that were* **b** he gave sight. *5185*
7:22 how that the **b** see, the lame walk, *5185*
14:13 call the poor, the maimed, the lame, the **b**: *5185*
14:21 and the maimed, and the halt, and the **b**. *5185*
18:35 a certain **b man** sat by the way side *5185*
Jn 5: 3 lay a great multitude of impotent *folk*, of **b**, *5185*
9: 1 he saw a man *which was* **b** from *his* birth. *5185*
9: 2 or his parents, that he was born **b**? *5185*
9: 6 he anointed the eyes of the **b man** with *5185*
9: 8 which before had seen him that he was **b**, *5185*
9:13 to the Pharisees him that aforetime was **b**. *5185*
9:17 They say unto the **b man** again, *5185*
9:18 that he had been **b**, and received his sight, *5185*
9:19 Is this your son, who ye say was born **b**? *5185*
9:20 that this is our son, and that he was born **b**: *5185*
9:24 Then again called they the man that was **b**, *5185*
9:25 I know, that, whereas I was **b**, now I see. *5185*
9:32 opened the eyes of one that was born **b**. *5185*
9:39 and that they which see might be made **b**. *5185*
9:40 and said unto him, Are we **b** also? *5185*
9:41 Jesus said unto them, If ye were **b**, *5185*
10:21 a devil. Can a devil open the eyes of the **b**? *5185*
11:37 this *man*, which opened the eyes of the **b**, *5185*
Ac 13:11 and thou shalt be **b**, not seeing the sun for a *5185*
Ro 2:19 that thou thyself art a guide of the **b**, *5185*
2Pe 1: 9 But he that lacketh these *things* is **b**, and *5185*
Rev 3:17 and miserable, and poor, and **b**, and naked: *5185*

BLINDED (5) [BLIND]
Jn 12:40 He hath **b** their eyes, and hardened their *5186*

Ro 11: 7 hath obtained *it,* and the rest were **b**, *4456*
2Co 3:14 But their minds were **b**: for until this day *4456*
4: 4 In whom the god of this world hath **b** *5186*
1Jn 2:11 because that darkness hath **b** his eyes. *5186*

BLINDETH (1) [BLIND]

Ex 23: 8 for the gift **b** the wise, and perverteth 5786

BLINDFOLDED (1) [BLIND]

Lk 22:64 And when they had **b** him, they stroke him *4028*

BLINDNESS (7) [BLIND]

Ge 19:11 that *were at* the door of the house with **b**, 5575
Dt 28:28 and **b**, and astonishment of heart: 5788
2Ki 6:18 said, Smite this people, I pray thee, with **b**. 5575
6:18 he smote them with **b** according to 5575
Zec 12: 4 will smite every horse of the people with **b**. 5788
Ro 11:25 that **b** in part is happened to Israel, until *4457*
Eph 4:18 is in them, because of the **b** of their heart: *4457*

BLOCKED See FENCED

BLOOD (447) [BLOODGUILTINESS, BLOODTHIRSTY, BLOODY]

Ge 4:10 the voice of thy brother's **b** crieth unto me 1818
4:11 to receive thy brother's **b** from thy hand. 1818
9: 4 *which is* the **b** thereof, shall you not eat. 1818
9: 5 surely your **b** of your lives will I require; 1818
9: 6 Whoso sheddeth man's **b**, by man shall his 1818
9: 6 man's blood, by man shall his **b** be shed: 1818
37:22 Shed no **b**, *but* cast him into this pit that *is* 1818
37:26 *it* if we slay our brother, and conceal his **b**? 1818
37:31 of the goats, and dipped the coat in the **b**; 1818
42:22 therefore, behold, also his **b** is required. 1818
49:11 in wine, and his clothes in the **b** of grapes: 1818
Ex 4: 9 the river shall become **b** upon the dry *land.* 1818
7:17 in the river, and they shall be turned to **b**. 1818
7:19 pools of water, that they may become **b**; 1818
7:19 *that* there may be **b** throughout all the land 1818
7:20 that *were* in the river were turned to **b**. 1818
7:21 there was **b** throughout all the land of 1818
12: 7 they shall take of the **b**, and strike *it* on 1818
12:13 the **b** shall be to you for a token upon 1818
12:13 where you *are:* and when I see the **b**, 1818
12:22 dip *it* in the **b** that *is* in the bason, and 1818
12:22 the two side posts with the **b** that *is* in 1818
12:23 when he seeth the **b** upon the lintel, and 1818
22: 2 he die, *there shall* no **b** *be shed* for him. 1818
22: 3 upon him, *there shall be* **b** *shed* for him; 1818
23:18 Thou shalt not offer the **b** of my sacrifice 1818
24: 6 Moses took half of the **b**, and put *it* in 1818
24: 6 and half of the **b** he sprinkled on the altar. 1818
24: 8 Moses took the **b**, and sprinkled *it* on 1818
24: 8 and said, Behold the **b** of the covenant, 1818
29:12 thou shalt take of the **b** of the bullock, and 1818
29:12 pour all the **b** beside the bottom of the altar. 1818
29:16 thou shalt take his **b**, and sprinkle *it* round 1818
29:20 take of his **b**, and put *it* upon the tip of 1818
29:20 sprinkle the **b** upon the altar round about. 1818
29:21 thou shalt take of the **b** that *is* upon 1818
30:10 the **b** of the sin offering of atonements: 1818
34:25 Thou shalt not offer the **b** of my sacrifice 1818
Lev 1: 5 shall bring the **b**, and sprinkle the blood 1818
1: 5 sprinkle the **b** round about upon the altar 1818
1:11 shall sprinkle his **b** round about upon 1818
1:15 the **b** thereof shall be wrung out at the side 1818
3: 2 Aaron's sons the priests shall sprinkle the **b** 1818
3: 8 Aaron's sons shall sprinkle the **b** thereof 1818
3:13 the sons of Aaron shall sprinkle the **b** 1818
3:17 your dwellings, *that* ye eat neither fat nor **b**. 1818
4: 5 is anointed shall take of the bullock's **b**, 1818
4: 6 the priest shall dip his finger in the **b**, and 1818
4: 6 sprinkle of the **b** seven times before 1818
4: 7 the priest shall put *some* of the **b** upon 1818
4: 7 shall pour all the **b** of the bullock at 1818
4:16 **b** to the tabernacle of the congregation: 1818
4:17 priest shall dip his finger *in some* of the **b**, 1818
4:18 he shall put *some* of the **b** upon the horns 1818
4:18 shall pour out all the **b** at the bottom of 1818
4:25 the priest shall take of the **b** of the sin 1818
4:25 shall pour out his **b** at the bottom of 1818
4:30 the priest shall take of the **b** thereof with 1818
4:30 shall pour out all the **b** thereof at 1818
4:34 the priest shall take of the **b** of the sin 1818
4:34 shall pour out all the **b** thereof at 1818
5: 9 he shall sprinkle of the **b** of the sin offering 1818
5: 9 the rest of the **b** shall be wrung out at 1818
6:27 when there is sprinkled of the **b** thereof 1818
6:30 whereof *any* of the **b** is brought into 1818
7: 2 the **b** thereof shall he sprinkle round about 1818
7:14 it shall be the priest's that sprinkleth the **b** 1818
7:26 Moreover ye shall eat no *manner of* **b**, 1818
7:27 soul *it be* that eateth any *manner of* **b**, 1818
7:33 that offereth the **b** of the peace offerings, 1818
8:15 he slew *it;* and Moses took the **b**, and put *it* 1818
8:15 poured the **b** at the bottom of the altar, and 1818
8:19 Moses sprinkled the **b** upon the altar round 1818
8:23 he slew *it;* and Moses took of the **b** of it, 1818
8:24 Moses put of the **b** upon the tip of their 1818
8:24 Moses sprinkled the **b** upon the altar round 1818
8:30 of the **b** which *was* upon the altar, and 1818
9: 9 the sons of Aaron brought the **b** unto him: 1818
9: 9 he dipt his finger in the **b**, and put *it* upon 1818
9: 9 poured out the **b** at the bottom of the altar: 1818
9:12 Aaron's sons presented unto him the **b**, 1818
9:18 Aaron's sons presented unto him the **b**, 1818
10:18 the **b** of it was not brought in within 1818
12: 4 continue in the **b** of her purifying three and 1818
12: 5 she shall continue in the **b** of her purifying 1818
12: 7 shall be cleansed from the issue of her **b**. 1818
14: 6 the living bird in the **b** of the bird *that was* 1818
14:14 the priest shall take *some* of the **b** of 1818
14:17 upon the **b** of the trespass offering: 1818
14:25 the priest shall take *some* of the **b** of 1818
14:28 upon the place of the **b** of the trespass 1818
14:51 dip them in the **b** of the slain bird, and 1818
14:52 he shall cleanse the house with the **b** of 1818
15:19 an issue, *and* her issue in her flesh be **b**, 1818
15:25 if a woman have an issue of her **b** many 1818
16:14 he shall take of the **b** of the bullock, and 1818
16:14 of the **b** with his finger seven times. 1818
16:15 bring his **b** within the vail, and do with that 1818
16:15 do with that **b** as he did with the blood of 1818
16:15 do with that blood as he did with the **b** of 1818
16:18 shall take of the **b** of the bullock, and of 1818
16:18 of the **b** of the goat, and put *it* upon 1818
16:19 he shall sprinkle of the **b** upon it with his 1818
16:27 whose **b** was brought in to make atonement 1818
17: 4 **b** shall be imputed unto that man; he hath 1818
17: 4 he hath shed **b**; and that man shall be cut 1818
17: 6 the priest shall sprinkle the **b** upon the altar 1818
17:10 among you, that eateth any *manner of* **b**; 1818
17:10 set my face against *that* soul that eateth **b**, 1818
17:11 For the life of the flesh *is* in the **b**: and 1818
17:11 for it *is* the **b** *that* maketh an atonement for 1818
17:12 of Israel, No soul of you shall eat **b**, 1818
17:12 stranger that sojourneth among you eat **b**. 1818
17:13 he shall even pour out the **b** thereof, and 1818
17:14 of all flesh; the **b** of it *is* for the life thereof: 1818
17:14 Ye shall eat the **b** of no *manner of* flesh: 1818
17:14 for the life of all flesh *is* the **b** thereof: 1818
19:16 neither shalt thou stand against the **b** of thy 1818
19:26 Ye shall not eat *any thing* with the **b**: 1818
20: 9 or his mother; his **b** *shall be* upon him. 1818
20:11 be put to death; their **b** *shall be* upon them. 1818
20:12 their **b** *shall be* upon them. 1818
20:13 be put to death; their **b** *shall be* upon them. 1818
20:16 be put to death; their **b** *shall be* upon them. 1818
20:18 she hath uncovered the fountain of her **b**: 1818
20:27 with stones: their **b** *shall be* upon them. 1818
Nu 18:17 thou shalt sprinkle their **b** upon the altar, 1818
19: 4 Eleazar the priest shall take of her **b** with 1818
19: 4 sprinkle of her **b** directly before 1818
19: 5 her skin, and her flesh, and her **b**, with her 1818
23:24 eat *of* the prey, and drink the **b** of the slain. 1818
35:19 The revenger of **b** himself shall slay 1818
35:21 the revenger of **b** shall slay the murderer, 1818
35:24 the revenger of **b** according to these 1818
35:25 slayer out of the hand of the revenger of **b**, 1818
35:27 the revenger of **b** find him without 1818
35:27 and the revenger of **b** kill the slayer; 1818
35:27 kill the slayer; he shall not be guilty of **b**: 1818
35:33 wherein ye *are:* for **b** it defileth the land: 1818
35:33 the land cannot be cleansed of the **b** that is 1818
35:33 but by the **b** of him that shed it. 1818
Dt 12:16 Only ye shall not eat the **b**; ye shall pour it 1818
12:23 Only be sure that thou eat not the **b**: for 1818
12:23 for the **b** *is* the life; and thou mayest not eat 1818

Dt 12:27 the flesh and the **b**, upon the altar of 1818
12:27 the **b** of thy sacrifices shall be poured out 1818
15:23 Only thou shalt not eat the **b** thereof; 1818
17: 8 between **b** and blood, between plea and 1818
17: 8 between blood and **b**, between plea and 1818
19: 6 Lest the avenger of the **b** pursue the slayer, 1818
19:10 That innocent **b** be not shed in thy land, 1818
19:10 *for* an inheritance, and *so* **b** be upon thee. 1818
19:12 him into the hand of the avenger of **b**, 1818
19:13 thou shalt put away *the guilt of* innocent **b** 1818
21: 7 and say, Our hands have not shed this **b**, 1818
21: 8 lay not innocent **b** unto thy people of 1818
21: 8 And the **b** shall be forgiven them. 1818
21: 9 the *guilt of* innocent **b** from among you, 1818
22: 8 that thou bring not **b** upon thine house, 1818
32:14 thou didst drink the pure **b** of the grape. 1818
32:42 I will make mine arrows drunk with **b**, and 1818
32:42 *and that* with the **b** of the slain and of 1818
32:43 for he will avenge the **b** of his servants, and 1818
Jos 2:19 his **b** *shall be* upon his head, and we *will be* 1818
2:19 his **b** *shall be* on our head, if *any* hand be 1818
20: 3 shall be your refuge from the avenger of **b**. 1818
20: 5 if the avenger of **b** pursue after him, then 1818
20: 9 not die by the hand of the avenger of **b**, 1818
Jdg 9:24 their **b** be laid upon Abimelech their 1818
1Sa 14:32 and the people did eat *them* with the **b**. 1818
14:33 the LORD, in that they eat with the **b**. 1818
14:34 not against the LORD in eating with the **b**. 1818
19: 5 then wilt thou sin against innocent **b**, 1818
25:26 withholden thee from coming to *shed* **b**, 1818
25:31 either that thou hast shed **b** causeless, or 1818
25:33 kept me this day from coming to *shed* **b**, 1818
26:20 let not my **b** fall to the earth before the face 1818
2Sa 1:16 said unto him, Thy **b** *be* upon thy head; 1818
1:22 From the **b** of the slain, from the fat of 1818
3:27 that he died, for the **b** of Asahel his brother. 1818
3:28 ever from the **b** of Abner the son of Ner: 1818
4:11 therefore now require his **b** of your hand, 1818
14:11 the revengers of **b** to destroy any more, 1818
16: 8 upon thee all the **b** of the house of Saul, 1818
20:12 Amasa wallowed in **b** in the midst of 1818
23:17 *is not this* the **b** of the men that went in 1818
1Ki 2: 5 shed the **b** of war in peace, and put 1818
2: 5 put the **b** of war upon his girdle that *was* 1818
2: 9 head bring thou down *to* the grave with **b**. 1818
2:31 that thou mayest take away the innocent **b**, 1818
2:32 the LORD shall return his **b** upon his own 1818
2:33 Their **b** shall therefore return upon the head 1818
2:37 thy **b** shall be upon thine own head. 1818
18:28 till the **b** gushed out upon them. 1818
21:19 In the place where dogs licked the **b** of 1818
21:19 the blood of Naboth shall dogs lick thy **b**, 1818
22:35 the **b** ran out of the wound into the midst of 1818
22:38 the dogs licked up his **b**; and they washed 1818
2Ki 3:22 saw the water on the other side *as* red as **b**: 1818
3:23 they said, This *is* **b**: the kings are surely 1818
9: 7 that I may avenge the **b** of my servants 1818
9: 7 the **b** of all the servants of the LORD, 1818
9:26 Surely I have seen yesterday the **b** of 1818
9:26 and the **b** of his sons, saith the LORD; 1818
9:33 *some* of her **b** was sprinkled on the wall, 1818
16:13 sprinkled the **b** of his peace offerings, 1818
16:15 sprinkle upon it all the **b** of the burnt 1818
16:15 burnt offering, and all the **b** of the sacrifice: 1818
21:16 Moreover Manasseh shed innocent **b** very 1818
24: 4 also *for* the innocent **b** that he shed: for he 1818
24: 4 for he filled Jerusalem *with* innocent **b**; 1818
1Ch 11:19 *I* should do this *thing:* shall I drink the **b** 1818
22: 8 Thou hast shed **b** abundantly, and 1818
22: 8 thou hast shed much **b** upon the earth in my 1818
28: 3 *hast been* a man of war, and hast shed **b**. 1818
2Ch 19:10 between **b** and blood, between law and 1818
19:10 between blood and **b**, between law and 1818
24:25 for the **b** of the sons of Jehoiada the priest, 1818
29:22 the priests received the **b**, and sprinkled *it* 1818
29:22 they sprinkled the **b** upon the altar: 1818
29:22 and they sprinkled the **b** upon the altar. 1818
29:24 they made reconciliation with their **b** upon 1818
30:16 the priests sprinkled the **b**, *which they* 1818
35:11 the priests sprinkled *the* **b** from their hands, NIH
Job 16:18 cover not thou my **b**, and let my cry have 1818
39:30 Her young ones also suck up **b**: and where 1818
Ps 9:12 When he maketh inquisition for **b**, he 1818
16: 4 their drink offerings of **b** will I not offer, 1818
30: 9 What profit *is there* in my **b**, when I go 1818
50:13 the flesh of bulls, or drink the **b** of goats? 1818
58:10 he shall wash his feet in the **b** of 1818
68:23 That thy foot may be dipped in the **b** of 1818
72:14 and precious shall their **b** be in his sight. 1818
78:44 had turned their rivers into **b**; and 1818
79: 3 Their **b** have they shed like water round 1818
79:10 of the **b** of thy servants which is shed. 1818
94:21 the righteous, and condemn the innocent **b**. 1818
105:29 He turned their waters into **b**, and 1818
106:38 shed innocent **b**, *even* the blood of their 1818
106:38 *even* the **b** of their sons and of their 1818
106:38 and the land was polluted with **b**. 1818
Pr 1:11 Come with us, let us lay wait for **b**, 1818
1:16 feet run to evil, and make haste to shed **b**. 1818
1:18 they lay wait for their own **b**; they lurk 1818
6:17 and hands that shed innocent **b**, 1818
12: 6 words of the wicked *are* to lie in wait *for* **b**: 1818
28:17 A man that doeth violence to the **b** of *any* 1818
30:33 the wringing of the nose bringeth forth **b**: 1818
Isa 1:11 I delight not in the **b** of bullocks, or 1818
1:15 I will not hear: your hands are full *of* **b**. 1818
4: 4 shall have purged the **b** of Jerusalem from 1818
9: 5 confused noise, and garments rolled in **b**; 1818
15: 9 For the waters of Dimon shall be full *of* **b**: 1818
26:21 the earth also shall disclose her **b**, and 1818
33:15 that stoppeth his ears from hearing of **b**, 1818
34: 3 the mountains shall be melted with their **b**. 1818
34: 6 The sword of the LORD is filled *with* **b**, 1818
34: 6 *and* with the **b** of lambs and goats, 1818
34: 7 their land shall be soaked with **b**, and 1818
49:26 they shall be drunken with their own **b**, 1818
59: 3 For your hands are defiled with **b**, and 1818
59: 7 and they make haste to shed innocent **b**: 1818
63: 3 their **b** shall be sprinkled upon my 5332
66: 3 an oblation, *as if he offered* swine's **b**; 1818
Jer 2:34 Also in thy skirts is found the **b** of the souls 1818
7: 6 and shed not innocent **b** in this place, 1818
18:21 pour out their *b* by the force of the sword; NIH
19: 4 have filled this place *with* the **b** of 1818
22: 3 neither shed innocent **b** in this place. 1818
22:17 for to shed innocent **b**, and for oppression, 1818
26:15 ye shall surely bring innocent **b** upon 1818
46:10 be satiate and made drunk with their **b**: 1818
48:10 *be* he that keepeth back his sword from **b**. 1818
51:35 my **b** upon the inhabitants of Chaldea, 1818
La 4:13 that *have* shed the **b** of the just in the midst 1818
4:14 they have polluted themselves with **b**, so 1818
Eze 3:18 but his **b** will I require at thine hand. 1818
3:20 but his **b** will I require at thine hand. 1818
5:17 pestilence and **b** shall pass through thee; 1818
9: 9 the land is full *of* **b**, and the city full *of* 1818
14:19 pour out my fury upon it in **b**, to cut off 1818
16: 6 and saw thee polluted in thine own **b**, 1818
16: 6 I said unto thee *when thou wast* in thy **b**, 1818
16: 6 I said unto thee *when thou wast* in thy **b**, 1818
16: 9 I throughly washed away thy **b** from thee, 1818
16:22 and bare, *and* wast polluted in thy **b**. 1818
16:36 by the **b** of thy children, which thou didst 1818
16:38 that break wedlock and shed **b** are judged; 1818
16:38 and I will give thee **b** in fury and jealousy. 1818
18:10 a shedder of **b**, and *that* doeth the like to 1818
18:13 he shall surely die; his **b** shall be upon him. 1818
19:10 Thy mother *is* like a vine in thy **b**, 1818
21:32 thy **b** shall be in the midst of the land; 1818
22: 3 The city sheddeth **b** in the midst of it, 1818
22: 4 Thou art become guilty in thy **b** that thou 1818
22: 6 one were in thee to their power to shed **b**. 1818
22: 9 In thee are men that carry tales to shed **b**: 1818
22:12 In thee have they taken gifts to shed **b**; 1818
22:13 at thy **b** which hath been in the midst of 1818
22:27 to shed **b**, *and* to destroy souls, to get 1818
23:37 **b** *is* in their hands, and with their idols have 1818
23:45 and after the manner of *women* that shed **b**; 1818
23:45 *are* adulteresses, and **b** *is* in their hands. 1818
24: 7 For her **b** is in the midst of her; she set it 1818
24: 8 I have set her **b** upon the top of a rock, 1818
28:23 into her pestilence, and **b** into her streets; 1818
32: 6 I will also water with thy **b** the land 1818
33: 4 his **b** shall be upon his own head. 1818
33: 5 took not warning; his **b** shall be upon him. 1818
33: 6 his **b** will I require at the watchman's hand. 1818
33: 8 but his **b** will I require at thine hand. 1818
33:25 Ye eat with the **b**, and lift up your eyes 1818

B

Eze	33:25	up your eyes toward your idols, and shed **b**:	1818
	35: 5	hast shed *the **b** of* the children of Israel by	NIH
	35: 6	I will prepare thee unto **b**, and blood shall	1818
	35: 6	thee unto blood, and **b** shall pursue thee:	1818
	35: 6	sith thou hast not hated **b**, even blood shall	1818
	35: 6	not hated blood, even **b** shall pursue thee.	1818
	36:18	for the **b** that they had shed upon the land,	1818
	38:22	against him with pestilence and with **b**;	1818
	39:17	of Israel, that ye may eat flesh, and drink **b**.	1818
	39:18	drink the **b** of the princes of the earth,	1818
	39:19	*ye* be full, and drink **b** till *ye* be drunken,	1818
	43:18	and to sprinkle **b** thereon.	1818
	43:20	thou shalt take of the **b** thereof, and put *it*	1818
	44: 7	the fat and the **b**, and they have broken my	1818
	44:15	me to offer unto me the fat and the **b**,	1818
	45:19	the priest shall take of the **b** of the sin	1818
Hos	1: 4	I will avenge the **b** of Jezreel upon	1818
	4: 2	they break out, and **b** toucheth blood.	1818
	4: 2	they break out, and blood toucheth **b**.	1818
	6: 8	that work iniquity, *and is* polluted with **b**.	1818
	12:14	therefore shall he leave his **b** upon him, and	1818
Joel	2:30	the earth, **b**, and fire, and pillars of smoke.	1818
	2:31	the moon into **b**, before the great and	1818
	3:19	they have shed innocent **b** in their land.	1818
	3:21	For I will cleanse their **b** *that* I have not	1818
Jnh	1:14	man's life, and lay not upon us innocent **b**:	1818
Mic	3:10	They build up Zion with **b**, and	1818
	7: 2	they all lie in wait for **b**; they hunt every	1818
Hab	2: 8	because of men's **b**, and *for* the violence of	1818
	2:12	Woe to him that buildeth a town with **b**,	1818
	2:17	because of men's **b**, and *for* the violence of	1818
Zep	1:17	their **b** shall be poured out as dust, and	1818
Zec	9: 7	I will take away his **b** out of his mouth,	1818
	9:11	by the **b** of thy covenant I have sent forth	1818
Mt	9:20	which was **diseased with an issue of b**	*131*
	16:17	for flesh and **b** hath not revealed *it* unto thee,	*129*
	23:30	partakers with them in the **b** of the prophets.	*129*
	23:35	That upon you may come all the righteous **b**	*129*
	23:35	from the **b** of righteous Abel unto the blood	*129*
	23:35	from the blood of righteous Abel unto the **b**	*129*
	26:28	For this is my **b** of the new testament,	*129*
	27: 4	sinned in that I have betrayed *the* innocent **b**.	*129*
	27: 6	into the treasury, because it is the price of **b**.	*129*
	27: 8	was called, The field of **b**, unto this day.	*129*
	27:24	I am innocent of the **b** of this just *person:*	*129*
	27:25	said, His **b** *be* on us, and on our children.	*129*
Mk	5:25	which had an issue of **b** twelve years,	*129*
	5:29	And straightway the fountain of her **b** was	*129*
	14:24	This is my **b** of the new testament,	*129*
Lk	8:43	And a woman having an issue of **b** twelve	*129*
	8:44	and immediately her issue of **b** stanched.	*129*
	11:50	That the **b** of all the prophets, which was	*129*
	11:51	From the **b** of Abel unto the blood of	*129*
	11:51	From the blood of Abel unto the **b** of	*129*
	13: 1	whose **b** Pilate had mingled with their	*129*
	22:20	This cup *is* the new testament in my **b**,	*129*
	22:44	his sweat was as it were great drops of **b**	*129*
Jn	1:13	Which were born, not of **b**, nor of the will of	*129*
	6:53	and drink his **b**, ye have no life in you.	*129*
	6:54	and drinketh my **b**, hath eternal life;	*129*
	6:55	is meat indeed, and my **b** is drink indeed.	*129*
	6:56	and drinketh my **b**, dwelleth in me, and I in	*129*
	19:34	and forthwith came there out **b** and water.	*129*
Ac	1:19	Aceldama, that is to say, The field of **b**.	*129*
	2:19	**b**, and fire, and vapour of smoke:	*129*
	2:20	and the moon into **b**, before *that* great and	*129*
	5:28	and intend to bring this man's **b** upon us.	*129*
	15:20	and *from* things strangled, and *from* **b**.	*129*
	15:29	and from **b**, and from things strangled, and	*129*
	17:26	And hath made of one **b** all nations of men	*129*
	18: 6	unto them, Your **b** *be* upon your own heads;	*129*
	20:26	that I *am* pure from the **b** of all *men.*	*129*
	20:28	which he hath purchased with his own **b**.	*129*
	21:25	and from **b**, and from strangled, and	*129*
	22:20	And when the **b** of thy martyr Stephen was	*129*
Ro	3:15	Their feet *are* swift to shed **b**:	*129*
	3:25	*to be* a propitiation through faith in his **b**,	*129*
	5: 9	more then, being now justified by his **b**,	*129*
1Co	10:16	is it not the communion of the **b** of Christ?	*129*
	11:25	This cup is the new testament in my **b**:	*129*
	11:27	shall be guilty of the body and **b** of the Lord.	*129*
	15:50	and **b** cannot inherit the kingdom of God;	*129*
Gal	1:16	I conferred not with flesh and **b**:	*129*
Eph	1: 7	In whom we have redemption through his **b**,	*129*
	2:13	far off are made nigh by the **b** of Christ.	*129*
	6:12	For we wrestle not against flesh and **b**, but	*129*
Col	1:14	In whom we have redemption through his **b**,	*129*
	1:20	having made peace through the **b** of his	*129*
Heb	2:14	as the children are partakers of flesh and **b**,	*129*
	9: 7	not without **b**, which he offered for himself,	*129*
	9:12	Neither by the **b** of goats and calves,	*129*
	9:12	by his own **b** he entered in once into	*129*
	9:13	For if the **b** of bulls and of goats, and	*129*
	9:14	How much more shall the **b** of Christ,	*129*
	9:18	the first *testament* was dedicated without **b**.	*129*
	9:19	he took the **b** of calves and of goats,	*129*
	9:20	This *is* the **b** of the testament which God	*129*
	9:21	Moreover he sprinkled with **b** both	*129*
	9:22	all *things* are by the law purged with **b**;	*129*
	9:22	and without **shedding of b** is no remission.	*130*
	9:25	the holy *place* every year with **b** of others;	*129*
	10: 4	For *it is* not possible that the **b** of bulls and	*129*
	10:19	boldness to enter into the holiest by the **b** of	*129*
	10:29	and hath counted the **b** of the covenant,	*129*
	11:28	he kept the passover, and the sprinkling of **b**,	*129*
	12: 4	Ye have not yet resisted unto **b**,	*129*
	12:24	and to the **b** of sprinkling, that speaketh	*129*
	13:11	whose **b** is brought into the sanctuary by	*129*
	13:12	he might sanctify the people with his own **b**,	*129*
	13:20	through the **b** of the everlasting covenant,	*129*
1Pe	1: 2	and sprinkling of the **b** of Jesus Christ:	*129*
	1:19	But with the precious **b** of Christ, as of a	*129*
1Jn	1: 7	the **b** of Jesus Christ his Son cleanseth us	*129*
	5: 6	This is he that came by water and **b**,	*129*
	5: 6	not by water only, but by water and **b**.	*129*
	5: 8	in earth, the Spirit, and the water, and the **b**:	*129*
Rev	1: 5	and washed us from our sins in his own **b**,	*129*
	5: 9	hast redeemed us to God by thy **b** out of	*129*
	6:10	avenge our **b** on them that dwell on	*129*
	6:12	sackcloth of hair, and the moon became as **b**;	*129*
	7:14	and made them white in the **b** of the Lamb.	*129*
	8: 7	there followed hail and fire mingled with **b**,	*129*
	8: 8	and the third *part* of the sea became **b**;	*129*
	11: 6	have power over waters to turn them to **b**,	*129*
	12:11	And they overcame him by the **b** of	*129*
	14:20	and **b** came out of the winepress, *even* unto	*129*
	16: 3	and it became as the **b** of a dead *man:* and	*129*
	16: 4	and fountains of waters; and they became **b**.	*129*
	16: 6	For they have shed the **b** of saints and	*129*
	16: 6	and thou hast given them **b** to drink;	*129*
	17: 6	And I saw the woman drunken with the **b** of	*129*
	17: 6	and with the **b** of the martyrs of Jesus:	*129*
	18:24	And in her was found the **b** of prophets, and	*129*
	19: 2	hath avenged the **b** of his servants at her	*129*
	19:13	And he *was* clothed with a vesture dipt in **b**:	*129*

BLOOD GUILT See BLOODGUILTINESS

BLOOD RELATIVES See KINDRED; KINDREDS

BLOODGUILTINESS (1) [BLOOD, GUILT]

Ps	51:14	Deliver me from **b**, O God, thou God of my	1818

BLOODTHIRSTY (1) [BLOOD, THIRST]

Pr	29:10	The **b** hate the upright: but the just	376+1818

BLOODY (16) [BLOOD]

Ex	4:25	and said, Surely a **b** husband *art* thou to me.	1818
	4:26	A **b** husband *thou art,* because of	1818
2Sa	16: 7	thou **b** man, and thou man of Belial:	1818
	16: 8	to thy mischief, because thou *art* a **b** man.	1818
	21: 1	for *his* **b** house, because he slew	1818
Ps	5: 6	the LORD will abhor the **b** and	1818
	26: 9	soul with sinners, nor my life with **b** men:	1818
	55:23	**b** and deceitful men shall not live out half	1818
	59: 2	of iniquity, and save me from **b** men.	1818
	139:19	depart from me therefore, ye **b** men.	1818
Eze	7:23	for the land is full *of* **b** crimes, and the city	1818
	22: 2	wilt thou judge, wilt thou judge the **b** city?	1818
	24: 6	Woe to the **b** city, to the pot whose scum *is*	1818
	24: 9	saith the Lord GOD; Woe to the **b** city!	1818
Na	3: 1	Woe to the **b** city! it *is* all full *of* lies *and*	1818
Ac	28: 8	Publius lay sick of a fever and of a **b** flixe:	*1420*

BLOOMED (1)

Nu	17: 8	and **b** blossoms, and yielded almonds.	6692

BLOSSOM (6) [BLOSSOMED, BLOSSOMS]

Nu	17: 5	man's rod, whom I shall choose, shall **b**:	6524

Isa 5:24 and their **b** shall go up as dust: 6525
27: 6 Israel shall **b** and bud, and fill the face of 6692
35: 1 the desert shall rejoice, and **b** as the rose. 6524
35: 2 It shall **b abundantly** and 6524+6524
Hab 3:17 Although the fig tree shall not **b**, 6524

BLOSSOMED (1) [BLOSSOM]
Eze 7:10 the rod hath **b**, pride hath budded. 6692

BLOSSOMS (2) [BLOSSOM]
Ge 40:10 as though it budded, *and* her **b** shot forth; 5322
Nu 17: 8 and bloomed **b**, and yielded almonds. 6731

BLOT (13) [BLOTTED, BLOTTETH, BLOTTING]
Ex 32:32 if not, **b** me, I pray thee, out of thy book 4229
32:33 against me, him will I **b out** of my book. 4229
Nu 5:23 he shall **b** *them* **out** with the bitter water: 4229
Dt 9:14 and **b out** their name from under heaven: 4229
25:19 *that* thou shalt **b out** the remembrance of 4229
29:20 the Lord shall **b out** his name from 4229
2Ki 14:27 the Lord said not that *he* would **b out** 4229
Job 31: 7 and *if any* **b** hath cleaved to my hands; 3971
Ps 51: 1 thy tender mercies **b out** my transgressions. 4229
51: 9 from my sins, and **b out** all mine iniquities. 4229
Pr 9: 7 rebuketh a wicked *man getteth* himself a **b**. 3971
Jer 18:23 neither **b out** their sin from thy sight, but 4229
Rev 3: 5 I will not **b out** his name out of the book of *1813*

BLOTTED (6) [BLOT]
Ne 4: 5 let not their sin be **b out** from before thee: 4229
Ps 69:28 Let them be **b out** of the book of the living, 4229
109:13 following let their name be **b out**. 4229
109:14 and let not the sin of his mother be **b out**. 4229
Isa 44:22 I have **b out**, as a thick cloud, 4229
Ac 3:19 be converted, that your sins may be **b out**, *1813*

BLOTTETH (1) [BLOT]
Isa 43:25 *am* he that **b out** thy transgressions for 4229

BLOTTING (1) [BLOT]
Col 2:14 **B out** the handwriting of ordinances that *1813*

BLOW (39) [BLEW, BLOWETH, BLOWING, BLOWN]
Ex 15:10 Thou didst **b** with thy wind, the sea covered 5398
Nu 10: 3 when they shall **b** with them, all 8628
10: 4 if they **b** *but* with one *trumpet,* then 8628
10: 5 When ye **b** an alarm, then the camps that 8628
10: 6 When you **b** an alarm the second time, then 8628
10: 6 they shall **b** an alarm for their journeys. 8628
10: 7 you shall **b**, but you shall not sound an 8628
10: 8 the priests, shall **b** with the trumpets; 8628
10: 9 then ye shall **b an alarm** with the trumpets; 7321
10:10 ye shall **b** with the trumpets over your 8628
31: 6 and the trumpets to **b** in his hand. 8643
Jos 6: 4 and the priests shall **b** with the trumpets. 8628
Jdg 7:18 When I **b** with a trumpet, I and all that *are* 8628
7:18 **b** ye the trumpets also on every side of all 8628
7:20 the trumpets in their right hands to **b** 8628
1Ki 1:34 **b** ye with the trumpet, and say, God save 8628
1Ch 15:24 did **b** with the trumpets before the ark of 2690
Ps 39:10 I am consumed by the **b** of thine hand. 8409
78:26 He **caused** an east wind **to b** in the heaven: 5265
81: 3 **B up** the trumpet in the new moon, in 8628
147:18 he **causeth** his wind **to b**, *and* the waters 5380
SS 4:16 **b** upon my garden, *that* the spices thereof 6315
Isa 40:24 he shall also **b** upon them, and they shall 5398
Jer 4: 5 and say, **B** ye the trumpet in the land: 8628
6: 1 **b** the trumpet in Tekoa, and set up a sign of 8628
14:17 *with* a great breach, *with* a very grievous **b**. 4347
51:27 **b** the trumpet among the nations, 8628
Eze 21:31 I will **b** against thee in the fire of my wrath, 6315
22:20 to **b** the fire upon it, to melt *it;* so will I 5301
22:21 **b** upon you in the fire of my wrath, and 5301
33: 3 he **b** the trumpet, and warn the people; 8628
33: 6 **b** not the trumpet, and the people be not 8628
Hos 5: 8 **B** ye the cornet in Gibeah, *and* the trumpet 8628
Joel 2: 1 **B** ye the trumpet in Zion, and sound an 8628
2:15 **B** the trumpet in Zion, sanctify a fast, call a 8628
Hag 1: 9 when ye brought *it* home, I did **b** upon it. 5301
Zec 9:14 the Lord God shall **b** the trumpet, and 8628
Lk 12:55 And when *ye see* the south wind **b**, ye say, *4154*
Rev 7: 1 that the wind should not **b** on the earth, *4154*

BLOWETH (4) [BLOW]
Isa 18: 3 and when *he* **b** a trumpet, hear ye. 8628
40: 7 because the spirit of the Lord **b** upon it: 5380
54:16 I have created the smith that **b** the coals in 5301
Jn 3: 8 The wind **b** where it listeth, and *4154*

BLOWING (4) [BLOW]
Lev 23:24 a memorial of **b of trumpets**, a holy 8643
Nu 29: 1 it is a day of **b** the **trumpets** unto you. 8643
Jos 6: 9 *priests* going on, and **b** with the trumpets. 8628
6:13 *priests* going on, and **b** with the trumpets. 8628

BLOWN (4) [BLOW]
Job 20:26 a fire not **b** shall consume him; it shall go 5301
Isa 27:13 *that* the great trumpet shall be **b**, and 8628
Eze 7:14 They have **b** the trumpet, even to make all 8628
Am 3: 6 Shall a trumpet be **b** in the city, and 8628

BLOWS See STRIPE; STRIPES

BLUE (50) [BLUENESS]
Ex 25: 4 **b**, and purple, and scarlet, and fine linen, 8504
26: 1 twined linen, and **b**, and purple, and scarlet: 8504
26: 4 thou shalt make loops of **b** upon the edge of 8504
26:31 thou shalt make a vail *of* **b**, and purple, 8504
26:36 *of* **b**, and purple, and scarlet, and 8504
27:16 *of* **b**, and purple, and scarlet, and 8504
28: 5 **b**, and purple, and scarlet, and fine linen. 8504
28: 6 *of* **b**, and *of* purple, *of* scarlet, and 8504
28: 8 *of* **b**, and purple, and scarlet, and 8504
28:15 *of* **b**, and *of* purple, and *of* scarlet, and 8504
28:28 unto the rings of the ephod with a lace of **b**, 8504
28:31 shalt make the robe of the ephod all of **b**. 8504
28:33 of it thou shalt make pomegranates of **b**, 8504
28:37 thou shalt put it on a **b** lace, that it may be 8504
35: 6 **b**, and purple, and scarlet, and fine linen, 8504
35:23 with whom was found **b**, and purple, and 8504
35:25 *both* of **b**, and of purple, *and* of scarlet, 8504
35:35 in **b**, and in purple, in scarlet, and in fine 8504
36: 8 twined linen, and **b**, and purple, and scarlet: 8504
36:11 he made loops of **b** on the edge of one 8504
36:35 he made a vail *of* **b**, and purple, and scarlet, 8504
36:37 a hanging for the tabernacle door *of* **b**, 8504
38:18 *of* **b**, and purple, and scarlet, and 8504
38:23 an embroiderer in **b**, and in purple, and 8504
39: 1 of the **b**, and purple, and scarlet, they made 8504
39: 2 **b**, and purple, and scarlet, and fine twined 8504
39: 3 to work *it* in the **b**, and in the purple, and 8504
39: 5 **b**, and purple, and scarlet, and fine twined 8504
39: 8 **b**, and purple, and scarlet, and fine twined 8504
39:21 unto the rings of the ephod with a lace of **b**, 8504
39:22 robe of the ephod *of* woven work, all of **b**. 8504
39:24 the hems of the robe pomegranates of **b**, 8504
39:29 **b**, and purple, and scarlet, *of* needlework; 8504
39:31 they tied unto it a lace of **b**, to fasten *it* on 8504
Nu 4: 6 shall spread over *it* a cloth wholly of **b**, and 8504
4: 7 of shewbread they shall spread a cloth of **b**, 8504
4: 9 they shall take a cloth of **b**, and cover 8504
4:11 golden altar they shall spread a cloth of **b**, 8504
4:12 put *them* in a cloth of **b**, and cover them 8504
15:38 the fringe of the borders a ribband of **b**: 8504
2Ch 2: 7 **b**, and that can skill to grave with 8504
2:14 in **b**, and in fine linen, and in crimson; 8504
3:14 he made the vail *of* **b**, and purple, and 8504
Est 1: 6 **b** *hangings,* fastened with cords of fine 8504
1: 6 of red, and **b**, and white, and black **marble**. 8336
8:15 presence of the king in royal apparel *of* **b** 8504
Jer 10: 9 **b** and purple *is* their clothing: they *are* all 8504
Eze 23: 6 *Which were* clothed with **b**, captains and 8504
27: 7 **b** and purple from the isles of Elishah was 8504
27:24 in **b** clothes, and broidered work, and 8504

BLUENESS (1) [BLUE]
Pr 20:30 The **b** of a wound cleanseth away evil: so 2250

BLUNT (1)
Ecc 10:10 If the iron be **b**, and he do not whet 6949

BLUSH (3)
Ezr 9: 6 and **b** to lift up my face to thee, 3637
Jer 6:15 not at all ashamed, neither could they **b**: 3637
8:12 not at all ashamed, neither could they **b**: 3637

BOANERGES (1)
Mk 3:17 (and he surnamed them **B**, which is, *993*

BOAR (1)
Ps 80:13 The **b** out of the wood doth waste it, and 2386

BOARD (17) [BOARDS]
Ex 26:16 Ten cubits *shall be* the length of a **b**, and 7175
26:16 and a half *shall be* the breadth of one **b**. 7175
26:17 Two tenons *shall there be* in one **b**, set in 7175
26:19 two sockets under one **b** for his two tenons, 7175
26:19 two sockets under another **b** for his two 7175
26:21 two sockets under one **b**, and two sockets 7175
26:21 and two sockets under another **b**. 7175
26:25 two sockets under one **b**, and two sockets 7175
26:25 and two sockets under another **b**. 7175
36:21 The length of a **b** *was* ten cubits, and 7175
36:21 and the breadth of a **b** one cubit and a half. 7175
36:22 One **b** had two tenons, equally distant one 7175
36:24 two sockets under one **b** for his two tenons, 7175
36:24 two sockets under another **b** for his two 7175
36:26 two sockets under one **b**, and two sockets 7175
36:26 and two sockets under another **b**. 7175
36:30 *of* silver, under every **b** two sockets. 7175

BOARDS (41) [BOARD]
Ex 26:15 thou shalt make **b** for the tabernacle *of* 7175
26:17 thus shalt thou make for all the **b** of 7175
26:18 thou shalt make the **b** for the tabernacle, 7175
26:18 twenty **b** on the south side southward. 7175
26:19 forty sockets of silver under the twenty **b**; 7175
26:20 on the north side *there shall be* twenty **b**: 7175
26:22 tabernacle westward thou shalt make six **b**. 7175
26:23 two **b** shalt thou make for the corners of 7175
26:25 they shall be eight **b**, and their sockets *of* 7175
26:26 five for the **b** of the one side of 7175
26:27 five bars for the **b** of the other side of 7175
26:27 five bars for the **b** of the side of 7175
26:28 the middle bar in the midst of the **b** shall 7175
26:29 thou shalt overlay the **b** with gold, and 7175
27: 8 Hollow with **b** shalt thou make it: as it was 3871
35:11 his taches, and his **b**, his bars, his pillars, 7175
36:20 he made **b** for the tabernacle *of* shittim 7175
36:22 thus did he make for all the **b** of 7175
36:23 he made **b** for the tabernacle; twenty boards 7175
36:23 twenty **b** for the south side southward: 7175
36:24 of silver he made under the twenty **b**; 7175
36:25 toward the north corner, he made twenty **b**, 7175
36:27 of the tabernacle westward he made six **b**. 7175
36:28 two **b** made he for the corners of 7175
36:30 there were eight **b**; and their sockets *were* 7175
36:31 five for the **b** of the one side of 7175
36:32 five bars for the **b** of the other side of 7175
36:32 five bars for the **b** of the tabernacle for 7175
36:33 through the **b** from the one end to the other. 7175
36:34 he overlaid the **b** with gold, and made their 7175
38: 7 it withal; he made *the altar* hollow with **b**. 3871
39:33 his **b**, his bars, and his pillars, and 7175
40:18 set up the **b** thereof, and put in the bars 7175
Nu 3:36 charge of the sons of Merari *shall be* the **b** 7175
4:31 the **b** of the tabernacle, and the bars 7175
1Ki 6: 9 the house with beams and **b** of cedar. 7713
6:15 walls of the house within with **b** of cedar, 6763
6:16 both the floor and the walls with **b** of cedar: 6763
SS 8: 9 a door, we will inclose her with **b** of cedar. 3871
Eze 27: 5 They have made all thy *ship* **b** of fir trees 3871
Ac 27:44 some on **b**, and some on broken pieces of *4548*

BOAST (20) [BOASTED, BOASTERS, BOASTEST, BOASTETH, BOASTING, BOASTINGS]
1Ki 20:11 *harness* **b** himself as he that putteth *it* off. 1984
2Ch 25:19 and thine heart lifteth thee up to **b**: 3513
Ps 34: 2 My soul shall **make** her **b** in the LORD: 1984
44: 8 In God we **b** all the day long, and praise thy 1984
49: 6 **b** themselves in the multitude of their 1984
94: 4 *and* all the workers of iniquity **b** themselves? 559
97: 7 graven images, that **b** themselves of idols: 1984
Pr 27: 1 **B** not thyself of to morrow; for thou 1984
Isa 10:15 Shall the axe **b** itself against him that 6286
61: 6 and in their glory shall you **b** yourselves. 3235
Ro 2:17 in the law, and **makest** thy **b** of God, *2744*
2:23 Thou that **makest** thy **b** of the law, *2744*
11:18 **B** not **against** the branches: but if thou *2620*
11:18 but if thou **b**, thou bearest not the root, but *2620*
2Co 9: 2 for which I **b** of you to them of Macedonia, *2744*
10: 8 For though I should **b** somewhat more of *2744*
10:13 But we will not **b** of *things* without *our* *2744*
10:16 not to **b** in another *man's* line of *things* *2744*
11:16 fool receive me, that I may **b** myself a little. *2744*
Eph 2: 9 Not of works, lest any *man* should **b**. *2744*

BOASTED (2) [BOAST]
Eze 35:13 Thus with your mouth ye have **b** against 1431
2Co 7:14 For if I have **b** any *thing* to him of you, *2744*

BOASTERS (2) [BOAST]
Ro 1:30 haters of God, despiteful, proud, **b**, *213*
2Ti 3: 2 covetous, **b**, proud, blasphemers, *213*

BOASTEST (1) [BOAST]
Ps 52: 1 Why **b** thou thyself in mischief, O mighty 1984

BOASTETH (4) [BOAST]
Ps 10: 3 For the wicked **b** of his heart's desire, and 1984
Pr 20:14 but when he is gone his way, then he **b**. 1984
25:14 Whoso **b** himself of a false gift *is like* 1984
Jas 3: 5 is a little member, and **b** great things. *3166*

BOASTING (9) [BOAST]
Ac 5:36 up Theudas, **b** himself to be somebody; *3004*
Ro 3:27 Where *is* **b** then? It is excluded. By what *2746*
2Co 7:14 even so our **b**, which *I made* before Titus, *2746*
8:24 of your love, and of our **b** on your behalf. *2746*
9: 3 lest our **b** of you should be in vain in this *2745*
9: 4 be ashamed in this *same* confident **b**. *2746*
10:15 Not **b** of *things* without *our* measure, *2744*
11:10 no *man* shall stop me of this **b** in *2746*
11:17 as *it were* foolishly, in this confidence of **b**. *2746*

BOASTINGS (1) [BOAST]
Jas 4:16 But now ye rejoice in your **b**: all such *212*

BOAT (6) [BOATS]
2Sa 19:18 there went over a **ferry b** to carry over 5679
Jn 6:22 sea saw that there was none other **b** there, *4142*
6:22 Jesus went not with his disciples into the **b**, *4142*
Ac 27:16 we had much work to come by the **b**: *4627*
27:30 when they had let down the **b** into the sea, *4627*
27:32 Then the soldiers cut off the ropes of the **b**, *4627*

BOATS (1) [BOAT]
Jn 6:23 (Howbeit there came other **b** from Tiberias *4142*

BOAZ (24) [BOOZ]
Ru 2: 1 family of Elimelech; and his name *was* **B**. 1162
2: 3 on a part of the field *belonging* unto **B**, 1162
2: 4 **B** came from Beth-lehem, and said unto 1162
2: 5 said **B** unto his servant that was set over 1162
2: 8 said **B** unto Ruth, Hearest thou not, 1162
2:11 **B** answered and said unto her, It hath fully 1162
2:14 **B** said unto her, At mealtime come thou 1162
2:15 **B** commanded his young men, saying, 1162
2:19 name with whom I wrought to day *is* **B**. 1162
2:23 So she kept fast by the maidens of **B** to 1162
3: 2 now *is* not **B** of our kindred, with whose 1162
3: 7 when **B** had eaten and drunk, and his heart 1162
4: 1 went **B** up *to* the gate, and sat him down 1162
4: 1 the kinsman of whom **B** spake came by; 1162
4: 5 said **B**, What day thou buyest the field of 1162
4: 8 Therefore the kinsman said unto **B**, Buy *it* 1162
4: 9 **B** said unto the elders, and *unto* all 1162
4:13 So **B** took Ruth, and she was his wife: and 1162
4:21 Salmon begat **B**, and Boaz begat Obed, 1162
4:21 Salmon begat Boaz, and **B** begat Obed, 1162
1Ki 7:21 left pillar, and called the name thereof **B**. 1162
1Ch 2:11 Nahshon begat Salma, and Salma begat **B**, 1162
2:12 And **B** begat Obed, and Obed begat Jesse, 1162
2Ch 3:17 and the name of *that on* the left **B**. 1162

BOCHERU (2)
1Ch 8:38 **B**, and Ishmael, and Sheariah, and Obadiah, 1074
9:44 **B**, and Ishmael, and Sheariah, and Obadiah, 1074

BOCHIM (2)
Jdg 2: 1 of the LORD came up from Gilgal to **B**, 1066
2: 5 they called the name of that place **B**: and 1066

BODIES (33) [BODY]
Ge 47:18 sight of my lord, but our **b**, and our lands: 1472
1Sa 31:12 the **b** of his sons from the wall of 1472
1Ch 10:12 the **b** of his sons, and brought them to 1480
2Ch 20:24 they *were* **dead b** fallen to the earth, and 6297

2Ch 20:25 in abundance both riches with the **dead b**, 6297
Ne 9:37 also they have dominion over our **b**, and 1472
Job 13:12 like unto ashes, your **b** to bodies of clay. 1354
13:12 like unto ashes, your bodies to **b** of clay. 1354
Ps 79: 2 The **dead b** of thy servants have they given 5038
110: 6 he shall fill *the places with* the **dead b**; 1472
Jer 31:40 the whole valley of the **dead b**, and of 6297
33: 5 *it is* to fill them with the **dead b** of men, 6297
34:20 their **dead b** shall be for meat unto 5038
41: 9 Ishmael had cast all the **dead b** of the men, 6297
Eze 1:11 one to another, and two covered their **b**. 1472
1:23 which covered on that *side,* their **b**. 1472
Da 3:27 upon whose **b** the fire had no power, 1655
3:28 the king's word, and yielded their **b**, 1655
Am 8: 3 *there shall be* many **dead b** in every place; 6297
Mt 27:52 and many **b** of saints which slept arose, 4983
Jn 19:31 that the **b** should not remain upon the cross 4983
Ro 1:24 to dishonour their own **b** between 4983
8:11 mortal **b** by his Spirit that dwelleth in you. 4983
12: 1 that *ye* present your **b** a living sacrifice, 4983
1Co 6:15 Know ye not that your **b** are the members 4983
15:40 *There are* also celestial **b**, and 4983
15:40 *are* also celestial bodies, and **b** terrestrial: 4983
Eph 5:28 men to love their wives as their own **b**. 4983
Heb 10:22 and *our* **b** washed with pure water. 4983
13:11 For the **b** of those beasts, whose blood is 4983
Rev 11: 8 And their **dead b** *shall lie* in the street of 4430
11: 9 nations shall see their **dead b** three days 4430
11: 9 shall not suffer their **dead b** to be put in 4430

BODILY (4) [BODY]
Lk 3:22 And the Holy Ghost descended in a **b** shape 4984
2Co 10:10 but *his* **b** presence *is* weak, and *his* speech 4983
Col 2: 9 dwelleth all the fulness of the Godhead **b**. 4985
1Ti 4: 8 For **b** exercise profiteth little: 4984

BODY (174) [BODIES, BODILY, BODY'S, BUSYBODIES, BUSYBODY]
Ex 24:10 as it were the **b** of heaven in *his* clearness. 6106
Lev 21:11 Neither shall he go in to any dead **b**, 5315
Nu 6: 6 the LORD he shall come at no dead **b**. 5315
9: 6 who were defiled by the **dead b** of a man, 5315
9: 7 We *are* defiled by the **dead b** of a man: 5315
9:10 shall be unclean by reason of a **dead b**, 5315
19:11 He that toucheth the dead ***b*** of any man NIH
19:13 Whosoever toucheth the dead ***b*** of *any* man NIH
19:16 or a dead ***b***, or a bone of a man, or a grave, NIH
Dt 21:23 His **b** shall not remain all night upon 5038
28: 4 Blessed *shall be* the fruit of thy **b**, and 990
28:11 in the fruit of thy **b**, and in the fruit of thy 990
28:18 Cursed *shall be* the fruit of thy **b**, and 990
28:53 thou shalt eat the fruit of thine own **b**, 990
30: 9 in the fruit of thy **b**, and in the fruit of thy 990
Jdg 8:30 and ten sons of his **b** begotten: 3409
1Sa 31:10 they fastened his **b** to the wall of 1472
31:12 took the **b** of Saul and the bodies of his 1472
2Ki 8: 5 king how he had restored a dead ***b*** to life, NIH
1Ch 10:12 took away the **b** of Saul, and the bodies of 1480
Job 19:17 for the children's *sake* of mine *own* **b**. 990
19:26 *though* after my skin *worms* destroy this ***b***, NIH
20:25 It is drawn, and cometh out of the **b**; yea, 1465
Ps 132:11 Of the fruit of thy **b** will I set upon thy 990
Pr 5:11 when thy flesh and thy **b** are consumed, 7607
Isa 10:18 and of his fruitful field, both soul and **b**: 1320
26:19 *together with* my **dead b** shall they arise. 5038
51:23 thou hast laid thy **b** as the ground, and 1460
Jer 26:23 cast his **dead b** into the graves of 5038
36:30 his **dead b** shall be cast out in the day to 5038
La 4: 7 they were more ruddy *in* **b** than rubies, 6106
Eze 10:12 their whole **b**, and their backs, and 1320
Da 4:33 and his **b** was wet with the dew of heaven, 1655
5:21 and his **b** was wet with the dew of heaven; 1655
7:11 his **b** destroyed, and given to the burning 1655
7:15 grieved in my spirit in the midst of *my* **b**, 5085
10: 6 His **b** also *was* like the beryl, and his face 1472
Mic 6: 7 the fruit of my **b** *for* the sin of my soul? 990
Hag 2:13 If *one that is* unclean *by* a **dead b** touch 5315
Mt 5:29 not *that* thy whole **b** should be cast into 4983
5:30 not *that* thy whole **b** should be cast into 4983
6:22 The light of the **b** is the eye: if therefore 4983
6:22 be single, thy whole **b** shall be full of light. 4983
6:23 thy whole **b** shall be full of darkness. 4983
6:25 nor yet for your **b**, what ye shall put on. 4983
6:25 more than meat, and the **b** than raiment? 4983
10:28 And fear not them which kill the **b**, but 4983
10:28 is able to destroy both soul and **b** in hell. 4983
14:12 And his disciples came, and took up the **b**, 4983
26:12 that she hath poured this ointment on my **b**, 4983
26:26 and said, Take, eat; this is my **b**. 4983
27:58 went to Pilate, and begged the **b** of Jesus. 4983
27:58 Then Pilate commanded the **b** to be 4983
27:59 And when Joseph had taken the **b**, 4983
Mk 5:29 she felt in *her* **b** that she was healed of *that* 4983
14: 8 she is come aforehand to anoint my **b** to 4983
14:22 to them, and said, Take, eat: this is my **b**. 4983
14:51 having a linen cloth cast about *his* naked **b**; NIG
15:43 unto Pilate, and craved the **b** of Jesus. 4983
15:45 *it* of the centurion, he gave the **b** to Joseph. 4983
Lk 11:34 The light of the **b** is the eye: 4983
11:34 is single, thy whole **b** also is full of light; 4983
11:34 *eye* is evil, thy **b** also *is* full of darkness. 4983
11:36 If thy whole **b** therefore *be* full of light, 4983
12: 4 Be not afraid of them that kill the **b**, and 4983
12:22 neither for the **b**, what ye shall put on. 4983
12:23 than meat, and the **b** *is more* than raiment. 4983
17:37 Wheresoever the **b** *is,* thither will 4983
22:19 This is my **b** which is given for you: 4983
23:52 went unto Pilate, and begged the **b** of Jesus. 4983
23:55 the sepulchre, and how his **b** was laid. 4983
24: 3 and found not the **b** of the Lord Jesus. 4983
24:23 And when they found not his **b**, they came, 4983
Jn 2:21 But he spake of the temple of his **b**. 4983
19:38 that he might take away the **b** of Jesus: 4983
19:38 He came therefore, and took the **b** of Jesus. 4983
19:40 Then took they the **b** of Jesus, and wound it 4983
20:12 at the feet, where the **b** of Jesus had lain. 4983
Ac 9:40 and turning *him* to the **b** said, Tabitha, 4983
19:12 So that from his **b** were brought unto 5559
Ro 4:19 he considered not his own **b** now dead, 4983
6: 6 *him,* that the **b** of sin might be destroyed, 4983
6:12 Let not sin therefore reign in your mortal **b**, 4983
7: 4 ye also are become dead to the law by the **b** 4983
7:24 who shall deliver me from the **b** of this 4983
8:10 *be* in you, the **b** *is* dead because of sin; 4983
8:13 the Spirit do mortify the deeds of the **b**, 4983
8:23 *to wit,* the redemption of our **b**. 4983
12: 4 For as we have many members in one **b**, 4983
12: 5 are one **b** in Christ, and every one members 4983
1Co 5: 3 I verily, as absent in **b**, but present in spirit, 4983
6:13 Now the **b** *is* not for fornication, but for 4983
6:13 but for the Lord; and the Lord for the **b**. 4983
6:16 that he which is joined to a harlot is one **b**? 4983
6:18 Every sin that a man doeth is without the **b**; 4983
6:18 fornication sinneth against his own **b**. 4983
6:19 know ye not that your **b** is the temple of 4983
6:20 therefore glorify God in your **b**, and in your 4983
7: 4 The wife hath not power of her own **b**, but 4983
7: 4 the husband hath not power of his own **b**, 4983
7:34 that she may be holy both in **b** and in spirit: 4983
9:27 But I keep under my **b**, and bring *it* into 4983
10:16 is it not the communion of the **b** of Christ? 4983
10:17 we being many are one bread, *and* one **b**: 4983
11:24 this is my **b**, which is broken for you: 4983
11:27 shall be guilty of the **b** and blood of 4983
11:29 to himself, not discerning the Lord's **b**. 4983
12:12 For as the **b** is one, and hath many 4983
12:12 and all the members of *that* one **b**, 4983
12:12 of *that* one body, being many, are one **b**: 4983
12:13 by one Spirit are we all baptized into one **b**, 4983
12:14 For the **b** is not one member, but many. 4983
12:15 I am not the hand, I am not of the **b**; 4983
12:15 not of the body; is it therefore not of the **b**? 4983
12:16 Because I am not the eye, I am not of the **b**; 4983
12:16 not of the body; is it therefore not of the **b**? 4983
12:17 If the whole **b** *were* an eye, where *were* 4983
12:18 set the members every one of them in the **b**, 4983
12:19 were all one member, where *were* the **b**? 4983
12:20 now *are they* many members, yet *but* one **b**. 4983
12:22 Nay, much more those members of the **b**, 4983
12:23 And those *members* of the **b**, which we 4983
12:24 but God hath tempered the **b** together, 4983
12:25 That there should be no schism in the **b**; but 4983
12:27 Now ye are the **b** of Christ, and members in 4983
13: 3 and though I give my **b** to be burned, 4983
15:35 raised up? and with what **b** do they come? 4983
15:37 thou sowest not that **b** that shall be, but 4983
15:38 But God giveth it a **b** as it hath pleased 4983
15:38 pleased him, and to every seed his own **b**. 4983

B

1Co 15:44 It is sown a natural **b**; it is raised a spiritual *4983*
15:44 a natural body; it is raised a spiritual **b**. *4983*
15:44 There is a natural **b**, and there is a spiritual *4983*
15:44 is a natural body, and there is a spiritual **b**. *4983*
2Co 4:10 Always bearing about in the **b** the dying of *4983*
4:10 of Jesus might be made manifest in our **b**. *4983*
5: 6 whilst we are at home in the **b**, *4983*
5: 8 and willing rather to be absent from the **b**, *4983*
5:10 one may receive the *things done* in *his* **b**, *4983*
12: 2 years ago, (whether in the **b**, I cannot tell; *4983*
12: 2 or whether out of the **b**, I cannot tell: *4983*
12: 3 (whether in the **b**, or out of the body, *4983*
12: 3 in the body, or out of the **b**, I cannot tell: *4983*
Gal 6:17 for I bear in my **b** the marks of the Lord *4983*
Eph 1:23 Which is his **b**, the fulness of him that *4983*
2:16 both unto God in one **b** by the cross, *4983*
3: 6 and **of the same b**, and partakers of his *4954*
4: 4 *There is* one **b**, and one Spirit, even as ye *4983*
4:12 for the edifying of the **b** of Christ: *4983*
4:16 From whom the whole **b** fitly joined *4983*
4:16 maketh increase of the **b** unto the edifying *4983*
5:23 the church: and he is the saviour of the **b**. *4983*
5:30 For we are members of his **b**, of his flesh, *4983*
Php 1:20 now also Christ shall be magnified in my **b**, *4983*
3:21 Who shall change our vile **b**, that it may be *4983*
3:21 may be fashioned like unto his glorious **b**, *4983*
Col 1:18 And he is the head of the **b**, the church: *4983*
1:22 In the **b** of his flesh through death, *4983*
2:11 in putting off the **b** of the sins of the flesh, *4983*
2:17 of *things* to come; but the **b** *is* of Christ. *4983*
2:19 from which all the **b** by joints and *4983*
2:23 and humility, and neglecting of the **b**, *4983*
3:15 to the which also ye are called in one **b**; *4983*
1Th 5:23 **b** be preserved blameless unto the coming *4983*
Heb 10: 5 but a **b** hast thou prepared me: *4983*
10:10 of the **b** of Jesus Christ once for all. *4983*
13: 3 as being yourselves also in the **b**. *4983*
Jas 2:16 not those *things which are* needful to the **b**; *4983*
2:26 For as the **b** without the spirit is dead, so *4983*
3: 2 *and* able also to bridle the whole **b**. *4983*
3: 3 obey us; and we turn about their whole **b**. *4983*
3: 6 that it defileth the whole **b**, and setteth on *4983*
1Pe 2:24 self bare our sins in his own **b** on the tree, *4983*
Jude 1: 9 the devil he disputed about the **b** of Moses, *4983*

BODY'S (1) [BODY]
Col 1:24 of Christ in my flesh for his **b** sake, *4983*

BOHAN (2)
Jos 15: 6 the border went up *to* the stone of **B** the son 932
18:17 descended *to* the stone of **B** the son of 932

BOIL (16) [BOILED, BOILING, BOILS]
Ex 9: 9 shall be a **b** breaking forth *with* blains upon 7822
9:10 it became a **b** breaking forth *with* blains 7822
9:11 for the **b** was upon the magicians, and 7822
Lev 8:31 **B** the flesh *at* the door of the tabernacle of 1310
13:18 in the skin thereof, was a **b**, and is healed, 7822
13:19 in the place of the **b** there be a white rising, 7822
13:20 it *is* a plague of leprosy broken out of the **b**. 7822
13:23 his place, *and* spread not, it *is* a burning **b**; 7822
2Ki 20: 7 they took and laid *it* on the **b**, and 7822
Job 41:31 He **maketh** the deep **to b** like a pot: 7570
Isa 38:21 lay *it* for a plaister upon the **b**, and he shall 7822
64: 2 the fire **causeth** the waters **to b**, 1158
Eze 24: 5 *and* **make** it **b well**, and let them 7570+7571
46:20 This *is* the place where the priests shall **b** 1310
46:24 These *are* the places of them that **b**, 1310
46:24 where the ministers of the house shall **b** 1310

BOILED (3) [BOIL]
1Ki 19:21 **b** their flesh with the instruments of 1310
2Ki 6:29 So we **b** my son, and did eat him: and I said 1310
Job 30:27 My bowels **b**, and rested not: the days of 7570

BOILING (1) [BOIL]
Eze 46:23 *it was* made *with* **b places** under the rows 4018

BOILS (2) [BOIL]
Ex 9:11 not stand before Moses because of the **b**; 7822
Job 2: 7 smote Job with sore **b** from the sole of his 7822

BOKERU See BOCHERU

BOKIM See BOCHIM

BOLD (11) [BOLDLY, BOLDNESS, EMBOLDENED, EMBOLDENETH]
Pr 28: 1 but the righteous are **b** as a lion. 982
Ac 13:46 Then Paul and Barnabas **waxed b**, and said, *3955*
Ro 10:20 But Esaias is **very b**, and saith, I was found *662*
2Co 10: 1 but being absent am **b** toward you: *2292*
10: 2 But I beseech *you,* that I may not be **b** *2292*
10: 2 wherewith I think to be **b** against some, *5111*
11:21 Howbeit whereinsoever any is **b**, (I speak *5111*
11:21 any is bold, (I speak foolishly,) I am **b** also. *5111*
Php 1:14 are much more **b** to speak the word without *5111*
1Th 2: 2 we were **b** in our God to speak unto you *3955*
Phm 1: 8 though I might be much **b** in Christ to *3954*

BOLDLY (13) [BOLD]
Ge 34:25 came upon the city **b**, and slew all the males. 983
Mk 15:43 and went in **b** unto Pilate, and craved *5111*
Jn 7:26 he speaketh **b**, and they say nothing unto *3954*
Ac 9:27 how he had **preached b** at Damascus in *3955*
9:29 And he spake **b** in the name of the Lord *3955*
14: 3 abode they **speaking b** in the Lord, *3955*
18:26 And he began to **speak b** in the synagogue: *3955*
19: 8 and **spake b** for the space of three months, *3955*
Ro 15:15 I have written the **more b** unto you in some *5112*
Eph 6:19 that *I* may open my mouth **b**, *1722+3954*
6:20 that therein I may **speak b**, as I ought to *3955*
Heb 4:16 come **b** unto the throne of grace, *3326+3954*
13: 6 So that we may **b** say, The Lord *is* my *2292*

BOLDNESS (10) [BOLD]
Ecc 8: 1 and the **b** of his face shall be changed. 5797
Ac 4:13 Now when they saw the **b** of Peter and *3954*
4:29 that with all **b** *they* may speak thy word, *3954*
4:31 and they spake the word of God with **b**. *3954*
2Co 7: 4 Great *is* my **b of speech** toward you, *3954*
Eph 3:12 In whom we have **b** and access with *3954*
Php 1:20 but *that* with all **b**, as always, *so* now also *3954*
1Ti 3:13 great **b** in the faith which is in Christ Jesus. *3954*
Heb 10:19 **b** to enter into the holiest by the blood of *3954*
1Jn 4:17 that we may have **b** in the day of judgment: *3954*

BOLLED (1)
Ex 9:31 barley *was* in the ear, and the flax *was* **b**. 1392

BOLSTER (6)
1Sa 19:13 put a pillow of goats' *hair for* his **b**, and 4763
19:16 with a pillow of goats' *hair for* his **b**. 4763
26: 7 and his spear stuck in the ground *at* his **b**: 4763
26:11 take thou now the spear that *is at* his **b**, and 4763
26:12 and the cruse of water from Saul's **b**; 4763
26:16 and the cruse of water that *was at* his **b**. 4763

BOLT (1) [BOLTED]
2Sa 13:17 out from me, and **b** the door after her. 5274

BOLTED (1) [BOLT]
2Sa 13:18 brought her out, and **b** the door after her. 5274

BOLTS See LOCKS

BOND (19) [BONDAGE, BONDMAID, BONDMAIDS, BONDMAN, BONDMEN, BONDS, BONDSERVANT, BONDSERVICE, BONDWOMAN, BONDWOMEN]
Nu 30: 2 or swear an oath to bind his soul with a **b**; 632
30: 3 bind *herself by* a **b**, *being* in her father's 632
30: 4 her **b** wherewith she hath bound her soul, 632
30: 4 every **b** wherewith she hath bound her soul 632
30:10 or bound her soul by a **b** with an oath; 632
30:11 every **b** wherewith she bound her soul shall 632
30:12 or concerning the **b** of her soul, shall not 632
Job 12:18 He looseth the **b** of kings, and girdeth their 4148
Eze 20:37 I will bring you into the **b** of the covenant: 4562
Lk 13:16 be loosed from this **b** on the sabbath day? *1199*
Ac 8:23 gall of bitterness, and *in* the **b** of iniquity. *4886*
1Co 12:13 or Gentiles, whether *we be* **b** or free; *1401*
Gal 3:28 Jew nor Greek, there is neither **b** nor free, *1401*
Eph 4: 3 the unity of the Spirit in the **b** of peace. *4886*
6: 8 of the Lord, whether *he be* **b** or free. *1401*
Col 3:11 barbarian, Scythian, **b** *nor* free: *1401*
3:14 *on* charity, which is the **b** of perfectness. *4886*
Rev 13:16 and great, rich and poor, free and **b**, *1401*
19:18 and the flesh of all *men,* both free and **b**, *1401*

BONDAGE (39) [BOND]
Ex 1:14 they made their lives bitter with hard **b**, 5656

Ex 2:23 children of Israel sighed by reason of the **b**, 5656
2:23 cry came up unto God by reason of the **b**. 5656
6: 5 of Israel, whom the Egyptians **keep in b**; 5647
6: 6 I will rid you out of their **b**, and I will 5656
6: 9 Moses for anguish of spirit, and for cruel **b**. 5656
13: 3 came out from Egypt, out of the house of **b**; 5650
13:14 us out from Egypt, from the house of **b**: 5650
20: 2 of the land of Egypt, out of the house of **b**. 5650
Dt 5: 6 of the land of Egypt, from the house of **b**. 5650
6:12 of the land of Egypt, from the house of **b**. 5650
8:14 of the land of Egypt, from the house of **b**; 5650
13: 5 and redeemed you out of the house of **b**, 5650
13:10 of the land of Egypt, from the house of **b**. 5650
26: 6 and afflicted us, and laid upon us hard **b**: 5656
Jos 24:17 from the house of **b**, and which did those 5650
Jdg 6: 8 and brought you forth out of the house of **b**; 5650
Ezr 9: 8 and give us a little reviving in our **b**. 5659
9: 9 yet our God hath not forsaken us in our **b**, 5659
Ne 5: 5 we **bring into b** our sons and our daughters 3533
5: 5 *some* of our daughters are **brought unto b** 3533
5:18 because the **b** was heavy upon this people. 5656
9:17 appointed a captain to return to their **b**: 5659
Isa 14: 3 from the hard **b** wherein thou wast made to 5656
Jn 8:33 were never **in b** to any *man:* how sayest *1398*
Ac 7: 6 and that they should **bring** them **into b**, and *1402*
7: 7 And the nation to whom they shall be **in b** *1398*
Ro 8:15 For ye have not received the spirit of **b** *1397*
8:21 **b** of corruption into the glorious liberty of *1397*
1Co 7:15 or a sister is not **under b** in such *cases:* but *1402*
2Co 11:20 For ye suffer, if a man **bring** you **into b**, *2615*
Gal 2: 4 that they might **bring** us **into b**: *2615*
4: 3 were **in b** under the elements of the world: *1402*
4: 9 whereunto ye desire again to be **in b**? *1398*
4:24 which gendereth to **b**, which is Agar. *1397*
4:25 which now is, and is **in b** with her children. *1398*
5: 1 be not entangled again with the yoke of **b**. *1397*
Heb 2:15 of death were all their lifetime subject to **b**. *1397*
2Pe 2:19 of the same is he **brought in b**. *1402*

BONDMAID (2) [BOND, MAID]
Lev 19:20 lieth carnally with a woman that *is* a **b**, 8198
Gal 4:22 the one by a **b**, the other by a freewoman. *3814*

BONDMAIDS (2) [BOND, MAID]
Lev 25:44 Both thy bondmen, and thy **b**, which thou 519
25:44 of them shall ye buy bondmen and **b**. 519

BONDMAN (7) [BOND, MAN]
Ge 44:33 let thy servant abide instead of the lad a **b** 5650
Dt 15:15 thou shalt remember that thou wast a **b** in 5650
16:12 thou shalt remember that thou wast a **b** in 5650
24:18 thou shalt remember that thou wast a **b** in 5650
24:22 thou shalt remember that thou wast a **b** in 5650
1Ki 9:22 children of Israel did Solomon make no **b**: 5650
Rev 6:15 and the mighty *men,* and every **b**, and *1401*

BONDMEN (16) [BOND, MAN]
Ge 43:18 upon us, and take us for **b**, and our asses. 5650
44: 9 him die, and we also will be my lord's **b**. 5650
Lev 25:42 land of Egypt: they shall not be sold as **b**. 5650
25:44 Both thy **b**, and thy bondmaids, which thou 5650
25:44 of them shall ye buy **b** and bondmaids. 5650
25:46 a possession; they shall be your **b** for ever: 5647
26:13 land of Egypt, that *ye* should not be their **b**; 5650
Dt 6:21 thy son, We were Pharaoh's **b** in Egypt; 5650
7: 8 redeemed you out of the house of **b**, 5650
28:68 ye shall be sold unto your enemies for **b** 5650
Jos 9:23 shall none of you be freed from being **b**, 5650
2Ki 4: 1 come to take unto him my two sons to be **b**. 5650
2Ch 28:10 Jerusalem for **b** and bondwomen unto you: 5650
Ezr 9: 9 For we *were* **b**; yet our God hath not 5650
Est 7: 4 if we had been sold for **b** and bondwomen, 5650
Jer 34:13 of Egypt, out of the house of **b**, saying, 5650

BONDS (26) [BOND]
Nu 30: 5 of her **b** wherewith she hath bound her soul, 632
30: 7 her **b** wherewith she bound her soul shall 632
30:14 her vows, or all her **b**, which *are* upon her: 632
Ps 116:16 of thy handmaid: thou hast loosed my **b**. 4147
Jer 5: 5 altogether broken the yoke, *and* burst the **b**. 4147
27: 2 Make thee **b** and yokes, and put them upon 4147
30: 8 will burst thy **b**, and strangers shall no 4147
Na 1:13 off thee, and will burst thy **b** in sunder. 4147
Ac 20:23 saying that **b** and afflictions abide me. *1199*
23:29 laid to his charge worthy of death or of **b**. *1199*
25:14 There is a certain man left in **b** by Felix: *1198*
26:29 altogether such as I am, except these **b**. *1199*
26:31 man doeth nothing worthy of death or of **b**. *1199*
Eph 6:20 For which I am an ambassador in **b**: *254*
Php 1: 7 inasmuch as both in my **b**, and *in* *1199*
1:13 So that my **b** in Christ are manifest in all *1199*
1:14 in the Lord, waxing confident by my **b**, *1199*
1:16 supposing to add affliction to my **b**: *1199*
Col 4: 3 mystery of Christ, for which I am also **in b**: *1210*
4:18 Remember my **b**. Grace *be* with you. *1199*
2Ti 2: 9 suffer trouble, as an evil doer, *even* unto **b**; *1199*
Phm 1:10 whom I have begotten in my **b**: *1199*
1:13 ministered unto me in the **b** of the gospel: *1199*
Heb 10:34 For ye had compassion *of me* in my **b**, *1199*
11:36 yea, moreover of **b** and imprisonment: *1199*
13: 3 Remember *them that are* **in b**, as bound *1198*

BONDSERVANT (1) [BOND, SERVE]
Lev 25:39 thou shalt not compel him to serve as a **b**: 5650

BONDSERVICE (1) [BOND, SERVE]
1Ki 9:21 upon those did Solomon levy a tribute of **b** 5647

BONDWOMAN (8) [BOND, WOMAN]
Ge 21:10 unto Abraham, Cast out this **b** and her son: 519
21:10 for the son of this **b** shall not be heir with my 519
21:12 because of the lad, and because of thy **b**; 519
21:13 also of the son of the **b** will I make a nation, 519
Gal 4:23 But he who was of the **b** was born after *3814*
4:30 Cast out the **b** and her son: for the son of *3814*
4:30 for the son of the **b** shall not be heir with *3814*
4:31 we are not children of *the* **b**, but of the free. *3814*

BONDWOMEN (3) [BOND, WOMAN]
Dt 28:68 sold unto your enemies for bondmen and **b**, 8198
2Ch 28:10 Jerusalem for bondmen and **b** unto you: 8198
Est 7: 4 if we had been sold for bondmen and **b**, 8198

BONE (20) [BONES, JAWBONE]
Ge 2:23 This *is* now **b** of my bones, and flesh of my 6106
29:14 to him, Surely thou *art* my **b** and my flesh. 6106
Ex 12:46 neither shall ye break a **b** thereof. 6106
Lev 3: 9 it shall he take off hard by the **back b**; 6096
Nu 9:12 it unto the morning, nor break any **b** of it: 6106
19:16 or a dead *body,* or a **b** of a man, or a grave, 6106
19:18 and upon him that touched a **b**, or one slain, 6106
Jdg 9: 2 remember also that I *am* your **b** and 6106
2Sa 5: 1 Behold, we *are* thy **b** and thy flesh. 6106
19:13 *Art* thou not *of* my **b**, and *of* my flesh? 6106
1Ch 11: 1 Behold, we *are* thy **b** and thy flesh. 6106
Job 2: 5 touch his **b** and his flesh, and he will curse 6106
19:20 My **b** cleaveth to my skin and to my flesh, 6106
31:22 and mine arm be broken from the **b**. 7070
Ps 3: 7 smitten all mine enemies *upon* the **cheek b**; 3895
Pr 25:15 and a soft tongue breaketh the **b**. 1634
Eze 37: 7 and the bones came together, **b** to his bone. 6106
37: 7 and the bones came together, bone to his **b**. 6106
39:15 when *any* seeth a man's **b**, then shall he set 6106
Jn 19:36 be fulfilled, A **b** of him shall not be broken. *3747*

BONES (99) [BONE]
Ge 2:23 This *is* now bone of my **b**, and flesh of my 6106
50:25 and ye shall carry up my **b** from hence. 6106
Ex 13:19 Moses took the **b** of Joseph with him: 6106
13:19 ye shall carry up my **b** away hence with 6106
Nu 24: 8 shall break their **b**, and pierce *them* through 6106
Jos 24:32 the **b** of Joseph, which the children of Israel 6106
Jdg 19:29 divided her, *together* with her **b**, 6106
1Sa 31:13 they took their **b**, and buried *them* under a 6106
2Sa 19:12 *are* my brethren, ye *are* my **b** and my flesh: 6106
21:12 David went and took the **b** of Saul and 6106
21:12 the **b** of Jonathan his son from the men of 6106
21:13 he brought up from thence the **b** of Saul 6106
21:13 of Saul and the **b** of Jonathan his son; 6106
21:13 they gathered the **b** of them that were 6106
21:14 the **b** of Saul and Jonathan his son buried 6106
1Ki 13: 2 and men's **b** shall be burnt upon thee. 6106
13:31 God *is* buried; lay my **b** beside his bones: 6106
13:31 God *is* buried; lay my bones beside his **b**: 6106
2Ki 13:21 touched the **b** of Elisha, he revived, and 6106
23:14 and filled their places *with* the **b** of men. 6106
23:16 took the **b** out of the sepulchres, and 6106
23:18 Let him alone; let no man move his **b**. 6106
23:18 So they let his **b** alone, with the bones of 6106

2Ki 23:18 with the **b** of the prophet that came out of 6106
23:20 burnt men's **b** upon them, and returned *to* 6106
1Ch 10:12 buried their **b** under the oak in Jabesh, and 6106
2Ch 34: 5 he burnt the **b** of the priests upon their 6106
Job 4:14 trembling, which made all my **b** to shake. 6106
10:11 and hast fenced me with **b** and sinews. 6106
20:11 His **b** are full *of the sin of* his youth, 6106
21:24 and his **b** are moistened with marrow. 6106
30:17 My **b** are pierced in me in the night season: 6106
30:30 upon me, and my **b** are burnt with heat. 6106
33:19 and the multitude of his **b** *with* strong *pain:* 6106
33:21 and his **b** *that* were not seen stick out. 6106
40:18 His **b** *are as* strong pieces of brass; 6106
40:18 pieces of brass; his **b** *are* like bars of iron. 1634
Ps 6: 2 O LORD, heal me; for my **b** are vexed. 6106
22:14 out like water, and all my **b** are out of joint: 6106
22:17 I may tell all my **b**: they look *and* 6106
31:10 of mine iniquity, and my **b** are consumed. 6106
32: 3 my **b** waxed old through my roaring all 6106
34:20 He keepeth all his **b**: not one of them is 6106
35:10 All my **b** shall say, LORD, who *is* like 6106
38: 3 neither *is there any* rest in my **b** because 6106
42:10 *As* with a sword in my **b**, mine enemies 6106
51: 8 *that* the **b** *which* thou hast broken may 6106
53: 5 for God hath scattered the **b** of him that 6106
102: 3 like smoke, and my **b** are burnt as a hearth. 6106
102: 5 reason of the voice of my groaning my **b** 6106
109:18 bowels like water, and like oil into his **b**. 6106
141: 7 Our **b** are scattered at the grave's mouth, 6106
Pr 3: 8 be health to thy navel, and marrow to thy **b**. 6106
12: 4 maketh ashamed *is* as rottenness in his **b**. 6106
14:30 the flesh: but envy the rottenness of the **b**. 6106
15:30 *and* a good report maketh the **b** fat. 6106
16:24 sweet to the soul, and health to the **b**. 6106
17:22 a medicine: but a broken spirit drieth the **b**. 1634
Ecc 11: 5 *nor* how the **b** *do grow* in the womb of her 6106
Isa 38:13 *that,* as a lion, so will he break all my **b**: 6106
58:11 thy soul in drought, and make fat thy **b**: 6106
66:14 and your **b** shall flourish like an herb: 6106
Jer 8: 1 they shall bring out the **b** of the kings of 6106
8: 1 the **b** of his princes, and the bones of 6106
8: 1 the **b** of the priests, and the bones of 6106
8: 1 the **b** of the prophets, and the bones of 6106
8: 1 the **b** of the inhabitants of Jerusalem, out of 6106
20: 9 heart as a burning fire shut up in my **b**, 6106
23: 9 because of the prophets; all my **b** shake; 6106
50:17 king of Babylon hath **broken** his **b**. 6105
La 1:13 From above hath he sent fire into my **b**, and 6106
3: 4 hath he made old; he hath broken my **b**. 6106
4: 8 their skin cleaveth to their **b**; it is withered, 6106
Eze 6: 5 I will scatter your **b** round about your 6106
24: 4 and the shoulder; fill *it with* the choice **b**. 6106
24: 5 burn also the **b** under it, *and* make it boil 6106
24: 5 and let them seethe the **b** of it therein. 6106
24:10 and spice it well, and let the **b** be burnt. 6106
32:27 but their iniquities shall be upon their **b**, 6106
37: 1 the midst of the valley which *was* full *of* **b**, 6106
37: 3 said unto me, Son of man, can these **b** live? 6106
37: 4 Prophesy upon these **b**, and say unto them, 6106
37: 4 these bones, and say unto them, O ye dry **b**, 6106
37: 5 Thus saith the Lord GOD unto these **b**; 6106
37: 7 and the **b** came together, bone to his bone. 6106
37:11 these **b** *are* the whole house of Israel: 6106
37:11 Our **b** are dried, and our hope is lost: 6106
Da 6:24 brake all their **b** in pieces or ever they came 1635
Am 2: 1 he burnt the **b** of the king of Edom into 6106
6:10 to bring out the **b** out of the house, and 6106
Mic 3: 2 off them, and their flesh from off their **b**; 6106
3: 3 they break their **b**, and chop *them* in pieces, 6106
Hab 3:16 rottenness entered into my **b**, and 6106
Zep 3: 3 they **gnaw** not the **b** till the morrow. 1633
Mt 23:27 but are within full of dead *men's* **b**, and *3747*
Lk 24:39 for a spirit hath not flesh and **b**, as ye see *3747*
Ac 3: 7 his feet and ankle **b** received strength, NIG
Eph 5:30 of his body, of his flesh, and of his **b**. *3747*
Heb 11:22 and gave commandment concerning his **b**. *3747*

BONNETS (6)

Ex 28:40 **b** shalt thou make for them, for glory and 4021
29: 9 Aaron and his sons, and put the **b** on them: 4021
39:28 goodly **b** *of* fine linen, and linen breeches 4021
Lev 8:13 them *with* girdles, and put **b** upon them; 4021
Isa 3:20 The **b**, and the ornaments of the legs, and 6287
Eze 44:18 They shall have linen **b** upon their heads, 6287

BOOK (188) [BOOKS]

Ge 5: 1 This *is* the **b** of the generations of Adam. 5612
Ex 17:14 Write this *for* a memorial in a **b**, and 5612
24: 7 he took the **b** of the covenant, and read in 5612
32:32 out of thy **b** which thou hast written. 5612
32:33 against me, him will I blot out of my **b**. 5612
Nu 5:23 the priest shall write these curses in a **b**, 5612
21:14 Wherefore it is said in the **b** of the wars of 5612
Dt 17:18 **b** out of *that which is* before the priests 5612
28:58 words of this law that are written in this **b**, 5612
28:61 which *is* not written in the **b** of this law, 5612
29:20 all the curses that are written in this **b** shall 5612
29:21 that are written in this **b** of the law: 5612
29:27 it all the curses that are written in this **b**: 5612
30:10 his statutes which are written in this **b** of 5612
31:24 end of writing the words of this law in a **b**, 5612
31:26 Take this **b** of the law, and put it in the side 5612
Jos 1: 8 This **b** of the law shall not depart out of thy 5612
8:31 as it is written in the **b** of the law of Moses, 5612
8:34 according to all that is written in the **b** of 5612
10:13 *Is* not this written in the **b** of Jasher? So 5612
18: 9 described it by cities into seven parts in a **b**, 5612
23: 6 to do all that is written in the **b** of the law 5612
24:26 Joshua wrote these words in the **b** of 5612
1Sa 10:25 wrote *it* in a **b**, and laid *it* up before 5612
2Sa 1:18 behold, *it is* written in the **b** of Jasher.) 5612
1Ki 11:41 *are* they not written in the **b** of the acts of 5612
14:19 behold they *are* written in the **b** of 5612
14:29 *are* they not written in the **b** of 5612
15: 7 *are* they not written in the **b** of 5612
15:23 *are* they not written in the **b** of 5612
15:31 *are* they not written in the **b** of 5612
16: 5 *are* they not written in the **b** of 5612
16:14 *are* they not written in the **b** of 5612
16:20 *are* they not written in the **b** of 5612
16:27 *are* they not written in the **b** of 5612
22:39 *are* they not written in the **b** of 5612
22:45 *are* they not written in the **b** of 5612
2Ki 1:18 *are* they not written in the **b** of 5612
8:23 *are* they not written in the **b** of 5612
10:34 *are* they not written in the **b** of 5612
12:19 *are* they not written in the **b** of 5612
13: 8 *are* they not written in the **b** of 5612
13:12 *are* they not written in the **b** of 5612
14: 6 is written in the **b** of the law of Moses, 5612
14:15 *are* they not written in the **b** of 5612
14:18 *are* they not written in the **b** of 5612
14:28 *are* they not written in the **b** of 5612
15: 6 *are* they not written in the **b** of 5612
15:11 they *are* written in the **b** of the chronicles of 5612
15:15 they *are* written in the **b** of the chronicles of 5612
15:21 *are* they not written in the **b** of 5612
15:26 they *are* written in the **b** of the chronicles of 5612
15:31 they *are* written in the **b** of the chronicles of 5612
15:36 *are* they not written in the **b** of 5612
16:19 *are* they not written in the **b** of 5612
20:20 *are* they not written in the **b** of 5612
21:17 *are* they not written in the **b** of 5612
21:25 *are* they not written in the **b** of 5612
22: 8 I have found the **b** of the law in the house 5612
22: 8 Hilkiah gave the **b** to Shaphan, and he read 5612
22:10 Hilkiah the priest hath delivered me a **b**. 5612
22:11 when the king had heard the words of the **b** 5612
22:13 concerning the words of this **b** that is 5612
22:13 not hearkened unto the words of this **b**, 5612
22:16 *even* all the words of the **b** which the king 5612
23: 2 he read in their ears all the words of the **b** 5612
23: 3 of this covenant that were written in this **b**. 5612
23:21 as it is written in the **b** of this covenant. 5612
23:24 **b** that Hilkiah the priest found *in* the house 5612
23:28 *are* they not written in the **b** of 5612
24: 5 *are* they not written in the **b** of 5612
1Ch 9: 1 they *were* written in the **b** of the kings of 5612
29:29 they *are* written in the **b** of Samuel the seer, 1697
29:29 in the **b** of Nathan the prophet, and in 1697
29:29 the prophet, and in the **b** of Gad the seer, 1697
2Ch 9:29 *are* they not written in the **b** of Nathan 1697
12:15 *are* they not written in the **b** of Shemaiah 1697
16:11 they *are* written in the **b** of the kings of 5612
17: 9 *had* the **b** of the law of the LORD with 5612
20:34 behold they *are* written in the **b** of Jehu 1697
20:34 who is mentioned in the **b** of the kings of 5612
24:27 behold they *are* written in the story of the **b** 5612

2Ch 25: 4 *did* as it is written in the law in the **b** of 5612
25:26 *are* they not written in the **b** of the kings of 5612
27: 7 lo they *are* written in the **b** of the kings of 5612
28:26 they *are* written in the **b** of the kings of 5612
32:32 *and* in the **b** of the kings of Judah and 5612
33:18 they *are written* in the **b** of the kings of 1697
34:14 Hilkiah the priest found a **b** of the law of 5612
34:15 I have found the **b** of the law in the house 5612
34:15 And Hilkiah delivered the **b** to Shaphan. 5612
34:16 Shaphan carried the **b** to the king, and 5612
34:18 Hilkiah the priest hath given me a **b**. 5612
34:21 concerning the words of the **b** that is found: 5612
34:21 to do after all that is written in this **b**. 5612
34:24 *even* all the curses that are written in the **b** 5612
34:30 he read in their ears all the words of the **b** 5612
34:31 of the covenant which are written in this **b**. 5612
35:12 as it is written in the **b** of Moses. 5612
35:27 they *are* written in the **b** of the kings of 5612
36: 8 they *are* written in the **b** of the kings of 5612
Ezr 4:15 That search may be made in the **b** of 5609
4:15 so shalt thou find in the **b** of the records, 5609
6:18 as it is written in the **b** of Moses. 5609
Ne 8: 1 scribe to bring the **b** of the law of Moses, 5612
8: 3 people *were attentive* unto the **b** of the law. 5612
8: 5 Ezra opened the **b** in the sight of all 5612
8: 8 So they read in the **b** in the law of God 5612
8:18 last day, he read in the **b** of the law of God. 5612
9: 3 read in the **b** of the law of the LORD their 5612
12:23 *were* written in the **b** of the chronicles, 5612
13: 1 On that day they read in the **b** of Moses in 5612
Est 2:23 it was written in the **b** of the chronicles 5612
6: 1 he commanded to bring the **b** of records of 5612
9:32 of Purim; and *it was* written in the **b**. 5612
10: 2 *are* they not written in the **b** of 5612
Job 19:23 O that they were printed in a **b**! 5612
31:35 and *that* mine adversary had written a **b**. 5612
Ps 40: 7 in the volume of the **b** *it is* written of me, 5612
56: 8 tears into thy bottle: *are they* not in thy **b**? 5612
69:28 Let them be blotted out of the **b** of 5612
139:16 in thy **b** all *my members* were written, 5612
Isa 29:11 unto you as the words of a **b** that is sealed, 5612
29:12 the **b** is delivered to *him* that is not learned, 5612
29:18 day shall the deaf hear the words of the **b**, 5612
30: 8 it before them in a table, and note it in a **b**, 5612
34:16 Seek ye out of the **b** of the LORD, and 5612
Jer 25:13 *even* all that is written in this **b**, which 5612
30: 2 words that I have spoken unto thee in a **b**. 5612
32:12 that subscribed the **b** of the purchase, 5612
36: 2 Take thee a roll of a **b**, and write therein all 5612
36: 4 he had spoken unto him, upon a roll of a **b**. 5612
36: 8 reading in the **b** the words of the LORD *in* 5612
36:10 read Baruch in the **b** the words of Jeremiah 5612
36:11 had heard out of the **b** all the words of 5612
36:13 when Baruch read the **b** in the ears of 5612
36:18 and I wrote *them* with ink in the **b**. 5612
36:32 **b** which Jehoiakim king of Judah had burnt 5612
45: 1 when he had written these words in a **b** at 5612
51:60 So Jeremiah wrote in a **b** all the evil that 5612
51:63 thou hast made an end of reading this **b**, 5612
Eze 2: 9 unto me; and lo, a roll of a **b** *was* therein; 5612
Da 12: 1 one that *shall* be found written in the **b**. 5612
12: 4 O Daniel, shut up the words, and seal the **b**, 5612
Na 1: 1 The **b** of the vision of Nahum 5612
Mal 3:16 a **b** of remembrance was written before him 5612
Mt 1: 1 The **b** of the generation of Jesus Christ, *976*
Mk 12:26 have ye not read in the **b** of Moses, how in *976*
Lk 3: 4 As it is written in the **b** of the words of *976*
4:17 And there was delivered unto him the **b** of *975*
4:17 And when he had opened the **b**, he found *975*
4:20 And he closed the **b**, and he gave *it* again to *975*
20:42 And David himself saith in the **b** of Psalms, *976*
Jn 20:30 his disciples, which are not written in this **b**: *975*
Ac 1:20 For it is written in the **b** of Psalms, Let his *976*
7:42 as it is written in the **b** of the prophets, O *ye* *976*
Gal 3:10 are written in the **b** of the law to do them. *975*
Php 4: 3 whose names *are* in the **b** of life. *976*
Heb 9:19 and sprinkled both the **b**, and all the people, *975*
10: 7 I come (in the volume of the **b** it is written of *975*
Rev 1:11 write in a **b**, and send *it* unto the seven *975*
3: 5 I will not blot out his name out of the **b** of *976*
5: 1 him that sat on the throne a **b** written within *975*
5: 2 Who is worthy to open the **b**, and to loose *975*
5: 3 under the earth, was able to open the **b**, *975*
5: 4 was found worthy to open and to read the **b**, *975*
5: 5 hath prevailed to open the **b**, and to loose *975*
5: 7 took the **b** out of the right hand of him that *975*
5: 8 And when he had taken the **b**, the four beasts *975*
5: 9 Thou art worthy to take the **b**, and to open *975*
10: 2 And he had in his hand a **little b** open: and *974*
10: 8 take the **little b** which is open in the hand of *974*
10: 9 and said unto him, Give me the **little b**. *974*
10:10 And I took the **little b** out of the angel's *974*
13: 8 whose names are not written in the **b** of life *976*
17: 8 whose names were not written in the **b** of *975*
20:12 and another **b** was opened, which is *the book* *975*
20:12 book was opened, which is *the b* of life: NIG
20:15 in the **b** of life was cast into the lake of fire. *976*
21:27 they which are written in the Lamb's **b** of *975*
22: 7 the sayings of the prophecy of this **b**. *975*
22: 9 of them which keep the sayings of this **b**: *975*
22:10 not the sayings of the prophecy of this **b**: *975*
22:18 heareth the words of the prophecy of this **b**, *975*
22:18 him the plagues that are written in this **b**: *975*
22:19 from the words of the **b** of this prophecy, *976*
22:19 God shall take away his part out of the **b** of *976*
22:19 *from the things* which are written in this **b**. *975*

BOOKS (8) [BOOK]
Ecc 12:12 of making many **b** *there is* no end; and 5612
Da 7:10 judgment was set, and the **b** were opened. 5609
9: 2 understood by **b** the number of the years, 5612
Jn 21:25 not contain the **b** that should be written. *975*
Ac 19:19 used curious arts brought their **b** together, *976*
2Ti 4:13 bring *with thee,* and the **b**, *but* especially *975*
Rev 20:12 stand before God; and the **b** were opened: *975*
20:12 of those *things* which were written in the **b**, *975*

BOOTH (2) [BOOTHS]
Job 27:18 a moth, and as a **b** *that* the keeper maketh. 5521
Jnh 4: 5 there made him a **b**, and sat under it in 5521

BOOTHS (9) [BOOTH]
Ge 33:17 him a house, and made **b** for his cattle: 5521
Lev 23:42 Ye shall dwell in **b** seven days; all that are 5521
23:42 all that are Israelites born shall dwell in **b**: 5521
23:43 I made the children of Israel to dwell in **b**, 5521
Ne 8:14 that the children of Israel should dwell in **b** 5521
8:15 of thick trees, to make **b**, as it is written. 5521
8:16 and brought *them,* and made themselves **b**, 5521
8:17 come again out of the captivity made **b**, 5521
8:17 captivity made booths, and sat under the **b**: 5521

BOOTIES (1) [BOOTY]
Hab 2: 7 and thou shalt be for **b** unto them? 4933

BOOTY (3) [BOOTIES]
Nu 31:32 the **b**, *being* the rest of the prey which 4455
Jer 49:32 their camels shall be a **b**, and the multitude 957
Zep 1:13 Therefore their goods shall become a **b**, 4933

BOOZ (3) [BOAZ]
Mt 1: 5 And Salmon begat **B** of Rachab; and *1003*
1: 5 and **B** begat Obed of Ruth; and Obed begat *1003*
Lk 3:32 *the son* of Obed, which was *the son* of **B**, *1003*

BOR ASHAN See CHOR-ASHAN

BORDER (158) [BORDERS]
Ge 10:19 the **b** of the Canaanites was from Sidon, 1366
49:13 of ships; and his **b** *shall be* unto Zidon. 3411
Ex 19:12 *not* up into the mount, or touch the **b** of it: 7097
25:25 thou shalt make unto it a **b** of a 4526
25:25 thou shalt make a golden crown to the **b** 4526
25:27 Over against the **b** shall the rings be for 4526
28:26 two ends of the breastplate in the **b** thereof, 8193
37:12 Also he made thereunto a **b** of a 4526
37:12 made a crown of gold for the **b** thereof 4526
37:14 Over against the **b** were the rings, 4526
39:19 upon the **b** of it, which *was* on the side of 8193
Nu 20:16 in Kadesh, a city in the uttermost of thy **b**: 1366
20:21 to give Israel passage through his **b**: 1366
21:13 for Arnon *is* the **b** of Moab, between Moab 1366
21:15 of Ar, and lieth upon the **b** of Moab. 1366
21:23 not suffer Israel to pass through his **b**: 1366
21:24 for the **b** of the children of Ammon *was* 1366
22:36 which *is* in the **b** of Arnon, which *is* in 1366
33:44 and pitched in Ije-abarim, in the **b** of Moab. 1366
34: 3 your south **b** shall be the outmost coast of 1366
34: 4 your **b** shall turn from the south to 1366

Nu 34: 5 the **b** shall fetch a compass from Azmon 1366
34: 6 *as for* the western **b**, you shall even have 1366
34: 6 you shall even have the great sea for a **b**: 1366
34: 6 sea for a border: this shall be your west **b**. 1366
34: 7 this shall be your north **b**: from the great 1366
34: 8 From mount Hor ye shall point out *your* **b** NIH
34: 8 the goings forth of the **b** shall be to Zedad: 1366
34: 9 the **b** shall go on to Ziphron, and the goings 1366
34: 9 be at Hazar-enan: this shall be your north **b**. 1366
34:10 ye shall point out your east **b** from 1366
34:11 the **b** shall descend, and shall reach unto 1366
34:12 the **b** shall go down to Jordan, and 1366
35:26 *without* the **b** of the city of his refuge, 1366
Dt 3:16 half the valley, and the **b**, even unto 1366
3:16 *which is* the **b** of the children of Ammon; 1366
12:20 the LORD thy God shall enlarge thy **b**, 1366
Jos 4:19 in Gilgal, in the east **b** of Jericho. 7097
12: 2 *which is* the **b** of the children of Ammon; 1366
12: 5 unto the **b** of the Geshurites and 1366
12: 5 the **b** of Sihon king of Heshbon. 1366
13:10 unto the **b** of the children of Ammon; 1366
13:11 the **b** of the Geshurites and Maachathites, 1366
13:23 the **b** of the children of Reuben was Jordan, 1366
13:23 the **b** *thereof.* This *was* the inheritance of 1366
13:26 and from Mahanaim unto the **b** of Debir; 1366
13:27 Sihon king of Heshbon, Jordan and *his* **b**, 1366
15: 1 *even* to the **b** of Edom, the wilderness of 1366
15: 2 their south **b** was from the shore of the salt 1366
15: 5 the east **b** *was* the salt sea, *even* unto 1366
15: 5 *their* **b** in the north quarter *was* from 1366
15: 6 the **b** went up *to* Beth-hogla, and 1366
15: 6 the **b** went up *to* the stone of Bohan the son 1366
15: 7 the **b** went up toward Debir from the valley 1366
15: 7 the **b** passed towards the waters of 1366
15: 8 the **b** went up *by* the valley of the son of 1366
15: 8 the **b** went up to the top of the mountain 1366
15: 9 the **b** was drawn from the top of the hill 1366
15: 9 the **b** was drawn *to* Baalah, which *is* 1366
15:10 the **b** compassed from Baalah westward 1366
15:11 the **b** went out unto the side of Ekron 1366
15:11 the **b** was drawn to Shicron, and 1366
15:11 and the goings out of the **b** were at the sea. 1366
15:12 the west **b** *was* to the great sea, and 1366
15:47 and the great sea, and the **b** *thereof.* 1366
16: 5 the **b** of the children of Ephraim according 1366
16: 5 **b** of their inheritance on the east side was 1366
16: 6 the **b** went out toward the sea *to* 1366
16: 6 the **b** went about eastward *unto* 1366
16: 8 The **b** went *out* from Tappuah westward 1366
17: 7 the **b** went *along* on the right hand unto 1366
17: 8 Tappuah on the **b** of Manasseh *belonged* to 1366
17:10 *it was* Manasseh's, and the sea is his **b**; 1366
18:12 their **b** on the north side was from Jordan; 1366
18:12 the **b** went up to the side of Jericho on 1366
18:13 the **b** went over from thence toward Luz, 1366
18:13 the **b** descended *to* Ataroth-adar, near 1366
18:14 the **b** was drawn *thence,* and compassed 1366
18:15 the **b** went out on the west, and went out to 1366
18:16 the **b** came down to the end of 1366
18:19 the **b** passed along to the side of 1366
18:19 the outgoings of the **b** were at the north bay 1366
18:20 Jordan was the **b** of it on the east side. 1379
19:10 the **b** of their inheritance was unto Sarid: 1366
19:11 their **b** went up toward the sea, and 1366
19:12 the sunrising unto the **b** of Chisloth-tabor, 1366
19:14 the **b** compasseth it on the north side *to* 1366
19:18 their **b** was toward Jezreel, and Chesulloth, 1366
19:22 and the outgoings of their **b** were *at* Jordan: 1366
19:25 their **b** was Helkath, and Hali, and Beten, 1366
19:46 and Rakkon, with the **b** before Japho. 1366
22:25 For the LORD hath made Jordan a **b** 1366
24:30 they buried him in the **b** of his inheritance 1366
Jdg 2: 9 they buried him in the **b** of his inheritance 1366
7:22 *and* to the **b** of Abel-meholah, 8193
11:18 but came not within the **b** of Moab: 1366
11:18 of Moab: for Arnon *was* the **b** of Moab. 1366
1Sa 6:12 after them unto the **b** of Beth-shemesh. 1366
10: 2 sepulchre in the **b** of Benjamin at Zelzah; 1366
13:18 another company turned *to* the way of the **b** 1366
2Sa 8: 3 as he went to recover his **b** at the river 3027
1Ki 4:21 of the Philistines, and unto the **b** of Egypt: 1366
2Ki 3:21 on armour, and upward, and stood in the **b**. 1366
2Ch 9:26 of the Philistines, and to the **b** of Egypt. 1366
Ps 78:54 he brought them to the **b** of his sanctuary, 1366
Pr 15:25 but he will establish the **b** of the widow. 1366
Isa 19:19 and a pillar at the **b** thereof to the LORD. 1366
37:24 I will enter *into* the height of his **b**, *and* 7093
Jer 31:17 children shall come again to their own **b**. 1366
50:26 Come against her from the **utmost b**, 7093
Eze 11:10 I will judge you in the **b** of Israel; and 1366
11:11 *but* I will judge you in the **b** of Israel: 1366
29:10 from the tower of Syene even unto the **b** of 1366
43:13 the **b** thereof by the edge thereof round 1366
43:17 the **b** about it *shall be* half a cubit; and 1366
43:20 of the settle, and upon the **b** round about: 1366
45: 7 from the west **b** unto the east border. 1366
45: 7 from the west border unto the east **b**. 1366
47:13 This *shall be* the **b**, whereby ye shall inherit 1366
47:15 this *shall be* the **b** of the land toward 1366
47:16 which *is* between the **b** of Damascus and 1366
47:16 border of Damascus and the **b** of Hamath; 1366
47:17 the **b** from the sea shall be Hazar-enan, 1366
47:17 the **b** of Damascus, and the north 1366
47:17 the north northward, and the **b** of Hamath. 1366
47:18 *by* Jordan, from the **b** unto the east sea. 1366
47:20 side also *shall be* the great sea from the **b**, 1366
48: 1 Hazar-enan, the **b** of Damascus northward, 1366
48: 2 by the **b** of Dan, from the east side unto 1366
48: 3 by the **b** of Asher, from the east side even 1366
48: 4 by the **b** of Naphtali, from the east side 1366
48: 5 by the **b** of Manasseh, from the east side 1366
48: 6 by the **b** of Ephraim, from the east side 1366
48: 7 by the **b** of Reuben, from the east side unto 1366
48: 8 by the **b** of Judah, from the east side unto 1366
48:12 *a thing* most holy by the **b** of the Levites. 1366
48:13 over against the **b** of the priests, the Levites 1366
48:21 thousand of the oblation toward the east **b**, 1366
48:21 and twenty thousand toward the west **b**, 1366
48:22 between the **b** of Judah and the border of 1366
48:22 the border of Judah and the **b** of Benjamin, 1366
48:24 by the **b** of Benjamin, from the east side 1366
48:25 by the **b** of Simeon, from the east side unto 1366
48:26 by the **b** of Issachar, from the east side unto 1366
48:27 by the **b** of Zebulun, from the east side unto 1366
48:28 by the **b** of Gad, at the south side 1366
48:28 the **b** shall be even from Tamar *unto* 1366
Joel 3: 6 that *ye* might remove them far from their **b**. 1366
Am 1:13 at Gilead, that *they* might enlarge their **b**: 1366
6: 2 or their **b** greater than your border? 1366
6: 2 or their border greater than your **b**? 1366
Ob 1: 7 have brought thee *even* to the **b**: 1366
Zep 2: 8 and magnified *themselves* against their **b**. 1366
Zec 9: 2 Hamath also shall **b** thereby; Tyrus, and 1379
Mal 1: 4 shall call them, The **b** of wickedness, and, 1366
1: 5 The LORD will be magnified from the **b** 1366
Mk 6:56 touch if it were but the **b** of his garment: *2899*
Lk 8:44 and touched the **b** of his garment: *2899*

BORDERS (43) [BORDER]

Ge 23:17 that *were* in all the **b** round about, 1366
47:21 **b** of Egypt even to the *other* end thereof. 1366
Ex 8: 2 behold, I will smite all thy **b** with frogs: 1366
16:35 until they came unto the **b** of the land of 7097
34:24 the nations before thee, and enlarge thy **b**: 1366
Nu 15:38 **b** of their garments throughout their 3671
15:38 that they put upon the fringe of the **b** a 3671
20:17 nor *to* the left, until we have passed thy **b**. 1366
21:22 the king's *high* way, until we be past thy **b**. 1366
35:27 him without the **b** of the city of his refuge, 1366
Jos 11: 2 the valley, and in the **b** of Dor on the west, 5299
13: 2 all the **b** of the Philistines, and all Geshuri, 1552
13: 3 even unto the **b** of Ekron northward, 1366
13: 4 unto Aphek, to the **b** of the Amorites: 1366
16: 2 passeth along unto the **b** of Archi *to* 1366
22:10 when they came unto the **b** of Jordan, 1552
22:11 in the **b** of Jordan, at the passage of 1552
1Ki 7:28 the bases *was on* this *manner:* they had **b**, 4526
7:28 and the **b** *were* between the ledges: 4526
7:29 on the **b** that *were* between the ledges *were* 4526
7:31 the mouth of it *were* gravings with their **b**, 4526
7:32 under the **b** *were* four wheels; and 4526
7:35 and the **b** thereof *were* of the same. 4526
7:36 on the **b** thereof, he graved cherubims, 4526
2Ki 16:17 king Ahaz cut off the **b** of the bases, and 4526
18: 8 *even* unto Gaza, and the **b** thereof, 1366
19:23 I will enter *into* the lodgings of his **b**, *and* 7093
1Ch 5:16 in all the suburbs of Sharon, upon their **b**. 8444
7:29 by the **b** of the children of Manasseh, 3027

Ps	74:17	Thou hast set all the **b** of the earth:	1367
	147:14	He maketh peace *in* thy **b**, *and* filleth thee	1366
SS	1:11	We will make thee **b** of gold with studs of	8447
Isa	15: 8	For the cry is gone round about the **b** of	1366
	54:12	and all thy **b** of pleasant stones.	1366
	60:18	wasting nor destruction within thy **b**;	1366
Jer	15:13	and *that* for all thy sins, even in all thy **b**.	1366
	17: 3	high places for sin, throughout all thy **b**.	1366
Eze	27: 4	Thy **b** *are* in the midst of the seas,	1366
	45: 1	This *shall be* holy in all the **b** thereof round	1366
Mic	5: 6	and when he treadeth within our **b**.	1366
Mt	4:13	in the **b** of Zabulon and Nephthalim:	*3725*
	23: 5	and enlarge the **b** of their garments,	*2899*
Mk	7:24	and went into the **b** of Tyre and Sidon, and	*3181*

BORE (2) [BORED]

Ex	21: 6	his master shall **b** his ear **through** with an	7527
Job	41: 2	or **b** his jaw **through** with a thorn?	5344

BORED (1) [BORE]

2Ki	12: 9	**b** a hole in the lid of it, and set it beside	5344

BORN (154) [BEAR]

Ge	4:18	unto Enoch was **b** Irad: and Irad begat	3205
	4:26	to Seth, *to* him also there was **b** a son; and	3205
	6: 1	the earth, and daughters were **b** unto them,	3205
	10: 1	and unto them were sons **b** after the flood.	3205
	10:21	the elder, even to him were *children* **b**.	3205
	10:25	unto Eber were **b** two sons: the name of	3205
	14:14	he armed his trained *servants,* **b** in his own	3211
	15: 3	and lo, **one b** in my house is mine heir.	1121
	17:12	he **that is b** in the house, or bought with	3211
	17:13	He **that is b** in thy house, and he that is	3211
	17:17	Shall *a child* be **b** unto him that is an	3205
	17:23	all **that were b** in his house, and all that	3211
	17:27	**b** in the house, and bought with money of	3211
	21: 3	the name of his son that was **b** unto him,	3205
	21: 5	when his son Isaac was **b** unto him.	3205
	21: 7	for I have **b** *him* a son in his old age.	3205
	21: 9	which she had **b** unto Abraham, mocking.	3205
	22:20	she hath also **b** children unto thy brother	3205
	24:15	who was **b** to Bethuel, son of Milcah,	3205
	29:34	unto me, because I have **b** him three sons:	3205
	30:20	with me, because I have **b** him six sons:	3205
	30:25	it came to pass, when Rachel had **b** Joseph,	3205
	31:43	or unto their children which they have **b**?	3205
	35:26	which were **b** to him in Padan-aram.	3205
	36: 5	which were **b** unto him in the land of	3205
	41:50	unto Joseph were **b** two sons before	3205
	46:20	unto Joseph in the land of Egypt were **b**	3205
	46:22	the sons of Rachel, which were **b** to Jacob:	3205
	46:27	which were **b** him in Egypt, *were* two	3205
	48: 5	which were **b** unto thee in the land of Egypt	3205
Ex	1:22	Every son that is **b** ye shall cast into	3209
	12:19	whether he be a stranger, or **b** in the land.	249
	12:48	and he shall be as one that is **b** in the land:	249
	21: 4	and she have **b** him sons or daughters;	3205
Lev	12: 2	have conceived seed, and **b** a man child:	3205
	12: 7	This *is* the law for her that hath **b** a male or	3205
	18: 9	*whether she be* **b** at home, or born abroad,	4138
	18: 9	*whether she be* born at home, or **b** abroad,	4138
	19:34	shall be unto you as **one b amongst** you,	249
	22:11	shall eat of it, and **he that is b** in his house:	3211
	23:42	all that are Israelites **b** shall dwell in booths:	249
	24:16	well the stranger, as he **that is b in the land,**	249
Nu	9:14	and for him **that was b** in the land.	249
	15:13	All that are **b of the country** shall do these	249
	15:29	*both for* him **that is b** amongst the children	249
	15:30	*whether he be* **b in the land,** or a stranger,	249
	26:60	unto Aaron was **b** Nadab, and Abihu,	3205
Dt	21:15	and they have **b** him children,	3205
Jos	5: 5	all the people *that were* **b** in the wilderness	3209
	8:33	the stranger, as he that was **b among** them;	249
Jdg	13: 8	we shall do unto the child that shall be **b**.	3205
	18:29	of Dan their father, who was **b** unto Israel:	3205
Ru	4:15	better to thee than seven sons, hath **b** him.	3205
	4:17	a name, saying, There is a son **b** to Naomi;	3205
1Sa	2: 5	so that the barren hath **b** seven; and she that	3205
	4:20	*unto her,* Fear not; for thou hast **b** a son.	3205
2Sa	3: 2	unto David were sons **b** in Hebron: and	3205
	3: 5	These were **b** to David in Hebron.	3205
	5:13	were yet sons and daughters **b** to David.	3205
	5:14	these *be* the names of those that were **b**	3209
	12:14	the child also that is **b** unto thee shall surely	3209
	14:27	unto Absalom there were **b** three sons, and	3205
	21:20	*in* number; and he also was **b** to the giant.	3205
	21:22	These four were **b** to the giant in Gath, and	3205
1Ki	13: 2	a child *shall be* **b** unto the house of David,	3205
1Ch	1:19	unto Eber were **b** two sons: the name of	3205
	2: 3	*which* three were **b** unto him of	3205
	2: 9	sons also of Hezron, that were **b** unto him;	3205
	3: 1	which were **b** unto him in Hebron;	3205
	3: 4	*These* six were **b** unto him in Hebron; and	3205
	3: 5	these were **b** unto him in Jerusalem;	3205
	7:21	whom the men of Gath that were **b** in *that*	3205
	20: 8	These were **b** unto the giant in Gath; and	3205
	22: 9	Behold, a son *shall be* **b** to thee, who shall	3205
	26: 6	Also unto Shemaiah his son were sons **b**,	3205
Ezr	10: 3	such as are **b** of them, according to	3205
Job	1: 2	there were **b** unto him seven sons and	3205
	3: 3	Let the day perish wherein I was **b**, and	3205
	5: 7	Yet man is **b** unto trouble, as the sparks fly	3205
	11:12	though man be **b** *like* a wild ass's colt.	3205
	14: 1	Man *that is* **b** of a woman *is* of few days,	3205
	15: 7	*Art* thou the first man *that* was **b**? or	3205
	15:14	*he which is* **b** of a woman, that he should	3205
	25: 4	how can he be clean *that is* **b** of a woman?	3205
	38:21	Knowest thou *it,* because thou wast then **b**?	3205
Ps	22:31	righteousness unto a people that *shall be* **b**,	3205
	58: 3	they go astray **as soon as** they be **b**,	990+4480
	78: 6	*them, even* the children *which* should be **b**;	3205
	87: 4	Tyre, with Ethiopia; this *man* was **b** there.	3205
	87: 5	be said, This and that man was **b** in her:	3205
	87: 6	*up* the people, *that* this *man* was **b** there.	3205
Pr	17:17	at all times, and a brother is **b** for adversity.	3205
Ecc	2: 7	maidens, and had servants **b** in *my* house;	1121
	3: 2	A time to be **b**, and a time to die; a time to	3205
	4:14	whereas also *he that is* **b** in his kingdom	3205
Isa	9: 6	For unto us a child is **b**, unto us a Son is	3205
	66: 8	*or* shall a nation be **b** at once? for as soon	3205
Jer	16: 3	concerning the daughters that are **b** in this	3209
	20:14	Cursed *be* the day wherein I was **b**: let not	3205
	20:15	saying, A man child is **b** unto thee;	3205
	22:26	into another country, where ye were not **b**;	3205
Eze	16: 4	in the day thou wast **b** thy navel was not	3205
	16: 5	of thy person, in the day that thou wast **b**.	3205
	47:22	they shall be unto you as **b in the country**	249
Hos	2: 3	and set her as *in* the day that she was **b**, and	3205
Mt	1:16	of whom was **b** Jesus, who is called Christ.	*1080*
	2: 1	Now when Jesus was **b** in Bethlehem of	*1080*
	2: 2	Where is he that is **b** King of the Jews?	*5088*
	2: 4	of them where Christ should be **b**.	*1080*
	11:11	Among *them that are* **b** of women there	*1084*
	19:12	so **b** from *their* mother's womb:	*1080*
	26:24	good for that man if he had not been **b**.	*1080*
Mk	14:21	were it for that man if he had never been **b**.	*1080*
Lk	1:35	also *that* holy thing which shall be **b** of thee	*1080*
	2:11	For unto you is **b** this day in the city of	*5088*
	7:28	Among *those that are* **b** of women there is	*1084*
Jn	1:13	Which were **b**, not of blood, nor of the will	*1080*
	3: 3	I say unto thee, Except a man be **b** again,	*1080*
	3: 4	How can a man be **b** when he is old?	*1080*
	3: 4	time into his mother's womb, and be **b**?	*1080*
	3: 5	Except a man be **b** of water and *of*	*1080*
	3: 6	That which is **b** of the flesh is flesh; and	*1080*
	3: 6	and that which is **b** of the Spirit is spirit.	*1080*
	3: 7	that I said unto thee, Ye must be **b** again.	*1080*
	3: 8	so is every one that is **b** of the Spirit.	*1080*
	8:41	they to him, We be not **b** of fornication;	*1080*
	9: 2	or his parents, that he was **b** blind?	*1080*
	9:19	Is this your son, who ye say was **b** blind?	*1080*
	9:20	that this is our son, and that he was **b** blind:	*1080*
	9:32	opened the eyes of one that was **b** blind.	*1080*
	9:34	Thou wast altogether **b** in sins, and	*1080*
	16:21	for joy that a man is **b** into the world.	*1080*
	18:37	To this end was I **b**, and for this cause came	*1080*
Ac	2: 8	in our own tongue, wherein we were **b**?	*1080*
	7:20	In which time Moses was **b**, and	*1080*
	18: 2	**b** in Pontus, lately come from Italy,	*1085*
	18:24	**b** at Alexandria, an eloquent man, *and*	*1085*
	22: 3	*am* a Jew, **b** in Tarsus, *a city* in Cilicia,	*1080*
	22:28	And Paul said, But I was *free* **b**.	*1080*
Ro	9:11	(For *the children* being not yet **b**,	*1080*
1Co	15: 8	of me also, as of one **b out of due time**.	*1626*
Gal	4:23	But he who was of the bondwoman was **b**	*1080*
	4:29	he that was **b** after the flesh persecuted him	*1080*
	4:29	persecuted him that was ***b*** after the Spirit,	NIG
Heb	11:23	By faith Moses, when he was **b**, was hid	*1080*

1Pe 1:23 Being **b again**, not of corruptible seed, but *313*
1Jn 2:29 one which doeth righteousness is **b** of him. *1080*
3: 9 Whosoever is **b** of God doth not commit *1080*
3: 9 and he cannot sin, because he is **b** of God. *1080*
4: 7 and every one that loveth is **b** of God, and *1080*
5: 1 that Jesus is the Christ is **b** of God: *1080*
5: 4 For whatsoever is **b** of God overcometh *1080*
5:18 We know that whosoever is **b** of God *1080*
Rev 12: 4 for to devour her child as soon as it was **b**. *5088*

BORN OF A FORBIDDEN MARRIAGE See BASTARD; BASTARDS

BORNE (31) [BEAR]
Ex 25:14 of the ark, that the ark may be **b** with them. 5375
25:28 that the table may be **b** with them. 5375
Jdg 16:29 on which it was **b up**, of the one with his 5564
Job 34:31 I have **b** *chastisement,* I will not offend 5375
Ps 55:12 I could have **b** *it:* neither *was it* he that 5375
69: 7 Because for thy sake I have **b** reproach; 5375
Isa 46: 3 which are **b** *by me* from the belly, 6006
53: 4 Surely he hath **b** our griefs, and carried our 5375
66:12 ye shall be **b** upon *her* sides, and 5375
Jer 10: 5 they **must needs be b**, because 5375+5375
15: 9 She that hath **b** seven languisheth: she hath 3205
15:10 that thou hast **b** me a man of strife and 3205
La 3:28 because he hath **b** *it* upon him. 5190
5: 7 *and are* not; *and* we have **b** their iniquities. 5445
Eze 16:20 whom thou hast **b** unto me, and these hast 3205
16:58 Thou hast **b** thy lewdness and thine 5375
32:24 yet have they **b** their shame with them that 5375
32:25 yet have they **b** their shame with them that 5375
36: 6 ye have **b** the shame of the heathen: 5375
39:26 After that they have **b** their shame, and all 5375
Am 5:26 ye have **b** the tabernacle of your Moloch 5375
Mt 20:12 which have **b** the burden and heat of the day. *941*
23: 4 bind heavy burdens and **grievous to be b**, *1419*
Mk 2: 3 one sick of the palsy, *which was* **b** of four. *142*
Lk 11:46 ye lade men *with* burdens **grievous to be b**, *1419*
Jn 5:37 which hath sent me, hath **b witness** of me. *3140*
20:15 if thou have **b** him *hence,* tell me where thou *941*
Ac 21:35 that he was **b** of the soldiers for the violence *941*
1Co 15:49 And as we have **b** the image of the earthy, *5409*
3Jn 1: 6 Which have **b witness** of thy charity before *3140*
Rev 2: 3 And hast **b**, and hast patience, and for my *941*

BORROW (8) [BORROWED, BORROWER, BORROWETH]
Ex 3:22 every woman shall **b** of her neighbour, and 7592
11: 2 let every man **b** of his neighbour, and 7592
22:14 if a man **b** *ought* of his neighbour, and it be 7592
Dt 15: 6 unto many nations, but thou shalt not **b**; 5670
28:12 unto many nations, and thou shalt not **b**. 3867
2Ki 4: 3 **b** thee vessels abroad of all thy neighbours, 7592
4: 3 *even* empty vessels; **b** not a few. NIH
Mt 5:42 from him that would **b** of thee turn not thou *1155*

BORROWED (3) [BORROW]
Ex 12:35 they **b** of the Egyptians jewels of silver, 7592
2Ki 6: 5 and said, Alas, master, for it *was* **b**. 7592
Ne 5: 4 We have **b** money for the king's tribute, 3867

BORROWER (2) [BORROW]
Pr 22: 7 the poor, and the **b** *is* servant to the lender. 3867
Isa 24: 2 the seller; as *with* the lender, so *with* the **b**; 3867

BORROWETH (1) [BORROW]
Ps 37:21 The wicked **b**, and payeth not again: but 3867

BOSCATH (1)
2Ki 22: 1 *was* Jedidah, the daughter of Adaiah of **B**. 1218

BOSOM (41)
Ge 16: 5 I have given my maid into thy **b**; and 2436
Ex 4: 6 unto him, Put now thine hand into thy **b**. 2436
4: 6 he put his hand into his **b**: and when he 2436
4: 7 he said, Put thine hand into thy **b** again. 2436
4: 7 he put his hand into his **b** again; and 2436
4: 7 plucked it out of his **b**, and behold, it was 2436
Nu 11:12 shouldest say unto me, Carry them in thy **b**, 2436
Dt 13: 6 or the wife of thy **b**, or thy friend, 2436
28:54 toward the wife of his **b**, and towards 2436
28:56 shall be evil towards the husband of her **b**, 2436
Ru 4:16 laid it in her **b**, and became nurse unto it. 2436
2Sa 12: 3 lay in his **b**, and was unto him as a 2436
12: 8 thy master's wives into thy **b**, and 2436
1Ki 1: 2 let her cherish him, and let her lie in thy **b**, 2436
3:20 laid it in her **b**, and laid her dead child in 2436
3:20 her bosom, and laid her dead child in my **b**. 2436
17:19 he took him out of her **b**, and carried him 2436
Job 31:33 as Adam, by hiding mine iniquity in my **b**: 2243
Ps 35:13 and my prayer returned into mine own **b**. 2436
74:11 even thy right hand? pluck *it* out of thy **b**. 2436
79:12 sevenfold into their **b** their reproach, 2436
89:50 *how* I do bear in my **b** *the reproach of* all 2436
129: 7 his hand; nor he that bindeth sheaves his **b**. 2683
Pr 5:20 and embrace the **b** of a stranger? 2436
6:27 Can a man take fire in his **b**, and his clothes 2436
17:23 A wicked *man* taketh a gift out of the **b** to 2436
19:24 A slothful *man* hideth his hand in *his* **b**, and 6747
21:14 and a reward in the **b** strong wrath. 2436
26:15 The slothful hideth his hand in *his* **b**; 6747
Ecc 7: 9 be angry: for anger resteth in the **b** of fools. 2436
Isa 40:11 carry *them* in his **b**, *and* shall gently lead 2436
65: 6 even recompense into their **b**, 2436
65: 7 I measure their former work into their **b**. 2436
Jer 32:18 into the **b** of their children after them: 2436
La 2:12 soul was poured out into their mothers' **b**. 2436
Mic 7: 5 of thy mouth from her that lieth in thy **b**. 2436
Lk 6:38 running over, shall *men* give into your **b**. *2859*
16:22 carried by the angels into Abraham's **b**: *2859*
16:23 Abraham afar off, and Lazarus in his **b**. *2859*
Jn 1:18 which is in the **b** of the Father, he hath *2859*
13:23 Now there was leaning on Jesus' **b** one of *2859*

BOSOR (1) [BEOR]
2Pe 2:15 following the way of Balaam *the son* of **B**, *1007*

BOSSES (1)
Job 15:26 *his* neck, upon the thick **b** of his bucklers: 1354

BOTCH (2)
Dt 28:27 The LORD will smite thee with the **b** of 7822
28:35 with a sore **b** that cannot be healed, 7822

BOTH (361) See Index

BOTTLE (15) [BOTTLES]
Ge 21:14 and a **b** of water, and gave *it* unto Hagar, 2573
21:15 the water was spent in the **b**, and she cast 2573
21:19 filled the **b** *with* water, and gave the lad 2573
Jdg 4:19 she opened a **b** of milk, and gave him 4997
1Sa 1:24 a **b** of wine, and brought him *unto* 5035
10: 3 of bread, and another carrying a **b** of wine: 5035
16:20 a **b** of wine, and a kid, and sent *them* by 4997
2Sa 16: 1 hundred of summer fruits, and a **b** of wine. 5035
Ps 56: 8 put thou my tears into thy **b**: *are they* not in 4997
119:83 For I am become like a **b** in the smoke; 4997
Jer 13:12 of Israel, Every **b** shall be filled *with* wine: 5035
13:12 Do we not certainly know that every **b** shall 5035
19: 1 Go and get a potter's earthen **b**, and *take* of 1228
19:10 shalt thou break the **b** in the sight of 1228
Hab 2:15 that puttest thy **b** to *him,* and makest *him* 2573

BOTTLES (19) [BOTTLE]
Jos 9: 4 and wine **b**, old, and rent, and bound up; 4997
9:13 these **b** of wine, which we filled, *were* new; 4997
1Sa 25:18 two **b** of wine, and five sheep ready 5035
Job 32:19 hath no vent; it is ready to burst like new **b**. 178
38:37 or who can stay the **b** of heaven, 5035
Jer 48:12 shall empty his vessels, and break their **b**. 5035
Hos 7: 5 princes have made *him* sick *with* **b** of wine; 2534
Mt 9:17 Neither do *men* put new wine into old **b**: *779*
9:17 else the **b** break, and the wine runneth out, *779*
9:17 and the wine runneth out, and the **b** perish: *779*
9:17 but they put new wine into new **b**, and *779*
Mk 2:22 And no *man* putteth new wine into old **b**: *779*
2:22 else the new wine doth burst the **b**, and *779*
2:22 the wine is spilled, and the **b** will be marred: *779*
2:22 but new wine must be put into new **b**. *779*
Lk 5:37 And no *man* putteth new wine into old **b**; *779*
5:37 else the new wine will burst the **b**, and *779*
5:37 and be spilled, and the **b** shall perish. *779*
5:38 But new wine must be put into new **b**; and *779*

BOTTOM (20) [BOTTOMLESS, BOTTOMS]
Ex 15: 5 they sank into the **b** as a stone. 4688
29:12 pour all the blood beside the **b** of the altar. 3247
Lev 4: 7 at the **b** of the altar of the burnt offering, 3247
4:18 shall pour out all the blood at the **b** of 3247
4:25 shall pour out his blood at the **b** of the altar 3247

Lev 4:30 shall pour out all the blood thereof at the **b** 3247
4:34 shall pour out all the blood thereof at the **b** 3247
5: 9 shall be wrung out at the **b** of the altar: 3247
8:15 poured the blood at the **b** of the altar, and 3247
9: 9 poured out the blood at the **b** of the altar: 3247
Job 36:30 light upon it, and covereth the **b** of the sea. 8328
SS 3:10 the **b** thereof *of* gold, the covering of it *of* 7507
Eze 43:13 even the **b** *shall be* a cubit, and the breadth 2436
43:14 from the **b** *upon* the ground *even* to 2436
43:17 and the **b** thereof *shall be* a cubit about; and 2436
Da 6:24 or ever they came at the **b** of the den. 773
Am 9: 3 though they be hid from my sight in the **b** 7172
Zec 1: 8 among the myrtle trees that *were* in the **b**; 4699
Mt 27:51 was rent in twain from the top to the **b**; *2736*
Mk 15:38 was rent in twain from the top to the **b**. *2736*

BOTTOMLESS (7) [BOTTOM]
Rev 9: 1 and to him was given the key of the **b** pit. *12*
9: 2 And he opened the **b** pit; and there arose a *12*
9:11 *which is* the angel of the **b** *pit*, whose name in *12*
11: 7 the beast that ascendeth out of the **b** *pit* shall *12*
17: 8 and shall ascend out of the **b** *pit*, and go into *12*
20: 1 having the key of the **b** *pit* and a great chain *12*
20: 3 And cast him into the **b** *pit*, and shut him up, *12*

BOTTOMS (1) [BOTTOM]
Jnh 2: 6 I went down to the **b** of the mountains; 7095

BOUGH (7) [BOUGHS]
Ge 49:22 Joseph *is* a **fruitful b**, *even* a fruitful 1121+6509
49:22 *even* a **fruitful b** by a well; 1121+6509
Jdg 9:48 cut down a **b** from the trees, and took it, 7754
9:49 people likewise cut down every man his **b**, 7754
Isa 10:33 LORD of hosts, shall lop the **b** with terror: 6288
17: 6 three berries in the top of the **uppermost b**, 534
17: 9 shall his strong cities be as a forsaken **b**, 2793

BOUGHS (18) [BOUGH]
Lev 23:40 ye shall take you on the first day the **b** of 6529
23:40 the **b** of thick trees, and willows of 6057
Dt 24:20 thou shalt not **go over the b** again: 6286
2Sa 18: 9 the mule went under the **thick b** of a great 7730
Job 14: 9 it will bud, and bring forth **b** like a plant. 7105
Ps 80:10 the **b** thereof *were like* the goodly cedars. 6057
80:11 She sent out her **b** unto the sea, and 7105
SS 7: 8 palm tree, I will take hold of the **b** thereof: 5577
Isa 27:11 When the **b** thereof are withered, they shall 7105
Eze 17:23 and it shall bring forth **b**, and bear fruit, and 6057
31: 3 and his top was among the **thick b**. 5688
31: 5 his **b** were multiplied, and his branches 5634
31: 6 fowls of heaven made their nests in his **b**, 5589
31: 8 the fir trees were not like his **b**, and 5589
31:10 he hath shot up his top among the **thick b**, 5688
31:12 his **b** are broken by all the rivers of 6288
31:14 shoot up their top among the **thick b**, 5688
Da 4:12 the fowls of the heaven dwelt in the **b** 6056

BOUGHT (44) [BUY]
Ge 17:12 or **b** with money of any stranger, which *is* 4736
17:13 he **that is b** with thy money, must needs be 4736
17:23 and all **that were b** with his money, 4736
17:27 and **b** with money of the stranger, 4736
33:19 he **b** a parcel of a field, where he had 7069
39: 1 **b** him of the hand of the Ishmeelites, 7069
47:14 land of Canaan, for the corn which they **b**: 7666
47:20 Joseph **b** all the land of Egypt for Pharaoh; 7069
47:22 Only the land of the priests **b** he not; for 7069
47:23 I have **b** you *this* day and your land for 7069
49:30 which Abraham **b** with the field of Ephron 7069
50:13 which Abraham **b** with the field for a 7069
Ex 12:44 every man's servant that is **b** for money, 4736
Lev 25:28 of him that hath **b** it until the year of jubile: 7069
25:30 to him that **b** it throughout his generations: 7069
25:50 he shall reckon with him that **b** him from 7069
25:51 out of the money that he was **b** for. 4736
27:22 unto the LORD a field which he hath **b**, 4736
27:24 shall return unto him of whom it was **b**, 7069
Dt 32: 6 *is* not he thy father *that* hath **b** thee? hath he 7069
Jos 24:32 in a parcel of ground which Jacob **b** of 7069
Ru 4: 9 that I have **b** all that *was* Elimelech's, and 7069
2Sa 12: 3 which he had **b** and nourished up: 7069
24:24 So David **b** the threshingfloor and the oxen 7069
1Ki 16:24 he **b** the hill Samaria of Shemer for two 7069
Ne 5:16 work of this wall, neither **b** we *any* land: 7069
Isa 43:24 Thou hast **b** me no sweet cane with money, 7069
Jer 32: 9 I **b** the field of Hanameel my uncle's son, 7069
32:43 fields shall be **b** in this land, whereof ye 7069
Hos 3: 2 So I **b** her to me for fifteen *pieces* of silver, 3739
Mt 13:46 went and sold all that he had, and **b** it. *59*
21:12 cast out all them that sold and **b** in the temple, *59*
27: 7 and **b** with them the potter's field, to bury *59*
Mk 11:15 to cast out them that sold and **b** in the temple, *59*
15:46 And he **b** fine linen, and took him down, and *59*
16: 1 and Salome, had **b** *sweet* spices, that they *59*
Lk 14:18 I have **b** a piece of ground, and I must needs *59*
14:19 I have **b** five yoke of oxen, and I go to prove *59*
17:28 they did eat, they drank, they **b**, they sold, *59*
19:45 out them that sold therein, and *them that* **b**; *59*
Ac 7:16 laid in the sepulchre that Abraham **b** for a *5608*
1Co 6:20 For ye are **b** with a price: therefore *59*
7:23 Ye are **b** with a price; be not ye the servants *59*
2Pe 2: 1 even denying the Lord that **b** them, and *59*

BOUND (104) [BIND, BOUNDS]
Ge 22: 9 **b** Isaac his son, and laid him on the altar 6123
38:28 and **b** upon his hand a scarlet thread, 7194
39:20 a place where the king's prisoners *were* **b**: 631
40: 3 the prison, the place where Joseph *was* **b**. 631
40: 5 king of Egypt, which *were* **b** in the prison. 631
42:19 brethren be **b** in the house of your prison: 631
42:24 them Simeon, and **b** him before their eyes. 631
44:30 seeing that his life *is* **b up** in *the lad's* life; 7194
49:26 unto the **utmost b** of the everlasting hills: 8379
Ex 12:34 their kneadingtroughs being **b up** in their 6887
Lev 8: 7 of the ephod, and **b** *it* unto him therewith. 640
Nu 19:15 which hath no covering **b** upon it, 6616
30: 4 and her bond wherewith she hath **b** her soul, 631
30: 4 every bond wherewith she hath **b** her soul 631
30: 5 of her bonds wherewith she hath **b** her soul, 631
30: 6 out of her lips, wherewith she **b** her soul; 631
30: 7 her bonds wherewith she **b** her soul shall 631
30: 8 wherewith she **b** her soul, of none effect: 631
30: 9 wherewith they have **b** their souls, 631
30:10 or **b** her soul by a bond with an oath; 631
30:11 every bond wherewith she **b** her soul shall 631
Jos 2:21 and she **b** the scarlet line in the window. 7194
9: 4 and wine bottles, old, and rent, and **b up**; 6887
Jdg 15:13 they **b** him with two new cords, and 631
16: 6 wherewith thou mightest be **b** to afflict thee. 631
16: 8 had not been dried, and she **b** him with them. 631
16:10 I pray thee, wherewith thou mightest be **b**. 631
16:12 and **b** him therewith, and said unto him, 631
16:13 tell me wherewith thou mightest be **b**. 631
16:21 to Gaza, and **b** him with fetters of brass; 631
1Sa 25:29 the soul of my lord shall be **b** in the bundle 6887
2Sa 3:34 Thy hands *were* not **b**, nor thy feet put into 631
2Ki 5:23 and **b** two talents of silver in two bags, 6696
17: 4 of Assyria shut him up, and **b** him *in* prison. 631
25: 7 **b** him with fetters of brass, and carried him 631
2Ch 33:11 **b** him with fetters, and carried him to 631
36: 6 **b** him in fetters, to carry him to Babylon. 631
Job 36: 8 if *they be* **b** in fetters, *and* be holden in cords 631
38:20 That thou shouldest take it to the **b** thereof, 1366
Ps 68: 6 he bringeth out those which are **b** with 615
104: 9 Thou hast set a **b** *that* they may not pass 1366
107:10 of death, *being* **b** in affliction and iron; 615
Pr 22:15 Foolishness *is* **b** in the heart of a child; *but* 7194
30: 4 who hath **b** the waters in a garment? 6887
Isa 1: 6 they have not been closed, neither **b up**, 2280
22: 3 are fled together, they are **b** by the archers: 631
22: 3 all that are found in thee are **b** together, 631
61: 1 the opening of the prison to *them that are* **b**; 631
Jer 5:22 which have placed the sand *for* the **b** of 1366
30:13 plead thy cause, that thou mayest be **b up**: 4205
39: 7 **b** him with chains to carry him to Babylon. 631
40: 1 when he had taken him being **b** in chains 631
52:11 and the king of Babylon **b** him in chains, and 631
La 1:14 The yoke of my transgressions is **b** by his 8244
Eze 27:24 **b** with cords, and made of cedar, 2280
30:21 lo, it shall not be **b up** to be healed, to put a 2280
34: 4 neither have ye **b up** that which was 2280
Da 3:21 these men were **b** in their coats, 3729
3:23 fell down **b** into the midst of the burning 3729
3:24 Did not we cast three men **b** into the midst 3729
Hos 4:19 The wind hath **b** her **up** in her wings, and 6887
5:10 of Judah were like them that remove the **b**: 1366
7:15 Though I have **b** *and* strengthened their 3256
13:12 The iniquity of Ephraim *is* **b up**; his sin *is* 6887

Na 3:10 and all her great *men* were **b** in chains. 7576
Mt 14: 3 and **b** him, and put *him* in prison for *1210*
16:19 shalt bind on earth shall be **b** in heaven: *1210*
18:18 ye shall bind on earth shall be **b** in heaven: *1210*
27: 2 And when they had **b** him, they led *him* *1210*
Mk 5: 4 Because that he had been often **b** with *1210*
6:17 and **b** him in prison for Herodias' sake, *1210*
15: 1 and **b** Jesus, and carried *him* away, and *1210*
15: 7 *which lay* **b** with them that had made *1210*
Lk 8:29 and he was kept **b** with chains and *1196*
10:34 And went to *him,* and **b up** his wounds, *2611*
13:16 whom Satan hath **b**, lo *these* eighteen years, *1210*
Jn 11:44 **b** hand and foot with graveclothes: *1210*
11:44 and his face was **b about** with a napkin. *4019*
18:12 officers of the Jews took Jesus, and **b** him, *1210*
18:24 Now Annas had sent him **b** unto Caiaphas *1210*
Ac 9: 2 he might bring *them* **b** unto Jerusalem. *1210*
9:21 might bring them **b** unto the chief priests? *1210*
12: 6 between two soldiers, **b** with two chains: *1210*
20:22 I go **b** in the spirit unto Jerusalem, *1210*
21:11 and **b** his *own* hands and feet, and said, *1210*
21:13 for I am ready not to be **b** only, but also to *1210*
21:33 commanded *him* to be **b** with two chains; *1210*
22: 5 **b** unto Jerusalem, for to be punished. *1210*
22:25 And as they **b** him with thongs, Paul said *4385*
22:29 was a Roman, and because he had **b** him. *1210*
23:12 and **b** themselves **under a curse**, *332*
23:14 have **b** ourselves **under a great curse**, *331+332*
23:21 which have **b** themselves **with an oath**, *332*
24:27 to shew the Jews a pleasure, left Paul **b**. *1210*
28:20 that for the hope of Israel I am **b with** this *4029*
Ro 7: 2 For the woman which hath a husband is **b** *1210*
1Co 7:27 Art thou **b** unto a wife? seek not to be *1210*
7:39 The wife is **b** by the law as long as her *1210*
2Th 1: 3 We are **b** to thank God always for you, *3784*
2:13 But we are **b** to give thanks alway to God *3784*
2Ti 2: 9 unto bonds; but the word of God is not **b**. *1210*
Heb 13: 3 as **b with** *them; and* them which suffer *4887*
Rev 9:14 Loose the four angels which are **b** in *1210*
20: 2 and Satan, and **b** him a thousand years, *1210*

BOUNDARY STONE See LANDMARK

BOUNDLESS See INFINITE

BOUNDS (8) [BOUND]

Ex 19:12 thou shalt **set b** unto the people round 1379
19:23 **Set b about** the mount, and sanctify it. 1379
23:31 I will set thy **b** from the Red sea even unto 1366
Dt 32: 8 he set the **b** of the people according to 1367
Job 14: 5 thou hast appointed his **b** that he cannot 2706
26:10 He hath compassed the waters with **b**, 2706
Isa 10:13 I have removed the **b** of the people, and 1367
Ac 17:26 and the **b** of their habitation; *3734*

BOUNTIFUL (2) [BOUNTY]

Pr 22: 9 He that hath a **b** eye shall be blessed; for he 2896
Isa 32: 5 called liberal, nor the churl said *to be* **b**. 7771

BOUNTIFULLY (6) [BOUNTY]

Ps 13: 6 because he hath **dealt b** with me. 1580
116: 7 for the LORD hath **dealt b** with thee. 1580
119:17 **Deal b** with thy servant, *that* I may live, 1580
142: 7 me about; for thou shalt **deal b** with me. 1580
2Co 9: 6 he which soweth **b** shall reap also *1909+2129*
9: 6 soweth bountifully shall reap also **b**. *1909+2129*

BOUNTIFULNESS (1) [BOUNTY]

2Co 9:11 Being enriched in every *thing* to all **b**, *572*

BOUNTY (3) [BOUNTIFUL, BOUNTIFULLY, BOUNTIFULNESS]

1Ki 10:13 *that* which Solomon gave her of his royal **b**. 3027
2Co 9: 5 and make up beforehand your **b**, *2129*
9: 5 as *a matter of* **b**, and not as *of* *2129*

BOW (99) [BOWED, BOWETH, BOWING, BOWMEN, BOWS, BOWSHOT, RAINBOW]

Ge 9:13 I do set my **b** in the cloud, and it shall be 7198
9:14 that the **b** shall be seen in the cloud: 7198
9:16 the **b** shall be in the cloud; and I will look 7198
27: 3 thy quiver and thy **b**, and go out to 7198
27:29 serve thee, and nations **b down** to thee: 7812
27:29 and let thy mother's sons **b down** to thee: 7812
37:10 thy brethren indeed come to **b down** 7812
41:43 and they cried before him, **B the knee**: 86
48:22 the Amorite with my sword and with my **b**. 7198
49: 8 thy father's children shall **b down** before 7812
49:24 his **b** abode in strength, and the arms of his 7198
Ex 11: 8 **b down** themselves unto me, saying, 7812
20: 5 Thou shalt not **b down** thyself to them, 7812
23:24 Thou shalt not **b down** to their gods, 7812
Lev 26: 1 of stone in your land, to **b down** unto it: 7812
Dt 5: 9 Thou shalt not **b down** thyself unto them, 7812
Jos 23: 7 serve them, nor **b** yourselves unto them. 7812
24:12 *but* not with thy sword, nor with thy **b**. 7198
Jdg 2:19 to serve them, and to **b down** unto them; 7812
1Sa 18: 4 to his sword, and to his **b**, and to his girdle. 7198
2Sa 1:18 teach the children of Judah the *use of the* **b**: 7198
1:22 the **b** of Jonathan turned not back, and 7198
22:35 so that a **b** of steel is broken *by* mine arms. 7198
1Ki 22:34 a *certain* man drew a **b** at a venture, 7198
2Ki 5:18 and I **b** myself *in* the house of Rimmon: 7812
5:18 when I **b down** myself *in* the house of 7812
6:22 captive with thy sword and with thy **b**? 7198
9:24 Jehu drew a **b** with his full strength, and 7198
13:15 Elisha said unto him, Take **b** and arrows. 7198
13:15 And he took unto him **b** and arrows. 7198
13:16 king of Israel, Put thine hand upon the **b**. 7198
17:35 nor **b** yourselves to them, nor serve them, 7812
19:16 LORD, **b down** thine ear, and hear: open, 5186
1Ch 5:18 and to shoot with **b**, and skilful in war, 7198
12: 2 and *shooting* arrows out of a **b**, 7198
2Ch 17:17 with him armed *men* with **b** and shield two 7198
18:33 a *certain* man drew a **b** at a venture, 7198
Job 20:24 *and* the **b** of steel shall strike him through. 7198
29:20 in me, and my **b** was renewed in my hand. 7198
31:10 and let others **b down** upon her. 3766
39: 3 They **b** themselves, they bring forth their 3766
Ps 7:12 he hath bent his **b**, and made it ready. 7198
11: 2 For lo, the wicked bend *their* **b**, they make 7198
18:34 so that a **b** of steel is broken *by* mine arms. 7198
22:29 all they that go down to the dust shall **b** 3766
31: 2 **B down** thine ear to me; deliver me 5186
37:14 and have bent their **b**, to cast down the poor 7198
44: 6 For I will not trust in my **b**, neither shall 7198
46: 9 he breaketh the **b**, and cutteth the spear in 7198
58: 7 *when* he bendeth *his* **b** *to shoot* his arrows, NIH
72: 9 They that dwell in the wilderness shall **b** 3766
76: 3 There brake he the arrows of the **b**, 7198
78:57 they were turned aside like a deceitful **b**. 7198
86: 1 **B down** thine ear, O LORD, hear me: 5186
95: 6 O come, let us worship and **b down**: let us 3766
144: 5 **B** thy heavens, O LORD, and come down: 5186
Pr 5: 1 *and* **b** thine ear to my understanding: 5186
14:19 The evil **b** before the good; and the wicked 7817
22:17 **B down** thine ear, and hear the words of 5186
Ecc 12: 3 the strong men shall **b** themselves, and 5791
Isa 10: 4 Without me they shall **b down** under 3766
21:15 from the bent **b**, and from the grievousness 7198
41: 2 *to* his sword, *and* as driven stubble *to* his **b**. 7198
45:23 not return, That unto me every knee shall **b**, 3766
46: 2 They stoop, they **b down** together; 3766
49:23 they shall **b down** to thee *with their* face 7812
51:23 to thy soul, **B down**, that we may go over: 7812
58: 5 *is it* to **b down** his head as a bulrush, and 3721
60:14 **b** themselves **down** at the soles of thy feet; 7812
65:12 and ye shall all **b down** to the slaughter: 3766
66:19 Pul, and Lud, that draw the **b**, *to* Tubal, and 7198
Jer 6:23 They shall lay hold on **b** and spear; they *are* 7198
9: 3 they bend their tongues *like* their **b** *for* lies: 7198
46: 9 the Lydians, that handle *and* bend the **b**. 7198
49:35 Behold, I *will* break the **b** of Elam, 7198
50:14 all ye that bend the **b**, shoot at her, spare no 7198
50:29 all ye that bend the **b**, camp against it round 7198
50:42 They shall hold the **b** and the lance: 7198
51: 3 *him that* bendeth let the archer bend his **b**, 7198
La 2: 4 He hath bent his **b** like an enemy: *he* stood 7198
3:12 He hath bent his **b**, and set me as a mark 7198
Eze 1:28 As the appearance of the **b** that is in 7198
39: 3 I will smite thy **b** out of thy left hand, and 7198
Hos 1: 5 that I will break the **b** of Israel in the valley 7198
1: 7 will not save them by **b**, nor by sword, 7198
2:18 I will break the **b** and the sword and 7198
7:16 they are like a deceitful **b**: their princes 7198
Am 2:15 Neither shall he stand that handleth the **b**; 7198
Mic 6: 6 *and* **b** myself before the high God? 3721
Hab 3: 6 were scattered, the perpetual hills did **b**: 7817
3: 9 Thy **b** was made quite naked, *according to* 7198

Zec 9:10 and the battle **b** shall be cut off: 7198
9:13 filled the **b** *with* Ephraim, and raised up thy 7198
10: 4 out of him the nail, out of him the battle **b**, 7198
Ro 11:10 may not see, and **b down** their back alway. *4781*
14:11 every knee shall **b** to me, and every tongue *2578*
Eph 3:14 For this cause I **b** my knees unto the Father *2578*
Php 2:10 at the name of Jesus every knee should **b**, *2578*
Rev 6: 2 and he that sat on him had a **b**; and a crown *5115*

BOWED (78) [BOW]

Ge 18: 2 tent door, and **b** himself toward the ground, 7812
19: 1 he **b** himself with his face toward 7812
23: 7 and **b** himself to the people of the land, 7812
23:12 Abraham **b down** himself before the people 7812
24:26 the man **b down** his **head**, and 6915
24:48 I **b down** my **head**, and worshipped 6915
33: 3 and **b** himself to the ground seven times, 7812
33: 6 and their children, and they **b** themselves. 7812
33: 7 her children came near, and **b** themselves: 7812
33: 7 and Rachel, and they **b** themselves. 7812
42: 6 **b down** themselves before him *with* their 7812
43:26 and **b** themselves to him to the earth. 7812
43:28 they **b down** their **heads**, and 6915
47:31 And Israel **b** himself upon the bed's head. 7812
48:12 and he **b** himself with his face to the earth. 7812
49:15 **b** his shoulder to bear, and became a 5186
Ex 4:31 then they **b** their **heads** and worshipped. 6915
12:27 the people **b the head** and worshipped. 6915
34: 8 **b** his **head** toward the earth, and 6915
Nu 22:31 he **b down** his **head**, and fell flat on his 6915
25: 2 people did eat, and **b down** to their gods. 7812
Jos 23:16 other gods, and **b** yourselves to them; 7812
Jdg 2:12 **b** themselves unto them, and provoked 7812
2:17 other gods, and **b** themselves unto them: 7812
5:27 At her feet he **b**, he fell, he lay down: at her 3766
5:27 at her feet he **b**, he fell: where he bowed, 3766
5:27 where he **b**, there he fell down dead. 3766
7: 6 all the rest of the people **b down** upon their 3766
16:30 he **b** *himself* with *all his* might; and 5186
Ru 2:10 **b** herself to the ground, and said unto him, 7812
1Sa 4:19 were dead, she **b** herself and travailed; 3766
20:41 to the ground, and **b** himself three times: 7812
24: 8 *with his* face to the earth, and **b** himself. 7812
25:23 on her face, and **b** herself *to* the ground, 7812
25:41 **b** herself *on her* face to the earth, and said, 7812
28:14 *with his* face to the ground, and **b** himself. 7812
2Sa 9: 8 he **b** himself, and said, What *is* thy servant, 7812
14:22 and **b** himself, and thanked the king: 7812
14:33 **b** himself on his face to the ground before 7812
18:21 And Cushi **b** himself unto Joab, and ran. 7812
19:14 he **b** the heart of all the men of Judah, 5186
22:10 He **b** the heavens also, and came down; and 5186
24:20 **b** himself before the king *on* his face upon 7812
1Ki 1:16 Bath-sheba **b**, and did obeisance unto 6915
1:23 he **b** himself before the king with his face 7812
1:31 Bath-sheba **b** *with her* face *to* the earth, 6915
1:47 And the king **b** himself upon the bed. 7812
1:53 he came and **b** himself to king Solomon: 7812
2:19 **b** himself unto her, and sat down on his 7812
19:18 all the knees which have not **b** unto Baal, 3766
2Ki 2:15 and **b** themselves to the ground before him. 7812
4:37 **b** herself to the ground, and took up her 7812
1Ch 21:21 **b** himself to David *with his* face to 7812
29:20 **b down** their **heads**, and worshipped 6915
2Ch 7: 3 they **b** themselves *with their* faces to 3766
20:18 Jehoshaphat **b** his **head** *with his* face to 6915
25:14 **b down** himself before them, and 7812
29:29 all that were present with him **b** 3766
29:30 and they **b** their **heads** and worshipped. 6915
Ne 8: 6 they **b** their **heads**, and worshipped 6915
Est 3: 2 the king's gate, **b**, and reverenced Haman: 3766
3: 2 But Mordecai **b** not, nor did *him* reverence. 3766
3: 5 And when Haman saw that Mordecai **b** not, 3766
Ps 18: 9 He **b** the heavens also, and came down: and 5186
35:14 I **b down** heavily, as one that mourneth for 7817
38: 6 I am troubled; I am **b down** greatly; I go 7817
44:25 For our soul is **b down** to the dust: 7743
57: 6 a net for my steps; my soul is **b down**: 3721
145:14 and raiseth up all those that be **b down**. 3721
146: 8 the LORD raiseth them that are **b down**: 3721
Isa 2:11 the haughtiness of men shall be **b down**, 7817
2:17 the loftiness of man shall be **b down**, and 7817
21: 3 I was **b down** at the hearing *of it;* I was 5753
Mt 27:29 and they **b the knee** before him, and *1120*
Lk 13:11 and was **b together**, and could in no wise *4794*
24: 5 and **b down** *their* faces to the earth, *2827*
Jn 19:30 and he **b** *his* head, and gave up the ghost. *2827*
Ro 11: 4 who have not **b** the knee to *the image of* *2578*

BOWELS (39)

Ge 15: 4 he that shall come forth out of thine own **b** 4578
25:23 of people shall be separated from thy **b**; 4578
43:30 for his **b** did yern upon his brother: 7356
Nu 5:22 that causeth the curse shall go into thy **b**, 4578
2Sa 7:12 which shall proceed out of thy **b**, and I will 4578
16:11 Behold, my son, which came forth of my **b**, 4578
20:10 fifth *rib,* and shed out his **b** to the ground, 4578
1Ki 3:26 for her **b** yerned upon her son, and she said, 7356
2Ch 21:15 have great sickness by disease of thy **b**, 4578
21:15 until thy **b** fall out by reason of the sickness 4578
21:18 after all this the LORD smote him in his **b** 4578
21:19 his **b** fell out by reason of his sickness: 4578
32:21 they that came forth of his own **b** slew him 4578
Job 20:14 *Yet* his meat in his **b** is turned, *it is* the gall 4578
30:27 My **b** boiled, and rested not: the days of 4578
Ps 22:14 like wax; it is melted in the midst of my **b**. 4578
71: 6 art he that took me out of my mother's **b**: 4578
109:18 so let it come into his **b** like water, and 7130
SS 5: 4 *of the door,* and my **b** were moved for him. 4578
Isa 16:11 Wherefore my **b** shall sound like a harp for 4578
48:19 the offspring of thy **b** like the gravel 4578
49: 1 from the **b** of my mother hath he made 4578
63:15 the sounding of thy **b** and of thy mercies 4578
Jer 4:19 My **b**, my bowels! I am pained *at* my very 4578
4:19 My bowels, my **b**! I am pained *at* my very 4578
31:20 therefore my **b** are troubled for him; I will 4578
La 1:20 my **b** are troubled; mine heart is turned 4578
2:11 eyes do fail with tears, my **b** are troubled, 4578
Eze 3: 3 and fill thy **b** with this roll that I give thee. 4578
7:19 not satisfy their souls, neither fill their **b**: 4578
Ac 1:18 in the midst, and all his **b** gushed out. *4698*
2Co 6:12 in us, but ye are straitened in your own **b**. *4698*
Php 1: 8 how *greatly* I long after you all in the **b** of *4698*
2: 1 of the Spirit, if any **b** and mercies, *4698*
Col 3:12 holy and beloved, **b** of mercies, kindness, *4698*
Phm 1: 7 the **b** of the saints are refreshed by thee, *4698*
1:12 therefore receive him, that is, mine own **b**: *4698*
1:20 thee in the Lord: refresh my **b** in the Lord. *4698*
1Jn 3:17 shutteth up his **b** *of compassion* from him, *4698*

BOWETH (3) [BOW]

Jdg 7: 5 likewise every one that **b down** upon his 3766
Isa 2: 9 the mean man **b down**, and the great man 7817
46: 1 Bel **b down**, Nebo stoopeth, their idols 3766

BOWING (4) [BOW]

Ge 24:52 the LORD, ***b** himself* to the earth. NIH
Ps 17:11 they have set their eyes **b down** to 5186
62: 3 as a **b** wall *shall ye be, and as* a tottering 5186
Mk 15:19 and **b** *their* knees worshipped him. *5087*

BOWL (17) [BOWLS]

Nu 7:13 thirty *shekels,* one silver **b** of seventy 4219
7:19 thirty *shekels,* one silver **b** of seventy 4219
7:25 thirty *shekels,* one silver **b** of seventy 4219
7:31 thirty *shekels,* one silver **b** of seventy 4219
7:37 thirty *shekels,* one silver **b** of seventy 4219
7:43 thirty *shekels,* a silver **b** of seventy shekels, 4219
7:49 thirty *shekels,* one silver **b** of seventy 4219
7:55 thirty *shekels,* one silver **b** of seventy 4219
7:61 thirty *shekels,* one silver **b** of seventy 4219
7:67 thirty *shekels,* one silver **b** of seventy 4219
7:73 thirty *shekels,* one silver **b** of seventy 4219
7:79 thirty *shekels,* one silver **b** of seventy 4219
7:85 and thirty *shekels,* each **b** seventy: 4219
Jdg 6:38 the dew out of the fleece, a **b** full *of* water. 5602
Ecc 12: 6 or the golden **b** be broken, or the pitcher be 1543
Zec 4: 2 with a **b** upon the top of it, and his seven 1531
4: 3 one upon the right *side* of the **b**, and 1543

BOWLS (24) [BOWL]

Ex 25:29 and covers thereof, and **b** thereof, 4518
25:31 his **b**, his knops, and his flowers, 1375
25:33 Three **b** made like unto almonds, *with* a 1375
25:33 three **b** made like almonds in the other 1375
25:34 in the candlestick *shall be* four **b** made like 1375
37:16 and his **b**, and *his* covers to cover withal, 4518
37:17 his **b**, his knops, and his flowers, 1375

Ex 37:19 Three **b** made after the fashion of almonds 1375
37:19 three **b** made like almonds in another 1375
37:20 in the candlestick *were* four **b** made like 1375
Nu 4: 7 and the **b**, and covers to cover withal: 4518
7:84 twelve silver **b**, twelve spoons of gold: 4219
1Ki 7:41 the two **b** of the chapiters that *were* on 1543
7:41 to cover the two **b** of the chapiters which 1543
7:42 to cover the two **b** of the chapiters that 1543
7:50 And the **b**, and the snuffers, and the basons, 5592
2Ki 12:13 *for* the house of the LORD **b** of silver, 5592
25:15 the **b**, *and* such *things* as *were of* gold, 4219
1Ch 28:17 *for* the fleshhooks, and the **b**, and the cups: 4219
Jer 52:18 the **b**, and the spoons, and all the vessels of 4219
52:19 the **b**, and the caldrons, and 4219
Am 6: 6 That drink wine in **b**, and 4219
Zec 9:15 they shall be filled like **b**, *and* as 4219
14:20 house shall be like the **b** before the altar. 4219

BOWMEN (1) [BOW, MAN]
Jer 4:29 for the noise of the horsemen and **b**; 7198+7411

BOWS (14) [BOW]
1Sa 2: 4 The **b** of the mighty *men are* broken, and 7198
1Ch 12: 2 *They were* armed with **b**, and could use 7198
2Ch 14: 8 that bare shields and drew **b**, two hundred 7198
26:14 and **b**, and slings to cast stones. 7198
Ne 4:13 with their swords, their spears, and their **b**. 7198
4:16 the shields, and the **b**, and the habergeons; 7198
Ps 37:15 their own heart, and their **b** shall be broken. 7198
64: 3 *and* bend *their* **b** *to shoot* their arrows, NIH
78: 9 of Ephraim, *being* armed, *and* carrying **b**, 7198
Isa 5:28 arrows *are* sharp, and all their **b** bent, 7198
7:24 and with **b** shall *men* come thither; 7198
13:18 *Their* **b** also shall dash the young men to 7198
Jer 51:56 are taken, *every one of* their **b** is broken: 7198
Eze 39: 9 the **b** and the arrows, and the handstaves, 7198

BOWSHOT (1) [BOW, SHOOT]
Ge 21:16 *him* a good way off, as it were a **b**: 2909+7198

BOX (8)
2Ki 9: 1 take this **b** of oil in thine hand, and go *to* 6378
9: 3 take the **b** of oil, and pour *it* on his head, 6378
Isa 41:19 *and* the pine, and the **b tree** together: 8391
60:13 fir tree, the pine tree, and the **b** together, 8391
Mt 26: 7 an **alabaster b** of very precious ointment, *211*
Mk 14: 3 there came a woman having an **alabaster b** *211*
14: 3 and she brake the **b**, and poured *it* on his *211*
Lk 7:37 brought an **alabaster b** of ointment, *211*

BOY (1) [BOYS]
Joel 3: 3 have given a **b** for a harlot, and sold a girl 3206

BOYS (2) [BOY]
Ge 25:27 the **b** grew: and Esau was a cunning hunter, 5288
Zec 8: 5 the streets of the city shall be full *of* **b** and 3206

BOYSTEROUS (1)
Mt 14:30 But when he saw the wind **b**, he was afraid; *2478*

BOZEZ (1)
1Sa 14: 4 the name of the one *was* **B**, and the name of 949

BOZKATH (1)
Jos 15:39 Lachish, and **B**, and Eglon, 1218

BOZRAH (9)
Ge 36:33 Jobab the son of Zerah of **B** reigned in his 1224
1Ch 1:44 Jobab the son of Zerah of **B** reigned in his 1224
Isa 34: 6 for the LORD hath a sacrifice in **B**, and 1224
63: 1 from Edom, with dyed garments from **B**? 1224
Jer 48:24 upon **B**, and upon all the cities of the land 1224
49:13 that **B** shall become a desolation, a 1224
49:22 as the eagle, and spread his wings over **B**: 1224
Am 1:12 which shall devour the palaces of **B**. 1224
Mic 2:12 I will put them together as the sheep of **B**, 1223

BRACELET (1) [BRACELETS]
2Sa 1:10 the **b** that *was* on his arm, and have brought 685

BRACELETS (10) [BRACELET]
Ge 24:22 two **b** for her hands of ten *shekels* weight 6781
24:30 the earring and **b** upon his sister's hands, 6781
24:47 upon her face, and the **b** upon her hands. 6781
38:18 thy **b**, and thy staff that *is* in thine hand. 6616
38:25 *are* these, the signet, and **b**, and staff. 6616
Ex 35:22 *and* brought **b**, and earrings, and rings, and 2397
Nu 31:50 chains, and **b**, rings, earrings, and tablets, 6781
Isa 3:19 The chains, and the **b**, and the mufflers, 8285
Eze 16:11 I put **b** upon thine hands, and a chain on thy 6781
23:42 which put **b** upon their hands, and 6781

BRAIDED See BROIDED; PLAITING

BRAIDS See LOCKS

BRAKE (73) [BREAK]
Ex 9:25 of the field, and **b** every tree of the field. 7665
32: 3 all the people **b off** the golden earrings 6561
32:19 his hands, and **b** them beneath the mount. 7665
Dt 9:17 two hands, and **b** them before your eyes. 7665
Jdg 7:19 and **b** the pitchers that *were* in their hands. 5310
7:20 **b** the pitchers, and held the lamps in their 7665
9:53 Abimelech's head, and **all to b** his skull. 7533
16: 9 he **b** the withs, as a thread of tow is broken 5423
16:12 he **b** them from off his arms like a thread. 5423
1Sa 4:18 of the gate, and his neck **b**, and he died: 7665
2Sa 23:16 the three mighty *men* **b** through the host of 1234
1Ki 19:11 **b in pieces** the rocks before the LORD; 7665
2Ki 10:27 they **b down** the image of Baal, and 5422
10:27 **b down** the house of Baal, and made it a 5422
11:18 went *into* the house of Baal, and **b** it **down**; 5422
11:18 and his images **b** they **in pieces** throughly, 7665
14:13 **b down** the wall of Jerusalem from the gate 6555
18: 4 **b** the images, and cut down the groves, and 7665
18: 4 **b in pieces** the brasen serpent that Moses 3807
23: 7 he **b down** the houses of the sodomites, 5422
23: 8 **b down** the high places of the gates that 5422
23:12 **b** *them* **down** from thence, and cast the dust 7323
23:14 he **b in pieces** the images, and cut down 7665
23:15 that altar and the high place he **b down**, 5422
25:10 **b down** the walls of Jerusalem round 5422
1Ch 11:18 the three **b** through the host of 1234
2Ch 14: 3 **b down** the images, and cut down 7665
21:17 **b into** it, and carried away all the substance 1234
23:17 **b** it **down**, and brake his altars and his 5422
23:17 **b** his altars and his images **in pieces**, and 7665
25:23 **b down** the wall of Jerusalem from the gate 6555
26: 6 **b down** the wall of Gath, and the wall of 6555
31: 1 **b** the images *in pieces*, and cut down 7665
34: 4 they **b down** the altars of Baalim in his 5422
34: 4 he **b** *in pieces*, and made dust *of them*, and 7665
36:19 **b down** the wall of Jerusalem, and burnt all 5422
Job 29:17 I **b** the jaws of the wicked, and pluckt 7665
38: 8 shut up the sea with doors, when it **b forth**, 1518
38:10 **b up** for it my decreed *place*, and set bars 7665
Ps 76: 3 There **b** he the arrows of the bow, 7665
105:16 the land: he **b** the whole staff of bread. 7665
105:33 fig trees; and **b** the trees of their coasts. 7665
106:29 and the plague **b in** upon them. 6555
107:14 of death, and **b** their bands **in sunder**. 5423
Jer 28:10 off the prophet Jeremiah's neck, and **b** it. 7665
31:32 which my covenant they **b**, although I was 6565
39: 8 and **b down** the walls of Jerusalem. 5422
52:14 **b down** all the walls of Jerusalem round 5422
52:17 the Chaldeans **b**, and carried all the brass of 7665
Eze 17:16 oath he despised, and whose covenant he **b**, 6565
Da 2: 1 was troubled, and his sleep **b** from him. 1961
2:34 of iron and clay, and **b** them **in pieces**. 1855
2:45 *that* it **b in pieces** the iron, the brass, 1855
6:24 **b** all their bones **in pieces** or ever they 1855
7: 7 it devoured and **b in pieces**, and 1855
7:19 **b in pieces**, and stamped the residue with 1855
8: 7 and smote the ram, and **b** his two horns: 7665
Mt 14:19 and **b**, and gave the loaves to *his* disciples, *2806*
15:36 and **b** *them,* and gave to his disciples, and *2806*
26:26 and blessed *it,* and **b** *it,* and gave *it* to *2806*
Mk 6:41 and **b** the loaves, and gave *them* to his *2622*
8: 6 and **b**, and gave to his disciples to set *2806*
8:19 When I **b** the five loaves among five *2806*
14: 3 and she **b** the box, and poured *it* on his *4937*
14:22 and **b** *it,* and gave to them, and said, Take, *2806*
Lk 5: 6 a great multitude of fishes: and their net **b**. *1284*
8:29 and he **b** the bands, and was driven of *1284*
9:16 and **b**, and gave to the disciples to set *2622*
22:19 and **b** *it,* and gave unto them, saying, *2806*
24:30 and blessed *it,* and **b**, and gave to them. *2806*
Jn 19:32 and **b** the legs of the first, and of the other *2608*
19:33 he was dead already, they **b** not his legs: *2608*

1Co 11:24 given thanks, he **b** *it,* and said, Take, eat: *2806*

BRAKEST (5) [BREAK]

Ex 34: 1 that were in the first tables, which thou **b**. 7665
Dt 10: 2 that were in the first tables which thou **b**, 7665
Ps 74:13 thou **b** the heads of the dragons in 7665
74:14 Thou **b** the heads of leviathan **in pieces**, 7533
Eze 29: 7 thou **b**, and madest all their loins to be at a 7665

BRAMBLE (4) [BRAMBLES]

Jdg 9:14 said all the trees unto the **b**, Come thou, 329
9:15 the **b** said unto the trees, If in truth ye anoint 329
9:15 let fire come out of the **b**, and devour 329
Lk 6:44 nor of a **b bush** gather they grapes. *942*

BRAMBLES (1) [BRAMBLE]

Isa 34:13 nettles and **b** in the fortresses thereof: 2336

BRANCH (37) [BRANCHES]

Ex 25:33 *with* a knop and a flower in one **b**; 7070
25:33 bowls made like almonds in the other **b**, 7070
37:17 his shaft, and his **b**, his bowls, his knops, 7070
37:19 made after the fashion of almonds in one **b**, 7070
37:19 bowls made like almonds in another **b**, 7070
Nu 13:23 cut down from thence a **b** with one cluster 2156
Job 8:16 and his **b** shooteth forth in his garden, 3127
14: 7 and that the **tender b** thereof will not cease. 3127
15:32 his time, and his **b** shall not be green. 3712
18:16 and above shall his **b** be cut off. 7105
29:19 and the dew lay all night upon my **b**. 7105
Ps 80:15 the **b** *that* thou madest strong for thyself. 1121
Pr 11:28 but the righteous shall flourish as a **b**. 5929
Isa 4: 2 In that day shall the **b** of the LORD be 6780
9:14 off from Israel head and tail, **b** and rush, 3712
11: 1 and a **B** shall grow out of his roots: 5342
14:19 cast out of thy grave like an abominable **b**, 5342
17: 9 and an uppermost **b**, which they left because 534
19:15 which the head or tail, **b** or rush, may do. 3712
25: 5 the **b** of the terrible ones shall be brought 2159
60:21 the **b** of my planting, the work of my 5342
Jer 23: 5 that I will raise unto David a righteous **B**, 6780
33:15 will I cause the **B** of righteousness to grow 6780
Eze 8:17 and lo, they put the **b** to their nose. 2156
15: 2 *than* a **b** which is among the trees of 2156
17: 3 and took the **highest b** of the cedar: 6788
17:22 I will also take of the **highest b** of the high 6788
Da 11: 7 out of a **b** of her roots shall *one* stand up *in* 5342
Zec 3: 8 I *will* bring forth my servant the **B**. 6780
6:12 Behold the man whose name *is* The **B**; 6780
Mal 4: 1 that it shall leave them neither root nor **b**. 6057
Mt 24:32 When his **b** is yet tender, and putteth forth *2798*
Mk 13:28 When her **b** is yet tender, and putteth forth *2798*
Jn 15: 2 Every **b** in me that beareth not fruit he *2814*
15: 2 and every *b* that beareth fruit, he purgeth it, NIG
15: 4 As the **b** cannot bear fruit of itself, except it *2814*
15: 6 he is cast forth as a **b**, and is withered; *2814*

BRANCHES (75) [BRANCH]

Ge 40:10 in the vine *were* three **b**: and it *was* as 8299
40:12 of it: The three **b** *are* three days: 8299
49:22 by a well; *whose* **b** run over the wall. 1323
Ex 25:31 his shaft, and his **b**, his bowls, his knops, 7070
25:32 six **b** shall come out of the sides of it; 7070
25:32 three **b** of the candlestick out of the one 7070
25:32 three **b** of the candlestick out of the other 7070
25:33 in the six **b** that come out of 7070
25:35 *there shall be* a knop under two **b** of 7070
25:35 a knop under two **b** of the same, and a knop 7070
25:35 and a knop under two **b** of the same, 7070
25:35 according to the six **b** that proceed out of 7070
25:36 and their **b** shall be of the same: 7070
37:18 six **b** going out of the sides thereof; 7070
37:18 three **b** of the candlestick out of the one 7070
37:18 three **b** of the candlestick out of the other 7070
37:19 throughout the six **b** going out of 7070
37:21 a knop under two **b** of the same, and a knop 7070
37:21 a knop under two **b** of the same, and a knop 7070
37:21 and a knop under two **b** of the same, 7070
37:21 according to the six **b** going out of it. 7070
37:22 Their knops and their **b** were of the same: 7070
Lev 23:40 **b** of palm trees, and the boughs of thick 3709
Ne 8:15 fetch olive **b**, and pine branches, and 5929
8:15 pine **b**, and myrtle branches, and 6086
8:15 myrtle **b**, and palm branches, and 5929
8:15 palm **b**, and branches of thick trees, 5929
8:15 palm branches, and **b** of thick trees, 5929
Job 15:30 the flame shall dry up his **b**, and by 3127
Ps 80:11 unto the sea, and her **b** unto the river. 3127
104:12 their habitation, *which* sing among the **b**. 6073
Isa 16: 8 her **b** are stretched out, they are gone over 7976
17: 6 *or* five in the outmost fruitful **b** thereof, 5585
18: 5 and take away *and* cut down the **b**. 5189
27:10 he lie down, and consume the **b** thereof. 5585
Jer 11:16 fire upon it, and the **b** of it are broken. 1808
Eze 17: 6 whose **b** turned toward him, and the roots 1808
17: 6 and brought forth **b**, and shot forth sprigs. 905
17: 7 and shot forth her **b** toward him, 1808
17: 8 that *it* might bring forth **b**, and that *it* might 6057
17:23 in the shadow of the **b** thereof shall they 1808
19:10 and **full of b** by reason of many waters. 6058
19:11 her stature was exalted among the **thick b**, 5688
19:11 in her height with the multitude of her **b**. 1808
19:14 fire is gone out of a rod of her **b**, *which* hath 905
31: 3 *was* a cedar in Lebanon with fair **b**, 6057
31: 5 his **b** became long because of the multitude 6288
31: 6 under his **b** did all the beasts of the field 6288
31: 7 fair in his greatness, in the length of his **b**: 1808
31: 8 and the chesnut trees were not like his **b**; 6288
31: 9 made him fair by the multitude of his **b**: 1808
31:12 and in all the valleys his **b** are fallen, 1808
31:13 the beasts of the field shall be upon his **b**: 6288
36: 8 ye shall shoot forth your **b**, and yield your 6057
Da 4:14 Hew down the tree, and cut off his **b**, 6056
4:14 from under it, and the fowls from his **b**: 6056
4:21 upon whose **b** the fowls of the heaven had 6056
Hos 11: 6 shall consume his **b**, and devour *them,* 905
14: 6 His **b** shall spread, and his beauty shall be 3127
Joel 1: 7 cast *it* away; the **b** thereof are made white. 8299
Na 2: 2 emptied them out, and marred their **vine b**. 2156
Zec 4:12 What *be these* two olive **b** which through 7641
Mt 13:32 of the air come and lodge in the **b** thereof. *2798*
21: 8 others cut down **b** from the trees, and *2798*
Mk 4:32 than all herbs, and shooteth out great **b**; *2798*
11: 8 and others cut down **b** off the trees, *4746*
Lk 13:19 the fowls of the air lodged in the **b** of it. *2798*
Jn 12:13 Took **b** of palm trees, and went forth to meet *902*
15: 5 I am the vine, ye *are* the **b**: He that abideth *2814*
Ro 11:16 and if the root *be* holy, so *are* the **b**. *2798*
11:17 And if some of the **b** be broken off, and *2798*
11:18 Boast not against the **b**: but if thou boast, *2798*
11:19 Thou wilt say then, The **b** were broken off, *2798*
11:21 For if God spared not the natural **b**, *2798*
11:24 which be the natural *b*, be graffed into their NIG

BRAND (1) [BRANDS, FIREBRAND, FIREBRANDS]

Zec 3: 2 *is* not this a **b** pluckt out of the fire? 181

BRANDISH (1)

Eze 32:10 when I shall **b** my sword before them; 5774

BRANDS (1) [BRAND]

Jdg 15: 5 when he had set the **b** on fire, he let *them* 3940

BRASEN (29) [BRASS]

Ex 27: 4 upon the net shalt thou make four **b** rings in 5178
35:16 The altar of burnt offering with his **b** grate, 5178
38: 4 he made for the altar a **b** grate of network 5178
38:10 *were* twenty, and their **b** sockets twenty; 5178
38:30 the **b** altar, and the brasen grate for it, and 5178
38:30 the **b** grate for it, and all the vessels of 5178
39:39 The **b** altar, and his grate of brass, his 5178
Lev 6:28 if it be sodden in a **b** pot, it shall be both 5178
Nu 16:39 Eleazar the priest took the **b** censers, 5178
1Ki 4:13 great cities *with* walls and **b** bars: 5178
7:30 every base had four **b** wheels, and plates of 5178
8:64 the **b** altar that *was* before the LORD *was* 5178
14:27 king Rehoboam made in their stead **b** 5178
2Ki 16:14 he brought also the **b** altar, which *was* 5178
16:15 the **b** altar shall be for me to inquire *by.* 5178
16:17 took down the sea from off the **b** oxen that 5178
18: 4 brake in pieces the **b** serpent that Moses 5178
25:13 the **b** sea that *was* in the house of 5178
1Ch 18: 8 wherewith Solomon made the **b** sea, and 5178
2Ch 1: 5 Moreover the **b** altar, that Bezaleel the son 5178
1: 6 Solomon went up thither to the **b** altar 5178
6:13 For Solomon had made a **b** scaffold, of five 5178
7: 7 the **b** altar which Solomon had made was 5178
Jer 1:18 and **b** walls against the whole land, 5178

Jer 15:20 I will make thee unto this people a fenced **b** 5178
52:17 the **b** sea that *was* in the house of 5178
52:20 twelve **b** bulls that *were* under the bases, 5178
Eze 9: 2 they went in, and stood beside the **b** altar. 5178
Mk 7: 4 of cups, and pots, **b vessels**, and of tables. *5473*

BRASS (126) [BRASEN]
Ge 4:22 an instructor of every artificer in **b** and 5178
Ex 25: 3 shall take of them; gold, and silver, and **b**, 5178
26:11 thou shalt make fifty taches of **b**, and 5178
26:37 thou shalt cast five sockets of **b** for them. 5178
27: 2 the same: and thou shalt overlay it with **b**. 5178
27: 3 all the vessels thereof thou shalt make *of* **b**. 5178
27: 4 shalt make for it a grate of network *of* **b**; 5178
27: 6 of shittim wood, and overlay them with **b**. 5178
27:10 and their twenty sockets *shall be of* **b**; 5178
27:11 twenty pillars and their twenty sockets *of* **b**; 5178
27:17 *shall be of* silver, and their sockets *of* **b**. 5178
27:18 *of* fine twined linen, and their sockets *of* **b**. 5178
27:19 and all the pins of the court, *shall be of* **b**. 5178
30:18 Thou shalt also make a laver *of* **b**, and 5178
30:18 his foot *also of* **b**, to wash *withal:* and 5178
31: 4 to work in gold, and in silver, and in **b**, 5178
35: 5 of the LORD; gold, and silver, and **b**, 5178
35:24 and **b** brought the LORD'S offering: 5178
35:32 to work in gold, and in silver, and in **b**, 5178
36:18 he made fifty taches of **b** to couple the tent 5178
36:38 with gold: but their five sockets *were of* **b**. 5178
38: 2 were of the same: and he overlaid it with **b**. 5178
38: 3 all the vessels thereof made he *of* **b**. 5178
38: 5 rings for the four ends of the grate of **b**, 5178
38: 6 *of* shittim wood, and overlaid them with **b**. 5178
38: 8 he made the laver *of* **b**, and the foot of it *of* 5178
38: 8 the laver *of* brass, and the foot of it *of* **b**, 5178
38:11 *were* twenty, and their sockets *of* **b** twenty; 5178
38:17 the sockets for the pillars *were of* **b**; 5178
38:19 *were* four, and their sockets *of* **b** four; 5178
38:20 and of the court round about, *were of* **b**. 5178
38:29 the **b** of the offering *was* seventy talents, 5178
39:39 his grate of **b**, his staves, and all his 5178
Lev 26:19 your heaven as iron, and your earth as **b**: 5154
Nu 21: 9 Moses made a serpent of **b**, and put it upon 5178
21: 9 when he beheld the serpent of **b**, he lived. 5178
31:22 the **b**, the iron, the tin, and the lead, 5178
Dt 8: 9 and out of whose hills thou mayest dig **b**. 5178
28:23 thy heaven that *is* over thy head shall be **b**, 5178
33:25 Thy shoes *shall be* iron and **b**; and as thy 5178
Jos 6:19 and gold, and vessels of **b** and iron, 5178
6:24 the gold, and the vessels of **b** and of iron, 5178
22: 8 with **b**, and with iron, and with very much 5178
Jdg 16:21 to Gaza, and bound him with **fetters of b**; 5178
1Sa 17: 5 *he had* a helmet of **b** upon his head, and 5178
17: 5 of the coat *was* five thousand shekels *of* **b**. 5178
17: 6 *he had* greaves of **b** upon his legs, and 5178
17: 6 and a target of **b** between his shoulders. 5178
17:38 and he put a helmet of **b** upon his head; 5178
2Sa 8: 8 king David took exceeding much **b**. 5178
8:10 and vessels of gold, and vessels of **b**: 5178
21:16 three hundred *shekels* of **b** *in* weight, 5178
1Ki 7:14 his father *was* a man of Tyre, a worker in **b**: 5178
7:14 and cunning to work all works in **b**. 5178
7:15 For he cast two pillars *of* **b**, of eighteen 5178
7:16 he made two chapiters *of* molten **b**, to set 5178
7:27 he made ten bases of **b**; four cubits *was* 5178
7:30 had four brasen wheels, and plates of **b**: 5178
7:38 made he ten lavers of **b**: one laver 5178
7:45 the house of the LORD, *were of* bright **b**. 5178
7:47 neither was the weight of the **b** found out. 5178
2Ki 25: 7 bound him with **fetters of b**, and 5178
25:13 the pillars of **b** that *were in* the house of 5178
25:13 and carried the **b** of them to Babylon. 5178
25:14 all the vessels of **b** wherewith they 5178
25:16 the **b** of all these vessels was without 5178
25:17 and the chapiter upon it *was* **b**: 5178
25:17 upon the chapiter round about, all *of* **b**: 5178
1Ch 15:19 *were appointed* to sound with cymbals of **b**; 5178
18: 8 of Hadarezer, brought David very much **b**, 5178
18: 8 and the pillars, and the vessels of **b**. 5178
18:10 *manner of* vessels of gold and silver and **b**. 5178
22: 3 and **b** in abundance without weight; 5178
22:14 of **b** and iron without weight; for it is in 5178
22:16 the gold, the silver, and the **b**, and the iron, 5178
29: 2 the **b** for *things of* brass, the iron for *things* 5178
29: 2 the brass for *things of* **b**, the iron for *things* 5178
29: 7 *of* **b** eighteen thousand talents, and 5178
2Ch 2: 7 in **b**, and in iron, and in purple, and 5178
2:14 in **b**, in iron, in stone, and in timber, 5178
4: 1 Moreover he made an altar of **b**, 5178
4: 9 and overlaid the doors of them with **b**. 5178
4:16 for the house of the LORD *of* bright **b**. 5178
4:18 for the weight of the **b** could not be found 5178
12:10 which king Rehoboam made shields of **b**, 5178
24:12 and **b** to mend the house of the LORD. 5178
Job 6:12 the strength of stones? or *is* my flesh of **b**? 5153
28: 2 the earth, and **b** *is* molten *out of* the stone. 5154
40:18 His bones *are as* strong pieces of **b**; 5154
41:27 iron as straw, *and* **b** as rotten wood. 5154
Ps 107:16 For he hath broken the gates of **b**, and 5178
Isa 45: 2 I will break in pieces the gates of **b**, and 5154
48: 4 thy neck *is* an iron sinew, and thy brow **b**: 5154
60:17 For **b** I will bring gold, and for iron I will 5178
60:17 and for wood **b**, and for stones iron: 5178
Jer 6:28 *they are* **b** and iron; they *are* all corrupters. 5178
52:17 Also the pillars of **b** that *were* in the house 5178
52:17 and carried all the **b** of them to Babylon. 5178
52:18 all the vessels of **b** wherewith they 5178
52:20 the **b** of all these vessels was without 5178
52:22 a chapiter of **b** *was* upon it; and the height 5178
52:22 upon the chapiters round about, all *of* **b**. 5178
Eze 1: 7 sparkled like the colour of burnished **b**. 5178
22:18 all they *are* **b**, and tin, and iron, and lead, 5178
22:20 and **b**, and iron, and lead, and tin, 5178
24:11 that the **b** of it may be hot, and may burn, 5178
27:13 of men and vessels of **b** in thy market. 5178
40: 3 appearance *was* like the appearance of **b**, 5178
Da 2:32 arms of silver, his belly and his thighs of **b**, 5174
2:35 the clay, the **b**, the silver, and the gold, 5174
2:39 another third kingdom of **b**, which shall 5174
2:45 the **b**, the clay, the silver, and the gold; 5174
4:15 even with a band of iron and **b**, in 5174
4:23 even with a band of iron and **b**, in 5174
5: 4 of **b**, of iron, of wood, and of stone. 5174
5:23 gold, of **b**, iron, wood, and stone, which see 5174
7:19 whose teeth *were of* iron, and his nails *of* **b**; 5174
10: 6 and his feet like in colour to polished **b**, 5178
Mic 4:13 horn iron, and I will make thy hoofs **b**: 5154
Zec 6: 1 and the mountains *were* mountains of **b**. 5178
Mt 10: 9 nor silver, nor **b** in your purses; *5475*
1Co 13: 1 I am become *as* sounding **b**, or a tinkling *5475*
Rev 1:15 And his feet like unto **fine b**, as if they *5474*
2:18 a flame of fire, and his feet *are* like **fine b**; *5474*
9:20 idols of gold, and silver, and **b**, and stone, *5470*
18:12 and of **b**, and iron, and marble, *5475*

BRAVE See VALIANT; VALOUR

BRAVERY (1)
Isa 3:18 In that day the Lord will take away the **b** of 8597

BRAWLER (1) [BRAWLERS, BRAWLING]
1Ti 3: 3 but patient, **not a b**, not covetous; *269*

BRAWLERS (1) [BRAWLER]
Tit 3: 2 To speak evil of no *man,* to be **no b**, *but* *269*

BRAWLING (2) [BRAWLER]
Pr 21: 9 than with a **b** woman in a wide house. 4066
25:24 than with a **b** woman and in a wide house. 4066

BRAY (2) [BRAYED]
Job 6: 5 Doth the wild ass **b** when he hath grass? or 5101
Pr 27:22 Though thou shouldest **b** a fool in a mortar 3806

BRAYED (1) [BRAY]
Job 30: 7 Among the bushes they **b**; under the nettles 5101

BRAZEN See IMPUDENT

BREACH (22) [BREACHES]
Ge 38:29 *this* **b** *be* upon thee: therefore his name was 6556
Lev 24:20 **B** for breach, eye for eye, tooth for tooth: 7667
24:20 Breach for **b**, eye for eye, tooth for tooth: 7667
Nu 14:34 and ye shall know my **b of promise**. 8569
Jdg 21:15 that the LORD had made a **b** in the tribes 6556
2Sa 5:20 enemies before me, as the **b** of waters. 6556
6: 8 LORD had **made a b** upon Uzzah: 6555+6556
2Ki 12: 5 the house, wheresoever any **b** shall be found. 919
1Ch 13:11 LORD had **made a b** upon Uzza: 6555+6556
15:13 the LORD our God **made a b** upon us, 6555

Ne 6: 1 and *that* there was no **b** left therein; 6556
Job 16:14 He breaketh me *with* **b** upon breach, 6556
16:14 He breaketh me *with* breach upon **b**, 6556
Ps 106:23 his chosen stood before him in the **b**, 6556
Pr 15: 4 but perverseness therein *is* a **b** in the spirit. 7667
Isa 7: 6 let us **make a b** therein for us, and set a 1234
30:13 iniquity shall be to you as a **b** ready to fall, 6556
30:26 in the day that the LORD bindeth up the **b** 7667
58:12 thou shalt be called, The repairer of the **b**, 6556
Jer 14:17 of my people is broken *with* a great **b**, 7667
La 2:13 for thy **b** *is* great like the sea: who can heal 7667
Eze 26:10 men enter into a city wherein is **made a b**. 1234

BREACHES (15) [BREACH]
Jdg 5:17 on the sea shore, and abode in his **b**. 4664
1Ki 11:27 repaired the **b** of the city of David his 6556
2Ki 12: 5 let them repair the **b** of the house, 919
12: 6 priests had not repaired the **b** of the house. 919
12: 7 Why repair ye not the **b** of the house? 919
12: 7 but deliver it for the **b** of the house. 919
12: 8 neither to repair the **b** of the house. 919
12:12 hewed stone to repair the **b** of the house of 919
22: 5 of the LORD, to repair the **b** of the house, 919
Ne 4: 7 *and* that the **b** began to be stopped, then 6555
Ps 60: 2 broken it: heal the **b** thereof; for it shaketh. 7667
Isa 22: 9 Ye have seen also the **b** of the city of 1233
Am 4: 3 ye shall go out *at* the **b**, every *cow at that* 6556
6:11 he will smite the great house *with* **b**, and 7447
9:11 that is fallen, and close up the **b** thereof; 6556

BREAD (361) [SHEWBREAD]
Ge 3:19 In the sweat of thy face shalt thou eat **b**, 3899
14:18 Melchizedek king of Salem brought forth **b** 3899
18: 5 I will fetch a morsel of **b**, and comfort ye 3899
19: 3 did bake **unleavened b**, and they did eat. 4682
21:14 took **b**, and a bottle of water, and gave *it* 3899
25:34 Jacob gave Esau **b** and pottage of lentiles; 3899
27:17 she gave the savoury meat and the **b**, 3899
28:20 will give me **b** to eat, and raiment to put on, 3899
31:54 the mount, and called his brethren to eat **b**: 3899
31:54 they did eat **b**, and tarried all night in 3899
37:25 they sat down to eat **b**: and they lift up their 3899
39: 6 ought he had, save the **b** which he did eat. 3899
41:54 but in all the land of Egypt there was **b**. 3899
41:55 the people cried to Pharaoh for **b**: 3899
43:25 for they heard that they should eat **b** there. 3899
43:31 and refrained himself, and said, Set on **b**. 3899
43:32 the Egyptians might not eat **b** with 3899
45:23 ten she asses laden with corn and **b** and 3899
47:12 and all his father's household, *with* **b**, 3899
47:13 *there was* no **b** in all the land; for 3899
47:15 came unto Joseph, and said, Give us **b**: 3899
47:17 Joseph gave them **b** *in exchange* for horses, 3899
47:17 he fed them with **b** for all their cattle for 3899
47:19 buy us and our land for **b**, and we and 3899
49:20 Out of Asher his **b** *shall be* fat, and he shall 3899
Ex 2:20 left the man? call him, that he may eat **b**. 3899
12: 8 roast with fire, and **unleavened b**; 4682
12:15 Seven days shall ye eat **unleavened b**; 4682
12:15 for whosoever eateth **leavened b** from 2557
12:17 ye shall observe the *feast of* **unleavened b**; 4682
12:18 ye shall eat **unleavened b**, until the one and 4682
12:20 your habitations shall ye eat **unleavened b**. 4682
13: 3 *place:* there shall no **leavened b** be eaten. 2557
13: 6 Seven days thou shalt eat **unleavened b**, 4682
13: 7 **Unleavened b** shall be eaten seven days; 4682
13: 7 there shall no **leavened b** be seen with thee, 2557
16: 3 *and* when we did eat **b** to the full; 3899
16: 4 Behold, I will rain **b** from heaven for you; 3899
16: 8 to eat, and in the morning **b** to the full; 3899
16:12 and in the morning ye shall be filled *with* **b**; 3899
16:15 This *is* the **b** which the LORD hath given 3899
16:22 sixth day they gathered twice as much **b**, 3899
16:29 he giveth you on the sixth day the **b** of two 3899
16:32 that they may see the **b** wherewith I have 3899
18:12 to eat **b** with Moses' father in law before 3899
23:15 Thou shalt keep the feast of **unleavened b**: 4682
23:15 thou shalt eat **unleavened b** seven days, 4682
23:18 the blood of my sacrifice with **leavened b**; 2557
23:25 and he shall bless thy **b**, and thy water; 3899
29: 2 unleavened **b**, and cakes unleavened 3899
29:23 one loaf of **b**, and one cake of oiled bread, 3899
29:23 one cake of oiled **b**, and one wafer out of 3899
29:23 **unleavened b** that *is* before the LORD: 4682
29:32 of the ram, and the **b** that *is* in the basket, 3899
29:34 or of the **b**, remain unto the morning, then 3899
34:18 The feast of **unleavened b** shalt thou keep: 4682
34:18 seven days thou shalt eat **unleavened b**, 4682
34:28 he did neither eat **b**, nor drink water. 3899
40:23 he set the **b** in order upon it before 3899
Lev 6:16 *with* **unleavened b** shall it be eaten in 4682
7:13 he shall offer *for* his offering leavened **b** 3899
8: 2 two rams, and a basket of **unleavened b**; 4682
8:26 out of the basket of **unleavened b**, that *was* 4682
8:26 a cake of oiled **b**, and one wafer, and 3899
8:31 there eat it with the **b** that *is* in the basket of 3899
8:32 and of the **b** shall ye burn with fire. 3899
21: 6 *and* the **b** of their God, they do offer: 3899
21: 8 for he offereth the **b** of thy God: 3899
21:17 let him not approach to offer the **b** of his 3899
21:21 he shall not come nigh to offer the **b** of his 3899
21:22 He shall eat the **b** of his God, *both* of 3899
22:25 ye offer the **b** of your God of any of these; 3899
23: 6 the feast of **unleavened b** unto the LORD: 4682
23: 6 seven days ye must eat **unleavened b**. 4682
23:14 ye shall eat neither **b**, nor parched *corn*, nor 3899
23:18 ye shall offer with the **b** seven lambs 3899
23:20 the priest shall wave them with the **b** of 3899
24: 7 that it may be on the **b** for a memorial, 3899
26: 5 ye shall eat your **b** to the full, and dwell in 3899
26:26 when I have broken the staff of your **b**, 3899
26:26 ten women shall bake your **b** in one oven, 3899
26:26 they shall deliver *you* your **b** again by 3899
Nu 4: 7 and the continual **b** shall be thereon: 3899
6:15 a basket of **unleavened b**, cakes *of* fine 4682
6:15 wafers of **unleavened b** anointed with oil, 4682
6:17 with the basket of **unleavened b**: 4682
9:11 *and* eat it with **unleavened b** and 4682
14: 9 the people of the land; for they *are* **b** for us: 3899
15:19 *that* when ye eat of the **b** of the land, 3899
21: 5 for *there is* no **b**, neither *is there any* water; 3899
21: 5 and our soul loatheth *this* light **b**. 3899
28: 2 *and* my **b** for my sacrifices made by fire, 3899
28:17 seven days shall **unleavened b** be eaten. 4682
Dt 8: 3 thee know that man doth not live by **b** only, 3899
8: 9 A land wherein thou shalt eat **b** without 3899
9: 9 I neither did eat **b** nor drink water: 3899
9:18 I did neither eat **b**, nor drink water, because 3899
16: 3 Thou shalt eat no **leavened b** with it; 2557
16: 3 seven days shalt thou eat **unleavened b** 4682
16: 3 bread therewith, *even* the **b** of affliction; 3899
16: 4 there shall be no **leavened b** seen with thee 7603
16: 8 Six days thou shalt eat **unleavened b**: and 4682
16:16 in the feast of **unleavened b**, and in 4682
23: 4 Because they met you not with **b** and 3899
29: 6 Ye have not eaten **b**, neither have you 3899
Jos 9: 5 all the **b** of their provision was dry *and* 3899
9:12 This our **b** we took hot for our provision 3899
Jdg 7:13 a cake of barley **b** tumbled into the host of 3899
8: 5 loaves of **b** unto the people that follow me; 3899
8: 6 that we should give **b** unto thine army? 3899
8:15 that we should give **b** unto thy men *that are* 3899
13:16 thou detain me, I will not eat of thy **b**: 3899
19: 5 Comfort thine heart *with* a morsel of **b**, and 3899
19:19 there is **b** and wine also for me, and for thy 3899
Ru 1: 6 had visited his people in giving them **b**. 3899
2:14 eat of the **b**, and dip thy morsel in 3899
1Sa 2: 5 *were* full have hired out themselves for **b**; 3899
2:36 him for a piece of silver and a morsel of **b**, 3899
2:36 priests' offices, that *I* may eat a piece of **b**. 3899
9: 7 for the **b** is spent in our vessels, and *there is* 3899
10: 3 another carrying three loaves of **b**, and 3899
10: 4 salute thee, and give thee two *loaves* of **b**; 3899
16:20 Jesse took an ass *laden* with **b**, and a bottle 3899
21: 3 give *me* five *loaves of* **b** in mine hand, or 3899
21: 4 *There is* no common **b** under mine hand, 3899
21: 4 under mine hand, but there is hallowed **b**; 3899
21: 5 and *the* **b** *is in* a manner common, yea, NIH
21: 6 So the priest gave him hallowed *b*: for there NIH
21: 6 hallowed *bread:* for there was no **b** there 3899
21: 6 to put hot **b** in the day when it was taken 3899
22:13 in that thou hast given him **b** and a sword, 3899
25:11 Shall I then take my **b**, and my water, and 3899
28:20 for he had eaten no **b** all the day, nor all 3899
28:22 and let me set a morsel of **b** before thee; 3899
28:24 and did bake **unleavened b** thereof: 4682
30:11 to David, and gave him **b**, and he did eat; 3899
30:12 for he had eaten no **b**, nor drunk *any* water, 3899

2Sa	3:29	that falleth on the sword, or that lacketh **b**.	3899
	3:35	and more also, if I taste **b**, or ought else,	3899
	6:19	to every one a cake of **b**, and a good piece	3899
	9: 7	and thou shalt eat **b** at my table continually.	3899
	9:10	Mephibosheth thy master's son shall eat **b**	3899
	12:17	would not, neither did he eat **b** with them.	3899
	12:20	they set **b** before him, and he did eat.	3899
	12:21	child was dead, thou didst rise and eat **b**.	3899
	16: 1	upon them two hundred *loaves of* **b**, and	3899
	16: 2	the **b** and summer fruit for the young men	3899
1Ki	13: 8	neither will I eat **b** nor drink water in this	3899
	13: 9	saying, Eat no **b**, nor drink water,	3899
	13:15	unto him, Come home with me, and eat **b**.	3899
	13:16	neither will I eat **b** nor drink water with	3899
	13:17	Thou shalt eat no **b** nor drink water there,	3899
	13:18	that he may eat **b** and drink water.	3899
	13:19	and did eat **b** in his house, and drank water.	3899
	13:22	hast eaten **b** and drunk water in the place,	3899
	13:22	say to thee, Eat no **b**, and drink no water;	3899
	13:23	after he had eaten **b**, and after he had	3899
	17: 6	the ravens brought him **b** and flesh in	3899
	17: 6	and **b** and flesh in the evening;	3899
	17:11	I pray thee, a morsel of **b** in thine hand.	3899
	18: 4	in a cave, and fed them *with* **b** and water.)	3899
	18:13	in a cave, and fed them *with* **b** and water?	3899
	21: 4	turned away his face, and would eat no **b**.	3899
	21: 5	is thy spirit so sad, that thou eatest no **b**?	3899
	21: 7	*and* eat **b**, and let thine heart be merry:	3899
	22:27	feed him with **b** of affliction and with water	3899
2Ki	4: 8	and she constrained him to eat **b**.	3899
	4: 8	he passed by, he turned in thither to eat **b**.	3899
	4:42	brought the man of God **b** of the firstfruits,	3899
	6:22	set **b** and water before them, that they may	3899
	18:32	and wine, a land of **b** and vineyards,	3899
	23: 9	they did eat of the **unleavened b** among	4682
	25: 3	there was no **b** for the people of the land.	3899
	25:29	he did eat **b** continually before him all	3899
1Ch	12:40	brought **b** on asses, and on camels, and	3899
	16: 3	to every one a loaf of **b**, and a good piece	3899
2Ch	8:13	*even* in the feast of **unleavened b**, and	4682
	18:26	feed him with **b** of affliction and with water	3899
	30:13	feast of **unleavened b** in the second month,	4682
	30:21	**unleavened b** seven days with great	4682
	35:17	the feast of **unleavened b** seven days.	4682
Ezr	6:22	kept the feast of **unleavened b** seven days	4682
	10: 6	he did eat no **b**, nor drink water:	3899
Ne	5:14	my brethren have not eaten the **b** of	3899
	5:15	had taken of them **b** and wine, beside forty	3899
	5:18	yet for *all* this required not I the **b** of	3899
	9:15	gavest them **b** from heaven for their	3899
	13: 2	they met not the children of Israel with **b**	3899
Job	15:23	He wandereth abroad for **b**, *saying,* Where	3899
	22: 7	thou hast withholden **b** from the hungry.	3899
	27:14	his offspring shall not be satisfied *with* **b**.	3899
	28: 5	*As for* the earth, out of it cometh **b**: and	3899
	33:20	So that his life abhorreth **b**, and his soul	3899
	42:11	and did eat **b** with him in his house:	3899
Ps	14: 4	who eat up my people *as* they eat **b**, *and*	3899
	37:25	righteous forsaken, nor his seed begging **b**.	3899
	41: 9	in whom I trusted, which did eat *of* my **b**,	3899
	53: 4	who eat up my people *as* they eat **b**:	3899
	78:20	the streams overflowed; can he give **b** also?	3899
	80: 5	Thou feedest them with the **b** of tears; and	3899
	102: 4	like grass; so that I forget to eat my **b**.	3899
	102: 9	For I have eaten ashes like **b**, and	3899
	104:15	and **b** *which* strengtheneth man's heart.	3899
	105:16	the land: he brake the whole staff of **b**.	3899
	105:40	and satisfied them *with* the **b** of heaven.	3899
	109:10	let them seek *their* **b** also out of their	NIH
	127: 2	to sit up late, to eat the **b** of sorrows:	3899
	132:15	her provision: I will satisfy her poor *with* **b**.	3899
Pr	4:17	For they eat the **b** of wickedness, and	3899
	6:26	woman *a man is brought* to a piece of **b**:	3899
	9: 5	eat of my **b**, and drink of the wine *which* I	3899
	9:17	are sweet, and **b** *eaten* in secret is pleasant.	3899
	12: 9	he that honoureth himself, and lacketh **b**.	3899
	12:11	that tilleth his land shall be satisfied *with* **b**:	3899
	20:13	*and* thou shalt be satisfied *with* **b**.	3899
	20:17	**B** of deceit *is* sweet to a man; but	3899
	22: 9	for he giveth of his **b** to the poor.	3899
	23: 6	Eat thou not the **b** of *him that hath* an evil	3899
	25:21	thine enemy *be* hungry, give him **b** to eat;	3899
	28:19	that tilleth his land shall have plenty *of* **b**:	3899
	28:21	for for a piece of **b** *that* man will transgress.	3899
	31:27	and eateth not the **b** of idleness.	3899
Ecc	9: 7	Go *thy way,* eat thy **b** with joy, and	3899
	9:11	to the strong, neither yet **b** to the wise,	3899
	11: 1	Cast thy **b** upon the waters: for thou shalt	3899
Isa	3: 1	the whole stay of **b**, and the whole stay of	3899
	3: 7	for in my house *is* neither **b** nor clothing:	3899
	4: 1	We will eat our own **b**, and wear our own	3899
	21:14	they prevented with their **b** him that fled.	3899
	28:28	**B** *corn* is bruised; because he will not ever	3899
	30:20	*though* the Lord give you the **b** of	3899
	30:23	**b** of the increase of the earth, and it shall be	3899
	33:16	**b** *shall be* given him; his waters *shall be*	3899
	36:17	and wine, a land of **b** and vineyards.	3899
	44:15	yea, he kindleth *it,* and baketh **b**; yea,	3899
	44:19	also I have baked **b** upon the coals thereof;	3899
	51:14	not die in the pit, nor that his **b** should fail.	3899
	55: 2	do ye spend money for *that which is* not **b**?	3899
	55:10	give seed to the sower, and **b** to the eater:	3899
	58: 7	*Is it* not to deal thy **b** to the hungry, and	3899
Jer	5:17	thy **b**, *which* thy sons and thy daughters	3899
	37:21	that *they* should give him daily a piece of **b**	3899
	37:21	until all the **b** in the city were spent.	3899
	38: 9	he is: for *there is* no more **b** in the city.	3899
	41: 1	and there they did eat **b** together in Mizpah.	3899
	42:14	sound of the trumpet, nor have hunger of **b**;	3899
	52: 6	that there was no **b** for the people of	3899
	52:33	he did continually eat **b** before him all	3899
La	1:11	All her people sigh, they seek **b**; they have	3899
	4: 4	the young children ask **b**, *and* no man	3899
	5: 6	*and* to the Assyrians, to be satisfied *with* **b**.	3899
	5: 9	We gat our **b** with *the peril of* our lives	3899
Eze	4: 9	in one vessel, and make thee **b** thereof,	3899
	4:13	eat their defiled **b** among the Gentiles,	3899
	4:15	and thou shalt prepare thy **b** therewith.	3899
	4:16	I will break the staff of **b** in Jerusalem:	3899
	4:16	they shall eat **b** by weight, and with care;	3899
	4:17	That they may want **b** and water, and	3899
	5:16	upon you, and will break your staff of **b**:	3899
	12:18	eat thy **b** with quaking, and drink thy water	3899
	12:19	They shall eat their **b** with carefulness, and	3899
	13:19	for handfuls of barley and for pieces of **b**,	3899
	14:13	will break the staff of the **b** thereof, and	3899
	16:49	fulness of **b**, and abundance of idleness was	3899
	18: 7	hath given his **b** to the hungry, and	3899
	18:16	*but* hath given his **b** to the hungry, and	3899
	24:17	cover not *thy* lips, and eat not the **b** of men.	3899
	24:22	not cover *your* lips, nor eat the **b** of men.	3899
	44: 3	he shall sit in it to eat **b** before the LORD;	3899
	44: 7	when ye offer my **b**, the fat and the blood,	3899
	45:21	of seven days; **unleavened b** shall be eaten.	4682
Da	10: 3	I ate no pleasant **b**, neither came flesh nor	3899
Hos	2: 5	that give *me* my **b** and my water, my wool	3899
	9: 4	their sacrifices *shall be* unto them as the **b**	3899
	9: 4	for their **b** for their soul shall not come *into*	3899
Am	4: 6	and want of **b** in all your places:	3899
	7:12	and there eat **b**, and prophesy there:	3899
	8:11	not a famine of **b**, nor a thirst for water, but	3899
Ob	1: 7	*they that eat* thy **b** have laid a wound under	3899
Hag	2:12	with his skirt do touch **b**, or pottage, or	3899
Mal	1: 7	*Ye* offer polluted **b** upon mine altar; and	3899
Mt	4: 3	command that these stones be made **b**.	*740*
	4: 4	Man shall not live by **b** alone, but by every	*740*
	6:11	Give us this day our daily **b**.	*740*
	7: 9	whom if his son ask **b**, will he give him a	*740*
	15: 2	they wash not their hands when they eat **b**.	*740*
	15:26	It is not meet to take the children's **b**, and	*740*
	15:33	should we have so much **b** in the wilderness,	*740*
	16: 5	the other side, they had forgotten to take **b**.	*740*
	16: 7	saying, *It is* because we have taken no **b**.	*740*
	16: 8	because ye have brought no **b**?	*740*
	16:11	that I spake *it* not to you concerning **b**,	*740*
	16:12	he bade *them* not beware of the leaven of **b**,	*740*
	26:17	*of* **unleavened b** the disciples came to Jesus,	*106*
	26:26	Jesus took **b**, and blessed *it,* and brake *it,* and	*740*
Mk	3:20	so that they could not so much as eat **b**.	*740*
	6: 8	no scrip, no **b**, no money in *their* purse:	*740*
	6:36	and *into* the villages, and buy themselves **b**:	*740*
	6:37	and buy two hundred pennyworth of **b**,	*740*
	7: 2	saw some of his disciples eat **b** with defiled,	*740*
	7: 5	the elders, but eat **b** with unwashen hands?	*740*
	7:27	for it is not meet to take the children's **b**, and	*740*
	8: 4	these *men* with **b** here in the wilderness?	*740*
	8:14	Now *the disciples* had forgotten to take **b**,	*740*
	8:16	saying, *It is* because we have no **b**.	*740*

Mk 8:17 Why reason ye, because ye have no **b**? *740*
14: 1 *feast of* the passover, and *of* **unleavened b**: *106*
14:12 And the first day of **unleavened b**, *106*
14:22 Jesus took **b**, and blessed, and brake *it,* and *740*
Lk 4: 3 command this stone that it be made **b**. *740*
4: 4 That man shall not live by **b** alone, but *740*
7:33 For John the Baptist came neither eating **b** *740*
9: 3 neither staves, nor scrip, neither **b**, *740*
11: 3 Give us day by day our daily **b**. *740*
11:11 *If* a son shall ask **b** of any of you that is a *740*
14: 1 chief Pharisees to eat **b** on the sabbath day, *740*
14:15 Blessed *is he* that shall eat **b** in the kingdom *740*
15:17 hired *servants* of my father's have **b** enough *740*
22: 1 Now the feast of **unleavened b** drew nigh, *106*
22: 7 Then came the day of **unleavened b**, *106*
22:19 And he took **b**, and gave thanks, and *740*
24:30 he took **b**, and blessed *it,* and brake, and *740*
24:35 how he was known of them in breaking of **b**. *740*
Jn 6: 5 Whence shall we buy **b**, that these may eat? *740*
6: 7 Two hundred pennyworth of **b** is not *740*
6:23 nigh unto the place where they did eat **b**, *740*
6:31 He gave them **b** from heaven to eat. *740*
6:32 Moses gave you not *that* **b** from heaven; *740*
6:32 my Father giveth you the true **b** from *740*
6:33 For the **b** of God is he which cometh down *740*
6:34 unto him, Lord, evermore give us this **b**. *740*
6:35 And Jesus said unto them, I am the **b** of life: *740*
6:41 I am the **b** which came down from heaven. *740*
6:48 I am *that* **b** of life. *740*
6:50 This is the **b** which cometh down from *740*
6:51 I am the living **b** which came down from *740*
6:51 if any *man* eat of this **b**, he shall live for *740*
6:51 and the **b** that I will give is my flesh, which I *740*
6:58 This is *that* **b** which came down from *740*
6:58 he that eateth *of* this **b** shall live for ever. *740*
13:18 He that eateth **b** with me hath lift up his heel *740*
21: 9 of coals there, and fish laid thereon, and **b**. *740*
21:13 and taketh **b**, and giveth them, and *740*
Ac 2:42 and in breaking of **b**, and in prayers. *740*
2:46 and breaking **b** from house to house, did eat *740*
12: 3 (Then were the days of **unleavened b**.) *106*
20: 6 Philippi after the days of **unleavened b**, *106*
20: 7 when the disciples came together to break **b**, *740*
20:11 was come up *again,* and had broken **b**, *740*
27:35 he took **b**, and gave thanks to God in *740*
1Co 5: 8 but with the **unleavened b** of sincerity and *106*
10:16 The **b** which we break, is it not *740*
10:17 For we being many are one **b**, *and* one body: *740*
10:17 for we are all partakers of *that* one **b**. *740*
11:23 *same* night in which he was betrayed took **b**: *740*
11:26 For as often as ye eat this **b**, and drink this *740*
11:27 Wherefore whosoever shall eat this **b**, and *740*
11:28 and so let him eat of *that* **b**, and drink of *that* *740*
2Co 9:10 to the sower both minister **b** for *your* food, *740*
2Th 3: 8 Neither did we eat any *man's* **b** for nought; *740*
3:12 quietness they work, and eat their own **b**. *740*

BREAD OF THE PRESENCE See SHEWBREAD

BREADTH (87) [BROAD, HANDBREADTH]

Ge 6:15 the **b** of it fifty cubits, and the height of it 7341
13:17 the land in the length of it and in the **b** of it; 7341
Ex 25:10 a cubit and a half the **b** thereof, and a cubit 7341
25:17 and a cubit and a half the **b** thereof. 7341
25:23 a cubit the **b** thereof, and a cubit and a half 7341
26: 2 and the **b** of one curtain four cubits: 7341
26: 8 and the **b** of one curtain four cubits: 7341
26:16 and a half *shall be* the **b** of one board. 7341
27:12 *for* the **b** of the court on the west side *shall* 7341
27:13 the **b** of the court on the east side eastward 7341
27:18 the **b** fifty every where, and the height five 7341
28:16 and a span *shall be* the **b** thereof. 7341
30: 2 the length thereof, and a cubit the **b** thereof; 7341
36: 9 and the **b** of one curtain four cubits: 7341
36:15 and four cubits *was* the **b** of one curtain: 7341
36:21 and the **b** of a board one cubit and a half. 7341
37: 1 a cubit and a half the **b** of it, and a cubit 7341
37: 6 and one cubit and a half the **b** thereof. 7341
37:10 a cubit the **b** thereof, and a cubit and a half 7341
37:25 of it *was* a cubit, and the **b** of it a cubit; 7341
38: 1 and five cubits the **b** thereof; 7341
38:18 and the height in the **b** *was* five cubits, 7341
39: 9 and a span the **b** thereof, *being* doubled. 7341
Dt 2: 5 of their land, no, not so much as a foot **b**; 4096
3:11 four cubits the **b** of it, after the cubit of a 7341
Jdg 20:16 every one could sling stones at a hair *b*, and NIH
1Ki 6: 2 the **b** thereof twenty *cubits,* and the height 7341
6: 3 according to the **b** of the house; 7341
6: 3 ten cubits *was* the **b** thereof before 7341
6:20 twenty cubits in **b**, and twenty cubits in 7341
7: 2 the **b** thereof fifty cubits, and the height 7341
7: 6 fifty cubits, and the **b** thereof thirty cubits: 7341
7:27 four cubits the **b** thereof, and three cubits 7341
2Ch 3: 3 threescore cubits, and the **b** twenty cubits. 7341
3: 4 *of it was* according to the **b** of the house, 7341
3: 8 the length whereof *was* according to the **b** 7341
3: 8 and the **b** thereof twenty cubits: 7341
4: 1 twenty cubits the **b** thereof, and ten cubits 7341
Ezr 6: 3 *and* the **b** thereof threescore cubits; 6613
Job 37:10 and the **b** of the waters is straitened. 7341
38:18 Hast thou perceived the **b** of the earth? 7338
Isa 8: 8 out of his wings shall fill the **b** of thy land, 7341
Eze 40: 5 six cubits *long* by the cubit and a **hand b**: 2948
40: 5 so he measured the **b** of the building, 7341
40:11 he measured the **b** of the entry of the gate, 7341
40:13 the **b** *was* five and twenty cubits, 7341
40:19 he measured the **b** from the forefront of 7341
40:20 the length thereof, and the **b** thereof. 7341
40:21 and the **b** five and twenty cubits. 7341
40:25 and the **b** five and twenty cubits. 7341
40:36 and the **b** five and twenty cubits. 7341
40:48 the **b** of the gate *was* three cubits on this 7341
40:49 *was* twenty cubits, and the **b** eleven cubits; 7341
41: 1 *which was* the **b** of the tabernacle. 7341
41: 2 the **b** of the door *was* ten cubits; and 7341
41: 2 forty cubits: and the **b**, twenty cubits. 7341
41: 3 and the **b** of the door, seven cubits. 7341
41: 4 and the **b**, twenty cubits, before the temple: 7341
41: 5 the **b** of *every* side chamber, four cubits, 7341
41: 7 the **b** of the house *was still* upward, 7341
41:11 the **b** of the place that was left *was* five 7341
41:14 Also the **b** of the face of the house, and 7341
42: 2 the north door, and the **b** *was* fifty cubits. 7341
42: 4 *was* a walk of ten cubits **b** inward, 7341
43:13 The cubit *is* a cubit and a **hand b**; even 2948
43:13 the **b** a cubit, and the border thereof by 7341
43:14 *shall be* two cubits, and the **b** one cubit; 7341
43:14 *shall be* four cubits, and the **b** *one* cubit. 7341
45: 1 and the **b** *shall be* ten thousand. 7341
45: 2 with five hundred *in b*, square round about; NIH
45: 3 twenty thousand, and the **b** of ten thousand: 7341
45: 5 *the* ten thousand of **b**, shall also 7341
48: 8 *of* five and twenty thousand *reeds in* **b**, 7341
48: 9 *in* length, and *of* ten thousand *in* **b**. 7341
48:10 and toward the west ten thousand *in* **b**, 7341
48:10 toward the east ten thousand *in* **b**, and 7341
48:13 thousand *in* length, and ten thousand *in* **b**: 7341
48:13 twenty thousand, and the **b** ten thousand. 7341
48:15 that are left in the **b** over against the five 7341
Da 3: 1 *and* the **b** thereof six cubits: 6613
Hab 1: 6 which *shall* march through the **b** of 4800
Zec 2: 2 to see what *is* the **b** thereof, and what *is* 7341
5: 2 twenty cubits, and the **b** thereof ten cubits. 7341
Eph 3:18 to comprehend with all saints what *is* the **b**, *4114*
Rev 20: 9 And they went up on the **b** of the earth, and *4114*
21:16 and the length is as large as the **b**: *4114*
21:16 The length and the **b** and the height of it are *4114*

BREAK (140) [BRAKE, BRAKEST, BREAKER, BREAKEST, BREAKETH, BREAKING, BREAKINGS, BROKEN, BROKEN-HEARTED, BROKENFOOTED, BROKENHANDED, COVENANT-BREAKERS, TRUCEBREAKERS]

Ge 19: 9 *even* Lot, and came near to **b** the door. 7665
27:40 that thou shalt **b** his yoke from off thy 6561
Ex 12:46 the house; neither shall ye **b** a bone thereof. 7665
13:13 not redeem *it,* then thou shalt **b** his **neck**: 6202
19:21 lest they **b through** unto the LORD to 2040
19:22 lest the LORD **b forth** upon them. 6555
19:24 the people **b through** to come up unto 2040
19:24 the LORD, lest he **b forth** upon them. 6555
22: 6 If fire **b out**, and catch in thorns, so that 3318
23:24 and **quite b down** their images. 7665+7665
32: 2 said unto them, **B off** the golden earrings, 6561
32:24 Whosoever hath *any* gold, let them **b** *it* **off**. 6561
34:13 **b** their images, and cut down their groves: 7665
34:20 redeem *him* not, then shalt thou **b** his **neck**. 6202
Lev 11:33 *is* in it shall be unclean; and ye shall **b** it. 7665

B

Lev 13:12 if a leprosy **b out abroad** in the skin, 6524+6524
14:43 plague come again, and **b out** in the house, 6524
14:45 he shall **b down** the house, the stones of it, 5422
26:15 *but* that ye **b** my covenant: 6565
26:19 I will **b** the pride of your power; and I will 7665
26:44 and to **b** my covenant with them: 6565
Nu 9:12 of it unto the morning, nor **b** any bone of it: 7665
24: 8 shall **b** their bones, and pierce *them* 1633
30: 2 he shall not **b** his word, he shall do 2490
Dt 7: 5 **b down** their images, and cut down their 7665
12: 3 **b** their pillars, and burn their groves with 7665
31:16 **b** my covenant which I have made with 6565
31:20 and provoke me, and **b** my covenant. 6565
Jdg 2: 1 I said, I will never **b** my covenant with you. 6565
8: 9 again in peace, I will **b down** this tower. 5422
1Sa 25:10 that **b away** every man from his master. 6555
2Sa 2:32 and they came to Hebron **at b of day**. 215
1Ki 15:19 **b** thy league with Baasha king of Israel, 6565
2Ki 3:26 to **b through** *even* unto the king of Edom: 1234
25:13 did the Chaldees **b** *in pieces,* and 7665
2Ch 16: 3 go, **b** thy league with Baasha king of Israel, 6565
Ezr 9:14 Should we again **b** thy commandments, and 6565
Ne 4: 3 he shall even **b down** their stone wall. 6555
Job 13:25 Wilt thou **b** a leaf driven to and fro? and 6206
19: 2 my soul, and **b** me **in pieces** with words? 1792
34:24 He shall **b in pieces** mighty *men* without 7489
39:15 or *that* the wild beast may **b** them. 1758
Ps 2: 3 Let us **b** their bands **asunder**, and 5423
2: 9 Thou shalt **b** them with a rod of iron; 7489
10:15 **B** thou the arm of the wicked and the evil 7665
58: 6 **B** their teeth, O God, in their mouth: 2040
58: 6 **b out** the great teeth of the young lions, 5422
72: 4 and shall **b in pieces** the oppressor. 1792
74: 6 now they **b down** the carved work thereof 1986
89:31 If they **b** my statutes, and keep not my 2490
89:34 My covenant will I not **b**, nor alter 2490
94: 5 They **b in pieces** thy people, O LORD, 1792
141: 5 an excellent oil, *which* shall not **b** my head: 5106
Ecc 3: 3 a time to **b down**, and a time to build *up;* 6555
SS 2:17 Until the day **b**, and the shadows flee away, 6315
4: 6 Until the day **b**, and the shadows flee away, 6315
Isa 5: 5 *and* **b down** the wall thereof, and it shall be 6555
14: 7 *and* is quiet: they **b forth** *into* singing. 6476
14:25 That *I* will **b** the Assyrian in my land, and 7665
28:24 he open and **b the clods** of his ground? 7702
28:28 nor **b** *it with* the wheel of his cart, 2000
30:14 he shall **b** it as the breaking of the potters' 7665
35: 6 for in the wilderness shall waters **b out**, and 1234
38:13 *that,* as a lion, so will he **b** all my bones: 7665
42: 3 A bruised reed shall he not **b**, and 7665
44:23 **b forth** *into* singing, ye mountains, 6476
45: 2 I will **b in pieces** the gates of brass, and 7665
49:13 and **b forth** *into* singing, O mountains: 6476
52: 9 **B forth** into joy, sing together, ye waste 6476
54: 1 **b forth** *into* singing, and cry aloud, 6476
54: 3 For thou shalt **b forth** *on* the right hand and 6555
55:12 the hills shall **b forth** before you *into* 6476
58: 6 go free, and *that* ye **b** every yoke? 5423
58: 8 shall thy light **b forth** as the morning, and 1234
Jer 1:14 Out of the north an evil shall **b forth** upon 6605
4: 3 **B up** your fallow ground, and sow not 5214
14:21 remember, **b** not thy covenant with us. 6565
15:12 Shall iron **b** the northern iron and the steel? 7489
19:10 shalt thou **b** the bottle in the sight of 7665
19:11 Even so will I **b** this people and this city, as 7665
28: 4 for I will **b** the yoke of the king of Babylon. 7665
28:11 will I **b** the yoke of Nebuchadnezzar king 7665
30: 8 *that* I will **b** his yoke from off thy neck, and 7665
31:28 to **b down**, and to throw down, and 5422
33:20 If you can **b** my covenant of the day, and 6565
43:13 He shall **b** also the images of 7665
45: 4 *that* which I have built *will* I **b down**, and 2040
48:12 shall empty his vessels, and **b** their bottles. 5310
49:35 Behold, I *will* **b** the bow of Elam, the chief 7665
51:20 for with thee will I **b in pieces** the nations, 5310
51:21 with thee will I **b in pieces** the horse and 5310
51:21 with thee will I **b in pieces** the chariot and 5310
51:22 With thee also will I **b in pieces** man and 5310
51:22 with thee will I **b in pieces** old and young; 5310
51:22 with thee will I **b in pieces** the young man 5310
51:23 I will also **b in pieces** with thee 5310
51:23 with thee will I **b in pieces** the husbandman 5310
51:23 with thee will I **b in pieces** captains and 5310
Eze 4:16 I will **b** the staff of bread in Jerusalem: 7665
5:16 upon you, and will **b** your staff of bread: 7665
13:14 So will I **b down** the wall that ye have 2040
14:13 will **b** the staff of the bread thereof, and 7665
16:38 as *women* that **b wedlock** and shed blood 5003
16:39 and shall **b down** thy high places: 5422
17:15 such *things?* or shall he **b** the covenant, 6565
23:34 thou shalt **b** the sherds thereof, and 1633
26: 4 the walls of Tyrus, and **b down** her towers: 2040
26: 9 with his axes he shall **b down** thy towers. 5422
26:12 they shall **b down** thy walls, and 2040
29: 7 thou didst **b**, and rent all their shoulder: 7533
30:18 when I shall **b** there the yokes of Egypt: 7665
30:22 will **b** his arms, the strong, and that which 7665
30:24 I will **b** Pharaoh's arms, and he shall groan 7665
Da 2:40 all these, shall it **b in pieces** and bruise. 1855
2:44 *but* it shall **b in pieces** and consume all 1855
4:27 **b off** thy sins by righteousness, and 6562
7:23 and shall tread it down, and **b** it **in pieces**. 1855
Hos 1: 5 that I will **b** the bow of Israel in the valley 7665
2:18 I will **b** the bow and the sword and 7665
4: 2 they **b out**, and blood toucheth blood. 6555
10: 2 he shall **b down** their altars, he shall spoil 6202
10:11 shall plow, *and* Jacob shall **b** his **clods**. 7702
10:12 reap in mercy; **b up** your fallow ground: 5214
Joel 2: 7 his ways, and they shall not **b** their ranks: 5670
Am 1: 5 I will **b** also the bar of Damascus, and 7665
5: 6 lest he **b out** like fire *in* the house of 6743
Mic 3: 3 they **b** their bones, and chop *them* in 6476
Na 1:13 For now will I **b** his yoke from off thee, 7665
Zec 11:10 that *I* might **b** my covenant which I had 6565
11:14 that I might **b** the brotherhood between 6565
Mt 5:19 shall **b** one of these least commandments, *3089*
6:19 and where thieves **b through** and steal: *1358*
6:20 where thieves do not **b through** nor steal: *1358*
9:17 else the bottles **b**, and the wine runneth out, *4486*
12:20 A bruised reed shall he not **b**, and *2608*
Ac 20: 7 when the disciples came together to **b** *2806*
20:11 *even* till **b of day**, so he departed. *827*
21:13 mean ye to weep and to **b** mine heart? *4919*
1Co 10:16 The bread which we **b**, is it not *2806*
Gal 4:27 **b forth** and cry, thou that travailest not: *4486*

BREAKER (2) [BREAK]

Mic 2:13 The **b** is come up before them: they have 6555
Ro 2:25 but if thou be a **b** of the law, *3848*

BREAKEST (1) [BREAK]

Ps 48: 7 Thou **b** the ships of Tarshish with an east 7665

BREAKETH (17) [BREAK]

Ge 32:26 he said, Let me go, for the day **b**. And he 5927
Job 9:17 For he **b** me with a tempest, and 7779
12:14 he **b down**, and it cannot be built *again:* he 2040
16:14 He **b** me *with* breach upon breach, 6555
28: 4 The flood **b out** from the inhabitant; *even* 6555
Ps 29: 5 The voice of the LORD **b** the cedars; yea, 7665
29: 5 yea, the LORD **b** the cedars of Lebanon. 7665
46: 9 he **b** the bow, and cutteth the spear in 7665
119:20 My soul **b** for the longing *that it hath* unto 1638
Pr 25:15 and a soft tongue **b** the bone. 7665
Ecc 10: 8 whoso **b** a hedge, a serpent shall bite him. 6555
Isa 59: 5 that which is crushed **b out** *into* a viper. 1234
Jer 19:11 this city, as *one* **b** a potter's vessel, 7665
23:29 like a hammer *that* **b** the rock **in pieces?** 6327
La 4: 4 ask bread, *and* no man **b** *it* unto them. 6566
Da 2:40 forasmuch as iron **b in pieces** and 1855
2:40 all *things:* and as iron that **b** all these, 7490

BREAKING (18) [BREAK]

Ge 32:24 there wrestled a man with him until the **b** of 5927
Ex 9: 9 shall be a boil **b forth** *with* blains upon 6524
9:10 it became a boil **b forth** *with* blains upon 6524
22: 2 If a thief be found **b up**, and be smitten that 4290
1Ch 14:11 by mine hand like the **b forth** of waters: 6556
Job 30:14 They came *upon me* as a wide **b in** *of* 6556
Ps 144:14 *that there be* no **b in**, nor going out; 6556
Isa 22: 5 **b down** the walls, and of crying to 6979
30:13 whose **b** cometh suddenly at an instant. 7667
30:14 he shall break it as the **b** of the potters' 7667
Eze 16:59 which hast despised the oath in **b** 6565
17:18 Seeing he despised the oath by **b** 6565
21: 6 thou son of man, with the **b** of *thy* loins; 7670
Hos 13:13 long in *the place of* the **b forth** of children. 4866
Lk 24:35 how he was known of them in **b** of bread. *2800*

Ac 2:42 and in **b** of bread, and in prayers. *2800*
2:46 and **b** bread from house to house, did eat *2806*
Ro 2:23 through **b** the law dishonourest thou God? *3847*

BREAKINGS (1) [BREAK]
Job 41:25 by reason of **b** they purify themselves. 7667

BREAST (18) [BREASTPLATE, BREASTPLATES, BREASTS]
Ex 29:26 thou shalt take the **b** of the ram of Aaron's 2373
29:27 thou shalt sanctify the **b** of the wave 2373
Lev 7:30 by fire, the fat with the **b**, it shall he bring, 2373
7:30 that the **b** may be waved *for* a wave 2373
7:31 but the **b** shall be Aaron's and his sons'. 2373
7:34 For the wave **b** and the heave shoulder 2373
8:29 Moses took the **b**, and waved it *for* a wave 2373
10:14 the wave **b** and heave shoulder shall ye eat 2373
10:15 the wave **b** shall they bring with 2373
Nu 6:20 with the wave **b** and heave shoulder: 2373
18:18 as the wave **b** and as the right shoulder are 2373
Job 24: 9 They pluck the fatherless from the **b**, and 7699
Isa 60:16 the Gentiles, and shalt suck the **b** of kings: 7699
La 4: 3 Even the sea monsters draw out the **b**, 7699
Da 2:32 his **b** and his arms of silver, his belly and 2306
Lk 18:13 unto heaven, but smote upon his **b**, saying, *4738*
Jn 13:25 He then lying on Jesus' **b** saith unto him, *4738*
21:20 which also leaned on his **b** at supper, and *4738*

BREASTPLATE (28) [BREAST, PLATE]
Ex 25: 7 stones to be set in the ephod, and in the **b**. 2833
28: 4 a **b**, and an ephod, and a robe, and 2833
28:15 thou shalt make the **b** of judgment *with* 2833
28:22 thou shalt make upon the **b** chains at 2833
28:23 thou shalt make upon the **b** two rings of 2833
28:23 put the two rings on the two ends of the **b**. 2833
28:24 two rings *which are* on the ends of the **b**. 2833
28:26 the two ends of the **b** in the border thereof, 2833
28:28 they shall bind the **b** by the rings thereof 2833
28:28 that the **b** be not loosed from the ephod. 2833
28:29 Israel in the **b** of judgment upon his heart, 2833
28:30 thou shalt put in the **b** of judgment 2833
29: 5 the **b**, and gird him with the curious girdle 2833
35: 9 stones to be set for the ephod, and for the **b**. 2833
35:27 to be set, for the ephod, and for the **b**; 2833
39: 8 he made the **b** *of* cunning work, like 2833
39: 9 It was foursquare; they made the **b** double: 2833
39:15 they made upon the **b** chains at the ends, 2833
39:16 put the two rings in the two ends of the **b**. 2833
39:17 gold in the two rings on the ends of the **b**. 2833
39:19 put *them* on the two ends of the **b**, upon 2833
39:21 they did bind the **b** by his rings unto 2833
39:21 that the **b** might not be loosed from 2833
Lev 8: 8 he put the **b** upon him: also he put in 2833
8: 8 also he put in the **b** the Urim and 2833
Isa 59:17 For he put on righteousness as a **b**, and 8302
Eph 6:14 and having on the **b** of righteousness; *2382*
1Th 5: 8 be sober, putting on the **b** of faith and love; *2382*

BREASTPLATES (3) [BREAST, PLATE]
Rev 9: 9 And they had **b**, as *it were* breastplates of *2382*
9: 9 they had breastplates, as *it were* **b** of iron; *2382*
9:17 having **b** of fire, and of jacinth, and *2382*

BREASTS (27) [BREAST]
Ge 49:25 blessings of the **b**, and of the womb: 7699
Lev 9:20 they put the fat upon the **b**, and he burnt 2373
9:21 the **b** and the right shoulder Aaron waved 2373
Job 3:12 or why the **b** that I should suck? 7699
21:24 His **b** are full *of* milk, and his bones are 5845
Ps 22: 9 me hope *when I was* upon my mother's **b**. 7699
Pr 5:19 let her **b** satisfy thee at all times; and 1717
SS 1:13 unto me; he shall lie all night betwixt my **b**. 7699
4: 5 Thy two **b** *are* like two young roes *that are* 7699
7: 3 Thy two **b** *are* like two young roes *that are* 7699
7: 7 a palm tree, and thy **b** to clusters *of grapes*. 7699
7: 8 now also thy **b** shall be as clusters of 7699
8: 1 that sucked the **b** of my mother! 7699
8: 8 We have a little sister, and she hath no **b**: 7699
8:10 I *am* a wall, and my **b** like towers: then 7699
Isa 28: 9 from the milk, *and* drawn from the **b**. 7699
66:11 be satisfied with the **b** of her consolations; 7699
Eze 16: 7 *thy* **b** are fashioned, and thine hair is 7699
23: 3 there were their **b** pressed, and there they 7699
23: 8 they bruised the **b** of her virginity, and 1717
23:34 sheards thereof, and pluck off thine own **b**: 7699
Hos 2: 2 and her adulteries from between her **b**; 7699
9:14 give them a miscarrying womb and dry **b**. 7699
Joel 2:16 the children, and those that suck the **b**: 7699
Na 2: 7 the voice of doves, tabring upon their **b**. 3824
Lk 23:48 were done, smote their **b**, and returned. *4738*
Rev 15: 6 having their **b** girded with golden girdles. *4738*

BREATH (42) [BREATHE]
Ge 2: 7 and breathed into his nostrils the **b** of life; 5397
6:17 to destroy all flesh, wherein *is* the **b** of life, 7307
7:15 and two of all flesh, wherein *is* the **b** of life. 7307
7:22 All in whose nostrils *was* the **b** of 5397+7307
2Sa 22:16 at the blast of the **b** of his nostrils. 7307
1Ki 17:17 so sore, that there was no **b** left in him. 5397
Job 4: 9 by the **b** of his nostrils are they consumed. 7307
9:18 He will not suffer me to take my **b**, but 7307
12:10 living *thing,* and the **b** of all mankind. 7307
15:30 and by the **b** of his mouth shall he go away. 7307
17: 1 My **b** is corrupt, my days are extinct, 7307
19:17 My **b** is strange to my wife, though I 7307
27: 3 All the while my **b** *is* in me, and the spirit 5397
33: 4 the **b** of the Almighty hath given me life. 5397
34:14 he gather unto himself his spirit and his **b**; 5397
37:10 By the **b** of God frost is given: and 5397
41:21 His **b** kindleth coals, and a flame goeth out 5315
Ps 18:15 at the blast of the **b** of thy nostrils. 7307
33: 6 all the host of them by the **b** of his mouth. 7307
104:29 thou takest away their **b**, they die, and 7307
135:17 neither is there *any* **b** in their mouths. 7307
146: 4 His **b** goeth forth, he returneth to his earth; 7307
150: 6 Let every *thing that hath* **b** praise 5397
Ecc 3:19 yea, they have all one **b**; so that a man hath 7307
Isa 2:22 ye from man, whose **b** *is* in his nostrils: 5397
11: 4 with the **b** of his lips shall he slay 7307
30:28 his **b**, as an overflowing stream, shall reach 7307
30:33 the **b** of the LORD, like a stream of 5397
33:11 your **b**, *as* fire, shall devour you. 7307
42: 5 he that giveth **b** unto the people upon it, 5397
Jer 10:14 *is* falsehood, and *there is* no **b** in them. 7307
51:17 *is* falsehood, and *there is* no **b** in them. 7307
La 4:20 The **b** of our nostrils, the anointed of 7307
Eze 37: 5 I *will* cause **b** to enter into you, and ye shall 7307
37: 6 and put **b** in you, and ye shall live; 7307
37: 8 them above: but *there was* no **b** in them. 7307
37: 9 O **b**, and breathe upon these slain, that they 7307
37:10 the **b** came into them, and they lived, and 7307
Da 5:23 the God in whose hand thy **b** *is,* and 5396
10:17 strength in me, neither is there **b** left in me. 5397
Hab 2:19 and *there is* no **b** at all in the midst of it. 7307
Ac 17:25 he giveth to all life, and **b**, and all *things;* *4157*

BREATHE (4) [BREATH, BREATHED, BREATHETH, BREATHING]
Jos 11:11 *them:* there was not any left to **b**: 5397
11:14 destroyed them, neither left they any to **b**. 5397
Ps 27:12 up against me, and such as **b out** cruelty. 3307
Eze 37: 9 O breath, and **b** upon these slain, that they 5301

BREATHED (4) [BREATHE]
Ge 2: 7 and **b** into his nostrils the breath of life; 5301
Jos 10:40 but utterly destroyed all that **b**, 5397
1Ki 15:29 he left not to Jeroboam any that **b**, until *he* 5397
Jn 20:22 he **b on** *them,* and saith unto them, *1720*

BREATHETH (1) [BREATHE]
Dt 20:16 thou shalt save alive nothing that **b**: 5397

BREATHING (2) [BREATHE]
La 3:56 hide not thine ear at my **b**, at my cry. 7309
Ac 9: 1 yet **b out** threatenings and slaughter against *1709*

BRED (1) [BREED]
Ex 16:20 the morning, and it **b** worms, and stank: 7311

BREECHES (5)
Ex 28:42 thou shalt make them linen **b** to cover *their* 4370
39:28 fine linen, and linen **b** *of* fine twined linen, 4370
Lev 6:10 *his* linen **b** shall he put upon his flesh, and 4370
16: 4 and he shall have the linen **b** upon his flesh, 4370
Eze 44:18 and shall have linen **b** upon their loins; 4370

BREED (2) [BRED, BREEDING]
Ge 8:17 that they may **b abundantly** in the earth, 8317
Dt 32:14 and rams of the **b** of Bashan, and goats, 1121

BREEDING (1) [BREED]
Zep 2: 9 *even* the **b** of nettles, and saltpits, and 4476

BRETHREN (563) [BROTHER]
Ge 9:22 of his father, and told his two **b** without. 251
9:25 a servant of servants shall he be unto his **b**. 251
13: 8 my herdmen and thy herdmen; for we *be* **b**. 251
16:12 he shall dwell in the presence of all his **b**. 251
19: 7 And said, I pray you, **b**, do not *so* wickedly. 251
24:27 led me to the house of my master's **b**. 251
25:18 *and* he died in the presence of all his **b**. 251
27:29 be lord over thy **b**, and let thy mother's sons 251
27:37 all his **b** have I given to him for servants; 251
29: 4 Jacob said unto them, My **b**, whence *be* ye? 251
31:23 he took his **b** with him, and pursued after 251
31:25 Laban with his **b** pitched in the mount of 251
31:32 before our **b** discern thou what *is* thine with 251
31:37 set *it* here before my **b** and thy brethren, 251
31:37 set *it* here before my brethren and thy **b**, 251
31:46 Jacob said unto his **b**, Gather stones; and 251
31:54 the mount, and called his **b** to eat bread: 251
34:11 Shechem said unto her father and unto her **b**, 251
34:25 Simeon and Levi, Dinah's **b**, took each man 251
37: 2 years old, was feeding the flock with his **b**; 251
37: 4 when his **b** saw that their father loved him 251
37: 4 their father loved him more than all his **b**, 251
37: 5 dreamed a dream, and he told *it* his **b**: 251
37: 8 his **b** said to him, Shalt thou indeed reign 251
37: 9 told it his **b**, and said, Behold, I have 251
37:10 And he told *it* to his father, and to his **b**: and 251
37:10 thy **b** indeed come to bow down ourselves to 251
37:11 his **b** envied him; but his father observed 251
37:12 his **b** went to feed their father's flock in 251
37:13 Do not thy **b** feed *the flock* in Shechem? 251
37:14 see whether it be well with thy **b**, and well 251
37:16 he said, I seek my **b**: tell me, I pray thee, 251
37:17 Joseph went after his **b**, and found them in 251
37:23 to pass, when Joseph was come unto his **b**, 251
37:26 Judah said unto his **b**, What profit *is it* if we 251
37:27 *and* our flesh. And his **b** were content. 251
37:30 he returned unto his **b**, and said, The child *is* 251
38: 1 that Judah went down from his **b**, and 251
38:11 as his **b** *did*. And Tamar went and dwelt *in* 251
42: 3 Joseph's ten **b** went down to buy corn in 251
42: 4 Joseph's brother, Jacob sent not with his **b**; 251
42: 6 Joseph's **b** came, and bowed down 251
42: 7 Joseph saw his **b**, and he knew them, but 251
42: 8 Joseph knew his **b**, but they knew not him. 251
42:13 they said, Thy servants *are* twelve **b**, 251
42:19 If ye *be* true *men*, let one of your **b** be bound 251
42:28 he said unto his **b**, My money is restored; 251
42:32 We *be* twelve **b**, sons of our father; one *is* 251
42:33 true *men*; leave one of your **b** *here* with me, 251
44:14 and his **b** came to Joseph's house; 251
44:33 to my lord; and let the lad go up with his **b**. 251
45: 1 Joseph made himself known unto his **b**. 251
45: 3 Joseph said unto his **b**, I *am* Joseph; doth my 251
45: 3 his **b** could not answer him; for they were 251
45: 4 Joseph said unto his **b**, Come near to me, 251
45:15 Moreover he kissed all his **b**, and wept upon 251
45:15 and after that his **b** talked with him. 251
45:16 saying, Joseph's **b** are come: 251
45:17 said unto Joseph, Say unto thy **b**, This do ye; 251
45:24 So he sent his **b** away, and they departed: 251
46:31 Joseph said unto his **b**, and unto his father's 251
46:31 say unto him, My **b**, and my father's house, 251
47: 1 My father and my **b**, and their flocks, and 251
47: 2 he took some of his **b**, *even* five men, and 251
47: 3 Pharaoh said unto his **b**, What *is* your 251
47: 5 Thy father and thy **b** are come unto thee: 251
47: 6 of the land make thy father and **b** to dwell; 251
47:11 Joseph placed his father and his **b**, and 251
47:12 his **b**, and all his father's household, 251
48: 6 shall be called after the name of their **b** in 251
48:22 I have given to thee one portion above thy **b**, 251
49: 5 Simeon and Levi *are* **b**; instruments of 251
49: 8 Judah, thou *art he* whom thy **b** shall praise: 251
49:26 the head of him *that was* separate from his **b**. 251
50: 8 of Joseph, and his **b**, and his father's house: 251
50:14 he, and his **b**, and all that went up with him 251
50:15 when Joseph's **b** saw that their father was 251
50:17 thee now, the trespass of thy **b**, and their sin; 251
50:18 his **b** also went and fell down before his 251
50:24 Joseph said unto his **b**, I die: and God will 251
Ex 1: 6 and all his **b**, and all that generation. 251
2:11 that he went out unto his **b**, and looked on 251
2:11 an Egyptian smiting a Hebrew, *one* of his **b**. 251
4:18 return unto my **b** which *are* in Egypt, and 251
Lev 10: 4 carry your **b** from before the sanctuary out 251
10: 6 let your **b**, the whole house of Israel, 251
21:10 *he that is* the high priest among his **b**, 251
25:46 over your **b** the children of Israel, ye shall 251
25:48 one of his **b** may redeem him: 251
Nu 8:26 shall minister with their **b** in the tabernacle 251
16:10 and all thy **b** the sons of Levi with thee: 251
18: 2 thy **b** also *of* the tribe of Levi, the tribe of 251
18: 6 I have taken your **b** the Levites from among 251
20: 3 Would God that we had died when our **b** 251
25: 6 brought unto his **b** a Midianitish *woman* in 251
27: 4 a possession among the **b** of our father. 251
27: 7 of an inheritance among their father's **b**; 251
27: 9 then ye shall give his inheritance unto his **b**. 251
27:10 if he have no **b**, then ye shall give his 251
27:10 shall give his inheritance unto his father's **b**. 251
27:11 if his father have no **b**, then ye shall give his 251
32: 6 Shall your **b** go to war, and shall ye sit here? 251
Dt 1:16 Hear *the causes* between your **b**, and 251
1:28 our **b** have discouraged our heart, saying, 251
2: 4 Ye are to pass through the coast of your **b** 251
2: 8 when we passed by from our **b** the children 251
3:18 ye shall pass over armed before your **b** 251
3:20 the LORD have given rest unto your **b**, 251
10: 9 Levi hath no part nor inheritance with his **b**; 251
15: 7 **b** within any of thy gates in thy land which 251
17:15 *one* from among thy **b** shalt thou set king 251
17:20 That his heart be not lifted up above his **b**, 251
18: 2 shall they have no inheritance among their **b**: 251
18: 7 as all his **b** the Levites *do*, which stand there 251
18:15 the midst of thee, of thy **b**, like unto me; 251
18:18 raise them up a Prophet from among their **b**, 251
24: 7 If a man be found stealing any of his **b** of 251
24:14 *whether he be* of thy **b**, or of thy strangers 251
25: 5 If **b** dwell together, and one of them die, and 251
33: 9 neither did he acknowledge his **b**, nor knew 251
33:16 head of him *that was* separated from his **b**. 251
33:24 let him be acceptable to his **b**, and let him 251
Jos 1:14 ye shall pass before your **b** armed, all 251
1:15 Until the LORD have given your **b** rest, 251
2:13 my **b**, and my sisters, and all that they have, 251
2:18 and thy **b**, and all thy father's household, 251
6:23 her mother, and her **b**, and all that she had; 251
14: 8 Nevertheless my **b** that went up with me 251
17: 4 to give us an inheritance among our **b**. 251
17: 4 an inheritance among the **b** of their father. 251
22: 3 Ye have not left your **b** these many days 251
22: 4 your God hath given rest unto your **b**, 251
22: 7 among their **b** on *this* side Jordan westward. 251
22: 8 divide the spoil of your enemies with your **b**. 251
Jdg 8:19 he said, They *were* my **b**, *even* the sons of 251
9: 1 went to Shechem unto his mother's **b**, 251
9: 3 his mother's **b** spake of him in the ears of all 251
9: 5 slew his **b** the sons of Jerubbaal, 251
9:24 which aided him in the killing of his **b**. 251
9:26 Gaal the son of Ebed came with his **b**, and 251
9:31 son of Ebed and his **b** be come to Shechem; 251
9:41 Zebul thrust out Gaal and his **b**, that *they* 251
9:56 did unto his father, in slaying his seventy **b**: 251
11: 3 Jephthah fled from his **b**, and dwelt in 251
14: 3 a woman among the daughters of thy **b**, 251
16:31 his **b** and all the house of his father came 251
18: 8 they came unto their **b** *to* Zorah and Eshtaol: 251
18: 8 and their **b** said unto them, What *say* ye? 251
18:14 said unto their **b**, Do ye know that there is in 251
19:23 said unto them, Nay, my **b**, *nay*, I pray you, 251
20:13 to the voice of their **b** the children of Israel: 251
21:22 or their **b** come unto us to complain, 251
Ru 4:10 of the dead be not cut off from among his **b**, 251
1Sa 16:13 and anointed him in the midst of his **b**; 251
17:17 Take now for thy **b** an ephah of this parched 251
17:17 ten loaves, and run *to* the camp to thy **b**; 251
17:18 look how thy **b** fare, and take their pledge. 251
17:22 *into* the army, and came and saluted his **b**. 251
20:29 let me get away, I pray thee, and see my **b**. 251
22: 1 when his **b** and all his father's house heard 251
30:23 said David, Ye shall not do so, my **b**, 251
2Sa 2:26 bid the people return from following their **b**? 251
3: 8 to his **b**, and to his friends, and have not 251

2Sa	15:20	I may, return thou, and take back thy **b**:	251
	19:12	Ye *are* my **b**, ye *are* my bones and my flesh:	251
	19:41	Why have our **b** the men of Judah stolen	251
1Ki	1: 9	called all his **b** the king's sons, and all	251
	12:24	nor fight against your **b** the children of	251
2Ki	9: 2	make him arise up from among his **b**, and	251
	10:13	Jehu met with the **b** of Ahaziah king of	251
	10:13	they answered, We *are* the **b** of Ahaziah;	251
	23: 9	eat of the unleavened bread among their **b**.	251
1Ch	4: 9	And Jabez was more honourable than his **b**:	251
	4:27	his **b** had not many children, neither did all	251
	5: 2	For Judah prevailed above his **b**, and of him	251
	5: 7	his **b** by their families, when the genealogy	251
	5:13	their **b** of the house of their fathers *were,*	251
	6:44	their **b** the sons of Merari *stood* on the left	251
	6:48	Their **b** also the Levites *were* appointed unto	251
	7: 5	their **b** among all the families of Issachar	251
	7:22	many days, and his **b** came to comfort him.	251
	8:32	these also dwelt with their **b** in Jerusalem,	251
	9: 6	Jeuel, and their **b**, six hundred and ninety.	251
	9: 9	their **b**, according to their generations,	251
	9:13	their **b**, heads of the house of their fathers,	251
	9:17	and Talmon, and Ahiman, and their **b**:	251
	9:19	son of Ebiasaph, the son of Korah, and his **b**,	251
	9:25	their **b**, *which were* in their villages, *were* to	251
	9:32	*other* of their **b**, of the sons of	251
	9:38	they also dwelt with their **b** at Jerusalem,	251
	9:38	brethren at Jerusalem, over against their **b**.	251
	12: 2	out of a bow, *even* of Saul's **b** of Benjamin.	251
	12:32	and all their **b** *were* at their commandment.	251
	12:39	drinking: for their **b** had prepared for them.	251
	13: 2	let us send abroad unto our **b** every where,	251
	15: 5	the chief, and his **b** an hundred and twenty:	251
	15: 6	the chief, and his **b** two hundred and twenty:	251
	15: 7	the chief, and his **b** an hundred and thirty:	251
	15: 8	Shemaiah the chief, and his **b** two hundred:	251
	15: 9	Eliel the chief, and his **b** fourscore:	251
	15:10	the chief, and his **b** an hundred and twelve.	251
	15:12	sanctify yourselves, *both* ye and your **b**,	251
	15:16	**b** *to be* the singers with instruments of	251
	15:17	of his **b**, Asaph the son of Berechiah; and	251
	15:17	of the sons of Merari their **b**, Ethan the son	251
	15:18	And with them their **b** of the second degree,	251
	16: 7	LORD into the hand of Asaph and his **b**.	251
	16:37	the covenant of the LORD Asaph and his **b**,	251
	16:38	And Obed-edom with their **b**, threescore and	251
	16:39	Zadok the priest, and his **b** the priests, before	251
	23:22	and their **b** the sons of Kish took them.	251
	23:32	and the charge of the sons of Aaron their **b**,	251
	24:31	These likewise cast lots over against their **b**	251
	24:31	fathers over against their younger **b**.	251
	25: 7	with their **b** *that were* instructed in the songs	251
	25: 9	who with his **b** and sons *were* twelve:	251
	25:10	*he,* his sons, and his **b**, *were* twelve:	251
	25:11	to Izri, *he,* his sons, and his **b**, *were* twelve:	251
	25:12	*he,* his sons, and his **b**, *were* twelve:	251
	25:13	*he,* his sons, and his **b**, *were* twelve:	251
	25:14	*he,* his sons, and his **b**, *were* twelve:	251
	25:15	*he,* his sons, and his **b**, *were* twelve:	251
	25:16	*he,* his sons, and his **b**, *were* twelve:	251
	25:17	*he,* his sons, and his **b**, *were* twelve:	251
	25:18	*he,* his sons, and his **b**, *were* twelve:	251
	25:19	*he,* his sons, and his **b**, *were* twelve:	251
	25:20	*he,* his sons, and his **b**, *were* twelve:	251
	25:21	*he,* his sons, and his **b**, *were* twelve:	251
	25:22	*he,* his sons, and his **b**, *were* twelve:	251
	25:23	*he,* his sons, and his **b**, *were* twelve:	251
	25:24	*he,* his sons, and his **b**, *were* twelve:	251
	25:25	*he,* his sons, and his **b**, *were* twelve:	251
	25:26	*he,* his sons, and his **b**, *were* twelve:	251
	25:27	*he,* his sons, and his **b**, *were* twelve:	251
	25:28	*he,* his sons, and his **b**, *were* twelve:	251
	25:29	*he,* his sons, and his **b**, *were* twelve:	251
	25:30	*he,* his sons, and his **b**, *were* twelve:	251
	25:31	*he,* his sons, and his **b**, *were* twelve.	251
	26: 7	whose **b** *were* strong men, Elihu, and	251
	26: 8	they and their sons and their **b**, able men for	251
	26: 9	Meshelemiah had sons and **b**, strong men,	251
	26:11	all the sons and **b** of Hosah *were* thirteen.	251
	26:25	And his **b** by Eliezer; Rehabiah his son, and	251
	26:26	his **b** *were* over all the treasures of	251
	26:28	under the hand of Shelomith, and of his **b**.	251
	26:30	Hashabiah and his **b**, men of valour,	251
	26:32	his **b**, men of valour, *were* two thousand	251
	27:18	Of Judah, Elihu, *one* of the **b** of David:	251
	28: 2	and said, Hear me, my **b**, and my people:	251
2Ch	5:12	of Jeduthun, with their sons and their **b**,	251
	11: 4	Ye shall not go up, nor fight against your **b**:	251
	11:22	Maachah the chief, to be ruler among his **b**:	251
	19:10	to you of your **b** that dwell in their cities,	251
	19:10	*so* wrath come upon you, and upon your **b**:	251
	21: 2	he had **b** the sons of Jehoshaphat, Azariah,	251
	21: 4	slew all his **b** with the sword, and *divers* also	251
	21:13	also hast slain thy **b** of thy father's house,	251
	22: 8	the sons of the **b** of Ahaziah, that ministered	251
	28: 8	captive of their **b** two hundred thousand,	251
	28:11	which ye have taken captive of your **b**:	251
	28:15	*to* Jericho, the city of palm trees, to their **b**:	251
	29:15	they gathered their **b**, and	251
	29:34	wherefore their **b** the Levites did help them,	251
	30: 7	be not ye like your fathers, and like your **b**,	251
	30: 9	your **b** and your children *shall find*	251
	31:15	*their* set office, to give to their **b** by courses,	251
	35: 5	families of the fathers of your **b** the people,	251
	35: 6	and sanctify yourselves, and prepare your **b**,	251
	35: 9	his **b**, and Hashabiah and Jeiel and Jozabad,	251
	35:15	for their **b** the Levites prepared for them.	251
Ezr	3: 2	his **b** the priests, and Zerubbabel the son of	251
	3: 2	his **b**, and builded the altar of the God of	251
	3: 8	the remnant of their **b** the priests and	251
	3: 9	stood Jeshua *with* his sons and his **b**,	251
	3: 9	*with* their sons and their **b** the Levites.	251
	6:20	for their **b** the priests, and for themselves.	251
	7:18	and to thy **b**, to do with the rest of the silver	252
	8:17	*and to* his **b** the Nethinims, at the place	251
	8:18	Sherebiah, with his sons and his **b**, eighteen;	251
	8:19	sons of Merari, his **b** and their sons, twenty;	251
	8:24	Hashabiah, and ten of their **b** with them,	251
	10:18	sons of Jeshua the son of Jozadak, and his **b**;	251
Ne	1: 2	one of my **b**, came, he and *certain* men of	251
	3: 1	Eliashib the high priest rose up with his **b**	251
	3:18	After him repaired their **b**, Bavai the son of	251
	4: 2	he spake before his **b** and the army of	251
	4:14	*is* great and terrible, and fight for your **b**,	251
	4:23	So neither I, nor my **b**, nor my servants,	251
	5: 1	and of their wives against their **b** the Jews.	251
	5: 5	Yet now our flesh *is* as the flesh of our **b**,	251
	5: 8	We after our ability have redeemed our **b**	251
	5: 8	the heathen; and will you even sell your **b**?	251
	5:10	I likewise, *and* my **b**, and my servants,	251
	5:14	my **b** have not eaten the bread of	251
	10:10	their **b**, Shebaniah, Hodijah, Kelita, Pelaiah,	251
	10:29	They clave to their **b**, their nobles, and	251
	11:12	their **b** that did the work of the house *were*	251
	11:13	his **b**, chief of the fathers, two hundred forty	251
	11:14	their **b**, mighty *men* of valour, an hundred	251
	11:17	and Bakbukiah the second among his **b**, and	251
	11:19	Talmon, and their **b** that kept the gates,	251
	12: 7	and of their **b** in the days of Jeshua.	251
	12: 8	*was* over the thanksgiving, he and his **b**.	251
	12: 9	Also Bakbukiah and Unni, their **b**, *were* over	251
	12:24	with their **b** over against them, to praise *and*	251
	12:36	his **b**, Shemaiah, and Azarael, Milalai,	251
	13:13	their office *was* to distribute unto their **b**.	251
Est	10: 3	and accepted of the multitude of his **b**,	251
Job	6:15	My **b** have dealt deceitfully as a brook, *and*	251
	19:13	He hath put my **b** far from me, and	251
	42:11	came there unto him all his **b**, and all his	251
	42:15	father gave them inheritance among their **b**.	251
Ps	22:22	I will declare thy name unto my **b**: in	251
	69: 8	I am become a stranger unto my **b**, and	251
	122: 8	For my **b** and companions' sakes, I will now	251
	133: 1	how pleasant *it is* for **b** to dwell together in	251
Pr	6:19	and he that soweth discord among **b**.	251
	17: 2	have part of the inheritance among the **b**.	251
	19: 7	All the **b** of the poor do hate him: how much	251
Isa	66: 5	Your **b** that hated you, that cast you out for	251
	66:20	they shall bring all your **b** *for* an offering	251
Jer	7:15	as I have cast out all your **b**, *even* the whole	251
	12: 6	For even thy **b**, and the house of thy father,	251
	29:16	*of* your **b** that are not gone forth with you	251
	35: 3	his **b**, and all his sons, and the whole house	251
	41: 8	he forbare, and slew them not among their **b**.	251
	49:10	and his **b**, and his neighbours, and he *is* not.	251
Eze	11:15	Son of man, thy **b**, *even* thy brethren,	251
	11:15	Son of man, thy brethren, *even* thy **b**,	251
Hos	2: 1	Say ye unto your **b**, Ammi; and to your	251
	13:15	Though he be fruitful among *his* **b**, an east	251

Mic 5: 3 the remnant of his **b** shall return unto 251
Mt 1: 2 begat Jacob; and Jacob begat Judas and his **b**; *80*
1:11 And Josias begat Jechonias and his **b**, *80*
4:18 saw two **b**, Simon called Peter, and *80*
4:21 he saw other two **b**, James the *son* of *80*
5:47 And if ye salute your **b** only, what do ye more *80*
12:46 behold, *his* mother and his **b** stood without, *80*
12:47 Behold, thy mother and thy **b** stand without, *80*
12:48 Who is my mother? and who are my **b**? *80*
12:49 and said, Behold my mother and my **b**. *80*
13:55 called Mary? and his **b**, James, and Joses, *80*
19:29 or **b**, or sisters, or father, or mother, or wife, *80*
20:24 moved with indignation against the two **b**. *80*
22:25 Now there were with us seven **b**: and the first, *80*
23: 8 is your Master, *even* Christ; and all ye are **b**. *80*
25:40 done *it* unto one of the least of these my **b**, *80*
28:10 go tell my **b** that they go into Galilee, and *80*
Mk 3:31 There came then *his* **b** and his mother, and, *80*
3:32 thy mother and thy **b** without seek for thee. *80*
3:33 saying, Who is my mother, or my **b**? *80*
3:34 and said, Behold my mother and my **b**. *80*
10:29 or **b**, or sisters, or father, or mother, or wife, *80*
10:30 and **b**, and sisters, and mothers, and children, *80*
12:20 Now there were seven **b**: and the first took a *80*
Lk 8:19 Then came to him *his* mother and his **b**, and *80*
8:20 Thy mother and thy **b** stand without, *80*
8:21 my **b** are these which hear the word of God, *80*
14:12 or a supper, call not thy friends, nor thy **b**, *80*
14:26 and wife, and children, and **b**, and sisters, yea, *80*
16:28 For I have five **b**; that he may testify unto *80*
18:29 or parents, or **b**, or wife, or children, for *80*
20:29 There were therefore seven **b**: and the first *80*
21:16 by parents, and **b**, and kinsfolks, and friends; *80*
22:32 when thou art converted, strengthen thy **b**. *80*
Jn 2:12 and his mother, and his **b**, and his disciples: *80*
7: 3 His **b** therefore said unto him, Depart hence, *80*
7: 5 For neither did his **b** believe in him. *80*
7:10 But when his **b** were gone up, then went he *80*
20:17 but go to my **b**, and say unto them, I ascend *80*
21:23 Then went this saying abroad among the **b**, *80*
Ac 1:14 and Mary the mother of Jesus, and with his **b**. *80*
1:16 Men *and* **b**, this scripture must needs have *80*
2:29 Men *and* **b**, let *me* freely speak unto you of *80*
2:37 of the apostles, Men *and* **b**, what shall we do? *80*
3:17 And now, **b**, I wot that through ignorance ye *80*
3:22 Lord your God raise up unto you of your **b**, *80*
6: 3 Wherefore, **b**, look ye out among you seven *80*
7: 2 And he said, Men, **b**, and fathers, hearken; *80*
7:13 second time Joseph was made known to his **b**; *80*
7:23 it came into his heart to visit his **b** *80*
7:25 For he supposed his **b** would have understood *80*
7:26 set them at one *again,* saying, Sirs, ye are **b**; *80*
7:37 Lord your God raise up unto you of your **b**, *80*
9:30 Which when the **b** knew, they brought him *80*
10:23 and certain **b** from Joppa accompanied him. *80*
11: 1 **b** that were in Judea heard that the Gentiles *80*
11:12 Moreover these six **b** accompanied me, and *80*
11:29 determined to send relief unto the **b** which *80*
12:17 shew these *things* unto James, and to the **b**. *80*
13:15 saying, *Ye* men *and* **b**, if ye have *any* word of *80*
13:26 Men *and* **b**, children of the stock of Abraham, *80*
13:38 Be it known unto you therefore, men *and* **b**, *80*
14: 2 made their minds evil affected against the **b**. *80*
15: 1 which came down from Judea taught the **b**, *80*
15: 3 and they caused great joy unto all the **b**. *80*
15: 7 Peter rose up, and said unto them, Men *and* **b**, *80*
15:13 James answered, saying, Men *and* **b**, *80*
15:22 and Silas, chief *men* among the **b**: *80*
15:23 **b** *send* greeting unto the brethren which are of *80*
15:23 brethren *send* greeting unto the **b** which are of *80*
15:32 exhorted the **b** with many words, and *80*
15:33 they were let go in peace from the **b** unto *80*
15:36 visit our **b** in every city where we have *80*
15:40 being recommended by the **b** unto the grace *80*
16: 2 Which was well reported of by the **b** that were *80*
16:40 and when they had seen the **b**, they comforted *80*
17: 6 and certain **b** unto the rulers of the city, *80*
17:10 And the **b** immediately sent away Paul and *80*
17:14 immediately the **b** sent away Paul to go as *it* *80*
18:18 and then took his leave of the **b**, and *80*
18:27 the **b** wrote, exhorting the disciples to receive *80*
20:32 And now, **b**, I commend you to God, and *80*
21: 7 and saluted the **b**, and abode with them one *80*
21:17 come to Jerusalem, the **b** received us gladly. *80*
22: 1 Men, **b**, and fathers, hear ye my defence *80*
22: 5 from whom also I received letters unto the **b**, *80*
23: 1 beholding the council, said, Men *and* **b**, *80*
23: 5 Then said Paul, I wist not, **b**, that he was *80*
23: 6 Men *and* **b**, I am a Pharisee, the son of a *80*
28:14 Where we found **b**, and were desired to tarry *80*
28:15 And from thence, when the **b** heard of us, *80*
28:17 come together, he said unto them, Men *and* **b**, *80*
28:21 neither any of the **b** that came shewed or *80*
Ro 1:13 Now I would not have you ignorant, **b**, *80*
7: 1 Know ye not, **b**, (for I speak to them that *80*
7: 4 Wherefore, my **b**, ye also are become dead to *80*
8:12 Therefore, **b**, we are debtors, not to the flesh, *80*
8:29 he might be the firstborn amongst many **b**. *80*
9: 3 myself were accursed from Christ for my **b**, *80*
10: 1 **B**, my heart's desire and prayer to God for *80*
11:25 For I would not, **b**, that ye should be ignorant *80*
12: 1 you therefore, **b**, by the mercies of God, *80*
15:14 my **b**, that ye also are full of goodness, *80*
15:15 Nevertheless, **b**, I have written the more *80*
15:30 Now I beseech you, **b**, for the Lord Jesus *80*
16:14 Hermes, and the **b** which are with them. *80*
16:17 Now I beseech you, **b**, mark them which *80*
1Co 1:10 Now I beseech you, **b**, by the name of our *80*
1:11 my **b**, by them which are of the *house* of *80*
1:26 For ye see your calling, **b**, how that not many *80*
2: 1 And I, **b**, when I came to you, came not with *80*
3: 1 And I, **b**, could not speak unto you as unto *80*
4: 6 And these *things,* **b**, I have in a figure *80*
6: 5 one that shall be able to judge between his **b**? *80*
6: 8 you do wrong, and defraud, and that *your* **b**. *80*
7:24 **B**, let every man, wherein he is called, *80*
7:29 But this I say, **b**, the time *is* short: *80*
8:12 But when ye sin so against the **b**, and *80*
9: 5 and *as* the **b** of the Lord, and Cephas? *80*
10: 1 Moreover, **b**, I would not that ye should be *80*
11: 2 Now I praise you, **b**, that you remember me in *80*
11:33 Wherefore, my **b**, when ye come together to *80*
12: 1 Now concerning spiritual *gifts,* **b**, I would not *80*
14: 6 Now, **b**, if I come unto you speaking with *80*
14:20 **B**, be not children in understanding: *80*
14:26 How is it then, **b**? when ye come together, *80*
14:39 Wherefore, **b**, covet to prophesy, and *80*
15: 1 Moreover, **b**, I declare unto you the gospel *80*
15: 6 he was seen of above five hundred **b** at once; *80*
15:50 **b**, that flesh and blood cannot inherit *80*
15:58 Therefore, my beloved **b**, be ye stedfast, *80*
16:11 come unto me: for I look for him with the **b**. *80*
16:12 desired him to come unto you with the **b**: *80*
16:15 I beseech you, **b**, (ye know the house of *80*
16:20 All the **b** greet you. Greet ye one another with *80*
2Co 1: 8 For we would not, **b**, have you ignorant of our *80*
8: 1 Moreover, **b**, we do you to wit of the grace of *80*
8:23 our **b** *be inquired of, they are* the messengers *80*
9: 3 Yet have I sent the **b**, lest our boasting of you *80*
9: 5 I thought it necessary to exhort the **b**, *80*
11: 9 the **b** which came from Macedonia supplied: *80*
11:26 *in* perils in the sea, *in* perils among **false b**; *5569*
13:11 Finally, **b**, farewell. Be perfect, be of good *80*
Gal 1: 2 And all the **b** which are with me, unto *80*
1:11 But I certify you, **b**, that the gospel which was *80*
2: 4 because of **false b** unawares brought in, *5569*
3:15 **B**, I speak after the manner of men; Though *it* *80*
4:12 **B**, I beseech you, be as I *am;* for I *am* as ye *80*
4:28 Now we, **b**, as Isaac was, are the children of *80*
4:31 So then, **b**, we are not children of *80*
5:11 And I, **b**, if I yet preach circumcision, why do *80*
5:13 For, **b**, ye have been called unto liberty; *80*
6: 1 **B**, if a man be overtaken in a fault, ye which *80*
6:18 **B**, the grace of our Lord Jesus Christ *be* with *80*
Eph 6:10 Finally, my **b**, be strong in the Lord, and *80*
6:23 Peace *be* to the **b**, and love with faith, *80*
Php 1:12 But I would ye should understand, **b**, that *80*
1:14 And many of the **b** in the Lord, *80*
3: 1 Finally, my **b**, rejoice in the Lord. To write *80*
3:13 **B**, I count not myself to have apprehended: *80*
3:17 **B**, be followers together of me, and *80*
4: 1 my **b** dearly beloved and longed for, my joy *80*
4: 8 Finally, **b**, whatsoever *things* are true, *80*
4:21 The **b** which are with me greet you. *80*
Col 1: 2 and faithful **b** in Christ which are at Colosse: *80*
4:15 Salute the **b** which are in Laodicea, and *80*
1Th 1: 4 Knowing, **b** beloved, your election of God. *80*
2: 1 For yourselves, **b**, know our entrance in unto *80*

1Th 2: 9 For ye remember, **b**, our labour and travail: *80*
2:14 For ye, **b**, became followers of the churches *80*
2:17 But we, **b**, being taken from you for a short *80*
3: 7 Therefore, **b**, we were comforted over you in *80*
4: 1 **b**, and exhort *you* by the Lord Jesus, *80*
4:10 And indeed ye do it towards all the **b** which *80*
4:10 but we beseech you, **b**, that *ye* increase more *80*
4:13 **b**, concerning them which are asleep, that ye *80*
5: 1 But of the times and the seasons, **b**, ye have *80*
5: 4 But ye, **b**, are not in darkness, that *that* day *80*
5:12 And we beseech you, **b**, to know them which *80*
5:14 Now we exhort you, **b**, warn *them that are* *80*
5:25 **B**, pray for us. *80*
5:26 Greet all the **b** with a holy kiss. *80*
5:27 that *this* epistle be read unto all the holy **b**. *80*
2Th 1: 3 **b**, as it is meet, because that your faith *80*
2: 1 Now we beseech you, **b**, by the coming of our *80*
2:13 **b** beloved of the Lord, because God hath from *80*
2:15 **b**, stand fast, and hold the traditions which ye *80*
3: 1 Finally, **b**, pray for us, that the word of *80*
3: 6 Now we command you, **b**, in the name of our *80*
3:13 But ye, **b**, be not weary in well doing. *80*
1Ti 4: 6 If thou put the **b** in remembrance of these *80*
5: 1 *him* as a father; *and* the younger *men* as **b**; *80*
6: 2 let them not despise *them*, because they are **b**; *80*
2Ti 4:21 Pudens, and Linus, and Claudia, and all the **b**. *80*
Heb 2:11 which cause he is not ashamed to call them **b**, *80*
2:12 Saying, I will declare thy name unto my **b**, *80*
2:17 it behoved him to be made like unto *his* **b**, *80*
3: 1 Wherefore, holy **b**, partakers of the heavenly *80*
3:12 Take heed, **b**, lest there be in any of you an *80*
7: 5 that is, of their **b**, though they come out of *80*
10:19 Having therefore, **b**, boldness to enter into *80*
13:22 And I beseech you, **b**, suffer the word of *80*
Jas 1: 2 My **b**, count *it* all joy when ye fall into divers *80*
1:16 Do not err, my beloved **b**. *80*
1:19 Wherefore, my beloved **b**, let every man be *80*
2: 1 My **b**, have not the faith of our Lord Jesus *80*
2: 5 Hearken, my beloved **b**, Hath not God chosen *80*
2:14 What *doth it* profit, my **b**, though a man say *80*
3: 1 My **b**, be not many masters, knowing that we *80*
3:10 cursing. My **b**, these *things* ought not so to be. *80*
3:12 Can the fig tree, my **b**, bear olive berries? *80*
4:11 Speak not evil one of another, **b**. He that *80*
5: 7 Be patient therefore, **b**, unto the coming of *80*
5: 9 one against another, **b**, lest ye be condemned: *80*
5:10 Take, my **b**, the prophets, who have spoken in *80*
5:12 But above all *things*, my **b**, swear not, *80*
5:19 **B**, if any of you do err from the truth, and *80*
1Pe 1:22 the Spirit unto unfeigned **love of** the **b**, *5360*
3: 8 **love as b**, *be* pitiful, *be* courteous: *5361*
5: 9 accomplished in your **b** that are in the world. *81*
2Pe 1:10 Wherefore the rather, **b**, give diligence to *80*
1Jn 2: 7 **B**, I write no new commandment unto you, *80*
3:13 Marvel not, my **b**, if the world hate you. *80*
3:14 from death unto life, because we love the **b**. *80*
3:16 and we ought to lay down *our* lives for the **b**. *80*
3Jn 1: 3 when *the* **b** came and testified of the truth *that* *80*
1: 5 faithfully whatsoever thou doest to the **b**, *80*
1:10 neither doth he himself receive the **b**, and *80*
Rev 6:11 until their fellowservants also and their **b**, *80*
12:10 for the accuser of our **b** is cast down, *80*
19:10 and of thy **b** that have the testimony of Jesus: *80*
22: 9 and of thy **b** the prophets, and of them which *80*

BRETHREN'S (1) [BROTHER]
Dt 20: 8 lest his **b** heart faint as well as his heart. 251

BRIBE (2) [BRIBERY, BRIBES]
1Sa 12: 3 of whose hand have I received *any* **b** to 3724
Am 5:12 they take a **b**, and they turn aside the poor 3724

BRIBERY (1) [BRIBE]
Job 15:34 and fire shall consume the tabernacles of **b**. 7810

BRIBES (3) [BRIBE]
1Sa 8: 3 and took **b**, and perverted judgment. 7810
Ps 26:10 *is* mischief, and their right hand is full *of* **b**. 7810
Isa 33:15 that shaketh his hands from holding of **b**, 7810

BRICK (7) [BRICKKILN, BRICKS]
Ge 11: 3 **make b**, and burn *them* thoroughly. 3835+3843
11: 3 they had **b** for stone, and slime had they for 3843
Ex 1:14 in **b**, and in all manner of service in 3843
5: 7 give the people straw to **make b**, 3835+3843
5:14 your task in **making b** both yesterday 3835
5:16 thy servants, and they say to us, Make **b**: 3843
Isa 65: 3 and burneth incense upon **altars of b**; 3843

BRICKKILN (3) [BRICK]
2Sa 12:31 of iron, and made them pass through the **b**: 4404
Jer 43: 9 and hide them in the clay in the **b**, 4404
Na 3:14 and tread the morter, make strong the **b**. 4404

BRICKS (4) [BRICK]
Ex 5: 8 the tale of the **b**, which they did make 3843
5:18 given you, yet shall ye deliver the tale of **b**. 3843
5:19 Ye shall not minish *ought* from your **b** of 3843
Isa 9:10 The **b** are fallen down, but we will build 3843

BRIDE (14) [BRIDECHAMBER, BRIDEGROOM, BRIDEGROOM'S]
Isa 49:18 and bind them *on thee*, as a **b** *doth*. 3618
61:10 and as a **b** adorneth *herself* with her jewels. 3618
62: 5 *as* the bridegroom rejoiceth over the **b**, *so* 3618
Jer 2:32 forget her ornaments, *or* a **b** her attire? 3618
7:34 of the bridegroom, and the voice of the **b**: 3618
16: 9 of the bridegroom, and the voice of the **b**. 3618
25:10 the voice of the **b**, the sound of 3618
33:11 of the bridegroom, and the voice of the **b**, 3618
Joel 2:16 of his chamber, and the **b** out of her closet. 3618
Jn 3:29 He that hath the **b** is the bridegroom: but *3565*
Rev 18:23 of the **b** shall be heard no more at all in *3565*
21: 2 prepared as a **b** adorned for her husband. *3565*
21: 9 saying, *Come* hither, I will shew thee the **b**, *3565*
22:17 And the Spirit and the **b** say, Come. And let *3565*

BRIDECHAMBER (3) [BRIDE]
Mt 9:15 Can the children of the **b** mourn, *3567*
Mk 2:19 unto them, Can the children of the **b** fast, *3567*
Lk 5:34 Can ye make the children of the **b** fast, *3567*

BRIDEGROOM (23) [BRIDE]
Ps 19: 5 Which *is* as a **b** coming out of his chamber, 2860
Isa 61:10 as a **b** decketh *himself* with ornaments, and 2860
62: 5 *as* the **b** rejoiceth over the bride, *so* 2860
Jer 7:34 the voice of the **b**, and the voice of 2860
16: 9 the voice of the **b**, and the voice of 2860
25:10 the voice of the **b**, and the voice of 2860
33:11 the voice of the **b**, and the voice of 2860
Joel 2:16 let the **b** go forth of his chamber, and 2860
Mt 9:15 as long as the **b** is with them? *3566*
9:15 when the **b** shall be taken from them, and *3566*
25: 1 their lamps, and went forth to meet the **b**. *3566*
25: 5 While the **b** tarried, they all slumbered and *3566*
25: 6 was a cry made, Behold, the **b** cometh; *3566*
25:10 And while they went to buy, the **b** came; *3566*
Mk 2:19 while the **b** is with them? *3566*
2:19 as long as they have the **b** with them, *3566*
2:20 when the **b** shall be taken away from them, *3566*
Lk 5:34 while the **b** is with them? *3566*
5:35 when the **b** shall be taken away from them, *3566*
Jn 2: 9 the governor of the feast called the **b**, *3566*
3:29 He that hath the bride is the **b**: but *3566*
3:29 but the friend of the **b**, which standeth and *3566*
Rev 18:23 and the voice of the **b** and of the bride shall *3566*

BRIDEGROOM'S (1) [BRIDE]
Jn 3:29 rejoiceth greatly because of the **b** voice: *3566*

BRIDE-PRICE See DOWRY

BRIDLE (9) [BRIDLES, BRIDLETH]
2Ki 19:28 my **b** in thy lips, and I will turn thee back 4964
Job 30:11 they have also let loose the **b** before me. 7448
41:13 *or* who can come *to him* with his double **b**? 7448
Ps 32: 9 mouth must be held in with bit and **b**, 7448
39: 1 I will keep my mouth with a **b**, while 4269
Pr 26: 3 a **b** for the ass, and a rod for the fools' 4964
Isa 30:28 *there shall be* a **b** in the jaws of the people, 7448
37:29 my **b** in thy lips, and I will turn thee back 4964
Jas 3: 2 *and* able also to **b** the whole body. *5468*

BRIDLES (1) [BRIDLE]
Rev 14:20 *even* unto the horse **b**, by the space of a *5469*

BRIDLETH (1) [BRIDLE]
Jas 1:26 and **b** not his tongue, but deceiveth his own *5468*

B

BRIEFLY (2)
Ro 13: 9 it is **b comprehended** in this saying, *346*
1Pe 5:12 I have written **b**, exhorting, and *1223+3641*

BRIER (3) [BRIERS]
Isa 55:13 instead of the **b** shall come up the myrtle 5636
Eze 28:24 there shall be no more a pricking **b** unto 5544
Mic 7: 4 The best of them *is* as a **b**: the *most* upright 2312

BRIERS (12) [BRIER]
Jdg 8: 7 the thorns of the wilderness and with **b**. 1303
8:16 thorns of the wilderness and **b**, and 1303
Isa 5: 6 but there shall come up **b** and thorns: 8068
7:23 it shall *even* be for **b** and thorns. 8068
7:24 all the land shall become **b** and thorns. 8068
7:25 there shall not come thither the fear of **b** 8068
9:18 it shall devour the **b** and thorns, and 8068
10:17 and devour his thorns and his **b** in one day; 8068
27: 4 who would set the **b** *and* thorns against me 8068
32:13 of my people shall come up thorns *and* **b**; 8068
Eze 2: 6 though **b** and thorns *be* with thee, and 5621
Heb 6: 8 that which beareth thorns and **b** *is* rejected, *5146*

BRIGANDINE (1) [BRIGANDINES]
Jer 51: 3 against *him that* lifteth himself up in his **b**: 5630

BRIGANDINES (1) [BRIGANDINE]
Jer 46: 4 furbish the spears, *and* put on the **b**. 5630

BRIGHT (29) [BRIGHTNESS]
Lev 13: 2 or **b spot**, and it be in the skin of his flesh 934
13: 4 If the **b spot** *be* white in the skin of his flesh, 934
13:19 or a **b spot**, white, *and* somewhat reddish, 934
13:23 if the **b spot** stay in his place, *and* 934
13:24 quick *flesh* that burneth have a white **b spot**, 934
13:25 *if* the hair in the **b spot** be turned white, and 934
13:26 *there be* no white hair in the **b spot**, and it *be* 934
13:28 if the **b spot** stay in his place, *and* spread not 934
13:38 have in the skin of their flesh **b spots**, 934
13:38 their flesh bright spots, *even* white **b spots**; 934
13:39 *if* the **b spots** in the skin of their flesh *be* 934
14:56 for a rising, and for a scab, and for a **b spot**: 934
1Ki 7:45 the house of the LORD, *were of* **b** brass. 4803
2Ch 4:16 for the house of the LORD *of* **b** brass. 4838
Job 37:11 the thick cloud: he scattereth his **b** cloud: 216
37:21 now *men* see not the **b** light which *is* in 925
SS 5:14 his belly *is as* **b** ivory overlaid *with* 6247
Jer 51:11 **Make b** the arrows: gather the shields: 1305
Eze 1:13 the fire was **b**, and out of the fire went forth 5051
21:15 ah, *it is* made **b**, *it is* wrapt up for 1300
21:21 he **made** *his* arrows **b**, he consulted with 7043
27:19 **b** iron, cassia, and calamus, were in thy 6219
32: 8 All the **b** lights of heaven will I make dark 3974
Na 3: 3 The horseman lifteth up both the **b** sword 3851
Zec 10: 1 *so* the LORD *shall* make **b clouds**, and 2385
Mt 17: 5 behold, a **b** cloud overshadowed them: *5460*
Lk 11:36 as when the **b shining** of a candle doth give *796*
Ac 10:30 a man stood before me in **b** clothing, *2986*
Rev 22:16 of David, *and* the **b** and morning star. *2986*

BRIGHTNESS (22) [BRIGHT]
2Sa 22:13 Through the **b** before him were coals of fire 5051
Job 31:26 when it shined, or the moon walking *in* **b**; 3368
Ps 18:12 At the **b** *that was* before him his thick 5051
Isa 59: 9 for **b**, *but* we walk in darkness. 5054
60: 3 to thy light, and kings to the **b** of thy rising. 5051
60:19 neither for **b** shall the moon give light unto 5051
62: 1 the righteousness thereof go forth as **b**, 5051
Eze 1: 4 a **b** *was* about it, and out of the midst 5051
1:27 of fire, and it had **b** round about. 5051
1:28 so *was* the appearance of the **b** round about. 5051
8: 2 as the appearance of **b**, as the colour of 2096
10: 4 the court was full of the **b** of the LORD'S 5051
28: 7 of thy wisdom, and they shall defile thy **b**. 3314
28:17 corrupted thy wisdom by reason of thy **b**: 3314
Da 2:31 This great image, whose **b** *was* excellent, 2122
4:36 mine honour and **b** returned unto me; 2122
12: 3 they that be wise shall shine as the **b** of 2096
Am 5:20 not light? even very dark, and no **b** in it? 5051
Hab 3: 4 *his* **b** was as the light; he had horns *coming* 5051
Ac 26:13 above the **b** of the sun, shining round about *2987*
2Th 2: 8 and shall destroy with the **b** of his coming: *2015*
Heb 1: 3 Who being the **b** of *his* glory, and *541*

BRIM (10) [BRIMSTONE]
Jos 3:15 the ark were dipped in the **b** of the water, 7097
1Ki 7:23 ten cubits from the one **b** to the other: 8193
7:24 under the **b** of it round about *there were* 8193
7:26 the **b** thereof was wrought like the brim of 8193
7:26 the brim thereof was wrought like the **b** of 8193
2Ch 4: 2 a molten sea of ten cubits from **b** to brim, 8193
4: 2 a molten sea of ten cubits from brim to **b**, 8193
4: 5 the **b** of it like the work of the brim of a 8193
4: 5 the brim of it like the work of the **b** of a 8193
Jn 2: 7 with water. And they filled them up to **the b**. *507*

BRIMSTONE (15) [BRIM, STONE]
Ge 19:24 upon Gomorrah **b** and fire from 1614
Dt 29:23 *And that* the whole land thereof *is* **b**, and 1614
Job 18:15 **b** shall be scattered upon his habitation. 1614
Ps 11: 6 fire and **b**, and a horrible tempest: 1614
Isa 30:33 like a stream of **b**, doth kindle it. 1614
34: 9 the dust thereof into **b**, and the land thereof 1614
Eze 38:22 and great hailstones, fire, and **b**. 1614
Lk 17:29 of Sodom it rained fire and **b** from heaven, *2303*
Rev 9:17 breastplates of fire, and of jacinth, and **b**: *2306*
9:17 their mouths issued fire and smoke and **b**. *2303*
9:18 by the fire, and by the smoke, and by the **b**, *2303*
14:10 and **b** in the presence of the holy angels, *2303*
19:20 cast alive into a lake of fire burning with **b**. *2303*
20:10 them was cast into the lake of fire and **b**, *2303*
21: 8 in the lake which burneth with fire and **b**: *2303*

BRING (727) [BRINGERS, BRINGEST, BRINGETH, BRINGING, BROUGHT, BROUGHTEST] See Index

BRINGERS (1) [BRING] See Index

BRINGEST (5) [BRING] See Index

BRINGETH (79) [BRING] See Index

BRINGING (24) [BRING] See Index

BRINK (6)
Ge 41: 3 stood by the *other* kine upon the **b** of 8193
Ex 2: 3 she laid *it* in the flags by the river's **b**. 8193
7:15 thou shalt stand by the river's **b** against he 8193
Dt 2:36 which *is* by the **b** of the river of Arnon, and 8193
Jos 3: 8 When ye are come to the **b** of the water of 7097
Eze 47: 6 caused me to return to the **b** of the river. 8193

BROAD (36) [BREADTH, BROADER]
Ex 27: 1 five cubits long, and five cubits **b**; 7341
Nu 16:38 let them make them **b** plates *for* a covering 7555
16:39 they were **made b** *plates for* a covering of 7554
1Ki 6: 6 The nethermost chamber *was* five cubits **b**, 7341
6: 6 the middle *was* six cubits **b**, and the third 7341
6: 6 and the third *was* seven cubits **b**: 7341
2Ch 6:13 and five cubits **b**, and three cubits high, and 7341
Ne 3: 8 they fortified Jerusalem unto the **b** wall. 7342
12:38 tower of the furnaces even unto the **b** wall; 7342
Job 36:16 thee out of the strait *into* a **b place**, 7338
Ps 119:96 *but* thy commandment *is* exceeding **b**. 7342
SS 3: 2 the city in the streets and in the **b ways**, 7339
Isa 33:21 *will be* unto us a place of **b** rivers 3027+7342
Jer 5: 1 and know, and seek in the **b places** thereof, 7339
51:58 The **b** walls of Babylon shall be utterly 7342
Eze 40: 6 of the gate, *which was* one reed **b**; 7341
40: 6 *of the gate, which was* one reed **b**. 7341
40: 7 *was* one reed long, and one reed **b**; 7341
40:29 cubits long, and five and twenty cubits **b**. 7341
40:30 and twenty cubits long, and five cubits **b**. 7341
40:33 cubits long, and five and twenty cubits **b**. 7341
40:42 and a cubit and a half **b**, and one cubit high: 7341
40:43 a **hand b**, fastened round about: 2948
40:47 and an hundred cubits **b**, foursquare; 7341
41: 1 six cubits **b** on the one side, and six cubits 7341
41: 1 one side, and six cubits **b** on the other side, 7341
41:12 end toward the west *was* seventy cubits **b**; 7341
42:11 the north, as long as they, *and* as **b** as they: 7341
42:20 hundred *reeds* long, and five hundred **b**, 7341
43:16 twelve **b**, square in the four squares thereof. 7341
43:17 and fourteen **b** in the four squares thereof; 7341
45: 6 the possession of the city five thousand **b**, 7341
46:22 joined *of* forty *cubits* long and thirty **b**: 7341
Na 2: 4 justle one against another in the **b ways**: 7339
Mt 7:13 for wide *is* the gate, and **b** *is* the way, *2149*
23: 5 they **make b** their phylacteries, and *4115*

BROADER (1) [BROAD]
Job 11: 9 *is* longer than the earth, and **b** than the sea. 7342

BROIDED (1) [BROIDERED]
1Ti 2: 9 and sobriety; not with **b hair**, *4117*

BROIDERED (8) [BROIDED]
Ex 28: 4 a robe, and a **b** coat, a mitre, and a girdle: 8665
Eze 16:10 I clothed thee also with **b work**, and 7553
16:13 *was of* fine linen, and silk, and **b work**; 7553
16:18 tookest thy **b** garments, and 7553
26:16 their robes, and put off their **b** garments: 7553
27: 7 Fine linen with **b work** from Egypt was 7553
27:16 **b work**, and fine linen, and coral, and 7553
27:24 and **b work**, and in chests of rich apparel, 7553

BROILED (1)
Lk 24:42 And they gave him a piece of a **b** fish, and *3702*

BROKEN (186) [BREAK]
Ge 7:11 all the fountains of the great deep **b up**, 1234
17:14 off from his people; he hath **b** my covenant. 6565
38:29 she said, How hast thou **b forth**? 6555
Lev 6:28 vessel wherein it is sodden shall be **b**: 7665
11:35 or ranges for pots, they shall be **b down**: 5422
13:20 it *is* a plague of leprosy **b out** of the boil. 6524
13:25 it *is* a leprosy **b out** of the burning: 6524
15:12 toucheth which hath the issue, shall be **b**: 7665
21:20 be scurvy, or scabbed, or hath his stones **b**; 4790
22:22 or **b**, or maimed, or having a wen, or 7665
22:24 which is bruised, or crushed, or **b**, or cut; 5423
26:13 I have **b** the bands of your yoke, and 7665
26:26 *And* when I have **b** the staff of your bread, 7665
Nu 15:31 hath **b** his commandment, that soul shall 6565
Jdg 5:22 were the horsehoofs **b** by the means of 1986
16: 9 as a thread of tow is **b** when it toucheth 5423
1Sa 2: 4 The bows of the mighty *men are* **b**, and 2844
2:10 of the LORD shall be **b to pieces**; 2865
2Sa 5:20 The LORD hath **b forth** upon mine 6555
22:35 so that a bow of steel is **b** *by* mine arms. 5181
1Ki 18:30 the altar of the LORD that was **b down**. 2040
22:48 for the ships were **b** at Ezion-geber. 7665
2Ki 11: 6 watch of the house, that it be **not b down**. 4535
25: 4 the city was **b up**, and all the men of war 1234
1Ch 14:11 God hath **b in upon** mine enemies by mine 6555
2Ch 20:37 the LORD hath **b** thy works. 6555
20:37 the ships were **b**, that they were not able to 7665
24: 7 wicked woman, had **b up** the house of God; 6555
25:12 of the rock, that they all were **b in pieces**. 1234
32: 5 built up all the wall that was **b**, and raised *it* 6555
33: 3 which Hezekiah his father had **b down**, 5422
34: 7 when he had **b down** the altars and 5422
Ne 1: 3 the wall of Jerusalem also *is* **b down**, and 6555
2:13 which were **b down**, and the gates thereof 6555
Job 4:10 and the teeth of the young lions, are **b**. 5421
7: 5 my skin is **b**, and become loathsome. 7280
16:12 I was at ease, but he hath **b** me **asunder**: 6565
17:11 My days are past, my purposes are **b off**, 5423
22: 9 and the arms of the fatherless have been **b**. 1792
24:20 and wickedness shall be **b** as a tree. 7665
31:22 and mine arm be **b** from the bone. 7665
38:15 is withholden, and the high arm shall be **b**. 7665
Ps 3: 7 thou hast **b** the teeth of the ungodly. 7665
18:34 so that a bow of steel is **b** *by* mine arms. 5181
31:12 as a dead man out of mind: I am like a **b** vessel. 6
34:18 *is* nigh unto them that are of a **b** heart; 7665
34:20 keepeth all his bones: not one of them is **b**. 7665
37:15 their own heart, and their bows shall be **b**. 7665
37:17 For the arms of the wicked shall be **b**: but 7665
38: 8 I am feeble and sore **b**: I have roared by 1794
44:19 Though thou hast **sore b** us in the place of 1794
51: 8 *that* the bones *which* thou hast **b** may 1794
51:17 The sacrifices of God *are* a **b** spirit: 7665
51:17 a **b** and a contrite heart, O God, thou wilt 7665
55:20 at peace with him: he hath **b** his covenant. 2490
60: 2 made the earth to tremble; thou hast **b** it: 6480
69:20 Reproach hath **b** my heart; and I am full of 7665
80:12 Why hast thou *then* **b down** her hedges, so 6555
89:10 Thou hast **b** Rahab **in pieces**, as one that is 1792
89:40 Thou hast **b down** all his hedges; thou hast 6555
107:16 For he hath **b** the gates of brass, and cut 7665
109:16 that *he* might even slay the **b** in heart. 3512
124: 7 the snare is **b**, and we are escaped. 7665
147: 3 He healeth the **b** in heart, and bindeth up 7665
Pr 3:20 By his knowledge the depths are **b up**, and 1234
6:15 suddenly shall he be **b** without remedy. 7665
15:13 but by sorrow of the heart the spirit *is* **b**. 5218
17:22 a medicine: but a **b** spirit drieth the bones. 5218
24:31 and the stone wall thereof was **b down**. 2040
25:19 *man* in time of trouble *is like* a **b** tooth, 7465
25:28 his own spirit *is like* a city *that is* **b down**, 6555
Ecc 4:12 and a threefold cord is not quickly **b**. 5423
12: 6 or the golden bowl be **b**, or the pitcher be 7533
12: 6 or the pitcher be **b** at the fountain, or 7665
12: 6 the fountain, or the wheel **b** at the cistern. 7533
Isa 5:27 nor the latchet of their shoes be **b**: 5423
7: 8 and five years shall Ephraim be **b**, 2865
8: 9 O ye people, and ye shall be **b in pieces**; 2865
8: 9 gird yourselves, and ye shall be **b in pieces**; 2865
8: 9 gird yourselves, and ye shall be **b in pieces**. 2865
8:15 fall, and be **b**, and be snared, and be taken. 7665
9: 4 For thou hast **b** the yoke of his burden, and 2865
14: 5 The LORD hath **b** the staff of the wicked, 7665
14:29 because the rod of him that smote thee is **b**: 7665
16: 8 the lords of the heathen have **b down** 1986
19:10 they shall be **b** *in* the purposes thereof, 1792
21: 9 all the graven images of her gods he hath **b** 7665
22:10 the houses have ye **b down** to fortify 5422
24: 5 the ordinance, **b** the everlasting covenant. 6565
24:10 The city of confusion is **b down**: 7665
24:19 The earth is **utterly b down**, 7489+7489
27:11 thereof are withered, they shall be **b off**: 7665
28:13 and be **b**, and snared, and taken. 7665
30:14 of the potters' vessel that is **b in pieces**; 3807
33: 8 he hath **b** the covenant, he hath despised 6565
33:20 neither shall any of the cords thereof be **b**. 5423
36: 6 Lo, thou trustest in the staff of this **b** reed, 7533
Jer 2:13 **b** cisterns, that can hold no water. 7665
2:16 Tahapanes have **b** the crown of thy head. 7462
2:20 For of old time I have **b** thy yoke, *and* 7665
4:26 all the cities thereof were **b down** at 5422
5: 5 these have altogether **b** the yoke, *and* 7665
10:20 is spoiled, and all my cords are **b**: 5423
11:10 the house of Judah have **b** my covenant 6565
11:16 fire upon it, and the branches of it are **b**. 7489
14:17 for the virgin daughter of my people is **b** 7665
22:28 *Is* this man Coniah a despised **b** idol? *is he* 5310
23: 9 Mine heart within me is **b** because of 7665
28: 2 I have **b** the yoke of the king of Babylon. 7665
28:12 **b** the yoke from off the neck of the prophet 7665
28:13 Thou hast **b** the yokes of wood; but 7665
33:21 *Then* may also my covenant be **b** with 6565
37:11 **b up** from Jerusalem for fear of Pharaoh's 5927
39: 2 ninth *day* of the month, the city was **b up**. 1234
48:17 How is the strong staff **b**, *and* the beautiful 7665
48:20 Moab is confounded; for it is **b down**: howl 2865
48:25 cut off, and his arm is **b**, saith the LORD. 7665
48:38 for I have **b** Moab like a vessel wherein *is* 7665
48:39 They shall howl, *saying*, How is it **b down**! 2865
50: 2 is confounded, Merodach is **b in pieces**; 2865
50: 2 are confounded, her images are **b in pieces**. 2865
50:17 king of Babylon hath **b** his **bones**. 6105
50:23 of the whole earth cut asunder and **b**! 7665
51:30 burnt her dwelling places; her bars are **b**. 7665
51:56 *men* are taken, *every one of* their bows is **b**: 2865
51:58 walls of Babylon shall be **utterly b**, 6209+6209
52: 7 the city was **b up**, and all the men of war 1234
La 2: 9 he hath destroyed and **b** her bars: 7665
3: 4 skin hath he made old; he hath **b** my bones. 7665
3:16 He hath also **b** my teeth with gravel stones, 1638
Eze 6: 4 be desolate, and your images shall be **b**: 7665
6: 6 your idols may be **b** and cease, and 7665
6: 9 because I am **b** with their whorish heart, 7665
17:19 and my covenant that he hath **b**, 6331
19:12 her strong rods were **b** and withered; 6561
26: 2 she is **b** *that was* the gates of the people: 7665
27:26 the east wind hath **b** thee in the midst of 7665
27:34 *In* the time when *thou shalt be* **b** by the seas 7665
30: 4 and her foundations shall be **b down**. 2040
30:21 I have **b** the arm of Pharaoh king of Egypt; 7665
30:22 his arms, the strong, and that which was **b**; 7665
31:12 his boughs are **b** by all the rivers of 7665
32:28 thou shalt be **b** in the midst of 7665
34: 4 neither have ye bound up that which was **b**, 7665
34:16 will bind up that which was **b**, and 7665
34:27 when I have **b** the bands of their yoke, and 7665
44: 7 they have **b** my covenant because of all 6565
Da 2:35 **b to pieces** together, and became like 1855

Da 2:42 shall be partly strong, and partly **b**. 8406
8: 8 when he was strong, the great horn was **b**; 7665
8:22 Now that being **b**, whereas four stood up 7665
8:25 of princes; but he shall be **b** without hand. 7665
11: 4 his kingdom shall be **b**, and shall be 7665
11:22 overflown from before him, and shall be **b**; 7665
Hos 5:11 Ephraim *is* oppressed *and* **b** in judgment, 7533
8: 6 but the calf of Samaria shall be **b in pieces**. 7616
Joel 1:17 are laid desolate, the barns are **b down**; 2040
Jnh 1: 4 in the sea, so that the ship was like to be **b**. 7665
Mic 2:13 they have **b up**, and have passed through 6555
Zec 11:11 it was **b** in that day: and so the poor of 6565
11:16 nor heal that that is **b**, nor feed that that 7665
Mt 15:37 they took up of the **b** *meat* that was left *2801*
21:44 shall fall on this stone shall be **b**: *4917*
24:43 not have suffered his house to be **b up**. *1358*
Mk 2: 4 and when they had **b** *it* **up**, they let down *1846*
5: 4 asunder by him, and the fetters **b in pieces**: *4937*
8: 8 they took up of the **b** *meat* that was left *2801*
Lk 12:39 have suffered his house to be **b through**. *1358*
20:18 shall fall upon that stone shall be **b**; *4917*
Jn 5:18 because he not only had **b** the sabbath, but *3089*
7:23 that the law of Moses should not be **b**; *3089*
10:35 of God came, and the scripture cannot be **b**; *3089*
19:31 besought Pilate that their legs might be **b**, *2608*
19:36 be fulfilled, A bone of him shall not be **b**. *4937*
21:11 there were so many, *yet* was not the net **b**. *4977*
Ac 13:43 Now when the congregation was **b up**, *3089*
20:11 was come up *again,* and had **b** bread, *2806*
27:35 and when he had **b** *it,* he began to eat. *2806*
27:41 the hinder part was **b** with the violence of *3089*
27:44 and some on **b**ˢ **pieces** of the ship. *5100*
Ro 11:17 And if some of the branches be **b off**, and *1575*
11:19 wilt say then, The branches were **b off**, *1575*
11:20 because of unbelief they were **b off**, and *1575*
1Co 11:24 this is my body, which is **b** for you: this do *2806*
Eph 2:14 hath **b down** the middle wall of partition *3089*
Rev 2:27 of a potter *shall* they be **b to shivers**: *4937*

BROKENFOOTED (1) [BREAK, FOOT]
Lev 21:19 Or a man that is **b**, or brokenhanded, 7272+7667

BROKENHANDED (1) [BREAK, HAND]
Lev 21:19 Or a man that is brokenfooted, or **b**, 3027+7667

BROKEN-HEARTED (2) [BREAK, HEART]
Isa 61: 1 he hath sent me to bind up the **b**, to 3820+7665
Lk 4:18 he hath sent me to heal the **b**, to preach *4937*

BRONZE See BRASEN; BRASS; STEEL

BROOD (1)
Lk 13:34 as a hen *doth gather* her **b** under *her* wings, *3555*

BROOK (39) [BROOKS]
Ge 32:23 sent them over the **b**, and sent over that he 5158
Lev 23:40 boughs of thick trees, and willows of the **b**; 5158
Nu 13:23 they came unto the **b** of Eshcol, and 5158
13:24 The place was called the **b** Eshcol, because 5158
Dt 2:13 *said I,* and get you over the **b** Zered. 5158
2:13 And we went over the **b** Zered. 5158
2:14 until we were come over the **b** Zered, 5158
9:21 I cast the dust thereof into the **b** that 5158
1Sa 17:40 chose him five smooth stones out of the **b**, 5158
30: 9 *were* with him, and came to the **b** Besor, 5158
30:10 faint that they could not go over the **b** 5158
30:21 whom they had made also to abide at the **b** 5158
2Sa 15:23 the king also *himself* passed over the **b** 5158
17:20 They be gone over the **b** of water. 4323
1Ki 2:37 goest out, and passest over the **b** Kidron, 5158
15:13 her idol, and burnt *it* by the **b** Kidron. 5158
17: 3 and hide thyself by the **b** Cherith, 5158
17: 4 it shall be, *that* thou shalt drink of the **b**; 5158
17: 5 for he went and dwelt by the **b** Cherith, 5158
17: 6 flesh in the evening; and he drank of the **b**. 5158
17: 7 that the **b** dried up, because there had been 5158
18:40 Elijah brought them down to the **b** Kishon, 5158
2Ki 23: 6 unto the **b** Kidron, and burnt it at the brook 5158
23: 6 burnt it at the **b** Kidron, and stampt *it* small 5158
23:12 and cast the dust of them into the **b** Kidron. 5158
2Ch 15:16 and stamped *it,* and burnt *it* at the **b** Kidron. 5158
20:16 ye shall find them at the end of the **b**, 5158
29:16 *it,* to carry *it* out abroad into the **b** Kidron. 5158
30:14 they away, and cast *them* into the **b** Kidron. 5158
32: 4 the **b** that ran through the midst of the land, 5158
Ne 2:15 went I up in the night by the **b**, and viewed 5158
Job 6:15 My brethren have dealt deceitfully as a **b**, 5158
40:22 the willows of the **b** compass him about. 5158
Ps 83: 9 as *to* Sisera, as *to* Jabin, at the **b** of Kison: 5158
110: 7 He shall drink of the **b** in the way: therefore 5158
Pr 18: 4 the wellspring of wisdom *as* a flowing **b**. 5158
Isa 15: 7 shall they carry away to the **b** of 5158
Jer 31:40 and all the fields unto the **b** of Kidron, 5158
Jn 18: 1 forth with his disciples over the **b** Cedron, *5493*

BROOKS (15) [BROOK]
Nu 21:14 did in the Red sea, and *in* the **b** of Arnon, 5158
21:15 *at* the stream of the **b** that goeth down to 5158
Dt 8: 7 a land of **b** of water, of fountains and 5158
2Sa 23:30 the Pirathonite, Hiddai of the **b** of Gaash, 5158
1Ki 18: 5 unto all fountains of water, and unto all **b**: 5158
1Ch 11:32 Hurai of the **b** of Gaash, Abiel 5158
Job 6:15 *and* as the stream of **b** they pass away; 5158
20:17 the floods, the **b** of honey and butter. 5158
22:24 and *the gold of* Ophir as the stones of the **b**. 5158
Ps 42: 1 As the hart panteth after the water **b**, so 650
Isa 19: 6 *and* the **b** of defence shall be emptied and 2975
19: 7 The paper reeds by the **b**, by the mouth of 2975
19: 7 by the mouth of the **b**, and every thing 2975
19: 7 and every thing sown by the **b**, shall wither, 2975
19: 8 all they that cast angle into the **b** shall 2975

BROOM See BESOM

BROTH (3)
Jdg 6:19 he put the **b** in a pot, and brought *it* out 4839
6:20 lay *them* upon this rock, and pour out the **b**. 4839
Isa 65: 4 **b** of abominable *things is in* their vessels; 4839

BROTHER (367) [BRETHREN, BRETHREN'S, BROTHER'S, BROTHERHOOD, BROTHERLY, BROTHERS']
Ge 4: 2 she again bare his **b** Abel. And Abel was a 251
4: 8 Cain talked with Abel his **b**: and it came to 251
4: 8 that Cain rose up against Abel his **b**, and 251
4: 9 said unto Cain, Where *is* Abel thy **b**? 251
9: 5 at the hand of every man's **b** will I require 251
10:21 the **b** of Japheth the elder, even to him were 251
14:13 **b** of Eshcol, and brother of Aner: 251
14:13 brother of Eshcol, and **b** of Aner: 251
14:14 when Abram heard that his **b** was taken 251
14:16 also brought again his **b** Lot, and his goods, 251
20: 5 she, even she herself said, He *is* my **b**: in 251
20:13 we shall come, say of me, He *is* my **b**. 251
20:16 I have given thy **b** a thousand *pieces* of 251
22:20 she hath also born children unto thy **b** 251
22:21 Buz his **b**, and Kemuel the father of Aram, 251
22:23 Milcah did bear to Nahor, Abraham's **b**. 251
24:15 of Milcah, the wife of Nahor, Abraham's **b**, 251
24:29 Rebekah had a **b**, and his name *was* Laban: 251
24:53 he gave also to her **b** and to her mother 251
24:55 her **b** and her mother said, Let the damsel 251
25:26 after that came his **b** out, and his hand took 251
27: 6 I heard thy father speak unto Esau thy **b**, 251
27:11 Esau my **b** *is* a hairy man, and I *am* a smooth 251
27:23 his hands were hairy, as his **b** Esau's hands: 251
27:30 that Esau his **b** came in from his hunting. 251
27:35 Thy **b** came with subtilty, and hath taken 251
27:40 sword shalt thou live, and shalt serve thy **b**; 251
27:41 are at hand; then will I slay my **b** Jacob. 251
27:42 said unto him, Behold, thy **b** Esau, 251
27:43 and arise, flee thou to Laban my **b** to Haran; 251
28: 2 of the daughters of Laban thy mother's **b**. 251
28: 5 the **b** of Rebekah, Jacob's and 251
29:10 the daughter of Laban his mother's **b**, 251
29:10 the sheep of Laban his mother's **b**, 251
29:10 watered the flock of Laban his mother's **b**. 251
29:12 Jacob told Rachel that he *was* her father's **b**, 251
29:15 Because thou *art* my **b**, shouldest thou 251
32: 3 him to Esau his **b** unto the land of Seir, 251
32: 6 We came to thy **b** Esau, and also he cometh 251
32:11 I pray thee, from the hand of my **b**, 251
32:13 came to his hand a present for Esau his **b**; 251
32:17 When Esau my **b** meeteth thee, and 251
33: 3 seven times, until he came near to his **b**. 251
33: 9 Esau said, I have enough, my **b**; keep that 251
35: 1 thou fleddest from the face of Esau thy **b**. 251
35: 7 when he fled from the face of his **b**. 251
36: 6 went into the country from the face of his **b** 251
37:26 What profit *is it* if we slay our **b**, and 251

Ge	37:27	be upon him; for he *is* our **b** *and* our flesh.	251
	38: 8	and marry her, and raise up seed to thy **b**.	251
	38: 9	lest that he should give seed to his **b**.	251
	38:29	back his hand, that, behold, his **b** came out:	251
	38:30	afterward came out his **b**, that had the scarlet	251
	42: 4	Benjamin, Joseph's **b**, Jacob sent not with	251
	42:15	except your youngest **b** come hither.	251
	42:16	let him fetch your **b**, and ye shall be kept in	251
	42:20	bring your youngest **b** unto me; so shall your	251
	42:21	We *are* verily guilty concerning our **b**,	251
	42:34	bring your youngest **b** unto me: then shall I	251
	42:34	ye *are* true *men: so* will I deliver you your **b**,	251
	42:38	for his **b** is dead, and he is left alone:	251
	43: 3	not see my face, except your **b** *be* with you.	251
	43: 4	If thou wilt send our **b** with us, we will go	251
	43: 5	not see my face, except your **b** *be* with you.	251
	43: 6	*as* to tell the man whether ye had yet a **b**?	251
	43: 7	have ye *another* **b**? and we told him	251
	43: 7	know that he would say, Bring your **b** down?	251
	43:13	Take also your **b**, and arise, go again unto	251
	43:14	that he may send away your other **b**, and	251
	43:29	saw his **b** Benjamin, his mother's son, and	251
	43:29	and said, *Is* this your younger **b**,	251
	43:30	for his bowels did yern upon his **b**:	251
	44:19	saying, Have ye a father, or a **b**?	251
	44:20	his **b** is dead, and he alone is left of his	251
	44:23	Except your youngest **b** come down with	251
	44:26	if our youngest **b** be with us, then will we go	251
	44:26	except our youngest **b** *be* with us.	251
	45: 4	he said, I *am* Joseph your **b**, whom ye sold	251
	45:12	eyes see, and the eyes of my **b** Benjamin,	251
	45:14	And he fell upon his **b** Benjamin's neck, and	251
	48:19	truly his younger **b** shall be greater than he,	251
Ex	4:14	and he said, Is not Aaron the Levite thy **b**?	251
	7: 1	and Aaron thy **b** shall be thy prophet.	251
	7: 2	Aaron thy **b** shall speak unto Pharaoh,	251
	28: 1	take thou unto thee Aaron thy **b**, and his	251
	28: 2	shalt make holy garments for Aaron thy **b**,	251
	28: 4	shall make holy garments for Aaron thy **b**,	251
	28:41	thou shalt put them upon Aaron thy **b**, and	251
	32:27	slay every man his **b**, and every man his	251
	32:29	every man upon his son, and upon his **b**;	251
Lev	16: 2	said unto Moses, Speak unto Aaron thy **b**,	251
	18:14	not uncover the nakedness of thy father's **b**,	251
	19:17	Thou shalt not hate thy **b** in thine heart:	251
	21: 2	his son, and for his daughter, and for his **b**,	251
	25:25	If thy **b** be waxen poor, and hath sold away	251
	25:25	then shall he redeem that which his **b** sold.	251
	25:35	if thy **b** be waxen poor, and fallen in decay	251
	25:36	fear thy God; that thy **b** may live with thee.	251
	25:39	if thy **b** *that dwelleth* by thee be waxen poor,	251
	25:47	thy **b** *that dwelleth* by him wax poor, and	251
Nu	6: 7	for his **b**, or for his sister, when they die:	251
	20: 8	Aaron thy **b**, and speak ye unto the rock	251
	20:14	Thus saith thy **b** Israel, Thou knowest all	251
	27:13	thy people, as Aaron thy **b** was gathered.	251
	36: 2	of Zelophehad our **b** unto his daughters.	251
Dt	1:16	righteously between every man and his **b**,	251
	13: 6	If thy **b**, the son of thy mother, or thy son, or	251
	15: 2	not exact *it* of his neighbour, or of his **b**;	251
	15: 3	*that* which is thine with thy **b** thine hand	251
	15: 7	nor shut thine hand from thy poor **b**:	251
	15: 9	and thine eye be evil against thy poor **b**, and	251
	15:11	Thou shalt open thine hand wide unto thy **b**,	251
	15:12	*And* if thy **b**, a Hebrew man, or a Hebrew	251
	17:15	set a stranger over thee, which *is* not thy **b**.	251
	19:18	*and* hath testified falsely against his **b**;	251
	19:19	as he had thought to have done unto his **b**:	251
	22: 1	in any case bring them again unto thy **b**.	251
	22: 2	if thy **b** *be* not nigh unto thee, or *if* thou	251
	22: 2	it shall be with thee until thy **b** seek after it,	251
	23: 7	shalt not abhor an Edomite; for he *is* thy **b**:	251
	23:19	Thou shalt not lend upon usury to thy **b**;	251
	23:20	unto thy **b** thou shalt not lend upon usury:	251
	24:10	When thou dost lend thy **b** any thing,	7453
	25: 3	then thy **b** should seem vile unto thee.	251
	25: 5	her **husband's b** shall go in unto her, and	2993
	25: 5	**perform the duty of a husband's b** unto	2992
	25: 6	succeed in the name of his **b** which is dead,	251
	25: 7	My **husband's b** refuseth to raise up unto	2993
	25: 7	to raise up unto his **b** a name in Israel,	251
	25: 7	not **perform the duty of my husband's b**.	2992
	28:54	his eye shall be evil toward his **b**, and	251
	32:50	as Aaron thy **b** died in mount Hor, and	251
Jos	15:17	the son of Kenaz, the **b** of Caleb, took it:	251
Jdg	1: 3	Judah said unto Simeon his **b**, Come up with	251
	1:13	the son of Kenaz, Caleb's younger **b**, took it:	251
	1:17	Judah went with Simeon his **b**, and they slew	251
	3: 9	the son of Kenaz, Caleb's younger **b**.	251
	9: 3	follow Abimelech; for they said, He *is* our **b**.	251
	9:18	the men of Shechem, because he *is* your **b**;)	251
	9:21	and dwelt there, for fear of Abimelech his **b**.	251
	9:24	their blood be laid upon Abimelech their **b**,	251
	20:23	against the children of Benjamin my **b**?	251
	20:28	against the children of Benjamin my **b**,	251
	21: 6	of Israel repented them for Benjamin their **b**,	251
Ru	4: 3	parcel of land, which *was* our **b** Elimelech's:	251
1Sa	14: 3	Ahiah, the son of Ahitub, Ichabod's **b**,	251
	17:28	Eliab his eldest **b** heard when he spake unto	251
	20:29	my **b**, he hath commanded me *to be there:*	251
	26: 6	the son of Zeruiah, **b** to Joab, saying,	251
2Sa	1:26	I am distressed for thee, my **b** Jonathan:	251
	2:22	then should I hold up my face to Joab thy **b**?	251
	2:27	had gone up every one from following his **b**.	251
	3:27	that he died, for the blood of Asahel his **b**.	251
	3:30	So Joab and Abishai his **b** slew Abner,	251
	3:30	he had slain their **b** Asahel at Gibeon in	251
	4: 6	and Rechab and Baanah his **b** escaped.	251
	4: 9	David answered Rechab and Baanah his **b**,	251
	10:10	he delivered into the hand of Abishai his **b**,	251
	13: 3	*was* Jonadab, the son of Shimeah David's **b**:	251
	13: 4	I love Tamar, my **b** Absalom's sister.	251
	13: 7	Go now *to* thy **b** Amnon's house, and	251
	13: 8	So Tamar went *to* her **b** Amnon's house; and	251
	13:10	*them* into the chamber to Amnon her **b**.	251
	13:12	answered him, Nay, my **b**, do not force me;	251
	13:20	Absalom her **b** said unto her, Hath Amnon	251
	13:20	unto her, Hath Amnon thy **b** been with thee?	251
	13:20	he *is* thy **b**; regard not this thing. So Tamar	251
	13:20	So Tamar remained desolate *in* her **b**	251
	13:22	Absalom spake unto his **b** Amnon neither	NIH
	13:26	I pray thee, let my **b** Amnon go with us.	251
	13:32	the son of Shimeah David's **b**, answered and	251
	14: 7	they said, Deliver him that smote his **b**,	251
	14: 7	kill him, for the life of his **b** whom he slew;	251
	18: 2	Joab's **b**, and a third part under the hand of	251
	20: 9	said to Amasa, *Art* thou in health, my **b**?	251
	20:10	Abishai his **b** pursued after Sheba the son of	251
	21:19	slew *the* **b** *of* Goliath the Gittite,	NIH
	21:21	Jonathan the son of Shimea the **b** of David	251
	23:18	Abishai, the **b** of Joab, the son of Zeruiah,	251
	23:24	Asahel the **b** of Joab *was* one of the thirty;	251
1Ki	1:10	and the mighty *men*, and Solomon his **b**,	251
	2: 7	to me when I fled because of Absalom thy **b**.	251
	2:21	be given to Adonijah thy **b** to wife.	251
	2:22	for he *is* mine elder **b**; even for him, and	251
	9:13	*are* these which thou hast given me, my **b**?	251
	13:30	they mourned over him, *saying*, Alas, my **b**.	251
	20:32	And he said, *Is* he yet alive? he *is* my **b**.	251
	20:33	catch *it:* and they said, Thy **b** Ben-hadad.	251
2Ki	24:17	Mattaniah his **father's b** king in his stead,	1730
1Ch	2:32	the sons of Jada the **b** of Shammai; Jether,	251
	2:42	Now the sons of Caleb the **b** of Jerahmeel	251
	4:11	Chelub the **b** of Shuah begat Mehir,	251
	6:39	his **b** Asaph, who stood on his right hand,	251
	7:16	the name of his **b** *was* Sheresh; and his sons	251
	7:35	the son of his **b** Helem; Zophah, and Imna,	251
	8:39	the sons of Eshek his **b** *were*, Ulam his	251
	11:20	Abishai the **b** of Joab, he was chief of	251
	11:26	of the armies *were*, Asahel the **b** of Joab,	251
	11:38	Joel the **b** of Nathan, Mibhar the son of	251
	11:45	the son of Shimri, and Joha his **b**, the Tizite,	251
	19:11	he delivered unto the hand of Abishai his **b**,	251
	19:15	they likewise fled before Abishai his **b**, and	251
	20: 5	Elhanan the son of Jair slew Lahmi the **b** of	251
	20: 7	Jonathan the son of Shimea David's **b** slew	251
	24:25	The **b** of Michah *was* Isshiah: of the sons of	251
	26:22	Zetham, and Joel his **b**, *which were* over	251
	27: 7	the fourth month *was* Asahel the **b** of Joab,	251
2Ch	31:12	*was* ruler, and Shimei his **b** *was* the next.	251
	31:13	the hand of Cononiah and Shimei his **b**,	251
	36: 4	the king of Egypt made Eliakim his **b** king	251
	36: 4	Necho took Jehoahaz his **b**, and carried him	251
	36:10	made Zedekiah his **b** king over Judah and	251
Ne	5: 7	You exact usury, every one of his **b**.	251
	7: 2	That I gave my **b** Hanani, and Hananiah	251
Job	22: 6	For thou hast taken a pledge from thy **b** for	251
	30:29	I am a **b** to dragons, and a companion to	251

Ps 35:14 as though *he had been* my friend *or* **b**: 251
49: 7 *of them* can by any means redeem *his* **b**, 251
50:20 Thou sittest *and* speakest against thy **b**; 251
Pr 17:17 at all times, and a **b** is born for adversity. 251
18: 9 He also that is slothful in his work *is* **b** to 251
18:19 A **b** offended *is harder to be won* than a 251
18:24 there is a friend *that* sticketh closer than a **b**. 251
27:10 *for* better *is* a neighbour *that is* near than a **b** 251
Ecc 4: 8 a second; yea, he hath neither child nor **b**: 251
SS 8: 1 O that thou *wert* as my **b**, that sucked 251
Isa 3: 6 When a man shall take hold of his **b** *of* 251
9:19 the fuel of the fire: no man shall spare his **b**. 251
19: 2 they shall fight every one against his **b**, and 251
41: 6 *every one* said to his **b**, Be of good courage. 251
Jer 9: 4 of his neighbour, and trust ye not in any **b**: 251
9: 4 for every **b** will utterly supplant, and 251
22:18 shall not lament for him, *saying,* Ah my **b**! 251
23:35 every one to his **b**, What hath the LORD 251
31:34 every man his **b**, saying, Know the LORD: 251
34: 9 serve himself of them, *to wit,* of a Jew his **b**. 251
34:14 years let ye go every man his **b** a Hebrew, 251
34:17 every one to his **b**, and every man to his 251
Eze 18:18 spoiled *his* **b** by violence, and did *that* which 251
33:30 every one to his **b**, saying, Come, I pray you, 251
38:21 every man's sword shall be against his **b**. 251
44:25 for **b**, or for sister that hath had no husband, 251
Hos 12: 3 He took his **b** by the heel in the womb, and 251
Am 1:11 because he did pursue his **b** with the sword, 251
Ob 1:10 For *thy* violence against thy **b** Jacob shame 251
1:12 of thy **b** in the day that he became a stranger; 251
Mic 7: 2 they hunt every man his **b** *with* a net. 251
Hag 2:22 come down, every one by the sword of his **b**. 251
Zec 7: 9 and compassions every man to his **b**: 251
7:10 let none of you imagine evil against his **b** in 251
Mal 1: 2 *was* not Esau Jacob's **b**? saith the LORD: 251
2:10 deal treacherously every man against his **b**, 251
Mt 4:18 Simon called Peter, and Andrew his **b**, *80*
4:21 James the *son* of Zebedee, and John his **b**, *80*
5:22 That whosoever is angry with his **b** without a *80*
5:22 and whosoever shall say to his **b**, Raca, *80*
5:23 there rememberest that thy **b** hath ought *80*
5:24 first be reconciled to thy **b**, and then come *80*
7: 4 Or how wilt thou say to thy **b**, Let me pull out *80*
10: 2 who is called Peter, and Andrew his **b**; *80*
10: 2 the *son* of Zebedee, and John his **b**; *80*
10:21 And the **b** shall deliver up the brother to *80*
10:21 And the brother shall deliver up the **b** to *80*
12:50 the same is my **b**, and sister, and mother. *80*
14: 3 prison for Herodias' sake, his **b** Philip's wife. *80*
17: 1 and John his **b**, and bringeth them up into a *80*
18:15 Moreover if thy **b** shall trespass against thee, *80*
18:15 if he shall hear thee, thou hast gained thy **b**. *80*
18:21 how oft shall my **b** sin against me, and I *80*
18:35 forgive not every one his **b** their trespasses. *80*
22:24 his **b** shall marry his wife, and raise up seed *80*
22:24 marry his wife, and raise up seed unto his **b**. *80*
22:25 and, having no issue, left his wife unto his **b**: *80*
Mk 1:16 and Andrew his **b** casting a net into the sea: *80*
1:19 James the *son* of Zebedee, and John his **b**, *80*
3:17 the *son* of Zebedee, and John the **b** of James; *80*
3:35 the same is my **b**, and my sister, and mother. *80*
5:37 and James, and John the **b** of James. *80*
6: 3 the **b** of James, and Joses, and of Juda, and *80*
6:17 prison for Herodias' sake, his **b** Philip's wife: *80*
12:19 If a man's **b** die, and leave *his* wife *behind* *80*
12:19 that his **b** should take his wife, and raise up *80*
12:19 take his wife, and raise up seed unto his **b**. *80*
13:12 Now the **b** shall betray the brother to death, *80*
13:12 Now the brother shall betray the **b** to death, *80*
Lk 3: 1 and his **b** Philip tetrarch of Iturea and of *80*
3:19 being reproved by him for Herodias his **b** *80*
6:14 and Andrew his **b**, James and John, Philip and *80*
6:16 *And* Judas *the* **b** of James, and NIG
6:42 Either how canst thou say to thy **b**, Brother, *80*
6:42 Either how canst thou say to thy brother, **B**, *80*
12:13 Master, speak to my **b**, that *he* divide *80*
15:27 And he said unto him, Thy **b** is come; *80*
15:32 for this thy **b** was dead, and is alive again; and *80*
17: 3 If thy **b** trespass against thee, rebuke him; and *80*
20:28 If any *man's* **b** die, having a wife, and he die *80*
20:28 that his **b** should take *his* wife, and raise up *80*
20:28 take *his* wife, and raise up seed unto his **b**. *80*
Jn 1:40 followed him, was Andrew, Simon Peter's **b**. *80*
1:41 He first findeth his own **b** Simon, and *80*
6: 8 Andrew, Simon Peter's **b**, saith unto him, *80*
11: 2 feet with her hair, whose **b** Lazarus was sick.) *80*
11:19 Mary, to comfort them concerning their **b**. *80*
11:21 if thou hadst been here, my **b** had not died. *80*
11:23 Jesus saith unto her, Thy **b** shall rise again. *80*
11:32 if thou hadst been here, my **b** had not died. *80*
Ac 1:13 Simon Zelotes, and Judas *the* **b** of James. NIG
9:17 on him said, **B** Saul, the Lord, *even* Jesus, *80*
12: 2 And he killed James the **b** of John with *80*
21:20 the Lord, and said unto him, Thou seest, **b**, *80*
22:13 unto me, and stood, and said unto me, **B** Saul, *80*
Ro 14:10 But why dost thou judge thy **b**? or why dost *80*
14:10 or why dost thou set at nought thy **b**? for we *80*
14:15 But if thy **b** be grieved with *thy* meat, *80*
14:21 nor *any thing* whereby thy **b** stumbleth, or *80*
16:23 of the city saluteth you, and Quartus a **b**. *80*
1Co 1: 1 through the will of God, and Sosthenes *our* **b**, *80*
5:11 if any *man that is* called a **b** be a fornicator, or *80*
6: 6 But **b** goeth to law with brother, and *80*
6: 6 But brother goeth to law with **b**, and *80*
7:12 If any **b** hath a wife that believeth not, and *80*
7:15 A **b** or a sister is not under bondage in such *80*
8:11 And through thy knowledge shall the weak **b** *80*
8:13 Wherefore, if meat make my **b** to offend, *80*
8:13 world standeth, lest I make my **b** to offend. *80*
16:12 As touching *our* **b** Apollos, I greatly desired *80*
2Co 1: 1 and Timothy *our* **b**, unto the church of God *80*
2:13 in my spirit, because I found not Titus my **b**: *80*
8:18 And we have sent with him the **b**, *80*
8:22 And we have sent with them our **b**, whom we *80*
12:18 I desired Titus, and with *him* I sent a **b**. *80*
Gal 1:19 apostles saw I none, save James the Lord's **b**. *80*
Eph 6:21 a beloved **b** and faithful minister in the Lord, *80*
Php 2:25 my **b**, and companion in labour, and *80*
Col 1: 1 by the will of God, and Timotheus *our* **b**, *80*
4: 7 *who is* a beloved **b**, and a faithful minister *80*
4: 9 With Onesimus, a faithful and beloved **b**, *80*
1Th 3: 2 our **b**, and minister of God, and *80*
4: 6 go beyond and defraud his **b** in *any* matter: *80*
2Th 3: 6 that ye withdraw yourselves from every **b** that *80*
3:15 not as an enemy, but admonish *him* as a **b**. *80*
Phm 1: 1 a prisoner of Jesus Christ, and Timothy *our* **b**, *80*
1: 7 bowels of the saints are refreshed by thee, **b**. *80*
1:16 a **b** beloved, specially to me, but how much *80*
1:20 Yea, **b**, let me have joy of thee in the Lord: *80*
Heb 8:11 and every man his **b**, saying, Know the Lord: *80*
13:23 Know ye that *our* **b** Timothy is set at liberty; *80*
Jas 1: 9 Let the **b** of low degree rejoice in that he is *80*
2:15 If a **b** or sister be naked, and destitute of daily *80*
4:11 He that speaketh evil of *his* **b**, and judgeth his *80*
4:11 and judgeth his **b**, speaketh evil of the law, *80*
1Pe 5:12 By Silvanus, a faithful **b** unto you, as I *80*
2Pe 3:15 even as our beloved **b** Paul also according to *80*
1Jn 2: 9 and hateth his **b**, is in darkness *even* until *80*
2:10 He that loveth his **b** abideth in the light, and *80*
2:11 But he that hateth his **b** is in darkness, and *80*
3:10 is not of God, neither he that loveth not his **b**. *80*
3:12 *who* was of *that* wicked one, and slew his **b**. *80*
3:14 He that loveth not *his* **b** abideth in death. *80*
3:15 Whosoever hateth his **b** is a murderer: and *80*
3:17 and seeth his **b** hath need, and shutteth up his *80*
4:20 I love God, and hateth his **b**, he is a liar: *80*
4:20 for he that loveth not his **b** whom he hath *80*
4:21 That he who loveth God love his **b** also. *80*
5:16 If any *man* see his **b** sin a sin *which is* not *80*
Jude 1: 1 the servant of Jesus Christ, and **b** of James, *80*
Rev 1: 9 who also am your **b**, and companion in *80*

BROTHER'S (35) [BROTHER]

Ge 4: 9 And he said, I know not: *Am* I my **b** keeper? 251
4:10 the voice of thy **b** blood crieth unto me from 251
4:11 mouth to receive thy **b** blood from thy hand. 251
4:21 his **b** name *was* Jubal: he was the father of 251
10:25 earth divided; and his **b** name *was* Joktan. 251
12: 5 Lot his **b** son, and all their substance that 251
14:12 they took Lot, Abram's **b** son, who dwelt in 251
24:48 to take my master's **b** daughter unto his son. 251
27:44 him a few days, until thy **b** fury turn away; 251
27:45 Until thy **b** anger turn away from thee, and 251
38: 8 Go in unto thy **b** wife, and marry her, and 251
38: 9 to pass, when he went in unto his **b** wife, 251
Lev 18:16 not uncover the nakedness of thy **b** wife: 251
18:16 of thy brother's wife: it *is* thy **b** nakedness. 251
20:21 if a man shall take his **b** wife, it *is* an 251

Lev 20:21 he hath uncovered his **b** nakedness; 251
Dt 22: 1 Thou shalt not see thy **b** ox or his sheep go 251
22: 3 with all lost *thing* of thy **b**, which he hath 251
22: 4 Thou shalt not see thy **b** ass or his ox fall 251
25: 7 if the man like not to take his **b wife**, then 2994
25: 7 let his **b wife** go up to the gate unto 2994
25: 9 shall his **b wife** come unto him in 2994
25: 9 *that* man that will not build up his **b** house. 251
1Ki 2:15 turned about, and is become my **b**: 251+3807.1
1Ch 1:19 was divided: and his **b** name *was* Joktan. 251
Job 1:13 and drinking wine in their eldest **b** house: 251
1:18 and drinking wine in their eldest **b** house: 251
Pr 27:10 neither go *into* thy **b** house in the day of thy 251
Mt 7: 3 beholdest thou the mote that is in thy **b** eye, *80*
7: 5 clearly to cast out the mote out of thy **b** eye. *80*
Mk 6:18 It is not lawful for thee to have thy **b** wife. *80*
Lk 6:41 beholdest thou the mote that is in thy **b** eye, *80*
6:42 to pull out the mote that is in thy **b** eye. *80*
Ro 14:13 or an occasion to fall in *his* **b** way. *80*
1Jn 3:12 his own works were evil, and his **b** righteous. *80*

BROTHERHOOD (2) [BROTHER]
Zec 11:14 that I might break the **b** between Judah and 264
1Pe 2:17 Honour all *men.* Love the **b**. Fear God. *81*

BROTHERLY (6) [BROTHER]
Am 1: 9 and remembered not the **b** covenant: 251
Ro 12:10 affectioned one to another with **b love**; *5360*
1Th 4: 9 But as touching **b love** ye need not that *I* *5360*
Heb 13: 1 Let **b love** continue. *5360*
2Pe 1: 7 And to godliness **b kindness**; and *5360*
1: 7 and to **b kindness** charity. *5360*

BROTHERS See BRETHREN

BROTHERS' (1) [BROTHER]
Nu 36:11 were married unto their **father's b** sons: 1730

BROUGHT (864) [BRING] See Index

BROUGHTEST (13) [BRING] See Index

BROW (2) [EYEBROWS]
Isa 48: 4 thy neck *is* an iron sinew, and thy **b** brass: 4696
Lk 4:29 led him unto the **b** of the hill whereon their *3790*

BROWN (4)
Ge 30:32 all the **b** cattle among the sheep, and 2345
30:33 the goats, and **b** amongst the sheep, 2345
30:35 all the **b** amongst the sheep, and gave *them* 2345
30:40 and all the **b** in the flock of Laban; 2345

BRUISE See STRIPE; STRIPES

BRUISE (8) [BRUISED, BRUISES, BRUISING, BRUIT]
Ge 3:15 it shall **b** thy head, and thou shalt bruise his 7779
3:15 bruise thy head, and thou shalt **b** his heel. 7779
Isa 28:28 of his cart, nor **b** it *with* his horsemen. 1854
53:10 Yet it pleased the LORD to **b** him; he hath 1792
Jer 30:12 Thy **b** *is* incurable, *and* thy wound *is* 7667
Da 2:40 all these, shall it break in pieces and **b**. 7490
Na 3:19 *There is* no healing of thy **b**; thy wound *is* 7667
Ro 16:20 And the God of peace shall **b** Satan under *4937*

BRUISED (9) [BRUISE]
Lev 22:24 not offer unto the LORD that which is **b**, 4600
2Ki 18:21 thou trustest upon the staff of this **b** reed, 7533
Isa 28:28 Bread *corn* is **b**; because he will not ever be 1854
42: 3 A **b** reed shall he not break, and 7533
53: 5 *he was* **b** for our iniquities: 1792
Eze 23: 3 and there they **b** the teats of their virginity. 6213
23: 8 they **b** the breasts of her virginity, and 6213
Mt 12:20 A **b** reed shall he not break, and *4937*
Lk 4:18 to the blind, to set at liberty *them that are* **b**, *2352*

BRUISES (1) [BRUISE]
Isa 1: 6 *but* wounds, and **b**, and putrifying sores: 2250

BRUISING (2) [BRUISE]
Eze 23:21 in **b** thy teats by the Egyptians for the paps 6213
Lk 9:39 and **b** him hardly departeth from him. *4937*

BRUIT (2) [BRUISE]
Jer 10:22 the noise of the **b** is come, and a great 8052
Na 3:19 all that hear the **b** of thee shall clap 8088

BRUTE (2) [BRUTISH]
2Pe 2:12 But these, as natural **b** beasts, made to be *249*
Jude 1:10 but what they know naturally, as **b** beasts, *249*

BRUTISH (11) [BRUTE]
Ps 49:10 likewise the fool and the **b person** perish, 1198
92: 6 A **b** man knoweth not; neither doth a fool 1198
94: 8 Understand, ye **b** among the people: and 1197
Pr 12: 1 but he that hateth reproof *is* **b**. 1198
30: 2 Surely I *am* more **b** than *any* man, and 1198
Isa 19:11 wise counsellers of Pharaoh is become **b**: 1197
Jer 10: 8 they are altogether **b** and foolish: the stock 1197
10:14 Every man is **b** in *his* knowledge: 1197
10:21 For the pastors are become **b**, and have not 1197
51:17 Every man is **b** by *his* knowledge; 1197
Eze 21:31 deliver thee into the hand of **b** men, *and* 1197

BUBASTIS See PHI-BESETH

BUCKET (1) [BUCKETS]
Isa 40:15 the nations *are* as a drop of a **b**, and 1805

BUCKETS (1) [BUCKET]
Nu 24: 7 He shall pour the water out of his **b**, and 1805

BUCKLER (11) [BUCKLERS]
2Sa 22:31 he *is* a **b** to all them that trust in him. 4043
1Ch 5:18 men *able to* bear **b** and sword, and to shoot 4043
12: 8 the battle, that could handle shield and **b**, 7420
Ps 18: 2 my **b**, and the horn of my salvation, *and* 4043
18:30 he *is* a **b** to all those that trust in him. 4043
35: 2 Take hold of shield and **b**, and stand up for 6793
91: 4 his truth *shall be thy* shield and **b**. 5507
Pr 2: 7 *he is* a **b** to them that walk uprightly. 4043
Jer 46: 3 Order ye the **b** and shield, and draw near to 4043
Eze 23:24 *which* shall set against thee **b** and shield 6793
26: 8 against thee, and lift up the **b** against thee. 6793

BUCKLERS (5) [BUCKLER]
2Ch 23: 9 **b**, and shields, that *had been* king David's, 4043
Job 15:26 on *his* neck, upon the thick bosses of his **b**: 4043
SS 4: 4 whereon there hang a thousand **b**, 4043
Eze 38: 4 *of armour, even* a great company *with* **b** 6793
39: 9 both the shields and the **b**, the bows and 6793

BUD (11) [BUDDED, BUDS]
Job 14: 9 *Yet* through the sent of water it will **b**, and 6524
38:27 to cause the **b** of the tender herb to spring 4161
Ps 132:17 There will I **make** the horn of David **to b**: 6779
SS 7:12 *and* the pomegranates **b forth**: 5340
Isa 18: 5 when the **b** is perfect, and the sour grape is 6525
27: 6 Israel shall blossom and **b**, and fill the face 6524
55:10 the earth, and maketh it bring forth and **b**, 6779
61:11 For as the earth bringeth forth her **b**, and 6780
Eze 16: 7 I have caused thee to multiply as the **b** of 6780
29:21 **cause** the horn of the house of Israel **to b forth**, 6779
Hos 8: 7 the **b** shall yield no meal: if so be it yield, 6780

BUDDED (5) [BUD]
Ge 40:10 it *was* as though it **b**, *and* her blossoms shot 6524
Nu 17: 8 rod of Aaron for the house of Levi was **b**, 6524
SS 6:11 vine flourished, *and* the pomegranates **b**. 5340
Eze 7:10 the rod hath blossomed, pride hath **b**. 6524
Heb 9: 4 and Aaron's rod that **b**, and the tables of *985*

BUDS (1) [BUD]
Nu 17: 8 brought forth **b**, and bloomed blossoms, 6525

BUFFET (2) [BUFFETED]
Mk 14:65 and to **b** him, and to say unto him, *2852*
2Co 12: 7 the messenger of Satan to **b** me, lest I *2852*

BUFFETED (3) [BUFFET]
Mt 26:67 Then did they spit in his face, and **b** him; *2852*
1Co 4:11 and are **b**, and have no certain dwelling *2852*
1Pe 2:20 glory *is it*, if, when ye be **b** for your faults, *2852*

BUILD (162) [BUILDED, BUILDEDST, BUILDER, BUILDERS, BUILDEST, BUILDETH, BUILDING, BUILDINGS, BUILT, MASTERBUILDER]
Ge 11: 4 Go to, let us **b** us a city and a tower, 1129
11: 8 all the earth: and they left off to **b** the city. 1129
Ex 20:25 of stone, thou shalt not **b** it *of* hewn stone: 1129
Nu 23: 1 **B** me here seven altars, and prepare me 1129

B

Nu 23:29 **B** me here seven altars, and prepare me 1129
32:16 We will **b** sheepfolds here for our cattle, 1129
32:24 **B** ye cities for your little ones, and folds for 1129
Dt 20:20 thou shalt **b** bulwarks against the city that 1129
25: 9 man that will not **b up** his brother's house. 1129
27: 5 there shalt thou **b** an altar unto the LORD 1129
27: 6 Thou shalt **b** the altar of the LORD thy 1129
28:30 thou shalt **b** a house, and thou shalt not 1129
Jos 22:26 Let us now prepare to **b** us an altar, 1129
22:29 to **b** an altar for burnt offerings, for meat 1129
Jdg 6:26 **b** an altar unto the LORD thy God upon 1129
Ru 4:11 which two did **b** the house of Israel: 1129
1Sa 2:35 I will **b** him a sure house; and he shall walk 1129
2Sa 7: 5 Shalt thou **b** me a house for me to dwell in? 1129
7: 7 Why **b** ye not me a house of cedar? 1129
7:13 He shall **b** a house for my name, and I will 1129
7:27 to thy servant, saying, I will **b** thee a house: 1129
24:21 of thee, to **b** an altar unto the LORD, 1129
1Ki 2:36 **B** thee a house in Jerusalem, and 1129
5: 3 **b** a house unto the name of the LORD his 1129
5: 5 I purpose to **b** a house unto the name of 1129
5: 5 thy room, he shall **b** a house unto my name. 1129
5:18 prepared timber and stones to **b** the house. 1129
6: 1 that he *began* to **b** the house of the LORD. 1129
8:16 out of all the tribes of Israel to **b** a house, 1129
8:17 it was in the heart of David my father to **b** a 1129
8:18 Whereas it was in thine heart to **b** a house 1129
8:19 Nevertheless thou shalt not **b** the house; but 1129
8:19 he shall **b** the house unto my name. 1129
9:15 for to **b** the house of the LORD, and his 1129
9:19 that which Solomon desired to **b** in 1129
9:24 had built for her: then did he **b** Millo. 1129
11: 7 did Solomon **b** a high place for Chemosh, 1129
11:38 **b** thee a sure house, as I built for David, 1129
16:34 In his days did Hiel the Bethelite **b** Jericho: 1129
1Ch 14: 1 and carpenters, to **b** him a house. 1129
17: 4 Thou shalt not **b** me a house to dwell in: 1129
17:10 thee that the LORD will **b** thee a house. 1129
17:12 He shall **b** me a house, and I will stablish 1129
17:25 hast told thy servant that *thou* wilt **b** him a 1129
21:22 that I may **b** an altar therein unto 1129
22: 2 he set masons to hew wrought stones to **b** 1129
22: 6 charged him to **b** a house for the LORD 1129
22: 7 it was in my mind to **b** a house unto 1129
22: 8 thou shalt not **b** a house unto my name, 1129
22:10 He shall **b** a house for my name; and 1129
22:11 and **b** the house of the LORD thy God, 1129
22:19 and **b** ye the sanctuary of the LORD God, 1129
28: 2 *As for me,* I *had* in mine heart to **b** a house 1129
28: 3 Thou shalt not **b** a house for my name, 1129
28: 6 he shall **b** my house and my courts: 1129
28:10 for the LORD hath chosen thee to **b** a 1129
29:16 all this store that we have prepared to **b** 1129
29:19 to do all *these things,* and to **b** the palace, 1129
2Ch 2: 1 Solomon determined to **b** a house for 1129
2: 3 didst send him cedars to **b** him a house to 1129
2: 4 I **b** a house to the name of the LORD my 1129
2: 5 the house which I **b** *is* great: for great *is* our 1129
2: 6 who is able to **b** him a house, seeing 1129
2: 6 who *am* I then, that I should **b** him a house, 1129
2: 9 for the house which I am about to **b** *shall* 1129
2:12 that might **b** a house for the LORD, and 1129
3: 1 Solomon began to **b** the house of 1129
3: 2 he began to **b** in the second *day* of 1129
6: 5 **b** a house *in,* that my name might be there; 1129
6: 7 **b** a house for the name of the LORD God 1129
6: 8 Forasmuch as it was in thine heart to **b** a 1129
6: 9 Notwithstanding thou shalt not **b** the house; 1129
6: 9 thy loins, he shall **b** the house for my name. 1129
8: 6 all that Solomon desired to **b** in Jerusalem, 1129
14: 7 Let us **b** these cities, and make about *them* 1129
35: 3 the son of David king of Israel did **b**; 1129
36:23 he hath charged me to **b** him a house in 1129
Ezr 1: 2 he hath charged me to **b** him a house at 1129
1: 3 **b** the house of the LORD God of Israel, 1129
1: 5 to go up to **b** the house of the LORD 1129
4: 2 and said unto them, Let us **b** with you: 1129
4: 3 You have nothing to do with us to **b** a 1129
4: 3 we ourselves together will **b** unto 1129
5: 2 began to **b** the house of God which *is* at 1124
5: 3 Who hath commanded you to **b** this house, 1124
5: 9 Who commanded you to **b** this house, and 1124
5:11 **b** the house that was builded these many 1124
5:13 made a decree to **b** this house of God. 1124
5:17 king to **b** this house of God at Jerusalem, 1124
6: 7 the elders of the Jews **b** this house of God 1124
Ne 2: 5 of my fathers' sepulchres, that I may **b** it. 1129
2:17 come, and let us **b** *up* the wall of Jerusalem, 1129
2:18 they said, Let us rise up and **b**. So they 1129
2:20 therefore we his servants will arise and **b**: 1129
3: 3 the fish gate did the sons of Hassenaah **b**, 1129
4: 3 he said, Even *that* which they **b**, if a fox go 1129
4:10 so that we are not able to **b** the wall. 1129
Ps 28: 5 he shall destroy them, and not **b** them **up**. 1129
51:18 unto Zion: **b** thou the walls of Jerusalem. 1129
69:35 save Zion, and will **b** the cities of Judah: 1129
89: 4 and **b up** thy throne to all generations. 1129
102:16 When the LORD shall **b up** Zion, he shall 1129
127: 1 Except the LORD **b** the house, 1129
127: 1 the house, they labour in vain that **b** it: 1129
147: 2 The LORD doth **b up** Jerusalem: 1129
Pr 24:27 in the field; and afterwards **b** thine house. 1129
Ecc 3: 3 a time to break down, and a time to **b** *up;* 1129
SS 8: 9 we will **b** upon her a palace of silver: 1129
Isa 9:10 but we will **b** *with* hewn stones: 1129
45:13 he shall **b** my city, and he shall let go my 1129
58:12 *they that shall be* of thee shall **b** the old 1129
60:10 the sons of strangers shall **b up** thy walls, 1129
61: 4 they shall **b** the old wastes, they shall raise 1129
65:21 they shall **b** houses, and inhabit *them;* and 1129
65:22 They shall not **b**, and another inhabit; 1129
66: 1 where *is* the house that ye **b** unto me? 1129
Jer 1:10 and to throw down, to **b**, and to plant. 1129
18: 9 concerning a kingdom, to **b** and to plant *it;* 1129
22:14 I will **b** me a wide house and 1129
24: 6 I will **b** them, and not pull *them* down; and 1129
29: 5 **B** ye houses, and dwell *in them;* and 1129
29:28 **b** ye houses, and dwell *in them;* and 1129
31: 4 Again I will **b** thee, and thou shalt be built, 1129
31:28 to **b**, and to plant, saith the LORD. 1129
33: 7 to return, and will **b** them, as at the first. 1129
35: 7 Neither shall ye **b** house, nor sow seed, 1129
35: 9 Nor to **b** houses for us to dwell in: 1129
42:10 will I **b** you, and not pull *you* down, and 1129
Eze 4: 2 **b** a fort against it, and cast a mount against 1129
11: 3 Which say, *It is* not near; *let us* **b** houses: 1129
21:22 the gates, to cast a mount, *and* to **b** a fort. 1129
28:26 shall **b** houses, and plant vineyards; 1129
36:36 know that I the LORD **b** the ruined *places,* 1129
Da 9:25 to **b** Jerusalem unto the Messiah the Prince 1129
Am 9:11 and I will **b** it as *in* the days of old: 1129
9:14 they shall **b** the waste cities, and 1129
Mic 3:10 They **b up** Zion with blood, and 1129
Zep 1:13 they shall also **b** houses, but not inhabit 1129
Hag 1: 8 and bring wood, and **b** the house; 1129
Zec 5:11 To **b** it a house in the land of Shinar: 1129
6:12 and he shall **b** the temple of the LORD: 1129
6:13 Even he shall **b** the temple of the LORD; 1129
6:15 and **b** in the temple of the LORD, 1129
9: 3 Tyrus did **b** herself a strong hold, and 1129
Mal 1: 4 we will return and **b** the desolate places; 1129
1: 4 They shall **b**, but I will throw down; 1129
Mt 16:18 and upon this rock I will **b** my church; *3618*
23:29 because ye **b** the tombs of the prophets, and *3618*
26:61 the temple of God, and to **b** it in three days. *3618*
Mk 14:58 within three days I will **b** another made *3618*
Lk 11:47 for ye **b** the sepulchres of the prophets, and *3618*
11:48 killed them, and ye **b** their sepulchres. *3618*
12:18 I will pull down my barns, and **b** greater; *3618*
14:28 For which of you, intending to **b** a tower, *3618*
14:30 This man began to **b**, and was not able to *3618*
Ac 7:49 what house will ye **b** me? saith the Lord: or *3618*
15:16 and will **b again** the tabernacle of David, *456*
15:16 and I will **b again** the ruins thereof, and *456*
20:32 which is able to **b** *you* up, and to give you *2026*
Ro 15:20 lest I should **b** upon another *man's* *3618*
1Co 3:12 Now if any *man* **b** upon this foundation *2026*
Gal 2:18 For if I **b** again the *things* which I *3618*

BUILDED (49) [BUILD]

Ge 4:17 he **b** a city, and called the name of the city, 1129
8:20 Noah **b** an altar unto the LORD; and 1129
10:11 **b** Nineveh, and the city Rehoboth, and 1129
11: 5 and the tower, which the children of men **b**. 1129
12: 7 there **b** he an altar unto the LORD, 1129
12: 8 there he **b** an altar unto the LORD, and 1129
26:25 he **b** an altar there, and called upon 1129
Ex 24: 4 **b** an altar under the hill, and twelve pillars, 1129

Nu 32:38 other names unto the cities which they **b**. 1129
Jos 22:16 in that ye have **b** you an altar, that ye might 1129
1Ki 8:27 how much less this house that I have **b**? 1129
8:43 which I have **b**, is called by thy name. 1129
15:22 timber thereof, where*with* Baasha had **b**; 1129
2Ki 23:13 which Solomon the king of Israel had **b** for 1129
1Ch 22: 5 the house *that is* to be **b** for the LORD 1129
Ezr 3: 2 and **b** the altar of the God of Israel, 1129
4: 1 **b** the temple unto the LORD God of 1129
4:13 if this city be **b**, and the walls set up *again*, 1124
4:16 if this city be **b** *again*, and the walls thereof 1124
4:21 *that* this city be not **b**, until *another* 1124
5: 8 which *is* **b** *with* great stones, and timber *is* 1124
5:11 build the house that was **b** these many 1124
5:11 which a great king of Israel **b** and set up. 1124
5:15 and let the house of God be **b** in his place. 1124
6: 3 Let the house be **b**, the place where they 1124
6:14 the elders of the Jews **b**, and they prospered 1124
6:14 they **b**, and finished *it*, according to 1124
Ne 3: 2 next unto him **b** the men of Jericho. 1129
3: 2 And next to them **b** Zaccur the son of Imri. 1129
4: 1 that when Sanballat heard that we **b** 1129
4:17 They which **b** on the wall, and they that 1129
4:18 had his sword girded by his side, and *so* **b**. 1129
6: 1 heard that I had **b** the wall, and *that* there 1129
7: 4 few therein, and the houses *were* not **b**, 1129
12:29 for the singers had **b** them villages round 1129
Job 20:19 taken away a house which he **b** not; 1129
Ps 122: 3 Jerusalem *is* **b** as a city that is compact 1129
Pr 9: 1 Wisdom hath **b** her house, she hath hewn 1129
24: 3 Through wisdom is a house **b**; and 1129
Ecc 2: 4 I **b** me houses; I planted me vineyards: 1129
SS 4: 4 Thy neck *is* like the tower of David **b** for 1129
Jer 30:18 the city shall be **b** upon her own heap, and 1129
La 3: 5 He hath **b** against me, and compassed *me* 1129
Eze 36:10 be inhabited, and the wastes shall be **b**: 1129
36:33 in the cities, and the wastes shall be **b**. 1129
Lk 17:28 they sold, they planted, they **b**; *3618*
Eph 2:22 In whom you also are **b together** for a *4925*
Heb 3: 3 inasmuch as he who hath **b** the house hath *2680*
3: 4 For every house is **b** by some *man;* but *2680*

BUILDEDST (1) [BUILD]
Dt 6:10 and goodly cities, which thou **b** not, 1129

BUILDER (1) [BUILD]
Heb 11:10 whose **b** and maker *is* God. *5079*

BUILDERS (15) [BUILD]
1Ki 5:18 Solomon's **b** and Hiram's builders did hew 1129
5:18 Hiram's **b** did hew *them*, and 1129
2Ki 12:11 they laid it out to the carpenters and **b**, 1129
22: 6 **b**, and masons, and to buy timber and 1129
2Ch 34:11 and **b** gave they *it*, to buy hewn stone, 1129
Ezr 3:10 when the **b** laid the foundation of 1129
Ne 4: 5 have provoked *thee* to anger before the **b**. 1129
4:18 For the **b**, every one had his sword girded 1129
Ps 118:22 The stone *which* the **b** refused is become 1129
Eze 27: 4 the seas, thy **b** have perfected thy beauty. 1129
Mt 21:42 The stone which the **b** rejected, *3618*
Mk 12:10 The stone which the **b** rejected is become *3618*
Lk 20:17 is written, The stone which the **b** rejected, *3618*
Ac 4:11 the stone which was set at nought of you **b**, *3618*
1Pe 2: 7 the stone which the **b** disallowed, *3618*

BUILDEST (5) [BUILD]
Dt 22: 8 When thou **b** a new house, then thou shalt 1129
Ne 6: 6 for which cause thou **b** the wall, that thou 1129
Eze 16:31 In that thou **b** thine eminent place in 1129
Mt 27:40 and **b** *it* in three days, save thyself. *3618*
Mk 15:29 the temple, and **b** *it* in three days, *3618*

BUILDETH (9) [BUILD]
Jos 6:26 that riseth up and **b** this city Jericho: 1129
Job 27:18 He **b** his house as a moth, and as a booth 1129
Pr 14: 1 Every wise woman **b** her house: but 1129
Jer 22:13 Woe unto him that **b** his house by 1129
Hos 8:14 hath forgotten his Maker, and **b** temples; 1129
Am 9: 6 *It is* he that **b** his stories in the heaven, and 1129
Hab 2:12 Woe to him that **b** a town with blood, and 1129
1Co 3:10 laid the foundation, and another **b thereon**. *2026*
3:10 every man take heed how he **b thereupon**. *2026*

BUILDING (37) [BUILD]
Jos 22:19 in **b** you an altar beside the altar of 1129
1Ki 3: 1 until he had made an end of **b** his own 1129
6: 7 the house, when it was **in b**, was built *of* 1129
6: 7 iron heard in the house, while it was **in b**. 1129
6:12 *Concerning* this house which thou art in **b**, 1129
6:38 fashion of it. So was he seven years in **b** it. 1129
7: 1 Solomon was **b** his own house thirteen 1129
9: 1 when Solomon had finished the **b** of 1129
15:21 Baasha heard *thereof*, that he left off **b** 1129
1Ch 28: 2 of our God, and had made ready for the **b**: 1129
2Ch 3: 3 instructed for the **b** of the house of God. 1129
16: 5 when Baasha heard *it*, that he left off **b** of 1129
16: 6 timber thereof, where*with* Baasha was a **b**; 1129
Ezr 4: 4 people of Judah, and troubled them in **b**, 1129
4:12 **b** the rebellious and the bad city, and 1124
5: 4 are the names of the men that make this **b**? 1147
5:16 that time even until now *hath it been* in **b**, 1124
6: 8 these Jews for the **b** of this house of God: 1124
Ecc 10:18 By much slothfulness the **b** decayeth; and 4746
Eze 17:17 by casting up mounts, and **b** forts, to cut off 1129
40: 5 so he measured the breadth of the **b**, 1146
41:12 Now the **b** that *was* before the separate 1146
41:12 the wall of the **b** *was* five cubits thick 1146
41:13 the separate place, and the **b**, with the walls 1140
41:15 he measured the length of the **b** over 1146
42: 1 which *was* before the **b** toward the north. 1146
42: 5 and than the middlemost of the **b**. 1146
42: 6 *the* **b** was straitened more than the lowest NIH
42:10 the separate place, and over against the **b**. 1146
46:23 *there was* a row *of* **b** round about in them, NIH
Jn 2:20 Forty and six years was this temple in **b**, *3618*
1Co 3: 9 ye are God's husbandry, *ye are* God's **b**. *3619*
2Co 5: 1 we have a **b** of God, a house not made with *3619*
Eph 2:21 In whom all the **b** fitly framed together *3619*
Heb 9:11 with hands, that is to say, not of this **b**, *2937*
Jude 1:20 **b up** yourselves on your most holy faith, *2026*
Rev 21:18 And the **b** of the wall of it was *of* jasper: *1739*

BUILDINGS (3) [BUILD]
Mt 24: 1 to *him* for to shew him the **b** of the temple. *3619*
Mk 13: 1 manner of stones and what **b** *are here*. *3619*
13: 2 said unto him, Seest thou these great **b**? *3619*

BUILT (171) [BUILD]
Ge 13:18 and **b** there an altar unto the LORD. 1129
22: 9 Abraham **b** an altar there, and laid 1129
33:17 **b** him a house, and made booths for his 1129
35: 7 he **b** there an altar, and called the place 1129
Ex 1:11 they **b** for Pharaoh treasure cities, Pithom 1129
17:15 Moses **b** an altar, and called the name of it 1129
32: 5 when Aaron saw *it*, he **b** an altar before it; 1129
Nu 13:22 *were*. (Now Hebron was **b** seven years 1129
21:27 let the city of Sihon be **b** and prepared: 1129
23:14 **b** seven altars, and offered a bullock and 1129
32:34 the children of Gad **b** Dibon, and Ataroth, 1129
32:37 the children of Reuben **b** Heshbon, and 1129
Dt 8:12 hast **b** goodly houses, and dwelt *therein;* 1129
13:16 be a heap for ever; it shall not be **b** again. 1129
20: 5 What man *is there* that hath **b** a new house, 1129
Jos 8:30 Joshua **b** an altar unto the LORD God of 1129
19:50 and he **b** the city, and dwelt therein. 1129
22:10 the half tribe of Manasseh **b** there an altar 1129
22:11 the half tribe of Manasseh have **b** an altar 1129
22:23 That we have **b** us an altar to turn from 1129
24:13 cities which ye **b** not, and ye dwell in them; 1129
Jdg 1:26 **b** a city, and called the name thereof Luz: 1129
6:24 Gideon **b** an altar there unto the LORD, 1129
6:28 was offered upon the altar that was **b**. 1129
18:28 And they **b** a city, and dwelt therein. 1129
21: 4 **b** there an altar, and offered burnt offerings 1129
1Sa 7:17 and there he **b** an altar unto the LORD. 1129
14:35 Saul **b** an altar unto the LORD: the same 1129
14:35 the same was the first altar that he **b** unto 1129
2Sa 5: 9 David **b** round about from Millo and 1129
5:11 masons: and they **b** David a house. 1129
24:25 David **b** there an altar unto the LORD, 1129
1Ki 3: 2 there was no house **b** unto the name of 1129
6: 2 the house which king Solomon **b** for 1129
6: 5 against the wall of the house he **b** chambers 1129
6: 7 was **b** *of* stone made ready *before it was* 1129
6: 9 So he **b** the house, and finished it; and 1129
6:10 *then* he **b** chambers against all the house, 1129
6:14 So Solomon **b** the house, and finished it. 1129
6:15 he **b** the walls of the house within with 1129
6:16 he **b** twenty cubits on the sides of 1129

1Ki 6:16 he even **b** *them* for it within, *even* for 1129
6:36 he **b** the inner court *with* three rows of 1129
7: 2 He **b** also the house of the forest of 1129
8:13 I have **surely b** thee a house to dwell 1129+1129
8:20 have **b** a house for the name of the LORD 1129
8:44 *toward* the house that I have **b** for thy 1129
8:48 and the house which I have **b** for thy name: 1129
9: 3 hallowed this house, which thou hast **b**, 1129
9:10 when Solomon had **b** the two houses, 1129
9:17 Solomon **b** Gezer, and Beth-horon 1129
9:24 her house which *Solomon* had **b** for her: 1129
9:25 peace offerings upon the altar which he **b** 1129
10: 4 and the house that he had **b**, 1129
11:27 Solomon **b** Millo, *and* repaired the breaches 1129
11:38 as I **b** for David, and will give Israel unto 1129
12:25 Jeroboam **b** Shechem in mount Ephraim, 1129
12:25 went out from thence, and **b** Penuel. 1129
14:23 For they also **b** them high places, and 1129
15:17 **b** Ramah, that *he* might not suffer *any* to go 1129
15:22 king Asa **b** with them Geba of Benjamin, 1129
15:23 all that he did, and the cities which he **b**, 1129
16:24 **b** *on* the hill, and called the name of 1129
16:24 and called the name of the city which he **b**, 1129
16:32 house of Baal, which he had **b** in Samaria. 1129
18:32 *with* the stones he **b** an altar in the name of 1129
22:39 which he made, and all the cities that he **b**, 1129
2Ki 14:22 He **b** Elath, and restored it to Judah, 1129
15:35 He **b** the higher gate of the house of 1129
16:11 Urijah the priest **b** an altar according to all 1129
16:18 the covert for the sabbath that they had **b** in 1129
17: 9 they **b** them high places in all their cities, 1129
21: 3 For he **b** *up* again the high places which 1129
21: 4 And he **b** altars in the house of the LORD, 1129
21: 5 he **b** altars for all the host of heaven in 1129
25: 1 and they **b** forts against it round about. 1129
1Ch 6:10 in the temple that Solomon **b** in Jerusalem:) 1129
6:32 until Solomon had **b** the house of 1129
7:24 who **b** Beth-horon the nether, and 1129
8:12 and Shamed, who **b** Ono, and Lod, 1129
11: 8 he **b** the city round about, even from Millo 1129
17: 6 Why have ye not **b** me a house of cedars? 1129
21:26 David **b** there an altar unto the LORD, 1129
22:19 into the house that is *to be* **b** to the name of 1129
2Ch 6: 2 I have **b** a house of habitation for thee, and 1129
6:10 have **b** the house for the name of 1129
6:18 how much less this house which I have **b**? 1129
6:33 may know that this house which I have **b** is 1129
6:34 the house which I have **b** for thy name; 1129
6:38 toward the house which I have **b** for thy 1129
8: 1 wherein Solomon had **b** the house of 1129
8: 2 Solomon **b** them, and caused the children 1129
8: 4 he **b** Tadmor in the wilderness, and all 1129
8: 4 all the store cities, which he **b** in Hamath. 1129
8: 5 Also he **b** Beth-horon the upper, and 1129
8:11 David unto the house that he had **b** for her: 1129
8:12 which he had **b** before the porch, 1129
9: 3 of Solomon, and the house that he had **b**, 1129
11: 5 and **b** cities for defence in Judah. 1129
11: 6 He **b** even Beth-lehem, and Etam, and 1129
14: 6 he **b** fenced cities in Judah: for the land had 1129
14: 7 rest on every side. So they **b** and prospered. 1129
16: 1 **b** Ramah, to the intent that *he* might let 1129
16: 6 and he **b** therewith Geba and Mizpah. 1129
17:12 he **b** in Judah castles, and cities of store. 1129
20: 8 have **b** thee a sanctuary therein for thy 1129
26: 2 He **b** Eloth, and restored it to Judah, 1129
26: 6 **b** cities about Ashdod, and among 1129
26: 9 Moreover Uzziah **b** towers in Jerusalem at 1129
26:10 Also he **b** towers in the desert, and 1129
27: 3 He **b** the high gate of the house of 1129
27: 3 and on the wall of Ophel he **b** much. 1129
27: 4 Moreover he **b** cities in the mountains of 1129
27: 4 and in the forests he **b** castles and towers. 1129
32: 5 **b up** all the wall that was broken, and 1129
33: 3 For he **b** again the high places which 1129
33: 4 Also he **b** altars in the house of 1129
33: 5 he **b** altars for all the host of heaven in 1129
33:14 Now after this he **b** a wall without the city 1129
33:15 all the altars that he had **b** in the mount of 1129
33:19 the places wherein he **b** high places, and 1129
Ne 3: 1 the priests, and they **b** the sheep gate; 1129
3:13 they **b** it, and set up the doors thereof, 1129
3:14 he **b** it, and set up the doors thereof, 1129
3:15 he **b** it, and covered it, and set up the doors 1129
4: 6 So **b** we the wall; and all the wall was 1129
7: 1 when the wall was **b**, and I had set up 1129
Job 3:14 which **b** desolate places for themselves; 1129
12:14 it cannot be **b** *again:* he shutteth up a man, 1129
22:23 thou shalt be **b** *up,* thou shalt put away 1129
Ps 78:69 he **b** his sanctuary like high *palaces,* like 1129
89: 2 I have said, Mercy shall be **b up** for ever: 1129
Ecc 9:14 besieged it, and **b** great bulwarks against it: 1129
Isa 5: 2 **b** a tower in the midst of it, and also made a 1129
25: 2 strangers to be no city; it shall never be **b**. 1129
44:26 Ye shall be **b**, and I will raise up 1129
44:28 even saying to Jerusalem, Thou shalt be **b**; 1129
Jer 7:31 they have **b** the high places of Tophet, 1129
12:16 shall they be **b** in the midst of my people. 1129
19: 5 They have **b** also the high places of Baal, 1129
31: 4 and thou shalt be **b**, O virgin of Israel: 1129
31:38 that the city shall be **b** to the LORD from 1129
32:31 of my fury from the day that they **b** it even 1129
32:35 they **b** the high places of Baal, which *are* in 1129
45: 4 *that* which I have **b** *will* I break down, and 1129
52: 4 and **b** forts against it round about. 1129
Eze 13:10 one **b up** a wall, and lo, others daubed it 1129
16:24 *That* thou hast also **b** unto thee an eminent 1129
16:25 Thou hast **b** thy high place at every head of 1129
26:14 spread nets upon; thou shalt be **b** no more: 1129
Da 4:30 that I have **b** for the house of the kingdom 1124
9:25 the street shall be **b** again, and the wall, 1129
Am 5:11 ye have **b** houses of hewn stone, but 1129
Mic 7:11 *In* the day that thy walls are *to be* **b**, *in* that 1129
Hag 1: 2 time that the LORD's house should be **b**. 1129
Zec 1:16 my house shall be **b** in it, saith the LORD 1129
8: 9 hosts was laid, that the temple might be **b**. 1129
Mt 7:24 a wise man, which **b** his house upon a rock: *3618*
7:26 which **b** his house upon the sand: *3618*
21:33 and **b** a tower, and let it out to husbandmen, *3618*
Mk 12: 1 and **b** a tower, and let it out to husbandmen, *3618*
Lk 4:29 brow of the hill whereon their city was **b**, *3618*
6:48 He is like a man which **b** a house, and *3618*
6:49 is like a man that without a foundation **b** a *3618*
7: 5 our nation, and he hath **b** us a synagogue. *3618*
Ac 7:47 But Solomon **b** him a house. *3618*
1Co 3:14 work abide which he hath **b thereupon**, *2026*
Eph 2:20 And are **b** upon the foundation of *2026*
Col 2: 7 Rooted and **b up** in him, and stablished in *2026*
Heb 3: 4 some *man;* but he that **b** all *things is* God. *2680*
1Pe 2: 5 as lively stones, are **b** *up* a spiritual house, *3618*

BUKKI (5)

Nu 34:22 of the children of Dan, **B** the son of Jogli. 1231
1Ch 6: 5 Abishua begat **B**, and Bukki begat Uzzi, 1231
6: 5 Abishua begat Bukki, and **B** begat Uzzi, 1231
6:51 **B** his son, Uzzi his son, Zerahiah his son, 1231
Ezr 7: 4 of Zerahiah, the son of Uzzi, the son of **B**, 1231

BUKKIAH (2)

1Ch 25: 4 **B**, Mattaniah, Uzziel, Shebuel, and 1232
25:13 The sixth *to* **B**, *he,* his sons, and 1232

BUL (1)

1Ki 6:38 in the eleventh year, in the month **B**, 945

BULL (2) [BULLOCK, BULLOCK'S, BULLOCKS, BULLS]

Job 21:10 Their **b** gendereth, and faileth not; 7794
Isa 51:20 head of all the streets, as a **wild b** *in* a net: 8377

BULLOCK (104) [BULL]

Ex 29: 1 Take one young **b**, and two rams 1241+6499
29: 3 in the basket, with the **b** and the two rams. 6499
29:10 thou shalt cause a **b** to be brought before 6499
29:10 shall put their hands upon the head of the **b**. 6499
29:11 thou shalt kill the **b** before the LORD, 6499
29:12 thou shalt take of the blood of the **b**, and 6499
29:14 the flesh of the **b**, and his skin, and his 6499
29:36 thou shalt offer every day a **b** *for* a sin 6499
Lev 1: 5 he shall kill the **b** before the LORD: 1121+1241
4: 3 a young **b** without blemish unto 1241+6499
4: 4 he shall bring the **b** unto the door of 6499
4: 4 and kill the **b** before the LORD. 6499
4: 7 shall pour all the blood of the **b** at 6499
4: 8 he shall take off from it all the fat of the **b** 6499
4:10 As it was taken off from the **b** of 7794
4:11 the skin of the **b**, and all his flesh, with his 6499
4:12 Even the whole **b** shall he carry forth 6499
4:14 shall offer a young **b** for the sin, 1241+6499

Lev 4:15 upon the head of the **b** before the LORD: 6499
4:15 and the **b** shall be killed before the LORD. 6499
4:20 he shall do with the **b** as he did with 6499
4:20 as he did with the **b** for a sin offering, 6499
4:21 he shall carry forth the **b** without the camp, 6499
4:21 and burn him as he burned the first **b**: 6499
8: 2 a **b** *for* the sin offering, and two rams, and 6499
8:14 he brought the **b** *for* the sin offering: and 6499
8:14 upon the head of the **b** *for* the sin offering. 6499
8:17 the **b**, and his hide, his flesh, and his dung, 6499
9: 4 Also a **b** and a ram for peace offerings, 7794
9:18 He slew also the **b** and the ram *for* a 7794
9:19 the fat of the **b** and of the ram, the rump, 7794
16: 3 with a young **b** for a sin offering, 1241+6499
16: 6 Aaron shall offer *his* **b** of the sin offering, 6499
16:11 Aaron shall bring the **b** of the sin offering, 6499
16:11 shall kill the **b** of the sin offering which *is* 6499
16:14 he shall take of the blood of the **b**, and 6499
16:15 that blood as he did with the blood of the **b**, 6499
16:18 shall take of the blood of the **b**, and of 6499
16:27 the **b** for the sin offering, and the goat for 6499
22:23 Either a **b** or a lamb that hath any thing 7794
22:27 When a **b**, or a sheep, or a goat, is brought 7794
23:18 and one young **b**, and two rams: 1241+6499
Nu 7:15 One young **b**, one ram, one lamb of 1241+6499
7:21 One young **b**, one ram, one lamb of 1241+6499
7:27 One young **b**, one ram, one lamb of 1241+6499
7:33 One young **b**, one ram, one lamb of 1241+6499
7:39 One young **b**, one ram, one lamb of 1241+6499
7:45 One young **b**, one ram, one lamb of 1241+6499
7:51 One young **b**, one ram, one lamb of 1241+6499
7:57 One young **b**, one ram, one lamb of 1241+6499
7:63 One young **b**, one ram, one lamb of 1241+6499
7:69 One young **b**, one ram, one lamb of 1241+6499
7:75 One young **b**, one ram, one lamb of 1241+6499
7:81 One young **b**, one ram, one lamb of 1241+6499
8: 8 let them take a young **b** with his 1241+6499
8: 8 another young **b** shalt thou take for a 1241+6499
15: 8 when thou preparest a **b** *for* a burnt 1121+1241
15: 9 shall he bring with a **b** a meat 1121+1241
15:11 Thus shall it be done for one **b**, or for one 7794
15:24 one young **b** for a burnt offering, 1241+6499
23: 2 and Balaam offered on *every* altar a **b** and 6499
23: 4 I have offered upon *every* altar a **b** and 6499
23:14 and offered a **b** and a ram on *every* altar. 6499
23:30 and offered a **b** and a ram on *every* altar. 6499
28:12 meat offering, mingled with oil, for one **b**; 6499
28:14 shall be half a hin of wine unto a **b**, 6499
28:20 three tenth deals shall ye offer for a **b**, and 6499
28:28 three tenth deals unto one **b**, two tenth 6499
29: 2 one young **b**, one ram, *and* 1241+6499
29: 3 three tenth deals for a **b**, *and* two tenth 6499
29: 8 one young **b**, one ram, *and* 1241+6499
29: 9 three tenth deals to a **b**, *and* two tenth deals 6499
29:14 three tenth deals unto every **b** of 6499
29:36 one **b**, one ram, seven lambs of the first 6499
29:37 and their drink offerings for the **b**, 6499
Dt 15:19 shalt do no work with the firstling of thy **b**, 7794
17: 1 sacrifice unto the LORD thy God *any* **b**, 7794
33:17 His glory *is like* the firstling of his **b**, and 7794
Jdg 6:25 said unto him, Take thy father's young **b**, 7794
6:25 even the second **b** of seven years old, and 6499
6:26 take the second **b**, and offer a burnt 6499
6:28 the second **b** was offered upon the altar that 6499
1Sa 1:25 they slew a **b**, and brought the child to Eli. 6499
1Ki 18:23 let them choose one **b** for themselves, and 6499
18:23 no fire *under:* and I will dress the other **b**, 6499
18:25 Choose you one **b** for yourselves, and 6499
18:26 they took the **b** which was given them, and 6499
18:33 cut the **b** in pieces, and laid *him* on 6499
2Ch 13: 9 to consecrate himself with a young **b** 1241+6499
Ps 50: 9 I will take no **b** out of thy house, *nor* he 6499
69:31 than an ox *or* **b** that hath horns *and* hoofs. 6499
Isa 65:25 and the lion shall eat straw like the **b**: 1241
Jer 31:18 as a **b** unaccustomed *to the yoke;* turn thou 5695
Eze 43:19 a young **b** for a sin offering. 1241+6499
43:21 Thou shalt take the **b** also of the sin 6499
43:22 the altar, as they did cleanse *it* with the **b**. 6499
43:23 offer a young **b** without blemish, 1241+6499
43:25 they shall also prepare a young **b**, 1241+6499
45:18 thou shalt take a young **b** without 1241+6499
45:22 for all the people of the land a **b** *for* a sin 6499
45:24 prepare a meat offering *of* an ephah for a **b**, 6499
46: 6 *shall be* a young **b** without blemish, 1241+6499
46: 7 an ephah for a **b**, and an ephah for a ram, 6499
46:11 the meat offering shall be an ephah to a **b**, 6499

BULLOCK'S (3) [BULL]

Lev 4: 4 shall lay his hand upon the **b** head, and 6499
4: 5 the priest that is anointed shall take of the **b** 6499
4:16 **b** blood to the tabernacle of 6499

BULLOCKS (45) [BULL]

Nu 7:87 oxen for the burnt offering *were* twelve **b**, 6499
7:88 the peace offerings *were* twenty and four **b**, 6499
8:12 lay their hands upon the heads of the **b**: 6499
23:29 prepare me here seven **b** and seven rams. 6499
28:11 two young **b**, and one ram, 1241+6499
28:19 two young **b**, and one ram, and 1241+6499
28:27 two young **b**, one ram, seven lambs 1241+6499
29:13 thirteen young **b**, two rams, *and* 1241+6499
29:14 deals unto every bullock of the thirteen **b**, 6499
29:17 day *ye shall offer* twelve young **b**, 1241+6499
29:18 and their drink offerings for the **b**, 6499
29:20 on the third day eleven **b**, two rams, 6499
29:21 and their drink offerings for the **b**, 6499
29:23 on the fourth day ten **b**, two rams, *and* 6499
29:24 and their drink offerings for the **b**, 6499
29:26 on the fifth day nine **b**, two rams, *and* 6499
29:27 and their drink offerings for the **b**, 6499
29:29 And on the sixth day eight **b**, two rams, *and* 6499
29:30 and their drink offerings for the **b**, 6499
29:32 on the seventh day seven **b**, two rams, *and* 6499
29:33 and their drink offerings for the **b**, 6499
1Sa 1:24 with three **b**, and one ephah of flour, and 6499
1Ki 18:23 Let them therefore give us two **b**; and 6499
1Ch 15:26 that they offered seven **b** and seven rams. 6499
29:21 *even* a thousand **b**, a thousand rams, *and* 6499
2Ch 29:21 they brought seven **b**, and seven rams, and 6499
29:22 So they killed the **b**, and the priests 1241
29:32 was threescore and ten **b**, an hundred rams, 1241
30:24 did give to the congregation a thousand **b** 6499
30:24 gave to the congregation a thousand **b** 6499
35: 7 of thirty thousand, and three thousand **b**: 1241
Ezr 6: 9 both young **b**, and rams, and lambs, 8450
6:17 of this house of God an hundred **b**, 8450
7:17 mayest buy speedily with this money **b**, 8450
8:35 twelve **b** for all Israel, ninety and six rams, 6499
Job 42: 8 Therefore take unto you now seven **b** and 6499
Ps 51:19 then shall they offer **b** upon thine altar. 6499
66:15 incense of rams; I will offer **b** with goats. 1241
Isa 1:11 I delight not in the blood of **b**, or of lambs, 6499
34: 7 down with them, and the **b** with the bulls; 6499
Jer 46:21 men *are* in the midst of her like fatted **b**; 5695
50:27 Slay all her **b**; let them go down to 6499
Eze 39:18 of rams, of lambs, and of goats, of **b**, all of 6499
45:23 seven **b** and seven rams without blemish 6499
Hos 12:11 they sacrifice **b** in Gilgal; yea, their altars 7794

BULLS (10) [BULL]

Ge 32:15 forty kine, and ten **b**, twenty she asses, and 6499
Ps 22:12 Many **b** have compassed me: strong *bulls* 6499
22:12 strong *b* of Bashan have beset me round. NIH
50:13 Will I eat the flesh of **b**, or drink the blood of 47
68:30 the multitude of the **b**, with the calves of 47
Isa 34: 7 down with them, and the bullocks with the **b**; 47
Jer 50:11 fat as the heifer at grass, and bellow as **b**; 47
52:20 twelve brasen **b** that *were* under the bases, 1241
Heb 9:13 For if the blood of **b** and of goats, and *5022*
10: 4 For *it is* not possible that the blood of **b** and *5022*

BULRUSH (1) [BULRUSHES, RUSH]

Isa 58: 5 *is it* to bow down his head as a **b**, and 100

BULRUSHES (2) [BULRUSH, RUSH]

Ex 2: 3 she took for him an ark of **b**, and daubed it 1573
Isa 18: 2 even in vessels of **b** upon the waters, 1573

BULWARKS (5)

Dt 20:20 thou shalt build **b** against the city that 4692
2Ch 26:15 *men,* to be on the towers and upon the **b**, 6438
Ps 48:13 Mark ye well her **b**, consider her palaces; 2430
Ecc 9:14 and besieged it, and built great **b** against it: 4685
Isa 26: 1 salvation will *God* appoint *for* walls and **b**. 2426

BUNAH (1)

1Ch 2:25 and **B**, and Oren, and Ozem, *and* Ahijah. 946

B

BUNCH (1) [BUNCHES]
Ex 12:22 ye shall take a **b** of hyssop, and dip *it* in 92

BUNCHES (3) [BUNCH]
2Sa 16: 1 an hundred **b of raisins**, and an hundred of 6778
1Ch 12:40 cakes *of figs*, and **b of raisins**, and wine, 6778
Isa 30: 6 their treasures upon the **b** of camels, to a 1707

BUNDLE (4) [BUNDLES]
Ge 42:35 every man's **b** of money *was* in his sack: 6872
1Sa 25:29 the soul of my lord shall be bound in the **b** 6872
SS 1:13 A **b** of myrrh *is* my well-beloved unto me; 6872
Ac 28: 3 And when Paul had gathered a **b** of sticks, *4128*

BUNDLES (2) [BUNDLE]
Ge 42:35 and their father saw the **b** of money, 6872
Mt 13:30 the tares, and bind them in **b** to burn them: *1197*

BUNNI (3)
Ne 9: 4 **B**, Sherebiah, Bani, *and* Chenani, and 1138
10:15 **B**, Azgad, Bebai, 1138
11:15 the son of Hashabiah, the son of **B**; 1138

BURDEN (69) [BURDENED, BURDENS, BURDENSOME]
Ex 18:22 and they shall bear *the* **b** with thee. NIH
23: 5 of him that hateth thee lying under his **b**, 4853
Nu 4:15 These *things are* the **b** of the sons of 4853
4:19 them every one to his service and to his **b**: 4853
4:31 this *is* the charge of their **b**, according to all 4853
4:32 the instruments of the charge of their **b**. 4853
4:47 the service of the **b** in the tabernacle of 4853
4:49 to his service, and according to his **b**: 4853
11:11 that *thou* layest the **b** of all this people upon 4853
11:17 they shall bear the **b** of the people with 4853
Dt 1:12 and your **b**, and your strife? 4853
2Sa 15:33 on with me, then thou shalt be a **b** unto me: 4853
19:35 should thy servant be yet a **b** unto my lord 4853
2Ki 5:17 be given to thy servant two mules' **b** of 4853
8: 9 forty camels' **b**, and came and stood before 4853
9:25 his father, the LORD laid this **b** upon him; 4853
2Ch 35: 3 *it shall* not *be* a **b** upon your shoulders: 4853
Ne 13:19 *that* there should no **b** be brought in on 4853
Job 7:20 against thee, so that I am a **b** to myself? 4853
Ps 38: 4 as a heavy **b** they are too heavy for me. 4853
55:22 Cast thy **b** upon the LORD, and he shall 3053
81: 6 I removed his shoulder from the **b**: 5447
Ecc 12: 5 the grasshopper shall be a **b**, and desire 5445
Isa 9: 4 For thou hast broken the yoke of his **b**, and 5448
10:27 *that* his **b** shall be taken away from off thy 5448
13: 1 The **b** of Babylon, which Isaiah the son of 4853
14:25 and his **b** depart from off their shoulders. 5448
14:28 In the year that king Ahaz died was this **b**. 4853
15: 1 The **b** of Moab. Because in the night Ar of 4853
17: 1 The **b** of Damascus. Behold, Damascus *is* 4853
19: 1 The **b** of Egypt. Behold, the LORD rideth 4853
21: 1 The **b** of the desert of the sea. 4853
21:11 The **b** of Dumah. He calleth to me out of 4853
21:13 The **b** upon Arabia. In the forest in Arabia 4853
22: 1 The **b** of the valley of vision. What aileth 4853
22:25 and the **b** that *was* upon it shall be cut off: 4853
23: 1 The **b** of Tyre. Howl, ye ships of Tarshish; 4853
30: 6 The **b** of the beasts of the south: into 4853
30:27 *with* his anger, and the **b** *thereof is* heavy: 4858
46: 1 *they are* a **b** to the weary *beast*. 4853
46: 2 they could not deliver the **b**, but 4853
Jer 17:21 bear no **b** on the sabbath day, 4853
17:22 Neither carry forth a **b** out of your houses 4853
17:24 to bring in no **b** through the gates of this 4853
17:27 not to bear a **b**, even entering in at the gates 4853
23:33 saying, What *is* the **b** of the LORD? 4853
23:33 thou shalt then say unto them, What **b**? 4853
23:34 that shall say, The **b** of the LORD, 4853
23:36 the **b** of the LORD shall ye mention no 4853
23:36 for every man's word shall be his **b**; for ye 4853
23:38 sith ye say, The **b** of the LORD; therefore 4853
23:38 The **b** of the LORD, and I have sent unto 4853
23:38 Ye shall not say, The **b** of the LORD; 4853
Eze 12:10 This **b** *concerneth* the prince in Jerusalem, 4853
Hos 8:10 they shall sorrow a little for the **b** of 4853
Na 1: 1 The **b** of Nineveh. The book of the vision 4853
Hab 1: 1 The **b** which Habakkuk the prophet did see. 4853
Zep 3:18 of thee, *to whom* the reproach of it *was* a **b**. 4864
Zec 9: 1 The **b** of the word of the LORD in 4853
12: 1 The **b** of the word of the LORD for Israel, 4853
12: 3 all that **b** themselves with it shall be cut in 6006
Mal 1: 1 The **b** of the word of the LORD to Israel 4853
Mt 11:30 For my yoke *is* easy, and my **b** is light. *5413*
20:12 which have borne the **b** and heat of the day. *922*
Ac 15:28 to lay upon you no greater **b** than these *922*
21: 3 for there the ship was to unlade *her* **b**. *1117*
2Co 12:16 But be it so, I did not **b** you: nevertheless, *2599*
Gal 6: 5 For every man shall bear his own **b**. *5413*
Rev 2:24 they speak; I will put upon you none other **b**. *922*

BURDENED (2) [BURDEN]
2Co 5: 4 that are in *this* tabernacle do groan, being **b**: *916*
8:13 not that other *men* be eased, and you **b**: *2347*

BURDENS (25) [BURDEN]
Ge 49:14 a strong ass couching down between **two b**: 4942
Ex 1:11 taskmasters to afflict them with their **b**. 5450
2:11 unto his brethren, and looked on their **b**: 5450
5: 4 from their works? get you unto your **b**. 5450
5: 5 and you make them rest from their **b**. 5450
6: 6 I will bring you out from under the **b** of 5450
6: 7 which bringeth you out from under the **b** of 5450
Nu 4:24 of the Gershonites, to serve, and for **b**: 4853
4:27 in all their **b**, and in all their service: 4853
4:27 appoint unto them in charge all their **b**. 4853
1Ki 5:15 and ten thousand that bare **b**, 5449
2Ch 2: 2 and ten thousand men to bear **b**, 5449
2:18 ten thousand of them *to be* **bearers of b**, 5449
24:27 the greatness of the **b** *laid* upon him, and 4853
34:13 Also *they were* over the **bearers of b**, and 5449
Ne 4:10 The strength of the **bearers of b** is 5449
4:17 and they that bare **b**, *with* those that laded, 5447
13:15 grapes, and figs, and all *manner of* **b**, 4853
Isa 58: 6 to undo the heavy **b**, and to let the oppressed 92
La 2:14 have seen for thee false **b** and causes of 4864
Am 5:11 the poor, and ye take from him **b** of wheat: 4864
Mt 23: 4 For they bind heavy **b** and grievous to be *5413*
Lk 11:46 for ye lade men *with* **b** grievous to be *5413*
11:46 ye yourselves touch not the **b** with one of *5413*
Gal 6: 2 Bear ye one another's **b**, and so fulfil the law *922*

BURDENSOME (5) [BURDEN]
Zec 12: 3 in that day will I make Jerusalem a **b** stone 4614
2Co 11: 9 in all *things* I have kept myself **from being b** *4*
12:13 except *it be* that I myself was not **b** to you? *2655*
12:14 to come to you; and I will not be **b** to you: *2655*
1Th 2: 6 when we might have been **b**, *922+1722*

BURIAL (6) [BURY]
2Ch 26:23 field of the **b** which *belonged* to the kings; 6900
Ecc 6: 3 with good, and also *that* he have no **b**; 6900
Isa 14:20 Thou shalt not be joined with them in **b**, 6900
Jer 22:19 He shall be buried *with* the **b** of an ass, 6900
Mt 26:12 ointment on my body, she did *it* for my **b**. *1779*
Ac 8: 2 And devout men carried Stephen *to his* **b**, NIG

BURIED (106) [BURY]
Ge 15:15 in peace; thou shalt be **b** in a good old age. 6912
23:19 Abraham **b** Sarah his wife in the cave of 6912
25: 9 Ishmael **b** him in the cave of Machpelah, 6912
25:10 there was Abraham **b**, and Sarah his wife. 6912
35: 8 she was **b** beneath Beth-el under an oak: 6912
35:19 and was **b** in the way to Ephrath, 6912
35:29 and his sons Esau and Jacob **b** him. 6912
48: 7 I **b** her there in the way of Ephrath; 6912
49:31 There they **b** Abraham and Sarah his wife; 6912
49:31 there they **b** Isaac and Rebekah his wife; 6912
49:31 and Rebekah his wife; and there I **b** Leah. 6912
50:13 **b** him in the cave of the field of 6912
50:14 to bury his father, after he had **b** his father. 6912
Nu 11:34 because there they **b** the people that lusted. 6912
20: 1 and Miriam died there, and was **b** there. 6912
33: 4 For the Egyptians **b** all *their* firstborn, 6912
Dt 10: 6 there Aaron died, and there he was **b**; 6912
34: 6 he **b** him in a valley in the land of Moab, 6912
Jos 24:30 they **b** him in the border of his inheritance 6912
24:32 up out of Egypt, **b** they in Shechem, 6912
24:33 they **b** him in a hill that pertained to 6912
Jdg 2: 9 they **b** him in the border of his inheritance 6912
8:32 was **b** in the sepulchre of Joash his father, 6912
10: 2 three years, and died, and was **b** in Shamir. 6912
10: 5 And Jair died, and was **b** in Camon. 6912
12: 7 and was **b** in *one of* the cities of Gilead. 6912
12:10 Then died Ibzan, and was **b** at Beth-lehem. 6912

Jdg 12:12 was **b** in Aijalon in the country of Zebulun. 6912
12:15 was **b** in Pirathon in the land of Ephraim, 6912
16:31 **b** him between Zorah and Eshtaol in 6912
Ru 1:17 thou diest, will I die, and there will I be **b**: 6912
1Sa 25: 1 and **b** him in his house at Ramah. 6912
28: 3 and **b** him in Ramah, even in his own city. 6912
31:13 **b** *them* under a tree at Jabesh, and 6912
2Sa 2: 4 men of Jabesh-gilead *were they* that **b** Saul. 6912
2: 5 your lord, *even* unto Saul, and have **b** him. 6912
2:32 and **b** him in the sepulchre of his father, 6912
3:32 they **b** Abner in Hebron: and the king lift 6912
4:12 **b** *it* in the sepulchre of Abner in Hebron. 6912
17:23 and was **b** in the sepulchre of his father. 6912
19:37 *and be* **b** by the grave of my father and NIH
21:14 Jonathan his son **b** they in the country of 6912
1Ki 2:10 his fathers, and was **b** in the city of David. 6912
2:34 he was **b** in his own house in 6912
11:43 and was **b** in the city of David his father: 6912
13:31 it came to pass, after he had **b** him, that he 6912
13:31 the sepulchre wherein the man of God *is* **b**; 6912
14:18 they **b** him; and all Israel mourned for him, 6912
14:31 was **b** with his fathers in the city of David. 6912
15: 8 and they **b** him in the city of David: 6912
15:24 was **b** with his fathers in the city of David 6912
16: 6 slept with his fathers, and was **b** in Tirzah: 6912
16:28 with his fathers, and was **b** in Samaria: 6912
22:37 *to* Samaria; and they **b** the king in Samaria. 6912
22:50 was **b** with his fathers in the city of David 6912
2Ki 8:24 was **b** with his fathers in the city of David: 6912
9:28 **b** him in his sepulchre with his fathers in 6912
10:35 they **b** him in Samaria. And Jehoahaz his 6912
12:21 they **b** him with his fathers in the city of 6912
13: 9 with his fathers; and they **b** him in Samaria: 6912
13:13 Joash was **b** in Samaria with the kings of 6912
13:20 Elisha died, and they **b** him. And the bands 6912
14:16 was **b** in Samaria with the kings of Israel; 6912
14:20 he was **b** at Jerusalem with his fathers in 6912
15: 7 they **b** him with his fathers in the city of 6912
15:38 was **b** with his fathers in the city of David 6912
16:20 was **b** with his fathers in the city of David: 6912
21:18 was **b** in the garden of his own house, 6912
21:26 he was **b** in his sepulchre in the garden of 6912
23:30 and **b** him in his own sepulchre. 6912
1Ch 10:12 **b** their bones under the oak in Jabesh, and 6912
2Ch 9:31 and he was **b** in the city of David his father: 6912
12:16 his fathers, and was **b** in the city of David: 6912
14: 1 and they **b** him in the city of David: 6912
16:14 they **b** him in his own sepulchres, which he 6912
21: 1 was **b** with his fathers in the city of David. 6912
21:20 Howbeit they **b** him in the city of David, 6912
22: 9 when they had slain him, they **b** him: 6912
24:16 they **b** him in the city of David among 6912
24:25 they **b** him in the city of David, but 6912
24:25 they **b** him not in the sepulchres of 6912
25:28 **b** him with his fathers in the city of Judah. 6912
26:23 they **b** him with his fathers in the field of 6912
27: 9 and they **b** him in the city of David: 6912
28:27 they **b** him in the city, *even* in Jerusalem: 6912
32:33 they **b** him in the chiefest of the sepulchres 6912
33:20 and they **b** him *in* his own house: 6912
35:24 was **b** in *one of the* sepulchres of his 6912
Job 27:15 Those that remain of him shall be **b** in 6912
Ecc 8:10 so I saw the wicked **b**, who had come and 6912
Jer 8: 2 they shall not be gathered, nor be **b**; 6912
16: 4 neither shall they be **b**; *but* they shall be as 6912
16: 6 they shall not be **b**, neither shall *men* 6912
20: 6 shalt be **b** there, thou, and all thy friends, 6912
22:19 He shall be **b** *with* the burial of an ass, 6912
25:33 not be lamented, neither gathered, nor **b**; 6912
Eze 39:15 till the buriers have **b** it in the valley of 6912
Mt 14:12 the body, and **b** it, and went and told Jesus. *2290*
Lk 16:22 the rich *man* also died, and was **b**; *2290*
Ac 2:29 that he is both dead and **b**, and *2290*
5: 6 him up, and carried *him* out, and **b** *him*. *2290*
5: 9 the feet of them which have **b** thy husband *2290*
5:10 carrying *her* forth, **b** *her* by her husband. *2290*
Ro 6: 4 Therefore we are **b with** him by baptism *4916*
1Co 15: 4 And that he was **b**, and that he rose *again* *2290*
Col 2:12 **B with** him in baptism, wherein also you *4916*

BURIERS (1) [BURY]
Eze 39:15 till the **b** have buried it in the valley of 6912

BURN (138) [BURNED, BURNETH, BURNING, BURNINGS, BURNT]
Ge 11: 3 **b** *them* **thoroughly**. 8313+8316+3807.1
44:18 let not thine anger **b** against thy servant: 2734
Ex 12:10 of it until the morning ye shall **b** with fire. 8313
27:20 for the light, to **cause** the lamp **to b** always. 5927
29:13 *is* upon them, and **b** *them* upon the altar. 6999
29:14 shalt thou **b** with fire without the camp: 8313
29:18 thou shalt **b** the whole ram upon the altar: 6999
29:25 **b** *them* upon the altar for a burnt offering, 6999
29:34 then thou shalt **b** the remainder with fire: 8313
30: 1 thou shalt make an altar to **b** incense upon: 4729
30: 7 Aaron shall **b** thereon sweet incense every 6999
30: 7 the lamps, he shall **b incense** upon it. 6999
30: 8 lamps at even, he shall **b incense** upon it, 6999
30:20 to **b** offering made by fire unto 6999
Lev 1: 9 the priest shall **b** all on the altar, *to be* a 6999
1:13 shall bring *it* all, and **b** *it* upon the altar: 6999
1:15 and wring off his head, and **b** *it* on the altar; 6999
1:17 the priest shall **b** it upon the altar, upon 6999
2: 2 the priest shall **b** the memorial of it upon 6999
2: 9 and shall **b** *it* upon the altar: 6999
2:11 for ye shall **b** no leaven, nor any honey, 6999
2:16 the priest shall **b** the memorial of it, *part* of 6999
3: 5 Aaron's sons shall **b** it on the altar upon 6999
3:11 the priest shall **b** it upon the altar: *it is* 6999
3:16 the priest shall **b** them upon the altar: *it is* 6999
4:10 the priest shall **b** them upon the altar of 6999
4:12 and **b** him on the wood with fire: 8313
4:19 all his fat from him, and **b** *it* upon the altar. 6999
4:21 and **b** him as he burned the first bullock: 8313
4:26 he shall **b** all his fat upon the altar, as 6999
4:31 the priest shall **b** *it* upon the altar for a 6999
4:35 the priest shall **b** them upon the altar, 6999
5:12 a memorial thereof, and **b** *it* on the altar, 6999
6:12 the priest shall **b** wood on it every morning, 1197
6:12 he shall **b** thereon the fat of the peace 6999
6:15 shall **b** *it upon* the altar *for* a sweet savour, 6999
7: 5 the priest shall **b** them upon the altar *for* an 6999
7:31 the priest shall **b** the fat upon the altar: but 6999
8:32 and of the bread shall ye **b** with fire. 8313
13:52 He shall therefore **b** *that* garment, 8313
13:55 it *is* unclean; thou shalt **b** it in the fire; it *is* 8313
13:57 it *is* a spreading *plague:* thou shalt **b** that 8313
16:25 the fat of the sin offering shall he **b** upon 6999
16:27 they shall **b** in the fire their skins, and their 8313
17: 6 **b** the fat for a sweet savour unto 6999
24: 2 to **cause** the lamps **to b** continually. 5927
Nu 5:26 **b** *it* upon the altar, and afterward shall 6999
18:17 shalt **b** their fat *for* an offering made by 6999
19: 5 *one* shall **b** the heifer in his sight; her skin, 8313
19: 5 and her blood, with her dung, shall he **b**: 8313
Dt 5:23 (for the mountain did **b** with fire,) 1197
7: 5 and **b** their graven images with fire. 8313
7:25 The graven images of their gods shall ye **b** 8313
12: 3 their pillars, and **b** their groves with fire; 8313
13:16 shalt **b** with fire the city, and all the spoil 8313
32:22 shall **b** unto the lowest hell, and 3344
Jos 11: 6 their horses, and **b** their chariots with fire. 8313
11:13 save Hazor only; *that* did Joshua **b**. 8313
Jdg 9:52 went hard unto the door of the tower to **b** it 8313
12: 1 we will **b** thine house upon thee with fire. 8313
14:15 lest we **b** thee and thy father's house with 8313
1Sa 2:16 Let them **not fail to b** the fat 6999+6999
2:28 to offer upon mine altar, to **b** incense, 6999
1Ki 13: 1 Jeroboam stood by the altar to **b incense**. 6999
13: 2 of the high places that **b incense** upon thee, 6999
2Ki 16:15 Upon the great altar **b** the morning burnt 6999
18: 4 the children of Israel did **b incense** to it: 6999
23: 5 **b incense** in the high places in the cities of 6999
1Ch 23:13 for ever, to **b incense** before the LORD, 6999
2Ch 2: 4 *and* to **b** before him sweet incense, and 6999
2: 6 save only to **b sacrifice** before him? 6999
4:20 that they should **b** after the manner before 1197
13:11 And they **b** unto the LORD every morning 6999
13:11 with the lamps thereof, to **b** every evening: 1197
26:16 to **b incense** upon the altar of incense. 6999
26:18 to **b incense** unto the LORD, but to 6999
26:18 of Aaron, that are consecrated to **b incense**: 6999
26:19 and *had* a censer in his hand to **b incense**: 6999
28:25 high places to **b incense** unto other gods, 6999
29:11 should minister unto him, and **b incense**. 6999
32:12 before one altar, and **b incense** upon it? 6999

Ne 10:34 to **b** upon the altar of the LORD our God, 1197
Ps 79: 5 for ever? shall thy jealousy **b** like fire? 1197
89:46 for ever? shall thy wrath **b** like fire? 1197
Isa 1:31 they shall both **b** together, and none shall 1197
10:17 it shall **b** and devour his thorns and 1197
27: 4 go through them, I would **b** them together. 6702
40:16 Lebanon *is* not sufficient to **b**, nor 1197
44:15 shall it be for a man to **b**: for he will take 1197
47:14 shall be as stubble; the fire shall **b** them; 8313
Jer 4: 4 **b** that none can quench *it,* because of 1197
7: 9 **b incense** unto Baal, and walk after other 6999
7:20 and it shall **b**, and shall not be quenched. 1197
7:31 to **b** their sons and their daughters in 8313
11:13 *even* altars to **b incense** unto Baal. 6999
15:14 in mine anger, *which* shall **b** upon you. 3344
17: 4 a fire in mine anger, *which* shall **b** for ever. 3344
19: 5 to **b** their sons with fire *for* burnt offerings 8313
21:10 king of Babylon, and he shall **b** it with fire. 8313
21:12 **b** that none can quench *it,* because of 1197
32:29 fire on this city, and **b** it with the houses, 8313
34: 2 king of Babylon, and he shall **b** it with fire: 8313
34: 5 before thee, so shall they **b** *odours* for thee; 8313
34:22 against it, and take it, and **b** it with fire: 8313
36:25 to the king that *he* would not **b** the roll: 8313
37: 8 this city, and take it, and **b** it with fire. 8313
37:10 man in his tent, and **b** this city with fire. 8313
38:18 they shall **b** it with fire, and thou shalt not 8313
43:12 he shall **b** them, and carry them away 8313
43:13 gods of the Egyptians shall he **b** with fire. 8313
44: 3 in that *they* went to **b incense**, *and* to serve 6999
44: 5 to **b** no **incense** unto other gods. 6999
44:17 to **b incense** unto the queen of heaven, and 6999
44:18 since we left off to **b incense** to the queen 6999
44:25 to **b incense** to the queen of heaven, and 6999
Eze 5: 2 Thou shalt **b** with fire a third *part* in 1197
5: 4 the midst of the fire, and **b** them in the fire; 8313
16:41 they shall **b** thine houses with fire, and 8313
23:47 and **b up** their houses with fire. 8313
24: 5 **b** also the bones under it, *and* make it boil 1752
24:11 may **b**, and *that* the filthiness of it may be 2787
39: 9 shall set on fire and **b** the weapons, 5400
39: 9 and they shall **b** them with fire seven years: 1197
39:10 for they shall **b** the weapons with fire: 1197
43:21 he shall **b** it in the appointed place of 8313
Hos 4:13 **b incense** upon the hills, under oaks and 6999
Na 2:13 I will **b** her chariots in the smoke, and 1197
Hab 1:16 their net, and **b incense** unto their drag; 6999
Mal 4: 1 the day cometh, that *shall* **b** as an oven; 1197
4: 1 the day that cometh shall **b** them **up**, saith 3857
Mt 3:12 will **b up** the chaff with unquenchable fire. *2618*
13:30 and bind them in bundles to **b** them: *2618*
Lk 1: 9 his lot was to **b incense** when he went into *2370*
3:17 the chaff he will **b** with fire unquenchable. *2618*
24:32 to another, Did not our heart **b** within us, *2545*
1Co 7: 9 for it is better to marry than to **b**. *4448*
2Co 11:29 am not weak? who is offended, and I **b** not? *4448*
Rev 17:16 and shall eat her flesh, and **b** her with fire. *2618*

BURNED (22) [BURN]

Ex 3: 2 the bush **b** with fire, and the bush was not 1197
Lev 4:21 and burn him as he **b** the first bullock: 8313
8:16 and their fat, and Moses **b** *it* upon the altar. 6999
Dt 9:15 from the mount, and the mount **b** with fire: 1197
Jos 7:25 him *with* stones, and **b** them with fire, 8313
11:13 Israel **b** none of them, save Hazor only; 8313
2Ch 25:14 before them, and **b incense** unto them. 6999
34:25 and have **b incense** unto other gods, 6999
Est 1:12 the king very wroth, and his anger **b** in him. 1197
Ps 39: 3 within me, while I was musing the fire **b**: 1197
Isa 24: 6 therefore the inhabitants of the earth are **b**, 2787
42:25 and it **b** him, yet he laid *it* not to heart. 1197
La 2: 3 he **b** against Jacob like a flaming fire, 1197
Eze 15: 5 when the fire hath devoured it, and it is **b**? 2787
Hos 11: 2 and **b incense** to graven images. 6999
Jn 15: 6 and cast *them* into the fire, and they are **b**. *2545*
Ac 19:19 and **b** *them* before all *men:* and *2618*
Ro 1:27 **b** in their lust one towards another; *1572*
1Co 13: 3 and though I give my body to be **b**, *2545*
Heb 6: 8 *is* nigh unto cursing; whose end *is* to be **b**. *2740*
12:18 and that **b** with fire, nor unto blackness, *2545*
Rev 1:15 unto fine brass, as if they **b** in a furnace; *4448*

BURNETH (18) [BURN]

Lev 13:24 the quick *flesh* that **b** have a white bright 4348
16:28 he that **b** them shall wash his clothes, and 8313
Nu 19: 8 he that **b** her shall wash his clothes in 8313
Ps 46: 9 spear in sunder; he **b** the chariot in the fire. 8313
83:14 As the fire **b** a wood, and as the flame 1197
97: 3 and **b up** his enemies round about. 3857
Isa 9:18 For wickedness **b** as the fire: it shall devour 1197
44:16 He **b** part thereof in the fire; with part 8313
62: 1 and the salvation thereof as a lamp *that* **b**. 1197
64: 2 As *when* the melting fire **b**, the fire causeth 6919
65: 3 and **b incense** upon altars of brick; 6999
65: 5 smoke in my nose, a fire that **b** all the day. 3344
66: 3 he that **b** incense, *as if* he blessed an idol. 2142
Jer 48:35 and him that **b incense** to his gods. 6999
Hos 7: 6 *in* the morning it **b** as a flaming fire. 1197
Joel 2: 3 before them; and behind them a flame **b**: 3857
Am 6:10 uncle shall take him up, and he that **b** him, 5635
Rev 21: 8 shall have their part in the lake which **b** *2545*

BURNING (60) [BURN]

Ge 15:17 a **b** lamp that passed between those pieces. 784
Ex 21:25 **B** for burning, wound for wound, stripe for 3555
21:25 Burning for **b**, wound for wound, stripe for 3555
Lev 6: 9 of the **b** upon the altar all night unto 4169
6: 9 and the fire of the altar shall be **b** in it. 3344
6:12 the fire upon the altar shall be **b** in it; 3344
6:13 The fire shall ever be **b** upon the altar; 3344
10: 6 bewail the **b** which the LORD hath 8316
13:23 in his place, *and* spread not, it *is* a **b** boil; 6867
13:24 in the skin whereof *there is* a hot **b**, and 4348
13:25 the skin; it *is* a leprosy broken out of the **b**: 4348
13:28 it *is* a rising of the **b**, and the priest shall 4348
13:28 for it *is* an inflammation of the **b**. 4348
16:12 he shall take a censer full of **b coals** of fire 1513
26:16 consumption, and the **b ague**, that shall 6920
Nu 16:37 that he take up the censers out of the **b**, and 8316
19: 6 cast *it* into the midst of the **b** of the heifer. 8316
Dt 28:22 and with an **extreme b**, and with the sword, 2746
29:23 salt, *and* **b**, *that* it is not sown, nor beareth, 8316
32:24 devoured with **b heat**, and with bitter 7565
2Ch 16:14 they **made a** very great **b** for him. 8313+8316
21:19 his people made no **b** for him, like 8316
21:19 no burning for him, like the **b** of his fathers. 8316
Job 41:19 Out of his mouth go **b lamps**, *and* sparks of 3940
Ps 140:10 Let **b coals** fall upon them: let them be cast 1513
Pr 16:27 up evil: and in his lips *there is* as a **b** fire. 6867
26:21 *As* coals *are* to **b coals**, and wood to fire; so 1513
26:23 **B** lips and a wicked heart *are like* a 1814
Isa 3:24 of sackcloth; *and* **b** instead of beauty. 3587
4: 4 spirit of judgment, and by the spirit of **b**. 1197
9: 5 but *this* shall be with **b** *and* fuel of fire. 8316
10:16 under his glory he shall kindle a **b** like 3350
10:16 he shall kindle a burning like the **b** of a fire. 3350
30:27 **b** *with* his anger, and the burden *thereof is* 1197
34: 9 and the land thereof shall become **b** pitch. 1197
Jer 20: 9 *his word* was in mine heart as a **b** fire shut 1197
36:22 *there was a fire on* the hearth **b** before him. 1197
44: 8 **b incense** unto other gods in the land of 6999
Eze 1:13 their appearance *was* like **b** coals of fire, 1197
Da 3: 6 be cast into the midst of a **b** fiery furnace. 3345
3:11 *that* he should be cast into the midst of a **b** 3345
3:15 hour into the midst of a **b** fiery furnace; 3345
3:17 able to deliver us from the **b** fiery furnace, 3345
3:20 *and* to cast *them* into the **b** fiery furnace. 3345
3:21 were cast into the midst of the **b** fiery 3345
3:23 fell down bound into the midst of the **b** 3345
3:26 near to the mouth of the **b** fiery furnace, 3345
7: 9 the fiery flame, *and* his wheels *as* **b** fire. 1815
7:11 body destroyed, and given to the **b** flame. 3346
Am 4:11 ye were as a firebrand pluckt out of the **b**: 8316
Hab 3: 5 and **b coals** went forth at his feet. 7565
Lk 12:35 loins be girded about, and *your* lights **b**; *2545*
Jn 5:35 He was a **b** and a shining light: and ye were *2545*
Jas 1:11 the sun is no sooner risen with a **b heat**, *2742*
Rev 4: 5 *there were* seven lamps of fire **b** before *2545*
8: 8 as *it were* a great mountain **b** with fire was *2545*
8:10 **b** as *it were* a lamp, and it fell upon *2545*
18: 9 when they shall see the smoke of her **b**, *4451*
18:18 cried when they saw the smoke of her **b**, *4451*
19:20 alive into a lake of fire **b** with brimstone. *2545*

BURNINGS (3) [BURN]

Isa 33:12 the people shall be *as* the **b** of lime: 4955
33:14 amongst us shall dwell *with* everlasting **b**? 4168
Jer 34: 5 with the **b** of thy fathers, the former kings 4955

BURNISHED (1)
Eze 1: 7 and they sparkled like the colour of **b** brass. 7044

BURNT (442) [BURN]
Ge 8:20 and offered **b offerings** on the altar. 5930
22: 2 offer him there for a **b offering** upon one of 5930
22: 3 clave the wood for the **b offering**, and 5930
22: 6 Abraham took the wood of the **b offering**, 5930
22: 7 but where *is* the lamb for a **b offering**? 5930
22: 8 provide himself a lamb for a **b offering**: 5930
22:13 offered him up for a **b offering** in the stead 5930
38:24 Bring her forth, and let her be **b**. 8313
Ex 3: 3 see this great sight, why the bush is not **b**. 1197
10:25 give us also sacrifices and **b offerings**, 5930
18:12 took a **b offering** and sacrifices for God: 5930
20:24 shalt sacrifice thereon thy **b offerings**, and 5930
24: 5 which offered **b offerings**, and 5930
29:18 it *is* a **b offering** unto the LORD: it *is* a 5930
29:25 burn *them* upon the altar for a **b offering**, 5930
29:42 *This shall be* a continual **b offering** 5930
30: 9 nor **b sacrifice**, nor meat offering; 5930
30:28 the altar of **b offering** with all his vessels, 5930
31: 9 the altar of **b offering** with all his furniture, 5930
32: 6 offered **b offerings**, and brought peace 5930
32:20 and **b** *it* in the fire, and ground *it* to powder, 8313
35:16 The altar of **b offering** with his brasen 5930
38: 1 he made the altar of **b offering** *of* shittim 5930
40: 6 thou shalt set the altar of the **b offering** 5930
40:10 thou shalt anoint the altar of the **b offering**, 5930
40:27 he **b** sweet incense thereon; as the LORD 6999
40:29 he put the altar of **b offering** *by* the door of 5930
40:29 offered upon it the **b offering** and the meat 5930
Lev 1: 3 If his offering *be* a **b sacrifice** of the herd, 5930
1: 4 his hand upon the head of the **b offering**; 5930
1: 6 he shall flay the **b offering**, and cut it into 5930
1: 9 *to be* a **b sacrifice**, an offering made by 5930
1:10 the sheep, or of the goats, for a **b sacrifice**; 5930
1:13 it *is* a **b sacrifice**, an offering made by fire, 5930
1:14 if the **b sacrifice** for his offering to 5930
1:17 it *is* a **b sacrifice**, an offering made by fire, 5930
2:12 they shall not be **b** on the altar for a sweet 5927
3: 5 burn it on the altar upon the **b sacrifice**, 5930
4: 7 at the bottom of the altar of the **b offering**, 5930
4:10 burn them upon the altar of the **b offering**. 5930
4:12 the ashes are poured out shall he be **b**. 8313
4:18 at the bottom of the altar of the **b offering**, 5930
4:24 they kill the **b offering** before the LORD: 5930
4:25 *it* upon the horns of the altar of **b offering**, 5930
4:25 at the bottom of the altar of **b offering**. 5930
4:29 sin offering in the place of the **b offering**. 5930
4:30 *it* upon the horns of the altar of **b offering**, 5930
4:33 in the place where they kill the **b offering**. 5930
4:34 *it* upon the horns of the altar of **b offering**, 5930
5: 7 sin offering, and the other for a **b offering**. 5930
5:10 he shall offer the second *for* a **b offering**, 5930
6: 9 This *is* the law of the **b offering**: 5930
6: 9 It *is* the **b offering**, because of the burning 5930
6:10 consumed with the **b offering** on the altar, 5930
6:12 lay the **b offering** in order upon it; 5930
6:22 ever unto the LORD; it shall be wholly **b**. 6999
6:23 shall be wholly *b*: it shall not be eaten. NIH
6:25 In the place where the **b offering** is killed 5930
6:30 shall be eaten: it shall be **b** in the fire. 8313
7: 2 In the place where they kill the **b offering** 5930
7: 8 priest that offereth *any* man's **b offering**, 5930
7: 8 of the **b offering** which he hath offered. 5930
7:17 on the third day shall be **b** with fire. 8313
7:19 shall not be eaten; it shall be **b** with fire: 8313
7:37 This *is* the law of the **b offering**, of 5930
8:17 his dung, he **b** with fire without the camp; 8313
8:18 he brought the ram for the **b offering**: and 5930
8:20 Moses **b** the head, and the pieces, and 6999
8:21 and Moses **b** the whole ram upon the altar: 6999
8:21 it *was* a **b sacrifice** for a sweet savour, *and* 5930
8:28 **b** *them* on the altar upon the burnt offering: 6999
8:28 burnt *them* on the altar upon the **b offering**: 5930
9: 2 a ram for a **b offering**, without blemish, 5930
9: 3 without blemish, for a **b offering**; 5930
9: 7 thy **b offering**, and make an atonement for 5930
9:10 liver of the sin offering, he **b** upon the altar; 6999
9:11 the hide he **b** with fire without the camp. 8313
9:12 he slew the **b offering**; and Aaron's sons 5930
9:13 they presented the **b offering** unto him, 5930
9:13 and the head: and he **b** *them* upon the altar. 6999
9:14 **b** *them* upon the burnt offering on the altar. 6999
9:14 burnt *them* upon the **b offering** on the altar. 5930
9:16 he brought the **b offering**, and offered it 5930
9:17 a handful thereof, and **b** *it* upon the altar, 6999
9:17 beside the **b sacrifice** of the morning. 5930
9:20 the breasts, and he **b** the fat upon the altar: 6999
9:22 and the **b offering**, and peace offerings. 5930
9:24 consumed upon the altar the **b offering** and 5930
10:16 of the sin offering, and behold, it was **b**: 8313
10:19 and their **b offering** before the LORD; 5930
12: 6 a lamb of the first year for a **b offering**, 5930
12: 8 the one for the **b offering**, and the other for 5930
13:52 *is* a fretting leprosy; it shall be **b** in the fire. 8313
14:13 kill the sin offering and the **b offering**, 5930
14:19 and afterward he shall kill the **b offering**: 5930
14:20 the priest shall offer the **b offering** and 5930
14:22 a sin offering, and the other a **b offering**. 5930
14:31 the other *for* a **b offering**, with the meat 5930
15:15 sin offering, and the other *for* a **b offering**; 5930
15:30 sin offering, and the other *for* a **b offering**; 5930
16: 3 a sin offering, and a ram for a **b offering**. 5930
16: 5 a sin offering, and one ram for a **b offering**. 5930
16:24 offer his **b offering**, and the burnt offering 5930
16:24 the **b offering** of the people, and make an 5930
17: 8 that offereth a **b offering** or sacrifice, 5930
19: 6 until the third day, it shall be **b** in the fire. 8313
20:14 they shall be **b** with fire, both he and they; 8313
21: 9 her father: she shall be **b** with fire. 8313
22:18 will offer unto the LORD for a **b offering**; 5930
23:12 first year for a **b offering** unto the LORD. 5930
23:18 they shall be *for* a **b offering** unto 5930
23:37 a **b offering**, and a meat offering, 5930
Nu 6:11 the other for a **b offering**, and make an 5930
6:14 first year without blemish for a **b offering**, 5930
6:16 offer his sin offering, and his **b offering**: 5930
7:15 one lamb of the first year, for a **b offering**: 5930
7:21 one lamb of the first year, for a **b offering**: 5930
7:27 one lamb of the first year, for a **b offering**: 5930
7:33 one lamb of the first year, for a **b offering**: 5930
7:39 one lamb of the first year, for a **b offering**: 5930
7:45 one lamb of the first year, for a **b offering**: 5930
7:51 one lamb of the first year, for a **b offering**: 5930
7:57 one lamb of the first year, for a **b offering**: 5930
7:63 one lamb of the first year, for a **b offering**: 5930
7:69 one lamb of the first year, for a **b offering**: 5930
7:75 one lamb of the first year, for a **b offering**: 5930
7:81 one lamb of the first year, for a **b offering**: 5930
7:87 All the oxen for the **b offering** *were* twelve 5930
8:12 the other *for* a **b offering**, unto the LORD, 5930
10:10 with the trumpets over your **b offerings**, 5930
11: 1 the fire of the LORD **b** among them, and 1197
11: 3 the fire of the LORD **b** among them. 1197
15: 3 a **b offering**, or a sacrifice in performing a 5930
15: 5 shalt thou prepare with the **b offering** 5930
15: 8 thou preparest a bullock *for* a **b offering**, 5930
15:24 offer one young bullock for a **b offering**, 5930
16:39 wherewith they that were **b** had offered; 8313
19:17 ashes of the **b** *heifer* of purification for sin, 8316
23: 3 Stand by thy **b offering**, and I will go: 5930
23: 6 lo, *he* stood by his **b sacrifice**, he, and 5930
23:15 unto Balak, Stand here by thy **b offering**, 5930
23:17 he stood by his **b offering**, and the princes 5930
28: 3 spot day by day, *for* a continual **b offering**. 5930
28: 6 *It is* a continual **b offering**, which was 5930
28:10 *This is* the **b offering** of every sabbath, 5930
28:10 beside the continual **b offering**, and 5930
28:11 shall offer a **b offering** unto the LORD; 5930
28:13 *for* a **b offering** *of* a sweet savour, 5930
28:14 this *is* the **b offering** of every month 5930
28:15 besides the continual **b offering**, and 5930
28:19 by fire *for* a **b offering** unto the LORD; 5930
28:23 Ye shall offer these beside the **b offering** in 5930
28:23 which *is* for a continual **b offering**. 5930
28:24 be offered beside the continual **b offering**, 5930
28:27 ye shall offer the **b offering** for a sweet 5930
28:31 offer *them* besides the continual **b offering**, 5930
29: 2 ye shall offer a **b offering** for a sweet 5930
29: 6 Beside the **b offering** of the month, and 5930
29: 6 the daily **b offering**, and his meat offering, 5930
29: 8 ye shall offer a **b offering** unto the LORD 5930
29:11 the continual **b offering**, and the meat 5930
29:13 ye shall offer a **b offering**, a sacrifice made 5930
29:16 beside the continual **b offering**, his meat 5930

B

Nu 29:19 beside the continual **b offering**, and 5930
29:22 beside the continual **b offering**, and 5930
29:25 beside the continual **b offering**, his meat 5930
29:28 beside the continual **b offering**, and 5930
29:31 beside the continual **b offering**, his meat 5930
29:34 beside the continual **b offering**, his meat 5930
29:36 ye shall offer a **b offering**, a sacrifice made 5930
29:38 beside the continual **b offering**, and 5930
29:39 for your **b offerings**, and for your meat 5930
31:10 they **b** all their cities wherein they dwelt, 8313
Dt 4:11 the mountain **b** with fire unto the midst of 1197
9:21 **b** it with fire, and stamped it, *and* ground *it* 8313
12: 6 thither ye shall bring your **b offerings**, and 5930
12:11 your **b offerings**, and your sacrifices, 5930
12:13 **b offerings** in every place that thou seest: 5930
12:14 there thou shalt offer thy **b offerings**, and 5930
12:27 thou shalt offer thy **b offerings**, the flesh 5930
12:31 their daughters they have **b** in the fire to 8313
27: 6 thou shalt offer **b offerings** thereon unto 5930
32:24 *They shall be* **b** with hunger, and 4198
33:10 and whole *b sacrifice* upon thine altar. NIH
Jos 6:24 they **b** the city with fire, and all that *was* 8313
7:15 with the accursed thing shall be **b** with fire, 8313
8:28 Joshua **b** Ai, and made it a heap for ever, 8313
8:31 they offered thereon **b offerings** unto 5930
11: 9 their horses, and **b** their chariots with fire. 8313
11:11 left to breathe: and he **b** Hazor with fire. 8313
22:23 or if to offer thereon **b offering** or 5930
22:26 not for **b offering**, nor for sacrifice: 5930
22:27 LORD before him with our **b offerings**, 5930
22:28 not for **b offerings**, nor for sacrifices; 5930
22:29 to build an altar for **b offerings**, for meat 5930
Jdg 6:26 offer a **b sacrifice** with the wood of 5930
11:31 and I will offer it up *for* a **b offering**. 5930
13:16 if thou wilt offer a **b offering**, thou must 5930
13:23 he would not have received a **b offering** 5930
15: 5 **b up** both the shocks, and also the standing 1197
15: 6 came up, and **b** her and her father with fire. 8313
15:14 arms became as flax that was **b** with fire, 1197
18:27 edge of the sword, and **b** the city with fire. 8313
20:26 offered **b offerings** and peace offerings 5930
21: 4 offered **b offerings** and peace offerings. 5930
1Sa 2:15 Also before they **b** the fat, the priest's 6999
6:14 offered the kine a **b offering** unto 5930
6:15 men of Beth-shemesh offered **b offerings** 5930
7: 9 offered it *for* a **b offering** wholly unto 5930
7:10 as Samuel was offering up the **b offering**, 5930
10: 8 to offer **b offerings**, *and* to sacrifice 5930
13: 9 Bring hither a **b offering** to me, and peace 5930
13: 9 And he offered the **b offering**. 5930
13:10 had made an end of offering the **b offering**, 5930
13:12 myself therefore, and offered a **b offering**. 5930
15:22 the LORD *as great* delight in **b offerings** 5930
30: 1 and smitten Ziklag, and **b** it with fire; 8313
30: 3 to the city, and behold, *it was* **b** with fire; 8313
30:14 south of Caleb; and we **b** Ziklag with fire. 8313
31:12 and came to Jabesh, and **b** them there. 8313
2Sa 5:21 and David and his men **b** them. 5375
6:17 David offered **b offerings** and 5930
6:18 had made an end of offering **b offerings** 5930
23: 7 they shall be **utterly b** with fire in 8313+8313
24:22 *here be* oxen for **b sacrifice**, and threshing 5930
24:24 neither will I offer **b offerings** unto 5930
24:25 offered **b offerings** and peace offerings. 5930
1Ki 3: 3 he sacrificed and **b incense** in high places. 6999
3: 4 a thousand **b offerings** did Solomon offer 5930
3:15 offered up **b offerings**, and offered peace 5930
8:64 for there he offered **b offerings**, and meat 5930
8:64 *was* too little to receive the **b offerings**, 5930
9:16 **b** it with fire, and slain the Canaanites that 8313
9:25 in a year did Solomon offer **b offerings** 5930
9:25 he **b incense** upon the altar that *was* before 6999
11: 8 which **b incense** and sacrificed unto their 6999
12:33 he offered upon the altar, and **b incense**. 6999
13: 2 and men's bones shall be **b** upon thee. 8313
15:13 her idol, and **b** *it* by the brook Kidron. 8313
16:18 **b** the king's house over him with fire, and 8313
18:33 pour *it* on the **b sacrifice**, and on the wood. 5930
18:38 consumed the **b sacrifice**, and the wood, 5930
22:43 and **b incense** yet in the high places. 6999
2Ki 1:14 **b up** the two captains of the former fifties 398
3:27 offered him *for* a **b offering** upon the wall. 5930
5:17 **b offering** nor sacrifice unto other gods, 5930
10:24 went in to offer sacrifices and **b offerings**, 5930
10:25 had made an end of offering the **b offering**, 5930
10:26 out of the house of Baal, and **b** them. 8313
12: 3 and **b incense** in the high places. 6999
14: 4 and **b incense** on the high places. 6999
15: 4 and **b incense** still on the high places. 6999
15:35 and **b incense** still in the high places. 6999
16: 4 and **b incense** in the high places, 6999
16:13 he **b** his burnt offering and his meat 6999
16:13 he burnt his **b offering** and his meat 5930
16:15 the great altar burn the morning **b offering**, 5930
16:15 the king's **b sacrifice**, and his meat 5930
16:15 with the **b offering** of all the people of 5930
16:15 upon it all the blood of the **b offering**, 5930
17:11 there they **b incense** in all the high places, 6999
17:31 the Sepharvites **b** their children in fire to 8313
22:17 and have **b incense** unto other gods, 6999
23: 4 he **b** them without Jerusalem in the fields 8313
23: 5 them also that **b incense** unto Baal, to 6999
23: 6 **b** it at the brook Kidron, and stampt *it* small 8313
23: 8 places where the priests had **b incense**, 6999
23:11 and **b** the chariots of the sun with fire. 8313
23:15 **b** the high place, *and* stampt *it* small to 8313
23:15 stampt *it* small to powder, and **b** the grove. 8313
23:16 and **b** *them* upon the altar, and polluted it, 8313
23:20 **b** men's bones upon them, and returned *to* 8313
25: 9 he **b** the house of the LORD, and 8313
25: 9 and every great *man's* house **b** he with fire. 8313
1Ch 6:49 offered upon the altar of the **b offering**, 5930
14:12 a commandment, and they were **b** with fire. 8313
16: 1 they offered **b sacrifices** and 5930
16: 2 made an end of offering the **b offerings** 5930
16:40 To offer **b offerings** unto the LORD upon 5930
16:40 altar of the **b offering** continually morning 5930
21:23 lo, I give *thee* the oxen *also* for **b offerings**, 5930
21:24 nor offer **b offerings** without cost. 5930
21:26 offered **b offerings** and peace offerings, 5930
21:26 heaven by fire upon the altar of **b offering**. 5930
21:29 and the altar of the **b offering**, 5930
22: 1 this *is* the altar of the **b offering** for Israel. 5930
23:31 to offer all **b sacrifices** unto the LORD in 5930
29:21 offered **b offerings** unto the LORD, 5930
2Ch 1: 6 and offered a thousand **b offerings** upon it. 5930
2: 4 *for* the **b offerings** morning and evening, 5930
4: 6 for the **b offering** they washed in them; 5930
7: 1 consumed the **b offering** and the sacrifices; 5930
7: 7 for there he offered **b offerings**, and the fat 5930
7: 7 was not able to receive the **b offerings**, 5930
8:12 Solomon offered **b offerings** unto 5930
13:11 every evening **b sacrifices** and 5930
15:16 stamped *it*, and **b** *it* at the brook Kidron. 8313
23:18 to offer the **b offerings** of the LORD, as it 5930
24:14 they offered **b offerings** in the house of 5930
28: 3 Moreover he **b incense** in the valley of 6999
28: 3 **b** his children in the fire after 1197
28: 4 and **b incense** in the high places, 6999
29: 7 have not **b incense** nor offered burnt 6999+7004
29: 7 **b offerings** in the holy *place* unto the God 5930
29:18 the altar of **b offering**, with all the vessels 5930
29:24 for the king commanded *that* the **b offering** 5930
29:27 to offer the **b offering** upon the altar. 5930
29:27 when the **b offering** began, the song of 5930
29:28 all *this continued* until the **b offering** was 5930
29:31 as many as were of a free heart **b offerings**. 5930
29:32 the number of the **b offerings**, which 5930
29:32 all these *were* for a **b offering** to 5930
29:34 that they could not flay all the **b offerings**: 5930
29:35 also the **b offerings** *were* in abundance, 5930
29:35 the drink offerings for *every* **b offering**. 5930
30:15 brought in the **b offerings** *into* the house of 5930
31: 2 the priests and Levites for **b offerings** and 5930
31: 3 portion of his substance for the **b offerings**, 5930
31: 3 for the morning and evening **b offerings**, 5930
31: 3 the **b offerings** for the sabbaths, and for 5930
34: 5 he **b** the bones of the priests upon their 8313
35:12 they removed the **b offerings**, that they 5930
35:14 *were busied* in offering of **b offerings** 5930
35:16 to offer **b offerings** upon the altar of 5930
36:19 they **b** the house of God, and brake down 8313
36:19 **b** all the palaces thereof with fire, and 8313
Ezr 3: 2 to offer **b offerings** thereon, 5930
3: 3 they offered **b offerings** thereon unto 5930
3: 3 *even* **b offerings** morning and evening. 5930
3: 4 *offered* the daily **b offerings** by number, 5930
3: 5 afterward *offered* the continual **b offering**, 5930

Ezr	3: 6	they to offer **b offerings** unto the LORD.	5930
	6: 9	for the **b offerings** of the God of heaven,	5928
	8:35	offered **b offerings** unto the God of Israel,	5930
	8:35	all *this was* a **b offering** unto the LORD.	5930
Ne	1: 3	and the gates thereof are **b** with fire.	3341
	2:17	and the gates thereof are **b** with fire:	3341
	4: 2	out of the heaps of the rubbish which are **b**?	8313
	10:33	for the continual **b offering**, of	5930
Job	1: 5	offered **b offerings** *according to*	5930
	1:16	hath **b up** the sheep, and the servants, and	1197
	30:30	upon me, and my bones are **b** with heat.	2787
	42: 8	and offer up for yourselves a **b offering**;	5930
Ps	20: 3	all thy offerings, and accept thy **b sacrifice**.	5930
	40: 6	**b offering** and sin offering hast thou not	5930
	50: 8	thee for thy sacrifices or thy **b offerings**,	5930
	51:16	I give *it:* thou delightest not in **b offering**.	5930
	51:19	with **b offering** and whole *burnt offering:*	5930
	51:19	burnt offering and whole *b offering:* then	NIH
	66:13	I will go *into* thy house with **b offerings**:	5930
	66:15	I will offer unto thee **b sacrifices** of	5930
	74: 8	they have **b up** all the synagogues of God	8313
	80:16	*It is* **b** with fire, *it is* cut down: they perish	8313
	102: 3	like smoke, and my bones are **b** as a hearth.	2787
	106:18	their company; the flame **b up** the wicked.	3857
Pr	6:27	fire in his bosom, and his clothes not be **b**?	8313
	6:28	go upon hot coals, and his feet not be **b**?	3554
Isa	1: 7	*is* desolate, your cities *are* **b** *with* fire:	8313
	1:11	I am full *of* the **b offerings** of rams, and	5930
	33:12	*as* thorns cut up shall they be **b** in the fire.	3341
	40:16	beasts thereof sufficient *for* a **b offering**.	5930
	43: 2	through the fire, thou shalt not be **b**;	3554
	43:23	me the small cattle of thy **b offerings**;	5930
	44:19	to say, I have **b** part of it in the fire;	8313
	56: 7	their **b offerings** and their sacrifices *shall*	5930
	61: 8	I hate robbery for **b offering**;	5930
	64:11	our fathers praised thee, is **b up** with fire:	8316
	65: 7	which have **b incense** upon the mountains,	6999
Jer	1:16	have **b incense** unto other gods, and	6999
	2:15	his cities are **b** without inhabitant.	3341
	6:20	your **b offerings** *are* not acceptable,	5930
	6:29	The bellows are **b**, the lead is consumed of	2787
	7:21	Put your **b offerings** unto your sacrifices,	5930
	7:22	concerning **b offerings** or sacrifices:	5930
	9:10	because they are **b up**, so that none can	3341
	9:12	*and* is **b up** like a wilderness,	3341
	14:12	when they offer **b offering** and an oblation,	5930
	17:26	bringing **b offerings**, and sacrifices, and	5930
	18:15	they have **b incense** to vanity, and	6999
	19: 4	and have **b incense** in it unto other gods,	6999
	19: 5	to burn their sons with fire *for* **b offerings**	5930
	19:13	have **b incense** unto all the host of heaven,	6999
	33:18	want a man before me to offer **b offerings**,	5930
	36:27	after that the king had **b** the roll, and	8313
	36:28	which Jehoiakim the king of Judah hath **b**.	8313
	36:29	Thou hast **b** this roll, saying, Why hast thou	8313
	36:32	Jehoiakim king of Judah had **b** in the fire:	8313
	38:17	and this city shall not be **b** with fire;	8313
	38:23	thou shalt **cause** this city **to be b** with fire.	8313
	39: 8	the Chaldeans **b** the king's house, and	8313
	44:15	their wives had **b incense** unto other gods,	6999
	44:19	when we **b incense** to the queen of heaven,	6999
	44:21	The incense that ye **b** in the cities of Judah,	6999
	44:23	Because you have **b incense**, and because	6999
	49: 2	and her daughters shall be **b** with fire:	3341
	51:25	the rocks, and will make thee a **b mountain**.	8316
	51:30	they have **b** her dwelling places; her bars	3341
	51:32	the reeds they have **b** with fire, and the men	8313
	51:58	her high gates shall be **b** with fire;	3341
	52:13	**b** the house of the LORD, and the king's	8313
	52:13	all the houses of the great *men*, **b** he with	8313
Eze	15: 4	both the ends of it, and the midst of it is **b**.	2787
	20:47	the south to the north shall be **b** therein.	6866
	24:10	and spice it well, and let the bones be **b**.	2787
	40:38	where they washed the **b offering**.	5930
	40:39	to slay thereon the **b offering** and the sin	5930
	40:42	*were* of hewn stone for the **b offering**,	5930
	40:42	wherewith they slew the **b offering**	5930
	43:18	to offer **b offerings** thereon, and to sprinkle	5930
	43:24	they shall offer them up *for* a **b offering**	5930
	43:27	the priests shall make your **b offerings**	5930
	44:11	they shall slay the **b offering** and	5930
	45:15	for a **b offering**, and for peace offerings,	5930
	45:17	be the prince's part *to give* **b offerings**,	5930
	45:17	and the **b offering**, and the peace offerings,	5930
	45:23	he shall prepare a **b offering** to the LORD,	5930
	45:25	according to the **b offering**, and	5930
	46: 2	the priests shall prepare his **b offering** and	5930
	46: 4	the **b offering** that the prince shall offer	5930
	46:12	prince shall prepare a voluntary **b offering**	5930
	46:12	he shall prepare his **b offering** and his	5930
	46:13	Thou shalt daily prepare a **b offering** unto	5930
	46:15	every morning *for* a continual **b offering**.	5930
Hos	2:13	where*in* she **b incense** to them, and	6999
	6: 6	knowledge of God more than **b offerings**.	5930
Joel	1:19	the flame hath **b** all the trees of the field.	3857
Am	2: 1	he **b** the bones of the king of Edom into	8313
	5:22	Though ye offer me **b offerings** and	5930
Mic	1: 7	all the hires thereof shall be **b** with the fire,	8313
	6: 6	shall I come before him with **b offerings**,	5930
Na	1: 5	the earth is **b** at his presence, yea,	5375
Mt	13:40	the tares are gathered and **b** in the fire;	*2618*
	22: 7	those murderers, and **b up** their city.	*1714*
Mk	12:33	is more than all **whole b offerings** and	*3646*
1Co	3:15	If any *man's* work shall be **b**, he shall	*2618*
Heb	10: 6	In **b offerings** and *sacrifices* for sin thou	*3646*
	10: 8	Sacrifice and offering and **b offerings** and	*3646*
	13:11	high priest for sin, are **b** without the camp.	*2618*
2Pe	3:10	the works that are therein shall be **b up**.	*2618*
Rev	8: 7	and the third *part* of trees was **b up**, and all	*2618*
	8: 7	was burnt up, and all green grass was **b up**.	*2618*
	18: 8	famine; and she shall be **utterly b** with fire:	*2618*

BURST (9) [BURSTING]

Job	32:19	no vent; it is **ready to b** like new bottles.	1234
Pr	3:10	and thy presses shall **b out** with new wine.	6555
Jer	2:20	I have broken thy yoke, *and* **b** thy bands;	5423
	5: 5	broken the yoke, *and* **b** the bonds.	5423
	30: 8	will **b** thy bonds, and strangers shall no	5423
Na	1:13	off thee, and will **b** thy bonds **in sunder**.	5423
Mk	2:22	else the new wine doth **b** the bottles, and	*4486*
Lk	5:37	else the new wine will **b** the bottles, and	*4486*
Ac	1:18	he **b asunder** in the midst, and all his	*2997*

BURSTING (1) [BURST]

Isa	30:14	that there shall not be found in the **b** of it a	4386

BURY (39) [BURIAL, BURIED, BURIERS, BURYING, BURYINGPLACE]

Ge	23: 4	that I may **b** my dead out of my sight.	6912
	23: 6	in the choice of our sepulchres **b** thy dead;	6912
	23: 6	but that thou mayest **b** thy dead.	6912
	23: 8	If it be your mind that I should **b** my dead	6912
	23:11	sons of my people give I it thee: **b** thy dead.	6912
	23:13	take *it* of me, and I will **b** my dead there.	6912
	23:15	betwixt me and thee? **b** therefore thy dead.	6912
	47:29	with me; **b** me not, I pray thee, in Egypt:	6912
	47:30	of Egypt, and **b** me in their buryingplace.	6912
	49:29	**b** me with my fathers in the cave that *is* in	6912
	50: 5	the land of Canaan, there shalt thou **b** me.	6912
	50: 5	and **b** my father, and I will come again.	6912
	50: 6	Pharaoh said, Go up, and **b** thy father,	6912
	50: 7	Joseph went up to **b** his father: and	6912
	50:14	all that went up with him to **b** his father,	6912
Dt	21:23	shalt **in any wise b** him that day;	6912+6912
1Ki	2:31	he hath said, and fall upon him, and **b** him;	6912
	11:15	of the host was gone up to **b** the slain,	6912
	13:29	came to the city, to mourn and to **b** him.	6912
	13:31	**b** me in the sepulchre wherein the man of	6912
	14:13	all Israel shall mourn for him, and **b** him:	6912
2Ki	9:10	*there shall be* none to **b** *her*. And he opened	6912
	9:34	Go, see now this cursed *woman*, and **b** her:	6912
	9:35	they went to **b** her: but they found no more	6912
Ps	79: 3	and *there was* none to **b** *them*.	6912
Jer	7:32	for they shall **b** in Tophet, till there be no	6912
	14:16	they *shall* have none to **b** them, them,	6912
	19:11	they shall **b** *them* in Tophet, till *there be* no	6912
	19:11	*them* in Tophet, till *there be* no place to **b**.	6912
Eze	39:11	there shall they **b** Gog and all his	6912
	39:13	all the people of the land shall **b** *them;* and	6912
	39:14	passing through the land to **b** with	6912
Hos	9: 6	gather them up, Memphis shall **b** them:	6912
Mt	8:21	Lord, suffer me first to go and **b** my father.	*2290*
	8:22	Follow me; and let the dead **b** their dead.	*2290*
	27: 7	them the potter's field, to **b** strangers in.	*5027*
Lk	9:59	Lord, suffer me first to go and **b** my father.	*2290*
	9:60	said unto him, Let the dead **b** their dead:	*2290*
Jn	19:40	as the manner of the Jews is to **b**.	*1779*

BURYING (4) [BURY]
2Ki 13:21 to pass, as they were **b** a man, that behold, 6912
Eze 39:12 seven months shall the house of Israel be **b** 6912
Mk 14: 8 come aforehand to anoint my body to the **b**. *1780*
Jn 12: 7 against the day of my **b** hath she kept this. *1780*

BURYINGPLACE (7) [BURY, PLACE]
Ge 23: 4 give me a possession of a **b** with you, that I 6913
23: 9 it me for a possession of a **b** amongst you. 6913
23:20 for a possession of a **b** by the sons of Heth. 6913
47:30 me out of Egypt, and bury me in their **b**. 6900
49:30 Ephron the Hittite for a possession of a **b**. 6913
50:13 a possession of a **b** of Ephron the Hittite, 6913
Jdg 16:31 and Eshtaol in the **b** of Manoah his father. 6913

BUSH (11) [BUSHES, BUSHY]
Ex 3: 2 in a flame of fire out of the midst of a **b**: 5572
3: 2 the **b** burned with fire, and the bush was 5572
3: 2 with fire, and the **b** was not consumed. 5572
3: 3 see this great sight, why the **b** is not burnt. 5572
3: 4 called unto him out of the midst of the **b**, 5572
Dt 33:16 *for* the good will of him that dwelt in the **b**: 5572
Mk 12:26 how in the **b** God spake unto him, saying, *942*
Lk 6:44 nor of a **bramble b** gather they grapes. *942*
20:37 dead are raised, even Moses shewed at the **b**, *942*
Ac 7:30 an angel of the Lord in a flame of fire in a **b**. *942*
7:35 of the angel which appeared to him in the **b**. *942*

BUSHEL (3)
Mt 5:15 and put it under a **b**, but on a candlestick; *3426*
Mk 4:21 Is a candle brought to be put under a **b**, or *3426*
Lk 11:33 neither under a **b**, but on a candlestick, *3426*

BUSHES (3) [BUSH]
Job 30: 4 Who cut up mallows by the **b**, and 7880
30: 7 Among the **b** they brayed; under the nettles 7880
Isa 7:19 and upon all thorns, and upon all **b**. 5097

BUSHY (1) [BUSH]
SS 5:11 his locks *are* **b**, *and* black as a raven. 8534

BUSIED (1) [BUSY]
2Ch 35:14 the priests the sons of Aaron *were* **b** in NIH

BUSINESS (29) [BUSY]
Ge 39:11 that *Joseph* went into the house to do his **b**; 4399
Dt 24: 5 neither shall he be charged with any **b**: 1697
Jos 2:14 Our life for yours, if ye utter not this our **b**. 1697
2:20 if thou utter this our **b**, then we will be quit 1697
Jdg 18: 7 the Zidonians, and had no **b** with *any* man. 1697
18:28 and they had no **b** with *any* man; 1697
1Sa 20:19 didst hide thyself when the **b** was *in hand,* 4639
21: 2 The king hath commanded me a **b**, and 1697
21: 2 Let no man know any thing of the **b** 1697
21: 8 because the king's **b** required haste. 1697
1Ch 26:29 his sons *were* for the outward **b** over Israel, 4399
26:30 Jordan westward in all the **b** of the LORD, 4399
2Ch 13:10 of Aaron, and the Levites *wait* upon *their* **b**: 4399
17:13 he had much **b** in the cities of Judah: and 4399
32:31 Howbeit in *the* **b** *of* the ambassadors of NIH
Ne 11:16 had the oversight of the outward **b** of 4399
11:22 the singers *were* over the **b** of the house of 4399
13:30 and the Levites, every one in his **b**; 4399
Est 3: 9 of those that have the charge of the **b**, 4399
Ps 107:23 to the sea in ships, that do **b** in great waters; 4399
Pr 22:29 Seest thou a man diligent in his **b**? he shall 4399
Ecc 5: 3 a dream cometh through the multitude of **b**; 6045
8:16 and to see the **b** that is done upon the earth: 6045
Da 8:27 afterward I rose up, and did the king's **b**; 4399
Lk 2:49 ye not that I must be about my Father's *b*? NIG
Ac 6: 3 wisdom, whom we may appoint over this **b**. *5532*
Ro 12:11 Not slothful in **b**; fervent in spirit; *4710*
16: 2 *that* ye assist her in whatsoever **b** she hath *4229*
1Th 4:11 and to do your own *b*, and to work with NIG

BUSY (1) [BUSIED, BUSINESS, BUSYBODIES, BUSYBODY]
1Ki 20:40 as thy servant was **b** here and there, he was 6213

BUSYBODIES (2) [BUSY, BODY]
2Th 3:11 working not at all, but are **b**. *4020*
1Ti 5:13 and not only idle, but tattlers also and **b**, *4021*

BUSYBODY (1) [BUSY, BODY]
1Pe 4:15 or as a **b in other men's matters**. *244*

BUT (3994) See Index

BUTLER (8) [BUTLERS, BUTLERSHIP]
Ge 40: 1 *that* the **b** of the king of Egypt and *his* 8248
40: 5 the **b** and the baker of the king of Egypt, 8248
40: 9 the chief **b** told his dream to Joseph, and 8248
40:13 the former manner when thou wast his **b**. 8248
40:20 he lifted up the head of the chief **b** and of 8248
40:21 he restored the chief **b** unto his butlership 8248
40:23 Yet did not the chief **b** remember Joseph, 8248
41: 9 spake the chief **b** unto Pharaoh, saying, 8248

BUTLERS (1) [BUTLER]
Ge 40: 2 against the chief of the **b**, and against 8248

BUTLERSHIP (1) [BUTLER]
Ge 40:21 he restored the chief butler unto his **b** 4945

BUTTER (11)
Ge 18: 8 he took **b**, and milk, and the calf which he 2529
Dt 32:14 **B** of kine, and milk of sheep, with fat of 2529
Jdg 5:25 she brought forth **b** in a lordly dish. 2529
2Sa 17:29 **b**, and sheep, and cheese of kine, for David, 2529
Job 20:17 the floods, the brooks of honey and **b**. 2529
29: 6 When *I* washed my steps with **b**, and 2529
Ps 55:21 *words of* his mouth were smoother than **b**, 4260
Pr 30:33 the churning of milk bringeth forth **b**, 2529
Isa 7:15 **B** and honey shall he eat, that he may know 2529
7:22 of milk *that they* shall give he shall eat **b**: 2529
7:22 for **b** and honey shall every one eat that is 2529

BUTTOCKS (3)
2Sa 10: 4 *even* to their **b**, and sent them away. 8357
1Ch 19: 4 their garments in the midst hard by *their* **b**, 4667
Isa 20: 4 and barefoot, even with *their* **b** uncovered, 8357

BUY (56) [BOUGHT, BUYER, BUYEST, BUYETH]
Ge 41:57 came into Egypt to Joseph for to **b** *corn;* 7666
42: 2 you down thither, and **b** for us from thence; 7666
42: 3 Joseph's ten brethren went down to **b** corn 7666
42: 5 the sons of Israel came to **b** *corn* among 7666
42: 7 From the land of Canaan to **b** food. 7666
42:10 but to **b** food are thy servants come. 7666
43: 2 said unto them, Go again, **b** us a little food. 7666
43: 4 with us, we will go down and **b** thee food: 7666
43:20 we came indeed down at the first time to **b** 7666
43:22 we brought down in our hands to **b** food: 7666
44:25 father said, Go again, *and* **b** us a little food. 7666
47:19 **b** us and our land for bread, and we and 7069
Ex 21: 2 If thou **b** a Hebrew servant, six years he 7069
Lev 22:11 if the priest **b** *any* soul with his 7069+7075
25:15 the jubile thou shalt **b** of thy neighbour, 7069
25:44 of them shall ye **b** bondmen and 7069
25:45 of them shall ye **b**, and of their families that 7069
Dt 2: 6 Ye shall **b** meat of them for money, that ye 7666
2: 6 ye shall also **b** water of them for money, 3739
28:68 and bondwomen, and no man shall **b** *you.* 7069
Ru 4: 4 **B** *it* before the inhabitants, and before 7069
4: 5 thou must **b** *it* also of Ruth the Moabitess, 7069
4: 8 the kinsman said unto Boaz, **B** *it* for thee. 7069
2Sa 24:21 David said, To **b** the threshingfloor of thee, 7069
24:24 I will **surely b** *it* of thee at a price: 7069+7069
2Ki 12:12 to **b** timber and hewed stone to repair 7069
22: 6 to **b** timber and hewn stone to repair 7069
1Ch 21:24 I will **verily b** *it* for the full price: 7069+7069
2Ch 34:11 and builders gave they *it,* to **b** hewn stone, 7069
Ezr 7:17 That thou mayest **b** speedily with this 7069
Ne 5: 3 houses, that we might **b** corn, because 3947
10:31 *that* we would not **b** *it* of them on 3947
Pr 23:23 **B** the truth, and sell *it* not; *also* wisdom, 7069
Isa 55: 1 come ye, **b**, and eat; yea, come, buy wine 7666
55: 1 **b** wine and milk without money and 7666
Jer 32: 7 **B** thee my field that *is* in Anathoth: 7069
32: 7 for the right of redemption *is* thine to **b** *it.* 7069
32: 8 said unto me, **B** my field, I pray thee, that *is* 7069
32: 8 and the redemption *is* thine; **b** *it* for thyself. 7069
32:25 **B** thee the field for money, and 7069
32:44 *Men* shall **b** fields for money, and 7069
Am 8: 6 That *we* may **b** the poor for silver, and 7069
Mt 14:15 into the villages, and **b** themselves victuals. *59*
25: 9 rather to them that sell, and **b** for yourselves. *59*
25:10 And while they went to **b**, the bridegroom *59*
Mk 6:36 and *into* the villages, and **b** themselves bread: *59*
6:37 and **b** two hundred pennyworth of bread, *59*

Lk 9:13 we should go and **b** meat for all this people. *59*
22:36 no sword, let him sell his garment, and **b** one. *59*
Jn 4: 8 were gone away unto the city to **b** meat.) *59*
6: 5 Whence shall we **b** bread, that these may eat? *59*
13:29 **B** *those things* that we have need of against *59*
1Co 7:30 and they that **b**, as though they possessed not; *59*
Jas 4:13 there a year, and **b and sell**, and get gain: *1710*
Rev 3:18 I counsel thee to **b** of me gold tried in the fire, *59*
13:17 And that no *man* might **b** or sell, save he that *59*

BUYER (3) [BUY]
Pr 20:14 *It is* naught, *it is* naught, saith the **b**: but 7069
Isa 24: 2 as *with* the **b**, so *with* the seller; 7069
Eze 7:12 let not the **b** rejoice, nor the seller mourn: 7069

BUYEST (2) [BUY]
Lev 25:14 or **b** *ought* of thy neighbour's hand, ye shall 7069
Ru 4: 5 What day thou **b** the field of the hand of 7069

BUYETH (3) [BUY]
Pr 31:16 She considereth a field, and **b** it: with 3947
Mt 13:44 and selleth all that he hath, and **b** that field. *59*
Rev 18:11 for no *man* **b** their merchandise any more: *59*

BUZ (3)
Ge 22:21 **B** his brother, and Kemuel the father of 938
1Ch 5:14 of Jeshishai, the son of Jahdo, the son of **B**; 938
Jer 25:23 and **B**, and all *that are* in the utmost corners, 938

BUZI (1)
Eze 1: 3 the son of **B**, in the land of the Chaldeans by 941

BUZITE (2)
Job 32: 2 the wrath of Elihu the son of Barachel the **B**, 940
32: 6 Elihu the son of Barachel the **B** answered 940

BY (2633) [HEREBY, THEREBY, WHEREBY] See Index

BYWAYS (1) [WAY]
Jdg 5: 6 and the travellers walked *through* **b**. 734+6128

BYWORD (6) [WORD]
Dt 28:37 an astonishment, a proverb, and a **b**, 8148
1Ki 9: 7 be a proverb and a **b** among all people: 8148
2Ch 7:20 to be a proverb and a **b** among all nations. 8148
Job 17: 6 He hath made me also a **b** of the people; 4914
30: 9 And now am I their song, yea, I am their **b**. 4405
Ps 44:14 Thou makest us a **b** among the heathen, 4912

C

CABBON (1)
Jos 15:40 And **C**, and Lahmam, and Kithlish, 3522

CABINS (1)
Jer 37:16 into the **c**, and Jeremiah had remained there 2588

CABUL (2)
Jos 19:27 Neiel, and goeth out to **C** on the left hand, 3521
1Ki 9:13 he called them the land of **C** unto this day. 3521

CAESAR; CAESAR'S See CESAR; CESAR'S

CAESAREA See CESAREA

CAGE (2)
Jer 5:27 As a **c** *is* full *of* birds, so *are* their houses 3619
Rev 18: 2 and a **c** of every unclean and hateful bird. *5438*

CAIAPHAS (9)
Mt 26: 3 palace of the high priest, who was called **C**, *2533*
26:57 on Jesus led *him* away to **C** the high priest, *2533*
Lk 3: 2 Annas and **C** being the high priests, *2533*
Jn 11:49 And one of them, *named* **C**, being the high *2533*
18:13 for he was father in law to **C**, which was *2533*
18:14 Now **C** was he, which gave counsel to *2533*
18:24 Now Annas had sent him bound unto **C** *2533*
18:28 Then led they Jesus from **C** unto the hall of *2533*
Ac 4: 6 and **C**, and John, and Alexander, and *2533*

CAIN (20)
Ge 4: 1 she conceived, and bare **C**, and said, I have 7014
4: 2 of sheep, but **C** was a tiller of the ground. 7014
4: 3 that **C** brought of the fruit of the ground an 7014
4: 5 unto **C** and to his offering he had not 7014
4: 5 **C** was very wroth, and his countenance fell. 7014
4: 6 the LORD said unto **C**, Why art thou 7014
4: 8 **C** talked with Abel his brother: and it came 7014
4: 8 that **C** rose up against Abel his brother, and 7014
4: 9 the LORD said unto **C**, Where *is* Abel thy 7014
4:13 **C** said unto the LORD, My punishment *is* 7014
4:15 unto him, Therefore whosoever slayeth **C**, 7014
4:15 the LORD set a mark upon **C**, lest any 7014
4:16 **C** went out from the presence of 7014
4:17 **C** knew his wife; and she conceived, and 7014
4:24 If **C** shall be avenged sevenfold, 7014
4:25 seed instead of Abel, whom **C** slew. 7014
Jos 15:57 **C**, Gibeah, and Timnah; ten cities with 7014
Heb 11: 4 unto God a more excellent sacrifice than **C**, *2535*
1Jn 3:12 Not as **C**, *who* was of *that* wicked one, and *2535*
Jude 1:11 for they have gone in the way of **C**, and *2535*

CAINAN (7)
Ge 5: 9 And Enos lived ninety years, and begat **C**: 7018
5:10 Enos lived after he begat **C** eight hundred 7018
5:12 **C** lived seventy years, and 7018
5:13 **C** lived after he begat Mahalaleel eight 7018
5:14 all the days of **C** were nine hundred 7018
Lk 3:36 Which was *the son* of **C**, which was *the son* *2536*
3:37 *son* of Maleleel, which was *the son* of **C**, *2536*

CAKE (13) [CAKES]
Ex 29:23 one **c** of oiled bread, and one wafer out of 2471
Lev 8:26 he took one unleavened **c**, and a cake of 2471
8:26 a **c** of oiled bread, and one wafer, and 2471
24: 5 two tenth deals shall be *in* one **c**. 2471
Nu 6:19 one unleavened **c** out of the basket, and 2471
15:20 Ye shall offer up a **c** *of* the first of your 2471
Jdg 7:13 a **c** of barley bread tumbled into the host of 6742
1Sa 30:12 they gave him a piece of a **c** *of figs*, and 1690
2Sa 6:19 to every one a **c** of bread, and a good piece 2471
1Ki 17:12 I have not a **c**, but a handful of meal in a 4580
17:13 make me thereof a little **c** first, and bring *it* 5692
19: 6 *there was* a **c** baken on the coals, and 5692
Hos 7: 8 the people; Ephraim is a **c** not turned. 5692

CAKES (25) [CAKE]
Ge 18: 6 knead *it*, and make **c** upon the hearth. 5692
Ex 12:39 they baked unleavened **c** of the dough 5692
29: 2 **c** unleavened tempered with oil, and 2471
Lev 2: 4 *it shall be* unleavened **c** of fine flour 2471
7:12 unleavened **c** mingled with oil, 2471
7:12 and **c** mingled with oil, of fine flour, fried. 2471
7:13 Besides the **c**, he shall offer *for* his offering 2471
24: 5 take fine flour, and bake twelve **c** thereof: 2471
Nu 6:15 **c** *of* fine flour mingled with oil, and 2471
11: 8 and baked *it* in pans, and made **c** *of* it: 5692
Jos 5:11 unleavened *c*, and parched *corn* in NIH
Jdg 6:19 and unleavened *c of* an ephah of flour: NIH
6:20 Take the flesh and the unleavened *c*, and NIH
6:21 touched the flesh and the unleavened *c*; and NIH
6:21 the unleavened *c*. Then the angel of NIH
1Sa 25:18 two hundred **c** *of figs*, and laid *them* on 1690
2Sa 13: 6 **make** *me* a couple of **c** in my sight, 3823+3834
13: 8 kneaded *it*, and **made c** in his sight, and 3823
13: 8 made cakes in his sight, and did bake the **c**. 3834
13:10 Tamar took the **c** which she had made, and 3834
1Ch 12:40 **c** *of figs*, and bunches of raisins, and wine, 1690
23:29 for the unleavened **c**, and for *that which is* 7550
Jer 7:18 to make **c** to the queen of heaven, and 3561
44:19 did we make her **c** to worship her, and 3561
Eze 4:12 thou shalt eat it *as* barley **c**, and thou shalt 5692

CALAH (2)
Ge 10:11 and the city Rehoboth, and **C**, 3625
10:12 Resen between Nineveh and **C**: the same *is* 3625

CALAMITIES (3) [CALAMITY]
Ps 57: 1 I make my refuge, until *these* **c** be overpast. 1942
141: 5 for yet my prayer also *shall be* in their **c**. 7451
Pr 17: 5 he that is glad at **c** shall not be unpunished. 343

CALAMITY (19) [CALAMITIES]
Dt 32:35 for the day of their **c** *is* at hand, and 343

2Sa 22:19 They prevented me in the day of my **c**: but 343
Job 6: 2 my **c** laid in the balances together! 1942
30:13 They mar my path, they set forward my **c**, 1942
Ps 18:18 They prevented me in the day of my **c**: but 343
Pr 1:26 I also will laugh at your **c**; I will mock when 343
6:15 Therefore shall his **c** come suddenly; 343
19:13 A foolish son *is* the **c** of his father: and 1942
24:22 For their **c** shall rise suddenly; and 343
27:10 *into* thy brother's house in the day of thy **c**: 343
Jer 18:17 and not the face, in the day of their **c**. 343
46:21 the day of their **c** was come upon them, 343
48:16 The **c** of Moab *is* near to come, and 343
49: 8 for I will bring the **c** of Esau upon him, 343
49:32 and I will bring their **c** from all sides thereof, 343
Eze 35: 5 the force of the sword in the time of their **c**, 343
Ob 1:13 the gate of my people in the day of their **c**: 343
1:13 on their affliction in the day of their **c**, 343
1:13 on their substance in the day of their **c**; 343

CALAMUS (3)
Ex 30:23 and of sweet **c** two hundred and 7070
SS 4:14 **c** and cinnamon, with all trees of 7070
Eze 27:19 bright iron, cassia, and **c**, were in thy 7070

CALCOL (1) [CHALCOL]
1Ch 2: 6 and Ethan, and Heman, and **C**, and Dara: 3633

CALDRON (6) [CALDRONS]
1Sa 2:14 *it* into the pan, or kettle, or **c**, or pot; 7037
Job 41:20 goeth smoke, as *out of* a seething pot or **c**. 100
Eze 11: 3 this *city is* the **c**, and we *be* the flesh. 5518
11: 7 they *are* the flesh, and this *city is* the **c**: 5518
11:11 This *city* shall not be your **c**, neither shall 5518
Mic 3: 3 as for the pot, and as flesh within the **c**. 7037

CALDRONS (3) [CALDRON]
2Ch 35:13 in **c**, and in pans, and divided *them* speedily 1731
Jer 52:18 The **c** also, and the shovels, and 5518
52:19 the **c**, and the candlesticks, and the spoons, 5518

CALEB (32) [CALEB'S, CALEB-EPHRATAH]
Nu 13: 6 the tribe of Judah, **C** the son of Jephunneh. 3612
13:30 **C** stilled the people before Moses, and said, 3612
14: 6 son of Nun, and **C** the son of Jephunneh, 3612
14:24 my servant **C**, because he had another spirit 3612
14:30 save **C** the son of Jephunneh, and 3612
14:38 son of Nun, and **C** the son of Jephunneh, 3612
26:65 save **C** the son of Jephunneh, and 3612
32:12 Save **C** the son of Jephunneh the Kenezite, 3612
34:19 the tribe of Judah, **C** the son of Jephunneh. 3612
Dt 1:36 Save **C** the son of Jephunneh, he shall see 3612
Jos 14: 6 **C** the son of Jephunneh the Kenezite said 3612
14:13 gave unto **C** the son of Jephunneh Hebron 3612
14:14 became the inheritance of **C** the son of 3612
15:13 unto **C** the son of Jephunneh he gave a part 3612
15:14 And **C** drove thence the three sons of Anak, 3612
15:16 **C** said, He that smiteth Kirjath-sepher, and 3612
15:17 the son of Kenaz, the brother of **C**, took it: 3612
15:18 and **C** said unto her, What wouldest thou? 3612
21:12 gave they to **C** the son of Jephunneh for his 3612
Jdg 1:12 **C** said, He that smiteth Kirjath-sepher, and 3612
1:14 and **C** said unto her, What wilt thou? 3612
1:15 **C** gave her the upper springs and the nether 3612
1:20 they gave Hebron unto **C**, as Moses said: 3612
1Sa 25: 3 his doings; and he *was* **of the house of C**. 3614
30:14 to Judah, and upon the south of **C**; 3612
1Ch 2:18 **C** the son of Hezron begat *children* of 3612
2:19 **C** took unto him Ephrath, which bare him 3612
2:42 Now the sons of **C** the brother of Jerahmeel 3612
2:49 and the daughter of **C** *was* Achsah. 3612
2:50 These were the sons of **C** the son of Hur, 3612
4:15 the sons of **C** the son of Jephunneh; Iru, 3612
6:56 they gave to **C** the son of Jephunneh. 3612

CALEB'S (4) [CALEB]
Jdg 1:13 son of Kenaz, **C** younger brother, took it: 3612
3: 9 the son of Kenaz, **C** younger brother. 3612
1Ch 2:46 **C** concubine, bare Haran, and Moza, and 3612
2:48 Maachah, **C** concubine, bare Sheber, and 3612

CALEB-EPHRATAH (1) [CALEB, EPHRATAH]
1Ch 2:24 after that Hezron was dead in **C**, then 3613

CALF (29) [CALF'S, CALVE, CALVED, CALVES, CALVETH]
Ge 18: 7 fetcht a **c** tender and good, and 1121+1241
18: 8 the **c** which he had dressed, and set *it* 1121+1241
Ex 32: 4 after he had made it a molten **c**: 5695
32: 8 they have made them a molten **c**, and 5695
32:19 that he saw the **c**, and the dancing: 5695
32:20 he took the **c** which they had made, and 5695
32:24 it into the fire, and there came out this **c**. 5695
32:35 because they made the **c**, which Aaron 5695
Lev 9: 2 Take thee a young **c** for a sin 1241+5695
9: 3 a **c** and a lamb, both of the first year, 5695
9: 8 the altar, and slew the **c** of the sin offering, 5695
Dt 9:16 your God, *and* had made you a molten **c**: 5695
9:21 the **c** which ye had made, and burnt it with 5695
1Sa 28:24 the woman had a fat **c** in the house; and 5695
Ne 9:18 when they had made them a molten **c**, and 5695
Job 21:10 their cow calveth, and **casteth** not **her c**. 7921
Ps 29: 6 He maketh them also to skip like a **c**; 5695
106:19 They made a **c** in Horeb, and 5695
Isa 11: 6 the **c** and the young lion and the fatling 5695
27:10 there shall the **c** feed, and there shall he lie 5695
Jer 34:18 when they cut the **c** in twain, and 5695
34:19 which passed between the parts of the **c**; 5695
Hos 8: 5 Thy **c**, O Samaria, hath cast *thee* off; 5695
8: 6 the **c** of Samaria shall be broken in pieces. 5695
Lk 15:23 And bring hither the fatted **c**, and kill *it;* *3448*
15:27 and thy father hath killed the fatted **c**, *3448*
15:30 thou hast killed for him the fatted **c**. *3448*
Ac 7:41 And they **made a c** in those days, and *3447*
Rev 4: 7 and the second beast like a **c**, and the third *3448*

CALF'S (1) [CALF]
Eze 1: 7 the sole of their feet *was* like the sole of a **c** 5695

CALKERS (2)
Eze 27: 9 wise *men* thereof were in thee thy **c**: 919+2388
27:27 thy **c**, and the occupiers of thy 919+2388

CALL (196) [CALLED, CALLEDST, CALLEST, CALLETH, CALLING]
Ge 2:19 unto Adam to see what he would **c** them: 7121
4:26 began *men* to **c** upon the name of 7121
16:11 bear a son, and shalt **c** his name Ishmael; 7121
17:15 thou shalt not **c** her name Sarai, but 7121
17:19 son indeed; and thou shalt **c** his name Isaac: 7121
24:57 We will **c** the damsel, and inquire at her 7121
30:13 am I, for the daughters will **c** me **blessed**: 833
46:33 when Pharaoh shall **c** you, and shall say, 7121
Ex 2: 7 **c** to thee a nurse of the Hebrew women, 7121
2:20 left the man? **c** him, that he may eat bread. 7121
34:15 and *one* **c** thee, and thou eat of his sacrifice; 7121
Nu 16:12 Moses sent to **c** Dathan and Abiram, 7121
22: 5 to **c** him, saying, Behold, there is a people 7121
22:20 If the men come to **c** thee, rise up, *and* 7121
22:37 Did I not earnestly send unto thee to **c** thee? 7121
Dt 2:11 but the Moabites **c** them Emims. 7121
2:20 and the Ammonites **c** them Zamzummims; 7121
3: 9 (*Which* Hermon the Sidonians **c** Sirion; and 7121
3: 9 call Sirion; and the Amorites **c** it Shenir;) 7121
4: 7 *is* in all *things that* we **c** upon him *for?* 7121
4:26 I **c** heaven and earth **to witness** against you 5749
25: 8 the elders of his city shall **c** him, and 7121
30: 1 thou shalt **c** *them* to mind among all 7725
30:19 I **c** heaven and earth **to record** *this* day 5749
31:14 **c** Joshua, and present yourselves in 7121
31:28 **c** heaven and earth **to record** against them. 5749
33:19 They shall **c** the people *unto* the mountain; 7121
Jdg 12: 1 and didst not **c** us to go with thee? 7121
16:25 that they said, **C** for Samson, that he may 7121
21:13 and to **c** peaceably unto them. 7121
Ru 1:20 unto them, **C** me not Naomi, call me Mara: 7121
1:20 unto them, Call me not Naomi, **c** me Mara: 7121
1:21 why *then* **c** ye me Naomi, seeing 7121
1Sa 3: 6 and said, Here *am* I; for thou didst **c** me. 7121
3: 8 and said, Here *am* I; for thou didst **c** me. 7121
3: 9 it shall be, if he **c** thee, that thou shalt say, 7121
12:17 I will **c** unto the LORD, and he shall send 7121
16: 3 **c** Jesse to the sacrifice, and I will shew thee 7121
22:11 the king sent to **c** Ahimelech the priest, 7121
2Sa 17: 5 **C** now Hushai the Archite also, and let us 7121
22: 4 I will **c on** the LORD, who is *worthy* to be 7121
1Ki 1:28 and said, **C** me Bath-sheba. 7121
1:32 **C** me Zadok the priest, and Nathan 7121
8:52 to hearken unto them in all that they **c for** 7121
17:18 unto me to **c** my sin **to remembrance**, 2142
18:24 **c** ye on the name of your gods, and I will 7121

1Ki 18:24 and I will **c** on the name of the LORD: 7121
18:25 **c** on the name of your gods, but put no fire 7121
22:13 the messenger that was gone to **c** Micaiah 7121
2Ki 4:12 to Gehazi his servant, **C** this Shunammite. 7121
4:15 he said, **C** her. And when he had called her, 7121
4:36 and said, **C** this Shunammite. 7121
5:11 **c** on the name of the LORD his God, and 7121
10:19 **c** unto me all the prophets of Baal, 7121
1Ch 16: 8 thanks unto the LORD, **c** upon his name, 7121
2Ch 18:12 the messenger that went to **c** Micaiah spake 7121
Job 5: 1 **C** now, if there be *any* that will answer 7121
13:22 **c** thou, and I will answer: or let me speak, 7121
14:15 Thou shalt **c**, and I will answer thee: 7121
27:10 the Almighty? will he always **c upon** God? 7121
Ps 4: 1 Hear me when I **c**, O God of my 7121
4: 3 the LORD will hear when I **c** unto him. 7121
14: 4 they eat bread, *and* **c** not **upon** the LORD. 7121
18: 3 I will **c upon** the LORD, who is *worthy* to 7121
20: 9 LORD: let the king hear us when we **c**. 7121
49:11 they **c** *their* lands after their own names. 7121
50: 4 He shall **c** to the heavens from above, and 7121
50:15 **c upon** me in the day of trouble: I will 7121
55:16 *As for* me, I will **c** upon God; and 7121
72:17 in him: all nations shall **c** him **blessed**. 833
77: 6 I **c to remembrance** my song in the night: 2142
80:18 quicken us, and we will **c** upon thy name. 7121
86: 5 in mercy unto all them that **c upon** thee. 7121
86: 7 In the day of my trouble I will **c upon** thee: 7121
91:15 He shall **c upon** me, and I will answer him: 7121
99: 6 Samuel among them that **c upon** his name; 7121
102: 2 in the day *when* I **c** answer me speedily. 7121
105: 1 thanks unto the LORD; **c** upon his name: 7121
116: 2 will I **c upon** *him* as long as I live. 7121
116:13 and **c** upon the name of the LORD. 7121
116:17 and will **c** upon the name of the LORD. 7121
145:18 *is* nigh unto all them that **c upon** him, 7121
145:18 upon him, to all that **c upon** him in truth. 7121
Pr 1:28 shall they **c upon** me, but I will not answer; 7121
7: 4 and **c** understanding *thy* kinswoman: 7121
8: 4 Unto you, O men, I **c**; and my voice *is* to 7121
9:15 To **c** passengers who go right *on* their 7121
31:28 Her children arise up, and **c** her **blessed**; 833
Isa 5:20 Woe unto them that **c** evil good, and good 559
7:14 bear a Son, and shall **c** his name Immanuel. 7121
8: 3 to me, **C** his name Maher-shalal-hash-baz. 7121
12: 4 Praise the LORD, **c** upon his name, 7121
22:12 in that day did the Lord GOD of hosts **c** to 7121
22:20 that I will **c** my servant Eliakim the son of 7121
31: 2 bring evil, and will not **c back** his words: 5493
34:12 They shall **c** the nobles thereof *to* 7121
41:25 from the rising of the sun shall he **c** upon 7121
44: 5 another shall **c** *himself* by the name of 7121
44: 7 shall **c**, and shall declare it, and set it in 7121
45: 3 the LORD, which **c** *thee* by thy name, 7121
48: 2 For they **c** themselves of the holy city, and 7121
48:13 *when* I **c** unto them, they stand *up* together. 7121
55: 5 thou shalt **c** a nation *that* thou knowest not, 7121
55: 6 be found, **c** ye **upon** him while he is near: 7121
58: 5 and ashes *under him?* wilt thou **c** this a fast, 7121
58: 9 shalt thou **c**, and the LORD shall answer; 7121
58:13 **c** the sabbath a delight, the holy of 7121
60:14 they shall **c** thee, The city of the LORD, 7121
60:18 thou shalt **c** thy walls Salvation, and 7121
61: 6 *men* shall **c** you the Ministers of our God: 559
62:12 they shall **c** them, The holy people, 7121
65:15 and **c** his servants by another name: 7121
65:24 to pass, that before they **c**, I will answer; 7121
Jer 1:15 I will **c** all the families of the kingdoms of 7121
3:17 At that time they shall **c** Jerusalem 7121
3:19 I said, Thou shalt **c** me, My father; and 7121
6:30 Reprobate silver shall *men* **c** them, because 7121
7:27 thou shalt also **c** unto them; but they will 7121
9:17 **c** for the mourning *women,* that they may 7121
10:25 upon the families that **c** not on thy name: 7121
25:29 for I *will* **c** for a sword upon all 7121
29:12 shall ye **c upon** me, and ye shall go and 7121
33: 3 **C** unto me, and I will answer thee, and 7121
50:29 **C together** the archers against Babylon: 8085
51:27 **c together** against her the kingdoms of 8085
La 2:15 *saying, Is* this the city that *men* **c** The 559
Eze 21:23 he will **c to remembrance** the iniquity, 2142
36:29 I will **c** for the corn, and will increase it, 7121
38:21 I will **c** *for* a sword against him throughout 7121
39:11 they shall **c** *it* The valley of Hamon-gog. 7121

Da 2: 2 the king commanded to **c** the magicians, 7121
Hos 1: 4 LORD said unto him, **C** his name Jezreel; 7121
1: 6 said unto him, **C** her name Lo-ruhamah: 7121
1: 9 said *God,* **C** his name Lo-ammi: for ye *are* 7121
2:16 saith the LORD, *that* thou shalt **c** *me* Ishi; 7121
2:16 call *me* Ishi; and shalt **c** me no more Baali. 7121
7:11 they **c** *to* Egypt, they go *to* Assyria. 7121
Joel 1:14 **c** a solemn assembly, gather the elders *and* 7121
2:15 sanctify a fast, **c** a solemn assembly: 7121
2:32 *that* whosoever shall **c** on the name of 7121
2:32 in the remnant whom the LORD *shall* **c**. 7121
Am 5:16 they shall **c** the husbandman to mourning, 7121
Jnh 1: 6 **c** upon thy God, if so be that God will think 7121
Zep 3: 9 that they may all **c** upon the name of 7121
Zec 3:10 shall ye **c** every man his neighbour, under 7121
13: 9 they shall **c** on my name, and I will hear 7121
Mal 1: 4 they shall **c** them, The border of 7121
3:12 all nations shall **c** you **blessed**: for ye shall 833
3:15 now we **c** the proud **happy**; yea, they that 833
Mt 1:21 a son, and thou shalt **c** his name JESUS: *2564*
1:23 a son, and they shall **c** his name Emmanuel, *2564*
9:13 for I am not come to **c** *the* righteous, but *2564*
10:25 how much more *shall they* **c** them of his NIG
20: 8 **C** the labourers, and give them *their* hire, *2564*
22: 3 And sent forth his servants to **c** them that *2564*
22:43 How then doth David in spirit **c** him Lord, *2564*
22:45 If David then **c** him Lord, how is he his *2564*
23: 9 And **c** no *man* your father upon the earth: *2564*
Mk 2:17 I came not to **c** *the* righteous, but sinners to *2564*
10:49 And they **c** the blind man, saying unto him, *5455*
15:12 *that* I shall do *unto him* whom ye **c** *3004*
15:16 and they **c together** the whole band. *4779*
Lk 1:13 thee a son, and thou shalt **c** his name John. *2564*
1:31 forth a son, and shalt **c** his name JESUS. *2564*
1:48 all generations shall **c** me **blessed**. *3106*
5:32 I came not to **c** *the* righteous, but sinners to *2564*
6:46 And why **c** ye me, Lord, Lord, and do not *2564*
14:12 a dinner or a supper, **c** not thy friends, *5455*
14:13 **c** the poor, the maimed, the lame, the blind: *2564*
Jn 4:16 Go, **c** thy husband, and come hither. *5455*
13:13 Ye **c** me Master and Lord: and ye say well; *5455*
15:15 Henceforth I **c** you not servants; for *3004*
Ac 2:21 *that* whosoever shall **c on** the name of *1941*
2:39 *even* as many as the Lord our God shall **c**. *4341*
9:14 chief priests to bind all that **c on** thy name. *1941*
10: 5 and **c for** *one* Simon, whose surname is *3343*
10:15 hath cleansed, *that* **c** not thou **common**. *2840*
10:28 God hath shewed me that *I* should not **c** any *3004*
10:32 therefore to Joppa, and **c hither** Simon, *3333*
11: 9 hath cleansed, *that* **c** not thou **common**. *2840*
11:13 Send men to Joppa, and **c for** Simon, *3343*
19:13 took upon them to **c** over them which had *3687*
24:14 that after the way which they **c** heresy, so *3004*
24:25 have a convenient season, I will **c for** thee. *3333*
Ro 9:25 saith also in Osee, I will **c** *them* my people, *2564*
10:12 over all *is* rich unto all that **c upon** him. *1941*
10:13 For whosoever shall **c upon** the name of *1941*
10:14 shall they **c on** *him* in whom they have not *1941*
1Co 1: 2 with all that in every place **c upon** *1941*
2Co 1:23 Moreover I **c** God **for** a record upon my *1941*
2Ti 1: 5 When I **c** to remembrance the unfeigned *2983*
2:22 with them that **c on** the Lord out of a pure *1941*
Heb 2:11 for which cause he is not ashamed to **c** *2564*
10:32 But **c to remembrance** the former days, *363*
Jas 5:14 let him **c for** the elders of the church; and *4341*
1Pe 1:17 And if ye **c on** the Father, who without *1941*

CALLED (623) [CALL]

Ge 1: 5 God **c** the light Day, and the darkness he 7121
1: 5 the light Day, and the darkness he **c** Night. 7121
1: 8 God **c** the firmament Heaven. And 7121
1:10 God **c** the dry *land* Earth; and the gathering 7121
1:10 the gathering together of the waters **c** he 7121
2:19 whatsoever Adam **c** every living creature, 7121
2:23 she shall be **c** Woman, because she was 7121
3: 9 the LORD God **c** unto Adam, and 7121
3:20 Adam **c** his wife's name Eve; because 7121
4:17 builded a city, and **c** the name of the city, 7121
4:25 she bare a son, and **c** his name Seth: 7121
4:26 he **c** his name Enos; then began *men* to call 7121
5: 2 blessed them, and **c** their name Adam, 7121
5: 3 after his image; and **c** his name Seth: 7121
5:29 he **c** his name Noah, saying, This *same* 7121
11: 9 Therefore is the name of it **c** Babel; 7121

Ge	12: 8	and **c** upon the name of the LORD.	7121
	12:18	Pharaoh **c** Abram, and said, What *is* this	7121
	13: 4	there Abram **c** on the name of the LORD.	7121
	16:13	she **c** the name of the LORD that spake	7121
	16:14	Wherefore the well was **c** Beer-lahai-roi;	7121
	16:15	Abram **c** his son's name, which Hagar bare,	7121
	17: 5	Neither shall thy name any more be **c**	7121
	19: 5	they **c** unto Lot, and said unto him,	7121
	19:22	Therefore the name of the city was **c** Zoar.	7121
	19:37	firstborn bare a son, and **c** his name Moab:	7121
	19:38	also bare a son, and **c** his name Ben-ammi:	7121
	20: 8	**c** all his servants, and told all these things	7121
	20: 9	Abimelech **c** Abraham, and said unto him,	7121
	21: 3	Abraham **c** the name of his son that was	7121
	21:12	her voice; for in Isaac shall thy seed be **c**.	7121
	21:17	the angel of God **c** to Hagar out of heaven,	7121
	21:31	Wherefore he **c** that place Beer-sheba;	7121
	21:33	**c** there on the name of the LORD,	7121
	22:11	the angel of the LORD **c** unto him out of	7121
	22:14	Abraham **c** the name of that place	7121
	22:15	the angel of the LORD **c** unto Abraham	7121
	24:58	they **c** Rebekah, and said unto her, Wilt	7121
	25:25	a hairy garment; and they **c** his name Esau.	7121
	25:26	on Esau's heel; and his name was **c** Jacob:	7121
	25:30	I *am* faint: therefore was his name **c** Edom.	7121
	26: 9	Abimelech **c** Isaac, and said, Behold, of a	7121
	26:18	he **c** their names after the names by which	7121
	26:18	the names by which his father had **c** them.	7121
	26:20	he **c** the name of the well Esek; because	7121
	26:21	for that also: and he **c** the name of it Sitnah.	7121
	26:22	he **c** the name of it Rehoboth; and he said,	7121
	26:25	**c** upon the name of the LORD, and	7121
	26:33	he **c** it Shebah: therefore the name of	7121
	27: 1	he **c** Esau his eldest son, and said unto him,	7121
	27:42	she sent and **c** Jacob her younger son, and	7121
	28: 1	Isaac **c** Jacob, and blessed him, and	7121
	28:19	he **c** the name of that place Beth-el: but	7121
	28:19	the name of *that* city *was* **c** Luz at the first.	NIH
	29:32	and bare a son, and she **c** his name Reuben:	7121
	29:33	this *son* also: and she **c** his name Simeon.	7121
	29:34	three sons: therefore was his name **c** Levi.	7121
	29:35	therefore she **c** his name Judah; and	7121
	30: 6	me a son: therefore **c** she his name Dan.	7121
	30: 8	and she **c** his name Naphtali.	7121
	30:11	A troop cometh: and she **c** his name Gad.	7121
	30:13	call me blessed: and she **c** his name Asher.	7121
	30:18	my husband: and she **c** his name Issachar.	7121
	30:20	him six sons: and she **c** his name Zebulun.	7121
	30:21	she bare a daughter, and **c** her name Dinah.	7121
	30:24	she **c** his name Joseph; and said,	7121
	31: 4	Jacob sent and **c** Rachel and Leah to	7121
	31:47	Laban **c** it Jegar-sahadutha: but	7121
	31:47	it Jegar-sahadutha: but Jacob **c** it Galeed.	7121
	31:48	Therefore was the name of it **c** Galeed;	7121
	31:54	the mount, and **c** his brethren to eat bread:	7121
	32: 2	and he **c** the name of that place Mahanaim.	7121
	32:28	Thy name shall be **c** no more Jacob, but	559
	32:30	Jacob **c** the name of the place Peniel: for I	7121
	33:17	the name of the place is **c** Succoth.	7121
	33:20	there an altar, and **c** it El-Elohe-Israel.	7121
	35: 7	there an altar, and **c** the place El-beth-el:	7121
	35: 8	and the name of it was **c** Allon-bachuth.	7121
	35:10	thy name shall not be **c** any more Jacob, but	7121
	35:10	shall be thy name: and he **c** his name Israel.	7121
	35:15	Jacob **c** the name of the place where God	7121
	35:18	(for she died) that she **c** his name Ben-oni:	7121
	35:18	but his father **c** him Benjamin.	7121
	38: 3	and bare a son; and he **c** his name Er.	7121
	38: 4	and bare a son; and she **c** his name Onan.	7121
	38: 5	and bare a son; and **c** his name Shelah:	7121
	38:29	therefore his name was **c** Pharez.	7121
	38:30	upon his hand: and his name was **c** Zarah.	7121
	39:14	That she **c** unto the men of her house, and	7121
	41: 8	and **c** for all the magicians of Egypt,	7121
	41:14	Pharaoh sent and **c** Joseph, and	7121
	41:45	Pharaoh **c** Joseph's name	7121
	41:51	Joseph **c** the name of the firstborn	7121
	41:52	the name of the second **c** he Ephraim:	7121
	47:29	he **c** his son Joseph, and said unto him,	7121
	48: 6	shall be **c** after the name of their brethren in	7121
	49: 1	Jacob **c** unto his sons, and said,	7121
	50:11	wherefore the name of it was **c**	7121
Ex	1:18	the king of Egypt **c** for the midwives, and	7121
	2: 8	the maid went and **c** the child's mother.	7121
	2:10	she **c** his name Moses: and she said,	7121
	2:22	*him* a son, and he **c** his name Gershom:	7121
	3: 4	God **c** unto him out of the midst of	7121
	7:11	Pharaoh also **c** the wise men and	7121
	8: 8	Pharaoh **c** for Moses and Aaron, and said,	7121
	8:25	Pharaoh **c** for Moses and for Aaron, and	7121
	9:27	**c** for Moses and Aaron, and said unto them,	7121
	10:16	Pharaoh **c** for Moses and Aaron in haste;	7121
	10:24	Pharaoh **c** unto Moses, and said, Go ye,	7121
	12:21	Moses **c** for all the elders of Israel, and	7121
	12:31	he **c** for Moses and Aaron by night, and	7121
	15:23	the name of it was **c** Marah.	7121
	16:31	the house of Israel **c** the name thereof	7121
	17: 7	he **c** the name of the place Massah, and	7121
	17:15	an altar, and **c** the name of it Jehovah-nissi:	7121
	19: 3	the LORD **c** unto him out of the mountain,	7121
	19: 7	and **c** for the elders of the people,	7121
	19:20	the LORD **c** Moses *up* to the top of	7121
	24:16	the seventh day he **c** unto Moses out of	7121
	31: 2	I have **c** by name Bezaleel the son of Uri,	7121
	33: 7	**c** it the Tabernacle of the Congregation.	7121
	34:31	Moses **c** unto them; and Aaron and all	7121
	35:30	the LORD hath **c** by name Bezaleel	7121
	36: 2	Moses **c** Bezaleel and Aholiab, and every	7121
Lev	1: 1	the LORD **c** unto Moses, and spake unto	7121
	9: 1	*that* Moses **c** Aaron and his sons, and	7121
	10: 4	Moses **c** Mishael and Elzaphan, the sons of	7121
Nu	11: 3	he **c** the name of the place Taberah:	7121
	11:34	he **c** the name of that place	7121
	12: 5	of the tabernacle, and **c** Aaron and Miriam:	7121
	13:16	Moses **c** Oshea the son of Nun, Jehoshua.	7121
	13:24	The place was **c** the brook Eshcol, because	7121
	21: 3	and he **c** the name of the place Hormah.	7121
	24:10	I **c** thee to curse mine enemies, and behold,	7121
	25: 2	they **c** the people unto the sacrifices of their	7121
	32:41	towns thereof, and **c** them Havoth-jair.	7121
	32:42	and **c** it Nobah, after his own name.	7121
Dt	3:13	all Bashan, which was **c** the land of giants.	7121
	3:14	**c** them after his own name,	7121
	5: 1	Moses **c** all Israel, and said unto them,	7121
	15: 2	because it is **c** the LORD'S release.	7121
	25:10	his name shall be **c** in Israel, The house of	7121
	28:10	that thou art **c** by the name of the LORD;	7121
	29: 2	Moses **c** unto all Israel, and said unto them,	7121
	31: 7	Moses **c** unto Joshua, and said unto him in	7121
Jos	4: 4	Joshua **c** the twelve men, whom he had	7121
	5: 9	Wherefore the name of the place is **c** Gilgal	7121
	6: 6	Joshua the son of Nun **c** the priests, and	7121
	7:26	Wherefore the name of that place was **c**,	7121
	8:16	all the people that *were* in Ai were **c**	2199
	9:22	Joshua **c** for them, and he spake unto them,	7121
	10:24	that Joshua **c** for all the men of Israel, and	7121
	19:47	and dwelt therein, and **c** Leshem, Dan,	7121
	22: 1	Joshua **c** the Reubenites, and the Gadites,	7121
	22:34	the children of Gad **c** the altar *Ed*: for it	7121
	23: 2	Joshua **c** for all Israel, *and* for their elders,	7121
	24: 1	**c** for the elders of Israel, and for their	7121
	24: 9	and **c** Balaam the son of Beor to curse you:	7121
Jdg	1:17	and the name of the city was **c** Hormah.	7121
	1:26	built a city, and **c** the name thereof Luz:	7121
	2: 5	they **c** the name of that place Bochim: and	7121
	4: 6	**c** Barak the son of Abinoam out of	7121
	4:10	Barak **c** Zebulun and Naphtali to Kedesh;	2199
	6:24	unto the LORD, and **c** it Jehovah-shalom:	7121
	6:32	Therefore on that day he **c** him Jerubbaal,	7121
	8:31	him a son, whose name he **c** Abimelech.	7760
	9:54	he **c** hastily unto the young man his	7121
	10: 4	which are **c** Havoth-jair unto this day,	7121
	12: 2	when I **c** you, ye delivered me not out of	2199
	13:24	woman bare a son, and **c** his name Samson:	7121
	14:15	have ye **c** us to take that we have? *is it* not	7121
	15:17	of his hand, and **c** that place Ramath-lehi.	7121
	15:18	sore athirst, and **c** on the LORD, and said,	7121
	15:19	wherefore he **c** the name thereof	7121
	16:18	and **c** for the lords of the Philistines,	7121
	16:19	she **c** for a man, and she caused *him* to	7121
	16:25	they **c** for Samson out of the prison house;	7121
	16:28	Samson **c** unto the LORD, and said,	7121
	18:12	wherefore they **c** that place Mahaneh-dan	7121
	18:29	they **c** the name of the city Dan, after	7121
Ru	4:17	born to Naomi; and they **c** his name Obed:	7121
1Sa	1:20	that she bare a son, and **c** his name Samuel,	7121
	3: 4	That the LORD **c** Samuel: and	7121
	3: 5	he said, I **c** not; lie down again. And he	7121

1Sa 3: 6 the LORD **c** yet again, Samuel. 7121
3: 6 he answered, I **c** not, my son; lie down 7121
3: 8 the LORD **c** Samuel again the third time. 7121
3: 8 Eli perceived that the LORD had **c** 7121
3:10 stood, and **c** as at other times, Samuel, 7121
3:16 Eli **c** Samuel, and said, Samuel, my son. 7121
6: 2 the Philistines **c** for the priests and 7121
7:12 and Shen, and **c** the name of it Eben-ezer, 7121
9: 9 for *he that is* now **c** a Prophet was NIH
9: 9 *called* a Prophet was beforetime **c** a Seer.) 7121
9:26 that Samuel **c** Saul to the top of the house, 7121
10:17 Samuel **c** the people **together** unto 6817
12:18 So Samuel **c** unto the LORD; and 7121
13: 4 the people were **c together** after Saul *to* 6817
16: 5 and his sons, and **c** them to the sacrifice. 7121
16: 8 Jesse **c** Abinadab, and made him pass 7121
19: 7 Jonathan **c** David, and Jonathan shewed 7121
23: 8 Saul **c** all the people **together** to war, to go 8085
23:28 they **c** that place Sela-hammahlekoth. 7121
28:15 therefore I have **c** thee, that *thou* mayest 7121
29: 6 Achish **c** David, and said unto him, Surely, 7121
2Sa 1: 7 behind him, he saw me, and **c** unto me. 7121
1:15 David **c** one of the young men, and said, 7121
2:16 wherefore that place was **c** 7121
2:26 Abner **c** to Joab, and said, Shall the sword 7121
5: 9 dwelt in the fort, and **c** it the city of David. 7121
5:20 Therefore he **c** the name of that place 7121
6: 2 whose name is **c** *by* the name of 7121
6: 8 he **c** *the name* of the place Perez-uzzah to 7121
9: 2 when they had **c** him unto David, the king 7121
9: 9 the king **c** to Ziba, Saul's servant, and 7121
11:13 when David had **c** him, he did eat and 7121
12:24 she bare a son, and he **c** his name Solomon: 7121
12:25 he **c** his name Jedidiah, because of 7121
12:28 I take the city, and it be **c** after my name. 7121
13:17 he **c** his servant that ministered unto him, 7121
14:33 when he had **c** for Absalom, he came to 7121
15: 2 Absalom **c** unto him, and said, Of what city 7121
15:11 hundred men out of Jerusalem, *that were* **c**; 7121
18:18 he **c** the pillar after his own name: and it is 7121
18:18 and it is **c** unto this day, Absalom's place. 7121
18:26 the watchman **c** unto the porter, and said, 7121
18:28 Ahimaaz **c**, and said unto the king, All is 7121
21: 2 the king **c** the Gibeonites, and said unto 7121
22: 7 In my distress I **c upon** the LORD, and 7121
1Ki 1: 9 **c** all his brethren the king's sons, and all 7121
1:10 and Solomon his brother, he **c** not. 7121
1:19 hath **c** all the sons of the king, and Abiathar 7121
1:19 but Solomon thy servant hath he not **c**. 7121
1:25 hath **c** all the king's sons, and the captains 7121
1:26 and thy servant Solomon, hath he not **c**. 7121
2:36 the king sent and **c** for Shimei, and 7121
2:42 the king sent and **c** for Shimei, and 7121
7:21 right pillar, and **c** the name thereof Jachin: 7121
7:21 the left pillar, and **c** the name thereof Boaz. 7121
8:43 which I have builded, is **c** by thy name. 7121
9:13 he **c** them the land of Cabul unto this day. 7121
12: 3 That they sent and **c** him. And Jeroboam 7121
12:20 they sent and **c** him unto the congregation, 7121
16:24 and **c** the name of the city which he built, 7121
17:10 he **c** to her, and said, Fetch me, I pray thee, 7121
17:11 as she was going to fetch *it,* he **c** to her, 7121
18: 3 Ahab **c** Obadiah, which *was* the governor 7121
18:26 **c** on the name of Baal from morning even 7121
20: 7 the king of Israel **c** all the elders of 7121
22: 9 the king of Israel **c** an officer, and said, 7121
2Ki 3:10 that the LORD hath **c** these three kings 7121
3:13 for the LORD hath **c** these three kings 7121
4:12 when he had **c** her, she stood before him. 7121
4:15 when he had **c** her, she stood in the door. 7121
4:22 she **c** unto her husband, and said, Send me, 7121
4:36 he **c** Gehazi, and said, Call this 7121
4:36 So he **c** her. And when she was come in 7121
6:11 he **c** his servants, and said unto them, Will 7121
7:10 they came and **c** unto the porter of the city: 7121
7:11 he **c** the porters; and they told *it to* 7121
8: 1 for the LORD hath **c** for a famine; and 7121
9: 1 Elisha the prophet **c** one of the children of 7121
12: 7 Then king Jehoash **c** for Jehoiada the priest, 7121
14: 7 and **c** the name of it Joktheel unto this day. 7121
18: 4 burn incense to it: and he **c** it Nehushtan. 7121
18:18 when they had **c** to the king, there came out 7121
1Ch 4: 9 his mother **c** his name Jabez, saying, 7121
4:10 Jabez **c** on the God of Israel, saying, 7121
6:65 these cities, which are **c** by *their* names. 7121
7:16 bare a son, and she **c** his name Peresh; 7121
7:23 he **c** his name Beriah, because it went evil 7121
11: 7 therefore they **c** it the city of David. 7121
13: 6 the cherubims, whose name is **c** *on it.* 7121
13:11 wherefore that place is **c** Perez-uzza to this 7121
14:11 they **c** the name of that place Baal-perazim. 7121
15:11 David **c** for Zadok and Abiathar the priests, 7121
21:26 peace offerings, and **c** upon the LORD; 7121
22: 6 he **c** for Solomon his son, and charged him 7121
2Ch 3:17 **c** the name of *that on* the right hand Jachin, 7121
6:33 house which I have built is **c** by thy name. 7121
7:14 If my people, which are **c** by my name, 7121
10: 3 they sent and **c** him. So Jeroboam and 7121
18: 8 the king of Israel **c** for one *of his* officers, 7121
20:26 therefore the name of the same place was **c**, 7121
24: 6 the king **c** for Jehoiada the chief, and 7121
Ezr 2:61 the Gileadite, and was **c** after their name: 7121
Ne 5:12 I **c** the priests, and took an oath of them, 7121
7:63 *to* wife, and was **c** after their name. 7121
Est 2:14 in her, and *that* she were **c** by name. 7121
3:12 were the king's scribes **c** on the thirteenth 7121
4: 5 **c** Esther for Hatach, *one* of the king's 7121
4:11 who is not **c**, *there is* one law of his to put 7121
4:11 I have not been **c** to come in unto the king 7121
5:10 he sent and **c for** his friends, and Zeresh his 935
8: 9 were the king's scribes **c** at that time in 7121
9:26 Wherefore they **c** these days Purim after 7121
Job 1: 4 sent and **c** for their three sisters to eat and 7121
9:16 If I had **c**, and he had answered me; 7121
19:16 I **c** my servant, and he gave *me* no answer; 7121
42:14 And he **c** the name of the first, Jemima; and 7121
Ps 17: 6 I have **c upon** thee, for thou wilt hear me, 7121
18: 6 In my distress I **c upon** the LORD, and 7121
31:17 O LORD; for I have **c upon** thee: 7121
50: 1 **c** the earth from the rising of the sun unto 7121
53: 4 they eat bread: they have not **c upon** God. 7121
79: 6 upon the kingdoms that have not **c** upon thy 7121
88: 9 LORD, I have **c** daily **upon** thee, I have 7121
99: 6 they **c** upon the LORD, and he answered 7121
105:16 Moreover, he **c** *for* a famine upon the land: 7121
116: 4 **c** I upon the name of the LORD; 7121
118: 5 I **c upon** the LORD in distress: 7121
Pr 1:24 Because I have **c**, and ye refused; I have 7121
16:21 The wise in heart shall be **c** prudent: and 7121
24: 8 He that deviseth to do evil shall be **c** a 7121
SS 5: 6 I **c** him, but he gave me no answer. 7121
Isa 1:26 afterward thou shalt be **c**, The city of 7121
4: 1 only let us be **c** by thy name, to take away 7121
4: 3 that remaineth in Jerusalem, shall be **c** holy, 559
9: 6 his name shall be **c** Wonderful, Counseller, 7121
13: 3 I have also **c** my mighty ones for mine 7121
19:18 one shall be **c**, The city of destruction. 559
31: 4 when a multitude of shepherds is **c forth** 7121
32: 5 The vile person shall be no more **c** liberal, 7121
35: 8 and it shall be **c** The way of holiness; 7121
41: 2 **c** him to his foot, gave the nations before 7121
41: 9 **c** thee from the chief men thereof, and 7121
42: 6 I the LORD have **c** thee in righteousness, 7121
43: 1 redeemed thee, I have **c** *thee* by thy name; 7121
43: 7 *Even* every one that is **c** by my name: for I 7121
43:22 thou hast not **c upon** me, O Jacob; but 7121
45: 4 mine elect, I have even **c** thee by thy name: 7121
47: 1 for thou shalt no more be **c** tender and 7121
47: 5 for thou shalt no more be **c**, The lady of 7121
48: 1 which are **c** by the name of Israel, and 7121
48: 8 wast **c** a transgressor from the womb. 7121
48:12 Hearken unto me, O Jacob, and Israel my **c**; 7121
48:15 I, *even* I, have spoken; yea, I have **c** him: 7121
49: 1 The LORD hath **c** me from the womb; 7121
50: 2 when I **c**, *was there* none to answer? Is my 7121
51: 2 for I **c** him alone, and blessed him, and 7121
54: 5 The God of the whole earth shall he be **c**. 7121
54: 6 For the LORD hath **c** thee as a woman 7121
56: 7 for mine house shall be **c** a house of prayer 7121
58:12 thou shalt be **c**, The repairer of the breach, 7121
61: 3 that they might be **c** trees of righteousness, 7121
62: 2 thou shalt be **c** by a new name, which 7121
62: 4 thou shalt be **c** Hephzi-bah, and thy land 7121
62:12 thou shalt be **c**, Sought out, A city not 7121
63:19 over them; they were not **c** by thy name. 7121
65: 1 unto a nation *that* was not **c** by my name. 7121
65:12 because when I **c**, ye did not answer; 7121
66: 4 because when I **c**, none did answer; when I 7121

C

Jer 7:10 this house, which is **c** by my name, and say, 7121
7:11 Is this house, which is **c** by my name, 7121
7:13 heard not; and I **c** you, but ye answered not; 7121
7:14 which is **c** by my name, wherein ye trust, 7121
7:30 in the house which is **c** by my name, 7121
7:32 that it shall no more be **c** Tophet, 559
11:16 The LORD **c** thy name, A green olive 7121
12: 6 yea, they have **c** a multitude after thee: 7121
14: 9 the midst of us, and we are **c** by thy name; 7121
15:16 for I am **c** by thy name, O LORD God of 7121
19: 6 that this place shall no more be **c** Tophet, 7121
20: 3 The LORD hath not **c** thy name Pashur, 7121
23: 6 this *is* his name whereby he shall be **c**, 7121
25:29 I begin to bring evil on the city which is **c** 7121
30:17 because they **c** thee an Outcast, 7121
32:34 which is **c** by my name, to defile it. 7121
33:16 this *is the name* wherewith she shall be **c**, 7121
34:15 me in the house which is **c** by my name. 7121
35:17 I have **c** unto them, but they have not 7121
36: 4 Jeremiah **c** Baruch the son of Neriah: and 7121
42: 8 **c** he Johanan the son of Kareah, and all 7121
La 1:15 he hath **c** an assembly against me to crush 7121
1:19 I **c** for my lovers, *but* they deceived me: 7121
1:21 *it:* thou wilt bring the day *that* thou hast **c**, 7121
2:22 Thou hast **c** as *in* a solemn day my terrors 7121
3:55 I **c upon** thy name, O LORD, out of 7121
3:57 Thou drewest near in the day *that* I **c upon** 7121
Eze 9: 3 he **c** to the man clothed *with* linen, 7121
20:29 the name thereof is **c** Bamah unto this day. 7121
Da 5:12 now let Daniel be **c**, and he will shew 7123
8:16 which **c**, and said, Gabriel, make this *man* 7121
9:18 and the city which is **c** by thy name: 7121
9:19 thy city and thy people are **c** by thy name. 7121
10: 1 whose name was **c** Belteshazzar; 7121
Hos 11: 1 I loved him, and **c** my son out of Egypt. 7121
11: 2 *As* they **c** them, so they went from them: 7121
11: 7 though they **c** them to the most High, 7121
Am 7: 4 the Lord GOD **c** to contend by fire, and 7121
9:12 of all the heathen, which are **c** by my name, 7121
Hag 1:11 I **c** *for* a drought upon the land, and 7121
Zec 8: 3 Jerusalem shall be **c** a city of truth; and 7121
11: 7 the one I **c** Beauty, and the other I called 7121
11: 7 I called Beauty, and the other I **c** Bands; 7121
Mt 1:16 of whom was born Jesus, who is **c** Christ. *3004*
1:25 firstborn son: and *he* **c** his name JESUS. *2564*
2: 7 when he had privily **c** the wise men, *2564*
2:15 saying, Out of Egypt have I **c** my son. *2564*
2:23 he came and dwelt in a city **c** Nazareth: *3004*
2:23 by the prophets, He shall be **c** a Nazarene. *2564*
4:18 Simon **c** Peter, and Andrew his brother, *3004*
4:21 mending their nets; and he **c** them. *2564*
5: 9 for they shall be **c** the children of God. *2564*
5:19 he shall be **c** the least in the kingdom of *2564*
5:19 teach *them,* the same shall be **c** great in *2564*
10: 1 And when he had **c unto** *him* his twelve *4341*
10: 2 who is **c** Peter, and Andrew his brother; *3004*
10:25 If they have **c** the master of the house *2564*
13:55 is not his mother **c** Mary? and his brethren, *3004*
15:10 And he **c** the multitude, and said unto them, *4341*
15:32 Then Jesus **c** his disciples **unto** *him,* and *4341*
18: 2 And Jesus **c** a little child **unto** *him,* and *4341*
18:32 Then his lord, after that he had **c** him, *4341*
20:16 the first last: for many be **c**, but few chosen. *2822*
20:25 But Jesus **c** them **unto** *him,* and said, *4341*
20:32 And Jesus stood still, and **c** them, and said, *5455*
21:13 My house shall be **c** the house of prayer; *2564*
22:14 For many are **c**, but few *are* chosen. *2822*
23: 7 and to be **c** of men, Rabbi, Rabbi. *2564*
23: 8 But be not ye **c** Rabbi: for one is your *2564*
23:10 Neither be ye **c** masters: for one is your *2564*
25:14 *who* **c** his own servants, and delivered unto *2564*
26: 3 of the high priest, who was **c** Caiaphas, *3004*
26:14 Then one of the twelve, **c** Judas Iscariot, *3004*
26:36 with them unto a place **c** Gethsemane, *3004*
27: 8 Wherefore that field was **c**, The field of *2564*
27:16 then a notable prisoner, **c** Barabbas. *3004*
27:17 Barabbas, or Jesus which is **c** Christ? *3004*
27:22 shall I do then with Jesus which is **c** Christ? *3004*
27:33 And when they were come unto a place **c** *3004*
Mk 1:20 And straightway he **c** them: and they left *2564*
3:23 And he **c** them **unto** *him,* and said unto *4341*
7:14 And when he had **c** all the people **unto** *4341*
8: 1 Jesus **c** his disciples **unto** *him,* and *4341*
8:34 And when he had **c** the people **unto** *him* *4341*
9:35 and **c** the twelve, and saith unto them, *5455*
10:42 But Jesus **c** them **to** *him,* and saith unto *4341*
10:49 stood still, and commanded him to be **c**. *5455*
11:17 My house shall be **c** of all nations the house *2564*
12:43 And he **c unto** *him* his disciples, and *4341*
14:72 And Peter **c to mind** the word that Jesus said *363*
15:16 led him away into the hall, **c** Pretorium; *3739*
Lk 1:32 and shall be **c** the Son of the Highest: *2564*
1:35 be born of thee shall be **c** the Son of God. *2564*
1:36 the sixth month with her, who was **c** barren. *2564*
1:59 and they **c** him Zacharias, after the name of *2564*
1:60 and said, Not *so;* but he shall be **c** John. *2564*
1:61 There is none of thy kindred that is **c** by *2564*
1:62 to his father, how he would have him **c**. *2564*
1:76 child, shalt be **c** the prophet of the Highest: *2564*
2: 4 the city of David, which is **c** Bethlehem; *2564*
2:21 his name was **c** JESUS, which was *so* *2564*
2:23 the womb shall be **c** holy to the Lord;) *2564*
6:13 it was day, he **c unto** *him* his disciples: *4377*
6:15 the *son* of Alpheus, and Simon **c** Zelotes, *2564*
7:11 *day* after, *that* he went into a city **c** Nain; *2564*
8: 2 and infirmities, Mary **c** Magdalene, *2564*
8:54 her by the hand, and **c**, saying, Maid, arise. *5455*
9: 1 Then he **c** his twelve disciples **together**, *4779*
9:10 place belonging to the city **c** Bethsaida. *2564*
10:39 And she had a sister **c** Mary, which also sat *2564*
13:12 he **c** *her* **to** *him,* and said unto her, Woman, *4377*
15:19 And am no more worthy to be **c** thy son: *2564*
15:21 and am no more worthy to be **c** thy son. *2564*
15:26 And he **c** one of the servants, and *4341*
16: 2 And he **c** him, and said unto him, How *is* it *5455*
16: 5 So he **c** every one of his lord's debtors **unto** *4341*
18:16 But Jesus **c** them **unto** *him,* and said, *4341*
19:13 And he **c** his ten servants, and *2564*
19:15 he commanded these servants to be **c** unto *5455*
19:29 at the mount **c** *the mount* of Olives, *2564*
21:37 abode in the mount that is **c** *the mount* of *2564*
22: 1 bread drew nigh, which is **c** the Passover. *3004*
22:25 they that exercise authority upon them are **c** *2564*
22:47 and he that was **c** Judas, one of the twelve, *3004*
23:13 when he had **c together** the chief priests *4779*
23:33 which is **c** Calvary, there they crucified *2564*
24:13 went *that* same day to a village **c** Emmaus, *3686*
Jn 1:42 thou shalt be **c** Cephas, which is by *2564*
1:48 said unto him, Before that Philip **c** thee, *5455*
2: 2 And both Jesus was **c**, and his disciples, *2564*
2: 9 the governor of the feast **c** the bridegroom, *5455*
4: 5 he to a city of Samaria, which is **c** Sychar, *3004*
4:25 that Messias cometh, which is **c** Christ: *3004*
5: 2 which is **c** in the Hebrew tongue Bethesda, *1951*
9:11 A man *that is* **c** Jesus made clay, and *3004*
9:18 until they **c** the parents of him that had *5455*
9:24 Then again **c** they the man that was blind, *5455*
10:35 If he **c** them gods, unto whom the word of *3004*
11:16 Then said Thomas, which is **c** Didymus, *3004*
11:28 and **c** Mary her sister secretly, saying, *5455*
11:54 into a city **c** Ephraim, and there continued *3004*
12:17 that was with him when he **c** Lazarus out of *5455*
15:15 but I have **c** you friends; for all *things* that I *3004*
18:33 and **c** Jesus, and said unto him, Art thou *5455*
19:13 seat in a place *that is* **c** the Pavement, *3004*
19:17 forth into a place **c** *the place* of a skull, *3004*
19:17 a skull, which is **c** in the Hebrew Golgotha: *3004*
20:24 But Thomas, one of the twelve, **c** Didymus, *3004*
21: 2 and Thomas **c** Didymus, and Nathanael of *3004*
Ac 1:12 unto Jerusalem from the mount **c** Olivet, *2564*
1:19 insomuch as that field is **c** in their proper *2564*
1:23 they appointed two, Joseph **c** Barsabas, *2564*
3: 2 the gate of the temple which is **c** Beautiful, *3004*
3:11 unto them in the porch that is **c** Solomon's, *2564*
4:18 And they **c** them, and commanded them not *2564*
5:21 and **c** the council **together**, and all *4779*
5:40 and when they had **c** the apostles, and *4341*
6: 2 **c** the multitude of the disciples **unto** *them,* *4341*
6: 9 which is **c** *the synagogue* of the Libertines, *3004*
7:14 and **c** his father Jacob to *him,* and all his *3333*
8: 9 But there was a certain man, **c** Simon, *3686*
9:11 and go into the street which is **c** Straight, *2564*
9:11 inquire in the house of Judas for *one* **c** Saul, *3686*
9:21 not this he that destroyed them which **c on** *1941*
9:36 which by interpretation is **c** Dorcas: *3004*
9:41 and when he had **c** the saints and widows, *5455*
10: 1 There was a certain man in Cesarea **c** *3686*
10: 1 a centurion of the band **c** the Italian *band,* *2564*

Ac 10: 7 he **c** two of his household servants, and *5455*
10:18 And **c**, and asked whether Simon, *5455*
10:23 Then **c** he them **in**, and lodged *them.* And *1528*
10:24 and had **c together** his kinsmen and near *4779*
11:26 the disciples were **c** Christians first in *5537*
13: 1 and Simeon that was **c** Niger, and Lucius of *2564*
13: 2 Saul for the work whereunto I have **c** them. *4341*
13: 7 who **c for** Barnabas and Saul, and *4341*
13: 9 Then Saul, (who also *is* **c** Paul,) filled with NIG
14:12 And they **c** Barnabas, Jupiter; and Paul, *2564*
15:17 upon whom my name is **c**, saith the Lord, *1941*
16:10 assuredly gathering that the Lord had **c** us *4341*
16:29 Then he **c for** a light, and sprang in, and *154*
19:25 Whom he **c together** with the workmen of *4867*
19:40 For we are in danger to be **c in question** for *1458*
20: 1 Paul **c unto** *him* the disciples, and *4341*
20:17 to Ephesus, and **c** the elders of the church. *3333*
23: 6 resurrection of the dead I am **c in question**. *2919*
23:17 Then Paul **c** one of the centurions **unto** *4341*
23:18 Paul the prisoner **c** me **unto** *him,* and *4341*
23:23 And he **c unto** *him* two centurions, saying, *4341*
24: 2 And when he was **c** *forth,* Tertullus began *2564*
24:21 dead I am **c in question** by you this day. *2919*
27: 8 came unto a place *which is* **c** The fair *2564*
27:14 it a tempestuous wind, **c** Euroclydon. *2564*
27:16 under a certain island *which is* **c** Clauda, *2564*
28: 1 then they knew that the island was **c** Melita. *2564*
28:17 days Paul **c** the chief of the Jews **together**: *4779*
28:20 For this cause therefore have I **c for** you, *3870*
Ro 1: 1 a servant of Jesus Christ, **c** *to be* an apostle, *2822*
1: 6 Among whom are ye also *the* **c** of Jesus *2822*
1: 7 be in Rome, beloved of God, **c** *to be* saints: *2822*
2:17 thou art **c** a Jew, and restest in the law, and *2028*
7: 3 to another man, she shall be **c** an adulteress: *5537*
8:28 to them who are *the* **c** according to *his* *2822*
8:30 whom he did predestinate, them he also **c**: *2564*
8:30 and whom he **c**, them he also justified: and *2564*
9: 7 but, In Isaac shall thy seed be **c**. *2564*
9:24 Even us, whom he hath **c**, not of the Jews *2564*
9:26 there shall they be **c** the children of *2564*
1Co 1: 1 **c** *to be* an apostle of Jesus Christ through *2822*
1: 2 are sanctified in Christ Jesus, **c** *to be* saints, *2822*
1: 9 by whom ye were **c** unto the fellowship of *2564*
1:24 But unto them which are **c**, both Jews and *2822*
1:26 not many mighty, not many noble, *are* **c**: NIG
5:11 if any *man that is* **c** a brother be a *3687*
7:15 in such *cases:* but God hath **c** us to peace. *2564*
7:17 as the Lord hath **c** every one, so let him *2564*
7:18 Is any *man* **c** being circumcised? let him *2564*
7:18 Is any **c** in uncircumcision? let him not be *2564*
7:20 abide in the same calling wherein he was **c**. *2564*
7:21 Art thou **c** *being* a servant? care not for it: *2564*
7:22 For he that is **c** in the Lord, *being* a servant, *2564*
7:22 likewise also he that is **c**, *being* free, *2564*
7:24 Brethren, let every man, wherein he is **c**, *2564*
8: 5 For though there be that are **c** gods, *3004*
15: 9 that am not meet to be **c** an apostle, because *2564*
Gal 1: 6 soon removed from him that **c** you into *2564*
1:15 my mother's womb, and **c** *me* by his grace, *2564*
5:13 For, brethren, ye have been **c** unto liberty; *2564*
Eph 2:11 who are **c** Uncircumcision by that which is *3004*
2:11 **c** the Circumcision in the flesh made by *3004*
4: 1 worthy of the vocation wherewith ye are **c**, *2564*
4: 4 even as ye are **c** in one hope of your *2564*
Col 3:15 to the which also ye are **c** in one body; *2564*
4:11 And Jesus, which is **c** Justus, who are of *3004*
1Th 2:12 who hath **c** you unto his kingdom and *2564*
4: 7 For God hath not **c** us unto uncleanness, but *2564*
2Th 2: 4 and exalteth himself above all that is **c** God, *3004*
2:14 Whereunto he **c** you by our gospel, to *2564*
1Ti 6:12 whereunto thou art also **c**, and *2564*
6:20 and oppositions of science **falsely** so **c**: *5581*
2Ti 1: 9 hath saved us, and **c** *us* with a holy calling, *2564*
Heb 3:13 one another daily, while it is **c** To day; *2564*
5: 4 but he that is **c** of God, as *was* Aaron. *2564*
5:10 **C** of God a high priest after the order of *4316*
7:11 and not be **c** after the order of Aaron? *3004*
9: 2 the shewbread; which is **c** the sanctuary. *3004*
9: 3 the tabernacle which is **c** the holiest of all; *3004*
9:15 they which are **c** might receive the promise *2564*
11: 8 when he was **c** to go out into a place which *2564*
11:16 wherefore God is not ashamed to be **c** their *1941*
11:18 was said, That in Isaac shall thy seed be **c**: *2564*
11:24 refused to be **c** the son of Pharaoh's *3004*
Jas 2: 7 *that* worthy name by the which ye are **c**? *1941*
2:23 and he was **c** the Friend of God. *2564*
1Pe 1:15 But as he which hath **c** you is holy, so be ye *2564*
2: 9 **c** you out of darkness into his marvellous *2564*
2:21 For *even* hereunto were ye **c**: because *2564*
3: 9 knowing that ye are thereunto **c**, that ye *2564*
5:10 who hath **c** us into his eternal glory by *2564*
2Pe 1: 3 through the knowledge of him that hath **c** *2564*
1Jn 3: 1 that we should be **c** the sons of God: *2564*
Jude 1: 1 and preserved *in* Jesus Christ, *and* **c**: *2822*
Rev 1: 9 was in the isle that is **c** Patmos, for *2564*
8:11 And the name of the star is **c** Wormwood: *3004*
11: 8 which spiritually is **c** Sodom and Egypt, *2564*
12: 9 **c** the devil, and Satan, which deceiveth *2564*
16:16 place **c** in the Hebrew tongue Armageddon. *2564*
17:14 and they that are with him *are* **c**, and *2822*
19: 9 Blessed *are* they which are **c** unto *2564*
19:11 and he that sat upon him *was* **c** Faithful and *2564*
19:13 and his name is **c** The Word of God. *2564*

CALLEDST (4) [CALL]

Jdg 8: 1 hast thou served us thus, that *thou* **c** us not, 7121
1Sa 3: 5 and said, Here *am* I; for thou **c** me. 7121
Ps 81: 7 Thou **c** in trouble, and I delivered thee; 7121
Eze 23:21 Thus thou **c to remembrance** the lewdness 6485

CALLEST (3) [CALL]

Mt 19:17 he said unto him, Why **c** thou me good? *3004*
Mk 10:18 Jesus said unto him, Why **c** thou me good? *3004*
Lk 18:19 Jesus said unto him, Why **c** thou me good? *3004*

CALLETH (31) [CALL]

1Ki 8:43 do according to all that the stranger **c** to 7121
2Ch 6:33 do according to all that the stranger **c** to 7121
Job 12: 4 who **c** upon God, and he answereth him: 7121
Ps 42: 7 Deep **c** unto deep at the noise of thy 7121
147: 4 of the stars; he **c** them all *by their* names. 7121
Pr 18: 6 and his mouth **c** for strokes. 7121
Isa 21:11 He **c** to me out of Seir, Watchman, what of 7121
40:26 he **c** them all by names by the greatness of 7121
59: 4 None **c** for justice, nor any pleadeth for 7121
64: 7 *there is* none that **c** upon thy name, 7121
Hos 7: 7 *there is* none among them that **c** unto me. 7121
Am 5: 8 that **c** for the waters of the sea, and 7121
9: 6 he that **c** for the waters of the sea, and 7121
Mt 27:47 they heard *that,* said, This *man* **c** for Elias. *5455*
Mk 3:13 and **c unto** *him* whom he would: *4341*
6: 7 And he **c unto** *him* the twelve, and *4341*
10:49 Be of good comfort, rise; he **c** thee. *5455*
12:37 David therefore himself **c** him Lord; and *3004*
15:35 when they heard *it,* said, Behold, he **c** Elias. *5455*
Lk 15: 6 he **c together** *his* friends and neighbours, *4779*
15: 9 **c** *her* friends and *her* neighbours **together**, *4779*
20:37 when he **c** the Lord the God of Abraham, *3004*
20:44 David therefore **c** him Lord, how is he then *2564*
Jn 10: 3 and he **c** his own sheep by name, and *2564*
11:28 saying, The Master is come, and **c for** thee. *5455*
Ro 4:17 **c** those *things* which be not as though they *2564*
9:11 not of works, but of him that **c**;) *2564*
1Co 12: 3 that no *man* speaking by the Spirit of God **c** *3004*
Gal 5: 8 *This* persuasion *cometh* not of him that **c** *2564*
1Th 5:24 Faithful *is* he that **c** you, who also will do *2564*
Rev 2:20 which **c** herself a prophetess, to teach and *3004*

CALLING (24) [CALL]

Nu 10: 2 that thou mayest use them for the **c** of 4744
Isa 1:13 and sabbaths, the **c** of assemblies, 7121
41: 4 done *it,* **c** the generations from 7121
46:11 **C** a ravenous bird from the east, the man 7121
Eze 23:19 in **c to remembrance** the days of her 2142
Mt 11:16 in the markets, and **c unto** their fellows, *4377*
Mk 3:31 and, standing without, sent unto him, **c** him. *5455*
11:21 And Peter **c to remembrance** saith unto *363*
15:44 and **c unto** *him* the centurion, he asked him *4341*
Lk 7:19 And John **c unto** *him* two of his disciples *4341*
7:32 and **c** one **to another**, and saying, We have *4377*
Ac 7:59 **c upon** *God,* and saying, Lord Jesus, *1941*
22:16 away thy sins, **c on** the name of the Lord. *1941*
Ro 11:29 and **c** of God *are* without repentance. *2821*
1Co 1:26 For ye see your **c**, brethren, how that not *2821*
7:20 Let every man abide in the same **c** wherein *2821*
Eph 1:18 that ye may know what is the hope of his **c**, *2821*
4: 4 even as ye are called in one hope of your **c**; *2821*
Php 3:14 prize of the high **c** of God in Christ Jesus. *2821*

2Th 1:11 our God would count you worthy of *this* **c**, *2821*
2Ti 1: 9 hath saved us, and called *us* with a holy **c**, *2821*
Heb 3: 1 holy brethren, partakers of the heavenly **c**, *2821*
1Pe 3: 6 *Even* as Sara obeyed Abraham, **c** him lord: *2564*
2Pe 1:10 give diligence to make your **c** and *2821*

CALLOUS See FAT; FATNESS

CALLOUSED See GROSS

CALM (6)
Ps 107:29 He maketh the storm a **c**, so that the waves 1827
Jnh 1:11 do unto thee, that the sea may be **c** unto us? 8367
1:12 into the sea; so shall the sea be **c** unto you: 8367
Mt 8:26 and the sea; and there was a great **c**. *1055*
Mk 4:39 the wind ceased, and there was a great **c**. *1055*
Lk 8:24 and they ceased, and there was a **c**. *1055*

CALNEH (2)
Ge 10:10 Erech, and Accad, and **C**, in the land of 3641
Am 6: 2 Pass ye *unto* **C**, and see; and from thence 3641

CALNO (1)
Isa 10: 9 *Is* not **C** as Carchemish? *is* not Hamath as 3641

CALVARY (1) [GOLGOTHA]
Lk 23:33 which is called **C**, there they crucified him, *2898*

CALVE (2) [CALF]
Job 39: 1 *or* canst thou mark when the hinds do **c**? 2342
Ps 29: 9 voice of the LORD **maketh** the hinds **to c**, 2342

CALVED (1) [CALF]
Jer 14: 5 the hind also **c** in the field, and forsook *it,* 3205

CALVES (18) [CALF]
1Sa 6: 7 the cart, and bring their **c** home from them: 1121
6:10 to the cart, and shut up their **c** at home: 1121
14:32 and **c**, and slew *them* on the ground: 1121+1241
1Ki 12:28 made two **c** of gold, and said unto them, 5695
12:32 sacrificing unto the **c** that he had made: 5695
2Ki 10:29 *to wit,* the golden **c** that *were in* Beth-el, 5695
17:16 *even* two **c**, and made a grove, and 5695
2Ch 11:15 and for the **c** which he had made. 5695
13: 8 and *there are* with you golden **c**, 5695
Ps 68:30 of the bulls, with the **c** of the people, 5695
Hos 10: 5 shall fear because of the **c** of Beth-aven: 5697
13: 2 Let the men that sacrifice kiss the **c**. 5695
14: 2 so will we render the **c** of our lips. 6499
Am 6: 4 and the **c** out of the midst of the stall; 5695
Mic 6: 6 with burnt offerings, with **c** of a year old? 5695
Mal 4: 2 shall go forth, and grow up as **c** of the stall. 5695
Heb 9:12 Neither by the blood of goats and **c**, *3448*
9:19 he took the blood of **c** and of goats, *3448*

CALVETH (1) [CALF]
Job 21:10 their cow **c**, and casteth not her calf. 6403

CAME (2096) [COME] See Index

CAMEL (9) [CAMEL'S, CAMELS, CAMELS']
Ge 24:64 when she saw Isaac, she lighted off the **c**. 1581
Lev 11: 4 *as* the **c**, because he cheweth the cud, but 1581
Dt 14: 7 *as* the **c**, and the hare, and the coney: 1581
1Sa 15: 3 and suckling, ox and sheep, **c** and ass. 1581
Zec 14:15 of the **c**, and of the ass, and of all the beasts 1581
Mt 19:24 It is easier for a **c** to go through the eye of a *2574*
23:24 which strain out a gnat, and swallow a **c**. *2574*
Mk 10:25 It is easier for a **c** to go through the eye of a *2574*
Lk 18:25 For it is easier for a **c** to go through a *2574*

CAMEL'S (3) [CAMEL]
Ge 31:34 put them in the **c** furniture, and sat upon 1581
Mt 3: 4 And the same John had his raiment of **c** *2574*
Mk 1: 6 And John was clothed with **c** hair, and *2574*

CAMELS (47) [CAMEL]
Ge 12:16 and maidservants, and she asses, and **c**. 1581
24:10 the servant took ten **c** of the camels of his 1581
24:10 the servant took ten camels of the **c** of his 1581
24:11 he made *his* **c** to kneel down without 1581
24:14 Drink, and I will give thy **c** drink also: 1581
24:19 she said, I will draw *water* for thy **c** also, 1581
24:20 well to draw *water,* and drew for all his **c**. 1581
24:22 it came to pass, as the **c** had done drinking, 1581
24:30 and behold, he stood by the **c** at the well. 1581
24:31 prepared the house, and room for the **c**. 1581
24:32 he ungirded *his* **c**, and gave straw and 1581
24:32 and gave straw and provender for the **c**, and 1581
24:35 and maidservants, and **c**, and asses. 1581
24:44 drink thou, and I will also draw for thy **c**: 1581
24:46 said, Drink, and I will give thy **c** drink also: 1581
24:46 so I drank, and she made the **c** drink also. 1581
24:61 they rode upon the **c**, and followed 1581
24:63 and saw, and behold, the **c** *were* coming. 1581
30:43 and menservants, and **c**, and asses. 1581
31:17 and set his sons and his wives upon **c**; 1581
32: 7 the flocks, and herds, and the **c**, into two 1581
32:15 Thirty milch **c** with their colts, forty kine, 1581
37:25 from Gilead with their **c** bearing spicery 1581
Ex 9: 3 upon the **c**, upon the oxen, and upon 1581
Jdg 6: 5 both they and their **c** were without number: 1581
7:12 their **c** *were* without number, as the sand by 1581
1Sa 27: 9 the **c**, and the apparel, and returned, and 1581
30:17 young men, which rode upon **c**, and fled. 1581
1Ki 10: 2 *with* **c** that bare spices, and very much 1581
1Ch 5:21 *of* their **c** fifty thousand, and *of* sheep two 1581
12:40 on **c**, and on mules, and on oxen, *and* meat, 1581
27:30 Over the **c** also *was* Obil the Ishmaelite: 1581
2Ch 9: 1 **c** that bare spices, and gold in abundance, 1581
14:15 and carried away sheep and **c** in abundance, 1581
Ezr 2:67 Their **c**, four hundred thirty and five; 1581
Ne 7:69 *Their* **c**, four hundred thirty and five: 1581
Est 8:10 riders on mules, **c**, *and* young dromedaries: 327
8:14 posts that rode upon mules *and* **c** went out, 327
Job 1: 3 three thousand **c**, and five hundred yoke of 1581
1:17 fell upon the **c**, and have carried them 1581
42:12 six thousand **c**, and a thousand yoke of 1581
Isa 21: 7 a chariot of asses, *and* a chariot of **c**; 1581
30: 6 their treasures upon the bunches of **c**, to a 1581
60: 6 The multitude of **c** shall cover thee, 1581
Jer 49:29 and all their vessels, and their **c**; 1581
49:32 their **c** shall be a booty, and the multitude 1581
Eze 25: 5 I will make Rabbah a stable for **c**, and 1581

CAMELS' (3) [CAMEL]
Jdg 8:21 the ornaments that *were* on their **c** necks. 1581
8:26 beside the chains that *were* about their **c** 1581
2Ki 8: 9 forty **c** burden, and came and stood before 1581

CAMEST (28) [COME] See Index

CAMON (1)
Jdg 10: 5 And Jair died, and was buried in **C**. 7056

CAMP (136) [CAMPED, CAMPS, ENCAMP, ENCAMPED, ENCAMPETH, ENCAMPING]
Ex 14:19 which went before the **c** of Israel, removed 4264
14:20 it came between the **c** of the Egyptians and 4264
14:20 camp of the Egyptians and the **c** of Israel; 4264
16:13 even the quails came up, and covered the **c**: 4264
19:16 that all the people that *was* in the **c** 4264
19:17 Moses brought forth the people out of the **c** 4264
29:14 shalt thou burn with fire without the **c**: 4264
32:17 *There is* a noise of war in the **c**. 4264
32:19 as soon as he came nigh unto the **c**, that he 4264
32:26 Moses stood in the gate of the **c**, and said, 4264
32:27 and out from gate to gate throughout the **c**, 4264
33: 7 pitched it without the **c**, afar off from 4264
33: 7 afar off from the **c**, and called it 4264
33: 7 the Congregation, which *was* without the **c**. 4264
33:11 he turned again into the **c**: but his servant 4264
36: 6 caused it to be proclaimed throughout the **c**, 4264
Lev 4:12 carry forth without the **c** unto a clean place, 4264
4:21 shall carry forth the bullock without the **c**, 4264
6:11 carry forth the ashes without the **c** unto a 4264
8:17 his dung, he burnt with fire without the **c**; 4264
9:11 the hide he burnt with fire without the **c**. 4264
10: 4 from before the sanctuary out of the **c**. 4264
10: 5 and carried them in their coats out of the **c**; 4264
13:46 without the **c** *shall* his habitation *be.* 4264
14: 3 the priest shall go forth out of the **c**; and 4264
14: 8 after *that* he shall come into the **c**, and 4264
16:26 in water, and afterward come into the **c**. 4264
16:27 *place,* shall *one* carry forth without the **c**; 4264
16:28 and afterward he shall come into the **c**. 4264
17: 3 in the **c**, or that killeth *it* out of the camp, 4264
17: 3 in the camp, or that killeth *it* out of the **c**, 4264
24:10 and a man of Israel strove together in the **c**; 4264
24:14 forth him that hath cursed without the **c**; 4264

Lev 24:23 bring forth him that had cursed out of the **c**, 4264
Nu 1:52 every man by his own **c**, and every man by 4264
2: 3 **c** of Judah pitch throughout their armies: 4264
2: 9 All that were numbered in the **c** of Judah 4264
2:10 the **c** of Reuben according to their armies: 4264
2:16 All that were numbered in the **c** of Reuben 4264
2:17 **c** of the Levites in the midst of the camp: 4264
2:17 camp of the Levites in the midst of the **c**: 4264
2:18 the **c** of Ephraim according to their armies: 4264
2:24 All that were numbered of the **c** of Ephraim 4264
2:25 The standard of the **c** of Dan *shall be* on 4264
2:31 All they that were numbered in the **c** of 4264
4: 5 when the **c** setteth forward, Aaron shall 4264
4:15 of the sanctuary, as the **c** is to set forward; 4264
5: 2 that they put out of the **c** every leper, and 4264
5: 3 ye put out, without the **c** shall ye put them; 4264
5: 4 did so, and put them out without the **c**: 4264
10:14 In the first *place* went the standard of the **c** 4264
10:18 the standard of the **c** of Reuben set forward 4264
10:22 the standard of the **c** of the children of 4264
10:25 the standard of the **c** of the children of Dan 4264
10:34 them by day, when they went out of the **c**. 4264
11: 1 *that were* in the uttermost parts of the **c**. 4264
11: 9 when the dew fell upon the **c** in the night, 4264
11:26 there remained two *of the* men in the **c**, 4264
11:26 and they prophesied in the **c**. 4264
11:27 Eldad and Medad do prophesy in the **c**. 4264
11:30 Moses gat him into the **c**, he and the elders 4264
11:31 from the sea, and let *them* fall by the **c**, 4264
11:31 round about the **c**, and as it were two cubits 4264
11:32 all abroad for themselves round about the **c**. 4264
12:14 let her be shut out from the **c** seven days, 4264
12:15 Miriam was shut out from the **c** seven days: 4264
14:44 and Moses, departed not out of the **c**. 4264
15:35 shall stone him with stones without the **c**. 4264
15:36 the congregation brought him without the **c**, 4264
19: 3 that he may bring her forth without the **c**, 4264
19: 7 afterward he shall come into the **c**, and 4264
19: 9 lay *them* up without the **c** in a clean place, 4264
31:12 unto the **c** at the plains of Moab, which *are* 4264
31:13 went forth to meet them without the **c**. 4264
31:19 do ye abide without the **c** seven days: 4264
31:24 and afterward ye shall come into the **c**. 4264
Dt 23:10 shall he go abroad out of the **c**, he shall not 4264
23:10 of the camp, he shall not come within the **c**: 4264
23:11 is down, he shall come into the **c** *again*. 4264
23:12 Thou shalt have a place also without the **c**, 4264
23:14 thy God walketh in the midst of thy **c**, 4264
23:14 before thee; therefore shall thy **c** be holy: 4264
29:11 your wives, and thy stranger that *is* in thy **c**, 4264
Jos 5: 8 that they abode in their places in the **c**, 4264
6:11 they came *into* the **c**, and lodged in 4264
6:11 came *into* the camp, and lodged in the **c**. 4264
6:14 the city once, and returned *into* the **c**: 4264
6:18 make the **c** of Israel a curse, and trouble it. 4264
6:23 and left them without the **c** of Israel. 4264
9: 6 they went to Joshua unto the **c** *at* Gilgal, 4264
10: 6 the men of Gibeon sent unto Joshua to the **c** 4264
10:15 and all Israel with him, unto the **c** to Gilgal. 4264
10:21 all the people returned to the **c** to Joshua *at* 4264
10:43 and all Israel with him, unto the **c** to Gilgal. 4264
Jdg 7:17 behold, when I come to the outside of the **c**, 4264
7:18 the trumpets also on every side of all the **c**, 4264
7:19 came unto the outside of the **c** *in* 4264
7:21 every man in his place round about the **c**: 4264
13:25 began to move him at times in the **c** of Dan, 4264
21: 8 there came none to the **c** from 4264
21:12 they brought them unto the **c** *to* Shiloh, 4264
1Sa 4: 3 when the people were come into the **c**, 4264
4: 5 covenant of the LORD came into the **c**, 4264
4: 6 of this great shout in the **c** of the Hebrews? 4264
4: 6 the ark of the LORD was come into the **c**. 4264
4: 7 for they said, God is come into the **c**. 4264
13:17 the spoilers came out of the **c** of 4264
14:21 which went up with them into the **c** *from* 4264
17: 4 there went out a champion out of the **c** of 4264
17:17 ten loaves, and run *to* the **c** to thy brethren; 4264
26: 6 will go down with me to Saul to the **c**? 4264
2Sa 1: 2 a man came out of the **c** from Saul with his 4264
1: 3 Out of the **c** of Israel am I escaped. 4264
1Ki 16:16 the host, king over Israel that day in the **c**. 4264
2Ki 3:24 when they came to the **c** of Israel, 4264
6: 8 In such and such a place *shall be* my **c**. 8466
7: 5 the twilight, to go unto the **c** of the Syrians: 4264
7: 5 come to the uttermost part of the **c** of Syria, 4264
7: 7 *even* the **c** as it *was*, and fled for their life. 4264
7: 8 lepers came to the uttermost part of the **c**, 4264
7:10 We came to the **c** of the Syrians, and 4264
7:12 are they gone out of the **c** to hide 4264
19:35 smote in the **c** of the Assyrians an hundred 4264
2Ch 22: 1 Arabians to the **c** had slain all the eldest. 4264
32:21 and captains in the **c** of the king of Assyria. 4264
Ps 78:28 he let *it* fall in the midst of their **c**, 4264
106:16 They envied Moses also in the **c**, *and* 4264
Isa 29: 3 I will **c** against thee round about, and 2583
37:36 smote in the **c** of the Assyrians an hundred 4264
Jer 50:29 that bend the bow, **c** against it round about; 2583
Eze 4: 2 set the **c** also against it, and set *battering* 4264
Joel 2:11 for his **c** *is* very great: for *he is* strong that 4264
Na 3:17 which **c** in the hedges in the cold day, *but* 2583
Heb 13:11 high priest for sin, are burnt without the **c**. *3925*
13:13 go forth therefore unto him without the **c**, *3925*
Rev 20: 9 and compassed the **c** of the saints about, *3925*

CAMPED (1) [CAMP]
Ex 19: 2 and there Israel **c** before the mount. 2583

CAMPFIRES See SHEEPFOLD

CAMPHIRE (2)
SS 1:14 My beloved *is* unto me *as* a cluster of **c** in 3724
4:13 with pleasant fruits; **c**, with spikenard, 3724

CAMPS (7) [CAMP]
Nu 2:32 all those that were numbered of the **c** 4264
5: 3 that they defile not their **c**, in the midst 4264
10: 2 and for the journeying of the **c**. 4264
10: 5 the **c** that lie on the east parts shall go 4264
10: 6 the **c** that lie on the south side shall take 4264
10:25 *which was* the rereward of all the **c** 4264
Am 4:10 I have made the stink of your **c** to come up 4264

CAN (235) [CANNOT, CANST] See Index

CANA (4)
Jn 2: 1 And the third day there was a marriage in **C** *2580*
2:11 This beginning of miracles did Jesus in **C** *2580*
4:46 So Jesus came again into **C** of Galilee, *2580*
21: 2 and Nathanael of **C** in Galilee, and the *sons* *2580*

CANAAN (93) [CANAANITE, CANAANITES, CANAANITESS, CANAANITISH]
Ge 9:18 and Japheth: and Ham *is* the father of **C**. 3667
9:22 Ham, the father of **C**, saw the nakedness of 3667
9:25 he said, Cursed *be* **C**; a servant of servants 3667
9:26 God of Shem; and **C** shall be his servant. 3667
9:27 tents of Shem; and **C** shall be his servant. 3667
10: 6 Cush, and Mizraim, and Phut, and **C**. 3667
10:15 And **C** begat Sidon his firstborn, and Heth, 3667
11:31 of the Chaldees, to go into the land of **C**; 3667
12: 5 they went forth to go into the land of **C**; 3667
12: 5 and into the land of **C** they came. 3667
13:12 Abram dwelled in the land of **C**, and 3667
16: 3 Abram had dwelt ten years in the land of **C**, 3667
17: 8 all the land of **C**, for an everlasting 3667
23: 2 the same *is* Hebron in the land of **C**: 3667
23:19 the same *is* Hebron in the land of **C**. 3667
28: 1 shalt not take a wife of the daughters of **C**. 3667
28: 6 shalt not take a wife of the daughters of **C**; 3667
28: 8 Esau seeing that the daughters of **C** pleased 3667
31:18 for to go to Isaac his father in the land of **C**. 3667
33:18 city of Shechem, which *is* in the land of **C**, 3667
35: 6 which *is* in the land of **C**, that *is*, Beth-el, 3667
36: 2 Esau took his wives of the daughters of **C**; 3667
36: 5 which were born unto him in the land of **C**. 3667
36: 6 which he had got in the land of **C**; 3667
37: 1 his father was a stranger, in the land of **C**. 3667
42: 5 for the famine was in the land of **C**. 3667
42: 7 they said, From the land of **C** to buy food. 3667
42:13 the sons of one man in the land of **C**; 3667
42:29 unto Jacob their father unto the land of **C**, 3667
42:32 *is this* day with our father in the land of **C**. 3667
44: 8 again unto thee out of the land of **C**: 3667
45:17 and go, get you unto the land of **C**; 3667
45:25 came *into* the land of **C** unto Jacob their 3667
46: 6 which they had gotten in the land of **C**, and 3667
46:12 Er and Onan died in the land of **C**. And 3667
46:31 which *were* in the land of **C**, are come unto 3667
47: 1 they have, are come out of the land of **C**; 3667

Ge 47: 4 for the famine *is* sore in the land of **C**: 3667
47:13 *all* the land of **C** fainted by reason of 3667
47:14 in the land of **C**, for the corn which they 3667
47:15 in the land of **C**, all the Egyptians came 3667
48: 3 appeared unto me at Luz in the land of **C**, 3667
48: 7 Rachel died by me in the land of **C** in 3667
49:30 which *is* before Mamre, in the land of **C**, 3667
50: 5 I have digged for me in the land of **C**, 3667
50:13 For his sons carried him into the land of **C**, 3667
Ex 6: 4 to give them the land of **C**, the land of their 3667
15:15 all the inhabitants of **C** shall melt away. 3667
16:35 came unto the borders of the land of **C**. 3667
Lev 14:34 When ye be come into the land of **C**, 3667
18: 3 after the doings of the land of **C**, whither I 3667
25:38 to give you the land of **C**, *and* to be your 3667
Nu 13: 2 that they may search the land of **C**, 3667
13:17 Moses sent them to spy out the land of **C**, 3667
26:19 and Er and Onan died in the land of **C**. 3667
32:30 possessions among you in the land of **C**. 3667
32:32 before the LORD *into* the land of **C**, 3667
33:40 which dwelt in the south in the land of **C**, 3667
33:51 are passed over Jordan into the land of **C**; 3667
34: 2 When ye come into the land of **C**; 3667
34: 2 *even* the land of **C** with the coasts thereof:) 3667
34:29 unto the children of Israel in the land of **C**. 3667
35:10 ye be come over Jordan into the land of **C**; 3667
35:14 three cities shall ye give in the land of **C**, 3667
Dt 32:49 behold the land of **C**, which I give unto 3667
Jos 5:12 they did eat of the fruit of the land of **C** that 3667
14: 1 children of Israel inherited in the land of **C**, 3667
21: 2 spake unto them at Shiloh in the land of **C**, 3667
22: 9 which *is* in the land of **C**, to go unto 3667
22:10 that *are* in the land of **C**, the children of 3667
22:11 built an altar over against the land of **C**, 3667
22:32 unto the land of **C**, to the children of Israel, 3667
24: 3 led him throughout all the land of **C**, and 3667
Jdg 3: 1 *Israel* as had not known all the wars of **C**; 3667
4: 2 sold them into the hand of Jabin king of **C**, 3667
4:23 the king of **C** before the children of Israel. 3667
4:24 prevailed against Jabin the king of **C**, 3667
4:24 until they had destroyed Jabin king of **C**. 3667
5:19 fought the kings of **C** in Taanach by 3667
21:12 camp *to* Shiloh, which *is* in the land of **C**. 3667
1Ch 1: 8 of Ham; Cush, and Mizraim, Put, and **C**. 3667
1:13 And **C** begat Zidon his firstborn, and Heth, 3667
16:18 Saying, Unto thee will I give the land of **C**, 3667
Ps 105:11 Saying, Unto thee will I give the land of **C**, 3667
106:38 whom they sacrificed unto the idols of **C**: 3667
135:11 king of Bashan, and all the kingdoms of **C**: 3667
Isa 19:18 the land of Egypt speak the language of **C**, 3667
Eze 16: 3 and thy nativity *is* of the land of **C**; 3669
16:29 fornication in the land of **C** unto Chaldea; 3667
Zep 2: 5 O **C**, the land of the Philistines, I will even 3667
Mt 15:22 a woman **of C** came out of the same coasts, *5478*
Ac 7:11 a dearth over all the land of Egypt and **C**, *5477*
13:19 destroyed seven nations in the land of **C**, *5477*

CANAANITE (14) [CANAAN]

Ge 12: 6 of Moreh. And the **C** *was* then in the land. 3669
13: 7 the **C** and the Perizzite dwelled then in 3669
38: 2 Judah saw there a daughter of a certain **C**, 3669
Ex 23:28 the **C**, and the Hittite, from before thee. 3669
33: 2 I will drive out the **C**, the Amorite, and 3669
34:11 and the **C**, and the Hittite, and the Perizzite, 3669
Nu 21: 1 *when* king Arad the **C**, which dwelt *in* 3669
33:40 king Arad the **C**, which dwelt in the south 3669
Jos 9: 1 the Hittite, and the Amorite, the **C**, 3669
11: 3 *And to* the **C** on the east and on the west, 3669
13: 3 *which* is counted to the **C**: 3669
Zec 14:21 in that day there shall be no more the **C** in 3669
Mt 10: 4 Simon the **C**, and Judas Iscariot, who also *2581*
Mk 3:18 and Thaddeus, and Simon the **C**, *2581*

CANAANITES (55) [CANAAN]

Ge 10:18 afterward were the families of the **C** spread 3669
10:19 the border of the **C** was from Sidon, as thou 3669
15:21 the **C**, and the Girgashites, and 3669
24: 3 wife unto my son of the daughters of the **C**, 3669
24:37 a wife to my son of the daughters of the **C**, 3669
34:30 the land, amongst the **C** and the Perizzites: 3669
50:11 when the inhabitants of the land, the **C**, 3669
Ex 3: 8 unto the place of the **C**, and the Hittites, 3669
3:17 affliction of Egypt unto the land of the **C**, 3669
13: 5 shall bring thee into the land of the **C**, 3669
13:11 shall bring thee into the land of the **C**, 3669
23:23 and the **C**, the Hivites, and the Jebusites: 3669
Nu 13:29 the **C** dwell by the sea, and by the coast of 3669
14:25 and the **C** dwelt in the valley.) 3669
14:43 and the **C** *are* there before you, 3669
14:45 the **C** which dwelt in that hill, and 3669
21: 3 the voice of Israel, and delivered up the **C**; 3669
Dt 1: 7 *to* the land of the **C**, and *unto* Lebanon, 3669
7: 1 the **C**, and the Perizzites, and the Hivites, 3669
11:30 the sun goeth down, in the land of the **C**, 3669
20:17 the **C**, and the Perizzites, the Hivites, and 3669
Jos 3:10 fail drive out from before you the **C**, 3669
5: 1 all the kings of the **C**, which *were* by 3669
7: 9 For the **C** and all the inhabitants of the land 3669
12: 8 the Amorites, and the **C**, the Perizzites, 3669
13: 4 all the land of the **C**, and Mearah that *is* 3669
16:10 they drave not out the **C** that dwelt in 3669
16:10 the **C** dwell among the Ephraimites unto 3669
17:12 but the **C** would dwell in that land. 3669
17:13 waxen strong, that they put the **C** to tribute; 3669
17:16 all the **C** that dwell in the land of the valley 3669
17:18 for thou shalt drive out the **C**, though they 3669
24:11 the **C**, and the Hittites, and the Girgashites, 3669
Jdg 1: 1 Who shall go up for us against the **C** first, 3669
1: 3 my lot, that we may fight against the **C**; 3669
1: 4 the LORD delivered the **C** and 3669
1: 5 and they slew the **C** and the Perizzites. 3669
1: 9 of Judah went down to fight against the **C**, 3669
1:10 Judah went against the **C** that dwelt in 3669
1:17 they slew the **C** that inhabited Zephath, and 3669
1:27 but the **C** would dwell in that land. 3669
1:28 that they put the **C** to tribute, and did not 3669
1:29 Neither did Ephraim drive out the **C** that 3669
1:29 but the **C** dwelt in Gezer among them. 3669
1:30 the **C** dwelt among them, and 3669
1:32 the Asherites dwelt among the **C**, 3669
1:33 he dwelt among the **C**, the inhabitants of 3669
3: 3 all the **C**, and the Sidonians, and 3669
3: 5 the children of Israel dwelt among the **C**, 3669
2Sa 24: 7 *to* all the cities of the Hivites, and of the **C**: 3669
1Ki 9:16 slain the **C** that dwelt in the city, and 3669
Ezr 9: 1 *even* of the **C**, the Hittites, the Perizzites, 3669
Ne 9: 8 with him to give the land of the **C**, 3669
9:24 the **C**, and gavest them into their hands, 3669
Ob 1:20 of Israel *shall possess* that of the **C**, 3669

CANAANITESS (1) [CANAAN]

1Ch 2: 3 unto him of the daughter of Shua the **C**. 3669

CANAANITISH (2) [CANAAN]

Ge 46:10 Zohar, and Shaul the son of a **C** woman. 3669
Ex 6:15 Zohar, and Shaul the son of a **C woman**: 3669

CANDACE (1)

Ac 8:27 an eunuch of great authority under **C** queen *2582*

CANDLE (16) [CANDLES, CANDLESTICK, CANDLESTICKS]

Job 18: 6 and his **c** shall be put out with him. 5216
21:17 How oft is the **c** of the wicked put out! and 5216
29: 3 When his **c** shined upon my head, *and* 5216
Ps 18:28 For thou wilt light my **c**: the LORD my 5216
Pr 20:27 The spirit of man *is* the **c** of the LORD, 5216
24:20 *man;* the **c** of the wicked shall be put out. 5216
31:18 *is* good: her **c** goeth not out by night. 5216
Jer 25:10 of the millstones, and the light of the **c**. 5216
Mt 5:15 Neither do men light a **c**, and put it under a *3088*
Mk 4:21 Is a **c** brought to be put under a bushel, or *3088*
Lk 8:16 No *man*, when he hath lighted a **c**, *3088*
11:33 No *man*, when he hath lighted a **c**, putteth *it* *3088*
11:36 as when the bright shining of a **c** doth give *3088*
15: 8 doth not light a **c**, and sweep the house, *3088*
Rev 18:23 And the light of a **c** shall shine no more at *3088*
22: 5 and they need no **c**, neither light of the sun; *3088*

CANDLES (1) [CANDLE]

Zep 1:12 *that* I will search Jerusalem with **c**, and 5216

CANDLESTICK (41) [CANDLE, STICK]

Ex 25:31 thou shalt make a **c** of pure gold: *of* beaten 4501
25:31 *of* beaten work shall the **c** be made: 4501
25:32 three branches of the **c** out of the one side, 4501
25:32 three branches of the **c** out of the other side: 4501
25:33 in the six branches that come out of the **c**. 4501
25:34 in the **c** *shall be* four bowls made like unto 4501
25:35 the six branches that proceed out of the **c**. 4501

Ex 26:35 the **c** over against the table on the side of 4501
30:27 the **c** and his vessels, and the altar of 4501
31: 8 the pure **c** with all his furniture, and 4501
35:14 The **c** also for the light, and his furniture, 4501
37:17 he made the **c** *of* pure gold: *of* beaten work 4501
37:17 *of* beaten work made he the **c**; his shaft, 4501
37:18 three branches of the **c** out of the one side 4501
37:18 three branches of the **c** out of the other side 4501
37:19 the six branches going out of the **c**. 4501
37:20 in the **c** *were* four bowls made like 4501
39:37 The pure **c**, *with* the lamps thereof, 4501
40: 4 thou shalt bring in the **c**, and light 4501
40:24 he put the **c** in the tent of the congregation, 4501
Lev 24: 4 He shall order the lamps upon the pure **c** 4501
Nu 3:31 the **c**, and the altars, and the vessels of 4501
4: 9 cover the **c** of the light, and his lamps, and 4501
8: 2 lamps shall give light over against the **c**. 4501
8: 3 lighted the lamps thereof over against the **c**, 4501
8: 4 this work of the **c** *was of* beaten gold, 4501
8: 4 had shewed Moses, so he made the **c**. 4501
2Ki 4:10 a bed, and a table, and a stool, and a **c**: 4501
1Ch 28:15 by weight for **every c**, 4501+4501+2050.1
28:15 *both* for the **c**, and *also for* the lamps 4501
28:15 to the use of **every c**. 4501+4501+2050.1
2Ch 13:11 the **c** of gold with the lamps thereof, 4501
Da 5: 5 wrote over against the **c** upon the plaister of 5043
Zec 4: 2 I have looked, and behold, a **c** all of gold, 4501
4:11 two olive trees upon the right *side* of the **c** 4501
Mt 5:15 and put it under a bushel, but on a **c**; *3087*
Mk 4:21 or under a bed? *and* not to be set on a **c**? *3087*
Lk 8:16 but setteth *it* on a **c**, that they which enter in *3087*
11:33 neither under a bushel, but on a **c**, *3087*
Heb 9: 2 wherein *was* the **c**, and the table, and *3087*
Rev 2: 5 and will remove thy **c** out of his place, *3087*

CANDLESTICKS (12) [CANDLE, STICK]
1Ki 7:49 the **c** *of* pure gold, five on the right side, 4501
1Ch 28:15 Even the weight for the **c** of gold, and 4501
28:15 for the **c** of silver by weight, *both* for 4501
2Ch 4: 7 he made ten **c** of gold according to their 4501
4:20 Moreover the **c** with their lamps, that they 4501
Jer 52:19 and the **c**, and the spoons, and the cups; 4501
Rev 1:12 And being turned, I saw seven golden **c**; *3087*
1:13 And in the midst of the seven **c** one like *3087*
1:20 in my right hand, and the seven golden **c**. *3087*
1:20 the seven **c** which thou sawest are the seven *3087*
2: 1 walketh in the midst of the seven golden **c**; *3087*
11: 4 the two **c** standing before the God of *3087*

CANE (2)
Isa 43:24 Thou hast bought me no **sweet c** with 7070
Jer 6:20 and the sweet **c** from a far country? 7070

CANKER (1) [CANKERED]
2Ti 2:17 And their word will eat as *doth* a **c**: *1044*

CANKERED (1) [CANKER]
Jas 5: 3 Your gold and silver is **c**; and the rust of *2728*

CANKERWORM (6) [WORM]
Joel 1: 4 that which the locust hath left hath the **c** 3218
1: 4 that which the **c** hath left hath 3218
2:25 the **c**, and the caterpillar, and 3218
Na 3:15 cut thee off, it shall eat thee up like the **c**: 3218
3:15 make thyself many as the **c**, make thyself 3218
3:16 of heaven: the **c** spoileth, and flieth away. 3218

CANNEH (1)
Eze 27:23 Haran, and **C**, and Eden, the merchants of 3656

CANNOT (184) [CAN] See Index

CANNOT SPEAK See DUMB

CANST (51) [CAN] See Index

CAPABLE See VALOUR

CAPERNAUM (16)
Mt 4:13 leaving Nazareth, he came and dwelt in **C**, *2584*
8: 5 And when Jesus was entered into **C**, *2584*
11:23 And thou, **C**, which art exalted unto *2584*
17:24 And when they were come to **C**, they that *2584*
Mk 1:21 And they went into **C**; and straightway on *2584*
2: 1 And again he entered into **C** after *some* *2584*
9:33 And he came to **C**: and being in the house *2584*
Lk 4:23 whatsoever we have heard done in **C**, *2584*
4:31 And came down to **C**, a city of Galilee, and *2584*
7: 1 audience of the people, he entered into **C**. *2584*
10:15 And thou, **C**, which art exalted to heaven, *2584*
Jn 2:12 After this he went down to **C**, he, and *2584*
4:46 certain nobleman, whose son was sick at **C**. *2584*
6:17 a ship, and went over the sea towards **C**. *2584*
6:24 and came to **C**, seeking for Jesus. *2584*
6:59 said he in the synagogue, as he taught in **C**. *2584*

CAPHTHORIM (1) [CAPHTOR]
1Ch 1:12 (of whom came the Philistines,) and **C**. 3732

CAPHTOR (3) [CAPHTHORIM, CAPHTORIM, CAPHTORIMS]
Dt 2:23 which came forth out of **C**, destroyed them, 3731
Jer 47: 4 the remnant of the country of **C**. 3731
Am 9: 7 the Philistines from **C**, and the Syrians 3731

CAPHTORIM (1) [CAPHTOR]
Ge 10:14 (out of whom came Philistim) and **C**. 3732

CAPHTORIMS (1) [CAPHTOR]
Dt 2:23 *even* unto Azzah, the **C**, which came forth 3732

CAPITAL; CAPITALS See CHAPITER; CHAPITERS

CAPPADOCIA (2)
Ac 2: 9 and in Judea, and **C**, in Pontus, and Asia, *2587*
1Pe 1: 1 Galatia, **C**, Asia, and Bithynia, *2587*

CAPTAIN (139) [CAPTAINS]
Ge 21:22 Phichol the **chief c** of his host spake unto 8269
21:32 Phichol the **chief c** of his host, and 8269
26:26 and Phichol the **chief c** of his army. 8269
37:36 an officer of Pharaoh's, *and* **c** of the guard. 8269
39: 1 of Pharaoh, **c** of the guard, an Egyptian, 8269
40: 3 he put them in ward *in* the house of the **c** of 8269
40: 4 the **c** of the guard charged Joseph with 8269
41:10 put me in ward *in* the **c** of the guard's 8269
41:12 a Hebrew, servant to the **c** of the guard; 8269
Nu 2: 3 Nahshon the son of Amminadab *shall be* **c** 5387
2: 5 Nethaneel the son of Zuar *shall be* **c** of 5387
2: 7 Eliab the son of Helon *shall be* **c** of 5387
2:10 the **c** of the children of Reuben *shall be* 5387
2:12 the **c** of the children of Simeon *shall be* 5387
2:14 the **c** of the sons of Gad *shall be* Eliasaph 5387
2:18 the **c** of the sons of Ephraim *shall be* 5387
2:20 the **c** of the children of Manasseh *shall be* 5387
2:22 the **c** of the sons of Benjamin *shall be* 5387
2:25 the **c** of the children of Dan *shall be* 5387
2:27 the **c** of the children of Asher *shall be* 5387
2:29 the **c** of the children of Naphtali *shall be* 5387
14: 4 Let us make a **c**, and let us return into 7218
Jos 5:14 *as* **c** of the host of the LORD am I now 8269
5:15 the **c** of the LORD'S host said unto 8269
Jdg 4: 2 the **c** of whose host *was* Sisera, which 8269
4: 7 the **c** of Jabin's army, with his chariots and 8269
11: 6 said unto Jephthah, Come, and be our **c**, 7101
11:11 the people made him head and **c** over them: 7101
1Sa 9:16 thou shalt anoint him to be **c** over my 5057
10: 1 the LORD hath anointed thee to be **c** over 5057
12: 9 **c** of the host of Hazor, and into the hand of 8269
13:14 the LORD hath commanded him to be **c** 5057
14:50 the name of the **c** of his host *was* Abner, 8269
17:18 carry these ten cheeses unto the **c** of *their* 8269
17:55 said unto Abner, the **c** of the host, Abner, 8269
18:13 and made him his **c** over a thousand; 8269
22: 2 unto him; and he became a **c** over them: 8269
26: 5 and Abner the son of Ner, the **c** of his host: 8269
2Sa 2: 8 Abner the son of Ner, **c** of Saul's host, 8269
5: 2 and thou shalt be a **c** over Israel. 5057
5: 8 *he shall be chief and* **c**. Wherefore they said, NIH
10:16 Shobach the **c** of the host of Hadarezer 8269
10:18 smote Shobach the **c** of their host, who died 8269
17:25 Absalom made Amasa **cs of** the host 5921
19:13 if thou be not **c** of the host before me 8269
23:19 therefore he was their **c**: howbeit he 8269
24: 2 For the king said to Joab the **c** of the host, 8269
1Ki 1:19 the priest, and Joab the **c** of the host: 8269
2:32 **c** of the host of Israel, and Amasa the son 8269
2:32 the son of Jether, **c** of the host of Judah. 8269
11:15 Joab the **c** of the host was gone up to bury 8269
11:21 that Joab the **c** of the host was dead, 8269
11:24 men unto him, and became **c** over a band, 8269
16: 9 **c** of half *his* chariots, conspired against 8269

1Ki 16:16 all Israel made Omri, the **c** of the host, 8269
2Ki 1: 9 the king sent unto him a **c** of fifty with his 8269
1:10 Elijah answered and said to the **c** of fifty, 8269
1:11 Again also he sent unto him another **c** of 8269
1:13 he sent again a **c** of the third fifty with his 8269
1:13 the third **c** of fifty went up, and came and 8269
4:13 for to the king, or to the **c** of the host? 8269
5: 1 **c** of the host of the king of Syria, 8269
9: 5 and he said, I have an errand to thee, O **c**. 8269
9: 5 which of all us? And he said, To thee, O **c**. 8269
9:25 said *Jehu* to Bidkar his **c**, Take up, *and* 7991
15:25 a **c** of his, conspired against him, and 7991
18:24 wilt thou turn away the face of one **c** of 6346
20: 5 and tell Hezekiah the **c** of my people, 5057
25: 8 came Nebuzar-adan, **c** of the guard, 7227
25:10 that *were with* the **c** of the guard, 7227
25:11 did Nebuzar-adan the **c** of the guard carry 7227
25:12 the **c** of the guard left of the poor of 7227
25:15 *in* silver, the **c** of the guard took *away*. 7227
25:18 the **c** of the guard took Seraiah the chief 7227
25:20 Nebuzar-adan **c** of the guard took these, 7227
1Ch 11: 6 the Jebusites first shall be chief and **c**. 8269
11:21 honourable than the two; for he was their **c**: 8269
11:42 a **c** of the Reubenites, and thirty with him, 7218
19:16 Shophach the **c** of the host of Hadarezer 8269
19:18 killed Shophach the **c** of the host. 8269
27: 5 The third **c** of the host for the third month 8269
27: 7 The fourth *c* for the fourth month *was* NIH
27: 8 The fifth **c** for the fifth month *was* 8269
27: 9 The sixth *c* for the sixth month *was* Ira NIH
27:10 The seventh *c* for the seventh month *was* NIH
27:11 The eighth *c* for the eighth month *was* NIH
27:12 The ninth *c* for the ninth month *was* Abiezer NIH
27:13 The tenth *c* for the tenth month *was* NIH
27:14 The eleventh *c* for the eleventh month *was* NIH
27:15 The twelfth *c* for the twelfth month *was* NIH
2Ch 13:12 God *himself is* with us for *our* **c**, and 7218
17:15 next to him *was* Jehohanan the **c**, and 8269
Ne 9:17 in their rebellion appointed a **c** to return to 7218
Isa 3: 3 The **c** of fifty, and the honourable *man*, and 8269
36: 9 wilt thou turn away the face of one **c** of 6346
Jer 37:13 a **c** of the ward *was* there, whose name *was* 1167
39: 9 Nebuzar-adan the **c** of the guard carried 7227
39:10 Nebuzar-adan the **c** of the guard left of 7227
39:11 to Nebuzar-adan the **c** of the guard, 7227
39:13 So Nebuzar-adan the **c** of the guard sent, 7227
40: 1 after that Nebuzar-adan the **c** of the guard 7227
40: 2 the **c** of the guard took Jeremiah, and 7227
40: 5 So the **c** of the guard gave him victuals and 7227
41:10 whom Nebuzar-adan the **c** of the guard had 7227
43: 6 every person that Nebuzar-adan the **c** of 7227
51:27 and Ashchenaz; appoint a **c** against her; 2951
52:12 came Nebuzar-adan, **c** of the guard, 7227
52:14 that *were* with the **c** of the guard, 7227
52:15 Nebuzar-adan the **c** of the guard carried 7227
52:16 Nebuzar-adan the **c** of the guard left *certain* 7227
52:19 *in* silver, took the **c** of the guard *away*. 7227
52:24 the **c** of the guard took Seraiah the chief 7227
52:26 So Nebuzar-adan the **c** of the guard took 7227
52:30 **c** of the guard carried away captive *of* 7227
Da 2:14 wisdom to Arioch the **c** of the king's guard, 7229
2:15 and said to Arioch the king's **c**, 7990
Jn 18:12 Then the band and the **c** and officers of *5506*
Ac 4: 1 and the **c** of the temple, and the Sadducees, *4755*
5:24 the *high* priest and the **c** of the temple and *4755*
5:26 Then went the **c** with the officers, and *4755*
21:31 tidings came unto the **chief c** of the band, *5506*
21:32 and when they saw the **chief c** and *5506*
21:33 Then the **chief c** came near, and took him, *5506*
21:37 he said unto the **chief c**, May I speak unto *5506*
22:24 The **chief c** commanded him to be brought *5506*
22:26 heard *that*, he went and told the **chief c**, *5506*
22:27 Then the **chief c** came, and said unto him, *5506*
22:28 And the **chief c** answered, With a great sum *5506*
22:29 and the **chief c** also was afraid, after he *5506*
23:10 there arose a great dissension, the **chief c**, *5506*
23:15 ye with the council signify to the **chief c** *5506*
23:17 said, Bring this young man unto the **chief c**: *5506*
23:18 and brought *him* to the **chief c**, and said, *5506*
23:19 Then the **chief c** took him by the hand, and *5506*
23:22 So the **chief c** then let the young man *5506*
24: 7 But the **chief c** Lysias came *upon us*, and *5506*
24:22 When Lysias the **chief c** shall come down, *5506*
28:16 the prisoners to the **c of the guard**: *4759*

Heb 2:10 to make the **c** of their salvation perfect *747*

CAPTAINS (119) [CAPTAIN]

Ex 14: 7 of Egypt, and **c** over every one of them. 7991
15: 4 his chosen **c** also are drowned in the Red 7991
Nu 31:14 *with* the **c** over thousands, and 8269
31:14 **c** over hundreds, which came from 8269
31:48 the **c** of thousands, and captains of 8269
31:48 and **c** of hundreds, came near unto Moses: 8269
31:52 of the **c** of thousands, and of the captains of 8269
31:52 of thousands, and of the **c** of hundreds, 8269
31:54 Eleazar the priest took the gold of the **c** of 8269
Dt 1:15 **c** over thousands, and captains over 8269
1:15 **c** over hundreds, and captains over fifties, 8269
1:15 **c** over fifties, and captains over tens, and 8269
1:15 **c** over tens, and officers among your tribes. 8269
20: 9 that they shall make **c** of the armies to lead 8269
29:10 your **c** of your tribes, your elders, and 7218
Jos 10:24 said unto the **c** of the men of war which 7101
1Sa 8:12 he will appoint him **c** over thousands, and 8269
8:12 captains over thousands, and **c** over fifties; 8269
22: 7 *and* make you all **c** of thousands, and 8269
22: 7 captains of thousands, and **c** of hundreds; 8269
2Sa 4: 2 Saul's son had two men *that were* **c** of 8269
18: 1 set **c** of thousands and captains of hundreds 8269
18: 1 of thousands and **c** of hundreds over them. 8269
18: 5 gave all the **c** charge concerning Absalom. 8269
23: 8 that sat in the seat, chief among the **c**; 7991
24: 4 against Joab, and against the **c** of the host. 8269
24: 4 the **c** of the host went out from the presence 8269
1Ki 1:25 the **c** of the host, and Abiathar the priest; 8269
2: 5 what he did to the two **c** of the hosts of 8269
9:22 his **c**, and rulers of his chariots, and 7991
15:20 sent the **c** of the hosts which he had against 8269
20:24 out of his place, and put **c** in their rooms: 6346
22:31 and two **c** that had rule over *his* chariots, 8269
22:32 when the **c** of the chariots saw Jehoshaphat, 8269
22:33 when the **c** of the chariots perceived that it 8269
2Ki 1:14 burnt up the two **c** of the former fifties with 8269
8:21 him about, and the **c** of the chariots: 8269
9: 5 behold, the **c** of the host *were* sitting; 8269
10:25 that Jehu said to the guard and to the **c**, 7991
10:25 the guard and the **c** cast *them* out, and 7991
11: 4 with the **c** and the guard, and brought them 3746
11: 9 the **c** over the hundreds did according to all 8269
11:10 to the **c** over hundreds did the priest give 8269
11:15 Jehoiada the priest commanded the **c** of 8269
11:19 the **c**, and the guard, and all the people of 3746
25:23 when all the **c** of the armies, they and 8269
25:26 and great, and the **c** of the armies, 8269
1Ch 4:42 having for their **c** Pelatiah, and Neariah, 7218
11:11 a Hachmonite, the chief of the **c**: 7991
11:15 Now three of the thirty **c** went down to 7218
12:14 *were* of the sons of Gad, **c** of the host: 7218
12:18 *who was* chief of the **c**, *and he said*, Thine 7970
12:18 and made them **c** of the band. 7218
12:20 **c** of the thousands that *were* of Manasseh. 7218
12:21 *men* of valour, and were **c** in the host. 8269
12:28 and *of* his father's house twenty and two **c**. 8269
12:34 of Naphtali a thousand **c**, and with them 8269
13: 1 David consulted with the **c** of thousands 8269
15:25 elders of Israel, and the **c** over thousands, 8269
25: 1 the **c** of the host separated to the service of 8269
26:26 the **c** over thousands and hundreds, and 8269
26:26 and hundreds, and the **c** of the host, 8269
27: 1 and **c** of thousands and hundreds, 8269
27: 3 of all the **c** of the host for the first month. 8269
28: 1 the **c** of the companies that ministered to 8269
28: 1 the **c** over the thousands, and captains over 8269
28: 1 **c** over the hundreds, and the stewards over 8269
29: 6 and the **c** of thousands and of hundreds, 8269
2Ch 1: 2 to the **c** of thousands and of hundreds, and 8269
8: 9 chief of his **c**, and captains of his chariots 7991
8: 9 and **c** of his chariots and horsemen. 8269
11:11 put **c** in them, and store of victual, and 5057
16: 4 sent the **c** of his armies against the cities of 8269
17:14 Of Judah, the **c** of thousands; Adnah 8269
18:30 the **c** of the chariots that *were* with him, 8269
18:31 when the **c** of the chariots saw Jehoshaphat, 8269
18:32 that when the **c** of the chariots perceived 8269
21: 9 compassed him in, and the **c** of the chariots. 8269
23: 1 took the **c** of hundreds, Azariah the son of 8269
23: 9 priest delivered to the **c** of hundreds spears, 8269
23:14 Jehoiada the priest brought out the **c** of 8269

2Ch 23:20 he took the **c** of hundreds, and the nobles, 8269
25: 5 made them **c** over thousands, and captains 8269
25: 5 over thousands, and **c** over hundreds, 8269
26:11 the hand of Hananiah, *one* of the king's **c**. 8269
32: 6 he set **c** of war over the people, and 8269
32:21 and **c** in the camp of the king of Assyria. 8269
33:11 the **c** of the host of the king of Assyria, 8269
33:14 put **c** of war in all the fenced cities of 8269
Ne 2: 9 Now the king had sent **c** of the army and 8269
Job 39:25 the thunder of the **c**, and the shouting. 8269
Jer 13:21 for thou hast taught them *to be* **c**, *and* 441
40: 7 *Now* when all the **c** of the forces which 8269
40:13 all the **c** of the forces that *were* in the fields, 8269
41:11 all the **c** of the forces that *were* with him, 8269
41:13 all the **c** of the forces that *were* with him, 8269
41:16 all the **c** of the forces that *were* with him, 8269
42: 1 all the **c** of the forces, and Johanan the son 8269
42: 8 all the **c** of the forces which *were* with him, 8269
43: 4 all the **c** of the forces, and all the people, 8269
43: 5 all the **c** of the forces, took all the remnant 8269
51:23 with thee will I break in pieces **c** and rulers. 6346
51:28 the **c** thereof, and all the rulers thereof, and 6346
51:57 her wise *men,* her **c**, and her rulers, and 6346
Eze 21:22 to appoint **c**, to open the mouth in 3733
23: 6 *Which were* clothed with blue, **c** and rulers, 6346
23:12 **c** and rulers clothed most gorgeously, 6346
23:23 **c** and rulers, great lords and renowned, 6346
Da 3: 2 and the **c**, the judges, the treasurers, 6347
3: 3 the governors and **c**, the judges, 6347
3:27 **c**, and the king's counsellers, 6347
6: 7 and the princes, the counsellers and the **c**, 6347
Na 3:17 and thy **c** as the great grasshoppers, 2951
Mk 6:21 **high c**, and chief *estates* of Galilee; *5506*
Lk 22: 4 and communed with the chief priests and **c**, *4755*
22:52 and **c** of the temple, and the elders, *4755*
Ac 25:23 with the **chief c**, and principal men of *5506*
Rev 6:15 and the rich *men,* and the **chief c**, and *5506*
19:18 and the flesh of **c**, and the flesh of mighty *5506*

CAPTIVE (59) [CAPTIVES, CAPTIVITY]

Ge 14:14 Abram heard that his brother was **taken c**, 7617
34:29 their wives **took** they **c**, and spoiled even 7617
Ex 12:29 firstborn of the **c** that *was* in the dungeon; 7628
Nu 24:22 until Asshur shall **carry** thee **away c**. 7617
Dt 21:10 and thou hast **taken** them **c**, 7617+7628
Jdg 5:12 arise, Barak, and **lead** thy captivity **c**, 7617
1Ki 8:48 which **led** them **away c**, and pray unto thee 7617
8:50 before them who **carried** them **c**, 7617
2Ki 5: 2 had **brought away c** out of the land of 7617
6:22 whom thou hast **taken c** with thy sword 7617
15:29 of Naphtali, and **carried** them **c** to Assyria. 1540
16: 9 **carried** *the people of* it **c** to Kir, and slew 1540
24:16 even them the king of Babylon brought **c** to 1473
1Ch 5: 6 king of Assyria **carried away c**: 1540
2Ch 6:37 in the land whither they are **carried c**, 7617
25:12 did the children of Judah **carry away c**, 7617
28: 8 the children of Israel **carried away c** of 7617
28:11 which ye have **taken c** of your brethren: 7617
30: 9 compassion before them that **lead** them **c**, 7617
Ps 68:18 ascended on high, thou hast **led** captivity **c**: 7617
137: 3 For there they that **carried** us **away c** 7617
Isa 49:21 *am* desolate, a **c**, and removing to and fro? 1540
49:24 from the mighty, or the lawful **c** delivered? 7628
51:14 The **c exile** hasteneth that *he* may be 6808
52: 2 bands of thy neck, O **c** daughter of Zion. 7628
Jer 1: 3 unto the **carrying away** of Jerusalem **c** in 1540
13:17 the LORD's flock is **carried away c**. 7617
13:19 Judah shall be **carried away c** all of it, 1540
13:19 all of it, it shall be wholly **carried away c**. 1540
20: 4 he shall **carry** them **c** into Babylon, and 1540
22:12 in the place whither they have **led** him **c**, 1540
24: 1 **carried away c** Jeconiah the son of 1540
24: 5 them that are **carried away c** of Judah, 1546
27:20 when he **carried away c** Jeconiah the son 1540
28: 6 all that is **carried away c**, from Babylon 1473
29: 1 **carried away c** from Jerusalem to 1540
29:14 I **caused** you **to be carried away c**. 1540
39: 9 **carried away c** *into* Babylon the remnant 1540
40: 1 all that were **carried away c** of Jerusalem 1546
40: 1 which were **carried away c** unto Babylon. 1540
40: 7 of *them* that were not **carried away c** to 1540
41:10 Ishmael **carried away c** all the residue of 7617
41:10 the son of Nethaniah **carried** them **away c**, 7617
41:14 **carried away c** from Mizpah cast about 7617
52:15 **carried away c** *certain* of the poor of 1540
52:27 Thus Judah was **carried away c** out of his 1540
52:28 whom Nebuchadrezzar **carried away c**: 1540
52:29 **carried away c** from Jerusalem eight 1540
52:30 **carried away c** *of* the Jews seven hundred 1540
Am 1: 6 they **carried away c** the whole captivity, 1540
6: 7 Therefore now shall they **go c** with the first 1540
6: 7 shall they go captive with the first that **go c**, 1540
7:11 Israel shall **surely** be **led away c** out 1540+1540
Ob 1:11 in the day that the strangers **carried away c** 7617
Na 2: 7 Huzzab shall be **led away c**, she shall be 1540
Lk 21:24 and shall be **led away c** into all nations: *163*
Eph 4: 8 he **led** captivity **c**, and gave gifts unto men. *162*
2Ti 2:26 *who are* **taken c** by him at his will. *2221*
3: 6 and **lead c** silly women laden with sins, *162*

CAPTIVES (43) [CAPTIVE]

Ge 31:26 my daughters, as **c** taken with the sword? 7617
Nu 31: 9 of Israel **took** *all* the women of Midian **c**, 7617
31:12 they brought the **c**, and the prey, and 7628
31:19 *both* yourselves and your **c** on the third day, 7628
Dt 21:11 seest among the **c** a beautiful woman, and 7633
32:42 *that* with the blood of the slain and of the **c**, 7633
1Sa 30: 2 had **taken** the women **c**, that *were* therein: 7617
30: 3 and their daughters, were **taken c**. 7617
30: 5 David's two wives were **taken c**, 7617
1Ki 8:46 that they **carry** them **away c** unto 7617+7617
8:47 in the land whither they were **carried c**, 7617
8:47 in the land of them *that* **carried** them **c**, 7617
2Ki 24:14 *even* ten thousand **c**, and all the craftsmen 1540
2Ch 6:36 they **carry** them **away c** unto a land 7617+7617
6:38 whither they have **carried** them **c**, and 7617
28: 5 **carried away** a great multitude of them **c**, 7617+7633
28:11 hear me therefore, and deliver the **c** again, 7633
28:13 Ye shall not bring in the **c** hither: 7633
28:14 So the armed men left the **c** and the spoil 7633
28:15 took the **c**, and with the spoil clothed all 7633
28:17 and smitten Judah, and carried away **c**. 7628
Ps 106:46 to be pitied of all those that **carried** them **c**. 7617
Isa 14: 2 they shall **take** them **c**, whose captives they 7617
14: 2 take them captives, whose **c** they were; 7617
20: 4 the Ethiopians **c**, young and old, naked and 1546
45:13 build my city, and he shall let go my **c**, 1546
49:25 Even the **c** of the mighty shall be taken 7628
61: 1 to proclaim liberty to the **c**, and the opening 7617
Jer 28: 4 with all the **c** of Judah, that went into 1546
29: 1 of the elders which were **carried away c**, 1473
29: 4 of Israel, unto all that are **carried away c**, 1473
29: 7 I have **caused** you **to be carried away c**, 1540
43: 3 and **carry** us **away c** *into* Babylon. 1540
43:12 shall burn them, and **carry** them **away c**: 7617
48:46 for thy sons are taken **c**, and thy daughters 7628
48:46 are taken captives, and thy daughters **c**. 7633
50:33 all that **took** them **c** held them fast; 7617
Eze 1: 1 as I *was* among the **c** by the river of 1473
6: 9 the nations whither they shall be **carried c**, 7617
16:53 *will I bring again* the captivity of thy **c** in 7622
Da 2:25 I have found a man of the **c** of Judah, 1123+1547
11: 8 shall also carry **c** *into* Egypt their gods, 7628
Lk 4:18 to preach deliverance to the **c**, and *164*

CAPTIVITY (127) [CAPTIVE]

Nu 21:29 his daughters into **c** unto Sihon king of 7622
Dt 21:13 she shall put the raiment of her **c** from off 7628
28:41 not enjoy them; for they shall go into **c**. 7628
30: 3 then the LORD thy God will turn thy **c**, 7622
Jdg 5:12 arise, Barak, and lead thy **c** captive, 7628
18:30 of Dan until the day of the **c** of the land. 1540
2Ki 24:15 *those* carried he *into* **c** from Jerusalem to 1473
25:27 thirtieth year of the **c** of Jehoiachin king of 1546
1Ch 5:22 And they dwelt in their steads until the **c**. 1473
6:15 Jehozadak went *into* **c**, when the LORD NIH
2Ch 6:37 and pray unto thee in the land of their **c**, 7628
6:38 and with all their soul in the land of their **c**, 7628
29: 9 and our wives *are* in **c** for this. 7628
Ezr 1:11 **c** that were brought up from Babylon unto 1473
2: 1 of the province that went up out of the **c**, 7628
3: 8 all they that were come out of the **c** *unto* 7628
4: 1 Benjamin heard that the children of the **c** 1473
6:16 and the rest of the children of the **c**, 1547
6:19 the children of the **c** kept the passover upon 1473
6:20 the passover for all the children of the **c**, 1473
6:21 which were come again out of **c**, and 1473

Ezr 8:35 which were come out of the **c**, offered burnt 7628
9: 7 to **c**, and to a spoil, and to confusion of 7628
10: 7 and Jerusalem unto all the children of the **c**, 1473
10:16 the children of the **c** did so. And Ezra 1473
Ne 1: 2 which were left of the **c**, and 7628
1: 3 The remnant that are left of the **c** there in 7628
4: 4 and give them for a prey in the land of **c**: 7633
7: 6 that went up out of the **c**, *of* those that had 7628
8:17 were come again out of the **c** made booths, 7628
Est 2: 6 **c** which had been carried away with 1473
Job 42:10 the LORD turned the **c** of Job, when he 7622
Ps 14: 7 when the LORD bringeth back the **c** of his 7622
53: 6 When God bringeth back the **c** of his 7622
68:18 ascended on high, thou hast led **c** captive: 7628
78:61 delivered his strength into **c**, and his glory 7628
85: 1 thou hast brought back the **c** of Jacob. 7622
126: 1 When the LORD turned again the **c** of 7870
126: 4 Turn again our **c**, O LORD, as the streams 7622
Isa 5:13 Therefore my people are **gone into c**, 1540
22:17 will carry thee away with a mighty **c**, 2925
46: 2 the burden, but themselves are gone into **c**. 7628
Jer 15: 2 and such as *are* for the **c**, to the captivity. 7628
15: 2 and such as *are* for the captivity, to the **c**. 7628
20: 6 all that dwell in thine house shall go into **c**: 7628
22:22 thy pastors, and thy lovers shall go into **c**: 7628
29:14 I will turn away your **c**, and I will gather 7622
29:16 that are not gone forth with you into **c**; 1473
29:20 the word of the LORD, all *ye of* the **c**, 1473
29:22 by all the **c** of Judah which *are* in Babylon, 1546
29:28 unto us *in* Babylon, saying, This *c is* long: NIH
29:31 Send to all them of the **c**, saying, Thus saith 1473
30: 3 that I will bring again the **c** of my people 7622
30:10 and thy seed from the land of their **c**; 7628
30:16 every one of them, shall go into **c**; 7628
30:18 I *will* bring again the **c** of Jacob's tents, and 7622
31:23 when I shall bring again their **c**; 7622
32:44 for I will cause their **c** to return, saith 7622
33: 7 I will cause the **c** of Judah and the captivity 7622
33: 7 of Judah and the **c** of Israel to return, 7622
33:11 For I will cause to return the **c** of the land 7622
33:26 for I will cause their **c** to return, and 7622
43:11 such *as are* for **c** to captivity; and such *as* 7628
43:11 such *as are* for captivity to **c**; and such *as* 7628
46:19 in Egypt, furnish thyself to **go into c**: 1473
46:27 and thy seed from the land of their **c**; 7628
48: 7 Chemosh shall go forth into **c** *with* his 1473
48:11 vessel to vessel, neither hath he gone into **c**: 1473
48:47 Yet will I bring again the **c** of Moab in 7622
49: 3 for their king shall go into **c**, *and* his priests 1473
49: 6 afterward I will bring again the **c** of 7622
49:39 *that* I will bring again the **c** of Elam, 7622
52:31 thirtieth year of the **c** of Jehoiachin king of 1546
La 1: 3 Judah is **gone into c** because of affliction, 1540
1: 5 her children are gone *into* **c** before 7628
1:18 and my young men are gone into **c**. 7628
2:14 thine iniquity, to turn away thy **c**; 7622
4:22 he will no more **carry** thee **away into c**: 1540
Eze 1: 2 *was* the fifth year of king Jehoiachin's **c**, 1546
3:11 go, get thee to them of the **c**, unto 1473
3:15 I came to them of the **c** *at* Tel-abib, 1473
11:24 of God into Chaldea, to them of the **c**. 1473
11:25 I spake unto them of the **c** all the things that 1473
12: 4 in their sight, as they that go forth into **c**. 1473
12: 7 as stuff for **c**, and in the even I digged 1473
12:11 unto them: they shall remove *and* go into **c**. 7628
16:53 When I shall bring again their **c**, 7622
16:53 the **c** of Sodom and her daughters, and 7622
16:53 the **c** of Samaria and her daughters, then 7622
16:53 *will I bring again* the **c** of thy captives in 7622
25: 3 the house of Judah, when they went into **c**; 1473
29:14 I will bring again the **c** of Egypt, and 7622
30:17 the sword: and these *cities* shall go into **c**. 7628
30:18 cover her, and her daughters shall go into **c**. 7628
33:21 it came to pass in the twelfth year of our **c**, 1546
39:23 of Israel **went into c** for their iniquity: 1540
39:25 Now will I bring again the **c** of Jacob, and 7622
39:28 which **caused** them **to be led into c** among 1540
40: 1 In the five and twentieth year of our **c**, 1546
Da 5:13 which *art* of the children of the **c** of Judah, 1547
6:13 which *is* of the children of the **c** of Judah, 1547
11:33 by flame, by **c**, and by spoil, *many* days. 7628
Hos 6:11 when I returned the **c** of my people. 7622
Joel 3: 1 when I shall bring again the **c** of Judah and 7622
Am 1: 5 the people of Syria shall **go into c** unto Kir, 1540
1: 6 they carried away captive the whole **c**, 1546
1: 9 they delivered up the whole **c** to Edom, 1546
1:15 their king shall go into **c**, he and his princes 1473
5: 5 for Gilgal shall **surely go into c**, 1540+1540
5:27 Therefore will I **cause** you **to go into c** 1540
7:17 Israel shall **surely go into c** forth of 1540+1540
9: 4 though they go into **c** before their enemies, 7628
9:14 I will bring again the **c** of my people of 7622
Ob 1:20 the **c** of this host of the children of Israel 1546
1:20 the **c** of Jerusalem, which *is* in Sepharad, 1546
Mic 1:16 for they are **gone into c** from thee. 1540
Na 3:10 Yet *was* she carried away, she went into **c**: 7628
Hab 1: 9 and they shall gather the **c** as the sand. 7628
Zep 2: 7 God shall visit them, and turn away their **c**. 7622
3:20 when I turn back your **c** before your eyes, 7622
Zec 6:10 Take of *them of* the **c**, *even* of Heldai, of 1473
14: 2 and half of the city shall go forth into **c**, and 1473
Ro 7:23 **bringing** me **into c** to the law of sin which is *163*
2Co 10: 5 **bringing into c** every thought to *163*
Eph 4: 8 he led **c** captive, and gave gifts unto men. *161*
Rev 13:10 He that leadeth into **c** *shall* go into captivity: *161*
13:10 He that leadeth into captivity *shall* go into **c**: *161*

CAPTURE See FETCH; FETCHED

CARAWAY See FITCHES

CARBUNCLE (3) [CARBUNCLES]

Ex 28:17 *first* row *shall be* a sardius, a topaz, and a **c**: 1304
39:10 *the first* row *was* a sardius, a topaz, and a **c**: 1304
Eze 28:13 the emerald, and the **c**, and gold: 1304

CARBUNCLES (1) [CARBUNCLE]

Isa 54:12 thy gates of **c**, and all thy borders of 68+688

CARCAS (1)

Est 1:10 Bigtha, and Abagtha, Zethar, and **C**, 3752

CARCASE (34) [CARCASES]

Lev 5: 2 whether *it be* a **c** of an unclean beast, or a 5038
5: 2 or a **c** of unclean cattle, or the carcase of 5038
5: 2 or the **c** of unclean creeping things, and *if* it 5038
11: 8 ye not eat, and their **c** shall ye not touch; 5038
11:24 whosoever toucheth the **c** of them shall be 5038
11:25 whosoever beareth *ought* of the **c** of them 5038
11:27 whoso toucheth their **c** shall be unclean 5038
11:28 he that beareth the **c** of them shall wash his 5038
11:35 every *thing* whereupon *any part* of their **c** 5038
11:36 that which toucheth their **c** shall be 5038
11:37 if *any part* of their **c** fall upon any sowing 5038
11:38 *any part* of their **c** fall thereon, it *shall be* 5038
11:39 he that toucheth the **c** thereof shall be 5038
11:40 he that eateth of the **c** of it shall wash his 5038
11:40 he also that beareth the **c** of it shall wash 5038
Dt 14: 8 eat of their flesh, nor touch their **dead c**. 5038
28:26 thy **c** shall be meat unto all fowls of the air, 5038
Jos 8:29 they should take his **c** down from the tree, 5038
Jdg 14: 8 and he turned aside to see the **c** of the lion: 4658
14: 8 of bees and honey in the **c** of the lion. 1472
14: 9 had taken the honey out of the **c** of the lion. 1472
1Ki 13:22 thy **c** shall not come unto the sepulchre of 5038
13:24 his **c** was cast in the way, and the ass stood 5038
13:24 ass stood by it, the lion also stood by the **c**. 5038
13:25 saw the **c** cast in the way, and the lion 5038
13:25 in the way, and the lion standing by the **c**: 5038
13:28 he went and found his **c** cast in the way, 5038
13:28 and the ass and the lion standing by the **c**: 5038
13:28 the lion had not eaten the **c**, nor torn 5038
13:29 the prophet took up the **c** of the man of 5038
13:30 he laid his **c** in his own grave; and 5038
2Ki 9:37 the **c** of Jezebel shall be as dung upon 5038
Isa 14:19 stones of the pit; as a **c** trodden under feet. 6297
Mt 24:28 For wheresoever the **c** is, there will *4430*

CARCASES (22) [CARCASE]

Ge 15:11 And when the fowls came down upon the **c**, 6297
Lev 11:11 but you shall have their **c** in abomination. 5038
11:26 *The* **c** of every beast which divideth NIH
26:30 cast your **c** upon the carcases of your idols, 6297
26:30 cast your carcases upon the **c** of your idols, 6297
Nu 14:29 Your **c** shall fall in this wilderness; and 6297
14:32 *as for* you, your **c**, they shall fall in this 6297
14:33 until your **c** be wasted in the wilderness. 6297
1Sa 17:46 I will give the **c** of the host of 6297
Isa 5:25 their **c** were torn in the midst of the streets. 5038

Isa 34: 3 their stink shall come up *out of* their **c**, and 6297
66:24 look upon the **c** of the men that have 6297
Jer 7:33 the **c** of this people shall be meat for 5038
9:22 Even the **c** of men shall fall as dung upon 5038
16: 4 their **c** shall be meat for the fowls of 5038
16:18 they have filled mine inheritance with the **c** 5038
19: 7 their **c** will I give to be meat for the fowls 5038
Eze 6: 5 I will lay the **dead c** of the children of 6297
43: 7 nor by the **c** of their kings *in* their high 6297
43: 9 the **c** of their kings, far from me, and I will 6297
Na 3: 3 multitude of slain, and a great number of **c**; 6297
Heb 3:17 had sinned, whose **c** fell in the wilderness? *2966*

CARCASS; CARCASSES See CARCASE; CARCASES

CARCHEMISH (3)
2Ch 35:20 came up to fight against **C** by Euphrates: 3751
Isa 10: 9 *Is* not Calno as **C**? *is* not Hamath as Arpad? 3751
Jer 46: 2 which was by the river Euphrates in **C**, 3751

CARE (20) [CARED, CAREFUL, CAREFULLY, CAREFULNESS, CARELESS, CARELESSLY, CARES, CAREST, CARETH, CARING]
1Sa 10: 2 lo, thy father hath left the **c** of the asses, 1697
2Sa 18: 3 for if we flee away, they will not **c** 3820+7760
18: 3 if half of us die, will they **c** for us: 3820+7760
2Ki 4:13 thou hast been careful for us with all this **c**; 2731
Jer 49:31 that dwelleth **without c**, saith the LORD, 983
Eze 4:16 they shall eat bread by weight, and with **c**; 1674
Mt 13:22 and the **c** of this world, and *3308*
Lk 10:34 brought him to an inn, and **took c of** him. *1959*
10:35 the host, and said unto him, **Take c of** him; *1959*
10:40 dost thou not **c** that my sister hath left me *3199*
1Co 7:21 Art thou called *being* a servant? **c** not **for** it: *3199*
9: 9 out the corn. Doth God **take c for** oxen? *3199*
12:25 *that* the members should **have** the same **c** *3309*
2Co 7:12 that our **c** for you in the sight of God might *4710*
8:16 which put the same **earnest c** into the heart *4710*
11:28 upon me daily, the **c** of all the churches. *3308*
Php 2:20 who will naturally **c for** your state. *3309*
4:10 that now at the last your **c** of me hath *5426*
1Ti 3: 5 how shall he **take c of** the church of God?) *1959*
1Pe 5: 7 Casting all your **c** upon him; for he careth *3308*

CAREAH (1)
2Ki 25:23 Johanan the son of **C**, and Seraiah the son 7143

CARED (3) [CARE]
Ps 142: 4 refuge failed me; no man **c** for my soul. 1875
Jn 12: 6 This he said, not that he **c** for the poor; but *3199*
Ac 18:17 And Gallio **c for** none of those *things*. *3199*

CAREFUL (7) [CARE]
2Ki 4:13 thou hast been **c** for us with all this care; 2729
Jer 17: 8 shall not be **c** in the year of drought, 1672
Da 3:16 we *are* not **c** to answer thee in this matter. 2818
Lk 10:41 thou art **c** and troubled about many *things*: *3309*
Php 4: 6 Be **c** for nothing; but in every *thing* by *3309*
4:10 wherein ye were also **c**, but ye lacked *5426*
Tit 3: 8 in God might be **c** to maintain good works. *5431*

CAREFULLY (4) [CARE]
Dt 15: 5 Only if thou **c hearken** unto 8085+8085
Mic 1:12 For the inhabitant of Maroth **waited c** for 2342
Php 2:28 I sent him therefore the **more c**, that, *4708*
Heb 12:17 though he **sought** it **c** with tears. *1567*

CAREFULNESS (4) [CARE]
Eze 12:18 drink thy water with trembling and with **c**; 1674
12:19 They shall eat their bread with **c**, and 1674
1Co 7:32 But I would have you **without c**. He *that is* *275*
2Co 7:11 what **c** it wrought in you, yea, *4710*

CARELESS (5) [CARE]
Jdg 18: 7 people that *were* therein, how they dwelt **c**, 983
Isa 32: 9 ye **c** daughters, give ear unto my speech. 982
32:10 ye **c** *women*: for the vintage shall fail, 982
32:11 that are at ease; be troubled, ye **c** ones: 982
Eze 30: 9 me in ships to make the **c** Ethiopians afraid, 983

CARELESSLY (3) [CARE]
Isa 47: 8 that dwellest **c**, that sayest in thine 983+3807.1
Eze 39: 6 among them that dwell **c** in the isles: 983+3807.1
Zep 2:15 *is* the rejoicing city that dwelt **c**, 983+3807.1

CARES (3) [CARE]
Mk 4:19 And the **c** of this world, and *3308*
Lk 8:14 and are choked with **c** and riches and *3308*
21:34 and **c** of *this* life, and *so* that day come *3308*

CARESSING See SPORTING

CAREST (3) [CARE]
Mt 22:16 neither **c** thou for any *man*: for thou *3199*
Mk 4:38 Master, **c** thou not that we perish? *3199*
12:14 **c** for no *man*: for thou regardest not *3199*

CARETH (7) [CARE]
Dt 11:12 A land which the LORD thy God **c for**: 1875
Jn 10:13 he is a hireling, and **c** not for the sheep. *3199*
1Co 7:32 He *that is* unmarried **c for** the *things* that *3309*
7:33 But he that is married **c for** the *things that* *3309*
7:34 The unmarried *woman* **c for** the *things* of *3309*
7:34 she that is married **c for** the *things* of *3309*
1Pe 5: 7 all your care upon him; for he **c** for you. *3199*

CARING (1) [CARE]
1Sa 9: 5 lest my father leave *c* for the asses, and NIH

CARMEL (26) [CARMELITE, CARMELITESS]
Jos 12:22 one; the king of Jokneam of **C**, one; 3760
15:55 Maon, **C**, and Ziph, and Juttah, 3760
19:26 reacheth to **C** westward, and 3760
1Sa 15:12 Saul came to **C**, and behold, 3760
25: 2 in Maon, whose possessions *were* in **C**; 3760
25: 2 and he was shearing his sheep in **C**. 3760
25: 5 Get you up to **C**, and go to Nabal, and 3760
25: 7 unto them, all the while they were in **C**. 3760
25:40 of David were come to Abigail to **C**, 3760
1Ki 18:19 *and* gather to me all Israel unto mount **C**, 3760
18:20 the prophets together unto mount **C**. 3760
18:42 Elijah went up to the top of **C**; and he cast 3760
2Ki 2:25 he went from thence to mount **C**, and 3760
4:25 and came unto the man of God to mount **C**. 3760
19:23 of his borders, *and into* the forest of his **C**. 3760
2Ch 26:10 vinedressers in the mountains, and in **C**: 3760
SS 7: 5 Thine head upon thee *is* like **C**, and the hair 3760
Isa 33: 9 and Bashan and **C** shake off *their fruits*. 3760
35: 2 the excellency of **C** and Sharon, they shall 3760
37:24 height of his border, *and* the forest of his **C**. 3760
Jer 46:18 and as **C** by the sea, *so* shall he come. 3760
50:19 he shall feed on **C** and Bashan, and his soul 3760
Am 1: 2 shall mourn, and the top of **C** shall wither. 3760
9: 3 they hide themselves in the top of **C**, 3760
Mic 7:14 solitarily *in* the wood, in the midst of **C**: 3760
Na 1: 4 **C**, and the flower of Lebanon languisheth. 3760

CARMELITE (5) [CARMEL]
1Sa 30: 5 and Abigail the wife of Nabal the **C**. 3761
2Sa 2: 2 and Abigail Nabal's wife the **C**. 3761
3: 3 of Abigail the wife of Nabal the **C**; 3761
23:35 Hezrai the **C**, Paarai the Arbite, 3761
1Ch 11:37 Hezro the **C**, Naarai the son of Ezbai, 3761

CARMELITESS (2) [CARMEL]
1Sa 27: 3 and Abigail the **C**, Nabal's wife. 3761
1Ch 3: 1 the second Daniel, of Abigail the **C**: 3761

CARMI (8) [CARMITES]
Ge 46: 9 Hanoch, and Phallu, and Hezron, and **C**. 3756
Ex 6:14 Hanoch, and Pallu, Hezron, and **C**: 3756
Nu 26: 6 of **C**, the family of the Carmites. 3756
Jos 7: 1 for Achan, the son of **C**, the son of Zabdi, 3756
7:18 Achan, the son of **C**, the son of Zabdi, 3756
1Ch 2: 7 the sons of **C**; Achar, the troubler of Israel, 3756
4: 1 Hezron, and **C**, and Hur, and Shobal. 3756
5: 3 *were*, Hanoch, and Pallu, Hezron, and **C**. 3756

CARMITE See CARMITES

CARMITES (1) [CARMI]
Nu 26: 6 of Carmi, the family of the **C**. 3757

CARNAL (11) [CARNALLY]
Ro 7:14 law is spiritual: but I am **c**, sold under sin. *4559*
8: 7 Because the **c** mind *is* enmity against God: *4561*
15:27 is also to minister unto them in **c** *things*. *4559*
1Co 3: 1 but as unto **c**, *even* as unto babes in Christ. *4559*
3: 3 For ye are yet **c**: for whereas *there is* among *4559*
3: 3 divisions, are ye not **c**, and walk as men? *4559*

1Co 3: 4 and another, I *am* of Apollos; are ye not **c**? *4559*
9:11 a great *thing* if we shall reap your **c** *things?* *4559*
2Co 10: 4 (For the weapons of our warfare *are* not **c**, *4559*
Heb 7:16 not after the law of a **c** commandment, but *4559*
9:10 and divers washings, and **c** ordinances, *4561*

CARNALLY (4) [CARNAL]
Lev 18:20 **lie c** with thy 2233+5414+7903+3807.1
19:20 **lieth c with** a woman that 854+2233+7901+7902
Nu 5:13 a **man** lie with her **c**, and it be 376+2233+7902
Ro 8: 6 For to be **c** minded *is* death; *4561*

CARNELIAN See SARDINE

CARPENTER (3) [CARPENTER'S, CARPENTERS]
Isa 41: 7 So the **c** encouraged the goldsmith, *and* 2796
44:13 The **c** stretcheth out *his* rule; 2796+6086
Mk 6: 3 Is not this the **c**, the son of Mary, *5045*

CARPENTER'S (1) [CARPENTER]
Mt 13:55 Is not this the **c** son? is not his mother *5045*

CARPENTERS (9) [CARPENTER]
2Sa 5:11 and cedar trees, and **c**, and masons: 2796+6086
2Ki 12:11 they laid it out to the **c** and builders, 2796+6086
22: 6 Unto **c**, and builders, and masons, and 2796
1Ch 14: 1 timber of cedars, with masons and **c**, 2796+6086
2Ch 24:12 and **c** to repair the house of the LORD, 2796
Ezr 3: 7 money also unto the masons, and to the **c**; 2796
Jer 24: 1 with the **c** and smiths, from Jerusalem, and 2796
29: 2 and Jerusalem, and the **c**, and the smiths, 2796
Zec 1:20 And the LORD shewed me four **c**. 2796

CARPUS (1)
2Ti 4:13 The cloke that I left at Troas with **C**, *2591*

CARRIAGE (3) [CARRIAGES]
Jdg 18:21 and the cattle and the **c** before them. 3520
1Sa 17:22 David left his **c** in the hand of the keeper of 3627
17:22 carriage in the hand of the keeper of the **c**, 3627

CARRIAGES (3) [CARRIAGE]
Isa 10:28 at Michmash he hath laid up his **c**: 3627
46: 1 your **c** *were* heavy loaden; *they are* a 5385
Ac 21:15 And after those days we **took up** our **c**, and *643*

CARRIED (145) [CARRY]
Ge 31:18 he **c away** all his cattle, and all his goods 5090
31:26 **c away** my daughters, as captives taken 5090
46: 5 the sons of Israel **c** Jacob their father, and 5375
50:13 For his sons **c** him into the land of Canaan, 5375
Lev 10: 5 and **c** them in their coats out of the camp; 5375
Jos 4: 8 **c** them **over** with them unto the place 5674
Jdg 16: 3 **c** them **up** to the top of a hill that *is* before 5927
1Sa 5: 8 Let the ark of the God of Israel be **c about** 5437
5: 8 they **c** the ark of the God of Israel **about** 5437
5: 9 it was *so,* that after they had **c** it **about**, 5437
30: 2 but **c** *them* **away**, and went on their way. 5090
30:18 all that the Amalekites had **c away**: 3947
2Sa 6:10 David **c** it **aside** *into* the house of 5186
15:29 Abiathar **c** the ark of God **again** *to* 7725
1Ki 8:47 in the land whither they were **c captives**, 7617
8:47 in the land of them *that* **c** them **captives**, 7617
8:50 before them who **c** them **captive**, 7617
17:19 **c** him **up** into a loft, where he abode, and 5927
21:13 they **c** him **forth** out of the city, and 3318
2Ki 7: 8 **c** thence silver, and gold, and raiment, and 5375
7: 8 and **c** thence *also,* and went and hid *it.* 5375
9:28 his servants **c** him *in a chariot* to Jerusalem, 7392
15:29 of Naphtali, and **c** them **captive** to Assyria. 1540
16: 9 **c** *the people of* it **captive** to Kir, and slew 1540
17: 6 **c** Israel **away** into Assyria, and placed them 1540
17:11 whom the LORD **c away** before them; 1540
17:23 So was Israel **c away** out of their own land 1540
17:28 one of the priests whom they had **c away** 1540
17:33 the nations whom they **c away** from thence. 1540
20:17 store unto this day, shall be **c** unto Babylon: 5375
23: 4 and **c** the ashes of them *unto* Beth-el. 5375
23:30 his servants **c** him *in a chariot* dead from 7392
24:13 he **c out** thence all the treasures of 3318
24:14 he **c away** all Jerusalem, and all 1540
24:15 he **c away** Jehoiachin to Babylon, and 1540
24:15 *those* **c** he *into* captivity from Jerusalem to 1980
25: 7 with fetters of brass, and **c** him *to* Babylon. 935
25:13 and **c** the brass of them to Babylon. 5375
25:21 So Judah was **c away** out of their land. 1540
1Ch 5: 6 king of Assyria **c away captive**: 1540
5:26 he **c** them **away**, even the Reubenites, and 1540
6:15 *captivity,* when the LORD **c away** Judah 1540
9: 1 *who* were **c away** to Babylon for their 1540
13: 7 they **c** the ark of God in a new cart out of 7392
13:13 **c** it **aside** into the house of Obed-edom 5186
2Ch 6:37 in the land whither they are **c captive**, 7617
6:38 whither they have **c** them **captives**, and 7617
12: 9 he **c away** also the shields of gold which 3947
14:13 his host; and they **c away** very much spoil. 5375
14:15 **c away** sheep and camels in abundance, 7617
16: 6 they **c away** the stones of Ramah, and 5375
21:17 **c away** all the substance that was found in 7617
24:11 and took it, and **c** it to his place **again**. 7725
28: 5 **c away** a great multitude of them **captives**, 7617+7633
28: 8 the children of Israel **c away captive** of 7617
28:15 **c** all the feeble of them upon asses, 5095
28:17 and smitten Judah, and **c away** captives. 7617
33:11 him with fetters, and **c** him to Babylon. 1980
34:16 Shaphan **c** the book to the king, and 935
36: 4 Jehoahaz his brother, and **c** him to Egypt. 935
36: 7 Nebuchadnezzar also **c** of the vessels of 935
36:20 from the sword **c** he **away** to Babylon; 1540
Ezr 2: 1 *of* **those** which had been **c away**, 1473
2: 1 king of Babylon had **c away** unto Babylon, 1540
5:12 and **c** the people **away** into Babylon. 1541
8:35 the children of those that had been **c away**, 1473
9: 4 of those that had been **c away**; 1473
10: 6 of **them** that had been **c away**. 1473
10: 8 of **those** that had been **c away**. 1473
Ne 7: 6 *of* **those** that had been **c away**, 1473
7: 6 the king of Babylon had **c away**, 1540
Est 2: 6 Who had been **c away** from Jerusalem with 1540
2: 6 been **c away** with Jeconiah king of Judah, 1540
2: 6 the king of Babylon had **c away**. 1540
Job 1:17 have **c** them **away**, yea, and slain 3947
5:13 the counsel of the froward is **c headlong**. 4116
10:19 I should have been **c** from the womb to 2986
Ps 46: 2 though the mountains be **c** into the midst of 4131
106:46 be pitied of all those that **c** them **captives**. 7617
137: 3 For there they that **c** us **away captive** 7617
Isa 39: 6 store until this day, shall be **c** *to* Babylon: 5375
46: 3 from the belly, which are **c** from the womb: 5375
49:22 thy daughters shall be **c** upon *their* 5375
53: 4 he hath borne our griefs, and **c** our sorrows: 5445
63: 9 bare them, and **c** them all the days of old. 5375
Jer 13:17 the LORD'S flock is **c away captive**. 7617
13:19 Judah shall be **c away captive** all of it, 1540
13:19 all of it, it shall be wholly **c away captive**. 1540
24: 1 **c away captive** Jeconiah the son of 1540
24: 5 them that are **c away captive** of Judah, 1546
27:20 when he **c away captive** Jeconiah the son 1540
27:22 They shall be **c** to Babylon, and there shall 935
28: 3 from this place, and **c** them *to* Babylon: 935
28: 6 all that is **c away captive**, from Babylon 1473
29: 1 of the elders which were **c away captives**, 1473
29: 1 **c away captive** from Jerusalem to 1540
29: 4 of Israel, unto all that are **c away captives**, 1473
29: 4 whom I have **caused to be c away** from 1540
29: 7 I have **caused** you **to be c away captives**, 1540
29:14 whence I **caused** you **to be c away captive**. 1540
39: 9 **c away captive** *into* Babylon the remnant 1540
40: 1 all that were **c away captive** of Jerusalem 1546
40: 1 which were **c away captive** unto Babylon. 1540
40: 7 of *them* that were not **c away captive** to 1540
41:10 Ishmael **c away captive** all the residue of 7617
41:10 the son of Nethaniah **c** them **away captive**, 7617
41:14 **c away captive** from Mizpah cast about 7617
52: 9 **c** him **up** unto the king of Babylon to 5927
52:11 **c** him to Babylon, and put him in prison till 935
52:15 **c away captive** *certain* of the poor of 1540
52:17 and **c** all the brass of them to Babylon. 5375
52:27 Thus Judah was **c away captive** out of his 1540
52:28 whom Nebuchadrezzar **c away captive**: 1540
52:29 **c away captive** from Jerusalem eight 1540
52:30 **c away captive** *of* the Jews seven hundred 1540
Eze 6: 9 nations whither they shall be **c captives**, 7617
17: 4 young twigs, and **c** it into a land of traffick; 935
37: 1 **c** me **out** in the spirit of the LORD, and 3318
Da 1: 2 which he **c** *into* the land of Shinar *to* 935
2:35 the wind **c** them **away**, that no place was 5376
Hos 10: 6 It shall be also **c** unto Assyria *for* a present 2986

Hos 12: 1 with the Assyrians, and oil is **c** into Egypt. 2986
Joel 3: 5 have **c** **into** your temples my goodly pleasant 935
Am 1: 6 they **c** **away captive** the whole captivity, 1540
Ob 1:11 in the day that the strangers **c** **away captive** 7617
Na 3:10 Yet *was* she **c** away, she went into 3807.1
Mt 1:11 about the time they were **c** **away** to *3350*
Mk 15: 1 and **c** *him* **away**, and delivered *him* to Pilate. *667*
Lk 7:12 behold, there was a dead man **c** **out**, *1580*
16:22 was **c** by the angels into Abraham's bosom: *667*
24:51 was parted from them, and **c** **up** into heaven. *399*
Ac 3: 2 man lame from his mother's womb was **c**, *941*
5: 6 him up, and **c** *him* **out**, and buried *him.* *1627*
7:16 And were **c** **over** into Sychem, and laid in *3346*
8: 2 And devout men **c** Stephen *to his burial,* *4792*
21:34 he commanded him to be **c** into the castle. *71*
1Co 12: 2 **c** **away** unto *these* dumb idols, *even* as ye *520*
Gal 2:13 also was **c** **away with** their dissimulation. *4879*
Eph 4:14 and **c** **about** with every wind of doctrine, *4064*
Heb 13: 9 Be not **c** **about** with divers and *4064*
2Pe 2:17 clouds that are **c** with a tempest; *1643*
Jude 1:12 *they are* without water, **c** **about** of winds; *4064*
Rev 12:15 might cause her to be **c** **away of the flood**. *4216*
17: 3 So he **c** me **away** in the spirit into *667*
21:10 And he **c** me **away** in the spirit to a great and *667*

CARRIEST (1) [CARRY]
Ps 90: 5 Thou **c** them **away as with a flood**; 2229

CARRIETH (3) [CARRY]
Job 21:18 and as chaff that the storm **c** **away**. 1589
27:21 The east wind **c** him **away**, and 5375
Rev 17: 7 and of the beast that **c** her, which hath *941*

CARRY (90) [CARRIED, CARRIEST, CARRIETH, CARRYING]
Ge 37:25 and myrrh, going to **c** *it* **down** to Egypt. 3381
42:19 go ye, **c** corn *for* the famine of your houses: 935
43:11 and **c** **down** the man a present, a little balm, 3381
43:12 of your sacks, **c** *it* **again** in your hand; 7725
44: 1 as much as they can **c**, and put every man's 5375
45:27 the wagons which Joseph had sent to **c** him, 5375
46: 5 in the wagons which Pharaoh had sent to **c** 5375
47:30 thou shalt **c** me out of Egypt, and bury me 5375
50:25 and ye shall **c** **up** my bones from hence. 5927
Ex 12:46 thou shalt not **c** **forth** *ought* of the flesh 3318
13:19 ye shall **c** **up** my bones away hence with 5927
14:11 thus with us, to **c** **us forth** out of Egypt? 3318
33:15 If thy presence go not *with me,* **c** us not **up** 5927
Lev 4:12 Even the whole bullock shall he **c** **forth** 3318
4:21 he shall **c** **forth** the bullock without 3318
6:11 **c** **forth** the ashes without the camp unto a 3318
10: 4 **c** your brethren from before the sanctuary 5375
14:45 he shall **c** *them* **forth** out of the city into an 3318
16:27 *place,* shall *one* **c** **forth** without the camp; 3318
Nu 11:12 say unto me, **C** them in thy bosom, 5375
24:22 until Asshur shall **c** thee **away captive**. 7617
Dt 14:24 for thee, so that thou art not able to **c** it; 5375
28:38 Thou shalt **c** much seed **out** *into* the field, 3318
Jos 4: 3 ye shall **c** them **over** with you, and 5674
1Sa 17:18 **c** these ten cheeses unto the captain of *their* 935
20:40 and said unto him, Go, **c** *them to* the city. 935
2Sa 15:25 **C** **back** the ark of God *into* the city: 7725
19:18 there went over a ferry boat to **c** **over** 5674
1Ki 8:46 that they **c** them **away captives** unto 7617+7617
18:12 that the spirit of the LORD shall **c** thee 5375
21:10 *then* **c** him **out**, and stone him, that he may 3318
22:26 **c** him **back** unto Amon the governor of 7725
22:34 Turn thine hand, and **c** me **out** of the host; 3318
2Ki 4:19 And he said to a lad, **C** him to his mother. 5375
9: 2 his brethren, and **c** him *to* an inner chamber: 935
17:27 **C** thither one of the priests whom ye 1980
18:11 the king of Assyria did **c** **away** Israel unto 1540
25:11 the captain of the guard **c** **away**. 1540
1Ch 10: 9 to **c** **tidings** unto their idols, and to 1319
15: 2 None ought to **c** the ark of God but 5375
15: 2 for them hath the LORD chosen to **c** 5375
23:26 *they* shall no *more* **c** the tabernacle, nor any 5375
2Ch 2:16 and thou shalt **c** it **up** *to* Jerusalem. 5927
6:36 they **c** them **away captives** unto a 7617+7617
18:25 **c** him **back** to Amon the governor of 7725
18:33 that thou mayest **c** me **out** of the host; 3318
20:25 more than they could **c** **away**: 4853
25:12 did the children of Judah **c** **away captive**, 7617
29: 5 **c** **forth** the filthiness out of the holy *place.* 3318
29:16 the Levites took *it,* to **c** *it* **out** abroad into 3318
36: 6 bound him in fetters, to **c** him to Babylon. 1980
Ezr 5:15 **c** them into the temple that *is* in Jerusalem, 5182
7:15 And to **c** the silver and gold, which the king 2987
Job 15:12 Why doth thine heart **c** thee **away**? and 3947
Ps 49:17 For when he dieth he shall **c** nothing **away**: 3947
Ecc 5:15 which he may **c** **away** in his hand. 1980
10:20 for a bird of the air shall **c** the voice, and 1980
Isa 5:29 shall **c** *it* **away safe**, and none shall deliver 6403
15: 7 shall they **c** **away** to the brook of 5375
22:17 the LORD will **c** thee **away** with a mighty 2904
23: 7 her own feet shall **c** her afar off to sojourn. 2986
30: 6 they will **c** their riches upon the shoulders 5375
40:11 **c** *them* in his bosom, *and* shall gently lead 5375
41:16 the wind shall **c** them **away**, and 5375
46: 4 *even* to hoar hairs will I **c** *you:* I have 5445
46: 4 even I will **c**, and will deliver *you.* 5445
46: 7 they **c** him, and set him in his place, and 5445
57:13 the wind shall **c** them all **away**; vanity shall 5375
Jer 17:22 Neither **c** **forth** a burden **out** of your 3318
20: 4 he shall **c** them **captive** into Babylon, and 1540
20: 5 and take them, and **c** them to Babylon. 935
39: 7 bound him with chains to **c** him to Babylon. 935
39:14 son of Shaphan, that *he* should **c** him home: 3318
43: 3 and **c** us **away captives** *into* Babylon. 1540
43:12 shall burn them, and **c** them **away captives**: 7617
La 4:22 he will no more **c** thee **away into captivity**: 1540
Eze 12: 5 the wall in their sight, and **c** **out** thereby. 3318
12: 6 *thy* shoulders, *and* **c** *it* **forth** in the twilight: 3318
12:12 they shall dig through the wall to **c** **out** 3318
22: 9 In thee are men that **c** **tales** to shed blood: 7400
38:13 to **c** **away** silver and gold, to take *away* 5375
Da 11: 8 shall also **c** captives *into* Egypt their gods, 935
Mk 6:55 began to **c** **about** in beds those that were *4064*
11:16 should **c** *any* vessel through the temple. *1308*
Lk 10: 4 **C** neither purse, nor scrip, nor shoes: and *941*
Jn 5:10 it is not lawful for thee to **c** *thy* bed. *142*
21:18 and **c** *thee* whither thou wouldest not. *5342*
Ac 5: 9 *are* at the door, and shall **c** thee **out**. *1627*
7:43 and I will **c** you **away** beyond Babylon. *3351*
1Ti 6: 7 *and it is* certain we can **c** nothing **out**. *1627*

CARRYING (8) [CARRY]
1Sa 10: 3 one **c** three kids, and another carrying three 5375
10: 3 another **c** three loaves of bread, and 5375
10: 3 of bread, and another **c** a bottle of wine: 5375
Ps 78: 9 of Ephraim, *being* armed, *and* **c** bows, 7411
Jer 1: 3 unto the **c** **away** of Jerusalem **captive** in 1540
Mt 1:17 from David until the **c** **away** into Babylon *3350*
1:17 from the **c** **away** into Babylon unto Christ *3350*
Ac 5:10 and found her dead, and, **c** *her* **forth**, *1627*

CARSHENA (1)
Est 1:14 the next unto him *was* **C**, Shethar, 3771

CART (15)
1Sa 6: 7 Now therefore make a new **c**, and take two 5699
6: 7 tie the kine to the **c**, and bring their calves 5699
6: 8 ark of the LORD, and lay it upon the **c**; 5699
6:10 tied them to the **c**, and shut up their calves 5699
6:11 they laid the ark of the LORD upon the **c**, 5699
6:14 the **c** came into the field of Joshua, 5699
6:14 they clave the wood of the **c**, and offered 5699
2Sa 6: 3 they set the ark of God upon a new **c**, and 5699
6: 3 the sons of Abinadab, drave the new **c**. 5699
1Ch 13: 7 they carried the ark of God in a new **c** out 5699
13: 7 and Uzza and Ahio drave the **c**. 5699
Isa 5:18 of vanity, and sin as it were with a **c** rope: 5699
28:27 is a **c** wheel turned about upon the cummin; 5699
28:28 nor break *it with* the wheel of his **c**, 5699
Am 2:13 as a **c** is pressed *that is* full *of* sheaves. 5699

CARVED (13) [CARVING]
Jdg 18:18 fetched the **c** **image**, the ephod, and 6459
1Ki 6:18 the cedar of the house within *was* **c** with 4734
6:29 he **c** all the walls of the house round about 7049
6:29 about *with* **c** **figures** of cherubims 4734+6603
6:32 he **c** upon them carvings of cherubims and 7049
6:35 he **c** *thereon* cherubims and palm trees and 7049
6:35 *them* with gold fitted upon the **c** **work**. 2707
2Ch 33: 7 he set a **c** **image**, the idol which he had 6459
33:22 for Amon sacrificed unto all the **c** **images** 6456
34: 3 and the **c** **images**, and the molten images. 6456
34: 4 and the **c** **images**, and the molten images, 6456
Ps 74: 6 now they break down the **c** **work** thereof at 6603

Pr 7:16 *with* **c** *works, with* fine linen of Egypt. 2405

CARVING (2) [CARVED, CARVINGS]
Ex 31: 5 of stones, to set *them,* and in **c** of timber, 2799
35:33 of stones, to set *them,* and in **c** of wood, 2799

CARVINGS (1) [CARVING]
1Ki 6:32 he carved upon them **c** of cherubims and 4734

CASE (8) [CASES]
Ex 5:19 see *that* they *were* in evil **c**, after it was said, NIH
Dt 19: 4 this *is* the **c** of the slayer, which shall flee 1697
22: 1 thou shalt **in any c bring** them **again** 7725+7725
24:13 **In any c** thou shalt **deliver** him the pledge **again** 7725+7725
Ps 144:15 Happy *is that* people, that is **in such a c**: 3602
Mt 5:20 ye shall **in no c** enter into the kingdom of *3364*
19:10 If the **c** of the man be so with *his* wife, it is *156*
Jn 5: 6 now a long time *in that c*, he saith unto him, NIG

CASEMENT (1)
Pr 7: 6 window of my house I looked through my **c**, 822

CASES (1) [CASE]
1Co 7:15 or a sister is not under bondage in such **c**: NIG

CASIPHIA (2)
Ezr 8:17 unto Iddo the chief at the place **C**, 3703
8:17 his brethren the Nethinims, at the place **C**, 3703

CASLUHIM (2)
Ge 10:14 Pathrusim, and **C**, (out of whom came 3695
1Ch 1:12 Pathrusim, and **C**, (of whom came 3695

CASLUHITES See CASLUHIM

CASSIA (3)
Ex 30:24 of **c** five hundred *shekels,* after the shekel 6916
Ps 45: 8 and aloes, *and* **c**, out of the ivory palaces, 7102
Eze 27:19 bright iron, **c**, and calamus, were in thy 6916

CAST (501) [CASTAWAY, CASTEDST, CASTEST, CASTETH, CASTING, OUTCAST, OUTCASTS] See Index

CASTAWAY (1) [AWAY, CAST]
1Co 9:27 preached to others, I myself should be a **c**. *96*

CASTEDST (1) [CAST]
Ps 73:18 *places:* thou **c** them **down** into destruction. 5307

CASTEST (3) [CAST]
Job 15: 4 thou **c off** fear, and restrainest prayer 6565
Ps 50:17 and **c** my words behind thee. 7993
88:14 LORD, why **c** thou **off** my soul? 2186

CASTETH (16) [CAST]
Job 21:10 their cow calveth, and **c** not **her calf**. 7921
Ps 147: 6 he **c** the wicked **down** to the ground. 8213
147:17 He **c forth** his ice like morsels: who can 7993
Pr 10: 3 but he **c away** the substance of the wicked. 1920
19:15 Slothfulness **c into** a deep sleep; and 5307
21:22 **c down** the strength of the confidence 3381
26:18 As a mad *man* who **c** firebrands, arrows, 3384
Isa 40:19 it over with gold, and **c** silver chains. 6884
Jer 6: 7 As a fountain **c out** her waters, so 6979
6: 7 her waters, so she **c out** her wickedness: 6979
Mt 9:34 He **c out** the devils through the prince of *1544*
Mk 3:22 by the prince of the devils **c** he **out** devils. *1544*
Lk 11:15 He **c out** devils through Beelzebub *1544*
1Jn 4:18 is no fear in love; but perfect love **c** out fear: *906*
3Jn 1:10 that would, and **c** *them* out of the church. *1544*
Rev 6:13 *even* as a fig tree **c** her untimely figs, when *906*

CASTING (21) [CAST]
2Sa 8: 2 with a line, **c** them **down** to the ground; 7901
1Ki 7:37 all of them had one **c**, one measure, *and* 4165
Ezr 10: 1 **c** himself **down** before the house of God, 5307
Job 6:21 ye see *my* **c down**, and are afraid. 2866
Ps 74: 7 they have defiled *by* **c** *down* the dwelling NIH
89:39 thou hast profaned his crown *by* **c** *it* to NIH
Eze 17:17 by **c up** mounts, and building forts, to cut 8210
Mic 6:14 thy **c down** *shall be* in the midst of thee; 3445
Mt 4:18 and Andrew his brother, **c** a net into the sea: *906*
27:35 and parted his garments, **c** lots: *906*
Mk 1:16 and Andrew his brother **c** a net into the sea: *906*
9:38 we saw one **c out** devils in thy name, and *1544*
10:50 **c away** his garment, rose, and came to Jesus. *577*
15:24 they parted his garments, **c** lots upon them, *906*
Lk 9:49 we saw one **c out** devils in thy name; *1544*
11:14 And he was **c out** a devil, and it was dumb. *1544*
21: 1 saw the rich *men* **c** their gifts into *906*
21: 2 And he saw also a certain poor widow **c** in *906*
Ro 11:15 For if the **c away** of them *be* the reconciling *580*
2Co 10: 5 **C down** imaginations, and every high thing *2507*
1Pe 5: 7 **C** all your care upon him; for he careth for *1977*

CASTLE (9) [CASTLES]
1Ch 11: 5 Nevertheless David took the **c** of Zion, 4686
11: 7 David dwelt in the **c**; therefore they called 4679
Pr 18:19 and *their* contentions *are* like the bars of a **c**. 759
Ac 21:34 he commanded him to be carried into the **c**. *3925*
21:37 And as Paul was to be led into the **c**, *3925*
22:24 commanded him to be brought into the **c**, *3925*
23:10 among them, and to bring *him* into the **c**. *3925*
23:16 he went and entered into the **c**, and *3925*
23:32 to go with him, and returned to the **c**: *3925*

CASTLES (6) [CASTLE]
Ge 25:16 their names, by their towns, and by their **c**; 2918
Nu 31:10 they dwelt, and all their **goodly c**, with fire. 2918
1Ch 6:54 places throughout their **c** in their coasts, 2918
27:25 the cities, and in the villages, and in the **c**, 4026
2Ch 17:12 he built in Judah **c**, and cities of store. 1003
27: 4 and in the forests he built **c** and towers. 1003

CASTOR (1)
Ac 28:11 in the isle, *whose* sign *was* **C and Pollux**. *1359*

CATCH (15) [CATCHETH, CAUGHT]
Ex 22: 6 **c** in thorns, so that the stacks of corn, or 4672
Jdg 21:21 **c** you every man his wife of the daughters 2414
1Ki 20:33 did hastily **c** *it:* and they said, Thy brother 2480
2Ki 7:12 we shall **c** them alive, and get into the city. 8610
Ps 10: 9 he lieth in wait to **c** the poor: he doth catch 2414
10: 9 he doth **c** the poor, when he draweth him 2414
35: 8 and let his net that he hath hid **c** himself: 3920
109:11 Let the extortioner **c** all that he hath; and 5367
Jer 5:26 setteth snares; they set a trap, they **c** men. 3920
Eze 19: 3 a young lion, and it learned to **c** the prey; 2963
19: 6 learned to **c** the prey, *and* devoured men. 2963
Hab 1:15 they **c** them in their net, and gather them in 1641
Mk 12:13 and of the Herodians, to **c** him in *his* words. *64*
Lk 5:10 Fear not; from henceforth thou shalt **c** men. *2221*
11:54 seeking to **c** something out of his mouth, *2340*

CATCHETH (3) [CATCH]
Lev 17:13 which hunteth and **c** *any* beast or fowl that 6718
Mt 13:19 **c away** that which was sown in his heart. *726*
Jn 10:12 and the wolf **c** them, and scattereth *726*

CATERPILLAR (5) [CATERPILLARS]
1Ki 8:37 blasting, mildew, locust, *or* if there be **c**; 2625
Ps 78:46 He gave also their increase unto the **c**, and 2625
Isa 33: 4 shall be gathered *like* the gathering of the **c**: 2625
Joel 1: 4 the cankerworm hath left hath the **c** eaten. 2625
2:25 and the **c**, and the palmerworm, 2625

CATERPILLARS (4) [CATERPILLAR]
2Ch 6:28 there be blasting, or mildew, locusts, or **c**; 2625
Ps 105:34 and **c**, and that without number, 3218
Jer 51:14 Surely I will fill thee *with* men, as *with* **c**; 3218
51:27 cause the horses to come up as the rough **c**. 3218

CATTLE (153)
Ge 1:24 **c**, and creeping thing, and beast of the earth 929
1:25 **c** after their kind, and every thing that 929
1:26 over the **c**, and over all the earth, and 929
2:20 Adam gave names to all **c**, and to the fowl of 929
3:14 thou *art* cursed above all **c**, and above every 929
4:20 as dwell in tents, and *of such as have* **c**. 4735
6:20 after their kind, and of **c** after their kind, 929
7:14 all the **c** after their kind, and every creeping 929
7:21 of **c**, and of beast, and of every creeping 929
7:23 **c**, and the creeping things, and the fowl of 929
8: 1 and all the **c** that *was* with him in the ark: 929
8:17 of **c**, and of every creeping thing that 929
9:10 of the **c**, and of every beast of the earth with 929
13: 2 Abram *was* very rich in **c**, in silver, and 4735
13: 7 a strife between the herdmen of Abram's **c** 4735
13: 7 Abram's cattle and the herdmen of Lot's **c**: 4735
29: 7 neither *is it* time that the **c** should be 4735

Ge 30:29 served thee, and how thy c was with me. 4735
30:32 from thence all the speckled and spotted c, 7716
30:32 all the brown c among the sheep, and 7716
30:39 brought forth c ringstraked, speckled, and 6629
30:40 put them not unto Laban's c. 6629
30:41 whensoever the stronger c did conceive, 6629
30:41 rods before the eyes of the c in the gutters, 6629
30:42 when the c were feeble, he put them not in: 6629
30:43 had much c, and maidservants, and 6629
31: 8 be thy wages; then all the c bare speckled: 6629
31: 8 be thy hire; then bare all the c ringstraked. 6629
31: 9 Thus God hath taken away the c of your 4735
31:10 it came to pass at the time that the c 6629
31:10 the rams which leaped upon the c were 6629
31:12 all the rams which leap upon the c are 6629
31:18 he carried away all his c, and all his goods 4735
31:18 which he had gotten, the c of his getting, 4735
31:41 thy two daughters, and six years for thy c: 6629
31:43 these c are my cattle, and all that thou seest 6629
31:43 these cattle are my c, and all that thou seest 6629
33:14 according as the c that goeth before me and 4399
33:17 him a house, and made booths for his c: 4735
34: 5 now his sons were with his c in the field: 4735
34:23 Shall not their c and their substance and 4735
36: 6 his c, and all his beasts, and all his 4735
36: 7 could not bear them because of their c. 4735
46: 6 they took their c, and their goods, 4735
46:32 for their trade hath been to feed c; 376+4735
46:34 Thy servants' trade hath been about c 376+4735
47: 6 then make them rulers over my c. 4735
47:16 Joseph said, Give your c; and I will give 4735
47:16 I will give you for your c, if money fail. 4735
47:17 they brought their c unto Joseph: and 4735
47:17 and for the c of the herds, and for the asses: 4735
47:17 he fed them with bread for all their c for 4735
47:18 is spent; my lord also had our herds of c; 929
Ex 9: 3 the hand of the LORD is upon thy c which 4735
9: 4 the LORD shall sever between the c of 4735
9: 4 the cattle of Israel and the c of Egypt: 4735
9: 6 on the morrow, and all the c of Egypt died: 4735
9: 6 of the c of the children of Israel died not 4735
9: 7 there was not one of the c of the Israelites 4735
9:19 and gather thy c, and all that thou hast in 4735
9:20 his servants and his c flee into the houses: 4735
9:21 left his servants and his c in the field. 4735
10:26 Our c also shall go with us; there shall not a 4735
12:29 in the dungeon; and all the firstborn of c. 929
12:38 and flocks, and herds, even very much c. 4735
17: 3 and our children and our c with thirst? 4735
20:10 nor thy maidservant, nor thy c, 929
34:19 every firstling amongst thy c, whether ox 4735
Lev 1: 2 ye shall bring your offering of the c, even of 929
5: 2 or a carcase of unclean c, or the carcase of 929
19:19 Thou shalt not let thy c gender with a diverse 929
25: 7 for thy c, and for the beast that are in thy 929
26:22 destroy your c, and make you few in 929
Nu 3:41 the c of the Levites instead of all 929
3:41 among the c of the children of Israel. 929
3:45 the c of the Levites instead of their cattle; 929
3:45 the cattle of the Levites instead of their c; 929
20: 4 that we and our c should die there? 1165
20:19 if I and my c drink of thy water, then I will 4735
31: 9 took the spoil of all their c, and all their 929
32: 1 of Gad had a very great multitude of c: 4735
32: 1 that behold, the place was a place for c; 4735
32: 4 is a land for c, and thy servants have cattle: 4735
32: 4 is a land for cattle, and thy servants have c: 4735
32:16 We will build sheepfolds here for our c, 4735
32:26 our wives, our flocks, and all our c, 929
35: 3 the suburbs of them shall be for their c, and 929
Dt 2:35 Only the c we took for a prey unto ourselves, 929
3: 7 all the c, and the spoil of the cities, we took 929
3:19 your wives, and your little ones, and your c, 4735
3:19 (for I know that ye have much c,) 4735
5:14 nor thine ox, nor thine ass, nor any of thy c, 929
7:14 female barren among you, or among your c. 929
11:15 I will send grass in thy fields for thy c, 929
13:15 and all that is therein, and the c thereof, 929
20:14 and the c, and all that is in the city, 929
28: 4 the fruit of thy ground, and the fruit of thy c, 929
28:11 in the fruit of thy c, and in the fruit of thy 929
28:51 he shall eat the fruit of thy c, and the fruit of 929
30: 9 in the fruit of thy c, and in the fruit of thy 929
Jos 1:14 Your wives, your little ones, and your c, 4735
8: 2 only the spoil thereof, and the c thereof, 929
8:27 Only the c and the spoil of that city Israel 929
11:14 all the spoil of these cities, and the c, 929
14: 4 to dwell in, with their suburbs for their c 4735
21: 2 dwell in, with the suburbs thereof for our c. 929
22: 8 with very much c, with silver, and 4735
Jdg 6: 5 For they came up with their c and 4735
18:21 put the little ones and the c and the carriage 4735
1Sa 23: 5 brought away their c, and smote them with 4735
30:20 which they drave before those other c, and 4735
1Ki 1: 9 oxen and fat c by the stone of Zoheleth, 4806
1:19 and fat c and sheep in abundance, 4806
1:25 hath slain oxen and fat c and sheep in 4806
2Ki 3: 9 the host, and for the c that followed them. 929
3:17 both ye, and your c, and your beasts. 4735
1Ch 5: 9 their c were multiplied in the land of 4735
5:21 they took away their c; of their camels fifty 4735
7:21 they came down to take away their c. 4735
2Ch 14:15 They smote also the tents of c, and 4735
26:10 for he had much c, both in the low country, 4735
35: 8 six hundred small c, and three hundred NIH
35: 9 for passover offerings five thousand small c, NIH
Ne 9:37 over our c, at their pleasure, and we are in 929
10:36 of our c, as it is written in the law, and 929
Job 36:33 the c also concerning the vapour. 4735
Ps 50:10 is mine, and the c upon a thousand hills. 929
78:48 He gave up their c also to the hail, and 1165
104:14 He causeth the grass to grow for the c, and 929
107:38 and suffereth not their c to decrease. 929
148:10 Beasts, and all c; creeping things, and 929
Ecc 2: 7 I had great possessions of great and small c 1241
Isa 7:25 of oxen, and for the treading of lesser c. 7716
30:23 in that day shall thy c feed in large 4735
43:23 Thou hast not brought me the small c of 7716
46: 1 idols were upon the beasts, and upon the c: 929
Jer 9:10 neither can men hear the voice of the c; 4735
49:32 a booty, and the multitude of their c a spoil: 4735
Eze 34:17 Behold, I judge between c and cattle, 7716
34:17 Behold, I judge between cattle and c, 7716
34:20 will judge between the fat c and 7716
34:20 the fat cattle and between the lean c. 7716
34:22 and I will judge between c and cattle. 7716
34:22 and I will judge between cattle and c. 7716
38:12 which have gotten c and goods, that dwell 4735
38:13 and gold, to take away c and goods, 4735
Joel 1:18 the herds of c are perplexed, because 1241
Jnh 4:11 and their left hand; and also much c? 929
Hag 1:11 upon c, and upon all the labour of the hands. 929
Zec 2: 4 walls for the multitude of men and c therein: 929
13: 5 for man taught me to keep c from my youth. NIH
Lk 17: 7 having a servant plowing or feeding c, 4165
Jn 4:12 thereof himself, and his children, and his c? 2353

CAUDA See CLAUDA

CAUGHT (37) [CATCH]
Ge 22:13 behold behind him a ram c in a thicket by his 270
39:12 she c him by his garment, saying, Lie with 8610
Ex 4: 4 and c it, and it became a rod in his hand: 2388
Nu 31:32 rest of the prey which the men of war had c, 962
Jdg 1: 6 c him, and cut off his thumbs and his great 270
8:14 c a young man of the men of Succoth, and 3920
15: 4 Samson went and c three hundred foxes, 3920
21:23 of them that danced, whom they c: 1497
1Sa 17:35 I c him by his beard, and smote him, and 2388
2Sa 2:16 they c every one his fellow by the head, 2388
18: 9 his head c hold of the oak, and he was 2388
1Ki 1:50 went, and c hold on the horns of the altar. 2388
1:51 he hath c hold on the horns of the altar, 270
2:28 and c hold on the horns of the altar. 2388
11:30 Ahijah c the new garment that was on him, 8610
2Ki 4:27 of God to the hill, she c him by the feet: 2388
2Ch 22: 9 and they c him, (for he was hid in Samaria,) 3920
Pr 7:13 So she c him, and kissed him, and with an 2388
Ecc 9:12 and as the birds that are c in the snare; 270
Jer 50:24 also c, because thou hast striven against 8610
Mt 14:31 and c him, and said unto him, O thou of 1949
21:39 And they c him, and cast him out of 2983
Mk 12: 3 And they c him, and beat him, and sent him 2983
Lk 8:29 For oftentimes it had c him: and he was 4884
Jn 21: 3 and that night they c nothing. 4084
21:10 Bring of the fish which ye have now c. 4084
Ac 6:12 and came upon him, and c him, and 4884
8:39 the Spirit of the Lord c away Philip, that 726

Ac 16:19 they **c** Paul and Silas, and drew *them* into *1949*
19:29 and having **c** Gaius and Aristarchus, men of *4884*
26:21 For these causes the Jews **c** me in *4815*
27:15 And when the ship was **c**, and could not *4884*
2Co 12: 2 such a one **c up** to the third heaven. *726*
12: 4 How that he was **c up** into paradise, and *726*
12:16 being crafty, I **c** you with guile. *2983*
1Th 4:17 remain shall be **c up** together with them in *726*
Rev 12: 5 and her child was **c up** unto God, and *to* his *726*

CAUL (12) [CAULS]
Ex 29:13 the **c** *that is* above the liver, and the two 3508
29:22 the **c** *above* the liver, and the two kidneys, 3508
Lev 3: 4 the **c** above the liver, with the kidneys, 3508
3:10 the **c** above the liver, with the kidneys, 3508
3:15 the **c** above the liver, with the kidneys, 3508
4: 9 the **c** above the liver, with the kidneys, 3508
7: 4 the **c** *that is* above the liver, with 3508
8:16 the **c** *above* the liver, and the two kidneys, 3508
8:25 the **c** *above* the liver, and the two kidneys, 3508
9:10 and the **c** above the liver of the sin offering, 3508
9:19 and the kidneys, and the **c** *above* the liver: 3508
Hos 13: 8 will rent the **c** of their heart, and there will I 5458

CAULS (1) [CAUL]
Isa 3:18 ornaments *about their feet,* and *their* **c**, 7636

CAUSE (328) [CAUSED, CAUSELESS, CAUSES, CAUSEST, CAUSETH, CAUSEWAY, CAUSING] See Index

CAUSED (94) [CAUSE] See Index

CAUSELESS (2) [CAUSE]
1Sa 25:31 either that thou hast shed blood **c**, or 2600
Pr 26: 2 by flying, so the curse **c** shall not come. 2600

CAUSES (7) [CAUSE] See Index

CAUSEST (2) [CAUSE] See Index

CAUSETH (32) [CAUSE] See Index

CAUSEWAY (2) [CAUSE]
1Ch 26:16 by the **c** of the going up, ward against ward. 4546
26:18 four at the **c**, *and* two at Parbar. 4546

CAUSING (4) [CAUSE]
SS 7: 9 **c** the lips of *those that are* asleep **to speak**. 1680
Isa 30:28 in the jaws of the people, **c** *them* **to err**. 8582
Jer 29:10 in **c** you **to return** to this place. 7725
33:12 of shepherds **c** *their* flocks **to lie down**. 7257

CAVE (33) [CAVE'S, CAVES]
Ge 19:30 he dwelt in a **c**, he and his two daughters. 4631
23: 9 That he may give me the **c** of Machpelah, 4631
23:11 and the **c** that *is* therein, I give it thee; 4631
23:17 the **c** which *was* therein, and all the trees 4631
23:19 Abraham buried Sarah his wife in the **c** of 4631
23:20 the field, and the **c** that *is* therein, were 4631
25: 9 Ishmael buried him in the **c** of Machpelah, 4631
49:29 bury me with my fathers in the **c** that *is* in 4631
49:30 In the **c** that *is* in the field of Machpelah, 4631
49:32 of the **c** that *is* therein *was* from 4631
50:13 buried him in the **c** of the field of 4631
Jos 10:16 and hid themselves in a **c** at Makkedah. 4631
10:17 The five kings are found hid in a **c** at 4631
10:18 Roll great stones upon the mouth of the **c**, 4631
10:22 Open the mouth of the **c**, and bring out 4631
10:22 out those five kings unto me out of the **c**. 4631
10:23 forth those five kings unto him out of the **c**, 4631
10:27 cast them into the **c** wherein they had been 4631
1Sa 22: 1 and escaped to the **c** Adullam: 4631
24: 3 the sheepcotes by the way, where *was* a **c**; 4631
24: 3 and his men remained in the sides of the **c**. 4631
24: 7 Saul rose up out of the **c**, and went on *his* 4631
24: 8 went out of the **c**, and cried after Saul, 4631
24:10 thee to day into mine hand in the **c**: 4631
2Sa 23:13 in the harvest time unto the **c** of Adullam: 4631
1Ki 18: 4 hid them *by* fifty in a **c**, and fed them *with* 4631
18:13 of the LORD'S prophets by fifty in a **c**, 4631
19: 9 he came thither unto a **c**, and lodged there; 4631
19:13 and stood *in* the entering in of the **c**. 4631
1Ch 11:15 to the rock to David, into the **c** of Adullam; 4631
Ps 57: T of David, when he fled from Saul in the **c**. 4631
142: T of David; A Prayer when he was in the **c**. 4631
Jn 11:38 It was a **c**, and a stone lay upon it. *4693*

CAVE'S (1) [CAVE]
Jos 10:27 laid great stones in the **c** mouth, 4631

CAVES (6) [CAVE]
Jdg 6: 2 in the mountains, and **c**, and strong holds. 4631
1Sa 13: 6 the people did hide themselves in **c**, and 4631
Job 30: 6 *in* **c** of the earth, and *in* the rocks. 2356
Isa 2:19 into the **c** of the earth, for fear of 4247
Eze 33:27 and in the **c** shall die of the pestilence. 4631
Heb 11:38 and *in* dens and **c** of the earth. *3692*

CEASE (70) [CEASED, CEASETH, CEASING]
Ge 8:22 and winter, and day and night shall not **c**. 7673
Ex 9:29 *and* the thunder shall **c**, neither shall there 2308
Nu 8:25 from the age of fifty years they shall **c** 7725
11:25 upon them, they prophesied, and did not **c**. 3254
17: 5 I will **make to c** from me the murmurings 7918
Dt 15:11 For the poor shall never **c** out of the land: 2308
32:26 **make** the remembrance of them **to c** from 7673
Jos 22:25 shall your children **make** our children **c** 7673
Jdg 15: 7 I be avenged of you, and after *that* I will **c**. 2308
20:28 of Benjamin my brother, or shall I **c**? 2308
1Sa 7: 8 **C** not to cry unto the LORD our God for 2790
2Ch 16: 5 off building of Ramah, and let his work **c**. 7673
Ezr 4:21 now commandment to **cause** these men **to c**, 989
4:23 and **made** them **to c** by force and power. 989
5: 5 that they could not **cause** them **to c**, till 989
Ne 4:11 and slay them, and **cause** the work **to c**. 7673
6: 3 why should the work **c**, whilst I leave it, 7673
Job 3:17 There the wicked **c** *from* troubling; and 2308
10:20 **c** then, and let me alone, that I may take 2308
14: 7 that the tender branch thereof will not **c**. 2308
Ps 37: 8 **C** from anger, and forsake wrath: fret not 7503
46: 9 He **maketh** wars **to c** unto the end of 7673
85: 4 and **cause** thine anger towards us **to c**. 6565
89:44 Thou hast **made** his glory **to c**, and cast his 7673
Pr 18:18 The lot **causeth** contentions **to c**, and 7673
19:27 **C**, my son, to hear the instruction *that* 2308
20: 3 *It is* an honour for a man to **c** from strife: 7674
22:10 go out; yea, strife and reproach shall **c**. 7673
23: 4 not to be rich: **c** from thine own wisdom. 2308
Ecc 12: 3 and the grinders **c** because they are few, and 988
Isa 1:16 doings from before mine eyes; **c** to do evil; 2308
2:22 **C** ye from man, whose breath *is* in his 2308
10:25 the indignation shall **c**, and mine anger in 3615
13:11 will **cause** the arrogancy of the proud **to c**, 7673
16:10 I have **made** *their vintage* shouting **to c**. 7673
17: 3 The fortress also shall **c** from Ephraim, and 7673
21: 2 all the sighing thereof have I **made to c**. 7673
30:11 **cause** the Holy One of Israel **to c** from 7673
33: 1 when thou shalt **c** to spoil, thou shalt be 8552
Jer 7:34 will I **cause to c** from the cities of Judah, 7673
14:17 *with* tears night and day, and let them not **c**: 1820
16: 9 I will **cause to c** out of this place in your 7673
17: 8 neither shall **c** from yielding fruit. 4185
31:36 the seed of Israel also shall **c** from being a 7673
36:29 shall **cause to c** from thence man and 7673
48:35 Moreover I will **cause to c** in Moab, 7673
La 2:18 no rest; let not the apple of thine eye **c**. 1826
Eze 6: 6 your idols may be broken and **c**, and 7673
7:24 will also **make** the pomp of the strong **to c**; 7673
12:23 I will **make** this proverb **to c**, and 7673
16:41 I will **cause** thee **to c** from playing 7673
23:27 Thus will I **make** thy lewdness **to c** from 7673
23:48 Thus will I **cause** lewdness **to c** out of 7673
26:13 I will **cause** the noise of thy songs **to c**; 7673
30:10 **make** the multitude of Egypt **to c** by 7673
30:13 I will **cause** *their* images **to c** out of Noph; 7673
30:18 the pomp of her strength shall **c** in her: 7673
33:28 the pomp of her strength shall **c**; 7673
34:10 and **cause** them **to c** from feeding the flock; 7673
34:25 will **cause** the evil beasts **to c** out of 7673
Da 9:27 **cause** the sacrifice and the oblation **to c**, 7673
11:18 **cause** the reproach offered by him **to c**; 7673
Hos 1: 4 will **cause to c** the kingdom of the house of 7673
2:11 I will also **cause** all her mirth **to c**, her feast 7673
Am 7: 5 said I, O Lord GOD, **c**, I beseech thee: 2308
Ac 13:10 wilt thou not **c** to pervert the right ways of *3973*
1Co 13: 8 whether *there be* tongues, they shall **c**; *3973*
Eph 1:16 **C** not to give thanks for you, *3973*
Col 1: 9 since the day we heard *it,* do not **c** to pray *3973*
2Pe 2:14 full of adultery and that **cannot c from** sin; *180*

CEASED (33) [CEASE]
Ge 18:11 it **c** to be with Sarah after the manner of 2308
Ex 9:33 the thunders and hail **c**, and the rain was 2308
9:34 and the hail and the thunders were **c**, 2308
Jos 5:12 the manna **c** on the morrow after they had 7673
Jdg 2:19 they **c** not from their own doings, nor from 5307
5: 7 *The inhabitants of* the villages **c**, 2308
5: 7 they **c** in Israel, until that I Deborah arose, 2308
1Sa 2: 5 for bread; and *they that were* hungry **c**: 2308
25: 9 those words in the name of David, and **c**. 5117
Ezr 4:24 **c** the work of the house of the God which *is* 989
4:24 So it **c** unto the second year of the reign of 989
Job 32: 1 So these three men **c** to answer Job, 7673
Ps 35:15 I knew *it* not; they did tear *me*, and **c** not: 1826
77: 2 my sore ran in the night, and **c** not: my soul 6313
Isa 14: 4 and say, How hath the oppressor **c**! 7673
14: 4 the oppressor ceased! the golden city **c**! 7673
La 5:14 The elders have **c** from the gate, the young 7673
5:15 The joy of our heart is **c**; our dance is 7673
Jnh 1:15 into the sea: and the sea **c** from her raging. 5975
Mt 14:32 they were come into the ship, the wind **c**. *2869*
Mk 4:39 And the wind **c**, and there was a great calm. *2869*
6:51 up unto them into the ship; and the wind **c**: *2869*
Lk 7:45 time I came in hath not **c** to kiss my feet. *1257*
8:24 the water: and they **c**, and there was a calm. *3973*
11: 1 when he **c**, one of his disciples said unto *3973*
Ac 5:42 they **c** not to teach and preach Jesus Christ. *3973*
20: 1 And after the uproar was **c**, Paul called unto *3973*
20:31 that *by the space of* three years I **c** not to *3973*
21:14 we **c**, saying, The will of the Lord be done. *2270*
Gal 5:11 then is the offence of the cross **c**. *2673*
Heb 4:10 he also hath **c** from his own works, as God *2664*
10: 2 then would they not have **c** to be offered? *3973*
1Pe 4: 1 for he that hath suffered in the flesh hath **c** *3973*

CEASETH (10) [CEASE]
Ps 12: 1 Help, LORD; for the godly *man* **c**; for 1584
49: 8 of their soul is precious, and it **c** for ever:) 2308
Pr 26:20 so where *there is* no talebearer, the strife **c**. 8367
Isa 16: 4 the extortioner is at an end, the spoiler **c**, 3615
24: 8 The mirth of tabrets **c**, the noise of them 7673
24: 8 that rejoice endeth, the joy of the harp **c**. 7673
33: 8 highways lie waste, the wayfaring man **c**: 7673
La 3:49 Mine eye trickleth down, and **c** not, without 1820
Hos 7: 4 *who* **c** from raising after *he* hath kneaded 7673
Ac 6:13 This man **c** not to speak blasphemous *3973*

CEASING (7) [CEASE]
1Sa 12:23 sin against the LORD in **c** to pray for you: 2308
Ac 12: 5 prayer was made **without c** of the church *1618*
Ro 1: 9 that **without c** I make mention of you, *89*
1Th 1: 3 Remembering **without c** your work of faith, *89*
2:13 For this cause also thank we God **without c**, *89*
5:17 Pray **without c**. *89*
2Ti 1: 3 that **without c** I have remembrance of thee in *88*

CEDAR (51) [CEDARS]
Lev 14: 4 clean, and **c** wood, and scarlet, and hyssop: 730
14: 6 the **c** wood, and the scarlet, and the hyssop, 730
14:49 and **c** wood, and scarlet, and hyssop: 730
14:51 he shall take the **c** wood, and the hyssop, 730
14:52 with the **c** wood, and with the hyssop, and 730
Nu 19: 6 the priest shall take **c** wood, and hyssop, 730
24: 6 *and* as **c trees** beside the waters. 730
2Sa 5:11 and **c** trees, and carpenters, and masons: 730
7: 2 I dwell in a house of **c**, but the ark of God 730
7: 7 Why build ye not me a house of **c**? 730
1Ki 4:33 from the **c tree** that *is* in Lebanon even unto 730
5: 6 command thou that they hew me **c trees** out 730
5: 8 will do all thy desire concerning timber of **c**, 730
5:10 So Hiram gave Solomon **c** trees and fir trees 730
6: 9 the house with beams and boards of **c**. 730
6:10 they rested on the house with timber of **c**. 730
6:15 walls of the house within with boards of **c**, 730
6:16 both the floor and the walls with boards of **c**: 730
6:18 the **c** of the house within *was* carved with 730
6:18 all *was* **c**; there was no stone seen. 730
6:20 and *so* covered the altar *which was of* **c**. 730
6:36 rows of hewed stone, and a row of **c** beams. 730
7: 2 thirty cubits, upon four rows of **c** pillars, 730
7: 2 cedar pillars, with **c** beams upon the pillars. 730
7: 3 *it was* covered with **c** above upon the beams, 730
7: 7 *it was* covered with **c** from one side of 730
7:12 a row of **c** beams, both for the inner court of 730
9:11 of Tyre had furnished Solomon with **c** trees 730
2Ki 14: 9 The thistle that *was* in Lebanon sent to the **c** 730
19:23 will cut down the tall **c trees** thereof, *and* 730
1Ch 22: 4 Also **c** trees in abundance: for the Zidonians 730
22: 4 they of Tyre brought much **c** wood to David. 730
2Ch 1:15 **c trees** made he as the sycomore trees that 730
2: 8 Send me also **c** trees, fir trees, and 730
9:27 **c trees** made he as the sycomore trees that 730
25:18 The thistle that *was* in Lebanon sent to the **c** 730
Ezr 3: 7 to bring **c** trees from Lebanon to the sea of 730
Job 40:17 He moveth his tail like a **c**: the sinews of his 730
Ps 92:12 palm tree: he shall grow like a **c** in Lebanon. 730
SS 1:17 The beams of our house *are* **c**, *and* 730
8: 9 a door, we will inclose her with boards of **c**. 730
Isa 41:19 I will plant in the wilderness the **c**, 730
Jer 22:14 *it is* cieled with **c**, and painted with 730
22:15 thou reign, because thou closest *thyself* in **c**? 730
Eze 17: 3 and took the highest branch of the **c**: 730
17:22 also take of the highest branch of the high **c**, 730
17:23 and bear fruit, and be a goodly **c**: 730
27:24 bound with cords, and **made of c**, 729
31: 3 the Assyrian *was* a **c** in Lebanon with fair 730
Zep 2:14 for he shall uncover the **c work**. 731
Zec 11: 2 Howl, fir tree; for the **c** is fallen; because 730

CEDARS (24) [CEDAR]
Jdg 9:15 of the bramble, and devour the **c** of Lebanon. 730
1Ki 7:11 after the measures of hewed stones, and **c**. 730
10:27 **c** made he *to be* as the sycomore trees that 730
1Ch 14: 1 and timber of **c**, with masons and carpenters, 730
17: 1 I dwell in a house of **c**, but the ark of 730
17: 6 Why have ye not built me a house of **c**? 730
2Ch 2: 3 didst send him **c** to build him a house to 730
Ps 29: 5 The voice of the LORD breaketh the **c**; yea, 730
29: 5 yea, the LORD breaketh the **c** of Lebanon. 730
80:10 the boughs thereof *were like* the goodly **c**. 730
104:16 The trees of the LORD are full *of sap;* the **c** 730
148: 9 all hills; fruitful trees, and all **c**: 730
SS 5:15 *is* as Lebanon, excellent as the **c**. 730
Isa 2:13 And upon all the **c** of Lebanon, that are high 730
9:10 cut down, but we will change *them into* **c**. 730
14: 8 trees rejoice at thee, *and* the **c** of Lebanon, 730
37:24 I will cut down the tall **c** thereof, *and* 730
44:14 *He* heweth him down **c**, and taketh 730
Jer 22: 7 they shall cut down thy choice **c**, and 730
22:23 of Lebanon, that makest thy nest in the **c**, 730
Eze 27: 5 they have taken **c** from Lebanon to make 730
31: 8 The **c** in the garden of God could not hide 730
Am 2: 9 whose height *was* like the height of the **c**, 730
Zec 11: 1 O Lebanon, that the fire may devour thy **c**. 730

CEDRON (1)
Jn 18: 1 forth with his disciples over the brook **C**, *2748*

CELEBRATE (3)
Lev 23:32 unto even, shall ye **c** your **sabbath**. 7673+7676
23:41 ye shall **c** it in the seventh month. 2287
Isa 38:18 cannot praise thee, death can *not* **c** thee: 1984

CELESTIAL (2)
1Co 15:40 *There are* also **c** bodies, and *2032*
15:40 but the glory of the **c** *is* one, and the *glory* *2032*

CELLARS (2)
1Ch 27:27 for the wine **c** *was* Zabdi the Shiphmite: 214
27:28 the Gederite: and over the **c** of oil *was* Joash: 214

CENCHREA (3)
Ac 18:18 having shorn *his* head in **C**: for he had a *2747*
Ro 16: 1 is a servant of the church which is at **C**: *2747*
16: S *sent* by Phebe servant of the church at **C**. *2747*

CENSER (12) [CENSERS]
Lev 10: 1 took either of them his **c**, and put fire 4289
16:12 he shall take a **c** full of burning coals of fire 4289
Nu 16:17 take every man his **c**, and put incense in 4289
16:17 ye before the LORD every man his **c**, 4289
16:17 thou also, and Aaron, each *of you* his **c**. 4289
16:18 they took every man his **c**, and put fire in 4289
16:46 Take a **c**, and put fire therein from off 4289
2Ch 26:19 and *had* a **c** in his hand to burn incense: 4730
Eze 8:11 with every man his **c** in his hand; 4730
Heb 9: 4 Which had the golden **c**, and the ark of *2369*
Rev 8: 3 and stood at the altar, having a golden **c**; *3031*
8: 5 And the angel took the **c**, and filled it with *3031*

C

CENSERS (8) [CENSER]
Nu 4:14 *even* the c, the fleshhooks, and the shovels, 4289
16: 6 Take you c, Korah, and all his company; 4289
16:17 man his censer, two hundred and fifty c; 4289
16:37 that he take up the c out of the burning, and 4289
16:38 The c of these sinners against their own 4289
16:39 Eleazar the priest took the brasen c, 4289
1Ki 7:50 and the spoons, and the c *of* pure gold; 4289
2Ch 4:22 the basons, and the spoons, and the c, 4289

CENSUS See NUMBER; SUM; TAXING

CENTURION (20) [CENTURION'S, CENTURIONS]
Mt 8: 5 there came unto him a c, beseeching him, *1543*
8: 8 The c answered and said, Lord, I am not *1543*
8:13 And Jesus said unto the c, Go thy way; and *1543*
27:54 Now when the c, and they that were with *1543*
Mk 15:39 And when the c, which stood over against *2760*
15:44 and calling unto *him* the c, he asked him *2760*
15:45 And when he knew *it* of the c, he gave *2760*
Lk 7: 6 the c sent friends to him, saying unto him, *1543*
23:47 Now when the c saw what was done, *1543*
Ac 10: 1 a c of the band called the Italian *band*, *1543*
10:22 Cornelius the c, a just man, and one that *1543*
22:25 Paul said unto the c that stood *by*, Is it *1543*
22:26 When the c heard *that*, he went and told *1543*
24:23 And he commanded a c to keep Paul, *1543*
27: 1 *one* named Julius, a c of Augustus' band. *1543*
27: 6 And there the c found a ship of Alexandria *1543*
27:11 Nevertheless the c believed the master and *1543*
27:31 Paul said to the c and to the soldiers, *1543*
27:43 But the c, willing to save Paul, kept them *1543*
28:16 the c delivered the prisoners to the captain *1543*

CENTURION'S (1) [CENTURION]
Lk 7: 2 And a certain c servant, who was dear unto *1543*

CENTURIONS (3) [CENTURION]
Ac 21:32 Who immediately took soldiers and c, and *1543*
23:17 Then Paul called one of the c unto *him*, and *1543*
23:23 And he called unto *him* two c, saying, *1543*

CEPHAS (6) [PETER]
Jn 1:42 thou shalt be called C, which is by *2786*
1Co 1:12 I of Apollos; and I of C; and I of Christ. *2786*
3:22 or C, or the world, or life, or death, or *2786*
9: 5 and *as* the brethren of the Lord, and C? *2786*
15: 5 And that he was seen of C, then of *2786*
Gal 2: 9 And when James, C, and John, *2786*

CEREMONIES (1)
Nu 9: 3 according to all the c thereof, shall ye keep 4941

CERTAIN (196) [CERTAINLY, CERTAINTY, UNCERTAIN]
Ge 28:11 he lighted upon a *c* place, and tarried there NIH
37:15 a *c* man found him, and behold, *he was* NIH
38: 1 turned in to a c Adullamite, whose name *was* 376
38: 2 Judah saw there a daughter of a c Canaanite, 376
Ex 16: 4 shall go out and gather a **c rate** every day, 1697
Nu 9: 6 there were *c* men, who were defiled by NIH
16: 2 with c of the children of Israel, two hundred 376
Dt 13:13 C men, the children of Belial, are gone out NIH
13:14 behold, *if it be* truth, *and* the thing c, *that* 3559
17: 4 and behold, *it is* true, *and* the thing c, 3559
25: 2 according to his fault, by a *c* number. NIH
Jdg 9:53 a c woman cast a piece of a millstone upon 259
13: 2 there was a c man of Zorah, of the family of 259
19: 1 that there was a c Levite sojourning on 376
19:22 behold, the men of the city, c sons of Belial, 376
Ru 1: 1 a *c* man of Beth-lehem-judah went to NIH
1Sa 1: 1 Now there was a c man of 259
21: 7 Now a *c* man of the servants of Saul *was* NIH
2Sa 18:10 And a c man saw *it*, and told Joab, and said, 259
1Ki 2:37 thou shalt **know for c** that thou shalt 3045+3045
2:42 unto thee, saying, **Know for a c**, 3045+3045
7:29 oxen *were c* additions made of thin work. NIH
11:17 c Edomites of his father's servants with him, 376
20:35 a c man of the sons of the prophets said unto 259
22:34 a *c* man drew a bow at a venture, and NIH
2Ki 4: 1 Now there cried a c woman of the wives of 259
8: 6 So the king appointed unto her a c officer, 259
1Ch 9:28 *c* of them had the charge of the ministering NIH
16: 4 he appointed *c* of the Levites to minister NIH
19: 5 there went *c*, and told David how the men NIH
2Ch 8:13 Even after a **c rate** every day, offering 1697
18: 2 after *c* years he went down to Ahab to NIH
18:33 a *c* man drew a bow at a venture, and NIH
28:12 c of the heads of the children of Ephraim, 376
Ezr 10:16 Ezra the priest, *with* c chief of the fathers, 376
Ne 1: 2 my brethren, came, he and c men of Judah; NIH
1: 4 mourned *c* days, and fasted, and NIH
11: 4 at Jerusalem dwelt *c* of the children of NIH
11:23 that a **c portion** *should be* for the singers, 548
12:35 *c* of the priests' sons with trumpets; NIH
13: 6 and after c days obtained I *leave* of the king: NIH
13:25 smote c of them, and pluckt off their hair, 376
Est 2: 5 *Now* in Shushan the palace there was a c 376
3: 8 There is a c people scattered abroad and 259
Jer 26:15 **know** ye **for c**, that if ye put me to 3045+3045
26:17 Then rose up c of the elders of the land, and 376
26:22 of Achbor, and c men with him into Egypt. NIH
41: 5 That there came c from Shechem, 376
52:15 away captive *c* of the poor of the people, NIH
52:16 Nebuzar-adan the captain of the guard left *c* NIH
Eze 14: 1 Then came c of the elders of Israel unto me, 376
20: 1 *that* c of the elders of Israel came to inquire 376
Da 1: 3 that *he* should bring *c* of the children of NIH
2:45 the dream *is* c, and the interpretation 3330
3: 8 Wherefore at that time c Chaldeans came 1400
3:12 There are c Jews whom thou hast set over 1400
8:13 another saint said unto that c *saint* which 6422
8:27 I Daniel fainted, and was sick *c* days; NIH
10: 5 looked, and behold, a c man clothed *in* linen, 259
11:13 shall certainly come after c years with a 6256
Mt 8:19 And a c scribe came, and said unto him, *1520*
9: 3 c of the scribes said within themselves, *5100*
9:18 there came a *c* ruler, and worshipped him, NIG
12:38 Then c of the scribes and of the Pharisees *5100*
17:14 there came to him a *c* man, kneeling down NIG
18:23 the kingdom of heaven likened unto a c king, *444*
20:20 and desiring a c *thing* of him. *5100*
21:28 A *c* man had two sons; and he came to NIG
21:33 There was a c householder, which planted a *5100*
22: 2 The kingdom of heaven is like unto a c king, *444*
Mk 2: 6 But there were c of the scribes sitting there, *5100*
5:25 And a c woman, which had an issue of *5100*
5:35 ruler of the synagogue's *house* c which said, NIG
7: 1 and c of the scribes, which came from *5100*
7:25 For a c woman, whose young daughter had NIG
11: 5 And c of them that stood there said unto *5100*
12: 1 A *c* man planted a vineyard, and set a hedge NIG
12:13 And they send unto him c of the Pharisees *5100*
12:42 And there came a c poor widow, and *1520*
14:51 And there followed him a c young man, *5100*
14:57 And there arose c, and bare false witness *5100*
Lk 1: 5 king of Judea, a c priest named Zacharias, *5100*
5:12 it came to pass, when he was in a c city, *1520*
5:17 And it came to pass on a c day, as he was *1520*
6: 2 And c of the Pharisees said unto them, *5100*
7: 2 And a c centurion's servant, who was dear *5100*
7:41 There was a c creditor which had two *5100*
8: 2 And c women, which had been healed of *5100*
8:20 And it was told him *by c* which said, NIG
8:22 Now it came to pass on a c day, that he *1520*
8:27 there met him out of the city a c man, *5100*
9:57 a c *man* said unto him, Lord, I will follow *5100*
10:25 a c lawyer stood up, and tempted him, *5100*
10:30 A c man went down from Jerusalem to *5100*
10:31 And by chance there came down a c priest *5100*
10:33 But a c Samaritan, as he journeyed, *5100*
10:38 they went, that he entered into a c village: *5100*
10:38 a c woman named Martha received him *5100*
11: 1 to pass *that*, as he was praying in a c place, *5100*
11:27 as he spake these *things*, a c woman of *5100*
11:37 a c Pharisee besought him to dine with him: *5100*
12:16 The ground of a c rich man brought forth *5100*
13: 6 A c *man* had a fig tree planted in his *5100*
13:31 The same day there came c *of* *5100*
14: 2 And behold, there was a c man before him, *5100*
14:16 A c man made a great supper, and *5100*
15:11 And he said, A c man had two sons: *5100*
16: 1 There was a c rich man, which had a *5100*
16:19 There was a c rich man, which was clothed *5100*
16:20 And there was a c beggar named Lazarus, *5100*
17:12 And as he entered into a c village, *5100*
18: 9 And he spake this parable unto c which *5100*
18:18 And a c ruler asked him, saying, *5100*
18:35 a c blind man sat by the way side begging: *5100*
19:12 A c nobleman went into a far country to *5100*

Lk 20: 9 A **c** man planted a vineyard, and let it forth 5100
20:27 Then came to *him* **c** of the Sadducees, 5100
20:39 Then **c** of the scribes answering said, 5100
21: 2 And he saw also a **c** poor widow casting in 5100
22:56 But a **c** maid beheld him as he sat by 5100
23:19 (Who for a **c** sedition made in the city, and 5100
24: 1 they had prepared, and **c** *others* with them. 5100
24:22 **c** women *also* of our company made us 5100
24:24 And **c** of them which were with us went to 5100
Jn 4:46 And there was a **c** nobleman, whose son 5100
5: 4 For an angel went down at a *c* season into NIG
5: 5 And a **c** man was there, which had an 5100
11: 1 Now a **c** *man* was sick, *named* Lazarus, 5100
12:20 And there were **c** Greeks among them that 5100
Ac 3: 2 And a **c** man lame from his mother's womb 5100
5: 1 But a **c** man named Ananias, with Sapphira 5100
5: 2 also being privy *to it,* and brought a **c** part, 5100
6: 9 Then there arose **c** of the synagogue, 5100
8: 9 But there was a **c** man, called Simon, 5100
8:36 on *their* way, they came unto a **c** water: 5100
9:10 And there was a **c** disciple at Damascus, 5100
9:19 Then was Saul **c** days with the disciples 5100
9:33 And there he found a **c** man named Aeneas, 5100
9:36 Now there was at Joppa a **c** disciple named 5100
10: 1 There was a **c** man in Cesarea called 5100
10:11 and a **c** vessel descending unto him, 5100
10:23 **c** brethren from Joppa accompanied him. 5100
10:48 Then prayed they him to tarry **c** days. 5100
11: 5 a trance I saw a vision, A **c** vessel descend, 5100
12: 1 forth *his* hands to vex **c** of the church. 5100
13: 1 the church that was at Antioch **c** prophets 5100
13: 6 they found a **c** sorcerer, a false prophet, 5100
14: 8 And there sat a **c** man at Lystra, impotent in 5100
14:19 And there came thither *c* Jews from Antioch NIG
15: 1 And **c** *men* which came down from Judea 5100
15: 2 and Barnabas, and **c** other of them, 5100
15: 5 But there rose up **c** of the sect of 5100
15:24 that **c** which went out from us have 5100
16: 1 and behold, a **c** disciple was there, 5100
16: 1 named Timotheus, the son of a **c** woman, 5100
16:12 and we were in that city abiding **c** days. 5100
16:14 And a **c** woman named Lydia, a seller of 5100
16:16 a **c** damsel possessed with a spirit of 5100
17: 5 took unto *them* **c** lewd fellows of the baser 5100
17: 6 and **c** brethren unto the rulers of the city, 5100
17:18 Then **c** philosophers of the Epicureans, and 5100
17:20 For thou bringest **c** strange *things* to our 5100
17:28 as **c** also of your own poets have said, 5100
17:34 Howbeit **c** men clave unto him, and 5100
18: 2 And found a **c** Jew named Aquila, born in 5100
18: 7 and entered into a **c** *man's* house, 5100
18:24 And a **c** Jew named Apollos, born at 5100
19: 1 came to Ephesus: and finding **c** disciples, 5100
19:13 Then **c** of the vagabond Jews, exorcists, 5100
19:24 For a **c** *man* named Demetrius, 5100
19:31 And **c** of the chief of Asia, which were his 5100
20: 9 And there sat in a window a **c** young man 5100
21:10 there came down from Judea a **c** prophet, 5100
21:16 There went with us also *c* of the disciples of NIG
23:12 it was day, **c** of the Jews banded together, 5100
23:17 for he hath a **c** *thing* to tell him. 5100
24: 1 and *with* a **c** orator *named* Tertullus, 5100
24:18 Whereupon **c** Jews from Asia found me 5100
24:24 And after **c** days, when Felix came with his 5100
25:13 And after **c** days king Agrippa and 5100
25:14 There is a **c** man left in bonds by Felix: 5100
25:19 But had **c** questions against him of their 5100
25:26 Of whom I have no **c** *thing* to write unto *my* *804*
27: 1 **c** other prisoners unto *one* named Julius, 5100
27:16 And running under a **c** island *which is* 5100
27:26 Howbeit we must be cast upon a **c** island. 5100
27:39 but they discovered a **c** creek with a shore, 5100
Ro 15:26 Achaia to make a **c** contribution for 5100
1Co 4:11 are buffeted, and **have no c dwelling place**; *790*
Gal 2:12 For before that **c** came from James, he did 5100
1Ti 6: 7 *and it is* **c** we can carry nothing out. *1212*
Heb 2: 6 But one in **a c place** testified, saying, *4225*
4: 4 For *he* spake in **a c place** of the seventh *4225*
4: 7 Again he limiteth a **c** day, saying in David, 5100
10:27 But a **c** fearful looking for of judgment and 5100
Jude 1: 4 For there are **c** men crept in unawares, 5100

CERTAINLY (31) [CERTAIN]

Ge 18:10 I will **c return** unto thee according 7725+7725
26:28 **saw c** that the LORD was with 7200+7200
43: 7 could we **c know** that he would say, 3045+3045
44:15 that such a man as I can **c divine**? 5172+5172
50:15 will **c requite** us all the evil which 7725+7725
Ex 3:12 he said, **C** I will be with thee; and this *shall* 3588
22: 4 If the theft be **c found** in his hand 4672+4672
Lev 5:19 hath **c trespassed** against the LORD. 816+816
24:16 the congregation shall **c stone** him: 7275+7275
Jos 9:24 Because it was **c told** thy servants, 5046+5046
Jdg 14:12 if you can **c declare** it me *within* 5046+5046
1Sa 20: 3 Thy father **c knoweth** that I have 3045+3045
20: 9 for if I **knew c** that evil were 3045+3045
23:10 thy servant hath **c heard** that Saul 8085+8085
25:28 for the LORD will **c make** my lord 6213+6213
1Ki 1:30 in my stead; even so will I **c** do this day. 3651
2Ki 8:10 unto him, Thou mayest **c recover**: 2421+2421
2Ch 18:27 If thou **c return** in peace, *then* 7725+7725
Pr 23: 5 for *riches* **c make** themselves wings; 6213+6213
Jer 8: 8 **c** in vain made he *it;* the pen of the scribes *is* 403
13:12 Do we not **c know** that every bottle 3045+3045
25:28 LORD of hosts; Ye shall **c drink**. 8354+8354
36:29 The king of Babylon shall **c come** 935+935
40:14 Dost thou **c know** that Baalis 3045+3045
42:19 **know c** that I have admonished you 3045+3045
42:22 **know c** that ye shall die by 3045+3045
44:17 we will **c do** whatsoever thing goeth 6213+6213
La 2:16 **c** this *is* the day that we looked for; we have 389
Da 11:10 *one* shall **c come**, and overflow, and 935+935
11:13 shall **c come** after certain years with a 935+935
Lk 23:47 saying, **C** this was a righteous man. *3689*

CERTAINTY (7) [CERTAIN]

Jos 23:13 **Know for a c** that the LORD your 3045+3045
1Sa 23:23 come ye again to me with the **c**, and I will 3559
Pr 22:21 That *I* might make thee know the **c** of 7189
Da 2: 8 I know of **c** that ye would gain the time, 3330
Lk 1: 4 That thou mightest know the **c** of *those* *803*
Ac 21:34 when he could not know the **c** for the tumult, *804*
22:30 he would have known the **c** wherefore he *804*

CERTIFIED (2) [CERTIFY]

Ezr 4:14 therefore have we sent and **c** the king; 3046
Est 2:22 Esther **c** the king *thereof* in Mordecai's 559

CERTIFY (5) [CERTIFIED]

2Sa 15:28 until there come word from you to **c** me. 5046
Ezr 4:16 We **c** the king that, if this city be builded 3046
5:10 We asked their names also, to **c** thee, 3046
7:24 Also *we* **c** you, that *touching* any of 3046
Gal 1:11 But I **c** you, brethren, that the gospel which *1107*

CESAR (21) [CESAR'S]

Mt 22:17 Is it lawful to give tribute unto **C**, or not? *2541*
22:21 unto **C** the *things* which are Cesar's; *2541*
Mk 12:14 Is it lawful to give tribute to **C**, or not? *2541*
12:17 Render to **C** the *things* that are Cesar's, and *2541*
Lk 2: 1 *that* there went out a decree from **C** *2541*
3: 1 the fifteenth year of the reign of Tiberius **C**, *2541*
20:22 Is it lawful for us to give tribute unto **C**, or *2541*
20:25 unto **C** the *things* which be Cesar's, *2541*
23: 2 and forbidding to give tribute to **C**, saying *2541*
Jn 19:12 maketh himself a king speaketh against **C**. *2541*
19:15 priests answered, We have no king but **C**. *2541*
Ac 11:28 came to pass in the days of Claudius **C**. *2541*
17: 7 these all do contrary to the decrees of **C**, *2541*
25: 8 against the temple, nor *yet* against **C**, *2541*
25:11 may deliver me unto them. I appeal unto **C**. *2541*
25:12 answered, Hast thou appealed unto **C**? *2541*
25:12 appealed unto Cesar? unto **C** shalt thou go. *2541*
25:21 him to be kept till I might send him to **C**. *2541*
26:32 set at liberty, if he had not appealed unto **C**. *2541*
27:24 Paul; thou must be brought before **C**: *2541*
28:19 *it,* I was constrained to appeal unto **C**; *2541*

CESAR'S (9) [CESAR]

Mt 22:21 They say unto him, **C**. Then saith he unto *2541*
22:21 unto Cesar the *things* which are **C**; *2541*
Mk 12:16 And they said unto him, **C**. *2541*
12:17 Render to Cesar the *things* that are **C**, and *2541*
Lk 20:24 hath it? They answered and said, **C**. *2541*
20:25 therefore unto Cesar the *things* which be **C**, *2541*
Jn 19:12 thou let this *man* go, thou art not **C** friend: *2541*
Ac 25:10 Then said Paul, I stand at **C** judgment seat, *2541*
Php 4:22 chiefly they that are of **C** household. *2541*

C

CESAREA (17)
Mt 16:13 When Jesus came into the coasts of **C** *2542*
Mk 8:27 his disciples, into the towns of **C** Philippi: *2542*
Ac 8:40 preached in all the cities, till he came to **C**. *2542*
9:30 they brought him down to **C**, and sent him *2542*
10: 1 There was a certain man in **C** called *2542*
10:24 And the morrow *after* they entered into **C**. *2542*
11:11 house where I was, sent from **C** unto me. *2542*
12:19 And he went down from Judea to **C**, and *2542*
18:22 And when he had landed at **C**, and gone up, *2542*
21: 8 company departed, and came unto **C**: *2542*
21:16 with us also *certain* of the disciples of **C**, *2542*
23:23 ready two hundred soldiers to go to **C**, *2542*
23:33 when they came to **C**, and delivered *2542*
25: 1 after three days he ascended from **C** to *2542*
25: 4 that Paul should be kept at **C**, and that he *2542*
25: 6 more than ten days, he went down unto **C**; *2542*
25:13 and Bernice came unto **C** to salute Festus. *2542*

CHAFED (1)
2Sa 17: 8 mighty *men,* and they *be* **c** in their minds, 4751

CHAFF (14)
Job 21:18 and as **c** that the storm carrieth away. 4671
Ps 1: 4 *are* like the **c** which the wind driveth away. 4671
35: 5 Let them be as **c** before the wind: and 4671
Isa 5:24 the flame consumeth the **c**, *so* their root 2842
17:13 shall be chased as the **c** of the mountains 4671
29: 5 ones *shall be* as **c** that passeth away: 4671
33:11 Ye shall conceive **c**, ye shall bring forth 2842
41:15 *them* small, and shalt make the hills as **c**. 4671
Jer 23:28 What *is* the **c** to the wheat? saith 8401
Da 2:35 became like the **c** of the summer 5784
Hos 13: 3 as the **c** *that* is driven with a whirlwind out 4671
Zep 2: 2 bring forth, *before* the day pass as the **c**, 4671
Mt 3:12 will burn up the **c** with unquenchable fire. *892*
Lk 3:17 the **c** he will burn with fire unquenchable. *892*

CHAIN (13) [CHAINS]
Ge 41:42 fine linen, and put a gold **c** about his neck; 7242
1Ki 7:17 of checker work, *and* wreaths of **c** work, 8333
Ps 73: 6 pride **compasseth** them **about as a c**; 6059
SS 4: 9 one of thine eyes, with one **c** of thy neck. 6060
La 3: 7 I cannot get out: he hath made my **c** heavy. 5178
Eze 7:23 Make a **c**: for the land is full *of* bloody 7569
16:11 upon thine hands, and a **c** on thy neck. 7242
Da 5: 7 *have* a **c** of gold about his neck, and 2002
5:16 *have* a **c** of gold about thy neck, and 2002
5:29 *put* a **c** of gold about his neck, and made a 2002
Ac 28:20 for the hope of Israel I am bound with this **c**. *254*
2Ti 1:16 refreshed me, and was not ashamed of my **c**: *254*
Rev 20: 1 the bottomless *pit* and a great **c** in his hand. *254*

CHAINS (37) [CHAIN]
Ex 28:14 two **c** *of* pure gold at the ends; *of* wreathen 8333
28:14 and fasten the wreathen **c** to the ouches. 8333
28:22 thou shalt make upon the breastplate **c** at 8331
28:24 thou shalt put the two wreathen *c of* gold in NIH
28:25 *the other* two ends of the two wreathen *c* NIH
39:15 they made upon the breastplate **c** at 8333
39:17 they put the two wreathen *c of* gold in NIH
39:18 the two ends of the two wreathen *c* they NIH
Nu 31:50 **c**, and bracelets, rings, earrings, and tablets, 685
Jdg 8:26 beside the **c** that *were* about their camels' 6060
1Ki 6:21 he made a partition by the **c** of gold before 7572
2Ch 3: 5 fine gold, and set thereon palm trees and **c**. 8333
3:16 he made **c**, *as* in the oracle, and put *them* on 8333
3:16 and put *them* on the **c**. 8333
Ps 68: 6 bringeth out those which are bound with **c**: 3574
149: 8 To bind their kings with **c**, and their nobles 2131
Pr 1: 9 grace unto thy head, and **c** about thy neck. 6060
SS 1:10 rows *of jewels,* thy neck with **c** *of gold.* 2737
Isa 3:19 The **c**, and the bracelets, and the mufflers, 5188
40:19 it over with gold, and casteth silver **c**. 7577
45:14 in **c** they shall come over, and they shall 2131
Jer 39: 7 bound him with **c** to carry him to Babylon. 5178
40: 1 when he had taken him being bound in **c** 246
40: 4 I loose thee *this* day from the **c** which *were* 246
52:11 the king of Babylon bound him in **c**, and 5178
Eze 19: 4 they brought him with **c** unto the land of 2397
19: 9 they put him in ward in **c**, and brought him 2397
Na 3:10 and all her great *men* were bound in **c**. 2131
Mk 5: 3 and no *man* could bind him, no, not with **c**: *254*
5: 4 he had been often bound with fetters and **c**, *254*
5: 4 and the **c** had been plucked asunder by him, *254*
Lk 8:29 and he was kept bound with **c** and in fetters; *254*
Ac 12: 6 between two soldiers, bound with two **c**: *254*
12: 7 up quickly. And his **c** fell off from *his* hands. *254*
21:33 commanded *him* to be bound with two **c**; *254*
2Pe 2: 4 and delivered *them* into **c** of darkness, *4577*
Jude 1: 6 he hath reserved in everlasting **c** under *1199*

CHALCEDONY (1)
Rev 21:19 the second, sapphire; the third, a **c**; *5472*

CHALCOL (1) [CALCOL]
1Ki 4:31 Heman, and **C**, and Darda, the sons of 3633

CHALDEA (7) [CHALDEAN, CHALDEANS, CHALDEANS', CHALDEES, CHALDEES']
Jer 50:10 **C** shall be a spoil: all that spoil her shall be 3778
51:24 to all the inhabitants of **C** all their evil that 3778
51:35 my blood upon the inhabitants of **C**, 3778
Eze 11:24 me in vision by the Spirit of God into **C**, 3778
16:29 fornication in the land of Canaan unto **C**; 3778
23:15 *after* the manner of the Babylonians of **C**, 3778
23:16 and sent messengers unto them into **C**. 3778

CHALDEAN (2) [CHALDEA]
Ezr 5:12 the **C**, who destroyed this house, 3679
Da 2:10 things at any magician, or astrologer, or **C**. 3779

CHALDEANS (66) [CHALDEA]
Job 1:17 The **C** made out three bands, and fell upon 3778
Isa 23:13 Behold the land of the **C**; this people was 3778
43:14 and the **C**, whose cry *is* in the ships. 3778
47: 1 *there is* no throne, O daughter of the **C**; 3778
47: 5 get thee into darkness, O daughter of the **C**: 3778
48:14 on Babylon, and his arm *shall be on* the **C**. 3778
48:20 Go ye forth of Babylon, flee ye from the **C**, 3778
Jer 21: 4 against the **C**, which besiege you without 3778
21: 9 falleth to the **C** that besiege you, he shall 3778
22:25 of Babylon, and into the hand of the **C**. 3778
24: 5 place *into* the land of the **C** for *their* good. 3778
25:12 the land of the **C**, and will make it 3778
32: 4 shall not escape out of the hand of the **C**, 3778
32: 5 though ye fight with the **C**, ye shall not 3778
32:24 the city is given into the hand of the **C**, 3778
32:25 for the city is given into the hand of the **C**. 3778
32:28 I *will* give this city into the hand of the **C**, 3778
32:29 the **C**, that fight against this city, 3778
32:43 or beast; it is given into the hand of the **C**. 3778
33: 5 They come to fight with the **C**, but *it is* to 3778
35:11 *to* Jerusalem for fear of the army of the **C**, 3778
37: 5 when the **C** that besieged Jerusalem heard 3778
37: 8 the **C** shall come again, and fight against 3778
37: 9 The **C** shall surely depart from us: 3778
37:10 whole army of the **C** that fight against you, 3778
37:11 *that* when the army of the **C** was broken up 3778
37:13 saying, Thou fallest away to the **C**. 3778
37:14 *It is* false; I fall not away to the **C**. 3778
38: 2 he that goeth forth to the **C** shall live; 3778
38:18 this city be given into the hand of the **C**, 3778
38:19 afraid of the Jews that are fallen to the **C**, 3778
38:23 out all thy wives and thy children to the **C**: 3778
39: 8 the **C** burnt the king's house, and 3778
40: 9 their men, saying, Fear not to serve the **C**: 3778
40:10 I *will* dwell at Mizpah to serve the **C**, 3778
41: 3 the **C** that were found there, *and* the men of 3778
41:18 Because of the **C**: for they were afraid of 3778
43: 3 for to deliver us into the hand of the **C**, 3778
50: 1 against the land of the **C** by Jeremiah 3778
50: 8 go forth out of the land of the **C**, and be as 3778
50:25 Lord GOD of hosts in the land of the **C**. 3778
50:35 A sword *is* upon the **C**, saith the LORD, 3778
50:45 he hath purposed against the land of the **C**: 3778
51: 4 Thus the slain shall fall in the land of the **C**, 3778
51:54 great destruction from the land of the **C**: 3778
52: 7 (now the **C** *were* by the city round about:) 3778
52: 8 the army of the **C** pursued after the king, 3778
52:14 all the army of the **C**, that *were* with 3778
52:17 the **C** brake, and carried all the brass of 3778
Eze 1: 3 in the land of the **C** by the river Chebar; 3778
12:13 bring him to Babylon *to* the land of the **C**; 3778
23:14 the images of the **C** pourtrayed with 3778
23:23 all the **C**, Pekod, and Shoa, and Koa, 3778
Da 1: 4 teach the learning and the tongue of the **C**. 3778
2: 2 and the sorcerers, and the **C**, 3778

Da 2: 4 spake the **C** to the king in Syriack, O king, 3778
2: 5 The king answered and said to the **C**, 3779
2:10 The **C** answered before the king, and said, 3779
3: 8 Wherefore at that time certain **C** came near, 3779
4: 7 the astrologers, the **C**, and the soothsayers: 3779
5: 7 the astrologers, the **C**, and the soothsayers. 3779
5:11 astrologers, **C**, *and* soothsayers; 3779
5:30 *was* Belshazzar the king of the **C** slain. 3778
9: 1 was made king over the realm of the **C**; 3778
Hab 1: 6 For lo, I raise up the **C**, *that* bitter and hasty 3778
Ac 7: 4 Then came he out of the land of the **C**, and *5466*

CHALDEANS' (1) [CHALDEA]
Jer 39: 5 the **C** army pursued after them, and 3778

CHALDEES (13) [CHALDEA]
Ge 11:28 in the land of his nativity, in Ur of the **C**. 3778
11:31 went forth with them from Ur of the **C**, 3778
15: 7 that brought thee out of Ur of the **C**, 3778
2Ki 24: 2 LORD sent against him bands of the **C**, 3778
25: 4 (now the **C** *were* against the city round 3778
25: 5 the army of the **C** pursued after the king, 3778
25:10 all the army of the **C**, that *were with* 3778
25:13 did the **C** break *in pieces*, and carried 3778
25:24 Fear not to be the servants of the **C**: 3778
25:25 and the **C** that were with him at Mizpah. 3778
25:26 *to* Egypt: for they were afraid of the **C**. 3778
2Ch 36:17 he brought upon them the king of the **C**, 3778
Ne 9: 7 broughtest him forth out of Ur of the **C**, 3778

CHALDEES' (1) [CHALDEA]
Isa 13:19 the beauty of the **C** excellency, 3778

CHALKSTONES (1) [STONE]
Isa 27: 9 the altar as **c** that are beaten in sunder, 68+1615

CHALLENGETH (1)
Ex 22: 9 for any manner of lost *thing*, which *another* **c** 559

CHAMBER (52) [BEDCHAMBER, CHAMBERING, CHAMBERLAIN, CHAMBERLAINS, CHAMBERS, GUESTCHAMBER]
Ge 43:30 and he entered into *his* **c**, and wept there. 2315
Jdg 3:24 Surely he covereth his feet in *his* summer **c**. 2315
15: 1 he said, I will go in to my wife into the **c**. 2315
16: 9 men lying in wait, abiding with her in the **c**. 2315
16:12 *there were* liers in wait abiding in the **c**. 2315
2Sa 13:10 Bring the meat *into* the **c**, that I may eat of 2315
13:10 brought *them* into the **c** to Amnon her 2315
18:33 went up to the **c** over the gate, and wept: 5944
1Ki 1:15 Bath-sheba went in unto the king into the **c**: 2315
6: 6 The nethermost **c** *was* five cubits broad, 3326
6: 8 The door for the middle **c** *was* in the right 6763
6: 8 up with winding stairs into the middle **c**, NIH
14:28 and brought them back into the guard **c**. 8372
17:23 brought him down out of the **c** into 5944
20:30 into the city, into an **inner c**. 2315+2315+871.1
22:25 into an **inner c** to hide thyself. 2315+2315+871.1
2Ki 1: 2 a lattice in his **upper c** that *was* in Samaria, 5944
4:10 Let us make a little **c**, I pray thee, on 5944
4:11 he turned into the **c**, and lay there. 5944
9: 2 and carry him *to* an **inner c**: 2315+2315+871.1
23:11 by the **c** of Nathan-melech the chamberlain, 3957
23:12 *were* on the top of the **upper c** of Ahaz, 5944
2Ch 12:11 and brought them again into the guard **c**. 8372
18:24 into an **inner c** to hide thyself. 2315+2315+871.1
Ezr 10: 6 went into the **c** of Johanan the son of 3957
Ne 3:30 the son of Berechiah over against his **c**. 5393
13: 4 having the oversight of the **c** of the house 3957
13: 5 he had prepared for him a great **c**, where 3957
13: 7 in preparing him a **c** in the courts of 5393
13: 8 the household stuff of Tobiah out of the **c**. 3957
Ps 19: 5 *is* as a bridegroom coming out of his **c**, 2646
SS 3: 4 and into the **c** of her that conceived me. 2315
Jer 35: 4 into the **c** of the sons of Hanan, the son of 3957
35: 4 of God, which *was* by the **c** of the princes, 3957
35: 4 which *was* above the **c** of Maaseiah the son 3957
36:10 in the **c** of Gemariah the son of Shaphan 3957
36:12 *into* the king's house, into the scribe's **c**: 3957
36:20 they laid up the roll in the **c** of Elishama 3957
36:21 he took it out of Elishama the scribe's **c**. 3957
Eze 40: 7 *every* **little c** *was* one reed long, and 8372
40:13 the gate from the roof of *one* **little c** to 8372
40:45 he said unto me, This **c**, whose prospect *is* 3957
40:46 the **c** whose prospect *is* toward the north *is* 3957
41: 5 the breadth of *every* **side c**, four cubits, 6763
41: 7 increased *from* the lowest **c** to the highest NIH
41: 9 which *was* for the **side c** without, *was* five 6763
42: 1 he brought me into the **c** that *was* over 3957
Da 6:10 his windows being open in his **c** toward 5952
Joel 2:16 let the bridegroom go forth of his **c**, and 2315
Ac 9:37 had washed, they laid *her* in an **upper c**. *5253*
9:39 they brought him into the **upper c**: *5253*
20: 8 And there were many lights in the **upper c**, *5253*

CHAMBERING (1) [CHAMBER]
Ro 13:13 not in **c** and wantonness, not in strife and *2845*

CHAMBERLAIN (6) [CHAMBER]
2Ki 23:11 by the chamber of Nathan-melech the **c**, 5631
Est 2: 3 unto the custody of Hege the king's **c**, 5631
2:14 the king's **c**, which kept the concubines: 5631
2:15 but what Hegai the king's **c**, 5631
Ac 12:20 the king's **c** their friend, *1909+2846+3588*
Ro 16:23 Erastus the **c** of the city saluteth you, and *3623*

CHAMBERLAINS (9) [CHAMBER]
Est 1:10 the seven **c** that served in the presence of 5631
1:12 come at the king's commandment by *his* **c**: 5631
1:15 of the king Ahasuerus by the **c**? 5631
2:21 two of the king's **c**, Bigthan and Teresh, 5631
4: 4 and her **c** came and told *it* her. 5631
4: 5 Esther for Hatach, *one* of the king's **c**, 5631
6: 2 and Teresh, two of the king's **c**, 5631
6:14 came the king's **c**, and hasted to bring 5631
7: 9 Harbonah, one of the **c**, said before 5631

CHAMBERS (66) [CHAMBER]
1Ki 6: 5 against the wall of the house he built **c** 3326
6: 5 of the oracle: and he made **c** round about: 6763
6:10 *then* he built **c** against all the house, 3326
1Ch 9:26 were over the **c** and treasuries of the house 3957
9:33 *who remaining* in the **c** *were* free: 3957
23:28 in the **c**, and in the purifying of all holy 3957
28:11 of the **upper c** thereof, and of the inner 5944
28:12 of all the **c** round about, of the treasuries of 3957
2Ch 3: 9 And he overlaid the **upper c** with gold. 5944
31:11 Hezekiah commanded to prepare **c** in 3957
Ezr 8:29 *in* the **c** of the house of the LORD. 3957
Ne 10:37 the priests, to the **c** of the house of our God; 3957
10:38 our God, to the **c**, into the treasure house. 3957
10:39 of the new wine, and the oil, unto the **c**, 3957
12:44 at that time were some appointed over the **c** 5393
13: 9 I commanded, and they cleansed the **c**: 3957
Job 9: 9 Orion, and Pleiades, and the **c** of the south. 2315
Ps 104: 3 Who layeth the beams of his **c** in 5944
104:13 He watereth the hills from his **c**: the earth is 5944
105:30 frogs in abundance, in the **c** of their kings. 2315
Pr 7:27 way to hell, going down to the **c** of death. 2315
24: 4 by knowledge shall the **c** be filled *with* all 2315
SS 1: 4 the king hath brought me *into* his **c**: we will 2315
Isa 26:20 enter thou into thy **c**, and shut thy doors 2315
Jer 22:13 by unrighteousness, and his **c** by wrong; 5944
22:14 I will build me a wide house and large **c**, 5944
35: 2 into one of the **c**, and give them wine to 3957
Eze 8:12 every man in the **c** of his imagery? 2315
21:14 *are* slain, which **entereth into** their **privy c**. 2314
40: 7 between the **little c** *were* five cubits; and 8372
40:10 the **little c** of the gate eastward *were* three 8372
40:12 The space also before the **little c** *was* one 8372
40:12 the **little c** *were* six cubits on this side, and 8372
40:16 *there were* narrow windows to the **little c**, 8372
40:17 lo, *there were* **c**, and a pavement made for 3957
40:17 thirty **c** *were* upon the pavement. 3957
40:21 the **little c** thereof *were* three on this side 8372
40:29 the **little c** thereof, and the posts thereof, 8372
40:33 the **little c** thereof, and the posts thereof, 8372
40:36 The **little c** thereof, the posts thereof, and 8372
40:38 the **c** and the entries thereof *were* by 3957
40:44 without the inner gate *were* the **c** of 3957
41: 6 the **side c** *were* three, one over another, 6763
41: 6 *was* of the house for the **side c** round about, 6763
41: 7 a winding about still upward to the **side c**: 6763
41: 8 the foundations of the **side c** *were* a full 6763
41: 9 *was* the place of the **side c** that *were* within. 6763
41:10 between the **c** *was* the wideness of twenty 3957
41:11 the doors of the **side c** *were* toward 6763
41:26 *upon* the **side c** of the house, and thick 6763

Eze 42: 4 before the **c** *was* a walk of ten cubits 3957
42: 5 Now the upper **c** *were* shorter: for 3957
42: 7 the wall that *was* without over against the **c**, 3957
42: 7 the utter court on the forepart of the **c**, 3957
42: 8 For the length of the **c** that *were* in the utter 3957
42: 9 from under these **c** *was* the entry on the east 3957
42:10 The **c** *were* in the thickness of the wall of 3957
42:11 of the **c** which *were* toward the north, 3957
42:12 according to the doors of the **c** that *were* 3957
42:13 The north **c** *and* the south chambers, 3957
42:13 The north chambers *and* the south **c**, 3957
42:13 before the separate place, they *be* holy **c**, 3957
44:19 lay them in the holy **c**, and they shall put on 3957
45: 5 for a possession *for* twenty **c**. 3957
46:19 into the holy **c** of the priests, which looked 3957
Mt 24:26 behold, *he is* in the **secret c**; believe *it* not. *5009*

CHAMELEON (1)
Lev 11:30 the **c**, and the lizard, and the snail, and 3581

CHAMOIS (1)
Dt 14: 5 and the pygarg, and the wild ox, and the **c**. 2169

CHAMPAIGN (1)
Dt 11:30 which dwell in the **c** over against Gilgal, 6160

CHAMPION (3)
1Sa 17: 4 there went out a **c** out of 376+1143+1886.1
17:23 behold, there came up the **c**, 376+1143+1886.1
17:51 when the Philistines saw their **c** was dead, 1368

CHANCE (6) [CHANCETH]
Dt 22: 6 If a bird's nest **c to be** before thee in 7122
1Sa 6: 9 smote us; it *was* a **c** *that* happened to us. 4745
2Sa 1: 6 As I **happened by c** upon mount Gilboa, 7122
Ecc 9:11 but time and **c** happeneth to them all. 6294
Lk 10:31 And by **c** there came down a certain priest *4795*
1Co 15:37 **it may c** of wheat, or of some other *1487+5177*

CHANCELLOR (3)
Ezr 4: 8 Rehum the **c** and Shimshai the scribe 1169+2942
4: 9 *wrote* Rehum the **c**, and Shimshai 1169+2942
4:17 king an answer unto Rehum the **c**, 1169+2942

CHANCETH (1) [CHANCE]
Dt 23:10 reason of *uncleanness* that **c** him by night, 7137

CHANGE (26) [CHANGEABLE, CHANGED, CHANGERS, CHANGERS', CHANGES, CHANGEST, CHANGETH, CHANGING, UNCHANGEABLE]
Ge 35: 2 and be clean, and **c** your garments: 2498
Lev 27:10 nor **c** it, a good for a bad, or a bad for a 4171
27:10 if he shall **at all c** beast for beast, 4171+4171
27:33 it be good or bad, neither shall he **c** it: 4171
27:33 if he **c** it **at all**, then both it and 4171+4171
27:33 both it and the **c** thereof shall be holy; 8545
Jdg 14:12 you thirty sheets and thirty **c** of garments: 2487
14:13 me thirty sheets and thirty **c** of garments. 2487
14:19 gave **c** *of garments* unto them which 2487
Job 14:14 appointed time will I wait, till my **c** come. 2487
17:12 They **c** the night into day: the light *is* short, 7760
Ps 102:26 as a vesture shalt thou **c** them, and 2498
Pr 24:21 meddle not with them that are **given to c**: 8138
Isa 9:10 cut down, but we will **c** *them into* cedars. 2498
Jer 2:36 gaddest thou about *so* much to **c** thy way? 8138
13:23 Can the Ethiopian **c** his skin, or the leopard 2015
Da 7:25 most High, and think to **c** times and laws: 8133
Hos 4: 7 *therefore* will I **c** their glory into shame. 4171
Hab 1:11 shall *his* mind **c**, and he shall pass over, 2498
Zec 3: 4 and *I will* clothe thee with **c of raiment**. 4254
Mal 3: 6 For I *am* the LORD, I **c** not; therefore 8138
Ac 6:14 shall **c** the customs which Moses delivered *236*
Ro 1:26 for even their women did **c** the natural use *3337*
Gal 4:20 be present with you now, and to **c** my voice; *236*
Php 3:21 Who shall **c** our vile body, that it may be *3345*
Heb 7:12 there is made of necessity a **c** also of *3331*

CHANGEABLE (1) [CHANGE]
Isa 3:22 The **c suits of apparel**, and the mantles, 4254

CHANGED (43) [CHANGE]
Ge 31: 7 deceived me, and **c** my wages ten times; 2498
31:41 and thou hast **c** my wages ten times. 2498
41:14 he shaved *himself*, and **c** his raiment, and 2498
Lev 13:16 be **c** unto white, he shall come unto 2015
13:55 *if* the plague have not **c** his colour, and 2015
Nu 32:38 and Baal-meon, (*their* names being **c**,) 5437
1Sa 21:13 he **c** his behaviour before them, and 8138
2Sa 12:20 and anointed *himself*, and **c** his apparel, and 2498
2Ki 24:17 in his stead, and **c** his name *to* Zedekiah. 5437
25:29 **c** his prison garments: and he did eat bread 8132
Job 30:18 great force *of my disease* is my garment **c**: 2664
Ps 34: T when he **c** his behaviour before Abimelech; 8138
102:26 shalt thou change them, and they shall be **c**: 2498
106:20 Thus they **c** their glory into the similitude 4171
Ecc 8: 1 and the boldness of his face shall be **c**. 8132
Isa 24: 5 have transgressed the laws, **c** the ordinance, 2498
Jer 2:11 Hath a nation **c** *their* gods, which *are* yet no 3235
2:11 my people have **c** their glory for *that which* 4171
48:11 taste remained in him, and his sent is not **c**. 4171
52:33 **c** his prison garments: and he did 8138
La 4: 1 *how* is the most fine gold **c**! the stones of 8132
Eze 5: 6 she hath **c** my judgments into wickedness 4784
Da 2: 9 words to speak before me, till the time be **c**: 8133
3:19 the form of his visage was **c** against 8133
3:27 head singed, neither were their coats **c**, 8133
3:28 have **c** the king's word, and yielded their 8133
4:16 Let his heart be **c** from man's, and let a 8133
5: 6 the king's countenance was **c**, and 8133
5: 9 his countenance *was* **c** in him, and his lords 8133
5:10 trouble thee, nor let thy countenance be **c**. 8133
6: 8 and sign the writing, that *it* be not **c**, 8133
6:15 which the king establisheth may be **c**. 8133
6:17 that the purpose might not be **c** concerning 8133
7:28 troubled me, and my countenance **c** in me: 8133
Mic 2: 4 he hath **c** the portion of my people: 4171
Ac 28: 6 they **c** *their minds*, and said that he was a *3328*
Ro 1:23 And **c** the glory of the uncorruptible God *236*
1:25 Who **c** the truth of God into a lie, and *3337*
1Co 15:51 We shall not all sleep, but we shall all be **c**, *236*
15:52 be raised incorruptible, and we shall be **c**. *236*
2Co 3:18 are **c** *into* the same image from glory to *3339*
Heb 1:12 shalt thou fold them up, and they shall be **c**: *236*
7:12 For the priesthood being **c**, there is made of *3346*

CHANGERS (1) [CHANGE]
Jn 2:14 and doves, and the **c of money** sitting: *2773*

CHANGERS' (1) [CHANGE]
Jn 2:15 and poured out the **c** money, and *2855*

CHANGES (7) [CHANGE]
Ge 45:22 To all of them he gave each man **c** of 2487
45:22 *pieces* of silver, and five **c** of raiment. 2487
2Ki 5: 5 *pieces* of gold, and ten **c** of raiment. 2487
5:22 a talent of silver, and two **c** of garments. 2487
5:23 with two **c** of garments, and laid *them* upon 2487
Job 10:17 upon me; **c** and war *are* against me. 2487
Ps 55:19 Because they have no **c**, therefore they fear 2487

CHANGEST (1) [CHANGE]
Job 14:20 thou **c** his countenance, and sendest him 8138

CHANGETH (2) [CHANGE]
Ps 15: 4 *He that* sweareth to *his own* hurt, and **c** not. 4171
Da 2:21 he **c** the times and the seasons: he removeth 8133

CHANGING (1) [CHANGE]
Ru 4: 7 concerning redeeming and concerning **c**, 8545

CHANNEL (1) [CHANNELS]
Isa 27:12 *that* the LORD shall beat off from the **c** of 7641

CHANNELS (3) [CHANNEL]
2Sa 22:16 the **c** of the sea appeared, the foundations of 650
Ps 18:15 the **c** of waters were seen, and 650
Isa 8: 7 he shall come up over all his **c**, and go over 650

CHANT (1)
Am 6: 5 That **c** to the sound of the viol, *and* 6527

CHAPEL (1)
Am 7:13 for it *is* the king's **c**, and it *is* the king's 4720

CHAPITER (13) [CHAPITERS]
1Ki 7:16 the height of the one **c** *was* five cubits, and 3805
7:16 the height of the other **c** *was* five cubits: 3805
7:17 seven for the one **c**, and seven for the other 3805
7:17 the one chapiter, and seven for the other **c**. 3805
7:18 and so did he for the other **c**. 3805

1Ki 7:20 *in* rows round about upon the other **c**. 3805
7:31 the mouth of it within the **c** and above *was* 3805
2Ki 25:17 eighteen cubits, and the **c** upon it *was* brass: 3805
25:17 the height of the **c** three cubits; and 3805
25:17 pomegranates upon the **c** round about, all 3805
2Ch 3:15 the **c** that *was* on the top *of each* of them 6858
Jer 52:22 a **c** of brass *was* upon it; and the height of 3805
52:22 the height of one **c** *was* five cubits, 3805

CHAPITERS (16) [CHAPITER]
Ex 36:38 he overlaid their **c** and their fillets with 7218
38:17 the overlaying of their **c** *of* silver; and all 7218
38:19 the overlaying of their **c** and their fillets *of* 7218
38:28 and overlaid their **c**, and filleted them. 7218
1Ki 7:16 he made two **c** *of* molten brass, to set upon 3805
7:17 for the **c** which *were* upon the top of 3805
7:18 to cover the **c** that *were* upon the top, *with* 3805
7:19 (And the **c** that *were* upon the top of 3805
7:20 the **c** upon the two pillars *had* 3805
7:41 the two bowls of the **c** that *were* on the top 3805
7:41 to cover the two bowls of the **c** which *were* 3805
7:42 to cover the two bowls of the **c** that *were* 3805
2Ch 4:12 the **c** *which were* on the top of the two 3805
4:12 the **c** which *were* on the top of the pillars; 3805
4:13 to cover the two pommels of the **c** which 3805
Jer 52:22 and pomegranates upon the **c** round about, 3805

CHAPMEN (1) [MAN]
2Ch 9:14 Besides *that which* **c** and merchants 376+1886.1

CHAPT (1)
Jer 14: 4 Because the ground is **c**, for there was no 2865

CHARASHIM (1)
1Ch 4:14 begat Joab, the father of the valley of **C**; 2798

CHARGE (102) [CHARGEABLE, CHARGED, CHARGEDST, CHARGES, CHARGEST, CHARGING, OVERCHARGE]
Ge 26: 5 kept my **c**, my commandments, my statutes, 4931
28: 6 that as he blessed him he **gave** him **a c**, 6680
Ex 6:13 **gave** them **a c** unto the children of Israel, 6680
19:21 said unto Moses, Go down, **c** the people, 5749
Lev 8:35 keep the **c** of the LORD, that ye die not: 4931
Nu 1:53 the Levites shall keep the **c** of 4931
3: 7 they shall keep his **c**, and the charge of 4931
3: 7 the **c** of the whole congregation before 4931
3: 8 the **c** of the children of Israel, to do 4931
3:25 the **c** of the sons of Gershon in 4931
3:28 six hundred, keeping the **c** of the sanctuary. 4931
3:31 their **c** *shall be* the ark, and the table, and 4931
3:32 *have* the oversight of them that keep the **c** 4931
3:36 **c of** the sons of Merari *shall be* the boards 4931
3:38 keeping the **c** of the sanctuary for 4931
3:38 sanctuary for the **c** of the children of Israel; 4931
4:27 ye shall appoint unto them in **c** all their 4931
4:28 their **c** *shall be* under the hand of Ithamar 4931
4:31 this *is* the **c** of their burden, according to all 4931
4:32 the instruments of the **c** of their burden. 4931
5:19 the priest shall **c** her **by an oath**, and 7650
5:21 **c** the woman **with an oath** of 7621+7650+871.1
8:26 to keep the **c**, and shall do no service. 4931
8:26 thou do unto the Levites touching their **c**. 4931
9:19 the children of Israel kept the **c** of 4931
9:23 they kept the **c** of the LORD, at 4931
18: 3 they shall keep thy **c**, and the charge of all 4931
18: 3 thy charge, and the **c** of all the tabernacle: 4931
18: 4 keep the **c** of the tabernacle of 4931
18: 5 ye shall keep the **c** of the sanctuary, and 4931
18: 5 of the sanctuary, and the **c** of the altar: 4931
18: 8 I also have given thee the **c** of mine heave 4931
27:19 and **give** him **a c** in their sight. 6680
27:23 laid his hands upon him, and **gave** him **a c**, 6680
31:30 which keep the **c** of the tabernacle of 4931
31:47 which kept the **c** of the tabernacle of 4931
31:49 of the men of war which *are* under our **c**, 3027
Dt 3:28 **c** Joshua, and encourage him, and 6680
11: 1 keep his **c**, and his statutes, and 4931
21: 8 blood unto thy people of Israel's **c**. 7130
31:14 the congregation, that I may **give** him **a c**. 6680
31:23 he **gave** Joshua the son of Nun **a c**, 6680
Jos 22: 3 have kept the **c** of the commandment of 4931
2Sa 14: 8 and I will **give c** concerning thee. 6680
18: 5 **gave** all the captains **c** concerning 6680
1Ki 2: 3 keep the **c** of the LORD thy God, to walk 4931
4:28 *officers* were, every man according to his **c**. 4941
11:28 he made him ruler over all the **c** of 5447
2Ki 7:17 hand he leaned to **have the c of** the gate: 5921
1Ch 9:27 because the **c** *was* upon them, and 4931
9:28 *certain* of them had the **c of** the ministering 5921
22:12 and **give** thee **c** concerning Israel, 6680
23:32 that they should keep the **c** of 4931
23:32 the **c** of the holy *place,* and the charge of 4931
23:32 the **c** of the sons of Aaron their brethren, 4931
2Ch 13:11 for we keep the **c** of the LORD our God; 4931
30:17 the Levites **had the c of** the killing of 5921
Ne 7: 2 **gave** my brother Hanani, and Hananiah the ruler of the palace, **c** 6680
10:32 to **c** ourselves yearly with the third *part* of a 5414
Est 3: 9 of those that have the **c** of the business, 6213
4: 8 to **c** her that *she* should go in unto the king, 6680
Job 34:13 Who hath **given** him **a c** over the earth? 6485
Ps 35:11 they **laid to** my **c** *things* that I knew not. 7592
91:11 For he shall **give** his angels **c** over thee, 6680
SS 2: 7 I **c** you, O ye daughters of Jerusalem, 7650
3: 5 I **c** you, O ye daughters of Jerusalem, 7650
5: 8 I **c** you, O daughters of Jerusalem, if ye 7650
5: 9 *another* beloved, that thou dost so **c** us? 7650
8: 4 I **c** you, O daughters of Jerusalem, that ye 7650
Isa 10: 6 the people of my wrath will I **give** him **a c**, 6680
Jer 39:11 **gave c** concerning Jeremiah to 6680
47: 7 seeing the LORD hath **given it a c** against 6680
52:25 which had the **c** of the men of war; 6496
Eze 9: 1 Cause them **that have c over** the city to 6486
40:45 the keepers of the **c** of the house. 4931
40:46 the priests, the keepers of the **c** of the altar: 4931
44: 8 ye have not kept the **c** of mine holy *things:* 4931
44: 8 ye have set keepers of my **c** in my 4931
44:11 *having* **c** at the gates of the house, and 6486
44:14 I will make them keepers of the **c** of 4931
44:15 that kept the **c** of my sanctuary when 4931
44:16 minister unto me, and they shall keep my **c**. 4931
48:11 which have kept my **c**, which went not 4931
Zec 3: 7 if thou wilt keep my **c**, then thou shalt also 4931
Mt 4: 6 He shall **give** his angels **c** concerning thee: *1781*
Mk 9:25 *Thou* dumb and deaf spirit, I **c** thee, *2004*
Lk 4:10 He shall **give** his angels **c** over thee, to keep *1781*
Ac 7:60 loud voice, Lord, **lay** not this sin **to** their **c**. *2476*
8:27 who had the **c of** all her treasure, and had *1909*
16:24 Who, having received such a **c**, thrust them *3852*
23:29 to have nothing **laid to** his **c** worthy of *1462*
Ro 8:33 Who shall **lay** any thing **to the c** of God's *1458*
1Co 9:18 I may make the gospel of Christ **without c**, *77*
1Th 5:27 I **c** you by the Lord that *this* epistle be read *3726*
1Ti 1: 3 that thou mightest **c** some that *they* teach *3853*
1:18 This **c** I commit unto thee, son Timothy, *3852*
5: 7 And these *things* **give in c**, that they may *3853*
5:21 I **c** *thee* before God, and the Lord Jesus *1263*
6:13 I **give** thee **c** in the sight of God, *3853*
6:17 **C** *them that are* rich in this world, that *they* *3853*
2Ti 4: 1 I **c** *thee* therefore before God, and the Lord *1263*
4:16 *I pray God* that it may not be **laid to** their **c**. *3049*

CHARGEABLE (5) [CHARGE]
2Sa 13:25 let us not all now go, lest we be **c** unto thee. 3513
Ne 5:15 *had been* before me were **c** unto the people, 3513
2Co 11: 9 I was **c to** no *man:* for that which was *2655*
1Th 2: 9 because *we* would not be **c** unto any of you, *1912*
2Th 3: 8 day, that *we* might not be **c** to any of you: *1912*

CHARGED (51) [CHARGE]
Ge 26:11 Abimelech **c** all *his* people, saying, He that 6680
28: 1 blessed him, and **c** him, and said unto him, 6680
40: 4 the captain of the guard **c** Joseph with 6485
49:29 he **c** them, and said unto them, I *am to be* 6680
Ex 1:22 Pharaoh **c** all his people, saying, Every son 6680
Dt 1:16 I **c** your judges at that time, saying, 6680
24: 5 shall he be **c** with any business: 5674+5921
27:11 Moses **c** the people the same day, saying, 6680
Jos 18: 8 Joshua **c** them that went to describe 6680
22: 5 which Moses the servant of the LORD **c** 6680
Ru 2: 9 have I not **c** the young men that *they* shall 6680
1Sa 14:27 when his father **c** the people **with the oath**: 7650
14:28 **straitly c** the people **with an oath**, 7650+7650
2Sa 11:19 **c** the messenger, saying, When thou hast 6680
18:12 for in our hearing the king **c** thee and 6680
1Ki 2: 1 and he **c** Solomon his son, saying, 6680
2:43 the commandment that I have **c** thee with? 6680
13: 9 so was it **c** me by the word of the LORD, 6680

2Ki 17:15 *concerning* whom the LORD had c them, 6680
17:35 c them, saying, Ye shall not fear other 6680
1Ch 22: 6 c him to build a house for the LORD God 6680
22:13 judgments which the LORD c Moses with 6680
2Ch 19: 9 he c them, saying, Thus shall ye do in 6680
36:23 he hath c me to build him a house in 6485
Ezr 1: 2 he hath c me to build him a house at 6485
Ne 13:19 c that they should not be opened till after 559
Est 2:10 for Mordecai had c her that she should not 6680
2:20 nor her people; as Mordecai had c her: 6680
Job 1:22 all this Job sinned not, nor c God foolishly. 5414
4:18 his servants; and his angels he c with folly: 7760
Jer 32:13 And I c Baruch before them, saying, 6680
35: 8 of Rechab our father in all that he hath c us, 6680
Mt 9:30 and Jesus **straitly** c them, saying, See *that* *1690*
12:16 And c them that they should not make him *2008*
16:20 Then c he his disciples that they should tell *1291*
17: 9 from the mountain, Jesus c them, saying, *1781*
Mk 1:43 And he **straitly** c him, and forthwith sent *1690*
3:12 And he straitly c them that they should not *2008*
5:43 And he c them straitly that no *man* should *1291*
7:36 And he c them that they should tell no *man:* *1291*
7:36 should tell no *man:* but the more he c them, *1291*
8:15 And he c them, saying, Take heed, *1291*
8:30 And he c them that they should tell no *man* *2008*
9: 9 he c them that they should tell no *man* what *1291*
10:48 And many c him that he should hold his *2008*
Lk 5:14 And he c him to tell no *man:* but go, and *3853*
8:56 he c them that they should tell no *man* what *3853*
9:21 And he **straitly** c them, and *2008*
Ac 23:22 c *him, See thou* tell no *man* that thou hast *3853*
1Th 2:11 and comforted and c every one of you, *3143*
1Ti 5:16 relieve them, and let not the church be c; *916*

CHARGEDST (1) [CHARGE]
Ex 19:23 for thou c us, saying, Set bounds about 5749

CHARGER (17) [CHARGERS]
Nu 7:13 his offering *was* one silver c, the weight 7086
7:19 He offered *for* his offering one silver c, 7086
7:25 His offering *was* one silver c, the weight 7086
7:31 His offering *was* one silver c of the weight 7086
7:37 His offering *was* one silver c, the weight 7086
7:43 His offering *was* one silver c of the weight 7086
7:49 His offering *was* one silver c, the weight 7086
7:55 His offering *was* one silver c of the weight 7086
7:61 His offering *was* one silver c, the weight 7086
7:67 His offering *was* one silver c, the weight 7086
7:73 His offering *was* one silver c, the weight 7086
7:79 His offering *was* one silver c, the weight 7086
7:85 Each c of silver *weighing* an hundred and 7086
Mt 14: 8 Give me here John Baptist's head in a c. *4094*
14:11 And his head was brought in a c, and *4094*
Mk 6:25 and by in a c the head of John the Baptist. *4094*
6:28 And brought his head in a c, and gave it to *4094*

CHARGERS (3) [CHARGER]
Nu 7:84 twelve c of silver, twelve silver bowls, 7086
Ezr 1: 9 thirty c of gold, a thousand chargers of 105
1: 9 a thousand c of silver, nine and 105

CHARGES (6) [CHARGE]
2Ch 8:14 the Levites to their c, to praise and minister 4931
31:16 *his* daily portion for their service in their c 4931
31:17 and upward, in their c by their courses; 4931
35: 2 he set the priests in their c, and 4931
Ac 21:24 thyself with them, and be at c with them, *1159*
1Co 9: 7 goeth a warfare any time at his own c? *3800*

CHARGEST (1) [CHARGE]
2Sa 3: 8 that thou c me to day with a fault 6485

CHARGING (2) [CHARGE]
Ac 16:23 into prison, c the jailor to keep them safely: *3853*
2Ti 2:14 c *them* before the Lord that *they* strive not *1263*

CHARIOT (64) [CHARIOTS]
Ge 41:43 he made him to ride in the second c which 4818
46:29 Joseph made ready his c, and went up to 4818
Ex 14: 6 he made ready his c, and took his people 7393
14:25 took off their c wheels, that they drave 4818
Jdg 4:15 so that Sisera lighted down off *his* c, and 4818
5:28 the lattice, Why is his c *so* long in coming? 7393
2Sa 8: 4 David houghed all the c *horses,* but 7393
1Ki 7:33 the wheels *was* like the work of a c wheel: 4818
10:29 a c came up and went out of Egypt for six 4818
12:18 made speed to get *him* up to *his* c, 4818
18:44 Prepare *thy* c, and get thee down, NIH
20:25 hast lost, horse for horse, and c for chariot: 7393
20:25 hast lost, horse for horse, and chariot for c: 7393
20:33 and he caused him to come up into the c. 4818
22:34 wherefore he said unto the **driver of** his c, 7395
22:35 the king was stayed up in *his* c against 4818
22:35 ran out of the wound into the midst of the c. 7393
22:38 *one* washed the c in the pool of Samaria; 7393
2Ki 2:11 *there appeared* a c of fire, and horses of 7393
2:12 the c of Israel, and the horsemen thereof. 7393
5: 9 came with his horses and with his c, 7393
5:21 he lighted down from the c to meet him, 4818
5:26 man turned *again* from his c to meet thee? 4818
7:14 They took therefore two c horses; and 7393
9:16 So Jehu rode *in a* c, and went to Jezreel; NIH
9:21 his c was made ready. And Joram king of 7393
9:21 each in his c, and they went out against 7393
9:24 out at his heart, and he sunk down in his c. 7393
9:27 after him, and said, Smite him also in the c. 4818
9:28 his servants carried him *in a* c to Jerusalem, NIH
10:15 and he took him up to him into the c. 4818
10:16 So they made him ride in his c. 7393
13:14 the c of Israel, and the horsemen thereof. 7393
23:30 his servants carried him *in a* c dead from NIH
1Ch 18: 4 David also houghed all the c *horses,* but 7393
28:18 gold for the pattern of the c of 4818
2Ch 1:14 which he placed in the c cities, and with 7393
1:17 brought forth out of Egypt a c for six 4818
8: 6 all the c cities, and the cities of 7393
9:25 whom he bestowed in the c cities, and 7393
10:18 made speed to get *him* up to *his* c, 4818
18:33 therefore he said to *his* **c man**, Turn thine 7395
18:34 in *his* c against the Syrians until the even: 4818
35:24 therefore took him out of *that* c, 4818
35:24 and put him in the second c that he had; 7393
Ps 46: 9 spear in sunder; he burneth the c in the fire. 5699
76: 6 both the c and horse *are* cast into a dead 7393
104: 3 who maketh the clouds his c: who walketh 7398
SS 3: 9 King Solomon made himself a c of the wood 668
Isa 21: 7 he saw a c *with* a couple of horsemen, 7393
21: 7 a c of asses, *and* a chariot of camels; 7393
21: 7 a chariot of asses, *and* a c of camels; 7393
21: 9 behold, here cometh a c of men, *with* a 7393
43:17 Which bringeth forth the c and horse, 7393
Jer 51:21 with thee will I break in pieces the c and 7393
Mic 1:13 of Lachish, bind the c to the swift beast: 4818
Zec 6: 2 In the first c *were* red horses; and in 4818
6: 2 and in the second c black horses; 4818
6: 3 in the third c white horses; and in the fourth 4818
6: 3 and in the fourth c grisled *and* bay horses. 4818
9:10 I will cut off the c from Ephraim, and 7393
Ac 8:28 and sitting in his c read Esaias the prophet. *716*
8:29 Go near, and join thyself to this c. *716*
8:38 And he commanded the c to stand still: and *716*

CHARIOTS (113) [CHARIOT]
Ge 50: 9 there went up with him both c and 7393
Ex 14: 7 he took six hundred chosen c, and all 7393
14: 7 all the c of Egypt, and captains over every 7393
14: 9 after them (all the horses *and* c of Pharaoh, 7393
14:17 upon his c, and upon his horsemen. 7393
14:18 upon his c, and upon his horsemen. 7393
14:23 Pharaoh's horses, his c, and his horsemen. 7393
14:26 upon their c, and upon their horsemen. 7393
14:28 covered the c, and the horsemen, and all 7393
15: 4 Pharaoh's c and his host hath he cast into 4818
15:19 For the horse of Pharaoh went in with his c 7393
Dt 11: 4 of Egypt, unto their horses, and to their c; 7393
20: 1 and c, *and* a people more than thou, 7393
Jos 11: 4 in multitude, with horses and c very many. 7393
11: 6 their horses, and burn their c with fire. 4818
11: 9 their horses, and burnt their c with fire. 4818
17:16 in the land of the valley have c of iron, 7393
17:18 though they have iron c, *and* though they *be* 7393
24: 6 Egyptians pursued after your fathers with c 7393
Jdg 1:19 of the valley, because they had c of iron. 7393
4: 3 for he had nine hundred c of iron; and 7393
4: 7 Jabin's army, with his c and his multitude; 7393
4:13 Sisera gathered together all his c, *even* nine 7393
4:13 *even* nine hundred c of iron, and all 7393
4:15 and all *his* c, and all *his* host, 7393
4:16 Barak pursued after the c, and after 7393

Jdg 5:28 in coming? why tarry the wheels of his **c**? 4818
1Sa 8:11 for his **c**, and to be his horsemen; 4818
8:11 and *some* shall run before his **c**. 4818
8:12 of war, and instruments of his **c**. 7393
13: 5 thirty thousand **c**, and six thousand 7393
2Sa 1: 6 the **c** and horsemen followed hard after 7393
8: 4 And David took from him a thousand **c**, and NIH
8: 4 but reserved of them *for* an hundred **c**. 7393
10:18 David slew *the men of* seven hundred **c** of 7393
15: 1 that Absalom prepared him **c** and horses, 4818
1Ki 1: 5 he prepared him **c** and horsemen, and 7393
4:26 had forty thousand stalls of horses for his **c**, 4817
9:19 cities for his **c**, and cities for his horsemen, 7393
9:22 and rulers of his **c**, and his horsemen. 7393
10:26 Solomon gathered together **c** and 7393
10:26 he had a thousand and four hundred **c**, and 7393
10:26 whom he bestowed in the cities for **c**, and 7393
16: 9 captain of half *his* **c**, conspired against him, 7393
20: 1 and two kings with him, and horses, and **c**: 7393
20:21 smote the horses and **c**, and slew 7393
22:31 and two captains that had rule over *his* **c**, 7393
22:32 when the captains of the **c** saw 7393
22:33 when the captains of the **c** perceived that it 7393
2Ki 6:14 he thither horses, and **c**, and a great host: 7393
6:15 compassed the city both with horses and **c**. 7393
6:17 *of* horses and **c** of fire round about Elisha. 7393
7: 6 the host of the Syrians to hear a noise of **c**, 7393
8:21 went over to Zair, and all the **c** with him: 7393
8:21 him about, and the captains of the **c**: 7393
10: 2 *there are* with you **c** and horses, a fenced 7393
13: 7 and ten **c**, and ten thousand footmen; 7393
18:24 put thy trust on Egypt for **c** and 7393
19:23 With the multitude of my **c** I am come up 7393
23:11 and burnt the **c** of the sun with fire. 4818
1Ch 18: 4 David took from him a thousand **c**, and 7393
18: 4 but reserved of them an hundred **c**. 7393
19: 6 a thousand talents of silver to hire them **c** 7393
19: 7 So they hired thirty and two thousand **c**, 7393
19:18 seven thousand *men which fought in* **c**, 7393
2Ch 1:14 Solomon gathered **c** and horsemen: and 7393
1:14 he had a thousand and four hundred **c**, and 7393
8: 9 and captains of his **c** and horsemen. 7393
9:25 had four thousand stalls for horses and **c**, 4818
12: 3 With twelve hundred **c**, and threescore 7393
14: 9 a thousand thousand, and three hundred **c**; 4818
16: 8 with very many **c** and horsemen? 7393
18:30 the captains of the **c** that *were* with him, 7393
18:31 when the captains of the **c** saw 7393
18:32 that when the captains of the **c** perceived 7393
21: 9 with his princes, and all *his* **c** with him: 7393
21: 9 him in, and the captains of the **c**. 7393
Ps 20: 7 Some *trust* in **c**, and some in horses: but 7393
68:17 The **c** of God *are* twenty thousand, 7393
SS 1: 9 to a company of horses in Pharaoh's **c**. 7393
6:12 my soul made me *like* the **c** of 4818
Isa 2: 7 neither *is there any* end of their **c**: 4818
22: 6 Elam bare the quiver with **c** of men *and* 7393
22: 7 *that* thy choicest valleys shall be full *of* **c**, 7393
22:18 there the **c** of thy glory *shall be* the shame 4818
31: 1 and trust in **c**, because *they are* many; 7393
36: 9 put thy trust on Egypt for **c** and 7393
37:24 By the multitude of my **c** am I come up *to* 7393
66:15 with his **c** like a whirlwind, to render his 4818
66:20 in **c**, and in litters, and upon mules, and 7393
Jer 4:13 as clouds, and his **c** *shall be* as a whirlwind: 4818
17:25 riding in **c** and on horses, they, and 7393
22: 4 riding in **c** and on horses, he, and 7393
46: 9 rage, ye **c**; and let the mighty *men* come 7393
47: 3 of his strong *horses*, at the rushing of his **c**, 7393
50:37 upon their **c**, and upon all the mingled 7393
Eze 23:24 they shall come against thee *with* **c**, 2021
26: 7 with **c**, and with horsemen, and companies, 7393
26:10 of the wheels, and of the **c**, when he shall 7393
27:20 *was* thy merchant in precious clothes for **c**. 7396
39:20 be filled at my table *with* horses and **c**, 7393
Da 11:40 with **c**, and with horsemen, and with many 7393
Joel 2: 5 Like the noise of **c** on the tops of mountains 4818
Mic 5:10 the midst of thee, and I will destroy thy **c**: 4818
Na 2: 3 the **c** *shall be* with flaming torches in 7393
2: 4 The **c** shall rage in the streets, they shall 7393
2:13 I will burn her **c** in the smoke, and 7393
3: 2 the pransing horses, and of the jumping **c**. 4818
Hab 3: 8 upon thine horses *and* thy **c** of salvation? 4818
Hag 2:22 I will overthrow the **c**, and those that ride in 4818
Zec 6: 1 there came four **c** out from between two 4818
Rev 9: 9 sound of **c** of many horses running to battle. *716*
18:13 horses, and **c**, and slaves, and souls of men. *4480*

CHARITABLY (1) [CHARITY]
Ro 14:15 with *thy* meat, now walkest thou not **c**. *26+2596*

CHARITY (28) [CHARITABLY]
1Co 8: 1 Knowledge puffeth up, but **c** edifieth. *26*
13: 1 tongues of men and of angels, and have not **c**, *26*
13: 2 and have no **c**, I am nothing. *26*
13: 3 and have not **c**, it profiteth me nothing. *26*
13: 4 **C** suffereth long, *and* is kind; charity envieth *26*
13: 4 suffereth long, *and* is kind; **c** envieth not; *26*
13: 4 **c** vaunteth not itself, is not puffed up, *26*
13: 8 **C** never faileth: *26*
13:13 And now abideth faith, hope, **c**, these three; *26*
13:13 these three; but the greatest of these *is* **c**. *26*
14: 1 Follow after **c**, and desire spiritual *gifts*, but *26*
16:14 Let all your *things* be done with **c**. *26*
Col 3:14 And above all these *things put on* **c**, which is *26*
1Th 3: 6 brought us good tidings of your faith and **c**, *26*
2Th 1: 3 the **c** of every one of you all towards each *26*
1Ti 1: 5 Now the end of the commandment is **c** out of *26*
2:15 in faith and **c** and holiness with sobriety. *26*
4:12 in **c**, in spirit, in faith, in purity. *26*
2Ti 2:22 but follow righteousness, faith, **c**, peace, *26*
3:10 purpose, faith, longsuffering, **c**, patience, *26*
Tit 2: 2 temperate, sound in faith, in **c**, in patience. *26*
1Pe 4: 8 And above all *things* have fervent **c** among *26*
4: 8 for **c** shall cover the multitude of sins. *26*
5:14 Greet ye one another with a kiss of **c**. *26*
2Pe 1: 7 and to brotherly kindness **c**. *26*
3Jn 1: 6 Which have borne witness of thy **c** before *26*
Jude 1:12 These are spots in your **feasts of c** when they *26*
Rev 2:19 I know thy works, and **c**, and service, *26*

CHARMED (1) [CHARMER, CHARMERS, CHARMING]
Jer 8:17 which *will* not *be* **c**, and they shall bite you, 3908

CHARMER (1) [CHARMED]
Dt 18:11 Or a **c**, or a consulter with familiar 2266+2267

CHARMERS (2) [CHARMED]
Ps 58: 5 Which will not hearken to the voice of **c**, 3907
Isa 19: 3 to the **c**, and to them that have familiar 328

CHARMING (1) [CHARMED]
Ps 58: 5 voice of charmers, **c** *never so* wisely. 2266+2267

CHARRAN (2) [HARAN]
Ac 7: 2 was in Mesopotamia, before he dwelt in **C**, *5488*
7: 4 the land of the Chaldeans, and dwelt in **C**: *5488*

CHASE (6) [CHASED, CHASETH, CHASING]
Lev 26: 7 ye shall **c** your enemies, and they shall fall 7291
26: 8 five of you shall **c** an hundred, and 7291
26:36 the sound of a shaken leaf shall **c** them; and 7291
Dt 32:30 How should one **c** a thousand, and two put 7291
Jos 23:10 One man of you shall **c** a thousand: for 7291
Ps 35: 5 and let the angel of the LORD **c** *them*. 1760

CHASED (13) [CHASE]
Dt 1:44 **c** you, as bees do, and destroyed you in 7291
Jos 7: 5 for they **c** them *from* before the gate *even* 7291
8:24 in the wilderness wherein they **c** them, and 7291
10:10 **c** them *along* the way that goeth up to 7291
11: 8 **c** them unto great Zidon, and 7291
Jdg 9:40 Abimelech **c** him, and he fled before him, 7291
20:43 *and* **c** them, *and* trode them down with ease 7291
Ne 13:28 the Horonite: therefore I **c** him from me. 1272
Job 18:18 light into darkness, and **c** out of the world. 5074
20: 8 he shall be **c away** as a vision of the night. 5074
Isa 13:14 it shall be as the **c** roe, and as a sheep that 5080
17:13 shall be **c** as the chaff of the mountains 7291
La 3:52 Mine enemies **c** me **sore**, like a bird, 6679+6679

CHASETH (1) [CHASE]
Pr 19:26 wasteth *his* father, *and* **c away** *his* mother, 1272

CHASING (1) [CHASE]
1Sa 17:53 the children of Israel returned from **c** after 1814

CHASTE (3)
2Co 11: 2 that *I* may present *you as* a **c** virgin to Christ. *53*

Tit 2: 5 *To be* discreet, **c**, keepers at home, good, *53*
1Pe 3: 2 While they behold your **c** conversation *53*

CHASTEN (6) [CHASTENED, CHASTENEST, CHASTENETH, CHASTENING]
2Sa 7:14 I will **c** him with the rod of men, and 3198
Ps 6: 1 neither **c** me in thy hot displeasure. 3256
38: 1 neither **c** me in thy hot displeasure. 3256
Pr 19:18 **C** thy son while there is hope, and let not 3256
Da 10:12 to **c** thyself before thy God, thy words were 6031
Rev 3:19 As many as I love, I rebuke and **c**: *3811*

CHASTENED (8) [CHASTEN]
Dt 21:18 his mother, and *that,* when they have **c** him, 3256
Job 33:19 He is **c** also with pain upon his bed, and 3198
Ps 69:10 When I wept, *and* **c** my soul with fasting, NIH
73:14 have I been plagued, and **c** every morning. 8433
118:18 The LORD hath **c** me **sore**: but 3256+3256
1Co 11:32 when we are judged, we are **c** of the Lord, *3811*
2Co 6: 9 and behold, we live; as **c**, and not killed; *3811*
Heb 12:10 For they verily for a few days **c** *us* after *3811*

CHASTENEST (1) [CHASTEN]
Ps 94:12 Blessed *is* the man whom thou **c**, 3256

CHASTENETH (5) [CHASTEN]
Dt 8: 5 as a man **c** his son, *so* the LORD thy God 3256
8: 5 his son, *so* the LORD thy God **c** thee. 3256
Pr 13:24 but he that loveth him **c** him betimes. 4148
Heb 12: 6 For whom the Lord loveth he **c**, and *3811*
12: 7 for what son is *he* whom the father **c** not? *3811*

CHASTENING (6) [CHASTEN]
Job 5:17 despise not thou the **c** of the Almighty: 4148
Pr 3:11 My son, despise not the **c** of the LORD; 4148
Isa 26:16 they poured out a prayer *when* thy **c** *was* 4148
Heb 12: 5 My son, despise not thou the **c** of the Lord, *3809*
12: 7 If ye endure **c**, God dealeth with you as *3809*
12:11 Now no **c** for the present seemeth to be *3809*

CHASTISE (10) [CHASTISED, CHASTISEMENT, CHASTISETH]
Lev 26:28 even I, will **c** you seven *times* for your sins. 3256
Dt 22:18 of that city shall take *that* man and **c** him; 3256
1Ki 12:11 with whips, but I will **c** you with scorpions. 3256
12:14 with whips, but I will **c** you with scorpions. 3256
2Ch 10:11 with whips, but I *will* **c** *you* with scorpions. NIH
10:14 with whips, but I *will* **c** *you* with scorpions. NIH
Hos 7:12 I will **c** them, as their congregation hath 3256
10:10 *It is* in my desire that I should **c** them; and 3256
Lk 23:16 I will therefore **c** him, and release *him.* *3811*
23:22 I will therefore **c** him, and let *him* go. *3811*

CHASTISED (6) [CHASTISE]
1Ki 12:11 my father hath **c** you with whips, but I will 3256
12:14 my father *also* **c** you with whips, but I will 3256
2Ch 10:11 my father **c** you with whips, but I *will* 3256
10:14 my father **c** you with whips, but I *will* 3256
Jer 31:18 bemoaning himself *thus;* Thou hast **c** me, 3256
31:18 I was **c**, as a bullock unaccustomed *to* 3256

CHASTISEMENT (5) [CHASTISE]
Dt 11: 2 which have not seen the **c** of the LORD 4148
Job 34:31 I have borne *c*, I will not offend *any more:* NIH
Isa 53: 5 the **c** of our peace *was* upon him; and 4148
Jer 30:14 *with* the **c** of a cruel one, for the multitude 4148
Heb 12: 8 But if ye be without **c**, whereof all are *3809*

CHASTISETH (1) [CHASTISE]
Ps 94:10 He that **c** the heathen, shall not he correct? 3256

CHATTER (1)
Isa 38:14 Like a crane *or* a swallow, so did I **c**: I did 6850

CHEBAR (8)
Eze 1: 1 I *was* among the captives by the river of **C**, 3529
1: 3 in the land of the Chaldeans by the river **C**; 3529
3:15 that dwelt by the river of **C**, and I sat where 3529
3:23 as the glory which I saw by the river of **C**: 3529
10:15 living creature that I saw by the river of **C**. 3529
10:20 under the God of Israel by the river of **C**; 3529
10:22 same faces which I saw by the river of **C**, 3529
43: 3 like the vision that I saw by the river **C**; 3529

CHECK (1)
Job 20: 3 I have heard the **c** of my reproach, and 4148

CHECKER (1)
1Ki 7:17 *And* nets of **c** work, *and* wreaths of chain 7639

CHEDORLAOMER (5)
Ge 14: 1 **C** king of Elam, and Tidal king of nations; 3540
14: 4 Twelve years they served **C**, and *in* 3540
14: 5 in the fourteenth year came **C**, and 3540
14: 9 With **C** the king of Elam, and *with* Tidal 3540
14:17 him after his return from the slaughter of **C**, 3540

CHEEK (8) [CHEEK-TEETH, CHEEKS]
1Ki 22:24 and smote Micaiah on the **c**, and said, 3895
2Ch 18:23 and smote Micaiah upon the **c**, and said, 3895
Job 16:10 they have smitten me upon the **c** 3895
Ps 3: 7 smitten all mine enemies *upon* the **c bone**; 3895
La 3:30 He giveth *his* **c** to him that smiteth him: 3895
Mic 5: 1 the judge of Israel with a rod upon the **c**. 3895
Mt 5:39 whosoever shall smite thee on thy right **c**, *4600*
Lk 6:29 *And* unto him that smiteth thee on the *one* **c** *4600*

CHEEKS (5) [CHEEK]
Dt 18: 3 the shoulder, and the **two c**, and the maw. 3895
SS 1:10 Thy **c** are comely with rows *of jewels,* thy 3895
5:13 His **c** *are* as a bed of spices, *as* sweet 3895
Isa 50: 6 and my **c** to them that plucked off the hair: 3895
La 1: 2 sore in the night, and her tears *are* on her **c**: 3895

CHEEK-TEETH (1) [CHEEK, TOOTH]
Joel 1: 6 of a lion, and he hath the **c** of a great lion. 4973

CHEER (10) [CHEERETH, CHEERFUL, CHEERFULLY, CHEERFULNESS]
Dt 24: 5 shall **c up** his wife which he hath taken. 8055
Ecc 11: 9 let thy heart **c** thee in the days of thy youth, 2895
Mt 9: 2 Son, **be of good c**; thy sins be forgiven *2293*
14:27 spake unto them, saying, **Be of good c**; *2293*
Mk 6:50 and saith unto them, **Be of good c**: *2293*
Jn 16:33 but **be of good c**; I have overcome *2293*
Ac 23:11 stood by him, and said, **Be of good c**, Paul: *2293*
27:22 And now I exhort you to **be of good c**: *2114*
27:25 Wherefore, sirs, **be of good c**: for I believe *2114*
27:36 Then were they all **of good c**, and they also *2115*

CHEERETH (1) [CHEER]
Jdg 9:13 which **c** God and man, and go to be 8055

CHEERFUL (4) [CHEER]
Pr 15:13 A merry heart **maketh** a **c** countenance: but 3190
Zec 8:19 of Judah joy and gladness, and **c** feasts; 2896
9:17 corn shall **make** the young men **c**, and 5107
2Co 9: 7 or of necessity: for God loveth a **c** giver. *2431*

CHEERFULLY (1) [CHEER]
Ac 24:10 I do the **more c** answer for myself: *2115*

CHEERFULNESS (1) [CHEER]
Ro 12: 8 he that sheweth mercy, with **c**. *2432*

CHEESE (2) [CHEESES]
2Sa 17:29 butter, and sheep, and **c** of kine, for David, 8194
Job 10:10 me out as milk, and cruddled me like **c**? 1385

CHEESES (1) [CHEESE]
1Sa 17:18 carry these ten **c** unto the captain of 2461+2757

CHELAL (1)
Ezr 10:30 Adna, and **C**, Benaiah, Maaseiah, 3636

CHELLUH (1)
Ezr 10:35 Benaiah, Bedeiah, **C**, 3622

CHELUB (2)
1Ch 4:11 **C** the brother of Shuah begat Mehir, 3620
27:26 tillage of the ground *was* Ezri the son of **C**: 3620

CHELUBAI (1)
1Ch 2: 9 born unto him; Jerahmeel, and Ram, and **C**. 3621

CHEMARIMS (1)
Zep 1: 4 *and* the name of the **C** with the priests; 3649

CHEMOSH (8)
Nu 21:29 thou art undone, O people of **C**: he hath 3645
Jdg 11:24 Wilt not thou possess that which **C** thy god 3645
1Ki 11: 7 did Solomon build a high place for **C**, 3645
11:33 **C** the god of the Moabites, and Milcom 3645

2Ki 23:13 for **C** the abomination of the Moabites, and 3645
Jer 48: 7 **C** shall go forth into captivity *with* his 3645
48:13 Moab shall be ashamed of **C**, as the house 3645
48:46 the people of **C** perisheth: for thy sons are 3645

CHENAANAH (5)
1Ki 22:11 Zedekiah the son of **C** made him horns of 3668
22:24 Zedekiah the son of **C** went near, and 3668
1Ch 7:10 **C**, and Zethan, and Tharshish, and 3668
2Ch 18:10 Zedekiah the son of **C** had made him horns 3668
18:23 Zedekiah the son of **C** came near, and 3668

CHENANI (1)
Ne 9: 4 *and* **C**, and cried with a loud voice unto 3662

CHENANIAH (3)
1Ch 15:22 **C**, chief of the Levites, *was* for song: 3663
15:27 **C** the master of the song *with* the singers: 3663
26:29 **C** and his sons *were* for the outward 3663

CHEPHAR-HAAMMONAI (1)
Jos 18:24 **C**, and Ophni, and Gaba; twelve cities with 3726

CHEPHIRAH (4)
Jos 9:17 and **C**, and Beeroth, and Kirjath-jearim. 3716
18:26 And Mizpeh, and **C**, and Mozah, 3716
Ezr 2:25 **C**, and Beeroth, seven hundred and forty 3716
Ne 7:29 **C**, and Beeroth, seven hundred forty and 3716

CHERAN (2)
Ge 36:26 Hemdan, and Eshban, and Ithran, and **C**. 3763
1Ch 1:41 Amram, and Eshban, and Ithran, and **C**. 3763

CHERETHIMS (1) [CHERETHITES]
Eze 25:16 I will cut off the **C**, and destroy 3774

CHERETHITES (9) [CHERETHIMS]
1Sa 30:14 made an invasion *upon* the south of the **C**, 3774
2Sa 8:18 the son of Jehoiada *was over* both the **C** 3774
15:18 all the **C**, and all the Pelethites, and all 3774
20: 7 the **C**, and the Pelethites, and all the mighty 3774
20:23 Benaiah the son of Jehoiada *was* over the **C** 3774
1Ki 1:38 the **C**, and the Pelethites, went down, and 3774
1:44 the **C**, and the Pelethites, and they have 3774
1Ch 18:17 Benaiah the son of Jehoiada *was* over the **C** 3774
Zep 2: 5 of the sea coast, the nation of the **C**! 3774

CHERISH (1) [CHERISHED, CHERISHETH]
1Ki 1: 2 let her **c** him, and let her lie in thy 1961+5532

CHERISHED (1) [CHERISH]
1Ki 1: 4 **c** the king, and ministered to him: 1961+5532

CHERISHETH (2) [CHERISH]
Eph 5:29 but nourisheth and **c** it, even as the Lord *2282*
1Th 2: 7 among you, *even* as a nurse **c** her children: *2282*

CHERITH (2)
1Ki 17: 3 and hide thyself by the brook **C**, 3747
17: 5 for he went and dwelt by the brook **C**, 3747

CHERUB (30) [CHERUBIMS, CHERUBIMS']
Ex 25:19 make one **c** on the one end, and the other 3742
25:19 one end, and the other **c** on the other end: 3742
37: 8 One **c** on the end on this side, and 3742
37: 8 and another **c** on the *other* end on that side: 3742
2Sa 22:11 he rode upon a **c**, and did fly: and he was 3742
1Ki 6:24 five cubits *was* the one wing of the **c**, and 3742
6:24 and five cubits the other wing of the **c**: 3742
6:25 the other **c** *was* ten cubits: both 3742
6:26 The height of the one **c** *was* ten cubits, and 3742
6:26 *was* ten cubits, and so *was it* of the other **c**. 3742
6:27 the wing of the other **c** touched the other 3742
2Ch 3:11 *one* wing of the one *c was* five cubits, NIH
3:11 reaching to the wing of the other **c**. 3742
3:12 *one* wing of the other **c** *was* five cubits, 3742
3:12 *also,* joining to the wing of the other **c**. 3742
Ezr 2:59 Tel-harsa, **C**, Addan, *and* Immer: 3743
Ne 7:61 Tel-haresha, **C**, Addon, and Immer: 3743
Ps 18:10 he rode upon a **c**, and did fly: yea, he did 3742
Eze 9: 3 the God of Israel was gone up from the **c**, 3742
10: 2 *even* under the **c**, and fill thine hand *with* 3742
10: 4 glory of the LORD went up from the **c**, 3742
10: 7 *one* **c** stretched forth his hand from between 3742
10: 9 one wheel by one **c**, and another wheel by 3742
10: 9 and another wheel by another **c**: 3742
10:14 the first face *was* the face of a **c**, and 3742
28:14 Thou *art* the anointed **c** that covereth; and 3742
28:16 I will destroy thee, O covering **c**, from 3742
41:18 so that a palm tree *was* between a **c** and a 3742
41:18 a palm tree *was* between a cherub and a **c**; 3742
41:18 and a cherub; and *every* **c** had two faces; 3742

CHERUBIMS (64) [CHERUB]
Ge 3:24 placed at the east of the garden of Eden **C**, 3742
Ex 25:18 thou shalt make two **c** *of* gold, *of* beaten 3742
25:19 *even* of the mercy seat shall ye make the **c** 3742
25:20 the **c** shall stretch forth *their* wings on high, 3742
25:20 the mercy seat shall the faces of the **c** be. 3742
25:22 from between the two **c** which *are* upon 3742
26: 1 *with* **c** *of* cunning work shalt thou make 3742
26:31 *of* cunning work: *with* **c** shall it be made: 3742
36: 8 *with* **c** *of* cunning work made he them. 3742
36:35 *with* **c** made he it *of* cunning work. 3742
37: 7 he made two **c** *of* gold, beaten out of one 3742
37: 8 out of the mercy seat made he the **c** on 3742
37: 9 the **c** spread out *their* wings on high, 3742
37: 9 the mercy seatward were the faces of the **c**. 3742
Nu 7:89 ark of Testimony, from between the two **c**: 3742
1Sa 4: 4 of hosts, which dwelleth *between* the **c**: 3742
2Sa 6: 2 of hosts that dwelleth *between* the **c**. 3742
1Ki 6:23 within the oracle he made two **c** *of* olive 3742
6:25 both the **c** *were* of one measure and 3742
6:27 And he set the **c** within the inner house: and 3742
6:27 they stretched forth the wings of the **c**, so 3742
6:28 And he overlaid the **c** with gold. 3742
6:29 house round about *with* carved figures of **c** 3742
6:32 he carved upon them carvings of **c** and 3742
6:32 spread gold upon the **c**, and upon the palm 3742
6:35 And he carved *thereon* **c** and palm trees and 3742
7:29 between the ledges *were* lions, oxen, and **c**: 3742
7:36 he graved **c**, lions, and palm trees, 3742
8: 6 holy *place,* even under the wings of the **c**. 3742
8: 7 For the **c** spread forth *their* two wings over 3742
8: 7 the **c** covered the ark and the staves thereof 3742
2Ki 19:15 which dwellest *between* the **c**, thou *art* 3742
1Ch 13: 6 that dwelleth *between* the **c**, whose name is 3742
28:18 gold for the pattern of the chariot of the **c**, 3742
2Ch 3: 7 with gold; and graved **c** on the walls. 3742
3:10 in the most holy house he made two **c** of 3742
3:11 the wings of the **c** *were* twenty cubits long: 3742
3:13 The wings of these **c** spread themselves 3742
3:14 and fine linen, and wrought **c** thereon. 3742
5: 7 holy *place,* even under the wings of the **c**: 3742
5: 8 For the **c** spread forth *their* wings over 3742
5: 8 the **c** covered the ark and the staves thereof 3742
Ps 80: 1 thou that dwellest *between* the **c**, 3742
99: 1 he sitteth *between* the **c**; let the earth be 3742
Isa 37:16 God of Israel, that dwellest *between* the **c**, 3742
Eze 10: 1 **c** there appeared over them as it were a 3742
10: 2 hand *with* coals of fire from between the **c**, 3742
10: 3 Now the **c** stood on the right side of 3742
10: 6 between the wheels, from between the **c**; 3742
10: 7 **c** unto the fire that *was* between 3742
10: 7 unto the fire that *was* between the **c**, 3742
10: 8 there appeared in the **c** the form of a man's 3742
10: 9 I looked, behold the four wheels by the **c**, 3742
10:15 the **c** were lifted up. This *is* the living 3742
10:16 when the **c** went, the wheels went by them: 3742
10:16 when the **c** lift up their wings to mount up 3742
10:18 of the house, and stood over the **c**. 3742
10:19 the **c** lift up their wings, and mounted up 3742
10:20 of Chebar; and I knew that they *were the* **c**. 3742
11:22 did the **c** lift up their wings, and the wheels 3742
41:18 *it was* made *with* **c** and palm trees, so that a 3742
41:20 the ground unto above the door *were* **c** 3742
41:25 the doors of the temple, **c** and palm trees, 3742
Heb 9: 5 And over it the **c** of glory shadowing *5502*

CHERUBIMS' (1) [CHERUB]
Eze 10: 5 the sound of the **c** wings was heard *even* to 3742

CHESALON (1)
Jos 15:10 which *is* **C**, on the north side, and 3693

CHESED (1)
Ge 22:22 **C**, and Hazo, and Pildash, and Jidlaph, and 3777

CHESIL (1)
Jos 15:30 And Eltolad, and **C**, and Hormah, 3686

CHESNUT (2)
Ge 30:37 of green poplar, and of the hazel and **c tree;** 6196
Eze 31: 8 and the **c trees** were not like his branches; 6196

CHEST (6) [CHESTS]
2Ki 12: 9 Jehoiada the priest took a **c**, and bored a hole 727
12:10 saw that *there was* much money in the **c**, 727
2Ch 24: 8 at the king's commandment they made a **c**, 727
24:10 and brought in, and cast into the **c**, 727
24:11 that at *what* time the **c** was brought unto 727
24:11 high priest's officer came and emptied the **c**, 727

CHESTS (1) [CHEST]
Eze 27:24 broidered work, and in **c** of rich apparel, 1595

CHESULLOTH (1)
Jos 19:18 was toward Jezreel, and **C**, and Shunem, 3694

CHEW (3) [CHEWED, CHEWETH]
Lev 11: 4 these shall ye not eat of them that **c** the cud, 5927
Dt 14: 7 these ye shall not eat of them that **c** the cud, 5927
14: 7 for they **c** the cud, but divide not the hoof; 5927

CHEWED (1) [CHEW]
Nu 11:33 *was* yet between their teeth, ere it was **c**, 3772

CHEWETH (8) [CHEW]
Lev 11: 3 *is* clovenfooted, *and* **c** cud, among 5927
11: 4 because he **c** the cud, but divideth not 5927
11: 5 because he **c** the cud, but divideth not 5927
11: 6 because he **c** the cud, but divideth not 5927
11: 7 and *be* clovenfooted, yet he **c** not the cud; 1641
11:26 *is* not clovenfooted, nor **c** the cud, 5927
Dt 14: 6 *and* **c** the cud amongst the beasts: 5927
14: 8 it divideth the hoof, yet *c* not the cud, NIH

CHEZIB (1)
Ge 38: 5 and he was at **C**, when she bare him. 3580

CHICKENS (1)
Mt 23:37 even as a hen gathereth her **c** under *her* *3556*

CHICKS See BROOD; CHICKENS

CHIDE (4) [CHIDING]
Ex 17: 2 Wherefore the people did **c** with Moses, 7378
17: 2 Moses said unto them, Why **c** you with me? 7378
Jdg 8: 1 And they did **c** with him sharply. 7378
Ps 103: 9 He will not always **c**: neither will he keep 7378

CHIDING (1) [CHIDE]
Ex 17: 7 because of the **c** of the children of Israel, 7379

CHIDON (1)
1Ch 13: 9 they came unto the threshingfloor of **C**, 3592

CHIEF (338) [CHIEFEST, CHIEFLY]
Ge 21:22 Phichol the **c captain** of his host spake 8269
21:32 Phichol the **c captain** of his host, and 8269
26:26 and Phichol the **c captain** of his army. 8269
40: 2 against the **c** of the butlers, and against 8269
40: 2 the butlers, and against the **c** of the bakers. 8269
40: 9 the **c** butler told his dream to Joseph, and 8269
40:16 When the **c** baker saw that 8269
40:20 he lifted up the head of the **c** butler and of 8269
40:20 and of the **c** baker among his servants. 8269
40:21 he restored the **c** butler unto his butlership 8269
40:22 he hanged the **c** baker: as Joseph had 8269
40:23 Yet did not the **c** butler remember Joseph, 8269
41: 9 spake the **c** butler unto Pharaoh, saying, 8269
41:10 the guard's house, *both* me and the **c** baker: 8269
Lev 21: 4 *being* a **c man** among his people, 1167
Nu 3:24 the **c** of the house of the father of 5387
3:30 the **c** of the house of the father of 5387
3:32 *shall be* **c over** the chief of the Levites, 5387
3:32 *shall be* chief over the **c** of the Levites, 5387
3:35 the **c** of the house of the father of 5387
4:34 the **c** of the congregation numbered 5387
4:46 and Aaron and the **c** of Israel numbered, 5387
25:14 a prince of a **c** house among the Simeonites. 1
25:15 head over a people, *and* of a **c** house in Midian. 1
31:26 and the **c** fathers of the congregation: 7218
32:28 the **c** fathers of the tribes of the children of 7218
36: 1 the **c** fathers of the families of the children 7218
36: 1 the **c** fathers of the children of Israel: 7218
Dt 1:15 So I took the **c** of your tribes, wise men, 7218
33:15 for the **c things** of the ancient mountains, 7218
Jos 22:14 of each **c** house a prince throughout all 5387
Jdg 20: 2 the **c** of all the people, *even* of all the tribes 6438
1Sa 14:38 Draw ye near hither, all the **c** of the people: 6438
15:21 the **c** of the things which should have been 7225
2Sa 5: 8 *he shall be c and captain.* Wherefore they NIH
8:18 and David's sons were **c rulers**. 3548
20:26 Ira also the Jairite was a **c ruler** about 3548
23: 8 that sat in the seat, **c** among the captains; 7218
23:13 three of the thirty **c** went down, and 7218
23:18 the son of Zeruiah, *was* **c** among three. 7218
1Ki 5:16 Besides the **c** of Solomon's officers which 8269
8: 1 the **c** of the fathers of the children of Israel, 5387
9:23 These *were* the **c** of the officers that *were* 8269
14:27 committed *them* unto the hands of the **c** of 8269
2Ki 25:18 the captain of the guard took Seraiah the **c** 7218
1Ch 5: 2 his brethren, and of him *came* the **c ruler;** 5057
5: 7 *were* the **c**, Jeiel, and Zechariah, 7218
5:12 Joel the **c**, and Shapham the next, and 7218
5:15 son of Guni, **c** of the house of their fathers. 7218
7: 3 and Joel, Ishiah, five: all of them **c** *men.* 7218
7:40 *and* mighty *men* of valour, **c** of the princes. 7218
8:28 **c** *men.* These dwelt in Jerusalem. 7218
9: 9 All these men *were* **c** of the fathers in 7218
9:17 and their brethren: Shallum *was* the **c;** 7218
9:26 For these Levites, the four **c** porters, 1368
9:33 the singers, **c** of the fathers of the Levites, 7218
9:34 These **c** fathers of the Levites *were* chief 7218
9:34 These chief fathers of the Levites *were* **c** 7218
11: 6 smiteth the Jebusites first shall be **c** 7218
11: 6 the son of Zeruiah went first up, and was **c**. 7218
11:10 These also *are* the **c** of the mighty *men* 7218
11:11 a Hachmonite, the **c** of the captains: 7218
11:20 the brother of Joab, he was **c** of the three: 7218
12: 3 The **c** *was* Ahiezer, then Joash, the sons of 7218
12:18 *who was* **c** of the captains, *and he said,* 7218
15: 5 Uriel the **c**, and his brethren an hundred and 8269
15: 6 Asaiah the **c**, and his brethren two hundred 8269
15: 7 Joel the **c**, and his brethren an hundred and 8269
15: 8 Shemaiah the **c**, and his brethren two 8269
15: 9 Eliel the **c**, and his brethren fourscore: 8269
15:10 Amminadab the **c**, and his brethren an 8269
15:12 Ye *are* the **c** of the fathers of the Levites: 7218
15:16 David spake to the **c** of the Levites to 8269
15:22 **c** of the Levites, *was* for song: 8269
16: 5 Asaph the **c**, and next to him Zechariah, 7218
18:17 the sons of David *were* **c** about the king. 7223
23: 8 the **c** *was* Jehiel, and Zetham, and Joel, 7218
23: 9 These *were* the **c** of the fathers of Laadan. 7218
23:11 Jahath was the **c**, and Zizah the second: 7218
23:16 *Of* the sons of Gershom, Shebuel *was* the **c**. 7218
23:17 the sons of Eliezer *were,* Rehabiah the **c**. 7218
23:18 *Of* the sons of Izhar; Shelomith the **c**. 7218
23:24 *even* the **c** of the fathers, as they were 7218
24: 4 there were moe **c** men found of the sons of 7218
24: 4 sixteen **c** *men* of the house of *their* fathers, 7218
24: 6 *before* the **c** of the fathers of the priests and 7218
24:31 the **c** of the fathers of the priests and 7218
26:10 Simri the **c**, (for *though* he was not 7218
26:10 yet his father made him the **c**;) 7218
26:12 *even* among the **c** men, *having* wards one 7218
26:21 **c** fathers, *even* of Laadan the Gershonite, 7218
26:26 the **c** fathers, the captains over thousands 7218
26:31 Among the Hebronites *was* Jerijah the **c**, 7218
26:32 two thousand and seven hundred **c** fathers, 7218
27: 1 *to wit,* the **c** fathers and captains of 7218
27: 3 Of the children of Perez *was* the **c** of all 7218
27: 5 *was* Benaiah the son of Jehoiada, a **c** priest: 7218
29: 6 the **c** of the fathers and princes of the tribes 8269
29:22 *him* unto the LORD to be the **c governor**, 5057
2Ch 1: 2 governor in all Israel, the **c** of the fathers. 7218
5: 2 the **c** of the fathers of the children of Israel, 5387
8: 9 **c** of his captains, and captains of his 8269
8:10 these *were* the **c** of king Solomon's 8269
11:22 made Abijah the son of Maachah the **c**, 7218
12:10 committed *them* to the hands of the **c** of 8269
17:14 Adnah the **c**, and with him mighty *men* of 8269
19: 8 and of the **c** of the fathers of Israel, 7218
19:11 Amariah the **c** priest *is* over you in all 7218
23: 2 the **c** of the fathers of Israel, and they came 7218
24: 6 the king called for Jehoiada the **c**, and 7218
26:12 The whole number of the **c** of the fathers of 7218
26:20 And Azariah the **c** priest, and all the priests, 7218
31:10 Azariah the **c** priest of the house of Zadok 7218

2Ch	35: 9	and Jeiel and Jozabad, **c** of the Levites,	8269
	36:14	Moreover all the **c** of the priests, and	8269
Ezr	1: 5	rose up the **c** of the fathers of Judah and	7218
	2:68	*some* of the **c** of the fathers, when they	7218
	3:12	the priests and Levites and **c** of the fathers,	7218
	4: 2	to the **c** of the fathers, and said unto them,	7218
	4: 3	and the rest of the **c** of the fathers of Israel,	7218
	5:10	names of the men that *were* the **c** of them.	7217
	7: 5	of Eleazar, the son of Aaron the **c** priest:	7218
	7:28	I gathered together out of Israel **c** *men* to go	7218
	8: 1	These *are* now the **c** of their fathers, and	7218
	8:16	**c** *men;* also for Joiarib, and for Elnathan,	7218
	8:17	unto Iddo the **c** at the place Casiphia,	7218
	8:24	I separated twelve of the **c** of the priests,	8269
	8:29	keep *them,* until ye weigh *them* before the **c**	8269
	8:29	the Levites, and **c** of the fathers of Israel,	8269
	9: 2	and rulers hath been **c** in this trespass.	7223
	10: 5	made the **c** priests, the Levites, and	8269
	10:16	Ezra the priest, *with* certain **c** of the fathers,	7218
Ne	7:70	some of the **c** of the fathers gave unto	7218
	7:71	*some* of the **c** of the fathers gave to	7218
	8:13	the **c** of the fathers of all the people,	7218
	10:14	The **c** of the people; Parosh, Pahath-moab,	7218
	11: 3	Now these *are* the **c** of the province that	7218
	11:13	his brethren, **c** of the fathers, two hundred	7218
	11:16	and Jozabad, of the **c** of the Levites,	7218
	12: 7	These *were* the **c** of the priests and of their	7218
	12:12	of Joiakim were priests, the **c** of the fathers:	7218
	12:22	and Jaddua, *were* recorded **c** of the fathers:	7218
	12:23	The sons of Levi, the **c** of the fathers,	7218
	12:24	the **c** of the Levites: Hashabiah, Sherebiah,	7218
	12:46	Asaph of old *there were* **c** of the singers,	7218
Job	12:24	He taketh away the heart of the **c** of	7218
	29:25	and sat **c**, and dwelt as a king in the army,	7218
	40:19	He *is* the **c** of the ways of God: he that	7225
Ps	4: T	To the **c** **Musician** on Neginoth, A Psalm	5329
	5: T	To the **c** **Musician** upon Nehiloth, A Psalm	5329
	6: T	To the **c** **Musician** on Neginoth upon	5329
	8: T	To the **c** **Musician** upon Gittith, A Psalm of	5329
	9: T	To the **c** **Musician** upon Muth-labben, A	5329
	11: T	To the **c** **Musician**, *A Psalm* of David.	5329
	12: T	To the **c** **Musician** upon Sheminith,	5329
	13: T	To the **c** **Musician**, A Psalm of David.	5329
	14: T	To the **c** **Musician**, *A Psalm* of David.	5329
	18: T	To the **c** **Musician**, *A Psalm* of David,	5329
	19: T	To the **c** **Musician**, A Psalm of David.	5329
	20: T	To the **c** **Musician**, A Psalm of David.	5329
	21: T	To the **c** **Musician**, A Psalm of David.	5329
	22: T	To the **c** **Musician** upon Aijeleth Shahar,	5329
	31: T	To the **c** **Musician**, A Psalm of David.	5329
	36: T	To the **c** **Musician**, *A Psalm* of David	5329
	39: T	To the **c** **Musician**, *even* to Jeduthun,	5329
	40: T	To the **c** **Musician**, A Psalm of David.	5329
	41: T	To the **c** **Musician**, A Psalm of David.	5329
	42: T	To the **c** **Musician**, Maschil, for the sons of	5329
	44: T	To the **c** **Musician** for the sons of Korah,	5329
	45: T	To the **c** **Musician** upon Shoshannim,	5329
	46: T	To the **c** **Musician** for the sons of Korah,	5329
	47: T	To the **c** **Musician**, A Psalm for the sons of	5329
	49: T	To the **c** **Musician**, A Psalm for the sons of	5329
	51: T	To the **c** **Musician**, A Psalm of David,	5329
	52: T	To the **c** **Musician**, Maschil, *A Psalm* of	5329
	53: T	To the **c** **Musician** upon Mahalath,	5329
	54: T	To the **c** **Musician** on Neginoth, Maschil,	5329
	55: T	To the **c** **Musician** on Neginoth, Maschil,	5329
	56: T	To the **c** **Musician** upon	5329
	57: T	To the **c** **Musician**, Al-taschith,	5329
	58: T	To the **c** **Musician**, Al-taschith,	5329
	59: T	To the **c** **Musician**, Al-taschith,	5329
	60: T	To the **c** **Musician** upon Shushan-eduth,	5329
	61: T	To the **c** **Musician** upon Neginah, *A Psalm*	5329
	62: T	To the **c** **Musician**, to Jeduthun, A Psalm	5329
	64: T	To the **c** **Musician**, A Psalm of David.	5329
	65: T	To the **c** **Musician**, A Psalm *and* Song of	5329
	66: T	To the **c** **Musician**, A Song *or* Psalm.	5329
	67: T	To the **c** **Musician** on Neginoth, A Psalm	5329
	68: T	To the **c** **Musician**, A Psalm *or* Song of	5329
	69: T	To the **c** **Musician** upon Shoshannim,	5329
	70: T	To the **c** **Musician**, *A Psalm* of David,	5329
	75: T	To the **c** **Musician**, Al-taschith, A Psalm *or*	5329
	76: T	To the **c** **Musician** on Neginoth, A Psalm	5329
	77: T	To the **c** **Musician**, to Jeduthun, A Psalm	5329
	78:51	the **c** of *their* strength in the tabernacles of	7225
	80: T	To the **c** **Musician** upon	5329
	81: T	To the **c** **Musician** upon Gittith, *A Psalm* of	5329
	84: T	To the **c** **Musician** upon Gittith, A Psalm	5329
	85: T	To the **c** **Musician**, A Psalm for the sons of	5329
	88: T	To the **c** **Musician** upon Mahalath	5329
	105:36	in their land, the **c** of all their strength.	7225
	109: T	To the **c** **Musician**, A Psalm of David.	5329
	137: 6	if I prefer not Jerusalem above my **c** joy.	7218
	139: T	To the **c** **Musician**, A Psalm of David.	5329
	140: T	To the **c** **Musician**, A Psalm of David.	5329
Pr	1:21	She crieth in the **c** **place** of concourse,	7218
	16:28	and a whisperer separateth **c** **friends**.	441
SS	4:14	myrrh and aloes, with all the **c** spices:	7218
Isa	14: 9	for thee, *even* all the **c** **ones** of the earth;	6260
	41: 9	called thee from the **c** **men** thereof, and	678
Jer	13:21	them *to be* captains, *and* as **c** over thee:	7218
	20: 1	who *was* also **c** governor in the house of	5057
	31: 7	and shout among the **c** of the nations:	7218
	49:35	break the bow of Elam, the **c** of their might.	7225
	52:24	the captain of the guard took Seraiah the **c**	7218
La	1: 5	Her adversaries are the **c**, her enemies	7218
Eze	27:22	they occupied in thy fairs with **c** of all	7218
	38: 2	the **c** prince of Meshech and Tubal, and	7218
	38: 3	O Gog, the **c** prince of Meshech and Tubal:	7218
	39: 1	O Gog, the **c** prince of Meshech and Tubal:	7218
Da	2:48	**c** of the governors over all the wise *men* of	7229
	10:13	lo, Michael, one of the **c** princes, came to	7223
	11:41	Moab, and the **c** of the children of Ammon.	7225
Am	6: 1	*which are* named **c** of the nations,	7225
	6: 6	and anoint themselves *with* the **c** ointments:	7225
Hab	3:19	To the **c** **singer** on my stringed instruments.	5329
Mt	2: 4	And when he had gathered all the **c** **priests**	*749*
	16:21	*things* of the elders and **c** **priests** and scribes,	*749*
	20:18	of man shall be betrayed unto the **c** **priests**	*749*
	20:27	And whosoever will be **c** among you,	*4413*
	21:15	And when the **c** **priests** and scribes saw	*749*
	21:23	the **c** **priests** and the elders of the people	*749*
	21:45	And when the **c** **priests** and Pharisees had	*749*
	23: 6	at feasts, and the **c** **seats** in the synagogues,	*4410*
	26: 3	Then assembled together the **c** **priests**, and	*749*
	26:14	called Judas Iscariot, went unto the **c** **priests**,	*749*
	26:47	from the **c** **priests** and elders of the people.	*749*
	26:59	Now the **c** **priests**, and elders, and all	*749*
	27: 1	all the **c** **priests** and elders of the people took	*749*
	27: 3	the thirty pieces of silver to the **c** **priests**	*749*
	27: 6	And the **c** **priests** took the silver pieces, and	*749*
	27:12	And when he was accused of the **c** **priests**	*749*
	27:20	But the **c** **priests** and elders persuaded	*749*
	27:41	Likewise also the **c** **priests** mocking *him,*	*749*
	27:62	the **c** **priests** and Pharisees came together	*749*
	28:11	shewed unto the **c** **priests** all the *things* that	*749*
Mk	6:21	high captains, and **c** *estates* of Galilee;	*4413*
	8:31	the elders, and *of* the **c** **priests**, and scribes,	*749*
	10:33	of man shall be delivered unto the **c** **priests**,	*749*
	11:18	And the scribes and **c** **priests** heard *it,* and	*749*
	11:27	there come to him the **c** **priests**, and	*749*
	12:39	And the **c** **seats** in the synagogues, and	*4410*
	14: 1	and the **c** **priests** and the scribes sought how	*749*
	14:10	one of the twelve, went unto the **c** **priests**,	*749*
	14:43	from the **c** **priests** and the scribes and	*749*
	14:53	with him were assembled all the **c** **priests**	*749*
	14:55	And the **c** **priests** and all the council sought	*749*
	15: 1	And straightway in the morning the **c** **priests**	*749*
	15: 3	And the **c** **priests** accused him of many	*749*
	15:10	For he knew that the **c** **priests** had delivered	*749*
	15:11	But the **c** **priests** moved the people, that he	*749*
	15:31	Likewise also the **c** **priests** mocking said	*749*
Lk	9:22	of the elders and **c** **priests** and scribes,	*749*
	11:15	devils through Beelzebub the **c** of the devils.	*758*
	14: 1	as he went into the house of one of the **c**	*758*
	14: 7	he marked how they chose out the **c** **rooms**;	*4411*
	19: 2	which was *the* **c** **among** the **publicans**, and	*754*
	19:47	But the **c** **priests** and the scribes and	*749*
	19:47	the **c** of the people sought to destroy him,	*4413*
	20: 1	the **c** **priests** and the scribes came upon *him*	*749*
	20:19	And the **c** **priests** and the scribes the same	*749*
	20:46	the synagogues, and the **c** **rooms** at feasts;	*4411*
	22: 2	And the **c** **priests** and scribes sought how	*749*
	22: 4	and communed with the **c** **priests** and	*749*
	22:26	and he that is **c**, as he that doth serve.	*2233*
	22:52	Then Jesus said unto the **c** **priests**, and	*749*
	22:66	the elders of the people and the **c** **priests** and	*749*
	23: 4	Then said Pilate to the **c** **priests** and *to*	*749*
	23:10	And the **c** **priests** and scribes stood and	*749*
	23:13	when he had called together the **c** **priests**	*749*

C

Lk 23:23 of them and of the **c priests** prevailed. *749*
24:20 And how the **c priests** and our rulers *749*
Jn 7:32 and the **c priests** sent officers to take him. *749*
7:45 Then came the officers to the **c priests** and *749*
11:47 Then gathered the **c priests** and the *749*
11:57 Now both the *c* priests and the Pharisees NIG
12:10 But the **c priests** consulted that they might *749*
12:42 Nevertheless among the *c* rulers also many NIG
18: 3 and officers from the **c priests** and *749*
18:35 the **c priests** have delivered thee unto me: *749*
19: 6 When the **c priests** therefore and officers *749*
19:15 The **c priests** answered, We have no king *749*
19:21 Then said the **c priests** of the Jews to Pilate, *749*
Ac 4:23 and reported all that the **c priests** and elders *749*
5:24 and the **c priests** heard these things, *749*
9:14 here he hath authority from the **c priests** *749*
9:21 might bring them bound unto the **c priests**? *749*
13:50 and the **c** *men* of the city, and *4413*
14:12 Mercurius, because he was the **c** speaker. *2233*
15:22 and Silas, **c** *men* among the brethren: *2233*
16:12 which is the **c** city of *that* part of *4413*
17: 4 and of the **c** women not a few. *4413*
18: 8 And Crispus, the *c* ruler of the synagogue, NIG
18:17 the *c* ruler of the synagogue, and beat *him* NIG
19:14 a Jew, *and* **c of the priests**, which did so. *749*
19:31 And certain of the **c of Asia**, which were his *775*
21:31 tidings came unto the **c captain** of *5506*
21:32 and when they saw the **c captain** and *5506*
21:33 Then the **c captain** came near, and *5506*
21:37 he said unto the **c captain**, May I speak *5506*
22:24 The **c captain** commanded him to be *5506*
22:26 heard *that,* he went and told the **c captain**, *5506*
22:27 Then the **c captain** came, and said unto *5506*
22:28 And the **c captain** answered, With a great *5506*
22:29 and the **c captain** also was afraid, after he *5506*
22:30 and commanded the **c priests** and all their *749*
23:10 arose a great dissension, the **c captain**, *5506*
23:14 And they came to the **c priests** and elders, *749*
23:15 ye with the council signify to the **c captain** *5506*
23:17 Bring this young man unto the **c captain**: *5506*
23:18 and brought *him* to the **c captain**, and said, *5506*
23:19 Then the **c captain** took him by the hand, *5506*
23:22 So the **c captain** then let the young man *5506*
24: 7 But the **c captain** Lysias came *upon us,* and *5506*
24:22 When Lysias the **c captain** shall come *5506*
25: 2 the **c** of the Jews informed him against *4413*
25:15 the **c priests** and the elders of the Jews *749*
25:23 with the **c captains**, and principal men of *5506*
26:10 having received authority from the **c priests**; *749*
26:12 and commission from the **c priests**, *749*
28: 7 were possessions of the **c** *man* of the island, *4413*
28:17 that after three days Paul called the **c** of *4413*
Eph 2:20 Jesus Christ himself being the **c corner** *204*
1Ti 1:15 the world to save sinners; of whom I am **c**. *4413*
1Pe 2: 6 Behold, I lay in Sion a **c corner** stone, elect, *204*
5: 4 And when the **c Shepherd** shall appear, *750*
Rev 6:15 and the rich *men,* and the **c captains**, and *5506*

CHIEFEST (9) [CHIEF]

1Sa 2:29 to make yourselves fat with the **c** of all 7225
9:22 made them sit in the **c** place among them 7218
21: 7 the **c** of the herdmen that *belonged* to Saul. 47
2Ch 32:33 they buried him in the **c** of the sepulchres 4608
SS 5:10 and ruddy, the **c** among ten thousand. 1713
Mk 10:44 And whosoever of you will be the **c**, *4413*
2Co 11: 5 *I* was not a whit behind the very **c** apostles. *3029*
12:11 for *in* nothing am I behind the very **c** *3029*
1Ti 6: S which is the **c city** of Phrygia Pacatiana. *3390*

CHIEFLY (3) [CHIEF]

Ro 3: 2 **c**, because that unto them were committed *4412*
Php 4:22 **c** they that are of Cesar's household. *3122*
2Pe 2:10 But **c** them that walk after the flesh in *3122*

CHILD (201) [CHILD'S, CHILDBEARING, CHILDHOOD, CHILDISH, CHILDLESS, CHILDREN, CHILDREN'S]

Ge 11:30 But Sarai was barren; she had no **c**. 2056
16:11 thou *art* **with c**, and shalt bear a son, and 2030
17:10 Every man *c* among you shall be NIH
17:12 every man *c* in your generations, he that is NIH
17:14 the uncircumcised man *c* whose flesh of his NIH
17:17 Shall *a c* be born unto him that is an NIH
18:13 Shall I of a surety bear *a c*, which am old? NIH
19:36 Thus were both the daughters of Lot **with c** 2029
21: 8 the **c** grew, and was weaned: and 3206
21:14 her shoulder, and the **c**, and sent her away: 3206
21:15 and she cast the **c** under one of the shrubs. 3206
21:16 she said, Let me not see the death of the **c**. 3206
37:30 unto his brethren, and said, The **c** *is* not; 3206
38:24 also, behold, she *is* **with c** by whoredom. 2030
38:25 By the man, whose these *are, am* I **with c**: 2030
42:22 unto you, saying, Do not sin against the **c**; 3206
44:20 old man, and a **c** of *his* old age, a little one; 3206
Ex 2: 2 when she saw him that he *was a* goodly *c,* NIH
2: 3 and with pitch, and put the **c** therein; 3206
2: 6 when she had opened *it,* she saw the **c**: and 3206
2: 7 that she may nurse the **c** for thee? 3206
2: 9 Take this **c** away, and nurse it for me, and 3206
2: 9 And the woman took the **c**, and nursed it. 3206
2:10 the **c** grew, and she brought him unto 3206
21:22 hurt a woman with **c**, so that her fruit 2030
22:22 shall not afflict any widow, or **fatherless c**. 3490
Lev 12: 2 have conceived seed, and born a **man c**: 2145
12: 5 if she bear a **maid c**, then she shall be 5347
22:13 have no **c**, and is returned unto her father's 2233
Nu 11:12 as a nursing father beareth the **sucking c**, 3243
Dt 25: 5 and one of them die, and have no **c**, 1121
Jdg 11:34 she *was his* only **c**; beside her he had 3173
13: 5 for the **c** shall be a Nazarite unto God from 5288
13: 7 neither eat any unclean *thing:* for the **c** shall 5288
13: 8 teach us what we shall do unto the **c** that 5288
13:12 How shall we order the **c**, and *how* shall we 5288
13:24 the **c** grew, and the LORD blessed him. 5288
Ru 4:16 Naomi took the **c**, and laid it in her bosom, 3206
1Sa 1:11 wilt give unto thine handmaid a man **c**, then 2233
1:22 *I will not go up* until the **c** be weaned, and 5288
1:24 the LORD *in* Shiloh: and the **c** *was* young. 5288
1:25 slew a bullock, and brought the **c** to Eli. 5288
1:27 For this **c** I prayed; and the LORD hath 5288
2:11 the **c** did minister unto the LORD before 5288
2:18 *being* a **c**, girded *with* a linen ephod. 5288
2:21 And the **c** Samuel grew before the LORD. 5288
2:26 the **c** Samuel grew on, and was in favour 5288
3: 1 the **c** Samuel ministered unto the LORD 5288
3: 8 perceived that the LORD had called the **c**. 5288
4:19 Phinehas' wife, was **with c**, *near* to be 2030
4:21 she named the **c** Ichabod, saying, The glory 5288
2Sa 6:23 of Saul had no **c** unto the day of her death. 2056
11: 5 sent and told David, and said, I *am* **with c**. 2030
12:14 the **c** also that is born unto thee shall surely 1121
12:15 the LORD strake the **c** that Uriah's wife 3206
12:16 David therefore besought God for the **c**; 5288
12:18 to pass on the seventh day, that the **c** died. 3206
12:18 feared to tell him that the **c** was dead: 3206
12:18 they said, Behold, while the **c** was *yet* alive, 3206
12:18 if we tell him *that* the **c** is dead? 3206
12:19 David perceived that the **c** was dead: 3206
12:19 David said unto his servants, Is the **c** dead? 3206
12:21 thou didst fast and weep for the **c**, *while it* 3206
12:21 when the **c** was dead, thou didst rise and 3206
12:22 While the **c** *was* yet alive, I fasted and 3206
12:22 will be gracious to me, that the **c** may live? 3206
1Ki 3: 7 *I am but* a little **c**: I know not *how* to go out 5288
3:17 I was **delivered of a c** with her in 3205
3:19 this woman's **c** died in the night; because 1121
3:20 and laid her dead **c** in my bosom. 1121
3:21 when I rose in the morning to give my **c** 1121
3:25 Divide the living **c** in two, and give half to 3206
3:26 spake the woman whose the living **c** *was* 1121
3:26 give her the living **c**, and in no wise slay it. 3205
3:27 Give her the living **c**, and in no wise slay it: 3205
11:17 to go *into* Egypt; Hadad *being yet* a little **c**. 5288
13: 2 a **c** *shall be* born unto the house of David, 1121
14: 3 shall tell thee what shall become of the **c**. 5288
14:12 thy feet enter into the city, the **c** shall die. 3206
14:17 to the threshold of the door, the **c** died; 5288
17:21 he stretched himself upon the **c** three times, 3206
17:22 the soul of the **c** came into him again, and 3206
17:23 Elijah took the **c**, and brought him down 3206
2Ki 4:14 Verily she hath no **c**, and her husband is 1121
4:18 when the **c** was grown, it fell on a day, 3206
4:26 *is it* well with the **c**? And she answered, 3206
4:29 and lay my staff upon the face of the **c**. 5288
4:30 the mother of the **c** said, *As* the LORD 5288
4:31 and laid the staff upon the face of the **c**; 5288
4:31 and told him, saying, The **c** is not awaked. 5288
4:32 the **c** was dead, *and* laid upon his bed. 5288
4:34 lay upon the **c**, and put his mouth upon his 3206

2Ki 4:34 he stretched himself upon the c^s; and 2050.2
4:34 and the flesh of the c waxed warm. 3206
4:35 the c neesed seven times, and the child 5288
4:35 seven times, and the c opened his eyes. 5288
5:14 came again like unto the flesh of a little c, 5288
8:12 and rip up their **women with** c. 2030
15:16 all the **women** therein that were **with** c he 2030
Job 3: 3 *it was* said, There is a **man** c conceived. 1397
Ps 131: 2 as a c that is **weaned** of his mother: 1580
131: 2 his mother: my soul *is even* as a **weaned** c. 1580
Pr 20:11 Even a c is known by his doings, 5288
22: 6 Train up a c in the way he should go: and 5288
22:15 Foolishness *is* bound in the heart of a c; *but* 5288
23:13 Withhold not correction from the c: for *if* 5288
23:24 he that begetteth a wise *c* shall have joy of NIH
29:15 a c left *to himself* bringeth his mother to 5288
29:21 c shall have him become *his* son at 5290
Ecc 4: 8 a second; yea, he hath neither c nor brother: 1121
4:13 and a wise c than an old and foolish king, 3206
4:15 with the second c that shall stand *up* in his 3206
10:16 when thy king *is* a c, and thy princes eat in 5288
11: 5 *do grow* in the womb of her that is **with** c: 4392
Isa 3: 5 the c shall behave himself proudly against 5288
7:16 For before the c shall know to refuse 5288
8: 4 For before the c shall have knowledge to 5288
9: 6 For unto us a c is born, unto us a Son is 3206
10:19 forest shall be few, that a c may write them. 5288
11: 6 and a little c shall lead them. 5288
11: 8 the **sucking** c shall play on the hole of 3243
11: 8 the **weaned** c shall put his hand on 1580
26:17 Like as a woman **with** c, *that* draweth near 2030
26:18 We have been **with** c, we have been in 2029
49:15 Can a woman forget her **sucking** c, that *she* 5764
54: 1 thou *that* didst not **travail with** c: 2342
65:20 for the c shall die an hundred years old; but 5288
66: 7 pain came, she was delivered of a **man** c. 2145
Jer 1: 6 behold, I cannot speak: for I *am* a c. 5288
1: 7 the LORD said unto me, Say not, I *am* a c: 5288
4:31 as of her that **bringeth forth** her **first** c, 1069
20:15 saying, A man c is born unto thee; 1121
30: 6 and see whether a man doth **travail with** c? 3205
31: 8 the woman **with** c and her that travaileth 2030
31: 8 and her that **travaileth with** c together: 3205
31:20 *is he* a pleasant c? for since I spake against 3206
44: 7 from you man and woman, c and suckling, 5768
La 4: 4 The tongue of the **sucking** c cleaveth to 3243
Hos 11: 1 When Israel *was* a c, then I loved him, and 5288
13:16 and their **women with** c shall be ript up. 2030
Am 1:13 they have ript up the **women with** c at 2030
Mt 1:18 **with** c of the Holy Ghost. *1064+1722+2192*
1:23 a virgin shall be **with** c, and *1064+1722+2192*
2: 8 Go and search diligently for the **young** c; *3813*
2: 9 and stood over where the **young** c was. *3813*
2:11 they saw the **young** c with Mary his *3813*
2:13 and take the **young** c and his mother, and *3813*
2:13 for Herod will seek the **young** c to destroy *3813*
2:14 he took the **young** c and his mother by *3813*
2:20 and take the **young** c and his mother, and *3813*
2:21 and took the **young** c and his mother, and *3813*
10:21 up the brother to death, and the father the c: *5043*
17:18 and the c was cured from that *very* hour. *3816*
18: 2 And Jesus called a **little** c unto *him,* and *3813*
18: 4 shall humble himself as this **little** c, *3813*
18: 5 And whoso shall receive one such **little** c in *3813*
23:15 ye make him twofold more *the* c of hell *5207*
24:19 woe unto them that are **with** c, *1064+1722+2192*
Mk 9:21 this came unto him? And he said, **Of a** c. *3812*
9:24 And straightway the father of the c cried *3813*
9:36 And he took a c, and set him in the midst of *3813*
10:15 receive the kingdom of God as a **little** c, *3813*
13:17 But woe to them that are with c, and *1064*
Lk 1: 7 And they had no c, because that Elisabeth *5043*
1:59 eighth day they came to circumcise the c; *3813*
1:66 saying, What *manner of* c shall this be! *3813*
1:76 And thou, c, shalt be called the prophet of *3813*
1:80 And the c grew, and waxed strong in spirit, *3813*
2: 5 his espoused wife, being **great with** c. *1471*
2:17 which was told them concerning this c. *3813*
2:21 accomplished for the circumcising of the c, *3813*
2:27 when the parents brought in the c Jesus, *3813*
2:34 this *c* is set for the fall and rising again of NIG
2:40 And the c grew, and waxed strong in spirit, *3813*
2:43 the c Jesus tarried behind in Jerusalem; *3816*
9:38 look upon my son: for he is mine **only** c. *3439*
9:42 and healed the c, and delivered him again *3816*
9:47 of their heart, took a c, and set him by him, *3813*
9:48 Whosoever shall receive this c in my name *3813*
18:17 as a **little** c shall in no wise enter therein. *3813*
21:23 woe unto them that are **with** c, *1064+1722+2192*
Jn 4:49 unto him, Sir, come down ere my c die. *3813*
16:21 but as soon as she is delivered of the c, *3813*
Ac 4:27 For of a truth against thy holy c Jesus, *3816*
4:30 be done by the name of thy holy c Jesus. *3816*
7: 5 his seed after him, when *as yet* he had no c. *5043*
13:10 and all mischief, *thou* c of the devil, *5207*
1Co 13:11 When I was a c, I spake as a child, *3516*
13:11 When I was a child, I spake as a c, *3516*
13:11 I spake as a child, I understood as a c, *3516*
13:11 I understood as a child, I thought as a c: *3516*
Gal 4: 1 I say, *That* the heir, as long as he is a c, *3516*
1Th 5: 3 travail upon a *woman* **with** c; *1064+1722+2192*
2Ti 3:15 And that from a c thou hast known the holy *1025*
Heb 11:11 was **delivered of a** c when *she* was past *5088*
11:23 because they saw *he was* a proper c; *3813*
Rev 12: 2 And she being with c cried, travailing in *1064*
12: 4 for to devour her c as soon as it was born. *5043*
12: 5 And she brought forth a man c, who was to *5207*
12: 5 and her c was caught up unto God, and *5043*
12:13 the woman which brought forth the man c. NIG

CHILD'S (4) [CHILD]

Ex 2: 8 And the maid went and called the c mother. 3206
1Ki 17:21 let this c soul come into him again. 3206
Job 33:25 His flesh shall be fresher than a c: he shall 5290
Mt 2:20 for they are dead which sought the **young** c *3813*

CHILDBEARING (1) [BEAR, CHILD]

1Ti 2:15 Notwithstanding she shall be saved in c, *5042*

CHILDHOOD (2) [CHILD]

1Sa 12: 2 I have walked before you from my c unto 5271
Ecc 11:10 from thy flesh: for c and youth *are* vanity. 3208

CHILDISH (1) [CHILD]

1Co 13:11 when I became a man, I put away c *things.* *3516*

CHILDLESS (7) [CHILD]

Ge 15: 2 seeing I go c, and the steward of my house 6185
Lev 20:20 they shall bear their sin; they shall die c. 6185
20:21 his brother's nakedness; they shall be c. 6185
1Sa 15:33 As thy sword hath **made** women c, so 7921
15:33 so shall thy mother be c among women. 7921
Jer 22:30 saith the LORD, Write ye this man c, 6185
Lk 20:30 the second took her to wife, and he died c. *815*

CHILDREN (1803) [CHILD]

Ge 3:16 in sorrow thou shalt bring forth c; and 1121
6: 4 they bare c to them, the same *became* NIH
10:21 Shem also, the father of all the c of Eber, 1121
10:21 Japheth the elder, even to him were *c* born. NIH
10:22 The c of Shem; Elam, and Asshur, and 1121
10:23 the c of Aram; Uz, and Hul, and Gether, 1121
11: 5 and the tower, which the c of men builded. 1121
16: 1 Now Sarai Abram's wife bare him no c: and NIH
16: 2 it may be that I may **obtain** c by her. 1129
18:19 that he will command his c and his 1121
19:38 the same *is* the father of the c of Ammon 1121
20:17 and his maidservants; and they bare *c.* NIH
21: 7 that Sarah should have given c suck? 1121
22:20 she hath also born c unto thy brother 1121
23: 5 the c of Heth answered Abraham, saying 1121
23: 7 people of the land, *even* to the c of Heth. 1121
23:10 Ephron dwelt amongst the c of Heth: and 1121
23:10 Abraham in the audience of the c of Heth, 1121
23:18 possession in the presence of the c of Heth, 1121
25: 4 Eldaah. All these *were* the c of Keturah. 1121
25:22 the c struggled together within her; and 1121
30: 1 when Rachel saw that she bare Jacob no *c,* NIH
30: 1 said unto Jacob, Give me c, or else I die. 1121
30: 3 my knees, that I may also **have** c by her. 1129
30:26 Give *me* my wives and my c, for whom I 3206
31:43 *these* c *are* my children, and *these* 1121+3807.1
31:43 *these* children *are* my c, and *these* cattle *are* 1121
31:43 or unto their c which they have born? 1121
32:11 and smite me, *and* the mother with the c. 1121
32:32 Therefore the c of Israel eat not *of* 1121
33: 1 he divided the c unto Leah, and 3206
33: 2 he put the handmaids and their c foremost, 3206
33: 2 Leah and her c after, and Rachel and 3206

Ge	33: 5	up his eyes, and saw the women and the **c**;	3206
	33: 5	The **c** which God hath graciously given thy	3206
	33: 6	they and their **c**, and they bowed	3206
	33: 7	Leah also with her **c** came near, and	3206
	33:13	My lord knoweth that the **c** *are* tender, and	3206
	33:14	before me and the **c** be able to endure,	3206
	33:19	at the hand of the **c** of Hamor,	1121
	36:21	the **c** of Seir in the land of Edom.	1121
	36:22	the **c** of Lotan were Hori and Hemam; and	1121
	36:23	the **c** of Shobal *were* these; Alvan, and	1121
	36:24	these *are* the **c** of Zibeon; both Aiah, and	1121
	36:25	the **c** of Anah *were* these; Dishon, and	1121
	36:26	these *are* the **c** of Dishon; Hemdan, and	1121
	36:27	The **c** of Ezer *are* these; Bilhan, and	1121
	36:28	The **c** of Dishan *are* these; Uz, and Aran.	1121
	36:31	before there reigned *any* king over the **c** of	1121
	37: 3	Israel loved Joseph more than all his **c**,	1121
	42:36	unto them, Me have ye **bereaved of** my **c**:	7921
	43:14	If I be **bereaved of** my **c**, I am bereaved.	7921
	45:10	thy **c**, and thy children's children, and	1121
	45:10	thy children's **c**, and thy flocks, and	1121
	45:21	the **c** of Israel did so: and Joseph gave them	1121
	46: 8	these *are* the names of the **c** of Israel,	1121
	49: 8	thy father's **c** shall bow down before thee.	1121
	49:32	of the cave that *is* therein *was* from the **c** of	1121
	50:23	Joseph saw Ephraim's **c** of the third	1121
	50:23	**c** also of Machir the son of Manasseh were	1121
	50:25	Joseph took an oath of the **c** of Israel,	1121
Ex	1: 1	Now these *are* the names of the **c** of Israel,	1121
	1: 7	the **c** of Israel were fruitful, and	1121
	1: 9	the people of the **c** of Israel *are* moe and	1121
	1:12	were grieved because of the **c** of Israel.	1121
	1:13	the Egyptians made the **c** of Israel to serve	1121
	1:17	but saved the **men c** alive.	3206
	1:18	this thing, and have saved the **men c** alive?	3206
	2: 6	and said, This *is one* of the Hebrews' **c**.	3206
	2:23	the **c** of Israel sighed by reason of	1121
	2:25	God looked upon the **c** of Israel, and	1121
	3: 9	the cry of the **c** of Israel is come unto me:	1121
	3:10	my people the **c** of Israel out of Egypt.	1121
	3:11	that I should bring forth the **c** of Israel out	1121
	3:13	*when* I come unto the **c** of Israel, and	1121
	3:14	Thus shalt thou say unto the **c** of Israel,	1121
	3:15	Thus shalt thou say unto the **c** of Israel,	1121
	4:29	gathered together all the elders of the **c** of	1121
	4:31	that the LORD had visited the **c** of Israel,	1121
	5:14	the officers of the **c** of Israel,	1121
	5:15	the officers of the **c** of Israel came and	1121
	5:19	the officers of the **c** of Israel did see *that*	1121
	6: 5	I have also heard the groaning of the **c** of	1121
	6: 6	Wherefore say unto the **c** of Israel, I *am*	1121
	6: 9	Moses spake so unto the **c** of Israel: but	1121
	6:11	that he let the **c** of Israel go out of his land.	1121
	6:12	the **c** of Israel have not hearkened unto me;	1121
	6:13	gave them a charge unto the **c** of Israel, and	1121
	6:13	to bring the **c** of Israel out of the land of	1121
	6:26	Bring out the **c** of Israel from the land of	1121
	6:27	to bring out the **c** of Israel from Egypt:	1121
	7: 2	that he send the **c** of Israel out of his land.	1121
	7: 4	mine armies, *and* my people the **c** of Israel,	1121
	7: 5	bring out the **c** of Israel from among them.	1121
	9: 6	of the cattle of the **c** of Israel died not one.	1121
	9:26	where the **c** of Israel *were,* was there no	1121
	9:35	neither would he let the **c** of Israel go;	1121
	10:20	so that he would not let the **c** of Israel go.	1121
	10:23	all the **c** of Israel had light in their	1121
	11: 7	against any of the **c** of Israel shall not a dog	1121
	11:10	that he would not let the **c** of Israel go out	1121
	12:26	to pass, when your **c** shall say unto you,	1121
	12:27	who passed over the houses of the **c** of	1121
	12:28	the **c** of Israel went away, and did as	1121
	12:31	my people, both you and the **c** of Israel;	1121
	12:35	the **c** of Israel did according to the word of	1121
	12:37	the **c** of Israel journeyed from Rameses to	1121
	12:37	thousand on foot *that were* men, beside **c**.	2945
	12:40	Now the sojourning of the **c** of Israel,	1121
	12:42	of all the **c** of Israel in their generations.	1121
	12:50	Thus did all the **c** of Israel; as the LORD	1121
	12:51	*that* the LORD did bring the **c** of Israel out	1121
	13: 2	whatsoever openeth the womb among the **c**	1121
	13:13	all the firstborn of man amongst thy **c** shalt	1121
	13:15	but all the firstborn of my **c** I redeem.	1121
	13:18	the **c** of Israel went up harnessed out of	1121
	13:19	for he had straitly sworn the **c** of Israel,	1121
	14: 2	Speak unto the **c** of Israel, that they turn	1121
	14: 3	For Pharaoh will say of the **c** of Israel,	1121
	14: 8	and he pursued after the **c** of Israel:	1121
	14: 8	the **c** of Israel went out with a high hand.	1121
	14:10	the **c** of Israel lift up their eyes, and behold,	1121
	14:10	the **c** of Israel cried out unto the LORD.	1121
	14:15	speak unto the **c** of Israel, that they go	1121
	14:16	the **c** of Israel shall go on dry *ground*	1121
	14:22	the **c** of Israel went into the midst of the sea	1121
	14:29	the **c** of Israel walked upon dry *land* in	1121
	15: 1	the **c** of Israel this song unto the LORD,	1121
	15:19	the **c** of Israel went on dry *land* in the midst	1121
	16: 1	all the congregation of the **c** of Israel came	1121
	16: 2	the whole congregation of the **c** of Israel	1121
	16: 3	the **c** of Israel said unto them, Would to	1121
	16: 6	and Aaron said unto all the **c** of Israel,	1121
	16: 9	Say unto all the congregation of the **c** of	1121
	16:10	the whole congregation of the **c** of Israel,	1121
	16:12	I have heard the murmurings of the **c** of	1121
	16:15	when the **c** of Israel saw *it,* they said one to	1121
	16:17	the **c** of Israel did so, and gathered,	1121
	16:35	the **c** of Israel did eat manna forty years,	1121
	17: 1	all the congregation of the **c** of Israel	1121
	17: 3	to kill us and our **c** and our cattle with	1121
	17: 7	because of the chiding of the **c** of Israel,	1121
	19: 1	when the **c** of Israel were gone forth out of	1121
	19: 3	the house of Jacob, and tell the **c** of Israel;	1121
	19: 6	which thou shalt speak unto the **c** of Israel.	1121
	20: 5	of the fathers upon the **c** unto the third	1121
	20:22	Thus thou shalt say unto the **c** of Israel,	1121
	21: 4	the wife and her **c** shall be her master's,	3206
	21: 5	I love my master, my wife, and my **c**;	1121
	22:24	shall be widows, and your **c** fatherless.	1121
	24: 5	he sent young men of the **c** of Israel,	1121
	24:11	upon the nobles of the **c** of Israel he laid	1121
	24:17	of the mount in the eyes of the **c** of Israel.	1121
	25: 2	Speak unto the **c** of Israel, that they bring	1121
	25:22	thee in commandment unto the **c** of Israel.	1121
	27:20	thou shalt command the **c** of Israel,	1121
	27:21	generations on the behalf of the **c** of Israel.	1121
	28: 1	sons with him, from among the **c** of Israel,	1121
	28: 9	grave on them the names of the **c** of Israel:	1121
	28:11	stones with the names of the **c** of Israel:	1121
	28:12	*for* stones of memorial unto the **c** of Israel:	1121
	28:21	the stones shall be with the names of the **c**	1121
	28:29	Aaron shall bear the names of the **c** of	1121
	28:30	Aaron shall bear the judgment of the **c** of	1121
	28:38	**c** of Israel shall hallow in all their holy	1121
	29:28	his sons' by a statute for ever from the **c** of	1121
	29:28	it shall be a heave offering from the **c** of	1121
	29:43	there I will meet with the **c** of Israel, and	1121
	29:45	I will dwell amongst the **c** of Israel, and	1121
	30:12	When thou takest the sum of the **c** of Israel	1121
	30:16	take the atonement money of the **c** of Israel,	1121
	30:16	that it may be a memorial unto the **c** of	1121
	30:31	thou shalt speak unto the **c** of Israel, saying,	1121
	31:13	Speak thou also unto the **c** of Israel, saying,	1121
	31:16	Wherefore the **c** of Israel shall keep	1121
	31:17	between me and the **c** of Israel for ever:	1121
	32:20	and made the **c** of Israel drink *of it.*	1121
	32:28	the **c** of Levi did according to the word of	1121
	33: 5	Say unto the **c** of Israel, Ye *are* a	1121
	33: 6	the **c** of Israel stript themselves of their	1121
	34: 7	the iniquity of the fathers upon the **c**,	1121
	34: 7	upon the children's **c**, unto the third and	1121
	34:23	Thrice in the year shall all your **men c**	2138
	34:30	and all the **c** of Israel saw Moses,	1121
	34:32	afterward all the **c** of Israel came nigh: and	1121
	34:34	spake unto the **c** of Israel *that* which he was	1121
	34:35	the **c** of Israel saw the face of Moses,	1121
	35: 1	the congregation of the **c** of Israel together,	1121
	35: 4	unto all the congregation of the **c** of Israel,	1121
	35:20	all the congregation of the **c** of Israel	1121
	35:29	The **c** of Israel brought a willing offering	1121
	35:30	Moses said unto the **c** of Israel, See,	1121
	36: 3	which the **c** of Israel had brought for	1121
	39: 6	with the names of the **c** of Israel.	1121
	39: 7	*be* stones for a memorial to the **c** of Israel;	1121
	39:14	according to the names of the **c** of Israel,	1121
	39:32	the **c** of Israel did according to all that	1121
	39:42	so the **c** of Israel made all the work.	1121
	40:36	the **c** of Israel went onward in all their	1121
Lev	1: 2	Speak unto the **c** of Israel, and say unto	1121
	4: 2	Speak unto the **c** of Israel, saying, If a soul	1121

C

Lev	6:18	All the males among the c of Aaron shall	1121
	7:23	Speak unto the c of Israel, saying, Ye shall	1121
	7:29	Speak unto the c of Israel, saying, He that	1121
	7:34	the heave shoulder have I taken of the c of	1121
	7:34	statute for ever from among the c of Israel.	1121
	7:36	to be given them of the c of Israel,	1121
	7:38	in the day that he commanded the c of	1121
	9: 3	unto the c of Israel thou shalt speak, saying,	1121
	10:11	that *ye* may teach the c of Israel all	1121
	10:14	of peace offerings of the c of Israel.	1121
	11: 2	Speak unto the c of Israel, saying,	1121
	12: 2	Speak unto the c of Israel, saying, If a	1121
	15: 2	Speak unto the c of Israel, and say unto	1121
	15:31	Thus shall ye separate the c of Israel from	1121
	16: 5	he shall take of the congregation of the c of	1121
	16:16	of the uncleanness of the c of Israel,	1121
	16:19	hallow it from the uncleanness of the c of	1121
	16:21	confess over him all the iniquities of the c	1121
	16:34	to make an atonement for the c of Israel for	1121
	17: 2	unto all the c of Israel, and say unto them;	1121
	17: 5	To the end that the c of Israel may bring	1121
	17:12	Therefore I said unto the c of Israel, No	1121
	17:13	whatsoever man *there be* of the c of Israel,	1121
	17:14	therefore I said unto the c of Israel,	1121
	18: 2	Speak unto the c of Israel, and say unto	1121
	19: 2	Speak unto all the congregation of the c of	1121
	19:18	nor bear any grudge against the c of thy	1121
	20: 2	Again, thou shalt say to the c of Israel,	1121
	20: 2	Whosoever *he be* of the c of Israel, or	1121
	21:24	and to his sons, and unto all the c of Israel.	1121
	22: 2	from the holy *things* of the c of Israel,	1121
	22: 3	that goeth unto the holy *things* which the c	1121
	22:15	profane the holy *things* of the c of Israel,	1121
	22:18	unto all the c of Israel, and say unto them,	1121
	22:32	I will be hallowed among the c of Israel:	1121
	23: 2	Speak unto the c of Israel, and say unto	1121
	23:10	Speak unto the c of Israel, and say unto	1121
	23:24	Speak unto the c of Israel, saying, In	1121
	23:34	Speak unto the c of Israel, saying, The	1121
	23:43	I made the c of Israel to dwell in booths,	1121
	23:44	Moses declared unto the c of Israel	1121
	24: 2	Command the c of Israel, that they bring	1121
	24: 8	*being taken* from the c of Israel *by* an	1121
	24:10	went out among the c of Israel:	1121
	24:15	thou shalt speak unto the c of Israel, saying,	1121
	24:23	Moses spake to the c of Israel, that they	1121
	24:23	the c of Israel did as the LORD	1121
	25: 2	Speak unto the c of Israel, and say unto	1121
	25:33	*are* their possession among the c of Israel.	1121
	25:41	*both* he and his c with him, and shall return	1121
	25:45	Moreover of the c of the strangers that do	1121
	25:46	them as an inheritance for your c after you,	1121
	25:46	over your brethren the c of Israel, ye shall	1121
	25:54	year of jubile, *both* he, and his c with him.	1121
	25:55	For unto me the c of Israel *are* servants;	1121
	26:22	which shall **rob** you **of** your c, and	7921
	26:46	the c of Israel in mount Sinai by the hand	1121
	27: 2	Speak unto the c of Israel, and say unto	1121
	27:34	Moses for the c of Israel in mount Sinai.	1121
Nu	1: 2	of all the congregation of the c of Israel,	1121
	1:10	Of the c of Joseph: of Ephraim;	1121
	1:20	the c of Reuben, Israel's eldest son, *by* their	1121
	1:22	Of the c of Simeon, *by* their generations,	1121
	1:24	Of the c of Gad, *by* their generations,	1121
	1:26	Of the c of Judah, *by* their generations,	1121
	1:28	Of the c of Issachar, *by* their generations,	1121
	1:30	Of the c of Zebulun, *by* their generations,	1121
	1:32	Of the c of Joseph, *namely,* of the children	1121
	1:32	*namely,* of the c of Ephraim, *by* their	1121
	1:34	Of the c of Manasseh, *by* their generations,	1121
	1:36	Of the c of Benjamin, *by* their generations,	1121
	1:38	Of the c of Dan, *by* their generations,	1121
	1:40	Of the c of Asher, *by* their generations,	1121
	1:42	*Of* the c of Naphtali, *throughout* their	1121
	1:45	those that were numbered of the c of Israel,	1121
	1:49	neither take the sum of them among the c	1121
	1:52	the c of Israel shall pitch their tents,	1121
	1:53	upon the congregation of the c of Israel:	1121
	1:54	the c of Israel did according to all that	1121
	2: 2	Every man of the c of Israel shall pitch by	1121
	2: 3	*shall be* captain of the c of Judah.	1121
	2: 5	of Zuar *shall be* captain of the c of Issachar.	1121
	2: 7	Helon *shall be* captain of the c of Zebulun.	1121
	2:10	the captain of the c of Reuben *shall be*	1121
	2:12	the captain of the c of Simeon *shall be*	1121
	2:20	the captain of the c of Manasseh *shall be*	1121
	2:25	the captain of the c of Dan *shall be* Ahiezer	1121
	2:27	the captain of the c of Asher *shall be* Pagiel	1121
	2:29	the captain of the c of Naphtali *shall be*	1121
	2:32	the c of Israel by the house of their fathers:	1121
	2:33	the Levites were not numbered among the c	1121
	2:34	the c of Israel did according to all that	1121
	3: 4	the wilderness of Sinai, and they had no c:	1121
	3: 8	the charge of the c of Israel, to do	1121
	3: 9	they *are* wholly given unto him out of the c	1121
	3:12	I have taken the Levites from among the c	1121
	3:12	openeth the matrix among the c of Israel:	1121
	3:15	Number the c of Levi after the house of	1121
	3:38	sanctuary for the charge of the c of Israel;	1121
	3:40	males of the c of Israel from a month old	1121
	3:41	instead of all the firstborn among the c of	1121
	3:41	firstlings among the cattle of the c of Israel.	1121
	3:42	all the firstborn among the c of Israel.	1121
	3:45	of all the firstborn among the c of Israel,	1121
	3:46	thirteen of the firstborn of the c of Israel,	1121
	3:50	Of the firstborn of the c of Israel took he	1121
	5: 2	Command the c of Israel, that they put out	1121
	5: 4	the c of Israel did so, and put them out	1121
	5: 4	spake unto Moses, so did the c of Israel.	1121
	5: 6	Speak unto the c of Israel, When a man or	1121
	5: 9	every offering of all the holy *things* of the c	1121
	5:12	Speak unto the c of Israel, and say unto	1121
	6: 2	Speak unto the c of Israel, and say unto	1121
	6:23	On this wise ye shall bless the c of Israel,	1121
	6:27	they shall put my name upon the c of Israel;	1121
	7:24	prince of the c of Zebulun, *did offer:*	1121
	7:30	prince of the c of Reuben, *did offer:*	1121
	7:36	prince of the c of Simeon, *did offer:*	1121
	7:42	of Deuel, prince of the c of Gad, *offered:*	1121
	7:48	prince of the c of Ephraim, *offered:*	1121
	7:54	of Pedahzur, prince of the c of Manasseh:	1121
	7:60	prince of the c of Benjamin, *offered:*	1121
	7:66	prince of the c of Dan, *offered:*	1121
	7:72	of Ocran, prince of the c of Asher, *offered:*	1121
	7:78	prince of the c of Naphtali, *offered:*	1121
	8: 6	Take the Levites from among the c of	1121
	8: 9	whole assembly of the c of Israel together:	1121
	8:10	the c of Israel shall put their hands upon	1121
	8:11	LORD *for* an offering of the c of Israel,	1121
	8:14	the Levites from among the c of Israel:	1121
	8:16	given unto me from among the c of Israel;	1121
	8:16	*even instead of* the firstborn of all the c of	1121
	8:17	For all the firstborn of the c of Israel *are*	1121
	8:18	for all the firstborn of the c of Israel.	1121
	8:19	and to his sons from among the c of Israel,	1121
	8:19	to do the service of the c of Israel in	1121
	8:19	to make an atonement for the c of Israel:	1121
	8:19	that there be no plague among the c of	1121
	8:19	when the c of Israel come nigh unto	1121
	8:20	and all the congregation of the c of Israel,	1121
	8:20	the Levites, so did the c of Israel unto them.	1121
	9: 2	Let the c of Israel also keep the passover at	1121
	9: 4	Moses spake unto the c of Israel, that they	1121
	9: 5	commanded Moses, so did the c of Israel.	1121
	9: 7	his appointed season among the c of Israel?	1121
	9:10	Speak unto the c of Israel, saying, If any	1121
	9:17	then after that the c of Israel journeyed:	1121
	9:17	there the c of Israel pitched their tents.	1121
	9:18	At the commandment of the LORD the c	1121
	9:19	the c of Israel kept the charge of	1121
	9:22	the c of Israel abode in their tents, and	1121
	10:12	the c of Israel took their journeys out of	1121
	10:14	of the c of Judah according to their armies:	1121
	10:15	over the host of the tribe of the c of	1121
	10:16	over the host of the tribe of the c of	1121
	10:19	over the host of the tribe of the c of Simeon	1121
	10:20	over the host of the tribe of the c of Gad	1121
	10:22	the standard of the camp of the c of	1121
	10:23	over the host of the tribe of the c of	1121
	10:24	over the host of the tribe of the c of	1121
	10:25	the standard of the camp of the c of Dan set	1121
	10:26	over the host of the tribe of the c of Asher	1121
	10:27	over the host of the tribe of the c of	1121
	10:28	Thus *were* the journeyings of the c of Israel	1121
	11: 4	the c of Israel also wept again, and said,	1121
	13: 2	which I give unto the c of Israel:	1121
	13: 3	all those men *were* heads of the c of Israel.	1121
	13:22	Sheshai, and Talmai, the c of Anak,	3211

Nu 13:24 of the cluster of grapes which the **c** of Israel 1121
13:26 to all the congregation of the **c** of Israel, 1121
13:28 and moreover we saw the **c** of Anak there. 3211
13:32 they had searched unto the **c** of Israel, 1121
14: 2 all the **c** of Israel murmured against Moses 1121
14: 3 *that* our wives and our **c** should be a prey? 2945
14: 5 of the congregation of the **c** of Israel. 1121
14: 7 they spake unto all the company of the **c** of 1121
14:10 the congregation before all the **c** of Israel. 1121
14:18 of the fathers upon the **c** unto the third 1121
14:27 I have heard the murmurings of the **c** of 1121
14:33 your **c** shall wander in the wilderness forty 1121
14:39 Moses told these sayings unto all the **c** of 1121
15: 2 Speak unto the **c** of Israel, and say unto 1121
15:18 Speak unto the **c** of Israel, and say unto 1121
15:25 for all the congregation of the **c** of Israel, 1121
15:26 all the congregation of the **c** of Israel, 1121
15:29 *both for* him that is born amongst the **c** of 1121
15:32 while the **c** of Israel were in the wilderness, 1121
15:38 Speak unto the **c** of Israel, and bid them 1121
16: 2 with certain of the **c** of Israel, two hundred 1121
16:27 and their sons, and their **little c**. 2945
16:38 and they shall be a sign unto the **c** of Israel. 1121
16:40 *To be* a memorial unto the **c** of Israel, that 1121
16:41 on the morrow all the congregation of the **c** 1121
17: 2 Speak unto the **c** of Israel, and take of 1121
17: 5 from me the murmurings of the **c** of Israel, 1121
17: 6 Moses spake unto the **c** of Israel, and 1121
17: 9 before the Lord unto all the **c** of Israel: 1121
17:12 the **c** of Israel spake unto Moses, saying, 1121
18: 5 that there be no wrath any more upon the **c** 1121
18: 6 the Levites from among the **c** of Israel: 1121
18: 8 of all the hallowed *things* of the **c** of Israel; 1121
18:11 with all the wave offerings of the **c** of 1121
18:19 which the **c** of Israel offer unto the Lord, 1121
18:20 and thine inheritance among the **c** of Israel. 1121
18:21 I have given the **c** of Levi all the tenth in 1121
18:22 Neither must the **c** of Israel henceforth 1121
18:23 that among the **c** of Israel they have no 1121
18:24 the tithes of the **c** of Israel, which they offer 1121
18:24 Among the **c** of Israel they shall have no 1121
18:26 When ye take of the **c** of Israel the tithes 1121
18:28 which ye receive of the **c** of Israel; 1121
18:32 ye pollute the holy *things* of the **c** of Israel, 1121
19: 2 saying, Speak unto the **c** of Israel, that they 1121
19: 9 it shall be kept for the congregation of the **c** 1121
19:10 it shall be unto the **c** of Israel, and unto 1121
20: 1 came the **c** of Israel, *even* the whole 1121
20:12 to sanctify me in the eyes of the **c** of Israel, 1121
20:13 the **c** of Israel strove with the Lord, 1121
20:19 the **c** of Israel said unto him, We will go by 1121
20:22 the **c** of Israel, *even* the whole 1121
20:24 which I have given unto the **c** of Israel, 1121
21:10 the **c** of Israel set forward, and pitched in 1121
21:24 unto Jabbok, *even* unto the **c** of Ammon: 1121
21:24 for the border of the **c** of Ammon *was* 1121
22: 1 the **c** of Israel set forward, and pitched in 1121
22: 3 was distressed because of the **c** of Israel. 1121
22: 5 which *is* by the river *of* the land of the **c** of 1121
24:17 of Moab, and destroy all the **c** of Sheth. 1121
25: 6 one of the **c** of Israel came and 1121
25: 6 in the sight of all the congregation of the **c** 1121
25: 8 So the plague was stayed from the **c** of 1121
25:11 hath turned my wrath away from the **c** of 1121
25:11 that I consumed not the **c** of Israel in my 1121
25:13 and made an atonement for the **c** of Israel. 1121
26: 2 of all the congregation of the **c** of Israel, 1121
26: 4 commanded Moses and the **c** of Israel, 1121
26: 5 the **c** of Reuben; Hanoch, *of whom cometh* 1121
26:11 Notwithstanding the **c** of Korah died not. 1121
26:15 The **c** of Gad after their families: 1121
26:18 These *are* the families of the **c** of Gad 1121
26:44 *Of* the **c** of Asher after their families: 1121
26:51 These *were* the numbered of the **c** of Israel, 1121
26:62 for they were not numbered among the **c** of 1121
26:62 given them among the **c** of Israel. 1121
26:63 who numbered the **c** of Israel in the plains 1121
26:64 when they numbered the **c** of Israel in 1121
27: 8 thou shalt speak unto the **c** of Israel, saying, 1121
27:11 it shall be unto the **c** of Israel a statute of 1121
27:12 see the land which I have given unto the **c** 1121
27:20 that all the congregation of the **c** of Israel 1121
27:21 *both* he, and all the **c** of Israel with him, 1121
28: 2 Command the **c** of Israel, and say unto 1121
29:40 Moses told the **c** of Israel according to all 1121
30: 1 of the tribes concerning the **c** of Israel, 1121
31: 2 Avenge the **c** of Israel of the Midianites: 1121
31: 9 the **c** of Israel took *all* the women of 1121
31:12 and unto the congregation of the **c** of Israel, 1121
31:16 Behold, these caused the **c** of Israel, 1121
31:18 all the women **c**, that have not known a 2945
31:30 of the **c** of Israel's half, thou shalt take one 1121
31:42 of the **c** of Israel's half, which Moses 1121
31:47 Even of the **c** of Israel's half, Moses took 1121
31:54 *for* a memorial for the **c** of Israel before 1121
32: 1 Now the **c** of Reuben and the children of 1121
32: 1 the **c** of Gad had a very great multitude of 1121
32: 2 The **c** of Gad and the children of Reuben 1121
32: 2 the **c** of Reuben came and spake unto 1121
32: 6 Moses said unto the **c** of Gad and to 1121
32: 6 the children of Gad and to the **c** of Reuben, 1121
32: 7 wherefore discourage ye the heart of the **c** 1121
32: 9 they discouraged the heart of the **c** of Israel, 1121
32:17 will go ready armed before the **c** of Israel, 1121
32:18 until the **c** of Israel have inherited every 1121
32:25 the **c** of Gad and the children of Reuben 1121
32:25 and the **c** of Reuben spake unto Moses, 1121
32:28 the chief fathers of the tribes of the **c** of 1121
32:29 If the **c** of Gad and the children of Reuben 1121
32:29 the **c** of Reuben will pass with you over 1121
32:31 the **c** of Gad and the children of Reuben 1121
32:31 of Gad and the **c** of Reuben answered, 1121
32:33 *even* to the **c** of Gad, and to the children of 1121
32:33 to the **c** of Reuben, and unto half the tribe 1121
32:34 the **c** of Gad built Dibon, and Ataroth, and 1121
32:37 the **c** of Reuben built Heshbon, and 1121
32:39 the **c** of Machir the son of Manasseh went 1121
33: 1 These *are* the journeys of the **c** of Israel, 1121
33: 3 on the morrow after the passover the **c** of 1121
33: 5 the **c** of Israel removed from Rameses, and 1121
33:38 in the fortieth year after the **c** of Israel were 1121
33:40 heard of the coming of the **c** of Israel. 1121
33:51 Speak unto the **c** of Israel, and say unto 1121
34: 2 Command the **c** of Israel, and say unto 1121
34:13 Moses commanded the **c** of Israel, saying, 1121
34:14 For the tribe of the **c** of Reuben according 1121
34:14 the tribe of the **c** of Gad according to 1121
34:20 of the tribe of the **c** of Simeon, Shemuel 1121
34:22 the prince of the tribe of the **c** of Dan, 1121
34:23 The prince of the **c** of Joseph, for the tribe 1121
34:23 for the tribe of the **c** of Manasseh, 1121
34:24 the prince of the tribe of the **c** of Ephraim, 1121
34:25 the prince of the tribe of the **c** of Zebulun, 1121
34:26 the prince of the tribe of the **c** of Issachar, 1121
34:27 the prince of the tribe of the **c** of Asher, 1121
34:28 the prince of the tribe of the **c** of Naphtali, 1121
34:29 unto the **c** of Israel in the land of Canaan. 1121
35: 2 Command the **c** of Israel, that they give 1121
35: 8 *shall be* of the possession of the **c** of Israel: 1121
35:10 Speak unto the **c** of Israel, and say unto 1121
35:15 *both* for the **c** of Israel, and for the stranger, 1121
35:34 for I the Lord dwell among the **c** of 1121
36: 1 the chief fathers of the families of the **c** of 1121
36: 1 the chief fathers of the **c** of Israel: 1121
36: 2 for an inheritance by lot to the **c** of Israel: 1121
36: 3 sons of the *other* tribes of the **c** of Israel, 1121
36: 4 when the jubile of the **c** of Israel shall be, 1121
36: 5 Moses commanded the **c** of Israel 1121
36: 7 So shall not the inheritance of the **c** of 1121
36: 7 for every one of the **c** of Israel shall keep 1121
36: 8 an inheritance in any tribe of the **c** of Israel, 1121
36: 8 that the **c** of Israel may enjoy every man 1121
36: 9 every one of the tribes of the **c** of Israel 1121
36:13 **c** of Israel in the plains of Moab by Jordan 1121
Dt 1: 3 *that* Moses spake unto the **c** of Israel, 1121
1:36 to his **c**, because he hath wholly followed 1121
1:39 which ye said should be a prey, and your **c**, 1121
2: 4 the coast of your brethren the **c** of Esau, 1121
2: 8 when we passed by from our brethren the **c** 1121
2: 9 I have given Ar unto the **c** of Lot *for* a 1121
2:12 the **c** of Esau succeeded them, when they 1121
2:19 *when* thou comest nigh over against the **c** 1121
2:19 for I will not give thee of the land of the **c** 1121
2:19 I have given it unto the **c** of Lot *for* a 1121
2:22 As he did to the **c** of Esau, which dwelt in 1121
2:29 (As the **c** of Esau which dwell in Seir, and 1121
2:37 Only unto the land of the **c** of Ammon thou 1121
3: 6 the men, women, and **c**, of every city. 2945

Dt	3:11	*is* it not in Rabbath of the **c** of Ammon?	1121
	3:16	*which is* the border of the **c** of Ammon;	1121
	3:18	armed before your brethren the **c** of Israel,	1121
	4:10	the earth, and *that* they may teach their **c**.	1121
	4:25	When thou shalt beget **c**, and	1121
	4:25	children's **c**, and ye shall have remained	1121
	4:40	with thy **c** after thee, and that thou mayest	1121
	4:44	this *is* the law which Moses set before the **c**	1121
	4:45	which Moses spake unto the **c** of Israel,	1121
	4:46	whom Moses and the **c** of Israel smote,	1121
	5: 9	the iniquity of the fathers upon the **c**	1121
	5:29	well with them, and with their **c** for ever!	1121
	6: 7	thou shalt teach them diligently unto thy **c**,	1121
	9: 2	people great and tall, the **c** of the Anakims,	1121
	9: 2	*say,* Who can stand before the **c** of Anak!	1121
	10: 6	the **c** of Israel took their journey from	1121
	10: 6	from Beeroth of the **c** of Jaakan *to* Mosera:	1121
	11: 2	for *I speak* not with your **c** which have not	1121
	11:19	ye shall teach them your **c**, speaking of	1121
	11:21	may be multiplied, and the days of your **c**,	1121
	12:25	go well with thee, and with thy **c** after thee,	1121
	12:28	with thee, and with thy **c** after thee for ever,	1121
	13:13	*Certain* men, the **c** of Belial, are gone out	1121
	14: 1	Ye *are* the **c** of the LORD your God:	1121
	17:20	he, and his **c**, in the midst of Israel.	1121
	21:15	another hated, and they have born him **c**,	1121
	23: 8	The **c** that are begotten of them shall enter	1121
	24: 7	any of his brethren of the **c** of Israel,	1121
	24:16	fathers shall not be put to death for the **c**,	1121
	24:16	neither shall the **c** be put to death for	1121
	28:54	towards the remnant of his **c** which he shall	1121
	28:55	of the flesh of his **c** whom he shall eat:	1121
	28:57	and towards her **c** which she shall bear:	1121
	29: 1	with the **c** of Israel in the land of Moab,	1121
	29:22	So that the generation to come of your **c**	1121
	29:29	*belong* unto us and to our **c** for ever,	1121
	30: 2	thou and thy **c**, with all thine heart, and	1121
	31:12	**c**, and thy stranger that *is* within thy gates,	2945
	31:13	*that* their **c**, which have not known *any*	1121
	31:19	song for you, and teach it the **c** of Israel:	1121
	31:19	be a witness for me against the **c** of Israel.	1121
	31:22	the same day, and taught it the **c** of Israel.	1121
	31:23	for thou shalt bring the **c** of Israel into	1121
	32: 5	their spot *is* not *the spot* of his **c**:	1121
	32: 8	according to the number of the **c** of Israel.	1121
	32:20	froward generation, **c** in whom *is* no faith.	1121
	32:46	which ye shall command your **c** to observe	1121
	32:49	which I give unto the **c** of Israel for a	1121
	32:51	**c** of Israel at the waters of	1121
	32:51	ye sanctified me not in the midst of the **c** of	1121
	32:52	unto the land which I give the **c** of Israel.	1121
	33: 1	God blessed the **c** of Israel before his death.	1121
	33: 9	his brethren, nor knew his own **c**:	1121
	33:24	Asher he said, *Let* Asher *be* blessed with **c**;	1121
	34: 8	the **c** of Israel wept for Moses in the plains	1121
	34: 9	the **c** of Israel hearkened unto him, and	1121
Jos	1: 2	I do give to them, *even* to the **c** of Israel.	1121
	2: 2	there came men in hither to night of the **c**	1121
	3: 1	he and all the **c** of Israel, and lodged there	1121
	3: 9	Joshua said unto the **c** of Israel,	1121
	4: 4	whom he had prepared of the **c** of Israel,	1121
	4: 5	the number of the tribes of the **c** of Israel:	1121
	4: 6	*that* when your **c** ask *their fathers* in time to	1121
	4: 7	for a memorial unto the **c** of Israel for ever.	1121
	4: 8	the **c** of Israel did so as Joshua commanded,	1121
	4: 8	the number of the tribes of the **c** of Israel,	1121
	4:12	the **c** of Reuben, and the children of Gad,	1121
	4:12	the **c** of Gad, and half the tribe of	1121
	4:12	passed over armed before the **c** of Israel,	1121
	4:21	he spake unto the **c** of Israel, saying,	1121
	4:21	When your **c** shall ask their fathers in time	1121
	4:22	ye shall let your **c** know, saying,	1121
	5: 1	waters of Jordan from before the **c** of Israel,	1121
	5: 1	them any more, because of the **c** of Israel.	1121
	5: 2	circumcise again the **c** of Israel the second	1121
	5: 3	circumcised the **c** of Israel at the hill of	1121
	5: 6	For the **c** of Israel walked forty years in	1121
	5: 7	their **c**, *whom* he raised up in their stead,	1121
	5:10	the **c** of Israel encamped in Gilgal, and	1121
	5:12	neither had the **c** of Israel manna any more;	1121
	6: 1	straitly shut up because of the **c** of Israel:	1121
	7: 1	the **c** of Israel committed a trespass in	1121
	7: 1	LORD was kindled against the **c** of Israel.	1121
	7:12	Therefore the **c** of Israel could not stand	1121
	7:23	unto all the **c** of Israel, and laid them out	1121
	8:31	of the LORD commanded the **c** of Israel,	1121
	8:32	which he wrote in the presence of the **c** of	1121
	9:17	the **c** of Israel journeyed, and came unto	1121
	9:18	And the **c** of Israel smote them not, because	1121
	9:26	delivered them out of the hand of the **c** of	1121
	10: 4	peace with Joshua and with the **c** of Israel.	1121
	10:11	whom the **c** of Israel slew with the sword.	1121
	10:12	up the Amorites before the **c** of Israel,	1121
	10:20	the **c** of Israel had made an end of slaying	1121
	10:21	none moved his tongue against any of the **c**	1121
	11:14	the **c** of Israel took for a prey unto	1121
	11:19	a city that made peace with the **c** of Israel,	1121
	11:22	Anakims left in the land of the **c** of Israel:	1121
	12: 1	which the **c** of Israel smote, and	1121
	12: 2	*which is* the border of the **c** of Ammon;	1121
	12: 6	of the LORD and the **c** of Israel smite:	1121
	12: 7	the **c** of Israel smote on *this* side Jordan on	1121
	13: 6	them will I drive out from before the **c** of	1121
	13:10	unto the border of the **c** of Ammon;	1121
	13:13	(Nevertheless the **c** of Israel expelled not	1121
	13:15	Moses gave unto the tribe of the **c** of	1121
	13:22	did the **c** of Israel slay with the sword	1121
	13:23	the border of the **c** of Reuben was Jordan,	1121
	13:23	of the **c** of Reuben after their families,	1121
	13:24	*even* unto the **c** of Gad according to their	1121
	13:25	and half the land of the **c** of Ammon,	1121
	13:28	This *is* the inheritance of the **c** of Gad after	1121
	13:29	tribe of the **c** of Manasseh by their families.	1121
	13:31	*were pertaining* unto the **c** of Machir	1121
	13:31	*even* to the one half of the **c** of Machir by	1121
	14: 1	these *are the countries* which the **c** of Israel	1121
	14: 1	the heads of the fathers of the tribes of the **c**	1121
	14: 4	For the **c** of Joseph were two tribes,	1121
	14: 5	so the **c** of Israel did, and they divided	1121
	14: 6	the **c** of Judah came unto Joshua in Gilgal:	1121
	14:10	while *the c of* Israel wandered in	NIH
	15: 1	was the lot of the tribe of the **c** of Judah by	1121
	15:12	the coast *thereof.* This *is* the coast of the **c**	1121
	15:13	he gave a part among the **c** of Judah,	1121
	15:14	and Ahiman, and Talmai, the **c** of Anak.	3211
	15:20	This *is* the inheritance of the tribe of the **c**	1121
	15:21	the uttermost cities of the tribe of the **c** of	1121
	15:63	the **c** of Judah could not drive them out:	1121
	15:63	the Jebusites dwell with the **c** of Judah at	1121
	16: 1	the lot of the **c** of Joseph fell from Jordan	1121
	16: 4	So the **c** of Joseph, Manasseh and Ephraim,	1121
	16: 5	the border of the **c** of Ephraim according to	1121
	16: 8	This *is* the inheritance of the tribe of the **c**	1121
	16: 9	the separate cities for the **c** of Ephraim	1121
	16: 9	the inheritance of the **c** of Manasseh,	1121
	17: 2	There was also *a lot* for the rest of the **c** of	1121
	17: 2	for the **c** of Abiezer, and for the children of	1121
	17: 2	for the **c** of Helek, and for the children of	1121
	17: 2	for the **c** of Asriel, and for the children of	1121
	17: 2	for the **c** of Shechem, and for the children	1121
	17: 2	for the **c** of Hepher, and for the children of	1121
	17: 2	of Hepher, and for the **c** of Shemida:	1121
	17: 2	these *were* the male **c** of Manasseh the son	1121
	17: 8	of Manasseh *belonged* to the **c** of Ephraim;	1121
	17:12	Yet the **c** of Manasseh could not drive out	1121
	17:13	when the **c** of Israel were waxen strong,	1121
	17:14	the **c** of Joseph spake unto Joshua, saying,	1121
	17:16	the **c** of Joseph said, The hill is not enough	1121
	18: 1	the whole congregation of the **c** of Israel	1121
	18: 2	there remained among the **c** of Israel seven	1121
	18: 3	Joshua said unto the **c** of Israel, How long	1121
	18:10	there Joshua divided the land unto the **c** of	1121
	18:11	the lot of the tribe of the **c** of Benjamin	1121
	18:11	their lot came forth between the **c** of Judah	1121
	18:11	the children of Judah and the **c** of Joseph.	1121
	18:14	*is* Kirjath-jearim, a city of the **c** of Judah:	1121
	18:20	This *was* the inheritance of the **c** of	1121
	18:21	Now the cities of the tribe of the **c** of	1121
	18:28	This *is* the inheritance of the **c** of Benjamin	1121
	19: 1	*even* for the tribe of the **c** of Simeon	1121
	19: 1	within the inheritance of the **c** of Judah.	1121
	19: 8	This *is* the inheritance of the tribe of the **c**	1121
	19: 9	Out of the portion of the **c** of Judah *was*	1121
	19: 9	*was* the inheritance of the **c** of Simeon:	1121
	19: 9	for the part of the **c** of Judah was too much	1121
	19: 9	the **c** of Simeon had their inheritance within	1121
	19:10	the third lot came up for the **c** of Zebulun	1121
	19:16	This *is* the inheritance of the **c** of Zebulun	1121

Jos	19:17	for the **c** of Issachar according to their	1121
	19:23	This *is* the inheritance of the tribe of the **c**	1121
	19:24	the fifth lot came out for the tribe of the **c**	1121
	19:31	This *is* the inheritance of the tribe of the **c**	1121
	19:32	The sixth lot came out to the **c** of Naphtali,	1121
	19:32	*even* for the **c** of Naphtali according to their	1121
	19:39	This *is* the inheritance of the tribe of the **c**	1121
	19:40	of the **c** of Dan according to their families.	1121
	19:47	the coast of the **c** of Dan went out *too little*	1121
	19:47	the **c** of Dan went up to fight against	1121
	19:48	This *is* the inheritance of the tribe of the **c**	1121
	19:49	the **c** of Israel gave an inheritance to Joshua	1121
	19:51	the heads of the fathers of the tribes of the **c**	1121
	20: 2	Speak to the **c** of Israel, saying,	1121
	20: 9	These were the cities appointed for all the **c**	1121
	21: 1	of the fathers of the tribes of the **c** of Israel;	1121
	21: 3	the **c** of Israel gave unto the Levites out of	1121
	21: 4	the **c** of Aaron the priest, *which were* of	1121
	21: 5	the rest of the **c** of Kohath had by lot out of	1121
	21: 6	the **c** of Gershon *had* by lot out of	1121
	21: 7	The **c** of Merari by their families *had* out of	1121
	21: 8	the **c** of Israel gave by lot unto the Levites	1121
	21: 9	they gave out of the tribe of the **c** of Judah,	1121
	21: 9	out of the tribe of the **c** of Simeon, these	1121
	21:10	Which the **c** of Aaron, *being* of the families	1121
	21:10	*who were* of the **c** of Levi, had:	1121
	21:13	Thus they gave to the **c** of Aaron the priest	1121
	21:19	All the cities of the **c** of Aaron, the priests,	1121
	21:20	the families of the **c** of Kohath, the Levites	1121
	21:20	the Levites which remained of the **c** of	1121
	21:26	families of the **c** of Kohath that remained.	1121
	21:27	unto the **c** of Gershon, of the families of	1121
	21:34	unto the families of the **c** of Merari, the rest	1121
	21:40	So all the cities for the **c** of Merari by their	1121
	21:41	the possession of the **c** of Israel *were* forty	1121
	22: 9	the **c** of Reuben and the children of Gad	1121
	22: 9	children of Reuben and the **c** of Gad and	1121
	22: 9	departed from the **c** of Israel out of Shiloh,	1121
	22:10	the **c** of Reuben and the children of Gad	1121
	22:10	children of Reuben and the **c** of Gad and	1121
	22:11	the **c** of Israel heard say, Behold,	1121
	22:11	the **c** of Reuben and the children of Gad	1121
	22:11	children of Reuben and the **c** of Gad and	1121
	22:11	of Jordan, at the passage of the **c** of Israel.	1121
	22:12	when the **c** of Israel heard *of it,* the whole	1121
	22:12	**c** of Israel gathered themselves together *at*	1121
	22:13	the **c** of Israel sent unto the children of	1121
	22:13	the children of Israel sent unto the **c** of	1121
	22:13	to the **c** of Gad, and to the half tribe of	1121
	22:15	they came unto the **c** of Reuben, and to	1121
	22:15	to the **c** of Gad, and to the half tribe of	1121
	22:21	the **c** of Reuben and the children of Gad	1121
	22:21	children of Reuben and the **c** of Gad and	1121
	22:24	In time to come your **c** might speak unto	1121
	22:24	come your children might speak unto our **c**,	1121
	22:25	ye **c** of Reuben and children of Gad;	1121
	22:25	ye children of Reuben and **c** of Gad;	1121
	22:25	shall your **c** make our children cease from	1121
	22:25	shall your children make our **c** cease from	1121
	22:27	that your **c** may not say to our children in	1121
	22:27	that your children may not say to our **c** in	1121
	22:30	heard the words that the **c** of Reuben and	1121
	22:30	the **c** of Gad and the children of Manasseh	1121
	22:30	of Gad and the **c** of Manasseh spake,	1121
	22:31	the priest said unto the **c** of Reuben,	1121
	22:31	to the **c** of Gad, and to the children of	1121
	22:31	children of Gad, and to the **c** of Manasseh,	1121
	22:31	now ye have delivered the **c** of Israel out of	1121
	22:32	returned from the **c** of Reuben, and	1121
	22:32	from the **c** of Gad, out of the land of	1121
	22:32	to the **c** of Israel, and brought them word	1121
	22:33	the thing pleased the **c** of Israel; and	1121
	22:33	the **c** of Israel blessed God, and did not	1121
	22:33	to destroy the land wherein the **c** of Reuben	1121
	22:34	the **c** of Reuben and the children of Gad	1121
	22:34	the **c** of Gad called the altar *Ed:* for it *shall*	1121
	24: 4	Jacob and his **c** went down *into* Egypt.	1121
	24:32	which the **c** of Israel brought up out of	1121
	24:32	it became the inheritance of the **c** of Joseph.	1121
Jdg	1: 1	that the **c** of Israel asked the LORD,	1121
	1: 8	Now the **c** of Judah had fought against	1121
	1: 9	afterward the **c** of Judah went down to fight	1121
	1:16	the **c** of the Kenite, Moses' father in law,	1121
	1:16	the **c** of Judah *into* the wilderness of Judah,	1121
	1:21	the **c** of Benjamin did not drive out	1121
	1:21	the Jebusites dwell with the **c** of Benjamin	1121
	1:34	the Amorites forced the **c** of Dan into	1121
	2: 4	spake these words unto all the **c** of Israel,	1121
	2: 6	the **c** of Israel went every man unto his	1121
	2:11	the **c** of Israel did evil in the sight of	1121
	3: 2	Only that the generations of the **c** of Israel	1121
	3: 5	the **c** of Israel dwelt among the Canaanites,	1121
	3: 7	the **c** of Israel did evil in the sight of	1121
	3: 8	the **c** of Israel served Chushan-rishathaim	1121
	3: 9	when the **c** of Israel cried unto the LORD,	1121
	3: 9	the LORD raised up a deliverer to the **c** of	1121
	3:12	the **c** of Israel did evil again in the sight of	1121
	3:13	he gathered unto him the **c** of Ammon and	1121
	3:14	So the **c** of Israel served Eglon the king of	1121
	3:15	when the **c** of Israel cried unto the LORD,	1121
	3:15	by him the **c** of Israel sent a present unto	1121
	3:27	the **c** of Israel went down with him from	1121
	4: 1	the **c** of Israel again did evil in the sight of	1121
	4: 3	the **c** of Israel cried unto the LORD: for he	1121
	4: 3	twenty years he mightily oppressed the **c** of	1121
	4: 5	the **c** of Israel came up to her for judgment.	1121
	4: 6	take with thee ten thousand men of the **c** of	1121
	4: 6	of Naphtali and of the **c** of Zebulun?	1121
	4:11	*which was* of the **c** of Hobab the father in	1121
	4:23	the king of Canaan before the **c** of Israel.	1121
	4:24	the hand of the **c** of Israel prospered,	1121
	6: 1	the **c** of Israel did evil in the sight of	1121
	6: 2	of the Midianites the **c** of Israel made them	1121
	6: 3	and the Amalekites, and the **c** of the east,	1121
	6: 6	and the **c** of Israel cried unto the LORD.	1121
	6: 7	when the **c** of Israel cried unto the LORD	1121
	6: 8	That the LORD sent a prophet unto the **c**	1121
	6:33	the **c** of the east were gathered together,	1121
	7:12	all the **c** of the east lay along in the valley	1121
	8:10	were left of all the hosts of the **c** of the east:	1121
	8:18	*each* one resembled the **c** of a king.	1121
	8:28	Thus was Midian subdued before the **c** of	1121
	8:33	that the **c** of Israel turned again, and went a	1121
	8:34	the **c** of Israel remembered not the LORD	1121
	10: 6	the **c** of Israel did evil again in the sight of	1121
	10: 6	the gods of the **c** of Ammon, and the gods	1121
	10: 7	and into the hands of the **c** of Ammon.	1121
	10: 8	they vexed and oppressed the **c** of Israel:	1121
	10: 8	all the **c** of Israel that *were* on the *other* side	1121
	10: 9	Moreover the **c** of Ammon passed over	1121
	10:10	the **c** of Israel cried unto the LORD,	1121
	10:11	the LORD said unto the **c** of Israel, *Did*	1121
	10:11	from the **c** of Ammon, and from	1121
	10:15	the **c** of Israel said unto the LORD,	1121
	10:17	the **c** of Ammon were gathered together,	1121
	10:17	the **c** of Israel assembled themselves	1121
	10:18	will begin to fight against the **c** of Ammon?	1121
	11: 4	that the **c** of Ammon made war against	1121
	11: 5	that when the **c** of Ammon made war	1121
	11: 6	that we may fight with the **c** of Ammon.	1121
	11: 8	fight against the **c** of Ammon, and be our	1121
	11: 9	again to fight against the **c** of Ammon,	1121
	11:12	unto the king of the **c** of Ammon,	1121
	11:13	the king of the **c** of Ammon answered unto	1121
	11:14	again unto the king of the **c** of Ammon:	1121
	11:15	of Moab, nor the land of the **c** of Ammon:	1121
	11:27	be judge *this* day between the **c** of Israel	1121
	11:27	the children of Israel and the **c** of Ammon.	1121
	11:28	Howbeit the king of the **c** of Ammon	1121
	11:29	he passed over *unto* the **c** of Ammon.	1121
	11:30	If thou shalt without fail deliver the **c** of	1121
	11:31	when I return in peace from the **c** of	1121
	11:32	So Jephthah passed over unto the **c** of	1121
	11:33	Thus the **c** of Ammon were subdued before	1121
	11:33	were subdued before the **c** of Israel.	1121
	11:36	of thine enemies, *even* of the **c** of Ammon.	1121
	12: 1	thou over to fight against the **c** of Ammon,	1121
	12: 2	my people were at great strife with the **c** of	1121
	12: 3	passed over against the **c** of Ammon, and	1121
	13: 1	the **c** of Israel did evil again in the sight of	1121
	14:16	thou hast put forth a riddle unto the **c** of my	1121
	14:17	she told the riddle to the **c** of her people.	1121
	18: 2	the **c** of Dan sent of their family five men	1121
	18:16	which *were* of the **c** of Dan, stood *by*	1121
	18:22	and overtook the **c** of Dan.	1121
	18:23	they cried unto the **c** of Dan. And they	1121
	18:25	the **c** of Dan said unto him, Let not thy	1121
	18:26	the **c** of Dan went their way: and	1121

Jdg 18:30 the c of Dan set up the graven image: and 1121
19:12 of a stranger, that *is* not of the c of Israel; 1121
19:30 c of Israel came up out of the land of Egypt 1121
20: 1 all the c of Israel went out, and 1121
20: 3 (Now the c of Benjamin heard that 1121
20: 3 the c of Israel were gone up *to* Mizpeh.) 1121
20: 3 said the c of Israel, Tell *us,* how was this 1121
20: 7 Behold, ye *are* all c of Israel; give here 1121
20:13 deliver *us* the men, the c of Belial, 1121
20:13 the c of Benjamin would not hearken to 1121
20:13 to the voice of their brethren the c of Israel: 1121
20:14 the c of Benjamin gathered themselves 1121
20:14 to go out to battle against the c of Israel. 1121
20:15 the c of Benjamin were numbered at that 1121
20:18 the c of Israel arose, and went up *to* 1121
20:18 first to the battle against the c of Benjamin? 1121
20:19 the c of Israel rose up in the morning, and 1121
20:21 the c of Benjamin came forth out of 1121
20:23 (And the c of Israel went up and 1121
20:23 Shall I go *up* again to battle against the c of 1121
20:24 the c of Israel came near against 1121
20:24 children of Israel came near against the c 1121
20:25 destroyed *down* to the ground of the c of 1121
20:26 all the c of Israel, and all the people, 1121
20:27 the c of Israel inquired of the LORD, 1121
20:28 against the c of Benjamin my brother, 1121
20:30 the c of Israel went up against the children 1121
20:30 the children of Israel went up against the c 1121
20:31 the c of Benjamin went out against 1121
20:32 the c of Benjamin said, They *are* smitten 1121
20:32 the c of Israel said, Let us flee, and 1121
20:35 the c of Israel destroyed of the Benjamites 1121
20:36 So the c of Benjamin saw that they were 1121
20:48 the men of Israel turned again upon the c of 1121
21: 5 the c of Israel said, Who *is there* among all 1121
21: 6 the c of Israel repented them for Benjamin 1121
21:10 of the sword, with the women and the c. 2945
21:13 c of Benjamin that *were* in the rock 1121
21:18 for the c of Israel have sworn, saying, 1121
21:20 Therefore they commanded the c of 1121
21:23 the c of Benjamin did so, and took *them* 1121
21:24 the c of Israel departed thence at that time, 1121
1Sa 1: 2 Peninnah had c, but Hannah had no 3206
1: 2 had children, but Hannah had no c. 3206
2: 5 and she that hath many c is waxed feeble. 1121
2:28 offerings made by fire of the c of Israel? 1121
7: 4 the c of Israel did put away Baalim and 1121
7: 6 Samuel judged the c of Israel in Mizpeh. 1121
7: 7 when the Philistines heard that the c of 1121
7: 7 when the c of Israel heard *it,* they were 1121
7: 8 the c of Israel said to Samuel, Cease not to 1121
9: 2 *there was* not among the c of Israel a 1121
10:18 said unto the c of Israel, Thus saith 1121
10:27 the c of Belial said, How shall this *man* 1121
11: 8 the c of Israel were three hundred thousand, 1121
12:12 when ye saw that Nahash the king of the c 1121
14:18 of God was at that time with the c of Israel. 1121
14:47 against the c of Ammon, and against Edom, 1121
15: 6 for ye shewed kindness to all the c of 1121
16:11 Samuel said unto Jesse, Are here all *thy* c? 5288
17:53 the c of Israel returned from chasing after 1121
22:19 c and sucklings, and oxen, and asses, and 5768
26:19 if *they be* the c of men, cursed *be* they 1121
30:22 save *to* every man his wife and his c, 1121
2Sa 1:18 (Also he bade *them* teach the c of Judah 1121
2:25 the c of Benjamin gathered themselves 1121
4: 2 a Beerothite, of the c of Benjamin: 1121
7: 6 I brought up the c of Israel out of Egypt, 1121
7: 7 c of Israel spake I a word with any of 1121
7:10 neither shall the c of wickedness afflict 1121
7:14 and with the stripes of the c of men: 1121
8:12 of the c of Ammon, and of the Philistines, 1121
10: 1 that the king of the c of Ammon died, and 1121
10: 2 David's servants came *into* the land of the c 1121
10: 3 the princes of the c of Ammon said unto 1121
10: 6 when the c of Ammon saw that they stank 1121
10: 6 the c of Ammon sent and hired the Syrians 1121
10: 8 the c of Ammon came out, and put 1121
10:10 put *them* in array against the c of Ammon. 1121
10:11 if the c of Ammon be too strong for thee, 1121
10:14 when the c of Ammon saw that the Syrians 1121
10:14 So Joab returned from the c of Ammon, 1121
10:19 So the Syrians feared to help the c of 1121
11: 1 they destroyed the c of Ammon, and 1121
12: 3 grew up together with him, and with his c; 1121
12: 9 hast slain him with the sword of the c of 1121
12:26 Joab fought against Rabbah of the c of 1121
12:31 thus did he unto all the cities of the c of 1121
17:27 of Nahash of Rabbah of the c of Ammon, 1121
21: 2 (now the Gibeonites *were* not of the c of 1121
21: 2 and the c of Israel had sworn unto them: 1121
21: 2 Saul sought to slay them in his zeal to the c 1121
23:29 Ittai the son of Ribai out of Gibeah of the c 1121
1Ki 2: 4 saying, If thy c take heed to their way, 1121
4:30 the wisdom of all the c of the east country, 1121
6: 1 eightieth year after the c of Israel were 1121
6:13 I will dwell among the c of Israel, and 1121
8: 1 the chief of the fathers of the c of Israel, 1121
8: 9 made *a covenant* with the c of Israel, 1121
8:25 so that thy c take heed to their way, 1121
8:39 knowest the hearts of all the c of men;) 1121
8:63 all the c of Israel dedicated the house of 1121
9: 6 you or your c, and will not keep my 1121
9:20 which *were* not of the c of Israel, 1121
9:21 Their c that were left after them in the land, 1121
9:21 whom the c of Israel also were not able 1121
9:22 of the c of Israel did Solomon make no 1121
11: 2 which the LORD said unto the c of Israel, 1121
11: 7 the abomination of the c of Ammon. 1121
11:33 Milcom the god of the c of Ammon, and 1121
12:17 *as for* the c of Israel which dwelt in 1121
12:24 nor fight against your brethren the c of 1121
12:33 and ordained a feast unto the c of Israel: 1121
14:24 the LORD cast out before the c of Israel. 1121
18:20 So Ahab sent unto all the c of Israel, and 1121
19:10 for the c of Israel have forsaken thy 1121
19:14 the c of Israel have forsaken thy covenant, 1121
20: 3 thy wives also and thy c, *even* 1121
20: 5 and thy gold, and thy wives, and thy c; 1121
20: 7 for my c, and for my silver, and for my 1121
20:15 *even* all the c of Israel, *being* seven 1121
20:27 the c of Israel were numbered, and were all 1121
20:27 the c of Israel pitched before them like two 1121
20:29 the c of Israel slew *of* the Syrians an 1121
21:13 in two men, c of Belial, and sat before him: 1121
21:26 whom the LORD cast out before the c of 1121
2Ki 2:23 there came forth little c out of the city, and 5288
2:24 the wood, and tare forty and two c of them. 3206
4: 7 thy debt, and live thou and thy c of the rest. 1121
8:12 evil that thou wilt do unto the c of Israel: 1121
8:12 wilt dash their c, and rip up their women 5768
8:19 to give to him alway a light, *and* to his c. 1121
9: 1 Elisha the prophet called one of the c of 1121
10: 1 to them that brought up Ahab's c, saying, NIH
10: 5 the bringers up *of the* c, sent to Jehu, NIH
10:13 we go down to salute the c of the king and 1121
10:13 children of the king and the c of the queen. 1121
10:30 thy c of the fourth *generation* shall sit on 1121
13: 5 the c of Israel dwelt in their tents, 1121
14: 6 the c of the murderers he slew not: 1121
14: 6 fathers shall not be put to death for the c, 1121
14: 6 nor the c be put to death for the fathers; 1121
16: 3 LORD cast out from before the c of Israel. 1121
17: 7 that the c of Israel had sinned against 1121
17: 8 LORD cast out from before the c of Israel, 1121
17: 9 the c of Israel did secretly *those* things that 1121
17:22 For the c of Israel walked in all the sins of 1121
17:24 cities of Samaria instead of the c of Israel: 1121
17:31 the Sepharvites burnt their c in fire to 1121
17:34 the LORD commanded the c of Jacob, 1121
17:41 both their c, and their children's children: 1121
17:41 both their children, and their children's c: 1121
18: 4 for unto those days the c of Israel did burn 1121
19: 3 for the c are come to the birth, and *there is* 1121
19:12 and the c of Eden which *were* in Thelasar? 1121
21: 2 whom the LORD cast out before the c of 1121
21: 9 LORD destroyed before the c of Israel. 1121
23: 6 upon the graves of the c of the people. 1121
23:10 which *is* in the valley of the c of Hinnom, 1121
23:13 for Milcom the abomination of the c of 1121
24: 2 bands of the c of Ammon, and sent them 1121
1Ch 1:43 before *any* king reigned over the c of Israel; 1121
2:10 begat Nahshon, prince of the c of Judah; 1121
2:18 Caleb the son of Hezron begat c of Azubah NIH
2:30 and Appaim: but Seled died without c. 1121
2:31 Sheshan. And the c of Sheshan; Ahlai. 1121
2:32 and Jonathan: and Jether died without c. 1121
4:27 his brethren had not many c, neither did all 1121

1Ch 4:27 their family multiply, like to the **c** of Judah. 1121
5:11 the **c** of Gad dwelt over against them, in 1121
5:14 These *are* the **c** of Abihail the son of Huri, 1121
5:23 the **c** of the half tribe of Manasseh dwelt in 1121
6: 3 the **c** of Amram; Aaron, and Moses, and 1121
6:33 these *are* they that waited with their **c**. 1121
6:64 the **c** of Israel gave to the Levites *these* 1121
6:65 they gave by lot out of the tribe of the **c** of 1121
6:65 out of the tribe of the **c** of Simeon, and 1121
6:65 out of the tribe of the **c** of Benjamin, these 1121
6:77 Unto the rest of the **c** of Merari *were given* 1121
7:12 and Huppim, the **c** of Ir, *and* Hushim, 1121
7:29 by the borders of the **c** of Manasseh, 1121
7:29 In these dwelt the **c** of Joseph the son of 1121
7:33 and Ashvath. These *are* the **c** of Japhlet. 1121
7:40 All these *were* the **c** of Asher, heads of 1121
8: 8 Shaharaim begat *c* in the country of Moab, NIH
9: 3 in Jerusalem dwelt of the **c** of Judah, and 1121
9: 3 of the **c** of Benjamin, and of the children of 1121
9: 3 and of the **c** of Ephraim, and Manasseh; 1121
9: 4 of Bani, of the **c** of Pharez the son of Judah. 1121
9:18 they *were* porters in the companies of the **c** 1121
9:23 their **c** had the oversight of the gates of 1121
11:31 that pertained to the **c** of Benjamin, 1121
12:16 there came of the **c** of Benjamin and 1121
12:24 The **c** of Judah that bare shield and 1121
12:25 Of the **c** of Simeon, mighty *men* of valour 1121
12:26 Of the **c** of Levi four thousand and 1121
12:29 of the **c** of Benjamin, the kindred of Saul, 1121
12:30 of the **c** of Ephraim twenty thousand and 1121
12:32 of the **c** of Issachar, *which were men* that 1121
14: 4 Now these *are* the names of *his* **c** which he 3205
15: 4 David assembled the **c** of Aaron, and 1121
15:15 the **c** of the Levites bare the ark of God 1121
16:13 his servant, ye **c** of Jacob, his chosen *ones.* 1121
17: 9 neither shall the **c** of wickedness waste 1121
18:11 from the **c** of Ammon, and from 1121
19: 1 that Nahash the king of the **c** of Ammon 1121
19: 2 into the land of the **c** of Ammon to Hanun, 1121
19: 3 the princes of the **c** of Ammon said to 1121
19: 6 when the **c** of Ammon saw that they had 1121
19: 6 the **c** of Ammon sent a thousand talents of 1121
19: 7 the **c** of Ammon gathered themselves 1121
19: 9 the **c** of Ammon came out, and put 1121
19:11 they set *themselves* in array against the **c** of 1121
19:12 if the **c** of Ammon be too strong for thee, 1121
19:15 when the **c** of Ammon saw that the Syrians 1121
19:19 neither would the Syrians help the **c** of 1121
20: 1 wasted the country of the **c** of Ammon, and 1121
20: 3 dealt David with all the cities of the **c** of 1121
20: 4 slew Sippai, *that was* of the **c** of the giant: 3211
24: 2 died before their father, and had no **c**: 1121
26:10 Also Hosah, of the **c** of Merari, had sons; 1121
27: 1 Now the **c** of Israel after their number, 1121
27: 3 Of the **c** of Perez *was* the chief of all 1121
27:10 Helez the Pelonite, of the **c** of Ephraim: 1121
27:14 the Pirathonite, of the **c** of Ephraim: 1121
27:20 Of the **c** of Ephraim, Hoshea the son of 1121
28: 8 leave *it* for an inheritance for your **c** after 1121
2Ch 5: 2 the chief of the fathers of the **c** of Israel, 1121
5:10 made *a covenant* with the **c** of Israel, 1121
6:11 that he made with the **c** of Israel. 1121
6:16 that thy **c** take heed to their way to walk in 1121
6:30 (for thou only knowest the hearts of the **c** of 1121
7: 3 when all the **c** of Israel saw how the fire 1121
8: 2 and caused the **c** of Israel to dwell there. 1121
8: 8 *But* of their **c**, who were left after them in 1121
8: 8 whom the **c** of Israel consumed not, 1121
8: 9 of the **c** of Israel did Solomon make no 1121
10:17 *as for* the **c** of Israel that dwelt in the cities 1121
10:18 the **c** of Israel stoned him with stones, 1121
11:19 Which bare him **c**; Jeush, and Shamariah, 1121
11:23 dispersed of all his **c** throughout all 1121
13: 7 the **c** of Belial, and have strengthened 1121
13:12 O **c** of Israel, fight ye not against 1121
13:16 the **c** of Israel fled before Judah: and 1121
13:18 Thus the **c** of Israel were brought under at 1121
13:18 the **c** of Judah prevailed, because 1121
20: 1 *that* the **c** of Moab, and the children of 1121
20: 1 the **c** of Ammon, and with them *other* 1121
20:10 the **c** of Ammon and Moab and mount Seir, 1121
20:13 their little ones, their wives, and their **c**. 1121
20:19 of the **c** of the Kohathites, and of 1121
20:19 the Kohathites, and of the **c** of the Korhites, 1121
20:22 the LORD set ambushments against the **c** 1121
20:23 For the **c** of Ammon and Moab stood up 1121
21:14 and thy **c**, and thy wives, and all thy goods: 1121
25: 4 he slew not their **c**, but *did* as it is written in 1121
25: 4 saying, The fathers shall not die for the **c**, 1121
25: 4 neither shall the **c** die for the fathers, but 1121
25: 7 *to wit, with* all the **c** of Ephraim. 1121
25:11 and smote *of* the **c** of Seir ten thousand. 1121
25:12 *other* ten thousand *left* alive did the **c** of 1121
25:14 that he brought the gods of the **c** of Seir, 1121
27: 5 the **c** of Ammon gave him the same year an 1121
27: 5 So much did the **c** of Ammon pay unto 1121
28: 3 burnt his **c** in the fire after the abominations 1121
28: 3 LORD had cast out before the **c** of Israel. 1121
28: 8 the **c** of Israel carried away captive of their 1121
28:10 now ye purpose to keep under the **c** of 1121
28:12 certain of the heads of the **c** of Ephraim, 1121
30: 6 of the king, saying, Ye **c** of Israel, 1121
30: 9 your **c** *shall find* compassion before them 1121
30:21 the **c** of Israel that were present at 1121
31: 1 *them all.* Then all the **c** of Israel returned, 1121
31: 5 the **c** of Israel brought in abundance 1121
31: 6 *concerning* the **c** of Israel and Judah, 1121
33: 2 whom the LORD had cast out before the **c** 1121
33: 6 he caused his **c** to pass through the fire in 1121
33: 9 had destroyed before the **c** of Israel. 1121
34:33 countries that *pertained* to the **c** of Israel, 1121
35:17 the **c** of Israel that were present kept 1121
Ezr 2: 1 Now these *are* the **c** of the province that 1121
2: 3 The **c** of Parosh, two thousand an hundred 1121
2: 4 The **c** of Shephatiah, three hundred seventy 1121
2: 5 The **c** of Arah, seven hundred seventy and 1121
2: 6 The **c** of Pahath-moab, of the children of 1121
2: 6 of the **c** of Jeshua *and* Joab, two thousand 1121
2: 7 The **c** of Elam, a thousand two hundred 1121
2: 8 The **c** of Zattu, nine hundred forty and five. 1121
2: 9 The **c** of Zaccai, seven hundred and 1121
2:10 The **c** of Bani, six hundred forty and two. 1121
2:11 The **c** of Bebai, six hundred twenty and 1121
2:12 The **c** of Azgad, a thousand two hundred 1121
2:13 The **c** of Adonikam, six hundred sixty and 1121
2:14 The **c** of Bigvai, two thousand fifty and six. 1121
2:15 The **c** of Adin, four hundred fifty and four. 1121
2:16 The **c** of Ater of Hezekiah, ninety and 1121
2:17 The **c** of Bezai, three hundred twenty and 1121
2:18 The **c** of Jorah, an hundred and twelve. 1121
2:19 The **c** of Hashum, two hundred twenty and 1121
2:20 The **c** of Gibbar, ninety and five. 1121
2:21 The **c** of Beth-lehem, an hundred twenty 1121
2:24 The **c** of Azmaveth, forty and two. 1121
2:25 The **c** of Kirjath-arim, Chephirah, and 1121
2:26 The **c** of Ramah and Gaba, six hundred 1121
2:29 The **c** of Nebo, fifty and two. 1121
2:30 The **c** of Magbish, an hundred fifty and six. 1121
2:31 The **c** of the other Elam, a thousand two 1121
2:32 The **c** of Harim, three hundred and twenty. 1121
2:33 The **c** of Lod, Hadid, and Ono, 1121
2:34 The **c** of Jericho, three hundred forty and 1121
2:35 The **c** of Senaah, three thousand and 1121
2:36 the **c** of Jedaiah, of the house of Jeshua, 1121
2:37 The **c** of Immer, a thousand fifty and two. 1121
2:38 The **c** of Pashur, a thousand two hundred 1121
2:39 The **c** of Harim, a thousand and seventeen. 1121
2:40 the **c** of Jeshua and Kadmiel, of 1121
2:40 of the **c** of Hodaviah, seventy and four. 1121
2:41 the **c** of Asaph, an hundred twenty and 1121
2:42 The **c** of the porters: the children of 1121
2:42 the **c** of Shallum, the children of Ater, 1121
2:42 the **c** of Ater, the children of Talmon, 1121
2:42 the children of Ater, the **c** of Talmon, 1121
2:42 the **c** of Akkub, the children of Hatita, 1121
2:42 the children of Akkub, the **c** of Hatita, 1121
2:42 the children of Hatita, the **c** of Shobai, 1121
2:43 the **c** of Ziha, the children of Hasupha, 1121
2:43 the children of Ziha, the **c** of Hasupha, 1121
2:43 the children of Hasupha, the **c** of Tabbaoth, 1121
2:44 The **c** of Keros, the children of Siaha, 1121
2:44 the **c** of Siaha, the children of Padon, 1121
2:44 the children of Siaha, the **c** of Padon, 1121
2:45 The **c** of Lebanah, the children of Hagabah, 1121
2:45 the **c** of Hagabah, the children of Akkub, 1121
2:45 the children of Hagabah, the **c** of Akkub, 1121
2:46 The **c** of Hagab, the children of Shalmai, 1121
2:46 the **c** of Shalmai, the children of Hanan, 1121

Ezr 2:46 the children of Shalmai, the **c** of Hanan, 1121
2:47 The **c** of Giddel, the children of Gahar, 1121
2:47 the **c** of Gahar, the children of Reaiah, 1121
2:47 the children of Gahar, the **c** of Reaiah, 1121
2:48 The **c** of Rezin, the children of Nekoda, 1121
2:48 The children of Rezin, the **c** of Nekoda, 1121
2:48 the children of Nekoda, the **c** of Gazzam, 1121
2:49 The **c** of Uzza, the children of Paseah, 1121
2:49 the **c** of Paseah, the children of Besai, 1121
2:49 the children of Paseah, the **c** of Besai, 1121
2:50 The **c** of Asnah, the children of Mehunim, 1121
2:50 The children of Asnah, the **c** of Mehunim, 1121
2:50 children of Mehunim, the **c** of Nephusim, 1121
2:51 The **c** of Bakbuk, the children of Hakupha, 1121
2:51 the **c** of Hakupha, the children of Harhur, 1121
2:51 the children of Hakupha, the **c** of Harhur, 1121
2:52 The **c** of Bazluth, the children of Mehida, 1121
2:52 the **c** of Mehida, the children of Harsha, 1121
2:52 the children of Mehida, the **c** of Harsha, 1121
2:53 The **c** of Barkos, the children of Sisera, 1121
2:53 The children of Barkos, the **c** of Sisera, 1121
2:53 the children of Sisera, the **c** of Thamah, 1121
2:54 The **c** of Neziah, the children of Hatipha. 1121
2:54 The children of Neziah, the **c** of Hatipha. 1121
2:55 The **c** of Solomon's servants: the children 1121
2:55 the **c** of Sotai, the children of Sophereth, 1121
2:55 the children of Sotai, the **c** of Sophereth, 1121
2:55 the children of Sophereth, the **c** of Peruda, 1121
2:56 The **c** of Jaalah, the children of Darkon, 1121
2:56 the **c** of Darkon, the children of Giddel, 1121
2:56 the children of Darkon, the **c** of Giddel, 1121
2:57 The **c** of Shephatiah, the children of Hattil, 1121
2:57 The children of Shephatiah, the **c** of Hattil, 1121
2:57 the **c** of Pochereth of Zebaim, the children 1121
2:57 of Pochereth of Zebaim, the **c** of Ami. 1121
2:58 and the **c** of Solomon's servants, 1121
2:60 The **c** of Delaiah, the children of Tobiah, 1121
2:60 the **c** of Tobiah, the children of Nekoda, 1121
2:60 the **c** of Nekoda, six hundred fifty and two. 1121
2:61 of the **c** of the priests: the children of 1121
2:61 the **c** of Habaiah, the children of Koz, 1121
2:61 the children of Habaiah, the **c** of Koz, 1121
2:61 the children of Koz, the **c** of Barzillai; 1121
3: 1 and the **c** of Israel *were* in the cities, 1121
4: 1 Benjamin heard that the **c** of the captivity 1121
6:16 the **c** of Israel, the priests, and the Levites, 1123
6:16 and the rest of the **c** of the captivity, 1123
6:19 the **c** of the captivity kept the passover 1121
6:20 killed the passover for all the **c** of 1121
6:21 the **c** of Israel, which were come again out 1121
7: 7 there went up *some* of the **c** of Israel, and 1121
8:35 *Also* the **c** of those that had been carried 1121
9:12 leave *it* for an inheritance to your **c** for 1121
10: 1 congregation *of* men and women and **c**: 3206
10: 7 Jerusalem unto all the **c** of the captivity, 1121
10:16 the **c** of the captivity did so. And Ezra 1121
10:44 of them had wives by *whom* they had **c**. 1121
Ne 1: 6 for the **c** of Israel thy servants, and 1121
1: 6 confess the sins of the **c** of Israel, which we 1121
2:10 a man to seek the welfare of the **c** of Israel. 1121
5: 5 of our brethren, our **c** as their children: 1121
5: 5 of our brethren, our children as their **c**: 1121
7: 6 These *are* the **c** of the province, that went 1121
7: 8 The **c** of Parosh, two thousand an hundred 1121
7: 9 The **c** of Shephatiah, three hundred seventy 1121
7:10 The **c** of Arah, six hundred fifty and two. 1121
7:11 The **c** of Pahath-moab, of the children of 1121
7:11 of the **c** of Jeshua and Joab, two thousand 1121
7:12 The **c** of Elam, a thousand two hundred 1121
7:13 The **c** of Zattu, eight hundred forty and 1121
7:14 The **c** of Zaccai, seven hundred and 1121
7:15 The **c** of Binnui, six hundred forty and 1121
7:16 The **c** of Bebai, six hundred twenty and 1121
7:17 The **c** of Azgad, two thousand three 1121
7:18 The **c** of Adonikam, six hundred threescore 1121
7:19 The **c** of Bigvai, two thousand threescore 1121
7:20 The **c** of Adin, six hundred fifty and five. 1121
7:21 The **c** of Ater of Hezekiah, ninety and 1121
7:22 The **c** of Hashum, three hundred twenty 1121
7:23 The **c** of Bezai, three hundred twenty and 1121
7:24 The **c** of Hariph, an hundred *and* twelve. 1121
7:25 The **c** of Gibeon, ninety and five. 1121
7:34 The **c** of the other Elam, a thousand two 1121
7:35 The **c** of Harim, three hundred and twenty. 1121
7:36 The **c** of Jericho, three hundred forty and 1121
7:37 The **c** of Lod, Hadid, and Ono, 1121
7:38 The **c** of Senaah, three thousand nine 1121
7:39 the **c** of Jedaiah, of the house of Jeshua, 1121
7:40 The **c** of Immer, a thousand fifty and two. 1121
7:41 The **c** of Pashur, a thousand two hundred 1121
7:42 The **c** of Harim, a thousand *and* seventeen. 1121
7:43 the **c** of Jeshua, of Kadmiel, *and* of 1121
7:43 *and* of the **c** of Hodevah, seventy and four. 1121
7:44 the **c** of Asaph, an hundred forty and eight. 1121
7:45 the **c** of Shallum, the children of Ater, 1121
7:45 the **c** of Ater, the children of Talmon, 1121
7:45 the children of Ater, the **c** of Talmon, 1121
7:45 the **c** of Akkub, the children of Hatita, 1121
7:45 the children of Akkub, the **c** of Hatita, 1121
7:45 the **c** of Shobai, an hundred thirty and 1121
7:46 the **c** of Ziha, the children of Hashupha, 1121
7:46 the children of Ziha, the **c** of Hashupha, 1121
7:46 children of Hashupha, the **c** of Tabbaoth, 1121
7:47 The **c** of Keros, the children of Sia, 1121
7:47 the **c** of Sia, the children of Padon, 1121
7:47 the children of Sia, the **c** of Padon, 1121
7:48 The **c** of Lebana, the children of Hagaba, 1121
7:48 The children of Lebana, the **c** of Hagaba, 1121
7:48 the children of Hagaba, the **c** of Shalmai, 1121
7:49 The **c** of Hanan, the children of Giddel, 1121
7:49 the **c** of Giddel, the children of Gahar, 1121
7:49 the children of Giddel, the **c** of Gahar, 1121
7:50 The **c** of Reaiah, the children of Rezin, 1121
7:50 the **c** of Rezin, the children of Nekoda, 1121
7:50 the children of Rezin, the **c** of Nekoda, 1121
7:51 The **c** of Gazzam, the children of Uzza, 1121
7:51 the **c** of Uzza, the children of Phaseah, 1121
7:51 the children of Uzza, the **c** of Phaseah, 1121
7:52 The **c** of Besai, the children of Meunim, 1121
7:52 The children of Besai, the **c** of Meunim, 1121
7:52 children of Meunim, the **c** of Nephishesim, 1121
7:53 The **c** of Bakbuk, the children of Hakupha, 1121
7:53 the **c** of Hakupha, the children of Harhur, 1121
7:53 the children of Hakupha, the **c** of Harhur, 1121
7:54 The **c** of Bazlith, the children of Mehida, 1121
7:54 the **c** of Mehida, the children of Harsha, 1121
7:54 the children of Mehida, the **c** of Harsha, 1121
7:55 The **c** of Barkos, the children of Sisera, 1121
7:55 the **c** of Sisera, the children of Tamah, 1121
7:55 the children of Sisera, the **c** of Tamah, 1121
7:56 The **c** of Neziah, the children of Hatipha. 1121
7:56 The children of Neziah, the **c** of Hatipha. 1121
7:57 The **c** of Solomon's servants: the children 1121
7:57 the **c** of Sotai, the children of Sophereth, 1121
7:57 the children of Sotai, the **c** of Sophereth, 1121
7:57 the children of Sophereth, the **c** of Perida, 1121
7:58 The **c** of Jaala, the children of Darkon, 1121
7:58 The children of Jaala, the **c** of Darkon, 1121
7:58 the children of Darkon, the **c** of Giddel, 1121
7:59 The **c** of Shephatiah, the children of Hattil, 1121
7:59 The children of Shephatiah, the **c** of Hattil, 1121
7:59 of Hattil, the **c** of Pochereth Zebaim, 1121
7:59 of Pochereth Zebaim, the **c** of Amon. 1121
7:60 and the **c** of Solomon's servants, 1121
7:62 The **c** of Delaiah, the children of Tobiah, 1121
7:62 the **c** of Tobiah, the children of Nekoda, 1121
7:62 the **c** of Nekoda, six hundred forty and two. 1121
7:63 the **c** of Habaiah, the children of Koz, 1121
7:63 the children of Habaiah, the **c** of Koz, 1121
7:63 the children of Koz, the **c** of Barzillai, 1121
7:73 the **c** of Israel *were* in their cities. 1121
8:14 that the **c** of Israel should dwell in booths in 1121
8:17 that day had not the **c** of Israel done so. 1121
9: 1 fourth day of this month the **c** of Israel 1121
9:23 Their **c** also multipliedst thou as the stars of 1121
9:24 So the **c** went in and possessed the land, 1121
10:39 For the **c** of Israel and the children of Levi 1121
10:39 the **c** of Levi shall bring the offering of 1121
11: 3 and the **c** of Solomon's servants. 1121
11: 4 at Jerusalem dwelt *certain* of the **c** of Judah, 1121
11: 4 of Judah, and of the **c** of Benjamin. 1121
11: 4 Of the **c** of Judah; Athaiah the son of 1121
11: 4 the son of Mahalaleel, of the **c** of Perez; 1121
11:24 of the **c** of Zerah the son of Judah, 1121
11:25 *some* of the **c** of Judah dwelt at 1121
11:31 The **c** also of Benjamin from Geba *dwelt at* 1121
12:43 the wives also and the **c** rejoiced: so 3206
12:47 the Levites sanctified *them* unto the **c** of 1121

C

Ne	13: 2	Because they met not the **c** of Israel with	1121
	13:16	and sold on the sabbath unto the **c** of Judah,	1121
	13:24	their **c** spake half in the speech of Ashdod,	1121
Est	3:13	both young and old, **little c** and women,	2945
	5:11	the multitude of his **c**, and all *the things*	1121
Job	5: 4	His **c** are far from safety, and they are	1121
	8: 4	If thy **c** have sinned against him, and	1121
	17: 5	*his* friends, even the eyes of his **c** shall fail.	1121
	19:18	Yea, **young c** despised me; I arose, and	5759
	20:10	His **c** shall *seek to* please the poor, and	1121
	21:11	little ones like a flock, and their **c** dance.	3206
	21:19	God layeth up his iniquity for his **c**:	1121
	24: 5	*yieldeth* food for them *and* for *their* **c**.	5288
	27:14	If his **c** be multiplied, *it is* for the sword:	1121
	29: 5	yet with me, *when* my **c** *were* about me;	5288
	30: 8	*They were* **c** of fools, yea, children of base	1121
	30: 8	*were* children of fools, yea, **c** of base men:	1121
	41:34	*things:* he *is* a king over all the **c** of pride.	1121
Ps	11: 4	eyes behold, his eyelids try, the **c** of men.	1121
	12: 1	for the faithful fail from among the **c** of	1121
	14: 2	down from heaven upon the **c** of men,	1121
	17:14	*with* thy hid *treasure:* they are full *of* **c**,	1121
	21:10	and their seed from among the **c** of men.	1121
	34:11	Come, ye **c**, hearken unto me: I will teach	1121
	36: 7	the **c** of men put their trust under	1121
	45: 2	Thou art fairer than the **c** of men: grace is	1121
	45:16	Instead of thy fathers shall be thy **c**,	1121
	53: 2	God looked down from heaven upon the **c**	1121
	66: 5	*he is* terrible *in his* doing toward the **c** of	1121
	69: 8	and an alien unto my mother's **c**.	1121
	72: 4	he shall save the **c** of the needy, and	1121
	73:15	offend *against* the generation of thy **c**.	1121
	78: 4	We will not hide *them* from their **c**,	1121
	78: 5	*they* should make them known to their **c**:	1121
	78: 6	*them, even* the **c** *which* should be born;	1121
	78: 6	should arise and declare *them* to their **c**:	1121
	78: 9	The **c** of Ephraim, *being* armed, *and*	1121
	82: 6	and all of you *are* **c** of the most High.	1121
	83: 8	they have holpen the **c** of Lot. Selah.	1121
	89:30	If his **c** forsake my law, and walk not in my	1121
	90: 3	and sayest, Return, ye **c** of men.	1121
	90:16	thy servants, and thy glory unto their **c**.	1121
	102:28	The **c** of thy servants shall continue, and	1121
	103: 7	unto Moses, his acts unto the **c** of Israel.	1121
	103:13	Like as a father pitieth *his* **c**, *so* the LORD	1121
	103:17	and his righteousness unto children's **c**;	1121
	105: 6	his servant, ye **c** of Jacob, his chosen.	1121
	107: 8	*for* his wonderful works to the **c** of men!	1121
	107:15	*for* his wonderful works to the **c** of men!	1121
	107:21	*for* his wonderful works to the **c** of men!	1121
	107:31	*for* his wonderful works to the **c** of men!	1121
	109: 9	Let his **c** be fatherless, and his wife a	1121
	109:10	Let his **c** be continually vagabonds,	1121
	109:12	let there be any to favour his **fatherless c**.	3490
	113: 9	to keep house, *to be* a joyful mother of **c**.	1121
	115:14	you more and more, you and your **c**.	1121
	115:16	but the earth hath he given to the **c** of men.	1121
	127: 3	Lo, **c** *are* an heritage of the LORD: *and*	1121
	127: 4	of a mighty *man;* so *are* **c** of the youth.	1121
	128: 3	thy **c** like olive plants round about thy	1121
	128: 6	thou shalt see thy children's **c**, *and*	1121
	132:12	If thy **c** will keep my covenant and	1121
	132:12	their **c** also shall sit upon thy throne for	1121
	137: 7	the **c** of Edom *in* the day of Jerusalem;	1121
	144: 7	of great waters, from the hand of strange **c**;	1121
	144:11	and deliver me from the hand of strange **c**,	1121
	147:13	thy gates; he hath blessed thy **c** within thee.	1121
	148:12	young men, and maidens; old men, and **c**:	5288
	148:14	*even* of the **c** of Israel, a people near unto	1121
	149: 2	let the **c** of Zion be joyful in their King.	1121
Pr	4: 1	Hear, ye **c**, the instruction of a father, and	1121
	5: 7	O ye **c**, and depart not from the words of	1121
	7:24	O ye **c**, and attend to the words of my	1121
	8:32	Now therefore hearken unto me, O ye **c**:	1121
	13:22	leaveth an inheritance to *his* children's **c**:	1121
	14:26	and his **c** shall have a place of refuge.	1121
	15:11	much more then the hearts of the **c** of men?	1121
	17: 6	Children's **c** *are* the crown of old men; and	1121
	17: 6	and the glory of **c** *are* their fathers.	1121
	20: 7	in his integrity: his **c** *are* blessed after him.	1121
	31:28	Her **c** arise up, and call her blessed;	1121
Ecc	6: 3	If a man beget an hundred **c**, and live many	NIH
SS	1: 6	my mother's **c** were angry with me;	1121
Isa	1: 2	I have nourished and brought up **c**, and	1121
	1: 4	a seed of evildoers, **c** that are corrupters:	1121
	2: 6	they please themselves in the **c** of strangers.	3206
	3: 4	I will give **c** *to be* their princes, and	5288
	3:12	**c** *are* their oppressors, and women rule over	5953
	8:18	the **c** whom the LORD hath given me *are*	3206
	11:14	and the **c** of Ammon shall obey them.	1121
	13:16	Their **c** also shall be dashed to pieces	5768
	13:18	of the womb; their eye shall not spare **c**.	1121
	14:21	Prepare slaughter for his **c** for the iniquity	1121
	17: 3	they shall be as the glory of the **c** of Israel,	1121
	17: 9	which they left because of the **c** of Israel:	1121
	21:17	the mighty *men* of the **c** of Kedar, shall be	1121
	23: 4	saying, I travail not, nor **bring forth c**,	3205
	27:12	be gathered one by one, O ye **c** of Israel.	1121
	29:23	when he seeth his **c**, the work of mine	3206
	30: 1	Woe to the rebellious **c**, saith the LORD,	1121
	30: 9	That this *is* a rebellious people, lying **c**,	1121
	30: 9	**c** *that* will not hear the law of the LORD:	1121
	31: 6	Turn ye unto *him from* whom the **c** of	1121
	37: 3	for the **c** are come to the birth, and *there is*	1121
	37:12	and the **c** of Eden which *were* in Telassar?	1121
	38:19	the father to the **c** shall make known thy	1121
	47: 8	a widow, neither shall I know the **loss of c**:	7908
	47: 9	in one day, the **loss of c**, and widowhood:	7908
	49:17	Thy **c** shall make haste; thy destroyers and	1121
	49:20	The **c** which thou shalt have, after thou hast	1121
	49:21	seeing I have **lost** my **c**, and *am* desolate,	7921
	49:25	contendeth with thee, and I will save thy **c**.	1121
	54: 1	for more *are* the **c** of the desolate than	1121
	54: 1	the desolate than the **c** of the married wife,	1121
	54:13	And all thy **c** *shall be* taught of the LORD;	1121
	54:13	and great *shall be* the peace of thy **c**.	1121
	57: 4	*are* ye not **c** of transgression, a seed of	3206
	57: 5	slaying the **c** in the valleys under the clifts	3206
	63: 8	they *are* my people, **c** *that* will not lie:	1121
	66: 8	as Zion travailed, she brought forth her **c**.	1121
	66:20	as the **c** of Israel bring an offering in a	1121
Jer	2: 9	and with your children's **c** will I plead.	1121
	2:16	Also the **c** of Noph and Tahapanes have	1121
	2:30	In vain have I smitten your **c**; they received	1121
	3:14	Turn, O backsliding **c**, saith the LORD;	1121
	3:19	How shall I put thee among the **c**, and	1121
	3:21	*and* supplications of the **c** of Israel:	1121
	3:22	ye backsliding **c**, *and* I will heal your	1121
	4:22	they *are* sottish **c**, and they have none	1121
	5: 7	thy **c** have forsaken me, and sworn by *them*	1121
	6: 1	O ye **c** of Benjamin, gather yourselves to	1121
	6:11	I *will* pour *it* out upon the **c** abroad, and	5768
	7:18	The **c** gather wood, and the fathers kindle	1121
	7:30	For the **c** of Judah have done evil in my	1121
	9:21	to cut off the **c** from without, *and* the young	5768
	9:26	the **c** of Ammon, and Moab, and all *that are*	1121
	10:20	my **c** are gone forth *of* me, and they *are* not:	1121
	15: 7	I will **bereave** *them* **of c**, I will destroy my	7921
	16:14	that brought up the **c** of Israel out of	1121
	16:15	that brought up the **c** of Israel from the land	1121
	17: 2	Whilst their **c** remember their altars and	1121
	17:19	and stand in the gate of the **c** of the people,	1121
	18:21	Therefore deliver up their **c** to the famine,	1121
	18:21	let their wives be **bereaved of** their **c**, and	7909
	23: 7	which brought up the **c** of Israel out of	1121
	25:21	Edom, and Moab, and the **c** of Ammon,	1121
	30:20	Their **c** also shall be as aforetime, and	1121
	31:15	Rahel weeping for her **c** refused to be	1121
	31:15	children refused to be comforted for her **c**,	1121
	31:17	that *thy* **c** shall come again to their own	1121
	32:18	fathers into the bosom of their **c** after them:	1121
	32:30	For the **c** of Israel and the children of Judah	1121
	32:30	the **c** of Judah have only done evil before	1121
	32:30	for the **c** of Israel have only provoked me to	1121
	32:32	Because of all the evil of the **c** of Israel and	1121
	32:32	the children of Israel and of the **c** of Judah,	1121
	32:39	the good of them, and of their **c** after them:	1121
	38:23	all thy wives and thy **c** to the Chaldeans:	1121
	40: 7	women, and **c**, and of the poor of the land,	2945
	41:16	and the women, and the **c**, and the eunuchs,	2945
	43: 6	**c**, and the king's daughters, and every	2945
	47: 3	the fathers shall not look back to *their* **c** for	1121
	49: 6	again the captivity of the **c** of Ammon,	1121
	49:11	Leave thy **fatherless c**, I will preserve *them*	3490
	50: 4	the **c** of Israel shall come, they and	1121
	50: 4	they and the **c** of Judah together, going and	1121
	50:33	The **c** of Israel and the children of Judah	1121
	50:33	and the **c** of Judah *were* oppressed together:	1121

La 1: 5 her **c** are gone *into* captivity before 5768
1:16 my **c** are desolate, because the enemy 1121
2:11 because the **c** and the sucklings swoon in 5768
2:19 toward him for the life of thy **young c**, 5768
2:20 women eat their fruit, *and* **c** of a span long? 5768
3:33 not afflict willingly nor grieve the **c** of men. 1121
4: 4 the **young c** ask bread, *and* no man 5768
4:10 the pitiful women have sodden their own **c**: 3206
5:13 men to grind, and the **c** fell under the wood. 5288
Eze 2: 3 Son of man, I send thee to the **c** of Israel, 1121
2: 4 For *they are* impudent **c** and stiff hearted. 1121
3:11 unto the **c** of thy people, and speak unto 1121
4:13 Even thus shall the **c** of Israel eat their 1121
6: 5 I will lay the dead carcases of the **c** of 1121
9: 6 both maids, and **little c**, and women: 2945
16:21 That thou hast slain my **c**, and 1121
16:36 by the blood of thy **c**, which thou didst give 1121
16:45 that lotheth her husband and her **c**; 1121
16:45 which lothed their husbands and their **c**: 1121
20:18 I said unto their **c** in the wilderness, 1121
20:21 Notwithstanding the **c** rebelled against me: 1121
23:39 For when they had slain their **c** to their 1121
31:14 of the earth, in the midst of the **c** of men, 1121
33: 2 speak to the **c** of thy people, and say unto 1121
33:12 son of man, say unto the **c** of thy people, 1121
33:17 Yet the **c** of thy people say, The way of 1121
33:30 the **c** of thy people still are talking against 1121
35: 5 hast shed *the blood of* the **c** of Israel by 1121
37:16 and for the **c** of Israel his companions: 1121
37:18 when the **c** of thy people shall speak unto 1121
37:21 I *will* take the **c** of Israel from among 1121
37:25 their **c**, and their children's children for 1121
37:25 and their children's **c** for ever: 1121
43: 7 where I will dwell in the midst of the **c** of 1121
44: 9 of any stranger that *is* among the **c** of 1121
44:15 when the **c** of Israel went astray from me, 1121
47:22 which shall beget **c** among you: 1121
47:22 born in the country among the **c** of Israel; 1121
48:11 which went not astray when the **c** of Israel 1121
Da 1: 3 that *he* should bring *certain* of the **c** of 1121
1: 4 **C** in whom *was* no blemish, but 3206
1: 6 Now among these were of the **c** of Judah, 1121
1:10 liking than the **c** which *are* of your sort? 3206
1:13 the countenance of the **c** that eat *of* 3206
1:15 fatter in flesh than all the **c** which did eat 3206
1:17 As for these four **c**, God gave them 3206
2:38 wheresoever the **c** of men dwell, the beasts 1123
5:13 which *art* of the **c** of the captivity of Judah, 1123
6:13 which *is* of the **c** of the captivity of Judah, 1123
6:24 den of lions, them, their **c**, and their wives; 1123
11:41 Moab, and the chief of the **c** of Ammon. 1121
12: 1 the great prince which standeth for the **c** of 1121
Hos 1: 2 a wife of whoredoms and **c** of whoredoms: 3206
1:10 Yet the number of the **c** of Israel shall be as 1121
1:11 shall the **c** of Judah and the children of 1121
1:11 and the **c** of Israel be gathered together, 1121
2: 4 I will not have mercy upon her **c**; for they 1121
2: 4 for they *be the* **c** of whoredoms. 1121
3: 1 love of the LORD toward the **c** of Israel, 1121
3: 4 For the **c** of Israel shall abide many days 1121
3: 5 Afterward shall the **c** of Israel return, and 1121
4: 1 the word of the LORD, ye **c** of Israel: 1121
4: 6 the law of thy God, I will also forget thy **c**. 1121
5: 7 for they have begotten strange **c**: now shall 1121
9:12 Though they bring up their **c**, yet will I 1121
9:13 Ephraim *shall* bring forth his **c** to 1121
10: 9 the battle in Gibeah against the **c** of iniquity 1121
10:14 mother was dashed in pieces upon *her* **c**. 1121
11:10 then the **c** shall tremble from the west. 1121
13:13 long in *the place of* the breaking forth of **c**. 1121
Joel 1: 3 Tell ye your **c** of it, and *let* your children 1121
1: 3 *let* your **c** *tell* their children, and 1121
1: 3 *let* your children *tell* their **c**, and 1121
1: 3 and their **c** another generation. 1121
2:16 gather the **c**, and those that suck the breasts: 5768
2:23 ye **c** of Zion, and rejoice in the LORD 1121
3: 6 The **c** also of Judah and the children of 1121
3: 6 the **c** of Jerusalem have ye sold unto 1121
3: 8 your daughters into the hand of the **c** of 1121
3:16 and the strength of the **c** of Israel. 1121
3:19 for the violence against the **c** of Judah, 1121
Am 1:13 For three transgressions of the **c** of 1121
2:11 *Is it* not even thus, O ye **c** of Israel? 1121
3: 1 hath spoken against you, O **c** of Israel, 1121
3:12 shall the **c** of Israel be taken out that dwell 1121
4: 5 for this liketh you, O ye **c** of Israel, 1121
9: 7 *Are* ye not as **c** of the Ethiopians unto me, 1121
9: 7 of the Ethiopians unto me, O **c** of Israel? 1121
Ob 1:12 **c** of Judah in the day of their destruction; 1121
1:20 the captivity of this host of the **c** of Israel 1121
Mic 1:16 thee bald, and poll thee for thy delicate **c**; 1121
2: 9 from their **c** have ye taken *away* my glory 5768
5: 3 his brethren shall return unto the **c** of Israel. 1121
Na 3:10 her **young c** also were dashed in pieces at 5768
Zep 1: 8 the king's **c**, and all such as are clothed 1121
2: 8 and the revilings of the **c** of Ammon, 1121
2: 9 the **c** of Ammon as Gomorrah, *even* 1121
Zec 10: 7 yea, their **c** shall see *it*, and be glad; 1121
10: 9 they shall live with their **c**, and turn again. 1121
Mal 4: 6 shall turn the heart of the fathers to the **c**, 1121
4: 6 the heart of the **c** to their fathers, lest I 1121
Mt 2:16 and slew all the **c** that were in Bethlehem, *3816*
2:18 Rachel weeping for her **c**, and would not be *5043*
3: 9 that God is able of these stones to raise up **c** *5043*
5: 9 for they shall be called the **c** of God. *5207*
5:45 That ye may be the **c** of your Father which *5207*
7:11 know how to give good gifts unto your **c**, *5043*
8:12 But the **c** of the kingdom shall be cast out *5207*
9:15 Can the **c** of the bridechamber mourn, *5207*
10:21 and the **c** shall rise up against *their* parents, *5043*
11:16 It is like unto **c** sitting in the markets, and *3808*
11:19 sinners. But wisdom is justified of her **c**. *5043*
12:27 by whom do your **c** cast *them* out? *5207*
13:38 the good seed are the **c** of the kingdom; but *5207*
13:38 but the tares are the **c** of the wicked one; *5207*
14:21 five thousand men, beside women and **c**. *3813*
15:38 four thousand men, beside women and **c**. *3813*
17:25 or tribute? of their own **c**, or of strangers? *5207*
17:26 Jesus saith unto him, Then are the **c** free. *5207*
18: 3 ye be converted, and become as **little c**, *3813*
18:25 and **c**, and all that he had, and payment to *5043*
19:13 Then were there brought unto him **little c**, *3813*
19:14 Suffer **little c**, and forbid them not, *3813*
19:29 or father, or mother, or wife, or **c**, or lands, *5043*
20:20 the mother of Zebedee's **c** with her sons, *5207*
21:15 and the **c** crying in the temple, and saying, *3816*
22:24 Moses said, If a man die, having no **c**, *5043*
23:31 that ye are the **c** of them which killed *5207*
23:37 how often would I have gathered thy **c** *5043*
27: 9 whom they of the **c** of Israel did value; *5207*
27:25 and said, His blood *be* on us, and on our **c**. *5043*
27:56 and Joses, and the mother of Zebedee's **c**. *5207*
Mk 2:19 Can the **c** of the bridechamber fast, *5207*
7:27 Jesus said unto her, Let the **c** first be filled: *5043*
9:37 Whosoever shall receive one of such **c** in *3813*
10:13 And they brought **young c** to him, that he *3813*
10:14 Suffer the **little c** to come unto me, and *3813*
10:24 answereth again, and saith unto them, **C**, *5043*
10:29 or father, or mother, or wife, or **c**, or lands, *5043*
10:30 and sisters, and mothers, and **c**, and lands, *5043*
12:19 leave *his* wife *behind him*, and leave no **c**, *5043*
13:12 and **c** shall rise up against *their* parents, and *5043*
Lk 1:16 And many of the **c** of Israel shall he turn to *5207*
1:17 to turn the hearts of the fathers to the **c**, and *5043*
3: 8 of these stones to raise up **c** unto Abraham. *5043*
5:34 Can ye make the **c** of the bridechamber *5207*
6:35 and ye shall be the **c** of the Highest: *5207*
7:32 They are like unto **c** sitting in *3813*
7:35 But wisdom is justified of all her **c**. *5043*
11: 7 is now shut, and my **c** are with me in bed; *3813*
11:13 know how to give good gifts unto your **c**: *5043*
13:34 how often would I have gathered thy **c** *5043*
14:26 and **c**, and brethren, and sisters, yea, *5043*
16: 8 for the **c** of this world are in their *5207*
16: 8 in their generation wiser than the **c** of light. *5207*
18:16 Suffer **little c** to come unto me, and *3813*
18:29 or parents, or brethren, or wife, or **c**, for *5043*
19:44 with the ground, and thy **c** within thee: *5043*
20:28 having a wife, and he die **without c**, *815*
20:29 and the first took a wife, and died **without c**. *815*
20:31 the seven also: and they left no **c**, and died. *5043*
20:34 The **c** of this world marry, and are given in *5207*
20:36 and are the **c** of God, being the children of *5207*
20:36 of God, being the **c** of the resurrection. *5207*
23:28 but weep for yourselves, and for your **c**. *5043*
Jn 4:12 thereof himself, and his **c**, and his cattle? *5207*
8:39 saith unto them, If ye were Abraham's **c**, *5043*
11:52 the **c** of God that were scattered abroad. *5043*

Jn 12:36 in the light, that ye may be the **c** of light. *5207*
13:33 **Little c**, yet a little while I am with you. *5040*
21: 5 saith unto them, **C**, have ye any meat? *3813*
Ac 2:39 and to your **c**, and to all that are afar off, *5043*
3:25 Ye are the **c** of the prophets, and of *5207*
5:21 and all the senate of the **c** of Israel, and *5207*
7:19 so that *they* cast out their **young c**, *1025*
7:23 his heart to visit his brethren the **c** of Israel. *5207*
7:37 *that* Moses, which said unto the **c** of Israel, *5207*
9:15 the Gentiles, and kings, and the **c** of Israel: *5207*
10:36 The word which *God* sent unto the **c** of *5207*
13:26 **c** of the stock of Abraham, and *5207*
13:33 God hath fulfilled the same unto us their **c**, *5043*
21: 5 with wives and **c**, till *we were* out of *5043*
21:21 that they *ought* not to circumcise *their* **c**, *5043*
Ro 8:16 with our spirit, that we are the **c** of God: *5043*
8:17 And if **c**, then heirs; heirs of God, and *5043*
8:21 into the glorious liberty of the **c** of God. *5043*
9: 7 are the seed of Abraham, *are they* all **c**: *5043*
9: 8 That is, *They which are* the **c** of the flesh, *5043*
9: 8 of the flesh, these *are* not the **c** of God: *5043*
9: 8 the **c** of the promise are counted for *5043*
9:11 (For *the* **c** being not yet born, neither having NIG
9:26 there shall they be called the **c** of the living *5207*
9:27 Though the number of the **c** of Israel be as *5207*
1Co 7:14 else were your **c** unclean; but now are they *5043*
14:20 Brethren, be not **c** in understanding: *3813*
14:20 howbeit in malice be ye **c**, *3515*
2Co 3: 7 that the **c** of Israel could not stedfastly *5207*
3:13 that the **c** of Israel could not stedfastly look *5207*
6:13 in the same, (I speak as unto *my* **c**,) *5043*
12:14 for the **c** ought not to lay up for the parents, *5043*
12:14 up for the parents, but the parents for the **c**. *5043*
Gal 3: 7 are of faith, the same are the **c** of Abraham. *5207*
3:26 For ye are all the **c** of God by faith in Christ *5207*
4: 3 Even so we, when we were **c**, were in *3516*
4:19 My **little c**, of whom I travail in birth again *5040*
4:25 which now is, and is in bondage with her **c**. *5043*
4:27 for the desolate hath many moe **c** than she *5043*
4:28 as Isaac was, are the **c** of promise. *5043*
4:31 we are not **c** of *the* bondwoman, but of *5043*
Eph 1: 5 **adoption of c** by Jesus Christ to himself, *5206*
2: 2 the spirit that now worketh in the **c** of *5207*
2: 3 and were by nature the **c** of wrath, even as *5043*
4:14 That we *henceforth* be no more **c**, tossed to *3516*
5: 1 Be ye therefore followers of God, as dear **c**; *5043*
5: 6 wrath of God upon the **c** of disobedience. *5207*
5: 8 *are ye* light in the Lord: walk as **c** of light: *5043*
6: 1 **C**, obey your parents in the Lord: for this is *5043*
6: 4 ye fathers, provoke not your **c** to wrath: *5043*
Col 3: 6 of God cometh on the **c** of disobedience: *5207*
3:20 **C**, obey *your* parents in all *things:* for this *5043*
3:21 provoke not your **c** *to anger,* lest they be *5043*
1Th 2: 7 *even* as a nurse cherisheth her **c**: *5043*
2:11 every one of you, as a father *doth* his **c**, *5043*
5: 5 Ye are all the **c** of light, and the children of *5207*
5: 5 the children of light, and the **c** of the day: *5207*
1Ti 3: 4 having *his* **c** in subjection with all gravity; *5043*
3:12 ruling *their* **c** and their own houses well. *5043*
5: 4 But if any widow have **c** or nephews, *5043*
5:10 if she have **brought up c**, if she have *5044*
5:14 *women* marry, **bear c**, guide the house, *5041*
Tit 1: 6 having faithful **c** not accused of riot or *5043*
2: 4 to love their husbands, to **love** their **c**, *5388*
Heb 2:13 I, and the **c** which God hath given me. *3813*
2:14 then as the **c** are partakers of flesh and *3813*
11:22 made mention of the departing of the **c** of *5207*
12: 5 which speaketh unto you as unto **c**, *5207*
1Pe 1:14 As obedient **c**, not fashioning yourselves *5043*
2Pe 2:14 exercised with covetous practices; cursed **c**: *5043*
1Jn 2: 1 My **little c**, these *things* write I unto you, *5040*
2:12 **little c**, because *your* sins are forgiven you *5040*
2:13 **little c**, because ye have known the Father. *3813*
2:18 **Little c**, it is the last time: and as ye have *3813*
2:28 And now, **little c**, abide in him; that, *5040*
3: 7 **Little c**, let no *man* deceive you: he that *5040*
3:10 In this the **c** of God are manifest, and *5043*
3:10 of God are manifest, and the **c** of the devil: *5043*
3:18 My **little c**, let us not love in word, *5040*
4: 4 of God, **little c**, and have overcome them: *5040*
5: 2 By this we know that we love the **c** of God, *5043*
5:21 **Little c**, keep yourselves from idols. Amen. *5040*
2Jn 1: 1 The elder unto the elect lady and her **c**, *5043*
1: 4 I rejoiced greatly that I found of thy **c** *5043*
1:13 The **c** of thy elect sister greet thee. Amen. *5043*
3Jn 1: 4 I have no greater joy than to hear that my **c** *5043*
Rev 2:14 cast a stumblingblock before the **c** of Israel, *5207*
2:23 And I will kill her **c** with death; and all *5043*
7: 4 four thousand of all the tribes of the **c** of *5207*
21:12 *names* of the twelve tribes of the **c** of Israel: *5207*

CHILDREN'S (19) [CHILD]
Ge 31:16 from our father, that *is* ours, and our **c**: 1121
45:10 thy **c** children, and thy flocks, and 1121
Ex 9: 4 there shall nothing die of all *that is* the **c** of 1121
34: 7 upon the **c** children, unto the third and 1121
Dt 4:25 **c** children, and ye shall have remained long 1121
Jos 14: 9 thy **c** for ever, because thou hast wholly 1121
2Ki 17:41 both their children, and their **c** children: 1121
Job 19:17 though I intreated for the **c** *sake* of mine 1121
Ps 103:17 and his righteousness unto **c** children; 1121
128: 6 thou shalt see thy **c** children, *and* 1121+3807.1
Pr 13:22 A good *man* leaveth an inheritance to *his* **c** 1121
17: 6 **C** children *are* the crown of old men; and 1121
Jer 2: 9 and with your **c** children will I plead. 1121
31:29 sour grape, and the **c** teeth are set on edge. 1121
Eze 18: 2 sour grapes, and the **c** teeth are set on edge? 1121
37:25 their children, and their **c** children for ever: 1121
Mt 15:26 It is not meet to take the **c** bread, and *5043*
Mk 7:27 for it is not meet to take the **c** bread, and *5043*
7:28 yet the dogs under the table eat of the **c** *3813*

CHILEAB (1)
2Sa 3: 3 his second, **C**, of Abigail the wife of Nabal 3609

CHILION (2) [CHILION'S]
Ru 1: 2 the name of his two sons Mahlon and **C**, 3630
1: 5 Mahlon and **C** died also both of them; and 3630

CHILION'S (1) [CHILION]
Ru 4: 9 all that *was* **C** and Mahlon's, of the hand of 3630

CHILMAD (1)
Eze 27:23 Asshur, *and* **C**, *were* thy merchants. 3638

CHIMHAM (4)
2Sa 19:37 behold thy servant **C**; let him go over with 3643
19:38 **C** shall go over with me, and I will do to 3643
19:40 went on to Gilgal, and **C** went on with him: 3643
Jer 41:17 and dwelt in the habitation of **C**, 3643

CHIMNEY (1)
Hos 13: 3 of the floor, and as the smoke out of the **c**. 699

CHINNERETH (3) [CINNEROTH]
Nu 34:11 shall reach unto the side of the sea of **C** 3672
Dt 3:17 the coast *thereof,* from **C** even unto the sea 3672
Jos 19:35 Zer, and Hammath, Rakkath, and **C**, 3672

CHIOS (1)
Ac 20:15 and came the next *day* over against **C**; *5508*

CHISEL See HEW

CHISELS See PLANES

CHISLEU (2)
Ne 1: 1 it came to pass in the month **C**, *in* 3691
Zec 7: 1 fourth *day* of the ninth month, *even* in **C**; 3691

CHISLON (1)
Nu 34:21 the tribe of Benjamin, Elidad the son of **C**. 3692

CHISLOTH-TABOR (1) [TABOR]
Jos 19:12 *toward* the sunrising unto the border of **C**, 3696

CHITTIM (6)
Nu 24:24 ships *shall come* from the coast of **C**, and 3794
Isa 23: 1 from the land of **C** it is revealed to them. 3794
23:12 arise, pass over *to* **C**; there also shalt thou 3794
Jer 2:10 For pass over the isles of **C**, and see; and 3794
Eze 27: 6 *of* ivory, *brought* out of the isles of **C**. 3794
Da 11:30 For *the* ships of **C** shall come against him: 3794

CHIUN (1)
Am 5:26 of your Moloch and **C** your images, 3594

CHLOE (1)
1Co 1:11 by them which are of the *house* of **C**, *5514*

CHODE (2)
Ge 31:36 Jacob was wroth, and **c** with Laban: and 7378
Nu 20: 3 the people **c** with Moses, and spake, saying, 7378

CHOICE (21) [CHOOSE]
Ge 23: 6 in the **c** of our sepulchres bury thy dead; 4005
49:11 the vine, and his ass's colt unto the **c vine**; 8322
Dt 12:11 all your **c** vows which ye vow unto 4005
1Sa 9: 2 *was* Saul, a **c** *young man,* and a goodly: 970
2Sa 10: 9 he chose of all the **c** *men* of Israel, and 977
2Ki 3:19 every **c** city, and shall fell every good tree, 4004
19:23 trees thereof, *and* the **c** fir trees thereof: 4004
1Ch 7:40 **c** *and* mighty *men* of valour, chief of 1305
19:10 he chose out of all the **c** of Israel, and 977
2Ch 25: 5 found them three hundred thousand **c** *men,* 977
Ne 5:18 *for me* daily *was* one ox *and* six **c** sheep; 1305
Pr 8:10 not silver; and knowledge rather than **c** gold. 977
8:19 than fine gold; and my revenue than **c** silver. 977
10:20 The tongue of the just *is as* **c** silver: the heart 977
SS 6: 9 she *is* the **c** one of her that bare her. 1249
Isa 37:24 cedars thereof, *and* the **c** fir trees thereof: 4005
Jer 22: 7 they shall cut down thy **c** cedars, and 4005
Eze 24: 4 and the shoulder; fill *it with* the **c** bones. 4005
24: 5 Take the **c** of the flock, and burn also 4005
31:16 the **c** and best of Lebanon, all that drink 4005
Ac 15: 7 a good while ago God **made c** among us, *1586*

CHOICEST (2) [CHOOSE]
Isa 5: 2 planted it *with* the **c vine**, and built a tower 8321
22: 7 *that* thy **c** valleys shall be full *of* chariots, 4005

CHOKE (2) [CHOKED]
Mt 13:22 **c** the word, and he becometh unfruitful. *4846*
Mk 4:19 **c** the word, and it becometh unfruitful. *4846*

CHOKED (6) [CHOKE]
Mt 13: 7 and the thorns sprung up, and **c** them: *638*
Mk 4: 7 grew up, and **c** it, and it yielded no fruit. *4846*
5:13 about two thousand,) and were **c** in the sea. *4155*
Lk 8: 7 and the thorns sprang up with *it,* and **c** it. *638*
8:14 and are **c** with cares and riches and *4846*
8:33 down a steep place into the lake, and were **c**. *638*

CHOLER (2)
Da 8: 7 he was **moved with c** against him, and 4843
11:11 king of the south shall be **moved with c**, 4843

CHOOSE (59) [CHOICE, CHOICEST, CHOOSEST, CHOOSETH, CHOOSING, CHOSE, CHOSEN]
Ex 17: 9 **C** us **out** men, and go out, fight with 977
Nu 16: 7 be *that* the man whom the LORD doth **c**, 977
17: 5 man's rod, whom I shall **c**, shall blossom: 977
Dt 7: 7 nor **c** you, because ye were moe in number 977
12: 5 **c** out of all your tribes to put his name there, 977
12:11 God shall **c** to cause his name to dwell there; 977
12:14 in the place which the LORD shall **c** in one 977
12:18 the place which the LORD thy God shall **c**, 977
12:26 go unto the place which the LORD shall **c**: 977
14:23 in the place which he shall **c** to place his 977
14:24 which the LORD thy God shall **c** to set his 977
14:25 the place which the LORD thy God shall **c**: 977
15:20 year in the place which the LORD shall **c**, 977
16: 2 in the place which the LORD shall **c** to 977
16: 6 the place which the LORD thy God shall **c** 977
16: 7 the place which the LORD thy God shall **c**: 977
16:15 God in the place which the LORD shall **c**: 977
16:16 thy God in the place which he shall **c**; 977
17: 8 the place which the LORD thy God shall **c**; 977
17:10 which the LORD shall **c** shall shew thee; 977
17:15 whom the LORD thy God shall **c**: 977
18: 6 unto the place which the LORD shall **c**; 977
23:16 in *that* place which he shall **c** in one of thy 977
26: 2 thy God shall **c** to place his name there. 977
30:19 therefore **c** life, that *both* thou and thy seed 977
31:11 thy God in the place which he shall **c**, 977
Jos 9:27 unto this day, in the place which he should **c**. 977
24:15 **c** you *this* day whom you will serve; 977
1Sa 2:28 did I **c** him out of all the tribes of Israel to be 977
17: 8 **c** you a man for you, and let him come 1262
2Sa 16:18 **c**, his will I be, and with him will I abide. 977
17: 1 Let me now **c out** twelve thousand men, and 977
21: 6 in Gibeah of Saul, whom the LORD did **c**. 972
24:12 I offer thee three *things;* **c** thee one of them, 977
1Ki 14:21 the city which the LORD did **c** out of all 977
18:23 let them **c** one bullock for themselves, and 977
18:25 **C** you one bullock for yourselves, and 977
1Ch 21:10 I offer thee three *things:* **c** thee one of them, 977
21:11 unto him, Thus saith the LORD, **C** thee 6901
Ne 9: 7 who didst **c** Abram, and broughtest him forth 977
Job 9:14 *and* **c out** my words *to reason* with him? 977
34: 4 Let us **c** to us judgment: let us know among 977
34:33 whether thou refuse, or whether thou **c**; 977
Ps 25:12 him shall he teach in the way *that* he shall **c**. 977
47: 4 He shall **c** our inheritance for us, 977
Pr 1:29 and did not **c** the fear of the LORD: 977
3:31 not the oppressor, and **c** none of his ways. 977
Isa 7:15 may know to refuse the evil, and **c** the good. 977
7:16 shall know to refuse the evil, and **c** the good, 977
14: 1 will yet **c** Israel, and set them in their own 977
49: 7 the Holy One of Israel, and he shall **c** thee. 977
56: 4 **c** *the things* that please me, and take hold of 977
65:12 and did **c** *that* wherein I delighted not. 977
66: 4 I also will **c** their delusions, and will bring 977
Eze 21:19 **c** thou a place, choose *it,* at the head of 1254
21:19 **c** *it,* at the head of the way to the city. 1254
Zec 1:17 yet comfort Zion, and shall yet **c** Jerusalem. 977
2:12 in the holy land, and shall **c** Jerusalem again. 977
Php 1:22 of my labour: yet what I shall **c** I wot not. *138*

CHOOSEST (2) [CHOOSE]
Job 15: 5 and thou **c** the tongue of the crafty. 977
Ps 65: 4 Blessed *is the man whom* thou **c**, and 977

CHOOSETH (3) [CHOOSE]
Job 7:15 So that my soul **c** strangling, *and* 977
Isa 40:20 impoverished that he hath no oblation **c** a 977
41:24 of nought: an abomination *is he that* **c** you. 977

CHOOSING (1) [CHOOSE]
Heb 11:25 **C** rather to suffer affliction with the people *138*

CHOP (1)
Mic 3: 3 **c** *them* **in pieces**, as for the pot, and as flesh 6566

CHOR-ASHAN (1)
1Sa 30:30 to *them* which *were* in **C**, and to *them* 3565

CHORAZIN (2)
Mt 11:21 unto thee, **C**, woe unto thee, Bethsaida: *5523*
Lk 10:13 unto thee, **C**, woe unto thee, Bethsaida: *5523*

CHOSE (29) [CHOOSE]
Ge 6: 2 they took them wives of all which they **c**. 977
13:11 Lot **c** him all the plain of Jordan; and 977
Ex 18:25 Moses **c** able men out of all Israel, and 977
Dt 4:37 therefore he **c** their seed after them, and 977
10:15 he **c** their seed after them, *even* you above 977
Jos 8: 3 Joshua **c out** thirty thousand mighty *men* of 977
Jdg 5: 8 They **c** new gods; then *was* war in the gates: 977
1Sa 13: 2 Saul **c** him three thousand *men* of Israel; 977
17:40 **c** him five smooth stones out of the brook, 977
2Sa 6:21 which **c** me before thy father, and before all 977
10: 9 he **c** of all the choice *men* of Israel, and 977
1Ki 8:16 I **c** no city out of all the tribes of Israel to 977
8:16 but I **c** David to be over my people Israel. 977
11:34 whom I **c**, because he kept my 977
1Ch 19:10 he **c** out of all the choice of Israel, and 977
28: 4 Howbeit the LORD God of Israel **c** me 977
2Ch 6: 5 **c** no city among all the tribes of Israel to 977
6: 5 neither **c** I any man to be a ruler over my 977
Job 29:25 I **c out** their way, and sat chief, and dwelt as 977
Ps 78:67 of Joseph, and **c** not the tribe of Ephraim: 977
78:68 **c** the tribe of Judah, the mount Zion which 977
78:70 He **c** David also his servant, and took him 977
Isa 66: 4 and **c** *that* in which I delighted not. 977
Eze 20: 5 In the day when I **c** Israel, and lifted up mine 977
Lk 6:13 and of them he **c** twelve, whom also he *1586*
14: 7 when he marked how they **c out** the chief *1586*
Ac 6: 5 and they **c** Stephen, a man full of faith and *1586*
13:17 The God of this people of Israel **c** our *1586*
15:40 And Paul **c** Silas, and departed, *1951*

CHOSEN (123) [CHOOSE]
Ex 14: 7 he took six hundred **c** chariots, and all 977
15: 4 his **c** captains also are drowned in the Red 4005
Nu 16: 5 even *him* whom he hath **c** will he cause to 977
Dt 7: 6 the LORD thy God hath **c** thee to be a 977
12:21 **c** to put his name there be too far from thee, 977
14: 2 the LORD hath **c** thee to be a peculiar 977

Dt 16:11 thy God hath **c** to place his name there. 977
18: 5 For the LORD thy God hath **c** him out of 977
21: 5 for them the LORD thy God hath **c** to 977
Jos 24:22 yourselves that ye have **c** you the LORD, 977
Jdg 10:14 Go and cry unto the gods which ye have **c**; 977
20:15 *which* were numbered seven hundred **c** men. 977
20:16 *there were* seven hundred **c** men lefthanded; 977
20:34 there came against Gibeah ten thousand **c** 977
1Sa 8:18 of your king which ye shall have **c** you; 977
10:24 See ye him whom the LORD hath **c**, 977
12:13 therefore behold the king whom ye have **c**, 977
16: 8 And he said, Neither hath the LORD **c** this. 977
16: 9 And he said, Neither hath the LORD **c** this. 977
16:10 unto Jesse, The LORD hath not **c** these. 977
20:30 **c** the son of Jesse to thine own confusion, 977
24: 2 Saul took three thousand **c** men out of all 977
26: 2 having three thousand **c** men of Israel with 977
2Sa 6: 1 David gathered together all the **c** *men* of 977
1Ki 3: 8 in the midst of thy people which thou hast **c**, 977
8:44 LORD toward the city which thou hast **c**, 977
8:48 the city which thou hast **c**, and the house 977
11:13 and for Jerusalem's sake, which I have **c**. 977
11:32 the city which I have **c** out of all the tribes of 977
11:36 the city which I have **c** me to put my name 977
12:21 fourscore thousand **c** *men,* which were 977
2Ki 21: 7 which I have **c** out of all tribes of Israel, 977
23:27 cast off this city Jerusalem which I have **c**, 977
1Ch 9:22 All these which were **c** to be porters in 1305
15: 2 for them hath the LORD **c** to carry the ark 977
16:13 his servant, ye children of Jacob, his **c** *ones.* 972
16:41 and Jeduthun, and the rest that were **c**, 1305
28: 4 for he hath **c** Judah to be the ruler; and of 977
28: 5 he hath **c** Solomon my son to sit upon 977
28: 6 for I have **c** him to be my son, and I will be 977
28:10 for the LORD hath **c** thee to build a house 977
29: 1 whom alone God hath **c**, *is yet* young and 977
2Ch 6: 6 I have **c** Jerusalem, that my name might be 977
6: 6 have **c** David to be over my people Israel. 977
6:34 unto thee toward this city which thou hast **c**, 977
6:38 *toward* the city which thou hast **c**, and 977
7:12 have **c** this place to myself for a house of 977
7:16 For now have I **c** and sanctified this house, 977
11: 1 fourscore thousand **c** *men,* which were 977
12:13 the city which the LORD had **c** out of all 977
13: 3 of war, *even* four hundred thousand **c** men: 977
13: 3 him with eight hundred thousand **c** men, 977
13:17 slain of Israel five hundred thousand **c** men. 977
29:11 for the LORD hath **c** you to stand before 977
33: 7 which I have **c** before all the tribes of Israel, 977
Ne 1: 9 will bring them unto the place that I have **c** 977
Job 36:21 for this hast thou **c** rather than affliction. 977
Ps 33:12 the people *whom* he hath **c** for his own 977
78:31 of them, and smote down the **c** *men* of Israel. 970
89: 3 I have made a covenant with my **c**, I have 972
89:19 I have exalted *one* **c** out of the people. 977
105: 6 his servant, ye children of Jacob, his **c**. 972
105:26 his servant; *and* Aaron whom he had **c**. 977
105:43 his people with joy, *and* his **c** with gladness: 972
106: 5 That *I* may see the good of thy **c**, that *I* may 972
106:23 had not Moses his **c** stood before him in 972
119:30 I have **c** the way of truth: thy judgments 977
119:173 hand help me; for I have **c** thy precepts. 977
132:13 For the LORD hath **c** Zion; he hath desired 977
135: 4 For the LORD hath **c** Jacob unto himself, 977
Pr 16:16 to get understanding rather to be **c** than 977
22: 1 A *good* name *is* rather to be **c** than great 977
Isa 1:29 confounded for the gardens that ye have **c**. 977
41: 8 Israel, *art* my servant, Jacob whom I have **c**, 977
41: 9 I have **c** thee, and not cast thee away. 977
43:10 the LORD, and my servant whom I have **c**: 977
43:20 the desert, to give drink to my people, my **c**. 972
44: 1 Jacob my servant; and Israel, whom I have **c**: 977
44: 2 and *thou,* Jeshurun, whom I have **c**. 977
48:10 I have **c** thee in the furnace of affliction. 977
58: 5 Is it such a fast that I have **c**? a day for a man 977
58: 6 *Is* not this the fast that I have **c**? to loose 977
65:15 shall leave your name for a curse unto my **c**: 972
66: 3 they have **c** their own ways, and their soul 977
Jer 8: 3 death shall be **c** rather than life by all 977
33:24 The two families which the LORD hath **c**, 977
48:15 his **c** young men are gone down to 4005
49:19 who *is a* **c** *man, that* I may appoint over her? 977
50:44 who *is a* **c** *man, that* I may appoint over her? 977
Eze 23: 7 *with* all them *that were* the **c** men of 4005
Da 11:15 shall not withstand, neither his **c** people, 4005
Hag 2:23 for I have **c** thee, saith the LORD of hosts. 977
Zec 3: 2 even the LORD that hath **c** Jerusalem 977
Mt 12:18 Behold my servant, whom I have **c**; my *140*
20:16 the first last: for many be called, but few **c**. *1588*
22:14 For many are called, but few *are* **c**. *1588*
Mk 13:20 but for the elect's sake, whom he hath **c**, *1586*
Lk 10:42 and Mary hath **c** *that* good part, which shall *1586*
23:35 save himself, if he be Christ, the **c** of God. *1588*
Jn 6:70 Have not I **c** you twelve, and one of you is *1586*
13:18 I know whom I have **c**: but that *1586*
15:16 Ye have not **c** me, but I have chosen you, *1586*
15:16 but I have **c** you, and ordained you, *1586*
15:19 but I have **c** you out of the world, therefore *1586*
Ac 1: 2 unto the Apostles whom he had **c**: *1586*
1:24 shew whether of these two thou hast **c**, *1586*
9:15 Go *thy way:* for he is a **c** vessel unto me, *1589*
10:41 but unto witnesses **c before** of God, *even* to *4401*
15:22 to send **c** men of their own company to *1586*
15:25 to send **c** men unto you with our beloved *1586*
22:14 he said, The God of our fathers hath **c** thee, *4400*
Ro 16:13 Salute Rufus **c** in the Lord, and his mother *1588*
1Co 1:27 But God hath **c** the foolish *things* of *1586*
1:27 God hath **c** the weak *things* of the world to *1586*
1:28 hath God **c**, *yea,* and *things* which are not, *1586*
2Co 8:19 who was also **c** of the churches to travel *5500*
Eph 1: 4 According as he hath **c** us in him before *1586*
2Th 2:13 God hath from the beginning **c** you to *138*
2Ti 2: 4 please him who hath **c** *him* **to be a soldier**. *4758*
Jas 2: 5 Hath not God **c** the poor of this world rich *1586*
1Pe 2: 4 indeed of men, but **c** of God, *and* precious, *1588*
2: 9 But ye *are* a **c** generation, a royal *1588*
Rev 17:14 are with him *are* called, and **c**, and faithful. *1588*

CHOZEBA (1)
1Ch 4:22 and the men of **C**, and Joash, and Saraph, 3578

CHRIST (555) [ANTICHRIST, ANTICHRISTS, CHRIST'S, CHRISTIAN, CHRISTIANS, CHRISTS]
Mt 1: 1 The book of the generation of Jesus **C**, *5547*
1:16 of whom was born Jesus, who is called **C**. *5547*
1:17 Babylon unto **C** *are* fourteen generations. *5547*
1:18 Now the birth of Jesus **C** was on this wise: *5547*
2: 4 he demanded of them where **C** should be *5547*
11: 2 had heard in the prison the works of **C**, *5547*
16:16 Peter answered and said, Thou art the **C**, *5547*
16:20 should tell no *man* that he was Jesus the **C**. *5547*
22:42 Saying, What think ye of **C**? whose son is *5547*
23: 8 for one is your Master, *even* **C**; *5547*
23:10 for one is your Master, *even* **C**. *5547*
24: 5 shall come in my name, saying, I am **C**; *5547*
24:23 shall say unto you, Lo, here *is* **C**, or there; *5547*
26:63 that thou tell us whether thou be the **C**, *5547*
26:68 Saying, Prophesy unto us, *thou* **C**, Who is *5547*
27:17 Barabbas, or Jesus which is called **C**? *5547*
27:22 I do then with Jesus which is called **C**? *5547*
Mk 1: 1 The beginning of the gospel of Jesus **C**, *5547*
8:29 and saith unto him, Thou art the **C**. *5547*
9:41 because ye belong to **C**, verily I say unto *5547*
12:35 How say the scribes that **C** is the Son of *5547*
13: 6 saying, I am **C**; and shall deceive many. NIG
13:21 if any *man* shall say to you, Lo, here *is* **C**; *5547*
14:61 and said unto him, Art thou the **C**, the Son *5547*
15:32 Let **C** the King of Israel descend now from *5547*
Lk 2:11 of David a Saviour, which is **C** the Lord. *5547*
2:26 see death, before he had seen the Lord's **C**. *5547*
3:15 of John, whether he were the **C**, or not; *5547*
4:41 and saying, Thou art **C** the Son of God. *5547*
4:41 not to speak: for they knew that he was **C**. *5547*
9:20 I am? Peter answering said, The **C** of God. *5547*
20:41 How say they that **C** is David's son? *5547*
21: 8 saying, I am **C**; and the time draweth near: NIG
22:67 Art thou the **C**? tell us. And he said unto *5547*
23: 2 saying that he himself is **C** a King. *5547*
23:35 save himself, if he be **C**, the chosen of God. *5547*
23:39 saying, If thou be **C**, save thyself and us. *5547*
24:26 Ought not **C** to have suffered these *things,* *5547*
24:46 and thus it behoved **C** to suffer, and to rise *5547*
Jn 1:17 *but* grace and truth came by Jesus **C**. *5547*
1:20 denied not; but confessed, I am not the **C**. *5547*
1:25 if thou be not *that* **C**, nor Elias, neither *that* *5547*
1:41 which is, being interpreted, the **C**. *5547*
3:28 I am not the **C**, but that I am sent before *5547*
4:25 that Messias cometh, which is called **C**: *5547*

Jn 4:29 all *things* that ever I did: is not this the **C**? *5547*
4:42 and know that this is indeed the **C**, *5547*
6:69 we believe and are sure that thou art *that* **C**, *5547*
7:26 rulers know indeed that this is the very **C**? *5547*
7:27 but when **C** cometh, no *man* knoweth *5547*
7:31 believed on him, and said, When **C** cometh, *5547*
7:41 Others said, This is the **C**. But some said, *5547*
7:41 some said, Shall **C** come out of Galilee? *5547*
7:42 That **C** cometh of the seed of David, and *5547*
9:22 that if any *man* did confess that he *was* **C**, *5547*
10:24 to doubt? If thou be the **C**, tell us plainly. *5547*
11:27 I believe that thou art the **C**, the Son of *5547*
12:34 We have heard out of the law that **C** *5547*
17: 3 and Jesus **C**, whom thou hast sent. *5547*
20:31 that ye might believe that Jesus is the **C**, *5547*
Ac 2:30 *he* would raise up **C** to sit on his throne; *5547*
2:31 *this* before, spake of the resurrection of **C**, *5547*
2:36 whom ye have crucified, both Lord and **C**. *5547*
2:38 name of Jesus **C** for the remission of sins, *5547*
3: 6 In the name of Jesus **C** of Nazareth rise up *5547*
3:18 that **C** should suffer, he hath so fulfilled. *5547*
3:20 And he shall send Jesus **C**, which before *5547*
4:10 that by the name of Jesus **C** of Nazareth, *5547*
4:26 against the Lord, and against his **C**. *5547*
5:42 ceased not to teach and preach Jesus **C**. *5547*
8: 5 city of Samaria, and preached **C** unto them. *5547*
8:12 and the name of Jesus **C**, they were *5547*
8:37 I believe that Jesus **C** is the Son of God. *5547*
9:20 And straightway he preached **C** in *5547*
9:22 at Damascus, proving that this is *very* **C**. *5547*
9:34 Aeneas, Jesus **C** maketh thee whole: *5547*
10:36 of Israel, preaching peace by Jesus **C**: *5547*
11:17 unto us, who believed on the Lord Jesus **C**; *5547*
15:11 of the Lord Jesus **C** *we* shall be saved, *5547*
15:26 lives for the name of our Lord Jesus **C**. *5547*
16:18 I command thee in the name of Jesus **C** to *5547*
16:31 Believe on the Lord Jesus **C**, and thou shalt *5547*
17: 3 that **C** must needs have suffered, and *5547*
17: 3 this Jesus, whom I preach unto you, is **C**. *5547*
18: 5 and testified to the Jews *that* Jesus *was* **C**. *5547*
18:28 shewing by the scriptures that Jesus was **C**. *5547*
19: 4 should come after him, that is, on **C** Jesus. *5547*
20:21 and faith toward our Lord Jesus **C**. *5547*
24:24 and heard him concerning the faith in **C**. *5547*
26:23 That **C** should suffer, *and* that he *should be* *5547*
28:31 *things* which concern the Lord Jesus **C**, *5547*
Ro 1: 1 Paul, a servant of Jesus **C**, called *to be* an *5547*
1: 3 Concerning his Son Jesus **C** our Lord, *5547*
1: 6 whom are ye also *the* called of Jesus **C**: *5547*
1: 7 from God our Father, and the Lord Jesus **C**. *5547*
1: 8 I thank my God through Jesus **C** for you *5547*
1:16 For I am not ashamed of the gospel of **C**: *5547*
2:16 of men by Jesus **C** according to my gospel. *5547*
3:22 of God *which is* by faith of Jesus **C** unto all *5547*
3:24 through the redemption that is in **C** Jesus: *5547*
5: 1 peace with God through our Lord Jesus **C**: *5547*
5: 6 in due time **C** died for the ungodly. *5547*
5: 8 while we were yet sinners, **C** died for us. *5547*
5:11 also joy in God through our Lord Jesus **C**, *5547*
5:15 by grace, which is by one man, Jesus **C**, *5547*
5:17 shall reign in life by one, Jesus **C**. *5547*
5:21 unto eternal life by Jesus **C** our Lord. *5547*
6: 3 many of us as were baptized into Jesus **C** *5547*
6: 4 that like as **C** was raised up from the dead *5547*
6: 8 Now if we be dead with **C**, we believe that *5547*
6: 9 Knowing that **C** being raised from the dead *5547*
6:11 alive unto God through Jesus **C** our Lord. *5547*
6:23 *is* eternal life through Jesus **C** our Lord. *5547*
7: 4 become dead to the law by the body of **C**; *5547*
7:25 I thank God through Jesus **C** our Lord. So *5547*
8: 1 *are* in **C** Jesus who walk not after the flesh, *5547*
8: 2 For the law of the Spirit of life in **C** Jesus *5547*
8: 9 Now if any *man* have not the Spirit of **C**, *5547*
8:10 And if **C** *be* in you, the body *is* dead *5547*
8:11 he that raised up **C** from the dead shall also *5547*
8:17 heirs of God, and joint-heirs with **C**; if so *5547*
8:34 *It is* **C** that died, yea rather, that is risen *5547*
8:35 Who shall separate us from the love of **C**? *5547*
8:39 love of God, which is in **C** Jesus our Lord. *5547*
9: 1 I say the truth in **C**, I lie not, my conscience *5547*
9: 3 were accursed from **C** for my brethren, *5547*
9: 5 of whom as concerning the flesh **C** *came,* *5547*
10: 4 For **C** *is* the end of the law for *5547*
10: 6 (that is, to bring **C** down *from above:*) *5547*
10: 7 (that is, to bring up **C** again from the dead.) *5547*
12: 5 are one body in **C**, and every one members *5547*
13:14 But put ye on the Lord Jesus **C**, and *5547*
14: 9 For to this end **C** both died, and rose, *5547*
14:10 all stand before the judgment seat of **C**. *5547*
14:15 not him with thy meat, for whom **C** died. *5547*
14:18 For he that in these *things* serveth **C** *is* *5547*
15: 3 For even **C** pleased not himself; but, as it is *5547*
15: 5 one towards another according to **C** Jesus: *5547*
15: 6 even the Father of our Lord Jesus **C**. *5547*
15: 7 as **C** also received us, to the glory of God. *5547*
15: 8 Now I say that Jesus **C** was a minister of *5547*
15:16 That I should be the minister of Jesus **C** to *5547*
15:17 whereof *I* may glory through Jesus **C** *in* *5547*
15:18 *things* which **C** hath not wrought by me, *5547*
15:19 I have fully preached the gospel of **C**. *5547*
15:20 preach the gospel, not where **C** was named, *5547*
15:29 fulness of the blessing of the gospel of **C**. *5547*
16: 3 and Aquila my helpers in **C** Jesus: *5547*
16: 5 who is the firstfruits of Achaia unto **C**. *5547*
16: 7 the apostles, who also were in **C** before me. *5547*
16: 9 Salute Urban our helper in **C**, and *5547*
16:10 Salute Apelles approved in **C**. Salute them *5547*
16:16 a holy kiss. The churches of **C** salute you. *5547*
16:18 *that are* such serve not our Lord Jesus **C**, *5547*
16:20 The grace of our Lord Jesus **C** *be* with you. *5547*
16:24 The grace of our Lord Jesus **C** *be* with you *5547*
16:25 and the preaching of Jesus **C**, according to *5547*
16:27 *be* glory through Jesus **C** for ever. *5547*
1Co 1: 1 called *to be* an apostle of Jesus **C** through *5547*
1: 2 to them that are sanctified in **C** Jesus, *5547*
1: 2 call upon the name of Jesus **C** our Lord, *5547*
1: 3 God our Father, and *from* the Lord Jesus **C**. *5547*
1: 4 of God which is given you by Jesus **C**; *5547*
1: 6 Even as the testimony of **C** was confirmed *5547*
1: 7 for the coming of our Lord Jesus **C**: *5547*
1: 8 blameless in the day of our Lord Jesus **C**. *5547*
1: 9 the fellowship of his Son Jesus **C** our Lord. *5547*
1:10 brethren, by the name of our Lord Jesus **C**, *5547*
1:12 I of Apollos; and I of Cephas; and I of **C**. *5547*
1:13 Is **C** divided? was Paul crucified for you? *5547*
1:17 For **C** sent me not to baptize, but to preach *5547*
1:17 lest the cross of **C** should be made of none *5547*
1:23 But we preach **C** crucified, unto the Jews a *5547*
1:24 **C** the power of God, and the wisdom of *5547*
1:30 But of him are ye in **C** Jesus, who of God is *5547*
2: 2 save Jesus **C**, and him crucified. *5547*
2:16 instruct him? But we have the mind of **C**. *5547*
3: 1 but as unto carnal, *even* as unto babes in **C**. *5547*
3:11 *man* lay than that is laid, which is Jesus **C**. *5547*
3:23 And ye *are* Christ's; and **C** *is* God's. *5547*
4: 1 as of the ministers of **C**, and stewards of *5547*
4:10 for Christ's sake, but ye *are* wise in **C**; *5547*
4:15 you have ten thousand instructors in **C**, *5547*
4:15 for in **C** Jesus I have begotten you through *5547*
4:17 remembrance of my ways which be in **C**, *5547*
5: 4 In the name of our Lord Jesus **C**, when ye *5547*
5: 4 with the power of our Lord Jesus **C**, *5547*
5: 7 For even **C** our passover is sacrificed for *5547*
6:15 not that your bodies are the members of **C**? *5547*
6:15 shall I then take the members of **C**, and *5547*
8: 6 and one Lord Jesus **C**, by whom *are* all *5547*
8:11 the weak brother perish, for whom **C** died? *5547*
8:12 their weak conscience, ye sin against **C**. *5547*
9: 1 have I not seen Jesus **C** our Lord? are not *5547*
9:12 lest we should hinder the gospel of **C**. *5547*
9:18 I may make the gospel of **C** without charge, *5547*
9:21 law to God, but under the law to **C**,) *5547*
10: 4 that followed *them:* and *that* Rock was **C**. *5547*
10: 9 Neither let us tempt **C**, as some of them *5547*
10:16 is it not the communion of the blood of **C**? *5547*
10:16 is it not the communion of the body of **C**? *5547*
11: 1 ye followers of me, even as I also *am* of **C**. *5547*
11: 3 you know, that the head of every man is **C**; *5547*
11: 3 *is* the man; and the head of **C** *is* God. *5547*
12:12 being many, are one body: so also *is* **C**. *5547*
12:27 Now ye are the body of **C**, and members in *5547*
15: 3 how that **C** died for our sins according to *5547*
15:12 Now if **C** be preached that he rose from *5547*
15:13 resurrection of the dead, then is **C** not risen: *5547*
15:14 And if **C** be not risen, then *is* our preaching *5547*
15:15 have testified of God that he raised up **C**: *5547*
15:16 if the dead rise not, then is not **C** raised: *5547*
15:17 And if **C** be not raised, your faith *is* vain; *5547*

1Co	15:18	Then they also which are fallen asleep in **C**	*5547*
	15:19	If in this life only we have hope in **C**,	*5547*
	15:20	But now is **C** risen from the dead, *and*	*5547*
	15:22	all die, even so in **C** shall all be made alive.	*5547*
	15:23	**C** the firstfruits; afterward they that are	*5547*
	15:31	rejoicing which I have in **C** Jesus our Lord,	*5547*
	15:57	us the victory through our Lord Jesus **C**.	*5547*
	16:22	If any *man* love not the Lord Jesus **C**,	*5547*
	16:23	The grace of *our* Lord Jesus **C** *be* with you.	*5547*
	16:24	My love *be* with you all in **C** Jesus. Amen.	*5547*
2Co	1: 1	an apostle of Jesus **C** by the will of God,	*5547*
	1: 2	God our Father, and *from* the Lord Jesus **C**.	*5547*
	1: 3	even the Father of our Lord Jesus **C**,	*5547*
	1: 5	For as the sufferings of **C** abound in us, so	*5547*
	1: 5	so our consolation also aboundeth by **C**.	*5547*
	1:19	For the Son of God, Jesus **C**, who was	*5547*
	1:21	Now he which stablisheth us with you in **C**,	*5547*
	2:10	your sakes *forgave I it* in the person of **C**;	*5547*
	2:14	which always causeth us to triumph in **C**,	*5547*
	2:15	For we are unto God a sweet savour of **C**,	*5547*
	2:17	of God, in the sight of God speak we in **C**.	*5547*
	3: 3	to be the epistle of **C** ministered by us,	*5547*
	3: 4	And such trust have we through **C** to	*5547*
	3:14	which *vail* is done away in **C**.	*5547*
	4: 4	lest the light of the glorious gospel of **C**,	*5547*
	4: 5	preach not ourselves, but **C** Jesus the Lord;	*5547*
	4: 6	of the glory of God in the face of Jesus **C**.	*5547*
	5:10	all appear before the judgment seat of **C**;	*5547*
	5:14	For the love of **C** constraineth us; because	*5547*
	5:16	though we have known **C** after the flesh,	*5547*
	5:17	Therefore if any *man be* in **C**, *he is* a new	*5547*
	5:18	hath reconciled us to himself by Jesus **C**,	*5547*
	5:19	that God was in **C** reconciling the world	*5547*
	5:20	*Now* then we are ambassadors for **C**,	*5547*
	6:15	And what concord hath **C** with Belial? or	*5547*
	8: 9	For ye know the grace of our Lord Jesus **C**,	*5547*
	8:23	of the churches, *and* the glory of **C**.	*5547*
	9:13	professed subjection unto the gospel of **C**,	*5547*
	10: 1	you by the meekness and gentleness of **C**,	*5547*
	10: 5	every thought to the obedience of **C**;	*5547*
	10:14	as to you also in *preaching* the gospel of **C**:	*5547*
	11: 2	*I* may present *you as* a chaste virgin to **C**.	*5547*
	11: 3	corrupted from the simplicity that is in **C**.	*5547*
	11:10	*As* the truth of **C** is in me, no *man* shall	*5547*
	11:13	themselves into the apostles of **C**.	*5547*
	11:23	Are they ministers of **C**? (I speak as a fool)	*5547*
	11:31	The God and Father of our Lord Jesus **C**,	*5547*
	12: 2	I knew a man in **C** above fourteen years	*5547*
	12: 9	that the power of **C** may rest upon me.	*5547*
	12:19	we speak before God in **C**: but *we do* all	*5547*
	13: 3	Since ye seek a proof of **C** speaking in me,	*5547*
	13: 5	how that Jesus **C** is in you, except ye be	*5547*
	13:14	The grace of the Lord Jesus **C**, and the love	*5547*
Gal	1: 1	but by Jesus **C**, and God the Father,	*5547*
	1: 3	God the Father, and *from* our Lord Jesus **C**,	*5547*
	1: 6	into the grace of **C** unto another gospel:	*5547*
	1: 7	and would pervert the gospel of **C**.	*5547*
	1:10	I should not be the servant of **C**.	*5547*
	1:12	I taught *it*, but by the revelation of Jesus **C**.	*5547*
	1:22	the churches of Judea which were in **C**:	*5547*
	2: 4	out our liberty which we have in **C** Jesus,	*5547*
	2:16	but by the faith of Jesus **C**, even we have	*5547*
	2:16	even we have believed in Jesus **C**,	*5547*
	2:16	that we might be justified by the faith of **C**,	*5547*
	2:17	But if, while we seek to be justified by **C**,	*5547*
	2:17	*is* therefore **C** the minister of sin?	*5547*
	2:20	I am crucified with **C**: nevertheless I live;	*5547*
	2:20	I live; yet not I, but **C** liveth in me:	*5547*
	2:21	*come* by the law, then **C** is dead in vain.	*5547*
	3: 1	before whose eyes Jesus **C** hath been	*5547*
	3:13	**C** hath redeemed us from the curse of	*5547*
	3:14	come on the Gentiles through Jesus **C**;	*5547*
	3:16	but as of one, And to thy seed, which is **C**.	*5547*
	3:17	that was confirmed before of God in **C**,	*5547*
	3:22	that the promise by faith of Jesus **C** might	*5547*
	3:24	was our schoolmaster *to bring us* unto **C**,	*5547*
	3:26	all the children of God by faith in **C** Jesus.	*5547*
	3:27	been baptized into **C** have put on Christ.	*5547*
	3:27	been baptized into Christ have put on **C**.	*5547*
	3:28	nor female: for ye are all one in **C** Jesus.	*5547*
	4: 7	and if a son, then an heir of God through **C**.	*5547*
	4:14	me as an angel of God, *even* as **C** Jesus.	*5547*
	4:19	of whom I travail in birth again until **C** be	*5547*
	5: 1	in the liberty wherewith **C** hath made us	*5547*
	5: 2	be circumcised, **C** shall profit you nothing.	*5547*
	5: 4	**C** is become of no effect unto you,	*5547*
	5: 6	For in Jesus **C** neither circumcision	*5547*
	6: 2	and so fulfil the law of **C**.	*5547*
	6:12	suffer persecution for the cross of **C**.	*5547*
	6:14	save in the cross of our Lord Jesus **C**,	*5547*
	6:15	For in **C** Jesus neither circumcision	*5547*
	6:18	the grace of our Lord Jesus **C** *be* with your	*5547*
Eph	1: 1	an apostle of Jesus **C** by the will of God,	*5547*
	1: 1	at Ephesus, and to the faithful in **C** Jesus:	*5547*
	1: 2	God our Father, and *from* the Lord Jesus **C**.	*5547*
	1: 3	*be* the God and Father of our Lord Jesus **C**,	*5547*
	1: 3	spiritual blessings in heavenly *places* in **C**:	*5547*
	1: 5	adoption of children by Jesus **C** to himself,	*5547*
	1:10	might gather together in one all *things* in **C**,	*5547*
	1:12	praise of his glory, who first trusted in **C**:	*5547*
	1:17	That the God of our Lord Jesus **C**,	*5547*
	1:20	Which he wrought in **C**, when he raised	*5547*
	2: 5	hath quickened *us* together with **C**, (by	*5547*
	2: 6	sit together in heavenly *places* in **C** Jesus:	*5547*
	2: 7	in *his* kindness towards us through **C** Jesus.	*5547*
	2:10	created in **C** Jesus unto good works,	*5547*
	2:12	That at that time ye were without **C**,	*5547*
	2:13	But now in **C** Jesus ye who sometimes	*5547*
	2:13	far off are made nigh by the blood of **C**.	*5547*
	2:20	Jesus **C** himself being the chief corner	*5547*
	3: 1	the prisoner of Jesus **C** for you Gentiles,	*5547*
	3: 4	my knowledge in the mystery of **C**)	*5547*
	3: 6	partakers of his promise in **C** by the gospel:	*5547*
	3: 8	the Gentiles the unsearchable riches of **C**;	*5547*
	3: 9	in God, who created all *things* by Jesus **C**:	*5547*
	3:11	which he purposed in **C** Jesus our Lord:	*5547*
	3:14	knees unto the Father of our Lord Jesus **C**,	*5547*
	3:17	That **C** may dwell in your hearts by faith;	*5547*
	3:19	And to know the love of **C**, which passeth	*5547*
	3:21	Unto him *be* glory in the church by **C** Jesus	*5547*
	4: 7	according to the measure of the gift of **C**.	*5547*
	4:12	for the edifying of the body of **C**:	*5547*
	4:13	measure of the stature of the fulness of **C**:	*5547*
	4:15	*in* all *things*, which is the head, *even* **C**:	*5547*
	4:20	But ye have not so learned **C**;	*5547*
	5: 2	as **C** also hath loved us, and hath given	*5547*
	5: 5	hath *any* inheritance in the kingdom of **C**	*5547*
	5:14	from the dead, and **C** shall give thee light.	*5547*
	5:20	the Father in the name of our Lord Jesus **C**;	*5547*
	5:23	even as **C** *is* the head of the church:	*5547*
	5:24	Therefore as the church is subject unto **C**,	*5547*
	5:25	even as **C** also loved the church, and	*5547*
	5:32	but I speak concerning **C** and the church.	*5547*
	6: 5	in singleness of your heart, as unto **C**;	*5547*
	6: 6	but as the servants of **C**, doing the will of	*5547*
	6:23	from God the Father and the Lord Jesus **C**.	*5547*
	6:24	that love our Lord Jesus **C** in sincerity.	*5547*
Php	1: 1	and Timotheus, the servants of Jesus **C**,	*5547*
	1: 1	to all the saints in **C** Jesus which are at	*5547*
	1: 2	God our Father, and *from* the Lord Jesus **C**.	*5547*
	1: 6	you will perform *it* until the day of Jesus **C**:	*5547*
	1: 8	long after you all in the bowels of Jesus **C**.	*5547*
	1:10	and without offence till the day of **C**;	*5547*
	1:11	which are by Jesus **C** unto the glory and	*5547*
	1:13	So that my bonds in **C** are manifest in all	*5547*
	1:15	Some indeed preach **C** even of envy and	*5547*
	1:16	The one preach **C** of contention,	*5547*
	1:18	in pretence, or in truth, **C** is preached;	*5547*
	1:19	and the supply of the Spirit of Jesus **C**,	*5547*
	1:20	now also **C** shall be magnified in my body,	*5547*
	1:21	For to me to live *is* **C**, and to die *is* gain.	*5547*
	1:23	having a desire to depart, and to be with **C**;	*5547*
	1:26	Jesus **C** for me by my coming to you again.	*5547*
	1:27	be as it becometh the gospel of **C**:	*5547*
	1:29	For unto you it is given in the behalf of **C**,	*5547*
	2: 1	If *there be* therefore any consolation in **C**,	*5547*
	2: 5	mind be in you, which *was* also in **C** Jesus:	*5547*
	2:11	tongue should confess that Jesus **C** *is* Lord,	*5547*
	2:16	that I may rejoice in the day of **C**, that I	*5547*
	2:30	Because for the work of **C** he was nigh	*5547*
	3: 3	and rejoice in **C** Jesus, and have no	*5547*
	3: 7	were gain to me, those I counted loss for **C**.	*5547*
	3: 8	of the knowledge of **C** Jesus my Lord:	*5547*
	3: 8	do count *them but* dung, that I may win **C**,	*5547*
	3: 9	but that which is through the faith of **C**,	*5547*
	3:12	which also I am apprehended of **C** Jesus.	*5547*
	3:14	prize of the high calling of God in **C** Jesus.	*5547*
	3:18	*that they are* the enemies of the cross of **C**:	*5547*

Php	3:20	we look for the Saviour, the Lord Jesus **C**:	*5547*
	4: 7	your hearts and minds through **C** Jesus.	*5547*
	4:13	I can do all *things* through **C** which	*5547*
	4:19	according to his riches in glory by **C** Jesus.	*5547*
	4:21	Salute every saint in **C** Jesus. The brethren	*5547*
	4:23	The grace of our Lord Jesus **C** *be* with you	*5547*
Col	1: 1	an apostle of Jesus **C** by the will of God,	*5547*
	1: 2	faithful brethren in **C** which are at Colosse:	*5547*
	1: 2	from God our Father and the Lord Jesus **C**.	*5547*
	1: 3	to God and the Father of our Lord Jesus **C**,	*5547*
	1: 4	Since we heard of your faith in **C** Jesus,	*5547*
	1: 7	who is for you a faithful minister of **C**;	*5547*
	1:24	of **C** in my flesh for his body's sake,	*5547*
	1:27	which is **C** in you, the hope of glory:	*5547*
	1:28	that we may present every man perfect in **C**	*5547*
	2: 2	of God and of the Father, and of **C**;	*5547*
	2: 5	and the stedfastness of your faith in **C**.	*5547*
	2: 6	therefore received **C** Jesus the Lord,	*5547*
	2: 8	the rudiments of the world, and not after **C**.	*5547*
	2:11	sins of the flesh, by the circumcision of **C**:	*5547*
	2:17	of *things* to come; but the body *is* of **C**.	*5547*
	2:20	Wherefore if ye be dead with **C** from	*5547*
	3: 1	If ye then be risen with **C**, seek those *things*	*5547*
	3: 1	where **C** sitteth on the right hand of God.	*5547*
	3: 3	and your life is hid with **C** in God.	*5547*
	3: 4	When **C**, *who is* our life, shall appear, then	*5547*
	3:11	bond *nor* free: but **C** *is* all, and in all.	*5547*
	3:13	even as **C** forgave you, so also *do* ye.	*5547*
	3:16	Let the word of **C** dwell in you richly in all	*5547*
	3:24	of the inheritance: for ye serve the Lord **C**.	*5547*
	4: 3	to speak the mystery of **C**, for which I am	*5547*
	4:12	is *one* of you, a servant of **C**, saluteth you,	*5547*
1Th	1: 1	in God the Father and *in* the Lord Jesus **C**:	*5547*
	1: 1	from God our Father, and the Lord Jesus **C**.	*5547*
	1: 3	and patience of hope in our Lord Jesus **C**,	*5547*
	2: 6	been burdensome, as *the* apostles of **C**.	*5547*
	2:14	of God which in Judea are in **C** Jesus:	*5547*
	2:19	of our Lord Jesus **C** at his coming?	*5547*
	3: 2	and our fellowlabourer in the gospel of **C**,	*5547*
	3:11	and our Father, and our Lord Jesus **C**,	*5547*
	3:13	at the coming of our Lord Jesus **C** with all	*5547*
	4:16	of God: and the dead in **C** shall rise first:	*5547*
	5: 9	but to obtain salvation by our Lord Jesus **C**,	*5547*
	5:18	for this *is* the will of God in **C** Jesus	*5547*
	5:23	unto the coming of our Lord Jesus **C**.	*5547*
	5:28	The grace of our Lord Jesus **C** *be* with you.	*5547*
2Th	1: 1	in God our Father and the Lord Jesus **C**:	*5547*
	1: 2	from God our Father and the Lord Jesus **C**.	*5547*
	1: 8	obey not the gospel of our Lord Jesus **C**:	*5547*
	1:12	That the name of our Lord Jesus **C** may be	*5547*
	1:12	the grace of our God and the Lord Jesus **C**.	*5547*
	2: 1	by the coming of our Lord Jesus **C**, and	*5547*
	2: 2	as from us, as that the day of **C** is at hand.	*5547*
	2:14	obtaining of the glory of our Lord Jesus **C**.	*5547*
	2:16	Now our Lord Jesus **C** himself, and God,	*5547*
	3: 5	of God, and into the patient waiting for **C**.	*5547*
	3: 6	brethren, in the name of our Lord Jesus **C**,	*5547*
	3:12	and exhort by our Lord Jesus **C**,	*5547*
	3:18	The grace of our Lord Jesus **C** *be* with you	*5547*
1Ti	1: 1	an apostle of Jesus **C** by the commandment	*5547*
	1: 1	and Lord Jesus **C**, *which is* our hope;	*5547*
	1: 2	from God our Father and Jesus **C** our Lord.	*5547*
	1:12	And I thank **C** Jesus our Lord, who hath	*5547*
	1:14	with faith and love which is in **C** Jesus.	*5547*
	1:15	that **C** Jesus came into the world to save	*5547*
	1:16	that in me first Jesus **C** might shew forth all	*5547*
	2: 5	between God and men, *the* man **C** Jesus;	*5547*
	2: 7	(I speak the truth in **C**, *and* lie not;)	*5547*
	3:13	great boldness in the faith which is in **C**	*5547*
	4: 6	thou shalt be a good minister of Jesus **C**,	*5547*
	5:11	they have *begun to* wax wanton against **C**,	*5547*
	5:21	and the Lord Jesus **C**, and the elect angels,	*5547*
	6: 3	*even* the *words* of our Lord Jesus **C**, and	*5547*
	6:13	quickeneth all *things,* and *before* **C** Jesus,	*5547*
	6:14	until the appearing of our Lord Jesus **C**:	*5547*
2Ti	1: 1	an apostle of Jesus **C** by the will of God,	*5547*
	1: 1	to the promise of life which is in **C** Jesus,	*5547*
	1: 2	from God the Father and **C** Jesus our Lord.	*5547*
	1: 9	which was given us in **C** Jesus before	*5547*
	1:10	by the appearing of our Saviour Jesus **C**,	*5547*
	1:13	of me, in faith and love which is in **C** Jesus.	*5547*
	2: 1	be strong in the grace that is in **C** Jesus.	*5547*
	2: 3	as a good soldier of Jesus **C**.	*5547*
	2: 8	Remember that Jesus **C** of the seed of	*5547*
	2:10	which is in **C** Jesus with eternal glory.	*5547*
	2:19	Let every one that nameth the name of **C**	*5547*
	3:12	all that will live godly in **C** Jesus shall	*5547*
	3:15	salvation through faith which is in **C** Jesus.	*5547*
	4: 1	therefore before God, and the Lord Jesus **C**,	*5547*
	4:22	The Lord Jesus **C** *be* with thy spirit. Grace	*5547*
Tit	1: 1	a servant of God, and an apostle of Jesus **C**,	*5547*
	1: 4	and the Lord Jesus **C** our Saviour.	*5547*
	2:13	of the great God and our Saviour Jesus **C**;	*5547*
	3: 6	us abundantly through Jesus **C** our Saviour;	*5547*
Phm	1: 1	a prisoner of Jesus **C**, and Timothy *our*	*5547*
	1: 3	from God our Father and the Lord Jesus **C**.	*5547*
	1: 6	good *thing* which is in you in **C** Jesus.	*5547*
	1: 8	though I might be much bold in **C** to enjoin	*5547*
	1: 9	and now also a prisoner of Jesus **C**.	*5547*
	1:23	my fellowprisoner in **C** Jesus;	*5547*
	1:25	The grace of our Lord Jesus **C** *be* with your	*5547*
Heb	3: 1	and High Priest of our profession, **C** Jesus;	*5547*
	3: 6	But **C** as a Son over his own house;	*5547*
	3:14	For we are made partakers of **C**, if we hold	*5547*
	5: 5	So also **C** glorified not himself to be made	*5547*
	6: 1	leaving the principles of the doctrine of **C**,	*5547*
	9:11	But **C** being come a high priest of good	*5547*
	9:14	How much more shall the blood of **C**,	*5547*
	9:24	For **C** is not entered into the holy *places*	*5547*
	9:28	So **C** was once offered to bear the sins of	*5547*
	10:10	offering of the body of Jesus **C** once for all.	*5547*
	11:26	Esteeming the reproach of **C** greater riches	*5547*
	13: 8	Jesus **C** the same yesterday, and to day, and	*5547*
	13:21	well pleasing in his sight, through Jesus **C**;	*5547*
Jas	1: 1	a servant of God and of the Lord Jesus **C**,	*5547*
	2: 1	have not the faith of our Lord Jesus **C**,	*5547*
1Pe	1: 1	Peter, an apostle of Jesus **C**, to	*5547*
	1: 2	and sprinkling of the blood of Jesus **C**:	*5547*
	1: 3	*be* the God and Father of our Lord Jesus **C**,	*5547*
	1: 3	the resurrection of Jesus **C** from the dead,	*5547*
	1: 7	and glory at the appearing of Jesus **C**:	*5547*
	1:11	what manner of time the Spirit of **C** which	*5547*
	1:11	it testified beforehand the sufferings of **C**,	*5547*
	1:13	unto you at the revelation of Jesus **C**;	*5547*
	1:19	But with the precious blood of **C**, as of a	*5547*
	2: 5	acceptable to God by Jesus **C**.	*5547*
	2:21	because **C** also suffered for us, leaving us	*5547*
	3:16	falsely accuse your good conversation in **C**.	*5547*
	3:18	For **C** also hath once suffered for sins,	*5547*
	3:21	by the resurrection of Jesus **C**:	*5547*
	4: 1	then as **C** hath suffered for us in the flesh,	*5547*
	4:11	all *things* may be glorified through Jesus **C**,	*5547*
	4:14	If ye be reproached for the name of **C**,	*5547*
	5: 1	and a witness of the sufferings of **C**, and	*5547*
	5:10	called us into his eternal glory by **C** Jesus,	*5547*
	5:14	Peace *be* with you all that are in **C** Jesus.	*5547*
2Pe	1: 1	a servant and an apostle of Jesus **C**,	*5547*
	1: 1	of God and our Saviour Jesus **C**:	*5547*
	1: 8	in the knowledge of our Lord Jesus **C**.	*5547*
	1:11	kingdom of our Lord and Saviour Jesus **C**.	*5547*
	1:14	even as our Lord Jesus **C** hath shewed me.	*5547*
	1:16	the power and coming of our Lord Jesus **C**,	*5547*
	2:20	of the Lord and Saviour Jesus **C**,	*5547*
	3:18	of our Lord and Saviour Jesus **C**.	*5547*
1Jn	1: 3	with the Father, and with his Son Jesus **C**.	*5547*
	1: 7	the blood of Jesus **C** his Son cleanseth us	*5547*
	2: 1	with the Father, Jesus **C** *the* righteous:	*5547*
	2:22	but he that denieth that Jesus is the **C**?	*5547*
	3:23	believe on the name of his Son Jesus **C**,	*5547*
	4: 2	Every spirit that confesseth that Jesus **C** is	*5547*
	4: 3	Jesus **C** is come in the flesh is not of God:	*5547*
	5: 1	Whosoever believeth that Jesus is the **C** is	*5547*
	5: 6	came by water and blood, *even* Jesus **C**;	*5547*
	5:20	in him *that is* true, *even* in his Son Jesus **C**.	*5547*
2Jn	1: 3	God the Father, and from the Lord Jesus **C**,	*5547*
	1: 7	who confess not that Jesus **C** is come in	*5547*
	1: 9	and abideth not in the doctrine of **C**,	*5547*
	1: 9	He that abideth in the doctrine of **C**,	*5547*
Jude	1: 1	the servant of Jesus **C**, and brother of	*5547*
	1: 1	and preserved *in* Jesus **C**, *and* called:	*5547*
	1: 4	the only Lord God, and our Lord Jesus **C**.	*5547*
	1:17	before of the apostles of our Lord Jesus **C**;	*5547*
	1:21	looking for the mercy of our Lord Jesus **C**	*5547*
Rev	1: 1	The Revelation of Jesus **C**, which God	*5547*
	1: 2	and of the testimony of Jesus **C**, and of all	*5547*
	1: 5	And from Jesus **C**, *who is* the faithful	*5547*
	1: 9	in the kingdom and patience of Jesus **C**,	*5547*
	1: 9	of God, and for the testimony of Jesus **C**.	*5547*

Rev 11:15 *the kingdoms* of our Lord, and of his **C**; *5547*
12:10 of our God, and the power of his **C**: *5547*
12:17 of God, and have the testimony of Jesus **C**. *5547*
20: 4 and reigned with **C** a thousand years. *5547*
20: 6 but they shall be priests of God and of **C**, *5547*
22:21 The grace of our Lord Jesus **C** *be* with you *5547*

CHRIST'S (16) [CHRIST]
Ro 15:30 for the Lord Jesus **C** sake, and for the love *5547*
1Co 3:23 And ye *are* **C**; and Christ *is* God's. *5547*
4:10 We *are* fools for **C** sake, but ye *are* wise in *5547*
7:22 he that is called, *being* free, is **C** servant. *5547*
15:23 afterward they that are **C** at his coming. *5547*
2Co 2:12 when I came to Troas to *preach* **C** gospel, *5547*
5:20 we pray *you* in **C** stead, be ye reconciled to *5547*
10: 7 If any *man* trust to himself that *he* is **C**, *5547*
10: 7 that, as he *is* **C**, even so *are* we Christ's. *5547*
10: 7 that, as he *is* Christ's, even so *are* we **C**. *5547*
12:10 in persecutions, in distresses for **C** sake: *5547*
Gal 3:29 And if ye *be* **C**, then are ye Abraham's *5547*
5:24 And they that are **C** have crucified the flesh *5547*
Eph 4:32 even as God for **C** sake hath forgiven you. *5547*
Php 2:21 their own, not the *things which are* Jesus **C**. *5547*
1Pe 4:13 inasmuch as ye are partakers of **C** *5547*

CHRISTIAN (2) [CHRIST]
Ac 26:28 Almost thou persuadest me to be a **C**. *5546*
1Pe 4:16 Yet if *any man suffer* as a **C**, let him not be *5546*

CHRISTIANS (1) [CHRIST]
Ac 11:26 the disciples were called **C** first in Antioch. *5546*

CHRISTS (2) [CHRIST]
Mt 24:24 For there shall arise **false C**, and *5580*
Mk 13:22 For **false C** and false prophets shall rise, *5580*

CHRONICLES (38)
1Ki 14:19 book of the **c** of the kings of Israel. 1697+3117
14:29 book of the **c** of the kings of Judah? 1697+3117
15: 7 book of the **c** of the kings of Judah? 1697+3117
15:23 book of the **c** of the kings of Judah? 1697+3117
15:31 book of the **c** of the kings of Israel? 1697+3117
16: 5 book of the **c** of the kings of Israel? 1697+3117
16:14 book of the **c** of the kings of Israel? 1697+3117
16:20 book of the **c** of the kings of Israel? 1697+3117
16:27 book of the **c** of the kings of Israel? 1697+3117
22:39 book of the **c** of the kings of Israel? 1697+3117
22:45 book of the **c** of the kings of Judah? 1697+3117
2Ki 1:18 book of the **c** of the kings of Israel? 1697+3117
8:23 book of the **c** of the kings of Judah? 1697+3117
10:34 book of the **c** of the kings of Israel? 1697+3117
12:19 book of the **c** of the kings of Judah? 1697+3117
13: 8 book of the **c** of the kings of Israel? 1697+3117
13:12 book of the **c** of the kings of Israel? 1697+3117
14:15 book of the **c** of the kings of Israel? 1697+3117
14:18 book of the **c** of the kings of Judah? 1697+3117
14:28 book of the **c** of the kings of Israel? 1697+3117
15: 6 book of the **c** of the kings of Judah? 1697+3117
15:11 they *are* written in the book of the **c** 1697+3117
15:15 they *are* written in the book of the **c** 1697+3117
15:21 book of the **c** of the kings of Israel? 1697+3117
15:26 they *are* written in the book of the **c** 1697+3117
15:31 they *are* written in the book of the **c** 1697+3117
15:36 book of the **c** of the kings of Judah? 1697+3117
16:19 book of the **c** of the kings of Judah? 1697+3117
20:20 book of the **c** of the kings of Judah? 1697+3117
21:17 book of the **c** of the kings of Judah? 1697+3117
21:25 book of the **c** of the kings of Judah? 1697+3117
23:28 book of the **c** of the kings of Judah? 1697+3117
24: 5 book of the **c** of the kings of Judah? 1697+3117
1Ch 27:24 of the **c** of king David. 1697+3117+1886.1
Ne 12:23 written in the book of the **c**, 1697+3117+1886.1
Est 2:23 of the **c** before the king. 1697+3117+1886.1
6: 1 the book of records of the **c**; 1697+3117+1886.1
10: 2 the **c** of the kings of Media 1697+3117+1886.1

CHRYSOLITE (1)
Rev 21:20 sardonyx; the sixth, sardius; the seventh, **c**; *5555*

CHRYSOPRASE See CHRYSOPRASUS

CHRYSOPRASUS (1)
Rev 21:20 beryl; the ninth, a topaz; the tenth, a **c**; *5556*

CHUB (1)
Eze 30: 5 **C**, and the men of the land that is in league, 3552

CHUN (1)
1Ch 18: 8 and from **C**, cities of Hadarezer, 3560

CHURCH (80) [CHURCHES]
Mt 16:18 and upon this rock I will build my **c**; *1577*
18:17 shall neglect to hear them, tell *it* unto the **c**: *1577*
18:17 but if he neglect to hear the **c**, let him be *1577*
Ac 2:47 And the Lord added to the **c** daily such as *1577*
5:11 And great fear came upon all the **c**, and *1577*
7:38 that was in the **c** in the wilderness with *1577*
8: 1 against the **c** which was at Jerusalem; *1577*
8: 3 As for Saul, he made havock of the **c**, *1577*
11:22 the ears of the **c** which was in Jerusalem: *1577*
11:26 year they assembled themselves with the **c**, *1577*
12: 1 forth *his* hands to vex certain of the **c**. *1577*
12: 5 prayer was made without ceasing of the **c** *1577*
13: 1 Now there were in the **c** that was at Antioch *1577*
14:23 had ordained them elders **in every c**, *1577+2596*
14:27 and had gathered the **c** together, *1577*
15: 3 And being brought on their way by the **c**, *1577*
15: 4 they were received of the **c**, and *of* *1577*
15:22 it the apostles and elders, with the whole **c**, *1577*
18:22 and gone up, and saluted the **c**, he went *1577*
20:17 to Ephesus, and called the elders of the **c**. *1577*
20:28 to feed the **c** of God, which he hath *1577*
Ro 16: 1 which is a servant of the **c** which is at *1577*
16: 5 Likewise *greet* the **c** that is in their house. *1577*
16:23 mine host, and of the whole **c**, saluteth you. *1577*
16: S *sent* by Phebe servant of the **c** at Cenchrea. *1577*
1Co 1: 2 Unto the **c** of God which is at Corinth, *1577*
4:17 in Christ, as I teach every where in every **c**. *1577*
6: 4 to judge who are least esteemed in the **c**. *1577*
10:32 nor to the Gentiles, nor to the **c** of God: *1577*
11:18 first of all, when ye come together in the **c**, *1577*
11:22 and to drink *in?* or despise ye the **c** of God, *1577*
12:28 And God hath set some in the **c**, *1577*
14: 4 but he that prophesieth edifieth *the* **c**. *1577*
14: 5 that the **c** may receive edifying. *1577*
14:12 that ye may excel to the edifying of the **c**. *1577*
14:19 Yet in the **c** I had rather speak five words *1577*
14:23 the whole **c** be come together into one *1577*
14:28 no interpreter, let him keep silence in the **c**; *1577*
14:35 it is a shame for women to speak in the **c**. *1577*
15: 9 because I persecuted the **c** of God. *1577*
16:19 in the Lord, with the **c** that is in their house. *1577*
2Co 1: 1 unto the **c** of God which is at Corinth, *1577*
Gal 1:13 how that beyond measure I persecuted the **c** *1577*
Eph 1:22 him *to be* the head over all *things* to the **c**, *1577*
3:10 by the **c** the manifold wisdom of God, *1577*
3:21 Unto him *be* glory in the **c** by Christ Jesus *1577*
5:23 the wife, even as Christ *is* the head of the **c**: *1577*
5:24 Therefore as the **c** is subject unto Christ, so *1577*
5:25 even as Christ also loved the **c**, and *1577*
5:27 he might present it to himself a glorious **c**, *1577*
5:29 and cherisheth it, even as the Lord the **c**: *1577*
5:32 but I speak concerning Christ and the **c**. *1577*
Php 3: 6 Concerning zeal, persecuting the **c**; *1577*
4:15 no **c** communicated with me as concerning *1577*
Col 1:18 And he is the head of the body, the **c**: *1577*
1:24 flesh for his body's sake, which is the **c**: *1577*
4:15 Nymphas, and the **c** which is in his house. *1577*
4:16 cause that it be read also in the **c** of *1577*
1Th 1: 1 unto the **c** of the Thessalonians *which is* in *1577*
2Th 1: 1 unto the **c** of the Thessalonians in God our *1577*
1Ti 3: 5 how shall he take care of the **c** of God?) *1577*
3:15 which is the **c** of the living God, the pillar *1577*
5:16 relieve them, and let not the **c** be charged; *1577*
2Ti 4: S ordained the first bishop of the **c** of *1577*
Tit 3: S ordained the first bishop of the **c** of *1577*
Phm 1: 2 our fellowsoldier, and to the **c** in thy house: *1577*
Heb 2:12 in the midst of the **c** will I sing praise unto *1577*
12:23 the general assembly, and **c** of the firstborn, *1577*
Jas 5:14 let him call for the elders of the **c**; and *1577*
1Pe 5:13 The *c that is* at Babylon, elected together NIG
3Jn 1: 6 borne witness of thy charity before the **c**: *1577*
1: 9 I wrote unto the **c**: but Diotrephes, *1577*
1:10 that would, and casteth *them* out of the **c**. *1577*
Rev 2: 1 Unto the angel of the **c** of Ephesus write; *1577*
2: 8 And unto the angel of the **c** in Smyrna *1577*
2:12 And to the angel of the **c** in Pergamos *1577*
2:18 And unto the angel of the **c** in Thyatira *1577*

Rev 3: 1 And unto the angel of the **c** in Sardis write; *1577*
3: 7 And to the angel of the **c** in Philadelphia *1577*
3:14 And unto the angel of the **c** of *1577*

CHURCHES (37) [CHURCH]
Ac 9:31 Then had the **c** rest throughout all Judea *1577*
15:41 through Syria and Cilicia, confirming the **c**. *1577*
16: 5 And so were the **c** established in the faith, *1577*
19:37 *which are* neither **robbers of c**, nor yet *2417*
Ro 16: 4 but also all the **c** of the Gentiles. *1577*
16:16 with a holy kiss. The **c** of Christ salute you. *1577*
1Co 7:17 so let him walk. And so ordain I in all **c**. *1577*
11:16 have no such custom, neither the **c** of God. *1577*
14:33 but of peace, as in all **c** of the saints. *1577*
14:34 Let your women keep silence in the **c**: for it *1577*
16: 1 as I have given order to the **c** of Galatia, *1577*
16:19 The **c** of Asia salute you. Aquila and *1577*
2Co 8: 1 of God bestowed on the **c** of Macedonia; *1577*
8:18 praise *is* in the gospel throughout all the **c**; *1577*
8:19 who was also chosen of the **c** to travel with *1577*
8:23 *of, they are* the messengers of the **c**, *1577*
8:24 and before the **c**, the proof of your love, *1577*
11: 8 I robbed other **c**, taking wages *of them,* to *1577*
11:28 cometh upon me daily, the care of all the **c**. *1577*
12:13 is it wherein ye were inferior to other **c**, *1577*
Gal 1: 2 which are with me, unto the **c** of Galatia: *1577*
1:22 And was unknown by face unto the **c** of *1577*
1Th 2:14 became followers of the **c** of God which in *1577*
2Th 1: 4 So that we ourselves glory in you in the **c** *1577*
Rev 1: 4 John to the seven **c** which are in Asia: *1577*
1:11 send *it* unto the seven **c** which are in Asia; *1577*
1:20 seven stars are the angels of the seven **c**: *1577*
1:20 which thou sawest are the seven **c**. *1577*
2: 7 let him hear what the Spirit saith unto the **c**; *1577*
2:11 let him hear what the Spirit saith unto the **c**; *1577*
2:17 let him hear what the Spirit saith unto the **c**; *1577*
2:23 all the **c** shall know that I am he which *1577*
2:29 let him hear what the Spirit saith unto the **c**. *1577*
3: 6 let him hear what the Spirit saith unto the **c**. *1577*
3:13 let him hear what the Spirit saith unto the **c**. *1577*
3:22 let him hear what the Spirit saith unto the **c**. *1577*
22:16 to testify unto you these *things* in the **c**. *1577*

CHURL (2) [CHURLISH]
Isa 32: 5 called liberal, nor the **c** said *to be* bountiful. 3596
32: 7 The instruments also of the **c** *are* evil: 3596

CHURLISH (1) [CHURL]
1Sa 25: 3 the man *was* **c** and evil *in* his doings; and 7186

CHURNING (1)
Pr 30:33 Surely the **c** of milk bringeth forth butter, 4330

CHUSHAN-RISHATHAIM (4)
Jdg 3: 8 he sold them into the hand of **C** king of 3573
3: 8 the children of Israel served **C** eight years. 3573
3:10 the LORD delivered **C** king of 3573
3:10 his hand; and his hand prevailed against **C**. 3573

CHUZA (1)
Lk 8: 3 And Joanna the wife of **C** Herod's steward, *5529*

CIELED (4) [CIELING]
2Ch 3: 5 the greater house he **c** with fir tree, 2645
Jer 22:14 *it is* **c** with cedar, and painted with 5603
Eze 41:16 **c** with wood round about, and *from* 7824
Hag 1: 4 to dwell in your **c** houses, and this house *lie* 5603

CIELING (1) [CIELED]
1Ki 6:15 floor of the house, and the walls of the **c**: 5604

CILICIA (8)
Ac 6: 9 and of them of **C** and of Asia, *2791*
15:23 of the Gentiles in Antioch and Syria and **C**: *2791*
15:41 And he went through Syria and **C**, *2791*
21:39 *a city* in **C**, a citizen of no mean city: *2791*
22: 3 *am* a Jew, born in Tarsus, *a city* in **C**, *2791*
23:34 and when he understood that *he was* of **C**; *2791*
27: 5 And when we had sailed over the sea of **C** *2791*
Gal 1:21 I came into the regions of Syria and **C**; *2791*

CINNAMON (4)
Ex 30:23 and of sweet **c** half so much, 7076
Pr 7:17 perfumed my bed *with* myrrh, aloes, and **c**. 7076
SS 4:14 calamus and **c**, with all trees of 7076

Rev 18:13 And **c**, and odours, and ointments, and *2792*

CINNERETH (1) [CINNEROTH]
Jos 13:27 *even* unto the edge of the sea of **C** on 3672

CINNEROTH (3) [CINNERETH, CHINNERETH]
Jos 11: 2 of the plains south of **C**, and in the valley, 3672
12: 3 *from* the plain to the sea of **C** on the east, 3672
1Ki 15:20 and Abel-beth-maachah, and all **C**, 3672

CIRCLE (1)
Isa 40:22 *It is* he that sitteth upon the **c** of the earth, 2329

CIRCUIT (3) [CIRCUITS]
1Sa 7:16 he went from year to year in **c** *to* Beth-el, 5437
Job 22:14 and he walketh *in* the **c** of heaven. 2329
Ps 19: 6 of the heaven, and his **c** unto the ends of it: 8622

CIRCUITS (1) [CIRCUIT]
Ecc 1: 6 the wind returneth *again* according to his **c**. 5439

CIRCUMCISE (10) [CIRCUMCISED, CIRCUMCISING, CIRCUMCISION, UNCIRCUMCISED]
Ge 17:11 ye shall **c** the flesh of your foreskin; and 5243
Dt 10:16 **C** therefore the foreskin of your heart, and 4135
30: 6 the LORD thy God will **c** thine heart, and 4135
Jos 5: 2 **c** again the children of Israel the second 4135
5: 4 this *is* the cause why Joshua did **c**: All 4135
Jer 4: 4 **C** yourselves to the LORD, and take away 4135
Lk 1:59 *that* on the eighth day they came to **c** *4059*
Jn 7:22 and ye on the sabbath day **c** a man. *4059*
Ac 15: 5 That it was needful to **c** them, and *4059*
21:21 saying that they *ought* not to **c** *their* *4059*

CIRCUMCISED (39) [CIRCUMCISE]
Ge 17:10 Every man *child* among you shall be **c**. 4135
17:12 he that is eight days old shall be **c** among 4135
17:13 with thy money, **must needs be c**: 4135+4135
17:14 *child* whose flesh of his foreskin is not **c**, 4135
17:23 **c** the flesh of their foreskin in the selfsame 4135
17:24 when he was **c** *in* the flesh of his foreskin. 4135
17:25 when he was **c** in the flesh of his foreskin. 4135
17:26 In the selfsame day was Abraham **c**, and 4135
17:27 money of the stranger, were **c** with him. 4135
21: 4 Abraham **c** his son Isaac being eight days 4135
34:15 be as we *be*, that every male of you be **c**; 4135
34:17 if ye will not hearken unto us, to be **c**; then 4135
34:22 be one people, if every male among us be **c**, 4135
34:22 among us be circumcised, as they *are* **c**. 4135
34:24 every male was **c**, all that went out of 4135
Ex 12:44 when thou hast **c** him, then shall he eat 4135
12:48 let all his males be **c**, and then let him come 4135
Lev 12: 3 day the flesh of his foreskin shall be **c**. 4135
Jos 5: 3 **c** the children of Israel at the hill of 4135
5: 5 Now all the people that came out were **c**: 4135
5: 5 forth out of Egypt, *them* they had not **c**. 4135
5: 7 he raised up in their stead, them Joshua **c**: 4135
5: 7 because they had not **c** them by the way. 4135
Jer 9:25 that I will punish all *them which are* **c** with 4135
Ac 7: 8 begat Isaac, and **c** him the eighth day; *4059*
15: 1 *said,* Except ye be **c** after the manner of *4059*
15:24 saying, *Ye must* be **c**, and keep the law: *4059*
16: 3 and took and **c** him because of the Jews *4059*
Ro 4:11 all them that believe, though they be **not c**; *203*
1Co 7:18 Is any *man* called being **c**? let him not *4059*
7:18 called in uncircumcision? let him not be **c**. *4059*
Gal 2: 3 being a Greek, was compelled to be **c**: *4059*
5: 2 Behold, I Paul say unto you, that if ye be **c**, *4059*
5: 3 For I testify again to every man that is **c**, *4059*
6:12 in the flesh, they constrain you to be **c**; *4059*
6:13 For neither they themselves who are **c** keep *4059*
6:13 but desire to have you **c**, that they may *4059*
Php 3: 5 **C** the eighth day, of the stock of Israel, *4061*
Col 2:11 In whom also ye are **c** with *4059*

CIRCUMCISING (2) [CIRCUMCISE]
Jos 5: 8 when they had done **c** all the people, 4135
Lk 2:21 were accomplished for the **c** of the child, *4059*

CIRCUMCISION (36) [CIRCUMCISE]
Ex 4:26 bloody husband *thou art,* because of the **c**. 4139
Jn 7:22 Moses therefore gave unto you **c**, not *4061*
7:23 If a man on the sabbath day receive **c**, *4061*
Ac 7: 8 And he gave him the covenant of **c**: and so *4061*
10:45 And they of the **c** which believed were *4061*

C

Ac 11: 2 they that were of the **c** contended with him, *4061*
Ro 2:25 For **c** verily profiteth, if thou keep the law: *4061*
2:25 of the law, thy **c** is made uncircumcision. *4061*
2:26 not his uncircumcision be counted for **c**? *4061*
2:27 by the letter and **c** dost transgress the law? *4061*
2:28 neither *is that* **c**, which is outward in *4061*
2:29 and **c** *is that* of the heart, in the spirit, *and* *4061*
3: 1 hath the Jew? or what profit *is there* of **c**? *4061*
3:30 which shall justify the **c** by faith, and *4061*
4: 9 this blessedness then upon the **c** *only,* or *4061*
4:10 when he was in **c**, or in uncircumcision? *4061*
4:10 Not in **c**, but in uncircumcision. *4061*
4:11 And he received the sign of **c**, a seal of *4061*
4:12 And the father of **c** to them who are not of *4061*
4:12 to them who are not of the **c** only, *4061*
15: 8 was a minister of the **c** for the truth of God, *4061*
1Co 7:19 **C** is nothing, and uncircumcision is *4061*
Gal 2: 7 as *the gospel* of the **c** *was* unto Peter; *4061*
2: 8 in Peter to the apostleship of the **c**, *4061*
2: 9 *go* unto the heathen, and they unto the **c**. *4061*
2:12 fearing them which were of the **c**. *4061*
5: 6 For in Jesus Christ neither **c** availeth any *4061*
5:11 And I, brethren, if I yet preach **c**, why do I *4061*
6:15 For in Christ Jesus neither **c** availeth any *4061*
Eph 2:11 is called the **C** in the flesh made by hands; *4061*
Php 3: 3 For we are the **c**, which worship God in *4061*
Col 2:11 In whom also ye are circumcised with the **c** *4061*
2:11 of the sins of the flesh, by the **c** of Christ: *4061*
3:11 **c** nor uncircumcision, barbarian, Scythian, *4061*
4:11 which is called Justus, who are of the **c**. *4061*
Tit 1:10 and deceivers, specially they of the **c**: *4061*

CIRCUMSPECT (1) [CIRCUMSPECTLY]
Ex 23:13 in all *things* that I have said unto you be **c**: 8104

CIRCUMSPECTLY (1) [CIRCUMSPECT]
Eph 5:15 See then that ye walk **c**, not as fools, but *199*

CIRCUMSTANCES See DEGREE; DEGREES

CIS (1)
Ac 13:21 and God gave unto them Saul the son of **C**, *2797*

CISTERN (4) [CISTERNS]
2Ki 18:31 and drink ye every one the waters of his **c**: 953
Pr 5:15 Drink waters out of thine own **c**, and 953
Ecc 12: 6 at the fountain, or the wheel broken at the **c**. 953
Isa 36:16 drink ye every one the waters of his own **c**; 953

CISTERNS (2) [CISTERN]
Jer 2:13 hewed them out **c**, broken cisterns, that can 953
2:13 broken **c**, that can hold no water. 953

CITIES (448) [CITY]
Ge 13:12 Lot dwelled in the **c** of the plain, and 5892
19:25 he overthrew those **c**, and all the plain, and 5892
19:25 all the inhabitants of the **c**, and that which 5892
19:29 when God destroyed the **c** of the plain, 5892
19:29 when he overthrew the **c** in the which Lot 5892
35: 5 the terror of God was upon the **c** that *were* 5892
41:35 of Pharaoh, and let them keep food in the **c**. 5892
41:48 land of Egypt, and laid up the food in the **c**: 5892
47:21 he removed them to **c** from *one* end of 5892
Ex 1:11 they built for Pharaoh treasure **c**, Pithom 5892
Lev 25:32 Notwithstanding the **c** of the Levites, *and* 5892
25:32 *and* the houses of the **c** of their possession, 5892
25:33 for the houses of the **c** of the Levites *are* 5892
25:34 the field of the suburbs of their **c** may not 5892
26:25 ye are gathered together within your **c**, 5892
26:31 I will make your **c** waste, and bring your 5892
26:33 land shall be desolate, and your **c** waste. 5892
Nu 13:19 what **c** *they be* that they dwell in, whether 5892
13:28 and the **c** *are* walled, *and* very great: 5892
21: 2 my hand, then I will utterly destroy their **c**. 5892
21: 3 and they utterly destroyed them and their **c**: 5892
21:25 Israel took all these **c**: and Israel dwelt in 5892
21:25 Israel dwelt in all the **c** of the Amorites, 5892
31:10 they burnt all their **c** wherein they dwelt, 5892
32:16 here for our cattle, and **c** for our little ones: 5892
32:17 our little ones shall dwell in the fenced **c** 5892
32:24 Build ye **c** for your little ones, and folds for 5892
32:26 our cattle, shall be there in the **c** of Gilead: 5892
32:33 the land, with the **c** thereof in the coasts, 5892
32:33 *even* the **c** of the country round about. 5892
32:36 and Beth-haran, fenced **c**: 5892
32:38 gave other names unto the **c** which they 5892
35: 2 of their possession **c** to dwell in; 5892
35: 2 Levites suburbs for the **c** round about them. 5892
35: 3 the **c** shall they have to dwell in; and 5892
35: 4 the suburbs of the **c**, which ye shall give 5892
35: 5 this shall be to them the suburbs of the **c**. 5892
35: 6 *among* the **c** which ye shall give unto 5892
35: 6 the Levites *there shall be* six **c** for refuge, 5892
35: 6 to them ye shall add forty and two **c**. 5892
35: 7 *So* all the **c** which ye shall give to 5892
35: 7 to the Levites *shall be* forty and eight **c**: 5892
35: 8 the **c** which ye shall give *shall be* of 5892
35: 8 every one shall give of his **c** unto 5892
35:11 ye shall appoint you **c** to be cities of refuge 5892
35:11 ye shall appoint you cities to be **c** of refuge 5892
35:12 they shall be unto you **c** for refuge from 5892
35:13 *of these* **c** which ye shall give six cities 5892
35:13 *of these* cities which ye shall give six **c** 5892
35:14 Ye shall give three **c** on *this* side Jordan, 5892
35:14 three **c** shall ye give in the land of Canaan, 5892
35:14 land of Canaan, *which* shall be **c** of refuge. 5892
35:15 These six **c** shall be a refuge, *both* for 5892
Dt 1:22 must go up, and into what **c** we shall come. 5892
1:28 the **c** *are* great and walled up to heaven; and 5892
2:34 we took all his **c** at that time, and 5892
2:35 and the spoil of the **c** which we took. 5892
2:37 nor *unto* the **c** in the mountains, 5892
3: 4 we took all his **c** at that time, there was not 5892
3: 4 threescore **c**, all the region of Argob, 5892
3: 5 All these **c** *were* fenced *with* high walls, 5892
3: 7 all the cattle, and the spoil of the **c**, we took 5892
3:10 All the **c** of the plain, and all Gilead, and 5892
3:10 Edrei, **c** of the kingdom of Og in Bashan. 5892
3:12 half mount Gilead, and the **c** thereof, gave I 5892
3:19 shall abide in your **c** which I have given 5892
4:41 Moses severed three **c** on *this* side Jordan 5892
4:42 that fleeing unto one of these **c** he might 5892
6:10 to Jacob, to give thee great and goodly **c**, 5892
9: 1 **c** great and fenced up to heaven, 5892
13:12 If thou shalt hear *say* in one of thy **c**, 5892
19: 1 and dwellest in their **c**, and in their houses; 5892
19: 2 Thou shalt separate three **c** for thee in 5892
19: 5 he shall flee unto one of those **c**, and live: 5892
19: 7 Thou shalt separate three **c** for thee. 5892
19: 9 shalt thou add three **c** moe for thee, 5892
19:11 that he die, and fleeth into one of these **c**: 5892
20:15 Thus shalt thou do unto all the **c** *which are* 5892
20:15 which *are* not of the **c** of these nations. 5892
20:16 of the **c** of these people, which the LORD 5892
21: 2 they shall measure unto the **c** which *are* 5892
Jos 9:17 and came unto their **c** on the third day. 5892
9:17 Now their **c** *were* Gibeon, and Chephirah, 5892
10: 2 as one of the royal **c**, and because it *was* 5892
10:19 suffer them not to enter into their **c**: 5892
10:20 remained of them entered into fenced **c**. 5892
10:37 all the **c** thereof, and all the souls that *were* 5892
10:39 and the king thereof, and all the **c** thereof; 5892
11:12 all the **c** of those kings, and all the kings of 5892
11:13 *as for* the **c** that stood still in their strength, 5892
11:14 all the spoil of these **c**, and the cattle, 5892
11:21 Joshua destroyed them utterly with their **c**. 5892
13:10 all the **c** of Sihon king of the Amorites, 5892
13:17 Heshbon, and all her **c** that *are* in the plain; 5892
13:21 all the **c** of the plain, and all the kingdom of 5892
13:23 their families, the **c** and villages thereof. 5892
13:25 all the **c** of Gilead, and half the land of 5892
13:28 after their families, the **c**, and their villages. 5892
13:30 of Jair, which *are* in Bashan, threescore **c**: 5892
13:31 Edrei, **c** of the kingdom of Og in Bashan, 5892
14: 4 save **c** to dwell *in,* with their suburbs for 5892
14:12 and *that* the **c** *were* great *and* fenced: 5892
15: 9 and went out to the **c** of mount Ephron; 5892
15:21 the uttermost **c** of the tribe of the children 5892
15:32 all the **c** *are* twenty and nine, with their 5892
15:36 Gederothaim; fourteen **c** with their villages. 5892
15:41 Makkedah; sixteen **c** with their villages. 5892
15:44 and Mareshah; nine **c** with their villages. 5892
15:51 and Giloh; eleven **c** with their villages. 5892
15:54 and Zior; nine **c** with their villages. 5892
15:57 and Timnah; ten **c** with their villages. 5892
15:59 and Eltekon; six **c** with their villages. 5892
15:60 and Rabbah; two **c** with their villages. 5892
15:62 and En-gedi; six **c** with their villages. 5892
16: 9 the separate **c** for the children of Ephraim 5892

Jos 16: 9 of Manasseh, all the **c** with their villages. 5892
17: 9 these **c** of Ephraim *are* among the cities of 5892
17: 9 these cities of Ephraim *are* among the **c** of 5892
17:12 not drive out *the inhabitants of* those **c**; 5892
18: 9 described it by **c** into seven parts in a book, 5892
18:21 Now the **c** of the tribe of the children of 5892
18:24 and Gaba; twelve **c** with their villages. 5892
18:28 *and* Kirjath; fourteen **c** with their villages. 5892
19: 6 and Sharuhen; thirteen **c** and their villages: 5892
19: 7 Ether, and Ashan; four **c** and their villages: 5892
19: 8 *were* round about these **c** to Baalath-beer, 5892
19:15 Beth-lehem: twelve **c** with their villages. 5892
19:16 to their families, these **c** with their villages. 5892
19:22 *at* Jordan: sixteen **c** with their villages. 5892
19:23 to their families, the **c** and their villages. 5892
19:30 twenty and two **c** with their villages. 5892
19:31 to their families, these **c** with their villages. 5892
19:35 the fenced **c** *are* Ziddim, Zer, and 5892
19:38 nineteen **c** with their villages. 5892
19:39 to their families, the **c** and their villages. 5892
19:48 to their families, these **c** with their villages. 5892
20: 2 Appoint out for you **c** of refuge, 5892
20: 4 when he that doth flee unto one of those **c** 5892
20: 9 These were the **c** appointed for all 5892
21: 2 the hand of Moses to give us **c** to dwell in, 5892
21: 3 of the LORD, these **c** and their suburbs. 5892
21: 4 and out of the tribe of Benjamin, thirteen **c**. 5892
21: 5 and out of the half tribe of Manasseh, ten **c**. 5892
21: 6 tribe of Manasseh in Bashan, thirteen **c**. 5892
21: 7 and out of the tribe of Zebulun, twelve **c**. 5892
21: 8 unto the Levites these **c** with their suburbs, 5892
21: 9 these **c** which are *here* mentioned by name, 5892
21:16 her suburbs; nine **c** out of those two tribes. 5892
21:18 and Almon with her suburbs; four **c**. 5892
21:19 All the **c** of the children of Aaron, 5892
21:19 *were* thirteen **c** with their suburbs. 5892
21:20 even they had the **c** of their lot out of 5892
21:22 and Beth-horon with her suburbs; four **c**. 5892
21:24 Gath-rimmon with her suburbs; four **c**. 5892
21:25 and Gath-rimmon with her suburbs; two **c**. 5892
21:26 All the **c** *were* ten with their suburbs for 5892
21:27 and Beeshterah with her suburbs; two **c**. 5892
21:29 En-gannim with her suburbs; four **c**. 5892
21:31 and Rehob with her suburbs; four **c**. 5892
21:32 and Kartan with her suburbs; three **c**. 5892
21:33 All the **c** of the Gershonites according to 5892
21:33 families *were* thirteen **c** with their suburbs. 5892
21:35 Nahalal with her suburbs; four **c**. 5892
21:37 and Mephaath with her suburbs; four **c**. 5892
21:39 Jazer with her suburbs; four **c** in all. 5892
21:40 So all the **c** for the children of Merari by 5892
21:40 of the Levites, were *by* their lot twelve **c**. 5892
21:41 All the **c** of the Levites within 5892
21:41 *were* forty and eight **c** with their suburbs. 5892
21:42 These **c** were **every one** with their 5892+5892
21:42 round about them: thus *were* all these **c**. 5892
24:13 **c** which ye built not, and ye dwell in them; 5892
Jdg 10: 4 they had thirty **c**, which are called 5892
11:26 in all the **c** that *be* along by the coasts of 5892
11:33 *even* twenty **c**, and unto the plain of 5892
12: 7 and was buried in *one of* the **c** of Gilead. 5892
20:14 together out of the **c** unto Gibeah, 5892
20:15 numbered at that time out of the **c** twenty 5892
20:42 them which *came* out of the **c** they 5892
20:48 also they set on fire all the **c** that they came 5892
21:23 and repaired the **c**, and dwelt in them. 5892
1Sa 6:18 *according to* the number of all the **c** of 5892
6:18 *both* of fenced **c**, and of country villages, 5892
7:14 the **c** which the Philistines had taken from 5892
18: 6 that the women came out of all **c** of Israel, 5892
30:29 to *them* which *were* in the **c** of 5892
30:29 to *them* which *were* in the **c** of the Kenites, 5892
31: 7 were dead, they forsook the **c**, and fled; 5892
2Sa 2: 1 Shall I go up into any of the **c** of Judah? 5892
2: 3 and they dwelt in the **c** of Hebron. 5892
8: 8 and from Berothai, **c** of Hadadezer, 5892
10:12 for our people, and for the **c** of our God: 5892
12:31 thus did he unto all the **c** of the children of 5892
20: 6 lest he get him fenced **c**, and escape us. 5892
24: 7 *to* all the **c** of the Hivites, and of 5892
1Ki 4:13 threescore great **c** *with* walls and 5892
8:37 enemy besiege them in the land of their **c**; 8179
9:11 king Solomon gave Hiram twenty **c** in 5892
9:12 Hiram came out from Tyre to see the **c** 5892
9:13 What **c** *are* these which thou hast given me, 5892
9:19 all the **c** of store that Solomon had, 5892
9:19 **c** for his chariots, and cities for his 5892
9:19 **c** for his horsemen, and that which 5892
10:26 whom he bestowed in the **c** for chariots, 5892
12:17 of Israel which dwelt in the **c** of Judah, 5892
13:32 high places which *are* in the **c** of Samaria, 5892
15:20 hosts which he had against the **c** of Israel, 5892
15:23 and all that he did, and the **c** which he built, 5892
20:34 *Ben-hadad* said unto him, The **c**, which my 5892
22:39 which he made, and all the **c** that he built, 5892
2Ki 3:25 they beat down the **c**, and *on* every good 5892
13:25 hand of Ben-hadad the son of Hazael the **c**, 5892
13:25 beat him, and recovered the **c** of Israel. 5892
17: 6 river of Gozan, and in the **c** of the Medes. 5892
17: 9 they built them high places in all their **c**, 5892
17:24 placed *them* in the **c** of Samaria instead of 5892
17:24 and dwelt in the **c** thereof. 5892
17:26 and placed in the **c** of Samaria, 5892
17:29 every nation in their **c** wherein they dwelt. 5892
18:11 river of Gozan, and in the **c** of the Medes: 5892
18:13 come up against all the fenced **c** of Judah, 5892
19:25 that thou shouldest be to lay waste fenced **c** 5892
23: 5 incense in the high places in the **c** of Judah, 5892
23: 8 he brought all the priests out of the **c** of 5892
23:19 high places that *were* in the **c** of Samaria, 5892
1Ch 2:22 and twenty **c** in the land of Gilead. 5892
2:23 and the towns thereof, *even* threescore **c**. 5892
4:31 These *were* their **c** unto the reign of David. 5892
4:32 Rimmon, and Tochen, and Ashan, five **c**: 5892
4:33 villages that *were* round about the same **c**, 5892
6:57 to the sons of Aaron they gave the **c** of 5892
6:60 All their **c** throughout their families *were* 5892
6:60 throughout their families *were* thirteen **c**. 5892
6:61 *were* **c** *given* out of the half tribe, NIH
6:61 *of* the half *tribe* of Manasseh, by lot, ten **c**. 5892
6:62 the tribe of Manasseh in Bashan, thirteen **c**. 5892
6:63 and out of the tribe of Zebulun, twelve **c**. 5892
6:64 to the Levites *these* **c** with their suburbs. 5892
6:65 these **c**, which are called by *their* names. 5892
6:66 **c** of their coasts out of the tribe of Ephraim. 5892
6:67 they gave unto them, *of* the **c** of refuge, 5892
9: 2 possessions in their **c** *were,* the Israelites, 5892
10: 7 then they forsook their **c**, and fled: 5892
13: 2 Levites *which are* in their **c** *and* suburbs, 5892
18: 8 and from Chun, **c** of Hadarezer, 5892
19: 7 gathered themselves together from their **c**, 5892
19:13 for our people, and for the **c** of our God: 5892
20: 3 dealt David with all the **c** of the children of 5892
27:25 in the **c**, and in the villages, and in 5892
2Ch 1:14 which he placed in the chariot **c**, and 5892
6:28 if their enemies besiege them in the **c** of 8179
8: 2 That the **c** which Huram had restored to 5892
8: 4 all the store **c**, which he built in Hamath. 5892
8: 5 fenced **c**, *with* walls, gates, and bars; 5892
8: 6 all the store **c** that Solomon had, and all 5892
8: 6 all the chariot **c**, and the cities of 5892
8: 6 the **c** of the horsemen, and all that Solomon 5892
9:25 whom he bestowed in the chariot **c**, and 5892
10:17 of Israel that dwelt in the **c** of Judah, 5892
11: 5 and built **c** for defence in Judah. 5892
11:10 *are* in Judah and in Benjamin, fenced **c**. 5892
12: 4 he took the fenced **c** which *pertained* to 5892
13:19 took **c** from him, Beth-el with the towns 5892
14: 5 Also he took away out of all the **c** of Judah 5892
14: 6 he built fenced **c** in Judah: for the land had 5892
14: 7 Let us build these **c**, and make about *them* 5892
14:14 they smote all the **c** round about Gerar; 5892
14:14 they spoiled all the **c**; for there was 5892
15: 8 out of the **c** which he had taken from mount 5892
16: 4 sent the captains of his armies against the **c** 5892
16: 4 and all the store **c** of Naphtali. 5892
17: 2 he placed forces in all the fenced **c** of 5892
17: 2 in the **c** of Ephraim, which Asa his father 5892
17: 7 and to Michaiah, to teach in the **c** of Judah. 5892
17: 9 went about throughout all the **c** of Judah, 5892
17:12 he built in Judah castles, and **c** of store. 5892
17:13 he had much business in the **c** of Judah: 5892
17:19 put in the fenced **c** throughout all Judah. 5892
19: 5 land throughout all the fenced **c** of Judah, 5892
19:10 to you of your brethren that dwell in their **c**, 5892
20: 4 even out of all the **c** of Judah they came to 5892
21: 3 of precious things, with fenced **c** in Judah: 5892
23: 2 gathered the Levites out of all the **c** of 5892

2Ch 24: 5 Go out unto the **c** of Judah, and gather of 5892
25:13 fell upon the **c** of Judah, from Samaria even 5892
26: 6 built **c** about Ashdod, and among 5892
27: 4 Moreover he built **c** in the mountains of 5892
28:18 The Philistines also had invaded the **c** of 5892
31: 1 all Israel that were present went out to the **c** 5892
31: 1 man to his possession, into their own **c**. 5892
31: 6 and Judah, that dwelt in the **c** of Judah, 5892
31:15 and Shecaniah, in the **c** of the priests, 5892
31:19 *were* in the fields of the suburbs of their **c**, 5892
32: 1 encamped against the fenced **c**, and 5892
32:29 Moreover he provided him **c**, and 5892
33:14 put captains of war in all the fenced **c** of 5892
34: 6 *so did he* in the **c** of Manasseh, and 5892
Ezr 2:70 dwelt in their **c**, and all Israel in their cities. 5892
2:70 dwelt in their cities, and all Israel in their **c**. 5892
3: 1 and the children of Israel *were* in the **c**, 5892
4:10 set in the **c** of Samaria, and the rest *that are* 7149
10:14 wives in our **c** come at appointed times, 5892
Ne 7:73 and all Israel, dwelt in their **c**; 5892
7:73 the children of Israel *were* in their **c**. 5892
8:15 should publish and proclaim in all their **c**, 5892
9:25 they took strong **c**, and a fat land, and 5892
10:37 have the tithes in all the **c** of our tillage. 5892
11: 1 holy city, and nine parts *to dwell* in *other* **c**. 5892
11: 3 in the **c** of Judah dwelt every one in his 5892
11: 3 dwelt every one in his possession in their **c**, 5892
11:20 *and* the Levites, *were* in all the **c** of Judah, 5892
12:44 to gather into them out of the fields of the **c** 5892
Est 9: 2 **c** throughout all the provinces of the king 5892
Job 15:28 he dwelleth in desolate **c**, *and* in houses 5892
Ps 9: 6 thou hast destroyed **c**; their memorial is 5892
69:35 save Zion, and will build the **c** of Judah: 5892
Isa 1: 7 *is* desolate, your **c** *are* burnt *with* fire: 5892
6:11 Until the **c** be wasted without inhabitant, 5892
14:17 a wilderness, and destroyed the **c** thereof; 5892
14:21 nor fill the face of the world *with* **c**. 5892
17: 2 The **c** of Aroer *are* forsaken: they shall be 5892
17: 9 In that day shall his strong **c** be as a 5892
19:18 In that day shall five **c** in the land of Egypt 5892
33: 8 he hath despised the **c**, he regardeth no 5892
36: 1 up against all the defenced **c** of Judah, 5892
37:26 to lay waste defenced **c** *into* ruinous heaps. 5892
40: 9 say unto the **c** of Judah, Behold your God. 5892
42:11 the **c** thereof lift up *their voice,* the villages 5892
44:26 to the **c** of Judah, Ye shall be built, and 5892
54: 3 and make the desolate **c** to be inhabited. 5892
61: 4 they shall repair the waste **c**, 5892
64:10 Thy holy **c** are a wilderness, Zion is a 5892
Jer 1:15 round about, and against all the **c** of Judah. 5892
2:15 his **c** are burnt without inhabitant. 5892
2:28 for *according* to the number of thy **c** are thy 5892
4: 5 and let us go into the defenced **c**. 5892
4: 7 *and* thy **c** shall be laid waste, without an 5892
4:16 give out their voice against the **c** of Judah. 5892
4:26 all the **c** thereof were broken down at 5892
5: 6 a leopard shall watch over their **c**: 5892
5:17 they shall impoverish thy fenced **c**, 5892
7:17 Seest thou not what they do in the **c** of 5892
7:34 will I cause to cease from the **c** of Judah, 5892
8:14 let us enter into the defenced **c**, and let us 5892
9:11 I will make the **c** of Judah desolate, 5892
10:22 to make the **c** of Judah desolate, *and* a den 5892
11: 6 Proclaim all these words in the **c** of Judah, 5892
11:12 shall the **c** of Judah and inhabitants of 5892
11:13 For *according to* the number of thy **c** were 5892
13:19 The **c** of the south shall be shut up, and 5892
17:26 they shall come from the **c** of Judah, and 5892
20:16 let that man be as the **c** which the LORD 5892
22: 6 a wilderness *and* **c** *which* are not inhabited. 5892
25:18 the **c** of Judah, and the kings thereof, *and* 5892
26: 2 and speak unto all the **c** of Judah, 5892
31:21 O virgin of Israel, turn again to these thy **c**, 5892
31:23 in the land of Judah and in the **c** thereof, 5892
31:24 *in* all the **c** thereof together, husbandmen, 5892
32:44 in the **c** of Judah, and in the cities of 5892
32:44 in the **c** of the mountains, and in the cities 5892
32:44 in the **c** of the valley, and in the cities of 5892
32:44 of the valley, and in the **c** of the south: 5892
33:10 *even* in the **c** of Judah, and in the streets of 5892
33:12 and without beast, and in all the **c** thereof, 5892
33:13 In the **c** of the mountains, in the cities of 5892
33:13 in the **c** of the vale, and in the cities of 5892
33:13 in the **c** of the south, and in the land of 5892
33:13 about Jerusalem, and in the **c** of Judah, 5892
34: 1 and against all the **c** thereof, saying, 5892
34: 7 against all the **c** of Judah that were left, 5892
34: 7 for these defenced **c** remained of the cities 5892
34: 7 for these defenced cities remained of the **c** 5892
34:22 I will make the **c** of Judah a desolation 5892
36: 6 ears of all Judah that come out of their **c**. 5892
36: 9 *to* all the people that came from the **c** of 5892
40: 5 hath made governor over the **c** of Judah, 5892
40:10 and dwell in your **c** that ye have taken. 5892
44: 2 and upon all the **c** of Judah; 5892
44: 6 was kindled in the **c** of Judah and in 5892
44:17 in the **c** of Judah, and in the streets of 5892
44:21 The incense that ye burnt in the **c** of Judah, 5892
48: 9 for the **c** thereof shall be desolate, without 5892
48:15 gone up *out of* her **c**, and his chosen young 5892
48:24 upon all the **c** of the land of Moab, far or 5892
48:28 leave the **c**, and dwell in the rock, and 5892
49: 1 inherit Gad, and his people dwell in his **c**? 5892
49:13 all the **c** thereof shall be perpetual wastes. 5892
49:18 and Gomorrah and the neighbour *c* thereof, NIH
50:32 I will kindle a fire in his **c**, and it shall 5892
50:40 and Gomorrah and the neighbour *c* thereof, NIH
51:43 Her **c** are a desolation, a dry land, and 5892
La 5:11 in Zion, *and* the maids in the **c** of Judah. 5892
Eze 6: 6 In all your dwelling places the **c** shall be 5892
12:20 the **c** that are inhabited shall be laid waste, 5892
19: 7 desolate palaces, and he laid waste their **c**; 5892
25: 9 I *will* open the side of Moab from the **c**, 5892
25: 9 from his **c** *which are* on his frontiers, 5892
26:19 like the **c** that are not inhabited; 5892
29:12 her **c** among the cities *that are* laid waste 5892
29:12 her cities among the **c** *that are* laid waste 5892
30: 7 her **c** shall be in the midst of the cities *that* 5892
30: 7 her cities shall be in the midst of the **c** *that* 5892
30:17 and these *c* shall go into captivity. NIH
35: 4 I will lay thy **c** waste, and thou shalt be 5892
35: 9 and thy **c** shall not return: 5892
36: 4 to the **c** that are forsaken, which became a 5892
36:10 the **c** shall be inhabited, and the wastes 5892
36:33 I will also cause *you* to dwell in the **c**, and 5892
36:35 and ruined **c** *are become* fenced, 5892
36:38 shall the waste **c** be filled *with* flocks of 5892
39: 9 they that dwell in the **c** of Israel shall go 5892
Da 11:15 up a mount, and take the most fenced **c**: 5892
Hos 8:14 and Judah hath multiplied fenced **c**: 5892
8:14 I will send a fire upon his **c**, and it shall 5892
11: 6 the sword shall abide on his **c**, and 5892
13:10 *is any other* that may save thee in all thy **c**? 5892
Am 4: 6 given you cleanness of teeth in all your **c**, 5892
4: 8 So two *or* three **c** wandered unto one city, 5892
9:14 they shall build the waste **c**, and 5892
Ob 1:20 shall possess the **c** of the south. 5892
Mic 5:11 I will cut off the **c** of thy land, and 5892
5:14 of the midst of thee: so will I destroy thy **c**. 5892
7:12 *from* the fortified **c**, and from the fortress 5892
Zep 1:16 the trumpet and alarm against the fenced **c**, 5892
3: 6 their **c** are destroyed, so that there is no 5892
Zec 1:12 mercy on Jerusalem and on the **c** of Judah, 5892
1:17 My **c** through prosperity shall yet be spread 5892
7: 7 and the **c** thereof round about her, 5892
8:20 and the inhabitants of many **c**: 5892
Mt 9:35 And Jesus went about all the **c** and villages, *4172*
10:23 Ye shall not have gone over the **c** of Israel, *4172*
11: 1 thence to teach and to preach in their **c**. *4172*
11:20 Then began he to upbraid the **c** wherein *4172*
14:13 they followed him on foot out of the **c**. *4172*
Mk 6:33 and ran afoot thither out of all **c**, and *4172*
6:56 he entered, into villages, or **c**, or country, *4172*
Lk 4:43 preach the kingdom of God to other **c** also: *4172*
13:22 And he went through the **c** and villages, *4172*
19:17 a very little, have thou authority over ten **c**. *4172*
19:19 likewise to him, Be thou also over five **c**. *4172*
Ac 5:16 There came also a multitude *out of* the **c** *4172*
8:40 passing through he preached in all the **c**, *4172*
14: 6 **c** of Lycaonia, and *unto* the region that lieth *4172*
16: 4 And as they went through the **c**, *4172*
26:11 I persecuted *them* even unto strange **c**. *4172*
2Pe 2: 6 And turning the **c** of Sodom and *4172*
Jude 1: 7 and Gomorrha, and the **c** about them, *4172*
Rev 16:19 three parts, and the **c** of the nations fell: *4172*

CITIZEN (2) [CITIZENS, FELLOWCITIZENS]

Lk 15:15 and joined himself to a **c** of that country; *4177*

Ac 21:39 *a city* in Cilicia, a **c** of no mean city: 4177

CITIZENS (1) [CITIZEN]

Lk 19:14 But his **c** hated him, and sent a message 4177

CITIZENSHIP See COMMONWEALTH

CITRON See THYINE

CITY (870) [CITIES]

Ge 4:17 he builded a **c**, and called the name of 5892
4:17 builded a city, and called the name of the **c**, 5892
10:11 and the **c** Rehoboth, and Calah, 5892
10:12 and Calah: the same *is* a great **c**. 5892
11: 4 Go to, let us build us a **c** and a tower, 5892
11: 5 the LORD came down to see the **c** and 5892
11: 8 all the earth: and they left off to build the **c**. 5892
18:24 there be fifty righteous within the **c**: 5892
18:26 I find in Sodom fifty righteous within the **c**, 5892
18:28 wilt thou destroy all the **c** for *lack of* five? 5892
19: 4 the men of the **c**, *even* the men of Sodom, 5892
19:12 and whatsoever thou hast in the **c**, 5892
19:14 for the LORD will destroy this **c**. 5892
19:15 thou be consumed in the iniquity of the **c**. 5892
19:16 him forth, and set him without the **c**. 5892
19:20 this **c** *is* near to flee unto, and it *is* a little 5892
19:21 that I will not overthrow *this* **c**, for 5892
19:22 Therefore the name of the **c** was called 5892
23:10 *even* of all that went in *at* the gate of his **c**, 5892
23:18 before all that went in *at* the gate of his **c**. 5892
24:10 went to Mesopotamia, unto the **c** of Nahor. 5892
24:11 **c** by a well of water at the time of 5892
24:13 the daughters of the men of the **c** come out 5892
26:33 the name of the **c** *is* Beer-sheba unto this 5892
28:19 the name of *that* **c** *was called* Luz at 5892
33:18 Jacob came to Shalem, a **c** of Shechem, 5892
33:18 and pitched his tent before the **c**. 5892
34:20 his son came unto the gate of their **c**, 5892
34:20 communed with the men of their **c**, saying, 5892
34:24 all that went out of the gate of his **c**; 5892
34:24 all that went out of the gate of his **c**. 5892
34:25 came upon the **c** boldly, and slew all 5892
34:27 spoiled the **c**, because they had defiled their 5892
34:28 that which *was* in the **c**, and that which *was* 5892
35:27 unto the **c** of Arbah, which *is* Hebron, 7151
36:32 and the name of his **c** *was* Dinhabah. 5892
36:35 his stead: and the name of his **c** *was* Avith. 5892
36:39 the name of his **c** *was* Pau; and his wife's 5892
41:48 the field, which *was* round about every **c**, 5892
44: 4 *And* when they were gone out of the **c**, *and* 5892
44:13 every man his ass, and returned to the **c**. 5892
Ex 9:29 As soon as I am gone out of the **c**, 5892
9:33 And Moses went out of the **c** from Pharaoh, 5892
Lev 14:40 them into an unclean place without the **c**: 5892
14:41 off without the **c** into an unclean place: 5892
14:45 he shall carry *them* forth out of the **c** into 5892
14:53 he shall let go the living bird out of the **c** 5892
25:29 if a man sell a dwelling house in a walled **c**, 5892
25:30 the house that *is* in the walled **c** shall be 5892
25:33 that was sold, and the **c** of his possession, 5892
Nu 20:16 a **c** in the uttermost of thy border: 5892
21:26 For Heshbon *was* the **c** of Sihon the king of 5892
21:27 let the **c** of Sihon be built and prepared: 5892
21:28 of Heshbon, a flame from the **c** of Sihon: 7151
22:36 he went out to meet him unto a **c** of Moab, 5892
24:19 shall destroy him that remaineth of the **c**. 5892
35: 4 *shall reach* from the wall of the **c** and 5892
35: 5 ye shall measure from without the **c** *on* 5892
35: 5 and the **c** *shall be* in the midst: 5892
35:25 the congregation shall restore him to the **c** 5892
35:26 *without* the border of the **c** of his refuge, 5892
35:27 without the borders of the **c** of his refuge, 5892
35:28 Because he should have remained in the **c** 5892
35:32 for him that is fled to the **c** of his refuge, 5892
Dt 2:34 the women, and the little ones, of every **c**, 5892
2:36 *from* the **c** that *is* by the river, even unto 5892
2:36 there was not one **c** too strong for us: 7151
3: 4 there was not a **c** which we took not from 7151
3: 6 the men, women, and children, of every **c**. 5892
13:13 have withdrawn the inhabitants of their **c**, 5892
13:15 of that **c** with the edge of the sword, 5892
13:16 shalt burn with fire the **c**, and all the spoil 5892
19:12 the elders of his **c** shall send and fetch him 5892
20:10 When thou comest nigh unto a **c** to fight 5892
20:14 and the cattle, and all that is in the **c**, 5892
20:19 When thou shalt besiege a **c** a long time, 5892
20:20 thou shalt build bulwarks against the **c** that 5892
21: 3 *that* the **c** *which is* next unto the slain *man*, 5892
21: 3 even the elders of that **c** shall take a heifer, 5892
21: 4 the elders of that **c** shall bring down 5892
21: 6 all the elders of that **c**, *that are* next unto 5892
21:19 bring him out unto the elders of his **c**, and 5892
21:20 they shall say unto the elders of his **c**, 5892
21:21 all the men of his **c** shall stone him with 5892
22:15 virginity unto the elders of the **c** in the gate: 5892
22:17 spread the cloth before the elders of the **c**. 5892
22:18 the elders of that **c** shall take *that* man and 5892
22:21 the men of her **c** shall stone her with stones 5892
22:23 a man find her in the **c**, and lie with her; 5892
22:24 bring them both out unto the gate of that **c**, 5892
22:24 because she cried not, *being* in the **c**; 5892
25: 8 the elders of his **c** shall call him, and 5892
28: 3 Blessed *shalt* thou *be* in the **c**, and 5892
28:16 Cursed *shalt* thou *be* in the **c**, and 5892
34: 3 of Jericho, the **c** of palm trees, unto Zoar. 5892
Jos 3:16 from the **c** Adam, that *is* beside Zaretan: 5892
6: 3 ye shall compass the **c**, all *ye* men of war, 5892
6: 3 men of war, *and* go round about the **c** once. 5892
6: 4 the seventh day ye shall compass the **c** 5892
6: 5 the wall of the **c** shall fall down flat, 5892
6: 7 compass the **c**, and let him that is armed 5892
6:11 So the ark of the LORD compassed the **c**, 5892
6:14 the second day they compassed the **c** once, 5892
6:15 compassed the **c** after the same manner 5892
6:15 only on that day they compassed the **c** 5892
6:16 Shout; for the LORD hath given you the **c**. 5892
6:17 the **c** shall be accursed, *even* it, and all that 5892
6:20 so that the people went up into the **c**, 5892
6:20 straight before him, and they took the **c**. 5892
6:21 they utterly destroyed all that *was* in the **c**, 5892
6:24 they burnt the **c** with fire, and all that *was* 5892
6:26 that riseth up and buildeth this **c** Jericho: 5892
8: 1 and his people, and his **c**, and his land: 5892
8: 2 lay thee an ambush for the **c** behind it. 5892
8: 4 Behold, ye shall lie in wait against the **c**, 5892
8: 4 in wait against the city, *even* behind the **c**: 5892
8: 4 go not very far from the **c**, but be ye all 5892
8: 5 that *are* with me, will approach unto the **c**: 5892
8: 6 till we have drawn them from the **c**; 5892
8: 7 up from the ambush, and seize upon the **c**: 5892
8: 8 it shall be, when ye have taken the **c**, 5892
8: 8 taken the city, *that* ye shall set the **c** on fire: 5892
8:11 came before the **c**, and pitched on the north 5892
8:12 and Ai, on the west side of the **c**. 5892
8:13 all the host that *was* on the north of the **c**, 5892
8:13 and their liers in wait on the west of the **c**, 5892
8:14 the men of the **c** went out against Israel to 5892
8:14 liers in ambush against him behind the **c**. 5892
8:16 and were drawn away from the **c**. 5892
8:17 they left the **c** open, and pursued after 5892
8:18 spear that *he had* in his hand toward the **c**. 5892
8:19 they entered *into* the **c**, and took it, and 5892
8:19 and took it, and hasted and set the **c** on fire. 5892
8:20 the smoke of the **c** ascended up to heaven, 5892
8:21 Israel saw that the ambush had taken the **c**, 5892
8:21 that the smoke of the **c** ascended, then 5892
8:22 the other issued out of the **c** against them; 5892
8:27 the spoil of that **c** Israel took for a prey 5892
8:29 cast it at the entering of the gate of the **c**, 5892
10: 2 because Gibeon *was* a great **c**, 5892
11:19 There was not a **c** that made peace with 5892
13: 9 the **c** that *is* in the midst of the river, and 5892
13:16 the **c** that *is* in the midst of the river, and 5892
15:13 *even* the **c** of Arba the father of Anak, 7151
15:13 Arba the father of Anak, which **c** *is* Hebron. NIH
15:62 and the **c** of salt, and En-gedi; 5892
18:14 a **c** of the children of Judah: 5892
19:29 turneth *to* Ramah, and to the strong **c** Tyre; 5892
19:50 they gave him the **c** which he asked, 5892
19:50 and he built the **c**, and dwelt therein. 5892
20: 4 stand *at* the entering of the gate of the **c**, 5892
20: 4 his cause in the ears of the elders of that **c**, 5892
20: 4 they shall take him into the **c** unto them, 5892
20: 6 he shall dwell in that **c**, until he stand 5892
20: 6 come unto his own **c**, and unto his own 5892
20: 6 own house, unto the **c** from whence he fled. 5892
21:11 they gave them the **c** of Arbah the father of 7151
21:11 which **c** *is* Hebron, in the hill *country* of NIH
21:12 the fields of the **c**, and the villages thereof, 5892

C

Jos 21:13 *to be* a **c** of refuge for the slayer; 5892
21:21 *to be* a **c** of refuge for the slayer; 5892
21:27 *to be* a **c** of refuge for the slayer; 5892
21:32 *to be* a **c** of refuge for the slayer; 5892
21:38 *to be* a **c** of refuge for the slayer; 5892
Jdg 1: 8 the edge of the sword, and set the **c** on fire. 5892
1:16 went up out of the **c** of palm trees with 5892
1:17 and the name of the **c** was called Hormah. 5892
1:23 (Now the name of the **c** before *was* Luz.) 5892
1:24 the spies saw a man come forth out of the **c**, 5892
1:24 the entrance into the **c**, and we will shew 5892
1:25 he shewed them the entrance into the **c**, 5892
1:25 they smote the **c** with the edge of 5892
1:26 built a **c**, and called the name thereof Luz: 5892
3:13 and possessed the **c** of palm trees. 5892
6:27 the men of the **c**, that *he* could not do *it* by 5892
6:28 when the men of the **c** arose early in 5892
6:30 the men of the **c** said unto Joash, Bring out 5892
8:16 he took the elders of the **c**, and thorns of 5892
8:17 tower of Penuel, and slew the men of the **c**. 5892
8:27 and put it in his **c**, *even* in Ophrah: 5892
9:30 when Zebul the ruler of the **c** heard 5892
9:31 and behold, they fortify the **c** against thee. 5892
9:33 thou shalt rise early, and set upon the **c**: 5892
9:35 stood *in* the entering of the gate of the **c**: 5892
9:43 the people *were* come forth out of the **c**; 5892
9:44 stood *in* the entering of the gate of the **c**: 5892
9:45 Abimelech fought against the **c** all that day; 5892
9:45 he took the **c**, and slew the people that *was* 5892
9:45 beat down the **c**, and sowed it *with* salt. 5892
9:51 there was a strong tower within the **c**, and 5892
9:51 all they of the **c**, and shut *it* to them, and 5892
14:18 the men of the **c** said unto him on 5892
16: 2 wait for him all night in the gate of the **c**, 5892
16: 3 took the doors of the gate of the **c**, and 5892
17: 8 the man departed out of the **c** from 5892
18:27 edge of the sword, and burnt the **c** with fire. 5892
18:28 And they built a **c**, and dwelt therein, 5892
18:29 they called the name of the **c** Dan, after 5892
18:29 howbeit the name of the **c** *was* Laish at 5892
19:11 and let us turn in into this **c** of the Jebusites, 5892
19:12 We will not turn aside hither into the **c** of a 5892
19:15 he sat him down in a street of the **c**: 5892
19:17 saw a wayfaring man in the street of the **c**: 5892
19:22 behold, the men of the **c**, certain sons of 5892
20:11 men of Israel were gathered against the **c**, 5892
20:31 *and* were drawn away from the **c**; 5892
20:32 draw them from the **c** unto the highways. 5892
20:37 smote all the **c** with the edge of the sword. 5892
20:38 great flame with smoke rise up out of the **c**. 5892
20:40 arise up out of the **c** *with* a pillar of smoke, 5892
20:40 the flame of the **c** ascended up to heaven. 5892
20:48 as well the men of *every* **c**, as the beast, and 5892
Ru 1:19 that all the **c** was moved about them, and 5892
2:18 she took *it* up, and went *into* the **c**: and 5892
3:11 for all the **c** of my people doth know that 8179
3:15 and laid *it* on her: and he went *into* the **c**. 5892
4: 2 he took ten men of the elders of the **c**, and 5892
1Sa 1: 3 this man went up out of his **c** yearly to 5892
4:13 when the man came into the **c**, and told *it*, 5892
4:13 into the city, and told *it*, all the **c** cried out. 5892
5: 9 the hand of the LORD was against the **c** 5892
5: 9 he smote the men of the **c**, both small and 5892
5:11 a deadly destruction throughout all the **c**; 5892
5:12 and the cry of the **c** went up *to* heaven. 5892
8:22 men of Israel, Go ye every man unto his **c**. 5892
9: 6 *there is* in this **c** a man of God, and *he is* an 5892
9:10 So they went unto the **c** where the man of 5892
9:11 *And* as they went up the hill to the **c**, they 5892
9:12 haste now, for he came to day to the **c**; 5892
9:13 As soon as ye be come *into* the **c**, ye shall 5892
9:14 they went up *into* the **c**: *and* when they 5892
9:14 *and* when they were come into the **c**, 5892
9:25 come down from the high place *into* the **c**, 5892
9:27 they were going down to the end of the **c**, 5892
10: 5 to pass, when thou art come thither *to* the **c**, 5892
15: 5 Saul came to a **c** of Amalek, and laid wait 5892
20: 6 me that *he* might run *to* Beth-lehem his **c**: 5892
20:29 for our family hath a sacrifice in the **c**; and 5892
20:40 and said unto him, Go, carry *them to* the **c**. 5892
20:42 and departed: and Jonathan went *into* the **c**. 5892
22:19 Nob, the **c** of the priests, smote he with 5892
23:10 to Keilah, to destroy the **c** for my sake. 5892
27: 5 thy servant dwell in the royal **c** with thee? 5892
28: 3 buried him in Ramah, even in his own **c**. 5892
30: 3 So David and his men came to the **c**, and 5892
2Sa 5: 7 hold of Zion: the same *is* the **c** of David. 5892
5: 9 in the fort, and called it the **c** of David. 5892
6:10 the LORD unto him into the **c** of David: 5892
6:12 *into* the **c** of David with gladness. 5892
6:16 as the ark of the LORD came *into* the **c** of 5892
10: 3 to search the **c**, and to spy it out, and 5892
10:14 *also* before Abishai, and entered *into* the **c**. 5892
11:16 it came to pass, when Joab observed the **c**, 5892
11:17 the men of the **c** went out, and fought with 5892
11:20 *so* nigh unto the **c** when *ye* did fight? 5892
11:25 make thy battle *more* strong against the **c**, 5892
12: 1 unto him, There were two men in one **c**; 5892
12:26 children of Ammon, and took the royal **c**. 5892
12:27 and have taken the **c** of waters. 5892
12:28 and encamp against the **c**, and take it: 5892
12:28 lest I take the **c**, and it be called after my 5892
12:30 he brought forth the spoil of the **c** in great 5892
15: 2 unto him, and said, Of what **c** *art* thou? 5892
15:12 from his **c**, *even* from Giloh, 5892
15:14 and smite the **c** with the edge of the sword. 5892
15:24 all the people had done passing out of the **c**. 5892
15:25 Carry back the ark of God *into* the **c**: 5892
15:27 return *into* the **c** in peace, and your two 5892
15:34 if thou return *to* the **c**, and say unto 5892
15:37 So Hushai David's friend came *into* the **c**, 5892
17:13 if he be gotten into a **c**, then shall all Israel 5892
17:13 shall all Israel bring ropes to that **c**, and 5892
17:17 they might not be seen to come into the **c**: 5892
17:23 to his **c**, and put his household in order, 5892
18: 3 *it is* better that thou succour us out of the **c**. 5892
19: 3 gat them by stealth that day *into* the **c**, 5892
19:37 that I may die in mine own **c**, *and be buried* 5892
20:15 they cast up a bank against the **c**, and 5892
20:16 cried a wise woman out of the **c**, Hear, 5892
20:19 thou seekest to destroy a **c** and a mother in 5892
20:21 him only, and I will depart from the **c**. 5892
20:22 they retired from the **c**, every man to his 5892
24: 5 *on* the right side of the **c** that *lieth* in 5892
1Ki 1:41 Wherefore *is this* noise of the **c** being in an 7151
1:45 thence rejoicing, so that the **c** rang again. 7151
2:10 and was buried in the **c** of David. 5892
3: 1 and brought her into the **c** of David, 5892
8: 1 of the LORD out of the **c** of David, 5892
8:16 I chose no **c** out of all the tribes of Israel to 5892
8:44 shall pray unto the LORD toward the **c** 5892
8:48 the **c** which thou hast chosen, and the house 5892
9:16 slain the Canaanites that dwelt in the **c**, and 5892
9:24 Pharaoh's daughter came up out of the **c** of 5892
11:27 repaired the breaches of the **c** of David his 5892
11:32 the **c** which I have chosen out of all 5892
11:36 the **c** which I have chosen me to put my 5892
11:43 and was buried in the **c** of David his father: 5892
13:25 told *it* in the **c** where the old prophet dwelt. 5892
13:29 the old prophet came to the **c**, to mourn and 5892
14:11 Him that dieth of Jeroboam in the **c** shall 5892
14:12 *and* when thy feet enter into the **c**, the child 5892
14:21 the **c** which the LORD did choose out of 5892
14:31 was buried with his fathers in the **c** of 5892
15: 8 and they buried him in the **c** of David: 5892
15:24 was buried with his fathers in the **c** of 5892
16: 4 Him that dieth of Baasha in the **c** shall 5892
16:18 when Zimri saw that the **c** was taken, 5892
16:24 and called the name of the **c** which he built, 5892
17:10 when he came to the gate of the **c**, behold, 5892
20: 2 to Ahab king of Israel into the **c**, 5892
20:12 they set *themselves in array* against the **c**. 5892
20:19 princes of the provinces came out of the **c**, 5892
20:30 the rest fled to Aphek, into the **c**; and 5892
20:30 Ben-hadad fled, and came into the **c**, 5892
21: 8 and to the nobles that *were* in his **c**, 5892
21:11 the men of his **c**, *even* the elders and 5892
21:11 nobles who *were* the inhabitants in his **c**, 5892
21:13 they carried him forth out of the **c**, and 5892
21:24 Him that dieth of Ahab in the **c** the dogs 5892
22:26 him back unto Amon the governor of the **c**, 5892
22:36 Every man to his **c**, and every man to his 5892
22:50 was buried with his fathers in the **c** of 5892
2Ki 2:19 the men of the **c** said unto Elisha, Behold, 5892
2:19 pray thee, the situation of *this* **c** *is* pleasant, 5892
2:23 there came forth little children out of the **c**, 5892
3:19 ye shall smite every fenced **c**, and 5892
3:19 every choice **c**, and shall fell every good 5892

2Ki	6:14	came by night, and compassed the **c** about.	5892
	6:15	a host compassed the **c** both with horses	5892
	6:19	This *is* not the way, neither *is* this the **c**:	5892
	7: 4	We will enter *into* the **c**, then the famine *is*	5892
	7: 4	the famine *is* in the **c**, and we shall die	5892
	7:10	and called unto the porter of the **c**:	5892
	7:12	saying, When they come out of the **c**, we	5892
	7:12	shall catch them alive, and get into the **c**.	5892
	7:13	which are left in **the c**s, (behold,	1886.3
	8:24	was buried with his fathers in the **c** of	5892
	9:15	let none go forth *nor* escape out of the **c** to	5892
	9:28	sepulchre with his fathers in the **c** of David.	5892
	10: 2	and horses, a fenced **c** also, and armour;	5892
	10: 5	*he* that *was* over the **c**, the elders also, and	5892
	10: 6	*were* with the great *men* of the **c**,	5892
	10:25	and went to the **c** of the house of Baal.	5892
	11:20	of the land rejoiced, and the **c** was in quiet:	5892
	12:21	they buried him with his fathers in the **c** of	5892
	14:20	with his fathers in the **c** of David.	5892
	15: 7	they buried him with his fathers in the **c** of	5892
	15:38	was buried with his fathers in the **c** of	5892
	16:20	was buried with his fathers in the **c** of	5892
	17: 9	the tower of the watchmen to the fenced **c**.	5892
	18: 8	the tower of the watchmen to the fenced **c**.	5892
	18:30	this **c** shall not be delivered into the hand of	5892
	19:13	the king of the **c** of Sepharvaim, *of* Hena,	5892
	19:32	He shall not come into this **c**, nor shoot an	5892
	19:33	shall not come into this **c**, saith	5892
	19:34	For I will defend this **c**, to save it, for mine	5892
	20: 6	this **c** out of the hand of the king of	5892
	20: 6	I will defend this **c** for mine own sake, and	5892
	20:20	and a conduit, and brought water into the **c**,	5892
	23: 8	of the gate of Joshua the governor of the **c**,	5892
	23: 8	on a man's left hand at the gate of the **c**.	5892
	23:17	the men of the **c** told him, *It is*	5892
	23:27	will cast off this **c** Jerusalem which I have	5892
	24:10	*against* Jerusalem, and the **c** was besieged.	5892
	24:11	king of Babylon came against the **c**,	5892
	25: 2	the **c** was besieged unto the eleventh year	5892
	25: 3	*fourth* month the famine prevailed in the **c**,	5892
	25: 4	the **c** was broken up, and all the men of war	5892
	25: 4	(now the Chaldees *were* against the **c** round	5892
	25:11	the rest of the people that were left in the **c**,	5892
	25:19	out of the **c** he took an officer that was set	5892
	25:19	which were found in the **c**, and	5892
	25:19	people of the land that were found in the **c**:	5892
1Ch	1:43	and the name of his **c** *was* Dinhabah.	5892
	1:46	his stead: and the name of his **c** *was* Avith.	5892
	1:50	the name of his **c** *was* Pai; and his wife's	5892
	6:56	the fields of the **c**, and the villages thereof,	5892
	6:57	*the* **c** of refuge, and Libnah with her	NIH
	11: 5	the castle of Zion, which *is* the **c** of David.	5892
	11: 7	they called it the **c** of David.	5892
	11: 8	he built the **c** round about, even from Millo	5892
	11: 8	and Joab repaired the rest of the **c**.	5892
	13:13	the ark *home* to himself to the **c** of David,	5892
	15: 1	*David* made him houses in the **c** of David,	5892
	15:29	of the LORD came to the **c** of David,	5892
	19: 9	the battle in array *before* the gate of the **c**:	5892
	19:15	Abishai his brother, and entered into the **c**.	5892
	20: 2	also exceeding much spoil *out* of the **c**.	5892
2Ch	5: 2	of the LORD out of the **c** of David,	5892
	6: 5	**c** among all the tribes of Israel to build a	5892
	6:34	they pray unto thee toward this **c** which	5892
	6:38	*toward* the **c** which thou hast chosen, and	5892
	8:11	**c** of David unto the house that he had built	5892
	9:31	he was buried in the **c** of David his father:	5892
	11:12	in every **several c** *he put*	5892+5892+2050.1
	11:23	and Benjamin, unto every fenced **c**:	5892
	12:13	the **c** which the LORD had chosen out of	5892
	12:16	and was buried in the **c** of David:	5892
	14: 1	and they buried him in the **c** of David:	5892
	15: 6	was destroyed of nation, and **c** of city:	5892
	15: 6	was destroyed of nation, and city of **c**:	5892
	16:14	which he had made for himself in the **c** of	5892
	18:25	him back to Amon the governor of the **c**,	5892
	19: 5	all the fenced cities of Judah, **c** by city,	5892
	19: 5	all the fenced cities of Judah, city by **c**,	5892
	21: 1	was buried with his fathers in the **c** of	5892
	21:20	Howbeit they buried him in the **c** of David,	5892
	23:21	the **c** was quiet, after that they had slain	5892
	24:16	they buried him in the **c** of David among	5892
	24:25	they buried him in the **c** of David, but	5892
	25:28	buried him with his fathers in the **c** of	5892
	27: 9	and they buried him in the **c** of David:	5892
	28:15	the **c** of palm trees, to their brethren:	5892
	28:25	in every **several c** of Judah	5892+5892+2050.1
	28:27	they buried him in the **c**, *even* in Jerusalem:	5892
	29:20	gathered the rulers of the **c**, and went up *to*	5892
	30:10	So the posts passed from **c** to city through	5892
	30:10	So the posts passed from city to **c** through	5892
	31:19	in every **several c**, the men	5892+5892+2050.1
	32: 3	of the fountains which *were* without the **c**:	5892
	32: 5	repaired Millo *in* the **c** of David, and	5892
	32: 6	to him in the street of the gate of the **c**,	5892
	32:18	to trouble them; that they might take the **c**.	5892
	32:30	down to the west *side* of the **c** of David.	5892
	33:14	Now after this he built a wall without the **c**	5892
	33:15	in Jerusalem, and cast *them* out of the **c**.	5892
	34: 8	Maaseiah the governor of the **c**, and Joah	5892
Ezr	2: 1	and Judah, every one unto his **c**;	5892
	4:12	building the rebellious and the bad **c**, and	7149
	4:13	if this **c** be builded, and the walls set up	7149
	4:15	and know that this **c** *is* a rebellious city, and	7149
	4:15	and know that this city *is* a rebellious **c**, and	7149
	4:15	for which *cause* was this **c** destroyed.	7149
	4:16	if this **c** be builded *again*, and the walls	7149
	4:19	it is found that this **c** of old time *hath* made	7149
	4:21	*that* this **c** be not builded, until *another*	7149
	10:14	them the elders of **every c**,	5892+5892+2050.1
Ne	2: 3	when the **c**, the place of my fathers'	5892
	2: 5	unto the **c** of my fathers' sepulchres, that I	5892
	2: 8	for the wall of the **c**, and for the house that	5892
	3:15	unto the stairs that go down from the **c** of	5892
	7: 4	Now the **c** *was* large and great: but	5892
	7: 6	and to Judah, every one unto his **c**;	5892
	11: 1	one of ten to dwell in Jerusalem the holy **c**,	5892
	11: 9	the son of Senuah *was* second over the **c**.	5892
	11:18	All the Levites in the holy **c** *were* two	5892
	12:37	they went up by the stairs of the **c** of David,	5892
	13:18	bring all this evil upon us, and upon this **c**?	5892
Est	3:15	to drink; but the **c** Shushan was perplexed.	5892
	4: 1	went out into the midst of the **c**, and	5892
	4: 6	forth to Mordecai unto the street of the **c**,	5892
	6: 9	on horseback through the street of the **c**,	5892
	6:11	on horseback through the street of the **c**,	5892
	8:11	**every c** to gather	3605+5892+5892+2050.1
	8:15	and the **c** of Shushan rejoiced and was glad.	5892
	8:17	in **every c**,	3605+5892+5892+2050.1
	9:28	every province, and **every c**;	5892+5892+2050.1
Job	24:12	Men groan from out of the **c**, and the soul	5892
	29: 7	When I went out *to* the gate through the **c**,	7176
	39: 7	He scorneth the multitude of the **c**,	7151
Ps	31:21	me his marvellous kindness in a strong **c**.	5892
	46: 4	the streams whereof shall make glad the **c**	5892
	48: 1	greatly to be praised in the **c** of our God,	5892
	48: 2	sides of the north, the **c** of the great King.	7151
	48: 8	have we seen in the **c** of the LORD of	5892
	48: 8	of the LORD of hosts, in the **c** of our God:	5892
	55: 9	for I have seen violence and strife in the **c**.	5892
	59: 6	noise like a dog, and go round about the **c**.	5892
	59:14	noise like a dog, and go round about the **c**.	5892
	60: 9	Who will bring me *into* the strong **c**?	5892
	72:16	*they* of the **c** shall flourish like grass of	5892
	87: 3	*things* are spoken of thee, O **c** of God.	5892
	101: 8	all wicked doers from the **c** of the LORD.	5892
	107: 4	a solitary way; they found no **c** to dwell in.	5892
	107: 7	that *they* might go to a **c** of habitation.	5892
	107:36	that they may prepare a **c** for habitation;	5892
	108:10	Who will bring me *into* the strong **c**?	5892
	122: 3	Jerusalem *is* builded as a **c** that is compact	5892
	127: 1	except the LORD keep the **c**,	5892
Pr	1:21	in the **c** she uttereth her words, *saying*,	5892
	8: 3	She crieth at the gates, at the entry of the **c**,	7176
	9: 3	she crieth upon the highest places of the **c**,	7176
	9:14	on a seat in the high places of the **c**,	7176
	10:15	The rich *man's* wealth *is* his strong **c**:	7151
	11:10	well with the righteous, the **c** rejoiceth:	7151
	11:11	By the blessing of the upright the **c** is	7176
	16:32	that ruleth his spirit than he that taketh a **c**.	5892
	18:11	The rich *man's* wealth *is* his strong **c**, and	7151
	18:19	*is harder to be won* than a strong **c**:	7151
	21:22	A wise *man* scaleth the **c** of the mighty, and	5892
	25:28	own spirit *is like* a **c** *that is* broken down,	5892
	29: 8	Scornful men bring a **c** into a snare: but	7151
Ecc	7:19	than ten mighty *men* which are in the **c**.	5892
	8:10	they were forgotten in the **c** where they had	5892
	9:14	*There was* a little **c**, and few men within it;	5892

Ecc	9:15	and he by his wisdom delivered the **c**;	5892
	10:15	because he knoweth not how to go to the **c**.	5892
SS	3: 2	go about the **c** in the streets and in	5892
	3: 3	The watchmen that go about the **c** found	5892
	5: 7	The watchmen that went about the **c** found	5892
Isa	1: 8	in a garden of cucumbers, as a besieged **c**.	5892
	1:21	How is the faithful **c** become a harlot!	7151
	1:26	The **c** of righteousness, the faithful city.	5892
	1:26	The city of righteousness, the faithful **c**.	7151
	14: 4	the oppressor ceased! the **golden c** ceased!	4062
	14:31	cry, O **c**; thou, whole Palestina,	5892
	17: 1	Damascus *is* taken away from *being* a **c**,	5892
	19: 2	**c** against city, *and* kingdom against	5892
	19: 2	city against **c**, *and* kingdom against	5892
	19:18	one shall be called, The **c** of destruction.	5892
	22: 2	full *of* stirs, a tumultuous **c**, a joyous city:	5892
	22: 2	full *of* stirs, a tumultuous city, a joyous **c**:	7151
	22: 9	Ye have seen also the breaches of the **c** of	5892
	23: 7	*Is* this your joyous *c*, whose antiquity *is* of	NIH
	23: 8	the crowning *c*, whose merchants *are*	NIH
	23:11	*c*, to destroy the strong holds thereof.	NIH
	23:16	Take a harp, go about the **c**, thou harlot that	5892
	24:10	The **c** of confusion is broken down:	7151
	24:12	In the **c** is left desolation, and the gate is	5892
	25: 2	For thou hast made of a **c** a heap; *of* a	5892
	25: 2	of a city a heap; *of* a defenced **c** a ruin:	7151
	25: 2	a palace of strangers to be no **c**; it shall	5892
	25: 3	the **c** of the terrible nations shall fear thee.	7151
	26: 1	We have a strong **c**; salvation will *God*	5892
	26: 5	the lofty **c**, he layeth it low; he layeth it	7151
	27:10	Yet the defenced **c** *shall be* desolate, *and*	5892
	29: 1	to Ariel, to Ariel, the **c** *where* David dwelt!	7151
	32:13	upon all the houses of joy *in* the joyous **c**:	7151
	32:14	the multitude of the **c** shall be left; the forts	5892
	32:19	and the **c** shall be low in a low place.	5892
	33:20	Look upon Zion, the **c** of our solemnities:	7151
	36:15	this **c** shall not be delivered into the hand of	5892
	37:13	the king of the **c** of Sepharvaim, Hena, and	5892
	37:33	He shall not come into this **c**, nor shoot an	5892
	37:34	shall not come into this **c**, saith	5892
	37:35	For I will defend this **c** to save it for mine	5892
	38: 6	this **c** out of the hand of the king of	5892
	38: 6	king of Assyria: and I will defend this **c**.	5892
	45:13	he shall build my **c**, and he shall let go my	5892
	48: 2	For they call themselves of the holy **c**, and	5892
	52: 1	O Jerusalem, the holy **c**:	5892
	60:14	they shall call thee, The **c** of the LORD,	5892
	62:12	be called, Sought out, A **c** not forsaken.	5892
	66: 6	A voice of noise from the **c**, a voice from	5892
Jer	1:18	I have made thee *this* day a defenced **c**, and	5892
	3:14	I will take you one of a **c**, and two of a	5892
	4:29	The whole **c** shall flee for the noise of	5892
	4:29	every **c** *shall be* forsaken, and not a man	5892
	6: 6	this is the **c** to be visited; she *is* wholly	5892
	8:16	is in it; the **c**, and those that dwell therein.	5892
	14:18	if I enter *into* the **c**, then behold them that	5892
	15: 8	upon it suddenly, and terrors *upon* the **c**.	5892
	17:24	the gates of this **c** on the sabbath day,	5892
	17:25	shall there enter into the gates of this **c**	5892
	17:25	and this **c** shall remain for ever.	5892
	19: 8	I will make this **c** desolate, and a hissing;	5892
	19:11	Even so will I break this people and this **c**,	5892
	19:12	and *even* make this **c** as Tophet:	5892
	19:15	I will bring upon this **c** and upon all her	5892
	20: 5	I will deliver all the strength of this **c**,	5892
	21: 4	will assemble them into the midst of this **c**.	5892
	21: 6	I will smite the inhabitants of this **c**, both	5892
	21: 7	such as are left in this **c** from the pestilence,	5892
	21: 9	He that abideth in this **c** shall die by	5892
	21:10	For I have set my face against this **c** for	5892
	22: 8	many nations shall pass by this **c**, and	5892
	22: 8	the LORD done thus unto this great **c**?	5892
	23:39	the **c** that I gave you and your fathers, *and*	5892
	25:29	I begin to bring evil on the **c** which is	5892
	26: 6	will make this **c** a curse to all the nations of	5892
	26: 9	this **c** shall be desolate without an	5892
	26:11	for he hath prophesied against this **c**, as ye	5892
	26:12	against this **c** all the words that ye have	5892
	26:15	upon this **c**, and upon the inhabitants	5892
	26:20	who prophesied against this **c** and	5892
	27:17	live: wherefore should this **c** be laid waste?	5892
	27:19	residue of the vessels that remain in this **c**,	5892
	29: 7	seek the peace of the **c** whither I have	5892
	29:16	of all the people that dwelleth in this **c**,	5892
	30:18	the **c** shall be builded upon her own heap,	5892
	31:38	that the **c** shall be built to the LORD from	5892
	32: 3	I *will* give this **c** into the hand of the king	5892
	32:24	they are come *unto* the **c** to take it;	5892
	32:24	the **c** is given into the hand of	5892
	32:25	for the **c** is given into the hand of	5892
	32:28	I *will* give this **c** into the hand of	5892
	32:29	that fight against this **c**, shall come and	5892
	32:29	shall come and set fire on this **c**, and burn it	5892
	32:31	For this **c** hath been to me *as* a provocation	5892
	32:36	of Israel, concerning this **c**, whereof ye say,	5892
	33: 4	concerning the houses of this **c**,	5892
	33: 5	wickedness I have hid my face from this **c**.	5892
	34: 2	I *will* give this **c** into the hand of the king	5892
	34:22	and cause them to return to this **c**;	5892
	37: 8	fight against this **c**, and take it, and burn it	5892
	37:10	man in his tent, and burn this **c** with fire.	5892
	37:21	until all the bread in the **c** were spent.	5892
	38: 2	He that remaineth in this **c** shall die by	5892
	38: 3	This **c** shall surely be given into the hand of	5892
	38: 4	of the men of war that remain in this **c**,	5892
	38: 9	he is: for *there is* no more bread in the **c**.	5892
	38:17	and this **c** shall not be burnt with fire;	5892
	38:18	shall this **c** be given into the hand of	5892
	38:23	thou shalt cause this **c** to be burnt with fire.	5892
	39: 2	*day* of the month, the **c** was broken up.	5892
	39: 4	and went forth out of the **c** by night,	5892
	39: 9	of the people that remained in the **c**,	5892
	39:16	I *will* bring my words upon this **c** for evil,	5892
	41: 7	*so,* when they came into the midst of the **c**,	5892
	46: 8	I will destroy the **c** and the inhabitants	5892
	47: 2	the **c**, and them that dwell therein:	5892
	48: 8	the spoiler shall come upon every **c**, and	5892
	48: 8	upon every city, and no **c** shall escape:	5892
	49:25	How is the **c** of praise not left, the city of	5892
	49:25	the city of praise not left, the **c** of my joy!	7151
	51:31	to shew the king of Babylon that his **c** is	5892
	52: 5	So the **c** was besieged unto the eleventh	5892
	52: 6	the famine was sore in the **c**, so that there	5892
	52: 7	the **c** was broken up, and all the men of war	5892
	52: 7	went forth out of the **c** by night *by* the way	5892
	52: 7	(now the Chaldeans *were* by the **c** round	5892
	52:15	residue of the people that remained in the **c**,	5892
	52:25	He took also out of the **c** an eunuch,	5892
	52:25	king's person, which were found in the **c**;	5892
	52:25	that were found in the midst of the **c**.	5892
La	1: 1	How doth the **c** sit solitary, *that was* full of	5892
	1:19	and mine elders gave up the ghost in the **c**,	5892
	2:11	the sucklings swoon in the streets of the **c**.	7151
	2:12	as the wounded in the streets of the **c**,	5892
	2:15	*saying, Is* this the **c** that *men* call The	5892
	3:51	because of all the daughters of my **c**.	5892
Eze	4: 1	and pourtray upon it *the* **c**, *even* Jerusalem:	5892
	4: 3	it *for* a wall of iron between thee and the **c**:	5892
	5: 2	with fire a third *part* in the midst of the **c**,	5892
	7:15	he that *is* in the **c**, famine and	5892
	7:23	bloody crimes, and the **c** is full *of* violence.	5892
	9: 1	Cause them that have charge over the **c** to	5892
	9: 4	Go through the midst of the **c** through	5892
	9: 5	Go ye after him through the **c**, and smite:	5892
	9: 7	And they went forth, and slew in the **c**.	5892
	9: 9	full *of* blood, and the **c** full *of* perverseness:	5892
	10: 2	the cherubims, and scatter *them* over the **c**.	5892
	11: 2	and give wicked counsel in this **c**:	5892
	11: 3	this *c is* the caldron, and we *be* the flesh.	NIH
	11: 6	Ye have multiplied your slain in this **c**,	5892
	11: 7	they *are* the flesh, and this *c is* the caldron:	NIH
	11:11	This *c* shall not be your caldron,	NIH
	11:23	LORD went up from the midst of the **c**,	5892
	11:23	mountain which *is* on the east side of the **c**.	5892
	17: 4	of traffick; he set it in a **c** of merchants.	5892
	21:19	choose *it,* at the head of the way to the **c**.	5892
	22: 2	thou judge, wilt thou judge the bloody **c**?	5892
	22: 3	The **c** sheddeth blood in the midst of it,	5892
	24: 6	Woe to the bloody **c**, to the pot whose scum	5892
	24: 9	saith the Lord GOD; Woe to the bloody **c**!	5892
	26:10	as men enter into a **c** wherein is made a	5892
	26:17	the renowned **c**, which wast strong in	5892
	26:19	When I shall make thee a desolate **c**,	5892
	27:32	over thee, *saying,* What *c is* like Tyrus,	NIH
	33:21	came unto me, saying, The **c** is smitten.	5892
	39:16	also the name of the **c** *shall be* Hamonah.	5892
	40: 1	in the fourteenth year after that the **c** was	5892
	40: 2	by which *was* as the frame of a **c** on	5892

Eze 43: 3 that I saw when I came to destroy the **c**: 5892
45: 6 ye shall appoint the possession of the **c** five 5892
45: 7 holy *portion,* and of the possession of the **c**, 5892
45: 7 and before the possession of the **c**, 5892
48:15 *shall be* a profane *place* for the **c**, 5892
48:15 and the **c** shall be in the midst thereof. 5892
48:17 the suburbs of the **c** shall be toward 5892
48:18 shall be for food unto them that serve the **c**. 5892
48:19 they that serve the **c** shall serve it out of all 5892
48:20 with the possession of the **c**. 5892
48:21 of the possession of the **c**, over against 5892
48:22 *and* from the possession of the **c**, 5892
48:30 these *are* the goings out of the **c**: on 5892
48:31 the gates of the **c** *shall be* after the names of 5892
48:35 the name of the **c** from *that* day *shall be,* 5892
Da 9:16 thy fury be turned away from thy **c** 5892
9:18 and the **c** which is called by thy name: 5892
9:19 for thy **c** and thy people are called by thy 5892
9:24 upon thy people and upon thy holy **c**, 5892
9:26 prince that *shall* come shall destroy the **c** 5892
Hos 6: 8 Gilead *is* a **c** of them that work iniquity, 7151
11: 9 midst of thee: and I will not enter into the **c**. 5892
Joel 2: 9 They shall run to and fro in the **c**; they shall 5892
Am 3: 6 Shall a trumpet be blown in the **c**, and 5892
3: 6 shall there be evil in a **c**, and the LORD 5892
4: 7 I caused it to rain upon one **c**, and caused it 5892
4: 7 and caused it not to rain upon another **c**: 5892
4: 8 So two *or* three cities wandered unto one **c**, 5892
5: 3 The **c** that went out *by* a thousand shall 5892
6: 8 will I deliver up the **c** with all that is 5892
7:17 Thy wife shall be a harlot in the **c**, and 5892
Jnh 1: 2 to Nineveh, *that* great **c**, and cry against it; 5892
3: 2 *that* great **c**, and preach unto it 5892
3: 3 Now Nineveh was an exceeding great **c** of 5892
3: 4 Jonah began to enter into the **c** a day's 5892
4: 5 So Jonah went out of the **c**, and sat on 5892
4: 5 sat on the east side of the **c**, and there made 5892
4: 5 he might see what would become of the **c**. 5892
4:11 should not I spare Nineveh, *that* great **c**, 5892
Mic 4:10 for now shalt thou go forth out of the **c**, and 7151
6: 9 The LORD'S voice crieth unto the **c**, and 5892
Na 3: 1 Woe to the bloody **c**! it *is* all full *of* lies *and* 5892
Hab 2: 8 *of* the **c**, and *of* all that dwell therein. 7151
2:12 with blood, and stablisheth a **c** by iniquity! 7151
2:17 *of* the **c**, and *of* all that dwell therein. 7151
Zep 2:15 This *is* the rejoicing **c** that dwelt carelessly, 5892
3: 1 is filthy and polluted, to the oppressing **c**! 5892
Zec 8: 3 Jerusalem shall be called a **c** of truth; and 5892
8: 5 the streets of the **c** shall be full *of* boys and 5892
8:21 the inhabitants of one **c** shall go to another, NIH
14: 2 the **c** shall be taken, and the houses rifled, 5892
14: 2 half of the **c** shall go forth into captivity, 5892
14: 2 of the people shall not be cut off from the **c**. 5892
Mt 2:23 he came and dwelt in a **c** called Nazareth: *4172*
4: 5 the devil taketh him *up* into the holy **c**, *4172*
5:14 A **c** that is set on a hill cannot be hid. *4172*
5:35 for it is the **c** of the great King. *4172*
8:33 and went their ways into the **c**, and *4172*
8:34 the whole **c** came out to meet Jesus: *4172*
9: 1 and passed over, and came into his own **c**. *4172*
10: 5 into *any* **c** of the Samaritans enter ye not: *4172*
10:11 And into whatsoever **c** or town ye shall *4172*
10:14 when ye depart out of that house or **c**, *4172*
10:15 in the day of judgment, than for that **c**. *4172*
10:23 But when they persecute you in this **c**, *4172*
12:25 and every **c** or house divided against itself *4172*
21:10 all the **c** was moved, saying, Who is this? *4172*
21:17 and went out of the **c** into Bethany; *4172*
21:18 in the morning as he returned into the **c**, *4172*
22: 7 those murderers, and burnt up their **c**. *4172*
23:34 and persecute *them* from **c** to city: *4172*
23:34 and persecute *them* from city to **c**: *4172*
26:18 Go into the **c** to such a man, and say unto *4172*
27:53 and went into the holy **c**, and appeared unto *4172*
28:11 some of the watch came into the **c**, and *4172*
Mk 1:33 And all the **c** was gathered together at *4172*
1:45 *Jesus* could no more openly enter into the **c**, *4172*
5:14 and told *it* in the **c**, and in the country. *4172*
6:11 in the day of judgment, than for that **c**. *4172*
11:19 when even was come, he went out of the **c**. *4172*
14:13 Go ye into the **c**, and there shall meet you a *4172*
14:16 and came into the **c**, and found as he had *4172*
Lk 1:26 was sent from God unto a **c** of Galilee, *4172*
1:39 the hill country with haste, into a **c** of Juda; *4172*
2: 3 went to be taxed, every one into his own **c**. *4172*
2: 4 out of the **c** of Nazareth, into Judea, *4172*
2: 4 into Judea, unto the **c** of David, *4172*
2:11 For unto you is born this day in the **c** of *4172*
2:39 into Galilee, to their own **c** Nazareth. *4172*
4:26 save unto Sarepta, *a* **c** of Sidon, unto a NIG
4:29 and thrust him out of the **c**, and led him *4172*
4:29 brow of the hill whereon their **c** was built, *4172*
4:31 a **c** of Galilee, and taught them on *4172*
5:12 it came to pass, when he was in a certain **c**, *4172*
7:11 *day* after, *that* he went into a **c** called Nain; *4172*
7:12 when he came nigh to the gate of the **c**, *4172*
7:12 and much people of the **c** was with her. *4172*
7:37 And behold, a woman in the **c**, which was a *4172*
8: 1 that he went throughout every **c** and *4172*
8: 4 and were come to him out of every **c**, *4172*
8:27 there met him out of the **c** a certain man, *4172*
8:34 and went and told *it* in the **c** and in *4172*
8:39 published throughout the whole **c** how *4172*
9: 5 not receive you, when ye go out of that **c**, *4172*
9:10 place belonging to the **c** called Bethsaida. *4172*
10: 1 and two before his face into every **c** and *4172*
10: 8 And into whatsoever **c** ye enter, and *4172*
10:10 But into whatsoever **c** ye enter, and *4172*
10:11 Even the *very* dust of your **c**, *4172*
10:12 in that day for Sodom, than for that **c**. *4172*
14:21 quickly into the streets and lanes of the **c**, *4172*
18: 2 Saying, There was in a **c** a judge, *4172*
18: 3 And there was a widow in that **c**; and *4172*
19:41 he beheld the **c**, and wept over it, *4172*
22:10 Behold, when ye are entered into the **c**, *4172*
23:19 (Who for a certain sedition made in the **c**, *4172*
23:51 *he was* of Arimathea, a **c** of the Jews: *4172*
24:49 but tarry ye in the **c** of Jerusalem, until ye *4172*
Jn 1:44 of Bethsaida, the **c** of Andrew and Peter. *4172*
4: 5 Then cometh he to a **c** of Samaria, which is *4172*
4: 8 were gone away unto the **c** to buy meat.) *4172*
4:28 and went her way into the **c**, and saith to *4172*
4:30 Then they went out of the **c**, and came unto *4172*
4:39 And many of the Samaritans of that **c** *4172*
11:54 into a **c** called Ephraim, and there *4172*
19:20 Jesus was crucified was nigh to the **c**: *4172*
Ac 7:58 And cast *him* out of the **c**, and stoned *him:* *4172*
8: 5 Then Philip went down to the **c** of Samaria, *4172*
8: 8 And there was great joy in that **c**. *4172*
8: 9 which beforetime in the *same* **c** used *4172*
9: 6 and go into the **c**, and it shall be told thee *4172*
10: 9 on their journey, and drew nigh unto the **c**, *4172*
11: 5 I was in the **c** of Joppa praying: and in a *4172*
12:10 unto the iron gate that leadeth unto the **c**; *4172*
13:44 whole **c** together to hear the word of God. *4172*
13:50 and the chief *men* of the **c**, and *4172*
14: 4 But the multitude of the **c** was divided: and *4172*
14:13 which was before their **c**, brought oxen and *4172*
14:19 having stoned Paul, drew *him* out of the **c**, *4172*
14:20 about him, he rose up, and came into the **c**: *4172*
14:21 they had preached the gospel to that **c**, *4172*
15:21 For Moses of old time hath in every **c** them *4172*
15:36 visit our brethren in every **c** where we have *4172*
16:12 which is the chief **c** of *that* part of *4172*
16:12 and we were in that **c** abiding certain days. *4172*
16:13 And on the sabbath we went out of the **c** by *4172*
16:14 a seller of purple, of the **c** of Thyatira, *4172*
16:20 being Jews, do exceedingly trouble our **c**, *4172*
16:39 and desired *them* to depart out of the **c**. *4172*
17: 5 and set all the **c** on an uproar, and assaulted *4172*
17: 6 certain brethren unto the **rulers of the c**, *4173*
17: 8 troubled the people and the **rulers of the c**, *4173*
17:16 when he saw the **c** wholly given to idolatry. *4172*
18:10 hurt thee: for I have much people in this **c**. *4172*
19:29 And the whole **c** was filled with confusion: *4172*
19:35 **c** of the Ephesians is a worshipper of *4172*
20:23 that the Holy Ghost witnesseth in every **c**, *4172*
21: 5 and children, till *we were* out of the **c**: *4172*
21:29 (For they had seen before with him in the **c** *4172*
21:30 And all the **c** was moved, and the people *4172*
21:39 *a* **c** in Cilicia, a citizen of no mean city: NIG
21:39 *a city* in Cilicia, a citizen of no mean **c**: *4172*
22: 3 *am* a Jew, born in Tarsus, *a* **c** in Cilicia, NIG
22: 3 yet brought up in this **c** at the feet of *4172*
24:12 neither in the synagogues, nor in the **c**: *4172*
25:23 chief captains, and principal men of the **c**, *4172*
27: 5 Pamphylia, we came to Myra, *a* **c** of Lycia. NIG
27: 8 nigh whereunto was the **c** *of* Lasea. *4172*

C

Ro 16:23 Erastus the chamberlain of the c saluteth 4172
2Co 11:26 *in* perils by the heathen, *in* perils in the c, 4172
11:32 c of the Damascenes *with a garrison,* 4172
13: S *a* c of Macedonia, by Titus and Lucas. NIG
1Ti 6: S which is the **chiefest** c of Phrygia 3390
Tit 1: 5 and ordain elders in every c, as I had 4172
Heb 11:10 For he looked for a c which hath 4172
11:16 for he hath prepared for them a c. 4172
12:22 and unto the c of the living God, 4172
13:14 For here have we no continuing c, but 4172
Jas 4:13 or to morrow we will go into such a c, 4172
Rev 3:12 and the name of the c of my God, *which is* 4172
11: 2 the holy c shall they tread under foot forty 4172
11: 8 bodies *shall lie* in the street of the great c, 4172
11:13 and the tenth *part* of the c fell, and in 4172
14: 8 Babylon is fallen, is fallen, *that* great c, 4172
14:20 the winepress was trodden without the c, 4172
16:19 And the great c was *divided* into three 4172
17:18 woman which thou sawest is *that* great c, 4172
18:10 saying, Alas, alas, *that* great c Babylon, 4172
18:10 alas, *that* great city Babylon, *that* mighty c! 4172
18:16 And saying, Alas, alas, *that* great c, 4172
18:18 saying, What c *is* like unto *this* great city? NIG
18:18 saying, What *city is* like unto *this* great c? 4172
18:19 and wailing, saying, Alas, alas, *that* great c, 4172
18:21 Thus with violence shall *that* great c 4172
20: 9 camp of the saints about, and the beloved c: 4172
21: 2 And I John saw the holy c, new Jerusalem, 4172
21:10 high mountain, and shewed me *that* great c, 4172
21:14 And the wall of the c had twelve 4172
21:15 me had a golden reed to measure the c, 4172
21:16 And the c lieth foursquare, and the length is 4172
21:16 and he measured the c with the reed, 4172
21:18 and the c *was* pure gold, like unto clear 4172
21:19 And the foundations of the wall of the c 4172
21:21 and the street of the c *was* pure gold, as *it* 4172
21:23 And the c had no need of the sun, neither of 4172
22:14 may enter in through the gates into the c. 4172
22:19 and out of the holy c, and *from* the *things* 4172

CITY CLERK See TOWNCLERK

CLAD (2)
1Ki 11:29 he had c himself with a new garment; and 3680
Isa 59:17 *for* clothing, and was c **with** zeal as a cloke. 5844

CLAMOROUS (1) [CLAMOUR]
Pr 9:13 A foolish woman *is* c: *she is* simple, and 1993

CLAMOUR (1) [CLAMOROUS]
Eph 4:31 wrath, and anger, and c, and evil speaking, 2906

CLAN See KINDRED; KINDREDS

CLANGING See TINKLING

CLAP (6) [CLAPPED, CLAPPETH, CLAPT]
Job 27:23 *Men* shall c their hands at him, and 5606
Ps 47: 1 O c *your* hands, all ye people; shout unto 8628
98: 8 Let the floods c *their* hands: let the hills be 4222
Isa 55:12 all the trees of the field shall c *their* hands. 4222
La 2:15 All that pass by c *their* hands at thee; 5606
Na 3:19 all that hear the bruit of thee shall c 8628

CLAPPED (1) [CLAP]
Eze 25: 6 Because thou hast c *thine* hands, and 4222

CLAPPETH (1) [CLAP]
Job 34:37 he c *his hands* amongst us, and 5606

CLAPT (1) [CLAP]
2Ki 11:12 they c their hands, and said, God save 5221

CLASP See TACHES

CLAUDA (1)
Ac 27:16 under a certain island *which is* called C, 2802

CLAUDIA (1)
2Ti 4:21 and Linus, and C, and all the brethren. 2803

CLAUDIUS (3)
Ac 11:28 which came to pass in the days of C Cesar. 2804
18: 2 that C had commanded all Jews to depart 2804
23:26 C Lysias unto the most excellent governor 2804

CLAVE (14) [CLEAVE]
Ge 22: 3 c the wood for the burnt offering, and 1234
34: 3 his soul c unto Dinah the daughter of Jacob, 1692
Nu 16:31 that the ground c **asunder** that *was* under 1234
Jdg 15:19 God c a hollow place that *was* in the jaw, 1234
Ru 1:14 her mother in law; but Ruth c unto her. 1692
1Sa 6:14 they c the wood of the cart, and offered 1234
2Sa 20: 2 the men of Judah c unto their king, 1692
23:10 was weary, and his hand c unto the sword: 1692
1Ki 11: 2 their gods: Solomon c unto these in love. 1692
2Ki 18: 6 For he c to the LORD, *and* departed not 1692
Ne 10:29 They c to their brethren, their nobles, and 2388
Ps 78:15 He c the rocks in the wilderness, and 1234
Isa 48:21 he c the rock also, and the waters gushed 1234
Ac 17:34 Howbeit certain men c unto him, and 2853

CLAWS (3)
Dt 14: 6 cleaveth the cleft *into* two c, *and* 6541
Da 4:33 eagles' *feathers,* and his nails like birds' c. NIH
Zec 11:16 flesh of the fat, and tear their c in pieces. 6541

CLAY (33)
1Ki 7:46 in the c ground between Succoth and 4568
2Ch 4:17 in the c ground between Succoth and 5645
Job 4:19 much less *in* them that dwell in houses of c, 2563
10: 9 that thou hast made me as the c; 2563
13:12 like unto ashes, your bodies to bodies of c. 2563
27:16 as the dust, and prepare raiment as the c; 2563
33: 6 God's stead: I also am formed out of the c. 2563
38:14 It is turned as c *to* the seal; and they stand 2563
Ps 40: 2 out of the miry c, and set my feet upon a 2916
Isa 29:16 down shall be esteemed as the potter's c: 2563
41:25 as *upon* morter, and as the potter treadeth c. 2916
45: 9 Shall the c say to him that fashioneth it, 2563
64: 8 we *are* the c, and thou our potter; and we all 2563
Jer 18: 4 the vessel that he made of c was marred in 2563
18: 6 as the c *is* in the potter's hand, so *are* ye in 2563
43: 9 and hide them in the c in the brickkiln, 4423
Da 2:33 of iron, his feet part of iron and part of c. 2635
2:34 image upon his feet *that were* of iron and c, 2635
2:35 the c, the brass, the silver, and the gold, 2635
2:41 and toes, part of potter's c, and part of iron, 2635
2:41 as thou sawest the iron mixed with miry c. 2635
2:42 part of c, *so* the kingdom shall be partly 2635
2:43 whereas thou sawest iron mixt with miry c, 2635
2:43 to another, even as iron is not mixed with c. 2635
2:45 the brass, the c, the silver, and the gold; 2635
Na 3:14 go into c, and tread the morter, make strong 2916
Hab 2: 6 and to him that ladeth himself with **thick** c! 5671
Jn 9: 6 and made c of the spittle, and he anointed 4081
9: 6 the eyes of the blind man with the c, 4081
9:11 A man *that is* called Jesus made c, and 4081
9:14 the sabbath day when Jesus made the c, 4081
9:15 He put c upon mine eyes, and I washed, 4081
Ro 9:21 Hath not the potter power over the c, of 4081

CLEAN (133) [CLEANNESS, CLEANSE, CLEANSED, CLEANSETH, CLEANSING, UNCLEAN]
Ge 7: 2 Of every c beast thou shalt take to thee by 2889
7: 2 and of beasts that *are* not c by two, the male 2889
7: 8 Of c beasts, and of beasts that *are* not clean, 2889
7: 8 of beasts that *are* not c, and of fowls, and 2889
8:20 took of every c beast, and of every clean 2889
8:20 of every c fowl, and offered burnt offerings 2889
35: 2 and be c, and change your garments: 2891
Lev 4:12 carry forth without the camp unto a c place, 2889
6:11 the ashes without the camp unto a c place. 2889
7:19 *for* the flesh, all that be c shall eat thereof. 2889
10:10 and unholy, and between unclean and c; 2889
10:14 and heave shoulder shall ye eat in a c place; 2889
11:36 *wherein there is* plenty of water, shall be c: 2889
11:37 seed which is to be sown, it *shall be* c. 2889
11:47 a difference between the unclean and the c, 2889
12: 8 an atonement for her, and she shall be c. 2891
13: 6 the skin, the priest shall **pronounce** him c: 2891
13: 6 and he shall wash his clothes, and be c. 2891
13:13 he shall **pronounce** *him* c *that hath* 2891
13:13 the plague: it is all turned white: he *is* c. 2889
13:17 the priest shall **pronounce** *him* c *that hath* 2891
13:17 *him* clean *that hath* the plague: he *is* c. 2889
13:23 and the priest shall **pronounce** him c. 2891
13:28 and the priest shall **pronounce** him c: 2891
13:34 then the priest shall **pronounce** him c: 2891
13:34 and he shall wash his clothes, and be c. 2891

Lev 13:37 up therein; the scall is healed, he *is* **c**: 2889
13:37 and the priest shall **pronounce** him **c**. 2891
13:39 spot *that* groweth in the skin: he *is* **c**. 2889
13:40 is fallen off his head, he *is* bald: *yet is* he **c**. 2889
13:41 his face, he *is* forehead bald: *yet is* he **c**. 2889
13:58 be washed the second time, and shall be **c**. 2891
13:59 to **pronounce** it **c**, or to pronounce it 2891
14: 4 that is to be cleansed two birds alive *and* **c**, 2889
14: 7 shall **pronounce** him **c**, and shall let 2891
14: 8 wash *himself* in water, that he may be **c**: 2891
14: 9 wash his flesh in water, and he shall be **c**. 2891
14:11 the priest that **maketh** *him* **c** shall present 2891
14:11 shall present the man that is to be **made c**, 2891
14:20 an atonement for him, and he shall be **c**. 2891
14:48 the priest shall **pronounce** the house **c**, 2891
14:53 atonement for the house: and it shall be **c**. 2891
14:57 teach when *it is* unclean, and when *it is* **c**: 2889
15: 8 that hath the issue spit upon him that is **c**; 2889
15:13 his flesh in running water, and shall be **c**. 2891
15:28 seven days, and after *that* she shall be **c**. 2891
16:30 *that* ye may be **c** from all your sins before 2891
17:15 unclean until the even: then shall he be **c**. 2891
20:25 put difference between **c** beasts 2889
20:25 and between unclean fowls and **c**: 2889
22: 4 not eat of the holy *things*, until he be **c**. 2891
22: 7 he shall be **c**, and shall afterward eat of 2891
23:22 thou shalt not **make c riddance** of 3615
Nu 5:28 if the woman be not defiled, but *be* **c**; then 2889
8: 7 their clothes, and *so* **make** themselves **c**. 2891
9:13 the man that *is* **c**, and is not in a journey, 2889
18:11 every one *that is* **c** in thy house shall eat of 2889
18:13 every one *that is* **c** in thine house shall eat 2889
19: 9 a man *that is* **c** shall gather up the ashes of 2889
19: 9 lay *them* up without the camp in a **c** place, 2889
19:12 and on the seventh day he shall be **c**: 2891
19:12 then the seventh day he shall not be **c**. 2891
19:18 a **c** person shall take hyssop, and dip *it* in 2889
19:19 the **c** *person* shall sprinkle upon the unclean 2889
19:19 *himself* in water, and shall be **c** at even. 2891
31:23 *it* go through the fire, and it shall be **c**: 2891
31:24 ye shall be **c**, and afterward ye shall come 2891
Dt 12:15 the unclean and the **c** may eat thereof, as of 2889
12:22 and the **c** shall eat of them alike. 2889
14:11 *Of* all **c** birds ye shall eat. 2889
14:20 *But* of all **c** fowls ye may eat. 2889
15:22 and the **c** *person shall eat it* alike, 2889
23:10 that is not **c** by reason of *uncleanness* that 2889
Jos 3:17 all the people were passed **c** over Jordan. 8552
4: 1 when all the people were **c** passed over 8552
4:11 when all the people were **c** passed over, 8552
1Sa 20:26 Something hath befallen him, he *is* not **c**; 2889
20:26 he *is* not clean; surely *he is* not **c**. 2889
2Ki 5:10 come again to thee, and thou shalt be **c**. 2891
5:12 may I not wash in them, and be **c**? So he 2891
5:13 when he saith to thee, Wash, and be **c**? 2891
5:14 unto the flesh of a little child, and he was **c**. 2891
2Ch 30:17 the passovers for every one *that was* not **c**, 2889
Job 9:30 **make** my hands **never so c**; 1253+2141+871.1
11: 4 doctrine *is* pure, and I am **c** in thine eyes. 1249
14: 4 Who can bring a **c** *thing* out of an unclean? 2889
15:14 What *is* man, that he should be **c**? and 2135
15:15 yea, the heavens are not **c** in his sight. 2141
17: 9 he that hath **c** hands shall be stronger and 2889
25: 4 how can he be **c** *that is* born of a woman? 2135
33: 9 I am **c** without transgression, I *am* 2134
Ps 19: 9 The fear of the LORD *is* **c**, enduring for 2889
24: 4 He that hath **c** hands, and a pure heart; 5355
51: 7 Purge me with hyssop, and I shall be **c**: 2891
51:10 Create in me a **c** heart, O God; and renew a 2889
73: 1 to Israel, *even* to such as are of a **c** heart. 1249
77: 8 Is his mercy **c gone** for ever? doth *his* 656
Pr 14: 4 Where no oxen *are*, the crib *is* **c**: but 1249
16: 2 All the ways of a man *are* **c** in his own 2134
20: 9 Who can say, I have **made** my heart **c**, I am 2135
Ecc 9: 2 to the good and to the **c**, and to the unclean; 2889
Isa 1:16 Wash ye, **make** you **c**; put away the evil of 2135
24:19 the earth is **c dissolved**, the earth is 6565+6565
28: 8 *and* filthiness, *so that there is* no place **c**. NIH
30:24 that ear the ground shall eat **c** provender, 2548
52:11 be ye **c**, that bear the vessels of 1305
66:20 in a **c** vessel *into* the house of the LORD. 2889
Jer 13:27 wilt thou not be **made c**? when *shall it* 2891
Eze 22:26 *difference* between the unclean and the **c**, 2889
36:25 will I sprinkle **c** water upon you, and 2889
36:25 clean water upon you, and ye shall be **c**: 2891
44:23 to discern between the unclean and the **c**. 2889
Joel 1: 7 he hath **made** it **c** bare, and cast *it* away; 2834
Zec 11:17 his arm shall be **c dried up**, and 3001+3001
Mt 8: 2 Lord, if thou wilt, thou canst **make** me **c**. *2511*
8: 3 and touched him, saying, I will; be thou **c**. *2511*
23:25 for ye **make c** the outside of the cup and *2511*
23:26 that the outside of them may be **c** also. *2513*
27:59 the body, he wrapped it in a **c** linen cloth, *2513*
Mk 1:40 If thou wilt, thou canst **make** me **c**. *2511*
1:41 and saith unto him, I will; be thou **c**. *2511*
Lk 5:12 Lord, if thou wilt, thou canst **make** me **c**. *2511*
5:13 be thou **c**. And immediately the leprosy *2511*
11:39 Now do ye Pharisees **make c** the outside of *2511*
11:41 and behold, all *things* are **c** unto you. *2513*
Jn 13:10 save to wash *his* feet, but is **c** every whit: *2513*
13:10 clean every whit: and ye are **c**, but not all. *2513*
13:11 therefore said he, Ye are not all **c**. *2513*
15: 3 Now ye are **c** through the word which I *2513*
Ac 18: 6 blood *be* upon your own heads; I *am* **c**: *2513*
2Pe 2:18 those that were **c** escaped from them who *3689*
Rev 19: 8 should be arrayed in fine linen, **c** and white: *2513*
19:14 clothed in fine linen, white and **c**. *2513*

CLEANNESS (5) [CLEAN]
2Sa 22:21 according to the **c** of my hands hath he 1252
22:25 according to my **c** in his eye sight. 1252
Ps 18:20 according to the **c** of my hands hath he 1252
18:24 according to the **c** of my hands in his 1252
Am 4: 6 I also have given you **c** of teeth in all your 5356

CLEANSE (33) [CLEAN]
Ex 29:36 thou shalt **c** the altar, when thou hast made 2398
Lev 14:49 he shall take to **c** the house two birds, and 2398
14:52 he shall **c** the house with the blood of 2398
16:19 **c** it, and hallow it from the uncleanness of 2891
16:30 to **c** you, *that* ye may be clean from all your 2891
Nu 8: 6 among the children of Israel, and **c** them. 2891
8: 7 thus shalt thou do unto them, to **c** them: 2891
8:15 thou shalt **c** them, and offer them *for* an 2891
8:21 Aaron made an atonement for them to **c** 2891
2Ch 29:15 the LORD, to **c** the house of the LORD. 2891
29:16 to **c** *it*, and brought out all the uncleanness 2891
Ne 13:22 I commanded the Levites that they should **c** 2891
Ps 19:12 *his* errors? **c** thou me from secret *faults*. 5352
51: 2 from mine iniquity, and **c** me from my sin. 2891
119: 9 Wherewithal shall a young man **c** his way? 2135
Jer 4:11 daughter of my people, not to fan, nor to **c**, 1305
33: 8 I will **c** them from all their iniquity, 2891
Eze 36:25 and from all your idols, will I **c** you. 2891
37:23 wherein they have sinned, and will **c** them: 2891
39:12 burying of them, that *they* may **c** the land. 2891
39:14 remain upon the face of the earth, to **c** it: 2891
39:16 *be* Hamonah. Thus shall they **c** the land. 2891
43:20 round about: thus shalt thou **c** and purge it. 2398
43:22 they shall **c** the altar, as they did cleanse *it* 2398
43:22 the altar, as they did **c** *it* with the bullock. 2398
45:18 without blemish, and **c** the sanctuary: 2398
Joel 3:21 For I will **c** their blood *that* I have not 5352
Mt 10: 8 Heal the sick, **c** the lepers, raise the dead, *2511*
23:26 **c** first that *which is* within the cup and *2511*
2Co 7: 1 let us **c** ourselves from all filthiness of *2511*
Eph 5:26 **c** *it* with the washing of water by the word, *2511*
Jas 4: 8 **C** *your* hands, *ye* sinners; and purify *your* *2511*
1Jn 1: 9 and to **c** us from all unrighteousness. *2511*

CLEANSED (39) [CLEAN]
Lev 11:32 be unclean until the even; so it shall be **c**. 2891
12: 7 she shall be **c** from the issue of her blood. 2891
14: 4 take for him that is to be **c** two birds alive 2891
14: 7 he shall sprinkle upon him that is to be **c** 2891
14: 8 he that is to be **c** shall wash his clothes, 2891
14:14 the tip of the right ear of him that is to be **c**, 2891
14:17 the tip of the right ear of him that is to be **c**, 2891
14:18 pour upon the head of him that is to be **c**: 2891
14:19 make an atonement for him that is to be **c** 2891
14:25 the tip of the right ear of him that is to be **c**, 2891
14:28 the tip of the right ear of him that is to be **c**, 2891
14:29 put upon the head of him that is to be **c**, 2891
14:31 for him that is to be **c** before the LORD. 2891
15:13 when he that hath an issue is **c** of his issue; 2891
15:28 if she be **c** of her issue, then she shall 2891
Nu 35:33 the land cannot be **c** of the blood that is 3722
Jos 22:17 from which we are not **c** until this day, 2891

C

2Ch 29:18 We have **c** all the house of the LORD, and 2891
30:18 and Zebulun, had not **c** themselves, 2891
30:19 though *he be* not **c** according to NIH
34: 5 their altars, and **c** Judah and Jerusalem. 2891
Ne 13: 9 I commanded, and they **c** the chambers: 2891
13:30 Thus **c** I them from all strangers, and 2891
Job 35: 3 profit shall I have, *if I be* **c** from my sin? NIH
Ps 73:13 Verily I have **c** my heart *in* vain, and 2135
Eze 22:24 say unto her, Thou *art* the land that is not **c**, 2891
36:33 In the day that I shall have **c** you from all 2891
44:26 after he is **c**, they shall reckon unto him 2893
Da 8:14 hundred days; then shall the sanctuary be **c**. 6663
Joel 3:21 I will cleanse their blood *that* I have not **c**: 5352
Mt 8: 3 And immediately his leprosy was **c**. *2511*
11: 5 the lepers are **c**, and the deaf hear, *2511*
Mk 1:42 leprosy departed from him, and he was **c**. *2511*
Lk 4:27 and none of them was **c**, saving Naaman *2511*
7:22 lame walk, the lepers are **c**, the deaf hear, *2511*
17:14 to pass *that,* as they went, they were **c**. *2511*
17:17 Jesus answering said, Were there not ten **c**? *2511*
Ac 10:15 What God hath **c**, *that* call not thou *2511*
11: 9 What God hath **c**, *that* call not thou *2511*

CLEANSETH (3) [CLEAN]
Job 37:21 but the wind passeth, and **c** them. 2891
Pr 20:30 The blueness of a wound **c away** evil: so 8562
1Jn 1: 7 the blood of Jesus Christ his Son **c** us from *2511*

CLEANSING (10) [CLEAN]
Lev 13: 7 he hath been seen of the priest for his **c**, 2893
13:35 the scall spread much in the skin after his **c**; 2893
14: 2 be the law of the leper in the day of his **c**: 2893
14:23 on the eighth day for his **c** unto the priest, 2893
14:32 able to get *that which pertaineth* to his **c**. 2893
15:13 number to himself seven days for his **c**, 2893
Nu 6: 9 he shall shave his head in the day of his **c**, 2893
Eze 43:23 When thou hast made an end of **c** *it,* thou 2398
Mk 1:44 offer for thy **c** *those things* which Moses *2512*
Lk 5:14 thyself to the priest, and offer for thy **c**, *2512*

CLEAR (15) [CLEARER, CLEARING, CLEARLY, CLEARNESS]
Ge 24: 8 then thou shalt be **c** from this my oath: 5352
24:41 shalt thou be **c** from *this* my oath, 5352
24:41 if they give not thee *one,* thou shalt be **c** 5355
44:16 or how shall we **c** ourselves? God hath 6663
Ex 34: 7 *that* will by no means **c** *the guilty;* 5352+5352
2Sa 23: 4 out of the earth by **c shining** after rain. 5051
Ps 51: 4 thou speakest, *and* be **c** when thou judgest. 2135
SS 6:10 **c** as the sun, *and* terrible as *an army* with 1249
Isa 18: 4 I will consider in my dwelling place like a **c** 6703
Am 8: 9 and I will darken the earth in the **c** day: 216
Zec 14: 6 *that* the light shall not be **c**, *nor* dark: 3368
2Co 7:11 approved yourselves to be **c** in *this* matter. *53*
Rev 21:11 *even* like a jasper stone, **c as crystal**; *2929*
21:18 the city *was* pure gold, like unto **c** glass. *2513*
22: 1 **c** as crystal, proceeding out of the throne of *2986*

CLEARER (1) [CLEAR]
Job 11:17 *thine* age shall be **c** than the noonday; 6965

CLEARING (2) [CLEAR]
Nu 14:18 by no means **c** *the guilty,* visiting 5352+5352
2Co 7:11 yea, *what* **c** of yourselves, yea, *627*

CLEARLY (5) [CLEAR]
Job 33: 3 and my lips shall utter knowledge **c**. 1305
Mt 7: 5 shalt thou **see c** to cast out the mote out of *1227*
Mk 8:25 and he was restored, and saw every *man* **c**. *5081*
Lk 6:42 shalt thou **see c** to pull out the mote that is *1227*
Ro 1:20 from the creation of the world are **c seen**, *2529*

CLEARNESS (1) [CLEAR]
Ex 24:10 and as it were the body of heaven in *his* **c**. 2892

CLEAVE (30) [CLAVE, CLEAVED, CLEAVETH, CLOVEN, CLOVENFOOTED]
Ge 2:24 and his mother, and shall **c** unto his wife: 1692
Lev 1:17 And he shall **c** it with the wings thereof, *but* 8156
Dt 4: 4 ye that did **c** unto the LORD your God *are* 1695
10:20 to him shalt thou **c**, and swear by his name. 1692
11:22 to walk in all his ways, and to **c** unto him; 1692
13: 4 and you shall serve him, and **c** unto him. 1692
13:17 there shall **c** nought of the cursed thing to 1692
28:21 The LORD shall **make** the pestilence **c** 1692
28:60 wast afraid of; and they shall **c** unto thee. 1692
30:20 his voice, and that thou mayest **c** unto him: 1692
Jos 22: 5 to **c** unto him, and to serve him with all 1692
23: 8 **c** unto the LORD your God, as ye have 1692
23:12 **c** unto the remnant of these nations, 1692
2Ki 5:27 therefore of Naaman shall **c** unto thee, 1692
Job 38:38 and the clods **c fast together**? 1692
Ps 74:15 Thou didst **c** the fountain and the flood: 1234
101: 3 of them that turn aside; *it* shall not **c** to me. 1692
102: 5 of my groaning my bones **c to** my skin. 1692
137: 6 let my tongue **c** to the roof of my mouth; 1692
Isa 14: 1 and they shall **c** to the house of Jacob. 5596
Jer 13:11 have I **caused to c** unto me the whole 1692
Eze 3:26 I will **make** thy tongue **c** to the roof of thy 1692
Da 2:43 they shall not **c** one to another, even as iron 1693
11:34 but many shall **c** to them with flatteries. 3867
Hab 3: 9 Selah. Thou didst **c** the earth *with* rivers. 1234
Zec 14: 4 the mount of Olives shall **c** in the midst 1234
Mt 19: 5 and mother, and shall **c to** his wife: *4347*
Mk 10: 7 his father and mother, and **c** to his wife; *4347*
Ac 11:23 of heart *they* would **c unto** the Lord. *4357*
Ro 12: 9 *that which* is evil; **c** to *that which is* good. *2853*

CLEAVED (3) [CLEAVE]
2Ki 3: 3 Nevertheless he **c** unto the sins of Jeroboam 1692
Job 29:10 their tongue **c** to the roof of their mouth. 1692
31: 7 and *if any* blot hath **c** to my hands; 1692

CLEAVETH (13) [CLEAVE]
Dt 14: 6 **c** the cleft *into* two claws, *and* cheweth 8156
Job 16:13 he **c** my reins **asunder**, and doth not spare; 6398
19:20 My bone **c** to my skin and to my flesh, and 1692
Ps 22:15 my tongue **c** *to* my jaws; and thou hast 1692
41: 8 An evil disease, *say they,* **c fast** unto him: 3332
44:25 down to the dust: our belly **c** unto the earth. 1692
119:25 My soul **c** unto the dust: quicken thou me 1692
141: 7 one cutteth and **c** *wood* upon the earth. 1234
Ecc 10: 9 he that **c** wood shall be endangered thereby. 1234
Jer 13:11 For as the girdle **c** to the loins of a man, so 1692
La 4: 4 The tongue of the sucking child **c** to 1692
4: 8 their skin **c** to their bones; it is withered, 6821
Lk 10:11 which **c on** us, we do wipe off against you: *2853*

CLEFT (2) [CLEFTS]
Dt 14: 6 cleaveth the **c** *into* two claws, *and* 8157
Mic 1: 4 the valleys shall be **c**, as wax before 1234

CLEFTS (4) [CLEFT]
SS 2:14 O my dove, *that art* in the **c** of the rock, 2288
Jer 49:16 O thou that dwellest in the **c** of the rock, 2288
Am 6:11 *with* breaches, and the little house *with* **c**. 1233
Ob 1: 3 thou that dwellest in the **c** of the rock, 2288

CLEMENCY (1)
Ac 24: 4 thou wouldest hear us of thy **c** a few words. *1932*

CLEMENT (1)
Php 4: 3 with **C** also, and *with* other my *2815*

CLEOPAS (1)
Lk 24:18 And the one *of them,* whose name *was* **C**, *2810*

CLEOPHAS (1)
Jn 19:25 Mary the *wife* of **C**, and Mary Magdalene. *2832*

CLIFF (1) [CLIFT, CLIFTS]
2Ch 20:16 behold, they come up by the **c** of Ziz; and 4608

CLIFT (1) [CLIFF]
Ex 33:22 that I will put thee in a **c** of the rock, and 5366

CLIFTS (3) [CLIFF]
Job 30: 6 To dwell in the **c** of the valleys, *in* caves of 6178
Isa 2:21 To go into the **c** of the rocks, and into 5366
57: 5 in the valleys under the **c** of the rocks? 5585

CLIMB (4) [CLIMBED, CLIMBETH]
Jer 4:29 go into thickets, and **c up** upon the rocks: 5927
Joel 2: 7 *men;* they shall **c** the wall like men of war; 5927
2: 9 the wall, they shall **c up** upon the houses; 5927
Am 9: 2 though they **c up** *to* heaven, thence will I 5927

CLIMBED (2) [CLIMB]
1Sa 14:13 Jonathan **c up** upon his hands and upon his 5927
Lk 19: 4 and **c up** into a sycomore tree to see him: *305*

CLIMBETH (1) [CLIMB]
Jn 10: 1 but **c up** some other way, the same is a thief *305*

CLING See CLEAVE; CLEAVED; CLEAVETH

CLIP OFF See MAR

CLIPT (1)
Jer 48:37 every head *shall be* bald, and every beard **c**: 1639

CLOAK See CLOKE; GARMENT; RAIMENT; VESTURE

CLODS (6)
Job 7: 5 flesh is clothed with worms and **c** of dust; 1487
21:33 The **c** of the valley shall be sweet unto him, 7263
38:38 and the **c** cleave fast together? 7263
Isa 28:24 he open and **break the c** of his ground? 7702
Hos 10:11 shall plow, *and* Jacob shall **break** his **c**. 7702
Joel 1:17 The seed is rotten under their **c**, the garners 4053

CLOKE (7)
Isa 59:17 *for* clothing, and was clad with zeal as a **c**. 4598
Mt 5:40 take *away* thy coat, let him have *thy* **c** also. *2440*
Lk 6:29 him that taketh away thy **c** forbid not *to* *2440*
Jn 15:22 but now they have no **c** for their sin. *4392*
1Th 2: 5 as ye know, nor a **c** of covetousness; *4392*
2Ti 4:13 The **c** that I left at Troas with Carpus, *5341*
1Pe 2:16 not using *your* liberty for a **c** of *1942*

CLOPAS See CLEOPHAS

CLOSE (11) [CLOSED, CLOSER, CLOSEST]
Nu 5:13 be **kept c**, and she be defiled, and *there be* 5641
2Sa 22:46 they shall be afraid out of their **c places**. 4526
1Ch 12: 1 while he yet **kept** himself **c** because of Saul 6113
Job 28:21 and **kept c** from the fowls of the air. 5641
41:15 *his* pride, shut up *together as with* a **c** seal. 6862
Ps 18:45 and be afraid out of their **c places**. 4526
Jer 42:16 shall **follow c** after you there *in* Egypt; 1692
Da 8: 7 I saw him **come c** unto the ram, and he was 5060
Am 9:11 that is fallen, and **c up** the breaches thereof; 1443
Lk 9:36 And they **kept** *it* **c**, and told no *man* in *4601*
Ac 27:13 loosing *thence*, they sailed **c by** Crete. *788*

CLOSED (11) [CLOSE]
Ge 2:21 his ribs, and **c up** the flesh instead thereof; 5462
20:18 For the LORD had **fast c up** all 6113+6113
Nu 16:33 into the pit, and the earth **c** upon them: 3680
Jdg 3:22 the fat **c** upon the blade, so that he could 5462
Isa 1: 6 they have not been **c**, neither bound up, 2115
29:10 spirit of deep sleep, and hath **c** your eyes: 6105
Da 12: 9 for the words *are* **c up** and sealed till 5640
Jnh 2: 5 the depth **c** me **round about**, the weeds 5437
Mt 13:15 dull of hearing, and their eyes they have **c**; *2576*
Lk 4:20 And he **c** the book, and he gave *it* again to *4428*
Ac 28:27 dull of hearing, and their eyes have they **c**; *2576*

CLOSER (1) [CLOSE]
Pr 18:24 there is a friend *that* **sticketh c** than a 1695

CLOSEST (1) [CLOSE]
Jer 22:15 thou reign, because thou **c** *thyself* in cedar? 8474

CLOSET (2) [CLOSETS]
Joel 2:16 of his chamber, and the bride out of her **c**. 2646
Mt 6: 6 enter into thy **c**, and when thou hast shut *5009*

CLOSETS (1) [CLOSET]
Lk 12: 3 *that* which ye have spoken in the ear in **c** *5009*

CLOTH (18) [CLOTHE, SACKCLOTH, SACKCLOTHES]
Nu 4: 6 shall spread over *it* a **c** wholly of blue, and 899
4: 7 of shewbread they shall spread a **c** of blue, 899
4: 8 they shall spread upon them a **c** of scarlet, 899
4: 9 they shall take a **c** of blue, and cover 899
4:11 upon the golden altar they shall spread a **c** of 899
4:12 put *them* in a **c** of blue, and cover them with 899
4:13 from the altar, and spread a purple **c** thereon: 899
Dt 22:17 they shall spread the **c** before the elders of 8071
1Sa 19:13 *hair for* his bolster, and covered *it* with a **c**. 899
21: 9 it *is here* wrapt in a **c** behind the ephod: 8071
2Sa 20:12 *into* the field, and cast a **c** upon him, 899
2Ki 8:15 that he took a **thick c**, and dipt *it* in water, 4346
Isa 30:22 shalt cast them away as a **menstruous c**; 1739
Mt 9:16 No *man* putteth a piece of new **c** unto an *4470*
27:59 the body, he wrapped it in a clean **linen c**, *4616*
Mk 2:21 No *man* also seweth a piece of new **c** on an *4470*
14:51 having a **linen c** cast about *his* naked *body*; *4616*
14:52 And he left the **linen c**, and fled from them *4616*

CLOTHE (16) [CLOTH, CLOTHED, CLOTHES, CLOTHEST, CLOTHING, GRAVECLOTHES, UNCLOTHED]
Ex 40:14 shalt bring his sons, and **c** them with coats: 3847
Est 4: 4 she sent raiment to **c** Mordecai, and to take 3847
Ps 132:16 I will also **c** her priests **with** salvation: and 3847
132:18 His enemies will I **c with** shame: but 3847
Pr 23:21 and drowsiness shall **c** *a man* **with** rags. 3847
Isa 22:21 I will **c** him with thy robe, and 3847
49:18 thou shalt surely **c** thee **with** them all, 3847
50: 3 I **c** the heavens **with** blackness, and I make 3847
Eze 26:16 they shall **c** themselves **with** trembling; 3847
34: 3 Ye eat the fat, and ye **c** you **with** the wool, 3847
Hag 1: 6 *ye* **c** you, but there is none warm; and he 3847
Zec 3: 4 and *I will* **c** thee **with** change of raiment. 3847
Mt 6:30 Wherefore, if God so **c** the grass of the field, *294*
6:30 *shall he* not much more **c** you, O ye of little NIG
Lk 12:28 If then God so **c** the grass, which is to day in *294*
12:28 how much more *will he* **c** you, O ye of little NIG

CLOTHED (73) [CLOTHE]
Ge 3:21 God make coats of skins, and **c** them. 3847
Lev 8: 7 **c** him with the robe, and put the ephod 3847
2Sa 1:24 weep over Saul, who **c** you **in** scarlet, 3847
1Ch 15:27 David *was* **c** with a robe of fine linen, and 3736
21:16 the elders *of Israel, who were* **c** in 3680
2Ch 6:41 be **c** *with* salvation, and let thy saints 3847
18: 9 **c in** *their* robes, and they sat in a void place 3847
28:15 with the spoil **c** all *that were* naked among 3847
Est 4: 2 for none might enter into the king's gate **c** 3830
Job 7: 5 My flesh is **c with** worms and clods of 3847
8:22 They that hate thee shall be **c with** shame; 3847
10:11 Thou hast **c** me **with** skin and flesh, and 3847
29:14 I put on righteousness, and it **c** me: 3847
39:19 hast thou **c** his neck with thunder? 3847
Ps 35:26 let them be **c** with shame and 3847
65:13 The pastures are **c** with flocks; the valleys 3847
93: 1 The LORD reigneth, he is **c with** majesty; 3847
93: 1 the LORD is **c with** strength, 3847
104: 1 thou art **c with** honour and majesty. 3847
109:18 As he **c** himself **with** cursing like as with 3847
109:29 Let mine adversaries be **c with** shame, and 3847
132: 9 Let thy priests be **c** *with* righteousness; and 3847
Pr 31:21 for all her household *are* **c with** scarlet. 3847
Isa 61:10 for he hath **c** me **with** the garments of 3847
Eze 7:27 the prince shall be **c with** desolation, and 3847
9: 2 one man among them *was* **c** *with* linen, 3847
9: 3 he called to the man **c** *with* linen, 3847
9:11 behold, the man **c with** linen, which *had* 3847
10: 2 he spake unto the man **c with** linen, and 3847
10: 6 he had commanded the man **c with** linen, 3847
10: 7 put *it* into the hands of *him that was* **c with** 3847
16:10 I **c** thee also **with** broidered work, and 3847
23: 6 *Which were* **c with** blue, captains and 3847
23:12 captains and rulers **c** most gorgeously, 3847
38: 4 all of them **c with** all sorts *of armour, even* 3847
44:17 they shall be **c with** linen garments; 3847
Da 5: 7 shall be **c with** scarlet, and *have* a chain of 3848
5:16 thou shalt be **c with** scarlet, and *have* a 3848
5:29 they **c** Daniel **with** scarlet, and *put* a chain 3848
10: 5 and behold, a certain man **c** *in* linen, 3847
12: 6 *one* said to the man **c in** linen, which *was* 3847
12: 7 I heard the man **c in** linen, which *was* upon 3847
Zep 1: 8 and all such as are **c** with strange apparel. 3847
Zec 3: 3 Now Joshua was **c** with filthy garments, 3847
3: 5 upon his head, and **c** him **with** garments. 3847
Mt 6:31 we drink? or, Wherewithal shall we be **c**? *4016*
11: 8 A man **c** in soft raiment? behold, they that *294*
25:36 Naked, and ye **c** me: I was sick, and *4016*
25:38 and took *thee* in? or naked, and **c** *thee*? *4016*
25:43 naked, and ye **c** me not: sick, and in prison, *4016*
Mk 1: 6 And John was **c with** camel's hair, and *1746*
5:15 sitting, and **c**, and in his right mind: *2439*
15:17 And they **c** him **with** purple, and platted a *1746*
16: 5 on the right side, **c in** a long white garment; *4016*
Lk 7:25 A man **c** in soft raiment? Behold, they which *294*
8:35 at the feet of Jesus, **c**, and in his right mind: *2439*
16:19 which was **c in** purple and fine linen, and *1737*
2Co 5: 2 earnestly desiring to be **c upon with** our *1902*
5: 3 be that being **c** we shall not be found *1746*
5: 4 that we would be unclothed, but **c upon**, *1902*

C

1Pe 5: 5 one to another, and be **c with** humility: *1463*
Rev 1:13 **c with a garment** down to the foot, and *1746*
3: 5 the same shall be **c** in white raiment; *4016*
3:18 that thou mayest be **c**, and *that* the shame of *4016*
4: 4 twenty elders sitting, **c** in white raiment; *4016*
7: 9 **c** with white robes, and palms in their *4016*
10: 1 come down from heaven, **c with** a cloud: *4016*
11: 3 *and* threescore days, **c in** sackcloth. *4016*
12: 1 a woman **c with** the sun, and the moon *4016*
15: 6 **c in** pure and white linen, and having their *1746*
18:16 that was **c in** fine linen, and purple, and *4016*
19:13 And he *was* **c with** a vesture dipt in blood: *4016*
19:14 **c in** fine linen, white and clean. *1746*

CLOTHES (105) [CLOTHE]

Ge 37:29 Joseph *was* not in the pit; and he rent his **c**. 899
37:34 Jacob rent his **c**, and put sackcloth upon his 8071
44:13 they rent their **c**, and laded every man his 8071
49:11 in wine, and his **c** in the blood of grapes: 5497
Ex 12:34 bound up in their **c** upon their shoulders. 8071
19:10 and to morrow, and let them wash their **c**, 8071
19:14 the people; and they washed their **c**. 8071
31:10 the **c** of service, and the holy garments for 899
35:19 The **c** of service, to do service in the holy 899
39: 1 and scarlet, they made **c** of service, 899
39:41 The **c** of service to do service in the holy 899
Lev 10: 6 Uncover not your heads, neither rend your **c**; 899
11:25 of the carcase of them shall wash his **c**, 899
11:28 beareth the carcase of them shall wash his **c**, 899
11:40 eateth of the carcase of it shall wash his **c**, 899
11:40 that beareth the carcase of it shall wash his **c**, 899
13: 6 a scab: and he shall wash his **c**, and be clean. 899
13:34 and he shall wash his **c**, and be clean. 899
13:45 the leper in whom the plague *is,* his **c** shall 899
14: 8 he that is to be cleansed shall wash his **c**, 899
14: 9 he shall wash his **c**, also he shall wash his 899
14:47 he that lieth in the house shall wash his **c**; 899
14:47 he that eateth in the house shall wash his **c**. 899
15: 5 whosoever toucheth his bed shall wash his **c**, 899
15: 6 he sat that hath the issue shall wash his **c**, 899
15: 7 of him that hath the issue shall wash his **c**, 899
15: 8 he shall wash his **c**, and bathe *himself* in 899
15:10 beareth *any of* those *things* shall wash his **c**, 899
15:11 he shall wash his **c**, and bathe *himself* in 899
15:13 wash his **c**, and bathe his flesh in running 899
15:21 whosoever toucheth her bed shall wash his **c**, 899
15:22 any thing that she sat upon shall wash his **c**, 899
15:27 shall wash his **c**, and bathe *himself* in water, 899
16:26 the goat for the scapegoat shall wash his **c**, 899
16:28 he that burneth them shall wash his **c**, and 899
16:32 shall put on the linen **c**, *even* the holy 899
17:15 he shall both wash his **c**, and bathe *himself* 899
21:10 shall not uncover his head, nor rend his **c**; 899
Nu 8: 7 let them wash their **c**, and *so* 899
8:21 were purified, and they washed their **c**; 899
14: 6 of them that searched the land, rent their **c**: 899
19: 7 the priest shall wash his **c**, and he shall bathe 899
19: 8 he that burneth her shall wash his **c** in water, 899
19:10 the ashes of the heifer shall wash his **c**, 899
19:19 day he shall purify him*self,* and wash his **c**, 899
19:21 the water of separation shall wash his **c**; 899
31:24 ye shall wash your **c** on the seventh day, 899
Dt 29: 5 your **c** are not waxen old upon you, and 8008
Jos 7: 6 Joshua rent his **c**, and fell to the earth upon 8071
Jdg 11:35 that he rent his **c**, and said, Alas, 899
1Sa 4:12 came *to* Shiloh the same day with his **c** 4055
19:24 he stript off his **c** also, and prophesied before 899
2Sa 1: 2 out of the camp from Saul with his **c** rent, 899
1:11 David took hold on his **c**, and rent them; 899
3:31 Rent your **c**, and gird you with sackcloth, 899
13:31 all his servants stood *by* with their **c** rent. 899
19:24 nor trimmed his beard, nor washed his **c**, 899
1Ki 1: 1 they covered him with **c**, but he gat no heat. 899
21:27 that he rent his **c**, and put sackcloth upon his 899
2Ki 2:12 he took hold of his own **c**, and rent them in 899
5: 7 that he rent his **c**, and said, *Am* I God, to kill 899
5: 8 heard that the king of Israel had rent his **c**, 899
5: 8 saying, Wherefore hast thou rent thy **c**? 899
6:30 the words of the woman, that he rent his **c**; 899
11:14 Athaliah rent her **c**, and cried, Treason, 899
18:37 to Hezekiah with *their* **c** rent, and told him 899
19: 1 king Hezekiah heard *it,* that he rent his **c**, 899
22:11 of the book of the law, that he rent his **c**. 899
22:19 and hast rent thy **c**, and wept before me; 899
2Ch 23:13 Then Athaliah rent her **c**, and said, Treason, 899
34:19 heard the words of the law, that he rent his **c**. 899
34:27 and didst rend thy **c**, and weep before me; 899
Ne 4:23 which followed me, none of us put off our **c**, 899
9:21 their **c** waxed not old, and their feet swelled 8008
Est 4: 1 Mordecai rent his **c**, and put on sackcloth 899
Job 9:31 the ditch, and mine own **c** shall abhor me. 8008
Pr 6:27 fire in his bosom, and his **c** not be burnt? 899
Isa 36:22 to Hezekiah with *their* **c** rent, and told him 899
37: 1 king Hezekiah heard *it,* that he rent his **c**, 899
Jer 41: 5 their **c** rent, and having cut themselves, 899
Eze 16:39 they shall strip thee also of thy **c**, and 899
23:26 They shall also strip thee out of thy **c**, and 899
27:20 Dedan *was* thy merchant in precious **c** for 899
27:24 in blue **c**, and broidered work, and in chests 1545
Am 2: 8 they lay *themselves* down upon **c** laid to 899
Mt 21: 7 and the colt, and put on them their **c**, *2440*
24:18 is in the field return back to take his **c**. *2440*
26:65 Then the high priest rent his **c**, saying, *2440*
Mk 5:28 For she said, If I may touch but his **c**, *2440*
5:30 in the press, and said, Who touched my **c**? *2440*
14:63 Then the high priest rent his **c**, and saith, *5509*
15:20 and put his own **c** on him, and led him out *2440*
Lk 2: 7 and **wrapped** him **in swaddling c**, and *4683*
2:12 find *the* babe **wrapped in swaddling c**, *4683*
8:27 and ware no **c**, neither abode in *any* house, *2440*
19:36 as he went, they spread their **c** in the way. *2440*
24:12 he beheld the **linen c** laid by themselves, *3608*
Jn 19:40 and wound it in **linen c** with the spices, *3608*
20: 5 and looking in, saw the **linen c** lying; *3608*
20: 6 into the sepulchre, and seeth the **linen c** lie, *3608*
20: 7 not lying with the **linen c**, but *3608*
Ac 7:58 the witnesses laid down their **c** at a young *2440*
14:14 heard *of,* they rent their **c**, and ran in among *2440*
16:22 and the magistrates rent off their **c**, and *2440*
22:23 and cast *off their* **c**, and threw dust into *2440*

CLOTHEST (1) [CLOTHE]

Jer 4:30 Though thou **c** thyself **with** crimson, 3847

CLOTHING (19) [CLOTHE]

Job 22: 6 for nought, and stripped the naked of their **c**. 899
24: 7 They cause the naked to lodge without **c**, 3830
24:10 They cause *him* to go naked without **c**, and 3830
31:19 If I have seen *any* perish for want of **c**, or 3830
Ps 35:13 when they were sick, my **c** *was* sackcloth: 3830
45:13 glorious within: her **c** *is* of wrought gold. 3830
Pr 27:26 The lambs *are* for thy **c**, and the goats *are* 3830
31:22 of tapestry; her **c** *is* silk and purple. 3830
31:25 Strength and honour *are* her **c**; and she shall 3830
Isa 3: 6 *saying,* Thou hast **c**, be thou our ruler, and 8071
3: 7 for in my house *is* neither bread nor **c**: 8071
23:18 to eat sufficiently, and for durable **c**. 4374
59:17 **put on** the garments of vengeance
for **c**, 3847+8516
Jer 10: 9 blue and purple *is* their **c**: they *are* all 3830
Mt 7:15 which come to you in sheep's **c**, but *1742*
11: 8 they that wear soft *c* are in kings' houses. NIG
Mk 12:38 which love to go in **long c**, and *4749*
Ac 10:30 behold, a man stood before me in bright **c**, *2066*
Jas 2: 3 have respect to him that weareth the gay **c**, *2066*

CLOUD (107) [CLOUDS, CLOUDY]

Ge 9:13 I do set my bow in the **c**, and it shall be for 6051
9:14 when I **bring a c** over the earth, 6049+6051
9:14 that the bow shall be seen in the **c**: 6051
9:16 the bow shall be in the **c**; and I will look 6051
Ex 13:21 went before them by day in a pillar of a **c**, 6051
13:22 He took not away the pillar of the **c** by day, 6051
14:19 the pillar of the **c** went from before their 6051
14:20 it was a **c** and darkness *to them,* but it gave 6051
14:24 through the pillar of fire and of the **c**, 6051
16:10 the glory of the LORD appeared in the **c**. 6051
19: 9 Lo, I come unto thee in a thick **c**, 6051
19:16 a thick **c** upon the mount, and the voice of 6051
24:15 into the mount, and a **c** covered the mount. 6051
24:16 mount Sinai, and the **c** covered it six days: 6051
24:16 called unto Moses out of the midst of the **c**. 6051
24:18 Moses went into the midst of the **c**, and 6051
34: 5 the LORD descended in the **c**, and 6051
40:34 a **c** covered the tent of the congregation, 6051
40:35 because the **c** abode thereon, and the glory 6051
40:36 when the **c** was taken up from over 6051
40:37 if the **c** were not taken up, then 6051

Ex 40:38 For the **c** of the LORD *was* upon 6051
Lev 16: 2 for I will appear in the **c** upon the mercy 6051
16:13 that the **c** of the incense may cover 6051
Nu 9:15 the **c** covered the tabernacle, *namely,* 6051
9:16 the **c** covered it *by day,* and the appearance 6051
9:17 when the **c** was taken up from 6051
9:17 in the place where the **c** abode, there 6051
9:18 as long as the **c** abode upon the tabernacle 6051
9:19 when the **c** tarried long upon the tabernacle 6051
9:20 when the **c** was a few days upon 6051
9:21 when the **c** abode from even unto 6051
9:21 *that* the **c** was taken up in the morning, then 6051
9:21 by day or by night that the **c** was taken up, 6051
9:22 that the **c** tarried upon the tabernacle, 6051
10:11 *that* the **c** was taken up from off 6051
10:12 and the **c** rested in the wilderness of Paran. 6051
10:34 the **c** of the LORD *was* upon them by day, 6051
11:25 the LORD came down in a **c**, and 6051
12: 5 LORD came down in the pillar of the **c**, 6051
12:10 the **c** departed from off the tabernacle; and 6051
14:14 *that* thy **c** standeth over them, and *that* thou 6051
14:14 by day time in a pillar of a **c**, and in a pillar 6051
16:42 the **c** covered it, and the glory of 6051
Dt 1:33 what way ye should go, and in a **c** by day. 6051
5:22 of the **c**, and of the thick darkness, *with* a 6051
31:15 appeared in the tabernacle in a pillar of a **c**: 6051
31:15 the pillar of the **c** stood over the door of 6051
1Ki 8:10 that the **c** filled the house of the LORD, 6051
8:11 not stand to minister because of the **c**: 6051
18:44 there ariseth a little **c** out of the sea, 5645
2Ch 5:13 that *then* the house was filled *with* a **c**, 6051
5:14 not stand to minister by reason of the **c**: 6051
Ne 9:19 the pillar of the **c** departed not from them 6051
Job 3: 5 of death stain it; let a **c** dwell upon it; 6053
7: 9 *As* the **c** is consumed and vanisheth away: 6051
22:13 can he judge through the dark **c**? NIH
26: 8 and the **c** is not rent under them. 6051
26: 9 of *his* throne, *and* spreadeth his **c** upon it. 6051
30:15 and my welfare passeth away as a **c**. 5645
36:32 commandeth it *not to shine* by *the* **c** that NIH
37:11 Also by watering he wearieth the **thick c**: 5645
37:11 the thick cloud: he scattereth his bright **c**: 6051
37:15 and caused the light of his **c** to shine? 6051
38: 9 When I made the **c** the garment thereof, and 6051
Ps 78:14 In the daytime also he led them with a **c**, 6051
105:39 He spread a **c** for a covering; and fire to 6051
Pr 16:15 and his favour *is* as a **c** of the latter rain. 5645
Isa 4: 5 a **c** and smoke by day, and the shining of a 6051
18: 4 *and* like a **c** of dew in the heat of harvest. 5645
19: 1 the LORD rideth upon a swift **c**, and 5645
25: 5 *even* the heat with the shadow of a **c**: 5645
44:22 I have blotted out, as a **thick c**, 5645
44:22 thy transgressions, and, as a **c**, thy sins: 6051
60: 8 Who *are* these *that* fly as a **c**, and as 5645
La 2: 1 **covered** the daughter of Zion **with a c** in 5743
3:44 Thou hast covered thyself with a **c**, that *our* 6051
Eze 1: 4 a great **c**, and a fire infolding itself, and 6051
1:28 the appearance of the bow that is in the **c** 6051
8:11 his hand; and a thick **c** of incense went up. 6051
10: 3 went in; and the **c** filled the inner court. 6051
10: 4 the house was filled with the **c**, and 6051
30:18 a **c** shall cover her, and her daughters shall 6051
32: 7 I will cover the sun with a **c**, and the moon 6051
38: 9 thou shalt be like a **c** to cover the land, 6051
38:16 people of Israel, as a **c** to cover the land; 6051
Hos 6: 4 for your goodness *is* as a morning **c**, and 6051
13: 3 Therefore they shall be as the morning **c**, 6051
Mt 17: 5 behold, a bright **c** overshadowed them: *3507*
17: 5 and behold a voice out of the **c**, which said, *3507*
Mk 9: 7 And there was a **c** that overshadowed them: *3507*
9: 7 and a voice came out of the **c**, saying, *3507*
Lk 9:34 there came a **c**, and overshadowed them: *3507*
9:34 and they feared as they entered into the **c**. *3507*
9:35 And there came a voice out of the **c**, saying, *3507*
12:54 When ye see a **c** rise out of the west, *3507*
21:27 shall they see the Son of man coming in a **c** *3507*
Ac 1: 9 and a **c** received him out of their sight. *3507*
1Co 10: 1 how that all our fathers were under the **c**, *3507*
10: 2 And were all baptized unto Moses in the **c** *3507*
Heb 12: 1 about with so great a **c** of witnesses, *3509*
Rev 10: 1 come down from heaven, clothed with a **c**: *3507*
11:12 And they ascended up to heaven in a **c**; and *3507*
14:14 and behold a white **c**, and upon the cloud *3507*
14:14 upon the **c** one sat like unto the Son of man, *3507*
14:15 with a loud voice to him that sat on the **c**, *3507*
14:16 And he that sat on the **c** thrust in his sickle *3507*

CLOUDS (49) [CLOUD]
Dt 4:11 *with* darkness, **c**, and thick darkness. 6051
Jdg 5: 4 heavens dropped, the **c** also dropped water. 5645
2Sa 22:12 dark waters, *and* **thick c** of the skies. 5645
23: 4 the sun riseth, *even* a morning without **c**; 5645
1Ki 18:45 that the heaven was black *with* **c** and wind, 5645
Job 20: 6 the heavens, and his head reach unto the **c**; 5645
22:14 **Thick c** *are* a covering to him, that he seeth 5645
26: 8 He bindeth up the waters in his **thick c**; and 5645
35: 5 behold the **c** *which* are higher than thou. 7834
36:28 Which the **c** do drop *and* distil upon man 7834
36:29 can *any* understand the spreadings of the **c**, 5645
36:32 With **c** he covereth the light; and 3709
37:16 Dost thou know the balancings of the **c**, 5645
37:21 see not the bright light which *is* in the **c**: 7834
38:34 Canst thou lift up thy voice to the **c**, 5645
38:37 Who can number the **c** in wisdom? or 7834
Ps 18:11 *were* dark waters *and* **thick c** of the skies. 5645
18:12 *that was* before him his **thick c** passed, 5645
36: 5 *and* thy faithfulness *reacheth* unto the **c**. 7834
57:10 unto the heavens, and thy truth unto the **c**. 7834
68:34 *is* over Israel, and his strength *is* in the **c**. 7834
77:17 The **c** poured out water: the skies sent out a 5645
78:23 Though he had commanded the **c** from 7834
97: 2 **C** and darkness *are* round about him: 6051
104: 3 who maketh the **c** his chariot: who walketh 5645
108: 4 and thy truth *reacheth* unto the **c**. 7834
147: 8 Who covereth the heaven with **c**, 5645
Pr 3:20 broken up, and the **c** drop down the dew. 7834
8:28 When he established the **c** above: when *he* 7834
25:14 boasteth himself of a false gift *is like* **c** 5387
Ecc 11: 3 If the **c** be full *of* rain, they empty 5645
11: 4 and he that regardeth the **c** shall not reap. 5645
12: 2 not darkened, nor the **c** return after the rain: 5645
Isa 5: 6 I will also command the **c** that they rain no 5645
14:14 I will ascend above the heights of the **c**; 5645
Jer 4:13 he shall come up as **c**, and his chariots *shall* 6051
Da 7:13 *one* like the Son of man came with the **c** of 6050
Joel 2: 2 a day of **c** and of thick darkness, 6051
Na 1: 3 the storm, and the **c** *are* the dust of his feet. 6051
Zep 1:15 gloominess, a day of **c** and thick darkness, 6051
Zec 10: 1 *so* the LORD *shall* make **bright c**, and 2385
Mt 24:30 man coming in the **c** of heaven with power *3507*
26:64 of power, and coming in the **c** of heaven. *3507*
Mk 13:26 of man coming in *the* **c** with great power *3507*
14:62 of power, and coming in the **c** of heaven. *3507*
1Th 4:17 be caught up together with them in the **c**, *3507*
2Pe 2:17 **c** that are carried with a tempest; *3507*
Jude 1:12 **c** *they are* without water, carried about of *3507*
Rev 1: 7 Behold, he cometh with **c**; and every eye *3507*

CLOUDY (6) [CLOUD]
Ex 33: 9 the **c** pillar descended, and stood *at* the door 6051
33:10 all the people saw the **c** pillar stand *at* 6051
Ne 9:12 thou leddest them in the day by a **c** pillar; 6051
Ps 99: 7 He spake unto them in the **c** pillar: 6051
Eze 30: 3 even the day of the LORD *is* near, a **c** day; 6051
34:12 where they have been scattered in the **c** 6051

CLOUTED (1) [CLOUTS]
Jos 9: 5 old shoes and **c** upon their feet, and 2921

CLOUTS (2) [CLOUTED]
Jer 38:11 took thence old **cast c** and old rotten rags, 5499
38:12 Put now *these* old **cast c** and rotten rags 5499

CLOVEN (2) [CLEAVE]
Dt 14: 7 the cud, or of them that divide the **c** hoof; 8156
Ac 2: 3 And there appeared unto them **c** tongues *1266*

CLOVENFOOTED (3) [CLEAVE, FOOT]
Lev 11: 3 *is* **c**, *and* cheweth cud, 6541+8156+8157
11: 7 he divide the hoof, and *be* **c**, 6541+8156+8157
11:26 *is* not **c**, nor cheweth the cud, 8156+8157

CLUB See DARTS

CLUBS See STAVES

CLUNG See CLAVE; CLEAVE; CLEAVED; CLEAVETH

CLUSTER (5) [CLUSTERS]
Nu 13:23 cut down from thence a branch with one **c** of 811

Nu 13:24 of the **c of grapes** which the children of 811
SS 1:14 My beloved *is* unto me *as* a **c** of camphire in 811
Isa 65: 8 As the new wine is found in the **c**, and 811
Mic 7: 1 *there is* no **c** to eat: my soul desired 811

CLUSTERS (7) [CLUSTER]
Ge 40:10 *and* the **c** thereof brought forth ripe grapes: 811
Dt 32:32 grapes *are* grapes of gall, their **c** *are* bitter: 811
1Sa 25:18 parched *corn,* and an hundred **c of raisins**, 6778
30:12 of a cake *of figs,* and two **c of raisins**: 6778
SS 7: 7 a palm tree, and thy breasts to **c** *of grapes.* 811
7: 8 now also thy breasts shall be as **c** of the vine, 811
Rev 14:18 and gather the **c** of the vine of the earth; *1009*

CNIDUS (1)
Ac 27: 7 and scarce were come over against **C**, *2834*

COAL (4) [COALS]
2Sa 14: 7 and *so* they shall quench my **c** which is left, 1513
Isa 6: 6 unto me, having a **live c** in his hand, 7531
47:14 *there shall* not *be* a **c** to warm at, *nor* fire to 1513
La 4: 8 Their visage is blacker than a **c**; they are 7815

COALS (26) [COAL]
Lev 16:12 he shall take a censer full of **burning c** of 1513
2Sa 22: 9 his mouth devoured: **c** were kindled by it. 1513
22:13 Through the brightness before him were **c** 1513
1Ki 19: 6 *there was* a cake **baken on the c**, and 7529
Job 41:21 His breath kindleth **c**, and a flame goeth out 1513
Ps 18: 8 his mouth devoured: **c** were kindled by it. 1513
18:12 clouds passed, hail-*stones* and **c** of fire. 1513
18:13 gave his voice; hail-*stones* and **c** of fire. 1513
120: 4 arrows of the mighty, with **c** of juniper. 1513
140:10 Let **burning c** fall upon them: let them be 1513
Pr 6:28 Can one go upon **hot c**, and his feet not be 1513
25:22 For thou shalt heap **c of fire** upon his head, 1513
26:21 *As* **c** *are* to burning coals, and wood to fire; 6352
26:21 *As* coals *are* to **burning c**, and wood to 1513
SS 8: 6 the **c** thereof *are* coals of fire, *which hath* a 7565
8: 6 the coals thereof *are* **c** of fire, *which hath* a 7565
Isa 44:12 smith *with* the tongs both worketh in the **c**, 6352
44:19 also I have baked bread upon the **c** thereof; 1513
54:16 I have created the smith that bloweth the **c** 6352
Eze 1:13 their appearance *was* like burning **c** of fire, 1513
10: 2 fill thine hand *with* **c** of fire from between 1513
24:11 set it empty upon the **c** thereof, that 1513
Hab 3: 5 and **burning c** went forth at his feet. 7565
Jn 18:18 stood *there,* who had made a **fire of c**; *439*
21: 9 they saw a **fire of c** there, and fish laid *439*
Ro 12:20 doing thou shalt heap **c** of fire on his head. *440*

COARSE JOKING See JESTING

COAST (62) [COASTS]
Ex 10: 4 morrow will I bring the locusts into thy **c**: 1366
Nu 13:29 dwell by the sea, and by the **c** of Jordan. 3027
20:23 by the **c** of the land of Edom, saying, 1366
22:36 border of Arnon, which *is* in the utmost **c**. 1366
24:24 And ships *shall come* from the **c** of Chittim, 3027
34: 3 wilderness of Zin along by the **c** of Edom, 1366
34: 3 **outmost c** of the salt sea eastward: 4480+7097
34:11 the **c** shall go down from Shepham *to* 1366
Dt 2: 4 Ye are to pass through the **c** of your 1366
2:18 over *through* Ar, the **c** of Moab, *this* day: 1366
3:17 the **c** *thereof,* from Chinnereth even unto 1366
11:24 even unto the uttermost sea shall your **c** be. 1366
16: 4 bread seen with thee in all thy **c** seven days; 1366
19: 8 if the LORD thy God enlarge thy **c**, as he 1366
Jos 1: 4 the going down of the sun, shall be your **c**. 1366
12: 4 the **c** of Og king of Bashan, *which was* of 1366
12:23 The king of Dor in the **c** of Dor, one; 5299
13:16 their **c** was from Aroer, that *is* on the bank 1366
13:25 their **c** was Jazer, and all the cities of 1366
13:30 their **c** was from Mahanaim, all Bashan, 1366
15: 1 *was* the uttermost part of the south **c**. NIH
15: 4 and the goings out of that **c** were at the sea: 1366
15: 4 were at the sea: this shall be your south **c**. 1366
15:12 the **c** *thereof.* This *is* the coast of 1366
15:12 the coast *thereof.* This *is* the **c** of 1366
15:21 the **c** of Edom southward were Kabzeel, 1366
16: 3 goeth down westward to the **c** of Japhleti, 1366
16: 3 unto the **c** of Beth-horon the nether, and 1366
17: 7 the **c** of Manasseh was from Asher *to* 1366
17: 9 the **c** descended *unto* the river Kanah, 1366
17: 9 the **c** of Manasseh also *was* on the north 1366
18: 5 Judah shall abide in their **c** on the south, 1366
18:11 the **c** of their lot came forth between 1366
18:19 south end of Jordan: this *was* the south **c**. 1366
19:22 the **c** reacheth to Tabor, and Shahazimah, 1366
19:29 *then* the **c** turneth *to* Ramah, and to 1366
19:29 the **c** turneth *to* Hosah; and the outgoings 1366
19:29 thereof are at the sea from the **c** to Achzib: 2256
19:33 their **c** was from Heleph, from Allon to 1366
19:34 the **c** turneth westward *to* Aznoth-tabor, 1366
19:41 the **c** of their inheritance was Zorah, and 1366
19:47 the **c** of the children of Dan went out *too* 1366
Jdg 1:18 Also Judah took Gaza with the **c** thereof, 1366
1:18 Askelon with the **c** thereof, and Ekron with 1366
1:18 coast thereof, and Ekron with the **c** thereof. 1366
1:36 the **c** of the Amorites *was* from the going 1366
11:20 trusted not Israel to pass through his **c**: 1366
1Sa 6: 9 if it goeth up *by* the way of his own **c** *to* 1366
7:13 and they came no more into the **c** of Israel: 1366
27: 1 to seek me any more in any **c** of Israel: 1366
30:14 upon *the* **c** which *belongeth* to Judah, and NIH
2Ki 14:25 He restored the **c** of Israel from the entering 1366
1Ch 4:10 enlarge my **c**, and that thine hand might be 1366
Eze 25:16 and destroy the remnant of the sea **c**. 2348
47:16 which *is* by the **c** of Hauran. 1366
48: 1 From the north end to the **c** of the way of 3027
48: 1 Damascus northward, to the **c** of Hamath; 3027
Zep 2: 5 Woe unto the inhabitants of the sea **c**, 2256
2: 6 the sea **c** shall be dwellings *and* cottages for 2256
2: 7 the **c** shall be for the remnant of the house 2256
Mt 4:13 in Capernaum, which is **upon the sea c**, *3864*
Lk 6:17 and *from* the **sea c** of Tyre and Sidon, *3882*

COASTS (51) [COAST]
Ex 10:14 of Egypt, and rested in all the **c** of Egypt: 1366
10:19 there remained not one locust in all the **c** of 1366
Nu 21:13 that cometh out of the **c** of the Amorites: 1366
32:33 the land, with the cities thereof in the **c**, 1367
34: 2 *even* the land of Canaan with the **c** thereof:) 1367
34:12 this shall be your land with the **c** thereof 1367
Dt 3:14 the country of Argob unto the **c** of Geshuri 1366
19: 3 thee a way, and divide the **c** of thy land, 1366
28:40 shalt have olive trees throughout all thy **c**, 1366
Jos 9: 1 in all the **c** of the great sea over against 2348
18: 5 the house of Joseph shall abide in their **c** on 1366
18:20 by the **c** thereof round about, according to 1367
19:49 dividing the land for inheritance by their **c**, 1367
Jdg 11:22 they possessed all the **c** of the Amorites, 1366
11:26 in all the cities that *be* along by the **c** of 3027
18: 2 sent of their family five men from their **c**, 7098
19:29 and sent her into all the **c** of Israel. 1366
1Sa 5: 6 *even* Ashdod and the **c** thereof. 1366
7:14 the **c** thereof did Israel deliver out of 1366
11: 3 that we may send messengers unto all the **c** 1366
11: 7 sent *them* throughout all the **c** of Israel by 1366
2Sa 21: 5 from remaining in any of the **c** of Israel, 1366
1Ki 1: 3 a fair damsel throughout all the **c** of Israel, 1366
2Ki 10:32 Hazael smote them in all the **c** of Israel; 1366
15:16 *were* therein, and the **c** thereof from Tirzah: 1366
1Ch 6:54 places throughout their castles in their **c**, 1366
6:66 cities of their **c** out of the tribe of Ephraim. 1366
21:12 destroying throughout all the **c** of Israel. 1366
2Ch 11:13 all Israel resorted to him out of all their **c**. 1366
Ps 105:31 divers sorts *of flies, and* lice in all their **c**. 1366
105:33 their fig trees; and brake the trees of their **c**. 1366
Jer 25:32 shall be raised up from the **c** of the earth. 3411
31: 8 and gather them from the **c** of the earth, *and* 3411
50:41 many kings shall be raised up from the **c** of 3411
Eze 33: 2 the people of the land take a man of their **c**, 7097
Joel 3: 4 and Zidon, and all the **c** of Palestine? 1552
Mt 2:16 and in all the **c** thereof, from two years old *3725*
8:34 *him* that he would depart out of their **c**. *3725*
15:21 and departed into the **c** of Tyre and Sidon. *3313*
15:22 woman of Canaan came out of the same **c**, *3725*
15:39 took ship, and came into the **c** of Magdala. *3725*
16:13 When Jesus came into the **c** of Cesarea *3313*
19: 1 came into the **c** of Judea beyond Jordan; *3725*
Mk 5:17 began to pray him to depart out of their **c**. *3725*
7:31 departing from the **c** of Tyre and Sidon, *3725*
7:31 through the midst of the **c** of Decapolis. *3725*
10: 1 cometh into the **c** of Judea by the farther *3725*
Ac 13:50 Barnabas, and expelled them out of their **c**. *3725*
19: 1 Paul having passed through the upper **c** *3313*
26:20 and throughout all the **c** of Judea, and *then* *5561*
27: 2 meaning to sail by the **c** of Asia; *5117*

COAT (25) [COATS]
Ge 37: 3 and he made him a c of many colours. 3801
37:23 that they stript Joseph out of his c, 3801
37:23 *his* c of many colours that *was* on him; 3801
37:31 they took Joseph's c, and killed a kid of 3801
37:31 of the goats, and dipped the c in the blood; 3801
37:32 they sent the c of many colours, and 3801
37:32 know now whether it *be* thy son's c or no. 3801
37:33 he knew it, and said, *It is* my son's c; 3801
Ex 28: 4 a robe, and a broidered c, a mitre, and 3801
28:39 thou shalt embroider the c of fine linen, 3801
29: 5 put upon Aaron the c, and the robe of 3801
Lev 8: 7 he put upon him the c, and girded him with 3801
16: 4 He shall put on the holy linen c, and 3801
1Sa 2:19 Moreover his mother made him a little c, 4598
17: 5 and he *was* armed with a c of mail; 8302
17: 5 the weight of the c *was* five thousand 8302
17:38 also he armed him with a c *of mail*. 8302
2Sa 15:32 Archite *came* to meet him with his c rent, 3801
Job 30:18 it bindeth me about as the collar of my c. 3801
SS 5: 3 I have put off my c; how shall I put it on? 3801
Mt 5:40 and take *away* thy c, let him have *thy* cloke 5509
Lk 6:29 away thy cloke forbid not *to take thy* c also. 5509
Jn 19:23 to every soldier a part; and *also his* c: 5509
19:23 now the c was without seam, woven from 5509
21: 7 he girt *his* **fisher's c** unto him, (for he was 1903

COAT OF ARMOR See HABERGEONS

COATS (14) [COAT]
Ge 3:21 to his wife did the LORD God make c of 3801
Ex 28:40 for Aaron's sons thou shalt make c, and 3801
29: 8 shalt bring his sons, and put c upon them. 3801
39:27 they made c *of* fine linen *of* woven work 3801
40:14 shalt bring his sons, and clothe them with c: 3801
Lev 8:13 put c upon them, and girded them *with* 3801
10: 5 and carried them in their c out of the camp; 3801
Da 3:21 these men were bound in their c, 5622
3:27 head singed, neither were their c changed, 5622
Mt 10:10 neither two c, neither shoes, nor yet staves: 5509
Mk 6: 9 *be* shod with sandals; and not put on two c. 5509
Lk 3:11 and saith unto them, He that hath two c, 5509
9: 3 neither money; neither have two c apiece. 5509
Ac 9:39 and shewing the c and garments which 5509

COBRA See ASP; ASPS

COCK (12) [COCKCROWING]
Mt 26:34 unto thee, That this night, before *the* c crow, 220
26:74 not the man. And immediately *the* c crew. 220
26:75 which said unto him, Before *the* c crow, 220
Mk 14:30 *even* in this night, before *the* c crow twice, 220
14:68 he went out into the porch; and *the* c crew. 220
14:72 And the second time *the* c crew. And Peter 220
14:72 Before *the* c crow twice, thou shalt deny me 220
Lk 22:34 tell thee, Peter, *the* c shall not crow this day, 220
22:60 while he yet spake, the c crew. 220
22:61 Before *the* c crow, thou shalt deny me thrice. 220
Jn 13:38 verily, I say unto thee, *The* c shall not crow, 220
18:27 denied again: and immediately *the* c crew. 220

COCKATRICE (1) [COCKATRICE', COCKATRICES]
Isa 14:29 of the serpent's root shall come forth a c, 6848

COCKATRICE' (2) [COCKATRICE]
Isa 11: 8 the weaned child shall put his hand on the c 6848
59: 5 They hatch c eggs, and weave the spider's 6848

COCKATRICES (1) [COCKATRICE]
Jer 8:17 I will send serpents, c, among you, 6848

COCKCROWING (1) [COCK, CROW]
Mk 13:35 or at midnight, or at the c, or in the morning: 219

COCKLE (1)
Job 31:40 instead of wheat, and c instead of barley. 890

COFFER (3)
1Sa 6: 8 a trespass offering, in a c by the side thereof; 712
6:11 the c with the mice of gold and the images of 712
6:15 the c that *was* with it, wherein the jewels of 712

COFFIN (1)
Ge 50:26 and he was put in a c in Egypt. 727

COGITATIONS (1)
Da 7:28 my c much troubled me, and 7476

COINS See PENCE

COLD (18)
Ge 8:22 c and heat, and summer and winter, and 7120
Job 24: 7 that *they have* no covering in the c. 7135
37: 9 the whirlwind: and c out of the north. 7135
Ps 147:17 like morsels: who can stand before his c? 7135
Pr 20: 4 sluggard will not plow by reason of the c; 2779
25:13 As the c of snow in the time of harvest, *so* 6793
25:20 *As* he that taketh away a garment in c 7135
25:25 *As* c waters to a thirsty soul, so *is* good 7119
Jer 18:14 shall the c flowing waters that come from 7119
Na 3:17 which camp in the hedges in the c day, *but* 7135
Mt 10:42 of c *water* only in the name of a disciple, 5593
24:12 shall abound, the love of many shall **wax c**. 5594
Jn 18:18 who had made a fire of coals; for it was c: 5592
Ac 28: 2 of the present rain, and because of the c. 5592
2Co 11:27 thirst, in fastings often, in c and nakedness. 5592
Rev 3:15 thy works, that thou art neither c nor hot: 5593
3:15 cold nor hot: I would thou wert c or hot. 5593
3:16 thou art lukewarm, and neither c nor hot, 5593

COL-HOZEH (2)
Ne 3:15 the fountain repaired Shallun the son of C, 3626
11: 5 the son of C, the son of Hazaiah, the son of 3626

COLLAR (1) [COLLARS]
Job 30:18 it bindeth me about as the c of my coat. 6310

COLLARS (1) [COLLAR]
Jdg 8:26 c, and purple raiment that *was* on the kings 5188

COLLECTION (3)
2Ch 24: 6 in out of Judah and out of Jerusalem the c, 4864
24: 9 to bring in to the LORD the c that Moses 4864
1Co 16: 1 Now concerning the c for the saints, as I 3048

COLLEGE (2)
2Ki 22:14 (now she dwelt in Jerusalem in the c;) and 4932
2Ch 34:22 (now she dwelt in Jerusalem in the c:) and 4932

COLLOPS (1)
Job 15:27 and maketh **c of fat** on *his* flanks. 6371

COLONY (1)
Ac 16:12 city of *that* part of Macedonia, *and* a c: 2862

COLORFUL See DIVERS; DIVERSE

COLOSSE (1) [COLOSSIANS]
Col 1: 2 faithful brethren in Christ which are at C: 2857

COLOSSIANS (1) [COLOSSE]
Col 4: S Written from Rome to the C by Tychicus 2858

COLOUR (14) [COLOURED, COLOURS]
Lev 13:55 *if* the plague have not changed his c, and 5869
Nu 11: 7 and the c thereof as the colour of bdellium. 5869
11: 7 and the colour thereof as the c of bdellium. 5869
Pr 23:31 when it giveth his c in the cup, *when* it 5869
Eze 1: 4 out of the midst thereof as the c of amber, 5869
1: 7 they sparkled like the c of burnished brass. 5869
1:16 their work *was* like unto the c of a beryl: 5869
1:22 creature *was* as the c of the terrible crystal, 5869
1:27 I saw as the c of amber, as the appearance 5869
8: 2 appearance of brightness, as the c of amber. 5869
10: 9 the appearance of the wheels *was* as the c 5869
Da 10: 6 and his feet like in c to polished brass, 5869
Ac 27:30 **under c** as though they would have cast 4392
Rev 17: 4 woman was arrayed in purple and **scarlet c**, 2847

COLOURED (1) [COLOUR]
Rev 17: 3 I saw a woman sit upon a **scarlet c** beast, 2847

COLOURS (12) [COLOUR]
Ge 37: 3 old age: and he made him a coat **of many c**. 6446
37:23 *his* coat **of many c** that *was* on him; 6446
37:32 they sent the coat **of many c**, and 6446
Jdg 5:30 to Sisera a prey of **divers c**, a prey of divers 6648
5:30 a prey of **divers c** of needlework, 6648
5:30 of **divers c** of needlework on both sides, 6648
2Sa 13:18 *she had* a garment of **divers c** upon her: 6446
13:19 rent her garment of **divers c** that *was* on 6446

1Ch	29: 2	of **divers c**, and all *manner of* precious	7553
Isa	54:11	I will lay thy stones with **fair c**, and lay thy	6320
Eze	16:16	deckedst thy high places with **divers c**, and	2921
	17: 3	full *of* feathers, which had **divers c**,	7553

COLT (15) [COLTS]

Ge	49:11	and his ass's **c** unto the choice vine;	1121
Job	11:12	though man be born *like* a wild ass's **c**.	5895
Zec	9: 9	upon an ass, and upon a **c** the foal of an ass.	5895
Mt	21: 2	ye shall find an ass tied, and a **c** with her:	*4454*
	21: 5	upon an ass, and a **c** the foal of an ass.	*4454*
	21: 7	and the **c**, and put on them their clothes,	*4454*
Mk	11: 2	ye shall find a **c** tied, whereon never man	*4454*
	11: 4	found the **c** tied by the door without in a	*4454*
	11: 5	said unto them, What do ye, loosing the **c**?	*4454*
	11: 7	And they brought the **c** to Jesus, and	*4454*
Lk	19:30	at your entering ye shall find a **c** tied,	*4454*
	19:33	And as they were loosing the **c**, the owners	*4454*
	19:33	thereof said unto them, Why loose ye the **c**?	*4454*
	19:35	and they cast their garments upon the **c**, and	*4454*
Jn	12:15	thy King cometh, sitting on an ass's **c**.	*4454*

COLTS (3) [COLT]

Ge	32:15	Thirty milch camels with their **c**, forty kine,	1121
Jdg	10: 4	he had thirty sons that rode on thirty **ass c**,	5895
	12:14	that rode on threescore and ten **ass c**:	5895

COME (1972) [CAME, CAMEST, COMERS, COMEST, COMETH, COMING, COMINGS] See Index

COME O LORD See MARAN-ATHA

COMELINESS (5) [COMELY, UNCOMELY]

Isa	53: 2	he hath no form nor **c**; and when we shall	1926
Eze	16:14	for it *was* perfect through my **c**, which I	1926
	27:10	and helmet in thee; they set forth thy **c**.	1926
Da	10: 8	for my **c** was turned in me into corruption,	1935
1Co	12:23	our uncomely *parts* have more abundant **c**.	*2157*

COMELY (16) [COMELINESS]

1Sa	16:18	a **c** person, and the LORD *is* with him.	8389
Job	41:12	nor *his* power, nor his **c** proportion.	2433
Ps	33: 1	ye righteous: *for* praise is **c** for the upright.	5000
	147: 1	our God; for *it is* pleasant; *and* praise is **c**.	5000
Pr	30:29	which go well, yea, four are **c** in going:	3190
Ecc	5:18	*it is* good and **c** *for one* to eat and to drink,	3303
SS	1: 5	I *am* black, but **c**, O ye daughters of	5000
	1:10	Thy cheeks are **c** with rows *of jewels,* thy	4998
	2:14	*is* thy voice, and thy countenance *is* **c**.	5000
	4: 3	like a thread of scarlet, and thy speech *is* **c**:	5000
	6: 4	O my love, as Tirzah, **c** as Jerusalem,	5000
Isa	4: 2	**c** for them that are escaped of	8597+3807.1
Jer	6: 2	I have likened the daughter of Zion *to* a **c**	5116
1Co	7:35	but for *that which is* **c**, and that you may	*2158*
	11:13	is it **c** that a woman pray unto God	*4241*
	12:24	For our **c** *parts* have no need:	*2158*

COMERS (1) [COME]

Heb	10: 1	continually make the **c** *thereunto* perfect.	*4334*

COMEST (29) [COME] See Index

COMETH (282) [COME] See Index

COMFORT (66) [COMFORTABLE, COMFORTABLY, COMFORTED, COMFORTEDST, COMFORTER, COMFORTERS, COMFORTETH, COMFORTLESS, COMFORTS]

Ge	5:29	This *same* shall **c** us concerning our work	5162
	18: 5	a morsel of bread, and **c** ye your hearts;	5582
	27:42	as touching thee, doth **c** himself,	5162
	37:35	and all his daughters rose up to **c** him;	5162
Jdg	19: 5	**C** thine heart *with* a morsel of bread, and	5582
	19: 8	father said, **C** thine heart, I pray thee.	5582
2Sa	10: 2	David sent to **c** him by the hand of his	5162
1Ch	7:22	many days, and his brethren came to **c** him.	5162
	19: 2	David sent messengers to **c** him concerning	5162
	19: 2	the children of Ammon to Hanun, to **c** him.	5162
Job	2:11	to come to mourn with him and to **c** him.	5162
	6:10	should I yet have **c**; yea, I would harden	5165
	7:13	When I say, My bed shall **c** me, my couch	5162
	9:27	I will leave off my heaviness, and **c** myself:	1082
	10:20	and let me alone, that I may **take c** a little,	1082
	21:34	How then **c** ye me in vain, seeing *in* your	5162
Ps	23: 4	*art* with me; thy rod and thy staff they **c** me.	5162
	71:21	my greatness, and **c** me on every side.	5162
	119:50	This *is* my **c** in my affliction: for thy word	5165
	119:76	thy merciful kindness be for my **c**,	5162
	119:82	for thy word, saying, When wilt thou **c** me?	5162
SS	2: 5	Stay me with flagons, **c** me with apples:	7502
Isa	22: 4	labour not to **c** me, because of the spoiling	5162
	40: 1	**C** ye, comfort ye my people, saith your	5162
	40: 1	Comfort ye, **c** ye my people, saith your	5162
	51: 3	For the LORD shall **c** Zion: he will	5162
	51: 3	he will **c** all her waste places; and he will	5162
	51:19	and the sword: *by* whom shall I **c** thee?	5162
	57: 6	meat offering. Should I **receive c** in these?	5162
	61: 2	vengeance of our God; to **c** all that mourn;	5162
	66:13	his mother comforteth, so will I **c** you;	5162
Jer	8:18	*When* I would **c** myself against sorrow,	4010
	16: 7	them in mourning, to **c** them for the dead;	5162
	31:13	will **c** them, and make them rejoice from	5162
La	1: 2	among all her lovers she hath none to **c** *her:*	5162
	1:17	forth her hands, *and there is* none to **c** her:	5162
	1:21	heard that I sigh; *there is* none to **c** me:	5162
	2:13	what shall I equal to thee, that I may **c** thee,	5162
Eze	14:23	they shall **c** you, when ye see their ways	5162
	16:54	hast done, in that thou art a **c** unto them.	5162
Zec	1:17	the LORD shall yet **c** Zion, and shall yet	5162
	10: 2	and have told false dreams; they **c** in vain:	5162
Mt	9:22	saw her, he said, Daughter, **be of good c**;	*2293*
Mk	10:49	saying unto him, **Be of good c**, rise;	*2293*
Lk	8:48	he said unto her, Daughter, **be of good c**:	*2293*
Jn	11:19	Mary, to **c** them concerning their brother.	*3888*
Ac	9:31	and in the **c** of the Holy Ghost,	*3874*
Ro	15: 4	and **c** of the scriptures might have hope.	*3874*
1Co	14: 3	men *to* edification, and exhortation, and **c**.	*3889*
2Co	1: 3	the Father of mercies, and the God of all **c**;	*3874*
	1: 4	that we may be able to **c** them which are in	*3870*
	1: 4	by the **c** wherewith we ourselves are	*3874*
	2: 7	**c** *him,* lest perhaps such a one should be	*3870*
	7: 4	I am filled with **c**, I am exceeding joyful in	*3874*
	7:13	Therefore we were comforted in your **c**:	*3874*
	13:11	Be perfect, be **of good c**, be of one mind,	*3870*
Eph	6:22	our affairs, and *that* he might **c** your hearts.	*3870*
Php	2: 1	any consolation in Christ, if any **c** of love,	*3890*
	2:19	that I also may be **of good c**, when I know	*2174*
Col	4: 8	might know your estate, and **c** your hearts;	*3870*
	4:11	of God, which have been a **c** unto me.	*3931*
1Th	3: 2	and to **c** you concerning your faith:	*3870*
	4:18	Wherefore **c** one another with these words.	*3870*
	5:11	Wherefore **c** yourselves together, and	*3870*
	5:14	**c** the feebleminded, support the weak,	*3888*
2Th	2:17	**C** your hearts, and stablish you in every	*3870*

COMFORTABLE (2) [COMFORT]

2Sa	14:17	word of my lord the king shall now be **c**:	4496
Zec	1:13	with me *with* good words *and* **c** words.	5150

COMFORTABLY (5) [COMFORT]

2Sa	19: 7	and speak **c** unto thy servants:	3820+5921
2Ch	30:22	Hezekiah spake **c** unto all the Levites	3820+5921
	32: 6	the city, and spake **c** to them, saying,	3824+5921
Isa	40: 2	Speak ye **c** to Jerusalem, and	3820+5921
Hos	2:14	the wilderness, and speak **c** unto her.	3820+5921

COMFORTED (36) [COMFORT]

Ge	24:67	and Isaac was **c** after his mother's *death.*	5162
	37:35	he refused to be **c**; and he said, For I will	5162
	38:12	Judah was **c**, and went up unto his	5162
	50:21	he **c** them, and spake kindly unto them.	5162
Ru	2:13	for that thou hast **c** me, and for that thou	5162
2Sa	12:24	David **c** Bath-sheba his wife, and went in	5162
	13:39	for he was **c** concerning Amnon, seeing he	5162
Job	42:11	**c** him over all the evil that the LORD had	5162
Ps	77: 2	and ceased not: my soul refused to be **c**.	5162
	86:17	thou, LORD, hast holpen me, and **c** me.	5162
	119:52	of old, O LORD; and have **c** myself.	5162
Isa	49:13	for the LORD hath **c** his people, and	5162
	52: 9	for the LORD hath **c** his people, he hath	5162
	54:11	tossed with tempest, *and* not **c**, behold,	5162
	66:13	and ye shall be **c** in Jerusalem.	5162
Jer	31:15	children refused to be **c** for her children,	5162
Eze	5:13	my fury to rest upon them, and I will be **c**:	5162
	14:22	ye shall be **c** concerning the evil that I have	5162
	31:16	shall be **c** in the nether parts of the earth.	5162
	32:31	shall be **c** over all his multitude,	5162
Mt	2:18	and would not be **c**, because they are not.	*3870*
	5: 4	*are* they that mourn: for they shall be **c**.	*3870*

Lk 16:25 Lazarus evil *things:* but now he is c, 3870
Jn 11:31 and c her, when they saw Mary, that she 3888
Ac 16:40 the brethren, they c them, and departed. 3870
20:12 the young man alive, and were not a little c. 3870
Ro 1:12 that *I* may be c **together** with you by 4837
1Co 14:31 by one, that all may learn, and all may be c. 3870
2Co 1: 4 wherewith we ourselves are c of God. 3870
1: 6 or whether we be c, *it is* for your 3870
7: 6 *are* cast down, c us by the coming of Titus; 3870
7: 7 by the consolation wherewith he was c in 3870
7:13 Therefore we were c in your comfort: *yea,* 3870
Col 2: 2 That their hearts might be c, being knit 3870
1Th 2:11 and c and charged every one of you, 3888
3: 7 we were c over you in all our affliction and 3870

COMFORTEDST (1) [COMFORT]
Isa 12: 1 thine anger is turned away, and thou c me. 5162

COMFORTER (8) [COMFORT]
Ecc 4: 1 such as were oppressed, and they had no c; 5162
4: 1 *there was* power; but they had no c. 5162
La 1: 9 she had no c. O LORD, behold my 5162
1:16 the c that *should* relieve my soul is far from 5162
Jn 14:16 the Father, and he shall give you another C, 3875
14:26 But the C, *which is* the Holy Ghost, 3875
15:26 But when the C is come, whom I will send 3875
16: 7 go not away, the C will not come unto you; 3875

COMFORTERS (5) [COMFORT]
2Sa 10: 3 thy father, that he hath sent c unto thee? 5162
1Ch 19: 3 thy father, that he hath sent c unto thee? 5162
Job 16: 2 I have heard many such *things:* miserable c 5162
Ps 69:20 *there was* none; and for c, but I found none. 5162
Na 3: 7 whence shall I seek c for thee? 5162

COMFORTETH (5) [COMFORT]
Job 29:25 in the army, as *one that* c the mourners. 5162
Isa 51:12 I, *even* I, *am* he that c you: who *art* thou, 5162
66:13 As one whom his mother c, so will I 5162
2Co 1: 4 Who c us in all our tribulation, that we may 3870
7: 6 that c *those that are* cast down, 3870

COMFORTLESS (1) [COMFORT]
Jn 14:18 I will not leave you c: I will come to you. 3737

COMFORTS (2) [COMFORT]
Ps 94:19 thoughts within me thy c delight my soul. 8575
Isa 57:18 and restore c unto him and to his mourners. 5150

COMING (100) [COME] See Index

COMINGS (1) [COME] See Index

COMMAND (104) [COMMANDED, COMMANDEDST, COMMANDER, COMMANDEST, COMMANDETH, COMMANDING, COMMANDMENT, COMMANDMENTS]
Ge 18:19 that he will c his children and his 6680
27: 8 obey my voice according to *that* which I c 6680
50:16 Thy father did c before he died, saying, 6680
Ex 7: 2 Thou shalt speak all that I c thee: and 6680
8:27 to the LORD our God, as he shall c us. 559
18:23 God c thee *so,* then thou shalt be able to 6680
27:20 thou shalt c the children of Israel, that they 6680
34:11 Observe thou that which I c thee *this* day: 6680
Lev 6: 9 C Aaron and his sons, saying, This *is* 6680
13:54 the priest shall c that they wash *the thing* 6680
14: 4 shall the priest c to take for him that is to be 6680
14: 5 the priest shall c that one of the birds be 6680
14:36 the priest shall c that they empty the house, 6680
14:40 the priest shall c that they take away 6680
24: 2 C the children of Israel, that they bring 6680
25:21 I will c my blessing upon you in the sixth 6680
Nu 5: 2 C the children of Israel, that they put out of 6680
9: 8 I will hear what the LORD will c 6680
28: 2 C the children of Israel, and say unto them, 6680
34: 2 C the children of Israel, and say unto them, 6680
35: 2 C the children of Israel, that they give unto 6680
36: 6 This *is* the thing which the LORD doth c 6680
Dt 2: 4 c thou the people, saying, Ye are to pass 6680
4: 2 Ye shall not add unto the word which I c 6680
4: 2 of the LORD your God which I c you. 6680
4:40 his commandments, which I c thee *this* day, 6680
6: 2 which I c thee, thou, and thy son, and 6680
6: 6 these words, which I c thee *this* day, 6680
7:11 which I c thee *this* day, to do them. 6680
8: 1 All the commandments which I c thee *this* 6680
8:11 and his statutes, which I c thee *this* day: 6680
10:13 which I c thee *this* day for thy good? 6680
11: 8 the commandments which I c you *this* day, 6680
11:13 my commandments which I c you *this* day, 6680
11:22 all these commandments which I c you, 6680
11:27 LORD your God, which I c you *this* day: 6680
11:28 turn aside out of the way which I c you *this* 6680
12:11 thither shall ye bring all that I c you; 6680
12:14 and there thou shalt do all that I c thee. 6680
12:28 and hear all these words which I c thee, 6680
12:32 What thing soever I c you, observe to do it: 6680
13:18 to keep all his commandments which I c 6680
15: 5 commandments which I c thee *this* day. 6680
15:11 therefore I c thee, saying, Thou shalt open 6680
15:15 therefore I c thee this thing to day. 6680
18:18 he shall speak unto them all that I shall c 6680
19: 7 Wherefore I c thee, saying, Thou shalt 6680
19: 9 which I c thee *this* day, to love the LORD 6680
24:18 therefore I c thee to do this thing. 6680
24:22 of Egypt: therefore I c thee to do this thing. 6680
27: 1 Keep all the commandments which I c you 6680
27: 4 which I c you *this* day, in mount Ebal, and 6680
27:10 and his statutes, which I c thee *this* day. 6680
28: 1 to do all his commandments which I c thee 6680
28: 8 The LORD shall c the blessing upon thee 6680
28:13 which I c thee *this* day, to observe and 6680
28:14 any of the words which I c thee *this* day, 6680
28:15 and his statutes which I c thee *this* day; 6680
30: 2 shalt obey his voice according to all that I c 6680
30: 8 do all his commandments which I c thee 6680
30:11 For this commandment which I c thee *this* 6680
30:16 In that I c thee *this* day to love the LORD 6680
32:46 which ye shall c your children to observe to 6680
Jos 1:11 c the people, saying, Prepare you victuals; 6680
3: 8 thou shalt c the priests that bear the ark of 6680
4: 3 c you them, saying, Take you hence out of 6680
4:16 C the priests that bear the ark of 6680
11:15 so did Moses c Joshua, and so did Joshua; 6680
1Sa 16:16 Let our lord now c thy servants *which are* 559
1Ki 5: 6 c thou that they hew me cedar trees out of 6680
11:38 if thou wilt hearken unto all that I c thee, 6680
2Ch 7:13 or if I c the locusts to devour the land, or 6680
Job 39:27 Doth the eagle mount up at thy c, and make 6310
Ps 42: 8 *Yet* the LORD will c his lovingkindness 6680
44: 4 my King, O God: c deliverances for Jacob. 6680
Isa 5: 6 I will also c the clouds that they rain no 6680
45:11 concerning the work of my hands c ye me. 6680
Jer 1: 7 and whatsoever I c thee thou shalt speak. 6680
1:17 arise, and speak unto them all that I c thee: 6680
11: 4 do them, according to all which I c you: 6680
26: 2 all the words that I c thee to speak unto 6680
27: 4 c them to say unto their masters, Thus saith 6680
34:22 Behold, I *will* c, saith the LORD, and 6680
La 1:10 whom thou didst c *that* they should not 6680
Am 9: 3 thence will I c the serpent, and he shall bite 6680
9: 4 thence will I c the sword, and it shall slay 6680
9: 9 I will c, and I will sift the house of Israel 6680
Mt 4: 3 of God, c that these stones be made bread. 3004
19: 7 then c to give a writing of divorcement, 1781
27:64 C therefore that the sepulchre be made sure 2753
Mk 10: 3 and said unto them, What did Moses c you? 1781
Lk 4: 3 of God, c this stone that it be made bread. 3004
8:31 And they besought him that he would not c 2004
9:54 wilt thou *that* we c fire to come down from 3004
Jn 15:14 are my friends, if ye do whatsoever I c you. 1781
15:17 These *things* I c you, that ye love one 1781
Ac 5:28 Did not we **straitly** c you that *you* 3852+3853
15: 5 and to c *them* to keep the law of Moses. 3853
16:18 I c thee in the name of Jesus Christ to come 3853
1Co 7:10 And unto the married I c, *yet* not I, but 3853
2Th 3: 4 and will do *the things* which we c you. 3853
3: 6 Now we c you, brethren, in the name of our 3853
3:12 Now *them that are* such we c and exhort by 3853
1Ti 4:11 These *things* c and teach. 3853

COMMANDED (443) [COMMAND]
Ge 2:16 the LORD God c the man, saying, 6680
3:11 whereof I c thee that thou shouldest not 6680
3:17 eaten of the tree, of which I c thee, saying, 6680
6:22 according to all that God c him, so did he. 6680
7: 5 according unto all that the LORD c him. 6680
7: 9 and the female, as God had c Noah. 6680
7:16 and female of all flesh, as God had c him: 6680

Ge	12:20	Pharaoh **c** *his* men concerning him: and	6680
	21: 4	being eight days old, as God had **c** him.	6680
	32: 4	he **c** them, saying, Thus shall ye speak unto	6680
	32:17	he **c** the foremost, saying, When Esau my	6680
	32:19	so **c** he the second, and the third, and all	6680
	42:25	Joseph **c** to fill their sacks *with* corn, and	6680
	44: 1	he **c** the steward of his house, saying,	6680
	45:19	Now thou art **c**, this do ye; take you	6680
	47:11	in the land of Rameses, as Pharaoh had **c**.	6680
	50: 2	Joseph **c** his servants the physicians to	6680
	50:12	his sons did unto him according as he **c**	6680
Ex	1:17	and did not as the king of Egypt **c** them, but	1696
	4:28	and all the signs which he had **c** him.	6680
	5: 6	Pharaoh **c** the same day the taskmasters of	6680
	7: 6	and Aaron did as the LORD **c** them,	6680
	7:10	and they did so as the LORD had **c**:	6680
	7:20	and Aaron did so, as the LORD **c**;	6680
	12:28	did as the LORD had **c** Moses and Aaron,	6680
	12:50	as the LORD **c** Moses and Aaron, so	6680
	16:16	This *is* the thing which the LORD hath **c**,	6680
	16:34	As the LORD **c** Moses, so Aaron laid it up	6680
	19: 7	all these words which the LORD **c** him.	6680
	23:15	as I **c** thee, in the time appointed of	6680
	29:35	according to all *things* which I have **c** thee:	6680
	31: 6	that they may make all that I have **c** thee;	6680
	31:11	to all that I have **c** thee shall they do.	6680
	32: 8	quickly out of the way which I **c** them:	6680
	34: 4	as the LORD had **c** him, and took in his	6680
	34:18	as I **c** thee, in the time of the month Abib:	6680
	34:34	the children of Israel *that* which he was **c**.	6680
	35: 1	*are* the words which the LORD hath **c**,	6680
	35: 4	This *is* the thing which the LORD **c**,	6680
	35:10	and make all that the LORD hath **c**;	6680
	35:29	which the LORD had **c** to be made by	6680
	36: 1	according to all that the LORD had **c**.	6680
	36: 5	of the work, which the LORD **c** to make.	6680
	38:22	made all that the LORD **c** Moses.	6680
	39: 1	for Aaron; as the LORD **c** Moses.	6680
	39: 5	fine twined linen; as the LORD **c** Moses.	6680
	39: 7	children of Israel; as the LORD **c** Moses.	6680
	39:21	from the ephod; as the LORD **c** Moses.	6680
	39:26	robe to minister *in;* as the LORD **c** Moses.	6680
	39:29	*of* needlework; as the LORD **c** Moses.	6680
	39:31	upon the mitre; as the LORD **c** Moses.	6680
	39:32	according to all that the LORD **c** Moses,	6680
	39:42	According to all that the LORD **c** Moses,	6680
	39:43	they had done it as the LORD had **c**, *even*	6680
	40:16	according to all that the LORD **c** him, so	6680
	40:19	tent above upon it; as the LORD **c** Moses.	6680
	40:21	of the Testimony; as the LORD **c** Moses.	6680
	40:23	the LORD; as the LORD had **c** Moses.	6680
	40:25	the LORD; as the LORD **c** Moses.	6680
	40:27	incense thereon; as the LORD **c** Moses.	6680
	40:29	the meat offering; as the LORD **c** Moses.	6680
	40:32	they washed; as the LORD **c** Moses.	6680
Lev	7:36	Which the LORD **c** to be given them of	6680
	7:38	Which the LORD **c** Moses in mount Sinai,	6680
	7:38	in the day that he **c** the children of Israel to	6680
	8: 4	Moses did as the LORD **c** him; and	6680
	8: 5	This *is* the thing which the LORD **c** to be	6680
	8: 9	the holy crown; as the LORD **c** Moses.	6680
	8:13	upon them; as the LORD **c** Moses.	6680
	8:17	without the camp; as the LORD **c** Moses.	6680
	8:21	unto the LORD; as the LORD **c** Moses.	6680
	8:29	it was Moses' part; as the LORD **c** Moses.	6680
	8:31	as I **c**, saying, Aaron and his sons shall eat	6680
	8:34	done this day, *so* the LORD hath **c** to do,	6680
	8:35	the LORD, that ye die not: for so I am **c**.	6680
	8:36	his sons did all things which the LORD **c**	6680
	9: 5	they brought *that* which Moses **c** before	6680
	9: 6	This *is* the thing which the LORD **c** *that*	6680
	9: 7	an atonement for them; as the LORD **c**.	6680
	9:10	upon the altar; as the LORD **c** Moses.	6680
	9:21	offering before the LORD; as Moses **c**.	6680
	10: 1	before the LORD, which he **c** them not.	6680
	10:13	of the LORD made by fire: for so I am **c**.	6680
	10:15	by a statute for ever; as the LORD hath **c**.	6680
	10:18	have eaten it in the holy *place,* as I **c**.	6680
	16:34	a year. And he did as the LORD **c** Moses.	6680
	17: 2	This *is* the thing which the LORD hath **c**,	6680
	24:23	the children of Israel did as the LORD **c**	6680
	27:34	which the LORD **c** Moses for the children	6680
Nu	1:19	As the LORD **c** Moses, so he numbered	6680
	1:54	according to all that the LORD **c** Moses,	6680
	2:33	children of Israel; as the LORD **c** Moses.	6680
	2:34	according to all that the LORD **c** Moses:	6680
	3:16	to the word of the LORD, as he was **c**.	6680
	3:42	Moses numbered, as the LORD **c** him,	6680
	3:51	of the LORD, as the LORD **c** Moses.	6680
	4:49	numbered of him, as the LORD **c** Moses.	6680
	8: 3	the candlestick, as the LORD **c** Moses.	6680
	8:20	LORD **c** Moses concerning the Levites,	6680
	8:22	as the LORD had **c** Moses concerning	6680
	9: 5	according to all that the LORD **c** Moses,	6680
	15:23	*Even* all that the LORD hath **c** you by	6680
	15:23	from the day that the LORD **c** *Moses,* and	6680
	15:36	and he died; as the LORD **c** Moses.	6680
	16:47	Aaron took as Moses **c**, and ran into	1696
	17:11	Moses did *so:* as the LORD **c** him, so	6680
	19: 2	of the law which the LORD hath **c**,	6680
	20: 9	rod from before the LORD, as he **c** him.	6680
	20:27	Moses did as the LORD **c**: and they went	6680
	26: 4	as the LORD **c** Moses and the children of	6680
	27:11	of judgment, as the LORD **c** Moses.	6680
	27:22	Moses did as the LORD **c** him: and	6680
	27:23	as the LORD **c** by the hand of Moses.	1696
	29:40	according to all that the LORD **c** Moses.	6680
	30: 1	This *is* the thing which the LORD hath **c**.	6680
	30:16	which the LORD **c** Moses, between a man	6680
	31: 7	the Midianites, as the LORD **c** Moses;	6680
	31:21	of the law which the LORD **c** Moses;	6680
	31:31	Eleazar the priest did as the LORD **c**	6680
	31:41	Eleazar the priest, as the LORD **c** Moses.	6680
	31:47	of the LORD; as the LORD **c** Moses.	6680
	32:28	So concerning them Moses **c** Eleazar	6680
	34:13	Moses **c** the children of Israel, saying,	6680
	34:13	which the LORD **c** to give unto the nine	6680
	34:29	These *are they* whom the LORD **c** to	6680
	36: 2	The LORD **c** my lord to give the land for	6680
	36: 2	my lord was **c** by the LORD to give	6680
	36: 5	Moses **c** the children of Israel according to	6680
	36:10	Even as the LORD **c** Moses, so did	6680
	36:13	which the LORD **c** by the hand of Moses	6680
Dt	1:18	I **c** you at that time all the things which ye	6680
	1:19	the Amorites, as the LORD our God **c** us;	6680
	1:41	according to all that the LORD our God **c**	6680
	3:18	I **c** you at that time, saying, The LORD	6680
	3:21	I **c** Joshua at that time, saying, Thine eyes	6680
	4: 5	even as the LORD my God **c** me,	6680
	4:13	which he **c** you to perform, *even* ten	6680
	4:14	the LORD **c** me at that time to teach you	6680
	5:12	as the LORD thy God hath **c** thee.	6680
	5:15	the LORD thy God **c** thee to keep	6680
	5:16	as the LORD thy God hath **c** thee;	6680
	5:32	as the LORD your God hath **c** you:	6680
	5:33	which the LORD your God hath **c** you,	6680
	6: 1	which the LORD your God **c** to teach you,	6680
	6:17	and his statutes, which he hath **c** thee.	6680
	6:20	which the LORD our God hath **c** you?	6680
	6:24	the LORD **c** us to do all these statutes,	6680
	6:25	the LORD our God, as he hath **c** us.	6680
	9:12	turned aside out of the way which I **c** them;	6680
	9:16	of the way which the LORD had **c** you.	6680
	10: 5	and there they be, as the LORD **c** me.	6680
	12:21	as I have **c** thee, and thou shalt eat in thy	6680
	13: 5	the LORD thy God **c** thee to walk in.	6680
	17: 3	of the host of heaven, which I have not **c**;	6680
	18:20	which I have not **c** him to speak, or	6680
	20:17	as the LORD thy God hath **c** thee:	6680
	24: 8	as I **c** them, *so* ye shall observe to do.	6680
	26:13	thy commandments which thou hast **c** me:	6680
	26:14	have done according to all that thou hast **c**	6680
	26:16	This day the LORD thy God hath **c** thee to	6680
	27: 1	Moses with the elders of Israel **c**	6680
	28:45	and his statutes which he **c** thee:	6680
	29: 1	which the LORD **c** Moses to make with	6680
	31: 5	all the commandments which I have **c** you.	6680
	31:10	Moses **c** them, saying, At the end of *every*	6680
	31:25	That Moses **c** the Levites, which bare	6680
	31:29	turn aside from the way which I have **c**	6680
	33: 4	Moses **c** us a law, *even* the inheritance of	6680
	34: 9	unto him, and did as the LORD **c** Moses.	6680
Jos	1: 7	all the law, which Moses my servant **c** thee:	6680
	1: 9	Have not I **c** thee? Be strong and of a good	6680
	1:10	Joshua **c** the officers of the people, saying,	6680
	1:13	Moses the servant of the LORD **c** you,	6680
	3: 3	they **c** the people, saying, When ye see	6680
	4: 8	the children of Israel did so as Joshua **c**,	6680

C

Jos	4:10	Lord **c** Joshua to speak unto the people,	6680
	4:10	according to all that Moses **c** Joshua:	6680
	4:17	Joshua therefore **c** the priests, saying,	6680
	6:10	Joshua had **c** the people, saying, Ye shall	6680
	7:11	transgressed my covenant which I **c** them:	6680
	8: 4	he **c** them, saying, Behold, ye shall lie in	6680
	8: 8	the Lord shall ye do. See, I have **c** you.	6680
	8:27	the word of the Lord which he **c** Joshua.	6680
	8:29	Joshua **c** that they should take his carcase	6680
	8:31	As Moses the servant of the Lord **c**	6680
	8:33	as Moses the servant of the Lord had **c**	6680
	8:35	There was not a word of all that Moses **c**,	6680
	9:24	how that the Lord thy God **c** his servant	6680
	10:27	*that* Joshua **c**, and they took them down off	6680
	10:40	as the Lord God of Israel **c**.	6680
	11:12	as Moses the servant of the Lord **c**.	6680
	11:15	As the Lord **c** Moses his servant, so	6680
	11:15	undone of all that the Lord **c** Moses.	6680
	11:20	destroy them, as the Lord **c** Moses.	6680
	13: 6	for an inheritance, as I have **c** thee.	6680
	14: 2	as the Lord **c** by the hand of Moses,	6680
	14: 5	As the Lord **c** Moses, so the children of	6680
	17: 4	The Lord **c** Moses to give us an	6680
	21: 2	The Lord **c** by the hand of Moses to give	6680
	21: 8	as the Lord **c** by the hand of Moses.	6680
	22: 2	Moses the servant of the Lord **c** you,	6680
	22: 2	have obeyed my voice in all that I **c** you:	6680
	23:16	which he **c** you, and have gone and	6680
Jdg	2:20	my covenant which I **c** their fathers,	6680
	3: 4	which he **c** their fathers by the hand of	6680
	4: 6	Hath not the Lord God of Israel **c**,	6680
	13:14	nor eat any unclean *thing*: all that I **c** her let	6680
	21:10	**c** them, saying, Go and smite	6680
	21:20	Therefore they **c** the children of Benjamin,	6680
Ru	2:15	up to glean, Boaz **c** his young men, saying,	6680
1Sa	2:29	which I have **c** *in my* habitation;	6680
	13:13	of the Lord thy God, which he **c** thee:	6680
	13:14	the Lord hath **c** him to be captain over	6680
	13:14	thou hast not kept *that* which the Lord **c**	6680
	17:20	and took, and went, as Jesse had **c** him;	6680
	18:22	Saul **c** his servants, *saying*, Commune with	6680
	20:29	he hath **c** me *to be there*: and now,	6680
	21: 2	The king hath **c** me a business, and	6680
	21: 2	I send thee, and what I have **c** thee:	6680
2Sa	4:12	David **c** *his* young men, and they slew	6680
	5:25	David did so, as the Lord had **c** him;	6680
	7: 7	whom I **c** to feed my people Israel, saying,	6680
	7:11	*as* since the time that I **c** judges *to be* over	6680
	9:11	all that my lord the king hath **c** his servant,	6680
	13:28	Now Absalom had **c** his servants, saying,	6680
	13:28	have not I **c** you? be courageous, and	6680
	13:29	did unto Amnon as Absalom had **c**.	6680
	18: 5	the king **c** Joab and Abishai and Ittai,	6680
	21:14	they performed all that the king **c**.	6680
	24:19	saying of Gad, went up as the Lord **c**.	6680
1Ki	2:46	So the king **c** Benaiah the son of Jehoiada;	6680
	5:17	the king **c**, and they brought great stones,	6680
	8:58	and his judgments, which he **c** our fathers.	6680
	9: 4	to do according to all that I have **c** thee, *and*	6680
	11:10	had **c** him concerning this thing, that *he*	6680
	11:10	but he kept not *that* which the Lord **c**.	6680
	11:11	and my statutes, which I have **c** thee,	6680
	13:21	which the Lord thy God **c** thee,	6680
	15: 5	turned not aside from any *thing* that he **c**	6680
	17: 4	and I have **c** the ravens to feed thee there.	6680
	17: 9	I have **c** a widow woman there to sustain	6680
	22:31	the king of Syria **c** his thirty and	6680
2Ki	11: 5	he **c** them, saying, This *is* the thing that ye	6680
	11: 9	to all *things* that Jehoiada the priest **c**:	6680
	11:15	Jehoiada the priest **c** the captains of	6680
	14: 6	where*in* the Lord **c**, saying, The fathers	6680
	16:15	king Ahaz **c** Urijah the priest, saying,	6680
	16:16	the priest, according to all that king Ahaz **c**.	6680
	17:13	according to all the law which I **c** your	6680
	17:27	the king of Assyria **c**, saying, Carry thither	6680
	17:34	commandment which the Lord **c**	6680
	18: 6	which the Lord **c** Moses.	6680
	18:12	all that Moses the servant of the Lord **c**,	6680
	21: 8	to do according to all that I have **c** them,	6680
	21: 8	all the law that my servant Moses **c** them.	6680
	22:12	the king **c** Hilkiah the priest, and Ahikam	6680
	23: 4	the king **c** Hilkiah the high priest, and	6680
	23:21	the king **c** all the people, saying, Keep	6680
1Ch	6:49	to all that Moses the servant of God had **c**.	6680
	14:16	David therefore did as God **c** him: and	6680
	15:15	as Moses **c** according to the word of	6680
	16:15	the word *which* he **c** to a thousand	6680
	16:40	in the law of the Lord, which he **c** Israel;	6680
	17: 6	whom I **c** to feed my people, saying,	6680
	17:10	since the time that I **c** judges *to be* over my	6680
	21:17	*Is it* not I *that* **c** the people to be numbered?	559
	21:18	the angel of the Lord **c** Gad to say to	559
	21:27	the Lord **c** the angel; and he put up his	559
	22: 2	David **c** to gather together the strangers that	559
	22:17	David also **c** all the princes of Israel to help	6680
	23:31	according to the **order** **c** unto them,	4941
	24:19	as the Lord God of Israel had **c** him.	6680
2Ch	7:17	do according to all that I have **c** thee, and	6680
	8:14	for so had David the man of God **c**.	4687
	14: 4	**c** Judah to seek the Lord God of their	559
	18:30	Now the king of Syria had **c** the captains of	6680
	23: 8	to all *things* that Jehoiada the priest had **c**,	6680
	25: 4	where the Lord **c**, saying, The fathers	6680
	29:21	he **c** the priests the sons of Aaron to offer	559
	29:24	for the king **c** *that* the burnt offering and	559
	29:27	Hezekiah **c** to offer the burnt offering upon	559
	29:30	the princes **c** the Levites to *sing* praise unto	559
	31: 4	Moreover he **c** the people that dwelt in	559
	31:11	Hezekiah **c** to prepare chambers in the house	559
	32:12	and **c** Judah and Jerusalem, saying,	559
	33: 8	will take heed to do all that I have **c** them,	6680
	33:16	**c** Judah to serve the Lord God of Israel.	559
	34:20	the king **c** Hilkiah, and Ahikam the son of	6680
	35:21	for God **c** me to make haste: forbear thee	559
Ezr	4: 3	as king Cyrus the king of Persia hath **c** us.	6680
	4:19	I **c**, and search hath been made, and	2942+7761
	5: 3	Who hath **c** you to build this house,	2942+7761
	5: 9	Who **c** you to build this house, and	2942+7761
	7:23	Whatsoever *is* **c** by the God of heaven, let it	2941
	9:11	Which thou hast **c** by thy servants	6680
Ne	8: 1	which the Lord had **c** to Israel.	6680
	8:14	the law which the Lord had **c** by Moses,	6680
	13: 5	which was **c** *to be given* to the Levites, and	4687
	13: 9	I **c**, and they cleansed the chambers: and	559
	13:19	I **c** that the gates should be shut, and	559
	13:22	I **c** the Levites that they should cleanse	559
Est	1:10	he **c** Mehuman, Biztha, Harbona, Bigtha,	559
	1:17	The king Ahasuerus **c** Vashti the queen to be	559
	3: 2	for the king had so **c** concerning him.	6680
	3:12	Haman had **c** unto the king's lieutenants,	6680
	4:13	Mordecai **c** to answer Esther, Think not with	559
	4:17	did according to all that Esther had **c** him.	6680
	6: 1	he **c** to bring the book of records of	559
	8: 9	to all that Mordecai **c** unto the Jews,	6680
	9:14	the king **c** it so to be done: and the decree	559
	9:25	he **c** by letters *that* his wicked device,	559
Job	38:12	Hast thou **c** the morning since thy days; *and*	6680
	42: 9	and did according as the Lord **c** them:	1696
Ps	7: 6	for me *to* the judgment *that* thou hast **c**.	6680
	33: 9	and it was *done*; he **c**, and it stood fast.	6680
	68:28	Thy God hath **c** thy strength: strengthen,	6680
	78: 5	a law in Israel, which he **c** our fathers,	6680
	78:23	Though he had **c** the clouds from above,	6680
	105: 8	the word *which* he **c** to a thousand	6680
	106:34	*concerning* whom the Lord **c** them:	559
	111: 9	he hath **c** his covenant for ever: holy and	6680
	119: 4	Thou hast **c** *us* to keep thy precepts	6680
	119:138	Thy testimonies *that* thou hast **c** *are*	6680
	133: 3	for there the Lord **c** the blessing,	6680
	148: 5	for he **c**, and they were created.	6680
Isa	13: 3	I have **c** my sanctified ones, I have also	6680
	34:16	for my mouth it hath **c**, and his spirit it hath	6680
	45:12	out the heavens, and all their host have I **c**.	6680
	48: 5	and my molten image, hath **c** them.	6680
Jer	7:22	nor **c** them in the day that I brought them	6680
	7:23	this thing **c** I them, saying, Obey my voice,	6680
	7:23	walk ye in all the ways that I have **c** you,	6680
	7:31	which I **c** *them* not, neither came it into my	6680
	11: 4	Which I **c** your fathers in the day that I	6680
	11: 8	of this covenant, which I **c** *them* to do;	6680
	13: 5	hid it by Euphrates, as the Lord **c** me.	6680
	13: 6	from thence, which I **c** thee to hide there.	6680
	14:14	I sent them not, neither have I **c** them,	6680
	17:22	ye the sabbath day, as I **c** your fathers.	6680
	19: 5	which I **c** not, nor spake *it*, neither came *it*	6680
	23:32	yet I sent them not, nor **c** them:	6680
	26: 8	had **c** *him* to speak unto all the people,	6680
	29:23	in my name, which I have not **c** them;	6680

Jer 32:35 which I **c** them not, neither came it into my 6680
35: 6 for Jonadab the son of Rechab our father **c** 6680
35:10 to all that Jonadab our father **c** us. 6680
35:14 that he **c** his sons not to drink wine, 6680
35:16 of their father, which he **c** them; 6680
35:18 done according unto all that he hath **c** you: 6680
36: 5 Jeremiah **c** Baruch, saying, I *am* shut up; 6680
36: 8 to all that Jeremiah the prophet **c** him, 6680
36:26 the king **c** Jerahmeel the son of 6680
37:21 Zedekiah the king **c** that they should 6680
38:10 the king **c** Ebed-melech the Ethiopian, 6680
38:27 to all these words that the king had **c**. 6680
50:21 and do according to all that I have **c** thee. 6680
51:59 The word which Jeremiah the prophet **c** 6680
La 1:17 the LORD hath **c** concerning Jacob, 6680
2:17 he hath fulfilled his word that he had **c** in 6680
Eze 9:11 I have done as thou hast **c** me. 6680
10: 6 *that* when he had **c** the man clothed with 6680
12: 7 I did so as I was **c**: I brought forth my stuff 6680
24:18 and I did in the morning as I was **c**. 6680
37: 7 So I prophesied as I was **c**: and as I 6680
37:10 So I prophesied as he **c** me, and the breath 6680
Da 2: 2 the king **c** to call the magicians, and 559
2:12 **c** to destroy all the wise *men* of Babylon. 560
2:46 **c** that *they* should offer an oblation and 560
3: 4 To you it is **c**, O people, nations, 560
3:13 in *his* rage and fury **c** to bring Shadrach, 560
3:19 **c** that *they* should heat the furnace one seven 560
3:20 he **c** the most mighty men that *were* in his 560
4:26 whereas they **c** to leave the stump of the tree 560
5: 2 **c** to bring the golden and silver vessels 560
5:29 **c** Belshazzar, and they clothed Daniel with 560
6:16 the king **c**, and they brought Daniel, and 560
6:23 **c** that *they* should take Daniel up out of 560
6:24 the king **c**, and they brought those men 560
Am 2:12 **c** the prophets, saying, Prophesy not. 6680
Zec 1: 6 which I **c** my servants the prophets, 6680
Mal 4: 4 which I **c** unto him in Horeb for all Israel, 6680
Mt 8: 4 offer the gift that Moses **c** for a testimony *4367*
10: 5 twelve Jesus sent forth, and **c** them, saying, *3853*
14: 9 with him at meat, he **c** *it* to be given *her*. *2753*
14:19 And he **c** the multitude to sit down on *2753*
15: 4 For God **c**, saying, Honour thy father and *1781*
15:35 And he **c** the multitude to sit down on *2753*
18:25 his lord **c** him to be sold, and his wife, and *2753*
21: 6 the disciples went, and did as Jesus **c** them, *4367*
27:58 Then Pilate **c** the body to be delivered. *2753*
28:20 observe all *things* whatsoever I have **c** you: *1781*
Mk 1:44 thy cleansing *those things* which Moses **c**, *4367*
5:43 **c** that *something* should be given her to eat. *3004*
6: 8 And **c** them that they should take nothing *3853*
6:27 and **c** his head to be brought: *2004*
6:39 And he **c** them to make all sit down by *2004*
8: 6 And he **c** the people to sit down on *3853*
8: 7 and **c** to set them also before *them*. *3004*
10:49 Jesus stood still, and **c** him to be called. *3004*
11: 6 they said unto them even as Jesus had **c**: *1781*
13:34 man his work, and **c** the porter to watch. *1781*
Lk 5:14 for thy cleansing, according as Moses **c**, *4367*
8:29 (For he had **c** the unclean spirit to come out *3853*
8:55 and he **c** to give her meat. *1299*
9:21 and **c** *them* to tell no *man* that *thing*; *3853*
14:22 it is done as thou hast **c**, and yet there is *2004*
17: 9 because he did the *things* that were **c** him? *1299*
17:10 have done all those *things* which are **c** you, *1299*
18:40 and **c** him to be brought unto him: *2753*
19:15 he **c** these servants to be called unto him, *3004*
Jn 8: 5 Now Moses in the law **c** us, that such *1781*
Ac 1: 4 **c** them that *they* should not depart from *3853*
4:15 But when they had **c** them to go aside out *2753*
4:18 **c** them not to speak at all nor teach in *3853*
5:34 and **c** to put the apostles forth a little space; *2753*
5:40 beaten *them*, they **c** that *they* should not *3853*
8:38 And he **c** the chariot to stand still: and *2753*
10:33 to hear all *things* that are **c** thee of God. *4367*
10:42 And he **c** us to preach unto the people, and *3853*
10:48 And he **c** them to be baptized in the name *4367*
12:19 and **c** that *they* should be put to death. *2753*
13:47 For so hath the Lord **c** us, *saying*, I have set *1781*
16:22 rent off their clothes, and **c** to beat *them*. *2753*
18: 2 that Claudius had **c** all Jews to depart from *1299*
21:33 and **c** *him* to be bound with two chains; *2753*
21:34 he **c** him to be carried into the castle. *2753*
22:24 The chief captain **c** him to be brought into *2753*
22:30 and **c** the chief priests and all their council *2753*
23: 2 And the high priest Ananias **c** them that *2004*
23:10 **c** the soldiers to go down, and to take him *2753*
23:31 as it was **c** them, took Paul, and *1299*
23:35 And he **c** him to be kept in Herod's *2753*
24:23 And he **c** a centurion to keep Paul, *1299*
25: 6 in the judgment seat, **c** Paul to be brought. *2753*
25:17 and **c** the man to be brought *forth*. *2753*
25:21 I **c** him to be kept till I might send him to *2753*
27:43 **c** that they which could swim should cast *2753*
1Co 14:34 but *they are* **c** to be under obedience, as also NIG
2Co 4: 6 who **c** the light to shine out of darkness, *3004*
1Th 4:11 to work with your own hands, as we **c** you; *3853*
2Th 3:10 this we **c** you, that if any would not work, *3853*
Heb 12:20 they could not endure that which was **c**, *1291*
Rev 9: 4 And it was **c** them that they should not hurt *3004*

COMMANDEDST (4) [COMMAND]

Ne 1: 7 which thou **c** thy servant Moses. 6680
1: 8 the word that thou **c** thy servant Moses, 6680
9:14 **c** them precepts, statutes, and laws, by 6680
Jer 32:23 they have done nothing of all that thou **c** 6680

COMMANDER (1) [COMMAND]

Isa 55: 4 to the people, a leader and **c** to the people. 6680

COMMANDEST (3) [COMMAND]

Jos 1:16 All that thou **c** us we will do, and 6680
1:18 unto thy words in all that thou **c** him, 6680
Ac 23: 3 and **c** me to be smitten contrary to the law? *2753*

COMMANDETH (13) [COMMAND]

Ex 16:32 This *is* the thing which the LORD **c**, 6680
Nu 32:25 Thy servants will do as my lord **c**. 6680
Job 9: 7 Which **c** the sun, and it riseth not; and 559
36:10 and **c** that they return from iniquity. 559
36:32 **c** it *not to shine* by *the cloud* that cometh 6680
37:12 that they may do whatsoever he **c** them 6680
Ps 107:25 For he **c**, and raiseth the stormy wind, 559
La 3:37 it cometh to pass, *when* the Lord **c** *it* not? 6680
Am 6:11 the LORD **c**, and he will smite the great 6680
Mk 1:27 for with authority **c** he even the unclean *2004*
Lk 4:36 and power he **c** the unclean spirits, *2004*
8:25 for he **c** even the winds and water, and *2004*
Ac 17:30 but now **c** all men every where to repent: *3853*

COMMANDING (4) [COMMAND]

Ge 49:33 when Jacob had made an end of **c** his sons, 6680
Mt 11: 1 when Jesus had made an end of **c** his *1299*
Ac 24: 8 **C** his accusers to come unto thee: *2753*
1Ti 4: 3 to marry, *and* **c** to abstain from meats, NIG

COMMANDMENT (177) [COMMAND]

Ge 45:21 according to the **c** of Pharaoh, and 6310
Ex 17: 1 according to the **c** of the LORD, and 6310
25:22 of all *things* which I will **give** thee **in c** unto 6680
34:32 he **gave** them **in c** all that the LORD had 6680
36: 6 Moses **gave c**, and they caused it to be 6680
38:21 was counted, according to the **c** of Moses, 6310
Nu 3:39 Aaron numbered at the **c** of the LORD, 6310
4:37 Aaron did number according to the **c** of 6310
4:41 Aaron did number according to the **c** of 6310
4:49 According to the **c** of the LORD they 6310
9:18 At the **c** of the LORD the children of 6310
9:18 and at the **c** of the LORD they pitched: 6310
9:20 according to the **c** of the LORD they 6310
9:20 according to the **c** of the LORD they 6310
9:23 At the **c** of the LORD they rested in 6310
9:23 and at the **c** of the LORD they journeyed: 6310
9:23 at the **c** of the LORD by the hand of 6310
10:13 the **c** of the LORD by the hand of Moses. 6310
13: 3 Moses by the **c** of the LORD sent them 6310
14:41 Wherefore now do ye transgress the **c** of 6310
15:31 hath broken his **c**, that soul shall utterly be 4687
23:20 Behold, I have received **c** to bless: and NIH
24:13 I cannot go beyond the **c** of the LORD, 6310
27:14 For ye rebelled against my **c** in the desert of 6310
33: 2 to their journeys by the **c** of the LORD: 6310
33:38 up into mount Hor at the **c** of the LORD, 6310
Dt 1: 3 the LORD had **given** him **in c** unto them; 6680
1:26 rebelled against the **c** of the LORD your 6310
1:43 rebelled against the **c** of the LORD, and 6310
9:23 you rebelled against the **c** of the LORD 6310
17:20 that *he* turn not aside from the **c**, *to* 4687
30:11 For this **c** which I command thee *this* day, 4687

Jos 1:18 *he be* that doth rebel against thy **c**, 6310
8: 8 according to the **c** of the LORD shall ye 1697
15:13 according to the **c** of the LORD to Joshua, 6310
17: 4 Therefore according to the **c** of the LORD 6310
21: 3 at the **c** of the LORD, these cities and 6310
22: 3 have kept the charge of the **c** of the LORD 4687
22: 5 take diligent heed to do the **c** and the law, 4687
1Sa 12:14 not rebel against the **c** of the LORD, then 6310
12:15 rebel against the **c** of the LORD, then 6310
13:13 thou hast not kept the **c** of the LORD thy 4687
15:13 I have performed the **c** of the LORD. 1697
15:24 for I have transgressed the **c** of the LORD, 6310
2Sa 12: 9 Wherefore hast thou despised the **c** of 1697
1Ki 2:43 and the **c** that I have charged thee with? 4687
13:21 hast not kept the **c** which the LORD thy 4687
2Ki 17:34 **c** which the LORD commanded 4687
17:37 and the ordinances, and the law, and the **c**, 4687
18:36 for the king's **c** was, saying, Answer him 4687
23:35 the money according to the **c** of Pharaoh: 6310
24: 3 Surely at the **c** of the LORD came *this* 6310
1Ch 12:32 and all their brethren *were* at their **c**. 6310
14:12 David **gave a c**, and they were burnt with 559
28:21 and all the people *will be* wholly at thy **c**. 1697
2Ch 8:13 offering according to the **c** of Moses, on 4687
8:15 they departed not *from* the **c** of the king 4687
14: 4 of their fathers, and to do the law and the **c**. 4687
19:10 and blood, between law and **c**, 4687
24: 6 *according to the* **c** of Moses the servant of NIH
24: 8 at the king's **c** they made a chest, and set it 559
24:21 stoned him *with* stones at the **c** of the king 4687
29:15 and came, according to the **c** of the king, 4687
29:25 according to the **c** of David, and of Gad 4687
29:25 *so was* the **c** of the LORD by his prophets. 4687
30: 6 Judah, and according to the **c** of the king, 4687
30:12 give them one heart to do the **c** of the king 4687
31: 5 as soon as the **c** came abroad, the children 1697
31:13 at the **c** of Hezekiah the king, and 4662
35:10 in their courses, according to the king's **c**. 4687
35:15 according to the **c** of David, and Asaph, 4687
35:16 according to the **c** of king Josiah. 4687
Ezr 4:21 Give ye now **c** to cause these men to cease, 2942
4:21 until *another* **c** shall be given from me. 2941
6:14 finished *it*, according to the **c** of the God of 2941
6:14 according to the **c** of Cyrus, and Darius, 2942
8:17 I **sent** them **with c** unto Iddo the chief at 6680
10: 3 of those that tremble at the **c** of our God; 4687
Ne 11:23 For *it was* the king's **c** concerning them, 4687
12:24 according to the **c** of David the man of 4687
12:45 according to the **c** of David, *and* 4687
Est 1:12 come at the king's **c** by *his* chamberlains: 1697
1:15 she hath not performed the **c** of the king 3982
1:19 let there go a royal **c** from him, and let it be 1697
2: 8 when the king's **c** and his decree was heard, 1697
2:20 for Esther did the **c** of Mordecai, like as 3982
3: 3 Why transgressest thou the king's **c**? 4687
3:14 The copy of the writing for a **c** to be given 1881
3:15 being hastened by the king's **c**, and 1697
4: 3 whithersoever the king's **c** and his decree 1697
4: 5 **gave** him **a c** to Mordecai, to know what it 6680
4:10 and **gave** him **c** unto Mordecai: 6680
8:13 The copy of the writing for a **c** to be given 1881
8:14 and pressed on by the king's **c**, 1697
8:17 whithersoever the king's **c** and his decree 1697
9: 1 when the king's **c** and his decree drew near 1697
Job 23:12 Neither have I gone back from the **c** of his 4687
Ps 19: 8 the **c** of the LORD *is* pure, 4687
71: 3 thou hast **given c** to save me; for thou *art* 6680
119:96 all perfection: *but* thy **c** *is* exceeding broad. 4687
147:15 He sendeth forth his **c** *upon* earth: his word 565
Pr 6:20 keep thy father's **c**, and forsake not the law 4687
6:23 For the **c** *is* a lamp; and the law *is* light; and 4687
8:29 that the waters should not pass his **c**; 6310
13:13 he that feareth the **c** shall be rewarded. 4687
19:16 He that keepeth the **c** keepeth his own soul; 4687
Ecc 8: 2 I *counsel thee* to keep the king's **c**, and 6310
8: 5 Whoso keepeth the **c** shall feel no evil 4687
Isa 23:11 the LORD hath **given a c** against 6680
36:21 for the king's **c** was, saying, Answer him 4687
Jer 35:14 they drink none, but obey their father's **c**: 4687
35:16 have performed the **c** of their father, 4687
35:18 Because ye have obeyed the **c** of Jonadab 4687
La 1:18 for I have rebelled against his **c**: 6310
Da 3:22 Therefore because the king's **c** *was* urgent, 4406
9:23 At the beginning of thy supplications the **c** 1697
9:25 *that* from the going forth of the **c** to restore 1697
Hos 5:11 because he willingly walked after the **c**. 6673
Na 1:14 the LORD hath **given a c** concerning thee, 6680
Mal 2: 1 And now, O ye priests, this **c** *is* for you. 4687
2: 4 ye shall know that I have sent this **c** unto 4687
Mt 8:18 he **gave c** to depart unto the other side. *2753*
15: 3 Why do you also transgress the **c** of God by *1785*
15: 6 *he shall be free.* Thus have ye made the **c** of *1785*
22:36 Master, which *is* the great **c** in the law? *1785*
22:38 This is the first and great **c**. *1785*
Mk 7: 8 For laying aside the **c** of God, ye hold *1785*
7: 9 unto them, Full well ye reject the **c** of God, *1785*
12:28 asked him, Which is the first **c** of all? *1785*
12:30 and with all thy strength: this *is* the first **c**. *1785*
12:31 There is none other **c** greater than these. *1785*
Lk 15:29 neither transgressed I at any time thy **c**: *1785*
23:56 rested the sabbath day according to the **c**. *1785*
Jn 10:18 This **c** have I received of my Father. *1785*
11:57 and the Pharisees had given a **c**, *1785*
12:49 he gave me a **c**, what I should say, and *1785*
12:50 And I know that his **c** is life everlasting: *1785*
13:34 A new **c** I give unto you, That ye love one *1785*
14:31 and as the Father **gave** me **c**, *even* so I do. *1781*
15:12 This is my **c**, That ye love one another, as I *1785*
Ac 15:24 keep the law: to whom we **gave** no *such* **c**: *1291*
17:15 and receiving a **c** unto Silas and Timotheus *1785*
23:30 **gave c** to *his* accusers also to say before *3853*
25:23 at Festus' **c** Paul was brought *forth*. *2753*
Ro 7: 8 But sin, taking occasion by the **c**, *1785*
7: 9 but when the **c** came, sin revived, and *1785*
7:10 And the **c**, which was *ordained* to life, *1785*
7:11 For sin, taking occasion by the **c**, *1785*
7:12 *is* holy, and the **c** holy, and just, and good. *1785*
7:13 that sin by the **c** might become exceeding *1785*
13: 9 and if *there be* any other **c**, it is briefly *1785*
16:26 according to the **c** of the everlasting God, *2003*
1Co 7: 6 I speak this by permission, *and* not of **c**. *2003*
7:25 Now concerning virgins I have no **c** of *2003*
2Co 8: 8 I speak not by **c**, but by occasion of *2003*
Eph 6: 2 (which is the first **c** with promise;) *1785*
1Ti 1: 1 an apostle of Jesus Christ by the **c** of God *2003*
1: 5 Now the end of the **c** is charity out of a *3852*
6:14 That thou keep *this* **c** without spot, *1785*
Tit 1: 3 me according to the **c** of God our Saviour; *2003*
Heb 7: 5 **c** to take tithes of the people according to *1785*
7:16 not after the law of a carnal **c**, but after *1785*
7:18 For there is verily a disannulling of the **c** *1785*
11:22 of Israel; and **gave c** concerning his bones. *1781*
11:23 and they were not afraid of the king's **c**. *1297*
2Pe 2:21 to turn from the holy **c** delivered unto them. *1785*
3: 2 of the **c** of us the apostles of the Lord and *1785*
1Jn 2: 7 I write no new **c** unto you, but an old *1785*
2: 7 an old **c** which ye had from the beginning. *1785*
2: 7 The old **c** is the word which ye have heard *1785*
2: 8 Again, a new **c** I write unto you, *1785*
3:23 And this is his **c**, That we should believe on *1785*
3:23 and love one another, as he gave us **c**. *1785*
4:21 And this **c** have we from him, That he who *1785*
2Jn 1: 4 as we have received a **c** from the Father. *1785*
1: 5 not as though I wrote a new **c** unto thee, but *1785*
1: 6 This is the **c**, That, as ye have heard from *1785*

COMMANDMENTS (171) [COMMAND]

Ge 26: 5 my charge, my **c**, my statutes, and my laws. 4687
Ex 15:26 wilt give ear to his **c**, and keep all his 4687
16:28 How long refuse ye to keep my **c** and 4687
20: 6 of them that love me, and keep my **c**. 4687
24:12 and a law, and **c** which I have written; 4687
34:28 tables the words of the covenant, the ten **c**. 1697
Lev 4: 2 **c** of the LORD (*concerning things* which 4687
4:13 **c** of the LORD *concerning things* which 4687
4:22 **c** of the LORD his God *concerning things* 4687
4:27 **c** of the LORD *concerning things* which 4687
5:17 to be done by the **c** of the LORD; 4687
22:31 Therefore shall ye keep my **c**, and do them: 4687
26: 3 in my statutes, and keep my **c**, and do them; 4687
26:14 unto me, and will not do all these **c**; 4687
26:15 so that *ye* will not do all my **c**, *but* that ye 4687
27:34 These *are* the **c**, which the LORD 4687
Nu 15:22 ye have erred, and not observed all these **c**, 4687
15:39 remember all the **c** of the LORD, and 4687
15:40 do all my **c**, and be holy unto your God. 4687
36:13 These *are* the **c** and the judgments, 4687
Dt 4: 2 that *ye* may keep the **c** of the LORD your 4687

Dt 4:13 he commanded you to perform, *even* ten **c**; 1697
4:40 shalt keep therefore his statutes, and his **c**, 4687
5:10 of them that love me and keep my **c**. 4687
5:29 would fear me, and keep all my **c** always, 4687
5:31 I will speak unto thee all the **c**, and 4687
6: 1 Now these *are* the **c**, the statutes, and 4687
6: 2 to keep all his statutes and his **c**, which I 4687
6:17 You shall diligently keep the **c** of 4687
6:25 if we observe to do all these **c** before 4687
7: 9 and keep his **c** to a thousand generations; 4687
7:11 Thou shalt therefore keep the **c**, and 4687
8: 1 All the **c** which I command thee *this* day 4687
8: 2 whether thou wouldest keep his **c**, or no. 4687
8: 6 Therefore thou shalt keep the **c** of 4687
8:11 in not keeping his **c**, and his judgments, and 4687
10: 4 according to the first writing, the ten **c**, 1697
10:13 To keep the **c** of the LORD, and his 4687
11: 1 and his judgments, and his **c** alway. 4687
11: 8 Therefore shall ye keep all the **c** which I 4687
11:13 if you shall hearken diligently unto my **c** 4687
11:22 For if ye shall diligently keep all these **c** 4687
11:27 if ye obey the **c** of the LORD your God, 4687
11:28 if ye will not obey the **c** of the LORD 4687
13: 4 keep his **c**, and obey his voice, and 4687
13:18 to keep all his **c** which I command thee *this* 4687
15: 5 to observe to do all these **c** which I 4687
19: 9 If thou shalt keep all these **c** to do them, 4687
26:13 according to all thy **c** which thou hast 4687
26:13 I have not transgressed thy **c**, neither have 4687
26:17 his **c**, and his judgments, and to hearken 4687
26:18 and that *thou* shouldest keep all his **c**; 4687
27: 1 Keep all the **c** which I command you *this* 4687
27:10 do his **c** and his statutes, which I command 4687
28: 1 to do all his **c** which I command thee *this* 4687
28: 9 if thou shalt keep the **c** of the LORD thy 4687
28:13 if that thou hearken unto the **c** of 4687
28:15 to observe to do all his **c** and his statutes 4687
28:45 to keep his **c** and his statutes which he 4687
30: 8 do all his **c** which I command thee *this* day. 4687
30:10 to keep his **c** and his statutes which are 4687
30:16 to keep his **c** and his statutes and 4687
31: 5 all the **c** which I have commanded you. 4687
Jos 22: 5 to keep his **c**, and to cleave unto him, and 4687
Jdg 2:17 walked in, obeying the **c** of the LORD; 4687
3: 4 would hearken unto the **c** of the LORD, 4687
1Sa 15:11 and hath not performed my **c**. 1697
1Ki 2: 3 *and* his **c**, and his judgments, and 4687
3:14 to keep my statutes and my **c**, as thy father 4687
6:12 and keep all my **c** to walk in them; 4687
8:58 to keep his **c**, and his statutes, and 4687
8:61 his statutes, and to keep his **c**, as at this day. 4687
9: 6 will not keep my **c** *and* my statutes which I 4687
11:34 he kept my **c** and my statutes: 4687
11:38 to keep my statutes and my **c**, as David my 4687
14: 8 who kept my **c**, and who followed me with 4687
18:18 in that ye have forsaken the **c** of 4687
2Ki 17:13 evil ways, and keep my **c** *and* my statutes, 4687
17:16 they left all the **c** of the LORD their God, 4687
17:19 Also Judah kept not the **c** of the LORD 4687
18: 6 not from following him, but kept his **c**, 4687
23: 3 to keep his **c** and his testimonies and his 4687
1Ch 28: 7 if he be constant to do my **c** and 4687
28: 8 seek for all the **c** of the LORD your God: 4687
29:19 to keep thy **c**, thy testimonies, and 4687
2Ch 7:19 and forsake my statutes and my **c**, 4687
17: 4 walked in his **c**, and not after the doings of 4687
24:20 Why transgress ye the **c** of the LORD, 4687
31:21 in the law, and in the **c**, to seek his God, 4687
34:31 to keep his **c**, and his testimonies, and 4687
Ezr 7:11 *even* a scribe of the words of the **c** of 4687
9:10 say after this? for we have forsaken thy **c**, 4687
9:14 Should we again break thy **c**, and join in 4687
Ne 1: 5 for them that love him and observe his **c**: 4687
1: 7 have not kept the **c**, nor the statutes, nor 4687
1: 9 turn unto me, and keep my **c**, and do them; 4687
9:13 and true laws, good statutes and **c**: 4687
9:16 their necks, and hearkened not to thy **c**, 4687
9:29 hearkened not unto thy **c**, but 4687
9:34 nor hearkened unto thy **c** and thy 4687
10:29 and do all the **c** of the LORD our Lord, 4687
Ps 78: 7 not forget the works of God, but keep his **c**: 4687
89:31 they break my statutes, and keep not my **c**; 4687
103:18 to those that remember his **c** to do them. 6490
103:20 that excel in strength, that do his **c**, 1697
111: 7 *are* verity and judgment; all his **c** *are* sure. 6490
111:10 that do *his* **c**: his praise endureth for ever. NIH
112: 1 the LORD, *that* delighteth greatly in his **c**. 4687
119: 6 when I have respect unto all thy **c**. 4687
119:10 O let me not wander from thy **c**. 4687
119:19 in the earth: hide not thy **c** from me. 4687
119:21 *that are* cursed, which do err from thy **c**. 4687
119:32 I will run the way of thy **c**, when thou shalt 4687
119:35 Make me to go in the path of thy **c**; 4687
119:47 I will delight myself in thy **c**, which I have 4687
119:48 My hands also will I lift up unto thy **c**, 4687
119:60 I made haste, and delayed not to keep thy **c**. 4687
119:66 and knowledge: for I have believed thy **c**. 4687
119:73 me understanding, that I may learn thy **c**. 4687
119:86 All thy **c** *are* faithful: they persecute me 4687
119:98 Thou *through* thy **c** hast made me wiser 4687
119:115 for I will keep the **c** of my God. 4687
119:127 Therefore I love thy **c** above gold; yea, 4687
119:131 and panted: for I longed for thy **c**. 4687
119:143 taken hold on me: *yet* thy **c** *are* my delights. 4687
119:151 *art* near, O LORD; and all thy **c** *are* truth. 4687
119:166 hoped for thy salvation, and done thy **c**. 4687
119:172 of thy word: for all thy **c** *are* righteousness. 4687
119:176 seek thy servant; for I do not forget thy **c**. 4687
Pr 2: 1 receive my words, and hide my **c** with thee; 4687
3: 1 not my law; but let thine heart keep my **c**: 4687
4: 4 heart retain my words: keep my **c**, and live. 4687
7: 1 keep my words, and lay up my **c** with thee. 4687
7: 2 Keep my **c**, and live; and my law as 4687
10: 8 The wise in heart will receive **c**: but 4687
Ecc 12:13 Fear God, and keep his **c**: for this *is* 4687
Isa 48:18 O that thou hadst hearkened to my **c**! then 4687
Da 9: 4 that love him, and to them that keep his **c**; 4687
Am 2: 4 have not kept his **c**, and their lies caused 2706
Mt 5:19 therefore shall break one of these least **c**, *1785*
15: 9 teaching for doctrines the **c** of men. *1778*
19:17 but if thou wilt enter into life, keep the **c**. *1785*
22:40 On these two **c** hang all the law and *1785*
Mk 7: 7 teaching for doctrines the **c** of men. *1778*
10:19 Thou knowest the **c**, Do not commit *1785*
12:29 The first of all the **c** *is*, Hear, O Israel; *1785*
Lk 1: 6 walking in all the **c** and ordinances of *1785*
18:20 Thou knowest the **c**, Do not commit *1785*
Jn 14:15 If ye love me, keep my **c**. *1785*
14:21 He that hath my **c**, and keepeth them, he it *1785*
15:10 If ye keep my **c**, ye shall abide in my love; *1785*
15:10 even as I have kept my Father's **c**, and *1785*
Ac 1: 2 **given c** unto the Apostles whom he had *1781*
1Co 7:19 is nothing, but the keeping of the **c** of God. *1785*
14:37 that I write unto you are the **c** of the Lord. *1785*
Eph 2:15 *even* the law of **c** *contained* in ordinances; *1785*
Col 2:22 after the **c** and doctrines of men? *1778*
4:10 (touching whom ye received **c**: *1785*
1Th 4: 2 For ye know what **c** we gave you by *3852*
Tit 1:14 and **c** of men, that turn from the truth. *1785*
1Jn 2: 3 know that we know him, if we keep his **c**. *1785*
2: 4 and keepeth not his **c**, is a liar, and the truth *1785*
3:22 because we keep his **c**, and do those *things* *1785*
3:24 And he that keepeth his **c** dwelleth in him, *1785*
5: 2 of God, when we love God, and keep his **c**. *1785*
5: 3 this is the love of God, that we keep his **c**: *1785*
5: 3 and his **c** are not grievous. *1785*
2Jn 1: 6 And this is love, that we walk after his **c**. *1785*
Rev 12:17 which keep the **c** of God, and have *1785*
14:12 here *are* they that keep the **c** of God, and *1785*
22:14 Blessed *are* they that do his **c**, that they *1785*

COMMEND (7) [COMMENDATION, COMMENDED, COMMENDETH, COMMENDING]

Lk 23:46 he said, Father, into thy hands I **c** my spirit: *3908*
Ac 20:32 I **c** you to God, and to the word of his *3908*
Ro 3: 5 But if our unrighteousness **c** *4921*
16: 1 I **c** unto you Phebe our sister, which is a *4921*
2Co 3: 1 Do we begin again to **c** ourselves? or need *4921*
5:12 For we **c** not ourselves again unto you, but *4921*
10:12 compare ourselves with some that **c** *4921*

COMMENDABLE See THANKWORTHY

COMMENDATION (2) [COMMEND]

2Co 3: 1 as some *others,* epistles of **c** to you, or *4956*
3: 1 to you, or *letters* of **c** from you? *4956*

COMMENDED (6) [COMMEND]
Ge 12:15 Pharaoh saw her, and **c** her before Pharaoh: 1984
Pr 12: 8 A man shall be **c** according to his wisdom: 1984
Ecc 8:15 I **c** mirth, because a man hath no better 7623
Lk 16: 8 And the lord **c** the unjust steward, because *1867*
Ac 14:23 they **c** them to the Lord, on whom they *3908*
2Co 12:11 for I ought to have been **c** of you: for *in* *4921*

COMMENDETH (4) [COMMEND]
Ro 5: 8 But God **c** his love toward us, in that, *4921*
1Co 8: 8 But meat **c** us not to God: for neither, if we *3936*
2Co 10:18 For not he that **c** himself is approved, but *4921*
10:18 himself is approved, but whom the Lord **c**. *4921*

COMMENDING (1) [COMMEND]
2Co 4: 2 by manifestation of the truth **c** ourselves to *4921*

COMMISSION (1) [COMMISSIONS]
Ac 26:12 with authority and **c** from the chief priests, *2011*

COMMISSIONS (1) [COMMISSION]
Ezr 8:36 they delivered the king's **c** unto the king's 1881

COMMIT (75) [COMMITTED, COMMITTEST, COMMITTETH, COMMITTING]
Ex 20:14 Thou shalt not **c adultery**. 5003
Lev 5:15 If a soul **c a trespass**, and 4603+4604
5:17 **c** any *of these things* which are forbidden to 6213
6: 2 **c a trespass** against the LORD, and 4603+4604
18:26 and shall not **c** any of these abominations; 6213
18:29 For whosoever shall **c** any of these 6213
18:29 even the souls that **c** *them* shall be cut off 6213
18:30 that *ye* **c** not *any one* of *these* abominable 6213
20: 5 to **c** whoredom with Molech, from among NIH
Nu 5: 6 or woman shall **c** any sin that men commit, 6213
5: 6 or woman shall commit any sin that men **c**, NIH
5:12 and **c a trespass** against him, 4603+4604
25: 1 the people begun to **c whoredom** with 2181
31:16 to **c** trespass against the LORD in 4560
Dt 5:18 Neither shalt thou **c adultery**. 5003
19:20 shall henceforth **c** no more any such evil 6213
Jos 22:20 **c a trespass** in the accursed thing, 4603+4604
2Sa 7:14 If he **c iniquity**, I will chasten him with 5753
2Ch 21:11 **caused** the inhabitants of Jerusalem **to c fornication**, 2181
Job 5: 8 and unto God would I **c** my cause: 7760
34:10 the Almighty, *that he should* **c** iniquity. NIH
Ps 31: 5 Into thine hand I **c** my spirit: thou hast 6485
37: 5 **C** thy way unto the LORD; trust also in 1556
Pr 16: 3 **C** thy works unto the LORD, and 1556
16:12 *It is* an abomination to kings to **c** 6213
Isa 22:21 and I will **c** thy government into his hand: 5414
23:17 shall **c fornication** with all the kingdoms of 2181
Jer 7: 9 **c adultery**, and swear falsely, and 5003
9: 5 *and* weary themselves to **c iniquity**. 5753
23:14 *they* **c adultery**, and walk in lies: 5003
37:21 **c** Jeremiah into the court of the prison, 6485
44: 7 Wherefore **c** ye *this* great evil against your 6213
Eze 3:20 **c** iniquity, and I lay a stumblingblock 6213
8:17 **c** the abominations which they commit 6213
8:17 the abominations which they **c** here? 6213
16:17 of men, and didst **c whoredom** with them, 2181
16:34 none followeth thee to **c whoredoms**: 2181
16:43 thou shalt not **c** *this* lewdness above all 6213
20:30 **c** ye **whoredom** after their abominations? 2181
22: 9 in the midst of thee they **c** lewdness. 6213
23:43 Will they now **c whoredoms** with 2181+8457
33:13 to his own righteousness, and **c** iniquity, 6213
Hos 4:10 they shall **c whoredom**, and shall not 2181
4:13 your daughters shall **c whoredom**, 2181
4:13 and your spouses shall **c adultery**. 5003
4:14 your daughters when they **c whoredom**, 2181
4:14 nor your spouses when they **c adultery**: 5003
6: 9 *in* the way by consent: for they **c** lewdness. 6213
7: 1 for they **c** falsehood; and the thief cometh 6466
Mt 5:27 of old time, Thou shalt not **c adultery**: *3431*
5:32 of fornication, causeth her to **c adultery**: *3429*
19: 9 her *which is* put away doth **c adultery**. *3429*
19:18 Thou shalt not **c adultery**, Thou shalt not *3431*
Mk 10:19 Do not **c adultery**, Do not kill, Do not *3431*
Lk 12:48 and did **c** *things* worthy of stripes, *4160*
16:11 who will **c to your trust** the true *riches?* *4100*
18:20 Do not **c adultery**, Do not kill, Do not *3431*
Jn 2:24 But Jesus did not **c** himself unto them, *4100*
Ro 1:32 that they which **c** such *things* are worthy of *4238*
2: 2 to truth against them which **c** such *things*. *4238*
2:22 that sayest *a man* should not **c adultery**, *3431*
2:22 not commit adultery, dost thou **c adultery**? *3431*
2:22 that abhorrest idols, dost thou **c sacrilege**? *2416*
13: 9 For *this*, Thou shalt not **c adultery**, *3431*
1Co 10: 8 Neither let us **c fornication**, as some of *4203*
1Ti 1:18 This charge I **c** unto thee, son Timothy, *3908*
2Ti 2: 2 the same **c** thou to faithful men, who shall *3908*
Jas 2: 9 ye **c** sin, and are convinced of the law as *2038*
2:11 Do not **c adultery**, said also, Do not kill. *3431*
2:11 Now if thou **c** no **adultery**, yet *if* thou kill, *3431*
1Pe 4:19 **c the keeping** of their souls to *him* in well *3908*
1Jn 3: 9 Whosoever is born of God doth not **c** sin; *4160*
Rev 2:14 sacrificed unto idols, and to **c fornication**. *4203*
2:20 and to seduce my servants to **c fornication**, *4203*
2:22 them that **c adultery** with her into great *3431*

COMMITTED (92) [COMMIT]
Ge 39: 8 and he hath **c** all that he hath to my hand; 5414
39:22 the keeper of the prison **c** to Joseph's hand 5414
Lev 4:35 an atonement for his sin that he hath **c**, 2398
5: 7 which he hath **c**, two turtledoves, or 2398
18:30 which were **c** before you, and that ye defile 6213
20:13 both of them have **c** an abomination: 6213
20:23 for they **c** all these *things*, and therefore 6213
Nu 15:24 if *ought* be **c** by ignorance without 6213
Dt 17: 5 which have **c** that wicked thing, 6213
21:22 if a man have **c a sin** worthy of death, and 2399
Jos 7: 1 the children of Israel **c a trespass** in 4603+4604
22:16 What trespass *is* this that ye have **c** against 4603
22:31 ye have not **c** this **trespass** against 4603+4604
Jdg 20: 6 for they have **c** lewdness and folly in Israel. 6213
1Ki 8:47 done perversely, we have **c wickedness**; 7561
14:22 to jealousy with their sins which they had **c**, 2398
14:27 **c** *them* unto the hands of the chief of 6485
1Ch 10:13 **transgression** which he **c** against 4603+4604
2Ch 12:10 **c** *them* to the hands of the chief of 6485
34:16 saying, All that was **c** to thy servants, 5414
Ps 106: 6 we have **c iniquity**, we have done 5753
Jer 2:13 For my people have **c** two evils; they have 6213
3: 8 Israel **c adultery** I had put her away, 5003
3: 9 and **c adultery** with stones and with stocks. 5003
5: 7 they then **c adultery**, and 5003
5:30 and horrible thing is **c** in the land; 1961
6:15 Were they ashamed when they had **c** 6213
8:12 Were they ashamed when they had **c** 6213
16:10 what *is* our **sin** that we have **c** against 2398+2403
29:23 Because they have **c** villany in Israel, and 6213
29:23 have **c adultery** with their neighbours' 5003
39:14 **c** him unto Gedaliah the son of Ahikam 5414
40: 7 had **c** unto him men, and women, and 6485
41:10 guard had **c** to Gedaliah the son of Ahikam: 6485
44: 3 which they have **c** to provoke me to anger, 6213
44: 9 which they have **c** in the land of Judah, and 6213
44:22 of the abominations which ye have **c**; 6213
Eze 6: 9 which they have **c** in all their abominations. 6213
15: 8 because they have **c a trespass**, saith 4603+4604
16:26 Thou hast also **c fornication** with 2181
16:50 and **c** abomination before me: 6213
16:51 Neither hath Samaria **c** half of thy sins; but 2398
16:52 **sins** that thou hast **c** more abominable than 2403
18:12 up his eyes to the idols, hath **c** abomination, 6213
18:21 will turn from all his sins that he hath **c**, 6213
18:22 All his transgressions that he hath **c**, 6213
18:27 away from his wickedness that he hath **c**, 6213
18:28 from all his transgressions that he hath **c**, 6213
20:27 they have **c a trespass** against me. 4603+4604
20:43 own sight for all your evils that ye have **c**. 6213
22:11 one hath **c** abomination with his 6213
23: 3 they **c whoredoms** in Egypt; 2181
23: 3 in Egypt; they **c whoredoms** in their youth: 2181
23: 7 Thus she **c** her whoredoms with them, 5414
23:37 That they have **c adultery**, and blood *is* in 5003
23:37 with their idols have they **c adultery**, and 5003
33:13 for his iniquity that he hath **c**, he shall die 6213
33:16 None of his sins that he hath **c** shall be 2398
33:29 of all their abominations which they have **c**. 6213
43: 8 by their abominations that they have **c**: 6213
44:13 and their abominations which they have **c**. 6213
Da 9: 5 have **c iniquity**, and have done wickedly, 5753
Hos 1: 2 for the land hath **c great whoredom**, 2181+2181
4:18 they have **c whoredom continually**: 2181+2181
Mal 2:11 an abomination is **c** in Israel and 6213

C

Mt 5:28 c adultery with her already in his heart. 3431
Mk 15: 7 *him,* who had c murder in the insurrection. 4160
Lk 12:48 and to whom *men* have c much, of him 3908
Jn 5:22 but hath c all judgment unto the Son: 1325
Ac 8: 3 haling men and women c *them* to prison. 3860
25:11 or have c any *thing* worthy of death, 4238
25:25 But when I found that he had c nothing 4238
27:40 they c *themselves* unto the sea, and 1439
28:17 though I have c nothing against the people, 4160
Ro 3: 2 that unto them were c the oracles of God. 4100
1Co 9:17 a dispensation *of the gospel* is c unto me. 4100
10: 8 as some of them c, and fell in one day three 4203
2Co 5:19 hath c unto us the word of reconciliation. 5087
11: 7 Have I c an offence in abasing myself that 4160
12:21 and lasciviousness which they have c. 4238
Gal 2: 7 of the uncircumcision was c unto me, 4100
1Ti 1:11 the blessed God, which was c to my trust. 4100
6:20 keep that which is c to *thy* trust, 3872
2Ti 1:12 which I have c unto *him* against that day. 3866
1:14 *That* good thing which was c unto *thee* 3872
Tit 1: 3 which is c unto me according to 4100
Jas 5:15 and if he have c sins, they shall be forgiven 4160
1Pe 2:23 c *himself* to him that judgeth righteously: 3860
Jude 1:15 ungodly deeds which they have ungodly c, 764
Rev 17: 2 the kings of the earth have c fornication, 4203
18: 3 the kings of the earth have c fornication 4203
18: 9 who have c fornication and 4203

COMMITTEST (1) [COMMIT]
Hos 5: 3 thou c whoredom, *and* Israel is defiled. 2181

COMMITTETH (19) [COMMIT]
Lev 20:10 the man that c adultery with *another* man's 5003
20:10 *even he* that c adultery with his 5003
Ps 10:14 the poor c *himself* unto thee; thou art 5800
Pr 6:32 *But* whoso c adultery with a woman 5003
Eze 8: 6 that the house of Israel c here, 6213
16:32 *But as* a wife that c adultery, *which* taketh 5003
18:24 c iniquity, *and* doeth according to all 6213
18:26 and c iniquity, and dieth in them; 6213
33:18 and c iniquity, he shall even die thereby. 6213
Mt 5:32 shall marry her that is divorced c adultery. 3429
19: 9 and shall marry another, c adultery: 3429
Mk 10:11 and marry another, c adultery against her. 3429
10:12 and be married to another, she c adultery. 3429
Lk 16:18 his wife, and marrieth another, c adultery: 3431
16:18 is put away from *her* husband c adultery. 3431
Jn 8:34 Whosoever c sin is the servant of sin. 4160
1Co 6:18 he that c fornication sinneth against his 4203
1Jn 3: 4 Whosoever c sin transgresseth also the law: 4160
3: 8 He that c sin is of the devil; for the devil 4160

COMMITTING (2) [COMMIT]
Eze 33:15 in the statutes of life, without c iniquity; 6213
Hos 4: 2 and killing, and stealing, and c adultery, 5003

COMMODIOUS (1)
Ac 27:12 because the haven was not c to winter in, 428

COMMON (21) [COMMONLY]
Lev 4:27 if any one of the c people sin through 776
Nu 16:29 If these *men* die the c death of all men, or 3509.1
1Sa 21: 4 *There is* no c bread under mine hand, but 2455
21: 5 and *the bread is in* a manner c, yea, 2455
Ecc 6: 1 seen under the sun, and it *is* c among men: 7227
Jer 26:23 cast his dead body into the graves of the c 1121
31: 5 shall plant, and shall eat *them* as c things. 2490
Eze 23:42 with the men of the c sort *were* brought 7230
Mt 27:27 of the governor took Jesus into the c hall, 4232
Mk 12:37 his son? And the c people heard him gladly. 4183
Ac 2:44 were together, and had all *things* c; 2839
4:32 was his own; but they had all *things* c. 2839
5:18 the apostles, and put them in the c prison. 1219
10:14 for I have never eaten any *thing that is* c or 2839
10:15 God hath cleansed, *that* call not thou c. 2840
10:28 shewed me that *I* should not call any man c 2839
11: 8 for nothing c or unclean hath at any time 2839
11: 9 God hath cleansed, *that* call not thou c. 2840
1Co 10:13 taken you but such as is c to man: 442
Tit 1: 4 To Titus, *mine* own son after the c faith: 2839
Jude 1: 3 to write unto you of the c salvation, 2839

COMMONLY (2) [COMMON]
Mt 28:15 this saying is c reported among the Jews 1310
1Co 5: 1 It is reported c *that there is* fornication 3654

COMMONWEALTH (1)
Eph 2:12 being aliens from the c of Israel, and 4174

COMMOTION (1) [COMMOTIONS]
Jer 10:22 and a great c out of the north country, 7494

COMMOTIONS (1) [COMMOTION]
Lk 21: 9 But when ye shall hear of wars and c, be not 181

COMMUNE (8) [COMMUNED, COMMUNING, COMMUNION]
Ge 34: 6 went out unto Jacob to c with him. 1696
Ex 25:22 I will c with thee from above the mercy 1696
1Sa 18:22 *saying,* C with David secretly, and say, 1696
19: 3 thou *art,* and I will c with my father of thee; 1696
Job 4: 2 *If we* assay to c with thee, wilt thou be 1697
Ps 4: 4 c with your own heart upon your bed, and 559
64: 5 they c of laying snares privily; they say, 5608
77: 6 I c with mine own heart: and my spirit 7878

COMMUNED (18) [COMMUNE]
Ge 23: 8 he c with them, saying, If it be your mind 1696
34: 8 Hamor c with them, saying, The soul of my 1696
34:20 and c with the men of their city, saying, 1696
42:24 returned to them *again,* and c with them, 1696
43:19 they c with him *at* the door of the house, 1696
Jdg 9: 1 c with them, and with all the family of 1696
1Sa 9:25 *Samuel* c with Saul upon the top of 1696
25:39 David sent and c with Abigail, to take her 1696
1Ki 10: 2 she c with him of all that was in her heart. 1696
2Ki 22:14 in the college;) and they c with her. 1696
2Ch 9: 1 she c with him of all that was in her heart. 1696
Ecc 1:16 I c with mine own heart, saying, Lo, I am 1696
Da 1:19 the king c with them; and among them all 1696
Zec 1:14 So the angel that c with me said unto me, 1696
Lk 6:11 c one with another what they might do to 1255
22: 4 and c with the chief priests and captains, 4814
24:15 that while they c *together* and reasoned, 3656
Ac 24:26 he sent for him the oftener, and c with him. 3656

COMMUNICATE (4) [COMMUNICATED, COMMUNICATION, COMMUNICATIONS]
Gal 6: 6 Let him that is taught in the word c unto 2841
Php 4:14 well done, that ye did c with my affliction. 4790
1Ti 6:18 ready to distribute, willing to c; 2843
Heb 13:16 But to do good and to c forget not: for with 2842

COMMUNICATED (2) [COMMUNICATE]
Gal 2: 2 c unto them *that* gospel which I preach 394
Php 4:15 no church c with me as concerning giving 2841

COMMUNICATION (6) [COMMUNICATE]
2Sa 3:17 Abner had c with the elders of Israel, 1697
2Ki 9:11 unto them, Ye know the man, and his c. 7879
Mt 5:37 But let your c be, Yea, yea; Nay, nay: 3056
Eph 4:29 Let no corrupt c proceed out of your mouth, 3056
Col 3: 8 blasphemy, filthy c out of your mouth. 148
Phm 1: 6 That the c of thy faith may become 2842

COMMUNICATIONS (2) [COMMUNICATE]
Lk 24:17 What *manner of* c *are* these that ye have 3056
1Co 15:33 not deceived: evil c corrupt good manners. 3657

COMMUNING (2) [COMMUNE]
Ge 18:33 as soon as he had left c with Abraham: 1696
Ex 31:18 when he had made an end of c with him 1696

COMMUNION (4) [COMMUNE]
1Co 10:16 is it not the c of the blood of Christ? 2842
10:16 is it not the c of the body of Christ? 2842
2Co 6:14 and what c hath light with darkness? 2842
13:14 and the c of the Holy Ghost, *be* with you 2842

COMPACT (1) [COMPACTED]
Ps 122: 3 Jerusalem *is* builded as a city that is c 2266

COMPACTED (1) [COMPACT]
Eph 4:16 and c by that which every joint supplieth, 4822

COMPANIED (1) [COMPANY]
Ac 1:21 Wherefore of these men which have c with 4905

COMPANIES (17) [COMPANY]
Jdg 7:16 divided the three hundred men *into* three c, 7218
7:20 the three c blew the trumpets, and brake 7218

Jdg 9:34 they laid wait against Shechem *in* four **c**. 7218
9:43 divided them into three **c**, and laid wait in 7218
9:44 the two *other* **c** ran upon all *the people* that 7218
1Sa 11:11 that Saul put the people *in* three **c**; 7218
13:17 out of the camp of the Philistines *in* three **c**: 7218
2Ki 5: 2 the Syrians had gone out *by* **c**, and 1416
1Ch 9:18 they *were* porters in the **c** of the children of 4264
28: 1 the **c** that ministered to the king **by course**, 4256
Ne 12:31 appointed two great **c** *of them that gave* NIH
12:40 So stood the two **c** *of them that gave* thanks NIH
Job 6:19 the **c** of Sheba waited for them. 1979
Isa 21:13 ye lodge, O ye **travelling c** of Dedanim. 736
57:13 When thou criest, let thy **c** deliver thee; but 6899
Eze 26: 7 with horsemen, and **c**, and much people. 6951
Mk 6:39 sit down **by c** upon the green grass. *4849+4849*

COMPANION (13) [COMPANIONS, COMPANIONS']

Ex 32:27 every man his **c**, and every man his 7453
Jdg 14:20 Samson's wife was *given* to his **c**, whom he 4828
15: 2 hated her; therefore I gave her to thy **c**: 4828
15: 6 had taken his wife, and given her to his **c**. 4828
1Ch 27:33 and Hushai the Archite *was* the king's **c**: 7453
Job 30:29 I am a brother to dragons, and a **c** to owls. 7453
Ps 119:63 I *am* a **c** of all *them* that fear thee, and 2270
Pr 13:20 be wise: but a **c** of fools shall be destroyed. 7462
28: 7 he that is a **c** of riotous *men* shameth his 7462
28:24 the same *is* the **c** of a destroyer. 2270
Mal 2:14 yet *is* she thy **c**, and the wife of thy 2278
Php 2:25 and **c in labour**, and fellowsoldier, but *4904*
Rev 1: 9 and **c** in tribulation, and in the kingdom and *4791*

COMPANIONS (21) [COMPANION]

Jdg 11:38 she went with her **c**, and bewailed her 7464
14:11 that they brought thirty **c** to be with him. 4828
Ezr 4: 7 Mithredath, Tabeel, and the rest of their **c**, 3674
4: 9 Shimshai the scribe, and the rest of their **c**; 3675
4:17 *to* the rest of their **c** that dwell in Samaria, 3675
4:23 Shimshai the scribe, and their **c**, they went 3675
5: 3 and their **c**, and said thus unto them, 3675
5: 6 and his **c** the Apharsachites, 3675
6: 6 and your **c** the Apharsachites, 3675
6:13 side the river, Shethar-boznai, and their **c**, 3675
Job 35: 4 I will answer thee, and thy **c** with thee. 7453
41: 6 Shall the **c** make a banquet of him? 2271
Ps 45:14 the virgins her **c** that follow her *shall be* 7464
SS 1: 7 that turneth aside by the flocks of thy **c**? 2270
8:13 in the gardens, the **c** hearken to thy voice: 2270
Isa 1:23 Thy princes *are* rebellious, and **c** of thieves: 2270
Eze 37:16 and for the children of Israel his **c**: 2270
37:16 and *for* all the house of Israel his **c**: 2270
Da 2:17 to Hananiah, Mishael, and Azariah, his **c**: 2269
Ac 19:29 men of Macedonia, Paul's **c in travel**, *4898*
Heb 10:33 whilst ye became **c** of them that were so *2844*

COMPANIONS' (1) [COMPANION]

Ps 122: 8 For my brethren and **c** sakes, I will now 7453

COMPANY (86) [COMPANIED, COMPANIED]

Ge 32: 8 If Esau come to the one **c**, and smite it, then 4264
32: 8 then the *other* **c** which is left shall escape. 4264
32:21 and himself lodged that night in the **c**. 4264
35:11 a nation and a **c** of nations shall be of thee, 6951
37:25 a **c** of Ishmeelites came from Gilead with 736
50: 9 and horsemen: and it was a very great **c**. 4264
Nu 14: 7 they spake unto all the **c** of the children of 5712
16: 5 And he spake unto Korah and unto all his **c**, 5712
16: 6 Take you censers, Korah, and all his **c**; 5712
16:11 all thy **c** *are* gathered together against 5712
16:16 Be thou and all thy **c** before the LORD, 5712
16:40 that he be not as Korah, and as his **c**: 5712
22: 4 Now shall *this* **c** lick up all *that are* round 6951
26: 9 and against Aaron in the **c** of Korah, 5712
26:10 when that **c** died, what time the fire 5712
27: 3 he was not in the **c** of them that gathered 5712
27: 3 against the LORD in the **c** of Korah; 5712
Jdg 9:37 another **c** come along by the plain of 7218
9:44 the **c** that *was* with him, rushed forward, 7218
18:23 aileth thee, that thou **comest with** such **a c**? 2199
1Sa 10: 5 that thou shalt meet a **c** of prophets coming 2256
10:10 to the hill, behold, a **c** of prophets met him; 2256
13:17 one **c** turned unto the way that leadeth to 7218
13:18 another **c** turned the way to Beth-horon: 7218
13:18 another **c** turned *to* the way of the border 7218
19:20 when they saw the **c** of the prophets 3862
30:15 to him, Canst thou bring me down to this **c**? 1416
30:15 and I will bring thee down to this **c**. 1416
30:23 delivered the **c** that came against us into 1416
2Ki 5:15 he and all his **c**, and came, and stood before 4264
9:17 he spied the **c** of Jehu as he came, and said, 8229
9:17 of Jehu as he came, and said, I see a **c**. 8229
2Ch 9: 1 with a very great **c**, and camels that bare 2428
20:12 for we have no might against this great **c** 1995
24:24 of the Syrians came with a small **c** of men, NIH
Ne 12:38 the other **c** *of them that gave* thanks went NIH
Job 16: 7 thou hast made desolate all my **c**. 5712
34: 8 Which goeth in **c** with the workers of 2274
Ps 55:14 *and* walked unto the house of God in **c**. 7285
68:11 great *was* the **c** of those that published *it*. 6635
68:30 Rebuke the **c** of spearmen, the multitude of 2416
106:17 up Dathan, and covered the **c** of Abiram. 5712
106:18 a fire was kindled in their **c**; the flame burnt 5712
Pr 29: 3 he that **keepeth c with** harlots spendeth *his* 7462
SS 1: 9 to a **c of horses** in Pharaoh's chariots. 5484
6:13 As it were the **c** of two armies. 4246
Jer 31: 8 child together: a great **c** shall return thither. 6951
Eze 16:40 They shall also bring up a **c** against thee, 6951
17:17 and great **c** make for him in the war, 6951
23:46 *I will* bring up a **c** upon them, and *will* give 6951
23:47 the **c** shall stone them with stones, and 6951
27: 6 the **c** of the Ashurites have made thy 1323
27:27 in all thy **c** which *is* in the midst of thee, 6951
27:34 and all thy **c** in the midst of thee shall fall. 6951
32: 3 spread out my net over thee with a **c** of 6951
32:22 Asshur *is* there and all her **c**: his graves *are* 6951
32:23 the pit, and her **c** is round about her grave: 6951
38: 4 *of armour, even* a great **c** *with* bucklers 6951
38: 7 all thy **c** that are assembled unto thee, and 6951
38:13 hast thou gathered thy **c** to take a prey? to 6951
38:15 upon horses, a great **c**, and a mighty army: 6951
Hos 6: 9 the **c** of priests murder *in* the way by 2267
Lk 2:44 supposing him to have been in the **c**, *4923*
5:29 and there was a great **c** of publicans and *3793*
6:17 and the **c** of his disciples, and a great *3793*
6:22 when they shall separate you *from their* **c**, NIG
9:14 Make them sit down by fifties in a **c**. *2828*
9:38 a man of the **c** cried out, saying, Master, *3793*
11:27 a certain woman of the **c** lift up her voice, *3793*
12:13 And one of the **c** said unto him, Master, *3793*
23:27 And there followed him a great **c** of people, *4128*
24:22 certain women *also* **of** our **c** made us *1537*
Jn 6: 5 *his* eyes, and saw a great **c** come unto him, *3793*
Ac 4:23 they went to their own **c**, and reported all NIG
6: 7 a great **c** of the priests were obedient to *3793*
10:28 *thing* for a man *that is* a Jew to **keep c**, *2853*
13:13 and his **c** loosed from Paphos, *3588+4012*
15:22 to send chosen men of **their own c** to *846*
17: 5 and **gathered a c**, and set all the city on an *3792*
21: 8 And the next day we that were **of** Paul's **c** *4012*
Ro 15:24 if first I be somewhat filled with your *c*. NIG
1Co 5: 9 I wrote unto you in an epistle not to **c with** *4874*
5:11 now I have written unto you not to **keep c**, *4874*
2Th 3:14 note that *man*, and **have** no **c with** him, *4874*
Heb 12:22 and to an **innumerable c** of angels, *3461*
Rev 18:17 every shipmaster, and all the **c** in ships, *3658*

COMPARABLE (1) [COMPARE]

La 4: 2 The precious sons of Zion, **c** to fine gold, 5537

COMPARE (4) [COMPARABLE, COMPARED, COMPARING, COMPARISON]

Isa 40:18 or what likeness will ye **c** unto him? 6186
46: 5 make *me* equal, and **c** me, that we may be 4911
Mk 4:30 or with what comparison shall we **c** it? *3846*
2Co 10:12 **c** ourselves **with** some that commend *4793*

COMPARED (5) [COMPARE]

Ps 89: 6 For who in the heaven can be **c** unto 6186
Pr 3:15 thou canst desire are not to be **c** unto her. 7737
8:11 that may be desired are not to be **c** to it. 7737
SS 1: 9 I have **c** thee, O my love, to a company of 1819
Ro 8:18 **c with** the glory which shall be revealed in *4314*

COMPARING (2) [COMPARE]

1Co 2:13 **c** spiritual *things* with spiritual. *4793*
2Co 10:12 and **c** themselves **amongst** themselves, *4793*

COMPARISON (4) [COMPARE]

Jdg 8: 2 What have I done now **in c of** you? 3509.1

Jdg 8: 3 what was I able to do **in c of** you? 3509.1
Hag 2: 3 *is it* not in your eyes **in c of** it as nothing? 3644
Mk 4:30 or with what **c** shall we compare it? *3850*

COMPASS (39) [COMPASSED, COMPASSEST, COMPASSETH, COMPASSING]

Ex 27: 5 thou shalt put it under the **c** of the altar 3749
38: 4 the **c** thereof beneath unto the midst of it. 3749
Nu 21: 4 way of the Red sea, to **c** the land of Edom: 5437
34: 5 the border shall **fetch a c** from Azmon unto 5437
Jos 6: 3 ye shall **c** the city, all *ye* men of war, 5437
6: 4 the seventh day ye shall **c** the city seven 5437
6: 7 **c** the city, and let him that is armed pass on 5437
15: 3 up to Adar, and **fetched a c** to Karkaa: 5437
2Sa 5:23 *but* **fetch a c** behind them, and come upon 5437
1Ki 7:15 of twelve cubits did **c** either of them **about**. 5437
7:23 of thirty cubits did **c** it **round about**. 5437+5439
7:35 in the top of the base *was there* a round **c** of 5439
2Ki 3: 9 they **fetcht a c** of seven days' journey: and 5437
11: 8 ye shall **c** the king round about, every man 5362
2Ch 4: 2 round **in c**, and five cubits the height 5439
4: 2 a line of thirty cubits did **c** it round about. 5437
4: 3 of oxen, which did **c** it round about: 5437
23: 7 the Levites shall **c** the king round about, 5362
Job 16:13 His archers **c** me **round about**, he cleaveth 5437
40:22 the willows of the brook **c** him **about**. 5437
Ps 5:12 *with* favour wilt thou **c** him as *with* a 5849
7: 7 congregation of the people **c** thee **about**: 5437
17: 9 *from* my deadly enemies, *who* **c** me **about**. 5362
26: 6 so will I **c** thine altar, O LORD: 5437
32: 7 thou shalt **c** me **about** *with* songs of 5437
32:10 in the LORD, mercy shall **c** him **about**. 5437
49: 5 the iniquity of my heels shall **c** me **about**? 5437
140: 9 *As for* the head of those that **c** me **about**, 4524
142: 7 the righteous shall **c** me **about**; for thou 3803
Pr 8:27 when he set a **c** upon the face of the depth: 2329
Isa 44:13 he marketh it out with the **c**, and maketh it 4230
50:11 a fire, that **c** *yourselves* **about** with sparks: 247
Jer 31:22 *thing* in the earth, A woman shall **c** a man. 5437
31:39 the hill Gareb, and shall **c about** to Goath. 5437
52:21 a fillet of twelve cubits did **c** it; and 5437
Hab 1: 4 for the wicked doth **c about** the righteous; 3803
Mt 23:15 for ye **c** sea and land to make one *4013*
Lk 19:43 and **c** thee **round**, and keep thee in on *4033*
Ac 28:13 And from thence we **fet a c**, *4022*

COMPASSED (44) [COMPASS]

Ge 19: 4 **c** the house **round**, both old and young, 5437
Dt 2: 1 unto me: and we **c** mount Seir many days. 5437
2: 3 Ye have **c** this mountain long enough: 5437
Jos 6:11 So the ark of the LORD **c** the city, 5437
6:14 the second day they **c** the city once, 5437
6:15 **c** the city after the same manner seven 5437
6:15 only on that day they **c** the city seven times. 5437
15:10 the border **c** from Baalah westward unto 5437
18:14 and **c** the corner of the sea southward, 5437
Jdg 11:18 **c** the land of Edom, and the land of Moab, 5437
16: 2 they **c** *him* **in**, and laid wait for him all 5437
1Sa 23:26 his men **c** David and his men **round about** 5849
2Sa 18:15 young men that bare Joab's armour **c about** 5437
22: 5 When the waves of death **c** me, the floods of 661
22: 6 The sorrows of hell **c** me **about**; the snares 5437
2Ki 6:14 they came by night, and **c** the city **about**. 5362
6:15 a host **c** the city both with horses and 5437
8:21 smote the Edomites which **c** him **about**, 5437
2Ch 18:31 Therefore they **c** about him to fight: but 5437
21: 9 smote the Edomites which **c** him **in**, and 5437
33:14 **c** about Ophel, and raised it up a very great 5437
Job 19: 6 overthrown me, and hath **c** me with his net. 5362
26:10 He hath **c** the waters **with** 2328+5921+6440
Ps 17:11 They have now **c** us *in* our steps: they have 5437
18: 4 The sorrows of death **c** me, and the floods of 661
18: 5 The sorrows of hell **c** me **about**: the snares 5437
22:12 Many bulls have **c** me: strong *bulls* of 5437
22:16 For dogs have **c** me: the assembly of 5437
40:12 For innumerable evils have **c** me **about**: 661
88:17 daily like water; they **c** me **about** together. 5362
109: 3 They **c** me **about** also *with* words of 5437
116: 3 The sorrows of death **c** me, and the pains of 661
118:10 All nations **c** me **about**: but in the name of 5437
118:11 They **c** me **about**; yea, they compassed me 5437
118:11 me about; yea, they **c** me **about**: 5437
118:12 They **c** me **about** like bees; they are 5437
La 3: 5 against me, and **c** *me* with gall and travail. 5362
Jnh 2: 3 of the seas; and the floods **c** me **about**: 5437
2: 5 The waters **c** me **about**, *even* to the soul: 661
Lk 21:20 And when ye shall see Jerusalem **c** with *2944*
Heb 5: 2 for that he himself also is **c with** infirmity. *4029*
11:30 after they were **c about** seven days. *2944*
12: 1 Wherefore seeing we also are **c about** with *4029*
Rev 20: 9 and **c** the camp of the saints **about**, and *2944*

COMPASSEST (1) [COMPASS]

Ps 139: 3 Thou **c** my path and my lying down, and 2219

COMPASSETH (5) [COMPASS]

Ge 2:11 that *is it* which **c** the whole land of Havilah, 5437
2:13 the same *is it* that **c** the whole land of 5437
Jos 19:14 the border **c** it on the north side *to* 5437
Ps 73: 6 Therefore pride **c** them **about as a chain**; 6059
Hos 11:12 Ephraim **c** me **about** with lies, and 5437

COMPASSING (3) [COMPASS]

1Ki 7:24 it **round about** *there were* knops **c** it, 5437+5439
7:24 ten in a cubit, **c** the sea round about: 5362
2Ch 4: 3 ten in a cubit, **c** the sea round about. 5362

COMPASSION (41) [COMPASSIONS]

Ex 2: 6 she **had c** on him, and said, This *is one* of 2550
Dt 13:17 and **have c** upon thee, and multiply thee, 7355
30: 3 **have c** upon thee, and will return and 7355
1Sa 23:21 *be* ye of the LORD; for ye **have c** on me. 2550
1Ki 8:50 give them **c** before them who carried them 7356
8:50 that they may **have c** on them: 7355
2Ki 13:23 **had c** on them, and had respect unto them, 7355
2Ch 30: 9 your children *shall find* **c** before them that 7356
36:15 because he **had c** on his people, and on his 2550
36:17 **had** no **c** upon young man or maiden, 2550
Ps 78:38 he, *being* **full of c**, forgave *their* iniquity, 7349
86:15 O Lord, *art* a God **full of c**, and gracious, 7349
111: 4 the LORD *is* gracious and **full of c**. 7349
112: 4 *he is* gracious, and **full of c**, and righteous. 7349
145: 8 The LORD *is* gracious, and **full of c**; 7349
Isa 49:15 that *she* should not **have c** on the son of her 7355
Jer 12:15 **have c** on them, and will bring them again, 7355
La 3:32 yet will he **have c** according to 7355
Eze 16: 5 any of these unto thee, to **have c** upon thee; 2550
Mic 7:19 He will turn again, he will **have c** upon us; 7355
Mt 9:36 he was **moved with c** on them, because *4697*
14:14 and was **moved with c** toward them, and *4697*
15:32 and said, I **have c** on the multitude, *4697*
18:27 the lord of that servant was **moved with c**, *4697*
18:33 Shouldest not thou also have **had c** on thy *1653*
20:34 So Jesus **had c** *on them,* and touched their *4697*
Mk 1:41 And Jesus, **moved with c**, put forth *his* *4697*
5:19 hath done for thee, and hath **had c** on thee. *1653*
6:34 and was **moved with c** toward them, *4697*
8: 2 I **have c** on the multitude, because *4697*
9:22 but if thou canst do any *thing*, **have c** on us, *4697*
Lk 7:13 he **had c** on her, and said unto her, *4697*
10:33 and when he saw him, he **had c** *on him,* *4697*
15:20 and **had c**, and ran, and fell on his neck, *4697*
Ro 9:15 I will **have c** on whom I will have *3627*
9:15 have compassion on whom I will **have c**. *3627*
Heb 5: 2 Who can **have c** on the ignorant, and *3356*
10:34 For ye **had c** *of me* in my bonds, *4834*
1Pe 3: 8 having **c one of another**, love as brethren, *4835*
1Jn 3:17 and shutteth up his bowels *of* **c** from him, NIG
Jude 1:22 And of some **have c**, making a difference: *1653*

COMPASSIONATE See TENDERHEARTED

COMPASSIONS (2) [COMPASSION]

La 3:22 are not consumed, because his **c** fail not. 7356
Zec 7: 9 shew mercy and **c** every man to his brother: 7356

COMPEL (5) [COMPELLED, COMPELLEST]

Lev 25:39 thou shalt not **c** him **to serve** as a 5647+5656
Est 1: 8 *was* according to the law; none did **c**: 597
Mt 5:41 And whosoever shall **c** thee **to go** a mile, *29*
Mk 15:21 And they **c** one Simon a Cyrenian, *29*
Lk 14:23 and hedges, and **c** *them* to come in, *315*

COMPELLED (6) [COMPEL]

1Sa 28:23 together with the woman, **c** him; 6555
2Ch 21:11 to commit fornication, and **c** Judah *thereto*. 5080
Mt 27:32 Simon by name: him they **c** to bear his cross. *29*
Ac 26:11 every synagogue, and **c** *them* to blaspheme; *315*
2Co 12:11 am become a fool in glorying; ye have **c** me: *315*

Gal 2: 3 being a Greek, was **c** to be circumcised: *315*

COMPELLEST (1) [COMPEL]
Gal 2:14 why **c** thou the Gentiles to live as do *315*

COMPLAIN (4) [COMPLAINED, COMPLAINERS, COMPLAINING, COMPLAINT, COMPLAINTS]
Jdg 21:22 or their brethren come unto us to **c**, 7378
Job 7:11 I will **c** in the bitterness of my soul. 7878
31:38 or that the furrows likewise thereof **c**; 1058
La 3:39 Wherefore doth a living man **c**, a man for 596

COMPLAINED (2) [COMPLAIN]
Nu 11: 1 *when* the people **c**, it displeased the LORD: 596
Ps 77: 3 I **c**, and my spirit was overwhelmed. Selah. 7878

COMPLAINERS (1) [COMPLAIN]
Jude 1:16 These are murmurers, **c**, walking after their *3202*

COMPLAINING (1) [COMPLAIN]
Ps 144:14 going out; that *there be* no **c** in our streets. 6682

COMPLAINT (9) [COMPLAIN]
1Sa 1:16 for out of the abundance of my **c** and 7879
Job 7:13 comfort me, my couch shall ease my **c**; 7879
9:27 If I say, I will forget my **c**, I will leave off 7879
10: 1 of my life; I will leave my **c** upon myself; 7879
21: 4 *As for* me, *is* my **c** to man? and if *it were* 7879
23: 2 Even to day *is* my **c** bitter: my stroke is 7879
Ps 55: 2 I mourn in my **c**, and make a noise; 7879
102: T and poureth out his **c** before the LORD. 7879
142: 2 I poured out my **c** before him; I shewed 7879

COMPLAINTS (1) [COMPLAIN]
Ac 25: 7 and laid many and grievous **c** against Paul, *157*

COMPLETE (3)
Lev 23:15 wave offering; seven sabbaths shall be **c**: 8549
Col 2:10 And ye are **c** in him, which is the head of *4137*
4:12 stand perfect and **c** in all the will of God. *4137*

COMPLETELY See UTTERMOST

COMPOSITION (2)
Ex 30:32 ye make *any other* like it, after the **c** of it: 4971
30:37 to yourselves according to the **c** thereof: 4971

COMPOUND (1) [COMPOUNDETH]
Ex 30:25 an ointment **c** *after* the art of 4842

COMPOUNDETH (1) [COMPOUND]
Ex 30:33 Whosoever **c** *any* like it, or 7543

COMPREHEND (2) [COMPREHENDED]
Job 37: 5 great *things* doeth he, which we cannot **c**. 3045
Eph 3:18 May be able to **c** with all saints what *is* *2638*

COMPREHENDED (3) [COMPREHEND]
Isa 40:12 and **c** the dust of the earth in a measure, and 3557
Jn 1: 5 in darkness; and the darkness **c** it not. *2638*
Ro 13: 9 it is **briefly c** in this saying, namely, *346*

CONANIAH (1)
2Ch 35: 9 **C** also, and Shemaiah and Nethaneel, 3562

CONCEAL (6) [CONCEALED, CONCEALETH]
Ge 37:26 *is it* if we slay our brother, and **c** his blood? 3680
Dt 13: 8 shalt thou spare, neither shalt thou **c** him: 3680
Job 27:11 *that* which *is* with the Almighty will I not **c**. 3582
41:12 I will not **c** his parts, nor *his* power, nor his 2790
Pr 25: 2 *It is* the glory of God to **c** a thing: but 5641
Jer 50: 2 and set up a standard; publish, *and* **c** not: 3582

CONCEALED (2) [CONCEAL]
Job 6:10 for I have not **c** the words of the Holy One. 3582
Ps 40:10 I have not **c** thy lovingkindness and 3582

CONCEALETH (2) [CONCEAL]
Pr 11:13 he that is of a faithful spirit **c** the matter. 3680
12:23 A prudent man **c** knowledge: but the heart 3680

CONCEIT (5) [CONCEITS]
Pr 18:11 strong city, and as a high wall in his own **c**. 4906
26: 5 to his folly, lest he be wise in his own **c**. 5869
26:12 Seest thou a man wise in his own **c**? 5869
26:16 The sluggard *is* wiser in his own **c** than 5869
28:11 The rich man *is* wise in his own **c**; but 5869

CONCEITED See HIGH-MINDED

CONCEITS (2) [CONCEIT]
Ro 11:25 lest ye should be wise in your own **c**; NIG
12:16 of low estate. Be not wise in your own **c**. NIG

CONCEIVE (14) [CONCEIVED, CONCEIVING, CONCEPTION]
Ge 30:38 that they should **c** when they came to drink. 3179
30:41 whensoever the stronger cattle did **c**, 3179
30:41 that they might **c** among the rods. 3179
Nu 5:28 she shall be free, and shall **c seed**. 2232+2233
Jdg 13: 3 bearest not: but thou shalt **c**, and bear a son. 2029
13: 5 For lo, thou *shalt* **c**, and bear a son; and 2030
13: 7 Behold, thou *shalt* **c**, and bear a son; 2030
Job 15:35 They **c** mischief, and bring forth vanity, 2029
Ps 51: 5 in iniquity; and in sin did my mother **c** me. 3179
Isa 7:14 a Virgin shall **c**, and bear a Son, and 2030
33:11 Ye shall **c** chaff, ye shall bring forth 2029
59: 4 *they* **c** mischief, and bring forth iniquity. 2029
Lk 1:31 thou shalt **c** in *thy* womb, and bring forth a *4815*
Heb 11:11 Sara herself received strength to **c** seed, *2602*

CONCEIVED (46) [CONCEIVE]
Ge 4: 1 she **c**, and bare Cain, and said, I have 2029
4:17 knew his wife; and she **c**, and bare Enoch: 2029
16: 4 he went in unto Hagar, and she **c**: and 2029
16: 4 when she saw that she had **c**, her mistress 2029
16: 5 when she saw that she had **c**, I was 2029
21: 2 For Sarah **c**, and bare Abraham a son in his 2029
25:21 intreated of him, and Rebekah his wife **c**. 2029
29:32 Leah **c**, and bare a son, and she called his 2029
29:33 she **c** again, and bare a son; and said, 2029
29:34 she **c** again, and bare a son; and said, 2029
29:35 she **c** again, and bare a son: and she said, 2029
30: 5 And Bilhah **c**, and bare Jacob a son. 2029
30: 7 Bilhah Rachel's maid **c** again, and 2029
30:17 and she **c**, and bare Jacob the fifth son. 2029
30:19 Leah **c** again, and bare Jacob the sixth son. 2029
30:23 she **c**, and bare a son; and said, God hath 2029
30:39 the flocks **c** before the rods, and 3179
31:10 it came to pass at the time that the cattle **c**, 3179
38: 3 she **c**, and bare a son; and he called his 2029
38: 4 she **c** again, and bare a son; and she called 2029
38: 5 she yet again **c**, and bare a son; and NIH
38:18 and came in unto her, and she **c** by him. 2029
Ex 2: 2 the woman **c**, and bare a son: and when she 2029
Lev 12: 2 If a woman have **c seed**, and born a man 2232
Nu 11:12 Have I **c** all this people? have I begotten 2029
1Sa 1:20 time was come about after Hannah had **c**, 2029
2:21 so that she **c**, and bare three sons and 2029
2Sa 11: 5 the woman **c**, and sent and told David, and 2029
2Ki 4:17 the woman **c**, and bare a son at that season 2029
1Ch 7:23 she **c**, and bare a son, and he called his 2029
Job 3: 3 *in which it was* said, There is a man child **c**. 2029
Ps 7:14 hath **c** mischief, and brought forth 2029
SS 3: 4 and into the chamber of her that **c** me. 2029
Isa 8: 3 the prophetess; and she **c**, and bare a son. 2029
Jer 49:30 and hath **c** a purpose against you. 2803
Hos 1: 3 of Diblaim; which **c**, and bare him a son. 2029
1: 6 she **c** again, and bare a daughter. And *God* 2029
1: 8 weaned Lo-ruhamah, she **c**, and bare a son. 2029
2: 5 she that **c** them hath done shamefully: 2029
Mt 1:20 for that which is **c** in her is of the Holy *1080*
Lk 1:24 And after those days his wife Elisabeth **c**, *4815*
1:36 she hath also **c** a son in her old age: *4815*
2:21 named of the angel before he was **c** in *4815*
Ac 5: 4 why hast thou **c** this thing in thine heart? *5087*
Ro 9:10 but when Rebecca also had **c** by one, *2845*
Jas 1:15 Then when lust hath **c**, it bringeth forth sin: *4815*

CONCEIVING (1) [CONCEIVE]
Isa 59:13 **c** and uttering from the heart words of 2029

CONCEPTION (3) [CONCEIVE]
Ge 3:16 I will greatly multiply thy sorrow and thy **c**; 2032
Ru 4:13 the LORD gave her **c**, and she bare a son. 2032
Hos 9:11 and from the womb, and from the **c**. 2032

CONCERN (2) [CONCERNETH, CONCERNING]
Ac 28:31 teaching those *things* which **c** the Lord *4012*
2Co 11:30 I will glory of the *things* which **c** mine NIG

CONCERNETH (2) [CONCERN]
Ps 138: 8 The LORD will perfect that which **c** me: 1157
Eze 12:10 This burden *c* the prince in Jerusalem, and NIH

C

CONCERNING (242) [CONCERN] See Index

CONCISION (1)
Php 3: 2 beware of evil workers, beware of the **c**. *2699*

CONCLUDE (1) [CONCLUDED, CONCLUSION]
Ro 3:28 Therefore we **c** that a man is justified by *3049*

CONCLUDED (3) [CONCLUDE]
Ac 21:25 **c** that they observe no such *thing,* save only *2919*
Ro 11:32 For God hath **c** *them* all in unbelief, that he *4788*
Gal 3:22 But the scripture hath **c** all under sin, *4788*

CONCLUSION (1) [CONCLUDE]
Ecc 12:13 Let us hear the **c** of the whole matter: 5490

CONCORD (1)
2Co 6:15 And what **c** hath Christ with Belial? or *4857*

CONCOURSE (2)
Pr 1:21 She crieth in the chief place of **c**, in 1993
Ac 19:40 whereby we may give an account of this **c**. *4963*

CONCUBINE (22) [CONCUBINES]
Ge 22:24 his **c**, whose name *was* Reumah, she bare 6370
35:22 and lay with Bilhah his father's **c**: 6370
36:12 Timna was **c** to Eliphaz Esau's son; and 6370
Jdg 8:31 his **c** that *was* in Shechem, she also bare 6370
19: 1 who took to him a **c** out of 6370
19: 2 his **c** played the whore against him, and 6370
19: 9 he, and his **c**, and his servant, his father in 6370
19:10 two asses saddled, his **c** also *was* with him. 6370
19:24 *here is* my daughter a maiden, and his **c**; 6370
19:25 so the man took his **c**, and brought *her* forth 6370
19:27 the woman his **c** *was* fallen down *at* 6370
19:29 and laid hold on his **c**, and divided her, 6370
20: 4 to Benjamin, I and my **c**, to lodge. 6370
20: 5 and my **c** have they forced, that she is dead. 6370
20: 6 I took my **c**, and cut her in pieces, and 6370
2Sa 3: 7 Saul had a **c**, whose name *was* Rizpah, 6370
3: 7 hast thou gone in unto my father's **c**? 6370
21:11 daughter of Aiah, the **c** of Saul, had done. 6370
1Ch 1:32 Now the sons of Keturah, Abraham's **c**: 6370
2:46 Caleb's **c**, bare Haran, and Moza, and 6370
2:48 Maachah, Caleb's **c**, bare Sheber, and 6370
7:14 his **c** the Aramitess bare Machir the father 6370

CONCUBINES (17) [CONCUBINE]
Ge 25: 6 unto the sons of the **c**, which Abraham had, 6370
2Sa 5:13 David took *him* mo **c** and wives out of 6370
15:16 *which were* **c**, to keep the house. 6370
16:21 unto Absalom, Go in unto thy father's **c**, 6370
16:22 Absalom went in unto his father's **c** in 6370
19: 5 lives of thy wives, and the lives of thy **c**; 6370
20: 3 the king took the ten women *his* **c**, 6370
1Ki 11: 3 princesses, and three hundred **c**: 6370
1Ch 3: 9 beside the sons of the **c**, and Tamar their 6370
2Ch 11:21 of Absalom above all his wives and his **c**: 6370
11:21 he took eighteen wives, and threescore **c**; 6370
Est 2:14 the king's chamberlain, which kept the **c**: 6370
SS 6: 8 fourscore **c**, and virgins without number. 6370
6: 9 *yea,* the queens and the **c**, and they praised 6370
Da 5: 2 and his princes, his wives, and his **c**, 3904
5: 3 and his princes, his wives, and his **c**, 3904
5:23 thou, and thy lords, thy wives, and thy **c**, 3904

CONCUPISCENCE (3)
Ro 7: 8 wrought in me all *manner of* **c**. *1939*
Col 3: 5 evil **c**, and covetousness, which is idolatry: *1939*
1Th 4: 5 Not in the lust of **c**, even as the Gentiles *1939*

CONDEMN (24) [CONDEMNATION, CONDEMNED, CONDEMNEST, CONDEMNETH, CONDEMNING, UNCONDEMNED]
Ex 22: 9 *and* whom the judges shall **c**, he shall pay 7561
Dt 25: 1 justify the righteous, and **c** the wicked. 7561
Job 9:20 justify myself, mine own mouth shall **c** me: 7561
10: 2 I will say unto God, Do not **c** me; shew me 7561
34:17 and wilt thou **c** him that is most just? 7561
40: 8 wilt thou **c** me, that thou mayest be 7561
Ps 37:33 in his hand, nor **c** him when he is judged. 7561
94:21 of the righteous, and **c** the innocent blood. 7561
109:31 to save *him* from those that **c** his soul. 8199
Pr 12: 2 but a man of wicked devices will he **c**. 7561
Isa 50: 9 will help me; who *is* he *that* shall **c** me? 7561
54:17 rise against thee in judgment thou shalt **c**. 7561
Mt 12:41 with this generation, and shall **c** it: *2632*
12:42 with this generation, and shall **c** it: *2632*
20:18 *the* scribes, and they shall **c** him to death, *2632*
Mk 10:33 and they shall **c** him to death, and *2632*
Lk 6:37 **c** not, and ye shall not be condemned: *2613*
11:31 the men of this generation, and **c** them: *2632*
11:32 with this generation, and shall **c** it: *2632*
Jn 3:17 For God sent not his Son into the world to **c** *2919*
8:11 Jesus said unto her, Neither do I **c** thee: *2632*
2Co 7: 3 I speak not *this* to **c** *you:* for I have said *2633*
1Jn 3:20 For if *our* heart **c** us, God is greater than *2607*
3:21 if our heart **c** us not, *then* have we *2607*

CONDEMNATION (12) [CONDEMN]
Lk 23:40 fear God, seeing thou art in the same **c**? *2917*
Jn 3:19 And this is the **c**, that light is come into *2920*
5:24 everlasting life, and shall not come into **c**; *2920*
Ro 5:16 for the judgment *was* by one to **c**, but *2631*
5:18 of one *judgment came* upon all men to **c**; *2631*
8: 1 now no **c** to them *which are* in Christ Jesus *2631*
1Co 11:34 at home; that ye come not together unto **c**. *2917*
2Co 3: 9 For if the ministration of **c** *be* glory, *2633*
1Ti 3: 6 up with pride he fall into the **c** of the devil. *2917*
Jas 3: 1 knowing that we shall receive the greater **c**. *2917*
5:12 and *your* nay, nay; lest ye fall into **c**. *2920*
Jude 1: 4 who were before of old ordained to this **c**, *2917*

CONDEMNED (21) [CONDEMN]
2Ch 36: 3 **c** the land in an hundred talents of silver 6064
Job 32: 3 had found no answer, and *yet* had **c** Job. 7561
Ps 109: 7 When he shall be judged, let him be **c**: and 7563
Am 2: 8 they drink the wine of the **c** *in* the house of 6064
Mt 12: 7 ye would not have **c** the guiltless. *2613*
12:37 and by thy words thou shalt be **c**. *2613*
27: 3 when he saw that he was **c**, *2632*
Mk 14:64 And they all **c** him to be guilty of death. *2632*
Lk 6:37 condemn not, and ye shall not be **c**: forgive, *2613*
24:20 our rulers delivered him to be **c** to death, *2917*
Jn 3:18 He that believeth on him is not **c**: but *2919*
3:18 but he that believeth not is **c** already, *2919*
8:10 those thine accusers? hath no *man* **c** thee? *2632*
Ro 8: 3 sinful flesh, and for sin, **c** sin in the flesh: *2632*
1Co 11:32 that we should not be **c** with the world. *2632*
Tit 2: 8 Sound speech that **cannot be c**; that he that *176*
3:11 is subverted, and sinneth, being **c of himself**. *843*
Heb 11: 7 by the which he **c** the world, and *2632*
Jas 5: 6 Ye have **c** *and* killed the just; *and* he doth *2613*
5: 9 one against another, brethren, lest ye be **c**: *2632*
2Pe 2: 6 Gomorrha into ashes **c** *them* with an *2632*

CONDEMNEST (1) [CONDEMN]
Ro 2: 1 thou judgest another, thou **c** thyself; *2632*

CONDEMNETH (4) [CONDEMN]
Job 15: 6 Thine own mouth **c** thee, and not I; yea, 7561
Pr 17:15 justifieth the wicked, and he that **c** the just, 7561
Ro 8:34 Who *is* he that **c**? *It is* Christ that died, *2632*
14:22 Happy *is* he that **c** not himself in *that thing* *2919*

CONDEMNING (2) [CONDEMN]
1Ki 8:32 do, and judge thy servants, **c** the wicked, 7561
Ac 13:27 they have fulfilled *them* in **c** *him.* *2919*

CONDESCEND (1)
Ro 12:16 not high *things,* but **c to** *men* of low estate. *4879*

CONDITION (1) [CONDITIONS]
1Sa 11: 2 On this **c** will I make *a covenant* with you, NIH

CONDITIONS (1) [CONDITION]
Lk 14:32 an ambassage, and desireth **c** of peace. *3588*

CONDUCT (3) [CONDUCTED]
2Sa 19:15 to meet the king, to **c** the king **over** Jordan. 5674
19:31 Jordan with the king, to **c** him *over* Jordan. 7971
1Co 16:11 but **c** him **forth** in peace, that he may come *4311*

CONDUCTED (2) [CONDUCT]
2Sa 19:40 all the people of Judah **c** the king, and 5674
Ac 17:15 And they that **c** Paul brought him unto *2525*

CONDUIT (4)
2Ki 18:17 and stood by the **c** of the upper pool, 8585
20:20 and a **c**, and brought water into the city, 8585

Isa 7: 3 at the end of the **c** of the upper pool in 8585
36: 2 he stood by the **c** of the upper pool in 8585

CONEY (1) [CONIES, CONY]
Dt 14: 7 *as* the camel, and the hare, and the **c**: 8227

CONFECTION (1) [CONFECTIONARIES]
Ex 30:35 a **c** *after* the art of the apothecary, 7545

CONFECTIONARIES (1) [CONFECTION]
1Sa 8:13 he will take your daughters to be **c**, and 7548

CONFEDERACY (3) [CONFEDERATE]
Isa 8:12 Say ye not, A **c**, to all *them to* whom this 7195
8:12 all *them to* whom this people shall say, A **c**; 7195
Ob 1: 7 All the men of thy **c** have brought thee *even* 1285

CONFEDERATE (3) [CONFEDERACY]
Ge 14:13 and these *were* **c** with Abram. 1167+1285
Ps 83: 5 *with one* consent: they are **c** against thee: 1285
Isa 7: 2 of David, saying, Syria is **c** with Ephraim. 5117

CONFERENCE (1) [CONFERRED]
Gal 2: 6 *to be somewhat* **in c added** nothing to me: *4323*

CONFERRED (4) [CONFERENCE]
1Ki 1: 7 he **c** with Joab the son of Zeruiah, 1697+1961
Ac 4:15 of the council, they **c** among themselves, *4820*
25:12 when he had **c** with the council, answered, *4814*
Gal 1:16 immediately I **c** not with flesh and blood: *4323*

CONFESS (28) [CONFESSED, CONFESSETH, CONFESSING, CONFESSION]
Lev 5: 5 he shall **c** that he hath sinned in that *thing:* 3034
16:21 **c** over him all the iniquities of the children 3034
26:40 If they shall **c** their iniquity, and 3034
Nu 5: 7 they shall **c** their sin which they have done: 3034
1Ki 8:33 **c** thy name, and pray, and 3034
8:35 **c** thy name, and turn from their sin, 3034
2Ch 6:24 shall return and **c** thy name, and pray and 3034
6:26 **c** thy name, *and* turn from their sin, 3034
Ne 1: 6 **c** the sins of the children of Israel, 3034
Job 40:14 will I also **c** unto thee that thine own right 3034
Ps 32: 5 I will **c** my transgressions unto the LORD; 3034
Mt 10:32 therefore shall **c** me before men, *3670*
10:32 him will I **c** also before my Father which is *3670*
Lk 12: 8 Whosoever shall **c** me before men, *3670*
12: 8 him shall the Son of man also **c** before *3670*
Jn 9:22 that if any *man* did **c** that he *was* Christ, *3670*
12:42 of the Pharisees they did not **c** *him,* lest *3670*
Ac 23: 8 angel nor spirit: but the Pharisees **c** both. *3670*
24:14 But this I **c** unto thee, that after the way *3670*
Ro 10: 9 That if thou shalt **c** with thy mouth the Lord *3670*
14:11 to me, and every tongue shall **c** to God. *1843*
15: 9 For this cause I will **c** to thee among *1843*
Php 2:11 And *that* every tongue should **c** that Jesus *1843*
Jas 5:16 **C** *your* faults one to another, and pray one *1843*
1Jn 1: 9 If we **c** our sins, he is faithful and just to *3670*
4:15 Whosoever shall **c** that Jesus is the Son of *3670*
2Jn 1: 7 who **c** not that Jesus Christ is come in *3670*
Rev 3: 5 but I will **c** his name before my Father, and *1843*

CONFESSED (7) [CONFESS]
Ezr 10: 1 when he had **c**, weeping and 3034
Ne 9: 2 stood and **c** their sins, and the iniquities of 3034
9: 3 *another* fourth *part* they **c**, and 3034
Jn 1:20 And he **c**, and denied not; but confessed, I *3670*
1:20 and denied not; but **c**, I am not the Christ. *3670*
Ac 19:18 and **c**, and shewed their deeds. *1843*
Heb 11:13 and **c** that they were strangers and *3670*

CONFESSETH (3) [CONFESS]
Pr 28:13 whoso **c** and forsaketh *them* shall have 3034
1Jn 4: 2 Every spirit that **c** that Jesus Christ is come *3670*
4: 3 And every spirit that **c** not that Jesus Christ *3670*

CONFESSING (3) [CONFESS]
Da 9:20 **c** my sin and the sin of my people Israel, 3034
Mt 3: 6 were baptized of him in Jordan, **c** their sins. *1843*
Mk 1: 5 of him in the river *of* Jordan, **c** their sins. *1843*

CONFESSION (6) [CONFESS]
Jos 7:19 God of Israel, and make **c** unto him; 8426
2Ch 30:22 **making c** to the LORD God of their 3034
Ezr 10:11 make **c** unto the LORD God of your 8426
Da 9: 4 **made** my **c**, and said, O Lord, the great and 3034
Ro 10:10 with the mouth **c** is **made** unto salvation. *3670*
1Ti 6:13 before Pontius Pilate witnessed a good **c**; *3671*

CONFIDENCE (38) [CONFIDENT]
Jdg 9:26 and the men of Shechem **put** their **c** in him. 982
2Ki 18:19 What **c** *is* this where*in* thou trustest? 986
Job 4: 6 *Is* not *this* thy fear, thy **c**, thy hope; and 3690
18:14 His **c** shall be rooted out of his tabernacle, 4009
31:24 or have said to the fine gold, *Thou art* my **c**; 4009
Ps 65: 5 *who art* the **c** of all the ends of the earth, 4009
118: 8 to trust in the LORD than to **put c** in man. 982
118: 9 trust in the LORD than to **put c** in princes. 982
Pr 3:26 For the LORD shall be thy **c**, and 3689
14:26 In the fear of the LORD *is* strong **c**: and 4009
21:22 casteth down the strength of the **c** thereof. 4009
25:19 **C** in an unfaithful *man* in time of trouble *is* 4009
Isa 30:15 in quietness and in **c** shall be your strength: 985
36: 4 What **c** *is* this where*in* thou trustest? 986
Jer 48:13 of Israel was ashamed of Beth-el their **c**. 4009
Eze 28:26 yea, they shall dwell with **c**, when I have 983
29:16 it shall be no more the **c** of the house of 4009
Mic 7: 5 ye not in a friend, **put** ye not **c** in a guide: 982
Ac 28:31 with all **c**, no man forbidding him. *3954*
2Co 1:15 And in this **c** I was minded to come unto *4006*
2: 3 having **c** in you all, that my joy is *the joy* of *3982*
7:16 therefore that I **have c** in you in all *things.* *2292*
8:22 upon the great **c** which *I have* in you. *4006*
10: 2 not be bold when I am present with *that* **c**, *4006*
11:17 as *it were* foolishly, in this **c** of boasting. *5287*
Gal 5:10 I have **c** in you through the Lord, that you *3982*
Eph 3:12 and access with **c** by the faith of him. *4006*
Php 1:25 And **having** this **c**, I know that I shall abide *3982*
3: 3 in Christ Jesus, and **have** no **c** in the flesh. *3982*
3: 4 Though I *might* also have **c** in the flesh. *4006*
2Th 3: 4 And we have **c** in the Lord touching you, *3982*
Phm 1:21 **Having c** in thy obedience I wrote unto *3982*
Heb 3: 6 if we hold fast the **c** and the rejoicing of *3954*
3:14 if we hold the beginning of *our* **c** stedfast *5287*
10:35 Cast not away therefore your **c**, which hath *3954*
1Jn 2:28 we may have **c**, and not be ashamed before *3954*
3:21 us not, *then* have we **c** towards God. *3954*
5:14 And this is the **c** that we have in him, that, *3954*

CONFIDENCES (1) [CONFIDENCE, CONFIDENCES, CONFIDENT]
Jer 2:37 for the LORD hath rejected thy **c**, and 4009

CONFIDENT (8) [CONFIDENTLY]
Ps 27: 3 should rise against me, in this *will* I *be* **c**. 982
Pr 14:16 from evil: but the fool rageth, and *is* **c**. 982
Ro 2:19 And art **c** that thou thyself art a guide of *3982*
2Co 5: 6 Therefore *we are* always **c**, knowing that, *2292*
5: 8 We are **c**, I say, and willing rather to be *2292*
9: 4 should be ashamed in this *same* **c** boasting. *5287*
Php 1: 6 Being **c** of this very *thing,* that he which *3982*
1:14 in the Lord, **waxing c** by my bonds, *3982*

CONFIDENTLY (1) [CONFIDENT]
Lk 22:59 space of one hour after another **c affirmed,** *1340*

CONFIRM (13) [CONFIRMATION, CONFIRMED, CONFIRMETH, CONFIRMING]
Ru 4: 7 concerning changing, for to **c** all things; 6965
1Ki 1:14 will come in after thee, and **c** thy words. 4390
2Ki 15:19 that his hand might be with him to **c** 2388
Est 9:29 to **c** this second letter of Purim. 6965
9:31 To **c** these days of Purim in their times 6965
Ps 68: 9 whereby thou didst **c** thine inheritance, 3559
Isa 35: 3 ye the weak hands, and **c** the feeble knees. 553
Eze 13: 6 *others* to hope that *they* would **c** the word. 6965
Da 9:27 he shall **c** the covenant with many *for* one 1396
11: 1 *even* I, stood to **c** and to strengthen him. 2388
Ro 15: 8 to **c** the promises made unto the fathers: *950*
1Co 1: 8 Who shall also **c** you unto the end, *that ye* *950*
2Co 2: 8 Wherefore I beseech you that *you* would **c** *2964*

CONFIRMATION (2) [CONFIRM]
Php 1: 7 and *in* the defence and **c** of the gospel, *951*
Heb 6:16 an oath for **c** *is* to them an end of all strife. *951*

CONFIRMED (13) [CONFIRM]
2Sa 7:24 For thou hast **c** to thyself thy people Israel 3559
2Ki 14: 5 as soon as the kingdom was **c** in his hand, 2388

C

C

1Ch 14: 2 David perceived that the LORD had **c** him 3559
16:17 hath **c** the same to Jacob for a law, *and* 5975
Est 9:32 the decree of Esther **c** these matters of 6965
Ps 105:10 **c** the same unto Jacob for a law, *and* 5975
Da 9:12 he hath **c** his words, which he spake against 6965
Ac 15:32 the brethren with many words, and **c** *them.* *1991*
1Co 1: 6 Even as the testimony of Christ was **c** in *950*
Gal 3:15 *it be* but a man's covenant, *yet if it be* **c**, *2964*
3:17 that was **c before** of God in Christ, the law, *4300*
Heb 2: 3 and was **c** unto us by them that heard *him;* *950*
6:17 immutability of his counsel, **c** *it* by an oath: *3315*

CONFIRMETH (3) [CONFIRM]

Nu 30:14 he **c** them, because he held his peace at her 6965
Dt 27:26 Cursed *be* he that **c** not *all* the words of this 6965
Isa 44:26 That **c** the word of his servant, and 6965

CONFIRMING (3) [CONFIRM]

Mk 16:20 and **c** the word with signs following. *950*
Ac 14:22 **C** the souls of the disciples, *and* *1991*
15:41 through Syria and Cilicia, **c** the churches. *1991*

CONFISCATION (1)

Ezr 7:26 or to **c** of goods, or to imprisonment. 6065

CONFLICT (2)

Php 1:30 Having the same **c** which ye saw in me, and *73*
Col 2: 1 For I would that ye knew what great **c** I have *73*

CONFORMABLE (1) [CONFORMED]

Php 3:10 his sufferings, being **made c** unto his death; *4833*

CONFORMED (2) [CONFORMABLE]

Ro 8:29 he also did predestinate *to be* **c to** the image *4832*
12: 2 And be not **c to** this world: but be ye *4964*

CONFOUND (5) [CONFOUNDED]

Ge 11: 7 let us go down, and there **c** their language, 1101
11: 9 the LORD did there **c** the language of all 1101
Jer 1:17 at their faces, lest I **c** thee before them. 2865
1Co 1:27 foolish *things* of the world to **c** the wise; *2617*
1:27 the world to **c** the *things which are* mighty; *2617*

CONFOUNDED (50) [CONFOUND]

2Ki 19:26 of small power, they were dismayed and **c**; 954
Job 6:20 They were **c** because they had hoped; 954
Ps 22: 5 they trusted in thee, and were not **c**. 954
35: 4 Let them be **c** and put to shame that seek 954
40:14 **c** together that seek after my soul to destroy 2659
69: 6 let not those that seek thee be **c** for my 3637
70: 2 be ashamed and **c** that seek after my soul: 2659
71:13 Let them be **c** *and* consumed that are 954
71:24 for they are **c**, for they are brought unto 954
83:17 Let them be **c** and troubled for ever; yea, 954
97: 7 **C** be all they that serve graven images, 954
129: 5 Let them all be **c** and turned back that hate 954
Isa 1:29 ye shall be **c** for the gardens that ye have 2659
19: 9 and they that weave networks, shall be **c**. 954
24:23 the moon shall be **c**, and the sun ashamed, 2659
37:27 of small power, they were dismayed and **c**: 954
41:11 against thee shall be ashamed and **c**: 3637
45:16 shall be ashamed, and also **c**, all of them: 3637
45:17 ye shall not be ashamed nor **c** world 3637
50: 7 will help me; therefore shall I not be **c**: 3637
54: 4 neither be thou **c**; for thou shalt not be put 3637
Jer 9:19 we are greatly **c**, because we have forsaken 954
10:14 every founder is **c** by the graven image: 954
14: 3 they were ashamed and **c**, and covered their 3637
15: 9 she hath been ashamed and **c**: and 2659
17:18 Let them be **c** that persecute me, but let not 954
17:18 that persecute me, but let not me be **c**: 954
22:22 be ashamed and **c** for all thy wickedness. 3637
31:19 yea, even **c**, because I did bear the reproach 3637
46:24 The daughter of Egypt shall be **c**; she shall 954
48: 1 Kiriathaim is **c** *and* taken: Misgab is 954
48: 1 *and* taken: Misgab is **c** and dismayed. 954
48:20 Moab is **c**; for it is broken down: howl and 954
49:23 Hamath is **c**, and Arpad: for they have heard 954
50: 2 say, Babylon is taken, Bel is **c**, Merodach is 954
50: 2 her idols are **c**, her images are broken in 954
50:12 Your mother shall be sore **c**; she that bare 954
51:17 every founder is **c** by the graven image: 954
51:47 her whole land shall be **c**, and all her slain 954
51:51 We are **c**, because we have heard reproach: 954
Eze 16:52 yea, be thou **c** also, and bear thy shame, 954
16:54 mayest be **c** in all that thou hast done, 3637
16:63 be **c**, and never open thy mouth any more, 954
36:32 be ashamed and **c** for your own ways, 3637
Mic 3: 7 the seers be ashamed, and the diviners **c**: 2659
7:16 nations shall see and be **c** at all their might: 954
Zec 10: 5 and the riders on horses shall be **c**. 3001
Ac 2: 6 and were **c**, because that every man heard *4797*
9:22 and **c** the Jews which dwelt at Damascus, *4797*
1Pe 2: 6 and he that believeth on him shall not be **c**. *2617*

CONFUSED (2) [CONFUSION]

Isa 9: 5 every battle of the warrior *is* with **c noise**, 7494
Ac 19:32 for the assembly was **c**; and **the more part** *4797*

CONFUSION (26) [CONFUSED]

Lev 18:23 before a beast to lie down thereto: it *is* **c**. 8397
20:12 they have wrought **c**; their blood *shall be* 8397
1Sa 20:30 hast chosen the son of Jesse to thine own **c**, 1322
20:30 and unto the **c** of thy mother's nakedness? 1322
Ezr 9: 7 to captivity, and to a spoil, and to **c** of face, 1322
Job 10:15 *I am* full of **c**; therefore see thou mine 7036
Ps 35: 4 and **brought to c** that devise my hurt. 2659
35:26 **brought to c** together that rejoice at mine 2659
44:15 My **c** *is* continually before me, and 3639
70: 2 and **put to c**, that desire my hurt. 3637
71: 1 do I put my trust: let me never be **put to c**. 954
109:29 let them cover *themselves with* their own **c**, 1322
Isa 24:10 The city of **c** is broken down: every house 8414
30: 3 and the trust in the shadow of Egypt *your* **c**. 3639
34:11 and he shall stretch out upon it the line of **c**, 8414
41:29 their molten images *are* wind and **c**. 8414
45:16 they shall go to **c** together *that are* makers 3639
61: 7 and *for* **c** they shall rejoice in their portion: 3639
Jer 3:25 down in our shame, and our **c** covereth us: 3639
7:19 *do they* not *provoke* themselves to the **c** of 1322
20:11 *their* everlasting **c** shall never be forgotten. 3639
Da 9: 7 but unto us **c** of faces, as *at* this day; 1322
9: 8 O Lord, to us *belongeth* **c** of face, to our 1322
Ac 19:29 And the whole city was filled with **c**: and *4799*
1Co 14:33 For God is not *the author* of **c**, but of peace, *181*
Jas 3:16 and strife *is*, there *is* **c** and every evil work. *181*

CONGEALED (1)

Ex 15: 8 the depths were **c** in the heart of the sea. 7087

CONGRATULATE (1)

1Ch 18:10 to **c** him, because he had fought against 1288

CONGREGATION (364) [CONGREGATIONS]

Ex 12: 3 Speak ye unto all the **c** of Israel, saying, 5712
12: 6 the whole assembly of the **c** of Israel shall 5712
12:19 even that soul shall be cut off from the **c** of 5712
12:47 All the **c** of Israel shall keep it. 5712
16: 1 all the **c** of the children of Israel came unto 5712
16: 2 the whole **c** of the children of Israel 5712
16: 9 Say unto all the **c** of the children of Israel, 5712
16:10 as Aaron spake unto the whole **c** of 5712
16:22 all the rulers of the **c** came and told Moses. 5712
17: 1 all the **c** of the children of Israel journeyed 5712
27:21 In the tabernacle of the **c** without the vail, 4150
28:43 they come in unto the tabernacle of the **c**, 4150
29: 4 unto the door of the tabernacle of the **c**, 4150
29:10 to be brought before the tabernacle of the **c**: 4150
29:11 *by* the door of the tabernacle of the **c**. 4150
29:30 of the **c** to minister in the holy *place*. 4150
29:32 *by* the door of the tabernacle of the **c**. 4150
29:42 the tabernacle of the **c** before the LORD: 4150
29:44 I will sanctify the tabernacle of the **c**, and 4150
30:16 it for the service of the tabernacle of the **c**; 4150
30:18 shalt put it between the tabernacle of the **c** 4150
30:20 When they go into the tabernacle of the **c**, 4150
30:26 thou shalt anoint the tabernacle of the **c** 4150
30:36 the Testimony in the tabernacle of the **c**, 4150
31: 7 The tabernacle of the **c**, and the ark of 4150
33: 7 and called it the Tabernacle of the **C**. 4150
33: 7 went out unto the Tabernacle of the **C**, 4150
34:31 all the rulers of the **c** returned unto him: 5712
35: 1 Moses gathered all the **c** of the children of 5712
35: 4 Moses spake unto all the **c** of the children 5712
35:20 all the **c** of the children of Israel departed 5712
35:21 to the work of the tabernacle of the **c**, 4150
38: 8 *at* the door of the tabernacle of the **c**. 4150
38:25 numbered of the **c** *was* an hundred talents, 5712
38:30 to the door of the tabernacle of the **c**, 4150

Ex 39:32 the tabernacle of the tent of the **c** finished: 4150
39:40 of the tabernacle, for the tent of the **c**, 4150
40: 2 set up the tabernacle of the tent of the **c**. 4150
40: 6 door of the tabernacle of the tent of the **c**. 4150
40: 7 shalt set the laver between the tent of the **c** 4150
40:12 unto the door of the tabernacle of the **c**, 4150
40:22 he put the table in the tent of the **c**, 4150
40:24 he put the candlestick in the tent of the **c**, 4150
40:26 he put the golden altar in the tent of the **c** 4150
40:29 door of the tabernacle of the tent of the **c**, 4150
40:30 he set the laver between the tent of the **c** 4150
40:32 When they went into the tent of the **c**, and 4150
40:34 a cloud covered the tent of the **c**, and 4150
40:35 was not able to enter into the tent of the **c**, 4150
Lev 1: 1 unto him out of the tabernacle of the **c**, 4150
1: 3 the tabernacle of the **c** before the LORD. 4150
1: 5 *is by* the door of the tabernacle of the **c**. 4150
3: 2 kill it *at* the door of the tabernacle of the **c**: 4150
3: 8 and kill it before the tabernacle of the **c**: 4150
3:13 and kill it before the tabernacle of the **c**: 4150
4: 4 the tabernacle of the **c** before the LORD; 4150
4: 5 and bring it to the tabernacle of the **c**: 4150
4: 7 which *is* in the tabernacle of the **c**; 4150
4: 7 *is at* the door of the tabernacle of the **c**. 4150
4:13 if the whole **c** of Israel sin through 5712
4:14 the **c** shall offer a young bullock for the sin, 6951
4:14 bring him before the tabernacle of the **c**. 4150
4:15 the elders of the **c** shall lay their hands 5712
4:16 bullock's blood to the tabernacle of the **c**: 4150
4:18 that *is* in the tabernacle of the **c**, and shall 4150
4:18 *is at* the door of the tabernacle of the **c**. 4150
4:21 first bullock: it *is* a sin offering for the **c**. 6951
6:16 in the court of the tabernacle of the **c** they 4150
6:26 in the court of the tabernacle of the **c**. 4150
6:30 **c** to reconcile *withal* in the holy *place*, shall 4150
8: 3 gather thou all the **c** together unto the door 5712
8: 3 unto the door of the tabernacle of the **c**. 4150
8: 4 unto the door of the tabernacle of the **c**. 4150
8: 5 Moses said unto the **c**, This *is* the thing 5712
8:31 flesh *at* the door of the tabernacle of the **c**: 4150
8:33 of the tabernacle of the **c** *in* seven days, 4150
8:35 *at* the door of the tabernacle of the **c** day 4150
9: 5 commanded before the tabernacle of the **c**: 4150
9: 5 all the **c** drew near and stood before 5712
9:23 and Aaron went into the tabernacle of the **c**, 4150
10: 7 out from the door of the tabernacle of the **c**, 4150
10: 9 when ye go into the tabernacle of the **c**, 4150
10:17 given it you to bear the iniquity of the **c**, 5712
12: 6 unto the door of the tabernacle of the **c**, 4150
14:11 *at* the door of the tabernacle of the **c**: 4150
14:23 unto the door of the tabernacle of the **c**, 4150
15:14 unto the door of the tabernacle of the **c**, 4150
15:29 to the door of the tabernacle of the **c**. 4150
16: 5 he shall take of the **c** of the children of 5712
16: 7 *at* the door of the tabernacle of the **c**. 4150
16:16 so shall he do for the tabernacle of the **c**, 4150
16:17 **c** when he goeth in to make an atonement 4150
16:17 for his household, and for all the **c** of Israel. 6951
16:20 the holy *place*, and the tabernacle of the **c**, 4150
16:23 shall come into the tabernacle of the **c**, 4150
16:33 an atonement for the tabernacle of the **c**, 4150
16:33 the priests, and for all the people of the **c**. 6951
17: 4 not unto the door of the tabernacle of the **c**, 4150
17: 5 unto the door of the tabernacle of the **c**, 4150
17: 6 *at* the door of the tabernacle of the **c**, 4150
17: 9 not unto the door of the tabernacle of the **c**, 4150
19: 2 Speak unto all the **c** of the children of 5712
19:21 unto the door of the tabernacle of the **c**, 4150
24: 3 of the Testimony, in the tabernacle of the **c**, 4150
24:14 upon his head, and let all the **c** stone him. 5712
24:16 all the **c** shall certainly stone him: 5712
Nu 1: 1 in the tabernacle of the **c**, on the first *day* of 4150
1: 2 Take ye the sum of all the **c** of the children 5712
1:16 These *were* the renowned of the **c**, 5712
1:18 they assembled all the **c** together on 5712
1:53 that there be no wrath upon the **c** of 5712
2: 2 far off about the tabernacle of the **c** shall 4150
2:17 the tabernacle of the **c** shall set forward 4150
3: 7 the charge of the whole **c** before 5712
3: 7 congregation before the tabernacle of the **c**, 4150
3: 8 the instruments of the tabernacle of the **c**, 4150
3:25 tabernacle of the **c** *shall be* the tabernacle, 4150
3:25 for the door of the tabernacle of the **c**, 4150
3:38 *even* before the tabernacle of the **c** 4150
4: 3 to do the work in the tabernacle of the **c**. 4150
4: 4 sons of Kohath in the tabernacle of the **c**, 4150
4:15 sons of Kohath in the tabernacle of the **c**. 4150
4:23 to do the work in the tabernacle of the **c**. 4150
4:25 the tabernacle of the **c**, his covering, and 4150
4:25 for the door of the tabernacle of the **c**, 4150
4:28 sons of Gershon in the tabernacle of the **c**: 4150
4:30 to do the work of the tabernacle of the **c**. 4150
4:31 to all their service in the tabernacle of the **c**; 4150
4:33 all their service, in the tabernacle of the **c**, 4150
4:34 the chief of the **c** numbered the sons of 5712
4:35 for the work in the tabernacle of the **c**: 4150
4:37 *might* do service in the tabernacle of the **c**, 4150
4:39 for the work in the tabernacle of the **c**, 4150
4:41 *might* do service in the tabernacle of the **c**, 4150
4:43 for the work in the tabernacle of the **c**, 4150
4:47 of the burden in the tabernacle of the **c**, 4150
6:10 to the door of the tabernacle of the **c**: 4150
6:13 unto the door of the tabernacle of the **c**: 4150
6:18 *at* the door of the tabernacle of the **c**, 4150
7: 5 to do the service of the tabernacle of the **c**; 4150
7:89 the tabernacle of the **c** to speak with him, 4150
8: 9 the Levites before the tabernacle of the **c**: 4150
8:15 to do the service of the tabernacle of the **c**: 4150
8:19 children of Israel in the tabernacle of the **c**, 4150
8:20 and all the **c** of the children of Israel, 5712
8:22 in the tabernacle of the **c** before Aaron, 4150
8:24 upon the service of the tabernacle of the **c**: 4150
8:26 their brethren in the tabernacle of the **c**, 4150
10: 3 thee at the door of the tabernacle of the **c**. 4150
10: 7 when the **c** is to be gathered together, you 6951
11:16 bring them unto the tabernacle of the **c**, 4150
12: 4 out ye three unto the tabernacle of the **c**. 4150
13:26 and to all the **c** of the children of Israel, 5712
13:26 unto all the **c**, and shewed them the fruit of 5712
14: 1 all the **c** lifted up their voice, and cried; 5712
14: 2 the whole **c** said unto them, Would God 5712
14: 5 assembly of the **c** of the children of Israel. 5712
14:10 all the **c** bade stone them with stones. 5712
14:10 of the **c** before all the children of Israel. 4150
14:27 How long *shall I bear* with this evil **c**, 5712
14:35 I will surely do it unto all this evil **c**, 5712
14:36 and made all the **c** to murmur against him, 5712
15:15 ordinance *shall be both* for you *of* the **c**, 6951
15:24 ignorance without the knowledge of the **c**, 5712
15:24 that all the **c** shall offer one young bullock 5712
15:25 for all the **c** of the children of Israel, 5712
15:26 it shall be forgiven all the **c** of the children 5712
15:33 unto Moses and Aaron, and unto all the **c**. 5712
15:35 all the **c** shall stone him with stones without 5712
15:36 all the **c** brought him without the camp, 5712
16: 2 famous in the **c**, men of renown: 4150
16: 3 seeing all the **c** *are* holy, every one of them, 5712
16: 3 lift you up yourselves above the **c** of 6951
16: 9 hath separated you from the **c** of Israel, 5712
16: 9 to stand before the **c** to minister unto them? 5712
16:18 stood *in* the door of the tabernacle of the **c** 4150
16:19 Korah gathered all the **c** against them unto 5712
16:19 unto the door of the tabernacle of the **c**: 4150
16:19 of the LORD appeared unto all the **c**. 5712
16:21 Separate yourselves from among this **c**, that 5712
16:22 and wilt thou be wroth with all the **c**? 5712
16:24 Speak unto the **c**, saying, Get you up from 5712
16:26 he spake unto the **c**, saying, Depart, I pray 5712
16:33 and they perished from among the **c**. 6951
16:41 on the morrow all the **c** of the children of 5712
16:42 when the **c** was gathered against Moses and 5712
16:42 they looked toward the tabernacle of the **c**: 4150
16:43 Aaron came before the tabernacle of the **c**. 4150
16:45 Get you up from among this **c**, that I may 5712
16:46 go quickly unto the **c**, and make an 5712
16:47 and ran into the midst of the **c**; 6951
16:50 unto the door of the tabernacle of the **c**: 4150
17: 4 tabernacle of the **c** before the Testimony, 4150
18: 4 keep the charge of the tabernacle of the **c**, 4150
18: 6 to do the service of the tabernacle of the **c**. 4150
18:21 *even* the service of the tabernacle of the **c**. 4150
18:22 come nigh the tabernacle of the **c**, 4150
18:23 do the service of the tabernacle of the **c**, 4150
18:31 for your service in the tabernacle of the **c**. 4150
19: 4 before the tabernacle of the **c** seven times: 4150
19: 9 it shall be kept for the **c** of the children of 5712
19:20 that soul shall be cut off from among the **c**, 6951
20: 1 the children of Israel, *even* the whole **c**, 5712

Nu 20: 2 there was no water for the **c**: and 5712
20: 4 why have ye brought up the **c** of 6951
20: 6 unto the door of the tabernacle of the **c**, 4150
20: 8 so thou shalt give the **c** and their beasts 5712
20:10 Aaron gathered the **c** together before 6951
20:11 and the **c** drank, and their beasts *also.* 5712
20:12 ye shall not bring this **c** into the land which 6951
20:22 *even* the whole **c**, journeyed from Kadesh, 5712
20:27 up into mount Hor in the sight of all the **c**. 5712
20:29 when all the **c** saw that Aaron was dead, 5712
25: 6 in the sight of all the **c** of the children of 5712
25: 6 *before* the door of the tabernacle of the **c**. 4150
25: 7 saw *it,* he rose up from amongst the **c**, and 5712
26: 2 Take the sum of all the **c** of the children of 5712
26: 9 and Abiram, *which were* famous in the **c**, 5712
27: 2 and before the princes and all the **c**, 5712
27: 2 *by* the door of the tabernacle of the **c**, 4150
27:14 in the strife of the **c**, to sanctify me at 5712
27:16 the spirits of all flesh, set a man over the **c**, 5712
27:17 that the **c** of the LORD be not as sheep 5712
27:19 Eleazar the priest, and before all the **c**; 5712
27:20 that all the **c** of the children of Israel may 5712
27:21 children of Israel with him, even all the **c**. 5712
27:22 Eleazar the priest, and before all the **c**: 5712
31:12 and unto the **c** of the children of Israel, 5712
31:13 the priest, and all the princes of the **c**, 5712
31:16 there was a plague among the **c** of 5712
31:26 the priest, and the chief fathers of the **c**: 5712
31:27 went out to battle, and between all the **c**: 5712
31:43 (Now the half that pertained unto the **c** was 5712
31:54 and brought it into the tabernacle of the **c**, 4150
32: 2 and unto the princes of the **c**, saying, 5712
32: 4 the LORD smote before the **c** of Israel, 5712
35:12 until he stand before the **c** in judgment. 5712
35:24 the **c** shall judge between the slayer and 5712
35:25 the **c** shall deliver the slayer out of the hand 5712
35:25 the **c** shall restore him to the city of his 5712
Dt 23: 1 shall not enter into the **c** of the LORD. 6951
23: 2 A bastard shall not enter into the **c** of 6951
23: 2 shall he not enter into the **c** of the LORD. 6951
23: 3 Moabite shall not enter into the **c** of 6951
23: 3 not enter into the **c** of the LORD for ever: 6951
23: 8 **c** of the LORD *in* their third generation. 6951
31:14 yourselves in the tabernacle of the **c**, 4150
31:14 themselves in the tabernacle of the **c**. 4150
31:30 Moses spake in the ears of all the **c** of Israel 6951
33: 4 *even* the inheritance of the **c** of Jacob. 6952
Jos 8:35 which Joshua read not before all the **c** of 6951
9:15 and the princes of the **c** sware unto them. 5712
9:18 the princes of the **c** had sworn unto them by 5712
9:18 And all the **c** murmured against the princes. 5712
9:19 all the princes said unto all the **c**, We have 5712
9:21 and drawers of water unto all the **c**; 5712
9:27 of wood and drawers of water for the **c**, 5712
18: 1 the whole **c** of the children of Israel 5712
18: 1 and set up the tabernacle of the **c** there. 4150
19:51 *at* the door of the tabernacle of the **c**. 4150
20: 6 until he stand before the **c** for judgment, 5712
20: 9 of blood, until he stood before the **c**. 5712
22:12 **c** of the children of Israel gathered 5712
22:16 Thus saith the whole **c** of the LORD, 5712
22:17 although there was a plague in the **c** of 5712
22:18 he will be wroth with the whole **c** of Israel. 5712
22:20 and wrath fell on all the **c** of Israel? 5712
22:30 the princes of the **c** and heads of 5712
Jdg 20: 1 the **c** was gathered together as one man, 5712
21: 5 came not up with the **c** unto the LORD? 6951
21:10 the **c** sent thither twelve thousand men of 5712
21:13 the whole **c** sent *some* to speak to 5712
21:16 the elders of the **c** said, How shall we do 5712
1Sa 2:22 *at* the door of the tabernacle of the **c**. 4150
1Ki 8: 4 the tabernacle of the **c**, and all the holy 4150
8: 5 king Solomon, and all the **c** of Israel, 5712
8:14 face about, and blessed all the **c** of Israel: 6951
8:14 of Israel: (and all the **c** of Israel stood;) 6951
8:22 in the presence of all the **c** of Israel, 6951
8:55 blessed all the **c** of Israel *with* a loud voice, 6951
8:65 a feast, and all Israel with him, a great **c**, 6951
12: 3 Jeroboam and all the **c** of Israel came, and 6951
12:20 that they sent and called him unto the **c**, 5712
1Ch 6:32 of the tabernacle of the **c** with singing, 4150
9:21 porter of the door of the tabernacle of the **c**. 4150
13: 2 David said unto all the **c** of Israel, If *it seem* 6951
13: 4 all the **c** said that *they* would do so: for 6951
23:32 keep the charge of the tabernacle of the **c**, 4150
28: 8 in the sight of all Israel the **c** of 6951
29: 1 David the king said unto all the **c**, 6951
29:10 David blessed the LORD before all the **c**: 6951
29:20 David said to all the **c**, Now bless 6951
29:20 all the **c** blessed the LORD God of their 6951
2Ch 1: 3 So Solomon, and all the **c** with him, went to 6951
1: 3 for there was the tabernacle of the **c** of 4150
1: 5 and Solomon and the **c** sought *unto* it. 6951
1: 6 which *was* at the tabernacle of the **c**, and 4150
1:13 from before the tabernacle of the **c**, and 4150
5: 5 the tabernacle of the **c**, and all the holy 4150
5: 6 all the **c** of Israel that were assembled unto 5712
6: 3 his face, and blessed the whole **c** of Israel: 6951
6: 3 of Israel: and all the **c** of Israel stood. 6951
6:12 in the presence of all the **c** of Israel, 6951
6:13 upon his knees before all the **c** of Israel, 6951
7: 8 all Israel with him, a very great **c**, from 6951
20: 5 Jehoshaphat stood in the **c** of Judah and 6951
20:14 spirit of the LORD in the midst of the **c**; 6951
23: 3 all the **c** made a covenant with the king in 6951
24: 6 of the **c** of Israel, for the tabernacle of 6951
28:14 the spoil before the princes and all the **c**. 6951
29:23 the sin offering before the king and the **c**; 6951
29:28 all the **c** worshipped, and the singers sang, 6951
29:31 the **c** brought in sacrifices and 6951
29:32 which the **c** brought, was threescore and 6951
30: 2 and his princes, and all the **c** in Jerusalem, 6951
30: 4 the thing pleased the king and all the **c**. 6951
30:13 bread in the second month, a very great **c**. 6951
30:17 For *there were* many in the **c** that were not 6951
30:24 Judah did give to the **c** a thousand bullocks 6951
30:24 the princes gave to the **c** a thousand 6951
30:25 all the **c** of Judah, with the priests and 6951
30:25 all the **c** that came out of Israel, and 6951
31:18 and their daughters, through all the **c**: 6951
Ezr 2:64 The whole **c** together *was* forty *and* 6951
10: 1 unto him out of Israel a very great **c** *of* men 6951
10: 8 himself separated from the **c** of those that 6951
10:12 all the **c** answered and said *with* a loud 6951
10:14 Let now our rulers of all the **c** stand, and 6951
Ne 5:13 all the **c** said, Amen, and praised 6951
7:66 The whole **c** together *was* forty *and* 6951
8: 2 Ezra the priest brought the law before the **c** 6951
8:17 all the **c** of them that were come again out 6951
13: 1 the Moabite should not come into the **c** of 6951
Job 15:34 For the **c** of hypocrites *shall be* desolate, 5712
30:28 the sun: I stood up, *and* I cried in the **c**. 6951
Ps 1: 5 nor sinners in the **c** of the righteous. 5712
7: 7 So shall the **c** of the people compass thee 5712
22:22 in the midst of the **c** will I praise thee. 6951
22:25 My praise *shall be* of thee in the great **c**: 6951
26: 5 I have hated the **c** of evildoers; and will not 6951
35:18 I will give thee thanks in the great **c**: I will 6951
40: 9 have preached righteousness in the great **c**: 6951
40:10 and thy truth from the great **c**. 6951
58: 1 Do ye indeed speak righteousness, O **c**? 482
68:10 Thy **c** hath dwelt therein: thou, O God, 2416
74: 2 Remember thy **c**, *which* thou hast 5712
74:19 forget not the **c** of thy poor for ever. 2416
75: 2 When I shall receive the **c** I will judge 4150
82: 1 God standeth in the **c** of the mighty; 5712
89: 5 thy faithfulness also in the **c** of the saints. 6951
107:32 Let them exalt him also in the **c** of 6951
111: 1 in the assembly of the upright, and *in* the **c**. 5712
149: 1 a new song, *and* his praise in the **c** of saints. 6951
Pr 5:14 I was almost in all evil in the midst of the **c** 6951
21:16 shall remain in the **c** of the dead. 6951
26:26 shall be shewed before the *whole* **c**. 6951
Isa 14:13 I will sit also upon the mount of the **c**, 4150
Jer 6:18 Therefore hear, ye nations, and know, O **c**, 5712
30:20 their **c** shall be established before me, and 5712
La 1:10 *that* they should not enter into thy **c**. 6951
Hos 7:12 I will chastise them, as their **c** hath heard. 5712
Joel 2:16 Gather the people, sanctify the **c**, 6951
Mic 2: 5 cast a cord by lot in the **c** of the LORD. 6951
Ac 13:43 Now when the **c** was broken up, many of *4864*

CONGREGATIONS (3) [CONGREGATION]

Ps 26:12 even place: in the **c** will I bless the LORD. 4721
68:26 Bless ye God in the **c**, *even* the Lord, 4721
74: 4 Thine enemies roar in the midst of thy **c**; 4150

CONIAH (3) [JEHOIACHIN]
Jer 22:24 though **C** the son of Jehoiakim king of 3659
22:28 *Is* this man **C** a despised broken idol? *is he* 3659
37: 1 reigned instead of **C** the son of Jehoiakim, 3659

CONIES (2) [CONEY]
Ps 104:18 for the wild goats; *and* the rocks for the **c**. 8227
Pr 30:26 The **c** *are but* a feeble folk, yet make they 8227

CONONIAH (2)
2Ch 31:12 over which **C** the Levite *was* ruler, and 3562
31:13 *were* overseers under the hand of **C** and 3562

CONQUER (1) [CONQUERING, CONQUERORS]
Rev 6: 2 and he went forth conquering, and to **c**. *3528*

CONQUERING (1) [CONQUER]
Rev 6: 2 and he went forth **c**, and to conquer. *3528*

CONQUERORS (1) [CONQUER]
Ro 8:37 in all these *things* we are **more than c** *5245*

CONSCIENCE (31) [CONSCIENCES]
Jn 8: 9 heard *it,* being convicted by *their own* **c**, *4893*
Ac 23: 1 I have lived in all good **c** before God until *4893*
24:16 to have always a **c** void of offence toward *4893*
Ro 2:15 their **c** also bearing witness, and *their* *4893*
9: 1 my **c** also bearing me witness in the Holy *4893*
13: 5 not only for wrath, but also for **c** sake. *4893*
1Co 8: 7 for some with **c** of the idol unto this hour, *4893*
8: 7 an idol; and their **c** being weak is defiled. *4893*
8:10 shall not the **c** of him which is weak be *4893*
8:12 the brethren, and wound their weak **c**, *4893*
10:25 *that* eat, asking no question for **c** sake: *4893*
10:27 eat, asking no question for **c** sake. *4893*
10:28 and *for* **c** *sake:* for the earth *is* the Lord's, *4893*
10:29 **C**, I say, not thine own, but of the other's: *4893*
10:29 is my liberty judged of another *man's* **c**? *4893*
2Co 1:12 the testimony of our **c**, that in simplicity *4893*
4: 2 to every man's **c** in the sight of God. *4893*
1Ti 1: 5 and *of* a good **c**, and *of* faith unfeigned: *4893*
1:19 Holding faith, and a good **c**; which some *4893*
3: 9 Holding the mystery of the faith in a pure **c**. *4893*
4: 2 having their **c** seared with a hot iron; *4893*
2Ti 1: 3 I serve from *my* forefathers with pure **c**, *4893*
Tit 1:15 but even their mind and **c** is defiled. *4893*
Heb 9: 9 the service perfect, as pertaining to the **c**; *4893*
9:14 purge your **c** from dead works to serve *4893*
10: 2 purged should have had no more **c** of sins. *4893*
10:22 having *our* hearts sprinkled from an evil **c**, *4893*
13:18 for we trust we have a good **c**, in all *things* *4893*
1Pe 2:19 if a man for **c** toward God endure grief, *4893*
3:16 Having a good **c**; that, whereas they speak *4893*
3:21 but the answer of a good **c** toward God,) *4893*

CONSCIENCES (1) [CONSCIENCE]
2Co 5:11 and I trust also are made manifest in your **c**. *4893*

CONSECRATE (14) [CONSECRATED, CONSECRATION, CONSECRATIONS]
Ex 28: 3 that they may make Aaron's garments to **c** 6942
28:41 and **c** them, and sanctify them, 853+3027+4390
29: 9 and thou shalt **c** Aaron and his sons. 3027+4390
29:33 to **c** *and* to sanctify them: 853+3027+4390
29:35 seven days shalt thou **c** them. 3027+4390
30:30 anoint Aaron and his sons, and **c** them, 6942
32:29 **C** yourselves to day to the LORD, 3027+4390
Lev 8:33 for seven days shall he **c** you. 853+3027+4390
16:32 whom he shall **c** to minister in 853+3027+4390
Nu 6:12 he shall **c** unto the LORD the days of his 5144
1Ch 29: 5 is willing to **c** his service *this* day unto 4390
2Ch 13: 9 that whosoever cometh to **c** himself 3027+4390
Eze 43:26 purify it; and they shall **c** themselves. 3027+4390
Mic 4:13 and I will **c** their gain unto the LORD, and 2763

CONSECRATED (14) [CONSECRATE]
Ex 29:29 and to be **c** in them. 853+3027+4390
Lev 21:10 that is **c** to put on the garments, 853+3027+4390
Nu 3: 3 he **c** to minister in the priest's office. 3027+4390
Jos 6:19 of brass and iron, *are* **c** unto the LORD: 6944
Jdg 17: 5 teraphim, and **c** one of his sons, 853+3027+4390
17:12 Micah **c** the Levite; and 853+3027+4390
1Ki 13:33 he **c** him, and he became *one of* 853+3027+4390
2Ch 26:18 sons of Aaron, that are **c** to burn incense: 6942
29:31 Now ye have **c** yourselves unto 3027+4390
29:33 the **c** *things were* six hundred oxen and 6944
31: 6 the tithe of holy *things* which were **c** unto 6942
Ezr 3: 5 all the set feasts of the LORD that were **c**, 6942
Heb 7:28 *maketh* the Son, who is **c** for evermore. *5048*
10:20 and living way, which he hath **c** for us, *1457*

CONSECRATION (8) [CONSECRATE]
Ex 29:22 and the right shoulder; for it *is* a ram of **c**: 4394
29:27 and which is heaved up, of the ram of the **c**, 4394
29:31 thou shalt take the ram of the **c**, and 4394
Lev 8:22 he brought the other ram, the ram of **c**: and 4394
8:29 *for* of the ram of **c** it was Moses' part; 4394
8:33 until the days of your **c** be at an end: 4394
Nu 6: 7 because the **c** of his God *is* upon his head. 5145
6: 9 and he hath defiled the head of his **c**; 5145

CONSECRATIONS (5) [CONSECRATE]
Ex 29:26 take the breast of the ram of Aaron's **c**, 4394
29:34 if *ought* of the flesh of the **c**, or of 4394
Lev 7:37 of the **c**, and of the sacrifice of the peace 4394
8:28 they *were* **c** for a sweet savour: it *is* an 4394
8:31 it with the bread that *is* in the basket of **c**, 4394

CONSENT (15) [CONSENTED, CONSENTEDST, CONSENTING]
Ge 34:15 in this will we **c** unto you: If ye will be as we 225
34:22 Only herein will the men **c** unto us for to 225
34:23 only let us **c** unto them, and they will dwell 225
Dt 13: 8 Thou shalt not **c** unto him, nor hearken unto 14
Jdg 11:17 he would not **c**: and Israel abode in Kadesh. 14
1Sa 11: 7 on the people, and they came out with one **c**. 376
1Ki 20: 8 said unto him, Hearken not *unto him,* nor **c**. 14
Ps 83: 5 they have consulted together *with one* **c**: 3820
Pr 1:10 My son, if sinners entice thee, **c** thou not. 14
Hos 6: 9 company of priests murder *in* the way by **c**: 7926
Zep 3: 9 of the LORD, to serve him *with* one **c**. 7926
Lk 14:18 And they all with one *c* began to make NIG
Ro 7:16 I would not, I **c** unto the law that *it is* good. *4852*
1Co 7: 5 one the other, except *it be* with **c** for a time, *4859*
1Ti 6: 3 and **c** not **to** wholesome words, *4334*

CONSENTED (4) [CONSENT]
2Ki 12: 8 the priests **c** to receive no *more* money of 225
Da 1:14 So he **c** to them in this matter, and 8085
Lk 23:51 (The same had not **c** to the counsel and *4784*
Ac 18:20 to tarry longer time with them, he **c** not; *1962*

CONSENTEDST (1) [CONSENT]
Ps 50:18 thou **c** with him, and hast been partaker 7521

CONSENTING (2) [CONSENT]
Ac 8: 1 And Saul was **c** unto his death. And at that *4909*
22:20 and **c** unto his death, and kept the raiment *4909*

CONSIDER (67) [CONSIDERED, CONSIDEREST, CONSIDERETH, CONSIDERING]
Ex 33:13 and **c** that this nation *is* thy people. 7200
Lev 13:13 the priest shall **c**: and behold, *if* the leprosy 7200
Dt 4:39 therefore *this* day, and **c** *it* in thine heart, 7725
8: 5 Thou shalt also **c** in thine heart, that, as a 3045
32: 7 days of old, **c** the years of many generations: 995
32:29 *that* they would **c** their latter end! 995
Jdg 18:14 now therefore **c** what ye have to do. 3045
19:30 **c** of it, take advice, and speak *your* 7760+3807.1
1Sa 12:24 for **c** how great things he hath done for you. 7200
25:17 therefore know and **c** what thou wilt do; 7200
2Ki 5: 7 wherefore **c**, I pray you, and see how he 3045
Job 11:11 seeth wickedness also; will he not then **c** *it?* 995
23:15 at his presence: when I **c**, I am afraid of him. 995
34:27 from him, and would not **c** any of his ways: 7919
37:14 and **c** the wondrous works of God. 995
Ps 5: 1 to my words, O LORD, **c** my meditation. 995
8: 3 When I **c** thy heavens, the work of thy 7200
9:13 **c** my trouble *which I suffer* of them that 7200
13: 3 **C** *and* hear me, O LORD my God: 5027
25:19 **C** mine enemies; for they are many; and 7200
37:10 thou shalt **diligently c** his place, and it *shall* 995
45:10 O daughter, and **c**, and incline thine ear; 7200
48:13 Mark ye well her bulwarks, **c** her palaces; 6448
50:22 Now **c** this, ye that forget God, lest I tear 995
64: 9 of God; for they shall **wisely c** of his doing. 7919
119:95 to destroy me: *but* I will **c** thy testimonies. 995
119:153 **C** mine affliction, and deliver me: for I do 7200
119:159 **C** how I love thy precepts: quicken me, 7200

C

Pr 6: 6 thou sluggard; **c** her ways, and be wise: 7200
23: 1 a ruler, **c diligently** what *is* before thee: 995+995
24:12 doth not he that pondereth the heart **c** *it?* and 995
Ecc 5: 1 of fools: for they **c** not that *they* do evil. 3045
7:13 **C** the work of God: for who can make *that* 7200
7:14 be joyful, but in the day of adversity **c**: 7200
Isa 1: 3 Israel doth not know, my people doth not **c**. 995
5:12 neither **c** the operation of his hands. 7200
14:16 shall narrowly look upon thee, *and* **c** thee, 995
18: 4 I will **c** in my dwelling place like a clear 5027
41:20 and know, and **c**, and understand together, 7760
41:22 what they *be,* that we may **c** *them,* 3820+7760
43:18 the former *things,* neither **c** the *things* of old. 995
52:15 *that* which they had not heard shall they **c**. 995
Jer 2:10 **c** diligently, and see if there be such a *thing.* 995
9:17 **C** ye, and call for the mourning *women,* that 995
23:20 in the latter days ye shall **c** it **perfectly**. 995+998
30:24 of his heart: in the latter days ye shall **c** it. 995
La 1:11 see, O LORD, and **c**; for I am become 5027
2:20 and **c** to whom thou hast done this. 5027
5: 1 come upon us: **c**, and behold our reproach. 5027
Eze 12: 3 it may be they will **c**, though they *be* a 7200
Da 9:23 understand the matter, and **c** the vision. 995
Hos 7: 2 they **c** not in their hearts *that* I remember all 559
Hag 1: 5 the LORD of hosts; **C** your ways. 3824+7760
1: 7 the LORD of hosts; **C** your ways. 3824+7760
2:15 **c** from this day and upward, 3824+7760
2:18 **C** now from this day and upward, 3824+7760
2:18 the LORD's temple was laid, **c** *it.* 3824+7760
Mt 6:28 **C** the lilies of the field, how they grow; *2648*
Lk 12:24 **C** the ravens: for they neither sow nor reap; *2657*
12:27 **C** the lilies how they grow: they toil not, *2657*
Jn 11:50 Nor **c** that it is expedient for us, that one *1260*
Ac 15: 6 elders came together for to **c** of this matter. *1492*
2Ti 2: 7 **C** what I say; and the Lord give thee *3539*
Heb 3: 1 **c** the Apostle and High Priest of our *2657*
7: 4 Now **c** how great this *man was,* unto whom *2334*
10:24 And let us **c** one another to provoke unto *2657*
12: 3 For **c** him that endured such contradiction of *357*

CONSIDERED (16) [CONSIDER]

1Ki 3:21 when I had **c** it in the morning, behold, 413+995
5: 8 I have **c** *the things* which thou sentest to me 8085
Job 1: 8 Hast thou **c** my servant Job, 3820+7760
2: 3 Hast thou **c** my servant Job, 3820+7760
Ps 31: 7 for thou hast **c** my trouble; thou hast known 7200
77: 5 I have **c** the days of old, the years of 2803
Pr 24:32 I saw, *and* **c** *it* well: I looked upon *it,* 3820+7896
Ecc 4: 1 **c** all the oppressions that *are* done under 7200
4: 4 Again, I **c** all travail, and every right work, 7200
4:15 I **c** all the living which walk under the sun, 7200
9: 1 For all this I **c** in my heart even to declare 5414
Da 7: 8 I **c** the horns, and behold, there came up 7920
Mk 6:52 For they **c** not *the miracle* of the loaves: *4920*
Ac 11: 6 I **c**, and saw fourfooted beasts of the earth, *2657*
12:12 And when he had **c** *the thing,* he came to *4894*
Ro 4:19 in faith, he **c** not his own body now dead, *2657*

CONSIDEREST (2) [CONSIDER]

Jer 33:24 **C** thou not what this people have spoken, 7200
Mt 7: 3 but **c** not the beam that is in thine own eye? *2657*

CONSIDERETH (9) [CONSIDER]

Ps 33:15 their hearts alike; he **c** all their works. 995
41: 1 Blessed *is* he that **c** the poor: the LORD 7919
Pr 21:12 The righteous *man* **wisely c** the house of 7919
28:22 and **c** not that poverty shall come *upon* him. 3045
29: 7 The righteous **c** the cause of the poor: *but* 3045
31:16 She **c** a field, and buyeth it: with the fruit of 2161
Isa 44:19 none **c** in his heart, neither *is there* 7725
Eze 18:14 hath done, and **c**, and doeth not such like, 7200
18:28 Because he **c**, and turneth away from all his 7200

CONSIDERING (4) [CONSIDER]

Isa 57: 1 none **c** that the righteous is taken away from 995
Da 8: 5 as I was **c**, behold, a he goat came from 995
Gal 6: 1 **c** thyself, lest thou also be tempted. *4648*
Heb 13: 7 faith follow, **c** the end of *their* conversation. *333*

CONSIST (1) [CONSISTETH]

Col 1:17 is before all *things,* and by him all *things* **c**. *4921*

CONSISTETH (1) [CONSIST]

Lk 12:15 for a man's life **c** not in the abundance of *1510*

CONSOLATION (15) [CONSOLATIONS]

Jer 16: 7 neither shall *men* give them the cup of **c** to 8575
Lk 2:25 and devout, waiting for the **c** of Israel: *3874*
6:24 that are rich: for ye have received your **c**. *3874*
Ac 4:36 (which is, being interpreted, The son of **c**,) *3874*
15:31 when they had read, they rejoiced for the **c**. *3874*
Ro 15: 5 **c** grant you to be likeminded one towards *3874*
2Co 1: 5 in us, so our **c** also aboundeth by Christ. *3874*
1: 6 be afflicted, *it is* for your **c** and salvation, *3874*
1: 6 be comforted, *it is* for your **c** and salvation. *3874*
1: 7 the sufferings, so *shall ye be* also of the **c**. *3874*
7: 7 by the **c** wherewith he was comforted in *3874*
Php 2: 1 If *there be* therefore any **c** in Christ, if any *3874*
2Th 2:16 and hath given *us* everlasting **c** and *3874*
Phm 1: 7 For we have great joy and **c** in thy love, *3874*
Heb 6:18 for God to lie, we might have a strong **c**, *3874*

CONSOLATIONS (3) [CONSOLATION]

Job 15:11 *Are* the **c** of God small with thee? is there 8575
21: 2 diligently my speech, and let this be your **c**. 8575
Isa 66:11 and be satisfied with the breasts of her **c**; 8575

CONSORTED (1)

Ac 17: 4 them believed, and **c with** Paul and Silas; *4345*

CONSPIRACY (10) [CONSPIRATORS, CONSPIRED]

2Sa 15:12 the **c** was strong; for the people increased 7195
2Ki 12:20 **made a c**, and slew Joash *in* 7194+7195
14:19 Now they **made a c** against him in 7194+7195
15:15 and his **c** which he **made**, behold, 7194+7195
15:30 Hoshea the son of Elah **made a c** 7194+7195
17: 4 the king of Assyria found **c** in Hoshea: 7195
2Ch 25:27 **made a c** against him in Jerusalem; 7194+7195
Jer 11: 9 A **c** is found among the men of Judah, and 7195
Eze 22:25 *There is* a **c** of her prophets in the midst 7195
Ac 23:13 more *than* forty which had made this **c**. *4945*

CONSPIRATORS (1) [CONSPIRACY]

2Sa 15:31 Ahithophel *is* among the **c** with Absalom. 7194

CONSPIRED (19) [CONSPIRACY]

Ge 37:18 unto them, they **c against** him to slay him. 5230
1Sa 22: 8 That all of you have **c** against me, and 7194
22:13 Why have ye **c** against me, thou and 7194
1Ki 15:27 of the house of Issachar, **c** against him; 7194
16: 9 **c** against him, as he *was* in Tirzah, 7194
16:16 Zimri hath **c**, and hath also slain the king: 7194
2Ki 9:14 the son of Nimshi **c** against Joram. 7194
10: 9 I **c** against my master, and slew him: 7194
15:10 Shallum the son of Jabesh **c** against him, 7194
15:25 **c** against him, and smote him in Samaria, 7194
21:23 the servants of Amon **c** against him, and 7194
21:24 all them that had **c** against king Amon; 7194
2Ch 24:21 they **c** against him, and stoned him *with* 7194
24:25 his own servants **c** against him for 7194
24:26 these *are* they that **c** against him; Zabad 7194
33:24 his servants **c** against him, and slew him in 7194
33:25 all them that had **c** against king Amon; 7194
Ne 4: 8 **c** all of them together to come *and* to fight 7194
Am 7:10 Amos hath **c** against thee in the midst of 7194

CONSTANT (1) [CONSTANTLY]

1Ch 28: 7 if he be **c** to do my commandments and 2388

CONSTANTLY (3) [CONSTANT]

Pr 21:28 the man that heareth, speaketh **c**. 5331+3807.1
Ac 12:15 But she **c affirmed** that it was *even* so. *1340*
Tit 3: 8 and these *things* I will that thou **affirm c**, *1226*

CONSTELLATIONS (1)

Isa 13:10 and the **c** thereof shall not give their light: 3685

CONSTRAIN (1) [CONSTRAINED, CONSTRAINETH, CONSTRAINT]

Gal 6:12 in the flesh, they **c** you to be circumcised; *315*

CONSTRAINED (6) [CONSTRAIN]

2Ki 4: 8 a great woman; and she **c** him to eat bread. 2388
Mt 14:22 And straightway Jesus **c** his disciples to get *315*
Mk 6:45 And straightway he **c** his disciples to get into *315*
Lk 24:29 But they **c** him, saying, Abide with us: *3849*
Ac 16:15 my house, and abide *there.* And she **c** us. *3849*
28:19 But when the Jews spake against *it,* I was **c** *315*

C

CONSTRAINETH (2) [CONSTRAIN]
Job 32:18 am full *of* matter, the spirit within me c me. 6693
2Co 5:14 For the love of Christ c us; because we thus *4912*

CONSTRAINT (1) [CONSTRAIN]
1Pe 5: 2 taking the oversight *thereof,* not by c, but *317*

CONSULT (1) [CONSULTATION, CONSULTED, CONSULTER, CONSULTETH]
Ps 62: 4 They only c to cast *him* down from his 3289

CONSULTATION (1) [CONSULT]
Mk 15: 1 the chief priests held a c with the elders *4824*

CONSULTED (13) [CONSULT]
1Ki 12: 6 king Rehoboam c with the old men, 3289
12: 8 c with the young men that were grown up 3289
1Ch 13: 1 David c with the captains of thousands and 3289
2Ch 20:21 when he had c with the people, he 3289
Ne 5: 7 I c with myself, and I rebuked the nobles, 4427
Ps 83: 3 thy people, and c against thy hidden ones. 3289
83: 5 For they have c together *with one* consent: 3289
Eze 21:21 he c with images, he looked in the liver. 7592
Da 6: 7 have c together to establish a royal statute, 3272
Mic 6: 5 remember now what Balak king of Moab c, 3289
Hab 2:10 Thou hast c shame to thy house by cutting 3289
Mt 26: 4 And c that they might take Jesus by *4823*
Jn 12:10 But the chief priests c that they might put *1011*

CONSULTER (1) [CONSULT]
Dt 18:11 or a c with familiar spirits, or a wizard, or 7592

CONSULTETH (1) [CONSULT]
Lk 14:31 c whether he be able with ten thousand to *1011*

CONSULTS THE DEAD See NECROMANCER

CONSUME (56) [CONSUMED, CONSUMETH, CONSUMING, CONSUMPTION]
Ge 41:30 of Egypt; and the famine shall c the land; 3615
Ex 32:10 hot against them, and that I may c them: 3615
32:12 and to c them from the face of the earth? 3615
33: 3 stiffnecked people: lest I c thee in the way. 3615
33: 5 the midst of thee in a moment, and c thee: 3615
Lev 26:16 that shall c the eyes, and cause sorrow of 3615
Nu 16:21 that I may c them in a moment. 3615
16:45 that I may c them as in a moment. 3615
Dt 5:25 for this great fire will c us: if we hear 398
7:16 thou shalt c all the people which the LORD 398
7:22 thou mayest not c them at once, lest 3615
28:38 *but* little in; for the locust shall c it. 2628
28:42 and fruit of thy land shall the locust c. 3423
32:22 shall c the earth with her increase, and set on 398
Jos 24:20 he will turn and do you hurt, and c you, 3615
1Sa 2:33 *shall be* to c thine eyes, and to grieve thine 3615
2Ki 1:10 down from heaven, and c thee and thy fifty. 398
1:12 down from heaven, and c thee and thy fifty. 398
Ne 9:31 mercies' sake thou didst not utterly c them, 3617
Est 9:24 *is,* the lot, to c them, and to destroy them; 2000
Job 15:34 and fire shall c the tabernacles of bribery. 398
20:26 a fire not blown shall c him; it shall go ill 398
24:19 Drought and heat c the snow waters: *so* 1497
Ps 37:20 they shall c; into smoke shall they 3615
37:20 into smoke shall they c *away.* 3615
39:11 thou makest his beauty to c away like a 4529
49:14 their beauty shall c *in* the grave from their 1086
59:13 C *them* in wrath, consume *them,* that they 3615
59:13 c *them,* that they *may* not *be:* and let them 3615
78:33 Therefore their days did he c in vanity, and 3615
Isa 7:20 hair of the feet: and it shall also c the beard. 5595
10:18 shall c the glory of his forest, and of his 3615
27:10 he lie down, and c the branches thereof. 3615
Jer 8:13 I will surely c them, saith 622+5486
14:12 I will c them by the sword, and by 3615
49:27 and it shall c the palaces of Ben-hadad. 398
Eze 4:17 with another, and c away for their iniquity. 4743
13:13 and great hailstones in *my* fury to c *it.* 3617
20:13 upon them in the wilderness, to c them. 3615
21:28 *it is* furbished, to c because of the glittering: 398
22:15 and will c thy filthiness out of thee. 8552
24:10 c the flesh, and spice it well, and let 8552
35:12 They are laid desolate, they are given us to c. 402
Da 2:44 break in pieces and c all these kingdoms, 5487
7:26 to c and to destroy *it* unto the end. 8046
Hos 11: 6 shall c his branches, and devour *them,* 3615
Zep 1: 2 I will utterly c all *things* from off the land, 5486
1: 3 I will c man and beast; I will consume 5486
1: 3 I will c the fowls of the heaven, and 5486
Zec 5: 4 shall c it with the timber thereof and 3615
14:12 Their flesh *shall* c away while they stand 4743
14:12 their eyes shall c away in their holes, and 4743
14:12 their tongue shall c away in their mouth. 4743
Lk 9:54 from heaven, and c them, even as Elias did? *355*
2Th 2: 8 whom the Lord shall c with the spirit of his *355*
Jas 4: 3 ask amiss, that ye may c *it* upon your lusts. *1159*

CONSUMED (96) [CONSUME]
Ge 19:15 lest thou be c in the iniquity of the city. 5595
19:17 escape to the mountain, lest thou be c. 5595
31:40 the drought c me, and the frost by night; 398
Ex 3: 2 burned with fire, and the bush was not c. 398
15: 7 forth thy wrath, *which* c them as stubble. 398
22: 6 be c *therewith;* he that kindled the fire shall 398
Lev 6:10 take up the ashes which the fire hath c with 398
9:24 c upon the altar the burnt offering and 398
Nu 11: 1 c *them that were* in the uttermost parts of 398
12:12 of whom the flesh is half c when he cometh 398
14:35 in this wilderness they shall be c, and 8552
16:26 of theirs, lest ye be c in all their sins. 5595
16:35 c the two hundred and fifty men that offered 398
17:13 LORD shall die: shall we be c with dying? 8552
21:28 it hath c Ar of Moab, *and* the lords of 398
25:11 that I c not the children of Israel in my 3615
32:13 done evil in the sight of the LORD, was c. 8552
Dt 2:15 from among the host, until they were c. 8552
2:16 when all the men of war were c and 8552
28:21 until he have c thee from off the land, 3615
Jos 5: 6 were c, because they obeyed not the voice 8552
8:24 until they were c, that all the Israelites 8552
10:20 till they were c, that the rest *which* 8552
Jdg 6:21 c the flesh and the unleavened *cakes.* Then 398
1Sa 12:25 ye shall be c, both ye and your king. 5595
15:18 and fight against them until they be c. 3615
2Sa 21: 5 The man that c us, and that devised against 3615
22:38 and turned not again until I had c them. 3615
22:39 I have c them, and wounded them, that they 3615
1Ki 18:38 c the burnt sacrifice, and the wood, and 398
22:11 push the Syrians, until *thou* have c them. 3615
2Ki 1:10 fire from heaven, and c him and his fifty. 398
1:12 down from heaven, and c him and his fifty. 398
7:13 all the multitude of the Israelites that are c:) 8552
13:17 Syrians in Aphek, till *thou* have c *them.* 3615
13:19 hadst thou smitten Syria till *thou* hadst c *it:* 3615
2Ch 7: 1 and c the burnt offering and the sacrifices; 398
8: 8 the land, whom the children of Israel c not, 3615
18:10 these thou shalt push Syria until they be c. 3615
Ezr 9:14 not be angry with us till *thou* hadst c *us,* 3615
Ne 2: 3 and the gates thereof are c with fire? 398
2:13 and the gates thereof were c with fire. 398
Job 1:16 up the sheep, and the servants, and c them; 398
4: 9 and by the breath of his nostrils are they c. 3615
6:17 when it is hot, they are c out of their place. 1846
7: 9 *As* the cloud is c and vanisheth away: so 3615
19:27 *though* my reins be c within me. 3615
33:21 His flesh is c away, that it cannot be seen; 3615
Ps 6: 7 Mine eye is c because of grief; it waxeth 6244
18:37 neither did I turn again till they were c. 3615
31: 9 mine eye is c with grief, *yea,* my soul and 6244
31:10 of mine iniquity, and my bones are c. 6244
39:10 from me: I am c by the blow of thine hand. 3615
71:13 *and* c that are adversaries to my soul; 3615
73:19 *in* a moment! they are utterly c with terrors. 5486
78:63 The fire c their young men; and 398
90: 7 For we are c by thine anger, and by thy 3615
102: 3 For my days are c like smoke, and 3615
104:35 Let the sinners be c out of the earth, and 8552
119:87 They had almost c me upon earth; but 3615
119:139 My zeal hath c me, because mine enemies 6789
Pr 5:11 the last, when thy flesh and thy body are c, 3615
Isa 1:28 and they that forsake the LORD shall be c. 3615
16: 4 the oppressors are c out of the land. 8552
29:20 the scorner is c, and all that watch for 3615
64: 7 and hast c us, because of our iniquities. 4127
66:17 and the mouse, shall be c together, 5486
Jer 5: 3 thou hast c them, *but* they have refused to 3615
6:29 bellows are burnt, the lead is c of the fire; 8552
9:16 send a sword after them, till I have c them. 3615
10:25 c him, and have made his habitation 3615
12: 4 the beasts are c, and the birds; because 5595

C

Jer 14:15 and famine shall those prophets be **c**. 8552
16: 4 they shall be **c** by the sword, and 3615
20:18 that my days should be **c** with shame? 3615
24:10 till they be **c** from off the land that I gave 8552
27: 8 until I have **c** them by his hand. 8552
36:23 until all the roll was **c** in the fire that *was* 8552
44:12 they shall all be **c**, *and* fall in the land of 8552
44:12 they shall *even* be **c** by the sword, *and* 8552
44:18 have been **c** by the sword and by 8552
44:27 in the land of Egypt shall be **c** by the sword 8552
49:37 the sword after them, till I have **c** them: 3615
La 2:22 and brought up hath mine enemy **c**. 3615
3:22 *of* the LORD'S mercies that we are not **c**, 8552
Eze 5:12 with famine shall they be **c** in the midst of 3615
13:14 and ye shall be **c** in the midst thereof: 3615
19:12 were broken and withered; the fire **c** them. 398
22:31 I have **c** them with the fire of my wrath: 3615
24:11 molten in it, *that* the scum of it may be **c**. 8552
34:29 they shall be no more **c** with hunger in 622
43: 8 wherefore I have **c** them in mine anger. 3615
47:12 not fade, neither shall the fruit thereof be **c**: 8552
Da 11:16 glorious land, which by his hand shall be **c**. 3617
Mal 3: 6 therefore ye sons of Jacob are not **c**. 3615
Gal 5:15 take heed ye be not **c** one of another. *355*

CONSUMETH (4) [CONSUME]
Job 13:28 he, as a rotten thing, **c**, as a garment that is 1086
22:20 cut down, but the remnant of them the fire **c**. 398
31:12 For it *is* a fire *that* **c** to destruction, and 398
Isa 5:24 the flame **c** the chaff, *so* their root shall be 7503

CONSUMING (3) [CONSUME]
Dt 4:24 For the LORD thy God *is* a **c** fire, *even* a 398
9: 3 *as* a **c** fire he shall destroy them, and he shall 398
Heb 12:29 For our God *is* a **c** fire. *2654*

CONSUMMATION (1)
Da 9:27 even until the **c**, and that determined shall 3617

CONSUMPTION (5) [CONSUME]
Lev 26:16 **c**, and the burning ague, that shall consume 7829
Dt 28:22 The LORD shall smite thee with a **c**, and 7829
Isa 10:22 the **c** decreed shall overflow *with* 3631
10:23 For the Lord GOD of hosts shall make a **c**, 3617
28:22 heard from the Lord GOD of hosts a **c**, 3617

CONTAIN (7) [CONTAINED, CONTAINETH, CONTAINING]
1Ki 8:27 and heaven of heavens cannot **c** thee; 3557
18:32 as great as would **c** two measures of seed. 1004
2Ch 2: 6 and heaven of heavens cannot **c** him? 3557
6:18 and the heaven of heavens cannot **c** thee; 3557
Eze 45:11 that the bath may **c** the tenth part of a 5375
Jn 21:25 not **c** the books that should be written. *5562*
1Co 7: 9 But if they cannot **c**, let them marry: for it *1467*

CONTAINED (5) [CONTAIN]
1Ki 7:26 flowers of lilies: it **c** two thousand baths. 3557
7:38 one laver **c** forty baths: *and* every laver was 3557
Ro 2:14 do by nature the *things* **c** in the law, these, NIG
Eph 2:15 *even* the law of commandments *c* in NIG
1Pe 2: 6 Wherefore also it is **c** in the scripture, *4023*

CONTAINETH (1) [CONTAIN]
Eze 23:32 to scorn and had in derision; *it* **c** much. 3557

CONTAINING (1) [CONTAIN]
Jn 2: 6 of the Jews, **c** two or three firkins apiece. *5562*

CONTEMN (2) [CONTEMNED, CONTEMNETH]
Ps 10:13 Wherefore doth the wicked **c** God? he hath 5006
Eze 21:13 and what if *the sword* **c** even the rod? 3988

CONTEMNED (4) [CONTEMN]
Ps 15: 4 In whose eyes a vile *person* is **c**; but he 959
107:11 of God, and **c** the counsel of the most High: 5006
SS 8: 7 house for love, it would **utterly** be **c**. 936+936
Isa 16:14 a hireling, and the glory of Moab shall be **c**, 7034

CONTEMNETH (1) [CONTEMN]
Eze 21:10 it **c** the rod of my son, *as* every tree. 3988

CONTEMPT (10) [CONTEMPTIBLE, CONTEMPTUOUSLY]
Est 1:18 Thus *shall there arise* too much **c** and wrath. 963
Job 12:21 He poureth **c** upon princes, and 937
31:34 or did the **c** of families terrify me, that I kept 937
Ps 107:40 He poureth **c** upon princes, and causeth them 937
119:22 Remove from me reproach and **c**; for I have 937
123: 3 for we are exceedingly filled *with* **c**. 937
123: 4 that are at ease, *and with* the **c** of the proud. 937
Pr 18: 3 *then* cometh also **c**, and with ignominy 937
Isa 23: 9 to **bring into c** all the honourable of 7043
Da 12: 2 and some to shame *and* everlasting **c**. 1860

CONTEMPTIBLE (4) [CONTEMPT]
Mal 1: 7 In that ye say, The table of the LORD *is* **c**. 959
1:12 the fruit thereof, *even* his meat, *is* **c**. 959
2: 9 Therefore have I also made you **c** and 959
2Co 10:10 bodily presence *is* weak, and *his* speech **c**. *1848*

CONTEMPTUOUSLY (1) [CONTEMPT]
Ps 31:18 things proudly and **c** against the righteous. 937

CONTEND (14) [CONTENDED, CONTENDEST, CONTENDETH, CONTENDING]
Dt 2: 9 the Moabites, neither **c** with them *in* battle: 1624
2:24 begin to possess *it,* and **c** with him *in* battle. 1624
Job 9: 3 If he will **c** with him, he cannot answer him 7378
13: 8 ye accept his person? will ye **c** for God? 7378
Pr 28: 4 but such as keep the law **c** with them. 1624
Ecc 6:10 neither may he **c** with him that *is* mightier 1777
Isa 49:25 for I will **c with** him that contendeth with 7378
50: 8 near that justifieth me; who will **c** with me? 7378
57:16 For I will not **c** for ever, neither will I be 7378
Jer 12: 5 then how canst thou **c** with horses? 8474
18:19 hearken to the voice of them that **c with** 3401
Am 7: 4 the Lord GOD called to **c** by fire, and 7378
Mic 6: 1 **c** thou before the mountains, and let 7378
Jude 1: 3 exhort *you* that *ye* should **earnestly c for** *1864*

CONTENDED (6) [CONTEND]
Ne 13:11 **c** I with the rulers, and said, Why is 7378
13:17 I **c** with the nobles of Judah, and said unto 7378
13:25 I **c** with them, and cursed them, and 7378
Job 31:13 of my maidservant, when they **c** with me; 7379
Isa 41:12 not find them, *even* them that **c with** thee: 4695
Ac 11: 2 they that were of the circumcision **c** with *1252*

CONTENDEST (1) [CONTEND]
Job 10: 2 shew me wherefore thou **c** with me. 7378

CONTENDETH (3) [CONTEND]
Job 40: 2 Shall he that **c** with the Almighty instruct 7378
Pr 29: 9 If a wise man **c** with a foolish man, 8199
Isa 49:25 for I will contend with him that **c with** thee, 3401

CONTENDING (1) [CONTEND]
Jude 1: 9 when **c** with the devil he disputed about *1252*

CONTENT (16) [CONTENTMENT]
Ge 37:27 *and* our flesh. And his brethren were **c**. 8085
Ex 2:21 Moses was **c** to dwell with the man: and 2974
Lev 10:20 Moses heard *that,* he was **c**. 3190+5869+871.1
Jos 7: 7 would to God we had been **c**, and dwelt on 2974
Jdg 17:11 the Levite was **c** to dwell with the man; 2974
19: 6 Be **c**, I pray thee, and tarry all night, and 2974
2Ki 5:23 Naaman said, Be **c**, take two talents. 2974
6: 3 Be **c**, I pray thee, and go with thy servants. 2974
Job 6:28 Now therefore be **c**, look upon me; for *it is* 2974
Pr 6:35 neither will he **rest c**, though thou givest 14
Mk 15:15 And *so* Pilate, willing to **c** *2425+4160*
Lk 3:14 *any* falsely; and be **c** with your wages. *714*
Php 4:11 in whatsoever *state* I am, *therewith* to be **c**. *842*
1Ti 6: 8 and raiment let us be therewith **c**. *714*
Heb 13: 5 *and be* **c** with such *things* as ye have: *714*
3Jn 1:10 and not **c** therewith, neither doth he himself *714*

CONTENTION (9) [CONTENTIONS, CONTENTIOUS]
Pr 13:10 Only by pride cometh **c**: but with the well 4683
17:14 therefore leave off **c**, before *it* be meddled 7379
18: 6 A fool's lips enter into **c**, and his mouth 7379
22:10 Cast out the scorner, and **c** shall go out; 4066
Jer 15:10 of strife and a man of **c** to the whole earth! 4066
Hab 1: 3 and there are *that* raise up strife and **c**. 4066
Ac 15:39 And the **c** was so **sharp** *between them,* that *3948*
Php 1:16 The one preach Christ of **c**, not sincerely, *2052*
1Th 2: 2 unto you the gospel of God with much **c**. *73*

CONTENTIONS (6) [CONTENTION]
Pr 18:18 The lot causeth **c** to cease, and 4066
18:19 and *their* **c** *are* like the bars of a castle. 4066

Pr 19:13 the c of a wife *are* a continual dropping. 4066
23:29 who hath c? who hath babbling? who hath 4066
1Co 1:11 *house* of Chloe, that there are c among you. *2054*
Tit 3: 9 and c, and strivings about the law; *2054*

CONTENTIOUS (5) [CONTENTION]
Pr 21:19 than with a c and an angry woman. 4066
26:21 wood to fire; so *is* a c man to kindle strife. 4066
27:15 a very rainy day and a c woman are alike. 4066
Ro 2: 8 But unto them that are c, *2052*
1Co 11:16 But if any *man* seem to be c, we have no *5380*

CONTENTMENT (1) [CONTENT]
1Ti 6: 6 But godliness with c is great gain. *841*

CONTINUAL (33) [CONTINUE]
Ex 29:42 *This shall be* a c burnt offering throughout 8548
Nu 4: 7 and the c bread shall be thereon: 8548
28: 3 spot day by day, *for* a c burnt offering. 8548
28: 6 *It is* a c burnt offering, which was ordained 8548
28:10 beside the c burnt offering, and his drink 8548
28:15 besides the c burnt offering, and his drink 8548
28:23 which *is* for a c burnt offering. 8548
28:24 it shall be offered beside the c burnt 8548
28:31 Ye shall offer *them* besides the c burnt 8548
29:11 the c burnt offering, and the meat offering 8548
29:16 beside the c burnt offering, his meat 8548
29:19 beside the c burnt offering, and the meat 8548
29:22 beside the c burnt offering, and his meat 8548
29:25 beside the c burnt offering, his meat 8548
29:28 beside the c burnt offering, and his meat 8548
29:31 beside the c burnt offering, his meat 8548
29:34 beside the c burnt offering, his meat 8548
29:38 beside the c burnt offering, and his meat 8548
2Ki 25:30 his allowance was a c allowance given him 8548
2Ch 2: 4 *for* the c shewbread, and *for* the burnt 8548
Ezr 3: 5 afterward *offered* the c burnt offering, 8548
Ne 10:33 *for* the c meat offering, and for 8548
10:33 for the c burnt offering, of the sabbaths, 8548
Pr 15:15 but *he that is* of a merry heart *hath* a c feast. 8548
19:13 the contentions of a wife *are* a c dropping. 2956
27:15 A c **dropping** in a very rainy day 1812+2956
Isa 14: 6 the people in wrath *with* a c stroke, 1115+5627
Jer 48: 5 up of Luhith c **weeping** shall go up; 1065+1065
52:34 there was a c diet given him of the king of 8548
Eze 39:14 they shall sever out men of c **employment**, 8548
46:15 every morning *for* a c burnt offering. 8548
Lk 18: 5 lest **by** her c coming she weary me. *1519+5056*
Ro 9: 2 great heaviness and c sorrow in my heart. *88*

CONTINUALLY (81) [CONTINUE]
Ge 6: 5 of his heart *was* only evil c. 3117+3605+1886.1
8: 3 returned from off the earth c: 1980+7725+2050.1
8: 5 the waters decreased c until the tenth 1980
Ex 28:29 *place,* for a memorial before the LORD c. 8548
28:30 Israel upon his heart before the LORD c. 8548
29:38 two lambs of the first year day by day c. 8548
Lev 24: 2 for the light, to cause the lamps to burn c. 8548
24: 3 unto the morning before the LORD c: 8548
24: 4 the pure candlestick before the LORD c. 8548
24: 8 he shall set it in order before the LORD c, 8548
Jos 6:13 the ark of the LORD **went on** c, 1980+1980
1Sa 18:29 became David's enemy c. 3117+3605+1886.1
2Sa 9: 7 and thou shalt eat bread at my table c. 8548
9:13 for he did eat c at the king's table; and *was* 8548
15:12 for the people increased c with Absalom. 1980
19:13 me c in the room of Joab. 3117+3605+1886.1
1Ki 10: 8 which stand c before thee, *and* that hear thy 8548
2Ki 4: 9 a holy man of God, which passeth by us c. 8548
25:29 he did eat bread c before him all the days of 8548
1Ch 16: 6 Jahaziel the priests with trumpets c before 8548
16:11 and his strength, seek his face c. 8548
16:37 his brethren, to minister before the ark c, 8548
16:40 the altar of the burnt offering c morning 8548
23:31 unto them, c before the LORD: 8548
2Ch 9: 7 which stand c before thee, and hear thy 8548
12:15 and Jeroboam c. 3117+3605+1886.1
24:14 of the LORD c all the days of Jehoiada. 8548
Job 1: 5 their hearts. Thus did Job c. 3117+3605+1886.1
Ps 34: 1 all times: his praise *shall* c *be* in my mouth. 8548
35:27 yea, let them say c, Let the LORD be 8548
38:17 to halt, and my sorrow *is* c before me. 8548
40:11 and thy truth c preserve me. 8548
40:16 let such as love thy salvation say c, 8548
42: 3 while *they* c say unto me, 3117+3605+1886.1
44:15 My confusion *is* c before 3117+3605+1886.1
50: 8 burnt offerings, *to have been* c before me. 8548
52: 1 goodness of God *endureth* c. 3117+3605+1886.1
58: 7 Let them melt away as waters *which* **run** c: 1980
69:23 see not; and make their loins c to shake. 8548
70: 4 let such as love thy salvation say c, 8548
71: 3 strong habitation, whereunto *I* may c resort: 8548
71: 6 my praise *shall be* c of thee. 8548
71:14 I will hope c, and will yet praise thee more 8548
72:15 prayer also shall be made for him c; *and* 8548
73:23 Nevertheless I *am* c with thee: thou hast 8548
74:23 those that rise up against thee increaseth c. 8548
109:10 Let his children be c **vagabonds**, 5128+5128
109:15 Let them be before the LORD c, that he 8548
109:19 and for a girdle where*with* he is girded c. 8548
119:44 So shall I keep thy law c for ever and ever. 8548
119:109 My soul *is* c in my hand: yet do I not forget 8548
119:117 and I will have respect unto thy statutes c. 8548
140: 2 c are they gathered together *for* war. 3117+3605
Pr 6:14 he deviseth mischief c; 3605+6256+871.1
6:21 Bind them c upon thine heart, *and* tie them 8548
Ecc 1: 6 it **whirleth about** c, and 1980+5437+5437
Isa 21: 8 I stand c upon the watchtower in 8548
49:16 of *my* hands; thy walls *are* c before me. 8548
51:13 hast feared c every day because of the fury 8548
52: 5 and my name c every day *is* blasphemed. 8548
58:11 the LORD shall guide thee c, and 8548
60:11 Therefore thy gates shall be open c; 8548
65: 3 A people that provoketh me to anger c to 8548
Jer 6: 7 in her; before me c *is* grief and wounds. 8548
33:18 and to do sacrifice c. 3117+3605+1886.1
52:33 he did c eat bread before him all the days of 8548
Eze 46:14 a meat offering c *by* a perpetual ordinance 8548
Da 6:16 Thy God whom thou servest c, 0.2+8411+871.2
6:20 thy God, whom thou servest c, 0.2+8411+871.2
Hos 4:18 they have **committed whoredom** c: 2181+2181
12: 6 and judgment, and wait on thy God c. 8548
Ob 1:16 *so* shall all the heathen drink c, yea, 8548
Na 3:19 whom hath not thy wickedness passed c? 8548
Hab 1:17 and not spare c to slay the nations? 8548
Lk 24:53 And were c in the temple, praising and *1275*
Ac 6: 4 But we will **give** ourselves c **to** prayer, and *4342*
10: 7 soldier of them that **waited on** him c; *4342*
Ro 13: 6 **attending** c upon this very *thing.* *4342*
Heb 7: 3 Son of God; abideth a priest c. *1336+1519+3588*
10: 1 c make the comers *thereunto* *1336+1519+3588*
13:15 offer the sacrifice of praise to God c, *1223+3956*

CONTINUANCE (5) [CONTINUE]
Dt 28:59 of **long** c, and sore sicknesses, and of long 539
28:59 and sore sicknesses, and of **long** c. 539
Ps 139:16 *which* in c were fashioned, when *as yet* 3117
Isa 64: 5 in those is c, and we shall be saved. 5769
Ro 2: 7 To them who by **patient** c in well doing *5281*

CONTINUE (38) [CONTINUAL, CONTINUALLY, CONTINUANCE, CONTINUED, CONTINUETH, CONTINUING]
Ex 21:21 Notwithstanding, if he c a day or two, 5975
Lev 12: 4 c in the blood of her purifying three and 3427
12: 5 she shall c in the blood of her purifying 3427
1Sa 12:14 also the king that reigneth over you c 1961
13:14 now thy kingdom shall not c: the LORD 6965
2Sa 7:29 that *it* may c for ever before thee: 1961
1Ki 2: 4 That the LORD may c his word which he 6965
Job 15:29 not be rich, neither shall his substance c, 6965
17: 2 *doth not* mine eye c in their provocation? 3885
Ps 36:10 O c thy lovingkindness unto them that 4900
49:11 *thought is, that* their houses *shall* c for ever, NIH
102:28 The children of thy servants shall c, and 7931
119:91 They c *this* day according to thine 5975
Isa 5:11 that c until night, *till* wine inflame them! 309
Jer 32:14 earthen vessel, that they may c many days. 5975
Da 11: 8 he shall c *more* years than the king of 5975
Mt 15:32 because they c with me now three days, and *4357*
Jn 8:31 If ye c in my word, *then* are ye my disciples *3306*
15: 9 so have I loved you: c ye in my love. *3306*
Ac 13:43 persuaded them to c in the grace of God. *1961*
14:22 *and* exhorting *them* to c **in** the faith, and *1696*
26:22 obtained help of God, I c unto this day, *2476*
Ro 6: 1 Shall we c **in** sin, that grace may abound? *1961*
11:22 goodness, if thou c **in** *his* goodness: *1961*
Gal 2: 5 that the truth of the gospel might c with *1265*

C

Php 1:25 and **c with** you all for your furtherance and *4839*
Col 1:23 If ye **c in** the faith grounded and settled, *1961*
4: 2 **C in** prayer, and watch in the same with *4342*
1Ti 2:15 if they **c** in faith and charity and *3306*
4:16 and unto the doctrine; **c in** them: *1961*
2Ti 3:14 But **c** thou in *the things* which thou hast *3306*
Heb 7:23 *they* were not suffered to **c** by reason of *3887*
13: 1 Let brotherly love **c**. *3306*
Jas 4:13 and **c** there a year, and buy and sell, and *4160*
2Pe 3: 4 all *things* **c** as *they were* from the beginning *1265*
1Jn 2:24 ye also shall **c** in the Son, and in the Father. *3306*
Rev 13: 5 power was given unto him to **c** forty *and* *4160*
17:10 when he cometh, he must **c** a short *space.* *3306*

CONTINUED (29) [CONTINUE]
Ge 40: 4 served them: and they **c** a season in ward. 1961
Jdg 5:17 Asher **c** on the sea shore, and abode in his 3427
Ru 1: 2 came *into* the country of Moab, and **c** there. 1961
2: 7 hath **c** even from the morning until now, 5975
1Sa 1:12 as she **c** praying before the LORD, 7235
2Sa 6:11 the ark of the LORD **c** *in* the house of 3427
1Ki 22: 1 they **c** three years without war between 3427
2Ch 29:28 all *this* **c** until the burnt offering was NIH
Ne 5:16 Yea also I **c** in the work of this wall, 2388
Job 27: 1 Moreover Job **c** his parable, and said, 3254+5375
29: 1 Moreover Job **c** his parable, and said, 3254+5375
Ps 72:17 his name shall be **c** as long as the sun: and 5125
Da 1:21 Daniel **c** *even* unto the first year of king 1961
Lk 6:12 to pray, and **c** all night in prayer to God. *1510*
22:28 Ye are they which have **c** with me in my *1265*
Jn 2:12 and they **c** there not many days. *3306*
8: 7 So when they **c** asking him, he lift up *1961*
11:54 and there **c** with his disciples. *1304*
Ac 1:14 These all **c** with one accord in prayer and *4342*
2:42 And they **c stedfastly** in the apostles' *4342*
8:13 he **c** with Philip, and wondered, *4342*
12:16 But Peter **c** knocking: and when they had *1961*
15:35 Paul also and Barnabas **c** in Antioch, *1304*
18:11 And he **c** *there* a year and six months, *2523*
19:10 And this **c** by the space of two years; so *1096*
20: 7 and **c** *his* speech until midnight. *3905*
27:33 day that ye have tarried and **c** fasting, *1300*
Heb 8: 9 because they **c** not in my covenant, and I *1696*
1Jn 2:19 of us, they would *no doubt* have **c** with us: *3306*

CONTINUETH (5) [CONTINUE]
Job 14: 2 he fleeth also as a shadow, and **c** not. 5975
Gal 3:10 Cursed *is* every one that **c** not in all *things* *1696*
1Ti 5: 5 and **c** in supplications and prayers night and *4357*
Heb 7:24 But this *man,* because he **c** ever, hath an *3306*
Jas 1:25 **c** *therein,* he being not a forgetful hearer, *3887*

CONTINUING (4) [CONTINUE]
Jer 30:23 goeth forth *with* fury, a **c** whirlwind: 1641
Ac 2:46 **c** daily with one accord in the temple, and *4342*
Ro 12:12 patient in tribulation; **c instant** in prayer; *4342*
Heb 13:14 For here have we no **c** city, but we seek one *3306*

CONTRADICTING (1) [CONTRADICTION]
Ac 13:45 were spoken by Paul, **c** and blaspheming. *483*

CONTRADICTION (2) [CONTRADICTING]
Heb 7: 7 And without all **c** the less is blessed of *485*
12: 3 For consider him that endured such **c** of *485*

CONTRARIWISE (3) [CONTRARY]
2Co 2: 7 So that **c** ye *ought* rather to forgive *him,* *5121*
Gal 2: 7 But **c**, when they saw that the gospel of *5121*
1Pe 3: 9 but **c** blessing; knowing that ye are *5121*

CONTRARY (24) [CONTRARIWISE]
Lev 26:21 if ye walk **c** unto me, and will not hearken 7147
26:23 by these *things,* but will walk **c** unto me; 7147
26:24 will I also walk **c** unto you, and will punish 7147
26:27 this hearken unto me, but walk **c** unto me; 7147
26:28 I will walk **c** unto you also in fury; and 7147
26:40 and that also they have walked **c** unto me; 7147
26:41 *And that* I also have walked **c** unto them, 7147
Est 9: 1 (though it was turned *to the* **c**, that the Jews NIH
Eze 16:34 the **c** is in thee from *other* women in thy 2016
16:34 is given unto thee, therefore thou art **c**. 2016
Mt 14:24 tossed with waves: for the wind was **c**. *1727*
Mk 6:48 in rowing; for the wind was **c** unto them: *1727*
Ac 17: 7 and these all do **c** to the decrees of Cesar, *561*
18:13 men to worship God **c to** the law. *3844*
23: 3 commandest me to be smitten **c to the law?** *3891*
26: 9 that *I* ought to do many *things* **c** to *1727*
27: 4 under Cyprus, because the winds were **c**. *1727*
Ro 11:24 wert graffed **c to** nature into a good olive *3844*
16:17 offences **c to** the doctrine which ye have *3844*
Gal 5:17 and these are **c** the one to the other: so *480*
Col 2:14 which was **c** to us, and took it out of *5227*
1Th 2:15 they please not God, and are **c** to all men: *1727*
1Ti 1:10 if *there be* any other *thing that* is **c** to sound *480*
Tit 2: 8 that he that is of the **c** *part* may be ashamed, *1727*

CONTRIBUTION (1)
Ro 15:26 Achaia to make a certain **c** for the poor *2842*

CONTRITE (5)
Ps 34:18 and saveth such as be of a **c** spirit. 1793
51:17 a broken and a **c** heart, O God, thou wilt 1794
Isa 57:15 holy *place,* with him also *that is* of a **c** and 1793
57:15 and to revive the heart of the **c ones**. 1792
66: 2 *even* to *him that is* poor and of a **c** spirit, 5223

CONTROVERSIES (1) [CONTROVERSY]
2Ch 19: 8 for the judgment of the LORD, and for **c**, 7379

CONTROVERSY (13) [CONTROVERSIES]
Dt 17: 8 stroke, *being* matters of **c** within thy gates: 7379
19:17 between whom the **c** *is,* shall stand before 7379
21: 5 by their word shall every **c** and 7379
25: 1 If there be a **c** between men, and they come 7379
2Sa 15: 2 *that when* any man that had a **c** came to 7379
Isa 34: 8 the year of recompences for the **c** of Zion. 7379
Jer 25:31 for the LORD hath a **c** with the nations, 7379
Eze 44:24 in **c** they shall stand in judgment; *and* 7379
Hos 4: 1 for the LORD hath a **c** with 7379
12: 2 The LORD hath also a **c** with Judah, and 7379
Mic 6: 2 the LORD'S **c**, and ye strong foundations 7379
6: 2 for the LORD hath a **c** with his people, 7379
1Ti 3:16 And **without c** great is the mystery of *3672*

CONVENIENT (9) [CONVENIENTLY]
Pr 30: 8 nor riches; feed me with food **c** for me: 2706
Jer 40: 4 and **c for** thee to go, 413+3477+1886.1
40: 5 go wheresoever it seemeth **c** unto thee to 3477
Mk 6:21 And when a **c** day was come, that Herod on *2121*
Ac 24:25 when I have a **c season**, I will call for thee. *2540*
Ro 1:28 to do those *things* which are not **c**; *2520*
1Co 16:12 he will come when he shall **have c time**. *2119*
Eph 5: 4 foolish talking, nor jesting, which are not **c**: *433*
Phm 1: 8 bold in Christ to enjoin thee that which is **c**, *433*

CONVENIENTLY (1) [CONVENIENT]
Mk 14:11 And he sought how he might **c** betray him. *2122*

CONVERSANT (2)
Jos 8:35 and the strangers that were **c** among them. 1980
1Sa 25:15 as long as we were **c** with them, when we 1980

CONVERSATION (20)
Ps 37:14 needy, *and* to slay such as be of upright **c**. 1870
50:23 to him that ordereth *his* **c** *aright* will I shew 1870
2Co 1:12 we have **had** our **c** in the world, and *390*
Gal 1:13 For ye have heard of my **c** in time past in *391*
Eph 2: 3 Among whom also we all **had** our **c** in times *390*
4:22 That ye put off concerning the former **c** *391*
Php 1:27 Only let your **c** be as it becometh the gospel *4176*
3:20 For our **c** is in heaven; from whence also *4175*
1Ti 4:12 in word, in **c**, in charity, in spirit, in faith, *391*
Heb 13: 5 *Let your* **c** *be* without covetousness; *and* *5158*
13: 7 faith follow, considering the end of *their* **c**. *391*
Jas 3:13 let him shew out of a good **c** his works with *391*
1Pe 1:15 you is holy, so be ye holy in all *manner of* **c**; *391*
1:18 from your vain **c** received by tradition from *391*
2:12 Having your **c** honest among the Gentiles: *391*
3: 1 the word be won by the **c** of the wives; *391*
3: 2 While they behold your chaste **c** *coupled* *391*
3:16 that falsely accuse your good **c** in Christ. *391*
2Pe 2: 7 vexed with the filthy **c** of the wicked: *391*
3:11 *of persons* ought ye to be in all holy **c** *391*

CONVERSION (1) [CONVERT]
Ac 15: 3 Samaria, declaring the **c** of the Gentiles: *1995*

CONVERT (2) [CONVERSION, CONVERTED, CONVERTETH, CONVERTING, CONVERTS]
Isa 6:10 *with* their heart, and **c**, and be healed. 7725

Jas 5:19 of you do err from the truth, and one **c** him; *1994*

CONVERTED (9) [CONVERT]
Ps 51:13 thy ways; and sinners shall be **c** unto thee. 7725
Isa 60: 5 the abundance of the sea shall be **c** unto 2015
Mt 13:15 and should be **c**, and I should heal them. *1994*
18: 3 Except ye be **c**, and become as little *4762*
Mk 4:12 lest at any time they should be **c**, and *1994*
Lk 22:32 and when thou art **c**, strengthen thy *1994*
Jn 12:40 and be **c**, and I should heal them. *1994*
Ac 3:19 Repent ye therefore, and be **c**, that your *1994*
28:27 and should be **c**, and I should heal them. *1994*

CONVERTETH (1) [CONVERT]
Jas 5:20 that he which **c** the sinner from the error of *1994*

CONVERTING (1) [CONVERT]
Ps 19: 7 law of the LORD *is* perfect, **c** the soul: 7725

CONVERTS (1) [CONVERT]
Isa 1:27 and her **c** with righteousness. 7725

CONVEY (2) [CONVEYED]
1Ki 5: 9 I will **c** them by sea *in* flotes unto the place 7760
Ne 2: 7 that they may **c** me over till I come into 5674

CONVEYED (1) [CONVEY]
Jn 5:13 for Jesus had **c** himself away, a multitude *1593*

CONVICT See REPROOF; REPROVE

CONVICTED (1)
Jn 8: 9 And they which heard *it,* being **c** by *their* *1651*

CONVINCE (2) [CONVINCED, CONVINCETH]
Tit 1: 9 both to exhort and to **c** the gainsayers. *1651*
Jude 1:15 to **c** all *that are* ungodly among them of all *1827*

CONVINCED (4) [CONVINCE]
Job 32:12 *there was* none of you that **c** Job, *or* 3198
Ac 18:28 For he mightily **c** the Jews, *and* *1246*
1Co 14:24 or *one* unlearned, he is **c** of all, he is judged *1651*
Jas 2: 9 and are **c** of the law as transgressors. *1651*

CONVINCETH (1) [CONVINCE]
Jn 8:46 Which of you **c** me of sin? And if I say *1651*

CONVINCING See INFALLIBLE

CONVOCATION (16) [CONVOCATIONS]
Ex 12:16 in the first day *there shall be* a holy **c**, and 4744
12:16 in the seventh day there shall be a holy **c** to 4744
Lev 23: 3 seventh day *is* the sabbath of rest, a holy **c**; 4744
23: 7 In the first day ye shall have a holy **c**: 4744
23: 8 in the seventh day *is* a holy **c**: ye shall do 4744
23:21 *that* it may be a holy **c** unto you: 4744
23:24 memorial of blowing of trumpets, a holy **c**. 4744
23:27 it shall be a holy **c** unto you; and ye shall 4744
23:35 On the first day *shall be* a holy **c**: ye shall 4744
23:36 on the eighth day shall be a holy **c** unto 4744
Nu 28:18 In the first day *shall be* a holy **c**; ye shall 4744
28:25 on the seventh day ye shall have a holy **c**; 4744
28:26 your weeks *be out,* ye shall have a holy **c**; 4744
29: 1 *day* of the month, ye shall have a holy **c**; 4744
29: 7 tenth *day* of this seventh month a holy **c**; 4744
29:12 of the seventh month ye shall have a holy **c**; 4744

CONVOCATIONS (3) [CONVOCATION]
Lev 23: 2 which ye shall proclaim *to be* holy **c**, 4744
23: 4 *are* the feasts of the LORD, *even* holy **c**, 4744
23:37 which ye shall proclaim *to be* holy **c**, 4744

CONVULSION See TARE

CONY (1) [CONEY]
Lev 11: 5 the **c**, because he cheweth the cud, but 8227

COOK (2) [COOKS]
1Sa 9:23 Samuel said unto the **c**, Bring the portion 2876
9:24 the **c** took up the shoulder, and *that* which 2876

COOKED See SOD; SODDEN

COOKING See SOD; SODDEN

COOKS (1) [COOK]
1Sa 8:13 and to be **c**, and to be bakers. 2879

COOL (2)
Ge 3: 8 walking in the garden in the **c** of the day: 7307
Lk 16:24 tip of his finger in water, and **c** my tongue; *2711*

COPIED (1) [COPY]
Pr 25: 1 the men of Hezekiah king of Judah **c** out. 6275

COPING (1)
1Ki 7: 9 even from the foundation unto the **c**, and *so* 2947

COPPER (1) [COPPERSMITH]
Ezr 8:27 and two vessels of fine **c**, precious as gold. 5178

COPPERSMITH (1) [COPPER, SMITH]
2Ti 4:14 Alexander the **c** did me much evil: the Lord *5471*

COPULATION (3)
Lev 15:16 if any man's seed of **c** go out from him, 7902
15:17 and every skin, whereon is the seed of **c**, 7902
15:18 with whom man shall lie *with* seed of **c**, 7902

COPY (9) [COPIED]
Dt 17:18 that he shall write him a **c** of this law in a 4932
Jos 8:32 he wrote there upon the stones a **c** of 4932
Ezr 4:11 This *is* the **c** of the letter that they sent unto 6573
4:23 Now when the **c** of king Artaxerxes' letter 6573
5: 6 The **c** of the letter that Tatnai, governor on 6573
7:11 Now this *is* the **c** of the letter that the king 6572
Est 3:14 The **c** of the writing for a commandment to 6572
4: 8 Also he gave him the **c** of the writing of 6572
8:13 The **c** of the writing for a commandment to 6572

COR (1)
Eze 45:14 *offer* the tenth part of a bath out of the **c**, 3734

CORAL (2)
Job 28:18 No mention shall be made of **c**, or 7215
Eze 27:16 and fine linen, and **c**, and agate. 7215

CORBAN (1)
Mk 7:11 shall say to *his* father or mother, *It is* **C**, *2878*

CORD (6) [CORDS]
Jos 2:15 she let them down by a **c** through 2256
Job 30:11 Because he hath loosed my **c**, and 3499
41: 1 his tongue with a **c** *which* thou lettest 2256
Ecc 4:12 and a threefold **c** is not quickly broken. 2339
12: 6 Or ever the silver **c** be loosed, or the golden 2256
Mic 2: 5 **c** by lot in the congregation of the LORD. 2256

CORDS (26) [CORD]
Ex 35:18 and the pins of the court, and their **c**, 4340
39:40 his **c**, and his pins, and all the vessels of 4340
Nu 3:26 and the **c** of it for all the service thereof. 4340
3:37 their sockets, and their pins, and their **c**. 4340
4:26 their **c**, and all the instruments of their 4340
4:32 their sockets, and their pins, and their **c**, 4340
Jdg 15:13 they bound him with two new **c**, and 5688
15:14 the **c** that *were* upon his arms became as 5688
Est 1: 6 blue *hangings,* fastened with **c** of fine linen 2256
Job 36: 8 in fetters, *and* be holden in **c** of affliction; 2256
Ps 2: 3 and cast away their **c** from us. 5688
118:27 bind the sacrifice with **c**, *even* unto 5688
129: 4 he hath cut asunder the **c** of the wicked. 5688
140: 5 The proud have hid a snare for me, and **c**; 2256
Pr 5:22 he shall be holden with the **c** of his sins. 2256
Isa 5:18 Woe unto them that draw iniquity with **c** of 2256
33:20 neither shall any of the **c** thereof be broken. 2256
54: 2 lengthen thy **c**, and strengthen thy stakes; 4340
Jer 10:20 is spoiled, and all my **c** are broken: 4340
38: 6 they let down Jeremiah with **c**. And in 2256
38:11 let them down by **c** into the dungeon to 2256
38:12 rags under thine armholes under the **c**. 2256
38:13 So they drew up Jeremiah with **c**, and 2256
Eze 27:24 bound with **c**, and made of cedar, 2256
Hos 11: 4 I drew them with **c** of a man, with bands of 2256
Jn 2:15 when he had made a scourge of small **c**, *4979*

CORE (1)
Jude 1:11 and perished in the gainsaying of **C**. *2879*

CORIANDER (2)
Ex 16:31 it *was* like **c** seed, white; and the taste of it 1407
Nu 11: 7 the manna *was* as **c** seed, and the colour 1407

C

CORINTH (6) [CORINTHIANS, CORINTHUS]

Ac 18: 1 Paul departed from Athens, and came to **C**; *2882*
19: 1 came to pass that, while Apollos was at **C**, *2882*
1Co 1: 2 Unto the church of God which is at **C**, *2882*
2Co 1: 1 unto the church of God which is at **C**, *2882*
1:23 that to spare you I came not as yet unto **C**. *2882*
2Ti 4:20 Erastus abode at **C**: but Trophimus have I *2882*

CORINTHIANS (4) [CORINTH]

Ac 18: 8 and many of the **C** hearing believed, and *2881*
1Co 16: S The first *epistle* to the **C** was written from *2881*
2Co 6:11 O *ye* **C**, our mouth is open unto you, *2881*
13: S The second *epistle* to the **C** was written *2881*

CORINTHUS (1) [CORINTH]

Ro 16: S Written to the Romans from **C**, *and sent* by *2882*

CORMORANT (4)

Lev 11:17 the little owl, and the **c**, and the great owl, 7994
Dt 14:17 the pelican, and the gier eagle, and the **c**, 7994
Isa 34:11 the **c** and the bittern shall possess it; 6893
Zep 2:14 both the **c** and the bittern shall lodge in 6893

CORN (102) [CORNFLOOR]

Ge 27:28 of the earth, and plenty of **c** and wine: 1715
27:37 and with **c** and wine have I sustained him: 1715
41: 5 seven **ears of c** came up upon one stalk, 7641
41:35 lay up **c** under the hand of Pharaoh, and 1250
41:49 Joseph gathered **c** as the sand of the sea, 1250
41:57 came into Egypt to Joseph for to buy *c*; NIH
42: 1 Now when Jacob saw that there was **c** in 7668
42: 2 I have heard that there is **c** in Egypt: 7668
42: 3 Joseph's ten brethren went down to buy **c** 1250
42: 5 the sons of Israel came to buy *c* among NIH
42:19 carry **c** *for* the famine of your houses: 7668
42:25 commanded to fill their sacks *with* **c**, 1250
42:26 they laded their asses with the **c**, and 7668
43: 2 when they had eaten up the **c** which they 7668
44: 2 mouth of the youngest, and his **c** money. 7668
45:23 ten she asses laden with **c** and bread and 1250
47:14 of Canaan, for the **c** which they bought: 7668
Ex 22: 6 so that the **stacks of c**, or the standing corn, 1430
22: 6 of corn, or the **standing c**, or the field, 7054
Lev 2:14 firstfruits **green ears of c** dried by the fire, 24
2:14 by the fire, *even* **c** beaten out **of full ears**. 3759
2:16 *part* of the **beaten c** thereof, and *part* of 1643
23:14 neither bread, nor parched *c*, nor green ears, NIH
Nu 18:27 as though it were the **c** of 1715
Dt 7:13 thy land, thy **c**, and thy wine, and thine oil, 1715
11:14 that thou mayest gather in thy **c**, and 1715
12:17 not eat within thy gates the tithe of thy **c**, 1715
14:23 the tithe of thy **c**, of thy wine, and of thine 1715
16: 9 *as thou* beginnest *to put* the sickle to the **c**. 7054
16:13 after that thou hast gathered in thy **c** and 1637
18: 4 The firstfruit *also* of thy **c**, of thy wine, and 1715
23:25 When thou comest into the **standing c** of 7054
23:25 a sickle unto thy neighbour's **standing c**. 7054
25: 4 muzzle the ox when he treadeth out *the c*. NIH
28:51 which *also* shall not leave thee *either* **c**, 1715
33:28 fountain of Jacob *shall be* upon a land of **c** 1715
Jos 5:11 they did eat of the **old c** of the land on 5669
5:11 and parched *c* in the selfsame day. NIH
5:12 after they had eaten of the **old c** of the land; 5669
Jdg 15: 5 he let *them* go into the **standing c** of 7054
15: 5 also the **standing c**, with the vineyards *and* 7054
Ru 2: 2 glean **ears of c** after *him* in whose sight I 7641
2:14 he reached her parched *c*, and she did eat, NIH
3: 7 went to lie down at the end of the heap *of c*: NIH
1Sa 17:17 for thy brethren an ephah of this parched *c*, NIH
25:18 five measures of parched *c*, and an hundred NIH
2Sa 17:19 and spread **ground c** thereon; 7383
17:28 parched *c*, and beans, and lentiles, and NIH
2Ki 4:42 and **full ears of c** in the husk thereof. 3759
18:32 a land of **c** and wine, a land of bread and 1715
19:26 and *as c* blasted before it be grown up. NIH
2Ch 31: 5 brought in abundance the firstfruits of **c**, 1715
32:28 Storehouses also for the increase of **c**, and 1715
Ne 5: 2 we take up **c** *for them*, that we may eat, 1715
5: 3 houses, that we might buy **c**, because of 1715
5:10 *might* exact of them money and **c**: 1715
5:11 *of* the **c**, the wine, and the oil, that ye exact 1715
10:39 of Levi shall bring the offering of the **c**, 1715
13: 5 the vessels, and the tithes of the **c**, the new 1715
13:12 brought all Judah the tithe of the **c** and 1715
Job 5:26 like as a **shock of c** cometh in in his season. 1430
24: 6 They reap *every one* his **c** in the field: and 1098
24:24 and cut off as the tops of the **ears of c**. 7641
39: 4 are in good liking, they grow up with **c**; 1250
Ps 4: 7 more than *in* the time *that* their **c** and 1715
65: 9 thou preparest them **c**, when thou hast so 1715
65:13 the valleys also are covered over with **c**; 1250
72:16 There shall be a handful of **c** in the earth 1250
78:24 and had given them *of* the **c** of heaven. 1715
Pr 11:26 He that withholdeth **c**, the people shall 1250
Isa 17: 5 be as when the harvestman gathereth the **c**, 7054
21:10 O my threshing, and the **c** of my floor: 1121
28:28 Bread *c* is bruised; because he will not ever NIH
36:17 a land of **c** and wine, a land of bread and 1715
37:27 and *as c* blasted before it be grown up. NIH
62: 8 Surely I will no more give thy **c** *to be* meat 1715
La 2:12 say to their mothers, Where *is* **c** and wine? 1715
Eze 36:29 I will call for the **c**, and will increase it, and 1715
Hos 2: 8 For she did not know that I gave her **c**, and 1715
2: 9 and take *away* my **c** in the time thereof, and 1715
2:22 And the earth shall hear the **c**, and the wine, 1715
7:14 they assemble themselves for **c** and wine, 1715
10:11 *and* loveth to tread out *the c*; but I passed NIH
14: 7 they shall revive *as* the **c**, and grow as 1715
Joel 1:10 for the **c** is wasted, the new wine is dried 1715
1:17 are broken down; for the **c** is withered. 1715
2:19 I *will* send you **c**, and wine, and oil, and 1715
Am 8: 5 the new moon be gone, that we may sell **c**? 7668
9: 9 like as *c* is sifted in a sieve, yet shall not NIH
Hag 1:11 and upon the **c**, and upon the new wine, and 1715
Zec 9:17 **c** shall make the young men cheerful, and 1715
Mt 12: 1 went on the sabbath day through the **c**; *4702*
12: 1 and began to pluck the **ears of c**, and to eat. *4719*
Mk 2:23 that he went through the **c fields** on *4702*
2:23 as they went, to pluck the **ears of c**. *4719*
4:28 then the ear, after that the full **c** in the ear. *4621*
Lk 6: 1 the first, that he went through the **c fields**; *4702*
6: 1 and his disciples plucked the **ears of c**, and *4719*
Jn 12:24 Except a **c** of wheat fall into the ground and *2848*
Ac 7:12 But when Jacob heard that there was **c** in *4621*
1Co 9: 9 the mouth of the ox that **treadeth out the c**. *248*
1Ti 5:18 not muzzle the ox that **treadeth out the c**. *248*

CORNELIUS (10)

Ac 10: 1 was a certain man in Cesarea called **C**, *2883*
10: 3 coming in to him, and saying unto him, **C**. *2883*
10: 7 And when the angel which spake unto **C** *2883*
10:17 the men which were sent from **C** had made *2883*
10:21 the men which were sent unto him from **C**; *2883*
10:22 **C** the centurion, a just man, and one that *2883*
10:24 And **C** waited for them, and had called *2883*
10:25 **C** met him, and fell down at *his* feet, and *2883*
10:30 And **C** said, Four days ago I was fasting *2883*
10:31 And said, **C**, thy prayer is heard, and *2883*

CORNER (37)

Ex 36:25 *which is* toward the north **c**, he made 6285
Lev 21: 5 neither shall they shave off the **c** of their 6285
Jos 18:14 and compassed the **c** of the sea southward, 6285
2Ki 11:11 from the right **c** of the temple to the left 3802
11:11 of the temple to the left **c** of the temple, 3802
14:13 from the gate of Ephraim unto the **c** gate, 6438
2Ch 25:23 from the gate of Ephraim to the **c** gate, 6437
26: 9 built towers in Jerusalem at the **c** gate, 6438
28:24 he made him altars in every **c** of Jerusalem. 6438
Ne 3:24 the turning *of the wall*, even unto the **c**. 6438
3:31 gate Miphkad, and to the going up of the **c**. 6438
3:32 between the going up of the **c** unto 6438
Job 38: 6 or who laid the **c** stone thereof; 6438
Ps 118:22 refused is become the head *stone* of the **c**. 6438
144:12 *that* our daughters *may be* as **c stones**, 2106
Pr 7: 8 Passing through the street near her **c**; and 6434
7:12 in the streets, and lieth in wait at every **c**.) 6438
21: 9 *It is* better to dwell in a **c** of the housetop, 6438
25:24 *It is* better to dwell in a **c** of the housetop, 6438
Isa 28:16 a precious **c** *stone*, a sure foundation: 6438
30:20 thy teachers be **removed into a c** any more, 3670
Jer 31:38 tower of Hananeel unto the gate of the **c**. 6438
31:40 unto the **c** of the horse gate towards 6438
48:45 shall devour the **c** of Moab, and the crown 6285
51:26 they shall not take of thee a stone for a **c**, 6438
Eze 46:21 **every c** of the court *there was* a 4740+4740
Am 3:12 out that dwell in Samaria in the **c** of a bed, 6285
Zec 10: 4 Out of him came forth the **c**, out of him 6438

Zec 14:10 unto the **c** gate, and *from* the tower of 6434
Mt 21:42 the same is become the head of the **c**: *1137*
Mk 12:10 rejected is become the head of the **c**: *1137*
Lk 20:17 the same is become the head of the **c**? *1137*
Ac 4:11 which is become the head of the **c**. *1137*
26:26 for this *thing* was not done in a **c**. *1137*
Eph 2:20 Jesus Christ himself being the **chief c** *stone;* *204*
1Pe 2: 6 Behold, I lay in Sion a **chief c** stone, elect, *204*
2: 7 the same is made the head of the **c**, *1137*

CORNER DEFENSES See BULWARKS

CORNERS (39)
Ex 25:12 for it, and put *them* in the four **c** thereof; 6471
25:26 put the rings in the four **c** that *are* on 6285
26:23 two boards shalt thou make for the **c** of 4742
26:24 for them both; they shall be for the two **c**. 4740
27: 2 the horns of it upon the four **c** thereof: 6438
27: 4 four brasen rings in the four **c** thereof. 7098
30: 4 by the two **c** thereof, upon the two sides of 6763
36:28 two boards made he for the **c** of 4742
36:29 thus he did to both of them in both the **c**. 4740
37: 3 rings of gold, *to be set* by the four **c** of it; 6471
37:13 put the rings upon the four **c** that *were* in 6285
37:27 by the two **c** of it, upon the two sides 6763
38: 2 he made the horns thereof on the four **c** of 6438
Lev 19: 9 thou shalt not wholly reap the **c** of thy field, 6285
19:27 Ye shall not round the **c** of your heads, 6285
19:27 neither shalt thou mar the **c** of thy beard. 6285
23:22 thou shalt not make clean riddance of the **c** 6285
Nu 24:17 shall smite the **c** of Moab, and destroy all 6285
Dt 32:26 I said, I would **scatter** them **into c**, I would 6284
1Ki 7:30 the four **c** thereof had undersetters: under 6471
7:34 *there were* four undersetters to the four **c** of 6438
Ne 9:22 and nations, and didst divide them into **c**: 6285
Job 1:19 smote the four **c** of the house, and it fell 6438
Isa 11:12 of Judah from the four **c** of the earth. 3671
Jer 9:26 and Moab, and all *that are* in the utmost **c**, 6285
25:23 and Buz, and all *that are* in the utmost **c**, 6285
49:32 into all winds them *that are* in the utmost **c**; 6285
Eze 7: 2 the end is come upon the four **c** of the land. 3671
41:22 the **c** thereof, and the length thereof, and 4740
43:20 on the four **c** of the settle, and upon 6438
45:19 and upon the four **c** of the settle of the altar, 6438
46:21 caused me to pass by the four **c** of 4740
46:22 In the four **c** of the court *there were* courts 4740
46:22 these four **c** *were* of one measure. 7106
Zec 9:15 filled like bowls, *and* as the **c** of the altar. 2106
Mt 6: 5 the synagogues and in the **c** of the streets, *1137*
Ac 10:11 as *it had been* a great sheet knit at the four **c**, *746*
11: 5 great sheet, let down from heaven by four **c**; *746*
Rev 7: 1 angels standing on the four **c** of the earth, *1137*

CORNET (7)
1Ch 15:28 with sound of the **c**, and with trumpets, and 7782
Ps 98: 6 sound of **c** make a joyful noise before 7782
Da 3: 5 at what time ye hear the sound of the **c**, 7162
3: 7 all the people heard the sound of the **c**, 7162
3:10 man that shall hear the sound of the **c**, 7162
3:15 that at what time ye hear the sound of the **c**, 7162
Hos 5: 8 Blow ye the **c** in Gibeah, *and* the trumpet in 7782

CORNETS (2)
2Sa 6: 5 and on timbrels, and on **c**, and on cymbals. 4517
2Ch 15:14 and with trumpets, and with **c**. 7782

CORNFLOOR (1) [CORN, FLOOR]
Hos 9: 1 hast loved a reward upon every **c**. 1637+1715

CORPSE (1) [CORPSES]
Mk 6:29 heard *of it,* they came and took up his **c**, *4430*

CORPSES (4) [CORPSE]
2Ki 19:35 the morning, behold, they *were* all dead **c**. 6297
Isa 37:36 the morning, behold, they *were* all dead **c**. 6297
Na 3: 3 of carcases; and *there is* none end of *their* **c**; 1472
3: 3 of *their* corpses; they stumble upon their **c**: 1472

CORRECT (7) [CORRECTED, CORRECTETH, CORRECTION]
Ps 39:11 When thou with rebukes dost **c** man for 3256
94:10 that chastiseth the heathen, shall not he **c**? 3198
Pr 29:17 **C** thy son, and he shall give thee rest; yea, 3256
Jer 2:19 Thine own wickedness shall **c** thee, and 3256
10:24 O LORD, **c** me, but with judgment; not in 3256
30:11 I will **c** thee in measure, and will not leave 3256
46:28 a full end of thee, but **c** thee in measure; 3256

CORRECTED (2) [CORRECT]
Pr 29:19 A servant will not be **c** by words: 3256
Heb 12: 9 have had fathers of our flesh which **c** *us,* *3810*

CORRECTETH (2) [CORRECT]
Job 5:17 Behold, happy *is* the man whom God **c**: 3198
Pr 3:12 For whom the LORD loveth he **c**; even as 3198

CORRECTION (12) [CORRECT]
Job 37:13 whether for **c**, or for his land, or for mercy. 7626
Pr 3:11 of the LORD; neither be weary of his **c**: 8433
7:22 or as a fool to the **c** of the stocks; 4148
15:10 **C** *is* grievous unto him that forsaketh 4148
22:15 *but* the rod of **c** shall drive it far from him. 4148
23:13 Withhold not **c** from the child: for *if* thou 4148
Jer 2:30 I smitten your children; they received no **c**: 4148
5: 3 *but* they have refused to receive **c**: 4148
7:28 of the LORD their God, nor receiveth **c**: 4148
Hab 1:12 thou hast established them for **c**. 3198
Zep 3: 2 obeyed not the voice; she received not **c**; 4148
2Ti 3:16 *is* profitable for doctrine, for reproof, for **c**, *1882*

CORRUPT (33) [CORRUPTED, CORRUPTERS, CORRUPTETH, CORRUPTIBLE, CORRUPTING, CORRUPTION, CORRUPTLY, UNCORRUPTIBLE]
Ge 6:11 The earth also was **c** before God, and 7843
6:12 looked upon the earth, and behold, it was **c**; 7843
Dt 4:16 Lest ye **c** *yourselves,* and make you a 7843
4:25 shall **c** *yourselves,* and make a graven 7843
31:29 death ye will **utterly c** *yourselves,* 7843+7843
Job 17: 1 My breath is **c**, my days are extinct, 2254
Ps 14: 1 They are **c**, they have done abominable 7843
38: 5 My wounds stink *and* are **c** because of my 4743
53: 1 **C** are they, and have done abominable 7843
73: 8 They are **c**, and speak wickedly *concerning* 4167
Pr 25:26 *is as* a troubled fountain, and a **c** spring. 7843
Eze 20:44 nor according to your **c** doings, O ye house 7843
23:11 was more **c** in her inordinate love than she, 7843
Da 2: 9 and **c** words to speak before me, 7844
11:32 against the covenant shall he **c** by flatteries: 2610
Mal 1:14 sacrificeth unto the Lord a **c** *thing:* for I *am* 7843
2: 3 I *will* **c** your seed, and spread dung upon 1605
Mt 6:19 where moth and rust doth **c**, and *853*
6:20 where neither moth nor rust doth **c**, and *853*
7:17 but a **c** tree bringeth forth evil fruit. *4550*
7:18 neither *can* a **c** tree bring forth good fruit. *4550*
12:33 or else make the tree **c**, and his fruit *4550*
12:33 else make the tree corrupt, and his fruit **c**: *4550*
Lk 6:43 For a good tree bringeth not forth **c** fruit; *4550*
6:43 neither doth a **c** tree bring forth good fruit. *4550*
1Co 15:33 evil communications **c** good manners. *5351*
2Co 2:17 are not as many, which **c** the word of God: *2585*
Eph 4:22 which is **c** according to the deceitful lusts; *5351*
4:29 Let no **c** communication proceed out of *4550*
1Ti 6: 5 Perverse disputings of men of **c** minds, and *1311*
2Ti 3: 8 men of **c** minds, reprobate concerning *2704*
Jude 1:10 in those *things* they **c** themselves. *5351*
Rev 19: 2 which did **c** the earth with her fornication, *5351*

CORRUPTED (14) [CORRUPT]
Ge 6:12 for all flesh had **c** his way upon the earth. 7843
Ex 8:24 the land was **c** by reason of the swarm *of* 7843
32: 7 of the land of Egypt, have **c** *themselves:* 7843
Dt 9:12 **c** *themselves;* they are quickly turned aside 7843
32: 5 They have **c** themselves, their spot *is* not 7843
Jdg 2:19 and **c** *themselves* more than their fathers, 7843
Eze 16:47 thou wast **c** more than they in all thy ways. 7843
28:17 thou hast **c** thy wisdom by reason of thy 7843
Hos 9: 9 They have deeply **c** *themselves,* as *in* 7843
Zep 3: 7 but they rose early, *and* **c** all their doings. 7843
Mal 2: 8 ye have **c** the covenant of Levi, saith 7843
2Co 7: 2 we have wronged no *man,* we have **c** no *5351*
11: 3 your minds should be **c** from the simplicity *5351*
Jas 5: 2 Your riches are **c**, and your garments are *4595*

CORRUPTERS (2) [CORRUPT]
Isa 1: 4 a seed of evildoers, children that are **c**: 7843
Jer 6:28 *they are* brass and iron; they *are* all **c**. 7843

CORRUPTETH (1) [CORRUPT]
Lk 12:33 where no thief approacheth, neither moth **c**. *1311*

CORRUPTIBLE (7) [CORRUPT]
Ro 1:23 God into an image made like to **c** man, *5349*
1Co 9:25 *things.* Now they *do it* to obtain a **c** crown; *5349*
15:53 For this **c** must put on incorruption, and *5349*
15:54 So when this **c** shall have put on *5349*
1Pe 1:18 were not redeemed with **c** *things, as* silver *5349*
1:23 not of **c** seed, but *of* incorruptible, *5349*
3: 4 in *that which is* **not c**, *even the ornament* of *862*

CORRUPTING (1) [CORRUPT]
Da 11:17 give him the daughter of women, **c** her: 7843

CORRUPTION (21) [CORRUPT]
Lev 22:25 because their **c** *is* in them, *and* blemishes *be* 4893
2Ki 23:13 *were* on the right hand of the mount of **c**, 4889
Job 17:14 I have said to **c**, Thou *art* my father: to 7845
Ps 16:10 wilt thou suffer thine Holy One to see **c**. 7845
49: 9 he should still live for ever, *and* not see **c**. 7845
Isa 38:17 to my soul *delivered it* from the pit of **c**: 1097
Da 10: 8 for my comeliness was turned in me into **c**, 4889
Jnh 2: 6 yet hast thou brought up my life from **c**, 7845
Ac 2:27 wilt thou suffer thine Holy One to see **c**. *1312*
2:31 not left in hell, neither his flesh did see **c**. *1312*
13:34 *now* no more to return to **c**, he said on this *1312*
13:35 shalt not suffer thine Holy One to see **c**. *1312*
13:36 and was laid unto his fathers, and saw **c**: *1312*
13:37 But he, whom God raised *again,* saw no **c**. *1312*
Ro 8:21 **c** into the glorious liberty of the children of *5356*
1Co 15:42 It is sown in **c**; it is raised in incorruption: *5356*
15:50 of God; neither doth **c** inherit incorruption. *5356*
Gal 6: 8 soweth to his flesh shall of the flesh reap **c**; *5356*
2Pe 1: 4 having escaped the **c** that is in the world *5356*
2:12 and shall utterly perish in their own **c**; *5356*
2:19 they themselves are the servants of **c**: *5356*

CORRUPTLY (2) [CORRUPT]
2Ch 27: 2 of the LORD. And the people did yet **c**. 7843
Ne 1: 7 We have **dealt very c** against thee, 2254+2254

COS (1)
Ac 21: 1 we came with a straight course unto **C**, and *2972*

COSAM (1)
Lk 3:28 *the son* of Addi, which was *the son* of **C**, *2973*

COST (4) [COSTLINESS, COSTLY]
2Sa 19:42 have we eaten at all of the king's *c*? or NIH
24:24 my God of that which doth **c** me **nothing**. 2600
1Ch 21:24 nor offer burnt offerings **without c**. 2600
Lk 14:28 sitteth not down first, and counteth the **c**, *1160*

COSTLINESS (1) [COST]
Rev 18:19 that had ships in the sea by reason of her **c**: *5094*

COSTLY (6) [COST]
1Ki 5:17 great stones, **c** stones, *and* hewed stones, 3368
7: 9 All these *were of* **c** stones, according to 3368
7:10 the foundation *was of* **c** stones, *even* great 3368
7:11 above *were* **c** stones, after the measures of 3368
Jn 12: 3 **very c**, and anointed the feet of Jesus, and *4186*
1Ti 2: 9 broided hair, or gold, or pearls, or **c** array; *4185*

COTES (1)
2Ch 32:28 for all *manner of* beasts, and **c** for flocks. 220

COTTAGE (2) [COTTAGES]
Isa 1: 8 the daughter of Zion is left as a **c** in a 5521
24:20 a drunkard, and shall be removed like a **c**; 4412

COTTAGES (1) [COTTAGE]
Zep 2: 6 shall be dwellings *and* **c** for shepherds, 3741

COUCH (7) [COUCHED, COUCHES, COUCHETH, COUCHING]
Ge 49: 4 then defiledst thou *it:* he went up to my **c**. 3326
Job 7:13 comfort me, my **c** shall ease my complaint; 4904
38:40 When they **c** in *their* dens, *and* abide in 7817
Ps 6: 6 bed to swim; I water my **c** with my tears. 6210
Am 3:12 the corner of a bed, and in Damascus *in* a **c**. 6210
Lk 5:19 let him down through the tiling with *his* **c** *2826*
5:24 and take up thy **c**, and go into thine house. *2826*

COUCHED (2) [COUCH]
Ge 49: 9 he **c** as a lion, and as an old lion; 7257
Nu 24: 9 He **c**, he lay down as a lion, and as a great 3766

COUCHES (2) [COUCH]
Am 6: 4 stretch themselves upon their **c**, and eat 6210
Ac 5:15 the streets, and laid *them* on beds and **c**, *2895*

COUCHETH (1) [COUCH]
Dt 33:13 for the dew, and for the deep that **c** beneath, 7257

COUCHING (2) [COUCH]
Ge 49:14 Issachar *is* a strong ass **c down** between 7257
Eze 25: 5 and the Ammonites a **c place** for flocks: 4769

COULD (166) [COULDEST] See Index

COULD NOT TALK See DUMB

COULDEST (5) [COULD] See Index

COULTER (1) [COULTERS]
1Sa 13:20 and his **c**, and his axe, and his mattock. 855

COULTERS (1) [COULTER]
1Sa 13:21 for the **c**, and for the forks, and for the axes, 855

COUNCIL (23) [COUNCILS]
Ps 68:27 the princes of Judah *and* their **c**, the princes 7277
Mt 5:22 Raca, shall be in danger of the **c**: *4892*
12:14 went out, and held a **c** against him, *4824*
26:59 the chief priests, and elders, and all the **c**, *4892*
Mk 14:55 all the **c** sought for witness against Jesus to *4892*
15: 1 with the elders and scribes and the whole **c**, *4892*
Lk 22:66 and led him into their **c**, saying, *4892*
Jn 11:47 the chief priests and the Pharisees a **c**, *4892*
Ac 4:15 commanded them to go aside out of the **c**, *4892*
5:21 and called the **c** together, and all the senate *4892*
5:27 brought them, they set *them* before the **c**: *4892*
5:34 Then stood there up one in the **c**, *4892*
5:41 they departed from the presence of the **c**, *4892*
6:12 and caught him, and brought *him* to the **c**, *4892*
6:15 And all that sat in the **c**, looking stedfastly *4892*
22:30 the chief priests and all their **c** to appear, *4892*
23: 1 earnestly beholding the **c**, said, Men *and* *4892*
23: 6 he cried out in the **c**, Men *and* brethren, *4892*
23:15 ye with the **c** signify to the chief captain *4892*
23:20 bring down Paul to morrow into the **c**, *4892*
23:28 I brought him forth into their **c**: *4892*
24:20 evil doing in me, while I stood before the **c**, *4892*
25:12 when he had conferred with the **c**, *4824*

COUNCILS (2) [COUNCIL]
Mt 10:17 for they will deliver you up to the **c**, and *4892*
Mk 13: 9 for they shall deliver you up to **c**; and in *4892*

COUNSEL (143) [COUNSELLED, COUNSELLER, COUNSELLERS, COUNSELS]
Ex 18:19 I will **give** thee **c**, and God shall be with 3289
Nu 27:21 who shall ask *c* for him after the judgment NIH
31:16 children of Israel, through the **c** of Balaam, 1697
Dt 32:28 For they *are* a nation void of **c**, neither *is* 6098
Jos 9:14 and asked not *c* at the mouth of the LORD. NIH
Jdg 18: 5 said unto him, Ask *c*, we pray thee, of God, NIH
20: 7 of Israel; give here your advice and **c**. 6098
20:18 house of God, and asked *c* of God, and said, NIH
20:23 and asked *c* of the LORD, saying, NIH
1Sa 14:37 Saul asked *c* of God, Shall I go down after NIH
2Sa 15:31 turn the **c** of Ahithophel into foolishness. 6098
15:34 mayest thou for me defeat the **c** of 6098
16:20 Give **c** among you what we shall do. 6098
16:23 the **c** of Ahithophel, which he counselled in 6098
16:23 *was* all the **c** of Ahithophel both with David 6098
17: 7 The **c** that Ahithophel hath **given** *is* 3289+6098
17:11 Therefore I **c** *that* all Israel be generally 3289
17:14 The **c** of Hushai the Archite *is* better than 6098
17:14 Archite *is* better than the **c** of Ahithophel. 6098
17:14 to defeat the good **c** of Ahithophel, 6098
17:15 thus did Ahithophel **c** Absalom and 3289
17:23 when Ahithophel saw that his **c** was not 6098
20:18 They shall surely ask *c* at Abel: NIH
1Ki 1:12 come, let me, I pray thee, **give** thee **c**, 3289+6098
12: 8 **c** of the old men, which they had **given** 3289+6098
12: 9 What **c give** ye that we may answer this 3289
12:13 the old men's **c** that they **gave** him; 3289+6098
12:14 spake to them after the **c** of the young men, 6098
12:28 Whereupon the king **took c**, and made two 3289
2Ki 6: 8 **took c** with his servants, saying, In such 3289
18:20 *I have* **c** and strength for the war. 6098

1Ch 10:13 also for asking *c* of *one that had* a familiar NIH
2Ch 10: 6 king Rehoboam **took c with** the old men 3289
10: 6 What **c give** ye *me* to return answer to this 3289
10: 8 the **c** which the old men **gave** him, 3289+6098
10: 8 **took c with** the young men that were 3289
10:13 king Rehoboam forsook the **c** of the old 6098
22: 5 He walked also after their **c**, and went with 6098
25:16 unto him, Art thou made of the king's **c**? 3289
25:16 and hast not hearkened unto my **c**. 6098
30: 2 For the king had **taken c**, and his princes, 3289
30:23 the whole assembly **took c** to keep other 3289
32: 3 He **took c** with his princes and his mighty 3289
Ezr 10: 3 according to the **c** of my lord, and of those 6098
10: 8 according to the **c** of the princes and 6098
Ne 4:15 God had brought their **c** to nought, that we 6098
6: 7 now therefore, and let us **take c** together. 3289
Job 5:13 the **c** of the froward is carried headlong. 6098
10: 3 and shine upon the **c** of the wicked? 6098
12:13 and strength, he hath **c** and understanding. 6098
18: 7 and his own **c** shall cast him down. 6098
21:16 the **c** of the wicked is far from me. 6098
22:18 but the **c** of the wicked is far from me. 6098
29:21 and waited, and kept silence at my **c**. 6098
38: 2 Who *is* this that darkeneth **c** by words 6098
42: 3 Who *is* he that hideth **c** without 6098
Ps 1: 1 Blessed *is* the man that walketh not in the **c** 6098
2: 2 the rulers **take c** together, against 3245
13: 2 How long shall I take **c** in my soul, 6098
14: 6 You have shamed the **c** of the poor, 6098
16: 7 bless the LORD, who hath **given** me **c**: 3289
20: 4 to thine own heart, and fulfil all thy **c**. 6098
31:13 while they **took c** together against me, 3245
33:10 The LORD bringeth the **c** of the heathen 6098
33:11 The **c** of the LORD standeth for ever, 6098
55:14 We took sweet **c** together, *and* walked unto 5475
64: 2 Hide me from the **secret c** of the wicked; 5475
71:10 they that lay wait for my soul **take c** 3289
73:24 Thou shalt guide me with thy **c**, and 6098
83: 3 They have taken crafty **c** against thy 5475
106:13 forgat his works; they waited not for his **c**: 6098
106:43 they provoked *him* with their **c**, and 6098
107:11 and contemned the **c** of the most High: 6098
Pr 1:25 ye have set at nought all my **c**, and 6098
1:30 They would none of my **c**: they despised all 6098
8:14 **C** *is* mine, and sound wisdom: I *am* 6098
11:14 Where no **c** *is*, the people fall: but in 8458
12:15 but he that hearkeneth unto **c** *is* wise. 6098
15:22 Without **c** purposes *are* disappointed: but 5475
19:20 Hear **c**, and receive instruction, that thou 6098
19:21 nevertheless the **c** of the LORD, that shall 6098
20: 5 **C** in the heart of man *is like* deep water; 6098
20:18 Every purpose is established by **c**: and 6098
21:30 *is* no wisdom nor understanding nor **c** 6098
24: 6 For by **wise c** thou shalt make thy war: and 8458
27: 9 the sweetness of a man's friend by hearty **c**. 6098
Ecc 8: 2 I *c thee* to keep the king's commandment, NIH
Isa 5:19 let the **c** of the Holy One of Israel draw 6098
7: 5 have **taken** evil **c** against thee, saying, 3289
8:10 **Take c together**, and it shall come to 5779+6098
11: 2 understanding, the spirit of **c** and might, 6098
16: 3 Take **c**, execute judgment; make thy 6098
19: 3 and I will destroy the **c** thereof: 6098
19:11 the **c** of the wise counsellers of Pharaoh is 6098
19:17 because of the **c** of the LORD of hosts, 6098
23: 8 Who hath **taken** this **c** against Tyre, 3289
28:29 which is wonderful in **c**, *and* excellent in 6098
29:15 seek deep to hide *their* **c** from the LORD, 6098
30: 1 saith the LORD, that take **c**, but not of me; 6098
36: 5 vain words) *I have* **c** and strength for war: 6098
40:14 With whom **took** he **c**, and *who* instructed 3289
44:26 and performeth the **c** of his messengers; 6098
45:21 *them* near; yea, let them **take c** together: 3289
46:10 My **c** shall stand, and I will do all my 6098
46:11 the man that executeth my **c** from a far 6098
Jer 18:18 nor **c** from the wise, nor the word from 6098
18:23 thou knowest all their **c** against me to slay 6098
19: 7 I will make void the **c** of Judah and 6098
23:18 For who hath stood in the **c** of the LORD, 5475
23:22 if they had stood in my **c**, and had caused 5475
32:19 Great in **c**, and mighty in work: for thine 6098
38:15 if I **give** thee **c**, wilt thou not hearken unto 3289
49: 7 is **c** perished from the prudent? is their 6098
49:20 Therefore hear the **c** of the LORD, that he 6098
49:30 of Babylon hath **taken c** against you, 3289+6098
50:45 Therefore hear ye the **c** of the LORD, 6098
Eze 7:26 from the priest, and **c** from the ancients. 6098
11: 2 and **give** wicked **c** in this city: 3289+6098
Da 2:14 Daniel answered with **c** and wisdom to 5843
4:27 let my **c** be acceptable unto thee, and 4431
Hos 4:12 My people ask **c** at their stocks, and NIH
10: 6 and Israel shall be ashamed of his own **c**. 6098
Mic 4:12 the LORD, neither understand they his **c**: 6098
Zec 6:13 the **c** of peace shall be between them both. 6098
Mt 22:15 took **c** how they might entangle him in *his* *4824*
27: 1 elders of the people took **c** against Jesus to *4824*
27: 7 And they took **c**, and bought with them *4824*
28:12 and had taken **c**, they gave large money *4824*
Mk 3: 6 straightway took **c** with the Herodians *4824*
Lk 7:30 lawyers rejected the **c** of God against *1012*
23:51 (The same had not consented to the **c** and *1012*
Jn 11:53 **took c together** for to put him to death. *4823*
18:14 Caiaphas was he, which **gave c** to the Jews, *4823*
Ac 2:23 being delivered by the determinate **c** and *1012*
4:28 and thy **c** determined before to be done. *1012*
5:33 cut *to the heart*, and **took c** to slay them. *1011*
5:38 for if this **c** or this work be of men, it will *1012*
9:23 were fulfilled, the Jews **took c** to kill him: *4823*
20:27 to declare unto you all the **c** of God. *1012*
27:42 And the soldiers' **c** was to kill *1012*
Eph 1:11 all *things* after the **c** of his own will: *1012*
Heb 6:17 heirs of promise the immutability of his **c**, *1012*
Rev 3:18 **I c thee to buy of me gold tried in the fire,** *4823*

COUNSELLED (4) [COUNSEL]

2Sa 16:23 of Ahithophel, which he **c** in those days, 3289
17:15 elders of Israel; and thus and thus have I **c**. 3289
17:21 for thus hath Ahithophel **c** against you. 3289
Job 26: 3 How hast thou **c** *him that hath* no wisdom? 3289

COUNSELLER (14) [COUNSEL]

2Sa 15:12 David's **c**, from his city, *even* from Giloh, 3289
1Ch 26:14 Zechariah his son, a wise **c**, they cast lots; 3289
27:32 Also Jonathan David's uncle *was* a **c**, 3289
27:33 Ahithophel *was* the king's **c**: and 3289
2Ch 22: 3 for his mother was his **c** to do wickedly. 3289
Isa 3: 3 the honourable *man*, and the **c**, and 3289
9: 6 **C**, The mighty God, The everlasting Father, 3289
40:13 or *being* his **c** hath taught him? 376+6098
41:28 amongst them, and *there was* no **c**, that, 3289
Mic 4: 9 is thy **c** perished? for pangs have taken thee 3289
Na 1:11 evil against the LORD, a wicked **c**. 3289
Mk 15:43 Joseph of Arimathea, an honourable **c**, *1010*
Lk 23:50 *there was* a man named Joseph, a **c**; *1010*
Ro 11:34 mind of the Lord? or who hath been his **c**? *4825*

COUNSELLERS (21) [COUNSEL]

2Ch 22: 4 for they were his **c** after the death of his 3289
Ezr 4: 5 hired **c** against them, to frustrate their 3289
7:14 of his seven **c**, to inquire concerning Judah 3272
7:15 his **c** have freely offered unto the God of 3272
7:28 his **c**, and before all the king's mighty 3289
8:25 his **c**, and his lords, and all Israel *there* 3289
Job 3:14 With kings and **c** of the earth, which built 3289
12:17 He leadeth **c** away spoiled, and maketh 3289
Ps 119:24 also *are* my delight *and* my **c**. 376+6098
Pr 11:14 but in the multitude of **c** *there is* safety. 3289
12:20 imagine evil: but to the **c** of peace *is* joy. 3289
15:22 in the multitude of **c** *they* are established. 3289
24: 6 and in multitude of **c** *there is* safety. 3289
Isa 1:26 as at the first, and thy **c** as at the beginning: 3289
19:11 the counsel of the wise **c** of Pharaoh is 3289
Da 3: 2 the **c**, the sheriffs, and all the rulers of 1884
3: 3 the **c**, the sheriffs, and all the rulers of 1884
3:24 up in haste, *and* spake, and said unto his **c**, 1907
3:27 governors, and captains, and the king's **c**, 1907
4:36 and my **c** and my lords sought unto me; and 1907
6: 7 and the princes, the **c** and the captains, 1907

COUNSELS (12) [COUNSEL]

Job 37:12 it is turned round about by his **c**: that they 8458
Ps 5:10 O God; let them fall by their own **c**; 4156
81:12 heart's lust: *and* they walked in their own **c**. 4156
Pr 1: 5 of understanding shall attain unto **wise c**: 8458
12: 5 *are* right: *but* the **c** of the wicked *are* deceit. 8458
22:20 not I written to thee excellent things in **c** 4156
Isa 25: 1 *thy* **c** of old *are* faithfulness *and* truth. 6098
47:13 Thou art wearied in the multitude of thy **c**. 6098
Jer 7:24 walked in the **c** *and* in the imagination of 4156

Hos 11: 6 and devour *them,* because of their own **c**. 4156
Mic 6:16 the house of Ahab, and ye walk in their **c**; 4156
1Co 4: 5 and will make manifest the **c** of the hearts: *1012*

COUNT (26) [COUNTED, COUNTETH, COUNTING]
Ex 12: 4 his eating shall **make** your **c** for the lamb. 3699
Lev 19:23 **c** the fruit thereof **as uncircumcised**: 6188+6190
23:15 ye shall **c** unto you from the morrow after 5608
25:27 let him **c** the years of the sale thereof, and 2803
25:52 he shall **c** with him, *and* according unto his 2803
Nu 23:10 Who can **c** the dust of Jacob, and 4487
1Sa 1:16 **C** not thine handmaid for a daughter of 5414
Job 19:15 and my maidens, **c** me for a stranger: 2803
31: 4 not he see my ways, and **c** all my steps? 5608
Ps 87: 6 The LORD shall **c**, when he writeth *up* 5608
139:18 *If* I should **c** them, they are moe in number 5608
139:22 I **c** them mine enemies. 1961+3807.1
Mic 6:11 Shall I **c** *them* **pure** with the wicked 2135
Ac 20:24 neither **c** I my life dear unto myself, so *2192*
Php 3: 8 and I **c** all *things but* loss for *2233*
3: 8 loss of all *things,* and do **c** *them but* dung, *2233*
3:13 I **c** not myself to have apprehended: *3049*
2Th 1:11 that our God would **c** you **worthy** of *this* *515*
3:15 Yet **c** *him* not as an enemy, but *2233*
1Ti 6: 1 **c** their own masters worthy of all honour, *2233*
Phm 1:17 If thou **c** me therefore a partner, *2192*
Jas 1: 2 **c** *it* all joy when ye fall into divers *2233*
5:11 Behold, we **c** them **happy** which endure. *3106*
2Pe 2:13 *as* they that **c** it pleasure to riot in the day *2233*
3: 9 *his* promise, as some *men* **c** slackness; *2233*
Rev 13:18 Let him that hath understanding **c** *5585*

COUNTED (40) [COUNT]
Ge 15: 6 and he **c** it to him *for* righteousness. 2803
30:33 the sheep, that *shall be* **c** stolen with me. NIH
31:15 Are we not **c** of him strangers? for he hath 2803
Ex 38:21 of the tabernacle of Testimony, as it was **c**, 6485
Lev 25:31 them shall be **c** as the fields of the country: 2803
Nu 18:30 it shall be **c** unto the Levites as the increase 2803
Jos 13: 3 *which* is **c** to the Canaanite: 2803
1Ki 1:21 and my son Solomon shall be **c** offenders. NIH
3: 8 that cannot be numbered nor **c** for 5608
1Ch 21: 6 and Benjamin **c** he not among them: 6485
23:24 as they were **c** by number of names by their 6485
Ne 13:13 for they were **c** faithful, and their office 2803
Job 18: 3 Wherefore are we **c** as beasts, *and* 2803
41:29 Darts are **c** as stubble: he laugheth at 2803
Ps 44:22 we are **c** as sheep for the slaughter. 2803
88: 4 I am **c** with them that go down into the pit: 2803
106:31 *that* was **c** unto him for righteousness unto 2803
Pr 17:28 a fool, when he holdeth his peace, is **c** wise: 2803
27:14 in the morning, it shall be **c** a curse to him. 2803
Isa 5:28 their horses' hoofs shall be **c** like flint, and 2803
32:15 and the fruitful field be **c** for a forest. 2803
33:18 the receiver? where *is* he that **c** the towers? 5608
40:15 and are **c** as the small dust of the balance: 2803
40:17 they are **c** to him less than nothing, and 2803
Hos 8:12 my law, *but* they were **c** as a strange *thing.* 2803
Mt 14: 5 because they **c** him as a prophet. *2192*
Mk 11:32 for all *men* **c** John, that he was a prophet *2192*
Ac 5:41 rejoicing that they were **c** **worthy** to suffer *2661*
19:19 all *men:* and they **c** the price of them, *4860*
Ro 2:26 shall not his uncircumcision be **c** for *3049*
4: 3 and it was **c** unto him for righteousness. *3049*
4: 5 the ungodly, his faith is **c** for righteousness. *3049*
9: 8 the children of the promise are **c** for *3049*
Php 3: 7 were gain to me, those I **c** loss for Christ. *2233*
2Th 1: 5 that ye may be **c** **worthy** of the kingdom of *2661*
1Ti 1:12 hath enabled me, for that he **c** me faithful, *2233*
5:17 Let the elders that rule well be **c** **worthy** of *515*
Heb 3: 3 For this *man* was **c** **worthy** of more glory *515*
7: 6 But he whose **descent** is not **c** from them *1075*
10:29 and hath **c** the blood of the covenant, *2233*

COUNTENANCE (53) [COUNTENANCES]
Ge 4: 5 And Cain was very wroth, and his **c** fell. 6440
4: 6 art thou wroth? and why is thy **c** fallen? 6440
31: 2 Jacob beheld the **c** of Laban, and behold, 6440
31: 5 said unto them, I see your father's **c**, that it 6440
Ex 23: 3 Neither shalt thou **c** a poor *man* in his 1921
Nu 6:26 The LORD lift up his **c** upon thee, and 6440
Dt 28:50 A nation of fierce **c**, which shall not regard 6440
Jdg 13: 6 his **c** *was* like the countenance of an angel 4758
13: 6 his countenance *was* like the **c** of an angel 4758
1Sa 1:18 and did eat, and her **c** was no more *sad.* 6440
16: 7 Look not on his **c**, or on the height of his 4758
16:12 *and* withal of a beautiful **c**, and goodly to 5869
17:42 *but* a youth, and ruddy, and of a fair **c**. 4758
25: 3 of good understanding, and of a beautiful **c**: 8389
2Sa 14:27 *was* Tamar: she was a woman of a fair **c**. 4758
2Ki 8:11 he settled his **c** stedfastly, until *he* was 6440
Ne 2: 2 Why *is* thy **c** sad, seeing thou *art* not sick? 6440
2: 3 why should not my **c** be sad, when the city, 6440
Job 14:20 thou changest his **c**, and sendest him away. 6440
29:24 and the light of my **c** they cast not down. 6440
Ps 4: 6 lift thou up the light of thy **c** upon us. 6440
10: 4 The wicked, through the pride of his **c**, 639
11: 7 his **c** doth behold the upright. 6440
21: 6 hast made him exceeding glad with thy **c**. 6440
42: 5 I shall yet praise him *for* the help of his **c**. 6440
42:11 *who is* the health of my **c**, and my God. 6440
43: 5 *who is* the health of my **c**, and my God. 6440
44: 3 the light of thy **c**, because thou hadst a 6440
80:16 they perish at the rebuke of thy **c**. 6440
89:15 shall walk, O LORD, in the light of thy **c**. 6440
90: 8 our secret *sins* in the light of thy **c**. 6440
Pr 15:13 A merry heart maketh a cheerful **c**: but 6440
16:15 In the light of the king's **c** *is* life; and 6440
25:23 so *doth* an angry **c** a backbiting tongue. 6440
27:17 so a man sharpeneth the **c** of his friend. 6440
Ecc 7: 3 for by the sadness of the **c** the heart is made 6440
SS 2:14 let me see thy **c**, let me hear thy voice; 4758
2:14 for sweet *is* thy voice, and thy **c** *is* comely. 4758
5:15 his **c** *is* as Lebanon, excellent as the cedars. 4758
Isa 3: 9 The shew of their **c** doth witness against 6440
Eze 27:35 sore afraid, they shall be troubled *in their* **c**. 6440
Da 1:13 the **c** of the children that eat *of* the portion 4758
5: 6 the king's **c** was changed, and his thoughts 2122
5: 9 his **c** *was* changed in him, and his lords 2122
5:10 trouble thee, nor let thy **c** be changed. 2122
7:28 troubled me, and my **c** changed in me: 2122
8:23 a king of fierce **c**, and understanding dark 6440
Mt 6:16 ye fast, be not as the hypocrites, of a **sad** **c**: *4659*
28: 3 His **c** was like lightning, and his raiment *2397*
Lk 9:29 the fashion of his **c** was altered, and *4383*
Ac 2:28 thou shalt make me full of joy with thy **c**. *4383*
2Co 3: 7 the face of Moses for the glory of his **c**; *4383*
Rev 1:16 his **c** *was* as the sun shineth in his strength. *3799*

COUNTENANCES (2) [COUNTENANCE]
Da 1:13 let our **c** be looked upon before thee, and 4758
1:15 at the end of ten days their **c** appeared fairer 4758

COUNTERVAIL (1)
Est 7: 4 although the enemy could not **c** the king's 7737

COUNTETH (3) [COUNT]
Job 19:11 he **c** me unto him as *one of* his enemies. 2803
33:10 against me, he **c** me for his enemy, 2803
Lk 14:28 sitteth not down first, and **c** the cost, *5585*

COUNTING (1) [COUNT]
Ecc 7:27 I found, saith the Preacher, *c* one by one, NIH

COUNTRIES (55) [COUNTRY]
Ge 10:20 their tongues, in their **c**, *and* in their nations. 776
26: 3 I will give all these **c**, and I will perform 776
26: 4 and will give unto thy seed all these **c**; 776
41:57 all **c** came into Egypt to Joseph for to buy 776
Jos 13:32 These *are the* **c** which Moses did distribute NIH
14: 1 these *are the* **c** which the children of Israel NIH
17:11 of Megiddo and her towns, *even* three **c**. 5316
2Ki 18:35 Who *are they* among all the gods of the **c**, 776
1Ch 22: 5 of fame and of glory throughout all **c**: 776
29:30 and over all the kingdoms of the **c**. 776
2Ch 11:23 all his children throughout all the **c** of Judah 776
12: 8 and the service of the kingdoms of the **c**. 776
15: 5 *were* upon all the inhabitants of the **c**. 776
20:29 of God was on all the kingdoms of *those* **c**, 776
34:33 the **c** that *pertained* to the children of Israel, 776
Ezr 3: 3 upon them because of the people of *those* **c**: 776
4:20 which have ruled over all **c** beyond NIH
Ps 110: 6 he shall wound the heads over many **c**. 776
Isa 8: 9 broken in pieces; and give ear, all ye of far **c**: 776
37:18 have laid waste all the nations, and their **c**, 776
Jer 23: 3 flock out of all **c** whither I have driven them, 776
23: 8 and from all **c** whither I had driven them; 776
28: 8 thee of old prophesied both against many **c**, 776

Jer 32:37 Behold, I *will* gather them out of all **c**, 776
40:11 in Edom, and that *were* in all the **c**, 776
Eze 5: 5 of the nations and **c** *that are* round about her. 776
5: 6 my statutes more than the **c** that *are* round 776
6: 8 when ye shall be scattered through the **c**. 776
11:16 although I have scattered them among the **c**, 776
11:16 sanctuary in the **c** where they shall come. 776
11:17 assemble you out of the **c** where ye have 776
12:15 the nations, and disperse them in the **c**. 776
20:23 and disperse them through the **c**; 776
20:32 as the families of the **c**, to serve wood and 776
20:34 will gather you out of the **c** wherein ye are 776
20:41 gather you out of the **c** wherein ye have been 776
22: 4 unto the heathen, and a mocking to all **c**. 776
22:15 disperse thee in the **c**, and will consume thy 776
25: 7 and I will cause thee to perish out of the **c**: 776
29:12 in the midst of the **c** *that are* desolate, 776
29:12 and will disperse them through the **c**. 776
30: 7 they shall be desolate in the midst of the **c** 776
30:23 and will disperse them through the **c**. 776
30:26 the nations, and disperse them among the **c**; 776
32: 9 into the **c** which thou hast not known. 776
34:13 gather them from the **c**, and will bring them 776
35:10 two nations and these two **c** shall be mine, 776
36:19 and they were dispersed through the **c**: 776
36:24 gather you out of all **c**, and will bring you 776
Da 9: 7 through all the **c** whither thou hast driven 776
11:40 he shall enter into the **c**, and shall overflow 776
11:41 and many *c* shall be overthrown: NIH
11:42 shall stretch forth his hand also upon the **c**: 776
Zec 10: 9 they shall remember me in **far c**; and 4801
Lk 21:21 let not them that are in the **c** enter thereinto. *5561*

COUNTRY (179) [COUNTRIES, COUNTRYMEN]

Ge 12: 1 Get thee out of thy **c**, and from thy kindred, 776
14: 7 smote all the **c** of the Amalekites, and 7704
19:28 the smoke of the **c** went up as the smoke of a 776
20: 1 journeyed from thence toward the south **c**, 776
24: 4 thou shalt go unto my **c**, and to my kindred, 776
24:62 well Lahai-roi; for he dwelt in the south **c**. 776
25: 6 while he yet lived, eastward, unto the east **c**. 776
29:26 Laban said, It must not be so done in our **c**, 4725
30:25 I may go unto mine own place, and to my **c**. 776
32: 3 unto the land of Seir, the **c** of Edom. 7704
32: 9 Return unto thy **c**, and to thy kindred, and 776
34: 2 prince of the **c**, saw her, he took her, and 776
36: 6 went into the **c** from the face of his brother 776
42:30 roughly to us, and took us for spies of the **c**. 776
42:33 And the man, the lord of the **c**, said unto us, 776
47:27 in the land of Egypt, in the **c** of Goshen; 776
Lev 16:29 work *at all, whether it be* one of **your own c**, 249
17:15 *beasts, whether it be* one of **your own c**, 249
24:22 for the stranger, as for **one of** your **own c**: 249
25:31 them shall be counted as the fields of the **c**: 776
Nu 15:13 All that are **born of the c** shall do these 249
20:17 Let us pass, I pray thee, through thy **c**: 776
21:20 that *is* in the **c** of Moab, *to* the top of 7704
32: 4 *Even* the **c** which the LORD smote before 776
32:33 *even* the cities of the **c** round about. 776
Dt 3:14 Jair the son of Manasseh took all the **c** of 2256
4:43 in the plain **c**, of the Reubenites; 776
26: 3 that I am come unto the **c** which the LORD 776
Jos 2: 2 of the children of Israel to search out the **c**. 776
2: 3 for they be come to search out all the **c**. 776
2:24 for even all the inhabitants of the **c** do faint 776
6:22 unto the two men that had spied out the **c**, 776
6:27 and his fame was *noised* throughout all the **c**. 776
7: 2 unto them, saying, Go up and view the **c**. 776
9: 6 the men of Israel, We be come from a far **c**: 776
9: 9 From a very far **c** thy servants are come 776
9:11 and all the inhabitants of our **c** spake to us, 776
10:40 So Joshua smote all the **c** of the hills, and 776
10:41 and all the **c** of Goshen, even unto Gibeon. 776
11:16 all the south *c*, and all the land of Goshen, NIH
12: 7 these *are* the kings of the **c** which Joshua 776
12: 8 in the south *c*; the Hittites, the Amorites, NIH
13: 6 All the inhabitants of the **hill c** from 2022
13:21 *were* dukes of Sihon, dwelling in the **c**. 776
17:15 *then* get thee up to the wood *c*, and NIH
19:51 So they made an end of dividing the **c**. 776
21:11 which *city is* Hebron, in the hill *c* of Judah, NIH
22: 9 to go unto the **c** of Gilead, to the land of 776
Jdg 8:28 the **c** was in quietness forty years in the days 776
11:21 of the Amorites, the inhabitants of that **c**. 776
12:12 was buried in Aijalon in the **c** of Zebulun. 776
16:24 the destroyer of our **c**, which slew many of 776
18:14 five men that went to spy out the **c** of Laish, 776
20: 6 sent her throughout all the **c** of 7704
Ru 1: 1 went to sojourn in the **c** of Moab, 7704
1: 2 they came *into* the **c** of Moab, and 7704
1: 6 that she might return from the **c** of Moab: 7704
1: 6 for she had heard in the **c** of Moab how that 7704
1:22 which returned out of the **c** of Moab: 7704
2: 6 back with Naomi out of the **c** of Moab: 7704
4: 3 that is come again out of the **c** of Moab, 7704
1Sa 6: 1 the ark of the LORD was in the **c** of 7704
6:18 *both* of fenced cities, and of **c** villages, 6521
14:21 them into the camp *from the c* round about, NIH
27: 5 them give me a place in some town in the **c**, 7704
27: 7 the time that David dwelt in the **c** of 7704
27:11 while he dwelleth in the **c** of the Philistines. 7704
2Sa 15:23 all the **c** wept *with* a loud voice, and all 776
18: 8 was there scattered over the face of all the **c**: 776
21:14 Jonathan his son buried they in the **c** of 776
1Ki 4:19 Geber the son of Uri *was* in the **c** of Gilead, 776
4:19 *in* the **c** of Sihon king of the Amorites, and 776
4:30 the wisdom of all the children of the **east c**, 6924
8:41 cometh out of a far **c** for thy name's sake; 776
10:13 So she turned and went to her own **c**, she and 776
10:15 of Arabia, and *of* the governors of the **c**. 776
11:21 Let me depart, that I may go to mine own **c**. 776
11:22 thou seekest to go to thine own **c**? 776
20:27 flocks of kids; but the Syrians filled the **c**. 776
22:36 man to his city, and every man to his own **c**. 776
2Ki 3:20 of Edom, and the **c** was filled with water. 776
3:24 smiting the Moabites, even in their **c**s. 1886.3
18:35 that have delivered their **c** out of mine hand, 776
20:14 Hezekiah said, They are come from a far **c**, 776
1Ch 8: 8 Shaharaim begat *children* in the **c** of Moab, 7704
20: 1 and wasted the **c** of the children of Ammon, 776
2Ch 6:32 is come from a far **c** for thy great name's 776
9:14 governors of the **c** brought gold and silver to 776
26:10 both in the **low c**, and in the plains: 8219
28:18 also had invaded the cities of the **low c**, 8219
30:10 from city to city through the **c** of Ephraim 776
Ne 12:28 both out of the **plain c** round about 3603
Pr 25:25 a thirsty soul, so *is* good news from a far **c**. 776
Isa 1: 7 Your **c** *is* desolate, your cities *are* burnt *with* 776
13: 5 They come from a far **c**, from the end of 776
22:18 and toss thee like a ball into a large **c**: 776
39: 3 They are come from a far **c** unto me, 776
46:11 man that executeth my counsel from a far **c**: 776
Jer 2: 7 I brought you into a plentiful **c**, to eat 776
4:16 *that* watchers come from a far **c**, and 776
6:20 from Sheba, and the sweet cane from a far **c**? 776
6:22 a people cometh from the north **c**, and 776
8:19 because of them that dwell in a far **c**: 776
10:22 and a great commotion out of the north **c**, 776
22:10 he shall return no more, nor see his native **c**. 776
22:26 into another **c**, where ye were not born; 776
23: 8 seed of the house of Israel out of the north **c**, 776
31: 8 I *will* bring them from the north **c**, and 776
32: 8 in Anathoth, which *is* in the **c** of Benjamin: 776
44: 1 and at Noph, and in the **c** of Pathros, saying, 776
46:10 in the north **c** by the river Euphrates. 776
47: 4 the remnant of the **c** of Caphtor. 339
48:21 judgment is come upon the plain **c**; 776
50: 9 assembly of great nations from the north **c**: 776
51: 9 and let us go every one into his own **c**: 776
Eze 20:38 I will bring them forth out of the **c** where 776
20:42 into the **c** *for* the which I lifted up mine hand 776
25: 9 the glory of the **c**, Beth-jeshimoth, 776
32:15 the **c** shall be destitute of that whereof it was 776
34:13 and in all the inhabited places of the **c**. 776
47: 8 These waters issue out toward the east **c**, 1552
47:22 they shall be unto you as **born in the c** 249
Hos 12:12 Jacob fled *into* the **c** of Syria, and 7704
Jnh 1: 8 what *is* thy **c**? and of what people *art* thou? 776
4: 2 not this my saying, when I was yet in my **c**? 127
Zec 6: 6 which *are* therein go forth into the north **c**; 776
6: 6 and the grisled go forth toward the south **c**. 776
6: 8 these that go toward the north **c** have quieted 776
6: 8 country have quieted my spirit in the north **c**. 776
8: 7 I *will* save my people from the east **c**, and 776
8: 7 from the east country, and from the west **c**; 776
Mt 2:12 they departed into their own **c** another way. *5561*
8:28 the other side into the **c** of the Gergesenes, *5561*
9:31 spread abroad his fame in all that **c**. *1093*

C

Mt 13:54 And when he was come into his own **c**, 3968
13:57 save in his own **c**, and in his own house. 3968
14:35 they sent out into all that **c round about**, 4066
21:33 it out to husbandmen, and **went into a far c**: 589
25:14 *of heaven is* as a man **travelling into a far c**, 589
Mk 5: 1 side of the sea, into the **c** of the Gadarenes. 5561
5:10 he would not send them away out of the **c**. 5561
5:14 swine fled, and told *it* in the city, and in the **c**. 68
6: 1 out from thence, and came into his own **c**; 3968
6: 4 but in his own **c**, and among his own kin, 3968
6:36 that they may go into the **c** round about, and 68
6:56 he entered, into villages, or cities, or **c**, 68
12: 1 it out to husbandmen, and **went into a far c**. 589
15:21 who passed by, coming out of the **c**, the father 68
16:12 of them, as they walked, and went into the **c**. 68
Lk 1:39 and went into the **hill c** with haste, into a 3714
1:65 abroad throughout all the **hill c** of Judea. 3714
2: 8 **in** the same **c** shepherds **abiding** in the field, 63
3: 3 And he came into all the **c about** Jordan, 4066
4:23 done in Capernaum, do also here in thy **c**. 3968
4:24 No prophet is accepted in his own **c**. 3968
4:37 out into every place of the **c round about**. 4066
8:26 And they arrived at the **c** of the Gadarenes, 5561
8:34 and went and told *it* in the city and in the **c**. 68
8:37 **c** of the Gadarenes **round about** besought 4066
9:12 they may go into the towns and **c** round about, 68
15:13 and took his journey into a far **c**, and 5561
15:15 and joined himself to a citizen of that **c**; 5561
19:12 A certain nobleman went into a far **c** to 5561
20: 9 and **went into a far c** for a long time. 589
23:26 coming out of the **c**, and on him they laid 68
Jn 4:44 that a prophet hath no honour in his own **c**. 3968
11:54 went thence unto a **c** near to the wilderness, 5561
11:55 many went out of the **c** up to Jerusalem 5561
Ac 4:36 a Levite, *and* **of the c of** Cyprus, 1085
7: 3 Get thee out of thy **c**, and from thy kindred, 1093
12:20 their **c** was nourished by the king's 5561
12:20 their country was nourished by the king's *c*. NIG
13: 7 Which was with the deputy *of the c*, Sergius NIG
18:23 and went over *all* the **c** of Galatia and 5561
27:27 deemed that they drew near to some **c**; 5561
Heb 11: 9 as *in* a strange *c*, dwelling in tabernacles NIG
11:14 *things* declare plainly that they seek a **c**. 3968
11:15 if they had been mindful of that *c* from NIG
11:16 But now they desire a better *c*, that is, NIG

COUNTRYMEN (2) [COUNTRY, MAN]
2Co 11:26 *in* perils of robbers, *in* perils by *my own* **c**, 1085
1Th 2:14 have suffered like *things* of your own **c**, 4853

COUPLE (10) [COUPLED, COUPLETH, COUPLING, COUPLINGS]
Ex 26: 6 and **c** the curtains together with the taches: 2266
26: 9 thou shalt **c** five curtains by themselves, 2266
26:11 and **c** the tent **together**, that it may be one. 2266
36:18 fifty taches of brass to **c** the tent **together**, 2266
39: 4 made shoulderpieces for it, to **c** *it* **together**: 2266
Jdg 19: 3 his servant with him, and a **c** of asses: 6776
2Sa 13: 6 make *me* a **c** of cakes in my sight, that I 8147
16: 1 with a **c** of asses saddled, and upon them 6776
Isa 21: 7 he saw a chariot *with* a **c** of horsemen, 6776
21: 9 a chariot of men, *with* a **c** of horsemen. 6776

COUPLED (12) [COUPLE]
Ex 26: 3 The five curtains shall be **c together** one to 2266
26: 3 *other* five curtains *shall be* **c** one to another. 2266
26:24 they shall be **c together** beneath, and 8382
26:24 they shall be **c together** above 3162+8535
36:10 And he **c** the five curtains one unto another: 2266
36:10 *the other* five curtains he **c** one unto 2266
36:13 **c** the curtains one unto another with 2266
36:16 he **c** five curtains by themselves, and six 2266
36:29 they were **c** beneath, and coupled together 8382
36:29 **c** together at the head thereof, to one 1961+8535
39: 4 by the two edges was it **c together**. 2266
1Pe 3: 2 behold your chaste conversation *c* with fear. NIG

COUPLETH (2) [COUPLE]
Ex 26:10 the edge of the curtain which **c** the second. 2279
36:17 the edge of the curtain which **c** the second. 2279

COUPLING (10) [COUPLE]
Ex 26: 4 the one curtain from the selvedge in the **c**; 2279
26: 4 of *another* curtain, in the **c** of the second. 4225
26: 5 of the curtain that *is* in the **c** of the second; 4225
26:10 of the one curtain *that is* outmost in the **c**, 2279
28:27 over against *the other* **c** thereof, 4225
36:11 of one curtain from the selvedge in the **c**: 4225
36:11 of *another* curtain, in the **c** of the second. 4225
36:12 curtain which *was* in the **c** of the second: 4225
36:17 the uttermost edge of the curtain in the **c**, 4225
39:20 of it, over against the *other* **c** thereof, 4225

COUPLINGS (1) [COUPLE]
2Ch 34:11 timber for **c**, and to floor the houses which 4226

COURAGE (20) [COURAGEOUS, COURAGEOUSLY]
Nu 13:20 be ye **of good c**, and bring of the fruit of 2388
Dt 31: 6 Be strong and **of a good c**, fear not, nor be 553
31: 7 sight of all Israel, Be strong and **of a good c**: 553
31:23 and said, Be strong and **of a good c**: 553
Jos 1: 6 Be strong and **of a good c**: for unto this 553
1: 9 Be strong and **of a good c**; be not afraid, 553
1:18 put to death: only be strong and **of a good c**. 553
2:11 neither did there remain any more **c** in any 7307
10:25 nor be dismayed, be strong and **of good c**: 553
2Sa 10:12 Be **of good c**, and let us play the men for 2388
1Ch 19:13 Be **of good c**, and let us behave ourselves 2388
22:13 be strong, and **of good c**; dread not, nor be 553
28:20 Be strong and **of good c**, and do *it:* fear not, 553
2Ch 15: 8 he **took c**, and put away the abominable 2388
Ezr 10: 4 *will be* with thee: be **of good c**, and do *it.* 2388
Ps 27:14 be **of good c**, and he shall strengthen thine 2388
31:24 Be **of good c**, and he shall strengthen your 2388
Isa 41: 6 *every one* said to his brother, Be of **good c**. 2388
Da 11:25 his **c** against the king of the south with a 3824
Ac 28:15 Paul saw, he thanked God, and took **c**. 2294

COURAGEOUS (5) [COURAGE]
Jos 1: 7 Only be thou strong and very **c**, that *thou* 553
23: 6 Be ye therefore very **c** to keep and to do all 2388
2Sa 13:28 not I commanded you? be **c**, and be valiant. 2388
2Ch 32: 7 Be strong and **c**, be not afraid nor dismayed 553
Am 2:16 he *that is* **c** among the mighty shall 533+3820

COURAGEOUSLY (1) [COURAGE]
2Ch 19:11 Deal **c**, and the LORD shall be with 2388

COURSE (35) [COURSES]
1Ch 27: 1 *of* every **c** *were* twenty and four thousand. 4256
27: 2 Over the first **c** for the first month *was* 4256
27: 2 and in his **c** *were* twenty and four thousand. 4256
27: 4 over the **c** of the second month *was* Dodai 4256
27: 4 and *of* his **c** *was* Mikloth also the ruler: 4256
27: 4 in his **c** likewise *were* twenty and 4256
27: 5 and in his **c** *were* twenty and four thousand. 4256
27: 6 and *in* his **c** *was* Ammizabad his son. 4256
27: 7 and in his **c** *were* twenty and four thousand. 4256
27: 8 and in his **c** *were* twenty and four thousand. 4256
27: 9 and in his **c** *were* twenty and four thousand. 4256
27:10 and in his **c** *were* twenty and four thousand. 4256
27:11 and in his **c** *were* twenty and four thousand. 4256
27:12 and in his **c** *were* twenty and four thousand. 4256
27:13 and in his **c** *were* twenty and four thousand. 4256
27:14 and in his **c** *were* twenty and four thousand. 4256
27:15 and in his **c** *were* twenty and four thousand. 4256
28: 1 **companies** that ministered to the king **by c**, 4256
2Ch 5:11 were sanctified, *and* did not *then* wait by **c**: 4256
Ezr 3:11 And they sung together by **c** in praising and NIH
Ps 82: 5 all the foundations of the earth are **out of c**. 4131
Jer 8: 6 every one turned to his **c**, as the horse 4794
23:10 their **c** is evil, and their force *is* not right. 4794
Lk 1: 5 priest named Zacharias, of the **c** of Abia: 2183
1: 8 office before God in the order of his **c**, 2183
Ac 13:25 And as John fulfilled *his* **c**, he said, 1408
16:11 we **came with a straight c** to Samothracia, 2113
20:24 so that *I* might finish my **c** with joy, and 1408
21: 1 we came with a **straight c** unto Cos, and 2113
21: 7 And when we had finished *our* **c** from Tyre, 4144
1Co 14:27 or at the most *by* three, and *that* **by c**; 303+3313
Eph 2: 2 ye walked according to the **c** of this world, 165
2Th 3: 1 that the word of the Lord may have *free* **c**, 5143
2Ti 4: 7 I have finished *my* **c**, I have kept the faith: 1408
Jas 3: 6 and setteth on fire the **c** of nature; 5164

COURSES (18) [COURSE]
Jdg 5:20 the stars in their **c** fought against Sisera. 4546
1Ki 5:14 to Lebanon, ten thousand a month *by* **c**: 2487
1Ch 23: 6 David divided them *into* **c** among the sons 4256

1Ch 27: 1 that served the king in any matter of the **c**, 4256
28:13 Also for the **c** of the priests and the Levites, 4256
28:21 the **c** of the priests and the Levites, 4256
2Ch 8:14 the **c** of the priests to their service, and 4256
8:14 the porters also by their **c** at every gate: for 4256
23: 8 for Jehoiada the priest dismissed not the **c**. 4256
31: 2 And Hezekiah appointed the **c** of the priests 4256
31: 2 of the priests and the Levites after their **c**, 4256
31:15 set office, to give to their brethren by **c**, 4256
31:16 service in their charges according to their **c**; 4256
31:17 and upward, in their charges by their **c**; 4256
35: 4 after your **c**, according to the writing of 4256
35:10 in their place, and the Levites in their **c**, 4256
Ezr 6:18 the Levites in their **c**, for the service of 4255
Isa 44: 4 among the grass, as willows by the water **c**. 2988

COURT (122) [COURTS]

Ex 27: 9 thou shalt make the **c** of the tabernacle: 2691
27: 9 **c** *of* fine twined linen of an hundred cubits 2691
27:12 *for* the breadth of the **c** on the west side 2691
27:13 the breadth of the **c** on the east side 2691
27:16 for the gate of the **c** *shall be* a hanging of 2691
27:17 All the pillars round about the **c** *shall be* 2691
27:18 The length of the **c** *shall be* an hundred 2691
27:19 and all the pins of the **c**, *shall be of* brass. 2691
35:17 The hangings of the **c**, his pillars, and 2691
35:17 and the hanging for the door of the **c**, 2691
35:18 and the pins of the **c**, and their cords, 2691
38: 9 he made the **c**: on the south side southward 2691
38: 9 hangings of the **c** *were of* fine twined linen, 2691
38:15 for the other side of the **c** gate, on this hand 2691
38:16 All the hangings of the **c** round about *were* 2691
38:17 all the pillars of the **c** *were* filleted *with* 2691
38:18 the hanging for the gate of the **c** *was* 2691
38:18 answerable to the hangings of the **c**. 2691
38:20 and of the **c** round about, *were of* brass. 2691
38:31 the sockets of the **c** round about, and 2691
38:31 the sockets of the **c** gate, and all the pins of 2691
38:31 and all the pins of the **c** round about. 2691
39:40 The hangings of the **c**, his pillars, and his 2691
39:40 the hanging for the **c** gate, his cords, and 2691
40: 8 thou shalt set up the **c** round about, and 2691
40: 8 and hang up the hanging at the **c** gate. 2691
40:33 he reared up the **c** round about 2691
40:33 and set up the hanging of the **c** gate. 2691
Lev 6:16 in the **c** of the tabernacle of 2691
6:26 in the **c** of the tabernacle of 2691
Nu 3:26 the hangings of the **c**, and the curtain for 2691
3:26 the curtain for the door of the **c**, which *is* by 2691
3:37 the pillars of the **c** round about, and 2691
4:26 the hangings of the **c**, and the hanging for 2691
4:26 hanging for the door of the gate of the **c**, 2691
4:32 the pillars of the **c** round about, and 2691
2Sa 17:18 in Bahurim, which had a well in his **c**; 2691
1Ki 6:36 he built the inner **c** *with* three rows of 2691
7: 8 his house where he dwelt *had* another **c** 2691
7: 9 and *so* on the outside toward the great **c**. 2691
7:12 the great **c** round about *was with* three rows 2691
7:12 both for the inner **c** of the house of 2691
8:64 **c** that *was* before the house of the LORD: 2691
2Ki 20: 4 afore Isaiah was gone out *into* the middle **c**, 2691
2Ch 4: 9 Furthermore he made the **c** of the priests, 2691
4: 9 the great **c**, and doors for the court, and 5835
4: 9 doors for the **c**, and overlaid the doors of 5835
6:13 and had set it in the midst of the **c**: 5835
7: 7 **c** that *was* before the house of the LORD: 2691
20: 5 the house of the LORD, before the new **c**, 2691
24:21 king in the **c** of the house of the LORD. 2691
29:16 into the **c** of the house of the LORD. 2691
Ne 3:25 high house, that *was* by the **c** of the prison. 2691
Est 1: 5 in the **c** of the garden of the king's palace; 2691
2:11 Mordecai walked every day before the **c** of 2691
4:11 shall come unto the king into the inner **c**, 2691
5: 1 and stood in the inner **c** of the king's house, 2691
5: 2 king saw Esther the queen standing in the **c**, 2691
6: 4 the king said, Who *is* in the **c**? Now Haman 2691
6: 4 Now Haman was come into the outward **c** 2691
6: 5 unto him, Behold, Haman standeth in the **c**. 2691
Isa 34:13 be a habitation of dragons, *and* a **c** for owls. 2681
Jer 19:14 he stood in the **c** of the LORD's house; 2691
26: 2 Stand in the **c** of the LORD's house, and 2691
32: 2 Jeremiah the prophet was shut up in the **c** 2691
32: 8 **c** of the prison according to the word of 2691
32:12 before all the Jews that sat in the **c** of 2691
33: 1 while he was yet shut up in the **c** of 2691
36:10 in the higher **c** *at* the entry of the new gate 2691
36:20 they went in to the king into the **c**, but 2691
37:21 commit Jeremiah into the **c** of the prison, 2691
37:21 Thus Jeremiah remained in the **c** of 2691
38: 6 that *was* in the **c** of the prison: 2691
38:13 Jeremiah remained in the **c** of the prison. 2691
38:28 So Jeremiah abode in the **c** of the prison 2691
39:14 took Jeremiah out of the **c** of the prison, 2691
39:15 while he was shut up in the **c** of the prison, 2691
Eze 8: 7 And he brought me to the door of the **c**; and 2691
8:16 he brought me into the inner **c** of 2691
10: 3 went in; and the cloud filled the inner **c**. 2691
10: 4 the **c** was full of the brightness of 2691
10: 5 wings was heard *even* to the utter **c**, 2691
40:14 even unto the post of the **c** round about 2691
40:17 Then brought he me into the outward **c**, and 2691
40:17 a pavement made for the **c** round about: 2691
40:19 unto the forefront of the inner **c** without, 2691
40:20 the gate of the outward **c** that looked 2691
40:23 the gate of the inner **c** *was* over against 2691
40:27 *there was* a gate in the inner **c** toward 2691
40:28 he brought me to the inner **c** by the south 2691
40:31 the arches thereof *were* toward the utter **c**; 2691
40:32 he brought me into the inner **c** toward 2691
40:34 arches thereof *were* toward the outward **c**; 2691
40:37 the posts thereof *were* toward the utter **c**; 2691
40:44 the chambers of the singers in the inner **c**, 2691
40:47 So he measured the **c**, an hundred cubits 2691
41:15 the inner temple, and the porches of the **c**; 2691
42: 1 he brought me forth into the utter **c**, 2691
42: 3 twenty *cubits* which *were* for the inner **c**, 2691
42: 3 the pavement which *was* for the utter **c**, 2691
42: 7 towards the utter **c** on the forepart of 2691
42: 8 that *were* in the utter **c** *was* fifty cubits: 2691
42: 9 as one goeth into them from the utter **c**. 2691
42:10 of the wall of the **c** toward the east, 2691
42:14 not go out of the holy *place* into the utter **c**, 2691
43: 5 me up, and brought me into the inner **c**; 2691
44:17 they enter in at the gates of the inner **c**, 2691
44:17 they minister in the gates of the inner **c**, 2691
44:19 when they go forth into the utter **c**, 2691
44:19 *even* into the utter **c** to the people, 2691
44:21 when they enter into the inner **c**. 2691
44:27 unto the inner **c**, to minister in 2691
45:19 upon the posts of the gate of the inner **c**. 2691
46: 1 The gate of the inner **c** that looketh *toward* 2691
46:20 that *they* bear *them* not out into the utter **c**, 2691
46:21 he brought me forth into the utter **c**, 2691
46:21 me to pass by the four corners of the **c**; 2691
46:21 in every corner of the **c** *there was* a court. 2691
46:21 in every corner of the court *there was* a **c**. 2691
46:22 In the four corners of the **c** *there were* 2691
Am 7:13 it *is* the king's chapel, and it *is* the king's **c**. 1004
Rev 11: 2 But the **c** which is without the temple leave *833*

COURTEOUS (1) [COURTEOUSLY]

1Pe 3: 8 of another, love as brethren, *be* pitiful, *be* **c**: *5391*

COURTEOUSLY (2) [COURTEOUS]

Ac 27: 3 And Julius **c** entreated Paul, and gave *him* *5364*
28: 7 received us, and lodged *us* three days **c**. *5390*

COURTS (25) [COURT]

2Ki 21: 5 in the two **c** of the house of the LORD. 2691
23:12 in the two **c** of the house of the LORD, 2691
1Ch 23:28 in the **c**, and in the chambers, and in 2691
28: 6 thy son, he shall build my house and my **c**: 2691
28:12 of the **c** of the house of the LORD, and 2691
2Ch 23: 5 all the people *shall be* in the **c** of the house 2691
33: 5 in the two **c** of the house of the LORD. 2691
Ne 8:16 in their **c**, and in the courts of the house of 2691
8:16 in the **c** of the house of God, and in 2691
13: 7 in preparing him a chamber in the **c** of 2691
Ps 65: 4 *unto thee, that* he may dwell *in* thy **c**: 2691
84: 2 yea, even fainteth for the **c** of the LORD: 2691
84:10 For a day in thy **c** *is* better than a thousand. 2691
92:13 LORD shall flourish in the **c** of our God. 2691
96: 8 bring an offering, and come into his **c**. 2691
100: 4 *and* into his **c** with praise: 2691
116:19 In the **c** of the LORD's house, in 2691
135: 2 in the **c** of the house of our God, 2691
Isa 1:12 required this at your hand, to tread my **c**? 2691
62: 9 shall drink it in the **c** of my holiness. 2691

Eze 9: 7 the house, and fill the **c** *with* the slain: 2691
42: 6 but had not pillars as the pillars of the **c**: 2691
46:22 In the four corners of the court *there were* **c** 2691
Zec 3: 7 shalt also keep my **c**, and I will give thee 2691
Lk 7:25 and live delicately, are in **kings' c**. *933*

COUSIN (1) [COUSINS]
Lk 1:36 And behold, thy **c** Elisabeth, she hath also *4773*

COUSINS (1) [COUSIN]
Lk 1:58 her **c** heard how the Lord had shewed great *4773*

COVENANT (292) [COVENANT-BREAKERS, COVENANTED, COVENANTS]
Ge 6:18 with thee will I establish my **c**; and 1285
9: 9 behold I establish my **c** with you and 1285
9:11 I will establish my **c** with you; neither shall 1285
9:12 This *is* the token of the **c** which I make 1285
9:13 it shall be for a token of a **c** between me 1285
9:15 I will remember my **c**, which *is* between me 1285
9:16 that I may remember the everlasting **c** 1285
9:17 said unto Noah, This *is* the token of the **c**, 1285
15:18 In the same day the LORD made a **c** with 1285
17: 2 I will make my **c** between me and thee, 1285
17: 4 my **c** *is* with thee, and thou shalt be a father 1285
17: 7 I will establish my **c** between me and thee 1285
17: 7 in their generations for an everlasting **c**, 1285
17: 9 Thou shalt keep my **c** therefore, thou, and 1285
17:10 This *is* my **c**, which ye shall keep, 1285
17:11 it shall be a token of the **c** betwixt me and 1285
17:13 my **c** shall be in your flesh for an 1285
17:13 shall be in your flesh for an everlasting **c**. 1285
17:14 off from his people; he hath broken my **c**. 1285
17:19 I will establish my **c** with him for an 1285
17:19 my covenant with him for an everlasting **c**, 1285
17:21 my **c** will I establish with Isaac, 1285
21:27 and both of them made a **c**. 1285
21:32 Thus they made a **c** at Beer-sheba: then 1285
26:28 and thee, and let us make a **c** with thee; 1285
31:44 come thou, let us make a **c**, I and thou; 1285
Ex 2:24 God remembered his **c** with Abraham, 1285
6: 4 I have also established my **c** with them, 1285
6: 5 in bondage; and I have remembered my **c**. 1285
19: 5 keep my **c**, then ye shall be a peculiar 1285
23:32 Thou shalt make no **c** with them, nor with 1285
24: 7 he took the book of the **c**, and read in 1285
24: 8 and said, Behold the blood of the **c**, 1285
31:16 their generations, *for* a perpetual **c**. 1285
34:10 he said, Behold, I make a **c**: before all thy 1285
34:12 lest thou make a **c** with the inhabitants of 1285
34:15 Lest thou make a **c** with the inhabitants of 1285
34:27 of these words I have made a **c** with thee 1285
34:28 he wrote upon the tables the words of the **c**, 1285
Lev 2:13 neither shalt thou suffer the salt of the **c** of 1285
24: 8 the children of Israel *by* an everlasting **c**. 1285
26: 9 multiply you, and establish my **c** with you. 1285
26:15 my commandments, *but* that ye break my **c**: 1285
26:25 that shall avenge the quarrel of *my* **c**: 1285
26:42 will I remember my **c** with Jacob, and 1285
26:42 also my **c** with Isaac, and also my covenant 1285
26:42 also my **c** with Abraham will I remember; 1285
26:44 them utterly, and to break my **c** with them: 1285
26:45 I will for their sakes remember the **c** of 1285
Nu 10:33 the ark of the **c** of the LORD went before 1285
14:44 nevertheless the ark of the **c** of the LORD, 1285
18:19 it *is* a **c** of salt for ever before the LORD 1285
25:12 Behold, I give unto him my **c** of peace: 1285
25:13 *even* the **c** of an everlasting priesthood; 1285
Dt 4:13 he declared unto you his **c**, which he 1285
4:23 lest ye forget the **c** of the LORD your 1285
4:31 nor forget the **c** of thy fathers which he 1285
5: 2 The LORD our God made a **c** with us in 1285
5: 3 The LORD made not this **c** with our 1285
7: 2 thou shalt make no **c** with them, nor shew 1285
7: 9 which keepeth **c** and mercy with them that 1285
7:12 LORD thy God shall keep unto thee the **c** 1285
8:18 that he may establish his **c** which he sware 1285
9: 9 *even* the tables of the **c** which the LORD 1285
9:11 two tables of stone, *even* the tables of the **c**. 1285
9:15 the two tables of the **c** *were* in my two 1285
10: 8 to bear the ark of the **c** of the LORD, 1285
17: 2 the LORD thy God, in transgressing his **c**, 1285
29: 1 These *are* the words of the **c**, which 1285
29: 1 beside the **c** which he made with them in 1285
29: 9 Keep therefore the words of this **c**, and 1285
29:12 That thou shouldest enter into **c** with 1285
29:14 Neither with you only do I make this **c** 1285
29:21 according to all the curses of the **c** that are 1285
29:25 Because they have forsaken the **c** of 1285
31: 9 which bare the ark of the **c** of the LORD, 1285
31:16 break my **c** which I have made with them. 1285
31:20 and provoke me, and break my **c**. 1285
31:25 which bare the ark of the **c** of the LORD, 1285
31:26 put it in the side of the ark of the **c** of 1285
33: 9 have observed thy word, and kept thy **c**. 1285
Jos 3: 3 When ye see the ark of the **c** of the LORD 1285
3: 6 Take up the ark of the **c**, and pass over 1285
3: 6 they took up the ark of the **c**, and 1285
3: 8 the priests that bear the ark of the **c**, 1285
3:11 Behold, the ark of the **c**, *even* the Lord of 1285
3:14 the priests bearing the ark *of* the **c** before 1285
3:17 the priests that bare the ark *of* the **c** of 1285
4: 7 off before the ark of the **c** of the LORD; 1285
4: 9 priests which bare the ark of the **c** stood: 1285
4:18 when the priests that bare the ark of the **c** of 1285
6: 6 Take up the ark of the **c**, and let seven 1285
6: 8 the ark of the **c** of the LORD followed 1285
7:11 they have also transgressed my **c** which I 1285
7:15 he hath transgressed the **c** of the LORD, 1285
8:33 which bare the ark of the **c** of the LORD, 1285
23:16 When ye have transgressed the **c** of 1285
24:25 So Joshua made a **c** with the people that 1285
Jdg 2: 1 I said, I will never break my **c** with you. 1285
2:20 my **c** which I commanded their fathers, 1285
20:27 (for the ark of the **c** of God *was* there in 1285
1Sa 4: 3 Let us fetch the ark of the **c** of the LORD 1285
4: 4 the ark of the **c** of the LORD of hosts, 1285
4: 4 *were* there with the ark of the **c** of God. 1285
4: 5 when the ark of the **c** of the LORD came 1285
11: 1 Make a **c** with us, and we will serve thee. 1285
11: 2 On this *condition* will I make *a* **c** with you, NIH
18: 3 Jonathan and David made a **c**, because 1285
20: 8 for thou hast brought thy servant into a **c** of 1285
20:16 So Jonathan made *a* **c** with the house of NIH
23:18 they two made a **c** before the LORD: and 1285
2Sa 15:24 with him, bearing the ark of the **c** of God: 1285
23: 5 yet he hath made with me an everlasting **c**, 1285
1Ki 3:15 stood before the ark of the **c** of the LORD, 1285
6:19 to set there the ark of the **c** of the LORD. 1285
8: 1 that *they* might bring up the ark of the **c** of 1285
8: 6 the priests brought in the ark of the **c** of 1285
8: 9 when the LORD made *a* **c** with NIH
8:21 wherein *is* the **c** of the LORD, which he 1285
8:23 who keepest **c** and mercy with thy servants 1285
11:11 thou hast not kept my **c** and my statutes, 1285
19:10 the children of Israel have forsaken thy **c**, 1285
19:14 the children of Israel have forsaken thy **c**, 1285
20:34 *Ahab,* I will send thee away with *this* **c**. 1285
20:34 So he made a **c** with him, and sent him 1285
2Ki 11: 4 made a **c** with them, and took an oath of 1285
11:17 Jehoiada made a **c** between the LORD 1285
13:23 because of his **c** with Abraham, Isaac, and 1285
17:15 his **c** that he made with their fathers, and 1285
17:35 With whom the LORD had made a **c**, and 1285
17:38 the **c** that I have made with you ye shall not 1285
18:12 transgressed his **c**, *and* all that Moses 1285
23: 2 **c** which was found in the house of 1285
23: 3 made a **c** before the LORD, to walk after 1285
23: 3 to perform the words of this **c** that were 1285
23: 3 this book. And all the people stood to the **c**. 1285
23:21 as it is written in the book of this **c**. 1285
1Ch 11: 3 David made a **c** with them in Hebron 1285
15:25 went to bring up the ark of the **c** of 1285
15:26 that bare the ark of the **c** of the LORD, 1285
15:28 Thus all Israel brought up the ark of the **c** 1285
15:29 *as* the ark of the **c** of the LORD came to 1285
16: 6 continually before the ark of the **c** of God. 1285
16:15 Be ye mindful always of his **c**; the word 1285
16:16 *Even of the* **c** which he made with NIH
16:17 for a law, *and* to Israel *for* an everlasting **c**, 1285
16:37 So he left there before the ark of the **c** of 1285
17: 1 the ark of the **c** of the LORD *remaineth* 1285
22:19 to bring the ark of the **c** of the LORD, and 1285
28: 2 of rest for the ark of the **c** of the LORD, 1285
28:18 and covered the ark of the **c** of the LORD. 1285
2Ch 5: 2 to bring up the ark of the **c** of the LORD 1285
5: 7 the priests brought in the ark of the **c** of 1285
5:10 when the LORD made *a* **c** with NIH

2Ch 6:11 put the ark, wherein *is* the **c** of the LORD, 1285
6:14 which keepest **c**, and *shewest* mercy unto 1285
13: 5 *even* to him and to his sons *by* a **c** of salt? 1285
15:12 they entered into a **c** to seek the LORD 1285
21: 7 of the **c** that he had made with David, 1285
23: 1 the son of Zichri, into **c** with him. 1285
23: 3 all the congregation made a **c** with the king 1285
23:16 Jehoiada made a **c** between him, and 1285
29:10 Now *it is* in mine heart to make a **c** with 1285
34:30 **c** that was found *in* the house of 1285
34:31 made a **c** before the LORD, to walk after 1285
34:31 to perform the words of the **c** which are 1285
34:32 of Jerusalem did according to the **c** of God, 1285
Ezr 10: 3 let us make a **c** with our God to put away 1285
Ne 1: 5 that keepeth **c** and mercy for them that love 1285
9: 8 madest a **c** with him to give the land of 1285
9:32 the terrible God, who keepest **c** and mercy, 1285
9:38 because of all this we **make a** sure **c**, and 3772
13:29 the **c** of the priesthood, and of the Levites. 1285
Job 31: 1 I made a **c** with mine eyes; why then 1285
41: 4 Will he make a **c** with thee? wilt thou take 1285
Ps 25:10 truth unto such as keep his **c** and 1285
25:14 that fear him; and he will shew them his **c**. 1285
44:17 neither have we dealt falsely in thy **c**. 1285
50: 5 those that have made a **c** with me by 1285
50:16 *that* thou shouldest take my **c** in thy mouth? 1285
55:20 be at peace with him: he hath broken his **c**. 1285
74:20 Have respect unto the **c**: for the dark places 1285
78:10 They kept not the **c** of God, and refused to 1285
78:37 neither were they stedfast in his **c**. 1285
89: 3 I have made a **c** with my chosen, I have 1285
89:28 and my **c** *shall* stand fast with him. 1285
89:34 My **c** will I not break, nor alter the thing 1285
89:39 Thou hast made void the **c** of thy servant: 1285
103:18 To such as keep his **c**, and to those that 1285
105: 8 He hath remembered his **c** for ever, 1285
105: 9 Which *c* he made with Abraham, and NIH
105:10 for a law, *and* to Israel *for* an everlasting **c**: 1285
106:45 he remembered for them his **c**, and 1285
111: 5 fear him: he will ever be mindful of his **c**. 1285
111: 9 he hath commanded his **c** for ever: holy and 1285
132:12 If thy children will keep my **c** and 1285
Pr 2:17 her youth, and forgetteth the **c** of her God. 1285
Isa 24: 5 the ordinance, broken the everlasting **c**. 1285
28:15 We have made a **c** with death, and with hell 1285
28:18 your **c** with death shall be disannulled, and 1285
33: 8 he hath broken the **c**, he hath despised 1285
42: 6 and give thee for a **c** of the people, 1285
49: 8 and give thee for a **c** of the people, 1285
54:10 neither shall the **c** of my peace be removed, 1285
55: 3 I will make an everlasting **c** with you, 1285
56: 4 that please me, and take hold of my **c**; 1285
56: 6 from polluting it, and taketh hold of my **c**; 1285
57: 8 thy bed, and made thee *a c* with them; NIH
59:21 As for me, this *is* my **c** with them, saith 1285
61: 8 and I will make an everlasting **c** with them. 1285
Jer 3:16 no more, The ark of the **c** of the LORD: 1285
11: 2 Hear ye the words of this **c**, and speak unto 1285
11: 3 man that obeyeth not the words of this **c**, 1285
11: 6 Hear ye the words of this **c**, and do them. 1285
11: 8 will bring upon them all the words of this **c**, 1285
11:10 the house of Judah have broken my **c** which 1285
14:21 remember, break not thy **c** with us. 1285
22: 9 Because they have forsaken the **c** of 1285
31:31 that I will make a new **c** with the house of 1285
31:32 Not according to the **c** that I made with 1285
31:32 which my **c** they brake, although I was a 1285
31:33 this *shall be* the **c** that I will make with 1285
32:40 And I will make an everlasting **c** with them, 1285
33:20 If you can break my **c** of the day, and my 1285
33:20 my **c** of the night, and that there should not 1285
33:21 *Then* may also my **c** be broken with David 1285
33:25 If my **c** *be* not with day and night, *and if* I 1285
34: 8 after that the king Zedekiah had made a **c** 1285
34:10 all the people, which had entered into the **c**, 1285
34:13 I made a **c** with your fathers in the day that 1285
34:15 ye had made a **c** before me in the house 1285
34:18 give the men that have transgressed my **c**, 1285
34:18 of the **c** which they had made before me, 1285
50: 5 *in* a perpetual **c** *that* shall not be forgotten. 1285
Eze 16: 8 unto thee, and entered into a **c** with thee, 1285
16:59 hast despised the oath in breaking the **c**. 1285
16:60 Nevertheless I will remember my **c** with 1285
16:60 I will establish unto thee an everlasting **c**. 1285
16:61 unto thee for daughters, but not by thy **c**. 1285
16:62 I will establish my **c** with thee; and 1285
17:13 made a **c** with him, and hath taken an oath 1285
17:14 *but* that by keeping of his **c** it might stand. 1285
17:15 doeth such *things?* or shall he break the **c**, 1285
17:16 oath he despised, and whose **c** he brake, 1285
17:18 he despised the oath by breaking the **c**, 1285
17:19 and my **c** that he hath broken, 1285
20:37 and I will bring you into the bond of the **c**: 1285
34:25 I will make with them a **c** of peace, and 1285
37:26 Moreover I will make a **c** of peace with 1285
37:26 it shall be an everlasting **c** with them: 1285
44: 7 they have broken my **c** because of all your 1285
Da 9: 4 keeping the **c** and mercy to them that love 1285
9:27 he shall confirm the **c** with many *for* one 1285
11:22 be broken; yea also, the prince of the **c**. 1285
11:28 his heart *shall be* against the holy **c**; and 1285
11:30 and have indignation against the holy **c**: 1285
11:30 with them that forsake the holy **c**. 1285
11:32 such as do wickedly against the **c** shall he 1285
Hos 2:18 in that day will I make a **c** for them with 1285
6: 7 they like men have transgressed the **c**: 1285
8: 1 because they have transgressed my **c**, and 1285
10: 4 swearing falsely in making a **c**: 1285
12: 1 they do make a **c** with the Assyrians, and 1285
Am 1: 9 and remembered not the brotherly **c**: 1285
Zec 9:11 by the blood of thy **c** I have sent forth thy 1285
11:10 that *I* might break my **c** which I had made 1285
Mal 2: 4 that my **c** might be with Levi, saith 1285
2: 5 My **c** was with him of life and peace; and 1285
2: 8 ye have corrupted the **c** of Levi, saith 1285
2:10 by profaning the **c** of our fathers? 1285
2:14 *is* she thy companion, and the wife of thy **c**. 1285
3: 1 even the messenger of the **c**, whom ye 1285
Lk 1:72 to our fathers, and to remember his holy **c**; *1242*
Ac 3:25 of the **c** which God made with our fathers, *1242*
7: 8 And he gave him the **c** of circumcision: and *1242*
Ro 11:27 For this *is* my **c** unto them, when I shall *1242*
Gal 3:15 Though *it be* but a man's **c**, *yet if it be* *1242*
3:17 And this I say, *that* the **c**, that was *1242*
Heb 8: 6 much also he is the mediator of a better **c**, *1242*
8: 7 For if that first *c* had been faultless, *then* NIG
8: 8 when I will make a new **c** with the house of *1242*
8: 9 Not according to the **c** that I made with *1242*
8: 9 because they continued not in my **c**, and I *1242*
8:10 For this *is* the **c** that I will make with *1242*
8:13 A new *c*, he hath made the first old. NIG
9: 1 Then verily the first *c* had also ordinances NIG
9: 4 the ark of the **c** overlaid round about with *1242*
9: 4 rod that budded, and the tables of the **c**; *1242*
10:16 This *is* the **c** that I will make with them *1242*
10:29 and hath counted the blood of the **c**, *1242*
12:24 And to Jesus the mediator of the new **c**, and *1242*
13:20 through the blood of the everlasting **c**, *1242*

COVENANT-BREAKERS (1) [BREAK, COVENANT]

Ro 1:31 Without understanding, **c**, without natural *802*

COVENANTED (4) [COVENANT]

2Ch 7:18 according as I have **c** with David thy father, 3772
Hag 2: 5 *According to* the word that I **c** with you 3772
Mt 26:15 And they **c** with him for thirty pieces of *2476*
Lk 22: 5 they were glad, and **c** to give him money. *4934*

COVENANTS (3) [COVENANT]

Ro 9: 4 and the **c**, and the giving of the law, and *1242*
Gal 4:24 for these are the two **c**; the one from *1242*
Eph 2:12 and strangers from the **c** of promise, *1242*

COVER (72) [COVERED, COVEREDST, COVEREST, COVERETH, COVERING, COVERINGS, COVERS, UNCOVER]

Ex 10: 5 they shall **c** the face of the earth, that *one* 3680
21:33 and not **c** it, and an ox or an ass fall therein; 3680
25:29 and bowls thereof, to **c** withal: 5258
26:13 on this side and on that side, to **c** it. 3680
28:42 thou shalt make them linen breeches to **c** 3680
33:22 will **c** thee with my hand while I pass by: 5526
37:16 and his bowls, and *his* covers to **c** withal, 5258
40: 3 the Testimony, and **c** the ark with the vail. 5526
Lev 13:12 the leprosy **c** all the skin of *him that hath* 3680
16:13 that the cloud of the incense may **c** 3680
17:13 out the blood thereof, and **c** it with dust. 3680
Nu 4: 5 and **c** the ark of Testimony with it: 3680
4: 7 and the bowls, and covers to **c withal**: 5262

C

Nu 4: 8 **c** the same with a covering of badgers' 3680
4: 9 **c** the candlestick of the light, and his lamps, 3680
4:11 **c** it with a covering of badgers' skins, and 3680
4:12 **c** them with a covering of badgers' skins, 3680
22: 5 they **c** the face of the earth, and they abide 3680
Dt 23:13 and **c** that which cometh from thee: 3680
33:12 *the* LORD shall **c** him all the day long, 2653
1Sa 24: 3 *was* a cave; and Saul went in to **c** his feet: 5526
1Ki 7:18 to **c** the chapiters that *were* upon the top, 3680
7:41 to **c** the two bowls of the chapiters which 3680
7:42 to **c** the two bowls of the chapiters that 3680
2Ch 4:12 the two wreaths to **c** the two pommels of 3680
4:13 to **c** the two pommels of the chapiters 3680
Ne 4: 5 **c** not their iniquity, and let not their sin be 3680
Job 16:18 **c** not thou my blood, and let my cry have 3680
21:26 in the dust, and the worms shall **c** them. 3680
22:11 not see; and abundance of waters **c** thee. 3680
38:34 that abundance of waters may **c** thee? 3680
40:22 The shady trees **c** him *with* their shadow; 5526
Ps 91: 4 He shall **c** thee with his feathers, and 5526
104: 9 *that* they turn not again to **c** the earth. 3680
109:29 let them **c** *themselves with* their own 5844
139:11 If I say, Surely the darkness shall **c** me; 7779
140: 9 let the mischief of their own lips **c** them. 3680
Isa 11: 9 of the LORD, as the waters **c** the sea. 3680
14:11 is spread under thee, and the worms **c** thee. 4374
22:17 and will **surely** **c** thee. 5844+5844
26:21 her blood, and shall no more **c** her slain. 3680
30: 1 that **c** *with* a covering, but not of my Spirit, 5258
58: 7 when thou seest the naked, that thou **c** him; 3680
59: 6 neither shall they **c** themselves with their 3680
60: 2 the darkness shall **c** the earth, and 3680
60: 6 The multitude of camels shall **c** thee, 3680
Jer 46: 8 he saith, I will go up, *and* will **c** the earth; 3680
Eze 7:18 with sackcloth, and horror shall **c** them; 3680
12: 6 thou shalt **c** thy face, that thou see not 3680
12:12 he shall **c** his face, that he see not 3680
24: 7 it not upon the ground, to **c** it with dust; 3680
24:17 **c** not *thy* lips, and eat not the bread of men. 5844
24:22 ye shall not **c** *your* lips, nor eat the bread of 5844
26:10 of his horses their dust shall **c** thee: 3680
26:19 upon thee, and great waters shall **c** thee; 3680
30:18 a cloud shall **c** her, and her daughters shall 3680
32: 7 I will **c** the heaven, and make the stars 3680
32: 7 I will **c** the sun with a cloud, and the moon 3680
37: 6 **c** you **with** skin, and put breath in you, and 7159
38: 9 thou shalt be like a cloud to **c** the land, 3680
38:16 people of Israel, as a cloud to **c** the land; 3680
Hos 2: 9 and my flax *given* to **c** her nakedness. 3680
10: 8 they shall say to the mountains, **C** us; and 3680
Ob 1:10 thy brother Jacob shame shall **c** thee, 3680
Mic 3: 7 yea, they shall all **c** their lips; for *there is* no 5844
7:10 and shame shall **c** her which said unto me, 3680
Hab 2:14 of the LORD, as the waters **c** the sea. 3680
2:17 For the violence of Lebanon shall **c** thee, 3680
Mk 14:65 and to **c** his face, and to buffet him, and *4028*
Lk 23:30 Fall on us; and to the hills, **C** us. *2572*
1Co 11: 7 For a man indeed ought not to **c** *his* head, *2619*
1Pe 4: 8 for charity shall **c** the multitude of sins. *2572*

COVERED (105) [COVER]
Ge 7:19 that *were* under the whole heaven, were **c**. 3680
7:20 waters prevail; and the mountains were **c**. 3680
9:23 and **c** the nakedness of their father; 3680
24:65 therefore she took a vail, and **c** herself. 3680
38:14 **c** her with a vail, and wrapped herself, and 3680
38:15 to be a harlot; because she had **c** her face. 3680
Ex 8: 6 the frogs came up, and **c** the land of Egypt. 3680
10:15 For they **c** the face of the whole earth, so 3680
14:28 **c** the chariots, and the horsemen, and all 3680
15: 5 The depths have **c** them: they sank into 3680
15:10 didst blow with thy wind, the sea **c** them: 3680
16:13 at even the quails came up, and **c** the camp: 3680
24:15 up into the mount, and a cloud **c** the mount. 3680
24:16 mount Sinai, and the cloud **c** it six days: 3680
37: 9 *and* **c** with their wings over the mercy seat, 5526
40:21 and **c** the ark of the Testimony; 5526
40:34 a cloud **c** the tent of the congregation, and 3680
Lev 13:13 behold, *if* the leprosy have **c** all his flesh, 3680
Nu 4:20 not go in to see when the holy *things* are **c**, 1104
7: 3 six **c** wagons, and twelve oxen; 6632
9:15 the cloud **c** the tabernacle, *namely,* the tent 3680
9:16 the cloud **c** it *by day,* and the appearance of 3680
16:42 the cloud **c** it, and the glory of the LORD 3680
Dt 32:15 thou art **c** *with fatness;* then he forsook God 3780
Jos 24: 7 and brought the sea upon them, and **c** them; 3680
Jdg 4:18 her into the tent, she **c** him with a mantle. 3680
4:19 of milk, and gave him drink, and **c** him. 3680
1Sa 19:13 *hair for* his bolster, and **c** *it* with a cloth. 3680
28:14 man cometh up; and he *is* **c** **with** a mantle. 5844
2Sa 15:30 and had his head **c**, and he went barefoot: 2645
15:30 all the people that *was* with him **c** every 2645
19: 4 the king **c** his face, and the king cried *with* 3813
1Ki 1: 1 they **c** him with clothes, but he gat no heat. 3680
6: 9 **c** the house with beams and boards of 5603
6:15 *and* he **c** *them* on the inside with wood, and 6823
6:15 **c** the floor of the house with planks of fir. 6823
6:20 and *so* **c** the altar *which was of* cedar. 6823
6:35 **c** *them* with gold fitted upon the carved 6823
7: 3 *it was* **c** with cedar above upon the beams, 5603
7: 7 *it was* **c** with cedar from one side of 5603
8: 7 the cherubims **c** the ark and the staves 5526
2Ki 19: 1 **c** himself with sackcloth, and went *into* 3680
19: 2 the elders of the priests, **c** with sackcloth, 3680
1Ch 28:18 **c** the ark of the covenant of the LORD. 5526
2Ch 5: 8 the cherubims **c** the ark and the staves 3680
Ne 3:15 and **c** it, and set up the doors thereof, 2926
Est 6:12 his house mourning, and having his head **c**. 2645
7: 8 of the king's mouth, they **c** Haman's face. 2645
Job 23:17 *neither* hath he **c** the darkness from my 3680
31:33 If I **c** my transgressions as Adam, by hiding 3680
Ps 32: 1 transgression *is* forgiven, whose sin *is* **c**. 3680
44:15 and the shame of my face hath **c** me, 3680
44:19 and **c** us with the shadow of death. 3680
65:13 the valleys also are **c** **over** with corn; 5848
68:13 *yet shall ye be as* the wings of a dove **c** 2645
69: 7 borne reproach; shame hath **c** my face. 3680
71:13 let them be **c** *with* reproach and 5844
80:10 The hills were **c** *with* the shadow of it, and 3680
85: 2 of thy people, thou hast **c** all their sin. 3680
89:45 thou hast **c** him **with** shame. Selah. 5844
106:11 the waters **c** their enemies: there was not 3680
106:17 up Dathan, and **c** the company of Abiram. 3680
139:13 thou hast **c** me in my mother's womb. 5526
140: 7 thou hast **c** my head in the day of battle. 5526
Pr 24:31 *and* nettles had **c** the face thereof, and 3680
26:23 a wicked heart *are like* a potsherd **c** with 6823
26:26 *Whose* hatred is **c** by deceit, his wickedness 3680
Ecc 6: 4 and his name shall be **c** with darkness. 3680
Isa 6: 2 with twain he **c** his face, and with twain he 3680
6: 2 with twain he **c** his feet, and with twain he 3680
29:10 and your rulers, the seers hath he **c**. 3680
37: 1 **c** himself with sackcloth, and went *into* 3680
37: 2 the elders of the priests **c** with sackcloth, 3680
51:16 have **c** thee in the shadow of mine hand, 3680
61:10 he hath **c** me **with** the robe of 3271
Jer 14: 3 and confounded, and **c** their heads. 2645
14: 4 plowmen were ashamed, they **c** their heads. 2645
51:42 she is **c** with the multitude of the waves 3680
51:51 shame hath **c** our faces: for strangers are 3680
La 2: 1 **c** the daughter of Zion **with a cloud** in his 5743
3:16 with gravel stones, he hath **c** me with ashes. 3728
3:43 Thou hast **c** with anger, and persecuted us: 5526
3:44 Thou hast **c** thyself with a cloud, that *our* 5526
Eze 1:11 one to another, and two **c** their bodies. 3680
1:23 which **c** on this *side,* and every one had 3680
1:23 had two, which **c** on that *side,* their bodies. 3680
16: 8 my skirt over thee, and **c** thy nakedness: 3680
16:10 about with fine linen, and I **c** thee *with* silk. 3680
18: 7 and hath **c** the naked with a garment; 3680
18:16 and hath **c** the naked with a garment, 3680
24: 8 the top of a rock, that *it* should not be **c**. 3680
27: 7 the isles of Elishah was that which **c** thee. 4374
31:15 I **c** the deep for him, and I restrained 3680
37: 8 up upon them, and the skin **c** them above: 7159
41:16 to the windows, and the windows *were* **c**; 3680
Jnh 3: 6 and **c** *him* with sackcloth, and sat in ashes. 3680
3: 8 let man and beast be **c** with sackcloth, and 3680
Hab 3: 3 His glory **c** the heavens, and the earth was 3680
Mt 8:24 insomuch that the ship was **c** with *2572*
10:26 for there is nothing **c**, that shall not be *2572*
Lk 12: 2 For there is nothing **c**, that shall not be *4780*
Ro 4: 7 are forgiven, and whose sins are **c**. *1943*
1Co 11: 4 or prophesying, having *his* head **c**, *2596*
11: 6 For if the woman be not **c**, let her also be *2619*
11: 6 woman to be shorn or shaven, let her be **c**. *2619*

COVEREDST (2) [COVER]
Ps 104: 6 Thou c it *with* the deep as *with* a garment: 3680
Eze 16:18 tookest thy broidered garments, and c them: 3680

COVEREST (2) [COVER]
Dt 22:12 of thy vesture, wherewith thou c *thyself.* 3680
Ps 104: 2 Who c *thyself with* light as *with* a garment: 5844

COVERETH (27) [COVER]
Ex 29:13 thou shalt take all the fat that c the inwards, 3680
29:22 the fat that c the inwards, and the caul 3680
Lev 3: 3 the fat that c the inwards, and all the fat that 3680
3: 9 the fat that c the inwards, and all the fat that 3680
3:14 the fat that c the inwards, and all the fat that 3680
4: 8 the fat that c the inwards, and all the fat that 3680
7: 3 the rump, and the fat that c the inwards, 3680
9:19 that which c *the inwards,* and the kidneys, 4374
Nu 22:11 out of Egypt, which c the face of the earth: 3680
Jdg 3:24 Surely he c his feet in *his* summer chamber. 5526
Job 9:24 he c the faces of the judges thereof; if not, 3680
15:27 Because he c his face with his fatness, and 3680
36:30 light upon it, and c the bottom of the sea. 3680
36:32 With clouds he c the light; and 3680
Ps 73: 6 as a chain; violence c them *as* a garment. 5848
109:19 Let it be unto him as the garment *which* c 5844
147: 8 Who c the heaven with clouds, 3680
Pr 10: 6 but violence c the mouth of the wicked. 3680
10:11 but violence c the mouth of the wicked. 3680
10:12 Hatred stirreth up strifes: but love c all sins. 3680
12:16 but a prudent *man* c shame. 3680
17: 9 He that c a transgression seeketh love; but 3680
28:13 He that c his sins shall not prosper: but 3680
Jer 3:25 down in our shame, and our confusion c us: 3680
Eze 28:14 Thou *art* the anointed cherub that c; and 5526
Mal 2:16 for *one* c violence with his garment, 3680
Lk 8:16 c it with a vessel, or putteth *it* under a bed; *2572*

COVERING (48) [COVER]
Ge 8:13 Noah removed the c of the ark, and looked, 4372
20:16 behold, he *is* to thee a c of the eyes, unto all 3682
Ex 22:27 For that *is* his c only, it *is* his raiment for 3682
25:20 c the mercy seat with their wings, and 5526
26: 7 *of* goats' *hair* to be a c upon the tabernacle: 168
26:14 thou shalt make a c for the tent *of* rams' 4372
26:14 dyed red, and a c above of badgers' skins. 4372
35:11 his tent, and his c, his taches, and 4372
35:12 *with* the mercy seat, and the vail of the c, 4539
36:19 he made a c for the tent *of* rams' skins dyed 4372
36:19 and a c of badgers' skins above *that.* 4372
39:34 the c of rams' skins dyed red, and 4372
39:34 the c of badgers' skins, and the vail of 4372
39:34 of badgers' skins, and the vail of the c, 4539
40:19 and put the c of the tent above upon it; 4372
40:21 set up the vail of the c, and covered the ark 4539
Lev 13:45 he shall **put a c** upon *his* upper lip, and 5844
Nu 3:25 the c thereof, and the hanging for the door 4372
4: 5 they shall take down the c vail, and 4539
4: 6 shall put thereon the c of badgers' skins, 3681
4: 8 cover the same with a c of badgers' skins, 4372
4:10 all the vessels thereof within a c of 4372
4:11 cover it with a c of badgers' skins, and 4372
4:12 cover them with a c of badgers' skins, and 4372
4:14 they shall spread upon it a c of badgers' 3681
4:15 his sons have made an end of c 3680
4:25 his c, and the covering of the badgers' skins 4372
4:25 the c of the badgers' skins that *is* above 4372
16:38 let them make them broad plates *for* a c of 6826
16:39 they were made broad *plates for* a c of 6826
19:15 which hath no c bound upon it, *is* unclean. 6781
2Sa 17:19 and spread a c over the well's mouth, 4539
Job 22:14 Thick clouds *are* a c to him, that he seeth 5643
24: 7 that *they have* no c in the cold. 3682
26: 6 before him, and destruction hath no c. 3682
31:19 for want of clothing, or *any* poor without c; 3682
Ps 105:39 He spread a cloud for a c; and fire to give 4539
SS 3:10 bottom thereof *of* gold, the c of it *of* purple, 4817
Isa 22: 8 he discovered the c of Judah, and thou didst 4539
25: 7 the face of the c cast over all people, 3875
28:20 the c narrower than that *he* can wrap 4541
30: 1 that cover *with* a c, but not of my Spirit, 4541
30:22 Ye shall defile also the c of thy graven 6826
50: 3 and I make sackcloth their c. 3682
Eze 28:13 every precious stone *was* thy c, the sardius, 4540
28:16 I will destroy thee, O c cherub, from 5526
Mal 2:13 c the altar of the LORD *with* tears, *with* 3680
1Co 11:15 to her: for *her* hair is given her for a c. *4018*

COVERINGS (2) [COVER]
Pr 7:16 I have deckt my bed *with* c **of tapestry,** 4765
31:22 She maketh herself c **of tapestry;** 4765

COVERS (3) [COVER]
Ex 25:29 and c thereof, and bowls thereof, 7184
37:16 and his bowls, and *his* c to cover withal, 7184
Nu 4: 7 and the bowls, and c to cover withal: 7184

COVERT (9)
1Sa 25:20 that she came down by the c of the hill, and 5643
2Ki 16:18 the c for the sabbath that they had built in 4329
Job 38:40 *their* dens, *and* abide in the c to lie in wait? 5521
40:21 shady trees, in the c of the reed, and fens. 5643
Ps 61: 4 I will trust in the c of thy wings. Selah. 5643
Isa 4: 6 and for a c from storm and from rain. 4563
16: 4 be thou a c to them from the face of 5643
32: 2 from the wind, and a c from the tempest; 5643
Jer 25:38 He hath forsaken his c, as the lion: for their 5520

COVET (8) [COVETED, COVETETH, COVETOUS, COVETOUSNESS]
Ex 20:17 Thou shalt not c thy neighbour's house, 2530
20:17 thou shalt not c thy neighbour's wife, 2530
Dt 5:21 neither shalt thou c thy neighbour's house, 183
Mic 2: 2 they c fields, and take *them* by violence; 2530
Ro 7: 7 except the law had said, Thou shalt not c. *1937*
13: 9 not bear false witness, Thou shalt not c; *1937*
1Co 12:31 But c **earnestly** the best gifts: and yet shew *2206*
14:39 c to prophesy, and forbid not to speak with *2206*

COVETED (3) [COVET]
Jos 7:21 then I c them, and took them; 2530
Ac 20:33 I have c no *man's* silver, or gold, or *1937*
1Ti 6:10 which while some c **after,** they have erred *3713*

COVETETH (2) [COVET]
Pr 21:26 He c **greedily** all the day long: but 183+8378
Hab 2: 9 Woe to him that c an evil covetousness to 1214

COVETOUS (9) [COVET]
Ps 10: 3 blesseth the c, *whom* the LORD 1214
Lk 16:14 who were c, heard all these *things:* and *5366*
1Co 5:10 or with the c, or extortioners, or *4123*
5:11 or c, or an idolater, or a railer, or *4123*
6:10 Nor thieves, nor c, nor drunkards, *4123*
Eph 5: 5 nor unclean *person,* nor c **man** who is an *4123*
1Ti 3: 3 filthy lucre; but patient, not a brawler, **not c;** *866*
2Ti 3: 2 c, boasters, proud, blasphemers, *5366*
2Pe 2:14 heart they have exercised with c **practices;** *4124*

COVETOUSNESS (19) [COVET]
Ex 18:21 such as fear God, men of truth, hating c; 1215
Ps 119:36 my heart unto thy testimonies, and not to c. 1215
Pr 28:16 *but* he that hateth c shall prolong *his* days. 1215
Isa 57:17 For the iniquity of his c was I wroth, and 1215
Jer 6:13 of them every one is **given to c;** 1214+1215
8:10 least even unto the greatest is given to c, 1215
22:17 and thine heart *are* not but for thy c, 1215
51:13 thine end is come, *and* the measure of thy c. 1215
Eze 33:31 *but* their heart goeth after their c. 1215
Hab 2: 9 Woe to him that coveteth an evil c to his 1215
Mk 7:22 Thefts, c, wickedness, deceit, *4124*
Lk 12:15 unto them, Take heed, and beware of c: *4124*
Ro 1:29 fornication, wickedness, c, maliciousness; *4124*
2Co 9: 5 as *a matter of* bounty, and not as *of* c. *4124*
Eph 5: 3 But fornication, and all uncleanness, or c, *4124*
Col 3: 5 and c, which is idolatry: *4124*
1Th 2: 5 as ye know, nor a cloke of c; *4124*
Heb 13: 5 *Let your* conversation *be* **without c;** *and* *866*
2Pe 2: 3 And through c shall they with feigned *4124*

COW (6) [COW'S]
Lev 22:28 *whether it be* c or ewe, ye shall not kill it 7794
Nu 18:17 the firstling of a c, or the firstling of a 7794
Job 21:10 their c calveth, and casteth not her calf. 6510
Isa 7:21 *that* a man shall nourish a **young** c, 1241+5697
11: 7 the c and the bear shall feed; their young 6510
Am 4: 3 every c *at that which is* before her; NIH

COW'S (1) [COW]
Eze 4:15 I have given thee c dung for man's dung, 1241

C

C

COWS THAT HAVE CALVED See MILCH

COZ (1)
1Ch 4: 8 C begat Anub, and Zobebah, and 6976

COZBI (2)
Nu 25:15 Midianitish woman that was slain *was* C, 3579
25:18 in the matter of C, the daughter of a prince 3579

COZEBA See CHOZEBA

CRACKLING (1)
Ecc 7: 6 For as the c of thorns under a pot, so *is* 6963

CRACKNELS (1)
1Ki 14: 3 and c, and a cruse of honey, and go to him: 5350

CRAFT (6) [CRAFTINESS, CRAFTSMAN, CRAFTSMEN, CRAFTY, WITCHCRAFT, WITCHCRAFTS]
Da 8:25 through his policy also he shall cause c to 4820
Mk 14: 1 sought how they might take him by c, *1388*
Ac 18: 3 And because *he* was of the **same** c, *3673*
19:25 ye know that by this c we have our wealth. *2039*
19:27 So *that* not only this our c is in danger to be *3313*
Rev 18:22 of whatsoever c *he be,* shall be found any *5078*

CRAFTINESS (5) [CRAFT]
Job 5:13 He taketh the wise in their own c: and 6193
Lk 20:23 But he perceived their c, and said unto *3834*
1Co 3:19 He taketh the wise in their own c. *3834*
2Co 4: 2 not walking in c, nor handling the word of *3834*
Eph 4:14 by the sleight of men, and **cunning** c, *3834*

CRAFTSMAN (2) [CRAFT, MAN]
Dt 27:15 the work of the hands of the c, and 2796
Rev 18:22 and no c, of whatsoever craft *he be,* shall be *5079*

CRAFTSMEN (7) [CRAFT, MAN]
2Ki 24:14 thousand captives, and all the c and smiths: 2796
24:16 c and smiths a thousand, all *that were* 2796
1Ch 4:14 of the valley of Charashim; for they were c. 2796
Ne 11:35 Lod, and Ono, the valley of c. 2791
Hos 13: 2 all of it the work of the c: 2796
Ac 19:24 for Diana, brought no small gain unto the c; *5079*
19:38 if Demetrius, and the c which are with him, *5079*

CRAFTY (4) [CRAFT]
Job 5:12 He disappointeth the devices of the c, so 6175
15: 5 and thou choosest the tongue of the c. 6175
Ps 83: 3 They have **taken** c counsel against thy 6191
2Co 12:16 nevertheless, being c, I caught you with *3835*

CRAG (1)
Job 39:28 upon the c of the rock, and the strong place. 8127

CRANE (2)
Isa 38:14 Like a c *or* a swallow, so did I chatter: I did 5483
Jer 8: 7 the turtle and the c and the swallow observe 5483

CRASHING (1)
Zep 1:10 the second, and a great c from the hills. 7667

CRAVED (1) [CRAVETH]
Mk 15:43 boldly unto Pilate, and c the body of Jesus. *154*

CRAVETH (1) [CRAVED]
Pr 16:26 for himself; for his mouth c it of him. 404

CREATE (8) [CREATED, CREATETH, CREATION, CREATOR, CREATURE, CREATURES]
Ps 51:10 C in me a clean heart, O God; and renew a 1254
Isa 4: 5 the LORD will c upon every dwelling 1254
45: 7 I form the light, and c darkness: I make 1254
45: 7 I make peace, and c evil: I the LORD do 1254
57:19 I c the fruit of the lips; Peace, peace to *him* 1254
65:17 behold, I c new heavens and a new earth: 1254
65:18 and rejoice for ever *in that* which I c: 1254
65:18 I c Jerusalem a rejoicing, and her people a 1254

CREATED (45) [CREATE]
Ge 1: 1 In the beginning God c the heaven and 1254
1:21 God c great whales, and every living 1254
1:27 So God c man in his own image, in 1254
1:27 own image, in the image of God c he him; 1254
1:27 created he him; male and female c he them. 1254
2: 3 had rested from all his work which God c 1254
2: 4 and of the earth when they were c, 1254
5: 1 In the day that God c man, in the likeness 1254
5: 2 Male and female c he them; and 1254
5: 2 name Adam, in the day when they were c. 1254
6: 7 I will destroy man whom I have c from 1254
Dt 4:32 since the day that God c man upon 1254
Ps 89:12 The north and the south thou hast c them: 1254
102:18 the people which *shall be* c shall praise 1254
104:30 Thou sendest forth thy spirit, they are c: 1254
148: 5 for he commanded, and they were c. 1254
Isa 40:26 behold who hath c these *things,* that 1254
41:20 and the Holy One of Israel hath c it. 1254
42: 5 he that c the heavens, and stretched them 1254
43: 1 now thus saith the LORD that c thee, 1254
43: 7 for I have c him for my glory, I have 1254
45: 8 spring up together; I the LORD have c it. 1254
45:12 I have made the earth, and c man upon it: I, 1254
45:18 For thus saith the LORD that c 1254
45:18 he hath established it, he c it not in vain, 1254
48: 7 They are c now, and not from 1254
54:16 I have c the smith that bloweth the coals in 1254
54:16 and I have c the waster to destroy. 1254
Jer 31:22 for the LORD hath c a new *thing* in 1254
Eze 21:30 judge thee in the place where thou wast c, 1254
28:13 prepared in thee in the day that thou wast c. 1254
28:15 in thy ways from the day that thou wast c, 1254
Mal 2:10 hath not one God c us? why do we deal 1254
Mk 13:19 of the creation which God c unto this time, *2936*
1Co 11: 9 Neither was the man c for the woman; but *2936*
Eph 2:10 c in Christ Jesus unto good works, *2936*
3: 9 in God, who c all *things* by Jesus Christ: *2936*
4:24 which after God is c in righteousness and *2936*
Col 1:16 For by him were all *things* c, that are in *2936*
1:16 all *things* were c by him, and for him: *2936*
3:10 after the image of him that c him: *2936*
1Ti 4: 3 which God hath c to be received with *2936*
Rev 4:11 for thou hast c all *things,* and for thy *2936*
4:11 and for thy pleasure they are and were c. *2936*
10: 6 who c heaven, and the *things* that therein *2936*

CREATETH (1) [CREATE]
Am 4:13 c the wind, and declareth unto man what *is* 1254

CREATION (6) [CREATE]
Mk 10: 6 But from the beginning of the c God made *2937*
13:19 such as was not from the beginning of the c *2937*
Ro 1:20 For the invisible *things* of him from the c of *2937*
8:22 For we know that the whole c groaneth and *2937*
2Pe 3: 4 as *they were* from the beginning of the c. *2937*
Rev 3:14 true witness, the beginning of the c of God; *2937*

CREATOR (5) [CREATE]
Ecc 12: 1 Remember now thy C in the days of thy 1254
Isa 40:28 the C of the ends of the earth, fainteth not, 1254
43:15 your Holy One, the c of Israel, your King. 1254
Ro 1:25 and served the creature more than the C, *2936*
1Pe 4:19 *to him* in well doing, as unto a faithful C. *2939*

CREATURE (29) [CREATE]
Ge 1:20 abundantly the **moving** c that hath life, 5315
1:21 and every living c that moveth, 5315
1:24 Let the earth bring forth the living c after 5315
2:19 and whatsoever Adam called every living c, 5315
9:10 with every living c that *is* with you, of 5315
9:12 and you and every living c that *is* with you, 5315
9:15 and you and every living c of all flesh; 5315
9:16 every living c of all flesh that *is* upon 5315
Lev 11:46 of every living c that moveth in the waters, 5315
11:46 and of every c that creepeth upon the earth: 5315
Eze 1:20 for the spirit of the **living** c *was* in 2416
1:21 for the spirit of the **living** c *was* in 2416
1:22 **living** c *was* as the colour of the terrible 2416
10:15 This *is* the **living** c that I saw by the river of 2416
10:17 for the spirit of the **living** c *was* in them. 2416
10:20 This *is* the **living** c that I saw under 2416
Mk 16:15 the world, and preach the gospel to every c. *2937*
Ro 1:25 and served the c more than the Creator, *2937*
8:19 For the earnest expectation of the c waiteth *2937*
8:20 For the c was made subject to vanity, *2937*
8:21 Because the c itself also shall be delivered *2937*
8:39 Nor height, nor depth, nor any other c, *2937*
2Co 5:17 if any *man be* in Christ, *he is* a new c: *2937*
Gal 6:15 any *thing,* nor uncircumcision, but a new c. *2937*
Col 1:15 the invisible God, the firstborn of every c: *2937*

Col 1:23 which was preached to every **c** which is *2937*
1Ti 4: 4 For every **c** of God *is* good, and nothing to *2938*
Heb 4:13 Neither is there any **c** *that is* not manifest in *2937*
Rev 5:13 And every **c** which is in heaven, and on *2938*

CREATURES (12) [CREATE]
Isa 13:21 their houses shall be full *of* **doleful c**; and 255
Eze 1: 5 thereof *came* the likeness of four **living c**. 2416
1:13 As for the likeness of the **living c**, 2416
1:13 it went up and down among the **living c**; 2416
1:14 the **living c** ran and returned as 2416
1:15 Now as I beheld the **living c**, behold one 2416
1:15 one wheel upon the earth by the **living c**, 2416
1:19 when the **living c** went, the wheels went by 2416
1:19 when the **living c** were lift up from 2416
3:13 of the **living c** that touched one another, 2416
Jas 1:18 we should be a kind of firstfruits of his **c**. *2938*
Rev 8: 9 And the third *part* of the **c** which were in *2938*

CREDIT; CREDITED; CREDITS See IMPUTE; IMPUTED; IMPUTETH; IMPUTING

CREDITOR (3) [CREDITORS]
Dt 15: 2 Every **c** that lendeth *ought* 1167+3027+4874
2Ki 4: 1 the **c** is come to take unto him my two sons 5383
Lk 7:41 There was a certain **c** which had two *1157*

CREDITORS (1) [CREDITOR]
Isa 50: 1 which of my **c** *is it* to whom I have sold 5383

CREEK (1)
Ac 27:39 but they discovered a certain **c** with a shore, *2859*

CREEP (7) [CREEPETH, CREEPING, CREPT]
Lev 11:20 All fowls that **c**, going upon *all* four, 8318
11:29 the creeping things that **c** upon the earth; 8317
11:31 These *are* unclean to you among all that **c**: 8318
11:42 all creeping things that **c** upon the earth, 8317
Ps 104:20 wherein all the beasts of the forest do **c** 7430
Eze 38:20 all creeping things that **c** upon the earth, 7430
2Ti 3: 6 For of this sort are they which **c** into *1744*

CREEPETH (14) [CREEP]
Ge 1:25 every **thing that c** upon the earth after his 7431
1:26 over every creeping thing that **c** upon 7430
1:30 to every *thing* that **c** upon the earth, 7430
7: 8 and of every *thing* that **c** upon the earth, 7430
7:14 every creeping thing that **c** upon the earth 7430
7:21 of every creeping thing that **c** upon 8317
8:17 of every creeping thing that **c** upon 7430
8:19 *and* whatsoever **c** upon the earth, 7430
Lev 11:41 every creeping thing that **c** upon the earth 8317
11:43 abominable with any creeping thing that **c**, 8317
11:44 *of* creeping thing that **c** upon the earth. 7430
11:46 and of every creature that **c** upon the earth: 8317
20:25 by any *manner of living thing* that **c** *on* 7430
Dt 4:18 The likeness of any *thing* that **c** on 7430

CREEPING (29) [CREEP]
Ge 1:24 **c thing**, and beast of the earth after his 7431
1:26 over every **c thing** that creepeth upon 7431
6: 7 and the **c thing**, and the fowls of the air; 7431
6:20 of every **c thing** of the earth after his kind, 7431
7:14 every **c thing** that creepeth upon the earth 7431
7:21 of every **c thing** that creepeth upon 8318
7:23 the **c things**, and the fowl of the heaven; 7431
8:17 of every **c thing** that creepeth upon 7431
8:19 every **c thing**, and every fowl, *and* 7431
Lev 5: 2 or the carcase of unclean **c things**, and *if* it 8318
11:21 flying **c thing** that goeth upon *all* four, 8318
11:23 all *other* flying **c things**, which have four 8318
11:29 the **c things** that creep upon the earth; 8318
11:41 every **c thing** that creepeth upon the earth 8318
11:42 all **c things** that creep upon the earth, 8318
11:43 abominable with any **c thing** that creepeth, 8318
11:44 *of* **c thing** that creepeth upon the earth. 8318
22: 5 Or whosoever toucheth any **c thing**, 8318
Dt 14:19 every **c thing** that flieth *is* unclean unto 8318
1Ki 4:33 and of fowl, and of **c things**, and of fishes. 7431
Ps 104:25 wherein *are* **things c** innumerable, 7431
148:10 all cattle; **c things**, and flying fowl: 7431
Eze 8:10 behold every form of **c things**, and 7431
38:20 all **c things** that creep upon the earth, and 7431
Hos 2:18 and *with* the **c things** of the ground: 7431
Hab 1:14 as the **c things**, *that have* no ruler over 7431

Ac 10:12 and **c things**, and fowls of the air. *2062*
11: 6 and **c things**, and fowls of the air. *2062*
Ro 1:23 and fourfooted beasts, and **c things**. *2062*

CREPT (1) [CREEP]
Jude 1: 4 For there are certain men **c in unawares**, *3921*

CRESCENS (1)
2Ti 4:10 **C** to Galatia, Titus unto Dalmatia. *2913*

CRETANS See CRETES; CRETIANS

CRETE (5) [CRETES, CRETIANS]
Ac 27: 7 we sailed under **C**, over against Salmone; *2914*
27:12 *which is* a haven of **C**, and lieth toward *2914*
27:13 loosing *thence,* they sailed close by **C**. *2914*
27:21 and not have loosed from **C**, and to have *2914*
Tit 1: 5 For this cause left I thee in **C**, that thou *2914*

CRETES (1) [CRETE]
Ac 2:11 **C** and Arabians, we do hear them speak in *2912*

CRETIANS (2) [CRETE]
Tit 1:12 said, The **C** *are* alway liars, evil beasts, *2912*
3: S the first bishop of the church of the **C**, *2912*

CREW (5) [CROW]
Mt 26:74 not the man. And immediately *the* cock **c**. *5455*
Mk 14:68 he went out into the porch; and *the* cock **c**. *5455*
14:72 And the second time *the* cock **c**. And Peter *5455*
Lk 22:60 while he yet spake, the cock **c**. *5455*
Jn 18:27 denied again: and immediately *the* cock **c**. *5455*

CRIB (3)
Job 39: 9 be willing to serve thee, or abide by thy **c**? 18
Pr 14: 4 Where no oxen *are,* the **c** *is* clean: but 18
Isa 1: 3 knoweth his owner, and the ass his master's **c**: 18

CRICKET See BEETLE

CRIED (199) [CRY]
Ge 27:34 he **c** with a great and exceeding bitter cry, 6817
39:14 to lie with me, and I **c** with a loud voice: 7121
39:15 he heard that I lifted up my voice and **c**, 7121
39:18 it came to pass, as I lift up my voice and **c**, 7121
41:43 and they **c** before him, Bow the knee: 7121
41:55 the people **c** to Pharaoh for bread: 6817
45: 1 he **c**, Cause every man to go out from me. 7121
Ex 2:23 they **c**, and their cry came up unto God by 2199
5:15 children of Israel came and **c** unto Pharaoh, 6817
8:12 Moses **c** unto the LORD because of 6817
14:10 the children of Israel **c out** unto 6817
15:25 he **c** unto the LORD; and the LORD 6817
17: 4 Moses **c** unto the LORD, saying, 6817
Nu 11: 2 the people **c** unto Moses; and when Moses 6817
12:13 Moses **c** unto the LORD, saying, Heal her 6817
14: 1 congregation lifted up their voice, and **c**; 5414
20:16 when we **c** unto the LORD, he heard our 6817
Dt 22:24 the damsel, because she **c** not, *being* in 6817
22:27 *and* the betrothed damsel **c**, and *there was* 6817
26: 7 when we **c** unto the LORD God of our 6817
Jos 24: 7 when they **c** unto the LORD, he put 6817
Jdg 3: 9 when the children of Israel **c** unto 2199
3:15 when the children of Israel **c** unto 2199
4: 3 the children of Israel **c** unto the LORD: 6817
5:28 **c** through the lattice, Why is his chariot *so* 2980
6: 6 the children of Israel **c** unto the LORD. 2199
6: 7 when the children of Israel **c** unto 2199
7:20 their right hands to blow *withal:* and they **c**, 7121
7:21 and all the host ran, and **c**, and fled. 7321
9: 7 lift up his voice, and **c**, and said unto them, 7121
10:10 the children of Israel **c** unto the LORD, 2199
10:12 ye **c** to me, and I delivered you out of their 6817
18:23 they **c** unto the children of Dan. And they 7121
1Sa 4:13 into the city, and told *it,* all the city **c out**. 2199
5:10 *to* Ekron, that the Ekronites **c out**, saying, 2199
7: 9 Samuel **c** unto the LORD for Israel; and 2199
12: 8 your fathers **c** unto the LORD, then 2199
12:10 they **c** unto the LORD, and said, We have 2199
15:11 and he **c** unto the LORD all night. 2199
17: 8 he stood and **c** unto the armies of Israel, 7121
20:37 Jonathan **c** after the lad, and said, *Is* not 7121
20:38 Jonathan **c** after the lad, Make speed, haste, 7121
24: 8 and **c** after Saul, saying, My lord the king. 7121
26:14 David **c** to the people, and to Abner the son 7121
28:12 saw Samuel, she **c** with a loud voice: 2199

C

2Sa	18:25	the watchman **c**, and told the king. And	7121
	19: 4	the king **c** *with* a loud voice, O my son	2199
	20:16	**c** a wise woman out of the city, Hear, hear;	7121
	22: 7	called upon the LORD, and **c** to my God:	7121
1Ki	13: 2	he **c** against the altar in the word of	7121
	13: 4	which had **c** against the altar in Beth-el,	7121
	13:21	he **c** unto the man of God that came from	7121
	13:32	For the saying which he **c** by the word of	7121
	17:20	he **c** unto the LORD, and said, O LORD	7121
	17:21	**c** unto the LORD, and said, O LORD my	7121
	18:28	they **c** loud, and cut themselves after their	7121
	20:39	as the king passed by, he **c** unto the king:	6817
	22:32	to fight against him: and Jehoshaphat **c out**.	2199
2Ki	2:12	Elisha saw *it,* and he **c**, My father,	6817
	4: 1	Now there **c** a certain woman of the wives	6817
	4:40	that they **c out**, and said, O thou man of	6817
	6: 5	he **c**, and said, Alas, master, for it *was*	6817
	6:26	there **c** a woman unto him, saying, Help,	6817
	8: 5	**c** to the king for her house and for her land.	6817
	11:14	rent her clothes, and **c**, Treason, Treason.	7121
	18:28	**c** with a loud voice in the Jews' language,	7121
	20:11	Isaiah the prophet **c** unto the LORD: and	7121
1Ch	5:20	for they **c** to God in the battle, and he was	2199
2Ch	13:14	they **c** unto the LORD, and the priests	6817
	14:11	Asa **c** unto the LORD his God, and said,	7121
	18:31	Jehoshaphat **c out**, and the LORD helped	2199
	32:18	they **c** with a loud voice in the Jews' speech	7121
	32:20	the son of Amoz, prayed and **c** *to* heaven.	2199
Ne	9: 4	**c** with a loud voice unto the LORD their	2199
	9:27	time of their trouble, when they **c** unto thee,	6817
	9:28	yet when they returned, and **c** unto thee,	2199
Est	4: 1	the city, and **c** *with* a loud and a bitter cry;	2199
Job	29:12	Because I delivered the poor that **c**, and	7768
	30: 5	(they **c** after them as *after* a thief;)	7321
	30:28	I stood up, *and* I **c** in the congregation.	7768
Ps	3: 4	I **c** unto the LORD *with* my voice, and	7121
	18: 6	upon the LORD, and **c** unto my God:	7768
	18:41	They **c**, but *there was* none to save *them:*	7768
	22: 5	They **c** unto thee, and were delivered:	2199
	22:24	but when he **c** unto him, he heard.	7768
	30: 2	I **c** unto thee, and thou hast healed me.	7768
	30: 8	I **c** to thee, O LORD; and unto	7121
	31:22	of my supplications when I **c** unto thee.	7768
	34: 6	This poor *man* **c**, and the LORD heard	7121
	66:17	I **c** unto him *with* my mouth, and *he was*	7121
	77: 1	I **c** unto God *with* my voice, *even* unto God	6817
	88: 1	I have **c** day *and* night before thee:	6817
	88:13	unto thee have I **c**, O LORD; and in	7768
	107: 6	they **c** unto the LORD in their trouble,	6817
	107:13	they **c** unto the LORD in their trouble,	2199
	119:145	I **c** with *my* whole heart; hear me,	7121
	119:146	I **c unto** thee; save me, and I shall keep thy	7121
	119:147	the dawning of the morning, and **c**:	7768
	120: 1	In my distress I **c unto** the LORD, and	7121
	130: 1	Out of the depths have I **c unto** thee,	7121
	138: 3	In the day when I **c** thou answeredst me,	7121
	142: 1	I **c** unto the LORD *with* my voice;	2199
	142: 5	I **c** unto thee, O LORD: I said, Thou *art*	2199
Isa	6: 3	one **c** unto another, and said, Holy, holy,	7121
	6: 4	the door moved at the voice of him that **c**,	7121
	21: 8	he **c**, A lion: My lord, I stand continually	7121
	30: 7	therefore have I **c** concerning this,	7121
	36:13	**c** with a loud voice in the Jews' language,	7121
Jer	4:20	Destruction upon destruction is **c**; for	7121
	20: 8	I spake, I **c out**, I cried violence and spoil;	2199
	20: 8	I spake, I cried out, I **c** violence and spoil;	7121
La	2:18	Their heart **c** unto the Lord, O wall of	6817
	4:15	They **c** unto them, Depart ye; *it is* unclean;	7121
Eze	9: 1	He **c** also in mine ears *with* a loud voice,	7121
	9: 8	my face, and **c**, and said, Ah Lord GOD,	2199
	10:13	it was **c** unto them in my hearing, O wheel.	7121
	11:13	**c** *with* a loud voice, and said, Ah Lord	2199
Da	3: 4	a herald **c** aloud, To you it is commanded,	7123
	4:14	He **c** aloud, and said thus, Hew down	7123
	5: 7	The king **c** aloud to bring in the astrologers,	7123
	6:20	he **c** with a lamentable voice unto Daniel:	2200
Hos	7:14	they have not **c** unto me with their heart,	2199
Jnh	1: 5	**c** every man unto his god, and cast forth	2199
	1:14	Wherefore they **c** unto the LORD, and	7121
	2: 2	I **c** by reason of mine affliction unto	7121
	2: 2	out of the belly of hell **c** I, *and*	7768
	3: 4	he **c**, and said, Yet forty days, and	7121
Zec	1: 4	unto whom the former prophets have **c**,	7121
	6: 8	**c** he upon me, and spake unto me, saying,	2199
	7: 7	the LORD hath **c** by the former prophets,	7121
	7:13	*that* as he **c**, and they would not hear;	7121
	7:13	so they **c**, and I would not hear, saith	7121
Mt	8:29	And behold, they **c out**, saying, What have	*2896*
	14:26	It is a spirit; and they **c out** for fear.	*2896*
	14:30	to sink, he **c**, saying, Lord, save me.	*2896*
	15:22	and **c** unto him, saying, Have mercy on me,	*2905*
	20:30	**c out**, saying, Have mercy on us, O Lord,	*2896*
	20:31	but they **c** the more, saying, Have mercy on	*2896*
	21: 9	and that followed, **c**, saying, Hosanna to	*2896*
	27:23	But they **c out** the more, saying, Let him be	*2896*
	27:46	And about the ninth hour Jesus **c** with a loud	*310*
	27:50	when he had **c** again with a loud voice,	*2896*
Mk	1:23	a man with an unclean spirit; and he **c out**,	*349*
	1:26	and **c** with a loud voice, he came out of	*2896*
	3:11	fell down before him, and **c**, saying,	*2896*
	5: 7	And **c** with a loud voice, and said,	*2896*
	6:49	they supposed *it* had been a spirit, and **c out**:	*349*
	9:24	straightway the father of the child **c out**,	*2896*
	9:26	And *the spirit* **c**, and rent him sore, and	*2896*
	10:48	but he **c** the more a great deal, *Thou* Son of	*2896*
	11: 9	and they that followed, **c**, saying, Hosanna;	*2896*
	15:13	And they **c out** again, Crucify him.	*2896*
	15:14	And they **c out** the more exceedingly,	*2896*
	15:34	And at the ninth hour Jesus **c** with a loud	*994*
	15:37	And Jesus **c** with a loud voice, and gave up	*863*
	15:39	saw that he so **c out**, and gave up the ghost,	*2896*
Lk	4:33	unclean devil, and **c out** with a loud voice,	*349*
	8: 8	And when he said these *things,* he **c**,	*5455*
	8:28	he **c out**, and fell down before him, and	*349*
	9:38	a man of the company **c out**, saying, Master,	*310*
	16:24	And he **c** and said, Father Abraham,	*5455*
	18:38	And he **c**, saying, Jesus, *thou* Son of David,	*994*
	18:39	but he **c** *so* much the more, *Thou* Son of	*2896*
	23:18	And they **c out** all at once, saying,	*349*
	23:21	But they **c**, saying, Crucify *him,* crucify	*2019*
	23:46	And when Jesus had **c** with a loud voice,	*5455*
Jn	1:15	John bare witness of him, and **c**, saying,	*2896*
	7:28	Then **c** Jesus in the temple as he taught,	*2896*
	7:37	Jesus stood and **c**, saying, If any *man* thirst,	*2896*
	11:43	he **c** with a loud voice, Lazarus, come forth.	*2905*
	12:13	went forth to meet him, and **c**, Hosanna:	*2896*
	12:44	Jesus **c** and said, He that believeth on me,	*2896*
	18:40	Then **c** they all again, saying, Not this *man,*	*2905*
	19: 6	and officers saw him, they **c out**, saying,	*2905*
	19:12	but the Jews **c out**, saying, If thou let this	*2896*
	19:15	But they **c out**, Away with *him,* away with	*2905*
Ac	7:57	Then they **c out** with a loud voice, and	*2896*
	7:60	and **c** with a loud voice, Lord,	*2896*
	16:17	The same followed Paul and us, and **c**,	*2896*
	16:28	But Paul **c** with a loud voice, saying,	*5455*
	19:28	and **c out**, saying, Great *is* Diana of	*2896*
	19:32	Some therefore **c** one *thing,* and	*2896*
	19:34	voice about the space of two hours **c out**,	*2896*
	21:34	And some **c** one *thing,* some another,	*994*
	22:23	And as they **c out**, and cast *off their*	*2905*
	22:24	he might know wherefore they **c** so **against**	*2019*
	23: 6	he **c out** in the council, Men *and* brethren,	*2896*
	24:21	one voice, that I **c** standing among them,	*2896*
Rev	6:10	And they **c** with a loud voice, saying,	*2896*
	7: 2	he **c** with a loud voice to the four angels,	*2896*
	7:10	And **c** with a loud voice, saying, Salvation	*2896*
	10: 3	And **c** with a loud voice, as *when* a lion	*2896*
	10: 3	and when he had **c**, seven thunders uttered	*2896*
	12: 2	And she being with child **c**, travailing in	*2896*
	14:18	**c** with a loud cry to him that had the sharp	*5455*
	18: 2	And he **c** mightily with a strong voice,	*2896*
	18:18	And **c** when they saw the smoke of her	*2896*
	18:19	and **c**, weeping and wailing, saying, Alas,	*2896*
	19:17	and he **c** with a loud voice, saying to all	*2896*

CRIES (1) [CRY]

Jas	5: 4	the **c** of them which have reaped are entered	*995*

CRIEST (5) [CRY]

Ex	14:15	unto Moses, Wherefore **c** thou unto me?	6817
1Sa	26:14	and said, Who *art* thou *that* **c** to the king?	7121
Pr	2: 3	if thou **c** after knowledge, *and* liftest up thy	7121
Isa	57:13	When thou **c**, let thy companies deliver	2199
Jer	30:15	Why **c** thou for thine affliction? thy sorrow	2199

CRIETH (17) [CRY]

Ge	4:10	the voice of thy brother's blood **c** unto me	6817
Ex	22:27	to pass, when he **c** unto me, that I will hear;	6817

Job 24:12 the city, and the soul of the wounded **c out**: 7768
Ps 72:12 For he shall deliver the needy when he **c**; 7768
84: 2 and my flesh **c out** for the living God. 7442
Pr 1:20 Wisdom **c** without; she uttereth her voice in 7442
1:21 She **c** in the chief place of concourse, in 7121
8: 3 She **c** at the gates, at the entry of the city, 7442
9: 3 she **c** upon the highest places of the city, 7121
Isa 26:17 is in pain, *and* **c out** in her pangs; 2199
40: 3 The voice of him that **c** in the wilderness, 7121
Jer 12: 8 the forest; it **c out** against me: 5414+6963+871.1
Mic 6: 9 The LORD's voice **c** unto the city, and 7121
Mt 15:23 saying, Send her away; for she **c** after us. *2896*
Lk 9:39 a spirit taketh him, and he suddenly **c out**; *2896*
Ro 9:27 Esaias also **c** concerning Israel, Though *2896*
Jas 5: 4 which is of you kept back by fraud, **c**: *2896*

CRIME (2) [CRIMES]
Job 31:11 For this *is* a **heinous c**; yea, it *is* an iniquity 2154
Ac 25:16 himself concerning the **c laid** *against him*. *1462*

CRIMES (2) [CRIME]
Eze 7:23 for the land is full *of* bloody **c**, and the city 4941
Ac 25:27 not withal to signify the **c** *laid* against him. *156*

CRIMINAL; CRIMINALS See MALEFACTOR; MALEFACTORS

CRIMSON (5)
2Ch 2: 7 **c**, and blue, and that can skill to grave with 3758
2:14 in blue, and in fine linen, and in **c**; 3758
3:14 **c**, and fine linen, and wrought cherubims 3758
Isa 1:18 though they be red like **c**, they shall be as 8438
Jer 4:30 Though thou clothest thyself with **c**, 8144

CRIPPLE (1)
Ac 14: 8 *his* feet, being a **c** from his mother's womb, *5560*

CRISPING (1)
Isa 3:22 and the wimples, and the **c pins**, 2754

CRISPUS (2)
Ac 18: 8 And **C**, the *chief* ruler of the synagogue, *2921*
1Co 1:14 I baptized none of you, but **C** and Gaius; *2921*

CROOKBACKT (1) [BACK, CROOKED]
Lev 21:20 Or **c**, or a dwarf, or that hath a blemish in 1384

CROOKED (14) [CROOKBACKT]
Dt 32: 5 *they are* a perverse and **c** generation. 6618
Job 26:13 his hand hath formed the **c** serpent. 1281
Ps 125: 5 As for such as turn aside *unto* their **c ways**, 6128
Pr 2:15 Whose ways *are* **c**, and *they* froward in 6141
Ecc 1:15 *That which is* **c** cannot be made straight: 5791
7:13 make *that* straight, which he hath **made c**? 5791
Isa 27: 1 even leviathan *that* **c** serpent; 6129
40: 4 the **c** shall be made straight, and the rough 6121
42:16 light before them, and **c things** straight. 4625
45: 2 before thee, and make the **c places** straight: 1921
59: 8 they have **made** them **c** paths: whosoever 6140
La 3: 9 with hewn stone, he hath **made** my paths **c**. 5753
Lk 3: 5 and the **c** shall be made straight, and *4646*
Php 2:15 in the midst of a **c** and perverse nation, *4646*

CROP (2) [CROPT]
Lev 1:16 he shall pluck away his **c** with his feathers, 4760
Eze 17:22 will set *it*; I will **c off** from the top of his 6998

CROPT (1) [CROP]
Eze 17: 4 He **c off** the top of his young twigs, and 6998

CROSS (28) [CROSSWAY]
Mt 10:38 And he that taketh not his **c**, and *4716*
16:24 and take up his **c**, and follow me. *4716*
27:32 by name: him they compelled to bear his **c**. *4716*
27:40 be the Son of God, come down from the **c**. *4716*
27:42 let him now come down from the **c**, and *4716*
Mk 8:34 and take up his **c**, and follow me. *4716*
10:21 and come, take up the **c**, and follow me. *4716*
15:21 of Alexander and Rufus, to bear his **c**. *4716*
15:30 Save thyself, and come down from the **c**. *4716*
15:32 the King of Israel descend now from the **c**, *4716*
Lk 9:23 him deny himself, and take up his **c** daily, *4716*
14:27 And whosoever doth not bear his **c**, and *4716*
23:26 of the country, and on him they laid the **c**, *4716*
Jn 19:17 And he bearing his **c** went forth into a place *4716*
19:19 And Pilate wrote a title, and put *it* on the **c**. *4716*
19:25 Now there stood by the **c** of Jesus his *4716*
19:31 not remain upon the **c** on the sabbath day, *4716*
1Co 1:17 lest the **c** of Christ should be made of none *4716*
1:18 For the preaching of the **c** is to them that *4716*
Gal 5:11 then is the offence of the **c** ceased. *4716*
6:12 suffer persecution for the **c** of Christ. *4716*
6:14 save in the **c** of our Lord Jesus Christ, *4716*
Eph 2:16 both unto God in one body by the **c**, *4716*
Php 2: 8 unto death, even the death of the **c**. *4716*
3:18 *that they are* the enemies of the **c** of Christ: *4716*
Col 1:20 made peace through the blood of his **c**, *4716*
2:14 took it out of the way, nailing it to *his* **c**; *4716*
Heb 12: 2 joy that was set before him endured the **c**, *4716*

CROSSWAY (1) [CROSS]
Ob 1:14 Neither shouldest thou have stood in the **c**, 6563

CROUCH (1) [CROUCHETH]
1Sa 2:36 **c** to him for a piece of silver and a morsel 7812

CROUCHETH (1) [CROUCH]
Ps 10:10 He **c**, *and* humbleth himself, that the poor 1794

CROW (7) [COCKCROWING, CREW]
Mt 26:34 That this night, before *the* cock **c**, *5455*
26:75 which said unto him, Before *the* cock **c**, *5455*
Mk 14:30 *even* in this night, before *the* cock **c** twice, *5455*
14:72 Before *the* cock **c** twice, thou shalt deny me *5455*
Lk 22:34 Peter, *the* cock shall not **c** this day, *5455*
22:61 Before *the* cock **c**, thou shalt deny me *5455*
Jn 13:38 verily, I say unto thee, *The* cock shall not **c**, *5455*

CROWING See COCKCROWING

CROWN (66) [CROWNED, CROWNEDST, CROWNEST, CROWNETH, CROWNING, CROWNS]
Ge 49:26 on the **c of the head** of him *that was* 6936
Ex 25:11 shalt make upon it a **c** *of* gold round about. 2213
25:24 and make thereto a **c** *of* gold round about. 2213
25:25 thou shalt make a golden **c** to the border 2213
29: 6 his head, and put the holy **c** upon the mitre. 5145
30: 3 thou shalt make unto it a **c** *of* gold round 2213
30: 4 rings shalt thou make to it under the **c** of it, 2213
37: 2 and made a **c** *of* gold to it round about. 2213
37:11 made thereunto a **c** *of* gold round about. 2213
37:12 made a **c** of gold for the border thereof 2213
37:26 also he made unto it a **c** *of* gold round 2213
37:27 he made two rings of gold for it under the **c** 2213
39:30 they made the plate of the holy **c** *of* pure 5145
Lev 8: 9 did he put the golden plate, the holy **c**; 5145
21:12 for the **c** of the anointing oil of his God *is* 5145
Dt 33:20 and teareth the arm with the **c of the head**. 6936
2Sa 1:10 and I took the **c** that *was* upon his head, and 5145
12:30 he took their king's **c** from off his head, 5850
14:25 **c of** his **head** there was no blemish in him. 6936
2Ki 11:12 put the **c** upon him, and *gave him* 5145
1Ch 20: 2 David took the **c** of their king from off his 5850
2Ch 23:11 put upon him the **c**, and *gave him* 5145
Est 1:11 the queen before the king with the **c** royal, 3804
2:17 so that he set the royal **c** upon her head, and 3804
6: 8 the **c** royal which is set upon his head: 3804
8:15 *with* a great **c** of gold, and *with* a garment 5850
Job 2: 7 boils from the sole of his foot unto his **c**. 6936
19: 9 of my glory, and taken the **c** *from* my head. 5850
31:36 upon my shoulder, *and* bind it *as* a **c** to me. 5850
Ps 21: 3 thou settest a **c** of pure gold on his head. 5850
89:39 thou hast profaned his **c** *by casting it* to 5145
132:18 but upon himself shall his **c** flourish. 5145
Pr 4: 9 a **c** of glory shall she deliver *to* thee. 5850
12: 4 A virtuous woman *is* a **c** to her husband: 5850
14:24 The **c** of the wise *is* their riches: *but* 5850
16:31 The hoary head *is* a **c** of glory, *if* it be 5850
17: 6 Children's children *are* the **c** of old men; 5850
27:24 and doth the **c** *endure* to every generation? 5145
SS 3:11 behold king Solomon with the **c** where*with* 5850
Isa 3:17 the **c of the head** of the daughters of Zion, 6936
28: 1 Woe to the **c** of pride, to the drunkards of 5850
28: 3 The **c** of pride, the drunkards of Ephraim, 5850
28: 5 the LORD of hosts be for a **c** of glory, 5850
62: 3 Thou shalt also be a **c** of glory in the hand 5850
Jer 2:16 Tahapanes have broken the **c of** thy **head**. 6936
13:18 shall come down, *even* the **c** of your glory. 5850
48:45 the **c of the head** of the tumultuous ones. 6936
La 5:16 The **c** is fallen *from* our head: woe unto us, 5850
Eze 16:12 and a beautiful **c** upon thine head. 5850
21:26 Remove the diadem, and take off the **c**: 5850

Zec 9:16 for they shall be as the stones of a c, 5145
Mt 27:29 And when they had platted a c of thorns, 4735
Mk 15:17 and platted a c of thorns, and put it about 4735
Jn 19: 2 And the soldiers platted a c of thorns, and 4735
19: 5 wearing the c of thorns, and the purple 4735
1Co 9:25 Now they do it to obtain a corruptible c; 4735
Php 4: 1 my joy and c, so stand fast in the Lord, 4735
1Th 2:19 what is our hope, or joy, or c of rejoicing? 4735
2Ti 4: 8 Henceforth there is laid up for me a c of 4735
Jas 1:12 he is tried, he shall receive the c of life, 4735
1Pe 5: 4 ye shall receive a c of glory that fadeth not 4735
Rev 2:10 unto death, and I will give thee a c of life. 4735
3:11 which thou hast, that no man take thy c. 4735
6: 2 had a bow; and a c was given unto him: 4735
12: 1 and upon her head a c of twelve stars: 4735
14:14 having on his head a golden c, and in his 4735

C

CROWNED (6) [CROWN]
Ps 8: 5 and hast c him with glory and honour. 5849
Pr 14:18 but the prudent are c with knowledge. 3803
SS 3:11 mother c him in the day of his espousals, 5849
Na 3:17 Thy c are as the locusts, and thy captains as 4502
2Ti 2: 5 yet is he not c, except he strive lawfully. 4737
Heb 2: 9 suffering of death, c with glory and honour; 4737

CROWNEDST (1) [CROWN]
Heb 2: 7 thou c him with glory and honour, and 4737

CROWNEST (1) [CROWN]
Ps 65:11 Thou c the year with thy goodness; and 5849

CROWNETH (1) [CROWN]
Ps 103: 4 who c thee with lovingkindness and 5849

CROWNING (1) [CROWN]
Isa 23: 8 the c city, whose merchants are princes, 5849

CROWNS (9) [CROWN]
Eze 23:42 and beautiful c upon their heads. 5850
Zec 6:11 make c, and set them upon the head of 5850
6:14 the c shall be to Helem, and to Tobijah, 5850
Rev 4: 4 and they had on their heads c of gold. 4735
4:10 and ever, and cast their c before the throne, 4735
9: 7 on their heads were as it were c like gold, 4735
12: 3 and ten horns, and seven c upon his heads. 1238
13: 1 and upon his horns ten c, and upon his 1238
19:12 flame of fire, and on his head were many c; 1238

CRUCIBLE See FINING POT

CRUCIFIED (37) [CRUCIFY]
Mt 26: 2 and the Son of man is betrayed to be c. 4717
27:22 They all say unto him, Let him be c. 4717
27:23 cried out the more, saying, Let him be c. 4717
27:26 scourged Jesus, he delivered him to be c. 4717
27:35 And they c him, and parted his garments, 4717
27:38 Then were there two thieves c with him, 4717
27:44 The thieves also, which were c with 4957
28: 5 for I know that ye seek Jesus, which was c. 4717
Mk 15:15 when he had scourged him, to be c. 4717
15:24 And when they had c him, they parted his 4717
15:25 And it was the third hour, and they c him. 4717
15:32 that were c with him reviled him. 4957
16: 6 Ye seek Jesus of Nazareth, which was c: 4717
Lk 23:23 loud voices, requiring that he might be c. 4717
23:33 there they c him, and the malefactors, 4717
24: 7 and be c, and the third day rise again. 4717
24:20 to be condemned to death, and have c him. 4717
Jn 19:16 he him therefore unto them to be c. 4717
19:18 Where they c him, and two other with him, 4717
19:20 for the place where Jesus was c was nigh to 4717
19:23 Then the soldiers, when they had c Jesus, 4717
19:32 and of the other which was c with him. 4957
19:41 Now in the place where he was c there was 4717
Ac 2:23 and by wicked hands have c and slain: 4362
2:36 whom ye have c, both Lord and Christ. 4717
4:10 whom ye c, whom God raised from 4717
Ro 6: 6 that our old man is c with him, that 4957
1Co 1:13 was Paul c for you? or were ye baptized in 4717
1:23 But we preach Christ c, unto the Jews a 4717
2: 2 among you, save Jesus Christ, and him c. 4717
2: 8 it, they would not have c the Lord of glory. 4717
2Co 13: 4 For though he was c through weakness, 4717
Gal 2:20 I am c with Christ: nevertheless I live; 4957
3: 1 hath been evidently set forth, c among you? 4717
5:24 And they that are Christ's have c the flesh 4717
6:14 by whom the world is c unto me, and I unto 4717
Rev 11: 8 and Egypt, where also our Lord was c. 4717

CRUCIFY (16) [CRUCIFIED]
Mt 20:19 and to c him: and the third day he shall rise 4717
23:34 and some of them ye shall kill and c; and 4717
27:31 on him, and led him away to c him. 4717
Mk 15:13 And they cried out again, C him. 4717
15:14 cried out the more exceedingly, C him. 4717
15:20 clothes on him, and led him out to c him. 4717
15:27 And with him they c two thieves; the one 4717
Lk 23:21 But they cried, saying, C him, crucify him. 4717
23:21 But they cried, saying, Crucify him, c him. 4717
Jn 19: 6 C him, crucify him. Pilate saith unto them, 4717
19: 6 Crucify him, c him. Pilate saith unto them, 4717
19: 6 and c him: for I find no fault in him. 4717
19:10 knowest thou not that I have power to c 4717
19:15 Away with him, away with him, c him. 4717
19:15 Pilate saith unto them, Shall I c your King? 4717
Heb 6: 6 they c to themselves the Son of God afresh, 388

CRUDDLED (1)
Job 10:10 me out as milk, and c me like cheese? 7087

CRUEL (19) [CRUELLY, CRUELTY]
Ge 49: 7 it was fierce; and their wrath, for it was c: 7185
Ex 6: 9 for anguish of spirit, and for c bondage. 7186
Dt 32:33 poison of dragons, and the c venom of asps. 393
Job 30:21 Thou art become c to me: with thy strong 393
Ps 25:19 and they hate me with c hatred. 2555+8135
71: 4 of the hand of the unrighteous and c man. 2556
Pr 5: 9 honour unto others, and thy years unto the c: 394
11:17 but he that is c troubleth his own flesh. 394
12:10 but the tender mercies of the wicked are c. 394
17:11 a c messenger shall be sent against him. 394
27: 4 Wrath is c, and anger is outrageous; but 395
SS 8: 6 strong as death; jealousy is c as the grave: 7186
Isa 13: 9 c both with wrath and fierce anger, to lay 394
19: 4 will I give over into the hand of a c lord; 7186
Jer 6:23 and spear; they are c, and have no mercy; 394
30:14 with the chastisement of a c one, for 394
50:42 they are c, and will not shew mercy: 394
La 4: 3 the daughter of my people is become c, 393
Heb 11:36 And others had trial of c mockings and NIG

CRUELLY (1) [CRUEL]
Eze 18:18 his father, because he c oppressed, 6231+6233

CRUELTY (5) [CRUEL]
Ge 49: 5 instruments of c are in their habitations. 2555
Jdg 9:24 That the c done to the threescore and 2555
Ps 27:12 up against me, and such as breathe out c. 2555
74:20 of the earth are full of the habitations of c. 2555
Eze 34: 4 with force and with c have ye ruled them. 6531

CRUMBLES See NOUGHT

CRUMBS (3)
Mt 15:27 yet the dogs eat of the c which fall from 5589
Mk 7:28 dogs under the table eat of the children's c. 5589
Lk 16:21 And desiring to be fed with the c which fell 5589

CRUSE (9)
1Sa 26:11 and the c of water, and let us go. 6835
26:12 and the c of water from Saul's bolster; 6835
26:16 and the c of water that was at his bolster. 6835
1Ki 14: 3 cracknels, and a c of honey, and go to him: 1228
17:12 of meal in a barrel, and a little oil in a c: 6835
17:14 not waste, neither shall the c of oil fail, 6835
17:16 wasted not, neither did the c of oil fail, 6835
19: 6 on the coals, and a c of water at his head. 6835
2Ki 2:20 Bring me a new c, and put salt therein. 6746

CRUSH (4) [CRUSHED, CRUSHT]
Job 39:15 forgetteth that the foot may c them, or 2115
La 1:15 he hath called an assembly against me to c 7665
3:34 To c under his feet all the prisoners of 1792
Am 4: 1 which oppress the poor, which c the needy, 7533

CRUSHED (6) [CRUSH]
Lev 22:24 which is bruised, or c, or broken, or cut; 3807
Dt 28:33 thou shalt be only oppressed and c alway: 7533
Job 4:19 is in the dust, which are c before the moth? 1792
5: 4 far from safety, and they are c in the gate, 1792

Isa 59: 5 that which is c breaketh out *into* a viper. 2116
Jer 51:34 he hath c me, he hath made me an empty 2000

CRUSHT (1) [CRUSH]
Nu 22:25 and c Balaam's foot against the wall: 3905

CRY (181) [CRIED, CRIES, CRIEST, CRIETH, CRYING]
Ge 18:20 Because the c of Sodom and Gomorrah is 2201
18:21 done altogether according to the c of it, 6818
19:13 the c of them is waxen great before the face 6818
27:34 he cried with a great and exceeding bitter c, 6818
Ex 2:23 their c came up unto God by reason of 7775
3: 7 have heard their c by reason of their 6818
3: 9 the c of the children of Israel is come unto 6818
5: 8 therefore they c, saying, Let us go *and* 6817
11: 6 there shall be a great c throughout all 6818
12:30 and there was a great c in Egypt; 6818
22:23 they c **at all** unto me, I will surely 6817+6817
22:23 cry at all unto me, I will surely hear their c; 6818
32:18 neither *is it* the voice of *them that* c for 6030
Lev 13:45 *his* upper lip, and shall c, Unclean, unclean. 7121
Nu 16:34 round about them fled at the c of them: 6963
Dt 15: 9 he c unto the LORD against thee, and it be 7121
24:15 lest he c against thee unto the LORD, and 7121
Jdg 10:14 and c unto the gods which ye have chosen; 2199
1Sa 5:12 and the c of the city went up *to* heaven. 7775
7: 8 Cease not to c unto the LORD our God for 2199
8:18 ye shall c **out** in that day because of your 2199
9:16 because their c is come unto me. 6818
2Sa 19:28 have I yet to c any more unto the king? 2199
22: 7 his temple, and my c *did enter* into his ears. 7775
1Ki 8:28 to hearken unto the c and to the prayer, 7440
18:27 that Elijah mocked them, and said, C aloud: 7121
2Ki 8: 3 she went forth to c unto the king for her 6817
2Ch 6:19 to hearken unto the c and the prayer which 7440
13:12 sounding trumpets to c **alarm** against you. 7321
20: 9 c unto thee in our affliction, then thou wilt 2199
Ne 5: 1 there was a great c of the people and 6818
5: 6 I was very angry when I heard their c and 2201
9: 9 and heardest their c by the Red sea; 2201
Est 4: 1 and cried *with* a loud and a bitter c; 2201
9:31 the matters of the fastings and their c. 2201
Job 16:18 thou my blood, and let my c have no place. 2201
19: 7 I c **out** *of* wrong, but I am not heard: 6817
19: 7 I c **aloud**, but *there is* no judgment. 7768
27: 9 Will God hear his c when trouble cometh 6818
30:20 I c unto thee, and thou dost not hear me: 7768
30:24 the grave, though *they* c in his destruction. 7769
31:38 If my land c against me, or that the furrows 2199
34:28 So that *they* cause the c of the poor to come 6818
34:28 and he heareth the c of the afflicted. 6818
35: 9 oppressions they **make** *the oppressed* **to** c: 2199
35: 9 they c **out** by reason of the arm of 7768
35:12 There they c, but none giveth answer, 6817
36:13 up wrath: they c not when he bindeth them. 7768
38:41 when his young ones c unto God, 7768
Ps 5: 2 Hearken unto the voice of my c, my King, 7773
9:12 he forgetteth not the c of the humble. 6818
17: 1 the right, O LORD, attend unto my c, 7440
18: 6 my c came before him, *even* into his ears. 7775
22: 2 I c in the daytime, but thou hearest not; 7121
27: 7 Hear, O LORD, *when* I c *with* my voice: 7121
28: 1 Unto thee will I c, O LORD, my rock; 7121
28: 2 of my supplications, when I c unto thee, 7768
34:15 and his ears *are open* unto their c. 7775
34:17 *The righteous* c, and the LORD heareth, 6817
39:12 O LORD, and give ear unto my c; 7775
40: 1 and he inclined unto me, and heard my c. 7775
55:17 and at noon, will I pray, and c **aloud**: 1993
56: 9 When I c *unto thee,* then shall mine 7121
57: 2 I will c unto God most High; unto God that 7121
61: 1 Hear my c, O God; attend unto my prayer. 7440
61: 2 From the end of the earth will I c unto thee, 7121
86: 3 unto me, O Lord: for I c unto thee daily. 7121
88: 2 before thee: incline thine ear unto my c; 7440
89:26 He shall c **unto** me, Thou *art* my Father, 7121
102: 1 O LORD, and let my c come unto thee. 7775
106:44 their affliction, when he heard their c: 7440
107:19 they c unto the LORD in their trouble, 2199
107:28 they c unto the LORD in their trouble, 6817
119:169 Let my c come near before thee, 7440
141: 1 LORD, I c **unto** thee: make haste unto 7121
141: 1 give ear unto my voice, when I c unto thee. 7121
142: 6 Attend unto my c; for I am brought very 7440
145:19 he also will hear their c, and will save 7775
147: 9 his food, *and* to the young ravens which c. 7121
Pr 8: 1 Doth not wisdom c? and understanding put 7121
21:13 Whoso stoppeth his ears at the c of 2201
21:13 he also shall c himself, but shall not be 7121
Ecc 9:17 more than the c of him that ruleth among 2201
Isa 5: 7 for righteousness, but behold a c. 6818
8: 4 before the child shall have knowledge to c, 7121
12: 6 C **out** and shout, thou inhabitant of Zion: 6670
13:22 the wild beasts of the islands shall c in their 6030
14:31 c, O city; thou, whole Palestina, 2199
15: 4 Heshbon shall c, and Elealeh: their voice 2199
15: 4 the armed soldiers of Moab shall c **out**; 7321
15: 5 My heart shall c **out** for Moab; his fugitives 2199
15: 5 they shall raise up a c of destruction. 2201
15: 8 For the c is gone round about the borders of 2201
19:20 for they shall c unto the LORD because of 6817
24:14 they shall c **aloud** from the sea. 6670
29: 9 and wonder; c **ye out**, and cry: 8173
29: 9 and wonder; cry ye out, and c: 8173
30:19 gracious unto thee at the voice of thy c; 2199
33: 7 Behold, their valiant ones shall c without: 6817
34:14 and the satyr shall c to his fellow; 7121
40: 2 c unto her, that her warfare is 7121
40: 6 The voice said, C. And he said, What shall 7121
40: 6 he said, What shall I c? All flesh *is* grass, 7121
42: 2 He shall not c, nor lift up, nor cause his 6817
42:13 he shall c, yea, roar; he shall prevail against 7321
42:14 *now* will I c like a travailing woman; I will 6463
43:14 and the Chaldeans, whose c *is* in the ships. 7440
46: 7 yea, *one* shall c unto him, yet can he not 6817
54: 1 break forth *into* singing, and c **aloud**, 6670
58: 1 C aloud, spare not, lift up thy voice like a 7121
58: 9 thou shalt c, and he shall say, Here I *am.* If 7768
65:14 ye shall c for sorrow of heart, and 6817
Jer 2: 2 Go and c in the ears of Jerusalem, saying, 7121
3: 4 Wilt thou not from this time c unto me, 7121
4: 5 c, gather together, and say, 7121
7:16 neither lift up c nor prayer for them, 7440
8:19 Behold the voice of the c of the daughter of 7775
11:11 though they shall c unto me, I will not 2199
11:12 c unto the gods unto whom they offer 2199
11:14 neither lift up a c or prayer for them: 7440
11:14 time that they c unto me for their trouble. 7121
14: 2 and the c of Jerusalem is gone up. 6682
14:12 When they fast, I will not hear their c; and 7440
18:22 Let a c be heard from their houses, 2201
20:16 let him hear the c in the morning, and 2201
22:20 Go up *to* Lebanon, and c; and lift up thy 6817
22:20 voice in Bashan, and c from the passages: 6817
25:34 Howl, ye shepherds, and c; and 2199
25:36 A voice of the c of the shepherds, and 6818
31: 6 watchmen upon the mount Ephraim shall c, 7121
46:12 *of* thy shame, and thy c hath filled the land: 6682
46:17 They did c there, Pharaoh king of Egypt *is* 7121
47: 2 the men shall c, and all the inhabitants of 2199
48: 4 her little ones have caused a c to be heard. 2201
48: 5 the enemies have heard a c of destruction. 6818
48:20 howl and c; tell ye *it* in Arnon, that Moab is 2199
48:31 for Moab, and I will c **out** for all Moab; 2199
48:34 From the c of Heshbon *even* unto Elealeh, 2201
49: 3 c, ye daughters of Rabbah, gird ye with 6817
49:21 *at* the c, the noise thereof was heard in 6818
49:29 they shall c unto them, Fear *is* on every 7121
50:46 and the c is heard among the nations. 2201
51:54 A sound of a c *cometh* from Babylon, and 2201
La 2:19 Arise, c **out** in the night: in the beginning 7442
3: 8 Also when I c and shout, he shutteth out 2199
3:56 hide not thine ear at my breathing, at my c. 7775
Eze 8:18 though they c in mine ears *with* a loud 7121
9: 4 that c for all the abominations that be done 602
21:12 C and howl, son of man: for it shall be 2199
24:17 Forbear to c, make no mourning *for* 602
26:15 at the sound of thy fall, when the wounded c, 602
27:28 shake at the sound of the c of thy pilots. 2201
27:30 shall c bitterly, and shall cast up dust upon 2199
Hos 5: 8 c **aloud** *at* Beth-aven, after thee, 7321
8: 2 Israel shall c unto me, My God, we know 2199
Joel 1:14 LORD your God, and c unto the LORD, 2199
1:19 O LORD, to thee will I c: for the fire hath 7121
1:20 The beasts of the field c also unto thee: 6165
Am 3: 4 will a young lion c out of his den, 5414+6963
Jnh 1: 2 to Nineveh, *that* great city, and c against it; 7121

Jnh 3: 8	with sackcloth, and **c** mightily unto God:	7121
Mic 3: 4	shall they **c** unto the LORD, but he will	2199
3: 5	that bite with their teeth, and **c**, Peace;	7121
4: 9	Now why dost thou **c out aloud**? *is*	7321+7452
Na 2: 8	stand, *shall they c*; but none shall look back.	NIH
Hab 1: 2	how long shall I **c**, and thou wilt not hear?	7768
1: 2	*even* **c out** unto thee *of* violence, and	2199
2:11	For the stone shall **c out** of the wall, and	2199
Zep 1:10	*that there shall be* the noise of a **c** from	6818
1:14	the mighty *man* shall **c** there bitterly.	6873
Zec 1:14	**C** thou, saying, Thus saith the LORD of	7121
1:17	**C** yet, saying, Thus saith the LORD of	7121
Mt 12:19	He shall not strive, nor **c**; neither shall any	*2905*
25: 6	And at midnight there was a **c** made,	*2906*
Mk 10:47	he began to **c out**, and say, Jesus, *thou* Son	*2896*
Lk 18: 7	which **c** day and night unto him, though he	*994*
19:40	the stones would immediately **c out**.	*2896*
Ac 23: 9	And there arose a great **c**: and the scribes	*2906*
Ro 8:15	of adoption, whereby we **c**, Abba, Father.	*2896*
Gal 4:27	break forth and **c**, thou that travailest not:	*994*
Rev 14:18	cried with a loud **c** to him that had	*2906*

CRYING (31) [CRY]

1Sa 4:14	when Eli heard the noise of the **c**, he said,	6818
2Sa 13:19	laid her hand on her head, and went on **c**.	2199
Job 39: 7	neither regardeth he the **c** of the driver.	8663
Ps 69: 3	I am weary of my **c**: my throat is dried:	7121
Pr 19:18	is hope, and let not thy soul spare for his **c**.	4191
30:15	hath two daughters, *c*, Give, give.	NIH
Isa 22: 5	down the walls, and of **c** to the mountains.	7771
24:11	*There is* a **c** for wine in the streets; all joy is	6682
65:19	be no more heard in her, nor the voice of **c**.	2201
Jer 48: 3	A voice of **c** *shall be* from Horonaim,	6818
Zec 4: 7	*with* shoutings, *c*, Grace, grace unto it.	NIH
Mal 2:13	*with* tears, *with* weeping, and *with* **c out**,	603
Mt 3: 3	saying, The voice of one **c** in the wilderness,	*994*
9:27	**c**, and saying, *Thou* Son of David,	*2896*
21:15	and the children **c** in the temple, and	*2896*
Mk 1: 3	The voice of one **c** in the wilderness,	*994*
5: 5	**c**, and cutting himself with stones.	*2896*
15: 8	And the multitude **c aloud** began to desire	*310*
Lk 3: 4	saying, The voice of one **c** in the wilderness,	*994*
4:41	And devils also came out of many, **c out**,	*2896*
Jn 1:23	I *am* the voice of one **c** in the wilderness,	*994*
Ac 8: 7	For unclean spirits, **c** with loud voice,	*994*
14:14	and ran in among the people, **c out**,	*2896*
17: 6	certain brethren unto the rulers of the city, **c**,	*994*
21:28	**C out**, Men of Israel, help: This is the man,	*2896*
21:36	multitude of the people followed *after*, **c**,	*2896*
25:24	**c** that he ought not to live any longer.	*1916*
Gal 4: 6	of his Son into your hearts, **c**, Abba, Father.	*2896*
Heb 5: 7	and supplications with strong **c** and	*2906*
Rev 14:15	**c** with a loud voice to him that sat on	*2896*
21: 4	be no more death, neither sorrow, nor **c**,	*2906*

CRYSTAL (5)

Job 28:17	The gold and the **c** cannot equal it: and	2137
Eze 1:22	creature *was* as the colour of the terrible **c**,	7140
Rev 4: 6	throne *there was* a sea of glass like unto **c**:	*2930*
21:11	*even* like a jasper stone, **clear as c**;	*2929*
22: 1	clear as **c**, proceeding out of the throne of	*2930*

CUB; CUBS See WHELP; WHELPS

CUBIT (45) [CUBITS]

Ge 6:16	the ark, and in a **c** shalt thou finish it above;	520
Ex 25:10	a **c** and a half the breadth thereof, and a cubit	520
25:10	and a **c** and a half the height thereof.	520
25:17	and a **c** and a half the breadth thereof.	520
25:23	a **c** the breadth thereof, and a cubit and a half	520
25:23	and a **c** and a half the height thereof.	520
26:13	a **c** on the one side, and a cubit on the other	520
26:13	a **c** on the other side of that which remaineth	520
26:16	a **c** and a half *shall be* the breadth of one	520
30: 2	A **c** *shall be* the length thereof, and a cubit	520
30: 2	length thereof, and a **c** the breadth thereof;	520
36:21	and the breadth of a board one **c** and a half.	520
37: 1	a **c** and a half the breadth of it, and a cubit	520
37: 1	of it, and a **c** and a half the height of it:	520
37: 6	and one **c** and a half the breadth thereof.	520
37:10	a **c** the breadth thereof, and a cubit and a half	520
37:10	and a **c** and a half the height thereof:	520
37:25	the length of it *was* a **c**, and the breadth of it	520
37:25	of it *was* a cubit, and the breadth of it a **c**;	520
Dt 3:11	cubits the breadth of it, after the **c** of a man.	520
Jdg 3:16	dagger which had two edges, of a **c** length;	1574
1Ki 7:24	ten in a **c**, compassing the sea round about:	520
7:31	of it within the chapiter and above *was* a **c**:	520
7:31	*after* the work of the base, a **c** and a half:	520
7:32	the height of a wheel *was* a **c** and half a	520
7:32	height of a wheel *was* a cubit and half a **c**.	520
7:35	*was there* a round compass of half a **c** high:	520
2Ch 4: 3	ten in a **c**, compassing the sea round about.	520
Eze 40: 5	a measuring reed of six cubits *long* by the **c**	520
40:12	the little chambers *was* one **c** *on this side*,	520
40:12	and the space *was* one **c** on that side:	520
40:42	of a **c** and a half long, and a cubit and a half	520
40:42	and a **c** and a half broad, and one cubit high:	520
40:42	and a cubit and a half broad, and one **c** high:	520
42: 4	of ten cubits breadth inward, a way of one **c**;	520
43:13	The **c** *is* a cubit and a hand breadth; even	520
43:13	The cubit *is* a **c** and a hand breadth; even	520
43:13	even the bottom *shall be* a **c**, and the breadth	520
43:13	the breadth a **c**, and the border thereof by	520
43:14	*shall be* two cubits, and the breadth one **c**;	520
43:14	*shall be* four cubits, and the breadth *one* **c**.	520
43:17	and the border about it *shall be* half a **c**; and	520
43:17	the bottom thereof *shall be* a **c** about; and	520
Mt 6:27	thought can add one **c** unto his stature?	*4083*
Lk 12:25	taking thought can add to his stature one **c**?	*4083*

CUBITS (213) [CUBIT]

Ge 6:15	length of the ark *shall be* three hundred **c**,	520
6:15	the breadth of it fifty **c**, and the height of it	520
6:15	of it fifty cubits, and the height of it thirty **c**.	520
7:20	Fifteen **c** upward did the waters prevail; and	520
Ex 25:10	**two c** and a half *shall be* the length thereof,	520
25:17	**two c** and a half *shall be* the length thereof,	520
25:23	**two c** *shall be* the length thereof, and a cubit	520
26: 2	of one curtain *shall be* eight and twenty **c**,	520
26: 2	and the breadth of one curtain four **c**:	520
26: 8	The length of one curtain *shall be* thirty **c**,	520
26: 8	and the breadth of one curtain four **c**:	520
26:16	Ten **c** *shall be* the length of a board, and	520
27: 1	five **c** long, and five cubits broad;	520
27: 1	five cubits long, and five **c** broad;	520
27: 1	and the height thereof *shall be* three **c**.	520
27: 9	linen of an hundred **c** long for one side:	520
27:11	*shall be* hangings of an hundred *c* long,	NIH
27:12	on the west side *shall be* hangings of fifty **c**:	520
27:13	on the east side eastward *shall be* fifty **c**.	520
27:14	of *one* side *of the gate shall be* fifteen **c**:	520
27:15	fifteen *c*: their pillars three, and	NIH
27:16	of the court *shall be* a hanging of twenty **c**,	520
27:18	length of the court *shall be* an hundred **c**,	520
27:18	the height five **c** *of* fine twined linen, and	520
30: 2	**two c** *shall be* the height thereof: the horns	520
36: 9	length of one curtain *was* twenty and eight **c**,	520
36: 9	and the breadth of one curtain four **c**:	520
36:15	The length of one curtain *was* thirty **c**, and	520
36:15	and four **c** *was* the breadth of one curtain:	520
36:21	The length of a board *was* ten **c**, and	520
37: 1	**two c** and a half *was* the length of it, and	520
37: 6	**two c** and a half *was* the length thereof, and	520
37:10	**two c** *was* the length thereof, and a cubit	520
37:25	and **two c** *was* the height of it;	520
38: 1	five **c** *was* the length thereof, and five cubits	520
38: 1	and five **c** the breadth thereof;	520
38: 1	and three **c** the height thereof.	520
38: 9	*were of* fine twined linen, an hundred **c**:	520
38:11	north side *the hangings were* an hundred **c**,	520
38:12	for the west side *were* hangings of fifty **c**,	520
38:13	And for the east side eastward fifty **c**.	520
38:14	of the *one* side *of the gate were* fifteen **c**;	520
38:15	and that hand, *were* hangings of fifteen **c**;	520
38:18	twenty **c** *was* the length, and the height in	520
38:18	and the height in the breadth *was* five **c**,	520
Nu 11:31	as it were **two c** *high* upon the face of	520
35: 4	and outward a thousand **c** round about.	520
35: 5	the city *on* the east side two thousand **c**,	520
35: 5	*on* the south side two thousand **c**, and *on*	520
35: 5	*on* the west side two thousand **c**, and *on*	520
35: 5	and *on* the north side two thousand **c**;	520
Dt 3:11	nine **c** *was* the length thereof, and four cubits	520
3:11	four **c** the breadth of it, after the cubit of a	520
Jos 3: 4	and it, about two thousand **c** by measure:	520
1Sa 17: 4	of Gath, whose height *was* six **c** and a span.	520
1Ki 6: 2	the length thereof *was* threescore **c**, and	520

1Ki 6: 2 the breadth thereof twenty *c*, and the height NIH
6: 2 twenty *cubits,* and the height thereof thirty c. 520
6: 3 twenty c *was* the length thereof, according to 520
6: 3 ten c *was* the breadth thereof before 520
6: 6 The nethermost chamber *was* five c broad, 520
6: 6 the middle *was* six c broad, and the third *was* 520
6: 6 and the third *was* seven c broad: 520
6:10 chambers against all the house, five c high: 520
6:16 he built twenty c on the sides of the house, 520
6:17 *is,* the temple before it, was forty c *long.* 520
6:20 the oracle in the forepart *was* twenty c in 520
6:20 twenty c in breadth, and twenty cubits in 520
6:20 and twenty c in the height thereof: 520
6:23 two cherubims *of* olive tree, each ten c high. 520
6:24 five c *was* the one wing of the cherub, and 520
6:24 and five c the other wing of the cherub: 520
6:24 the uttermost part of the other *were* ten c. 520
6:25 the other cherub *was* ten c: both 520
6:26 The height of the one cherub *was* ten c, and 520
7: 2 the length thereof *was* an hundred c, and 520
7: 2 the breadth thereof fifty c, and the height 520
7: 2 fifty cubits, and the height thereof thirty c, 520
7: 6 the length thereof *was* fifty c, and 520
7: 6 fifty cubits, and the breadth thereof thirty c: 520
7:10 stones of ten c, and stones of eight cubits. 520
7:10 stones of ten cubits, and stones of eight c. 520
7:15 pillars *of* brass, of eighteen c high apiece: 520
7:15 a line of twelve c did compass either of them 520
7:16 the height of the one chapiter *was* five c, and 520
7:16 the height of the other chapiter *was* five c: 520
7:19 *were* of lily work in the porch, four c). 520
7:23 ten c from the one brim to the other: 520
7:23 round all about, and his height *was* five c: 520
7:23 a line of thirty c did compass it round about. 520
7:27 four c *was* the length of one base, and 520
7:27 four c the breadth thereof, and three cubits 520
7:27 breadth thereof, and three c the height of it. 520
7:38 *and* every laver was four c: *and* upon every 520
2Ki 14:13 unto the corner gate, four hundred c. 520
25:17 The height of the one pillar *was* eighteen c, 520
25:17 the height of the chapiter three c; and 520
1Ch 11:23 five c *high;* and in the Egyptian's hand *was* a 520
2Ch 3: 3 The length *by* c after the first measure *was* 520
3: 3 after the first measure *was* threescore c, 520
3: 3 threescore cubits, and the breadth twenty c. 520
3: 4 twenty c, and the height *was* an hundred and 520
3: 8 twenty c, and the breadth thereof twenty 520
3: 8 and the breadth thereof twenty c: 520
3:11 the wings of the cherubims *were* twenty c 520
3:11 *one* wing of the one *cherub was* five c, 520
3:11 the other wing *was likewise* five c, 520
3:12 And *one* wing of the other cherub *was* five c, 520
3:12 the other wing *was* five c *also,* joining to 520
3:13 cherubims spread themselves forth twenty c: 520
3:15 house two pillars of thirty and five c high, 520
3:15 *was* on the top *of each* of them *was* five c. 520
4: 1 twenty c the length thereof, and 520
4: 1 twenty c the breadth thereof, and ten cubits 520
4: 1 breadth thereof, and ten c the height thereof. 520
4: 2 Also he made a molten sea of ten c from 520
4: 2 in compass, and five c the height thereof; 520
4: 2 a line of thirty c did compass it round about. 520
6:13 of five c long, and five cubits broad, 520
6:13 five c broad, and three cubits high, and 520
6:13 three c high, and had set it in the midst of 520
25:23 Ephraim to the corner gate, four hundred c. 520
Ezr 6: 3 the height thereof threescore c, *and* 521
6: 3 *and* the breadth thereof threescore c; 521
Ne 3:13 a thousand c on the wall unto the dung gate. 520
Est 5:14 Let a gallows be made of fifty c high, and to 520
7: 9 Behold also, the gallows fifty c high, 520
Jer 52:21 the height of one pillar *was* eighteen c; 520
52:21 a fillet of twelve c did compass it; and 520
52:22 the height of one chapiter *was* five c, 520
Eze 40: 5 in the man's hand a measuring reed of six c 520
40: 7 and between the little chambers *were* five c; 520
40: 9 measured he the porch of the gate, eight c; 520
40: 9 the posts thereof, two c; and the porch of 520
40:11 the breadth of the entry of the gate, ten c; 520
40:11 *and* the length of the gate, thirteen c. 520
40:12 the little chambers *were* six c on this side, 520
40:12 six cubits on this side, and six c on that side. 520
40:13 the breadth *was* five and twenty c, 520
40:14 He made also posts *of* threescore c, 520
40:15 of the porch of the inner gate *were* fifty c. 520
40:19 an hundred c east*ward* and north*ward.* 520
40:21 the length thereof *was* fifty c, and 520
40:21 and the breadth five and twenty c. 520
40:23 he measured from gate to gate an hundred c. 520
40:25 the length *was* fifty c, and the breadth five 520
40:25 and the breadth five and twenty c. 520
40:27 gate to gate toward the south an hundred c. 520
40:29 *it was* fifty c long, and five and 520
40:29 cubits long, and five and twenty c broad. 520
40:30 round about *were* five and twenty c long, 520
40:30 and twenty cubits long, and five c broad. 520
40:33 *it was* fifty c long, and five and 520
40:33 cubits long, and five and twenty c broad. 520
40:36 the length *was* fifty c, and the breadth five 520
40:36 and the breadth five and twenty c. 520
40:47 an hundred c long, and an hundred cubits 520
40:47 and an hundred c broad, foursquare; 520
40:48 five c on this side, and five cubits on that 520
40:48 cubits on this side, and five c on that side: 520
40:48 the breadth of the gate *was* three c on this 520
40:48 cubits on this side, and three c on that side. 520
40:49 The length of the porch *was* twenty c, and 520
40:49 *was* twenty cubits, and the breadth eleven c; 520
41: 1 six c broad on the one side, and six cubits 520
41: 1 one side, and six c broad on the other side, 520
41: 2 the breadth of the door *was* ten c; and 520
41: 2 the sides of the door *were* five c on the one 520
41: 2 on the one side, and five c on the other side: 520
41: 2 he measured the length thereof, forty c: and 520
41: 2 forty cubits: and the breadth, twenty c. 520
41: 3 measured the post of the door, two c; 520
41: 3 the door, six c; and the breadth of the door, 520
41: 3 and the breadth of the door, seven c. 520
41: 4 So he measured the length thereof, twenty c; 520
41: 4 and the breadth, twenty c, before the temple: 520
41: 5 he measured the wall of the house, six c; 520
41: 5 the breadth of *every* side chamber, four c, 520
41: 8 side chambers *were* a full reed of six great c. 520
41: 9 for the side chamber without, *was* five c: 520
41:10 c round about the house on every side. 520
41:11 place that was left *was* five c round about. 520
41:12 end toward the west *was* seventy c broad; 520
41:12 the wall of the building *was* five c thick 520
41:12 round about, and the length thereof ninety c. 520
41:13 he measured the house, an hundred c long; 520
41:13 with the walls thereof, an hundred c long; 520
41:14 separate place toward the east, an hundred c. 520
41:15 one side and on the other side, an hundred c, 520
41:22 The altar *of* wood *was* three c high, and 520
41:22 cubits high, and the length thereof two c; 520
42: 2 Before the length of an hundred c *was* 520
42: 2 the north door, and the breadth *was* fifty c. 520
42: 3 Over against the twenty *c* which *were* for NIH
42: 4 before the chambers *was* a walk of ten c 520
42: 7 the chambers, the length thereof *was* fifty c. 520
42: 8 that *were* in the utter court *was* fifty c: 520
42: 8 and lo, before the temple *were* an hundred c. 520
43:13 these *are* the measures of the altar after the c: 520
43:14 *even* to the lower settle *shall be* two c, 520
43:14 *even* to the greater settle *shall be* four c, 520
43:15 So the altar *shall be* four c; and from 520
43:16 the altar *shall be* twelve *c* long, twelve NIH
43:17 the settle *shall be* fourteen *c* long and NIH
45: 2 fifty c round about *for* the suburbs thereof. 520
46:22 *there were* courts joined *of* forty *c* long NIH
47: 3 forth east*ward,* he measured a thousand c, 520
Da 3: 1 whose height *was* threescore c, *and* 521
3: 1 *and* the breadth thereof six c: 521
Zec 5: 2 the length thereof *is* twenty c, and 520
5: 2 twenty cubits, and the breadth thereof ten c. 520
Jn 21: 8 from land, but as it were two hundred c,) *4083*
Rev 21:17 an hundred *and* forty *and* four c, *4083*

CUCKOW (2)

Lev 11:16 and the c, and the hawk after his kind, 7828
Dt 14:15 and the c, and the hawk after his kind, 7828

CUCUMBERS (2)

Nu 11: 5 the c, and the melons, and the leeks, and 7180
Isa 1: 8 as a lodge in a **garden of c**, as a besieged 4750

CUD (11)

Lev 11: 3 *is* clovenfooted, *and* cheweth c, among 1625

Lev 11: 4 shall ye not eat of them that chew the **c**, 1625
11: 4 because he cheweth the **c**, but divideth not 1625
11: 5 because he cheweth the **c**, but divideth not 1625
11: 6 because he cheweth the **c**, but divideth not 1625
11: 7 *be* clovenfooted, yet he cheweth not the **c**; 1625
11:26 *is* not clovenfooted, nor cheweth the **c**, 1625
Dt 14: 6 *and* cheweth the **c** amongst the beasts: 1625
14: 7 ye shall not eat of them that chew the **c**, 1625
14: 7 for they chew the **c**, but divide not the hoof; 1625
14: 8 it divideth the hoof, yet *cheweth* not the **c**, 1625

CULTIVATED See TILLED; TILLER; TILLEST; TILLETH

CUMBERED (1) [CUMBRANCE]
Lk 10:40 But Martha was **c** about much serving, and *4049*

CUMBERETH (1) [CUMBRANCE]
Lk 13: 7 find none: cut it down; why **c** it the ground? *2673*

CUMBRANCE (1) [CUMBERETH, CUMBERED]
Dt 1:12 How can I myself alone bear your **c**, and 2960

CUMI (1)
Mk 5:41 the hand, and said unto her, TALITHA **C**; *2891*

CUMMIN (4)
Isa 28:25 scatter the **c**, and cast in the principal wheat 3646
28:27 is a cart wheel turned about upon the **c**; 3646
28:27 beaten out with a staff, and the **c** with a rod. 3646
Mt 23:23 for ye pay tithe of mint and anise and **c**, and *2951*

CUN See CHUN

CUNNING (33) [CUNNINGLY]
Ge 25:27 Esau was a **c** hunter, a man of the field; and 3045
Ex 26: 1 *with* cherubims *of* **c** work shalt thou make 2803
26:31 scarlet, and fine twined linen *of* **c** work: 2803
28: 6 and fine twined linen, *with* **c** work. 2803
28:15 the breastplate of judgment *with* **c** work; 2803
31: 4 To devise **c works**, to work in gold, and 4284
35:33 of wood, to make any *manner of* **c** work. 4284
35:35 of the **c workman**, and of the embroiderer, 2803
35:35 and of **those that devise c work**. 2803+4284
36: 8 *with* cherubims *of* **c** work made he them. 2803
36:35 *with* cherubims made he it *of* **c** work. 2803
38:23 a **c workman**, and an embroiderer in blue, 2803
39: 3 and in the fine linen, *with* **c** work. 2803
39: 8 he made the breastplate *of* **c** work, like 2803
1Sa 16:16 seek out a man, *who is* a **c** player on a harp: 3045
16:18 *that is* **c** in playing, and a mighty valiant 3045
1Ki 7:14 and **c** to work all works in brass. 1847
1Ch 22:15 all *manner of* **c** *men* for every *manner of* 2450
25: 7 *even* all that were **c**, was two hundred 995
2Ch 2: 7 me now therefore a man **c** to work in gold, 2450
2: 7 that can skill to grave with the **c** *men* that 2450
2:13 now I have sent a **c** man, endued with 2450
2:14 with thy **c** *men,* and with the cunning *men* 2450
2:14 with the **c** *men* of my lord David thy father. 2450
26:15 invented by **c** *men,* to be on the towers and 2803
Ps 137: 5 O Jerusalem, let my right hand forget *her* **c**. NIH
SS 7: 1 the work of the hands of a **c workman**. 542
Isa 3: 3 and the **c** artificer, and the eloquent orator. 2450
40:20 he seeketh unto him a **c** workman to 2450
Jer 9:17 and send for **c** *women,* that they may come: 2450
10: 9 they *are* all the work of **c** *men.* 2450
Da 1: 4 **c** in knowledge, and understanding science, 3045
Eph 4:14 by the sleight of men, and **c craftiness**, *3834*

CUNNINGLY (1) [CUNNING]
2Pe 1:16 For we have not followed **c devised** fables, *4679*

CUP (68) [CUPBEARER, CUPBEARERS, CUPS]
Ge 40:11 Pharaoh's **c** *was* in my hand: and I took 3563
40:11 pressed them into Pharaoh's **c**, and I gave 3563
40:11 and I gave the **c** into Pharaoh's hand. 3563
40:13 thou shalt deliver Pharaoh's **c** into his hand, 3563
40:21 and he gave the **c** into Pharaoh's hand: 3563
44: 2 put my **c**, the silver cup, in the sack's 1375
44: 2 put my cup, the silver **c**, in the sack's 1375
44:12 and the **c** was found in Benjamin's sack. 1375
44:16 and *he* also with whom the **c** is found. 1375
44:17 *but* the man in whose hand the **c** is found, 1375
2Sa 12: 3 drank of his own **c**, and lay in his bosom, 3563
1Ki 7:26 thereof was wrought like the brim of a **c**, 3563
2Ch 4: 5 brim of it like the work of the brim of a **c**, 3563
Ps 11: 6 *this shall be* the portion of their **c**. 3563
16: 5 portion of mine inheritance and of my **c**: 3563
23: 5 my head with oil; my **c** runneth over. 3563
73:10 and waters of a full *c* are wrung out to them. NIH
75: 8 For in the hand of the LORD *there is* a **c**, 3563
116:13 I will take the **c** of salvation, and call upon 3563
Pr 23:31 when it giveth his colour in the **c**, *when* it 3563
Isa 51:17 at the hand of the LORD the **c** of his fury; 3563
51:17 thou hast drunken the dregs of the **c** of 3563
51:22 I have taken out of thine hand the **c** of 3563
51:22 *even* the dregs of the **c** of my fury; 3563
Jer 16: 7 neither shall *men* give them the **c** of 3563
25:15 Take the wine **c** of this fury at mine hand, 3563
25:17 took I the **c** at the LORD's hand, and 3563
25:28 if they refuse to take the **c** at thine hand to 3563
49:12 to drink of the **c** have assuredly drunken; 3563
51: 7 Babylon *hath been* a golden **c** in 3563
La 4:21 the **c** also shall pass through unto thee: 3563
Eze 23:31 therefore will I give her **c** into thine hand. 3563
23:32 Thou shalt drink *of* thy sister's **c** deep and 3563
23:33 *with* the **c** of astonishment and desolation, 3563
23:33 desolation, *with* the **c** of thy sister Samaria. 3563
Hab 2:16 the **c** of the LORD's right hand shall be 3563
Zec 12: 2 I *will* make Jerusalem a **c** of trembling unto 5592
Mt 10:42 **c** of cold *water* only in the name of a *4221*
20:22 Are ye able to drink *of* the **c** that I shall *4221*
20:23 Ye shall drink indeed *of* my **c**, and *4221*
23:25 for ye make clean the outside of the **c** and *4221*
23:26 cleanse first that *which is* within the **c** and *4221*
26:27 And he took the **c**, and gave thanks, and *4221*
26:39 if it be possible, let this **c** pass from me: *4221*
26:42 if this **c** may not pass away from me, *4221*
Mk 9:41 For whosoever shall give you a **c** of water *4221*
10:38 can ye drink *of* the **c** that I drink *of*? and be *4221*
10:39 Ye shall indeed drink *of* the **c** that I drink *4221*
14:23 And he took the **c**, and when he had given *4221*
14:36 unto thee; take away this **c** from me: *4221*
Lk 11:39 Pharisees make clean the outside of the **c** *4221*
22:17 And he took *the* **c**, and gave thanks, and *4221*
22:20 Likewise also the **c** after supper, saying, *4221*
22:20 This **c** *is* the new testament in my blood, *4221*
22:42 if thou be willing, remove this **c** from me: *4221*
Jn 18:11 the **c** which my Father hath given me, *4221*
1Co 10:16 The **c** of blessing which we bless, is it not *4221*
10:21 Ye cannot drink the **c** of the Lord, and *4221*
10:21 the cup of the Lord, and the **c** of devils: *4221*
11:25 After the same manner also *he took* the **c**, *4221*
11:25 This **c** is the new testament in my blood: *4221*
11:26 often as ye eat this bread, and drink this **c**, *4221*
11:27 and drink *this* **c** of the Lord unworthily, *4221*
11:28 him eat of *that* bread, and drink of *that* **c**. *4221*
Rev 14:10 mixture into the **c** of his indignation; *4221*
16:19 to give unto her the **c** of the wine of *4221*
17: 4 having a golden **c** in her hand full of *4221*
18: 6 in the **c** which she hath filled fill to her *4221*

CUPBEARER (1) [BEAR, CUP]
Ne 1:11 sight of this man. For I was the king's **c**. 8248

CUPBEARERS (2) [BEAR, CUP]
1Ki 10: 5 his **c**, and his ascent *by* which he went up 8248
2Ch 9: 4 his **c** also, and their apparel; and his ascent 8248

CUPS (6) [CUP]
1Ch 28:17 the fleshhooks, and the bowls, and the **c**: 7184
Isa 22:24 of small quantity, from the vessels of **c**, 101
Jer 35: 5 and **c**, and I said unto them, Drink ye wine. 3563
52:19 the candlesticks, and the spoons, and the **c**; 4518
Mk 7: 4 *as* the washing of **c**, and pots, *4221*
7: 8 of men, *as* the washing of pots and **c**: *4221*

CURE (5) [CURED, CURES]
Jer 33: 6 I *will* bring it health and **c**, and I will cure 4832
33: 6 I will **c** them, and will reveal unto them 7495
Hos 5:13 yet could he not heal you nor **c** you of your 1455
Mt 17:16 to thy disciples, and they could not **c** him. *2323*
Lk 9: 1 authority over all devils, and to **c** diseases. *2323*

CURED (4) [CURE]
Jer 46:11 many medicines; *for* thou shalt not be **c**. 8585
Mt 17:18 and the child was **c** from that *very* hour. *2323*
Lk 7:21 And in that *same* hour he **c** many of *their* *2323*
Jn 5:10 therefore said unto him that was **c**, *2323*

CURES (1) [CURE]
Lk 13:32 and I do **c** to day and to morrow, and *2392*

CURIOUS (10) [CURIOUSLY]
Ex 28: 8 the **c girdle** of the ephod, which *is* upon it, 2805
28:27 above the **c girdle** of the ephod. 2805
28:28 that *it* may be above the **c girdle** of 2805
29: 5 and gird him with the **c girdle** of the ephod: 2805
35:32 to devise **c works**, to work in gold, and 4284
39: 5 the **c girdle** of his ephod, that *was* upon it, 2805
39:20 above the **c girdle** of the ephod. 2805
39:21 that *it* might be above the **c girdle** of 2805
Lev 8: 7 he girded him with the **c girdle** of 2805
Ac 19:19 Many also of them which used **c arts** *4021*

CURIOUSLY (1) [CURIOUS]
Ps 139:15 **c wrought** in the lowest parts of the earth. 7551

CURRENT (1)
Ge 23:16 of silver, **c** *money* with the merchant. 5674

CURRY FAVOR See INTREAT; INTREATED; INTREATIES; INTREATY

CURSE (101) [ACCURSED, CURSED, CURSEDST, CURSES, CURSEST, CURSETH, CURSING, CURSINGS]
Ge 8:21 I will not again **c** the ground any more for 7043
12: 3 that bless thee, and **c** him that curseth thee: 779
27:12 I shall bring a **c** upon me, and not a 7045
27:13 said unto him, Upon me *be* thy **c**, my son: 7045
Ex 22:28 revile the gods, nor **c** the ruler of thy people. 779
Lev 19:14 Thou shalt not **c** the deaf, nor put a 7043
Nu 5:18 his hand the bitter water that **causeth** the **c**: 779
5:19 free from this bitter water that **causeth the c**: 779
5:21 The LORD make thee a **c** and an oath 423
5:22 this water that **causeth the c** shall go into 779
5:24 to drink the bitter water that **causeth the c**: 779
5:24 the water that **causeth the c** shall enter into 779
5:27 that the water that **causeth the c** shall enter 779
5:27 the woman shall be a **c** among her people. 423
22: 6 now therefore, I pray thee, **c** me this people; 779
22:11 come now, **c** me them; peradventure I shall 6895
22:12 go with them; thou shalt not **c** the people: 779
22:17 I pray thee, **c** me this people. 6895
23: 7 **c** me Jacob, and come, defy Israel. 779
23: 8 How shall I **c**, whom God hath not cursed? 5344
23:11 I took thee to **c** mine enemies, and behold, 6895
23:13 see them all: and **c** me them from thence. 6895
23:25 **c** them **at all**, nor bless them at all. 5344+5344
23:27 that thou mayest **c** me them from thence. 6895
24:10 I called thee to **c** mine enemies, and behold, 6895
Dt 11:26 I set before you *this* day a blessing and a **c**; 7045
11:28 a **c**, if ye will not obey the commandments 7045
11:29 mount Gerizim, and the **c** upon mount Ebal. 7045
23: 4 Beor of Pethor of Mesopotamia, to **c** thee. 7043
23: 5 the LORD thy God turned the **c** into a 7045
27:13 these shall stand upon mount Ebal to **c**; 7045
29:19 to pass, when he heareth the words of this **c**, 423
30: 1 the blessing and the **c**, which I have set 7045
Jos 6:18 make the camp of Israel a **c**, and trouble it. 2764
24: 9 and called Balaam the son of Beor to **c** you: 7043
Jdg 5:23 **C** ye Meroz, said the angel of the LORD, 779
5:23 **c** ye bitterly the inhabitants thereof; 779
9:57 upon them came the **c** of Jotham the son of 7045
2Sa 16: 9 Why should this dead dog **c** my lord 7043
16:10 so let him **c**, because the LORD hath said 7043
16:10 the LORD hath said unto him, **C** David. 7043
16:11 *do it?* let him alone, and let him **c**; 7043
1Ki 2: 8 which cursed me *with* a grievous **c** in 7045
2Ki 22:19 *they* should become a desolation and a **c**, 7045
Ne 10:29 and entered into a **c**, and into an oath, 423
13: 2 against them, that *he* should **c** them: 7043
13: 2 howbeit our God turned the **c** into a 7045
Job 1:11 that he hath, and he will **c** thee to thy face. 1288
2: 5 and his flesh, and he will **c** thee to thy face. 1288
2: 9 still retain thine integrity? **c** God, and die. 1288
3: 8 Let them **c** it that curse the day, who are 5344
3: 8 Let them curse it that **c** the day, who are 779
31:30 my mouth to sin by wishing a **c** to his soul.) 423
Ps 62: 4 bless with their mouth, but they **c** inwardly. 7043
109:28 Let them **c**, but bless thou: when they arise, 7043
Pr 3:33 The **c** of the LORD *is* in the house of 3994
11:26 withholdeth corn, the people shall **c** him: 5344
24:24 him shall the people **c**, nations shall abhor 5344
26: 2 by flying, so the **c** causeless shall not come. 7045
27:14 the morning, it shall be counted a **c** to him. 7045
28:27 he that hideth his eyes shall have many a **c**. 3994
30:10 lest he **c** thee, and thou be found guilty. 7043
Ecc 7:21 lest thou hear thy servant **c** thee: 7043
10:20 **C** not the king, no not in thy thought; and 7043
10:20 and **c** not the rich in thy bedchamber: 7043
Isa 8:21 **c** their king and their God, and 7043
24: 6 Therefore hath the **c** devoured the earth, and 423
34: 5 and upon the people of my **c**, to judgment. 2764
43:28 have given Jacob to the **c**, and Israel to 2764
65:15 ye shall leave your name for a **c** unto my 7621
Jer 15:10 on usury; *yet* every one of them doth **c** me. 7043
24: 9 a reproach and a proverb, a taunt and a **c**, 7045
25:18 an astonishment, a hissing, and a **c**; 7045
26: 6 will make this city a **c** to all the nations of 7045
29:18 to be a **c**, and an astonishment, and a hissing, 423
29:22 of them shall be taken up a **c** by all 7045
42:18 an astonishment, and a **c**, and a reproach; 7045
44: 8 that *ye* might be a **c** and a reproach among 7045
44:12 an astonishment, and a **c**, and a reproach. 7045
44:22 an astonishment, and a **c**, without an 7045
49:13 a desolation, a reproach, a waste, and a **c**; 7045
La 3:65 Give them sorrow of heart, thy **c** unto them. 8381
Da 9:11 therefore the **c** is poured upon us, and 423
Zec 5: 3 This *is* the **c** that goeth forth over the face of 423
8:13 *that* as ye were a **c** among the heathen, 7045
Mal 2: 2 I will even send a **c** upon you, and 3994
2: 2 a curse upon you, and will **c** your blessings: 779
3: 9 Ye *are* cursed with a **c**: for ye *have* robbed 3994
4: 6 lest I come and smite the earth *with* a **c**. 2764
Mt 5:44 Love your enemies, bless them that **c** you, *2672*
26:74 Then began he to **c** and to swear, *saying,* I *2653*
Mk 14:71 But he began to **c** and to swear, *saying,* I *332*
Lk 6:28 Bless them that **c** you, and pray for them *2672*
Ac 23:12 and **bound** themselves **under a c**, *332*
23:14 have **bound** ourselves **under a great c**, *331+332*
Ro 12:14 them which persecute you: bless, and **c** not. *2672*
Gal 3:10 are of the works of the law are under the **c**: *2671*
3:13 Christ hath redeemed us from the **c** of *2671*
3:13 the curse of the law, being made a **c** for us: *2671*
Jas 3: 9 and therewith **c** we men, which are made *2672*
Rev 22: 3 And there shall be no more **c**: but *2652*

CURSED (72) [CURSE]
Ge 3:14 thou *art* **c** above all cattle, and above every 779
3:17 **c** *is* the ground for thy sake; in sorrow shalt 779
4:11 now *art* thou **c** from the earth, which hath 779
5:29 of the ground which the LORD hath **c**. 779
9:25 he said, **C** *be* Canaan; a servant of servants 779
27:29 **c** *be* every one that curseth thee, and 779
49: 7 **C** *be* their anger, for *it was* fierce; and 779
Lev 20: 9 he hath **c** his father or his mother; his blood 7043
24:11 blasphemed the name *of the* LORD, and **c**. 7043
24:14 Bring forth him that hath **c** without 7043
24:23 that they should bring forth him that had **c** 7043
Nu 22: 6 *is* blessed, and *he* whom thou cursest is **c**. 779
23: 8 How shall I curse, whom God hath not **c**? 6895
24: 9 blesseth thee, and **c** *is* he that curseth thee. 779
Dt 7:26 thine house, lest thou be a **c thing** like it: 2764
7:26 shalt utterly abhor it; for it *is* a **c thing**. 2764
13:17 there shall cleave nought of the **c thing** to 2764
27:15 **C** *be* the man that maketh *any* graven or 779
27:16 **C** *be* he that setteth light by his father or 779
27:17 **C** *be* he that removeth his neighbour's 779
27:18 **C** *be* he that maketh the blind to wander out 779
27:19 **C** *be* he that perverteth the judgment of 779
27:20 **C** *be* he that lieth with his father's wife; 779
27:21 **C** *be* he that lieth with any *manner of* beast. 779
27:22 **C** *be* he that lieth with his sister, 779
27:23 **C** *be* he that lieth with his mother in law. 779
27:24 **C** *be* he that smiteth his neighbour secretly. 779
27:25 **C** *be* he that taketh reward to slay an 779
27:26 **C** *be* he that confirmeth not *all* the words of 779
28:16 **C** *shalt* thou *be* in the city, and cursed *shalt* 779
28:16 *be* in the city, and **c** *shalt* thou *be* in the field. 779
28:17 **C** *shall be* thy basket and thy store. 779
28:18 **C** *shall be* the fruit of thy body, and the fruit 779
28:19 **C** *shalt* thou *be* when thou comest in, and 779
28:19 and **c** *shalt* thou *be* when thou goest out. 779
Jos 6:26 saying, **C** *be* the man before the LORD, 779
9:23 Now therefore ye *are* **c**, and there shall none 779
Jdg 9:27 and did eat and drink, and **c** Abimelech. 7043
21:18 **C** *be* he that giveth a wife to Benjamin. 779
1Sa 14:24 **C** *be* the man that eateth *any* food until 779
14:28 **C** *be* the man that eateth *any* food *this* day. 779
17:43 And the Philistine **c** David by his gods. 7043

1Sa 26:19 of men, c *be* they before the LORD; 779
2Sa 16: 5 he came forth, and c still as he came. 7043
16: 7 And thus said Shimei when he c, Come out, 7043
16:13 c as he went, and threw stones at him, and 7043
19:21 because he c me the LORD'S anointed? 7043
1Ki 2: 8 which c me *with* a grievous curse in the day 7043
2Ki 2:24 and c them in the name of the LORD. 7043
9:34 Go, see now this c *woman,* and bury her: 779
Ne 13:25 c them, and smote certain of them, and 7043
Job 1: 5 sons have sinned, and c God in their hearts. 1288
3: 1 this opened Job his mouth, and c his day. 7043
5: 3 taking root: but suddenly I c his habitation. 5344
24:18 as the waters; their portion is c in the earth: 7043
Ps 37:22 and they that be c of him shall be cut off. 7043
119:21 Thou hast rebuked the proud *that are* c, 779
Ecc 7:22 that thou thyself likewise hast c others. 7043
Jer 11: 3 C *be* the man that obeyeth not the words of 779
17: 5 C *be* the man that trusteth in man, and 779
20:14 C *be* the day wherein I was born: let not 779
20:15 C *be* the man who brought tidings to my 779
48:10 C *be* he that doeth the work of the LORD 779
48:10 c *be* he that keepeth back his sword from 779
Mal 1:14 c *be* the deceiver, which hath in his flock a 779
2: 2 yea, I have c them already, because ye do 779
3: 9 Ye *are* c with a curse: for ye *have* robbed 779
Mt 25:41 Depart from me, ye c, into everlasting fire, *2672*
Jn 7:49 this people who knoweth not the law are c. *1944*
Gal 3:10 C *is* every one that continueth not in all *1944*
3:13 C *is* every one that hangeth on a tree: *1944*
2Pe 2:14 with covetous practices; c children: *2671*

CURSEDST (2) [CURSE]
Jdg 17: 2 about which thou c, and spakest of also in 422
Mk 11:21 the fig tree which thou c is withered away. *2672*

CURSES (8) [CURSE]
Nu 5:23 the priest shall write these c in a book, and 423
Dt 28:15 that all these c shall come upon thee, and 7045
28:45 Moreover all these c shall come upon thee, 7045
29:20 all the c that are written in this book shall lie 423
29:21 according to all the c of the covenant that are 423
29:27 to bring upon it all the c that are written in 7045
30: 7 the LORD thy God will put all these c upon 423
2Ch 34:24 *even* all the c that are written in the book 423

CURSEST (1) [CURSE]
Nu 22: 6 *is* blessed, and *he* whom thou c is cursed. 779

CURSETH (10) [CURSE]
Ge 12: 3 that bless thee, and curse him that c thee: 7043
27:29 cursed *be* every one that c thee, and 779
Ex 21:17 he that c his father, or his mother, 7043
Lev 20: 9 For every one that c his father or his mother 7043
24:15 Whosoever c his God shall bear his sin. 7043
Nu 24: 9 blesseth thee, and cursed *is* he that c thee. 779
Pr 20:20 Whoso c his father or his mother, his lamp 7043
30:11 *There is* a generation *that* c their father, and 7043
Mt 15: 4 and, He that c father or mother, let him die *2551*
Mk 7:10 and, Whoso c father or mother, let him die *2551*

CURSING (12) [CURSE]
Nu 5:21 shall charge the woman with an oath of c, 423
Dt 28:20 The LORD shall send upon thee c, 3994
30:19 before you life and death, blessing and c: 7045
2Sa 16:12 will requite me good for his c this day. 7045
Ps 10: 7 His mouth is full *of* c and deceit and fraud: 423
59:12 and for c and lying *which* they speak. 423
109:17 As he loved c, so let it come *unto* him: as 7045
109:18 As he clothed himself with c like as with 7045
Pr 29:24 own soul: he heareth c, and bewrayeth *it* not. 423
Ro 3:14 Whose mouth is full of c and bitterness: *685*
Heb 6: 8 and briers *is* rejected, and *is* nigh unto c; *2671*
Jas 3:10 the same mouth proceedeth blessing and c. *2671*

CURSINGS (1) [CURSE]
Jos 8:34 the words of the law, the blessings and c, 7045

CURTAIN (26) [CURTAINS]
Ex 26: 2 The length of one c *shall be* eight and 3407
26: 2 and the breadth of one c four cubits: 3407
26: 4 the one c from the selvedge in the coupling; 3407
26: 4 make in the uttermost edge of *another* c, 3407
26: 5 Fifty loops shalt thou make in the one c, 3407
26: 5 the c that *is* in the coupling of the second; 3407
26: 8 The length of one c *shall be* thirty cubits, 3407
26: 8 and the breadth of one c four cubits: 3407
26: 9 shalt double the sixth c in the forefront of 3407
26:10 of the one c *that is* outmost in the coupling, 3407
26:10 fifty loops in the edge of the c which 3407
26:12 the half c that remaineth, shall hang over 3407
36: 9 The length of one c *was* twenty and 3407
36: 9 and the breadth of one c four cubits: 3407
36:11 he made loops of blue on the edge of one c 3407
36:11 he made in the uttermost side of *another* c, 3407
36:12 Fifty loops made he in one c, and 3407
36:12 fifty loops made he in the edge of the c 3407
36:12 the second: the loops held one c to another. NIH
36:15 The length of one c *was* thirty cubits, and 3407
36:15 and four cubits *was* the breadth of one c: 3407
36:17 the uttermost edge of the c in the coupling, 3407
36:17 fifty loops made he upon the edge of the c 3407
Nu 3:26 the c for the door of the court, which *is* by 4539
Ps 104: 2 who stretchest out the heavens like a c: 3407
Isa 40:22 that stretcheth out the heavens as a c, and 1852

CURTAINS (31) [CURTAIN]
Ex 26: 1 tabernacle *with* ten c *of* fine twined linen, 3407
26: 2 every one of the c shall have one measure. 3407
26: 3 The five c shall be coupled together one to 3407
26: 3 *other* five c *shall be* coupled one to another. 3407
26: 6 and couple the c together with the taches: 3407
26: 7 thou shalt make c *of* goats' *hair* to be a 3407
26: 7 the tabernacle: eleven c shalt thou make. 3407
26: 8 the eleven c *shall be all* of one measure. 3407
26: 9 And thou shalt couple five c by themselves, 3407
26: 9 six c by themselves, and shalt double 3407
26:12 the remnant that remaineth of the c of 3407
26:13 remaineth in the length of the c of the tent, 3407
36: 8 tabernacle made ten c *of* fine twined linen, 3407
36: 9 four cubits: the c *were* all of one size. 3407
36:10 And he coupled the five c one unto another: 3407
36:10 *the other* five c he coupled one unto 3407
36:13 coupled the c one unto another with 3407
36:14 he made c *of* goats' *hair* for the tent over 3407
36:14 over the tabernacle: eleven c he made them. 3407
36:15 one curtain: the eleven c *were* of one size. 3407
36:16 he coupled five c by themselves, and six 3407
36:16 by themselves, and six c by themselves. 3407
Nu 4:25 they shall bear the c of the tabernacle, and 3407
2Sa 7: 2 but the ark of God dwelleth within c. 3407
1Ch 17: 1 covenant of the LORD *remaineth* under c. 3407
SS 1: 5 as the tents of Kedar, as the c of Solomon. 3407
Isa 54: 2 let them stretch forth the c of thine 3407
Jer 4:20 my tents spoiled, *and* my c in a moment. 3407
10:20 forth my tent any more, and to set up my c. 3407
49:29 *away:* they shall take to themselves their c, 3407
Hab 3: 7 *and* the c of the land of Midian did tremble. 3407

CUSH (8)
Ge 10: 6 C, and Mizraim, and Phut, and Canaan. 3568
10: 7 the sons of C; Seba, and Havilah, and 3568
10: 8 C begat Nimrod: he began to be a mighty 3568
1Ch 1: 8 of Ham; C, and Mizraim, Put, and Canaan. 3568
1: 9 the sons of C; Seba, and Havilah, and 3568
1:10 C begat Nimrod: he began to be mighty 3568
Ps 7: T concerning the words of C the Benjamite. 3568
Isa 11:11 from C, and from Elam, and from Shinar, 3568

CUSHAN (1)
Hab 3: 7 I saw the tents of C in affliction: *and* 3572

CUSHAN-RISHATHAIM See CHUSHAN-RISHATHAIM

CUSHI (10)
2Sa 18:21 said Joab to C, Go tell the king what thou 3569
18:21 And C bowed himself unto Joab, and ran. 3569
18:22 let me, I pray thee, also run after C. 3569
18:23 ran *by* the way of the plain, and overran C. 3569
18:31 behold, C came; and Cushi said, Tidings, 3569
18:31 and C said, Tidings, my lord the king: 3569
18:32 the king said unto C, *Is* the young man 3569
18:32 C answered, The enemies of my lord 3569
Jer 36:14 the son of C, unto Baruch, saying, 3569
Zep 1: 1 which came unto Zephaniah the son of C, 3569

CUSTODY (5)
Nu 3:36 under the c and charge of the sons of 6486
Est 2: 3 unto the c of Hege the king's chamberlain, 3027
2: 8 to the c of Hegai, that Esther was brought 3027
2: 8 to the c of Hegai, keeper of the women. 3027

Est 2:14 to the **c** of Shaashgaz, the king's 3027

CUSTOM (20) [ACCUSTOMED, CUSTOMS]

Ge 31:35 before thee; for the **c** of women *is* upon me. 1870
Jdg 11:39 she knew no man. And it was a **c** in Israel, 2706
1Sa 2:13 the priests' **c** with the people *was, that* 4941
Ezr 3: 4 **according to the c**, as the duty of every 3509.1
4:13 **c**, and *so* thou shalt endamage the revenue 1983
4:20 and toll, tribute, and **c**, *was* paid unto them. 1983
7:24 to impose toll, tribute, or **c**, upon them. 1983
Jer 32:11 was sealed *according to* the law and **c**, 2706
Mt 9: 9 named Matthew, sitting at the **receipt of c**: *5058*
17:25 of whom do the kings of the earth take **c** or *5056*
Mk 2:14 *son* of Alpheus sitting at the **receipt of c**, *5058*
Lk 1: 9 According to the **c** of the priest's office, *1485*
2:27 to do for him after the **c** of the law, *1480*
2:42 they went up to Jerusalem after the **c** of *1485*
4:16 and, as his **c** was, he went into *1486*
5:27 named Levi, sitting at the **receipt of c**: *5058*
Jn 18:39 But ye have a **c**, that I should release unto *4914*
Ro 13: 7 tribute to whom tribute *is due;* **c** to whom *5056*
13: 7 to whom tribute *is due;* custom to whom **c**; *5056*
1Co 11:16 we have no such **c**, neither the churches of *4914*

CUSTOMS (7) [CUSTOM]

Lev 18:30 commit not *any one* of *these* abominable **c**, 2708
Jer 10: 3 For the **c** of the people *are* vain: for *one* 2708
Ac 6:14 shall change the **c** which Moses delivered *1485*
16:21 And teach **c**, which are not lawful for us to *1485*
21:21 *their* children, neither to walk after the **c**. *1485*
26: 3 *I know* thee to be expert in all **c** and *1485*
28:17 against the people, or **c** of our fathers, *1485*

CUT (320) [CUTTEST, CUTTETH, CUTTING, CUTTINGS]

Ge 9:11 neither shall all flesh be **c off** any more by 3772
17:14 that soul shall be **c off** from his people; 3772
Ex 4:25 **c off** the foreskin of her son, and cast *it* at 3772
9:15 and thou shalt be **c off** from the earth. 3582
12:15 that soul shall be **c off** from Israel. 3772
12:19 even that soul shall be **c off** from 3772
23:23 and the Jebusites: and I will **c** them **off**. 3582
29:17 thou shalt **c** the ram in pieces, and wash 5408
30:33 shall even be **c off** from his people. 3772
30:38 shall even be **c off** from his people. 3772
31:14 that soul shall be **c off** from amongst his 3772
34:13 their images, and **c down** their groves: 3772
39: 3 **c** *it into* wires, to work *it* in the blue, and 7112
Lev 1: 6 the burnt offering, and **c** it into his pieces. 5408
1:12 he shall **c** it into his pieces, with his head 5408
7:20 even that soul shall be **c off** from his 3772
7:21 even that soul shall be **c off** from his 3772
7:25 even the soul that eateth *it* shall be **c off** 3772
7:27 even that soul shall be **c off** from his 3772
8:20 he **c** the ram into pieces; and Moses burnt 5408
17: 4 that man shall be **c off** from among his 3772
17: 9 even that man shall be **c off** from among 3772
17:10 and will **c** him **off** from among his people. 3772
17:14 whosoever eateth it shall be **c off**. 3772
18:29 shall be **c off** from among their people. 3772
19: 8 that soul shall be **c off** from among his 3772
20: 3 and will **c** him **off** from among his people; 3772
20: 5 will **c** him **off**, and all that go a whoring 3772
20: 6 and will **c** him **off** from among his people. 3772
20:17 they shall be **c off** in the sight of their 3772
20:18 both of them shall be **c off** from among 3772
22: 3 that soul shall be **c off** from my presence: 3772
22:24 is bruised, or crushed, or broken, or **c**; 3772
23:29 he shall be **c off** from among his people. 3772
26:30 **c down** your images, and cast your 3772
Nu 4:18 **C** ye not **off** the tribe of the families of 3772
9:13 even the same soul shall be **c off** from 3772
13:23 **c down** from thence a branch with one 3772
13:24 the children of Israel **c down** from thence. 3772
15:30 that soul shall be **c off** from among his 3772
15:31 that soul shall **utterly** be **c off**; 3772+3772
19:13 and that soul shall be **c off** from Israel: 3772
19:20 that soul shall be **c off** from among 3772
Dt 7: 5 **c down** their groves, and burn their graven 1438
12:29 When the LORD thy God shall **c off** 3772
14: 1 ye shall not **c** yourselves, nor make *any* 1413
19: 1 When the LORD thy God hath **c off** 3772
19: 5 a stroke with the axe to **c down** the tree, 3772
20:19 thou shalt not **c** them **down** (for the tree of 3772
20:20 thou shalt destroy and **c** them **down**; 3772
23: 1 the stones, or hath *his* privy member **c off**, 3772
25:12 thou shalt **c off** her hand, thine eye shall 7112
Jos 3:13 *that* the waters of Jordan shall be **c off** *from* 3772
3:16 *even* the salt sea, failed, *and* were **c off**: 3772
4: 7 That the waters of Jordan were **c off** before 3772
4: 7 the waters of Jordan were **c off**: 3772
7: 9 and **c off** our name from the earth: 3772
11:21 **c off** the Anakims from the mountains, 3772
17:15 **c down** for thyself there in the land of 1254
17:18 for it *is* a wood, and thou shalt **c** it **down**: 1254
23: 4 with all the nations that I have **c off**, 3772
Jdg 1: 6 and **c off** his thumbs and his great toes. 7112
1: 7 their thumbs and their great toes **c off**, 7112
6:25 and **c down** the grove that *is* by it: 3772
6:26 of the grove which thou shalt **c down**. 3772
6:28 the grove was **c down** that *was* by it, and 3772
6:30 he hath **c down** the grove that *was* by it. 3772
9:48 **c down** a bough from the trees, and took it, 3772
9:49 all the people likewise **c down** every man 3772
20: 6 **c** her **in pieces**, and sent her throughout all 5408
21: 6 There is one tribe **c off** from Israel *this* day. 1438
Ru 4:10 that the name of the dead be not **c off** from 3772
1Sa 2:31 that I will **c off** thine arm, and the arm of 1438
2:33 *whom* I shall not **c off** from mine altar, 3772
5: 4 both the palms of his hands *were* **c off** upon 3772
17:51 and slew him, and **c off** his head therewith. 3772
20:15 *also* thou shalt not **c off** thy kindness from 3772
20:15 not when the LORD hath **c off** 3772
24: 4 and **c off** the skirt of Saul's robe privily. 3772
24: 5 because he had **c off** Saul's skirt. 3772
24:11 for in that I **c off** the skirt of thy robe, and 3772
24:21 that thou wilt not **c off** my seed after me, 3772
28: 9 how he hath **c off** those that have familiar 3772
31: 9 they **c off** his head, and stripped off his 3772
2Sa 4:12 **c off** their hands and their feet, and 7112
7: 9 have **c off** all thine enemies out of thy 3772
10: 4 **c off** their garments in the middle, *even* to 3772
20:22 they **c off** the head of Sheba the son of 3772
1Ki 9: 7 will I **c off** Israel out of the land which I 3772
11:16 until he had **c off** every male in Edom:) 3772
13:34 even to **c** *it* **off**, and to destroy *it* from off 3582
14:10 will **c off** from Jeroboam *him that* pisseth 3772
14:14 who shall **c off** the house of Jeroboam that 3772
18: 4 when Jezebel **c off** the prophets of 3772
18:23 **c** it **in pieces**, and lay *it* on wood, and 5408
18:28 **c** themselves after their manner with knives 1413
18:33 **c** the bullock **in pieces**, and laid *him* on 5408
21:21 will **c off** from Ahab *him that* pisseth 3772
2Ki 6: 4 they came to Jordan, they **c down** wood. 1504
6: 6 he **c down** a stick, and cast *it* in thither; 7094
9: 8 I will **c off** from Ahab *him that* pisseth 3772
10:32 days the LORD began to **c** Israel **short**: 7096
16:17 king Ahaz **c off** the borders of the bases, 7112
18: 4 **c down** the groves, and brake in pieces 3772
18:16 At that time did Hezekiah **c off** *the gold* 7112
19:23 will **c down** the tall cedar trees thereof, *and* 3772
23:14 **c down** the groves, and filled their places 3772
24:13 **c in pieces** all the vessels of gold which 7112
1Ch 17: 8 have **c off** all thine enemies from before 3772
19: 4 **c off** their garments in the midst hard by 3772
20: 3 **c** *them* with saws, and with harrows of iron, 7787
2Ch 2: 8 for I know that thy servants can skill to **c** 3772
2:10 to thy servants, the hewers that **c** timber, 3772
2:16 we will **c** wood out of Lebanon, as much as 3772
14: 3 down the images, and **c down** the groves: 1438
15:16 Asa **c down** her idol, and stamped *it,* and 3772
22: 7 whom the LORD had anointed to **c off** 3772
26:21 for he was **c off** from the house of 1504
28:24 **c in pieces** the vessels of the house of God, 7112
31: 1 images *in pieces,* and **c down** the groves, 1438
32:21 which **c off** all the mighty *men* of valour, 3582
34: 4 that *were* on high above them, he **c down**; 1438
34: 7 **c down** all the idols throughout all the land 1438
Job 4: 7 or where were the righteous **c off**? 3582
6: 9 he would let loose his hand, and **c** me **off**! 1214
8:12 it *is* yet in his greenness, *and* not **c down**, 6998
8:14 Whose hope shall be **c off**, and whose trust 6990
11:10 If he **c off**, and shut up, or gather together, 2498
14: 2 cometh forth like a flower, and is **c down**: 5243
14: 7 if it be **c down**, that it will sprout again, 3772
18:16 above shall his branch be **c off**. 5243
21:21 number of his months is **c off in the midst**? 2686
22:16 Which were **c down** out of time, 7059
22:20 Whereas our substance is not **c down**, but 3582

Job	23:17	Because I was not **c off** before	6789
	24:24	and **c off** as the tops of the ears of corn.	5243
	30: 4	Who **c up** mallows by the bushes, and	6998
	36:20	when people are **c off** in their place.	5927
Ps	12: 3	The LORD shall **c off** all flattering lips,	3772
	31:22	my haste, I am **c off** from before thine eyes:	1629
	34:16	to **c off** the remembrance of them from	3772
	37: 2	For they shall soon be **c down** like	5243
	37: 9	For evildoers shall be **c off**: but those that	3772
	37:22	they that be cursed of him shall be **c off**.	3772
	37:28	but the seed of the wicked shall be **c off**.	3772
	37:34	when the wicked are **c off**, thou shalt see	3772
	37:38	the end of the wicked shall be **c off**.	3772
	54: 5	unto mine enemies: **c** them **off** in thy truth.	6789
	58: 7	*shoot* his arrows, let them be as **c in pieces**.	4135
	75:10	All the horns of the wicked also will I **c off**;	1438
	76:12	He shall **c off** the spirit of princes: *he is*	1219
	80:16	*It is* burnt with fire, *it is* **c down**:	3683
	83: 4	and let us **c** them **off** from *being* a nation;	3582
	88: 5	no more: and they are **c off** from thy hand.	1504
	88:16	goeth over me; thy terrors have **c** me **off**.	6789
	90: 6	in the evening it is **c down**, and withereth.	4135
	90:10	for it is soon **c off**, and we fly away.	1468
	94:23	shall **c** them **off** in their own wickedness;	6789
	94:23	*yea,* the LORD our God shall **c** them **off**.	6789
	101: 5	slandereth his neighbour, him will I **c off**:	6789
	101: 8	that *I* may **c off** all wicked doers from	3772
	107:16	of brass, and **c** the bars of iron **in sunder**.	1438
	109:13	Let his posterity be **c off**; *and* in	3772
	109:15	that he may **c off** the memory of them from	3772
	129: 4	he hath **c asunder** the cords of the wicked.	7112
	143:12	of thy mercy **c off** mine enemies, and	6789
Pr	2:22	the wicked shall be **c off** from the earth,	3772
	10:31	but the froward tongue shall be **c out**.	3772
	23:18	and thine expectation shall not be **c off**.	3772
	24:14	and thy expectation shall not be **c off**.	3772
Isa	9:10	the sycomores are **c down**, but we will	1438
	9:14	Therefore the LORD will **c off** from Israel	3772
	10: 7	heart to destroy and **c off** nations not a few.	3772
	10:34	he shall **c down** the thickets of the forest	5362
	11:13	and the adversaries of Judah shall be **c off**:	3772
	14:12	*how* art thou **c down** to the ground,	1438
	14:22	**c off** from Babylon the name, and remnant,	3772
	15: 2	*shall be* baldness, *and* every beard **c off**.	1438
	18: 5	he shall both **c off** the sprigs with pruning	3772
	18: 5	and take away *and* **c down** the branches.	8456
	22:25	place be removed, and be **c down**, and fall;	1438
	22:25	the burden that *was* upon it shall be **c off**:	3772
	29:20	and all that watch for iniquity are **c off**:	3772
	33:12	*as* thorns **c up** shall they be burnt in	3683
	37:24	I will **c down** the tall cedars thereof, *and*	3772
	38:12	I have **c off** like a weaver my life: he will	7088
	38:12	he will **c** me **off** with pining sickness:	1214
	45: 2	of brass, and **c in sunder** the bars of iron:	1438
	48: 9	will I refrain for thee, that *I* **c** thee not **off**.	3772
	48:19	his name should not have been **c off** nor	3772
	51: 9	*Art* thou not it that hath **c** Rahab, *and*	2672
	53: 8	for he was **c off** out of the land of	1504
	55:13	an everlasting sign *that* shall not be **c off**.	3772
	56: 5	an everlasting name, that shall not be **c off**.	3772
	66: 3	a lamb, *as if* he **c off** a dog's **neck**;	6202
Jer	7:28	is perished, and is **c off** from their mouth.	3772
	7:29	**C off** thine hair, *O Jerusalem,* and cast *it*	1494
	9:21	to **c off** the children from without, *and*	3772
	11:19	let us **c** him **off** from the land of the living,	3772
	16: 6	*men* lament for them, nor **c** themselves,	1413
	22: 7	they shall **c down** thy choice cedars, and	3772
	25:37	the peaceable habitations are **c down**	1826
	34:18	when they **c** the calf in twain, and	3772
	36:23	he **c** it with the penknife, and cast *it* into	7167
	41: 5	having **c** themselves, with offerings and	1413
	44: 7	to **c off** from you man and woman, child	3772
	44: 8	that ye might **c** yourselves **off**, and that *ye*	3772
	44:11	against you for evil, and to **c off** all Judah.	3772
	46:23	They shall **c down** her forest, saith	3772
	47: 4	*and* to **c off** from Tyrus and Zidon every	3772
	47: 5	Ashkelon is **c off** *with* the remnant of their	1820
	47: 5	their valley: how long wilt thou **c** thyself?	1413
	48: 2	and let us **c** it **off** from *being* a nation.	3772
	48: 2	Also thou shalt be **c down**, O Madmen;	1826
	48:25	The horn of Moab is **c off**, and his arm is	1438
	49:26	all the men of war shall be **c off** in that day,	1826
	50:16	**C off** the sower from Babylon, and him that	3772
	50:23	is the hammer of the whole earth **c asunder**	1438
	50:30	all her men of war shall be **c off** in that day,	1826
	51: 6	be not **c off** in her iniquity; for this *is*	1826
	51:62	to **c** it **off**, that none shall remain in it,	3772
La	2: 3	He hath **c off** in *his* fierce anger all the horn	1438
	3:53	They have **c off** my life in the dungeon, and	6789
	3:54	over mine head; *then* I said, I am **c off**.	1504
Eze	6: 6	your images may be **c down**, and	1438
	14: 8	I will **c** him **off** from the midst of my	3772
	14:13	and will **c off** man and beast from it:	3772
	14:17	so that I **c off** man and beast from it:	3772
	14:19	it in blood, to **c off** from it man and beast:	3772
	14:21	to **c off** from it man and beast?	3772
	16: 4	the day thou wast born thy navel was not **c**,	3772
	17: 9	and **c off** the fruit thereof, that it wither?	7082
	17:17	and building forts, to **c off** many persons:	3772
	21: 3	will **c off** from thee the righteous and	3772
	21: 4	that I will **c off** from thee the righteous and	3772
	25: 7	I will **c** thee **off** from the people, and I will	3772
	25:13	and will **c off** man and beast from it;	3772
	25:16	I will **c off** the Cherethims, and destroy	3772
	29: 8	and **c off** man and beast out of thee.	3772
	30:15	and I will **c off** the multitude of No.	3772
	31:12	have **c** him **off**, and have left him:	3772
	35: 7	**c off** from it him that passeth out and	3772
	37:11	our hope is lost: we are **c off** for our parts.	1504
	39:10	neither **c down** *any* out of the forests;	2404
Da	2: 5	ye shall be **c** in pieces, and your houses	5648
	2:34	Thou sawest till that a stone was **c out**	1505
	2:45	was **c out** of the mountain without hands,	1505
	3:29	shall be **c** in pieces, and their houses shall	5648
	4:14	Hew down the tree, and **c off** his branches,	7113
	9:26	and two weeks shall Messiah be **c off**,	3772
Hos	8: 4	made them idols, that they may be **c off**.	3772
	10: 7	her king is **c off** as the foam upon	1820
	10:15	the king of Israel **utterly** be **c off**.	1820+1820
Joel	1: 5	new wine, for it is **c off** from your mouth.	3772
	1: 9	the drink offering is **c off** from the house of	3772
	1:16	Is not the meat **c off** before our eyes,	3772
Am	1: 5	**c off** the inhabitant from the plain of Aven,	3772
	1: 8	I will **c off** the inhabitant from Ashdod,	3772
	2: 3	I will **c off** the judge from the midst	3772
	3:14	the horns of the altar shall be **c off**, and	1438
	9: 1	**c** them in the head, all of them; and I will	1214
Ob	1: 5	if robbers by night, (how art thou **c off**!)	1820
	1: 9	mount of Esau may be **c off** by slaughter.	3772
	1:10	cover thee, and thou shalt be **c off** for ever.	3772
	1:14	to **c off** those of his that did escape;	3772
Mic	5: 9	and all thine enemies shall be **c off**.	3772
	5:10	that I will **c off** thy horses out of the midst	3772
	5:11	I will **c off** the cities of thy land, and	3772
	5:12	I will **c off** witchcrafts out of thine hand;	3772
	5:13	Thy graven images also will I **c off**, and	3772
Na	1:12	yet thus shall they be **c down**,	1494
	1:14	out of the house of thy gods will I **c off**	3772
	1:15	more pass through thee; he is utterly **c off**.	3772
	2:13	I will **c off** thy prey from the earth, and	3772
	3:15	the sword shall **c** thee **off**, it shall eat thee	3772
Hab	3:17	the flock shall be **c off** from the fold, and	1504
Zep	1: 3	I will **c off** man from off the land, saith	3772
	1: 4	I will **c off** the remnant of Baal from this	3772
	1:11	for all the merchant people are **c down**;	1820
	1:11	cut down; all they that bear silver are **c off**.	3772
	3: 6	I have **c off** *the* nations: their towers are	3772
	3: 7	so their dwelling should not be **c off**,	3772
Zec	5: 3	for every one that stealeth shall be **c off** *as*	5352
	5: 3	every one that sweareth shall be **c off** *as* on	5352
	9: 6	and I will **c off** the pride of the Philistines.	3772
	9:10	I will **c off** the chariot from Ephraim, and	3772
	9:10	and the battle bow shall be **c off**:	3772
	11: 8	Three shepherds also I **c off** in one month;	3582
	11: 9	that that is to be **c off**, let it be cut off; and	3582
	11: 9	that that is to be cut off, let it be **c off**; and	3582
	11:10	my staff, *even* Beauty, and **c** it **asunder**,	1438
	11:14	I **c asunder** mine other staff, *even* Bands,	1438
	11:16	*which* shall not visit those that be **c off**,	3582
	12: 3	with it shall be **c in pieces**,	8295+8295
	13: 2	*that* I will **c off** the names of the idols out	3772
	13: 8	two parts therein shall be **c off** *and* die;	3772
	14: 2	the residue of the people shall not be **c off**	3772
Mal	2:12	The LORD will **c off** the man that doth	3772
Mt	5:30	offend thee, **c** it **off**, and cast *it* from thee:	*1581*
	18: 8	**c** them **off**, and cast *them* from thee:	*1581*
	21: 8	others **c down** branches from the trees, and	*2875*
	24:51	And shall **c** him **asunder**, and appoint *him*	*1371*

Mk 9:43 And if thy hand offend thee, c it off: it is 609
9:45 And if thy foot offend thee, c it off: it is 609
11: 8 and others c down branches off the trees, 2875
14:47 a servant of the high priest, and c off his ear. 851
Lk 12:46 and will c him in sunder, and will appoint 1371
13: 7 c it down; why cumbereth it the ground? 1581
13: 9 if not, then after that thou shalt c it down. 1581
22:50 of the high priest, and c off his right ear. 851
Jn 18:10 high priest's servant, and c off his right ear. 609
18:26 being his kinsman whose ear Peter c off, 609
Ac 5:33 When they heard that, they were c to 1282
7:54 When they heard these things, they were c 1282
27:32 Then the soldiers c off the ropes of the boat, 609
Ro 9:28 the work, and c it short in righteousness: 4932
11:22 otherwise thou also shalt be c off. 1581
11:24 For if thou wert c out of the olive tree 1581
2Co 11:12 that I may c off occasion from them which 1581
Gal 5:12 I would they were even c off which trouble 609

CUTH (1) [CUTHAH]
2Ki 17:30 the men of C made Nergal, and the men of 3575

CUTHAH (1) [CUTH]
2Ki 17:24 from C, and from Ava, and from Hamath, 3575

CUTTEST (1) [CUT]
Dt 24:19 When thou c down thine harvest in 7105+7114

CUTTETH (6) [CUT]
Job 28:10 He c out rivers among the rocks; and 1234
Ps 46: 9 the bow, and c the spear in sunder; 7112
141: 7 as when one c and cleaveth wood upon 6398
Pr 26: 6 message by the hand of a fool c off the feet, 7096
Jer 10: 3 for one c a tree out of the forest, the work 3772
22:14 large chambers, and c him out windows; 7167

CUTTING (5) [CUT]
Ex 31: 5 in c of stones, to set them, and in carving of 2799
35:33 in the c of stones, to set them, and 2799
Isa 38:10 I said, in the c off of my days, I shall go to 1824
Hab 2:10 shame to thy house by c off many people, 7096
Mk 5: 5 crying, and c himself with stones. 2629

CUTTINGS (3) [CUT]
Lev 19:28 Ye shall not make any c in your flesh for 8296
21: 5 nor make any c in their flesh. 8295+8296
Jer 48:37 upon all the hands shall be c, and upon 1417

CUZ See CHUZA

CYMBAL (1) [CYMBALS]
1Co 13: 1 become as sounding brass, or a tinkling c. 2950

CYMBALS (16) [CYMBAL]
2Sa 6: 5 and on timbrels, and on cornets, and on c. 6767
1Ch 13: 8 and with c, and with trumpets. 4700
15:16 psalteries and harps and c, sounding, 4700
15:19 were appointed to sound with c of brass; 4700
15:28 the cornet, and with trumpets, and with c, 4700
16: 5 with harps; but Asaph made a sound with c; 4700
16:42 and c for those that should make a sound, 4700
25: 1 with harps, with psalteries, and with c: 4700
25: 6 with c, psalteries, and harps, for the service 4700
2Ch 5:12 having c and psalteries and harps, 4700
5:13 and c and instruments of musick, 4700
29:25 Levites in the house of the LORD with c, 4700
Ezr 3:10 the Levites the sons of Asaph with c, 4700
Ne 12:27 with c, psalteries, and with harps. 4700
Ps 150: 5 Praise him upon the loud c: praise him 6767
150: 5 praise him upon the high sounding c. 6767

CYPRESS (1)
Isa 44:14 down cedars, and taketh the c and the oak, 8645

CYPRUS (8)
Ac 4:36 a Levite, and of the country of C, 2953
11:19 and C, and Antioch, preaching the word to 2954
11:20 And some of them were men of C and 2953
13: 4 and from thence they sailed to C. 2954
15:39 so Barnabas took Mark, and sailed unto C; 2954
21: 3 Now when we had discovered C, we left it 2954
21:16 and brought with them one Mnason of C, 2953
27: 4 we sailed under C, because the winds were 2954

CYRENE (4) [CYRENIAN, CYRENIANS]
Mt 27:32 they found a man of C, Simon by name: 2956
Ac 2:10 and in the parts of Libya about C, and 2957
11:20 some of them were men of Cyprus and C, 2956
13: 1 called Niger, and Lucius of C, and Manaen, 2956

CYRENIAN (2) [CYRENE]
Mk 15:21 And they compel one Simon a C, 2956
Lk 23:26 a C, coming out of the country, and on him 2956

CYRENIANS (1) [CYRENE]
Ac 6: 9 and C, and Alexandrians, and of them of 2956

CYRENIUS (1)
Lk 2: 2 (And this taxing was first made when C 2958

CYRUS (23)
2Ch 36:22 Now in the first year of C king of Persia, 3566
36:22 the LORD stirred up the spirit of C king 3566
36:23 Thus saith C king of Persia, All 3566
Ezr 1: 1 Now in the first year of C king of Persia, 3566
1: 1 the LORD stirred up the spirit of C king 3566
1: 2 Thus saith C king of Persia, The LORD 3566
1: 7 Also C the king brought forth the vessels of 3566
1: 8 Even those did C king of Persia bring forth 3566
3: 7 according to the grant that they had of C 3566
4: 3 as king C the king of Persia hath 3566
4: 5 all the days of C king of Persia, 3566
5:13 in the first year of C the king of Babylon 3567
5:13 C made a decree to build this house of 3567
5:14 those did C the king take out of the temple 3567
5:17 that a decree was made of C the king to 3567
6: 3 In the first year of C the king the same 3567
6: 3 C the king made a decree concerning 3567
6:14 according to the commandment of C, and 3567
Isa 44:28 That saith of C, He is my shepherd, and 3566
45: 1 to C, whose right hand I have holden, to 3566
Da 1:21 even unto the first year of king C. 3566
6:28 of Darius, and in the reign of C the Persian. 3567
10: 1 In the third year of C king of Persia a thing 3566

D

DABAREH (1)
Jos 21:28 with her suburbs, D with her suburbs, 1705

DABBASHETH (1)
Jos 19:11 reached to D, and reached to the river that 1708

DABBESHETH See DABBASHETH

DABERATH (2)
Jos 19:12 then goeth out to D, and goeth up to Japhia, 1705
1Ch 6:72 with her suburbs, D with her suburbs, 1705

DAGGER (3)
Jdg 3:16 Ehud made him a d which had two edges, 2719
3:21 took the d from his right thigh, and thrust it 2719
3:22 that he could not draw the d out of his 2719

DAGON (12) [BETH-DAGON, DAGON'S]
Jdg 16:23 to offer a great sacrifice unto D their god, 1712
1Sa 5: 2 they brought it into the house of D, and 1712
5: 2 it into the house of Dagon, and set it by D. 1712
5: 3 D was fallen upon his face to the earth 1712
5: 3 they took D, and set him in his place again. 1712
5: 4 D was fallen upon his face to the ground 1712
5: 4 the head of D and both the palms of his 1712
5: 4 only the stump of D was left to him. 1712
5: 5 Therefore neither the priests of D, nor any 1712
5: 5 tread on the threshold of D in Ashdod unto 1712
5: 7 hand is sore upon us, and upon D our god. 1712
1Ch 10:10 and fastened his head in the temple of D. 1712

DAGON'S (1) [DAGON]
1Sa 5: 5 of Dagon, nor any that come into D house, 1712

DAILY (63) [DAY]
Ex 5:13 Fulfil your works, your d 3117+3117+871.1
5:19 your bricks of your d task. 3117+3117+871.1

Ex 16: 5 be twice as much as they gather **d**. 3117+3117
Nu 4:16 the **d** meat offering, and the anointing oil, 8548
28:24 manner ye shall offer **d**, 3117+1886.1+3807.1
29: 6 the **d** burnt offering, and his meat offering, 8548
Jdg 16:16 when she pressed him **d** with 3117+3605+1886.1
2Ki 25:30 a **d** rate for every day, all the days of his 3117
2Ch 31:16 *his* **d** portion for their service 3117+3117+871.1
Ezr 3: 4 **d** burnt offerings by number, 3117+3117+871.1
Ne 5:18 prepared *for me* **d** *was* one ox 259+3117+3807.1
Est 3: 4 when they spake **d** unto him, 3117+3117+2050.1
Ps 13: 2 in my soul, *having* sorrow in my heart **d**? 3119
42:10 while they say **d** unto me, 3117+3605+1886.1
56: 1 he fighting **d** oppresseth me. 3117+3605+1886.1
56: 2 Mine enemies would **d** 3117+3605+1886.1
61: 8 that I may **d** perform my vows. 3117+3117
68:19 *who* **d** loadeth us *with benefits, even* 3117+3117
72:15 *and* **d** shall he be praised. 3117+3605+1886.1
74:22 *man* reproacheth thee **d**. 3117+3605+1886.1
86: 3 for I cry unto thee **d**. 3117+3605+1886.1
88: 9 LORD, I have called **d** upon 3117+3605+871.1
88:17 came round about me **d** 3117+3605+1886.1
Pr 8:30 up *with him:* and I was **d** *his* delight, 3117+3117
8:34 watching **d** at my gates, waiting at 3117+3117
Isa 58: 2 Yet they seek me **d**, and delight to 3117+3117
Jer 7:25 **d** rising up early and sending *them:* 3117
20: 7 **d**, every one mocketh me. 3117+3605+1886.1
20: 8 unto me, and a derision, **d**. 3117+3605+1886.1
37:21 **d** a piece of bread out of 3117+1886.1+3807.1
Eze 30:16 and Noph *shall have* distresses **d**. 3119
45:23 blemish **d** the seven days; 3117+1886.1+3807.1
45:23 goats **d** *for* a sin offering. 3117+1886.1+3807.1
46:13 Thou shalt **d** prepare a 3117+1886.1+3807.1
Da 1: 5 the king appointed them a **d** 3117+3117+871.1
8:11 by him the **d** *sacrifice* was taken away, and 8548
8:12 a host was given *him* against the **d** *sacrifice* 8548
8:13 *be* the vision *concerning* the **d** *sacrifice,* 8548
11:31 shall take away the **d** *sacrifice,* and 8548
12:11 from the time *that* the **d** *sacrifice* shall be 8548
Hos 12: 1 he **d** increaseth lies and 3117+3605+1886.1
Mt 6:11 Give us this day our **d** bread. *1967*
26:55 I sat **d** with you teaching in *2250+2596*
Mk 14:49 I was **d** with you in the temple *2250+2596*
Lk 9:23 and take up his cross **d**, *2250+2596*
11: 3 Give us day by day our **d** bread. *1967*
19:47 And he taught **d** in the temple. *2250+2596*
22:53 When I was **d** with you in *2250+2596*
Ac 2:46 continuing **d** with one accord in *2250+2596*
2:47 And the Lord added to the church **d** *2250+2596*
3: 2 whom they laid **d** at the gate of *2250+2596*
5:42 And **d** in the temple, and in every *2250+3956*
6: 1 their widows were neglected in the **d** *2522*
16: 5 the faith, and increased in number **d**. *2250+2596*
17:11 and searched the scriptures **d**, *2250+2596*
17:17 in the market **d** with them that *2250+2596+3956*
19: 9 **d** in the school of one Tyrannus. *2250+2596*
1Co 15:31 in Christ Jesus our Lord, I die **d**. *2250+2596*
2Co 11:28 that which cometh upon me **d**, *2250+2596*
Heb 3:13 But exhort one another **d**, *1538+2250+2596*
7:27 Who needeth not **d**, as *those* high *2250+2596*
10:11 And every priest standeth **d** *2250+2596*
Jas 2:15 or sister be naked, and destitute of **d** food, *2184*

DAINTIES (3) [DAINTY]
Ge 49:20 *shall be* fat, and he shall yield royal **d**. 4574
Ps 141: 4 work iniquity: and let me not eat of their **d**. 4516
Pr 23: 3 Be not desirous of his **d**: for they *are* 4303

DAINTY (3) [DAINTIES]
Job 33:20 life abhorreth bread, and his soul **d** meat. 8378
Pr 23: 6 an evil eye, neither desire thou his **d meats**: 4303
Rev 18:14 and all *things which were* **d** and goodly are *3045*

DALAIAH (1)
1Ch 3:24 and Johanan, and **D**, and Anani, seven. 1806

DALE (2)
Ge 14:17 the valley of Shaveh, which *is* the king's **d**. 6010
2Sa 18:18 himself a pillar, which *is* in the king's **d**: 6010

DALMANUTHA (1)
Mk 8:10 his disciples, and came into the parts of **D**. *1148*

DALMATIA (1)
2Ti 4:10 Crescens to Galatia, Titus unto **D**. *1149*

DALPHON (1)
Est 9: 7 And Parshandatha, and **D**, and Aspatha, 1813

DAM (5)
Ex 22:30 seven days it shall be with his **d**; on 517
Lev 22:27 then it shall be seven days under the **d**; 517
Dt 22: 6 the **d** sitting upon the young, or upon 517
22: 6 thou shalt not take the **d** with the young: 517
22: 7 *But* thou shalt in any wise let the **d** go, 517

DAMAGE (6) [ENDAMAGE]
Ezr 4:22 why should **d** grow to the hurt of the kings? 2257
Est 7: 4 enemy could not countervail the king's **d**. 5143
Pr 26: 6 of a fool cutteth off the feet, *and* drinketh **d**. 2555
Da 6: 2 unto them, and the king should have no **d**. 5142
Ac 27:10 *this* voyage will be with hurt and much **d**, *2209*
2Co 7: 9 that ye might **receive d** by us in nothing. *2210*

DAMARIS (1)
Ac 17:34 and a woman named **D**, and others with *1152*

DAMASCENES (1) [DAMASCUS]
2Co 11:32 **D** *with a garrison,* desirous to apprehend *1153*

DAMASCUS (60) [DAMASCENES, SYRIA-DAMASCUS]
Ge 14:15 unto Hobah, which *is* on the left hand of **D**. 1834
15: 2 steward of my house *is* this Eliezer of **D**? 1834
2Sa 8: 5 when the Syrians of **D** came to succour 1834
8: 6 David put garrisons in Syria of **D**: and 1834
1Ki 11:24 slew them *of Zobah:* and they went *to* **D**, 1834
11:24 and dwelt therein, and reigned in **D**. 1834
15:18 king of Syria, that dwelt at **D**, saying, 1834
19:15 return on thy way to the wilderness of **D**: 1834
20:34 thou shalt make streets for thee in **D**, as my 1834
2Ki 5:12 *Are* not Abana and Pharpar, rivers of **D**, 1834
8: 7 Elisha came *to* **D**; and Ben-hadad the king 1834
8: 9 even *of* every good thing of **D**, 1834
14:28 and how he recovered **D**, and Hamath, 1834
16: 9 for the king of Assyria went up against **D**, 1834
16:10 king Ahaz went *to* **D** to meet 1834
16:10 of Assyria, and saw an altar that *was* at **D**: 1834
16:11 to all that king Ahaz had sent from **D**: 1834
16:11 made *it* against king Ahaz came from **D**. 1834
16:12 when the king was come from **D**, the king 1834
1Ch 18: 5 when the Syrians of **D** came to help 1834
2Ch 16: 2 king of Syria, that dwelt at **D**, saying, 1834
24:23 all the spoil of them unto the king of **D**. 1834
28: 5 of them captives, and brought *them to* **D**. 1834
28:23 For he sacrificed unto the gods of **D**, 1834
SS 7: 4 tower of Lebanon which looketh toward **D**. 1834
Isa 7: 8 For the head of Syria *is* **D**, and the head of 1834
7: 8 *is* Damascus, and the head of **D** *is* Rezin; 1834
8: 4 the riches of **D** and the spoil of Samaria 1834
10: 9 not Hamath as Arpad? *is* not Samaria as **D**? 1834
17: 1 The burden of **D**. Behold, Damascus *is* 1834
17: 1 **D** *is* taken away from *being* a city, and 1834
17: 3 the kingdom from **D**, and the remnant of 1834
Jer 49:23 Concerning **D**. Hamath is confounded, and 1834
49:24 **D** is waxed feeble, *and* turneth herself to 1834
49:27 I will kindle a fire in the wall of **D**, and 1834
Eze 27:18 **D** *was* thy merchant in the multitude of 1834
47:16 which *is* between the border of **D** and 1834
47:17 the border of **D**, and the north northward, 1834
47:18 from **D**, and from Gilead, and from the land 1834
48: 1 Hazar-enan, the border of **D** northward, to 1834
Am 1: 3 For three transgressions of **D**, and for four, 1834
1: 5 I will break also the bar of **D**, and cut off 1834
3:12 in the corner of a bed, and in **D** *in* a couch. 1833
5:27 I cause you to go into captivity beyond **D**, 1834
Zec 9: 1 of Hadrach, and **D** *shall be* the rest thereof: 1834
Ac 9: 2 And desired of him letters to **D** to *1154*
9: 3 And as *he* journeyed, he came near **D**: and *1154*
9: 8 him by the hand, and brought *him* into **D**. *1154*
9:10 And there was a certain disciple at **D**, *1154*
9:19 days with the disciples which were at **D**. *1154*
9:22 and confounded the Jews which dwelt at **D**, *1154*
9:27 how he had preached boldly at **D** in *1154*
22: 5 and went to **D**, to bring them which were *1154*
22: 6 and was come nigh unto **D** about noon, *1154*
22:10 Lord said unto me, Arise, and go into **D**; *1154*
22:11 of them that were with me, I came into **D**. *1154*
26:12 Whereupon as I went to **D** with authority *1154*
26:20 But shewed first unto them of **D**, *1154*
2Co 11:32 In **D** the governor under Aretas the king *1154*

Gal 1:17 into Arabia, and returned again unto **D**. *1154*

DAMNABLE (1) [DAMNATION]
2Pe 2: 1 who privily shall bring in **d** heresies, *684*

DAMNATION (11) [DAMNABLE, DAMNED]
Mt 23:14 therefore ye shall receive the greater **d**. *2917*
23:33 of vipers, how can ye escape the **d** of hell? *2920*
Mk 3:29 but is in danger of eternal **d**. *2920*
12:40 long prayers: these shall receive greater **d**. *2917*
Lk 20:47 the same shall receive greater **d**. *2917*
Jn 5:29 have done evil, unto the resurrection of **d**. *2920*
Ro 3: 8 that good may come? whose **d** is just. *2917*
13: 2 that resist shall receive to themselves **d**. *2917*
1Co 11:29 eateth and drinketh **d** to himself, *2917*
1Ti 5:12 Having **d**, because they have cast off *their* *2917*
2Pe 2: 3 lingereth not, and their **d** slumbereth not. *684*

DAMNED (3) [DAMNATION]
Mk 16:16 but he that believeth not shall be **d**. *2632*
Ro 14:23 And he that doubteth is **d** if he eat, because *2632*
2Th 2:12 That they all might be **d** who believed not *2919*

DAMSEL (40) [DAMSEL'S, DAMSELS]
Ge 24:14 *that* the **d** to whom I shall say, Let down 5291
24:16 the **d** *was* very fair to look upon, a virgin, 5291
24:28 the **d** ran, and told *them of* her mother's 5291
24:55 Let the **d** abide with us *a few* days, at 5291
24:57 We will call the **d**, and inquire at her 5291
34: 3 he loved the **d**, and spake kindly unto 5291
34: 3 the damsel, and spake kindly unto the **d**. 5291
34: 4 saying, Get me this **d** to wife. 3207
34:12 say unto me: but give me the **d** to wife. 5291
Dt 22:15 shall the father of the **d**, and her mother, 5291
22:19 give *them* unto the father of the **d**, because 5291
22:20 *tokens of* virginity be not found for the **d**: 5291
22:21 they shall bring out the **d** to the door of her 5291
22:23 If a **d** *that is* a virgin be betrothed unto a 5291
22:24 the **d**, because she cried not, *being* in 5291
22:25 if a man find a betrothed **d** in the field, and 5291
22:26 unto the **d** thou shalt do nothing; *there is* in 5291
22:26 *there is* in the **d** no sin *worthy* of death: 5291
22:27 *and* the betrothed **d** cried, and *there was* 5291
22:28 If a man find a **d** *that is* a virgin, which is 5291
Jdg 5:30 divided the prey; to every man a **d** *or* two; 7356
19: 3 when the father of the **d** saw him, 5291
Ru 2: 5 was set over the reapers, Whose **d** *is* this? 5291
2: 6 It *is* the Moabitish **d** that came back with 5291
1Ki 1: 3 So they sought for a fair **d** throughout all 5291
1: 4 the **d** *was* very fair, and cherished the king, 5291
Mt 14:11 brought in a charger, and given to the **d**: *2877*
26:69 and a **d** came unto him, saying, Thou also *3814*
Mk 5:39 and weep? the **d** is not dead, but sleepeth. *3813*
5:40 he taketh the father and the mother of the **d**, *3813*
5:40 and entereth in where the **d** was lying. *3813*
5:41 And he took the **d** by the hand, and *3813*
5:41 being interpreted, **D** (I say unto thee) *2877*
5:42 And straightway the **d** arose, and walked; *2877*
6:22 that sat with *him,* the king said unto the **d**, *2877*
6:28 his head in a charger, and gave it to the **d**: *2877*
6:28 the damsel: and the **d** gave it to her mother. *2877*
Jn 18:17 Then saith the **d** that kept the door unto *3814*
Ac 12:13 a **d** came to hearken, named Rhoda. *3814*
16:16 a certain **d** possessed with a spirit of *3814*

DAMSEL'S (8) [DAMSEL]
Dt 22:15 bring forth *the tokens of* the **d** virginity 5291
22:16 the **d** father shall say unto the elders, I gave 5291
22:29 give unto the **d** father fifty *shekels* of silver, 5291
Jdg 19: 4 his father in law, the **d** father, retained him; 5291
19: 5 the **d** father said unto his son in law, 5291
19: 6 for the **d** father had said unto the man, 5291
19: 8 the **d** father said, Comfort thine heart, 5291
19: 9 the **d** father, said unto him, Behold now, 5291

DAMSELS (3) [DAMSEL]
Ge 24:61 her **d**, and they rode upon the camels, and 5291
1Sa 25:42 with five **d** of hers that went after her; 5291
Ps 68:25 among *them were* the **d** playing with 5959

DAN (72) [DAN-JAAN, DANITES, LESHEM, MAHANEH-DAN]
Ge 14:14 and eighteen, and pursued *them* unto **D**. 1835
30: 6 me a son: therefore called she his name **D**. 1835
35:25 Rachel's handmaid; **D**, and Naphtali: 1835
46:23 And the sons of **D**; Hushim. 1835
49:16 **D** shall judge his people, as one of 1835
49:17 **D** shall be a serpent by the way, an adder in 1835
Ex 1: 4 **D**, and Naphtali, Gad, and Asher. 1835
31: 6 the son of Ahisamach, of the tribe of **D**: 1835
35:34 the son of Ahisamach, of the tribe of **D**. 1835
38:23 of the tribe of **D**, an engraver, and 1835
Lev 24:11 the daughter of Dibri, of the tribe of **D**:) 1835
Nu 1:12 Of **D**; Ahiezer the son of Ammishaddai. 1835
1:38 Of the children of **D**, *by* their generations, 1835
1:39 *even* of the tribe of **D**, *were* threescore and 1835
2:25 The standard of the camp of **D** *shall be* on 1835
2:25 the captain of the children of **D** *shall be* 1835
2:31 in the camp of **D** *were* an hundred thousand 1835
7:66 prince of the children of **D**, *offered:* 1835
10:25 the camp of the children of **D** set forward, 1835
13:12 Of the tribe of **D**, Ammiel the son of 1835
26:42 These *are* the sons of **D** after their families: 1835
26:42 These *are* the families of **D** after their 1835
34:22 the prince of the tribe of the children of **D**, 1835
Dt 27:13 and Asher, and Zebulun, **D**, and Naphtali. 1835
33:22 of **D** he said, Dan *is* a lion's whelp: he shall 1835
33:22 of Dan he said, **D** *is* a lion's whelp: he shall 1835
34: 1 shewed him all the land of Gilead, unto **D**, 1835
Jos 19:40 children of **D** according to their families. 1835
19:47 the coast of the children of **D** went out *too* 1835
19:47 the children of **D** went up to fight against 1835
19:47 and dwelt therein, and called Leshem, **D**, 1835
19:47 Dan, after the name of **D** their father. 1835
19:48 children of **D** according to their families, 1835
21: 5 out of the tribe of **D**, and out of the half 1835
21:23 out of the tribe of **D**, Eltekeh with her 1835
Jdg 1:34 the Amorites forced the children of **D** into 1835
5:17 why did **D** remain *in* ships? 1835
13:25 to move him at times in the camp of **D**, 1835
18: 2 the children of **D** sent of their family five 1835
18:16 which *were* of the children of **D**, stood *by* 1835
18:22 and overtook the children of **D**. 1835
18:23 they cried unto the children of **D**. And they 1835
18:25 the children of **D** said unto him, Let not thy 1835
18:26 the children of **D** went their way: and 1835
18:29 they called the name of the city **D**, after 1835
18:29 after the name of **D** their father, who was 1835
18:30 the children of **D** set up the graven image: 1835
18:30 his sons were priests to the tribe of **D** until 1839
20: 1 from **D** even to Beer-sheba, with the land 1835
1Sa 3:20 all Israel from **D** even to Beer-sheba knew 1835
2Sa 3:10 over Judah, from **D** even to Beer-sheba. 1835
17:11 from **D** even to Beer-sheba, as the sand that 1835
24: 2 from **D** even to Beer-sheba, and number ye 1835
24:15 there died of the people from **D** even to 1835
1Ki 4:25 his fig tree, from **D** even to Beer-sheba, 1835
12:29 one in Beth-el, and the other put he in **D**. 1835
12:30 *to worship* before the one, *even* unto **D**. 1835
15:20 **D**, and Abel-beth-maachah, and all 1835
2Ki 10:29 that *were in* Beth-el, and that *were* in **D**. 1835
1Ch 2: 2 **D**, Joseph, and Benjamin, Naphtali, Gad, 1835
21: 2 number Israel from Beer-sheba even to **D**; 1835
27:22 Of **D**, Azareel the son of Jeroham. 1835
2Ch 2:14 The son of a woman of the daughters of **D**, 1835
16: 4 **D**, and Abel-maim, and all the store cities 1835
30: 5 all Israel, from Beer-sheba even to **D**, 1835
Jer 4:15 For a voice declareth from **D**, and 1835
8:16 snorting of his horses was heard from **D**: 1835
Eze 27:19 **D** also and Javan going to and fro occupied 1835
48: 1 are his sides east *and* west; a *portion for* **D**. 1835
48: 2 by the border of **D**, from the east side unto 1835
48:32 one gate of Benjamin, one gate of **D**. 1835
Am 8:14 of Samaria, and say, Thy god, O **D**, liveth; 1835

DANCE (8) [DANCED, DANCES, DANCING]
Jdg 21:21 if the daughters of Shiloh come out to **d** in 2342
Job 21:11 little ones like a flock, and their children **d**. 7540
Ps 149: 3 Let them praise his name in the **d**: let them 4234
150: 4 Praise him with the timbrel and **d**: 4234
Ecc 3: 4 to laugh; a time to mourn, and a time to **d**; 7540
Isa 13:21 shall dwell there, and satyrs shall **d** there. 7540
Jer 31:13 shall the virgin rejoice in the **d**, both young 4234
La 5:15 is ceased; our **d** is turned into mourning. 4234

DANCED (6) [DANCE]
Jdg 21:23 of them that **d**, whom they caught: 2342
2Sa 6:14 David **d** before the LORD with all *his* 3769
Mt 11:17 have piped unto you, and ye have not **d**; *3738*
14: 6 the daughter of Herodias **d** before them, *3738*

D

Mk 6:22 and **d**, and pleased Herod and them that sat *3738*
Lk 7:32 have piped unto you, and ye have not **d**; *3738*

DANCES (6) [DANCE]
Ex 15:20 went out after her with timbrels and with **d**. 4246
Jdg 11:34 out to meet him with timbrels and with **d**: 4246
21:21 daughters of Shiloh come out to dance in **d**, 4246
1Sa 21:11 they not sing one to another of him in **d**, 4246
29: 5 of whom they sang one to another in **d**, 4246
Jer 31: 4 shalt go forth in the **d** of them that make 4234

DANCING (7) [DANCE]
Ex 32:19 the camp, that he saw the calf, and the **d**: 4246
1Sa 18: 6 singing and **d**, to meet king Saul, 4246
30:16 **d**, because of all the great spoil that they 2287
2Sa 6:16 David leaping and **d** before the LORD; 3769
1Ch 15:29 looking out at a window saw king David **d** 7540
Ps 30:11 hast turned for me my mourning into **d**: 4234
Lk 15:25 nigh to the house, he heard musick and **d**. *5525*

DANDLED (1)
Isa 66:12 upon *her* sides, and be **d** upon *her* knees. 8173

DANGER (7) [DANGEROUS]
Mt 5:21 whosoever shall kill shall be **in d** of *1777*
5:22 a cause shall be **in d** of the judgment: *1777*
5:22 Raca, shall be **in d** of the council: *1777*
5:22 *Thou* fool, shall be **in d** of hell fire. *1777*
Mk 3:29 but is in **d** of eternal damnation. *1777*
Ac 19:27 So *that* not only this our craft is **in d** to be *2793*
19:40 For we are **in d** to be called in question for *2793*

DANGEROUS (1) [DANGER]
Ac 27: 9 and when sailing was now **d**, because *2000*

DANIEL (83) [BELTESHAZZAR]
1Ch 3: 1 the second **D**, of Abigail the Carmelitess: 1840
Ezr 8: 2 of the sons of Ithamar; **D**: of the sons of 1840
Ne 10: 6 **D**, Ginnethon, Baruch, 1840
Eze 14:14 Noah, **D**, and Job, were in it, they should 1840
14:20 **D**, and Job, *were* in it, *as* I live, 1840
28: 3 Behold, thou *art* wiser than **D**; *there is* no 1840
Da 1: 6 **D**, Hananiah, Mishael, and Azariah: 1840
1: 7 for he gave unto **D** *the name of* 1840
1: 8 **D** purposed in his heart that he would not 1840
1: 9 Now God had brought **D** into favour and 1840
1:10 the prince of the eunuchs said unto **D**, I fear 1840
1:11 said **D** to Melzar, whom the prince of 1840
1:11 the prince of the eunuchs had set over **D**, 1840
1:17 **D** had understanding in all visions and 1840
1:19 among them all was found none like **D**, 1840
1:21 **D** continued *even* unto the first year of king 1840
2:13 they sought **D** and his fellows to be slain. 1841
2:14 **D** answered with counsel and wisdom to 1841
2:15 Then Arioch made the thing known to **D**. 1841
2:16 **D** went in, and desired of the king that he 1841
2:17 **D** went to his house, and made the thing 1841
2:18 that **D** and his fellows should not perish 1841
2:19 *was* the secret revealed unto **D** in a night 1841
2:19 Then **D** blessed the God of heaven. 1841
2:20 **D** answered and said, Blessed be the name 1841
2:24 Therefore **D** went in unto Arioch, 1841
2:25 Arioch brought in **D** before the king in 1841
2:26 The king answered and said to **D**, 1841
2:27 **D** answered in the presence of the king, and 1841
2:46 worshipped **D**, and commanded that *they* 1841
2:47 The king answered unto **D**, and said, Of a 1841
2:48 the king made **D** a great man, and gave him 1841
2:49 **D** requested of the king, and he set 1841
2:49 but **D** *sat* in the gate of the king. 1841
4: 8 at the last **D** came in before me, 1841
4:19 **D**, whose name *was* Belteshazzar, 1841
5:12 of doubts, were found in the same **D**, 1841
5:12 now let **D** be called, and he will shew 1841
5:13 was **D** brought in before the king. *And* 1841
5:13 *And* the king spake and said unto **D**, 1841
5:13 and said unto Daniel, *Art* thou that **D**, 1841
5:17 **D** answered and said before the king, 1841
5:29 they clothed **D** with scarlet, and *put* a chain 1841
6: 2 three presidents; of whom **D** *was* first: 1841
6: 3 this **D** was preferred above the presidents 1841
6: 4 princes sought to find occasion against **D** 1841
6: 5 shall not find any occasion against this **D**, 1841
6:10 Now when **D** knew that the writing *was* 1841
6:11 found **D** praying and making supplication 1841
6:13 and said before the king, *That* **D**, 1841
6:14 and set *his* heart on **D** to deliver him: 1841
6:16 they brought **D**, and cast *him* into the den 1841
6:16 *Now* the king spake and said unto **D**, 1841
6:17 might not be changed concerning **D**. 1841
6:20 he cried with a lamentable voice unto **D**: 1841
6:20 *and* the king spake and said to **D**, O Daniel, 1841
6:20 *and* the king spake and said to Daniel, O **D**, 1841
6:21 said **D** unto the king, O king, live for ever. 1841
6:23 commanded that *they* should take **D** up out 1841
6:23 So **D** was taken up out of the den, and 1841
6:24 brought those men which had accused **D**, 1841
6:26 *men* tremble and fear before the God of **D**: 1841
6:27 who hath delivered **D** from the power of 1841
6:28 So this **D** prospered in the reign of Darius, 1841
7: 1 Belshazzar king of Babylon **D** had a dream 1841
7: 2 **D** spake and said, I saw in my vision by 1841
7:15 I **D** was grieved in my spirit in the midst of 1841
7:28 *As for* me **D**, my cogitations much troubled 1841
8: 1 *even unto* me **D**, after that which appeared 1840
8:15 when I, *even* I **D**, had seen the vision, and 1840
8:27 I **D** fainted, and was sick *certain* days; 1840
9: 2 In the first year of his reign I **D** understood 1840
9:22 and talked with me, and said, O **D**, 1840
10: 1 king of Persia a thing was revealed unto **D**, 1840
10: 2 In those days I **D** was mourning three full 1840
10: 7 I **D** alone saw the vision: for the men that 1840
10:11 he said unto me, O **D**, a man greatly 1840
10:12 said he unto me, Fear not, **D**: for from 1840
12: 4 thou, O **D**, shut up the words, and seal 1840
12: 5 I **D** looked, and behold, there stood other 1840
12: 9 he said, Go thy way, **D**: for the words *are* 1840
Mt 24:15 spoken of by **D** the prophet, stand in *1158*
Mk 13:14 spoken of by **D** the prophet, standing where *1158*

DANITES (4) [DAN]
Jdg 13: 2 of the family of the **D**, whose name *was* 1839
18: 1 in those days the tribe of the **D** sought them 1839
18:11 went from thence of the family of the **D**, 1839
1Ch 12:35 of the **D** expert in war twenty and 1839

DAN-JAAN (1) [DAN]
2Sa 24: 6 and they came to **D**, and about to Zidon, 1842

DANNAH (1)
Jos 15:49 And **D**, and Kirjath-sannah, which *is* Debir, 1837

DAPPLED See GRISLED

DARA (1)
1Ch 2: 6 and Ethan, and Heman, and Calcol, and **D**: 1873

DARDA (1)
1Ki 4:31 Heman, and Chalcol, and **D**, the sons of 1862

DARE (5) [DURST]
Job 41:10 None *is so* fierce that **d stir** him **up**: who 5782
Ro 5: 7 for a good *man* some would even **d** to die. *5111*
15:18 For I will not **d** to speak of any of *those* *5111*
1Co 6: 1 **D** any of you, having a matter against *5111*
2Co 10:12 For we **d** not make *ourselves* of *5111*

DARE; DARED See DURST

DARICS See DRAMS

DARING See DURST

DARIUS (25)
Ezr 4: 5 even until the reign of **D** king of Persia. 1867
4:24 year of the reign of **D** king of Persia. 1868
5: 5 them to cease, till the matter came to **D**: 1868
5: 6 on *this* side the river, sent unto **D** the king: 1868
5: 7 written thus: Unto **D** the king, all peace. 1868
6: 1 **D** the king made a decree, and search was 1868
6:12 I **D** have made a decree; let it be done with 1868
6:13 according to that which **D** the king had 1868
6:14 and **D**, and Artaxerxes king of Persia. 1868
6:15 *in* the sixth year of the reign of **D** the king. 1868
Ne 12:22 the priests, to the reign of **D** the Persian. 1867
Da 5:31 **D** the Median took the kingdom, 1868
6: 1 It pleased **D** to set over the kingdom an 1868
6: 6 said thus unto him, King **D**, live for ever. 1868
6: 9 Wherefore king **D** signed the writing and 1868
6:25 king **D** wrote unto all people, nations, 1868
6:28 So this Daniel prospered in the reign of **D**, 1868

Da 9: 1 In the first year of **D** the son of Ahasuerus, 1867
11: 1 Also I in the first year of **D** the Mede, 1867
Hag 1: 1 In the second year of **D** the king, in 1867
1:15 in the second year of **D** the king. 1867
2:10 of the ninth *month,* in the second year of **D,** 1867
Zec 1: 1 the eighth month, in the second year of **D,** 1867
1: 7 *is* the month Sebat, in the second year of **D,** 1867
7: 1 it came to pass in the fourth year of king **D,** 1867

DARK (43)
Ge 15:17 that, when the sun went down, and it was **d,** 5939
Lev 13: 6 *if* the plague *be* **somewhat d,** and 3544
13:21 lower than the skin, but *be* **somewhat d;** 3544
13:26 than the *other* skin, but *be* **somewhat d;** 3544
13:28 not in the skin, but it *be* **somewhat d;** 3544
13:56 the plague *be* **somewhat d** after 3544
Nu 12: 8 even apparently, and not in **d speeches;** 2420
Jos 2: 5 when it was **d,** that the men went out: 2822
2Sa 22:12 **d** waters, *and* thick clouds of the skies. 2841
Ne 13:19 Jerusalem began to be **d** before the sabbath, 6751
Job 3: 9 Let the stars of the twilight thereof be **d;** 2821
12:25 They grope *in* the **d** without light, and 2822
18: 6 The light shall be **d** in his tabernacle, and 2821
22:13 can he judge through the **d** *cloud?* 6205
24:16 In the **d** *they* dig *through* houses, 2822
Ps 18:11 his pavilion round about him *were* **d** waters 2824
35: 6 Let their way be **d** and slippery: and let 2822
49: 4 I will open my **d saying** upon the harp. 2420
74:20 for the **d places** of the earth are full *of* 4285
78: 2 in a parable: I will utter **d sayings** of old: 2420
88:12 Shall thy wonders be known in the **d?** and 2822
105:28 He sent darkness, and **made** it **d;** and 2821
Pr 1: 6 the words of the wise, and their **d sayings.** 2420
7: 9 in the evening, in the black and **d** night: 653
Isa 29:15 their works are in the **d,** and they say, 4285
45:19 spoken in secret, in a **d** place of the earth: 2822
Jer 13:16 before your feet stumble upon the **d** 5399
La 3: 6 He hath set me in **d places,** as they that be 4285
Eze 8:12 ancients of the house of Israel do in the **d,** 2822
32: 7 the heaven, and **make** the stars thereof **d;** 6937
32: 8 the bright lights of heaven will I **make d** 6937
34:12 been scattered in the cloudy and **d** day. 6205
Da 8:23 understanding **d sentences,** shall stand up. 2420
Joel 2:10 the sun and the moon shall be **d,** and 6937
Am 5: 8 and **maketh** the day **d** *with* night: 2821
5:20 even **very d,** and no brightness in it? 651
Mic 3: 6 it shall be **d** unto you, that *ye* shall not 2821
3: 6 and the day shall be **d** over them. 6937
Zec 14: 6 *that* the light shall not be clear, *nor* **d:** 7087
Lk 11:36 therefore *be* full of light, having no part **d,** *4652*
Jn 6:17 And it was now **d,** and Jesus was not come *4653*
20: 1 when it was yet **d,** unto the sepulchre, and *4653*
2Pe 1:19 as unto a light that shineth in a **d** place, *850*

DARKEN (1) [DARKENED, DARKENETH, DARKISH, DARKLY, DARKNESS]
Am 8: 9 and I will **d** the earth in the clear day: 2821

DARKENED (19) [DARKEN]
Ex 10:15 of the whole earth, so that the land was **d;** 2821
Ps 69:23 Let their eyes be **d,** that *they* see not; and 2821
Ecc 12: 2 the light, or the moon, or the stars, be not **d,** 2821
12: 3 those that look out of the windows be **d,** 2821
Isa 5:30 and the light is **d** in the heavens thereof. 2821
9:19 wrath of the LORD of hosts is the land **d,** 6272
13:10 the sun shall be **d** in his going forth, and 2821
24:11 all joy is **d,** the mirth of the land is gone. 6150
Eze 30:18 At Tehaphnehes also the day shall be **d,** 2821
Joel 3:15 The sun and the moon shall be **d,** and 6937
Zec 11:17 his right eye shall be **utterly d.** 3543+3543
Mt 24:29 tribulation of those days shall the sun be **d,** *4654*
Mk 13:24 the sun shall be **d,** and the moon shall not *4654*
Lk 23:45 And the sun was **d,** and the vail of *4654*
Ro 1:21 and their foolish heart was **d.** *4654*
11:10 Let their eyes be **d,** that *they* may not see, *4654*
Eph 4:18 Having the understanding **d,** *4654*
Rev 8:12 so as the third *part* of them was **d** and *4654*
9: 2 the air were **d** by reason of the smoke of *4654*

DARKENETH (1) [DARKEN]
Job 38: 2 Who *is* this that **d** counsel by words 2821

DARKISH (1) [DARKEN]
Lev 13:39 spots in the skin of their flesh *be* **d** white; 3544

DARKLY (1) [DARKEN]
1Co 13:12 For now we see through a glass, **d;** *135+1722*

DARKNESS (162) [DARKEN]
Ge 1: 2 void; and **d** *was* upon the face of the deep. 2822
1: 4 and God divided the light from the **d.** 2822
1: 5 the light Day, and the **d** he called Night. 2822
1:18 the night, and to divide the light from the **d:** 2822
15:12 and, lo, a horror of great **d** fell upon him. 2825
Ex 10:21 that there may be **d** over the land of Egypt, 2822
10:21 land of Egypt, even **d** *which* may be felt. 2822
10:22 there was a thick **d** in all the land of Egypt 2822
14:20 it was a cloud and **d** *to them,* but it gave 2822
20:21 Moses drew near unto the **thick d** where 6205
Dt 4:11 *with* **d,** clouds, and thick darkness. 2822
4:11 *with* darkness, clouds, and **thick d.** 6205
5:22 of the cloud, and of the **thick d,** *with* a 6205
5:23 ye heard the voice out of the midst of the **d,** 2822
28:29 as the blind gropeth in **d,** and thou shalt not 653
Jos 24: 7 he put **d** between you and the Egyptians, 3990
1Sa 2: 9 and the wicked shall be silent in **d;** 2822
2Sa 22:10 and came down; and **d** *was* under his feet. 6205
22:12 he made **d** pavilions round about him, 2822
22:29 and the LORD will lighten my **d.** 2822
1Ki 8:12 said that *he* would dwell in the **thick d.** 6205
2Ch 6: 1 said that *he* would dwell in the **thick d.** 6205
Job 3: 4 Let that day be **d;** let not God regard it 2822
3: 5 Let **d** and the shadow of death stain it; let a 2822
3: 6 *As for* that night, let **d** seize upon it; let it not 652
5:14 They meet with **d** in the daytime, and 2822
10:21 *even* to the land of **d** and the shadow of 2822
10:22 A land of **d,** as darkness itself; *and of* 5890
10:22 A land of darkness, as **d** itself; *and of* 652
10:22 any order, and *where* the light is as **d.** 652
12:22 He discovereth deep *things* out of **d,** and 2822
15:22 believeth not that *he* shall return out of **d,** 2822
15:23 that the day of **d** is ready at his hand. 2822
15:30 He shall not depart out of **d;** the flame shall 2822
17:12 into day: the light *is* short, because of **d.** 2822
17:13 mine house: I have made my bed in the **d.** 2822
18:18 He shall be driven from light into **d,** and 2822
19: 8 cannot pass, and he hath set **d** in my paths. 2822
20:26 All **d** *shall be* hid in his secret places: a fire 2822
22:11 Or **d,** *that* thou canst not see; and 2822
23:17 Because I was not cut off before the **d,** 2822
23:17 *neither* hath he covered the **d** from my face. 652
28: 3 He setteth an end to **d,** and searcheth out all 2822
28: 3 the stones of **d,** and the shadow of death. 652
29: 3 *and when* by his light I walked *through* **d;** 2822
30:26 and when I waited for light, there came **d.** 652
34:22 *There is* no **d,** nor shadow of death, 2822
37:19 we cannot order *our speech* by reason of **d.** 2822
38: 9 and **thick d** a swaddling band for it, 6205
38:19 and *as for* **d,** where *is* the place thereof, 2822
Ps 18: 9 and came down: and **d** *was* under his feet. 6205
18:11 He made **d** his secret place; his pavilion 2822
18:28 the LORD my God will enlighten my **d.** 2822
82: 5 will they understand; they walk on in **d:** 2825
88: 6 laid me in the lowest pit, in **d,** in the deeps. 4285
88:18 far from me, *and* mine acquaintance *into* **d.** 4285
91: 6 *Nor* for the pestilence *that* walketh in **d;** 652
97: 2 Clouds and **d** *are* round about him: 6205
104:20 Thou makest **d,** and it is night: wherein all 2822
105:28 He sent **d,** and made it dark; and 2822
107:10 Such as sit in **d** and in the shadow of death, 2822
107:14 He brought them out of **d** and the shadow 2822
112: 4 Unto the upright there ariseth light in the **d:** 2822
139:11 If I say, Surely the **d** shall cover me; 2822
139:12 Yea, the **d** hideth not from thee; but 2822
139:12 the **d** and the light *are* both alike *to thee.* 2825
143: 3 he hath made me to dwell in **d,** as those that 4285
Pr 2:13 of uprightness, to walk in the ways of **d;** 2822
4:19 The way of the wicked *is* as **d:** they know 653
20:20 his lamp shall be put out in obscure **d.** 2822
Ecc 2:13 excelleth folly, as far as light excelleth **d.** 2822
2:14 *are* in his head; but the fool walketh in **d:** 2822
5:17 All his days also he eateth in **d,** and *he hath* 2822
6: 4 departeth in **d,** and his name shall be 2822
6: 4 and his name shall be covered with **d.** 2822
11: 8 yet let him remember the days of **d;** 2822
Isa 5:20 that put **d** for light, and light for darkness; 2822
5:20 that put darkness for light, and light for **d;** 2822

D

Isa 5:30 behold **d** *and* sorrow, and the light is 2822
8:22 behold trouble and **d**, dimness of anguish; 2825
8:22 of anguish; and *they shall be* driven *to* **d**. 653
9: 2 The people that walked in **d** have seen a 2822
29:18 shall see out of obscurity, and out of **d**, 2822
42: 7 them that sit in **d** out of the prison house. 2822
42:16 I will make **d** light before them, and 4285
45: 3 I will give thee the treasures of **d**, and 2822
45: 7 I form the light, and create **d**: I make peace, 2822
47: 5 Sit thou silent, and get thee into **d**, 2822
49: 9 to *them* that *are* in **d**, Shew yourselves. 2822
50:10 that walketh *in* **d**, and hath no light? 2825
58:10 in obscurity, and thy **d** *be* as the noonday: 653
59: 9 for brightness, *but* we walk in **d**. 653
60: 2 the **d** shall cover the earth, and 2822
60: 2 cover the earth, and **gross d** the people: 6205
Jer 2:31 a land of **d**? wherefore say my people, 3991
13:16 before he **cause d**, and before your feet 2821
13:16 the shadow of death, *and* make *it* **gross d**. 6205
23:12 shall be unto them as slippery *ways* in the **d**: 653
La 3: 2 and brought *me into* **d**, but not *into* light. 2822
Eze 32: 8 set **d** upon thy land, saith the Lord God. 2822
Da 2:22 secret *things*: he knoweth what *is* in the **d**, 2816
Joel 2: 2 A day of **d** and of gloominess, a day of 2822
2: 2 a day of clouds and of **thick d**, 6205
2:31 The sun shall be turned into **d**, and 2822
Am 4:13 that maketh the morning **d**, and 5890
5:18 the day of the Lord *is* **d**, and not light. 2822
5:20 *Shall* not the day of the Lord *be* **d**, and 2822
Mic 7: 8 when I sit in **d**, the Lord *shall be* a light 2822
Na 1: 8 and **d** shall pursue his enemies. 2822
Zep 1:15 and desolation, a day of **d** and gloominess, 2822
1:15 gloominess, a day of clouds and **thick d**, 6205
Mt 4:16 The people which sat in **d** saw great light; *4655*
6:23 be evil, thy whole body shall be **full of d**. *4652*
6:23 If therefore the light that is in thee be **d**, *4655*
6:23 is in thee be darkness, how great *is* that **d**? *4655*
8:12 the kingdom shall be cast out into outer **d**: *4655*
10:27 What I tell you in **d**, *that* speak ye in light: *4653*
22:13 take him away, and cast *him* into outer **d**; *4655*
25:30 ye the unprofitable servant into outer **d**: *4655*
27:45 Now from the sixth hour there was **d** over *4655*
Mk 15:33 there was **d** over the whole land until *4655*
Lk 1:79 To give light to them that sit in **d** and *in* *4655*
11:34 *thine eye* is evil, thy body also *is* **full of d**. *4652*
11:35 that the light which is in thee be not **d**. *4655*
12: 3 Therefore whatsoever ye have spoken in **d** *4653*
22:53 but this is your hour, and the power of **d**. *4655*
23:44 there was a **d** over all the earth until *4655*
Jn 1: 5 And the light shineth in **d**; and the darkness *4653*
1: 5 in darkness; and the **d** comprehended it not. *4653*
3:19 and men loved **d** rather than light, because *4655*
8:12 he that followeth me shall not walk in **d**, *4653*
12:35 ye have the light, lest **d** come upon you: *4653*
12:35 for he that walketh in **d** knoweth not *4653*
12:46 believeth on me should not abide in **d**. *4653*
Ac 2:20 The sun shall be turned into **d**, and *4655*
13:11 there fell on him a mist and a **d**; *4655*
26:18 *and* to turn *them* from **d** to light, and *4655*
Ro 2:19 of the blind, a light of them which are in **d**, *4655*
13:12 let us therefore cast off the works of **d**, and *4655*
1Co 4: 5 will bring to light the hidden *things* of **d**, *4655*
2Co 4: 6 who commanded the light to shine out of **d**, *4655*
6:14 and what communion hath light with **d**? *4655*
Eph 5: 8 For ye were sometimes **d**, but now *are ye* *4655*
5:11 fellowship with the unfruitful works of **d**, *4655*
6:12 against the rulers of the **d** of this world, *4655*
Col 1:13 Who hath delivered us from the power of **d**, *4655*
1Th 5: 4 But ye, brethren, are not in **d**, that *that* day *4655*
5: 5 of the day: we are not of the night, nor of **d**. *4655*
Heb 12:18 burned with fire, nor unto blackness, and **d**, *4655*
1Pe 2: 9 you out of **d** into his marvellous light: *4655*
2Pe 2: 4 to hell, and delivered *them* into chains of **d**, *2217*
2:17 to whom the mist of **d** is reserved for ever. *4655*
1Jn 1: 5 that God is light, and in him is no **d** at all. *4653*
1: 6 and walk in **d**, we lie, and do not the truth: *4655*
2: 8 because the **d** is past, and the true light now *4653*
2: 9 hateth his brother, is in **d** *even* until now. *4653*
2:11 But he that hateth his brother is in **d**, and *4653*
2:11 and walketh in **d**, and knoweth not whither *4653*
2:11 because that **d** hath blinded his eyes. *4653*
Jude 1: 6 under **d** unto the judgment of the great day. *2217*
1:13 to whom is reserved the blackness of **d** for *4655*
Rev 16:10 and his kingdom was **full of d**; and *4656*

DARKON (2)
Ezr 2:56 the children of **D**, the children of Giddel, 1874
Ne 7:58 The children of Jaala, the children of **D**, 1874

DARLING (2)
Ps 22:20 the sword; my **d** from the power of the dog. 3173
35:17 their destructions, my **d** from the lions. 3173

DART (3) [DARTS]
Job 41:26 the spear, the **d**, nor the habergeon. 4551
Pr 7:23 Till a **d** strike through his liver; as a bird 2671
Heb 12:20 shall be stoned, or thrust through with a **d**: *1002*

DARTS (4) [DART]
2Sa 18:14 he took three **d** in his hand, and thrust them 7626
2Ch 32: 5 and made **d** and shields in abundance. 7973
Job 41:29 **D** are counted as stubble: he laugheth at 8455
Eph 6:16 able to quench all the fiery **d** of the wicked. *956*

DASH (7) [DASHED, DASHETH]
2Ki 8:12 wilt **d** their children, and rip up their 7376
Ps 2: 9 thou shalt **d** them **in pieces** like a potter's 5310
91:12 lest thou **d** thy foot against a stone. 5062
Isa 13:18 bows also shall **d** the young men **to pieces**; 7376
Jer 13:14 I will **d** them one against another, even 5310
Mt 4: 6 lest at any time thou **d** thy foot against a *4350*
Lk 4:11 lest at any time thou **d** thy foot against a *4350*

DASHED (5) [DASH]
Ex 15: 6 O Lord, hath **d in pieces** the enemy. 7492
Isa 13:16 Their children also shall be **d to pieces** 7376
Hos 10:14 the mother was **d in pieces** upon *her* 7376
13:16 their infants shall be **d in pieces**, and 7376
Na 3:10 her young children also were **d in pieces** at 7376

DASHETH (2) [DASH]
Ps 137: 9 and **d** thy little ones against the stones. 5310
Na 2: 1 He that **d in pieces** is come up before thy 6327

DATHAN (10)
Nu 16: 1 the son of Levi, and **D** and Abiram, 1885
16:12 Moses sent to call **D** and Abiram, the sons 1885
16:24 the tabernacle of Korah, **D**, and Abiram. 1885
16:25 rose up and went unto **D** and Abiram; 1885
16:27 of Korah, **D**, and Abiram, on every side: 1885
16:27 **D** and Abiram came out, and stood *in* 1885
26: 9 sons of Eliab; Nemuel, and **D**, and Abiram. 1885
26: 9 This *is that* **D** and Abiram, *which were* 1885
Dt 11: 6 what he did unto **D** and Abiram, the sons of 1885
Ps 106:17 The earth opened and swallowed up **D**, and 1885

DAUB (1) [DAUBED, DAUBING]
Eze 13:11 Say unto them which **d** *it with* untempered 2902

DAUBED (7) [DAUB]
Ex 2: 3 **d** it with slime and with pitch, and put 2560
Eze 13:10 and lo, others **d** it *with* untempered *morter:* 2902
13:12 Where *is* the daubing where*with* ye have **d** 2902
13:14 that ye have **d** *with* untempered *morter,* 2902
13:15 upon them that have **d** it *with* untempered 2902
13:15 The wall *is* no *more,* neither they that **d** it; 2902
22:28 her prophets have **d** them *with* untempered 2902

DAUBING (1) [DAUB]
Eze 13:12 Where *is* the **d** where*with* ye have daubed 2915

DAUGHTER (324) [DAUGHTER'S, DAUGHTERS]
Ge 11:29 Milcah, the **d** of Haran, the father of 1323
11:31 Sarai his **d in law**, his son Abram's wife; 3618
20:12 she *is* the **d** of my father, but not 1323
20:12 of my father, but not the **d** of my mother; 1323
24:23 said, Whose **d** *art* thou? tell me, I pray thee: 1323
24:24 I *am* the **d** of Bethuel the son of Milcah, 1323
24:47 I asked her, and said, Whose **d** *art* thou? 1323
24:47 she said, The **d** of Bethuel, Nahor's son, 1323
24:48 take my master's brother's **d** unto his son. 1323
25:20 the **d** of Bethuel the Syrian of Padan-aram, 1323
26:34 to wife Judith the **d** of Beeri the Hittite, 1323
26:34 and Bashemath the **d** of Elon the Hittite: 1323
28: 9 Mahalath the **d** of Ishmael Abraham's son, 1323
29: 6 Rachel his **d** cometh with the sheep. 1323
29:10 when Jacob saw Rachel the **d** of Laban his 1323
29:18 thee seven years for Rachel thy younger **d**. 1323
29:23 that he took Leah his **d**, and brought her to 1323
29:24 Laban gave unto his **d** Leah Zilpah his 1323

Ge	29:28	and he gave him Rachel his **d** to wife *also*.	1323
	29:29	Laban gave to Rachel his **d** Bilhah his	1323
	30:21	afterwards she bare a **d**, and called her	1323
	34: 1	Dinah the **d** of Leah, which she bare unto	1323
	34: 3	his soul clave unto Dinah the **d** of Jacob,	1323
	34: 5	heard that he had defiled Dinah his **d**:	1323
	34: 7	folly in Israel in lying with Jacob's **d**;	1323
	34: 8	of my son Shechem longeth for your **d**:	1323
	34:17	will we take our **d**, and we will be gone.	1323
	34:19	because he had delight in Jacob's **d**:	1323
	36: 2	Adah the **d** of Elon the Hittite, and	1323
	36: 2	Aholibamah the **d** of Anah the daughter of	1323
	36: 2	Aholibamah the daughter of Anah the **d** of	1323
	36: 3	Bashemath Ishmael's **d**, sister of Nebajoth.	1323
	36:14	the **d** of Anah, daughter of Zibeon,	1323
	36:14	of Anah, **d** of Zibeon, Esau's wife:	1323
	36:18	*that came* of Aholibamah the **d** of Anah,	1323
	36:25	Dishon, and Aholibamah the **d** of Anah.	1323
	36:39	the **d** of Matred, the daughter of Mezahab.	1323
	36:39	the daughter of Matred, the **d** of Mezahab.	1323
	38: 2	Judah saw there a **d** of a certain Canaanite,	1323
	38:11	said Judah to Tamar his **d in law**, Remain a	3618
	38:12	in process of time the **d** of Shuah Judah's	1323
	38:16	(for he knew not that she *was* his **d in law**:)	3618
	38:24	Tamar thy **d in law** hath played the harlot;	3618
	41:45	he gave him to wife Asenath the **d** of	1323
	41:50	which Asenath the **d** of Poti-pherah priest	1323
	46:15	Jacob in Padan-aram, with his **d** Dinah:	1323
	46:18	whom Laban gave to Leah his **d**, and	1323
	46:20	which Asenath the **d** of Poti-pherah priest	1323
	46:25	which Laban gave unto Rachel his **d**, and	1323
Ex	1:16	kill him: but if it *be* a **d**, then she shall live.	1323
	1:22	the river, and every **d** ye shall save alive.	1323
	2: 1	house of Levi, and took *to wife* a **d** of Levi.	1323
	2: 5	the **d** of Pharaoh came down to wash	1323
	2: 7	said his sister to Pharaoh's **d**, Shall I go	1323
	2: 8	Pharaoh's **d** said to her, Go. And the maid	1323
	2: 9	Pharaoh's **d** said unto her, Take this child	1323
	2:10	she brought him unto Pharaoh's **d**, and	1323
	2:21	and he gave Moses Zipporah his **d**.	1323
	6:23	**d** of Amminadab, sister of Naashon,	1323
	20:10	thou, nor thy son, nor thy **d**,	1323
	21: 7	if a man sell his **d** to be a maidservant,	1323
	21:31	he have gored a son, or have gored a **d**,	1323
Lev	12: 6	purifying are fulfilled, for a son, or for a **d**,	1323
	18: 9	the **d** of thy father, or daughter of thy	1323
	18: 9	daughter of thy father, or **d** of thy mother,	1323
	18:10	The nakedness of thy son's **d**, or of thy	1323
	18:10	thy son's daughter, or of thy daughter's **d**,	1323
	18:11	The nakedness of thy father's wife's **d**,	1323
	18:15	not uncover the nakedness of thy **d in law**:	3618
	18:17	the nakedness of a woman and her **d**,	1323
	18:17	neither shalt thou take her son's **d**, or	1323
	18:17	or her daughter's **d**, to uncover her	1323
	19:29	Do not prostitute thy **d**, to cause her to be a	1323
	20:12	if a man lie with his **d in law**, both of them	3618
	20:17	his father's **d**, or his mother's daughter, and	1323
	20:17	or his mother's **d**, and see her nakedness,	1323
	21: 2	his son, and for his **d**, and for his brother,	1323
	21: 9	the **d** of any priest, if she profane herself by	1323
	22:12	If the priest's **d** also be *married* unto a	1323
	22:13	if the priest's **d** be a widow, or divorced,	1323
	24:11	the **d** of Dibri, of the tribe of Dan:)	1323
Nu	25:15	that was slain *was* Cozbi, the **d** of Zur;	1323
	25:18	the **d** of a prince of Midian, their sister,	1323
	26:46	And the name of the **d** of Asher *was* Sarah.	1323
	26:59	the **d** of Levi, whom *her mother* bare to	1323
	27: 8	cause his inheritance to pass unto his **d**.	1323
	27: 9	if he have no **d**, then ye shall give his	1323
	30:16	and his wife, between the father and his **d**,	1323
	36: 8	every **d**, that possesseth an inheritance in	1323
Dt	5:14	thou, nor thy son, nor thy **d**, nor thy	1323
	7: 3	thy **d** thou shalt not give unto his son,	1323
	7: 3	nor his **d** shalt thou take unto thy son.	1323
	12:18	thy **d**, and thy manservant, and	1323
	13: 6	or thy **d**, or the wife of thy bosom, or	1323
	16:11	thy **d**, and thy manservant, and	1323
	16:14	thy **d**, and thy manservant, and	1323
	18:10	his son or his **d** to pass through the fire,	1323
	22:16	I gave my **d** unto this man to wife, and	1323
	22:17	*her*, saying, I found not thy **d** a maid;	1323
	27:22	the **d** of his father, or the daughter of his	1323
	27:22	of his father, or the **d** of his mother.	1323
	28:56	and towards her son, and towards her **d**,	1323
Jos	15:16	to him will I give Achsah my **d** to wife.	1323
	15:17	and he gave him Achsah his **d** to wife.	1323
Jdg	1:12	to him will I give Achsah my **d** to wife.	1323
	1:13	and he gave him Achsah his **d** to wife.	1323
	11:34	his **d** came out to meet him with timbrels	1323
	11:34	beside her he had neither son nor **d**.	1323
	11:35	he rent his clothes, and said, Alas, my **d**,	1323
	11:40	**d** of Jephthah the Gileadite four days in a	1323
	19:24	*here is* my **d** a maiden, and his concubine;	1323
	21: 1	There shall not any of us give his **d** unto	1323
Ru	1:22	Ruth the Moabitess, her **d in law**, with her,	3618
	2: 2	And she said unto her, Go, my **d**.	1323
	2: 8	Boaz unto Ruth, Hearest thou not, my **d**?	1323
	2:20	Naomi said unto her **d in law**, Blessed *be*	3618
	2:22	Naomi said unto Ruth her **d in law**, *It is*	3618
	2:22	*It is* good, my **d**, that thou go out with his	1323
	3: 1	My **d**, shall I not seek rest for thee, that it	1323
	3:10	Blessed *be* thou of the LORD, my **d**:	1323
	3:11	now, my **d**, fear not; I will do to thee all	1323
	3:16	in law, she said, Who *art* thou, my **d**?	1323
	3:18	said she, Sit still, my **d**, until thou know	1323
	4:15	for thy **d in law**, which loveth thee,	3618
1Sa	1:16	Count not thine handmaid for a **d** of Belial:	1323
	4:19	his **d in law**, Phinehas' wife, was with	3618
	14:50	wife *was* Ahinoam, the **d** of Ahimaaz:	1323
	17:25	will give him his **d**, and make his father's	1323
	18:17	said to David, Behold my elder **d** Merab,	1323
	18:19	Saul's **d** should have been given to David,	1323
	18:20	Michal Saul's **d** loved David: and they told	1323
	18:27	And Saul gave him Michal his **d** to wife.	1323
	18:28	and *that* Michal Saul's **d** loved him.	1323
	25:44	Saul had given Michal his **d**, David's wife,	1323
2Sa	3: 3	Absalom the son of Maacah the **d** of	1323
	3: 7	whose name *was* Rizpah, the **d** of Aiah:	1323
	3:13	except thou first bring Michal Saul's **d**,	1323
	6:16	Michal Saul's **d** looked through a window,	1323
	6:20	Michal the **d** of Saul came out to meet	1323
	6:23	Therefore Michal the **d** of Saul had no	1323
	11: 3	*Is* not this Bath-sheba, the **d** of Eliam,	1323
	12: 3	lay in his bosom, and was unto him as a **d**.	1323
	14:27	and one **d**, whose name *was* Tamar:	1323
	17:25	that went in to Abigail the **d** of Nahash,	1323
	21: 8	the king took the two sons of Rizpah the **d**	1323
	21: 8	the five sons of Michal the **d** of Saul,	1323
	21:10	Rizpah the **d** of Aiah took sackcloth, and	1323
	21:11	it was told David what Rizpah the **d** of	1323
1Ki	3: 1	took Pharaoh's **d**, and brought her into	1323
	4:11	which had Taphath the **d** of Solomon to	1323
	4:15	he also took Basmath the **d** of Solomon to	1323
	7: 8	made also a house for Pharaoh's **d**,	1323
	9:16	given it *for* a present unto his **d**,	1323
	9:24	Pharaoh's **d** came up out of the city of	1323
	11: 1	together with the **d** of Pharaoh, *women of*	1323
	15: 2	name *was* Maachah, the **d** of Abishalom.	1323
	15:10	name *was* Maachah, the **d** of Abishalom.	1323
	16:31	that he took *to* wife Jezebel the **d** of	1323
	22:42	his mother's name *was* Azubah the **d** of	1323
2Ki	8:18	for the **d** of Ahab was his wife: and he did	1323
	8:26	*was* Athaliah, the **d** of Omri king of Israel.	1323
	9:34	and bury her: for she *is* a king's **d**.	1323
	11: 2	Jehosheba, the **d** of king Joram, sister of	1323
	14: 9	Give thy **d** to my son to wife:	1323
	15:33	name *was* Jerusha, the **d** of Zadok.	1323
	18: 2	name also *was* Abi, the **d** of Zachariah.	1323
	19:21	The virgin the **d** of Zion hath despised thee,	1323
	19:21	the **d** of Jerusalem hath shaken her head at	1323
	21:19	the **d** of Haruz of Jotbah.	1323
	22: 1	*was* Jedidah, the **d** of Adaiah of Boscath.	1323
	23:10	or his **d** to pass through the fire to Molech.	1323
	23:31	*was* Hamutal, the **d** of Jeremiah of Libnah.	1323
	23:36	*was* Zebudah, the **d** of Pedaiah of Rumah.	1323
	24: 8	the **d** of Elnathan of Jerusalem.	1323
	24:18	*was* Hamutal, the **d** of Jeremiah of Libnah.	1323
1Ch	1:50	the **d** of Matred, the daughter of Mezahab.	1323
	1:50	the daughter of Matred, the **d** of Mezahab.	1323
	2: 3	*which* three were born unto him of the **d** of	1323
	2: 4	Tamar his **d in law** bare him Pharez and	3618
	2:21	afterward Hezron went in to the **d** of	1323
	2:35	Sheshan gave his **d** to Jarha his servant to	1323
	2:49	of Gibea: and the **d** of Caleb *was* Achsah.	1323
	3: 2	Absalom the son of Maachah the **d** of	1323
	3: 5	four, of Bath-shua the **d** of Ammiel:	1323
	4:18	these *are* the sons of Bithiah the **d** of	1323
	7:24	(And his **d** *was* Sherah, who built	1323

1Ch 15:29 that Michal the **d** of Saul looking out at a 1323
2Ch 8:11 Solomon brought up the **d** of Pharaoh out 1323
11:18 Rehoboam took him Mahalath the **d** of 1323
11:18 Abihail the **d** of Eliab the son of Jesse; 1323
11:20 after her he took Maachah the **d** of 1323
11:21 Rehoboam loved Maachah the **d** of 1323
13: 2 His mother's name also *was* Michaiah the **d** 1323
20:31 his mother's name *was* Azubah the **d** of 1323
21: 6 for he had the **d** of Ahab to wife: and 1323
22: 2 His mother's name also *was* Athaliah the **d** 1323
22:11 Jehoshabeath, the **d** of the king, took Joash 1323
22:11 So Jehoshabeath, the **d** of king Jehoram, 1323
25:18 Give thy **d** to my son to wife: 1323
27: 1 name also *was* Jerushah, the **d** of Zadok. 1323
29: 1 name *was* Abijah, the **d** of Zechariah. 1323
Ne 6:18 his son Johanan had taken the **d** of 1323
Est 2: 7 up Hadassah, that *is,* Esther, his uncle's **d**: 1323
2: 7 and mother were dead, took for his own **d**. 1323
2:15 the **d** of Abihail the uncle of Mordecai, 1323
2:15 who had taken *her* for his **d**, was come to 1323
9:29 the **d** of Abihail, and Mordecai the Jew, 1323
Ps 9:14 all thy praise in the gates of the **d** of Zion: 1323
45:10 O **d**, and consider, and incline thine ear; 1323
45:12 the **d** of Tyre *shall be there* with a gift; 1323
45:13 The king's **d** *is* all glorious within: 1323
137: 8 O **d** of Babylon, who art *to be* destroyed; 1323
SS 7: 1 are thy feet with shoes, O prince's **d**! 1323
Isa 1: 8 the **d** of Zion is left as a cottage in a 1323
10:30 Lift up thy voice, O **d** of Gallim: cause *it* to 1323
10:32 his hand *against* the mount of the **d** of Zion, 1323
16: 1 unto the mount of the **d** of Zion. 1323
22: 4 of the spoiling of the **d** of my people. 1323
23:10 thy land as a river, O **d** of Tarshish: 1323
23:12 O thou oppressed virgin, **d** of Zidon: 1323
37:22 The virgin, the **d** of Zion, hath despised 1323
37:22 the **d** of Jerusalem hath shaken her head at 1323
47: 1 and sit in the dust, O virgin **d** of Babylon, 1323
47: 1 *there is* no throne, O **d** of the Chaldeans: 1323
47: 5 thee into darkness, O **d** of the Chaldeans: 1323
52: 2 the bands of thy neck, O captive **d** of Zion. 1323
62:11 Say ye to the **d** of Zion, Behold, 1323
Jer 4:11 the wilderness toward the **d** of my people, 1323
4:31 the voice of the **d** of Zion, *that* bewaileth 1323
6: 2 I have likened the **d** of Zion *to* a comely 1323
6:14 They have healed also the hurt of *the d of* NIH
6:23 as men for war against thee, O **d** of Zion. 1323
6:26 O **d** of my people, gird *thee* with sackcloth, 1323
8:11 For they have healed the hurt of the **d** of 1323
8:19 Behold the voice of the cry of the **d** of my 1323
8:21 For the hurt of the **d** of my people am I 1323
8:22 is not the health of the **d** of my people 1323
9: 1 night for the slain of the **d** of my people! 1323
9: 7 for how shall I do for the **d** of my people? 1323
14:17 for the virgin **d** of my people is broken *with* 1323
31:22 wilt thou go about, O thou backsliding **d**? 1323
46:11 and take balm, O virgin, the **d** of Egypt: 1323
46:19 O thou **d** dwelling in Egypt, furnish thyself 1323
46:24 The **d** of Egypt shall be confounded; 1323
48:18 Thou **d** that dost inhabit Dibon, come down 1323
49: 4 thy flowing valley, O backsliding **d**? 1323
50:42 to the battle, against thee, O **d** of Babylon. 1323
51:33 The **d** of Babylon *is* like a threshingfloor, 1323
52: 1 his mother's name *was* Hamutal the **d** of 1323
La 1: 6 from the **d** of Zion all her beauty is 1323
1:15 the **d** of Judah, *as in* a winepress. 1323
2: 1 How hath the Lord covered the **d** of Zion 1323
2: 2 wrath the strong holds of the **d** of Judah; 1323
2: 4 the eye, in the tabernacle of the **d** of Zion: 1323
2: 5 hath increased in the **d** of Judah mourning 1323
2: 8 to destroy the wall of the **d** of Zion: 1323
2:10 The elders of the **d** of Zion sit upon 1323
2:11 for the destruction of the **d** of my people; 1323
2:13 shall I liken to thee, O **d** of Jerusalem? 1323
2:13 I may comfort thee, O virgin **d** of Zion? 1323
2:15 and wag their head at the **d** of Jerusalem, 1323
2:18 unto the Lord, O wall of the **d** of Zion, 1323
3:48 for the destruction of the **d** of my people. 1323
4: 3 the **d** of my people *is* become cruel, like 1323
4: 6 For the punishment of the iniquity of the **d** 1323
4:10 in the destruction of the **d** of my people. 1323
4:21 Rejoice and be glad, O **d** of Edom, 1323
4:22 thine iniquity is accomplished, O **d** of Zion; 1323
4:22 he will visit thine iniquity, O **d** of Edom; 1323
Eze 14:20 they shall deliver neither son nor **d**; 1323
16:44 saying, As *is* the mother, *so is* her **d**. 1323
16:45 Thou *art* thy mother's **d**, that lotheth her 1323
22:11 another hath lewdly defiled his **d in law**; 3618
22:11 thee hath humbled his sister, his father's **d**. 1323
44:25 or for mother, or for son, or for **d**, 1323
Da 11: 6 for the king's **d** of the south shall come to 1323
11:17 he shall give him the **d** of women, 1323
Hos 1: 3 he went and took Gomer the **d** of Diblaim; 1323
1: 6 she conceived again, and bare a **d**. 1323
Mic 1:13 she *is* the beginning of the sin to the **d** of 1323
4: 8 the flock, the strong hold of the **d** of Zion, 1323
4: 8 the kingdom shall come to the **d** of 1323
4:10 and labour to bring forth, O **d** of Zion, 1323
4:13 Arise and thresh, O **d** of Zion: for I will 1323
5: 1 Now gather thyself in troops, O **d** of troops: 1323
7: 6 the **d** riseth up against her mother, 1323
7: 6 the **d in law** against her mother in law; 3618
Zep 3:10 *even* the **d** of my dispersed, shall bring 1323
3:14 Sing, O **d** of Zion; shout, O Israel; be glad 1323
3:14 rejoice with all the heart, O **d** of Jerusalem. 1323
Zec 2: 7 that dwellest *with* the **d** of Babylon. 1323
2:10 Sing and rejoice, O **d** of Zion: for lo, 1323
9: 9 Rejoice greatly, O **d** of Zion; shout, 1323
9: 9 daughter of Zion; shout, O **d** of Jerusalem: 1323
Mal 2:11 and hath married the **d** of a strange god. 1323
Mt 9:18 saying, My **d** is even now dead: *2364*
9:22 and when he saw her, he said, **D**, be of *2364*
10:35 and the **d** against her mother, and *2364*
10:35 and the **d in law** against her mother in law. *3565*
10:37 or **d** more than me is not worthy of me. *2364*
14: 6 the **d** of Herodias danced before them, and *2364*
15:22 my **d** is grievously vexed with a devil. *2364*
15:28 And her **d** was made whole from that *very* *2364*
21: 5 Tell ye the **d** of Sion, Behold, thy King *2364*
Mk 5:23 My **little d** lieth at the point of death: *2365*
5:34 And he said unto her, **D**, thy faith hath *2364*
5:35 *house certain* which said, Thy **d** is dead: *2364*
6:22 And when the **d** of the said Herodias came *2364*
7:25 whose **young d** had an unclean spirit, *2365*
7:26 he would cast forth the devil out of her **d**. *2364*
7:29 go thy way; the devil is gone out of thy **d**. *2364*
7:30 devil gone out, and *her* **d** laid upon the bed. *2364*
Lk 2:36 a prophetess, the **d** of Phanuel, of the tribe *2364*
8:42 For he had one only **d**, about twelve years *2364*
8:48 he said unto her, **D**, be of good comfort: *2364*
8:49 *house,* saying to him, Thy **d** is dead; *2364*
12:53 the mother against the **d**, and the daughter *2364*
12:53 the daughter, and the **d** against the mother; *2364*
12:53 the mother in law against her **d in law**, and *3565*
12:53 and the **d in law** against her mother in law. *3565*
13:16 And ought not this *woman,* being a **d** of *2364*
Jn 12:15 Fear not, **d** of Sion: behold, thy King *2364*
Ac 7:21 Pharaoh's **d** took him up, and *2364*
Heb 11:24 refused to be called the son of Pharaoh's **d**; *2364*

DAUGHTER'S (3) [DAUGHTER]

Lev 18:10 of thy son's daughter, or of thy **d** daughter, 1323
18:17 or her **d** daughter, to uncover her 1323
Dt 22:17 *yet* these *are the tokens of* my **d** virginity. 1323

DAUGHTERS (254) [DAUGHTER]

Ge 5: 4 hundred years: and he begat sons and **d**: 1323
5: 7 seven years, and begat sons and **d**: 1323
5:10 fifteen years, and begat sons and **d**: 1323
5:13 forty years, and begat sons and **d**: 1323
5:16 thirty years, and begat sons and **d**: 1323
5:19 eight hundred years, and begat sons and **d**: 1323
5:22 three hundred years, and begat sons and **d**: 1323
5:26 and two years, and begat sons and **d**: 1323
5:30 and five years, and begat sons and **d**: 1323
6: 1 of the earth, and **d** were born unto them, 1323
6: 2 That the sons of God saw the **d** of men that 1323
6: 4 when the sons of God came in unto the **d** of 1323
11:11 five hundred years, and begat sons and **d**. 1323
11:13 three years, and begat sons and **d**. 1323
11:15 three years, and begat sons and **d**. 1323
11:17 thirty years, and begat sons and **d**. 1323
11:19 nine years, and begat sons and **d**. 1323
11:21 seven years, and begat sons and **d**. 1323
11:23 two hundred years, and begat sons and **d**. 1323
11:25 nineteen years, and begat sons and **d**. 1323
19: 8 I have two **d** which have not known man; 1323
19:12 thy **d**, and whatsoever thou hast in the city, 1323
19:14 which married his **d**, and said, Up, get ye 1323

Ge	19:15	saying, Arise, take thy wife, and thy two **d**,	1323
	19:16	of his wife, and upon the hand of his two **d**;	1323
	19:30	in the mountain, and his two **d** with him;	1323
	19:30	and he dwelt in a cave, he and his two **d**.	1323
	19:36	Thus were both the **d** of Lot with child by	1323
	24: 3	unto my son of the **d** of the Canaanites,	1323
	24:13	the **d** of the men of the city come out to	1323
	24:37	a wife to my son of the **d** of the Canaanites,	1323
	27:46	weary of my life because of the **d** of Heth:	1323
	27:46	if Jacob take a wife of the **d** of Heth,	1323
	27:46	such as these *which are* of the **d** of the land,	1323
	28: 1	Thou shalt not take a wife of the **d** of	1323
	28: 2	take thee a wife from thence of the **d** of	1323
	28: 6	Thou shalt not take a wife of the **d** of	1323
	28: 8	Esau seeing that the **d** of Canaan pleased	1323
	29:16	Laban had two **d**: the name of the elder *was*	1323
	30:13	Happy am I, for the **d** will call me blessed:	1323
	31:26	carried away my **d**, as captives taken with	1323
	31:28	not suffered me to kiss my sons and my **d**?	1323
	31:31	thou wouldest take by force thy **d** from me.	1323
	31:41	I served thee fourteen years for thy two **d**,	1323
	31:43	*These* **d** *are* my daughters, and *these*	1323
	31:43	*These* daughters *are* my **d**, and *these*	1323
	31:43	what can I do *this* day unto these my **d**, or	1323
	31:50	If thou shalt afflict my **d**, or if thou shalt	1323
	31:50	if thou shalt take *other* wives beside my **d**,	1323
	31:55	kissed his sons and his **d**, and blessed them:	1323
	34: 1	went out to see the **d** of the land.	1323
	34: 9	*and* give your **d** unto us, and take our	1323
	34: 9	daughters unto us, and take our **d** unto you.	1323
	34:16	will we give our **d** unto you, and we will	1323
	34:16	we will take your **d** to us, and we will dwell	1323
	34:21	let us take their **d** to us for wives, and let us	1323
	34:21	to us for wives, and let us give them our **d**.	1323
	36: 2	Esau took his wives of the **d** of Canaan;	1323
	36: 6	his **d**, and all the persons of his house, and	1323
	37:35	and all his **d** rose up to comfort him;	1323
	46: 7	his **d**, and his sons' daughters, and all his	1323
	46: 7	his sons' **d**, and all his seed brought he with	1323
	46:15	of his sons and his **d** *were* thirty and three.	1323
Ex	2:16	Now the priest of Midian had seven **d**: and	1323
	2:20	he said unto his **d**, And where *is* he? why *is*	1323
	3:22	put *them* upon your sons, and upon your **d**;	1323
	6:25	Eleazar Aaron's son took him *one* of the **d**	1323
	10: 9	with our old, with our sons and with our **d**,	1323
	21: 4	a wife, and she have born him sons or **d**;	1323
	21: 9	he shall deal with her after the manner of **d**.	1323
	32: 2	and of your **d**, and bring *them* unto me.	1323
	34:16	thou take of their **d** unto thy sons, and	1323
	34:16	their **d** go a whoring after their gods, and	1323
Lev	10:14	thou, and thy sons, and thy **d** with thee:	1323
	26:29	and the flesh of your **d** shall ye eat.	1323
Nu	18:11	to thy sons and to thy **d** with thee, by a	1323
	18:19	and thy sons and thy **d** with thee,	1323
	21:29	his **d** into captivity unto Sihon king of	1323
	25: 1	to commit whoredom with the **d** of Moab.	1323
	26:33	the son of Hepher had no sons, but **d**:	1323
	26:33	the names of the **d** of Zelophehad *were*	1323
	27: 1	came the **d** of Zelophehad, the son of	1323
	27: 1	these *are* the names of his **d**; Mahlah,	1323
	27: 7	The **d** of Zelophehad speak right: thou shalt	1323
	36: 2	of Zelophehad our brother unto his **d**.	1323
	36: 6	command concerning the **d** of Zelophehad,	1323
	36:10	so did the **d** of Zelophehad:	1323
	36:11	Milcah, and Noah, the **d** of Zelophehad,	1323
Dt	12:12	your **d**, and your menservants, and	1323
	12:31	their **d** they have burnt in the fire to their	1323
	23:17	There shall be no whore of the **d** of Israel,	1323
	28:32	thy **d** *shall be* given unto another people,	1323
	28:41	Thou shalt beget sons and **d**, but thou shalt	1323
	28:53	the flesh of thy sons and of thy **d**, which	1323
	32:19	of the provoking of his sons, and of his **d**.	1323
Jos	7:24	his **d**, and his oxen, and his asses, and his	1323
	17: 3	the son of Manasseh, had no sons, but **d**:	1323
	17: 3	these *are* the names of his **d**, Mahlah, and	1323
	17: 6	Because the **d** of Manasseh had an	1323
Jdg	3: 6	they took their **d** to be their wives, and	1323
	3: 6	gave their **d** to their sons, and served their	1323
	11:40	*That* the **d** of Israel went yearly to lament	1323
	12: 9	thirty **d**, *whom* he sent abroad, and took in	1323
	12: 9	took in thirty **d** from abroad for his sons.	1323
	14: 1	saw a woman in Timnath of the **d** of	1323
	14: 2	I have seen a woman in Timnath of the **d** of	1323
	14: 3	*Is there* never a woman among the **d** of thy	1323
	21: 7	*we* will not give them of our **d** to wives?	1323
	21:18	we may not give them wives of our **d**:	1323
	21:21	if the **d** of Shiloh come out to dance in	1323
	21:21	catch you every man his wife of the **d** of	1323
Ru	1: 6	she arose with her **d in law**, that she might	3618
	1: 7	she was, and her two **d in law** with her;	3618
	1: 8	Naomi said unto her two **d in law**, Go,	3618
	1:11	Naomi said, Turn again, my **d**: why will	1323
	1:12	Turn again, my **d**, go *your way;* for I am	1323
	1:13	nay, my **d**; for it grieveth me much for your	1323
1Sa	1: 4	and to all her sons and her **d**, portions:	1323
	2:21	and bare three sons and two **d**.	1323
	8:13	he will take your **d** to be confectionaries,	1323
	14:49	the names of his two **d** *were these;*	1323
	30: 3	their wives, and their sons, and their **d**,	1323
	30: 6	every man for his sons and for his **d**:	1323
	30:19	nor great, neither sons nor **d**, neither spoil,	1323
2Sa	1:20	lest the **d** of the Philistines rejoice, lest	1323
	1:20	lest the **d** of the uncircumcised triumph.	1323
	1:24	Ye **d** of Israel, weep over Saul,	1323
	5:13	there were yet sons and **d** born to David.	1323
	13:18	for with such robes were the king's **d** *that*	1323
	19: 5	the lives of thy sons and of thy **d**, and	1323
2Ki	17:17	and their **d** to pass through the fire,	1323
1Ch	2:34	Now Sheshan had no sons, but **d**.	1323
	4:27	Shimei had sixteen sons and six **d**; but his	1323
	7:15	*was* Zelophehad: and Zelophehad had **d**.	1323
	14: 3	and David begat moe sons and **d**.	1323
	23:22	Eleazar died, and had no sons, but **d**: and	1323
	25: 5	gave to Heman fourteen sons and three **d**.	1323
2Ch	2:14	The son of a woman of the **d** of Dan, and	1323
	11:21	and eight sons, and threescore **d**.)	1323
	13:21	begat twenty and two sons, and sixteen **d**.	1323
	24: 3	him two wives; and he begat sons and **d**.	1323
	28: 8	**d**, and took also away much spoil from	1323
	29: 9	our sons and our **d** and our wives *are* in	1323
	31:18	their wives, and their sons, and their **d**,	1323
Ezr	2:61	which took a wife of the **d** of Barzillai	1323
	9: 2	For they have taken of their **d** for	1323
	9:12	therefore give not your **d** unto their sons,	1323
	9:12	neither take their **d** unto your sons, nor seek	1323
Ne	3:12	of the half part of Jerusalem, he and his **d**.	1323
	4:14	your sons, and your **d**, your wives, and	1323
	5: 2	We, our sons, and our **d**, *are* many:	1323
	5: 5	bondage our sons and our **d** to be servants,	1323
	5: 5	*some* of our **d** are brought unto bondage	1323
	7:63	which took *one* of the **d** of Barzillai	1323
	10:28	their wives, their sons, and their **d**,	1323
	10:30	that we would not give our **d** unto	1323
	10:30	of the land, nor take their **d** for our sons:	1323
	13:25	*saying,* Ye shall not give your **d** unto their	1323
	13:25	nor take their **d** unto your sons, or	1323
Job	1: 2	were born unto him seven sons and three **d**.	1323
	1:13	when his sons and his **d** *were* eating and	1323
	1:18	Thy sons and thy **d** *were* eating and	1323
	42:13	He had also seven sons and three **d**.	1323
	42:15	no women found *so* fair as the **d** of Job:	1323
Ps	45: 9	Kings' **d** *were* among thy honourable	1323
	48:11	let the **d** of Judah be glad, because of thy	1323
	97: 8	the **d** of Judah rejoiced, because of thy	1323
	106:37	sacrificed their sons and their **d** unto devils,	1323
	106:38	*even* the blood of their sons and of their **d**,	1323
	144:12	*that* our **d** *may be* as corner stones,	1323
Pr	30:15	The horseleach hath two **d**, *crying,* Give,	1323
	31:29	Many **d** have done virtuously, but	1323
Ecc	12: 4	all the **d** of musick shall be brought low;	1323
SS	1: 5	*am* black, but comely, O ye **d** of Jerusalem,	1323
	2: 2	among thorns, so *is* my love among the **d**.	1323
	2: 7	O ye **d** of Jerusalem, by the roes, and	1323
	3: 5	O ye **d** of Jerusalem, by the roes, and	1323
	3:10	paved *with* love, for the **d** of Jerusalem.	1323
	3:11	O ye **d** of Zion, and behold king Solomon	1323
	5: 8	I charge you, O **d** of Jerusalem, if ye find	1323
	5:16	and this *is* my friend, O **d** of Jerusalem.	1323
	6: 9	The **d** saw her, and blessed her; *yea,*	1323
	8: 4	I charge you, O **d** of Jerusalem, that ye stir	1323
Isa	3:16	Because the **d** of Zion are haughty, and	1323
	3:17	scab the crown of the head of the **d** of Zion,	1323
	4: 4	washed away the filth of the **d** of Zion,	1323
	16: 2	the **d** of Moab shall be *at* the fords of	1323
	32: 9	ye careless **d**, give ear unto my speech.	1323
	43: 6	and my **d** from the ends of the earth;	1323
	49:22	thy **d** shall be carried upon *their* shoulders.	1323
	56: 5	and a name better than *of* sons and *of* **d**:	1323

Isa 60: 4 and thy **d** shall be nursed at *thy* side. 1323
Jer 3:24 and their herds, their sons and their **d**. 1323
5:17 *which* thy sons and thy **d** should eat: 1323
7:31 to burn their sons and their **d** in the fire; 1323
9:20 teach your **d** wailing, and every one her 1323
11:22 their sons and their **d** shall die by famine: 1323
14:16 their wives, nor their sons, nor their **d**: 1323
16: 2 neither shalt thou have sons nor **d** in this 1323
16: 3 concerning the **d** that are born in this place, 1323
19: 9 flesh of their sons and the flesh of their **d**, 1323
29: 6 Take ye wives, and beget sons and **d**; and 1323
29: 6 give your **d** to husbands, that they may bear 1323
29: 6 to husbands, that they may bear sons and **d**; 1323
32:35 their **d** to pass through *the fire* unto 1323
35: 8 we, our wives, our sons, nor our **d**; 1323
41:10 *even* the king's **d**, and all the people that 1323
43: 6 the king's **d**, and every person that 1323
48:46 sons are taken captives, and thy **d** captives. 1323
49: 2 and her **d** shall be burnt with fire: 1323
49: 3 cry, ye **d** of Rabbah, gird ye with sackcloth; 1323
La 3:51 mine heart because of all the **d** of my city. 1323
Eze 13:17 set thy face against the **d** of thy people, 1323
14:16 they shall deliver neither sons nor **d**; 1323
14:18 they shall deliver neither sons nor **d**, but 1323
14:22 that shall be brought forth, *both* sons and **d**: 1323
16:20 thou hast taken thy sons and thy **d**, 1323
16:27 the **d** of the Philistines, which are ashamed 1323
16:46 she and her **d** that dwell at thy left hand: 1323
16:46 at thy right hand, *is* Sodom and her **d**. 1323
16:48 she nor her **d**, as thou hast done, thou and 1323
16:48 as thou hast done, thou and thy **d**. 1323
16:49 of idleness was in her and in her **d**, 1323
16:53 the captivity of Sodom and her **d**, and 1323
16:53 and the captivity of Samaria and her **d**, then 1323
16:55 When thy sisters, Sodom and her **d**, 1323
16:55 and her **d** shall return to their former estate, 1323
16:55 and thy **d** shall return to your former estate. 1323
16:57 as *at* the time of *thy* reproach of the **d** of 1323
16:57 *are* round about her, the **d** of the Philistines, 1323
16:61 I will give them unto thee for **d**, but not by 1323
23: 2 were two women, the **d** of one mother: 1323
23: 4 they were mine, and they bare sons and **d**. 1323
23:10 they took her sons and her **d**, and slew her 1323
23:25 they shall take thy sons and thy **d**; and 1323
23:47 they shall slay their sons and their **d**, and 1323
24:21 your **d** whom ye have left shall fall by 1323
24:25 they set their minds, their sons and their **d**, 1323
26: 6 her **d** which *are* in the field shall be slain by 1323
26: 8 He shall slay with the sword thy **d** in 1323
30:18 cover her, and her **d** shall go into captivity. 1323
32:16 the **d** of the nations shall lament her: 1323
32:18 *even* her, and the **d** of the famous nations, 1323
Hos 4:13 therefore your **d** shall commit whoredom, 1323
4:14 I will not punish your **d** when they commit 1323
Joel 2:28 your sons and your **d** shall prophesy, 1323
3: 8 your **d** into the hand of the children of 1323
Am 7:17 thy sons and thy **d** shall fall by the sword, 1323
Lk 1: 5 and his wife *was* of the **d** of Aaron, and *2364*
23:28 said, **D** of Jerusalem, weep not for me, but *2364*
Ac 2:17 and your sons and your **d** shall prophesy, *2364*
21: 9 And the same *man* had four **d**, virgins, *2364*
2Co 6:18 and ye shall be my sons and **d**, saith *2364*
1Pe 3: 6 whose **d** ye are, as long as ye do well, and *5043*

DAVID (1085) [DAVID'S]

Ru 4:17 he *is* the father of Jesse, the father of **D**. 1732
4:22 And Obed begat Jesse, and Jesse begat **D**. 1732
1Sa 16:13 the spirit of the LORD came upon **D** from 1732
16:19 said, Send me **D** thy son, which *is* with 1732
16:20 and sent *them* by **D** his son unto Saul. 1732
16:21 **D** came to Saul, and stood before him: and 1732
16:22 Let **D**, I pray thee, stand before me; 1732
16:23 that **D** took a harp, and played with his 1732
17:12 Now **D** *was* the son of that Ephrathite of 1732
17:14 **D** *was* the youngest: and the three eldest 1732
17:15 **D** went and returned from Saul to feed his 1732
17:17 Jesse said unto **D** his son, Take now for thy 1732
17:20 **D** rose up early in the morning, and left 1732
17:22 **D** left his carriage in the hand of the keeper 1732
17:23 to the same words: and **D** heard *them*. 1732
17:26 **D** spake to the men that stood by him, 1732
17:28 Eliab's anger was kindled against **D**, and 1732
17:29 **D** said, What have I now done? *Is there* not 1732
17:31 when the words were heard which **D** spake, 1732
17:32 **D** said to Saul, Let no man's heart fail 1732
17:33 Saul said to **D**, Thou art not able to go 1732
17:34 **D** said unto Saul, Thy servant kept his 1732
17:37 **D** said moreover, The LORD that 1732
17:37 Saul said unto **D**, Go, and the LORD be 1732
17:38 Saul armed **D** with his armour, and he put a 1732
17:39 **D** girded his sword upon his armour, and 1732
17:39 for he had not proved *it*. And **D** said unto 1732
17:39 for I have not proved *them*. And **D** put 1732
17:41 Philistine came on and drew near unto **D**; 1732
17:42 looked about, and saw **D**, he disdained him: 1732
17:43 the Philistine said unto **D**, *Am* I a dog, 1732
17:43 And the Philistine cursed **D** by his gods. 1732
17:44 the Philistine said to **D**, Come to me, and 1732
17:45 said **D** to the Philistine, Thou comest to me 1732
17:48 came and drew nigh to meet **D**, that David 1732
17:48 that **D** hasted, and ran *toward* the army to 1732
17:49 **D** put his hand in *his* bag, and took thence a 1732
17:50 So **D** prevailed over the Philistine with a 1732
17:50 but *there was* no sword in the hand of **D**. 1732
17:51 Therefore **D** ran, and stood upon 1732
17:54 **D** took the head of the Philistine, and 1732
17:55 when Saul saw **D** go forth against 1732
17:57 as **D** returned from the slaughter of 1732
17:58 **D** answered, *I am* the son of thy servant 1732
18: 1 of Jonathan was knit with the soul of **D**, 1732
18: 3 Jonathan and **D** made a covenant, because 1732
18: 4 gave it to **D**, and his garments, even to his 1732
18: 5 **D** went out whithersoever Saul sent him, 1732
18: 6 when **D** was returned from the slaughter of 1732
18: 7 his thousands, and **D** his ten thousands. 1732
18: 8 They have ascribed unto **D** ten thousands, 1732
18: 9 Saul eyed **D** from that day and forward. 1732
18:10 **D** played with his hand, as at other times: 1732
18:11 I will smite **D** even to the wall *with it*. And 1732
18:11 And **D** avoided out of his presence twice. 1732
18:12 Saul was afraid of **D**, because the LORD 1732
18:14 **D** behaved himself wisely in all his ways; 1732
18:16 all Israel and Judah loved **D**, because 1732
18:17 Saul said to **D**, Behold my elder daughter 1732
18:18 **D** said unto Saul, Who *am* I? and what *is* 1732
18:19 daughter should have been given to **D**, 1732
18:20 Michal Saul's daughter loved **D**: and 1732
18:21 Wherefore Saul said to **D**, Thou shalt *this* 1732
18:22 *saying*, Commune with **D** secretly, and say, 1732
18:23 servants spake those words in the ears of **D**. 1732
18:23 **D** said, Seemeth it to you a light *thing* to be 1732
18:24 told him, saying, On this manner spake **D**. 1732
18:25 Saul said, Thus shall ye say to **D**, The king 1732
18:25 Saul thought to make **D** fall by the hand of 1732
18:26 when his servants told **D** these words, 1732
18:26 it pleased **D** well to be the king's son in 1732
18:27 Wherefore **D** arose and went, he and 1732
18:27 **D** brought their foreskins, and they gave 1732
18:28 and knew that the LORD *was* with **D**, 1732
18:29 Saul was yet the more afraid of **D**; and 1732
18:30 *that* **D** behaved himself more wisely than 1732
19: 1 to all his servants, that they should kill **D**. 1732
19: 2 Jonathan Saul's son delighted much in **D**: 1732
19: 2 Jonathan told **D**, saying, Saul my father 1732
19: 4 Jonathan spake good of **D** unto Saul his 1732
19: 4 the king sin against his servant, against **D**; 1732
19: 5 innocent blood, to slay **D** without a cause? 1732
19: 7 Jonathan called **D**, and Jonathan shewed 1732
19: 7 Jonathan brought **D** to Saul, and he was in 1732
19: 8 **D** went out, and fought with the Philistines, 1732
19: 9 in his hand: and **D** played with *his* hand. 1732
19:10 Saul sought to smite **D** even to the wall 1732
19:10 and **D** fled, and escaped that night. 1732
19:12 So Michal let **D** down through a window: 1732
19:14 when Saul sent messengers to take **D**, she 1732
19:15 Saul sent the messengers *again* to see **D**, 1732
19:18 So **D** fled, and escaped, and came to 1732
19:19 Behold, **D** *is* at Naioth in Ramah. 1732
19:20 Saul sent messengers to take **D**: and 1732
19:22 and said, Where *are* Samuel and **D**? 1732
20: 1 **D** fled from Naioth in Ramah, and came 1732
20: 3 **D** sware moreover, and said, Thy father 1732
20: 4 said Jonathan unto **D**, Whatsoever thy soul 1732
20: 5 **D** said unto Jonathan, Behold, to morrow *is* 1732
20: 6 **D** earnestly asked *leave* of me that *he* might 1732
20:10 said **D** to Jonathan, Who shall tell me? 1732
20:11 Jonathan said unto **D**, Come, and let us go 1732
20:12 Jonathan said unto **D**, O LORD God of 1732

D

1Sa 20:12 *if there be* good toward **D**, and I then 1732
20:15 of **D** every one from the face of the earth. 1732
20:16 made *a covenant* with the house of **D**, 1732
20:17 Jonathan caused **D** to swear again, because 1732
20:18 Jonathan said to *D*, To morrow *is* the new NIH
20:24 So **D** hid himself in the field: and when 1732
20:28 **D** earnestly asked *leave* of me *to go* to 1732
20:33 it was determined of his father to slay **D**. 1732
20:34 for he was grieved for **D**, because his father 1732
20:35 *into* the field at the time appointed with **D**, 1732
20:39 only Jonathan and **D** knew the matter. 1732
20:41 **D** arose out of *a place* toward the south, 1732
20:41 wept one with another, until **D** exceeded. 1732
20:42 Jonathan said to **D**, Go in peace, 1732
21: 1 came **D** to Nob to Ahimelech the priest: 1732
21: 1 Ahimelech was afraid at the meeting of **D**, 1732
21: 2 **D** said unto Ahimelech the priest, The king 1732
21: 4 the priest answered **D**, and said, *There is* no 1732
21: 5 **D** answered the priest, and said unto him, 1732
21: 8 **D** said unto Ahimelech, And is there not 1732
21: 9 **D** said, *There is* none like that; give it me. 1732
21:10 **D** arose, and fled that day for fear of Saul, 1732
21:11 unto him, *Is* not this **D** the king of the land? 1732
21:11 his thousands, and **D** his ten thousands? 1732
21:12 **D** laid up these words in his heart, and 1732
22: 1 **D** therefore departed thence, and escaped to 1732
22: 3 **D** went thence *to* Mizpeh of Moab: and 1732
22: 4 they dwelt with him all the while that **D** 1732
22: 5 the prophet Gad said unto **D**, Abide not in 1732
22: 5 **D** departed, and came *into* the forest of 1732
22: 6 When Saul heard that **D** was discovered, 1732
22:14 *so* faithful among all thy servants as **D**, 1732
22:17 because their hand also *is* with **D**, and 1732
22:20 named Abiathar, escaped, and fled after **D**. 1732
22:21 Abiathar shewed **D** that Saul had slain 1732
22:22 **D** said unto Abiathar, I knew *it* that day, 1732
23: 1 they told **D**, saying, Behold, the Philistines 1732
23: 2 Therefore **D** inquired of the LORD, 1732
23: 2 the LORD said unto **D**, Go, and smite 1732
23: 4 **D** inquired of the LORD yet again. 1732
23: 5 So **D** and his men went *to* Keilah, and 1732
23: 5 So **D** saved the inhabitants of Keilah. 1732
23: 6 the son of Ahimelech fled to **D** *to* Keilah, 1732
23: 7 it was told Saul that **D** was come *to* Keilah. 1732
23: 8 down *to* Keilah, to besiege **D** and his men. 1732
23: 9 **D** knew that Saul secretly practised 1732
23:10 said **D**, O LORD God of Israel, 1732
23:12 said **D**, Will the men of Keilah deliver me 1732
23:13 **D** and his men, *which were* about six 1732
23:13 it was told Saul that **D** was escaped from 1732
23:14 **D** abode in the wilderness in strong holds, 1732
23:15 **D** saw that Saul was come out to seek his 1732
23:15 **D** *was* in the wilderness of Ziph in a wood. 1732
23:16 went to **D** *into* the wood, and 1732
23:18 **D** abode in the wood, and Jonathan went to 1732
23:19 Doth not **D** hide himself with us in strong 1732
23:24 **D** and his men *were* in the wilderness of 1732
23:25 his men went to seek *him*. And they told **D**: 1732
23:25 when Saul heard *that*, he pursued after **D** *in* 1732
23:26 **D** and his men on that side of the mountain: 1732
23:26 **D** made haste to get away for fear of Saul; 1732
23:26 for Saul and his men compassed **D** and his 1732
23:28 Saul returned from pursuing after **D**, 1732
23:29 **D** went up from thence, and dwelt in strong 1732
24: 1 Behold, **D** *is* in the wilderness of En-gedi. 1732
24: 2 went to seek **D** and his men upon the rocks 1732
24: 3 **D** and his men remained in the sides of 1732
24: 4 the men of **D** said unto him, Behold the day 1732
24: 4 **D** arose, and cut off the skirt of Saul's robe 1732
24: 7 So **D** stayed his servants with *these* words, 1732
24: 8 **D** also rose afterward, and went out of 1732
24: 8 **D** stooped *with his* face to the earth, and 1732
24: 9 **D** said to Saul, Wherefore hearest thou 1732
24: 9 saying, Behold, **D** seeketh thy hurt? 1732
24:16 when **D** had made an end of speaking these 1732
24:16 that Saul said, *Is* this thy voice, my son **D**? 1732
24:17 he said to **D**, Thou *art* more righteous than 1732
24:22 **D** sware unto Saul. And Saul went home; 1732
24:22 **D** and his men gat them up unto the hold. 1732
25: 1 **D** arose, and went down to the wilderness 1732
25: 4 **D** heard in the wilderness that Nabal did 1732
25: 5 **D** sent out ten young men, and David said 1732
25: 5 **D** said unto the young men, Get you up to 1732
25: 8 hand unto thy servants, and to thy son **D**. 1732
25: 9 to all those words in the name of **D**, 1732
25:10 David's servants, and said, Who *is* **D**? 1732
25:13 **D** said unto his men, Gird you on every 1732
25:13 his sword; and **D** also girded on his sword: 1732
25:13 there went up after **D** about four hundred 1732
25:14 **D** sent messengers out of the wilderness to 1732
25:20 **D** and his men came down against her; 1732
25:21 Now **D** had said, Surely in vain have I kept 1732
25:22 more also do God unto the enemies of **D**, 1732
25:23 when Abigail saw **D**, she hasted, and 1732
25:23 fell before **D** on her face, and 1732
25:32 **D** said to Abigail, Blessed *be* the LORD 1732
25:35 So **D** received of her hand *that* which she 1732
25:39 when **D** heard that Nabal was dead, he said, 1732
25:39 **D** sent and communed with Abigail, to take 1732
25:40 when the servants of **D** were come to 1732
25:40 spake unto her, saying, **D** sent us unto thee, 1732
25:42 she went after the messengers of **D**, and 1732
25:43 **D** also took Ahinoam of Jezreel; and 1732
26: 1 Doth not **D** hide himself in the hill of 1732
26: 2 to seek **D** in the wilderness of Ziph. 1732
26: 3 **D** abode in the wilderness, and he saw that 1732
26: 4 **D** therefore sent out spies, and 1732
26: 5 **D** arose, and came to the place where Saul 1732
26: 5 **D** beheld the place where Saul lay, and 1732
26: 6 answered **D** and said to Ahimelech 1732
26: 7 So **D** and Abishai came to the people by 1732
26: 8 said Abishai to **D**, God hath delivered thine 1732
26: 9 **D** said to Abishai, Destroy him not: 1732
26:10 **D** said furthermore, *As* the LORD liveth, 1732
26:12 So **D** took the spear and the cruse of water 1732
26:13 **D** went over *to* the *other* side, and stood on 1732
26:14 **D** cried to the people, and to Abner the son 1732
26:15 **D** said to Abner, *Art* not thou a *valiant* 1732
26:17 and said, *Is* this thy voice, my son **D**? 1732
26:17 **D** said, *It is* my voice, my lord, O king. 1732
26:21 return, my son **D**: for I will no more do thee 1732
26:22 **D** answered and said, Behold, the king's 1732
26:25 Saul said to **D**, Blessed *be* thou, my son 1732
26:25 said to David, Blessed *be* thou, my son **D**: 1732
26:25 So **D** went on his way, and Saul returned to 1732
27: 1 **D** said in his heart, I shall now perish one 1732
27: 2 **D** arose, and he passed over with the six 1732
27: 3 **D** dwelt with Achish at Gath, he and 1732
27: 3 *even* **D** with his two wives, Ahinoam 1732
27: 4 it was told Saul that **D** was fled *to* Gath: 1732
27: 5 **D** said unto Achish, If I have now found 1732
27: 7 the time that **D** dwelt in the country of 1732
27: 8 **D** and his men went up, and invaded 1732
27: 9 **D** smote the land, and left neither man nor 1732
27:10 **D** said, Against the south of Judah, and 1732
27:11 **D** saved neither man nor woman alive, 1732
27:11 So did **D**, and so *will be* his manner all 1732
27:12 Achish believed **D**, saying, He hath made 1732
28: 1 Achish said unto **D**, Know thou assuredly, 1732
28: 2 **D** said to Achish, Surely thou shalt know 1732
28: 2 Achish said to **D**, Therefore will I make 1732
28:17 and given it to thy neighbour, *even* to **D**: 1732
29: 2 **D** and his men passed on in the rereward 1732
29: 3 *Is* not this **D**, the servant of Saul the king of 1732
29: 5 *Is* not this **D**, of whom they sang one to 1732
29: 5 his thousands, and **D** his ten thousands? 1732
29: 6 Achish called **D**, and said unto him, Surely, 1732
29: 8 **D** said unto Achish, But what have I done? 1732
29: 9 Achish answered and said to **D**, I know that 1732
29:11 So **D** and his men rose up early to depart in 1732
30: 1 when **D** and his men were come *to* Ziklag 1732
30: 3 So **D** and his men came to the city, and 1732
30: 4 **D** and the people that *were* with him lift up 1732
30: 6 **D** was greatly distressed; for the people 1732
30: 6 **D** encouraged himself in the LORD his 1732
30: 7 **D** said to Abiathar the priest, 1732
30: 7 Abiathar brought thither the ephod to **D**. 1732
30: 8 **D** inquired at the LORD, saying, Shall I 1732
30: 9 So **D** went, he and the six hundred men that 1732
30:10 **D** pursued, he and four hundred men: 1732
30:11 brought him to **D**, and gave him bread, and 1732
30:13 **D** said unto him, To whom *belongest* thou? 1732
30:15 **D** said to him, Canst thou bring me down to 1732
30:17 **D** smote them from the twilight even unto 1732
30:18 **D** recovered all that the Amalekites had 1732
30:18 carried away: and **D** rescued his two wives. 1732
30:19 they had taken to them: **D** recovered all. 1732
30:20 **D** took all the flocks and the herds, 1732

D

1Sa 30:21 **D** came to the two hundred men, 1732
30:21 so faint that they could not follow **D**, 1732
30:21 they went forth to meet **D**, and to meet 1732
30:21 when **D** came near to the people, he saluted 1732
30:22 of those that went with **D**, and said, 1732
30:23 said **D**, Ye shall not do so, my brethren, 1732
30:26 when **D** came to Ziklag, he sent of the spoil 1732
30:31 to all the places where **D** himself and 1732
2Sa 1: 1 when **D** was returned from the slaughter of 1732
1: 1 and **D** had abode two days in Ziklag; 1732
1: 2 *so* it was, when he came to **D**, that he fell to 1732
1: 3 **D** said unto him, From whence comest 1732
1: 4 **D** said unto him, How went the matter? 1732
1: 5 **D** said unto the young man that told him, 1732
1:11 **D** took hold on his clothes, and rent them; 1732
1:13 **D** said unto the young man that told him, 1732
1:14 **D** said unto him, How wast thou not afraid 1732
1:15 **D** called one of the young men, and said, 1732
1:16 **D** said unto him, Thy blood *be* upon thy 1732
1:17 **D** lamented with this lamentation over Saul 1732
2: 1 that **D** inquired of the LORD, saying, 1732
2: 1 **D** said, Whither shall I go up? And he said, 1732
2: 2 So **D** went up thither, and his two wives 1732
2: 3 his men that *were* with him did **D** bring up, 1732
2: 4 there they anointed **D** king over the house 1732
2: 4 they told **D**, saying, *That* the men of 1732
2: 5 **D** sent messengers unto the men of 1732
2:10 But the house of Judah followed **D**. 1732
2:11 the time that **D** was king in Hebron over 1732
2:13 the servants of **D**, went out, and 1732
2:15 of Saul, and twelve of the servants of **D**. 1732
2:17 the men of Israel, before the servants of **D**. 1732
2:31 the servants of **D** had smitten of Benjamin, 1732
3: 1 the house of Saul and the house of **D**: 1732
3: 1 **D** waxed stronger and stronger, and 1732
3: 2 unto **D** were sons born in Hebron: and 1732
3: 5 These were born to **D** in Hebron. 1732
3: 6 the house of Saul and the house of **D**, 1732
3: 8 have not delivered thee into the hand of **D**, 1732
3: 9 as the LORD hath sworn to **D**, even so 1732
3:10 to set up the throne of **D** over Israel and 1732
3:12 Abner sent messengers to **D** on his behalf, 1732
3:14 **D** sent messengers to Ish-bosheth Saul's 1732
3:17 Ye sought for **D** in times past to be king 1732
3:18 do *it:* for the LORD hath spoken of **D**, 1732
3:18 By the hand of my servant **D** I will save my 1732
3:19 Abner went also to speak in the ears of **D** in 1732
3:20 So Abner came to **D** *to* Hebron, and 1732
3:20 **D** made Abner and the men that *were* with 1732
3:21 Abner said unto **D**, I will arise and go, and 1732
3:21 **D** sent Abner away; and he went in peace. 1732
3:22 the servants of **D** and Joab came from 1732
3:22 Abner *was* not with **D** in Hebron; for he 1732
3:26 when Joab was come out from **D**, he sent 1732
3:26 from the well of Sirah: but **D** knew *it* not. 1732
3:28 afterward when **D** heard *it,* he said, I and 1732
3:31 **D** said to Joab, and to all the people that 1732
3:31 And king **D** *himself* followed the bier. 1732
3:35 when all the people came to cause **D** to eat 1732
3:35 **D** sware, saying, So do God to me, and 1732
4: 8 the head of Ish-bosheth unto **D** *to* Hebron, 1732
4: 9 **D** answered Rechab and Baanah his 1732
4:12 **D** commanded *his* young men, and 1732
5: 1 came all the tribes of Israel to **D** unto 1732
5: 3 king **D** made a league with them in Hebron 1732
5: 3 and they anointed **D** king over Israel. 1732
5: 4 **D** *was* thirty years old when he *began* to 1732
5: 6 which spake unto **D**, saying, Except thou 1732
5: 6 thinking, **D** cannot come in hither. 1732
5: 7 Nevertheless **D** took the strong hold of 1732
5: 7 hold of Zion: the same *is* the city of **D**. 1732
5: 8 **D** said on that day, Whosoever getteth up to 1732
5: 9 So **D** dwelt in the fort, and called it the city 1732
5: 9 dwelt in the fort, and called it the city of **D**. 1732
5: 9 **D** built round about from Millo and inward. 1732
5:10 **D** went on, and grew great, and the LORD 1732
5:11 Hiram king of Tyre sent messengers to **D**, 1732
5:11 masons: and they built **D** a house. 1732
5:12 **D** perceived that the LORD had 1732
5:13 **D** took *him* mo concubines and wives out 1732
5:13 were yet sons and daughters born to **D**. 1732
5:17 that they had anointed **D** king over Israel, 1732
5:17 all the Philistines came up to seek **D**; 1732
5:17 **D** heard *of it,* and went down to the hold. 1732
5:19 **D** inquired of the LORD, saying, Shall I 1732
5:19 the LORD said unto **D**, Go up: for I will 1732
5:20 **D** came to Baal-perazim, and David smote 1732
5:20 and **D** smote them there, and said, 1732
5:21 and **D** and his men burnt them. 1732
5:23 when **D** inquired of the LORD, he said, 1732
5:25 **D** did so, as the LORD had commanded 1732
6: 1 **D** gathered together all the chosen *men* of 1732
6: 2 **D** arose, and went with all the people that 1732
6: 5 **D** and all the house of Israel played before 1732
6: 8 **D** was displeased, because the LORD had 1732
6: 9 **D** was afraid of the LORD that day, 1732
6:10 So **D** would not remove the ark of 1732
6:10 of the LORD unto him into the city of **D**: 1732
6:10 **D** carried it aside *into* the house of 1732
6:12 it was told king **D**, saying, The LORD 1732
6:12 So **D** went and brought up the ark of God 1732
6:12 *into* the city of **D** with gladness. 1732
6:14 **D** danced before the LORD with all *his* 1732
6:14 and **D** *was* girded *with* a linen ephod. 1732
6:15 So **D** and all the house of Israel brought up 1732
6:16 ark of the LORD came *into* the city of **D**, 1732
6:16 saw king **D** leaping and dancing before 1732
6:17 in the midst of the tabernacle that **D** had 1732
6:17 **D** offered burnt offerings and 1732
6:18 as soon as **D** had made an end of offering 1732
6:20 **D** returned to bless his household. 1732
6:20 the daughter of Saul came out to meet **D**, 1732
6:21 **D** said unto Michal, *It was* before 1732
7: 5 Go and tell my servant **D**, Thus saith 1732
7: 8 so shalt thou say unto my servant **D**, 1732
7:17 all this vision, so did Nathan speak unto **D**. 1732
7:18 went king **D** in, and sat before the LORD, 1732
7:20 what can **D** say more unto thee? for thou, 1732
7:26 let the house of thy servant **D** be 1732
8: 1 that **D** smote the Philistines, and 1732
8: 1 **D** took Metheg-ammah out of the hand of 1732
8: 3 **D** smote also Hadadezer, the son of Rehob, 1732
8: 4 **D** took from him a thousand *chariots,* and 1732
8: 4 **D** houghed all the chariot *horses,* but 1732
8: 5 **D** slew of the Syrians two and 1732
8: 6 Then **D** put garrisons in Syria of Damascus: 1732
8: 6 the Syrians became servants to **D**, 1732
8: 6 the LORD preserved **D** whithersoever he 1732
8: 7 **D** took the shields of gold that were on 1732
8: 8 king **D** took exceeding much brass. 1732
8: 9 When Toi king of Hamath heard that **D** had 1732
8:10 Toi sent Joram his son unto king **D**, 1732
8:11 Which also king **D** did dedicate unto 1732
8:13 **D** gat *him* a name when he returned from 1732
8:14 the LORD preserved **D** whithersoever he 1732
8:15 **D** reigned over all Israel; and David 1732
8:15 **D** executed judgment and justice unto all 1732
9: 1 **D** said, Is there yet *any* that is left of 1732
9: 2 when they had called him unto **D**, the king 1732
9: 5 king **D** sent, and fet him out of the house of 1732
9: 6 the son of Saul, was come unto **D**, he fell 1732
9: 6 **D** said, Mephibosheth. And he answered, 1732
9: 7 **D** said unto him, Fear not: for I will surely 1732
10: 2 said **D**, I will shew kindness unto Hanun 1732
10: 2 **D** sent to comfort him by the hand of his 1732
10: 3 Thinkest thou that **D** doth honour thy 1732
10: 3 hath not **D** *rather* sent his servants unto 1732
10: 5 When they told *it* unto **D**, he sent to meet 1732
10: 6 of Ammon saw that they stank before **D**, 1732
10: 7 when **D** heard *of it,* he sent Joab, and all 1732
10:17 when it was told **D**, he gathered all Israel 1732
10:17 Syrians set *themselves* in array against **D**, 1732
10:18 **D** slew *the men of* seven hundred chariots 1732
11: 1 kings go forth *to battle,* that **D** sent Joab, 1732
11: 1 But **D** tarried *still* at Jerusalem. 1732
11: 2 that **D** arose from off his bed, and 1732
11: 3 **D** sent and inquired after the woman. 1732
11: 4 **D** sent messengers, and took her; and 1732
11: 5 sent and told **D**, and said, I *am* with child. 1732
11: 6 **D** sent to Joab, *saying,* Send me Uriah 1732
11: 6 Uriah the Hittite. And Joab sent Uriah to **D**. 1732
11: 7 **D** demanded *of him* how Joab did, and how 1732
11: 8 **D** said to Uriah, Go down to thy house, 1732
11:10 when they had told **D**, saying, Uriah went 1732
11:10 **D** said unto Uriah, Camest thou not from 1732
11:11 Uriah said unto **D**, The ark, and Israel, and 1732
11:12 **D** said to Uriah, Tarry here to day also, 1732
11:13 when **D** had called him, he did eat and 1732

2Sa 11:14 that **D** wrote a letter to Joab, and sent *it* by 1732
11:17 fell *some* of the people of the servants of **D**; 1732
11:18 told **D** all the things concerning the war; 1732
11:22 shewed **D** all that Joab had sent him for. 1732
11:23 the messenger said unto **D**, Surely the men 1732
11:25 **D** said unto the messenger, Thus shalt thou 1732
11:27 **D** sent and fet her to his house, and 1732
11:27 the thing that **D** had done displeased 1732
12: 1 the LORD sent Nathan unto **D**. And he 1732
12: 7 Nathan said to **D**, Thou *art* the man. 1732
12:13 **D** said unto Nathan, I have sinned against 1732
12:13 Nathan said unto **D**, The LORD also hath 1732
12:15 the child that Uriah's wife bare unto **D**, 1732
12:16 **D** therefore besought God for the child; and 1732
12:16 **D** fasted, and went in, and lay all night 1732
12:18 the servants of **D** feared to tell him that 1732
12:19 when **D** saw that his servants whispered, 1732
12:19 **D** perceived that the child was dead: 1732
12:19 therefore **D** said unto his servants, Is 1732
12:20 **D** arose from the earth, and washed, and 1732
12:24 **D** comforted Bath-sheba his wife, and 1732
12:27 Joab sent messengers to **D**, and said, I have 1732
12:29 And **D** gathered all the people together, and 1732
12:31 So **D** and all the people returned *unto* 1732
13: 1 that Absalom the son of **D** had a fair sister, 1732
13: 1 and Amnon the son of **D** loved her. 1732
13: 7 **D** sent home to Tamar, saying, Go now *to* 1732
13:21 when king **D** heard of all these things, he 1732
13:30 in the way, that tidings came to **D**, saying, 1732
13:37 And *D* mourned for his son every day. NIH
13:39 *the soul of* king **D** longed to go forth unto 1732
15:13 there came a messenger to **D**, saying, 1732
15:14 **D** said unto all his servants that *were* with 1732
15:22 **D** said to Ittai, Go and pass over. And Ittai 1732
15:30 **D** went up by the ascent of *mount* Olivet, 1732
15:31 *one* told **D**, saying, Ahithophel *is* among 1732
15:31 **D** said, O LORD, I pray thee, turn 1732
15:32 that *when* **D** was come to the top *of* 1732
15:33 Unto whom **D** said, If thou passest on with 1732
16: 1 when **D** was a little past the top *of the hill*, 1732
16: 5 when king **D** came to Bahurim, behold, 1732
16: 6 he cast stones at **D**, and at all the servants 1732
16: 6 at David, and at all the servants of king **D**: 1732
16:10 the LORD hath said unto him, Curse **D**. 1732
16:11 **D** said to Abishai, and to all his servants, 1732
16:13 as **D** and his men went by the way, Shimei 1732
16:23 all the counsel of Ahithophel both with **D** 1732
17: 1 I will arise and pursue after **D** *this* night: 1732
17:16 therefore send quickly, and tell **D**, saying, 1732
17:17 told them; and they went and told king **D**. 1732
17:21 went and told king **D**, and said unto David, 1732
17:21 said unto **D**, Arise, and pass quickly over 1732
17:22 **D** arose, and all the people that *were* with 1732
17:24 **D** came to Mahanaim. And Absalom 1732
17:27 to pass, when **D** was come to Mahanaim, 1732
17:29 for **D**, and for the people that *were* with 1732
18: 1 **D** numbered the people that *were* with him, 1732
18: 2 **D** sent forth a third part of the people under 1732
18: 7 Israel were slain before the servants of **D**, 1732
18: 9 Absalom met the servants of **D**. 1732
18:24 **D** sat between the two gates: and 1732
19:11 king **D** sent to Zadok and to Abiathar 1732
19:16 with the men of Judah to meet king **D**. 1732
19:22 **D** said, What have I to do with you, ye sons 1732
19:43 and we have also more *right* in **D** than ye: 1732
20: 1 a trumpet, and said, We have no part in **D**, 1732
20: 2 every man of Israel went up from after **D**, 1732
20: 3 **D** came to his house *at* Jerusalem; and 1732
20: 6 **D** said to Abishai, Now shall Sheba the son 1732
20:11 and he that *is* for **D**, *let him go* after Joab. 1732
20:21 his hand against the king, *even* against **D**: 1732
20:26 also the Jairite was a chief ruler about **D**. 1732
21: 1 there was a famine in the days of **D** three 1732
21: 1 after year; and **D** inquired of the LORD. 1732
21: 3 Wherefore **D** said unto the Gibeonites, 1732
21: 7 between **D** and Jonathan the son of Saul. 1732
21:11 it was told **D** what Rizpah the daughter of 1732
21:12 **D** went and took the bones of Saul and 1732
21:15 **D** went down, and his servants with him, 1732
21:15 against the Philistines: and **D** waxed faint. 1732
21:16 *with* a new *sword*, thought to have slain **D**. 1732
21:17 the men of **D** sware unto him, saying, 1732
21:21 the son of Shimea the brother of **D** 1732
21:22 fell by the hand of **D**, and by the hand of 1732
22: 1 **D** spake unto the LORD the words of this 1732
22:51 unto **D**, and to his seed for evermore. 1732
23: 1 Now these *be* the last words of **D**. 1732
23: 1 **D** the son of Jesse said, and the man *who* 1732
23: 8 the names of the mighty *men* whom **D** had: 1732
23: 9 *one* of the three mighty *men* with **D**, 1732
23:13 came to **D** in the harvest time unto the cave 1732
23:14 **D** *was* then in a hold, and the garrison of 1732
23:15 **D** longed, and said, Oh that one would give 1732
23:16 by the gate, and took *it*, and brought *it* to **D**: 1732
23:23 *first* three. And **D** set him over his guard. 1732
24: 1 he moved **D** against them to say, Go, 1732
24:10 **D** said unto the LORD, I have sinned 1732
24:11 For when **D** was up in the morning, 1732
24:12 Go and say unto **D**, Thus saith the LORD, 1732
24:13 So Gad came to **D**, and told him, and 1732
24:14 **D** said unto Gad, I am in a great strait: 1732
24:17 **D** spake unto the LORD when he saw 1732
24:18 Gad came that day to **D**, and said unto him, 1732
24:19 **D**, according to the saying of Gad, went up 1732
24:21 **D** said, To buy the threshingfloor of thee, 1732
24:22 Araunah said unto **D**, Let my lord the king 1732
24:24 So **D** bought the threshingfloor and 1732
24:25 **D** built there an altar unto the LORD, and 1732
1Ki 1: 1 Now king **D** was old *and* stricken in years; 1732
1: 8 and the mighty *men* which *belonged* to **D**, 1732
1:11 doth reign, and **D** our lord knoweth *it* not? 1732
1:13 Go and get thee in unto king **D**, and 1732
1:28 king **D** answered and said, Call me 1732
1:31 and said, Let my lord king **D** live for ever. 1732
1:32 king **D** said, Call me Zadok the priest, and 1732
1:37 greater than the throne of my lord king **D**. 1732
1:43 Verily our lord king **D** hath made Solomon 1732
1:47 servants came to bless our lord king **D**, 1732
2: 1 Now the days of **D** drew nigh that *he* 1732
2:10 So **D** slept with his fathers, and was buried 1732
2:10 his fathers, and was buried in the city of **D**. 1732
2:11 the days that **D** reigned over Israel *were* 1732
2:12 sat Solomon upon the throne of **D** his 1732
2:24 set me on the throne of **D** my father, and 1732
2:26 ark of the Lord GOD before **D** my father, 1732
2:32 my father **D** not knowing *thereof, to wit,* 1732
2:33 upon **D**, and upon his seed, and upon his 1732
2:44 is privy to, that thou didst to **D** my father: 1732
2:45 the throne of **D** shall be established before 1732
3: 1 and brought her into the city of **D**, 1732
3: 3 walking in the statutes of **D** his father: 1732
3: 6 Thou hast shewed unto thy servant **D** my 1732
3: 7 thy servant king instead of **D** my father: 1732
3:14 as thy father **D** did walk, then I will 1732
5: 1 his father: for Hiram was ever a lover of **D**. 1732
5: 3 Thou knowest how that **D** my father could 1732
5: 5 as the LORD spake unto **D** my father, 1732
5: 7 which hath given unto **D** a wise son over 1732
6:12 with thee, which I spake unto **D** thy father: 1732
7:51 Solomon brought in the *things* which **D** his 1732
8: 1 of the LORD out of the city of **D**, 1732
8:15 which spake with his mouth unto **D** my 1732
8:16 but I chose **D** to be over my people Israel. 1732
8:17 it was in the heart of **D** my father to build a 1732
8:18 the LORD said unto **D** my father, 1732
8:20 I am risen up in the room of **D** my father, 1732
8:24 Who hast kept with thy servant **D** my father 1732
8:25 keep with thy servant **D** my father that thou 1732
8:26 which thou spakest unto thy servant **D** my 1732
8:66 that the LORD had done for **D** his servant, 1732
9: 4 as **D** thy father walked, in integrity of heart, 1732
9: 5 as I promised to **D** thy father, saying, 1732
9:24 **D** unto her house which *Solomon* had built 1732
11: 4 his God, as *was* the heart of **D** his father. 1732
11: 6 fully after the LORD, as *did* **D** his father. 1732
11:12 days I will not do it for **D** thy father's sake: 1732
11:13 will give one tribe to thy son for **D** my 1732
11:15 when **D** was in Edom, and Joab the captain 1732
11:21 when Hadad heard in Egypt that **D** slept 1732
11:24 when **D** slew them *of Zobah:* and they went 1732
11:27 repaired the breaches of the city of **D** his 1732
11:33 and my judgments, as *did* **D** his father. 1732
11:34 the days of his life for **D** my servant's sake, 1732
11:36 that **D** my servant may have a light alway 1732
11:38 my commandments, as **D** my servant did; 1732
11:38 as I built for **D**, and will give Israel unto 1732
11:39 I will for this afflict the seed of **D**, but 1732
11:43 and was buried in the city of **D** his father: 1732

D

1Ki 12:16 saying, What portion have we in **D**? 1732
12:16 now see to thine own house, **D**. So Israel 1732
12:19 So Israel rebelled against the house of **D** 1732
12:20 was none that followed the house of **D**, 1732
12:26 shall the kingdom return to the house of **D**: 1732
13: 2 a child *shall be* born unto the house of **D**, 1732
14: 8 the kingdom away from the house of **D**, 1732
14: 8 *yet* thou hast not been as my servant **D**, 1732
14:31 was buried with his fathers in the city of **D**. 1732
15: 3 his God, as the heart of **D** his father. 1732
15: 5 Because **D** did *that* which *was* right in 1732
15: 8 and they buried him in the city of **D**: 1732
15:11 the eyes of the LORD, as *did* **D** his father. 1732
15:24 was buried with his fathers in the city of **D** 1732
22:50 was buried with his fathers in the city of **D** 1732
2Ki 8:19 not destroy Judah for **D** his servant's sake, 1732
8:24 was buried with his fathers in the city of **D**: 1732
9:28 sepulchre with his fathers in the city of **D**. 1732
12:21 buried him with his fathers in the city of **D**: 1732
14: 3 of the LORD, yet not like **D** his father: 1732
14:20 Jerusalem with his fathers in the city of **D**. 1732
15: 7 buried him with his fathers in the city of **D**: 1732
15:38 was buried with his fathers in the city of **D** 1732
16: 2 of the LORD his God, like **D** his father. 1732
16:20 was buried with his fathers in the city of **D**: 1732
17:21 For he rent Israel from the house of **D**; and 1732
18: 3 according to all that **D** his father did. 1732
20: 5 saith the LORD, the God of **D** thy father, 1732
21: 7 of which the LORD said to **D**, and 1732
22: 2 walked in all the way of **D** his father, and 1732
1Ch 2:15 Ozem the sixth, **D** the seventh: 1732
3: 1 Now these were the sons of **D**, which were 1732
3: 9 *These were* all the sons of **D**, beside 1732
4:31 These *were* their cities unto the reign of **D**. 1732
6:31 these *are they* whom **D** set over the service 1732
7: 2 whose number *was* in the days of **D** two 1732
9:22 whom **D** and Samuel the seer did ordain in 1732
10:14 turned the kingdom unto **D** the son of Jesse. 1732
11: 1 all Israel gathered themselves to **D** unto 1732
11: 3 **D** made a covenant with them in Hebron 1732
11: 3 they anointed **D** king over Israel, 1732
11: 4 **D** and all Israel went *to* Jerusalem, which *is* 1732
11: 5 the inhabitants of Jebus said to **D**, 1732
11: 5 Nevertheless **D** took the castle of Zion, 1732
11: 5 the castle of Zion, which *is* the city of **D**. 1732
11: 6 **D** said, Whosoever smiteth the Jebusites 1732
11: 7 **D** dwelt in the castle; therefore they called 1732
11: 7 therefore they called it the city of **D**. 1732
11: 9 So **D** waxed greater and greater: for 1732
11:10 the chief of the mighty *men* whom **D** had, 1732
11:11 number of the mighty *men* whom **D** had; 1732
11:13 He was with **D** at Pas-dammim, and 1732
11:15 thirty captains went down to the rock to **D**, 1732
11:16 **D** *was* then in the hold, and the Philistines' 1732
11:17 **D** longed, and said, Oh that one would give 1732
11:18 by the gate, and took *it*, and brought *it* to **D**: 1732
11:18 **D** would not drink *of* it, but poured it out to 1732
11:25 *first* three: and **D** set him over his guard. 1732
12: 1 Now these *are* they that came to **D** to 1732
12: 8 **D** into the hold to the wilderness men of 1732
12:16 of Benjamin and Judah to the hold unto **D**. 1732
12:17 **D** went out to meet them, and answered 1732
12:18 *and he said,* Thine *are we*, **D**, and on thy 1732
12:18 **D** received them, and made them captains 1732
12:19 there fell *some* of Manasseh to **D**, when he 1732
12:21 they helped **D** against the band *of* 1732
12:22 For at *that* time day by day there came to **D** 1732
12:23 *and* came to **D** to Hebron, to turn 1732
12:31 by name, to come and make **D** king. 1732
12:38 to Hebron, to make **D** king over all Israel: 1732
12:38 of Israel *were of* one heart to make **D** king. 1732
12:39 there they were with **D** three days, eating 1732
13: 1 **D** consulted with the captains of thousands 1732
13: 2 **D** said unto all the congregation of Israel, 1732
13: 5 So **D** gathered all Israel together, 1732
13: 6 **D** went up, and all Israel, to Baalah, *that is,* 1732
13: 8 **D** and all Israel played before God with all 1732
13:11 **D** was displeased, because the LORD had 1732
13:12 **D** was afraid of God that day, saying, 1732
13:13 So **D** brought not the ark *home* to himself 1732
13:13 not the ark *home* to himself to the city of **D**, 1732
14: 1 Hiram king of Tyre sent messengers to **D**, 1732
14: 2 **D** perceived that the LORD had 1732
14: 3 **D** took moe wives at Jerusalem: and 1732
14: 3 and **D** begat moe sons and daughters. 1732
14: 8 when the Philistines heard that **D** was 1732
14: 8 all the Philistines went up to seek **D**. 1732
14: 8 **D** heard *of it,* and went out against them. 1732
14:10 **D** inquired of God, saying, Shall I go up 1732
14:11 to Baal-perazim; and **D** smote them there. 1732
14:11 **D** said, God hath broken in upon mine 1732
14:12 **D** gave a commandment, and they were 1732
14:14 Therefore **D** inquired again of God; and 1732
14:16 **D** therefore did as God commanded him: 1732
14:17 the fame of **D** went out into all lands; and 1732
15: 1 *D* made him houses in the city of David, NIH
15: 1 *David* made him houses in the city of **D**, 1732
15: 2 **D** said, None ought to carry the ark of God 1732
15: 3 **D** gathered all Israel together to Jerusalem, 1732
15: 4 **D** assembled the children of Aaron, and 1732
15:11 **D** called for Zadok and Abiathar 1732
15:16 **D** spake to the chief of the Levites to 1732
15:25 So **D**, and the elders of Israel, and 1732
15:27 **D** *was* clothed with a robe of fine linen, 1732
15:27 **D** also *had* upon him an ephod of linen. 1732
15:29 of the LORD came to the city of **D**, 1732
15:29 out at a window saw king **D** dancing 1732
16: 1 set it in the midst of the tent that **D** had 1732
16: 2 when **D** had made an end of offering 1732
16: 7 on that day **D** delivered first *this psalm* to 1732
16:43 and **D** returned to bless his house. 1732
17: 1 Now it came to pass, as **D** sat in his house, 1732
17: 1 that **D** said to Nathan the prophet, Lo, 1732
17: 2 Nathan said unto **D**, Do all that *is* in thine 1732
17: 4 Go and tell **D** my servant, Thus saith 1732
17: 7 thus shalt thou say unto my servant **D**, 1732
17:15 all this vision, so did Nathan speak unto **D**. 1732
17:16 **D** the king came and sat before 1732
17:18 What can **D** *speak* more to thee for 1732
17:24 *let* the house of **D** thy servant *be* 1732
18: 1 that **D** smote the Philistines, and 1732
18: 3 **D** smote Hadarezer king of Zobah unto 1732
18: 4 **D** took from him a thousand chariots, and 1732
18: 4 **D** also houghed all the chariot *horses,* but 1732
18: 5 **D** slew of the Syrians two and 1732
18: 6 **D** put *garrisons* in Syria-damascus; 1732
18: 6 Thus the LORD preserved **D** 1732
18: 7 **D** took the shields of gold that were on 1732
18: 8 of Hadarezer, brought **D** very much brass, 1732
18: 9 **D** had smitten all the host of Hadarezer 1732
18:10 He sent Hadoram his son to king **D**, 1732
18:11 Them also king **D** dedicated unto 1732
18:13 Thus the LORD preserved **D** 1732
18:14 So **D** reigned over all Israel, and executed 1732
18:17 the sons of **D** *were* chief about the king. 1732
19: 2 **D** said, I will shew kindness unto Hanun 1732
19: 2 **D** sent messengers to comfort him 1732
19: 2 So the servants of **D** came into the land of 1732
19: 3 Thinkest thou that **D** doth honour thy 1732
19: 5 and told **D** how the men were served. 1732
19: 6 that they had made themselves odious to **D**, 1732
19: 8 when **D** heard *of it,* he sent Joab, and all 1732
19:17 it was told **D**; and he gathered all Israel, 1732
19:17 So when **D** had put the battle in array 1732
19:18 **D** slew of the Syrians seven thousand *men* 1732
19:19 they made peace with **D**, and became his 1732
20: 1 **D** tarried at Jerusalem. And Joab smote 1732
20: 2 **D** took the crown of their king from off his 1732
20: 3 dealt **D** with all the cities of the children of 1732
20: 3 **D** and all the people returned *to* Jerusalem. 1732
20: 8 they fell by the hand of **D**, and by the hand 1732
21: 1 and provoked **D** to number Israel. 1732
21: 2 **D** said to Joab and to the rulers of 1732
21: 5 sum of the number of the people unto **D**. 1732
21: 8 **D** said unto God, I have sinned greatly, 1732
21:10 Go and tell **D**, saying, Thus saith 1732
21:11 So Gad came to **D**, and said unto him, 1732
21:13 **D** said unto Gad, I am in a great strait: 1732
21:16 **D** lift up his eyes, and saw the angel of 1732
21:16 **D** and the elders *of Israel, who were* 1732
21:17 **D** said unto God, *Is it* not I *that* 1732
21:18 the LORD commanded Gad to say to **D**, 1732
21:18 that **D** should go up, and set up an altar 1732
21:19 **D** went up at the saying of Gad, which he 1732
21:21 And as **D** came to Ornan, Ornan looked and 1732
21:21 Ornan looked and saw **D**, and went out of 1732
21:21 bowed himself to **D** *with his* face to 1732
21:22 **D** said to Ornan, Grant me the place of *this* 1732

1Ch 21:23 And Ornan said unto **D**, Take *it* to thee, and 1732
21:24 king **D** said to Ornan, Nay; but I will verily 1732
21:25 So **D** gave to Ornan for the place six 1732
21:26 **D** built there an altar unto the LORD, and 1732
21:28 At that time when **D** saw that the LORD 1732
21:30 **D** could not go before it to inquire of God: 1732
22: 1 **D** said, This *is* the house of the LORD 1732
22: 2 **D** commanded to gather together 1732
22: 3 **D** prepared iron in abundance for the nails 1732
22: 4 of Tyre brought much cedar wood to **D**. 1732
22: 5 **D** said, Solomon my son *is* young and 1732
22: 5 So **D** prepared abundantly before his death. 1732
22: 7 **D** said to Solomon, My son, *as for* me, 1732
22:17 **D** also commanded all the princes of Israel 1732
23: 1 So when **D** was old and full *of* days, 1732
23: 5 which I made, *said* **D**, to praise *therewith*. NIH
23: 6 **D** divided them *into* courses among 1732
23:25 For **D** said, The LORD God of Israel hath 1732
23:27 For by the last words of **D**, the Levites 1732
24: 3 **D** distributed them, both Zadok of the sons 1732
24:31 of Aaron in the presence of **D** the king, 1732
25: 1 Moreover **D** and the captains of the host 1732
26:26 of the dedicate *things*, which **D** the king, 1732
26:31 In the fortieth year of the reign of **D** they 1732
26:32 whom king **D** made rulers over 1732
27:18 Of Judah, Elihu, *one* of the brethren of **D**: 1732
27:23 **D** took not the number of them from twenty 1732
27:24 in the account of the chronicles of king **D**. 1732
28: 1 **D** assembled all the princes of Israel, 1732
28: 2 Then **D** the king stood up upon his feet, and 1732
28:11 **D** gave to Solomon his son the pattern of 1732
28:19 All *this, said* **D**, the LORD made me NIH
28:20 **D** said to Solomon his son, Be strong and 1732
29: 1 Furthermore **D** the king said unto all 1732
29: 9 and **D** the king also rejoiced *with* great joy. 1732
29:10 Wherefore **D** blessed the LORD before all 1732
29:10 **D** said, Blessed *be* thou, LORD God of 1732
29:20 **D** said to all the congregation, Now bless 1732
29:22 they made Solomon the son of **D** king 1732
29:23 the LORD as king instead of **D** his father, 1732
29:24 and all the sons likewise of king **D**, 1732
29:26 Thus **D** the son of Jesse reigned over all 1732
29:29 Now the acts of **D** the king, first and last, 1732
2Ch 1: 1 Solomon the son of **D** was strengthened in 1732
1: 4 the ark of God had **D** brought up from 1732
1: 4 to *the place which* **D** had prepared for it: 1732
1: 8 Thou hast shewed great mercy unto **D** my 1732
1: 9 let thy promise unto **D** my father be 1732
2: 3 As thou didst deal with **D** my father, and 1732
2: 7 whom **D** my father did provide. 1732
2:12 who hath given to **D** the king a wise son, 1732
2:14 with the cunning *men* of my lord **D** thy 1732
2:17 after the numbering where*with* **D** his father 1732
3: 1 where *the LORD* appeared unto **D** his 1732
3: 1 in the place that **D** had prepared in 1732
5: 1 Solomon brought in *all the things* that **D** his 1732
5: 2 of the LORD out of the city of **D**, 1732
6: 4 he spake with his mouth to my father **D**, 1732
6: 6 have chosen **D** to be over my people Israel. 1732
6: 7 Now it was in the heart of **D** my father to 1732
6: 8 the LORD said to **D** my father, 1732
6:10 for I am risen up in the room of **D** my 1732
6:15 Thou which hast kept with thy servant **D** 1732
6:16 keep with thy servant **D** my father *that* 1732
6:17 which thou hast spoken unto thy servant **D**. 1732
6:42 remember the mercies of **D** thy servant. 1732
7: 6 which **D** the king had made to praise 1732
7: 6 for ever, when **D** praised by their ministry; 1732
7:10 that the LORD had shewed unto **D**, 1732
7:17 as **D** thy father walked, and do according to 1732
7:18 according as I have covenanted with **D** thy 1732
8:11 **D** unto the house that he had built for her: 1732
8:11 My wife shall not dwell in the house of **D** 1732
8:14 according to the order of **D** his father, 1732
8:14 so had **D** the man of God commanded. 1732
9:31 he was buried in the city of **D** his father: 1732
10:16 saying, What portion have we in **D**? 1732
10:16 *and* now, **D**, see to thine own house. So all 1732
10:19 Israel rebelled against the house of **D** unto 1732
11:17 for three years they walked in the way of **D** 1732
11:18 daughter of Jerimoth the son of **D** *to* wife, 1732
12:16 his fathers, and was buried in the city of **D**: 1732
13: 5 gave the kingdom over Israel to **D** for ever, 1732
13: 6 the servant of Solomon the son of **D**, 1732
13: 8 of the LORD in the hand of the sons of **D**; 1732
14: 1 and they buried him in the city of **D**: 1732
16:14 he had made for himself in the city of **D**, 1732
17: 3 he walked in the first ways of his father **D**, 1732
21: 1 was buried with his fathers in the city of **D**. 1732
21: 7 LORD would not destroy the house of **D**, 1732
21: 7 of the covenant that he had made with **D**, 1732
21:12 Thus saith the LORD God of **D** thy father, 1732
21:20 Howbeit they buried him in the city of **D**, 1732
23: 3 as the LORD hath said of the sons of **D**. 1732
23:18 whom **D** had distributed in the house of 1732
23:18 and with singing, as it was ordained by **D**. 1732
24:16 they buried him in the city of **D** among 1732
24:25 they buried him in the city of **D**, but 1732
27: 9 and they buried him in the city of **D**: 1732
28: 1 the sight of the LORD, like **D** his father: 1732
29: 2 according to all that **D** his father had done. 1732
29:25 according to the commandment of **D**, and 1732
29:26 the Levites stood with the instruments of **D**, 1732
29:27 with the instruments ordained by **D** king of 1732
29:30 unto the LORD with the words of **D**, 1732
30:26 for since the time of Solomon the son of **D** 1732
32: 5 repaired Millo *in* the city of **D**, and 1732
32:30 down to the west *side* of the city of **D**. 1732
32:33 chiefest of the sepulchres of the sons of **D**: 1732
33: 7 of which God had said to **D** and 1732
33:14 this he built a wall without the city of **D**, 1732
34: 2 walked in the ways of **D** his father, and 1732
34: 3 he began to seek after the God of **D** his 1732
35: 3 the son of **D** king of Israel did build; 1732
35: 4 according to the writing of **D** king of Israel, 1732
35:15 according to the commandment of **D**, and 1732
Ezr 3:10 after the ordinance of **D** king of Israel. 1732
8: 2 Daniel: of the sons of **D**; Hattush. 1732
8:20 whom **D** and the princes had appointed for 1732
Ne 3:15 the stairs that go down from the city of **D**. 1732
3:16 *the place* over against the sepulchres of **D**, 1732
12:24 according to the commandment of **D** 1732
12:36 with the musical instruments of **D** the man 1732
12:37 they went up by the stairs of the city of **D**, 1732
12:37 going up of the wall, above the house of **D**, 1732
12:45 according to the commandment of **D**, *and* 1732
12:46 For in the days of **D** and Asaph of old *there* 1732
Ps 3: T A Psalm of **D**, when he fled from Absalom 1732
4: T chief Musician on Neginoth, A Psalm of **D**. 1732
5: T Musician upon Nehiloth, A Psalm of **D**. 1732
6: T Neginoth upon Sheminith, A Psalm of **D**. 1732
7: T Shiggaion of **D**, which he sang unto 1732
8: T chief Musician upon Gittith, A Psalm of **D**. 1732
9: T upon Muth-labben, A Psalm of **D**. 1732
11: T To the chief Musician, *A Psalm* of **D**. 1732
12: T Musician upon Sheminith, A Psalm of **D**. 1732
13: T To the chief Musician, A Psalm of **D**. 1732
14: T To the chief Musician, *A Psalm* of **D**. 1732
15: T A Psalm of **D**. 1732
16: T Michtam of **D**. 1732
17: T A Prayer of **D**. 1732
18: T To the chief Musician, *A Psalm* of **D**, 1732
18:50 to **D**, and to his seed for evermore. 1732
19: T To the chief Musician, A Psalm of **D**. 1732
20: T To the chief Musician, A Psalm of **D**. 1732
21: T To the chief Musician, A Psalm of **D**. 1732
22: T upon Aijeleth Shahar, A Psalm of **D**. 1732
23: T A Psalm of **D**. 1732
24: T A Psalm of **D**. 1732
25: T *A Psalm* of **D**. 1732
26: T *A Psalm* of **D**. 1732
27: T *A Psalm* of **D**. 1732
28: T *A Psalm* of **D**. 1732
29: T A Psalm of **D**. 1732
30: T Song *at* the dedication of the house of **D**. 1732
31: T To the chief Musician, A Psalm of **D**. 1732
32: T *A Psalm* of **D**, Maschil. 1732
34: T *A Psalm* of **D**, when he changed his 1732
35: T *A Psalm* of **D**. 1732
36: T *A Psalm* of **D** the servant of the LORD. 1732
37: T *A Psalm* of **D**. 1732
38: T A Psalm of **D**, to bring to remembrance. 1732
39: T *even* to Jeduthun, A Psalm of **D**. 1732
40: T To the chief Musician, A Psalm of **D**. 1732
41: T To the chief Musician, A Psalm of **D**. 1732
51: T To the chief Musician, A Psalm of **D**, 1732
52: T the chief Musician, Maschil, *A Psalm* of **D**, 1732
52: T **D** is come to the house of Ahimelech. 1732

D

Ps	53: T	upon Mahalath, Maschil, *A Psalm* of **D**.	1732
	54: T	Maschil, *A Psalm* of **D**, when the Ziphims	1732
	54: T	to Saul, Doth not **D** hide himself with us?	1732
	55: T	on Neginoth, Maschil, *A Psalm* of **D**.	1732
	56: T	Michtam of **D**, when the Philistines took	1732
	57: T	chief Musician, Al-taschith, Michtam of **D**,	1732
	58: T	chief Musician, Al-taschith, Michtam of **D**.	1732
	59: T	chief Musician, Al-taschith, Michtam of **D**;	1732
	60: T	Michtam of **D**, to teach;	1732
	61: T	Musician upon Neginah, *A Psalm* of **D**.	1732
	62: T	chief Musician, to Jeduthun, A Psalm of **D**.	1732
	63: T	A Psalm of **D**, when he was in	1732
	64: T	To the chief Musician, A Psalm of **D**.	1732
	65: T	chief Musician, A Psalm *and* Song of **D**.	1732
	68: T	the chief Musician, A Psalm *or* Song of **D**.	1732
	69: T	Musician upon Shoshannim, *A Psalm* of **D**.	1732
	70: T	To the chief Musician, *A Psalm* of **D**,	1732
	72:20	The prayers of **D** the son of Jesse are	1732
	78:70	He chose **D** also his servant, and took him	1732
	86: T	A Prayer of **D**.	1732
	89: 3	I have sworn unto **D** my servant,	1732
	89:20	I have found **D** my servant; with my holy	1732
	89:35	by my holiness that I will not lie unto **D**.	1732
	89:49	*which* thou swarest unto **D** in thy truth?	1732
	101: T	A Psalm of **D**.	1732
	103: T	*A Psalm* of **D**.	1732
	108: T	A Song *or* Psalm of **D**.	1732
	109: T	To the chief Musician, A Psalm of **D**.	1732
	110: T	A Psalm of **D**.	1732
	122: T	A Song of degrees of **D**.	1732
	122: 5	of judgment, the thrones of the house of **D**.	1732
	124: T	A Song of degrees of **D**.	1732
	131: T	A Song of degrees of **D**.	1732
	132: 1	remember **D**, *and* all his afflictions:	1732
	132:11	The LORD hath sworn *in* truth unto **D**;	1732
	132:17	There will I make the horn of **D** to bud:	1732
	133: T	A Song of degrees of **D**.	1732
	138: T	*A Psalm* of **D**.	1732
	139: T	To the chief Musician, A Psalm of **D**.	1732
	140: T	To the chief Musician, A Psalm of **D**.	1732
	141: T	A Psalm of **D**.	1732
	142: T	Maschil of **D**; A Prayer when he was in	1732
	143: T	A Psalm of **D**.	1732
	144: T	*A Psalm* of **D**.	1732
	144:10	who delivereth **D** his servant from	1732
Pr	1: 1	The proverbs of Solomon the son of **D**,	1732
Ecc	1: 1	the son of **D**, king in Jerusalem.	1732
SS	4: 4	Thy neck *is* like the tower of **D** builded for	1732
Isa	7: 2	it was told the house of **D**, saying, Syria is	1732
	7:13	he said, Hear ye now, O house of **D**; *Is it* a	1732
	9: 7	upon the throne of **D**, and upon his	1732
	16: 5	sit upon it in truth in the tabernacle of **D**,	1732
	22: 9	seen also the breaches of the city of **D**,	1732
	22:22	the key of the house of **D** will I lay upon	1732
	29: 1	to Ariel, to Ariel, the city *where* **D** dwelt!	1732
	38: 5	saith the LORD, the God of **D** thy father,	1732
	55: 3	with you, *even* the sure mercies of **D**.	1732
Jer	17:25	and princes sitting upon the throne of **D**,	1732
	21:12	O house of **D**, thus saith the LORD;	1732
	22: 2	that sittest upon the throne of **D**, thou, and	1732
	22: 4	house kings sitting upon the throne of **D**,	1732
	22:30	sitting upon the throne of **D**, and ruling any	1732
	23: 5	that I will raise unto **D** a righteous Branch,	1732
	29:16	the king that sitteth upon the throne of **D**,	1732
	30: 9	**D** their king, whom I will raise up unto	1732
	33:15	Branch of righteousness to grow up unto **D**;	1732
	33:17	**D** shall never want a man to sit upon	1732
	33:21	my covenant be broken with **D** my servant,	1732
	33:22	so will I multiply the seed of **D** my servant,	1732
	33:26	**D** my servant, *so* that *I* will not take *any* of	1732
	36:30	shall have none to sit upon the throne of **D**:	1732
Eze	34:23	and he shall feed them, *even* my servant **D**;	1732
	34:24	and my servant **D** a prince among them;	1732
	37:24	**D** my servant *shall be* king over them; and	1732
	37:25	my servant **D** *shall be* their prince for ever.	1732
Hos	3: 5	the LORD their God, and **D** their king;	1732
Am	6: 5	themselves instruments of musick, like **D**;	1732
	9:11	I raise up the tabernacle of **D** that is fallen,	1732
Zec	12: 7	that the glory of the house of **D** and	1732
	12: 8	among them at that day shall be as **D**;	1732
	12: 8	the house of **D** *shall be* as God, as the angel	1732
	12:10	I will pour upon the house of **D**, and	1732
	12:12	the family of the house of **D** apart, and	1732
	13: 1	be a fountain opened to the house of **D**	1732

Mt	1: 1	the son of **D**, the son of Abraham.	*1138*
	1: 6	And Jesse begat **D** the king; and David	*1138*
	1: 6	**D** the king begat Solomon of *her that had*	*1138*
	1:17	So all the generations from Abraham to **D**	*1138*
	1:17	from **D** until the carrying away into	*1138*
	1:20	saying, Joseph, *thou* son of **D**, fear not to	*1138*
	9:27	crying, and saying, *Thou* Son of **D**,	*1138*
	12: 3	unto them, Have ye not read what **D** did,	*1138*
	12:23	were amazed, and said, Is this the son of **D**?	*1138*
	15:22	Have mercy on me, O Lord, *thou* Son of **D**;	*1138*
	20:30	Have mercy on us, O Lord, *thou* Son of **D**.	*1138*
	20:31	Have mercy on us, O Lord, *thou* Son of **D**.	*1138*
	21: 9	cried, saying, Hosanna to the Son of **D**:	*1138*
	21:15	and saying, Hosanna to the Son of **D**;	*1138*
	22:42	is he? They say unto him, *The Son* of **D**.	*1138*
	22:43	How then doth **D** in spirit call him Lord,	*1138*
	22:45	If **D** then call him Lord, how is he his son?	*1138*
Mk	2:25	Have ye never read what **D** did, when he	*1138*
	10:47	and say, Jesus, *thou* Son of **D**, have mercy	*1138*
	10:48	*Thou* Son of **D**, have mercy on me.	*1138*
	11:10	Blessed *be* the kingdom of our father **D**,	*1138*
	12:35	say the scribes that Christ is the Son of **D**?	*1138*
	12:36	For **D** himself said by the Holy Ghost,	*1138*
	12:37	**D** therefore himself calleth him Lord; and	*1138*
Lk	1:27	whose name was Joseph, of the house of **D**;	*1138*
	1:32	give unto him the throne of his father **D**:	*1138*
	1:69	for us in the house of his servant **D**;	*1138*
	2: 4	of Nazareth, into Judea, unto the city of **D**,	*1138*
	2: 4	he was of the house and lineage of **D**:)	*1138*
	2:11	is born this day in the city of **D** a Saviour,	*1138*
	3:31	*the son* of Nathan, which was *the son* of **D**,	*1138*
	6: 3	ye not read so much as this, what **D** did,	*1138*
	18:38	And he cried, saying, Jesus, *thou* Son of **D**,	*1138*
	18:39	he cried *so* much the more, *Thou* Son of **D**,	*1138*
	20:42	And **D** himself saith in the book of Psalms,	*1138*
	20:44	**D** therefore calleth him Lord, how is he	*1138*
Jn	7:42	That Christ cometh of the seed of **D**, and	*1138*
	7:42	of the town of Bethlehem, where **D** was?	*1138*
Ac	1:16	which the Holy Ghost by the mouth of **D**	*1138*
	2:25	For **D** speaketh concerning him, I foresaw	*1138*
	2:29	freely speak unto you of the patriarch **D**,	*1138*
	2:34	For **D** is not ascended into the heavens: but	*1138*
	4:25	Who by the mouth of thy servant **D** hast	*1138*
	7:45	the face of our fathers, unto the days of **D**;	*1138*
	13:22	he raised up unto them **D** to be their king;	*1138*
	13:22	and said, I have found **D** the *son* of Jesse,	*1138*
	13:34	I will give you the sure mercies of **D**.	*1138*
	13:36	For **D**, after he had served his own	*1138*
	15:16	and will build again the tabernacle of **D**,	*1138*
Ro	1: 3	which was made of the seed of **D** according	*1138*
	4: 6	Even as **D** also describeth the blessedness	*1138*
	11: 9	And **D** saith, Let their table be made a	*1138*
2Ti	2: 8	that Jesus Christ of the seed of **D**	*1138*
Heb	4: 7	saying in **D**, To day, after so long a time;	*1138*
	11:32	*of* **D** also, and Samuel, and *of* the prophets:	*1138*
Rev	3: 7	he *that is* true, he that hath the key of **D**,	*1138*
	5: 5	the Lion of the tribe of Juda, the root of **D**,	*1138*
	22:16	I am the root and the offspring of **D**, *and*	*1138*

DAVID'S (54) [DAVID]

1Sa	18:29	and Saul became **D** enemy continually.	1732
	19:11	Saul also sent messengers unto **D** house,	1732
	19:11	Michal **D** wife told him, saying, If thou	1732
	20:16	even require *it* at the hand of **D** enemies.	1732
	20:25	sat by Saul's side, and **D** place was empty.	1732
	20:27	*day* of the month, that **D** place was empty:	1732
	23: 3	**D** men said unto him, Behold, we *be* afraid	1732
	24: 5	that **D** heart smote him, because he had cut	1732
	25: 9	when **D** young men came, they spake to	1732
	25:10	Nabal answered **D** servants, and said,	1732
	25:12	So **D** young men turned their way, and	1732
	25:44	**D** wife, to Phalti the son of Laish,	1732
	26:17	Saul knew **D** voice, and said, *Is* this thy	1732
	30: 5	**D** two wives were taken captives,	1732
	30:20	those *other* cattle, and said, This *is* **D** spoil.	1732
2Sa	2:30	there lacked of **D** servants nineteen men	1732
	3: 5	the sixth, Ithream, by Eglah **D** wife.	1732
	5: 8	and the blind, *that are* hated of **D** soul,	1732
	8: 2	*so* the Moabites became **D** servants, and	1732
	8:14	and all they of Edom became **D** servants.	1732
	8:18	the Pelethites; and **D** sons were chief rulers.	1732
	10: 2	**D** servants came *into* the land of	1732
	10: 4	Wherefore Hanun took **D** servants, and	1732
	12: 5	**D** anger was greatly kindled against	1732

2Sa 12:30 it was *set* on **D** head. And he brought forth 1732
13: 3 the son of Shimeah **D** brother: 1732
13:32 the son of Shimeah **D** brother, answered 1732
15:12 **D** counseller, from his city, *even* from 1732
15:37 So Hushai **D** friend came *into* the city, and 1732
16:16 **D** friend, was come unto Absalom, 1732
19:41 and all **D** men with him, over Jordan? 1732
24:10 **D** heart smote him after that he had 1732
24:11 came unto the prophet Gad, **D** seer, saying, 1732
1Ki 1:38 caused Solomon to ride upon king **D** mule, 1732
11:32 shall have one tribe for my servant **D** sake, 1732
15: 4 Nevertheless for **D** sake did the LORD his 1732
2Ki 11:10 hundreds did the priest give king **D** spears 1732
19:34 mine own sake, and for my servant **D** sake. 1732
20: 6 mine own sake, and for my servant **D** sake. 1732
1Ch 18: 2 the Moabites became **D** servants, and 1732
18: 6 the Syrians became **D** servants, and 1732
18:13 and all the Edomites became **D** servants. 1732
19: 4 Wherefore Hanun took **D** servants, and 1732
20: 2 stones in it; and it was *set* upon **D** head: 1732
20: 7 Jonathan the son of Shimea **D** brother slew 1732
21: 9 LORD spake unto Gad, **D** seer, saying, 1732
27:31 of the substance which *was* king **D**. 1732+3807.1
27:32 Also Jonathan **D** uncle *was* a counseller, 1732
2Ch 23: 9 and shields, that *had been* king **D**, 1732+3807.1
Ps 132:10 For thy servant **D** sake turn not away 1732
145: T **D** *Psalm of* praise. 1732
Isa 37:35 mine own sake, and for my servant **D** sake. 1732
Jer 13:13 even the kings that sit upon **D** 1732+3807.1
Lk 20:41 How say they that Christ is **D** son? *1138*

DAWN (2) [DAWNING]
Mt 28: 1 as it began to **d** towards the first *day* of *2020*
2Pe 1:19 until the day **d**, and the day star arise in *1306*

DAWNING (5) [DAWN]
Jos 6:15 that they rose early about the **d** of the day, 5927
Jdg 19:26 came the woman in the **d** of the day, and 6437
Job 3: 9 neither let it see the **d** of the day: 6079
7: 4 *of* tossings to and fro unto the **d of the day**. 5399
Ps119:147 I prevented the **d of the morning**, and 5399

DAY (1732) [BIRTHDAY, DAILY, DAY'S, DAYS, DAYS', DAYSMAN, DAYSPRING, DAYTIME, HOLYDAY, MIDDAY, NOONDAY, NOONDAYS, YESTERDAY]
Ge 1: 5 God called the light **D**, and the darkness he 3117
1: 5 and the morning were the first **d**. 3117
1: 8 and the morning were the second **d**. 3117
1:13 and the morning were the third **d**. 3117
1:14 the heaven to divide the **d** from the night; 3117
1:16 the greater light to rule the **d**, and the lesser 3117
1:18 to rule over the **d** and over the night, and 3117
1:19 and the morning were the fourth **d**. 3117
1:23 and the morning were the fifth **d**. 3117
1:31 and the morning were the sixth **d**. 3117
2: 2 on the seventh **d** God ended his work 3117
2: 2 he rested on the seventh **d** from all his work 3117
2: 3 God blessed the seventh **d**, and 3117
2: 4 in the **d** that the LORD God made 3117
2:17 for in the **d** that thou eatest thereof thou 3117
3: 5 For God doth know that in the **d** ye eat 3117
3: 8 walking in the garden in the cool of the **d**: 3117
4:14 thou hast driven me out *this* **d** from the face 3117
5: 1 In the **d** that God created man, in 3117
5: 2 in the **d** when they were created. 3117
7:11 the seventeenth **d** of the month, 3117
7:11 the same **d** were all the fountains of 3117
7:13 In the selfsame **d** entered Noah, and Shem, 3117
8: 4 on the seventeenth **d** of the month, upon 3117
8: 5 in the tenth *month,* on the first *d* of NIH
8:13 in the first *month,* the first *d* of the month, NIH
8:14 on the seven and twentieth **d** of the month, 3117
8:22 and winter, and **d** and night shall not cease. 3117
15:18 In the same **d** the LORD made a covenant 3117
17:23 the flesh of their foreskin in the selfsame **d**, 3117
17:26 In the selfsame **d** was Abraham 3117
18: 1 he sat *in* the tent door in the heat of the **d**; 3117
19:37 *is* the father of the Moabites unto *this* **d**. 3117
19:38 of the children of Ammon unto *this* **d**. 3117
21: 8 Abraham made a great feast the *same* **d** that 3117
21:26 neither yet heard I *of it,* but **to d**. 3117+1886.1
22: 4 on the third **d** Abraham lift up his eyes, 3117
22:14 as it is said *to this* **d**, In the mount of 3117
24:12 send me good speed *this* **d**, and 3117
24:42 I came this **d** unto the well, and said, 3117
25:31 Jacob said, Sell me *this* **d** thy birthright. 3117
25:33 Jacob said, Swear to me *this* **d**; and 3117
26:32 it came to pass the same **d**, that Isaac's 3117
26:33 name of the city *is* Beer-sheba unto this **d**. 3117
27: 2 I am old, I know not the **d** of my death: 3117
27:45 I be deprived also of you both *in* one **d**? 3117
29: 7 he said, Lo, *it is* yet high **d**, neither *is it* 3117
30:32 will pass through all thy flock **to d**, 3117+1886.1
30:35 he removed that **d** the he goats that were 3117
31:22 it was told Laban on the third **d** that Jacob 3117
31:39 *whether* stolen by **d**, or stolen by night. 3117
31:40 *Thus* I was in the **d**, the drought consumed 3117
31:43 what can I do *this* **d** unto these my 3117
31:48 *is* a witness between me and thee *this* **d**. 3117
32:24 a man with him until the breaking of the **d**. 7837
32:26 he said, Let me go, for the **d** breaketh. 7837
32:32 *is* upon the hollow of the thigh, unto this **d**: 3117
33:13 if *men* should overdrive them one **d**, all 3117
33:16 So Esau returned that **d** on his way unto 3117
34:25 it came to pass on the third **d**, when they 3117
35: 3 who answered me in the **d** of my distress, 3117
35:20 *is* the pillar of Rachel's grave unto *this* **d**. 3117
39:10 to pass, as she spake to Joseph **d** by day, 3117
39:10 to pass, as she spake to Joseph day by **d**, 3117
40: 7 Wherefore look ye *so* sadly **to d**? 3117+1886.1
40:20 it came to pass the third **d**, *which was* 3117
41: 9 I do remember my faults *this* **d**: 3117
42:13 the youngest *is this* **d** with our father, and 3117
42:18 Joseph said unto them the third **d**, This do, 3117
42:32 the youngest *is this* **d** with our father in 3117
47:23 I have bought you *this* **d** and your land for 3117
47:26 it a law over the land of Egypt unto this **d**, 3117
48:15 which fed me all my life long unto this **d**, 3117
48:20 he blessed them that **d**, saying, In thee shall 3117
50:20 it unto good, to bring to pass, as *it is* this **d**, 3117
Ex 2:13 when he went out the second **d**, behold, 3117
2:18 *is it that* you are come so soon **d**? 3117+1886.1
5: 6 Pharaoh commanded the same **d** 3117
5:14 brick both yesterday and **to d**, 3117+1886.1
6:28 it came to pass on the **d** *when* the LORD 3117
8:22 I will sever in that **d** the land of Goshen, 3117
10: 6 since the **d** that they were upon the earth 3117
10: 6 that they were upon the earth unto this **d**. 3117
10:13 an east wind upon the land all that **d**, 3117
10:28 for in *that* **d** thou seest my face thou shalt 3117
12: 3 In the tenth *d* of this month they shall take NIH
12: 6 ye shall keep it *up* until the fourteenth **d** of 3117
12:14 this **d** shall be unto you for a memorial; 3117
12:15 even the first **d** ye shall put away leaven 3117
12:15 bread from the first **d** until the seventh day, 3117
12:15 bread from the first day until the seventh **d**, 3117
12:16 in the first **d** *there shall be* a holy 3117
12:16 in the seventh **d** there shall be a holy 3117
12:17 for in this selfsame **d** have I brought your 3117
12:17 shall ye observe this **d** in your generations 3117
12:18 In the first *month,* on the fourteenth **d** of 3117
12:18 and twentieth **d** of the month at even. 3117
12:41 even the selfsame **d** it came to pass, 3117
12:51 it came to pass the selfsame **d**, *that* 3117
13: 3 said unto the people, Remember this **d**, 3117
13: 4 *This* **d** came ye out in the month Abib. 3117
13: 6 in the seventh **d** *shall be* a feast to 3117
13: 8 thou shalt shew thy son in that **d**, saying, 3117
13:21 the LORD went before them **by d** in a 3119
13:21 to give them light; to go **by d** and night: 3119
13:22 took not away the pillar of the cloud **by d**, 3119
14:13 which he will shew to you **to d**: 3117+1886.1
14:13 Egyptians whom ye have seen **to d**, 3117+1886.1
14:30 Thus the LORD saved Israel that **d** out of 3117
16: 1 on the fifteenth **d** of the second month after 3117
16: 4 gather a certain rate **every d**, 3117+3117+871.1
16: 5 that on the sixth **d** they shall prepare *that* 3117
16:22 *that* on the sixth **d** they gathered twice as 3117
16:23 bake *that* which you will bake *to d*, and NIH
16:25 Moses said, Eat that **to d**; for to 3117+1886.1
16:25 **to d** *is* a sabbath unto the LORD: 3117+1886.1
16:25 *is* a sabbath unto the LORD: **to d** 3117+1886.1
16:26 on the seventh **d**, *which is* the sabbath, in it 3117
16:27 of the people on the seventh **d** for to gather, 3117
16:29 he giveth you on the sixth **d** the bread of 3117
16:29 man go out of his place on the seventh **d**. 3117
16:30 So the people rested on the seventh **d**. 3117
19: 1 the same **d** came they *into* the wilderness of 3117

Ex	19:10	sanctify them **to d** and to morrow,	3117+1886.1
	19:11	be ready against the third **d**: for the third	3117
	19:11	for the third **d** the LORD will come down	3117
	19:15	the people, Be ready against the third **d**:	3117
	19:16	it came to pass on the third **d** in	3117
	20: 8	Remember the sabbath **d**, to keep it holy.	3117
	20:10	the seventh **d** *is* the sabbath of the LORD	3117
	20:11	all that in them *is*, and rested the seventh **d**:	3117
	20:11	the LORD blessed the sabbath **d**,	3117
	21:21	Notwithstanding, if he continue a **d** or two,	3117
	22:30	on the eighth **d** thou shalt give it me.	3117
	23:12	and on the seventh **d** thou shalt rest:	3117
	24:16	the seventh **d** he called unto Moses out of	3117
	29:36	thou shalt offer every **d** a bullock *for* a sin	3117
	29:38	year **d by day** continually.	3117+1886.1+3807.1
	29:38	year **day by d** continually.	3117+1886.1+3807.1
	31:15	doeth *any* work in the sabbath **d**,	3117
	31:17	on the seventh **d** he rested, and	3117
	32:28	there fell of the people that **d** about three	3117
	32:29	yourselves **to d** to the LORD,	3117+1886.1
	32:29	he may bestow upon you a blessing *this* **d**.	3117
	32:34	nevertheless in the **d** when I visit, I will	3117
	34:11	thou that which I command thee *this* **d**:	3117
	34:21	but on the seventh **d** thou shalt rest:	3117
	35: 2	on the seventh **d** there shall be to you a	3117
	35: 2	a holy *d*, a sabbath of rest to the LORD:	NIH
	35: 3	your habitations upon the sabbath **d**.	3117
	40: 2	On the first **d** of the first month shalt thou	3117
	40:17	on the first *d* of the month, *that*	NIH
	40:37	they journeyed not till the **d** that it was	3117
	40:38	the LORD *was* upon the tabernacle **by d**,	3119
Lev	6: 5	in the **d** of his trespass offering.	3117
	6:20	the LORD in the **d** when he is anointed;	3117
	7:15	shall be eaten the same **d** that it is offered;	3117
	7:16	it shall be eaten the *same* **d** that he offereth	3117
	7:17	on the third **d** shall be burnt with fire.	3117
	7:18	offerings be eaten at all on the third **d**,	3117
	7:35	in the **d** *when* he presented them to minister	3117
	7:36	in the **d** that he anointed them, *by* a statute	3117
	7:38	in the **d** that he commanded the children of	3117
	8:34	As he hath done this **d**, *so* the LORD hath	3117
	8:35	door of the tabernacle of the congregation **d**	3119
	9: 1	it came to pass on the eighth **d**, *that* Moses	3117
	9: 4	**to d** the LORD will appear unto	3117+1886.1
	10:19	*this* **d** have they offered their sin offering	3117
	10:19	*if* I had eaten the sin offering to **d**,	3117+1886.1
	12: 3	in the eighth **d** the flesh of his foreskin	3117
	13: 5	the priest shall look on him the seventh **d**:	3117
	13: 6	shall look on him again the seventh **d**:	3117
	13:27	priest shall look upon him the seventh **d**:	3117
	13:32	in the seventh **d** the priest shall look on	3117
	13:34	in the seventh **d** the priest shall look on	3117
	13:51	shall look on the plague on the seventh **d**:	3117
	14: 2	This shall be the law of the leper in the **d** of	3117
	14: 9	it shall be on the seventh **d**, *that* he shall	3117
	14:10	on the eighth **d** he shall take two he lambs	3117
	14:23	he shall bring them on the eighth **d** for his	3117
	14:39	the priest shall come again the seventh **d**,	3117
	15:14	on the eighth **d** he shall take to him two	3117
	15:29	on the eighth **d** she shall take unto her two	3117
	16:29	on the tenth *d* of the month, ye shall afflict	NIH
	16:30	For on that **d** shall *the priest* make an	3117
	19: 6	It shall be eaten the *same* **d** ye offer it, and	3117
	19: 6	if ought remain until the third **d**, it shall be	3117
	19: 7	if it be eaten at all on the third **d**, it *is*	3117
	22:27	from the eighth **d** and thenceforth it shall	3117
	22:28	shall not kill it and her young both in one **d**.	3117
	22:30	On the same **d** it shall be eaten up; ye shall	3117
	23: 3	the seventh **d** *is* the sabbath of rest, a holy	3117
	23: 5	In the fourteenth *d* of the first month at even	NIH
	23: 6	on the fifteenth **d** of the same month *is*	3117
	23: 7	In the first **d** ye shall have a holy	3117
	23: 8	in the seventh **d** *is* a holy convocation:	3117
	23:12	ye shall offer that **d** when ye wave	3117
	23:14	until the selfsame **d** that ye have brought an	3117
	23:15	from the **d** that ye brought the sheaf of	3117
	23:21	ye shall proclaim on the selfsame **d**, *that* it	3117
	23:24	seventh month, in the first *d* of the month,	NIH
	23:27	Also on the tenth *d* of this seventh month	NIH
	23:27	month *there shall be* a **d** of atonement:	3117
	23:28	ye shall do no work in that same **d**: for it *is*	3117
	23:28	for it *is* a **d** of atonement, to make an	3117
	23:29	*be* that shall not be afflicted in that same **d**,	3117
	23:30	*it be* that doeth any work in that same **d**,	3117
	23:32	in the ninth *d* of the month at even,	NIH
	23:34	The fifteenth **d** of this seventh month *shall*	3117
	23:35	On the first **d** *shall be* a holy convocation:	3117
	23:36	on the eighth **d** shall be a holy convocation	3117
	23:37	every thing **upon** his **d**:	3117+3117+871.1
	23:39	Also in the fifteenth **d** of the seventh	3117
	23:39	on the first **d** *shall be* a sabbath, and on	3117
	23:39	and on the eighth **d** *shall be* a sabbath.	3117
	23:40	ye shall take you on the first **d** the boughs	3117
	25: 9	sound on the tenth *d* of the seventh month,	NIH
	25: 9	in the **d** of atonement shall ye make	3117
	27:23	he shall give thine estimation in that **d**, *as* a	3117
Nu	1: 1	on the first *d* of the second month,	NIH
	1:18	together on the first *d* of the second month,	NIH
	3: 1	Moses in the **d** that the LORD spake with	3117
	3:13	*for* on the **d** that I smote all the firstborn in	3117
	6: 9	he shall shave his head in the **d** of his	3117
	6: 9	on the seventh **d** shall he shave it.	3117
	6:10	on the eighth **d** he shall bring two turtles,	3117
	6:11	and shall hallow his head that *same* **d**.	3117
	7: 1	it came to pass on the **d** that Moses had	3117
	7:10	of the altar in the **d** that it was anointed,	3117
	7:11	each prince on *his* **d**, for the dedicating of	3117
	7:12	he that offered his offering the first **d** was	3117
	7:18	On the second **d** Nethaneel the son of Zuar,	3117
	7:24	On the third **d** Eliab the son of Helon,	3117
	7:30	On the fourth **d** Elizur the son of Shedeur,	3117
	7:36	On the fifth **d** Shelumiel the son of	3117
	7:42	On the sixth **d** Eliasaph the son of Deuel,	3117
	7:48	On the seventh **d** Elishama the son of	3117
	7:54	On the eighth **d** *offered* Gamaliel the son of	3117
	7:60	On the ninth **d** Abidan the son of Gideoni,	3117
	7:66	On the tenth **d** Ahiezer the son of	3117
	7:72	On the eleventh **d** Pagiel the son of Ocran,	3117
	7:78	On the twelfth **d** Ahira the son of Enan,	3117
	7:84	in the **d** when it was anointed, by	3117
	8:17	on the **d** that I smote every firstborn in	3117
	9: 3	In the fourteenth **d** of this month, at even,	3117
	9: 5	they kept the passover on the fourteenth **d**	3117
	9: 6	they could not keep the passover on that **d**:	3117
	9: 6	before Moses and before Aaron on that **d**:	3117
	9:11	The fourteenth **d** of the second month at	3117
	9:15	on the **d** that the tabernacle was reared up,	3117
	9:16	the cloud covered it *by d*, and	NIH
	9:21	whether *it was* **by d** or by night that	3119
	10:10	Also in the **d** of your gladness, and in your	3117
	10:11	it came to pass on the twentieth *d* of	NIH
	10:34	cloud of the LORD *was* upon them **by d**,	3119
	11:19	Ye shall not eat one **d**, nor two days,	3117
	11:32	the people stood up all that **d**, and all *that*	3117
	11:32	all the next **d**, and they gathered the quails:	3117
	14:14	**by d time** in a pillar of a cloud, and in a	3119
	14:34	*even* forty days, each **d** for a year, shall ye	3117
	15:23	from the **d** that the LORD commanded	3117
	15:32	that gathered sticks upon the sabbath **d**.	3117
	19:12	shall purify himself with it on the third **d**,	3117
	19:12	and on the seventh **d** he shall be clean:	3117
	19:12	if he purify not himself the third **d**, then	3117
	19:12	then the seventh **d** he shall not be clean.	3117
	19:19	sprinkle upon the unclean on the third **d**,	3117
	19:19	on the third day, and on the seventh **d**:	3117
	19:19	on the seventh **d** he shall purify him*self*,	3117
	22:30	ridden ever since *I was* thine unto this **d**?	3117
	25:18	which was slain in the **d** of the plague for	3117
	28: 3	without spot **d by day**,	3117+1886.1+3807.1
	28: 3	without spot **day by d**,	3117+1886.1+3807.1
	28: 9	on the sabbath **d** two lambs of the first year	3117
	28:16	in the fourteenth **d** of the first month *is*	3117
	28:17	in the fifteenth **d** of this month *is* the feast:	3117
	28:18	In the first **d** *shall be* a holy convocation;	3117
	28:25	on the seventh **d** ye shall have a holy	3117
	28:26	Also in the **d** of the firstfruits, when ye	3117
	29: 1	seventh month, on the first *d* of the month,	NIH
	29: 1	it is a **d** of blowing the trumpets unto you.	3117
	29: 7	ye shall have on the tenth *d* of this seventh	NIH
	29:12	on the fifteenth **d** of the seventh month ye	3117
	29:17	on the second **d** *ye shall offer* twelve young	3117
	29:20	on the third **d** eleven bullocks, two rams,	3117
	29:23	And on the fourth **d** ten bullocks, two rams,	3117
	29:26	on the fifth **d** nine bullocks, two rams, *and*	3117
	29:29	on the sixth **d** eight bullocks, two rams,	3117
	29:32	on the seventh **d** seven bullocks, two rams,	3117
	29:35	On the eighth **d** ye shall have a solemn	3117
	30: 5	if her father disallow her in the **d** that he	3117

Nu 30: 7 held his peace at her in the **d** that he heard 3117
30: 8 if her husband disallow her on the **d** that he 3117
30:12 made them void on the **d** he heard *them;* 3117
30:14 hold his peace at her from **d** to day; 3117
30:14 hold his peace at her from day to **d**; 3117
30:14 he held his peace at her in the **d** that he 3117
31:19 and your captives on the third **d**, 3117
31:19 on the third day, and on the seventh **d**. 3117
31:24 shall wash your clothes on the seventh **d**, 3117
33: 3 on the fifteenth **d** of the first month; 3117
33:38 of Egypt, in the first ***d*** of the fifth month. NIH
Dt 1: 3 eleventh month, on the first ***d*** of the month, NIH
1:10 you *are this* **d** as the stars of heaven for 3117
1:33 way ye should go, and in a cloud **by d**. 3119
1:39 which *in that* **d** had no knowledge between 3117
2:18 over *through* Ar, the coast of Moab, *this* **d**: 3117
2:22 and dwelt in their stead *even* unto this **d**: 3117
2:25 This **d** will I begin to put the dread of thee 3117
2:30 him into thy hand, as *appeareth* this **d**. 3117
3:14 own name, Bashan-havoth-jair, unto this **d**. 3117
4: 4 your God *are* alive every one of you *this* **d**. 3117
4: 8 all this law, which I set before you *this* **d**? 3117
4:10 *Specially* the **d** that thou stoodest before 3117
4:15 for ye saw no *manner of* similitude on the **d** 3117
4:20 a people of inheritance, as *ye are* this **d**. 3117
4:26 and earth to witness against you *this* **d**, 3117
4:32 since the **d** that God created man upon 3117
4:38 their land *for* an inheritance, as *it is* this **d**. 3117
4:39 Know therefore *this* **d**, and consider *it* in 3117
4:40 which I command thee *this* **d**, 3117
5: 1 which I speak in your ears *this* **d**, 3117
5: 3 *even* us, who *are* all of us here alive *this* **d**. 3117
5:12 Keep the sabbath **d** to sanctify it, as 3117
5:14 the seventh **d** *is* the sabbath of the LORD 3117
5:15 commanded thee to keep the sabbath **d**. 3117
5:24 we have seen this **d** that God doth talk with 3117
6: 6 these words, which I command thee *this* **d**, 3117
6:24 he might preserve us alive, as *it is at* this **d**. 3117
7:11 which I command thee *this* **d**, to do them. 3117
8: 1 command thee *this* **d** shall ye observe to do, 3117
8:11 his statutes, which I command thee *this* **d**: 3117
8:18 he sware unto thy fathers, as *it is* this **d**. 3117
8:19 I testify against you *this* **d** that ye shall 3117
9: 1 Thou art to pass over Jordan *this* **d**, to go in 3117
9: 3 Understand therefore *this* **d**, that 3117
9: 7 from the **d** that thou didst depart out of 3117
9:10 midst of the fire in the **d** of the assembly. 3117
9:24 the LORD from the **d** that I knew you. 3117
10: 4 midst of the fire in the **d** of the assembly: 3117
10: 8 and to bless in his name, unto this **d**. 3117
10:13 which I command thee *this* **d** for thy good? 3117
10:15 *even* you above all people, as *it is* this **d**. 3117
11: 2 know you *this* **d**: for *I speak* not with your 3117
11: 4 LORD hath destroyed them unto this **d**; 3117
11: 8 which I command you *this* **d**, 3117
11:13 which I command you *this* **d**, 3117
11:26 I set before you *this* **d** a blessing and 3117
11:27 your God, which I command you *this* **d**: 3117
11:28 of the way which I command you *this* **d**, 3117
11:32 judgments which I set before you *this* **d**. 3117
12: 8 after all *the things* that we do here *this* **d**, 3117
13:18 which I command thee *this* **d**, 3117
15: 5 which I command thee *this* **d**. 3117
15:15 I command thee this thing **to d**. 3117+1886.1
16: 3 that thou mayest remember the **d** when 3117
16: 4 which thou sacrificedst the first **d** at even, 3117
16: 8 on the seventh **d** *shall be* a solemn 3117
18:16 thy God in Horeb in the **d** of the assembly, 3117
19: 9 which I command thee *this* **d**, to love 3117
20: 3 you approach *this* **d** unto battle against your 3117
21:23 but thou shalt in any wise bury him that **d**; 3117
24:15 At his **d** thou shalt give *him* his hire, 3117
26: 3 I profess *this* **d** unto the LORD thy God, 3117
26:16 This **d** the LORD thy God hath 3117
26:17 Thou hast avouched the LORD *this* **d** to 3117
26:18 the LORD hath avouched thee *this* **d** to be 3117
27: 1 which I command you *this* **d**. 3117
27: 2 it shall be on the **d** when you shall pass 3117
27: 4 which I command you *this* **d**, in mount 3117
27: 9 this **d** thou art become the people of 3117
27:10 his statutes, which I command thee *this* **d**. 3117
27:11 Moses charged the people the same **d**, 3117
28: 1 which I command thee *this* **d**, 3117
28:13 which I command thee *this* **d**, to observe 3117
28:14 of the words which I command thee *this* **d**, 3117
28:15 his statutes which I command thee *this* **d**; 3117
28:32 fail *with longing* for them all the **d** long: 3117
28:66 thou shalt fear **d** and night, and shalt have 3119
29: 4 eyes to see, and ears to hear, unto this **d**. 3117
29:10 Ye stand *this* **d** all of you before 3117
29:12 LORD thy God maketh with thee *this* **d**: 3117
29:13 That he may establish thee **to d** for 3117+1886.1
29:15 with *him* that standeth here with us *this* **d** 3117
29:15 also with *him* that *is* not here with us *this* **d**: 3117
29:18 whose heart turneth away *this* **d** from 3117
29:28 cast them into another land, as *it is* this **d**. 3117
30: 2 according to all that I command thee *this* **d**, 3117
30: 8 which I command thee *this* **d**. 3117
30:11 which I command thee *this* **d**, 3117
30:15 I have set before thee *this* **d** life and good, 3117
30:16 In that I command thee *this* **d** to love 3117
30:18 I denounce unto you *this* **d**, that ye shall 3117
30:19 and earth to record *this* **d** against you, 3117
31: 2 *am* an hundred and twenty years old *this* **d**; 3117
31:17 shall be kindled against them in that **d**, 3117
31:17 so that they will say in that **d**, Are not these 3117
31:18 I will surely hide my face in that **d** for all 3117
31:22 wrote this song the same **d**, 3117
31:27 while I am yet alive with you *this* **d**, 3117
32:35 for the **d** of their calamity *is* at hand, and 3117
32:46 the words which I testify among you *this* **d**, 3117
32:48 LORD spake unto Moses that selfsame **d**, 3117
33:12 *the* LORD shall cover him all the **d** long, 3117
34: 6 man knoweth of his sepulchre unto this **d**. 3117
Jos 1: 8 thou shalt meditate therein **d** and night, that 3119
3: 7 This **d** will I begin to magnify thee in 3117
4: 9 and they are there unto this **d**. 3117
4:14 On that **d** the LORD magnified Joshua in 3117
4:19 of Jordan on the tenth ***d*** of the first month, NIH
5: 9 *This* **d** have I rolled away the reproach of 3117
5: 9 of the place is called Gilgal unto this **d**. 3117
5:10 kept the passover on the fourteenth **d** of 3117
5:11 and parched *corn* in the selfsame **d**. 3117
6: 4 the seventh **d** ye shall compass the city 3117
6:10 of your mouth, until the **d** I bid you shout; 3117
6:14 the second **d** they compassed the city once, 3117
6:15 it came to pass on the seventh **d**, that they 3117
6:15 they rose early about the dawning of the **d**, 7837
6:15 only on that **d** they compassed the city 3117
6:25 she dwelleth in Israel *even* unto this **d**; 3117
7:25 the LORD shall trouble thee this **d**. 3117
7:26 over him a great heap of stones unto this **d**. 3117
7:26 The valley of Achor, unto this **d**. 3117
8:25 *so* it was, *that* all that fell that **d**, both of 3117
8:28 heap for ever, *even* a desolation unto this **d**. 3117
8:29 heap of stones, *that remaineth* unto this **d**. 3117
9:12 on the **d** we came forth to go unto you; 3117
9:17 and came unto their cities on the third **d**. 3117
9:27 Joshua made them that **d** hewers of wood 3117
9:27 the altar of the LORD, *even* unto this **d**, 3117
10:12 spake Joshua to the LORD in the **d** when 3117
10:13 and hasted not to go down about a whole **d**. 3117
10:14 there was no **d** like that before it or after it, 3117
10:27 *which remain* until this very **d**. 3117
10:28 that **d** Joshua took Makkedah, and smote it 3117
10:32 which took it on the second **d**, and smote it 3117
10:35 they took it on that **d**, and smote it with 3117
10:35 *were* therein he utterly destroyed that **d**, 3117
13:13 dwell among the Israelites until this **d**.) 3117
14: 9 Moses sware on that **d**, saying, Surely 3117
14:10 I *am this* **d** fourscore and five years old. 3117
14:11 As yet I *am as* strong *this* **d** as *I was* in 3117
14:11 day as *I was* in the **d** that Moses sent me: 3117
14:12 whereof the LORD spake in that **d**; 3117
14:12 for thou heardest in that **d** how 3117
14:14 son of Jephunneh the Kenezite unto this **d**, 3117
15:63 children of Judah at Jerusalem unto this **d**. 3117
16:10 dwell among the Ephraimites unto this **d**, 3117
22: 3 your brethren these many days unto this **d**, 3117
22:16 to turn away *this* **d** from following 3117
22:16 that ye might rebel *this* **d** against 3117
22:17 from which we are not cleansed until this **d**, 3117
22:18 that ye must turn away *this* **d** from 3117
22:18 ye rebel **to d** against the LORD, 3117+1886.1
22:22 against the LORD, (save us not this **d**,) 3117
22:29 turn *this* **d** from following the LORD, 3117
22:31 *This* **d** we perceive that the LORD *is* 3117
23: 8 your God, as ye have done unto this **d**. 3117

D

D

Jos 23: 9 *been able to* stand before you unto this **d**. 3117
23:14 *this* **d** I am going the way of all the earth: 3117
24:15 choose you *this* **d** whom you will serve; 3117
24:25 made a covenant with the people that **d**, 3117
Jdg 1:21 of Benjamin in Jerusalem unto this **d**. 3117
1:26 which *is* the name thereof unto this **d**. 3117
3:30 So Moab was subdued that **d** under 3117
4:14 for this *is* the **d** in which the LORD hath 3117
4:23 So God subdued on that **d** Jabin the king of 3117
5: 1 and Barak the son of Abinoam on that **d**, 3117
6:24 unto this **d** it *is* yet in Ophrah of 3117
6:27 of the city, that *he* could not do *it* **by d**, 3119
6:32 Therefore on that **d** he called him 3117
9:18 risen up against my father's house *this* **d**, 3117
9:19 with Jerubbaal and with his house this **d**, 3117
9:45 fought against the city all that **d**; 3117
10: 4 which are called Havoth-jair unto this **d**, 3117
10:15 deliver us only, we pray thee, this **d**. 3117
11:27 the LORD the Judge be judge *this* **d** 3117
12: 3 are ye come up unto me this **d**, 3117
13: 7 God from the womb to the **d** of his death. 3117
13:10 unto me, that came unto me the *other* **d**. 3117
14:15 it came to pass on the seventh **d**, that they 3117
14:17 it came to pass on the seventh **d**, that he 3117
14:18 on the seventh **d** before the sun went down, 3117
15:19 which *is* in Lehi unto this **d**. 3117
16: 2 saying, In the morning, when it is **d**, we shall 216
18: 1 **d** *all their* inheritance had not fallen unto 3117
18:12 called that place Mahaneh-dan unto this **d**: 3117
18:30 Dan until the **d** of the captivity of the land. 3117
19: 5 it came to pass on the fourth **d**, when they 3117
19: 8 he arose early in the morning on the fifth **d** 3117
19: 9 the **d** draweth towards evening, 3117
19: 9 behold, the **d** groweth to an end, 3117
19:11 they *were* by Jebus, the **d** was far spent; 3117
19:25 when the **d began** to spring, they let her go. 7837
19:26 came the woman in the dawning of the **d**, 1242
19:30 **d** that the children of Israel came up out of 3117
19:30 up out of the land of Egypt unto this **d**: 3117
20:21 to the ground of the Israelites that **d** twenty 3117
20:22 they put *themselves* in array the first **d**. 3117
20:24 the children of Benjamin the second **d**. 3117
20:25 against them out of Gibeah the second **d**, 3117
20:26 fasted that **d** until even, and offered burnt 3117
20:30 the children of Benjamin on the third **d**, 3117
20:35 destroyed of the Benjamites that **d** twenty 3117
20:46 So that all which fell that **d** of Benjamin 3117
21: 3 that there should be **to d** one tribe 3117+1886.1
21: 6 There is one tribe cut off from Israel *this* **d**. 3117
Ru 2:19 Where hast thou gleaned **to d**? 3117+1886.1
2:19 with whom I wrought **to d** *is* Boaz. 3117+1886.1
3:18 until he have finished the thing *this* **d**. 3117
4: 5 What **d** thou buyest the field of the hand of 3117
4: 9 *unto* all the people, Ye *are* witnesses *this* **d**, 3117
4:10 gate of his place: ye *are* witnesses *this* **d**. 3117
4:14 which hath not left thee *this* **d** without a 3117
1Sa 2:34 in one **d** they shall die both of them. 3117
3:12 In that **d** I will perform against Eli all 3117
4: 3 us **to d** before the Philistines? 3117+1886.1
4:12 came *to* Shiloh the same **d** with his clothes 3117
4:16 and I fled **to d** out of the army. 3117+1886.1
5: 5 threshold of Dagon in Ashdod unto this **d**. 3117
6:15 sacrificed sacrifices the same **d** unto 3117
6:16 seen *it*, they returned *to* Ekron the same **d**. 3117
6:18 *which stone remaineth* unto this **d** in 3117
7: 6 and fasted on that **d**, and said there, 3117
7:10 great thunder on that **d** upon the Philistines, 3117
8: 8 **d** that I brought them up out of Egypt even 3117
8: 8 them up out of Egypt even unto this **d**, 3117
8:18 ye shall cry out in that **d** because of your 3117
8:18 and the LORD will not hear you in that **d**. 3117
9:12 for he came **to d** to the city; 3117+1886.1
9:12 the people **to d** in the high place: 3117+1886.1
9:15 Samuel in his ear a **d** before Saul came, 3117
9:19 for ye shall eat with me **to d**, and 3117+1886.1
9:24 So Saul did eat with Samuel that **d**. 3117
9:26 it came to pass about the spring of the **d**, 7837
10: 2 thou art departed from me **to d**, 3117+1886.1
10: 9 and all those signs came to pass that **d**. 3117
10:19 ye have *this* **d** rejected your God, 3117
11:11 slew the Ammonites until the heat of the **d**: 3117
11:13 shall not a man be put to death this **d**: 3117
11:13 for **to d** the LORD hath wrought 3117+1886.1
12: 2 before you from my childhood unto this **d**. 3117
12: 5 and his anointed *is* witness this **d**, 3117
12:17 *Is it* not wheat harvest **to d**? I will 3117+1886.1
12:18 the LORD sent thunder and rain that **d**: 3117
13:22 So it came to pass in the **d** of battle, 3117
14: 1 Now it came to pass upon a **d**, 3117
14:23 So the LORD saved Israel that **d**: and 3117
14:24 the men of Israel were distressed that **d**: 3117
14:28 *be* the man that eateth *any* food *this* **d**. 3117
14:30 **to d** of the spoil of their enemies 3117+1886.1
14:31 they smote the Philistines that **d** from 3117
14:33 roll a great stone unto me *this* **d**. 3117
14:37 of Israel? But he answered him not that **d**. 3117
14:38 and see wherein this sin hath been *this* **d**. 3117
14:45 for he hath wrought with God this **d**. 3117
15:28 rent the kingdom of Israel from thee *this* **d**, 3117
15:35 no more to see Saul until the **d** of his death: 3117
16:13 came upon David from that **d** forward. 3117
17:10 I defy the armies of Israel this **d**; 3117
17:46 This **d** will the LORD deliver thee into 3117
17:46 Philistines this **d** unto the fowls of the air, 3117
18: 2 Saul took him that **d**, and would let him go 3117
18: 9 Saul eyed David from that **d** and forward. 3117
18:21 Thou shalt *this* **d** be my son in law in 3117
19:24 lay down naked all that **d** and all *that* night. 3117
20: 5 myself in the fields unto the third *d* at even. NIH
20:12 *or* the third *d*, and behold, *if there be* good NIH
20:26 Saul spake not any thing that **d**: 3117
20:27 *which was* the second *d* of the month, NIH
20:27 neither yesterday, nor **to d**? 3117+1886.1
20:34 did eat no meat the second **d** of the month: 3117
21: 5 though it were sanctified *this* **d** in 3117
21: 6 to put hot bread in the **d** when it was taken 3117
21: 7 of the servants of Saul *was* there that **d**, 3117
21:10 fled that **d** for fear of Saul, and went to 3117
22: 8 against me, to lie in wait, as at this **d**? 3117
22:13 rise against me, to lie in wait, as at this **d**? 3117
22:18 slew on that **d** fourscore and five persons 3117
22:22 David said unto Abiathar, I knew *it* that **d**, 3117
23:14 Saul sought him every **d**, but God delivered 3117
24: 4 Behold the **d** of which the LORD said 3117
24:10 this **d** thine eyes have seen how that 3117
24:10 **to d** into mine hand in the cave: 3117+1886.1
24:18 thou hast shewed *this* **d** how that thou hast 3117
24:19 good for that thou hast done unto me this **d**. 3117
25: 8 for we come in a good **d**: give, I pray thee, 3117
25:16 were a wall unto us both by night and **d**, 3119
25:32 of Israel, which sent thee this **d** to meet me: 3117
25:33 which hast kept me this **d** from coming to 3117
26: 8 thine enemy into thine hand *this* **d**: 3117
26:10 or his **d** shall come to die; or he shall 3117
26:19 for they have driven me out *this* **d** from 3117
26:21 my soul was precious in thine eyes this **d**: 3117
26:23 delivered thee into *my* hand **to d**, 3117+1886.1
26:24 as thy life was much set by this **d** in mine 3117
27: 1 I shall now perish one **d** by the hand of 3117
27: 6 Achish gave him Ziklag that **d**: wherefore 3117
27: 6 unto the kings of Judah unto this **d**. 3117
27:10 Whither have ye made a road **to d**? 3117+1886.1
28:18 the LORD done this thing unto thee this **d**. 3117
28:20 for he had eaten no bread all the **d**, nor all 3117
29: 3 in him since he fell *unto me* unto this **d**? 3117
29: 6 for I have not found evil in thee since the **d** 3117
29: 6 the day of thy coming unto me unto this **d**: 3117
29: 8 so long as I have been with thee unto this **d**, 3117
30: 1 his men were come *to* Ziklag on the third **d**, 3117
30:17 even unto the evening of the **next d**: 4283
30:25 it was *so* from that **d** forward, that he made 3117
30:25 and an ordinance for Israel unto this **d**. 3117
31: 6 all his men, that *same* **d** together. 3117
2Sa 1: 2 It came even to pass on the third **d**, that 3117
2:17 there was a very sore battle that **d**; 3117
2:32 and they came to Hebron **at break of d**. 215
3: 8 *this* **d** unto the house of Saul thy father, 3117
3: 8 that thou chargest me **to d** with a 3117+1886.1
3:35 cause David to eat meat while it was yet **d**, 3117
3:37 all Israel understood that **d** that it was not 3117
3:38 and a great *man* fallen this **d** in Israel? 3117
3:39 I *am this* **d** weak, though anointed king; 3117
4: 3 and were sojourners there until this **d**.) 3117
4: 5 came about the heat of the **d** to the house of 3117
4: 8 avenged my lord the king this **d** of Saul, 3117
5: 8 David said on that **d**, Whosoever getteth up 3117
6: 8 *the name* of the place Perez-uzzah to this **d**. 3117
6: 9 David was afraid of the LORD that **d**, 3117

2Sa	6:20	was the king of Israel **to d**,	3117+1886.1
	6:20	who uncovered himself **to d** in	3117+1886.1
	6:23	Saul had no child unto the **d** of her death.	3117
	7: 6	even to this **d**, but have walked in a tent	3117
	11:12	Tarry here **to d** also, and	3117+1886.1
	11:12	So Uriah abode in Jerusalem that **d**, and	3117
	12:18	it came to pass on the seventh **d**, that	3117
	13: 4	*being* the king's son, lean from **d** to day?	1242
	13: 4	*being* the king's son, lean from day to **d**?	1242
	13:32	from the **d** that he forced his sister Tamar.	3117
	13:37	And *David* mourned for his son every **d**.	3117
	14:22	**To d** thy servant knoweth that I	3117+1886.1
	15:20	should I *this* **d** make thee go up and	3117
	16: 3	for he said, **To d** shall the house of	3117+1886.1
	16:12	will requite me good for his cursing this **d**.	3117
	18: 7	there was there a great slaughter that **d** *of*	3117
	18: 8	the wood devoured more people that **d** than	3117
	18:18	it is called unto this **d**, Absalom's place.	3117
	18:20	Thou *shalt* not bear tidings this **d**, but	3117
	18:20	but thou shalt bear tidings another **d**:	3117
	18:20	this **d** thou shalt bear no tidings, because	3117
	18:31	for the LORD hath avenged thee *this* **d** of	3117
	19: 2	the victory that **d** was *turned* into mourning	3117
	19: 2	for the people heard say that **d** *how*	3117
	19: 3	the people gat them by stealth that **d** *into*	3117
	19: 5	Thou hast shamed *this* **d** the faces of all thy	3117
	19: 5	which *this* **d** have saved thy life, and	3117
	19: 6	for thou hast declared *this* **d**, that thou	3117
	19: 6	for *this* **d** I perceive, that if Absalom had	3117
	19: 6	all we had died *this* **d**, then it had pleased	3117
	19:19	**d** that my lord the king went out of	3117
	19:20	I am come the first *this* **d** of all the house of	3117
	19:22	that ye should *this* **d** be adversaries unto	3117
	19:22	shall there any man be put to death *this* **d** in	3117
	19:22	for do not I know that I *am this* **d** king over	3117
	19:24	from the **d** the king departed until the day	3117
	19:24	from the day the king departed until the **d**	3117
	19:35	I *am this* **d** fourscore years old: *and* can I	3117
	20: 3	So they were shut up unto the **d** of their	3117
	21:10	the birds of the air to rest on them **by d**,	3119
	22: 1	**d** *that* the LORD had delivered him out of	3117
	22:19	They prevented me in the **d** of my	3117
	23:10	the LORD wrought a great victory that **d**;	3117
	24:18	Gad came that **d** to David, and said unto	3117
1Ki	1:25	For he is gone down *this* **d**, and hath slain	3117
	1:30	my stead; even so will I certainly do this **d**.	3117
	1:48	hath given *one* to sit on my throne *this* **d**,	3117
	1:51	**to d** that he will not slay his	3117+1886.1
	2: 8	curse in the **d** when I went *to* Mahanaim:	3117
	2:24	Adonijah shall be put to death *this* **d**.	3117
	2:37	*that* on the **d** thou goest out, and	3117
	2:42	on the **d** thou goest out, and walkest *abroad*	3117
	3: 6	him a son to sit on his throne, as *it is* this **d**.	3117
	3:18	it came to pass the third **d** after that I was	3117
	4:22	Solomon's provision for one **d** was thirty	3117
	5: 7	and said, Blessed *be* the LORD *this* **d**,	3117
	8: 8	seen without: and there they are unto this **d**.	3117
	8:16	Since the **d** that I brought forth my people	3117
	8:24	fulfilled *it* with thine hand, as *it is* this **d**.	3117
	8:28	servant prayeth before thee **to d**:	3117+1886.1
	8:29	may be open toward this house night and **d**,	3117
	8:59	be nigh unto the LORD our God **d** and	3119
	8:61	to keep his commandments, as at this **d**.	3117
	8:64	The same **d** did the king hallow the middle	3117
	8:66	On the eighth **d** he sent the people away:	3117
	9:13	called them the land of Cabul unto this **d**.	3117
	9:21	levy a tribute of bondservice unto this **d**.	3117
	10:12	such almug trees, nor were seen unto this **d**.	3117
	12: 7	wilt be a servant unto this people *this* **d**,	3117
	12:12	the people came to Rehoboam the third **d**,	3117
	12:12	saying, Come to me again the third **d**.	3117
	12:19	against the house of David unto this **d**.	3117
	12:32	on the fifteenth **d** of the month, like unto	3117
	12:33	Beth-el the fifteenth **d** of the eighth month,	3117
	13: 3	he gave a sign the same **d**, saying, This *is*	3117
	13:11	the man of God had done *that* **d** in Beth-el:	3117
	14:14	shall cut off the house of Jeroboam that **d**:	3117
	16:16	king over Israel that **d** in the camp.	3117
	17:14	until the **d** *that* the LORD sendeth rain	3117
	18:15	surely shew myself unto him **to d**.	3117+1886.1
	18:36	let it be known *this* **d** that thou *art* God in	3117
	20:13	I will deliver it into thine hand *this* **d**;	3117
	20:29	that in the seventh **d** the battle was joined:	3117
	20:29	an hundred thousand footmen in one **d**.	3117
	22: 5	at the word of the LORD **to d**.	3117+1886.1
	22:25	Behold, thou shalt see in that **d**,	3117
	22:35	the battle increased that **d**: and the king was	3117
2Ki	2: 3	thy master from thy head **to d**?	3117+1886.1
	2: 5	thy master from thy head **to d**?	3117+1886.1
	2:22	So the waters were healed unto this **d**,	3117
	4: 8	it fell on a **d**, that Elisha passed to Shunem,	3117
	4:11	it fell on a **d**, that he came thither, and	3117
	4:18	when the child was grown, it fell on a **d**,	3117
	4:23	wilt thou go to him **to d**?	3117+1886.1
	6:28	that we may eat him **to d**, and we	3117+1886.1
	6:29	I said unto her on the next **d**, Give thy son,	3117
	6:31	son of Shaphat shall stand on him *this* **d**.	3117
	7: 9	this **d** *is* a day of good tidings, and we hold	3117
	7: 9	this day *is* a **d** of good tidings, and we hold	3117
	8: 6	all the fruits of the field since the **d** that she	3117
	8:22	from under the hand of Judah unto this **d**.	3117
	10:27	and made it a draught house unto *this* **d**.	3117
	14: 7	called the name of it Joktheel unto this **d**.	3117
	15: 5	that he was a leper unto the **d** of his death,	3117
	16: 6	came *to* Elath, and dwelt there unto this **d**.	3117
	17:23	out of their own land to Assyria unto this **d**.	3117
	17:34	Unto this **d** they do after the former	3117
	17:41	as did their fathers, *so* do they unto this **d**.	3117
	19: 3	This **d** *is* a day of trouble, and of rebuke,	3117
	19: 3	This day *is* a **d** of trouble, and of rebuke,	3117
	20: 5	on the third **d** thou shalt go up *unto*	3117
	20: 8	*into* the house of the LORD the third **d**?	3117
	20:17	thy fathers have laid up in store unto this **d**,	3117
	21:15	since the **d** their fathers came forth out of	3117
	21:15	came forth out of Egypt, even unto this **d**.	3117
	25: 1	the tenth month, in the tenth *d* of the month,	NIH
	25: 3	on the ninth *d* of the *fourth* month	NIH
	25: 8	fifth month, on the seventh *d* of the month,	NIH
	25:27	on the seven and twentieth *d* of the month,	NIH
	25:30	a daily rate for every **d**, all the days of his	3117
1Ch	4:41	destroyed them utterly unto this **d**, and	3117
	4:43	were escaped, and dwelt there unto this **d**.	3117
	5:26	Hara, and to the river Gozan, unto this **d**.	3117
	9:33	for they were employed in *that* work **d** and	3119
	11:22	and slew a lion in a pit in a snowy **d**.	3117
	12:22	For at *that* time **d** by day there came to	3117
	12:22	For at *that* time day by **d** there came to	3117
	13:11	that place is called Perez-uzza to this **d**.	3117
	13:12	David was afraid of God that **d**, saying,	3117
	16: 7	on that **d** David delivered first *this psalm* to	3117
	16:23	shew forth from **d** to day his salvation.	3117
	16:23	shew forth from day to **d** his salvation.	3117
	17: 5	For I have not dwelt in a house since the **d**	3117
	17: 5	the day that I brought up Israel unto this **d**;	3117
	26:17	northward four a **d**, southward four a day,	3117
	26:17	southward four a **d**, and toward Asuppim	3117
	28: 7	and my judgments, as *at* this **d**.	3117
	29: 5	is willing to consecrate his service *this* **d**	3117
	29:21	on the morrow after that **d**, *even* a thousand	3117
	29:22	drink before the LORD on that **d** with	3117
2Ch	3: 2	he began to build in the second *d* of	NIH
	5: 9	not seen without. And there it is unto this **d**.	3117
	6: 5	Since the **d** that I brought forth my people	3117
	6:15	fulfilled *it* with thine hand, as *it is* this **d**.	3117
	6:20	thine eyes may be open upon this house **d**	3119
	7: 9	in the eighth **d** they made a solemn	3117
	7:10	twentieth **d** of the seventh month he sent	3117
	8: 8	Solomon make to pay tribute until this **d**.	3117
	8:13	after a certain rate **every d**,	3117+3117+871.1
	8:14	the duty of **every d** required:	3117+3117+871.1
	8:16	**d** of the foundation of the house of	3117
	10:12	people came to Rehoboam on the third **d**,	3117
	10:12	saying, Come again to me on the third **d**.	3117
	10:19	against the house of David unto this **d**.	3117
	18: 4	at the word of the LORD **to d**.	3117+1886.1
	18:24	thou shalt see on that **d** when thou shalt go	3117
	18:34	the battle increased that **d**: howbeit the king	3117
	20:26	on the fourth **d** they assembled themselves	3117
	20:26	The valley of Berachah, unto *this* **d**.	3117
	21:10	from under the hand of Judah unto this **d**.	3117
	21:15	fall out by reason of the sickness **d** by day.	3117
	21:15	fall out by reason of the sickness day by **d**.	3117
	24:11	Thus they did **d** by day, and	3117
	24:11	Thus they did day by **d**, and	3117
	26:21	Uzziah the king was a leper unto the **d** of	3117
	28: 6	an hundred and twenty thousand in one **d**,	3117
	29:17	Now they began on the first *d* of the first	NIH
	29:17	on the eighth **d** of the month came they to	3117

2Ch	29:17	in the sixteenth **d** of the first month they	3117
	30:15	they killed the passover on the fourteenth *d*	NIH
	30:21	the priests praised the LORD **d** by day,	3117
	30:21	the priests praised the LORD day by **d**,	3117
	35:1	they killed the passover on the fourteenth *d*	NIH
	35:16	of the LORD was prepared the same **d**,	3117
	35:21	*I come* not against thee *this* **d**, but	3117
	35:25	of Josiah in their lamentations to *this* **d**,	3117
Ezr	3:4	the duty of **every d** required;	3117+3117+871.1
	3:6	From the first **d** of the seventh month	3117
	6:9	let *it* be given them **d** by day without fail:	3118
	6:9	let *it* be given them day by **d** without fail:	3118
	6:15	this house was finished on the third **d** of	3118
	6:19	upon the fourteenth *d* of the first month.	NIH
	7:9	For upon the first *d* of the first month began	NIH
	7:9	on the first *d* of the fifth month came he to	NIH
	8:31	of Ahava on the twelfth *d* of the first month,	NIH
	8:33	Now on the fourth **d** was the silver and	3117
	9:7	we *been* in a great trespass unto this **d**;	3117
	9:7	and to confusion of face, as *it is* this **d**.	3117
	9:15	for we remain *yet* escaped, as *it is* this **d**:	3117
	10:9	on the twentieth *d* of the month;	NIH
	10:13	neither *is this* a work of one **d** or two:	3117
	10:16	sat down in the first **d** of the tenth month to	3117
	10:17	wives by the first **d** of the first month.	3117
Ne	1:6	which I pray before thee now, **d** and night,	3119
	1:11	thy servant *this* **d**, and grant him mercy in	3117
	4:2	will they make an end in a **d**? will they	3117
	4:9	set a watch against them **d** and night,	3119
	4:22	may be a guard to us, and labour on the **d**.	3117
	5:11	Restore, I pray you, to them, even *this* **d**,	3117
	6:15	in the twenty and fifth *d* of *the month* Elul,	NIH
	8:2	upon the first **d** of the seventh month.	3117
	8:9	*This* **d** *is* holy unto the LORD your God;	3117
	8:10	for *this* **d** *is* holy unto our Lord: neither be	3117
	8:11	Hold your peace, for the **d** *is* holy;	3117
	8:13	on the second **d** were gathered together	3117
	8:17	**d** had not the children of Israel done so.	3117
	8:18	Also **d** by day, from the first day unto	3117
	8:18	Also day by **d**, from the first day unto	3117
	8:18	by day, from the first **d** unto the last day,	3117
	8:18	by day, from the first day unto the last **d**,	3117
	8:18	and on the eighth **d** *was* a solemn assembly,	3117
	9:1	fourth **d** of this month the children of Israel	3117
	9:3	LORD their God *one* fourth *part* of the **d**;	3117
	9:10	So didst thou get thee a name, as *it is* this **d**.	3117
	9:12	Moreover thou leddest them in the **d** by a	3119
	9:19	of the cloud departed not from them by **d**,	3119
	9:32	the time of the kings of Assyria unto this **d**.	3117
	9:36	we *are* servants *this* **d**, and *for* the land that	3117
	10:31	or any victuals on the sabbath **d** to sell,	3117
	10:31	*it* of them on the sabbath, or on the holy **d**:	3117
	11:23	the singers, due **for every d**.	3117+3117+871.1
	12:43	Also that **d** they offered great sacrifices,	3117
	12:47	**every d** his portion:	3117+3117+871.1
	13:1	On that **d** they read in the book of Moses in	3117
	13:15	brought *into* Jerusalem on the sabbath **d**:	3117
	13:15	I testified *against them* in the **d** wherein	3117
	13:17	this that ye do, and profane the sabbath **d**?	3117
	13:19	no burden be brought in on the sabbath **d**.	3117
	13:22	keep the gates, to sanctify the sabbath **d**.	3117
Est	1:10	On the seventh **d**, when the heart of	3117
	1:18	Media say this **d** unto all the king's princes,	3117
	2:11	**every d** before	3117+3117+3605+2050.1
	3:7	before Haman from **d** to day, and	3117
	3:7	before Haman from day to **d**, and	3117
	3:12	called on the thirteenth **d** of the first month,	3117
	3:13	little children and women, in one **d**,	3117
	3:13	*even* upon the thirteenth *d* of the twelfth	NIH
	3:14	that *they* should be ready against that **d**.	3117
	4:16	neither eat nor drink three days, night or **d**;	3117
	5:1	Now it came to pass on the third **d**,	3117
	5:4	Haman come *this* **d** unto the banquet that I	3117
	5:9	went Haman forth that **d** joyful and with a	3117
	7:2	on the second **d** at the banquet of wine,	3117
	8:1	On that **d** did the king Ahasuerus give	3117
	8:9	on the three and twentieth *d* thereof;	NIH
	8:12	Upon one **d** in all the provinces of king	3117
	8:12	*namely,* upon the thirteenth *d* of the twelfth	NIH
	8:13	that the Jews should be ready against that **d**	3117
	8:17	had joy and gladness, a feast and a good **d**.	3117
	9:1	on the thirteenth **d** of the same,	3117
	9:1	in the **d** that the enemies of the Jews hoped	3117
	9:11	On that **d** the number of those that were	3117
	9:15	on the fourteenth **d** also of the month Adar,	3117
	9:17	On the thirteenth **d** of the month Adar; and	3117
	9:17	on the fourteenth *d* of the same rested they,	NIH
	9:17	and made it a **d** of feasting and gladness.	3117
	9:18	together on the thirteenth *d* thereof,	NIH
	9:18	on the fifteenth *d* of the same they rested,	NIH
	9:18	and made it a **d** of feasting and gladness.	3117
	9:19	made the fourteenth **d** of the month Adar *a*	3117
	9:19	day of the month Adar *a d of* gladness	NIH
	9:19	a good **d**, and *of* sending portions one to	3117
	9:21	that they should keep the fourteenth **d** of	3117
	9:21	and the fifteenth **d** of the same, yearly,	3117
	9:22	to joy, and from mourning into a good **d**:	3117
Job	1:4	and feasted *in their* houses, every one his **d**;	3117
	1:6	Now there was a **d** when the sons of God	3117
	1:13	there was a **d** when his sons and	3117
	2:1	Again there was a **d** when the sons of God	3117
	3:1	opened Job his mouth, and cursed his **d**.	3117
	3:3	Let the **d** perish wherein I was born, and	3117
	3:4	Let that **d** be darkness; let not God regard it	3117
	3:5	upon it; let the blackness of the **d** terrify it.	3117
	3:8	Let them curse it that curse the **d**, who are	3117
	3:9	neither let it see the dawning of the **d**:	7837
	7:4	and fro unto the **dawning of the d**.	5399
	14:6	till he shall accomplish, as a hireling, his **d**.	3117
	15:23	*saying,* Where *is it?* he knoweth that the **d**	3117
	17:12	They change the night into **d**: the light *is*	3117
	18:20	come after *him* shall be astonied at his **d**,	3117
	19:25	*that* he shall stand *at* the latter *d* upon	NIH
	20:28	*his goods shall* flow away in the **d** of his	3117
	21:30	That the wicked is reserved to the **d** of	3117
	21:30	they shall be brought forth to the **d** of	3117
	23:2	Even **to d** *is* my complaint bitter:	3117+1886.1
	26:10	until the **d** and night come to an end.	216
	38:23	of trouble, against the **d** of battle and war?	3117
Ps	1:2	and in his law doth he meditate **d** and night.	3119
	2:7	*art* my Son; *this* **d** have I begotten thee.	3117
	7:11	and God is angry *with the wicked* every **d**.	3117
	18:T	**d** *that* the LORD delivered him from	3117
	18:18	They prevented me in the **d** of my	3117
	19:2	**D** unto day uttereth speech, and night unto	3117
	19:2	Day unto **d** uttereth speech, and night unto	3117
	20:1	The LORD hear thee in the **d** of trouble;	3117
	25:5	of my salvation; on thee do I wait all the **d**.	3117
	32:3	old through my roaring all the **d** long.	3117
	32:4	For **d** and night thy hand was heavy upon	3119
	35:28	*and* of thy praise all the **d** long.	3117
	37:13	at him: for he seeth that his **d** is coming.	3117
	38:6	down greatly; I go mourning all the **d** long.	3117
	38:12	and imagine deceits all the **d** long.	3117
	42:3	My tears have been my meat **d** and night,	3119
	44:8	In God we boast all the **d** long, and	3117
	44:22	for thy sake are we killed all the **d** long;	3117
	50:15	call upon me in the **d** of trouble: I will	3117
	55:10	**D** and night they go about it upon the walls	3119
	56:5	Every **d** they wrest my words: all their	3117
	59:16	and refuge in the **d** of my trouble.	3117
	71:8	thy praise *and with* thy honour all the **d**.	3117
	71:15	*and* thy salvation all the **d**;	3117
	71:24	talk of thy righteousness all the **d** long:	3117
	73:14	For all the **d** long have I been plagued, and	3117
	74:16	The **d** *is* thine, the night also *is* thine:	3117
	77:2	In the **d** of my trouble I sought the Lord:	3117
	78:9	turned *back* in the **d** of battle.	3117
	78:42	*nor* the **d** when he delivered them from	3117
	81:3	the time appointed, on our solemn feast **d**.	3117
	84:10	For a **d** in thy courts *is* better than a	3117
	86:7	In the **d** of my trouble I will call upon thee:	3117
	88:1	I have cried **d** *and* night before thee:	3117
	89:16	In thy name shall they rejoice all the **d**: and	3117
	91:5	by night; *nor* for the arrow *that* flieth **by d**;	3119
	92:T	A Psalm *or* Song for the sabbath **d**.	3117
	95:7	**To d** if ye will hear his voice,	3117+1886.1
	95:8	as *in* the **d** of temptation in the wilderness:	3117
	96:2	shew forth his salvation from **d** to day.	3117
	96:2	shew forth his salvation from day to **d**.	3117
	102:2	Hide not thy face from me in the **d** *when* I	3117
	102:2	in the **d** *when* I call answer me speedily.	3117
	102:8	Mine enemies reproach me all the **d**; *and*	3117
	110:3	Thy people *shall be* willing in the **d** of thy	3117
	110:5	strike through kings in the **d** of his wrath.	3117
	118:24	This *is* the **d** *which* the LORD hath made;	3117
	119:91	They continue *this* **d** according to thine	3117
	119:97	love I thy law! it *is* my meditation all the **d**.	3117

Ps119:164 Seven *times* a **d** do I praise thee because 3117
121: 6 The sun shall not smite thee **by d**, nor 3119
136: 8 The sun to rule by **d**: for his mercy 3117
137: 7 the children of Edom *in* the **d** of Jerusalem; 3117
138: 3 In the **d** when I cried thou answeredst me, 3117
139:12 from thee; but the night shineth as the **d**: 3117
140: 7 thou hast covered my head in the **d** of 3117
145: 2 Every **d** will I bless thee; and I will praise 3117
146: 4 his earth; in that *very* **d** his thoughts perish. 3117
Pr 4:18 shineth more and more unto the perfect **d**. 3117
6:34 he will not spare in the **d** of vengeance. 3117
7:14 with me; *this* **d** have I payed my vows. 3117
7:20 will come home at the **d** appointed. 3117
11: 4 Riches profit not in the **d** of wrath: but 3117
16: 4 even the wicked for the **d** of evil. 3117
21:26 He coveteth greedily all the **d** long: but 3117
21:31 The horse *is* prepared against the **d** of 3117
22:19 I have made known to thee *this* **d**, even *to* 3117
23:17 *be thou* in the fear of the LORD all the **d** 3117
24:10 *If* thou faint in the **d** of adversity, 3117
27: 1 for thou knowest not what a **d** may bring 3117
27:10 neither go *into* thy brother's house in the **d** 3117
27:15 A continual dropping in a very rainy **d** and 3117
Ecc 7: 1 the **d** of death than the day of one's birth. 3117
7: 1 the day of death than the **d** of one's birth. 3117
7:14 In the **d** of prosperity be joyful, but in 3117
7:14 be joyful, but in the **d** of adversity consider: 3117
8: 8 neither *hath he* power in the **d** of death: 3117
8:16 (for also *there is that* neither **d** nor night 3117
12: 3 In the **d** when the keepers of the house shall 3117
SS 2:17 Until the **d** break, and the shadows flee 3117
3:11 crowned him in the **d** of his espousals, 3117
3:11 and in the **d** of the gladness of his heart. 3117
4: 6 Until the **d** break, and the shadows flee 3117
8: 8 what shall we do for our sister in the **d** 3117
Isa 2:11 the LORD alone shall be exalted in that **d**. 3117
2:12 For the **d** of the LORD of hosts *shall be* 3117
2:17 the LORD alone shall be exalted in that **d**. 3117
2:20 In that **d** a man shall cast his idols of silver, 3117
3: 7 In that **d** shall he swear, saying, I will not 3117
3:18 In that **d** the Lord will take away 3117
4: 1 in that **d** seven women shall take hold of 3117
4: 2 In that **d** shall the branch of the LORD be 3117
4: 5 a cloud and smoke **by d**, and the shining of 3119
5:30 in that **d** they shall roar against them like 3117
7:17 from the **d** that Ephraim departed from 3117
7:18 it shall come to pass in that **d**, *that* 3117
7:20 In the same **d** shall the Lord shave with a 3117
7:21 it shall come to pass in that **d**, *that* a man 3117
7:23 it shall come to pass in that **d**, *that* every 3117
9: 4 rod of his oppressor, as *in* the **d** of Midian. 3117
9:14 and tail, branch and rush, *in* one **d**. 3117
10: 3 what will ye do in the **d** of visitation, and 3117
10:17 devour his thorns and his briers in one **d**; 3117
10:20 it shall come to pass in that **d**, *that* 3117
10:27 it shall come to pass in that **d**, *that* his 3117
10:32 As yet shall *he* remain at Nob *that* **d**: 3117
11:10 in that **d** there shall be a root of Jesse, 3117
11:11 it shall come to pass in that **d**, *that* the Lord 3117
11:16 like as it was to Israel in the **d** that he came 3117
12: 1 in that **d** thou shalt say, O LORD, I will 3117
12: 4 in that **d** shall ye say, Praise the LORD, 3117
13: 6 for the **d** of the LORD *is* at hand; 3117
13: 9 Behold, the **d** of the LORD cometh, 3117
13:13 of hosts, and in the **d** of his fierce anger. 3117
14: 3 it shall come to pass in the **d** that 3117
17: 4 in that **d** it shall come to pass, *that* the glory 3117
17: 7 At that **d** shall a man look to his Maker, 3117
17: 9 In that **d** shall his strong cities be as a 3117
17:11 In the **d** shalt thou make thy plant to grow, 3117
17:11 the harvest *shall be* a heap in the **d** of grief 3117
19:16 In that **d** shall Egypt be like unto women: 3117
19:18 In that **d** shall five cities in the land of 3117
19:19 In that **d** shall there be an altar to 3117
19:21 Egyptians shall know the LORD in that **d**, 3117
19:23 In that **d** shall there be a highway out of 3117
19:24 In that **d** shall Israel be the third with Egypt 3117
20: 6 the inhabitant of this isle shall say in that **d**, 3117
22: 5 For *it is* a **d** of trouble, and of treading 3117
22: 8 thou didst look in that **d** to the armour of 3117
22:12 in that **d** did the Lord GOD of hosts call to 3117
22:20 it shall come to pass in that **d**, that I will 3117
22:25 In that **d**, saith the LORD of hosts, 3117
23:15 it shall come to pass in that **d**, that Tyre 3117
24:21 it shall come to pass in that **d**, *that* 3117
25: 9 it shall be said in that **d**, Lo, this *is* our 3117
26: 1 In that **d** shall this song be sung in the land 3117
27: 1 In that **d** the LORD with his sore and 3117
27: 2 In that **d** sing ye unto her, A vineyard of 3117
27: 3 lest *any* hurt it, I will keep it night and **d**. 3117
27: 8 he stayeth his rough wind in the **d** of 3117
27:12 it shall come to pass in that **d**, *that* 3117
27:13 it shall come to pass in that **d**, *that* the great 3117
28: 5 In that **d** shall the LORD of hosts be for a 3117
28:19 shall it pass over, by **d** and by night: 3117
28:24 Doth the plowman plow all **d** to sow? 3117
29:18 in that **d** shall the deaf hear the words of 3117
30:23 in that **d** shall thy cattle feed *in* large 3117
30:25 streams of waters in the **d** of the great 3117
30:26 in the **d** that the LORD bindeth up 3117
31: 7 For in that **d** every man shall cast away his 3117
34: 8 For *it is* the **d** of the LORD'S vengeance, 3117
34:10 It shall not be quenched night nor **d**; 3119
37: 3 This **d** *is* a day of trouble, and of rebuke, 3117
37: 3 This day *is* a **d** of trouble, and of rebuke, 3117
38:12 from **d** *even* to night wilt thou make an end 3117
38:13 from **d** *even* to night wilt thou make an end 3117
38:19 he shall praise thee, as I *do this* **d**: 3117
39: 6 thy fathers have laid up in store until this **d**, 3117
43:13 Yea, before the **d** *was* I *am* he; and *there is* 3117
47: 9 shall come to thee *in* a moment in one **d**, 3117
48: 7 even before the **d** when thou heardest them 3117
49: 8 and in a **d** of salvation have I helped thee: 3117
51:13 hast feared continually every **d** because of 3117
52: 5 my name continually every **d** *is* 3117
52: 6 *they shall know* in that **d** that I *am* he that 3117
56:12 to morrow shall be as this **d**, *and* 3117
58: 3 in the **d** of your fast you find pleasure, and 3117
58: 4 ye shall not fast as *ye do this* **d**, to make 3117
58: 5 a **d** for a man to afflict his soul? *is it* to bow 3117
58: 5 a fast, and an acceptable **d** to the LORD? 3117
58:13 *from* doing thy pleasure on my holy **d**; 3117
60:11 they shall not be shut **d** nor night; 3119
60:19 The sun shall be no more thy light **by d**; 3119
61: 2 and the **d** of vengeance of our God; 3117
62: 6 *which* shall never hold their peace **d** nor 3117
63: 4 For the **d** of vengeance *is* in mine heart, 3117
65: 2 I have spread out mine hands all the **d** unto 3117
65: 5 in my nose, a fire that burneth all the **d**. 3117
66: 8 the earth be made to bring forth in one **d**? 3117
Jer 1:10 I have this **d** set thee over the nations and 3117
1:18 I have made thee *this* **d** a defenced city, and 3117
3:25 from our youth even unto this **d**, and 3117
4: 9 it shall come to pass at that **d**, saith 3117
6: 4 for the **d** goeth away, for the shadows of 3117
7:22 nor commanded them in the **d** that I 3117
7:25 Since the **d** that your fathers came forth out 3117
7:25 forth out of the land of Egypt unto this **d**, 3117
9: 1 that I might weep **d** and night for the slain 3119
11: 4 Which I commanded your fathers in the **d** 3117
11: 5 flowing with milk and honey, as *it is* this **d**. 3117
11: 7 **d** that I brought them up out of the land of 3117
11: 7 *even* unto this **d**, rising early and 3117
12: 3 and prepare them for the **d** of slaughter. 3117
14:17 mine eyes run down *with* tears night and **d**, 3119
15: 9 her sun is gone down while *it was* yet **d**: 3119
16:13 there shall ye serve other gods **d** and night; 3119
16:19 and my refuge in the **d** of affliction, 3117
17:16 neither have I desired the woeful **d**; 3117
17:17 unto me: thou *art* my hope in the **d** of evil. 3117
17:18 bring upon them the **d** of evil, and 3117
17:21 bear no burden on the sabbath **d**, 3117
17:22 burden out of your houses on the sabbath **d**, 3117
17:22 ye any work, but hallow ye the sabbath **d**, 3117
17:24 the gates of this city on the sabbath **d**, 3117
17:24 hallow the sabbath **d**, to do no work 3117
17:27 hearken unto me to hallow the sabbath **d**, 3117
17:27 at the gates of Jerusalem on the sabbath **d**; 3117
18:17 and not the face, in the **d** of their calamity. 3117
20:14 Cursed *be* the **d** wherein I was born: let not 3117
20:14 let not the **d** wherein my mother bare me be 3117
25: 3 even unto this **d**, that *is* the three and 3117
25:18 a hissing, and a curse; as *it is* this **d**; 3117
25:33 the slain of the LORD shall be at that **d** 3117
27:22 there shall they be until the **d** that I visit 3117
30: 7 for that **d** *is* great, so that none *is* like it: 3117
30: 8 For it shall come to pass in that **d**, saith 3117
31: 6 For there shall be a **d**, *that* the watchmen 3117

Jer 31:32 in the **d** *that* I took them by the hand, 3117
31:35 which giveth the sun for a light **by d**, *and* 3119
32:20 *even* unto this **d**, and in Israel, and 3117
32:20 and hast made thee a name, as *at* this **d**; 3117
32:31 of my fury from the **d** that they built it even 3117
32:31 the day that they built it even unto this **d**; 3117
33:20 If you can break my covenant of the **d**, and 3117
33:20 that there should not be **d** and night in their 3119
33:25 If my covenant *be* not with **d** and night, *and* 3119
34:13 made a covenant with your fathers in the **d** 3117
35:14 for unto this **d** they drink none, but 3117
36: 2 the nations, from the **d** I spake unto thee, 3117
36: 2 from the days of Josiah, even unto this **d**. 3117
36: 6 *in* the LORD's house upon the fasting **d**: 3117
36:30 his dead body shall be cast out in the **d** to 3117
38:28 prison until the **d** that Jerusalem was taken: 3117
39: 2 the fourth month, the ninth *d* of the month, NIH
39:16 they shall be *accomplished* in that **d** before 3117
39:17 I will deliver thee in that **d**, saith 3117
40: 4 I loose thee *this* **d** from the chains which 3117
41: 4 it came to pass the second **d** after *he* had 3117
42:19 certainly that I have admonished you *this* **d**. 3117
42:21 *now* I have *this* **d** declared *it* to you; but 3117
44: 2 this **d** they *are* a desolation, and no man 3117
44: 6 they are wasted *and* desolate, as *at* this **d**. 3117
44:10 They are not humbled *even* unto this **d**, 3117
44:22 a curse, without an inhabitant, as *at* this **d**. 3117
44:23 this evil is happened unto you, as *at* this **d**. 3117
46:10 For this *is* the **d** of the Lord GOD of hosts, 3117
46:10 a **d** of vengeance, that *he* may avenge him 3117
46:21 the **d** of their calamity was come upon 3117
47: 4 Because of the **d** that cometh to spoil all 3117
48:41 the mighty *men's* hearts in Moab at that **d** 3117
49:22 at that **d** shall the heart of the mighty *men* 3117
49:26 all the men of war shall be cut off in that **d**, 3117
50:27 for their **d** is come, the time of their 3117
50:30 all her men of war shall be cut off in that **d**, 3117
50:31 for thy **d** is come, the time *that* I will visit 3117
51: 2 for in the **d** of trouble they shall be against 3117
52: 4 the tenth month, in the tenth *d* of the month, NIH
52: 6 fourth month, in the ninth *d* of the month, NIH
52:11 and put him in prison till the **d** of his death. 3117
52:12 the fifth month, in the tenth *d* of the month, NIH
52:31 in the five and twentieth *d* of the month, NIH
52:34 **every d** a portion until 3117+3117+871.1
52:34 every day a portion until the **d** of his death, 3117
La 1:12 afflicted *me* in the **d** of his fierce anger. 3117
1:13 hath made me desolate *and* faint all the **d**. 3117
1:21 thou wilt bring the **d** *that* thou hast called, 3117
2: 1 remembered not his footstool in the **d** of his 3117
2: 7 the LORD, as *in* the **d** of a solemn feast. 3117
2:16 certainly this *is* the **d** that we looked for; 3117
2:18 let tears run down like a river **d** and night: 3119
2:21 thou hast slain *them* in the **d** of thine anger; 3117
2:22 Thou hast called as *in* a solemn **d** my 3117
2:22 that in the **d** of the LORD's anger none 3117
3: 3 he turneth his hand *against me* all the **d**. 3117
3:14 to all my people; *and* their song all the **d**. 3117
3:57 Thou drewest near in the **d** *that* I called 3117
3:62 and their device against me all the **d**. 3117
Eze 1: 1 in the fourth *month,* in the fifth *d* of NIH
1: 2 In the fifth *d* of the month, which *was* NIH
1:28 the bow that is in the cloud in the **d** of rain, 3117
2: 3 against me, *even* unto this very **d**. 3117
4: 6 appointed thee **each d** for a year. 3117+3117
4:10 eat *shall be* by weight, twenty shekels a **d**: 3117
7: 7 the **d** of trouble *is* near, and not 3117
7:10 Behold the **d**, behold, it is come: 3117
7:12 The time is come, the **d** draweth near: 3117
7:19 them in the **d** of the wrath of the LORD: 3117
8: 1 in the sixth *month,* in the fifth *d* of NIH
12: 3 and remove **by d** in their sight; 3119
12: 4 shalt thou bring forth thy stuff **by d** in their 3119
12: 7 I brought forth my stuff **by d**, as stuff for 3119
13: 5 stand in the battle in the **d** of the LORD. 3117
16: 4 in the **d** thou wast born thy navel was not 3117
16: 5 of thy person, in the **d** that thou wast born. 3117
16:56 by thy mouth in the **d** of thy pride, 3117
20: 1 in the fifth *month,* the tenth *d* of the month, NIH
20: 5 In the **d** when I chose Israel, and lifted up 3117
20: 6 In the **d** *that* I lifted up mine hand unto 3117
20:29 name thereof is called Bamah unto this **d**. 3117
20:31 with all your idols, *even* unto *this* **d**: 3117
21:25 wicked prince of Israel, whose **d** is come, 3117
21:29 whose **d** is come, when *their* iniquity *shall* 3117
22:24 nor rained upon in the **d** of indignation. 3117
23:38 have defiled my sanctuary in the same **d**, 3117
23:39 they came the same **d** into my sanctuary to 3117
24: 1 the tenth month, in the tenth *d* of the month, NIH
24: 2 Son of man, write thee the name of the **d**, 3117
24: 2 the name of the day, *even* of this same **d**: 3117
24: 2 set himself against Jerusalem this same **d**. 3117
24:25 *shall it* not *be* in the **d** when I take from 3117
24:26 *That* he that escapeth in that **d** shall come 3117
24:27 In that **d** shall thy mouth be opened to him 3117
26: 1 eleventh year, in the first *d* of the month, NIH
26:18 Now shall the isles tremble *in* the **d** of thy 3117
27:27 shall fall into the midst of the seas in the **d** 3117
28:13 of thy pipes was prepared in thee in the **d** 3117
28:15 Thou *wast* perfect in thy ways from the **d** 3117
29: 1 in the tenth *month,* in the twelfth *d* of NIH
29:17 in the first *month,* in the first *d* of NIH
29:21 In that **d** will I cause the horn of the house 3117
30: 2 Lord GOD; Howl ye, Woe worth the **d**! 3117
30: 3 For the **d** *is* near, even the day of 3117
30: 3 even the **d** of the LORD *is* near, a cloudy 3117
30: 3 the day of the LORD *is* near, a cloudy **d**; 3117
30: 9 In that **d** shall messengers go forth from me 3117
30: 9 shall come upon them, as *in* the **d** of Egypt: 3117
30:18 At Tehaphnehes also the **d** shall be 3117
30:20 in the first *month,* in the seventh *d* of NIH
31: 1 in the third *month,* in the first *d* of NIH
31:15 In the **d** when he went down to the grave I 3117
32: 1 twelfth month, in the first *d* of the month, NIH
32:10 man for his own life, in the **d** of thy fall. 3117
32:17 twelfth year, in the fifteenth *d* of the month, NIH
33:12 deliver him in the **d** of his transgression: 3117
33:12 he shall not fall thereby in the **d** that he 3117
33:12 his *righteousness* in the **d** that he sinneth. 3117
33:21 in the tenth *month,* in the fifth *d* of NIH
34:12 As a shepherd seeketh out his flock in the **d** 3117
34:12 been scattered in the cloudy and dark **d**. 3117
36:33 In the **d** that I shall have cleansed you from 3117
38:14 In that **d** when my people of Israel dwelleth 3117
38:19 Surely in that **d** there shall be a great 3117
39: 8 this *is* the **d** whereof I have spoken. 3117
39:11 it shall come to pass in that **d**, *that* I will 3117
39:13 it shall be to them a renown the **d** that I 3117
39:22 that I *am* the LORD their God from that **d** 3117
40: 1 of the year, in the tenth *d* of the month, NIH
40: 1 in the selfsame **d** the hand of the LORD 3117
43:18 the altar in the **d** when *they* shall make it, 3117
43:22 on the second **d** thou shalt offer a kid of 3117
43:25 Seven days shalt thou prepare every **d** a 3117
43:27 *that* upon the eight **d**, and *so* forward, 3117
44:27 in the **d** that he goeth into the sanctuary, 3117
45:18 In the first *month,* in the first *d* of NIH
45:20 thou shalt do the seventh *d* of the month for NIH
45:21 In the first *month,* in the fourteenth **d** of 3117
45:22 upon that **d** shall the prince prepare for 3117
45:25 In the seventh *month,* in the fifteenth **d** of 3117
46: 1 in the **d** of the new moon it shall be opened. 3117
46: 4 **d** *shall be* six lambs without blemish, 3117
46: 6 in the **d** of the new moon *it shall be* a 3117
46:12 peace offerings, as he did on the sabbath **d**: 3117
48:35 the name of the city from *that* **d** *shall be,* 3117
Da 6:10 he kneeled upon his knees three times a **d**, 3118
6:13 but maketh his petition three times a **d**. 3118
9: 7 but unto us confusion of faces, as *at* this **d**; 3117
9:15 and hast gotten thee renown, as *at* this **d**; 3117
10: 4 the four and twentieth **d** of the first month, 3117
10:12 for from the first **d** that thou didst set thine 3117
Hos 1: 5 it shall come to pass at that **d**, that I will 3117
1:11 the land: for great *shall be* the **d** of Jezreel. 3117
2: 3 set her as *in* the **d** that she was born, and 3117
2:15 as *in* the **d** when she came up out of 3117
2:16 it shall be at that **d**, saith the LORD, 3117
2:18 in that **d** will I make a covenant for them 3117
2:21 it shall come to pass in that **d**, I will hear, 3117
4: 5 Therefore shalt thou fall *in* the **d**, and 3117
5: 9 Ephraim shall be desolate in the **d** of 3117
6: 2 in the third **d** he will raise us up, and 3117
7: 5 *In* the **d** of our king the princes have made 3117
9: 5 What will ye do in the solemn **d**, and in 3117
9: 5 and in the **d** of the feast of the LORD? 3117
10:14 as Shalman spoiled Beth-arbel in the **d** of 3117
Joel 1:15 Alas for the **d**! for the day of the LORD *is* 3117
1:15 for the **d** of the LORD *is* at hand, and as a 3117

Joel	2: 1	for the **d** of the LORD cometh, for *it is*	3117
	2: 2	A **d** of darkness and of gloominess, a day	3117
	2: 2	a **d** of clouds and of thick darkness,	3117
	2:11	for the **d** of the LORD *is* great and	3117
	2:31	and the terrible **d** of the LORD come.	3117
	3:14	for the **d** of the LORD *is* near in the valley	3117
	3:18	it shall come to pass in that **d**, *that*	3117
Am	1:14	with shouting in the **d** of battle,	3117
	1:14	with a tempest in the **d** of the whirlwind:	3117
	2:16	the mighty shall flee away naked in that **d**,	3117
	3:14	That in the **d** that I shall visit	3117
	5: 8	and maketh the **d** dark *with* night:	3117
	5:18	Woe unto *you* that desire the **d** of	3117
	5:18	the **d** of the LORD *is* darkness, and	3117
	5:20	*Shall* not the **d** of the LORD *be* darkness,	3117
	6: 3	Ye that put far away the evil **d**, and	3117
	8: 3	of the temple shall be howlings in that **d**,	3117
	8: 9	it shall come to pass in that **d**, saith	3117
	8: 9	and I will darken the earth in the clear **d**:	3117
	8:10	only *son,* and the end thereof as a bitter **d**.	3117
	8:13	In that **d** shall the fair virgins and young	3117
	9:11	In that **d** will I raise up the tabernacle of	3117
Ob	1: 8	Shall I not in that **d**, saith the LORD,	3117
	1:11	In the **d** that thou stoodest on the other side,	3117
	1:11	in the **d** that the strangers carried away	3117
	1:12	thou shouldest not have looked on the **d** of	3117
	1:12	brother in the **d** that he became a stranger;	3117
	1:12	of Judah in the **d** of their destruction;	3117
	1:12	have spoken proudly in the **d** of distress.	3117
	1:13	of my people in the **d** of their calamity:	3117
	1:13	on their affliction in the **d** of their calamity,	3117
	1:13	their substance in the **d** of their calamity;	3117
	1:14	of his that did remain in the **d** of distress.	3117
	1:15	For the **d** of the LORD *is* near upon all	3117
Jnh	4: 7	a worm when the morning rose the **next d**,	4283
Mic	2: 4	In that **d** shall *one* take up a parable against	3117
	3: 6	and the **d** shall be dark over them.	3117
	4: 6	In that **d**, saith the LORD, will I assemble	3117
	5:10	it shall come to pass in that **d**, saith	3117
	7: 4	the **d** of thy watchmen *and* thy visitation	3117
	7:11	*In* the **d** that thy walls are *to be* built, *in* that	3117
	7:11	*in* that **d** shall the decree be far removed.	3117
	7:12	*In* that **d** *also* he shall come even to thee	3117
Na	1: 7	*is* good, a strong hold in the **d** of trouble;	3117
	2: 3	flaming torches in the **d** of his preparation,	3117
	3:17	which camp in the hedges in the cold **d**, *but*	3117
Hab	3:16	that I might rest in the **d** of trouble:	3117
Zep	1: 7	for the **d** of the LORD *is* at hand: for	3117
	1: 8	it shall come to pass in the **d** of	3117
	1: 9	In the same **d** also will I punish all those	3117
	1:10	it shall come to pass in that **d**, saith	3117
	1:14	The great **d** of the LORD *is* near, *it is*	3117
	1:14	*even* the voice of the **d** of the LORD:	3117
	1:15	That **d** *is* a day of wrath, a day of trouble	3117
	1:15	That day *is* a **d** of wrath, a day of trouble	3117
	1:15	a **d** of trouble and distress, a day of	3117
	1:15	distress, a **d** of wasteness and desolation,	3117
	1:15	desolation, a **d** of darkness and gloominess,	3117
	1:15	a **d** of clouds and thick darkness,	3117
	1:16	A **d** of the trumpet and alarm against	3117
	1:18	them in the **d** of the LORD'S wrath;	3117
	2: 2	bring forth, *before* the **d** pass as the chaff,	3117
	2: 2	before the **d** of the LORD'S anger come	3117
	2: 3	it may be ye shall be hid in the **d** of	3117
	2: 4	they shall drive out Ashdod at the **noon d**,	6672
	3: 8	until the **d** that I rise up to the prey:	3117
	3:11	In that **d** shalt thou not be ashamed for all	3117
	3:16	In that **d** it shall be said to Jerusalem,	3117
Hag	1: 1	the sixth month, in the first **d** of the month,	3117
	1:15	the four and twentieth **d** of the sixth month,	3117
	2: 1	in the one and twentieth *d* of the month,	NIH
	2:10	twentieth *d* of the ninth *month,* in	NIH
	2:15	pray you, consider from this **d** and upward,	3117
	2:18	Consider now from this **d** and upward,	3117
	2:18	twentieth **d** of the ninth *month, even* from	3117
	2:18	**d** that the foundation of the LORD'S	3117
	2:19	brought forth: from this **d** will I bless *you.*	3117
	2:20	in the four and twentieth *d* of the month,	NIH
	2:23	In that **d**, saith the LORD of hosts, will I	3117
Zec	1: 7	and twentieth **d** of the eleventh month,	3117
	2:11	shall be joined to the LORD in that **d**,	3117
	3: 9	remove the iniquity of that land in one **d**.	3117
	3:10	In that **d**, saith the LORD of hosts,	3117
	4:10	For who hath despised the **d** of small	3117
	6:10	come thou the same **d**, and go *into*	3117
	7: 1	in the fourth *d* of the ninth month,	NIH
	8: 9	which *were* in the **d** *that* the foundation of	3117
	9:12	even **to d** do I declare *that* I will	3117+1886.1
	9:16	them in that **d** as the flock of his people:	3117
	11:11	it was broken in that **d**: and so the poor of	3117
	12: 3	in that **d** will I make Jerusalem a	3117
	12: 4	In that **d**, saith the LORD, I will smite	3117
	12: 6	In that **d** will I make the governors of Judah	3117
	12: 8	In that **d** shall the LORD defend	3117
	12: 8	he that is feeble among them at that **d** shall	3117
	12: 9	it shall come to pass in that **d**, *that* I will	3117
	12:11	In that **d** shall there be a great mourning in	3117
	13: 1	In that **d** there shall be a fountain opened to	3117
	13: 2	it shall come to pass in that **d**, saith	3117
	13: 4	it shall come to pass in that **d**, *that*	3117
	14: 1	the **d** of the LORD cometh, and thy spoil	3117
	14: 3	as when he fought in the **d** of battle.	3117
	14: 4	his feet shall stand in that **d** upon the mount	3117
	14: 6	it shall come to pass in that **d**, *that* the light	3117
	14: 7	it shall be one **d** which shall be known to	3117
	14: 7	be known to the LORD, not **d**, nor night:	3117
	14: 8	it shall be in that **d**, *that* living waters shall	3117
	14: 9	in that **d** shall there be one LORD, and	3117
	14:13	it shall come to pass in that **d**, *that* a great	3117
	14:20	In that **d** shall there be upon the bells of	3117
	14:21	in that **d** there shall be no more	3117
Mal	3: 2	who *may* abide the **d** of his coming? and	3117
	3:17	in that **d** when I make *up my* jewels;	3117
	4: 1	For behold, the **d** cometh, that *shall* burn as	3117
	4: 1	the **d** that cometh shall burn them up, saith	3117
	4: 3	**d** that I *shall* do *this,* saith the LORD of	3117
	4: 5	of the great and dreadful **d** of the LORD:	3117
Mt	6:11	Give us **this d** our daily bread.	*4594*
	6:30	which **to d** is, and to morrow is cast into	*4594*
	6:34	Sufficient unto the **d** *is* the evil thereof.	*2250*
	7:22	Many will say to me in that **d**, Lord, Lord,	*2250*
	10:15	and Gomorrha in the **d** of judgment,	*2250*
	11:22	for Tyre and Sidon at the **d** of judgment,	*2250*
	11:23	it would have remained until **this d**.	*4594*
	11:24	for the land of Sodom in the **d** of judgment,	*2250*
	12: 1	At that time Jesus went on the sabbath **d**	NIG
	12: 2	is not lawful to do upon the sabbath **d**.	NIG
	12: 8	Son of man is Lord even of the sabbath **d**.	NIG
	12:11	and if it fall into a pit on the sabbath **d**,	NIG
	12:36	they shall give account thereof in the **d** of	*2250*
	13: 1	The same **d** went Jesus out of the house,	*2250*
	16: 3	in the morning, *It will be* foul weather **to d**:	*4594*
	16:21	be killed, and be raised *again* the third **d**.	*2250*
	17:23	the third **d** he shall be raised *again.* And	*2250*
	20: 2	agreed with the labourers for a penny a **d**,	*2250*
	20: 6	Why stand ye here all the **d** idle?	*2250*
	20:12	have borne the burden and heat of the **d**.	*2250*
	20:19	and the third **d** he shall rise again.	*2250*
	21:28	said, Son, go work **to d** in my vineyard.	*4594*
	22:23	The same **d** came to him *the* Sadducees,	*2250*
	22:46	neither durst any *man* from that **d** forth ask	*2250*
	24:20	not in the winter, neither on the sabbath **d**:	NIG
	24:36	But of that **d** and hour knoweth no *man,* no,	*2250*
	24:38	until the **d** that Noe entered into the ark,	*2250*
	24:50	The lord of that servant shall come in a **d**	*2250*
	25:13	for ye know neither the **d** nor the hour	*2250*
	26: 5	Not on the feast *d*, lest there be an uproar	NIG
	26:17	Now the first *d* of the *feast of* unleavened	NIG
	26:29	until that **d** when I drink it new with you in	*2250*
	27: 8	was called, The field of blood, unto **this d**.	*4594*
	27:19	suffered many *things* **this d** in a dream	*4594*
	27:62	Now the **next d**, that followed the *day of*	*1887*
	27:62	that followed the *d of the* preparation,	NIG
	27:64	the sepulchre be made sure until the third **d**,	*2250*
	28: 1	as it began to dawn towards the first *d* of	NIG
	28:15	reported among the Jews until **this d**.	*4594*
Mk	1:21	straightway on the sabbath **d** he entered into	NIG
	1:35	rising up a great while **before d**, he went	*1773*
	2:23	through the corn fields on the sabbath **d**;	NIG
	2:24	why do they on the sabbath **d** *that* which is	NIG
	3: 2	he would heal him on the sabbath **d**;	NIG
	4:27	and rise night and **d**, and the seed should	*2250*
	4:35	And the same **d**, when the even was come,	*2250*
	5: 5	And always, night and **d**, he was in	*2250*
	6: 2	And when the sabbath **d** was come,	NIG
	6:11	and Gomorrha in the **d** of judgment,	*2250*
	6:21	And when a convenient **d** was come,	*2250*
	6:35	And when the **d** was now far spent,	*5610*

Mk 9:31 that he is killed, he shall rise the third **d**. *2250*
10:34 kill him: and the third **d** he shall rise again. *2250*
13:32 But of that **d** and *that* hour knoweth no *2250*
14: 2 Not on the feast *d*, lest there be an uproar of NIG
14:12 And the first **d** of unleavened bread, *2250*
14:25 until that **d** that I drink it new in *2250*
14:30 unto thee, That **this d**, *even* in this night, *4594*
15:42 that is, the **d before the sabbath**, *4315*
16: 2 And very early in the morning the first *d* of NIG
16: 9 Now when *Jesus* was risen early the first *d* NIG
Lk 1:20 until the **d** that these *things* shall be *2250*
1:59 *that* on the eighth **d** they came to *2250*
1:80 was in the deserts till the **d** of his shewing *2250*
2:11 For unto you is born **this d** in the city of *4594*
2:37 *God* with fastings and prayers night and **d**. *2250*
4:16 went into the synagogue on the sabbath **d**, *2250*
4:21 **This d** is this scripture fulfilled in your *4594*
4:42 And when it was **d**, he departed and *2250*
5:17 And it came to pass on a certain **d**, as he *2250*
5:26 saying, We have seen strange *things* **to d**. *4594*
6: 7 whether he would heal on the sabbath *d*; NIG
6:13 And when it was **d**, he called unto *him* his *2250*
6:23 Rejoice ye in that **d**, and leap *for joy*: for *2250*
7:11 And it came to pass the *d* after, *that* he went NIG
8:22 Now it came to pass on a certain **d**, that he *2250*
9:12 And *when* the **d** began to wear away, then *2250*
9:22 and be slain, and be raised the third **d**. *2250*
9:37 And it came to pass, *that* on the next **d**, *2250*
10:12 that it shall be more tolerable in that **d** for *2250*
11: 3 Give us **d by day** our daily bread. *2250+2596*
11: 3 Give us **day by d** our daily bread. *2250+2596*
12:28 which is **to d** in the field, and to morrow is *4594*
12:46 The lord of that servant will come in a **d** *2250*
13:14 that Jesus had healed on the sabbath *d*, NIG
13:14 and be healed, and not on the sabbath **d**. *2250*
13:16 be loosed from this bond on the sabbath **d**? *2250*
13:31 The same **d** there came certain *of* *2250*
13:32 and I do cures **to d** and to morrow, and *4594*
13:32 and the third *d* I shall be perfected. NIG
13:33 Nevertheless I must walk **to d**, and *4594*
13:33 to day, and to morrow, and the *d* following: NIG
14: 1 Pharisees to eat bread on the sabbath *d*, NIG
14: 3 saying, Is it lawful to heal on the sabbath *d*? NIG
14: 5 straightway pull him out on the sabbath **d**? *2250*
16:19 fine linen, and fared sumptuously every **d**: *2250*
17: 4 he trespass against thee seven times in a **d**, *2250*
17: 4 and seven times in a **d** turn again to thee, *2250*
17:24 so shall also the Son of man be in his **d**. *2250*
17:27 until the **d** that Noe entered into the ark, *2250*
17:29 But the *same* **d** that Lot went out of Sodom *2250*
17:30 Even thus shall it be in the **d** when the Son *2250*
17:31 In that **d**, he which shall be upon *2250*
18: 7 which cry **d** and night unto him, though he *2250*
18:33 to death: and the third **d** he shall rise again. *2250*
19: 5 for **to d** I must abide at thy house. *4594*
19: 9 **This d** is salvation come to this house, *4594*
19:42 even thou, at least in this thy **d**, *2250*
21:34 and *so* that **d** come upon you unawares. *2250*
21:37 And in the **d time** he was teaching in *2250*
22: 7 Then came the **d** of unleavened bread, *2250*
22:34 Peter, *the* cock shall not crow **this d**, *4594*
22:66 And as soon as it was **d**, the elders of *2250*
23:12 And the same **d** Pilate and Herod were *2250*
23:43 **To d** shalt thou be with me in paradise. *4594*
23:54 And *that* **d** was the preparation, and *2250*
23:56 rested the sabbath *d* according to NIG
24: 1 Now upon the first *d* of the week, very early NIG
24: 7 and be crucified, and the third **d** rise again. *2250*
24:13 two of them went *that* same **d** to a village *2250*
24:21 **to d** is the third day since these *things* were *4594*
24:21 to day is the third **d** since these *things* were *2250*
24:29 it is towards evening, and the **d** is far spent. *2250*
24:46 and to rise from the dead the third **d**: *2250*
Jn 1:29 The **next d** John seeth Jesus coming unto *1887*
1:35 Again the **next d** *after* John stood, and *1887*
1:39 where he dwelt, and abode with him that **d**: *2250*
1:43 The **d following** Jesus would go forth into *1887*
2: 1 And the third **d** there was a marriage in *2250*
2:23 in the feast *d*, many believed in his name, NIG
5: 9 walked: and on the same **d** was the sabbath. *2250*
5:10 unto him that was cured, It is the sabbath *d*: NIG
5:16 he had done these *things* on the sabbath *d*. NIG
6:22 The **d following**, when the people which *1887*
6:39 but should raise it up *again* at the last **d**. *2250*
6:40 and I will raise him up *at* the last **d**. *2250*
6:44 and I will raise him up *at* the last **d**. *2250*
6:54 and I will raise him up *at* the last **d**. *2250*
7:22 and ye on the sabbath *d* circumcise a man. NIG
7:23 If a man on the sabbath *d* receive NIG
7:23 a man every whit whole on the sabbath *d*? NIG
7:37 In the last **d**, *that* great *day* of the feast, *2250*
7:37 *that* great *d* of the feast, Jesus stood and NIG
8:56 Your father Abraham rejoiced to see my **d**: *2250*
9: 4 the works of him that sent me, while it is **d**: *2250*
9:14 And it was the sabbath **d** when Jesus made *2250*
9:16 because he keepeth not the sabbath *d*. NIG
11: 9 Are there not twelve hours in the **d**? *2250*
11: 9 If any *man* walk in the **d**, he stumbleth not, *2250*
11:24 rise again in the resurrection at the last **d**. *2250*
11:53 Then from that **d** forth they took counsel *2250*
12: 7 against the **d** of my burying hath she kept *2250*
12:12 On the **next d** much people that were come *1887*
12:48 the same shall judge him in the last **d**. *2250*
14:20 At that **d** ye shall know that I *am* in my *2250*
16:23 And in that **d** ye shall ask me nothing. *2250*
16:26 At that **d** ye shall ask in my name: and I say *2250*
19:31 not remain upon the cross on the sabbath *d*, NIG
19:31 (for that sabbath *d* was a high day,) NIG
19:31 (for that sabbath day was a high **d**,) *2250*
19:42 of the Jews' preparation *d*; for the sepulchre NIG
20: 1 The first *d* of the week cometh Mary NIG
20:19 Then the same **d** at evening, being the first *2250*
20:19 at evening, being the first *d* of the week, NIG
Ac 1: 2 Until the **d** *in* which he was taken up, *2250*
1:22 unto *that same* **d** that he was taken up from *2250*
2: 1 And when the **d** of Pentecost was fully *2250*
2:15 seeing it is *but* the third hour of the **d**. *2250*
2:20 *that* great and notable **d** of the Lord come: *2250*
2:29 and his sepulchre is with us unto this **d**. *2250*
2:41 the same **d** there were added *unto them* *2250*
4: 3 and put *them* in hold unto the **next d**: *839*
4: 9 If we **this d** be examined of the good deed *4594*
7: 8 and circumcised him the eighth **d**; *2250*
7:26 And the next **d** he shewed himself unto *2250*
9:24 And they watched the gates **d** and night to *2250*
10: 3 about the ninth hour of the **d**, *2250*
10:40 Him God raised up the third **d**, and *2250*
12:18 Now as soon as it was **d**, there was no *2250*
12:21 And upon a set **d** Herod, arrayed in royal *2250*
13:14 went into the synagogue on the sabbath **d**, *2250*
13:27 prophets which are read every sabbath *d*, NIG
13:33 art my Son, **this d** have I begotten thee. *4594*
13:44 And the next sabbath *d* came almost NIG
14:20 the **next d** he departed with Barnabas to *1887*
15:21 read in the synagogues every sabbath *d*. NIG
16:11 to Samothracia, and the next *d* to Neapolis; NIG
16:35 And when it was **d**, the magistrates sent *2250*
17:31 Because he hath appointed a **d**, in *2250*
20: 7 And upon the first *d* of the week, when NIG
20:11 *even* till **break of d**, so he departed. *827*
20:15 and came the next *d* over against Chios; NIG
20:15 and the next *d* we arrived at Samos, and NIG
20:15 and the next *d* we came to Miletus. NIG
20:16 to be at Jerusalem the **d** of Pentecost. *2250*
20:18 from the first **d** that I came into Asia, *2250*
20:26 I take you to record **this d**, *2250+4594*
20:31 to warn every one night and **d** with tears. *2250*
21: 1 and the *d* following unto Rhodes, and from NIG
21: 7 the brethren, and abode with them one **d**. *2250*
21: 8 And the **next d** we that were of Paul's *1887*
21:18 And the *d* following Paul went in with us NIG
21:26 the next **d** purifying himself with them *2250*
22: 3 zealous towards God, as ye all are **this d**. *4594*
23: 1 all good conscience before God until this **d**. *2250*
23:12 And when it was **d**, certain of the Jews *2250*
24:21 dead I am called in question by you **this d**. *4594*
25: 6 and the **next d** sitting in the judgment seat, *1887*
26: 2 I shall answer for myself **this d** before thee *4594*
26: 7 instantly serving *God* **d** and night, hope to *2250*
26:22 help of God, I continue unto this **d**, *2250*
26:29 but also all that hear me **this d**, were both *4594*
27: 3 And the next *d* we touched at Sidon. NIG
27:18 the next *d* they lightened the ship; NIG
27:19 And the third *d* we cast *out* with our own NIG
27:29 out of the stern, and wished for the **d**. *2250*
27:33 And while the **d** was coming on, Paul *2250*
27:33 **This d** is the fourteenth day that ye have *4594*
27:33 This day is the fourteenth **d** that ye have *2250*

Ac 27:39 And when it was **d**, they knew not the land: *2250*
28:13 and after one **d** the south wind blew, and *2250*
28:13 and we came the **next d** to Puteoli: *1206*
28:23 And when they had appointed him a **d**, *2250*
Ro 2: 5 up unto thyself wrath against the **d** of wrath *2250*
2:16 In the **d** when God shall judge the secrets *2250*
8:36 For thy sake we are killed all the **d** long; *2250*
10:21 All **d** long have I stretched forth my hands *2250*
11: 8 that *they* should not hear;) unto **this d**. *2250+4594*
13:12 The night is far spent, the **d** is at hand: *2250*
13:13 Let us walk honestly, as in the **d**; not in *2250*
14: 5 One man esteemeth one **d** above another: *2250*
14: 5 another esteemeth every **d** *alike.* Let every *2250*
14: 6 He that regardeth the **d**, regardeth *it* unto *2250*
14: 6 and he that regardeth not the **d**, to the Lord *2250*
1Co 1: 8 *that ye may be* blameless in the **d** of our *2250*
3:13 for the **d** shall declare *it,* because it shall be *2250*
4:13 *are* the offscouring of all *things* unto **this d**. *737*
5: 5 that the spirit may be saved in the **d** of *2250*
10: 8 and fell in one **d** three and twenty thousand. *2250*
15: 4 that he rose *again* the third **d** according to *2250*
16: 2 Upon the first *d* of the week let every one of NIG
2Co 1:14 even as ye also *are* ours in the **d** of the Lord *2250*
3:14 for until **this d** remaineth the same *2250+4594*
3:15 But *even* unto **this d**, when Moses is read, *4594*
4:16 yet the inward *man* is renewed **d** by day. *2250*
4:16 yet the inward *man* is renewed day by **d**. *2250*
6: 2 in the **d** of salvation have I succoured thee: *2250*
6: 2 behold, now *is* the **d** of salvation.) *2250*
11:25 **a night and a d** I have been in the deep; *3574*
Eph 4:30 whereby ye are sealed unto the **d** of *2250*
6:13 ye may be able to withstand in the evil **d**, *2250*
Php 1: 5 in the gospel from the first **d** until now; *2250*
1: 6 will perform *it* until the **d** of Jesus Christ: *2250*
1:10 and without offence till the **d** of Christ; *2250*
2:16 that I may rejoice in the **d** of Christ, that I *2250*
3: 5 Circumcised the **eighth d**, of the stock of *3637*
Col 1: 6 since the **d** ye heard of *it,* and knew *2250*
1: 9 since the **d** we heard *it,* do not cease to pray *2250*
1Th 2: 9 for labouring night and **d**, because *we* *2250*
3:10 **d** praying exceedingly that *we* might see *2250*
5: 2 For yourselves know perfectly that the **d** of *2250*
5: 4 that *that* **d** should overtake you as a thief. *2250*
5: 5 children of light, and the children of the **d**: *2250*
5: 8 But let us, who are of the **d**, be sober, *2250*
2Th 1:10 among you was believed) in that **d**. *2250*
2: 2 from us, as that the **d** of Christ is at hand. *2250*
2: 3 for *that d shall not come,* except there come NIG
3: 8 with labour and travail night and **d**, *2250*
1Ti 5: 5 in supplications and prayers night and **d**. *2250*
2Ti 1: 3 of thee in my prayers night and **d**; *2250*
1:12 I have committed unto *him* against that **d**. *2250*
1:18 *he* may find mercy of the Lord in that **d**: *2250*
4: 8 the righteous judge, shall give me at that **d**: *2250*
Heb 1: 5 art my Son, **this d** have I begotten thee? *4594*
3: 7 Ghost saith, **To d** if ye will hear his voice, *4594*
3: 8 in the **d** of temptation in the wilderness: *2250*
3:13 one another daily, while it is called **To d**; *4594*
3:15 it is said, **To d** if ye will hear his voice, *4594*
4: 4 a certain place of the seventh *d* on this wise, NIG
4: 4 And God did rest the seventh **d** from all his *2250*
4: 7 Again he limiteth a certain **d**, saying in *2250*
4: 7 saying in David, **To d**, after so long a time; *4594*
4: 7 as it is said, **To d** if ye will hear his voice, *4594*
4: 8 he not afterward have spoken of another **d**. *2250*
5: 5 Thou art my Son, **to d** have I begotten thee. *4594*
8: 9 **d** when I took them by the hand to lead *2250*
10:25 the more, as ye see the **d** approaching. *2250*
13: 8 the same yesterday, and **to d**, and for ever. *4594*
Jas 4:13 **To d** or to morrow we will go into such a *4594*
5: 5 your hearts, as in a **d** of slaughter. *2250*
1Pe 2:12 glorify God in the **d** of visitation. *2250*
2Pe 1:19 until the **d** dawn, and the day star arise in *2250*
1:19 and the **d star** arise in your hearts: *5459*
2: 8 vexed *his* righteous soul from **d** to day with *2250*
2: 8 vexed *his* righteous soul from day to **d** with *2250*
2: 9 to reserve the unjust unto the **d** of judgment *2250*
2:13 *as* they that count it pleasure to riot in the **d** *2250*
3: 7 reserved unto fire against the **d** of judgment *2250*
3: 8 be not ignorant of this one *thing,* that one **d** *2250*
3: 8 and a thousand years as one **d**. *2250*
3:10 But the **d** of the Lord will come as a thief in *2250*
3:12 hasting *unto* the coming of the **d** of God, *2250*
1Jn 4:17 that we may have boldness in the **d** of *2250*
Jude 1: 6 darkness unto the judgment of the great **d**. *2250*
Rev 1:10 I was in the spirit on the Lord's **d**, and *2250*
4: 8 and they rest not **d** and night, saying, Holy, *2250*
6:17 For the great **d** of his wrath is come; and *2250*
7:15 and serve him **d** and night in his temple: *2250*
8:12 and the **d** shone not for a third *part* of it, *2250*
9:15 and a **d**, and a month, and a year, for to slay *2250*
12:10 which accused them before our God **d** and *2250*
14:11 and they have no rest **d** nor night, *2250*
16:14 to gather them to the battle of that great **d** *2250*
18: 8 Therefore shall her plagues come in one **d**, *2250*
20:10 and shall be tormented **d** and night for ever *2250*
21:25 the gates of it shall not be shut at all by **d**: *2250*

DAY'S (9) [DAY]

Nu 11:31 as it were a **d** journey on this side, and as it 3117
11:31 as it were a **d** journey on the other side, 3117
1Ki 19: 4 he himself went a **d** journey into 3117
1Ch 16:37 as **every d** work required: 3117+3117+871.1
Est 9:13 morrow also according unto *this* **d** decree, 3117
Jnh 3: 4 Jonah began to enter into the city a **d** 3117
Lk 2:44 been in the company, went a **d** journey; *2250*
Ac 1:12 a **sabbath d journey**. *2192+3598+4521*
19:40 to be called in question for **this d** uproar, *4594*

DAYS (855) [DAY]

Ge 1:14 and for seasons, and for **d**, and years: 3117
3:14 and dust shalt thou eat all the **d** of thy life: 3117
3:17 in sorrow shalt thou eat *of* it all the **d** of thy 3117
5: 4 the **d** of Adam after he had begotten Seth 3117
5: 5 all the **d** that Adam lived were nine 3117
5: 8 all the **d** of Seth were nine hundred 3117
5:11 all the **d** of Enos were nine hundred 3117
5:14 all the **d** of Cainan were nine hundred 3117
5:17 all the **d** of Mahalaleel were eight hundred 3117
5:20 all the **d** of Jared were nine hundred sixty 3117
5:23 all the **d** of Enoch were three hundred sixty 3117
5:27 all the **d** of Methuselah were nine hundred 3117
5:31 all the **d** of Lamech were seven hundred 3117
6: 3 yet his **d** shall be an hundred and 3117
6: 4 There were giants in the earth in those **d**; 3117
7: 4 For yet seven **d**, *and* I will cause it to rain 3117
7: 4 I will cause it to rain upon the earth forty **d** 3117
7:10 it came to pass after seven **d**, that 3117
7:12 the rain was upon the earth forty **d** and 3117
7:17 the flood was forty **d** upon the earth; and 3117
7:24 upon the earth an hundred and fifty **d**. 3117
8: 3 and fifty **d** the waters were abated. 3117
8: 6 it came to pass at the end of forty **d**, 3117
8:10 he stayed yet other seven **d**; and again he 3117
8:12 he stayed yet other seven **d**; and sent forth 3117
9:29 all the **d** of Noah were nine hundred and 3117
10:25 for in his **d** was the earth divided; and 3117
11:32 the **d** of Terah were two hundred and 3117
14: 1 it came to pass in the **d** of Amraphel king 3117
17:12 he that is eight **d** old shall be circumcised 3117
21: 4 circumcised his son Isaac being eight **d** old, 3117
21:34 sojourned in the Philistines' land many **d**. 3117
24:55 Let the damsel abide with us *a few* **d**, at 3117
25: 7 these *are* the **d** of the years of Abraham's 3117
25:24 when her **d** to be delivered were fulfilled, 3117
26: 1 besides the first famine that was in the **d** of 3117
26:15 had digged in the **d** of Abraham his father, 3117
26:18 which they had digged in the **d** of Abraham 3117
27:41 The **d** of mourning for my father are at 3117
27:44 tarry with him a few **d**, until thy brother's 3117
29:20 they seemed unto him *but* a few **d**, for 3117
29:21 Give *me* my wife, for my **d** are fulfilled, 3117
30:14 Reuben went in the **d** of wheat harvest, 3117
35:28 the **d** of Isaac were an hundred 3117
35:29 unto his people, *being* old and full of **d**: 3117
37:34 his loins, and mourned for his son many **d**. 3117
40:12 of it: The three branches *are* three **d**: 3117
40:13 Yet within three **d** shall Pharaoh lift up 3117
40:18 The three baskets *are* three **d**: 3117
40:19 Yet within three **d** shall Pharaoh lift up thy 3117
42:17 he put them all together into ward three **d**. 3117
47: 9 The **d** of the years of my pilgrimage *are* an 3117
47: 9 evil have the **d** of the years of my life been, 3117
47: 9 have not attained unto the **d** of the years of 3117
47: 9 of my fathers in the **d** of their pilgrimage. 3117
49: 1 you *that* which shall befall you in the last **d**. 3117
50: 3 forty **d** were fulfilled for him; for so 3117
50: 3 are fulfilled the **d** of those which are 3117

D

Ge 50: 3 mourned for him threescore and ten **d**. 3117
50: 4 when the **d** of his mourning were past, 3117
50:10 he made a mourning for his father seven **d**. 3117
Ex 2:11 it came to pass in those **d**, when Moses was 3117
7:25 seven **d** were fulfilled, after *that* 3117
10:22 darkness in all the land of Egypt three **d**: 3117
10:23 neither rose any from his place for three **d**: 3117
12:15 Seven **d** shall ye eat unleavened bread; 3117
12:19 Seven **d** shall there be no leaven found in 3117
13: 6 Seven **d** thou shalt eat unleavened bread, 3117
13: 7 Unleavened bread shall be eaten seven **d**; 3117
15:22 they went three **d** in the wilderness, and 3117
16:26 Six **d** ye shall gather it; but on the seventh 3117
16:29 you on the sixth day the bread of **two d**; 3117
20: 9 Six **d** shalt thou labour, and do all thy 3117
20:11 For *in* six **d** the LORD made heaven and 3117
20:12 that thy **d** may be long upon the land which 3117
22:30 seven **d** it shall be with his dam; on 3117
23:12 Six **d** thou shalt do thy work, and on 3117
23:15 thou shalt eat unleavened bread seven **d**, 3117
23:26 thy land: the number of thy **d** I will fulfil. 3117
24:16 mount Sinai, and the cloud covered it six **d**: 3117
24:18 Moses was in the mount forty **d** and 3117
29:30 in his stead shall put them on seven **d**, 3117
29:35 seven **d** shalt thou consecrate them. 3117
29:37 Seven **d** thou shalt make an atonement for 3117
31:15 Six **d** may work be done; but in the seventh 3117
31:17 for *in* six **d** the LORD made heaven and 3117
34:18 seven **d** thou shalt eat unleavened bread, 3117
34:21 Six **d** thou shalt work, but on the seventh 3117
34:28 he was there with the LORD forty **d** and 3117
35: 2 Six **d** shall work be done, but on 3117
Lev 8:33 tabernacle of the congregation *in* seven **d**, 3117
8:33 until the **d** of your consecration be at an 3117
8:33 an end: for seven **d** shall he consecrate you. 3117
8:35 of the congregation day and night seven **d**, 3117
12: 2 she shall be unclean seven **d**; according to 3117
12: 2 according to the **d** of the separation for her 3117
12: 4 blood of her purifying three and thirty **d**; 3117
12: 4 until the **d** of her purifying be fulfilled. 3117
12: 5 blood of her purifying threescore and six **d**. 3117
12: 6 when the **d** of her purifying are fulfilled, 3117
13: 4 shut up *him that hath* the plague seven **d**: 3117
13: 5 the priest shall shut him up seven **d** more: 3117
13:21 then the priest shall shut him up seven **d**: 3117
13:26 then the priest shall shut him up seven **d**: 3117
13:31 *that hath* the plague of the scall seven **d**: 3117
13:33 up *him that hath* the scall seven **d** more: 3117
13:46 All the **d** wherein the plague *shall be* in him 3117
13:50 and shut up *it that hath* the plague seven **d**: 3117
13:54 and he shall shut it up seven **d** more: 3117
14: 8 shall tarry abroad out of his tent seven **d**. 3117
14:38 the house, and shut up the house seven **d**: 3117
15:13 he shall number to himself seven **d** for his 3117
15:19 be blood, she shall be put apart seven **d**: 3117
15:24 be upon him, he shall be unclean seven **d**; 3117
15:25 many **d** out of the time of her separation, 3117
15:25 all the **d** of the issue of her uncleanness 3117
15:25 shall be as the **d** of her separation: 3117
15:26 Every bed whereon she lieth all the **d** of her 3117
15:28 she shall number to herself seven **d**, and 3117
22:27 then it shall be seven **d** under the dam; 3117
23: 3 Six **d** shall work be done: but the seventh 3117
23: 6 seven **d** ye must eat unleavened bread. 3117
23: 8 made by fire unto the LORD seven **d**: 3117
23:16 the seventh sabbath shall ye number fifty **d**; 3117
23:34 of tabernacles *for* seven **d** unto the LORD. 3117
23:36 Seven **d** ye shall offer an offering made by 3117
23:39 shall keep a feast unto the LORD seven **d**: 3117
23:40 before the LORD your God seven **d**. 3117
23:41 feast unto the LORD seven **d** in the year. 3117
23:42 Ye shall dwell in booths seven **d**; all that 3117
Nu 6: 4 All the **d** of his separation shall he eat 3117
6: 5 All the **d** of the vow of his separation there 3117
6: 5 until the **d** be fulfilled, *in* the which he 3117
6: 6 All the **d** that he separateth *himself* unto 3117
6: 8 All the **d** of his separation he *is* holy unto 3117
6:12 he shall consecrate unto the LORD the **d** 3117
6:12 the **d** that were before shall be lost, because 3117
6:13 when the **d** of his separation are fulfilled: 3117
9:19 tarried long upon the tabernacle many **d**, 3117
9:20 when the cloud was a few **d** upon 3117
9:22 Or *whether it were* **two d**, or a month, or 3117
10:10 in your **solemn d**, and in the beginnings of 4150
11:19 nor **two d**, nor five days, neither ten days, 3117
11:19 nor two days, nor five **d**, neither ten days, 3117
11:19 nor two days, nor five days, neither ten **d**, 3117
11:19 five days, neither ten days, nor twenty **d**; 3117
12:14 should she not be ashamed seven **d**? 3117
12:14 let her be shut out from the camp seven **d**, 3117
12:15 was shut out from the camp seven **d**: 3117
13:25 from searching of the land after forty **d**. 3117
14:34 After the number of the **d** *in* which ye 3117
14:34 *even* forty **d**, each day for a year, shall ye 3117
19:11 *body* of any man shall be unclean seven **d**. 3117
19:14 that *is* in the tent, shall be unclean seven **d**. 3117
19:16 a man, or a grave, shall be unclean seven **d**. 3117
20:29 they mourned for Aaron thirty **d**, *even* all 3117
24:14 people shall do to thy people in the latter **d**. 3117
28:17 seven **d** shall unleavened bread be eaten. 3117
28:24 ye shall offer daily, *throughout* the seven **d**, 3117
29:12 shall keep a feast unto the LORD seven **d**: 3117
31:19 do ye abide without the camp seven **d**: 3117
Dt 1:46 So ye abode in Kadesh many **d**, 3117
1:46 according unto the **d** that ye abode *there*. 3117
2: 1 and we compassed mount Seir many **d**. 3117
4: 9 lest they depart from thy heart all the **d** of 3117
4:10 that they may learn to fear me all the **d** that 3117
4:26 ye shall not prolong *your* **d** upon it, but 3117
4:30 *even* in the latter **d**, if thou turn to 3117
4:32 For ask now of the **d** that are past, 3117
4:40 that thou mayest prolong *thy* **d** upon 3117
5:13 Six **d** thou shalt labour, and do all thy 3117
5:16 that thy **d** may be prolonged, and that it 3117
5:33 *that* ye may prolong *your* **d** in the land 3117
6: 2 and thy son's son, all the **d** of thy life; 3117
6: 2 thy life; and that thy **d** may be prolonged. 3117
9: 9 I abode in the mount forty **d** and 3117
9:11 it came to pass at the end of forty **d** and 3117
9:18 as at the first, forty **d** and forty nights: 3117
9:25 Thus I fell down before the LORD forty **d** 3117
10:10 to the first time, forty **d** and forty nights; 3117
11: 9 that ye may prolong *your* **d** in the land, 3117
11:21 That your **d** may be multiplied, and 3117
11:21 be multiplied, and the **d** of your children, 3117
11:21 as the **d** of heaven upon the earth. 3117
12: 1 all the **d** that ye live upon the earth. 3117
16: 3 seven **d** shalt thou eat unleavened bread 3117
16: 3 out of the land of Egypt all the **d** of thy life. 3117
16: 4 seen with thee in all thy coast seven **d**; 3117
16: 8 Six **d** thou shalt eat unleavened bread: and 3117
16:13 observe the feast of tabernacles seven **d**, 3117
16:15 Seven **d** shalt thou keep a solemn feast unto 3117
17: 9 unto the judge that shall be in those **d**, 3117
17:19 he shall read therein all the **d** of his life: 3117
17:20 to the end that he may prolong *his* **d** in his 3117
19:17 and the judges, which shall be in those **d**; 3117
22: 7 and *that* thou mayest prolong *thy* **d**. 3117
22:19 his wife; he may not put her away all his **d**. 3117
22:29 he may not put her away all his **d**. 3117
23: 6 peace nor their prosperity all thy **d** for ever. 3117
25:15 that thy **d** may be lengthened in the land 3117
26: 3 go unto the priest that shall be in those **d**, 3117
30:18 *that* ye shall not prolong *your* **d** upon 3117
30:20 for he *is* thy life, and the length of thy **d**: 3117
31:14 Behold, thy **d** approach that *thou* must die: 3117
31:29 evil will befall you in the latter **d**; because 3117
32: 7 Remember the **d** of old, consider the years 3117
32:47 through this thing ye shall prolong *your* **d** 3117
33:25 and as thy **d**, *so shall* thy strength *be*. 3117
34: 8 for Moses in the plains of Moab thirty **d**: 3117
34: 8 so the **d** of weeping *and* mourning for 3117
Jos 1: 5 *to* stand before thee all the **d** of thy life: 3117
1:11 for within three **d** ye shall pass over this 3117
2:16 hide yourselves there three **d**, until 3117
2:22 unto the mountain, and abode there three **d**, 3117
3: 2 it came to pass after three **d**, that 3117
4:14 as they feared Moses, all the **d** of his life. 3117
6: 3 the city once. Thus shalt thou do six **d**. 3117
6:14 returned *into* the camp: so they did six **d**. 3117
9:16 it came to pass at the end of three **d** after 3117
20: 6 of the high priest that shall be in those **d**: 3117
22: 3 have not left your brethren these many **d** 3117
24:31 Israel served the LORD all the **d** of 3117
24:31 all the **d** of the elders that overlived Joshua, 3117
Jdg 2: 7 the people served the LORD all the **d** of 3117
2: 7 all the **d** of the elders that outlived Joshua, 3117
2:18 hand of their enemies all the **d** of the judge: 3117

Jdg 5: 6 In the **d** of Shamgar the son of Anath, 3117
5: 6 in the **d** of Jael, the highways were 3117
8:28 in quietness forty years in the **d** of Gideon. 3117
11:40 of Jephthah the Gileadite four **d** in a year. 3117
14:12 it me *within* the seven **d** of the feast, 3117
14:14 they could not *in* three **d** expound 3117
14:17 she wept before him the seven **d**, 3117
15:20 he judged Israel in the **d** of the Philistines 3117
17: 6 In those **d** *there was* no king in Israel, *but* 3117
18: 1 In those **d** *there was* no king in Israel: and 3117
18: 1 in those **d** the tribe of the Danites sought 3117
19: 1 it came to pass in those **d**, when *there was* 3117
19: 4 and he abode with him three **d**: 3117
20:27 the covenant of God *was* there in those **d**, 3117
20:28 son of Aaron, stood before it in those **d**,) 3117
21:25 In those **d** *there was* no king in Israel: 3117
Ru 1: 1 Now it came to pass in the **d** when 3117
1Sa 1:11 I will give him unto the LORD all the **d** of 3117
2:31 Behold, the **d** come, that I will cut off thine 3117
3: 1 of the LORD was precious in those **d**; 3117
7:13 against the Philistines all the **d** of Samuel. 3117
7:15 Samuel judged Israel all the **d** of his life. 3117
9:20 as for thine asses that were lost three **d** ago, 3117
10: 8 seven **d** shalt thou tarry, till I come to thee, 3117
13: 8 he tarried seven **d**, according to the set time 3117
13:11 *that* thou camest not within the **d** 3117
14:52 war against the Philistines all the **d** of Saul: 3117
17:12 among men *for* an old man in the **d** of Saul. 3117
17:16 and evening, and presented himself forty **d**. 3117
18:26 son in law: and the **d** were not expired. 3117
20:19 *when* thou hast **stayed three d**, *then* 8027
21: 5 kept from us about **these three d**, 8032+8543
25:10 there be many servants **now a d** 3117+1886.1
25:28 evil hath not been found in thee *all* thy **d**. 3117
25:38 it came to pass about ten **d** *after*, that 3117
28: 1 it came to pass in those **d**, that 3117
29: 3 which hath been with me these **d**, or 3117
30:12 drunk *any* water, three **d** and three nights. 3117
30:13 left me, because three **d** agone I fell sick. 3117
31:13 under a tree at Jabesh, and fasted seven **d**. 3117
2Sa 1: 1 and David had abode two **d** in Ziklag; 3117
7:12 when thy **d** be fulfilled, and thou shalt sleep 3117
16:23 which he counselled in those **d**, 3117
20: 4 me the men of Judah *within* three **d**, 3117
21: 1 there was a famine in the **d** of David three 3117
21: 9 and were put to death in the **d** of harvest, 3117
21: 9 in the first *d*, in the beginning of barley NIH
24: 8 at the end of nine months and twenty **d**. 3117
1Ki 2: 1 Now the **d** of David drew nigh that *he* 3117
2:11 the **d** that David reigned over Israel *were* 3117
2:38 And Shimei dwelt in Jerusalem many **d**. 3117
3: 2 unto the name of the LORD, until those **d**. 3117
3:13 among the kings like unto thee all thy **d**. 3117
3:14 David did walk, then I will lengthen thy **d**. 3117
4:21 and served Solomon all the **d** of his life. 3117
4:25 even to Beer-sheba, all the **d** of Solomon. 3117
8:40 That they may fear thee all the **d** that they 3117
8:65 seven **d** and seven days, *even* fourteen 3117
8:65 seven days and seven **d**, *even* fourteen 3117
8:65 and seven days, *even* fourteen **d**. 3117
10:21 it was nothing accounted of in the **d** of 3117
11:12 Notwithstanding in thy **d** I will not do it for 3117
11:25 he was an adversary to Israel all the **d** of 3117
11:34 I will make him prince all the **d** of his life 3117
12: 5 Depart yet *for* three **d**, then come again to 3117
14:20 the **d** which Jeroboam reigned *were* two 3117
14:30 and Jeroboam all *their* **d**. 3117
15: 5 that he commanded him all the **d** of his life, 3117
15: 6 and Jeroboam all the **d** of his life. 3117
15:14 heart was perfect with the LORD all his **d**. 3117
15:16 and Baasha king of Israel all their **d**. 3117
15:32 and Baasha king of Israel all their **d**. 3117
16:15 of Judah did Zimri reign seven **d** in Tirzah. 3117
16:34 In his **d** did Hiel the Bethelite build 3117
17:15 she, and he, and her house, did eat *many* **d**. 3117
18: 1 it came to pass *after* many **d**, that the word 3117
19: 8 went in the strength of that meat forty **d** 3117
20:29 pitched one over against the other seven **d**. 3117
21:29 before me, I will not bring the evil in his **d**: 3117
21:29 in his son's **d** will I bring the evil upon his 3117
22:46 which remained in the **d** of his father Asa, 3117
2Ki 2:17 and they sought three **d**, but found him not. 3117
8:20 In his **d** Edom revolted from under 3117
10:32 In those **d** the LORD began to cut Israel 3117
12: 2 **d** where*in* Jehoiada the priest instructed 3117
13: 3 of Ben-hadad the son of Hazael, all *their* **d**. 3117
13:22 oppressed Israel all the **d** of Jehoahaz. 3117
15:18 he departed not all his **d** from the sins of 3117
15:29 In the **d** of Pekah king of Israel came 3117
15:37 In those **d** the LORD began to send 3117
18: 4 for unto those **d** the children of Israel did 3117
20: 1 In those **d** was Hezekiah sick unto death. 3117
20: 6 I will add unto thy **d** fifteen years; and 3117
20:17 Behold, the **d** come, that all that *is* in thine 3117
20:19 *it* not *good*, if peace and truth be in my **d**? 3117
23:22 from the **d** of the judges that judged Israel, 3117
23:22 nor *in* all the **d** of the kings of Israel, nor of 3117
23:29 In his **d** Pharaoh-nechoh king of Egypt 3117
24: 1 In his **d** Nebuchadnezzar king of Babylon 3117
25:29 continually before him all the **d** of his life. 3117
25:30 daily rate for every day, all the **d** of his life. 3117
1Ch 1:19 because in his **d** the earth was divided: 3117
4:41 these written by name came in the **d** of 3117
5:10 in the **d** of Saul they made war with 3117
5:17 in the **d** of Jotham king of Judah, 3117
5:17 and in the **d** of Jeroboam king of Israel. 3117
7: 2 whose number *was* in the **d** of David two 3117
7:22 Ephraim their father mourned many **d**, and 3117
9:25 *were* to come after seven **d** from time to 3117
10:12 under the oak in Jabesh, and fasted seven **d**. 3117
12:39 there they were with David three **d**, eating 3117
13: 3 for we inquired not *at* it in the **d** of Saul. 3117
17:11 when thy **d** be expired that *thou* must go *to* 3117
21:12 or else three **d** the sword of the LORD, 3117
22: 9 and quietness unto Israel in his **d**. 3117
23: 1 So when David was old and full *of* **d**, 3117
29:15 our **d** on the earth *are* as a shadow, and 3117
29:28 good old age, full of **d**, riches, and honour: 3117
2Ch 7: 8 same time Solomon kept the feast seven **d**, 3117
7: 9 kept the dedication of the altar seven **d**, 3117
7: 9 the altar seven days, and the feast seven **d**. 3117
9:20 it was *not* any thing accounted of in the **d** 3117
10: 5 Come again unto me after three **d**. 3117
13:20 recover strength again in the **d** of Abijah: 3117
14: 1 In his **d** the land was quiet ten years. 3117
15:17 the heart of Asa was perfect all his **d**. 3117
20:25 they were three **d** in gathering of the spoil, 3117
21: 8 In his **d** the Edomites revolted from under 3117
24: 2 the LORD all the **d** of Jehoiada the priest. 3117
24:14 LORD continually all the **d** of Jehoiada. 3117
24:15 waxed old, and was full *of* **d** when he died; 3117
26: 5 he sought God in the **d** of Zechariah, 3117
29:17 the house of the LORD in eight **d**; 3117
30:21 bread seven **d** with great gladness: 3117
30:22 they did eat throughout the feast seven **d**, 3117
30:23 took counsel to keep other seven **d**: 3117
30:23 and they kept *other* seven **d** *with* gladness. 3117
32:24 In those **d** Hezekiah was sick to the death, 3117
32:26 came not upon them in the **d** of Hezekiah. 3117
34:33 *And* all his **d** they departed not from 3117
35:17 the feast of unleavened bread seven **d**. 3117
35:18 kept in Israel from the **d** of Samuel 3117
36: 9 three months and ten **d** in Jerusalem: 3117
Ezr 4: 2 we do sacrifice unto him since the **d** of 3117
4: 5 all the **d** of Cyrus king of Persia, 3117
4: 7 in the **d** of Artaxerxes wrote Bishlam, 3117
6:22 kept the feast of unleavened bread seven **d** 3117
8:15 and there abode we in tents three **d**: 3117
8:32 came *to* Jerusalem, and abode there three **d**. 3117
9: 7 Since the **d** of our fathers *have* we *been* in a 3117
10: 8 whosoever would not come within three **d**, 3117
10: 9 together *unto* Jerusalem within three **d**. 3117
Ne 1: 4 mourned *certain* **d**, and fasted, and 3117
2:11 I came to Jerusalem, and was there three **d**. 3117
5:18 and once in ten **d** store of all *sorts of* wine: 3117
6:15 *day* of *the month* Elul, in fifty and two **d**. 3117
6:17 Moreover in those **d** the nobles of Judah 3117
8:17 for since the **d** of Jeshua the son of Nun 3117
8:18 they kept the feast seven **d**; and on 3117
12: 7 and of their brethren in the **d** of Jeshua. 3117
12:12 in the **d** of Joiakim were priests, the chief 3117
12:22 The Levites in the **d** of Eliashib, Joiada, 3117
12:23 even until the **d** of Johanan the son of 3117
12:26 These *were* in the **d** of Joiakim the son of 3117
12:26 in the **d** of Nehemiah the governor, and 3117
12:46 For in the **d** of David and Asaph of old 3117
12:47 all Israel in the **d** of Zerubbabel, and in 3117
12:47 in the **d** of Nehemiah, gave the portions of 3117

D

Ne 13: 6 after certain **d** obtained I *leave* of the king: 3117
13:15 In those **d** saw I in Judah *some* treading 3117
13:23 In those **d** also saw I Jews *that* had married 3117
Est 1: 1 Now it came to pass in the **d** of Ahasuerus, 3117
1: 2 *That* in those **d**, when the king Ahasuerus 3117
1: 4 the honour of his excellent majesty many **d**, 3117
1: 4 *even* an hundred and fourscore **d**. 3117
1: 5 when these **d** were expired, the king made a 3117
1: 5 both unto great and small, seven **d**, in 3117
2:12 were the **d** of their purifications 3117
2:21 In those **d**, while Mordecai sat in the king's 3117
4:11 to come in unto the king these thirty **d**. 3117
4:16 neither eat nor drink three **d**, night or day; 3117
9:22 As the **d** wherein the Jews rested from their 3117
9:22 that *they* should make them **d** of feasting 3117
9:26 Wherefore they called these **d** Purim after 3117
9:27 that they would keep these two **d** according 3117
9:28 *that* these **d** *should be* remembered and 3117
9:28 *that* these **d** of Purim should not fail from 3117
9:31 To confirm these **d** of Purim in their times 3117
Job 1: 5 when the **d** of *their* feasting were gone 3117
2:13 sat down with him upon the ground seven **d** 3117
3: 6 let it not be joined unto the **d** of the year, 3117
7: 1 *are not* his **d** also like the days of a 3117
7: 1 *are not* his days also like the **d** of a 3117
7: 6 My **d** are swifter than a weaver's shuttle, 3117
7:16 let me alone; for my **d** *are* vanity. 3117
8: 9 because our **d** upon earth *are* a shadow:) 3117
9:25 Now my **d** are swifter than a post: they flee 3117
10: 5 *Are* thy **d** as the days of man? *are* thy years 3117
10: 5 *Are* thy days as the **d** of man? *are* thy years 3117
10: 5 the days of man? *are* thy years as man's **d**, 3117
10:20 *Are* not my **d** few? cease then, and let me 3117
12:12 and *in* length of **d** understanding. 3117
14: 1 Man *that is* born of a woman *is* of few **d**, 3117
14: 5 Seeing his **d** *are* determined, the number of 3117
14:14 shall he live *again?* all the **d** of my 3117
15:20 wicked *man* travaileth with pain all his **d**, 3117
17: 1 My breath is corrupt, my **d** are extinct, 3117
17:11 My **d** are past, my purposes are broken off, 3117
21:13 They spend their **d** in wealth, and in a 3117
24: 1 do they that know him not see his **d**? 3117
29: 2 as *in* the **d** *when* God preserved me; 3117
29: 4 As I was in the **d** of my youth, when 3117
29:18 and I shall multiply *my* **d** as the sand. 3117
30:16 the **d** of affliction have taken hold upon me. 3117
30:27 rested not: the **d** of affliction prevented me. 3117
32: 7 **D** should speak, and multitude of years 3117
33:25 he shall return to the **d** of his youth: 3117
36:11 serve *him,* they shall spend their **d** in 3117
38:12 thou commanded the morning since thy **d**; 3117
38:21 or *because* the number of thy **d** *is* great? 3117
42:17 So Job died, *being* old and full of **d**. 3117
Ps 21: 4 *it* him, *even* length of **d** for ever and ever. 3117
23: 6 mercy shall follow me all the **d** of my life: 3117
27: 4 house of the LORD all the **d** of my life, 3117
34:12 *and* loveth *many* **d**, that *he* may see good? 3117
37:18 The LORD knoweth the **d** of the upright: 3117
37:19 in the **d** of famine they shall be satisfied. 3117
39: 4 know mine end, and the measure of my **d**, 3117
39: 5 thou hast made my **d** *as* a handbreadth; 3117
44: 1 *what* work thou didst in their **d**, in the times 3117
49: 5 Wherefore should I fear in the **d** of evil, 3117
55:23 deceitful men shall not live out half their **d**; 3117
72: 7 In his **d** shall the righteous flourish; and 3117
77: 5 I have considered the **d** of old, the years of 3117
78:33 Therefore their **d** did he consume in vanity, 3117
89:29 for ever, and his throne as the **d** of heaven. 3117
89:45 The **d** of his youth hast thou shortened: 3117
90: 9 For all our **d** are passed away in thy wrath: 3117
90:10 The **d** of our years *are* threescore years and 3117
90:12 So teach *us* to number our **d**, that we may 3117
90:14 that we may rejoice and be glad all our **d**. 3117
90:15 Make us glad according to the **d** *wherein* 3117
94:13 That *thou* mayest give him rest from the **d** 3117
102: 3 For my **d** are consumed like smoke, and 3117
102:11 My **d** *are* like a shadow that declineth; and 3117
102:23 my strength in the way; he shortened my **d**. 3117
102:24 take me not away in the midst of my **d**: 3117
103:15 *As for* man, his **d** *are* as grass: as a flower 3117
109: 8 Let his **d** be few; *and* let another take his 3117
119:84 How many *are* the **d** of thy servant? 3117
128: 5 the good of Jerusalem all the **d** of thy life. 3117
143: 5 I remember the **d** of old; I meditate on all 3117
144: 4 his **d** *are* as a shadow that passeth away. 3117
Pr 3: 2 For length of **d**, and long life, and peace, 3117
3:16 Length of **d** *is* in her right hand; and in her 3117
9:11 For by me thy **d** shall be multiplied, and 3117
10:27 The fear of the LORD prolongeth **d**: but 3117
15:15 All the **d** of the afflicted *are* evil: but 3117
28:16 hateth covetousness shall prolong *his* **d**. 3117
31:12 him good and not evil all the **d** of her life. 3117
Ecc 2: 3 do under the heaven all the **d** of their life. 3117
2:16 seeing *that* which now *is, in* the **d** to come 3117
2:23 For all his **d** *are* sorrows, and his travail 3117
5:17 All his **d** also he eateth in darkness, and 3117
5:18 he taketh under the sun all the **d** of his life, 3117
5:20 For he shall not much remember the **d** of 3117
6: 3 so that the **d** of his years be many, and 3117
6:12 all the **d** of his vain life which he spendeth 3117
7:10 What is *the cause* that the former **d** were 3117
7:15 All *things* have I seen in the **d** of my 3117
8:12 an hundred *times,* and his *d* be prolonged, NIH
8:13 neither shall he prolong *his* **d**, *which are* as 3117
8:15 with him of his labour the **d** of his life, 3117
9: 9 lovest all the **d** of the life of thy vanity, 3117
9: 9 thee under the sun, all the **d** of thy vanity: 3117
11: 1 for thou shalt find it after many **d**. 3117
11: 8 yet let him remember the **d** of darkness; 3117
11: 9 let thy heart cheer thee in the **d** of thy 3117
12: 1 Remember now thy Creator in the **d** of thy 3117
12: 1 while the evil **d** come not, nor the years 3117
Isa 1: 1 and Jerusalem in the **d** of Uzziah, 3117
2: 2 it shall come to pass in the last **d**, *that* 3117
7: 1 it came to pass in the **d** of Ahaz the son of 3117
7:17 thy father's house, **d** that have not come, 3117
13:22 to come, and her **d** shall not be prolonged. 3117
23: 7 *city,* whose antiquity *is* of ancient **d**? 3117
23:15 according to the **d** of one king: 3117
24:22 and after many **d** shall they be visited. 3117
30:26 shall be sevenfold, as the light of seven **d**, 3117
32:10 Many **d** and years shall ye be troubled, 3117
38: 1 In those **d** was Hezekiah sick unto death. 3117
38: 5 behold, I will add unto thy **d** fifteen years. 3117
38:10 I said, in the cutting off of my **d**, I shall go 3117
38:20 **d** of our life in the house of the LORD. 3117
39: 6 Behold, the **d** come, that all that *is* in thine 3117
39: 8 For there shall be peace and truth in my **d**. 3117
51: 9 awake, as *in* the ancient **d**, *in* 3117
53:10 he shall prolong *his* **d**, and the pleasure of 3117
60:20 and the **d** of thy mourning shall be ended. 3117
63: 9 bare them, and carried them all the **d** of old. 3117
63:11 he remembered the **d** of old, Moses, *and* 3117
65:20 shall be no more thence an infant of **d**, 3117
65:20 nor an old man that hath not filled his **d**: 3117
65:22 for as the **d** of a tree *are* the days of my 3117
65:22 for as the days of a tree *are* the **d** of my 3117
Jer 1: 2 **d** of Josiah the son of Amon king of Judah, 3117
1: 3 It came also in the **d** of Jehoiakim the son 3117
2:32 yet my people have forgotten me **d** without 3117
3: 6 The LORD said also unto me in the **d** of 3117
3:16 in the land, in those **d**, saith the LORD, 3117
3:18 In those **d** the house of Judah shall walk 3117
5:18 Nevertheless in those **d**, saith the LORD, 3117
6:11 be taken, the aged with *him that is* full of **d**. 3117
7:32 Therefore, behold, the **d** come, saith 3117
9:25 Behold, the **d** come, saith the LORD, 3117
13: 6 it came to pass after many **d**, that 3117
16: 9 in your **d**, the voice of mirth, and the voice 3117
16:14 the **d** come, saith the LORD, 3117
17:11 shall leave them in the midst of his **d**, and 3117
19: 6 the **d** come, saith the LORD, 3117
20:18 that my **d** should be consumed with shame? 3117
22:30 a man *that* shall not prosper in his **d**: 3117
23: 5 Behold, the **d** come, saith the LORD, 3117
23: 6 In his **d** Judah shall be saved, and 3117
23: 7 the **d** come, saith the LORD, 3117
23:20 in the latter **d** ye shall consider it perfectly. 3117
25:34 for the **d** of your slaughter and of your 3117
26:18 Micah the Morasthite prophesied in the **d** 3117
30: 3 For lo, the **d** come, saith the LORD, that I 3117
30:24 his heart: in the latter **d** ye shall consider it. 3117
31:27 Behold, the **d** come, saith the LORD, 3117
31:29 In those **d** they shall say no more, 3117
31:31 Behold, the **d** come, saith the LORD, 3117
31:33 After those **d**, saith the LORD, I will put 3117
31:38 Behold, the **d** come, saith the LORD, 3117
32:14 that they may continue many **d**. 3117

Jer 33:14 Behold, the **d** come, saith the LORD, 3117
33:15 In those **d**, and at that time, will I cause 3117
33:16 In those **d** shall Judah be saved, and 3117
35: 1 **d** of Jehoiakim the son of Josiah king of 3117
35: 7 but all your **d** ye shall dwell in tents; 3117
35: 7 that ye may live many **d** in the land where 3117
35: 8 to drink no wine all our **d**, we, our wives, 3117
36: 2 from the **d** of Josiah, even unto this day. 3117
37:16 and Jeremiah had remained there many **d**; 3117
42: 7 it came to pass after ten **d**, that the word of 3117
46:26 as *in* the **d** of old, saith the LORD. 3117
48:12 the **d** come, saith the LORD, 3117
48:47 again the captivity of Moab in the latter **d**, 3117
49: 2 the **d** come, saith the LORD, 3117
49:39 it shall come to pass in the latter **d**, *that* I 3117
50: 4 In those **d**, and in that time, saith 3117
50:20 In those **d**, and in that time, saith 3117
51:47 Therefore behold, the **d** come, that I will do 3117
51:52 the **d** come, saith the LORD, 3117
52:33 eat bread before him all the **d** of his life. 3117
52:34 the day of his death, all the **d** of his life. 3117
La 1: 7 Jerusalem remembered in the **d** of her 3117
1: 7 pleasant things that she had in the **d** of old, 3117
2:17 that he had commanded in the **d** of old: 3117
4:18 our end is near, our **d** are fulfilled; for our 3117
5:21 we shall be turned; renew our **d** as of old. 3117
Eze 3:15 there astonished among them seven **d**. 3117
3:16 it came to pass at the end of seven **d**, 3117
4: 4 *according to* the number of the **d** that thou 3117
4: 5 according to the number of the **d**, 3117
4: 5 of the days, three hundred and ninety **d**: 3117
4: 6 the iniquity of the house of Judah forty **d**: 3117
4: 8 till thou hast ended the **d** of thy siege. 3117
4: 9 *according to* the number of the **d** that thou 3117
4: 9 and ninety **d** shalt thou eat thereof. 3117
5: 2 when the **d** of the siege are fulfilled: 3117
12:22 The **d** are prolonged, and every vision 3117
12:23 The **d** are at hand, and the effect of every 3117
12:25 for in your **d**, O rebellious house, will I say 3117
12:27 The vision that he seeth *is* for many **d** *to* 3117
16:22 hast not remembered the **d** of thy youth, 3117
16:43 Because thou hast not remembered the **d** of 3117
16:60 covenant with thee in the **d** of thy youth, 3117
22: 4 thou hast caused thy **d** to draw near, and 3117
22:14 in the **d** that I shall deal with thee? 3117
23:19 in calling to remembrance the **d** of her 3117
38: 8 After many **d** thou shalt be visited: in 3117
38:16 it shall be in the latter **d**, and I will bring 3117
38:17 which prophesied in those **d** *many* years, 3117
43:25 Seven **d** shalt thou prepare every day a goat 3117
43:26 Seven **d** shall they purge the altar and 3117
43:27 when *these* **d** are expired, it shall be, 3117
44:26 they shall reckon unto him seven **d**. 3117
45:21 shall have the passover, a feast of seven **d**; 3117
45:23 seven **d** of the feast he shall prepare a burnt 3117
45:23 rams without blemish daily the seven **d**; 3117
45:25 he do the like in the feast *of* the seven **d**, 3117
46: 1 the east shall be shut the six working **d**; 3117
Da 1:12 Prove thy servants, I beseech thee, ten **d**; 3117
1:14 them in this matter, and proved them ten **d**. 3117
1:15 at the end of ten **d** their countenances 3117
1:18 Now at the end of the **d** that the king had 3117
2:28 what shall be in the latter **d**. 3118
2:44 in the **d** of these kings shall the God of 3118
4:34 at the end of the **d** I Nebuchadnezzar lift up 3118
5:11 in the **d** of thy father light and 3118
6: 7 a petition of any God or man for thirty **d**, 3118
6:12 *petition* of any God or man within thirty **d**, 3118
7: 9 cast *down*, and the Ancient of **d** did sit, 3118
7:13 came to the Ancient of **d**, and they brought 3118
7:22 Until the Ancient of **d** came, and 3118
8:14 two thousand and three hundred **d**; 1242+6153
8:26 up the vision; for *it shall be* for many **d**. 3117
8:27 I Daniel fainted, and was sick *certain* **d**; 3117
10: 2 In those **d** I Daniel was mourning three full 3117
10:13 of Persia withstood me one and twenty **d**: 3117
10:14 what shall befall thy people in the latter **d**: 3117
10:14 latter days: for yet the vision *is* for *many* **d**. 3117
11:20 within few **d** he shall be destroyed, 3117
11:33 by captivity, and by spoil, *many* **d**. 3117
12:11 *be* a thousand two hundred and ninety **d**. 3117
12:12 three hundred *and* five and thirty **d**. 3117
12:13 and stand in thy lot at the end of the **d**. 3117
Hos 1: 1 in the **d** of Uzziah, Jotham, Ahaz, *and* 3117
1: 1 in the **d** of Jeroboam the son of Joash, 3117
2:11 her feast *d*, her new moons, and NIH
2:13 I will visit upon her the **d** of Baalim, 3117
2:15 as *in* the **d** of her youth, and as *in* the day 3117
3: 3 unto her, Thou shalt abide for me many **d**; 3117
3: 4 of Israel shall abide many **d** without a king, 3117
3: 5 and his goodness in the latter **d**. 3117
6: 2 After **two d** will he revive us: in the third 3117
9: 7 The **d** of visitation are come, the days of 3117
9: 7 are come, the **d** of recompence are come; 3117
9: 9 *themselves,* as *in* the **d** of Gibeah: 3117
10: 9 thou hast sinned from the **d** of Gibeah: 3117
12: 9 as *in* the **d** of the solemn feast. 3117
Joel 1: 2 Hath this been in your **d**, or even in 3117
1: 2 your days, or even in the **d** of your fathers? 3117
2:29 upon the handmaids in those **d** will I pour 3117
3: 1 For behold, in those **d**, and in that time, 3117
Am 1: 1 which he saw concerning Israel in the **d** of 3117
1: 1 in the **d** of Jeroboam the son of Joash king 3117
4: 2 that lo, the **d** shall come upon you, that he 3117
5:21 I despise your feast *d*, and I will not smell NIH
8:11 Behold, the **d** come, saith the Lord GOD, 3117
9:11 and I will build it as *in* the **d** of old: 3117
9:13 Behold, the **d** come, saith the LORD, 3117
Jnh 1:17 Jonah was in the belly of the fish three **d** 3117
3: 4 Yet forty **d**, and Nineveh *shall be* 3117
Mic 1: 1 to Micah the Morasthite in the **d** of Jotham, 3117
4: 1 in the last **d** it shall come to pass, *that* 3117
7:14 *in* Bashan and Gilead, as *in* the **d** of old. 3117
7:15 According to the **d** of thy coming out of 3117
7:20 sworn unto our fathers from the **d** of old. 3117
Hab 1: 5 for *I will* work a work in your **d**, *which* ye 3117
Zep 1: 1 in the **d** of Josiah the son of Amon, king of 3117
Hag 2:16 Since those *d* were, when *one* came to a NIH
Zec 8: 6 of the remnant of this people in these **d**, 3117
8: 9 ye that hear in these **d** these words by 3117
8:10 For before these **d** there was no hire for 3117
8:11 residue of this people as *in* the former **d**, 3117
8:15 So again have I thought in these **d** to do 3117
8:23 In those **d** *it shall come to pass,* that ten 3117
14: 5 in the **d** of Uzziah king of Judah: 3117
Mal 3: 4 as *in* the **d** of old, and as *in* former years. 3117
3: 7 Even from the **d** of your fathers ye are gone 3117
Mt 2: 1 of Judea in the **d** of Herod the king, *2250*
3: 1 In those **d** came John the Baptist, *2250*
4: 2 And when he had fasted forty **d** and *2250*
9:15 but the **d** will come, when the bridegroom *2250*
11:12 And from the **d** of John the Baptist until *2250*
12: 5 how that on the sabbath **d** the priests in NIG
12:10 saying, Is it lawful to heal on the sabbath **d**? NIG
12:12 it is lawful to do well on the sabbath **d**. NIG
12:40 For as Jonas was three **d** and three nights in *2250*
12:40 so shall the Son of man be three **d** and *2250*
15:32 they continue with me now three **d**, *2250*
17: 1 And after six **d** Jesus taketh Peter, James, *2250*
23:30 If we had been in the **d** of our fathers, *2250*
24:19 and to them that give suck in those **d**. *2250*
24:22 And except those **d** should be shortened, *2250*
24:22 for the elect's sake those **d** shall be *2250*
24:29 Immediately after the tribulation of those **d** *2250*
24:37 But as the **d** of Noe *were,* so shall also *2250*
24:38 For as in the **d** that were before the flood *2250*
26: 2 Ye know that after two **d** is *the feast of* *2250*
26:61 temple of God, and to build it in three **d**. *2250*
27:40 and buildest *it* in three **d**, save thyself. *2250*
27:63 yet alive, After three **d** I will rise *again.* *2250*
Mk 1: 9 And it came to pass in those **d**, *that* Jesus *2250*
1:13 And he was there in the wilderness forty **d**, *2250*
2: 1 he entered into Capernaum after *some* **d**; *2250*
2:20 But the **d** will come, when the bridegroom *2250*
2:20 and then shall they fast in those **d**. *2250*
2:26 of God **in the d of** Abiathar the high priest, *1909*
3: 4 Is it lawful to do good on the sabbath **d**, or NIG
8: 1 In those **d** the multitude being very great, *2250*
8: 2 they have now been with me three **d**, *2250*
8:31 and be killed, and after three **d** rise again. *2250*
9: 2 And after six **d** Jesus taketh *with him* Peter, *2250*
13:17 and to them that give suck in those **d**. *2250*
13:19 For *in* those **d** shall be affliction, such as *2250*
13:20 except that the Lord had shortened *those* **d**, *2250*
13:20 he hath chosen, he hath shortened the **d**. *2250*
13:24 But in those **d**, after that tribulation, the sun *2250*
14: 1 After two **d** was *the feast of* the passover, *2250*
14:58 within three **d** I will build another made *2250*

Mk 15:29 the temple, and buildest *it* in three **d**, *2250*
Lk 1: 5 There was in the **d** of Herod, the king of *2250*
1:23 And it came to pass *that,* as soon as the **d** of *2250*
1:24 And after those **d** his wife Elisabeth *2250*
1:25 Thus hath the Lord dealt with me in the **d** *2250*
1:39 And Mary arose in those **d**, and went into *2250*
1:75 before him, all the **d** of our life. *2250*
2: 1 And it came to pass in those **d**, *that* there *2250*
2: 6 the **d** were accomplished that she should be *2250*
2:21 And when eight **d** were accomplished for *2250*
2:22 And when the **d** of her purification *2250*
2:43 And when they had fulfilled the **d**, as they *2250*
2:46 *that* after three **d** they found him in *2250*
4: 2 Being forty **d** tempted of the devil. And in *2250*
4: 2 And in those **d** he did eat nothing: and *2250*
4:25 many widows were in Israel in the **d** of *2250*
4:31 and taught them on the sabbath **d**. NIG
5:35 But the **d** will come, when the bridegroom *2250*
5:35 and then shall they fast in those **d**. *2250*
6: 2 which is not lawful to do on the sabbath **d**? NIG
6: 9 Is it lawful on the sabbath **d** to do good, NIG
6:12 And it came to pass in those **d**, *that* he went *2250*
9:28 And it came to pass about an eight **d** after *2250*
9:36 told no *man* in those **d** any of *those things* *2250*
13:14 There are six **d** in which *men* ought to *2250*
15:13 And not many **d** after the younger son *2250*
17:22 he said unto the disciples, The **d** will come, *2250*
17:22 when ye shall desire to see one of the **d** of *2250*
17:26 And as it was in the **d** of Noe, so shall it be *2250*
17:26 shall it be also in the **d** of the Son of man. *2250*
17:28 Likewise also as it was in the **d** of Lot; *2250*
19:43 For the **d** shall come upon thee, that thine *2250*
20: 1 And it came to pass, *that* on one of those **d**, *2250*
21: 6 *things* which ye behold, the **d** will come, *2250*
21:22 For these be *the* **d** of vengeance, that all *2250*
21:23 and to them that give suck, in those **d**, *2250*
23:29 For behold, the **d** are coming, in the which *2250*
24:18 which are come to pass there in these **d**? *2250*
Jn 2:12 and they continued there not many **d**. *2250*
2:19 this temple, and in three **d** I will raise it up. *2250*
2:20 and wilt thou rear it up in three **d**? *2250*
4:40 tarry with them: and he abode there two **d**. *2250*
4:43 Now after two **d** he departed thence, and *2250*
11: 6 he abode two **d** *still* in the *same* place *2250*
11:17 that he had *lien* in the grave four **d** already. *2250*
11:39 he stinketh: for he hath been *dead* **four d**. *5066*
12: 1 Then Jesus six **d** before the passover came *2250*
20:26 And after eight **d** again his disciples were *2250*
Ac 1: 3 being seen of them forty **d**, and speaking of *2250*
1: 5 with the Holy Ghost not many **d** hence. *2250*
1:15 And in those **d** Peter stood up in the midst *2250*
2:17 And it shall come to pass in the last **d**, *2250*
2:18 I will pour out in those **d** of my Spirit; *2250*
3:24 have likewise foretold of these **d**. *2250*
5:36 For before these **d** rose up Theudas, *2250*
5:37 up Judas of Galilee in the **d** of the taxing, *2250*
6: 1 And in those **d**, when the number of *2250*
7:41 And they made a calf in those **d**, and *2250*
7:45 the face of our fathers, unto the **d** of David; *2250*
9: 9 And he was three **d** without sight, and *2250*
9:19 Then was Saul certain **d** with the disciples *2250*
9:23 And after that many **d** were fulfilled, *2250*
9:37 And it came to pass in those **d**, that she was *2250*
9:43 that he tarried many **d** in Joppa with one *2250*
10:30 Four **d** ago I was fasting until this hour; *2250*
10:48 Then prayed they him to tarry certain **d**. *2250*
11:27 And in these **d** came prophets from *2250*
11:28 which came to pass in the **d** of Claudius NIG
12: 3 (Then were the **d** of unleavened bread.) *2250*
13:31 And he was seen many **d** of them which *2250*
13:41 for I work a work in your **d**, a work which *2250*
15:36 And some **d** after Paul said unto Barnabas, *2250*
16:12 and we were in that city abiding certain **d**. *2250*
16:18 And this did she many **d**. But Paul, *2250*
17: 2 three sabbath **d** reasoned with them out of NIG
20: 6 Philippi after the **d** of unleavened bread, *2250*
20: 6 and came unto them to Troas in five **d**; *2250*
20: 6 in five days; where we abode seven **d**. *2250*
21: 4 finding disciples, we tarried there seven **d**: *2250*
21: 5 And when we had accomplished *those* **d**, *2250*
21:10 And as we tarried *there* many **d**, there came *2250*
21:15 And after those **d** we took up our carriages, *2250*
21:26 to signify the accomplishment of the **d** of *2250*
21:27 And when the seven **d** were almost ended, *2250*
21:38 which before these **d** madest an uproar, and *2250*
24: 1 And after five **d** Ananias the high priest *2250*
24:11 twelve **d** since I went up to Jerusalem for to *2250*
24:24 And after certain **d**, when Felix came with *2250*
25: 1 after three **d** he ascended from Cesarea to *2250*
25: 6 he had tarried among them more than ten **d**, *2250*
25:13 And after certain **d** king Agrippa and *2250*
25:14 And when they had been there many **d**, *2250*
27: 7 And when we had sailed slowly many **d**, *2250*
27:20 And when neither sun nor stars in many **d** *2250*
28: 7 and lodged *us* three **d** courteously. *2250*
28:12 at Syracuse, we tarried *there* three **d**. *2250*
28:14 were desired to tarry with them seven **d**: *2250*
28:17 that after three **d** Paul called the chief of *2250*
Gal 1:18 to see Peter, and abode with him fifteen **d**. *2250*
4:10 Ye observe **d**, and months, and times, and *2250*
Eph 5:16 Redeeming the time, because the **d** are evil. *2250*
Col 2:16 or of the new moon, or of the **sabbath d**: *4521*
2Ti 3: 1 that in the last **d** perilous times shall come. *2250*
Heb 1: 2 Hath in these last **d** spoken unto us by *his* *2250*
5: 7 Who in the **d** of his flesh, when he had *2250*
7: 3 having neither beginning of **d**, nor end of *2250*
8: 8 *he* saith, Behold, the **d** come, saith *2250*
8:10 make with the house of Israel after those **d**, *2250*
10:16 that I will make with them after those **d**, *2250*
10:32 But call to remembrance the former **d**, *2250*
11:30 after they were compassed about seven **d**. *2250*
12:10 For they verily for a few **d** chastened *us* *2250*
Jas 5: 3 have heaped treasure together for the last **d**. *2250*
1Pe 3:10 For he that will love life, and see good **d**, *2250*
3:20 of God waited in the **d** of Noah, *2250*
2Pe 3: 3 that there shall come in the last **d** scoffers, *2250*
Rev 2:10 be tried; and ye shall have tribulation ten **d**: *2250*
2:13 even in *those* **d** wherein Antipas *was* my *2250*
9: 6 And in those **d** shall men seek death, and *2250*
10: 7 But in the **d** of the voice of the seventh *2250*
11: 3 a thousand two hundred *and* threescore **d**, *2250*
11: 6 that it rain not in the **d** of their prophecy: *2250*
11: 9 nations shall see their dead bodies three **d** *2250*
11:11 And after three **d** and a half the spirit of life *2250*
12: 6 a thousand two hundred *and* threescore **d**. *2250*

DAYS' (13) [DAY]
Ge 30:36 he set three **d** journey betwixt himself and 3117
31:23 and pursued after him seven **d** journey; 3117
Ex 3:18 three **d** journey into the wilderness, 3117
5: 3 three **d** journey into the desert, and 3117
8:27 We will go three **d** journey into 3117
Nu 10:33 the mount of the LORD three **d** journey: 3117
10:33 went before them *in* the three **d** journey, 3117
33: 8 went three **d** journey in the wilderness of 3117
Dt 1: 2 (*There are* eleven **d** *journey* from Horeb *by* 3117
1Sa 11: 3 said unto him, Give us seven **d** respite, 3117
2Sa 24:13 that there be three **d** pestilence in thy land? 3117
2Ki 3: 9 they fetcht a compass of seven **d** journey: 3117
Jnh 3: 3 an exceeding great city of three **d** journey. 3117

DAYSMAN (1) [DAY, MAN]
Job 9:33 Neither is there *any* **d** betwixt us, 3198

DAYSPRING (2) [DAY, SPRING]
Job 38:12 *and* caused the **d** to know his place; 7837
Lk 1:78 whereby the **d** from on high hath visited us, *395*

DAYTIME (7) [DAY, TIME]
Job 5:14 They meet with darkness **in** the **d**, and 3119
24:16 they had marked for themselves **in** the **d**: 3119
Ps 22: 2 I cry in the **d**, but thou hearest not; 3119
42: 8 will command his lovingkindness in the **d**, 3119
78:14 In the **d** also he led them with a cloud, and 3119
Isa 4: 6 for a shadow **in** the **d** from the heat, 3119
21: 8 continually upon the watchtower **in** the **d**, 3119

DEACON (2) [DEACONS]
1Ti 3:10 then let them **use the office of a d**, *1247*
3:13 For they that have **used the office of a d** *1247*

DEACONS (3) [DEACON]
Php 1: 1 are at Philippi, with the bishops and **d**: *1249*
1Ti 3: 8 Likewise *must* the **d** *be* grave, *1249*
3:12 Let the **d** be the husbands of one wife, *1249*

DEAD (364) [DIE]
Ge 20: 3 said to him, Behold, thou *art but* a **d** man, 4191
23: 3 Abraham stood up from before his **d**, and 4191

Ge	23: 4	that I may bury my **d** out of my sight.	4191
	23: 6	in the choice of our sepulchres bury thy **d**;	4191
	23: 6	but that thou mayest bury thy **d**.	4191
	23: 8	If it be your mind that I should bury my **d**	4191
	23:11	sons of my people give I it thee: bury thy **d**.	4191
	23:13	take *it* of me, and I will bury my **d** there.	4191
	23:15	betwixt me and thee? bury therefore thy **d**.	4191
	42:38	for his brother is **d**, and he is left alone:	4191
	44:20	his brother is **d**, and he alone is left of his	4191
	50:15	brethren saw that their father was **d**,	4191
Ex	4:19	for all the men are **d** which sought thy life.	4191
	9: 7	was not one of the cattle of the Israelites **d**.	4191
	12:30	*was* not a house where *there was* not one **d**.	4191
	12:33	in haste; for they said, We *be* all **d** *men.*	4191
	14:30	Israel saw the Egyptians **d** upon the sea	4191
	21:34	owner of them; and the **d** *beast* shall be his.	4191
	21:35	of it; and the **d** *ox* also they shall divide.	4191
	21:36	pay ox for ox; and the **d** shall be his own.	4191
Lev	11:31	doth touch them, when they be **d**,	4194
	11:32	when they are **d**, doth fall, it shall be	4194
	19:28	make any cuttings in your flesh for the **d**,	5315
	21: 1	There shall none be defiled for the **d** among	5315
	21:11	Neither shall he go in to any **d** body,	4191
	22: 4	toucheth any *thing that is* unclean *by* the **d**,	5315
Nu	5: 2	an issue, and whosoever is defiled by the **d**:	5315
	6: 6	the LORD he shall come at no **d** body.	4191
	6:11	for that he sinned by the **d**, and shall hallow	5315
	9: 6	who were defiled by the **d body** of a man,	5315
	9: 7	We *are* defiled by the **d body** of a man:	5315
	9:10	shall be unclean by reason of a **d body**,	5315
	12:12	Let her not be as one **d**, of whom the flesh	4191
	16:48	he stood between the **d** and the living; and	4191
	19:11	He that toucheth the **d** *body* of any man	4191
	19:13	Whosoever toucheth the **d** *body* of *any* man	4191
	19:13	the dead *body* of *any* man that is **d**,	4191
	19:16	or a **d** *body,* or a bone of a man, or a grave,	4191
	19:18	a bone, or one slain, or one **d**, or a grave:	4191
	20:29	all the congregation saw that Aaron was **d**,	1478
Dt	2:16	and **d** from among the people,	4191
	14: 1	*any* baldness between your eyes for the **d**.	4191
	14: 8	eat of their flesh, nor touch their **d carcase**.	5038
	25: 5	the wife of the **d** shall not marry without	4191
	25: 6	in the name of his brother which is **d**,	4191
	26:14	*use,* nor given *ought* thereof for the **d**:	4191
Jos	1: 2	Moses my servant is **d**; now therefore arise,	4191
Jdg	2:19	when the judge was **d**, *that* they returned,	4194
	3:25	their lord *was* fallen down **d** on the earth.	4191
	4: 1	the sight of the LORD, when Ehud was **d**.	4191
	4:22	Sisera lay **d**, and the nail *was* in his	4191
	5:27	where he bowed, there he fell down **d**.	7703
	8:33	it came to pass, as soon as Gideon was **d**,	4191
	9:55	men of Israel saw that Abimelech was **d**,	4191
	16:30	So the **d** which he slew at his death were	4191
	20: 5	concubine have they forced, that she is **d**.	4191
Ru	1: 8	as ye have dealt with the **d**, and with me.	4191
	2:20	off his kindness to the living and to the **d**.	4191
	4: 5	of Ruth the Moabitess, the wife of the **d**,	4191
	4: 5	to raise up the name of the **d** upon his	4191
	4:10	to raise up the name of the **d** upon his	4191
	4:10	that the name of the **d** be not cut off from	4191
1Sa	4:17	are **d**, and the ark of God is taken.	4191
	4:19	her father in law and her husband were **d**,	4191
	17:51	the Philistines saw their champion was **d**,	4191
	24:14	dost thou pursue? after a **d** dog, after a flea.	4191
	25:39	when David heard that Nabal was **d**,	4191
	28: 3	Now Samuel was **d**, and all Israel had	4191
	31: 5	his armourbearer saw that Saul was **d**,	4191
	31: 7	that Saul and his sons were **d**, they forsook	4191
2Sa	1: 4	many of the people also are fallen and **d**;	4191
	1: 4	and Saul and Jonathan his son are **d** also.	4191
	1: 5	thou that Saul and Jonathan his son be **d**?	4191
	2: 7	for your master Saul is **d**, and also	4191
	4: 1	when Saul's son heard that Abner was **d** in	4191
	4:10	one told me, saying, Behold, Saul is **d**,	4191
	9: 8	that thou shouldest look upon such a **d** dog	4191
	11:21	Thy servant Uriah the Hittite is **d** also.	4191
	11:24	*some* of the king's servants be **d**, and	4191
	11:24	and thy servant Uriah the Hittite is **d** also.	4191
	11:26	Uriah heard that Uriah her husband was **d**,	4191
	12:18	feared to tell him that the child was **d**:	4191
	12:18	if we tell him *that* the child is **d**?	4191
	12:19	David perceived that the child was **d**:	4191
	12:19	David said unto his servants, Is the child **d**?	4191
	12:19	Is the child dead? And they said, He is **d**.	4191
	12:21	when the child was **d**, thou didst rise and	4191
	12:23	now he is **d**, wherefore should I fast? can I	4191
	13:32	men the king's sons; for Amnon only is **d**:	4191
	13:33	to think *that* all the king's sons are **d**:	4191
	13:33	king's sons are dead: for Amnon only is **d**.	4191
	13:39	concerning Amnon, seeing he was **d**.	4191
	14: 2	*that had* a long time mourned for the **d**:	4191
	14: 5	a widow woman, and mine husband is **d**.	4191
	16: 9	Why should this **d** dog curse my lord	4191
	18:20	bear no tidings, because the king's son is **d**.	4191
	19:10	whom we anointed over us, is **d** in battle.	4191
	19:28	but **d** men before my lord the king:	4194
1Ki	3:20	and laid her **d** child in my bosom.	4191
	3:21	to give my child suck, behold, it was **d**:	4191
	3:22	the living *is* my son, and the **d** *is* thy son.	4191
	3:22	the **d** *is* thy son, and the living *is* my son.	4191
	3:23	*is* my son that liveth, and thy son *is* the **d**:	4191
	3:23	thy son *is* the **d**, and my son *is* the living.	4191
	11:21	that Joab the captain of the host was **d**,	4191
	13:31	When I am **d**, then bury me in	4191
	21:14	saying, Naboth is stoned, and is **d**.	4191
	21:15	and was **d**, that Jezebel said to Ahab, Arise,	4191
	21:15	for money: for Naboth is not alive, but **d**.	4191
	21:16	when Ahab heard that Naboth was **d**,	4191
2Ki	3: 5	it came to pass, when Ahab was **d**, that	4194
	4: 1	Thy servant my husband is **d**;	4191
	4:32	the child was **d**, *and* laid upon his bed.	4191
	8: 5	king how he had restored a **d** *body* to life,	4191
	11: 1	mother of Ahaziah saw that her son was **d**,	4191
	19:35	behold, they *were* all **d** corpses.	4191
	23:30	his servants carried him *in a chariot* **d** from	4191
1Ch	1:44	when Bela was **d**, Jobab the son of Zerah of	4191
	1:45	when Jobab was **d**, Husham of the land of	4191
	1:46	when Husham was **d**, Hadad the son of	4191
	1:47	when Hadad was **d**, Samlah of Masrekah	4191
	1:48	when Samlah was **d**, Shaul of Rehoboth *by*	4191
	1:49	when Shaul was **d**, Baal-hanan the son of	4191
	1:50	when Baal-hanan was **d**, Hadad reigned in	4191
	2:19	when Azubah was **d**, Caleb took unto him	4191
	2:24	after that Hezron was **d** in Caleb-ephratah,	4194
	10: 5	his armourbearer saw that Saul was **d**,	4191
	10: 7	that Saul and his sons were **d**, then	4191
2Ch	20:24	they *were* **d bodies** fallen to the earth, and	6297
	20:25	in abundance both riches with the **d bodies**,	6297
	22:10	mother of Ahaziah saw that her son was **d**,	4191
Est	2: 7	when her father and mother were **d**,	4194
Job	1:19	it fell upon the young men, and they are **d**;	4191
	26: 5	**D** *things* are formed from under the waters,	7496
Ps	31:12	I am forgotten as a **d man** out of mind:	4191
	76: 6	and horse *are* **cast into a d sleep**.	7290
	79: 2	The **d bodies** of thy servants have they	5038
	88: 5	Free among the **d**, like the slain that lie in	4191
	88:10	Wilt thou shew wonders to the **d**? shall	4191
	88:10	shall the **d** arise *and* praise thee? Selah.	7496
	106:28	and ate the sacrifices of the **d**.	4191
	110: 6	he shall fill *the places with* the **d bodies**;	1472
	115:17	The **d** praise not the LORD, neither any	4191
	143: 3	in darkness, as those that have been long **d**.	4191
Pr	2:18	unto death, and her paths unto the **d**.	7496
	9:18	But he knoweth not that the **d** *are* there; *and*	7496
	21:16	shall remain in the congregation of the **d**.	7496
Ecc	4: 2	Wherefore I praised the **d** which are	4191
	4: 2	**d** more than the living which are yet alive.	4191
	9: 3	they live, and after that *they go* to the **d**.	4191
	9: 4	for a living dog *is* better than a **d** lion.	4191
	9: 5	the **d** know not any thing, neither have they	4191
	10: 1	**D** flies cause the ointment of	4194
Isa	8:19	seek unto their God? for the living to the **d**?	4191
	14: 9	it stirreth up the **d** for thee, *even* all	7496
	22: 2	*are* not slain with the sword, nor **d** in battle.	4191
	26:14	*They are* **d**, they shall not live; *they are*	4191
	26:19	Thy **d** *men* shall live, *together with* my	4191
	26:19	*together with* my **d body** shall they arise.	5038
	26:19	of herbs, and the earth shall cast out the **d**.	7496
	37:36	behold, they *were* all **d** corpses.	4191
	59:10	*we are* in desolate places as **d** *men.*	4191
Jer	16: 7	in mourning, to comfort them for the **d**;	4191
	22:10	Weep ye not for the **d**, neither bemoan him:	4191
	26:23	cast his **d body** into the graves of	5038
	31:40	the whole valley of the **d bodies**, and of	6297
	33: 5	*it is* to fill them with the **d bodies** of men,	6297
	34:20	their **d bodies** shall be for meat unto	5038
	36:30	his **d body** shall be cast out in the day to	5038
	41: 9	had cast all the **d bodies** of the men,	6297

D

La 3: 6 me in dark places, as they that be **d** of old. 4191
Eze 6: 5 I will lay the **d carcases** of the children of 6297
24:17 to cry, make no mourning *for* the **d**, 4191
44:25 they shall come at no **d** person to defile 4191
44:31 shall not eat *of* any thing **that is d of itself**, 5038
Am 8: 3 *there shall be* many **d bodies** in every 6297
Hag 2:13 If *one that is* unclean *by* a **d body** touch 5315
Mt 2:19 But when Herod was **d**, behold, an angel of *5053*
2:20 for they are **d** which sought the young *2348*
8:22 Follow me; and let the **d** bury their dead. *3498*
8:22 Follow me; and let the dead bury their **d**. *3498*
9:18 saying, My daughter is even now **d**: *5053*
9:24 for the maid is not **d**, but sleepeth. And they *599*
10: 8 the lepers, raise the **d**, cast out devils: *3498*
11: 5 the **d** are raised up, and the poor have *3498*
14: 2 he is risen from the **d**; and therefore mighty *3498*
17: 9 the Son of man be risen again from the **d**. *3498*
22:31 But as touching the resurrection of the **d**, *3498*
22:32 God is not the God of the **d**, but of *3498*
23:27 but are within full of **d** *men's* bones, and *3498*
27:64 say unto the people, He is risen from the **d**: *3498*
28: 4 keepers did shake, and became as **d** *men*. *3498*
28: 7 tell his disciples that he is risen from the **d**; *3498*
Mk 5:35 *house certain* which said, Thy daughter is **d**: *599*
5:39 and weep? the damsel is not **d**, but sleepeth. *599*
6:14 That John the Baptist was risen from the **d**, *3498*
6:16 whom I beheaded: he is risen from the **d**. *3498*
9: 9 till the Son of man were risen from the **d**. *3498*
9:10 what the rising from the **d** should mean. *3498*
9:26 and came out of *him:* and he was as **one d**; *3498*
9:26 one dead; insomuch that many said, He is **d**. *599*
12:25 For when they shall rise from the **d**, *3498*
12:26 And as touching the **d**, that they rise: *3498*
12:27 He is not the God of the **d**, but the God of *3498*
15:44 And Pilate marvelled if he were already **d**: *2348*
15:44 asked him whether he had been any while **d**. *599*
Lk 7:12 behold, there was a **d man** carried out, *2348*
7:15 And he that was **d** sat up, and began to *3498*
7:22 are cleansed, the deaf hear, the **d** are raised, *3498*
8:49 *house,* saying to him, Thy daughter is **d**; *2348*
8:52 he said, Weep not; she is not **d**, but sleepeth. *599*
8:53 him to scorn, knowing that she was **d**. *599*
9: 7 of some, that John was risen from the **d**; *3498*
9:60 said unto him, Let the **d** bury their dead: *3498*
9:60 said unto him, Let the dead bury their **d**: *3498*
10:30 and departed, leaving *him* **half d**. *2253*
15:24 For this my son was **d**, and is alive again; *3498*
15:32 for this thy brother was **d**, and is alive *3498*
16:30 but if one went unto them from the **d**, *3498*
16:31 be persuaded, though one rose from the **d**. *3498*
20:35 and the resurrection from the **d**, *3498*
20:37 Now that the **d** are raised, even Moses *3498*
20:38 For he is not a God of the **d**, but of *3498*
24: 5 Why seek ye the living among the **d**? *3498*
24:46 and to rise from the **d** the third day: *3498*
Jn 2:22 When therefore he was risen from the **d**, *3498*
5:21 For as the Father raiseth up the **d**, and *3498*
5:25 when the **d** shall hear the voice of the Son *3498*
6:49 did eat manna in the wilderness, and are **d**. *599*
6:58 not as your fathers did eat manna, and are **d**: *599*
8:52 Abraham is **d**, and the prophets; and *599*
8:53 greater than our father Abraham, which is **d**? *599*
8:53 and the prophets are **d**: whom makest thou *599*
11:14 said Jesus unto them plainly, Lazarus is **d**. *599*
11:25 in me, though he were **d**, *yet* shall he live: *599*
11:39 Martha, the sister of him that was **d**, saith *2348*
11:39 he stinketh: for he hath been ***d*** four days. NIG
11:41 stone *from the place* where the **d** was laid. *2348*
11:44 And he that was **d** came forth, bound hand *2348*
12: 1 where Lazarus was which had been **d**, *2348*
12: 1 had been dead, whom he raised from the **d**. *3498*
12: 9 whom he had raised from the **d**. *3498*
12:17 and raised him from the **d**, bare record. *3498*
19:33 and saw that he was **d** already, they brake *2348*
20: 9 that he must rise again from the **d**. *3498*
21:14 after that he was risen from the **d**. *3498*
Ac 2:29 that he is both **d** and buried, and *5053*
3:15 of life, whom God hath raised from the **d**; *3498*
4: 2 through Jesus the resurrection from the **d**. *3498*
4:10 ye crucified, whom God raised from the **d**, *3498*
5:10 and found her **d**, and, carrying *her* forth, *3498*
7: 4 and from thence, when his father was **d**, *599*
10:41 and drink with him after he rose from the **d**. *3498*
10:42 of God *to be* the Judge of quick and **d**. *3498*
13:30 But God raised him from the **d**: *3498*
13:34 that he raised him up from the **d**, *3498*
14:19 out of the city, supposing he had been **d**. *2348*
17: 3 have suffered, and risen again from the **d**; *3498*
17:31 *men,* in that he hath raised him from the **d**. *3498*
17:32 they heard of the resurrection of the **d**, *3498*
20: 9 from the third loft, and was taken up **d**. *3498*
23: 6 resurrection of the **d** I am called in *3498*
24:15 that there shall be a resurrection of the **d**, *3498*
24:21 Touching the resurrection of the **d** I am *3498*
25:19 and of one Jesus, *which was* **d**, whom Paul *2348*
26: 8 with you, that God should raise the **d**? *3498*
26:23 *be* the first *that* should rise from the **d**, *3498*
28: 6 have swollen, or fallen down **d** suddenly: *3498*
Ro 1: 4 of holiness, by the resurrection from the **d**: *3498*
4:17 who quickeneth the **d**, and calleth those *3498*
4:19 he considered not his own body now **d**, *3499*
4:24 that raised up Jesus our Lord from the **d**; *3498*
5:15 For if through the offence of one many be **d**, *599*
6: 2 How shall we, that are **d** to sin, live any *599*
6: 4 that like as Christ was raised up from the **d** *3498*
6: 7 For he that is **d** is freed from sin. *599*
6: 8 Now if we be **d** with Christ, we believe that *599*
6: 9 being raised from the **d** dieth no more; *3498*
6:11 Likewise reckon ye also yourselves to be **d** *3498*
6:13 as *those that are* alive from the **d**, and *3498*
7: 2 but if the husband be **d**, she is loosed from *599*
7: 3 but if *her* husband be **d**, she is free from *that* *599*
7: 4 ye also are become **d** to the law by *2289*
7: 4 *even* to him who is raised from the **d**, *3498*
7: 6 the law, *that* being **d** wherein we were held; *599*
7: 8 For without the law sin *was* **d**. *3498*
8:10 *be* in you, the body *is* **d** because of sin; *3498*
8:11 raised up Jesus from the **d** dwell in you, *3498*
8:11 he that raised up Christ from the **d** shall *3498*
10: 7 to bring up Christ again from the **d**.) *3498*
10: 9 heart that God hath raised him from the **d**, *3498*
11:15 receiving *of them be,* but life from the **d**? *3498*
14: 9 that he might be Lord both of the **d** and *3498*
1Co 7:39 but if her husband be **d**, she is at liberty to *2837*
15:12 Christ be preached that he rose from the **d**, *3498*
15:12 you that there is no resurrection of the **d**? *3498*
15:13 But if there be no resurrection of the **d**, *3498*
15:15 he raised not up, if so be that the **d** rise not. *3498*
15:16 For if the **d** rise not, then is not Christ *3498*
15:20 But now is Christ risen from the **d**, *and* *3498*
15:21 by man *came* also the resurrection of the **d**. *3498*
15:29 shall they do which are baptized for the **d**, *3498*
15:29 for the dead, if the **d** rise not at all? *3498*
15:29 at all? why are they then baptized for the **d**? *3498*
15:32 what advantageth it me, if the **d** rise not? *3498*
15:35 *man* will say, How are the **d** raised up? *3498*
15:42 So also *is* the resurrection of the **d**. It is *3498*
15:52 and the **d** shall be raised incorruptible, and *3498*
2Co 1: 9 but in God which raiseth the **d**: *3498*
5:14 that if one died for all, then were all **d**: *599*
Gal 1: 1 the Father, who raised him from the **d**;) *3498*
2:19 For I through the law am **d** to the law, that I *599*
2:21 *come* by the law, then Christ is **d** in vain. *599*
Eph 1:20 when he raised him from the **d**, and *3498*
2: 1 And you *hath he quickened,* who were **d** in *3498*
2: 5 Even when we were **d** in sins, *3498*
5:14 and arise from the **d**, and Christ shall give *3498*
Php 3:11 I might attain unto the resurrection of the **d**. *3498*
Col 1:18 is the beginning, the firstborn from the **d**; *3498*
2:12 of God, who hath raised him from the **d**. *3498*
2:13 being **d** in *your* sins and the uncircumcision *3498*
2:20 Wherefore if ye be **d** with Christ from *599*
3: 3 For ye are **d**, and your life is hid with Christ *599*
1Th 1:10 whom he raised from the **d**, *even* Jesus, *3498*
4:16 of God: and the **d** in Christ shall rise first: *3498*
1Ti 5: 6 But she that liveth in pleasure is **d** while *2348*
2Ti 2: 8 raised from the **d** according to my gospel: *3498*
2:11 For if we be **d with** *him,* we shall also live *4880*
4: 1 and the **d** at his appearing and his kingdom; *3498*
Heb 6: 1 the foundation of repentance from **d** works, *3498*
6: 2 and of resurrection of the **d**, and of eternal *3498*
9:14 purge your conscience from **d** works to *3498*
9:17 For a testament *is* of force after *men* are **d**: *3498*
11: 4 his gifts: and by it he being **d** yet speaketh. *599*
11:12 and him **as good as d**, *so many* as the stars *3499*
11:19 *was* able to raise *him* up, even from the **d**; *3498*
11:35 Women received their **d** raised to life *3498*
13:20 that brought again from the **d** our Lord *3498*

Jas 2:17 if it hath not works, is **d**, *being* alone. *3498*
2:20 O vain man, that faith without works is **d**? *3498*
2:26 For as the body without the spirit is **d**, so *3498*
2:26 is dead, so faith without works is **d** also. *3498*
1Pe 1: 3 the resurrection of Jesus Christ from the **d**, *3498*
1:21 that raised him up from the **d**, and gave him *3498*
2:24 that we, being **d** to sins, should live unto *581*
4: 5 that is ready to judge the quick and the **d**. *3498*
4: 6 the gospel preached also to *them that are* **d**, *3498*
Jude 1:12 without fruit, twice **d**, plucked up by *599*
Rev 1: 5 *and* the first begotten of the **d**, and *3498*
1:17 And when I saw him, I fell at his feet as **d**. *3498*
1:18 I am he that liveth, and was **d**; and behold, *3498*
2: 8 and the last, which was **d**, and is alive; *3498*
3: 1 thou hast a name that thou livest, and art **d**. *3498*
11: 8 And their **d bodies** *shall lie* in the street of *4430*
11: 9 nations shall see their **d bodies** three days *4430*
11: 9 shall not suffer their **d bodies** to be put in *4430*
11:18 thy wrath is come, and the time of the **d**, *3498*
14:13 Blessed *are* the **d** which die in the Lord *3498*
16: 3 and it became as the blood of a **d** *man:* and *3498*
20: 5 But the rest of the **d** lived not again until *3498*
20:12 And I saw the **d**, small and great, stand *3498*
20:12 the **d** were judged out of those *things* which *3498*
20:13 And the sea gave up the **d** which were in it; *3498*
20:13 hell delivered up the **d** which were in them: *3498*

DEADLY (7) [DIE]
1Sa 5:11 for there was a **d** destruction throughout all 4194
Ps 17: 9 *from* my **d** enemies, *who* compass 5315+871.1
Eze 30:24 *with* the groanings of a **d wounded** *man.* 2491
Mk 16:18 if they drink any **d** *thing,* it shall not hurt *2286*
Jas 3: 8 *it is* an unruly evil, full of **d** poison. *2287*
Rev 13: 3 to death; and his **d** wound was healed: *2288*
13:12 the first beast, whose **d** wound was healed. *2288*

DEADNESS (1) [DIE]
Ro 4:19 year old, neither *yet* the **d** of Sara's womb: *3500*

DEAF (15)
Ex 4:11 the dumb, or **d**, or the seeing, or the blind? 2795
Lev 19:14 Thou shalt not curse the **d**, nor put a 2795
Ps 38:13 I, as a **d** *man,* heard not; and *I was* as a 2795
58: 4 *they are* like the **d** adder *that* stoppeth her 2795
Isa 29:18 in that day shall the **d** hear the words of 2795
35: 5 and the ears of the **d** shall be unstopped. 2795
42:18 Hear, ye **d**; and look, ye blind, that *ye* may 2795
42:19 or **d**, as my messenger *that* I sent? who *is* 2795
43: 8 that have eyes, and the **d** that have ears. 2795
Mic 7:16 upon *their* mouth, their ears shall be **d**. 2790
Mt 11: 5 and the **d** hear, the dead are raised up, and *2974*
Mk 7:32 And they bring unto him one *that was* **d**, *2974*
7:37 he maketh both the **d** to hear, and the dumb *2974*
9:25 *Thou* dumb and **d** spirit, I charge thee, *2974*
Lk 7:22 the **d** hear, the dead are raised, *2974*

DEAL (60) [DEALER, DEALERS, DEALEST, DEALETH, DEALING, DEALINGS, DEALS, DEALT]
Ge 19: 9 now will we **d worse** with thee, than with 7489
21:23 God that thou wilt not **d falsely** with me, 8266
24:49 now if ye will **d** kindly and truly with my 6213
32: 9 to thy kindred, and I will **d well** with thee: 3190
34:31 Should he **d with** our sister as with a 6213
47:29 my thigh, and **d** kindly and truly with me; 6213
Ex 1:10 Come on, let us **d wisely** with them; 2449
8:29 let not Pharaoh **d deceitfully** any more in 2048
21: 9 he shall **d** with her after the manner of 6213
23:11 In like manner thou shalt **d** with thy 6213
29:40 with the one lamb a **tenth d** of flour 6241
Lev 14:21 **one tenth d** of fine flour mingled with 259+6241
19:11 Ye shall not steal, neither **d falsely**, 3584
Nu 11:15 if thou **d** thus **with** me, kill me, I pray thee, 6213
15: 4 **tenth d** *of* flour mingled with the fourth 6241
28:13 a **several tenth d** of flour mingled 6241+6241
28:21 A **several tenth d** shalt thou offer 6241+6241
28:29 A **several tenth d** unto one lamb, 6241+6241
29: 4 one **tenth d** for one lamb, throughout 6241
29:10 A **several tenth d** for one lamb, 6241+6241
29:15 a **several tenth d** to each lamb of 6241+6241
Dt 7: 5 thus shall ye **d** with them; ye shall destroy 6213
Jos 2:14 that we will **d** kindly and truly with thee. 6213
Ru 1: 8 the LORD **d** kindly with you, as ye have 6213
1Sa 20: 8 Therefore thou shalt **d** kindly with thy 6213
2Sa 18: 5 *D* gently for my sake with the young man, NIH
2Ch 2: 3 As thou didst **d** with David my father, and 6213
2: 3 house to dwell therein, *even so* **d** *with me.* NIH
19:11 **D** courageously, and the LORD shall be 6213
Job 42: 8 lest *I* **d** with you *after your* folly, in that ye 6213
Ps 75: 4 I said unto the fools, **D** not **foolishly**: and 1984
105:25 his people, to **d subtilly** with his servants. 5230
119:17 **D bountifully** with thy servant, *that* I may 1580
119:124 **D** with thy servant according unto thy 6213
142: 7 for thou shalt **d bountifully** with me. 1580
Pr 12:22 but they that **d** truly *are* his delight. 6213
Isa 26:10 the land of uprightness will he **d unjustly**, 5765
33: 1 thou shalt make an end to **d treacherously**, 898
33: 1 they shall **d treacherously** with thee. 898
48: 8 thou wouldest **d very treacherously**, 898+898
52:13 Behold, my servant shall **d prudently**, 7919
58: 7 *Is it* not to **d** thy bread to the hungry, and 6536
Jer 12: 1 they happy that **d very treacherously**? 898+899
18:23 **d** *thus* with them in the time of thine anger. 6213
21: 2 be that the LORD will **d** with us 6213
Eze 8:18 Therefore will I also **d** in fury: mine eye 6213
16:59 I will even **d** with thee as thou hast done, 6213
18: 9 and hath kept my judgments, to **d** truly; 6213
22:14 in the days that I shall **d** with thee? 6213
23:25 and they shall **d** furiously with thee: 6213
23:29 they shall **d** with thee hatefully, and 6213
31:11 he shall **surely d** with him: 6213+6213
Da 1:13 and as thou seest, **d** with thy servants. 6213
11: 7 and shall **d** against them, and shall prevail: 6213
Hab 1:13 thou upon them that **d treacherously**, 898
Mal 2:10 why do we **d treacherously** every man 898
2:15 let none **d treacherously** against the wife of 898
2:16 to your spirit, that ye **d** not **treacherously**. 898
Mk 7:36 much the more a **great d** they published *it;* *4054*
10:48 but he cried the more a **great d**, *Thou* Son *4183*

DEALER (1) [DEAL]
Isa 21: 2 the **treacherous d** dealeth treacherously, and 898

DEALERS (2) [DEAL]
Isa 24:16 the **treacherous d** have dealt treacherously; 898
24:16 the **treacherous d** have dealt very 898

DEALEST (2) [DEAL]
Ex 5:15 Wherefore **d** thou thus with thy servants? 6213
Isa 33: 1 **d treacherously**, and they dealt not 898

DEALETH (10) [DEAL]
Jdg 18: 4 Thus and thus **d** Micah with me, and 6213
1Sa 23:22 it is told me *that* he **d very subtilly**. 6191+6191
Pr 10: 4 *He becometh* poor that **d** *with* a slack hand: 6213
13:16 Every prudent *man* **d** with knowledge: but 6213
14:17 *He that is* soon angry **d** foolishly: and 6213
21:24 scorner *is* his name, who **d** in proud wrath. 6213
Isa 21: 2 the treacherous dealer **d treacherously**, and 898
Jer 6:13 even unto the priest every one **d** falsely. 6213
8:10 even unto the priest every one **d** falsely. 6213
Heb 12: 7 God **d** with you as with sons; *4374*

DEALING (1) [DEAL]
Ps 7:16 his **violent d** shall come down upon his 2555

DEALINGS (2) [DEAL]
1Sa 2:23 for I hear of your evil **d** by all this people. 1697
Jn 4: 9 For the Jews **have** no **d with** *4798*

DEALS (19) [DEAL]
Lev 14:10 **three tenth d** of fine flour *for* a meat 6241+7969
23:13 two **tenth d** *of* fine flour mingled with oil, 6241
23:17 two wave loaves of two **tenth d**: 6241
24: 5 two **tenth d** shall be *in* one cake. 6241
Nu 15: 6 **tenth d** *of* flour mingled with the third *part* 6241
15: 9 **tenth d** *of* flour mingled with half a hin of 6241
28: 9 two **tenth d** *of* flour *for* a meat offering, 6241
28:12 three **tenth d** *of* flour *for* a meat offering, 6241
28:12 two **tenth d** *of* flour *for* a meat offering, 6241
28:20 three **tenth d** shall ye offer for a bullock, 6241
28:20 for a bullock, and two **tenth d** for a ram; 6241
28:28 three **tenth d** unto one bullock, two tenth 6241
28:28 one bullock, two **tenth d** unto one ram, 6241
29: 3 three **tenth d** for a bullock, *and* two tenth 6241
29: 3 for a bullock, *and* two **tenth d** for a ram, 6241
29: 9 three **tenth d** to a bullock, *and* two tenth 6241
29: 9 to a bullock, *and* two **tenth d** to one ram, 6241
29:14 three **tenth d** unto every bullock of 6241
29:14 two **tenth d** to each ram of the two rams, 6241

DEALT (57) [DEAL]
Ge 16: 6 when Sarai **d hardly with** her, she fled 6031
33:11 because God hath **d graciously** with me, 2603
43: 6 Israel said, Wherefore **d** ye *so* **ill** with me, 7489
Ex 1:20 Therefore God **d well** with the midwives: 3190
14:11 wherefore hast thou **d** thus with us, to carry 6213
18:11 for in the thing wherein they **d proudly** *he* 2102
21: 8 seeing he hath **d deceitfully** with her. 898
Jdg 9:16 if ye have **d** well with Jerubbaal and his 6213
9:19 If ye then have **d** truly and sincerely with 6213
9:23 the men of Shechem **d treacherously** with 898
Ru 1: 8 as ye have **d** with the dead, and with me. 6213
1:20 for the Almighty hath **d** very **bitterly** with 4843
1Sa 24:18 *this* day how that thou hast **d** well with me: 6213
25:31 when the LORD shall have **d well** with 3190
2Sa 6:19 he **d** among all the people, *even* among 2505
2Ki 12:15 on workmen: for they **d** faithfully. 6213
21: 6 and **d** with familiar spirits and wizards: 6213
22: 7 into their hand, because they **d** faithfully. 6213
1Ch 16: 3 he **d** to every one of Israel, both man and 2505
20: 3 **d** David with all the cities of the children of 6213
2Ch 6:37 we have done amiss, and have **d wickedly**; 7561
11:23 he **d wisely**, and dispersed of all his children 995
33: 6 **d** with a familiar spirit, and with wizards: 6213
Ne 1: 7 We have **d very corruptly** against 2254+2254
9:10 for thou knewest that they **d proudly** 2102
9:16 they and our fathers **d proudly**, and 2102
9:29 yet they **d proudly**, and hearkened not unto 2102
Job 6:15 My brethren have **d deceitfully** as a brook, 898
Ps 13: 6 because he hath **d bountifully** with me. 1580
44:17 neither have we **d falsely** in thy covenant. 8266
78:57 and **d unfaithfully** like their fathers: 898
103:10 He hath not **d with** us after our sins; 6213
116: 7 for the LORD hath **d bountifully** with 1580
119:65 Thou hast **d** well with thy servant, 6213
119:78 for they **d perversely with** me without a 5791
147:20 He hath not **d** so with any nation: and *as for* 6213
Isa 24:16 treacherous dealers have **d treacherously**; 898
24:16 dealers have **d very treacherously**. 898+899
33: 1 and they **d** not **treacherously** with thee! 898
Jer 3:20 so have you **d treacherously** with me, 898
5:11 have **d very treacherously** against me, 898+898
12: 6 even they have **d treacherously** with thee; 898
La 1: 2 her friends have **d treacherously** with her, 898
Eze 22: 7 in the midst of thee have they **d** by 6213
25:12 Because that Edom hath **d** against 6213
25:15 Because the Philistines have **d** by revenge, 6213
Hos 5: 7 They have **d treacherously** against 898
6: 7 there have they **d treacherously** against me. 898
Joel 2:26 that hath **d** wondrously with you: 6213
Zec 1: 6 to our doings, so hath he **d** with us. 6213
Mal 2:11 Judah hath **d treacherously**, and 898
2:14 against whom thou hast **d treacherously**: 898
Lk 1:25 Thus hath the Lord **d** with me in the days *4160*
2:48 Son, why hast thou thus **d** with us? *4160*
Ac 7:19 The same **d subtilly with** our kindred, and *2686*
25:24 the multitude of the Jews have **d with** me, *1793*
Ro 12: 3 according as God hath **d** to every man *3307*

DEAR (7) [DEARLY]
Jer 31:20 *Is* Ephraim my **d** son? *is he* a pleasant 3357
Lk 7: 2 who was **d** unto him, was sick, and ready to *1784*
Ac 20:24 neither count I my life **d** unto myself, so *5093*
Eph 5: 1 therefore followers of God, as **d** children; *27*
Col 1: 7 As ye also learned of Epaphras our **d** *27*
1:13 hath translated *us* into the kingdom of his **d** *26*
1Th 2: 8 our own souls, because ye were **d** unto us. *27*

DEARLY (10) [DEAR]
Jer 12: 7 I have given the **d beloved** of my soul into 3033
Ro 12:19 **D beloved**, avenge not yourselves, but *27*
1Co 10:14 Wherefore, my **d beloved**, flee from idolatry. *27*
2Co 7: 1 Having therefore these promises, **d beloved**, *27*
12:19 but *we do* all *things*, **d beloved**, for your *27*
Php 4: 1 my brethren **d beloved** and longed for, my joy *27*
4: 1 so stand fast in the Lord, *my* **d beloved**. *27*
2Ti 1: 2 To Timothy, *my* **d beloved** son: Grace, *27*
Phm 1: 1 unto Philemon *our* **d beloved**, and *27*
1Pe 2:11 **D beloved**, I beseech *you* as strangers and *27*

DEARTH (8)
Ge 41:54 the seven years of **d** began to come, 7458
41:54 the **d** was in all lands; but in all the land of 7458
2Ki 4:38 *there was* a **d** in the land; and the sons of 7458
2Ch 6:28 If there be **d** in the land, if there be 7458
Ne 5: 3 that we might buy corn, because of the **d**. 7458
Jer 14: 1 that came to Jeremiah concerning the **d**. 1226
Ac 7:11 Now there came a **d** over all the land of *3042*
11:28 should be great **d** throughout all the world: *3042*

DEATH (372) [DIE]
Ge 21:16 she said, Let me not see the **d** of the child. 4194
24:67 Isaac was comforted after his mother's **d**. NIH
25:11 And it came to pass after the **d** of Abraham, 4194
26:11 his wife shall **surely be put to d**. 4191+4191
26:18 had stopped them after the **d** of Abraham: 4194
27: 2 I am old, I know not the day of my **d**: 4194
27: 7 bless thee before the LORD before my **d**. 4194
27:10 and that he may bless thee before his **d**. 4194
Ex 10:17 that he may take away from me this **d** only. 4194
19:12 the mount shall be **surely put to d**: 4191+4191
21:12 that he die, shall be **surely put to d**. 4191+4191
21:15 his mother, shall be **surely put to d**. 4191+4191
21:16 his hand, he shall **surely** be **put to d**. 4191+4191
21:17 his mother, shall **surely** be **put to d**. 4191+4191
21:29 and his owner also shall be **put to d**. 4191
22:19 with a beast shall **surely** be **put to d**. 4191+4191
31:14 defileth it shall **surely** be **put to d**: 4191+4191
31:15 he shall **surely** be **put to d**. 4191+4191
35: 2 doeth work therein shall be **put to d**. 4191
Lev 16: 1 the LORD spake unto Moses after the **d** of 4194
19:20 they shall not be **put to d**, because she was 4191
20: 2 he shall **surely** be **put to d**: 4191+4191
20: 9 his mother shall be **surely put to d**: 4191+4191
20:10 adulteress shall **surely** be **put to d**. 4191+4191
20:11 of them shall **surely** be **put to d**; 4191+4191
20:12 of them shall **surely** be **put to d**: 4191+4191
20:13 they shall **surely** be **put to d**; their 4191+4191
20:15 a beast, he shall **surely** be **put to d**: 4191+4191
20:16 they shall **surely** be **put to d**; their 4191+4191
20:27 is a wizard, shall **surely** be **put to d**: 4191+4191
24:16 he shall **surely** be **put to d**, *and* 4191+4191
24:16 the name *of the LORD*, shall be **put to d**. 4191
24:17 any man shall **surely** be **put to d**. 4191+4191
24:21 he that killeth a man, he shall be **put to d**. 4191
27:29 *but* shall **surely** be **put to d**. 4191+4191
Nu 1:51 stranger that cometh nigh shall be **put to d**. 4191
3:10 stranger that cometh nigh shall be **put to d**. 4191
3:38 stranger that cometh nigh shall be **put to d**. 4191
15:35 The man shall be **surely put to d**: 4191+4191
16:29 If these *men* die the common **d** of all men, 4194
18: 7 stranger that cometh nigh shall be **put to d**. 4191
23:10 Let me die the **d** of the righteous, and 4194
35:16 murderer shall **surely** be **put to d**. 4191+4191
35:17 murderer shall **surely** be **put to d**. 4191+4191
35:18 murderer shall **surely** be **put to d**. 4191+4191
35:21 smote *him* shall **surely** be **put to d**; 4191+4191
35:25 he shall abide in it unto the **d** of the high 4194
35:28 of his refuge until the **d** of the high priest: 4194
35:28 after the **d** of the high priest the slayer shall 4194
35:30 the murderer shall be **put to d** by the mouth 7523
35:31 the life of a murderer, which *is* guilty of **d**: 4191
35:31 but he shall be **surely put to d**. 4191+4191
35:32 dwell in the land, until the **d** of the priest. 4194
Dt 13: 5 that dreamer of dreams, shall be **put to d**; 4191
13: 9 shall be first upon him to **put** him **to d**, 4191
17: 6 shall he that is *worthy* of **d** be put to death; 4191
17: 6 shall he that is *worthy* of death be **put to d**; 4191
17: 6 of one witness he shall not be **put to d**. 4191
17: 7 shall be first upon him to **put** him **to d**, 4191
19: 6 whereas he *was* not worthy of **d**, 4194
21:22 if a man have committed a sin worthy of **d**, 4194
21:22 he be *to be* **put to d**, and thou hang him on 4191
22:26 *there is* in the damsel no sin *worthy* of **d**: 4194
24:16 The fathers shall not be **put to d** for 4191
24:16 neither shall the children be **put to d** for 4191
24:16 every man shall be **put to d** for his own sin. 4191
30:15 thee *this* day life and good, and **d** and evil; 4194
30:19 *that* I have set before you life and **d**, 4194
31:27 and how much more after my **d**? 4194
31:29 For I know that after my **d** ye will utterly 4194
33: 1 blessed the children of Israel before his **d**. 4194
Jos 1: 1 Now after the **d** of Moses the servant of 4194
1:18 thou commandest him, he shall be **put to d**: 4191
2:13 that they have, and deliver our lives from **d**. 4194
20: 6 until the **d** of the high priest that shall be in 4194
Jdg 1: 1 Now after the **d** of Joshua it came to pass, 4194
5:18 unto the **d** in the high places of the field. 4191

Jdg	6:31	let him be **put to d** whilst *it is yet* morning:	4191
	13: 7	to God from the womb to the day of his **d**.	4194
	16:16	*so* that his soul was vexed unto **d**;	4191
	16:30	So the dead which he slew at his **d** were	4194
	20:13	that we may **put** them **to d**, and put away	4191
	21: 5	He shall **surely** be **put to d**.	4191+4191
Ru	1:17	more also, *if ought* but **d** part thee and me.	4194
	2:11	mother in law since the **d** of thine husband:	4194
1Sa	4:20	about the time of her **d** the *women* that	4191
	11:12	bring the men, that we may **put** them **to d**.	4191
	11:13	There shall not a man be **put to d** this day:	4191
	15:32	Surely the bitterness of **d** is past.	4194
	15:35	no more to see Saul until the day of his **d**:	4194
	20: 3	*there is* but a step between me and **d**.	4194
	22:22	I have occasioned *the* **d** of all the persons of	NIH
2Sa	1: 1	Now it came to pass after the **d** of Saul,	4194
	1:23	and in their **d** they were not divided:	4194
	6:23	of Saul had no child unto the day of her **d**.	4194
	8: 2	*with* two lines measured he to **put to d**,	4191
	15:21	whether in **d** or life, even there *also* will thy	4194
	19:21	said, Shall not Shimei be **put to d** for this,	4191
	19:22	shall there any man be **put to d** *this* day in	4191
	20: 3	they were shut up unto the day of their **d**,	4191
	21: 9	and were **put to d** in the days of harvest,	4191
	22: 5	When the waves of **d** compassed me,	4194
	22: 6	me about; the snares of **d** prevented me:	4194
1Ki	2: 8	I will not **put** thee **to d** with the sword.	4191
	2:24	Adonijah shall be **put to d** *this* day.	4191
	2:26	thine own fields; for thou *art* worthy of **d**:	4194
	2:26	I will not at this time **put** thee **to d**, because	4191
	11:40	and was in Egypt until the **d** of Solomon.	4194
2Ki	1: 1	Moab rebelled against Israel after the **d** of	4194
	2:21	there shall not be from thence any more **d**	4194
	4:40	O thou man of God, *there is* **d** in the pot.	4194
	14: 6	The fathers shall not be **put to d** for	4191
	14: 6	nor the children be **put to d** for the fathers;	4191
	14: 6	every man shall be **put to d** for his own sin.	4191
	14:17	**d** of Jehoash son of Jehoahaz king of Israel	4194
	15: 5	so that he was a leper unto the day of his **d**,	4194
	20: 1	In those days was Hezekiah sick unto **d**.	4191
1Ch	22: 5	So David prepared abundantly before his **d**.	4194
2Ch	15:13	LORD God of Israel should be **put to d**,	4191
	22: 4	for they were his counsellers after the **d** of	4194
	23: 7	cometh into the house, he shall be **put to d**:	4191
	24:17	Now after the **d** of Jehoiada came	4194
	25:25	**d** of Joash son of Jehoahaz king of Israel	4194
	26:21	the king was a leper unto the day of his **d**,	4194
	32:24	In those days Hezekiah was sick to the **d**,	4191
	32:33	of Jerusalem did him honour at his **d**.	4194
Ezr	7:26	whether *it be* unto **d**, or to banishment, or	4193
Est	4:11	*there is* one law of his to **put** *him* **to d**,	4191
Job	3: 5	Let darkness and the **shadow of d** stain it;	6757
	3:21	Which long for **d**, but it *cometh* not; and	4194
	5:20	In famine he shall redeem thee from **d**: and	4194
	7:15	*and* **d** rather than my life.	4194
	10:21	the land of darkness and the **shadow of d**;	6757
	10:22	*and of* the **shadow of d**, without any order,	6757
	12:22	and bringeth out to light the **shadow of d**.	6757
	16:16	and on mine eyelids *is* the **shadow of d**;	6757
	18:13	*even* the firstborn of **d** shall devour his	4194
	24:17	*is* to them even as the **shadow of d**:	6757
	24:17	*they are in* the terrors of the **shadow of d**.	6757
	27:15	that remain of him shall be buried in **d**:	4194
	28: 3	stones of darkness, and the **shadow of d**.	6757
	28:22	Destruction and **d** say, We have heard	4194
	30:23	For I know *that* thou wilt bring me *to* **d**,	4194
	34:22	*There is* no darkness, nor **shadow of d**,	6757
	38:17	Have the gates of **d** been opened unto thee?	4194
	38:17	thou seen the doors of the **shadow of d**?	6757
Ps	6: 5	For in **d** *there is* no remembrance of thee:	4194
	7:13	also prepared for him the instruments of **d**;	4194
	9:13	thou that liftest me up from the gates of **d**:	4194
	13: 3	mine eyes, lest I sleep the *sleep of* **d**;	4194
	18: 4	The sorrows of **d** compassed me, and	4194
	18: 5	me about: the snares of **d** prevented me.	4194
	22:15	and thou hast brought me into the dust of **d**.	4194
	23: 4	through the valley of the **shadow of d**,	6757
	33:19	To deliver their soul from **d**, and to keep	4194
	44:19	and covered us with the **shadow of d**.	6757
	48:14	and ever: he will be our guide *even* unto **d**.	4191
	49:14	**d** shall feed *on* them; and the upright shall	4194
	55: 4	and the terrors of **d** are fallen upon me.	4194
	55:15	Let **d** seize upon them, *and* let them go	4194
	56:13	For thou hast delivered my soul from **d**:	4194
	68:20	GOD the Lord *belong* the issues from **d**.	4194
	73: 4	For *there are* no bands in their **d**: but	4194
	78:50	he spared not their soul from **d**, but	4194
	89:48	man *is he that* liveth, and shall not see **d**?	4194
	102:20	loose those that are **appointed to d**;	1121+8546
	107:10	as sit in darkness and in the **shadow of d**,	6757
	107:14	them out of darkness and the **shadow of d**,	6757
	107:18	and they draw near unto the gates of **d**.	4194
	116: 3	The sorrows of **d** compassed me, and	4194
	116: 8	For thou hast delivered my soul from **d**,	4194
	116:15	Precious in the sight of the LORD *is* the **d**	4194
	118:18	but he hath not given me over unto **d**.	4194
Pr	2:18	For her house inclineth unto **d**, and	4194
	5: 5	Her feet go down *to* **d**; her steps take hold	4194
	7:27	to hell, going down to the chambers of **d**.	4194
	8:36	his own soul: all they that hate me love **d**.	4194
	10: 2	but righteousness delivereth from **d**.	4194
	11: 4	but righteousness delivereth from **d**.	4194
	11:19	that pursueth evil *pursueth it* to his own **d**.	4194
	12:28	and *in* the pathway *thereof there is* no **d**.	4194
	13:14	of life, to depart from the snares of **d**.	4194
	14:12	but the end thereof *are* the ways of **d**.	4194
	14:27	of life, to depart from the snares of **d**.	4194
	14:32	but the righteous hath hope in his **d**.	4194
	16:14	The wrath of a king *is as* messengers of **d**:	4194
	16:25	but the end thereof *are* the ways of **d**.	4194
	18:21	**D** and life *are* in the power of the tongue:	4194
	21: 6	vanity tossed to and fro of them that seek **d**.	4194
	24:11	to deliver *them that are* drawn unto **d**,	4194
	26:18	*man* who casteth firebrands, arrows, and **d**,	4194
Ecc	7: 1	and the day of **d** than the day of one's birth.	4194
	7:26	I find more bitter than **d** the woman,	4194
	8: 8	neither *hath he* power in the day of **d**:	4194
SS	8: 6	for love *is* strong as **d**; jealousy *is* cruel as	4194
Isa	9: 2	that dwell in the land of the **shadow of d**,	6757
	25: 8	He will swallow up **d** in victory; and	4194
	28:15	We have made a covenant with **d**, and	4194
	28:18	your covenant with **d** shall be disannulled,	4194
	38: 1	In those days was Hezekiah sick unto **d**.	4191
	38:18	cannot praise thee, **d** can *not* celebrate thee:	4194
	53: 9	with the wicked, and with the rich in his **d**;	4194
	53:12	because he hath poured out his soul unto **d**:	4194
Jer	2: 6	a land of drought, and of the **shadow of d**,	6757
	8: 3	**d** shall be chosen rather than life by all	4194
	9:21	For **d** is come up into our windows, *and*	4194
	13:16	he turn it into the **shadow of d**, *and* make *it*	6757
	15: 2	Such as *are* for **d**, to death; and such as *are*	4194
	15: 2	Such as *are* for death, to **d**; and such as *are*	4194
	18:21	and let their men be **put to d**;	2026+4194
	21: 8	you the way of life, and the way of **d**.	4194
	26:15	know ye for certain, that if ye **put** me **to d**,	4191
	26:19	and all Judah **put** him **at all to d**?	4191+4191
	26:21	his words, the king sought to **put** him **to d**:	4191
	26:24	into the hand of the people to **put** him **to d**.	4191
	38: 4	We beseech thee, let this man be **put to d**:	4191
	38:15	wilt thou not **surely put** me **to d**?	4191+4191
	38:16	made us this soul, I will not **put** thee **to d**,	4191
	38:25	not from us, and we will not **put** thee **to d**;	4191
	43: 3	that *they* might **put** us **to d**, and carry us	4191
	43:11	*and deliver* such *as are* for **d** to death;	4194
	43:11	*and deliver* such *as are* for death to **d**;	4194
	52:11	and put him in prison till the day of his **d**.	4194
	52:27	**put** them **to d** in Riblah in the land of	4191
	52:34	every day a portion until the day of his **d**,	4194
La	1:20	the sword bereaveth, at home *there is* as **d**.	4194
Eze	18:32	For I have no pleasure in the **d** of him that	4194
	31:14	for they are all delivered unto **d**, to	4194
	33:11	I have no pleasure in the **d** of the wicked;	4194
Hos	13:14	of the grave; I will redeem them from **d**:	4194
	13:14	O **d**, I will be thy plagues; O grave, I will	4194
Am	5: 8	turneth the **shadow of d** into the morning,	6757
Jnh	4: 9	he said, I do well to be angry, *even* unto **d**.	4194
Hab	2: 5	*is* as **d**, and cannot be satisfied, but	4194
Mt	2:15	And was there until the **d** of Herod: that it	*5054*
	4:16	and shadow of **d** light is sprung up.	*2288*
	10:21	the brother shall deliver up the brother to **d**,	*2288*
	10:21	and cause them to be **put to d**.	*2289*
	14: 5	And when he would have **put** him **to d**,	*615*
	15: 4	curseth father or mother, let him die the **d**.	*2288*
	16:28	standing here, which shall not taste of **d**,	*2288*
	20:18	and they shall condemn him to **d**,	*2288*
	26:38	soul is exceeding sorrowful, *even* unto **d**:	*2288*
	26:59	false witness against Jesus, to **put** him **to d**;	*2289*
	26:66	They answered and said, He is guilty of **d**.	*2288*

Mt 27: 1 took counsel against Jesus to **put him to d**: *2289*
Mk 5:23 daughter **lieth at the point of d**: *2079+2192*
7:10 curseth father or mother, let him die the **d**. 2288
9: 1 that stand here, which shall not taste of **d**, 2288
10:33 and they shall condemn him to **d**, and 2288
13:12 the brother shall betray the brother to **d**, 2288
13:12 and shall cause them to be **put to d**. *2289*
14: 1 might take him by craft, and **put** *him* **to d**. *615*
14:34 My soul is exceeding sorrowful unto **d**: 2288
14:55 for witness against Jesus to **put him to d**; *2289*
14:64 they all condemned him to be guilty of **d**. 2288
Lk 1:79 that sit in darkness and *in* the shadow of **d**, 2288
2:26 that *he* should not see **d**, before he had seen 2288
9:27 standing here, which shall not taste of **d**, 2288
18:33 they shall scourge *him*, and **put** him **to d**: *615*
21:16 *some* of you shall they cause to be **put to d**. *2289*
22:33 to go with thee, both into prison, and to **d**. 2288
23:15 lo, nothing worthy of **d** is done unto him. 2288
23:22 I have found no cause of **d** in him: I will 2288
23:32 malefactors, led with him to be **put to d**. *337*
24:20 rulers delivered him to be condemned to **d**, 2288
Jn 4:47 and heal his son: for he was at the point of **d**. *599*
5:24 but is passed from **d** unto life. 2288
8:51 a man keep my saying, he shall never see **d**. 2288
8:52 keep my saying, he shall never taste of **d**. 2288
11: 4 This sickness is not unto **d**, but for 2288
11:13 Howbeit Jesus spake of his **d**: but 2288
11:53 took counsel together for to **put him to d**. *615*
12:10 that they might **put** Lazarus also **to d**; *615*
12:33 he said, signifying what **d** he should die. 2288
18:31 It is not lawful for us to **put** any *man* **to d**: *615*
18:32 he spake, signifying what **d** he should die. 2288
21:19 signifying by what **d** he should glorify 2288
Ac 2:24 raised up, having loosed the pains of **d**: 2288
8: 1 And Saul was consenting unto his **d**. And at *336*
12:19 commanded that *they* should be **put to d**. *520*
13:28 And though they found no cause of **d** *in* 2288
22: 4 And I persecuted this way unto the **d**, 2288
22:20 and consenting unto his **d**, and kept *336*
23:29 have nothing laid to his charge worthy of **d** 2288
25:11 or have committed any *thing* worthy of **d**, 2288
25:25 that he had committed nothing worthy of **d**, 2288
26:10 and when they were **put to d**, I gave my *337*
26:31 This man doeth nothing worthy of **d** or 2288
28:18 because there was no cause of **d** in me. 2288
Ro 1:32 which commit such *things* are worthy of **d**, 2288
5:10 we were reconciled to God by the **d** of his 2288
5:12 sin entered into the world, and **d** by sin; 2288
5:12 and so **d** passed upon all men, for that all 2288
5:14 Nevertheless **d** reigned from Adam to 2288
5:17 For if by one man's offence **d** reigned by 2288
5:21 That as sin hath reigned unto **d**, even so 2288
6: 3 into Jesus Christ were baptized into his **d**? 2288
6: 4 we are buried with him by baptism into **d**: 2288
6: 5 planted together in the likeness of his **d**, 2288
6: 9 **d** hath no more dominion over him. 2288
6:16 whether of sin unto **d**, or of obedience unto 2288
6:21 for the end of those *things is* **d**. 2288
6:23 For the wages of sin *is* **d**; but the gift of 2288
7: 5 in our members to bring forth fruit unto **d**. 2288
7:10 was *ordained* to life, I found *to be* unto **d**. 2288
7:13 then that which is good made **d** unto me? 2288
7:13 working **d** in me by that which is good; 2288
7:24 shall deliver me from the body of this **d**? 2288
8: 2 made me free from the law of sin and **d**. 2288
8: 6 For to be carnally minded *is* **d**; 2288
8:38 that neither **d**, nor life, nor angels, 2288
1Co 3:22 or **d**, or *things* present, or *things* to come; 2288
4: 9 the apostles last, as *it were* **appointed to d**: *1935*
11:26 ye do shew the Lord's **d** till he come. 2288
15:21 For since by man *came* **d**, by man *came* 2288
15:26 The last enemy *that* shall be destroyed *is* **d**. 2288
15:54 is written, **D** is swallowed up in victory. 2288
15:55 O **d**, where *is* thy sting? O grave, where *is* 2288
15:56 The sting of **d** *is* sin; 2288
2Co 1: 9 But we had the sentence of **d** in ourselves, 2288
1:10 Who delivered us from so great a **d**, and 2288
2:16 To the one *we are* the savour of **d** unto 2288
2:16 the one *we are* the savour of death unto **d**; 2288
3: 7 But if the ministration of **d**, written *and* 2288
4:11 are alway delivered unto **d** for Jesus' sake, 2288
4:12 So then **d** worketh in us, but life in you. 2288
7:10 but the sorrow of the world worketh **d**. 2288
Php 1:20 in my body, whether *it be* by life, or by **d**. 2288
2: 8 and became obedient unto **d**, 2288
2: 8 unto death, even the **d** of the cross. 2288
2:27 For indeed he was sick nigh unto **d**: but 2288
2:30 for the work of Christ he was nigh unto **d**, 2288
3:10 being made conformable unto his **d**; 2288
Col 1:22 In the body of his flesh through **d**, 2288
2Ti 1:10 who hath abolished **d**, and hath brought life 2288
Heb 2: 9 for the suffering of **d**, crowned with glory 2288
2: 9 that he by the grace of God should taste **d** 2288
2:14 that through **d** he might destroy him that 2288
2:14 might destroy him that had the power of **d**, 2288
2:15 And deliver them who through fear of **d** 2288
5: 7 unto him that was able to save him from **d**, 2288
7:23 not suffered to continue by reason of **d**: 2288
9:15 of the new testament, that by means of **d**, 2288
9:16 also of necessity be the **d** of the testator. 2288
11: 5 was translated that *he* should not see **d**; 2288
Jas 1:15 when it is finished, bringeth forth **d**. 2288
5:20 error of his way shall save a soul from **d**, 2288
1Pe 3:18 being **put to d** in the flesh, but *2289*
1Jn 3:14 We know that we have passed from **d** unto 2288
3:14 He that loveth not *his* brother abideth in **d**. 2288
5:16 see his brother sin a sin *which is* not unto **d**, 2288
5:16 give him life for them that sin not unto **d**. 2288
5:16 There is a sin unto **d**: I do not say that he 2288
5:17 is sin: and there is a sin not unto **d**. 2288
Rev 1:18 and have the keys of hell and of **d**. 2288
2:10 be thou faithful unto **d**, and I will give thee 2288
2:11 shall not be hurt of the second **d**. 2288
2:23 And I will kill her children with **d**; and 2288
6: 8 and his name that sat on him *was* **D**, and 2288
6: 8 and with **d**, and with the beasts of the earth. 2288
9: 6 And in those days shall men seek **d**, and 2288
9: 6 desire to die, and **d** shall flee from them. 2288
12:11 and they loved not their lives unto the **d**. 2288
13: 3 one of his heads as *it were* wounded to **d**; 2288
18: 8 in one day, **d**, and mourning, and famine; 2288
20: 6 on such the second **d** hath no power, but 2288
20:13 and **d** and hell delivered up the dead which 2288
20:14 And **d** and hell were cast into the lake of 2288
20:14 into the lake of fire. This is the second **d**. 2288
21: 4 and there shall be no more **d**, 2288
21: 8 and brimstone: which is the second **d**. 2288

DEATHS (4) [DIE]
Jer 16: 4 They shall die of grievous **d**; they shall not 4463
Eze 28: 8 thou shalt die the **d** of *them that are* slain in 4463
28:10 Thou shalt die the **d** of the uncircumcised 4194
2Co 11:23 in prisons more frequent, in **d** oft. 2288

DEBASE (1)
Isa 57: 9 far off, and didst **d** *thyself even* unto hell. 8213

DEBATE (4) [DEBATES]
Pr 25: 9 **D** thy cause with thy neighbour *himself*; 7378
Isa 27: 8 when it shooteth forth, thou wilt **d with** it: 7378
58: 4 ye fast for strife and **d**, and to smite with 4683
Ro 1:29 full of envy, murder, **d**, deceit, malignity; *2054*

DEBATES (1) [DEBATE]
2Co 12:20 lest *there be* **d**, envyings, wraths, strifes, *2054*

DEBAUCHERY See LASCIVIOUSNESS

DEBIR (14) [KIRJATH-SANNAH, KIRJATH-SEPHER]
Jos 10: 3 and unto **D** king of Eglon, saying, 1688
10:38 and all Israel with him, to **D**; 1688
10:39 so he did to **D**, and to the king thereof; 1688
11:21 from **D**, from Anab, and from all 1688
12:13 The king of **D**, one; the king of Geder, one; 1688
13:26 and from Mahanaim unto the border of **D**; 1688
15: 7 the border went up toward **D** from 1688
15:15 he went up thence to the inhabitants of **D**: 1688
15:15 the name of **D** before *was* Kirjath-sepher. 1688
15:49 and Kirjath-sannah, which *is* **D**, 1688
21:15 with her suburbs, and **D** with her suburbs, 1688
Jdg 1:11 thence he went against the inhabitants of **D**: 1688
1:11 the name of **D** before *was* Kirjath-sepher. 1688
1Ch 6:58 Hilen with her suburbs, **D** with her suburbs, 1688

DEBORAH (10)
Ge 35: 8 **D** Rebekah's nurse died, and she was 1683
Jdg 4: 4 **D**, a prophetess, the wife of Lapidoth, 1683
4: 5 she dwelt under the palm tree of **D** between 1683
4: 9 **D** arose, and went with Barak to Kedesh. 1683

Jdg 4:10 men at his feet: and **D** went up with him. 1683
4:14 **D** said unto Barak, Up; for this *is* the day in 1683
5: 1 sang **D** and Barak the son of Abinoam on 1683
5: 7 they ceased in Israel, until that I **D** arose, 1683
5:12 Awake, awake, **D**: awake, awake, utter a 1683
5:15 the princes of Issachar *were* with **D**; 1683

DEBT (7) [DEBTOR, DEBTORS, DEBTS, INDEBTED]
1Sa 22: 2 every one that was in **d**, and every one *that* 5378
2Ki 4: 7 pay thy **d**, and live thou and thy children of 5386
Ne 10:31 and the **exaction of** every **d**. 3027+4853
Mt 18:27 and loosed him, and forgave him the **d**. *1156*
18:30 him into prison, till he should pay the **d**. *3784*
18:32 I forgave thee all that **d**, because *3782*
Ro 4: 4 the reward not reckoned of grace, but of **d**. *3783*

DEBTOR (4) [DEBT]
Eze 18: 7 *but* hath restored *to* the **d** his pledge, 2326
Mt 23:16 swear by the gold of the temple, he is a **d**. *3784*
Ro 1:14 I am **d** both to the Greeks, and to *3781*
Gal 5: 3 that he is a **d** to do the whole law. *3781*

DEBTORS (5) [DEBT]
Mt 6:12 forgive us our debts, as we forgive our **d**. *3781*
Lk 7:41 was a certain creditor which had two **d**: *5533*
16: 5 So he called every one of his lord's **d** unto *5533*
Ro 8:12 Therefore, brethren, we are **d**, not to *3781*
15:27 pleased them verily; and their **d** they are. *3781*

DEBTS (2) [DEBT]
Pr 22:26 *or* of them that are sureties for **d**. 4859
Mt 6:12 And forgive us our **d**, as we forgive *3783*

DECAPOLIS (3)
Mt 4:25 and *from* **D**, and *from* Jerusalem, and *1179*
Mk 5:20 began to publish in **D** how great *things* *1179*
7:31 through the midst of the coasts of **D**. *1179*

DECAY (1) [DECAYED, DECAYETH]
Lev 25:35 and **fallen in d** with thee; 3027+4131

DECAYED (2) [DECAY]
Ne 4:10 The strength of the bearers of burdens is **d**, 3782
Isa 44:26 and I will raise up the **d places** thereof: 2723

DECAYETH (3) [DECAY]
Job 14:11 from the sea, and the flood **d** and drieth up: 2717
Ecc 10:18 By much slothfulness the building **d**; and 4355
Heb 8:13 Now that which **d** and waxeth old *is* ready *3822*

DECEASE (2) [DECEASED]
Lk 9:31 spake of his **d** which he should accomplish *1841*
2Pe 1:15 **d** to have these *things* always in *1841*

DECEASED (2) [DECEASE]
Isa 26:14 shall not live; *they are* **d**, they shall not rise: 7496
Mt 22:25 when he had married *a wife,* **d**, and, *5053*

DECEIT (34) [DECEIVE]
Job 15:35 forth vanity, and their belly prepareth **d**. 4820
27: 4 speak wickedness, nor my tongue utter **d**. 7423
31: 5 with vanity, or *if* my foot hath hasted to **d**; 4820
Ps 10: 7 mouth is full *of* cursing and **d** and fraud: 4820
36: 3 The words of his mouth *are* iniquity and **d**: 4820
50:19 mouth to evil, and thy tongue frameth **d**. 4820
55:11 **d** and guile depart not from her streets. 8496
72:14 He shall redeem their soul from **d** and 8496
101: 7 He that worketh **d** shall not dwell within 7423
119:118 from thy statutes: for their **d** *is* falsehood. 8649
Pr 12: 5 *but* the counsels of the wicked *are* **d**. 4820
12:17 forth righteousness: but a false witness **d**. 4820
12:20 **D** *is* in the heart of them that imagine evil: 4820
14: 8 his way: but the folly of fools *is* **d**. 4820
20:17 Bread of **d** *is* sweet to a man; but 8267
26:24 with his lips, and layeth up **d** within him; 4820
26:26 *Whose* hatred is covered by **d**, 4860
Isa 53: 9 neither *was any* **d** in his mouth. 4820
Jer 5:27 *is* full *of* birds, so *are* their houses full *of* **d**: 4820
8: 5 they hold fast **d**, they refuse to return. 8649
9: 6 Thine habitation *is* in the midst of **d**; 4820
9: 6 through **d** they refuse to know me, saith 4820
9: 8 *is as* an arrow shot out; it speaketh **d**: 4820
14:14 a thing of nought, and the **d** of their heart. 8649
23:26 *they are* prophets of the **d** of their own 8649
Hos 11:12 with lies, and the house of Israel with **d**: 4820
12: 7 the balances of **d** *are* in his hand: 4820
Am 8: 5 and falsifying the balances by **d**? 4820
Zep 1: 9 their masters' houses *with* violence and **d**. 4820
Mk 7:22 Thefts, covetousness, wickedness, **d**, *1388*
Ro 1:29 full of envy, murder, debate, **d**, malignity; *1388*
3:13 with their tongues they have **used d**; *1387*
Col 2: 8 spoil you through philosophy and vain **d**, *539*
1Th 2: 3 For our exhortation *was* not of **d**, nor of *4106*

DECEITFUL (21) [DECEIVE]
Ps 5: 6 LORD will abhor the bloody and **d** man. 4820
35:20 they devise **d** matters against *them that are* 4820
43: 1 O deliver me from the **d** and unjust man. 4820
52: 4 all devouring words, O thou **d** tongue. 4820
55:23 and **d** men shall not live out half their days; 4820
78:57 they were turned aside like a **d** bow. 7423
109: 2 the mouth of the **d** are opened against me: 4820
120: 2 from lying lips, *and* from a **d** tongue. 7423
Pr 11:18 The wicked worketh a **d** work: but *to* him 8267
14:25 but a **d** *witness* speaketh lies. 4820
23: 3 desirous of his dainties: for they *are* **d** meat. 3577
27: 6 a friend; but the kisses of an enemy *are* **d**. 6280
29:13 The poor and the **d** man meet together: 8501
31:30 Favour *is* **d**, and beauty *is* vain: *but* 8267
Jer 17: 9 The heart *is* **d** above all *things,* and 6121
Hos 7:16 they are like a **d** bow: their princes shall 7423
Mic 6:11 and with the bag of **d** weights? 4820
6:12 and their tongue *is* **d** in their mouth. 7423
Zep 3:13 neither shall a **d** tongue be found in their 8649
2Co 11:13 For such *are* false apostles, **d** workers, *1386*
Eph 4:22 which is corrupt according to the **d** lusts; *539*

DECEITFULLY (11) [DECEIVE]
Ge 34:13 and Hamor his father **d**, 4820+871.1
Ex 8:29 let not Pharaoh **deal d** any more in not 2048
21: 8 no power, seeing he hath **dealt d** with her. 898
Lev 6: 4 or the thing which he hath **d gotten**, 6231+6233
Job 6:15 My brethren have **dealt d** as a brook, *and* 898
13: 7 wickedly for God? and talk **d** for him? 7423
Ps 24: 4 his soul unto vanity, nor sworn **d**. 4820+3807.1
52: 2 like a sharp rasor, working **d**. 7423
Jer 48:10 *be* he that doeth the work of the LORD **d**, 7423
Da 11:23 the league *made* with him he shall work **d**: 4820
2Co 4: 2 nor **handling** the word of God **d**; *1389*

DECEITFULNESS (3) [DECEIVE]
Mt 13:22 and the **d** of riches, choke the word, and *539*
Mk 4:19 and the **d** of riches, and the lusts of other *539*
Heb 3:13 lest any of you be hardened through the **d** of *539*

DECEITS (2) [DECEIVE]
Ps 38:12 and imagine **d** all the day long. 4820
Isa 30:10 speak unto us smooth *things,* prophesy **d**: 4123

DECEIVABLENESS (1) [DECEIVE]
2Th 2:10 And with all **d** of unrighteousness in them *539*

DECEIVE (27) [DECEIT, DECEITFUL, DECEITFULLY, DECEITFULNESS, DECEITS, DECEIVABLENESS, DECEIVED, DECEIVER, DECEIVERS, DECEIVETH, DECEIVING, DECEIVINGS]
2Sa 3:25 that he came to **d** thee, and to know thy 6601
2Ki 4:28 son of my lord? did I not say, Do not **d** me? 7952
18:29 saith the king, Let not Hezekiah **d** you: 5377
19:10 Let not thy God in whom thou trustest **d** 5377
2Ch 32:15 Now therefore let not Hezekiah **d** you, 5377
Pr 24:28 without cause; and **d** not with thy lips. 6601
Isa 36:14 saith the king, Let not Hezekiah **d** you: 5377
37:10 in whom thou trustest, **d** thee, saying, 5377
Jer 9: 5 they will **d** every one his neighbour, and 2048
29: 8 that *be* in the midst of you, **d** you, 5377
37: 9 **D** not yourselves, saying, The Chaldeans 5377
Zec 13: 4 shall they wear a rough garment to **d**: 3584
Mt 24: 4 unto them, Take heed that no *man* **d** you. *4105*
24: 5 saying, I am Christ; and shall **d** many. *4105*
24:11 false prophets shall rise, and shall **d** many. *4105*
24:24 *it were* possible, *they shall* **d** the very elect. *4105*
Mk 13: 5 to say, Take heed lest any *man* **d** you: *4105*
13: 6 saying, I am *Christ;* and shall **d** many. *4105*
Ro 16:18 and fair speeches **d** the hearts of the simple. *1818*
1Co 3:18 Let no *man* **d** himself. If any *man* among *1818*
Eph 4:14 whereby they lie in wait to **d**; *4106*
5: 6 Let no *man* **d** you with vain words: for *538*
2Th 2: 3 Let no *man* **d** you by any means: for *that* *1818*

D

1Jn 1: 8 we d ourselves, and the truth is not in us. 4105
3: 7 Little children, let no *man* d you: he that 4105
Rev 20: 3 that he should d the nations no more, 4105
20: 8 And shall go out to d the nations which are 4105

DECEIVED (34) [DECEIVE]
Ge 31: 7 your father hath d me, and changed my 2048
Lev 6: 2 away by violence, or hath d his neighbour; 6231
Dt 11:16 that your heart be not d, and ye turn aside, 6601
1Sa 19:17 Why hast thou d me so, and sent away 7411
28:12 spake to Saul, saying, Why hast thou d me? 7411
2Sa 19:26 My lord, O king, my servant d me: 7411
Job 12:16 and wisdom: the d and the deceiver *are* his. 7683
15:31 Let not him that is d trust in vanity: 8582
31: 9 If mine heart have been d by a woman, or 6601
Pr 20: 1 and whosoever is d thereby is not wise. 7686
Isa 19:13 become fools, the princes of Noph are d; 5377
44:20 a d heart hath turned him aside, that he 2048
Jer 4:10 surely thou hast **greatly** d this people 5377+5377
20: 7 thou hast d me, and I was deceived: 6601
20: 7 thou hast deceived me, and I was d: 6601
49:16 Thy terribleness hath d thee, *and* the pride 5377
La 1:19 I called for my lovers, *but* they d me: 7411
Eze 14: 9 if the prophet be d when he hath spoken a 6601
14: 9 I the LORD have d that prophet, and 6601
Ob 1: 3 The pride of thine heart hath d thee, 5377
1: 7 the men that were at peace with thee have d 5377
Lk 21: 8 And he said, Take heed that ye be not d: 4105
Jn 7:47 them the Pharisees, Are ye also d? 4105
Ro 7:11 d me, and by it slew *me*. 1818
1Co 6: 9 Be not d: neither fornicators, nor idolaters, 4105
15:33 Be not d: evil communications corrupt 4105
Gal 6: 7 Be not d; God is not mocked: 4105
1Ti 2:14 And Adam was not d, but the woman being 538
2:14 the woman being d was in the transgression. 538
2Ti 3:13 and worse, deceiving, and being d. 4105
Tit 3: 3 disobedient, d, serving divers lusts and 4105
Rev 18:23 for by thy sorceries were all nations d. 4105
19:20 with which he d them that had received 4105
20:10 And the devil that d them was cast into 4105

DECEIVER (5) [DECEIVE]
Ge 27:12 will feel me, and I shall seem to him as a d; 8591
Job 12:16 and wisdom: the deceived and the d *are* his. 7686
Mal 1:14 cursed *be* the d, which hath in his flock a 5230
Mt 27:63 Saying, Sir, we remember that that d said, 4108
2Jn 1: 7 in the flesh. This is a d and an antichrist. 4108

DECEIVERS (3) [DECEIVE]
2Co 6: 8 and good report: as d, and *yet* true; 4108
Tit 1:10 are many unruly and vain talkers and d, 5423
2Jn 1: 7 For many d are entered into the world, 4108

DECEIVETH (6) [DECEIVE]
Pr 26:19 So *is* the man *that* d his neighbour, and 7411
Jn 7:12 *man:* others said, Nay; but he d the people. 4105
Gal 6: 3 when he is nothing, he d himself. 5422
Jas 1:26 bridleth not his tongue, but d his own heart, 538
Rev 12: 9 and Satan, which d the whole world: 4105
13:14 And d them that dwell on the earth by 4105

DECEIVING (2) [DECEIVE]
2Ti 3:13 and worse, d, and being deceived. 4105
Jas 1:22 and not hearers only, d your own selves. 3884

DECEIVINGS (1) [DECEIVE]
2Pe 2:13 sporting themselves with their own d while 539

DECENCY See SHAMEFACEDNESS

DECENTLY (1)
1Co 14:40 Let all *things* be done d and in order. 2156

DECIDE See REPROOF; REPROVE

DECIDED (1) [DECISION]
1Ki 20:40 So *shall* thy judgment *be;* thyself hast d *it.* 2782

DECISION (2) [DECIDED]
Joel 3:14 Multitudes, multitudes in the valley of d: 2742
3:14 of the LORD *is* near in the valley of d. 2742

DECK (2) [DECKED, DECKEDST, DECKEST, DECKETH, DECKT]
Job 40:10 D thyself now with majesty and excellency; 5710
Jer 10: 4 They d it with silver and with gold; 3302

DECKED (5) [DECK]
Eze 16:11 I d thee also *with* ornaments, and I put 5710
16:13 Thus wast thou d *with* gold and silver; and 5710
Hos 2:13 she d herself with her earrings and 5710
Rev 17: 4 and d **with gold** and precious stone 5557+5558
18:16 and d with gold, and precious stones, and 5558

DECKEDST (2) [DECK]
Eze 16:16 d thy high places with divers colours, and 6213
23:40 and d thyself **with ornaments,** 5710+5716

DECKEST (1) [DECK]
Jer 4:30 though thou d thee **with** ornaments of gold, 5710

DECKETH (1) [DECK]
Isa 61:10 as a bridegroom d *himself* **with** ornaments, 3547

DECKT (1) [DECK]
Pr 7:16 I have d my bed *with* coverings of tapestry, 7234

DECLARATION (4) [DECLARE]
Est 10: 2 and the d of the greatness of Mordecai, 6575
Job 13:17 my speech, and my d with your ears. 262
Lk 1: 1 d of those things which are most surely 1335
2Co 8:19 of the same Lord, and *d of* your ready mind: NIG

DECLARE (95) [DECLARATION, DECLARED, DECLARETH, DECLARING]
Ge 41:24 but *there was* none that could d *it* to me. 5046
Dt 1: 5 of Moab, began Moses to d this law, saying, 874
Jos 20: 4 shall d his cause in the ears of the elders of 1696
Jdg 14:12 if you can **certainly** d it me *within* 5046+5046
14:13 if ye cannot d *it* me, then shall ye give me 5046
14:15 that he may d unto us the riddle, lest we 5046
1Ki 22:13 the words of the prophets *d* good unto NIH
1Ch 16:24 D his glory among the heathen; 5608
2Ch 18:12 the words of the prophets *d* good to the king NIH
Est 4: 8 to d *it* unto her, and to charge her that *she* 5046
Job 12: 8 and the fishes of the sea shall d unto thee. 5608
15:17 and that which I have seen I will d; 5608
21:31 Who shall d his way to his face? and 5046
28:27 did he see it, and d it; he prepared it, yea, 5608
31:37 I would d unto him the number of my 5046
38: 4 of the earth? d, if thou hast understanding. 5046
38:18 of the earth? d if thou knowest it all. 5046
40: 7 I will demand of thee, and d thou unto me. 3045
42: 4 I will demand of thee, and d thou unto me. 3045
Ps 2: 7 I will d the decree: the LORD hath said 5608
9:11 in Zion: d among the people his doings. 5046
19: 1 The heavens d the glory of God; and 5608
22:22 I will d thy name unto my brethren: in 5608
22:31 shall d his righteousness unto a people that 5046
30: 9 the dust praise thee? shall it d thy truth? 5046
38:18 For I will d mine iniquity; I will be sorry 5046
40: 5 *if* I would d and speak *of them,* they are 5046
50: 6 the heavens shall d his righteousness: 5046
50:16 What hast thou to do to d my statutes, or 5608
64: 9 shall fear, and shall d the work of God; 5046
66:16 and I will d what he hath done for my soul. 5608
73:28 the Lord GOD, that *I* may d all thy works. 5608
75: 1 thy name *is* near thy wondrous works d. 5608
75: 9 I will d for ever; I will sing *praises* to 5046
78: 6 should arise and d *them* to their children: 5608
96: 3 D his glory among the heathen, 5608
97: 6 The heavens d his righteousness, and 5046
102:21 To d the name of the LORD in Zion, and 5608
107:22 and d his works with rejoicing. 5608
118:17 but live, and d the works of the LORD. 5608
145: 4 to another, and shall d thy mighty acts. 5046
145: 6 thy terrible acts: and I will d thy greatness. 5608
Ecc 9: 1 all this I considered in my heart even to d 952
Isa 3: 9 they d their sin as Sodom, they hide *it* not. 5046
12: 4 his name, d his doings among the people, 3045
21: 6 set a watchman, let him d what he seeth. 5046
41:22 end of them; or d us *things* for to come. 8085
42: 9 are come to pass, and new *things* do I d: 5046
42:12 the LORD, and d his praise in the islands. 5046
43: 9 who among them can d this, and shew us 5046
43:26 d thou, that thou mayest be justified. 5608
44: 7 and shall d it, and set it in order for me, 5046
45:19 I d things that are right. 5046
48: 6 will not ye d *it?* I have shewed thee new 5046
48:20 with a voice of singing d ye, tell this, 5046
53: 8 who shall d his generation? for he was cut 7878

Isa 57:12 I will **d** thy righteousness, and thy works; 5046
66:19 they shall **d** my glory among the Gentiles. 5046
Jer 4: 5 **D** ye in Judah, and publish in Jerusalem; 5046
5:20 **D** this in the house of Jacob, and publish it 5046
9:12 that he may **d** it, for what the land perisheth 5046
31:10 and **d** *it* in the isles afar off, and say, 5046
38:15 said unto Zedekiah, If I **d** *it* unto thee, 5046
38:25 **D** unto us now what thou hast said unto 5046
42: 4 shall answer you, I will **d** *it* unto you; 5046
42:20 shall say, so **d** unto us, and we will do *it.* 5046
46:14 **D** ye in Egypt, and publish in Migdol, and 5046
50: 2 **D** ye among the nations, and publish, and 5046
50:28 to **d** in Zion the vengeance of the LORD 5046
51:10 let us **d** in Zion the work of the LORD our 5608
Eze 12:16 that they may **d** all their abominations 5608
23:36 yea, **d** unto them their abominations; 5046
40: 4 **d** all that thou seest to the house of Israel. 5046
Da 4:18 O Belteshazzar, **d** the interpretation thereof, 560
Mic 1:10 **D** ye *it* not at Gath, weep ye not at all: 5046
3: 8 to **d** unto Jacob his transgression, and 5046
Zec 9:12 even to day do I **d** *that* I will render double 5046
Mt 13:36 **D** unto us the parable of the tares of *5419*
15:15 and said unto him, **D** unto us this parable. *5419*
Jn 17:26 will **d** *it:* that the love where*with* thou hast *1107*
Ac 8:33 and who shall **d** his generation? for his life *1334*
13:32 And we **d** unto you **glad tidings**, how that *2097*
13:41 wise believe, though a man **d** it unto you. *1555*
17:23 ye ignorantly worship, him **d** I unto you. *2605*
20:27 For I have not shunned to **d** unto you all *312*
Ro 3:25 to **d** his righteousness for the remission of *1732*
3:26 To **d**, *I say,* at this time his righteousness: *1732*
1Co 3:13 for the day shall **d** *it,* because it shall be *1213*
11:17 Now in this that I **d** *unto you* I praise *you* *3853*
15: 1 I **d** unto you the gospel which I preached *1107*
Col 4: 7 All my state shall Tychicus **d** unto you, *1107*
Heb 2:12 Saying, I will **d** thy name unto my brethren, *518*
11:14 For they that say such *things* **d** **plainly** that *1718*
1Jn 1: 3 we have seen and heard **d** we unto you, *518*
1: 5 and **d** unto you, that God is light, and in him *312*

DECLARED (41) [DECLARE]
Ex 9:16 that my name may be **d** throughout all 5608
Lev 23:44 Moses **d** unto the children of Israel 1696
Nu 1:18 they **d** their **pedigrees** after their families, 3205
15:34 it was not **d** what should be done to him. 6567
Dt 4:13 he **d** unto you his covenant, which he 5046
2Sa 19: 6 for thou hast **d** *this* day, that thou regardest 5046
Ne 8:12 they had understood the words that were **d** 3045
Job 26: 3 *how* hast thou plentifully **d** the thing as it 3045
Ps 40:10 I have **d** thy faithfulness and thy salvation: 559
71:17 and hitherto have I **d** thy wondrous works. 5046
77:14 thou hast **d** thy strength among the people. 3045
88:11 Shall thy lovingkindness be **d** in the grave? 5608
119:13 With my lips have I **d** all the judgments of 5608
119:26 I have **d** my ways, and thou heardest me: 5608
Isa 21: 2 A grievous vision is **d** unto me; 5046
21:10 the God of Israel, have I **d** unto you. 5046
41:26 Who hath **d** from the beginning, that we 5046
43:12 I have **d**, and have saved, and I have 5046
44: 8 and have **d** *it?* ye *are* even my witnesses. 5046
45:21 who hath **d** this from ancient time? 8085
48: 3 I have **d** the former *things* from 5046
48: 5 I have even from the beginning **d** *it* to thee; 5046
48:14 which among them hath **d** these *things?* 5046
Jer 36:13 Michaiah **d** unto them all the words that he 5046
42:21 *now* I have *this* day **d** *it* to you; but ye have 5046
Lk 8:47 she **d** unto him before all the people for what *518*
Jn 1:18 in the bosom of the Father, he hath **d** *him.* *1834*
17:26 And I have **d** unto them thy name, and *1107*
Ac 9:27 **d** unto them how he had seen the Lord in *1334*
10: 8 And when he had **d** all *these things* unto *1834*
12:17 **d** unto them how the Lord had brought him *1334*
15: 4 they **d** all *things* that God had done with *312*
15:14 Simeon hath **d** how God at the first did visit *1834*
21:19 he **d** particularly what *things* God had *1834*
25:14 Festus **d** Paul's cause unto the king, saying, *394*
Ro 1: 4 *And* **d** *to be* the Son of God with power, *3724*
9:17 that my name might be **d** throughout all *1229*
1Co 1:11 For it hath been **d** unto me of you, *1213*
2Co 3: 3 Forasmuch as ye are **manifestly** **d** to be *5319*
Col 1: 8 Who also **d** unto us your love in the Spirit. *1213*
Rev 10: 7 as he hath **d** to his servants the prophets. *2097*

DECLARETH (4) [DECLARE]
Isa 41:26 that sheweth, yea, *there is* none that **d**, yea, 8085
Jer 4:15 For a voice **d** from Dan, and 5046
Hos 4:12 at their stocks, and their staff **d** unto them: 5046
Am 4:13 and **d** unto man what *is* his thought, 5046

DECLARING (4) [DECLARE]
Isa 46:10 **D** the end from the beginning, and 5046
Ac 15: 3 Samaria, **d** the conversion of the Gentiles: *1555*
15:12 **d** what miracles and wonders God had *1834*
1Co 2: 1 **d** unto you the testimony of God. *2605*

DECLINE (5) [DECLINED, DECLINETH]
Ex 23: 2 neither shalt thou speak in a cause to **d** 5186
Dt 17:11 thou shalt not **d** from the sentence which 5493
Ps119:157 *yet* do I not **d** from thy testimonies. 5186
Pr 4: 5 neither **d** from the words of my mouth. 5186
7:25 Let not thine heart **d** to her ways, go not 7847

DECLINED (4) [DECLINE]
2Ch 34: 2 **d** neither *to* the right hand, nor *to* the left. 5493
Job 23:11 his steps, his way have I kept, and not **d**. 5186
Ps 44:18 neither have our steps **d** from thy way; 5186
119:51 in derision: *yet* have I not **d** from thy law. 5186

DECLINETH (2) [DECLINE]
Ps 102:11 My days *are* like a shadow that **d**; and I am 5186
109:23 I am gone like the shadow when it **d**: I am 5186

DECREASE (2) [DECREASED]
Ps 107:38 and **suffereth** not their cattle **to d**. 4591
Jn 3:30 He must increase, but I *must* **d**. *1642*

DECREASED (1) [DECREASE]
Ge 8: 5 the waters **d** continually until the tenth 2637

DECREE (49) [DECREED, DECREES]
2Ch 30: 5 So they established a **d** to make 1697
Ezr 5:13 Cyrus made a **d** to build this house of God. 2942
5:17 that a **d** *was* made of Cyrus the king to 2942
6: 1 Darius the king made a **d**, and search was 2942
6: 3 **d** *concerning* the house of God at 2942
6: 8 Moreover I make a **d** what ye shall do to 2942
6:11 Also I have made a **d**, that whosoever shall 2942
6:12 I Darius have made a **d**; let it be done with 2942
7:13 I make a **d**, that all they of the people of 2942
7:21 do make a **d** to all the treasurers which *are* 2942
Est 1:20 when the king's **d** which he shall make 6599
2: 8 king's commandment and his **d** was heard, 1881
3:15 and the **d** was given in Shushan the palace. 1881
4: 3 the king's commandment and his **d** came, 1881
4: 8 **d** that was given at Shushan to destroy 1881
8:14 and the **d** was given at Shushan the palace. 1881
8:17 the king's commandment and his **d** came, 1881
9: 1 and his **d** drew near to be put in execution, 1881
9:13 to morrow also according unto *this* day's **d**, 1881
9:14 the **d** was given at Shushan; and they 1881
9:32 the **d** of Esther confirmed these matters of 3982
Job 22:28 Thou shalt also **d** a thing, and it shall be 1504
28:26 When he made a **d** for the rain, and a way 2706
Ps 2: 7 I will declare the **d**: the LORD hath said 2706
148: 6 he hath made a **d** which shall not pass. 2706
Pr 8:15 By me kings reign, and princes **d** justice. 2710
8:29 When he gave to the sea his **d**, that 2706
Isa 10: 1 Woe unto them that **d** unrighteous decrees, 2710
Jer 5:22 *for* the bound of the sea *by* a perpetual **d**, 2706
Da 2: 9 me the dream, *there is but* one **d** for you: 1882
2:13 the **d** went forth that the wise *men* should 1882
2:15 Why *is* the **d** *so* hasty from the king? 1882
3:10 Thou, O king, hast made a **d**, that every 2942
3:29 Therefore I make a **d**, That every people, 2942
4: 6 Therefore made I a **d** to bring in all 2942
4:17 *This* matter *is* by the **d** of the watchers, and 1510
4:24 O king, and this *is* the **d** of the most High, 1510
6: 7 to make a firm **d**, that whosoever shall ask a 633
6: 8 O king, establish the **d**, and sign the writing, 633
6: 9 king Darius signed the writing and the **d**. 633
6:12 before the king concerning the king's **d**; 633
6:12 Hast thou not signed a **d**, that every man that 633
6:13 nor the **d** that thou hast signed, but 633
6:15 Persians *is,* That no **d** nor statute which 633
6:26 I make a **d**, That in every dominion of my 2942
Jnh 3: 7 published through Nineveh by the **d** of 2940
Mic 7:11 *in* that day shall the **d** be far removed. 2706

Zep 2: 2 Before the **d** bring forth, *before* the day 2706
Lk 2: 1 *that* there went out a **d** from Cesar *1378*

DECREED (5) [DECREE]
Est 2: 1 she had done, and what was **d** against her. 1504
9:31 as they had **d** for themselves and for their 6965
Job 38:10 And brake up for it my **d** *place,* and set bars 2706
Isa 10:22 the consumption **d** shall overflow *with* 2782
1Co 7:37 so **d** in his heart that *he* will keep his virgin, *2919*

DECREES (3) [DECREE]
Isa 10: 1 Woe unto them that decree unrighteous **d**, 2711
Ac 16: 4 they delivered them the **d** for to keep, *1378*
17: 7 and these all do contrary to the **d** of Cesar, *1378*

DEDAN (11) [DEDANIM]
Ge 10: 7 and the sons of Raamah; Sheba, and **D**. 1719
25: 3 Jokshan begat Sheba, and **D**. And the sons 1719
25: 3 the sons of **D** were Asshurim, and 1719
1Ch 1: 9 And the sons of Raamah; Sheba, and **D**. 1719
1:32 And the sons of Jokshan; Sheba, and **D**. 1719
Jer 25:23 **D**, and Tema, and Buz, and all *that are* in 1719
49: 8 turn back, dwell deep, O inhabitants of **D**; 1719
Eze 25:13 and they of **D** shall fall by the sword. 1719
27:15 The men of **D** *were* thy merchants; 1719
27:20 **D** *was* thy merchant in precious clothes for 1719
38:13 and **D**, and the merchants of Tarshish, 1719

DEDANIM (1) [DEDAN]
Isa 21:13 ye lodge, O ye travelling companies of **D**. 1720

DEDANITES See DEDANIM

DEDICATE (11) [DEDICATED, DEDICATING, DEDICATION]
Dt 20: 5 he die in the battle, and another man **d** it. 2596
2Sa 8:11 Which also king David did **d** unto 6942
2Ki 12:18 had **d**, and his own hallowed *things,* and all 6942
1Ch 26:20 and over the treasures of the **d** *things.* 6944
26:26 of the **d** *things,* which David the king, 6944
26:27 Out of the spoils won in battles did they **d** 6942
28:12 and of the treasures of the **d** *things:* 6944
2Ch 2: 4 to **d** *it* to him, *and* to burn before him sweet 6942
24: 7 also all the **d** *things* of the house of 6944
31:12 and the tithes and the **d** *things* faithfully: 6944
Eze 44:29 and every **d thing** in Israel shall be theirs. 2764

DEDICATED (17) [DEDICATE]
Dt 20: 5 hath built a new house, and hath not **d** it? 2596
Jdg 17: 3 I had **wholly d** the silver unto 6942+6942
2Sa 8:11 gold that he had **d** of all nations which he 6942
1Ki 7:51 in the *things* which David his father had **d**; 6944
8:63 all the children of Israel **d** the house of 2596
15:15 in *the things* which his father had **d**, 6944
15:15 *the things* which himself had **d**, *into* 6944
2Ki 12: 4 All the money of the **d** *things* that is 6944
1Ch 18:11 Them also king David **d** unto the LORD, 6942
26:26 and the captains of the host, had **d**. 6942
26:28 of Ner, and Joab the son of Zeruiah, had **d**; 6942
26:28 whosoever had **d** *anything, it was* under 6942
2Ch 5: 1 in *all the things* that David his father had **d**; 6944
7: 5 and all the people **d** the house of God. 2596
15:18 of God *the things* that his father had **d**, 6944
15:18 that he himself had **d**, silver, and gold, and 6944
Heb 9:18 the first *testament* was **d** without blood. *1457*

DEDICATING (2) [DEDICATE]
Nu 7:10 the princes offered *for* **d** of the altar in 2598
7:11 prince on *his* day, for the **d** of the altar. 2598

DEDICATION (11) [DEDICATE]
Nu 7:84 This *was* the **d** of the altar, in the day when 2598
7:88 This *was* the **d** of the altar, after *that* it was 2598
2Ch 7: 9 for they kept the **d** of the altar seven days, 2598
Ezr 6:16 kept the **d** of this house of God with joy, 2597
6:17 offered at the **d** of this house of God an 2597
Ne 12:27 at the **d** of the wall of Jerusalem they 2598
12:27 to keep the **d** with gladness, both with 2598
Ps 30: T *and* Song *at* the **d** of the house of David. 2598
Da 3: 2 to come to the **d** of the image which 2597
3: 3 were gathered together unto the **d** of 2597
Jn 10:22 And it was at Jerusalem *the feast of* the **d**, *1456*

DEED (19) [DEEDS]
Ge 44:15 What **d** *is* this that ye have done? 4639
Ex 9:16 **in very d** for this cause have I raised thee 199
Jdg 19:30 There was no such **d** done nor seen from NIH
1Sa 25:34 For **in very d**, *as* the LORD God of Israel 199
26: 4 understood that Saul was come in **very d.** 3559
2Sa 12:14 by this **d** thou hast given great occasion to 1697
2Ch 6:18 will God **in very d** dwell with men on 552
Est 1:17 For *this* **d** of the queen shall come abroad 1697
1:18 which have heard of the **d** of the queen. 1697
Lk 23:51 consented to the counsel and **d** of them;) *4234*
24:19 which was a prophet mighty in **d** and *2041*
Ac 4: 9 If we this day be examined of the **good d** *2108*
Ro 15:18 make the Gentiles obedient, by word and **d**, *2041*
1Co 5: 2 that he that hath done this **d** might be taken *2041*
5: 3 *concerning* him that hath so done this **d**, NIG
2Co 10:11 such *will we be* also in **d** when we are *2041*
Col 3:17 And whatsoever ye do in word or **d**, *do* all *2041*
Jas 1:25 the work, this *man* shall be blessed in his **d**. *4162*
1Jn 3:18 neither in tongue; but in **d** and in truth. *2041*

DEEDS (33) [DEED]
Ge 20: 9 thou hast done **d** unto me that ought not to 4639
1Ch 16: 8 make known his **d** among the people. 5949
2Ch 35:27 his **d**, first and last, behold, they *are* written 1697
Ezr 9:13 after all that is come upon us for our evil **d**, 4639
Ne 6:19 Also they reported his **good d** before me, 2896
13:14 wipe not out my **good d** that I have done 2617
Ps 28: 4 Give them according to their **d**, and 6467
105: 1 make known his **d** among the people. 5949
Isa 59:18 According to *their* **d**, accordingly he will 1578
Jer 5:28 yea, they overpass the **d** of the wicked: 1697
25:14 will recompense them according to their **d**, 6467
Lk 11:48 Truly ye bear witness that ye allow the **d** of *2041*
23:41 for we receive the due reward of our **d**: *4238*
Jn 3:19 rather than light, because their **d** were evil. *2041*
3:20 to the light, lest his **d** should be reproved. *2041*
3:21 that his **d** may be made manifest, that they *2041*
8:41 Ye do the **d** of your father. Then said they *2041*
Ac 7:22 and was mighty in words and in **d**. *2041*
19:18 and confessed, and shewed their **d**. *4234*
24: 2 that **very worthy d** are done unto this *2735*
Ro 2: 6 will render to every *man* according to his **d**: *2041*
3:20 Therefore by the **d** of the law there shall no *2041*
3:28 justified by faith without the **d** of the law. *2041*
8:13 if ye through the Spirit do mortify the **d** of *4234*
2Co 12:12 in signs, and wonders, and **mighty d**. *1411*
Col 3: 9 that ye have put off the old man with his **d**; *4234*
2Pe 2: 8 from day to day with *their* unlawful **d**;) *2041*
2Jn 1:11 him God speed is partaker of his evil **d**. *2041*
3Jn 1:10 I will remember his **d** which he doeth, *2041*
Jude 1:15 **d** which they have ungodly committed, *2041*
Rev 2: 6 that thou hatest the **d** of the Nicolaitans, *2041*
2:22 except they repent of their **d**. *2041*
16:11 and their sores, and repented not of their **d**. *2041*

DEEMED (1)
Ac 27:27 about midnight the shipmen **d** that they *5282*

DEEP (65) [DEEPER, DEEPLY, DEEPNESS, DEEPS, DEPTH, DEPTHS]
Ge 1: 2 and darkness *was* upon the face of the **d**. 8415
2:21 the LORD God caused a **d sleep** to fall 8639
7:11 all the fountains of the great **d** broken up, 8415
8: 2 The fountains also of the **d** and 8415
15:12 going down, a **d sleep** fell upon Abram; 8639
49:25 blessings of the **d** that lieth under, 8415
Dt 33:13 and for the **d** that coucheth beneath, 8415
1Sa 26:12 a **d sleep** from the LORD was fallen upon 8639
Job 4:13 of the night, when **d sleep** falleth on men. 8639
12:22 He discovereth **d** *things* out of darkness, 6013
33:15 the night, when **d sleep** falleth upon men, 8639
38:30 *with* a stone, and the face of the **d** is frozen. 8415
41:31 He maketh the **d** to boil like a pot: 4688
41:32 *one* would think the **d** to be hoary. 8415
Ps 36: 6 thy judgments *are* a great **d**: 8415
42: 7 **D** calleth unto deep at the noise of thy 8415
42: 7 Deep calleth unto **d** at the noise of thy 8415
64: 6 of every one *of them,* and the heart, *is* **d**. 6013
69: 2 I sink in **d** mire, where *there is* no standing: 4688
69: 2 I am come into **d** waters, where the floods 4615
69:14 them that hate me, and out of the **d** waters. 4615
69:15 neither let the **d** swallow me up, and let not 4688
80: 9 didst **cause it to take d root**, and 8327+8328
92: 5 are thy works! *and* thy thoughts are very **d**. 6009
95: 4 In his hand *are* the **d places** of the earth: 4278
104: 6 Thou coveredst it *with* the **d** as *with* a 8415

Ps 107:24 of the LORD, and his wonders in the **d**. 4688
135: 6 and in earth, in the seas, and all **d places**. 8415
140:10 into **d pits**, *that* they rise not up again. 4113
Pr 8:28 *he* strengthened the fountains of the **d**: 8415
18: 4 The words of a man's mouth *are as* **d** 6013
19:15 Slothfulness casteth into a **d sleep**; and 8639
20: 5 Counsel in the heart of man *is like* **d** water; 6013
22:14 The mouth of strange *women is* a **d** pit: 6013
23:27 For a whore *is* a **d** ditch; and a strange 6013
Ecc 7:24 **exceeding d**, who can find it out? 6013+6013
Isa 29:10 poured out upon you the spirit of **d sleep**, 8639
29:15 Woe unto them that **seek d** to hide *their* 6009
30:33 it is prepared; he hath **made** *it* **d** *and* large: 6009
44:27 That saith to the **d**, Be dry, and I will dry 6683
51:10 hath dried the sea, the waters of the great **d**; 8415
63:13 That led them through the **d**, as a horse in 8415
Jer 49: 8 Flee ye, turn back, dwell **d**, O inhabitants 6009
49:30 Flee, get you far off, dwell **d**, O ye 6009
Eze 23:32 Thou shalt drink *of* thy sister's cup **d** and 6013
26:19 when *I* shall bring up the **d** upon thee, 8415
31: 4 the **d** set him up on high with her rivers 8415
31:15 I covered the **d** for him, and I restrained 8415
32:14 will I **make** their waters **d**, and cause their 8257
34:18 to have drunk of the **d** waters, but ye must 4950
Da 2:22 He revealeth the **d** and secret *things:* he 5994
8:18 I was **in a d sleep** on my face toward 7290
10: 9 was I **in a d sleep** on my face, and my face 7290
Am 7: 4 it devoured the great **d**, and did eat up a 8415
Jnh 2: 3 For thou hadst cast me *into* the **d**, in 4688
Hab 3:10 the **d** uttered his voice, *and* lift up his hands 8415
Lk 5: 4 Launch out into the **d**, and let down your *899*
6:48 and digged **d**, and laid the foundation on a *900*
8:31 not command them to go out into the **d**. *12*
Jn 4:11 hast nothing to draw with, and the well is **d**: *901*
Ac 20: 9 named Eutychus, being fallen into a **d** sleep: *901*
Ro 10: 7 Or, Who shall descend into the **d**? (that is, *12*
1Co 2:10 all *things,* yea, the **d things** of God. *899*
2Co 8: 2 their **d** poverty abounded unto *899+2596*
11:25 a night and a day I have been in the **d**; *1037*

DEEPER (9) [DEEP]
Lev 13: 3 the plague in sight *be* **d** than the skin of his 6013
13: 4 in sight *be* not **d** than the skin, and the hair 6013
13:25 and it *be* in sight **d** than the skin; 6013
13:30 behold, *if* it *be* in sight **d** than the skin; and 6013
13:31 it *be* not in sight **d** than the skin, and 6013
13:32 and the scall *be* not in sight **d** than the skin; 6013
13:34 in the skin, nor *be* in sight **d** than the skin; 6013
Job 11: 8 **d** than hell; what canst thou know? 6013
Isa 33:19 a people of a **d** speech than *thou* canst 6012

DEEPLY (3) [DEEP]
Isa 31: 6 the children of Israel have **d** revolted. 6009
Hos 9: 9 They have **d** corrupted *themselves,* as *in* 6009
Mk 8:12 And he **sighed d** in his spirit, and saith, *389*

DEEPNESS (1) [DEEP]
Mt 13: 5 sprung up, because *they* had no **d** of earth: *899*

DEEPS (4) [DEEP]
Ne 9:11 their persecutors thou threwest into the **d**, 4688
Ps 88: 6 me in the lowest pit, in darkness, in the **d**. 4688
148: 7 from the earth, ye dragons, and all **d**: 8415
Zec 10:11 and all the **d** of the river shall dry up: 4688

DEER (1)
Dt 14: 5 the **fallow d**, and the wild goat, and 3180

DEFAMED (1) [DEFAMING]
1Co 4:13 Being **d**, we intreat: we are made as the filth *987*

DEFAMING (1) [DEFAMED]
Jer 20:10 For I heard the **d** of many, fear on every 1681

DEFEAT (2)
2Sa 15:34 mayest thou for me **d** the counsel of 6565
17:14 For the LORD had appointed to **d** 6565

DEFENCE (22) [DEFEND]
Nu 14: 9 their **d** is departed from them, and 6738
2Ch 11: 5 in Jerusalem, and built cities for **d** in Judah. 4692
Job 22:25 the Almighty shall be thy **d**, and thou shalt 1220
Ps 7:10 My **d** *is* of God, which saveth the upright in 4043
31: 2 strong rock, for a house of **d** to save me. 4686
59: 9 will I wait upon thee: for God *is* my **d**. 4869
59:16 for thou hast been my **d** and refuge in 4869
59:17 for God *is* my **d**, *and* the God of my mercy. 4869
62: 2 *is* my rock and my salvation; *he is* my **d**; 4869
62: 6 *he is* my **d**; I shall not be moved. 4869
89:18 For the LORD *is* our **d**; and the Holy One 4043
94:22 the LORD is my **d**; and my God *is* 4869
Ecc 7:12 For wisdom *is* a **d**, *and* money *is* a defence: 6738
7:12 For wisdom *is* a defence, *and* money *is* a **d**: 6738
Isa 4: 5 by night: for upon all the glory *shall be* a **d**. 2646
19: 6 *and* the brooks of **d** shall be emptied and 4693
33:16 his **place of d** *shall be* the munitions of 4869
Na 2: 5 wall thereof, and the **d** shall be prepared. 5526
Ac 19:33 and would have **made** *his* **d** unto the people. *626*
22: 1 hear ye my **d** *which I make* now unto you. *627*
Php 1: 7 and in the **d** and confirmation of the gospel, *627*
1:17 knowing that I am set for the **d** of the gospel. *627*

DEFENCED (9) [DEFEND]
Isa 25: 2 made of a city a heap; *of* a **d** city a ruin: 1219
27:10 Yet the **d** city *shall be* desolate, *and* 1219
36: 1 came up against all the **d** cities of Judah, 1219
37:26 that thou shouldest be to lay waste **d** cities 1219
Jer 1:18 I have made thee this *day* a **d** city, and 4013
4: 5 and let us go into the **d** cities. 4013
8:14 let us enter into the **d** cities, and let us be 4013
34: 7 for these **d** cities remained of the cities of 4013
Eze 21:20 to Judah in Jerusalem the **d**. 1219

DEFEND (11) [DEFENCE, DEFENCED, DEFENDED, DEFENDEST, DEFENDING]
Jdg 10: 1 after Abimelech there arose to **d** Israel Tola 3467
2Ki 19:34 For I will **d** this city, to save it, for mine 1598
20: 6 I will **d** this city for mine own sake, and 1598
Ps 20: 1 the name of the God of Jacob **d** thee; 7682
59: 1 **d** me from them that rise up against me. 7682
82: 3 **D** the poor and fatherless: do justice to 8199
Isa 31: 5 so will the LORD of hosts **d** Jerusalem; 1598
37:35 For I will **d** this city to save it for mine own 1598
38: 6 of the king of Assyria: and I will **d** this city. 1598
Zec 9:15 The LORD of hosts shall **d** them; and 1598
12: 8 In that day shall the LORD **d** 1598

DEFENDED (2) [DEFEND]
2Sa 23:12 and **d** it, and slew the Philistines: 5337
Ac 7:24 he **d** *him,* and avenged him that was *292*

DEFENDEST (1) [DEFEND]
Ps 5:11 shout for joy, because thou **d** them: 5526+5921

DEFENDING (1) [DEFEND]
Isa 31: 5 **d** also he will deliver *it;* and passing over 1598

DEFER (3) [DEFERRED, DEFERRETH]
Ecc 5: 4 thou vowest a vow unto God, **d** not to pay it; 309
Isa 48: 9 For my name's sake will I **d** mine anger, and 748
Da 9:19 do; **d** not, for thine own sake, O my God: 309

DEFERRED (3) [DEFER]
Ge 34:19 the young man **d** not to do the thing, because 309
Pr 13:12 Hope **d** maketh the heart sick: but *when* 4900
Ac 24:22 he **d** them, and said, When Lysias the chief *306*

DEFERRETH (1) [DEFER]
Pr 19:11 The discretion of a man **d** his anger; and *it is* 748

DEFIED (6) [DEFY]
Nu 23: 8 shall I defy, *whom* the LORD hath not **d**? 2194
1Sa 17:36 seeing he hath **d** the armies of the living 2778
17:45 of the armies of Israel, whom thou hast **d**. 2778
2Sa 21:21 when he **d** Israel, Jonathan the son of 2778
23: 9 when they **d** the Philistines *that* were there 2778
1Ch 20: 7 when he **d** Israel, Jonathan the son of 2778

DEFILE (39) [DEFILED, DEFILEDST, DEFILETH, UNDEFILED]
Lev 11:44 neither shall ye **d** yourselves with any 2930
15:31 when they **d** my tabernacle that *is* among 2930
18:20 thy neighbour's wife, to **d** *thyself* with her. 2930
18:23 Neither shalt thou lie with any beast to **d** 2930
18:24 **D** not you yourselves in any of these 2930
18:28 land spue not you out also, when ye **d** it, 2930
18:30 and that ye **d** not **yourselves** therein: 2930
20: 3 to **d** my sanctuary, and to profane my holy 2930
21: 4 *But* he shall not **d** himself, *being* a chief 2930
21:11 nor **d** himself for his father, or for his 2930
22: 8 is torn *with beasts,* he shall not eat to **d** 2930

Nu 5: 3 that they **d** not their camps, in the midst 2930
35:34 **D** not therefore the land which ye shall 2930
2Ki 23:13 of the children of Ammon, did the king **d**. 2930
SS 5: 3 I have washed my feet; how shall I **d** them? 2936
Isa 30:22 Ye shall **d** also the covering of thy graven 2930
Jer 32:34 which is called by my name, to **d** it. 2930
Eze 7:22 for the robbers shall enter into it, and **d** it. 2490
9: 7 **D** the house, and fill the courts *with* 2930
20: 7 **d** not yourselves with the idols of Egypt: 2930
20:18 nor **d** yourselves with their idols: 2930
22: 3 maketh idols against herself to **d** *herself.* 2930
28: 7 and they shall **d** thy brightness. 2490
33:26 and ye **d** every one his neighbour's wife: 2930
37:23 Neither shall they **d** themselves any more 2930
43: 7 shall the house of Israel no more **d**, 2930
44:25 they shall come at no dead person to **d** 2930
44:25 had no husband, they may **d** themselves. 2930
Da 1: 8 **d** himself with the portion of the king's 1351
1: 8 of the eunuchs that he might not **d** himself. 1351
Mt 15:18 forth from the heart; and they **d** the man. *2840*
15:20 These are *the things* which **d** a man: but *2840*
Mk 7:15 a man, that entering into him can **d** him: *2840*
7:15 out of him, those are they that **d** the man. *2840*
7:18 entereth into the man, *it* cannot **d** him; *2840*
7:23 *things* come from within, and **d** the man. *2840*
1Co 3:17 If any *man* **d** the temple of God, him shall *5351*
1Ti 1:10 for **them that d** themselves **with mankind**, *733*
Jude 1: 8 Likewise also these *filthy* dreamers **d** *3392*

DEFILED (71) [DEFILE]

Ge 34: 2 he took her, and lay with her, and **d** her. 6031
34: 5 Jacob heard that he had **d** Dinah his 2930
34:13 said, because he had **d** Dinah their sister: 2930
34:27 the city, because they had **d** their sister. 2930
Lev 5: 3 *it be* that a man shall be **d** withal, 2930
11:43 with them, that ye should be **d** thereby. 2930
13:46 the plague *shall be* in him he shall be **d**; 2930
15:32 seed goeth from him, and is **d** therewith; 2930
18:24 nations are **d** which I cast out before you: 2930
18:25 the land is **d**: therefore I do visit 2930
18:27 which *were* before you, and the land is **d**;) 2930
19:31 neither seek after wizards, to be **d** by them: 2930
21: 1 There shall none be **d** for the dead among 2930
21: 3 hath had no husband; for her may he be **d**. 2930
Nu 5: 2 an issue, and whosoever is **d** by the dead: 2931
5:13 she be **d**, and *there be* no witness against 2930
5:14 and he be jealous of his wife, and she be **d**: 2930
5:14 he be jealous of his wife, and she be not **d**: 2930
5:20 if thou be **d**, and *some* man hath lain with 2930
5:27 *that,* if she be **d**, and have done trespass 2930
5:28 if the woman be not **d**, but *be* clean; then 2930
5:29 *to another* instead of her husband, and is **d**; 2930
6: 9 and he hath **d** the head of his consecration; 2930
6:12 shall be lost, because his separation was **d**. 2930
9: 6 who were **d** by the dead body of a man, 2931
9: 7 We *are* **d** by the dead body of a man: 2931
19:20 he hath **d** the sanctuary of the LORD: 2930
Dt 21:23 that thy land be not **d**, which the LORD 2930
22: 9 and the fruit of thy vineyard, be **d**. 6942
24: 4 her again to be his wife, after that she is **d**; 2930
2Ki 23: 8 **d** the high places where the priests had 2930
23:10 he **d** Topheth, which *is* in the valley of 2930
1Ch 5: 1 but, forasmuch as he **d** his father's bed, 2490
Ne 13:29 because they have **d** the priesthood, and 1352
Job 16:15 upon my skin, and **d** my horn in the dust. 5953
Ps 74: 7 they have **d** *by casting down* the dwelling 2490
79: 1 thy holy temple have they **d**; they have laid 2930
106:39 Thus were they **d** with their own works, 2930
Isa 24: 5 The earth also is **d** under the inhabitants 2610
59: 3 For your hands are **d** with blood, and 1351
Jer 2: 7 ye **d** my land, and made mine heritage an 2930
3: 9 that she **d** the land, and committed adultery 2610
16:18 because they have **d** my land, they have 2490
19:13 shall be **d** as the place of Tophet, because 2931
Eze 4:13 Israel eat their **d** bread among the Gentiles, 2931
5:11 thou hast **d** my sanctuary with all thy 2930
7:24 to cease; and their holy places shall be **d**. 2490
18: 6 neither hath **d** his neighbour's wife, 2930
18:11 the mountains, and **d** his neighbour's wife, 2930
18:15 of Israel, hath not **d** his neighbour's wife, 2930
20:43 all your doings, wherein ye have been **d**; 2930
22: 4 hast **d** *thyself* in thine idols which thou hast 2930
22:11 another hath lewdly **d** his daughter in law; 2930
23: 7 she doted: with all their idols she **d** herself. 2930
23:13 I saw that she was **d**, *that* they took both 2930
23:17 they **d** her with their whoredom, and 2930
23:38 they have **d** my sanctuary in the same day, 2930
28:18 Thou hast **d** thy sanctuaries by 2490
36:17 they **d** it by their own way and by their 2930
43: 8 they have even **d** my holy name by their 2930
Hos 5: 3 thou committest whoredom, *and* Israel is **d**. 2930
6:10 *is* the whoredom of Ephraim, Israel is **d**. 2930
Mic 4:11 Let her be **d**, and let our eye look upon 2610
Mk 7: 2 saw some of his disciples eat bread with **d**, *2839*
Jn 18:28 the judgment hall, lest they should be **d**; *3392*
1Co 8: 7 and their conscience being weak is **d**. *3435*
Tit 1:15 but unto them that are **d** and unbelieving *is* *3392*
1:15 but even their mind and conscience is **d**. *3392*
Heb 12:15 up trouble *you,* and thereby many be **d**; *3392*
Rev 3: 4 in Sardis, which have not **d** their garments; *3435*
14: 4 These are they which were not **d** with *3435*

DEFILEDST (1) [DEFILE]

Ge 49: 4 then **d** thou *it:* he went up to my couch. 2490

DEFILETH (9) [DEFILE]

Ex 31:14 *every* one that **d** it shall surely be put to 2490
Nu 19:13 **d** the tabernacle of the LORD; 2930
35:33 land wherein ye *are:* for blood it **d** the land: 2610
Mt 15:11 Not that which goeth into the mouth **d** a *2840*
15:11 cometh out of the mouth, this **d** a man. *2840*
15:20 to eat with unwashen hands **d** not a man. *2840*
Mk 7:20 cometh out of the man, that **d** the man. *2840*
Jas 3: 6 that it **d** the whole body, and setteth on fire *4695*
Rev 21:27 in no wise enter into it any *thing* that **d**, *2840*

DEFORMED See CORRUPTION; SUPERFLUOUS

DEFRAUD (5) [DEFRAUDED]

Lev 19:13 Thou shalt not **d** thy neighbour, neither rob 6231
Mk 10:19 **D** not, Honour thy father and mother. *650*
1Co 6: 8 you do wrong, and **d**, and that *your* brethren. *650*
7: 5 **D** you not one the other, except *it be* with *650*
1Th 4: 6 go beyond and **d** his brother in *any* matter: *4122*

DEFRAUDED (4) [DEFRAUD]

1Sa 12: 3 or whom have I **d**? whom have I 6231
12: 4 they said, Thou hast not **d** us, 6231
1Co 6: 7 do ye not rather *suffer yourselves to* be **d**? *650*
2Co 7: 2 have corrupted no *man,* we have **d** no *man.* *4122*

DEFY (5) [DEFIED]

Nu 23: 7 curse me Jacob, and come, **d** Israel. 2194
23: 8 or how shall I **d**, *whom* the LORD hath 2194
1Sa 17:10 I **d** the armies of Israel this day; 2778
17:25 surely to **d** Israel is he come up: and it shall 2778
17:26 that he should **d** the armies of the living 2778

DEGENERATE (1)

Jer 2:21 art thou turned *into* the **d** plant of a strange 5494

DEGREE (7) [DEGREES]

1Ch 15:18 with them their brethren of the **second d**, 4932
17:17 according to the estate of a man of **high d**, 4609
Ps 62: 9 Surely **men of low d** *are* vanity, *and* 120+1121
62: 9 *and* **men of high d** *are* a lie: 376+1121
Lk 1:52 from *their* seats, and exalted them of **low d**. *5011*
1Ti 3:13 well purchase to themselves a good **d**, *898*
Jas 1: 9 Let the brother of **low d** rejoice in that he is *5011*

DEGREES (24) [DEGREE]

2Ki 20: 9 shall the shadow go forward ten **d**, or 4609
20: 9 go forward ten degrees, or go back ten **d**? 4609
20:10 thing for the shadow to go down ten **d**: 4609
20:10 but let the shadow return backward ten **d**. 4609
20:11 he brought the shadow ten **d** backward, 4609
Ps 120: T A Song of **d**. 4609
121: T A Song of **d**. 4609
122: T A Song of **d** of David. 4609
123: T A Song of **d**. 4609
124: T A Song of **d** of David. 4609
125: T A Song of **d**. 4609
126: T A Song of **d**. 4609
127: T A Song of **d** for Solomon. 4609
128: T A Song of **d**. 4609
129: T A Song of **d**. 4609
130: T A Song of **d**. 4609
131: T A Song of **d** of David. 4609
132: T A Song of **d**. 4609

Ps 133: T A Song of **d** of David. 4609
134: T A Song of **d**. 4609
Isa 38: 8 I will bring again the shadow of the **d**, 4609
38: 8 in the sun dial of Ahaz, ten **d** backward. 4609
38: 8 So the sun returned ten **d**, by which degrees 4609
38: 8 ten degrees, by which **d** it was gone down. 4609

DEHAVITES (1)
Ezr 4: 9 the Susanchites, the **D**, *and* the Elamites, 1723

DEITY See GODHEAD

DEKAR (1)
1Ki 4: 9 The son of **D**, in Makaz, and in Shaalbim, 1857

DELAIAH (6)
1Ch 24:18 The three and twentieth to **D**, the four and 1806
Ezr 2:60 The children of **D**, the children of Tobiah, 1806
Ne 6:10 the son of **D** the son of Mehetabeel, 1806
7:62 The children of **D**, the children of Tobiah, 1806
Jer 36:12 **D** the son of Shemaiah, and Elnathan 1806
36:25 Nevertheless Elnathan and **D** and 1806

DELAY (3) [DELAYED, DELAYETH]
Ex 22:29 Thou shalt not **d** *to offer the first of* thy ripe 309
Ac 9:38 desiring *him* that *he* would not **d** to come to *3635*
25:17 they were come hither, without any **d**, *311+4160*

DELAYED (2) [DELAY]
Ex 32: 1 when the people saw that Moses **d** to come 954
Ps 119:60 and **d** not to keep thy commandments. 4102

DELAYETH (2) [DELAY]
Mt 24:48 say in his heart, My lord **d** his coming; *5549*
Lk 12:45 say in his heart, My lord **d** his coming; *5549*

DELECTABLE (1)
Isa 44: 9 their **d** *things* shall not profit; and they *are* 2530

DELEGATION See AMBASSAGE

DELICACIES (1)
Rev 18: 3 waxed rich through the abundance of her **d**. *4764*

DELICATE (5) [DELICATELY, DELICATENESS, DELICATES, DELICIOUSLY]
Dt 28:54 very **d**, his eye shall be evil toward his 6028
28:56 The tender and **d** *woman* among you, 6028
Isa 47: 1 thou shalt no more be called tender and **d**. 6028
Jer 6: 2 of Zion *to* a comely and **d** *woman*. 6026
Mic 1:16 thee bald, and poll thee for thy **d** children; 8588

DELICATELY (4) [DELICATE]
1Sa 15:32 Agag came unto him **d**. And Agag said, 4574
Pr 29:21 He that **d bringeth up** his servant from a 6445
La 4: 5 They that did feed **d** are desolate in 4574+3807.1
Lk 7:25 and live **d**, are in kings' courts. *5172*

DELICATENESS (1) [DELICATE]
Dt 28:56 the sole of her foot upon the ground for **d** 6026

DELICATES (1) [DELICATE]
Jer 51:34 he hath filled his belly with my **d**, he hath 5730

DELICIOUSLY (2) [DELICATE]
Rev 18: 7 and **lived d**, so much torment and *4763*
18: 9 committed fornication and **lived d** with her, *4763*

DELIGHT (51) [DELIGHTED, DELIGHTEST, DELIGHTETH, DELIGHTS, DELIGHTSOME]
Ge 34:19 because he had **d** in Jacob's daughter: 2654
Nu 14: 8 If the LORD **d** in us, then he will bring us 2654
Dt 10:15 Only the LORD **had a d** in thy fathers to 2836
21:14 if thou have no **d** in her, then thou shalt let 2654
1Sa 15:22 Hath the LORD *as great* **d** in burnt 2656
18:22 the king hath **d** in thee, and all his servants 2654
2Sa 15:26 if he thus say, I have no **d** in thee; behold, 2654
24: 3 why doth my lord the king **d** in this thing? 2654
Est 6: 6 To whom would the king **d** to do honour 2654
Job 22:26 then shalt thou **have** thy **d** in the Almighty, 6026
27:10 Will he **d** himself in the Almighty? will he 6026
34: 9 It profiteth a man nothing that he should **d** 7521
Ps 1: 2 his **d** *is* in the law of the LORD; and in his 2656
16: 3 *to* the excellent, in whom *is* all my **d**. 2656
37: 4 **D** thyself also in the LORD; and he shall 6026
37:11 shall **d** themselves in the abundance of 6026
40: 8 I **d** to do thy will, O my God: yea, thy law 2654
62: 4 they **d in** lies: they bless with their mouth, 7521
68:30 scatter thou the people *that* **d in** war. 2654
94:19 thoughts within me thy comforts **d** my soul. 8173
119:16 I will **d** myself in thy statutes: I will not 8173
119:24 Thy testimonies also *are* my **d** *and* 8191
119:35 of thy commandments; for therein do I **d**. 2654
119:47 I will **d** myself in thy commandments, 8173
119:70 heart is as fat as grease; *but* I **d** *in* thy law. 8173
119:77 that I may live: for thy law *is* my **d**. 8191
119:174 O LORD; and thy law *is* my **d**. 8191
Pr 1:22 the scorners **d in** their scorning, and 2530
2:14 *and* **d** in the frowardness of the wicked; 1523
8:30 brought up *with him:* and I was daily *his* **d**, 8191
11: 1 to the LORD: but a just weight *is* his **d**. 7522
11:20 *such as are* upright in *their* way *are* his **d**. 7522
12:22 but they that deal truly *are* his **d**. 7522
15: 8 but the prayer of the upright *is* his **d**. 7522
16:13 Righteous lips *are* the **d** of kings; and 7522
18: 2 A fool hath no **d** in understanding, but that 2654
19:10 **D** *is* not seemly for a fool; much less for a 8588
24:25 to them that rebuke *him* shall be **d**, and 5276
29:17 thee rest; yea, he shall give **d** unto thy soul. 4574
SS 2: 3 I sat down under his shadow **with great d**, 2530
Isa 1:11 I **d** not in the blood of bullocks, or 2654
13:17 and *as for* gold, they shall not **d** in it. 2654
55: 2 *is* good, and let your soul **d** itself in fatness. 6026
58: 2 seek me daily, and **d** to know my ways, 2654
58: 2 they **take d in** approaching to God. 2654
58:13 call the sabbath a **d**, the holy of 6027
58:14 shalt thou **d** thyself in the LORD; and 6026
Jer 6:10 unto them a reproach; they have no **d** in it. 2654
9:24 for in these *things* I **d**, saith the LORD. 2654
Mal 3: 1 messenger of the covenant, whom ye **d** in: 2655
Ro 7:22 For I **d in** the law of God after the inward *4913*

DELIGHTED (12) [DELIGHT]
1Sa 19: 2 Jonathan Saul's son **d** much in David: and 2654
2Sa 22:20 he delivered me, because he **d** in me. 2654
1Ki 10: 9 be the LORD thy God, which **d** in thee, 2654
2Ch 9: 8 which **d** in thee to set thee on his throne, 2654
Ne 9:25 and **d** themselves in thy great goodness. 5727
Est 2:14 except the king **d** in her, and *that* she were 2654
Ps 18:19 he delivered me, because he **d** in me. 2654
22: 8 let him deliver him, seeing he **d** in him. 2654
109:17 as he **d** not in blessing, so let it be far from 2654
Isa 65:12 and did choose *that* wherein I **d** not. 2654
66: 4 mine eyes, and chose *that* in which I **d** not. 2654
66:11 and be **d** with the abundance of her glory. 6026

DELIGHTEST (1) [DELIGHT]
Ps 51:16 else would I give *it:* thou **d** not **in** burnt 7521

DELIGHTETH (14) [DELIGHT]
Est 6: 6 unto the man whom the king **d** to honour? 2654
6: 7 *For* the man whom the king **d** to honour, 2654
6: 9 the man *withal* whom the king **d** to honour, 2654
6: 9 to the man whom the king **d** to honour. 2654
6:11 unto the man whom the king **d** to honour. 2654
Ps 37:23 by the LORD: and he **d** in his way. 2654
112: 1 *that* **d** greatly in his commandments. 2654
147:10 He **d** not in the strength of the horse: 2654
Pr 3:12 even as a father the son *in whom* he **d**. 7521
Isa 42: 1 I uphold; mine elect, *in whom* my soul **d**; 7521
62: 4 for the LORD **d** in thee, and thy land shall 2654
66: 3 and their soul **d** in their abominations. 2654
Mic 7:18 his anger for ever, because he **d** in mercy. 2654
Mal 2:17 the sight of the LORD, and he **d** in them; 2654

DELIGHTFUL See GOODLIER; GOODLIEST; GOODLY

DELIGHTS (6) [DELIGHT]
2Sa 1:24 who clothed you in scarlet, with *other* **d**, 5730
Ps 119:92 Unless thy law *had been* my **d**, I should 8191
119:143 on me: *yet* thy commandments *are* my **d**. 8191
Pr 8:31 and my **d** *were* with the sons of men. 8191
Ecc 2: 8 and the **d** of the sons of men, 8588
SS 7: 6 and how pleasant art thou, O love, for **d**! 8588

DELIGHTSOME (1) [DELIGHT]
Mal 3:12 for ye shall be a **d** land, saith the LORD of 2656

DELILAH (6)
Jdg 16: 4 in the valley of Sorek, whose name *was* **D**. 1807
16: 6 **D** said to Samson, Tell me, I pray thee, 1807

Jdg	16:10	**D** said unto Samson, Behold, thou hast	1807
	16:12	**D** therefore took new ropes, and bound him	1807
	16:13	**D** said unto Samson, Hitherto thou hast	1807
	16:18	when **D** saw that he had told her all his	1807

DELIVER (296) [DELIVERANCE, DELIVERANCES, DELIVERED, DELIVEREDST, DELIVERER, DELIVEREST, DELIVERETH, DELIVERING, DELIVERY]

Ge	32:11	**D** me, I pray thee, from the hand of my	5337
	37:22	their hands, **to d** him to his father again.	3807.1
	40:13	thou shalt **d** Pharaoh's cup into his hand,	5414
	42:34	*are* true *men: so* will I **d** you your brother,	5414
	42:37	**d** him into my hand, and I will bring him to	5414
Ex	3: 8	I am come down to **d** them out of the hand	5337
	5:18	given you, yet shall ye **d** the tale of bricks.	5414
	21:13	lie not in wait, but God **d** *him* into his hand;	579
	22: 7	If a man shall **d** unto his neighbour money	5414
	22:10	If a man **d** unto his neighbour an ass, or	5414
	22:26	thou shalt **d** it unto him by that the sun	7725
	23:31	for I will **d** the inhabitants of the land into	5414
Lev	26:26	they shall **d** *you* your bread **again** by	7725
Nu	21: 2	If thou wilt **indeed d** this people into	5414+5414
	35:25	the congregation shall **d** the slayer out of	5337
Dt	1:27	to **d** us into the hand of the Amorites,	5414
	2:30	that he might **d** him into thy hand,	5414
	3: 2	for I will **d** him, and all his people, and	5414
	7: 2	when the LORD thy God shall **d** them	5414
	7:16	which the LORD thy God shall **d** thee;	5414
	7:23	the LORD thy God shall **d** them unto thee,	5414
	7:24	he shall **d** their kings into thine hand, and	5414
	19:12	**d** him into the hand of the avenger of	5414
	23:14	to **d** thee, and to give up thine enemies	5337
	23:15	Thou shalt not **d** unto his master the servant	5462
	24:13	**In any case** thou shalt **d** him the pledge **again**	7725+7725
	25:11	the wife of the one draweth near for to **d**	5337
	32:39	neither *is there any* that can **d** out of my	5337
Jos	2:13	that they have, and **d** our lives from death.	5337
	7: 7	to **d** us into the hand of the Amorites,	5414
	8: 7	for the LORD your God will **d** it into your	5414
	11: 6	time will I **d** them **up** all slain before Israel:	5414
	20: 5	they shall not **d** the slayer **up** into his hand;	5462
Jdg	4: 7	and I will **d** him into thine hand.	5414
	7: 7	and **d** the Midianites into thine hand:	5414
	10:11	*Did* not *I d you* from the Egyptians, and	NIH
	10:13	other gods: wherefore I will **d** you no more.	3467
	10:14	let them **d** you in the time of your	3467
	10:15	unto thee; **d** us only, we pray thee, this day.	5337
	11: 9	the LORD **d** them before me, shall I be	5414
	11:30	If thou shalt **without fail d**	5414+5414
	13: 5	he shall begin to **d** Israel out of the hand of	3467
	15:12	that we may **d** thee into the hand of	5414
	15:13	bind thee fast, and **d** thee into their hand:	5414
	20:13	Now therefore **d** *us* the men, the children of	5414
	20:28	for to morrow I will **d** them into thine hand.	5414
1Sa	4: 8	who shall **d** us out of the hand of these	5337
	7: 3	he will **d** you out of the hand of	5337
	7:14	the coasts thereof did Israel **d** out of	5337
	12:10	now **d** us out of the hand of our enemies,	5337
	12:21	after vain *things,* which cannot profit nor **d**;	5337
	14:37	wilt thou **d** them into the hand of Israel?	5414
	17:37	he will **d** me out of the hand of this	5337
	17:46	This day will the LORD **d** thee into mine	5462
	23: 4	for I will **d** the Philistines into thine hand.	5414
	23:11	Will the men of Keilah **d** me **up** into his	5462
	23:12	Will the men of Keilah **d** me and my men	5462
	23:12	And the LORD said, They will **d** *thee* **up**.	5462
	23:20	our part *shall be* to **d** him into the king's	5462
	24: 4	I will **d** thine enemy into thine hand,	5414
	24:15	my cause, and **d** me out of thine hand.	8199
	26:24	and let him **d** me out of all tribulation.	5337
	28:19	Moreover the LORD will also **d** Israel	5414
	28:19	the LORD also shall **d** the host of Israel	5414
	30:15	nor **d** me into the hands of my master, and	5462
2Sa	3:14	Saul's son, saying, **D** *me* my wife Michal,	5414
	5:19	wilt thou **d** them into mine hand? And	5414
	5:19	for I will **doubtless d** the Philistines	5414+5414
	14: 7	and they said, **D** him that smote his brother,	5414
	14:16	to **d** his handmaid out of the hand of	5337
	20:21	**d** him only, and I will depart from the city.	5414
1Ki	8:46	**d** them to the enemy, so that they carry	5414
	18: 9	that thou wouldest **d** thy servant into	5414
	20: 5	Thou shalt **d** me thy silver, and thy gold,	5414
	20:13	behold, I will **d** it into thine hand *this* day;	5414
	20:28	will I **d** all this great multitude into thine	5414
	22: 6	for the Lord shall **d** *it* into the hand of	5414
	22:12	for the LORD shall **d** *it* into the king's	5414
	22:15	for the LORD shall **d** *it* into the hand of	5414
2Ki	3:10	*together,* to **d** them into the hand of Moab.	5414
	3:13	*together,* to **d** them into the hand of Moab.	5414
	3:18	he will **d** the Moabites also into your hand.	5414
	12: 7	but **d** it for the breaches of the house.	5414
	17:39	he shall **d** you out of the hand of all your	5337
	18:23	and I will **d** thee two thousand horses,	5414
	18:29	for he shall not be able to **d** you out of his	5337
	18:30	The LORD will **surely d** us, and	5337+5337
	18:32	saying, The LORD will **d** us.	5337
	18:35	that the LORD should **d** Jerusalem out of	5337
	20: 6	I will **d** thee and this city out of the hand of	5337
	21:14	and **d** them into the hand of their enemies;	5414
	22: 5	let them **d** it into the hand of the doers of	5414
1Ch	14:10	wilt thou **d** them into mine hand? And	5414
	14:10	Go up; for I will **d** them into thine hand.	5414
	16:35	us together, and **d** us from the heathen,	5337
2Ch	6:36	**d** them *over* before *their* enemies, and	5414
	18: 5	for God will **d** *it* into the king's hand.	5414
	18:11	for the LORD shall **d** *it* into the hand of	5414
	25:15	which could not **d** their own people out of	5337
	25:20	that *he* might **d** them into the hand *of their*	5414
	28:11	me therefore, and **d** the captives **again,**	7725
	32:11	The LORD our God shall **d** us out of	5337
	32:13	able to **d** their lands out of mine hand?	5337
	32:14	that could **d** his people out of mine hand,	5337
	32:14	that your God should be able to **d** you out	5337
	32:15	kingdom was able to **d** his people out of	5337
	32:15	how much less shall your God **d** you out of	5337
	32:17	shall not the God of Hezekiah **d** his people	5337
Ezr	7:19	*those* **d** thou before the God of Jerusalem.	8000
Ne	9:28	many times didst thou **d** them according to	5337
Job	5: 4	in the gate, neither *is there* any to **d** *them.*	5337
	5:19	He shall **d** thee in six troubles: yea,	5337
	6:23	Or, **D** me from the enemy's hand? or,	4422
	10: 7	*there is* none that can **d** out of thine hand.	5337
	22:30	He shall **d** the island of the innocent: and	4422
	33:24	saith, **D** him from going down *to* the pit:	6308
	33:28	He will **d** his soul from going into the pit,	6299
	36:18	then a great ransom cannot **d** thee.	5186
Ps	6: 4	Return, O LORD, **d** my soul: O save me	2502
	7: 1	from all them that persecute me, and **d** me:	5337
	7: 2	*it* in pieces, while *there is* none to **d**.	5337
	17:13	**d** my soul from the wicked, *which is* thy	6403
	22: 4	in thee: they trusted, and thou didst **d** them.	6403
	22: 8	He trusted on the LORD *that* he would **d**	6403
	22: 8	let him **d** him, seeing he delighted in him.	5337
	22:20	**D** my soul from the sword; my darling	5337
	25:20	O keep my soul, and **d** me: let me not be	5337
	27:12	**D** me not **over** unto the will of mine	5414
	31: 1	be ashamed: **d** me in thy righteousness.	6403
	31: 2	Bow down thine ear to me; **d** me speedily:	5337
	31:15	**d** me from the hand of mine enemies, and	5337
	33:17	neither shall he **d** *any* by his great strength.	4422
	33:19	To **d** their soul from death, and to keep	5337
	37:40	the LORD shall help them, and **d** them:	6403
	37:40	he shall **d** them from the wicked, and	6403
	39: 8	**D** me from all my transgressions: make me	5337
	40:13	Be pleased, O LORD, to **d** me: O LORD,	5337
	41: 1	the LORD will **d** him in time of trouble.	4422
	41: 2	thou wilt not **d** him unto the will of his	5414
	43: 1	O **d** me from the deceitful and unjust man.	6403
	50:15	I will **d** thee, and thou shalt glorify me.	2502
	50:22	I tear *you* in pieces, and *there be* none to **d**.	5337
	51:14	**D** me from bloodguiltiness, O God,	5337
	56:13	*wilt* not *thou d* my feet from falling, that *I*	NIH
	59: 1	**D** me from mine enemies, O my God:	5337
	59: 2	**D** me from the workers of iniquity, and	5337
	69:14	**D** me out of the mire, and let me not sink:	5337
	69:18	redeem it: **d** me because of mine enemies.	6299
	70: 1	*Make haste,* O God, to **d** me; make haste to	5337
	71: 2	**D** me in thy righteousness, and cause me to	5337
	71: 4	**D** me, O my God, out of the hand of	6403
	71:11	and take him; for *there is* none to **d** *him.*	5337
	72:12	For he shall **d** the needy when he crieth;	5337
	74:19	O **d** not the soul of thy turtledove unto	5414
	79: 9	**d** us, and purge away our sins, for thy	5337
	82: 4	**D** the poor and needy: rid *them* out of	6403
	89:48	shall he **d** his soul from the hand of	4422
	91: 3	Surely he shall **d** thee from the snare of	5337
	91:14	his love upon me, therefore will I **d** him:	6403

Ps 91:15 in trouble; I will **d** him, and honour him. 2502
106:43 Many times did he **d** them; but 5337
109:21 because thy mercy *is* good, **d** thou me. 5337
116: 4 O LORD, I beseech thee, **d** my soul. 4422
119:134 **D** me from the oppression of man: so will I 6299
119:153 Consider mine affliction, and **d** me: for I do 2502
119:154 Plead my cause, and **d** me: quicken me 1350
119:170 before thee: **d** me according to thy word. 5337
120: 2 **D** my soul, O LORD, from lying lips, *and* 5337
140: 1 **D** me, O LORD, from the evil man: 2502
142: 6 **d** me from my persecutors; for they are 5337
143: 9 **D** me, O LORD, from mine enemies: 5337
144: 7 rid me, and **d** me out of great waters, 5337
144:11 and **d** me from the hand of strange children, 5337
Pr 2:12 To **d** thee from the way of the evil *man,* 5337
2:16 To **d** thee from the strange woman, 5337
4: 9 a crown of glory shall she **d** *to* thee. 4042
6: 3 Do this now, my son, and **d** thyself, 5337
6: 5 **D** thyself as a roe from the hand *of* 5337
11: 6 The righteousness of the upright shall **d** 5337
12: 6 but the mouth of the upright shall **d** them. 5337
19:19 for if thou **d** *him,* yet thou must do *it* again. 5337
23:14 with the rod, and shalt **d** his soul from hell. 5337
24:11 If thou forbear to **d** *them that are* drawn 5337
Ecc 8: 8 neither shall wickedness **d** those that are 4422
Isa 5:29 carry *it* away safe, and none shall **d** *it.* 5337
19:20 and a great one, and he shall **d** them. 5337
29:11 which *men* **d** to one that is learned, saying, 5414
31: 5 defending also he will **d** *it;* and 5337
36:14 for he shall not be able to **d** you. 5337
36:15 The LORD will **surely d** us: 5337+5337
36:18 saying, The LORD will **d** us. 5337
36:20 that the LORD should **d** Jerusalem out of 5337
38: 6 I will **d** thee and this city out of the hand of 5337
43:13 *there is* none that can **d** out of my hand: 5337
44:17 and prayeth unto it, and saith, **D** me; 5337
44:20 that he cannot **d** his soul, nor say, *Is there* 5337
46: 2 they could not **d** the burden, but 4422
46: 4 will bear; even I will carry, and will **d** *you.* 4422
47:14 they shall not **d** themselves from the power 5337
50: 2 or have I no power to **d**? behold, at my 5337
57:13 When thou criest, let thy companies **d** thee; 5337
Jer 1: 8 for I *am* with thee to **d** thee, saith 5337
1:19 I *am* with thee, saith the LORD, to **d** thee. 5337
15: 9 the residue of them will I **d** to the sword 5414
15:20 I *am* with thee to save thee and to **d** thee, 5337
15:21 I will **d** thee out of the hand of the wicked, 5337
18:21 Therefore **d up** their children to the famine, 5414
20: 5 Moreover I will **d** all the strength of this 5414
21: 7 I will **d** Zedekiah king of Judah, and his 5414
21:12 **d** *him that is* spoiled out of the hand of 5337
22: 3 **d** the spoiled out of the hand of 5337
24: 9 I will **d** them to be removed into all 5414
29:18 will **d** them to be removed to all 5414
29:21 I will **d** them into the hand of 5414
38:19 lest they **d** me into their hand, and 5414
38:20 They shall not **d** *thee.* Obey, I beseech thee, 5414
39:17 I will **d** thee in that day, saith the LORD: 5337
39:18 For I will **surely d** thee, and 4422+4422
42:11 to save you, and to **d** you from his hand. 5337
43: 3 for to **d** us into the hand of the Chaldeans, 5414
43:11 *and* **d** such *as are* for death to death; NIH
46:26 I will **d** them into the hand of those that 5414
51: 6 of Babylon, and **d** every man his soul: 4422
51:45 **d** ye every man his soul from the fierce 4422
La 5: 8 *there is* none that doth **d** *us* out of their 6561
Eze 7:19 their gold shall not be able to **d** them in 5337
11: 9 **d** you into the hands of strangers, and 5414
13:21 **d** my people out of your hand, and 5337
13:23 for I will **d** my people out of your hand: 5337
14:14 they should **d** *but* their own souls by their 5337
14:16 they shall **d** neither sons nor daughters; 5337
14:18 they shall **d** neither sons nor daughters, but 5337
14:20 they shall **d** neither son nor daughter; 5337
14:20 **d** their own souls by their righteousness. 5337
21:31 **d** thee into the hand of brutish men, *and* 5414
23:28 I *will* **d** thee into the hand *of them* whom 5414
25: 4 I *will* **d** thee to the men of the east for a 5414
25: 7 and will **d** thee for a spoil to the heathen; 5414
33: 5 But he that taketh warning shall **d** his soul. 4422
33:12 not **d** him in the day of his transgression: 5337
34:10 for I will **d** my flock from their mouth, 5337
34:12 will **d** them out of all places where they 5337
Da 3:15 who *is* that God that shall **d** you out of my 7804
3:17 our God whom we serve *is* able to **d** us 7804
3:17 and he will **d** *us* out of thine hand, O king. 7804
3:29 there is no other God that can **d** after this 5338
6:14 and set *his* heart on Daniel to **d** him: 7804
6:14 till the going down of the sun to **d** him. 5338
6:16 thou servest continually, he will **d** thee. 7804
6:20 able to **d** thee from the lions? 7804
8: 4 neither *was there any* that could **d** out of his 5337
8: 7 there was none that could **d** the ram out of 5337
Hos 2:10 and none shall **d** her out of mine hand, 5337
11: 8 *how* shall I **d** thee, Israel? how shall I make 4042
Am 1: 6 the whole captivity, to **d** *them* **up** to Edom: 5462
2:14 neither shall the mighty **d** himself: 4422
2:15 *he that is* swift of foot shall not **d** *himself:* 4422
2:15 shall he that rideth the horse **d** himself. 4422
6: 8 will I **d up** the city with all that is therein. 5462
Jnh 4: 6 over his head, to **d** him from his grief. 5337
Mic 5: 6 thus shall he **d** *us* from the Assyrian, 5337
5: 8 and teareth in pieces, and none can **d**. 5337
6:14 thou shalt take hold, but shalt not **d**; and 6403
Zep 1:18 **d** them in the day of the LORD'S wrath; 5337
Zec 2: 7 **D** thyself, O Zion, that dwellest *with* 4422
11: 6 I *will* **d** the men every one into his 4672
11: 6 and out of their hand I will not **d** *them.* 5337
Mt 5:25 lest at any time the adversary **d** thee to *3860*
5:25 and the judge **d** thee to the officer, and *3860*
6:13 us not into temptation, but **d** us from evil: *4506*
10:17 for they will **d** you **up** to the councils, and *3860*
10:19 But when they **d** you **up**, take no thought *3860*
10:21 And the brother shall **d up** the brother to *3860*
20:19 And shall **d** him to the Gentiles to mock, *3860*
24: 9 Then shall they **d** you **up** to be afflicted, *3860*
26:15 will ye give me, and I will **d** him unto you? *3860*
27:43 let him **d** him now, if he will have him: *4506*
Mk 10:33 to death, and shall **d** him to the Gentiles: *3860*
13: 9 for they shall **d** you **up** to councils; and *3860*
13:11 when they shall lead *you,* and **d** you **up**, *3860*
Lk 11: 4 us not into temptation; but **d** us from evil. *4506*
12:58 and the judge **d** thee to the officer, and *3860*
20:20 *so they* might **d** him unto the power and *3860*
Ac 7:25 that God by his hand would **d** them: *1325+4991*
7:34 and am come down to **d** them. *1807*
21:11 shall **d** *him* into the hands of the Gentiles. *3860*
25:11 accuse me, no *man* may **d** me unto them. *5483*
25:16 It is not the manner of the Romans to **d** any *5483*
Ro 7:24 who shall **d** me from the body of this *4506*
1Co 5: 5 To **d** such a one unto Satan for *3860*
2Co 1:10 us from so great a death, and doth **d**: *4506*
1:10 in whom we trust that he will yet **d** *us;* *4506*
Gal 1: 4 that he might **d** us from *this* present evil *1807*
2Ti 4:18 And the Lord shall **d** me from every evil *4506*
Heb 2:15 And **d** them who through fear of death were *525*
2Pe 2: 9 The Lord knoweth *how* to **d** the godly out *4506*

DELIVERANCE (16) [DELIVER]

Ge 45: 7 and to save your lives by a great **d**. 6413
Jdg 15:18 Thou hast given this great **d** into the hand 8668
2Ki 5: 1 by him the LORD had given **d** unto Syria: 8668
13:17 The arrow of the LORD'S **d**, and 8668
13:17 and the arrow of **d** from Syria: 8668
1Ch 11:14 and the LORD saved *them by* a great **d**. 8668
2Ch 12: 7 destroy them, but I will grant them some **d**; 6413
Ezr 9:13 and hast given us *such* **d** as this; 6413
Est 4:14 and **d** arise to the Jews from another place; 2020
Ps 18:50 Great **d** giveth he to his king; and 3444
32: 7 shalt compass me about *with* songs of **d**. 6405
Isa 26:18 we have not wrought any **d** *in* the earth; 3444
Joel 2:32 in mount Zion and in Jerusalem shall be **d**, 6413
Ob 1:17 upon mount Zion shall be **d**, and there shall 6413
Lk 4:18 to preach **d** to the captives, and recovering of *859*
Heb 11:35 and others were tortured, not accepting **d**; *629*

DELIVERANCES (1) [DELIVER]

Ps 44: 4 *art* my King, O God: command **d** for Jacob. 3444

DELIVERED (291) [DELIVER]

Ge 9: 2 fishes of the sea; into your hand **are** they **d**. 5414
14:20 which hath **d** thine enemies into thy hand. 4042
25:24 when her days to be **d** were fulfilled, 3205
32:16 he **d** *them* into the hand of his servants, 5414
37:21 heard *it,* and he **d** him out of their hands; 5337
Ex 1:19 are **d** ere the midwives come in unto them. 3205
2:19 An Egyptian **d** us out of the hand of 5337
5:23 neither hast thou **d** thy people **at all**. 5337+5337

Ex 12:27 he smote the Egyptians, and **d** our houses. 5337
18: 4 and **d** me from the sword of Pharaoh: 5337
18: 8 by the way, and *how* the LORD **d** them. 5337
18: 9 whom he had **d** out of the hand of 5337
18:10 who hath **d** you out of the hand of 5337
18:10 who hath **d** the people from under the hand 5337
Lev 6: 2 in **that which was d** him **to keep,** 6487
6: 4 that which was **d** him **to keep,** 854+6485+6487
26:25 ye shall be **d** into the hand of the enemy. 5414
Nu 21: 3 voice of Israel, and **d up** the Canaanites; 5414
21:34 for I have **d** him into thy hand, and all his 5414
31: 5 So there were **d** out of the thousands of 4560
Dt 2:33 the LORD our God **d** him before us; and 5414
2:36 for us: the LORD our God **d** all unto us: 5414
3: 3 So the LORD our God **d** into our hands 5414
5:22 in two tables of stone, and **d** them unto me. 5414
9:10 the LORD **d** unto me two tables of stone 5414
20:13 when the LORD thy God hath **d** it into 5414
21:10 the LORD thy God hath **d** them into thine 5414
31: 9 **d** it unto the priests the sons of Levi, 5414
Jos 2:24 Truly the LORD hath **d** into our hands all 5414
9:26 **d** them out of the hand of the children of 5337
10: 8 for I have **d** them into thine hand; 5414
10:12 **d up** the Amorites before the children of 5414
10:19 for the LORD your God hath **d** them into 5414
10:30 the LORD **d** it also, and the king thereof, 5414
10:32 the LORD **d** Lachish into the hand of 5414
11: 8 the LORD **d** them into the hand of Israel, 5414
21:44 the LORD **d** all their enemies into their 5414
22:31 now ye have **d** the children of Israel out of 5337
24:10 blessed you still: so I **d** you out of his hand. 5337
24:11 the Jebusites; and I **d** them into your hand. 5414
Jdg 1: 2 behold, I have **d** the land into his hand. 5414
1: 4 the LORD **d** the Canaanites and 5414
2:14 he **d** them into the hands of spoilers that 5414
2:16 which **d** them out of the hand of those that 3467
2:18 **d** them out of the hand of their enemies all 3467
2:23 neither **d** he them into the hand of Joshua. 5414
3: 9 who **d** them, *even* Othniel the son of 3467
3:10 the LORD **d** Chushan-rishathaim king of 5414
3:28 for the LORD hath **d** your enemies 5414
3:31 men with an ox goad: and he also **d** Israel. 3467
4:14 the LORD hath **d** Sisera into thine hand: 5414
5:11 *They that are d* from the noise of archers in NIH
6: 1 the LORD **d** them into the hand of Midian 5414
6: 9 I **d** you out of the hand of the Egyptians, 5337
6:13 and **d** us into the hands of the Midianites. 5414
7: 9 the host; for I have **d** it into thine hand. 5414
7:14 *for* into his hand hath God **d** Midian, and 5414
7:15 for the LORD hath **d** into your hand 5414
8: 3 God hath **d** into your hands the princes of 5414
8: 7 Therefore when the LORD hath **d** Zebah 5414
8:22 for thou hast **d** us from the hand of Midian. 3467
8:34 who had **d** them out of the hands of all their 5337
9:17 and **d** you out of the hand of Midian: 5337
10:12 cried to me, and I **d** you out of their hand. 3467
11:21 the LORD God of Israel **d** Sihon and all 5414
11:32 and the LORD **d** them into his hands. 5414
12: 2 I called you, ye **d** me not out of their hands. 3467
12: 3 when I saw that ye **d** *me* not, I put my life 3467
12: 3 and the LORD **d** them into my hand: 5414
13: 1 the LORD **d** them into the hand of 5414
16:23 Our god hath **d** Samson our enemy into our 5414
16:24 Our god hath **d** into our hands our enemy, 5414
1Sa 4:19 was with child, *near* to be **d**: 3205
10:18 **d** you out of the hand of the Egyptians, and 5337
12:11 **d** you out of the hand of your enemies on 5337
14:10 for the LORD hath **d** them into our hand: 5414
14:12 for the LORD hath **d** them into the hand 5414
14:48 **d** Israel out of the hands of them that 5337
17:35 and smote him, and **d** *it* out of his mouth: 5337
17:37 The LORD that **d** me out of the paw of 5337
23: 7 Saul said, God hath **d** him into mine hand; 5234
23:14 every day, but God **d** him not into his hand. 5414
24:10 **d** thee to day into mine hand in the cave: 5414
24:18 forasmuch as when the LORD had **d** me 5462
26: 8 God hath **d** thine enemy into thine hand 5462
26:23 for the LORD **d** thee into *my* hand to day, 5414
30:23 **d** the company that came against us into 5414
2Sa 3: 8 and have not **d** thee into the hand of David, 4672
10:10 the rest of the people he **d** into the hand of 5414
12: 7 and I **d** thee out of the hand of Saul; 5337
16: 8 the LORD hath **d** the kingdom into 5414
18:28 which hath **d up** the men that lift up their 5462
19: 9 he **d** us out of the hand of the Philistines; 4422
21: 6 Let seven men of his sons be **d** unto us, and 5414
21: 9 he **d** them into the hands of the Gibeonites, 5414
22: 1 **d** him out of the hand of all his enemies, 5337
22:18 He **d** me from my strong enemy, *and* 5337
22:20 he **d** me, because he delighted in me. 2502
22:44 Thou also hast **d** me from the strivings of 6403
22:49 thou hast **d** me from the violent man. 5337
1Ki 3:17 I was **d of a child** with her in the house. 3205
3:18 to pass the third day after that I was **d**, 3205
3:18 was delivered, that this woman was **d** also: 3205
13:26 the LORD hath **d** him unto the lion, 5414
15:18 and **d** them into the hand of his servants: 5414
17:23 into the house, and **d** him unto his mother: 5414
2Ki 12:15 into whose hand they **d** the money to be 5414
13: 3 he **d** them into the hand of Hazael king of 5414
17:20 and **d** them into the hand of spoilers, 5414
18:30 this city shall not be **d** into the hand of 5414
18:33 **d at all** his land out of the hand of 5337+5337
18:34 have they **d** Samaria out of mine hand? 5337
18:35 that have **d** their country out of mine hand, 5337
19:10 Jerusalem shall not be **d** into the hand of 5414
19:11 them utterly: and shalt thou be **d**? 5337
19:12 Have the gods of the nations **d** them which 5337
22: 7 of the money that was **d** into their hand, 5414
22: 9 have **d** it into the hand of them that do 5414
22:10 saying, Hilkiah the priest hath **d** me a book. 5414
1Ch 5:20 the Hagarites were **d** into their hand, and 5414
11:14 and **d** it, and slew the Philistines; 5337
16: 7 on that day David **d** first *this psalm* to 5414
19:11 the rest of the people he **d** unto the hand of 5414
2Ch 13:16 and God **d** them into their hand. 5414
16: 8 on the LORD, he **d** them into thine hand. 5414
18:14 prosper, and they shall be **d** into your hand. 5414
23: 9 Moreover Jehoiada the priest **d** to 5414
24:24 the LORD **d** a very great host into their 5414
28: 5 Wherefore the LORD his God **d** him into 5414
28: 5 he was also **d** into the hand of the king of 5414
28: 9 he hath **d** them into your hand, and ye have 5414
29: 8 Jerusalem, and he hath **d** them to trouble, 5414
32:17 have not **d** their people out of mine hand, 5337
34: 9 they **d** the money that was brought *into* 5414
34:15 And Hilkiah **d** the book to Shaphan. 5414
34:17 and have **d** it into the hand of the overseers, 5414
Ezr 5:14 they *were* **d** unto *one,* whose name *was* 3052
8:31 he **d** us from the hand of the enemy, and 5337
8:36 they **d** the king's commissions unto 5414
9: 7 been **d** into the hand of the kings of 5414
Est 6: 9 horse be **d** to the hand of one of the king's 5414
Job 16:11 God hath **d** me to the ungodly, and 5462
22:30 and it is **d** by the pureness of thine hands. 4422
23: 7 so should I be **d** for ever from my judge. 6403
29:12 Because I **d** the poor that cried, and 4422
Ps 7: 4 I have **d** him that without cause is mine 2502
18: T **d** him from the hand of all his enemies, 5337
18:17 He **d** me from my strong enemy, and 5337
18:19 he **d** me, because he delighted in me. 2502
18:43 Thou hast **d** me from the strivings of 6403
18:48 thou hast **d** me from the violent man. 5337
22: 5 They cried unto thee, and were **d**: 4422
33:16 a mighty *man* is not **d** by much strength. 5337
34: 4 he heard me, and **d** me from all my fears. 5337
54: 7 For he hath **d** me out of all trouble: and 5337
55:18 He hath **d** my soul in peace from the battle 6299
56:13 For thou hast **d** my soul from death: *wilt* 5337
60: 5 That thy beloved may be **d**; save *with* thy 2502
69:14 let me be **d** from them that hate me, and 5337
78:42 *nor* the day when he **d** them from 6299
78:61 **d** his strength into captivity, and his glory 5414
81: 6 the burden: his hands were **d** from the pots. 5674
81: 7 Thou calledst in trouble, and I **d** thee; 2502
86:13 thou hast **d** my soul from the lowest hell. 5337
107: 6 *and* he **d** them out of their distresses. 5337
107:20 and **d** *them* from their destructions. 4422
108: 6 That thy beloved may be **d**: save *with* thy 2502
116: 8 For thou hast **d** my soul from death, mine 2502
Pr 11: 8 The righteous is **d** out of trouble, and 2502
11: 9 but through knowledge shall the just be **d**. 2502
11:21 but the seed of the righteous shall be **d**. 4422
28:26 but whoso walketh wisely, he shall be **d**. 4422
Ecc 9:15 wise man, and he by his wisdom **d** the city; 4422
Isa 20: 6 whither we flee for help to be **d** from 5337
29:12 the book is **d** to *him* that is not learned, 5414
34: 2 he hath **d** them to the slaughter. 5414

Isa 36:15 this city shall not be **d** into the hand of 5414
36:18 Hath any of the gods of the nations **d** his 5337
36:19 and have they **d** Samaria out of my hand? 5337
36:20 that have **d** their land out of my hand, 5337
37:11 them utterly; and shalt thou be **d**? 5337
37:12 Have the gods of the nations **d** them which 5337
38:17 thou hast in love to my soul *d it* from the pit NIH
49:24 from the mighty, or the lawful captive **d**? 4422
49:25 and the prey of the terrible shall be **d**: 4422
66: 7 her pain came, she was **d** of a man child. 4422
Jer 7:10 say, We are **d** to do all these abominations? 5337
20:13 for he hath **d** the soul of the poor from 5337
32: 4 shall **surely** be **d** into the hand of the king 5414
32:16 Now when I had **d** the evidence of 5414
32:36 It shall be **d** into the hand of the king of 5414
34: 3 shalt surely be taken, and **d** into his hand; 5414
37:17 thou shalt be **d** into the hand of the king of 5414
46:24 she shall be **d** into the hand of the people of 5414
La 1:14 to fall, the Lord hath **d** me into *their* hands, 5414
Eze 3:19 die in his iniquity; but thou hast **d** thy soul. 5337
3:21 he is warned; also thou hast **d** thy soul. 5337
14:16 they only shall be **d**, but the land shall be 5337
14:18 but they only shall be **d** themselves. 5337
16:21 **d** them to cause them to pass through 5414
16:27 **d** thee unto the will of them that hate thee, 5414
17:15 or shall he break the covenant, and be **d**? 4422
23: 9 Wherefore I have **d** her into the hand of her 5414
31:11 **d** him into the hand of the mighty one of 5414
31:14 for they are all **d** unto death, to the nether 5414
32:20 she is **d** *to* the sword: draw her and all her 5414
33: 9 die in his iniquity; but thou hast **d** thy soul. 5337
34:27 **d** them out of the hand of those that served 5337
Da 3:28 **d** his servants that trusted in him, and 7804
6:27 who hath **d** Daniel from the power of 7804
12: 1 at that time thy people shall be **d**, every one 4422
Joel 2:32 call on the name of the LORD shall be **d**: 4422
Am 1: 9 they **d up** the whole captivity to Edom, 5462
9: 1 and he that escapeth of them shall not be **d**. 4422
Ob 1:14 neither shouldest thou have **d up** those of 5462
Mic 4:10 go *even* to Babylon; there shalt thou be **d**; 5337
Hab 2: 9 that *he* may be **d** from the power of evil! 5337
Mal 3:15 set up; yea, *they that* tempt God are even **d**. 4422
Mt 11:27 All *things* are **d** unto me of my Father: and *3860*
18:34 was wroth, and **d** him to the tormentors, *3860*
25:14 own servants, and **d** unto them his goods. *3860*
27: 2 and **d** him to Pontius Pilate the governor. *3860*
27:18 For he knew that for envy they had **d** him. *3860*
27:26 scourged Jesus, he **d** *him* to be crucified. *3860*
27:58 Then Pilate commanded the body to be **d**. *591*
Mk 7:13 through your tradition, which ye have **d**: *3860*
9:31 The Son of man is **d** into the hands of men, *3860*
10:33 the Son of man shall be **d** unto the chief *3860*
15: 1 and carried *him* away, and **d** *him* to Pilate. *3860*
15:10 For he knew that the chief priests had **d** *3860*
15:15 released Barabbas unto them, and **d** Jesus, *3860*
Lk 1: 2 Even as they **d** *them* unto us, which from *3860*
1:57 full time came that she should be **d**; *5088*
1:74 that *we* being **d** out of the hand of our *4506*
2: 6 were accomplished that she should be **d**. *5088*
4: 6 for *that* is **d** unto me; and to whomsoever I *3860*
4:17 And there was **d** unto him the book of *1929*
7:15 to speak. And he **d** him to his mother. *1325*
9:42 the child, and **d** him **again** to his father. *591*
9:44 for the Son of man shall be **d** into the hands *3860*
10:22 All *things* are **d** to me of my Father: and *3860*
12:58 give diligence that *thou* mayest be **d** from *525*
18:32 For he shall be **d** unto the Gentiles, and *3860*
19:13 and **d** them ten pounds, and said unto them, *1325*
23:25 had desired; but he **d** Jesus to their will. *3860*
24: 7 The Son of man must be **d** into the hands of *3860*
24:20 our rulers **d** him to be condemned to death, *3860*
Jn 16:21 but as soon as she is **d** of the child, *1080*
18:30 we would not have **d** him **up** unto thee. *3860*
18:35 and the chief priests have **d** thee unto me: *3860*
18:36 that I should not be **d** to the Jews: *3860*
19:11 he that **d** me unto thee hath the greater sin. *3860*
19:16 Then **d** he him therefore unto them to be *3860*
Ac 2:23 being **d** by the determinate counsel and *1560*
3:13 whom ye **d up**, and denied him in *3860*
6:14 shall change the customs which Moses **d** *3860*
7:10 And **d** him out of all his afflictions, and *1807*
12: 4 **d** *him* to four quaternions of soldiers to *3860*
12:11 and hath **d** me out of the hand of Herod, *1807*
15:30 the multitude together, they **d** the epistle: *1929*
16: 4 they **d** them the decrees for to keep, *3860*
23:33 to Cesarea, and **d** the epistle to the governor, *325*
27: 1 they **d** Paul and certain other prisoners unto *3860*
28:16 the centurion **d** the prisoners to the captain *3860*
28:17 *yet* was I **d** prisoner from Jerusalem into *3860*
Ro 4:25 Who was **d** for our offences, and was raised *3860*
6:17 *that* form of doctrine which was **d** you. *3860*
7: 6 But now we are **d** from the law, *that* being *2673*
8:21 Because the creature itself also shall be **d** *1659*
8:32 not his own Son, but **d** him **up** for us all, *3860*
15:31 That I may be **d** from them that do not *4506*
1Co 11: 2 keep the ordinances, as I **d** *them* to you. *3860*
11:23 of the Lord *that* which also I **d** unto you, *3860*
15: 3 For I **d** unto you first *of all* that which I *3860*
15:24 when he shall have **d up** the kingdom to *3860*
2Co 1:10 Who **d** us from so great a death, and *4506*
4:11 For we which live are alway **d** unto death *3860*
Col 1:13 Who hath **d** us from the power of darkness, *4506*
1Th 1:10 which **d** us from the wrath to come. *4506*
2Th 3: 2 And that we may be **d** from unreasonable *4506*
1Ti 1:20 whom I have **d** unto Satan, that they may *3860*
2Ti 3:11 but out of *them* all the Lord **d** me. *4506*
4:17 and I was **d** out of the mouth of the lion. *4506*
Heb 11:11 was **d of a child** when *she* was past age, *5088*
2Pe 2: 4 to hell, and **d** *them* **into** chains of darkness, *3860*
2: 7 And **d** just Lot, vexed with the filthy *4506*
2:21 from the holy commandment **d** unto them. *3860*
Jude 1: 3 the faith which was once **d** unto the saints. *3860*
Rev 12: 2 travailing in birth, and pained to be **d**. *5088*
12: 4 before the woman which was ready to be **d**, *5088*
20:13 and hell **d up** the dead which were in them: *1325*

DELIVEREDST (3) [DELIVER]
Ne 9:27 Therefore thou **d** them into the hand of 5414
Mt 25:20 saying, Lord, thou **d** unto me five talents: *3860*
25:22 and said, Lord, thou **d** unto me two talents: *3860*

DELIVERER (10) [DELIVER]
Jdg 3: 9 the LORD raised up a **d** to the children of 3467
3:15 the LORD raised them up a **d**, Ehud 3467
18:28 *there was* no **d**, because it *was* far from 5337
2Sa 22: 2 *is* my rock, and my fortress, and my **d**; 6403
Ps 18: 2 *is* my rock, and my fortress, and my **d**; 6403
40:17 thou *art* my help and my **d**; make no 6403
70: 5 thou *art* my help and my **d**; O LORD, 6403
144: 2 my high tower, and my **d**; my shield, and 6403
Ac 7:35 a **d** by the hand of the angel which *3086*
Ro 11:26 There shall come out of Sion the **D**, and *4506*

DELIVEREST (2) [DELIVER]
Ps 35:10 which **d** the poor from him that is too 5337
Mic 6:14 *that* which thou **d** will I give up to 6403

DELIVERETH (13) [DELIVER]
Job 36:15 He **d** the poor in his affliction, and 2502
Ps 18:48 He **d** me from mine enemies: yea, 6403
34: 7 about them that fear him, and **d** them. 2502
34:17 and **d** them out of all their troubles. 5337
34:19 but the LORD **d** him out of them all. 5337
97:10 he **d** them out of the hand of the wicked. 5337
144:10 who **d** David his servant from the hurtful 6475
Pr 10: 2 but righteousness **d** from death. 5337
11: 4 of wrath: but righteousness **d** from death. 5337
14:25 A true witness **d** souls: but a deceitful 5337
31:24 selleth *it;* and **d** girdles unto the merchant. 5414
Isa 42:22 they are for a prey, and none **d**; *for* a spoil, 5337
Da 6:27 He **d** and rescueth, and he worketh signs 7804

DELIVERING (3) [DELIVER]
Lk 21:12 persecute *you,* **d** *you* **up** to *the* synagogues, *3860*
Ac 22: 4 binding and **d** into prisons both men and *3860*
26:17 **D** thee from the people, and *from* *1807*

DELIVERY (1) [DELIVER]
Isa 26:17 *that* draweth near the time of her **d**, is in 3205

DELUSION (1) [DELUSIONS]
2Th 2:11 for this cause God shall send them strong **d**, *4106*

DELUSIONS (1) [DELUSION]
Isa 66: 4 I also will choose their **d**, and will bring 8586

DEMAND (4) [DEMANDED]
Job 38: 3 for I will **d** of thee, and answer thou me. 7592
40: 7 I will **d** of thee, and declare thou unto me. 7592

D

Job 42: 4 I will **d** of thee, and declare thou unto me. 7592
Da 4:17 and the **d** *by* the word of the holy ones: 7595

DEMANDED (7) [DEMAND]
Ex 5:14 had set over them, were beaten, *and* **d**, 559
2Sa 11: 7 David **d** *of him* how Joab did, and how 7592
Da 2:27 The secret which the king hath **d** cannot 7593
Mt 2: 4 he **d** of them where Christ should be born. *4441*
Lk 3:14 And *the* soldiers likewise **d** of him, saying, *1905*
17:20 And when he was **d** of the Pharisees, *1905*
Ac 21:33 and **d** who he was, and what he had done. *4441*

DEMAS (3)
Col 4:14 the beloved physician, and **D**, greet you. *1214*
2Ti 4:10 For **D** hath forsaken me, having loved *this* *1214*
Phm 1:24 Marcus, Aristarchus, **D**, Lucas, *1214*

DEMETRIUS (3)
Ac 19:24 For a certain *man* named **D**, a silversmith, *1216*
19:38 Wherefore if **D**, and the craftsmen which *1216*
3Jn 1:12 **D** hath good report of all *men*, and of *1216*

DEMON; DEMONS See DEVIL; DEVILS

DEMONSTRATION (1)
1Co 2: 4 but in **d** of the Spirit and of power: *585*

DEN (19) [DENS]
Ps 10: 9 He lieth in wait secretly as a lion in his **d**: 5520
Isa 11: 8 shall put his hand on the cockatrice' **d**. 3975
Jer 7:11 become a **d** of robbers in your eyes? 4631
9:11 make Jerusalem heaps, *and* a **d** of dragons; 4583
10:22 cities of Judah desolate, *and* a **d** of dragons. 4583
Da 6: 7 O king, he shall be cast into the **d** of lions. 1358
6:12 O king, shall be cast into the **d** of lions? 1358
6:16 and cast *him* into the **d** of lions. 1358
6:17 and laid upon the mouth of the **d**; 1358
6:19 and went in haste unto the **d** of lions. 1358
6:20 when he came to the **d**, he cried with a 1358
6:23 *they* should take Daniel up out of the **d**. 1358
6:23 So Daniel was taken up out of the **d**, and 1358
6:24 and they cast *them* into the **d** of lions, them, 1358
6:24 or ever they came at the bottom of the **d**. 1358
Am 3: 4 will a young lion cry out of his **d**, if he 4585
Mt 21:13 but ye have made it a **d** of thieves. *4693*
Mk 11:17 but ye have made it a **d** of thieves. *4693*
Lk 19:46 but ye have made it a **d** of thieves. *4693*

DENARII See PENCE

DENARIUS See PENNY

DENIED (19) [DENY]
Ge 18:15 Sarah **d**, saying, I laughed not; for she was 3584
1Ki 20: 7 and for my gold; and I **d** him not. 4513
Job 31:28 for I should have **d** the God *that is* above. 3584
Mt 26:70 But he **d** before *them* all, saying, I know not *720*
26:72 And again he **d** with an oath, I do not know *720*
Mk 14:68 But he **d**, saying, I know not, neither *720*
14:70 And he **d** *it* again. And a little after, they that *720*
Lk 8:45 When all **d**, Peter and they that were with *720*
12: 9 But he that denieth me before men shall be **d** *533*
22:57 And he **d** him, saying, Woman, I know him *720*
Jn 1:20 And he confessed, and **d** not; but confessed, *720*
13:38 shall not crow, till thou hast **d** me thrice. *533*
18:25 of his disciples? He **d** *it*, and said, I am not. *720*
18:27 Peter then **d** again: and immediately *the* cock *720*
Ac 3:13 and **d** him in the presence of Pilate, *720*
3:14 But ye **d** the Holy One and the Just, and *720*
1Ti 5: 8 he hath **d** the faith, and is worse than an *720*
Rev 2:13 fast my name, and hast not **d** my faith, *720*
3: 8 hast kept my word, and hast not **d** my name. *720*

DENIETH (4) [DENY]
Lk 12: 9 But he that **d** me before men shall be denied *720*
1Jn 2:22 is a liar but he that **d** that Jesus is the Christ? *720*
2:22 is antichrist, that **d** the Father and the Son. *720*
2:23 Whosoever **d** the Son, the same hath not *720*

DENOUNCE (1)
Dt 30:18 I **d** unto you *this* day, that ye shall surely 5046

DENOUNCED See UPBRAID; UPBRAIDED; UPBRAIDETH

DENS (9) [DEN]
Jdg 6: 2 them the **d** which *are* in the mountains, 4492
Job 37: 8 the beasts go into **d**, and remain in their 695
38:40 When they couch in *their* **d**, *and* abide in 4585
Ps 104:22 and lay them down in their **d**. 4585
SS 4: 8 of Shenir and Hermon, from the lions' **d**, 4585
Isa 32:14 the forts and towers shall be for **d** for ever, 4631
Na 2:12 his holes *with* prey, and his **d** *with* ravin. 4585
Heb 11:38 and *in* **d** and caves of the earth. *4693*
Rev 6:15 every free *man*, hid themselves in the **d** and *4693*

DENY (24) [DENIED, DENIETH, DENYING]
Jos 24:27 a witness unto you, lest ye **d** your God. 3584
1Ki 2:16 I ask one petition of thee, **d** me not. 6440+7725
Job 8:18 *it* shall **d** him, *saying*, I have not seen thee. 3584
Pr 30: 7 of thee; **d** me *them* not before I die: 4513
30: 9 Lest I be full, and **d** *thee*, and say, Who *is* 3584
Mt 10:33 But whosoever shall **d** me before men, *720*
10:33 him will I also **d** before my Father which is *720*
16:24 let him **d** himself, and take up his cross, and *533*
26:34 before *the* cock crow, thou shalt **d** me thrice. *533*
26:35 I should die with thee, *yet* will I not **d** thee. *533*
26:75 Before *the* cock crow, thou shalt **d** me thrice. *533*
Mk 8:34 let him **d** himself, and take up his cross, and *533*
14:30 *the* cock crow twice, thou shalt **d** me thrice. *533*
14:31 die with thee, I will not **d** thee in any wise. *533*
14:72 *the* cock crow twice, thou shalt **d** me thrice. *533*
Lk 9:23 let him **d** himself, and take up his cross *533*
20:27 which **d** that there is any resurrection; *483*
22:34 before that thou shalt thrice **d** that *thou* *533*
22:61 Before *the* cock crow, thou shalt **d** me thrice. *533*
Ac 4:16 that dwell in Jerusalem; and we cannot **d** *it*. *720*
2Ti 2:12 we shall also reign with *him*: if we **d** *him*, he *720*
2:12 with *him*: if we deny *him*, he also will **d** us: *720*
2:13 *yet* he abideth faithful: he cannot **d** himself. *720*
Tit 1:16 but in works they **d** *him*, being abominable, *720*

DENYING (4) [DENY]
2Ti 3: 5 a form of godliness, but **d** the power thereof: *720*
Tit 2:12 Teaching us that **d** ungodliness and worldly *720*
2Pe 2: 1 even **d** the Lord that bought them, and *720*
Jude 1: 4 and **d** the only Lord God, and our Lord Jesus *720*

DEPART (125) [DEPARTED, DEPARTETH, DEPARTING, DEPARTURE]
Ge 13: 9 or if *thou* **d** *to* the right hand, then I will go NIH
49:10 The sceptre shall not **d** from Judah, nor a 5493
Ex 8:11 the frogs shall **d** from thee, and from thy 5493
8:29 the swarms *of flies* may **d** from Pharaoh, 5493
18:27 Moses let his father in law **d**; and he went 7971
21:22 so that her fruit **d** *from her*, and yet no 3318
33: 1 **D**, *and* go up hence, thou and 1980+4480
Lev 25:41 *then* shall he **d** from thee, *both* he and 3318
Nu 10:30 I will **d** to mine own land, and to my 1980
16:26 saying, **D**, I pray you, from the tents of 5493
Dt 4: 9 lest they **d** from thy heart all the days of thy 5493
9: 7 from the day that thou didst **d** out of 3318
Jos 1: 8 This book of the law shall not **d** out of thy 4185
24:28 So Joshua **let** the people **d**, every man unto 7971
Jdg 6:18 **D** not hence, I pray thee, until I come unto 4185
7: 3 him return and **d** **early** from mount Gilead. 6852
19: 5 early in the morning, that he rose up to **d**: 1980
19: 7 when the man rose up to **d**, his father in law 1980
19: 8 early in the morning on the fifth day to **d**: 1980
19: 9 when the man rose up to **d**, he, and 1980
1Sa 15: 6 Saul said unto the Kenites, Go, **d**, get you 5493
22: 5 **d**, and get thee *into* the land of Judah. 1980
29:10 up early in the morning, and have light, **d**. 1980
29:11 his men rose up early to **d** in the morning, 1980
30:22 that they may lead *them* away, and **d**. 1980
2Sa 7:15 my mercy shall not **d** **away** from him, as I 5493
11:12 to day also, and to morrow I will let thee **d**. 7971
12:10 the sword shall never **d** from thine house, 5493
15:14 make speed to **d**, lest he overtake us 1980
20:21 deliver him only, and I will **d** from the city. 1980
22:23 *as for* his statutes, I did not **d** from them. 5493
1Ki 11:21 Hadad said to Pharaoh, **Let** me **d**, that I 7971
12: 5 **D** yet *for* three days, then come again to 1980
12:24 the word of the LORD, and returned to **d**, 1980
15:19 king of Israel, that he may **d** from me. 5927
2Ch 16: 3 king of Israel, that he may **d** from me. 5927
18:31 and God moved them *to* **d** from him. NIH
35:15 they might not **d** from their service; 5493
Job 7:19 How long wilt thou not **d** from me, nor let 8159
15:30 He shall not **d** out of darkness; the flame 5493
20:28 The increase of his house shall **d**, *and* 1540

Job	21:14	Therefore they say unto God, **D** from us;	5493
	22:17	Which said unto God, **D** from us: and	5493
	28:28	and to **d** from evil *is* understanding.	5493
Ps	6: 8	**D** from me, all ye workers of iniquity;	5493
	34:14	**D** from evil, and do good; seek peace, and	5493
	37:27	**D** from evil, and do good; and dwell for	5493
	55:11	and guile **d** not from her streets.	4185
	101: 4	A froward heart shall **d** from me: I will not	5493
	119:115	**D** from me, ye evildoers: for I will keep	5493
	139:19	**d** from me therefore, ye bloody men.	5493
Pr	3: 7	fear the LORD, and **d** from evil.	5493
	3:21	My son, let not them **d** from thine eyes:	3868
	4:21	Let them not **d** from thine eyes; keep them	3868
	5: 7	and **d** not from the words of my mouth.	5493
	13:14	of life, to **d** from the snares of death.	5493
	13:19	but *it is* abomination to fools to **d** from evil.	5493
	14:27	of life, to **d** from the snares of death.	5493
	15:24	the wise, that *he* may **d** from hell beneath.	5493
	16: 6	by the fear of the LORD *men* **d** from evil.	5493
	16:17	The highway of the upright *is* to **d** from	5493
	17:13	for good, evil shall not **d** from his house.	4185
	22: 6	and when he is old, he will not **d** from it.	5493
	27:22	*yet* will not his foolishness **d** from him.	5493
Isa	11:13	The envy also of Ephraim shall **d**, and	5493
	14:25	shall his yoke **d** from off them, and	5493
	14:25	and his burden **d** from off their shoulders.	5493
	52:11	**D** ye, depart ye, go ye out from thence,	5493
	52:11	Depart ye, **d** ye, go ye out from thence,	5493
	54:10	For the mountains shall **d**, and the hills be	4185
	54:10	my kindness shall not **d** from thee,	4185
	59:21	shall not **d** out of thy mouth, nor out of	4185
Jer	6: 8	O Jerusalem, lest my soul **d** from thee;	3363
	17:13	they that **d** from me shall be written in	5493
	31:36	If those ordinances **d** from before me,	4185
	32:40	their hearts, that *they* shall not **d** from me.	5493
	37: 9	Chaldeans shall **surely d** from us:	1980+1980
	37: 9	surely depart from us: for they shall not **d**.	1980
	50: 3	they shall **d**, both man and beast.	1980
La	4:15	They cried unto them, **D** ye; *it is* unclean;	5493
	4:15	**d**, depart, touch not, when they fled away	5493
	4:15	depart, **d**, touch not, when they fled away	5493
Eze	16:42	my jealousy shall **d** from thee, and I will be	5493
Hos	9:12	woe also to them when I **d** from them!	5493
Mic	2:10	Arise ye, and **d**; for this *is* not *your* rest:	1980
Zec	10:11	and the sceptre of Egypt shall **d away**.	5493
Mt	7:23	knew you: **d** from me, ye that work iniquity.	*672*
	8:18	he gave commandment to **d** unto the other	*565*
	8:34	they besought *him* that he would **d** out of	*3327*
	10:14	when ye **d** out of that house or city,	*1831*
	14:16	But Jesus said unto them, They need not **d**;	*565*
	25:41	**D** from me, ye cursed, into everlasting fire,	*4198*
Mk	5:17	And they began to pray him to **d out** of their	*565*
	6:10	there abide till ye **d** from that place.	*1831*
	6:11	nor hear you, when ye **d** thence,	*1607*
Lk	2:29	now lettest thou thy servant **d** in peace,	*630*
	4:42	stayed him, that *he* should not **d** from them.	*4198*
	5: 8	down at Jesus' knees, saying, **D** from me;	*1831*
	8:37	round about besought him to **d** from them;	*565*
	9: 4	ye enter into, there abide, and thence **d**.	*1831*
	12:59	I tell thee, thou shalt not **d** thence, till thou	*1831*
	13:27	**d** from me, all *ye* workers of iniquity.	*868*
	13:31	saying unto him, Get *thee* out, and **d** hence:	*4198*
	21:21	let them which are in the midst of it **d out**;	*1633*
Jn	7: 3	said unto him, **D** hence, and go into Judea,	*3327*
	13: 1	should **d** out of this world unto the Father,	*3327*
	16: 7	but if I **d**, I will send him unto you.	*4198*
Ac	1: 4	commanded them that *they* should not **d**	*5563*
	16:36	you go: now therefore **d**, and go in peace.	*1831*
	16:39	and desired *them* to **d out** of the city.	*1831*
	18: 2	that Claudius had commanded all Jews to **d**	*5563*
	20: 7	unto them, ready to **d** on the morrow;	*1826*
	22:21	And he said unto me, **D**: for I will send thee	*4198*
	23:22	the chief captain then **let** the young man **d**,	*630*
	25: 4	and that he himself would **d** shortly *thither.*	*1607*
	27:12	the more part advised to **d** thence also,	*321*
1Co	7:10	Let not the wife **d** from *her* husband:	*5563*
	7:11	But and if she **d**, let her remain unmarried,	*5563*
	7:15	But if the unbelieving **d**, let him depart.	*5563*
	7:15	But if the unbelieving depart, let him **d**.	*5563*
2Co	12: 8	the Lord thrice, that it might **d** from me.	*868*
Php	1:23	having a desire to **d**, and to be with Christ;	*360*
1Ti	4: 1	that in the latter times some shall **d from**	*868*
2Ti	2:19	nameth the name of Christ **d** from iniquity.	*868*
Jas	2:16	**D** in peace, be you warmed and filled;	*5217*

DEPARTED (217) [DEPART]

Ge	12: 4	So Abram **d**, as the LORD had spoken	1980
	12: 4	and five years old when he **d** out of Haran.	3318
	14:12	who dwelt in Sodom, and his goods, and **d**.	1980
	21:14	she **d**, and wandered in the wilderness of	1980
	24:10	camels of the camels of his master, and **d**;	1980
	26:17	Isaac **d** thence, and pitched his tent in	1980
	26:31	them away, and they **d** from him in peace.	1980
	31:40	by night; and my sleep **d** from mine eyes.	5074
	31:55	and Laban **d**, and returned unto his place.	1980
	37:17	the man said, They are **d** hence; for I heard	5265
	42:26	their asses with the corn, and **d** thence.	1980
	45:24	So he sent his brethren away, and they **d**:	1980
Ex	19: 2	For they were **d** from Rephidim, and	5265
	33:11	a young man, **d** not out of the tabernacle.	4185
	35:20	of Israel **d** from the presence of Moses.	3318
Lev	13:58	if the plague be **d** from them, then it shall	5493
Nu	10:33	they **d** from the mount of the LORD three	5265
	12: 9	was kindled against them; and he **d**.	1980
	12:10	the cloud **d** from off the tabernacle; and	5493
	14: 9	their defence is **d** from them, and	5493
	14:44	and Moses, **d** not out of the camp.	4185
	22: 7	the elders of Midian **d** with the rewards of	1980
	33: 3	they **d** from Rameses in the first month,	5265
	33: 6	they **d** from Succoth, and pitched in Etham,	5265
	33: 8	they **d** from before *Pi*-hahiroth, and	5265
	33:13	they **d** from Dophkah, and encamped in	5265
	33:15	they **d** from Rephidim, and pitched in	5265
	33:17	they **d** from Kibroth-hattaavah, and	5265
	33:18	they **d** from Hazeroth, and pitched in	5265
	33:19	they **d** from Rithmah, and pitched at	5265
	33:20	they **d** from Rimmon-parez, and pitched in	5265
	33:27	they **d** from Tahath, and pitched at Tarah.	5265
	33:30	they **d** from Hashmonah, and encamped at	5265
	33:31	they **d** from Moseroth, and pitched in	5265
	33:35	they **d** from Ebronah, and encamped at	5265
	33:41	they **d** from mount Hor, and pitched in	5265
	33:42	they **d** from Zalmonah, and pitched in	5265
	33:43	they **d** from Punon, and pitched in Oboth.	5265
	33:44	they **d** from Oboth, and pitched in	5265
	33:45	they **d** from Iim, and pitched in Dibon-gad.	5265
	33:48	they **d** from the mountains of Abarim, and	5265
Dt	1:19	when we **d** from Horeb, we went *through*	5265
	24: 2	when she is **d** out of his house, she may go	3318
Jos	2:21	she sent them away, and they **d**: and	1980
	22: 9	**d** from the children of Israel out of Shiloh,	1980
Jdg	6:21	the angel of the LORD **d** out of his sight.	1980
	9:55	was dead, they **d** every man unto his place.	1980
	16:20	he wist not that the LORD was **d** from	5493
	17: 8	the man **d** out of the city from	1980
	18: 7	the five men **d**, and came to Laish, and	1980
	18:21	So they turned and **d**, and put the little ones	1980
	19:10	he rose up and **d**, and came over against	1980
	21:24	the children of Israel **d** thence at that	1980+4480
1Sa	4:21	saying, The glory is **d** from Israel:	1540
	4:22	she said, The glory is **d** from Israel: for	1540
	6: 6	did they not let the people go, and they **d**?	1980
	10: 2	When thou art **d** from me to day, then	1980
	15: 6	So the Kenites **d** from among	5493
	16:14	the spirit of the LORD **d** from Saul, and	5493
	16:23	was well, and the evil spirit **d** from him.	5493
	18:12	was with him, and was **d** from Saul.	5493
	20:42	he arose and **d**: and Jonathan went *into*	1980
	22: 1	David therefore **d** thence, and	1980+4480
	22: 5	David **d**, and came *into* the forest of	1980
	23:13	arose and **d** out of Keilah, and	3318
	28:15	God is **d** from me, and answereth me no	5493
	28:16	seeing the LORD is **d** from thee, and	5493
2Sa	6:19	a flagon *of wine.* So all the people **d** every	1980
	11: 8	Uriah **d** out of the king's house, and	3318
	12:15	Nathan **d** unto his house. And the LORD	1980
	17:21	it came to pass, after they were **d**, that they	1980
	19:24	from the day the king **d** until the day he	1980
	22:22	and have not **wickedly d** from my God.	7561
1Ki	12: 5	then come again to me. And the people **d**.	1980
	12:16	David. So Israel **d** unto their tents.	1980
	14:17	wife arose, and **d**, and came to Tirzah:	1980
	19:19	So he **d** thence, and found Elisha the son of	1980
	20: 9	the messengers **d**, and brought him word	1980
	20:36	behold, as soon as thou art **d** from me, a	1980
	20:36	as soon as he was **d** from him, a lion found	1980
	20:38	So the prophet **d**, and waited for the king	1980
2Ki	1: 4	gone up, but shalt surely die. And Elijah **d**.	1980

D

D

2Ki 3: 3 made Israel to sin; he **d** not therefrom. 5493
3:27 they **d** from him, and returned to *their own* 5265
5: 5 he **d**, and took with him ten talents of 1980
5:19 Go in peace. So he **d** from him a little way. 1980
5:24 and he let the men go, and they **d**. 1980
8:14 So he **d** from Elisha, and came to his 1980
10:12 he arose and **d**, and came *to* Samaria. *And* as 935
10:15 when he was **d** thence, he lighted on 1980+4480
10:29 Israel to sin, Jehu **d** not from after them, 5493
10:31 *for* he **d** not from the sins of Jeroboam, 5493
13: 2 made Israel to sin; he **d** not therefrom. 5493
13: 6 Nevertheless they **d** not from the sins of 5493
13:11 he **d** not from all the sins of Jeroboam 5493
14:24 he **d** not from all the sins of Jeroboam 5493
15: 9 he **d** not from the sins of Jeroboam the son 5493
15:18 he **d** not all his days from the sins of 5493
15:24 he **d** not from the sins of Jeroboam the son 5493
15:28 he **d** not from the sins of Jeroboam the son 5493
17:22 which he did; they **d** not from them; 5493
18: 6 *and* **d** not from following him, but kept his 5493
19: 8 for he had heard that he was **d** from 5265
19:36 So Sennacherib king of Assyria **d**, and 5265
1Ch 16:43 all the people **d** every man to his house: 1980
21: 4 Wherefore Joab **d**, and went throughout all 3318
2Ch 8:15 they **d** not *from* the commandment of 5493
10: 5 unto me after three days. And the people **d**. 1980
20:32 the way of Asa his father, and **d** not from it, 5493
21:20 eight years, and **d** without being desired. 1980
24:25 when they were **d** from him, (for they left 1980
34:33 *And* all his days they **d** not from following 5493
Ezr 8:31 we **d** from the river of Ahava on the twelfth 5265
Ne 9:19 the pillar of the cloud **d** not from them by 5493
Ps 18:21 and have not **wickedly** **d** from my God. 7561
34: T who drove him away, and he **d**. 1980
105:38 Egypt was glad when they **d**: for the fear of 3318
119:102 I have not **d** from thy judgments: for thou 5493
Isa 7:17 from the day that Ephraim **d** from Judah; 5493
37: 8 for he had heard that he was **d** from 5265
37:37 So Sennacherib king of Assyria **d**, and 5265
38:12 Mine age is **d**, and is removed from me as a 5265
Jer 29: 2 and the smiths, were **d** from Jerusalem;) 3318
37: 5 tidings of them, they **d** from Jerusalem. 5927
41:10 and **d** to go over to the Ammonites. 1980
41:17 they **d**, and dwelt in the habitation of 1980
La 1: 6 the daughter of Zion all her beauty is **d**: 3318
Eze 6: 9 which hath **d** from me, and with their eyes, 5493
10:18 the glory of the LORD **d** from off 3318
Da 4:31 it is spoken; The kingdom is **d** from thee. 5709
Hos 10: 5 for the glory thereof, because it is **d** from it. 1540
Mal 2: 8 ye are **d** out of the way; ye have caused 5493
Mt 2: 9 When they had heard the king, they **d**; and *4198*
2:12 they **d** into their own country another way. *402*
2:13 And when they were **d**, behold, *the* angel of *402*
2:14 and his mother by night, and **d** into Egypt: *402*
4:12 John was cast into prison, he **d** into Galilee; *402*
9: 7 And he arose, and **d** to his house. *565*
9:27 And when Jesus **d** thence, two blind men *3855*
9:31 But they, when they were **d**, spread abroad *1831*
11: 1 he **d** thence to teach and to preach in their *3327*
11: 7 And as they **d**, Jesus began to say unto *4198*
12: 9 And when he was **d** thence, he went into *3327*
13:53 had finished these parables, he **d** thence. *3332*
14:13 When Jesus heard *of it,* he **d** thence by ship *402*
15:21 and **d** into the coasts of Tyre and Sidon. *402*
15:29 And Jesus **d** from thence, and came nigh *3327*
16: 4 the prophet Jonas. And he left them, and **d**. *565*
17:18 rebuked the devil; and he **d** out of him: *1831*
19: 1 he **d** from Galilee, and came into the coasts *3332*
19:15 he laid *his* hands on them, and **d** thence. *4198*
20:29 And as they **d** from Jericho, a great *1607*
24: 1 And Jesus went out, and **d** from the temple: *4198*
27: 5 and **d**, and went and hanged himself. *402*
27:60 stone to the door of the sepulchre, and **d**. *565*
28: 8 And they **d** quickly from the sepulchre with *1831*
Mk 1:35 and **d** into a solitary place, and there prayed. *565*
1:42 immediately the leprosy **d** from him, and *565*
5:20 And he **d**, and began to publish in Decapolis *565*
6:32 And they **d** into a desert place by ship *565*
6:46 them away, he **d** into a mountain to pray. *565*
8:13 entering into the ship again **d** to the other *565*
9:30 And they **d** thence, and passed through *1831*
Lk 1:23 were accomplished, he **d** to his own house. *565*
1:38 to thy word. And the angel **d** from her. *565*
2:37 which **d** not from the temple, but served *God* *868*
4:13 the temptation, he **d** from him for a season. *868*
4:42 was day, he **d** and went into a desert place: *1831*
5:13 And immediately the leprosy **d** from him. *565*
5:25 and **d** to his own house, glorifying God. *565*
7:24 And when the messengers of John were **d**, *565*
8:35 the man, out of whom the devils were **d**, *1831*
8:38 **d** besought him that *he* might be with him: *1831*
9: 6 And they **d**, and went through the towns, *1831*
9:33 And it came to pass, as they **d** from him, *1316*
10:30 and wounded *him,* and **d**, leaving *him* half *565*
10:35 And on the morrow when he **d**, he took out *1831*
24:12 the linen clothes laid by themselves, and **d**, *565*
Jn 4: 3 He left Judea, and **d** again into Galilee. *565*
4:43 Now after two days he **d** thence, and *1831*
5:15 The man **d**, and told the Jews that it was *565*
6:15 he **d** again into a mountain himself alone. *402*
12:36 and **d**, and did hide himself from them. *565*
Ac 5:41 And they **d** from the presence of *4198*
10: 7 the angel which spake unto Cornelius was **d**, *565*
11:25 Then **d** Barnabas to Tarsus, for to seek *1831*
12:10 and forthwith the angel **d** from him. *868*
12:17 And he **d**, and went into another place. *1831*
13: 4 forth by the Holy Ghost, **d** unto Seleucia; *2718*
13:14 But when they **d** from Perga, they came to *1330*
14:20 the next day he **d** with Barnabas to Derbe. *1831*
15:38 *them,* who **d** from them from Pamphylia, *868*
15:39 sharp *between them,* that they **d** **asunder** *673*
15:40 And Paul chose Silas, and **d**, *1831*
16:40 the brethren, they comforted them, and **d**. *1831*
17:15 for to come to him with all speed, they **d**. *1826*
17:33 So Paul **d** from among them. *1831*
18: 1 After these *things* Paul **d** from Athens, and *5563*
18: 7 And he **d** thence, and entered into a certain *3327*
18:23 after he had spent some time *there,* he **d**, *1831*
19: 9 he **d** from them, and separated the disciples, *868*
19:12 and the diseases **d** from them, and the evil *525*
20: 1 and **d** for to go into Macedonia. *1831*
20:11 a long while, *even* till break of day, so he **d**. *1831*
21: 5 we **d** and went *our way;* and *they* all *1831*
21: 8 next day we that were of Paul's company **d**, *1831*
22:29 Then straightway they **d** from him which *868*
28:10 and when we **d**, they laded *us* with such *321*
28:11 And after three months we **d** in a ship of *321*
28:25 they **d**, after that Paul had spoken one word, *630*
28:29 when he had said these *words,* the Jews **d**, *565*
Php 4:15 of the gospel, when I **d** from Macedonia, *1831*
2Ti 4:10 present world, and is **d** unto Thessalonica; *4198*
Phm 1:15 For perhaps he therefore **d** for a season, *5563*
Rev 6:14 And the heaven **d** as a scrole when it is *673*
18:14 And the fruits that thy soul lusted after are **d** *565*
18:14 *were* dainty and goodly are **d** from thee, *565*

DEPARTETH (8) [DEPART]

Job 27:21 The east wind carrieth him away, and he **d**: 1980
Pr 14:16 A wise *man* feareth, and **d** from evil: but 5493
Ecc 6: 4 **d** in darkness, and his name shall be 1980
Isa 59:15 he *that* **d** from evil maketh himself a prey: 5493
Jer 3:20 Surely *as* a wife treacherously **d** **from** her 4480
17: 5 and whose heart **d** from the LORD. 5493
Na 3: 1 all full *of* lies *and* robbery; the prey **d** not; 4185
Lk 9:39 and bruising him hardly **d** from him. *672*

DEPARTING (12) [DEPART]

Ge 35:18 to pass, as her soul was **in** **d** (for she died) 3318
Ex 16: 1 month after their **d** out of the land of Egypt. 3318
Isa 59:13 **d** **away** from our God, speaking oppression 5253
Da 9: 5 even by **d** from thy precepts and from thy 5493
9:11 even by **d**, that *they* might not obey thy 5493
Hos 1: 2 great whoredom, *d* from the LORD. NIH
Mk 6:33 And the people saw them **d**, and *5217*
7:31 **d** from the coasts of Tyre and Sidon, *1831*
Ac 13:13 and John **d** from them returned to Jerusalem. *672*
20:29 that after my **d** shall grievous wolves enter *867*
Heb 3:12 heart of unbelief, in **d** from the living God. *868*
11:22 made mention of the **d** of the children of *1841*

DEPARTURE (2) [DEPART]

Eze 26:18 that *are* in the sea shall be troubled at thy **d**. 3318
2Ti 4: 6 be offered, and the time of my **d** is at hand. *359*

DEPOSED (1)

Da 5:20 he was **d** from his kingly throne, and 5182

DEPRAVED See REPROBATE; REPROBATES

DEPRIVE See SUBVERT

DEPRIVED (3)
Ge 27:45 why should I be **d** also of you both *in* one 7921
Job 39:17 Because God hath **d** her of wisdom, 5382
Isa 38:10 I am **d** of the residue of my years. 6485

DEPTH (12) [DEEP]
Job 28:14 The **d** saith, It *is* not in me: and the sea 8415
38:16 or hast thou walked in the search of the **d**? 8415
Ps 33: 7 as a heap: he layeth up the **d** in storehouses. 8415
Pr 8:27 he set a compass upon the face of the **d**: 8415
25: 3 the earth for **d**, and the heart of kings *is* 6011
Isa 7:11 ask it either in the **d**, or in the height above. 6009
Jnh 2: 5 the **d** closed me round about, the weeds 8415
Mt 18: 6 *that* he were drowned in the **d** of the sea. *3989*
Mk 4: 5 it sprang up, because *it* had no **d** of earth: *899*
Ro 8:39 Nor height, nor **d**, nor any other creature, *899*
11:33 O the **d** of the riches both of the wisdom and *899*
Eph 3:18 *is* the breadth, and length, and **d**, and height; *899*

DEPTHS (17) [DEEP]
Ex 15: 5 The **d** have covered them: they sank into 8415
15: 8 the **d** were congealed in the heart of 8415
Dt 8: 7 **d** that spring out of the valleys and hills; 8415
Ps 68:22 I will bring *my people* again from the **d** of 4688
71:20 shalt bring me up again from the **d** of 8415
77:16 they were afraid: the **d** also were troubled. 8415
78:15 and gave *them* drink as *out of* the great **d**. 8415
106: 9 so he led them through the **d**, as *through* 8415
107:26 *to* the heaven, they go down *again to* the **d**: 8415
130: 1 Out of the **d** have I cried unto thee, 4615
Pr 3:20 By his knowledge the **d** are broken up, and 8415
8:24 When *there were* no **d**, I was brought forth; 8415
9:18 *and that* her guests *are* in the **d** of hell. 6012
Isa 51:10 that hath made the **d** of the sea a way for 4615
Eze 27:34 *be* broken by the seas in the **d** of the waters, 4615
Mic 7:19 thou wilt cast all their sins into the **d** of 4688
Rev 2:24 and which have not known the **d** of Satan, *899*

DEPUTED (1) [DEPUTY]
2Sa 15: 3 *there is* no man *d* of the king to hear thee. NIH

DEPUTIES (3) [DEPUTY]
Est 8: 9 the **d** and rulers of the provinces which *are* 6346
9: 3 and the **d**, and officers of the king, 6346
Ac 19:38 any *man,* the law is open, and there are **d**: *446*

DEPUTY (5) [DEPUTED, DEPUTIES]
1Ki 22:47 then no king in Edom: a **d** *was* king. 5324
Ac 13: 7 Which was with the **d** *of the country,* *446*
13: 8 seeking to turn away the **d** from the faith. *446*
13:12 Then the **d**, when he saw what was done, *446*
18:12 And when Gallio was the **d** of Achaia, *445*

DERBE (4)
Ac 14: 6 were ware of *it,* and fled unto Lystra and **D**, *1191*
14:20 next day he departed with Barnabas to **D**. *1191*
16: 1 Then came he to **D** and Lystra: and behold, *1191*
20: 4 and Gaius **of D**, and Timotheus; and *1190*

DERIDE (1) [DERIDED, DERISION]
Hab 1:10 they shall **d** every strong hold; for they 7832

DERIDED (2) [DERIDE]
Lk 16:14 heard all these *things:* and they **d** him. *1592*
23:35 And the rulers also with them **d** *him,* *1592*

DERISION (15) [DERIDE]
Job 30: 1 *they that are* younger than I have me in **d**, 7832
Ps 2: 4 the LORD shall have them in **d**. 3932
44:13 and a **d** to them that are round about us. 7047
59: 8 thou shalt **have** all the heathen **in d**. 3932
79: 4 and **d** to them that are round about us. 7047
119:51 The proud have **had** me greatly in **d**: 3887
Jer 20: 7 I am in **d** daily, every one mocketh me. 7814
20: 8 made a reproach unto me, and a **d**, daily. 7047
48:26 in his vomit, and he also shall be in **d**. 7814
48:27 For was not Israel a **d** unto thee? was he 7814
48:39 so shall Moab be a **d** and a dismaying to all 7814
La 3:14 I was a **d** to all my people; *and* their song 7814
Eze 23:32 thou shalt be laughed to scorn and had in **d**; 3933
36: 4 **d** to the residue of the heathen that *are* 3933
Hos 7:16 this *shall be* their **d** in the land of Egypt. 3933

DESCEND (10) [DESCENDED, DESCENDETH, DESCENDING, DESCENT]
Nu 34:11 the border shall **d**, and shall reach unto 3381
1Sa 26:10 to die; or he shall **d** into battle, and perish. 3381
Ps 49:17 his glory shall not **d** after him. 3381
Isa 5:14 and he that rejoiceth, shall **d** into it. 3381
Eze 26:20 thee down with them that **d** into the pit, 3381
31:16 down to hell with them that **d** into the pit: 3381
Mk 15:32 Let Christ the King of Israel **d** now from *2597*
Ac 11: 5 a trance I saw a vision, A certain vessel **d**, *2597*
Ro 10: 7 Or, Who shall **d** into the deep? (that is, *2597*
1Th 4:16 For the Lord himself shall **d** from heaven *2597*

D

DESCENDED (19) [DESCEND]
Ex 19:18 the LORD **d** upon it in fire: 3381
33: 9 the cloudy pillar **d**, and stood *at* the door of 3381
34: 5 the LORD **d** in the cloud, and stood with 3381
Dt 9:21 I cast the dust thereof into the brook that **d** 3381
Jos 2:23 **d** from the mountain, and passed over, and 3381
17: 9 the coast **d** *unto* the river Kanah, 3381
18:13 the border **d** *to* Ataroth-adar, near the hill 3381
18:16 **d** *to* the valley of Hinnom, to the side of 3381
18:16 of Jebusi on the south, and **d** *to* En-rogel, 3381
18:17 **d** *to* the stone of Bohan the son of Reuben, 3381
Ps 133: 3 *as the dew* that **d** upon the mountains of 3381
Pr 30: 4 Who hath ascended up *into* heaven, or **d**? 3381
Mt 7:25 And the rain **d**, and the floods came, and *2597*
7:27 And the rain **d**, and the floods came, and *2597*
28: 2 for *the* angel of the Lord **d** from heaven, *2597*
Lk 3:22 And the Holy Ghost **d** in a bodily shape *2597*
Ac 24: 1 Ananias the high priest **d** with the elders, *2597*
Eph 4: 9 that he also **d** first into the lower parts of *2597*
4:10 He that **d** is the same also that ascended up *2597*

DESCENDETH (1) [DESCEND]
Jas 3:15 This wisdom **d** not from above, but *2718*

DESCENDING (8) [DESCEND]
Ge 28:12 the angels of God ascending and **d** on it. 3381
Mt 3:16 and he saw the Spirit of God **d** like a dove, *2597*
Mk 1:10 and the Spirit like a dove **d** upon him: *2597*
Jn 1:32 I saw the Spirit **d** from heaven like a dove, *2597*
1:33 Upon whom thou shalt see the Spirit **d**, and *2597*
1:51 God ascending and **d** upon the Son of man. *2597*
Ac 10:11 and a certain vessel **d** unto him, *2597*
Rev 21:10 holy Jerusalem, **d** out of heaven from God, *2597*

DESCENT (3) [DESCEND]
Lk 19:37 *even* now at the **d** of the mount of Olives, *2600*
Heb 7: 3 Without father, without mother, **without d**, *35*
7: 6 But he whose **d** is not **counted** from them *1075*

DESCRIBE (4) [DESCRIBED, DESCRIBETH, DESCRIPTION]
Jos 18: 4 **d** it according to the inheritance of them; 3789
18: 6 therefore **d** the land *into* seven parts, 3789
18: 8 Joshua charged them that went to **d** 3789
18: 8 the land, and **d** it, and come again to me, 3789

DESCRIBED (2) [DESCRIBE]
Jos 18: 9 **d** it by cities into seven parts in a book, and 3789
Jdg 8:14 he **d** unto him the princes of Succoth, and 3789

DESCRIBETH (2) [DESCRIBE]
Ro 4: 6 Even as David also **d** the blessedness of *3004*
10: 5 For Moses **d** the righteousness which is of *1125*

DESCRIPTION (1) [DESCRIBE]
Jos 18: 6 seven parts, and bring *the d* hither to me, NIH

DESCRY (1)
Jdg 1:23 the house of Joseph **sent to d** Beth-el. 8446

DESERT (42) [DESERTS]
Ex 3: 1 he led the flock to the backside of the **d**, 4057
5: 3 three days' journey into the **d**, and 4057
19: 2 were come *to* the **d** of Sinai, and 4057
23:31 and from the **d** unto the river: 4057
Nu 20: 1 *into* the **d** of Zin in the first month: 4057
27:14 against my commandment in the **d** of Zin, 4057
33:16 they removed from the **d** of Sinai, and 4057
Dt 32:10 He found him in a **d** land, and in the waste 4057
2Ch 26:10 Also he built towers in the **d**, and 4057
Job 24: 5 Behold, *as* wild asses in the **d**, go they forth 4057
Ps 28: 4 work of their hands; render to them their **d**. 1576
78:40 in the wilderness, *and* grieve him in the **d**! 3452

Ps 102: 6 of the wilderness: I am like an owl of the **d**. 2723
106:14 the wilderness, and tempted God in the **d**. 3452
Isa 13:21 **wild beasts of the d** shall lie there; and 6728
21: 1 The burden of the **d** of the sea. 4057
21: 1 *so* it cometh from the **d**, from a terrible 4057
34:14 The **wild beasts of the d** shall also meet 6728
35: 1 the **d** shall rejoice, and blossom as the rose. 6160
35: 6 shall waters break out, and streams in the **d**. 6160
40: 3 make straight in the **d** a highway for our 6160
41:19 I will set in the **d** the fir tree, *and* the pine, 6160
43:19 a way in the wilderness, *and* rivers in the **d**. 3452
43:20 *and* rivers in the **d**, to give drink to my 3452
51: 3 and her **d** like the garden of the LORD; 6160
Jer 17: 6 For he shall be like the heath in the **d**, and 6160
25:24 of the mingled people that dwell in the **d**, 4057
50:12 *shall be* a wilderness, a dry land, and a **d**. 6160
50:39 Therefore the **wild beasts of the d** with 6728
Eze 47: 8 and go down into the **d**, and go into the sea: 6160
Mt 14:13 thence by ship into a **d** place apart: *2048*
14:15 *This* is a **d** place, and the time is now past; *2048*
24:26 shall say unto you, Behold, he is in the **d**; *2048*
Mk 1:45 into the city, but was without in **d** places: *2048*
6:31 Come ye yourselves apart into a **d** place, *2048*
6:32 And they departed into a **d** place by ship *2048*
6:35 *This* is a **d** place, and now the time *is* far *2048*
Lk 4:42 he departed and went into a **d** place: *2048*
9:10 went aside privately into a **d** place *2048*
9:12 get victuals: for we are here in a **d** place. *2048*
Jn 6:31 Our fathers did eat manna in the **d**; as it is *2048*
Ac 8:26 from Jerusalem unto Gaza, which is **d**. *2048*

DESERTS (6) [DESERT]
Isa 48:21 not *when* he led them through the **d**: 2723
Jer 2: 6 through a land of **d** and of pits, through a 6160
Eze 7:27 and according to their **d** will I judge them; 4941
13: 4 thy prophets are like the foxes in the **d**. 2723
Lk 1:80 was in the **d** till the day of his shewing unto *2048*
Heb 11:38 they wandered in **d**, and *in* mountains, and *2047*

DESERVE (1) [DESERVETH, DESERVING]
Ezr 9:13 hast punished us less than our iniquities *d*, NIH

DESERVETH (1) [DESERVE]
Job 11: 6 exacteth of thee *less* than thine iniquity *d*. NIH

DESERVING (1) [DESERVE]
Jdg 9:16 have done unto him according to the **d** of 1576

DESIRABLE (3) [DESIRE]
Eze 23: 6 and rulers, all of them **d** young men, 2531
23:12 upon horses, all of them **d** young men. 2531
23:23 all of them **d** young men, captains and 2531

DESIRE (111) [DESIRABLE, DESIRED, DESIREDST, DESIRES, DESIREST, DESIRETH, DESIRING, DESIROUS]
Ge 3:16 thy **d** *shall be* to thy husband, and he shall 8669
4: 7 unto thee *shall be* his **d**, and thou shalt rule 8669
Ex 10:11 and serve the LORD; for that you did **d**. 1245
34:24 neither shall any man **d** thy land, when thou 2530
Dt 5:21 Neither shalt thou **d** thy neighbour's wife, 2530
7:25 thou shalt not **d** the silver or gold *that is* on 2530
18: 6 come with all the **d** of his mind unto 185
21:11 **hast a d** unto her, that thou wouldest have 2836
Jdg 8:24 I would **d a request** of you, 7592+7596
1Sa 9:20 on whom *is* all the **d** of Israel? *Is it* not on 2532
23:20 come down according to all the **d** of thy soul 185
2Sa 23: 5 for *this is* all my salvation, and all *my* **d**, 2656
1Ki 2:20 she said, I **d** one small petition of thee; 7592
5: 8 I will do all thy **d** concerning timber of 2656
5: 9 and thou shalt accomplish my **d**, 2656
5:10 and fir trees *according to* all his **d**. 2656
9: 1 all Solomon's **d** which he was pleased to 2837
9:11 and with gold, according to all his **d**,) 2656
10:13 gave unto the queen of Sheba all her **d**, 2656
2Ki 4:28 she said, Did I **d** a son of my lord? did I not 7592
2Ch 9:12 gave to the queen of Sheba all her **d**, 2656
15:15 and sought him with their whole **d**; 7522
Ne 1:11 of thy servants, who **d** to fear thy name: 2655
Job 13: 3 the Almighty, and I **d** to reason with God. 2654
14:15 thou wilt **have** a **d** to the work of thine 3700
21:14 for we **d** not the knowledge of thy ways. 2654
31:16 If I have withheld the poor from *their* **d**, or 2656
31:35 my **d** *is, that* the Almighty would answer 8420
33:32 answer me: speak, for I **d** to justify thee. 2654
34:36 **My d** *is that* Job may be tried unto the end 15
36:20 **D** not the night, when people are cut off in 7602
Ps 10: 3 For the wicked boasteth of his heart's **d**, 8378
10:17 thou hast heard the **d** of the humble: 8378
21: 2 Thou hast given him his heart's **d**, and 8378
38: 9 Lord, all my **d** *is* before thee; and 8378
40: 6 Sacrifice and offering thou didst not **d**; 2654
45:11 So shall the king **greatly d** thy beauty: for he 183
54: 7 mine eye hath seen *his* **d** upon mine NIH
59:10 God shall let me see *my* **d** upon mine NIH
70: 2 and put to confusion, that **d** my hurt. 2655
73:25 *there is* none upon earth *that* I **d** beside 2654
78:29 well filled: for he gave them their own **d**; 8378
92:11 Mine eye also shall see *my* **d** on mine NIH
92:11 mine ears shall hear *my* **d** of the wicked that NIH
112: 8 until he see *his* **d** upon his enemies. NIH
112:10 melt away: the **d** of the wicked shall perish. 8378
118: 7 shall I see *my* **d** upon them that hate me. NIH
145:16 and satisfiest the **d** of every living thing. 7522
145:19 He will fulfil the **d** of them that fear him: 7522
Pr 3:15 all the things thou canst **d** are not to be 2656
10:24 but the **d** of the righteous shall be granted. 8378
11:23 The **d** of the righteous *is* only good: *but* 8378
13:12 but *when* the **d** cometh, *it is* a tree of life. 8378
13:19 The **d** accomplished is sweet to the soul: 8378
18: 1 Through **d** a man, having separated 8378
19:22 The **d** of a man *is* his kindness: and a poor 8378
21:25 The **d** of the slothful killeth him; for his 8378
23: 6 an evil eye, neither **d** thou his dainty meats: 183
24: 1 against evil men, neither **d** to be with them. 183
Ecc 6: 9 of the eyes than the wandering of the **d**: 5315
12: 5 shall be a burden, and **d** shall fail: 35
SS 7:10 *am* my beloved's, and his **d** *is* towards me. 8669
Isa 26: 8 the **d** of *our* soul *is* to thy name, and to 8378
53: 2 *there is* no beauty that we should **d** him. 2530
Jer 22:27 to the land whereunto they **d** to 5315+5375
42:22 in the place whither ye **d** to go *and* 2654
44:14 to the which they **have a d** to return 5315+5375
Eze 24:16 I take away from thee the **d** of thine eyes 4261
24:21 the **d** of your eyes, and that which your 4261
24:25 the **d** of their eyes, and that whereupon they 4261
Da 2:18 That *they* would **d** mercies of the God of 1156
11:37 nor the **d** of women, nor regard any god: 2532
Hos 10:10 *It is* in my **d** that I should chastise them; and 185
Am 5:18 Woe unto *you* that **d** the day of the LORD! 183
Mic 7: 3 great *man,* he uttereth his mischievous **d**: 5315
Hab 2: 5 who enlargeth his **d** as hell, and *is* as death, 5315
Hag 2: 7 and the **d** of all nations shall come: 2532
Mk 9:35 saith unto them, If any *man* **d** to be first, *2309*
10:35 shouldest do for us whatsoever we shall **d**. *154*
11:24 What *things* soever ye **d**, when ye pray, *154*
15: 8 And the multitude crying aloud began to **d** *154*
Lk 17:22 when ye shall **d** to see one of the days of *1937*
20:46 which **d** to walk in long robes, and *2309*
22:15 With **d** I have desired to eat this passover *1939*
Ac 23:20 The Jews have agreed to **d** thee that thou *2065*
28:22 But we **d** to hear of thee what thou thinkest: *515*
Ro 10: 1 my heart's **d** and prayer to God for Israel *2107*
15:23 having a **great d** these many years to come *1974*
1Co 14: 1 and **d** spiritual *gifts,* but rather that ye may *2206*
2Co 7: 7 when he told us your **earnest d**, your *1972*
7:11 yea, *what* fear, yea, *what* **vehement d**, yea, *1972*
11:12 off occasion from them which **d** occasion; *2309*
12: 6 For though I would **d** to glory, I shall not *2309*
Gal 4: 9 whereunto ye **d** again to be in bondage? *2309*
4:20 I **d** to be present with you now, and *2309*
4:21 Tell me, ye that **d** to be under the law, *2309*
6:12 As many as **d** to make a fair shew in *2309*
6:13 but **d** to have you circumcised, that they *2309*
Eph 3:13 Wherefore I **d** that *ye* faint not at my *154*
Php 1:23 having a **d** to depart, and to be with Christ; *1939*
4:17 Not because I **d** a gift: but I desire fruit that *1934*
4:17 I **d** fruit that *may* abound to your account. *1934*
Col 1: 9 to **d** that ye might be filled *with* *154*
1Th 2:17 abundantly to see your face with great **d**. *1939*
1Ti 3: 1 If a man **d** the office of a bishop, *3713*
Heb 6:11 And we **d** that every one of you do shew *1937*
11:16 But now they **d** a better *country,* that is, *3713*
Jas 4: 2 ye kill, and **d** *to have,* and cannot obtain: *2206*
1Pe 1:12 which *things the* angels **d** to look into. *1937*
2: 2 **d** the sincere milk of the word, *1971*
Rev 9: 6 and shall **d** to die, and death shall flee from *1937*

DESIRED (50) [DESIRE]
Ge 3: 6 a tree to be **d** to make *one* wise, she took of 2530
1Sa 12:13 ye have chosen, *and* whom ye have **d**: 7592
1Ki 9:19 that which Solomon **d** to build in 2836+2837
2Ch 8: 6 Solomon **d** to build in Jerusalem, 2836+2837
11:23 in abundance. And he **d** many wives. 7592
21:20 eight years, and departed without being **d**. 2532
Est 2:13 whatsoever she **d** was given her to go with 559
Job 20:20 he shall not save of that which he **d**. 2530
Ps 19:10 More to be **d** *are they* than gold, yea, 2530
27: 4 One *thing* have I **d** of the LORD, that will 7592
107:30 so he bringeth them unto their **d** haven. 2656
132:13 chosen Zion; he hath **d** *it* for his habitation. 183
132:14 for ever: here will I dwell; for I have **d** it. 183
Pr 8:11 all the things that may be **d** are not to be 2656
21:20 *There is* treasure to be **d** and oil in 2530
Ecc 2:10 whatsoever mine eyes **d** I kept not from 7592
Isa 1:29 be ashamed of the oaks which ye have **d**, 2530
26: 9 *With* my soul have I **d** thee in the night; yea, 183
Jer 17:16 neither have I **d** the woeful day; 183
Da 2:16 **d** of the king that he would give him time, 1156
2:23 hast made known unto me now what we **d** 1156
Hos 6: 6 For I **d** mercy, and not sacrifice; and 2654
Mic 7: 1 no cluster to eat: my soul **d** the firstripe fruit. 183
Zep 2: 1 yea, gather together, O nation not **d**; 3700
Mt 13:17 righteous *men* have **d** to see *those things* *1937*
16: 1 tempting **d** him that *he* would shew them a *1905*
Mk 15: 6 unto them one prisoner, whomsoever they **d**. *154*
Lk 7:36 And one of the Pharisees **d** him that he *2065*
9: 9 of whom I hear such *things?* And he **d** to *2212*
10:24 kings have **d** to see *those things* which ye *2309*
22:15 With desire I have **d** to eat this passover *1937*
22:31 Simon, behold, Satan hath **d** *to have* you, *1809*
23:25 was cast into prison, whom they had **d**; *154*
Jn 12:21 and **d** him, saying, Sir, we would see Jesus. *2065*
Ac 3:14 and **d** a murderer to be granted unto you; *154*
7:46 **d** to find a tabernacle for the God of Jacob. *154*
8:31 And he **d** Philip that *he* would come up and *3870*
9: 2 And **d** of him letters to Damascus to *154*
12:20 the king's chamberlain their friend, **d** peace; *154*
13: 7 and Saul, and **d** to hear the word of God. *1934*
13:21 And afterward they **d** a king: and God gave *154*
13:28 *him, yet* **d** they Pilate that he should be slain. *154*
16:39 and **d** *them* to depart out of the city. *2065*
18:20 When they **d** *him* to tarry longer time with *2065*
25: 3 And **d** favour against him, that he would *154*
28:14 and were **d** to tarry with them seven days: *3870*
1Co 16:12 I greatly **d** him to come unto you with *3870*
2Co 8: 6 Insomuch that we **d** Titus, that as he had *3870*
12:18 I **d** Titus, and with *him* I sent a brother. *3870*
1Jn 5:15 we know that we have the petitions that we **d** *154*

DESIREDST (2) [DESIRE]
Dt 18:16 According to all that thou **d** of the LORD 7592
Mt 18:32 thee all that debt, because thou **d** me: *3870*

DESIRES (3) [DESIRE]
Ps 37: 4 and he shall give thee the **d** of thine heart. 4862
140: 8 Grant not, O LORD, the **d** of the wicked: 3970
Eph 2: 3 fulfilling the **d** of the flesh and of the mind; *2307*

DESIREST (2) [DESIRE]
Ps 51: 6 Behold, thou **d** truth in the inward parts: 2654
51:16 For thou **d** not sacrifice; else would I give 2654

DESIRETH (17) [DESIRE]
Dt 14:26 strong drink, or for whatsoever thy soul **d**: 7592
1Sa 2:16 *then* take *as much* as thy soul **d**; 183
18:25 The king **d** not *any* dowry, but an hundred 2656
20: 4 Whatsoever thy soul **d**, I will even do *it* for 559
2Sa 3:21 thou mayest reign over all that thine heart **d**. 183
1Ki 11:37 shalt reign according to all that thy soul **d**, 183
Job 7: 2 As a servant **earnestly d** the shadow, and 7602
23:13 and *what* his soul **d**, even *that* he doeth. 183
Ps 34:12 What man *is he that* **d** life, *and* loveth *many* 2655
68:16 *this is* the hill *which* God **d** to dwell in; yea, 2530
Pr 12:12 The wicked **d** the net of evil *men:* but 2530
13: 4 The soul of the sluggard **d**, and *hath* nothing: 183
21:10 The soul of the wicked **d** evil: his neighbour 183
Ecc 6: 2 wanteth nothing for his soul of all that he **d**, 183
Lk 5:39 having drunk old *wine* straightway **d** new: *2309*
14:32 an ambassage, and **d** conditions of peace. *2065*
1Ti 3: 1 the office of a bishop, he **d** a good work. *1937*

DESIRING (12) [DESIRE]
Mt 12:46 stood without, **d** to speak with him. *2212*
12:47 stand without, **d** to speak with thee. *2212*
20:20 and **d** a certain *thing* of him. *154*
Lk 8:20 thy brethren stand without, **d** to see thee. *2309*
16:21 And **d** to be fed with the crumbs which fell *1937*
Ac 9:38 **d** *him* that *he* would not delay to come to *3870*
19:31 **d** *him* that *he* would not adventure himself *3870*
25:15 the elders of the Jews informed *me,* **d** *to* *154*
2Co 5: 2 **earnestly d** to be clothed upon with our *1971*
1Th 3: 6 **d greatly** to see us, as we also *to see* you: *1971*
1Ti 1: 7 **D** to be teachers of the law; *2309*
2Ti 1: 4 **Greatly d** to see thee, being mindful of thy *1971*

DESIROUS (6) [DESIRE]
Pr 23: 3 Be not **d** of his dainties: for they *are* 183
Lk 23: 8 for he was **d** to see him of a long *season,* *2309*
Jn 16:19 Now Jesus knew that they were **d** to ask *2309*
2Co 11:32 *with a garrison,* **d** to apprehend me: *2309*
Gal 5:26 Let us not be **d** of vain glory, provoking one NIG
1Th 2: 8 So being **affectionately d** of you, we were *2442*

DESOLATE (148) [DESOLATION, DESOLATIONS]
Ge 47:19 and not die, that the land be not **d**. 3456
Ex 23:29 lest the land become **d**, and the beast of 8077
Lev 26:22 in number; and your *high* ways shall be **d**. 8074
26:33 your land shall be **d**, and your cities waste. 8077
26:34 as long as it **lieth d**, and ye *be* in your 8074
26:35 As long as it **lieth d** it shall rest; because 8074
26:43 while she **lieth d** without them: 8074
2Sa 13:20 So Tamar remained **d** *in* her brother 8074
2Ch 36:21 *for* as long as *she* **lay d** she kept sabbath, 8074
Job 3:14 which built **d places** for themselves; 2723
15:28 he dwelleth in **d** cities, *and* in houses which 3582
15:34 the congregation of hypocrites *shall be* **d**, 1565
16: 7 thou hast **made d** all my company. 8074
30: 3 flying *into* the wilderness in former time **d** 7722
38:27 To satisfy the **d** and waste *ground;* and 7722
Ps 25:16 mercy upon me; for I *am* **d** and afflicted. 3173
34:21 and they that hate the righteous shall be **d**. 816
34:22 and none of them that trust in him shall be **d**. 816
40:15 Let them be **d** for a reward of their shame 8074
69:25 Let their habitation be **d**; *and* let none dwell 8074
109:10 seek *their bread* also out of their **d places**. 2723
143: 4 within me; my heart within me is **d**. 8074
Isa 1: 7 Your country *is* **d**, your cities *are* burnt 8077
1: 7 and *it is* **d**, as overthrown by strangers. 8077
3:26 and she *being* **d** shall sit upon the ground. 5352
5: 9 Of a truth many houses shall be **d**, 8047
6:11 without man, and the land be utterly **d**, 7582
7:19 shall rest all of them in the **d** valleys, and 1327
13: 9 and fierce anger, to lay the land **d**: 8047
13:22 of the islands shall cry in their **d houses**, 490
15: 6 For the waters of Nimrim shall be **d**: for 4923
24: 6 the earth, and they that dwell therein are **d**: 816
27:10 Yet the defenced city *shall be* **d**, *and* 910
49: 8 the earth, to cause to inherit the **d** heritages; 8074
49:19 For thy waste and thy **d places**, and 8074
49:21 *am* **d**, a captive, and removing to and fro? 1565
54: 1 for more *are* the children of the **d** than 8074
54: 3 and make the **d** cities to be inhabited. 8074
59:10 the night; *we are* in **d places** as dead *men.* 820
62: 4 shall thy land any more be termed **D**: 8077
Jer 2:12 be ye very **d**, saith the LORD. 2717
4: 7 forth from his place to make thy land **d**; 8047
4:27 LORD said, The whole land shall be **d**; 8077
6: 8 lest I make thee **d**, a land not inhabited. 8077
7:34 voice of the bride: for the land shall be **d**. 2723
9:11 I will make the cities of Judah **d**, 8077
10:22 to make the cities of Judah **d**, *and* a den of 8077
10:25 and have **made** his habitation **d**. 8074
12:10 they have made my pleasant portion a **d** 8077
12:11 They have made it **d**, *and being* desolate it 8076
12:11 *and being* **d** it mourneth unto me; 8077
12:11 the whole land is **made d**, because no man 8074
18:16 To make their land **d**, *and* a perpetual 8047
19: 8 I will make this city **d**, and a hissing; 8047
25:38 for their land is **d** because of the fierceness 8047
26: 9 this city shall be **d** without an inhabitant? 2717
32:43 ye say, *It is* **d** without man or beast; 8077
33:10 which ye say *shall be* **d** without man and 2720
33:10 that are **d**, without man, and without 8074
33:12 *which is* **d** without man and without beast, 2720
44: 6 and they are wasted *and* **d**, as *at* this day. 8077

D

Jer 46:19 shall be waste and **d** without an inhabitant. 3341
48: 9 for the cities thereof shall be **d**, without any 8047
48:34 for the waters also of Nimrim shall be **d**. 4923
49: 2 it shall be a **d** heap, and her daughters shall 8077
49:20 surely he shall **make** their habitations **d** 8074
50: 3 which shall make her land **d**, and none shall 8047
50:13 not be inhabited, but it shall be wholly **d**: 8077
50:45 surely he shall **make** *their* habitation **d** with 8074
51:26 thou shalt be **d** for ever, saith the LORD. 8077
51:62 nor beast, but that it shall be **d** for ever. 8077
La 1: 4 all her gates are **d**: her priests sigh: 8074
1:13 he hath made me **d** *and* faint all the day. 8074
1:16 my children are **d**, because the enemy 8074
3:11 pulled me in pieces: he hath made me **d**. 8074
4: 5 They that did feed delicately are **d** in 8074
5:18 of Zion, which is **d**, the foxes walk upon it. 8074
Eze 6: 4 your altars shall be **d**, and your images 8074
6: 6 laid waste, and the high places shall be **d**; 3456
6: 6 your altars may be laid waste and **made d**, 816
6:14 hand upon them, and make the land **d**, yea, 8077
6:14 more **d** than the wilderness toward Diblath, 4923
12:19 that her land may be **d** from all that is 3456
12:20 shall be laid waste, and the land shall be **d**; 8077
14:15 they spoil it, so that it be **d**, that no man 8077
14:16 shall be delivered, but the land shall be **d**. 8077
15: 8 I will make the land **d**, because they have 8077
19: 7 he knew their **d palaces**, and he laid waste 490
19: 7 the land was **d**, and the fulness thereof, 3456
20:26 that I might **make** them **d**, to the end that 8074
25: 3 against the land of Israel, when it was **d**; 8074
25:13 I will make it **d** from Teman; and they of 2723
26:19 When I shall make thee a **d** city, like 2717
26:20 in **places d** of old, with them that go down 2723
29: 9 And the land of Egypt shall be **d** and waste; 8077
29:10 make the land of Egypt utterly waste *and* **d**, 8077
29:12 I will make the land of Egypt **d** in the midst 8077
29:12 in the midst of the countries *that are* **d**, 8074
29:12 *that are* laid waste shall be **d** forty years: 8077
30: 7 they shall be **d** in the midst of the countries 8074
30: 7 in the midst of the countries *that are* **d**, 8074
30:14 I will **make** Pathros **d**, and will set fire in 8074
32:15 When I shall make the land of Egypt **d**, and 8077
33:28 I will lay the land **most d**, 4923+8077+2050.1
33:28 the mountains of Israel shall be **d**, that none 8074
33:29 I have laid the land **most d** 4923+8077+2050.1
35: 3 and I will make thee **most d**. 4923+8077+2050.1
35: 4 thou shalt be **d**, and thou shalt know that I 8077
35: 7 I make mount Seir **most d**, 8077+8077+2050.1
35:12 saying, They are **laid d**, they are given us 8074
35:14 whole earth rejoiceth, I will make thee **d**. 8077
35:15 because it was **d**, so will I do unto thee: 8074
35:15 thou shalt be **d**, O mount Seir, and 8077
36: 3 Because *they* have **made** *you* **d**, and 8074
36: 4 to the **d** wastes, and to the cities that are 8074
36:34 the **d** land shall be tilled, whereas it lay 8074
36:34 whereas it lay **d** in the sight of all that 8077
36:35 This land that was **d** is become like 8074
36:35 the waste and **d** and ruined cities *are* 8074
36:36 the ruined *places, and* plant that that was **d**: 8074
38:12 to turn thine hand upon the **d places** *that* 2723
Da 9:17 face to shine upon thy sanctuary that is **d**, 8076
9:27 of abominations he *shall* **make** *it* **d**, 8074
9:27 that determined shall be poured upon the **d**. 8074
11:31 shall place the abomination that **maketh d**. 8074
12:11 the abomination that **maketh d** set up, 8074
Hos 5: 9 Ephraim shall be **d** in the day of rebuke: 8047
13:16 Samaria shall become **d**; for she hath 816
Joel 1:17 the garners are **laid d**, the barns are broken 8074
1:18 yea, the flocks of sheep are **made d**. 816
2: 3 and behind them a **d** wilderness; 8077
2:20 and will drive him into a land barren and **d**, 8077
3:19 and Edom shall be a **d** wilderness, 8077
Am 7: 9 the high places of Isaac shall be **d**, and 8074
Mic 1: 7 and all the idols thereof will I lay **d**: 8077
6:13 in **making** *thee* **d** because of thy sins. 8074
7:13 Notwithstanding the land shall be **d** 8077
Zep 3: 6 their towers are **d**; I made their streets 8074
Zec 7:14 thus the land was **d** after them, that no man 8074
7:14 for they laid the pleasant land **d**. 8047
Mal 1: 4 but we will return and build the **d places**; 2723
Mt 23:38 Behold, your house is left unto you **d**. *2048*
Lk 13:35 Behold, your house is left unto you **d**: and *2048*
Ac 1:20 Let his habitation be **d**, and let no man *2048*
Gal 4:27 for the **d** hath many moe children than she *2048*
1Ti 5: 5 and **d**, trusteth in God, and continueth in *3443*
Rev 17:16 and shall make her **d** and naked, and shall *2049*
18:19 for in one hour is she **made d**. *2049*

DESOLATION (46) [DESOLATE]

Lev 26:31 **bring** your sanctuaries **unto d**, and I will 8074
26:32 I will **bring** the land **into d**: and 8074
Jos 8:28 it a heap for ever, *even* a **d** unto this day. 8077
2Ki 22:19 that *they* should become a **d** and a curse, 8047
2Ch 30: 7 *who* therefore gave them up to **d**, as ye see. 8047
Job 30:14 in the **d** they rolled themselves *upon me.* 7722
Ps 73:19 How are they *brought* into **d**, as *in* a 8047
Pr 1:27 When your fear cometh as **d**, and 7722
3:25 neither of the **d** of the wicked, when it 7722
Isa 10: 3 and in the **d** *which* shall come from far? 7722
17: 9 the children of Israel: and there shall be **d**. 8077
24:12 In the city is left **d**, and the gate is smitten 8047
47:11 **d** shall come upon thee suddenly, 7722
51:19 **d**, and destruction, and the famine, and 7701
64:10 Zion is a wilderness, Jerusalem a **d**. 8077
Jer 22: 5 that this house shall become a **d**. 2723
25:11 this whole land shall be a **d**, *and* 2723
25:18 to make them a **d**, an astonishment, a 2723
34:22 I will make the cities of Judah a **d** without 8077
44: 2 this day they *are* a **d**, and no man dwelleth 2723
44:22 therefore is your land a **d**, and an 2723
49:13 that Bozrah shall become a **d**, a reproach, a 8047
49:17 Also Edom shall be a **d**: every one that 8047
49:33 be a dwelling for dragons, *and* a **d** for ever: 8077
50:23 how is Babylon become a **d** among 8047
51:29 to make the land of Babylon a **d** without an 8047
51:43 Her cities are a **d**, a dry land, and 8047
La 3:47 a snare is come upon us, **d** and destruction. 7612
Eze 7:27 the prince shall be clothed with **d**, and 8077
23:33 sorrow, *with* the cup of astonishment and **d**, 8077
Da 8:13 daily *sacrifice,* and the transgression of **d**, 8074
Hos 12: 1 he daily increaseth lies and **d**; and they do 7701
Joel 3:19 Egypt shall be a **d**, and Edom shall be a 8077
Mic 6:16 that I should make thee a **d**, and 8047
Zep 1:13 shall become a booty, and their houses a **d**: 8077
1:15 and distress, a day of wasteness and **d**, 4875
2: 4 Gaza shall be forsaken, and Ashkelon a **d**: 8077
2: 9 of nettles, and saltpits, and a perpetual **d**: 8077
2:13 will make Nineveh a **d**, *and* dry like a 8077
2:14 the windows; **d** *shall be* in the thresholds: 2721
2:15 how is she become a **d**, a place for beasts to 8047
Mt 12:25 divided against itself is **brought to d**; *2049*
24:15 therefore shall see the abomination of **d**, *2050*
Mk 13:14 But when ye shall see the abomination of **d**, *2050*
Lk 11:17 divided against itself is **brought to d**; *2049*
21:20 then know that the **d** thereof is nigh. *2050*

DESOLATIONS (11) [DESOLATE]

Ezr 9: 9 to repair the **d** thereof, and to give us a wall 2723
Ps 46: 8 what **d** he hath made in the earth. 8047
74: 3 Lift up thy feet unto the perpetual **d**; 4876
Isa 61: 4 they shall raise up the former **d**, and 8074
61: 4 the waste cities, the **d** of many generations. 8074
Jer 25: 9 and a hissing, and perpetual **d**. 2723
25:12 and will make it perpetual **d**. 8077
Eze 35: 9 I will make thee perpetual **d**, and thy cities 8077
Da 9: 2 seventy years in the **d** of Jerusalem. 2723
9:18 behold our **d**, and the city which is called 8074
9:26 unto the end of the war **d** *are* determined. 8074

DESPAIR (3) [DESPAIRED]

1Sa 27: 1 Saul shall **d** of me, to seek me any more in 2976
Ecc 2:20 **cause** my heart **to d** of all the labour which 2976
2Co 4: 8 *we are* perplexed, but not **in d**; *1820*

DESPAIRED (1) [DESPAIR]

2Co 1: 8 insomuch that we **d** even of life: *1820*

DESPERATE (2) [DESPERATELY]

Job 6:26 the speeches of one that is **d**, *which are* as 2976
Isa 17:11 *be* a heap in the day of grief and of **d** sorrow. 605

DESPERATELY (1) [DESPERATE]

Jer 17: 9 *is* deceitful above all *things,* and **d wicked**: 605

DESPISE (37) [DESPISED, DESPISERS, DESPISEST, DESPISETH, DESPISING]

Lev 26:15 if ye shall **d** my statutes, or if your soul 3988
1Sa 2:30 and they that **d** me shall be lightly esteemed. 959
2Sa 19:43 why then did ye **d** us, that our advice 7043

Est 1:17 that *they* shall **d** their husbands in their eyes, 959
Job 5:17 **d** not thou the chastening of the Almighty: 3988
9:21 I not know my soul: I would **d** my life. 3988
10: 3 that thou shouldest **d** the work of thine 3988
31:13 If I did **d** the cause of my manservant or 3988
Ps 51:17 and a contrite heart, O God, thou wilt not **d**. 959
73:20 when *thou* awakest, thou shalt **d** their image. 959
102:17 of the destitute, and not **d** their prayer. 959
Pr 1: 7 *but* fools **d** wisdom and instruction. 936
3:11 **d** not the chastening of the LORD; 3988
6:30 *Men* do not **d** a thief, if he steal to satisfy his 936
23: 9 for he will **d** the wisdom of thy words. 936
23:22 and **d** not thy mother when she is old. 936
Isa 30:12 Because ye **d** this word, and trust in 3988
Jer 4:30 *thy* lovers will **d** thee, they will seek thy 3988
23:17 They say still unto them that **d** me, 5006
La 1: 8 all that honoured her **d** her, because 2107
Eze 16:57 the Philistines, which **d** thee round about. 7590
28:26 all those that **d** them round about them; 7590
Am 5:21 I **d** your feast *days,* and I will not smell in 3988
Mal 1: 6 of hosts unto you, O priests, that **d** my name. 959
Mt 6:24 else he will hold to the one, and **d** the other. *2706*
18:10 Take heed that ye **d** not one of these little *2706*
Lk 16:13 else he will hold to the one, and **d** the other. *2706*
Ro 14: 3 Let not him that eateth **d** him that eateth *1848*
1Co 11:22 and to drink *in?* or **d** ye the church of God, *2706*
16:11 Let no *man* therefore **d** him: but *1848*
1Th 5:20 **D** not prophesyings. *1848*
1Ti 4:12 Let no *man* **d** thy youth; but be thou an *2706*
6: 2 let them not **d** *them,* because they are *2706*
Tit 2:15 with all authority. Let no *man* **d** thee. *4065*
Heb 12: 5 **d** not thou the chastening of the Lord, *3643*
2Pe 2:10 the lust of uncleanness, and **d** government. *2706*
Jude 1: 8 **d** dominion, and speak evil of dignities. *114*

DESPISED (60) [DESPISE]

Ge 16: 4 her mistress was **d** in her eyes. 7043
16: 5 that she had conceived, I was **d** in her eyes: 7043
25:34 and went his way: thus Esau **d** *his* birthright. 959
Lev 26:43 even because they **d** my judgments, and 3988
Nu 11:20 that ye have **d** the LORD which *is* among 3988
14:31 they shall know the land which ye have **d**. 3988
15:31 Because he hath **d** the word of the LORD, 959
Jdg 9:38 *is* not this the people that thou hast **d**? go 3988
1Sa 10:27 they **d** him, and brought him no presents. 959
2Sa 6:16 the LORD; and she **d** him in her heart. 959
12: 9 Wherefore hast thou **d** the commandment of 959
12:10 because thou hast **d** me, and hast taken 959
2Ki 19:21 The virgin the daughter of Zion hath **d** thee, 959
1Ch 15:29 and playing: and she **d** him in her heart. 959
2Ch 36:16 and **d** his words, and misused his prophets, 959
Ne 2:19 **d** us, and said, What *is* this thing that ye do? 959
4: 4 Hear, O our God; for we are **d**: and turn their 939
Job 12: 5 a lamp **d** in the thought of him that is at ease. 937
19:18 Yea, young children **d** me; I arose, and 3988
Ps 22: 6 a reproach of men, and **d** of the people. 959
22:24 For he hath not **d** nor abhorred the affliction 959
53: 5 *them* to shame, because God hath **d** them. 3988
106:24 Yea, they **d** the pleasant land, they believed 3988
119:141 I *am* small and **d**: *yet* do not I forget thy 959
Pr 1:30 none of my counsel: they **d** all my reproof. 5006
5:12 I hated instruction, and my heart **d** reproof; 5006
12: 8 but he that is of a perverse heart shall be **d**. 937
12: 9 *He that is* **d**, and hath a servant, *is* better 7034
Ecc 9:16 nevertheless the poor *man's* wisdom *is* **d**, 959
SS 8: 1 I would kiss thee; yea, I should not be **d**. 936
Isa 5:24 and **d** the word of the Holy One of Israel. 5006
33: 8 he hath **d** the cities, he regardeth no man. 3988
37:22 hath **d** thee, *and* laughed thee to scorn; 959
53: 3 He is **d** and rejected of men; a man of 959
53: 3 he was **d**, and we esteemed him not. 959
60:14 all they that **d** thee shall bow themselves 5006
Jer 22:28 *Is* this man Coniah a **d** broken idol? *is he* a 959
33:24 thus they have **d** my people, that *they* 5006
49:15 small among the heathen, *and* **d** among men. 959
La 2: 6 hath **d** in the indignation of his anger 5006
Eze 16:59 which hast **d** the oath in breaking 959
17:16 whose oath he **d**, and whose covenant he 959
17:18 Seeing he **d** the oath by breaking 959
17:19 surely mine oath that he hath **d**, and 959
20:13 they **d** my judgments, which *if* a man do, 3988
20:16 Because they **d** my judgments, and walked 3988
20:24 had **d** my statutes, and had polluted my 3988
22: 8 Thou hast **d** mine holy *things,* and hast 959
28:24 all *that are* round about them, that **d** them; 7590
Am 2: 4 because they have **d** the law of the LORD, 3988
Ob 1: 2 small among the heathen: thou *art* greatly **d**. 959
Zec 4:10 For who hath **d** the day of small *things?* for 936
Mal 1: 6 And ye say, Wherein have we **d** thy name? 959
Lk 18: 9 that they were righteous, and **d** other: *1848*
Ac 19:27 goddess Diana should be **d**, *1519+3049+3762*
1Co 1:28 and *things* which are **d**, hath God chosen, *1848*
4:10 *are* strong; ye *are* honourable, but we *are* **d**. *820*
Gal 4:14 temptation which was in my flesh ye **d** not, *1848*
Heb 10:28 He that **d** Moses' law died without mercy *114*
Jas 2: 6 But ye have **d** the poor. Do not rich *men* *818*

DESPISERS (2) [DESPISE]

Ac 13:41 Behold *ye* **d**, and wonder, and perish: for I *2707*
2Ti 3: 3 incontinent, fierce, **d of** *those that are* **good**, *865*

DESPISEST (1) [DESPISE]

Ro 2: 4 Or **d** thou the riches of his goodness and *2706*

DESPISETH (19) [DESPISE]

Job 36: 5 **d** not *any: he is* mighty in strength *and* 3988
Ps 69:33 heareth the poor, and **d** not his prisoners. 959
Pr 11:12 He that is void of wisdom **d** his neighbour: 936
13:13 Whoso **d** the word shall be destroyed: but 936
14: 2 but he that is perverse in his ways **d** him. 959
14:21 He that **d** his neighbour sinneth: but he that 936
15: 5 A fool **d** his father's instruction: but he that 5006
15:20 a glad father: but a foolish man **d** his mother. 959
15:32 He that refuseth instruction **d** his own soul: 3988
19:16 own soul; *but* he that **d** his ways shall die. 959
30:17 at *his* father, and **d** to obey *his* mother, 936
Isa 33:15 he that **d** the gain of oppressions, 3988
49: 7 *and* his Holy One, to him whom man **d**, 960
Lk 10:16 and he that **d** you despiseth me; and he that *114*
10:16 and he that despiseth you **d** me; and he that *114*
10:16 and he that **d** me despiseth him that sent me. *114*
10:16 and he that despiseth me **d** him that sent me. *114*
1Th 4: 8 He therefore that **d**, despiseth not man, but *114*
4: 8 therefore that despiseth, **d** not man, but God, *114*

DESPISING (1) [DESPISE]

Heb 12: 2 **d** the shame, and is set down at the right *2706*

DESPITE (2) [DESPITEFUL, DESPITEFULLY]

Eze 25: 6 rejoiced in heart with all thy **d** against 7589
Heb 10:29 and hath **done d unto** the Spirit of grace? *1796*

DESPITEFUL (3) [DESPITE]

Eze 25:15 have taken vengeance with a **d** heart, 7589
36: 5 with **d** minds, to cast it out for a prey. 7589
Ro 1:30 haters of God, **d**, proud, boasters, *5197*

DESPITEFULLY (3) [DESPITE]

Mt 5:44 and pray for them which **d use** you, and *1908*
Lk 6:28 and pray for them which **d use** you. *1908*
Ac 14: 5 to **use** *them* **d**, and to stone them, *5195*

DESTINY See END; EVENT; NUMBER; PATHS

DESTITUTE (8)

Ge 24:27 who hath not **left d** my master of his mercy 5800
Ps 102:17 He will regard the prayer of the **d**, and 6199
141: 8 in thee is my trust; **leave** not my soul **d**. 6168
Pr 15:21 Folly *is* joy to *him that is* **d** of wisdom: but 2638
Eze 32:15 the country shall be **d** of that whereof it 8074
1Ti 6: 5 and **d** of the truth, supposing that gain is *650*
Heb 11:37 being **d**, afflicted, tormented; *5302*
Jas 2:15 or sister be naked, and **d** of daily food, *3007*

DESTROY (261) [DESTROYED, DESTROYER, DESTROYERS, DESTROYEST, DESTROYETH, DESTROYING, DESTRUCTION, DESTRUCTIONS]

Ge 6: 7 I will **d** man whom I have created from 4229
6:13 and behold, I will **d** them with the earth. 7843
6:17 to **d** all flesh, wherein *is* the breath of life, 7843
7: 4 made will I **d** from off the face of the earth. 4229
9:11 neither shall there any more be a flood to **d** 7843
9:15 shall no more become a flood to **d** all flesh. 7843
18:23 Wilt thou also **d** the righteous with 5595
18:24 wilt thou also **d** and not spare the place for 5595
18:28 wilt thou **d** all the city for *lack of* five? And 7843
18:28 If I find there forty and five, I will not **d** *it.* 7843

Ge 18:31 he said, I will not **d** *it* for twenty's sake. 7843
18:32 And he said, I will not **d** *it* for ten's sake. 7843
19:13 For we will **d** this place, because the cry of 7843
19:13 and the LORD hath sent us to **d** it. 7843
19:14 this place; for the LORD will **d** this city. 7843
Ex 8: 9 to **d** the frogs from thee and thy houses, 3772
12:13 the plague shall not be upon you to **d** *you,* 4889
15: 9 will draw my sword, my hand shall **d** them. 3423
23:27 will **d** all the people to whom thou shalt 2000
34:13 ye shall **d** their altars, break their images, 5422
Lev 23:30 the same soul will I **d** from among his people. 6
26:22 **d** your cattle, and make you few in number; 3772
26:30 I will **d** your high places, and cut down 8045
26:44 to **d** them **utterly**, and to break my 3615
Nu 21: 2 my hand, then I will **utterly d** their cities. 2763
24:17 of Moab, and **d** all the children of Sheth. 6979
24:19 and shall **d** him that remaineth of the city. 6
32:15 and ye shall **d** all this people. 7843
33:52 **d** all their pictures, and destroy all their molten 6
33:52 **d** all their molten images, and quite pluck 6
Dt 1:27 us into the hand of the Amorites, to **d** us. 8045
2:15 to **d** them from among the host, until they 2000
4:31 he will not forsake thee, neither **d** thee, 7843
6:15 and **d** thee from off the face of the earth. 8045
7: 2 thou shalt smite them, *and* **utterly d** 2763+2763
7: 4 kindled against you, and **d** thee suddenly. 8045
7: 5 ye shall **d** their altars, and break down their 5422
7:10 them that hate him to their face, to **d** them: 6
7:23 shall **d** them *with* a mighty destruction, 1949
7:24 and thou shalt **d** their name from under heaven: 6
9: 3 *as* a consuming fire he shall **d** them, and 8045
9: 3 shalt thou drive them out, and **d** them quickly, 6
9:14 that I may **d** them, and blot out their name 8045
9:19 LORD was wroth against you to **d** you. 8045
9:25 the LORD had said he would **d** you. 8045
9:26 **d** not thy people and thine inheritance, 7843
10:10 *and* the LORD would not **d** thee. 7843
12: 2 Ye shall **utterly d** all the places, wherein 6+6
12: 3 and **d** the names of them out of that place. 6
20:17 thou shalt **utterly d** them; 2763+2763
20:19 thou shalt not **d** the trees thereof by forcing 7843
20:20 for meat, thou shalt **d** and cut them down; 7843
28:63 so the LORD will rejoice over you to **d** you, 6
31: 3 he will **d** these nations from before thee, 8045
32:25 shall **d** both the young man and the virgin, 7921
33:27 from before thee; and shall say, **D** *them.* 8045
Jos 7: 7 us into the hand of the Amorites, to **d** us? 6
7:12 except ye **d** the accursed from amongst 8045
9:24 to **d** all the inhabitants of the land from 8045
11:20 that *he* might **d** them **utterly**, *and* that they 2763
11:20 have no favour, but that *he* might **d** them, 8045
22:33 to **d** the land wherein the children of 7843
Jdg 6: 5 and they entered into the land to **d** it. 7843
21:11 Ye shall **utterly d** every male, and 2763
1Sa 15: 3 **utterly d** all that they have, and spare them 2763
15: 6 the Amalekites, lest I **d** you with them: 622
15: 9 *was* good, and would not **utterly d** them: 2763
15:18 and **utterly d** the sinners the Amalekites, 2763
23:10 come to Keilah, to **d** the city for my sake. 7843
24:21 that thou wilt not **d** my name out of my 8045
26: 9 David said to Abishai, **D** him not: for who 7843
26:15 for there came one of the people in to **d** 7843
2Sa 1:14 thine hand to **d** the LORD's anointed? 7843
14: 7 whom he slew; and we will **d** the heir also: 8045
14:11 the revengers of blood to **d** any more, 7843
14:11 to destroy any more, lest they **d** my son. 8045
14:16 out of the hand of the man *that would* **d** me 8045
20:19 thou seekest to **d** a city and a mother in 4191
20:20 it from me, that I should swallow up or **d**. 7843
22:41 that I might **d** them that hate me. 6789
24:16 out his hand *upon* Jerusalem to **d** it, 7843
1Ki 9:21 of Israel also were not able **utterly** to **d**, 2763
13:34 and to **d** *it* from off the face of the earth. 8045
16:12 Thus did Zimri **d** all the house of Baasha, 8045
2Ki 8:19 Yet the LORD would not **d** Judah for 7843
10:19 to the intent that *he* might **d** the worshippers of 6
13:23 Isaac, and Jacob, and would not **d** them, 7843
18:25 the LORD against this place to **d** it? 7843
18:25 to me, Go up against this land, and **d** it. 7843
24: 2 of Ammon, and sent them against Judah to **d** it, 6
1Ch 21:15 God sent an angel unto Jerusalem to **d** it: 7843
2Ch 12: 7 *therefore* I will not **d** them, but I will grant 7843
12:12 that *he* would not **d** *him* altogether: 7843
20:23 utterly to slay and **d** *them:* and when they 8045
20:23 of Seir, every one helped to **d** another. 4889
21: 7 Howbeit the LORD would not **d** the house 7843
25:16 I know that God hath determined to **d** thee, 7843
35:21 who *is* with me, that he **d** thee not. 7843
Ezr 6:12 caused his name to dwell there **d** all kings 4049
6:12 to **d** this house of God which *is* at 2255
Est 3: 6 wherefore Haman sought to **d** all the Jews 8045
3:13 to **d**, to kill, and to cause to perish, all Jews, 8045
4: 7 to the king's treasuries for the Jews, to **d** them. 6
4: 8 decree that was given at Shushan to **d** them, 8045
8: 5 which he wrote to **d** the Jews which *are* in all 6
8:11 to **d**, to slay, and to cause to perish, 8045
9:24 had devised against the Jews to **d** them, and 6
9:24 that *is,* the lot, to consume them, and to **d** them; 6
Job 2: 3 me against him, to **d** him without cause. 1104
6: 9 Even *that* it would please God to **d** me: 1792
8:18 If he **d** him from his place, then *it* shall 1104
10: 8 together round about; yet thou dost **d** me. 1104
19:26 *though* after my skin *worms* **d** this *body,* 5362
Ps 5: 6 Thou shalt **d** them that speak leasing: 6
5:10 **D** thou them, O God; let them fall by their 816
18:40 that I might **d** them that hate me. 6789
21:10 Their fruit shalt thou **d** from the earth, and 6
28: 5 he shall **d** them, and not build them up. 2040
40:14 together that seek after my soul to **d** it; 5595
52: 5 God shall likewise **d** thee for ever, he shall 5422
55: 9 **D**, O Lord, *and* divide their tongues: for I 1104
63: 9 to **d** *it,* shall go into the lower parts of 7722
69: 4 they that would **d** me, *being* mine enemies 6789
74: 8 said in their hearts, Let us **d** them together: 3238
101: 8 I will early **d** all the wicked of the land; 6789
106:23 Therefore he said that *he* would **d** them, 8045
106:23 turn away his wrath, lest *he* should **d** *them.* 7843
106:34 They did not **d** the nations, 8045
118:10 in the name of the LORD will I **d** them. 4135
118:11 in the name of the LORD I will **d** them. 4135
118:12 for in the name of the LORD I will **d** 4135
119:95 The wicked have waited for me to **d** me: *but* 6
143:12 and **d** all them that afflict my soul: 6
144: 6 shoot out thine arrows, and **d** them. 2000
145:20 that love him: but all the wicked will he **d**. 8045
Pr 1:32 and the prosperity of fools shall **d** them. 6
11: 3 the perverseness of transgressors shall **d** 7703
15:25 The LORD will **d** the house of the proud: 5255
21: 7 The robbery of the wicked shall **d** them; 1641
Ecc 5: 6 at thy voice, and **d** the work of thine hands? 2254
7:16 over wise: why shouldest thou **d** thyself? 8074
Isa 3:12 *thee* to err, and **d** the way of thy paths. 1104
10: 7 *it is* in his heart to **d** and cut off nations not 8045
11: 9 They shall not hurt nor **d** in all my holy 7843
11:15 the LORD shall **utterly d** the tongue of 2763
13: 5 of his indignation, to **d** the whole land. 2254
13: 9 and he shall **d** the sinners thereof out of it. 8045
19: 3 and I will **d** the counsel thereof: 1104
23:11 merchant *city,* to **d** the strong holds thereof. 8045
25: 7 he will **d** in this mountain the face of 1104
32: 7 he deviseth wicked devices to **d** the poor 2254
36:10 the LORD against this land to **d** it? 7843
36:10 unto me, Go up against this land, and **d** it. 7843
42:14 I will **d** and devour at once. 5395
51:13 of the oppressor, as if he were ready to **d**? 7843
54:16 and I have created the waster to **d**. 2254
65: 8 found in the cluster, and *one* saith, **D** it not; 7843
65: 8 servants' sakes, that *I* may not **d** them all. 7843
65:25 They shall not hurt nor **d** in all my holy 7843
Jer 1:10 to **d**, and to throw down, to build, and to plant. 6
5:10 Go ye up upon her walls, and **d**; but 7843
6: 5 let us go by night, and let us **d** her palaces. 7843
11:19 *saying,* Let us **d** the tree with the fruit 7843
12:17 I will utterly pluck up and **d** that nation, saith 6
13:14 nor spare, nor have mercy, but **d** them. 7843
15: 3 and the beasts of the earth, to devour and **d**. 7843
15: 6 out my hand against thee, and **d** thee; 7843
15: 7 bereave *them* of children, I will **d** my people, 6
17:18 of evil, and **d** them *with* double destruction. 7665
18: 7 to pluck up, and to pull down, and to **d** *it;* 6
23: 1 Woe be unto *the* pastors that **d** and scatter 6
25: 9 will **utterly d** them, and make them an 2763
31:28 and to throw down, and to **d**, and to afflict; 6
36:29 shall certainly come and **d** this land, 7843
46: 8 I will **d** the city and the inhabitants thereof. 6
48:18 upon thee, *and* he shall **d** thy strong holds. 7843
49: 9 by night, they will **d** till they have enough. 7843
49:38 will **d** from thence the king and the princes, 6

Jer	50:21	waste and **utterly d** after them, saith	2763
	50:26	cast her up as heaps, and **d** her **utterly**:	2763
	51: 3	her young men; **d** ye **utterly** all her host.	2763
	51:11	for his device *is* against Babylon, to **d** it;	7843
	51:20	and with thee will I **d** kingdoms:	7843
La	2: 8	The LORD hath purposed to **d** the wall of	7843
	3:66	**d** them in anger from under the heavens of	8045
Eze	5:16	*and* which I will send to **d** you:	7843
	6: 3	sword upon you, and I will **d** your high places.	6
	9: 8	*wilt* thou **d** all the residue of Israel in thy	7843
	14: 9	will **d** him from the midst of my people	8045
	21:31	the hand of brutish men, *and* skilful to **d**.	4889
	22:27	to shed blood, *and* to **d** souls, to get dishonest	6
	22:30	me for the land, that *I* should not **d** it:	7843
	25: 7	I will **d** thee; and thou shalt know that I *am*	8045
	25:15	a despiteful heart, to **d** *it for* the old hatred;	4889
	25:16	and **d** the remnant of the sea coast.	6
	26: 4	they shall **d** the walls of Tyrus, and	7843
	26:12	down thy walls, and **d** thy pleasant houses:	5422
	28:16	I will **d** thee, O covering cherub, from	6
	30:11	the nations, *shall be* brought to **d** the land:	7843
	30:13	I will also **d** the idols, and I will cause *their*	6
	32:13	I will **d** also all the beasts thereof from besides	6
	34:16	I will **d** the fat and the strong; I will feed	8045
	43: 3	vision that I saw when I came to **d** the city:	7843
Da	2:12	commanded to **d** all the wise *men* of Babylon.	7
	2:24	whom the king had ordained to **d** the wise *men*	7
	2:24	thus unto him; **D** not the wise *men* of Babylon:	7
	4:23	saying, Hew the tree down, and **d** it;	2255
	7:26	to consume and to **d** *it* unto the end.	7
	8:24	he shall **d** wonderfully, and shall prosper,	7843
	8:24	and shall **d** the mighty and the holy people.	7843
	8:25	in his heart, and by peace shall **d** many:	7843
	9:26	of the prince that *shall* come shall **d** the city	7843
	11:26	feed of the portion of his meat shall **d** him,	7665
	11:44	he shall go forth with great fury to **d**,	8045
Hos	2:12	I will **d** her vines and her fig trees,	8074
	4: 5	thee *in* the night, and I will **d** thy mother.	1820
	11: 9	mine anger, I will not return to **d** Ephraim:	7843
Am	9: 8	and I will **d** it from off the face of the earth;	8045
	9: 8	saving that I will not **utterly d**	8045+8045
Ob	1: 8	even **d** the wise *men* out of Edom, and	6
Mic	2:10	it shall **d** *you,* even *with* a sore destruction.	2254
	5:10	of the midst of thee, and I will **d** thy chariots:	6
	5:14	of the midst of thee: so will I **d** thy cities.	8045
Zep	2: 5	the land of the Philistines, I will even **d** thee,	6
	2:13	out his hand against the north, and **d** Assyria;	6
Hag	2:22	I will **d** the strength of the kingdoms of	8045
Zec	12: 9	*that* I will seek to **d** all the nations that	8045
Mal	3:11	and he shall not **d** the fruits of your ground;	7843
Mt	2:13	for Herod will seek the young child to **d**	*622*
	5:17	Think not that I am come to **d** the law, or	*2647*
	5:17	I am not come to **d**, but to fulfil.	*2647*
	10:28	rather fear him which is able to **d** both soul	*622*
	12:14	council against him, how they might **d** him.	*622*
	21:41	He will miserably **d** those wicked *men,* and	*622*
	26:61	I am able to **d** the temple of God, and	*2647*
	27:20	that they should ask Barabbas, and **d** Jesus.	*622*
Mk	1:24	art thou come to **d** us? I know thee who thou	*622*
	3: 6	against him, how they might **d** him.	*622*
	9:22	into the fire, and into the waters, to **d** him:	*622*
	11:18	heard *it,* and sought how they might **d** him:	*622*
	12: 9	he will come and **d** the husbandmen, and	*622*
	14:58	I will **d** this temple that is made with hands,	*2647*
Lk	4:34	art thou come to **d** us? I know thee who thou	*622*
	6: 9	or to do evil? to save life, or to **d** *it?*	*622*
	9:56	For the Son of man is not come to **d** men's	*622*
	19:47	and the chief of the people sought to **d** him,	*622*
	20:16	He shall come and **d** these husbandmen, and	*622*
Jn	2:19	**D** this temple, and in three days I will raise	*3089*
	10:10	but for to steal, and to kill, and to **d**:	*622*
Ac	6:14	that this Jesus of Nazareth shall **d** this	*2647*
Ro	14:15	**D** not him with thy meat, for whom Christ	*622*
	14:20	For meat **d** not the work of God. All *things*	*2647*
1Co	1:19	I will **d** the wisdom of the wise, and	*622*
	3:17	defile the temple of God, him shall God **d**;	*5351*
	6:13	but God shall **d** both it and them. Now	*2673*
2Th	2: 8	shall **d** with the brightness of his coming:	*2673*
Heb	2:14	that through death he might **d** him that had	*2673*
Jas	4:12	is one lawgiver, who is able to save and to **d**:	*622*
1Jn	3: 8	that he might **d** the works of the devil.	*3089*
Rev	11:18	shouldest **d** them which destroy the earth.	*1311*
	11:18	shouldest destroy them which **d** the earth.	*1311*

DESTROYED (167) [DESTROY]

Ge	7:23	every living substance was **d** which *was*	4229
	7:23	the heaven; and they were **d** from the earth:	4229
	13:10	before the LORD **d** Sodom and	7843
	19:29	to pass, when God **d** the cities of the plain,	7843
	34:30	slay me; and I shall be **d**, I and my house.	8045
Ex	10: 7	knowest thou not yet that Egypt is **d**?	6
	22:20	the LORD only, he shall be **utterly d**.	2763
Nu	21: 3	and they **utterly d** them and their cities:	2763
Dt	1:44	chased you, as bees do, and **d** you in Seir,	3807
	2:12	when they had **d** them from before them,	8045
	2:21	the LORD **d** them before them; and	8045
	2:22	when he **d** the Horims from before them;	8045
	2:23	**d** them, and dwelt in their stead.)	8045
	2:34	**utterly d** the men, and the women, and	2763
	3: 6	we **utterly d** them, as we did unto Sihon	2763
	4: 3	the LORD thy God hath **d** them from	8045
	4:26	days upon it, but shall utterly be **d**.	8045+8045
	7:20	are left, and hide themselves from thee, be **d**.	6
	7:23	*with* a mighty destruction, until they be **d**.	8045
	7:24	stand before thee, until thou have **d** them.	8045
	9: 8	LORD was angry with you to have **d** you.	8045
	9:20	was very angry with Aaron to have **d** him:	8045
	11: 4	and *how* the LORD hath **d** them unto this day;	6
	12:30	after that they be **d** from before thee;	8045
	28:20	until thou be **d**, and until thou perish	8045
	28:24	it come down upon thee, until thou be **d**.	8045
	28:45	and overtake thee, till thou be **d**;	8045
	28:48	of iron upon thy neck, until he have **d** thee.	8045
	28:51	and the fruit of thy land, until thou be **d**:	8045
	28:51	or flocks of thy sheep, until he have **d** thee.	6
	28:61	LORD bring upon thee, until thou be **d**.	8045
	31: 4	and unto the land of them, whom he **d**.	8045
Jos	2:10	Sihon and Og, whom ye **utterly d**.	2763
	6:21	they **utterly d** all that *was* in the city,	2763
	8:26	until *he* had **utterly d** all the inhabitants of	2763
	10: 1	Joshua had taken Ai, and had **utterly d** it;	2763
	10:28	the king thereof he **utterly d**, them,	2763
	10:35	all the souls that *were* therein he **utterly d**	2763
	10:37	**d** it **utterly**, and all the souls that *were*	2763
	10:39	**utterly d** all the souls that *were* therein;	2763
	10:40	but **utterly d** all that breathed,	2763
	11:12	edge of the sword, *and* he **utterly d** them,	2763
	11:14	until they had **d** them, neither left they any	8045
	11:21	Joshua **d** them **utterly** with their cities.	2763
	23:15	until he have **d** you from off this good land	8045
	24: 8	their land; and I **d** them from before you.	8045
Jdg	1:17	that inhabited Zephath, and **utterly d** it:	2763
	4:24	until they had **d** Jabin king of Canaan.	3772
	6: 4	**d** the increase of the earth, till thou come	7843
	20:21	**d** *down* to the ground of the Israelites that	7843
	20:25	**d** *down* to the ground of the children of	7843
	20:35	the children of Israel **d** of the Benjamites	7843
	20:42	them which *came* out of the cities they **d** in	7843
	21:16	seeing the women are **d** out of Benjamin?	8045
	21:17	that a tribe be not **d** out of Israel.	4229
1Sa	5: 6	he **d** them, and smote them with emerods,	8074
	15: 8	**utterly d** all the people with the edge of	2763
	15: 9	*was* vile and refuse, that they **d utterly**.	2763
	15:15	thy God; and the rest we have **utterly d**.	2763
	15:20	and have **utterly d** the Amalekites.	2763
	15:21	**things** which should have been **utterly d**,	2764
2Sa	11: 1	they **d** the children of Ammon, and	7843
	21: 5	that devised against us *that* we should be **d**	8045
	22:38	I have pursued mine enemies, and **d** them;	8045
	24:16	said to the angel that **d** the people, *It is*	7843
1Ki	15:13	Asa **d** her idol, and burnt *it* by the brook	3772
	15:29	until *he* had **d** him, according unto	8045
2Ki	10:17	till *he* had **d** him, according to the saying of	8045
	10:28	Thus Jehu **d** Baal out of Israel.	8045
	11: 1	was dead, she arose and **d** all the seed royal.	6
	13: 7	for the king of Syria had **d** them, and had made	6
	19:12	delivered them which my fathers have **d**;	7843
	19:17	the kings of Assyria have **d** the nations and	2717
	19:18	wood and stone: therefore they have **d** them.	6
	21: 3	high places which Hezekiah his father had **d**;	6
	21: 9	the LORD **d** before the children of Israel.	8045
1Ch	4:41	**d** them **utterly** unto this day, and dwelt in	2763
	5:25	of the land, whom God **d** before them.	8045
	20: 1	And Joab smote Rabbah, and **d** it.	2040
	21:12	or three months to be **d** before thy foes,	5595
	21:15	said to the angel that **d**, *It is* enough,	7843
2Ch	14:13	for they were **d** before the LORD, and	7665

D

2Ch 15: 6 nation was **d** of nation, and city of city: 3807
20:10 but they turned from them, and **d** them not; 8045
22:10 **d** all the seed royal of the house of Judah. 1696
24:23 **d** all the princes of the people from among 7843
31: 1 until *they* had **utterly d** *them all.* Then all 3615
32:14 of those nations that my fathers **utterly d**, 2763
33: 9 whom the LORD had **d** before 8045
34:11 the houses which the kings of Judah had **d**. 7843
36:19 and **d** all the goodly vessels thereof. 7843
Ezr 4:15 of old time: for which *cause* was this city **d**. 2718
5:12 who **d** this house, and carried the people 5642
Est 3: 9 the king, let it be written that they may be **d**: 6
4:14 but thou and thy father's house shall be **d**: 6
7: 4 to be **d**, to be slain, and to perish. 8045
9: 6 palace the Jews slew and **d** five hundred men. 6
9:12 and **d** five hundred men in Shushan the palace, 6
Job 4:20 They are **d** from morning to evening: 3807
19:10 He hath **d** me on every side, and I am gone: 5422
34:25 *them* in the night, so that they are **d**. 1792
Ps 9: 5 rebuked the heathen, thou hast **d** the wicked, 6
9: 6 thou hast **d** cities; their memorial is 5428
11: 3 If the foundations be **d**, what can 2040
37:38 the transgressors shall be **d** together: 8045
73:27 thou hast **d** all them that go a whoring from 6789
78:38 forgave *their* iniquity, and **d** *them* not: 7843
78:45 devoured them; and frogs, which **d** them. 7843
78:47 He **d** their vines with hail, and 2026
92: 7 *it is* that they shall be **d** for ever: 8045
137: 8 O daughter of Babylon, who art *to be* **d**; 7703
Pr 13:13 Whoso despiseth the word shall be **d**: 2254
13:20 but a companion of fools shall be **d**. 7489
13:23 but there is *that is* **d** for want of judgment. 5595
29: 1 shall suddenly be **d**, and that without 7665
Isa 9:16 to err; and *they that are* led of them *are* **d**. 1104
10:27 the yoke shall be **d** because of 2254
14:17 as a wilderness, and **d** the cities thereof; 2040
14:20 because thou hast **d** thy land, *and* slain thy 7843
26:14 therefore hast thou visited and **d** them, and 8045
34: 2 he hath **utterly d** them, he hath delivered 2763
37:12 delivered them which my fathers have **d**, 7843
37:19 wood and stone: therefore they have **d** them. 6
48:19 his name should not have been cut off nor **d** 8045
Jer 12:10 Many pastors have **d** my vineyard, 7843
22:20 from the passages: for all thy lovers are **d**. 7665
48: 4 Moab is **d**; her little ones have caused a cry 7665
48: 8 also shall perish, and the plain shall be **d**, 8045
48:42 Moab shall be **d** from *being* a people, 8045
51: 8 Babylon is suddenly fallen and **d**: howl for 7665
51:55 and **d** out of her the great voice; 6
La 2: 5 he hath **d** his strong holds, and 7843
2: 6 he hath **d** his places of the assembly: 7843
2: 9 into the ground; he hath **d** and broken her bars: 6
Eze 26:17 say to thee, How art thou **d**, *that wast* inhabited 6
27:32 like the **d** in the midst of the sea? 1822
30: 8 and *when* all her helpers shall be **d**. 7665
32:12 and all the multitude thereof shall be **d**. 8045
Da 2:44 set up a kingdom, which shall never be **d**: 2255
6:26 his kingdom *that* which shall not be **d**, and 2255
7:11 and his body **d**, and given to the burning flame. 7
7:14 and his kingdom *that* which shall not be **d**. 2255
11:20 within few days he shall be **d**, neither in 7665
Hos 4: 6 My people are **d** for lack of knowledge, 1820
10: 8 also of Aven, the sin of Israel, shall be **d**: 8045
13: 9 O Israel, *thou* hast **d** thyself; but in me *is* 7843
Am 2: 9 Yet **d** I the Amorite before them, 8045
2: 9 yet I **d** his fruit from above, and his roots 8045
Zep 3: 6 their cities are **d**, so that there is no man, 6658
Mt 22: 7 and **d** those murderers, and burnt up their *622*
Lk 17:27 the ark, and the flood came, and **d** *them* all. *622*
17:29 and brimstone from heaven, and **d** *them* all. *622*
Ac 3:23 shall be **d** from among the people. *1842*
9:21 Is not this he that **d** them which called on *4199*
13:19 And when he had **d** seven nations in *2507*
19:27 and her magnificence should be **d**, *2507*
Ro 6: 6 with *him,* that the body of sin might be **d**, *2673*
1Co 10: 9 them also tempted, and were **d** of serpents. *622*
10:10 also murmured, and were **d** of the destroyer. *622*
15:26 The last enemy *that* shall be **d** *is* death. *2673*
2Co 4: 9 but not forsaken; cast down, but not **d**; *622*
Gal 1:23 now preacheth the faith which once he **d**. *4199*
2:18 For if I build again the *things* which I **d**, *2647*
Heb 11:28 lest he that **d** the firstborn should touch *3645*
2Pe 2:12 brute beasts, made to be taken and **d**, *5356*
Jude 1: 5 of Egypt, afterward **d** them that believed not. *622*

Rev 8: 9 died; and the third *part* of the ships were **d**. *1311*

DESTROYER (7) [DESTROY]

Ex 12:23 will not suffer the **d** to come in unto your 7843
Jdg 16:24 the **d** of our country, which slew many of 2717
Job 15:21 in prosperity the **d** shall come *upon* him. 7703
Ps 17: 4 lips I have kept *me from* the paths of the **d**. 6530
Pr 28:24 the same *is* the companion of a **d**. 376+4889
Jer 4: 7 and the **d** of the Gentiles is on his way; 7843
1Co 10:10 and were destroyed of the **d**. *3644*

DESTROYERS (4) [DESTROY]

Job 33:22 near unto the grave, and his life to the **d**. 4191
Isa 49:17 thy **d** and they that made thee waste shall 2040
Jer 22: 7 I will prepare **d** against thee, every one 7843
50:11 O ye **d** of mine heritage, because ye are 8154

DESTROYEST (4) [DESTROY]

Job 14:19 dust of the earth; and thou **d** the hope of man. 6
Jer 51:25 saith the LORD, which **d** all the earth: 7843
Mt 27:40 *Thou* that **d** the temple, and buildest *it* in *2647*
Mk 15:29 *thou* that **d** the temple, and buildest *it* in *2647*

DESTROYETH (8) [DESTROY]

Dt 8:20 As the nations which the LORD **d** before your 6
Job 9:22 therefore I said *it,* He **d** the perfect and 3615
12:23 He increaseth the nations, and **d** them: 6
Pr 6:32 he *that* doeth it **d** his own soul. 7843
11: 9 A hypocrite with *his* mouth **d** his 7843
31: 3 nor thy ways to *that which* **d** kings. 4229
Ecc 7: 7 maketh a wise *man* mad; and a gift **d** the heart. 6
9:18 weapons of war: but one sinner **d** much good. 6

DESTROYING (14) [DESTROY]

Dt 3: 6 **utterly d** the men, women, and children, 2763
13:15 **d** it **utterly**, and all that *is* therein, and 2763
Jos 11:11 **utterly d** *them:* there was not any left to 2763
2Ki 19:11 have done to all lands, by **d** them **utterly**: 2763
1Ch 21:12 the angel of the LORD **d** throughout all 7843
21:15 as *he* was **d**, the LORD beheld, and 7843
Isa 28: 2 *which* as a tempest of hail *and* a **d** storm, 6986
37:11 have done to all lands by **d** them **utterly**; 2763
Jer 2:30 hath devoured your prophets, like a **d** lion. 7843
51: 1 of them that rise up against me, a **d** wind; 7843
51:25 Behold, I *am* against thee, O **d** mountain, 4889
La 2: 8 he hath not withdrawn his hand from **d**: 1104
Eze 9: 1 even every man *with* his **d** weapon in his 4892
20:17 Nevertheless mine eye spared them from **d** 7843

DESTRUCTION (94) [DESTROY]

Dt 7:23 shall destroy them *with* a mighty **d**, 4103
32:24 with burning heat, and with bitter **d**: 6986
1Sa 5: 9 was against the city *with* a very great **d**: 4103
5:11 for there was a deadly **d** throughout all 4103
1Ki 20:42 hand a man whom I **appointed to utter d**, 2764
2Ch 22: 4 after the death of his father to his **d**. 4889
22: 7 the **d** of Ahaziah was of God by coming to 8395
26:16 was strong, his heart was lifted up to *his* **d**: 7843
Est 8: 6 how can I endure to see the **d** of my kindred? 13
9: 5 **d**, and did what they would unto those that 12
Job 5:21 neither shalt thou be afraid of **d** when it 7701
5:22 At **d** and famine thou shalt laugh: 7701
18:12 and **d** *shall be* ready at his side. 343
21:17 *how oft* cometh their **d** upon them! 343
21:20 His eyes shall see his **d**, and he shall drink 3589
21:30 That the wicked is reserved to the day of **d**? 343
26: 6 *is* naked before him, and **d** hath no covering. 11
28:22 **D** and death say, We have heard the fame 11
30:12 they raise up against me the ways of their **d**. 343
30:24 hand to the grave, though *they* cry in his **d**. 6365
31: 3 *Is* not **d** to the wicked? and a strange 343
31:12 For it *is* a fire *that* consumeth to **d**, and 11
31:23 For **d** from God *was* a terror to me, and 343
31:29 If I rejoiced at the **d** of him that hated me, 6365
Ps 35: 8 Let **d** come upon him at unawares; and 7722
35: 8 catch himself: into that *very* **d** let him fall. 7722
55:23 shalt bring them down into the pit of **d**: 7845
73:18 *places:* thou castedst them down into **d**. 4876
88:11 in the grave? *or* thy faithfulness in **d**? 11
90: 3 Thou turnest man to **d**; and sayest, Return, 1793
91: 6 *nor* for the **d** *that* wasteth at noonday. 6986
103: 4 Who redeemeth thy life from **d**; 7845
Pr 1:27 and your **d** cometh as a whirlwind; 343
10:14 but the mouth of the foolish *is* near **d**. 4288
10:15 the **d** of the poor *is* their poverty. 4288

Pr 10:29 but **d** *shall be* to the workers of iniquity. 4288
13: 3 he that openeth wide his lips shall have **d**. 4288
14:28 in the want of people *is* the **d** of the prince. 4288
15:11 Hell and **d** *are* before the LORD: how much 11
16:18 Pride *goeth* before **d**, and a haughty spirit 7667
17:19 *and* he that exalteth his gate seeketh **d**. 7667
18: 7 A fool's mouth *is* his **d**, and his lips *are* 4288
18:12 Before **d** the heart of man is haughty, and 7667
21:15 but **d** *shall be* to the workers of iniquity. 4288
24: 2 For their heart studieth **d**, and their lips talk 7701
27:20 Hell and **d** are never full; so the eyes of man 10
31: 8 of all such as are **appointed to d**. 1121+2475
Isa 1:28 the **d** of the transgressors and of the sinners 7667
10:25 shall cease, and mine anger in their **d**. 8399
13: 6 it shall come as a **d** from the Almighty. 7701
14:23 I will sweep it with the besom of **d**, 8045
15: 5 of Horonaim they shall raise up a cry of **d**. 7667
19:18 of hosts: one shall be called, The city of **d**. 2041
24:12 and the gate is smitten *with* **d**. 7591
49:19 thy desolate places, and the land of thy **d**, 2035
51:19 and **d**, and the famine, and the sword: 7667
59: 7 of iniquity; wasting and **d** are in their paths. 7667
60:18 thy land, wasting nor **d** within thy borders; 7667
Jer 4: 6 bring evil from the north, and a great **d**. 7667
4:20 **D** upon destruction is cried; for the whole 7667
4:20 Destruction upon **d** is cried; for the whole 7667
6: 1 evil appeareth out of the north, and great **d**. 7667
17:18 of evil, and destroy them *with* double **d**. 7670
46:20 *is like* a very fair heifer, *but* **d** cometh; 7171
48: 3 *be* from Horonaim, spoiling and great **d**. 7667
48: 5 the enemies have heard a cry of **d**. 7667
50:22 of battle *is* in the land, and of great **d**. 7667
51:54 and great **d** from the land of the Chaldeans: 7667
La 2:11 for the **d** of the daughter of my people; 7667
3:47 a snare is come upon us, desolation and **d**. 7667
3:48 for the **d** of the daughter of my people. 7667
4:10 they were their meat in the **d** of 7667
Eze 5:16 which shall be for *their* **d**, *and* which I will 4889
7:25 **D** cometh; and they shall seek peace, and 7089
32: 9 when I shall bring thy **d** among the nations, 7667
Hos 7:13 **d** unto them! because they have 7701
9: 6 For lo, they are gone because of **d**: 7701
13:14 be thy plagues; O grave, I will be thy **d**: 6987
Joel 1:15 and as a **d** from the Almighty shall it come. 7701
Ob 1:12 over the children of Judah in the day of their **d**; 6
Mic 2:10 it shall destroy *you*, even *with* a sore **d**. 2256
Zec 14:11 in it, and there shall be no more **utter d**; 2764
Mt 7:13 that leadeth to **d**, and many there be which *684*
Ro 3:16 **D** and misery *are* in their ways: *4938*
9:22 longsuffering *the* vessels of wrath fitted to **d**: *684*
1Co 5: 5 To deliver such a one unto Satan for the **d** *3639*
2Co 10: 8 and not for your **d**, I should not be *2506*
13:10 hath given me to edification, and not to **d**. *2506*
Php 3:19 Whose end *is* **d**, whose God *is their* belly, *684*
1Th 5: 3 then sudden **d** cometh upon them, as travail *3639*
2Th 1: 9 Who shall be punished *with* everlasting **d** *3639*
1Ti 6: 9 which drown men in **d** and perdition. *3639*
2Pe 2: 1 and bring upon themselves swift **d**. *684*
3:16 also the other scriptures, unto their own **d**. *684*

DESTRUCTIONS (3) [DESTROY]
Ps 9: 6 thou enemy, **d** are come to a perpetual end: 2723
35:17 rescue my soul from their **d**, my darling 7722
107:20 and delivered *them* from their **d**. 7825

DETAIN (2) [DETAINED]
Jdg 13:15 I pray thee, let us **d** thee, until we shall 6113
13:16 Though thou **d** me, I will not eat of thy 6113

DETAINED (1) [DETAIN]
1Sa 21: 7 *was* there that day, **d** before the LORD; 6113

DETER See FORBAD

DETERMINATE (1) [DETERMINE]
Ac 2:23 being delivered by the **d** counsel and *3724*

DETERMINATION (1) [DETERMINE]
Zep 3: 8 for my **d** *is* to gather the nations, that I may 4941

DETERMINE (1) [DETERMINATE, DETERMINATION, DETERMINED]
Ex 21:22 upon him; and he shall pay as the judges **d**. NIH

DETERMINED (30) [DETERMINE]
1Sa 20: 7 *then* be sure that evil is **d** by him. 3615
20: 9 for if I knew certainly that evil were **d** by 3615
20:33 whereby Jonathan knew that it was **d** of his 3617
25:17 for evil is **d** against our master, and 3615
2Sa 13:32 **d** from the day that he forced his 1961+7760
2Ch 2: 1 Solomon **d** to build a house for the name of 559
25:16 I know that God hath **d** to destroy thee, 3289
Est 7: 7 for he saw that there was evil **d** against him 3615
Job 14: 5 Seeing his days *are* **d**, the number of his 2782
Isa 10:23 even **d**, *in* the midst of all *the land*. 2782
19:17 of hosts, which he hath **d** against it. 3289
28:22 even **d** upon the whole earth. 2782
Da 9:24 Seventy weeks are **d** upon thy people and 2852
9:26 unto the end of the war desolations *are* **d**. 2782
9:27 that **d** shall be poured upon the desolate. 2782
11:36 for that that is **d** shall be done. 2782
Lk 22:22 truly the Son of man goeth, as it was **d**: *3724*
Ac 3:13 of Pilate, when he was **d** to let *him* go. *2919*
4:28 and thy counsel **d before** to be done. *4309*
11:29 **d** to send relief unto the brethren which *3724*
15: 2 they **d** that Paul and Barnabas, and *5021*
15:37 And Barnabas **d** to take with *them* John, *1011*
17:26 and hath **d** the times before appointed, and *3724*
19:39 *matters*, it shall be **d** in a lawful assembly. *1956*
20:16 For Paul had **d** to sail by Ephesus, because *2919*
25:25 appealed to Augustus, I have **d** to send him. *2919*
27: 1 And when it was **d** that we should sail into *2919*
1Co 2: 2 For I **d** not to know any *thing* among you, *2919*
2Co 2: 1 But I **d** this with myself, that *I* would not *2919*
Tit 3:12 to Nicopolis: for I have **d** there to winter. *2919*

DETEST (1) [DETESTABLE]
Dt 7:26 *but* thou shalt **utterly d** it, and 8262+8262

DETESTABLE (6) [DETEST]
Jer 16:18 inheritance with the carcases of their **d** 8251
Eze 5:11 defiled my sanctuary with all thy **d things**, 8251
7:20 *and* of their **d things** therein: 8251
11:18 they shall take away all the **d things** 8251
11:21 walketh after the heart of their **d things** 8251
37:23 nor with their **d things**, nor with any of 8251

DEUEL (4) [REUEL]
Nu 1:14 Of Gad; Eliasaph the son of **D**. 1845
7:42 On the sixth day Eliasaph the son of **D**, 1845
7:47 *was* the offering of Eliasaph the son of **D**. 1845
10:20 children of Gad *was* Eliasaph the son of **D**. 1845

DEVICE (10) [DEVICES]
2Ch 2:14 to find out every **d** which shall be put to 4284
Est 8: 3 his **d** that he had devised against the Jews. 4284
9:25 he commanded by letters *that* his wicked **d**, 4284
Ps 21:11 they imagined a **mischievous d**, 4209
140: 8 further not his **wicked d**; *lest* they exalt 2162
Ecc 9:10 nor **d**, nor knowledge, nor wisdom, in 2808
Jer 18:11 against you, and devise a **d** against you: 4284
51:11 for his **d** *is* against Babylon, to destroy it; 4209
La 3:62 and their **d** against me all the day. 1902
Ac 17:29 silver, or stone, graven by art and man's **d**. *1761*

DEVICES (16) [DEVICE]
Job 5:12 He disappointeth the **d** of the crafty, so 4284
21:27 the **d** *which* ye wrongfully imagine against 4209
Ps 10: 2 let them be taken in the **d** that they have 4209
33:10 he maketh the **d** of the people of none 4284
37: 7 of the man who bringeth **wicked d** to pass. 4209
Pr 1:31 own way, and be filled with their own **d**. 4156
12: 2 but a man of **wicked d** will he condemn. 4209
14:17 and a man of **wicked d** is hated. 4209
19:21 *There are* many **d** in a man's heart; 4284
Isa 32: 7 he deviseth **wicked d** to destroy the poor 2154
Jer 11:19 I knew not that they had devised **d** against 4284
18:12 we will walk after our own **d**, and we will 4284
18:18 Come, and let us devise **d** against Jeremiah; 4284
Da 11:24 he shall forecast his **d** against the strong 4284
11:25 for they shall forecast **d** against him. 4284
2Co 2:11 of us: for we are not ignorant of his **d**. *3540*

DEVIL (61) [DEVILISH, DEVILS]
Mt 4: 1 into the wilderness to be tempted of the **d**. *1228*
4: 5 Then the **d** taketh him *up* into the holy city, *1228*
4: 8 the **d** taketh him *up* into an exceeding high *1228*
4:11 Then the **d** leaveth him, and behold, *1228*

D

Mt 9:32 to him a dumb man **possessed with a d**. *1139*
9:33 And when the **d** was cast out, the dumb *1140*
11:18 nor drinking, and they say, He hath a **d**. *1140*
12:22 brought unto him **one possessed with a d**, *1139*
13:39 The enemy that sowed them is the **d**; *1228*
15:22 my daughter is grievously **vexed with a d**. *1139*
17:18 And Jesus rebuked the **d**; and he departed *1140*
25:41 prepared for the **d** and his angels: *1228*
Mk 5:15 and see him that was **possessed with the d**, *1139*
5:16 to him that was **possessed with the d**, *1139*
5:18 he that had been **possessed with the d** *1139*
7:26 would cast forth the **d** out of her daughter. *1140*
7:29 thy way; the **d** is gone out of thy daughter. *1140*
7:30 she found the **d** gone out, and *her* daughter *1140*
Lk 4: 2 Being forty days tempted of the **d**. And in *1228*
4: 3 And the **d** said unto him, If thou be the Son *1228*
4: 5 And the **d**, taking him up into a high *1228*
4: 6 And the **d** said unto him, All this power *1228*
4:13 And when the **d** had ended all *1228*
4:33 which had a spirit of an unclean **d**, and *1140*
4:35 And when the **d** had thrown him in *1140*
7:33 nor drinking wine; and ye say, He hath a **d**. *1140*
8:12 then cometh the **d**, and taketh away *1228*
8:29 was driven of the **d** into the wilderness.) *1142*
9:42 the **d** threw him down, and tare *him*. And *1140*
11:14 And he was casting out a **d**, and it was *1140*
11:14 when the **d** was gone out, the dumb spake; *1140*
Jn 6:70 I chosen you twelve, and one of you is a **d**? *1228*
7:20 people answered and said, Thou hast a **d**: *1140*
8:44 Ye are of *your* father the **d**, and the lusts of *1228*
8:48 well that thou art a Samaritan, and hast a **d**? *1140*
8:49 Jesus answered, I have not a **d**; but *1140*
8:52 unto him, Now we know that thou hast a **d**. *1140*
10:20 of them said, He hath a **d**, and is mad; *1140*
10:21 are not the words of him that **hath a d**. *1139*
10:21 a devil. Can a **d** open the eyes of the blind? *1140*
13: 2 the **d** having now put into the heart of Judas *1228*
Ac 10:38 healing all that were oppressed of the **d**; *1228*
13:10 and all mischief, *thou* child of the **d**, *1228*
Eph 4:27 Neither give place to the **d**. *1228*
6:11 be able to stand against the wiles of the **d**. *1228*
1Ti 3: 6 he fall into the condemnation of the **d**. *1228*
3: 7 he fall into reproach and the snare of the **d**. *1228*
2Ti 2:26 themselves out of the snare of the **d**, *1228*
Heb 2:14 that had the power of death, that is, the **d**; *1228*
Jas 4: 7 Resist the **d**, and he will flee from you. *1228*
1Pe 5: 8 because your adversary the **d**, as a roaring *1228*
1Jn 3: 8 He that committeth sin is of the **d**; for *1228*
3: 8 for the **d** sinneth from the beginning. *1228*
3: 8 that he might destroy the works of the **d**. *1228*
3:10 God are manifest, and the children of the **d**: *1228*
Jude 1: 9 when contending with the **d** he disputed *1228*
Rev 2:10 the **d** shall cast *some* of you into prison, *1228*
12: 9 called the **d**, and Satan, which deceiveth *1228*
12:12 for the **d** is come down unto you, *1228*
20: 2 which is the **d**, and Satan, and bound him a *1228*
20:10 And the **d** that deceived them was cast into *1228*

DEVILISH (1) [DEVIL]

Jas 3:15 not from above, but *is* earthly, sensual, **d**. *1141*

DEVILS (55) [DEVIL]

Lev 17: 7 shall no more offer their sacrifices unto **d**, 8163
Dt 32:17 They sacrificed unto **d**, not *to* God; *to* gods 7700
2Ch 11:15 for the **d**, and for the calves which he had 8163
Ps 106:37 their sons and their daughters unto **d**, 7700
Mt 4:24 and those which were **possessed with d**, *1139*
7:22 thy name? and in thy name have cast out **d**? *1140*
8:16 unto him many *that were* **possessed with d**: *1139*
8:28 there met him two **possessed with d**, *1139*
8:31 So the **d** besought him, saying, If thou cast *1142*
8:33 was befallen to the **possessed of the d**. *1139*
9:34 He casteth out the **d** through the prince of *1140*
9:34 out the devils through the prince of the **d**. *1140*
10: 8 the lepers, raise the dead, cast out **d**: *1140*
12:24 This *fellow* doth not cast out **d**, but by *1140*
12:24 but by Beelzebub the prince of the **d**. *1140*
12:27 And if I by Beelzebub cast out **d**, by whom *1140*
12:28 But if I cast out **d** by the Spirit of God, then *1140*
Mk 1:32 and them that were **possessed with d**. *1139*
1:34 of divers diseases, and cast out many **d**; *1140*
1:34 and suffered not the **d** to speak, because *1140*
1:39 throughout all Galilee, and cast out **d**. *1140*
3:15 power to heal sicknesses, and to cast out **d**: *1140*
3:22 by the prince of the **d** casteth he out devils. *1140*
3:22 by the prince of the devils casteth he out **d**. *1140*
5:12 And all the **d** besought him, saying, *1142*
6:13 And they cast out many **d**, and *1140*
9:38 we saw one casting out **d** in thy name, and *1140*
16: 9 out of whom he had cast seven **d**. *1140*
16:17 In my name shall they cast out **d**; they shall *1140*
Lk 4:41 And **d** also came out of many, crying out, *1140*
8: 2 out of whom went seven **d**, *1140*
8:27 which had **d** long time, and ware no *1140*
8:30 because many **d** were entered into him. *1140*
8:33 Then went the **d** out of the man, and *1140*
8:35 the man, out of whom the **d** were departed, *1140*
8:36 he that was **possessed of the d** was healed. *1139*
8:38 Now the man out of whom the **d** were *1140*
9: 1 gave them power and authority over all **d**, *1140*
9:49 we saw one casting out **d** in thy name; *1140*
10:17 even the **d** are subject unto us through thy *1140*
11:15 He casteth out **d** through Beelzebub *1140*
11:15 devils through Beelzebub the chief of the **d**. *1140*
11:18 ye say that I cast out **d** through Beelzebub. *1140*
11:19 And if I by Beelzebub cast out **d**, by whom *1140*
11:20 But if I with the finger of God cast out **d**, *1140*
13:32 I cast out **d**, and I do cures to day and *1140*
1Co 10:20 they sacrifice to **d**, and not to God: *1140*
10:20 not that ye should have fellowship with **d**. *1140*
10:21 drink the cup of the Lord, and the cup of **d**: *1140*
10:21 of the Lord's table, and of the table of **d**. *1140*
1Ti 4: 1 heed to seducing spirits, and doctrines of **d**; *1140*
Jas 2:19 doest well: the **d** also believe, and tremble. *1140*
Rev 9:20 that they should not worship **d**, and idols of *1140*
16:14 For they are the spirits of **d**, working *1142*
18: 2 is fallen, and is become the habitation of **d**, *1142*

DEVIOUS See FROWARD

DEVISE (16) [DEVISED, DEVISETH]

Ex 31: 4 To **d** cunning works, to work in gold, and 2803
35:32 to **d** curious works, to work in gold, and 2803
35:35 and of **those that d cunning work**. 2803+4284
2Sa 14:14 yet doth he **d** means, that *his* banished be 2803
Ps 35: 4 and brought to confusion that **d** my hurt. 2803
35:20 they **d** deceitful matters against *them that* 2803
41: 7 against me: against me do they **d** my hurt. 2803
Pr 3:29 **D** not evil against thy neighbour, seeing he 2790
14:22 Do they not err that **d** evil? but mercy and 2790
14:22 and truth *shall be to* them that **d** good. 2790
16:30 He shutteth his eyes to **d** froward things: 2803
Jer 18:11 against you, and **d** a device against you: 2803
18:18 and let us **d** devices against Jeremiah; 2803
Eze 11: 2 these *are* the men that **d** mischief, and give 2803
Mic 2: 1 Woe to them that **d** iniquity, and work evil 2803
2: 3 Behold, against this family do I **d** an evil, 2803

DEVISED (12) [DEVISE]

2Sa 21: 5 that **d** against us *that* we should be 1819
1Ki 12:33 *even* in the month which he had **d** of his own 908
Est 8: 3 his device that he had **d** against the Jews. 2803
8: 5 let it be written to reverse the letters **d** by 4284
9:24 had **d** against the Jews to destroy them, and 2803
9:25 which he **d** against the Jews, should return 2803
Ps 31:13 against me, they **d** to take away my life. 2161
Jer 11:19 I knew not that they had **d** devices against 2803
48: 2 in Heshbon they have **d** evil against it; 2803
51:12 for the LORD hath both **d** and done that 2161
La 2:17 LORD hath done *that* which he had **d**; 2161
2Pe 1:16 For we have not followed **cunningly d** *4679*

DEVISETH (8) [DEVISE]

Ps 36: 4 He **d** mischief upon his bed; he setteth 2803
52: 2 Thy tongue **d** mischiefs; like a sharp rasor, 2803
Pr 6:14 *is* in his heart, he **d** mischief continually; 2790
6:18 A heart that **d** wicked imaginations, 2790
16: 9 A man's heart **d** his way: but the LORD 2803
24: 8 He that **d** to do evil shall be called a 2803
Isa 32: 7 he **d** wicked devices to destroy the poor 3289
32: 8 the liberal **d** liberal *things;* and by liberal 3289

DEVOTE (1) [DEVOTED, DEVOTIONS]

Lev 27:28 that a man shall **d** unto the LORD of all 2763

DEVOTED (7) [DEVOTE]

Lev 27:21 shall be holy unto the LORD, as a field **d**; 2764
27:28 Notwithstanding no **d thing**, that a man 2764
27:28 every **d thing** *is* most holy unto 2764

Lev 27:29 None **d**, which shall be devoted of men, 2764
27:29 None devoted, which shall be **d** of men, 2763
Nu 18:14 Every thing **d** in Israel shall be thine. 2764
Ps 119:38 word unto thy servant, who *is* **d** to thy fear. NIH

DEVOTIONS (1) [DEVOTE]
Ac 17:23 For as I passed by, and beheld your **d**, *4574*

DEVOUR (71) [DEVOURED, DEVOURER, DEVOUREST, DEVOURETH, DEVOURING]
Ge 49:27 in the morning he shall **d** the prey, and 398
Dt 32:42 with blood, and my sword shall **d** flesh; 398
Jdg 9:15 of the bramble, and **d** the cedars of Lebanon. 398
9:20 **d** the men of Shechem, and the house of 398
9:20 from the house of Millo, and **d** Abimelech. 398
2Sa 2:26 to Joab, and said, Shall the sword **d** for ever? 398
2Ch 7:13 or if I command the locusts to **d** the land, or 398
Job 18:13 It shall **d** the strength of his skin: *even* 398
18:13 *even* the firstborn of death shall **d** his 398
Ps 21:9 up in his wrath, and the fire shall **d** them. 398
50:3 a fire shall **d** before him, and it shall be very 398
80:13 and the wild beast of the field doth **d** it. 7462
Pr 30:14 to **d** the poor from off the earth, and 398
Isa 1:7 strangers **d** it in your presence, and *it is* 398
9:12 they shall **d** Israel with open mouth. 398
9:18 it shall **d** the briers and thorns, and 398
10:17 it shall burn and **d** his thorns and his briers 398
26:11 yea, the fire of thine enemies shall **d** them. 398
31:8 the sword, not of a mean man, shall **d** him: 398
33:11 your breath, *as* fire, shall **d** you. 398
42:14 I will destroy and **d** at once. 7602
56:9 All ye beasts of the field, come to **d**, *yea,* all 398
Jer 2:3 all that **d** him shall offend; evil shall come 398
5:14 and this people wood, and it shall **d** them. 398
12:9 all the beasts of the field, come to **d**. 402
12:12 for the sword of the LORD *shall* **d** from 398
15:3 and the beasts of the earth, to **d** and destroy. 398
17:27 it shall **d** the palaces of Jerusalem, and 398
21:14 and it shall **d** all things round about it. 398
30:16 Therefore all they that **d** thee shall be 398
46:10 the sword shall **d**, and it shall be satiate and 398
46:14 for the sword shall **d** round about thee. 398
48:45 shall **d** the corner of Moab, and the crown of 398
50:32 his cities, and it shall **d** all round about him. 398
Eze 7:15 the city, famine and pestilence shall **d** him. 398
15:7 from *one* fire, and *another* fire shall **d** them; 398
20:47 it shall **d** every green tree in thee, and 398
23:37 to pass for them through *the fire,* to **d** *them.* 402
28:18 it shall **d** thee, and I will bring thee to ashes 398
34:28 neither shall the beast of the land **d** them; 398
36:14 Therefore thou shalt **d** men no more, 398
Da 7:5 they said thus unto it, Arise, **d** much flesh. 399
7:23 shall **d** the whole earth, and shall tread it 399
Hos 5:7 now shall a month **d** them with their 398
8:14 his cities, and it shall **d** the palaces thereof. 398
11:6 and **d** *them,* because of their own counsels. 398
13:8 and there will I **d** them like a lion: 398
Am 1:4 which shall **d** the palaces of Ben-hadad. 398
1:7 of Gaza, which shall **d** the palaces thereof: 398
1:10 of Tyrus, which shall **d** the palaces thereof. 398
1:12 which shall **d** the palaces of Bozrah. 398
1:14 it shall **d** the palaces thereof, with shouting 398
2:2 and it shall **d** the palaces of Kerioth: 398
2:5 and it shall **d** the palaces of Jerusalem. 398
5:6 **d** *it,* and *there be* none to quench *it* in 398
Ob 1:18 and they shall kindle in them, and **d** them; 398
Na 2:13 and the sword shall **d** thy young lions: 398
3:13 unto thine enemies: the fire shall **d** thy bars. 398
3:15 There shall the fire **d** thee; the sword shall 398
Hab 3:14 their rejoicing *was* as to **d** the poor secretly. 398
Zec 9:15 they shall **d**, and subdue *with* sling stones; 398
11:1 O Lebanon, that the fire may **d** thy cedars. 398
12:6 they shall **d** all the people round about, 398
Mt 23:14 for ye **d** widows' houses, and for a pretence *2719*
Mk 12:40 Which **d** widows' houses, and for a *2719*
Lk 20:47 Which **d** widows' houses, and for a shew *2719*
2Co 11:20 if a man **d** *you,* if a man take *of you,* if a *2719*
Gal 5:15 But if ye bite and **d** one another, take heed *2719*
Heb 10:27 which shall **d** the adversaries. *2068*
1Pe 5:8 walketh about, seeking whom he may **d**: *2666*
Rev 12:4 for to **d** her child as soon as it was born. *2719*

DEVOURED (53) [DEVOUR]
Ge 31:15 and hath **quite d** also our money. 398+398
37:20 and we will say, *Some* evil beast hath **d** him: 398
37:33 *It is* my son's coat; an evil beast hath **d** him; 398
41:7 the seven thin ears **d** the seven rank and 1104
41:24 the thin ears **d** the seven good ears: 1104
Lev 10:2 **d** them, and they died before the LORD. 398
Nu 26:10 what time the fire **d** two hundred and 398
Dt 31:17 they shall be **d**, and many evils and 398
32:24 **d** with burning heat, and with bitter 3898
2Sa 18:8 the wood **d** more people that day than 398
18:8 more people that day than the sword **d**. 398
22:9 of his nostrils, and fire out of his mouth **d**: 398
Ps 18:8 of his nostrils, and fire out of his mouth **d**: 398
78:45 sorts *of flies* among them, which **d** them; 398
79:7 For they have **d** Jacob, and laid waste his 398
105:35 in their land, and **d** the fruit of their ground. 398
Isa 1:20 and rebel, ye shall be **d** *with* the sword: 398
24:6 Therefore hath the curse **d** the earth, and 398
Jer 2:30 your own sword hath **d** your prophets, like a 398
3:24 For shame hath **d** the labour of our fathers 398
8:16 and have **d** the land, and all that is in it; 398
10:25 **d** him, and consumed him, and have made 398
30:16 all they that devour thee shall be **d**; 398
50:7 All that found them have **d** them: and 398
50:17 first the king of Assyria hath **d** him; and last 398
51:34 Nebuchadrezzar the king of Babylon hath **d** 398
La 4:11 and it hath **d** the foundations thereof. 398
Eze 15:5 when the fire hath **d** it, and it is burned? 398
16:20 these hast thou sacrificed unto them to be **d**. 398
19:3 and it learned to catch the prey; it **d** men. 398
19:6 and learned to catch the prey, *and* **d** men. 398
19:14 *which* hath **d** her fruit, so that she hath no 398
22:25 they have **d** souls; they have taken 398
23:25 and thy residue shall be **d** by the fire. 398
33:27 open field will I give to the beasts to be **d**, 398
39:4 and *to* the beasts of the field to be **d**. 402
Da 7:7 it **d** and brake in pieces, and stamped 399
7:19 *which* **d**, brake in pieces, and stamped 399
Hos 7:7 all hot as an oven, and have **d** their judges; 398
7:9 Strangers have **d** his strength, and 398
Joel 1:19 for the fire hath **d** the pastures of 398
1:20 the fire hath **d** the pastures of the wilderness. 398
Am 4:9 the palmerworm **d** *them:* yet have ye not 398
7:4 and it **d** the great deep, and did eat up a part. 398
Na 1:10 they shall be **d** as stubble fully dry. 398
Zep 1:18 the whole land shall be **d** by the fire of his 398
3:8 for all the earth shall be **d** with the fire of my 398
Zec 9:4 in the sea; and she shall be **d** with fire. 398
Mt 13:4 and the fowls came and **d** them **up**: *2719*
Mk 4:4 and the fowls of the air came and **d** it **up**. *2719*
Lk 8:5 trodden down, and the fowls of the air **d** it. *2719*
15:30 which hath **d** thy living with harlots, *2719*
Rev 20:9 down from God out of heaven, and **d** them. *2719*

DEVOURER (1) [DEVOUR]
Mal 3:11 I will rebuke the **d** for your sakes, and 398

DEVOUREST (1) [DEVOUR]
Eze 36:13 Thou *land* **d up** men, and hast bereaved thy 398

DEVOURETH (10) [DEVOUR]
2Sa 11:25 for the sword **d** one as well as another: 398
Pr 19:28 and the mouth of the wicked **d** iniquity. 1104
20:25 *It is* a snare to the man *who* **d** *that which is* 3216
Isa 5:24 Therefore as the fire **d** the stubble, and 398
La 2:3 like a flaming fire, *which* **d** round about. 398
Eze 15:4 the fire **d** both the ends of it, and the midst 398
Joel 2:3 A fire **d** before them; and behind them a 398
2:5 like the noise of a flame of fire that **d** 398
Hab 1:13 holdest thy tongue when the wicked **d** 1104
Rev 11:5 out of their mouth, and **d** their enemies: *2719*

DEVOURING (6) [DEVOUR]
Ex 24:17 **d** fire on the top of the mount in the eyes of 398
Ps 52:4 Thou lovest all **d** words, O thou deceitful 1105
Isa 29:6 and tempest, and the flame of **d** fire. 398
30:27 *of* indignation, and his tongue as a **d** fire: 398
30:30 *with* the flame of a **d** fire, *with* scattering, 398
33:14 Who among us shall dwell *with* the **d** fire? 398

DEVOUT (9)
Lk 2:25 and the same man *was* just and **d**, *2126*
Ac 2:5 **d** men, out of every nation under heaven. *2126*
8:2 And **d** men carried Stephen *to his burial,* *2126*
10:2 A **d** *man,* and one that feared God with all *2152*

Ac 10: 7 a **d** soldier of them that waited on him *2152*
13:50 But the Jews stirred up the **d** and *4576*
17: 4 and of the **d** Greeks a great multitude, and *4576*
17:17 and with the **d** *persons,* and in the market *4576*
22:12 one Ananias, a **d** man according to the law, *2152*

DEW (37)

Ge 27:28 Therefore God give thee of the **d** of heaven, 2919
27:39 and of the **d** of heaven from above; 2919
Ex 16:13 in the morning the **d** lay round about 2919
16:14 when the **d** that lay was gone up, behold, 2919
Nu 11: 9 when the **d** fell upon the camp in the night, 2919
Dt 32: 2 as the rain, my speech shall distil as the **d**, 2919
33:13 for the **d**, and for the deep that coucheth 2919
33:28 wine; also his heavens shall drop down **d**. 2919
Jdg 6:37 *and* if the **d** be on the fleece only, and *it be* 2919
6:38 wringed the **d** out of the fleece, a bowl full 2919
6:39 upon all the ground let there be **d**. 2919
6:40 and there was **d** on all the ground. 2919
2Sa 1:21 Ye mountains of Gilboa, *let there be* no **d**, 2919
17:12 we *will light* upon him as the **d** falleth on 2919
1Ki 17: 1 there shall not be **d** nor rain these years, but 2919
Job 29:19 and the **d** lay all night upon my branch. 2919
38:28 or who hath begotten the drops of **d**? 2919
Ps 110: 3 the morning: thou hast the **d** of thy youth. 2919
133: 3 As the **d** of Hermon, *and as the dew* that 2919
133: 3 *as the* **d** that descended upon the mountains NIH
Pr 3:20 broken up, and the clouds drop down the **d**. 2919
19:12 a lion; but his favour *is* as **d** upon the grass. 2919
SS 5: 2 for my head is filled *with* **d**, *and* my locks 2919
Isa 18: 4 *and* like a cloud of **d** in the heat of harvest. 2919
26:19 for thy **d** *is as* the dew of herbs, and 2919
26:19 for thy dew *is as* the **d** of herbs, and 2919
Da 4:15 let it be wet with the **d** of heaven, and 2920
4:23 let it be wet with the **d** of heaven, and 2920
4:25 they *shall* wet thee with the **d** of heaven, 2920
4:33 and his body was wet with the **d** of heaven, 2920
5:21 and his body was wet with the **d** of heaven; 2920
Hos 6: 4 and as the early **d** *it* goeth away. 2919
13: 3 and as the early **d** that passeth away, 2919
14: 5 I will be as the **d** unto Israel: he shall grow 2919
Mic 5: 7 of many people as a **d** from the LORD, 2919
Hag 1:10 the heaven over you is stayed from **d**, 2919
Zec 8:12 and the heavens shall give their **d**; 2919

DIADEM (4)

Job 29:14 my judgment *was* as a robe and a **d**. 6797
Isa 28: 5 for a **d** of beauty, unto the residue of his 6843
62: 3 and a royal **d** in the hand of thy God. 6797
Eze 21:26 Remove the **d**, and take off the crown: 4701

DIAL (2)

2Ki 20:11 by which it had gone down in the **d** of 4609
Isa 38: 8 which is gone down in the sun **d** of Ahaz, 4609

DIAMOND (4)

Ex 28:18 *shall be* an emerald, a sapphire, and a **d**. 3095
39:11 an emerald, a sapphire, and a **d**. 3095
Jer 17: 1 a pen of iron, *and* with the point of a **d**: 8068
Eze 28:13 topaz, and the **d**, the beryl, the onyx, and 3095

DIANA (5)

Ac 19:24 which made silver shrines for **D**, *735*
19:27 also that the temple of the great goddess **D** *735*
19:28 saying, Great *is* **D** of the Ephesians. *735*
19:34 hours cried out, Great *is* **D** of the Ephesians. *735*
19:35 is a worshipper of the great goddess **D**, *735*

DIBLAH See DIBLATH

DIBLAIM (1)

Hos 1: 3 he went and took Gomer the daughter of **D**; 1691

DIBLATH (1)

Eze 6:14 desolate than the wilderness toward **D**, 1689

DIBON (9) [DIBON-GAD]

Nu 21:30 Heshbon is perished even unto **D**, and 1769
32: 3 **D**, and Jazer, and Nimrah, and Heshbon, 1769
32:34 the children of Gad built **D**, and Ataroth, 1769
Jos 13: 9 and all the plain of Medeba unto **D**; 1769
13:17 **D**, and Bamoth-baal, and Beth-baal-meon, 1769
Ne 11:25 at **D**, and *in* the villages thereof, and 1769
Isa 15: 2 and *to* **D**, the high places, to weep: 1769
Jer 48:18 Thou daughter that dost inhabit **D**, 1769
48:22 upon **D**, and upon Nebo, and 1769

DIBON-GAD (2) [DIBON, GAD]

Nu 33:45 they departed from Iim, and pitched in **D**. 1769
33:46 they removed from **D**, and encamped in 1769

DIBRI (1)

Lev 24:11 the daughter of **D**, of the tribe of Dan:) 1704

DID (1006) [DO] See Index

DIDST (123) [DO] See Index

DIDYMUS (3)

Jn 11:16 Then said Thomas, which is called **D**, *1324*
20:24 But Thomas, one of the twelve, called **D**, *1324*
21: 2 and Thomas called **D**, and Nathanael of *1324*

DIE (321) [DEAD, DEADLY, DEADNESS, DEATH, DEATHS, DIED, DIEST, DIETH]

Ge 2:17 eatest thereof thou shalt **surely d**. 4191+4191
3: 3 eat of it, neither shall ye touch it, lest ye **d**. 4191
3: 4 the woman, Ye shall not **surely d**: 4191+4191
6:17 *and* every *thing* that *is* in the earth shall **d**. 1478
19:19 lest *some* evil take me, and I **d**: 4191
20: 7 know thou that thou shalt **surely d**, 4191+4191
25:32 Esau said, Behold, I *am* at the point to **d**: 4191
26: 9 unto him, Because I said, Lest I **d** for her. 4191
27: 4 that my soul may bless thee before I **d**. 4191
30: 1 unto Jacob, Give me children, or else I **d**. 4191
33:13 them one day, all the flock will **d**. 4191
38:11 for he said, Lest peradventure he **d** also, 4191
42: 2 from thence; that we may live, and not **d**. 4191
42:20 your words be verified, and ye shall not **d**. 4191
43: 8 not **d**, both we, and thou, *and* also our little 4191
44: 9 both let him **d**, and we also will be my 4191
44:22 should leave his father, *his father* would **d**. 4191
44:31 that the lad *is* not *with us,* that he will **d**: 4191
45:28 yet alive: I will go and see him before I **d**. 4191
46:30 Now let me **d**, since I have seen thy face, 4191
47:15 for why should we **d** in thy presence? 4191
47:19 Wherefore shall we **d** before thine eyes, 4191
47:19 give *us* seed, that we may live, and not **d**, 4191
47:29 the time drew nigh that Israel must **d**: and 4191
48:21 Israel said unto Joseph, Behold, I **d**: but 4191
50: 5 My father made me swear, saying, Lo, I **d**: 4191
50:24 Joseph said unto his brethren, I **d**: and 4191
Ex 7:18 the fish that *is* in the river shall **d**, and 4191
9: 4 there shall nothing **d** of all *that is* 4191
9:19 come down upon them, and they shall **d**. 4191
10:28 in *that* day thou seest my face thou shalt **d**. 4191
11: 5 all the firstborn in the land of Egypt shall **d**, 4191
14:11 hast thou taken us away to **d** in 4191
14:12 than that we should **d** in the wilderness. 4191
20:19 but let not God speak with us, lest we **d**. 4191
21:12 He that smiteth a man, so that he **d**, shall be 4191
21:14 take him from mine altar, that he may **d**. 4191
21:18 *his* fist, and he **d** not, but keepeth *his* bed: 4191
21:20 with a rod, and he **d** under his hand; 4191
21:28 an ox gore a man or a woman, that they **d**: 4191
21:35 if one man's ox hurt another's, that he **d**; 4191
22: 2 breaking up, and be smitten that he **d**, 4191
22:10 it **d**, or be hurt, or driven away, no man 4191
22:14 it be hurt, or **d**, the owner thereof *being* not 4191
28:35 and when he cometh out, that he **d** not. 4191
28:43 *place;* that they bear not iniquity, and **d**: 4191
30:20 they shall wash *with* water, that they **d** not; 4191
30:21 their hands and their feet, that they **d** not: 4191
Lev 8:35 the charge of the LORD, that ye **d** not: 4191
10: 6 lest you **d**, and lest wrath come upon all 4191
10: 7 tabernacle of the congregation, lest you **d**: 4191
10: 9 tabernacle of the congregation, lest ye **d**: 4191
11:39 if any beast, of which ye may eat, **d**; he that 4191
15:31 that they **d** not in their uncleanness, 4191
16: 2 which *is* upon the ark; that he **d** not: 4191
16:13 that *is* upon the Testimony, that he **d** not: 4191
20:20 shall bear their sin; they shall **d** childless. 4191
22: 9 sin for it, and **d** therefore, if they profane it: 4191
Nu 4:15 shall not touch *any* holy *thing,* lest they **d**. 4191
4:19 do unto them, that they may live, and not **d**, 4191
4:20 the holy *things* are covered, lest they **d**. 4191
6: 7 his brother, or for his sister, when they **d**: 4194
6: 9 if any man **d** very suddenly by him, 4191+4191
14:35 shall be consumed, and there they shall **d**. 4191
16:29 If these *men* **d** the common death of all 4191

Nu	17:10	their murmurings from me, that they **d** not.	4191
	17:12	saying, Behold, we **d**, we perish, we all	1478
	17:13	unto the tabernacle of the LORD shall **d**:	4191
	18: 3	the altar, that neither they, nor you also, **d**.	4191
	18:22	the congregation, lest they bear sin, and **d**.	4191
	18:32	*things* of the children of Israel, lest ye **d**.	4191
	20: 4	that we and our cattle should **d** there?	4191
	20:26	gathered *unto his people*, and shall **d** there.	4191
	21: 5	us up out of Egypt to **d** in the wilderness?	4191
	23:10	Let me **d** the death of the righteous, and	4191
	26:65	shall **surely d** in the wilderness.	4191+4191
	27: 8	If a man **d**, and have no son, then ye shall	4191
	35:12	that the manslayer **d** not, until he stand	4191
	35:16	of iron, so that he **d**, he *is* a murderer:	4191
	35:17	wherewith he may **d**, and he die, he *is* a	4191
	35:17	he may die, and he **d**, he *is* a murderer:	4191
	35:18	wherewith he may **d**, and he die, he *is* a	4191
	35:18	he may die, and he **d**, he *is* a murderer:	4191
	35:20	or hurl at him by laying of wait, that he **d**;	4191
	35:21	enmity smite him with his hand, that he **d**:	4191
	35:23	wherewith *a man* may **d**, seeing *him* not,	4191
	35:23	that he **d**, and *was* not his enemy,	4191
	35:30	testify against *any* person *to cause him* to **d**.	4191
Dt	4:22	I *must* **d** in this land, I *must* not go over	4191
	5:25	Now therefore why should we **d**? for this	4191
	5:25	our God any more, then we shall **d**.	4191
	13:10	thou shalt stone him with stones, that he **d**;	4191
	17: 5	shalt stone them with stones, till they **d**.	4191
	17:12	or unto the judge, even that man shall **d**:	4191
	18:16	me see this great fire any more, that I **d** not.	4191
	18:20	of other gods, even that prophet shall **d**.	4191
	19: 5	and lighteth upon his neighbour, that he **d**;	4191
	19:11	smite him mortally that he **d**, and	4191
	19:12	of the avenger of blood, that he may **d**.	4191
	20: 5	lest he **d** in the battle, and another man	4191
	20: 6	lest he **d** in the battle, and another man eat	4191
	20: 7	lest he **d** in the battle, and another man take	4191
	21:21	city shall stone him with stones, that he **d**:	4191
	22:21	city shall stone her with stones that she **d**:	4191
	22:22	they shall both of them **d**, *both* the man that	4191
	22:24	ye shall stone them with stones that they **d**;	4191
	22:25	then the man only that lay with her shall **d**:	4191
	24: 3	or if the latter husband **d**, which took her *to*	4191
	24: 7	that thief shall **d**; and thou shalt put evil	4191
	25: 5	and one of them **d**, and have no child,	4191
	31:14	thy days approach that *thou* must **d**:	4191
	32:50	**d** in the mount whither thou goest up, and	4191
	33: 6	Let Reuben live, and not **d**; and let *not* his	4191
Jos	20: 9	not **d** by the hand of the avenger of blood,	4191
Jdg	6:23	*be* unto thee; fear not: thou shalt not **d**.	4191
	6:30	Bring out thy son, that he may **d**:	4191
	13:22	We shall **surely d**, because we have	4191+4191
	15:18	now shall I **d** for thirst, and fall into	4191
	16:30	Samson said, Let me **d** with the Philistines.	4191
Ru	1:17	will I **d**, and there will I be buried:	4191
1Sa	2:33	all the increase of thine house shall **d** in	4191
	2:34	in one day they shall **d** both of them.	4191
	12:19	unto the LORD thy God, that we **d** not:	4191
	14:39	Jonathan my son, he shall **surely d**.	4191+4191
	14:43	rod that *was* in mine hand, *and* lo, I must **d**.	4191
	14:44	for thou shalt **surely d**, Jonathan.	4191+4191
	14:45	the people said unto Saul, Shall Jonathan **d**,	4191
	20: 2	said unto him, God forbid; thou shalt not **d**:	4191
	20:14	the kindness of the LORD, that I **d** not:	4191
	20:31	him unto me, for he shall **surely d**.	1121+4194
	22:16	Thou shalt **surely d**, Ahimelech,	4191+4191
	26:10	or his day shall come to **d**; or he shall	4191
	26:16	ye *are* **worthy to d**, because ye have	1121+4194
	28: 9	thou a snare for my life, to **cause** me **to d**?	4191
2Sa	11:15	ye from him, that he may be smitten, and **d**.	4191
	12: 5	hath done this *thing* shall **surely d**:	1121+4194
	12:13	also hath put away thy sin; thou shalt not **d**.	4191
	12:14	that is born unto thee shall **surely d**.	4191+4191
	14:14	For we **must needs d**, and *are* as	4191+4191
	18: 3	neither if half of us **d**, will they care for us:	4191
	19:23	the king said unto Shimei, Thou shalt not **d**.	4191
	19:37	that I may **d** in mine own city, *and*	4191
1Ki	1:52	shall be found in him, he shall **d**.	4191
	2: 1	days of David drew nigh that *he* should **d**;	4191
	2:30	he said, Nay; but I will **d** here.	4191
	2:37	for certain that thou shalt **surely d**:	4191+4191
	2:42	that thou shalt **surely d**?	4191+4191
	14:12	thy feet enter into the city, the child shall **d**.	4191
	17:12	and my son, that we may eat it, and **d**.	4191
	19: 4	he requested for himself that he might **d**;	4191
	21:10	him out, and stone him, that he may **d**.	4191
2Ki	1: 4	thou art gone up, but shalt **surely d**.	4191+4191
	1: 6	thou art gone up, but shalt **surely d**.	4191+4191
	1:16	thou art gone up, but shalt **surely d**.	4191+4191
	7: 3	one to another, Why sit we here until we **d**?	4191
	7: 4	famine *is* in the city, and we shall **d** there:	4191
	7: 4	if we sit still here, we **d** also. Now therefore	4191
	7: 4	shall live; and if they kill us, we shall but **d**.	4191
	8:10	shewed me that he shall **surely d**.	4191+4191
	18:32	and of honey, that ye may live, and not **d**:	4191
	20: 1	in order; for thou shalt **d**, and not live.	4191
2Ch	25: 4	The fathers shall not **d** for the children,	4191
	25: 4	neither shall the children **d** for the fathers,	4191
	25: 4	but every man shall **d** for his own sin.	4191
	32:11	you to give over yourselves to **d** by famine	4191
Job	2: 9	retain thine integrity? curse God, and **d**.	4191
	4:21	go away? they **d**, even without wisdom.	4191
	12: 2	the people, and wisdom shall **d** with you.	4191
	14: 8	and the stock thereof **d** in the ground;	4191
	14:14	If a man **d**, shall he live *again?* all the days	4191
	27: 5	till I **d** I will not remove my integrity from	1478
	29:18	I shall **d** in my nest, and I shall multiply *my*	1478
	34:20	*In* a moment shall they **d**, and the people	4191
	36:12	and they shall **d** without knowledge.	1478
	36:14	They **d** in youth, and their life *is* among	4191
Ps	41: 5	When shall he **d**, and his name perish?	4191
	49:10	For he seeth *that* wise *men* **d**, likewise	4191
	79:11	thou those that are **appointed to d**;	1121+8546
	82: 7	ye shall **d** like men, and fall like one of	4191
	88:15	**ready to d** from *my* youth *up: while* I	1478
	104:29	their breath, they **d**, and return to their dust.	1478
	118:17	I shall not **d**, but live, and declare the works	4191
Pr	5:23	He shall **d** without instruction; and in	4191
	10:21	feed many: but fools **d** for want of wisdom.	4191
	15:10	the way: *and* he that hateth reproof shall **d**.	4191
	19:16	*but* he that despiseth his ways shall **d**.	4191
	23:13	beatest him with the rod, he shall not **d**.	4191
	30: 7	of thee; deny me *them* not before I **d**:	4191
Ecc	3: 2	A time to be born, and a time to **d**; a time to	4191
	7:17	why shouldest thou **d** before thy time?	4191
	9: 5	For the living know that they shall **d**: but	4191
Isa	22:13	us eat and drink; for to morrow we shall **d**.	4191
	22:14	shall not be purged from you till ye **d**,	4191
	22:18	there shalt thou **d**, and there the chariots of	4191
	38: 1	in order: for thou shalt **d**, and not live.	4191
	51: 6	they that dwell therein shall **d** in like	4191
	51:12	shouldest be afraid of a man *that* shall **d**,	4191
	51:14	that he should not **d** in the pit, nor that his	4191
	65:20	for the child shall **d** an hundred years old;	4191
	66:24	for their worm shall not **d**, neither shall	4191
Jer	11:21	of the LORD, that thou **d** not by our hand:	4191
	11:22	the young men shall **d** by the sword;	4191
	11:22	and their daughters shall **d** by famine:	4191
	16: 4	They shall **d** of grievous deaths; they shall	4191
	16: 6	the great and the small shall **d** in this land:	4191
	20: 6	there thou shalt **d**, and shalt be buried there,	4191
	21: 6	and beast: they shall **d** of a great pestilence.	4191
	21: 9	He that abideth in this city shall **d** by	4191
	22:12	he shall **d** in the place whither they have	4191
	22:26	ye were not born; and there shall ye **d**.	4191
	26: 8	saying, Thou shalt **surely d**.	4191+4191
	26:11	saying, This man *is* worthy to **d**;	4194
	26:16	the prophets; This man *is* not worthy to **d**:	4194
	27:13	Why will ye **d**, thou and thy people, by	4191
	28:16	*this* year thou *shalt* **d**, because thou hast	4191
	31:30	every one shall **d** for his own iniquity:	4191
	34: 4	of thee, Thou shalt not **d** by the sword:	4191
	34: 5	*But* thou shalt **d** in peace: and with	4191
	37:20	house of Jonathan the scribe, lest I **d** there.	4191
	38: 2	He that remaineth in this city shall **d** by	4191
	38: 9	he is like to **d** for hunger in the place where	4191
	38:10	prophet out of the dungeon, before he **d**.	4191
	38:24	know of these words, and thou shalt not **d**.	4191
	38:26	to return *to* Jonathan's house, to **d** there.	4191
	42:16	you there *in* Egypt; and there ye shall **d**.	4191
	42:17	they shall **d** by the sword, by the famine,	4191
	42:22	know certainly that ye shall **d** by the sword,	4191
	44:12	they shall **d**, from the least even unto	4191
Eze	3:18	the wicked, Thou shalt **surely d**;	4191+4191
	3:18	the same wicked *man* shall **d** in his	4191
	3:19	his wicked way, he shall **d** in his iniquity;	4191
	3:20	a stumblingblock before him, he shall **d**:	4191
	3:20	he shall **d** in his sin, and his righteousness	4191

Eze	5:12	A third *part* of thee shall **d** with	4191
	6:12	*He* that *is* far off shall **d** of the pestilence;	4191
	6:12	and is besieged shall **d** by the famine:	4191
	7:15	he that *is* in the field shall **d** with	4191
	12:13	shall he not see it, though he shall **d** there.	4191
	13:19	to slay the souls that should not **d**, and	4191
	17:16	him in the midst of Babylon he shall **d**.	4191
	18: 4	son *is* mine: the soul that sinneth, it shall **d**.	4191
	18:13	he shall **surely d**; his blood shall be	4191+4191
	18:17	he shall not **d** for the iniquity of his father,	4191
	18:18	lo, even he shall **d** in his iniquity.	4191
	18:20	The soul that sinneth, it shall **d**. The son	4191
	18:21	right, he shall surely live, he shall not **d**.	4191
	18:23	pleasure at all that the wicked should **d**?	4194
	18:24	sin that he hath sinned, in them shall he **d**.	4191
	18:26	for his iniquity that he hath done shall he **d**.	4191
	18:28	he shall surely live, he shall not **d**.	4191
	18:31	for why will ye **d**, O house of Israel?	4191
	28: 8	thou shalt **d** the deaths of *them that are*	4191
	28:10	Thou shalt **d** the deaths of	4191
	33: 8	O wicked *man,* thou shalt **surely d**;	4191+4191
	33: 8	that wicked *man* shall **d** in his iniquity;	4191
	33: 9	from his way, he shall **d** in his iniquity;	4191
	33:11	for why will ye **d**, O house of Israel?	4191
	33:13	that he hath committed, he shall **d** for it.	4191
	33:14	the wicked, Thou shalt **surely d**;	4191+4191
	33:15	he shall surely live, he shall not **d**.	4191
	33:18	he shall even **d** thereby.	4191
	33:27	and in the caves shall **d** of the pestilence.	4191
Am	2: 2	Moab shall **d** with tumult, with shouting,	4191
	6: 9	ten men in one house, that they shall **d**.	4191
	7:11	Jeroboam shall **d** by the sword, and	4191
	7:17	by line; and thou shalt **d** in a polluted land:	4191
	9:10	All the sinners of my people shall **d** by	4191
Jnh	4: 3	for *it is* better for me to **d** than to live.	4194
	4: 8	and wished in himself to **d**, and said,	4191
	4: 8	and said, *It is* better for me to **d** than to live.	4194
Hab	1:12	we shall not **d**. O LORD, thou hast	4191
Zec	11: 9	that that dieth, let it **d**; and that that is to be	4191
	13: 8	two parts therein shall be cut off *and* **d**;	1478
Mt	15: 4	or mother, let him **d** the death.	*5053*
	22:24	Saying, Master, Moses said, If a man **d**,	*599*
	26:35	said unto him, Though I should **d** with thee,	*599*
Mk	7:10	or mother, let him **d** the death.	*5053*
	12:19	If a man's brother **d**, and leave *his* wife	*599*
	14:31	If I should **d with** thee, I will not deny thee	*4880*
Lk	7: 2	dear unto him, was sick, and ready to **d**.	*5053*
	20:28	If any *man's* brother **d**, having a wife, and	*599*
	20:28	having a wife, and he **d** without children,	*599*
	20:36	Neither can they **d** any more: for they are	*599*
Jn	4:49	unto him, Sir, come down ere my child **d**.	*599*
	6:50	that a man may eat thereof, and not **d**.	*599*
	8:21	ye shall seek me, and shall **d** in your sins:	*599*
	8:24	unto you, that ye shall **d** in your sins:	*599*
	8:24	for if ye believe not that I am *he,* ye shall **d**	*599*
	11:16	Let us also go, that we may **d** with him.	*599*
	11:26	and believeth in me shall never **d**.	*599*
	11:50	that one man should **d** for the people, and	*599*
	11:51	he prophesied that Jesus should **d** for *that*	*599*
	12:24	a corn of wheat fall into the ground and **d**,	*599*
	12:24	but if it **d**, it bringeth forth much fruit.	*599*
	12:33	he said, signifying what death he should **d**.	*599*
	18:14	that it was expedient that one man should **d**	*622*
	18:32	he spake, signifying what death he should **d**.	*599*
	19: 7	and by our law he ought to **d**, because	*599*
	21:23	the brethren, that that disciple should not **d**:	*599*
	21:23	yet Jesus said not unto him, He shall not **d**;	*599*
Ac	21:13	also to **d** at Jerusalem for the name of	*599*
	25:11	any *thing* worthy of death, I refuse not to **d**:	*599*
	25:16	of the Romans to deliver any man to **d**,	*684*
Ro	5: 7	For scarcely for a righteous *man* will one **d**:	*599*
	5: 7	for a good *man* some would even dare to **d**.	*599*
	8:13	For if ye live after the flesh, ye shall **d**: but	*599*
	14: 8	and whether we **d**, we die unto the Lord:	*599*
	14: 8	and whether we die, we **d** unto the Lord:	*599*
	14: 8	we live therefore, or **d**, we are the Lord's.	*599*
1Co	9:15	for *it were* better for me to **d**, than that any	*599*
	15:22	For as in Adam all **d**, even so in Christ shall	*599*
	15:31	I have in Christ Jesus our Lord, I **d** daily.	*599*
	15:32	let us eat and drink; for to morrow we **d**.	*599*
	15:36	thou sowest is not quickened, except it **d**:	*599*
2Co	7: 3	that you are in our hearts to **d** and live with	*4880*
Php	1:21	For to me to live *is* Christ, and to **d** *is* gain.	*599*
Heb	7: 8	And here men that **d** receive tithes; but	*599*
	9:27	And as it is appointed unto men once to **d**,	*599*
Rev	3: 2	the *things* which remain, that are ready to **d**:	*599*
	9: 6	and shall desire to **d**, and death shall flee	*599*
	14:13	Blessed *are* the dead which **d** in the Lord	*599*

DIED (201) [DIE]

Ge	5: 5	nine hundred and thirty years: and he **d**.	4191
	5: 8	nine hundred and twelve years: and he **d**.	4191
	5:11	were nine hundred and five years: and he **d**.	4191
	5:14	were nine hundred and ten years: and he **d**.	4191
	5:17	hundred ninety and five years: and he **d**.	4191
	5:20	nine hundred sixty and two years: and he **d**.	4191
	5:27	hundred sixty and nine years: and he **d**.	4191
	5:31	hundred seventy and seven years: and he **d**.	4191
	7:21	all flesh **d** that moved upon the earth,	1478
	7:22	of life, of all that *was* in the dry *land,* **d**.	4191
	9:29	nine hundred and fifty years: and he **d**.	4191
	11:28	Haran **d** before his father Terah in the land	4191
	11:32	five years: and Terah **d** in Haran.	4191
	23: 2	Sarah **d** in Kirjath-arba; the same *is* Hebron	4191
	25: 8	**d** in a good old age, an old man, and full *of*	4191
	25:17	he gave up the ghost and **d**; and	4191
	25:18	*and* he **d** in the presence of all his brethren.	5307
	35: 8	Deborah Rebekah's nurse **d**, and she was	4191
	35:18	as her soul was in departing (for she **d**)	4191
	35:19	Rachel **d**, and was buried in the way to	4191
	35:29	**d**, and was gathered unto his people,	4191
	36:33	Bela **d**, and Jobab the son of Zerah of	4191
	36:34	Jobab **d**, and Husham of the land of Temani	4191
	36:35	Husham **d**, and Hadad the son of Bedad,	4191
	36:36	Hadad **d**, and Samlah of Masrekah reigned	4191
	36:37	Samlah **d**, and Saul of Rehoboth *by*	4191
	36:38	Saul **d**, and Baal-hanan the son of Achbor	4191
	36:39	Baal-hanan the son of Achbor **d**, and	4191
	38:12	time the daughter of Shuah Judah's wife **d**;	4191
	46:12	Er and Onan **d** in the land of Canaan.	4191
	48: 7	Rachel **d** by me in the land of Canaan in	4191
	50:16	Thy father did command before he **d**,	4194
	50:26	So Joseph **d**, *being* an hundred and	4191
Ex	1: 6	Joseph **d**, and all his brethren, and all that	4191
	2:23	in process of time, that the king of Egypt **d**:	4191
	7:21	the fish that *was* in the river **d**; and the river	4191
	8:13	the frogs **d** out of the houses, out of	4191
	9: 6	the morrow, and all the cattle of Egypt **d**:	4191
	9: 6	of the cattle of the children of Israel **d** not	4191
	16: 3	Would to God we had **d** by the hand of	4191
Lev	10: 2	and they **d** before the LORD.	4191
	16: 1	they offered before the LORD, and **d**;	4191
	17:15	soul that eateth **that which d of itself**,	5038
Nu	3: 4	and Abihu **d** before the LORD,	4191
	14: 2	Would God that we had **d** in the land of	4191
	14: 2	or would God we had **d** in this wilderness!	4191
	14:37	**d** by the plague before the LORD.	4191
	15:36	and stoned him with stones, and he **d**;	4191
	16:49	Now they that **d** in the plague were	4191
	16:49	beside them that **d** about the matter of	4191
	20: 1	and Miriam **d** there, and was buried there.	4191
	20: 3	Would God that we had **d** when our	1478
	20: 3	when our brethren **d** before the LORD!	1478
	20:28	and Aaron **d** there in the top of the mount:	4191
	21: 6	bit the people; and much people of Israel **d**.	4191
	25: 9	those that **d** in the plague were twenty and	4191
	26:10	when that company **d**, what time the fire	4194
	26:11	Notwithstanding the children of Korah **d**	4191
	26:19	and Er and Onan **d** in the land of Canaan.	4191
	26:61	Nadab and Abihu **d**, when they offered	4191
	27: 3	Our father **d** in the wilderness, and he was	4191
	27: 3	but **d** in his own sin, and had no sons.	4191
	33:38	**d** there, in the fortieth year after	4191
	33:39	three years old when he **d** in mount Hor.	4194
Dt	10: 6	there Aaron **d**, and there he was buried; and	4191
	32:50	as Aaron thy brother **d** in mount Hor,	4191
	34: 5	So Moses the servant of the LORD **d**	4191
	34: 7	and twenty years old when he **d**:	4194
Jos	5: 4	men of war, **d** in the wilderness by the way,	4191
	10:11	upon them unto Azekah, and they **d**:	4191
	10:11	*they were* moe which **d** with hailstones	4191
	24:29	**d**, *being* an hundred and ten years old.	4191
	24:33	Eleazar the son of Aaron **d**; and they buried	4191
Jdg	1: 7	brought him *to* Jerusalem, and there he **d**.	4191
	2: 8	**d**, *being* an hundred and ten years old.	4191
	2:21	of the nations which Joshua left when he **d**:	4191
	3:11	And Othniel the son of Kenaz **d**.	4191
	4:21	for he was fast asleep and weary. So he **d**.	4191

Jdg 8:32 Gideon the son of Joash **d** in a good old 4191
9:49 that all the men of the tower of Shechem **d** 4191
9:54 young man thrust him through, and he **d**. 4191
10: 2 and **d**, and was buried in Shamir. 4191
10: 5 And Jair **d**, and was buried in Camon. 4191
12: 7 **d** Jephthah the Gileadite, and was buried in 4191
12:10 **d** Ibzan, and was buried at Beth-lehem. 4191
12:12 Elon the Zebulonite **d**, and was buried in 4191
12:15 Abdon the son of Hillel the Pirathonite **d**, 4191
Ru 1: 3 Elimelech Naomi's husband **d**; and she was 4191
1: 5 and Chilion **d** also both of them; 4191
1Sa 4:18 of the gate, and his neck brake, and he **d**: 4191
5:12 the men that **d** not were smitten with 4191
14:45 the people rescued Jonathan, that he **d** not. 4191
25: 1 Samuel **d**; and all the Israelites were 4191
25:37 that his heart **d** within him, and he became 4191
25:38 that the LORD smote Nabal, that he **d**. 4191
31: 5 likewise upon his sword, and **d** with him. 4191
31: 6 So Saul **d**, and his three sons, and 4191
2Sa 1:15 fall upon him. And he smote him that he **d**. 4191
2:23 he fell down there, and **d** in the same place: 4191
2:23 where Asahel fell down and **d** stood still. 4191
2:31 *so that* three hundred and threescore men **d**. 4191
3:27 him there *under* the fifth *rib*, that he **d**, 4191
3:33 and said, **D** Abner as a fool dieth? 4191
6: 7 *his* error; and there he **d** by the ark of God. 4191
10: 1 that the king of the children of Ammon **d**, 4191
10:18 the captain of their host, who **d** there. 4191
11:17 of David; and Uriah the Hittite **d** also. 4191
11:21 him from the wall, that he **d** in Thebez? 4191
12:18 to pass on the seventh day, that the child **d**. 4191
17:23 **d**, and was buried in the sepulchre of his 4191
18:33 would God I had **d** for thee, O Absalom, 4191
19: 6 all we had **d** *this* day, then it had pleased 4191
20:10 and strake him not again; and he **d**. 4191
24:15 there **d** of the people from Dan even to 4191
1Ki 2:25 of Jehoiada; and he fell upon him that he **d**. 4191
2:46 went out, and fell upon him, that he **d**. 4191
3:19 this woman's child **d** in the night; because 4191
12:18 all Israel stoned him with stones, that he **d**. 4191
14:17 to the threshold of the door, the child **d**; 4191
16:18 the king's house over him with fire, and **d**, 4191
16:22 of Ginath: so Tibni **d**, and Omri reigned. 4191
21:13 and stoned him with stones, that he **d**. 4191
22:35 chariot against the Syrians, and **d** at even: 4191
22:37 So the king **d**, and was brought *to* Samaria; 4191
2Ki 1:17 So he **d** according to the word of 4191
4:20 he sat on her knees till noon, and *then* **d**. 4191
7:17 and he **d**, as the man of God had said, 4191
7:20 trode upon him in the gate, and he **d**. 4191
8:15 and spread *it* on his face, so that he **d**: 4191
9:27 And he fled *to* Megiddo, and **d** there. 4191
12:21 his servants, smote him, and he **d**; 4191
13:14 fallen sick of his sickness whereof he **d**. 4191
13:20 Elisha **d**, and they buried him. And 4191
13:24 So Hazael king of Syria **d**; and 4191
23:34 and he came *to* Egypt, and **d** there. 4191
25:25 that he **d**, and the Jews and the Chaldees 4191
1Ch 1:51 Hadad **d** also. And the dukes of Edom 4191
2:30 and Appaim: but Seled **d** without children. 4191
2:32 Jonathan: and Jether **d** without children. 4191
10: 5 he fell likewise on the sword, and **d**. 4191
10: 6 So Saul **d**, and his three sons, and all his 4191
10: 6 his three sons, and all his house **d** together. 4191
10:13 So Saul **d** for his transgression which he 4191
13:10 hand to the ark: and there he **d** before God. 4191
19: 1 the king of the children of Ammon **d**, 4191
23:22 Eleazar **d**, and had no sons, but daughters: 4191
24: 2 Nadab and Abihu **d** before their father, and 4191
29:28 he **d** in a good old age, full of days, riches, 4191
2Ch 10:18 of Israel stoned him with stones, that he **d**. 4191
13:20 and the LORD struck him, and he **d**. 4191
16:13 **d** in the one and fortieth year of his reign. 4191
18:34 about the time of the sun going down he **d**. 4191
21:19 so he **d** of sore diseases. And his people 4191
24:15 waxed old, and was full *of* days when he **d**; 4191
24:15 and thirty years old *was he* when he **d**. 4194
24:22 when he **d**, he said, The LORD look upon 4194
24:25 and slew him on his bed, and he **d**: 4191
35:24 he **d**, and was buried in *one of* 4191
Job 3:11 Why **d** I not from the womb? *why* did I *not* 4191
42:17 So Job **d**, *being* old and full of days. 4191
Isa 6: 1 In the year that king Uzziah **d** I saw also 4194
14:28 In the year that king Ahaz **d** was this 4194
Jer 28:17 So Hananiah the prophet **d** the same year in 4191
Eze 11:13 that Pelatiah the son of Benaiah **d**. 4191
24:18 at even my wife **d**; and I did in the morning 4191
Hos 13: 1 but when he offended in Baal, he **d**. 4191
Mt 22:27 And last of all the woman **d** also. *599*
Mk 12:21 took her, and **d**, neither left he *any* seed: *599*
12:22 left no seed: last of all the woman **d** also. *599*
Lk 16:22 And it came to pass that the beggar **d**, and *599*
16:22 the rich *man* also **d**, and was buried; *599*
20:29 the first took a wife, and **d** without children. *599*
20:30 second took her to wife, and he **d** childless. *599*
20:31 seven also: and they left no children, and **d**. *599*
20:32 Last of all the woman **d** also. *599*
Jn 11:21 thou hadst been here, my brother had not **d**. *2348*
11:32 thou hadst been here, my brother had not **d**. *599*
11:37 that even this *man* should not have **d**? *599*
Ac 7:15 into Egypt, and **d**, he, and our fathers, *5053*
9:37 pass in those days, that she was sick, and **d**: *599*
Ro 5: 6 in due time Christ **d** for the ungodly. *599*
5: 8 while we were yet sinners, Christ **d** for us. *599*
6:10 For in that he **d**, he died unto sin once: but *599*
6:10 For in that he died, he **d** unto sin once: but *599*
7: 9 commandment came, sin revived, and I **d**. *599*
8:34 *It is* Christ that **d**, yea rather, that is risen *599*
14: 9 For to this end Christ both **d**, and rose, *599*
14:15 not him with thy meat, for whom Christ **d**. *599*
1Co 8:11 the weak brother perish, for whom Christ **d**? *599*
15: 3 how that Christ **d** for our sins according to *599*
2Co 5:14 that if one **d** for all, then were all dead: *599*
5:15 And *that* he **d** for all, that they which live *599*
5:15 but unto him which **d** for them, and *599*
1Th 4:14 For if we believe that Jesus **d** and rose again, *599*
5:10 Who **d** for us, that, whether we wake or *599*
Heb 10:28 He that despised Moses' law **d** without *599*
11:13 These all **d** in faith, not having received *599*
11:22 By faith Joseph, when he **d**, made mention *5053*
Rev 8: 9 which were in the sea, and had life, **d**; *599*
8:11 and many men **d** of the waters, because *599*
16: 3 dead *man:* and every living soul **d** in the sea. *599*

DIEST (1) [DIE]
Ru 1:17 Where thou **d**, will I die, and there will I be 4191

DIET (2)
Jer 52:34 *for* his **d**, there was a continual diet given 737
52:34 there was a continual **d** given him of 737

DIETH (30) [DIE]
Lev 7:24 the fat of the **beast that d of itself**, and 5038
22: 8 **That which d of itself**, or is torn *with* 5038
Nu 19:14 This *is* the law, when a man **d** in a tent: 4191
Dt 14:21 Ye shall not eat of any thing that **d of itself**: 5038
2Sa 3:33 and said, Died Abner as a fool **d**? 4194
1Ki 14:11 Him that **d** of Jeroboam in the city shall 4191
14:11 him that **d** in the field shall the fowls of 4191
16: 4 Him that **d** of Baasha in the city shall 4191
16: 4 him that **d** of his in the fields shall 4191
21:24 Him that **d** of Ahab in the city the dogs 4191
21:24 him that **d** in the field shall the fowls of 4191
Job 14:10 man **d**, and wasteth away: yea, man giveth 4191
21:23 One **d** in his full strength, *being* wholly at 4191
21:25 another **d** in the bitterness of his soul, and 4191
Ps 49:17 For when he **d** he shall carry nothing away: 4194
Pr 11: 7 When a wicked man **d**, *his* expectation 4194
Ecc 2:16 And how **d** the wise *man?* as the fool. 4191
3:19 as the one **d**, so dieth the other; yea, 4194
3:19 as the one dieth, so **d** the other; yea, 4194
Isa 50: 2 because *there is* no water, and **d** for thirst. 4191
59: 5 he that eateth of their eggs **d**, and 4191
Eze 4:14 have I not eaten *of* that which **d of itself**, 5038
18:26 and committeth iniquity, and **d** in them; 4191
18:32 have no pleasure in the death of him that **d**, 4191
Zec 11: 9 that that **d**, let it die; and that that is to be 4191
Mk 9:44 Where their worm **d** not, and the fire is not *5053*
9:46 Where their worm **d** not, and the fire is not *5053*
9:48 Where their worm **d** not, and the fire is not *5053*
Ro 6: 9 Christ being raised from the dead **d** no more; *599*
14: 7 liveth to himself, and no *man* **d** to himself. *599*

DIFFER (1) [DIFFERENCE, DIFFERENCES, DIFFERETH, DIFFERING]
1Co 4: 7 For who **maketh** thee **to d** *from another?* *1252*

DIFFERENCE (12) [DIFFER]
Ex 11: 7 doth **put a d** between the Egyptians 6395
Lev 10:10 that *ye* may **put d** between holy and unholy, 914
11:47 To **make a d** between the unclean and 914
20:25 **put d** between clean beasts and unclean, 914
Eze 22:26 *things:* they have **put** no **d** between the holy 914
22:26 neither have they shewed **d** between NIH
44:23 they shall teach my people *the* **d** between NIH
Ac 15: 9 And **put** no **d** between us and them, *1252*
Ro 3:22 upon all them that believe: for there is no **d**: *1293*
10:12 For there is no **d** between the Jew and *1293*
1Co 7:34 There is **d** *also* **between** a wife and a *3307*
Jude 1:22 of some have compassion, **making a d**: *1252*

DIFFERENCES (1) [DIFFER]
1Co 12: 5 And there are **d** of administrations, but *1243*

DIFFERENT See DIVERS; DIVERSE

DIFFERETH (2) [DIFFER]
1Co 15:41 for *one* star **d from** *another* star in glory. *1308*
Gal 4: 1 as he is a child, **d** nothing **from** a servant, *1308*

DIFFERING (1) [DIFFER]
Ro 12: 6 gifts **d** according to the grace that is given *1313*

DIG (13) [DIGGED, DIGGEDST, DIGGETH]
Ex 21:33 or if a man shall **d** a pit, and not cover it, 3738
Dt 8: 9 and out of whose hills thou mayest **d** brass. 2672
23:13 thou shalt **d** therewith, and shalt turn back 2658
Job 3:21 and **d** for it more than for hid treasures; 2658
6:27 and you **d** *a pit* for your friend. 3738
11:18 thou shalt **d** *about thee, and* thou shalt take 2658
24:16 In the dark *they* **d** *through* houses, 2864
Eze 8: 8 he unto me, Son of man, **d** now in the wall: 2864
12: 5 **D** thou through the wall in their sight, and 2864
12:12 they shall **d** through the wall to carry out 2864
Am 9: 2 Though they **d** into hell, thence shall mine 2864
Lk 13: 8 year also, till I shall **d** about it, and dung *it:* *4626*
16: 3 I cannot **d**; to beg I am ashamed. *4626*

DIGGED (37) [DIG]
Ge 21:30 a witness unto me, that I have **d** this well. 2658
26:15 had **d** in the days of Abraham his father, 2658
26:18 Isaac **d** again the wells of water, which they 2658
26:18 which they had **d** in the days of Abraham 2658
26:19 Isaac's servants **d** in the valley, and 2658
26:21 they **d** another well, and strove for that 2658
26:22 removed from thence, and **d** another well; 2658
26:25 and there Isaac's servants **d** a well. 3738
26:32 him concerning the well which they had **d**, 2658
49: 6 and in their selfwill they **d down** a wall. 6131
50: 5 in my grave which I have **d** for me in 3738
Ex 7:24 all the Egyptians **d** round about the river 2658
Nu 21:18 The princes **d** the well, the nobles of 2658
21:18 the well, the nobles of the people **d** it, 3738
Dt 6:11 wells **d**, which thou diggedst not, vineyards 2672
2Ki 19:24 I have **d** and drunk strange waters, and 6979
2Ch 26:10 towers in the desert, and **d** many wells: 2672
Ne 9:25 wells **d**, vineyards, and oliveyards, and 2672
Ps 7:15 **d** it, and is fallen into the ditch *which* he 2658
35: 7 *which* without cause they have **d** for my 2658
57: 6 they have **d** a pit before me, into the midst 3738
94:13 until the pit be **d** for the wicked. 3738
119:85 The proud have **d** pits for me, which *are* 3738
Isa 5: 6 it shall not be pruned, nor **d**; but there shall 5737
7:25 *on* all hills that shall be **d** with the mattock, 5737
37:25 I have **d**, and drunk water; and with 6979
51: 1 and to the hole of the pit *whence* ye are **d**. 5365
Jer 13: 7 **d**, and took the girdle from the place where 2658
18:20 for they have **d** a pit for my soul. 3738
18:22 for they have **d** a pit to take me, and 3738
Eze 8: 8 when I had **d** in the wall, behold a door. 2864
12: 7 in the even I **d** through the wall with mine 2864
Mt 21:33 and **d** a winepress in it, and built a tower, *3736*
25:18 had received one went and **d** in the earth, *3736*
Mk 12: 1 about *it,* and **d** *a place for* the winefat, *3736*
Lk 6:48 and **d** deep, and laid the foundation on a *4626*
Ro 11: 3 thy prophets, and **d down** thine altars; *2679*

DIGGEDST (1) [DIG]
Dt 6:11 which thou **d** not, vineyards and olive trees, 2672

DIGGETH (3) [DIG]
Pr 16:27 An ungodly man **d up** evil: and in his lips 3738
26:27 Whoso **d** a pit shall fall therein: and he that 3738
Ecc 10: 8 He that **d** a pit shall fall into it; and 2658

DIGNITIES (2) [DIGNITY]
2Pe 2:10 they are not afraid to speak evil of **d**. *1391*
Jude 1: 8 despise dominion, and speak evil of **d**. *1391*

DIGNITY (4) [DIGNITIES]
Ge 49: 3 the excellency of **d**, and the excellency of 7613
Est 6: 3 and **d** hath been done to Mordecai for this? 1420
Ecc 10: 6 Folly is set in great **d**, and the rich sit in 4791
Hab 1: 7 and their **d** shall proceed of themselves. 7613

DIKLAH (2)
Ge 10:27 And Hadoram, and Uzal, and **D**, 1853
1Ch 1:21 Hadoram also, and Uzal, and **D**, 1853

DILEAN (1)
Jos 15:38 And **D**, and Mizpeh, and Joktheel, 1810

DILIGENCE (10) [DILIGENT]
Pr 4:23 Keep thy heart with all **d**; for out of it *are* 4929
Lk 12:58 give **d** that *thou* mayest be delivered from *2039*
Ro 12: 8 he that ruleth, with **d**; he that sheweth *4710*
2Co 8: 7 and *in* all **d**, and *in* your love to us, *4710*
2Ti 4: 9 **Do** thy **d** to come shortly unto me: *4704*
4:21 **Do** thy **d** to come before winter. *4704*
Heb 6:11 **d** to the full assurance of hope unto the end: *4710*
2Pe 1: 5 And beside this, giving all **d**, add to your *4710*
1:10 **give d** to make your calling and *4704*
Jude 1: 3 when I gave all **d** to write unto you of *4710*

DILIGENT (15) [DILIGENCE, DILIGENTLY]
Dt 19:18 the judges shall make **d** inquisition: and 3190
Jos 22: 5 take **d** heed to do the commandment and 3966
Ps 64: 6 out iniquities; they accomplish a **d** search: 2664
77: 6 own heart: and my spirit **made d search**. 2664
Pr 10: 4 but the hand of the **d** maketh rich. 2742
12:24 The hand of the **d** shall bear rule: but 2742
12:27 but the substance of a **d** man *is* precious. 2742
13: 4 but the soul of the **d** shall be made fat. 2742
21: 5 The thoughts of the **d** *tend* only to 2742
22:29 Seest thou a man **d** in his business? he shall 4106
27:23 Be thou **d to know** the state of thy 3045+3045
2Co 8:22 whom we have oftentimes proved **d** in *4707*
8:22 in many *things,* but now much more **d**, *4705*
Tit 3:12 be **d** to come unto me to Nicopolis: *4704*
2Pe 3:14 seeing that ye look for such *things,* be **d** *4704*

DILIGENTLY (37) [DILIGENT]
Ex 15:26 If thou wilt **d hearken** to the voice 8085+8085
Lev 10:16 Moses **d sought** the goat of the sin 1875+1875
Dt 4: 9 take heed to thyself, and keep thy soul **d**, 3966
6: 7 thou shalt **teach** them **d** unto thy children, 8150
6:17 You shall **d keep** the commandments 8104+8104
11:13 if you shall **hearken d** unto my 8085+8085
11:22 For if ye shall **d keep** all these 8104+8104
13:14 thou inquire, and make search, and ask **d**; 3190
17: 4 thou hast heard *of it,* and inquired **d**, and 3190
24: 8 that *thou* observe **d**, and do according to all 3966
28: 1 if thou shalt **hearken d** unto 8085+8085
1Ki 20:33 Now the men did **d observe** whether *any* 5172
Ezr 7:23 let it be **d** done for the house of the God of 149
Job 13:17 **Hear d** my speech, and 8085+8085
21: 2 **Hear d** my speech, and let this be 8085+8085
Ps 37:10 thou shalt **d consider** his place, and it *shall* 995
119: 4 hast commanded *us* to keep thy precepts **d**. 3966
Pr 7:15 **d** to **seek** thy face, and I have found thee. 7836
11:27 He that **d seeketh** good procureth favour: 7836
23: 1 a ruler, **consider d** what *is* before thee: 995+995
Isa 21: 7 he **hearkened d** *with* much heed: 7181+7182
55: 2 **hearken d** unto me, and eat ye *that which* 8085
Jer 2:10 consider **d**, and see if there be such a *thing.* 3966
12:16 if they will **d learn** the ways of my 3925+3925
17:24 **d hearken** unto me, saith 8085+8085
Zec 6:15 if ye will **d obey** the voice of 8085+8085
Mt 2: 7 **inquired** of them **d** what time the star *198*
2: 8 said, Go and search **d** for the young child; *199*
2:16 which he had **d inquired** of the wise men. *198*
Lk 15: 8 the house, and seek **d** till she find *it?* *1960*
Ac 18:25 he spake and taught **d** the *things* of the Lord, *199*
1Ti 5:10 if she have **d followed** every good work. *1872*
2Ti 1:17 he was in Rome, he sought me out **very d**, *4706*
Tit 3:13 the lawyer and Apollos on their journey **d**, *4709*
Heb 11: 6 *that* he is a rewarder of them that **d seek** *1567*

Heb 12:15 **Looking d** lest any *man* fail of the grace of 1983
1Pe 1:10 the prophets have inquired and **searched d**, 1830

DILL See ANISE

DIM (9) [DIMNESS]
Ge 27: 1 his eyes were **d**, so that he could not see, 3543
48:10 Now the eyes of Israel were **d** for age, *so* 3513
Dt 34: 7 his eye was not **d**, nor his natural force 3543
1Sa 3: 2 his eyes began *to wax* **d**, *that* he could not 3544
4:15 and his eyes were **d**, that he could not see. 6965
Job 17: 7 Mine eye also is **d** by reason of sorrow, and 3543
Isa 32: 3 the eyes of them that see shall not be **d**, 8159
La 4: 1 How is the gold **become d**! *how* is the most 6004
5:17 is faint; for these *things* our eyes are **d**. 2821

DIMINISH (8) [DIMINISHED, DIMINISHING]
Ex 5: 8 upon them; you shall not **d** *ought* thereof: 1639
21:10 and her duty of marriage, shall he not **d**. 1639
Lev 25:16 fewness of years thou shalt **d** the price of it: 4591
Dt 4: 2 neither shall you **d** *ought* from it, 1639
12:32 thou shalt not add thereto, nor **d** from it. 1639
Jer 26: 2 thee to speak unto them; **d** not a word: 1639
Eze 5:11 will I also **d** *thee;* neither shall mine eye 1639
29:15 for I will **d** them, that *they* shall no more 4591

DIMINISHED (5) [DIMINISH]
Ex 5:11 *it:* yet not ought of your work *shall be* **d**. 1639
Pr 13:11 Wealth *gotten* by vanity shall be **d**: but 4591
Isa 21:17 *men* of the children of Kedar, shall be **d**: 4591
Jer 29: 6 that ye may be increased there, and not **d**. 4591
Eze 16:27 have **d** thine ordinary *food,* and 1639

DIMINISHING (1) [DIMINISH]
Ro 11:12 and the **d** of them the riches of the Gentiles; *2275*

DIMNAH (1)
Jos 21:35 **D** with her suburbs, Nahalal with her 1829

DIMNESS (2) [DIM]
Isa 8:22 behold trouble and darkness, **d** of anguish; 4588
9: 1 Nevertheless the **d** *shall* not *be* such as *was* 4155

DIMON (2)
Isa 15: 9 For the waters of **D** shall be full *of* blood: 1775
15: 9 for I will bring more upon **D**, lions upon 1775

DIMONAH (1)
Jos 15:22 And Kinah, and **D**, and Adadah, 1776

DINAH (7) [DINAH'S]
Ge 30:21 she bare a daughter, and called her name **D**. 1783
34: 1 **D** the daughter of Leah, which she bare 1783
34: 3 his soul clave unto **D** the daughter of Jacob, 1783
34: 5 Jacob heard that he had defiled **D** his 1783
34:13 said, because he had defiled **D** their sister: 1783
34:26 took **D** out of Shechem's house, and 1783
46:15 Jacob in Padan-aram, with his daughter **D**: 1783

DINAH'S (1) [DINAH]
Ge 34:25 Simeon and Levi, **D** brethren, took each 1783

DINAITES (1)
Ezr 4: 9 the **D**, the Apharsathchites, the Tarpelites, 1784

DINE (3) [DINED, DINNER]
Ge 43:16 for *these* men shall **d** with me at noon. 398
Lk 11:37 a certain Pharisee besought him to **d** with *709*
Jn 21:12 Jesus saith unto them, Come *and* **d**. *709*

DINED (1) [DINE]
Jn 21:15 So when they had **d**, Jesus saith to Simon *709*

DINHABAH (2)
Ge 36:32 in Edom: and the name of his city *was* **D**. 1838
1Ch 1:43 of Beor: and the name of his city *was* **D**. 1838

DINNER (4) [DINE]
Pr 15:17 Better *is* a **d** of herbs where love is, than a 737
Mt 22: 4 are bidden, Behold, I have prepared my **d**: *712*
Lk 11:38 that he had not first washed before **d**. *712*
14:12 When thou makest a **d** or a supper, call not *712*

DIONYSIUS (1)
Ac 17:34 among the which *was* **D** the Areopagite, *1354*

DIOTREPHES (1)
3Jn 1: 9 but **D**, who loveth to have the preeminence *1361*

DIP (10) [DIPPED, DIPPETH, DIPT]
Ex 12:22 **d** *it* in the blood that *is* in the bason, and 2881
Lev 4: 6 the priest shall **d** his finger in the blood, 2881
4:17 the priest shall **d** his finger *in some* of 2881
14: 6 shall **d** them and the living bird in the blood 2881
14:16 the priest shall **d** his right finger in the oil 2881
14:51 **d** them in the blood of the slain bird, 2881
Nu 19:18 **d** *it* in the water, and sprinkle *it* upon 2881
Dt 33:24 to his brethren, and let him **d** his foot in oil. 2881
Ru 2:14 the bread, and **d** thy morsel in the vinegar. 2881
Lk 16:24 that he may **d** the tip of his finger in water, *911*

DIPPED (6) [DIP]
Ge 37:31 of the goats, and **d** the coat in the blood; 2881
Jos 3:15 the ark were **d** in the brim of the water, 2881
2Ki 5:14 and **d** *himself* seven times in Jordan, 2881
Ps 68:23 That thy foot may be **d** in the blood of *thine* 4272
Jn 13:26 when I have **d** *it.* And when he had dipped *911*
13:26 when I have dipped *it.* And when he had **d** *1686*

DIPPETH (2) [DIP]
Mt 26:23 He that **d** *his* hand with me in the dish, *1686*
Mk 14:20 of the twelve, that **d** with me in the dish. *1686*

DIPT (4) [DIP]
Lev 9: 9 he **d** his finger in the blood, and put *it* upon 2881
1Sa 14:27 **d** it in a honeycomb, and put his hand to his 2881
2Ki 8:15 **d** *it* in water, and spread *it* on his face, so 2881
Rev 19:13 And he *was* clothed with a vesture **d** in *911*

DIRECT (10) [DIRECTED, DIRECTETH, DIRECTION, DIRECTLY]
Ge 46:28 him unto Joseph, to **d** his face unto Goshen; 3384
Ps 5: 3 *in* the morning will I **d** *my prayer* unto 6186
Pr 3: 6 acknowledge him, and he shall **d** thy paths. 3474
11: 5 The righteousness of the perfect shall **d** his 3474
Ecc 10:10 but wisdom *is* profitable to **d**. 3787
Isa 45:13 in righteousness, and I will **d** all his ways: 3474
61: 8 I will **d** their work in truth, and I will make 5414
Jer 10:23 *it is* not in man that walketh to **d** his steps. 3559
1Th 3:11 our Lord Jesus Christ, **d** our way unto you. *2720*
2Th 3: 5 And the Lord **d** your hearts into the love of *2720*

DIRECTED (3) [DIRECT]
Job 32:14 Now he hath not **d** *his* words against me: 6186
Ps 119: 5 O that my ways were **d** to keep thy statutes! 3559
Isa 40:13 Who hath **d** the spirit of the LORD, or 8505

DIRECTETH (3) [DIRECT]
Job 37: 3 He **d** it under the whole heaven, and 3474
Pr 16: 9 his way: but the LORD **d** his steps. 3559
21:29 his face: but *as for* the upright, he **d** his way. 995

DIRECTION (1) [DIRECT]
Nu 21:18 **by the d of** the lawgiver, with their staves. 871.1

DIRECTLY (2) [DIRECT]
Nu 19: 4 sprinkle of her blood **d** before 413+5227
Eze 42:12 *even* the way **d** before the wall toward 1903

DIRT (3)
Jdg 3:22 dagger out of his belly; and the **d** came out. 6574
Ps 18:42 I did cast them out as the **d** in the streets. 2916
Isa 57:20 whose waters cast up mire and **d**. 2916

DISABLED See IMPOTENT

DISALLOW (2) [DISALLOWED]
Nu 30: 5 if her father **d** her in the day that he 5106
30: 8 if her husband **d** her on the day that he 5106

DISALLOWED (4) [DISALLOW]
Nu 30: 5 shall forgive her, because her father **d** her. 5106
30:11 and held his peace at her, *and* **d** her not: 5106
1Pe 2: 4 **d** indeed of men, but chosen of God, *and* *593*
2: 7 the stone which the builders **d**, *593*

DISANNUL (3) [DISANNULLED, DISANNULLETH, DISANNULLING]
Job 40: 8 Wilt thou also **d** my judgment? wilt thou 6565
Isa 14:27 who shall **d** *it?* and his hand *is* stretched 6565
Gal 3:17 hundred and thirty years after, cannot **d**, *208*

DISANNULLED (1) [DISANNUL]
Isa 28:18 your covenant with death shall be **d**, and 3722

DISANNULLETH (1) [DISANNUL]
Gal 3:15 *it be* confirmed, no *man* **d**, or added thereto. *114*

DISANNULLING (1) [DISANNUL]
Heb 7:18 For there is verily a **d** of the commandment *115*

DISAPPOINT (1) [DISAPPOINTED, DISAPPOINTETH]
Ps 17:13 Arise, O LORD, **d** him, cast him 6440+6923

DISAPPOINTED (1) [DISAPPOINT]
Pr 15:22 Without counsel purposes *are* **d**: but in 6565

DISAPPOINTETH (1) [DISAPPOINT]
Job 5:12 He **d** the devices of the crafty, so that their 6565

DISCERN (17) [DISCERNED, DISCERNER, DISCERNETH, DISCERNING]
Ge 31:32 before our brethren **d** thou what *is* thine 5234
38:25 she said, **D**, I pray thee, whose *are* these, 5234
2Sa 14:17 so *is* my lord the king to **d** good and bad: 8085
19:35 *and* can I **d** between good and evil? can thy 3045
1Ki 3: 9 that *I* may **d** between good and bad: 995
3:11 hast asked for thyself understanding to **d** 8085
Ezr 3:13 So that the people could not **d** the noise of 5234
Job 4:16 but I could not **d** the form thereof: 5234
6:30 cannot my taste **d** perverse things? 995
Eze 44:23 **cause** them **to d** between the unclean and 3045
Jnh 4:11 that cannot **d** between their right hand 3045
Mal 3:18 **d** between the righteous and the wicked, 7200
Mt 16: 3 *ye* hypocrites, ye can **d** the face of the sky; *1252*
16: 3 but can ye not ***d*** the signs of the times? NIG
Lk 12:56 ye can **d** the face of the sky and of *1381*
12:56 how *is it that* ye do not **d** this time? *1381+1492*
Heb 5:14 have their senses exercised to **d** both good *1253*

DISCERNED (4) [DISCERN]
Ge 27:23 he **d** him not, because his hands were hairy, 5234
1Ki 20:41 the king of Israel **d** him that he *was* of 5234
Pr 7: 7 the simple ones, I **d** among the youths, 995
1Co 2:14 know *them,* because they are spiritually **d**. *350*

DISCERNER (1) [DISCERN]
Heb 4:12 and *is* a **d** of the thoughts and intents of *2924*

DISCERNETH (1) [DISCERN]
Ecc 8: 5 a wise *man's* heart **d** *both* time and 3045

DISCERNING (2) [DISCERN]
1Co 11:29 to himself, not **d** the Lord's body. *1252*
12:10 to another prophecy; to another **d** of spirits; *1253*

DISCHARGE (1) [DISCHARGED]
Ecc 8: 8 *there is* no **d** in *that* war; neither shall 4917

DISCHARGED (1) [DISCHARGE]
1Ki 5: 9 will **cause** them **to be d** there, and 5310

DISCIPLE (29) [DISCIPLES, DISCIPLES', FELLOW-DISCIPLES]
Mt 10:24 The **d** is not above *his* master, nor *3101*
10:25 *It is* enough for the **d** that he be as his *3101*
10:42 a cup of cold *water* only in the name of a **d**, *3101*
27:57 who also himself was Jesus' **d**: *3100*
Lk 6:40 The **d** is not above his master: but *3101*
14:26 and his own life also, he cannot be my **d**. *3101*
14:27 and come after me, cannot be my **d**. *3101*
14:33 not all that he hath, he cannot be my **d**. *3101*
Jn 9:28 they reviled him, and said, Thou art his **d**; *3101*
18:15 Peter followed Jesus, and *so did* another **d**: *3101*
18:15 that **d** was known unto the high priest, and *3101*
18:16 Then went out *that* other **d**, which was *3101*
19:26 saw *his* mother, and the **d** standing by, *3101*
19:27 Then saith he to the **d**, Behold thy mother. *3101*
19:27 And from that hour *that* **d** took her unto his *3101*
19:38 being a **d** of Jesus, but secretly for fear of *3101*
20: 2 and to the other **d**, whom Jesus loved, and *3101*
20: 3 and *that* other **d**, and came to the sepulchre. *3101*
20: 4 and the other **d** did outrun Peter, and *3101*
20: 8 Then went in also *that* other **d**, which came *3101*
21: 7 Therefore that **d** whom Jesus loved saith *3101*
21:20 seeth the **d** whom Jesus loved following; *3101*
21:23 the brethren, that that **d** should not die: *3101*
21:24 This is the **d** which testifieth of these *3101*
Ac 9:10 And there was a certain **d** at Damascus, *3101*
9:26 of him, and believed not that he was a **d**. *3101*
9:36 Now there was at Joppa a certain **d** named *3102*
16: 1 and behold, a certain **d** was there, *3101*
21:16 an old **d**, with whom we should lodge. *3101*

DISCIPLES (243) [DISCIPLE]
Isa 8:16 up the testimony, seal the law among my **d**. 3928
Mt 5: 1 and when he was set, his **d** came unto him: *3101*
8:21 And another of his **d** said unto him, Lord, *3101*
8:23 was entered into a ship, his **d** followed him. *3101*
8:25 And his **d** came to *him,* and awoke him, *3101*
9:10 and sat down with him and his **d**. *3101*
9:11 the Pharisees saw *it,* they said unto his **d**, *3101*
9:14 Then came to him the **d** of John, saying, *3101*
9:14 the Pharisees fast oft, but thy **d** fast not? *3101*
9:19 and followed him, and *so did* his **d**. *3101*
9:37 Then saith he unto his **d**, The harvest truly *3101*
10: 1 when he had called unto *him* his twelve **d**, *3101*
11: 1 made an end of commanding his twelve **d**, *3101*
11: 2 the works of Christ, he sent two of his **d**, *3101*
12: 1 and his **d** were a hungred, and began to *3101*
12: 2 thy **d** do *that* which is not lawful to do upon *3101*
12:49 he stretched forth his hand toward his **d**, *3101*
13:10 And the **d** came, and said unto him, *3101*
13:36 and his **d** came unto him, saying, *3101*
14:12 And his **d** came, and took up the body, *3101*
14:15 his **d** came to him, saying, *This* is a desert *3101*
14:19 and gave the loaves to *his* **d**, and *3101*
14:19 to *his* disciples, and the **d** to the multitude. *3101*
14:22 And straightway Jesus constrained his **d** to *3101*
14:26 And when the **d** saw him walking on *3101*
15: 2 Why do thy **d** transgress the tradition of *3101*
15:12 Then came his **d**, and said unto him, *3101*
15:23 And his **d** came and besought him, saying, *3101*
15:32 Then Jesus called his **d** unto *him,* and said, *3101*
15:33 And his **d** say unto him, Whence should we *3101*
15:36 and brake *them,* and gave to his **d**, and *3101*
15:36 to his disciples, and the **d** to the multitude. *3101*
16: 5 And when his **d** were come to the other *3101*
16:13 he asked his **d**, saying, Whom do men say *3101*
16:20 Then charged he his **d** that they should tell *3101*
16:21 time forth began Jesus to shew unto his **d**, *3101*
16:24 Then said Jesus unto his **d**, If any *man* will *3101*
17: 6 And when the **d** heard *it,* they fell on their *3101*
17:10 And his **d** asked him, saying, Why then *3101*
17:13 Then the **d** understood that he spake unto *3101*
17:16 And I brought him to thy **d**, and they could *3101*
17:19 Then came the **d** to Jesus apart, *3101*
18: 1 At the same time came the **d** unto Jesus, *3101*
19:10 His **d** say unto him, If the case of the man *3101*
19:13 on them, and pray: and the **d** rebuked them. *3101*
19:23 Then said Jesus unto his **d**, Verily I say *3101*
19:25 When his **d** heard *it,* they were exceedingly *3101*
20:17 took the twelve **d** apart in the way, *3101*
21: 1 the mount of Olives, then sent Jesus two **d**, *3101*
21: 6 And the **d** went, and did as Jesus *3101*
21:20 And when the **d** saw *it,* they marvelled, *3101*
22:16 And they sent out unto him their **d** with *3101*
23: 1 spake Jesus to the multitude, and to his **d**, *3101*
24: 1 his **d** came to *him* for to shew him *3101*
24: 3 the **d** came unto him privately, saying, *3101*
26: 1 all these sayings, he said unto his **d**, *3101*
26: 8 But when his **d** saw *it,* they had *3101*
26:17 *of* unleavened bread the **d** came to Jesus, *3101*
26:18 keep the passover at thy house with my **d**. *3101*
26:19 And the **d** did as Jesus had appointed them; *3101*
26:26 blessed *it,* and brake *it,* and gave *it* to the **d**, *3101*
26:35 not deny thee. Likewise also said all the **d**. *3101*
26:36 and saith unto the **d**, Sit ye here, while I go *3101*
26:40 And he cometh unto the **d**, and *3101*
26:45 Then cometh he to his **d**, and saith unto *3101*
26:56 Then all the **d** forsook him, and fled. *3101*
27:64 lest his **d** come by night, and steal him *3101*
28: 7 and tell his **d** that he is risen from the dead; *3101*
28: 8 great joy; and did run to bring his **d** word. *3101*
28: 9 And as they went to tell his **d**, behold, Jesus *3101*
28:13 His **d** came by night, and stole him *away* *3101*
28:16 Then the eleven **d** went *away* into Galilee, *3101*
Mk 2:15 sat also together with Jesus and his **d**: *3101*
2:16 and sinners, they said unto his **d**, *3101*
2:18 And the **d** of John and of the Pharisees used *3101*

Mk 2:18 Why do the **d** of John and of the Pharisees 3101
2:18 and of the Pharisees fast, but thy **d** fast not? 3101
2:23 and his **d** began, as they went, to pluck 3101
3: 7 But Jesus withdrew himself with his **d** to 3101
3: 9 And he spake to his **d**, that a small ship 3101
4:34 he expounded all *things* to his **d**. 3101
5:31 And his **d** said unto him, Thou seest 3101
6: 1 into his own country; and his **d** follow him. 3101
6:29 And when his **d** heard *of it,* they came and 3101
6:35 his **d** came unto him, and said, *This* is a 3101
6:41 and gave *them* to his **d** to set before them; 3101
6:45 And straightway he constrained his **d** to get 3101
7: 2 And when they saw some of his **d** eat bread 3101
7: 5 Why walk not thy **d** according to 3101
7:17 his **d** asked him concerning the parable. 3101
8: 1 Jesus called his **d** unto *him,* and saith unto 3101
8: 4 And his **d** answered him, From whence can 3101
8: 6 and gave to his **d** to set before *them;* and 3101
8:10 he entered into a ship with his **d**, 3101
8:14 Now *the d* had forgotten to take bread, NIG
8:27 And Jesus went out, and his **d**, into 3101
8:27 and by the way he asked his **d**, saying unto 3101
8:33 he had turned about and looked on his **d**, 3101
8:34 called the people unto *him* with his **d** also, 3101
9:14 And when he came to *his* **d**, he saw a great 3101
9:18 I spake to thy **d** that they should cast him 3101
9:28 his **d** asked him privately, Why could not 3101
9:31 For he taught his **d**, and said unto them, 3101
10:10 And in the house his **d** asked him again of 3101
10:13 *his* **d** rebuked those that brought *them.* 3101
10:23 looked round about, and saith unto his **d**, 3101
10:24 And the **d** were astonished at his words. 3101
10:46 as he went out of Jericho with his **d** and 3101
11: 1 of Olives, he sendeth forth two of his **d**, 3101
11:14 thee hereafter for ever. And his **d** heard *it.* 3101
12:43 And he called unto *him* his **d**, and 3101
13: 1 one of his **d** saith unto him, Master, 3101
14:12 his **d** said unto him, Where wilt thou *that* 3101
14:13 And he sendeth forth two of his **d**, and 3101
14:14 where I shall eat the passover with my **d**? 3101
14:16 And his **d** went forth, and came into 3101
14:32 and he saith to his **d**, Sit ye here, while I 3101
16: 7 tell his **d** and Peter that he goeth before you 3101
Lk 5:30 and Pharisees murmured against his **d**, 3101
5:33 Why do the **d** of John fast often, and 3101
5:33 and likewise the *d* of the Pharisees; NIG
6: 1 and his **d** plucked the ears of corn, and 3101
6:13 when it was day, he called unto *him* his **d**: 3101
6:17 and the company of his **d**, and a great 3101
6:20 And he lifted up his eyes on his **d**, and said, 3101
7:11 and many of his **d** went with him, and 3101
7:18 And the **d** of John shewed him of all these 3101
7:19 And John calling unto *him* two of his **d** sent 3101
8: 9 And his **d** asked him, saying, What might 3101
8:22 that he went into a ship with his **d**: 3101
9: 1 Then he called his twelve **d** together, and 3101
9:14 And he said to his **d**, Make them sit down 3101
9:16 gave to the **d** to set before the multitude. 3101
9:18 he was alone praying, *his* **d** were with him: 3101
9:40 And I besought thy **d** to cast him out; and 3101
9:43 *things* which Jesus did, he said unto his **d**, 3101
9:54 And when his **d** James and John saw *this,* 3101
10:23 And he turned him unto *his* **d**, and 3101
11: 1 he ceased, one of his **d** said unto him, Lord, 3101
11: 1 teach us to pray, as John also taught his **d**. 3101
12: 1 he began to say unto his **d** first *of all,* 3101
12:22 And he said unto his **d**, Therefore I say 3101
16: 1 And he said also unto his **d**, There was a 3101
17: 1 Then said he unto the **d**, It is impossible but 3101
17:22 And he said unto the **d**, The days will 3101
18:15 but when *his* **d** saw *it,* they rebuked them. 3101
19:29 *the mount* of Olives, he sent two of his **d**, 3101
19:37 the whole multitude of the **d** began to 3101
19:39 said unto him, Master, rebuke thy **d**. 3101
20:45 of all the people he said unto his **d**, 3101
22:11 where I shall eat the passover with my **d**? 3101
22:39 of Olives; and his **d** also followed him. 3101
22:45 rose up from prayer, and was come to his **d**, 3101
Jn 1:35 next day *after* John stood, and two of his **d**; 3101
1:37 And the two **d** heard him speak, and 3101
2: 2 Jesus was called, and his **d**, to the marriage. 3101
2:11 forth his glory; and his **d** believed on him. 3101
2:12 and his mother, and his brethren, and his **d**: 3101
2:17 And his **d** remembered that it was written, 3101
2:22 his **d** remembered that he had said this unto 3101
3:22 came Jesus and his **d** into the land of Judea; 3101
3:25 arose a question between *some* of John's **d** 3101
4: 1 Jesus made and baptized moe **d** than John, 3101
4: 2 Jesus himself baptized not, but his **d**,) 3101
4: 8 (For his **d** were gone away unto the city to 3101
4:27 And upon this came his **d**, and 3101
4:31 In the mean while *his* **d** prayed him, saying, 3101
4:33 Therefore said the **d** one to another, 3101
6: 3 into a mountain, and there he sat with his **d**. 3101
6: 8 One of his **d**, Andrew, Simon Peter's 3101
6:11 he distributed to the **d**, and the disciples to 3101
6:11 and the **d** to them that were set down; 3101
6:12 When they were filled, he said unto his **d**, 3101
6:16 *now* come, his **d** went down unto the sea, 3101
6:22 save that one whereinto his **d** were entered, 3101
6:22 that Jesus went not with his **d** into the boat, 3101
6:22 but *that* his **d** were gone away alone; 3101
6:24 neither his **d**, they also took shipping, 3101
6:60 Many therefore of his **d**, when they had 3101
6:61 When Jesus knew in himself that his **d** 3101
6:66 From that *time* many of his **d** went back, 3101
7: 3 that thy **d** also may see the works that thou 3101
8:31 in my word, *then* are ye my **d** indeed; 3101
9: 2 And his **d** asked him, saying, Master, 3101
9:27 you hear *it* again? will ye also be his **d**? 3101
9:28 Thou art his disciple; but we are Moses' **d**. 3101
11: 7 Then after that saith he to *his* **d**, Let us go 3101
11: 8 *His* **d** say unto him, Master, the Jews of late 3101
11:12 Then said his **d**, Lord, if he sleep, he shall 3101
11:54 and there continued with his **d**. 3101
12: 4 Then saith one of his **d**, Judas Iscariot, 3101
12:16 These *things* understood not his **d** at 3101
13:22 Then the **d** looked one on another, 3101
13:23 was leaning on Jesus' bosom one of his **d**, 3101
13:35 this shall all *men* know that ye are my **d**, 3101
15: 8 ye bear much fruit; so shall ye be my **d**. 3101
16:17 Then said *some* of his **d** among themselves, 3101
16:29 His **d** said unto him, Lo, now speakest thou 3101
18: 1 forth with his **d** over the brook Cedron, 3101
18: 1 into the which he entered, and his **d**. 3101
18: 2 Jesus ofttimes resorted thither with his **d**. 3101
18:17 Art not thou also *one* of this man's **d**? 3101
18:19 The high priest then asked Jesus of his **d**, 3101
18:25 unto him, Art not thou also *one* of his **d**? 3101
20:10 Then the **d** went away again unto their own 3101
20:18 and told the **d** that she had seen the Lord, 3101
20:19 when the doors were shut where the **d** were 3101
20:20 Then were the **d** glad, when they saw 3101
20:25 The other **d** therefore said unto him, 3101
20:26 And after eight days again his **d** were 3101
20:30 truly did Jesus in the presence of his **d**, 3101
21: 1 himself again to the **d** at the sea of Tiberias; 3101
21: 2 the *sons* of Zebedee, and two other of his **d**. 3101
21: 4 but the **d** knew not that it was Jesus. 3101
21: 8 And the other **d** came in a little ship; 3101
21:12 And none of the **d** durst ask him, Who art 3101
21:14 time *that* Jesus shewed himself to his **d**, 3101
Ac 1:15 days Peter stood up in the midst of the **d**, 3101
6: 1 when the number of the **d** was multiplied, 3101
6: 2 called the multitude of the **d** unto *them,* 3101
6: 7 the number of the **d** multiplied in Jerusalem 3101
9: 1 and slaughter against the **d** of the Lord, 3101
9:19 Then was Saul certain days with the **d** 3101
9:25 Then the **d** took him by night, and let *him* 3101
9:26 he assayed to join himself to the **d**: 3101
9:38 and the **d** had heard that Peter was there, 3101
11:26 the **d** were called Christians first in 3101
11:29 Then the **d**, every man according to his 3101
13:52 And the **d** were filled with joy, and with 3101
14:20 Howbeit, as the **d** stood round about him, 3101
14:22 Confirming the souls of the **d**, *and* 3101
14:28 And there they abode long time with the **d**. 3101
15:10 to put a yoke upon the neck of the **d**, 3101
18:23 Phrygia in order, strengthening all the **d**. 3101
18:27 exhorting the **d** to receive him: 3101
19: 1 came to Ephesus: and finding certain **d**, 3101
19: 9 he departed from them, and separated the **d**, 3101
19:30 in unto the people, the **d** suffered him not. 3101
20: 1 Paul called unto *him* the **d**, and embraced 3101
20: 7 when the **d** came together to break bread, 3101
20:30 speaking perverse *things,* to draw away **d** 3101
21: 4 And finding **d**, we tarried there seven days: 3101
21:16 There went with us also *certain* of the **d** of 3101

DISCIPLES' (1) [DISCIPLE]
Jn 13: 5 and began to wash the **d** feet, and to wipe *3101*

DISCIPLINE (1)
Job 36:10 He openeth also their ear to **d**, and 4148

DISCLOSE (1)
Isa 26:21 the earth also shall **d** her blood, and 1540

DISCOMFITED (9) [DISCOMFITURE]
Ex 17:13 Joshua **d** Amalek and his people with 2522
Nu 14:45 smote them, and **d** them, *even* unto 3807
Jos 10:10 the LORD **d** them before Israel, and 2000
Jdg 4:15 the LORD **d** Sisera, and all *his* chariots, 2000
8:12 and Zalmunna, and **d** all the host. 2729
1Sa 7:10 that day upon the Philistines, and **d** them; 2000
2Sa 22:15 and scattered them; lightning, and **d** them. 2000
Ps 18:14 and he shot out lightnings, and **d** them. 2000
Isa 31: 8 the sword, and his young men shall be **d**. 4522

DISCOMFITURE (1) [DISCOMFITED]
1Sa 14:20 his fellow, *and there was* a very great **d**. 4103

DISCONTENTED (1)
1Sa 22: 2 in debt, and every one *that was* **d**, 4751+5315

DISCONTINUE (1)
Jer 17: 4 shalt **d** from thine heritage that I gave thee; 8058

DISCORD (2)
Pr 6:14 deviseth mischief continually; he soweth **d**. 4066
6:19 and he that soweth **d** among brethren. 4066

DISCOURAGE (1) [DISCOURAGED]
Nu 32: 7 wherefore **d** ye the heart of the children of 5106

DISCOURAGED (6) [DISCOURAGE]
Nu 21: 4 the soul of the people was much **d** because 7114
32: 9 they **d** the heart of the children of Israel, 5106
Dt 1:21 hath said unto thee; fear not, neither be **d**. 2865
1:28 our brethren have **d** our heart, saying, 4549
Isa 42: 4 He shall not fail nor be **d**, till he have set 7533
Col 3:21 not your children *to anger*, lest they be **d**. *120*

DISCOVER (12) [DISCOVERED, DISCOVERETH, DISCOVERING]
Dt 22:30 his father's wife, nor **d** his father's skirt. 1540
1Sa 14: 8 and we will **d** ourselves unto them. 1540
Job 41:13 Who can **d** the face of his garment? *or* 1540
Pr 18: 2 but that his heart may **d** itself. 1540
25: 9 and **d** not a secret *to* another: 1540
Isa 3:17 and the LORD will **d** their secret parts. 6168
Jer 13:26 Therefore will I **d** thy skirts upon thy face, 2834
La 4:22 O daughter of Edom; he will **d** thy sins. 1540
Eze 16:37 will **d** thy nakedness unto them, that they 1540
Hos 2:10 now will I **d** her lewdness in the sight of 1540
Mic 1: 6 and I will **d** the foundations thereof. 1540
Na 3: 5 I will **d** thy skirts upon thy face, and I will 1540

DISCOVERED (22) [DISCOVER]
Ex 20:26 that thy nakedness be not **d** thereon. 1540
Lev 20:18 he hath **d** her fountain, and she hath 6168
1Sa 14:11 both of them **d** themselves unto 1540
22: 6 When Saul heard that David was **d**, and 3045
2Sa 22:16 the foundations of the world were **d**, at 1540
Ps 18:15 the foundations of the world were **d** at thy 1540
Isa 22: 8 he **d** the covering of Judah, and thou didst 1540
57: 8 for thou hast **d** *thyself to another* than me, 1540
Jer 13:22 greatness of thine iniquity are thy skirts **d**, 1540
La 2:14 they have not **d** thine iniquity, to turn away 1540
Eze 13:14 so that the foundation thereof shall be **d**, 1540
16:36 thy nakedness **d** through thy whoredoms 1540
16:57 Before thy wickedness was **d**, as *at* the time 1540
21:24 in that your transgressions are **d**, so that in 1540
22:10 In thee have they **d** their father's 1540
23:10 These **d** her nakedness: they took her sons 1540
23:18 So she **d** her whoredoms, and 1540
23:18 her whoredoms, and **d** her nakedness: 1540
23:29 the nakedness of thy whoredoms shall be **d**, 1540
Hos 7: 1 the iniquity of Ephraim was **d**, and 1540
Ac 21: 3 Now when we had **d** Cyprus, we left it on *398*
27:39 but they **d** a certain creek with a shore, *2657*

DISCOVERETH (2) [DISCOVER]
Job 12:22 He **d** deep *things* out of darkness, and 1540
Ps 29: 9 the hinds to calve, and **d** the forests: 2834

DISCOVERING (1) [DISCOVER]
Hab 3:13 by **d** the foundation unto the neck. 6168

DISCREDIT See DISANNUL; DISANNULLED

DISCREET (3) [DISCREETLY, DISCRETION]
Ge 41:33 let Pharaoh look out a man **d** and wise, 995
41:39 *there is* none so **d** and wise as thou *art*: 995
Tit 2: 5 *To be* **d**, chaste, keepers at home, good, *4998*

DISCREETLY (1) [DISCREET]
Mk 12:34 And when Jesus saw that he answered **d**, *3562*

DISCRETION (9) [DISCREET]
Ps 112: 5 lendeth: he will guide his affairs with **d**. 4941
Pr 1: 4 to the young man knowledge and **d**. 4209
2:11 **D** shall preserve thee, understanding shall 4209
3:21 from thine eyes: keep sound wisdom and **d**: 4209
5: 2 That *thou* mayest regard **d**, and *that* thy lips 4209
11:22 *so is* a fair woman which is without **d**. 2940
19:11 The **d** of a man deferreth his anger; and *it is* 7922
Isa 28:26 For his God doth instruct him to **d**, *and* 4941
Jer 10:12 and hath stretched out the heavens by his **d**. 8394

DISDAINED (2)
1Sa 17:42 looked about, and saw David, he **d** him: 959
Job 30: 1 whose fathers I would have **d** to have set 3988

DISEASE (15) [DISEASED, DISEASES]
2Ki 1: 2 of Ekron whether I shall recover of this **d**. 2483
8: 8 by him, saying, Shall I recover of this **d**? 2483
8: 9 to thee, saying, Shall I recover of this **d**? 2483
2Ch 16:12 until his **d** *was* exceeding *great*: yet in his 2483
16:12 yet in his **d** he sought not *to* the LORD, 2483
21:15 thou *shalt* have great sickness by **d** of thy 4245
21:18 him in his bowels with an incurable **d**. 2483
Job 30:18 By the great force *of my* **d** is my garment NIH
Ps 38: 7 For my loins are filled *with* a loathsome **d**: NIH
41: 8 An evil **d**, *say they*, cleaveth fast unto him: 1697
Ecc 6: 2 eateth it: this *is* vanity, and it *is* an evil **d**. 2483
Mt 4:23 and all *manner of* **d** among the people. *3119*
9:35 and every **d** among the people. *3119*
10: 1 all *manner of* sickness and all *manner of* **d**. *3119*
Jn 5: 4 was made whole of whatsoever **d** he had. *3553*

DISEASED (8) [DISEASE]
1Ki 15:23 the time of his old age he was **d** in his feet. 2470
2Ch 16:12 and ninth year of his reign was **d** in his feet, 2456
Eze 34: 4 The **d** have ye not strengthened, 2470
34:21 and pusht all the **d** with your horns, 2470
Mt 9:20 which was **d with an issue of blood** twelve *131*
14:35 and brought unto him all that were **d**; *2192+2560*
Mk 1:32 they brought unto him all that were **d**, and *2560*
Jn 6: 2 miracles which he did on them that were **d**. *770*

DISEASES (13) [DISEASE]
Ex 15:26 I will put none of *these* **d** upon thee, 4245
Dt 7:15 will put none of the evil **d** of Egypt, 4064
28:60 Moreover he will bring upon thee all the **d** 4064
2Ch 21:19 so he died of sore **d**. And his people made 8463
24:25 from him, (for they left him in great **d**,) 4251
Ps 103: 3 all thine iniquities; who healeth all thy **d**; 8463
Mt 4:24 sick people that were taken with divers **d** *3554*
Mk 1:34 he healed many *that were* sick of divers **d**, *3554*
Lk 4:40 all they that had *any* sick with divers **d** *3554*
6:17 to hear him, and to be healed of their **d**; *3554*
9: 1 and authority over all devils, and to cure **d**. *3554*
Ac 19:12 and the **d** departed from them, and the evil *3554*
28: 9 which had **d** in the island, came, and *769*

DISFIGURE (1)
Mt 6:16 for they **d** their faces, that they may appear *853*

DISGRACE (1)
Jer 14:21 do not **d** the throne of thy glory: 5034

DISGUISE (3) [DISGUISED, DISGUISETH]
1Ki 14: 2 his wife, Arise, I pray thee, and **d** thyself, 8138
22:30 I will **d** myself, and enter into the battle; 2664
2Ch 18:29 I will **d** myself, and will go to the battle; 2664

DISGUISED (5) [DISGUISE]
1Sa 28: 8 Saul **d** himself, and put on other raiment, 2664
1Ki 20:38 and **d** himself with ashes upon his face. 2664

1Ki 22:30 the king of Israel **d** himself, and went into 2664
2Ch 18:29 So the king of Israel **d** himself; and 2664
35:22 **d** himself, that *he* might fight with him, and 2664

DISGUISETH (1) [DISGUISE]
Job 24:15 No eye shall see me: and **d** *his* face. 5643

DISH (4) [DISHES, SNUFFDISHES]
Jdg 5:25 she brought forth butter in a lordly **d**. 5602
2Ki 21:13 I will wipe Jerusalem as *a man* wipeth a **d**, 6747
Mt 26:23 He that dippeth *his* hand with me in the **d**, *5165*
Mk 14:20 of the twelve, that dippeth with me in the **d**. *5165*

DISHAN (5)
Ge 36:21 Dishon, and Ezer, and **D**: these *are* 1789
36:28 The children of **D** *are* these; Uz, and Aran. 1789
36:30 Duke Dishon, duke Ezer, duke **D**: these *are* 1789
1Ch 1:38 and Anah, and Dishon, and Ezer, and **D**. 1789
1:42 *and* Jakan. The sons of **D**; Uz, and Aran. 1789

DISHES (3) [DISH]
Ex 25:29 thou shalt make the **d** thereof, and 7086
37:16 his **d**, and his spoons, and his bowls, and 7086
Nu 4: 7 put thereon the **d**, and the spoons, and 7086

DISHON (7)
Ge 36:21 **D**, and Ezer, and Dishan: these *are* 1787
36:25 **D**, and Aholibamah the daughter of Anah. 1787
36:26 these *are* the children of **D**; Hemdan, and 1789
36:30 Duke **D**, duke Ezer, duke Dishan: these *are* 1787
1Ch 1:38 and Anah, and **D**, and Ezer, and Dishan. 1787
1:41 The sons of Anah; **D**. And the sons of 1787
1:41 the sons of **D**; Amram, and Eshban, and 1787

DISHONEST (2) [DISHONESTY]
Eze 22:13 I have smitten mine hand at thy **d gain** 1215
22:27 *and* to destroy souls, to **get d gain**. 1214+1215

DISHONESTY (1) [DISHONEST]
2Co 4: 2 But have renounced the hidden *things* of **d**, *152*

DISHONOUR (11) [DISHONOUREST, DISHONOURETH]
Ezr 4:14 *it was* not meet for us to see the king's **d**, 6173
Ps 35:26 and **d** that magnify *themselves* against me. 3639
69:19 my reproach, and my shame, and my **d**: 3639
71:13 *with* reproach and **d** that seek my hurt. 3639
Pr 6:33 A wound and **d** shall he get; and 7036
Jn 8:49 but I honour my Father, and ye do **d** me. *818*
Ro 1:24 to **d** their own bodies between themselves: *818*
9:21 one vessel unto honour, and another unto **d**? *819*
1Co 15:43 It is sown in **d**; it is raised in glory: it is *819*
2Co 6: 8 By honour and **d**, by evil report and *819*
2Ti 2:20 of earth; and some to honour, and some to **d**. *819*

DISHONOUREST (1) [DISHONOUR]
Ro 2:23 through breaking the law **d** thou God? *818*

DISHONOURETH (3) [DISHONOUR]
Mic 7: 6 For the son **d** the father, the daughter riseth 5034
1Co 11: 4 having *his* head covered, **d** his head. *2617*
11: 5 prophesieth with *her* head uncovered **d** her *2617*

DISINHERIT (1)
Nu 14:12 **d** them, and will make of thee a greater 3423

DISMAYED (31) [DISMAYING]
Dt 31: 8 neither forsake thee: fear not, neither be **d**. 2865
Jos 1: 9 be not afraid, neither be thou **d**: 2865
8: 1 unto Joshua, Fear not, neither be thou **d**: 2865
10:25 Fear not, nor be **d**, be strong and of good 2865
1Sa 17:11 they were **d**, and greatly afraid. 2865
2Ki 19:26 small power, they were **d** and confounded; 2865
1Ch 22:13 and of good courage; dread not, nor be **d**. 2865
28:20 good courage, and do *it*: fear not, nor be **d**: 2865
2Ch 20:15 Be not afraid nor **d** by reason of this great 2865
20:17 fear not, nor be **d**; to morrow go out against 2865
32: 7 be not afraid nor **d** for the king of Assyria, 2865
Isa 21: 3 the hearing *of it*; I was **d** at the seeing *of it*. 926
37:27 small power, they were **d** and confounded: 2865
41:10 be not **d**; for I *am* thy God: I will 8159
41:23 that we may be **d**, and behold *it* together. 8159
Jer 1:17 be not **d** at their faces, lest I confound thee 2865
8: 9 *men* are ashamed, they are **d** and taken: 2865
10: 2 and be not **d** at the signs of heaven; 2865
10: 2 of heaven; for the heathen are **d** at them. 2865
17:18 let them be **d**, but let not me be dismayed: 2865
17:18 let them be dismayed, but let not me be **d**: 2865
23: 4 they shall fear no more, nor be **d**, neither 2865
30:10 saith the LORD; neither be **d**, O Israel: 2865
46: 5 Wherefore have I seen them **d** *and* 2844
46:27 O my servant Jacob, and be not **d**, O Israel: 2865
48: 1 *and* taken: Misgab is confounded and **d**. 2865
49:37 For I will **cause** Elam **to be d** before their 2865
50:36 upon her mighty *men*; and they shall be **d**. 2865
Eze 2: 6 of their words, nor be **d** at their looks, 2865
3: 9 fear them not, neither be **d** at their looks, 2865
Ob 1: 9 thy mighty *men*, O Teman, shall be **d**, 2865

DISMAYING (1) [DISMAYED]
Jer 48:39 be a derision and a **d** to all them about him. 4288

DISMISSED (3)
2Ch 23: 8 for Jehoiada the priest **d** not the courses. 6362
Ac 15:30 So when they were **d**, they came to Antioch: *630*
19:41 when he had thus spoken, he **d** the assembly. *630*

DISOBEDIENCE (6) [DISOBEDIENT, DISOBEYED]
Ro 5:19 For as by one man's **d** many were made *3876*
2Co 10: 6 And having in a readiness to revenge all **d**, *3876*
Eph 2: 2 spirit that now worketh in the children of **d**: *543*
5: 6 the wrath of God upon the children of **d**. *543*
Col 3: 6 wrath of God cometh on the children of **d**: *543*
Heb 2: 2 **d** received a just recompence of reward; *3876*

DISOBEDIENT (13) [DISOBEDIENCE]
1Ki 13:26 who was **d** unto the word of the LORD: 4784
Ne 9:26 Nevertheless they were **d**, and 4784
Lk 1:17 and the **d** to the wisdom of the just; *545*
Ac 26:19 I was not **d** unto the heavenly vision: *545*
Ro 1:30 inventors of evil *things*, **d** to parents, *545*
10:21 have I stretched forth my hands unto a **d** *544*
1Ti 1: 9 a righteous *man*, but for the lawless and **d**, *506*
2Ti 3: 2 **d** to parents, unthankful, unholy, *545*
Tit 1:16 and **d**, and unto every good work reprobate. *545*
3: 3 **d**, deceived, serving divers lusts and *545*
1Pe 2: 7 but unto them which be **d**, the stone which *544*
2: 8 *to them* which stumble at the word, being **d**: *544*
3:20 Which sometime were **d**, when once *544*

DISOBEYED (1) [DISOBEDIENCE]
1Ki 13:21 Forasmuch as thou hast **d** the mouth of 4784

DISORDERLY (3)
2Th 3: 6 from every brother that walketh **d**, *814*
3: 7 for we **behaved** not ourselves **d** among you; *812*
3:11 *there are* some which walk among you **d**, *814*

DISPATCH (1)
Eze 23:47 with stones, and **d** them with their swords; 1254

DISPENSATION (4)
1Co 9:17 a **d** *of the gospel* is committed unto me. *3622*
Eph 1:10 That in the **d** of the fulness of times *he* *3622*
3: 2 If ye have heard of the **d** of the grace of *3622*
Col 1:25 according to the **d** of God which is given to *3622*

DISPERSE (8) [DISPERSED, DISPERSIONS]
1Sa 14:34 **D** yourselves among the people, and 6327
Pr 15: 7 The lips of the wise **d** knowledge: but 2219
Eze 12:15 the nations, and **d** them in the countries. 2219
20:23 and **d** them through the countries; 2219
22:15 **d** thee in the countries, and will consume 2219
29:12 and will **d** them through the countries. 2219
30:23 and will **d** them through the countries. 2219
30:26 and **d** them among the countries; 2219

DISPERSED (10) [DISPERSE]
2Ch 11:23 **d** of all his children throughout all 6555
Est 3: 8 **d** among the people in all the provinces of 6504
Ps 112: 9 He hath **d**, he hath given to the poor; 6340
Pr 5:16 Let thy fountains be **d** abroad, *and* rivers of 6327
Isa 11:12 gather together the **d** of Judah from the four 5310
Eze 36:19 and they were **d** through the countries: 2219
Zep 3:10 *even* the daughter of my **d**, shall bring mine 6327
Jn 7:35 will he go unto the **d among** the Gentiles, *1290*
Ac 5:37 all, *even* as many as obeyed him, were **d**. *1287*
2Co 9: 9 (As it is written, He hath **d abroad**; he hath *4650*

DISPERSIONS (1) [DISPERSE]
Jer 25:34 and of your **d** are accomplished. 8600

DISPLAYED (1)
Ps 60: 4 that *it* may be **d** because of the truth. 5127

DISPLEASE (5) [DISPLEASED, DISPLEASURE]
Ge 31:35 Let it not **d** my lord that I 2734+5869+871.1
Nu 22:34 now therefore, if it **d** thee, 5869+7489+871.1
1Sa 29: 7 **d** not the lords of 5869+6213+7451+871.1
2Sa 11:25 Let not this thing **d** thee, 3415+7489+871.1
Pr 24:18 the LORD see *it,* and it **d** 5869+7489+871.1

DISPLEASED (25) [DISPLEASE]
Ge 38:10 *the thing* which he did **d** 3415+5869+871.1
48:17 the head of Ephraim, it **d** him: 3415+5869+871.1
Nu 11: 1 it **d** the LORD: 241+7451+871.1
11:10 Moses also was **d**. 5869+7489+871.1
1Sa 8: 6 the thing **d** Samuel, 3415+5869+871.1
18: 8 and the saying **d** him; 3415+5869+871.1
2Sa 6: 8 David was **d**, because the LORD had 2734
11:27 had done **d** the LORD. 3415+7489+871.1
1Ki 1: 6 his father had not **d** him at any time in 6087
20:43 of Israel went to his house heavy and **d**, 2198
21: 4 came into his house heavy and **d** because 2198
1Ch 13:11 David was **d**, because the LORD had 2734
21: 7 God was **d** with this thing; 3415+5869+871.1
Ps 60: 1 thou hast scattered us, thou hast been **d**; 599
Isa 59:15 **d** him that *there was* no 3415+5869+871.1
Da 6:14 was sore **d** with himself, and set *his* heart on 888
Jnh 4: 1 it **d** Jonah **exceedingly**, and he 1419+3415+7451
Hab 3: 8 Was the LORD **d** against the rivers? 2734
Zec 1: 2 The LORD hath been **sore d** with 7107+7110
1:15 I am very **sore d** with the heathen 7107+7110
1:15 for I was *but* a little **d**, and they helped 7107
Mt 21:15 to the Son of David; they were **sore d**, *23*
Mk 10:14 But when Jesus saw *it,* he was **much d**, and *23*
10:41 heard *it,* they began to be **much d** with James *23*
Ac 12:20 And Herod was **highly d** with them of Tyre *2371*

DISPLEASURE (5) [DISPLEASE]
Dt 9:19 For I was afraid of the anger and **hot d**, 2534
Jdg 15: 3 than the Philistines, though I do them a **d**. 7451
Ps 2: 5 in his wrath, and vex them in his **sore d**. 2740
6: 1 neither chasten me in thy **hot d**. 2534
38: 1 thy wrath: neither chasten me in thy **hot d**. 2534

DISPOSED (4) [DISPOSITION]
Job 34:13 the earth? or who hath **d** the whole world? 7760
37:15 Dost thou know when God **d** them, and 7760
Ac 18:27 And when he was **d** to pass into Achaia, *1014*
1Co 10:27 not bid you *to a feast,* and ye be **d** to go; *2309*

DISPOSING (1) [DISPOSITION]
Pr 16:33 but the whole **d** thereof *is* of the LORD. 4941

DISPOSITION (1) [DISPOSED, DISPOSING]
Ac 7:53 Who have received the law by the **d** of *1296*

DISPOSSESS (2) [DISPOSSESSED]
Nu 33:53 ye shall **d** *the inhabitants of* the land, and 3423
Dt 7:17 nations *are* moe than I; how can I **d** them? 3423

DISPOSSESSED (2) [DISPOSSESS]
Nu 32:39 took it, and **d** the Amorite which *was* in it. 3423
Jdg 11:23 So now the LORD God of Israel hath **d** 3423

DISPUTATION (1) [DISPUTE]
Ac 15: 2 had no small dissension and **d** with them, *4803*

DISPUTATIONS (1) [DISPUTE]
Ro 14: 1 the faith receive you, *but* not to doubtful **d**. *1253*

DISPUTE (1) [DISPUTATION, DISPUTATIONS, DISPUTED, DISPUTER, DISPUTING, DISPUTINGS]
Job 23: 7 There the righteous *might* **d** with him; so 3198

DISPUTED (5) [DISPUTE]
Mk 9:33 What *was it that* ye **d** among yourselves by *1260*
9:34 for by the way they had **d** among *1256*
Ac 9:29 the Lord Jesus, and **d** against the Grecians: *4802*
17:17 Therefore **d** he in the synagogue with *1256*
Jude 1: 9 when contending with the devil he **d** about *1256*

DISPUTER (1) [DISPUTE]
1Co 1:20 where *is* the **d** of this world? hath not God *4804*

DISPUTING (5) [DISPUTE]
Ac 6: 9 of Cilicia and of Asia, **d** with Stephen. *4802*
15: 7 And when there had been much **d**, Peter *4803*
19: 8 **d** and persuading the *things* concerning *1256*
19: 9 **d** daily in the school of one Tyrannus. *1256*
24:12 And they neither found me in the temple **d** *1256*

DISPUTINGS (2) [DISPUTE]
Php 2:14 Do all *things* without murmurings and **d**: *1261*
1Ti 6: 5 **Perverse d** of men of corrupt minds, and *3859*

DISQUALIFIED See CASTAWAY

DISQUALIFY See BEGUILE; BEGUILED; BEGUILING

DISQUIET (1) [DISQUIETED, DISQUIETNESS]
Jer 50:34 the land, and **d** the inhabitants of Babylon. 7264

DISQUIETED (6) [DISQUIET]
1Sa 28:15 Why hast thou **d** me, to bring me up? 7264
Ps 39: 6 surely they are **d** in vain: he heapeth up 1993
42: 5 *why* art thou **d** in me? hope thou in God: 1993
42:11 why art thou **d** within me? hope thou in 1993
43: 5 why art thou **d** within me? hope in God: 1993
Pr 30:21 For three *things* the earth is **d**, and for four 7264

DISQUIETNESS (1) [DISQUIET]
Ps 38: 8 I have roared by reason of the **d** of my 5100

DISSEMBLED (3) [DISSEMBLERS, DISSEMBLETH]
Jos 7:11 **d** also, and they have put *it* even amongst 3584
Jer 42:20 For ye **d** in your hearts, when ye sent me 8582
Gal 2:13 And the other Jews **d** likewise **with** him; *4942*

DISSEMBLERS (1) [DISSEMBLED]
Ps 26: 4 vain persons, neither will I go in with **d**. 5956

DISSEMBLETH (1) [DISSEMBLED]
Pr 26:24 He that hateth **d** with his lips, and layeth up 5234

DISSENSION (3)
Ac 15: 2 and Barnabas had no small **d** and *4714*
23: 7 there arose a **d** between the Pharisees and *4714*
23:10 And when there arose a great **d**, the chief *4714*

DISSENSIONS See SEDITIONS

DISSIMULATION (2)
Ro 12: 9 *Let* love *be* **without d**. Abhor *that which is* *505*
Gal 2:13 also was carried away with their **d**. *5272*

DISSIPATION See SURFEITING

DISSOLVE (1) [DISSOLVED, DISSOLVEST, DISSOLVING]
Da 5:16 canst make interpretations, and **d** doubts: 8271

DISSOLVED (8) [DISSOLVE]
Ps 75: 3 and all the inhabitants thereof *are* **d**: 4127
Isa 14:31 cry, O city; thou, whole Palestina, *art* **d**: 4127
24:19 the earth is **clean d**, the earth is 6565+6565
34: 4 all the host of heaven shall be **d**, and 4743
Na 2: 6 shall be opened, and the palace shall be **d**. 4127
2Co 5: 1 our earthly house of *this* tabernacle were **d**, *2647*
2Pe 3:11 Seeing then that all these *things shall* be **d**, *3089*
3:12 the heavens being on fire shall be **d**, *3089*

DISSOLVEST (1) [DISSOLVE]
Job 30:22 me to ride *upon it,* and **d** my substance. 4127

DISSOLVING (1) [DISSOLVE]
Da 5:12 shewing of hard sentences, and **d** of doubts, 8271

DISTAFF (1)
Pr 31:19 to the spindle, and her hands hold the **d**. 6418

DISTANT (1)
Ex 36:22 two tenons, **equally d** one from another: 7947

DISTIL (2)
Dt 32: 2 as the rain, my speech shall **d** as the dew, 5140
Job 36:28 do drop *and* **d** upon man abundantly. 7491

DISTINCTION (1) [DISTINCTLY]
1Co 14: 7 or harp, except they give a **d** in the sounds, *1293*

DISTINCTLY (1) [DISTINCTION]
Ne 8: 8 they read in the book in the law of God **d**, 6567

DISTORT See WREST

DISTRACTED (1) [DISTRACTION]
Ps 88:15 youth *up: while* I suffer thy terrors I am **d**. 6323

DISTRACTION (1) [DISTRACTED]
1Co 7:35 you may attend upon the Lord **without d**. *563*

DISTRESS (33) [DISTRESSED, DISTRESSES]
Ge 35: 3 who answered me in the day of my **d**, and 6869
42:21 not hear; therefore is this **d** come upon us. 6869
Dt 2: 9 LORD said unto me, **D** not the Moabites, 6696
2:19 **d** them not, nor meddle with them: 6696
28:53 wherewith thine enemies shall **d** thee: 6693
28:55 wherewith thine enemies shall **d** thee in all 6693
28:57 wherewith thine enemy shall **d** thee in thy 6693
Jdg 11: 7 ye come unto me now when ye are in **d**? 6887
1Sa 22: 2 every one *that was* in **d**, and every one that 4689
2Sa 22: 7 In my **d** I called upon the LORD, and 6862
1Ki 1:29 that hath redeemed my soul out of all **d**, 6869
2Ch 28:22 in the time of his **d** did he trespass yet more 6887
Ne 2:17 I unto them, Ye see the **d** that we *are* in, 7451
9:37 at their pleasure, and we *are* in great **d**. 6869
Ps 4: 1 thou hast enlarged me *when I was* in **d**; 6862
18: 6 In my **d** I called upon the LORD, and 6862
118: 5 I called upon the LORD in **d**: the LORD 4712
120: 1 In my **d** I cried unto the LORD, and 6869
Pr 1:27 when **d** and anguish cometh upon you: 6869
Isa 25: 4 a strength to the needy in his **d**, a refuge 6862
29: 2 Yet I will **d** Ariel, and there shall be 6693
29: 7 and her munition, and that **d** her, 6693
Jer 10:18 and will **d** them, that they may find *it so*. 6887
La 1:20 Behold, O LORD; for I *am* in **d**: my 6887
Ob 1:12 thou have spoken proudly in the day of **d**. 6869
1:14 those of his that did remain in the day of **d**. 6869
Zep 1:15 a day of trouble and **d**, a day of wasteness 4691
1:17 I will **bring d** upon men, that they shall 6887
Lk 21:23 for there shall be great **d** in the land, and *318*
21:25 and upon the earth **d** of nations, *4928*
Ro 8:35 or **d**, or persecution, or famine, or *4730*
1Co 7:26 therefore that this is good for the present **d**, *318*
1Th 3: 7 over you in all our affliction and **d**, *318*

DISTRESSED (11) [DISTRESS]
Ge 32: 7 Jacob was greatly afraid and **d**: and he 3334
Nu 22: 3 Moab was **d** because of the children of 6973
Jdg 2:15 sworn unto them: and they were greatly **d**. 3334
10: 9 house of Ephraim; so that Israel was sore **d**. 3334
1Sa 13: 6 were in a strait, (for the people were **d**,) 5065
14:24 the men of Israel were **d** that day: for Saul 5065
28:15 Saul answered, I am sore **d**; for 6887
30: 6 David was greatly **d**; for the people spake 3334
2Sa 1:26 I am **d** for thee, my brother Jonathan: 6887
2Ch 28:20 and **d** him, but strengthened him not. 6696
2Co 4: 8 *We are* troubled on every *side*, yet not **d**; *4729*

DISTRESSES (8) [DISTRESS]
Ps 25:17 are enlarged: O bring thou me out of my **d**. 4691
107: 6 *and* he delivered them out of their **d**. 4691
107:13 *and* he saved them out of their **d**. 4691
107:19 their trouble, he saveth them out of their **d**. 4691
107:28 and he bringeth them out of their **d**. 4691
Eze 30:16 rent asunder, and Noph *shall have* **d** daily. 6862
2Co 6: 4 in afflictions, in necessities, in **d**, *4730*
12:10 in persecutions, in **d** for Christ's sake: *4730*

DISTRIBUTE (5) [DISTRIBUTED, DISTRIBUTETH, DISTRIBUTING, DISTRIBUTION]
Jos 13:32 **d for inheritance** in the plains of Moab, 5157
2Ch 31:14 to **d** the oblations of the LORD, and 5414
Ne 13:13 their office *was* to **d** unto their brethren. 2505
Lk 18:22 and **d** unto the poor, and thou shalt have *1239*
1Ti 6:18 **ready to d**, willing to communicate; *2130*

DISTRIBUTED (6) [DISTRIBUTE]
Jos 14: 1 of Israel, **d for inheritance** to them. 5157
1Ch 24: 3 David **d** them, both Zadok of the sons of 2505
2Ch 23:18 whom David had **d** in the house of 2505
Jn 6:11 he **d** to the disciples, and the disciples to *1239*
1Co 7:17 But as God hath **d** to every man, as *3307*
2Co 10:13 measure of the rule which God hath **d** to us, *3307*

DISTRIBUTETH (1) [DISTRIBUTE]
Job 21:17 upon them! *God* **d** sorrows in his anger. 2505

DISTRIBUTING (1) [DISTRIBUTE]
Ro 12:13 **D** to the necessity of saints; given to *2841*

DISTRIBUTION (2) [DISTRIBUTE]
Ac 4:35 **d** was made unto every man according as *1239*
2Co 9:13 and *for your* liberal **d** unto them, and unto *2842*

DITCH (6) [DITCHES]
Job 9:31 Yet shalt thou plunge me in the **d**, and 7845
Ps 7:15 and is fallen into the **d** *which* he made. 7845
Pr 23:27 For a whore *is* a deep **d**; and a strange 7745
Isa 22:11 Ye made also a **d** between the two walls for 4724
Mt 15:14 blind lead the blind, both shall fall into the **d**. *999*
Lk 6:39 the blind? shall they not both fall into the **d**? *999*

DITCHES (1) [DITCH]
2Ki 3:16 Make this valley **full of d**. 1356+1356

DIVERS (37) [DIVERSE]
Dt 22: 9 Thou shalt not sow thy vineyard with **d** 3610
22:11 Thou shalt not wear a **garment of d sorts**, 8162
25:13 not have in thy bag **d weights**, 68+68+2050.1
25:14 in thine house **d measures**, 374+374+2050.1
Jdg 5:30 to Sisera a prey of **d colours**, a prey of 6648
5:30 a prey of **d colours** of needlework, 6648
5:30 of **d colours** of needlework on both sides, 6648
2Sa 13:18 *she had* a garment of **d colours** upon her: 6446
13:19 rent her garment of **d colours** that *was* on 6446
1Ch 29: 2 of **d colours**, and all *manner of* precious 7553
2Ch 16:14 **d kinds** *of spices* prepared by 2177
21: 4 and *d* also of the princes of Israel. NIH
30:11 Nevertheless **d** of Asher and Manasseh and 376
Ps 78:45 He sent **d sorts** *of flies* among them, 6157
105:31 there came **d sorts** *of flies, and* lice in all 6157
Pr 20:10 **D weights**, *and* divers measures, 68+68+2050.1
20:10 *and* **d measures**, 374+374+2050.1
20:23 **D weights** *are* an abomination 68+68+2050.1
Ecc 5: 7 and many words *there are* also *d* vanities: NIH
Eze 16:16 deckedst thy high places with **d colours**, 2921
17: 3 full *of* feathers, which had **d colours**, 7553
Mt 4:24 sick people that were taken with **d** diseases *4164*
24: 7 pestilences, and earthquakes **in d** places. *2596*
Mk 1:34 And he healed many *that were* sick of **d** *4164*
8: 3 by the way: for **d** of them came from far. *5100*
13: 8 and there shall be earthquakes **in d** places, *2596*
Lk 4:40 all they that had *any* sick with **d** diseases *4164*
21:11 And great earthquakes shall be **in d** places, *2596*
Ac 19: 9 But when **d** were hardened, and *5100*
1Co 12:10 of spirits; to another *d* kinds of tongues; NIG
2Ti 3: 6 laden with sins, led away with **d** lusts, *4164*
Tit 3: 3 deceived, serving **d** lusts and pleasures, *4164*
Heb 1: 1 **in d** manners spake in time past unto **the** *3588*
2: 4 and with **d** miracles, and gifts of the Holy *4164*
9:10 and **d** washings, and carnal ordinances, *1313*
13: 9 Be not carried about with **d** and *4164*
Jas 1: 2 count *it* all joy when ye fall into **d** *4164*

DIVERSE (8) [DIVERS, DIVERSITIES]
Lev 19:19 shalt not let thy cattle gender with a **d kind**: 3610
Est 1: 7 (the vessels being **d** one from another,) 8138
3: 8 their laws *are* **d** from all people; 8138
Da 7: 3 came up from the sea, **d** one from another. 8133
7: 7 it *was* **d** from all the beasts that *were* before 8133
7:19 which was **d** from all the others, 8133
7:23 which shall be **d** from all kingdoms, 8133
7:24 he shall be **d** from the first, and he shall 8133

DIVERSITIES (3) [DIVERSE]
1Co 12: 4 Now there are **d** of gifts, but the same *1243*
12: 6 And there are **d** of operations, but it is *1243*
12:28 helps, governments, **d** of tongues. *1085*

DIVIDE (49) [DIVIDED, DIVIDER, DIVIDETH, DIVIDING, DIVISION, DIVISIONS]
Ge 1: 6 let it **d** the waters from the waters. 914
1:14 of the heaven to **d** the day from the night; 914
1:18 and to **d** the light from the darkness: 914
49: 7 I will **d** them in Jacob, and scatter them in 2505
49:27 the prey, and at night he shall **d** the spoil. 2505
Ex 14:16 stretch out thine hand over the sea, and **d** it: 1234
15: 9 I will overtake, I will **d** the spoil; 2505
21:35 shall sell the live ox, and **d** the money of it; 2673
21:35 of it; and the dead *ox* also they shall **d**. 2673
26:33 the vail shall **d** unto you between the holy 914

Lev 1:17 the wings thereof, but shall not d it asunder: 914
5: 8 from his neck, but shall not d it asunder: 914
11: 4 chew the cud, or of them that d the hoof: 6536
11: 7 though he d the hoof, and be clovenfooted, 6536
Nu 31:27 d the prey into two parts; between them 2673
33:54 d the land by lot for an inheritance among 5157
34:17 of the men which shall d the land unto you: 5157
34:18 of every tribe, to d the land by inheritance. 5157
34:29 d the inheritance unto the children of 5157
Dt 14: 7 the cud, or of them that d the cloven hoof; 6536
14: 7 for they chew the cud, but d not the hoof; 6536
19: 3 d the coasts of thy land, which the LORD thy God giveth thee to inherit, into three parts, 8027
Jos 1: 6 shalt thou d for an inheritance the land, 5157
13: 6 only d thou it by lot unto the Israelites for 5307
13: 7 d this land for an inheritance unto the nine 2505
18: 5 they shall d it into seven parts: Judah shall 2505
22: 8 d the spoil of your enemies with your 2505
2Sa 19:29 I have said, Thou and Ziba d the land. 2505
1Ki 3:25 D the living child in two, and give half to 1504
3:26 Let it be neither mine nor thine, but d it. 1504
Ne 9:11 thou didst d the sea before them, so 1234
9:22 and nations, and didst d them into corners: 2505
Job 27:17 put it on, and the innocent shall d the silver. 2505
Ps 55: 9 Destroy, O Lord, and d their tongues: for I 6385
60: 6 I will d Shechem, and mete out the valley 2505
74:13 Thou didst d the sea by thy strength: 6565
108: 7 I will d Shechem, and mete out the valley 2505
Pr 16:19 than to d the spoil with the proud. 2505
Isa 9: 3 and as men rejoice when they d the spoil. 2505
53:12 Therefore will I d him a portion with 2505
53:12 and he shall d the spoil with the strong; 2505
Eze 5: 1 take thee balances to weigh, and d the hair. 2505
45: 1 when ye shall d by lot the land for 5307
47:21 So shall ye d this land unto you according 2505
47:22 that ye shall d it by lot for an inheritance 5307
48:29 This is the land which ye shall d by lot unto 5307
Da 11:39 over many, and shall d the land for gain. 2505
Lk 12:13 that he d the inheritance with me. 3307
22:17 said, Take this, and d it among yourselves: 1266

DIVIDED (69) [DIVIDE]
Ge 1: 4 and God d the light from the darkness. 914
1: 7 d the waters which were under 914
10: 5 By these were the isles of the Gentiles d in 6504
10:25 for in his days was the earth d; and 6385
10:32 by these were the nations d in the earth 6504
14:15 he d himself against them, he and 2505
15:10 d them in the midst, and laid each piece 1334
15:10 one against another: but the birds d he not. 1334
32: 7 he d the people that was with him, and 2673
33: 1 he d the children unto Leah, and 2673
Ex 14:21 the sea dry land, and the waters were d. 1234
Nu 26:53 Unto these the land shall be d for an 2505
26:55 Notwithstanding the land shall be d by lot: 2505
26:56 the possession thereof be d between many 2505
31:42 which Moses d from the men that warred, 2673
Dt 4:19 which the LORD thy God hath d unto all 2505
32: 8 High d to the nations their inheritance, 5157
Jos 14: 5 children of Israel did, and they d the land. 2505
18:10 there Joshua d the land unto the children of 2505
19:51 d for an inheritance by lot in Shiloh 5157
23: 4 I have d unto you by lot these nations that 5307
Jdg 5:30 have they not d the prey; to every man a 2505
7:16 he d the three hundred men into three 2673
9:43 d them into three companies, and laid wait 2673
19:29 d her, together with her bones, into twelve 5408
2Sa 1:23 and in their death they were not d: 6504
1Ki 16:21 were the people of Israel d into two parts: 2505
18: 6 So they d the land between them to pass 2505
2Ki 2: 8 they were d hither and thither, so that they 2673
1Ch 1:19 because in his days the earth was d: 6385
23: 6 David d them into courses among the sons 2505
24: 4 the sons of Ithamar; and thus were they d. 2505
24: 5 Thus were they d by lot, one sort with 2505
2Ch 35:13 and d them speedily among all the people. 7323
Job 38:25 Who hath d a watercourse for 6385
Ps 68:12 she that tarried at home d the spoil. 2505
78:13 He d the sea, and caused them to pass 1234
78:55 d them an inheritance by line, and made 5307
136:13 To him which d the Red sea into parts: 1504
Isa 33:23 is the prey of a great spoil d; the lame take 2505
34:17 and his hand hath d it unto them by line: 2505
51:15 that d the sea, whose waves roared: 7280
La 4:16 The anger of the LORD hath d them; 2505
Eze 37:22 neither shall they be d into two kingdoms 2673
Da 2:41 and part of iron, the kingdom shall be d; 6386
5:28 Thy kingdom is d, and given to the Medes 6537
11: 4 shall be d toward the four winds of heaven; 2673
Hos 10: 2 Their heart is d; now shall they be found 2505
Am 7:17 the sword, and thy land shall be d by line; 2505
Mic 2: 4 from me! turning away he hath d our fields. 2505
Zec 14: 1 and thy spoil shall be d in the midst of thee. 2505
Mt 12:25 Every kingdom d against itself is brought 3307
12:25 or house d against itself shall not stand: 3307
12:26 cast out Satan, he is d against himself; 3307
Mk 3:24 And if a kingdom be d against itself, 3307
3:25 And if a house be d against itself, 3307
3:26 and be d, he cannot stand, but hath an end. 3307
6:41 and the two fishes d he among them all. 3307
Lk 11:17 Every kingdom d against itself is brought 1266
11:17 and a house d against a house falleth. NIG
11:18 If Satan also be d against himself, 1266
12:52 there shall be five in one house d, 1266
12:53 The father shall be d against the son, and 1266
15:12 to me. And he d unto them his living. 1244
Ac 13:19 of Canaan, he d their land to them by lot. 2624
14: 4 But the multitude of the city was d: and 4977
23: 7 the Sadducees: and the multitude was d. 4977
1Co 1:13 Is Christ d? was Paul crucified for you? or 3307
Rev 16:19 And the great city was d into three parts, NIG

DIVIDER (1) [DIVIDE]
Lk 12:14 who made me a judge or a d over you? 3312

DIVIDETH (10) [DIVIDE]
Lev 11: 4 he cheweth the cud, but d not the hoof; 6536
11: 5 he cheweth the cud, but d not the hoof; 6536
11: 6 he cheweth the cud, but d not the hoof; 6536
11:26 The carcases of every beast which d 6536
Dt 14: 8 the swine, because it d the hoof, 6536
Job 26:12 He d the sea with his power, and by his 7280
Ps 29: 7 The voice of the LORD d the flames of 2672
Jer 31:35 which d the sea when the waves thereof 7280
Mt 25:32 as a shepherd d his sheep from the goats: 873
Lk 11:22 armour wherein he trusted, and d his spoils. 1239

DIVIDING (7) [DIVIDE]
Jos 19:49 d the land for inheritance by their coasts, 5157
19:51 So they made an end of d the country. 2505
Isa 63:12 d the water before them, to make himself 1234
Da 7:25 until a time and times and the d of time. 6387
1Co 12:11 d to every man severally as he will. 1244
2Ti 2:15 to be ashamed, rightly d the word of truth. 3718
Heb 4:12 piercing even to the d asunder of soul and 3311

DIVINATION (12) [DIVINE]
Nu 22: 7 with the rewards of d in their hand; 7081
23:23 neither is there any d against Israel: 7081
Dt 18:10 or that useth d, or an observer of 7080+7081
2Ki 17:17 used d and enchantments, and 7080+7081
Jer 14:14 prophesy unto you a false vision and d, 7081
Eze 12:24 nor flattering d within the house of Israel. 4738
13: 6 They have seen vanity and lying d, saying, 7081
13: 7 have ye not spoken a lying d, whereas ye 4738
21:21 at the head of the two ways, to use d: 7080+7081
21:22 At his right hand was the d for Jerusalem, 7081
21:23 it shall be unto them as a false d in their 7080
Ac 16:16 certain damsel possessed with a spirit of d 4436

DIVINATIONS (1) [DIVINE]
Eze 13:23 ye shall see no more vanity, nor divine d: 7081

DIVINE (11) [DIVINATION, DIVINATIONS, DIVINERS, DIVINETH, DIVINING]
Ge 44:15 that such a man as I can certainly d? 5172+5172
1Sa 28: 8 d unto me by the familiar spirit, and 7080
Pr 16:10 A d sentence is in the lips of the king: 7081
Eze 13: 9 the prophets that see vanity, and that d lies: 7080
13:23 shall see no more vanity, nor d divinations: 7080
21:29 unto thee, whiles they d a lie unto thee, 7080
Mic 3: 6 shall be dark unto you, that ye shall not d; 7080
3:11 and the prophets thereof d for money: 7080
Heb 9: 1 covenant had also ordinances of d service, 2999
2Pe 1: 3 According as his d power hath given unto 2304
1: 4 you might be partakers of the d nature, 2304

DIVINE BEING See GODHEAD

DIVINERS (7) [DIVINE]
Dt 18:14 unto observers of times, and unto **d**: 7080
1Sa 6: 2 Philistines called for the priests and the **d**, 7080
Isa 44:25 the tokens of the liars, and maketh **d** mad; 7080
Jer 27: 9 nor to your **d**, nor to your dreamers, nor to 7080
29: 8 Let not your prophets and your **d**, that *be* in 7080
Mic 3: 7 seers be ashamed, and the **d** confounded: 7080
Zec 10: 2 the **d** have seen a lie, and have told false 7080

DIVINETH (1) [DIVINE]
Ge 44: 5 and whereby **indeed** he **d**? 5172+5172

DIVINING (1) [DIVINE]
Eze 22:28 **d** lies unto them, saying, Thus saith 7080

DIVISION (6) [DIVIDE]
Ex 8:23 I will put a **d** between my people and thy 6304
2Ch 35: 5 *after* the **d** of the families of the Levites. 2515
Lk 12:51 on earth? I tell you, Nay; but rather **d**: *1267*
Jn 7:43 So there was a **d** among the people because *4978*
9:16 And there was a **d** among them. *4978*
10:19 There was a **d** therefore again among *4978*

DIVISIONS (17) [DIVIDE]
Jos 11:23 Israel according to their **d** by their tribes. 4256
12: 7 Israel *for* a possession according to their **d**; 4256
18:10 the children of Israel according to their **d**. 4256
Jdg 5:15 For the **d** of Reuben *there were* great 6390
5:16 For the **d** of Reuben *there were* great 6390
1Ch 24: 1 Now *these are* the **d** of the sons of Aaron. 4256
26: 1 Concerning the **d** of the porters: Of 4256
26:12 Among these *were* the **d** of the porters, 4256
26:19 These *are* the **d** of the porters among 4256
2Ch 35: 5 stand in the holy *place* according to the **d** of 6391
35:12 that they might give according to the **d** of 4653
Ezr 6:18 they set the priests in their **d**, and 6392
Ne 11:36 of the Levites *were* **d** *in* Judah, *and* 4256
Ro 16:17 mark them which cause **d** and offences *1370*
1Co 1:10 and *that* there be no **d** among you; *4978*
3: 3 and strife, and **d**, are ye not carnal, and *1370*
11:18 I hear that there be **d** among you; *4978*

DIVISIVE PERSON See HERETICK

DIVORCE (1) [DIVORCED, DIVORCEMENT]
Jer 3: 8 had put her away, and given her a bill of **d**; 3748

DIVORCED (4) [DIVORCE]
Lev 21:14 or a **d** *woman,* or profane, *or* a harlot, 1644
22:13 or **d**, and have no child, and is returned 1644
Nu 30: 9 every vow of a widow, and of her that is **d**, 1644
Mt 5:32 whosoever shall marry her that is **d** *630*

DIVORCEMENT (6) [DIVORCE]
Dt 24: 1 let him write her a bill of **d**, and give *it* in 3748
24: 3 write her a bill of **d**, and giveth *it* in her 3748
Isa 50: 1 Where *is* the bill of your mother's **d**, 3748
Mt 5:31 his wife, let him give her a **writing of d**: *647*
19: 7 then command to give a writing of **d**, *647*
Mk 10: 4 Moses suffered to write a bill of **d**, and *647*

DIZAHAB (1)
Dt 1: 1 and Laban, and Hazeroth, and **D**. 1774

DO (1368) [DID, DIDST, DOER, DOERS, DOEST, DOETH, DOING, DOINGS, DONE, DOST, DOTH, UNDO] See Index

DO BEST See STUDY

DOCTOR (1) [DOCTORS]
Ac 5:34 a Pharisee, named Gamaliel, a **d of law**, *3547*

DOCTORS (2) [DOCTOR]
Lk 2:46 sitting in the midst of the **d**, both hearing *1320*
5:17 **d of the law** sitting *by,* which were come *3547*

DOCTRINE (51) [DOCTRINES]
Dt 32: 2 My **d** shall drop as the rain, my speech 3948
Job 11: 4 My **d** *is* pure, and I am clean in thine eyes. 3948
Pr 4: 2 For I give you good **d**, forsake you not my 3948
Isa 28: 9 whom shall he make to understand **d**? 8052
29:24 and they that murmured shall learn **d**. 3948
Jer 10: 8 and foolish: the stock *is* a **d** of vanities. 4148
Mt 7:28 the people were astonished at his **d**: *1322*
16:12 but of the **d** of the Pharisees and *of* *1322*
22:33 heard *this,* they were astonished at his **d**. *1322*
Mk 1:22 And they were astonished at his **d**: for he *1322*
1:27 what new **d** *is* this? for with authority *1322*
4: 2 by parables, and said unto them in his **d**, *1322*
11:18 all the people was astonished at his **d**. *1322*
12:38 And he said unto them in his **d**, Beware of *1322*
Lk 4:32 And they were astonished at his **d**: for his *1322*
Jn 7:16 said, My **d** is not mine, but his that sent me. *1322*
7:17 he shall know of the **d**, whether it be of *1322*
18:19 asked Jesus of his disciples, and of his **d**. *1322*
Ac 2:42 they continued stedfastly in the apostles' **d** *1322*
5:28 ye have filled Jerusalem with your **d**, and *1322*
13:12 being astonished at the **d** of the Lord. *1322*
17:19 saying, May we know what this new **d**, *1322*
Ro 6:17 *that* form of **d** which was delivered you. *1322*
16:17 offences contrary to the **d** which ye have *1322*
1Co 14: 6 by knowledge, or by prophesying, or by **d**? *1322*
14:26 hath a **d**, hath a tongue, hath a revelation, *1322*
Eph 4:14 fro, and carried about with every wind of **d**, *1319*
1Ti 1: 3 charge some that *they* **teach** no **other d**, *2085*
1:10 any other *thing that* is contrary to sound **d**; *1319*
4: 6 up in the words of faith and of good **d**, *1319*
4:13 attendance to reading, to exhortation, to **d**. *1319*
4:16 Take heed unto thyself, and unto the **d**; *1319*
5:17 they who labour in the word and **d**. *1319*
6: 1 name of God and *his* **d** be not blasphemed. *1319*
6: 3 to the **d** which is according to godliness; *1319*
2Ti 3:10 But thou hast fully known my **d**, manner of *1319*
3:16 and *is* profitable for **d**, for reproof, *1319*
4: 2 rebuke, exhort with all longsuffering and **d**. *1322*
4: 3 come when they will not endure sound **d**; *1319*
Tit 1: 9 that he may be able by sound **d** both to *1319*
2: 1 thou *the things* which become sound **d**: *1319*
2: 7 in **d** *shewing* uncorruptness, gravity, *1319*
2:10 that they may adorn the **d** of God our *1319*
Heb 6: 1 Therefore leaving the principles of the **d** of *3056*
6: 2 Of the **d** of baptisms, and of laying on of *1322*
2Jn 1: 9 and abideth not in the **d** of Christ, hath not *1322*
1: 9 He that abideth in the **d** of Christ, he hath *1322*
1:10 come any unto you, and bring not this **d**, *1322*
Rev 2:14 thou hast there them that hold the **d** of *1322*
2:15 So hast thou also them that hold the **d** of *1322*
2:24 as many as have not this **d**, and which have *1322*

DOCTRINES (5) [DOCTRINE]
Mt 15: 9 teaching for **d** the commandments of men. *1319*
Mk 7: 7 teaching for **d** the commandments of men. *1319*
Col 2:22 after the commandments and **d** of men? *1319*
1Ti 4: 1 heed to seducing spirits, and **d** of devils; *1319*
Heb 13: 9 not carried about with divers and strange **d**. *1322*

DODAI (1)
1Ch 27: 4 over the course of the second month *was* **D** 1737

DODANIM (2)
Ge 10: 4 Elishah, and Tarshish, Kittim, and **D**. 1721
1Ch 1: 7 Elishah, and Tarshish, Kittim, and **D**. 1721

DODAVAH (1)
2Ch 20:37 Eliezer the son of **D** of Mareshah 1735

DODAVAHU See DODAVAH

DODO (5)
Jdg 10: 1 of Puah, the son of **D**, a man of Issachar; 1734
2Sa 23: 9 after him *was* Eleazar the son of **D** 1734
23:24 Elhanan the son of **D** *of* Beth-lehem, 1734
1Ch 11:12 after him *was* Eleazar the son of **D**, 1734
11:26 Elhanan the son of **D** of Beth-lehem, 1734

DOE See HIND

DOEG (6)
1Sa 21: 7 his name *was* **D**, an Edomite, the chiefest 1673
22: 9 answered **D** the Edomite, which *was* set 1673
22:18 the king said to **D**, Turn thou, and fall upon 1673
22:18 **D** the Edomite turned, and he fell upon 1673
22:22 *it* that day, when **D** the Edomite *was* there, 1673
Ps 52: T when **D** the Edomite came and told Saul, 1673

DOER (8) [DO]
Ge 39:22 they did there, he was the **d** *of it.* 6213
2Sa 3:39 the LORD shall reward the **d** of evil 6213
Ps 31:23 and plentifully rewardeth the proud **d**. 6213
Pr 17: 4 A **wicked d** giveth heed to false lips; *and* 7489
2Ti 2: 9 as an **evil d**, *even* unto bonds; *2557*

Jas 1:23 if any be a hearer of the word, and not a **d**, *4163*
1:25 but a **d** of the work, this *man* shall be *4163*
4:11 thou art not a **d** of the law, but a judge. *4163*

DOERS (6) [DO]

2Ki 22: 5 let them deliver it into the hand of the **d** of 6213
22: 5 let them give it to the **d** of the work which 6213
Job 8:20 perfect *man,* neither will he help the **evil d**: 7489
Ps 101: 8 that *I* may cut off all wicked **d** from the city 6466
Ro 2:13 but the **d** of the law shall be justified. *4163*
Jas 1:22 But be ye **d** of the word, and not hearers *4163*

DOEST (45) [DO] See Index

DOETH (93) [DO] See Index

DOG (15) [DOG'S, DOGS]

Ex 11: 7 of Israel shall not a **d** move his tongue, 3611
Dt 23:18 the hire of a whore, or the price of a **d**, 3611
Jdg 7: 5 as a **d** lappeth, him shalt thou set by 3611
1Sa 17:43 the Philistine said unto David, *Am* I a **d**, 3611
24:14 thou pursue? after a dead **d**, after a flea. 3611
2Sa 9: 8 thou shouldest look upon such a dead **d** 3611
16: 9 Why should this dead **d** curse my lord 3611
2Ki 8:13 Hazael said, But what, *is* thy servant a **d**, 3611
Ps 22:20 my darling from the power of the **d**. 3611
59: 6 they make a noise like a **d**, and go round 3611
59:14 *and* let them make a noise like a **d**, and 3611
Pr 26:11 As a **d** returneth to his vomit, *so* a fool 3611
26:17 *is like* one that taketh a **d** by the ears. 3611
Ecc 9: 4 for a living **d** *is* better than a dead lion. 3611
2Pe 2:22 The **d** *is* turned to his own vomit again; *2965*

DOG'S (2) [DOG]

2Sa 3: 8 of Ish-bosheth, and said, *Am* I a **d** head, 3611
Isa 66: 3 sacrificeth a lamb, *as if* he cut off a **d** neck; 3611

DOGS (24) [DOG]

Ex 22:31 *beasts* in the field; ye shall cast it to the **d**. 3611
1Ki 14:11 dieth of Jeroboam in the city shall the **d** eat; 3611
16: 4 dieth of Baasha in the city shall the **d** eat; 3611
21:19 In the place where **d** licked the blood of 3611
21:19 the blood of Naboth shall **d** lick thy blood, 3611
21:23 The **d** shall eat Jezebel by the wall of 3611
21:24 Him that dieth of Ahab in the city the **d** 3611
22:38 the **d** licked up his blood; and they washed 3611
2Ki 9:10 the **d** shall eat Jezebel in the portion of 3611
9:36 In the portion of Jezreel shall **d** eat the flesh 3611
Job 30: 1 to have set with the **d** of my flock. 3611
Ps 22:16 For **d** have compassed me: the assembly of 3611
68:23 *and* the tongue of thy **d** in the same. 3611
Isa 56:10 they *are* all dumb **d**, they cannot bark; 3611
56:11 *they are* greedy **d** *which* can never have 3611
Jer 15: 3 the **d** to tear, and the fowls of the heaven, 3611
Mt 7: 6 Give not that which is holy unto the **d**, *2965*
15:26 take the children's bread, and to cast *it* to **d**. *2952*
15:27 yet the **d** eat of the crumbs which fall from *2952*
Mk 7:27 children's bread, and to cast *it* unto the **d**. *2952*
7:28 yet the **d** under the table eat of *2952*
Lk 16:21 moreover the **d** came and licked his sores. *2965*
Php 3: 2 Beware of **d**, beware of evil workers, *2965*
Rev 22:15 For without *are* **d**, and sorcerers, and *2965*

DOING (39) [DO] See Index

DOINGS (51) [DO] See Index

DOLEFUL (2)

Isa 13:21 and their houses shall be full *of* **d creatures**; 255
Mic 2: 4 lament with a **d lamentation**, *and* say, 5093

DOMINION (62) [DOMINIONS]

Ge 1:26 and let them **have d** over the fish of the sea, 7287
1:28 **have d** over the fish of the sea, and over 7287
27:40 come to pass when thou shalt have the **d**, 7300
37: 8 or shalt thou **indeed have d** over us? 4910+4910
Nu 24:19 of Jacob shall come *he* that shall have **d**, 7287
Jdg 5:13 he **made** him that remaineth **have d over** 7287
5:13 the LORD **made** me **have d over** 7287
14: 4 for at that time the Philistines **had d** over 4910
1Ki 4:24 For he had **d** over all *the region* on *this* side 7287
9:19 and in Lebanon, and in all the land of his **d**. 4475
2Ki 20:13 was nothing in his house, nor in all his **d**, 4475
1Ch 4:22 who had the **d** in Moab, and Jashubi-lehem. 1166
18: 3 as he went to stablish his **d** by the river 3027
2Ch 8: 6 and throughout all the land of his **d**. 4475
21: 8 revolted from under the **d** of Judah, 3027
Ne 9:28 so that they had the **d** over them: 7287
9:37 also they **have d** over our bodies, and 4910
Job 25: 2 **D** and fear *are* with him, he maketh peace 4910
38:33 canst thou set the **d** thereof in the earth? 4896
Ps 8: 6 Thou **madest** him **to have d** over the works 4910
19:13 *sins;* let them not **have d** over me: 4910
49:14 the upright shall have **d** over them in 7287
72: 8 He shall have **d** also from sea to sea, and 7287
103:22 all his works in all places of his **d**: 4475
114: 2 Judah was his sanctuary, *and* Israel his **d**. 4475
119:133 and let not any iniquity **have d** over me. 7980
145:13 thy **d** *endureth* throughout all generations. 4475
Isa 26:13 *other* lords besides thee have **had d over** 1166
39: 2 was nothing in his house, nor in all his **d**, 4475
Jer 34: 1 the kingdoms of the earth of his **d**, 3027+4475
51:28 the rulers thereof, and all the land of his **d**. 4475
Da 4: 3 and his **d** *is* from generation to generation. 7985
4:22 and thy **d** to the end of the earth. 7985
4:34 whose **d** *is* an everlasting dominion, and 7985
4:34 whose dominion *is* an everlasting **d**, and 7985
6:26 That in every **d** of my kingdom *men* 7985
6:26 and his **d** *shall be even* unto the end. 7985
7: 6 had also four heads; and **d** *was* given to it. 7985
7:12 of the beasts, they had their **d** taken away: 7985
7:14 there *was* given him **d**, and glory, and 7985
7:14 his **d** *is* an everlasting dominion, 7985
7:14 his dominion *is* an everlasting **d**, 7985
7:26 they shall take away his **d**, to consume and 7985
7:27 the kingdom and **d**, and the greatness of 7985
11: 3 that shall rule *with* great **d**, and 4474
11: 4 nor according to his **d** which he ruled: 4915
11: 5 he shall be strong above him, and **have d**; 4910
11: 5 his **d** *shall be* a great dominion. 4475
11: 5 his dominion *shall be* a great **d**. 4474
Mic 4: 8 unto thee shall it come, even the first **d**; 4475
Zec 9:10 his **d** *shall be* from sea *even* to sea, and 4915
Mt 20:25 of the Gentiles **exercise d over** them, *2634*
Ro 6: 9 no more; death hath no more **d over** him. *2961*
6:14 For sin shall not have **d** over you: for ye are NIG
7: 1 how that the law **hath d over** a man, *2961*
2Co 1:24 Not for that we **have d over** your faith, but *2961*
Eph 1:21 and **d**, and every name that is named, *2963*
1Pe 4:11 to whom be praise and **d** for ever and ever. *2904*
5:11 To him *be* glory and **d** for ever and ever. *2904*
Jude 1: 8 despise **d**, and speak evil of dignities. *2963*
1:25 *be* glory and majesty, **d** and power, *2904*
Rev 1: 6 to him *be* glory and **d** for ever and ever. *2904*

DOMINIONS (2) [DOMINION]

Da 7:27 and all **d** shall serve and obey him. 7985
Col 1:16 or **d**, or principalities, or powers: *2963*

DONE (565) [DO] See Index

DONKEY; DONKEYS See ASS; ASS'S; ASSES

DOOR (189) [DOORKEEPER, DOORKEEPERS, DOORS]

Ge 4: 7 if thou doest not well, sin lieth at the **d**. 6607
6:16 the **d** of the ark shalt thou set in the side 6607
18: 1 he sat *in* the tent **d** in the heat of the day; 6607
18: 2 *them,* he ran to meet them from the tent **d**, 6607
18:10 Sarah heard *it in* the tent **d**, which *was* 6607
19: 6 Lot went out at the **d** unto them, and 6607
19: 6 door unto them, and shut the **d** after him, 1817
19: 9 *even* Lot, and came near to break the **d**. 1817
19:10 into the house to them, and shut to the **d**. 1817
19:11 they smote the men that *were at* the **d** of 6607
19:11 that they wearied themselves to find the **d**. 6607
43:19 they communed with him *at* the **d** of 6607
Ex 12: 7 and on the **upper d post** of the houses, 4947
12:22 none of you shall go out at the **d** of his 6607
12:23 the LORD will pass over the **d**, and 6607
21: 6 he shall also bring him to the **d**, or unto 1817
21: 6 bring him to the door, or unto the **d post**; 4201
26:36 thou shalt make a hanging for the **d** of 6607
29: 4 his sons thou shalt bring unto the **d** of 6607
29:11 *by* the **d** of the tabernacle of 6607
29:32 *by* the **d** of the tabernacle of 6607
29:42 **d** of the tabernacle of the congregation 6607
33: 8 stood every man *at* his tent **d**, and 6607
33: 9 stood *at* the **d** of the tabernacle, and 6607
33:10 the cloudy pillar stand *at* the tabernacle **d**: 6607
33:10 and worshipped, every man *in* his tent **d**. 6607
35:15 the hanging for the **d** at the entering in of 6607

Ex 35:17 and the hanging for the **d** of the court, 8179
36:37 he made a hanging for the tabernacle **d** *of* 6607
38: 8 which assembled *at* the **d** of the tabernacle 6607
38:30 therewith he made the sockets to the **d** of 6607
39:38 and the hanging for the tabernacle **d**, 6607
40: 5 put the hanging of the **d** to the tabernacle. 6607
40: 6 **d** of the tabernacle of the tent of 6607
40:12 his sons unto the **d** of the tabernacle of 6607
40:28 he set up the hanging at the **d** of 6607
40:29 he put the altar of burnt offering *by* the **d** of 6607
Lev 1: 3 **d** of the tabernacle of the congregation 6607
1: 5 the **d** of the tabernacle of the congregation. 6607
3: 2 kill it *at* the **d** of the tabernacle of 6607
4: 4 he shall bring the bullock unto the **d** of 6607
4: 7 which *is at* the **d** of the tabernacle of 6607
4:18 which *is at* the **d** of the tabernacle of 6607
8: 3 the **d** of the tabernacle of the congregation. 6607
8: 4 the **d** of the tabernacle of the congregation. 6607
8:31 Boil the flesh *at* the **d** of the tabernacle of 6607
8:33 ye shall not go out of the **d** of 6607
8:35 Therefore shall ye abide *at* the **d** of 6607
10: 7 ye shall not go out from the **d** of 6607
12: 6 unto the **d** of the tabernacle of 6607
14:11 *at* the **d** of the tabernacle of 6607
14:23 unto the **d** of the tabernacle of 6607
14:38 the priest shall go out of the house to the **d** 6607
15:14 come before the LORD unto the **d** of 6607
15:29 to the **d** of the tabernacle of 6607
16: 7 present them before the LORD *at* the **d** of 6607
17: 4 bringeth it not unto the **d** of the tabernacle 6607
17: 5 unto the **d** of the tabernacle of 6607
17: 6 the **d** of the tabernacle of the congregation, 6607
17: 9 bringeth it not unto the **d** of the tabernacle 6607
19:21 unto the **d** of the tabernacle of 6607
Nu 3:25 the hanging for the **d** of the tabernacle of 6607
3:26 the curtain for the **d** of the court, which *is* 6607
4:25 the hanging for the **d** of the tabernacle of 6607
4:26 the hanging for the **d** of the gate of 6607
6:10 to the **d** of the tabernacle of 6607
6:13 he shall be brought unto the **d** of 6607
6:18 the **d** of the tabernacle of the congregation, 6607
10: 3 the **d** of the tabernacle of the congregation. 6607
11:10 every man in the **d** of his tent: 6607
12: 5 stood *in* the **d** of the tabernacle, and 6607
16:18 stood *in* the **d** of the tabernacle of 6607
16:19 the **d** of the tabernacle of the congregation: 6607
16:27 stood *in* the **d** of their tents, and 6607
16:50 Aaron returned unto Moses unto the **d** of 6607
20: 6 the **d** of the tabernacle of the congregation, 6607
25: 6 who *were* weeping *before* the **d** of 6607
27: 2 *by* the **d** of the tabernacle of 6607
Dt 11:20 thou shalt write them upon the **d posts** of 4201
15:17 thrust *it* through his ear unto the **d**, and 1817
22:21 they shall bring out the damsel to the **d** of 6607
31:15 the pillar of the cloud stood over the **d** of 6607
Jos 19:51 *at* the **d** of the tabernacle of 6607
Jdg 4:20 Stand *in* the **d** of the tent, and it shall be, 6607
9:52 went hard unto the **d** of the tower to burn it 6607
19:22 *and* beat at the **d**, and spake to the master of 1817
19:26 fell down *at* the **d** of the man's house where 6607
19:27 *was* fallen down *at* the **d** of the house, 6607
1Sa 2:22 the **d** of the tabernacle of the congregation. 6607
2Sa 11: 9 Uriah slept *at* the **d** of the king's house with 6607
13:17 out from me, and bolt the **d** after her. 1817
13:18 brought her out, and bolted the **d** after her. 1817
1Ki 6: 8 The **d** for the middle chamber *was* in 6607
6:33 So also made he for the **d** of the temple 6607
6:34 the two leaves of the one **d** *were* folding, 1817
6:34 the two leaves of the other **d** *were* folding. 1817
14: 6 as she came in at the **d**, that he said, 6607
14:17 when she came to the threshold of the **d**, 1004
14:27 which kept the **d** of the king's house. 6607
2Ki 4: 4 thou shalt shut the **d** upon thee and 1817
4: 5 and shut the **d** upon her and upon her sons, 1817
4:15 when he had called her, she stood in the **d**. 6607
4:21 and shut *the d* upon him, and went out. NIH
4:33 shut the **d** upon them twain, and 1817
5: 9 and stood *at* the **d** of the house of Elisha. 6607
6:32 shut the **d**, and hold him fast at the door: 1817
6:32 shut the door, and hold him fast at the **d**: 1817
9: 3 Then open the **d**, and flee, and tarry not. 1817
9:10 *be* none to bury *her*. And he opened the **d**, 1817
12: 9 the priests that kept the **d** put therein all 5592
22: 4 which the keepers of the **d** have gathered of 5592
23: 4 the keepers of the **d**, to bring forth out of 5592
25:18 and the three keepers of the **d**: 5592
1Ch 9:21 the **d** of the tabernacle of the congregation. 6607
Ne 3:20 from the turning *of the wall* unto the **d** of 6607
3:21 from the **d** of the house of Eliashib even to 6607
Est 2:21 and Teresh, of those which kept the **d**, 5592
6: 2 king's chamberlains, the keepers of the **d**, 5592
Job 31: 9 or *if* I have laid wait at my neighbour's **d**; 6607
31:34 I kept silence, *and* went not out *of* the **d**? 6607
Ps 141: 3 before my mouth; keep the **d** of my lips. 1817
Pr 5: 8 and come not nigh the **d** of her house: 6607
9:14 For she sitteth at the **d** of her house, on a 6607
26:14 *As* the **d** turneth upon his hinges, so 1817
SS 5: 4 beloved put in his hand by the hole *of the d*, NIH
8: 9 if she *be* a **d**, we will inclose her with 1817
Isa 6: 4 the posts of the **d** moved at the voice of 5592
Jer 35: 4 the son of Shallum, the keeper of the **d**: 5592
52:24 and the three keepers of the **d**: 5592
Eze 8: 3 to the **d** of the inner gate that looketh 6607
8: 7 he brought me to the **d** of the court; and 6607
8: 8 when I had digged in the wall, behold a **d**. 6607
8:14 he brought me to the **d** of the gate of 6607
8:16 *at* the **d** of the temple of the LORD, 6607
10:19 *every one* stood *at* the **d** of the east gate of 6607
11: 1 behold at the **d** of the gate five and 6607
40:13 *was* five and twenty cubits, **d** against door. 6607
40:13 *was* five and twenty cubits, door against **d**. 6607
41: 2 the breadth of the **d** *was* ten cubits; and 6607
41: 2 the sides of the **d** *were* five cubits on 6607
41: 3 measured the post of the **d**, two cubits; 6607
41: 3 the **d**, six cubits; and the breadth of 6607
41: 3 and the breadth of the **d**, seven cubits. 6607
41:11 one **d** toward the north, and another door 6607
41:11 the north, and another **d** toward the south: 6607
41:16 The **d posts**, and the narrow windows, and 5592
41:16 on their three *stories,* over against the **d**, 5592
41:17 To *that* above the **d**, even unto the inner 6607
41:20 From the ground unto above the **d** *were* 6607
41:24 two *leaves* for the one **d**, and two leaves 1817
41:24 one door, and two leaves for the other *d*. NIH
42: 2 of an hundred cubits *was* the north **d**, 6607
42:12 the south *was* a **d** in the head of the way, 6607
46: 3 **d** of this gate before the LORD in 6607
47: 1 Afterward he brought me again unto the **d** 6607
Hos 2:15 and the valley of Achor for a **d** of hope: 6607
Am 9: 1 he said, Smite the **lintel of the d**, that 3730
Mt 6: 6 thy closet, and when thou hast shut thy **d**, *2374*
25:10 him to the marriage: and the **d** was shut. *2374*
27:60 he rolled a great stone to the **d** of *2374*
28: 2 came and rolled back the stone from the **d**, *2374*
Mk 1:33 all the city was gathered together at the **d**. *2374*
2: 2 *them,* no, not so much as about the **d**: *2374*
11: 4 found the colt tied by the **d** without in a *2374*
15:46 rolled a stone unto the **d** of the sepulchre. *2374*
16: 3 Who shall roll us away the stone from the **d** *2374*
Lk 11: 7 the **d** is now shut, and my children are with *2374*
13:25 and hath shut to the **d**, and ye begin to *2374*
13:25 and to knock at the **d**, saying, Lord, Lord, *2374*
Jn 10: 1 He that entereth not by the **d** into *2374*
10: 2 But he that entereth in by the **d** is *2374*
10: 7 I say unto you, I am the **d** of the sheep. *2374*
10: 9 I am the **d**: by me if any *man* enter in, *2374*
18:16 But Peter stood at the **d** without. Then went *2374*
18:16 and spake unto her that **kept the d**, and *2377*
18:17 Then saith the damsel that **kept the d** unto *2377*
Ac 5: 9 which have buried thy husband *are* at the **d**, *2374*
12: 6 *the* keepers before the **d** kept the prison. *2374*
12:13 And as Peter knocked at the **d** of the gate, *2374*
12:16 and when they had opened *the d*, and NIG
14:27 how he had opened *the* **d** of faith unto *2374*
1Co 16: 9 For a great **d** and effectual is opened unto *2374*
2Co 2:12 and a **d** was opened unto me of the Lord, *2374*
Col 4: 3 that God would open unto us a **d** of *2374*
Jas 5: 9 the judge standeth before the **d**. *2374*
Rev 3: 8 I have set before thee an open **d**, and no *2374*
3:20 Behold, I stand at the **d**, and knock: if any *2374*
3:20 and open the **d**, I will come in to him, and *2374*
4: 1 and behold, a **d** *was* opened in heaven: *2374*

DOORKEEPER (1) [DOOR, KEEP]

Ps 84:10 I had rather be a **d** in the house of my God, 5605

DOORKEEPERS (2) [DOOR, KEEP]

1Ch 15:23 and Elkanah *were* **d** for the ark. 7778

1Ch 15:24 Obed-edom and Jehiah *were* **d** for the ark. 7778

DOORS (71) [DOOR]
Jos 2:19 *that* whosoever shall go out of the **d** of thy 1817
Jdg 3:23 shut the **d** of the parlour upon him, and 1817
3:24 the **d** of the parlour *were* locked, they said, 1817
3:25 behold, he opened not the **d** of the parlour; 1817
11:31 that whatsoever cometh forth of the **d** of 1817
16: 3 took the **d** of the gate of the city, and 1817
19:27 opened the **d** of the house, and went out to 1817
1Sa 3:15 opened the **d** of the house of the LORD. 1817
21:13 scrabled on the **d** of the gate, and let his 1817
1Ki 6:31 for the entering of the oracle he made **d** of 1817
6:32 The two **d** also *were* of olive tree; and 1817
6:34 the two **d** *were* of fir tree: the two leaves of 1817
7: 5 all the **d** and posts *were* square, *with* 6607
7:50 *of* gold, *both* for the **d** of the inner house, 1817
7:50 most holy *place, and* for the **d** of the house, 1817
2Ki 18:16 *from* the **d** of the temple of the LORD, 1817
1Ch 22: 3 for the nails for the **d** of the gates, 1817
2Ch 3: 7 walls thereof, and the **d** thereof, with gold; 1817
4: 9 **d** for the court, and overlaid the doors of 1817
4: 9 and overlaid the **d** of them with brass. 1817
4:22 the inner **d** thereof for the most holy *place,* 1817
4:22 and the **d** of the house of the temple, 1817
23: 4 and of the Levites, *shall be* porters of the **d**; 5592
28:24 shut up the **d** of the house of the LORD, 1817
29: 3 opened the **d** of the house of the LORD, 1817
29: 7 Also they have shut up the **d** of the porch, 1817
34: 9 which the Levites that kept the **d** had 5592
Ne 3: 1 they sanctified it, and set up the **d** of it; 1817
3: 3 set up the **d** thereof, the locks thereof, and 1817
3: 6 set up the **d** thereof, and the locks thereof, 1817
3:13 they built it, and set up the **d** thereof, 1817
3:14 he built it, and set up the **d** thereof, 1817
3:15 and covered it, and set up the **d** thereof, 1817
6: 1 (though at that time I had not set up the **d** 1817
6:10 and let us shut the **d** of the temple: 1817
7: 1 I had set up the **d**, and the porters and 1817
7: 3 let them shut the **d**, and bar *them:* and 1817
Job 3:10 Because it shut not up the **d** of my *mother's* 1817
31:32 *but* I opened my **d** to the traveller. 1817
38: 8 Or *who* shut up the sea with **d**, when it 1817
38:10 for it my decreed *place,* and set bars and **d**, 1817
38:17 hast thou seen the **d** of the shadow of 8179
41:14 Who can open the **d** of his face? his teeth 1817
Ps 24: 7 be ye lift up, ye everlasting **d**; and the King 6607
24: 9 even lift *them* up, ye everlasting **d**; and 6607
78:23 from above, and opened the **d** of heaven, 1817
Pr 8: 3 entry of the city, *at* the coming in at the **d**. 6607
8:34 at my gates, waiting at the posts of my **d**. 6607
Ecc 12: 4 the **d** shall be shut in the streets, when 1817
Isa 26:20 thy chambers, and shut thy **d** about thee: 1817
57: 8 Behind the **d** also and the posts hast thou 1817
Eze 33:30 thee by the walls and in the **d** of the houses, 6607
41:11 the **d** of the side chambers *were* toward 6607
41:23 the temple and the sanctuary had two **d**. 1817
41:24 the **d** had two leaves *apiece,* two turning 1817
41:25 on the **d** of the temple, cherubims and 1817
42: 4 of one cubit; and their **d** toward the north. 6607
42:11 to their fashions, and according to their **d**. 6607
42:12 according to the **d** of the chambers that 6607
Mic 7: 5 keep the **d** of thy mouth from her that lieth 6607
Zec 11: 1 Open thy **d**, O Lebanon, that the fire may 1817
Mal 1:10 **d** *for nought?* neither do ye kindle *fire on* 1817
Mt 24:33 *things,* know that it is near, *even* at the **d**. *2374*
Mk 13:29 to pass, know that it is nigh, *even* at the **d**. *2374*
Jn 20:19 when the **d** were shut where the disciples *2374*
20:26 *then* came Jesus, the **d** being shut, *2374*
Ac 5:19 of the Lord by night opened the prison **d**, *2374*
5:23 the keepers standing without before the **d**: *2374*
16:26 and immediately all the **d** were opened, and *2374*
16:27 and seeing the prison **d** open, he drew out *2374*
21:30 the temple: and forthwith the **d** were shut. *2374*

DOPHKAH (2)
Nu 33:12 the wilderness of Sin, and encamped in **D**. 1850
33:13 they departed from **D**, and encamped in 1850

DOR (7) [HAMMOTH-DOR]
Jos 11: 2 and in the borders of **D** on the west, 1756
12:23 The king of **D** in the coast of Dor, one; 1756
12:23 The king of Dor in the coast of **D**, one; 1756
17:11 the inhabitants of **D** and her towns, and 1756
Jdg 1:27 nor the inhabitants of **D** and her towns, 1756
1Ki 4:11 The son of Abinadab, *in* all the region of **D**; 1756
1Ch 7:29 Megiddo and her towns, **D** and her towns. 1756

DORCAS (2)
Ac 9:36 which by interpretation is called **D**: *1393*
9:39 the coats and garments which **D** made, *1393*

DOST (56) [DO] See Index

DOTE (1) [DOTED, DOTING]
Jer 50:36 A sword *is* upon the liars; and they shall **d**: 2973

DOTED (6) [DOTE]
Eze 23: 5 she **d** on her lovers, on the Assyrians *her* 5689
23: 7 of Assyria, and with all *on* whom she **d**: 5689
23: 9 hand of the Assyrians, upon whom she **d**. 5689
23:12 She **d** upon the Assyrians *her* neighbours, 5689
23:16 she **d** upon them, and sent messengers unto 5689
23:20 For she **d** upon their paramours, 5689

DOTH (210) [DO] See Index

DOTHAN (3)
Ge 37:17 for I heard *them* say, Let us go to **D**. 1886
37:17 after his brethren, and found them in **D**. 1886
2Ki 6:13 it was told him, saying, Behold, *he is* in **D**. 1886

DOTING (1) [DOTE]
1Ti 6: 4 but **d** about questions and strifes of words, *3552*

DOUBLE (26) [DOUBLED, DOUBLETONGUED]
Ge 43:12 take **d** money in your hand; and the money 4932
43:15 they took **d** money in their hand, and 4932
Ex 22: 4 it be ox, or ass, or sheep; he shall restore **d**. 8147
22: 7 if the thief be found, let him pay **d**. 8147
22: 9 he shall pay **d** unto his neighbour. 8147
26: 9 shalt **d** the sixth curtain in the forefront of 3717
39: 9 they made the breastplate **d**: 3717
Dt 15:18 for he hath been worth a **d** hired servant *to* 4932
21:17 by giving him a **d** portion of all that he 8147
2Ki 2: 9 let a **d** portion of thy spirit be upon me. 8147
1Ch 12:33 *they were* not of **d heart**. 3820+3820+2050.1
Job 11: 6 of wisdom, that *they are* **d** to that which is. 3718
41:13 *or* who can come *to him* with his **d** bridle? 3718
Ps 12: 2 a **d heart** do they speak. 3820+3820+2050.1
Isa 40: 2 of the LORD'S hand **d** for all her sins. 3718
61: 7 For your shame *you shall have* **d**; and 4932
61: 7 in their land they shall possess the **d**: 4932
Jer 16:18 recompense their iniquity and their sin **d**; 4932
17:18 and destroy them *with* **d** destruction. 4932
Zec 9:12 even to day do I declare *that* I will render **d** 4932
1Ti 5:17 rule well be counted worthy of **d** honour, *1362*
Jas 1: 8 A **d minded** man *is* unstable in all his *1374*
4: 8 and purify *your* hearts, *ye* **d minded**. *1374*
Rev 18: 6 **d** unto her double according to her works: *1363*
18: 6 double unto her **d** according to her works: *1362*
18: 6 in the cup which she hath filled fill to her **d**. *1362*

DOUBLED (4) [DOUBLE]
Ge 41:32 for that the dream was **d** unto Pharaoh 8138
Ex 28:16 Foursquare it shall be *being* **d**; a span *shall* 3717
39: 9 and a span the breadth thereof, *being* **d**. 3717
Eze 21:14 let the sword be **d** the third time, the sword 3717

DOUBLE-EDGED See TWOEDGED

DOUBLETONGUED (1) [DOUBLE, TONGUE]
1Ti 3: 8 not **d**, not given to much wine, not greedy *1351*

DOUBT (13) [DOUBTED, DOUBTETH, DOUBTFUL, DOUBTING, DOUBTLESS, DOUBTS]
Ge 37:33 Joseph is **without d rent in pieces**. 2963+2963
Dt 28:66 thy life shall **hang in d** before thee; and 8511
Job 12: 2 **No d** but ye *are* the people, and 551
Mt 14:31 thou of little faith, wherefore didst thou **d**? *1365*
21:21 I say unto you, If ye have faith, and **d** not, *1252*
Mk 11:23 and shall not **d** in his heart, but *1252*
Lk 11:20 **no d** the kingdom of God is come upon you. *686*
Jn 10:24 long dost thou **make us to d**? *142+3588+5590*
Ac 2:12 and were in **d**, saying one to another, *1280*
28: 4 **No d** this man is a murderer, whom, *3843*
1Co 9:10 For our sakes, **no d**, *this* is written: that he *1063*
Gal 4:20 to change my voice; for I **stand in d** of you. *639*
1Jn 2:19 they would *no d* have continued with us: NIG

DOUBTED (4) [DOUBT]
Mt 28:17 saw him, they worshipped him: but some **d**. *1365*
Ac 5:24 they **d** of them whereunto this would grow. *1280*
10:17 Now while Peter **d** in himself what *this* *1280*
25:20 because I **d** of such *manner of* questions, *639*

DOUBTETH (1) [DOUBT]
Ro 14:23 And he that **d** is damned if he eat, because *1252*

DOUBTFUL (2) [DOUBT]
Lk 12:29 ye shall drink, neither be ye of **d mind**. *3349*
Ro 14: 1 faith receive you, *but* not to **d** disputations. *1261*

DOUBTING (4) [DOUBT]
Jn 13:22 looked one on another, **d** of whom he spake. *639*
Ac 10:20 *thee* down, and go with them, **d** nothing: *1252*
11:12 the Spirit bade me go with them, nothing **d**. *1252*
1Ti 2: 8 lifting up holy hands, without wrath and **d**. *1261*

DOUBTLESS (7) [DOUBT]
Nu 14:30 **D** ye shall **not** come into the land, 518
2Sa 5:19 for I will **d deliver** the Philistines 5414+5414
Ps 126: 6 shall **d come again** with rejoicing, 935+935
Isa 63:16 **D** thou *art* our father, though Abraham be 3588
1Co 9: 2 apostle unto others, **yet d** I am to you: *235+1065*
2Co 12: 1 It is not expedient for me **d** to glory. I will *1211*
Php 3: 8 Yea **d**, and I count all *things but* loss for *3304*

DOUBTS (2) [DOUBT]
Da 5:12 of hard sentences, and dissolving of **d**, 7001
5:16 canst make interpretations, and dissolve **d**: 7001

DOUGH (8)
Ex 12:34 the people took their **d** before it was 1217
12:39 they baked unleavened cakes of the **d** 1217
Nu 15:20 *of* the first of your **d** *for* a heave offering: 6182
15:21 Of the first of your **d** ye shall give unto 6182
Ne 10:37 *that* we should bring the firstfruits of our **d**, 6182
Jer 7:18 the fire, and the women knead *their* **d**, 1217
Eze 44:30 also give unto the priest the first of your **d**, 6182
Hos 7: 4 from raising after *he* hath kneaded the **d**, 1217

DOVE (18) [DOVE'S, DOVES, DOVES']
Ge 8: 8 Also he sent forth a **d** from him, to see if 3123
8: 9 the **d** found no rest for the sole of her foot, 3123
8:10 and again he sent forth the **d** out of the ark; 3123
8:11 the **d** came in to him in the evening; and 3123
8:12 yet other seven days; and sent forth the **d**; 3123
Ps 55: 6 O that I had wings like a **d**, *for then* 3123
68:13 *yet shall ye be as* the wings of a **d** covered 3123
SS 2:14 O my **d**, *that art* in the clefts of the rock, 3123
5: 2 my sister, my love, my **d**, my undefiled: 3123
6: 9 My **d**, my undefiled *is but* one; she *is* 3123
Isa 38:14 I did mourn as a **d**: mine eyes fail *with* 3123
Jer 48:28 be like the **d** *that* maketh her nest in 3123
Hos 7:11 Ephraim also is like a silly **d**, without heart: 3123
11:11 and as a **d** out of the land of Assyria: 3123
Mt 3:16 saw the Spirit of God descending like a **d**, *4058*
Mk 1:10 the Spirit like a **d** descending upon him: *4058*
Lk 3:22 in a bodily shape like a **d** upon him, *4058*
Jn 1:32 the Spirit descending from heaven like a **d**, *4058*

DOVE'S (1) [DOVE]
2Ki 6:25 the fourth part of a kab of **d dung** for five 1686

DOVES (10) [DOVE]
SS 5:12 His eyes *are* as *the eyes of* **d** by the rivers 3123
Isa 59:11 roar all like bears, and mourn sore like **d**: 3123
60: 8 as a cloud, and as the **d** to their windows? 3123
Eze 7:16 shall be on the mountains like **d** of 3123
Na 2: 7 maids *shall* lead *her* as *with* the voice of **d**, 3123
Mt 10:16 wise as serpents, and harmless as **d**. *4058*
21:12 and the seats of them that sold **d**, *4058*
Mk 11:15 and the seats of them that sold **d**; *4058*
Jn 2:14 those that sold oxen and sheep and **d**, *4058*
2:16 And said unto them that sold **d**, Take these *4058*

DOVES' (2) [DOVE]
SS 1:15 behold, thou *art* fair; thou *hast* **d** eyes. 3123
4: 1 *art* fair; thou *hast* **d** eyes within thy locks: 3123

DOWN (1125) [DOWNSITTING, DOWNWARD] See Index

DOWNSITTING (1) [DOWN, SIT]
Ps 139: 2 Thou knowest my **d** and mine uprising, 3427

DOWNWARD (5) [DOWN]
2Ki 19:30 Judah shall *yet* again take root **d**, 4295+3807.1
Ecc 3:21 the spirit of the beast that goeth **d** 4295+3807.1
Isa 37:31 of Judah shall again take root **d**, 4295+3807.1
Eze 1:27 the appearance of his loins even **d**, 4295+3807.1
8: 2 the appearance of his loins even **d**, 4295+3807.1

DOWRY (4)
Ge 30:20 God hath endued me with a good **d**; 2065
34:12 Ask me never so much **d** and gift, and 4119
Ex 22:17 he shall pay money according to the **d** of 4119
1Sa 18:25 The king desireth not *any* **d**, but an hundred 4119

DRACHMAS See DRAMS

DRAG (2) [DRAGGING]
Hab 1:15 in their net, and gather them in their **d**: 4365
1:16 their net, and burn incense unto their **d**; 4365

DRAGGING (1) [DRAG]
Jn 21: 8 two hundred cubits,) **d** the net with fishes. *4951*

DRAGON (19) [DRAGONS]
Ne 2:13 even before the **d** well, and to the dung 8577
Ps 91:13 and the **d** shalt thou trample under feet. 8577
Isa 27: 1 and he shall slay the **d** that *is* in the sea. 8577
51: 9 it that hath cut Rahab, *and* wounded the **d**? 8577
Jer 51:34 he hath swallowed me up like a **d**, 8577
Eze 29: 3 the great **d** that lieth in the midst of his 8577
Rev 12: 3 and behold a great red **d**, having seven *1404*
12: 4 the **d** stood before the woman which was *1404*
12: 7 and his angels fought against the **d**; *1404*
12: 7 the dragon; and the **d** fought and his angels, *1404*
12: 9 And the great **d** was cast *out, that* old *1404*
12:13 And when the **d** saw that he was cast unto *1404*
12:16 swallowed up the flood which the **d** cast *1404*
12:17 And the **d** was wroth with the woman, and *1404*
13: 2 and the **d** gave him his power, and his seat, *1404*
13: 4 And they worshipped the **d** which gave *1404*
13:11 two horns like a lamb, and he spake as a **d**. *1404*
16:13 like frogs *come* out of the mouth of the **d**, *1404*
20: 2 And he laid hold on the **d**, *that* old serpent, *1404*

DRAGONS (16) [DRAGON]
Dt 32:33 Their wine *is* the poison of **d**, and the cruel 8577
Job 30:29 I am a brother to **d**, and a companion to 8577
Ps 44:19 thou hast sore broken us in the place of **d**, 8577
74:13 thou brakest the heads of the **d** in 8577
148: 7 LORD from the earth, ye **d**, and all deeps: 8577
Isa 13:22 and **d** in *their* pleasant palaces: 8577
34:13 it shall be a habitation of **d**, *and* a court for 8577
35: 7 in the habitation of **d**, where each lay, 8577
43:20 field shall honour me, the **d** and the owls: 8577
Jer 9:11 will make Jerusalem heaps, *and* a den of **d**; 8577
10:22 the cities of Judah desolate, *and* a den of **d**. 8577
14: 6 they snuffed up the wind like **d**; 8577
49:33 Hazor shall be a dwelling for **d**, *and* 8577
51:37 a dwelling place for **d**, an astonishment, 8577
Mic 1: 8 I will make a wailing like the **d**, and 8577
Mal 1: 3 his heritage waste for the **d** of 8577

DRAMS (6)
1Ch 29: 7 five thousand talents and ten thousand **d**, 150
Ezr 2:69 and one thousand **d** *of* gold, 1871
8:27 Also twenty basons of gold, of a thousand **d**; 150
Ne 7:70 gave to the treasure a thousand **d** *of* gold, 1871
7:71 of the work twenty thousand **d** *of* gold, 1871
7:72 gave *was* twenty thousand **d** *of* gold, 1871

DRANK (18) [DRINK]
Ge 9:21 he **d** of the wine, and was drunken; and 8354
24:46 so I **d**, and she made the camels drink also. 8354
27:25 did eat: and he brought him wine, and he **d**. 8354
Nu 20:11 the congregation **d**, and their beasts *also*. 8354
Dt 32:38 *and* **d** the wine of their drink offerings? 8354
2Sa 12: 3 **d** of his own cup, and lay in his bosom, and 8354
1Ki 13:19 and did eat bread in his house, and **d** water. 8354
17: 6 flesh in the evening; and he **d** of the brook. 8354
Da 1: 5 king's meat, and of the wine which he **d**: 4960
1: 8 king's meat, nor with the wine which he **d**: 4960
5: 1 his lords, and **d** wine before the thousand. 8355
5: 3 his wives, and his concubines, **d** in them. 8355
5: 4 They **d** wine, and praised the gods of gold, 8355
Mk 14:23 he gave *it* to them: and they all **d** of it. *4095*
Lk 17:27 They did eat, they **d**, they married *wives*, *4095*

Lk 17:28 they did eat, they **d**, they bought, they sold, *4095*
Jn 4:12 and **d** thereof himself, and his children, and *4095*
1Co 10: 4 for they **d** of *that* spiritual Rock that *4095*

DRAUGHT (5)
2Ki 10:27 and made it a **d house** unto *this* day. 4280
Mt 15:17 into the belly, and is cast out into the **d**? *856*
Mk 7:19 but into the belly, and goeth out into the **d**, *856*
Lk 5: 4 into the deep, and let down your nets for a **d**. *61*
5: 9 at the **d** of the fishes which they had taken: *61*

DRAVE (13) [DRIVE]
Ex 14:25 chariot wheels, that they **d** them heavily: 5090
Jos 16:10 they **d** not **out** the Canaanites that dwelt in 3423
24:12 which **d** them **out** from before you, 1644
24:18 the LORD **d out** from before us all 1644
Jdg 1:19 he **d out** *the inhabitants of* the mountain; 3423
6: 9 **d** them **out** from before you, and gave you 1644
1Sa 30:20 *which* they **d** before those *other* cattle, and 5090
2Sa 6: 3 Ahio, the sons of Abinadab, **d** the new cart. 5090
2Ki 16: 6 Elath to Syria, and **d** the Jews from Elath: 5394
17:21 Jeroboam **d** Israel from following 5080
1Ch 13: 7 of Abinadab: and Uzza and Ahio **d** the cart. 5090
Ac 7:45 whom God **d out** before the face of our *1856*
18:16 And he **d** them from the judgment seat. *556*

DRAW (76) [DRAWER, DRAWERS, DRAWETH, DRAWING, DRAWN, DREW, DREWEST]
Ge 24:11 *even* the time that *women* go out to **d** 7579
24:13 of the men of the city come out to **d** water: 7579
24:19 she said, I will **d** *water* for thy camels also, 7579
24:20 ran again unto the well to **d** *water,* and 7579
24:43 *that when* the virgin cometh forth to **d** 7579
24:44 drink thou, and I will also **d** for thy camels: 7579
Ex 3: 5 he said, **D** not **nigh** hither: put off thy shoes 7126
12:21 **D out** and take you a lamb according to 4900
15: 9 I will **d** my sword, my hand shall destroy 7324
Lev 26:33 and will **d out** a sword after you: 7324
Jdg 3:22 that he could not **d** the dagger out of his 8025
4: 6 *saying,* Go and **d** toward mount Tabor, and 4900
4: 7 I will **d** unto thee to the river Kishon 4900
9:54 said unto him, **D** thy sword, and slay me, 8025
19:13 let us **d near** to one of *these* places to lodge 7126
20:32 **d** them from the city unto the highways. 5423
1Sa 9:11 they found young maidens going out to **d** 7579
14:36 the priest, Let us **d near** hither unto God. 7126
14:38 Saul said, **D** ye **near** hither, all the chief of 5066
31: 4 **D** thy sword, and thrust me through 8025
2Sa 17:13 to that city, and we will **d** it into the river, 5498
1Ch 10: 4 **D** thy sword, and thrust me through 8025
Job 21:33 every man shall **d** after him, as *there are* 4900
40:23 he trusteth that he can **d up** Jordan into his 1518
41: 1 Canst thou **d out** leviathan with a hook? or 4900
Ps 28: 3 **D** me not **away** with the wicked, and 4900
35: 3 **D out** also the spear, and stop *the way* 7324
69:18 **D nigh** unto my soul, *and* redeem it: 7126
73:28 *it is* good for me to **d near** to God: I have 7132
85: 5 wilt thou **d out** thine anger to all 4900
107:18 and they **d near** unto the gates of death. 5060
119:150 They **d nigh** that follow after mischief: 7126
Pr 20: 5 but a man of understanding will **d** it **out**. 1802
Ecc 12: 1 nor the years **d nigh**, when thou shalt say, 5060
SS 1: 4 **D** me, we will run after thee: the king hath 4900
Isa 5:18 Woe unto them that **d** iniquity with cords 4900
5:19 counsel of the Holy One of Israel **d nigh** 7126
12: 3 Therefore with joy shall ye **d** water out of 7579
29:13 Forasmuch as this people **d near** *me* with 5066
45:20 **d near** together, ye *that are* escaped of 5066
57: 3 **d near** hither, ye sons of the sorceress, 7126
57: 4 ye a wide mouth, *and* **d out** the tongue? 748
58:10 *if* thou **d out** thy soul to the hungry, and 6329
66:19 Pul, and Lud, that **d** the bow, *to* Tubal, and 4900
Jer 30:21 I will **cause** him **to d near**, and he shall 7126
46: 3 the buckler and shield, and **d near** to battle. 5066
49:20 the least of the flock shall **d** them **out**: 5498
50:45 the least of the flock shall **d** them **out**: 5498
La 4: 3 Even the sea monsters **d out** the breast, 2502
Eze 5: 2 and I will **d out** a sword after them. 7324
5:12 and I will **d out** a sword after them. 7324
9: 1 **Cause** them that have charge over the city **to d near**, 7126
12:14 and I will **d out** the sword after them. 7324
21: 3 will **d forth** my sword out of his sheath, 3318
22: 4 thou hast **caused** thy days **to d near**, and 7126
28: 7 they shall **d** their swords against the beauty 7324
30:11 and they shall **d** their swords against Egypt, 7324
32:20 *to* the sword: **d** her and all her multitudes. 4900
Joel 3: 9 mighty *men,* let all the men of war **d near**; 5066
Na 3:14 **D** thee waters for the siege, fortify thy 7579
Hag 2:16 when *one* came to the pressfat for to **d out** 2834
Jn 2: 8 **D out** now, and bear unto the governor of *501*
4: 7 There cometh a woman of Samaria to **d** *501*
4:11 Sir, thou hast nothing to **d with**, and the well *502*
4:15 that I thirst not, neither come hither to **d**. *501*
6:44 except the Father which hath sent me **d** *1670*
12:32 up from the earth, will **d** all *men* unto me. *1670*
21: 6 now they were not able to **d** it for *1670*
Ac 20:30 speaking perverse *things,* to **d away** *645*
Heb 7:19 *did;* by the which we **d nigh** unto God. *1448*
10:22 Let us **d near** with a true heart in full *4334*
10:38 but if *any man* **d back**, my soul shall have *5288*
10:39 But we are not of *them* who **d back** unto *5289*
Jas 2: 6 and **d** you before the judgment seats? *1670*
4: 8 **D nigh** to God, and he will draw nigh to *1448*
4: 8 nigh to God, and he will **d nigh** to you. *1448*

DRAWER (1) [DRAW]
Dt 29:11 from the hewer of thy wood unto the **d** of 7579

DRAWERS (3) [DRAW]
Jos 9:21 and **d** of water unto all the congregation; 7579
9:23 and **d** of water for the house of my God. 7579
9:27 and **d** of water for the congregation, 7579

DRAWETH (12) [DRAW]
Dt 25:11 the wife of the one **d near** for to deliver her 7126
Jdg 19: 9 Behold now, the day **d** towards evening, 7503
Job 24:22 He **d** also the mighty with his power: 4900
33:22 his soul **d near** unto the grave, and his life 7126
Ps 10: 9 catch the poor, when he **d** him into his net. 4900
88: 3 and my life **d nigh** unto the grave. 5060
Isa 26:17 *that* **d near the time** of her delivery, is in 7126
Eze 7:12 The time is come, the day **d near**: let not 5060
Mt 15: 8 This people **d nigh** unto me with their *1448*
Lk 21: 8 saying, I am *Christ;* and the time **d near**: *1448*
21:28 up your heads; for your redemption **d nigh**. *1448*
Jas 5: 8 for the coming of the Lord **d nigh**. *1448*

DRAWING (2) [DRAW]
Jdg 5:11 **places of d** *water,* there shall they rehearse 4857
Jn 6:19 on the sea, and **d** nigh unto the ship: *1096*

DRAWN (28) [DRAW]
Nu 22:23 in the way, and his sword **d** in his hand: 8025
22:31 in the way, and his sword **d** in his hand: 8025
Dt 21: 3 *and* which hath not **d** in the yoke; 4900
30:17 shalt be **d away**, and worship other gods, 5080
Jos 5:13 against him with his sword **d** in his hand: 8025
8: 6 till we have **d** them from the city; for they 5423
8:16 and were **d away** from the city. 5423
15: 9 the border was **d** from the top of the hill 8388
15: 9 the border was **d** *to* Baalah, which *is* 8388
15:11 the border was **d** to Shicron, and 8388
18:14 the border was **d** *thence,* and 8388
18:17 was **d** from the north, and went forth *to* 8388
Jdg 20:31 the people, *and* were **d away** from the city; 5423
Ru 2: 9 drink of *that* which the young men have **d**. 7579
1Ch 21:16 having a **d** sword in his hand stretched out 8025
Job 20:25 It is **d**, and cometh out of the body; yea, 8025
Ps 37:14 The wicked have **d out** the sword, and 6605
55:21 softer than oil, yet *were* they **d swords**. 6609
Pr 24:11 to deliver *them that are* **d unto** death, 3947
Isa 21:15 from the **d** sword, and from the bent bow, 5203
28: 9 from the milk, *and* **d** from the breasts. 6267
Jer 22:19 **d** and cast forth beyond the gates of 5498
31: 3 *with* lovingkindness have I **d** thee. 4900
La 2: 3 he hath **d** back his right hand from before 7725
Eze 21: 5 have **d forth** my sword out of his sheath: 3318
21:28 even say thou, The sword, the sword *is* **d**: 6605
Ac 11:10 and all were **d up** again into heaven. *385*
Jas 1:14 when he is **d away** of his own lust, and *1828*

DREAD (9) [DREADFUL]
Ge 9: 2 the **d** of you shall be upon every beast of 2844
Ex 15:16 Fear and **d** shall fall upon them; by 6343
Dt 1:29 I said unto you, **D** not, neither be afraid of 6206
2:25 This day will I begin to put the **d** of thee 6343
11:25 the **d** of you upon all the land that ye shall 4172
1Ch 22:13 of good courage; **d** not, nor be dismayed. 3372

Job 13:11 make you afraid? and his **d** fall upon you? 6343
13:21 from me: and let not thy **d** make me afraid. 367
Isa 8:13 *let* him *be* your fear, and *let* him *be* your **d**. 6206

DREADFUL (9) [DREAD]

Ge 28:17 was afraid, and said, How **d** *is* this place! 3372
Job 15:21 A **d** sound *is* in his ears: in prosperity 6343
Eze 1:18 they were so high that they were **d**; 3374
Da 7: 7 **d** and terrible, and strong exceedingly; 1763
7:19 exceeding **d**, whose teeth *were of* iron, and 1763
9: 4 and said, O Lord, the great and **d** God, 3372
Hab 1: 7 They *are* terrible and **d**: their judgment and 3372
Mal 1:14 and my name *is* **d** among the heathen. 3372
4: 5 of the great and **d** day of the LORD: 3372

DREAM (74) [DREAMED, DREAMER, DREAMERS, DREAMETH, DREAMS]

Ge 20: 3 God came to Abimelech in a **d** by night, 2472
20: 6 God said unto him in a **d**, Yea, I know that 2472
31:10 up mine eyes, and saw in a **d**, and behold, 2472
31:11 the angel of God spake unto me in a **d**, 2472
31:24 God came to Laban the Syrian in a **d** by 2472
37: 5 Joseph dreamed a **d**, and he told *it* his 2472
37: 6 I pray you, this **d** which I have dreamed: 2472
37: 9 he dreamed yet another **d**, and told it his 2472
37: 9 and said, Behold, I have dreamed a **d** more; 2472
37:10 What *is* this **d** that thou hast dreamed? 2472
40: 5 they dreamed a **d** both of them, each man 2472
40: 5 both of them, each man his **d** in one night, 2472
40: 5 according to the interpretation of his **d**, 2472
40: 8 We have dreamed a **d**, and *there is* no 2472
40: 9 the chief butler told his **d** to Joseph, and 2472
40: 9 said to him, In my **d**, behold, a vine *was* 2472
40:16 I also *was* in my **d**, and behold, 2472
41: 7 Pharaoh awoke, and behold, *it was* a **d**. 2472
41: 8 Pharaoh told them his **d**; but *there was* 2472
41:11 we dreamed a **d** in one night, I and he; 2472
41:11 according to the interpretation of his **d**. 2472
41:12 to each man according to his **d** he did 2472
41:15 I have dreamed a **d**, and *there is* none that 2472
41:15 *that* thou canst understand a **d** to interpret 2472
41:17 Pharaoh said unto Joseph, In my **d**, behold, 2472
41:22 I saw in my **d**, and behold, seven ears came 2472
41:25 said unto Pharaoh, The **d** of Pharaoh *is* one: 2472
41:26 good ears *are* seven years: the **d** *is* one. 2472
41:32 for that the **d** was doubled unto Pharaoh 2472
Nu 12: 6 in a vision, *and* will speak unto him in a **d**. 2472
Jdg 7:13 *there was* a man that told a **d** unto his 2472
7:13 and said, Behold, I dreamed a **d**, and lo, 2472
7:15 *so,* when Gideon heard the telling of the **d**, 2472
1Ki 3: 5 appeared to Solomon in a **d** by night: 2472
3:15 Solomon awoke; and behold, *it was* a **d**. 2472
Job 20: 8 He shall fly away as a **d**, and shall not be 2472
33:15 In a **d**, *in* a vision of the night, when deep 2472
Ps 73:20 As a **d** when *one* awaketh; *so,* O Lord, 2472
126: 1 captivity of Zion, we were like them that **d**. 2492
Ecc 5: 3 For a **d** cometh through the multitude of 2472
Isa 29: 7 shall be as a **d** of a night vision. 2472
Jer 23:28 The prophet that hath a **d**, let him tell a 2472
23:28 prophet that hath a dream, let him tell a **d**; 2472
Da 2: 3 I have dreamed a **d**, and my spirit was 2472
2: 3 and my spirit was troubled to know the **d**. 2472
2: 4 tell thy servants the **d**, and we will shew 2493
2: 5 if ye will not make known unto me the **d**, 2493
2: 6 if ye shew the **d**, and the interpretation 2493
2: 6 therefore shew me the **d**, and 2493
2: 7 Let the king tell his servants the **d**, and 2493
2: 9 if ye will not make known unto me the **d**, 2493
2: 9 therefore tell me the **d**, and I shall know 2493
2:26 Art thou able to make known unto me the **d** 2493
2:28 Thy **d**, and the visions of thy head upon thy 2493
2:36 This *is* the **d**; and we will tell 2493
2:45 the **d** *is* certain, and the interpretation 2493
4: 5 I saw a **d** which made me afraid, and 2493
4: 6 known unto me the interpretation of the **d**. 2493
4: 7 I told the **d** before them; but they *did* not 2493
4: 8 and before him I told the **d**, *saying,* 2493
4: 9 tell *me* the visions of my **d** that I have seen, 2493
4:18 This **d** I king Nebuchadnezzar have seen. 2493
4:19 let not the **d**, or the interpretation thereof, 2493
4:19 the **d** *be* to them that hate thee, and 2493
7: 1 Belshazzar king of Babylon Daniel had a **d** 2493
7: 1 he wrote the **d**, *and* told the sum of 2493
Joel 2:28 your old men shall **d** dreams, 2492
Mt 1:20 angel of the Lord appeared unto him in a **d**, *3677*
2:12 And being warned of God in a **d** that *they* *3677*
2:13 of the Lord appeareth to Joseph in a **d**, *3677*
2:19 an angel of the Lord appeareth in a **d** to *3677*
2:22 being warned of God in a **d**, *3677*
27:19 I have suffered many *things* this day in a **d** *3677*
Ac 2:17 and your old men shall **d** dreams: *1797*

DREAMED (20) [DREAM]

Ge 28:12 he **d**, and behold a ladder set up on 2492
37: 5 Joseph **d** a dream, and he told *it* his 2492
37: 6 I pray you, this dream which I have **d**: 2492
37: 9 he **d** yet another dream, and told it his 2492
37: 9 and said, Behold, I have **d** a dream more; 2492
37:10 What *is* this dream that thou hast **d**? 2492
40: 5 they **d** a dream both of them, each man his 2492
40: 8 We have **d** a dream, and *there is* no 2492
41: 1 at the end of two full years, that Pharaoh **d**: 2492
41: 5 he slept and **d** the second time: and behold, 2492
41:11 we **d** a dream in one night, I and he; 2492
41:11 we **d** each man according to 2492
41:15 I have **d** a dream, and *there is* none that can 2492
42: 9 Joseph remembered the dreams which he **d** 2492
Jdg 7:13 and said, Behold, I **d** a dream, and lo, 2492
Jer 23:25 my name, saying, I have **d**, I have dreamed. 2492
23:25 my name, saying, I have dreamed, I have **d**. 2492
29: 8 to your dreams which ye **cause to be d**. 2492
Da 2: 1 Nebuchadnezzar **d** dreams, wherewith his 2492
2: 3 I have **d** a dream, and my spirit was 2492

DREAMER (4) [DREAM]

Ge 37:19 this **d** cometh. 1167+2472+1886.1
Dt 13: 1 or a **d** of dreams, and giveth thee a sign or 2492
13: 3 words of that prophet, or that **d** of dreams: 2492
13: 5 that prophet, or that **d** of dreams, shall be 2492

DREAMERS (2) [DREAM]

Jer 27: 9 nor to your diviners, nor to your **d**, nor to 2472
Jude 1: 8 Likewise also these *filthy* **d** defile the flesh, *1797*

DREAMETH (2) [DREAM]

Isa 29: 8 It shall even be as when a hungry *man* **d**, 2492
29: 8 or as when a thirsty *man* **d**, and behold, 2492

DREAMS (21) [DREAM]

Ge 37: 8 they hated him yet the more for his **d**, and 2472
37:20 and we shall see what will become of his **d**. 2472
41:12 we told him, and he interpreted to us our **d**; 2472
42: 9 Joseph remembered the **d** which he 2472
Dt 13: 1 or a dreamer of **d**, and giveth thee a sign or 2472
13: 3 words of that prophet, or that dreamer of **d**: 2472
13: 5 that prophet, or that dreamer of **d**, shall be 2472
1Sa 28: 6 neither by **d**, nor by Urim, nor by prophets. 2472
28:15 me no more, neither by prophets, nor by **d**: 2472
Job 7:14 thou scarest me with **d**, and terrifiest me 2472
Ecc 5: 7 For in the multitude of **d** and many words 2472
Jer 23:27 **d** which they tell every man to his 2472
23:32 I *am* against them that prophesy false **d**, 2472
29: 8 neither hearken to your **d** which ye cause to 2472
Da 1:17 had understanding in all visions and **d**. 2472
2: 1 Nebuchadnezzar dreamed **d**, wherewith his 2472
2: 2 the Chaldeans, for to shew the king his **d**. 2472
5:12 interpreting of **d**, and shewing of hard 2493
Joel 2:28 shall prophesy, your old men shall dream **d**, 2472
Zec 10: 2 have seen a lie, and have told false **d**; 2472
Ac 2:17 and your old men shall dream **d**: *1798*

DREGS (3)

Ps 75: 8 the **d** thereof, all the wicked of the earth 8105
Isa 51:17 thou hast drunken the **d** of the cup of 6907
51:22 *even* the **d** of the cup of my fury; 6907

DRESS (9) [DRESSED, DRESSER, DRESSETH, UNDRESSED, VINEDRESSERS]

Ge 2:15 put him into the garden of Eden to **d** it and 5647
18: 7 *it* unto a young man; and he hasted to **d** it. 6213
Dt 28:39 **d** *them,* but shalt neither drink *of* the wine, 5647
2Sa 12: 4 to **d** for the wayfaring man that was come 6213
13: 5 give me meat, and **d** the meat in my sight, 6213
13: 7 brother Amnon's house, and **d** him meat. 6213
1Ki 17:12 I may go in and **d** it for me and my son, 6213
18:23 fire *under:* and I will **d** the other bullock, 6213
18:25 one bullock for yourselves, and **d** *it* first; 6213

D

DRESSED (7) [DRESS]
Ge 18: 8 the calf which he had **d**, and set *it* before 6213
Lev 7: 9 all *that* is **d** in the fryingpan, and in the pan, 6213
1Sa 25:18 five sheep **ready d**, and five measures of 6213
2Sa 12: 4 and **d** it for the man that was come to him. 6213
19:24 had neither **d** his feet, nor trimmed his 6213
1Ki 18:26 they **d** *it,* and called on the name of Baal 6213
Heb 6: 7 forth herbs meet for them by whom it is **d**, *1090*

DRESSER (1) [DRESS]
Lk 13: 7 Then said he unto the **d of** his **vineyard**, *289*

DRESSETH (1) [DRESS]
Ex 30: 7 when he **d** the lamps, he shall burn incense 3190

DREW (85) [DRAW]
Ge 18:23 Abraham **d near**, and said, Wilt thou also 5066
24:20 well to draw *water,* and **d** for all his camels. 7579
24:45 **d** *water:* and I said unto her, Let me drink, 7579
37:28 they **d** and lift up Joseph out of the pit, and 4900
38:29 to pass, as he **d back** his hand, that, behold, 7725
47:29 the time **d nigh** that Israel must die: and 7126
Ex 2:10 she said, Because I **d** him out of the water. 4871
2:16 they came and **d water**, and filled 1802
2:19 also **d water enough** for us, and 1802+1802
14:10 when Pharaoh **d nigh**, the children of Israel 7126
20:21 Moses **d near** unto the thick darkness 5066
Lev 9: 5 all the congregation **d near** and 7126
Jos 8:11 **d nigh**, and came before the city, and 5066
8:26 For Joshua **d** not his hand **back**, 7725
Jdg 8:10 and twenty thousand men that **d** sword. 8025
8:20 the youth **d** not his sword: for he feared, 8025
20: 2 four hundred thousand footmen that **d** 8025
20:15 and six thousand men that **d** sword, 8025
20:17 four hundred thousand men that **d** sword: 8025
20:25 thousand men; all these **d** the sword. 8025
20:35 and an hundred men: all these **d** the sword. 8025
20:37 the liers in wait **d** *themselves* **along**, and 4900
20:46 and five thousand men that **d** the sword; 8025
Ru 4: 8 Buy *it* for thee. So he **d off** his shoe. 8025
1Sa 7: 6 **d** water, and poured *it* out before 7579
7:10 the Philistines **d near** to battle against 5066
9:18 Saul **d near** to Samuel in the gate, and 5066
17:16 the Philistine **d near** morning and evening, 5066
17:40 in his hand: and he **d near** to the Philistine. 5066
17:41 Philistine came on and **d near** unto David; 7131
17:48 came and **d nigh** to meet David, that David 7126
17:51 **d** it out of the sheath thereof, and slew him, 8025
2Sa 10:13 Joab **d nigh**, and the people that *were* with 5066
18:25 his mouth. And he came apace, and **d near**. 7131
22:17 he took me; he **d** me **out** of many waters; 4871
23:16 **d** water out of the well of Beth-lehem, 7579
24: 9 thousand valiant men that **d** the sword; 8025
1Ki 2: 1 Now the days of David **d nigh** that *he* 7126
8: 8 they **d out** the staves, that the ends of 748
22:34 a *certain* man **d** a bow at a venture, 4900
2Ki 3:26 he took with him seven hundred men that **d** 8025
9:24 **d** a bow **with** his **full strength**, 3027+4390+871.1
1Ch 11:18 **d** water out of the well of Beth-lehem, 7579
19:14 the people that *were* with him **d nigh** 5066
19:16 **d forth** the Syrians that *were* beyond 3318
21: 5 and an hundred thousand men that **d** sword: 8025
21: 5 and ten thousand men that **d** sword. 8025
2Ch 5: 9 they **d out** the staves *of the ark,* that the ends 748
14: 8 that bare shields and **d** bows, two hundred 1869
18:33 a *certain* man **d** a bow at a venture, 4900
Est 5: 2 So Esther **d near**, and touched the top of 7126
9: 1 his decree **d near** to be put in execution, 5060
Ps 18:16 he took me, he **d** me **out** of many waters. 4871
Isa 41: 5 of the earth were afraid, **d near**, and came. 7126
Jer 38:13 So they **d up** Jeremiah with cords, and 4900
Hos 11: 4 I **d** them with cords of a man, with bands of 4900
Zep 3: 2 in the LORD; she **d** not **near** to her God. 7126
Mt 13:48 they **d** to shore, and sat down, and *307*
21: 1 And when they **d nigh** unto Jerusalem, and *1448*
21:34 And when the time of the fruit **d near**, *1448*
26:51 and **d** his sword, and stroke a servant of *645*
Mk 6:53 the land of Genesaret, and **d to the shore**. *4358*
14:47 And one of them that stood by **d** a sword, *4685*
Lk 15: 1 Then **d near** unto him all the publicans and *1448*
15:25 and as he came and **d nigh** to the house, *1448*
22: 1 Now the feast of unleavened bread **d nigh**, *1448*
22:47 and **d near** unto Jesus to kiss him. *1448*
23:54 was the preparation, and the sabbath **d on**. *2020*
24:15 Jesus himself **d near**, and went with them. *1448*
24:28 And they **d nigh** unto the village, *1448*
Jn 2: 9 (but the servants which **d** the water knew;) *501*
18:10 Then Simon Peter having a sword **d** it, and *1670*
21:11 and **d** the net to land full of great fishes, *1670*
Ac 5:37 and **d away** much people after him: *868*
7:17 But when the time of the promise **d nigh**, *1448*
7:31 as he **d near** to behold *it,* the voice of *4334*
10: 9 on their journey, and **d nigh** unto the city, *1448*
14:19 having stoned Paul, **d** *him* out of the city, *4951*
16:19 **d** *them* into the market-place unto *1670*
16:27 he **d out** his sword, and would have killed *4685*
17: 6 they **d** Jason and certain brethren unto *4951*
19:33 And they **d** Alexander out of the multitude, *4264*
21:30 took Paul, and **d** him **out** of the temple: *1670*
27:27 deemed that they **d near** to some country; *4317*
Rev 12: 4 And his tail **d** the third *part* of the stars of *4951*

DREWEST (1) [DRAW]
La 3:57 Thou **d near** in the day *that* I called upon 7126

DRIED (39) [DRY]
Ge 8: 7 until the waters were **d up** from off 3001
8:13 the waters were **d up** from off the earth: 2717
8:14 day of the month, was the earth **d**. 3001
Lev 2:14 firstfruits green ears of corn **d** by the fire, 7033
Nu 6: 3 liquor of grapes, nor eat moist grapes, or **d**. 3002
11: 6 now our soul *is* **d away**: *there is* nothing at 3002
Jos 2:10 For we have heard how the LORD **d up** 3001
4:23 For the LORD your God **d up** the waters 3001
4:23 which he **d up** from before us, until we 3001
5: 1 heard that the LORD had **d up** the waters 3001
Jdg 16: 7 with seven green withs that were never **d**, 2717
16: 8 seven green withs which had not been **d**, 2717
1Ki 13: 4 **d up**, so that he could not pull it in again to 3001
17: 7 that the brook **d up**, because there had been 3001
2Ki 19:24 with the sole of my feet have I **d up** all 2717
Job 18:16 His roots shall be **d up** beneath, and 3001
28: 4 they are **d up**, they are gone away from 1809
Ps 22:15 My strength is **d up** like a potsherd; and 3001
69: 3 my throat is **d**: mine eyes fail while *I* wait 2787
106: 9 rebuked the Red sea also, and it was **d up**: 2717
Isa 5:13 and their multitude **d up** with thirst. 6704
19: 5 and the river shall be wasted and **d up**. 3001
19: 6 of defence shall be emptied and **d up**: 2717
37:25 with the sole of my feet have I **d up** all 2717
51:10 *Art* thou not it which hath **d** the sea, 2717
Jer 23:10 pleasant places of the wilderness are **d up**, 3001
50:38 *is* upon her waters; and they shall be **d up**: 3001
Eze 17:24 have **d up** the green tree, and have made 3001
19:12 and the east wind **d up** her fruit: 3001
37:11 Our bones are **d**, and our hope is lost: 3001
Hos 9:16 Ephraim is smitten, their root is **d up**, 3001
13:15 become dry, and his fountain shall be **d up**: 2717
Joel 1:10 the new wine is **d up**, the oil languisheth. 3001
1:12 The vine is **d up**, and the fig tree 3001
1:20 for the rivers of waters are **d up**, and 3001
Zec 11:17 his arm shall be **clean d up**, and 3001+3001
Mk 5:29 the fountain of her blood was **d up**; *3583*
11:20 they saw the fig tree **d up** from the roots. *3583*
Rev 16:12 and the water thereof was **d up**, that *3583*

DRIEDST (1) [DRY]
Ps 74:15 and the flood: thou **d up** mighty rivers. 3001

DRIETH (3) [DRY]
Job 14:11 the sea, and the flood decayeth and **d up**: 3001
Pr 17:22 a medicine: but a broken spirit **d** the bones. 3001
Na 1: 4 and maketh it dry, and **d up** all the rivers: 2717

DRINK (369) [DRANK, DRINKERS, DRINKETH, DRINKING, DRINKS, DRUNK, DRUNKARD, DRUNKARDS, DRUNKEN, DRUNKENNESS]
Ge 19:32 let us **make** our father **d** wine, and we will 8248
19:33 they **made** their father **d** wine that night: 8248
19:34 let us **make** him **d** wine this night also; and 8248
19:35 they **made** their father **d** wine that night 8248
21:19 the bottle *with* water, and **gave** the lad **d**. 8248
24:14 down thy pitcher, I pray thee, that I may **d**; 8354
24:14 **D**, and I will give thy camels drink also: 8354
24:14 Drink, and I will **give** thy camels **d** also: 8248
24:17 I pray thee, **d** a little water of thy pitcher. 1572
24:18 she said, **D**, my lord: and she hasted, and 8354
24:18 her pitcher upon her hand, and **gave** him **d**. 8248

Ge	24:19	when she had done **giving** him **d**, she said,	8248
	24:43	**Give** me, I pray thee, a little water of thy pitcher **to d**;	8248
	24:44	Both **d** thou, and I will also draw for thy	8354
	24:45	and I said unto her, Let me **d**, I pray thee.	8248
	24:46	**D**, and I will give thy camels drink also:	8354
	24:46	Drink, and I will **give** thy camels **d** also:	8248
	24:46	so I drank, and she **made** the camels **d** also.	8248
	24:54	they did eat and **d**, he and the men that	8354
	25:34	he did eat and **d**, and rose up, and went his	8354
	26:30	made them a feast, and they did eat and **d**.	8354
	30:38	troughs when the flocks came to **d**,	8354
	30:38	they should conceive when they came to **d**.	8354
	35:14	he poured a **d offering** thereon, and	5262
Ex	7:18	the Egyptians shall lothe to **d** of the water	8354
	7:21	the Egyptians could not **d** of the water of	8354
	7:24	digged round about the river *for* water to **d**;	8354
	7:24	for they could not **d** of the water of	8354
	15:23	they could not **d** of the waters of Marah,	8354
	15:24	against Moses, saying, What shall we **d**?	8354
	17: 1	and *there was* no water for the people to **d**.	8354
	17: 2	and said, Give us water that we may **d**.	8354
	17: 6	come water out of it, that the people may **d**.	8354
	24:11	also they saw God, and did eat and **d**.	8354
	29:40	*part* of a hin of wine *for* a **d offering**.	5262
	29:41	according to the **d offering** thereof, for a	5262
	30: 9	neither shall ye pour **d offering** thereon.	5262
	32: 6	and the people sat down to eat and to **d**, and	8354
	32:20	and **made** the children of Israel **d** *of it*.	8248
	34:28	he did neither eat bread, nor **d** water.	8354
Lev	10: 9	Do not **d** wine nor strong drink, thou,	8354
	10: 9	Do not drink wine nor **strong d**, thou,	7941
	11:34	all **d** that may be drunk in every *such* vessel	4945
	23:13	the **d offering** thereof *shall be of* wine,	5262
	23:18	their meat offering, and their **d offerings**,	5262
	23:37	meat offering, a sacrifice, and **d offerings**,	5262
Nu	5:24	he shall **cause** the woman **to d** the bitter	8248
	5:26	afterward shall **cause** the woman **to d**	8248
	5:27	And when he hath **made** her **to d** the water,	8248
	6: 3	separate *himself* from wine and **strong d**,	7941
	6: 3	*and* shall **d** no vinegar of wine, or	8354
	6: 3	no vinegar of wine, or vinegar of **strong d**,	7941
	6: 3	neither shall he **d** any liquor of grapes,	8354
	6:15	their meat offering, and their **d offerings**.	5262
	6:17	also his meat offering, and his **d offering**.	5262
	6:20	and after *that* the Nazarite may **d** wine.	8354
	15: 5	**d offering** shalt thou prepare with the burnt	5262
	15: 7	for a **d offering** thou shalt offer the third	5262
	15:10	thou shalt bring for a **d offering** half a hin	5262
	15:24	with his meat offering, and his **d offering**,	5262
	20: 5	neither *is there any* water to **d**.	8354
	20: 8	**give** the congregation and their beasts **d**.	8248
	20:17	neither will we **d** *of* the water of the wells:	8354
	20:19	if I and my cattle **d** *of* thy water, then I will	8354
	21:22	we will not **d** *of* the waters of the well:	8354
	23:24	eat *of* the prey, and **d** the blood of the slain.	8354
	28: 7	the **d offering** thereof *shall be* the fourth	5262
	28: 7	poured unto the LORD *for* a **d offering**.	5262
	28: 8	the morning, and as the **d offering** thereof,	5262
	28: 9	with oil, and the **d offering** thereof:	5262
	28:10	burnt offering, and his **d offering**.	5262
	28:14	their **d offerings** shall be half a hin of wine	5262
	28:15	burnt offering, and his **d offering**.	5262
	28:24	burnt offering, and his **d offering**.	5262
	28:31	you without blemish) and their **d offerings**.	5262
	29: 6	his meat offering, and their **d offerings**,	5262
	29:11	meat offering of it, and their **d offerings**.	5262
	29:16	his meat offering, and his **d offering**.	5262
	29:18	and their **d offerings** for the bullocks,	5262
	29:19	offering thereof, and their **d offerings**.	5262
	29:21	and their **d offerings** for the bullocks,	5262
	29:22	and his meat offering, and his **d offering**.	5262
	29:24	and their **d offerings** for the bullocks,	5262
	29:25	his meat offering, and his **d offering**.	5262
	29:27	and their **d offerings** for the bullocks,	5262
	29:28	and his meat offering, and his **d offering**.	5262
	29:30	and their **d offerings** for the bullocks,	5262
	29:31	his meat offering, and his **d offering**.	5262
	29:33	and their **d offerings** for the bullocks,	5262
	29:34	his meat offering, and his **d offering**.	5262
	29:37	and their **d offerings** for the bullock,	5262
	29:38	and his meat offering, and his **d offering**.	5262
	29:39	for your **d offerings**, and for your peace	5262
	33:14	where was no water for the people to **d**.	8354
Dt	2: 6	water of them for money, that ye may **d**.	8354
	2:28	and give me water for money, that I may **d**:	8354
	9: 9	I neither did eat bread nor **d** water:	8354
	9:18	nor **d** water, because of all your sins which	8354
	14:26	or for **strong d**, or for whatsoever thy soul	7941
	28:39	dress *them*, but shalt neither **d** *of* the wine,	8354
	29: 6	neither have you drunk wine or **strong d**:	7941
	32:14	thou didst **d** the pure blood of the grape.	8354
	32:38	*and* drank the wine of their **d offerings**?	5257
Jdg	4:19	**Give** me, I pray thee, a little water **to d**;	8248
	4:19	of milk, and **gave** him **d**, and covered him.	8248
	7: 5	one that boweth down upon his knees to **d**.	8354
	7: 6	bowed down upon their knees to **d** water.	8354
	9:27	and did eat and **d**, and cursed Abimelech.	8354
	13: 4	**d** not wine nor strong drink, and eat not	8354
	13: 4	drink not wine nor **strong d**, and eat not	7941
	13: 7	now **d** no wine nor strong drink, neither eat	8354
	13: 7	now drink no wine nor **strong d**, neither eat	7941
	13:14	neither let her **d** wine or strong drink,	8354
	13:14	neither let her drink wine or **strong d**,	7941
	19: 4	so they did eat and **d**, and lodged there.	8354
	19: 6	and did eat and **d** both of them together:	8354
	19:21	they washed their feet, and did eat and **d**.	8354
Ru	2: 9	**d** of *that* which the young men have drawn.	8354
1Sa	1:15	I have drunk neither wine nor **strong d**, but	7941
	30:11	and he did eat; and they **made** him **d** water;	8248
2Sa	11:11	to eat and to **d**, and to lie with my wife?	8354
	11:13	called him, he did eat and **d** before him;	8354
	16: 2	such as be faint in the wilderness may **d**.	8354
	19:35	can thy servant taste what I eat or what I **d**?	8354
	23:15	Oh that one would **give** me **d** *of* the water	8248
	23:16	nevertheless he would not **d** thereof, but	8354
	23:17	therefore he would not **d** it. These *things*	8354
1Ki	1:25	behold, they eat and **d** before him, and say,	8354
	13: 8	neither will I eat bread nor **d** water in this	8354
	13: 9	saying, Eat no bread, nor **d** water,	8354
	13:16	neither will I eat bread nor **d** water with	8354
	13:17	Thou shalt eat no bread nor **d** water there,	8354
	13:18	that he may eat bread and **d** water.	8354
	13:22	say to thee, Eat no bread, and **d** no water;	8354
	17: 4	it shall be, *that* thou shalt **d** of the brook;	8354
	17:10	a little water in a vessel, that I may **d**.	8354
	18:41	said unto Ahab, Get thee up, eat and **d**;	8354
	18:42	So Ahab went up to eat and to **d**.	8354
	19: 6	he did eat and **d**, and laid him down again.	8354
	19: 8	did eat and **d**, and went in the strength of	8354
2Ki	3:17	that ye may **d**, *both* ye, and your cattle, and	8354
	6:22	that they may eat and **d**, and go to their	8354
	7: 8	did eat and **d**, and carried thence silver, and	8354
	9:34	come in, he did eat and **d**, and said, Go,	8354
	16:13	poured his **d offering**, and sprinkled	5262
	16:15	their meat offering, and their **d offerings**;	5262
	18:27	own dung, and **d** their own piss with you?	8354
	18:31	**d** ye every one the waters of his cistern:	8354
1Ch	11:17	Oh that one would **give** me **d** *of* the water	8248
	11:18	David would not **d** *of* it, but poured it out to	8354
	11:19	that *I* should do this *thing*: shall I **d**	8354
	11:19	Therefore he would not **d** it. These *things*	8354
	29:21	with their **d offerings**, and sacrifices in	5262
	29:22	**d** before the LORD on that day with great	8354
2Ch	28:15	gave them to eat and to **d**, and	8248
	29:35	the **d offerings** for *every* burnt offering.	5262
Ezr	3: 7	meat, and **d**, and oil, unto them of Zidon,	4960
	7:17	their meat offerings and their **d offerings**,	5261
	10: 6	he did eat no bread, nor **d** water:	8354
Ne	8:10	**d** the sweet, and send portions unto *them*	8354
	8:12	to **d**, and to send portions, and to make	8354
Est	1: 7	*they* **gave** *them* **d** in vessels of gold,	8248
	3:15	And the king and Haman sat down to **d**; but	8354
	4:16	neither eat nor **d** three days, night or day;	8354
Job	1: 4	their three sisters to eat and to **d** with them.	8354
	21:20	and he shall **d** of the wrath of the Almighty.	8354
	22: 7	hast not **given** water to the weary **to d**,	8248
Ps	16: 4	their **d offerings** of blood will I not offer,	5262
	36: 8	thou shalt **make** them **d** *of* the river of thy	8248
	50:13	the flesh of bulls, or **d** the blood of goats?	8354
	60: 3	**made** us **to d** the wine *of* astonishment.	8248
	69:21	and in my thirst they **gave** me vinegar **to d**.	8248
	75: 8	the earth shall wring *them* out, *and* **d** *them*.	8354
	78:15	and **gave** *them* **d** as *out of* the great depths.	8248
	78:44	and their floods, *that* they could not **d**.	8354
	80: 5	and **givest** them tears **to d** *in great* measure.	8248
	102: 9	and mingled my **d** with weeping,	8249
	104:11	They **give d** to every beast of the field:	8248

Ps 110: 7 He shall **d** of the brook in the way: 8354
Pr 4:17 of wickedness, and **d** the wine of violence. 8354
5:15 **D** waters out of thine own cistern, and 8354
9: 5 and **d** of the wine *which* I have mingled. 8354
20: 1 Wine *is* a mocker, **strong d** *is* raging: and 7941
23: 7 Eat and **d**, saith he to thee; but his heart *is* 8354
25:21 and if he *be* thirsty, **give** him water **to d**: 8248
31: 4 O Lemuel, *it is* not for kings to **d** wine; 8354
31: 4 to drink wine; nor for princes **strong d**: 7941
31: 5 Lest they **d**, and forget the law, and 8354
31: 6 Give **strong d** unto him that is ready to 7941
31: 7 Let him **d**, and forget his poverty, and 8354
Ecc 2:24 *than* that he should eat and **d**, and *that* he 8354
3:13 also that every man should eat and **d**, and 8354
5:18 *is* good and comely *for one* to eat and to **d**, 8354
8:15 than to eat, and to **d**, and to be merry: 8354
9: 7 and **d** thy wine with a merry heart; 8354
SS 5: 1 **d**, yea, drink abundantly, O beloved. 8354
5: 1 drink, yea, **d abundantly**, O beloved. 7937
8: 2 I would **cause** thee **to d** of spiced wine, 8248
Isa 5:11 *that* they may follow **strong d**; 7941
5:22 Woe unto *them that are* mighty to **d** wine, 8354
5:22 and men of strength to mingle **strong d**: 7941
21: 5 the table, watch *in* the watchtower, eat, **d**: 8354
22:13 let us eat and **d**; for to morrow we shall die. 8354
24: 9 They shall not **d** wine with a song; 8354
24: 9 **strong d** shall be bitter to them that drink 7941
24: 9 strong drink shall be bitter to them that **d** it. 8354
28: 7 and through **strong d** are out of the way; 7941
28: 7 the prophet have erred through **strong d**, 7941
28: 7 they are out of the way through **strong d**; 7941
29: 9 they stagger, but not *with* **strong d**. 7941
32: 6 and he will cause the **d** of the thirsty to fail. 4945
36:12 own dung, and **d** their own piss with you? 8354
36:16 **d** ye every one the waters of his own 8354
43:20 to **give d** to my people, my chosen. 8248
51:22 of my fury; thou shalt no more **d** it again: 8354
56:12 and we will fill ourselves with **strong d**; 7941
57: 6 even to them hast thou poured a **d offering**, 5262
62: 8 the sons of the stranger shall not **d** thy 8354
62: 9 they that have brought it together shall **d** it 8354
65:11 that furnish the **d offering** unto *that* 4469
65:13 my servants shall **d**, but ye shall be thirsty: 8354
Jer 2:18 the way of Egypt, to **d** the waters of Sihor? 8354
2:18 of Assyria, to **d** the waters of the river? 8354
7:18 to pour out **d offerings** unto other gods, 5262
8:14 **given** us water of gall **to d**, because 8248
9:15 and **give** them water of gall **to d**. 8248
16: 7 **give** them the cup of consolation **to d** for 8248
16: 8 of feasting, to sit with them to eat and to **d**. 8354
19:13 have poured out **d offerings** unto other 5262
22:15 did not thy father eat and **d**, and 8354
23:15 and **make** them **d** the water of gall: 8248
25:15 **cause** all the nations, to whom I send thee, **to d** 8248
25:16 they shall **d**, and be moved, and be mad, 8354
25:17 **made** all the nations **to d**, unto whom 8248
25:26 and the king of Sheshach shall **d** after them. 8354
25:27 **D** ye, and be drunken, and spue, and fall, 8354
25:28 refuse to take the cup at thine hand to **d**, 8354
25:28 of hosts; Ye shall **certainly d**. 8354+8354
32:29 and poured out **d offerings** unto other gods, 5262
35: 2 of the chambers, and **give** them wine **to d**. 8248
35: 5 and cups, and I said unto them, **D** ye wine. 8354
35: 6 they said, We will **d** no wine: for Jonadab 8354
35: 6 saying, Ye shall **d** no wine, *neither* ye, 8354
35: 8 to **d** no wine all our days, we, our wives, 8354
35:14 that he commanded his sons not to **d** wine, 8354
35:14 for unto this day they **d** none, but 8354
44:17 to pour out **d offerings** unto her, as we 5262
44:18 to pour out **d offerings** unto her, we have 5262
44:19 poured out **d offerings** unto her, did we 5262
44:19 pour out **d offerings** unto her, without our 5262
44:25 and to pour out **d offerings** unto her: 5262
49:12 they whose judgment *was* not to **d** of 8354
49:12 but thou shalt **surely d** *of it*. 8354+8354
Eze 4:11 Thou shalt **d** also water by measure, 8354
4:11 of a hin: from time to time shalt thou **d**. 8354
4:16 they shall **d** water by measure, and 8354
12:18 **d** thy water with trembling and 8354
12:19 and **d** their water with astonishment, 8354
20:28 and poured out there their **d offerings**. 5262
23:32 Thou shalt **d** *of* thy sister's cup deep and 8354
23:34 Thou shalt even **d** it and suck *it* out, and 8354

25: 4 shall eat thy fruit, and they shall **d** thy milk. 8354
31:14 stand up in their height, all that **d** water: 8354
31:16 and best of Lebanon, all that **d** water, 8354
34:19 they **d** that which ye have fouled with your 8354
39:17 that ye may eat flesh, and **d** blood. 8354
39:18 **d** the blood of the princes of the earth, 8354
39:19 *ye* be full, and **d** blood till *ye* be drunken, 8354
44:21 Neither shall any priest **d** wine, when they 8354
45:17 **d offerings**, in the feasts, and in the new 5262
Da 1:10 who hath appointed your meat and your **d**: 4960
1:12 them give us pulse to eat, and water to **d**. 8354
1:16 their meat, and the wine that they should **d**; 4960
5: 2 and his concubines, might **d** therein. 8355
Hos 2: 5 my wool and my flax, mine oil and my **d**. 8250
4:18 Their **d** is sour; they have committed 5435
Joel 1: 9 the **d offering** is cut off from the house of 5262
1:13 the **d offering** is withholden from the house 5262
2:14 a **d offering** unto the LORD your God? 5262
3: 3 and sold a girl for wine, that they might **d**. 8354
Am 2: 8 they **d** the wine of the condemned *in* 8354
2:12 ye **gave** the Nazarites wine **to d**; 8248
4: 1 say to their masters, Bring, and let us **d**. 8354
4: 8 cities wandered unto one city, to **d** water; 8354
5:11 but ye shall not **d** wine of them. 8354
6: 6 That **d** wine in bowls, and 8354
9:14 plant vineyards, and **d** the wine thereof; 8354
Ob 1:16 *so* shall all the heathen **d** continually, yea, 8354
1:16 they shall **d**, and they shall swallow down, 8354
Jnh 3: 7 any thing: let them not feed, nor **d** water: 8354
Mic 2:11 unto thee of wine and of **strong d**; 7941
6:15 and sweet wine, but shalt not **d** wine. 8354
Hab 2:15 Woe unto him that **giveth** his neighbour **d**, 8248
2:16 **d** thou also, and let thy foreskin be 8354
Zep 1:13 plant vineyards, but not **d** the wine thereof. 8354
Hag 1: 6 *ye* **d**, but ye are not filled with drink; 8354
1: 6 *ye* drink, but ye are not **filled with d**; 7937
Zec 7: 6 when ye did eat, and when ye did **d**, did not 8354
7: 6 eat *for yourselves,* and **d** *for yourselves?* 8354
9:15 they shall **d**, *and* make a noise as *through* 8354
Mt 6:25 what ye shall eat, or what ye shall **d**; *4095*
6:31 or, What shall we **d**? or, Wherewithal shall *4095*
10:42 And whosoever shall **give** to **d** unto one of *4222*
20:22 Are ye able to **d** *of* the cup that I shall drink *4095*
20:22 Are ye able to drink *of* the cup that I shall **d** *4095*
20:23 Ye shall **d** indeed *of* my cup, and *4095*
24:49 and to eat and **d** with the drunken; *4095*
25:35 I was thirsty, and ye **gave** me **d**: I was a *4222*
25:37 and fed *thee?* or thirsty, and **gave** *thee* **d**? *4222*
25:42 I was thirsty, and ye **gave** me no **d**: *4222*
26:27 and gave *it* to them, saying, **D** ye all of it; *4095*
26:29 I will not **d** henceforth of this fruit of *4095*
26:29 until that day when I **d** it new with you in *4095*
26:42 from me, except I **d** it, thy will be done. *4095*
27:34 They gave him vinegar to **d** mingled with *4095*
27:34 when he had tasted *thereof,* he would not **d**. *4095*
27:48 and put *it* on a reed, and **gave** him **to d**. *4222*
Mk 9:41 **give** you a cup of water **to d** in my name, *4222*
10:38 can ye **d** *of* the cup that I drink *of?* and be *4095*
10:38 can ye drink *of* the cup that I **d** *of?* and be *4095*
10:39 Ye shall indeed **d** *of* the cup that I drink *of;* *4095*
10:39 Ye shall indeed drink *of* the cup that I **d** *of;* *4095*
14:25 I will **d** no more of the fruit of the vine, *4095*
14:25 until that day that I **d** it new in the kingdom *4095*
15:23 And they gave him to **d** wine mingled with *4095*
15:36 and **gave** him **to d**, saying, Let alone; *4222*
16:18 if they **d** any deadly *thing,* it shall not hurt *4095*
Lk 1:15 and shall **d** neither wine nor strong drink; *4095*
1:15 and shall drink neither wine nor **strong d**; *4608*
5:30 do ye eat and **d** with publicans and sinners? *4095*
5:33 of the Pharisees; but thine eat and **d**? *4095*
12:19 take thine ease, eat, **d**, *and* be merry. *4095*
12:29 or what ye shall **d**, neither be ye of doubtful *4095*
12:45 and to eat and **d**, and to be drunken; *4095*
17: 8 and afterward thou shalt eat and **d**? *4095*
22:18 I will not **d** of the fruit of the vine, *4095*
22:30 may eat and **d** at my table in my kingdom, *4095*
Jn 4: 7 Jesus saith unto her, Give me to **d**. *4095*
4: 9 *is it that* thou, being a Jew, askest **d** of me, *4095*
4:10 who it is that saith to thee, Give me to **d**; *4095*
6:53 and **d** his blood, ye have no life in you. *4095*
6:55 is meat indeed, and my blood is **d** indeed. *4213*
7:37 *man* thirst, let him come unto me, and **d**. *4095*
18:11 my Father hath given me, shall I not **d** it? *4095*
Ac 9: 9 without sight, and neither did eat nor **d**. *4095*

Ac 10:41 and **d with** him after he rose from the dead. *4844*
23:12 saying that *they* would neither eat nor **d** till *4095*
23:21 that *they* will neither eat nor **d** till they have *4095*
Ro 12:20 feed him; if he thirst, **give** him **d**: *4222*
14:17 For the kingdom of God is not meat and **d**; *4213*
14:21 *It is* good neither to eat flesh, nor to **d** wine, *4095*
1Co 9: 4 Have we not power to eat and to **d**? *4095*
10: 4 And did all **d** the same spiritual drink: *4095*
10: 4 And did all drink the same spiritual **d**: *4188*
10: 7 The people sat down to eat and **d**, and *4095*
10:21 Ye cannot **d** the cup of the Lord, and *4095*
10:31 therefore ye eat, or **d**, or whatsoever ye do, *4095*
11:22 have ye not houses to eat and to **d** *in?* or *4095*
11:25 as oft as ye **d** *it,* in remembrance of me. *4095*
11:26 as often as ye eat this bread, and **d** this cup, *4095*
11:27 and **d** *this* cup of the Lord unworthily, *4095*
11:28 let him eat of *that* bread, and **d** of *that* cup. *4095*
12:13 have been all **made to d** into one Spirit. *4222*
15:32 let us eat and **d**; for to morrow we die. *4095*
Col 2:16 or in **d**, or in respect of a holyday, or of *4213*
1Ti 5:23 **D** no longer **water**, but use a little wine for *5202*
Rev 14: 8 she **made** all nations **d** of the wine of *4222*
14:10 The same shall **d** of the wine of the wrath *4095*
16: 6 and thou hast given them blood to **d**; *4095*

DRINKERS (1) [DRINK]
Joel 1: 5 howl, all ye **d** of wine, because of the new 8354

DRINKETH (17) [DRINK]
Ge 44: 5 *Is* not this *it* in which my lord **d**, and 8354
Dt 11:11 valleys, *and* **d** water of the rain of heaven: 8354
Job 6: 4 the poison whereof **d up** my spirit: 8354
15:16 filthy *is* man, which **d** iniquity like water? 8354
34: 7 *is* like Job, *who* **d up** scorning like water? 8354
40:23 Behold, he **d up** a river, *and* hasteth not: 6231
Pr 26: 6 of a fool cutteth off the feet, *and* **d** damage. 8354
Isa 29: 8 a thirsty *man* dreameth, and behold, he **d**; 8354
44:12 strength faileth: he **d** no water, and is faint. 8354
Mk 2:16 he eateth and **d** with publicans and sinners? *4095*
Jn 4:13 Whosoever **d** of this water shall thirst *4095*
4:14 But whosoever **d** of the water that I shall *4095*
6:54 my flesh, and **d** my blood, hath eternal life; *4095*
6:56 and **d** my blood, dwelleth in me, and I in *4095*
1Co 11:29 For he that eateth and **d** unworthily, eateth *4095*
11:29 eateth and **d** damnation to himself, *4095*
Heb 6: 7 For the earth which **d** *in* the rain that *4095*

DRINKING (21) [DRINK]
Ge 24:19 for thy camels also, until they have done **d**. 8354
24:22 it came to pass, as the camels had done **d**, 8354
Ru 3: 3 until he shall have done eating and **d**. 8354
1Sa 30:16 eating and **d**, and dancing, because of all 8354
1Ki 4:20 eating and **d**, and making merry. 8354
10:21 all king Solomon's **d** vessels *were of* gold, 4945
16: 9 **d** *himself* drunk *in* the house of Arza 8354
20:12 as he *was* **d**, he and the kings in 8354
20:16 Ben-hadad *was* **d** *himself* drunk in 8354
1Ch 12:39 were with David three days, eating and **d**: 8354
2Ch 9:20 all the **d** vessels of king Solomon *were of* 4945
Est 1: 8 the **d** *was* according to the law; none did 8360
Job 1:13 and **d** wine in their eldest brother's house: 8354
1:18 and **d** wine in their eldest brother's house: 8354
Isa 22:13 and killing sheep, eating flesh, and **d** wine: 8354
Mt 11:18 For John came neither eating nor **d**, and *4095*
11:19 The Son of man came eating and **d**, and *4095*
24:38 before the flood they were eating and **d**, *4095*
Lk 7:33 came neither eating bread nor **d** wine; *4095*
7:34 The Son of man is come eating and **d**; and *4095*
10: 7 eating and **d** such *things* as they give: *4095*

DRINKS (1) [DRINK]
Heb 9:10 *Which stood* only in meats and **d**, and *4188*

DRIVE (57) [DRAVE, DRIVEN, DRIVER, DRIVETH, DRIVING, DROVE, OVERDRIVE]
Ex 6: 1 with a strong hand shall he **d** them **out** of 1644
23:28 which shall **d out** the Hivite, the Canaanite, 1644
23:29 I will not **d** them **out** from before thee in 1644
23:30 little I will **d** them **out** from before thee, 1644
23:31 thou shalt **d** them out before thee. 1644
33: 2 and I will **d out** the Canaanite, the Amorite, 1644
34:11 I **d out** before thee the Amorite, and 1644
Nu 22: 6 and *that* I may **d** them **out** of the land: 1644
22:11 be able to overcome them, and **d** them **out**. 1644
33:52 ye shall **d out** all the inhabitants of the land 3423
33:55 if ye will not **d out** the inhabitants of 3423
Dt 4:38 To **d out** nations from before thee greater 3423
9: 3 so shalt thou **d** them **out**, and destroy them 3423
9: 4 LORD doth **d** them **out** from before thee. 3423
9: 5 thy God doth **d** them **out** from before thee, 3423
11:23 will the LORD **d out** all these nations 3423
18:12 thy God doth **d** them **out** from before thee. 3423
Jos 3:10 *that* he will **without fail d out** from 3423+3423
13: 6 them will I **d out** from before the children 3423
14:12 I shall *be able to* **d** them **out**, as the LORD 3423
15:63 the children of Judah could not **d** them **out**: 3423
17:12 the children of Manasseh could not **d out** 3423
17:13 but did not **utterly d** them **out**. 3423+3423
17:18 for thou shalt **d out** the Canaanites, 3423
23: 5 and **d** them from out of your sight; 3423
23:13 **d out** *any of* these nations from before you; 3423
Jdg 1:19 could not **d out** the inhabitants of 3423
1:21 the children of Benjamin did not **d out** 3423
1:27 Neither did Manasseh **d out** *the inhabitants* 3423
1:28 and did not **utterly d** them **out**. 3423+3423
1:29 Neither did Ephraim **d out** the Canaanites 3423
1:30 Neither did Zebulun **d out** the inhabitants 3423
1:31 Neither did Asher **d out** the inhabitants of 3423
1:32 of the land: for they did not **d** them **out**. 3423
1:33 Neither did Naphtali **d out** the inhabitants 3423
2: 3 I will not **d** them **out** from before you; 1644
2:21 I also will not henceforth **d out** any from 3423
11:24 our God shall **d out** from before us, 3423
2Ki 4:24 **D**, and go *forward;* slack not *thy* riding for 5090
2Ch 20: 7 who didst **d out** the inhabitants of this land 3423
Job 18:11 on every side, and shall **d** him to his feet. 6327
24: 3 They **d away** the ass of the fatherless, 5090
Ps 44: 2 *How* thou didst **d out** the heathen *with* thy 3423
68: 2 As smoke is driven away, *so* **d** *them* **away**: 5086
Pr 22:15 the rod of correction shall **d** it **far** from 7368
Isa 22:19 I will **d** thee from thy station, and from thy 1920
Jer 24: 9 a curse, in all places whither I shall **d** them. 5080
27:10 *that* I should **d** you **out**, and ye should 5080
27:15 that I might **d** you **out**, and that ye might 5080
46:15 stood not, because the LORD did **d** them. 1920
Eze 4:13 among the Gentiles, whither I will **d** them. 5080
Da 4:25 That they *shall* **d** thee from men, and 2957
4:32 they *shall* **d** thee from men, and 2957
Hos 9:15 doings I will **d** them **out** of mine house, 1644
Joel 2:20 will **d** him into a land barren and desolate, 5080
Zep 2: 4 they shall **d out** Ashdod at the noon day, 1644
Ac 27:15 bear up into the wind, we **let** *her* **d**. *1929+5342*

DRIVEN (49) [DRIVE]
Ge 4:14 thou hast **d** me **out** *this* day from the face 1644
Ex 10:11 they were **d out** from Pharaoh's presence. 1644
22:10 it die, or be hurt, or **d away**, no man seeing 7617
Nu 32:21 until he hath **d out** his enemies from before 3423
Dt 4:19 shouldest be **d** to worship them, and 5080
30: 1 whither the LORD thy God hath **d** thee, 5080
30: 4 If *any* of thine be **d out** unto the outmost 5080
Jos 23: 9 For the LORD hath **d out** from before you 3423
1Sa 26:19 for they have **d** me **out** *this* day from 1644
Job 6:13 in me? and is wisdom **d** *quite* from me? 5080
13:25 Wilt thou break a leaf **d to and fro**? and 5086
18:18 He shall be **d** from light into darkness, and 1920
30: 5 They were **d forth** from among men, 1644
Ps 40:14 let them be **d** backward and put to shame 5472
68: 2 As smoke is **d away**, *so* drive *them* away: 5086
114: 3 sea saw *it,* and fled: Jordan was **d** back. 5437
114: 5 thou Jordan, *that* thou wast **d** back? 5437
Pr 14:32 The wicked is **d away** in his wickedness: 1760
Isa 8:22 of anguish; and *they shall be* **d** *to* darkness. 5080
19: 7 shall wither, be **d away**, and *be* no *more.* 5086
41: 2 *to* his sword, *and* as **d** stubble *to* his bow. 5086
Jer 8: 3 in all the places whither I have **d** them, 5080
16:15 from all the lands whither he had **d** them: 5080
23: 2 **d** them **away**, and have not visited them: 5080
23: 3 out of all countries whither I have **d** them, 5080
23: 8 from all countries whither I had **d** them; 5080
23:12 they shall be **d on**, and fall therein: for I 1760
29:14 from all the places whither I have **d** you, 5080
29:18 among all the nations whither I have **d** 5080
32:37 whither I have **d** them in mine anger, and 5080
40:12 out of all places whither they were **d**, 5080
43: 5 whither they had been **d**, to dwell in 5080
46:28 end of all the nations whither I have **d** thee: 5080
49: 5 ye shall be **d out** every man right forth; 5080

Jer 50:17 scattered sheep; the lions have **d** *him* **away**: 5080
Eze 31:11 I have **d** him **out** for his wickedness. 1644
34: 4 ye brought again that which was **d away**, 5080
34:16 bring again that which was **d away**, and 5080
Da 4:33 he *was* **d** from men, and did eat grass as 2957
5:21 he *was* **d** from the sons of men; and 2957
9: 7 all the countries whither thou hast **d** them, 5080
Hos 13: 3 as the chaff *that* is **d with a whirlwind** out 5590
Mic 4: 6 I will gather her that is **d out**, and *her* that I 5080
Zep 3:19 that halteth, and gather her that was **d out**; 5080
Lk 8:29 and was **d** of the devil into the wilderness.) *1643*
Ac 27:17 the quicksands, strake sail, and so were **d**. *5342*
27:27 as we were **d up and down** in Adria, *1308*
Jas 1: 6 is like a wave of the sea **d with the wind** *416*
3: 4 they be so great, and are **d** of fierce winds, *1643*

DRIVER (2) [DRIVE]
1Ki 22:34 wherefore he said unto the **d of** his **chariot**, 7395
Job 39: 7 neither regardeth he the crying of the **d**. 5065

DRIVETH (4) [DRIVE]
2Ki 9:20 Jehu the son of Nimshi; for he **d** furiously. 5090
Ps 1: 4 *are* like the chaff which the wind **d away**. 5086
Pr 25:23 The north wind **d away** rain: so *doth* an 2342
Mk 1:12 And immediately the Spirit **d** him into *1544*

DRIVING (4) [DRIVE]
Jdg 2:23 those nations, without **d** them **out** hastily; 3423
2Ki 9:20 the **d** *is* like the driving of Jehu the son of 4491
9:20 the driving *is* like the **d** of Jehu the son of 4491
1Ch 17:21 by **d out** nations from before thy people, 1644

DROMEDARIES (3) [DROMEDARY]
1Ki 4:28 **d** brought they unto the place where 7409
Est 8:10 *and* riders on mules, camels, *and* young **d**: 7424
Isa 60: 6 cover thee, the **d** of Midian and Ephah; 1070

DROMEDARY (1) [DROMEDARIES]
Jer 2:23 *thou art* a swift **d** traversing her ways; 1072

DROP (15) [DROPPED, DROPPETH, DROPPING, DROPS]
Dt 32: 2 My doctrine shall **d** as the rain, my speech 6201
33:28 wine; also his heavens shall **d down** dew. 6201
Job 36:28 Which the clouds do **d** *and* distil upon man 5140
Ps 65:11 with thy goodness; and thy paths **d** fatness. 7491
65:12 They **d** *upon* the pastures of the wilderness: 7491
Pr 3:20 broken up, and the clouds **d down** the dew. 7491
5: 3 For the lips of a strange *woman* **d** *as* a 5197
SS 4:11 O *my* spouse, **d** *as* the honeycomb: 5197
Isa 40:15 the nations *are* as a **d** of a bucket, and 4752
45: 8 **D down**, ye heavens, from above, and 7491
Eze 20:46 **d** *thy word* toward the south, and 5197
21: 2 **d** *thy word* toward the holy places, and 5197
Joel 3:18 *that* the mountains shall **d down** new wine, 5197
Am 7:16 **d** not *thy word* against the house of Isaac. 5197
9:13 the mountains shall **d** sweet wine, and 5197

DROPPED (7) [DROP]
Jdg 5: 4 the earth trembled, and the heavens **d**, 5197
5: 4 heavens dropped, the clouds also **d** water. 5197
1Sa 14:26 come into the wood, behold the honey **d**; 1982
2Sa 21:10 from the beginning of harvest until water **d** 5413
Job 29:22 not again; and my speech **d** upon them. 5197
Ps 68: 8 the heavens also **d** at the presence of God: 5197
SS 5: 5 my hands **d** *with* myrrh, and my fingers 5197

DROPPETH (1) [DROP]
Ecc 10:18 idleness of the hands the house **d through**. 1811

DROPPING (3) [DROP]
Pr 19:13 the contentions of a wife *are* a continual **d**. 1812
27:15 A **continual d** in a very rainy day 1812+2956
SS 5:13 his lips *like* lilies, **d** sweet smelling myrrh. 5197

DROPS (4) [DROP]
Job 36:27 For he maketh small the **d** of water: 5198
38:28 a father? or who hath begotten the **d** of dew? 96
SS 5: 2 *and* my locks *with* the **d** of the night. 7447
Lk 22:44 his sweat was as it were great **d** of blood *2361*

DROPSY (1)
Lk 14: 2 a certain man before him, which **had the d**. *5203*

DROSS (8)
Ps119:119 away all the wicked of the earth *like* **d**: 5509
Pr 25: 4 Take away the **d** from the silver, and 5509
26:23 *are like* a potsherd covered with silver **d**. 5509
Isa 1:22 Thy silver is become **d**, thy wine mixt with 5509
1:25 purely purge away thy **d**, and take away all 5509
Eze 22:18 the house of Israel is to me become **d**: 5509
22:18 of the furnace; they are *even the* **d** *of* silver. 5509
22:19 Because ye are all become **d**, 5509

DROUGHT (10)
Ge 31:40 the **d** consumed me, and the frost by night; 2721
Dt 8:15 scorpions, and **d**, where *there was* no water; 6774
Job 24:19 **D** and heat consume the snow waters: *so* 6723
Ps 32: 4 my moisture is turned into the **d** of 2725
Isa 58:11 satisfy thy soul in **d**, and make fat thy 6710
Jer 2: 6 through a land of **d**, and of the shadow of 6723
17: 8 shall not be careful in the year of **d**, 1226
50:38 A **d** *is* upon her waters; and they shall be 2721
Hos 13: 5 in the wilderness, in the land of **great d**. 8514
Hag 1:11 I called *for* a **d** upon the land, and upon 2721

DROVE (13) [DRIVE, DROVES]
Ge 3:24 So he **d out** the man; and he placed at 1644
15:11 upon the carcases, Abram **d** them **away**. 5380
32:16 his servants, **every d** by themselves; 5739+5739
32:16 and put a space betwixt **d** and drove. 5739
32:16 and put a space betwixt drove and **d**. 5739
33: 8 What meanest thou by all this **d** which I 4264
Ex 2:17 the shepherds came and **d** them **away**: but 1644
Nu 21:32 and **d out** the Amorites that *were* there. 3423
Jos 15:14 Caleb **d** thence the three sons of Anak, 3423
1Ch 8:13 who **d away** the inhabitants of Gath: 1272
Ps 34: T who **d** him **away**, and he departed. 1644
Hab 3: 6 he beheld, and **d asunder** the nations; and 5425
Jn 2:15 he **d** *them* all **out** of the temple, and *1544*

DROVES (1) [DROVE]
Ge 32:19 and all that followed the **d**, saying, 5739

DROWN (2) [DROWNED]
SS 8: 7 quench love, neither can the floods **d** it: 7857
1Ti 6: 9 which **d** men in destruction and perdition. *1036*

DROWNED (5) [DROWN]
Ex 15: 4 his chosen captains also are **d** in the Red 2883
Am 8: 8 it shall be cast out and **d**, as *by* the flood of 8257
9: 5 and shall be **d**, as *by* the flood of Egypt. 8257
Mt 18: 6 and *that* he were **d** in the depth of the sea. *2670*
Heb 11:29 which the Egyptians assaying to do were **d**. *2666*

DROWSINESS (1)
Pr 23:21 and **d** shall clothe *a man* with rags. 5124

DRUNK (31) [DRINK]
Ge 43:34 And they **d**, and were merry with him. 8354
Lev 11:34 all drink that may be **d** in every *such* vessel 8354
Dt 29: 6 neither have you **d** wine or strong drink: 8354
32:42 I will **make** mine arrows **d** with blood, and 7937
Jdg 15:19 when he had **d**, his spirit came again, and 8354
Ru 3: 7 when Boaz had eaten and **d**, and his heart 8354
1Sa 1: 9 had eaten in Shiloh, and after *they* had **d**. 8354
1:15 I have **d** neither wine nor strong drink, but 8354
30:12 nor **d** *any* water, three days and 8354
2Sa 11:13 and drink before him; and he **made** him **d**: 7937
1Ki 13:22 hast eaten bread and **d** water in the place, 8354
13:23 after he had eaten bread, and after he had **d**, 8354
16: 9 drinking *himself* **d** *in* the house of Arza 7910
20:16 Ben-hadad *was* drinking *himself* **d** in 7910
2Ki 6:23 when they had eaten and **d**, he sent them 8354
19:24 I have digged and **d** strange waters, and 8354
SS 5: 1 my honey; I have **d** my wine with my milk: 8354
Isa 37:25 I have digged, and **d** water; and with 8354
51:17 which hast **d** at the hand of the LORD 8354
63: 6 **make** them **d** in my fury, and I will bring 7937
Jer 46:10 be satiate and **made d** with their blood: 7301
51:57 I will **make d** her princes, and her wise 7937
Eze 34:18 to have **d** of the deep waters, but ye must 8354
Da 5:23 and thy concubines, *have* **d** wine in them; 8355
Ob 1:16 For as ye have **d** upon my holy mountain, 8354
Lk 5:39 No *man* also having **d** old *wine* straightway *4095*
13:26 We have eaten and **d** in thy presence, and *4095*
Jn 2:10 and when *men* have **well d**, then that which *3182*
Eph 5:18 And be not **d** with wine, wherein is excess; *3182*
Rev 17: 2 **made d** with the wine of her fornication. *3184*
18: 3 For all nations have **d** of the wine of *4095*

DRUNKARD (5) [DRINK]
Dt 21:20 not obey our voice; *he is* a glutton, and a **d**. 5433
Pr 23:21 For the **d** and the glutton shall come to 5433
26: 9 *As* a thorn goeth up into the hand of a **d**, so 7910
Isa 24:20 The earth shall reel to and fro like a **d**, and 7910
1Co 5:11 or a railer, or a **d**, or an extortioner; *3183*

DRUNKARDS (6) [DRINK]
Ps 69:12 and *I was* the song of the **d**. 7941+8354
Isa 28: 1 to the crown of pride, to the **d** of Ephraim, 7910
28: 3 The crown of pride, the **d** of Ephraim, 7910
Joel 1: 5 Awake, ye **d**, and weep; and howl, all ye 7910
Na 1:10 while they be drunken *as* **d**, they shall be 5435
1Co 6:10 nor covetous, nor **d**, nor revilers, *3183*

DRUNKEN (33) [DRINK]
Ge 9:21 he drank of the wine, and was **d**; and 7937
1Sa 1:13 therefore Eli thought she had been **d**. 7910
1:14 Eli said unto her, How long wilt thou be **d**? 7937
25:36 *was* merry within him, for he *was* very **d**: 7910
Job 12:25 he maketh them to stagger like a **d** *man*. 7910
Ps 107:27 stagger like a **d** *man*, and are at their wit's 7910
Isa 19:14 as a **d** *man* staggereth in his vomit. 7910
29: 9 they are **d**, but not *with* wine; they stagger, 7937
49:26 they shall be **d** with their own blood, 7937
51:17 thou hast **d** the dregs of the cup of 8354
51:21 thou afflicted, and **d**, but not with wine: 7937
Jer 23: 9 I am like a **d** man, and like a man whom 7910
25:27 be **d**, and spue, and fall, and rise no more, 7937
48:26 **Make** ye him **d**: for he magnified *himself* 7937
49:12 to drink of the cup have **assuredly d**; 8354+8354
51: 7 LORD'S hand, that **made** all the earth **d**: 7937
51: 7 the nations have **d** of her wine; therefore 8354
51:39 I will **make** them **d**, that they may rejoice, 7937
La 3:15 he hath **made** me **d** *with* wormwood. 7301
4:21 thou shalt be **d**, and shalt make thyself 7937
5: 4 We have **d** our water for money; our wood 8354
Eze 39:19 till *ye* be full, and drink blood till *ye* be **d**, 7943
Na 1:10 while they be **d** *as* drunkards, they shall be 5433
3:11 Thou also shalt be **d**: thou shalt be hid, 7937
Hab 2:15 thy bottle to *him*, and **makest** *him* **d** also, 7937
Mt 24:49 and to eat and drink with the **d**; *3184*
Lk 12:45 and to eat and drink, and to be **d**; *3182*
17: 8 and serve me, till I have eaten and **d**; *4095*
Ac 2:15 For these are not **d**, as ye suppose, seeing it *3184*
1Co 11:21 and one is hungry, and another is **d**. *3184*
1Th 5: 7 and they that be **d** are drunken in the night. *3182*
5: 7 and they that be drunken are **d** in the night. *3184*
Rev 17: 6 And I saw the woman **d** with the blood of *3184*

DRUNKENNESS (7) [DRINK]
Dt 29:19 of mine heart, to add **d** *to* thirst: 7302
Ecc 10:17 in due season, for strength, and not for **d**. 8358
Jer 13:13 and all the inhabitants of Jerusalem, *with* **d**. 7943
Eze 23:33 Thou shalt be filled *with* **d** and sorrow, 7943
Lk 21:34 and **d**, and cares of *this* life, and *so* that day *3178*
Ro 13:13 not in rioting and **d**, not in chambering and *3178*
Gal 5:21 Envyings, murders, **d**, revellings, and *3178*

DRUSILLA (1)
Ac 24:24 when Felix came with his wife **D**, *1409*

DRY (71) [DRIED, DRIEDST, DRIETH, DRYSHOD]
Ge 1: 9 unto one place, and let the **d** *land* appear: 3004
1:10 God called the **d** *land* Earth; and 3004
7:22 of life, of all that *was* in the **d** *land*, died. 2724
8:13 and behold, the face of the ground was **d**. 2717
Ex 4: 9 pour *it upon* the **d** *land*: and the water 3004
4: 9 river shall become blood upon the **d** *land*. 3006
14:16 the children of Israel shall go on **d** *ground* 3004
14:21 made the sea **d** *land*, and the waters were 2724
14:22 into the midst of the sea upon the **d** *ground*: 3004
14:29 the children of Israel walked upon **d** *land* in 3004
15:19 the children of Israel went on **d** *land* in 3004
Lev 7:10 meat offering, mingled with oil, and **d**, 2720
13:30 it *is* a **d scall**, *even* a leprosy upon the head 5424
Jos 3:17 firm on **d** *ground* in the midst of Jordan, 2724
3:17 all the Israelites passed over on **d** *ground*, 2724
4:18 **d** *land*, that the waters of Jordan returned 2724
4:22 Israel came over this Jordan on **d** *land*. 3004
9: 5 all the bread of their provision was **d** *and* 3001
9:12 but now, behold, it is **d**, and it is mouldy: 3001
Jdg 6:37 *it be* **d** upon all the earth *beside*, then shall I 2721
6:39 let it now be **d** only upon the fleece, 2721
6:40 for it was **d** upon the fleece only, and 2721
2Ki 2: 8 so that they two went over on **d** *ground*. 2724
Ne 9:11 through the midst of the sea on the **d** *land*; 3004
Job 12:15 he withholdeth the waters, and they **d up**: 3001
13:25 fro? and wilt thou pursue the **d** stubble? 3002
15:30 the flame shall **d up** his branches, and 3001
Ps 63: 1 in a **d** and thirsty land, where no water is; 6723
66: 6 He turned the sea into **d** *land*: they went 3004
68: 6 but the rebellious dwell *in* a **d** *land*. 6707
95: 5 made it: and his hands formed the **d** *land*. 3006
105:41 they ran in the **d** *places like* a river. 6723
107:33 and the watersprings into **d ground**; 6774
107:35 and **d** ground into watersprings; 6723
Pr 17: 1 Better *is* a **d** morsel, and 2720
Isa 25: 5 noise of strangers, as the heat in a **d place**; 6724
32: 2 as rivers of water in a **d place**, as 6724
41:18 of water, and the **d** land springs of water. 6723
42:15 and hills, and **d up** all their herbs; 3001
42:15 the rivers islands, and I will **d up** the pools. 3001
44: 3 floods upon the **d** *ground*: I will pour my 3004
44:27 the deep, Be **d**, and I will dry up thy rivers: 2717
44:27 the deep, Be dry, and I will **d up** thy rivers: 3001
50: 2 behold, at my rebuke I **d up** the sea, I make 2717
53: 2 and as a root out of a **d** ground: 6723
56: 3 let the eunuch say, Behold, I *am* a **d** tree. 3002
Jer 4:11 A **d** wind of the high places in 6703
50:12 *be* a wilderness, a **d land**, and a desert. 6723
51:36 I will **d up** her sea, and make her springs 2717
51:36 dry up her sea, and **make** her springs **d**. 3001
51:43 are a desolation, a **d** land, and a wilderness, 6723
Eze 17:24 and have made the **d** tree to flourish: 3002
19:13 in the wilderness, in a **d** and thirsty ground. 6723
20:47 every green tree in thee, and every **d** tree: 3002
30:12 I will make the rivers **d**, and sell the land 2724
37: 2 the open valley; and lo, *they were* very **d**. 3002
37: 4 and say unto them, O ye **d** bones, 3002
Hos 2: 3 set her like a **d** land, and slay her with 6723
9:14 them a miscarrying womb and **d** breasts. 6784
13:15 his spring shall become **d**, and his fountain 3001
Jnh 1: 9 which hath made the sea and the **d** *land*. 3004
2:10 and it vomited out Jonah upon the **d** *land*. 3004
Na 1: 4 **maketh** it **d**, and drieth up all the rivers: 3001
1:10 they shall be devoured as stubble fully **d**. 3002
Zep 2:13 a desolation, *and* **d** like a wilderness. 6723
Hag 2: 6 and the earth, and the sea, and the **d** *land*; 2724
Zec 10:11 and all the deeps of the river shall **d up**: 3001
Mt 12:43 he walketh through **d** places, seeking rest, *504*
Lk 11:24 he walketh through **d** places, seeking rest; *504*
23:31 in a green tree, what shall be done in the **d**? *3584*
Heb 11:29 **d** *land*: which the Egyptians assaying to do *3584*

DRYSHOD (1) [DRY]
Isa 11:15 seven streams, and make *men* go over **d**. 5275

DUE (31) [DUES]
Lev 10:13 because it *is* thy **d**, and thy sons' due, 2706
10:13 because it *is* thy due, and thy sons' **d**, 2706
10:14 for *they be* thy **d**, and thy sons' due, 2706
10:14 for *they be* thy due, and thy sons' **d**, 2706
26: 4 I will give you rain in **d season**, and 6256
Nu 28: 2 observe to offer unto me in their **d season**. 4150
Dt 11:14 *you* the rain of your land in his **d season**, 6256
18: 3 this shall be the priest's **d** from the people, 4941
32:35 recompence; their foot shall slide in **d** time: NIH
1Ch 15:13 that we sought him not after the **d order**. 4941
16:29 Give unto the LORD the glory **d** unto his NIH
Ne 11:23 *should be* for the singers, **d** for every day. 1697
Ps 29: 2 Give unto the LORD the glory **d** unto his NIH
96: 8 Give unto the LORD the glory **d** unto his NIH
104:27 mayest give *them* their meat in **d season**. 6256
145:15 thou givest them their meat in **d season**. 6256
Pr 3:27 not good from **them to whom** it **is d**, 1167
15:23 a word *spoken* in **d season**, how 6256+2050.2
Ecc 10:17 thy princes eat in **d season**, for strength, 6256
Mt 18:34 till he should pay all that was **d** unto him. *3784*
24:45 to give them meat in **d season**? *2540*
Lk 12:42 *them their* portion of meat in **d season**? *2540*
23:41 for we receive the **d reward** of our deeds: *514*
Ro 5: 6 **in d** time Christ died for the ungodly. *2596*
13: 7 tribute to whom tribute *is* **d**; custom to NIG
1Co 7: 3 Let the husband render unto the wife **d** *3784*
15: 8 of me also, as of one **born out of d time**. *1626*
Gal 6: 9 for in **d** season we shall reap, if we faint *2398*
1Ti 2: 6 a ransom for all, to be testified in **d** time. *2398*

Tit 1: 3 But hath in **d** times manifested his word *2398*
1Pe 5: 6 of God, that he may exalt you in **d** **time**: *2540*

DUES (1) [DUE]
Ro 13: 7 Render therefore to all *their* **d**: tribute to *3782*

DUKE (43) [DUKES]
Ge 36:15 **d** Teman, duke Omar, duke Zepho, 441
36:15 **d** Omar, duke Zepho, duke Kenaz, 441
36:15 duke Omar, **d** Zepho, duke Kenaz, 441
36:15 duke Omar, duke Zepho, **d** Kenaz, 441
36:16 **D** Korah, duke Gatam, *and* duke Amalek: 441
36:16 Duke Korah, **d** Gatam, *and* duke Amalek: 441
36:16 Duke Korah, duke Gatam, *and* **d** Amalek: 441
36:17 **d** Nahath, duke Zerah, duke Shammah, 441
36:17 duke Nahath, **d** Zerah, duke Shammah, 441
36:17 duke Nahath, duke Zerah, **d** Shammah, 441
36:17 duke Zerah, duke Shammah, **d** Mizzah: 441
36:18 **d** Jeush, duke Jaalam, duke Korah: 441
36:18 duke Jeush, **d** Jaalam, duke Korah: 441
36:18 duke Jeush, duke Jaalam, **d** Korah: 441
36:29 **d** Lotan, duke Shobal, duke Zibeon, 441
36:29 duke Lotan, **d** Shobal, duke Zibeon, 441
36:29 duke Shobal, **d** Zibeon, duke Anah, 441
36:29 duke Shobal, duke Zibeon, **d** Anah, 441
36:30 **D** Dishon, duke Ezer, duke Dishan: these *are* 441
36:30 Duke Dishon, **d** Ezer, duke Dishan: these *are* 441
36:30 Duke Dishon, duke Ezer, **d** Dishan: these *are* 441
36:40 **d** Timnah, duke Alvah, duke Jetheth, 441
36:40 duke Timnah, **d** Alvah, duke Jetheth, 441
36:40 duke Timnah, duke Alvah, **d** Jetheth, 441
36:41 **D** Aholibamah, duke Elah, duke Pinon, 441
36:41 Duke Aholibamah, **d** Elah, duke Pinon, 441
36:41 Duke Aholibamah, duke Elah, **d** Pinon, 441
36:42 **D** Kenaz, duke Teman, duke Mibzar, 441
36:42 Duke Kenaz, **d** Teman, duke Mibzar, 441
36:42 Duke Kenaz, duke Teman, **d** Mibzar, 441
36:43 **D** Magdiel, duke Iram: these *be* the dukes of 441
36:43 Duke Magdiel, **d** Iram: these *be* the dukes of 441
1Ch 1:51 **d** Timnah, duke Aliah, duke Jetheth, 441
1:51 duke Timnah, **d** Aliah, duke Jetheth, 441
1:51 duke Timnah, duke Aliah, **d** Jetheth, 441
1:52 **D** Aholibamah, duke Elah, duke Pinon, 441
1:52 Duke Aholibamah, **d** Elah, duke Pinon, 441
1:52 Duke Aholibamah, duke Elah, **d** Pinon, 441
1:53 **D** Kenaz, duke Teman, duke Mibzar, 441
1:53 Duke Kenaz, **d** Teman, duke Mibzar, 441
1:53 Duke Kenaz, duke Teman, **d** Mibzar, 441
1:54 **D** Magdiel, duke Iram. These *are* the dukes 441
1:54 Duke Magdiel, **d** Iram. These *are* the dukes 441

DUKES (15) [DUKE]
Ge 36:15 These *were* **d** of the sons of Esau: the sons 441
36:16 these *are* the **d** *that came* of Eliphaz in 441
36:17 these *are* the **d** *that came* of Reuel in the land 441
36:18 these *were* the **d** *that came* of Aholibamah 441
36:19 of Esau, who *is* Edom, and these *are* their **d**. 441
36:21 these *are* the **d** of the Horites, the children of 441
36:29 These *are* the **d** *that came* of the Horites; 441
36:30 these *are* the **d** *that came* of Hori, 441
36:30 of Hori, among their **d** in the land of Seir. 441
36:40 these *are* the names of the **d** *that came* of 441
36:43 these *be* the **d** of Edom, according to their 441
Ex 15:15 the **d** of Edom shall be amazed; the mighty 441
Jos 13:21 Hur, and Reba, *which were* **d** of Sihon, 5257
1Ch 1:51 the **d** of Edom were; duke Timnah, 441
1:54 duke Iram. These *are* the **d** of Edom. 441

DULCIMER (3)
Da 3: 5 psaltery, **d**, and all kinds of musick, 5481
3:10 psaltery, and **d**, and all kinds of musick, 5481
3:15 psaltery, and **d**, and all kinds of musick, 5481

DULL (3)
Mt 13:15 and *their* ears are **d** of hearing, and their eyes *917*
Ac 28:27 and *their* ears are **d** of hearing, and their eyes *917*
Heb 5:11 to be uttered, seeing ye are **d** of hearing. *3576*

DUMAH (4)
Ge 25:14 And Mishma, and **D**, and Massa, 1746
Jos 15:52 Arab, and **D**, and Eshean, 1746
1Ch 1:30 Mishma, and **D**, Massa, Hadad, and Tema, 1746
Isa 21:11 The burden of **D**. He calleth to me out of 1746

DUMB (29)
Ex 4:11 or who maketh the **d**, or deaf, or the seeing, 483
Ps 38:13 *I was* as a **d** *man that* openeth not his mouth. 483
39: 2 I was **d** *with* silence, I held my peace, 481
39: 9 I was **d**, I opened not my mouth; because 481
Pr 31: 8 Open thy mouth for the **d** in the cause of all 483
Isa 35: 6 leap as a hart, and the tongue of the **d** sing: 483
53: 7 as a sheep before her shearers is **d**, so 481
56:10 they *are* all **d** dogs, they cannot bark; 483
Eze 3:26 that thou shalt be **d**, and shalt not be to them 481
24:27 and thou shalt speak, and be no more **d**: 481
33:22 my mouth was opened, and I was no more **d**. 481
Da 10:15 my face toward the ground, and I **became** **d**. 481
Hab 2:18 of his work trusteth therein, to make **d** idols? 483
2:19 Awake; to the **d** stone, Arise, it shall teach! 1748
Mt 9:32 they brought to him a **d** man possessed *2974*
9:33 when the devil was cast out, the **d** spake: *2974*
12:22 one possessed with a devil, blind, and **d**: *2974*
12:22 that the blind and **d** both spake and saw. *2974*
15:30 blind, **d**, maimed, and many others, and *2974*
15:31 when they saw the **d** to speak, the maimed *2974*
Mk 7:37 both the deaf to hear, and the **d** to speak. *216*
9:17 unto thee my son, which hath a **d** spirit: *216*
9:25 *Thou* **d** and deaf spirit, I charge thee, *216*
Lk 1:20 thou shalt be **d**, and not able to speak, *4623*
11:14 he was casting out a devil, and it was **d**. *2974*
11:14 when the devil was gone out, the **d** spake; *2974*
Ac 8:32 and like a lamb **d** before his shearer, so *880*
1Co 12: 2 carried away unto *these* **d** idols, *even* as ye *880*
2Pe 2:16 the **d** ass speaking with man's voice forbad *880*

DUNG (28) [DUNGHILL, DUNGHILLS]
Ex 29:14 flesh of the bullock, and his skin, and his **d**, 6569
Lev 4:11 with his legs, and his inwards, and his **d**, 6569
8:17 and his hide, his flesh, and his **d**, 6569
16:27 fire their skins, and their flesh, and their **d**. 6569
Nu 19: 5 and her flesh, and her blood, with her **d**, 6569
1Ki 14:10 as *a man* taketh away **d**, till it be all gone. 1557
2Ki 6:25 the fourth part of a kab of **dove's** **d** for five 1686
9:37 the carcase of Jezebel shall be as **d** upon 1828
18:27 that *they* may eat their own **d**, and drink 6675
Ne 2:13 to the **d** port, and viewed the walls of 830
3:13 a thousand cubits on the wall unto the **d** 830
3:14 the **d** gate repaired Malchiah the son of 830
12:31 right hand upon the wall toward the **d** gate: 830
Job 20: 7 *Yet* he shall perish for ever like his own **d**: 1561
Ps 83:10 at En-dor: they became *as* **d** for the earth. 1828
Isa 36:12 that *they* may eat their own **d**, and drink 6675
Jer 8: 2 they shall be for **d** upon the face of 1828
9:22 Even the carcases of men shall fall as **d** 1828
16: 4 they shall be as **d** upon the face of 1828
25:33 nor buried; they shall be **d** upon the ground. 1828
Eze 4:12 thou shalt bake it with **d** that cometh out of 1561
4:15 I have given thee cow's **d** for man's dung, 6832
4:15 I have given thee cow's dung for man's **d**, 1561
Zep 1:17 poured out as dust, and their flesh as the **d**. 1561
Mal 2: 3 your seed, and spread **d** upon your faces, 6569
2: 3 *even* the **d** of your solemn feasts; 6569
Lk 13: 8 till I shall dig about it, and **d** *it*: *906+2874*
Php 3: 8 loss of all *things*, and do count *them but* **d**, *4657*

DUNGEON (13)
Ge 40:15 nothing that they should put me into the **d**. 953
41:14 and they brought him hastily out of the **d**: 953
Ex 12:29 of the captive that *was* in the **d**; 953+1004
Jer 37:16 was entered into the **d**, 953+1004+1886.1
38: 6 cast him into the **d** of Malchiah the son of 953
38: 6 And in the **d** *there was* no water, but mire: so 953
38: 7 heard that they had put Jeremiah in the **d**; 953
38: 9 the prophet, whom they have cast into the **d**; 953
38:10 take up Jeremiah the prophet out of the **d**, 953
38:11 let them down by cords into the **d** to 953
38:13 with cords, and took him up out of the **d**: 953
La 3:53 They have cut off my life in the **d**, and cast a 953
3:55 upon thy name, O LORD, out of the low **d**. 953

DUNGHILL (7) [DUNG, HILL]
1Sa 2: 8 *and* lifteth up the beggar from the **d**, to set 830
Ezr 6:11 let his house be made a **d** for this. 5122
Ps 113: 7 of the dust, *and* lifteth the needy out of the **d**; 830
Isa 25:10 *even* as straw is trodden down for the **d**. 4087
Da 2: 5 and your houses shall be made a **d**. 5122
3:29 and their houses shall be made a **d**: 5122
Lk 14:35 is neither fit for the land, nor yet for the **d**; *2874*

DUNGHILLS (1) [DUNG, HILL]
La 4: 5 that were brought up in scarlet embrace **d**. 830

DURA (1)
Da 3: 1 he set it up in the plain of **D**, in 1757

DURABLE (2) [DURETH]
Pr 8:18 with me; *yea,* **d** riches and righteousness. 6276
Isa 23:18 to eat sufficiently, and for **d** clothing. 6266

DURETH (1) [DURABLE]
Mt 13:21 he not root in himself, but **d** for a while: *1510*

DURST (9) [DARE]
Est 7: 5 *is* he, that **d presume** in his heart to do so? 4390
Job 32: 6 and **d not** shew you mine opinion. 3372
Mt 22:46 neither **d** any *man* from that day forth ask *5111*
Mk 12:34 And no *man* after that **d** ask him *any* *5111*
Lk 20:40 And after that they **d** not ask him any *5111*
Jn 21:12 And none of the disciples **d** ask him, *5111*
Ac 5:13 And of the rest **d** no *man* join himself to *5111*
7:32 Then Moses trembled, and **d** not behold. *5111*
Jude 1: 9 **d** not bring against *him* a railing *5111*

DUST (108)
Ge 2: 7 the LORD God formed man *of* the **d** of 6083
3:14 and **d** shalt thou eat all the days of thy life: 6083
3:19 for **d** thou *art,* and unto dust shalt thou 6083
3:19 dust thou *art,* and unto **d** shalt thou return. 6083
13:16 I will make thy seed as the **d** of the earth: 6083
13:16 that if a man can number the **d** of the earth, 6083
18:27 unto the Lord, which *am but* **d** and ashes: 6083
28:14 thy seed shall be as the **d** of the earth, and 6083
Ex 8:16 out thy rod, and smite the **d** of the land, 6083
8:17 smote the **d** of the earth, and it became lice 6083
8:17 all the **d** of the land became lice throughout 6083
9: 9 it shall become **small d** in all the land of 80
Lev 14:41 they shall pour out the **d** that they scrape 6083
17:13 out the blood thereof, and cover it with **d**. 6083
Nu 5:17 of the **d** that is in the floor of the tabernacle 6083
23:10 Who can count the **d** of Jacob, and 6083
Dt 9:21 very small, *even* until *it was as* small as **d**: 6083
9:21 I cast the **d** thereof into the brook that 6083
28:24 make the rain of thy land powder and **d**: 6083
32:24 with the poison of serpents of the **d**. 6083
Jos 7: 6 elders of Israel, and put **d** upon their heads. 6083
1Sa 2: 8 He raiseth up the poor out of the **d**, *and* 6083
2Sa 16:13 and threw stones at him, and cast **d**. 6083
22:43 did I beat them *as* small as the **d** of 6083
1Ki 16: 2 Forasmuch as I exalted thee out of the **d**, 6083
18:38 the **d**, and licked up the water that *was* in 6083
20:10 if the **d** of Samaria shall suffice for 6083
2Ki 13: 7 and had made them like the **d** by threshing. 6083
23:12 cast the **d** of them into the brook Kidron. 6083
2Ch 1: 9 a people like the **d** of the earth in multitude. 6083
34: 4 brake *in pieces,* and **made d** *of them,* 1854
Job 2:12 sprinkled **d** upon their heads toward 6083
4:19 whose foundation *is* in the **d**, which are 6083
5: 6 affliction cometh not forth of the **d**, 6083
7: 5 flesh is clothed with worms and clods of **d**; 6083
7:21 for now shall I sleep in the **d**; and 6083
10: 9 and wilt thou bring me into **d** again? 6083
14:19 things which grow out of the **d** of the earth; 6083
16:15 upon my skin, and defiled my horn in the **d**. 6083
17:16 of the pit, when *our* rest together *is* in the **d**. 6083
20:11 which shall lie down with him in the **d**. 6083
21:26 They shall lie down alike in the **d**, and 6083
22:24 shalt thou lay up gold as **d**, and *the gold of* 6083
27:16 Though he heap up silver as the **d**, and 6083
28: 6 place of sapphires: and it hath **d** of gold. 6083
30:19 the mire, and I am become like **d** and ashes. 6083
34:15 and man shall turn again unto **d**. 6083
38:38 When the **d** groweth into hardness, and 6083
39:14 eggs in the earth, and warmeth them in **d**, 6083
40:13 Hide them in the **d** together; *and* bind their 6083
42: 6 I abhor *myself,* and repent in **d** and ashes. 6083
Ps 7: 5 the earth, and lay mine honour in the **d**. 6083
18:42 did I beat them small as the **d** before 6083
22:15 thou hast brought me into the **d** of death. 6083
22:29 all they that go down to the **d** shall bow 6083
30: 9 Shall the **d** praise thee? shall it declare thy 6083
44:25 For our soul is bowed down to the **d**: 6083
72: 9 and his enemies shall lick the **d**. 6083
78:27 He rained flesh also upon them as **d**, and 6083
102:14 in her stones, and favour the **d** thereof. 6083
103:14 our frame; he remembereth that we *are* **d**. 6083
104:29 their breath, they die, and return to their **d**. 6083
113: 7 He raiseth up the poor out of the **d**, *and* 6083
119:25 My soul cleaveth unto the **d**: quicken thou 6083
Pr 8:26 nor the highest part of the **d** of the world. 6083
Ecc 3:20 all are of the **d**, and all turn to dust again. 6083
3:20 all are of the dust, and all turn to **d** again. 6083
12: 7 shall the **d** return to the earth as it was: 6083
Isa 2:10 Enter into the rock, and hide thee in the **d**, 6083
5:24 and their blossom shall go up as **d**: 80
25:12 *and* bring to the ground, *even* to the **d**. 6083
26: 5 to the ground; he bringeth it *even* to the **d**. 6083
26:19 Awake and sing, ye that dwell in **d**: for thy 6083
29: 4 thy speech shall be low out of the **d**, and 6083
29: 4 and thy speech shall whisper out of the **d**. 6083
29: 5 of thy strangers shall be like small **d**, 80
34: 7 and their **d** made fat with fatness. 6083
34: 9 the **d** thereof into brimstone, and the land 6083
40:12 comprehended the **d** of the earth in a 6083
40:15 are counted as the **small d** of the balance: 7834
41: 2 he gave *them* as the **d** *to* his sword, *and* 6083
47: 1 Come down, and sit in the **d**, O virgin 6083
49:23 the earth, and lick up the **d** of thy feet; 6083
52: 2 Shake thyself from the **d**; arise, *and* 6083
65:25 **d** *shall be* the serpent's meat. They shall 6083
La 2:10 they have cast up **d** upon their heads; 6083
3:29 He putteth his mouth in the **d**; if so be there 6083
Eze 24: 7 it not upon the ground, to cover it with **d**; 6083
26: 4 I will also scrape her **d** from her, and 6083
26:10 of his horses their **d** shall cover thee: 80
26:12 and thy **d** in the midst of the water. 6083
27:30 and shall cast up **d** upon their heads, 6083
Da 12: 2 many of them that sleep in the **d** of the earth 127
Am 2: 7 That pant after the **d** of the earth on 6083
Mic 1:10 in the house of Aphrah roll thyself *in* the **d**. 6083
7:17 They shall lick the **d** like a serpent, 6083
Na 1: 3 the storm, and the clouds *are* the **d** of his feet. 80
3:18 thy nobles shall dwell *in the* **d**: thy people is NIH
Hab 1:10 for they shall heap **d**, and take it. 6083
Zep 1:17 their blood shall be poured out as **d**, and 6083
Zec 9: 3 heaped up silver as the **d**, and fine gold as 6083
Mt 10:14 or city, shake off the **d** of your feet. *2868*
Mk 6:11 shake off the **d** under your feet for a *5522*
Lk 9: 5 shake off the very **d** from your feet for a *2868*
10:11 Even the *very* **d** of your city, *2868*
Ac 13:51 But they shook off the **d** of their feet *2868*
22:23 *off their* clothes, and threw **d** into the air, *2868*
Rev 18:19 And they cast **d** on their heads, and cried, *5522*

DUTIES (1) [DUTY]
Eze 18:11 that doeth not any of those **d**, but even hath NIH

DUTY (8) [DUTIES]
Ex 21:10 her raiment, and her **d of marriage**, 5772
Dt 25: 5 **perform the d of a husband's brother** 2992
25: 7 **perform the d of** my **husband's brother**. 2992
2Ch 8:14 the priests, as the **d** of every day **required**: 1697
Ezr 3: 4 the custom, as the **d** of every day required; 1697
Ecc 12:13 for this *is* the whole *d of* man. NIH
Lk 17:10 we have done *that* which was our **d** to do. *3784*
Ro 15:27 **d** is also to minister unto them in carnal *3784*

DWARF (1)
Lev 21:20 or a **d**, or that hath a blemish in his eye, or 1851

DWELL (338) [DWELLED, DWELLERS, DWELLEST, DWELLETH, DWELLING, DWELLINGS, DWELT]
Ge 4:20 he was the father of such as **d in** tents, and 3427
9:27 and he shall **d** in the tents of Shem; 7931
13: 6 to bear them, that they might **d** together: 3427
13: 6 was great, so that they could not **d** together. 3427
16:12 he shall **d** in the presence of all his 7931
19:30 with him; for he feared to **d** in Zoar: 3427
20:15 *is* before thee: **d** where it pleaseth thee. 3427
24: 3 of the Canaanites, amongst whom I **d**: 3427
24:37 of the Canaanites, in whose land I **d**: 3427
26: 2 **d** in the land which I shall tell thee of: 7931
30:20 now will my husband **d with** me, because 2082
34:10 ye shall **d** with us: and the land shall be 3427
34:10 **d** and trade you therein, and get you 3427
34:16 we will **d** with you, and we will become 3427
34:21 therefore let them **d** in the land, and 3427
34:22 the men consent unto us for to **d** with us, 3427

Ge 34:23 consent unto them, and they will **d** with us. 3427
35: 1 Arise, go up to Beth-el, and **d** there: 3427
36: 7 were more than that they might **d** together; 3427
45:10 And thou shalt **d** in the land of Goshen, and 3427
46:34 that ye may **d** in the land of Goshen; 3427
47: 4 let thy servants **d** in the land of Goshen. 3427
47: 6 the land **make** thy father and brethren **to d**; 3427
47: 6 to dwell; in the land of Goshen let them **d**: 3427
49:13 Zebulun shall **d** at the haven of the sea; and 7931
Ex 2:21 Moses was content to **d** with the man: and 3427
8:22 in which my people **d**, that no swarms *of* 5975
15:17 *which* thou hast made for thee to **d in**, 3427
23:33 They shall not **d** in thy land, lest they make 3427
25: 8 me a sanctuary; that I may **d** amongst them. 7931
29:45 I will **d** amongst the children of Israel, and 7931
29:46 land of Egypt, that I may **d** amongst them: 7931
Lev 13:46 he shall **d** alone; without the camp *shall* his 3427
20:22 the land, whither I bring you to **d** therein, 3427
23:42 Ye shall **d** in booths seven days; all that are 3427
23:42 all that are Israelites born shall **d** in booths: 3427
23:43 I **made** the children of Israel **to d** in booths, 3427
25:18 and ye shall **d** in the land in safety. 3427
25:19 shall eat *your* fill, and **d** therein in safety. 3427
26: 5 bread to the full, and **d** in your land safely. 3427
26:32 your enemies which **d** therein shall be 3427
Nu 5: 3 not their camps, in the midst whereof I **d**. 7931
13:19 what the land *is* that they **d** in, whether it *be* 3427
13:19 what cities *they be* that they **d** in, whether 3427
13:28 Nevertheless the people *be* strong that **d** in 3427
13:29 The Amalekites **d** in the land of the south: 3427
13:29 and the Amorites, **d** in the mountains: 3427
13:29 the Canaanites **d** by the sea, and by 3427
14:30 *concerning* which I sware to **make** you **d** 7931
23: 9 lo, the people shall **d** alone, and shall not be 7931
32:17 our little ones shall **d** in the fenced cities 3427
33:53 *the inhabitants of* the land, and **d** therein: 3427
33:55 and shall vex you in the land wherein ye **d**. 3427
35: 2 of their possession cities to **d in**; 3427
35: 3 the cities shall they have to **d in**; and 3427
35:32 that he should come again to **d** in the land, 3427
35:34 land which ye shall inhabit, wherein I **d**: 7931
35:34 for I the LORD **d** among the children of 7931
Dt 2: 4 the children of Esau, which **d** in Seir; 3427
2:29 (As the children of Esau which **d** in Seir, 3427
2:29 the Moabites which **d** in Ar, did unto me;) 3427
11:30 which **d** in the champaign over against 3427
11:31 and ye shall possess it, and **d** therein. 3427
12:10 **d** in the land which the LORD your God 3427
12:10 enemies round about, so that ye **d** in safety; 3427
12:11 shall choose to **cause** his name **to d** there; 7931
13:12 LORD thy God hath given thee to **d** there, 3427
17:14 and shalt **d** therein, and shalt say, 3427
23:16 He shall **d** with thee, *even* among you, 3427
25: 5 If brethren **d** together, and one of them die, 3427
28:30 build a house, and thou shalt not **d** therein: 3427
30:20 that thou mayest **d** in the land which 3427
33:12 The beloved of the LORD shall **d** in 7931
33:12 and he shall **d** between his shoulders. 7931
33:28 Israel then shall **d** *in* safety alone: 7931
Jos 9: 7 the Hivites, Peradventure ye **d** among us; 3427
9:22 very far from you; when ye **d** among us? 3427
10: 6 for all the kings of the Amorites that **d** in 3427
13:13 the Maachathites **d** among the Israelites 3427
14: 4 save cities to **d** *in*, with their suburbs for 3427
15:63 the Jebusites **d** with the children of Judah at 3427
16:10 the Canaanites **d** among the Ephraimites 3427
17:12 but the Canaanites would **d** in that land. 3427
17:16 all the Canaanites that **d** in the land of 3427
20: 4 him a place, that he may **d** among them. 3427
20: 6 he shall **d** in that city, until he stand before 3427
21: 2 the hand of Moses to give us cities to **d in**, 3427
24:13 cities which ye built not, and ye **d** in them; 3427
24:15 gods of the Amorites, in whose land ye **d**: 3427
Jdg 1:21 the Jebusites **d** with the children of 3427
1:27 but the Canaanites would **d** in that land. 3427
1:35 the Amorites would **d** in mount Heres in 3427
6:10 gods of the Amorites, in whose land ye **d**: 3427
9:41 that *they* should not **d** in Shechem. 3427
17:10 **D** with me, and be unto me a father and 3427
17:11 the Levite was content to **d** with the man; 3427
18: 1 **d** *in;* for unto that day *all their* inheritance 3427
1Sa 12: 8 of Egypt, and **made** them **d** in this place. 3427
27: 5 town in the country, that I may **d** there: 3427
27: 5 for why should thy servant **d** in the royal 3427

2Sa 7: 2 I **d** in a house of cedar, but the ark of God 3427
7: 5 Shalt thou build me a house for me to **d in**? 3427
7:10 that they may **d** in a place of their own, and 7931
1Ki 2:36 **d** there, and go not forth thence any 3427
3:17 my lord, I and this woman **d** in one house; 3427
6:13 I will **d** among the children of Israel, and 7931
8:12 The LORD said that *he* would **d** in 7931
8:13 I have surely built thee a house to **d in**, 2073
8:27 But will God indeed **d** on the earth? behold, 3427
17: 9 which *belongeth* to Zidon, and **d** there: 3427
2Ki 4:13 she answered, I **d** among mine own people. 3427
6: 1 the place where we **d** with thee is too strait 3427
6: 2 us make us a place there, where we may **d**. 3427
17:27 let them go and **d** there, and let him teach 3427
25:24 **d** in the land, and serve the king of 3427
1Ch 17: 1 I **d** in a house of cedars, but the ark of 3427
17: 4 Thou shalt not build me a house to **d in**: 3427
17: 9 they shall **d** in their place, and shall be 7931
23:25 that they may **d** in Jerusalem for ever: 7931
2Ch 2: 3 cedars to build him a house to **d** therein, 3427
6: 1 The LORD hath said that *he* would **d** in 7931
6:18 will God in very deed **d** with men on 3427
8: 2 and **caused** the children of Israel **to d** there. 3427
8:11 My wife shall not **d** in the house of David 3427
19:10 to you of your brethren that **d** in their cities, 3427
Ezr 4:17 *to* the rest of their companions that **d** in 3488
6:12 the God that hath **caused** his name **to d** 7932
Ne 8:14 that the children of Israel should **d** in 3427
11: 1 to bring one of ten to **d** in Jerusalem 3427
11: 1 holy city, and nine parts *to* **d** in *other* cities. NIH
11: 2 that willingly offered themselves to **d** at 3427
Job 3: 5 of death stain it; let a cloud **d** upon it; 7931
4:19 How much less *in* them that **d in** houses of 7931
11:14 and let not wickedness **d** in thy tabernacles. 7931
18:15 It shall **d** in his tabernacle, because *it is* 7931
19:15 They that **d** in mine house, and 1481
30: 6 To **d** in the clifts of the valleys, *in* caves of 7931
Ps 4: 8 LORD, only **makest** me **d** in safety. 3427
5: 4 neither shall evil **d** *with* thee. 1481
15: 1 who shall **d** in thy holy hill? 7931
23: 6 I will **d** in the house of the LORD for 3427
24: 1 the world, and they that **d** therein. 3427
25:13 His soul shall **d** at ease; and his seed shall 3885
27: 4 that I may **d** in the house of the LORD all 3427
37: 3 *so* shalt thou **d in** the land, and verily thou 7931
37:27 and do good; and **d** for evermore. 7931
37:29 inherit the land, and **d** therein for ever. 7931
65: 4 *unto thee, that* he may **d** *in* thy courts: 7931
65: 8 They also that **d** in the uttermost parts are 3427
68: 6 but the rebellious **d** *in* a dry *land.* 7931
68:16 *this is* the hill *which* God desireth to **d in**; 3427
68:16 yea, the LORD will **d** *in it* for ever. 7931
68:18 that the LORD God might **d** *among them.* 7931
69:25 be desolate; *and* let none **d** in their tents. 3427
69:35 that they may **d** there, and have it in 3427
69:36 and they that love his name shall **d** therein. 7931
72: 9 They **that d in the wilderness** shall bow 6728
78:55 **made** the tribes of Israel **to d** in their tents. 7931
84: 4 Blessed *are* they that **d in** thy house: 3427
84:10 than to **d** in the tents of wickedness. 1752
85: 9 that fear him; that glory may **d** in our land. 7931
98: 7 the world, and they that **d** therein. 3427
101: 6 of the land, that *they* may **d** with me: 3427
101: 7 He that worketh deceit shall not **d** within 3427
107: 4 a solitary way; they found no city to **d in**. 4186
107:34 for the wickedness of them that **d** therein. 3427
107:36 there he **maketh** the hungry **to d**, that they 3427
120: 5 *in* Mesech, *that* I **d** in the tents of Kedar! 7931
132:14 for ever: here will I **d**; for I have desired it. 3427
133: 1 how pleasant *it is* for brethren to **d** together 3427
139: 9 *and* **d** in the uttermost parts of the sea; 7931
140:13 the upright shall **d** in thy presence. 3427
143: 3 he hath **made** me **to d** in darkness, as those 3427
Pr 1:33 whoso hearkeneth unto me shall **d** safely, 7931
2:21 For the upright shall **d** *in* the land, and 7931
8:12 I wisdom **d** *with* prudence, and find out 7931
21: 9 *It is* better to **d** in a corner of the housetop, 3427
21:19 *It is* better to **d** in the wilderness, than with 3427
25:24 *It is* better to **d** in a corner of the housetop, 3427
Isa 6: 5 I **d** in the midst of a people of unclean lips: 3427
9: 2 they that **d** in the land of the shadow of 3427
11: 6 The wolf also shall **d** with the lamb, and 1481
13:21 owls shall **d** there, and satyrs shall dance 7931
16: 4 Let mine outcasts **d** with thee, Moab; 1481

Isa 23:13 it for **them that d in the wilderness**: 6728
23:18 for her merchandise shall be for them that **d** 3427
24: 6 and they that **d** therein are desolate: 3427
26: 5 For he bringeth down them that **d** on high; 3427
26:19 Awake and sing, ye that **d in** dust: for thy 7931
30:19 For the people shall **d** in Zion at Jerusalem: 3427
32:16 judgment shall **d** in the wilderness, and 7931
32:18 my people shall **d** in a peaceable habitation, 3427
33:14 Who among us shall **d** *with* the devouring 1481
33:14 who amongst us shall **d** *with* everlasting 1481
33:16 He shall **d** on high: his place of defence 7931
33:24 the people that **d** therein *shall be* forgiven 3427
34:11 the owl also and the raven shall **d** in it: 7931
34:17 from generation to generation shall they **d** 7931
40:22 and spreadeth them out as a tent to **d in**: 3427
49:20 strait for me: give place to me that I may **d**. 3427
51: 6 they that **d** therein shall die in like manner: 3427
57:15 I **d** *in* the high and holy *place,* with him 7931
58:12 of the breach, The restorer of paths to **d in**. 3427
65: 9 inherit it, and my servants shall **d** there. 7931
Jer 4:29 *shall be* forsaken, and not a man **d** therein. 3427
7: 3 and I will **cause** you **to d** in this place. 7931
7: 7 will I **cause** you **to d** in this place, in 7931
8:16 is in it; the city, and those that **d** therein. 3427
8:19 because of them that **d** in a far country: NIH
9:26 the utmost corners, that **d** in the wilderness: 3427
12: 4 for the wickedness of them that **d** therein? 3427
20: 6 all that **d in** thine house shall go into 3427
23: 6 shall be saved, and Israel shall **d** safely: 7931
23: 8 and they shall **d** in their own land. 3427
24: 8 and them that **d** in the land of Egypt: 3427
25: 5 **d** in the land that the LORD hath given 3427
25:24 all the kings of the mingled people that **d** in 7931
27:11 and they shall till it, and **d** therein. 3427
29: 5 **d** *in them;* and plant gardens, and eat 3427
29:28 **d** *in them;* and plant gardens, and eat 3427
29:32 he shall not have a man to **d** among this 3427
31:24 there shall **d** in Judah itself, and *in* all 3427
32:37 and I will **cause** them **to d** safely: 3427
33:16 be saved, and Jerusalem shall **d** safely: 7931
35: 7 but all your days ye shall **d** in tents; 3427
35: 9 Nor to build houses for us to **d in**: 3427
35:11 army of the Syrians: so we **d** at Jerusalem. 3427
35:15 ye shall **d** in the land which I have given to 3427
40: 5 and **d** with him among the people: 3427
40: 9 **d** in the land and serve the king of Babylon, 3427
40:10 I *will* **d** at Mizpah to serve the Chaldeans, 3427
40:10 and **d** in your cities that ye have taken. 3427
42:13 if ye say, We will not **d** in this land, neither 3427
42:14 have hunger of bread; and there will we **d**: 3427
43: 4 of the LORD, to **d** in the land of Judah. 3427
43: 5 had been driven, to **d** in the land of Judah: 1481
44: 1 all the Jews which **d** in the land of Egypt, 3427
44: 1 which **d** at Migdol, and at Tahpanhes, and 3427
44: 8 whither ye be gone to **d**, that ye might cut 1481
44:13 For I will punish them that **d** in the land of 3427
44:14 they have a desire to return to **d** there: 3427
44:26 all Judah that **d** in the land of Egypt; 3427
47: 2 is therein; the city, and them that **d** therein: 3427
48: 9 shall be desolate, without any to **d** therein. 3427
48:28 O ye that **d** in Moab, leave the cities, and 3427
48:28 **d** in the rock, and be like the dove *that* 7931
49: 1 inherit Gad, and his people **d** in his cities? 3427
49: 8 Flee ye, turn back, **d** deep, O inhabitants of 3427
49:18 neither shall a son of man **d** in it. 1481
49:30 Flee, get you far off, **d** deep, O ye 3427
49:31 have neither gates nor bars, *which* **d** alone. 7931
49:33 man abide there, nor *any* son of man **d** in it. 1481
50: 3 her land desolate, and none shall **d** therein: 3427
50:39 the wild beasts of the islands shall **d** *there,* 3427
50:39 dwell *there,* and the owls shall **d** therein: 3427
50:40 neither shall any son of man **d** therein. 1481
51: 1 against them that **d** in the midst of them 3427
Eze 2: 6 and thou dost **d** among scorpions: 3427
12:19 of the violence of all them that **d** therein. 3427
16:46 and her daughters that **d** at thy left hand: 3427
17:23 under it shall **d** all fowl of every wing; 7931
17:23 of the branches thereof shall they **d**. 7931
28:25 shall they **d** in their land that I have given 3427
28:26 they shall **d** safely therein, and shall build 3427
28:26 yea, they shall **d** with confidence, when I 3427
32:15 when I shall smite all them that **d** therein, 3427
34:25 they shall **d** safely in the wilderness, and 3427
34:28 they shall **d** safely, and none shall make 3427
36:28 ye shall **d** in the land that I gave to your 3427
36:33 I will also **cause** *you* **to d in** the cities, and 3427
37:25 they shall **d** in the land that I have given 3427
37:25 they shall **d** therein, *even* they, and 3427
38: 8 and they shall **d** safely all of them. 3427
38:11 go *to* them that are at rest, that **d** safely, 3427
38:12 and goods, that **d** in the midst of the land. 3427
39: 6 among them that **d** carelessly **in** the isles: 3427
39: 9 they that **d in** the cities of Israel shall go 3427
43: 7 where I will **d** in the midst of the children 7931
43: 9 and I will **d** in the midst of them for ever. 7931
Da 2:38 wheresoever the children of men **d**, 1753
4: 1 languages, that **d** in all the earth; 1753
6:25 languages, that **d** in all the earth; 1753
Hos 9: 3 They shall not **d** in the LORD'S land; but 3427
12: 9 will yet **make** thee **to d** in tabernacles, 3427
14: 7 They that **d** under his shadow shall return; 3427
Joel 3:20 Judah shall **d** for ever, and Jerusalem from 3427
Am 3:12 out that **d** in Samaria in the corner of a bed, 3427
5:11 of hewn stone, but ye shall not **d** in them; 3427
9: 5 and all that **d** therein shall mourn: 3427
Mic 4:10 thou shalt **d** in the field, and thou shalt go 7931
7:13 be desolate because of them that **d** therein, 3427
7:14 which **d** solitarily *in* the wood, in the midst 7931
Na 1: 5 yea, the world, and all that **d** therein. 3427
3:18 thy nobles shall **d** *in the dust:* thy people is 7931
Hab 2: 8 *of* the city, and *of* all that **d** therein. 3427
2:17 *of* the city, and *of* all that **d** therein. 3427
Zep 1:18 riddance of all them that **d in** the land. 3427
Hag 1: 4 to **d** in your cieled houses, and this house 3427
Zec 2:10 I come, and I will **d** in the midst of thee, 7931
2:11 I will **d** in the midst of thee, and thou shalt 7931
8: 3 and will **d** in the midst of Jerusalem: 7931
8: 4 old women **d** in the streets of Jerusalem, 3427
8: 8 and they shall **d** in the midst of Jerusalem: 7931
9: 6 a bastard shall **d** in Ashdod, and I will cut 3427
14:11 *men* shall **d** in it, and there shall be no more 3427
Mt 12:45 than himself, and they enter in and **d** there: *2730*
Lk 11:26 than himself; and they enter in, and **d** there: *2730*
21:35 them that **d** on the face of the whole earth. *2521*
Ac 1:20 be desolate, and let no man **d** therein: *2730*
2:14 of Judea, and all *ye* that **d** at Jerusalem, *2730*
4:16 *is* manifest to all them that **d** in Jerusalem; *2730*
7: 4 him into this land, wherein ye now **d**. *2730*
13:27 For they that **d** at Jerusalem, and *2730*
17:26 of men for to **d** on all the face of the earth, *2730*
28:16 Paul was suffered to **d** by himself with a *3306*
Ro 8: 9 if so be that the Spirit of God **d** in you. *3611*
8:11 that raised up Jesus from the dead **d** in you, *3611*
1Co 7:12 and she be pleased to **d** with him, let him *3611*
7:13 and *if* he be pleased to **d** with her, let her *3611*
2Co 6:16 I will **d** in them, and walk in *them;* and *1774*
Eph 3:17 That Christ may **d** in your hearts by faith; *2730*
Col 1:19 *the Father* that in him should all fulness **d**; *2730*
3:16 Let the word of Christ **d** in you richly in all *1774*
1Pe 3: 7 **d with** *them* according to knowledge, *4924*
1Jn 4:13 Hereby know we that we **d** in him, and *3306*
Rev 3:10 the world, to try them that **d** upon the earth. *2730*
6:10 avenge our blood on them that **d** on *2730*
7:15 he that sitteth on the throne shall **d** among *4637*
11:10 And they that **d** upon the earth shall rejoice *2730*
12:12 ye heavens, and ye that **d** in them. *4637*
13: 6 his tabernacle, and them that **d** in heaven. *4637*
13: 8 And all that **d** upon the earth shall worship *2730*
13:12 them which **d** therein to worship the first *2730*
13:14 And deceiveth them that **d** on the earth by *2730*
13:14 saying to them that **d** on the earth, that *they* *2730*
14: 6 to preach unto them that **d** on the earth, *2730*
17: 8 and they that **d** on the earth shall wonder, *2730*
21: 3 and he will **d** with them, and they shall be *4637*

DWELLED (6) [DWELL]

Ge 13: 7 and the Perizzite **d** then in the land. 3427
13:12 Abram **d** in the land of Canaan, and 3427
13:12 Lot **d** in the cities of the plain, and 3427
20: 1 **d** between Kadesh and Shur, and 3427
Ru 1: 4 and they **d** there about ten years. 3427
1Sa 12:11 your enemies on every side, and ye **d** safe. 3427

DWELLERS (3) [DWELL]

Isa 18: 3 of the world, and **d** on the earth, see ye, 7931
Ac 1:19 And it was known unto all the **d** at *2730*
2: 9 and the **d** in Mesopotamia, and in Judea, *2730*

D

DWELLEST (19) [DWELL]
Dt 12:29 thou succeedest them, and **d** in their land; 3427
19: 1 and **d** in their cities, and in their houses; 3427
26: 1 and possessest it, and **d** therein; 3427
2Ki 19:15 which **d** *between* the cherubims, thou *art* 3427
Ps 80: 1 thou that **d** *between* the cherubims, 3427
123: 1 up mine eyes, O thou that **d** in the heavens. 3427
SS 8:13 Thou that **d** in the gardens, the companions 3427
Isa 10:24 O my people that **d in** Zion, be not afraid of 3427
37:16 of Israel, that **d** *between* the cherubims, 3427
47: 8 that **d** carelessly, that sayest in thine heart, 3427
Jer 49:16 O thou that **d** in the clefts of the rock, 7931
51:13 O thou that **d** upon many waters, 7931
La 4:21 daughter of Edom, that **d** in the land of Uz; 3427
Eze 7: 7 come unto thee, O thou that **d in** the land: 3427
12: 2 thou **d** in the midst of a rebellious house, 3427
Ob 1: 3 thou that **d** in the clefts of the rock, 7931
Zec 2: 7 that **d** *with* the daughter of Babylon. 3427
Jn 1:38 being interpreted, Master,) where **d** thou? *3306*
Rev 2:13 I know thy works, and where thou **d**, *2730*

DWELLETH (58) [DWELL]
Lev 19:34 *But* the stranger that **d** with you shall be 1481
25:39 if thy brother *that* **d** by thee be waxen poor, NIH
25:47 and thy brother *that* **d** by him wax poor, and NIH
Nu 13:18 what it *is;* and the people that **d** therein, 3427
Dt 33:20 he **d** as a lion, and teareth the arm with 7931
Jos 6:25 she **d** in Israel *even* unto this day; because 3427
22:19 wherein the LORD'S tabernacle **d**, and 7931
1Sa 4: 4 of hosts, which **d** *between* the cherubims: 3427
27:11 *will be* his manner all the while he **d** in 3427
2Sa 6: 2 of hosts that **d** *between* the cherubims. 3427
7: 2 but the ark of God **d** within curtains. 3427
1Ch 13: 6 that **d** *between* the cherubims, whose name 3427
Job 15:28 he **d in** desolate cities, *and* in houses which 7931
38:19 Where *is* the way *where* light **d**? and *as for* 7931
39:28 She **d** and abideth on the rock, upon 7931
Ps 9:11 *praises* to the LORD, which **d in** Zion: 3427
26: 8 and the place **where** thine honour **d**. 4908
91: 1 He that **d** in the secret place of the most 3427
113: 5 unto the LORD our God, who **d** on high, 3427
135:21 LORD out of Zion, which **d** *at* Jerusalem. 7931
Pr 3:29 seeing he **d** securely by thee. 3427
Isa 8:18 LORD of hosts, which **d** in mount Zion. 7931
33: 5 The LORD *is* exalted; for he **d** on high: 7931
Jer 29:16 of all the people that **d** in this city, *and* 3427
44: 2 they *are* a desolation, and no man **d** therein, 3427
49:31 that **d** without care, saith the LORD, 3427
51:43 and a wilderness, a land wherein no man **d**, 3427
La 1: 3 she **d** among the heathen, she findeth no 3427
Eze 16:46 that **d** at thy right hand, *is* Sodom and 3427
17:16 surely in the place *where* the king **d** that NIH
38:14 In that day when my people of Israel **d** 3427
Da 2:22 *is* in the darkness, and the light **d** with him. 8271
Hos 4: 3 every one that **d** therein shall languish, 3427
Joel 3:21 not cleansed: for the LORD **d** in Zion. 7931
Am 8: 8 and every one mourn that **d** therein? 3427
Mt 23:21 sweareth by it, and by him that **d** therein. *2730*
Jn 6:56 drinketh my blood, **d** in me, and I in him. *3306*
14:10 but the Father that **d** in me, he doeth *3306*
14:17 for he **d** with you, and shall be in you. *3306*
Ac 7:48 Howbeit the most High **d** not in temples *2730*
17:24 earth, **d** not in temples made with hands; *2730*
Ro 7:17 is no more I that do it, but sin that **d** in me. *3611*
7:18 **d** no good *thing:* for to will is present with *3611*
7:20 is no more I that do it, but sin that **d** in me. *3611*
8:11 mortal bodies by his Spirit that **d** in you. *1774*
1Co 3:16 of God, and *that* the Spirit of God **d** in you? *3611*
Col 2: 9 For in him **d** all the fulness of the Godhead *2730*
2Ti 1:14 *thee* keep by the Holy Ghost which **d** in us. *1774*
Jas 4: 5 the spirit that **d** in us lusteth to envy? *2730*
2Pe 3:13 and a new earth, wherein **d** righteousness. *2730*
1Jn 3:17 from him, how **d** the love of God in him? *3306*
3:24 And he that keepeth his commandments **d** *3306*
4:12 God **d** in us, and his love is perfected in us. *3306*
4:15 Son of God, God **d** in him, and he in God. *3306*
4:16 and he that **d** in love dwelleth in God, and *3306*
4:16 and he that dwelleth in love **d** in God, and *3306*
2Jn 1: 2 which **d** in us, and shall be with us for ever. *3306*
Rev 2:13 who was slain among you, where Satan **d**. *2730*

DWELLING (60) [DWELL]
Ge 10:30 their **d** was from Mesha, as thou goest unto 4186
25:27 and Jacob *was* a plain man, **d** in tents. 3427
27:39 thy **d** shall be the fatness of the earth, and 4186
Lev 25:29 if a man sell a **d** house in a walled city, 4186
Nu 21:15 the brooks that goeth down to the **d** of Ar, 3427
24:21 Strong *is* thy **d place**, and thou puttest thy 4186
Jos 13:21 *were* dukes of Sihon, **d in** the country. 3427
1Ki 8:30 hear thou in heaven thy **d** place: and 3427
8:39 hear thou *in* heaven thy **d** place, and 3427
8:43 Hear thou *in* heaven thy **d** place, and 3427
8:49 their supplication *in* heaven thy **d** place, 3427
21: 8 nobles that *were* in his city, **d** with Naboth. 3427
2Ki 17:25 *so* it was at the beginning of their **d** there, 3427
1Ch 6:32 they ministered before the **d place** of 4908
6:54 Now these *are* their **d places** throughout 4186
2Ch 6: 2 for thee, and a place for thy **d** for ever. 3427
6:21 hear thou from thy **d** place, *even* from 3427
6:30 hear thou from heaven thy **d** place, and 3427
6:33 *even* from thy **d** place, and do according to 3427
6:39 *even* from thy **d** place, their prayer and 3427
30:27 their prayer came *up* to his **holy d** place, 6944
36:15 on his people, and on his **d place**: 4583
Job 8:22 the **d place** of the wicked shall come to 168
21:28 and where *are* the **d** places of the wicked? 4908
Ps 49:11 *and* their **d places** to all generations; 4908
49:14 shall consume *in* the grave from their **d**. 2073
52: 5 pluck thee out of *thy* **d place**, and root thee 168
74: 7 the **d place** of thy name to the ground. 4908
76: 2 is his tabernacle, and his **d place** in Zion. 4585
79: 7 devoured Jacob, and laid waste his **d place**. 5116
90: 1 thou hast been our **d place** in all 4583
91:10 neither shall *any* plague come nigh thy **d**. 168
Pr 21:20 to be desired and oil in the **d** of the wise; 5116
24:15 O wicked *man,* against the **d** of 5116
Isa 4: 5 the LORD will create upon every **d place** 4349
18: 4 I will consider in my **d place** like a clear 4349
Jer 30:18 and have mercy on his **d places**; 4908
46:19 O thou daughter **d** in Egypt, furnish thyself 3427
49:33 Hazor shall be a **d** for dragons, *and* 4583
51:30 they have burnt her **d places**; her bars are 4908
51:37 a **d place** for dragons, an astonishment, and 4583
Eze 6: 6 In all your **d places** the cities shall be laid 4186
37:23 I will save them out of all their **d places**, 4186
38:11 all of them **d** without walls, and 3427
48:15 *place* for the city, for **d**, and for suburbs: 4186
Da 2:11 except the gods, whose **d** is not with flesh. 4070
4:25 thy **d** shall be with the beasts of the field, 4070
4:32 thy **d** *shall be* with the beasts of the field: 4070
5:21 and his **d** *was* with the wild asses: 4070
Joel 3:17 that I *am* the LORD your God **d** in Zion, 7931
Na 2:11 Where *is* the **d** of the lions, and the feeding 4583
Hab 1: 6 to possess the **d places** *that are* not theirs. 4908
Zep 3: 7 so their **d** should not be cut off, 4583
Mk 5: 3 Who had *his* **d** among the tombs; *2731*
Ac 2: 5 And there were **d** at Jerusalem Jews, *2730*
19:17 all the Jews and Greeks also **d at** Ephesus; *2730*
1Co 4:11 are buffeted, and **have no certain d place**; *790*
1Ti 6:16 **d** in the light which no *man* can approach *3611*
Heb 11: 9 as *in* a strange *country,* **d** in tabernacles *2730*
2Pe 2: 8 (For *that* righteous *man* **d** among them, *1460*

DWELLINGS (17) [DWELL]
Ex 10:23 all the children of Israel had light in their **d**. 4186
Lev 3:17 for your generations throughout all your **d**, 4186
7:26 *it be* of fowl or of beast, in any of your **d**. 4186
23: 3 *is* the sabbath of the LORD in all your **d**. 4186
23:14 throughout your generations in all your **d**. 4186
23:21 in all your **d** throughout your generations. 4186
23:31 throughout your generations in all your **d**. 4186
Nu 35:29 throughout your generations in all your **d**. 4186
Job 18:19 his people, nor *any* remaining in his **d**. 4033
18:21 Surely such *are* the **d** of the wicked, and 4908
39: 6 the wilderness, and the barren *land* his **d**. 4908
Ps 55:15 for wickedness *is* in their **d**, *and* 4033
87: 2 gates of Zion more than all the **d** of Jacob. 4908
Isa 32:18 and in sure **d**, and in quiet resting places; 4908
Jer 9:19 the land, because our **d** have cast *us* out. 4908
Eze 25: 4 palaces in thee, and make their **d** in thee: 4908
Zep 2: 6 the sea coast shall be **d** *and* cottages for 5116

DWELT (226) [DWELL]
Ge 4:16 **d** in the land of Nod, on the east of Eden. 3427
11: 2 in the land of Shinar; and they **d** there. 3427
11:31 and they came unto Haran, and **d** there. 3427
13:18 came and **d** in the plain of Mamre, which *is* 3427
14: 7 also the Amorites, that **d** in Hazezon-tamar. 3427

Ge 14:12 who **d** in Sodom, and his goods, and 3427
14:13 for he **d** in the plain of Mamre the Amorite, 7931
16: 3 after Abram had **d** ten years in the land of 3427
19:29 he overthrew the cities in the which Lot **d**. 3427
19:30 **d** in the mountain, and his two daughters 3427
19:30 he **d** in a cave, he and his two daughters. 3427
21:20 **d** in the wilderness, and became an archer. 3427
21:21 he **d** in the wilderness of Paran: and 3427
22:19 and Abraham **d** at Beer-sheba. 3427
23:10 Ephron **d** amongst the children of Heth: 3427
24:62 for he **d** in the south country. 3427
25:11 and Isaac **d** by the well Lahai-roi. 3427
25:18 they **d** from Havilah unto Shur, that *is* 7931
26: 6 And Isaac **d** in Gerar: 3427
26:17 his tent in the valley of Gerar, and **d** there. 3427
35:22 when Israel **d** in that land, that Reuben 7931
36: 8 Thus **d** Esau in mount Seir: Esau *is* Edom. 3427
37: 1 Jacob **d** in the land wherein his father was a 3427
38:11 Tamar went and **d** *in* her father's house. 3427
47:27 Israel **d** in the land of Egypt, in the country 3427
50:22 Joseph **d** in Egypt, he, and his father's 3427
Ex 2:15 of Pharaoh, and **d** in the land of Midian: 3427
12:40 who **d** in Egypt, *was* four hundred and 3427
Lev 18: 3 of Egypt, wherein ye **d**, shall ye not do: 3427
26:35 rest in your sabbaths, when ye **d** upon it. 3427
Nu 14:25 and the Canaanites **d** in the valley.) 3427
14:45 the Canaanites which **d** in that hill, 3427
20:15 and we have **d** in Egypt a long time; 3427
21: 1 Arad the Canaanite, which **d** *in* the south, 3427
21:25 Israel **d** in all the cities of the Amorites, 3427
21:31 Thus Israel **d** in the land of the Amorites. 3427
21:34 king of the Amorites, which **d** at Heshbon. 3427
31:10 they burnt all their cities wherein they **d**, 4186
32:40 the son of Manasseh; and he **d** therein. 3427
33:40 which **d** in the south in the land of Canaan, 3427
Dt 1: 4 which **d** in Heshbon, and Og the king of 3427
1: 4 of Bashan, which **d** at Astaroth in Edrei: 3427
1: 6 Ye have **d** long enough in this mount: 3427
1:44 the Amorites, which **d** in that mountain, 3427
2: 8 which **d** in Seir, through the way of 3427
2:10 (The Emims **d** therein in times past, 3427
2:12 The Horims also **d** in Seir beforetime; but 3427
2:12 from before them, and **d** in their stead; 3427
2:20 giants **d** therein in old time; and 3427
2:21 they succeeded them, and **d** in their stead: 3427
2:22 did to the children of Esau, which **d** in Seir, 3427
2:22 and **d** in their stead *even* unto this day: 3427
2:23 the Avims which **d** in Hazerim, *even* unto 3427
2:23 destroyed them, and **d** in their stead.) 3427
3: 2 king of the Amorites, which **d** at Heshbon. 3427
4:46 who **d** at Heshbon, whom Moses and 3427
8:12 hast built goodly houses, and **d** *therein;* 3427
29:16 (For ye know how we have **d** in the land of 3427
33:16 *for* the good will of him that **d in** the bush: 7931
Jos 2:15 the town wall, and she **d** upon the wall. 3427
7: 7 and **d** on the *other* side Jordan! 3427
9:16 and *that* they **d** among them. 3427
12: 2 who **d** in Heshbon, *and* ruled from Aroer, 3427
12: 4 the giants, that **d** at Ashtaroth and at Edrei, 3427
16:10 they drave not out the Canaanites that **d** in 3427
19:47 and **d** therein, and called Leshem, Dan, 3427
19:50 and he built the city, and **d** therein. 3427
21:43 and they possessed it, and **d** therein. 3427
22:33 wherein the children of Reuben and Gad **d**. 3427
24: 2 Your fathers **d** on the *other* side of 3427
24: 7 and ye **d** in the wilderness a long season. 3427
24: 8 which **d** on the *other* side Jordan; 3427
24:18 even the Amorites which **d in** the land: 3427
Jdg 1: 9 that **d in** the mountain, and in the south, 3427
1:10 Judah went against the Canaanites that **d** in 3427
1:16 and they went and **d** among the people. 3427
1:29 drive out the Canaanites that **d** in Gezer; 3427
1:29 but the Canaanites **d** in Gezer among them. 3427
1:30 the Canaanites **d** among them, and 3427
1:32 the Asherites **d** among the Canaanites, 3427
1:33 he **d** among the Canaanites, the inhabitants 3427
3: 3 and the Hivites that **d in** mount Lebanon, 3427
3: 5 the children of Israel **d** among 3427
4: 2 which **d** in Harosheth of the Gentiles. 3427
4: 5 she **d** under the palm tree of Deborah 3427
8:11 Gideon went up *by* the way of them that **d** 7931
8:29 son of Joash went and **d** in his own house. 3427
9:21 and fled, and went to Beer, and **d** there, 3427
9:41 Abimelech **d** at Arumah: and Zebul thrust 3427
10: 1 and he **d** in Shamir in mount Ephraim. 3427
11: 3 from his brethren, and **d** in the land of Tob: 3427
11:26 While Israel **d** in Heshbon and her towns, 3427
15: 8 and **d** in the top of the rock Etam. 3427
18: 7 that *were* therein, how they **d** careless, 3427
18:28 And they built a city, and **d** therein, 3427
21:23 and repaired the cities, and **d** in them. 3427
Ru 2:23 and **d** with her mother in law. 3427
1Sa 19:18 And he and Samuel went and **d** in Naioth. 3427
22: 4 they **d** with him all the while that David 3427
23:29 and **d** in strong holds at En-gedi. 3427
27: 3 David **d** with Achish at Gath, he and 3427
27: 7 the time that David **d** in the country of 3427
31: 7 and the Philistines came and **d** in them. 3427
2Sa 2: 3 and they **d** in the cities of Hebron. 3427
5: 9 So David **d** in the fort, and called it the city 3427
7: 6 Whereas I have not **d** in *any* house since 3427
9:12 all that **d** in the house of Ziba *were* servants 4186
9:13 So Mephibosheth **d** in Jerusalem: for he did 3427
14:28 So Absalom **d** two full years in Jerusalem, 3427
1Ki 2:38 And Shimei **d** in Jerusalem many days. 3427
4:25 Judah and Israel **d** safely, every man under 3427
7: 8 his house where he **d** *had* another court 3427
9:16 slain the Canaanites that **d** in the city, and 3427
11:24 and **d** therein, and reigned in Damascus. 3427
12: 2 king Solomon, and Jeroboam **d** in Egypt;) 3427
12:17 *as for* the children of Israel which **d** in 3427
12:25 Shechem in mount Ephraim, and **d** therein; 3427
13:11 Now there **d** an old prophet in Beth-el; and 3427
13:25 told *it* in the city where the old prophet **d**. 3427
15:18 king of Syria, that **d** at Damascus, saying, 3427
15:21 left off building of Ramah, and **d** in Tirzah. 3427
17: 5 for he went and **d** by the brook Cherith, 3427
2Ki 13: 5 the children of Israel **d** in their tents, 3427
15: 5 day of his death, and **d** in a several house. 3427
16: 6 came *to* Elath, and **d** there unto this day. 3427
17:24 and **d** in the cities thereof. 3427
17:28 away from Samaria came and **d** in Beth-el, 3427
17:29 every nation in their cities wherein they **d**. 3427
19:36 and went and returned, and **d** at Nineveh. 3427
22:14 (now she **d** in Jerusalem in the college;) 3427
1Ch 2:55 the families of the scribes which **d at** 3427
4:23 those that **d amongst** plants and hedges: 3427
4:23 there they **d** with the king for his work. 3427
4:28 they **d** at Beer-sheba, and Moladah, and 3427
4:40 for *they* of Ham had **d** there of old. 3427
4:41 utterly unto this day, and **d** in their rooms: 3427
4:43 were escaped, and **d** there unto this day. 3427
5: 8 the son of Joel, who **d** in Aroer, even unto 3427
5:10 they **d** in their tents throughout all the east 3427
5:11 the children of Gad **d** over against them, 3427
5:16 they **d** in Gilead in Bashan, and in her 3427
5:22 they **d** in their steads until the captivity. 3427
5:23 the children of the half tribe of Manasseh **d** 3427
7:29 In these **d** the children of Joseph the son of 3427
8:28 chief *men*. These **d** in Jerusalem. 3427
8:29 at Gibeon **d** the father of Gibeon; 3427
8:32 these also **d** with their brethren in 3427
9: 2 Now the first inhabitants that *d* in their NIH
9: 3 in Jerusalem **d** of the children of Judah, 3427
9:16 that **d** in the villages of the Netophathites. 3427
9:34 their generations; these **d** at Jerusalem. 3427
9:35 in Gibeon **d** the father of Gibeon, Jehiel, 3427
9:38 they also **d with** their brethren at 3427
10: 7 and the Philistines came and **d** in them. 3427
11: 7 David **d** in the castle; therefore they called 3427
17: 5 For I have not **d** in a house since the day 3427
2Ch 10:17 *as for* the children of Israel that **d** in 3427
11: 5 Rehoboam **d** in Jerusalem, and built cities 3427
16: 2 king of Syria, that **d** at Damascus, saying, 3427
19: 4 Jehoshaphat **d** at Jerusalem: and he went 3427
20: 8 they **d** therein, and have built thee a 3427
26: 7 and against the Arabians that **d** in Gur-baal, 3427
26:21 and **d** *in* a several house, *being* a leper; 3427
28:18 and the villages thereof: and they **d** there. 3427
30:25 land of Israel, and that **d** in Judah, rejoiced. 3427
31: 4 **d in** Jerusalem to give the portion of 3427
31: 6 and Judah, that **d** in the cities of Judah, 3427
34:22 (now she **d** in Jerusalem in the college:) 3427
Ezr 2:70 **d** in their cities, and all Israel in their cities. 3427
Ne 3:26 Moreover the Nethinims **d** in Ophel, 3427
4:12 that when the Jews which **d** by them came, 3427
7:73 and all Israel, **d** in their cities; 3427
11: 1 And the rulers of the people **d** at Jerusalem: 3427

Ne 11: 3 chief of the province that **d** in Jerusalem: 3427
11: 3 in the cities of Judah **d** every one in his 3427
11: 4 at Jerusalem **d** *certain* of the children of 3427
11: 6 All the sons of Perez that **d** at Jerusalem 3427
11:21 the Nethinims **d** in Ophel: and Ziha and 3427
11:25 *some* of the children of Judah **d** at 3427
11:30 they **d** from Beer-sheba unto the valley of 2583
11:31 The children also of Benjamin from Geba *d* NIH
13:16 There **d** men of Tyre also therein, which 3427
Est 9:19 the villages, that **d** in the unwalled towns, 3427
Job 22: 8 the earth; and the honourable *man* **d** in it. 3427
29:25 and sat chief, and **d** as a king in the army, 7931
Ps 68:10 Thy congregation hath **d** therein: thou, 3427
74: 2 this mount Zion, wherein thou hast **d**. 7931
94:17 my help, my soul had almost **d** *in* silence. 7931
120: 6 My soul hath long **d** with him that hateth 7931
Isa 13:20 neither shall it be **d in** from generation to 7931
29: 1 to Ariel, to Ariel, the city *where* David **d**! 2583
37:37 and went and returned, and **d** at Nineveh. 3427
Jer 2: 6 man passed through, and where no man **d**? 3427
35:10 we have **d** in tents, and have obeyed, and 3427
39:14 carry him home: so he **d** among the people. 3427
40: 6 **d** with him among the people that were left 3427
41:17 and **d** in the habitation of Chimham, 3427
44:15 even all the people that **d** in the land of 3427
50:39 neither shall it be **d in** from generation to 7931
Eze 3:15 that **d** by the river of Chebar, and I sat 3427
31: 6 and under his shadow **d** all great nations. 3427
31:17 *that* **d** under his shadow in the midst of 3427
36:17 when the house of Israel **d** in their own 3427
37:25 my servant, wherein your fathers have **d**; 3427
39:26 when they **d** safely in their land, and 3427
Da 4:12 the fowls of the heaven **d** in the boughs 1753
4:21 under which the beasts of the field **d**, and 1753
Zep 2:15 This *is* the rejoicing city that **d** carelessly, 3427
Mt 2:23 he came and **d** in a city called Nazareth: *2730*
4:13 he came and **d** in Capernaum, *2730*
Lk 1:65 And fear came on all that **d round about** *4039*
13: 4 sinners above all men that **d** in Jerusalem? *2730*
Jn 1:14 and **d** among us, (and we beheld his glory, *4637*
1:39 They came and saw where he **d**, and *3306*
Ac 7: 2 in Mesopotamia, before he **d** in Charran, *2730*
7: 4 land of the Chaldeans, and **d** in Charran: *2730*
9:22 confounded the Jews which **d** at Damascus, *2730*
9:32 down also to the saints which **d** at Lydda. *2730*
9:35 And all that **d** at Lydda and Saron saw him, *2730*
11:29 relief unto the brethren which **d** in Judea: *2730*
13:17 *they* **d as strangers** in the land of Egypt, *3940*
19:10 that all they which **d in** Asia heard *2730*
22:12 a good report of all the Jews which **d** *there,* *2730*
28:30 And Paul **d** two whole years in his own *3306*
2Ti 1: 5 which **d** first in thy grandmother Lois, and *1774*
Rev 11:10 these two prophets tormented them that **d** *2730*

DYED (7) [DYING]
Ex 25: 5 rams' skins **d red**, and badgers' skins, and 119
26:14 a covering for the tent *of* rams' skins **d red**, 119
35: 7 rams' skins **d red**, and badgers' skins, and 119
36:19 a covering for the tent *of* rams' skins **d red**, 119
39:34 the covering of rams' skins **d red**, and 119
Isa 63: 1 from Edom, with **d** garments from Bozrah? 2556
Eze 23:15 **exceeding in d attire** upon their 2871+5628

DYING (6) [DYED]
Nu 17:13 shall die: shall we be consumed with **d**? 1478
Mk 12:20 and the first took a wife, and **d** left no seed. *599*
Lk 8:42 about twelve years of age, and she lay a **d**. *599*
2Co 4:10 Always bearing about in the body the **d** of *3500*
6: 9 as **d**, and behold, we live; as chastened, and *599*
Heb 11:21 By faith Jacob, when he was a **d**, *599*

DYSENTERY See FLUX

E

EACH (51) See Index

EAGERNESS See FORWARDNESS

EAGLE (23) [EAGLE'S, EAGLES, EAGLES']
Lev 11:13 the **e**, and the ossifrage, and the ospray, 5404
11:18 the swan, and the pelican, and the **gier e**, 7360
Dt 14:12 the **e**, and the ossifrage, and the ospray, 5404
14:17 and the **gier e**, and the cormorant, 7360
28:49 the end of the earth, *as swift* as the **e** flieth; 5404
32:11 As an **e** stirreth up her nest, fluttereth over 5404
Job 9:26 swift ships: as the **e** *that* hasteth to the prey. 5404
39:27 Doth the **e** mount up at thy command, and 5404
Pr 23: 5 they fly away as an **e** *toward* heaven. 5404
30:19 The way of an **e** in the air; the way of a 5404
Jer 48:40 he shall fly as an **e**, and shall spread his 5404
49:16 shouldest make thy nest as high as the **e**, 5404
49:22 he shall come up and fly as the **e**, and 5404
Eze 1:10 left side; they four also had the face of an **e**. 5404
10:14 of a lion, and the fourth the face of an **e**. 5404
17: 3 A great **e** with great wings, longwinged, 5404
17: 7 There was also another great **e** with great 5404
Hos 8: 1 *He shall come* as an **e** against the house of 5404
Ob 1: 4 Though thou exalt *thyself* as the **e**, and 5404
Mic 1:16 enlarge thy baldness as the **e**; 5404
Hab 1: 8 they shall fly as the **e** *that* hasteth to eat. 5404
Rev 4: 7 and the fourth beast *was* like a flying **e**. *105*
12:14 woman were given two wings of a great **e**, *105*

EAGLE'S (2) [EAGLE]
Ps 103: 5 *so that* thy youth is renewed like the **e**. 5404
Da 7: 4 The first *was* like a lion, and had **e** wings: I 5403

EAGLES (7) [EAGLE]
2Sa 1:23 they were swifter than **e**, they were stronger 5404
Pr 30:17 pick it out, and the young **e** shall eat it. 5404
Isa 40:31 they shall mount up *with* wings as **e**; 5404
Jer 4:13 his horses are swifter than **e**. Woe unto us! 5404
La 4:19 Our persecutors are swifter than the **e** of 5404
Mt 24:28 there will the **e** be gathered together. *105*
Lk 17:37 Wheresoever the body *is,* thither will the **e** *105*

EAGLES' (2) [EAGLE]
Ex 19: 4 *how* I bare you on **e** wings, and 5404
Da 4:33 till his hairs were grown like **e** *feathers,* and 5403

EAR (120) [EARED, EARING, EARRING, EARRINGS, EARS]
Ex 9:31 for the barley *was* **in the e**, and the flax *was* 24
15:26 wilt **give e** to his commandments, and 238
21: 6 his master shall bore his **e** through with an 241
29:20 put *it* upon the tip of the *right* **e** of Aaron, 241
29:20 upon the tip of the right **e** of his sons, and 241
Lev 8:23 put *it* upon the tip of Aaron's right **e**, and 241
8:24 put of the blood upon the tip of their right **e**, 241
14:14 of the right **e** of him that is to be cleansed, 241
14:17 of the right **e** of him that is to be cleansed, 241
14:25 put *it* upon the tip of the right **e** of him that is 241
14:28 of the right **e** of him that is to be cleansed, 241
Dt 1:45 hearken to your voice, nor **give e** unto you. 238
15:17 and thrust *it* through his **e** unto the door, and 241
32: 1 **Give e**, O ye heavens, and I will speak; and 238
Jdg 5: 3 **give e**, O ye princes; I, *even* I, will sing unto 238
1Sa 8:12 *will set them* to **e** his ground, and to reap 2790
9:15 Now the LORD had told Samuel in his **e** a 241
2Ki 19:16 LORD, bow down thine **e**, and hear: open, 241
2Ch 24:19 against them: but they would not **give e**. 238
Ne 1: 6 Let thine **e** now be attentive, and thine eyes 241
1:11 let now thine **e** be attentive to the prayer of 241
9:30 yet would they not **give e**: therefore 238
Job 4:12 to me, and mine **e** received a little thereof. 241
12:11 Doth not the **e** try words? and the mouth 241
13: 1 mine eye hath seen all *this,* mine **e** hath 241
29:11 When the **e** heard *me,* then it blessed me; 241
29:21 Unto me *men* **gave e**, and waited, and 8085
32:11 I **gave e** to your reasons, whilst you searched 238
34: 2 ye wise *men;* and **give e** unto me, 238
34: 3 For the **e** trieth words, as the mouth tasteth 241
36:10 He openeth also their **e** to discipline, and 241
42: 5 I have heard of thee by the hearing of the **e**: 241
Ps 5: 1 **Give e** to my words, O LORD, consider my 238
10:17 their heart, thou wilt cause thine **e** to hear: 241
17: 1 attend unto my cry, **give e** unto my prayer, 238
17: 6 incline thine **e** unto me, *and* hear my speech. 241
31: 2 Bow down thine **e** to me; deliver me 241
39:12 O LORD, and **give e** unto my cry; 238
45:10 and consider, and incline thine **e**; 241
49: 1 **give e**, all ye inhabitants of the world: 238
49: 4 I will incline mine **e** to a parable: I will open 241

Ps 54: 2 O God; **give e** to the words of my mouth. 238
55: 1 **Give e** to my prayer, O God; and hide not 238
58: 4 *are* like the deaf adder *that* stoppeth her **e**; 241
71: 2 incline thine **e** unto me, and save me. 241
77: 1 God *with* my voice; and he **gave e** unto me. 238
78: 1 **Give e**, O my people, to my law: 238
80: 1 **Give e**, O Shepherd of Israel, thou that 238
84: 8 my prayer: **give e**, O God of Jacob. Selah. 238
86: 1 Bow down thine **e**, O LORD, hear me: for I 241
86: 6 **Give e**, O LORD, unto my prayer; and 238
88: 2 before thee: incline thine **e** unto my cry; 241
94: 9 He that planted the **e**, shall he not hear? he 241
102: 2 I am in trouble; incline thine **e** unto me: 241
116: 2 Because he hath inclined his **e** unto me, 241
141: 1 **give e** unto my voice, when I cry unto thee. 238
143: 1 O LORD, **give e** to my supplications: 238
Pr 2: 2 So that *thou* incline thine **e** unto wisdom, 241
4:20 my words; incline thine **e** unto my sayings. 241
5: 1 *and* bow thine **e** to my understanding: 241
5:13 nor inclined mine **e** to them that instructed 241
15:31 The **e** that heareth the reproof of life abideth 241
17: 4 *and* a liar **giveth e** to a naughty tongue. 238
18:15 and the **e** of the wise seeketh knowledge. 241
20:12 The hearing **e**, and the seeing eye, 241
22:17 Bow down thine **e**, and hear the words of 241
25:12 *so is* a wise reprover upon an obedient **e**. 241
28: 9 He that turneth away his **e** from hearing 241
Ecc 1: 8 with seeing, nor the **e** filled with hearing. 241
Isa 1: 2 Hear, O heavens, and **give e**, O earth: for 238
1:10 **give e** unto the law of our God, ye people of 238
8: 9 in pieces; and **give e**, all ye of far countries: 238
28:23 **Give** ye **e**, and hear my voice; hearken, and 238
30:24 the young asses that **e** the ground shall eat 5647
32: 9 careless daughters, **give e** unto my speech. 238
37:17 Incline thine **e**, O LORD, and hear; 241
42:23 Who among you will **give e** to this? *who* will 238
48: 8 from that time *that* thine **e** was not opened: 241
50: 4 he wakeneth mine **e** to hear as the learned. 241
50: 5 The Lord GOD hath opened mine **e**, and 241
51: 4 and **give e** unto me, O my nation: 238
55: 3 Incline your **e**, and come unto me: hear, and 241
59: 1 neither his **e** heavy, that *it* cannot hear: 241
64: 4 nor **perceived by the e**, neither hath the eye 238
Jer 6:10 their **e** *is* uncircumcised, and they cannot 241
7:24 nor inclined their **e**, but walked in 241
7:26 nor inclined their **e**, but hardened their neck: 241
9:20 and let your **e** receive the word of his mouth, 241
11: 8 nor inclined their **e**, but walked every one in 241
13:15 Hear ye, and **give e**; be not proud: for 238
17:23 neither inclined their **e**, but made their neck 241
25: 4 not hearkened, nor inclined your **e** to hear. 241
34:14 not unto me, neither inclined their **e**. 241
35:15 ye have not inclined your **e**, nor hearkened 241
44: 5 nor inclined their **e** to turn from their 241
La 3:56 hide not thine **e** at my breathing, at my cry. 241
Da 9:18 O my God, incline thine **e**, and hear; 241
Hos 5: 1 of Israel; and **give** ye **e**, O house of the king; 238
Joel 1: 2 Hear this, ye old men, and **give e**, all ye 238
Am 3:12 of the lion two legs, or a piece of an **e**; 241
Mt 10:27 and what ye hear in the **e**, *that* preach ye *3775*
26:51 of the high priest's, and smote off his **e**. *5621*
Mk 4:28 first the blade, then the **e**, after that the full *4719*
4:28 then the ear, after that the full corn in the **e**. *4719*
14:47 servant of the high priest, and cut off his **e**. *5621*
Lk 12: 3 *that* which ye have spoken in the **e** in *3775*
22:50 of the high priest, and cut off his right **e**. *3775*
22:51 And he touched his **e**, and healed him. *5621*
Jn 18:10 high priest's servant, and cut off his right **e**. *5621*
18:26 being *his* kinsman whose **e** Peter cut off, *5621*
1Co 2: 9 it is written, Eye hath not seen, nor **e** heard, *3775*
12:16 And if the **e** shall say, Because I am not *3775*
Rev 2: 7 He that hath an **e**, let him hear what *3775*
2:11 He that hath an **e**, let him hear what *3775*
2:17 He that hath an **e**, let him hear what *3775*
2:29 He that hath an **e**, let him hear what *3775*
3: 6 He that hath an **e**, let him hear what *3775*
3:13 He that hath an **e**, let him hear what *3775*
3:22 He that hath an **e**, let him hear what *3775*
13: 9 If any *man* have an **e**, let him hear. *3775*

EARED (1) [EAR]
Dt 21: 4 which is neither **e** nor sown, and shall strike 5647

EARING (2) [EAR]
Ge 45: 6 *in* the which *there shall* neither *be* **e** nor 2758
Ex 34:21 in **e time** and in harvest thou shalt rest. 2758

EARLIER See HERETOFORE

EARLY (86)
Ge 19: 2 ye shall **rise up e**, and go on your ways. 7925
19:27 Abraham **gat up e** in the morning to 7925
20: 8 Therefore Abimelech **rose e** in 7925
21:14 Abraham **rose up e** in the morning, and 7925
22: 3 Abraham **rose up e** in the morning, and 7925
28:18 Jacob **rose up e** in the morning, and 7925
31:55 **e** in the morning Laban **rose up**, and 7925
Ex 8:20 **Rise up e** in the morning, and stand before 7925
9:13 **Rise up e** in the morning, and stand before 7925
24: 4 **rose up e** in the morning, and builded an 7925
32: 6 they **rose up e** on the morrow, and 7925
34: 4 Moses **rose up e** in the morning, and 7925
Nu 14:40 they **rose up e** in the morning, and 7925
Jos 3: 1 Joshua **rose e** in the morning; and 7925
6:12 Joshua **rose e** in the morning, and 7925
6:15 that they **rose e** about the dawning of 7925
7:16 So Joshua **rose up e** in the morning, and 7925
8:10 Joshua **rose up e** in the morning, and 7925
8:14 of Ai saw *it,* that they hasted and **rose up e**, 7925
Jdg 6:28 when the men of the city **arose e** in 7925
6:38 for he **rose up e** on the morrow, and 7925
7: 1 **rose up e**, and pitched beside the well of 7925
7: 3 and **depart e** from mount Gilead. 6852
9:33 thou shalt **rise e**, and set upon the city: 7925
19: 5 when they **arose e** in the morning, that he 7925
19: 8 he **arose e** in the morning on the fifth day 7925
19: 9 to morrow **get** you **e** on your way, that thou 7925
21: 4 that the people **rose e**, and built there an 7925
1Sa 1:19 they **rose up** in the morning **e**, and 7925
5: 3 when they of Ashdod **arose e** on 7925
5: 4 when they **arose e** on the morrow morning, 7925
9:26 they **arose e**: and it came to pass about 7925
15:12 when Samuel **rose e** to meet Saul in 7925
17:20 David **rose up e** in the morning, and 7925
29:10 Wherefore now **rise up e** in the morning 7925
29:10 as soon as ye **be up e** in the morning, and 7925
29:11 his men **rose up e** to depart in the morning, 7925
2Sa 15: 2 Absalom **rose up e**, and stood beside 7925
2Ki 3:22 they **rose up e** in the morning, and the sun 7925
6:15 the servant of the man of God was risen **e**, 7925
19:35 when they **arose e** in the morning, behold, 7925
2Ch 20:20 they **rose e** in the morning, and went forth 7925
29:20 Hezekiah the king **rose e**, and gathered 7925
Job 1: 5 **rose up e** in the morning, and offered burnt 7925
Ps 46: 5 God shall help her, *and that* right **e**. 1242
57: 8 and harp: I *myself* will awake **e**. 7837
63: 1 O God, thou *art* my God; **e** will I **seek** thee: 7836
78:34 they returned and **inquired e after** God. 7836
90:14 O satisfy us **e** *with* thy 1242+871.1+1886.1
101: 8 I will **e** destroy all 1242+1886.1+3807.1
108: 2 and harp: I *myself* will awake **e**. 7837
127: 2 *It is* vain for you to rise up **e**, to sit up late, 7925
Pr 1:28 they shall **seek** me **e**, but they shall not find 7836
8:17 and those that **seek** me **e** shall find me. 7836
27:14 **rising e** in the morning, it shall be counted 7925
SS 7:12 Let us **get up e** to the vineyards; let us see 7925
Isa 5:11 Woe unto them that **rise up e** in 7925
26: 9 *with* my spirit within me will I **seek** thee **e**: 7836
37:36 when they **arose e** in the morning, behold, 7925
Jer 7:13 **rising up e** and speaking, but ye heard not; 7925
7:25 daily **rising up e** and sending *them:* 7925
11: 7 **rising e** and protesting, saying, Obey my 7925
25: 3 spoken unto you, **rising e** and speaking; 7925
25: 4 **rising e** and sending *them;* but ye have not 7925
26: 5 both **rising up e**, and sending *them,* but 7925
29:19 **rising up e** and sending *them;* but ye would 7925
32:33 **rising up e** and teaching *them,* yet they 7925
35:14 spoken unto you, **rising e** and speaking; 7925
35:15 **rising up e** and sending *them,* saying, 7925
44: 4 **rising e** and sending *them,* saying, Oh, 7925
Da 6:19 the king arose **very e** in the morning, and 8238
Hos 5:15 in their affliction they will **seek** me **e**. 7836
6: 4 and as the **e** dew *it* goeth away. 7925
13: 3 and as the **e** dew that passeth away, 7925
Zep 3: 7 they **rose e**, *and* corrupted all their doings. 7925
Mt 20: 1 which went out **e in the morning** to *260+4404*
Mk 16: 2 And very **e in the morning** the first *day* of *4404*

E

Mk 16: 9 Now when *Jesus* was risen **e** the first *day* of *4404*
Lk 21:38 And all the people **came e in the morning** *3719*
24: 1 **very e in the morning**, they came *901+3722*
24:22 which were **e** at the sepulchre; *3721*
Jn 8: 2 And **e in the morning** he came again into *3722*
18:28 unto the hall of judgment: and it was **e**; *4405*
20: 1 of the week cometh Mary Magdalene **e**, *4404*
Ac 5:21 the temple **e in the morning**, *3588+3722+5259*
Jas 5: 7 for it, until he receive the **e** and latter rain. *4406*

EARNEST (8) [EARNESTLY]
Ro 8:19 For the **e expectation** of the creature waiteth *603*
2Co 1:22 and given the **e** of the Spirit in our hearts. *728*
5: 5 who also hath given unto us the **e** of *728*
7: 7 when he told us your **e desire**, your *1972*
8:16 which put the same **e care** into the heart of *4710*
Eph 1:14 Which is the **e** of our inheritance, until *728*
Php 1:20 According to my **e expectation** and *603*
Heb 2: 1 Therefore we ought to give the **more e** *4056*

EARNESTLY (16) [EARNEST]
Nu 22:37 I not **e send** unto thee to call thee? 7971+7971
1Sa 20: 6 David **e asked** *leave* of me that *he* 7592+7592
20:28 David **e asked** *leave* of me *to go* to 7592+7592
Ne 3:20 After him Baruch the son of Zabbai **e** 2734
Job 7: 2 As a servant **e desireth** the shadow, and 7602
Jer 11: 7 For I **e protested** unto your fathers 5749+5749
31:20 I do **e remember** him still: 2142+2142
Mic 7: 3 may do evil with both hands **e**, 3190+3807.1
Lk 22:44 And being in an agony he prayed **more e**: *1617*
22:56 and **e looked** upon him, and said, This *man* *816*
Ac 3:12 or why **look** ye *so* **e** on us, as though by our *816*
23: 1 **e beholding** the council, said, Men *and* *816*
1Co 12:31 But **covet e** the best gifts: and yet shew I *2206*
2Co 5: 2 **e desiring** to be clothed upon with our *1971*
Jas 5:17 he **prayed e** that it might not rain: *4335+4336*
Jude 1: 3 exhort *you* that *ye* should **e contend for** *1864*

EARNESTNESS See FORWARDNESS

EARNETH (2)
Hag 1: 6 he that **e wages** earneth wages *to put it* into 7936
1: 6 he that earneth wages **e wages** *to put it* into 7936

EARRING (5) [EAR, RING]
Ge 24:22 that the man took a golden **e** of half a 5141
24:30 when he saw the **e** and bracelets upon his 5141
24:47 I put the **e** upon her face, and the bracelets 5141
Job 42:11 piece of money, and every one an **e** of gold. 5141
Pr 25:12 *As* an **e** of gold, and an ornament of fine 5141

EARRINGS (12) [EAR, RING]
Ge 35: 4 and *all their* **e** which *were* in their ears; 5141
Ex 32: 2 said unto them, Break off the golden **e**, 5141
32: 3 all the people brake off the golden **e** which 5141
35:22 and **e**, and rings, and tablets, 5141
Nu 31:50 chains, and bracelets, rings, **e**, and tablets, 5694
Jdg 8:24 that you would give me every man the **e** of 5141
8:24 (For they had golden **e**, because they *were* 5141
8:25 did cast therein every man the **e** of his prey. 5141
8:26 the weight of the golden **e** that he requested 5141
Isa 3:20 the headbands, and the tablets, and the **e**, 3908
Eze 16:12 **e** in thine ears, and a beautiful crown upon 5694
Hos 2:13 she decked herself with her **e** and 5141

EARS (151) [EAR]
Ge 20: 8 and told all these things in their **e**: 241
35: 4 and *all their* earrings which *were* in their **e**; 241
41: 5 seven **e of corn** came up upon one stalk, 7641
41: 6 seven thin **e** and blasted with the east wind 7641
41: 7 the seven thin **e** devoured the seven rank 7641
41: 7 ears devoured the seven rank and full **e**. 7641
41:22 seven **e** came up in one stalk, full and good: 7641
41:23 seven **e**, withered, thin, *and* blasted with 7641
41:24 the thin **e** devoured the seven good ears: 7641
41:24 the thin ears devoured the seven good **e**: 7641
41:26 the seven good **e** *are* seven years: 7641
41:27 the seven empty **e** blasted with the east 7641
44:18 speak a word in my lord's **e**, and let not thine 241
50: 4 I pray you, in the **e** of Pharaoh, saying, 241
Ex 10: 2 And that thou mayest tell in the **e** of thy son, 241
11: 2 Speak now in the **e** of the people, and 241
17:14 in a book, and rehearse *it* in the **e** of Joshua: 241
32: 2 which *are* in the **e** of your wives, of your 241
32: 3 off the golden earrings which *were* in their **e**, 241
Lev 2:14 firstfruits **green e of corn** dried by the fire, 24
2:14 by the fire, *even* **corn** beaten out **of full e**. 3759
23:14 nor parched *corn*, nor **green e**, 3759
Nu 11:18 for you have wept in the **e** of the LORD, 241
14:28 as ye have spoken in mine **e**, so will I do to 241
Dt 5: 1 judgments which I speak in your **e** *this* day, 241
23:25 thou mayest pluck the **e** with thine hand; 4425
29: 4 and eyes to see, and **e** to hear, unto this day. 241
31:28 that I may speak these words in their **e**, 241
31:30 Moses spake in the **e** of all the congregation 241
32:44 spake all the words of this song in the **e** of 241
Jos 20: 4 shall declare his cause in the **e** of the elders 241
Jdg 7: 3 go to, proclaim in the **e** of the people, 241
9: 2 pray you, in the **e** of all the men of Shechem, 241
9: 3 his mother's brethren spake of him in the **e** 241
17: 2 spakest of also in mine **e**, behold, the silver 241
Ru 2: 2 glean **e of corn** after *him* in whose sight I 7641
1Sa 3:11 *at* which both the **e** of every one that heareth 241
8:21 he rehearsed them in the **e** of the LORD. 241
11: 4 and told the tidings in the **e** of the people: 241
15:14 then this bleating of the sheep in mine **e**, 241
18:23 Saul's servants spake those words in the **e** of 241
2Sa 3:19 And Abner also spake in the **e** of Benjamin: 241
3:19 Abner went also to speak in the **e** of David 241
7:22 to all that we have heard with our **e**. 241
22: 7 his temple, and my cry *did enter* into his **e**. 241
2Ki 4:42 and **full e of corn** in the husk thereof. 3759
18:26 in the **e** of the people that *are* on the wall. 241
19:28 and thy tumult is come up into mine **e**, 241
21:12 heareth of it, both his **e** shall tingle. 241
23: 2 he read in their **e** all the words of the book of 241
1Ch 17:20 to all that we have heard with our **e**. 241
2Ch 6:40 *let* thine **e** *be* attent unto the prayer *that is* 241
7:15 mine **e** attent unto the prayer *that is made* in 241
34:30 he read in their **e** all the words of the book of 241
Ne 8: 3 the **e** of all the people *were attentive* unto 241
Job 13:17 my speech, and my declaration with your **e**. 241
15:21 A dreadful sound *is* in his **e**: in prosperity 241
24:24 and cut off as the tops of the **e of corn**. 7641
28:22 We have heard the fame thereof with our **e**. 241
33:16 he openeth the **e** of men, and sealeth their 241
36:15 and openeth their **e** in oppression. 241
Ps 18: 6 and my cry came before him, *even* into his **e**. 241
34:15 and his **e** *are open* unto their cry. 241
40: 6 didst not desire; mine **e** hast thou opened: 241
44: 1 We have heard with our **e**, O God, 241
78: 1 incline your **e** to the words of my mouth. 241
92:11 mine **e** shall hear *my desire* of the wicked 241
115: 6 They have **e**, but they hear not: noses have 241
130: 2 let thine **e** be attentive to the voice of my 241
135:17 They have **e**, but they hear not; neither is 241
Pr 21:13 Whoso stoppeth his **e** at the cry of the poor, 241
23: 9 Speak not in the **e** of a fool: for he will 241
23:12 and thine **e** to the words of knowledge. 241
26:17 to him, *is like* one that taketh a dog by the **e**. 241
Isa 5: 9 In mine **e** *said* the LORD of hosts, Of a 241
6:10 and make their **e** heavy, and shut their eyes; 241
6:10 hear with their **e**, and understand *with* their 241
11: 3 neither reprove after the hearing of his **e**: 241
17: 5 the corn, and reapeth the **e** *with* his arm; 7641
17: 5 it shall be as he that gathereth **e** in 7641
22:14 it was revealed in mine **e** *by* the LORD of 241
30:21 thine **e** shall hear a word behind thee, saying, 241
32: 3 and the **e** of them that hear shall hearken. 241
33:15 that stoppeth his **e** from hearing of blood, 241
35: 5 and the **e** of the deaf shall be unstopped. 241
36:11 in the **e** of the people that *are* on the wall. 241
37:29 is come up into mine **e**, therefore will I put 241
42:20 opening the **e**, but he heareth not. 241
43: 8 that have eyes, and the deaf that have **e**. 241
49:20 hast lost the other, shall say again in thine **e**, 241
Jer 2: 2 Go and cry in the **e** of Jerusalem, saying, 241
5:21 and see not; which have **e**, and hear not: 241
19: 3 which whosoever heareth, his **e** shall tingle. 241
26:11 this city, as ye have heard with your **e**. 241
26:15 unto you to speak all these words in your **e**. 241
28: 7 thou now this word that I speak in thine **e**, 241
28: 7 in thine ears, and in the **e** of all the people. 241
29:29 Zephaniah the priest read this letter in the **e** 241
36: 6 the words of the LORD in the **e** of 241
36: 6 also thou shalt read them in the **e** of all 241
36:10 LORD'S house, in the **e** of all the people. 241
36:13 when Baruch read the book in the **e** of 241
36:14 wherein thou hast read in the **e** of the people, 241

Jer 36:15 unto him, Sit down now, and read it in our **e**. 241
36:15 it in our ears. So Baruch read *it* in their **e**. 241
36:20 and told all the words in the **e** of the king. 241
36:21 Jehudi read it in the **e** of the king, and in 241
36:21 in the **e** of all the princes which stood beside 241
Eze 3:10 receive in thine heart, and hear with thine **e**. 241
8:18 though they cry in mine **e** *with* a loud voice, 241
9: 1 He cried also in mine **e** *with* a loud voice, 241
12: 2 see not; they have **e** to hear, and hear not: 241
16:12 earrings in thine **e**, and a beautiful crown 241
23:25 they shall take away thy nose and thine **e**; 241
24:26 to cause *thee* to hear *it* with *thine* **e**? 241
40: 4 hear with thine **e**, and set thine heart upon all 241
44: 5 hear with thine **e** all that I say unto thee 241
Mic 7:16 hand upon *their* mouth, their **e** shall be deaf. 241
Zec 7:11 stopped their **e**, that *they* should not hear. 241
Mt 11:15 He that hath **e** to hear, let him hear. *3775*
12: 1 and began to pluck the **e of corn**, and *4719*
13: 9 Who hath **e** to hear, let him hear. *3775*
13:15 and *their* **e** are dull of hearing, and *3775*
13:15 see with *their* eyes, and hear with *their* **e**, *3775*
13:16 for they see: and your **e**, for they hear. *3775*
13:43 Who hath **e** to hear, let him hear. *3775*
28:14 And if this **come to** the governor's **e**, *191+1909*
Mk 2:23 as they went, to pluck the **e of corn**. *4719*
4: 9 He that hath **e** to hear, let him hear. *3775*
4:23 If any *man* have **e** to hear, let him hear. *3775*
7:16 If any *man* have **e** to hear, let him hear. *3775*
7:33 and put his fingers into his **e**, and he spit, *3775*
7:35 And straightway his **e** were opened, *189*
8:18 and having **e**, hear ye not? and do ye not *3775*
Lk 1:44 voice of thy salutation sounded in mine **e**, *3775*
4:21 This day is this scripture fulfilled in your **e**. *3775*
6: 1 and his disciples plucked the **e of corn**, and *4719*
8: 8 He that hath **e** to hear, let him hear. *3775*
9:44 Let these sayings sink down into your **e**: *3775*
14:35 it out. He that hath **e** to hear, let him hear. *3775*
Ac 7:51 and uncircumcised in heart and **e**, *3775*
7:57 and stopped their **e**, and ran upon him with *3775*
11:22 the **e** of the church which was in Jerusalem: *3775*
17:20 thou bringest certain strange *things* to our **e**: *189*
28:27 and *their* **e** are dull of hearing, and *3775*
28:27 and hear with *their* **e**, and understand with *3775*
Ro 11: 8 not see, and **e** that *they* should not hear;) *3775*
2Ti 4: 3 to themselves teachers, having itching **e**; *189*
4: 4 And they shall turn away *their* **e** from *189*
Jas 5: 4 entered into the **e** of the Lord of sabaoth. *3775*
1Pe 3:12 and his **e** *are open* unto their prayers: *3775*

EARTH (987) [EARTHEN, EARTHLY, EARTHQUAKE, EARTHQUAKES, EARTHY]

Ge 1: 1 beginning God created the heaven and the **e**. 776
1: 2 the **e** was without form, and void; and 776
1:10 God called the dry *land* **E**; and the gathering 776
1:11 God said, Let the **e** bring forth grass, 776
1:11 his kind, whose seed *is* in itself, upon the **e**: 776
1:12 the **e** brought forth grass, *and* herb yielding 776
1:15 of the heaven to give light upon the **e**: 776
1:17 of the heaven to give light upon the **e**, 776
1:20 fowl *that* may fly above the **e** in the open 776
1:22 in the seas, and let fowl multiply in the **e**. 776
1:24 Let the **e** bring forth the living creature after 776
1:24 and beast of the **e** after his kind: 776
1:25 God made the beast of the **e** after his kind, 776
1:25 every thing that creepeth upon the **e** after his 127
1:26 over all the **e**, and over every creeping thing 776
1:26 creeping thing that creepeth upon the **e**. 776
1:28 multiply, and replenish the **e**, and subdue it: 776
1:28 every living thing that moveth upon the **e**. 776
1:29 which *is* upon the face of all the **e**, and every 776
1:30 to every beast of the **e**, and to every fowl of 776
1:30 to every *thing* that creepeth upon the **e**, 776
2: 1 Thus the heavens and the **e** were finished, 776
2: 4 and of the **e** when they were created, 776
2: 4 in the day that the LORD God made the **e** 776
2: 5 every plant of the field before it was in the **e**, 776
2: 5 God had not caused it to rain upon the **e**, 776
2: 6 there went up a mist from the **e**, and 776
4:11 now *art* thou cursed from the **e**, which hath 127
4:12 and a vagabond shalt thou be in the **e**. 776
4:14 driven me out *this* day from the face of the **e**; 127
4:14 I shall be a fugitive and a vagabond in the **e**; 776
6: 1 men began to multiply on the face of the **e**, 127
6: 4 There were giants in the **e** in those days; and 776
6: 5 the wickedness of man *was* great in the **e**, 776
6: 6 the LORD that he had made man on the **e**, 776
6: 7 whom I have created from the face of the **e**; 127
6:11 The **e** also was corrupt before God, and 776
6:11 and the **e** was filled *with* violence. 776
6:12 God looked upon the **e**, and behold, it was 776
6:12 all flesh had corrupted his way upon the **e**. 776
6:13 for the **e** is filled *with* violence through 776
6:13 and behold, I will destroy them with the **e**. 776
6:17 even I, do bring a flood of waters upon the **e**, 776
6:17 *and* every *thing* that *is* in the **e** shall die. 776
6:20 of every creeping thing of the **e** after his 127
7: 3 to keep seed alive upon the face of all the **e**. 776
7: 4 I will cause it to rain upon the **e** forty days 776
7: 4 will I destroy from off the face of the **e**. 127
7: 6 old when the flood of waters was upon the **e**. 776
7: 8 and of every *thing* that creepeth upon the **e**, 127
7:10 that the waters of the flood were upon the **e**. 776
7:12 the rain was upon the **e** forty days and 776
7:14 every creeping thing that creepeth upon the **e** 776
7:17 And the flood was forty days upon the **e**; and 776
7:17 up the ark, and it was lift up above the **e**. 776
7:18 and were increased greatly upon the **e**; 776
7:19 the waters prevailed exceedingly upon the **e**; 776
7:21 all flesh died that moved upon the **e**, *both* of 776
7:21 creeping thing that creepeth upon the **e**, 776
7:23 and they were destroyed from the **e**: 776
7:24 the waters prevailed upon the **e** an hundred 776
8: 1 and God made a wind to pass over the **e**, and 776
8: 3 the waters returned from off the **e** 776
8: 7 until the waters were dried up from off the **e**. 776
8: 9 the waters *were* on the face of the whole **e**: 776
8:11 that the waters were abated from off the **e**. 776
8:13 the waters were dried up from off the **e**: 776
8:14 twentieth day of the month, was the **e** dried. 776
8:17 creeping thing that creepeth upon the **e**; 776
8:17 that they may breed abundantly in the **e**, and 776
8:17 and be fruitful, and multiply upon the **e**. 776
8:19 *and* whatsoever creepeth upon the **e**, 776
8:22 While the **e** remaineth, seedtime and harvest, 776
9: 1 Be fruitful, and multiply, and replenish the **e**. 776
9: 2 of you shall be upon every beast of the **e**, 776
9: 2 upon all that moveth *upon* the **e**, and 127
9: 7 bring forth abundantly in the **e**, and 776
9:10 and of every beast of the **e** with you; 776
9:10 that go out of the ark, to every beast of the **e**. 776
9:11 there any more be a flood to destroy the **e**. 776
9:13 a token of a covenant between me and the **e**. 776
9:14 to pass, when I bring a cloud over the **e**, 776
9:16 living creature of all flesh that *is* upon the **e**. 776
9:17 between me and all flesh that *is* upon the **e**. 776
9:19 and of them was the whole **e** overspread. 776
10: 8 he began to be a mighty *one* in the **e**. 776
10:25 for in his days was the **e** divided; and 776
10:32 by these were the nations divided in the **e** 776
11: 1 the whole **e** was *of* one language, and *of* one 776
11: 4 abroad upon the face of the whole **e**. 776
11: 8 from thence upon the face of all the **e**: 776
11: 9 did there confound the language of all the **e**: 776
11: 9 them abroad upon the face of all the **e**. 776
12: 3 in thee shall all families of the **e** be blessed. 127
13:16 And I will make thy seed as the dust of the **e**: 776
13:16 so that if a man can number the dust of the **e**, 776
14:19 most high God, possessor of heaven and **e**: 776
14:22 high God, the possessor of heaven and **e**, 776
18:18 all the nations of the **e** shall be blessed in 776
18:25 Shall not the Judge of all the **e** do right? 776
19:23 The sun was risen upon the **e** when Lot 776
19:31 *there is* not a man in the **e** to come in unto us 776
19:31 come in unto us after the manner of all the **e**: 776
22:18 in thy seed shall all the nations of the **e** be 776
24: 3 the God of heaven, and the God of the **e**, 776
24:52 the LORD, *bowing himself* to the **e**. 776
26: 4 in thy seed shall all the nations of the **e** be 776
26:15 had stopped them, and filled them *with* **e**. 6083
27:28 the fatness of the **e**, and plenty of corn and 776
27:39 thy dwelling shall be the fatness of the **e**, and 776
28:12 behold a ladder set up on the **e**, and the top 776
28:14 thy seed shall be as the dust of the **e**, and 776
28:14 in thy seed shall all the families of the **e** be 127
37:10 to bow down ourselves to thee to the **e**? 776
41:47 in the seven plenteous years the **e** brought 776
41:56 the famine was over all the face of the **e**: 776
42: 6 before him *with* their faces to the **e**. 776

E

Ge 43:26 and bowed themselves to him to the **e**. 776
45: 7 you to preserve you a posterity in the **e**, 776
48:12 and he bowed himself with his face to the **e**. 776
48:16 grow into a multitude in the midst of the **e**. 776
Ex 8:17 smote the dust of the **e**, and it became lice in 776
8:22 that I *am* the LORD in the midst of the **e**. 776
9:14 know that *there is* none like me in all the **e**. 776
9:15 and thou shalt be cut off from the **e**. 776
9:16 name may be declared throughout all the **e**. 776
9:29 that thou mayest know how that the **e** *is* 776
9:33 and the rain was not poured upon the **e**. 776
10: 5 they shall cover the face of the **e**, that *one* 776
10: 5 that *one* cannot be able to see the **e**: 776
10: 6 since the day that they were upon the **e** unto 127
10:15 For they covered the face of the whole **e**, so 776
15:12 out thy right hand, the **e** swallowed them. 776
19: 5 me above all people: for all the **e** *is* mine: 776
20: 4 or that *is* in the **e** beneath, or that *is* in 776
20: 4 or that *is* in the water under the **e**: 776
20:11 *in* six days the LORD made heaven and **e**, 776
20:24 An altar of **e** thou shalt make unto me, and 127
31:17 *in* six days the LORD made heaven and **e**, 776
32:12 and to consume them from the face of the **e**? 127
33:16 all the people that *are* upon the face of the **e**. 127
34: 8 bowed his head toward the **e**, and 776
34:10 such as have not been done in all the **e**, 776
Lev 11: 2 eat among all the beasts that *are* on the **e**. 776
11:21 above their feet, to leap withal upon the **e**; 776
11:29 the creeping things that creep upon the **e**; 776
11:41 every creeping thing that creepeth upon the **e** 776
11:42 all creeping things that creep upon the **e**, 776
11:44 *of* creeping thing that creepeth upon the **e**. 776
11:46 of every creature that creepeth upon the **e**: 776
15:12 the vessel of **e**, that he toucheth which hath 2789
26:19 your heaven as iron, and your **e** as brass: 776
Nu 11:31 were two cubits *high* upon the face of the **e**. 776
12: 3 the men which *were* upon the face of the **e**.) 127
14:21 all the **e** shall be filled *with* the glory of 776
16:30 the **e** open her mouth, and swallow them up, 127
16:32 the **e** opened her mouth, and 776
16:33 into the pit, and the **e** closed upon them: 776
16:34 for they said, Lest the **e** swallow us up *also*. 776
22: 5 they cover the face of the **e**, and they abide 776
22:11 of Egypt, which covereth the face of the **e**: 776
26:10 the **e** opened her mouth, and 776
Dt 3:24 for what God *is there* in heaven or in **e**, 776
4:10 all the days that they shall live upon the **e**, 127
4:17 The likeness of any beast that *is* on the **e**, 776
4:18 any fish that *is* in the waters beneath the **e**: 776
4:26 and **e** to witness against you *this* day, 776
4:32 the day that God created man upon the **e**, 776
4:36 and upon **e** he shewed thee his great fire; and 776
4:39 in heaven above, and upon the **e** beneath: 776
4:40 thou mayest prolong *thy* days upon the **e**, 127
5: 8 or that *is* in the **e** beneath, or that *is* in 776
5: 8 or that *is* in the waters beneath the **e**: 776
6:15 and destroy thee from off the face of the **e**. 127
7: 6 all people that *are* upon the face of the **e**. 127
10:14 thy God, the **e** *also*, with all that therein *is*. 776
11: 6 how the **e** opened her mouth, and 776
11:21 give them, as the days of heaven upon the **e**. 776
12: 1 all the days that ye live upon the **e**. 127
12:16 ye shall pour it upon the **e** as water. 776
12:19 the Levite as long as thou livest upon the **e**. 127
12:24 eat it; thou shalt pour it upon the **e** as water. 776
13: 7 from the *one* end of the **e** even unto the *other* 776
13: 7 of the earth even unto the *other* end of the **e**; 776
14: 2 above all the nations that *are* upon the **e**. 127
26: 2 shalt take of the first of all the fruit of the **e**, 127
28: 1 set thee on high above all nations of the **e**: 776
28:10 all people of the **e** shall see that thou art 776
28:23 and the **e** that *is* under thee *shall be* iron. 776
28:25 be removed into all the kingdoms of the **e**. 776
28:26 unto the beasts of the **e**, and no man shall 776
28:49 from the end of the **e**, *as swift* as the eagle 776
28:64 from the *one* end of the **e** even unto 776
30:19 and **e** to record *this* day against you, 776
31:28 and call heaven and **e** to record against them. 776
32: 1 and hear, O **e**, the words of my mouth. 776
32:13 made him ride on the high places of the **e**, 776
32:22 shall consume the **e** with her increase, and 776
33:16 for the precious things of the **e** and 776
33:17 push the people together *to* the ends of the **e**: 776
Jos 2:11 he *is* God in heaven above, and in **e** beneath. 776
3:11 *even* the Lord of all the **e** passeth over before 776
3:13 the Lord of all the **e**, shall rest in the waters 776
4:24 That all the people of the **e** might know 776
5:14 Joshua fell on his face to the **e**, and 776
7: 6 fell to the **e** upon his face before the ark of 776
7: 9 us round, and cut off our name from the **e**: 776
7:21 they *are* hid in the **e** in the midst of my tent, 776
23:14 *this* day I am going the way of all the **e**: 776
Jdg 3:25 their lord *was* fallen down dead on the **e**. 776
5: 4 the **e** trembled, and the heavens dropped, 776
6: 4 destroyed the increase of the **e**, till thou 776
6:37 *it be* dry upon all the **e** *beside*, then shall I 776
18:10 *there is* no want of any thing that *is* in the **e**. 776
1Sa 2: 8 for the pillars of the **e** *are* the LORD'S, and 776
2:10 the LORD shall judge the ends of the **e**; and 776
4: 5 *with* a great shout, so that the **e** rang again. 776
4:12 his clothes rent, and *with* **e** upon his head. 127
5: 3 Dagon *was* fallen upon his face to the **e** 776
14:15 they also trembled, and the **e** quaked: 776
17:46 of the air, and to the wild beasts of the **e**; 776
17:46 that all the **e** may know that there is a God in 776
17:49 and he fell upon his face to the **e**. 776
20:15 of David every one from the face of the **e**. 127
24: 8 David stooped *with his* face to the **e**, and 776
25:41 bowed herself *on her* face to the **e**, and said, 776
26: 8 with the spear even to the **e** at once, and 776
26:20 let not my blood fall to the **e** before the face 776
28:13 unto Saul, I saw gods ascending out of the **e**. 776
28:20 Then Saul fell straightway all along on the **e**, 776
28:23 So he arose from the **e**, and sat upon the bed. 776
30:16 *they were* spread abroad upon all the **e**, 776
2Sa 1: 2 with his clothes rent, and **e** upon his head: 127
1: 2 that he fell to the **e**, and did obeisance. 776
4:11 of your hand, and take you away from the **e**? 776
7: 9 the name of the great *men* that *are* in the **e**. 776
7:23 what one nation in the **e** *is* like thy people, 776
12:16 and went in, and lay all night upon the **e**. 776
12:17 *and went* to him, to raise him up from the **e**: 776
12:20 David arose from the **e**, and washed, and 776
13:31 and tare his garments, and lay on the **e**; 776
14: 7 *neither* name nor remainder upon the **e**. 127
14:11 shall not one hair of thy son fall to the **e**. 776
14:20 of God, to know all *things* that *are* in the **e**. 776
15:32 him with his coat rent, and **e** upon his head: 127
18: 9 was taken up between the heaven and the **e**; 776
18:28 he fell down to the **e** upon his face before 776
22: 8 the **e** shook and trembled; the foundations of 776
22:43 did I beat them *as* small as the dust of the **e**, 776
23: 4 *as* the tender grass *springing* out of the **e** by 776
1Ki 1:31 Bath-sheba bowed *with her* face *to* the **e**, 776
1:40 so that the **e** rent with the sound of them. 776
1:52 there shall not a hair of him fall to the **e**: 776
2: 2 I go the way of all the **e**: be thou strong 776
4:34 from all kings of the **e**, which had heard of 776
8:23 in heaven above, or on **e** beneath, 776
8:27 But will God indeed dwell on the **e**? behold, 776
8:43 that all people of the **e** may know thy name, 776
8:53 them from among all the people of the **e**, 776
8:60 That all the people of the **e** may know that 776
10:23 exceeded all the kings of the **e** for riches 776
10:24 all the **e** sought to Solomon, to hear his 776
13:34 and to destroy *it* from off the face of the **e**. 127
17:14 day *that* the LORD sendeth rain upon the **e**. 127
18: 1 unto Ahab; and I will send rain upon the **e**. 127
18:42 he cast himself down upon the **e**, and put his 776
2Ki 5:15 now I know that *there is* no God in all the **e**, 776
5:17 given to thy servant two mules' burden of **e**? 127
10:10 Know now that there shall fall unto the **e** 776
19:15 thou alone, of all the kingdoms of the **e**; 776
19:15 of the earth; thou hast made heaven and **e**. 776
19:19 that all the kingdoms of the **e** may know that 776
1Ch 1:10 he began to be mighty upon the **e**. 776
1:19 because in his days the **e** was divided: 776
16:14 our God; his judgments *are* in all the **e**. 776
16:23 Sing unto the LORD, all the **e**; shew forth 776
16:30 Fear before him, all the **e**: the world also 776
16:31 Let the heavens be glad, and let the **e** rejoice: 776
16:33 because he cometh to judge the **e**. 776
17: 8 the name of the great *men* that *are* in the **e**. 776
17:21 what one nation in the **e** *is* like thy people 776
21:16 the angel of the LORD stand between the **e** 776
22: 8 thou hast shed much blood upon the **e** in my 776
29:11 and in the **e** *is thine*; thine *is* the kingdom, 776
29:15 our days on the **e** *are* as a shadow, and 776

2Ch 1: 9 a people like the dust of the **e** in multitude. 776
2:12 God of Israel, that made heaven and **e**, 776
6:14 no God like thee in the heaven, nor in the **e**; 776
6:18 God in very deed dwell with men on the **e**? 776
6:33 that all people of the **e** may know thy name, 776
9:22 king Solomon passed all the kings of the **e** in 776
9:23 all the kings of the **e** sought the presence of 776
16: 9 run to and fro throughout the whole **e**, 776
20:24 they *were* dead bodies fallen to the **e**, and 776
32:19 as against the gods of the people of the **e**, 776
36:23 All the kingdoms of the **e** hath the LORD 776
Ezr 1: 2 hath given me all the kingdoms of the **e**; 776
5:11 are the servants of the God of heaven and **e**, 772
Ne 9: 1 and with sackclothes, and **e** upon them. 127
9: 6 the **e**, and all *things* that *are* therein, the seas, 776
Job 1: 7 From going to and fro in the **e**, and 776
1: 8 that *there is* none like him in the **e**, a perfect 776
2: 2 From going to and fro in the **e**, and 776
2: 3 that *there is* none like him in the **e**, a perfect 776
3:14 With kings and counsellers of the **e**, 776
5:10 Who giveth rain upon the **e**, and 776
5:22 shalt thou be afraid of the beasts of the **e**. 776
5:25 and thine offspring as the grass of the **e**. 776
7: 1 *there* not an appointed time to man upon **e**? 776
8: 9 because our days upon **e** *are* a shadow:) 776
8:19 his way, and out of the **e** shall others grow. 6083
9: 6 Which shaketh the **e** out of her place, and 776
9:24 The **e** is given into the hand of the wicked: 776
11: 9 The measure thereof *is* longer than the **e**, and 776
12: 8 Or speak to the **e**, and it shall teach thee: and 776
12:15 he sendeth them out, and they overturn the **e**. 776
12:24 the heart of the chief of the people of the **e**, 776
14: 8 Though the root thereof wax old in the **e**, 776
14:19 things which grow out of the dust of the **e**; 776
15:19 Unto whom alone the **e** was given, and 776
15:29 he prolong the perfection thereof upon the **e**. 776
16:18 O **e**, cover not thou my blood, and let my cry 776
18: 4 shall the **e** be forsaken for thee? and shall 776
18:17 His remembrance shall perish from the **e**, 776
19:25 he shall stand *at* the latter *day* upon the **e**: 6083
20: 4 *not* this of old, since man was placed upon **e**, 776
20:27 and the **e** shall rise up against him. 776
22: 8 But *as for* the mighty man, he had the **e**; and 776
24: 4 the poor of the **e** hide themselves together. 776
24:18 as the waters; their portion is cursed in the **e**: 776
26: 7 *and* hangeth the **e** upon nothing. 776
28: 2 Iron is taken out of the **e**, and brass *is* 6083
28: 5 *As for* the **e**, out of it cometh bread: and 776
28:24 For he looketh to the ends of the **e**, *and* 776
30: 6 *in* caves of the **e**, and *in* the rocks. 6083
30: 8 of base men: they were viler than the **e**. 776
34:13 Who hath given him a charge over the **e**? or 776
35:11 teacheth us more than the beasts of the **e**, 776
37: 3 and his lightning unto the ends of the **e**. 776
37: 6 For he saith to the snow, Be thou *on* the **e**; 776
37:12 them upon the face of the world in the **e**. 776
37:17 when he quieteth the **e** by the south *wind?* 776
38: 4 thou when I laid the foundations of the **e**? 776
38:13 That *it* might take hold of the ends of the **e**, 776
38:18 Hast thou perceived the breadth of the **e**? 776
38:24 *which* scattereth the east wind upon the **e**? 776
38:26 To cause it to rain on the **e**, *where* no man *is;* 776
38:33 canst thou set the dominion thereof in the **e**? 776
39:14 Which leaveth her eggs in the **e**, and 776
41:33 Upon **e** there is not his like, who is made 6083
Ps 2: 2 The kings of the **e** set themselves, and 776
2: 8 the uttermost parts of the **e** *for* thy 776
2:10 O ye kings: be instructed, ye judges of the **e**. 776
7: 5 let him tread down my life upon the **e**, and 776
8: 1 how excellent *is* thy name in all the **e**! 776
8: 9 how excellent *is* thy name in all the **e**! 776
10:18 that the man of the **e** may no more oppress. 776
12: 6 *as* silver tried in a furnace of **e**, 776
16: 3 *But* to the saints that *are* in the **e**, and *to* 776
17:11 have set their eyes bowing down to the **e**; 776
18: 7 the **e** shook and trembled; the foundations 776
19: 4 Their line is gone out through all the **e**, and 776
21:10 Their fruit shalt thou destroy from the **e**, and 776
22:29 All *they that be* fat upon **e** shall eat and 776
24: 1 The **e** *is* the LORD'S, and the fulness 776
25:13 dwell at ease; and his seed shall inherit the **e**. 776
33: 5 the **e** is full *of* the goodness of the LORD. 776
33: 8 Let all the **e** fear the LORD: let all 776
33:14 he looketh upon all the inhabitants of the **e**. 776
34:16 cut off the remembrance of them from the **e**. 776
37: 9 upon the LORD, they shall inherit the **e**. 776
37:11 the meek shall inherit the **e**; and shall delight 776
37:22 such as be blessed of him shall inherit the **e**; 776
41: 2 *and* he shall be blessed upon the **e**: 776
44:25 to the dust: our belly cleaveth unto the **e**. 776
45:16 whom thou mayest make princes in all the **e**. 776
46: 2 though the **e** be removed, and though 776
46: 6 he uttered his voice, the **e** melted. 776
46: 8 what desolations he hath made in the **e**. 776
46: 9 maketh wars to cease unto the end of the **e**; 776
46:10 among the heathen, I will be exalted in the **e**. 776
47: 2 *is* terrible; *he is* a great King over all the **e**. 776
47: 7 For God *is* the King of all the **e**: sing ye 776
47: 9 for the shields of the **e** *belong* unto God: 776
48: 2 the joy of the whole **e**, *is* mount Zion, 776
48:10 so *is* thy praise unto the ends of the **e**: 776
50: 1 called the **e** from the rising of the sun unto 776
50: 4 and to the **e**, that *he* may judge his people. 776
57: 5 the heavens; *let* thy glory *be* above all the **e**. 776
57:11 the heavens: *let* thy glory *be* above all the **e**. 776
58: 2 weigh the violence of your hands in the **e**. 776
58:11 verily he is a God that judgeth in the **e**. 776
59:13 God ruleth in Jacob unto the ends of the **e**. 776
60: 2 Thou hast made the **e** to tremble; thou hast 776
61: 2 From the end of the **e** will I cry unto thee, 776
63: 9 *it,* shall go into the lower parts of the **e**. 776
65: 5 *art* the confidence of all the ends of the **e**, 776
65: 9 Thou visitest the **e**, and waterest it: 776
66: 4 All the **e** shall worship thee, and shall sing 776
67: 2 That thy way may be known upon **e**, 776
67: 4 and govern the nations upon **e**. 776
67: 6 *Then* shall the **e** yield her increase; *and* God, 776
67: 7 and all the ends of the **e** shall fear him. 776
68: 8 The **e** shook, the heavens also dropped at 776
68:32 Sing unto God, ye kingdoms of the **e**; O sing 776
69:34 Let the heaven and **e** praise him, the seas, 776
71:20 bring me up again from the depths of the **e**. 776
72: 6 the mown grass: as showers that water the **e**. 776
72: 8 and from the river unto the ends of the **e**. 776
72:16 There shall be a handful of corn in the **e** 776
72:16 of the city shall flourish like grass of the **e**. 776
72:19 let the whole **e** be filled *with* his glory; 776
73: 9 and their tongue walketh through the **e**. 776
73:25 *there is* none upon **e** *that* I desire beside thee. 776
74:12 working salvation in the midst of the **e**. 776
74:17 Thou hast set all the borders of the **e**: 776
74:20 for the dark places of the **e** are full *of* 776
75: 3 The **e** and all the inhabitants thereof *are* 776
75: 8 all the wicked of the **e** shall wring *them* out, 776
76: 8 from heaven; the **e** feared, and was still, 776
76: 9 to judgment, to save all the meek of the **e**. 776
76:12 of princes: *he is* terrible to the kings of the **e**. 776
77:18 the world: the **e** trembled and shook. 776
78:69 like the **e** which he hath established for ever. 776
79: 2 flesh of thy saints unto the beasts of the **e**. 776
82: 5 all the foundations of the **e** are out of course. 776
82: 8 Arise, O God, judge the **e**: for thou shalt 776
83:10 at En-dor: they became *as* dung for the **e**. 127
83:18 *art* the most High over all the **e**. 776
85:11 Truth shall spring out of the **e**; and 776
89:11 The heavens *are* thine, the **e** also *is* thine: 776
89:27 *my* firstborn, higher than the kings of the **e**. 776
90: 2 or ever thou hadst formed the **e** and 776
94: 2 Lift up thyself, thou judge of the **e**: render a 776
95: 4 In his hand *are* the deep places of the **e**: 776
96: 1 a new song: sing unto the LORD, all the **e**. 776
96: 9 beauty of holiness: fear before him, all the **e**. 776
96:11 Let the heavens rejoice, and let the **e** be glad; 776
96:13 for he cometh, for he cometh to judge the **e**: 776
97: 1 The LORD reigneth; let the **e** rejoice; 776
97: 4 the world: the **e** saw, and trembled. 776
97: 5 at the presence of the Lord of the whole **e**. 776
97: 9 For thou, LORD, *art* High above all the **e**: 776
98: 3 all the ends of the **e** have seen the salvation 776
98: 4 a joyful noise unto the LORD, all the **e**: 776
98: 9 the LORD; for he cometh to judge the **e**: 776
99: 1 *between* the cherubims; let the **e** be moved. 776
102:15 and all the kings of the **e** thy glory. 776
102:19 from heaven did the LORD behold the **e**; 776
102:25 Of old hast thou laid the foundation of the **e**: 776
103:11 For as the heaven is high above the **e**, *so* 776
104: 5 *Who* laid the foundations of the **e**, *that* it 776
104: 9 *that* they turn not again to cover the **e**. 776

E

Ps 104:13 the **e** is satisfied with the fruit of thy works. 776
104:14 that *he* may bring forth food out of the **e**; 776
104:24 made them all: the **e** is full *of* thy riches. 776
104:30 and thou renewest the face of the **e**. 127
104:32 He looketh on the **e**, and it trembleth: 776
104:35 Let the sinners be consumed out of the **e**, 776
105: 7 our God: his judgments *are* in all the **e**. 776
106:17 The **e** opened and swallowed up Dathan, and 776
108: 5 the heavens: and thy glory above all the **e**. 776
109:15 may cut off the memory of them from the **e**. 776
112: 2 His seed shall be mighty upon **e**: 776
113: 6 *the things that are* in heaven, and in the **e**? 776
114: 7 Tremble, thou **e**, at the presence of the Lord, 776
115:15 of the LORD which made heaven and **e**. 776
115:16 the **e** hath he given to the children of men. 776
119:19 I *am* a stranger in the **e**: hide not thy 776
119:64 The **e**, O LORD, is full *of* thy mercy: 776
119:87 They had almost consumed me upon **e**; but 776
119:90 thou hast established the **e**, and it abideth. 776
119:119 Thou puttest away all the wicked of the **e** 776
121: 2 from the LORD, which made heaven and **e**. 776
124: 8 of the LORD, who made heaven and **e**. 776
134: 3 made heaven and **e** bless thee out of Zion. 776
135: 6 and in **e**, in the seas, and all deep places. 776
135: 7 the vapours to ascend from the ends of the **e**; 776
136: 6 To him that stretched out the **e** above 776
138: 4 All the kings of the **e** shall praise thee, 776
139:15 wrought in the lowest parts of the **e**. 776
140:11 not an evil speaker be established in the **e**: 776
141: 7 one cutteth and cleaveth *wood* upon the **e**. 776
146: 4 His breath goeth forth, he returneth to his **e**; 127
146: 6 and **e**, the sea, and all that therein is: 776
147: 8 with clouds, who prepareth rain for the **e**, 776
147:15 He sendeth forth his commandment *upon* **e**: 776
148: 7 Praise the LORD from the **e**, ye dragons, 776
148:11 Kings of the **e**, and all people; princes, and 776
148:11 all people; princes, and all judges of the **e**: 776
148:13 his glory *is* above the **e** and heaven. 776
Pr 2:22 the wicked shall be cut off from the **e**, and 776
3:19 The LORD by wisdom hath founded the **e**; 776
8:16 and nobles, *even* all the judges of the **e**. 776
8:23 from the beginning, or ever the **e** was. 776
8:26 While as yet he had not made the **e**, nor 776
8:29 when he appointed the foundations of the **e**: 776
8:31 Rejoicing in the habitable part of his **e**; and 776
10:30 but the wicked shall not inhabit the **e**. 776
11:31 the righteous shall be recompensed in the **e**: 776
17:24 but the eyes of a fool *are* in the ends of the **e**. 776
25: 3 the **e** for depth, and the heart of kings *is* 776
30: 4 who hath established all the ends of the **e**? 776
30:14 to devour the poor from off the **e**, and 776
30:16 the **e** *that* is not filled *with* water; and the fire 776
30:21 For three *things* the **e** is disquieted, and 776
30:24 be four *things which are* little upon the **e**, 776
Ecc 1: 4 but the **e** abideth for ever. 776
3:21 of the beast that goeth downward to the **e**? 776
5: 2 for God *is* in heaven, and thou upon **e**: 776
5: 9 Moreover the profit of the **e** *is* for all: 776
7:20 For *there is* not a just man upon **e**, that doeth 776
8:14 There is a vanity which is done upon the **e**; 776
8:16 to see the business that is done upon the **e**: 776
10: 7 and princes walking as servants upon the **e**. 776
11: 2 knowest not what evil shall be upon the **e**. 776
11: 3 *of* rain, they empty *themselves* upon the **e**: 776
12: 7 shall the dust return to the **e** as it was: and 776
SS 2:12 The flowers appear on the **e**; the time of 776
Isa 1: 2 Hear, O heavens, and give ear, O **e**: for 776
2:19 into the caves of the **e**, for fear of 6083
2:19 when he ariseth to shake terribly the **e**. 776
2:21 when he ariseth to shake terribly the **e**. 776
4: 2 the fruit of the **e** *shall be* excellent and 776
5: 8 may be placed alone in the midst of the **e**! 776
5:26 will hiss unto them from the end of the **e**: 776
6: 3 of hosts: the whole **e** *is* full of his glory. 776
8:22 they shall look unto the **e**; and 776
10:14 eggs *that are* left, have I gathered all the **e**; 776
11: 4 reprove with equity for the meek of the **e**: 776
11: 4 he shall smite the **e** with the rod of his 776
11: 9 for the **e** shall be full *of* the knowledge of 776
11:12 of Judah from the four corners of the **e**. 776
12: 5 excellent things: this *is* known in all the **e**. 776
13:13 and the **e** shall remove out of her place, 776
14: 7 The whole **e** is at rest, *and* is quiet: 776
14: 9 for thee, *even* all the chief ones of the **e**; 776
14:16 *saying, Is* this the man that made the **e** to 776
14:26 purpose that is purposed upon the whole **e**: 776
18: 3 of the world, and dwellers on the **e**, see ye, 776
18: 6 of the mountains, and to the beasts of the **e**: 776
18: 6 all the beasts of the **e** shall winter upon 776
23: 8 traffickers *are* the honourable of the **e**? 776
23: 9 into contempt all the honourable of the **e**. 776
23:17 of the world upon the face of the **e**. 127
24: 1 the LORD maketh the **e** empty, and 776
24: 4 The **e** mourneth *and* fadeth away, the world 776
24: 4 the haughty people of the **e** do languish. 776
24: 5 The **e** also is defiled under the inhabitants 776
24: 6 Therefore hath the curse devoured the **e**, and 776
24: 6 therefore the inhabitants of the **e** are burned, 776
24:16 From the uttermost part of the **e** have we 776
24:17 *are* upon thee, O inhabitant of the **e**. 776
24:18 and the foundations of the **e** do shake. 776
24:19 The **e** is utterly broken down, the earth is 776
24:19 the **e** is clean dissolved, the earth is moved 776
24:19 clean dissolved, the **e** is moved exceedingly. 776
24:20 The **e** shall reel to and fro like a drunkard, 776
24:21 and the kings of the **e** upon the earth. 127
24:21 and the kings of the earth upon the **e**. 127
25: 8 people shall he take away from off all the **e**: 776
26: 9 for when thy judgments *are* in the **e**, 776
26:15 removed *it* far *unto* all the ends of the **e**. 776
26:18 have not wrought any deliverance *in* the **e**; 776
26:19 of herbs, and the **e** shall cast out the dead. 776
26:21 the inhabitants of the **e** for their iniquity: 776
26:21 the **e** also shall disclose her blood, and 776
28: 2 shall cast down to the **e** with the hand. 776
28:22 even determined upon the whole **e**. 776
30:23 bread of the increase of the **e**, and it shall be 127
33: 9 The **e** mourneth *and* languisheth: Lebanon is 776
34: 1 let the **e** hear, and all that is therein; 776
37:16 thou alone, of all the kingdoms of the **e**: 776
37:16 of the earth: thou hast made heaven and **e**. 776
37:20 that all the kingdoms of the **e** may know that 776
40:12 comprehended the dust of the **e** in a measure, 776
40:21 understood *from* the foundations of the **e**? 776
40:22 *It is* he that sitteth upon the circle of the **e**, 776
40:23 he maketh the judges of the **e** as vanity. 776
40:24 yea, their stock shall not take root in the **e**: 776
40:28 the Creator of the ends of the **e**, fainteth not, 776
41: 5 the ends of the **e** were afraid, drew near, and 776
41: 9 whom I have taken from the ends of the **e**, 776
42: 4 till he have set judgment in the **e**: 776
42: 5 he that spread forth the **e**, and that which 776
42:10 *and* his praise from the end of the **e**, ye that 776
43: 6 and my daughters from the ends of the **e**; 776
44:23 hath done *it*: shout, ye lower parts of the **e**: 776
44:24 that spreadeth abroad the **e** by myself; 776
45: 8 let the **e** open, and let them bring forth 776
45: 9 potsherd *strive* with the potsherds of the **e**. 127
45:12 I have made the **e**, and created man upon it: 776
45:18 God himself that formed the **e** and made it; 776
45:19 not spoken in secret, in a dark place of the **e**: 776
45:22 and be ye saved, all the ends of the **e**: 776
48:13 hand also hath laid the foundation of the **e**, 776
48:20 tell this, utter it *even* to the end of the **e**; 776
49: 6 be my salvation unto the end of the **e**. 776
49: 8 a covenant of the people, to establish the **e**, 776
49:13 be joyful, O **e**; and break forth *into* singing, 776
49:23 down to thee *with their* face *toward* the **e**, 776
51: 6 to the heavens, and look upon the **e** beneath: 776
51: 6 the **e** shall wax old like a garment, and 776
51:13 and laid the foundations of the **e**; 776
51:16 lay the foundations of the **e**, and say unto 776
52:10 all the ends of the **e** shall see the salvation of 776
54: 5 The God of the whole **e** shall he be called. 776
54: 9 of Noah should no more go over the **e**; 776
55: 9 For *as* the heavens are higher than the **e**, so 776
55:10 but watereth the **e**, and maketh it bring forth 776
58:14 thee to ride upon the high places of the **e**, 776
60: 2 the darkness shall cover the **e**, and 776
61:11 For as the **e** bringeth forth her bud, and 776
62: 7 and till he make Jerusalem a praise in the **e**. 776
63: 6 and I will bring down their strength to the **e**. 776
65:16 That he who blesseth himself in the **e** shall 776
65:16 he that sweareth in the **e** shall swear by 776
65:17 behold, I create new heavens and a new **e**: 776
66: 1 *is* my throne, and the **e** *is* my footstool: 776
66: 8 the **e** be made to bring forth in one day? 776
66:22 For as the new heavens and the new **e**, which 776

Jer	4:23	I beheld the **e**, and lo, *it was* without form,	776
	4:28	For this shall the **e** mourn, and the heavens	776
	6:19	Hear, O **e**: behold, I will bring evil upon this	776
	6:22	nation shall be raised from the sides of the **e**.	776
	7:33	of the heaven, and for the beasts of the **e**;	776
	8: 2	they shall be for dung upon the face of the **e**.	127
	9: 3	they are not valiant for the truth upon the **e**;	776
	9:24	judgment, and righteousness, in the **e**:	776
	10:10	at his wrath the **e** shall tremble, and	776
	10:11	that have not made the heavens and the **e**,	778
	10:11	*even* they shall perish from the **e**, and	772
	10:12	He hath made the **e** by his power, he hath	776
	10:13	the vapours to ascend from the ends of the **e**;	776
	14: 4	for there was no rain in the **e**, the plowmen	776
	15: 3	the beasts of the **e**, to devour and destroy.	776
	15: 4	to be removed into all kingdoms of the **e**,	776
	15:10	and a man of contention to the whole **e**!	776
	16: 4	they shall be as dung upon the face of the **e**:	127
	16: 4	fowls of heaven, and for the beasts of the **e**.	776
	16:19	shall come unto thee from the ends of the **e**,	776
	17:13	that depart from me shall be written in the **e**,	776
	19: 7	of the heaven, and for the beasts of the **e**.	776
	22:29	O **e**, earth, earth, hear the word of	776
	22:29	O earth, **e**, earth, hear the word of	776
	22:29	O earth, earth, **e**, hear the word of	776
	23: 5	shall execute judgment and justice in the **e**.	776
	23:24	Do not I fill heaven and **e**? saith the LORD.	776
	24: 9	into all the kingdoms of the **e** for *their* hurt,	776
	25:26	the world, which *are* upon the face of the **e**:	127
	25:29	for a sword upon all the inhabitants of the **e**,	776
	25:30	*grapes,* against all the inhabitants of the **e**.	776
	25:31	A noise shall come *even* to the ends of the **e**;	776
	25:32	shall be raised up from the coasts of the **e**.	776
	25:33	of the **e** even unto the *other* end of the earth:	776
	25:33	of the earth even unto the *other* end of the **e**:	776
	26: 6	this city a curse to all the nations of the **e**.	776
	27: 5	I have made the **e**, the man and the beast that	776
	28:16	I will cast thee from off the face of the **e**:	127
	29:18	to be removed to all the kingdoms of the **e**,	776
	31: 8	and gather them from the coasts of the **e**, *and*	776
	31:22	LORD hath created a new *thing* in the **e**,	776
	31:37	the foundations of the **e** searched out	776
	32:17	the **e** by thy great power and stretched out	776
	33: 9	and an honour before all the nations of the **e**,	776
	33:25	appointed the ordinances of heaven and **e**;	776
	34: 1	all the kingdoms of the **e** of his dominion,	776
	34:17	to be removed into all the kingdoms of the **e**.	776
	34:20	of the heaven, and to the beasts of the **e**.	776
	44: 8	a reproach among all the nations of the **e**?	776
	46: 8	he saith, I will go up, *and* will cover the **e**;	776
	49:21	The **e** is moved at the noise of their fall,	776
	50:23	How is the hammer of the whole **e** cut	776
	50:41	shall be raised up from the coasts of the **e**.	776
	50:46	At the noise of the taking of Babylon the **e** is	776
	51: 7	LORD'S hand, that made all the **e** drunken:	776
	51:15	He hath made the **e** by his power, he hath	776
	51:16	the vapours to ascend from the ends of the **e**:	776
	51:25	saith the LORD, which destroyest all the **e**:	776
	51:41	*how* is the praise of the whole **e** surprised!	776
	51:48	the heaven and the **e**, and all that *is* therein,	776
	51:49	so at Babylon shall fall the slain of all the **e**.	776
La	2: 1	cast down from heaven *unto* the **e** the beauty	776
	2:11	are troubled, my liver is poured upon the **e**,	776
	2:15	perfection of beauty, The joy of the whole **e**?	776
	3:34	crush under his feet all the prisoners of the **e**,	776
	4:12	The kings of the **e**, and all the inhabitants of	776
Eze	1:15	behold one wheel upon the **e** by the living	776
	1:19	the living creatures were lift up from the **e**,	776
	1:21	when those were lifted up from the **e**,	776
	7:21	a prey, and to the wicked of the **e** for a spoil;	776
	8: 3	the spirit lift me up between the **e** and	776
	8:12	seeth us not; the LORD hath forsaken the **e**.	776
	9: 9	The LORD hath forsaken the **e**, and	776
	10:16	lift up their wings to mount up from the **e**,	776
	10:19	and mounted up from the **e** in my sight:	776
	26:20	shall set thee in the low parts of the **e**,	776
	27:33	thou didst enrich the kings of the **e** with	776
	28:18	I will bring thee to ashes upon the **e** in	776
	31:12	all the people of the **e** are gone down from	776
	31:14	to the nether parts of the **e**, in the midst of	776
	31:16	be comforted in the nether parts of the **e**.	776
	31:18	trees of Eden unto the nether parts of the **e**:	776
	32: 4	I will fill the beasts of the whole **e** with thee.	776
	32:18	unto the nether parts of the **e**, with them that	776
	32:24	uncircumcised into the nether parts of the **e**,	776
	34: 6	flock was scattered upon all the face of the **e**,	776
	34:27	the **e** shall yield her increase, and they shall	776
	35:14	When the whole **e** rejoiceth, I will make thee	776
	38:20	and all creeping things that creep upon the **e**,	127
	38:20	all the men that *are* upon the face of the **e**,	127
	39:14	those that remain upon the face of the **e**,	776
	39:18	drink the blood of the princes of the **e**,	776
	43: 2	and the **e** shined with his glory.	776
Da	2:10	There is not a man upon the **e** that can shew	3007
	2:35	a great mountain, and filled the whole **e**.	772
	2:39	of brass, which shall bear rule over all the **e**.	772
	4: 1	languages, that dwell in all the **e**;	772
	4:10	a tree in the midst of the **e**, and the height	772
	4:11	the sight thereof to the end of all the **e**:	772
	4:15	leave the stump of his roots in the **e**,	772
	4:15	*be* with the beasts in the grass of the **e**:	772
	4:20	the heaven, and the sight thereof to all the **e**;	772
	4:22	and thy dominion to the end of the **e**.	772
	4:23	leave the stump of the roots thereof in the **e**,	772
	4:35	all the inhabitants of the **e** *are* reputed as	772
	4:35	and *among* the inhabitants of the **e**:	772
	6:25	languages, that dwell in all the **e**;	772
	6:27	and wonders in heaven and in **e**,	772
	7: 4	it was lifted up from the **e**, and made stand	772
	7:17	*are* four kings, *which* shall arise out of the **e**.	772
	7:23	beast shall be the fourth kingdom upon **e**,	772
	7:23	shall devour the whole **e**, and shall tread it	772
	8: 5	from the west on the face of the whole **e**,	776
	12: 2	many of them that sleep in the dust of the **e**	6083
Hos	2:18	and the sword and the battle out of the **e**,	776
	2:21	hear the heavens, and they shall hear the **e**;	776
	2:22	the **e** shall hear the corn, and the wine, and	776
	2:23	I will sow her unto me in the **e**; and I will	776
	6: 3	as the latter *and* former rain *unto* the **e**.	776
Joel	2:10	The **e** shall quake before them; the heavens	776
	2:30	shew wonders in the heavens and in the **e**,	776
	3:16	and the heavens and the **e** shall shake:	776
Am	2: 7	That pant after the dust of the **e** on the head	776
	3: 2	have I known of all the families of the **e**:	127
	3: 5	Can a bird fall in a snare upon the **e**,	776
	3: 5	shall *one* take up a snare from the **e**, and	127
	4:13	treadeth upon the high places of the **e**,	776
	5: 7	and leave off righteousness in the **e**,	776
	5: 8	and poureth them out upon the face of the **e**:	776
	8: 9	and I will darken the **e** in the clear day:	776
	9: 6	and hath founded his troop in the **e**;	776
	9: 6	and poureth them out upon the face of the **e**:	776
	9: 8	I will destroy it from off the face of the **e**;	127
	9: 9	yet shall not the least grain fall *upon* the **e**.	776
Jnh	2: 6	the **e** *with* her bars *was* about me for ever:	776
Mic	1: 2	hearken, O **e**, and all that therein is:	776
	1: 3	and tread upon the high places of the **e**.	776
	4:13	their substance unto the Lord of the whole **e**.	776
	5: 4	now shall he be great unto the ends of the **e**.	776
	6: 2	and ye strong foundations of the **e**:	776
	7: 2	The good *man* is perished out of the **e**: and	776
	7:17	move out of their holes like worms of the **e**:	776
Na	1: 5	the **e** is burnt at his presence, yea, the world,	776
	2:13	I will cut off thy prey from the **e**, and	776
Hab	2:14	For the **e** shall be filled with the knowledge	776
	2:20	let all the **e** keep silence before him.	776
	3: 3	the heavens, and the **e** was full *of* his praise.	776
	3: 6	He stood, and measured the **e**: he beheld,	776
	3: 9	Selah. Thou didst cleave the **e** *with* rivers.	776
Zep	2: 3	Seek ye the LORD, all ye meek of the **e**,	776
	2:11	for he will famish all the gods of the **e**; and	776
	3: 8	for all the **e** shall be devoured with the fire	776
	3:20	and a praise among all people of the **e**,	776
Hag	1:10	from dew, and the **e** is stayed *from* her fruit.	776
	2: 6	and the **e**, and the sea, and the dry *land;*	776
	2:21	I *will* shake the heavens and the **e**;	776
Zec	1:10	hath sent to walk to and fro through the **e**.	776
	1:11	We have walked to and fro through the **e**,	776
	1:11	behold, all the **e** sitteth still, and is at rest.	776
	4:10	which run to and fro through the whole **e**.	776
	4:14	that stand by the Lord of the whole **e**.	776
	5: 3	that goeth forth over the face of the whole **e**:	776
	5: 6	This *is* their resemblance through all the **e**.	776
	5: 9	and they lift up the ephah between the **e** and	776
	6: 5	from standing before the Lord of all the **e**.	776
	6: 7	*they* might walk to and fro through the **e**:	776
	6: 7	Get ye *hence,* walk to and fro through the **e**.	776
	6: 7	So they walked to and fro through the **e**.	776

Zec	9:10	and from the river *even* to the ends of the **e**.	776
	12: 1	layeth the foundation of the **e**, and	776
	12: 3	though all the people of the **e** be gathered	776
	14: 9	And the LORD shall be king over all the **e**:	776
	14:17	of the **e** unto Jerusalem to worship the King,	776
Mal	4: 6	lest I come and smite the **e** *with* a curse.	776
Mt	5: 5	*are* the meek: for they shall inherit the **e**.	1093
	5:13	Ye are the salt of the **e**: but if the salt have	1093
	5:18	Till heaven and **e** pass, one jot or one tittle	1093
	5:35	Nor by the **e**; for it is his footstool: neither	1093
	6:10	Thy will be done in **e**, as *it is* in heaven.	1093
	6:19	Lay not up for yourselves treasures upon **e**,	1093
	9: 6	Son of man hath power on **e** to forgive sins,	1093
	10:34	not that I am come to send peace on **e**:	1093
	11:25	Lord of heaven and **e**, because thou hast hid	1093
	12:40	and three nights in the heart of the **e**.	1093
	12:42	of the **e** to hear the wisdom of Solomon;	1093
	13: 5	stony *places*, where they had not much **e**:	1093
	13: 5	because *they* had no deepness of **e**:	1093
	16:19	whatsoever thou shalt bind on **e** shall be	1093
	16:19	whatsoever thou shalt loose on **e** shall be	1093
	17:25	of whom do the kings of the **e** take custom	1093
	18:18	Whatsoever ye shall bind on **e** shall be	1093
	18:18	whatsoever ye shall loose on **e** shall be	1093
	18:19	That if two of you shall agree on **e** as	1093
	23: 9	And call no *man* your father upon the **e**:	1093
	23:35	all the righteous blood shed upon the **e**,	1093
	24:30	and then shall all the tribes of the **e** mourn,	1093
	24:35	Heaven and **e** shall pass away, but	1093
	25:18	had received one went and digged in the **e**,	1093
	25:25	and went and hid thy talent in the **e**:	1093
	27:51	and the **e** did quake, and the rocks rent;	1093
	28:18	power is given unto me in heaven and in **e**.	1093
Mk	2:10	Son of man hath power on **e** to forgive sins,	1093
	4: 5	on stony ground, where it had not much **e**;	1093
	4: 5	it sprang up, because *it* had no depth of **e**:	1093
	4:28	For the **e** bringeth forth fruit of herself;	1093
	4:31	which, when it is sown in the **e**,	1093
	4:31	is less than all the seeds that be in the **e**:	1093
	9: 3	so as no fuller on **e** can white *them*.	1093
	13:27	from the uttermost part of the **e** to	1093
	13:31	Heaven and **e** shall pass away: but	1093
Lk	2:14	and on **e** peace, good will towards men.	1093
	5:24	of man hath power upon **e** to forgive sins,	1093
	6:49	a foundation built a house upon the **e**;	1093
	10:21	thank thee, O Father, Lord of heaven and **e**,	1093
	11: 2	Thy will be done, as in heaven, so in **e**.	1093
	11:31	for she came from the utmost parts of the **e**	1093
	12:49	I am come to send fire on the **e**; and	1093
	12:51	ye that I am come to give peace on **e**?	1093
	12:56	can discern the face of the sky and of the **e**;	1093
	16:17	And it is easier for heaven and **e** to pass,	1093
	18: 8	of man cometh, shall he find faith on the **e**?	1093
	21:25	and upon the **e** distress of nations,	1093
	21:26	those *things* which are coming on the **e**:	3625
	21:33	Heaven and **e** shall pass away: but	1093
	21:35	them that dwell on the face of the whole **e**.	1093
	23:44	there was a darkness over all the **e** until	1093
	24: 5	and bowed down *their* faces to the **e**,	1093
Jn	3:31	is above all: he that is of the **e** is earthly,	1093
	3:31	the earth is earthly, and speaketh of the **e**:	1093
	12:32	And I, if I be lifted up from the **e**, will draw	1093
	17: 4	I have glorified thee on the **e**: I have	1093
Ac	1: 8	and unto the uttermost part of the **e**.	1093
	2:19	in heaven above, and signs in the **e** beneath;	1093
	3:25	shall all the kindreds of the **e** be blessed.	1093
	4:24	and **e**, and the sea, and all that in them is:	1093
	4:26	The kings of the **e** stood up, and the rulers	1093
	7:49	Heaven *is* my throne, and **e** *is* my footstool:	1093
	8:33	for his life is taken from the **e**.	1093
	9: 4	And he fell to the **e**, and heard a voice	1093
	9: 8	And Saul arose from the **e**; and when his	1093
	10:11	at the four corners, and let down to the **e**:	1093
	10:12	all *manner of* fourfooted beasts of the **e**,	1093
	11: 6	and saw fourfooted beasts of the **e**, and	1093
	13:47	be for salvation unto the ends of the **e**.	1093
	14:15	and **e**, and the sea, and all *things* that are	1093
	17:24	seeing that he is Lord of heaven and **e**,	1093
	17:26	of men for to dwell on all the face of the **e**,	1093
	22:22	said, Away with such *a fellow* from the **e**:	1093
	26:14	And when we were all fallen to the **e**,	1093
Ro	9:17	might be declared throughout all the **e**.	1093
	9:28	a short work will the Lord make upon the **e**.	1093
	10:18	their sound went into all the **e**, and	1093
1Co	8: 5	whether in heaven or in **e**, (as there be gods	1093
	10:26	For the **e** *is* the Lord's, and the fulness	1093
	10:28	*for* conscience *sake:* for the **e** *is* the Lord's,	1093
	15:47	The first man *is* of the **e**, earthy: the second	1093
Eph	1:10	which are in heaven, and which are on **e**;	1093
	3:15	the whole family in heaven and **e** is named,	1093
	4: 9	first into the lower parts of the **e**?	1093
	6: 3	and thou mayest live long on the **e**.	1093
Php	2:10	and *things* **in e**, and *things* under the earth;	1919
	2:10	and *things* in earth, and *things* **under the e**;	2709
Col	1:16	and that are in **e**, visible and invisible,	1093
	1:20	*I say,* whether *they be things* in **e**, or	1093
	3: 2	on *things* above, not on *things* on the **e**.	1093
	3: 5	your members which are upon the **e**;	1093
2Ti	2:20	and of silver, but also of wood and **of e**;	3749
Heb	1:10	beginning hast laid the foundation of the **e**;	1093
	6: 7	For the **e** which drinketh *in* the rain that	1093
	8: 4	For if he were on **e**, he should not be a	1093
	11:13	they were strangers and pilgrims on the **e**.	1093
	11:38	and *in* dens and caves of the **e**.	1093
	12:25	not who refused him that spake on **e**,	1093
	12:26	Whose voice then shook the **e**: but now he	1093
	12:26	Yet once *more* I shake not the **e** only, but	1093
Jas	5: 5	Ye have lived in pleasure on the **e**, and	1093
	5: 7	waiteth for the precious fruit of the **e**,	1093
	5:12	neither by heaven, neither by the **e**,	1093
	5:17	it rained not on the **e** *by the space of* three	1093
	5:18	gave rain, and the **e** brought forth her fruit.	1093
2Pe	3: 5	and the **e** standing out of the water and	1093
	3: 7	But the heavens and the **e**, which are now,	1093
	3:10	the **e** also and the works that are therein	1093
	3:13	look for new heavens and a new **e**,	1093
1Jn	5: 8	And there are three that bear witness in **e**,	1093
Rev	1: 5	and the prince of the kings of the **e**.	1093
	1: 7	and all kindreds of the **e** shall wail because	1093
	3:10	the world, to try them that dwell upon the **e**.	1093
	5: 3	in heaven, nor in **e**, neither under the earth,	1093
	5: 3	in heaven, nor in earth, neither under the **e**,	1093
	5: 6	seven spirits of God sent forth into all the **e**.	1093
	5:10	and priests: and we shall reign on the **e**.	1093
	5:13	and on the **e**, and under the earth, and	1093
	5:13	and under the **e**, and such as are in the sea,	1093
	6: 4	that sat thereon to take peace from the **e**,	1093
	6: 8	unto them over the fourth *part* of the **e**,	1093
	6: 8	and with death, and with the beasts of the **e**.	1093
	6:10	our blood on them that dwell on the **e**?	1093
	6:13	And the stars of heaven fell unto the **e**,	1093
	6:15	And the kings of the **e**, and the great men,	1093
	7: 1	angels standing on the four corners of the **e**,	1093
	7: 1	holding the four winds of the **e**, that	1093
	7: 1	that the wind should not blow on the **e**,	1093
	7: 2	to whom it was given to hurt the **e** and	1093
	7: 3	Saying, Hurt not the **e**, neither the sea,	1093
	8: 5	with fire of the altar, and cast *it* into the **e**:	1093
	8: 7	with blood, and they were cast upon the **e**:	1093
	8:13	to the inhabiters of the **e** by reason of	1093
	9: 1	and I saw a star fall from heaven unto the **e**:	1093
	9: 3	came out of the smoke locusts upon the **e**:	1093
	9: 3	as the scorpions of the **e** have power.	1093
	9: 4	that they should not hurt the grass of the **e**,	1093
	10: 2	foot upon the sea, and *his* left *foot* on the **e**,	1093
	10: 5	and upon the **e** lifted up his hand to heaven,	1093
	10: 6	and the **e**, and the *things* that therein are,	1093
	10: 8	standeth upon the sea and upon the **e**.	1093
	11: 4	standing before the God of the **e**.	1093
	11: 6	and to smite the **e** with all plagues, as often	1093
	11:10	And they that dwell upon the **e** shall rejoice	1093
	11:10	tormented them that dwelt on the **e**.	1093
	11:18	shouldest destroy them which destroy the **e**.	1093
	12: 4	stars of heaven, and did cast them to the **e**:	1093
	12: 9	he was cast *out* into the **e**, and his angels	1093
	12:12	Woe to the inhabiters of the **e** and of	1093
	12:13	the dragon saw that he was cast unto the **e**,	1093
	12:16	And the **e** helped the woman, and the earth	1093
	12:16	and the **e** opened her mouth, and	1093
	13: 8	And all that dwell upon the **e** shall worship	1093
	13:11	another beast coming up out of the **e**;	1093
	13:12	and causeth the **e** and them which dwell	1093
	13:13	from heaven on the **e** in the sight of men,	1093
	13:14	And deceiveth them that dwell on the **e** by	1093
	13:14	saying to them that dwell on the **e**, that *they*	1093
	14: 3	which were redeemed from the **e**.	1093
	14: 6	to preach unto them that dwell on the **e**,	1093
	14: 7	and **e**, and the sea, and the fountains of	1093

Rev 14:15 thee to reap; for the harvest of the **e** is ripe. *1093*
14:16 sat on the cloud thrust in his sickle on the **e**; *1093*
14:16 sickle on the earth; and the **e** was reaped. *1093*
14:18 and gather the clusters of the vine of the **e**; *1093*
14:19 And the angel thrust in his sickle into the **e**, *1093*
14:19 and gathered the vine of the **e**, and cast *it* *1093*
16: 1 the vials of the wrath of God upon the **e**. *1093*
16: 2 and poured out his vial upon the **e**; *1093*
16:14 which go forth unto the kings of the **e** and *1093*
16:18 such as was not since men were upon the **e**, *1093*
17: 2 With whom the kings of the **e** have *1093*
17: 2 the inhabiters of the **e** have been made *1093*
17: 5 AND ABOMINATIONS OF THE **E**. *1093*
17: 8 and they that dwell on the **e** shall wonder, *1093*
17:18 which reigneth over the kings of the **e**. *1093*
18: 1 and the **e** was lightened with his glory. *1093*
18: 3 the kings of the **e** have committed *1093*
18: 3 the merchants of the **e** are waxed rich *1093*
18: 9 And the kings of the **e**, who have *1093*
18:11 And the merchants of the **e** *shall* weep and *1093*
18:23 thy merchants were the great men of the **e**; *1093*
18:24 and of all that were slain upon the **e**. *1093*
19: 2 which did corrupt the **e** with her *1093*
19:19 and the kings of the **e**, and their armies, *1093*
20: 8 which are in the four quarters of the **e**, *1093*
20: 9 And they went up on the breadth of the **e**, *1093*
20:11 from whose face the **e** and the heaven fled *1093*
21: 1 And I saw a new heaven and a new **e**: *1093*
21: 1 and the first **e** were passed away; *1093*
21:24 the kings of the **e** do bring their glory and *1093*

EARTHEN (10) [EARTH]
Lev 6:28 the **e** vessel wherein it is sodden shall be 2789
11:33 every **e** vessel, whereinto *any* of them 2789
14: 5 be killed in an **e** vessel over running water: 2789
14:50 he shall kill the one of the birds in an **e** 2789
Nu 5:17 the priest shall take holy water in an **e** 2789
2Sa 17:28 **e** vessels, and wheat, and barley, and flour, 3335
Jer 19: 1 Go and get a potter's **e** bottle, and *take* of 2789
32:14 put them in an **e** vessel, that they may 2789
La 4: 2 how are they esteemed as **e** pitchers, 2789
2Co 4: 7 But we have this treasure in **e** vessels, *3749*

EARTHLY (5) [EARTH]
Jn 3:12 If I have told you **e** *things,* and ye believe *1919*
3:31 he that is of the earth is **e**, *1093+1537+3588*
2Co 5: 1 For we know that if our **e** house of *this* *1919*
Php 3:19 glory *is* in their shame, who mind **e** *things.*) *1919*
Jas 3:15 not from above, but *is* **e**, sensual, devilish. *1919*

EARTHQUAKE (16) [EARTH, QUAKE]
1Ki 19:11 after the wind an **e**; *but* the LORD *was* not 7494
19:11 *but* the LORD *was* not in the **e**: 7494
19:12 after the **e** a fire; *but* the LORD *was* not in 7494
Isa 29: 6 with **e**, and great noise, *with* storm and 7494
Am 1: 1 Joash king of Israel, two year before the **e**. 7494
Zec 14: 5 like as ye fled from before the **e** in the days 7494
Mt 27:54 saw the **e**, and *those things* that were done, *4578*
28: 2 And behold, there was a great **e**: for *4578*
Ac 16:26 And suddenly there was a great **e**, so *4578*
Rev 6:12 the sixth seal, and lo, there was a great **e**; *4578*
8: 5 and thunderings, and lightnings, and an **e**. *4578*
11:13 And the same hour was there a great **e**, and *4578*
11:13 in the **e** were slain of men seven thousand: *4578*
11:19 and thunderings, and an **e**, and great hail. *4578*
16:18 and there was a great **e**, such as was not *4578*
16:18 the earth, so mighty an **e**, *and* so great. *4578*

EARTHQUAKES (3) [EARTH, QUAKE]
Mt 24: 7 and pestilences, and **e** in divers places. *4578*
Mk 13: 8 and there shall be **e** in divers places, and *4578*
Lk 21:11 And great **e** shall be in divers places, and *4578*

EARTHY (4) [EARTH]
1Co 15:47 The first man *is* of the earth, **e**: the second *5517*
15:48 As *is* the **e**, such *are they* also *that are* *5517*
15:48 *is* the earthy, such *are they* also *that are* **e**: *5517*
15:49 And as we have borne the image of the **e**, *5517*

EASE (20) [EASED, EASIER, EASILY, EASY]
Dt 23:13 it shall be, when thou wilt **e** thyself abroad, 3427
28:65 among these nations shalt thou **find** no **e**, 7280
Jdg 20:43 trode them down **with e** over against 4496
2Ch 10: 4 **e** thou **somewhat** the grievous servitude of 7043
10: 9 **E somewhat** the yoke that thy father did 7043
Job 7:13 my couch shall **e** my complaint; 5375
12: 5 despised in the thought of him that is **at e**. 7600
16:12 I was **at e**, but he hath broken me asunder: 7961
21:23 full strength, *being* wholly **at e** and quiet. 7946
Ps 25:13 His soul shall dwell at **e**; and his seed shall 2896
123: 4 *with* the scorning of those that are **at e**, 7600
Isa 1:24 I will **e** me of mine adversaries, and 5162
32: 9 Rise up, ye women that are **at e**, hear my 7600
32:11 Tremble, ye *women* that are **at e**; 7600
Jer 46:27 be in rest and **at e**, and none shall make 7599
48:11 Moab hath been **at e** from his youth, and 7599
Eze 23:42 a voice of a multitude being **at e** *was* with 7961
Am 6: 1 Woe to them *that are* **at e** in Zion, and trust 7600
Zec 1:15 displeased with the heathen *that are* **at e**: 7600
Lk 12:19 **take** thine **e**, eat, drink, *and* be merry. *373*

EASED (2) [EASE]
Job 16: 6 *though* I forbear, what am I **e**? 4480+1980
2Co 8:13 For *I mean* not that other *men* be **e**, and *425*

EASIER (8) [EASE]
Ex 18:22 so shall it be **e** for thyself, and 4480+7043
Mt 9: 5 For whether is **e**, to say, *Thy* sins be *2123*
19:24 It is **e** for a camel to go through the eye of a *2123*
Mk 2: 9 Whether is it **e** to say to the sick of *2123*
10:25 It is **e** for a camel to go through the eye of a *2123*
Lk 5:23 Whether is **e**, to say, Thy sins be forgiven *2123*
16:17 And it is **e** for heaven and earth to pass, *2123*
18:25 For it is **e** for a camel to go through a *2123*

EASILY (2) [EASE]
1Co 13: 5 is not **e provoked**, thinketh no evil; *3947*
Heb 12: 1 and the sin which doth so **e beset** *us,* and *2139*

EAST (157) [EASTWARD]
Ge 2:14 that *is it* which goeth **toward** the **e** of 6926
3:24 he placed at the **e** of the garden of Eden 6924
4:16 dwelt in the land of Nod, on the **e** of Eden. 6926
10:30 as thou goest unto Sephar, a mount of the **e**. 6924
11: 2 came to pass, as they journeyed from the **e**, 6924
12: 8 thence unto a mountain on the **e** of Beth-el, 6924
12: 8 Beth-el on the west, and Hai on the **e**: 6924
13:11 all the plain of Jordan; and Lot journeyed **e**: 6924
25: 6 he yet lived, eastward, unto the **e** country. 6924
28:14 to the **e**, and to the north, and to the south: 6924
29: 1 came into the land of the people of the **e**. 6924
41: 6 blasted with the **e wind** sprang up after 6921
41:23 withered, thin, *and* blasted with the **e wind**, 6921
41:27 the **e wind** shall be seven years of famine. 6921
Ex 10:13 the LORD brought an **e** wind upon 6921
10:13 the **e** wind brought the locusts. 6921
14:21 to go *back* by a strong **e** wind all *that* night, 6921
27:13 the breadth of the court on the **e** side 6924
38:13 for the **e** side eastward fifty cubits. 6924+1886.5
Lev 1:16 cast it beside the altar on the **e part**, by 6924
Nu 2: 3 on the **e side** toward the rising of the sun 6924
3:38 encamp before the tabernacle toward the **e**, 6924
10: 5 the camps that lie on the **e parts** shall go 6924
23: 7 out of the mountains of the **e**, 6924
34:10 ye shall point out your **e** border 6924+1886.5
34:11 Shepham *to* Riblah, on the **e side** of Ain; 6924
35: 5 the city *on* the **e** side two thousand cubits, 6924
Jos 4:19 in Gilgal, in the **e** border of Jericho. 4217
7: 2 on the **e side** of Beth-el, and spake unto 6924
11: 3 *And to* the Canaanite on the **e** and on 4217
12: 1 mount Hermon, and all the plain on the **e**: 4217
12: 3 the plain to the sea of Cinneroth on the **e**, 4217
12: 3 sea of the plain, *even* the salt sea on the **e**, 4217
15: 5 the **e** border *was* the salt sea, 6924+1886.5
16: 1 unto the water of Jericho on the **e**, 4217
16: 5 on the **e side** was Ataroth-addar, 4217
16: 6 and passed by it on the **e** *to* Janohah; 4217
17:10 on the north, and in Issachar on the **e**. 4217
18: 7 their inheritance beyond Jordan on the **e**, 4217
18:20 Jordan was the border of it on the **e** 6924+1886.5
19:13 on the **e** to Gittah-hepher, 4217+6924+1886.5
Jdg 6: 3 the Amalekites, and the children of the **e**, 6924
6:33 the children of the **e** were gathered 6924
7:12 all the children of the **e** lay along in 6924
8:10 left of all the hosts of the children of the **e**: 6924
8:11 them that dwelt in tents on the **e** of Nobah 6924
11:18 by the **e side** of the land of Moab, 4217+8121
21:19 on **the e side** of the highway 4217+8121+1886.1
1Ki 4:30 wisdom of all the children of the **e country**, 6924

1Ki 7:25 the south, and three looking toward the **e**: 4217
1Ch 4:39 *even* unto the **e** *side* of the valley, to seek 4217
5:10 they dwelt in their tents throughout all the **e** 4217
6:78 Jordan *by* Jericho, on the **e** *side* of Jordan, 4217
9:24 toward the **e**, west, north, and south. 4217
12:15 *both* toward the **e**, and toward the west. 4217
2Ch 4: 4 the south, and three looking toward the **e**: 4217
4:10 he set the sea on the right side of the **e end**, 6924
5:12 stood *at* the **e** *end* of the altar, and 4217
29: 4 and gathered them together into the **e** street, 4217
31:14 Imnah the Levite, the porter toward the **e**, 4217
Ne 3:26 over against the water gate toward the **e**, 4217
3:29 son of Shechaniah, the keeper of the **e** gate. 4217
Job 1: 3 was the greatest of all the men of the **e**. 6924
15: 2 and fill his belly *with* the **e wind**? 6921
27:21 The **e wind** carrieth him away, and 6921
38:24 *which* scattereth the **e wind** upon the earth? 6921
Ps 48: 7 the ships of Tarshish with an **e** wind. 6921
75: 6 For promotion *cometh* neither from the **e**, 4161
78:26 He caused an **e wind** to blow in the heaven: 6921
103:12 As far as the **e** is from the west, *so* far hath 4217
107: 3 from the **e**, and from the west, from 4217
Isa 2: 6 because they be replenished from the **e**, and 6924
11:14 they shall spoil them of the **e** together: 6924
27: 8 his rough wind in the day of the **e wind**. 6921
41: 2 raised up the righteous *man* from the **e**, 4217
43: 5 I will bring thy seed from the **e**, and 4217
46:11 Calling a ravenous bird from the **e**, the man 4217
Jer 18:17 I will scatter them as *with* an **e** wind before 6921
19: 2 which *is by* the entry of the **e** gate, and 2777
31:40 the corner of the horse gate towards the **e**, 4217
49:28 go up to Kedar, and spoil the men of the **e**. 6924
Eze 8:16 the LORD, and their faces towards the **e**; 6924
8:16 and they worshipped the sun towards the **e**. 6924
10:19 *every one* stood *at* the door of the **e** gate of 6931
11: 1 brought me unto the **e** gate of 6931
11:23 mountain which *is* on the **e side** of the city. 6924
17:10 utterly wither, when the **e** wind toucheth it? 6921
19:12 and the **e** wind dried up her fruit: 6921
25: 4 I *will* deliver thee to the men of the **e** for a 6924
25:10 Unto the men of the **e** with the Ammonites, 6924
27:26 the **e** wind hath broken thee in the midst of 6921
39:11 the valley of the passengers *on* the **e** of 6926
40: 6 gate which looketh toward the **e**, 6921+1886.5
40:22 of the gate that looketh towards the **e**; 6921
40:23 the gate toward the north, and toward the **e**; 6921
40:32 me into the inner court toward the **e**: 6921
40:44 one at the side of the **e** gate *having* 6921
41:14 of the separate place toward the **e**, 6921
42: 9 these chambers *was* the entry on the **e side**, 6921
42:10 of the wall of the court toward the **e**, 6921
42:12 way directly before the wall toward the **e**, 6921
42:15 the gate whose prospect *is* toward the **e**, 6921
42:16 He measured the **e** side with the measuring 6921
43: 1 *even* the gate that looketh toward the **e**: 6921
43: 2 God of Israel came from the way of the **e**: 6921
43: 4 of the gate whose prospect *is* toward the **e**. 6921
43:17 and his stairs *shall* look toward the **e**. 6921
44: 1 sanctuary which looketh *toward* the **e**; 6921
45: 7 from the **e** side eastward: 6924+1886.5
45: 7 the west border unto the **e** border. 6921+1886.5
46: 1 the **e** shall be shut the six working days; 6921
46:12 open him the gate that looketh *toward* the **e**, 6921
47: 1 forefront of the house *stood toward* the **e**, 6921
47: 8 These waters issue out toward the **e** 6930
47:18 the **e** side ye shall measure from Hauran, 6921
47:18 *by* Jordan, from the border unto the **e** sea. 6931
47:18 the east sea. And *this is* the **e** side. 6921+1886.5
48: 1 for these are his sides **e** *and* west; a *portion* 6921
48: 2 from the **e** side unto the west side, a *portion* 6921
48: 3 from the **e** side even unto the west 6921+1886.5
48: 4 from the **e** side unto the west side, 6921+1886.5
48: 5 from the **e** side unto the west side, 6921+1886.5
48: 6 from the **e** side even unto the west side, 6921
48: 7 from the **e** side unto the west side, a *portion* 6921
48: 8 of Judah, from the **e** side unto the west side, 6921
48: 8 from the **e** side unto the west side: 6921+1886.5
48:10 toward the **e** ten thousand *in* breadth, and 6921
48:16 on the **e** side four thousand and 6921
48:17 and toward the **e** two hundred and fifty, and 6921
48:21 of the oblation toward the **e** border, 6921+1886.5
48:23 from the **e** side unto the west side, 6921+1886.5
48:24 from the **e** side unto the west side, 6921+1886.5
48:25 from the **e** side unto the west side, 6921+1886.5
48:26 from the **e** side unto the west side, 6921+1886.5
48:27 from the **e** side unto the west side, 6921+1886.5
48:32 at the **e** side four thousand and 6921+1886.5
Da 8: 9 toward the **e**, and toward the pleasant *land*. 4217
11:44 tidings out of the **e** and out of the north 4217
Hos 12: 1 on wind, and followeth after the **e wind**: 6921
13:15 among *his* brethren, an **e** wind shall come, 6921
Joel 2:20 with his face toward the **e** sea, and 6931
Am 8:12 from the north even to the **e**, they shall run 4217
Jnh 4: 5 sat on the **e side** of the city, and there made 6924
4: 8 that God prepared a vehement **e** wind; 6921
Hab 1: 9 their faces shall sup up *as* the **e wind**, and 6921
Zec 8: 7 I *will* save my people from the **e** country, 4217
14: 4 which *is* before Jerusalem on the **e**, and 6924
14: 4 cleave in the midst thereof toward the **e** 4217
Mt 2: 1 there came wise men from the **e** to *395*
2: 2 for we have seen his star in the **e**, and *395*
2: 9 and lo, the star, which they saw in the **e**, *395*
8:11 That many shall come from the **e** and west, *395*
24:27 For as the lightning cometh out of the **e**, and *395*
Lk 13:29 And they shall come from the **e**, and *395*
Rev 7: 2 another angel ascending from the **e**, *395+2246*
16:12 that the way of the kings of the **e** *395+2246*
21:13 On the **e** three gates; on the north three *395*

EASTER (1)
Ac 12: 4 intending after **E** to bring him forth to *3957*

EASTWARD (40) [EAST]
Ge 2: 8 the LORD God planted a garden **e** 4480+6924
13:14 southward, and **e**, and westward: 6924+1886.5
25: 6 while he yet lived, **e**, unto the east country. 6924
Ex 27:13 the east side **e** *shall be* fifty cubits. 4217+1886.5
38:13 And for the east side **e** fifty cubits. 4217+1886.5
Lev 16:14 his finger upon the mercy seat **e**; 6924+1886.5
Nu 3:38 tabernacle of the congregation **e**, 4217+1886.5
32:19 is fallen to us on *this* side Jordan **e**. 4217+1886.5
34: 3 the outmost coast of the salt sea **e**: 6924+1886.5
34:11 the side of the sea of Chinnereth **e**: 6924+1886.5
34:15 on *this* side Jordan *near* Jericho **e**, 6924+1886.5
Dt 3:17 salt sea, under Ashdoth-pisgah **e**. 4217+1886.5
3:27 **e**, and behold *it* with thine eyes: 4217+1886.5
4:49 all the plain on *this* side Jordan **e**, 4217+1886.5
Jos 11: 8 and unto the valley of Mizpeh **e**; 4217+1886.5
13: 8 gave them, beyond Jordan **e**, 4217+1886.5
13:27 on the *other* side Jordan **e**. 4217+1886.5
13:32 the *other* side Jordan, *by* Jericho, **e**. 4217+1886.5
16: 6 the border went about **e** *unto* 4217+1886.5
19:12 turned from Sarid **e** *toward* 6924+1886.5
20: 8 the *other* side Jordan *by* Jericho **e**, 4217+1886.5
1Sa 13: 5 pitched in Michmash, **e** from Beth-aven. 6926
1Ki 7:39 the house **e** over against the south. 6924+1886.5
17: 3 turn thee **e**, and hide thyself by 6924+1886.5
2Ki 10:33 From Jordan **e**, all the land 4217+8121+1886.1
13:17 he said, Open the window **e**. And 6924+1886.5
1Ch 5: 9 **e** he inhabited unto the entering in of 4217
7:28 **e** Naaran, and westward 4217+1886.1+3807.1
9:18 hitherto *waited* in the king's gate **e**: 4217+1886.5
26:14 the lot **e** fell to Shelemiah. 4217+1886.5
26:17 **E** *were* six Levites, northward four a day, 4217
Ne 12:37 of David, even unto the water gate **e**. 4217
Eze 11: 1 LORD'S house, which looketh **e**: 6921+1886.5
40:10 **e** *were* three on this side, 1870+6921+1886.1
40:19 an hundred cubits **e** and north*ward*. 6921
45: 7 and from the east side **e**: 6921+1886.5
47: 1 under the threshold of the house **e**: 6921+1886.5
47: 2 utter gate *by* the way that looketh **e**; 6921
47: 3 **e**, he measured a thousand cubits, 6921
48:18 *portion shall be* ten thousand **e**, 6921+1886.5

EASY (4) [EASE]
Pr 14: 6 knowledge *is* **e** unto him that 7043
Mt 11:30 For my yoke *is* **e**, and my burden is light. *5543*
1Co 14: 9 by the tongue words **e to be understood**, *2154*
Jas 3:17 peaceable, gentle, *and* **e to be intreated**, *2138*

EAT (655) [ATE, EATEN, EATER, EATERS, EATEST, EATETH, EATING, MOTHEATEN, MOTH-EATEN]
Ge 2:16 tree of the garden thou mayest **freely e**: 398+398
2:17 of good and evil, thou shalt not **e** of it: 398
3: 1 Ye shall not **e** of every tree of the garden? 398
3: 2 We may **e** of the fruit of the trees of 398
3: 3 God hath said, Ye shall not **e** of it, 398
3: 5 For God doth know that in the day ye **e** 398

Ge	3: 6	did **e**, and gave also unto her husband with	398
	3: 6	also unto her husband with her; and he did **e**.	398
	3:11	I commanded thee that thou shouldest not **e**?	398
	3:12	with me, she gave me of the tree, and I did **e**.	398
	3:13	The serpent beguiled me, and I did **e**.	398
	3:14	and dust shalt thou **e** all the days of thy life:	398
	3:17	saying, Thou shalt not **e** of it:	398
	3:17	in sorrow shalt thou **e** *of* it all the days of thy	398
	3:18	to thee; and thou shalt **e** the herb of the field;	398
	3:19	In the sweat of thy face shalt thou **e** bread,	398
	3:22	of the tree of life, and **e**, and live for ever:	398
	9: 4	*which is* the blood thereof, shall you not **e**.	398
	18: 8	stood by them under the tree, and they did **e**.	398
	19: 3	did bake unleavened bread, and they did **e**.	398
	24:33	there was set *meat* before him to **e**: but	398
	24:33	he said, I will not **e**, until I have told mine	398
	24:54	they did **e** and drink, he and the men that	398
	25:28	because he did **e** of *his* venison:	6310+871.1
	25:34	he did **e** and drink, and rose up, and went his	398
	26:30	made them a feast, and they did **e** and drink.	398
	27: 4	as I love, and bring *it* to me, that I may **e**;	398
	27: 7	that I may **e**, and bless thee before	398
	27:10	that he may **e**, and that he may bless thee	398
	27:19	arise, I pray thee, sit and **e** of my venison,	398
	27:25	near to me, and I will **e** of my son's venison,	398
	27:25	And he brought *it* near to him, and he did **e**:	398
	27:31	my father arise, and **e** of his son's venison,	398
	28:20	will give me bread to **e**, and raiment to put	398
	31:46	a heap: and they did **e** there upon the heap.	398
	31:54	the mount, and called his brethren to **e** bread:	398
	31:54	they did **e** bread, and tarried all night in	398
	32:32	Therefore the children of Israel **e** not *of*	398
	37:25	they sat down to **e** bread: and they lift up	398
	39: 6	ought he had, save the bread which he did **e**.	398
	40:17	the birds did **e** them out of the basket upon	398
	40:19	and the birds shall **e** thy flesh from off thee.	398
	41: 4	leanfleshed kine did **e up** the seven well	398
	41:20	the ill favoured kine did **e up** the first seven	398
	43:25	for they heard that they should **e** bread there.	398
	43:32	which did **e** with him, by themselves:	398
	43:32	the Egyptians might not **e** bread with	398
	45:18	of Egypt, and ye shall **e** the fat of the land.	398
	47:22	did **e** their portion which Pharaoh gave them:	398
Ex	2:20	left the man? call him, that he may **e** bread.	398
	10: 5	they shall **e** the residue of that which is	398
	10: 5	shall **e** every tree which groweth for you out	398
	10:12	**e** every herb of the land, *even* all that the hail	398
	10:15	they did **e** every herb of the land, and all	398
	12: 7	post of the houses, wherein they shall **e** it.	398
	12: 8	they shall **e** the flesh in that night, roast with	398
	12: 8	*and* with bitter *herbs* they shall **e** it.	398
	12: 9	**E** not of it raw, nor sodden at all with water,	398
	12:11	thus shall ye **e** it; *with* your loins girded,	398
	12:11	staff in your hand; and ye shall **e** it in haste:	398
	12:15	Seven days shall ye **e** unleavened bread;	398
	12:16	save *that* which every man must **e**, that only	398
	12:18	ye shall **e** unleavened bread, until the one	398
	12:20	Ye shall **e** nothing leavened; in all your	398
	12:20	in all your habitations shall ye **e** unleavened	398
	12:43	There shall no stranger **e** thereof:	398
	12:44	hast circumcised him, then shall he **e** thereof.	398
	12:45	and a hired servant shall not **e** thereof.	398
	12:48	for no uncircumcised person shall **e** thereof.	398
	13: 6	Seven days thou shalt **e** unleavened bread,	398
	16: 3	*and* when we did **e** bread to the full;	398
	16: 8	shall give you in the evening flesh to **e**,	398
	16:12	At even ye shall **e** flesh, and in the morning	398
	16:15	bread which the LORD hath given you to **e**.	402
	16:25	Moses said, **E** that to day; for to day *is* a	398
	16:35	the children of Israel did **e** manna forty	398
	16:35	they did **e** manna, until they came unto	398
	18:12	to **e** bread with Moses' father in law before	398
	22:31	neither shall ye **e** *any* flesh *that is* torn *of*	398
	23:11	lie still; that the poor of thy people may **e**:	398
	23:11	they leave the beasts of the field shall **e**.	398
	23:15	thou shalt **e** unleavened bread seven days,	398
	24:11	also they saw God, and did **e** and drink.	398
	29:32	and his sons shall **e** the flesh of the ram,	398
	29:33	they shall **e** those *things* wherewith	398
	29:33	a stranger shall not **e** *thereof,* because	398
	32: 6	the people sat down to **e** and to drink, and	398
	34:15	and *one* call thee, and thou **e** of his sacrifice;	398
	34:18	seven days thou shalt **e** unleavened bread,	398
	34:28	he did neither **e** bread, nor drink water.	398
Lev	3:17	*that* ye **e** neither fat nor blood.	398
	6:16	thereof shall Aaron and his sons **e**:	398
	6:16	tabernacle of the congregation they shall **e** it.	398
	6:18	among the children of Aaron shall **e** of it.	398
	6:26	The priest that offereth it for sin shall **e** it:	398
	6:29	All the males among the priests shall **e**	398
	7: 6	Every male among the priests shall **e** thereof:	398
	7:19	*for* the flesh, all that be clean shall **e** thereof.	398
	7:21	**e** of the flesh of the sacrifice of peace	398
	7:23	Ye shall **e** no *manner* fat, of ox, or of sheep,	398
	7:24	but ye shall **in no wise e** of it.	398+398+3808
	7:26	Moreover ye shall **e** no *manner of* blood,	398
	8:31	there **e** it with the bread that *is* in the basket	398
	8:31	Aaron and his sons shall **e** it.	398
	10:12	and **e** it without leaven beside the altar:	398
	10:13	ye shall **e** it in the holy place, because it *is*	398
	10:14	heave shoulder shall ye **e** in a clean place;	398
	11: 2	These *are* the beasts which ye shall **e** among	398
	11: 3	among the beasts, that shall ye **e**.	398
	11: 4	Nevertheless these shall ye not **e** of them	398
	11: 8	Of their flesh shall ye not **e**, and	398
	11: 9	These shall ye **e** of all that *are* in the waters:	398
	11: 9	in the seas, and in the rivers, them shall ye **e**.	398
	11:11	ye shall not **e** of their flesh, but you shall	398
	11:21	Yet these may ye **e** of every flying creeping	398
	11:22	*Even* these of them ye may **e**; the locust after	398
	11:39	if any beast, of which ye may **e**, die; he that	402
	11:42	creep upon the earth, them ye shall not **e**;	398
	17:12	of Israel, No soul of you shall **e** blood,	398
	17:12	stranger that sojourneth among you **e** blood.	398
	17:14	Ye shall **e** the blood of no *manner of* flesh:	398
	19:25	in the fifth year shall ye **e** of the fruit thereof,	398
	19:26	Ye shall not **e** *any thing* with the blood:	398
	21:22	He shall **e** the bread of his God, *both* of	398
	22: 4	he shall not **e** of the holy *things,* until he be	398
	22: 6	shall not **e** of the holy *things,* unless he wash	398
	22: 7	shall afterward **e** of the holy *things;* because	398
	22: 8	is torn *with beasts,* he shall not **e** to defile	398
	22:10	There shall no stranger **e** *of* the holy *thing:* a	398
	22:10	a hired servant, shall not **e** *of* the holy *thing.*	398
	22:11	he shall **e** of it, and he that is born in his	398
	22:11	is born in his house: they shall **e** of his meat.	398
	22:12	she may not **e** of an offering of the holy	398
	22:13	*in* her youth, she shall **e** of her father's meat:	398
	22:13	but there shall no stranger **e** thereof.	398
	22:14	And if a man **e** *of* the holy *thing* unwittingly,	398
	22:16	when they **e** their holy *things:* for I	398
	23: 6	seven days ye must **e** unleavened bread.	398
	23:14	ye shall **e** neither bread, nor parched *corn,*	398
	24: 9	and they shall **e** it in the holy place:	398
	25:12	ye shall **e** the increase thereof out of	398
	25:19	ye shall **e** *your* fill, and dwell therein in	398
	25:20	shall say, What shall we **e** the seventh year?	398
	25:22	and **e** *yet* of old fruit until the ninth year;	398
	25:22	until her fruits come in ye shall **e** *of* the old	398
	26: 5	ye shall **e** your bread to the full, and dwell in	398
	26:10	ye shall **e** old store, and bring forth the old	398
	26:16	your seed in vain, for your enemies shall **e** it.	398
	26:26	and ye shall **e**, and not be satisfied.	398
	26:29	ye shall **e** the flesh of your sons, and	398
	26:29	and the flesh of your daughters shall ye **e**.	398
	26:38	and the land of your enemies shall **e** you **up**.	398
Nu	6: 3	liquor of grapes, nor **e** moist grapes, or dried.	398
	6: 4	All the days of his separation shall he **e**	398
	9:11	*and* **e** it with unleavened bread and	398
	11: 4	and said, Who shall **give** us flesh **to e**?	398
	11: 5	the fish, which we did **e** in Egypt freely;	398
	11:13	saying, Give us flesh, that we may **e**.	398
	11:18	against to morrow, and ye shall **e** flesh:	398
	11:18	Who shall **give** us flesh **to e**?	398
	11:18	LORD will give you flesh, and ye shall **e**.	398
	11:19	Ye shall not **e** one day, nor two days,	398
	11:21	them flesh, that they may **e** a whole month.	398
	15:19	*that* when ye **e** of the bread of the land,	398
	18:10	In the most holy *place* shalt thou **e** it;	398
	18:10	*place* shalt thou eat it; every male shall **e** it:	398
	18:11	every one *that is* clean in thy house shall **e** of	398
	18:13	every one *that is* clean in thine house shall **e**	398
	18:31	ye shall **e** it in every place, ye and	398
	23:24	he shall not lie down until he **e** *of* the prey,	398
	24: 8	he shall **e up** the nations his enemies, and	398
	25: 2	the people did **e**, and bowed down to their	398
Dt	2: 6	buy meat of them for money, that ye may **e**;	398
	2:28	shalt sell me meat for money, that I may **e**;	398

E

Dt 4:28 which neither see, nor hear, nor **e**, nor smell. 398
8: 9 A land wherein thou shalt **e** bread without 398
9: 9 I neither did **e** bread nor drink water: 398
9:18 I did neither **e** bread, nor drink water, 398
11:15 for thy cattle, that thou mayest **e** and be full. 398
12: 7 there ye shall **e** before the LORD your God, 398
12:15 thou mayest kill and **e** flesh in all thy gates, 398
12:15 the unclean and the clean may **e** thereof, 398
12:16 Only ye shall not **e** the blood; ye shall pour it 398
12:17 Thou mayest not **e** within thy gates the tithe 398
12:18 thou must **e** them before the LORD thy 398
12:20 I will **e** flesh, because thy soul longeth to eat 398
12:20 eat flesh, because thy soul longeth to **e** flesh; 398
12:20 thou mayest **e** flesh, whatsoever thy soul 398
12:21 thou shalt **e** in thy gates whatsoever thy soul 398
12:22 and the hart is eaten, so thou shalt **e** them: 398
12:22 and the clean shall **e** of them alike. 398
12:23 Only be sure that thou **e** not the blood: 398
12:23 and thou mayest not **e** the life with the flesh. 398
12:24 Thou shalt not **e** it; thou shalt pour it upon 398
12:25 Thou shalt not **e** it; that it may go well with 398
12:27 LORD thy God, and thou shalt **e** the flesh. 398
14: 3 Thou shalt not **e** any abominable *thing.* 398
14: 4 These *are* the beasts which ye shall **e**: the ox, 398
14: 6 the cud amongst the beasts: that ye shall **e**. 398
14: 7 Nevertheless these ye shall not **e** of them 398
14: 8 ye shall not **e** of their flesh, nor touch their 398
14: 9 These ye shall **e** of all that *are* in the waters: 398
14: 9 all that have fins and scales shall ye **e**: 398
14:10 hath not fins and scales ye may not **e**; 398
14:11 *Of* all clean birds ye shall **e**. 398
14:12 these *are they* of which ye shall not **e**: 398
14:20 *But* of all clean fowls ye may **e**. 398
14:21 Ye shall not **e** of any thing that dieth of 398
14:21 stranger that *is* in thy gates, that he may **e** it; 398
14:23 And thou shalt **e** before the LORD thy God, 398
14:26 thou shalt **e** there before the LORD thy 398
14:29 shall come, and shall **e** and be satisfied; 398
15:20 Thou shalt **e** it before the LORD thy God 398
15:22 Thou shalt **e** it within thy gates: the unclean 398
15:22 and the clean *person shall* **e** *it* alike, NIH
15:23 Only thou shalt not **e** the blood thereof; 398
16: 3 Thou shalt **e** no leavened bread with it; 398
16: 3 seven days shalt thou **e** unleavened bread 398
16: 7 **e** *it* in the place which the LORD thy God 398
16: 8 Six days thou shalt **e** unleavened bread: and 398
18: 1 they shall **e** the offerings of the LORD 398
18: 8 They shall have like portions to **e**, beside 398
20: 6 he die in the battle, and another man **e** of it. 2490
20:14 thou shalt **e** the spoil of thine enemies, 398
20:19 for thou mayest **e** of them, and thou shalt not 398
23:24 thou mayest **e** grapes thy fill at thine own 398
26:12 that they may **e** within thy gates, and 398
27: 7 shalt **e** there, and rejoice before the LORD 398
28:31 thine eyes, and thou shalt not **e** thereof: 398
28:33 shall a nation which thou knowest not **e up**; 398
28:39 nor gather *the grapes;* for the worms shall **e** 398
28:51 he shall **e** the fruit of thy cattle, and the fruit 398
28:53 And thou shalt **e** the fruit of thine own body, 398
28:55 of the flesh of his children whom he shall **e**: 398
28:57 for she shall **e** them for want of all *things* 398
32:13 that he might **e** the increase of the fields; 398
32:38 Which did **e** the fat of their sacrifices, *and* 398
Jos 5:11 they did **e** of the old corn of the land on 398
5:12 they did **e** of the fruit of the land of Canaan 398
24:13 and oliveyards which ye planted not do ye **e**. 398
Jdg 9:27 and did **e** and drink, and cursed Abimelech. 398
13: 4 strong drink, and **e** not any unclean *thing:* 398
13: 7 neither **e** any unclean *thing:* for the child 398
13:14 She may not **e** of any *thing* that cometh of 398
13:14 nor **e** any unclean *thing:* all that I 398
13:16 thou detain me, I will not **e** of thy bread: 398
14: 9 and he gave them, and they did **e**: 398
19: 4 so they did **e** and drink, and lodged there. 398
19: 6 and did **e** and drink both of them together: 398
19: 8 until afternoon, and they did **e** both of them. 398
19:21 they washed their feet, and did **e** and drink. 398
Ru 2:14 **e** of the bread, and dip thy morsel in 398
2:14 he reached her parched *corn,* and she did **e**, 398
1Sa 1: 7 therefore she wept, and did not **e**. 398
1:18 did **e**, and her countenance was no more 398
2:36 priests' offices, that *I* may **e** a piece of bread. 398
9:13 before he go up to the high place to **e**: 398
9:13 for the people will not **e** until he come, 398
9:13 *and* afterwards they **e** that be bidden. 398
9:19 for ye shall **e** with me to day, and to morrow 398
9:24 that which is left; set *it* before thee, *and* **e**: 398
9:24 So Saul did **e** with Samuel that day. 398
14:32 and the people did **e** *them* with the blood. 398
14:33 the LORD, in that they **e** with the blood. 398
14:34 man his sheep, and slay *them* here, and **e**; 398
20:24 was come, the king sat him down to **e** meat. 398
20:34 did **e** no meat the second day of the month: 398
28:22 **e**, that thou mayest have strength, when thou 398
28:23 he refused, and said, I will not **e**. But his 398
28:25 and before his servants; and they did **e**. 398
30:11 to David, and gave him bread, and he did **e**; 398
2Sa 3:35 **cause** David **to e** meat while it was yet day, 1262
9: 7 thou shalt **e** bread at my table continually. 398
9:10 that thy master's son may have food to **e**: 398
9:10 Mephibosheth thy master's son shall **e** bread 398
9:11 *said the king,* he shall **e** at my table, 398
9:13 for he did **e** continually at the king's table; 398
11:11 to **e** and to drink, and to lie with my wife? 398
11:13 called him, he did **e** and drink before him; 398
12: 3 it did **e** of his own meat, and drank of his 398
12:17 neither did he **e** bread with them. 1262
12:20 they set bread before him, and he did **e**. 398
12:21 child was dead, thou didst rise and **e** bread. 398
13: 5 that I may see *it,* and **e** *it* at her hand. 398
13: 6 cakes in my sight, that I may **e** at her hand. 1262
13: 9 *them* out before him; but he refused to **e**. 398
13:10 the chamber, that I may **e** of thine hand. 1262
13:11 when she had brought *them* unto him to **e**, 398
16: 2 and summer fruit for the young men to **e**; 398
17:29 and for the people that *were* with him, to **e**: 398
19:28 among them that did **e** at thine own table. 398
19:35 can thy servant taste what I **e** or what I 398
1Ki 1:25 behold, they **e** and drink before him, and say, 398
2: 7 and let them be of *those* that **e** at thy table: 398
13: 8 neither will I **e** bread nor drink water in this 398
13: 9 **E** no bread, nor drink water, 398
13:15 unto him, Come home with me, and **e** bread. 398
13:16 neither will I **e** bread nor drink water with 398
13:17 Thou shalt **e** no bread nor drink water there, 398
13:18 that he may **e** bread and drink water. 398
13:19 did **e** bread in his house, and drank water. 398
13:22 say to thee, **E** no bread, and drink no water; 398
14:11 of Jeroboam in the city shall the dogs **e**; 398
14:11 dieth in the field shall the fowls of the air **e**: 398
16: 4 dieth of Baasha in the city shall the dogs **e**; 398
16: 4 his in the fields shall the fowls of the air **e**. 398
17:12 for me and my son, that we may **e** it, and die. 398
17:15 she, and he, and her house, did **e** *many* days. 398
18:19 four hundred, which **e** *at* Jezebel's table. 398
18:41 said unto Ahab, Get thee up, **e** and drink; 398
18:42 So Ahab went up to **e** and to drink. 398
19: 5 touched him, and said unto him, Arise *and* **e**. 398
19: 6 he did **e** and drink, and laid him down again. 398
19: 7 and touched him, and said, Arise *and* **e**; 398
19: 8 did **e** and drink, and went in the strength of 398
19:21 and gave unto the people, and they did **e**. 398
21: 4 turned away his face, and would **e** no bread. 398
21: 7 *and* **e** bread, and let thine heart be merry: 398
21:23 The dogs shall **e** Jezebel by the wall of 398
21:24 dieth of Ahab in the city the dogs shall **e**; 398
21:24 dieth in the field shall the fowls of the air **e**. 398
2Ki 4: 8 and she constrained him to **e** bread. 398
4: 8 he passed by, he turned in thither to **e** bread. 398
4:40 So they poured out for the men to **e**. And it 398
4:40 in the pot. And they could not **e** *thereof.* 398
4:41 Pour out for the people, that they may **e**. 398
4:42 Give unto the people, that they may **e**. 398
4:43 said again, Give the people, that they may **e**: 398
4:43 They shall **e**, and shall leave *thereof.* 398
4:44 they did **e**, and left *thereof,* according to 398
6:22 that they may **e** and drink, and go to their 398
6:28 that we may **e** him to day, and we will eat 398
6:28 him to day, and we will **e** my son to morrow. 398
6:29 So we boiled my son, and did **e** him: and 398
6:29 next day, Give thy son, that we may **e** him: 398
7: 2 see *it* with thine eyes, but shalt not **e** thereof. 398
7: 8 did **e** and drink, and carried thence silver, 398
7:19 see *it* with thine eyes, but shalt not **e** thereof. 398
9:10 the dogs shall **e** Jezebel in the portion of 398
9:34 come in, he did **e** and drink, and said, Go, 398
9:36 In the portion of Jezreel shall dogs **e** 398
18:27 that *they* may **e** their own dung, and drink 398

2Ki	18:31	*then* **e** ye every man of his own vine, and	398
	19:29	Ye shall **e** *this* year such things as grow of	398
	19:29	and plant vineyards, and **e** the fruits thereof.	398
	23: 9	they did **e** of the unleavened bread among	398
	25:29	he did **e** bread continually before him all	398
1Ch	29:22	did **e** and drink before the LORD on that	398
2Ch	28:15	**gave** them **to e** and to drink, and	398
	30:18	yet did they **e** the passover otherwise than it	398
	30:22	they did **e** throughout the feast seven days,	398
	31:10	*we* have had enough to **e**, and have left	398
Ezr	2:63	that they should not **e** of the most holy *things*	398
	6:21	to seek the LORD God of Israel, did **e**,	398
	9:12	**e** the good of the land, and leave *it* for an	398
	10: 6	he did **e** no bread, nor drink water:	398
Ne	5: 2	we take up corn *for them,* that we may **e**,	398
	7:65	that they should not **e** of the most holy	398
	8:10	Go *your way,* **e** the fat, and drink the sweet,	398
	8:12	all the people went *their way* to **e**, and	398
	9:25	so they did **e**, and were filled, and	398
	9:36	gavest unto our fathers to **e** the fruit thereof	398
Est	4:16	neither **e** nor drink three days, night or day;	398
Job	1: 4	sent and called for their three sisters to **e** and	398
	3:24	For my sighing cometh before I **e**, and	3899
	31: 8	*Then* let me sow, and let another **e**; yea,	398
	42:11	and did **e** bread with him in his house:	398
Ps	14: 4	who **e up** my people *as* they eat bread, *and*	398
	14: 4	who eat up my people *as* they **e** bread, *and*	398
	22:26	The meek shall **e** and be satisfied: they shall	398
	22:29	All *they that be* fat upon earth shall **e** and	398
	27: 2	my foes, came upon me to **e up** my flesh,	398
	41: 9	in whom I trusted, which did **e** *of* my bread,	398
	50:13	Will I **e** the flesh of bulls, or drink the blood	398
	53: 4	who **e up** my people *as* they eat bread:	398
	53: 4	who eat up my people *as* they **e** bread:	398
	78:24	And had rained down manna upon them to **e**,	398
	78:25	Man did **e** angels' food: he sent them meat to	398
	78:29	So they did **e**, and were well filled: for he	398
	102: 4	like grass; so that I forget to **e** my bread.	398
	105:35	did **e up** all the herbs in their land, and	398
	127: 2	to sit up late, to **e** the bread of sorrows:	398
	128: 2	For thou shalt **e** the labour of thine hands:	398
	141: 4	and let me not **e** of their dainties.	3898
Pr	1:31	Therefore shall they **e** of the fruit of their	398
	4:17	For they **e** the bread of wickedness, and	3898
	9: 5	**e** of my bread, and drink of the wine *which*	3898
	13: 2	A man shall **e** good by the fruit of *his* mouth:	398
	13: 2	the soul of the transgressors *shall* **e**	NIH
	18:21	and they that love it shall **e** the fruit thereof.	398
	23: 1	When thou sittest to **e** with a ruler,	3898
	23: 6	**E** thou not the bread of *him that hath* an	3898
	23: 7	**E** and drink, saith he to thee; but his heart *is*	398
	24:13	My son, **e** thou honey, because *it is* good;	398
	25:16	**e** so much as is sufficient for thee, lest thou	398
	25:21	thine enemy *be* hungry, **give** him bread **to e**;	398
	25:27	*It is* not good to **e** much honey: so *for men* to	398
	27:18	Whoso keepeth the fig tree shall **e** the fruit	398
	30:17	pick it out, and the young eagles shall **e** it.	398
Ecc	2:24	*than* that he should **e** and drink, and *that* he	398
	2:25	For who can **e**, or who else can hasten	398
	3:13	And also that every man should **e** and drink,	398
	5:11	they are increased that **e** them:	398
	5:12	*man is* sweet, whether he **e** little or much:	398
	5:18	*is* good and comely *for one* to **e** and to drink,	398
	5:19	hath given him power to **e** thereof, and	398
	6: 2	yet God giveth him not power to **e** thereof,	398
	8:15	than to **e**, and to drink, and to be merry:	398
	9: 7	Go *thy way,* **e** thy bread with joy, and	398
	10:16	*is* a child, and thy princes **e** in the morning.	398
	10:17	and thy princes **e** in due season, for strength,	398
SS	4:16	into his garden, and **e** his pleasant fruits.	398
	5: 1	**e**, O friends; drink, yea, drink abundantly,	398
Isa	1:19	and obedient, ye shall **e** the good of the land:	398
	3:10	that *it shall be* well *with him:* for they shall **e**	398
	4: 1	We will **e** our own bread, and wear our own	398
	5:17	waste places of the fat ones shall strangers **e**.	398
	7:15	Butter and honey shall he **e**, that he may	398
	7:22	of milk *that they* shall give he shall **e** butter:	398
	7:22	honey shall every one **e** that is left in	398
	9:20	he shall **e** on the left hand, and they shall not	398
	9:20	they shall **e** every man the flesh of his own	398
	11: 7	and the lion shall **e** straw like the ox.	398
	21: 5	the table, watch *in* the watchtower, **e**, drink:	398
	22:13	let us **e** and drink; for to morrow we shall	398
	23:18	to **e** sufficiently, and for durable clothing.	398
	30:24	the young asses that ear the ground shall **e**	398
	36:12	that *they* may **e** their own dung, and drink	398
	36:16	**e** ye every one *of* his vine, and every one *of*	398
	37:30	Ye shall **e** *this* year such as groweth of itself;	398
	37:30	and plant vineyards, and **e** the fruit thereof.	398
	50: 9	old as a garment; the moth shall **e** them **up**.	398
	51: 8	For the moth shall **e** them **up** like a garment,	398
	51: 8	and the worm shall **e** them like wool:	398
	55: 1	come ye, buy, and **e**; yea, come, buy wine	398
	55: 2	**e** ye *that which is* good, and let your soul	398
	61: 6	ye shall **e** the riches of the Gentiles, and	398
	62: 9	they that have gathered it shall **e** it, and	398
	65: 4	which **e** swine's flesh, and broth of	398
	65:13	my servants shall **e**, but ye shall be hungry:	398
	65:21	shall plant vineyards, and **e** the fruit of them.	398
	65:22	they shall not plant, and another **e**:	398
	65:25	and the lion shall **e** straw like the bullock:	398
Jer	2: 7	to **e** the fruit thereof and the goodness	398
	5:17	they shall **e up** thine harvest, and thy bread,	398
	5:17	*which* thy sons and thy daughters should **e**:	398
	5:17	they shall **e up** thy flocks and thine herds:	398
	5:17	they shall **e up** thy vines and thy fig trees:	398
	7:21	offerings unto your sacrifices, and **e** flesh.	398
	15:16	Thy words were found, and I did **e** them; and	398
	16: 8	of feasting, to sit with them to **e** and to drink.	398
	19: 9	I will **cause** them **to e** the flesh of their sons	398
	19: 9	they shall **e** every one the flesh of his friend	398
	22:15	did not thy father **e** and drink, and	398
	22:22	The wind shall **e up** all thy pastors, and	7462
	29: 5	and plant gardens, and **e** the fruit of them;	398
	29:28	and plant gardens, and **e** the fruit of them.	398
	31: 5	and shall **e** *them* **as common things.**	2490
	41: 1	there they did **e** bread together in Mizpah.	398
	52:33	he did continually **e** bread before him all	398
La	2:20	Shall the women **e** their fruit, *and* children of	398
Eze	2: 8	open thy mouth, and **e** that I give thee.	398
	3: 1	unto me, Son of man, **e** that thou findest;	398
	3: 1	**e** this roll, and go speak unto the house of	398
	3: 2	my mouth, and he **caused** me **to e** that roll.	398
	3: 3	**cause** thy belly **to e**, and fill thy bowels with	398
	3: 3	did I **e** *it;* and it was in my mouth as honey	398
	4: 9	and ninety days shalt thou **e** thereof.	398
	4:10	thy meat which thou shalt **e** *shall be* by	398
	4:10	a day: from time to time shalt thou **e** it.	398
	4:12	thou shalt **e** it *as* barley cakes, and thou shalt	398
	4:13	Even thus shall the children of Israel **e** their	398
	4:16	they shall **e** bread by weight, and with care;	398
	5:10	Therefore the fathers shall **e** the sons in	398
	5:10	of thee, and the sons shall **e** their fathers;	398
	12:18	**e** thy bread with quaking, and drink thy	398
	12:19	They shall **e** their bread with carefulness,	398
	16:13	thou didst **e** fine flour, and honey, and oil:	398
	22: 9	in thee they **e** upon the mountains: in	398
	24:17	not *thy* lips, and **e** not the bread of men.	398
	24:22	not cover *your* lips, nor **e** the bread of men.	398
	25: 4	they shall **e** thy fruit, and they shall drink thy	398
	33:25	Ye **e** with the blood, and lift up your eyes	398
	34: 3	Ye **e** the fat, and ye clothe you with	398
	34:19	they **e** that which ye have trodden with	7462
	39:17	that ye may **e** flesh, and drink blood.	398
	39:18	Ye shall **e** the flesh of the mighty, and	398
	39:19	ye shall **e** fat till *ye* be full, and drink blood	398
	42:13	**e** the most holy *things:* there shall they lay	398
	44: 3	he shall sit in it to **e** bread before	398
	44:29	They shall **e** the meat offering, and the sin	398
	44:31	The priests shall not **e** *of* any thing that is	398
Da	1:12	let them give us pulse to **e**, and water to	398
	1:13	the countenance of the children that **e** *of*	398
	1:15	which did **e** the portion of the king's meat.	398
	4:25	they shall **make** thee **to e** grass as oxen,	2939
	4:32	they shall **make** thee **to e** grass as oxen,	2939
	4:33	did **e** grass as oxen, and his body was wet	399
Hos	2:12	and the beasts of the field shall **e** them.	398
	4: 8	They **e** *up* the sin of my people, and they set	398
	4:10	For they shall **e**, and not have enough:	398
	8:13	and **e** *it; but* the LORD accepteth them not;	398
	9: 3	and they shall **e** unclean *things* in Assyria.	398
	9: 4	all that **e** thereof shall be polluted:	398
Joel	2:26	ye shall **e in plenty**, and be satisfied,	398+398
Am	6: 4	**e** the lambs out of the flock, and the calves	398
	7: 4	devoured the great deep, and did **e up** a part.	398
	7:12	and there **e** bread, and prophesy there:	398
	9:14	also make gardens, and **e** the fruit of them.	398
Ob	1: 7	*they that* **e** thy bread have laid a wound	NIH

Mic 3: 3 Who also e the flesh of my people, and 398
6:14 Thou shalt e, but not be satisfied; and 398
7: 1 *there is* no cluster to e: my soul desired 398
Na 3:15 it shall e thee up like the cankerworm: 398
Hab 1: 8 they shall fly as the eagle *that* hasteth to e. 398
Hag 1: 6 *ye* e, but ye have not enough; *ye* drink, but 398
Zec 7: 6 when ye did e, and when ye did drink, did 398
7: 6 did not ye e *for yourselves,* and drink *for* 398
11: 9 let the rest e every one the flesh of another. 398
11:16 he shall e the flesh of the fat, and tear their 398
Mt 6:25 what ye shall e, or what ye shall drink; 5315
6:31 take no thought, saying, What shall we e? 5315
12: 1 began to pluck the ears of corn, and to e. 2068
12: 4 and did e the shewbread, which was not 5315
12: 4 which was not lawful for him to e, 5315
14:16 They need not depart; give ye them to e. 5315
14:20 And they did all e, and were filled: and 5315
15: 2 for they wash not their hands when they e 2068
15:20 to e with unwashen hands defileth not a 5315
15:27 yet the dogs e of the crumbs which fall 2068
15:32 me now three days, and have nothing to e: 5315
15:37 And they did all e, and were filled: and 5315
15:38 And they that did e were four thousand 2068
24:49 and to e and drink with the drunken; 2068
26:17 *that* we prepare for thee to e the passover? 5315
26:21 And as they did e, he said, Verily I say unto 2068
26:26 gave *it* to the disciples, and said, Take, e; 5315
Mk 1: 6 and he did e locusts and wild honey; 2068
2:16 and Pharisees saw him e with publicans and 2068
2:26 and did e the shewbread, which is not 5315
2:26 which is not lawful to e but for the priests, 5315
3:20 so that they could not so much as e bread. 5315
5:43 that *something* should be given her to e. 5315
6:31 and they had no leisure so much as to e. 5315
6:36 for they have nothing to e. 5315
6:37 and said unto them, Give ye them to e. 5315
6:37 pennyworth of bread, and give them to e? 5315
6:42 And they did all e, and were filled. 5315
6:44 And they that did e *of* the loaves were 5315
7: 2 And when they saw some of his disciples e 2068
7: 3 except they wash *their* hands oft, e not, 2068
7: 4 the market, except they wash, they e not. 2068
7: 5 but e bread with unwashen hands? 2068
7:28 yet the dogs under the table e of 2068
8: 1 and having nothing to e, Jesus called his 5315
8: 2 with me three days, and have nothing to e: 5315
8: 8 So they did e, and were filled: and 5315
11:14 No *man* e fruit of thee hereafter for ever. 5315
14:12 prepare that thou mayest e the passover? 5315
14:14 where I shall e the passover with my 5315
14:18 And as they sat and did e, Jesus said, 2068
14:22 And as they did e, Jesus took bread, and 2068
14:22 and gave to them, and said, Take, e: 5315
Lk 4: 2 And in those days he did e nothing: and 5315
5:30 Why do ye e and drink with publicans and 2068
5:33 of the Pharisees; but thine e and drink? 2068
6: 1 and did e, rubbing *them* in *their* hands. 2068
6: 4 of God, and did take and e the shewbread, 5315
6: 4 which it is not lawful to e but for the priests 5315
7:36 desired him that he would e with him. 5315
9:13 But he said unto them, Give ye them to e. 5315
9:17 And they did e, and were all filled: and 5315
10: 8 e such *things* as are set before you: 2068
12:19 take thine ease, e, drink, *and* be merry. 5315
12:22 no thought for your life, what ye shall e; 5315
12:29 And seek not ye what ye shall e, or what ye 5315
12:45 and to e and drink, and to be drunken; 2068
14: 1 Pharisees to e bread on the sabbath day, 5315
14:15 Blessed *is he* that shall e bread in 5315
15:16 belly with the husks that the swine did e: 2068
15:23 and kill *it;* and let us e, and be merry: 5315
17: 8 and afterward thou shalt e and drink? 5315
17:27 They did e, they drank, they married *wives,* 2068
17:28 they did e, they drank, they bought, 2068
22: 8 and prepare us the passover, that we may e. 5315
22:11 where I shall e the passover with my 5315
22:15 With desire I have desired to e this 5315
22:16 say unto you, I will not any more e thereof, 5315
22:30 That ye may e and drink at my table in my 2068
24:43 And he took *it,* and did e before them. 5315
Jn 4:31 *his* disciples prayed him, saying, Master, e. 5315
4:32 I have meat to e that ye know not of. 5315
4:33 Hath any *man* brought him *ought* to e? 5315
6: 5 shall we buy bread, that these may e? 5315
6:23 nigh unto the place where they did e bread, 5315
6:26 but because ye did e of the loaves, and 5315
6:31 Our fathers did e manna in the desert; as it 5315
6:31 He gave them bread from heaven to e. 5315
6:49 Your fathers did e manna in the wilderness, 5315
6:50 from heaven, that a man may e thereof, 5315
6:51 if any *man* e of this bread, he shall live for 5315
6:52 How can this *man* give us *his* flesh to e? 5315
6:53 Except ye e the flesh of the Son of man, 5315
6:58 not as your fathers did e manna, and 5315
18:28 but that they might e the passover. 5315
Ac 2:46 did e *their* meat with gladness and 3335
9: 9 without sight, and neither did e nor drink. 5315
10:13 a voice to him, Rise, Peter; kill, and e. 5315
10:41 who did e and drink with him after he rose 4906
11: 3 men uncircumcised, and didst e with them. 4906
11: 7 saying unto me, Arise, Peter; slay and e. 5315
23:12 saying that *they* would neither e nor drink 5315
23:14 that *we* will e nothing until we have slain 1089
23:21 that *they* will neither e nor drink till they 5315
27:35 and when he had broken *it,* he began to e. 2068
Ro 14: 2 For one believeth that *he* may e all *things:* 5315
14:21 *It is* good neither to e flesh, nor to drink 5315
14:23 And he that doubteth is damned if he e, 5315
1Co 5:11 an extortioner; with such a one no not to e. 4906
8: 7 e *it* as a thing offered unto an idol; 2068
8: 8 for neither, if we e, are we the better; 5315
8: 8 neither, if we e not, are we the worse. 5315
8:10 to e those things which are offered to idols; 2068
8:13 I will e no flesh while the world standeth, 5315
9: 4 Have we not power to e and to drink? 5315
10: 3 And did all e the same spiritual meat; 5315
10: 7 The people sat down to e and drink, and 5315
10:18 are not they which e *of* the sacrifices 2068
10:25 Whatsoever is sold in the shambles, *that* e, 2068
10:27 whatsoever is set before you, e, asking no 2068
10:28 e not for his sake that shewed *it,* and 2068
10:31 Whether therefore ye e, or drink, or 2068
11:20 one place, *this* is not to e the Lord's supper. 5315
11:22 have ye not houses to e and to drink *in?* or 2068
11:24 given thanks, he brake *it,* and said, Take, e: 5315
11:26 For as often as ye e this bread, and 2068
11:27 Wherefore whosoever shall e this bread, 2068
11:28 and so let him e of *that* bread, and drink of 2068
11:33 my brethren, when ye come together to e, 5315
11:34 And if any *man* hunger, let him e at home; 2068
15:32 let us e and drink; for to morrow we die. 5315
Gal 2:12 from James, he did e with the Gentiles: 4906
2Th 3: 8 Neither did we e any *man's* bread for 5315
3:10 if any would not work, neither should he e. 2068
3:12 quietness they work, and e their own bread. 2068
2Ti 2:17 And their word will e as *doth* a 2192+3542
Heb 13:10 whereof they have no right to e which serve 5315
Jas 5: 3 and shall e your flesh as *it were* fire: 5315
Rev 2: 7 To him that overcometh will I give to e of 5315
2:14 to e things sacrificed unto idols, and 5315
2:17 To him that overcometh will I give to e of 5315
2:20 and to e things sacrificed unto idols. 5315
10: 9 And he said unto me, Take *it,* and e it up; 2719
17:16 and shall e her flesh, and burn her with fire. 5315
19:18 That ye may e the flesh of kings, and 5315

EATEN (104) [EAT]

Ge 3:11 Hast thou e of the tree, whereof I 398
3:17 hast e of the tree, of which I commanded 398
6:21 And take thou unto thee of all food that is e, 398
14:24 Save only that which the young men have e, 398
27:33 I have e of all before thou camest, and 398
31:38 and the rams of thy flock have I not e. 398
41:21 when they had e them up, it 413+935+7130
41:21 be known that they had e them; 413+935+7130
43: 2 when they had e up the corn which they had 398
Ex 12:46 In one house shall it be e; thou shalt not 398
13: 3 *place:* there shall no leavened bread be e. 398
13: 7 Unleavened bread shall be e seven days; and 398
21:28 be surely stoned, and his flesh shall not be e; 398
22: 5 man shall cause a field or vineyard to be e, 1197
29:34 with fire: it shall not be e, because it *is* holy. 398
Lev 6:16 *with* unleavened bread shall it be e in 398
6:23 priest shall be wholly *burnt:* it shall not be e. 398
6:26 in the holy place shall it be e, in the court of 398
6:30 reconcile *withal* in the holy *place,* shall be e: 398
7: 6 it shall be e in the holy place: it *is* most holy. 398

Lev 7:15 shall be **e** the same day that it is offered; 398
7:16 it shall be **e** the *same* day that he offereth his 398
7:16 morrow also the remainder of it shall be **e**: 398
7:18 offerings be **e at all** on the third day, 398+398
7:19 toucheth any unclean *thing* shall not be **e**; 398
10:17 Wherefore have ye not **e** the sin offering in 398
10:18 **indeed** have **e** it in the holy *place*, as I 398+398
10:19 *if* I had **e** the sin offering to day, should it 398
11:13 they shall not be **e**, they *are* an abomination: 398
11:34 Of all meat which may be **e**, *that* on which 398
11:41 *shall be* an abomination; it shall not be **e**. 398
11:47 between the beast that may be **e** and 398
11:47 be eaten and the beast that may not be **e**. 398
17:13 and catcheth *any* beast or fowl that may be **e**; 398
19: 6 It shall be **e** the *same* day ye offer it, and 398
19: 7 if it be **e at all** on the third day, it *is* 398+398
19:23 uncircumcised unto you: it shall not be **e** of. 398
22:30 On the same day it shall be **e up**; ye shall 398
Nu 28:17 seven days shall unleavened bread be **e**. 398
Dt 6:11 when thou shalt have **e** and be full; 398
8:10 When thou hast **e** and art full, then thou shalt 398
8:12 Lest *when* thou hast **e** and art full, and 398
12:22 Even as the roebuck and the hart is **e**, so 398
14:19 *is* unclean unto you: they shall not be **e**. 398
20: 6 planted a vineyard, and hath not *yet* **e** of it? 2490
26:14 I have not **e** thereof in my mourning, 398
29: 6 Ye have not **e** bread, neither have you drunk 398
31:20 they shall have **e** and filled *themselves,* and 398
Jos 5:12 after they had **e** of the old corn of the land; 398
Ru 3: 7 when Boaz had **e** and drunk, and his heart 398
1Sa 1: 9 So Hannah rose up after *they* had **e** in 398
14:30 if haply the people had **e freely** to day 398+398
28:20 for he had **e** no bread all the day, nor all 398
30:12 when he had **e**, his spirit came again to him: 398
30:12 for he had **e** no bread, nor drunk *any* water, 398
2Sa 19:42 have we **e at all** of the king's *cost?* or 398+398
1Ki 13:22 hast **e** bread and drunk water in the place, 398
13:23 after he had **e** bread, and after he had drunk, 398
13:28 the lion had not **e** the carcase, nor torn 398
2Ki 6:23 when they had **e** and drunk, he sent them 398
Ne 5:14 my brethren have not **e** the bread of 398
Job 6: 6 Can that which is unsavoury be **e** without 398
31:17 Or have **e** my morsel myself alone, and 398
31:17 and the fatherless hath not **e** thereof; 398
31:39 If I have **e** the fruits thereof without money, 398
Ps 69: 9 For the zeal of thine house hath **e** me **up**; 398
102: 9 For I have **e** ashes like bread, and 398
Pr 9:17 are sweet, and bread *e* in secret is pleasant. NIH
23: 8 The morsel *which* thou hast **e** shalt thou 398
SS 5: 1 I have **e** my honeycomb with my honey; 398
Isa 3:14 for ye have **e up** the vineyard; the spoil of 1197
5: 5 the hedge thereof, and it shall be **e up**; 1197
6:13 a tenth, and *it* shall return, and shall be **e**: 1197
44:19 **e** *it:* and shall I make the residue thereof an 398
Jer 10:25 for they have **e up** Jacob, and devoured him, 398
24: 2 which could not be **e**, they were so bad. 398
24: 3 very evil, that cannot be **e**, they are so evil. 398
24: 8 evil figs, which cannot be **e**, they are so evil; 398
29:17 vile figs, that cannot be **e**, they are so evil. 398
31:29 The fathers have **e** a sour grape, and 398
Eze 4:14 now have I not **e** *of* that which dieth of itself, 398
18: 2 The fathers have **e** sour grapes, and 398
18: 6 *And* hath not **e** upon the mountains, 398
18:11 but even hath **e** upon the mountains, 398
18:15 *That* hath not **e** upon the mountains, 398
34:18 unto you to have **e up** the good pasture, 7462
45:21 of seven days; unleavened bread shall be **e**. 398
Hos 10:13 reaped iniquity; ye have **e** the fruit of lies: 398
Joel 1: 4 the palmerworm hath left hath the locust **e**; 398
1: 4 the locust hath left hath the cankerworm **e**; 398
1: 4 cankerworm hath left hath the caterpillar **e**. 398
2:25 to you the years that the locust hath **e**, 398
Mt 14:21 And they that had **e** were about five *2068*
Mk 8: 9 And they that had **e** were about four *5315*
Lk 13:26 We have **e** and drunk in thy presence, and *5315*
17: 8 and serve me, till I have **e** and drunken; *5315*
Jn 2:17 The zeal of thine house hath **e** me **up**. *2719*
6:13 and above unto them that had **e**. *977*
Ac 10:10 he became very hungry, and would have **e**: *1089*
10:14 for I have never **e** any *thing that is* common *5315*
12:23 and he was **e of worms**, and gave up *4662*
20:11 and **e**, and talked a long while, *1089*
27:38 And when they had **e enough**, *2880+5160*
Rev 10:10 and as soon as I had **e** it, my belly was *5315*

EATER (3) [EAT]
Jdg 14:14 Out of the **e** came forth meat, and out of 398
Isa 55:10 give seed to the sower, and bread to the **e**: 398
Na 3:12 they shall even fall into the mouth of the **e**. 398

EATERS (1) [EAT]
Pr 23:20 amongst **riotous e** of flesh: 2151

EATEST (3) [EAT]
Ge 2:17 for in the day that thou **e** thereof thou shalt 398
1Sa 1: 8 why **e** thou not? and why is thy heart 398
1Ki 21: 5 is thy spirit so sad, that thou **e** no bread? 398

EATETH (56) [EAT]
Ex 12:15 for whosoever **e** leavened bread from 398
12:19 for whosoever **e** that which is leavened, 398
Lev 7:18 the soul that **e** of it shall bear his iniquity. 398
7:20 the soul that **e** *of* the flesh of the sacrifice of 398
7:25 For whosoever **e** the fat of the beast, 398
7:25 even the soul that **e** *it* shall be cut off from 398
7:27 Whatsoever soul *it be* that **e** any *manner of* 398
11:40 he that **e** of the carcase of it shall wash his 398
14:47 he that **e** in the house shall wash his clothes. 398
17:10 among you, that **e** any *manner of* blood; 398
17:10 will even set my face against *that* soul that **e** 398
17:14 whosoever **e** it shall be cut off. 398
17:15 every soul that **e** that which died of itself, 398
19: 8 Therefore *every one* that **e** it shall bear his 398
Nu 13:32 *is* a land that **e up** the inhabitants thereof; 398
1Sa 14:24 Cursed *be* the man that **e** *any* food until 398
14:28 Cursed *be* the man that **e** *any* food *this* day. 398
Job 5: 5 Whose harvest the hungry **e up**, and taketh it 398
21:25 of his soul, and never **e** with pleasure. 398
40:15 which I made with thee; he **e** grass as an ox. 398
Ps 106:20 into the similitude of an ox that **e** grass. 398
Pr 13:25 The righteous **e** to the satisfying of his soul: 398
30:20 she **e**, and wipeth her mouth, and saith, 398
31:27 and **e** not the bread of idleness. 398
Ecc 4: 5 his hands together, and **e** his own flesh. 398
5:17 All his days also he **e** in darkness, and 398
6: 2 not power to eat thereof, but a stranger **e** it: 398
Isa 28: 4 while it is yet in his hand he **e** it **up**. 1104
29: 8 a hungry *man* dreameth, and behold, he **e**; 398
44:16 with part thereof he **e** flesh; he roasteth roast, 398
59: 5 he that **e** of their eggs dieth, and that which 398
Jer 31:30 every man that **e** the sour grape, his teeth 398
Mt 9:11 Why **e** your Master with publicans and *2068*
Mk 2:16 How *is it* that he **e** and drinketh with *2068*
14:18 One of you which **e** with me shall betray *2068*
Lk 15: 2 *man* receiveth sinners, and **e with** them. *4906*
Jn 6:54 Whoso **e** my flesh, and drinketh my blood, *5176*
6:56 He that **e** my flesh, and drinketh my blood, *5176*
6:57 so he that **e** me, even he shall live by me. *5176*
6:58 he that **e** *of* this bread shall live for ever. *5176*
13:18 He that **e** bread with me hath lift up his heel *5176*
Ro 14: 2 all *things:* another, who is weak, **e** herbs. *2068*
14: 3 Let not him that **e** despise him that eateth *2068*
14: 3 Let not him that eateth despise him that **e** *2068*
14: 3 let not him which **e** not judge him that *2068*
14: 3 not him which eateth not judge him that **e**: *2068*
14: 6 to the Lord he doth not regard *it.* He that **e**, *2068*
14: 6 **e** to the Lord, for he giveth God thanks; *2068*
14: 6 and he that **e** not, to the Lord he eateth not, *2068*
14: 6 to the Lord he **e** not, and giveth God *2068*
14:20 *it is* evil for *that* man who **e** with offence. *2068*
14:23 damned if he eat, because *he e* not of faith: NIG
1Co 9: 7 a vineyard, and **e** not of the fruit thereof? *2068*
9: 7 a flock, and **e** not of the milk of the flock? *2068*
11:29 For he that **e** and drinketh unworthily, *2068*
11:29 **e** and drinketh damnation to himself, *2068*

EATING (27) [EAT]
Ex 12: 4 every man according to his **e** shall make 400
16:16 Gather of it every man according to his **e**, 400
16:18 they gathered every man according to his **e**. 400
16:21 every man according to his **e**: 400
Jdg 14: 9 went on **e**, and came to his father and 398
Ru 3: 3 until he shall have done **e** and drinking. 398
1Sa 14:34 sin not against the LORD in **e** with 398
30:16 **e** and drinking, and dancing, because of all 398
1Ki 1:41 him heard *it* as they had made an end of **e**. 398
4:20 **e** and drinking, and making merry. 398
2Ki 4:40 as they were **e** of the pottage, that they cried 398
1Ch 12:39 were with David three days, **e** and drinking: 398

Job 1:13 when his sons and his daughters *were* **e** and 398
1:18 Thy sons and thy daughters *were* **e** and 398
20:23 and shall rain *it* upon him while he is **e**. 3894
Isa 22:13 and killing sheep, **e** flesh, and drinking wine: 398
66:17 **e** swine's flesh, and the abomination, and 398
Am 7: 2 *that* when they had made an end of **e** 398
Mt 11:18 For John came neither **e** nor drinking, and *2068*
11:19 The Son of man came **e** and drinking, and *2068*
24:38 days that were before the flood they were **e** *5176*
26:26 And as they were **e**, Jesus took bread, and *2068*
Lk 7:33 For John the Baptist came neither **e** bread *2068*
7:34 The Son of man is come **e** and drinking; *2068*
10: 7 **e** and drinking such *things* as they give: *2068*
1Co 8: 4 the **e** of those things that are offered in *1035*
11:21 For in **e** every one taketh before *other* his *5315*

E

EBAL (8)
Ge 36:23 and Manahath, and **E**, Shepho, and Onam. 5858
Dt 11:29 and the curse upon mount **E**. 5858
27: 4 in mount **E**, and thou shalt plaister them 5858
27:13 these shall stand upon mount **E** to curse; 5858
Jos 8:30 unto the LORD God of Israel in mount **E**, 5858
8:33 and half of them over against mount **E**; 5858
1Ch 1:22 And **E**, and Abimael, and Sheba, 5858
1:40 and Manahath, and **E**, Shephi, and Onam. 5858

EBED (6)
Jdg 9:26 Gaal the son of **E** came with his brethren, 5651
9:28 Gaal the son of **E** said, Who *is* Abimelech, 5651
9:30 city heard the words of Gaal the son of **E**, 5651
9:31 Gaal the son of **E** and his brethren be come 5651
9:35 Gaal the son of **E** went out, and stood *in* 5651
Ezr 8: 6 **E** the son of Jonathan, and with him fifty 5651

EBED-MELECH (6)
Jer 38: 7 Now when **E** the Ethiopian, one of 5663
38: 8 **E** went forth out of the king's house, and 5663
38:10 the king commanded **E** the Ethiopian, 5663
38:11 So **E** took the men with him, and went *into* 5663
38:12 **E** the Ethiopian said unto Jeremiah, 5663
39:16 Go and speak to **E** the Ethiopian, saying, 5663

EBEN-EZER (3)
1Sa 4: 1 the Philistines to battle, and pitched beside **E**: 72
5: 1 of God, and brought it from **E** unto Ashdod. 72
7:12 and Shen, and called the name of it **E**, 72

EBENY (1)
Eze 27:15 thee *for* a present horns of ivory and **e**. 1894

EBER (13) [HEBER]
Ge 10:21 the father of all the children of **E**, 5677
10:24 Arphaxad begat Salah; and Salah begat **E**. 5677
10:25 unto **E** were born two sons: the name of 5677
11:14 And Salah lived thirty years, and begat **E**: 5677
11:15 Salah lived after he begat **E** four hundred 5677
11:16 **E** lived four and thirty years, and 5677
11:17 **E** lived after he begat Peleg four hundred 5677
Nu 24:24 shall afflict **E**, and he also shall perish for 5677
1Ch 1:18 begat Shelah, and Shelah begat **E**. 5677
1:19 unto **E** were born two sons: the name of 5677
1:25 **E**, Peleg, Rehu, 5677
8:12 **E**, and Misham, and Shamed, who built 5677
Ne 12:20 Of Sallai, Kallai; of Amok, **E**; 5677

EBEZ See ABEZ

EBIASAPH (3)
1Ch 6:23 his son, and **E** his son, and Assir his son, 43
6:37 the son of Assir, the son of **E**, the son of 43
9:19 the son of **E**, the son of Korah, and 43

EBRONAH (2)
Nu 33:34 from Jotbathah, and encamped at **E**. 5684
33:35 they departed from **E**, and encamped at 5684

ECBATANA See ACHMETHA

ED (1)
Jos 22:34 the children of Gad called the altar *E*: for it NIH

EDAR (1)
Ge 35:21 and spread his tent beyond the tower of **E**. 5740

EDEN (20)
Ge 2: 8 God planted a garden eastward in **E**; 5731
2:10 a river went out of **E** to water the garden; 5731
2:15 put him into the garden of **E** to dress it and 5731
3:23 God sent him forth from the garden of **E**, 5731
3:24 he placed at the east of the garden of **E** 5731
4:16 dwelt in the land of Nod, on the east of **E**. 5731
2Ki 19:12 the children of **E** which *were* in Thelasar? 5729
2Ch 29:12 the son of Zimmah, and **E** the son of Joah: 5731
31:15 next him *were* **E**, and Miniamin, and 5731
Isa 37:12 the children of **E** which *were* in Telassar? 5729
51: 3 and he will make her wilderness like **E**, and 5731
Eze 27:23 Haran, and Canneh, and **E**, the merchants 5729
28:13 Thou hast been in **E** the garden of God; 5731
31: 9 so that all the trees of **E**, that *were* in 5731
31:16 all the trees of **E**, the choice and best of 5731
31:18 and in greatness among the trees of **E**? 5731
31:18 trees of **E** unto the nether parts of the earth: 5731
36:35 desolate is become like the garden of **E**; 5731
Joel 2: 3 the land *is* as the garden of **E** before them, 5731
Am 1: 5 holdeth the sceptre from the house of **E**: 5729

EDER (3)
Jos 15:21 southward were Kabzeel, and **E**, and Jagur, 5740
1Ch 23:23 Mahli, and **E**, and Jeremoth, three. 5740
24:30 also of Mushi; Mahli, and **E**, and Jerimoth. 5740

EDGE (56) [EDGES, TWOEDGED]
Ge 34:26 Shechem his son with the **e** of the sword, 6310
Ex 13:20 in Etham, in the **e** of the wilderness. 7097
17:13 and his people with the **e** of the sword. 6310
26: 4 thou shalt make loops of blue upon the **e** of 8193
26: 4 likewise shalt thou make in the uttermost **e** 8193
26: 5 fifty loops shalt thou make in the **e** of 7097
26:10 thou shalt make fifty loops on the **e** of 8193
26:10 fifty loops in the **e** of the curtain which 8193
36:11 he made loops of blue on the **e** of one 8193
36:12 fifty loops made he in the **e** of the curtain 7097
36:17 he made fifty loops upon the uttermost **e** of 8193
36:17 fifty loops made he upon the **e** of 8193
Nu 21:24 Israel smote him with the **e** of the sword, 6310
33: 6 which *is* in the **e** of the wilderness. 7097
33:37 in mount Hor, in the **e** of the land of Edom. 7097
Dt 13:15 of that city with the **e** of the sword, 6310
13:15 the cattle thereof, with the **e** of the sword. 6310
20:13 every male thereof with the **e** of the sword: 6310
Jos 6:21 and sheep, and ass, with the **e** of the sword. 6310
8:24 *when* they were all fallen on the **e** of 6310
8:24 and smote it with the **e** of the sword. 6310
10:28 smote it with the **e** of the sword, and 6310
10:30 he smote it with the **e** of the sword, and all 6310
10:32 smote it with the **e** of the sword, and all 6310
10:35 smote it with the **e** of the sword, and all 6310
10:37 smote it with the **e** of the sword, and 6310
10:39 they smote them with the **e** of the sword, 6310
11:11 that *were* therein with the **e** of the sword, 6310
11:12 smote them with the **e** of the sword, *and* 6310
11:14 every man they smote with the **e** of 6310
13:27 *even* unto the **e** of the sea of Cinnereth on 7097
19:47 smote it with the **e** of the sword, and 6310
Jdg 1: 8 smitten it with the **e** of the sword, and set 6310
1:25 they smote the city with the **e** of the sword; 6310
4:15 with the **e** of the sword before Barak; 6310
4:16 all the host of Sisera fell upon the **e** of 6310
18:27 they smote them with the **e** of the sword, 6310
20:37 smote all the city with the **e** of the sword. 6310
20:48 smote them with the **e** of the sword, as well 6310
21:10 of Jabesh-gilead with the **e** of the sword, 6310
1Sa 15: 8 utterly destroyed all the people with the **e** 6310
22:19 smote he with the **e** of the sword, both men 6310
22:19 asses, and sheep, with the **e** of the sword. 6310
2Sa 15:14 and smite the city with the **e** of the sword. 6310
2Ki 10:25 they smote them with the **e** of the sword; 6310
Job 1:15 they have slain the servants with the **e** of 6310
1:17 slain the servants with the **e** of the sword; 6310
Ps 89:43 Thou hast also turned the **e** of his sword, 6697
Ecc 10:10 he do not whet the **e**, then must he put to 6440
Jer 21: 7 he shall smite them with the **e** of the sword; 6310
31:29 and the children's teeth are **set on e**. 6949
31:30 the sour grape, his teeth shall be **set on e**. 6949
Eze 18: 2 and the children's teeth are **set on e**? 6949
43:13 the border thereof by the **e** thereof round 8193
Lk 21:24 And they shall fall by the **e** of the sword, *4750*
Heb 11:34 violence of fire, escaped the **e** of the sword, *4750*

EDGES (4) [EDGE]
Ex 28: 7 *thereof* joined at the two **e** thereof; 7098
39: 4 by the two **e** was it coupled together. 7098
Jdg 3:16 Ehud made him a dagger which had two **e**, 6310
Rev 2:12 he which hath the sharp sword **with two e**; *1366*

EDIFICATION (4) [EDIFY]
Ro 15: 2 of us please *his* neighbour for *his* good to **e**. *3619*
1Co 14: 3 he that prophesieth speaketh unto men *to* **e**, *3619*
2Co 10: 8 which the Lord hath given us for **e**, and *3619*
13:10 power which the Lord hath given me to **e**, *3619*

EDIFIED (2) [EDIFY]
Ac 9:31 and Galilee and Samaria, and were **e**; *3618*
1Co 14:17 givest thanks well, but the other is not **e**. *3618*

EDIFIETH (3) [EDIFY]
1Co 8: 1 Knowledge puffeth up, but charity **e**. *3618*
14: 4 He that speaketh in an *unknown* tongue **e** *3618*
14: 4 but he that prophesieth **e** *the* church. *3618*

EDIFY (3) [EDIFICATION, EDIFIED, EDIFIETH, EDIFYING]
Ro 14:19 and *things* wherewith one may **e** another. *3619*
1Co 10:23 are lawful for me, but all *things* **e** not. *3618*
1Th 5:11 and **e** one another, even as also ye do. *3618*

EDIFYING (8) [EDIFY]
1Co 14: 5 he interpret, that the church may receive **e**. *3619*
14:12 that ye may excel to the **e** of the church. *3619*
14:26 Let all *things* be done unto **e**. *3619*
2Co 12:19 *we do* all *things*, dearly beloved, for your **e**. *3619*
Eph 4:12 the ministry, for the **e** of the body of Christ: *3619*
4:16 maketh increase of the body unto the **e** of *3619*
4:29 but that which *is* good to the use of **e**, that it *3619*
1Ti 1: 4 rather than godly **e** which is in faith: *3622*

EDOM (87) [EDOMITE, EDOMITES, ESAU]
Ge 25:30 I *am* faint: therefore was his name called **E**. 123
32: 3 unto the land of Seir, the country of **E**. 123
36: 1 these *are* the generations of Esau, who *is* **E**. 123
36: 8 Thus dwelt Esau in mount Seir: Esau *is* **E**. 123
36:16 dukes *that came* of Eliphaz in the land of **E**; 123
36:17 dukes *that came* of Reuel in the land of **E**; 123
36:19 of Esau, who *is* **E**, and these *are* their dukes. 123
36:21 the children of Seir in the land of **E**. 123
36:31 *are* the kings that reigned in the land of **E**, 123
36:32 Bela the son of Beor reigned in **E**: and 123
36:43 these *be* the dukes of **E**, according to their 123
Ex 15:15 the dukes of **E** shall be amazed; the mighty 123
Nu 20:14 messengers from Kadesh unto the king of **E**, 123
20:18 **E** said unto him, Thou shalt not pass by me, 123
20:20 **E** came out against him with much people, 123
20:21 Thus **E** refused to give Israel passage 123
20:23 by the coast of the land of **E**, saying, 123
21: 4 of the Red sea, to compass the land of **E**: 123
24:18 **E** shall be a possession, Seir also shall be a 123
33:37 in mount Hor, in the edge of the land of **E**. 123
34: 3 wilderness of Zin along by the coast of **E**, 123
Jos 15: 1 *even* to the border of **E**, the wilderness of 123
15:21 the coast of **E** southward were Kabzeel, 123
Jdg 5: 4 when thou marchedst out of the field of **E**, 123
11:17 Israel sent messengers unto the king of **E**, 123
11:17 the king of **E** would not hearken *thereto*. 123
11:18 compassed the land of **E**, and the land of 123
1Sa 14:47 against **E**, and against the kings of Zobah, 123
2Sa 8:14 he put garrisons in **E**; throughout all Edom 123
8:14 throughout all **E** put he garrisons, and 123
8:14 and all they of **E** became David's servants. 123
1Ki 9:26 on the shore of the Red sea, in the land of **E**. 123
11:14 the Edomite: he *was* of the king's seed in **E**. 123
11:15 when David was in **E**, and Joab the captain 123
11:15 after he had smitten every male in **E**; 123
11:16 until he had cut off every male in **E**:) 123
22:47 *There was* then no king in **E**: a deputy *was* 123
2Ki 3: 8 The way through the wilderness of **E**. 123
3: 9 and the king of Judah, and the king of **E**: 123
3:12 and the king of **E** went down to him. 123
3:20 there came water by the way of **E**, and 123
3:26 to break through *even* unto the king of **E**: 123
8:20 In his days **E** revolted from under the hand 123
8:22 Yet **E** revolted from under the hand of Judah 123
14: 7 He slew *of* **E** in the valley of salt ten 123
14:10 Thou hast indeed smitten **E**, and thine heart 123
1Ch 1:43 **E** before *any* king reigned over the children 123
1:51 the dukes of **E** were; duke Timnah, 123
1:54 duke Iram. These *are* the dukes of **E**. 123
18:11 from **E**, and from Moab, and from 123
18:13 he put garrisons in **E**; and all the Edomites 123
2Ch 8:17 and to Eloth, at the sea side in the land of **E**. 123
25:20 because they sought after the gods of **E**. 123
Ps 60: T smote of **E** in the valley of salt twelve 123
60: 8 my washpot; over **E** will I cast out my shoe: 123
60: 9 the strong city? who will lead me into **E**? 123
83: 6 The tabernacles of **E**, and the Ishmaelites; 123
108: 9 my washpot; over **E** will I cast out my shoe; 123
108:10 the strong city? who will lead me into **E**? 123
137: 7 the children of **E** *in* the day of Jerusalem; 123
Isa 11:14 they shall lay their hand upon **E** and Moab; 123
63: 1 Who *is* this *that* cometh from **E**, with dyed 123
Jer 9:26 **E**, and the children of Ammon, and Moab, 123
25:21 **E**, and Moab, and the children of Ammon, 123
27: 3 send them to the king of **E**, and to the king 123
40:11 in **E**, and that *were* in all the countries, 123
49: 7 Concerning **E**, thus saith the LORD of 123
49:17 Also **E** shall be a desolation: every one that 123
49:20 of the LORD, that he hath taken against **E**; 123
49:22 **E** be as the heart of a woman in her pangs. 123
La 4:21 Rejoice and be glad, O daughter of **E**, 123
4:22 he will visit thine iniquity, O daughter of **E**; 123
Eze 25:12 Because that **E** hath dealt against the house 123
25:13 I will also stretch out mine hand upon **E**, and 123
25:14 I will lay my vengeance upon **E** by the hand 123
25:14 they shall do in **E** according to mine anger 123
32:29 There *is* **E**, her kings, and all her princes, 123
Da 11:41 *even* **E**, and Moab, and the chief of 123
Joel 3:19 and **E** shall be a desolate wilderness, 123
Am 1: 6 the whole captivity, to deliver *them* up to **E**: 123
1: 9 they delivered up the whole captivity to **E**, 123
1:11 For three transgressions of **E**, and for four, 123
2: 1 he burnt the bones of the king of **E** into lime: 123
9:12 That they may possess the remnant of **E**, and 123
Ob 1: 1 Thus saith the Lord GOD concerning **E**; 123
1: 8 even destroy the wise *men* out of **E**, and 123
Mal 1: 4 Whereas **E** saith, We are impoverished, but 123

EDOMITE (7) [EDOM]
Dt 23: 7 Thou shalt not abhor an **E**; for he *is* thy 130
1Sa 21: 7 his name *was* Doeg, an **E**, the chiefest of 130
22: 9 answered Doeg the **E**, which *was* set over 130
22:18 Doeg the **E** turned, and he fell upon 130
22:22 *it* that day, when Doeg the **E** *was* there, 130
1Ki 11:14 up an adversary unto Solomon, Hadad the **E**: 130
Ps 52: T when Doeg the **E** came and told Saul, and 130

EDOMITES (13) [EDOM]
Ge 36: 9 of Esau the father of the **E** in mount Seir: 123
36:43 he *is* Esau the father of the **E**. 123
1Ki 11: 1 Ammonites, **E**, Zidonians, *and* Hittites; 130
11:17 certain **E** of his father's servants with him, 130
2Ki 8:21 smote the **E** which compassed him about, 123
1Ch 18:12 the **E** in the valley of salt eighteen thousand. 123
18:13 and all the **E** became David's servants. 123
2Ch 21: 8 In his days the **E** revolted from under 123
21: 9 smote the **E** which compassed him in, and 123
21:10 So the **E** revolted from under the hand of 123
25:14 was come from the slaughter of the **E**, 130
25:19 Thou sayest, Lo, thou hast smitten the **E**; 123
28:17 For again the **E** had come and smitten Judah, 130

EDREI (8)
Nu 21:33 he, and all his people, to the battle *at* **E**. 154
Dt 1: 4 of Bashan, which dwelt at Astaroth in **E**: 154
3: 1 he and all his people, to battle *at* **E**. 154
3:10 and all Bashan, unto Salchah and **E**, 154
Jos 12: 4 the giants, that dwelt at Ashtaroth and at **E**, 154
13:12 which reigned in Ashtaroth and in **E**, 154
13:31 half Gilead, and Ashtaroth, and **E**, cities of 154
19:37 And Kedesh, and **E**, and En-hazor, 154

EFFECT (14) [EFFECTED, EFFECTUAL, EFFECTUALLY]
Nu 30: 8 wherewith she bound her soul, of **none e**: 6565
2Ch 34:22 the college:) and they spake to her to that *e*. NIH
Ps 33:10 **maketh** the devices of the people **of none e**. 5106
Isa 32:17 the **e** of righteousness quietness and 5656
Jer 48:30 *it shall* not *be* so; his lies shall not so **e** *it*. 6213
Eze 12:23 days are at hand, and the **e** of every vision. 1697
Mt 15: 6 **made** the commandment of God **of none e** *208*
Mk 7:13 **Making** the word of God **of none e** through *208*

Ro 3: 3 unbelief **make** the faith of God **without e**? *2673*
4:14 and the promise **made of none e**: *2673*
9: 6 though the word of God hath **taken none e**. *1601*
1Co 1:17 cross of Christ should be **made of none e**. *2758*
Gal 3:17 that *it* should **make** the promise **of none e**. *2673*
5: 4 Christ is **become of no e** unto you, *2673*

EFFECTED (1) [EFFECT]
2Ch 7:11 and in his own house, he **prosperously e**. 6743

EFFECTUAL (6) [EFFECT]
1Co 16: 9 For a great door and **e** is opened unto me, *1756*
2Co 1: 6 which is **e** in the enduring of the same *1754*
Eph 3: 7 unto me by the **e working** of his power. *1753*
4:16 according to the **e working** in the measure *1753*
Phm 1: 6 **e** by the acknowledging of every good *1756*
Jas 5:16 The **e fervent** prayer of a righteous *man* *1754*

EFFECTUALLY (2) [EFFECT]
Gal 2: 8 (For he that **wrought e in** Peter to *1754*
1Th 2:13 which **e worketh** also in you that believe. *1754*

EFFEMINATE (1)
1Co 6: 9 nor idolaters, nor adulterers, nor **e**, *3120*

EGG (2) [EGGS]
Job 6: 6 or is there *any* taste in the white of an **e**? 2495
Lk 11:12 Or if he shall ask an **e**, will he offer him a *5609*

EGGS (7) [EGG]
Dt 22: 6 or **e**, and the dam sitting upon the young, or 1000
22: 6 dam sitting upon the young, or upon the **e**, 1000
Job 39:14 Which leaveth her **e** in the earth, and 1000
Isa 10:14 as *one* gathereth **e** *that are* left, have I 1000
59: 5 They hatch cockatrice' **e**, and weave 1000
59: 5 he that eateth of their **e** dieth, and 1000
Jer 17:11 *As* the partridge sitteth *on* **e**, and NIH

EGLAH (2)
2Sa 3: 5 the sixth, Ithream, by **E** David's wife. 5698
1Ch 3: 3 of Abital: the sixth, Ithream by **E** his wife. 5698

EGLAIM (1)
Isa 15: 8 the howling thereof unto **E**, and the howling 97

EGLON (13)
Jos 10: 3 and unto Debir king of **E**, saying, 5700
10: 5 the king of Lachish, the king of **E**, 5700
10:23 the king of Lachish, *and* the king of **E**. 5700
10:34 from Lachish Joshua passed unto **E**, and 5700
10:36 Joshua went up from **E**, and all Israel with 5700
10:37 according to all that he had done to **E**; 5700
12:12 The king of **E**, one; the king of Gezer, one; 5700
15:39 Lachish, and Bozkath, and **E**, 5700
Jdg 3:12 the LORD strengthened **E** the king of 5700
3:14 So the children of Israel served **E** the king 5700
3:15 sent a present unto **E** the king of Moab. 5700
3:17 he brought the present unto **E** king of 5700
3:17 king of Moab: and **E** *was* a very fat man. 5700

EGYPT (611) [EGYPTIAN, EGYPTIAN'S, EGYPTIANS]
Ge 12:10 Abram went down into **E** to sojourn there; 4714
12:11 when he was come near to enter into **E**, 4714
12:14 that, when Abram was come into **E**, 4714
13: 1 Abram went up out of **E**, he, and his wife, 4714
13:10 like the land of **E**, as thou comest unto 4714
15:18 from the river of **E** unto the great river, 4714
21:21 took him a wife out of the land of **E**. 4714
25:18 that *is* before **E**, as thou goest towards 4714
26: 2 unto him, and said, Go not down into **E**; 4714
37:25 and myrrh, going to carry *it* down to **E**. 4714
37:28 of silver: and they brought Joseph into **E**. 4714
37:36 the Medanites sold him into **E** unto 4714
39: 1 Joseph was brought down to **E**; and 4714
40: 1 *that* the butler of the king of **E** and *his* 4714
40: 1 baker had offended their lord the king of **E**. 4714
40: 5 the butler and the baker of the king of **E**, 4714
41: 8 and called for all the magicians of **E**, 4714
41:19 such as I never saw in all the land of **E** for 4714
41:29 of great plenty throughout all the land of **E**: 4714
41:30 plenty shall be forgotten in the land of **E**; 4714
41:33 and wise, and set him over the land of **E**. 4714
41:34 take up the fifth *part* of the land of **E** in 4714
41:36 of famine, which shall be in the land of **E**; 4714
41:41 See, I have set thee over all the land of **E**. 4714
41:43 he made him *ruler* over all the land of **E**. 4714
41:44 lift up his hand or foot in all the land of **E**. 4714
41:45 And Joseph went out over *all* the land of **E**. 4714
41:46 when he stood before Pharaoh king of **E**. 4714
41:46 and went throughout all the land of **E**. 4714
41:48 which were in the land of **E**, and laid up 4714
41:53 that was in the land of **E**, were ended. 4714
41:54 but in all the land of **E** there was bread. 4714
41:55 when all the land of **E** was famished, 4714
41:56 and the famine waxed sore in the land of **E**. 4714
41:57 all countries came into **E** to Joseph for to 4714
42: 1 when Jacob saw that there was corn in **E**, 4714
42: 2 Behold, I have heard that there is corn in **E**: 4714
42: 3 ten brethren went down to buy corn in **E**. 4714
43: 2 the corn which they had brought out of **E**, 4714
43:15 went down *to* **E**, and stood before Joseph. 4714
45: 4 Joseph your brother, whom ye sold into **E**. 4714
45: 8 and a ruler throughout all the land of **E**. 4714
45: 9 God hath made me lord of all **E**: 4714
45:13 shall tell my father of all my glory in **E**, 4714
45:18 I will give you the good of the land of **E**, 4714
45:19 take you wagons out of the land of **E** for 4714
45:20 for the good of all the land of **E** *is* yours. 4714
45:23 ten asses laden with the good things of **E**, 4714
45:25 they went up out of **E**, and came *into* 4714
45:26 and he *is* governor over all the land of **E**. 4714
46: 3 fear not to go down into **E**; for I will there 4714
46: 4 I will go down with thee into **E**; and I will 4714
46: 6 came into **E**, Jacob, and all his seed with 4714
46: 7 and all his seed brought he with him into **E**. 4714
46: 8 which came into **E**, Jacob and his sons: 4714
46:20 unto Joseph in the land of **E** were born 4714
46:26 All the souls that came with Jacob into **E**, 4714
46:27 which were born him in **E**, *were* two souls: 4714
46:27 which came into **E**, *were* threescore and 4714
47: 6 The land of **E** *is* before thee; in the best of 4714
47:11 gave them a possession in the land of **E**, 4714
47:13 so that the land of **E** and *all* the land of 4714
47:14 the money that was found in the land of **E**, 4714
47:15 when money failed in the land of **E**, and 4714
47:20 Joseph bought all the land of **E** for 4714
47:21 borders of **E** even to the *other* end thereof. 4714
47:26 Joseph made it a law over the land of **E** 4714
47:27 Israel dwelt in the land of **E**, in the country 4714
47:28 Jacob lived in the land of **E** seventeen 4714
47:29 with me; bury me not, I pray thee, in **E**: 4714
47:30 thou shalt carry me out of **E**, and bury me 4714
48: 5 which were born unto thee in the land of **E** 4714
48: 5 of Egypt before I came unto thee into **E**, 4714
50: 7 and all the elders of the land of **E**, 4714
50:14 Joseph returned into **E**, he, and 4714
50:22 Joseph dwelt in **E**, he, and his father's 4714
50:26 and he was put in a coffin in **E**. 4714
Ex 1: 1 the children of Israel, which came into **E**; 4714
1: 5 seventy souls: for Joseph was in **E** *already*. 4714
1: 8 Now there arose up a new king over **E**, 4714
1:15 the king of **E** spake to the Hebrew 4714
1:17 did not as the king of **E** commanded them, 4714
1:18 the king of **E** called for the midwives, and 4714
2:23 in process of time, that the king of **E** died: 4714
3: 7 the affliction of my people which *are* in **E**, 4714
3:10 my people the children of Israel out of **E**. 4714
3:11 bring forth the children of Israel out of **E**? 4714
3:12 thou hast brought forth the people out of **E**, 4714
3:16 and *seen* that which is done to you in **E**: 4714
3:17 I will bring you up out of the affliction of **E** 4714
3:18 unto the king of **E**, and you shall say unto 4714
3:19 I am sure that the king of **E** will not let you 4714
3:20 smite **E** with all my wonders which I will 4714
4:18 and return unto my brethren which *are* in **E**, 4714
4:19 unto Moses in Midian, Go, return *into* **E**: 4714
4:20 an ass, and he returned to the land of **E**: 4714
4:21 When thou goest to return into **E**, 4714
5: 4 the king of **E** said unto them, Wherefore do 4714
5:12 land of **E** to gather stubble instead of straw. 4714
6:11 Go in, speak unto Pharaoh king of **E**, 4714
6:13 of Israel, and unto Pharaoh king of **E**, 4714
6:13 the children of Israel out of the land of **E**. 4714
6:26 the land of **E** according to their armies. 4714
6:27 *are* they which spake to Pharaoh king of **E**, 4714
6:27 to bring out the children of Israel from **E**: 4714
6:28 LORD spake unto Moses in the land of **E**, 4714
6:29 speak thou unto Pharaoh king of **E** all that I 4714

Ex	7: 3	my signs and my wonders in the land of **E**.	4714
	7: 4	that I may lay my hand upon **E**, and	4714
	7: 4	out of the land of **E** by great judgments.	4714
	7: 5	when I stretch forth mine hand upon **E**, and	4714
	7:11	now the magicians of **E**, they also did in	4714
	7:19	stretch out thine hand upon the waters of **E**,	4714
	7:19	may be blood throughout all the land of **E**,	4714
	7:21	was blood throughout all the land of **E**.	4714
	7:22	the magicians of **E** did so with their	4714
	8: 5	cause frogs to come up upon the land of **E**.	4714
	8: 6	stretched out his hand over the waters of **E**;	4714
	8: 6	frogs came up, and covered the land of **E**.	4714
	8: 7	and brought up frogs upon the land of **E**.	4714
	8:16	become lice throughout all the land of **E**.	4714
	8:17	became lice throughout all the land of **E**.	4714
	8:24	servants' houses, and into all the land of **E**:	4714
	9: 4	the cattle of Israel and the cattle of **E**:	4714
	9: 6	on the morrow, and all the cattle of **E** died:	4714
	9: 9	shall become small dust in all the land of **E**,	4714
	9: 9	upon beast, throughout all the land of **E**.	4714
	9:18	such as hath not been in **E** since	4714
	9:22	that there may be hail in all the land of **E**,	4714
	9:22	herb of the field, throughout the land of **E**.	4714
	9:23	the LORD rained hail upon the land of **E**.	4714
	9:24	in all the land of **E** since it became a nation.	4714
	9:25	the hail smote throughout all the land of **E**	4714
	10: 2	what things I have wrought in **E**, and my	4714
	10: 7	knowest thou not yet that **E** is destroyed?	4714
	10:12	Stretch out thine hand over the land of **E**	4714
	10:12	that they may come up upon the land of **E**,	4714
	10:13	stretched forth his rod over the land of **E**,	4714
	10:14	the locusts went up over all the land of **E**,	4714
	10:14	of Egypt, and rested in all the coasts of **E**:	4714
	10:15	herbs of the field, through all the land of **E**.	4714
	10:19	not one locust in all the coasts of **E**.	4714
	10:21	there may be darkness over the land of **E**,	4714
	10:22	darkness in all the land of **E** three days:	4714
	11: 1	plague *more* upon Pharaoh, and upon **E**;	4714
	11: 3	man Moses *was* very great in the land of **E**,	4714
	11: 4	midnight will I go out into the midst of **E**:	4714
	11: 5	all the firstborn in the land of **E** shall die,	4714
	11: 6	be a great cry throughout all the land of **E**,	4714
	11: 9	may be multiplied in the land of **E**.	4714
	12: 1	unto Moses and Aaron in the land of **E**,	4714
	12:12	For I will pass through the land of **E** this	4714
	12:12	will smite all the firstborn in the land of **E**,	4714
	12:12	against all the gods of **E** I will execute	4714
	12:13	to destroy *you,* when I smite the land of **E**.	4714
	12:17	I brought your armies out of the land of **E**:	4714
	12:27	the houses of the children of Israel in **E**,	4714
	12:29	smote all the firstborn in the land of **E**,	4714
	12:30	and there was a great cry in **E**;	4714
	12:39	dough which they brought forth out of **E**,	4714
	12:39	because they were thrust out of **E**, and	4714
	12:40	who dwelt in **E**, *was* four hundred and	4714
	12:41	of the LORD went out from the land of **E**.	4714
	12:42	for bringing them out from the land of **E**:	4714
	12:51	Israel out of the land of **E** by their armies.	4714
	13: 3	this day, *in* which ye came out from **E**,	4714
	13: 8	did unto me when I came forth out of **E**.	4714
	13: 9	hath the LORD brought thee out of **E**.	4714
	13:14	of hand the LORD brought us out from **E**,	4714
	13:15	slew all the firstborn in the land of **E**,	4714
	13:16	hand the LORD brought us forth out of **E**.	4714
	13:17	when they see war, and they return to **E**:	4714
	13:18	went up harnessed out of the land of **E**.	4714
	14: 5	it was told the king of **E** that the people	4714
	14: 7	all the chariots of **E**, and captains over	4714
	14: 8	hardened the heart of Pharaoh king of **E**,	4714
	14:11	Because *there were* no graves in **E**,	4714
	14:11	thus with us, to carry us forth out of **E**?	4714
	14:12	not this the word that we did tell thee in **E**,	4714
	16: 1	after their departing out of the land of **E**.	4714
	16: 3	by the hand of the LORD in the land of **E**,	4714
	16: 6	hath brought you out from the land of **E**:	4714
	16:32	I brought you forth from the land of **E**.	4714
	17: 3	*is* this *that* thou hast brought us up out of **E**,	4714
	18: 1	the LORD had brought Israel out of **E**;	4714
	19: 1	Israel were gone forth out of the land of **E**,	4714
	20: 2	have brought thee out of the land of **E**,	4714
	22:21	for ye were strangers in the land of **E**.	4714
	23: 9	seeing ye were strangers in the land of **E**.	4714
	23:15	for in it thou camest out from **E**:	4714
	29:46	brought them forth out of the land of **E**,	4714
	32: 1	man that brought us up out of the land of **E**,	4714
	32: 4	which brought thee up out of the land of **E**.	4714
	32: 7	which thou broughtest out of the land of **E**,	4714
	32: 8	have brought thee up out of the land of **E**.	4714
	32:11	forth out of the land of **E** with great power,	4714
	32:23	man that brought us up out of the land of **E**,	4714
	33: 1	thou hast brought up out of the land of **E**,	4714
	34:18	in the month Abib thou camest out from **E**.	4714
Lev	11:45	that bringeth you up out of the land of **E**,	4714
	18: 3	After the doings of the land of **E**,	4714
	19:34	for ye were strangers in the land of **E**:	4714
	19:36	which brought you out of the land of **E**.	4714
	22:33	That brought you out of the land of **E**, to be	4714
	23:43	when I brought them out of the land of **E**:	4714
	25:38	brought you forth out of the land of **E**,	4714
	25:42	which I brought forth out of the land of **E**:	4714
	25:55	whom I brought forth out of the land of **E**:	4714
	26:13	brought you forth out of the land of **E**,	4714
	26:45	whom I brought forth out of the land of **E**	4714
Nu	1: 1	after they were come out of the land of **E**,	4714
	3:13	**E** I hallowed unto me all the firstborn in	4714
	8:17	I smote every firstborn in the land of **E**,	4714
	9: 1	after they were come out of the land of **E**,	4714
	11: 5	the fish, which we did eat in **E** freely;	4714
	11:18	for *it was* well with us in **E**: therefore	4714
	11:20	saying, Why came we forth out of **E**?	4714
	13:22	was built seven years before Zoan in **E**.)	4714
	14: 2	God that we had died in the land of **E**!	4714
	14: 3	were it not better for us to return into **E**?	4714
	14: 4	us make a captain, and let us return into **E**.	4714
	14:19	this people, from **E** even until now.	4714
	14:22	which I did in **E** and in the wilderness, and	4714
	15:41	which brought you out of the land of **E**,	4714
	20: 5	have ye made us to come up out of **E**,	4714
	20:15	How our fathers went down into **E**, and	4714
	20:15	and we have dwelt in **E** a long time;	4714
	20:16	and hath brought us forth out of **E**:	4714
	21: 5	Wherefore have ye brought us up out of **E**	4714
	22: 5	Behold, there is a people come out from **E**:	4714
	22:11	Behold, *there is* a people come out of **E**,	4714
	23:22	God brought them out of **E**; he hath as it	4714
	24: 8	God brought him forth out of **E**; he hath as	4714
	26: 4	which went forth out of the land of **E**.	4714
	26:59	whom *her mother* bare to Levi in **E**:	4714
	32:11	none of the men that came up out of **E**,	4714
	33: 1	which went forth out of the land of **E** with	4714
	33:38	of Israel were come out of the land of **E**,	4714
	34: 5	a compass from Azmon unto the river of **E**,	4714
Dt	1:27	hath brought us forth out of the land of **E**,	4714
	1:30	according to all that he did for you in **E**	4714
	4:20	*even* out of **E**, to be unto him a people of	4714
	4:34	God did for you in **E** before your eyes?	4714
	4:37	in his sight with his mighty power out of **E**;	4714
	4:45	of Israel, after they came forth out of **E**,	4714
	4:46	after they were come forth out of **E**:	4714
	5: 6	which brought thee out of the land of **E**,	4714
	5:15	that thou wast a servant in the land of **E**,	4714
	6:12	brought thee forth out of the land of **E**,	4714
	6:21	thy son, We were Pharaoh's bondmen in **E**;	4714
	6:21	the LORD brought us out of **E** with a	4714
	6:22	and wonders, great and sore, upon **E**,	4714
	7: 8	from the hand of Pharaoh king of **E**.	4714
	7:15	will put none of the evil diseases of **E**,	4714
	7:18	thy God did unto Pharaoh, and unto all **E**;	4714
	8:14	brought thee forth out of the land of **E**,	4714
	9: 7	that thou didst depart out of the land of **E**,	4714
	9:12	**E** have corrupted *themselves;* they are	4714
	9:26	which thou hast brought forth out of **E** with	4714
	10:19	for ye were strangers in the land of **E**.	4714
	10:22	Thy fathers went down into **E** with	4714
	11: 3	which he did in the midst of **E** unto	4714
	11: 3	midst of Egypt unto Pharaoh the king of **E**,	4714
	11: 4	what he did unto the army of **E**, unto their	4714
	11:10	*is* not as the land of **E**, from whence ye	4714
	13: 5	which brought you out of the land of **E**, and	4714
	13:10	which brought thee out of the land of **E**,	4714
	15:15	that thou wast a bondman in the land of **E**,	4714
	16: 1	God brought thee forth out of **E** by night.	4714
	16: 3	for thou camest forth out of the land of **E** in	4714
	16: 3	out of the land of **E** all the days of thy life.	4714
	16: 6	the season that thou camest forth out of **E**.	4714
	16:12	remember that thou wast a bondman in **E**:	4714
	17:16	nor cause the people to return to **E**, to	4714
	20: 1	which brought thee up out of the land of **E**.	4714

E

Dt 23: 4 in the way, when ye came forth out of **E**; 4714
24: 9 after that ye were come forth out of **E**. 4714
24:18 remember that thou wast a bondman in **E**, 4714
24:22 that thou wast a bondman in the land of **E**: 4714
25:17 when ye were come forth out of **E**; 4714
26: 5 he went down into **E**, and sojourned there 4714
26: 8 the LORD brought us forth out of **E** with 4714
28:27 LORD will smite thee with the botch of **E**, 4714
28:60 will bring upon thee all the diseases of **E**, 4714
28:68 the LORD shall bring thee *into* **E** again 4714
29: 2 your eyes in the land of **E** unto Pharaoh, 4714
29:16 know how we have dwelt in the land of **E**; 4714
29:25 he brought them forth out of the land of **E**: 4714
34:11 sent him to do in the land of **E** to Pharaoh, 4714
Jos 2:10 Red sea for you, when you came out of **E**; 4714
5: 4 All the people that came out of **E**, *that were* 4714
5: 4 by the way, after they came out of **E**. 4714
5: 5 by the way as they came forth out of **E**, 4714
5: 6 which came out of **E**, were consumed, 4714
5: 9 rolled away the reproach of **E** from off you. 4714
9: 9 the fame of him, and all that he did in **E**, 4714
13: 3 From Sihor, which *is* before **E**, even unto 4714
15: 4 and went out *unto* the river of **E**; 4714
15:47 unto the river of **E**, and the great sea, and 4714
24: 4 Jacob and his children went down *into* **E**. 4714
24: 5 Moses also and Aaron, and I plagued **E**, 4714
24: 6 I brought your fathers out of **E**: and 4714
24: 7 your eyes have seen what I have done in **E**: 4713
24:14 on the *other* side of the flood, and in **E**; 4714
24:17 us up and our fathers out of the land of **E**, 4714
24:32 the children of Israel brought up out of **E**, 4714
Jdg 2: 1 I made you to go up out of **E**, and 4714
2:12 which brought them out of the land of **E**, 4714
6: 8 I brought you up from **E**, and brought you 4714
6:13 Did not the LORD bring us up from **E**? 4714
11:13 when they came up out of **E**, from Arnon 4714
11:16 when Israel came up from **E**, and 4714
19:30 came up out of the land of **E** unto this day: 4714
1Sa 2:27 when they were in **E** in Pharaoh's house? 4714
8: 8 them up out of **E** even unto this day, 4714
10:18 I brought up Israel out of **E**, and 4714
12: 6 your fathers up out of the land of **E**. 4714
12: 8 When Jacob was come *into* **E**, and 4714
12: 8 which brought forth your fathers out of **E**, 4714
15: 2 him in the way, when he came up from **E**. 4714
15: 6 of Israel, when they came up out of **E**. 4714
15: 7 thou comest *to* Shur, that *is* over against **E**. 4714
27: 8 thou goest to Shur, even unto the land of **E**. 4714
30:13 he said, I *am* a young man **of E**, servant to 4713
2Sa 7: 6 I brought up the children of Israel out of **E**, 4714
7:23 which thou redeemedst to thee from **E**, 4714
1Ki 3: 1 made affinity with Pharaoh king of **E**, 4714
4:21 of the Philistines, and unto the border of **E**: 4714
4:30 the east country, and all the wisdom of **E**. 4714
6: 1 of Israel were come out of the land of **E**, 4714
8: 9 when they came out of the land of **E**. 4714
8:16 I brought forth my people Israel out of **E**, 4714
8:21 when he brought them out of the land of **E**. 4714
8:51 which thou broughtest forth out of **E**, 4714
8:53 when thou broughtest our fathers out of **E**, 4714
8:65 entering in of Hamath unto the river of **E**, 4714
9: 9 forth their fathers out of the land of **E**, 4714
9:16 *For* Pharaoh king of **E** had gone up, and 4714
10:28 Solomon had horses brought out of **E**, and 4714
10:29 went out of **E** for six hundred *shekels* of 4714
11:17 his father's servants with him, to go *into* **E**; 4714
11:18 they came *to* **E**, unto Pharaoh king of 4714
11:18 came *to* Egypt, unto Pharaoh king of **E**; 4714
11:21 when Hadad heard in **E** that David slept 4714
11:40 Jeroboam arose, and fled *into* **E**, 4714
11:40 unto Shishak king of **E**, and was in Egypt 4714
11:40 and was in **E** until the death of Solomon. 4714
12: 2 the son of Nebat, who was yet in **E**, 4714
12: 2 king Solomon, and Jeroboam dwelt in **E**;) 4714
12:28 which brought thee up out of the land of **E**. 4714
14:25 *that* Shishak king of **E** came up against 4714
2Ki 17: 4 for he had sent messengers to So king of **E**, 4714
17: 7 had brought them up out of the land of **E**, 4714
17: 7 from under the hand of Pharaoh king of **E**, 4714
17:36 who brought you up out of the land of **E** 4714
18:21 *even* upon **E**, on which if a man lean, it will 4714
18:21 *is* Pharaoh king of **E** unto all that trust on 4714
18:24 put thy trust on **E** for chariots and 4714
21:15 the day their fathers came forth out of **E**, 4714
23:29 In his days Pharaoh-nechoh king of **E** went 4714
23:34 took Jehoahaz *away:* and he came *to* **E**, and 4714
24: 7 the king of **E** came not again any more out 4714
24: 7 **E** unto the river Euphrates all that pertained 4714
24: 7 all that pertained to the king of **E**. 4714
25:26 of the armies, arose, and came *to* **E**: 4714
1Ch 13: 5 from Shihor of **E** even unto the entering of 4714
17:21 whom thou hast redeemed out of **E**? 4714
2Ch 1:16 Solomon had horses brought out of **E**, and 4714
1:17 brought forth out of **E** a chariot for six 4714
5:10 of Israel, when they came out of **E**. 4714
6: 5 **E** I chose no city among all the tribes of 4714
7: 8 entering in of Hamath unto the river of **E**. 4714
7:22 brought them forth out of the land of **E**, 4714
9:26 of the Philistines, and to the border of **E**. 4714
9:28 they brought unto Solomon horses out of **E**, 4714
10: 2 Jeroboam the son of Nebat, who *was* in **E**, 4714
10: 2 heard *it,* that Jeroboam returned out of **E**. 4714
12: 2 king of **E** came up against Jerusalem, 4714
12: 3 number that came with him out of **E**; 4714
12: 9 So Shishak king of **E** came up against 4714
20:10 when they came out of the land of **E**, but 4714
26: 8 spread abroad even to the entering in of **E**: 4714
35:20 Necho king of **E** came up to fight against 4714
36: 3 the king of **E** put him down at Jerusalem, 4714
36: 4 the king of **E** made Eliakim his brother 4714
36: 4 Jehoahaz his brother, and carried him to **E**. 4714
Ne 9: 9 didst see the affliction of our fathers in **E**, 4714
9:18 *is* thy God that brought thee up out of **E**, 4714
Ps 68:31 Princes shall come out of **E**; Ethiopia shall 4714
78:12 in the land of **E**, *in* the field of Zoan. 4714
78:43 How he had wrought his signs in **E**, and 4714
78:51 smote all the firstborn in **E**; the chief of 4714
80: 8 Thou hast brought a vine out of **E**: 4714
81: 5 when he went out through the land of **E**: 4714
81:10 which brought thee out of the land of **E**: 4714
105:23 Israel also came *into* **E**; and 4714
105:38 **E** was glad when they departed: for the fear 4714
106: 7 fathers understood not thy wonders in **E**; 4714
106:21 which had done great *things* in **E**; 4714
114: 1 When Israel went out of **E**, the house of 4714
135: 8 Who smote the firstborn of **E**, both of man 4714
135: 9 O **E**, upon Pharaoh, and upon all his 4714
136:10 To him that smote **E** in their firstborn: 4714
Pr 7:16 *with* carved *works, with* fine linen of **E**. 4714
Isa 7:18 *is* in the uttermost part of the rivers of **E**, 4714
10:24 his staff against thee, after the manner of **E**. 4714
10:26 so shall he lift it up after the manner of **E**. 4714
11:11 from **E**, and from Pathros, and from Cush, 4714
11:16 day that he came up out of the land of **E**. 4714
19: 1 The burden of **E**. Behold, the LORD 4714
19: 1 upon a swift cloud, and shall come *into* **E**: 4714
19: 1 the idols of **E** shall be moved at his 4714
19: 1 the heart of **E** shall melt in the midst of it. 4714
19: 3 the spirit of **E** shall fail in the midst thereof; 4714
19:12 the LORD of hosts hath purposed upon **E**. 4714
19:13 they have also seduced **E**, *even they that* 4714
19:14 they have caused **E** to err in every work 4714
19:15 Neither shall there be *any* work for **E**, 4714
19:16 In that day shall **E** be like unto women: and 4714
19:17 the land of Judah shall be a terror unto **E**, 4714
19:18 In that day shall five cities in the land of **E** 4714
19:19 to the LORD in the midst of the land of **E**, 4714
19:20 unto the LORD of hosts in the land of **E**: 4714
19:21 the LORD shall be known to **E**, and 4714
19:22 the LORD shall smite **E**: *he* shall smite 4714
19:23 there be a highway out of **E** to Assyria, 4714
19:23 the Assyrian shall come into **E**, and 4714
19:24 In that day shall Israel be the third with **E** 4714
19:25 Blessed *be* **E** my people, and Assyria 4714
20: 3 and wonder upon **E** and upon Ethiopia; 4714
20: 4 buttocks uncovered, *to* the shame of **E**. 4714
20: 5 their expectation, and of **E** their glory. 4714
23: 5 As *at* the report concerning **E**, so shall they 4714
27:12 channel of the river unto the stream of **E**, 4714
27:13 the outcasts in the land of **E**, and 4714
30: 2 That walk to go down *into* **E**, and have not 4714
30: 2 of Pharaoh, and to trust in the shadow of **E**. 4714
30: 3 the trust in the shadow of **E** *your* confusion. 4714
31: 1 Woe to them that go down *to* **E** for help; 4714
36: 6 in the staff of this broken reed, on **E**; 4714
36: 6 *is* Pharaoh king of **E** to all that trust in him. 4714
36: 9 put thy trust on **E** for chariots and 4714
43: 3 I gave **E** *for* thy ransom, Ethiopia and 4714

Isa 45:14 The labour of **E**, and merchandise of 4714
52: 4 My people went down aforetime *into* **E** to 4714
Jer 2: 6 that brought us up out of the land of **E**, 4714
2:18 now what hast thou to do in the way of **E**, 4714
2:36 thou also shalt be ashamed of **E**, as thou 4714
7:22 that I brought them out of the land of **E**, 4714
7:25 forth out of the land of **E** unto this day, 4714
9:26 **E**, and Judah, and Edom, and the children 4714
11: 4 I brought them forth out of the land of **E**, 4714
11: 7 that I brought them up out of the land of **E**, 4714
16:14 the children of Israel out of the land of **E**; 4714
23: 7 the children of Israel out of the land of **E**; 4714
24: 8 and them that dwell in the land of **E**: 4714
25:19 Pharaoh king of **E**, and his servants, and his 4714
26:21 *it*, he was afraid, and fled, and went *into* **E**; 4714
26:22 Jehoiakim the king sent men *into* **E**, 4714
26:22 and *certain* men with him into **E**. 4714
26:23 they fet forth Urijah out of **E**, and 4714
31:32 to bring them out of the land of **E**; 4714
32:20 hast set signs and wonders in the land of **E**, 4714
32:21 Israel out of the land of **E** with signs, 4714
34:13 I brought them forth out of the land of **E**, 4714
37: 5 Pharaoh's army was come forth out of **E**: 4714
37: 7 shall return *to* **E** into their own land. 4714
41:17 *is* by Beth-lehem, to go to enter *into* **E**, 4714
42:14 we will go *into* the land of **E**, where we 4714
42:15 If ye wholly set your faces to enter *into* **E**, 4714
42:16 shall overtake you there in the land of **E**, 4714
42:16 shall follow close after you there *in* **E**; 4714
42:17 set their faces to go *into* **E** to sojourn there; 4714
42:18 forth upon you, when ye shall enter *into* **E**: 4714
42:19 O ye remnant of Judah; Go ye not *into* **E**: 4714
43: 2 thee to say, Go not *into* **E** to sojourn there: 4714
43: 7 So they came *into* the land of **E**: for they 4714
43:11 he shall smite the land of **E**, *and* 4714
43:12 kindle a fire in the houses of the gods of **E**; 4714
43:12 he shall array himself with the land of **E**, 4714
43:13 of Beth-shemesh, that *is* in the land of **E**; 4714
44: 1 all the Jews which dwell in the land of **E**, 4714
44: 8 incense unto other gods in the land of **E**, 4714
44:12 to go *into* the land of **E** to sojourn there, 4714
44:12 all be consumed, *and* fall in the land of **E**; 4714
44:13 punish them that dwell in the land of **E**, 4714
44:14 which are gone into the land of **E** to 4714
44:15 all the people that dwelt in the land of **E**, 4714
44:24 all Judah that *are* in the land of **E**: 4714
44:26 all Judah that dwell in the land of **E**; 4714
44:26 of any man of Judah in all the land of **E**, 4714
44:27 land of **E** shall be consumed by the sword 4714
44:28 out of the land of **E** *into* the land of Judah, 4714
44:28 that are gone into the land of **E** to sojourn 4714
44:30 I *will* give Pharaoh-hophra king of **E** into 4714
46: 2 Against **E**, against the army of 4714
46: 2 the army of Pharaoh-necho king of **E**, 4714
46: 8 **E** riseth up like a flood, and *his* waters are 4714
46:11 and take balm, O virgin, the daughter of **E**: 4714
46:13 should come and smite the land of **E**. 4714
46:14 Declare ye in **E**, and publish in Migdol, and 4714
46:17 cry there, Pharaoh king of **E** *is but* a noise; 4714
46:19 O thou daughter dwelling in **E**, 4714
46:20 **E** *is like* a very fair heifer, *but* 4714
46:24 The daughter of **E** shall be confounded; 4714
46:25 Pharaoh, and **E**, with their gods, and their 4714
Eze 17:15 him in sending his ambassadors *into* **E**, 4714
19: 4 brought him with chains unto the land of **E**. 4714
20: 5 myself known unto them in the land of **E**, 4714
20: 6 to bring them forth of the land of **E** into a 4714
20: 7 defile not yourselves with the idols of **E**: 4714
20: 8 neither did they forsake the idols of **E**: 4714
20: 8 against them in the midst of the land of **E**. 4714
20: 9 in bringing them forth out of the land of **E**. 4714
20:10 them to go forth out of the land of **E**, 4714
20:36 fathers in the wilderness of the land of **E**, 4714
23: 3 they committed whoredoms in **E**; 4714
23: 8 left she her whoredoms *brought* from **E**: 4714
23:19 she had played the harlot in the land of **E**. 4714
23:27 thy whoredom *brought* from the land of **E**: 4714
23:27 eyes unto them, nor remember **E** any more. 4714
27: 7 Fine linen with broidered work from **E** was 4714
29: 2 set thy face against Pharaoh king of **E**, and 4714
29: 2 prophesy against him, and against all **E**: 4714
29: 3 I *am* against thee, Pharaoh king of **E**, 4714
29: 6 all the inhabitants of **E** shall know that I *am* 4714
29: 9 the land of **E** shall be desolate and waste; 4714
29:10 I will make the land of **E** utterly waste *and* 4714
29:12 I will make the land of **E** desolate in 4714
29:14 I will bring again the captivity of **E**, and 4714
29:19 I *will* give the land of **E** unto 4714
29:20 I have given him the land of **E** *for* his 4714
30: 4 the sword shall come upon **E**, and 4714
30: 4 when the slain shall fall in **E**, and they shall 4714
30: 6 They also that uphold **E** shall fall; and 4714
30: 8 when I have set a fire in **E**, and *when* all 4714
30: 9 shall come upon them, as *in* the day of **E**: 4714
30:10 I will also make the multitude of **E** to cease 4714
30:11 they shall draw their swords against **E**, and 4714
30:13 shall be no more a prince of the land of **E**: 4714
30:13 and I will put a fear in the land of **E**. 4714
30:15 pour my fury upon Sin, the strength of **E**; 4714
30:16 I will set fire in **E**: Sin shall have great 4714
30:18 when I shall break there the yokes of **E**: 4714
30:19 Thus will I execute judgments in **E**: and 4714
30:21 have broken the arm of Pharaoh king of **E**; 4714
30:22 I *am* against Pharaoh king of **E**, and 4714
30:25 he shall stretch it out upon the land of **E**. 4714
31: 2 speak unto Pharaoh king of **E**, and to his 4714
32: 2 up a lamentation for Pharaoh king of **E**, 4714
32:12 they shall spoil the pomp of **E**, and all 4714
32:15 When I shall make the land of **E** desolate, 4714
32:16 *even* for **E**, and for all her multitude, 4714
32:18 wail for the multitude of **E**, and cast them 4714
Da 9:15 out of the land of **E** with a mighty hand, 4714
11: 8 shall also carry captives *into* **E** their gods, 4714
11:42 and the land of **E** shall not escape. 4714
11:43 and over all the precious *things* of **E**: 4714
Hos 2:15 day when she came up out of the land of **E**. 4714
7:11 they call *to* **E**, they go *to* Assyria. 4714
7:16 this *shall be* their derision in the land of **E**. 4714
8:13 and visit their sins: they shall return *to* **E**. 4714
9: 3 Ephraim shall return *to* **E**, and they shall 4714
9: 6 **E** shall gather them up, Memphis shall bury 4714
11: 1 I loved him, and called my son out of **E**. 4714
11: 5 He shall not return into the land of **E**, but 4714
11:11 They shall tremble as a bird out of **E**, and 4714
12: 1 the Assyrians, and oil is carried into **E**. 4714
12: 9 **E** will yet make thee to dwell in 4714
12:13 the LORD brought Israel out of **E**, 4714
13: 4 *am* the LORD thy God from the land of **E**, 4714
Joel 3:19 **E** shall be a desolation, and Edom shall be 4714
Am 2:10 Also I brought you up from the land of **E**, 4714
3: 1 which I brought up from the land of **E**, 4714
3: 9 and in the palaces in the land of **E**, and say, 4714
4:10 you the pestilence after the manner of **E**: 4714
8: 8 cast out and drowned, as *by* the flood of **E**. 4714
9: 5 and shall be drowned, as *by* the flood of **E**. 4714
9: 7 not I brought up Israel out of the land of **E**? 4714
Mic 6: 4 For I brought thee up out of the land of **E**, 4714
7:15 **E** will I shew unto him marvellous *things*. 4714
Na 3: 9 Ethiopia and **E** *were* her strength, and 4714
Hag 2: 5 with you when ye came out of **E**, 4714
Zec 10:10 bring them again also out of the land of **E**, 4714
10:11 and the sceptre of **E** shall depart away. 4714
14:18 if the family of **E** go not up, and come not, 4714
14:19 This shall be the punishment of **E**, and 4714
Mt 2:13 and flee into **E**, and be thou there until I *125*
2:14 his mother by night, and departed into **E**: *125*
2:15 saying, Out of **E** have I called my son. *125*
2:19 Lord appeareth in a dream to Joseph in **E**, *125*
Ac 2:10 in **E**, and in the parts of Libya about Cyrene, *125*
7: 9 moved with envy, sold Joseph into **E**: *125*
7:10 wisdom in the sight of Pharaoh king of **E**; *125*
7:10 and he made him governor over **E** and all his *125*
7:11 there came a dearth over all the land of **E** *125*
7:12 when Jacob heard that there was corn in **E**, *125*
7:15 So Jacob went down into **E**, and died, he, *125*
7:17 the people grew and multiplied in **E**, *125*
7:34 the affliction of my people which is in **E**, *125*
7:34 And now come, I will send thee into **E**. *125*
7:36 shewed wonders and signs in the land of **E**, *125*
7:39 and in their hearts turned *back again* into **E**, *125*
7:40 which brought us out of the land of **E**, *125*
13:17 *they* dwelt as strangers in the land of **E**, *125*
Heb 3:16 howbeit not all that came out of **E** by Moses. *125*
8: 9 the hand to lead them out of the land of **E**; *125*
11:26 Christ greater riches than the treasures in **E**: *125*
11:27 By faith he forsook **E**, not fearing the wrath *125*
Jude 1: 5 having saved the people out of the land of **E**, *125*
Rev 11: 8 which spiritually is called Sodom and **E**, *125*

EGYPTIAN (23) [EGYPT]
Ge 16: 1 no *children:* and she had a handmaid, an **E**, 4713
16: 3 Abram's wife took Hagar her maid the **E**, 4713
21: 9 Sarah saw the son of Hagar the **E**, 4713
25:12 Abraham's son, whom Hagar the **E**, 4713
39: 1 of Pharaoh, captain of the guard, an **E**, 4713
39: 2 and he was in the house of his master the **E**. 4713
Ex 1:19 Hebrew women *are* not as the **E** women; 4713
2:11 he spied an **E** smiting a Hebrew, *one* of his 4713
2:12 he slew the **E**, and hid him in the sand. 4713
2:14 thou to kill me, as thou killedst the **E**? 4713
2:19 An **E** delivered us out of the hand of 4713
Lev 24:10 Israelitish woman, whose father *was* an **E**, 4713
Dt 23: 7 thou shalt not abhor an **E**; because 4713
1Sa 30:11 they found an **E** in the field, and 376+4713
2Sa 23:21 he slew an **E**, a goodly man: and 4713
23:21 the **E** had a spear in his hand; but he went 4713
1Ch 2:34 had a servant, an **E**, whose name *was* Jarha. 4713
11:23 he slew an **E**, a man of *great* 376+4713+1886.1
Isa 11:15 utterly destroy the tongue of the **E** sea; 4714
19:23 the **E** into Assyria, and the Egyptians shall 4714
Ac 7:24 him that was oppressed, and smote the **E**: *124*
7:28 thou kill me, as thou didst the **E** yesterday? *124*
21:38 Art not thou *that* **E**, which before these days *124*

EGYPTIAN'S (4) [EGYPT]
Ge 39: 5 that the LORD blessed the **E** house for 4713
2Sa 23:21 plucked the spear out of the **E** hand, and 4713
1Ch 11:23 in the **E** hand *was* a spear like a weaver's 4713
11:23 pluckt the spear out of the **E** hand, and 4713

EGYPTIANS (98) [EGYPT]
Ge 12:12 when the **E** shall see thee, that they shall 4714
12:14 the **E** beheld the woman that she *was* very 4713
41:55 Pharaoh said unto all the **E**, Go unto 4714
41:56 all the storehouses, and sold unto the **E**; 4714
43:32 for the **E**, which did eat with him, by 4713
43:32 the **E** might not eat bread with 4713
43:32 for that *is* an abomination unto the **E**. 4714
45: 2 and the **E** and the house of Pharaoh heard. 4714
46:34 shepherd *is* an abomination unto the **E**. 4714
47:15 all the **E** came unto Joseph, and said, 4714
47:20 for the **E** sold every man his field, because 4714
50: 3 the **E** mourned for him threescore and 4714
50:11 This *is* a grievous mourning to the **E**: 4714
Ex 1:13 the **E** made the children of Israel to serve 4714
3: 8 to deliver them out of the hand of the **E**, 4714
3: 9 oppression wherewith the **E** oppress them. 4714
3:21 this people favour in the sight of the **E**: 4714
3:22 your daughters; and ye shall spoil the **E**. 4714
6: 5 of Israel, whom the **E** keep in bondage; 4714
6: 6 you out from under the burdens of the **E**, 4714
6: 7 you out from under the burdens of the **E**. 4714
7: 5 the **E** shall know that I *am* the LORD, 4714
7:18 the **E** shall lothe to drink of the water of 4714
7:21 the **E** could not drink of the water of 4714
7:24 all the **E** digged round about the river *for* 4714
8:21 the houses of the **E** shall be full of swarms 4714
8:26 of the **E** to the LORD our God: 4714
8:26 shall we sacrifice the abomination of the **E** 4714
9:11 upon the magicians, and upon all the **E**. 4714
10: 6 all thy servants, and the houses of all the **E**; 4714
11: 3 gave the people favour in the sight of the **E**. 4714
11: 7 doth put a difference between the **E** 4714
12:23 LORD will pass through to smite the **E**; 4714
12:27 when he smote the **E**, and delivered our 4714
12:30 he, and all his servants, and all the **E**; 4714
12:33 the **E** were urgent upon the people, that 4714
12:35 and they borrowed of the **E** jewels of silver, 4714
12:36 gave the people favour in the sight of the **E**, 4714
12:36 *as they required.* And they spoiled the **E**. 4714
14: 4 that the **E** may know that I *am* the LORD. 4714
14: 9 the **E** pursued after them (all the horses *and* 4714
14:10 and behold, the **E** marched after them; 4714
14:12 Let us alone, that we may serve the **E**? 4714
14:12 For *it had been* better for us to serve the **E**, 4714
14:13 for the **E** whom ye have seen to day, 4714
14:17 I will harden the hearts of the **E**, and 4714
14:18 the **E** shall know that I *am* the LORD, 4714
14:20 And it came between the camp of the **E** and 4714
14:23 the **E** pursued, and went in after them to 4714
14:24 the host of the **E** through the pillar of fire 4714
14:24 of the cloud, and troubled the host of the **E**, 4714
14:25 so that the **E** said, Let us flee from the face 4714
14:25 the LORD fighteth for them against the **E**. 4714
14:26 that the waters may come again upon the **E**, 4714
14:27 the **E** fled against it; and the LORD 4714
14:27 the LORD overthrew the **E** in the midst of 4714
14:30 Israel that day out of the hand of the **E**; 4714
14:30 Israel saw the **E** dead upon the sea shore. 4714
14:31 work which the LORD did upon the **E**: 4714
15:26 which I have brought upon the **E**: 4714
18: 8 unto Pharaoh and to the **E** for Israel's sake, 4714
18: 9 he had delivered out of the hand of the **E**. 4714
18:10 hath delivered you out of the hand of the **E**, 4714
18:10 the people from under the hand of the **E**. 4714
19: 4 Ye have seen what I did unto the **E**, and 4714
32:12 Wherefore should the **E** speak, and say, 4714
Nu 14:13 the **E** shall hear *it,* (for thou broughtest up 4714
20:15 and the **E** vexed us, and our fathers: 4714
33: 3 with a high hand in the sight of all the **E**. 4714
33: 4 For the **E** buried all *their* firstborn, which 4714
Dt 26: 6 the **E** evil entreated us, and afflicted us, 4713
Jos 24: 6 the **E** pursued after your fathers with 4714
24: 7 he put darkness between you and the **E**, and 4714
Jdg 6: 9 I delivered you out of the hand of the **E**, 4714
10:11 *Did* not *I deliver you* from the **E**, and 4714
1Sa 4: 8 these *are* the Gods that smote the **E** with all 4714
6: 6 as the **E** and Pharaoh hardened their hearts? 4714
10:18 delivered you out of the hand of the **E**, and 4714
2Ki 7: 6 and the kings of the **E**, to come upon us. 4714
Ezr 9: 1 the Moabites, the **E**, and the Amorites. 4713
Isa 19: 2 I will set the **E** against the Egyptians: and 4714
19: 2 I will set the Egyptians against the **E**: and 4714
19: 4 the **E** will I give over into the hand of a 4714
19:21 the **E** shall know the LORD in that day, 4714
19:23 and the **E** shall serve *with* the Assyrians. 4714
20: 4 king of Assyria lead away the **E** prisoners, 4714
30: 7 For the **E** shall help in vain, and to no 4714
31: 3 Now the **E** *are* men, and not God; and 4714
Jer 43:13 the houses of the gods of the **E** shall he 4714
La 5: 6 We have given the hand *to* the **E**, *and to* 4714
Eze 16:26 with the **E** thy neighbours, 1121+4714
23:21 in bruising thy teats by the **E** for the paps 4714
29:12 I will scatter the **E** among the nations, and 4714
29:13 At the end of forty years will I gather the **E** 4714
30:23 I will scatter the **E** among the nations, and 4714
30:26 I will scatter the **E** among the nations, and 4714
Ac 7:22 was learned in all the wisdom of the **E**, *124*
Heb 11:29 which the **E** assaying to do were drowned. *124*

EHI (1)
Ge 46:21 Ashbel, Gera, and Naaman, **E**, and Rosh, 278

EHUD (10)
Jdg 3:15 **E** the son of Gera, a Benjamite, a man 164
3:16 **E** made him a dagger which had two edges, 164
3:20 **E** came unto him; and he was sitting in a 164
3:20 **E** said, I have a message from God unto 164
3:21 **E** put forth his left hand, and took the dagger 164
3:23 **E** went forth through the porch, and shut 164
3:26 **E** escaped while they tarried, and passed 164
4: 1 the sight of the LORD, when **E** was dead. 164
1Ch 7:10 **E**, and Chenaanah, and Zethan, and 164
8: 6 these *are* the sons of **E**: these *are* the heads 261

EIGHT (81) [EIGHTH]
Ge 5: 4 he had begotten Seth were **e** hundred years: 8083
5: 7 Seth lived after he begat Enos **e** hundred 8083
5:10 Enos lived after he begat Cainan **e** hundred 8083
5:13 Cainan lived after he begat Mahalaleel **e** 8083
5:16 Mahalaleel lived after he begat Jared **e** 8083
5:17 all the days of Mahalaleel were **e** hundred 8083
5:19 Jared lived after he begat Enoch **e** hundred 8083
17:12 he that is **e** days old shall be circumcised 8083
21: 4 Abraham circumcised his son Isaac being **e** 8083
22:23 these **e** Milcah did bear to Nahor, 8083
Ex 26: 2 The length of one curtain *shall be* **e** and 8083
26:25 they shall be **e** boards, and their sockets *of* 8083
36: 9 of one curtain *was* twenty and **e** cubits, 8083
36:30 there were **e** boards; and their sockets *were* 8083
Nu 2:24 and **e** thousand and an hundred, 8083
3:28 upward, *were* **e** thousand and six hundred, 8083
4:48 were **e** thousand and five hundred and 8083
7: 8 and **e** oxen he gave unto the sons of Merari, 8083
29:29 on the sixth day **e** bullocks, two rams, *and* 8083
35: 7 to the Levites *shall be* forty and **e** cities: 8083
Dt 2:14 the brook Zered, *was* thirty and **e** years; 8083

Jos	21:41	*were* forty and **e** cities with their suburbs.	8083
Jdg	3: 8	Israel served Chushan-rishathaim **e** years.	8083
	12:14	ten ass colts: and he judged Israel **e** years.	8083
1Sa	4:15	Now Eli *was* ninety and **e** years old; and	8083
	17:12	whose name *was* Jesse; and he had **e** sons:	8083
2Sa	23: 8	*he lift up his spear* against **e** hundred,	8083
	24: 9	there were in Israel **e** hundred thousand	8083
1Ki	7:10	stones of ten cubits, and stones of **e** cubits.	8083
2Ki	8:17	and he reigned **e** years in Jerusalem.	8083
	10:36	Israel in Samaria *was* twenty and **e** years.	8083
	22: 1	Josiah *was* **e** years old when he *began* to	8083
1Ch	12:24	and spear *were* six thousand and **e** hundred,	8083
	12:30	of Ephraim twenty thousand and **e** hundred,	8083
	12:35	and **e** thousand and six hundred.	8083
	16:38	with their brethren, threescore and **e**;	8083
	23: 3	man by man, was thirty and **e** thousand.	8083
	24: 4	**e** among the sons of Ithamar according to	8083
	25: 7	was two hundred fourscore and **e**.	8083
2Ch	11:21	begat twenty and **e** sons, and	8083
	13: 3	him with **e** hundred thousand chosen men,	8083
	21: 5	and he reigned **e** years in Jerusalem.	8083
	21:20	he reigned in Jerusalem **e** years, and	8083
	29:17	the house of the LORD in **e** days;	8083
	34: 1	Josiah *was* **e** years old when he *began* to	8083
	36: 9	Jehoiachin *was* **e** years old when he *began*	8083
Ezr	2: 6	Joab, two thousand **e** hundred and twelve.	8083
	2:16	children of Ater of Hezekiah, ninety and **e**.	8083
	2:23	men of Anathoth, an hundred twenty and **e**.	8083
	2:41	of Asaph, an hundred twenty and **e**.	8083
	8:11	of Bebai, and with him twenty and **e** males.	8083
Ne	7:11	two thousand and **e** hundred *and* eighteen.	8083
	7:13	children of Zattu, **e** hundred forty and five.	8083
	7:15	children of Binnui, six hundred forty and **e**.	8083
	7:16	of Bebai, six hundred twenty and **e**.	8083
	7:21	children of Ater of Hezekiah, ninety and **e**.	8083
	7:22	of Hashum, three hundred twenty and **e**.	8083
	7:26	and Netophah, an hundred fourscore and **e**.	8083
	7:27	men of Anathoth, an hundred twenty and **e**.	8083
	7:44	children of Asaph, an hundred forty and **e**.	8083
	7:45	children of Shobai, an hundred thirty and **e**.	8083
	11: 6	four hundred threescore and **e** valiant men.	8083
	11: 8	Sallai, nine hundred twenty and **e**.	8083
	11:12	work of the house *were* **e** hundred twenty	8083
	11:14	*men* of valour, an hundred twenty and **e**:	8083
Ecc	11: 2	Give a portion to seven, and also to **e**;	8083
Jer	41:15	escaped from Johanan with **e** men,	8083
	52:29	captive from Jerusalem **e** hundred thirty	8083
Eze	40: 9	measured he the porch of the gate, **e** cubits;	8083
	40:31	and the going up to it *had* **e** steps.	8083
	40:34	that side: and the going up to it *had* **e** steps.	8083
	40:37	that side: and the going up to it *had* **e** steps.	8083
	40:41	**e** tables, whereupon they slew *their*	8083
	43:27	*that* upon the **e** day, and *so* forward,	8066
Mic	5: 5	him seven shepherds, and **e** principal men.	8083
Lk	2:21	And when **e** days were accomplished for	*3638*
	9:28	And it came to pass about an **e** days after	*3638*
Jn	5: 5	which had an infirmity thirty *and* **e** years.	*3638*
	20:26	And after **e** days again his disciples were	*3638*
Ac	9:33	which had kept his bed **e** years, and was	*3638*
1Pe	3:20	that is, **e** souls were saved by water.	*3638*

EIGHTEEN (22) [EIGHTEENTH]

Ge	14:14	three hundred and **e**, and	6240+8083
Jdg	3:14	Eglon the king of Moab **e** years.	6240+8083
	10: 8	**e** years, all the children of Israel that	6240+8083
	20:25	of Israel again **e** thousand men;	6240+8083
	20:44	there fell of Benjamin **e** thousand	6240+8083
2Sa	8:13	valley of salt, *being* **e** thousand *men.*	6240+8083
1Ki	7:15	*of* brass, of **e** cubits high apiece:	6240+8083
2Ki	24: 8	Jehoiachin *was* **e** years old when he	6240+8083
	25:17	The height of the one pillar *was* **e**	6240+8083
1Ch	12:31	of the half tribe of Manasseh **e**	6240+8083
	18:12	in the valley of salt **e** thousand.	6240+8083
	26: 9	had sons and brethren, strong men, **e**.	6240+8083
	29: 7	*of* brass **e thousand**	505+7239+8083+2050.1
2Ch	11:21	(for he took **e** wives, and	6240+8083
Ezr	8: 9	with him two hundred and **e** males.	6240+8083
	8:18	with his sons and his brethren, **e**;	6240+8083
Ne	7:11	and eight hundred *and* **e**.	6240+8083
Jer	52:21	the height of one pillar *was* **e** cubits;	6240+8083
Eze	48:35	*It was* round about **e** thousand	6240+8083
Lk	13: 4	Or those **e**, upon whom the tower	*1176+2532+3638*
	13:11	a spirit of infirmity **e** years,	*1176+2532+3638*
	13:16	Satan hath bound, lo *these* **e**	*1176+2532+3638*

EIGHTEENTH (11) [EIGHTEEN]

1Ki	15: 1	Now in the **e** year of king Jeroboam	6240+8083
2Ki	3: 1	**e** year of Jehoshaphat king of Judah,	6240+8083
	22: 3	it came to pass in the **e** year of king	6240+8083
	23:23	in the **e** year of king Josiah,	6240+8083
1Ch	24:15	to Hezir, the **e** to Aphses,	6240+8083
	25:25	The **e** to Hanani, *he,* his sons, and	6240+8083
2Ch	13: 1	Now in the **e** year of king Jeroboam	6240+8083
	34: 8	Now in the **e** year of his reign,	6240+8083
	35:19	In the **e** year of the reign of Josiah	6240+8083
Jer	32: 1	*was* the **e** year of Nebuchadrezzar.	6240+8083
	52:29	In the **e** year of Nebuchadrezzar he	6240+8083

EIGHTH (38) [EIGHT]

Ex	22:30	his dam; on the **e** day thou shalt give it me.	8066
Lev	9: 1	it came to pass on the **e** day, *that* Moses	8066
	12: 3	in the **e** day the flesh of his foreskin shall	8066
	14:10	on the **e** day he shall take two he lambs	8066
	14:23	he shall bring them on the **e** day for his	8066
	15:14	on the **e** day he shall take to him two	8066
	15:29	on the **e** day she shall take unto her two	8066
	22:27	from the **e** day and thenceforth it shall be	8066
	23:36	on the **e** day shall be a holy convocation	8066
	23:39	and on the **e** day *shall be* a sabbath.	8066
	25:22	ye shall sow the **e** year, and eat *yet* of old	8066
Nu	6:10	on the **e** day he shall bring two turtles, or	8066
	7:54	On the **e** day *offered* Gamaliel the son of	8066
	29:35	On the **e** day ye shall have a solemn	8066
1Ki	6:38	in the month Bul, which *is* the **e** month,	8066
	8:66	On the **e** day he sent the people away: and	8066
	12:32	Jeroboam ordained a feast in the **e** month,	8066
	12:33	in Beth-el the fifteenth day of the **e** month,	8066
	16:29	**e** year of Asa king of Judah *began* Ahab	8083
2Ki	15: 8	**e** year of Azariah king of Judah did	8083
	24:12	the king of Babylon took him in the **e** year	8083
1Ch	12:12	Johanan the **e**, Elzabad the ninth,	8066
	24:10	The seventh to Hakkoz, the **e** to Abijah,	8066
	25:15	The **e** *to* Jeshaiah, *he,* his sons, and	8066
	26: 5	Issachar the seventh, Peulthai the **e**:	8066
	27:11	The **e** *captain* for the eighth month *was*	8066
	27:11	The eighth *captain* for the **e** month *was*	8066
2Ch	7: 9	in the **e** day they made a solemn assembly:	8066
	29:17	on the **e** day of the month came they to	8083
	34: 3	For in the **e** year of his reign, while he was	8083
Ne	8:18	on the **e** day *was* a solemn assembly,	8066
Zec	1: 1	In the **e** month, in the second year of	8066
Lk	1:59	*that* on the **e** day they came to circumcise	*3590*
Ac	7: 8	begat Isaac, and circumcised him the **e** day;	*3590*
Php	3: 5	Circumcised the **e day**, of the stock of	*3637*
2Pe	2: 5	saved Noah the **e** *person,* a preacher of	*3590*
Rev	17:11	even he is the **e**, and is of the seven, and	*3590*
	21:20	the **e**, beryl; the ninth, a topaz; the tenth,	*3590*

EIGHTIETH (1) [EIGHTY]

1Ki	6: 1	**e** year after the children of Israel were	8084

EIGHTY (3) [EIGHTIETH, FOURSCORE]

Ge	5:25	Methuselah lived an hundred **e** and seven	8084
	5:26	after he begat Lamech seven hundred **e**	8084
	5:28	Lamech lived an hundred **e** and two years,	8084

EITHER (41) See Index

EKER (1)

1Ch	2:27	Jerahmeel were, Maaz, and Jamin, and **E**.	6134

EKRON (22) [EKRONITES]

Jos	13: 3	even unto the borders of **E** northward,	6138
	15:11	the border went out unto the side of **E**	6138
	15:45	**E**, with her towns and her villages:	6138
	15:46	From **E** even unto the sea, all that *lay* near	6138
	19:43	And Elon, and Thimnathah, and **E**,	6138
Jdg	1:18	coast thereof, and **E** with the coast thereof.	6138
1Sa	5:10	Therefore they sent the ark of God *to* **E**.	6138
	5:10	came to pass, as the ark of God came *to* **E**,	6138
	6:16	seen *it,* they returned *to* **E** the same day.	6138
	6:17	for Askelon one, for Gath one, for **E** one;	6138
	7:14	restored to Israel, from **E** even unto Gath;	6138
	17:52	come *to* the valley, and to the gates of **E**.	6138
	17:52	to Shaaraim, even unto Gath, and unto **E**.	6138
2Ki	1: 2	inquire of Baal-zebub the god of **E** whether	6138
	1: 3	go to inquire of Baal-zebub the god of **E**?	6138
	1: 6	to inquire of Baal-zebub the god of **E**?	6138
	1:16	to inquire of Baal-zebub the god of **E**,	6138

Jer 25:20 and **E**, and the remnant of Ashdod: 6138
Am 1: 8 and I will turn mine hand against **E**: 6138
Zep 2: 4 at the noon day, and **E** shall be rooted up. 6138
Zec 9: 5 *shall see it,* and be very sorrowful, and **E**; 6138
9: 7 as a governor in Judah, and **E** as a Jebusite. 6138

EKRONITES (2) [EKRON]
Jos 13: 3 the Eshkalonites, the Gittites, and the **E**; 6139
1Sa 5:10 came *to* Ekron, that the **E** cried out, saying, 6139

ELADAH (1)
1Ch 7:20 his son, and **E** his son, and Tahath his son, 497

ELAH (17)
Ge 36:41 Duke Aholibamah, duke **E**, duke Pinon, 425
1Sa 17: 2 pitched by the valley of **E**, and set the battle 425
17:19 all the men of Israel, *were* in the valley of **E**, 425
21: 9 whom thou slewest in the valley of **E**, 425
1Ki 4:18 Shimei the son of **E**, in Benjamin: 414
16: 6 in Tirzah: and **E** his son reigned in his stead. 425
16: 8 sixth year of Asa king of Judah *began* **E** 425
16:13 the sins of **E** his son, *by* which they sinned, 425
16:14 Now the rest of the acts of **E**, and all that he 425
2Ki 15:30 Hoshea the son of **E** made a conspiracy 425
17: 1 **E** to reign in Samaria over Israel nine years. 425
18: 1 third year of Hoshea son of **E** king of Israel, 425
18: 9 year of Hoshea son of **E** king of Israel, 425
1Ch 1:52 Duke Aholibamah, duke **E**, duke Pinon, 425
4:15 the son of Jephunneh; Iru, **E**, and Naam: 425
4:15 and Naam: and the sons of **E**, even Kenaz. 425
9: 8 and **E** the son of Uzzi, the son of Michri, and 425

ELAM (28) [ELAMITES]
Ge 10:22 **E**, and Asshur, and Arphaxad, and Lud, and 5867
14: 1 Chedorlaomer king of **E**, and Tidal king of 5867
14: 9 With Chedorlaomer the king of **E**, and 5867
1Ch 1:17 **E**, and Asshur, and Arphaxad, and Lud, and 5867
8:24 And Hananiah, and **E**, and Antothijah, 5867
26: 3 **E** the fifth, Jehohanan the sixth, 5867
Ezr 2: 7 The children of **E**, a thousand two hundred 5867
2:31 The children of the other **E**, a thousand two 5867
8: 7 of the sons of **E**; Jeshaiah the son of 5867
10: 2 *one* of the sons of **E**, answered and 5867
10:26 of the sons of **E**; Mattaniah, Zechariah, 5867
Ne 7:12 The children of **E**, a thousand two hundred 5867
7:34 The children of the other **E**, a thousand two 5867
10:14 Parosh, Pahath-moab, **E**, Zatthu, Bani, 5867
12:42 and Malchijah, and **E**, and Ezer. 5867
Isa 11:11 from **E**, and from Shinar, and 5867
21: 2 Go up, O **E**: besiege, O Media; all 5867
22: 6 **E** bare the quiver with chariots of men *and* 5867
Jer 25:25 all the kings of **E**, and all the kings of 5867
49:34 **E** in the beginning of the reign of Zedekiah 5867
49:35 Behold, I *will* break the bow of **E**, the chief 5867
49:36 upon **E** will I bring the four winds from 5867
49:36 whither the outcasts of **E** shall not come. 5867
49:37 For I will cause **E** to be dismayed before 5867
49:38 I will set my throne in **E**, and will destroy 5867
49:39 *that* I will bring again the captivity of **E**, 5867
Eze 32:24 There *is* **E** and all her multitude round 5867
Da 8: 2 *in* the palace, which *is* in the province of **E**; 5867

ELAMITES (2) [ELAM]
Ezr 4: 9 the Susanchites, the Dehavites, *and* the **E**, 5962
Ac 2: 9 and **E**, and the dwellers in Mesopotamia, *1639*

ELAPSED See EXPIRED

ELASAH (2)
Ezr 10:22 Ishmael, Nethaneel, Jozabad, and **E**. 501
Jer 29: 3 By the hand of **E** the son of Shaphan, and 501

ELATH (5) [ELOTH]
Dt 2: 8 through the way of the plain from **E**, and 359
2Ki 14:22 He built **E**, and restored it to Judah, after that 359
16: 6 At that time Rezin king of Syria recovered **E** 359
16: 6 Elath to Syria, and drave the Jews from **E**: 359
16: 6 the Syrians came *to* **E**, and dwelt there unto 359

EL-BERITH See BERITH; GOD

EL-BETH-EL (1) [BETH-EL]
Ge 35: 7 built there an altar, and called the place **E**: 416

ELDAAH (2)
Ge 25: 4 and Epher, and Hanoch, and Abidah, and **E**. 420
1Ch 1:33 and Epher, and Henoch, and Abida, and **E**. 420

ELDAD (2)
Nu 11:26 the name of the one *was* **E**, and the name of 419
11:27 said, **E** and Medad do prophesy in the camp. 419

ELDER (20) [OLD]
Ge 10:21 the brother of Japheth the **e**, even to him 1419
25:23 and the **e** shall serve the younger. 7227
27:42 these words of Esau her **e** son were told to 1419
29:16 the name of the **e** *was* Leah, and the name 1419
1Sa 18:17 to David, Behold my **e** daughter Merab, 1419
1Ki 2:22 for he *is* mine **e** brother; even for 1419+4480
Job 15:10 and very aged men, much **e** than thy father. 3117
32: 4 because they *were* **e** than he. 2205+3117+3807.1
Eze 16:46 thine **e** sister *is* Samaria, she and 1419
16:61 receive thy sisters, thine **e** and thy younger: 1419
23: 4 the names of them *were* Aholah the **e**, and 1419
Lk 15:25 Now his **e** son was in the field: and as he *4245*
Ro 9:12 unto her, The **e** shall serve the younger. *3187*
1Ti 5: 1 Rebuke not an **e**, but intreat *him* as a father; *4245*
5: 2 The **e** *women* as mothers; the younger as *4245*
5:19 Against an **e** receive not an accusation, but *4245*
1Pe 5: 1 who am **also an e**, and a witness of *4850*
5: 5 *ye* younger, submit yourselves unto the **e**. *4245*
2Jn 1: 1 The **e** unto the elect lady and her children, *4245*
3Jn 1: 1 The **e** unto the wellbeloved Gaius, whom I *4245*

ELDERS (179) [OLD]
Ge 50: 7 the **e** of his house, and all the elders of 2205
50: 7 and all the **e** of the land of Egypt, 2205
Ex 3:16 gather the **e** of Israel together, and say unto 2205
3:18 thou shalt come, thou and the **e** of Israel, 2205
4:29 gathered together all the **e** of the children of 2205
12:21 Moses called for all the **e** of Israel, and 2205
17: 5 and take with thee of the **e** of Israel; 2205
17: 6 Moses did so in the sight of the **e** of Israel. 2205
18:12 Aaron came, and all the **e** of Israel, to eat 2205
19: 7 and called for the **e** of the people, 2205
24: 1 and Abihu, and seventy of the **e** of Israel; 2205
24: 9 and Abihu, and seventy of the **e** of Israel: 2205
24:14 he said unto the **e**, Tarry ye here for us, 2205
Lev 4:15 the **e** of the congregation shall lay their 2205
9: 1 and his sons, and the **e** of Israel; 2205
Nu 11:16 Gather unto me seventy men of the **e** of 2205
11:16 whom thou knowest to be the **e** of 2205
11:24 gathered the seventy men of the **e** of 2205
11:25 upon him, and gave *it* unto the seventy **e**: 2205
11:30 him into the camp, he and the **e** of Israel. 2205
16:25 Abiram; and the **e** of Israel followed him. 2205
22: 4 Moab said unto the **e** of Midian, Now shall 2205
22: 7 the **e** of Moab and the elders of Midian 2205
22: 7 the **e** of Midian departed with the rewards 2205
Dt 5:23 all the heads of your tribes, and your **e**; 2205
19:12 the **e** of his city shall send and fetch him 2205
21: 2 thy **e** and thy judges shall come forth, and 2205
21: 3 even the **e** of that city shall take a heifer, 2205
21: 4 the **e** of that city shall bring down the heifer 2205
21: 6 all the **e** of that city, *that are* next unto 2205
21:19 and bring him out unto the **e** of his city, and 2205
21:20 they shall say unto the **e** of his city, 2205
22:15 virginity unto the **e** of the city in the gate: 2205
22:16 the damsel's father shall say unto the **e**, 2205
22:17 they shall spread the cloth before the **e** of 2205
22:18 the **e** of that city shall take *that* man and 2205
25: 7 brother's wife go up to the gate unto the **e**, 2205
25: 8 the **e** of his city shall call him, and 2205
25: 9 come unto him in the presence of the **e**, 2205
27: 1 Moses with the **e** of Israel commanded 2205
29:10 your **e**, and your officers, *with* all the men 2205
31: 9 of the LORD, and unto all the **e** of Israel. 2205
31:28 Gather unto me all the **e** of your tribes, and 2205
32: 7 shew thee; thy **e**, and they will tell thee. 2205
Jos 7: 6 he and the **e** of Israel, and put dust upon 2205
8:10 and went up, he and the **e** of Israel, 2205
8:33 and their **e**, and officers, and their judges, 2205
9:11 Wherefore our **e** and all the inhabitants of 2205
20: 4 shall declare his cause in the ears of the **e** 2205
23: 2 *and* for their **e**, and for their heads, and 2205
24: 1 called for the **e** of Israel, and for their 2205
24:31 all the days of the **e** that overlived Joshua, 2205
Jdg 2: 7 all the days of the **e** that outlived Joshua, 2205
8:14 the **e** thereof, *even* threescore 2205
8:16 he took the **e** of the city, and thorns of 2205

Jdg 11: 5 the **e** of Gilead went to fetch Jephthah out 2205
11: 7 Jephthah said unto the **e** of Gilead, Did not 2205
11: 8 the **e** of Gilead said unto Jephthah, 2205
11: 9 Jephthah said unto the **e** of Gilead, If ye 2205
11:10 the **e** of Gilead said unto Jephthah, 2205
11:11 Jephthah went with the **e** of Gilead, and 2205
21:16 the **e** of the congregation said, How shall 2205
Ru 4: 2 he took ten men of the **e** of the city, and 2205
4: 4 and before the **e** of my people. 2205
4: 9 Boaz said unto the **e**, and *unto* all 2205
4:11 the gate, and the **e**, said, *We are* witnesses. 2205
1Sa 4: 3 come into the camp, the **e** of Israel said, 2205
8: 4 all the **e** of Israel gathered themselves 2205
11: 3 the **e** of Jabesh said unto him, Give us 2205
15:30 before the **e** of my people, and 2205
16: 4 the **e** of the town trembled at his coming, 2205
30:26 he sent of the spoil unto the **e** of Judah, 2205
2Sa 3:17 Abner had communication with the **e** of 2205
5: 3 So all the **e** of Israel came to the king to 2205
12:17 the **e** of his house arose, *and went* to him, 2205
17: 4 Absalom well, and all the **e** of Israel. 2205
17:15 counsel Absalom and the **e** of Israel; 2205
19:11 Speak unto the **e** of Judah, saying, 2205
1Ki 8: 1 Solomon assembled the **e** of Israel, 2205
8: 3 all the **e** of Israel came, and the priests took 2205
20: 7 the king of Israel called all the **e** of 2205
20: 8 all the **e** and all the people said unto him, 2205
21: 8 sent the letters unto the **e** and to the nobles 2205
21:11 *even* the **e** and the nobles who *were* 2205
2Ki 6:32 sat in his house, and the **e** sat with him; 2205
6:32 messenger came to him, he said to the **e**, 2205
10: 1 to the **e**, and to them that brought up 2205
10: 5 the **e** also, and the bringers up *of* 2205
19: 2 Shebna the scribe, and the **e** of the priests, 2205
23: 1 they gathered unto him all the **e** of Judah 2205
1Ch 11: 3 Therefore came all the **e** of Israel to 2205
15:25 the **e** of Israel, and the captains over 2205
21:16 the **e** *of Israel, who were* clothed in 2205
2Ch 5: 2 Solomon assembled the **e** of Israel, and 2205
5: 4 all the **e** of Israel came; and the Levites 2205
34:29 gathered together all the **e** of Judah and 2205
Ezr 5: 5 the eye of their God was upon the **e** of 7868
5: 9 asked we those **e**, *and* said unto them thus, 7868
6: 7 the **e** of the Jews build this house of God in 7868
6: 8 **e** of these Jews for the building of this 7868
6:14 the **e** of the Jews builded, and 7868
10: 8 to the counsel of the princes and the **e**, 2205
10:14 with them the **e** of every city, and 2205
Ps 107:32 and praise him in the assembly of the **e**. 2205
Pr 31:23 when he sitteth among the **e** of the land. 2205
Isa 37: 2 the **e** of the priests covered with sackcloth, 2205
Jer 26:17 rose up certain of the **e** of the land, and 2205
29: 1 of the **e** which were carried away captives, 2205
La 1:19 and mine **e** gave up the ghost in the city, 2205
2:10 The **e** of the daughter of Zion sit upon 2205
4:16 of the priests, they favoured not the **e**. 2205
5:12 the faces of **e** were not honoured. 2205
5:14 The **e** have ceased from the gate, the young 2205
Eze 8: 1 and the **e** of Judah sat before me, 2205
14: 1 came certain of the **e** of Israel unto me, 2205
20: 1 *that* certain of the **e** of Israel came to 2205
20: 3 speak unto the **e** of Israel, and say unto 2205
Joel 1:14 gather the **e** *and* all the inhabitants of 2205
2:16 assemble the **e**, gather the children, and 2205
Mt 15: 2 disciples transgress the tradition of the **e**? *4245*
16:21 and suffer many *things* of the **e** and *4245*
21:23 the **e** of the people came unto him as he *4245*
26: 3 and the scribes, and the **e** of the people, *4245*
26:47 from the chief priests and **e** of the people. *4245*
26:57 the scribes and the **e** were assembled. *4245*
26:59 the chief priests, and **e**, and all the council, *4245*
27: 1 **e** of the people took counsel against Jesus *4245*
27: 3 pieces of silver to the chief priests and **e**, *4245*
27:12 he was accused of the chief priests and **e**, *4245*
27:20 **e** persuaded the multitude that they should *4245*
27:41 priests mocking *him,* with the scribes and **e**, *4245*
28:12 And when they were assembled with the **e**, *4245*
Mk 7: 3 eat not, holding the tradition of the **e**. *4245*
7: 5 disciples according to the tradition of the **e**, *4245*
8:31 suffer many *things,* and be rejected of the **e**, *4245*
11:27 the chief priests, and the scribes, and the **e**, *4245*
14:43 the chief priests and the scribes and the **e**. *4245*
14:53 the chief priests and the **e** and the scribes. *4245*
15: 1 chief priests held a consultation with the **e** *4245*
Lk 7: 3 of Jesus, he sent unto him *the* **e** of the Jews, *4245*
9:22 and be rejected of the **e** and chief priests *4245*
20: 1 and the scribes came upon *him* with the **e**, *4245*
22:52 and captains of the temple, and the **e**, *4245*
22:66 the **e** of the people and the chief priests and *4244*
Ac 4: 5 that their rulers, and **e**, and scribes, *4245*
4: 8 Ye rulers of the people, and **e** of Israel, *4245*
4:23 the chief priests and **e** had said unto them. *4245*
6:12 and the **e**, and the scribes, and came upon *4245*
11:30 sent it to the **e** by the hands of Barnabas *4245*
14:23 And when they had ordained them **e** in *4245*
15: 2 unto the apostles and **e** about this question. *4245*
15: 4 and *of* the apostles and **e**, and they declared *4245*
15: 6 **e** came together for to consider of this *4245*
15:22 Then pleased it the apostles and **e**, with *4245*
15:23 The apostles and **e** and brethren *send* *4245*
16: 4 the apostles and **e** which were at Jerusalem. *4245*
20:17 to Ephesus, and called the **e** of the church. *4245*
21:18 us unto James; and all the **e** were present. *4245*
22: 5 bear me witness, and all the **estate of the e**: *4244*
23:14 And they came to the chief priests and **e**, *4245*
24: 1 the high priest descended with the **e**, *4245*
25:15 the **e** of the Jews informed *me,* desiring *to* *4245*
1Ti 5:17 Let the **e** that rule well be counted worthy *4245*
Tit 1: 5 and ordain **e** in every city, as I had *4245*
Heb 11: 2 For by it the **e** obtained a good report. *4245*
Jas 5:14 let him call for the **e** of the church; and *4245*
1Pe 5: 1 The **e** which are among you I exhort, *4245*
Rev 4: 4 the seats I saw four and twenty **e** sitting, *4245*
4:10 twenty **e** fall down before him that sat on *4245*
5: 5 And one of the **e** saith unto me, Weep not: *4245*
5: 6 of the four beasts, and in the midst of the **e**, *4245*
5: 8 *and* twenty **e** fell down before the Lamb, *4245*
5:11 about the throne and the beasts and the **e**: *4245*
5:14 And the four *and* twenty **e** fell down and *4245*
7:11 and *about* the **e** and the four beasts, and *4245*
7:13 And one of the **e** answered, saying unto me, *4245*
11:16 And the four and twenty **e**, which sat before *4245*
14: 3 and before the four beasts, and the **e**: *4245*
19: 4 And the four and twenty **e** and the four *4245*

ELDEST (14) [OLD]

Ge 24: 2 Abraham said unto his **e** servant of his 2205
27: 1 he called Esau his **e** son, and said unto him, 1419
27:15 Rebekah took goodly raiment of her **e** son 1419
44:12 *and* began at the **e**, and left at the youngest: 1419
Nu 1:20 Israel's **e son**, *by* their generations, 1060
26: 5 Reuben, the **e son** of Israel: the children of 1060
1Sa 17:13 the three **e** sons of Jesse went *and* 1419
17:14 the youngest: and the three **e** followed Saul. 1419
17:28 Eliab his **e** brother heard when he spake 1419
2Ki 3:27 he took his **e** son that should have reigned 1060
2Ch 22: 1 the Arabians to the camp had slain all the **e**. 7223
Job 1:13 drinking wine in their **e** brother's house: 1060
1:18 drinking wine in their **e** brother's house: 1060
Jn 8: 9 beginning at the **e**, *even* unto the last: *4245*

ELEAD (1)

1Ch 7:21 and Shuthelah his son, and Ezer, and **E**, 496

ELEADAH See ELADAH

ELEALEH (5)

Nu 32: 3 and **E**, and Shebam, and Nebo, and Beon, 500
32:37 built Heshbon, and **E**, and Kirjathaim, 500
Isa 15: 4 Heshbon shall cry, and **E**: their voice shall 500
16: 9 water thee *with* my tears, O Heshbon, and **E**: 500
Jer 48:34 From the cry of Heshbon *even* unto **E**, *and* 500

ELEASAH (4)

1Ch 2:39 Azariah begat Helez, and Helez begat **E**, 501
2:40 **E** begat Sisamai, and Sisamai begat 501
8:37 Rapha *was* his son, **E** his son, Azel his son: 501
9:43 Rephaiah his son, **E** his son, Azel his son. 501

ELEAZAR (74)

Ex 6:23 bare him Nadab, and Abihu, **E**, and Ithamar. 499
6:25 **E** Aaron's son took him *one* of the daughters 499
28: 1 Nadab and Abihu, **E** and Ithamar, 499
Lev 10: 6 unto **E** and unto Ithamar his sons, 499
10:12 unto **E** and unto Ithamar his sons that were 499
10:16 he was angry with **E** and Ithamar the sons of 499
Nu 3: 2 the firstborn, and Abihu, **E**, and Ithamar. 499
3: 4 **E** and Ithamar ministered in the priest's 499
3:32 **E** the son of Aaron the priest *shall be* chief 499

Nu 4:16 to the office of E the son of Aaron the priest 499
16:37 Speak unto E the son of Aaron the priest, 499
16:39 E the priest took the brasen censers, 499
19: 3 ye shall give her unto E the priest, that he 499
19: 4 E the priest shall take of her blood with his 499
20:25 Take Aaron and E his son, and bring them 499
20:26 his garments, and put them upon E his son: 499
20:28 his garments, and put them upon E his son; 499
20:28 Moses and E came down from the mount. 499
25: 7 when Phinehas, the son of E, the son of 499
25:11 Phinehas, the son of E, the son of Aaron 499
26: 1 and unto E the son of Aaron the priest, 499
26: 3 E the priest spake with them in the plains of 499
26:60 was born Nadab, and Abihu, E, and Ithamar. 499
26:63 were numbered by Moses and E the priest, 499
27: 2 before E the priest, and before the princes 499
27:19 set him before E the priest, and before all 499
27:21 he shall stand before E the priest, who shall 499
27:22 set him before E the priest, and before all 499
31: 6 them and Phinehas the son of E the priest, 499
31:12 E the priest, and unto the congregation of 499
31:13 E the priest, and all the princes of 499
31:21 E the priest said unto the men of war which 499
31:26 E the priest, and the chief fathers of 499
31:29 it of their half, and give it unto E the priest, 499
31:31 E the priest did as the LORD commanded 499
31:41 unto E the priest, as the LORD commanded 499
31:51 and E the priest took the gold of them, 499
31:54 E the priest took the gold of the captains of 499
32: 2 to E the priest, and unto the princes of 499
32:28 So concerning them Moses commanded E 499
34:17 E the priest, and Joshua the son of Nun. 499
Dt 10: 6 E his son ministered in the priest's office in 499
Jos 14: 1 which E the priest, and Joshua the son of 499
17: 4 And they came near before E the priest, and 499
19:51 which E the priest, and Joshua the son of 499
21: 1 the fathers of the Levites unto E the priest, 499
22:13 of Gilead, Phinehas the son of E the priest, 499
22:31 Phinehas the son of E the priest said unto 499
22:32 Phinehas the son of E the priest, and 499
24:33 E the son of Aaron died; and they buried 499
Jdg 20:28 Phinehas, the son of E, the son of Aaron, 499
1Sa 7: 1 sanctified E his son to keep the ark of 499
2Sa 23: 9 after him was E the son of Dodo 499
1Ch 6: 3 Nadab, and Abihu, E, and Ithamar. 499
6: 4 E begat Phinehas, Phinehas begat Abishua, 499
6:50 E his son, Phinehas his son, Abishua his son, 499
9:20 Phinehas the son of E was the ruler over 499
11:12 after him was E the son of Dodo, 499
23:21 and Mushi. The sons of Mahli; E, and Kish. 499
23:22 And E died, and had no sons, but daughters: 499
24: 1 Nadab, and Abihu, E, and Ithamar. 499
24: 2 therefore E and Ithamar executed the priest's 499
24: 3 both Zadok of the sons of E, and 499
24: 4 of the sons of E than of the sons of Ithamar; 499
24: 4 Among the sons of E there were sixteen 499
24: 5 were of the sons of E, and of the sons of 499
24: 6 one principal household being taken for E, 499
24:28 Of Mahli came E, who had no sons. 499
Ezr 7: 5 the son of Phinehas, the son of E, 499
8:33 and with him was E the son of Phinehas; and 499
10:25 Miamin, and E, and Malchijah, and Benaiah. 499
Ne 12:42 E, and Uzzi, and Jehohanan, and Malchijah, 499
Mt 1:15 And Eliud begat E; and Eleazar begat 1648
1:15 and E begat Matthan; and Matthan begat 1648

ELECT (17) [ELECT'S, ELECTED, ELECTION, ELECTS']
Isa 42: 1 mine e, in whom my soul delighteth; 972
45: 4 Jacob my servant's sake, and Israel mine e, 972
65: 9 mine e shall inherit it, and my servants shall 972
65:22 mine e shall long enjoy the work of their 972
Mt 24:24 were possible, they shall deceive the very e. 1588
24:31 they shall gather together his e from 1588
Mk 13:22 to seduce, if it were possible, even the e. 1588
13:27 shall gather together his e from the four 1588
Lk 18: 7 And shall not God avenge his own e, 1588
Ro 8:33 lay any thing to the charge of God's e? 1588
Col 3:12 as the e of God, holy and beloved, 1588
1Ti 5:21 and the Lord Jesus Christ, and the e angels, 1588
Tit 1: 1 according to the faith of God's e, and 1588
1Pe 1: 2 E according to the foreknowledge of God 1588
2: 6 lay in Sion a chief corner stone, e, precious: 1588
2Jn 1: 1 The elder unto the e lady and her children, 1588
1:13 The children of thy e sister greet thee. 1588

ELECT'S (2) [ELECT]
Mt 24:22 for the e sake those days shall be shortened. 1588
Mk 13:20 but for the e sake, whom he hath chosen, 1588

ELECTED (1) [ELECT]
1Pe 5:13 e together with you, saluteth you; 4899

ELECTION (6) [ELECT]
Ro 9:11 that the purpose of God according to e 1589
11: 5 is a remnant according to the e of grace. 1589
11: 7 but the e hath obtained it, and the rest were 1589
11:28 but as touching the e, they are beloved for 1589
1Th 1: 4 Knowing, brethren beloved, your e of God. 1589
2Pe 1:10 diligence to make your calling and e sure: 1589

ELECTS' (1) [ELECT]
2Ti 2:10 Therefore I endure all things for the e 1588

ELEGANT See GORGEOUS

EL-ELOHE-ISRAEL (1) [ISRAEL]
Ge 33:20 And he erected there an altar, and called it E. 415

ELEMENTS (4)
Gal 4: 3 were in bondage under the e of the world: 4747
4: 9 turn ye again to the weak and beggarly e, 4747
2Pe 3:10 and the e shall melt with fervent heat, 4747
3:12 and the e shall melt with fervent heat? 4747

ELEPH (1)
Jos 18:28 Zelah, E, and Jebusi, which is Jerusalem, 507

ELEUZAI (1)
1Ch 12: 5 E, and Jerimoth, and Bealiah, and 498

ELEVEN (24) [ELEVENTH]
Ge 32:22 his e sons, and passed over the ford 259+6240
37: 9 and the e stars made obeisance to me. 259+6240
Ex 26: 7 e curtains shalt thou make. 6240+6249
26: 8 e curtains shall be all of one 6240+6249
36:14 e curtains he made them. 6240+6249
36:15 the e curtains were of one size. 6240+6249
Nu 29:20 on the third day e bullocks, 6240+6249
Dt 1: 2 (There are e days' journey from Horeb 259+6240
Jos 15:51 and Giloh; e cities with their villages. 259+6240
Jdg 16: 5 us e hundred pieces of silver. 505+3967+2050.1
17: 2 The e hundred shekels of 505+3967+2050.1
17: 3 e hundred shekels of silver to 505+3967+2050.1
2Ki 23:36 and he reigned e years in Jerusalem. 259+6240
24:18 and he reigned e years in Jerusalem. 259+6240
2Ch 36: 5 and he reigned e years in Jerusalem: 259+6240
36:11 and reigned e years in Jerusalem. 259+6240
Jer 52: 1 and he reigned e years in Jerusalem. 259+6240
Eze 40:49 and the breadth e cubits; 6240+6249
Mt 28:16 Then the e disciples went away into 1733
Mk 16:14 Afterward he appeared unto the e as they 1733
Lk 24: 9 and told all these things unto the e, and 1733
24:33 and found the e gathered together, and 1733
Ac 1:26 and he was numbered with the e apostles. 1733
2:14 But Peter, standing up with the e, lift up his 1733

ELEVENTH (20) [ELEVEN]
Nu 7:72 On the e day Pagiel the son of Ocran, 6240+6249
Dt 1: 3 in the e month, on the first day of 6240+6249
1Ki 6:38 in the e year, in the month Bul, 259+6240
2Ki 9:29 in the e year of Joram the son of Ahab 259+6240
25: 2 the city was besieged unto the e year 6240+6249
1Ch 12:13 Jeremiah the tenth, Machbanai the e. 6240+6249
24:12 The e to Eliashib, the twelfth to 6240+6249
25:18 The e to Azareel, he, his sons, and 6240+6249
27:14 The e captain for the eleventh month 6240+6249
27:14 The eleventh captain for the e month 6240+6249
Jer 1: 3 unto the end of the e year of 6240+6249
39: 2 And in the e year of Zedekiah, in 6240+6249
52: 5 So the city was besieged unto the e 6240+6249
Eze 26: 1 it came to pass in the e year, in 6240+6249
30:20 it came to pass in the e year, in 259+6240
31: 1 it came to pass in the e year, in 259+6240
Zec 1: 7 and twentieth day of the e month, 6240+6249
Mt 20: 6 And about the e hour he went out, and 1734
20: 9 they came that were hired about the e hour, 1734
Rev 21:20 the e, a jacinth; the twelfth, an amethyst. 1734

ELHANAN (4)
2Sa 21:19 where E the son of Jaare-oregim, 445

2Sa 23:24 the thirty; **E** the son of Dodo *of* Beth-lehem, 445
1Ch 11:26 of Joab, **E** the son of Dodo of Beth-lehem, 445
20: 5 **E** the son of Jair slew Lahmi the brother of 445

ELI (34) [ELI'S, ELOI]
1Sa 1: 3 the two sons of **E**, Hophni and Phinehas, 5941
1: 9 Now **E** the priest sat upon a seat by a post 5941
1:12 the LORD, that **E** marked her mouth. 5941
1:13 therefore **E** thought she had been drunken. 5941
1:14 **E** said unto her, How long wilt thou be 5941
1:17 **E** answered and said, Go in peace: and 5941
1:25 slew a bullock, and brought the child to **E**. 5941
2:11 unto the LORD before **E** the priest. 5941
2:12 Now the sons of **E** *were* sons of Belial; 5941
2:20 **E** blessed Elkanah and his wife, and said, 5941
2:22 Now **E** was very old, and heard all that his 5941
2:27 there came a man of God unto **E**, and 5941
3: 1 ministered unto the LORD before **E**. 5941
3: 2 when **E** *was* laid down in his place, and 5941
3: 5 he ran unto **E**, and said, Here *am* I; for thou 5941
3: 6 Samuel arose and went to **E**, and said, 5941
3: 8 he arose and went to **E**, and said, Here *am* 5941
3: 8 **E** perceived that the LORD had called 5941
3: 9 Therefore **E** said unto Samuel, Go, 5941
3:12 In that day I will perform against **E** all 5941
3:14 I have sworn unto the house of **E**, 5941
3:15 And Samuel feared to shew **E** the vision. 5941
3:16 **E** called Samuel, and said, Samuel, my son. 5941
4: 4 the two sons of **E**, Hophni and Phinehas, 5941
4:11 the two sons of **E**, Hophni and Phinehas, 5941
4:13 **E** sat upon a seat *by* the wayside watching: 5941
4:14 when **E** heard the noise of the crying, he 5941
4:14 And the man came in hastily, and told **E**. 5941
4:15 Now **E** *was* ninety and eight years old; and 5941
4:16 the man said unto **E**, I *am* he that came out 5941
14: 3 the son of Phinehas, the son of **E**, 5941
1Ki 2:27 which he spake concerning the house of **E** 5941
Mt 27:46 saying, **E**, ELI, LAMA SABACHTHANI? *2241*
27:46 saying, ELI, **E**, LAMA SABACHTHANI? *2241*

ELI'S (1) [ELI]
1Sa 3:14 that the iniquity of **E** house shall not be 5941

ELIAB (20) [ELIAB'S]
Nu 1: 9 Of Zebulun; **E** the son of Helon. 446
2: 7 **E** the son of Helon *shall be* captain of 446
7:24 On the third day **E** the son of Helon, 446
7:29 this *was* the offering of **E** the son of Helon. 446
10:16 children of Zebulun *was* **E** the son of Helon. 446
16: 1 Dathan and Abiram, the sons of **E**, and On, 446
16:12 to call Dathan and Abiram, the sons of **E**: 446
26: 8 And the sons of Pallu; **E**. 446
26: 9 And the sons of **E**; Nemuel, and Dathan, and 446
Dt 11: 6 did unto Dathan and Abiram, the sons of **E**, 446
1Sa 16: 6 were come, that he looked on **E**, and said, 446
17:13 that went to the battle *were* **E** the firstborn, 446
17:28 **E** his eldest brother heard when he spake 446
1Ch 2:13 Jesse begat his firstborn **E**, and Abinadab 446
6:27 **E** his son, Jeroham his son, Elkanah his son. 446
12: 9 the first, Obadiah the second, **E** the third, 446
15:18 **E**, and Benaiah, and Maaseiah, and 446
15:20 Unni, and **E**, and Maaseiah, and Benaiah, 446
16: 5 and **E**, and Benaiah, and Obed-edom: 446
2Ch 11:18 Abihail the daughter of **E** the son of Jesse; 446

ELIAB'S (1) [ELIAB]
1Sa 17:28 and **E** anger was kindled against David, and 446

ELIADA (3)
2Sa 5:16 And Elishama, and **E**, and Eliphalet. 450
1Ch 3: 8 And Elishama, and **E**, and Eliphelet, nine. 450
2Ch 17:17 **E** a mighty *man* of valour, and with him 450

ELIADAH (1)
1Ki 11:23 up *another* adversary, Rezon the son of **E**, 450

ELIAH (2)
1Ch 8:27 Jaresiah, and **E**, and Zichri, the sons of 452
Ezr 10:26 and Jehiel, and Abdi, and Jeremoth, and **E**. 452

ELIAHBA (2)
2Sa 23:32 **E** the Shaalbonite, *of* the sons of Jashen, 455
1Ch 11:33 the Baharumite, **E** the Shaalbonite, 455

ELIAKIM (15) [JEHOIAKIM]
2Ki 18:18 there came out to them **E** the son of Hilkiah, 471
18:26 Then said **E** the son of Hilkiah, and Shebna, 471
18:37 came **E** the son of Hilkiah, which *was* over 471
19: 2 he sent **E**, which *was* over the household, 471
23:34 Pharaoh-nechoh made **E** the son of Josiah 471
2Ch 36: 4 the king of Egypt made **E** his brother king 471
Ne 12:41 **E**, Maaseiah, Miniamin, Michaiah, Elioenai, 471
Isa 22:20 that I will call my servant **E** the son of 471
36: 3 came forth unto him **E**, Hilkiah's son, 471
36:11 said **E** and Shebna and Joah unto 471
36:22 came **E**, the son of Hilkiah, that *was* over 471
37: 2 And he sent **E**, who *was* over the household, 471
Mt 1:13 and Abiud begat **E**; and Eliakim begat *1662*
1:13 Abiud begat Eliakim; and **E** begat Azor; *1662*
Lk 3:30 *the son* of Jonan, which was *the son* of **E**, *1662*

E

ELIAM (2)
2Sa 11: 3 *Is* not this Bath-sheba, the daughter of **E**, 463
23:34 **E** the son of Ahithophel the Gilonite, 463

ELIAS (30) [ELIJAH]
Mt 11:14 And if ye will receive *it*, this is **E**, *2243*
16:14 some, **E**; and others, Jeremias, or one of *2243*
17: 3 unto them Moses and **E** talking with him. *2243*
17: 4 for thee, and one for Moses, and one for **E**. *2243*
17:10 then say the scribes that **E** must first come? *2243*
17:11 **E** truly shall first come, and restore all *2243*
17:12 That **E** is come already, and they knew him *2243*
27:47 heard *that*, said, This *man* calleth for **E**. *2243*
27:49 let us see whether **E** will come to save him. *2243*
Mk 6:15 Others said, That it is **E**. And others said, *2243*
8:28 but some *say*, **E**; and others, One of *2243*
9: 4 And there appeared unto them **E** with *2243*
9: 5 for thee, and one for Moses, and one for **E**. *2243*
9:11 Why say the scribes that **E** must first *2243*
9:12 **E** verily cometh first, and restoreth all *2243*
9:13 That **E** is indeed come, and they have done *2243*
15:35 they heard *it*, said, Behold, he calleth **E**. *2243*
15:36 let us see whether **E** will come to take him *2243*
Lk 1:17 go before him in the spirit and power of **E**, *2243*
4:25 widows were in Israel in the days of **E**, *2243*
4:26 But unto none of them was **E** sent, *2243*
9: 8 And of some, that **E** had appeared; and *2243*
9:19 but some *say*, **E**; and others *say*, that one of *2243*
9:30 him two men, which were Moses and **E**: *2243*
9:33 for thee, and one for Moses, and one for **E**: *2243*
9:54 and consume them, even as **E** did? *2243*
Jn 1:21 Art thou **E**? And he saith, I am not. *2243*
1:25 not *that* Christ, nor **E**, neither *that* prophet? *2243*
Ro 11: 2 Wot ye not what the scripture saith of **E**? *2243*
Jas 5:17 **E** was a man subject to like passions as we *2243*

ELIASAPH (6)
Nu 1:14 Of Gad; **E** the son of Deuel. 460
2:14 the captain of the sons of Gad *shall be* **E** 460
3:24 of the Gershonites *shall be* **E** the son of Lael. 460
7:42 On the sixth day **E** the son of Deuel, 460
7:47 this *was* the offering of **E** the son of Deuel. 460
10:20 the children of Gad *was* **E** the son of Deuel. 460

ELIASHIB (17)
1Ch 3:24 **E**, and Pelaiah, and Akkub, and Johanan, 475
24:12 The eleventh to **E**, the twelfth to Jakim, 475
Ezr 10: 6 into the chamber of Johanan the son of **E**: 475
10:24 Of the singers also; **E**: and of the porters; 475
10:27 Elioenai, **E**, Mattaniah, and Jeremoth, and 475
10:36 Vaniah, Meremoth, **E**, 475
Ne 3: 1 **E** the high priest rose up with his brethren 475
3:20 the door of the house of **E** the high priest. 475
3:21 from the door of the house of **E** even to 475
3:21 of Eliashib even to the end of the house of **E**. 475
12:10 Joiakim also begat **E**, and Eliashib begat 475
12:10 also begat Eliashib, and **E** begat Joiada, 475
12:22 The Levites in the days of **E**, Joiada, and 475
12:23 even until the days of Johanan the son of **E**. 475
13: 4 before this, **E** the priest, having the oversight 475
13: 7 understood of the evil that **E** did for Tobiah, 475
13:28 sons of Joiada, the son of **E** the high priest, 475

ELIATHAH (2)
1Ch 25: 4 Hanani, **E**, Giddalti, and Romamti-ezer, 448
25:27 The twentieth to **E**, *he*, his sons, and 448

ELIDAD (1)
Nu 34:21 the tribe of Benjamin, **E** the son of Chislon. 449

ELIEHOENAI See ELIHOENAI

ELIEL (10)
1Ch 5:24 **E**, and Azriel, and Jeremiah, and Hodaviah, 447
6:34 of Jeroham, the son of **E**, the son of Toah, 447
8:20 And Elienai, and Zilthai, and **E**, 447
8:22 And Ishpan, and Heber, and **E**, 447
11:46 **E** the Mahavite, and Jeribai, and Joshaviah, 447
11:47 **E**, and Obed, and Jasiel the Mesobaite. 447
12:11 Attai the sixth, **E** the seventh, 447
15: 9 **E** the chief, and his brethren fourscore: 447
15:11 and Joel, Shemaiah, and **E**, and Amminadab, 447
2Ch 31:13 **E**, and Ismachiah, and Mahath, and Benaiah, 447

ELIENAI (1)
1Ch 8:20 And **E**, and Zilthai, and Eliel, 462

ELIEZER (15)
Ge 15: 2 the steward of my house *is* this **E** of 461
Ex 18: 4 the name of the other *was* **E**; for the God of 461
1Ch 7: 8 **E**, and Elioenai, and Omri, and Jerimoth, 461
15:24 Amasai, and Zechariah, and Benaiah, and **E**, 461
23:15 The sons of Moses *were*, Gershom, and **E**. 461
23:17 And the sons of **E** *were*, Rehabiah the chief. 461
23:17 **E** had none other sons; but the sons of 461
26:25 his brethren by **E**; Rehabiah his son, and 461
27:16 the ruler of the Reubenites *was* **E** the son of 461
2Ch 20:37 **E** the son of Dodavah of Mareshah 461
Ezr 8:16 sent I for **E**, for Ariel, for Shemaiah, and 461
10:18 Maaseiah, and **E**, and Jarib, and Gedaliah. 461
10:23 same *is* Kelita,) Pethahiah, Judah, and **E**. 461
10:31 **E**, Ishijah, Malchiah, Shemaiah, Shimeon, 461
Lk 3:29 *the son* of Jose, which was *the son* of **E**, *1663*

ELIHOENAI (1)
Ezr 8: 4 **E** the son of Zerahiah, and with him two 454

ELIHOREPH (1)
1Ki 4: 3 **E** and Ahiah, the sons of Shisha, scribes; 456

ELIHU (11)
1Sa 1: 1 the son of **E**, the son of Tohu, the son of 453
1Ch 12:20 Michael, and Jozabad, and **E**, and Zilthai, 453
26: 7 *were* strong men, **E**, and Semachiah. 453
27:18 Of Judah, **E**, *one* of the brethren of David: 453
Job 32: 2 was kindled the wrath of **E** the son of 453
32: 4 Now **E** had waited till Job had spoken, 453
32: 5 When **E** saw that *there was* no answer in 453
32: 6 **E** the son of Barachel the Buzite answered 453
34: 1 Furthermore **E** answered and said, 453
35: 1 **E** spake moreover, and said, 453
36: 1 **E** also proceeded, and said, 453

ELIJAH (69) [ELIAS]
1Ki 17: 1 **E** the Tishbite, *who was* of the inhabitants of 452
17:13 **E** said unto her, Fear not; go *and* do as thou 452
17:15 and did according to the saying of **E**: 452
17:16 word of the LORD, which he spake by **E**. 452
17:18 she said unto **E**, What have I to do with thee, 452
17:22 the LORD heard the voice of **E**; and 452
17:23 **E** took the child, and brought him down out 452
17:23 his mother: and **E** said, See, thy son liveth. 452
17:24 the woman said to **E**, Now *by* this I know 452
18: 1 that the word of the LORD came to **E** in 452
18: 2 **E** went to shew himself unto Ahab. 452
18: 7 Obadiah was in the way, behold **E** met him: 452
18: 7 his face, and said, *Art* thou that my lord **E**? 452
18: 8 I *am*: go, tell thy lord, Behold, **E** *is here*. 452
18:11 Go, tell thy lord, Behold, **E** *is here*. 452
18:14 Behold, **E** *is here*: and he shall slay me. 452
18:15 **E** said, *As* the LORD of hosts liveth, before 452
18:16 and told him: and Ahab went to meet **E**. 452
18:17 it came to pass, when Ahab saw **E**, 452
18:21 **E** came unto all the people, and said, How 452
18:22 said **E** unto the people, I, *even* I only, 452
18:25 **E** said unto the prophets of Baal, 452
18:27 that **E** mocked them, and said, Cry aloud: 452
18:30 **E** said unto all the people, Come near unto 452
18:31 **E** took twelve stones, according to 452
18:36 that **E** the prophet came near, and said, 452
18:40 **E** said unto them, Take the prophets of Baal; 452
18:40 **E** brought them down to the brook Kishon, 452
18:41 **E** said unto Ahab, Get thee up, eat and drink; 452
18:42 **E** went up to the top of Carmel; and he cast 452
18:46 the hand of the LORD was on **E**; and 452
19: 1 Ahab told Jezebel all that **E** had done, and 452
19: 2 Jezebel sent a messenger unto **E**, saying, 452
19: 9 he said unto him, What dost thou here, **E**? 452
19:13 when **E** heard *it*, that he wrapped his face in 452
19:13 unto him, and said, What dost thou here, **E**? 452
19:19 **E** passed by him, and cast his mantle upon 452
19:20 ran after **E**, and said, Let me, I pray thee, 452
19:21 and went after **E**, and ministered unto him. 452
21:17 the word of the LORD came to **E** 452
21:20 Ahab said to **E**, Hast thou found me, O mine 452
21:28 the word of the LORD came to **E** 452
2Ki 1: 3 the angel of the LORD said to **E** 452
1: 4 but shalt surely die. And **E** departed. 452
1: 8 his loins. And he said, It *is* **E** the Tishbite. 452
1:10 **E** answered and said to the captain of fifty, 452
1:12 **E** answered and said unto them, If I *be* a 452
1:13 and came and fell on his knees before **E**, and 452
1:15 the angel of the LORD said unto **E**, 452
1:17 word of the LORD which **E** had spoken. 452
2: 1 when the LORD would take up **E** *into* 452
2: 1 that **E** went with Elisha from Gilgal. 452
2: 2 **E** said unto Elisha, Tarry here, I pray thee; 452
2: 4 **E** said unto him, Elisha, tarry here, I pray 452
2: 6 **E** said unto him, Tarry, I pray thee, here; 452
2: 8 **E** took his mantle, and wrapt *it* together, 452
2: 9 they were gone over, that **E** said unto Elisha, 452
2:11 and **E** went up by a whirlwind *into* heaven. 452
2:13 He took up also the mantle of **E** that fell 452
2:14 he took the mantle of **E** that fell from him, 452
2:14 and said, Where *is* the LORD God of **E**? 452
2:15 they said, The spirit of **E** doth rest on Elisha. 452
3:11 which poured water on the hands of **E**. 452
9:36 which he spake by his servant **E** 452
10:10 done *that* which he spake by his servant **E**. 452
10:17 saying of the LORD, which he spake to **E**. 452
2Ch 21:12 there came a writing to him from **E** 452
Ezr 10:21 **E**, and Shemaiah, and Jehiel, and Uzziah. 452
Mal 4: 5 I *will* send you **E** the prophet before 452

ELIKA (1)
2Sa 23:25 Shammah the Harodite, **E** the Harodite, 470

ELIM (6) [BEER-ELIM]
Ex 15:27 they came to **E**, where *were* twelve wells of 362
16: 1 they took their journey from **E**, and all 362
16: 1 of Sin, which *is* between **E** and Sinai, 362
Nu 33: 9 they removed from Marah, and came unto **E**: 362
33: 9 and in **E** *were* twelve fountains of water, and 362
33:10 they removed from **E**, and encamped by 362

ELIMELECH (4) [ELIMELECH'S]
Ru 1: 2 the name of the man *was* **E**, and the name of 458
1: 3 **E** Naomi's husband died; and she was left, 458
2: 1 a mighty man of wealth, of the family of **E**; 458
2: 3 unto Boaz, who *was* of the kindred of **E**. 458

ELIMELECH'S (2) [ELIMELECH]
Ru 4: 3 a parcel of land, which *was* our brother **E**: 458
4: 9 that I have bought all that *was* **E**, and all that 458

ELIOENAI (8)
1Ch 3:23 **E**, and Hezekiah, and Azrikam, three. 454
3:24 the sons of **E** *were*, Hodaiah, and Eliashib, 454
4:36 **E**, and Jaakobah, and Jeshohaiah, and 454
7: 8 **E**, and Omri, and Jerimoth, and Abiah, and 454
26: 3 the fifth, Jehohanan the sixth, **E** the seventh. 454
Ezr 10:22 **E**, Maaseiah, Ishmael, Nethaneel, Jozabad, 454
10:27 **E**, Eliashib, Mattaniah, and Jeremoth, and 454
Ne 12:41 Eliakim, Maaseiah, Miniamin, Michaiah, **E**, 454

ELIPHAL (1)
1Ch 11:35 son of Sacar the Hararite, **E** the son of Ur, 465

ELIPHALET (2)
2Sa 5:16 And Elishama, and Eliada, and **E**. 467
1Ch 14: 7 And Elishama, and Beeliada, and **E**. 467

ELIPHAZ (15)
Ge 36: 4 Adah bare to Esau **E**; and Bashemath bare 464
36:10 **E** the son of Adah the wife of Esau, 464
36:11 the sons of **E** were Teman, Omar, Zepho, 464
36:12 And Timna was concubine to **E** Esau's son; 464

Ge 36:12 Esau's son; and she bare to E Amalek: 464
36:15 the sons of E the firstborn son of Esau; 464
36:16 these are the dukes that came of E in 464
1Ch 1:35 E, Reuel, and Jeush, and Jaalam, and Korah. 464
1:36 The sons of E; Teman, and Omar, Zephi, 464
Job 2:11 E the Temanite, and Bildad the Shuhite, and 464
4: 1 Then E the Temanite answered and said, 464
15: 1 Then answered E the Temanite, and said, 464
22: 1 Then E the Temanite answered and said, 464
42: 7 the LORD said to E the Temanite, 464
42: 9 So E the Temanite and Bildad the Shuhite 464

ELIPHELEH (2)
1Ch 15:18 E, and Mikneiah, and Obed-edom, and Jeiel, 466
15:21 E, and Mikneiah, and Obed-edom, and Jeiel, 466

ELIPHELEHU See ELIPHELEH

ELIPHELET (6)
2Sa 23:34 E the son of Ahasbai, the son of 467
1Ch 3: 6 Ibhar also, and Elishama, and E, 467
3: 8 And Elishama, and Eliada, and E, nine. 467
8:39 Jehush the second, and E the third. 467
Ezr 8:13 E, Jeiel, and Shemaiah, and with them 467
10:33 Zabad, E, Jeremai, Manasseh, and Shimei. 467

ELISABETH (8) [ELISABETH'S]
Lk 1: 5 daughters of Aaron, and her name was E. 1665
1: 7 because that E was barren, and they both 1665
1:13 and thy wife E shall bear thee a son, and 1665
1:24 And after those days his wife E conceived, 1665
1:36 And behold, thy cousin E, she hath also 1665
1:40 into the house of Zacharias, and saluted E. 1665
1:41 And it came to pass that, when E heard 1665
1:41 and E was filled with the Holy Ghost: 1665

ELISABETH'S (1) [ELISABETH]
Lk 1:57 Now E full time came that she should be 1665

ELISEUS (1) [ELISHA]
Lk 4:27 were in Israel in the time of E the prophet; 1666

ELISHA (58) [ELISEUS]
1Ki 19:16 E the son of Shaphat of Abel-meholah shalt 477
19:17 from the sword of Jehu shall E slay. 477
19:19 and found E the son of Shaphat, 477
2Ki 2: 1 that Elijah went with E from Gilgal. 477
2: 2 Elijah said unto E, Tarry here, I pray thee; 477
2: 2 And E said unto him, As the LORD liveth, 477
2: 3 that were at Beth-el came forth to E, 477
2: 4 said unto him, E, tarry here, I pray thee; 477
2: 5 the prophets that were at Jericho came to E, 477
2: 9 they were gone over, that Elijah said unto E, 477
2: 9 E said, I pray thee, let a double portion of 477
2:12 E saw it, and he cried, My father, my father, 477
2:14 parted hither and thither: and E went over. 477
2:15 they said, The spirit of Elijah doth rest on E. 477
2:19 And the men of the city said unto E, Behold, 477
2:22 according to the saying of E which he spake. 477
3:11 and said, Here is E the son of Shaphat, 477
3:13 E said unto the king of Israel, What have I to 477
3:14 E said, As the LORD of hosts liveth, before 477
4: 1 the wives of the sons of the prophets unto E, 477
4: 2 E said unto her, What shall I do for thee? 477
4: 8 it fell on a day, that E passed to Shunem, 477
4:17 bare a son at that season that E had said unto 477
4:32 when E was come into the house, behold, 477
4:38 E came again to Gilgal: and there was a 477
5: 8 when E the man of God had heard that 477
5: 9 and stood at the door of the house of E. 477
5:10 E sent a messenger unto him, saying, Go 477
5:20 the servant of E the man of God, said, 477
5:25 E said unto him, Whence comest thou, 477
6: 1 the sons of the prophets said unto E, 477
6:12 E, the prophet that is in Israel, telleth 477
6:17 E prayed, and said, LORD, I pray thee, 477
6:17 of horses and chariots of fire round about E. 477
6:18 E prayed unto the LORD, and said, 477
6:18 with blindness according to the word of E. 477
6:19 E said unto them, This is not the way, 477
6:20 come into Samaria, that E said, LORD, 477
6:21 the king of Israel said unto E, when he saw 477
6:31 if the head of E the son of Shaphat shall 477
6:32 E sat in his house, and the elders sat with 477
7: 1 E said, Hear ye the word of the LORD; 477
8: 1 spake E unto the woman, whose son he had 477
8: 4 all the great things that E hath done. 477
8: 5 and this is her son, whom E restored to life. 477
8: 7 E came to Damascus; and Ben-hadad 477
8:10 E said unto him, Go, say unto him, 477
8:13 E answered, The LORD hath shewed me 477
8:14 So he departed from E, and came to his 477
8:14 who said to him, What said E to thee? 477
9: 1 E the prophet called one of the children of 477
13:14 Now E was fallen sick of his sickness 477
13:15 And E said unto him, Take bow and arrows. 477
13:16 and E put his hands upon the king's hands. 477
13:17 he opened it. Then E said, Shoot. And he 477
13:20 E died, and they buried him. And the bands 477
13:21 they cast the man into the sepulchre of E: 477
13:21 and touched the bones of E, he revived, and 477

ELISHAH (3)
Ge 10: 4 E, and Tarshish, Kittim, and Dodanim. 473
1Ch 1: 7 E, and Tarshish, Kittim, and Dodanim. 473
Eze 27: 7 purple from the isles of E was that which 473

ELISHAMA (17)
Nu 1:10 of Ephraim; E the son of Ammihud: 476
2:18 the captain of the sons of Ephraim shall be E 476
7:48 On the seventh day E the son of Ammihud, 476
7:53 this was the offering of E the son of 476
10:22 over his host was E the son of Ammihud. 476
2Sa 5:16 And E, and Eliada, and Eliphalet. 476
2Ki 25:25 the son of E, of the seed royal, came, and 476
1Ch 2:41 begat Jekamiah, and Jekamiah begat E. 476
3: 6 Ibhar also, and E, and Eliphelet, 476
3: 8 And E, and Eliada, and Eliphelet, nine. 476
7:26 Laadan his son, Ammihud his son, E his son, 476
14: 7 And E, and Beeliada, and Eliphalet. 476
2Ch 17: 8 and with them E and Jehoram, priests. 476
Jer 36:12 even E the scribe, and Delaiah the son of 476
36:20 they laid up the roll in the chamber of E 476
36:21 and he took it out of E the scribe's chamber. 476
41: 1 Ishmael the son of Nethaniah the son of E, 476

ELISHAPHAT (1)
2Ch 23: 1 E the son of Zichri, into covenant with him. 478

ELISHEBA (1)
Ex 6:23 Aaron took him E, daughter of Amminadab, 472

ELISHUA (2)
2Sa 5:15 Ibhar also, and E, and Nepheg, and Japhia, 474
1Ch 14: 5 And Ibhar, and E, and Elpalet, 474

ELIUD (2)
Mt 1:14 Sadoc begat Achim; and Achim begat E; 1664
1:15 And E begat Eleazar; and Eleazar begat 1664

ELIZABETH See ELISABETH

ELIZAPHAN (4)
Nu 3:30 the Kohathites shall be E the son of Uzziel. 469
34:25 children of Zebulun, E the son of Parnach. 469
1Ch 15: 8 Of the sons of E; Shemaiah the chief, and 469
2Ch 29:13 And of the sons of E; Shimri, and Jeiel: and 469

ELIZUR (5)
Nu 1: 5 of the tribe of Reuben; E the son of Shedeur. 468
2:10 of Reuben shall be E the son of Shedeur. 468
7:30 On the fourth day E the son of Shedeur, 468
7:35 this was the offering of E the son of 468
10:18 and over his host was E the son of Shedeur. 468

ELKANAH (21)
Ex 6:24 sons of Korah; Assir, and E, and Abiasaph: 511
1Sa 1: 1 of mount Ephraim, and his name was E, 511
1: 4 when the time was that E offered, he gave to 511
1: 8 said E her husband to her, Hannah, why 511
1:19 E knew Hannah his wife; and the LORD 511
1:21 the man E, and all his house, went up to 511
1:23 E her husband said unto her, Do what 511
2:11 E went to Ramah to his house. And the child 511
2:20 Eli blessed E and his wife, and said, 511
1Ch 6:23 E his son, and Ebiasaph his son, and 511
6:25 And the sons of E; Amasai, and Ahimoth. 511
6:26 As for E: the sons of Elkanah; Zophai his 511
6:26 the sons of E; Zophai his son, and 511
6:27 Eliab his son, Jeroham his son, E his son. 511

1Ch 6:34 The son of **E**, the son of Jeroham, the son of 511
6:35 The son of Zuph, the son of **E**, the son of 511
6:36 The son of **E**, the son of Joel, the son of 511
9:16 and Berechiah the son of Asa, the son of **E**, 511
12: 6 **E**, and Jesiah, and Azareel, and Joezer, and 511
15:23 and **E** *were* doorkeepers for the ark. 511
2Ch 28: 7 of the house, and **E** *that was* next to the king. 511

ELKOSHITE (1)
Na 1: 1 The book of the vision of Nahum the **E**. 512

ELLASAR (2)
Ge 14: 1 Arioch king of **E**, Chedorlaomer king of 495
14: 9 king of Shinar, and Arioch king of **E**; 495

E

ELMADAM See ELMODAM

ELMODAM (1)
Lk 3:28 which was *the son* of **E**, which was *the son* *1678*

ELMS (1)
Hos 4:13 under oaks and poplars and **e**, because 424

ELNAAM (1)
1Ch 11:46 the sons of **E**, and Ithmah the Moabite, 493

ELNATHAN (7)
2Ki 24: 8 the daughter of **E** of Jerusalem. 494
Ezr 8:16 for **E**, and for Jarib, and for Elnathan, and 494
8:16 for **E**, and for Nathan, and for Zechariah, 494
8:16 for Joiarib, and for **E**, *men* of understanding. 494
Jer 26:22 *namely,* **E** the son of Achbor, and 494
36:12 **E** the son of Achbor, and Gemariah the son 494
36:25 Nevertheless **E** and Delaiah and 494

ELOI (2) [ELI]
Mk 15:34 saying, **E**, ELOI, *1682*
15:34 saying, ELOI, **E**, *1682*

ELON (7) [ELON-BETH-HANAN, ELONITES]
Ge 26:34 and Bashemath the daughter of **E** the Hittite: 356
36: 2 Adah the daughter of **E** the Hittite, and 356
46:14 sons of Zebulun; Sered, and **E**, and Jahleel. 440
Nu 26:26 of **E**, the family of the Elonites: of Jahleel, 356
Jos 19:43 And **E**, and Thimnathah, and Ekron, 356
Jdg 12:11 And after him **E**, a Zebulonite, judged Israel; 356
12:12 **E** the Zebulonite died, and was buried in 356

ELON-BETH-HANAN (1) [ELON, HANAN]
1Ki 4: 9 and in Shaalbim, and Beth-shemesh, and **E**: 358

ELONITES (1) [ELON]
Nu 26:26 of Elon, the family of the **E**: of Jahleel, 440

ELOQUENT (3)
Ex 4:10 I *am* not **e**, neither heretofore, 376+1697
Isa 3: 3 and the cunning artificer, and the **e** orator. 995
Ac 18:24 an **e** man, *and* mighty in the scriptures, *3052*

ELOTH (3) [ELATH]
1Ki 9:26 which *is* beside **E**, on the shore of the Red 359
2Ch 8:17 and to **E**, at the sea side in the land of Edom. 359
26: 2 He built **E**, and restored it to Judah, after that 359

ELPAAL (3)
1Ch 8:11 And of Hushim he begat Abitub, and **E**. 508
8:12 The sons of **E**; Eber, and Misham, and 508
8:18 and Jezliah, and Jobab, the sons of **E**; 508

ELPALET (1)
1Ch 14: 5 And Ibhar, and Elishua, and **E**, 467

EL-PARAN (1) [PARAN]
Ge 14: 6 unto **E**, which *is* by the wilderness. 364

ELPELET See ELPALET

ELSE (48) See Index

ELTEKEH (2)
Jos 19:44 And **E**, and Gibbethon, and Baalath, 514
21:23 out of the tribe of Dan, **E** with her suburbs, 514

ELTEKON (1)
Jos 15:59 Maarath, and Beth-anoth, and **E**; six cities 515

ELTOLAD (2)
Jos 15:30 And **E**, and Chesil, and Hormah, 513
19: 4 And **E**, and Bethul, and Hormah, 513

ELUL (1)
Ne 6:15 in the twenty and fifth *day* of the *month* **E**, 435

ELYMAS (1)
Ac 13: 8 But **E** the sorcerer (for so is his name by *1681*

ELZABAD (2)
1Ch 12:12 Johanan the eighth, **E** the ninth, 443
26: 7 Othni, and Rephael, and Obed, **E**, 443

ELZAPHAN (2)
Ex 6:22 sons of Uzziel; Mishael, and **E**, and Zithri. 469
Lev 10: 4 Moses called Mishael and **E**, the sons of 469

EMBALM (1) [EMBALMED]
Ge 50: 2 his servants the physicians to **e** his father: 2590

EMBALMED (3) [EMBALM]
Ge 50: 2 his father: and the physicians **e** Israel. 2590
50: 3 are fulfilled the days of those which are **e**: 2590
50:26 they **e** him, and he was put in a coffin in 2590

EMBOLDENED (1) [BOLD]
1Co 8:10 **e** to eat those things which are offered to *3618*

EMBOLDENETH (1) [BOLD]
Job 16: 3 an end? or what **e** thee that thou answerest? 4834

EMBRACE (8) [EMBRACED, EMBRACING]
2Ki 4:16 to the time of life, thou shalt **e** a son. 2263
Job 24: 8 and **e** the rock for want of a shelter. 2263
Pr 4: 8 bring thee to honour, when thou dost **e** her. 2263
5:20 and **e** the bosom of a stranger? 2263
Ecc 3: 5 a time to **e**, and a time to refrain from 2263
SS 2: 6 my head, and his right hand doth **e** me. 2263
8: 3 my head, and his right hand should **e** me. 2263
La 4: 5 they that were brought up in scarlet **e** 2263

EMBRACED (5) [EMBRACE]
Ge 29:13 **e** him, and kissed him, and brought him to 2263
33: 4 **e** him, and fell on his neck, and kissed him: 2263
48:10 unto him; and he kissed them, and **e** them. 2263
Ac 20: 1 and **e** *them,* and departed for to go into *782*
Heb 11:13 were persuaded of *them,* and **e** *them,* and *782*

EMBRACING (2) [EMBRACE]
Ecc 3: 5 to embrace, and a time to refrain from **e**; 2263
Ac 20:10 went down, and fell on him, and **e** *him* said, *4843*

EMBROIDER (1) [EMBROIDERER]
Ex 28:39 thou shalt **e** the coat of fine linen, and 7660

EMBROIDERED See DIVERS; DIVERSE

EMBROIDERER (2) [EMBROIDER]
Ex 35:35 of the **e**, in blue, and in purple, in scarlet, 7551
38:23 an **e** in blue, and in purple, and in scarlet, 7551

EMERALD (5) [EMERALDS]
Ex 28:18 the second row *shall be* an **e**, a sapphire, 5306
39:11 an **e**, a sapphire, and a diamond. 5306
Eze 28:13 the **e**, and the carbuncle, and gold: 5306
Rev 4: 3 about the throne, in sight like unto an **e**. *4664*
21:19 the third, a chalcedony; the fourth, an **e**; *4665*

EMERALDS (1) [EMERALD]
Eze 27:16 they occupied in thy fairs with **e**, purple, 5306

EMERODS (8)
Dt 28:27 with the **e**, and with the scab, and with 6076
1Sa 5: 6 smote them with **e**, *even* Ashdod and 2914
5: 9 and they had **e** in their secret parts. 2914
5:12 men that died not were smitten with the **e**: 2914
6: 4 Five golden **e**, and five golden mice, 2914
6: 5 Wherefore ye shall make images of your **e**, 2914
6:11 the mice of gold and the images of their **e**. 2914
6:17 these *are* the golden **e** which the Philistines 2914

EMIMS (3)
Ge 14: 5 in Ham, and the **E** in Shaveh Kiriathaim, 368
Dt 2:10 (The **E** dwelt therein in times past, a people 368
2:11 the Anakims; but the Moabites call them **E**. 368

EMINENT (4) [PREEMINENCE]
Eze 16:24 thou hast also built unto thee an **e place**, 1354
16:31 In that thou buildest thine **e place** in 1354
16:39 they shall throw down thine **e place**, and 1354
17:22 will plant *it* upon a high mountain and **e**: 8524

EMISSION See COPULATION

EMITES See EMIMS

EMMANUEL (1) [IMMANUEL]
Mt 1:23 forth a son, and they shall call his name **E**, *1694*

EMMAUS (1)
Lk 24:13 went *that* same day to a village called **E**, *1695*

EMMOR (1) [HAMOR]
Ac 7:16 of the sons of **E** the *father* of Sychem. *1697*

EMPIRE (1)
Est 1:20 shall be published throughout all his **e**, 4438

EMPLOY (1) [EMPLOYED, EMPLOYMENT]
Dt 20:19 to **e** *them* in the siege: 935+4480+6440

EMPLOYED (2) [EMPLOY]
1Ch 9:33 for they were **e** in *that* work day and night. 5921
Ezr 10:15 Jahaziah the son of Tikvah were **e** about 5975

EMPLOYMENT (1) [EMPLOY]
Eze 39:14 they shall sever out men of **continual e**, 8548

EMPTIED (8) [EMPTY]
Ge 24:20 **e** her pitcher into the trough, and ran again 6168
42:35 it came to pass as they **e** their sacks, 7324
2Ch 24:11 high priest's officer came and **e** the chest, 6168
Ne 5:13 even thus be he shaken out, and **e**. 7386
Isa 19: 6 *and* the brooks of defence shall be **e** and 1809
24: 3 The land shall be **utterly e**, 1238+1238
Jer 48:11 and hath not been **e** from vessel to vessel, 7324
Na 2: 2 for the emptiers have **e** them **out**, and 1238

EMPTIERS (1) [EMPTY]
Na 2: 2 for the **e** have emptied them out, and 1238

EMPTINESS (1) [EMPTY]
Isa 34:11 it the line of confusion, and the stones of **e**. 922

EMPTY (38) [EMPTIED, EMPTIERS, EMPTINESS]
Ge 31:42 surely thou hadst sent me away now **e**. 7387
37:24 and the pit *was* **e**, *there was* no water in it. 7386
41:27 the seven **e** ears blasted with the east wind 7386
Ex 3:21 to pass, that, when ye go, ye shall not go **e**: 7387
23:15 and none shall appear before me **e**: 7387
34:20 and none shall appear before me **e**. 7387
Lev 14:36 the priest shall command that they **e** 6437
Dt 15:13 from thee, thou shalt not let him go away **e**: 7387
16:16 they shall not appear before the LORD **e**: 7387
Jdg 7:16 with **e** pitchers, and lamps within 7386
Ru 1:21 the LORD hath brought me *home* again **e**: 7387
3:17 to me, Go not **e** unto thy mother in law. 7387
1Sa 6: 3 the ark of the God of Israel, send it not **e**; 7387
20:18 shalt be missed, because thy seat will be **e**. 6485
20:25 sat by Saul's side, and David's place was **e**. 6485
20:27 *day* of the month, that David's place was **e**: 6485
2Sa 1:22 and the sword of Saul returned not **e**. 7387
2Ki 4: 3 of all thy neighbours, *even* **e** vessels; 7386
Job 22: 9 Thou hast sent widows away **e**, and 7387
26: 7 He stretcheth out the north over the **e place**, 8414
Ecc 11: 3 *of* rain, they **e** *themselves* upon the earth: 7324
Isa 24: 1 the LORD **maketh** the earth **e**, and 1238
29: 8 he eateth; but he awaketh, and his soul *is* **e**: 7386
32: 6 to **make e** the soul of the hungry, and 7324
Jer 14: 3 no water; they returned *with* their vessels **e**; 7387
48:12 shall **e** his vessels, and break their bottles. 7324
51: 2 that shall fan her, and shall **e** her land: 1238
51:34 crushed me, he hath made me an **e** vessel, 7385
Eze 24:11 set it **e** upon the coals thereof, that the brass 7386
Hos 10: 1 Israel *is* an **e** vine, he bringeth forth fruit 1238
Na 2:10 She *is* **e**, and void, and waste: and the heart 950
Hab 1:17 Shall they therefore **e** their net, and 7324
Zec 4:12 pipes **e** the golden *oil* out of themselves? 7324
Mt 12:44 he findeth *it* **e**, swept, and garnished. *4980*
Mk 12: 3 and beat *him*, and sent *him* away **e**. *2756*
Lk 1:53 and the rich he hath sent **e** away. *2756*
20:10 beat him, and sent *him* away **e**. *2756*
20:11 *him* shamefully, and sent *him* away **e**. *2756*

EMULATION (1) [EMULATIONS]
Ro 11:14 If by any means I may **provoke to e** *them* *3863*

EMULATIONS (1) [EMULATION]
Gal 5:20 hatred, variance, **e**, wrath, strife, seditions, *2205*

ENABLED (1)
1Ti 1:12 who hath **e** me, for that he counted me *1743*

ENAM (1)
Jos 15:34 and En-gannim, Tappuah, and **E**, 5879

ENAN (5) [HAZAR-ENAN]
Nu 1:15 Of Naphtali; Ahira the son of **E**. 5881
2:29 of Naphtali *shall be* Ahira the son of **E**. 5881
7:78 On the twelfth day Ahira the son of **E**, 5881
7:83 this *was* the offering of Ahira the son of **E**. 5881
10:27 of Naphtali *was* Ahira the son of **E**. 5881

ENCAMP (11) [CAMP]
Ex 14: 2 that they turn and **e** before Pi-hahiroth, 2583
14: 2 before it shall ye **e** by the sea. 2583
Nu 1:50 and shall **e** round about the tabernacle. 2583
2:17 as they **e**, so shall they set forward, 2583
2:27 those that **e** by him *shall be* the tribe of 2583
3:38 those that **e** before the tabernacle toward 2583
10:31 forasmuch as thou knowest how we are to **e** 2583
2Sa 12:28 and **e** against the city, and take it: 2583
Job 19:12 and **e** round about my tabernacle. 2583
Ps 27: 3 Though a host should **e** against me, 2583
Zec 9: 8 I will **e about** mine house because of 2583

ENCAMPED (33) [CAMP]
Ex 13:20 **e** in Etham, in the edge of the wilderness. 2583
15:27 palm trees: and they **e** there by the waters. 2583
18: 5 where he **e** *at* the mount of God: 2583
Nu 33:10 removed from Elim, and **e** by the Red sea. 2583
33:11 the Red sea, and **e** in the wilderness of Sin. 2583
33:12 of the wilderness of Sin, and **e** in Dophkah. 2583
33:13 departed from Dophkah, and **e** in Alush. 2583
33:14 removed from Alush, and **e** at Rephidim, 2583
33:17 from Kibroth-hattaavah, and **e** at Hazeroth. 2583
33:24 from mount Shapher, and **e** in Haradah. 2583
33:26 removed from Makheloth, and **e** at Tahath. 2583
33:30 from Hashmonah, and **e** at Moseroth. 2583
33:32 from Bene-jaakan, and **e** at Hor-hagidgad. 2583
33:34 removed from Jotbathah, and **e** at Ebronah. 2583
33:35 from Ebronah, and **e** at Ezion-gaber. 2583
33:46 and **e** in Almon-diblathaim. 2583
Jos 4:19 **e** in Gilgal, in the east border of Jericho. 2583
5:10 the children of Israel **e** in Gilgal, and 2583
10: 5 **e** before Gibeon, and made war against it. 2583
10:31 and **e** against it, and fought against it: 2583
10:34 and they **e** against it, and fought against it: 2583
Jdg 6: 4 they **e** against them, and destroyed 2583
9:50 and **e** against Thebez, and took it. 2583
10:17 were gathered together, and **e** in Gilead. 2583
10:17 themselves together, and **e** in Mizpeh. 2583
20:19 up in the morning, and **e** against Gibeah. 2583
1Sa 11: 1 came up, and **e** against Jabesh-gilead: 2583
13:16 but the Philistines **e** in Michmash. 2583
2Sa 11:11 of my lord, are **e** in the open fields; 2583
1Ki 16:15 the people *were* **e** against Gibbethon, 2583
16:16 the people that *were* **e** heard say, Zimri hath 2583
1Ch 11:15 the host of the Philistines **e** in the valley of 2583
2Ch 32: 1 **e** against the fenced cities, and thought to 2583

ENCAMPETH (2) [CAMP]
Ps 34: 7 The angel of the LORD **e** round about 2583
53: 5 the bones of him that **e** *against* thee: 2583

ENCAMPING (1) [CAMP]
Ex 14: 9 overtook them **e** by the sea, 2583

ENCHANTER (1) [ENCHANTERS, ENCHANTMENT, ENCHANTMENTS]
Dt 18:10 an observer of times, or an **e**, or a witch, 5172

ENCHANTERS (1) [ENCHANTER]
Jer 27: 9 nor to your **e**, nor to your sorcerers, 6049

ENCHANTMENT (3) [ENCHANTER]
Lev 19:26 neither shall ye **use e**, nor observe times. 5172

Nu 23:23 Surely *there is* no **e** against Jacob, neither *is* 5173
Ecc 10:11 Surely the serpent will bite without **e**; and 3908

ENCHANTMENTS (10) [ENCHANTER]
Ex 7:11 they also did in like manner with their **e**. 3858
7:22 the magicians of Egypt did so with their **e**: 3909
8: 7 the magicians did so with their **e**, and 3909
8:18 so with their **e** to bring forth lice, 3909
Nu 24: 1 to seek for **e**, but he set his face toward 5173
2Ki 17:17 used divination and **e**, and sold themselves 5172
21: 6 **used e**, and dealt with familiar spirits and 5172
2Ch 33: 6 **used e**, and used witchcraft, and dealt with 5172
Isa 47: 9 *and* for the great abundance of thine **e**. 2267
47:12 Stand now with thine **e**, and with 2267

ENCLOSE See INCLOSE

ENCOUNTERED (1)
Ac 17:18 the Epicureans, and of the Stoicks, **e** him. *4820*

ENCOURAGE (4) [ENCOURAGED]
Dt 1:38 **e** him: for he shall cause Israel to inherit it. 2388
3:28 and **e** him, and strengthen him: 2388
2Sa 11:25 the city, and overthrow it: and **e** thou him. 2388
Ps 64: 5 They **e** themselves *in* an evil matter: 2388

ENCOURAGED (5) [ENCOURAGE]
Jdg 20:22 the people the men of Israel **e** themselves, 2388
1Sa 30: 6 but David **e** himself in the LORD his God. 2388
2Ch 31: 4 that they might be **e** in the law of 2388
35: 2 **e** them to the service of the house of 2388
Isa 41: 7 So the carpenter **e** the goldsmith, *and* 2388

END (307) [ENDED, ENDETH, ENDING, ENDLESS, ENDS]
Ge 6:13 The **e** of all flesh is come before me; 7093
8: 3 after the **e** of the hundred and fifty days 7097
8: 6 it came to pass at the **e** of forty days, 7093
23: 9 which he hath, which *is* in the **e** of his field; 7097
27:30 as soon as Isaac had **made an e** of blessing 3615
41: 1 it came to pass at the **e** of two full years, 7093
47:21 he removed them to cities from *one* **e** of 7097
47:21 of Egypt even to the *other* **e** thereof. 7097
49:33 when Jacob had **made an e** of commanding 3615
Ex 8:22 *of flies* shall be there; **to the e** 4616+3807.1
12:41 it came to pass at the **e** of the four hundred 7093
23:16 of ingathering, *which is* in the **e** of the year, 3318
25:19 make one cherub on the one **e**, and 7098
25:19 and the other cherub on the other **e**: 7098
26:28 of the boards shall reach from **e** to end. 7097
26:28 of the boards shall reach from end to **e**. 7097
31:18 when he had **made an e** of communing 3615
34:22 and the feast of ingathering *at* the year's **e**. 8622
36:33 the boards from the one **e** to the other. 7097
37: 8 One cherub on the **e** on this side, and 7098
37: 8 another cherub on the *other* **e** on that side: 7098
Lev 8:33 the days of your consecration be **at an e**: 4390
16:20 when he hath **made an e** of reconciling 3615
17: 5 **To the e** that the children of Israel 4616+3807.1
Nu 4:15 his sons have **made an e** of covering 3615
16:31 as he had **made an e** of speaking all these 3615
23:10 the righteous, and let my **last e** be like his! 319
24:20 his **latter e** *shall be* that he perish for ever. 319
Dt 8:16 prove thee, to do thee good at thy **latter e**; 319
9:11 it came to pass at the **e** of forty days and 7093
11:12 of the year even unto the **e** of the year. 319
13: 7 from the *one* **e** of the earth even unto 7097
13: 7 the earth even unto the *other* **e** of the earth; 7097
14:28 At the **e** of three years thou shalt bring forth 7097
15: 1 At the **e** of *every* seven years thou shalt 7093
17:16 to return to Egypt, **to the e that** 4616+3807.1
17:20 *to* the left: **to the e that** he may 4616+3807.1
20: 9 when the officers have **made an e** of 3615
26:12 When thou hast **made an e** of tithing all 3615
28:49 from the **e** of the earth, *as swift* as the eagle 7097
28:64 from the *one* **e** of the earth even unto 7097
31:10 saying, At the **e** of *every* seven years, 7093
31:24 when Moses had **made an e** of writing 3615
32:20 I will see what their **e** *shall be*: for they *are* a 319
32:29 *that* they would consider their **latter e**! 319
32:45 Moses **made an e** of speaking all these 3615
Jos 8:24 when Israel had **made an e** of slaying all 3615
9:16 it came to pass at the **e** of three days after 7097
10:20 the children of Israel had **made an e** of 3615
15: 5 *was* the salt sea, *even* unto the **e** of Jordan. 7097
15: 8 which *is* at the **e** of the valley of the giants 7097
18:15 the south quarter *was* from the **e** of 7097
18:16 the border came down to the **e** of 7097
18:19 bay of the salt sea at the south **e** of Jordan: 7097
19:49 When they had **made an e** of dividing 3615
19:51 So they **made an e** of dividing the country. 3615
Jdg 3:18 when he had **made an e** to offer 3615
6:21 the angel of the LORD put forth the **e** of 7097
11:39 it came to pass at the **e** of two months, 7093
15:17 when he had **made an e** of speaking, 3615
19: 9 behold, the day **groweth to an e**, 2583
Ru 2:23 Boaz to glean unto the **e** of barley harvest 3615
3: 7 he went to lie down at the **e** of the heap *of* 7097
3:10 in the **latter e** than at the beginning, 314
1Sa 3:12 when I begin, I will also **make an e**. 3615
9:27 *And* as they were going down to the **e** of 7097
10:13 when he had **made an e** of prophesying, 3615
13:10 that as soon as he had **made an e** of 3615
14:27 wherefore he put forth the **e** of the rod that 7097
14:43 taste a little honey with the **e** of the rod that 7097
18: 1 when he **made an e** of speaking unto Saul, 3615
24:16 when David had **made an e** of speaking 3615
2Sa 2:23 wherefore Abner with the **hinder e** of 310
2:26 not that it will be bitterness in the **latter e**? 314
6:18 as soon as David had **made an e** of offering 3615
11:19 When thou hast **made an e** of telling 3615
13:36 as soon as he had **made an e** of speaking, 3615
14:26 (for it was at every year's **e** that he polled 7093
24: 8 they came *to* Jerusalem at the **e** of nine 7097
1Ki 1:41 heard *it* as they had **made an e** of eating. 3615
2:39 it came to pass at the **e** of three years, 7093
3: 1 until he had **made an e** of building his own 3615
7:40 So Hiram **made an e** of doing all the work 3615
8:54 *that* when Solomon had **made an e** of 3615
9:10 it came to pass at the **e** of twenty years, 7097
2Ki 8: 3 it came to pass at the seven years' **e**, 7097
10:21 the house of Baal was full from **one e** to 6310
10:25 as soon as he had **made an e** of offering 3615
18:10 at the **e** of three years they took it: *even* in 7097
21:16 till he had filled Jerusalem from **one e** to 6310
1Ch 16: 2 when David had **made an e** of offering 3615
2Ch 4:10 he set the sea on the right side of the **east e**, 6924
5:12 stood *at* the east **e** of the altar, and NIH
7: 1 Now when Solomon had **made an e** of 3615
8: 1 it came to pass at the **e** of twenty years, 7093
20:16 ye shall find them at the **e** of the brook, 5490
20:23 when they had **made an e** of 3615
21:19 in process of time, after the **e** of two years, 7093
24:10 into the chest, until *they* had **made an e**. 3615
24:23 it came to pass at the **e** of the year, *that* 8622
29:17 day of the first month they **made an e**. 3615
29:29 when *they* had **made an e** of offering, 3615
Ezr 9:11 which have filled it from one **e** to another 6310
10:17 they **made an e** with all the men that had 3615
Ne 3:21 even to the **e** of the house of Eliashib. 8503
4: 2 will they **make an e** in a day? will they 3615
Job 6:11 what *is* mine **e**, that I should prolong my 7093
8: 7 yet thy **latter e** should greatly increase. 319
16: 3 Shall vain words **have an e**? or 7093
18: 2 How long *will it be ere* you make an **e** of 7078
26:10 until the day and night **come to an e**. 8503
28: 3 He setteth an **e** to darkness, and searcheth 7093
34:36 desire *is that* Job may be tried unto the **e** 5331
42:12 So the LORD blessed the **latter e** of Job 319
Ps 7: 9 wickedness of the wicked **come to an e**; 1584
9: 6 destructions are **come to** a perpetual **e**: 8552
19: 4 and their words to the **e** of the world. 7097
19: 6 His going forth *is* from the **e** of the heaven, 7097
30:12 **To the e that** *my* glory may sing 4616+3807.1
37:37 the upright: for the **e** of *that* man *is* peace. 319
37:38 the **e** of the wicked shall be cut off. 319
39: 4 make me to know mine **e**, and the measure 7093
46: 9 He maketh wars to cease unto the **e** of 7097
61: 2 From the **e** of the earth will I cry unto thee, 7097
73:17 sanctuary of God; *then* understood I their **e**. 319
102:27 *art* the same, and thy years shall have no **e**. 8552
107:27 and are **at their wit's e**. 1104+2451+3605
119:33 thy statutes; and I shall keep it *unto* the **e**. 6118
119:96 I have seen an **e** of all perfection: *but* 7093
119:112 perform thy statutes alway, *even unto* the **e**. 6118
Pr 5: 4 her **e** is bitter as wormwood, sharp as a 319
14:12 but the **e** thereof *are* the ways of death. 319
14:13 and the **e** of that mirth *is* heaviness. 319
16:25 but the **e** thereof *are* the ways of death. 319
19:20 that thou mayest be wise in thy **latter e**. 319

Pr 20:21 but the **e** thereof shall not be blessed. 319
23:18 For surely there is an **e**; and 319
25: 8 lest *thou know not* what to do in the **e** 319
Ecc 3:11 God maketh from the beginning to the **e**. 5490
4: 8 yet *is there* no **e** of all his labour; neither is 7093
4:16 *There is* no **e** of all the people, *even* of all 7093
7: 2 for that *is* the **e** of all men; and the living 5490
7: 8 Better *is* the **e** of a thing than the beginning 319
7:14 to the **e** that man should find nothing after 1700
10:13 and the **e** of his talk *is* mischievous madness. 319
12:12 of making many books *there is* no **e**; and 7093
Isa 2: 7 neither *is there any* **e** of their treasures; 7097
2: 7 neither *is there any* **e** of their chariots: 7097
5:26 will hiss unto them from the **e** of the earth: 7097
7: 3 at the **e** of the conduit of the upper pool in 7097
9: 7 and peace *there shall be* no **e**, 7093
13: 5 from the **e** of the heaven, *even* the LORD, 7097
16: 4 for the extortioner is **at an e**, the spoiler 656
23:15 after the **e** of seventy years shall Tyre sing 7093
23:17 it shall come to pass after the **e** of seventy 7093
33: 1 when thou shalt **make an e** to deal 5239
38:12 from day *even* to night wilt thou **make an e** 7999
38:13 from day *even* to night wilt thou **make an e** 7999
41:22 and know the **latter e** of them; 319
42:10 *and* his praise from the **e** of the earth, 7097
45:17 confounded **world without e**. 5703+5704+5769
46:10 Declaring the **e** from the beginning, and 319
47: 7 neither didst remember the **latter e** of it. 319
48:20 tell this, utter it *even* to the **e** of the earth; 7097
49: 6 that *thou* mayest be my salvation unto the **e** 7097
62:11 the LORD hath proclaimed unto the **e** of 7097
Jer 1: 3 unto the **e** of the eleventh year of Zedekiah 8552
3: 5 will he keep *it* to the **e**? Behold, thou hast 5331
4:27 be desolate; yet will I not make a **full e**. 3617
5:10 and destroy; but make not a **full e**: 3617
5:18 I will not make a **full e** with you. 3617
5:31 *it* so: and what will ye do in the **e** thereof? 319
12: 4 they said, He shall not see our **last e**. 319
12:12 **e** of the land even to the *other* end of 7097
12:12 of the land even to the *other* **e** of the land: 7097
17:11 midst of his days, and at his **e** shall be a fool. 319
25:33 **e** of the earth even unto the *other* end of 7097
25:33 the earth even unto the *other* **e** of the earth: 7097
26: 8 when Jeremiah had **made an e** of speaking 3615
29:11 and not of evil, to give you an expected **e**. 319
30:11 though I make a **full e** of all nations 3617
30:11 yet will I not make a **full e** of thee: 3617
31:17 there is hope in thine **e**, saith the LORD, 319
34:14 At the **e** of seven years let ye go every man 7093
43: 1 *that* when Jeremiah had **made an e** of 3615
44:27 by the famine, until there be an **e** of them. 3615
46:28 for I will make a **full e** of all the nations 3617
46:28 I will not make a **full e** of thee, but 3617
51:13 thine **e** is come, *and* the measure of thy 7093
51:31 of Babylon that his city is taken at *one* **e**, 7097
51:63 when thou hast **made an e** of reading this 3615
La 1: 9 she remembereth not her **last e**; therefore 319
4:18 our **e** is near, our days are fulfilled; for our 7093
4:18 our days are fulfilled; for our **e** is come. 7093
Eze 3:16 it came to pass at the **e** of seven days, 7097
7: 2 An **e**, the end is come upon the four corners 7093
7: 2 the **e** is come upon the four corners of 7093
7: 3 Now *is* the **e** *come* upon thee, and I will 7093
7: 6 An **e** is come, the end is come: it watcheth 7093
7: 6 An end is come, the **e** is come: it watcheth 7093
11:13 *wilt* thou make a **full e** of the remnant of 3617
20:17 neither did I make an **e** of them in 3617
20:26 might make them desolate, **to the e** 4616+3807.1
21:25 day is come, when iniquity *shall have* an **e**, 7093
21:29 when *their* iniquity *shall have* an **e**. 7093
29:13 At the **e** of forty years will I gather 7093
31:14 **To the e** that none of all the trees 4616+3807.1
35: 5 in the time *that their* iniquity *had* an **e**: 7093
39:14 after the **e** of seven months shall they 7097
41:12 **e** toward the west *was* seventy cubits broad; 6285
42:15 Now when he had **made an e** of measuring 3615
43:23 When thou hast **made an e** of cleansing *it,* 3615
48: 1 From the north **e** to the coast of the way of 7097
Da 1: 5 that at the **e** thereof they might stand before 7117
1:15 at the **e** of ten days their countenances 7117
1:18 Now at the **e** of the days that the king had 7117
4:11 the sight thereof to the **e** of all the earth: 5491
4:22 thy dominion to the **e** of the earth. 5491
4:29 At the **e** of twelve months he walked in 7118
4:34 at the **e** of the days I Nebuchadnezzar lift 7118
6:26 and his dominion *shall be even* unto the **e**. 5491
7:26 to consume and to destroy *it* unto the **e**. 5491
7:28 Hitherto *is* the **e** of the matter. *As for* me 5491
8:17 for at the time of the **e** *shall be* the vision. 7093
8:19 what shall be in the **last e** of the indignation: 319
8:19 for at the time appointed the **e** *shall be.* 7093
9:24 to **make an e** of sins, and to make 8552
9:26 the **e** thereof *shall be* with a flood, and 7093
9:26 unto the **e** of the war desolations *are* 7093
11: 6 in the **e** of years they shall join themselves 7093
11:27 for yet the **e** *shall be* at the time appointed. 7093
11:35 make *them* white, *even* to the time of the **e**: 7093
11:40 at the time of the **e** shall the king of 7093
11:45 yet he shall come to his **e**, and none shall 7093
12: 4 and seal the book, *even* to the time of the **e**: 7093
12: 6 How long *shall it be to* the **e** of *these* 7093
12: 8 my lord, what *shall be* the **e** of these *things?* 319
12: 9 closed up and sealed till the time of the **e**. 7093
12:13 go thou thy way till the **e** *be:* for thou shalt 7093
12:13 and stand in thy lot at the **e** of the days. 7093
Am 3:15 the great houses shall **have an e**, saith 5486
5:18 **to what e** *is* it for you? the day of 4100+3807.1
7: 2 *that* when they had **made an e** of eating 3615
8: 2 The **e** is come upon my people *of* Israel; 7093
8:10 an only *son,* and the **e** thereof as a bitter day. 319
Ob 1: 9 **to the e that** every one of 4616+3807.1
Na 1: 8 will make an **utter e** of the place thereof, 3617
1: 9 he *will* make an **utter e**: affliction shall not 3617
2: 9 for *there is* none **e** of the store *and* glory out 7097
3: 3 and *there is* none **e** of *their* corpses; 7097
Hab 2: 3 but at the **e** it shall speak, and not lie: 7093
Mt 10:22 but he that endureth to the **e** shall be saved. 5056
11: 1 when Jesus had **made an e** of commanding 5055
13:39 the harvest is the **e** of the world; and 4930
13:40 the fire; so shall it be in the **e** of this world. 4930
13:49 So shall it be at the **e** of the world: 4930
24: 3 of thy coming, and of the **e** of the world? 4930
24: 6 must come to pass, but the **e** is not yet. 5056
24:13 But he that shall endure unto the **e**, 5056
24:14 unto all nations; and then shall the **e** come. 5056
24:31 from one **e** of heaven to the other. 206
26:58 and sat with the servants, to see the **e**. 5056
28: 1 **In the e** of the sabbath, as it began to dawn 3796
28:20 you alway, *even* unto the **e** of the world. 4930
Mk 3:26 be divided, he cannot stand, but hath an **e**. 5056
13: 7 must needs be; but the **e** *shall* not *be* yet. 5056
13:13 but he that shall endure unto the **e**, the same 5056
Lk 1:33 and of his kingdom there shall be no **e**. 5056
18: 1 And he spake a parable unto them *to this* **e**, NIG
21: 9 come to pass; but the **e** *is* not by and by. 5056
22:37 for the *things* concerning me have an **e**. 5056
Jn 13: 1 in the world, he loved them unto the **e**. 5056
18:37 **To this e** was I born, and for this cause 1519
Ac 7:19 **to the e** *they* might not live. 1519+3588
Ro 1:11 **to the e** you may be established; 1519+3588
4:16 **to the e** the promise might be sure to 1519+3588
6:21 for the **e** of those *things is* death. 5056
6:22 unto holiness, and the **e** everlasting life. 5056
10: 4 For Christ *is* the **e** of the law for 5056
14: 9 For **to this e** Christ both died, and 1519+3778
1Co 1: 8 Who shall also confirm you unto the **e**, 5056
15:24 Then *cometh* the **e**, when he shall have 5056
2Co 1:13 I trust you shall acknowledge even to the **e**; 5056
2: 9 For **to this e** also did I write, that I 1519+3778
3:13 look to the **e** of that which is abolished: 5056
11:15 whose **e** shall be according to their works. 5056
Eph 3:21 all ages, **world without e**. 165+165+3588+3588
Php 3:19 Whose **e** *is* destruction, whose God *is their* 5056
1Th 3:13 **To the e** *he* may stablish your hearts 1519+3588
1Ti 1: 5 Now the **e** of the commandment is charity 5056
Heb 3: 6 the rejoicing of the hope firm unto the **e**. 5056
3:14 of *our* confidence stedfast unto the **e**; 5056
6: 8 nigh unto cursing; whose **e** *is* to be burned. 5056
6:11 to the full assurance of hope unto the **e**: 5056
6:16 an oath for confirmation *is* to them an **e** of 4009
7: 3 neither beginning of days, nor **e** of life; 5056
9:26 now once in the **e** of the world hath he 4930
13: 7 considering the **e** of *their* conversation. 1545
Jas 5:11 of Job, and have seen the **e** of the Lord; 5056
1Pe 1: 9 Receiving the **e** of your faith, *even* 5056
1:13 hope to the **e** for the grace that is *to be* 5049
4: 7 But the **e** of all *things* is at hand: be ye 5056
4:17 what *shall* the **e** *be* of them that obey not 5056

2Pe 2:20 the latter e is worse with them than NIG
Rev 2:26 and keepeth my works unto the e, *5056*
21: 6 and Omega, the beginning and the e. *5056*
22:13 the beginning and the e, the first and *5056*

ENDAMAGE (1) [DAMAGE]
Ezr 4:13 and *so* thou shalt e the revenue of the kings. 5142

ENDANGER (1) [ENDANGERED]
Da 1:10 shall ye **make** *me* e my head to the king. 2325

ENDANGERED (1) [ENDANGER]
Ecc 10: 9 he that cleaveth wood shall be e thereby. 5533

ENDEAVOUR (1) [ENDEAVOURED, ENDEAVOURING, ENDEAVOURS]
2Pe 1:15 Moreover I will e that you may be able *4704*

ENDEAVOURED (2) [ENDEAVOUR]
Ac 16:10 immediately we e to go into Macedonia, *2212*
1Th 2:17 e the more abundantly to see your face with *4704*

ENDEAVOURING (1) [ENDEAVOUR]
Eph 4: 3 E to keep the unity of the Spirit in the bond *4704*

ENDEAVOURS (1) [ENDEAVOUR]
Ps 28: 4 and according to the wickedness of their e: 4611

ENDED (21) [END]
Ge 2: 2 on the seventh day God e his work which 3615
41:53 that was in the land of Egypt, were e. 3615
47:18 When that year was e, they came unto him 8552
Dt 31:30 the words of this song, until they were e. 8552
34: 8 *and* mourning for Moses were e. 8552
Ru 2:21 until they have e all my harvest. 3615
2Sa 20:18 *counsel* at Abel: and so they e *the matter.* 8552
1Ki 7:51 So was e all the work that king Solomon 7999
2Ch 29:34 till the work was e, and until the *other* 3615
Job 31:40 instead of barley. The words of Job are e. 8552
Ps 72:20 The prayers of David the son of Jesse are e. 3615
Isa 60:20 and the days of thy mourning shall be e. 7999
Jer 8:20 the summer is e, and we are not saved. 3615
Eze 4: 8 till thou hast e the days of thy siege. 3615
Mt 7:28 to pass, when Jesus had e these sayings, *4931*
Lk 4: 2 and when they were e, he afterward *4931*
4:13 And when the devil had e all *4931*
7: 1 Now when he had e all his sayings in *4137*
Jn 13: 2 And supper being e, the devil having now *1096*
Ac 19:21 After these *things* were e, Paul purposed in *4137*
21:27 And when the seven days were almost e, *4931*

ENDETH (1) [END]
Isa 24: 8 the noise of them that rejoice e, the joy of 2308

ENDING (1) [END]
Rev 1: 8 and Omega, the beginning and the e, *5056*

ENDLESS (2) [END]
1Ti 1: 4 give heed to fables and e genealogies, *562*
Heb 7:16 but after the power of an e life. *179*

ENDOR, EN-DOR (3) [ENDOR]
Jos 17:11 the inhabitants of E and her towns, and 5874
1Sa 28: 7 *is* a woman that hath a familiar spirit at E. 5874
Ps 83:10 *Which* perished at E: they became *as* dung 5874

ENDOW (1)
Ex 22:16 he shall **surely** e her to be his wife. 4117+4117

ENDS (51) [END]
Ex 25:18 make them, in the two e of the mercy seat. 7098
25:19 make the cherubims on the two e thereof. 7098
28:14 two chains *of* pure gold at the e; 4020
28:22 at the e *of* wreathen work *of* pure gold. 1383
28:23 shalt put the two rings on the two e of 7098
28:24 rings *which are* on the e of the breastplate. 7098
28:25 *the other* two e of the two wreathen *chains* 7098
28:26 thou shalt put them upon the two e of 7098
37: 7 he them, on the two e of the mercy seat; 7098
37: 8 he the cherubims on the two e thereof. 7098
38: 5 he cast four rings for the four e of the grate 7099
39:15 made upon the breastplate chains **at the e**, 1383
39:16 put the two rings in the two e of 7098
39:17 in the two rings on the e of the breastplate. 7098
39:18 the two e of the two wreathen *chains* they 7098
39:19 put *them* on the two e of the breastplate, 7098
Dt 33:17 push the people together *to* the e of the earth: 657
1Sa 2:10 the LORD shall judge the e of the earth; 657
1Ki 8: 8 that the e of the staves were seen out in 7218
2Ch 5: 9 e of the staves were seen from the ark 7218
Job 28:24 For he looketh to the e of the earth, *and* 7098
37: 3 and his lightning unto the e of the earth. 3671
38:13 That *it* might take hold of the e of the earth, 3671
Ps 19: 6 the heaven, and his circuit unto the e of it: 7098
22:27 All the e of the world shall remember and 657
48:10 so *is* thy praise unto the e of the earth: 7099
59:13 God ruleth in Jacob unto the e of the earth. 657
65: 5 *who art* the confidence of all the e of 7099
67: 7 and all the e of the earth shall fear him. 657
72: 8 and from the river unto the e of the earth. 657
98: 3 all the e of the earth have seen the salvation 657
135: 7 vapours to ascend from the e of the earth; 7097
Pr 17:24 the eyes of a fool *are* in the e of the earth. 7097
30: 4 who hath established all the e of the earth? 657
Isa 26:15 thou hadst removed *it* far *unto* all the e of 7099
40:28 the Creator of the e of the earth, 7098
41: 5 the e of the earth were afraid, drew near, 7098
41: 9 *Thou* whom I have taken from the e of 7098
43: 6 and my daughters from the e of the earth; 7097
45:22 and be ye saved, all the e of the earth: 657
52:10 all the e of the earth shall see the salvation of 657
Jer 10:13 he causeth the vapours to ascend from the e 7097
16:19 the Gentiles shall come unto thee from the e 657
25:31 A noise shall come *even* to the e of 7097
51:16 he causeth the vapours to ascend from the e 7097
Eze 15: 4 the fire devoureth both the e of it, and 7098
Mic 5: 4 for now shall he be great unto the e of 657
Zec 9:10 and from the river *even* to the e of the earth. 657
Ac 13:47 be for salvation unto the e of the earth. *2078*
Ro 10:18 and their words unto the e of the world. *4009*
1Co 10:11 upon whom the e of the world are come. *5056*

ENDUED (5)
Ge 30:20 God hath e me with a good dowry; 2064
2Ch 2:12 e with prudence and understanding, 3045
2:13 e with understanding, of Huram my 3045
Lk 24:49 until ye be **e with** power from on high. *1746*
Jas 3:13 and e with knowledge amongst you? NIG

ENDURE (29) [ENDURED, ENDURETH, ENDURING]
Ge 33:14 and the children be **able to e**, 7272+3807.1
Ex 18:23 *so,* then thou shalt be able to e, 5975
Est 8: 6 For how can I e to see the evil that shall 3201
8: 6 how can I e to see the destruction of my 3201
Job 8:15 he shall hold it fast, but it shall not e. 6965
31:23 and by reason of his highness I **could** not e. 3201
Ps 9: 7 the LORD shall e for ever: he hath 3427
30: 5 weeping may e for a night, but joy *cometh* 3885
72: 5 thee as long as the sun and moon e, 6440+3807.1
72:17 His name shall e for ever: his name shall be 1961
89:29 His seed also will I make *to* e for ever, and NIH
89:36 His seed shall e for ever, and his throne as 1961
102:12 thou, O LORD, shalt e for ever; and 3427
102:26 They shall perish, but thou shalt e: yea, 5975
104:31 The glory of the LORD shall e for ever: 1961
Pr 27:24 and doth the crown e to every generation? NIH
Eze 22:14 Can thine heart e, or can thine hands be 5975
Mt 24:13 But he that shall e unto the end, the same *5278*
Mk 4:17 root in themselves, and so e but for a time; *1510*
13:13 but he that shall e unto the end, the same *5278*
2Th 1: 4 your persecutions and tribulations that ye e: *430*
2Ti 2: 3 Thou therefore e **hardness**, as a good *2553*
2:10 Therefore I e all *things* for the elects' sakes, *5278*
4: 3 For the time will come when they will not e *430*
4: 5 But watch thou in all *things,* **e afflictions**, *2553*
Heb 12: 7 If ye e chastening, God dealeth with you as *5278*
12:20 (For they could not e that which was *5342*
Jas 5:11 Behold, we count them happy which e. *5278*
1Pe 2:19 if a man for conscience toward God e grief, *5297*

ENDURED (8) [ENDURE]
Ps 81:15 but their time should have e for ever. 1961
Ro 9:22 e with much longsuffering *the* vessels of *5342*
2Ti 3:11 at Lystra; what persecutions I e: *5297*
Heb 6:15 And so, after he had **patiently** e, *3114*
10:32 ye e a great fight of afflictions; *5278*
11:27 for he e, as seeing *him who is* invisible. *2594*
12: 2 who for the joy that was set before him e *5278*
12: 3 For consider him that e such contradiction *5278*

ENDURETH (59) [ENDURE]

1Ch	16:34	for *he is* good; for his mercy *e* for ever.	NIH
	16:41	the LORD, because his mercy *e* for ever;	NIH
2Ch	5:13	For *he is* good; for his mercy *e* for ever:	NIH
	7: 3	For *he is* good; for his mercy *e* for ever.	NIH
	7: 6	because his mercy *e* for ever, when David	NIH
	20:21	Praise the LORD; for his mercy *e* for ever.	NIH
Ezr	3:11	for his mercy *e* for ever towards Israel.	NIH
Ps	30: 5	For his anger *e but* a moment; in his favour	NIH
	52: 1	O mighty *man?* the goodness of God *e*	NIH
	72: 7	of peace **so long as** the moon **e**.	1097+5704
	100: 5	his truth *e* to all generations.	NIH
	106: 1	for *he is* good: for his mercy *e* for ever.	NIH
	107: 1	for *he is* good: for his mercy *e* for ever.	NIH
	111: 3	glorious: and his righteousness **e** for ever.	5975
	111:10	*his commandments:* his praise **e** for ever.	5975
	112: 3	his house: and his righteousness **e** for ever.	5975
	112: 9	to the poor; his righteousness **e** for ever;	5975
	117: 2	the truth of the LORD *e* for ever. Praise ye	NIH
	118: 1	for *he is* good: because his mercy *e* for ever.	NIH
	118: 2	Israel now say, that his mercy *e* for ever.	NIH
	118: 3	of Aaron now say, that his mercy *e* for ever.	NIH
	118: 4	the LORD say, that his mercy *e* for ever.	NIH
	118:29	for *he is* good: for his mercy *e* for ever.	NIH
	119:160	every one of thy righteous judgments *e* for	NIH
	135:13	Thy name, O LORD, *e* for ever; *and*	NIH
	136: 1	for *he is* good: for his mercy *e* for ever.	NIH
	136: 2	the God of gods: for his mercy *e* for ever.	NIH
	136: 3	the Lord of lords: for his mercy *e* for ever.	NIH
	136: 4	great wonders: for his mercy *e* for ever.	NIH
	136: 5	made the heavens: for his mercy *e* for ever.	NIH
	136: 6	above the waters: for his mercy *e* for ever.	NIH
	136: 7	made great lights: for his mercy *e* for ever:	NIH
	136: 8	sun to rule by day: for his mercy *e* for ever:	NIH
	136: 9	to rule by night: for his mercy *e* for ever:	NIH
	136:10	in their firstborn: for his mercy *e* for ever:	NIH
	136:11	from among them: for his mercy *e* for ever:	NIH
	136:12	stretched out arm: for his mercy *e* for ever.	NIH
	136:13	Red sea into parts: for his mercy *e* for ever:	NIH
	136:14	the midst of it: for his mercy *e* for ever:	NIH
	136:15	host in the Red sea: for his mercy *e* for ever.	NIH
	136:16	the wilderness: for his mercy *e* for ever.	NIH
	136:17	smote great kings: for his mercy *e* for ever:	NIH
	136:18	slew famous kings: for his mercy *e* for ever:	NIH
	136:19	of the Amorites: for his mercy *e* for ever:	NIH
	136:20	the king of Bashan: for his mercy *e* for ever:	NIH
	136:21	for an heritage: for his mercy *e* for ever:	NIH
	136:22	Israel his servant: for his mercy *e* for ever.	NIH
	136:23	in our low estate: for his mercy *e* for ever:	NIH
	136:24	from our enemies: for his mercy *e* for ever.	NIH
	136:25	food to all flesh: for his mercy *e* for ever.	NIH
	136:26	the God of heaven: for his mercy *e* for ever.	NIH
	138: 8	thy mercy, O LORD, *e* for ever:	NIH
	145:13	thy dominion *e* throughout all generations.	NIH
Jer	33:11	LORD *is* good; for his mercy *e* for ever:	NIH
Mt	10:22	but he that **e** to the end shall be saved.	*5278*
Jn	6:27	for *that* meat which **e** unto everlasting life,	*3306*
1Co	13: 7	all *things,* hopeth all *things,* **e** all *things.*	*5278*
Jas	1:12	Blessed *is* the man that **e** temptation:	*5278*
1Pe	1:25	But the word of the Lord **e** for ever. And	*3306*

ENDURING (3) [ENDURE]

Ps	19: 9	The fear of the LORD *is* clean, **e** for ever:	5975
2Co	1: 6	which is effectual in the **e** of the same	*5281*
Heb	10:34	have in heaven a better and an **e** substance.	*3306*

EN-EGLAIM (1)

Eze	47:10	stand upon it from En-gedi even unto **E**;	5882

ENEMIES (267) [ENEMY]

Ge	14:20	which hath delivered thine **e** into thy hand.	6862
	22:17	and thy seed shall possess the gate of his **e**;	341
	49: 8	thy hand *shall be* in the neck of thine **e**;	341
Ex	1:10	they join also unto our **e**, and fight against	8130
	23:22	I will be an enemy unto thine **e**, and	341
	23:27	I will make all thine **e** turn their backs unto	341
	32:25	naked unto *their* shame amongst their **e**:)	6965
Lev	26: 7	ye shall chase your **e**, and they shall fall	341
	26: 8	your **e** shall fall before you by the sword.	341
	26:16	sow your seed in vain, for your **e** shall eat it.	341
	26:17	and ye shall be slain before your **e**;	341
	26:32	your **e** which dwell therein shall be	341
	26:36	into their hearts in the lands of their **e**;	341
	26:37	shall have no power to stand before your **e**.	341
	26:38	and the land of your **e** shall eat you up.	341
	26:41	have brought them into the land of their **e**;	341
	26:44	all that, when they be in the land of their **e**,	341
Nu	10: 9	your God, and ye shall be saved from your **e**.	341
	10:35	LORD, and let thine **e** be scattered;	341
	14:42	that ye be not smitten before your **e**.	341
	23:11	I took thee to curse mine **e**, and behold,	341
	24: 8	he shall eat up the nations his **e**, and	6862
	24:10	I called thee to curse mine **e**, and behold,	341
	24:18	Seir also shall be a possession for his **e**;	341
	32:21	until he hath driven out his **e** from before	341
Dt	1:42	among you; lest ye be smitten before your **e**.	341
	6:19	To cast out all thine **e** from before thee,	341
	12:10	*when* he giveth you rest from all your **e**	341
	20: 1	When thou goest out to battle against thine **e**,	341
	20: 3	approach *this* day unto battle against your **e**:	341
	20: 4	to fight for you against your **e**, to save you.	341
	20:14	thou shalt eat the spoil of thine **e**, which	341
	21:10	When thou goest forth to war against thine **e**,	341
	23: 9	When the host goeth forth against thine **e**,	341
	23:14	and to give up thine **e** before thee;	341
	25:19	given thee rest from all thine **e** round about,	341
	28: 7	The LORD shall cause thine **e** that rise up	341
	28:25	shall cause thee *to be* smitten before thine **e**:	341
	28:31	thy sheep *shall be* given unto thine **e**, and	341
	28:48	Therefore shalt thou serve thine **e** which	341
	28:53	wherewith thine **e** shall distress thee:	341
	28:55	wherewith thine **e** shall distress thee in all	341
	28:68	there ye shall be sold unto your **e** for	341
	30: 7	God will put all these curses upon thine **e**,	341
	32:31	even our **e** themselves *being* judges.	341
	32:41	I will render vengeance to mine **e**, and	6862
	33: 7	and be thou a help *to him* from his **e**.	6862
	33:29	thine **e** shall be found liars unto thee; and	341
Jos	7: 8	Israel turneth *their* backs before their **e**!	341
	7:12	of Israel could not stand before their **e**,	341
	7:12	*but* turned *their* backs before their **e**, because	341
	7:13	thou canst not stand before thine **e**, until ye	341
	10:13	people had avenged themselves upon their **e**.	341
	10:19	*but* pursue after your **e**, and smite	341
	10:25	for thus shall the LORD do to all your **e**	341
	21:44	there stood not a man of all their **e** before	341
	21:44	the LORD delivered all their **e** into their	341
	22: 8	divide the spoil of your **e** with your brethren.	341
	23: 1	rest unto Israel from all their **e** round about,	341
Jdg	2:14	he sold them into the hands of their **e** round	341
	2:14	could not any longer stand before their **e**.	341
	2:18	delivered them out of the hand of their **e** all	341
	3:28	for the LORD hath delivered your **e**	341
	5:31	So let all thine **e** perish, O LORD: but	341
	8:34	out of the hands of all their **e** on every side:	341
	11:36	hath taken vengeance for thee of thine **e**,	341
1Sa	2: 1	my mouth is enlarged over mine **e**; because	341
	4: 3	it may save us out of the hand of our **e**.	341
	12:10	now deliver us out of the hand of our **e**, and	341
	12:11	delivered you out of the hand of your **e** on	341
	14:24	that I may be avenged on mine **e**.	341
	14:30	day of the spoil of their **e** which they found?	341
	14:47	fought against all his **e** on every side,	341
	18:25	the Philistines, to be avenged of the king's **e**.	341
	20:15	not when the LORD hath cut off the **e** of	341
	20:16	even require *it* at the hand of David's **e**.	341
	25:22	and more also do God unto the **e** of David,	341
	25:26	now let thine **e**, and they that seek evil to my	341
	25:29	the souls of thine **e**, them shall he sling out	341
	29: 8	that I may not go fight against the **e** of my	341
	30:26	Behold a present for you of the spoil of the **e**	341
2Sa	3:18	and out of the hand of all their **e**.	341
	5:20	The LORD hath broken forth upon mine **e**	341
	7: 1	given him rest round about from all his **e**;	341
	7: 9	have cut off all thine **e** out of thy sight, and	341
	7:11	and have caused thee to rest from all thine **e**.	341
	12:14	to the **e** of the LORD to blaspheme,	341
	18:19	that the LORD hath avenged him of his **e**.	341
	18:32	The **e** of my lord the king, and all that rise	341
	19: 6	In that thou lovest thine **e**, and hatest thy	8130
	19: 9	The king saved us out of the hand of our **e**,	341
	22: 1	delivered him out of the hand of all his **e**,	341
	22: 4	be praised: so shall I be saved from mine **e**.	341
	22:38	I have pursued mine **e**, and destroyed them;	341
	22:41	Thou hast also given me the necks of mine **e**,	341
	22:49	that bringeth me forth from mine **e**: thou also	341
	24:13	wilt thou flee three months before thine **e**,	6862
1Ki	3:11	for thyself, nor hast asked the life of thine **e**;	341

E

E

1Ki	8:48	and with all their soul, in the land of their **e**,	341
2Ki	17:39	deliver you out of the hand of all your **e**.	341
	21:14	and deliver them into the hand of their **e**;	341
	21:14	shall become a prey and a spoil to all their **e**;	341
1Ch	12:17	if *ye be come* to betray me to mine **e**,	6862
	14:11	God hath broken in upon mine **e** by mine	341
	17: 8	and have cut off all thine **e** from before thee,	341
	17:10	Moreover I will subdue all thine **e**.	341
	21:12	while that the sword of thine **e** overtaketh	341
	22: 9	I will give him rest from all his **e** round	341
2Ch	1:11	wealth, or honour, nor the life of thine **e**,	8130
	6:28	if their **e** besiege them in the cities of their	341
	6:34	If thy people go out to war against their **e** by	341
	6:36	deliver them *over* before *their* **e**, and	341
	20:27	had made them to rejoice over their **e**.	341
	20:29	the LORD fought against the **e** of Israel.	341
	25:20	might deliver them into the hand *of their* **e**,	NIH
Ne	4:15	when our **e** heard that it was known unto us,	341
	5: 9	of the reproach of the heathen our **e**?	341
	6: 1	Geshem the Arabian, and the rest of our **e**,	341
	6:16	that when all our **e** heard *thereof,* and all	341
	9:27	deliveredst them into the hand of their **e**,	6862
	9:27	who saved them out of the hand of their **e**.	6862
	9:28	leftest thou them in the hand of their **e**,	341
Est	8:13	that day to avenge themselves on their **e**.	341
	9: 1	in the day that the **e** of the Jews hoped to	341
	9: 5	Thus the Jews smote all their **e** *with*	341
	9:16	had rest from their **e**, and slew of their foes	341
	9:22	days wherein the Jews rested from their **e**,	341
Job	19:11	he counteth me unto him as *one of* his **e**.	6862
Ps	3: 7	for thou hast smitten all mine **e** *upon*	341
	5: 8	in thy righteousness because of mine **e**;	8324
	6: 7	it waxeth old because of all mine **e**.	6887
	6:10	Let all mine **e** be ashamed and sore vexed:	341
	7: 6	up thyself because of the rage of mine **e**:	6887
	8: 2	thou ordained strength because of thine **e**,	6887
	9: 3	When mine **e** are turned back, they shall fall	341
	10: 5	his sight: *as for* all his **e**, he puffeth at them.	6887
	17: 9	*from* my deadly **e**, *who* compass me about.	341
	18: T	delivered him from the hand of all his **e**,	341
	18: 3	be praised: so shall I be saved from mine **e**.	341
	18:37	I have pursued mine **e**, and overtaken them:	341
	18:40	Thou hast also given me the necks of mine **e**;	341
	18:48	He delivereth me from mine **e**: yea,	341
	21: 8	Thine hand shall find out all thine **e**:	341
	23: 5	a table before me in the presence of mine **e**:	6887
	25: 2	be ashamed, let not mine **e** triumph over me.	341
	25:19	Consider mine **e**; for they are many; and	341
	27: 2	the wicked, *even* mine **e** and my foes,	6862
	27: 6	be lifted up above mine **e** round about me:	341
	27:11	lead me in a plain path, because of mine **e**.	8324
	27:12	me not over unto the will of mine **e**:	6862
	31:11	I was a reproach among all mine **e**, but	6887
	31:15	deliver me from the hand of mine **e**, and	341
	35:19	Let not them that are mine **e** wrongfully	341
	37:20	the **e** of the LORD *shall be* as the fat of	341
	38:19	mine **e** *are* lively, *and* they are strong: and	341
	41: 2	wilt not deliver him unto the will of his **e**.	341
	41: 5	Mine **e** speak evil of me, When shall he die,	341
	42:10	a sword in my bones, mine **e** reproach me;	6887
	44: 5	Through thee will we push down our **e**:	6862
	44: 7	thou hast saved us from our **e**, and hast put	6862
	45: 5	arrows *are* sharp in the heart of the king's **e**;	341
	54: 5	He shall reward evil unto mine **e**: cut them	8324
	54: 7	mine eye hath seen *his desire* upon mine **e**.	341
	56: 2	Mine **e** would daily swallow *me* up:	8324
	56: 9	I cry *unto thee,* then shall mine **e** turn back:	341
	59: 1	Deliver me from mine **e**, O my God:	341
	59:10	shall let me see *my desire* upon mine **e**.	8324
	60:12	for he *it is that* shall tread down our **e**.	6862
	66: 3	shall thine **e** submit themselves unto thee.	341
	68: 1	Let God arise, let his **e** be scattered: let them	341
	68:21	God shall wound the head of his **e**, *and*	341
	68:23	foot may be dipped in the blood of *thine* **e**,	341
	69: 4	*being* mine **e** wrongfully, are mighty:	341
	69:18	*and* redeem it: deliver me because of mine **e**.	341
	71:10	For mine **e** speak against me; and they that	341
	72: 9	bow before him; and his **e** shall lick the dust.	341
	74: 4	Thine **e** roar in the midst of thy	6887
	74:23	Forget not the voice of thine **e**: the tumult	6887
	78:53	feared not: but the sea overwhelmed their **e**.	341
	78:66	he smote his **e** in the hinder parts: he put	6862
	80: 6	and our **e** laugh among themselves.	341
	81:14	I should soon have subdued their **e**, and	341
	83: 2	For lo, thine **e** make a tumult: and they that	341
	89:10	thou hast scattered thine **e** with thy strong	341
	89:42	thou hast made all his **e** to rejoice.	341
	89:51	Wherewith thine **e** have reproached,	341
	92: 9	For lo, thine **e**, O LORD, for lo,	341
	92: 9	O LORD, for lo, thine **e** shall perish;	341
	92:11	eye also shall see *my desire* on mine **e**,	7790
	97: 3	and burneth up his **e** round about.	6862
	102: 8	Mine **e** reproach me all the day; *and*	341
	105:24	and made them stronger than their **e**.	6862
	106:11	the waters covered their **e**: there was not	6862
	106:42	Their **e** also oppressed them, and they were	341
	108:13	for he *it is that* shall tread down our **e**.	6862
	110: 1	right hand, until I make thine **e** thy footstool.	341
	110: 2	out of Zion: rule thou in the midst of thine **e**.	341
	112: 8	be afraid, until he see *his desire* upon his **e**.	6862
	119:98	hast made me wiser than mine **e**:	341
	119:139	because mine **e** have forgotten thy words.	6862
	119:157	Many *are* my persecutors and mine **e**;	6862
	127: 5	but they shall speak with the **e** in the gate.	341
	132:18	His **e** will I clothe with shame: but	341
	136:24	hath redeemed us from our **e**: for his mercy	6862
	138: 7	forth thine hand against the wrath of mine **e**,	341
	139:20	*and* thine **e** take *thy name* in vain.	6145
	139:22	*with* perfect hatred: I count them mine **e**.	341
	143: 9	Deliver me, O LORD, from mine **e**: I flee	341
	143:12	of thy mercy cut off mine **e**, and destroy all	341
Pr	16: 7	he maketh even his **e** to be at peace with	341
Isa	1:24	mine adversaries, and avenge me of mine **e**:	341
	9:11	of Rezin against him, and join his **e** together;	341
	26:11	yea, the fire of thine **e** shall devour them.	6862
	42:13	yea, roar; he shall prevail against his **e**.	341
	59:18	fury to his adversaries, recompence to his **e**;	341
	62: 8	no more give thy corn *to be* meat for thine **e**;	341
	66: 6	LORD that rendereth recompence to his **e**.	341
	66:14	and *his* indignation towards his **e**.	341
Jer	12: 7	beloved of my soul into the hand of her **e**.	341
	15: 9	will I deliver to the sword before their **e**,	341
	15:14	I will make *thee* to pass with thine **e** into a	341
	17: 4	I will cause thee to serve thine **e** in the land	341
	19: 7	them to fall by the sword before their **e**,	341
	19: 9	wherewith their **e**, and they that seek their	341
	20: 4	they shall fall by the sword of their **e**, and	341
	20: 5	of Judah will I give into the hand of their **e**,	341
	21: 7	into the hand of their **e**, and into the hand of	341
	34:20	I will even give them into the hand of their **e**,	341
	34:21	princes will I give into the hand of their **e**,	341
	44:30	king of Egypt into the hand of his **e**,	341
	48: 5	for in the going down of Horonaim the **e**	6862
	49:37	cause Elam to be dismayed before their **e**,	341
La	1: 2	with her, they are become her **e**.	341
	1: 5	Her adversaries are the chief, her **e** prosper;	341
	1:21	all mine **e** have heard of my trouble; they are	341
	2:16	All thine **e** have opened their mouth against	341
	3:46	All our **e** have opened their mouths against	341
	3:52	Mine **e** chased me sore, like a bird,	341
Eze	39:23	and gave them into the hand of their **e**:	6862
Da	4:19	and the interpretation thereof to thine **e**.	6146
Am	9: 4	though they go into captivity before their **e**,	341
Mic	4:10	shall redeem thee from the hand of thine **e**.	341
	5: 9	and all thine **e** shall be cut off.	341
	7: 6	a man's **e** *are* the men of his own house.	341
Na	1: 2	and he reserveth *wrath* for his **e**.	341
	1: 8	and darkness shall pursue his **e**.	341
	3:13	thy land shall be set wide open unto thine **e**:	341
Zec	10: 5	*their* **e** in the mire of the streets in the battle:	NIH
Mt	5:44	But I say unto you, Love your **e**, bless them	*2190*
	22:44	right hand, till I make thine **e** thy footstool?	*2190*
Mk	12:36	right hand, till I make thine **e** thy footstool.	*2190*
Lk	1:71	That *we* should be saved from our **e**, and	*2190*
	1:74	hand of our **e** might serve him without fear,	*2190*
	6:27	I say unto you which hear, Love your **e**,	*2190*
	6:35	But love ye your **e**, and do good, and lend,	*2190*
	19:27	But those mine **e**, which would not that I	*2190*
	19:43	that thine **e** shall cast a trench about thee,	*2190*
	20:43	Till I make thine **e** thy footstool.	*2190*
Ro	5:10	For if, when we were **e**, we were reconciled	*2190*
	11:28	the gospel, *they are* **e** for your sakes:	*2190*
1Co	15:25	till he hath put all **e** under his feet.	*2190*
Php	3:18	*that they are* the **e** of the cross of Christ:	*2190*
Col	1:21	and **e** in *your* mind by wicked works,	*2190*
Heb	1:13	until I make thine **e** thy footstool?	*2190*
	10:13	From henceforth expecting till his **e** be	*2190*
Rev	11: 5	out of their mouth, and devoureth their **e**:	*2190*

Rev 11:12 heaven in a cloud; and their **e** beheld them. *2190*

ENEMIES' (3) [ENEMY]
Lev 26:34 as it lieth desolate, and ye *be* in your **e** land; 341
26:39 pine away in their iniquity in your **e** lands; 341
Eze 39:27 gathered them out of their **e** lands, and 341

ENEMY (107) [ENEMIES, ENEMIES', ENEMY'S]
Ex 15: 6 O LORD, hath dashed in pieces the **e**. 341
15: 9 The **e** said, I will pursue, I will overtake, 341
23:22 I will be an **e** unto thine enemies, and 340
Lev 26:25 ye shall be delivered into the hand of the **e**. 341
Nu 10: 9 if ye go *to* war in your land against the **e** 6862
35:23 *it* upon him, that he die, and *was* not his **e**, 341
Dt 28:57 wherewith thine **e** shall distress thee in thy 341
32:27 Were it not that I feared the wrath of the **e**, 341
32:42 from the beginning of revenges upon the **e**. 341
33:27 he shall thrust out the **e** from before thee; 341
Jdg 16:23 Our god hath delivered Samson our **e** into 341
16:24 Our god hath delivered into our hands our **e**, 341
1Sa 2:32 thou shalt see an **e** *in my* habitation, in all 6862
18:29 and Saul became David's **e** continually. 341
19:17 and sent away mine **e**, that he is escaped? 341
24: 4 Behold, I will deliver thine **e** into thine hand, 341
24:19 For if a man find his **e**, will he let him go 341
26: 8 God hath delivered thine **e** into thine hand 341
28:16 departed from thee, and is become thine **e**? 6145
2Sa 4: 8 head of Ish-bosheth the son of Saul thine **e**, 341
22:18 He delivered me from my strong **e**, *and* 341
1Ki 8:33 people Israel be smitten down before the **e**, 341
8:37 if their **e** besiege them in the land of their 341
8:44 If thy people go out to battle against their **e**, 341
8:46 deliver them to the **e**, so that they carry them 341
8:46 them away captives unto the land of the **e**, 341
21:20 to Elijah, Hast thou found me, O mine **e**? 341
2Ch 6:24 Israel be put to the worse before the **e**, 341
25: 8 God shall make thee fall before the **e**: 341
26:13 mighty power, to help the king against the **e**. 341
Ezr 8:22 horsemen to help us against the **e** in the way: 341
8:31 he delivered us from the hand of the **e**, and 341
Est 3:10 of Hammedatha the Agagite, the Jews' **e**. 6887
7: 4 although the **e** could not countervail 6862
7: 6 The adversary and **e** *is* this wicked Haman. 341
8: 1 Haman the Jews' **e** unto Esther the queen. 6887
9:10 the **e** of the Jews, slew they; 6887
9:24 the Agagite, the **e** of all the Jews, 6887
Job 13:24 thou thy face, and holdest me for thine **e**? 341
16: 9 mine **e** sharpeneth his eyes upon me. 6862
27: 7 Let mine **e** be as the wicked, and he that 341
33:10 against me, he counteth me for his **e**, 341
Ps 7: 4 delivered him that without cause is mine **e**:) 6887
7: 5 Let the **e** persecute my soul, and take *it;* yea, 341
8: 2 that *thou* mightest still the **e** and the avenger. 341
9: 6 O thou **e**, destructions are come to a 341
13: 2 how long shall mine **e** be exalted over me? 341
13: 4 Lest mine **e** say, I have prevailed against 341
18:17 He delivered me from my strong **e**, and 341
31: 8 hast not shut me up into the hand of the **e**: 341
41:11 because mine **e** doth not triumph over me. 341
42: 9 because of the oppression of the **e**? 341
43: 2 because of the oppression of the **e**? 341
44:10 Thou makest us to turn back from the **e**: 6862
44:16 blasphemeth; by reason of the **e** and avenger. 341
55: 3 Because of the voice of the **e**, because of 341
55:12 For *it was* not an **e** *that* reproached me; then 341
61: 3 shelter for me, *and* a strong tower from the **e**. 341
64: 1 preserve my life from fear of the **e**. 341
74: 3 *even* all *that* the **e** hath done wickedly in 341
74:10 shall the **e** blaspheme thy name for ever? 341
74:18 *that* the **e** hath reproached, O LORD, and 341
78:42 the day when he delivered them from the **e**. 6862
89:22 The **e** shall not exact upon him; nor the son 341
106:10 and redeemed them from the hand of the **e**. 341
107: 2 he hath redeemed from the hand of the **e**; 6862
143: 3 For the **e** hath persecuted my soul; he hath 341
Pr 24:17 Rejoice not when thine **e** falleth, and let not 341
25:21 If thine **e** *be* hungry, give him bread to eat; 8130
27: 6 a friend; but the kisses of an **e** *are* deceitful. 8130
Isa 59:19 When the **e** shall come in like a flood, 6862
63:10 therefore he was turned to be their **e**, *and* 341
Jer 6:25 for the sword of the **e** *and* fear *is* on every 341
15:11 verily I will cause the **e** to entreat thee *well* 341
18:17 them as *with* an east wind before the **e**; 341
30:14 I have wounded thee *with* the wound of an **e**, 341
31:16 they shall come again from the land of the **e**. 341
44:30 of Babylon, his **e**, and that sought his life. 341
La 1: 5 are gone *into* captivity before the **e**. 6862
1: 7 when her people fell into the hand of the **e**, 6862
1: 9 for the **e** hath magnified *himself.* 341
1:16 are desolate, because the **e** prevailed. 341
2: 3 drawn back his right hand from before the **e**, 341
2: 4 He hath bent his bow like an **e**: *he* stood *with* 341
2: 5 The Lord was as an **e**: he hath swallowed up 341
2: 7 he hath given up into the hand of the **e** 341
2:17 he hath caused *thine* **e** to rejoice over thee, 341
2:22 and brought up hath mine **e** consumed. 341
4:12 the **e** should have entered into the gates of 341
Eze 36: 2 Because the **e** hath said against you, Aha, 341
Hos 8: 3 *the thing that is* good: the **e** shall pursue him. 341
Mic 2: 8 Even of late my people is risen up as an **e**: 341
7: 8 Rejoice not against me, O mine **e**: when I 341
7:10 she *that is* mine **e** shall see *it,* and 341
Na 3:11 also shalt seek strength because of the **e**. 341
Zep 3:15 away thy judgments, he hath cast out thine **e**: 341
Mt 5:43 shalt love thy neighbour, and hate thine **e**. *2190*
13:25 his **e** came and sowed tares among *2190*
13:28 He said unto them, An **e** hath done *444+2190*
13:39 The **e** that sowed them is the devil; *2190*
Lk 10:19 scorpions, and over all the power of the **e**: *2190*
Ac 13:10 of the devil, *thou* **e** of all righteousness, *2190*
Ro 12:20 Therefore if thine **e** hunger, feed him; if he *2190*
1Co 15:26 The last **e** *that* shall be destroyed *is* death. *2190*
Gal 4:16 Am I therefore become your **e**, because *2190*
2Th 3:15 Yet count *him* not as an **e**, but *2190*
Jas 4: 4 will be a friend of the world is the **e** of *2190*

ENEMY'S (3) [ENEMY]
Ex 23: 4 If thou meet thine **e** ox or his ass going 341
Job 6:23 Or, Deliver me from the **e** hand? or, 6862
Ps 78:61 into captivity, and his glory into the **e** hand. 6862

ENGAGED (1)
Jer 30:21 for who *is* this that **e** his heart to approach 6148

EN-GANNIM (3)
Jos 15:34 And Zanoah, and **E**, Tappuah, and Enam, 5873
19:21 and **E**, and En-haddah, and Beth-pazzez; 5873
21:29 with her suburbs, **E** with her suburbs; 5873

EN-GEDI (6)
Jos 15:62 Nibshan, and the city of salt, and **E**; 5872
1Sa 23:29 from thence, and dwelt in strong holds at **E**. 5872
24: 1 Behold, David *is* in the wilderness of **E**. 5872
2Ch 20: 2 they *be* in Hazazon-tamar, which *is* **E**. 5872
SS 1:14 a cluster of camphire in the vineyards of **E**. 5872
Eze 47:10 *that* the fishers shall stand upon it from **E** 5872

ENGINES (2)
2Ch 26:15 he made in Jerusalem **e**, invented by 2810
Eze 26: 9 he shall set **e** of war against thy walls, and 4239

ENGRAFTED (1)
Jas 1:21 and receive with meekness the **e** word, *1721*

ENGRAVE (2) [ENGRAVEN, ENGRAVER, ENGRAVINGS]
Ex 28:11 shalt thou **e** the two stones with the names 6605
Zec 3: 9 behold, I *will* **e** the graving thereof, 6605

ENGRAVED See GRAVED; GRAVEN

ENGRAVEN (1) [ENGRAVE]
2Co 3: 7 written *and* **e** in stones, was glorious, *1795*

ENGRAVER (3) [ENGRAVE]
Ex 28:11 *With* the work of an **e** in stone, *like* 2796
35:35 of the **e**, and of the cunning workman, and 2796
38:23 an **e**, and a cunning workman, and 2796

ENGRAVINGS (5) [ENGRAVE]
Ex 28:11 an engraver in stone, *like* the **e** of a signet, 6603
28:21 to their names, *like* the **e** of a signet; 6603
28:36 grave upon it, *like* the **e** of a signet, 6603
39:14 *like* the **e** of a signet, every one with his 6603
39:30 upon it a writing, *like to* the **e** of a signet, 6603

EN-HADDAH (1)
Jos 19:21 and En-gannim, and **E**, and Beth-pazzez; 5876

EN-HAKKORE (1)
Jdg 15:19 wherefore he called the name thereof **E**, 5875

ENHANCE See ABOUNDED; ABOUNDETH

EN-HAZOR (1)
Jos 19:37 And Kedesh, and Edrei, and E, 5877

ENJOIN (1) [ENJOINED]
Phm 1: 8 though I might be much bold in Christ to e *2004*

ENJOINED (3) [ENJOIN]
Est 9:31 and Esther the queen had e them, 5921+6965
Job 36:23 Who hath e him his way? or who can say, 6485
Heb 9:20 the testament which God hath e unto you. *1781*

ENJOY (14) [ENJOYED]
Lev 26:34 shall the land e her sabbaths, as long as it 7521
26:34 then shall the land rest, and e her sabbaths. 7521
26:43 be left of them, and shall e her sabbaths, 7521
Nu 36: 8 that the children of Israel may e every man 3423
Dt 28:41 but thou shalt not e them; 1961+3807.1
Jos 1:15 unto the land of your possession, and e it, 3423
Ecc 2: 1 prove thee with mirth, therefore e pleasure: 7200
2:24 *that* he should **make** his soul e good in his 7200
3:13 and drink, and e the good of all his labour, 7200
5:18 to e the good of all his labour that he taketh 7200
Isa 65:22 mine elect shall **long** e the work of their 1086
Ac 24: 2 Seeing that by thee we e great quietness, *5177*
1Ti 6:17 who giveth us richly all *things* to e; *619*
Heb 11:25 than to e the pleasures of sin for a season; *2192*

ENJOYED (1) [ENJOY]
2Ch 36:21 until the land had e her sabbaths: 7521

ENLARGE (10) [ENLARGED, ENLARGEMENT, ENLARGETH, ENLARGING]
Ge 9:27 God shall e Japheth, and he shall dwell in 6601
Ex 34:24 the nations before thee, and e thy borders: 7337
Dt 12:20 When the LORD thy God shall e thy 7337
19: 8 if the LORD thy God e thy coast, as he 7337
1Ch 4:10 e my coast, and that thine hand might be 7235
Ps 119:32 when thou shalt e my heart. 7337
Isa 54: 2 E the place of thy tent, and let them stretch 7337
Am 1:13 at Gilead, that *they* might e their border: 7337
Mic 1:16 e thy baldness as the eagle; 7337
Mt 23: 5 and e the borders of their garments, *3170*

ENLARGED (11) [ENLARGE]
1Sa 2: 1 my mouth is e over mine enemies; because 7337
2Sa 22:37 Thou hast e my steps under me; so that my 7337
Ps 4: 1 thou hast e me *when I was* in distress; 7337
18:36 Thou hast e my steps under me, that my 7337
25:17 The troubles of my heart are e: O bring 7337
Isa 5:14 Therefore hell hath e herself, and 7337
57: 8 thou hast e thy bed, and made thee *a* 7337
60: 5 and thine heart shall fear, and be e; 7337
2Co 6:11 our mouth is open unto you, our heart is e. *4115*
6:13 (I speak as unto *my* children,) be ye also e. *4115*
10:15 that *we* shall be e by you according to our *3170*

ENLARGEMENT (1) [ENLARGE]
Est 4:14 *then* shall there e and deliverance arise to 7305

ENLARGETH (3) [ENLARGE]
Dt 33:20 of Gad he said, Blessed *be* he that e Gad: 7337
Job 12:23 he e the nations, and straiteneth them 7849
Hab 2: 5 who e his desire as hell, and *is* as death, 7337

ENLARGING (1) [ENLARGE]
Eze 41: 7 *there was* an e, and a winding about still 7337

ENLIGHTEN (1) [LIGHT]
Ps 18:28 the LORD my God will e my darkness. 5050

ENLIGHTENED (6) [LIGHT]
1Sa 14:27 his hand to his mouth; and his eyes were e. 215
14:29 how mine eyes have been e, because I tasted 215
Job 33:30 the pit, to be e with the light of the living. 215
Ps 97: 4 His lightnings e the world: the earth saw, 215
Eph 1:18 The eyes of your understanding being e; *5461*
Heb 6: 4 *it is* impossible for those who were once e, *5461*

ENLIGHTENING (1) [LIGHT]
Ps 19: 8 of the LORD *is* pure, e the eyes. 215

EN-MISHPAT (1)
Ge 14: 7 came to E, which *is* Kadesh, and smote all 5880

ENMITY (8)
Ge 3:15 I will put e between thee and the woman, 342
Nu 35:21 Or in e smite him with his hand, that he die: 342
35:22 if he thrust him suddenly without e, or 342
Lk 23:12 for before they were at e between *2189*
Ro 8: 7 Because the carnal mind *is* e against God: *2189*
Eph 2:15 Having abolished in his flesh the e, *2189*
2:16 by the cross, having slain the e thereby: *2189*
Jas 4: 4 the friendship of the world is e with God? *2189*

ENOCH (12) [HENOCH]
Ge 4:17 his wife; and she conceived, and bare E: 2585
4:17 of the city, after the name of his son, E. 2585
4:18 unto E was born Irad: and Irad begat 2585
5:18 and two years, and he begat E: 2585
5:19 Jared lived after he begat E eight hundred 2585
5:21 E lived sixty and five years, and 2585
5:22 E walked with God after he begat 2585
5:23 all the days of E were three hundred sixty 2585
5:24 E walked with God: and he *was* not; 2585
Lk 3:37 which was *the son* of E, which was *the son* *1802*
Heb 11: 5 By faith E was translated that *he* should not *1802*
Jude 1:14 And E also, the seventh from Adam, *1802*

ENOS (7) [ENOSH]
Ge 4:26 he called his name E; then began *men* to call 583
5: 6 an hundred and five years, and begat E: 583
5: 7 Seth lived after he begat E eight hundred 583
5: 9 And E lived ninety years, and begat Cainan: 583
5:10 E lived after he begat Cainan eight hundred 583
5:11 And all the days of E were nine hundred and 583
Lk 3:38 Which was *the son* of E, which was *the son* *1800*

ENOSH (1) [ENOS]
1Ch 1: 1 Adam, Sheth, E, 583

ENOUGH (32)
Ge 24:25 We have both straw and provender e, and 7227
33: 9 Esau said, I have e, my brother; keep that 7227
33:11 graciously with me, and because I have e. 3605
34:21 behold, *it is* **large** e for them; 3027+7342
45:28 Israel said, *It is* e; Joseph my son *is* yet 7227
Ex 2:19 also **drew water** e for us, and 1802+1802
9:28 Intreat the LORD (for *it is* e) that there be 7227
36: 5 The people bring much more than e for 1767
Dt 1: 6 Ye have dwelt **long** e in this mount: 7227
2: 3 Ye have compassed this mountain **long** e: 7227
Jos 17:16 of Joseph said, The hill is not e for us: 4672
2Sa 24:16 the angel that destroyed the people, *It is* e: 7227
1Ki 19: 4 said, *It is* e; now, O LORD, take away my 7227
1Ch 21:15 that destroyed, *It is* e, stay now thine hand. 7227
2Ch 31:10 *we* have **had** e to eat, and have left plenty: 7646
Pr 27:27 *thou shalt have* goats' milk e for thy food, 1767
28:19 after vain *persons* shall **have** poverty e. 7646
30:15 *yea,* four *things* say not, *It is* e: 1952
30:16 and the fire *that* saith not, *It is* e. 1952
Isa 56:11 *are* greedy dogs *which* can never have e, 7654
Jer 49: 9 by night, they will destroy till they have e. 1767
Hos 4:10 For they shall eat, and not **have** e: 7646
Ob 1: 5 would they not have stolen till they had e? 1767
Na 2:12 The lion did tear in pieces e for his whelps, 1767
Hag 1: 6 *ye* eat, but ye have not e; *ye* drink, but 7654
Mal 3:10 that *there shall* not *be room* e *to receive it.* 1767
Mt 10:25 *It is* e for the disciple that he be as his *713*
25: 9 *Not so;* lest there be not e for us and you: *714*
Mk 14:41 it is e, the hour is come; behold, the Son of *568*
Lk 15:17 of my father's **have** bread e **and to spare,** *4052*
22:38 two swords. And he said unto them, It is e. *2425*
Ac 27:38 And when they had **eaten** e, *2880+5160*

ENRICH (2) [RICH]
1Sa 17:25 the king will e him *with* great riches, and 6238
Eze 27:33 thou didst e the kings of the earth with 6238

ENRICHED (2) [RICH]
1Co 1: 5 That in every *thing* ye are e by him, in all *4148*
2Co 9:11 Being e in every *thing* to all bountifulness, *4148*

ENRICHEST (1) [RICH]
Ps 65: 9 thou greatly e it *with* the river of God, 6238

EN-RIMMON (1)
Ne 11:29 And at E, and at Zareah, and at Jarmuth, 5884

EN-ROGEL (4)
Jos 15: 7 and the goings out thereof were at E: 5883
18:16 of Jebusi on the south, and descended to E, 5883
2Sa 17:17 Now Jonathan and Ahimaaz stayed by E; 5883
1Ki 1: 9 which is by E, and called all his brethren 5883

ENSAMPLE (3) [ENSAMPLES]
Php 3:17 them which walk so as ye have us for an e. 5179
2Th 3: 9 to make ourselves an e unto you to follow 5179
2Pe 2: 6 making them an e unto those that after 5262

ENSAMPLES (3) [ENSAMPLE]
1Co 10:11 all these things happened unto them for e: 5179
1Th 1: 7 So that ye were e to all that believe in 5179
1Pe 5: 3 God's heritage, but being e to the flock. 5179

EN-SHEMESH (2)
Jos 15: 7 the border passed towards the waters of E, 5885
18:17 went forth to E, and went forth toward 5885

ENSIGN (8) [ENSIGNS]
Nu 2: 2 with the e of their father's house: 226
Isa 5:26 he will lift up an e to the nations from far, 5251
11:10 which shall stand for an e of the people; 5251
11:12 And he shall set up an e for the nations, and 5251
18: 3 when he lifteth up an e on the mountains; 5251
30:17 the top of a mountain, and as an e on a hill. 5251
31: 9 his princes shall be afraid of the e, saith 5251
Zec 9:16 of a crown, lifted up as an e upon his land. 5264

ENSIGNS (1) [ENSIGN]
Ps 74: 4 they set up their e for signs. 226

ENSNARED (1) [SNARE]
Job 34:30 the hypocrite reign not, lest the people be e. 4170

ENSUE (1)
1Pe 3:11 and do good; let him seek peace, and e it. 1377

ENSURE See SURETY

ENTANGLE (1) [ENTANGLED, ENTANGLETH]
Mt 22:15 took counsel how they might e him in his 3802

ENTANGLED (3) [ENTANGLE]
Ex 14: 3 They are e in the land, the wilderness hath 943
Gal 5: 1 be not e again with the yoke of bondage. 1758
2Pe 2:20 they are again e therein, and overcome, 1707

ENTANGLETH (1) [ENTANGLE]
2Ti 2: 4 No man that warreth e himself with 1707

EN-TAPPUAH (1)
Jos 17: 7 on the right hand unto the inhabitants of E. 5887

ENTER (149) [ENTERED, ENTERETH, ENTERING, ENTRANCE, ENTRANCES]
Ge 12:11 when he was come near to e into Egypt, 935
Ex 40:35 Moses was not able to e into the tent of 935
Nu 4: 3 until fifty years old, all that e into the host, 935
4:23 all that e in to perform the service, to do 935
5:24 the water that causeth the curse shall e into 935
5:27 that the water that causeth the curse shall e 935
20:24 for he shall not e into the land which I have 935
Dt 23: 1 shall not e into the congregation of 935
23: 2 A bastard shall not e into the congregation of 935
23: 2 even to his tenth generation shall he not e 935
23: 3 Moabite shall not e into the congregation of 935
23: 3 e into the congregation of the LORD for 935
23: 8 children that are begotten of them shall e 935
29:12 That thou shouldest e into covenant with 5674
Jos 10:19 of them; suffer them not to e into their cities: 935
Jdg 18: 9 slothful to go, and to e to possess the land. 935
2Sa 22: 7 of his temple, and my cry did e into his ears. NIH
1Ki 14:12 and when thy feet e into the city, the child 935
22:30 I will disguise myself, and e into the battle; 935
2Ki 7: 4 We will e into the city, then the famine is in 935
11: 5 A third part of you that e in on the sabbath 935
19:23 and I will e into the lodgings of his borders, 935
2Ch 7: 2 the priests could not e into the house of 935
23:19 which was unclean in any thing should e in. 935
30: 8 e into his sanctuary, which he hath sanctified 935
Ne 2: 8 the city, and for the house that I shall e into. 935
Est 4: 2 for none might e into the king's gate clothed 935
Job 22: 4 of thee? will he e with thee into judgment? 935
34:23 that he should e into judgment with God. 1980
Ps 37:15 Their sword shall e into their own heart, and 935
45:15 they shall e into the king's palace. 935
95:11 my wrath that they should not e into my rest. 935
100: 4 E into his gates with thanksgiving, and 935
118:20 the LORD, into which the righteous shall e. 935
143: 2 e not into judgment with thy servant: for in 935
Pr 4:14 E not into the path of the wicked, and 935
18: 6 A fool's lips e into contention, and 935
23:10 and e not into the fields of the fatherless: 935
Isa 2:10 E into the rock, and hide thee in the dust, 935
3:14 The LORD will e into judgment with 935
26: 2 nation which keepeth the truth may e in. 935
26:20 e thou into thy chambers, and shut thy doors 935
37:24 and I will e into the height of his border, and 935
57: 2 He shall e into peace: they shall rest in their 935
59:14 is fallen in the street, and equity cannot e. 935
Jer 7: 2 that e in at these gates to worship 935
8:14 let us e into the defenced cities, and let us be 935
14:18 if I e into the city, then behold them that are 935
16: 5 E not into the house of mourning, 935
17:20 of Jerusalem, that e in by these gates: 935
17:25 shall there e into the gates of this city kings 935
21:13 or who shall e into our habitations? 935
22: 2 and thy people that e in by these gates: 935
22: 4 shall there e in by the gates of this house 935
41:17 is by Beth-lehem, to go to e into Egypt, 935
42:15 If ye wholly set your faces to e into Egypt, 935
42:18 forth upon you, when ye shall e into Egypt: 935
La 1:10 that they should not e into thy congregation. 935
3:13 He hath caused the arrows of his quiver to e 935
Eze 7:22 secret place: for the robbers shall e into it, 935
13: 9 neither shall they e into the land of Israel; 935
20:38 and they shall not e into the land of Israel: 935
26:10 the chariots, when he shall e into thy gates, 935
26:10 as men e into a city wherein is made a 3996
37: 5 I will cause breath to e into you, and ye shall 935
42:14 When the priests e therein, then shall they 935
44: 2 not be opened, and no man shall e in by it; 935
44: 3 he shall e by the way of the porch of that 935
44: 9 in flesh, shall e into my sanctuary, 935
44:16 They shall e into my sanctuary, and 935
44:17 that when they e in at the gates of the inner 935
44:21 drink wine, when they e into the inner court. 935
46: 2 the prince shall e by the way of the porch of 935
46: 8 when the prince shall e, he shall go in by 935
Da 11: 7 shall e into the fortress of the king of 935
11:17 He shall also set his face to e with 935
11:24 He shall e peaceably even upon the fattest 935
11:40 he shall e into the countries, and 935
11:41 He shall e also into the glorious land, and 935
Hos 11: 9 midst of thee: and I will not e into the city. 935
Joel 2: 9 they shall e in at the windows like a thief. 935
Am 5: 5 nor e into Gilgal, and pass not to Beer-sheba: 935
Jnh 3: 4 Jonah began to e into the city a day's 935
Zec 5: 4 and it shall e into the house of the thief, and 935
Mt 5:20 ye shall in no case e into the kingdom of 1525
6: 6 e into thy closet, and when thou hast shut 1525
7:13 E ye in at the strait gate: for wide is 1525
7:21 Lord, shall e into the kingdom of heaven; 1525
10: 5 into any city of the Samaritans e ye not: 1525
10:11 into whatsoever city or town ye shall e, 1525
12:29 Or else how can one e into a strong man's 1525
12:45 than himself, and they e in and dwell there: 1525
18: 3 ye shall not e into the kingdom of heaven. 1525
18: 8 it is better for thee to e into life halt or 1525
18: 9 it is better for thee to e into life with one 1525
19:17 but if thou wilt e into life, keep 1525
19:23 That a rich man shall hardly e into 1525
19:24 than for a rich man to e into the kingdom of 1525
25:21 many things: e thou into the joy of thy lord. 1525
25:23 many things: e thou into the joy of thy lord. 1525
26:41 and pray, that ye e not into temptation: 1525
Mk 1:45 Jesus could no more openly e into the city, 1525
3:27 No man can e into a strong man's house, 1525
5:12 us into the swine, that we may e into them. 1525
6:10 In what place soever ye e into a house, 1525
9:25 come out of him, and e no more into him. 1525
9:43 it is better for thee to e into life maimed, 1525
9:45 it is better for thee to e halt into life, 1525
9:47 it is better for thee to e into the kingdom of 1525
10:15 God as a little child, he shall not e therein. 1525
10:23 How hardly shall they that have riches e 1525
10:24 in riches to e into the kingdom of God! 1525

Mk 10:25 than for a rich *man* to **e** into the kingdom of 1525
13:15 neither **e** *therein,* to take any *thing* out of 1525
14:38 and pray, lest ye **e** into temptation. 1525
Lk 7: 6 for I am not worthy that thou shouldest **e** 1525
8:16 that they which **e in** may see the light. 1531
8:32 that he would suffer them to **e** into them. 1525
9: 4 And whatsoever house ye **e** into, 1525
10: 5 And into whatsoever house ye **e**, first say, 1525
10: 8 And into whatsoever city ye **e**, and 1525
10:10 But into whatsoever city ye **e**, and 1525
11:26 and they **e in**, and dwell there: 1525
13:24 Strive to **e in** at the strait gate: for many, 1525
13:24 will seek to **e in**, and shall not be able. 1525
18:17 as a little child shall in no wise **e** therein. 1525
18:24 How hardly shall they that have riches **e** 1525
18:25 than for a rich *man* to **e** into the kingdom of 1525
21:21 let not them that are in the countries **e** 1525
22:40 Pray that *ye* **e** not into temptation. 1525
22:46 rise and pray, lest ye **e** into temptation. 1525
24:26 these *things,* and to **e** into his glory? 1525
Jn 3: 4 can he **e** the second time into his mother's 1525
3: 5 he cannot **e** into the kingdom of God. 1525
10: 9 by me if any *man* **e in**, he shall be saved, 1525
Ac 14:22 that we must through much tribulation **e** 1525
20:29 shall grievous wolves **e** in among you, 1525
Heb 3:11 in my wrath, They shall not **e** into my rest. 1525
3:18 sware he that *they* should not **e** into his rest, 1525
3:19 So we see that they could not **e in** because 1525
4: 3 For we which have believed do **e** into rest, 1525
4: 3 in my wrath, if they shall **e** into my rest: 1525
4: 5 this *place* again, If they shall **e** into my rest. 1525
4: 6 it remaineth that some *must* **e** therein, 1525
4:11 Let us labour therefore to **e** into that rest, 1525
10:19 boldness to **e** into the holiest by the blood 1529
Rev 15: 8 and no *man* was able to **e** into the temple, 1525
21:27 And there shall in no wise **e** into it any 1525
22:14 may **e in through** the gates into the city. 1525

ENTERED (107) [ENTER]
Ge 7:13 In the selfsame day **e** Noah, and Shem, and 935
19: 3 turned in unto him, and **e** into his house; 935
19:23 The sun was risen upon the earth when Lot **e** 935
31:33 out of Leah's tent, and **e** into Rachel's tent. 935
43:30 and he **e** into *his* chamber, and wept there. 935
Ex 33: 9 came to pass, as Moses **e** into the tabernacle, 935
Jos 2: 3 come to thee, which are **e** into thine house: 935
8:19 they **e** *into* the city, and took it, and hasted 935
10:20 that the rest *which* remained of them **e** into 935
Jdg 6: 5 and they **e** into the land to destroy it. 935
9:46 **e** into a hold of the house of the god Berith. 935
2Sa 10:14 they *also* before Abishai, and **e** *into* the city. 935
2Ki 7: 8 **e** into another tent, and carried thence *also,* 935
9:31 as Jehu **e in** at the gate, she said, *Had* Zimri 935
1Ch 19:15 Abishai his brother, and **e** into the city. 935
2Ch 12:11 when the king **e** *into* the house of 935
15:12 they **e** into a covenant to seek the LORD 935
27: 2 howbeit he **e** not into the temple of 935
32: 1 **e** into Judah, and encamped against 935
Ne 2:15 **e** by the gate of the valley, and *so* returned. 935
10:29 and **e** into a curse, and into an oath, 935
Job 38:16 Hast thou **e** into the springs of the sea? or 935
38:22 Hast thou **e** into the treasures of the snow? or 935
Jer 2: 7 when ye **e**, ye defiled my land, and 935
9:21 *and* is **e** into our palaces, to cut off 935
34:10 the people, which had **e** into the covenant, 935
37:16 When Jeremiah was **e** into the dungeon, and 935
La 1:10 for she hath seen *that* the heathen **e into** her 935
4:12 the enemy should have **e** into the gates of 935
Eze 2: 2 the spirit **e** into me when he spake unto me, 935
3:24 the spirit **e** into me, and set me upon my feet, 935
16: 8 unto thee, and **e** into a covenant with thee, 935
36:20 when they **e** unto the heathen, whither they 935
41: 6 they **e** into the wall which *was* of the house 935
44: 2 hath **e in** by it, therefore it shall be shut. 935
Ob 1:11 foreigners **e** *into* his gates, and cast lots upon 935
1:13 Thou shouldest not have **e** into the gate of 935
Hab 3:16 rottenness **e** into my bones, and I trembled in 935
Mt 8: 5 And when Jesus was **e** into Capernaum, 1525
8:23 And when he was **e** into a ship, 1684
9: 1 And he **e** into a ship, and passed over, and 1684
12: 4 How he **e** into the house of God, and 1525
24:38 until the day that Noe **e** into the ark, 1525
Mk 1:21 straightway on the sabbath day he **e** into 1525
1:29 they **e** into the house of Simon and 2064
2: 1 And again he **e** into Capernaum after *some* 1525
3: 1 And he **e** again into the synagogue; and 1525
4: 1 so that he **e** into a ship, and sat in the sea; 1684
5:13 spirits went out, and **e** into the swine: 1525
6:56 And whithersoever he **e**, into villages, or 1531
7:17 And when he was **e** into *the* house from 1525
7:24 and **e** into a house, and would have no *man* 1525
8:10 And straightway he **e** into a ship with his 1684
11: 2 and as soon as ye be **e** into it, ye shall find a 1531
11:11 And Jesus **e** into Jerusalem, and into 1525
Lk 1:40 And **e** into the house of Zacharias, and 1525
4:38 the synagogue, and **e** into Simon's house. 1525
5: 3 And he **e** into one of the ships, which was 1684
6: 6 that he **e** into the synagogue and taught: 1525
7: 1 of the people, he **e** into Capernaum. 1525
7:44 I **e** into thine house, thou gavest me no 1525
8:30 because many devils were **e** into him. 1525
8:33 devils out of the man, and **e** into the swine: 1525
9:34 and they feared as they **e** into the cloud. 1525
9:52 and **e** into a village of the Samaritans, 1525
10:38 they went, that he **e** into a certain village: 1525
11:52 ye **e** not **in** yourselves, and them that were 1525
17:12 And as he **e** into a certain village, there met 1525
17:27 until the day that Noe **e** into the ark, and 1525
19: 1 And *Jesus* **e** and passed through Jericho. 1525
22: 3 Then **e** Satan into Judas surnamed Iscariot, 1525
22:10 Behold, when ye are **e** into the city, 1525
24: 3 And they **e in**, and found not the body of 1525
Jn 4:38 and ye are **e** into their labours. 1525
6:17 And **e** into a ship, and went over the sea 1684
6:22 that one whereinto his disciples were **e**, 1684
13:27 And after the sop Satan **e** into him. 1525
18: 1 into the which he **e**, and his disciples. 1525
18:33 Then Pilate **e** into the judgment hall again, 1525
21: 3 went forth, and **e** into a ship immediately; 305
Ac 3: 2 to ask alms of them that **e** into the temple; 1531
3: 8 walked, and **e** with them into the temple, 1525
5:21 And when they heard *that,* they **e** into 1525
9:17 Ananias went his way, and **e** into the house; 1525
10:24 And the morrow *after* they **e** into Cesarea. 1525
11: 8 unclean hath at any time **e** into my mouth. 1525
11:12 and we **e** into the man's house: 1525
16:40 of the prison, and **e** into *the house of* Lydia: 1525
18: 7 and **e** into a certain *man's* house, 2064
18:19 but he himself **e** into the synagogue, and 1525
19:30 And when Paul would have **e** in unto 1525
21: 8 we **e** into the house of Philip the evangelist, 1525
21:26 the next day purifying himself with them **e** 1524
23:16 he went and **e** into the castle, and told Paul. 1525
25:23 and were **e** into the place of hearing, 1525
28: 8 to whom Paul **e in**, and prayed, and laid *his* 1525
Ro 5:12 as by one man sin **e** into the world, and 1525
5:20 Moreover the law **e**, that the offence might 3922
1Co 2: 9 neither have **e** into the heart of man, 305
Heb 4: 6 they to whom it was first preached **e** not **in** 1525
4:10 For he that is **e** into his rest, he also hath 1525
6:20 Whither the forerunner is for us **e**, 1525
9:12 by his own blood he **e in** once into the holy 1525
9:24 For Christ is not **e** into the holy *places* 1525
Jas 5: 4 the cries of them which have reaped are **e** 1525
2Jn 1: 7 For many deceivers are **e** into the world, 1525
Rev 11:11 a half the spirit of life from God **e** into 1525

ENTERETH (20) [ENTER]
Nu 4:30 every one that **e** into the service, to do 935
4:35 years old, every one that **e** into the service, 935
4:39 years old, every one that **e** into the service, 935
4:43 years old, every one that **e** into the service, 935
2Ch 31:16 *even* unto every one that **e** into the house of 935
Pr 2:10 When wisdom **e** into thine heart, and 935
17:10 A reproof **e** more into a wise *man* than an 5181
Eze 21:14 which **e into** their **privy chambers.** 2314
42:12 the wall toward the east, as *one* **e into** them. 935
46: 9 he that **e in** *by* the way of the north gate to 935
46: 9 he that **e** *by* the way of the south gate shall 935
Mt 15:17 that whatsoever **e** in at the mouth goeth into 1531
Mk 5:40 and **e in** where the damsel was lying. 1531
7:18 that whatsoever *thing* from without **e** into 1531
7:19 Because it **e** not into his heart, but into 1531
Lk 22:10 follow him into the house where he **e in.** 1531
Jn 10: 1 He that **e** not by the door into 1525
10: 2 But he that **e in** by the door is the shepherd 1525
Heb 6:19 and which **e** into that within the vail; 1525
9:25 as the high priest **e** into the holy *place* 1525

ENTERING (46) [ENTER]
Ex 35:15 the hanging for the door at the **e** in of 6607
Jos 8:29 cast it at the **e** of the gate of the city, and 6607
13: 5 mount Hermon unto the **e** into Hamath. 935
20: 4 shall stand *at* the **e** of the gate of the city, 6607
Jdg 3: 3 from mount Baal-hermon unto the **e** in of 935
9:35 and stood *in* the **e** of the gate of the city: 6607
9:40 *and* wounded, *even* unto the **e** of the gate. 6607
9:44 and stood *in* the **e** of the gate of the city: 6607
18:16 children of Dan, stood *by* the **e** of the gate. 6607
18:17 the priest stood *in* the **e** of the gate with 6607
1Sa 23: 7 by **e** into a town that hath gates and bars. 935
2Sa 10: 8 put the battle in array *at* the **e** in of the gate: 6607
11:23 we were upon them *even* unto the **e** of 6607
1Ki 6:31 for the **e** of the oracle he made doors of 6607
8:65 from the **e** in of Hamath unto the river of 935
19:13 went out, and stood *in* the **e** in of the cave. 6607
2Ki 7: 3 there were four leprous men *at* the **e** in of 6607
10: 8 Lay ye them *in* two heaps *at* the **e** in of 6607
14:25 He restored the coast of Israel from the **e** of 935
23: 8 **e** in of the gate of Joshua the governor of 6607
23:11 at the **e** in of the house of the LORD, by 935
1Ch 5: 9 eastward he inhabited unto the **e** in of 935
13: 5 from Shihor of Egypt even unto the **e** of 935
2Ch 7: 8 from the **e** in of Hamath unto the river of 935
18: 9 they sat in a void place *at* the **e** in of 6607
23: 4 A third *part* of you **e** on the sabbath, of 935
23:13 the king stood at his pillar at the **e** in, and 3996
23:15 when she was come to the **e** of the horse 3996
26: 8 his name spread abroad even to the **e in** of 935
33:14 even to the **e in** at the fish gate, and 935
Isa 23: 1 laid waste, so that *there is* no house, no **e in**: 935
Jer 1:15 they shall set every one his throne *at* the **e** 6607
17:27 even **e in** at the gates of Jerusalem on 935
Eze 44: 5 mark well the **e in** of the house, with every 3996
Am 6:14 they shall afflict you from the **e in** of 935
Mt 23:13 neither suffer ye them that are **e** to go in. *1525*
Mk 4:19 and the lusts of other *things* **e in**, choke *1531*
7:15 a man, that **e** into him can defile him: *1531*
8:13 **e** into the ship again departed to the other *1684*
16: 5 And **e** into the sepulchre, they saw a young *1525*
Lk 11:52 and them that were **e in** ye hindered. *1525*
19:30 the which at your **e** ye shall find a colt tied, *1531*
Ac 8: 3 havock of the church, **e into** every house, *1531*
27: 2 And **e into** a ship of Adramyttium, *1910*
1Th 1: 9 of us what manner of **e in** we had unto you, *1529*
Heb 4: 1 a promise being left *us* of **e** into his rest, *1525*

ENTERPRISE (1)
Job 5:12 so that their hands cannot perform *their* **e**. 8454

ENTERTAIN (1) [ENTERTAINED]
Heb 13: 2 Be not forgetful to **e strangers**: for thereby *5381*

ENTERTAINED (1) [ENTERTAIN]
Heb 13: 2 for thereby some have **e** angels unawares. *3579*

ENTICE (8) [ENTICED, ENTICETH, ENTICING]
Ex 22:16 if a man **e** a maid that is not betrothed, and 6601
Dt 13: 6 **e** thee secretly, saying, Let us go and 5496
Jdg 14:15 said unto Samson's wife, **E** thy husband, 6601
16: 5 **E** him, and see wherein his great strength 6601
2Ch 18:19 Who shall **e** Ahab king of Israel, that he 6601
18:20 before the LORD, and said, I will **e** him. 6601
18:21 Thou shalt **e** *him*, and thou shalt also 6601
Pr 1:10 My son, if sinners **e** thee, consent thou not. 6601

ENTICED (3) [ENTICE]
Job 31:27 my heart hath been secretly **e**, or my mouth 6601
Jer 20:10 *saying*, Peradventure he will be **e**, and 6601
Jas 1:14 he is drawn away of his own lust, and **e**. *1185*

ENTICETH (1) [ENTICE]
Pr 16:29 A violent man **e** his neighbour, and 6601

ENTICING (2) [ENTICE]
1Co 2: 4 my preaching *was* not with **e** words of *3981*
Col 2: 4 any *man* should beguile you with **e words**. *4086*

ENTIRE (1)
Jas 1: 4 that ye may be perfect and **e**, *3648*

ENTRANCE (11) [ENTER]
Nu 34: 8 point out *your border* unto the **e** of Hamath; 935
Jdg 1:24 the **e** into the city, and we will shew thee 3996
1:25 when he shewed them the **e** into the city, 3996
1Ki 18:46 and ran before Ahab to the **e** of Jezreel. 935
22:10 in a void place *in* the **e** of the gate of 6607
1Ch 4:39 they went to the **e** of Gedor, *even* unto 3996
2Ch 12:10 that kept the **e** of the king's house. 6607
Ps119:130 The **e** of thy words giveth light; it giveth 6608
Eze 40:15 from the face of the gate of the **e** unto 2978
1Th 2: 1 brethren, know our **e in** unto you, *1529*
2Pe 1:11 an **e** shall be ministered unto you *1529*

ENTRANCES (1) [ENTER]
Mic 5: 6 and the land of Nimrod in the **e** thereof: 6607

ENTREAT (2) [ENTREATED, ENTREATETH, INTREAT]
Jer 15:11 verily I will **cause** the enemy **to e** thee *well* 6293
Ac 7: 6 and **e** *them* **evil** four hundred years. *2559*

ENTREATED (9) [ENTREAT]
Ge 12:16 he **e** Abram **well** for her sake: and he had 3190
Ex 5:22 wherefore hast thou *so* **evil e** this people? 7489
Dt 26: 6 the Egyptians **evil e** us, and afflicted us, 7489
Mt 22: 6 and **e** *them* **spitefully**, and slew *them*. *5195*
Lk 18:32 be mocked, and **spitefully e**, and spitted on: *5195*
20:11 and **e** *him* **shamefully**, and sent *him* away *818*
Ac 7:19 and **evil e** our fathers, so that *they* cast out *2559*
27: 3 And Julius courteously **e** Paul, and *5530*
1Th 2: 2 and were **shamefully e**, as ye know, *5195*

ENTREATETH (1) [ENTREAT]
Job 24:21 He **evil e** the barren *that* beareth not: and 7462

ENTREATY See INTREAT; INTREATED; INTREATIES; INTREATY

ENTRIES (1) [ENTRY]
Eze 40:38 the **e** thereof *were* by the posts of the gates, 6607

ENTRY (15) [ENTRIES]
2Ki 16:18 built in the house, and the king's **e** without, 3996
1Ch 9:19 host of the LORD, *were* keepers of the **e**. 3996
2Ch 4:22 the **e** of the house, the inner doors thereof 6607
Pr 8: 3 She crieth at the gates, at the **e** of the city, 6310
Jer 19: 2 which *is by* the **e** of the east gate, and 6607
26:10 sat down in the **e** of the new gate of 6607
36:10 in the higher court *at* the **e** of the new gate 6607
38:14 third **e** that *is* in the house of the LORD: 3996
43: 9 which *is* at the **e** of Pharaoh's house in 6607
Eze 8: 5 of the altar this image of jealousy in the **e**. 872
27: 3 O thou that art situate at the **e** of the sea, 3997
40:11 he measured the breadth of the **e** of 6607
40:40 as one goeth up to the **e** of the north gate, 6607
42: 9 from under these chambers *was* the **e** on 3996
46:19 After, he brought me through the **e**, 3996

ENVIED (6) [ENVY]
Ge 26:14 store of servants: and the Philistims **e** him. 7065
30: 1 bare Jacob no *children*, Rachel **e** her sister; 7065
37:11 his brethren **e** him; but his father observed 7065
Ps 106:16 They **e** Moses also in the camp, *and* 7065
Ecc 4: 4 that for this a man is **e** of his neighbour. 7068
Eze 31: 9 that *were* in the garden of God, **e** him. 7065

ENVIES (1) [ENVY]
1Pe 2: 1 hypocrisies, and **e**, and all evil speakings, *5355*

ENVIEST (1) [ENVY]
Nu 11:29 Moses said unto him, **E** thou for my sake? 7065

ENVIETH (1) [ENVY]
1Co 13: 4 suffereth long, *and* is kind; charity **e** not; *2206*

ENVIOUS (4) [ENVY]
Ps 37: 1 neither be thou **e** against the workers of 7065
73: 3 For I was **e** at the foolish, *when* I saw 7065
Pr 24: 1 Be not thou **e** against evil men, 7065
24:19 of evil *men*, neither be thou **e** at 7065

ENVIRON (1)
Jos 7: 9 land shall hear *of it*, and shall **e** us **round**, 5437

ENVY (20) [ENVIED, ENVIES, ENVIEST, ENVIETH, ENVIOUS, ENVYING, ENVYINGS]
Job 5: 2 the foolish man, and **e** slayeth the silly one. 7068
Pr 3:31 **E** thou not the oppressor, and choose none 7065
14:30 the flesh: but **e** the rottenness of the bones. 7068
23:17 Let not thine heart **e** sinners: but *be thou* in 7065
27: 4 but who is able to stand before **e**? 7068

Ecc 9: 6 their love, and their hatred, and their **e**, 7068
Isa 11:13 The **e** also of Ephraim shall depart, and 7068
11:13 Ephraim shall not **e** Judah, and Judah shall 7065
26:11 and be ashamed for *their* **e** at the people; 7068
Eze 35:11 according to thine **e** which thou hast used 7068
Mt 27:18 For he knew that for **e** they had delivered *5355*
Mk 15:10 the chief priests had delivered him for **e**. *5355*
Ac 7: 9 And the patriarchs, **moved with e**, *2206*
13:45 they were filled with **e**, and spake against *2205*
17: 5 Jews which believed not, **moved with e**, *2206*
Ro 1:29 full of **e**, murder, debate, deceit, malignity; *5355*
Php 1:15 Some indeed preach Christ even of **e** and *5355*
1Ti 6: 4 whereof cometh **e**, strife, railings, *5355*
Tit 3: 3 living in malice and **e**, hateful, *and* *5355*
Jas 4: 5 the spirit that dwelleth in us lusteth to **e**? *5355*

ENVYING (5) [ENVY]
Ro 13:13 and wantonness, not in strife and **e**. *2205*
1Co 3: 3 for whereas *there is* among you **e**, and *2205*
Gal 5:26 provoking one another, **e** one another. *5354*
Jas 3:14 But if ye have bitter **e** and strife in your *2205*
3:16 For where **e** and strife *is*, there *is* confusion *2205*

ENVYINGS (2) [ENVY]
2Co 12:20 **e**, wraths, strifes, backbitings, whisperings, *2205*
Gal 5:21 **E**, murders, drunkenness, revellings, and *5355*

EPAPHRAS (3)
Col 1: 7 As ye also learned of **E** our dear *1889*
4:12 **E**, who is *one* of you, a servant of Christ, *1889*
Phm 1:23 There salute thee **E**, my fellowprisoner in *1889*

EPAPHRODITUS (3)
Php 2:25 I supposed it necessary to send to you **E**, *1891*
4:18 having received of **E** the *things which were* *1891*
4: S written to the Philippians from Rome by **E**. *1891*

EPENETUS (1)
Ro 16: 5 Salute my wellbeloved **E**, who is *1866*

EPHAH (39)
Ge 25: 4 **E**, and Epher, and Hanoch, and Abidah, 5891
Ex 16:36 Now an omer *is* the tenth *part* of an **e**. 374
Lev 5:11 *part* of an **e** of fine flour for a sin offering; 374
6:20 the tenth *part* of an **e** of fine flour *for* a meat 374
19:36 just weights, a just **e**, and a just hin, shall ye 374
Nu 5:15 for her, the tenth *part* of an **e** of barley meal; 374
28: 5 a tenth *part* of an **e** *of* flour for a meat 374
Jdg 6:19 a kid, and unleavened *cakes of* an **e** of flour: 374
Ru 2:17 had gleaned: and it was about an **e** of barley. 374
1Sa 1:24 and one **e** of flour, and a bottle of wine, and 374
17:17 Take now for thy brethren an **e** of this 374
1Ch 1:33 **E**, and Epher, and Henoch, and Abida, and 5891
2:46 **E**, Caleb's concubine, bare Haran, and 5891
2:47 and Geshan, and Pelet, and **E**, and Shaaph. 5891
Isa 5:10 and the seed of a homer shall yield an **e**. 374
60: 6 the dromedaries of Midian and **E**; 5891
Eze 45:10 just balances, and a just **e**, and a just bath. 374
45:11 The **e** and the bath shall be of one measure, 374
45:11 a homer, and the **e** the tenth *part* of a homer: 374
45:13 the sixth *part* of an **e** of a homer of wheat, 374
45:13 ye shall give the sixth part of an **e** of a homer 374
45:24 he shall prepare a meat offering *of* an **e** for a 374
45:24 an **e** for a ram, and a hin of oil for an ephah. 374
45:24 an ephah for a ram, and a hin of oil for an **e**. 374
46: 5 the meat offering *shall be* an **e** for a ram, 374
46: 5 shall be able to give, and a hin of oil to an **e**. 374
46: 7 an **e** for a bullock, and an ephah for a ram, 374
46: 7 an **e** for a ram, and for the lambs according 374
46: 7 shall attain unto, and a hin of oil to an **e**. 374
46:11 the meat offering shall be an **e** to a bullock, 374
46:11 an **e** to a ram, and to the lambs as he is able 374
46:11 as he is able to give, and a hin of oil to an **e**. 374
46:14 the sixth *part* of an **e**, and the third *part* of a 374
Am 8: 5 making the **e** small, and the shekel great, and 374
Zec 5: 6 he said, This *is* an **e** that goeth forth. He said 374
5: 7 *is* a woman that sitteth in the midst of the **e**. 374
5: 8 he cast it into the midst of the **e**; and he cast 374
5: 9 they lift up the **e** between the earth and 374
5:10 talked with me, Whither do these bear the **e**? 374

EPHAI (1)
Jer 40: 8 the sons of **E** the Netophathite, and 5778

EPHER (4)
Ge 25: 4 **E**, and Hanoch, and Abidah, and Eldaah. 6081
1Ch 1:33 and **E**, and Henoch, and Abida, and Eldaah. 6081
4:17 *were,* Jether, and Mered, and **E**, and Jalon: 6081
5:24 even **E**, and Ishi, and Eliel, and Azriel, and 6081

EPHES-DAMMIM (1)
1Sa 17: 1 pitched between Shochoh and Azekah, in **E**. 658

EPHESIAN (1) [EPHESUS]
Ac 21:29 with him in the city Trophimus an **E**, *2180*

EPHESIANS (5) [EPHESUS]
Ac 19:28 cried out, saying, Great *is* Diana of the **E**. *2180*
19:34 hours cried out, Great *is* Diana of the **E**. *2180*
19:35 of the **E** is a worshipper of the great *2180*
Eph 6: S Written from Rome unto the **E** by *2180*
2Ti 4: S the first bishop of the church of the **E**, *2180*

EPHESUS (17) [EPHESIAN, EPHESIANS]
Ac 18:19 And he came to **E**, and left them there: but *2181*
18:21 if God will. And he sailed from **E**. *2181*
18:24 *and* mighty in the scriptures, came to **E**. *2181*
19: 1 passed through the upper coasts came to **E**: *2181*
19:17 all the Jews and Greeks also dwelling at **E**; *2181*
19:26 that not alone at **E**, but almost throughout *2181*
19:35 appeased the people, he said, *Ye* men **of E**, *2180*
20:16 For Paul had determined to sail by **E**, *2181*
20:17 And from Miletus he sent to **E**, and *2181*
1Co 15:32 of men I have fought with beasts at **E**, *2181*
16: 8 But I will tarry at **E** until Pentecost. *2181*
Eph 1: 1 to the saints which are at **E**, and to *2181*
1Ti 1: 3 As I besought thee to abide *still* at **E**, *2181*
2Ti 1:18 many *things* he ministered *unto me* at **E**, *2181*
4:12 And Tychicus have I sent to **E**. *2181*
Rev 1:11 unto **E**, and unto Smyrna, and *2181*
2: 1 Unto the angel of the church of **E** write; *2179*

EPHLAL (2)
1Ch 2:37 And Zabad begat **E**, and Ephlal begat Obed, 654
2:37 And Zabad begat Ephlal, and **E** begat Obed, 654

EPHOD (52)
Ex 25: 7 stones to be set in the **e**, and in 646
28: 4 an **e**, and a robe, and a broidered coat, 646
28: 6 they shall make the **e** *of* gold, *of* blue, and 646
28: 8 the curious girdle of the **e**, which *is* upon it, 642
28:12 **e** *for* stones of memorial unto the children of 646
28:15 after the work of the **e** thou shalt make it; 646
28:25 put *them* on the shoulderpieces of the **e** 646
28:26 which *is* in the side of the **e** inward. 646
28:27 shalt put them on the two sides of the **e** 646
28:27 above the curious girdle of the **e**. 646
28:28 unto the rings of the **e** with a lace of blue, 646
28:28 *it* may be above the curious girdle of the **e**, 646
28:28 that the breastplate be not loosed from the **e**. 646
28:31 thou shalt make the robe of the **e** all of blue. 646
29: 5 the robe of the **e**, and the ephod, and 646
29: 5 the **e**, and the breastplate, and gird him with 646
29: 5 and gird him with the curious girdle of the **e**: 646
35: 9 stones to be set for the **e**, and for 646
35:27 to be set, for the **e**, and for the breastplate; 646
39: 2 And he made the **e** *of* gold, blue, and purple, 646
39: 5 the curious girdle of his **e**, that *was* upon it, 642
39: 7 he put them on the shoulders of the **e**, 646
39: 8 *of* cunning work, like the work of the **e**; 646
39:18 and put them on the shoulderpieces of the **e**, 646
39:19 of it, which *was* on the side of the **e** inward. 646
39:20 put them on the two sides of the **e** 646
39:20 above the curious girdle of the **e**. 646
39:21 unto the rings of the **e** with a lace of blue, 646
39:21 *it* might be above the curious girdle of the **e**, 646
39:21 breastplate might not be loosed from the **e**; 646
39:22 he made the robe of the **e** *of* woven work, 646
Lev 8: 7 put the **e** upon him, and he girded him with 646
8: 7 girded him with the curious girdle of the **e**, 646
Nu 34:23 children of Manasseh, Hanniel the son of **E**. 641
Jdg 8:27 Gideon made an **e** thereof, and put it in his 646
17: 5 made an **e**, and teraphim, and 646
18:14 ye know that there is in these houses an **e**, 646
18:17 the **e**, and the teraphim, and the molten 646
18:18 the **e**, and the teraphim, and the molten 646
18:20 he took the **e**, and the teraphim, and 646
1Sa 2:18 *being* a child, girded *with* a linen **e**. 646

1Sa 2:28 to burn incense, to wear an **e** before me? 646
14: 3 the LORD'S priest in Shiloh, wearing an **e**. 646
21: 9 it *is here* wrapt in a cloth behind the **e**: 646
22:18 and five persons that did wear a linen **e**. 646
23: 6 *that* he came down *with* an **e** in his hand. 646
23: 9 to Abiathar the priest, Bring hither the **e**. 646
30: 7 I pray thee, bring me hither the **e**. 646
30: 7 And Abiathar brought thither the **e** to David. 646
2Sa 6:14 and David *was* girded *with* a linen **e**. 646
1Ch 15:27 David also *had* upon him an **e** of linen. 646
Hos 3: 4 and without an **e**, and *without* teraphim: 646

EPHPHATHA (1)
Mk 7:34 and saith unto him, **E**, that is, Be opened. *2188*

EPHRAIM (172) [EPHRAIM'S, EPHRAIMITE, EPHRAIMITES]
Ge 41:52 the name of the second called he **E**: For God 669
46:20 land of Egypt were born Manasseh and **E**, 669
48: 1 with him his two sons, Manasseh and **E**. 669
48: 5 now thy two sons, **E** and Manasseh, 669
48:13 **E** in his right hand toward Israel's left hand, 669
48:17 father laid his right hand upon the head of **E**, 669
48:20 God make thee as **E** and as Manasseh: 669
48:20 as Manasseh: and he set **E** before Manasseh. 669
Nu 1:10 of **E**; Elishama the son of Ammihud: 669
1:32 *namely*, of the children of **E**, *by* their 669
1:33 *even* of the tribe of **E**, *were* forty thousand 669
2:18 of the camp of **E** according to their armies: 669
2:18 the captain of the sons of **E** *shall be* 669
2:24 All that were numbered of the camp of **E** 669
7:48 prince of the children of **E**, *offered*: 669
10:22 the standard of the camp of the children of **E** 669
13: 8 Of the tribe of **E**, Oshea the son of Nun. 669
26:28 after their families *were* Manasseh and **E**. 669
26:35 These *are* the sons of **E** after their families: 669
26:37 These *are* the families of the sons of **E** 669
34:24 the prince of the tribe of the children of **E**, 669
Dt 33:17 they *are* the ten thousands of **E**, and they *are* 669
34: 2 the land of **E**, and Manasseh, and all the land 669
Jos 14: 4 of Joseph were two tribes, Manasseh and **E**: 669
16: 4 Manasseh and **E**, took their inheritance. 669
16: 5 the border of the children of **E** according to 669
16: 8 tribe of the children of **E** by their families. 669
16: 9 the separate cities for the children of **E** *were* 669
17: 8 of Manasseh *belonged* to the children of **E**; 669
17: 9 these cities of **E** *are* among the cities of 669
17:15 the giants, if mount **E** be too narrow for thee. 669
17:17 *even* to **E** and to Manasseh, saying, Thou *art* 669
19:50 he asked, *even* Timnath-serah in mount **E**: 669
20: 7 Shechem in mount **E**, and Kirjath-arba, 669
21: 5 by lot out of the families of the tribe of **E**, 669
21:20 the cities of their lot out of the tribe of **E**. 669
21:21 them Shechem with her suburbs in mount **E**, 669
24:30 which *is* in mount **E**, on the north side of 669
24:33 his son, which was given him in mount **E**. 669
Jdg 1:29 Neither did **E** drive out the Canaanites that 669
2: 9 in the mount of **E**, on the north side of 669
3:27 that he blew a trumpet in the mountain of **E**, 669
4: 5 between Ramah and Beth-el in mount **E**: 669
5:14 Out of **E** *was there* a root of them against 669
7:24 sent messengers throughout all mount **E**, 669
7:24 all the men of **E** gathered themselves 669
8: 1 the men of **E** said unto him, Why hast thou 669
8: 2 *Is* not the gleaning of the grapes of **E** better 669
10: 1 and he dwelt in Shamir in mount **E**. 669
10: 9 and against the house of **E**; 669
12: 1 the men of **E** gathered themselves together, 669
12: 4 all the men of Gilead, and fought with **E**: 669
12: 4 the men of Gilead smote **E**, because 669
12: 4 Ye Gileadites *are* fugitives of **E** among 669
12:15 was buried in Pirathon in the land of **E**, 669
17: 1 there was a man of mount **E**, whose name 669
17: 8 he came *to* mount **E** to the house of Micah, 669
18: 2 who when they came *to* mount **E**, to 669
18:13 they passed thence *unto* mount **E**, and 669
19: 1 Levite sojourning on the side of mount **E**, 669
19:16 field at even, which *was* also of mount **E**; 669
19:18 toward the side of mount **E**; 669
1Sa 1: 1 of mount **E**, and his name *was* Elkanah, 669
9: 4 he passed through mount **E**, and 669
14:22 Israel which had hid themselves in mount **E**, 669
2Sa 2: 9 over **E**, and over Benjamin, and over all 669
13:23 in Baal-hazor, which *is* beside **E**: 669
18: 6 and the battle was in the wood of **E**; 669
20:21 a man of mount **E**, Sheba the son of Bichri 669
1Ki 4: 8 *are* their names: The son of Hur, in mount **E**: 669
12:25 Jeroboam built Shechem in mount **E**, and 669
2Ki 5:22 **E** two young men of the sons of 669
14:13 from the gate of **E** unto the corner gate, 669
1Ch 6:66 had cities of their coasts out of the tribe of **E**. 669
6:67 Shechem in mount **E** with her suburbs; 669
7:20 the sons of **E**; Shuthelah, and Bered his son, 669
7:22 And **E** their father mourned many days, and 669
9: 3 and of the children of **E**, and Manasseh; 669
12:30 of the children of **E** twenty thousand and 669
27:10 *was* Helez the Pelonite, of the children of **E**: 669
27:14 Benaiah the Pirathonite, of the children of **E**: 669
27:20 Of the children of **E**, Hoshea the son of 669
2Ch 13: 4 which *is* in mount **E**, and said, Hear me, 669
15: 8 the cities which he had taken from mount **E**, 669
15: 9 the strangers with them out of **E** and 669
17: 2 in the cities of **E**, which Asa his father had 669
19: 4 the people from Beer-sheba to mount **E**, 669
25: 7 with Israel, *to wit, with* all the children of **E**. 669
25:10 the army that was come to him out of **E**, 669
25:23 from the gate of **E** to the corner gate, 669
28: 7 Zichri, a mighty *man* of **E**, slew Maaseiah 669
28:12 certain of the heads of the children of **E**, 669
30: 1 and wrote letters also to **E** and Manasseh, 669
30:10 from city to city through the country of **E** 669
30:18 *even* many of **E**, and Manasseh, Issachar, 669
31: 1 and Benjamin, in **E** also and Manasseh, 669
34: 6 and **E**, and Simeon, even unto Naphtali, 669
34: 9 had gathered of the hand of Manasseh and **E**, 669
Ne 8:16 water gate, and in the street of the gate of **E**. 669
12:39 from above the gate of **E**, and above the old 669
Ps 60: 7 *is* mine; **E** also *is* the strength of mine head; 669
78: 9 The children of **E**, *being* armed, *and* 669
78:67 of Joseph, and chose not the tribe of **E**: 669
80: 2 Before **E** and Benjamin and Manasseh stir 669
108: 8 *is* mine; **E** also *is* the strength of mine head; 669
Isa 7: 2 saying, Syria is confederate with **E**. 669
7: 5 Because Syria, **E**, and the son of Remaliah, 669
7: 8 and five years shall **E** be broken, 669
7: 9 the head of **E** *is* Samaria, and the head of 669
7:17 from the day that **E** departed from Judah; 669
9: 9 *even* **E** and the inhabitant of Samaria, 669
9:21 Manasseh, **E**; and Ephraim, Manasseh: *and* 669
9:21 Manasseh, Ephraim; and **E**, Manasseh: *and* 669
11:13 The envy also of **E** shall depart, and 669
11:13 **E** shall not envy Judah, and Judah shall not 669
11:13 not envy Judah, and Judah shall not vex **E**. 669
17: 3 The fortress also shall cease from **E**, and 669
28: 1 to the crown of pride, to the drunkards of **E**, 669
28: 3 The crown of pride, the drunkards of **E**, 669
Jer 4:15 and publisheth affliction from mount **E**. 669
7:15 all your brethren, *even* the whole seed of **E**. 669
31: 6 *that* the watchmen upon the mount **E** shall 669
31: 9 I am a father to Israel, and **E** *is* my firstborn. 669
31:18 I have surely heard **E** bemoaning himself 669
31:20 *Is* **E** my dear son? *is he* a pleasant child? 669
50:19 his soul shall be satisfied upon mount **E** and 669
Eze 37:16 the stick of **E**, and *for* all the house of Israel 669
37:19 which *is* in the hand of **E**, and the tribes of 669
48: 5 east side unto the west side, a *portion for* **E**. 669
48: 6 by the border of **E**, from the east side even 669
Hos 4:17 **E** *is* joined to idols: let him alone. 669
5: 3 I know **E**, and Israel is not hid from me: 669
5: 3 for now, O **E**, thou committest whoredom, 669
5: 5 shall Israel and **E** fall in their iniquity; 669
5: 9 **E** shall be desolate in the day of rebuke: 669
5:11 **E** *is* oppressed *and* broken in judgment, 669
5:12 Therefore *will* I *be* unto **E** as a moth, and 669
5:13 When **E** saw his sickness, and Judah *saw* his 669
5:13 went **E** to the Assyrian, and sent to king 669
5:14 For I *will be* unto **E** as a lion, and as a young 669
6: 4 O **E**, what shall I do unto thee? O Judah, 669
6:10 there *is* the whoredom of **E**, Israel is defiled. 669
7: 1 the iniquity of **E** was discovered, and 669
7: 8 **E**, he hath mixed himself among the people; 669
7: 8 among the people; **E** is a cake not turned. 669
7:11 **E** also is like a silly dove, without heart: 669
8: 9 ass alone by himself: **E** hath hired lovers. 669
8:11 Because **E** hath made many altars to sin, 669
9: 3 **E** shall return *to* Egypt, and they shall eat 669
9: 8 The watchman of **E** *was* with my God: *but* 669
9:11 *As for* **E**, their glory shall fly away like a 669
9:13 **E**, as I saw Tyrus, *is* planted in a pleasant 669

Hos 9:13 **E** *shall* bring forth his children to 669
9:16 **E** is smitten, their root is dried up, they shall 669
10: 6 **E** shall receive shame, and Israel shall be 669
10:11 **E** *is as* a heifer *that is* taught, *and* loveth to 669
10:11 I will make **E** to ride; Judah shall plow, *and* 669
11: 3 I taught **E** also to go, taking them by their 669
11: 8 How shall I give thee up, **E**? *how* shall I 669
11: 9 of mine anger, I will not return to destroy **E**: 669
11:12 **E** compasseth me about with lies, and 669
12: 1 **E** feedeth on wind, and followeth after 669
12: 8 **E** said, Yet I am become rich, I have found 669
12:14 **E** provoked *him* to anger most bitterly: 669
13: 1 When **E** spake trembling, he exalted *himself* 669
13:12 The iniquity of **E** *is* bound up; his sin *is* hid. 669
14: 8 **E** *shall say,* What have I to do any more with 669
Ob 1:19 they shall possess the fields of **E**, and 669
Zec 9:10 I will cut off the chariot from **E**, and 669
9:13 filled the bow *with* **E**, and raised up thy 669
10: 7 *they of* **E** shall be like a mighty *man,* and 669
Jn 11:54 into a city called **E**, and there continued *2187*

EPHRAIM'S (4) [EPHRAIM]

Ge 48:14 laid *it* upon **E** head, who *was* the younger, 669
48:17 to remove it from **E** head unto Manasseh's 669
50:23 Joseph saw **E** children of the third 669
Jos 17:10 Southward *it was* **E**, and 669+3807.1

EPHRAIMITE (1) [EPHRAIM]

Jdg 12: 5 men of Gilead said unto him, *Art* thou an **E**? 673

EPHRAIMITES (5) [EPHRAIM]

Jos 16:10 the Canaanites dwell among the **E** unto this 669
Jdg 12: 4 *are* fugitives of Ephraim among the **E**, 669
12: 5 took the passages of Jordan before the **E**: 669
12: 5 that when those **E** which were escaped said, 669
12: 6 there fell at that time of the **E** forty and 669

EPHRAIN (1)

2Ch 13:19 and **E** with the towns thereof. 6085

EPHRATAH (5) [CALEB-EPHRATAH, EPHRATH]

Ru 4:11 do thou worthily in **E**, and be famous in 672
1Ch 2:50 of Caleb the son of Hur, the firstborn of **E**; 672
4: 4 the firstborn of **E**, the father of Beth-lehem. 672
Ps 132: 6 Lo, we heard *of* it at **E**: we found it in 672
Mic 5: 2 thou, Beth-lehem **E**, *though thou* be little 672

EPHRATH (5) [EPHRATAH, EPHRATHITE, EPHRATHITES]

Ge 35:16 and there was but a little way to come to **E**: 672
35:19 Rachel died, and was buried in the way to **E**, 672
48: 7 *there was* but a little way to come unto **E**: 672
48: 7 I buried her there in the way of **E**; the same 672
1Ch 2:19 Caleb took unto him **E**, which bare him Hur. 672

EPHRATHITE (3) [EPHRATH]

1Sa 1: 1 the son of Tohu, the son of Zuph, an **E**: 673
17:12 Now David *was* the son of that **E** of 673
1Ki 11:26 an **E** of Zereda, Solomon's servant, 673

EPHRATHITES (1) [EPHRATH]

Ru 1: 2 and Chilion, **E** of Beth-lehem-judah. 673

EPHRON (13)

Ge 23: 8 and intreat for me to **E** the son of Zohar, 6085
23:10 **E** dwelt amongst the children of Heth: and 6085
23:10 **E** the Hittite answered Abraham in 6085
23:13 he spake unto **E** in the audience of 6085
23:14 **E** answered Abraham, saying unto him, 6085
23:16 Abraham hearkened unto **E**; and 6085
23:16 Abraham weighed to **E** the silver, which he 6085
23:17 the field of **E**, which *was* in Machpelah, 6085
25: 9 in the field of **E** the son of Zohar 6085
49:29 the cave that *is* in the field of **E** the Hittite, 6085
49:30 which Abraham bought with the field of **E** 6085
50:13 of a buryingplace of **E** the Hittite, 6085
Jos 15: 9 and went out to the cities of mount **E**; 6085

EPICUREANS (1)

Ac 17:18 Then certain philosophers of the **E**, and *1946*

EPISTLE (19) [EPISTLES]

Ac 15:30 the multitude together, they delivered the **e**: *1992*
23:33 and delivered the **e** to the governor, *1992*
Ro 16:22 I Tertius, who wrote *this* **e**, salute you in *1992*
1Co 5: 9 I wrote unto you in an **e** not to company *1992*
16: S The first *e* to the Corinthians was written NIG
2Co 3: 2 Ye are our **e** written in our hearts, known *1992*
3: 3 to be the **e** of Christ ministered by us, *1992*
7: 8 for I perceive that the same **e** hath made *1992*
13: S The second *e* to the Corinthians was written NIG
Col 4:16 And when *this* **e** is read amongst you, *1992*
4:16 that ye likewise read the **e** from Laodicea. NIG
1Th 5:27 I charge you by the Lord that *this* **e** be read *1992*
5: S The first *e* unto the Thessalonians was NIG
2Th 2:15 been taught, whether by word, or by our **e**. *1992*
3:14 if any *man* obey not our word by *this* **e**, *1992*
3:17 own hand, which is the token in every **e**: *1992*
3: S The second *e* to the Thessalonians was NIG
2Ti 4: S The second *e* unto Timotheus, ordained NIG
2Pe 3: 1 This second **e**, beloved, I now write unto *1992*

EPISTLES (2) [EPISTLE]

2Co 3: 1 as some *others,* **e** of commendation to you, *1992*
2Pe 3:16 As also in all *his* **e**, speaking in them of *1992*

EQUAL (21) [EQUALITY, EQUALLY, EQUALS, UNEQUAL]

Job 28:17 The gold and the crystal cannot **e** it: and 6186
28:19 The topaz of Ethiopia shall not **e** it, 6186
Ps 17: 2 let thine eyes behold the **things that are e**. 4339
55:13 a man mine **e**, my guide, and 6187+3509.1
Pr 26: 7 The legs of the lame are **not e**: so *is* a 1809
Isa 40:25 then will ye liken me, or shall I be **e**? 7737
46: 5 **make** *me* **e**, and compare me, that we may 7737
La 2:13 what shall I **e** to thee, that I may comfort 7737
Eze 18:25 Yet ye say, The way of the Lord is not **e**. 8505
18:25 O house of Israel; Is not my way **e**? 8505
18:29 of Israel, The way of the Lord is not **e**. 8505
18:29 O house of Israel, are not my ways **e**? 8505
33:17 people say, The way of the Lord is not **e**: 8505
33:17 but *as for* them, their way is not **e**. 8505
33:20 Yet ye say, The way of the Lord is not **e**. 8505
Mt 20:12 and thou hast made them **e** unto us, *2470*
Lk 20:36 for they are **e unto** *the* **angels**; and are *2465*
Jn 5:18 was his Father, making himself **e** with God. *2470*
Php 2: 6 thought it not robbery to be **e** with God: *2470*
Col 4: 1 unto *your* servants that which is just and **e**; *2471*
Rev 21:16 and the breadth and the height of it are **e**. *2470*

EQUALITY (2) [EQUAL]

2Co 8:14 But by an **e**, *that* now at *this* time your *2471*
8:14 *a supply* for your want: that there may be **e**: *2471*

EQUALLY (1) [EQUAL]

Ex 36:22 two tenons, **e distant** one from another: 7947

EQUALS (1) [EQUAL]

Gal 1:14 above many *my* **e** in mine own nation, *4915*

EQUITY (10)

Ps 98: 9 he judge the world, and the people with **e**. 4339
99: 4 thou dost establish **e**, thou executest 4339
Pr 1: 3 of wisdom, justice, and judgment, and **e**; 4339
2: 9 and judgment, and **e**; 4339
17:26 just *is* not good, *nor* to strike princes for **e**. 3476
Ecc 2:21 *is* in wisdom, and in knowledge, and in **e**; 3788
Isa 11: 4 reprove with **e** for the meek of the earth: 4334
59:14 is fallen in the street, and **e** cannot enter. 5229
Mic 3: 9 that abhor judgment, and pervert all **e**. 3477
Mal 2: 6 he walked with me in peace and **e**, and 4334

ER (11)

Ge 38: 3 and bare a son; and he called his name **E**. 6147
38: 6 Judah took a wife for **E** his firstborn, 6147
38: 7 **E**, Judah's firstborn, was wicked in 6147
46:12 **E**, and Onan, and Shelah, and Pharez, and 6147
46:12 **E** and Onan died in the land of Canaan. 6147
Nu 26:19 The sons of Judah *were* **E** and Onan: and 6147
26:19 and **E** and Onan died in the land of Canaan. 6147
1Ch 2: 3 sons of Judah; **E**, and Onan, and Shelah: 6147
2: 3 **E**, the firstborn of Judah, was evil in 6147
4:21 son of Judah *were,* **E** the father of Lecah, 6147
Lk 3:28 *son* of Elmodam, which was *the son* of **E**, *2262*

ERAN (1) [ERANITES]

Nu 26:36 of **E**, the family of the Eranites. 6197

ERANITES (1) [ERAN]

Nu 26:36 of Shuthelah: of Eran, the family of the **E**. 6198

ERASTUS (3)
Ac 19:22 that ministered unto him, Timotheus and **E**; *2037*
Ro 16:23 **E** the chamberlain of the city saluteth you, *2037*
2Ti 4:20 **E** abode at Corinth: but Trophimus have I *2037*

ERE (10)
Ex 1:19 are delivered **e** the midwives come 2962+871.1
Nu 11:33 yet between their teeth, **e** it was chewed, 2962
14:11 how long will it be **e** they believe me, 3808
1Sa 3: 3 **e** the lamp of God went out in the temple of 2962
2Sa 2:26 **e** thou bid the people return from following 3808
2Ki 6:32 **but e** the messenger came to him, he 2962+871.1
Job 18: 2 How long *will it be* **e** you make an end of NIH
Jer 47: 6 how long *will it be* **e** thou be quiet? 3808
Hos 8: 5 how long *will it be* **e** they attain to 3808
Jn 4:49 unto him, Sir, come down **e** my child die. *4250*

ERECH (1)
Ge 10:10 **E**, and Accad, and Calneh, in the land of 751

ERECTED (1)
Ge 33:20 he **e** there an altar, and called it 5324

ERI (2) [ERITES]
Ge 46:16 Shuni, and Ezbon, **E**, and Arodi, and Areli. 6179
Nu 26:16 the Oznites: of **E**, the family of the Erites: 6179

ERITES (1) [ERI]
Nu 26:16 of the Oznites: of Eri, the family of the **E**: 6180

ERR (24) [ERRED, ERRETH, ERROR, ERRORS]
2Ch 33: 9 **made** Judah and the inhabitants of Jerusalem **to e**, 8582
Ps 95:10 It *is* a people that do **e** in *their* heart, and 8582
119:21 which do **e** from thy commandments. 7686
119:118 Thou hast trodden down all them that **e** 7686
Pr 14:22 Do they not **e** that devise evil? but mercy 8582
19:27 to hear the instruction *that causeth* to **e** 7686
Isa 3:12 they which lead thee **cause** *thee* **to e**, and 8582
9:16 the leaders of this people **cause** *them* **to e**; 8582
19:14 they have **caused** Egypt **to e** in every work 8582
28: 7 they **e** in vision, they stumble *in* judgment. 7686
30:28 the jaws of the people, **causing** *them* **to e**. 8582
35: 8 though fools, shall not **e** *therein*. 8582
63:17 why hast thou **made** us **to e** from thy ways, 8582
Jer 23:13 in Baal, and **caused** my people Israel **to e**. 8582
23:32 **cause** my people **to e** by their lies, and 8582
Hos 4:12 spirit of whoredoms hath **caused** *them* **to e**, 8582
Am 2: 4 and their lies **caused** them **to e**, 8582
Mic 3: 5 the prophets that **make** my people **e**, 8582
Mt 22:29 and said unto them, Ye do **e**, *4105*
Mk 12:24 Do ye not therefore **e**, because ye know not *4105*
12:27 God of the living: ye therefore do greatly **e**. *4105*
Heb 3:10 and said, They do alway **e** in *their* heart; *4105*
Jas 1:16 Do not **e**, my beloved brethren. *4105*
5:19 if any of you do **e** from the truth, and *4105*

ERRAND (3)
Ge 24:33 I will not eat, until I have told mine **e**. 1697
Jdg 3:19 said, I have a secret **e** unto thee, O king: 1697
2Ki 9: 5 and he said, I have an **e** to thee, O captain. 1697

ERRED (12) [ERR]
Lev 5:18 him concerning his ignorance wherein he **e** 7683
Nu 15:22 if ye have **e**, and not observed all these 7686
1Sa 26:21 played the fool, and have **e** exceedingly. 7686
Job 6:24 cause me to understand wherein I have **e**. 7686
19: 4 be it indeed *that* I have **e**, mine error 7686
Ps119:110 snare for me: yet I **e** not from thy precepts. 8582
Isa 28: 7 they also have **e** through wine, and 7686
28: 7 the prophet have **e** through strong drink, 7686
29:24 They also that **e** in spirit shall come to 8582
1Ti 6:10 they have **e** from the faith, and *635*
6:21 Which some professing have **e** concerning *795*
2Ti 2:18 Who concerning the truth have **e**, saying that *795*

ERRETH (2) [ERR]
Pr 10:17 but he that refuseth reproof **e**. 8582
Eze 45:20 *day* of the month for every one that **e**, 7686

ERROR (13) [ERR]
2Sa 6: 7 God smote him there for *his* **e**; and there he 7944
Job 19: 4 I have erred, mine **e** remaineth with myself. 4879
Ecc 5: 6 say thou before the angel, that it *was* an **e**: 7684
10: 5 as an **e** *which* proceedeth from the ruler: 7684
Isa 32: 6 and to utter **e** against the LORD, 8442
Da 6: 4 neither was there any **e** or fault found in 7960
Mt 27:64 so the last **e** shall be worse than the first. *4106*
Ro 1:27 *that* recompence of their **e** which was meet. *4106*
Jas 5:20 **e** of his way shall save a soul from death, *4106*
2Pe 2:18 clean escaped from them who live in **e**. *4106*
3:17 being led away with the **e** of the wicked, *4106*
1Jn 4: 6 we the spirit of truth, and the spirit of **e**. *4106*
Jude 1:11 ran greedily after the **e** of Balaam for *4106*

ERRORS (4) [ERR]
Ps 19:12 Who can understand *his* **e**? cleanse thou 7691
Jer 10:15 They *are* vanity, *and* the work of **e**: in 8595
51:18 They *are* vanity, the work of **e**: in the time 8595
Heb 9: 7 for himself, and *for* the **e** of the people: *51*

ESAI (1) [ISAIAH]
2Ki 19: 2 to **E** the prophet the son of Amoz. 3470

ESAIAS (21) [ISAIAH]
Mt 3: 3 is he that was spoken of by the prophet **E**, *2268*
4:14 which was spoken by **E** the prophet, *2268*
8:17 which was spoken by **E** the prophet, *2268*
12:17 which was spoken by **E** the prophet, *2268*
13:14 And in them is fulfilled the prophecy of **E**, *2268*
15: 7 well did **E** prophesy of you, saying, *2268*
Mk 7: 6 Well hath **E** prophesied of you hypocrites, *2268*
Lk 3: 4 in the book of the words of **E** the prophet, *2268*
4:17 unto him the book of the prophet **E**. *2268*
Jn 1:23 the way of the Lord, as said the prophet **E**. *2268*
12:38 That the saying of **E** the prophet might be *2268*
12:39 not believe, because that **E** said again, *2268*
12:41 These *things* said **E**, when he saw his glory, *2268*
Ac 8:28 and sitting in his chariot read **E** the prophet. *2268*
8:30 to *him*, and heard him read the prophet **E**, *2268*
28:25 Well spake the Holy Ghost by **E** *2268*
Ro 9:27 **E** also crieth concerning Israel, Though *2268*
9:29 And as **E** said before, Except the Lord of *2268*
10:16 For **E** saith, Lord, who hath believed our *2268*
10:20 But **E** is very bold, and saith, I was found *2268*
15:12 And again **E** saith, There shall be a root of *2268*

ESARHADDON, ESAR-HADDON (3) [ESARHADDON]
2Ki 19:37 And **E** his son reigned in his stead. 634
Ezr 4: 2 we do sacrifice unto him since the days of **E** 634
Isa 37:38 and **E** his son reigned in his stead. 634

ESAU (88) [EDOM, ESAU'S]
Ge 25:25 hairy garment; and they called his name **E**. 6215
25:27 **E** was a cunning hunter, a man of the field; 6215
25:28 Isaac loved **E**, because he did eat of *his* 6215
25:29 **E** came from the field, and he *was* faint: 6215
25:30 **E** said to Jacob, Feed me, I pray thee, 6215
25:32 **E** said, Behold, I *am* at the point to die: 6215
25:34 Jacob gave **E** bread and pottage of lentiles; 6215
25:34 his way: thus **E** despised *his* birthright. 6215
26:34 **E** was forty years old when he took to wife 6215
27: 1 he called **E** his eldest son, and said unto 6215
27: 5 Rebekah heard when Isaac spake to **E** his 6215
27: 5 And **E** went to the field to hunt for venison, 6215
27: 6 I heard thy father speak unto **E** thy brother, 6215
27:11 **E** my brother *is* a hairy man, and I *am* a 6215
27:15 took goodly raiment of her eldest son **E**, 6215
27:19 said unto his father, I *am* **E** thy firstborn; 6215
27:21 whether thou *be* my very son **E** or not. 6215
27:22 but the hands *are* the hands of **E**. 6215
27:24 he said, *Art* thou my very son **E**? And he 6215
27:30 that **E** his brother came in from his hunting. 6215
27:32 And he said, I *am* thy son, thy firstborn **E**. 6215
27:34 when **E** heard the words of his father, he 6215
27:37 Isaac answered and said unto **E**, Behold, 6215
27:38 **E** said unto his father, Hast thou but one 6215
27:38 And **E** lift up his voice, and wept. 6215
27:41 **E** hated Jacob because of the blessing 6215
27:41 **E** said in his heart, The days of mourning 6215
27:42 these words of **E** her elder son were told to 6215
27:42 said unto him, Behold, thy brother **E**, 6215
28: 6 When **E** saw that Isaac had blessed Jacob, 6215
28: 8 **E** seeing that the daughters of Canaan 6215
28: 9 went **E** unto Ishmael, and took unto 6215
32: 3 Jacob sent messengers before him to **E** his 6215
32: 4 saying, Thus shall ye speak unto my lord **E**; 6215
32: 6 We came to thy brother **E**, and also he 6215
32: 8 If **E** come to the one company, and smite it, 6215

Ge 32:11 the hand of my brother, from the hand of **E**: 6215
32:13 to his hand a present for **E** his brother; 6215
32:17 When **E** my brother meeteth thee, and 6215
32:18 it *is* a present sent unto my lord **E**: 6215
32:19 On this manner shall you speak unto **E**, 6215
33: 1 **E** came, and with him four hundred men. 6215
33: 4 **E** ran to meet him, and embraced him, and 6215
33: 9 **E** said, I have enough, my brother; 6215
33:15 **E** said, Let me now leave with thee *some* of 6215
33:16 So **E** returned that day on his way unto 6215
35: 1 fleddest from the face of **E** thy brother. 6215
35:29 and his sons **E** and Jacob buried him. 6215
36: 1 Now these *are* the generations of **E**, who *is* 6215
36: 2 **E** took his wives of the daughters of 6215
36: 4 Adah bare to **E** Eliphaz; and 6215
36: 5 these *are* the sons of **E**, which were born 6215
36: 6 **E** took his wives, and his sons, and his 6215
36: 8 Thus dwelt **E** in mount Seir: Esau *is* Edom. 6215
36: 8 Thus dwelt Esau in mount Seir: **E** *is* Edom. 6215
36: 9 these *are* the generations of **E** the father of 6215
36:10 Eliphaz the son of Adah the wife of **E**, 6215
36:10 Reuel the son of Bashemath the wife of **E**. 6215
36:14 she bare to **E** Jeush, and Jaalam, and 6215
36:15 These *were* dukes of the sons of **E**: the sons 6215
36:15 the sons of Eliphaz the firstborn *son* of **E**; 6215
36:19 These *are* the sons of **E**, who *is* Edom, and 6215
36:40 *are* the names of the dukes *that came* of **E**, 6215
36:43 he *is* **E** the father of the Edomites. 6215
Dt 2: 4 the coast of your brethren the children of **E**, 6215
2: 5 I have given mount Seir unto **E** *for* a 6215
2: 8 by from our brethren the children of **E**, 6215
2:12 the children of **E** succeeded them, 6215
2:22 As he did to the children of **E**, which dwelt 6215
2:29 (As the children of **E** which dwell in Seir, 6215
Jos 24: 4 I gave unto Isaac Jacob and **E**: and I gave 6215
24: 4 I gave unto **E** mount Seir, to possess it; 6215
1Ch 1:34 begat Isaac. The sons of Isaac; **E** and Israel. 6215
1:35 The sons of **E**; Eliphaz, Reuel, and Jeush, 6215
Jer 49: 8 for I will bring the calamity of **E** upon him, 6215
49:10 I have made **E** bare, I have uncovered his 6215
Ob 1: 6 How are *the things of* **E** searched out! 6215
1: 8 and understanding out of the mount of **E**? 6215
1: 9 to the end that every one of the mount of **E** 6215
1:18 the house of **E** for stubble, and they shall 6215
1:18 not be *any* remaining of the house of **E**; 6215
1:19 *of* the south shall possess the mount of **E**; 6215
1:21 up on mount Zion to judge the mount of **E**; 6215
Mal 1: 2 *was* not **E** Jacob's brother? saith 6215
1: 3 I hated **E**, and laid his mountains and his 6215
Ro 9:13 Jacob have I loved, but **E** have I hated. *2269*
Heb 11:20 and **E** concerning *things* to come. *2269*
12:16 *be* any fornicator, or profane *person*, as **E**, *2269*

ESAU'S (12) [ESAU]

Ge 25:26 and his hand took hold on **E** heel; 6215
27:23 hands were hairy, as his brother **E** hands: 6215
28: 5 brother of Rebekah, Jacob's and **E** mother. 6215
36:10 These *are* the names of **E** sons; Eliphaz 6215
36:12 Timna was concubine to Eliphaz **E** son; 6215
36:12 these *were* the sons of Adah **E** wife. 6215
36:13 these were the sons of Bashemath **E** wife. 6215
36:14 of Anah, daughter of Zibeon, **E** wife: 6215
36:17 these *are* the sons of Reuel **E** son; 6215
36:17 these *are* the sons of Bashemath **E** wife. 6215
36:18 these *are* the sons of Aholibamah **E** wife; 6215
36:18 Aholibamah the daughter of Anah, **E** wife. 6215

ESCAPE (59) [ESCAPED, ESCAPETH, ESCAPING]

Ge 19:17 forth abroad, that he said, **E** for thy life; 4422
19:17 **e** to the mountain, lest thou be consumed. 4422
19:19 I cannot **e** to the mountain, lest *some* evil 4422
19:20 Oh, let me **e** thither, (*is* it not a little one?) 4422
19:22 Haste thee, **e** thither; for I cannot do any 4422
32: 8 the *other* company which is left shall **e**. 6413
Jos 8:22 so that *they* let none of them remain or **e**. 6412
1Sa 27: 1 **speedily e** into the land of 4422+4422
27: 1 coast of Israel: so shall I **e** out of his hand. 4422
2Sa 15:14 we shall not *else* **e** from Absalom. 1961+6413
20: 6 he get him fenced cities, and **e** us. 5337+5869
1Ki 18:40 the prophets of Baal; let not one of them **e**. 4422
2Ki 9:15 let none go forth *nor* **e** out of the city to go 6412
10:24 whom I *have* brought into your hands **e**, 4422
19:31 and **they that e** out of mount Zion: 6413
Ezr 9: 8 to leave us a **remnant to e**, and to give us a 6413
Est 4:13 Think not with thyself that *thou* shalt **e** *in* 4422
Job 11:20 they shall not **e**, and their hope *shall be as* 4498
Ps 55: 8 I would hasten my **e** from the windy storm 4655
56: 7 *Shall* they **e** by iniquity? in *thine* anger cast 6405
71: 2 me in thy righteousness, and **cause** me **to e**: 6403
141:10 into their own nets, whilst that I withal **e**. 5674
Pr 19: 5 and *he that* speaketh lies shall not **e**. 4422
Ecc 7:26 whoso pleaseth God shall **e** from her; but 4422
Isa 20: 6 the king of Assyria: and how shall we **e**? 4422
37:32 and **they that e** out of mount Zion: 6413
66:19 I will send those that **e** of them unto 6412
Jer 11:11 which they shall not be able to **e**; 3318
25:35 to flee, nor the principal of the flock to **e**. 6413
32: 4 Zedekiah king of Judah shall not **e** out of 4422
34: 3 thou shalt not **e** out of his hand, but 4422
38:18 and thou shalt not **e** out of their hand. 4422
38:23 thou shalt not **e** out of their hand, but 4422
42:17 **e** from the evil that I *will* bring upon them. 6412
44:14 shall **e** or remain, that *they* should 1961+6412
44:14 for none shall return but such as shall **e**. 6405
44:28 Yet a small number that **e** the sword shall 6412
46: 6 the swift flee away, nor the mighty *man* **e**; 4422
48: 8 come upon every city, and no city shall **e**: 4422
50:28 that flee and **e** out of the land of Babylon, 6405
50:29 against it round about; let none thereof **e**: 6413
Eze 6: 8 that ye may have *some* that shall **e** 6412
6: 9 they that **e** of you shall remember me 6412
7:16 they that **e** of them shall escape, and 6412
7:16 they that escape of them shall **e**, and 6403
17:15 shall he **e** that doeth such *things?* or 4422
17:18 hath done all these *things*, he shall not **e**. 4422
Da 11:41 these shall **e** out of his hand, *even* Edom, 4422
11:42 and the land of Egypt shall not **e**. 6413
Joel 2: 3 and nothing shall **e** them. 1961+6413
Ob 1:14 to cut off those of his that did **e**; 6412
Mt 23:33 how can ye **e** the damnation of hell? *5343*
Lk 21:36 that ye may be accounted worthy to **e** all *1628*
Ac 27:42 lest any *of them* should swim out, and **e**. *1309*
Ro 2: 3 that thou shalt **e** the judgment of God? *1628*
1Co 10:13 with the temptation also make a **way to e**, *1545*
1Th 5: 3 a *woman* with child; and they shall not **e**. *1628*
Heb 2: 3 How shall we **e**, if we neglect so *1628*
12:25 much more *shall not* we **e**, if we turn away NIG

ESCAPED (58) [ESCAPE]

Ge 14:13 there came one that had **e**, and told Abram 6412
Ex 10: 5 they shall eat the residue of that **which is e** 6413
Nu 21:29 he hath given his sons that **e**, and 6412
Dt 23:15 which is **e** from his master unto thee: 5337
Jdg 3:26 Ehud **e** while they tarried, and passed 4422
3:26 beyond the quarries, and **e** unto Seirath. 4422
3:29 all men of valour; and there **e** not a man. 4422
12: 5 that when those Ephraimites which were **e** 6412
21:17 for **them that be e** of Benjamin, 6413
1Sa 14:41 and Jonathan were taken: but the people **e**. 3318
19:10 the wall: and David fled, and **e** that night. 4422
19:12 a window: and he went, and fled, and **e**. 4422
19:17 and sent away mine enemy, that he is **e**? 4422
19:18 **e**, and came to Samuel to Ramah, and 4422
22: 1 departed thence, and **e** to the cave Adullam: 4422
22:20 named Abiathar, **e**, and fled after David. 4422
23:13 it was told Saul that David was **e** from 4422
30:17 there **e** not a man of them, save four 4422
2Sa 1: 3 unto him, Out of the camp of Israel am I **e**. 4422
4: 6 and Rechab and Baanah his brother **e**. 4422
1Ki 20:20 Ben-hadad the king of Syria **e** on a horse 4422
2Ki 19:30 the remnant **that is e** of the house of Judah 6413
19:37 they **e** *into* the land of Armenia. 4422
1Ch 4:43 the rest of the Amalekites that were **e**, 6413
2Ch 16: 7 is the host of the king of Syria **e** out of 4422
20:24 dead bodies fallen to the earth, and none **e**. 6413
30: 6 **that are e** out of the hand of the kings of 6413
36:20 them that had **e** from the sword carried he 7611
Ezr 9:15 for we remain *yet* **e**, as *it is* this day: 6413
Ne 1: 2 asked them concerning the Jews that had **e**, 6413
Job 1:15 and I only am **e** alone to tell thee. 4422
1:16 and I only am **e** alone to tell thee. 4422
1:17 and I only am **e** alone to tell thee. 4422
1:19 are dead; and I only am **e** alone to tell thee. 4422
19:20 and I am **e** with the skin of my teeth. 4422
Ps 124: 7 Our soul is **e** as a bird out of the snare of 4422
124: 7 the snare is broken, and we are **e**. 4422
Isa 4: 2 and comely for **them that are e** of Israel. 6413
10:20 and **such as are e** of the house of Jacob, 6413

Isa 37:31 the remnant that is e of the house of Judah 6413
37:38 and they e into the land of Armenia: 4422
45:20 near together, ye that are e of the nations: 6412
Jer 41:15 Ishmael the son of Nethaniah e from 4422
51:50 Ye that have e the sword, go away, stand 6405
La 2:22 the LORD'S anger none e nor remained: 6412
Eze 24:27 thy mouth be opened to him which is e, 6412
33:21 that one that had e out of Jerusalem came 6412
33:22 in the evening, afore he that was e came; 6412
Jn 10:39 to take him: but he e out of their hand, 1831
Ac 27:44 it came to pass, that they e all safe to land. 1295
28: 1 And when they were e, then they knew that 1295
28: 4 whom, though he hath e the sea, 1295
2Co 11:33 was I let down by the wall, and e his hands. 1628
Heb 11:34 violence of fire, e the edge of the sword, 5343
12:25 for if they e not who refused him that spake 5343
2Pe 1: 4 having e the corruption that is in the world 668
2:18 those that were clean e from them who live 668
2:20 For if after they have e the pollutions of 668

ESCAPETH (6) [ESCAPE]
1Ki 19:17 that him that e the sword of Hazael shall 4422
19:17 him that e from the sword of Jehu shall 4422
Isa 15: 9 lions upon him that e of Moab, and 6413
Jer 48:19 and her that e, and say, What is done? 4422
Eze 24:26 That he that e in that day shall come unto 6412
Am 9: 1 and he that e of them shall not be delivered. 6412

ESCAPING (1) [ESCAPE]
Ezr 9:14 so that there should be no remnant nor e? 6413

ESCHEW (1) [ESCHEWED, ESCHEWETH]
1Pe 3:11 Let him e evil, and do good; let him seek 1578

ESCHEWED (1) [ESCHEW]
Job 1: 1 and one that feared God, and e evil. 5493

ESCHEWETH (2) [ESCHEW]
Job 1: 8 one that feareth God, and e evil? 5493
2: 3 one that feareth God, and e evil? 5493

ESCORT See FETCH; FETCHED

ESEK (1)
Ge 26:20 he called the name of the well E; because 6230

ESHAN See ESHEAN

ESHBAAL (2) [ISH-BOSHETH]
1Ch 8:33 and Malchishua, and Abinadab, and E. 792
9:39 and Malchishua, and Abinadab, and E. 792

ESHBAN (2)
Ge 36:26 Hemdan, and E, and Ithran, and Cheran. 790
1Ch 1:41 Amram, and E, and Ithran, and Cheran. 790

ESHCOL (6)
Ge 14:13 brother of E, and brother of Aner: 812
14:24 which went with me, Aner, E, and Mamre; 812
Nu 13:23 they came unto the brook of E, and cut down 812
13:24 The place was called the brook E, because 812
32: 9 For when they went up unto the valley of E, 812
Dt 1:24 came unto the valley of E, and searched it 812

ESHEAN (1)
Jos 15:52 Arab, and Dumah, and E, 824

ESHEK (1)
1Ch 8:39 the sons of E his brother were, Ulam his 6232

ESHKALONITES (1) [ASHKELON]
Jos 13: 3 the E, the Gittites, and the Ekronites; 832

ESHTAOL (7)
Jos 15:33 in the valley, E, and Zoreah, and Ashnah, 847
19:41 was Zorah, and E, and Ir-shemesh, 847
Jdg 13:25 in the camp of Dan, between Zorah and E. 847
16:31 E in the buryingplace of Manoah his father. 847
18: 2 men of valour, from Zorah and from E, 847
18: 8 came unto their brethren to Zorah and E: 847
18:11 out of Zorah and out of E, six hundred men 847

ESHTAOLITES See ESHTAULITES

ESHTAULITES (1)
1Ch 2:53 of them came the Zareathites, and the E. 848

ESHTEMOA (5)
Jos 21:14 with her suburbs, and E with her suburbs, 851
1Sa 30:28 in Siphmoth, and to them which were in E, 851
1Ch 4:17 and Shammai, and Ishbah the father of E. 851
4:19 Keilah the Garmite, and E the Maachathite. 851
6:57 and Jattir, and E, with their suburbs, 851

ESHTEMOH (1)
Jos 15:50 And Anab, and E, and Anim, 851

ESHTON (2)
1Ch 4:11 begat Mehir, which was the father of E. 850
4:12 E begat Beth-rapha, and Paseah, and 850

ESLI (1)
Lk 3:25 the son of Naum, which was the son of E, 2069

ESPECIALLY (5) [SPECIAL]
Ps 31:11 e among my neighbours, and a fear to mine 3966
Ac 26: 3 E because I know thee to be expert in all 3122
Gal 6:10 let us do good unto all men, e unto them 3122
1Ti 5:17 e they who labour in the word and doctrine. 3122
2Ti 4:13 and the books, but e the parchments. 3122

ESPIED (2) [SPY]
Ge 42:27 ass provender in the inn, he e his money; 7200
Eze 20: 6 of Egypt into a land that I had e for them, 8446

ESPOUSALS (2) [ESPOUSED]
SS 3:11 his mother crowned him in the day of his e, 2861
Jer 2: 2 kindness of thy youth, the love of thine e, 3623

ESPOUSED (5) [ESPOUSALS]
2Sa 3:14 which I e to me for an hundred foreskins of 781
Mt 1:18 When as his mother Mary was e to Joseph, 3423
Lk 1:27 To a virgin e to a man whose name was 3423
2: 5 To be taxed with Mary his e wife, 3423
2Co 11: 2 for I have e you to one husband, that I may 718

ESPY (2) [SPY]
Jos 14: 7 me from Kadesh-barnea to e out the land; 7270
Jer 48:19 inhabitant of Aroer, stand by the way and e; 6822

ESROM (3) [HEZRON]
Mt 1: 3 and Phares begat E; and Esrom begat 2074
1: 3 Phares begat Esrom; and E begat Aram; 2074
Lk 3:33 the son of Aram, which was the son of E, 2074

ESTABLISH (41) [ESTABLISHED, ESTABLISHETH, ESTABLISHMENT]
Ge 6:18 with thee will I e my covenant; and 6965
9: 9 behold I e my covenant with you and 6965
9:11 I will e my covenant with you; neither shall 6965
17: 7 I will e my covenant between me and thee 6965
17:19 I will e my covenant with him for an 6965
17:21 my covenant will I e with Isaac, 6965
Lev 26: 9 multiply you, and e my covenant with you. 6965
Nu 30:13 her husband may e it, or her husband may 6965
Dt 8:18 that he may e his covenant which he sware 6965
28: 9 The LORD shall e thee a holy people unto 6965
29:13 That he may e thee to day for a people unto 6965
1Sa 1:23 weaned him; only the LORD e his word. 6965
2Sa 7:12 out of thy bowels, and I will e his kingdom. 3559
7:25 e it for ever, and do as thou hast said. 6965
1Ki 9: 5 I will e the throne of thy kingdom upon 6965
15: 4 set up his son after him, and to e Jerusalem: 5975
1Ch 22:10 I will e the throne of his kingdom over 3559
28: 7 Moreover I will e his kingdom for ever, 3559
2Ch 9: 8 to e them for ever, therefore made he thee 5975
Job 36: 7 he doth e them for ever, and they are 3427
Ps 7: 9 the wicked come to an end; but e the just: 3559
48: 8 of our God: God will e it for ever. Selah. 3559
87: 5 in her: and the Highest himself shall e her. 3559
89: 2 thy faithfulness shalt thou e in the very 3559
90:17 e thou the work of our hands upon us; yea, 355[illegible]
90:17 yea, the work of our hands e thou it. 35[illegible]
99: 4 thou dost e equity, thou executest judgment [illegible]
Pr 15:25 but he will e the border of the widow.
Isa 49: 8 for a covenant of the people, to e the earth
62: 7 till he e, and till he make Jerusalem a pra[illegible]
Jer 33: 2 the LORD that formed it, to e it;
Eze 16:60 I will e unto thee an everlasting cove[illegible]
16:62 I will e my covenant with thee; and
Da 6: 7 have consulted together to e a ro[illegible]
6: 8 O king, e the decree, and sign t[illegible]

E

Da	11:14	shall exalt themselves to **e** the vision;	5975
Am	5:15	love the good, and **e** judgment in the gate:	3322
Ro	3:31	God forbid: yea, we **e** the law.	*2476*
	10: 3	going about to **e** their own righteousness,	*2476*
1Th	3: 2	to **e** you, and to comfort you concerning	*4741*
Heb	10: 9	away the first, that he may **e** the second.	*2476*

ESTABLISHED (68) [ESTABLISH]

Ge	9:17	which I have **e** between me and all flesh	6965
	41:32	*it is* because the thing *is* **e** by God, and God	3559
Ex	6: 4	I have also **e** my covenant with them,	6965
	15:17	O Lord, *which* thy hands have **e**.	3559
Dt	32: 6	hath he *not* made thee, and **e** thee?	3559
1Sa	3:20	Samuel *was* **e** to be a prophet of the LORD.	539
	13:13	for now would the LORD have **e** thy	3559
	24:20	*that* the kingdom of Israel shall be **e** in	6965
2Sa	5:12	David perceived that the LORD had **e** him	3559
	7:26	let the house of thy servant David be **e**	3559
1Ki	2:12	his father; and his kingdom was **e** greatly.	3559
	2:24	which hath **e** me, and set me on the throne	3559
	2:45	the throne of David shall be **e** before	3559
	2:46	the kingdom was **e** in the hand of Solomon.	3559
1Ch	17:14	and his throne shall be **e** for evermore.	3559
	17:23	and concerning his house be **e** for ever,	539
	17:24	Let it even be **e**, that thy name may be	539
	17:24	*let* the house of David thy servant *be* **e**	3559
2Ch	1: 9	let thy promise unto David my father be **e**:	539
	12: 1	when Rehoboam had **e** the kingdom, and	3559
	20:20	in the LORD your God, so shall you be **e**;	539
	25: 3	to pass, when the kingdom was **e** to him,	2388
	30: 5	So they **e** a decree to make proclamation	5975
Job	21: 8	Their seed is **e** in their sight with them, and	3559
	22:28	decree a thing, and it shall be **e** unto thee:	6965
Ps	24: 2	it upon the seas, and **e** it upon the floods.	3559
	40: 2	set my feet upon a rock, *and* **e** my goings.	3559
	78: 5	For he **e** a testimony in Jacob, and	6965
	78:69	like the earth which he hath **e** for ever.	3245
	89:21	With whom my hand shall be **e**: mine arm	3559
	89:37	It shall be **e** for ever as the moon, and *as* a	3559
	93: 2	Thy throne is **e** of old: thou *art* from	3559
	96:10	the world also shall be **e** *that* it shall not be	3559
	102:28	and their seed shall be **e** before thee.	3559
	112: 8	His heart *is* **e**, he shall not be afraid,	5564
	119:90	thou hast **e** the earth, and it abideth.	3559
	140:11	Let not an evil speaker be **e** in the earth:	3559
Pr	3:19	by understanding hath he **e** the heavens.	3559
	4:26	path of thy feet, and let all thy ways be **e**.	3559
	8:28	When he **e** the clouds above: when *he*	553
	12: 3	A man shall not be **e** by wickedness: but	3559
	12:19	The lip of truth shall be **e** for ever: but	3559
	15:22	in the multitude of counsellers *they* are **e**.	6965
	16: 3	the LORD, and thy thoughts shall be **e**.	3559
	16:12	for the throne is **e** by righteousness.	3559
	20:18	Every purpose is **e** by counsel: and	3559
	24: 3	house builded; and by understanding it is **e**:	3559
	25: 5	and his throne shall be **e** in righteousness.	3559
	29:14	the poor, his throne shall be **e** for ever.	3559
	30: 4	who hath **e** all the ends of the earth? what *is*	6965
Isa	2: 2	shall be **e** in the top of the mountains,	3559
	7: 9	ye will not believe, surely ye shall not be **e**.	539
	16: 5	in mercy shall the throne be **e**: and he shall	3559
	45:18	he hath **e** it, he created it not in vain,	3559
	54:14	In righteousness shalt thou be **e**: thou shalt	3559
Jer	10:12	he hath **e** the world by his wisdom, and	3559
	30:20	and their congregation shall be **e** before me,	3559
	51:15	he hath **e** the world by his wisdom, and	3559
Da	4:36	I was **e** in my kingdom, and	8627
Mic	4: 1	shall be **e** in the top of the mountains,	3559
Hab	1:12	thou hast **e** them for correction.	3245
Zec	5:11	it shall be **e**, and set there upon her own	3559
Mt	18:16	or three witnesses every word may be **e**.	*2476*
Ac	16: 5	And so were the churches **e** in the faith, and	*4732*
Ro	1:11	spiritual gift, to the end you may be **e**;	*4741*
2Co	13: 1	or three witnesses shall every word be **e**.	*2476*
Heb	8: 6	which was **e** upon better promises.	*3549*
	13: 9	For *it is* a good *thing* that the heart be **e** with	*950*

ESTABLISHETH (2) [ESTABLISH]

Nu	30:14	he **e** all her vows, or all her bonds,	6965
Da	6:15	statute which the king **e** may be changed.	6966

ESTABLISHMENT (1) [ESTABLISH]

2Ch	32: 1	the **e** *thereof,* Sennacherib king of Assyria	571

ESTATE (17) [ESTATES]

1Ch	17:17	hast regarded me according to the **e** of a	8448
Est	1:19	let the king give her **royal e** unto another	4438
Ps	136:23	Who remembered us in our **low e**: for his	8216
Ecc	1:16	Lo, I am **come to great e**, and have gotten	1431
	3:18	I said in my heart concerning the **e** of	1700
Eze	16:55	shall return to their **former e**, and Samaria	6927
	16:55	her daughters shall return to their **former e**,	6927
	16:55	thy daughters shall return to your **former e**.	6927
Da	11: 7	of her roots shall *one* stand up *in* his **e**,	3653
	11:20	shall stand up in his **e** a raiser of taxes *in*	3653
	11:21	in his **e** shall stand up a vile person, to	3653
	11:38	in his **e** shall he honour the God of forces:	3653
Lk	1:48	For he hath regarded the **low e** of his	*5014*
Ac	22: 5	bear me witness, and all the **e of the elders**:	*4244*
Ro	12:16	*things,* but condescend to *men* **of low e**.	*5011*
Col	4: 8	that he might know your **e**, and	*4012*
Jude	1: 6	And the angels which kept not their **first e**,	*746*

ESTATES (2) [ESTATE]

Eze	36:11	I will settle you after your **old e**, and	6927
Mk	6:21	high captains, and chief *e* of Galilee;	NIG

ESTEEM (5) [ESTEEMED, ESTEEMETH, ESTEEMING]

Job	36:19	Will he **e** thy riches? *no,* not gold, nor all	6186
Ps	119:128	**e** all *thy* precepts concerning all *things* **to be right**;	3474
Isa	53: 4	yet we did **e** him stricken, smitten of God,	2803
Php	2: 3	in lowliness of mind *let* each **e** other better	*2233*
1Th	5:13	And to **e** them very highly in love for their	*2233*

ESTEEMED (11) [ESTEEM]

Dt	32:15	and **lightly e** the Rock of his salvation.	5034
1Sa	2:30	and they that despise me shall be **lightly e**.	7043
	18:23	seeing that I *am* a poor man, and **lightly e**?	7034
Job	23:12	I have **e** the words of his mouth more than	6845
Pr	17:28	he that shutteth his lips *is e a man* of	NIH
Isa	29:16	upside down shall be **e** as the potter's clay:	2803
	29:17	and the fruitful field shall be **e** as a forest?	2803
	53: 3	he was despised, and we **e** him not.	2803
La	4: 2	how are they **e** as earthen pitchers,	2803
Lk	16:15	for that which is **highly e** amongst men is	*5308*
1Co	6: 4	set them to judge who are **least e** in	*1848*

ESTEEMETH (4) [ESTEEM]

Job	41:27	He **e** iron as straw, *and* brass as rotten	2803
Ro	14: 5	One man **e** one day above another:	*2919*
	14: 5	another **e** every day *alike.* Let every man be	*2919*
	14:14	but to him that **e** any *thing* to be unclean,	*3049*

ESTEEMING (1) [ESTEEM]

Heb	11:26	**E** the reproach of Christ greater riches than	*2233*

ESTHER (53) [ESTHER'S, HADASSAH]

Est	2: 7	up Hadassah, that *is,* **E**, his uncle's daughter:	635
	2: 8	that **E** was brought *also* unto the king's	635
	2:10	**E** had not shewed her people nor her	635
	2:11	to know how **E** did, and what should become	635
	2:15	Now when the turn of **E**, the daughter of	635
	2:15	**E** obtained favour in the sight of all them	635
	2:16	So **E** was taken unto king Ahasuerus into his	635
	2:17	the king loved **E** above all the women, and	635
	2:20	**E** had not *yet* shewed her kindred nor her	635
	2:20	for **E** did the commandment of Mordecai,	635
	2:22	to Mordecai, who told *it* unto **E** the queen;	635
	2:22	**E** certified the king *thereof* in Mordecai's	635
	4: 5	called **E** for Hatach, *one* of the king's	635
	4: 8	to shew *it* unto **E**, and to declare *it* unto her,	635
	4: 9	and told **E** the words of Mordecai.	635
	4:10	Again **E** spake unto Hatach, and gave him	635
	4:13	Mordecai commanded to answer **E**,	635
	4:15	**E** bade *them* return Mordecai *this answer:*	635
	4:17	did according to all that **E** had commanded	635
	5: 1	that **E** put on *her* royal *apparel,* and stood in	635
	5: 2	when the king saw **E** the queen standing in	635
	5: 2	the king held out to **E** the golden sceptre that	635
	5: 2	So **E** drew near, and touched the top of	635
	5: 3	the king unto her, What wilt thou, queen **E**?	635
	5: 4	**E** answered, If *it seem* good unto the king,	635
	5: 5	to make haste, that *he* may do as **E** hath said.	635
	5: 5	Haman came to the banquet that **E** had	635
	5: 6	the king said unto **E** at the banquet of wine,	635
	5: 7	Then answered **E**, and said, My petition and	635
	5:12	**E** the queen did let no *man* come in with	635

Est 6:14 unto the banquet that E had prepared. 635
7: 1 Haman came to banquet with E the queen. 635
7: 2 the king said again unto E on the second day 635
7: 2 of wine, What *is* thy petition, queen E? 635
7: 3 E the queen answered and said, If I have 635
7: 5 and said unto E the queen, 635
7: 6 E said, The adversary and enemy *is* this 635
7: 7 to make request for his life to E the queen; 635
7: 8 Haman was fallen upon the bed whereon E 635
8: 1 Haman the Jews' enemy unto E the queen. 635
8: 1 for E had told what he *was* unto her. 635
8: 2 E set Mordecai over the house of Haman. 635
8: 3 E spake yet again before the king, and 635
8: 4 king held out the golden sceptre toward E. 635
8: 4 So E arose, and stood before the king, 635
8: 7 the king Ahasuerus said unto E the queen 635
8: 7 I have given E the house of Haman, and him 635
9:12 the king said unto E the queen, The Jews 635
9:13 said E, If it please the king, let it be granted 635
9:25 when *E* came before the king, NIH
9:29 E the queen, the daughter of Abihail, and 635
9:31 the Jew and E the queen had enjoined them, 635
9:32 the decree of E confirmed these matters of 635

ESTHER'S (3) [ESTHER]
Est 2:18 all his princes and his servants, *even* E feast; 635
4: 4 So E maids and her chamberlains came and 635
4:12 And they told to Mordecai E words. 635

ESTIMATE (2) [ESTIMATION, ESTIMATIONS]
Lev 27:14 the priest shall e it, whether it be good or 6186
27:14 as the priest shall e it, so shall it stand. 6186

ESTIMATION (23) [ESTIMATE]
Lev 5:15 with thy e *by* shekels of silver, after 6187
5:18 with thy e, for a trespass offering, unto 6187
6: 6 with thy e, for a trespass offering, unto 6187
27: 2 persons *shall be* for the LORD by thy e. 6187
27: 3 thy e shall be, of the male from twenty 6187
27: 3 even thy e shall be fifty shekels of silver, 6187
27: 4 a female, then thy e shall be thirty shekels. 6187
27: 5 thy e shall be of the male twenty shekels, 6187
27: 6 thy e shall be of the male five shekels of 6187
27: 6 for the female thy e *shall be* three shekels 6187
27: 7 thy e shall be fifteen shekels, and for 6187
27: 8 if he be poorer than thy e, then he shall 6187
27:13 he shall add a fifth *part* thereof unto thy e. 6187
27:15 the fifth *part* of the money of thy e unto it, 6187
27:16 thy e shall be according to the seed thereof: 6187
27:17 of jubile, according to thy e it shall stand. 6187
27:18 the jubile, and it shall be abated from thy e. 6187
27:19 the fifth *part* of the money of thy e unto it, 6187
27:23 shall reckon unto him the worth of thy e, 6187
27:23 he shall give thine e in that day, *as* a holy 6187
27:27 he shall redeem *it* according to thine e, and 6187
27:27 then it shall be sold according to thy e. 6187
Nu 18:16 according to thine e, *for* the money of five 6187

ESTIMATIONS (1) [ESTIMATE]
Lev 27:25 all thy e shall be according to the shekel of 6187

ESTRANGED (5)
Job 19:13 mine acquaintance are verily e from me. 2114
Ps 58: 3 The wicked are e from the womb: they go 2114
78:30 They were not e from their lust. But while 2114
Jer 19: 4 have e this place, and have burnt incense in 5234
Eze 14: 5 they are all e from me through their idols. 2114

ETAM (5)
Jdg 15: 8 and dwelt in the top of the rock E. 5862
15:11 men of Judah went to the top of the rock E, 5862
1Ch 4: 3 these *were of* the father of E; Jezreel, and 5862
4:32 their villages *were*, E, and Ain, Rimmon, 5862
2Ch 11: 6 built even Beth-lehem, and E, and Tekoa, 5862

ETERNAL (47) [ETERNITY]
Dt 33:27 The e God *is thy* refuge, and underneath *are* 6924
Isa 60:15 *thee,* I will make thee an e excellency, 5769
Mt 19:16 good *thing* shall I do, that I may have e life? *166*
25:46 but the righteous into life e. *166*
Mk 3:29 but is in danger of e damnation. *166*
10:17 what shall I do that I may inherit e life? *166*
10:30 and in the world to come e life. *166*
Lk 10:25 Master, what shall I do to inherit e life? *166*
18:18 what shall I do to inherit e life? *166*
Jn 3:15 in him should not perish, but have e life. *166*
4:36 and gathereth fruit unto life e: *166*
5:39 for in them ye think ye have e life: *166*
6:54 my flesh, and drinketh my blood, hath e life; *166*
6:68 shall we go? thou hast the words of e life. *166*
10:28 And I give unto them e life; and they shall *166*
12:25 his life in this world shall keep it unto life e. *166*
17: 2 that he should give e life to as many as thou *166*
17: 3 And this is life e, that they might know thee *166*
Ac 13:48 as many as were ordained to e life believed. *166*
Ro 1:20 are made, *even* his e power and Godhead; *126*
2: 7 for glory and honour and immortality, e life: *166*
5:21 unto e life by Jesus Christ our Lord. *166*
6:23 the gift of God *is* e life through Jesus Christ *166*
2Co 4:17 a far more exceeding *and* e weight of glory; *166*
4:18 but the *things* which are not seen *are* e. *166*
5: 1 house not made with hand, e in the heavens. *166*
Eph 3:11 According to the e purpose which he *165*
1Ti 1:17 Now unto the King e, immortal, invisible, *165*
6:12 the good fight of faith, lay hold on e life, *166*
6:19 to come, that they may lay hold on e life. *166*
2Ti 2:10 which is in Christ Jesus with e glory. *166*
Tit 1: 2 In hope of e life, which God, that cannot lie, *166*
3: 7 be made heirs according to the hope of e life. *166*
Heb 5: 9 he became the author of e salvation unto all *166*
6: 2 resurrection of the dead, and of e judgment. *166*
9:12 *place,* having obtained e redemption *for us.* *166*
9:14 who through the e Spirit offered himself *166*
9:15 might receive the promise of e inheritance. *166*
1Pe 5:10 who hath called us into his e glory by Christ *166*
1Jn 1: 2 bear witness, and shew unto you *that* e life, *166*
2:25 that he hath promised us, *even* e life. *166*
3:15 ye know that no murderer hath e life abiding *166*
5:11 that God hath given to us e life, and this life *166*
5:13 that ye may know that ye have e life, and *166*
5:20 Jesus Christ. This is the true God, and e life. *166*
Jude 1: 7 suffering the vengeance of e fire. *166*
1:21 mercy of our Lord Jesus Christ unto e life. *166*

ETERNITY (1) [ETERNAL]
Isa 57:15 the high and lofty One that inhabiteth e, 5703

ETH KAZIN See ITTAH-KAZIN

ETHAM (4)
Ex 13:20 encamped in E, in the edge of 864
Nu 33: 6 departed from Succoth, and pitched in E, 864
33: 7 they removed from E, and turned again unto 864
33: 8 three days' journey in the wilderness of E, 864

ETHAN (8)
1Ki 4:31 than E the Ezrahite, and Heman, and 387
1Ch 2: 6 and E, and Heman, and Calcol, and Dara: 387
2: 8 And the sons of E; Azariah. 387
6:42 The son of E, the son of Zimmah, the son of 387
6:44 E the son of Kishi, the son of Abdi, the son 387
15:17 Merari their brethren, E the son of Kushaiah; 387
15:19 So the singers, Heman, Asaph, and E, 387
Ps 89: T Maschil of E the Ezrahite. 387

ETHANIM (1)
1Ki 8: 2 king Solomon at the feast in the month E, 388

ETHBAAL (1)
1Ki 16:31 the daughter of E king of the Zidonians, 856

ETHER (2)
Jos 15:42 Libnah, and E, and Ashan, 6281
19: 7 Ain, Remmon, and E, and Ashan; 6281

ETHIOPIA (20) [ETHIOPIAN, ETHIOPIANS]
Ge 2:13 *is it* that compasseth the whole land of E. 3568
2Ki 19: 9 when he heard say of Tirhakah king of E, 3568
Est 1: 1 from India even unto E, *over* an hundred 3568
8: 9 the provinces which *are* from India unto E, 3568
Job 28:19 The topaz of E shall not equal it, 3568
Ps 68:31 E shall soon stretch out her hands unto 3568
87: 4 behold Philistia, and Tyre, with E; this *man* 3568
Isa 18: 1 which *is* beyond the rivers of E: 3568
20: 3 a sign and wonder upon Egypt and upon E; 3568
20: 5 and ashamed of E their expectation, 3568
37: 9 heard say concerning Tirhakah king of E, 3568
43: 3 Egypt *for* thy ransom, E and Seba for thee. 3568
45:14 merchandise of E and of the Sabeans, 3568
Eze 29:10 tower of Syene even unto the border of E. 3568

Eze 30: 4 great pain shall be in **E**, when the slain 3568
30: 5 **E**, and Libya, and Lydia, and all 3568
38: 5 Persia, **E**, and Libya with them; all of them 3568
Na 3: 9 **E** and Egypt *were* her strength, and *it was* 3568
Zep 3:10 From beyond the rivers of **E** my suppliants, 3568
Ac 8:27 and behold, a man of **E**, an eunuch of great *128*

ETHIOPIAN (8) [ETHIOPIA]
Nu 12: 1 of the **E** woman whom he had married: 3569
12: 1 for he had married an **E** woman. 3569
2Ch 14: 9 there came out against them Zerah the **E** 3569
Jer 13:23 Can the **E** change his skin, or the leopard 3569
38: 7 Now when Ebed-melech the **E**, one of 3569
38:10 the king commanded Ebed-melech the **E**, 3569
38:12 Ebed-melech the **E** said unto Jeremiah, 3569
39:16 Go and speak to Ebed-melech the **E**, 3569

ETHIOPIANS (13) [ETHIOPIA]
2Ch 12: 3 the Lubims, the Sukkiims, and the **E**. 3569
14:12 So the LORD smote the **E** before Asa, and 3569
14:12 and before Judah; and the **E** fled. 3569
14:13 the **E** were overthrown, that they could not 3569
16: 8 Were not the **E** and the Lubims a huge 3569
21:16 and of the Arabians, that *were* near the **E**: 3569
Isa 20: 4 the **E** captives, young and old, naked and 3568
Jer 46: 9 the **E** and the Libyans, that handle 3568
Eze 30: 9 me in ships to make the careless **E** afraid, 3568
Da 11:43 the Libyans and the **E** *shall be* at his steps. 3569
Am 9: 7 *Are* ye not as children of the **E** unto me, 3569
Zep 2:12 Ye **E** also, ye *shall be* slain by my sword. 3569
Ac 8:27 authority under Candace queen of the **E**, *128*

ETHNAN (1)
1Ch 4: 7 of Helah *were*, Zereth, and Jezoar, and **E**. 869

ETHNI (1)
1Ch 6:41 The son of **E**, the son of Zerah, the son of 867

EUBULUS (1)
2Ti 4:21 **E** greeteth thee, and Pudens, and Linus, and *2103*

EUNICE (1)
2Ti 1: 5 in thy grandmother Lois, and thy mother **E**; *2131*

EUNUCH (7) [EUNUCHS]
Isa 56: 3 neither let the **e** say, Behold, I *am* a dry 5631
Jer 52:25 He took also out of the city an **e**, which had 5631
Ac 8:27 an **e** of great authority under Candace *2135*
8:34 And the **e** answered Philip, and said, I pray *2135*
8:36 and the **e** said, See, *here is* water; what doth *2135*
8:38 both into the water, both Philip and the **e**; *2135*
8:39 away Philip, that the **e** saw him no more: *2135*

EUNUCHS (20) [EUNUCH]
2Ki 9:32 And there looked out to him two *or* three **e**. 5631
20:18 they shall be **e** in the palace of the king of 5631
Isa 39: 7 they shall be **e** in the palace of the king of 5631
56: 4 For thus saith the LORD unto the **e** that 5631
Jer 29: 2 the queen, and the **e**, the princes of Judah 5631
34:19 the **e**, and the priests, and all the people of 5631
38: 7 one of the **e** which *was* in the king's house, 5631
41:16 and the women, and the children, and the **e**, 5631
Da 1: 3 spake unto Ashpenaz the master of his **e**, 5631
1: 7 Unto whom the prince of the **e** gave names: 5631
1: 8 he requested of the prince of the **e** that he 5631
1: 9 and tender love with the prince of the **e**. 5631
1:10 the prince of the **e** said unto Daniel, I fear 5631
1:11 whom the prince of the **e** had set over 5631
1:18 the prince of the **e** brought them in before 5631
Mt 19:12 For there are *some* **e**, which were so *2135*
19:12 and there are *some* **e**, which were made *2135*
19:12 *some* eunuchs, which were **made e** of men: *2134*
19:12 and there be **e**, which have made *2135*
19:12 which have **made** themselves **e** for *2134*

EUODIAS (1)
Php 4: 2 I beseech **E**, and beseech Syntyche, *2136*

EUPHRATES (21)
Ge 2:14 east of Assyria. And the fourth river *is* **E**. 6578
15:18 of Egypt unto the great river, the river **E**: 6578
Dt 1: 7 unto the great river, the river **E**. 6578
11:24 and Lebanon, from the river, the river **E**, 6578
Jos 1: 4 the river **E**, all the land of the Hittites, and 6578
2Sa 8: 3 he went to recover his border at the river **E**. 6578
2Ki 23:29 against the king of Assyria to the river **E**: 6578
24: 7 **E** all that pertained to the king of Egypt. 6578
1Ch 5: 9 in of the wilderness from the river **E**: 6578
18: 3 to stablish his dominion by the river **E**. 6578
2Ch 35:20 came up to fight against Carchemish by **E**: 6578
Jer 13: 4 go to **E**, and hide it there in a hole of 6578
13: 5 So I went, and hid it by **E**, as the LORD 6578
13: 6 go to **E**, and take the girdle from thence, 6578
13: 7 I went to **E**, and digged, and took the girdle 6578
46: 2 which was by the river **E** in Carchemish, 6578
46: 6 and fall toward the north by the river **E**. 6578
46:10 sacrifice in the north country by the river **E**. 6578
51:63 a stone to it, and cast it into the midst of **E**: 6578
Rev 9:14 angels which are bound in the great river **E**. *2166*
16:12 poured out his vial upon the great river **E**; *2166*

EUROCLYDON (1)
Ac 27:14 against it a tempestuous wind, called **E**. *2148*

EUTYCHUS (1)
Ac 20: 9 in a window a certain young man named **E**, *2161*

EVANGELIST (2) [EVANGELISTS]
Ac 21: 8 we entered into the house of Philip the **e**, *2099*
2Ti 4: 5 do the work of an **e**, make full proof of thy *2099*

EVANGELISTS (1) [EVANGELIST]
Eph 4:11 and some, **e**; and some, pastors and *2099*

EVE (4)
Ge 3:20 Adam called his wife's name **E**; because 2332
4: 1 Adam knew **E** his wife; and she conceived, 2332
2Co 11: 3 as the serpent beguiled **E** through his *2096*
1Ti 2:13 For Adam was first formed, then **E**. *2096*

EVEN (1395) [EVENING, EVENINGS, EVENINGTIDE, EVENTIDE] See Index

EVENING (60) [EVEN]
Ge 1: 5 the **e** and the morning were the first day. 6153
1: 8 the **e** and the morning were the second day. 6153
1:13 the **e** and the morning were the third day. 6153
1:19 the **e** and the morning were the fourth day. 6153
1:23 the **e** and the morning were the fifth day. 6153
1:31 the **e** and the morning were the sixth day. 6153
8:11 the dove came in to him in the **e**; and lo, 6153
24:11 city by a well of water at the time of the **e**, 6153
29:23 it came to pass in the **e**, that he took Leah 6153
30:16 Jacob came out of the field in the **e**, and 6153
Ex 12: 6 congregation of Israel shall kill it in the **e**. 6153
16: 8 LORD shall give you in the **e** flesh to eat, 6153
18:13 by Moses from the morning unto the **e**. 6153
27:21 his sons shall order it from **e** to morning 6153
Lev 24: 3 shall Aaron order it from the **e** unto 6153
Dt 23:11 it shall be, when **e** cometh on, he shall wash 6153
Jos 10:26 were hanging upon the trees until the **e**. 6153
Jdg 19: 9 Behold now, the day draweth towards **e**, 6150
1Sa 14:24 *be* the man that eateth *any* food until **e**, 6153
17:16 the Philistine drew near morning and **e**, 6150
30:17 the twilight even unto the **e** of the next day: 6153
1Ki 17: 6 the morning, and bread and flesh in the **e**; 6153
18:29 *the time* of the offering of the **e** sacrifice, NIH
18:36 at *the time of* the offering of the **e** sacrifice, NIH
2Ki 16:15 the **e** meat offering, and the king's burnt 6153
1Ch 16:40 burnt offering continually morning and **e**, 6153
2Ch 2: 4 *for* the burnt offerings morning and **e**, 6153
13:11 every morning and **every e** 6153+6153+871.1+871.1+1886.1+1886.1
13:11 to burn **every e**: 6153+6153+871.1+871.1+1886.1+1886.1
31: 3 *wit*, for the morning and **e** burnt offerings, 6153
Ezr 3: 3 *even* burnt offerings morning and **e**. 6153
9: 4 and I sat astonied until the **e** sacrifice. 6153
9: 5 at the **e** sacrifice I arose up from my 6153
Est 2:14 In the **e** she went, and on the morrow she 6153
Job 4:20 They are destroyed from morning to **e**: 6153
Ps 55:17 **E**, and morning, and at noon, will I pray, 6153
59: 6 They return at **e**: they make a noise like a 6153
59:14 at **e** let them return; *and* let them make a 6153
65: 8 outgoings of the morning and **e** to rejoice. 6153
90: 6 in the **e** it is cut down, and withereth. 6153
104:23 unto his work and to his labour until the **e**. 6153
141: 2 the lifting up of my hands *as* the **e** sacrifice. 6153
Pr 7: 9 in the **e**, in the black and dark night: 6153
Ecc 11: 6 and in the **e** withhold not thine hand: 6153

Jer 6: 4 for the shadows of the **e** are stretched out. 6153
Eze 33:22 hand of the LORD was upon me in the **e**, 6153
46: 2 but the gate shall not be shut until the **e**. 6153
Da 8:26 the vision of the **e** and the morning which 6153
9:21 touched me about the time of the **e** 6153
Hab 1: 8 and are more fierce than the **e** wolves: 6153
Zep 2: 7 of Ashkelon shall they lie down in the **e**: 6153
3: 3 *are* roaring lions; her judges *are* **e** wolves; 6153
Zec 14: 7 come to pass, *that* at **e** time it shall be light. 6153
Mt 14:15 And when it was **e**, his disciples came to *3798*
14:23 and when the **e** was come, he was there *3798*
16: 2 and said unto them, When it is **e**, ye say, *3798*
Mk 14:17 And in the **e** he cometh with the twelve. *3798*
Lk 24:29 for it is towards **e**, and the day is far spent. *2073*
Jn 20:19 Then the same day at **e**, being the first *day* *3798*
Ac 28:23 *out of* the prophets, from morning till **e**. *2073*

EVENINGS (1) [EVEN]
Jer 5: 6 *and* a wolf of the **e** shall spoil them, 6160

EVENINGTIDE (2) [EVEN]
2Sa 11: 2 it came to pass in an **e**, that David 6153+6256
Isa 17:14 behold at **e** trouble; *and* before 6153+6256

EVENT (3)
Ecc 2:14 I myself perceived also that one **e** 4745
9: 2 *there is* one **e** to the righteous, and to 4745
9: 3 under the sun, that *there is* one **e** unto all: 4745

EVENTIDE (5) [EVEN]
Ge 24:63 out to meditate in the field at the **e**: 6153+6437
Jos 7: 6 before the ark of the LORD until the **e**, 6153
8:29 he hanged on a tree until **e**: 6153+6256+1886.1
Mk 11:11 and now the **e** was come, *3588+3798+5610*
Ac 4: 3 in hold unto the next day: for it was now **e**. *2073*

EVER (476) [EVERLASTING, EVERMORE, HOWSOEVER, SOEVER, WHATSOEVER, WHENSOEVER, WHEREINSOEVER, WHERESOEVER, WHITHERSOEVER, WHOMSOEVER, WHOSOEVER]
Ge 3:22 of the tree of life, and eat, and live for **e**: 5769
13:15 to thee will I give it, and to thy seed for **e**. 5769
43: 9 let me bear the blame **for e**: 3117+3605+1886.1
44:32 the blame to my father **for e**. 3117+3605+1886.1
Ex 3:15 this *is* my name for **e**, and this *is* my 5769
12:14 shall keep it a feast by an ordinance **for e**. 5769
12:17 in your generations by an ordinance **for e**. 5769
12:24 an ordinance to thee and to thy sons for **e**. 5769
14:13 ye shall see them again no more for **e**. 5769
15:18 The LORD shall reign for **e** and ever. 5769
15:18 The LORD shall reign for ever and **e**. 5703
19: 9 I speak with thee, and believe thee for **e**. 5769
21: 6 with an aul; and he shall serve him for **e**. 5769
27:21 *it shall be* a statute **for e** unto their 5769
28:43 *it shall be* a statute **for e** unto him and his 5769
29:28 his sons' by a statute **for e** from 5769
30:21 it shall be a statute **for e** to them, *even* to 5769
31:17 between me and the children of Israel for **e**: 5769
32:13 your seed, and they shall inherit *it* for **e**. 5769
Lev 6:13 The fire shall **e** be burning upon the altar; 8548
6:18 *It shall be* a statute **for e** in your 5769
6:22 *it is* a statute **for e** unto the LORD; it shall 5769
7:34 unto his sons by a statute **for e** from among 5769
7:36 *by* a statute for **e throughout** their 5769
10: 9 *it shall be* a statute for **e throughout** your 5769
10:15 and thy sons' with thee, by a statute **for e**; 5769
16:29 *this* shall be a statute **for e** unto you: *that* in 5769
16:31 shall afflict your souls, *by* a statute **for e**. 5769
17: 7 This shall be a statute **for e** unto them 5769
23:14 *it shall be* a statute **for e** throughout your 5769
23:21 **for e** in all your dwellings throughout your 5769
23:31 *it shall be* a statute **for e** throughout your 5769
23:41 *It shall be* a statute **for e** in your 5769
24: 3 *it shall be* a statute **for e** in your 5769
25:23 The land shall not be sold for **e**: for the land 6783
25:30 **e** to him that bought it throughout his 6783
25:46 they shall be your bondmen **for e**: 5769
Nu 10: 8 they shall be to you for an ordinance **for e** 5769
15:15 an ordinance **for e** in your generations: 5769
18: 8 and to thy sons, by an ordinance **for e**. 5769
18:11 thy daughters with thee, by a statute **for e**: 5769
18:19 thy daughters with thee, by a statute **for e**: 5769
18:19 it *is* a covenant of salt **for e** before 5769
18:23 *it shall be* a statute **for e** throughout your 5769
19:10 sojourneth among them, for a statute **for e**. 5769
22:30 upon which thou hast ridden **e since** 4480+5750
22:30 was I **e wont** to do so unto thee? 5532+5532
24:20 his latter end *shall be* that he perish **for e**. 5703
24:24 afflict Eber, and he also shall perish **for e**. 5703
Dt 4:33 Did **e** people hear the voice of God NIH
4:40 thy God giveth thee, **for e**. 3117+3605+1886.1
5:29 and with their children **for e**! 5769+3807.1
12:28 and with thy children after thee for **e**, 5769
13:16 it shall be a heap **for e**; it shall not be built 5769
15:17 the door, and he shall be thy servant **for e**. 5769
18: 5 him and his sons **for e**. 3117+3605+1886.1
19: 9 and to walk **e** in his ways; 3117+3605+1886.1
23: 3 into the congregation of the LORD for **e**: 5769
23: 6 peace nor their prosperity all thy days for **e**. 5769
28:46 and for a wonder, and upon thy seed for **e**. 5769
29:29 *belong* unto us and to our children for **e**, 5769
32:40 up my hand to heaven, and say, I live for **e**. 5769
Jos 4: 7 a memorial unto the children of Israel for **e**. 5769
4:24 the LORD your God **for e**. 3117+3605+1886.1
8:28 Joshua burnt Ai, and made it a heap **for e**, 5769
14: 9 thy children's for **e**, because thou hast 5769
Jdg 11:25 did he **e strive** against Israel, or 7378+7378
11:25 or did he **e fight** against them, 3898+3898
1Sa 1:22 before the LORD, and there abide for **e**. 5769
2:30 of thy father, should walk before me for **e**: 5769
2:32 old man in thine house **for e**. 3117+3605+1886.1
2:35 before mine anointed **for e**. 3117+3605+1886.1
3:13 for **e** for the iniquity which he knoweth; 5769
3:14 be purged with sacrifice nor offering for **e**. 5769
13:13 established thy kingdom upon Israel for **e**. 5769
20:15 cut off thy kindness from my house for **e**: 5769
20:23 the LORD *be* between thee and me for **e**. 5769
20:42 and between my seed and thy seed for **e**. 5769
27:12 therefore he shall be my servant **for e**. 5769
28: 2 keeper of mine head **for e**. 3117+3605+1886.1
2Sa 2:26 and said, Shall the sword devour for **e**? 5331
3:28 **e** from the blood of Abner the son of Ner: 5769
7:13 stablish the throne of his kingdom for **e**. 5769
7:16 thy kingdom shall be stablished for **e** before 5769
7:16 thy throne shall be stablished for **e**. 5769
7:24 people Israel to be a people unto thee for **e**; 5769
7:25 establish *it* for **e**, and do as thou hast said. 5769
7:26 let thy name be magnified for **e**, saying, 5769
7:29 that *it* may continue for **e** before thee: 5769
7:29 let the house of thy servant be blessed for **e**. 5769
1Ki 1:31 and said, Let my lord king David live for **e**. 5769
2:33 and upon the head of his seed for **e**: 5769
2:33 shall there be peace for **e** from the LORD. 5769
2:45 be established before the LORD for **e**. 5769
5: 1 was **e** a lover of David. 3117+3605+1886.1
8:13 a settled place for thee to abide in **for e**. 5769
9: 3 thou hast built, to put my name there for **e**; 5769
9: 5 the throne of thy kingdom upon Israel for **e**, 5769
10: 9 because the LORD loved Israel for **e**, 5769
11:39 seed of David, but not **for e**. 3117+3605+1886.1
12: 7 will be thy servants **for e**. 3117+3605+1886.1
2Ki 5:27 cleave unto thee, and unto thy seed for **e**. 5769
21: 7 of Israel, will I put my name **for e**: 5769+3807.1
1Ch 15: 2 ark of God, and to minister unto him for **e**. 5769
16:34 for *he is* good; for his mercy *endureth* for **e**. 5769
16:36 Blessed *be* the LORD God of Israel for **e** 5769
16:36 *be* the LORD God of Israel for ever and **e**. 5769
16:41 because his mercy *endureth* for **e**; 5769
17:12 a house, and I will stablish his throne for **e**. 5769
17:14 in mine house and in my kingdom for **e**: 5769
17:22 didst thou make thine own people for **e**; 5769
17:23 concerning his house be established for **e**, 5769
17:24 that thy name may be magnified for **e**, 5769
17:27 thy servant, that *it* may be before thee for **e**: 5769
17:27 O LORD, and *it shall be* blessed for **e**. 5769
22:10 the throne of his kingdom over Israel for **e**. 5769
23:13 the most holy *things,* he and his sons for **e**, 5769
23:13 unto him, and to bless in his name for **e**. 5769
23:25 they may dwell in Jerusalem for **e**: 5769+3807.1
28: 4 of my father to be king over Israel for **e**: 5769
28: 7 I will establish his kingdom for **e**, 5769
28: 8 for your children after you for **e**. 5769
28: 9 thou forsake him, he will cast thee off for **e**. 5703
29:10 God of Israel our father, for **e** and ever. 5769
29:10 God of Israel our father, for ever and **e**. 5769
29:18 keep this for **e** in the imagination of 5769
2Ch 2: 4 This *is an ordinance* for **e** to Israel. 5769
5:13 *he is* good; for his mercy *endureth* for **e**: 5769

2Ch	6: 2	for thee, and a place for thy dwelling **for e**.	5769
	7: 3	*he is* good; for his mercy *endureth* for **e**.	5769
	7: 6	because his mercy *endureth* for **e**,	5769
	7:16	that my name may be there for **e**:	5769
	9: 8	to establish them for **e**, therefore made he	5769
	10: 7	will be thy servants **for e**.	3117+3605+1886.1
	13: 5	the kingdom over Israel to David for **e**,	5769
	20: 7	it to the seed of Abraham thy friend for **e**?	5769
	20:21	the LORD; for his mercy *endureth* for **e**.	5769
	21: 7	to him and to his sons **for e**.	3117+3605+1886.1
	30: 8	which he hath sanctified for **e**:	5769
	33: 4	In Jerusalem shall my name be for **e**.	5769
	33: 7	tribes of Israel, will I put my name for **e**:	5865
Ezr	3:11	for his mercy *endureth* for **e** towards Israel.	5769
	9:12	nor seek their peace or their wealth for **e**:	5769
	9:12	*it* for an inheritance to your children for **e**.	5769
Ne	2: 3	said unto the king, Let the king live for **e**:	5769
	9: 5	*and* bless the LORD your God for **e** and	5769
	9: 5	bless the LORD your God for ever and **e**:	5769
	13: 1	come into the congregation of God for **e**;	5769
Job	4: 7	Remember, I pray thee, who **e** perished,	NIH
	4:20	they perish for **e** without *any* regarding *it*.	5331
	14:20	Thou prevailest for **e** against him, and	5331
	19:24	with an iron pen and lead in the rock for **e**!	5703
	20: 7	*Yet* he shall perish for **e** like his own dung:	5331
	23: 7	should I be delivered for **e** from my judge.	5331
	36: 7	he doth establish them for **e**, and they are	5331
	41: 4	wilt thou take him for a servant **for e**?	5769
Ps	5:11	let them **e** shout for joy, because	5769+3807.1
	9: 5	thou hast put out their name for **e** and ever.	5769
	9: 5	thou hast put out their name for ever and **e**.	5703
	9: 7	the LORD shall endure for **e**: he hath	5769
	9:18	of the poor shall *not* perish for **e**.	5703
	10:16	The LORD *is* King **for e** and ever:	5769
	10:16	The LORD *is* King for ever and **e**:	5703
	12: 7	preserve them from this generation for **e**.	5769
	13: 1	**for e**? how long wilt thou hide thy face	5331
	19: 9	fear of the LORD *is* clean, enduring for **e**:	5703
	21: 4	*it* him, *even* length of days **for e** and ever.	5769
	21: 4	*it* him, *even* length of days for ever and **e**.	5703
	21: 6	For thou hast made him most blessed for **e**:	5703
	22:26	that seek him: your heart shall live for **e**.	5703
	23: 6	in the house of the LORD for **e**.	753+3117
	25: 6	for they *have been* **e of old**.	4480+5769
	25:15	Mine eyes *are* **e** towards the LORD; for he	8548
	28: 9	feed them also, and lift them up for **e**.	5769
	29:10	yea, the LORD sitteth King for **e**.	5769
	30:12	my God, I will give thanks unto thee for **e**.	5769
	33:11	The counsel of the LORD standeth for **e**,	5769
	37:18	and their inheritance shall be for **e**.	5769
	37:26	*He is* **e** merciful, and	3117+3605+1886.1
	37:28	not his saints; they are preserved for **e**:	5769
	37:29	inherit the land, and dwell therein for **e**.	5703
	41:12	and settest me before thy face for **e**.	5769
	44: 8	all the day long, and praise thy name for **e**.	5769
	44:23	O Lord? arise, cast *us* not off for **e**.	5331
	45: 2	therefore God hath blessed thee for **e**.	5769
	45: 6	Thy throne, O God, *is* **for e** and ever:	5769
	45: 6	Thy throne, O God, *is* for ever and **e**:	5703
	45:17	shall the people praise thee for **e** and ever.	5769
	45:17	shall the people praise thee for ever and **e**.	5703
	48: 8	our God: God will establish it for **e**. Selah.	5769
	48:14	For this God *is* our God **for e** and ever:	5769
	48:14	For this God *is* our God for ever and **e**:	5703
	49: 8	their soul is precious, and it ceaseth for **e**:)	5769
	49: 9	That he should still live for **e**, *and* not see	5331
	49:11	*is, that* their houses *shall continue* for **e**,	5769
	51: 3	and my sin *is* **e** before me.	8548
	52: 5	God shall likewise destroy thee for **e**,	5331
	52: 8	I trust in the mercy of God **for e** and ever.	5769
	52: 8	I trust in the mercy of God for ever and **e**.	5703
	52: 9	I will praise thee for **e**, because thou hast	5769
	61: 4	I will abide in thy tabernacle **for e**: I will	5769
	61: 7	He shall abide before God **for e**: O prepare	5769
	61: 8	So will I sing *praise* unto thy name for **e**,	5703
	66: 7	He ruleth by his power **for e**; his eyes	5769
	68:16	yea, the LORD will dwell *in it* for **e**.	5331
	72:17	His name shall endure for **e**: his name shall	5769
	72:19	And blessed *be* his glorious name for **e**: and	5769
	73:26	strength of my heart, and my portion for **e**.	5769
	74: 1	O God, why hast thou cast *us* off for **e**?	5331
	74:10	shall the enemy blaspheme thy name for **e**?	5331
	74:19	not the congregation of thy poor for **e**.	5331
	75: 9	I will declare for **e**; I will sing *praises* to	5769
	77: 7	Will the Lord cast off for **e**? and will he be	5769
	77: 8	Is his mercy clean gone for **e**? doth *his*	5331
	78:69	the earth which he hath established for **e**.	5769
	79: 5	wilt thou be angry, for **e**? shall thy jealousy	5331
	79:13	of thy pasture will give thee thanks for **e**:	5769
	81:15	but their time should have endured for **e**.	5769
	83:17	Let them be confounded and troubled for **e**;	5703
	85: 5	Wilt thou be angry with us for **e**? wilt thou	5769
	89: 1	sing of the mercies of the LORD **for e**:	5769
	89: 2	I have said, Mercy shall be built up **for e**:	5769
	89: 4	Thy seed will I stablish for **e**, and build up	5769
	89:29	His seed also will I make *to endure* for **e**,	5703
	89:36	His seed shall endure for **e**, and his throne	5769
	89:37	It shall be established **for e** as the moon,	5769
	89:46	wilt thou hide thyself, for **e**? shall thy wrath	5331
	90: 2	or **e** thou hadst formed the earth and	NIH
	92: 7	*it is* that they shall be destroyed for **e**:	5703
	93: 5	thine house, O LORD, for **e**.	753+3117
	102:12	thou, O LORD, shalt endure for **e**; and	5769
	103: 9	neither will he keep *his anger* for **e**.	5769
	104: 5	should not be removed **for e**.	5703+5769+2050.1
	104:31	The glory of the LORD shall endure for **e**:	5769
	105: 8	He hath remembered his covenant for **e**,	5769
	106: 1	for *he is* good: for his mercy *endureth* for **e**.	5769
	107: 1	for *he is* good: for his mercy *endureth* for **e**.	5769
	110: 4	Thou *art* a priest for **e** after the order of	5769
	111: 3	and his righteousness endureth for **e**.	5703
	111: 5	will **e** be mindful of his covenant.	5769+3807.1
	111: 8	They stand fast for **e** and ever, *and are* done	5703
	111: 8	They stand fast for ever and **e**, *and*	5769+3807.1
	111: 9	he hath commanded his covenant for **e**:	5769
	111:10	*commandments:* his praise endureth for **e**.	5703
	112: 3	and his righteousness endureth for **e**.	5703
	112: 6	Surely he shall not be moved for **e**:	5769
	112: 9	the poor; his righteousness endureth for **e**;	5703
	117: 2	the truth of the LORD *endureth* for **e**.	5769
	118: 1	*is* good: because his mercy *endureth* for **e**.	5769
	118: 2	now say, that his mercy *endureth* for **e**.	5769
	118: 3	now say, that his mercy *endureth* for **e**.	5769
	118: 4	LORD say, that his mercy *endureth* for **e**.	5769
	118:29	for *he is* good: for his mercy *endureth* for **e**.	5769
	119:44	So shall I keep thy law continually for **e**	5769
	119:44	I keep thy law continually for ever and **e**.	5703
	119:89	For **e**, O LORD, thy word *is* settled in	5769
	119:98	for they *are* **e** with me.	5769+3807.1
	119:111	have I taken as an heritage for **e**:	5769
	119:152	of old that thou hast founded them for **e**.	5769
	119:160	of thy righteous judgments *endureth* for **e**.	5769
	125: 1	cannot be removed, *but* abideth for **e**.	5769
	125: 2	his people from henceforth even for **e**.	5769
	131: 3	in the LORD from henceforth and for **e**.	5769
	132:14	This *is* my rest for **e**: here will I dwell; for I	5703
	135:13	Thy name, O LORD, *endureth* for **e**; *and*	5769
	136: 1	for *he is* good: for his mercy *endureth* for **e**.	5769
	136: 2	God of gods: for his mercy *endureth* for **e**.	5769
	136: 3	Lord of lords: for his mercy *endureth* for **e**.	5769
	136: 4	for his mercy *endureth* for **e**.	5769
	136: 5	the heavens: for his mercy *endureth* for **e**:	5769
	136: 6	the waters: for his mercy *endureth* for **e**.	5769
	136: 7	great lights: for his mercy *endureth* for **e**:	5769
	136: 8	to rule by day: for his mercy *endureth* for **e**:	5769
	136: 9	rule by night: for his mercy *endureth* for **e**:	5769
	136:10	their firstborn: for his mercy *endureth* for **e**:	5769
	136:11	among them: for his mercy *endureth* for **e**:	5769
	136:12	out arm: for his mercy *endureth* for **e**.	5769
	136:13	sea into parts: for his mercy *endureth* for **e**:	5769
	136:14	the midst of it: for his mercy *endureth* for **e**:	5769
	136:15	the Red sea: for his mercy *endureth* for **e**.	5769
	136:16	for his mercy *endureth* for **e**.	5769
	136:17	great kings: for his mercy *endureth* for **e**:	5769
	136:18	famous kings: for his mercy *endureth* for **e**:	5769
	136:19	the Amorites: for his mercy *endureth* for **e**:	5769
	136:20	of Bashan: for his mercy *endureth* for **e**:	5769
	136:21	an heritage: for his mercy *endureth* for **e**:	5769
	136:22	his servant: for his mercy *endureth* for **e**.	5769
	136:23	low estate: for his mercy *endureth* for **e**:	5769
	136:24	our enemies: for his mercy *endureth* for **e**.	5769
	136:25	to all flesh: for his mercy *endureth* for **e**.	5769
	136:26	of heaven: for his mercy *endureth* for **e**.	5769
	138: 8	thy mercy, O LORD, *endureth* for **e**:	5769
	145: 1	and I will bless thy name for **e** and ever.	5769
	145: 1	and I will bless thy name for ever and **e**.	5703
	145: 2	and I will praise thy name for **e** and ever.	5769
	145: 2	and I will praise thy name for ever and **e**.	5703

Ps 145:21 let all flesh bless his holy name for **e** and 5769
145:21 all flesh bless his holy name for ever and **e**. 5703
146: 6 all that therein is: which keepeth truth for **e**: 5769
146:10 The LORD shall reign for **e**, *even* thy 5769
148: 6 He hath also stablished them for **e** and ever: 5703
148: 6 He hath also stablished them for ever and **e**: 5769
Pr 8:23 the beginning, **or e** the earth **was**. 4480+6924
12:19 The lip of truth shall be established for **e**: 5703
27:24 For riches *are* not for **e**: and doth the crown 5769
29:14 his throne shall be established for **e**. 5703
Ecc 1: 4 but the earth abideth for **e**. 5769
2:16 of the wise more than of the fool for **e**; 5769
3:14 whatsoever God doeth, it shall be for **e**: 5769
9: 6 neither have they any more a portion for **e** 5769
12: 6 **Or e** the silver cord be loosed, 834+3808+5704
SS 6:12 **Or e** I was aware, my soul made me *like* 3808
Isa 9: 7 and with justice from henceforth even for **e**. 5769
26: 4 Trust ye in the LORD for **e**: for in 5703
28:28 because he will not **e** be threshing 5331+3807.1
30: 8 that it may be for the time to come for **e** 5703
30: 8 may be for the time to come for ever and **e**: 5769
32:14 the forts and towers shall be for dens for **e**, 5769
32:17 and assurance for **e**. 5769
33:20 not one of the stakes thereof shall **e** 5331+3807.1
34:10 the smoke thereof shall go up for **e**: 5769
34:10 none shall pass through it for **e** and ever. 5331
34:10 none shall pass through it for ever and **e**. 5331
34:17 they shall possess it for **e**, from generation 5769
40: 8 but the word of our God shall stand for **e**. 5769
47: 7 thou saidst, I shall be a lady for **e**: *so* 5703+5769
51: 6 my salvation shall be for **e**, and 5769
51: 8 my righteousness shall be for **e**, and 5769
57:16 For I will not contend for **e**, neither will I 5769
59:21 the LORD, from henceforth and for **e**. 5769
60:21 they shall inherit the land for **e**, the branch 5769
64: 9 O LORD, neither remember iniquity for **e**: 5703
65:18 and rejoice for **e** *in that* which I create: 5703
Jer 3: 5 Will he reserve *his anger* for **e**? will he 5769
3:12 the LORD, *and* I will not keep *anger* for **e**. 5769
7: 7 I gave to your fathers, for **e** and ever. 4480+5769
7: 7 I gave to your fathers, for ever and **e**. 5704+5769
17: 4 a fire in mine anger, *which* shall burn for **e**. 5769
17:25 and this city shall remain for **e**. 5769
25: 5 unto you and to your fathers for **e** and ever: 5769
25: 5 and to your fathers for ever and **e**: 5704+5769
31:36 a nation before me **for e**. 3117+3605+1886.1
31:40 nor thrown down any more for **e**. 5769
32:39 that *they* may fear me **for e**, 3117+3605+1886.1
33:11 *is* good; for his mercy *endureth* for **e**: 5769
35: 6 no wine, *neither* ye, nor your sons for **e**: 5769
35:19 to stand before me **for e**. 3117+3605+1886.1
49:33 for dragons, *and* a desolation for **e**: 5769
50:39 it shall be no more inhabited for **e**; 5331
51:26 thou shalt be desolate **for e**, saith 5769
51:62 nor beast, but that it shall be desolate **for e**. 5769
La 3:31 For the Lord will not cast off for **e**: 5769
5:19 Thou, O LORD, remainest for **e**; 5769
5:20 Wherefore dost thou forget us for **e**, *and* 5331
Eze 37:25 and their children's children for **e**: 5769
37:25 servant David *shall be* their prince for **e**. 5769
43: 7 in the midst of the children of Israel for **e**, 5769
43: 9 and I will dwell in the midst of them for **e**. 5769
Da 2: 4 to the king in Syriack, O king, live for **e**: 5957
2:20 be the name of God for **e** and ever: 0.2+5957
2:20 the name of God for ever and **e**: 0.2+5705+5957
2:44 all these kingdoms, and it shall stand for **e**. 5957
3: 9 king Nebuchadnezzar, O king, live for **e**. 5957
4:34 and honoured him that liveth **for e**, 0.2+5957
5:10 the queen spake and said, O king, live for **e**: 5957
6: 6 said thus unto him, King Darius, live for **e**. 5957
6:21 Daniel unto the king, O king, live for **e**. 5957
6:24 or **e** they came at the bottom of the den. 3809
6:26 stedfast for **e**, and his kingdom *that* which 5957
7:18 possess the kingdom for **e**, even for ever 5957
7:18 the kingdom for ever, even for **e** and ever. 5957
7:18 the kingdom for ever, even for ever and **e**. 5957
12: 3 turn many to righteousness as the stars for **e** 5769
12: 3 to righteousness as the stars for ever and **e**. 5703
12: 7 sware by him that liveth **for e** that *it shall* 5769
Hos 2:19 I will betroth thee unto me for **e**; yea, I will 5769
Joel 2: 2 there hath not been **e** 4480+5769+1886.1
3:20 Judah shall dwell for **e**, and Jerusalem from 5769
Am 1:11 and he kept his wrath **for e**: 5331
Ob 1:10 cover thee, and thou shalt be cut off for **e**. 5769
Jnh 2: 6 the earth *with* her bars *was* about me for **e**: 5769
Mic 2: 9 have ye taken *away* my glory for **e**. 5769
4: 5 in the name of the LORD our God for **e** 5769
4: 5 of the LORD our God for ever and **e**. 5703
4: 7 in mount Zion from henceforth, even for **e**. 5769
7:18 he retaineth not his anger for **e**, because 5703
Zec 1: 5 and the prophets, do they live for **e**? 5769
Mal 1: 4 whom the LORD hath indignation for **e**. 5769
Mt 6:13 and the power, and the glory, for **e**. *165*
21:19 no fruit grow on thee henceforward for **e**. *165*
24:21 of the world to this time, no, **nor e** shall be. *3364*
Mk 11:14 No *man* eat fruit of thee hereafter for **e**. *165*
15: 8 desire *him to do* as he had **e** done unto them. *104*
Lk 1:33 he shall reign over the house of Jacob for **e**; *165*
1:55 to Abraham, and to his seed for **e**. *165*
15:31 thou art **e** with me, and all that I have is *3842*
Jn 4:29 which told me all *things* **that e** I did: *3745*
4:39 which testified, He told me all that **e** I did. *3745*
6:51 any *man* eat of this bread, he shall live for **e**: *165*
6:58 he that eateth *of* this bread shall live for **e**. *165*
8:35 the servant abideth not in the house for **e**: *165*
8:35 for ever: *but* the son abideth **e**. *165+1519+3588*
10: 8 All **that e** came before me are thieves and *3745*
12:34 heard out of the law that Christ abideth for **e**: *165*
14:16 that he may abide with you for **e**; *165*
18:20 I **e** taught in the synagogue, and in *3842*
Ac 23:15 and we, or **e** he come near, are ready *3588+4253*
Ro 1:25 more than the Creator, who is blessed for **e**. *165*
9: 5 *came,* who is over all, God blessed for **e**. *165*
11:36 *are* all *things:* to whom *be* glory for **e**. *165*
16:27 *be* glory through Jesus Christ for **e**. *165*
2Co 9: 9 the poor: his righteousness remaineth for **e**. *165*
Gal 1: 5 To whom *be* glory for **e** and ever. Amen. *165*
1: 5 To whom *be* glory for ever and **e**. Amen. *165*
Eph 5:29 For no *man* **e yet** hated his own flesh; but *4218*
Php 4:20 and our Father *be* glory for **e** and ever. *165*
4:20 and our Father *be* glory for ever and **e**. *165*
1Th 4:17 the air: and so shall we **e** be with the Lord. *3842*
5:15 any *man;* but **e** follow *that which is* good, *3842*
1Ti 1:17 *be* honour and glory for **e** and ever. *165*
1:17 *be* honour and glory for ever and **e**. *165*
2Ti 3: 7 **E** learning, and never able to come to *3842*
4:18 to whom *be* glory for **e** and ever. Amen. *165*
4:18 to whom *be* glory for ever and **e**. Amen. *165*
Phm 1:15 that thou shouldest receive him **for e**; *166*
Heb 1: 8 *saith,* Thy throne, O God, *is* for **e** and ever: *165*
1: 8 *saith,* Thy throne, O God, *is* for ever and **e**: *165*
5: 6 a priest for **e** after the order of Melchisedec. *165*
6:20 made a high priest for **e** after the order of *165*
7:17 Thou *art* a priest for **e** after the order of *165*
7:21 Thou *art* a priest for **e** after the order of *165*
7:24 because he continueth **e**, *165+1519+3588*
7:25 seeing he **e** liveth to make intercession for *3842*
10:12 one sacrifice for sins **for e**, *1336+1519+3588*
10:14 **for e** them that are sanctified. *1336+1519+3588*
13: 8 the same yesterday, and to day, and for **e**. *165*
13:21 to whom *be* glory for **e** and ever. *165*
13:21 to whom *be* glory for ever and **e**. *165*
1Pe 1:23 word of God, which liveth and abideth for **e**. *165*
1:25 But the word of the Lord endureth for **e**. And *165*
4:11 be praise and dominion for **e** and ever. *165*
4:11 be praise and dominion for ever and **e**. *165*
5:11 him *be* glory and dominion for **e** and ever. *165*
5:11 him *be* glory and dominion for ever and **e**. *165*
2Pe 2:17 whom the mist of darkness is reserved for **e**. *165*
3:18 *be* glory both now and for **e**. Amen. *165+2250*
1Jn 2:17 he that doeth the will of God abideth for **e**. *165*
2Jn 1: 2 dwelleth in us, and shall be with us for **e**. *165*
Jude 1:13 is reserved the blackness of darkness for **e**. *165*
1:25 power, both now and **e**. *165+1519+3588+3956*
Rev 1: 6 to him *be* glory and dominion for **e** and ever. *165*
1: 6 to him *be* glory and dominion for ever and **e**. *165*
4: 9 sat on the throne, who liveth for **e** and ever, *165*
4: 9 sat on the throne, who liveth for ever and **e**, *165*
4:10 and worship him that liveth for **e** and ever, *165*
4:10 and worship him that liveth for ever and **e**, *165*
5:13 the throne, and unto the Lamb for **e** and ever. *165*
5:13 the throne, and unto the Lamb for ever and **e**. *165*
5:14 and worshipped him that liveth for **e** and *165*
5:14 worshipped him that liveth for ever and **e**. *165*
7:12 and might, *be* unto our God for **e** and ever. *165*
7:12 and might, *be* unto our God for ever and **e**. *165*
10: 6 And sware by him that liveth for **e** and ever, *165*
10: 6 And sware by him that liveth for ever and **e**, *165*

Rev 11:15 his Christ; and he shall reign for **e** and ever. *165*
11:15 his Christ; and he shall reign for ever and **e**. *165*
14:11 smoke of their torment ascendeth up for **e** *165*
14:11 of their torment ascendeth up for ever and **e**: *165*
15: 7 the wrath of God, who liveth for **e** and ever. *165*
15: 7 the wrath of God, who liveth for ever and **e**. *165*
19: 3 And her smoke rose up for **e** and ever. *165*
19: 3 And her smoke rose up for ever and **e**. *165*
20:10 be tormented day and night for **e** and ever. *165*
20:10 be tormented day and night for ever and **e**. *165*
22: 5 and they shall reign for **e** and ever. *165*
22: 5 and they shall reign for ever and **e**. *165*

EVERLASTING (97) [EVER]

E

Ge 9:16 that I may remember the **e** covenant 5769
17: 7 thee in their generations for an **e** covenant, 5769
17: 8 all the land of Canaan, for an **e** possession; 5769
17:13 my covenant shall be in your flesh for an **e** 5769
17:19 my covenant with him for an **e** covenant, 5769
21:33 on the name of the LORD, the **e** God. 5769
48: 4 to thy seed after thee *for* an **e** possession. 5769
49:26 unto the utmost bound of the **e** hills: 5769
Ex 40:15 for their anointing shall surely be an **e** 5769
Lev 16:34 this shall be an **e** statute unto you, to make 5769
24: 8 the children of Israel *by* an **e** covenant. 5769
Nu 25:13 *even* the covenant of an **e** priesthood; 5769
Dt 33:27 *thy* refuge, and underneath *are* the **e** arms: 5769
2Sa 23: 5 yet he hath made with me an **e** covenant, 5769
1Ch 16:17 for a law, *and* to Israel *for* an **e** covenant, 5769
Ps 24: 7 be ye lift up, ye **e** doors; and the King of 5769
24: 9 even lift *them* up, ye **e** doors; and the King 5769
41:13 *be* the LORD God of Israel from **e**, 5769
41:13 God of Israel from everlasting, and to **e**. 5769
90: 2 and the world, even from **e** to everlasting, 5769
90: 2 and the world, even from everlasting to **e**, 5769
93: 2 throne is established of old: thou *art* from **e**. 5769
100: 5 his mercy *is* **e**; and his truth 5769+3807.1
103:17 the mercy of the LORD *is* from **e** to 5769
103:17 everlasting to **e** upon them that fear him, 5769
105:10 for a law, *and* to Israel *for* an **e** covenant: 5769
106:48 *be* the LORD God of Israel from **e** 5769
106:48 LORD God of Israel from everlasting to **e**: 5769
112: 6 the righteous shall be in **e** remembrance. 5769
119:142 Thy righteousness *is* an **e** 5769+3807.1
119:144 of thy testimonies *is* **e**: 5769+3807.1
139:24 way in me, and lead me in the way **e**. 5769
145:13 Thy kingdom *is* an **e** kingdom, and 3605+5769
Pr 8:23 I was set up from **e**, from the beginning, or 5769
10:25 but the righteous *is* an **e** foundation. 5769
Isa 9: 6 Counseller, The mighty God, The **e** Father, 5703
24: 5 the ordinance, broken the **e** covenant. 5769
26: 4 for in the LORD JEHOVAH *is* **e** strength: 5769
33:14 who amongst us shall dwell *with* **e** 5769
35:10 Zion with songs and **e** joy upon their heads: 5769
40:28 thou not heard, *that* the **e** God, the LORD, 5769
45:17 be saved in the LORD *with* an **e** salvation: 5769
51:11 and **e** joy *shall be* upon their head: 5769
54: 8 with **e** kindness will I have mercy on thee, 5769
55: 3 I will make an **e** covenant with you, 5769
55:13 for an **e** sign *that* shall not be cut off. 5769
56: 5 I will give them an **e** name, that shall not be 5769
60:19 the LORD shall be unto thee an **e** light, 5769
60:20 for the LORD shall be thine **e** light, and 5769
61: 7 the double: **e** joy shall be unto them. 5769
61: 8 and I will make an **e** covenant with them. 5769
63:12 before them, to make himself an **e** name? 5769
63:16 our redeemer; thy name *is* from **e**. 5769
Jer 10:10 he *is* the living God, and an **e** king: 5769
20:11 *their* **e** confusion shall never be forgotten. 5769
23:40 I will bring an **e** reproach upon you, and 5769
31: 3 I have loved thee *with* an **e** love; 5769
32:40 I will make an **e** covenant with them, that I 5769
Eze 16:60 and I will establish unto thee an **e** covenant. 5769
37:26 it shall be an **e** covenant with them: 5769
Da 4: 3 his kingdom *is* an **e** kingdom, and 5957
4:34 whose dominion *is* an **e** dominion, and 5957
7:14 his dominion *is* an **e** dominion, which shall 5957
7:27 whose kingdom *is* an **e** kingdom, and 5957
9:24 to bring in **e** righteousness, and to seal up 5769
12: 2 some to **e** life, and some to shame *and* 5769
12: 2 and some to shame *and* **e** contempt. 5769
Mic 5: 2 forth *have been* from of old, from **e**. 3117+5769
Hab 1:12 *Art* thou not from **e**, O LORD my God, 6924
3: 6 the **e** mountains were scattered, 5703
3: 6 the perpetual hills did bow: his ways *are* **e**. 5769
Mt 18: 8 two hands or two feet to be cast into **e** fire. *166*
19:29 an hundredfold, and shall inherit **e** life. *166*
25:41 Depart from me, ye cursed, into **e** fire, *166*
25:46 And these shall go away into **e** punishment: *166*
Lk 16: 9 they may receive you into **e** habitations. *166*
18:30 *present* time, and in the world to come life **e**. *166*
Jn 3:16 in him should not perish, but have **e** life. *166*
3:36 He that believeth on the Son hath **e** life: and *166*
4:14 him a well of water springing up into **e** life. *166*
5:24 hath **e** life, and shall not come into *166*
6:27 but for *that* meat which endureth unto **e** life, *166*
6:40 and believeth on him, may have **e** life: *166*
6:47 unto you, He that believeth on me hath **e** life. *166*
12:50 And I know that his commandment is life **e**: *166*
Ac 13:46 and judge yourselves unworthy of **e** life, *166*
Ro 6:22 your fruit unto holiness, and the end **e** life. *166*
16:26 according to the commandment of the **e** *166*
Gal 6: 8 to the Spirit shall of the Spirit reap life **e**. *166*
2Th 1: 9 Who shall be punished *with* **e** destruction *166*
2:16 and hath given *us* **e** consolation and *166*
1Ti 1:16 should hereafter believe on him to life **e**. *166*
6:16 to whom *be* honour and power **e**. Amen. *166*
Heb 13:20 through the blood of the **e** covenant, *166*
2Pe 1:11 abundantly into the **e** kingdom of our Lord *166*
Jude 1: 6 he hath reserved in **e** chains under darkness *126*
Rev 14: 6 having the **e** gospel to preach unto them that *166*

EVERMORE (26) [EVER]
Dt 28:29 and spoiled **e**, 3117+3605+1886.1
2Sa 22:51 unto David, and to his seed for **e**. 5769
2Ki 17:37 ye shall observe to do **for e**; 3117+3605+1886.1
1Ch 17:14 and his throne shall be established for **e**. 5769
Ps 16:11 at thy right hand *there are* pleasures **for e**. 5331
18:50 to David, and to his seed for **e**. 5769
37:27 from evil, and do good; and dwell for **e**. 5769
77: 8 doth *his* promise fail for **e**? 1755+1755+2050.1
86:12 my heart: and I will glorify thy name for **e**. 5769
89:28 My mercy will I keep for him for **e**, and 5769
89:52 Blessed *be* the LORD for **e**. Amen, and 5769
92: 8 But thou, LORD, *art most* high for **e**. 5769
105: 4 and his strength: seek his face **e**. 8548
106:31 for righteousness unto all generations for **e**. 5769
113: 2 the LORD from this time forth and for **e**. 5769
115:18 the LORD from this time forth and for **e**. 5769
121: 8 in from this time forth, and *even* for **e**. 5769
132:12 children also shall sit upon thy throne for **e**. 5703
133: 3 commanded the blessing, *even* life for **e**. 5769
Eze 37:26 set my sanctuary in the midst of them for **e**. 5769
37:28 shall be in the midst of them for **e**. 5769
Jn 6:34 they unto him, Lord, **e** give us this bread. *3842*
2Co 11:31 which is blessed for **e**, knoweth that I lie not. *165*
1Th 5:16 Rejoice **e**. *3842*
Heb 7:28 *maketh* the Son, who is consecrated for **e**. *165*
Rev 1:18 and behold, I am alive for **e**, Amen; *165+165*

EVERY (1238) See Index

EVI (2)
Nu 31: 8 *namely*, **E**, and Rekem, and Zur, and Hur, 189
Jos 13:21 **E**, and Rekem, and Zur, and Hur, and Reba, 189

EVIDENCE (7) [EVIDENCES]
Jer 32:10 I subscribed the **e**, and sealed *it*, and 5612
32:11 So I took the **e** of the purchase, *both* that 5612
32:12 I gave the **e** of the purchase unto Baruch 5612
32:14 this **e** of the purchase, both which is sealed, 5612
32:14 which is sealed, and this **e** which is open; 5612
32:16 Now when I had delivered the **e** of 5612
Heb 11: 1 *things* hoped for, the **e** of things not seen. *1650*

EVIDENCES (2) [EVIDENCE]
Jer 32:14 Take these **e**, this evidence of the purchase, 5612
32:44 subscribe **e**, and seal *them*, and 5612

EVIDENT (5) [EVIDENTLY]
Job 6:28 look upon me; for *it is* **e** unto you if I lie. 6440
Gal 3:11 by the law in the sight of God, *it is* **e**: *1212*
Php 1:28 which is to them an **e token** of perdition, *1732*
Heb 7:14 For *it is* **e** that our Lord sprang out of Juda; *4271*
7:15 And it is yet far more **e**: for that after *2612*

EVIDENTLY (2) [EVIDENT]
Ac 10: 3 He saw in a vision **e**, about the ninth hour *5320*
Gal 3: 1 eyes Jesus Christ hath been **e set forth**, *4270*

EVIL (613) [EVILDOER, EVILDOERS, EVILS]

Ge	2: 9	and the tree of knowledge of good and **e**.	7451
	2:17	of the tree of the knowledge of good and **e**,	7451
	3: 5	ye shall be as gods, knowing good and **e**.	7451
	3:22	become as one of us, to know good and **e**:	7451
	6: 5	of his heart *was* only **e** continually.	7451
	8:21	for the imagination of man's heart *is* **e** from	7451
	19:19	lest *some* **e** take me, and I die:	7451
	37: 2	Joseph brought unto his father their **e**	7451
	37:20	will say, *Some* **e** beast hath devoured him:	7451
	37:33	son's coat; an **e** beast hath devoured him;	7451
	44: 4	Wherefore have ye rewarded **e** for good?	7451
	44: 5	he divineth? ye have **done e** in *so* doing.	7489
	44:34	lest peradventure I see the **e** that shall come	7451
	47: 9	**e** have the days of the years of my life	7451
	48:16	The Angel which redeemed me from all **e**,	7451
	50:15	will certainly requite us all the **e** which we	7451
	50:17	and their sin; for they did unto thee **e**:	7451
	50:20	But as for you, ye thought **e** against me; *but*	7451
Ex	5:19	*that* they *were* in **e** *case,* after it was said,	7451
	5:22	hast thou *so* **e entreated** this people?	7489
	5:23	in thy name, he hath **done e** to this people;	7489
	10:10	little ones: look *to it;* for **e** *is* before you.	7451
	23: 2	Thou shalt not follow a multitude to *do* **e**;	7451
	32:12	and repent of *this* **e** against thy people.	7451
	32:14	the LORD repented of the **e** which he	7451
	33: 4	when the people heard these **e** tidings, they	7451
Lev	5: 4	pronouncing with *his* lips to **do e**, or to do	7489
	26: 6	I will rid **e** beasts out of the land,	7451
Nu	13:32	they brought up an **e report** of the land	1681
	14:27	How long *shall I bear* with this **e**	7451
	14:35	I will surely do it unto all this **e**	7451
	14:37	Even *those* men that did bring up the **e**	7451
	20: 5	of Egypt, to bring us in unto this **e** place?	7451
	32:13	that had done **e** in the sight of the LORD,	7451
Dt	1:35	men of this **e** generation see that good land,	7451
	1:39	day had no knowledge between good and **e**,	7451
	4:25	shall do **e** in the sight of the LORD thy	7451
	7:15	will put none of the **e** diseases of Egypt,	7451
	13: 5	So shalt thou put the **e** away from the midst	7451
	15: 9	thine eye be **e** against thy poor brother, and	7489
	17: 1	is blemish, *or* any **e favouredness**:	1697+7451
	17: 7	So thou shalt put the **e** away from among	7451
	17:12	and thou shalt put away the **e** from Israel.	7451
	19:19	shalt thou put the **e** away from among you.	7451
	19:20	henceforth commit no more any such **e**	7451
	21:21	so shalt thou put **e** away from among you;	7451
	22:14	bring up an **e** name upon her, and say, I	7451
	22:19	he hath brought up an **e** name upon a virgin	7451
	22:21	so shalt thou put **e** away from among you.	7451
	22:22	so shalt thou put away **e** from Israel.	7451
	22:24	so thou shalt put away **e** from among you.	7451
	24: 7	and thou shalt put **e** away from among you.	7451
	26: 6	the Egyptians **e entreated** us, and	7489
	28:54	his eye shall be **e** toward his brother, and	3415
	28:56	her eye shall be **e** towards the husband of	3415
	29:21	the LORD shall separate him unto **e** out of	7451
	30:15	*this* day life and good, and death and **e**;	7451
	31:29	**e** will befall you in the latter days; because	7451
	31:29	ye will do **e** in the sight of the LORD,	7451
Jos	23:15	shall the LORD bring upon you all **e**	7451
	24:15	if it seem **e** unto you to serve the LORD,	7489
Jdg	2:11	the children of Israel did **e** in the sight of	7451
	2:15	hand of the LORD was against them for **e**,	7451
	3: 7	the children of Israel did **e** in the sight of	7451
	3:12	the children of Israel did **e** again in	7451
	3:12	they had done **e** in the sight of the LORD.	7451
	4: 1	the children of Israel again did **e** in	7451
	6: 1	the children of Israel did **e** in the sight of	7451
	9:23	God sent an **e** spirit between Abimelech	7451
	9:57	all the **e** of the men of Shechem did God	7451
	10: 6	the children of Israel did **e** again in	7451
	13: 1	the children of Israel did **e** again in	7451
	20:13	them to death, and put away **e** from Israel.	7451
	20:34	but they knew not that **e** *was* near them.	7451
	20:41	for they saw that **e** was come upon them.	7451
1Sa	2:23	for I hear of your **e** dealings by all this	7451
	6: 9	*then* he hath done us this great **e**:	7451
	12:19	for we have added unto all our sins *this* **e**,	7451
	15:19	and didst **e** in the sight of the LORD?	7451
	16:14	an **e** spirit from the LORD troubled him.	7451
	16:15	an **e** spirit from God troubleth thee.	7451
	16:16	when the **e** spirit from God is upon thee,	7451
	16:23	when the **e** spirit from God was upon Saul,	NIH
	16:23	and the **e** spirit departed from him.	7451
	18:10	that the **e** spirit from God came upon Saul,	7451
	19: 9	the **e** spirit from the LORD was upon	7451
	20: 7	be sure that **e** is determined by him.	7451
	20: 9	for if I knew certainly that **e** were	7451
	20:13	*but* if it please my father *to do* thee **e**, then	7451
	24:11	see that *there is* neither **e** nor transgression	7451
	24:17	me good, whereas I have rewarded thee **e**.	7451
	25: 3	the man *was* churlish and **e** *in* his doings;	7451
	25:17	for **e** is determined against our master, and	7451
	25:21	and he hath requited me **e** for good.	7451
	25:26	they that seek **e** to my lord, be as Nabal.	7451
	25:28	**e** hath not been found in thee *all* thy days.	7451
	25:39	of Nabal, and hath kept his servant from **e**:	7451
	26:18	have I done? or what **e** *is* in mine hand?	7451
	29: 6	for I have not found **e** in thee since the day	7451
2Sa	3:39	the LORD shall reward the doer of **e**	7451
	12: 9	of the LORD, to do **e** in his sight?	7451
	12:11	I will raise up **e** against thee out of thine	7451
	13:16	this **e** in sending me away *is* greater than	7451
	15:14	bring **e** upon us, and smite the city with	7451
	17:14	to the intent that the LORD might bring **e**	7451
	19: 7	that *will be* worse unto thee than all the **e**	7451
	19:35	*and* can I discern between good and **e**? can	7451
	24:16	the LORD repented him of the **e**, and	7451
1Ki	5: 4	*that there is* neither adversary nor **e**	7451
	9: 9	the LORD brought upon them all this **e**.	7451
	11: 6	Solomon did **e** in the sight of the LORD,	7451
	13:33	Jeroboam returned not from his **e** way,	7451
	14: 9	hast done **e** above all that were before thee:	7489
	14:10	I will bring **e** upon the house of Jeroboam,	7451
	14:22	And Judah did **e** in the sight of the LORD,	7451
	15:26	he did **e** in the sight of the LORD, and	7451
	15:34	he did **e** in the sight of the LORD, and	7451
	16: 7	even for all the **e** that he did in the sight of	7451
	16:19	For his sins which he sinned in doing **e** in	7451
	16:25	Omri wrought **e** in the eyes of the LORD,	7451
	16:30	Ahab the son of Omri did **e** in the sight of	7451
	17:20	hast thou also **brought e** upon the widow	7489
	21:20	thou hast sold thyself to work **e** in the sight	7451
	21:21	I will bring **e** upon thee, and will take away	7451
	21:29	before me, I will not bring the **e** in his days:	7451
	21:29	in his son's days will I bring the **e** upon his	7451
	22: 8	not prophesy good concerning me, but **e**.	7451
	22:18	prophesy no good concerning me, but **e**?	7451
	22:23	the LORD hath spoken **e** concerning thee.	7451
	22:52	he did **e** in the sight of the LORD, and	7451
2Ki	3: 2	he wrought **e** in the sight of the LORD;	7451
	6:33	he said, Behold, this **e** *is* of the LORD;	7451
	8:12	Because I know the **e** that thou wilt do unto	7451
	8:18	and he did **e** in the sight of the LORD.	7451
	8:27	did **e** in the sight of the LORD, as *did*	7451
	13: 2	he did *that* which *was* **e** in the sight of	7451
	13:11	he did *that* which *was* **e** in the sight of	7451
	14:24	he did *that* which *was* **e** in the sight of	7451
	15: 9	he did *that* which *was* **e** in the sight of	7451
	15:18	he did *that* which *was* **e** in the sight of	7451
	15:24	he did *that* which *was* **e** in the sight of	7451
	15:28	he did *that* which *was* **e** in the sight of	7451
	17: 2	he did *that* which *was* **e** in the sight of	7451
	17:13	Turn ye from your **e** ways, and keep my	7451
	17:17	sold themselves to do **e** in the sight of	7451
	21: 2	he did *that* which *was* **e** in the sight of	7451
	21: 9	Manasseh seduced them to do more **e** than	7451
	21:12	I *am* bringing *such* **e** upon Jerusalem and	7451
	21:15	Because they have done *that* which *was* **e**	7451
	21:16	in doing *that* which *was* **e** in the sight of	7451
	21:20	he did *that* which *was* **e** in the sight of	7451
	22:16	I will bring **e** upon this place, and upon	7451
	22:20	thine eyes shall not see all the **e** which I	7451
	23:32	he did *that* which *was* **e** in the sight of	7451
	23:37	he did *that* which *was* **e** in the sight of	7451
	24: 9	he did *that* which *was* **e** in the sight of	7451
	24:19	he did *that* which *was* **e** in the sight of	7451
1Ch	2: 3	of Judah, was **e** in the sight of the LORD;	7451
	4:10	that thou wouldest keep *me* from **e**, that it	7451
	7:23	because it went **e** with his house.	7451
	21:15	he repented him of the **e**, and said to	7451
	21:17	that have sinned and **done e indeed**;	7489+7489
2Ch	7:22	hath he brought all this **e** upon them.	7451
	12:14	he did **e**, because he prepared not his heart	7451
	18: 7	prophesied good unto me, but always **e**:	7451
	18:17	would not prophesy good unto me, but **e**?	7451

2Ch	18:22	and the LORD hath spoken **e** against thee.	7451
	20: 9	If, *when* **e** cometh upon us, *as* the sword,	7451
	21: 6	he wrought *that* which *was* **e** in the eyes of	7451
	22: 4	Wherefore he did **e** in the sight of	7451
	29: 6	done *that* which *was* **e** in the eyes of	7451
	33: 2	did *that* which *was* **e** in the sight of	7451
	33: 6	he wrought much **e** in the sight of	7451
	33:22	he did *that* which *was* **e** in the sight of	7451
	34:24	I will bring **e** upon this place, and upon	7451
	34:28	neither shall thine eyes see all the **e** that I	7451
	36: 5	he did *that* which *was* **e** in the sight of	7451
	36: 9	he did *that* which *was* **e** in the sight of	7451
	36:12	he did *that* which *was* **e** in the sight of	7451
Ezr	9:13	after all that is come upon us for our **e**	7451
Ne	6:13	*that* they might have *matter* for an **e** report,	7451
	9:28	they had rest, they did **e** again before thee:	7451
	13: 7	understood of the **e** that Eliashib did for	7451
	13:17	What **e** thing *is* this that ye do, and	7451
	13:18	*did not* our God bring all this **e** upon us,	7451
	13:27	then hearken unto you to do all this great **e**,	7451
Est	7: 7	for he saw that there was **e** determined	7451
	8: 6	For how can I endure to see the **e** that shall	7451
Job	1: 1	and one that feared God, and eschewed **e**.	7451
	1: 8	one that feareth God, and escheweth **e**?	7451
	2: 3	one that feareth God, and escheweth **e**?	7451
	2:10	hand of God, and shall we not receive **e**?	7451
	2:11	heard of all this **e** that was come upon him,	7451
	5:19	yea, in seven there shall no **e** touch thee.	7451
	8:20	*man,* neither will he help the **e doers**:	7489
	24:21	He **e entreateth** the barren *that* beareth not:	7462
	28:28	and to depart from **e** *is* understanding.	7451
	30:26	**e** came *unto me:* and when I waited for	7451
	31:29	or lift up myself when **e** found him:	7451
	35:12	because of the pride of **e men**.	7451
	42:11	comforted him over all the **e** that	7451
Ps	5: 4	neither shall **e** dwell *with* thee.	7451
	7: 4	If I have rewarded **e** *unto* him that was at	7451
	10:15	the **e** *man:* seek out his wickedness *till* thou	7451
	15: 3	his tongue, nor doeth **e** to his neighbour,	7451
	21:11	For they intended **e** against thee:	7451
	23: 4	of the shadow of death, I will fear no **e**:	7451
	34:13	Keep thy tongue from **e**, and thy lips from	7451
	34:14	Depart from **e**, and do good; seek peace,	7451
	34:16	of the LORD *is* against them that do **e**,	7451
	34:21	**E** shall slay the wicked: and they that hate	7451
	35:12	They rewarded me **e** for good *to*	7451
	36: 4	a way *that is* not good; he abhorreth not **e**.	7451
	37: 8	fret not thyself in any wise to **do e**.	7489
	37:19	They shall not be ashamed in the **e** time:	7451
	37:27	Depart from **e**, and do good; and dwell for	7451
	38:20	They also that render **e** for good are mine	7451
	40:14	and put to shame that wish me **e**.	7451
	41: 5	Mine enemies speak **e** of me, When shall	7451
	41: 8	An **e** disease, *say they,* cleaveth fast unto	1100
	49: 5	Wherefore should I fear in the days of **e**,	7451
	50:19	Thou givest thy mouth to **e**, and thy tongue	7451
	51: 4	have I sinned, and done *this* **e** in thy sight:	7451
	52: 3	Thou lovest **e** more than good; *and*	7451
	54: 5	He shall reward **e** unto mine enemies:	7451
	56: 5	all their thoughts *are* against me for **e**.	7451
	64: 5	They encourage themselves *in* an **e** matter:	7451
	78:49	trouble, *by* sending **e** angels *among them.*	7451
	90:15	*and* the years *wherein* we have seen **e**.	7451
	91:10	There shall no **e** befall thee, neither shall	7451
	97:10	Ye that love the LORD, hate **e**:	7451
	109: 5	And they have rewarded me **e** for good, and	7451
	109:20	and of them that speak **e** against my soul.	7451
	112: 7	He shall not be afraid of **e** tidings: his heart	7451
	119:101	I have refrained my feet from every **e** way,	7451
	121: 7	The LORD shall preserve thee from all **e**:	7451
	140: 1	Deliver me, O LORD, from the **e** man:	7451
	140:11	Let not an **e speaker** be established in	376+3956
	140:11	**e** shall hunt the violent man to overthrow	7451
	141: 4	Incline not my heart to *any* **e** thing,	7451
Pr	1:16	For their feet run to **e**, and make haste to	7451
	1:33	and shall be quiet from fear of **e**.	7451
	2:12	To deliver thee from the way of the **e** *man,*	7451
	2:14	Who rejoice to do **e**, *and* delight in	7451
	3: 7	fear the LORD, and depart from **e**.	7451
	3:29	Devise not **e** against thy neighbour,	7451
	4:14	and go not in the way of **e** *men.*	7451
	4:27	nor *to* the left: remove thy foot from **e**.	7451
	5:14	I was almost in all **e** in the midst of	7451
	6:24	To keep thee from the **e** woman, from	7451
	8:13	The fear of the LORD *is* to hate **e**: pride,	7451
	8:13	the **e** way, and the froward mouth, do I	7451
	11:19	he that pursueth **e** *pursueth it* to his own	7451
	12:12	The wicked desireth the net of **e** *men:* but	7451
	12:20	*is* in the heart of them that imagine **e**:	7451
	12:21	There shall no **e** happen to the just: but	205
	13:19	*it is* abomination to fools to depart from **e**.	7451
	13:21	**E** pursueth sinners: but to the righteous	7451
	14:16	A wise *man* feareth, and departeth from **e**:	7451
	14:19	The **e** bow before the good; and the wicked	7451
	14:22	Do they not err that devise **e**? but mercy	7451
	15: 3	every place, beholding the **e** and the good.	7451
	15:15	All the days of the afflicted *are* **e**: but	7451
	15:28	the mouth of the wicked poureth out **e**	7451
	16: 4	even the wicked for the day of **e**.	7451
	16: 6	the fear of the LORD *men* depart from **e**.	7451
	16:17	highway of the upright *is* to depart from **e**:	7451
	16:27	An ungodly man diggeth up **e**: and in his	7451
	16:30	moving his lips he bringeth **e** to pass.	7451
	17:11	An **e** *man* seeketh only rebellion: therefore	7451
	17:13	Whoso rewardeth **e** for good, evil shall not	7451
	17:13	for good, **e** shall not depart from his house.	7451
	19:23	he shall not be visited *with* **e**.	7451
	20: 8	scattereth *away* all **e** with his eyes.	7451
	20:22	Say not thou, I will recompense **e**; *but*	7451
	20:30	The blueness of a wound cleanseth away **e**:	7451
	21:10	The soul of the wicked desireth **e**:	7451
	22: 3	A prudent *man* foreseeth the **e**, and	7451
	23: 6	Eat thou not the bread of *him that hath* an **e**	7451
	24: 1	Be not thou envious against **e** men,	7451
	24: 8	He that deviseth to **do e** shall be called a	7489
	24:19	of **e** *men,* neither be thou envious at	7489
	24:20	For there shall be no reward to the **e** *man;*	7451
	27:12	A prudent *man* foreseeth the **e**, *and*	7451
	28: 5	**E** men understand not judgment: but	7451
	28:10	the righteous to go astray in an **e** way,	7451
	28:22	He that hasteth to be rich *hath* an **e** eye, and	7451
	29: 6	In the transgression of an **e** man *there is* a	7451
	30:32	or if thou hast **thought e**, *lay thine* hand	2161
	31:12	him good and not **e** all the days of her life.	7451
Ecc	2:21	This also *is* vanity and a great **e**.	7451
	4: 3	who hath not seen the **e** work that is done	7451
	5: 1	for they consider not that *they* do **e**.	7451
	5:13	There is a sore **e** *which* I have seen under	7451
	5:14	those riches perish by **e** travail: and	7451
	5:16	this also *is* a sore **e**, *that* in all points as he	7451
	6: 1	There is an **e** which I have seen under	7451
	6: 2	this *is* vanity, and it *is* an **e** disease.	7451
	8: 3	stand not in an **e** thing; for he doeth	7451
	8: 5	the commandment shall feel no **e** thing:	7451
	8:11	Because sentence *against* an **e** work is not	7451
	8:11	the sons of men is fully set in them to do **e**.	7451
	8:12	Though a sinner do **e** an hundred *times,* and	7451
	9: 3	This *is* an **e** among all *things* that are done	7451
	9: 3	also the heart of the sons of men is full *of* **e**,	7451
	9:12	as the fishes that are taken in an **e** net, and	7451
	9:12	so *are* the sons of men snared in an **e** time,	7451
	10: 5	There is an **e** *which* I have seen under	7451
	11: 2	for thou knowest not what **e** shall be upon	7451
	11:10	thy heart, and put away **e** from thy flesh:	7451
	12: 1	while the **e** days come not, nor the years	7451
	12:14	whether *it be* good, or whether *it be* **e**.	7451
Isa	1:16	put away the **e** of your doings from before	7455
	1:16	from before mine eyes; cease to **do e**;	7489
	3: 9	for they have rewarded **e** unto themselves.	7451
	5:20	Woe unto them that call **e** good, and good	7451
	5:20	unto them that call evil good, and good **e**;	7451
	7: 5	have taken **e** counsel against thee, saying,	7451
	7:15	that he may know to refuse the **e**, and	7451
	7:16	before the child shall know to refuse the **e**,	7451
	13:11	I will punish the world for *their* **e**, and	7451
	31: 2	will bring **e**, and will not call back his	7451
	32: 7	The instruments also of the churl *are* **e**:	7451
	33:15	and shutteth his eyes from seeing **e**;	7451
	41:23	yea, do good, or **do e**, that we may be	7489
	45: 7	I make peace, and create **e**: I the LORD	7451
	47:11	Therefore shall **e** come upon thee;	7451
	56: 2	and keepeth his hand from doing any **e**.	7451
	57: 1	is taken away from the **e** *to come.*	7451
	59: 7	Their feet run to **e**, and they make haste to	7451
	59:15	he *that* departeth from **e** maketh himself a	7451
	65:12	did **e** before mine eyes, and did choose *that*	7451
	66: 4	they did **e** before mine eyes, and chose *that*	7451
Jer	1:14	Out of the north an **e** shall break forth upon	7451

Jer 2: 3 **e** shall come upon them, saith the LORD. 7451
2:19 and see that *it is* an **e** *thing* and bitter, 7451
3: 5 and done **e** *things* as thou couldest. 7451
3:17 more after the imagination of their **e** heart. 7451
4: 4 quench *it,* because of the **e** of your doings. 7455
4: 6 for I will bring **e** from the north, and a great 7451
4:22 they *are* wise to **do e**, but to do good they 7489
5:12 *It is* not he; neither shall **e** come upon us; 7451
6: 1 for **e** appeareth out of the north, and 7451
6:19 behold, I will bring **e** upon this people, 7451
7:24 *and* in the imagination of their **e** heart, 7451
7:30 For the children of Judah have done **e** in 7451
8: 3 residue of them that remain of this **e** family, 7451
9: 3 for they proceed from **e** to evil, and they 7451
9: 3 for they proceed from evil to **e**, and they 7451
10: 5 for they cannot **do e**, neither also *is it* in 7489
11: 8 one in the imagination of their **e** heart: 7451
11:11 Behold, I *will* bring **e** upon them, 7451
11:15 when thou **doest e**, then thou rejoicest. 7451
11:17 hath pronounced **e** against thee, 7451
11:17 for the **e** of the house of Israel and of 7451
11:23 for I will bring **e** upon the men of 7451
12:14 Thus saith the LORD against all mine **e** 7451
13:10 This **e** people, which refuse to hear my 7451
13:23 also do good, that are accustomed to **do e**. 7489
15:11 enemy to entreat thee *well* in the time of **e**, 7451
16:10 pronounced all this great **e** against us? 7451
16:12 one after the imagination of his **e** heart, 7451
17:17 unto me: thou *art* my hope in the day of **e**. 7451
17:18 bring upon them the day of **e**, and 7451
18: 8 whom I have pronounced, turn from their **e**, 7451
18: 8 I will repent of the **e** that I thought to do 7451
18:10 If it do **e** in my sight, that *it* obey not my 7451
18:11 I frame **e** against you, and devise a device 7451
18:11 return ye now every one from his **e** way, 7451
18:12 every one do the imagination of his **e** heart. 7451
18:20 Shall **e** be recompensed for good? for they 7451
19: 3 Behold, I *will* bring **e** upon this place, 7451
19:15 upon all her towns all the **e** that I have 7451
21:10 I have set my face against this city for **e**, 7451
21:12 quench *it,* because of the **e** of your doings. 7455
23: 2 I will visit upon you the **e** of your doings, 7455
23:10 their course is **e**, and their force *is* not right. 7451
23:12 for I will bring **e** upon them, *even* the year 7451
23:17 his own heart, No **e** shall come upon you. 7451
23:22 they should have turned them from their **e** 7451
23:22 evil way, and from the **e** of their doings. 7455
24: 3 the **e**, very evil, that cannot be eaten, 7451
24: 3 the evil, very **e**, that cannot be eaten, 7451
24: 3 that cannot be eaten, they are so **e**. 7455
24: 8 as the **e** figs, which cannot be eaten, 7451
24: 8 which cannot be eaten, they are so **e**; 7455
25: 5 Turn ye again now every one from his **e** 7451
25: 5 from the **e** of your doings, and dwell in 7455
25:29 I begin to **bring e** on the city which is 7489
25:32 **e** *shall* go forth from nation to nation, and 7451
26: 3 and turn every man from his **e** way, 7451
26: 3 that I may repent me of the **e**, which I 7451
26: 3 unto them because of the **e** of their doings. 7455
26:13 the LORD will repent him of the **e** that he 7451
26:19 the LORD repented him of the **e** which he 7451
26:19 Thus *might* we procure great **e** against our 7451
28: 8 of war, and of **e**, and of pestilence. 7451
29:11 thoughts of peace, and not of **e**, 7451
29:17 vile figs, that cannot be eaten, they are so **e**. 7455
32:23 thou hast caused all this **e** to come upon 7451
32:30 the children of Judah have only done **e** 7451
32:32 Because of all the **e** of the children of Israel 7451
32:42 Like as I have brought all this great **e** upon 7451
35:15 Return ye now every man from his **e** way, 7451
35:17 the **e** that I have pronounced against them: 7451
36: 3 all the **e** which I purpose to do unto them; 7451
36: 3 that they may return every man from his **e** 7451
36: 7 and will return every one from his **e** way: 7451
36:31 all the **e** that I have pronounced against 7451
38: 9 these men have **done e** in all that they have 7489
39:16 I *will* bring my words upon this city for **e**, 7451
40: 2 LORD thy God hath pronounced this **e** 7451
41:11 heard of all the **e** that Ishmael the son of 7451
42: 6 Whether *it be* good, or whether *it be* **e**, 7451
42:10 for I repent me of the **e** that I have done 7451
42:17 escape from the **e** that I *will* bring upon 7451
44: 2 Ye have seen all the **e** that I have brought 7451
44: 7 Wherefore commit ye *this* great **e** against 7451
44:11 I will set my face against you for **e**, and 7451
44:17 of victuals, and were well, and saw no **e**. 7451
44:22 because of the **e** of your doings, *and* 7455
44:23 therefore this **e** is happened unto you, as *at* 7451
44:27 I *will* watch over them for **e**, and not for 7451
44:29 words shall surely stand against you for **e**: 7451
45: 5 for behold, I *will* bring **e** upon all flesh, 7451
48: 2 in Heshbon they have devised **e** against it; 7451
49:23 for they have heard **e** tidings: they are 7451
49:37 I will bring **e** upon them, *even* my fierce 7451
51:24 to all the inhabitants of Chaldea all their **e** 7451
51:60 So Jeremiah wrote in a book all the **e** that 7451
51:64 shall not rise from the **e** that I *will* bring 7451
52: 2 he did *that* which *was* **e** in the eyes of 7451
La 3:38 mouth of the most High proceedeth not **e** 7451
Eze 5:16 When I shall send upon them the **e** arrows 7451
5:17 will I send upon you famine and **e** beasts, 7451
6:10 in vain that *I* would do this **e** unto them. 7451
6:11 Alas for all the **e** abominations of the house 7451
7: 5 An **e**, an only evil, behold, is come. 7451
7: 5 An evil, an only **e**, behold, is come. 7451
14:22 ye shall be comforted concerning the **e** that 7451
33:11 turn ye, turn ye from your **e** ways; for why 7451
34:25 will cause the **e** beasts to cease out of 7451
36:31 shall ye remember your own **e** ways, and 7451
38:10 thy mind, and thou shalt think an **e** thought: 7451
Da 9:12 judged us, by bringing upon us a great **e**: 7451
9:13 law of Moses, all this **e** is come upon us: 7451
9:14 hath the LORD watched upon the **e**, 7451
Joel 2:13 great kindness, and repenteth him of the **e**. 7451
Am 3: 6 shall there be **e** in a city, and the LORD 7451
5:13 keep silence in that time; for it *is* an **e** time. 7451
5:14 Seek good, and not **e**, that ye may live: and 7451
5:15 Hate the **e**, and love the good, and 7451
6: 3 Ye that put far away the **e** day, and 7451
9: 4 I will set mine eyes upon them for **e**, and 7451
9:10 The **e** shall not overtake nor prevent us. 7451
Jnh 1: 7 that we may know for whose cause this **e** *is* 7451
1: 8 for whose cause this **e** *is* upon us; 7451
3: 8 let them turn every one from his **e** way, and 7451
3:10 that they turned from their **e** way; 7451
3:10 God repented of the **e**, that he had said that 7451
4: 2 great kindness, and repentest thee of the **e**. 7451
Mic 1:12 **e** came down from the LORD unto 7451
2: 1 and work **e** upon their beds! 7451
2: 3 Behold, against this family do I devise an **e**, 7451
2: 3 shall ye go haughtily: for this time *is* **e**. 7451
3: 2 Who hate the good, and love the **e**; 7451
3:11 among us? none **e** can come upon us. 7451
7: 3 That *they* may do **e** with both hands 7451
Na 1:11 that imagineth **e** against the LORD, 7451
Hab 1:13 *Thou art* of purer eyes than to behold **e**, and 7451
2: 9 Woe to him that coveteth an **e** covetousness 7451
2: 9 *he* may be delivered from the power of **e**! 7451
Zep 1:12 will not do good, neither will he **do e**. 7489
3:15 of thee: thou shalt not see **e** any more. 7451
Zec 1: 4 Turn ye now from your **e** ways, and 7451
1: 4 your evil ways, and *from* your **e** doings: 7451
7:10 let none of you imagine **e** against his 7451
8:17 let none of you imagine **e** in your hearts 7451
Mal 1: 8 if ye offer the blind for sacrifice, *is it* not **e**? 7451
1: 8 and if ye offer the lame and sick, *is it* not **e**? 7451
2:17 Every one that doeth **e** *is* good in the sight 7451
Mt 5:11 shall say all manner of **e** against you *4190*
5:37 whatsoever is more than these cometh of **e**. *4190*
5:39 But I say unto you, That *ye* resist not **e**: but *4190*
5:45 for he maketh his sun to rise on the **e** and *4190*
6:13 not into temptation, but deliver us from **e**: *4190*
6:23 But if thine eye be **e**, thy whole body shall *4190*
6:34 Sufficient unto the day *is* the **e** thereof. *2549*
7:11 If ye then, being **e**, know how to give good *4190*
7:17 but a corrupt tree bringeth forth **e** fruit. *4190*
7:18 A good tree cannot bring forth **e** fruit, *4190*
9: 4 Wherefore think ye **e** in your hearts? *4190*
12:34 generation of vipers, how can ye, being **e**, *4190*
12:35 an **e** man out of the evil treasure bringeth *4190*
12:35 an evil man out of the **e** treasure bringeth *4190*
12:35 of the evil treasure bringeth forth **e** *things*. *4190*
12:39 An **e** and adulterous generation seeketh *4190*
15:19 For out of the heart proceed **e** thoughts, *4190*
20:15 what I will with mine own? Is thine eye **e**, *4190*
24:48 *and* if that **e** servant shall say in his heart, *2556*
27:23 governor said, Why, what **e** hath he done? *2556*
Mk 3: 4 to do good on the sabbath days, or to **do e**? *2554*

Mk 7:21 proceed **e** thoughts, adulteries, fornications, *2556*
7:22 an **e** eye, blasphemy, pride, foolishness: *4190*
7:23 All these **e** *things* come from within, and *4190*
9:39 in my name, that can lightly **speak e** of me. *2551*
15:14 said unto them, Why, what **e** hath he done? *2556*
Lk 6: 9 on the sabbath days to do good, or to **do e**? *2554*
6:22 reproach *you,* and cast out your name as **e**, *4190*
6:35 he is kind unto the unthankful and *to the* **e**. *4190*
6:45 an **e** man out of the evil treasure of his *4190*
6:45 an evil man out of the **e** treasure of his *4190*
6:45 of his heart bringeth forth that which is **e**: *4190*
7:21 and plagues, and of **e** spirits; *4190*
8: 2 which had been healed of **e** spirits and *4190*
11: 4 not into temptation; but deliver us from **e**. *4190*
11:13 If ye then, being **e**, know how to give good *4190*
11:29 he began to say, This is an **e** generation: *4190*
11:34 but when *thine eye* is **e**, thy body also *is* *4190*
16:25 and likewise Lazarus **e** *things:* but now he *2556*
23:22 the third time, Why, what **e** hath he done? *2556*
Jn 3:19 than light, because their deeds were **e**. *4190*
3:20 For every one that doeth **e** hateth the light, *5337*
5:29 and they that have done **e**, unto *5337*
7: 7 I testify of it, that the works thereof are **e**. *4190*
17:15 that thou shouldest keep them from the **e**. *4190*
18:23 Jesus answered him, If I have spoken **e**, *2560*
18:23 If I have spoken evil, bear witness of the **e**: *2556*
Ac 7: 6 and **entreat** *them* **e** four hundred years. *2559*
7:19 and **e entreated** our fathers, so that *they* *2559*
9:13 how much **e** he hath done to thy saints at *2556*
14: 2 **made** their minds **e affected** against *2559*
19: 9 **spake e** of *that* way before the multitude, *2551*
19:12 and the **e** spirits went out of them. *4190*
19:13 had **e** spirits the name of the Lord Jesus, *4190*
19:15 And the **e** spirit answered and said, Jesus I *4190*
19:16 And the man in whom the **e** spirit was leapt *4190*
23: 5 Thou shalt not speak **e** of the ruler of thy *2560*
23: 9 strove, saying, We find no **e** in this man: *2556*
24:20 if they have found any **e doing** in me, *92*
Ro 1:30 inventors of **e** *things,* disobedient to *2556*
2: 9 upon every soul of man that doeth **e**, *2556*
3: 8 we say,) Let us do **e**, that good may come? *2556*
7:19 but the **e** which I would not, that I do. *2556*
7:21 I would do good, **e** is present with me. *2556*
9:11 neither having done any good or **e**, *2556*
12: 9 Abhor *that which is* **e**; cleave to *that which* *4190*
12:17 Recompense to no *man* **e** for evil. *2556*
12:17 Recompense to no *man* evil for **e**. *2556*
12:21 Be not overcome of **e**, but overcome evil *2556*
12:21 of evil, but overcome **e** with good. *2556*
13: 3 are not a terror to good works, but to the **e**. *2556*
13: 4 But if thou do *that which is* **e**, be afraid; *2556*
13: 4 to *execute* wrath upon him that doeth **e**. *2556*
14:16 Let not then your good be **e spoken of**: *987*
14:20 *it is* **e** for *that* man who eateth with offence. *2556*
16:19 *which is* good, and simple concerning **e**. *2556*
1Co 10: 6 to the intent we should not lust after **e** *2556*
10:30 why am I **e spoken of** for *that for* which I *987*
13: 5 is not easily provoked, thinketh no **e**; *2556*
15:33 **e** communications corrupt good manners. *2556*
2Co 6: 8 dishonour, by **e report** and good report: *1426*
13: 7 Now I pray to God that ye do no **e**; not that *2556*
Gal 1: 4 that he might deliver us from *this* present **e** *4190*
Eph 4:31 and anger, and clamour, and **e speaking**, *988*
5:16 the time, because the days are **e**. *4190*
6:13 that ye may be able to withstand in the **e** *4190*
Php 3: 2 Beware of dogs, beware of **e** workers, *2556*
Col 3: 5 **e** concupiscence, and covetousness, *2556*
1Th 5:15 See that none render **e** for evil unto any *2556*
5:15 See that none render evil for **e** unto any *2556*
5:22 Abstain from all appearance of **e**. *4190*
2Th 3: 3 shall stablish you, and keep *you* from **e**. *4190*
1Ti 6: 4 cometh envy, strife, railings, **e** surmisings, *4190*
6:10 For the love of money is the root of all **e**: *2556*
2Ti 2: 9 as an **e doer**, *even* unto bonds; *2557*
3:13 But **e** men and seducers shall wax worse *4190*
4:14 Alexander the coppersmith did me much **e**: *2556*
4:18 And the Lord shall deliver me from every **e** *4190*
Tit 1:12 *are* alway liars, **e** beasts, slow bellies. *2556*
2: 8 having no **e** *thing* to say of you. *5337*
3: 2 To **speak e** of no *man,* to be no brawlers, *but* *987*
Heb 3:12 lest there be in any of you an **e** heart of *4190*
5:14 exercised to discern both good and **e**. *2556*
10:22 having *our* hearts sprinkled from an **e** *4190*
Jas 1:13 for God cannot be tempted with **e**, *2556*
2: 4 and are become judges of **e** thoughts? *4190*
3: 8 *it is* an unruly **e**, full of deadly poison. *2556*
3:16 *is,* there *is* confusion and every **e** work. *5337*
4:11 **Speak** not **e** one of another, brethren. *2635*
4:11 He that **speaketh e** of *his* brother, and *2635*
4:11 **speaketh e** of the law, and judgeth the law: *2635*
4:16 in your boastings: all such rejoicing is **e**. *4190*
1Pe 2: 1 and envies, and all **e speakings**, *2636*
3: 9 Not rendering **e** for evil, or railing for *2556*
3: 9 Not rendering evil for **e**, or railing for *2556*
3:10 let him refrain his tongue from **e**, and *2556*
3:11 Let him eschew **e**, and do good; let him *2556*
3:12 face of the Lord *is* against them that do **e**. *2556*
3:16 that, whereas they **speak e** of you, as of *2635*
3:17 *ye* suffer for well doing, than for **e doing**. *2554*
4: 4 the same excess of riot, **speaking e** *of you:* *987*
4:14 on their part he is **e spoken of**, but on your *987*
2Pe 2: 2 whom the way of truth shall be **e spoken of**. *987*
2:10 they are not afraid to **speak e** of dignities. *987*
2:12 **speak e** of *the things* that they understand *987*
1Jn 3:12 Because his own works were **e**, and his *4190*
2Jn 1:11 him God speed is partaker of his **e** deeds. *4190*
3Jn 1:11 follow not *that which is* **e**, but *that which is* *2556*
1:11 but he that **doeth e** hath not seen God. *2554*
Jude 1: 8 despise dominion, and **speak e** of dignities. *987*
1:10 But these **speak e** of those *things* which they *987*
Rev 2: 2 how thou canst not bear *them which are* **e**: *2556*

EVILDOER (2) [EVIL]
Isa 9:17 for every one *is* a hypocrite and an **e**, and 7489
1Pe 4:15 or *as* an **e**, or as a busybody in other men's *2555*

EVILDOERS (13) [EVIL]
Ps 26: 5 I have hated the congregation of **e**; and 7489
37: 1 Fret not thyself because of **e**, neither be 7489
37: 9 For **e** shall be cut off: but those that wait 7489
94:16 Who will rise up for me against the **e**? *or* 7489
119:115 Depart from me, ye **e**: for I will keep 7489
Isa 1: 4 a seed of **e**, children that are corrupters: 7489
14:20 the seed of **e** shall never be renowned. 7489
31: 2 but will arise against the house of the **e**, and 7489
Jer 20:13 the soul of the poor from the hand of **e**. 7489
23:14 they strengthen also the hands of **e**, 7489
1Pe 2:12 that, whereas they speak against you as **e**, *2555*
2:14 are sent by him for the punishment of **e**, *2555*
3:16 whereas they speak evil of you, as of **e**, *2555*

EVIL-MERODACH (2)
2Ki 25:27 *day* of the month, *that* **E** king of Babylon, 192
Jer 52:31 *that* **E** king of Babylon in the *first* year of his 192

EVILS (9) [EVIL]
Dt 31:17 and many **e** and troubles shall befall them; 7451
31:17 Are not these **e** come upon us, because our 7451
31:18 for all the **e** which they shall have wrought, 7451
31:21 when many **e** and troubles are befallen 7451
Ps 40:12 For innumerable **e** have compassed me 7451
Jer 2:13 For my people have committed two **e**; 7451
Eze 6: 9 they shall lothe themselves for the **e** which 7451
20:43 sight for all your **e** that ye have committed. 7451
Lk 3:19 and for all the **e** which Herod had done, *4190*

EWE (7) [EWES]
Ge 21:28 Abraham set seven **e lambs** of the flock by 3535
21:29 What *mean* these seven **e lambs** which 3535
21:30 For *these* seven **e lambs** shalt thou take of 3535
Lev 14:10 one **e lamb** of the first year without 3535
22:28 *whether it be* cow or **e**, ye shall not kill it 7716
Nu 6:14 one **e lamb** of the first year without 3535
2Sa 12: 3 save one little **e lamb**, which he had bought 3535

EWES (3) [EWE]
Ge 31:38 thy **e** and thy she goats have not cast their 7353
32:14 he goats, two hundred **e**, and twenty rams, 7353
Ps 78:71 From following the **e** great with young he NIH

EXACT (8) [EXACTED, EXACTETH, EXACTION, EXACTIONS, EXACTORS]
Dt 15: 2 release *it;* he shall not **e** *it* of his neighbour, 5065
15: 3 Of a foreigner thou mayest **e** *it again:* but 5065
Ne 5: 7 the rulers, and said unto them, You **e** usury, 5378
5:10 *might* **e** of them money and corn: 5383
5:11 the wine, and the oil, that ye **e** of them. 5383
Ps 89:22 The enemy shall not **e** upon him; nor 5378
Isa 58: 3 you find pleasure, and **e** all your labours. 5065

Lk 3:13 **E** no more than that which is appointed *4238*

EXACTED (2) [EXACT]
2Ki 15:20 Menahem **e** the money of Israel, *even* of all 3318
23:35 he **e** the silver and the gold of the people of 5065

EXACTETH (1) [EXACT]
Job 11: 6 that God **e** of thee *less* than thine iniquity 5382

EXACTION (1) [EXACT]
Ne 10:31 and the **e of** every **debt**. 3027+4853

EXACTIONS (1) [EXACT]
Eze 45: 9 justice, take away your **e** from my people, 1646

EXACTORS (1) [EXACT]
Isa 60:17 officers peace, and thine **e** righteousness. 5065

EXALT (26) [EXALTED, EXALTEST, EXALTETH]
Ex 15: 2 my father's God, and I will **e** him. 7311
1Sa 2:10 his king, and **e** the horn of his anointed. 7311
Job 17: 4 shalt thou not **e** *them.* 7311
Ps 34: 3 with me, and let us **e** his name together. 7311
37:34 and he shall **e** thee to inherit the land: 7311
66: 7 let not the rebellious **e** themselves. Selah. 7311
92:10 my horn shalt thou **e** like *the horn of* an 7311
99: 5 **E** ye the LORD our God, and worship at 7311
99: 9 **E** the LORD our God, and worship at his 7311
107:32 Let them **e** him also in the congregation of 7311
118:28 praise thee: *thou art* my God, I will **e** thee. 7311
140: 8 his wicked device; *lest* they **e** themselves. 7311
Pr 4: 8 **E** her, and she shall promote thee: she shall 5549
Isa 13: 2 **e** the voice unto them, shake the hand, 7311
14:13 I will **e** my throne above the stars of God: 7311
25: 1 I will **e** thee, I will praise thy name; 7311
Eze 21:26 **e** *him that is* low, and abase *him that is* 1361
29:15 neither shall it **e** itself any more above 5375
31:14 by the waters **e** themselves for their height, 1361
Da 11:14 also the robbers of thy people shall **e** 5375
11:36 he shall **e** himself, and magnify himself 7311
Hos 11: 7 to the most High, none at all would **e** *him.* 7311
Ob 1: 4 Though thou **e** *thyself* as the eagle, and 1361
Mt 23:12 And whosoever shall **e** himself shall be *5312*
2Co 11:20 if a man take *of you,* if a man **e** himself, *1869*
1Pe 5: 6 of God, that he may **e** you in due time: *5312*

EXALTED (64) [EXALT]
Nu 24: 7 than Agag, and his kingdom shall be **e**. 5375
1Sa 2: 1 the LORD, mine horn is **e** in the LORD: 7311
2Sa 5:12 that he had **e** his kingdom for his people 5375
22:47 **e** be the God of the rock of my salvation. 7311
1Ki 1: 5 Adonijah the son of Haggith **e** himself, 5375
14: 7 Forasmuch as I **e** thee from among 7311
16: 2 Forasmuch as I **e** thee out of the dust, and 7311
2Ki 19:22 against whom hast thou **e** *thy* voice, and 7311
1Ch 29:11 and *thou* art **e** as head **above** all. 5375
Ne 9: 5 which *is* **e** above all blessing and praise. 7311
Job 5:11 that those which mourn may be **e** *to* safety. 7682
24:24 They are **e** for a little while, but are gone 7426
36: 7 doth establish them for ever, and they are **e**. 1361
Ps 12: 8 on every side, when the vilest men are **e**. 7311
13: 2 how long shall mine enemy be **e** over me? 7311
18:46 and let the God of my salvation be **e**. 7311
21:13 Be thou **e**, LORD, in thine own strength: 7311
46:10 I will be **e** among the heathen, I will be 7311
46:10 among the heathen, I will be **e** in the earth. 7311
47: 9 the earth *belong* unto God: he is greatly **e**. 5927
57: 5 Be thou **e**, O God, above the heavens; 7311
57:11 Be thou **e**, O God, above the heavens: 7311
75:10 *but* the horns of the righteous shall be **e**. 7311
89:16 and in thy righteousness shall they be **e**. 7311
89:17 and in thy favour our horn shall be **e**. 7311
89:19 I have **e** *one* chosen out of the people. 7311
89:24 and in my name shall his horn be **e**. 7311
97: 9 all the earth: thou art **e** far above all gods. 5927
108: 5 Be thou **e**, O God, above the heavens: and 7311
112: 9 for ever; his horn shall be **e** with honour. 7311
118:16 The right hand of the LORD is **e**: the right 7426
Pr 11:11 By the blessing of the upright the city is **e**: 7311
Isa 2: 2 and *shall be* **e** above the hills; 5375
2:11 and the LORD alone shall be **e** in that day. 7682
2:17 and the LORD alone shall be **e** in that day. 7682
5:16 the LORD of hosts shall be **e** in judgment, 1361
12: 4 make mention that his name *is* **e**. 7682
30:18 unto you, and therefore will he be **e**, 7311
33: 5 The LORD *is* **e**; for he dwelleth on high: 7682
33:10 I rise, saith the LORD; now will I be **e**; 7426
37:23 against whom hast thou **e** *thy* voice, and 7311
40: 4 Every valley shall be **e**, and every mountain 5375
49:11 a way, and my highways shall be **e**. 7311
52:13 he shall be **e** and extolled, and be very high. 7311
Eze 17:24 have **e** the low tree, have dried up the green 1361
19:11 her stature was **e** among the thick branches, 1361
31: 5 Therefore his height was **e** above all 1361
Hos 13: 1 spake trembling, he **e** *himself* in Israel; 5375
13: 6 they were filled, and their heart was **e**; 7311
Mic 4: 1 and *it shall be* **e** above the hills; 5375
Mt 11:23 Capernaum, which art **e** unto heaven, *5312*
23:12 and he that shall humble himself shall be **e**. *5312*
Lk 1:52 from *their* seats, and **e** them of low degree. *5312*
10:15 Capernaum, which art **e** to heaven, *5312*
14:11 and he that humbleth himself shall be **e**. *5312*
18:14 and he that humbleth himself shall be **e**. *5312*
Ac 2:33 Therefore being by the right hand of God **e**, *5312*
5:31 Him hath God **e** with his right hand *to be* a *5312*
13:17 **e** the people when *they* dwelt as strangers *5312*
2Co 11: 7 in abasing myself that you might be **e**, *5312*
12: 7 And lest I should be **e above measure** *5229*
12: 7 lest I should be **e above measure.** *5229*
Php 2: 9 Wherefore God also hath **highly e** him, and *5251*
Jas 1: 9 brother of low degree rejoice in that he is **e**: *5311*

EXALTEST (1) [EXALT]
Ex 9:17 As yet **e** thou thyself against my people, 5549

EXALTETH (9) [EXALT]
Job 36:22 Behold, God **e** by his power: who teacheth 7682
Ps 148:14 He also **e** the horn of his people, the praise 7311
Pr 14:29 but *he that is* hasty of spirit **e** folly. 7311
14:34 Righteousness **e** a nation: but sin *is* a 7311
17:19 *and* he that **e** his gate seeketh destruction. 1361
Lk 14:11 For whosoever **e** himself shall be abased; *5312*
18:14 for every one that **e** himself shall be *5312*
2Co 10: 5 every high thing that **e** itself against *1869*
2Th 2: 4 and **e** himself above all that is called God, *5229*

EXAMINATION (1) [EXAMINE]
Ac 25:26 O king Agrippa, that, after **e** had, *351*

EXAMINE (5) [EXAMINATION, EXAMINED, EXAMINING]
Ezr 10:16 first day of the tenth month to **e** the matter. 1875
Ps 26: 2 **E** me, O LORD, and prove me; try my 974
1Co 9: 3 Mine answer to them that do **e** me is this: *350*
11:28 But let a man **e** himself, and so let him eat *1381*
2Co 13: 5 **E** yourselves, whether ye be in the faith; *3985*

EXAMINED (6) [EXAMINE]
Lk 23:14 and behold, I, having **e** *him* before you, *350*
Ac 4: 9 If we this day be **e** of the good deed done to *350*
12:19 he **e** the keepers, and commanded that *they* *350*
22:24 and bade that he should be **e** by scourging; *426*
22:29 departed from him which should have **e** him: *426*
28:18 Who, when they had **e** me, would have let *350*

EXAMINING (1) [EXAMINE]
Ac 24: 8 by **e** of whom thyself mayest take *350*

EXAMPLE (8) [EXAMPLES]
Mt 1:19 and not willing to **make her a publick e**, *3856*
Jn 13:15 For I have given you an **e**, that ye should do *5262*
1Ti 4:12 but be thou an **e** of the believers, in word, *5179*
Heb 4:11 lest any *man* fall after the same **e** of *5262*
8: 5 Who serve unto the **e** and shadow of *5262*
Jas 5:10 for an **e** of suffering affliction, and *5262*
1Pe 2:21 Christ also suffered for us, leaving us an **e**, *5261*
Jude 1: 7 after strange flesh, are set forth for an **e**, *1164*

EXAMPLES (1) [EXAMPLE]
1Co 10: 6 Now these *things* were our **e**, to the intent *5179*

EXCEED (4) [EXCEEDED, EXCEEDEST, EXCEEDETH, EXCEEDING, EXCEEDINGLY]
Dt 25: 3 Forty stripes he may give him, *and* not **e**: 3254
25: 3 *if* he should **e**, and beat him above these 3254
Mt 5:20 **e** *the righteousness* of the scribes *4052+4183*
2Co 3: 9 the ministration of righteousness **e** in glory. *4052*

EXCEEDED (3) [EXCEED]
1Sa 20:41 wept one with another, until David **e**. 1431
1Ki 10:23 So king Solomon **e** all the kings of 1431+4480

Job 36: 9 and their transgressions that they have **e**. 1396

EXCEEDEST (1) [EXCEED]
2Ch 9: 6 told me: *for* thou **e** the fame that I heard. 3254

EXCEEDETH (1) [EXCEED]
1Ki 10: 7 and prosperity **e** the fame which I heard. 3254

EXCEEDING (59) [EXCEED]
Ge 15: 1 I *am* thy shield, *and* thy **e** great reward. 3966
17: 6 I will make thee **e** fruitful, and 3966+3966+871.1
27:34 he cried with a great and **e** bitter cry, 3966+5704
Ex 1: 7 and waxed **e** mighty; 3966+3966+871.1
19:16 and the voice of the trumpet **e** loud; 3966
Nu 14: 7 to search it, *is* an **e** good land. 3966+3966
1Sa 2: 3 Talk no more *so* **e proudly**; let *not* 1364+1364
2Sa 8: 8 king David took **e** much brass. 3966
12: 2 The rich *man* had **e** many flocks and herds: 3966
1Ki 4:29 and understanding **e** much, 3966
7:47 because they were **e** many: 3966+3966
1Ch 20: 2 he brought also **e** much spoil *out* of 3966
22: 5 the LORD *must be* **e** magnifical, 4605+1886.5
2Ch 11:12 and spears, and made them **e** strong, 3966+7235
14:14 for there was **e** much spoil in them. NIH
16:12 until his disease *was* **e** 4605+1886.5+3807.1
32:27 Hezekiah had **e** much riches and honour: 3966
Ps 21: 6 thou hast made him **e** glad with thy 871.1
43: 4 unto the altar of God, unto God my **e** joy: 8057
119:96 *but* thy commandment *is* **e** broad. 3966
Pr 30:24 upon the earth, but they *are* **e wise**: 2449+2450
Ecc 7:24 and **e deep**, who can find it out? 6013+6013
Jer 48:29 heard the pride of Moab; *he is* **e** proud: 3966
Eze 9: 9 of Israel and Judah *is* **e** great, 3966+3966+871.1
16:13 thou wast **e** beautiful, and 3966+3966+871.1
23:15 **e in dyed attire** upon their heads, 2871+5628
37:10 up upon their feet, an **e** great army. 3966+3966
47:10 as the fish of the great sea, **e** many. 3966
Da 3:22 *was* urgent, and the furnace **e** hot, 3493
6:23 was the king **e** glad for him, and 7690
7:19 **e** dreadful, whose teeth *were of* iron, and 3493
8: 9 which waxed **e** great, toward the south, and 3499
Jnh 3: 3 Now Nineveh was an **e** great city of 430+3807.1
4: 6 Jonah was **e glad** of the gourd. 1419+8055+8057
Mt 2:10 saw the star, they rejoiced *with* **e** great joy. *4970*
2:16 was **e** wroth, and sent forth, and slew all *3029*
4: 8 the devil taketh him *up* into an **e** high *3029*
5:12 Rejoice, and be **e glad**: for great *is* your *21*
8:28 **e** fierce, so that no *man* might pass by that *3029*
17:23 be raised *again.* And they were **e** sorry. *4970*
26:22 And they were **e** sorrowful, and *4970*
26:38 My soul is **e sorrowful**, *even* unto death: *4036*
Mk 6:26 And the king was **e sorry**; *yet* for his oaths' *4036*
9: 3 raiment became shining, **e** white as snow; *3029*
14:34 My soul is **e sorrowful** unto death: *4036*
Lk 23: 8 And when Herod saw Jesus, he was **e** glad: *3029*
Ac 7:20 was born, and was **e fair**, *791+2316+3588*
Ro 7:13 might become **e** sinful. *2596+5236*
2Co 4:17 for us a **far more e** *1519+2596+5236+5236*
7: 4 I am **e** joyful in all our tribulation. *5248*
9:14 which long after you for the **e** grace of God *5235*
Eph 1:19 And what *is* the **e** greatness of his power to *5235*
2: 7 **e** riches of his grace in *his* kindness *5235*
3:20 Now unto him that is able to do **e** *5228*
1Ti 1:14 And the grace of our Lord was **e abundant** *5250*
1Pe 4:13 be revealed, ye may be glad also with **e joy**. *21*
2Pe 1: 4 Whereby are given unto us **e great** and *3176*
Jude 1:24 before the presence of his glory with **e joy**, *20*
Rev 16:21 the hail; for the plague thereof was **e** great. *4970*

EXCEEDINGLY (39) [EXCEED]
Ge 7:19 the waters prevailed **e** upon the earth; 3966+3966
13:13 and sinners before the LORD **e**. 3966
16:10 I will **multiply** thy seed **e**, that it 7235+7235
17: 2 and will multiply thee **e**. 3966+3966+871.1
17:20 will multiply him **e**; 3966+3966+871.1
27:33 Isaac trembled very **e**, and said, Who? 1419
30:43 the man increased **e**, and had much 3966+3966
47:27 and grew, and multiplied **e**. 3966
1Sa 26:21 played the fool, and have erred **e**. 3966+7235
2Sa 13:15 Amnon **hated** her **e**; so 1419+3966+8130+8135
2Ki 10: 4 they were **e** afraid, and said, Behold, 3966+3966
1Ch 29:25 **e** in the sight of all Israel, 4605+1886.5+3807.1
2Ch 1: 1 and magnified him **e**. 4605+1886.5+3807.1
17:12 waxed great **e**; 4605+5704+1886.5+3807.1
26: 8 *himself* **e**. 4605+5704+1886.5+3807.1
Ne 2:10 heard *of it,* it **grieved** them **e** 1419+7451+7489
Est 4: 4 was the queen **e** grieved; and she sent 3966
Job 3:22 Which **rejoice e**, *and* are glad, 413+1524+8056
Ps 68: 3 yea, let them **e rejoice**. 7797+8057+871.1
106:14 **lusted e** in the wilderness, and 183+8378
119:167 kept thy testimonies; and *I* love them **e**. 3966
123: 3 upon us: for we are **e** filled *with* contempt. 7227
123: 4 Our soul is **e** filled *with* the scorning of 7227
Isa 24:19 the earth is **moved e**. 4131+4131
Da 7: 7 dreadful and terrible, and strong **e**; 3493
Jnh 1:10 were the men **e afraid**, 1419+3372+3374
1:16 the men **feared** the LORD **e**, 1419+3372+3374
4: 1 it **displeased** Jonah **e**, and he 1419+3415+7451
Mt 19:25 When his disciples heard *it,* they were **e** *4970*
Mk 4:41 And they feared **e**, and said one to another, *3173*
15:14 And they cried out the **more e**, Crucify *4056*
Ac 16:20 being Jews, do **e trouble** our city, *1613*
26:11 and being **e** mad against them, I persecuted *4057*
27:18 And we being **e** tossed with a tempest, *4971*
2Co 7:13 **e** the more joyed we for the joy of Titus, *4056*
Gal 1:14 being **more e** zealous of the traditions of *4056*
1Th 3:10 **e** that *we* might see your face, *1537+4053+5228*
2Th 1: 3 because that your faith **groweth e**, and *5232*
Heb 12:21 *that* Moses said, I **e fear** and quake;) *1510+1630*

EXCEL (5) [EXCELLED, EXCELLENCY, EXCELLENT, EXCELLEST, EXCELLETH]
Ge 49: 4 Unstable as water, thou shalt not **e**; because 3498
1Ch 15:21 Azaziah, with harps on the Sheminith to **e**. 5329
Ps 103:20 ye his angels, that **e** in strength, 1368
Isa 10:10 whose graven images did **e** *them of* 4480
1Co 14:12 that ye may **e** to the edifying of the church. *4052*

EXCELLED (1) [EXCEL]
1Ki 4:30 Solomon's wisdom **e** the wisdom of all 7235

EXCELLENCY (26) [EXCEL]
Ge 49: 3 the **e** of dignity, and the excellency of 3499
49: 3 excellency of dignity, and the **e** of power: 3499
Ex 15: 7 in the greatness of thine **e** thou hast 1347
Dt 33:26 heaven in thy help, and in his **e** *on* the sky. 1346
33:29 of thy help, and who *is* the sword of thy **e**! 1346
Job 4:21 Doth not their **e** *which is* in them go away? 3499
13:11 Shall not his **e** make you afraid? and 7613
20: 6 Though his **e** mount up to the heavens, and 7863
37: 4 he thundereth with the voice of his **e**; and 1347
40:10 Deck thyself now with majesty and **e**; and 1363
Ps 47: 4 for us, the **e** of Jacob whom he loved. 1347
62: 4 only consult to cast *him* down from his **e**: 7613
68:34 his **e** *is* over Israel, and his strength *is* in 1346
Ecc 7:12 the **e** of knowledge *is, that* wisdom giveth 3504
Isa 13:19 of kingdoms, the beauty of the Chaldees' **e**, 1347
35: 2 the **e** of Carmel and Sharon, they shall see 1926
35: 2 glory of the LORD, *and* the **e** of our God. 1926
60:15 through *thee,* I will make thee an eternal **e**, 1347
Eze 24:21 the **e** of your strength, the desire of your 1347
Am 6: 8 I abhor the **e** of Jacob, and hate his palaces: 1347
8: 7 The LORD hath sworn by the **e** of Jacob, 1347
Na 2: 2 For the LORD hath turned *away* the **e** of 1347
2: 2 the excellency of Jacob, as the **e** of Israel: 1347
1Co 2: 1 came not with **e** of speech or of wisdom, *5247*
2Co 4: 7 that the **e** of the power may be of God, and *5236*
Php 3: 8 loss for the **e** of the knowledge of Christ *5242*

EXCELLENT (34) [EXCEL]
Est 1: 4 and the honour of his **e** majesty many days, 8597
Job 37:23 *he is* **e** in power, and *in* judgment, and 7689
Ps 8: 1 our Lord, how **e** *is* thy name in all the earth! 117
8: 9 our Lord, how **e** *is* thy name in all the earth! 117
16: 3 *to* the **e**, in whom *is* all my delight. 117
36: 7 How **e** *is* thy lovingkindness, O God! 3368
76: 4 *and* **e** than the mountains of prey. 117
141: 5 *it shall be* an **e** oil, *which* shall not break 7218
148:13 for his name alone *is* **e**; his glory *is* above 7682
150: 2 praise him according to his **e** greatness. 7230
Pr 8: 6 Hear, for I will speak of **e things**; and 5057
12:26 The righteous *is* more **e** than his neighbour: 8446
17: 7 **E** speech becometh not a fool: much less 3499
17:27 *and* a man of understanding is of an **e** spirit. 3368
22:20 Have not I written to thee **e things** in 7991
SS 5:15 countenance *is* as Lebanon, **e** as the cedars. 977
Isa 4: 2 the fruit of the earth *shall be* **e** and comely 1347
12: 5 the LORD; for he hath done **e things**: 1348

Isa 28:29 is wonderful in counsel, *and* **e** in working. 1431
Eze 16: 7 and thou art come to **e ornaments**: 5716+5716
Da 2:31 This great image, whose brightness *was* **e**, 3493
4:36 and **e** majesty was added unto me. 3493
5:12 Forasmuch as an **e** spirit, and knowledge, 3493
5:14 and **e** wisdom is found in thee. 3493
6: 3 and princes, because an **e** spirit *was* in him; 3493
Lk 1: 3 unto thee in order, **most e** Theophilus, *2903*
Ac 23:26 Claudius Lysias unto the **most e** governor *2903*
Ro 2:18 and approvest the *things* that are **more e**, *1308*
1Co 12:31 yet shew I unto you a **more e** way. *2596+5236*
Php 1:10 That ye may approve *things* that are **e**; *1308*
Heb 1: 4 as he hath by inheritance obtained a **more e** *1313*
8: 6 But now hath he obtained a **more e** *1313*
11: 4 By faith Abel offered unto God a **more e** *4183*
2Pe 1:17 came such a voice to him from the **e** glory, *3169*

EXCELLEST (1) [EXCEL]
Pr 31:29 have done virtuously, but thou **e** them all. 5927

EXCELLETH (3) [EXCEL]
Ecc 2:13 I saw that wisdom **e** folly, as far as light 3504
2:13 excelleth folly, as far as light **e** darkness. 3504
2Co 3:10 in this respect, by reason of the glory that **e**. *5235*

EXCEPT (74) [EXCEPTED] See Index

EXCEPTED (1) [EXCEPT] See Index

EXCESS (4)
Mt 23:25 but within they are full of extortion and **e**. *192*
Eph 5:18 And be not drunk with wine, wherein is **e**; *810*
1Pe 4: 3 lusts, **e of wine**, revellings, banquetings, *3632*
4: 4 you run not with *them* to the same **e** of riot, *401*

EXCESSIVE See OVERMUCH

EXCHANGE (6) [EXCHANGERS]
Ge 47:17 Joseph gave them bread *in* **e** for horses, and NIH
Lev 27:10 then it and the **e** thereof shall be holy. 8545
Job 28:17 the **e** of it *shall not be for* jewels of fine 8545
Eze 48:14 they shall not sell of it, neither **e**, 4171
Mt 16:26 or what shall a man give **in e for** his soul? *465*
Mk 8:37 Or what shall a man give **in e for** his soul? *465*

EXCHANGERS (1) [EXCHANGE]
Mt 25:27 therefore to have put my money to the **e**, *5133*

EXCLUDE (1) [EXCLUDED]
Gal 4:17 yea, they would **e** you, that you might *1576*

EXCLUDED (1) [EXCLUDE]
Ro 3:27 It is **e**. By what law? of works? Nay: but *1576*

EXCUSE (3) [EXCUSED, EXCUSING]
Lk 14:18 they all with one *consent* began to **make e**. *3868*
Ro 1:20 and Godhead; so that they are **without e**: *379*
2Co 12:19 think you that we **e ourselves** unto you? *626*

EXCUSED (2) [EXCUSE]
Lk 14:18 needs go and see it: I pray thee have me **e**. *3868*
14:19 I go to prove them: I pray thee have me **e**. *3868*

EXCUSING (1) [EXCUSE]
Ro 2:15 mean while accusing or else **e** one another;) *626*

EXECRATION (2)
Jer 42:18 ye shall be an **e**, and an astonishment, and 423
44:12 and they shall be an **e**, *and* an astonishment, 423

EXECUTE (32) [EXECUTED, EXECUTEDST, EXECUTEST, EXECUTETH, EXECUTING, EXECUTION, EXECUTIONER]
Ex 12:12 against all the gods of Egypt I will **e** 6213
Nu 5:30 and the priest shall **e** upon her all this law. 6213
8:11 that they may **e** the service of the LORD. 5647
Dt 10:18 He doth **e** the judgment of the fatherless 6213
1Ki 6:12 **e** my judgments, and keep all my 6213
Ps 119:84 when wilt thou **e** judgment on them that 6213
149: 7 To **e** vengeance upon the heathen, *and* 6213
149: 9 To **e** upon them the judgment written: 6213
Isa 16: 3 Take counsel, **e** judgment; make thy 6213
Jer 7: 5 if you **throughly e** judgment 6213+6213
21:12 **E** judgment in the morning, and 1777
22: 3 **E** ye judgment and righteousness, and 6213
23: 5 shall **e** judgment and justice in the earth. 6213
33:15 he shall **e** judgment and righteousness in 6213
Eze 5: 8 will **e** judgments in the midst of thee in 6213
5:10 I will **e** judgments in thee, and the whole 6213
5:15 when I shall **e** judgments in thee in anger 6213
11: 9 and will **e** judgments among you. 6213
16:41 **e** judgments upon thee in the sight of many 6213
25:11 I will **e** judgments upon Moab; and 6213
25:17 I will **e** great vengeance upon them with 6213
30:14 fire in Zoan, and will **e** judgments in No. 6213
30:19 Thus will I **e** judgments in Egypt: and 6213
45: 9 and spoil, and **e** judgment and justice, 6213
Hos 11: 9 I will not **e** the fierceness of mine anger, 6213
Mic 5:15 I will **e** vengeance in anger and fury upon 6213
7: 9 he plead my cause, and **e** judgment for me: 6213
Zec 7: 9 **E** true judgment, and shew mercy and 8199
8:16 **e the judgment** of truth and peace in 4941+8199
Jn 5:27 And hath given him authority to **e** judgment *4160*
Ro 13: 4 a revenger to *e* wrath upon him that doeth NIG
Jude 1:15 To **e** judgment upon all, and to convince all *4160*

EXECUTED (20) [EXECUTE]
Nu 33: 4 upon their gods also the LORD **e** 6213
Dt 33:21 he **e** the justice of the LORD, and 6213
2Sa 8:15 David **e** judgment and justice unto all his 6213
1Ch 6:10 (he *it is* that **e the priest's office** in 3547
18:14 **e** judgment and justice among all his 6213
24: 2 Eleazar and Ithamar **e the priest's office.** 3547
2Ch 24:24 So they **e** judgment against Joash. 6213
Ezr 7:26 let judgment be **e** speedily upon him, 5648
Ps 106:30 stood up Phinehas, and **e judgment**: and 6419
Ecc 8:11 *against* an evil work is not **e** speedily, 6213
Jer 23:20 until he have **e**, and till he have performed 6213
Eze 11:12 neither **e** my judgments, but have done 6213
18: 8 hath **e** true judgment between man and 6213
18:17 hath **e** my judgments, hath walked in my 6213
20:24 Because they had not **e** my judgments, but 6213
23:10 for they had **e** judgment upon her. 6213
28:22 when I shall have **e** judgments in her, and 6213
28:26 when I have **e** judgments upon all those 6213
39:21 shall see my judgment that I have **e**, 6213
Lk 1: 8 *that* while he **e the priest's office** before *2407*

EXECUTEDST (1) [EXECUTE]
1Sa 28:18 nor **e** his fierce wrath upon Amalek, 6213

EXECUTEST (1) [EXECUTE]
Ps 99: 4 thou **e** judgment and righteousness in 6213

EXECUTETH (6) [EXECUTE]
Ps 9:16 is known *by* the judgment *which* he **e**: 6213
103: 6 The LORD **e** righteousness and 6213
146: 7 Which **e** judgment for the oppressed: 6213
Isa 46:11 the man that **e** my counsel from a far NIH
Jer 5: 1 find a man, if there be *any* that **e** judgment, 6213
Joel 2:11 for *he is* strong that **e** his word: for the day 6213

EXECUTING (3) [EXECUTE]
2Ki 10:30 Because thou hast done well in **e** *that* which 6213
2Ch 11:14 from **e the priest's office** unto the LORD: 3547
22: 8 that when Jehu was **e judgment** upon 8199

EXECUTION (1) [EXECUTE]
Est 9: 1 and his decree drew near to be **put in e**, 6213

EXECUTIONER (1) [EXECUTE]
Mk 6:27 And immediately the king sent an **e**, and *4688*

EXEMPTED (1)
1Ki 15:22 throughout all Judah; none *was* **e**: 5355

EXERCISE (11) [EXERCISED, EXERCISETH]
Ps 131: 1 neither do I **e** myself in great *matters*, or 1980
Jer 9:24 that I *am* the LORD which **e** 6213
Mt 20:25 of the Gentiles **e dominion over** them, *2634*
20:25 they *that are* great **e authority upon** them. *2715*
Mk 10:42 over the Gentiles **e lordship over** them; *2634*
10:42 their great ones **e authority upon** them. *2715*
Lk 22:25 The kings of the Gentiles **e lordship over** *2961*
22:25 they that **e authority upon** them are called *1850*
Ac 24:16 And herein do I **e** myself, to have always a *778*
1Ti 4: 7 and **e** thyself *rather* unto godliness. *1128*
4: 8 For bodily **e** profiteth little: *1129*

EXERCISED (6) [EXERCISE]
Ecc 1:13 given to the sons of man to be **e** therewith. 6031
3:10 hath given to the sons of men to be **e** in it. 6031

E

Eze 22:29 e **robbery**, and have vexed the poor 1497+1498
Heb 5:14 use have their senses e to discern both good *1128*
12:11 unto them which are e thereby. *1128*
2Pe 2:14 a heart they have e with covetous practices; *1128*

EXERCISETH (1) [EXERCISE]
Rev 13:12 And he e all the power of the first beast *4160*

EXHORT (16) [EXHORTATION, EXHORTED, EXHORTETH, EXHORTING]
Ac 2:40 with many other words did he testify and e, *3870*
27:22 And now I e you to be of good cheer: *3867*
2Co 9: 5 Therefore I thought it necessary to e *3870*
1Th 4: 1 brethren, and e *you* by the Lord Jesus, *3870*
5:14 Now we e you, brethren, warn *them that* *3870*
2Th 3:12 and e by our Lord Jesus Christ, *3870*
1Ti 2: 1 I e therefore that, first of all, supplications, *3870*
6: 2 of the benefit. These *things* teach and e. *3870*
2Ti 4: 2 e with all longsuffering and doctrine. *3870*
Tit 1: 9 he may be able by sound doctrine both to e *3870*
2: 6 Young *men* likewise e to be sober minded. *3870*
2: 9 *E* servants to be obedient unto their own NIG
2:15 and e, and rebuke with all authority. *3870*
Heb 3:13 But e one another daily, while it is called *3870*
1Pe 5: 1 The elders which are among you I e, *3870*
Jude 1: 3 e *you* that *ye* should earnestly contend for *3870*

EXHORTATION (10) [EXHORT]
Lk 3:18 And many other *things* in his e preached he *3870*
Ac 13:15 if ye have *any* word of e for the people, *3874*
20: 2 and had **given** them much e, he came *3056+3870*
Ro 12: 8 Or he that exhorteth, on e: he that giveth, *3874*
1Co 14: 3 unto men *to* edification, and e, and comfort. *3874*
2Co 8:17 For indeed he accepted the e; but *3874*
1Th 2: 3 For our e *was* not of deceit, nor of *3874*
1Ti 4:13 give attendance to reading, to e, to doctrine. *3874*
Heb 12: 5 And ye have forgotten the e which speaketh *3874*
13:22 beseech you, brethren, suffer the word of e: *3874*

EXHORTED (3) [EXHORT]
Ac 11:23 the grace of God, was glad, and e *them* all, *3870*
15:32 e the brethren with many words, and *3870*
1Th 2:11 As you know how we e and comforted and *3870*

EXHORTETH (1) [EXHORT]
Ro 12: 8 Or he that e, on exhortation: he that giveth, *3870*

EXHORTING (4) [EXHORT]
Ac 14:22 *and* e *them* to continue in the faith, and *3870*
18:27 e the disciples to receive him: *4389*
Heb 10:25 but e *one another:* and so much the more, *3870*
1Pe 5:12 e, and testifying that this is the true grace of *3870*

EXILE (2)
2Sa 15:19 for thou *art* a stranger, and also an e. 1540
Isa 51:14 The **captive** e hasteneth that *he* may be 6808

EXORCISTS (1)
Ac 19:13 Then certain of the vagabond Jews, e, *1845*

EXPANSE See FIRMAMENT

EXPECTATION (14) [EXPECTED, EXPECTING]
Ps 9:18 the e of the poor shall *not* perish for ever. 8615
62: 5 thou only upon God; for my e *is* from him. 8615
Pr 10:28 but the e of the wicked shall perish. 8615
11: 7 a wicked man dieth, *his* e shall perish: 8615
11:23 only good: *but* the e of the wicked *is* wrath. 8615
23:18 is an end; and thine e shall not be cut off. 8615
24:14 be a reward, and thy e shall not be cut off. 8615
Isa 20: 5 be afraid and ashamed of Ethiopia their e, 4007
20: 6 shall say in that day, Behold, such *is* our e, 4007
Zec 9: 5 for her e shall be ashamed; and the king 4007
Lk 3:15 And as the people were **in** e, and all *men* *4328*
Ac 12:11 and *from* all the e of the people of the Jews. *4329*
Ro 8:19 For the **earnest** e of the creature waiteth for *603*
Php 1:20 According to my **earnest** e and *my* hope, *603*

EXPECTED (1) [EXPECTATION]
Jer 29:11 and not of evil, to give you an e end. 8615

EXPECTING (2) [EXPECTATION]
Ac 3: 5 unto them, e **to** receive something of them. *4328*
Heb 10:13 From henceforth e till his enemies be made *1551*

EXPEDIENT (7)
Jn 11:50 Nor consider that it is e for us, that one man *4851*
16: 7 you the truth; It is e for you that I go away: *4851*
18:14 that it was e that one man should die for *4851*
1Co 6:12 are lawful unto me, but all *things* are not e: *4851*
10:23 are lawful for me, but all *things* are not e: *4851*
2Co 8:10 for this is e for you, who have begun *4851*
12: 1 It is not e for me doubtless to glory. I will *4851*

EXPEL (2) [EXPELLED]
Jos 23: 5 he shall e them from before you, and 1920
Jdg 11: 7 and e me out of my father's house? 1644

EXPELLED (4) [EXPEL]
Jos 13:13 (Nevertheless the children of Israel e not 3423
Jdg 1:20 and he e thence the three sons of Anak. 3423
2Sa 14:14 that *his* banished be not e from him. 5080
Ac 13:50 Barnabas, and e them out of their coasts. *1544*

EXPENCES (2)
Ezr 6: 4 let the e be given out of the king's house: 5313
6: 8 forthwith e be given unto these men, 5313

EXPERIENCE (4)
Ge 30:27 *tarry: for* I have **learned by** e that 5172
Ecc 1:16 my heart **had** great e of wisdom and 7200
Ro 5: 4 And patience, e; and experience, hope: *1382*
5: 4 And patience, experience; and e, hope: *1382*

EXPERIMENT (1)
2Co 9:13 Whiles by the e of this ministration they *1382*

EXPERT (6)
1Ch 12:33 e in war, with all instruments of war, 6186
12:35 of the Danites e in war twenty and 6186
12:36 forth to battle, e in war, forty thousand. 6186
SS 3: 8 They all hold swords, *being* e in war: 3925
Jer 50: 9 their arrows *shall be* as of a mighty e *man;* 7919
Ac 26: 3 *I know* thee to be e in all customs and *1109*

EXPERT BUILDER See MASTERBUILDER

EXPIRED (9)
1Sa 18:26 king's son in law: and the days were not e. 4390
2Sa 11: 1 it came to pass, after the year was e, at 8666
1Ch 17:11 when thy days be e that *thou* must go *to be* 4390
20: 1 it came to pass, that after the year was e, 8666
2Ch 36:10 when the year was e, king Nebuchadnezzar 8666
Est 1: 5 when these days were e, the king made a 4390
Eze 43:27 when *these* days are e, it shall be, *that* upon 3615
Ac 7:30 And when forty years were e, *4137*
Rev 20: 7 And when the thousand years are e, Satan *5055*

EXPLOITS (2)
Da 11:28 he shall do e, and return to his own land. NIH
11:32 know their God shall be strong, and do e. NIH

EXPLORE See ESPIED; ESPY

EXPOSE See REPROOF; REPROVE

EXPOUND (1) [EXPOUNDED]
Jdg 14:14 they could not *in* three days e the riddle. 5046

EXPOUNDED (6) [EXPOUND]
Jdg 14:19 *of garments* unto them which e the riddle. 5046
Mk 4:34 *were* alone, he e all *things* to his disciples. *1956*
Lk 24:27 he e unto them in all the scriptures *1329*
Ac 11: 4 *and* e *it* by order unto them, saying, *1620*
18:26 e unto him the way of God more perfectly. *1620*
28:23 to whom he e and testified the kingdom of *1620*

EXPRESS (1) [EXPRESSED, EXPRESSLY]
Heb 1: 3 and the **e image** of his person, and *5481*

EXPRESSED (6) [EXPRESS]
Nu 1:17 Aaron took these men which are e by *their* 5344
1Ch 12:31 which were e by name, to come and make 5344
16:41 rest that were chosen, who were e by name, 5344
2Ch 28:15 the men which were e by name rose up, 5344
31:19 several city, the men that were e by name, 5344
Ezr 8:20 all of them were e by name. 5344

EXPRESSLY (3) [EXPRESS]
1Sa 20:21 If I **e say** unto the lad, Behold, 559+559
Eze 1: 3 The word of the LORD **came e** 1961+1961

1Ti 4: 1 Now the Spirit speaketh **e**, that in the latter *4490*

EXTEND (2) [EXTENDED, EXTENDETH]
Ps 109:12 Let there be none to **e** mercy **unto** him: 4900
Isa 66:12 I will **e** peace to her like a river, and 5186

EXTENDED (2) [EXTEND]
Ezr 7:28 hath **e** mercy unto me before the king, and 5186
9: 9 hath **e** mercy unto us in the sight of 5186

EXTENDETH (1) [EXTEND]
Ps 16: 2 *art* my Lord: my goodness **e** not to thee; NIH

EXTINCT (2)
Job 17: 1 My breath is corrupt, my days are **e**, 2193
Isa 43:17 they are **e**, they are quenched as tow. 1846

EXTINGUISHED See EXTINCT

EXTOL (4) [EXTOLLED]
Ps 30: 1 I will **e** thee, O LORD; for thou hast lifted 7311
68: 4 **e** him that rideth upon the heavens by his 5549
145: 1 I will **e** thee, my God, O king; and I will 7311
Da 4:37 and **e** and honour the King of heaven, 7313

EXTOLLED (2) [EXTOL]
Ps 66:17 my mouth, and *he was* **e** with my tongue. 7311
Isa 52:13 he shall be exalted and **e**, and be very high. 5375

EXTORTION (2) [EXTORTIONER, EXTORTIONERS]
Eze 22:12 hast greedily gained of thy neighbours by **e**, 6233
Mt 23:25 but within they are full of **e** and excess. *724*

EXTORTIONER (3) [EXTORTION]
Ps 109:11 Let the **e** catch all that he hath; and let 5383
Isa 16: 4 for the **e** is at an end, the spoiler ceaseth, 4160
1Co 5:11 an idolater, or a railer, or a drunkard, or an **e**; *727*

EXTORTIONERS (3) [EXTORTION]
Lk 18:11 that I am not as other men *are*, **e**, unjust, *727*
1Co 5:10 or with the covetous, or **e**, or with idolaters; *727*
6:10 nor drunkards, nor revilers, nor **e**, *727*

EXTREME (1) [EXTREMITY]
Dt 28:22 with an **e burning**, and with the sword, and 2746

EXTREMITY (1) [EXTREME]
Job 35:15 his anger; yet he knoweth *it* not in great **e**: 6580

EYE (116) [EYE'S, EYEBROWS, EYED, EYELIDS, EYES, EYESALVE, EYESERVICE, EYESIGHT, EYEWITNESSES]
Ex 21:24 **E** for eye, tooth for tooth, hand for hand, 5869
21:24 Eye for **e**, tooth for tooth, hand for hand, 5869
21:26 if a man smite the **e** of his servant, or 5869
21:26 or the **e** of his maid, that it perish; 5869
Lev 21:20 or that hath a blemish in his **e**, or be scurvy, 5869
24:20 for breach, **e** for eye, tooth for tooth: 5869
24:20 for breach, eye for **e**, tooth for tooth: 5869
Dt 7:16 thine **e** shall have no pity upon them: 5869
13: 8 neither shall thine **e** pity him, neither shalt 5869
15: 9 thine **e** be evil against thy poor brother, and 5869
19:13 Thine **e** shall not pity him, but thou shalt 5869
19:21 thine **e** shall not pity; *but* life *shall go* for 5869
19:21 **e** for eye, tooth for tooth, hand for hand, 5869
19:21 eye for **e**, tooth for tooth, hand for hand, 5869
25:12 cut off her hand, thine **e** shall not pity *her*. 5869
28:54 his **e** shall be evil toward his brother, and 5869
28:56 her **e** shall be evil towards the husband of 5869
32:10 he kept him as the apple of his **e**. 5869
34: 7 his **e** was not dim, nor his natural force 5869
1Sa 24:10 *mine* **e** spared thee; and I said, I will not put NIH
2Sa 22:25 according to my cleanness in his **e sight**. 5869
Ezr 5: 5 the **e** of their God was upon the elders of 5870
Job 7: 7 life *is* wind: mine **e** shall no more see good. 5869
7: 8 The **e** of him that hath seen me shall see me 5869
10:18 given up the ghost, and no **e** had seen me! 5869
13: 1 mine **e** hath seen all *this*, mine ear hath 5869
16:20 *but* mine **e** poureth out *tears* unto God. 5869
17: 2 *doth not* mine **e** continue in their 5869
17: 7 Mine **e** also is dim by reason of sorrow, and 5869
20: 9 The **e** also *which* saw him shall *see him* no 5869
24:15 The **e** also of the adulterer waiteth for 5869
24:15 for the twilight, saying, No **e** shall see me: 5869
28: 7 and which the vulture's **e** hath not seen: 5869
28:10 and his **e** seeth every precious thing. 5869
29:11 when the **e** saw *me*, it gave witness to me: 5869
42: 5 of the ear: but now mine **e** seeth thee. 5869
Ps 6: 7 Mine **e** is consumed because of grief; 5869
17: 8 Keep me as the apple of the **e**, hide me 5869
31: 9 mine **e** is consumed with grief, *yea*, my 5869
32: 8 thou shalt go: I will guide thee with mine **e**. 5869
33:18 the **e** of the LORD *is* upon them that fear 5869
35:19 *neither* let them wink *with* the **e** that hate 5869
35:21 *and* said, Aha, aha, our **e** hath seen *it*. 5869
54: 7 mine **e** hath seen *his desire* upon mine 5869
88: 9 Mine **e** mourneth by reason of affliction: 5869
92:11 Mine **e** also shall see *my desire* on mine 5869
94: 9 he that formed the **e**, shall he not see? 5869
Pr 7: 2 live; and my law as the apple of thine **e**. 5869
10:10 He that winketh *with* the **e** causeth sorrow: 5869
20:12 The hearing ear, and the seeing **e**, 5869
22: 9 He that hath a bountiful **e** shall be blessed; 5869
23: 6 not the bread of *him that hath* an evil **e**, 5869
28:22 He that hasteth to be rich *hath* an evil **e**, and 5869
30:17 The **e** *that* mocketh at *his* father, and 5869
Ecc 1: 8 man cannot utter *it*: the **e** is not satisfied 5869
4: 8 neither is his **e** satisfied *with* riches; 5869
Isa 13:18 the womb; their **e** shall not spare children. 5869
52: 8 for they shall see **e** to eye, when 5869
52: 8 for they shall see eye to **e**, when 5869
64: 4 neither hath the **e** seen, O God, 5869
Jer 13:17 mine **e** shall weep sore, and run down *with* 5869
La 1:16 mine **e**, mine eye runneth down *with* water, 5869
1:16 mine **e** runneth down *with* water, because 5869
2: 4 slew all *that were* pleasant to the **e**, in 5869
2:18 no rest; let not the apple of thine **e** cease. 5869
3:48 Mine **e** runneth down *with* rivers of water 5869
3:49 Mine **e** trickleth down, and ceaseth not, 5869
3:51 Mine **e** affecteth mine heart because of all 5869
Eze 5:11 diminish *thee*; neither shall mine **e** spare, 5869
7: 4 mine **e** shall not spare thee, neither will I 5869
7: 9 mine **e** shall not spare, neither will I have 5869
8:18 mine **e** shall not spare, neither will I have 5869
9: 5 let not your **e** spare, neither have ye pity: 5869
9:10 *as for* me also, mine **e** shall not spare, 5869
16: 5 None **e** pitied thee, to do any of these unto 5869
20:17 Nevertheless mine **e** spared them from 5869
Mic 4:11 be defiled, and let our **e** look upon Zion. 5869
Zec 2: 8 toucheth you toucheth the apple of his **e**. 5869
11:17 *shall be* upon his arm, and upon his right **e**: 5869
11:17 and his right **e** shall be utterly darkened. 5869
Mt 5:29 And if thy right **e** offend thee, pluck it out, *3788*
5:38 An **e** for an eye, and a tooth for a tooth: *3788*
5:38 An eye for an **e**, and a tooth for a tooth: *3788*
6:22 The light of the body is the **e**: if therefore *3788*
6:22 if therefore thine **e** be single, thy whole *3788*
6:23 But if thine **e** be evil, thy whole body shall *3788*
7: 3 thou the mote that is in thy brother's **e**, *3788*
7: 3 not the beam that is in thine own **e**? *3788*
7: 4 Let me pull out the mote out of thine **e**; *3788*
7: 4 and behold, a beam *is* in thine own **e**? *3788*
7: 5 first cast out the beam out of thine own **e**; *3788*
7: 5 to cast out the mote out of thy brother's **e**. *3788*
18: 9 And if thine **e** offend thee, pluck it out, and *3788*
18: 9 better for thee to enter into life with **one e**, *3442*
19:24 It is easier for a camel to go through the **e** *5169*
20:15 what I will with mine own? Is thine **e** evil, *3788*
Mk 7:22 an evil **e**, blasphemy, pride, foolishness: *3788*
9:47 And if thine **e** offend thee, pluck it out: it is *3788*
9:47 enter into the kingdom of God with **one e**, *3442*
10:25 It is easier for a camel to go through the **e** *5168*
Lk 6:41 thou the mote that is in thy brother's **e**, *3788*
6:41 not the beam that is in thine own **e**? *3788*
6:42 let me pull out the mote that is in thine **e**, *3788*
6:42 not the beam that is in thine own **e**? *3788*
6:42 cast out first the beam out of thine own **e**, *3788*
6:42 pull out the mote that is in thy brother's **e**. *3788*
11:34 The light of the body is the **e**: *3788*
11:34 therefore when thine **e** is single, thy whole *3788*
11:34 but when *thine* **e** is evil, thy body also *is* full NIG
18:25 for a camel to go through a needle's **e**, *5168*
1Co 2: 9 it is written, **E** hath not seen, nor ear heard, *3788*
12:16 Because I am not the **e**, I am not of *3788*
12:17 If the whole body *were* an **e**, where *were* *3788*
12:21 And the **e** cannot say unto the hand, I have *3788*
15:52 In a moment, in the twinkling of an **e**, at *3788*
Rev 1: 7 and every **e** shall see him, and they *also* *3788*

EYE'S (1) [EYE]
Ex 21:26 he shall let him go free for his **e** sake. 5869

EYEBROWS (1) [EYE, BROW]
Lev 14: 9 off his head and his beard and his **e**, 1354+5869

EYED (2) [EYE]
Ge 29:17 Leah was tender **e**; but Rachel was 5869
1Sa 18: 9 Saul **e** David from that day and forward. 5770

EYELIDS (9) [EYE]
Job 16:16 and on mine **e** *is* the shadow of death; 6079
41:18 and his eyes *are* like the **e** of the morning. 6079
Ps 11: 4 his eyes behold, his **e** try, the children of 6079
132: 4 sleep to mine eyes, *or* slumber to mine **e**, 6079
Pr 4:25 and let thine **e** look straight before thee. 6079
6: 4 sleep to thine eyes, nor slumber to thine **e**. 6079
6:25 neither let her take thee with her **e**. 6079
30:13 are their eyes! and their **e** are lifted up. 6079
Jer 9:18 *with* tears, and our **e** gush out with waters. 6079

EYES (501) [EYE]
Ge 3: 5 your **e** shall be opened, and ye shall be as 5869
3: 6 that it *was* pleasant to the **e**, and a tree to be 5869
3: 7 the **e** of them both were opened, and 5869
6: 8 Noah found grace in the **e** of the LORD. 5869
13:10 Lot lifted up his **e**, and beheld all the plain 5869
13:14 Lift up now thine **e**, and look from 5869
16: 4 her mistress was despised in her **e**. 5869
16: 5 she had conceived, I was despised in her **e**: 5869
18: 2 he lift up his **e** and looked, and lo, 5869
19: 8 and do ye to them as *is* good in your **e**: 5869
20:16 behold, he *is* to thee a covering of the **e**, 5869
21:19 God opened her **e**, and she saw a well of 5869
22: 4 on the third day Abraham lift up his **e**, 5869
22:13 Abraham lifted up his **e**, and looked, and 5869
24:63 he lift up his **e**, and saw, and, behold, 5869
24:64 Rebekah lift up her **e**, and when she saw 5869
27: 1 his **e** were dim, so that he could not see, 5869
30:27 pray thee, if I have found favour in thine **e**, 5869
30:41 that Jacob laid the rods before the **e** of 5869
31:10 that I lifted up mine **e**, and saw in a dream, 5869
31:12 he said, Lift up now thine **e**, and see, all 5869
31:40 and my sleep departed from mine **e**. 5869
33: 1 Jacob lifted up his **e**, and looked, and 5869
33: 5 he lift up his **e**, and saw the women and 5869
34:11 Let me find grace in your **e**, and what ye 5869
37:25 they lift up their **e** and looked, and behold, 5869
39: 7 that his master's wife cast her **e** upon 5869
41:37 the thing was good in the **e** of Pharaoh, 5869
41:37 of Pharaoh, and in the **e** of all his servants. 5869
42:24 and bound him before their **e**. 5869
43:29 he lift up his **e**, and saw his brother 5869
44:21 unto me, that I may set mine **e** upon him. 5869
45:12 your **e** see, and the eyes of my brother 5869
45:12 eyes see, and the **e** of my brother Benjamin, 5869
46: 4 and Joseph shall put his hand upon thine **e**. 5869
47:19 Wherefore shall we die before thine **e**, 5869
48:10 Now the **e** of Israel were dim for age, *so* 5869
49:12 *His* **e** *shall be* red with wine, and *his* teeth 5869
50: 4 If now I have found grace in your **e**, speak, 5869
Ex 5:21 savour to be abhorred in the **e** of Pharaoh, 5869
5:21 in the **e** of his servants, to put a sword in 5869
8:26 of the Egyptians before their **e**, 5869
13: 9 for a memorial between thine **e**, that 5869
13:16 and for frontlets between thine **e**: 5869
14:10 the children of Israel lift up their **e**, and 5869
24:17 the mount in the **e** of the children of Israel. 5869
Lev 4:13 the thing be hid from the **e** of the assembly, 5869
20: 4 do any ways hide their **e** from the man, 5869
26:16 that shall consume the **e**, and cause sorrow 5869
Nu 5:13 it be hid from the **e** of her husband, and 5869
10:31 and thou mayest be to us instead of **e**. 5869
11: 6 at all, beside *this* manna, *before* our **e**. 5869
15:39 not after your own heart and your own **e**, 5869
16:14 wilt thou put out the **e** of these men? 5869
20: 8 and speak ye unto the rock before their **e**; 5869
20:12 to sanctify me in the **e** of the children of 5869
22:31 the LORD opened the **e** of Balaam, and 5869
24: 2 Balaam lift up his **e**, and he saw Israel 5869
24: 3 and the man whose **e** are open hath said: 5869
24: 4 falling *into a trance*, but having his **e** open: 5869
24:15 and the man whose **e** are open hath said: 5869
24:16 falling *into a trance*, but having his **e** open: 5869
27:14 to sanctify me at the water before their **e**: 5869
33:55 let remain of them *shall be* pricks in your **e**, 5869
Dt 1:30 that he did for you in Egypt before your **e**; 5869
3:21 Thine **e** have seen all that the LORD your 5869
3:27 lift up thine **e** westward, and northward, 5869
3:27 eastward, and behold *it* with thine **e**: 5869
4: 3 Your **e** have seen what the LORD did 5869
4: 9 lest thou forget the things which thine **e** 5869
4:19 lest thou lift up thine **e** unto heaven, and 5869
4:34 God did for you in Egypt before your **e**? 5869
6: 8 they shall be as frontlets between thine **e**. 5869
6:22 and upon all his household, before our **e**: 5869
7:19 The great temptations which thine **e** saw, 5869
9:17 two hands, and brake them before your **e**. 5869
10:21 and terrible *things*, which thine **e** have seen. 5869
11: 7 your **e** have seen all the great acts of 5869
11:12 the **e** of the LORD thy God *are* always 5869
11:18 they may be as frontlets between your **e**. 5869
12: 8 every man whatsoever *is* right in his own **e**. 5869
13:18 to do *that which is* right in the **e** of 5869
14: 1 nor make *any* baldness between your **e** for 5869
16:19 for a gift doth blind the **e** of the wise, and 5869
21: 7 shed this blood, neither have our **e** seen *it*. 5869
24: 1 to pass that she find no favour in his **e**, 5869
28:31 Thine ox *shall be* slain before thine **e**, and 5869
28:32 thine **e** shall look, and fail *with longing* for 5869
28:34 for the sight of thine **e** which thou shalt see. 5869
28:65 and failing of **e**, and sorrow of mind: 5869
28:67 for the sight of thine **e** which thou shalt see. 5869
29: 2 your **e** in the land of Egypt unto Pharaoh, 5869
29: 3 The great temptations which thine **e** have 5869
29: 4 and **e** to see, and ears to hear, unto this day. 5869
34: 4 I have caused thee to see *it* with thine **e**, but 5869
Jos 5:13 that he lift up his **e** and looked, and behold, 5869
23:13 in your sides, and thorns in your **e**, 5869
24: 7 your **e** have seen what I have done in 5869
Jdg 16:21 put out his **e**, and brought him down to 5869
16:28 avenged of the Philistines for my two **e**. 5869
17: 6 man did *that* which *was* right in his own **e**. 5869
19:17 when he had lift up his **e**, he saw a 5869
21:25 man did *that* which *was* right in his own **e**. 5869
Ru 2: 9 *Let* thine **e** *be* on the field that they do reap, 5869
2:10 Why have I found grace in thine **e**, 5869
1Sa 2:33 *shall be* to consume thine **e**, and to grieve 5869
3: 2 his **e** began *to wax* dim, *that* he could not 5869
4:15 and his **e** were dim, that he could not see. 5869
6:13 they lifted up their **e**, and saw the ark, and 5869
11: 2 that *I* may thrust out all your right **e**, and 5869
12: 3 *any* bribe to blind mine **e** therewith? 5869
12:16 which the LORD will do before your **e**. 5869
14:27 to his mouth; and his **e** were enlightened. 5869
14:29 how mine **e** have been enlightened, because 5869
20: 3 knoweth that I have found grace in thine **e**; 5869
20:29 and now, if I have found favour in thine **e**, 5869
24:10 this day thine **e** have seen how that 5869
25: 8 let the young men find favour in thine **e**: 5869
26:21 my soul was precious in thine **e** this day: 5869
26:24 thy life was much set by this day in mine **e**, 5869
26:24 let my life be much set by in the **e** of 5869
27: 5 If I have now found grace in thine **e**, 5869
2Sa 6:20 who uncovered himself to day in the **e** of 5869
12:11 and I will take thy wives before thine **e**, and 5869
13:34 young man that kept the watch lift up his **e**, 5869
15:25 if I shall find favour in the **e** of the LORD, 5869
18:24 lift up his **e**, and looked, and behold a man 5869
19:27 do therefore what *is* good in thine **e**. 5869
22:28 thine **e** *are* upon the haughty, *that* thou 5869
24: 3 *that* the **e** of my lord the king may see *it*: 5869
1Ki 1:20 O king, the **e** of all Israel *are* upon thee, 5869
1:48 my throne *this* day, mine **e** even seeing *it*. 5869
8:29 That thine **e** may be open toward this house 5869
8:52 That thine **e** may be open unto 5869
9: 3 mine **e** and mine heart shall be there 5869
10: 7 I came, and mine **e** had seen *it*: and behold, 5869
11:33 to do *that* which *is* right in mine **e**, and 5869
14: 4 for his **e** were set by reason of his age. 5869
14: 8 to do *that* only which *was* right in mine **e**; 5869
15: 5 which *was* right in the **e** of the LORD, 5869
15:11 Asa did *that* which *was* right in the **e** of 5869
16:25 Omri wrought evil in the **e** of the LORD, 5869
20: 6 *that* whatsoever *is* pleasant in thine **e**, 5869
22:43 doing *that* which *was* right in the **e** of 5869
2Ki 4:34 his **e** upon his eyes, and his hands upon his 5869
4:34 his eyes upon his **e**, and his hands upon his 5869
4:35 seven times, and the child opened his **e**. 5869
6:17 said, LORD, I pray thee, open his **e**, 5869
6:17 the LORD opened the **e** of the young man; 5869

2Ki 6:20 open the **e** of these *men,* that they may see. 5869
6:20 the LORD opened their **e**, and they saw; 5869
7: 2 thou shalt see *it* with thine **e**, but shalt not 5869
7:19 thou shalt see *it* with thine **e**, but shalt not 5869
10: 5 do thou *that* which *is* good in thine **e**. 5869
10:30 in executing *that* which *is* right in mine **e**, 5869
19:16 open, LORD, thine **e**, and see: and 5869
19:22 *thy* voice, and lift up thine **e** on high? 5869
22:20 thine **e** shall not see all the evil which I will 5869
25: 7 they slew the sons of Zedekiah before his **e**, 5869
25: 7 put out the **e** of Zedekiah, and bound him 5869
1Ch 13: 4 for the thing was right in the **e** of all 5869
17:17 *yet* this was a small thing in thine **e**, O God; 5869
21:16 David lift up his **e**, and saw the angel of 5869
21:23 lord the king do *that* which *is* good in his **e**: 5869
2Ch 6:20 That thine **e** may be open upon this house 5869
6:40 thine **e** be open, and *let* thine ears *be* attent 5869
7:15 Now mine **e** shall be open, and mine ears 5869
7:16 mine **e** and mine heart shall be there 5869
9: 6 I came, and mine **e** had seen *it:* and behold, 5869
14: 2 and right in the **e** of the LORD his God: 5869
16: 9 For the **e** of the LORD run to and 5869
20:12 we what to do: but our **e** *are* upon thee. 5869
21: 6 he wrought *that* which *was* evil in the **e** of 5869
29: 6 done *that* which *was* evil in the **e** of 5869
29: 8 and to hissing, as ye see with your **e**. 5869
34:28 neither shall thine **e** see all the evil that I 5869
Ezr 3:12 of this house was laid before their **e**, 5869
9: 8 that our God may lighten our **e**, and give us 5869
Ne 1: 6 ear now be attentive, and thine **e** open, 5869
6:16 they were much cast down in their own **e**: 5869
Est 1:17 *they* shall despise their husbands in their **e**, 5869
8: 5 before the king, and I *be* pleasing in his **e**, 5869
Job 2:12 when they lift up their **e** afar off, and 5869
3:10 nor hid sorrow from mine **e**. 5869
4:16 an image *was* before mine **e**, *there was* 5869
7: 8 shall see me no *more:* thine **e** *are* upon me, 5869
10: 4 Hast thou **e** of flesh? or seest thou as man 5869
11: 4 doctrine *is* pure, and I am clean in thine **e**. 5869
11:20 the **e** of the wicked shall fail, and they shall 5869
14: 3 dost thou open thine **e** upon such a one, 5869
15:12 thee away? and what do thine **e** wink at, 5869
16: 9 mine enemy sharpeneth his **e** upon me. 5869
17: 5 even the **e** of his children shall fail. 5869
19:27 and mine **e** shall behold, and not another; 5869
21: 8 and their offspring before their **e**. 5869
21:20 His **e** shall see his destruction, and he shall 5869
24:23 he resteth; yet his **e** *are* upon their ways. 5869
27:19 be gathered: he openeth his **e**, and he *is* not. 5869
28:21 Seeing it is hid from the **e** of all living, and 5869
29:15 I was **e** to the blind, and feet *was* I to 5869
31: 1 I made a covenant with mine **e**; why then 5869
31: 7 mine heart walked after mine **e**, and *if any* 5869
31:16 or have caused the **e** of the widow to fail; 5869
32: 1 because he *was* righteous in his own **e**. 5869
34:21 For his **e** *are* upon the ways of man, and 5869
36: 7 He withdraweth not his **e** from 5869
39:29 seeketh the prey, *and* her **e** behold afar off. 5869
40:24 He taketh it with his **e**: *his* nose pierceth 5869
41:18 his **e** *are* like the eyelids of the morning. 5869
Ps 10: 8 his **e** are privily set against the poor. 5869
11: 4 his **e** behold, his eyelids try, the children of 5869
13: 3 lighten mine **e**, lest I sleep the *sleep of* 5869
15: 4 In whose **e** a vile *person* is contemned; but 5869
17: 2 let thine **e** behold the things that are equal. 5869
17:11 they have set their **e** bowing down to 5869
19: 8 of the LORD *is* pure, enlightening the **e**. 5869
25:15 Mine **e** *are* ever towards the LORD; for he 5869
26: 3 For thy lovingkindness *is* before mine **e**: 5869
31:22 my haste, I am cut off from before thine **e**: 5869
34:15 The **e** of the LORD *are* upon 5869
36: 1 *that there is* no fear of God before his **e**. 5869
36: 2 For he flattereth himself in his own **e**, 5869
38:10 as for the light of mine **e**, it also is gone 5869
50:21 and set *them* in order before thine **e**. 5869
66: 7 his power for ever; his **e** behold the nations: 5869
69: 3 mine **e** fail while *I* wait for my God. 5869
69:23 Let their **e** be darkened, that *they* see not; 5869
73: 7 Their **e** stand out with fatness: they have 5869
77: 4 Thou holdest mine **e** waking: I am *so* 5869
91: 8 Only with thine **e** shalt thou behold and 5869
101: 3 I will set no wicked thing before mine **e**: 5869
101: 6 Mine **e** *shall be* upon the faithful of 5869
115: 5 speak not: **e** have they, but they see not: 5869
116: 8 mine **e** from tears, *and* my feet from falling. 5869
118:23 LORD'S doing; it is marvellous in our **e**. 5869
119:18 Open thou mine **e**, that I may behold 5869
119:37 Turn away mine **e** from beholding vanity; 5869
119:82 Mine **e** fail for thy word, saying, When wilt 5869
119:123 Mine **e** fail for thy salvation, and for 5869
119:136 Rivers of waters run down mine **e**, because 5869
119:148 Mine **e** prevent the *night* watches, that *I* 5869
121: 1 I will lift up mine **e** unto the hills, 5869
123: 1 Unto thee lift I up mine **e**, O thou that 5869
123: 2 as the **e** of servants *look* unto the hand of 5869
123: 2 as the **e** of a maiden unto the hand of her 5869
123: 2 so our **e** *wait* upon the LORD our God, 5869
131: 1 my heart is not haughty, nor mine **e** lofty: 5869
132: 4 I will not give sleep to mine **e**, *or* 5869
135:16 speak not; **e** have they, but they see not; 5869
139:16 Thine **e** did see my substance, yet being 5869
141: 8 mine **e** *are* unto thee, O GOD the Lord: 5869
145:15 The **e** of all wait upon thee; and thou givest 5869
146: 8 The LORD openeth *the* **e** *of* the blind: NIH
Pr 3: 7 Be not wise in thine own **e**: fear 5869
3:21 My son, let not them depart from thine **e**: 5869
4:21 Let them not depart from thine **e**; 5869
4:25 Let thine **e** look right on, and let thine 5869
5:21 For the ways of man *are* before the **e** of 5869
6: 4 Give not sleep to thine **e**, nor slumber to 5869
6:13 He winketh with his **e**, he speaketh with his 5869
10:26 as smoke to the **e**, so *is* the sluggard to 5869
12:15 The way of a fool *is* right in his own **e**: but 5869
15: 3 The **e** of the LORD *are* in every place, 5869
15:30 The light of the **e** rejoiceth the heart: *and* 5869
16: 2 the ways of a man *are* clean in his own **e**; 5869
16:30 He shutteth his **e** to devise froward things: 5869
17: 8 A gift *is as* a precious stone in the **e** of him 5869
17:24 the **e** of a fool *are* in the ends of the earth. 5869
20: 8 scattereth *away* all evil with his **e**. 5869
20:13 open thine **e**, *and* thou shalt be satisfied 5869
21: 2 Every way of a man *is* right in his own **e**: 5869
21:10 his neighbour findeth no favour in his **e**. 5869
22:12 The **e** of the LORD preserve knowledge, 5869
23: 5 Wilt thou set thine **e** upon that which is 5869
23:26 and let thine **e** observe my ways. 5869
23:29 without cause? who hath redness of **e**? 5869
23:33 Thine **e** shall behold strange *women,* and 5869
25: 7 of the prince whom thine **e** have seen. 5869
27:20 so the **e** of man are never satisfied. 5869
28:27 he that hideth his **e** shall have many a 5869
29:13 the LORD lighteneth both their **e**. 5869
30:12 *is* a generation *that are* pure in their own **e**, 5869
30:13 *is* a generation, O how lofty are their **e**! 5869
Ecc 2:10 whatsoever mine **e** desired I kept not from 5869
2:14 The wise *man's* **e** *are* in his head; but 5869
5:11 saving the beholding *of them* with their **e**? 5869
6: 9 Better *is* the sight of the **e** than 5869
8:16 day nor night seeth sleep with his **e**:) 5869
11: 7 a pleasant *thing it is* for the **e** to behold 5869
11: 9 of thine heart, and in the sight of thine **e**: 5869
SS 1:15 behold, thou *art* fair; thou *hast* doves' **e**. 5869
4: 1 *art* fair; thou *hast* doves' **e** within thy locks: 5869
4: 9 hast ravished my heart with one of thine **e**, 5869
5:12 His **e** *are* as *the eyes of* doves by the rivers 5869
5:12 His eyes *are* as *the* **e** *of* doves by the rivers NIH
6: 5 Turn away thine **e** from me, for they have 5869
7: 4 thine **e** *like* the *fish*pools in Heshbon, 5869
8:10 then was I in his **e** as one that found favour. 5869
Isa 1:15 your hands, I will hide mine **e** from you: 5869
1:16 the evil of your doings from before mine **e**; 5869
3: 8 the LORD, to provoke the **e** of his glory. 5869
3:16 with stretched forth necks and wanton **e**, 5869
5:15 and the **e** of the lofty shall be humbled: 5869
5:21 Woe unto *them that are* wise in their own **e**, 5869
6: 5 for mine **e** have seen the King, the LORD 5869
6:10 and make their ears heavy, and shut their **e**; 5869
6:10 lest they see with their **e**, and hear with 5869
11: 3 he shall not judge after the sight of his **e**, 5869
13:16 shall be dashed to pieces before their **e**; 5869
17: 7 his **e** shall have respect to the Holy One of 5869
29:10 spirit of deep sleep, and hath closed your **e**: 5869
29:18 the **e** of the blind shall see out of obscurity, 5869
30:20 any more, but thine **e** shall see thy teachers: 5869
32: 3 the **e** of them that see shall not be dim, and 5869
33:15 and shutteth his **e** from seeing evil; 5869
33:17 Thine **e** shall see the king in his beauty: 5869
33:20 thine **e** shall see Jerusalem a quiet 5869

Isa 35: 5 Then the **e** of the blind shall be opened, and 5869
37:17 and hear; open thine **e**, O LORD, and see: 5869
37:23 *thy* voice, and lifted up thine **e** on high? 5869
38:14 mine **e** fail *with looking* upward: 5869
40:26 Lift up your **e** on high, and behold who 5869
42: 7 To open the blind **e**, to bring out 5869
43: 8 Bring forth the blind people that have **e**, 5869
44:18 for he hath shut their **e**, that *they* cannot 5869
49: 5 yet shall I be glorious in the **e** of 5869
49:18 Lift up thine **e** round about, and behold: 5869
51: 6 Lift up your **e** to the heavens, and 5869
52:10 bare his holy arm in the **e** of all the nations; 5869
59:10 the blind, and we grope as if *we had* no **e**: 5869
60: 4 Lift up thine **e** round about, and see: 5869
65:12 did evil before mine **e**, and did choose *that* 5869
65:16 and because they are hid from mine **e**. 5869
66: 4 they did evil before mine **e**, and chose *that* 5869
Jer 3: 2 Lift up thine **e** unto the high places, and 5869
5: 3 O LORD, *are* not thine **e** upon the truth? 5869
5:21 which have **e**, and see not; which have ears, 5869
7:11 become a den of robbers in your **e**? 5869
9: 1 mine **e** a fountain of tears, that I might 5869
9:18 that our **e** may run down *with* tears, and 5869
13:20 Lift up your **e**, and behold them that come 5869
14: 6 their **e** did fail, because *there was* no grass. 5869
14:17 Let mine **e** run down *with* tears night and 5869
16: 9 cause to cease out of this place in your **e**, 5869
16:17 For mine **e** *are* upon all their ways: they are 5869
16:17 neither is their iniquity hid from mine **e**. 5869
20: 4 thine **e** *shall* behold *it;* and I will give all 5869
22:17 thine **e** and thine heart *are* not but for thy 5869
24: 6 For I will set mine **e** upon them for good, 5869
29:21 and he shall slay them before your **e**; 5869
31:16 voice from weeping, and thine **e** from tears: 5869
32: 4 to mouth, and his **e** shall behold his eyes: 5869
32: 4 to mouth, and his eyes shall behold his **e**: 5869
32:19 for thine **e** *are* open upon all the ways of 5869
34: 3 thine **e** shall behold the eyes of the king of 5869
34: 3 thine eyes shall behold the **e** of the king of 5869
39: 6 the sons of Zedekiah in Riblah before his **e**: 5869
39: 7 Moreover he put out Zedekiah's **e**, and 5869
42: 2 *but* a few of many, as thine **e** do behold us:) 5869
52: 2 he did *that* which *was* evil in the **e** of 5869
52:10 slew the sons of Zedekiah before his **e**: 5869
52:11 he put out the **e** of Zedekiah; and the king 5869
La 2:11 Mine **e** do fail with tears, my bowels are 5869
4:17 for us, our **e** as yet failed for our vain help: 5869
5:17 heart is faint; for these *things* our **e** are dim. 5869
Eze 1:18 their rings *were* full *of* **e** round about them 5869
6: 9 hath departed from me, and with their **e**, 5869
8: 5 lift up thine **e** now the way towards 5869
8: 5 So I lift up mine **e** the way toward 5869
10:12 and the wheels, *were* full *of* **e** round about, 5869
12: 2 which have **e** to see, and see not; 5869
12:12 that he see not the ground with *his* **e**. 5869
18: 6 neither hath lift up his **e** to the idols of 5869
18:12 and hath lift up his **e** to the idols, 5869
18:15 neither hath lift up his **e** to the idols of 5869
20: 7 away every man the abominations of his **e**, 5869
20: 8 man cast away the abominations of their **e**, 5869
20:24 and their **e** were after their fathers' idols. 5869
21: 6 and with bitterness sigh before their **e**. 5869
22:26 have hid their **e** from my sabbaths, and 5869
23:16 as soon as she saw them with her **e**, 5869
23:27 that thou shalt not lift up thine **e** unto them, 5869
23:40 thou didst wash *thyself,* paintedst thy **e**, 5869
24:16 I take away from thee the desire of thine **e** 5869
24:21 the desire of your **e**, and that which your 5869
24:25 the desire of their **e**, and that whereupon 5869
33:25 lift up your **e** toward your idols, and 5869
36:23 I shall be sanctified in you before their **e**. 5869
37:20 writest shall be in thine hand before their **e**. 5869
38:16 be sanctified in thee, O Gog, before their **e**. 5869
38:23 I will be known in the **e** of many nations, 5869
40: 4 behold with thine **e**, and hear with thine 5869
44: 5 behold with thine **e**, and hear with thine 5869
Da 4:34 lift up mine **e** unto heaven, 5870
7: 8 in this horn *were* **e** like the eyes of man, 5870
7: 8 in this horn *were* eyes like the **e** of man, 5870
7:20 even *of* that horn that had **e**, and a mouth 5870
8: 3 I lifted up mine **e**, and saw, and behold, 5869
8: 5 the goat *had* a notable horn between his **e**. 5869
8:21 the great horn that *is* between his **e** *is* 5869
9:18 open thine **e**, and behold our desolations, 5869
10: 5 I lift up mine **e**, and looked, and behold, 5869
10: 6 his **e** as lamps of fire, and his arms and 5869
Hos 13:14 repentance shall be hid from mine **e**. 5869
Joel 1:16 Is not the meat cut off before our **e**, *yea,* joy 5869
Am 9: 4 I will set mine **e** upon them for evil, and 5869
9: 8 the **e** of the Lord GOD *are* upon the sinful 5869
Mic 7:10 mine **e** shall behold her: now shall she be 5869
Hab 1:13 *Thou art* of purer **e** than to behold evil, and 5869
Zep 3:20 I turn back your captivity before your **e**, 5869
Hag 2: 3 *is it* not in your **e** in comparison of it as 5869
Zec 1:18 lift I up mine **e**, and saw, and behold four 5869
2: 1 I lift up mine **e** again, and looked, and 5869
3: 9 upon one stone *shall be* seven **e**: 5869
4:10 they *are* the **e** of the LORD, which run to 5869
5: 1 lift up mine **e**, and looked, and behold, 5869
5: 5 Lift up now thine **e**, and see what *is* this 5869
5: 9 lift I up mine **e**, and looked, and behold, 5869
6: 1 and lift up mine **e**, and looked, and behold, 5869
8: 6 If it be marvellous in the **e** of the remnant 5869
8: 6 should it also be marvellous in my **e**? 5869
9: 1 when the **e** of man, as of all the tribes of 5869
9: 8 any more: for now have I seen with mine **e**. 5869
12: 4 I will open mine **e** upon the house of Judah, 5869
14:12 their **e** shall consume away in their holes, 5869
Mal 1: 5 your **e** shall see, and ye shall say, 5869
Mt 9:29 Then touched he their **e**, saying, *3788*
9:30 And their **e** were opened; and Jesus straitly *3788*
13:15 of hearing, and their **e** they have closed; *3788*
13:15 lest at any time they should see with *their* **e**, *3788*
13:16 But blessed *are* your **e**, for they see: and *3788*
17: 8 And when they had lift up their **e**, they saw *3788*
18: 9 rather than having two **e** to be cast into hell *3788*
20:33 unto him, Lord, that our **e** may be opened. *3788*
20:34 compassion *on them,* and touched their **e**: *3788*
20:34 and immediately their **e** received sight, and *3788*
21:42 Lord's doing, and it is marvellous in our **e**? *3788*
26:43 them asleep again: for their **e** were heavy. *3788*
Mk 8:18 Having **e**, see ye not? and having ears, *3788*
8:23 and when he had spit on his **e**, and put *his* *3659*
8:25 that he put *his* hands again upon his **e**, *3788*
9:47 than having two **e** to be cast into hell fire: *3788*
12:11 Lord's doing, and it is marvellous in our **e**? *3788*
14:40 them asleep again, (for their **e** were heavy,) *3788*
Lk 2:30 For mine **e** have seen thy salvation, *3788*
4:20 And the **e** of all *them that were* in *3788*
6:20 And he lifted up his **e** on his disciples, and *3788*
10:23 Blessed *are* the **e** which see *the things* that *3788*
16:23 And in hell he lift up his **e**, being in *3788*
18:13 not lift up so much as *his* **e** unto heaven, *3788*
19:42 but now they are hid from thine **e**. *3788*
24:16 But their **e** were holden that *they* should not *3788*
24:31 And their **e** were opened, and they knew *3788*
Jn 4:35 Lift up your **e**, and look on the fields; *3788*
6: 5 When Jesus then lift up *his* **e**, *3788*
9: 6 he anointed the **e** of the blind man with *3788*
9:10 they unto him, How were thine **e** opened? *3788*
9:11 and anointed mine **e**, and said unto me, Go *3788*
9:14 Jesus made the clay, and opened his **e**. *3788*
9:15 He put clay upon mine **e**, and I washed, *3788*
9:17 thou of him, that he hath opened thine **e**? *3788*
9:21 or who hath opened his **e**, we know not: *3788*
9:26 did he to thee? how opened he thine **e**? *3788*
9:30 he is, and *yet* he hath opened mine **e**. *3788*
9:32 opened the **e** of one that was born blind. *3788*
10:21 a devil. Can a devil open the **e** of the blind? *3788*
11:37 Could not this *man,* which opened the **e** of *3788*
11:41 And Jesus lift up *his* **e**, and said, Father, *3788*
12:40 He hath blinded their **e**, and hardened their *3788*
12:40 that they should not see with *their* **e**, *3788*
17: 1 and lift up his **e** to heaven, and said, Father, *3788*
Ac 3: 4 **fastening** his **e** upon him with John, said, *816*
9: 8 and when his **e** were opened, he saw no *3788*
9:18 And immediately there fell from his **e** as it *3788*
9:40 And she opened her **e**: and when she saw *3788*
11: 6 Upon the which when I had **fastened** mine **e**, *816*
13: 9 filled with the Holy Ghost, **set** his **e** on him, *816*
26:18 To open their **e**, *and* to turn *them* from *3788*
28:27 of hearing, and their **e** have they closed; *3788*
28:27 lest they should see with *their* **e**, and *3788*
Ro 3:18 There is no fear of God before their **e**. *3788*
11: 8 **e** that *they* should not see, and ears that *3788*
11:10 Let their **e** be darkened, that *they* may not *3788*
Gal 3: 1 before whose **e** Jesus Christ hath been *3788*
4:15 ye would have plucked out your own **e**, and *3788*

Eph 1:18 The **e** of your understanding being *3788*
Heb 4:13 opened unto the **e** of him with whom we *3788*
1Pe 3:12 For the **e** of the Lord *are* over the righteous, *3788*
2Pe 2:14 Having **e** full of adultery and that cannot *3788*
1Jn 1: 1 have heard, which we have seen with our **e**, *3788*
2:11 because that darkness hath blinded his **e**. *3788*
2:16 and the lust of the **e**, and the pride of life, *3788*
Rev 1:14 as snow; and his **e** *were* as a flame of fire; *3788*
2:18 who hath his **e** like unto a flame of fire, and *3788*
3:18 and anoint thine **e** *with* eyesalve, that thou *3788*
4: 6 *were* four beasts full of **e** before and *3788*
4: 8 about *him;* and *they were* full of **e** within: *3788*
5: 6 *been* slain, having seven horns and seven **e**, *3788*
7:17 God shall wipe away all tears from their **e**. *3788*
19:12 His **e** *were* as a flame of fire, and on his *3788*
21: 4 God shall wipe away all tears from their **e**; *3788*

EYESALVE (1) [EYE]
Rev 3:18 and anoint thine eyes *with* **e**, that thou *2854*

EYESERVICE (2) [EYE, SERVE]
Eph 6: 6 Not with **e**, as menpleasers; but as *3787*
Col 3:22 not with **e**, as menpleasers; but *3787*

EYESIGHT (1) [EYE, SEE]
Ps 18:24 to the cleanness of my hands in his **e**. 5869

EYEWITNESSES (2) [EYE, WITNESS]
Lk 1: 2 which from the beginning were **e**, and *845*
2Pe 1:16 Jesus Christ, but were **e** of his majesty. *2030*

EZBAI (1)
1Ch 11:37 Hezro the Carmelite, Naarai the son of **E**, 229

EZBON (2)
Ge 46:16 Shuni, and **E**, Eri, and Arodi, and Areli. 675
1Ch 7: 7 **E**, and Uzzi, and Uzziel, and Jerimoth, and 675

EZEKIAS (2) [HEZEKIAH]
Mt 1: 9 Joatham begat Achaz; and Achaz begat **E**; *1478*
1:10 And **E** begat Manasses; and *1478*

EZEKIEL (2)
Eze 1: 3 LORD came expressly unto **E** the priest, 3168
24:24 Thus **E** is unto you a sign: according to all 3168

EZEL (1) [BETH-EZEL]
1Sa 20:19 *in hand,* and shalt remain by the stone **E**. 237

EZEM (1)
1Ch 4:29 And at Bilhah, and at **E**, and at Tolad, 6107

EZER (10)
Ge 36:21 Dishon, and **E**, and Dishan: these *are* 687
36:27 The children of **E** *are* these; Bilhan, and 687
36:30 Duke Dishon, duke **E**, duke Dishan: 687
1Ch 1:38 and Anah, and Dishon, and **E**, and Dishan. 687
1:42 The sons of **E**; Bilhan, and Zavan, *and* 687
4: 4 of Gedor, and **E** the father of Hushah. 5829
7:21 and Shuthelah his son, and **E**, and Elead, 5827
12: 9 **E** the first, Obadiah the second, Eliab 5829
Ne 3:19 next to him repaired **E** the son of Jeshua, 5829
12:42 and Malchijah, and Elam, and **E**. 5829

EZION-GABER (3) [EZION-GEBER]
Nu 33:35 from Ebronah, and encamped at **E**. 6100
33:36 they removed from **E**, and pitched in 6100
Dt 2: 8 from **E**, we turned and passed *by* the way 6100

EZION-GEBER (4) [EZION-GABER]
1Ki 9:26 king Solomon made a navy *of ships* in **E**, 6100
22:48 went not; for the ships were broken at **E**. 6100
2Ch 8:17 went Solomon to **E**, and to Eloth, at the sea 6100
20:36 *to* Tarshish: and they made the ships in **E**. 6100

EZNITE (1)
2Sa 23: 8 the captains; the same *was* Adino the **E**: 6112

EZRA (26)
1Ch 4:17 the sons of **E** *were,* Jether, and Mered, and 5834
Ezr 7: 1 **E** the son of Seraiah, the son of Azariah, 5830
7: 6 This **E** went up from Babylon; and he *was* 5830
7:10 For **E** had prepared his heart to seek 5830
7:11 the king Artaxerxes gave unto **E** the priest, 5830
7:12 Artaxerxes, king of kings, unto **E** the priest, 5831
7:21 that whatsoever **E** the priest, the scribe of 5831
7:25 thou, **E**, after the wisdom of thy God, 5831
10: 1 Now when **E** had prayed, and when he had 5830
10: 2 sons of Elam, answered and said unto **E**, 5830
10: 5 arose **E**, and made the chief priests, 5830
10: 6 **E** rose up from before the house of God, 5830
10:10 **E** the priest stood up, and said unto them, 5830
10:16 **E** the priest, *with* certain chief of 5830
Ne 8: 1 they spake unto **E** the scribe to bring 5830
8: 2 **E** the priest brought the law before 5830
8: 4 **E** the scribe stood upon a pulpit of wood, 5830
8: 5 **E** opened the book in the sight of all 5830
8: 6 **E** blessed the LORD, the great God. 5830
8: 9 **E** the priest the scribe, and the Levites that 5830
8:13 and the Levites, unto **E** the scribe, 5830
12: 1 and Jeshua: Seraiah, Jeremiah, **E**, 5830
12:13 Of **E**, Meshullam; of Amariah, Jehohanan; 5830
12:26 the governor, and of **E** the priest, the scribe. 5830
12:33 And Azariah, **E**, and Meshullam, 5830
12:36 man of God, and **E** the scribe before them. 5830

EZRAHITE (3)
1Ki 4:31 than Ethan the **E**, and Heman, and Chalcol, 250
Ps 88: T Maschil of Heman the **E**. 250
89: T Maschil of Ethan the **E**. 250

EZRI (1)
1Ch 27:26 of the ground *was* **E** the son of Chelub: 5836

F

FABLES (5)
1Ti 1: 4 Neither give heed to **f** and *3454*
4: 7 But refuse profane and old wives' **f**, and *3454*
2Ti 4: 4 from the truth, and shall be turned unto **f**. *3454*
Tit 1:14 Not giving heed to Jewish **f**, and *3454*
2Pe 1:16 we have not followed cunningly devised **f**, *3454*

FACE (416) [FACES]
Ge 1: 2 and darkness *was* upon the **f** of the deep. 6440
1: 2 the Spirit of God moved upon the **f** of 6440
1:29 which *is* upon the **f** of all the earth, and 6440
2: 6 and watered the whole **f** of the ground. 6440
3:19 In the sweat of thy **f** shalt thou eat bread, 639
4:14 thou hast driven me out *this* day from the **f** 6440
4:14 from thy **f** shall I be hid; and I shall be a 6440
6: 1 when men began to multiply on the **f** of 6440
6: 7 I have created from the **f** of the earth; 6440
7: 3 to keep seed alive upon the **f** of all 6440
7: 4 will I destroy from off the **f** of the earth. 6440
7:18 and the ark went upon the **f** of the waters. 6440
7:23 which *was* upon the **f** of the ground, 6440
8: 8 were abated from off the **f** of the ground; 6440
8: 9 for the waters *were* on the **f** of the whole 6440
8:13 and behold, the **f** of the ground was dry. 6440
11: 4 lest we be scattered abroad upon the **f** of 6440
11: 8 from thence upon the **f** of all the earth: 6440
11: 9 them abroad upon the **f** of all the earth. 6440
16: 6 dealt hardly with her, she fled from her **f**. 6440
16: 8 I flee from the **f** of my mistress Sarai. 6440
17: 3 Abram fell on his **f**: and God talked with 6440
17:17 Abraham fell upon his **f**, and laughed, and 6440
19: 1 he bowed himself with his **f** toward 639
19:13 the cry of them is waxen great before the **f** 6440
24:47 I put the earring upon her **f**, and the bracelets 639
30:33 when it shall come for my hire before thy **f**: 6440
31:21 and set his **f** *toward* the mount Gilead. 6440
32:20 before me, and afterward I will see his **f**; 6440
32:30 for I have seen God **f** to face, and my life is 6440
32:30 for I have seen God face to **f**, and my life is 6440
33:10 for therefore I have seen thy **f**, as though I 6440
33:10 as though I had seen the **f** of God, and 6440
35: 1 fleddest from the **f** of Esau thy brother. 6440
35: 7 when he fled from the **f** of his brother. 6440
36: 6 went into the country from the **f** of his 6440
38:15 be a harlot; because she had covered her **f**. 6440
41:56 the famine was over all the **f** of the earth: 6440
43: 3 saying, Ye shall not see my **f**, except your 6440

Ge	43: 5	the man said unto us, Ye shall not see my f,	6440
	43:31	he washed his f, and went out, and	6440
	44:23	down with you, ye shall see my f no more.	6440
	44:26	for we may not see the man's f, except our	6440
	46:28	unto Joseph, to direct his f unto Goshen;	6440
	46:30	since I have seen thy f, because thou *art* yet	6440
	48:11	unto Joseph, I had not thought to see thy f:	6440
	48:12	and he bowed himself with his f to the earth.	639
	50: 1	Joseph fell upon his father's f, and	6440
	50:18	also went and fell down before his f;	6440
Ex	2:15	Moses fled from the f of Pharaoh, and	6440
	3: 6	Moses hid his f; for he was afraid to look	6440
	10: 5	they shall cover the f of the earth, that *one*	5869
	10:15	For they covered the f of the whole earth,	5869
	10:28	take heed to thyself, see my f no more;	6440
	10:28	for in *that* day thou seest my f thou shalt	6440
	10:29	spoken well, I will see thy f again no more.	6440
	14:19	pillar of the cloud went from **before** their f,	6440
	14:25	Let us flee from the f of Israel;	6440
	16:14	upon the f of the wilderness *there lay* a	6440
	32:12	to consume them from the f of the earth?	6440
	33:11	the LORD spake unto Moses f to face,	6440
	33:11	the LORD spake unto Moses face to f,	6440
	33:16	from all the people that *are* upon the f of	6440
	33:20	he said, Thou canst not see my f: for there	6440
	33:23	my back parts: but my f shall not be seen.	6440
	34:29	that Moses wist not that the skin of his f	6440
	34:30	saw Moses, behold, the skin of his f shone;	6440
	34:33	speaking with them, he put a vail on his f.	6440
	34:35	the children of Israel saw the f of Moses,	6440
	34:35	of Moses, that the skin of Moses' f shone:	6440
	34:35	Moses put the vail upon his f again, until he	6440
Lev	13:41	off from the part of *his head toward* his f,	6440
	17:10	I will even set my f against *that* soul that	6440
	19:32	honour the f of the old man, and fear thy	6440
	20: 3	I will set my f against that man, and	6440
	20: 5	I will set my f against that man, and	6440
	20: 6	I will even set my f against that soul, and	6440
	26:17	I will set my f against you, and ye shall be	6440
Nu	6:25	The LORD make his f shine upon thee,	6440
	11:31	as it were two cubits *high* upon the f of	6440
	12: 3	above all the men which *were* upon the f of	6440
	12:14	If her father had but spit in her f,	6440
	14:14	that thou LORD *art* seen f to face, and	5869
	14:14	that thou LORD *art* seen face to f, and	5869
	16: 4	when Moses heard *it,* he fell upon his f:	6440
	19: 3	and *one* shall slay her before his f:	6440
	22: 5	they cover the f of the earth, and they abide	5869
	22:11	of Egypt, which covereth the f of the earth:	5869
	22:31	bowed down his head, and fell flat on his f.	639
	24: 1	but he set his f toward the wilderness.	6440
Dt	1:17	you shall not be afraid of the f of man;	6440
	5: 4	The LORD talked with you f to face in	6440
	5: 4	The LORD talked with you face to f in	6440
	6:15	and destroy thee from off the f of the earth.	6440
	7: 6	above all people that *are* upon the f of	6440
	7:10	repayeth them that hate him to their f,	6440
	7:10	that hateth him, he will repay him to his f.	6440
	8:20	which the LORD destroyeth before your f,	6440
	9: 3	and he shall bring them down before thy f:	6440
	25: 2	to be beaten before his f, according to his	6440
	25: 9	and spit in his f, and shall answer and say,	6440
	28: 7	up against thee *to be* smitten before thy f:	6440
	28:31	*be* violently taken away from before thy f,	6440
	31: 5	LORD shall give them up before your f,	6440
	31:17	I will hide my f from them, and they shall	6440
	31:18	I will surely hide my f in that day for all	6440
	32:20	he said, I will hide my f from them, I will	6440
	34:10	whom the LORD knew f to face,	6440
	34:10	whom the LORD knew face to f,	6440
Jos	5:14	Joshua fell on his f to the earth, and	6440
	7: 6	fell to the earth upon his f before the ark of	6440
	7:10	wherefore liest thou thus upon thy f?	6440
Jdg	6:22	I have seen an angel of the LORD f to	6440
	6:22	have seen an angel of the LORD face to f.	6440
Ru	2:10	she fell on her f, and bowed herself to	6440
1Sa	5: 3	Dagon *was* fallen upon his f to the earth	6440
	5: 4	Dagon *was* fallen upon his f to the ground	6440
	17:49	and he fell upon his f to the earth.	6440
	20:15	of David every one from the f of the earth.	6440
	20:41	fell on his f to the ground, and	639
	24: 8	David stooped *with his* f to the earth, and	639
	25:23	fell before David on her f, and	6440
	25:41	bowed herself *on her* f to the earth, and said,	639
	26:20	fall to the earth before the f of the LORD:	6440
	28:14	and he stooped *with his* f to the ground, and	639
2Sa	2:22	should I hold up my f to Joab thy brother?	6440
	3:13	of thee, that is, Thou shalt not see my f,	6440
	3:13	when thou comest to see my f.	6440
	9: 6	he fell on his f, and did reverence.	6440
	14: 4	she fell on her f to the ground, and	639
	14:22	Joab fell to the ground on his f, and	6440
	14:24	to his own house, and let him not see my f.	6440
	14:24	to his own house, and saw not the king's f.	6440
	14:28	in Jerusalem, and saw not the king's f.	6440
	14:32	now therefore let me see the king's f; and	6440
	14:33	bowed himself on his f to the ground before	639
	18: 8	For the battle was there scattered over the f	6440
	18:28	he fell down to the earth upon his f before	639
	19: 4	the king covered his f, and the king cried	6440
	24:20	bowed himself before the king *on* his f upon	639
1Ki	1:23	he bowed himself before the king with his f	639
	1:31	Bath-sheba bowed *with her* f *to* the earth,	639
	8:14	the king turned his f about, and blessed all	6440
	13: 6	Intreat now the f of the LORD thy God,	6440
	13:34	and to destroy *it* from off the f of the earth.	6440
	18: 7	he knew him, and fell on his f, and said,	6440
	18:42	the earth, and put his f between his knees,	6440
	19:13	when Elijah heard *it,* that he wrapped his f	6440
	20:38	disguised himself with ashes upon his f.	5869
	20:41	and took the ashes away from his f;	5869
	21: 4	turned away his f, and would eat no bread.	6440
2Ki	4:29	and lay my staff upon the f of the child.	6440
	4:31	and laid the staff upon the f of the child;	6440
	8:15	and spread *it* on his f, so that he died:	6440
	9:30	Jezebel heard *of it;* and she painted her f,	5869
	9:32	he lift up his f to the window, and said,	6440
	9:37	the f of the field in the portion of Jezreel;	6440
	12:17	and Hazael set his f to go up to Jerusalem.	6440
	13:14	wept over his f, and said, O my father,	6440
	14: 8	Come, let us look one another *in* the f.	6440
	14:11	one another *in* the f at Beth-shemesh,	6440
	18:24	wilt thou turn away the f of one captain of	6440
	20: 2	he turned his f to the wall, and prayed unto	6440
1Ch	16:11	and his strength, seek his f continually.	6440
	21:21	bowed himself to David *with his* f to	639
2Ch	6: 3	the king turned his f, and blessed the whole	6440
	6:42	turn not away the f of thine anointed:	6440
	7:14	seek my f, and turn from their wicked	6440
	20:18	Jehoshaphat bowed his head *with his* f to	639
	25:17	Come, let us see one another *in* the f.	6440
	25:21	they saw one another *in* the f, *both* he and	6440
	30: 9	and will not turn away *his* f from you,	6440
	32:21	So he returned with shame of f to his own	6440
	35:22	Nevertheless Josiah would not turn his f	6440
Ezr	9: 6	and blush to lift up my f to thee,	6440
	9: 7	and to a spoil, and to confusion of f,	6440
Est	1:14	which saw the king's f, *and* which sat	6440
	7: 8	the king's mouth, they covered Haman's f.	6440
Job	1:11	that he hath, and he will curse thee to thy f.	6440
	2: 5	his flesh, and he will curse thee to thy f.	6440
	4:15	a spirit passed before my f; the hair of my	6440
	11:15	then shalt thou lift up thy f without spot;	6440
	13:24	Wherefore hidest thou thy f, and	6440
	15:27	Because he covereth his f with his fatness,	6440
	16: 8	rising up in me beareth witness to my f.	6440
	16:16	My f is foul with weeping, and on mine	6440
	21:31	Who shall declare his way to his f? and	6440
	22:26	and shalt lift up thy f unto God.	6440
	23:17	hath he covered the darkness from my f.	6440
	24:15	No eye shall see me: and disguiseth *his* f.	6440
	26: 9	He holdeth back the f of *his* throne, *and*	6440
	30:10	far from me, and spare not to spit in my f.	6440
	33:26	he shall see his f with joy: for he will	6440
	34:29	when he hideth *his* f, who then can behold	6440
	37:12	them upon the f of the world in the earth.	6440
	38:30	*with* a stone, and the f of the deep is frozen.	6440
	41:13	Who can discover the f of his garment? *or*	6440
	41:14	Who can open the doors of his f? his teeth	6440
Ps	5: 8	make thy way straight before my f.	6440
	10:11	he hideth his f; he will never see *it.*	6440
	13: 1	how long wilt thou hide thy f from me?	6440
	17:15	*for* me, I will behold thy f in righteousness:	6440
	21:12	upon thy strings against the f of them.	6440
	22:24	neither hath he hid his f from him; but	6440
	24: 6	that seek him, that seek thy f, O Jacob.	6440
	27: 8	*When thou saidst,* Seek ye my f; my heart	6440
	27: 8	said unto thee, Thy f, LORD, will I seek.	6440

Ps 27: 9 Hide not thy f *far* from me; put not thy 6440
30: 7 thou didst hide thy f, *and* I was troubled. 6440
31:16 Make thy f to shine upon thy servant: 6440
34:16 The f of the LORD *is* against them that do 6440
41:12 and settest me before thy f for ever. 6440
44:15 and the shame of my f hath covered me, 6440
44:24 Wherefore hidest thou thy f, *and* 6440
51: 9 Hide thy f from my sins, and blot out all 6440
67: 1 *and* cause his f to shine upon us; Selah. 6440
69: 7 borne reproach; shame hath covered my f. 6440
69:17 hide not thy f from thy servant; for I am in 6440
80: 3 us again, O God, and cause thy f to shine; 6440
80: 7 O God *of* hosts, and cause thy f to shine; 6440
80:19 LORD God *of* hosts, cause thy f to shine; 6440
84: 9 and look upon the f of thine anointed. 6440
88:14 my soul? *why* hidest thou thy f from me? 6440
89:14 mercy and truth shall go before thy f. 6440
89:23 I will beat down his foes before his f, and 6440
102: 2 Hide not thy f from me in the day *when* I 6440
104:15 *and* oil to make *his* f to shine, and 6440
104:29 Thou hidest thy f, they are troubled: 6440
104:30 and thou renewest the f of the earth. 6440
105: 4 and his strength: seek his f evermore. 6440
119:135 Make thy f to shine upon thy servant; and 6440
132:10 sake turn not away the f of thine anointed. 6440
143: 7 hide not thy f from me, lest I be like unto 6440
Pr 7:13 and with an impudent f said unto him, 6440
7:15 diligently to seek thy f, and I have found 6440
8:27 when he set a compass upon the f of 6440
21:29 A wicked man hardeneth his f: but *as for* 6440
24:31 *and* nettles had covered the f thereof, and 6440
27:19 As *in* water f *answereth* to face, so the heart 6440
27:19 As *in* water face *answereth* to f, so the heart 6440
Ecc 8: 1 a man's wisdom maketh his f to shine, and 6440
8: 1 and the boldness of his f shall be changed. 6440
Isa 6: 2 with twain he covered his f, and with twain 6440
8:17 that hideth his f from the house of Jacob, 6440
14:21 nor fill the f of the world *with* cities. 6440
16: 4 be thou a covert to them from the f of 6440
23:17 of the world upon the f of the earth. 6440
25: 7 he will destroy in this mountain the f of 6440
27: 6 bud, and fill the f of the world *with* fruit. 6440
28:25 When he hath made plain the f thereof, 6440
29:22 neither shall his f now wax pale. 6440
36: 9 wilt thou turn away the f of one captain of 6440
38: 2 Hezekiah turned his f toward the wall, 6440
49:23 they shall bow down to thee *with their* f 639
50: 6 I hid not my f from shame and spitting. 6440
50: 7 therefore have I set my f like a flint, and 6440
54: 8 In a little wrath I hid my f from thee for a 6440
59: 2 and your sins have hid *his* f from you, 6440
64: 7 for thou hast hid thy f from us, and 6440
65: 3 provoketh me to anger continually to my f; 6440
Jer 1:13 and the f thereof *is* towards the north. 6440
2:27 turned *their* back unto me, and not *their* f: 6440
4:30 though thou rentest thy f with painting, 5869
8: 2 they shall be for dung upon the f of 6440
13:26 will I discover thy skirts upon thy f, 6440
16: 4 they shall be as dung upon the f of 6440
16:17 they are not hid from my f, neither is their 6440
18:17 I will shew them the back, and not the f, 6440
21:10 For I have set my f against this city for evil, 6440
22:25 into the hand *of them* whose f thou fearest, 6440
25:26 which *are* upon the f of the earth: 6440
28:16 I will cast thee from off the f of the earth: 6440
32:31 that *I* should remove it from before my f, 6440
32:33 turned unto me the back, and not the f: 6440
33: 5 for all whose wickedness I have hid my f 6440
44:11 I will set my f against you for evil, and 6440
La 2:19 pour out thine heart like water before the f 6440
3:35 To turn aside the right of a man before the f 6440
Eze 1:10 they four had the f of a man, and the face of 6440
1:10 a man, and the f of a lion, on the right side: 6440
1:10 they four had the f of an ox on the left side; 6440
1:10 they four also had the f of an eagle. 6440
1:28 when I saw *it,* I fell upon my f, and I heard 6440
3: 8 I have made thy f strong against their faces, 6440
3:23 by the river of Chebar: and I fell on my f. 6440
4: 3 set thy f against it, and it shall be besieged, 6440
4: 7 Therefore thou shalt set thy f toward 6440
6: 2 set thy f towards the mountains of Israel, 6440
7:22 My f will I turn also from them, and 6440
9: 8 that I fell upon my f, and cried, and said, 6440
10:14 the first f *was* the face of a cherub, and 6440
10:14 the first face *was* the f of a cherub, and 6440
10:14 the second f *was* the face of a man, and 6440
10:14 the second face *was* the f of a man, and 6440
10:14 the third the f of a lion, and the fourth 6440
10:14 of a lion, and the fourth the f of an eagle. 6440
11:13 fell I down upon my f, and cried *with* a 6440
12: 6 thou shalt cover thy f, that thou see not 6440
12:12 he shall cover his f, that he see not 6440
13:17 set thy f against the daughters of thy 6440
14: 3 of their iniquity before their f: 6440
14: 4 stumblingblock of his iniquity before his f, 6440
14: 7 stumblingblock of his iniquity before his f, 6440
14: 8 I will set my f against that man, and 6440
15: 7 I will set my f against them; they shall go 6440
15: 7 the LORD, when I set my f against them. 6440
20:35 and there will I plead with you f to face. 6440
20:35 and there will I plead with you face to f. 6440
20:46 set thy f toward the south, and drop *thy* 6440
21: 2 set thy f toward Jerusalem, and drop *thy* 6440
21:16 on the left, whithersoever thy f *is* set. 6440
25: 2 set thy f against the Ammonites, 6440
28:21 set thy f against Zidon, and 6440
29: 2 set thy f against Pharaoh king of Egypt, and 6440
34: 6 my flock was scattered upon all the f of 6440
35: 2 set thy f against mount Seir, and 6440
38: 2 Son of man, set thy f against Gog, the land 6440
38:18 *that* my fury shall come up in my f. 639
38:20 all the men that *are* upon the f of the earth, 6440
39:14 those that remain upon the f of the earth, 6440
39:23 therefore hid I my f from them, and 6440
39:24 I done unto them, and hid my f from them. 6440
39:29 Neither will I hide my f any more from 6440
40:15 from the f of the gate of the entrance unto 6440
40:15 f of the porch of the inner gate *were* fifty 6440
41:14 Also the breadth of the f of the house, and 6440
41:19 So that the f of a man *was* toward the palm 6440
41:19 the f of a young lion toward the palm tree 6440
41:21 *were* squared, *and* the f of the sanctuary; 6440
41:25 *there were* thick planks upon the f of 6440
43: 3 by the river Chebar; and I fell upon my f. 6440
44: 4 house of the LORD: and I fell upon my f. 6440
Da 2:46 the king Nebuchadnezzar fell upon his f, 600
8: 5 a he goat came from the west on the f of 6440
8:17 he came, I was afraid, and fell upon my f: 6440
8:18 I was in a deep sleep on my f toward 6440
9: 3 I set my f unto the Lord God, to seek *by* 6440
9: 8 O Lord, to us *belongeth* confusion of f, 6440
9:17 cause thy f to shine upon thy sanctuary that 6440
10: 6 his f as the appearance of lightning, and 6440
10: 9 was I in a deep sleep on my f, and my face 6440
10: 9 on my face, and my f toward the ground. 6440
10:15 I set my f toward the ground, and I became 6440
11:17 He shall also set his f to enter with 6440
11:18 After this shall he turn his f unto the isles, 6440
11:19 he shall turn his f towards the fort of his 6440
Hos 5: 5 the pride of Israel doth testify to his f: 6440
5:15 acknowledge their offence, and seek my f: 6440
7: 2 beset them about; they are before my f. 6440
7:10 the pride of Israel testifieth to his f: and 6440
Joel 2: 6 Before their f *the* people shall be much 6440
2:20 with his f toward the east sea, and 6440
Am 5: 8 poureth them out upon the f of the earth: 6440
9: 6 poureth them out upon the f of the earth: 6440
9: 8 I will destroy it from off the f of the earth; 6440
Mic 3: 4 he will even hide his f from them at that 6440
Na 2: 1 dasheth in pieces is come up before thy f: 6440
3: 5 I will discover thy skirts upon thy f, and 6440
Zec 5: 3 This *is* the curse that goeth forth over the f 6440
Mt 6:17 anoint thine head, and wash thy f; *4383*
11:10 Behold, I send my messenger before thy f, *4383*
16: 3 ye can discern the f of the sky; *4383*
17: 2 and his f did shine as the sun, and *4383*
17: 6 the disciples heard *it,* they fell on their f, *4383*
18:10 the f of my Father which is in heaven. *4383*
26:39 and fell on his f, and prayed, saying, O my *4383*
26:67 Then did they spit in his f, and *4383*
Mk 1: 2 Behold, I send my messenger before thy f, *4383*
14:65 and to cover his f, and to buffet him, and *4383*
Lk 1:76 for thou shalt go before the f of the Lord to *4383*
2:31 Which thou hast prepared before the f of all *4383*
5:12 who seeing Jesus fell on *his* f, and *4383*
7:27 Behold, I send my messenger before thy f, *4383*
9:51 he stedfastly set his f to go to Jerusalem, *4383*
9:52 And sent messengers before his f: and *4383*

Lk 9:53 his f was *as though he* would go to 4383
10: 1 and two before his f into every city and 4383
12:56 ye can discern the f of the sky and of 4383
17:16 And fell down on *his* f at his feet, 4383
21:35 them that dwell on the f of the whole earth. 4383
22:64 they stroke him on the f, and asked him, 4383
Jn 11:44 and his f was bound about with a napkin. 3799
Ac 2:25 I foresaw the Lord always **before** my f, 1799
6:15 saw his f as it had been the face of an 4383
6:15 saw his face as it had been the f of an 4383
7:45 whom God drave out before the f of our 4383
17:26 of men for to dwell on all the f of the earth, 4383
20:25 kingdom of God, shall see my f no more. 4383
20:38 that they should see his f no more. 4383
25:16 accused have the accusers **f to face,** 2596+4383
25:16 accused have the accusers **face to f,** 2596+4383
1Co 13:12 through a glass, darkly; but then f to face: 4383
13:12 through a glass, darkly; but then face to f: 4383
14:25 falling down on *his* f he will worship God, 4383
2Co 3: 7 f of Moses for the glory of his countenance; 4383
3:13 not as Moses, *which* put a vail over his f, 4383
3:18 with open f beholding as in a glass 4383
4: 6 of the glory of God in the f of Jesus Christ. 4383
11:20 exalt himself, if a man smite you on the f. 4383
Gal 1:22 And was unknown by f unto the churches 4383
2:11 I withstood him to the f, because he was *to* 4383
Col 2: 1 *for* as many as have not seen my f in 4383
1Th 2:17 abundantly to see your f with great desire. 4383
3:10 exceedingly that *we* might see your f, 4383
Jas 1:23 he is like unto a man beholding his natural f 4383
1Pe 3:12 the f of the Lord *is* against them that do 4383
2Jn 1:12 and speak f to face, that our joy may be 4750
1:12 and speak face to f, that our joy may be 4750
3Jn 1:14 see thee, and we shall speak f to face. 4750
1:14 see thee, and we shall speak face to f. 4750
Rev 4: 7 and the third beast had a f as a man, and 4383
6:16 hide us from the f of him that sitteth on 4383
10: 1 and his f *was* as *it were* the sun, and his feet 4383
12:14 and half a time, from the f of the serpent. 4383
20:11 from whose f the earth and the heaven fled 4383
22: 4 And they shall see his f; and his name *shall* 4383

FACES (73) [FACE]

Ge 9:23 their f *were* backward, and they saw not 6440
18:22 the men **turned** their f from thence, and 6437
30:40 set the f of the flocks toward 6440
42: 6 before him *with* their f to the earth. 639
Ex 19: 7 laid before their f all these words which 6440
20:20 that his fear may be before your f, that ye 6440
25:20 and their f *shall look* one to another; 6440
25:20 toward the mercy seat shall the f of 6440
37: 9 the mercy seat, with their f one to another; 6440
37: 9 *even* to the mercy seatward were the f of 6440
Lev 9:24 they shouted, and fell on their f. 6440
Nu 14: 5 Aaron fell on their f before all the assembly 6440
16:22 they fell upon their f, and said, O God, 6440
16:45 as in a moment. And they fell upon their f. 6440
20: 6 the congregation, and they fell upon their f: 6440
Jdg 13:20 on *it,* and fell on their f to the ground. 6440
18:23 they turned their f, and said unto Micah, 6440
2Sa 19: 5 Thou hast shamed *this* day the f of all thy 6440
1Ki 2:15 *that* all Israel set their f on me, that *I* should 6440
18:39 all the people saw *it,* they fell on their f: 6440
1Ch 12: 8 whose f *were like* the faces of lions, and 6440
12: 8 whose faces *were like* the f of lions, and 6440
21:16 *were* clothed in sackcloth, fell upon their f. 6440
2Ch 3:13 stood on their feet, and their f *were* inward. 6440
7: 3 they bowed themselves *with their* f to 639
29: 6 have turned away their f from 6440
Ne 8: 6 worshipped the LORD *with their* f to 639
Job 9:24 he covereth the f of the judges thereof; 6440
40:13 the dust together; *and* bind their f in secret. 6440
Ps 34: 5 and their f were not ashamed. 6440
83:16 Fill their f *with* shame; that they may seek 6440
Isa 3:15 to pieces, and grind the f of the poor? 6440
13: 8 one at another; their f *shall be as* flames. 6440
25: 8 GOD will wipe away tears from off all f; 6440
53: 3 we hid as it were *our* f from him; he was 6440
Jer 1: 8 Be not afraid of their f: for I *am* with thee 6440
1:17 be not dismayed at their f, lest I confound 6440
5: 3 they have made their f harder than a rock; 6440
7:19 themselves to the confusion of their own f? 6440
30: 6 in travail, and all f are turned into paleness? 6440
42:15 If ye wholly set your f to enter *into* Egypt, 6440
42:17 set their f to go *into* Egypt to sojourn there; 6440
44:12 that have set their f to go *into* the land of 6440
50: 5 They shall ask the way *to* Zion with their f 6440
51:51 shame hath covered our f: for strangers are 6440
La 5:12 the f of elders were not honoured. 6440
Eze 1: 6 *every* one had four f, and every one had 6440
1: 8 and they four had their f and their wings. 6440
1:10 As for the likeness of their f, they four had 6440
1:11 Thus *were* their f: and their wings *were* 6440
1:15 by the living creatures, with his four f. 6440
3: 8 I have made thy face strong against their f, 6440
7:18 shame *shall be* upon all f, and 6440
8:16 of the LORD, and their f towards the east; 6440
10:14 *every* one had four f: the first face *was* 6440
10:21 Every one had four f apiece, and every one 6440
10:22 the likeness of their f *was* the same faces 6440
10:22 the likeness of their faces *was* the same f 6440
14: 6 turn away your f from all your 6440
20:47 all f from the south to the north shall be 6440
41:18 and a cherub; and *every* cherub had two f; 6440
Da 1:10 for why should he see your f worse liking 6440
9: 7 but unto us confusion of f, as *at* this day; 6440
Joel 2: 6 much pained: all f shall gather blackness. 6440
Na 2:10 the f of them all gather blackness. 6440
Hab 1: 9 their f shall sup up *as* the east wind, and 6440
Mal 2: 3 your seed, and spread dung upon your f, 6440
Mt 6:16 for they disfigure their f, that they may 4383
Lk 24: 5 and bowed down *their* f to the earth, 4383
Rev 7:11 and fell before the throne on their f, and 4383
9: 7 and their f *were* as the faces of men. 4383
9: 7 and their faces *were* as the f of men. 4383
11:16 fell upon their f, and worshipped God, 4383

FADE (6) [FADETH, FADING]

2Sa 22:46 Strangers shall **f away,** and they shall be 5034
Ps 18:45 The strangers shall **f away,** and be afraid 5034
Isa 64: 6 we all do f as a leaf; and our iniquities, 5034
Jer 8:13 nor figs on the fig tree, and the leaf shall f; 5034
Eze 47:12 all trees for meat, whose leaf shall not f, 5034
Jas 1:11 also shall the rich *man* **f away** in his ways. 3133

FADETH (7) [FADE]

Isa 1:30 For ye shall be as an oak whose leaf f, and 5034
24: 4 The earth mourneth *and* **f away,** the world 5034
24: 4 the world languisheth *and* **f away,** 5034
40: 7 The grass withereth, the flower f: because 5034
40: 8 The grass withereth, the flower f: but 5034
1Pe 1: 4 and undefiled, and that **f not away,** 263
5: 4 receive a crown of glory that **f not away.** 262

FADING (2) [FADE]

Isa 28: 1 whose glorious beauty *is* a f flower, 5034
28: 4 shall be a f flower, *and* as the hasty fruit 5034

FAIL (64) [FAILED, FAILETH, FAILING]

Ge 47:16 I will give you for your cattle, if money f. 656
Dt 28:32 f *with longing* for them all the day long: 3616
31: 6 he will not f thee, nor forsake thee. 7503
31: 8 he will be with thee, he will not f thee, 7503
Jos 1: 5 with thee: I will not f thee, nor forsake thee. 7503
3:10 *that* he will **without f drive out** from 3423+3423
Jdg 11:30 If thou shalt **without f deliver** 5414+5414
1Sa 2:16 Let them **not f to burn** the fat 6999+6999
17:32 Let no man's heart f because of him; 5307
20: 5 I should **not f to sit** with the king at meat: 3427
30: 8 and **without f recover** *all.* 5337+5337
2Sa 3:29 let there not f from the house of Joab one 3772
1Ki 2: 4 all their soul, there shall not f thee (said he) 3772
8:25 There shall not f thee a man in my sight to 3772
9: 5 There shall not f thee a man upon 3772+3807.1
17:14 not waste, neither shall the cruse of oil f, 2637
17:16 wasted not, neither did the cruse of oil f, 2638
1Ch 28:20 he will not f thee, nor forsake thee, 7503
2Ch 6:16 There shall not f thee a man in my sight to 3772
7:18 There shall not f thee a man *to be* ruler in 3772
Ezr 4:22 Take heed now that ye f not to do this: why 7960
6: 9 let *it* be given them day by day without f: 7960
Est 6:10 let nothing f of all that thou hast spoken. 5307
9:27 themselves unto them, so as it should not f, 5674
9:28 *that* these days of Purim should not f from 5674
Job 11:20 the eyes of the wicked shall f, and 3615
14:11 *As* the waters f from the sea, and the flood 235
17: 5 even the eyes of his children shall f. 3615
31:16 or have **caused** the eyes of the widow **to f;** 3615

Ps 12: 1 for the faithful f from among the children 6461
69: 3 mine eyes f while *I* wait for my God. 3615
77: 8 for ever? doth *his* promise f for evermore? 1584
89:33 from him, nor **suffer** my faithfulness **to** f. 8266
119:82 Mine eyes f for thy word, saying, 3615
119:123 Mine eyes f for thy salvation, and for 3615
Pr 22: 8 reap vanity: and the rod of his anger shall f. 3615
Ecc 12: 5 shall be a burden, and desire shall f: 6565
Isa 19: 3 the spirit of Egypt shall f in the midst 1238
19: 5 the waters shall f from the sea, and the river 5405
21:16 and all the glory of Kedar shall f: 3615
31: 3 fall down, and they all shall f together. 3615
32: 6 he will **cause** the drink of the thirsty **to** f. 2637
32:10 ye careless *women:* for the vintage shall f, 3615
34:16 no one of these shall f, none shall want her 5737
38:14 mine eyes f *with looking* upward: 1809
42: 4 He shall not f nor be discouraged, till he 3543
51:14 die in the pit, nor that his bread should f. 2637
57:16 for the spirit should f before me, and 5848
58:11 like a spring of water, whose waters f not. 3576
Jer 14: 6 their eyes did f, because *there was* no grass. 3615
15:18 unto me as a liar, *and as* waters *that* f? 539+3808
48:33 I have **caused** wine **to** f from the wine 7673
La 2:11 Mine eyes do f with tears, my bowels are 3615
3:22 because his compassions f not. 3615
Hos 9: 2 feed them, and the new wine shall f in her. 3584
Am 8: 4 even to **make** the poor of the land **to** f, 7673
Hab 3:17 the labour of the olive shall f, and the fields 3584
Lk 16: 9 that, when ye f, they may receive you into *1587*
16:17 earth to pass, than one tittle of the law to f. *4098*
22:32 I have prayed for thee, that thy faith f not: *1587*
1Co 13: 8 whether *there be* prophecies, they shall f; *2673*
Heb 1:12 thou art the same, and thy years shall not f. *1587*
11:32 for the time would f me to tell of Gedeon, *1952*
12:15 Looking diligently lest any *man* f of *5302*

FAILED (12) [FAIL]
Ge 42:28 and their heart f *them,* and they were afraid, 3318
47:15 when money f in the land of Egypt, and 8552
Jos 3:16 *even* the salt sea, f, *and* were cut off: 8552
21:45 There f not ought of any good thing which 5307
23:14 that not one thing hath f of all the good 5307
23:14 unto you, *and* not one thing hath f thereof. 5307
1Ki 8:56 there hath not f one word of all his good 5307
Job 19:14 My kinsfolk have f, and my familiar friends 2308
Ps 142: 4 refuge f me; no man cared for my soul. 6+4480
SS 5: 6 my soul f when he spake: I sought him, but 3318
Jer 51:30 their might hath f; they became as women: 5405
La 4:17 for us, our eyes as yet f for our vain help: 3615

FAILETH (19) [FAIL]
Ge 47:15 we die in thy presence? for the money f. 656
Job 21:10 Their bull gendereth, and f not; their cow 1602
Ps 31:10 my strength f because of mine iniquity, and 3782
38:10 My heart panteth, my strength f me: as for 5800
40:12 of mine head: therefore my heart f me. 5800
71: 9 forsake me not when my strength f. 3615
73:26 My flesh and my heart f: *but* God *is* 3615
109:24 through fasting; and my flesh f of fatness. 3584
143: 7 my spirit f: hide not thy face from me, lest I 3615
Ecc 10: 3 his wisdom f *him,* and he saith to every one 2638
Isa 15: 6 the grass f, there is no green thing. 3615
40:26 for that *he is* strong in power; not one f. 5737
41:17 *there is* none, *and* their tongue f for thirst, 5405
44:12 yea, he is hungry, and his strength f: 369
59:15 Yea, truth f; and he *that* departeth from evil 5737
Eze 12:22 The days are prolonged, and every vision f? 6
Zep 3: 5 he bring his judgment to light, he f not; 5737
Lk 12:33 a treasure in the heavens that f **not**, where no *413*
1Co 13: 8 Charity never f: *1601*

FAILING (2) [FAIL]
Dt 28:65 and f of eyes, and sorrow of mind: 3631
Lk 21:26 Men's **hearts** f them for fear, and *674*

FAIN (2)
Job 27:22 he **would** f **flee** out of his hand. 1272+1272
Lk 15:16 And he **would** f have filled his belly with *1937*

FAINT (41) [FAINTED, FAINTEST, FAINTETH, FAINTHEARTED, FAINTNESS]
Ge 25:29 and Esau came from the field, and he *was* f: 5889
25:30 with that same red *pottage;* for I *am* f: 5889
Dt 20: 3 let not your hearts f, fear not, and do not 7401
20: 8 lest his brethren's heart f as well as his 4549
25:18 behind thee, when thou *wast* f and weary; 5889
Jos 2: 9 that all the inhabitants of the land f because 4127
2:24 even all the inhabitants of the country do f 4127
Jdg 8: 4 that *were* with him, f, yet pursuing *them.* 5889
8: 5 for they *be* f, and I am pursuing after Zebah 5889
1Sa 14:28 *any* food *this* day. And the people were f. 5774
14:31 to Aijalon: and the people were very f. 5774
30:10 f that they could not go over the brook 6296
30:21 so f that they could not follow David, 6296
2Sa 16: 2 that such as be f in the wilderness may 3287
21:15 against the Philistines: and David **waxed** f. 5774
Pr 24:10 *If* thou f in the day of adversity, 7503
Isa 1: 5 whole head *is* sick, and the whole heart f. 1742
13: 7 Therefore shall all hands be f, and 7503
29: 8 behold, *he is* f, and his soul hath appetite: 5889
40:29 He giveth power to the f; and to *them that* 3287
40:30 Even the youths shall f and be weary, and 3286
40:31 be weary; *and* they shall walk, and not f. 3286
44:12 he drinketh no water, and is f. 3286
Jer 8:18 myself against sorrow, my heart *is* f in me. 1742
51:46 lest your heart f, and ye fear for the rumour 7401
La 1:13 he hath made me desolate *and* f all the day. 1739
1:22 for my sighs *are* many, and my heart *is* f. 1742
2:19 that f for hunger in the top of every street. 5848
5:17 For this our heart is f; for these *things* our 1739
Eze 21: 7 every spirit shall f, and all knees shall be 3543
21:15 that *their* heart may f, and *their* ruins be 4127
Am 8:13 the fair virgins and young men f for thirst. 5968
Mt 15:32 them away fasting, lest they f in the way. *1590*
Mk 8: 3 to their own houses, they will f by the way: *1590*
Lk 18: 1 *men* ought always to pray, and not to f; *1573*
2Co 4: 1 as we have received mercy, we f not; *1573*
4:16 For which cause we f not; but though our *1573*
Gal 6: 9 for in due season we shall reap, if we f not. *1590*
Eph 3:13 Wherefore I desire that *ye* f not at my *1573*
Heb 12: 3 lest ye be wearied and f in your minds. *1590*
12: 5 nor f when thou art rebuked of him: *1590*

FAINTED (12) [FAINT]
Ge 45:26 *Jacob's* heart f, for he believed them not. 6313
47:13 *all* the land of Canaan f by reason of 3856
Ps 27:13 *I had f,* unless I had believed to see NIH
107: 5 Hungry and thirsty, their soul f in them. 5848
Isa 51:20 Thy sons have f, they lie at the head of all 5968
Jer 45: 3 I f in my sighing, and I find no rest. 3021
Eze 31:15 and all the trees of the field f for him. 5969
Da 8:27 I Daniel f, and was sick *certain* days; 1961
Jnh 2: 7 When my soul f within me I remembered 5848
4: 8 that he f, and wished in himself to die, and 5968
Mt 9:36 with compassion on them, because they f, *1590*
Rev 2: 3 name's sake hast laboured, and hast not f. *2577*

FAINTEST (1) [FAINT]
Job 4: 5 now it is come upon thee, and thou f; 3811

FAINTETH (4) [FAINT]
Ps 84: 2 yea, even f for the courts of the LORD: 3615
119:81 My soul f for thy salvation: *but* I hope in 3615
Isa 10:18 they shall be as when a standard-bearer f. 4549
40:28 ends of the earth, f not, neither is weary? 3286

FAINTHEARTED (3) [FAINT, HEART]
Dt 20: 8 *is there that is* fearful and f? 3824+7390+1886.1
Isa 7: 4 neither be f for the two tails of these 3824+7401
Jer 49:23 they are f; *there is* sorrow on the sea; 4127

FAINTNESS (1) [FAINT]
Lev 26:36 f into their hearts in the lands of their 4816

FAIR (53) [FAIRER, FAIREST, FAIRS]
Ge 6: 2 saw the daughters of men that they *were* f; 2896
12:11 I know that thou *art* a f woman to look 3303
12:14 beheld the woman that she *was* very f. 3303
24:16 the damsel *was* very f to look upon, 2896
26: 7 because she *was* f to look upon. 2896
1Sa 17:42 a youth, and ruddy, and of a f countenance. 3303
2Sa 13: 1 that Absalom the son of David had a f 3303
14:27 she was a woman of a f countenance. 3303
1Ki 1: 3 So they sought for a f damsel throughout 3303
1: 4 the damsel *was* very f, and cherished 3303
Est 1:11 princes her beauty: for she *was* f to look on. 2896
2: 2 Let there be f young virgins sought 2896+4758
2: 3 f young virgins unto Shushan 2896+4758
2: 7 and the maid *was* f and beautiful; 3303+8389

Job 37:22 **F weather** cometh out of the north: 2091
42:15 women found *so* f as the daughters of Job: 3303
Pr 7:21 With her much f **speech** she caused him to 3948
11:22 *is* a f woman which is without discretion. 3303
26:25 When he speaketh f, believe him not: 2603
SS 1:15 Behold, thou *art* f, my love; behold, 3303
1:15 thou *art* fair, my love; behold, thou *art* f; 3303
1:16 Behold, thou *art* f, my beloved, yea, 3303
2:10 my love, my f **one**, and come away. 3303
2:13 Arise, my love, my f **one**, and come away. 3303
4: 1 Behold, thou *art* f, my love; behold, 3303
4: 1 thou *art* fair, my love; behold, thou *art* f; 3303
4: 7 Thou *art* all f, my love; *there is* no spot in 3303
4:10 How f is thy love, my sister, *my* spouse! 3302
6:10 f as the moon, clear as the sun, *and* 3303
7: 6 How f and how pleasant art thou, O love, 3302
Isa 5: 9 *even* great and f, without inhabitant. 2896
54:11 I will lay thy stones with f **colours**, and 6320
Jer 4:30 in vain shalt thou **make** thyself f; 3302
11:16 A green olive tree, f, *and* of goodly fruit: 3303
12: 6 though they speak f *words* unto thee. 2896
46:20 Egypt *is like* a **very** f heifer, *but* 3304
Eze 16:17 Thou hast also taken thy f jewels of my 8597
16:39 shall take thy f jewels, and leave thee naked 8597
23:26 of thy clothes, and take away thy f jewels. 8597
31: 3 the Assyrian *was* a cedar in Lebanon with f 3303
31: 7 Thus was he f in his greatness, in the length 3302
31: 9 I have made him f by the multitude of his 3303
Da 4:12 The leaves thereof *were* f, and the fruit 8209
4:21 Whose leaves *were* f, and the fruit thereof 8209
Hos 10:11 *the corn;* but I passed over upon her f neck: 2898
Am 8:13 In that day shall the f virgins and young 3303
Zec 3: 5 I said, Let them set a f mitre upon his head. 2889
3: 5 So they set a f mitre upon his head, and 2889
Mt 16: 2 it is evening, ye say, *It will be* f **weather**: *2105*
Ac 7:20 was born, and was **exceeding** f, *791+2316+3588*
27: 8 unto a place *which is* called The f **havens**; *2568*
Ro 16:18 f **speeches** deceive the hearts of the simple. *2129*
Gal 6:12 As many as desire to **make a** f **shew** in *2146*

FAIRER (3) [FAIR]
Jdg 15: 2 *is* not her younger sister f than she? 2896
Ps 45: 2 Thou art f than the children of men: 3302
Da 1:15 of ten days their countenances appeared f 2896

FAIREST (3) [FAIR]
SS 1: 8 If thou know not, O thou f among women, 3303
5: 9 *another* beloved, O thou f among women? 3303
6: 1 thy beloved gone, O thou f among women? 3303

FAIRS (6) [FAIR]
Eze 27:12 iron, tin, and lead, they traded in thy f. 5801
27:14 of Togarmah traded in thy f with horses 5801
27:16 they occupied in thy f with emeralds, 5801
27:19 Javan going to and fro occupied in thy f: 5801
27:22 they occupied in thy f with chief of all 5801
27:27 Thy riches, and thy f, thy merchandise, 5801

FAITH (246) [FAITHFUL, FAITHFULLY, FAITHFULNESS, FAITHLESS, UNFAITHFUL]
Dt 32:20 children in whom *is* no f. 529
Hab 2: 4 in him: but the just shall live by his f. 530
Mt 6:30 not much more *clothe* you, O ye **of little f**? *3640*
8:10 I have not found so great f, no not in Israel. *4102*
8:26 Why are ye fearful, O ye **of little f**? *3640*
9: 2 Jesus seeing their f said unto the sick of *4102*
9:22 good comfort; thy f hath made thee whole. *4102*
9:29 saying, According to your f be it unto you. *4102*
14:31 and said unto him, O thou **of little f**, *3640*
15:28 and said unto her, O woman, great *is* thy f: *4102*
16: 8 he said unto them, O ye **of little f**, *3640*
17:20 If ye have f as a grain of mustard seed, *4102*
21:21 I say unto you, If ye have f, and doubt not, *4102*
23:23 *matters* of the law, judgment, mercy, and f: *4102*
Mk 2: 5 When Jesus saw their f, he said unto *4102*
4:40 ye so fearful? how *is it that* you have no f? *4102*
5:34 Daughter, thy f hath made thee whole; *4102*
10:52 Go thy way; thy f hath made thee whole. *4102*
11:22 answering saith unto them, Have f in God. *4102*
Lk 5:20 And when he saw their f, he said unto him, *4102*
7: 9 I have not found so great f, no, not in Israel. *4102*
7:50 said to the woman, Thy f hath saved thee; *4102*
8:25 And he said unto them, Where is your f? *4102*
8:48 thy f hath made thee whole; go in peace.) *4102*
12:28 more *will he clothe* you, O ye **of little f**? *3640*
17: 5 apostles said unto the Lord, Increase our f. *4102*
17: 6 If ye had f as a grain of mustard seed, *4102*
17:19 go *thy way:* thy f hath made thee whole. *4102*
18: 8 of man cometh, shall he find f on the earth? *4102*
18:42 Receive thy sight: thy f hath saved thee. *4102*
22:32 I have prayed for thee, that thy f fail not: *4102*
Ac 3:16 And his name through f in his name hath *4102*
3:16 the f which is by him hath given him this *4102*
6: 5 a man full of f and of the Holy Ghost, and *4102*
6: 7 of the priests were obedient to the f. *4102*
6: 8 And Stephen, full of f and power, did great *4102*
11:24 and full of the Holy Ghost and of f: *4102*
13: 8 seeking to turn away the deputy from the f. *4102*
14: 9 and perceiving that he had f to be healed, *4102*
14:22 *and* exhorting *them* to continue in the f, and *4102*
14:27 how he had opened *the* door of f unto *4102*
15: 9 and them, purifying their hearts by f. *4102*
16: 5 so were the churches established in the f, *4102*
20:21 and f toward our Lord Jesus Christ. *4102*
24:24 and heard him concerning the f in Christ. *4102*
26:18 them which are sanctified by f that is in me. *4102*
Ro 1: 5 for obedience to the f among all nations, *4102*
1: 8 that your f is spoken of throughout *4102*
1:12 with you by the mutual f both of you *4102*
1:17 of God revealed from f to faith: *4102*
1:17 of God revealed from faith to f: *4102*
1:17 as it is written, The just shall live by f. *4102*
3: 3 shall their unbelief make the f of God *4102*
3:22 God *which is* by f of Jesus Christ unto all *4102*
3:25 *to be* a propitiation through f in his blood, *4102*
3:27 of works? Nay: but by the law of f. *4102*
3:28 justified by f without the deeds of the law. *4102*
3:30 which shall justify the circumcision by f, *4102*
3:30 by faith, and uncircumcision through f. *4102*
3:31 Do we then make void the law through f? *4102*
4: 5 his f is counted for righteousness. *4102*
4: 9 for we say that f was reckoned to Abraham *4102*
4:11 a seal of the righteousness of the f which he *4102*
4:12 who also walk in the steps of *that* f of our *4102*
4:13 the law, but through the righteousness of f. *4102*
4:14 f is made void, and the promise made of *4102*
4:16 Therefore *it is* of f, that *it might be* by *4102*
4:16 to that also which is of the f of Abraham; *4102*
4:19 And being not weak in f, he considered not *4102*
4:20 but was strong in f, giving glory to God; *4102*
5: 1 Therefore being justified by f, we have *4102*
5: 2 By whom also we have access by f into this *4102*
9:30 even the righteousness which is of f. *4102*
9:32 Because *they sought it* not by f, but as *it* *4102*
10: 6 But the righteousness which is of f *4102*
10: 8 that is, the word of f, which we preach; *4102*
10:17 So then f *cometh* by hearing, *4102*
11:20 were broken off, and thou standest by f. *4102*
12: 3 hath dealt to every man the measure of f. *4102*
12: 6 *prophesy* according to the proportion of f; *4102*
14: 1 Him that is weak in the f receive you, *but* *4102*
14:22 Hast thou f? have *it* to thyself before God. *4102*
14:23 if he eat, because *he eateth* not of f: *4102*
14:23 of faith: for whatsoever *is* not of f is sin. *4102*
16:26 known to all nations for the obedience of f: *4102*
1Co 2: 5 That your f should not stand in the wisdom *4102*
12: 9 To another f by the same Spirit; to another *4102*
13: 2 and though I have all f, so that *I* could *4102*
13:13 And now abideth f, hope, charity, *4102*
15:14 our preaching vain, and your f *is* also vain. *4102*
15:17 And if Christ be not raised, your f *is* vain; *4102*
16:13 Watch ye, stand fast in the f, quit you like *4102*
2Co 1:24 Not for that we have dominion over your f, *4102*
1:24 are helpers of your joy: for by f ye stand. *4102*
4:13 We having the same spirit of f, *4102*
5: 7 (For we walk by f, not by sight:) *4102*
8: 7 as ye abound in every *thing, in* f, and *4102*
10:15 but having hope, when your f is increased, *4102*
13: 5 Examine yourselves, whether ye be in the f; *4102*
Gal 1:23 preacheth the f which once he destroyed. *4102*
2:16 but by the f of Jesus Christ, even we have *4102*
2:16 that we might be justified by the f of Christ, *4102*
2:20 the flesh I live by the f of the Son of God, *4102*
3: 2 the works of the law, or by the hearing of f? *4102*
3: 5 the works of the law, or by the hearing of f? *4102*
3: 7 Know ye therefore that they which are of f, *4102*
3: 8 God would justify the heathen through f, *4102*
3: 9 they which be of f are blessed with faithful *4102*

Gal 3:11 *it is* evident: for, The just shall live by f. *4102*
3:12 And the law is not of f: but, The man that *4102*
3:14 receive the promise of the Spirit through f. *4102*
3:22 that the promise by f of Jesus Christ might *4102*
3:23 But before f came, we were kept under *4102*
3:23 shut up unto the f which should afterwards *4102*
3:24 unto Christ, that we might be justified by f. *4102*
3:25 But after that f is come, we are no longer *4102*
3:26 For ye are all the children of God by f in *4102*
5: 5 wait for the hope of righteousness by f. *4102*
5: 6 but f which worketh by love. *4102*
5:22 longsuffering, gentleness, goodness, f, *4102*
6:10 unto them who are of the household of f. *4102*
Eph 1:15 after I heard of your f in the Lord Jesus, *4102*
2: 8 For by grace are ye saved through f; and *4102*
3:12 and access with confidence by the f of him. *4102*
3:17 That Christ may dwell in your hearts by f; *4102*
4: 5 One Lord, one f, one baptism, *4102*
4:13 Till we all come in the unity of the f, and *4102*
6:16 Above all, taking the shield of f, *4102*
6:23 and love with f, from God the Father and *4102*
Php 1:25 you all for your furtherance and joy of f; *4102*
1:27 with one mind striving together for the f of *4102*
2:17 upon the sacrifice and service of your f, *4102*
3: 9 but that which is through the f of Christ, *4102*
3: 9 the righteousness which is of God by f: *4102*
Col 1: 4 Since we heard of your f in Christ Jesus, *4102*
1:23 If ye continue in the f grounded and settled, *4102*
2: 5 and the stedfastness of your f in Christ. *4102*
2: 7 and built up in him, and stablished in the f, *4102*
2:12 *him* through the f of the operation of God, *4102*
1Th 1: 3 without ceasing your work of f, *4102*
1: 8 also in every place your f to God-ward is *4102*
3: 2 and to comfort you concerning your f: *4102*
3: 5 no longer forbear, I sent to know your f, *4102*
3: 6 and brought us good tidings of your f and *4102*
3: 7 in all our affliction and distress, by your f: *4102*
3:10 perfect that which is lacking in your f? *4102*
5: 8 putting on the breastplate of f and love; *4102*
2Th 1: 3 because that your f groweth exceedingly, *4102*
1: 4 and f in all your persecutions and *4102*
1:11 *his* goodness, and the work of f with power: *4102*
3: 2 and wicked men: for all *men* have not f. *4102*
1Ti 1: 2 Unto Timothy, *my* own son in the f: Grace, *4102*
1: 4 rather than godly edifying which is in f: *4102*
1: 5 *of* a good conscience, and *of* f unfeigned: *4102*
1:14 of our Lord was exceeding abundant with f *4102*
1:19 Holding f, and a good conscience; *4102*
1:19 concerning f have made shipwrack: *4102*
2: 7 a teacher of the Gentiles in f and verity. *4102*
2:15 if they continue in f and charity and *4102*
3: 9 Holding the mystery of the f in a pure *4102*
3:13 great boldness in the f which is in Christ *4102*
4: 1 latter times some shall depart from the f, *4102*
4: 6 nourished up in the words of f and of good *4102*
4:12 in charity, in spirit, in f, in purity. *4102*
5: 8 he hath denied the f, and is worse than an *4102*
5:12 because they have cast off *their* first f. *4102*
6:10 they have erred from the f, and *4102*
6:11 godliness, f, love, patience, meekness. *4102*
6:12 Fight the good fight of f, lay hold on *4102*
6:21 professing have erred concerning the f. *4102*
2Ti 1: 5 the unfeigned f that is in thee, *4102*
1:13 in f and love which is in Christ Jesus. *4102*
2:18 past already; and overthrow the f of some. *4102*
2:22 but follow righteousness, f, charity, peace, *4102*
3: 8 corrupt minds, reprobate concerning the f. *4102*
3:10 f, longsuffering, charity, patience, *4102*
3:15 salvation through f which is in Christ Jesus. *4102*
4: 7 have finished *my* course, I have kept the f: *4102*
Tit 1: 1 according to the f of God's elect, and *4102*
1: 4 *mine* own son after the common f: *4102*
1:13 that they may be sound in the f; *4102*
2: 2 grave, temperate, sound in f, in charity, *4102*
3:15 Greet them that love us in the f. Grace *be* *4102*
Phm 1: 5 Hearing of thy love and f, which thou hast *4102*
1: 6 That the communication of thy f may *4102*
Heb 4: 2 not being mixed with f in them that heard *4102*
6: 1 from dead works, and of f towards God, *4102*
6:12 but followers of them who through f and *4102*
10:22 near with a true heart in full assurance of f, *4102*
10:38 Now the just shall live by f: but if *any man* *4102*
11: 1 Now f is the substance of *things* hoped for, *4102*
11: 3 Through f we understand that the worlds *4102*
11: 4 By f Abel offered unto God a more *4102*
11: 5 By f Enoch was translated that *he* should *4102*
11: 6 But without f *it is* impossible to please *him:* *4102*
11: 7 By f Noah, being warned of God of *things* *4102*
11: 7 heir of the righteousness which is by f. *4102*
11: 8 By f Abraham, when he was called to go *4102*
11: 9 By f he sojourned in the land of promise, *4102*
11:11 Through f also Sara herself received *4102*
11:13 These all died in f, not having received *4102*
11:17 By f Abraham, when he was tried, *4102*
11:20 By f Isaac blessed Jacob and Esau *4102*
11:21 By f Jacob, when he was a dying, *4102*
11:22 By f Joseph, when he died, made mention *4102*
11:23 By f Moses, when he was born, was hid *4102*
11:24 By f Moses, when he was come to years, *4102*
11:27 By f he forsook Egypt, not fearing *4102*
11:28 Through f he kept the passover, and *4102*
11:29 By f they passed through the Red sea as by *4102*
11:30 By f the walls of Jericho fell down, *4102*
11:31 By f the harlot Rahab perished not with *4102*
11:33 Who through f subdued kingdoms, *4102*
11:39 having obtained a good report through f, *4102*
12: 2 unto Jesus the author and finisher of *our* f; *4102*
13: 7 whose f follow, considering the end of *their* *4102*
Jas 1: 3 Knowing *this,* that the trying of your f *4102*
1: 6 But let him ask in f, nothing wavering: *4102*
2: 1 have not the f of our Lord Jesus Christ, *4102*
2: 5 God chosen the poor of this world rich in f, *4102*
2:14 though a man say *he* hath f, and have not *4102*
2:14 and have not works? can f save him? *4102*
2:17 Even so f, if it hath not works, is dead, *4102*
2:18 may say, Thou hast f, and I have works: *4102*
2:18 shew me thy f without thy works, and I will *4102*
2:18 and I will shew thee my f by my works. *4102*
2:20 O vain man, that f without works is dead? *4102*
2:22 Seest thou how f wrought with his works, *4102*
2:22 and by works was f made perfect? *4102*
2:24 works a man is justified, and not by f only. *4102*
2:26 is dead, so f without works is dead also. *4102*
5:15 And the prayer of f shall save the sick, and *4102*
1Pe 1: 5 f unto salvation ready to be revealed in *4102*
1: 7 That the trial of your f, *being* much more *4102*
1: 9 Receiving the end of your f, *even* *4102*
1:21 that your f and hope might be in God. *4102*
5: 9 Whom resist stedfast in the f, knowing that *4102*
2Pe 1: 1 to them that have obtained like precious f *4102*
1: 5 giving all diligence, add to your f virtue; *4102*
1Jn 5: 4 that overcometh the world, *even* our f. *4102*
Jude 1: 3 f which was once delivered unto the saints. *4102*
1:20 building up yourselves on your most holy f, *4102*
Rev 2:13 fast my name, and hast not denied my f, *4102*
2:19 thy works, and charity, and service, and f, *4102*
13:10 Here is the patience and the f of the saints. *4102*
14:12 commandments of God, and the f of Jesus. *4102*

FAITHFUL (82) [FAITH]

Nu 12: 7 Moses *is* not so, who *is* f in all mine house. 539
Dt 7: 9 he *is* God, the f God, which keepeth 539
1Sa 2:35 I will raise me up a f priest, *that* shall do 539
22:14 who *is so* f among all thy servants as David, 539
2Sa 20:19 *of them that are* peaceable *and* f in Israel: 539
Ne 7: 2 for he *was* a f man, and feared God above 571
9: 8 foundest his heart f before thee, and 539
13:13 for they were counted f, and their office *was* 539
Ps 12: 1 for the f fail from among the children of 539
31:23 *for* the LORD preserveth the f, and 529
89:37 as the moon, and *as* a f witness in heaven. 539
101: 6 Mine eyes *shall be* upon the f of the land, 539
119:86 All thy commandments *are* f: they persecute 530
119:138 hast commanded *are* righteous and very f. 530
Pr 11:13 he that is of a f spirit concealeth the matter. 539
13:17 into mischief: but a f ambassador *is* health. 529
14: 5 A f witness will not lie: but a false witness 529
20: 6 his own goodness: but a f man who can find? 529
25:13 *so is* a f messenger to them that send him: 539
27: 6 F *are* the wounds of a friend; but the kisses 539
28:20 A f man shall abound with blessings: but 530
Isa 1:21 How is the f city become a harlot! *it was* full 539
1:26 The city of righteousness, the f city. 539
8: 2 I took unto me f witnesses to record, Uriah 539
49: 7 because of the LORD that *is* f, *and* 539
Jer 42: 5 LORD be a true and f witness between us, 539
Da 6: 4 forasmuch as he *was* f, neither was there any 540
Hos 11:12 yet ruleth with God, and is f with the saints. 539

Mt 24:45 Who then is a f and wise servant, whom his *4103*
25:21 Well *done, thou* good and f servant: *4103*
25:21 thou hast been f over a few *things,* I will *4103*
25:23 unto him, Well *done,* good and f servant; *4103*
25:23 thou hast been f over a few *things,* I will *4103*
Lk 12:42 Who then is *that* f and wise steward, *4103*
16:10 He that is f in *that which is* least is faithful *4103*
16:10 He that is faithful in *that which is* least is f *4103*
16:11 ye have not been f in the unrighteous *4103*
16:12 And if ye have not been f in that which is *4103*
19:17 because thou hast been f in a very little, *4103*
Ac 16:15 If ye have judged me to be f to the Lord, *4103*
1Co 1: 9 God *is* f, by whom ye were called unto *4103*
4: 2 required in stewards, that a man be found f. *4103*
4:17 who is my beloved son, and f in the Lord, *4103*
7:25 hath obtained mercy of the Lord to be f. *4103*
10:13 but God *is* f, who will not suffer you to be *4103*
Gal 3: 9 they which be of faith are blessed with f *4103*
Eph 1: 1 are at Ephesus, and to the f in Christ Jesus: *4103*
6:21 beloved brother and f minister in the Lord, *4103*
Col 1: 2 f brethren in Christ which are at Colosse: *4103*
1: 7 who is for you a f minister of Christ; *4103*
4: 7 and a f minister and fellowservant in *4103*
4: 9 With Onesimus, a f and beloved brother, *4103*
1Th 5:24 F *is* he that calleth you, who also will do *it.* *4103*
2Th 3: 3 But the Lord is f, who shall stablish you, *4103*
1Ti 1:12 hath enabled me, for that he counted me f, *4103*
1:15 *This is* a f saying, and worthy of all *4103*
3:11 not slanderers, sober, f in all *things.* *4103*
4: 9 *This is* a f saying and worthy of all *4103*
6: 2 because they are f and beloved, *4103*
2Ti 2: 2 the same commit thou to f men, who shall *4103*
2:11 *It is* a f saying: For if we be dead with *him,* *4103*
2:13 If we believe not, *yet* he abideth f: *4103*
Tit 1: 6 having f children not accused of riot or *4103*
1: 9 Holding fast the f word as *he* hath been *4103*
3: 8 *This is* a f saying, and these *things* I will *4103*
Heb 2:17 f high priest *in things* pertaining to God, *4103*
3: 2 Who was f to him that appointed him, *4103*
3: 2 as also Moses *was f* in all his house. NIG
3: 5 And Moses verily *was* f in all his house, *4103*
10:23 (for he *is* f that promised;) *4103*
11:11 she judged him f who had promised. *4103*
1Pe 4:19 *to him* in well doing, as unto a f Creator. *4103*
5:12 By Silvanus, a f brother unto you, as I *4103*
1Jn 1: 9 he is f and just to forgive us *our* sins, and *4103*
Rev 1: 5 *who is* the f witness, *and* the first begotten *4103*
2:10 be thou f unto death, and I will give thee a *4103*
2:13 days wherein Antipas *was* my f martyr, *4103*
3:14 saith the Amen, the f and true witness, *4103*
17:14 are with him *are* called, and chosen, and f. *4103*
19:11 and he that sat upon him *was* called F and *4103*
21: 5 Write: for these words are true and f. *4103*
22: 6 said unto me, These sayings *are* f and true: *4103*

FAITHFULLY (8) [FAITH]
2Ki 12:15 on workmen: for they dealt f. 530+871.1
22: 7 into their hand, because they dealt f. 530+871.1
2Ch 19: 9 ye do in the fear of the LORD, f, 530+871.1
31:12 the tithes and the dedicate *things* f: 530+871.1
34:12 the men did the work f: and 530+871.1
Pr 29:14 The king that f judgeth the poor, his throne 571
Jer 23:28 that hath my word, let him speak my word f. 571
3Jn 1: 5 thou doest f whatsoever thou doest to *4103*

FAITHFULNESS (19) [FAITH]
1Sa 26:23 to every man his righteousness and his f: 530
Ps 5: 9 For *there is* no f in their mouth; 3559
36: 5 *and* thy f *reacheth* unto the clouds. 530
40:10 I have declared thy f and thy salvation: 530
88:11 in the grave? *or* thy f in destruction? 530
89: 1 with my mouth will I make known thy f to 530
89: 2 thy f shalt thou establish in the very heavens. 530
89: 5 thy f also in the congregation of the saints. 530
89: 8 like unto thee? or *to* thy f round about thee? 530
89:24 my f and my mercy *shall be* with him: and 530
89:33 utterly take from him, nor suffer my f to fail. 530
92: 2 in the morning, and thy f every night, 530
119:75 *are* right, and *that* thou *in* f hast afflicted me. 530
119:90 Thy f *is* unto all generations: thou hast 530
143: 1 in thy f answer me, *and* in thy righteousness. 530
Isa 11: 5 of his loins, and f the girdle of his reins. 530
25: 1 *thy* counsels of old *are* f *and* truth. 530
La 3:23 *They are* new every morning: great *is* thy f. 530

Hos 2:20 I will even betroth thee unto me in f: and 530

FAITHLESS (4) [FAITH]
Mt 17:17 and said, O f and perverse generation, *571*
Mk 9:19 He answereth him, and saith, O f generation, *571*
Lk 9:41 answering said, O f and perverse generation, *571*
Jn 20:27 *it* into my side: and be not f, but believing. *571*

FALL (252) [FALLEN, FALLEST, FALLETH, FALLING, FELL]
Ge 2:21 the LORD God **caused** a deep sleep **to f** 5307
43:18 f upon us, and take us for bondmen, and 5307
45:24 unto them, See that ye f not **out** by the way. 7264
49:17 so that his rider shall f backward. 5307
Ex 5: 3 lest he f **upon** us with pestilence, or 6293
15:16 Fear and dread shall f upon them; by 5307
21:33 not cover it, and an ox or an ass f therein; 5307
Lev 11:32 they are dead, doth f, it shall be unclean; 5307
11:37 if *any part* of their carcase f upon any 5307
11:38 *any part* of their carcase f thereon, it *shall* 5307
19:29 lest the land f **to whoredom**, and the land 2181
26: 7 and they shall f before you by the sword. 5307
26: 8 your enemies shall f before you by 5307
26:36 and they shall f when none pursueth. 5307
26:37 they shall f one upon another, as it were 3782
Nu 11:31 from the sea, and let *them* f by the camp, 5203
14: 3 to f by the sword, *that* our wives and 5307
14:29 Your carcases shall f in this wilderness; and 5307
14:32 they shall f in this wilderness. 5307
14:43 before you, and ye shall f by the sword: 5307
34: 2 (this *is* the land that shall f unto you for an 5307
Dt 22: 4 brother's ass or his ox f **down** by the way, 5307
22: 8 upon thine house, if any man f from thence. 5307
Jos 6: 5 the wall of the city shall f **down** flat, 5307
Jdg 8:21 Zalmunna said, Rise thou, and f upon us: 6293
15:12 that ye will not f **upon** me yourselves. 6293
15:18 and f into the hand of the uncircumcised? 5307
Ru 2:16 **let** f also *some* of the handfuls **of purpose** 7997+7997
3:18 until thou know how the matter will f: 5307
1Sa 3:19 did let none of his words f to the ground. 5307
14:45 there shall not one hair of his head f to 5307
18:25 Saul thought to **make** David f by the hand 5307
21:13 and **let** his spittle f **down** upon his beard. 3381
22:17 hand to f upon the priests of the LORD. 6293
22:18 to Doeg, Turn thou, and f upon the priests. 6293
26:20 let not my blood f to the earth before 5307
2Sa 1:15 and said, Go near, *and* f upon him. 6293
14:11 there shall not one hair of thy son f to 5307
24:14 let us f now into the hand of the LORD; 5307
24:14 and let me not f into the hand of man. 5307
1Ki 1:52 there shall not a hair of him f to the earth: 5307
2:29 son of Jehoiada, saying, Go, f upon him. 6293
2:31 he hath said, and f upon him, and bury him; 6293
22:20 that he may go up and f at Ramoth-gilead? 5307
2Ki 7: 4 and let us f unto the host of the Syrians: 5307
10:10 Know now that there shall f unto the earth 5307
14:10 that thou shouldest f, *even* thou, and 5307
19: 7 I will **cause** him **to** f by the sword in his 5307
1Ch 12:19 He will f to his master Saul to *the jeopardy* 5307
21:13 let me f now into the hand of the LORD; 5307
21:13 but let me not f into the hand of man. 5307
2Ch 18:19 that he may go up and f at Ramoth-gilead? 5307
21:15 until thy bowels f **out** by reason of 3318
25: 8 God shall **make** thee f before the enemy: 3782
25:19 that thou shouldest f, *even* thou, and 5307
Est 6:13 before whom thou hast begun to f, 5307
6:13 but shalt **surely** f before him. 5307+5307
Job 13:11 make you afraid? and his dread f upon you? 5307
31:22 *Then* let mine arm f from *my* shoulder 5307
Ps 5:10 O God; let them f by their own counsels; 5307
9: 3 they shall f and perish at thy presence. 3782
10:10 that the poor may f by his strong *ones.* 5307
35: 8 into that *very* destruction let him f. 5307
37:24 Though he f, he shall not be utterly cast 5307
45: 5 *whereby* the people f under thee. 5307
63:10 They shall f by the sword: they shall be a 5064
64: 8 So they shall **make** their own tongue **to** f 3782
72:11 Yea, all kings shall f **down** before him: 7812
78:28 he let *it* f in the midst of their camp, 5307
82: 7 die like men, and f like one of the princes. 5307
91: 7 A thousand shall f at thy side, and 5307
118:13 Thou hast thrust sore at me that *I* might f: 5307
140:10 Let burning coals f upon them: let them be 4131
141:10 Let the wicked f into their own nets, 5307

Ps 145:14 The LORD upholdeth all that f, and 5307
Pr 4:16 is taken away, unless they **cause** *some* **to** f. 3782
10: 8 but a prating fool shall f. 3832
10:10 causeth sorrow: but a prating fool shall f. 3832
11: 5 the wicked shall f by his own wickedness. 5307
11:14 Where no counsel *is,* the people f: but 5307
11:28 He that trusteth in his riches shall f: but 5307
16:18 and a haughty spirit before a f. 3783
22:14 he that is abhorred of the LORD shall f 5307
24:16 but the wicked shall f into mischief. 3782
26:27 Whoso diggeth a pit shall f therein: and 5307
28:10 he shall f himself into his own pit: 5307
28:14 he that hardeneth his heart shall f into 5307
28:18 *he that is* perverse in *his* ways shall f at 5307
29:16 but the righteous shall see their f. 4658
Ecc 4:10 For if they f, the one will lift up his fellow: 5307
10: 8 He that diggeth a pit shall f into it; and 5307
11: 3 if the tree f toward the south, or toward 5307
Isa 3:25 Thy men shall f by the sword, and 5307
8:15 f, and be broken, and be snared, and 5307
10: 4 and they shall f under the slain. 5307
10:34 and Lebanon shall f by a mighty one. 5307
13:15 every one that is joined *unto them* shall f by 5307
22:25 place be removed, and be cut down, and f; 5307
24:18 the noise of the fear shall f into the pit; 5307
24:20 upon it; and it shall f, and not rise again. 5307
28:13 f backward, and be broken, and snared, and 3782
30:13 shall be to you as a breach ready to f, 5307
30:25 of the great slaughter, when the towers f. 5307
31: 3 both he that helpeth shall f, and he that is 3782
31: 3 he that is holpen shall f **down**, and they all 5307
31: 8 shall the Assyrian f with the sword, not of a 5307
34: 4 all their host shall f **down**, as the leaf 5034
37: 7 I will **cause** him **to** f by the sword in his 5307
40:30 and the young men shall **utterly** f: 3782+3782
44:19 shall I f **down** to the stock of a tree? 5456
45:14 and they shall f **down** unto thee, 7812
46: 6 it a god: they f **down**, yea, they worship. 5456
47:11 mischief shall f upon thee; thou shalt not be 5307
54:15 together against thee shall f for thy sake. 5307
Jer 3:12 I will not **cause** mine anger **to** f upon you: 5307
6:15 therefore they shall f among them that fall: 5307
6:15 therefore they shall fall among them that f: 5307
6:21 and the sons together shall f upon them; 3782
8: 4 the LORD; Shall they f, and not arise? 5307
8:12 therefore shall they f among them that fall: 5307
8:12 therefore shall they fall among them that f: 5307
9:22 Even the carcases of men shall f as dung 5307
15: 8 I have **caused** *him* **to** f upon it suddenly, 5307
19: 7 I will **cause** them **to** f by the sword before 5307
20: 4 they shall f by the sword of their enemies, 5307
23:12 they shall be driven on, and f therein: for I 5307
23:19 it shall f **grievously** upon the head of 2342
25:27 spue, and f, and rise no more, because 5307
25:34 And ye shall f like a pleasant vessel. 5307
30:23 it shall f **with pain** upon the head of 2342
37:14 *It is* false; I f not **away** to the Chaldeans. 5307
39:18 thou shalt not f by the sword, but thy life 5307
44:12 all be consumed, *and* f in the land of Egypt; 5307
46: 6 f toward the north by the river Euphrates. 5307
46:16 He made many to f, yea, one fell upon 3782
48:44 He that fleeth from the fear shall f into 5307
49:21 The earth is moved at the noise of their f, 5307
49:26 Therefore her young men shall f in her 5307
50:30 Therefore shall her young men f in 5307
50:32 the most proud shall stumble and f, and 5307
51: 4 Thus the slain shall f in the land of 5307
51:44 unto him: yea, the wall of Babylon shall f. 5307
51:47 and all her slain shall f in the midst of her. 5307
51:49 Babylon *hath caused* the slain of Israel to f, 5307
51:49 at Babylon shall f the slain of all the earth. 5307
La 1:14 he hath **made** my strength **to** f, the Lord 3782
Eze 5:12 a third *part* shall f by the sword round about 5307
6: 7 the slain shall f in the midst of you, and 5307
6:11 for they shall f by the sword, by the famine, 5307
6:12 *he* that *is* near shall f by the sword; and 5307
11:10 Ye shall f by the sword; I will judge you in 5307
13:11 *it with* untempered *morter,* that it shall f: 5307
13:11 ye, O great hailstones, shall f; and a stormy 5307
13:14 it shall f, and ye shall be consumed in 5307
17:21 all his fugitives with all his bands shall f by 5307
23:25 and thy remnant shall f by the sword: 5307
24: 6 it out piece by piece; let no lot f upon it. 5307
24:21 your daughters whom ye have left shall f 5307
25:13 and they of Dedan shall f by the sword. 5307
26:15 not the isles shake at the sound of thy f, 4658
26:18 shall the isles tremble *in* the day of thy f; 4658
27:27 shall f into the midst of the seas in the day 5307
27:34 all thy company in the midst of thee shall f. 5307
29: 5 thou shalt f upon the open fields; thou shalt 5307
30: 4 when the slain shall f in Egypt, and 5307
30: 5 is in league, shall f with them by the sword. 5307
30: 6 They also that uphold Egypt shall f; and 5307
30: 6 from the tower of Syene shall they f in it by 5307
30:17 and of Phi-beseth shall f by the sword: 5307
30:22 I will **cause** the sword **to** f out of his hand. 5307
30:25 and the arms of Pharaoh shall f **down**; 5307
31:16 the nations to shake at the sound of his f, 4658
32:10 man for his own life, in the day of thy f. 4658
32:12 the mighty will I **cause** thy multitude **to** f, 5307
32:20 They shall f in the midst of *them that are* 5307
33:12 he shall not f thereby in the day that he 3782
33:27 surely *they* that *are* in the wastes shall f by 5307
35: 8 shall they f *that are* slain with the sword. 5307
36:15 neither shalt thou **cause** thy nations **to** f any 3782
38:20 the steep places shall f, and every wall shall 5307
38:20 and every wall shall f to the ground. 5307
39: 3 will **cause** thine arrows **to** f out of thy right 5307
39: 4 Thou shalt f upon the mountains of Israel, 5307
39: 5 Thou shalt f upon the open field: for I have 5307
44:12 **caused** the house of Israel **to** f into 4383
47:14 this land shall f unto you for inheritance. 5307
Da 3: 5 ye f **down** and worship the golden image 5308
3:10 shall f **down** and worship the golden 5308
3:15 ye f **down** and worship the image which I 5308
11:14 to establish the vision; but they shall f. 3782
11:19 he shall stumble and f, and not be found. 5307
11:26 and many shall f **down** slain. 5307
11:33 yet they shall f by the sword, and by flame, 3782
11:34 Now when they shall f, they shall be holpen 3782
11:35 *some* of them of understanding shall f, 3782
Hos 4: 5 Therefore shalt thou f *in* the day, and 3782
4: 5 the prophet also shall f with thee *in* 3782
4:14 the people *that* doth not understand shall f. 3832
5: 5 shall Israel and Ephraim f in their iniquity; 3782
5: 5 their iniquity; Judah also shall f with them. 3782
7:16 their princes shall f by the sword for 5307
10: 8 Cover us; and to the hills, F on us. 5307
13:16 they shall f by the sword: their infants shall 5307
14: 9 but the transgressors shall f therein. 3782
Joel 2: 8 *when* they f upon the sword, they shall not 5307
Am 3: 5 Can a bird f in a snare upon the earth, 5307
3:14 altar shall be cut off, and f to the ground. 5307
7:17 and thy daughters shall f by the sword, 5307
8:14 even they shall f, and never rise up again. 5307
9: 9 yet shall not the least grain f *upon* the earth. 5307
Mic 7: 8 when I f, I shall arise; when I sit in 5307
Na 3:12 they shall even f into the mouth of 5307
Mt 4: 9 if thou wilt f **down** and worship me. *4098*
7:27 and it fell: and great was the f of it. *4431*
10:29 one of them shall not f on the ground *4098*
12:11 and if it f into a pit on the sabbath day, *1706*
15:14 lead the blind, both shall f into the ditch. *4098*
15:27 yet the dogs eat of the crumbs which f from *4098*
21:44 And whosoever shall f on this stone shall *4098*
21:44 but on whomsoever it shall f, it will grind *4098*
24:29 and the stars shall f from heaven, and *4098*
Mk 13:25 And the stars of heaven shall f, *1601*
Lk 2:34 this *child* is set for the f and rising again of *4431*
6:39 shall they not both f into the ditch? *4098*
8:13 and in time of temptation f **away**. *868*
10:18 I beheld Satan as lightning f from heaven. *4098*
20:18 Whosoever shall f upon that stone shall be *4098*
20:18 but on whomsoever it shall f, it will grind *4098*
21:24 And they shall f by the edge of the sword, *4098*
23:30 they begin to say to the mountains, F on us; *4098*
Jn 12:24 Except a corn of wheat f into the ground *4098*
Ac 27:17 fearing lest they should f into *1601*
27:32 off the ropes of the boat, and let her f **off**. *1601*
27:34 for there shall not a hair f from the head of *4098*
Ro 11:11 Have they stumbled that they should f? *4098*
11:11 *rather* through their f salvation *is come* unto *3900*
11:12 Now if the f of them *be* the riches of *3900*
14:13 or an **occasion to** f in *his* brother's way. *4625*
1Co 10:12 that thinketh he standeth take heed lest he f. *4098*
1Ti 3: 6 lest being lifted up with pride he f into *1706*
3: 7 lest he f into reproach and the snare of *1706*
6: 9 But they that will be rich f into temptation *1706*

Heb	4:11	lest any *man* **f** after the same example of	*4098*
	6: 6	If they shall **f away**, to renew *them* again	3895
	10:31	*It is* a fearful *thing* to **f** into the hands of	*1706*
Jas	1: 2	count *it* all joy when ye **f into** divers	*4045*
	5:12	*your* nay, nay; lest ye **f** into condemnation.	*4098*
2Pe	1:10	for if ye do these *things,* ye shall never **f**:	*4417*
	3:17	the wicked, **f from** your own stedfastness.	*1601*
Rev	4:10	twenty elders **f down** before him that sat on	*4098*
	6:16	**F** on us, and hide us from the face of him	*4098*
	9: 1	I saw a star **f** from heaven unto the earth:	*4098*

FALLEN (79) [FALL]

Ge	4: 6	thou wroth? and why is thy countenance **f**?	5307
Lev	13:40	the man whose **hair** is **f off** his head, he *is*	4803
	13:41	he that hath his **hair f off** from the part of	4803
	25:35	and **f in decay** with thee;	3027+4131
Nu	32:19	our inheritance is **f** to us on *this* side Jordan	935
Jos	2: 9	that your terror is **f** upon us, and that all	5307
	8:24	*when* they were all **f** on the edge of	5307
Jdg	3:25	their lord *was* **f down** dead on the earth.	5307
	18: 1	not **f** unto them among the tribes of Israel.	5307
	19:27	the woman his concubine *was* **f down** *at*	5307
1Sa	5: 3	Dagon *was* **f** upon his face to the earth	5307
	5: 4	Dagon *was* **f** upon his face to the ground	5307
	26:12	a deep sleep from the LORD was **f** upon	5307
	31: 8	and his three sons **f** in mount Gilboa.	5307
2Sa	1: 4	and many of the people also are **f** and dead;	5307
	1:10	that he could not live after *that* he was **f**:	5307
	1:12	of Israel; because they were **f** by the sword.	5307
	1:19	upon thy high places: how are the mighty **f**!	5307
	1:25	How are the mighty **f** in the midst of	5307
	1:27	How are the mighty **f**, and the weapons of	5307
	3:38	and a great *man* **f** this day in Israel?	5307
	22:39	not arise: yea, they are **f** under my feet.	5307
2Ki	13:14	Now Elisha was **f sick** of his sickness	2470
1Ch	10: 8	found Saul and his sons **f** in mount Gilboa.	5307
2Ch	20:24	they *were* dead bodies **f** to the earth, and	5307
	29: 9	our fathers have **f** by the sword, and	5307
Est	7: 8	Haman was **f** upon the bed whereon Esther	5307
Job	1:16	The fire of God is **f** from heaven, and	5307
Ps	7:15	and is **f** into the ditch *which* he made.	5307
	16: 6	The lines are **f** unto me in pleasant *places;*	5307
	18:38	not able to rise: they are **f** under my feet.	5307
	20: 8	They are brought down and **f**: but we are	5307
	36:12	There are the workers of iniquity **f**: they are	5307
	55: 4	and the terrors of death are **f** upon me.	5307
	57: 6	into the midst whereof they are **f**	5307
	69: 9	of them that reproached thee are **f** upon me.	5307
Isa	3: 8	For Jerusalem is ruined, and Judah is **f**:	5307
	9:10	The bricks are **f down**, but we will build	5307
	14:12	How art thou **f** from heaven, O Lucifer,	5307
	16: 9	thy summer fruits and for thy harvest is **f**.	5307
	21: 9	he answered and said, Babylon is **f**,	5307
	21: 9	and said, Babylon is fallen, is **f**;	5307
	26:18	neither have the inhabitants of the world **f**.	5307
	59:14	for truth is **f** in the street, and equity cannot	3782
Jer	38:19	I am afraid of the Jews that are **f** to	5307
	46:12	the mighty, *and* they are **f** both together.	5307
	48:32	the spoiler is **f** upon thy summer fruits and	5307
	50:15	her foundations are **f**, her walls are thrown	5307
	51: 8	Babylon is suddenly **f** and destroyed:	5307
La	2:21	and my young men are **f** by the sword;	5307
	5:16	The crown is **f** *from* our head: woe unto us,	5307
Eze	13:12	Lo, when the wall is **f**, shall it not be said	5307
	31:12	and in all the valleys his branches are **f**,	5307
	32:22	about him: all of them slain, **f** by the sword:	5307
	32:23	all of them slain, **f** by the sword,	5307
	32:24	her grave, all of them slain, **f** by the sword,	5307
	32:27	they shall not lie with the mighty *that are* **f**	5307
Hos	7: 7	devoured their judges; all their kings are **f**:	5307
	14: 1	thy God; for thou hast **f** by thine iniquity.	3782
Am	5: 2	The virgin of Israel is **f**; she shall no more	5307
	9:11	I raise up the tabernacle of David that is **f**,	5307
Zec	11: 2	Howl, fir tree; for the cedar is **f**; because	5307
Lk	14: 5	you shall have an ass or an ox **f** into a pit,	*1706*
Ac	8:16	(For as yet he was **f upon** none of	*1968*
	15:16	the tabernacle of David, which is **f down**;	*4098*
	20: 9	named Eutychus, being **f into** a deep sleep:	*2702*
	26:14	And when we were all **f** to the earth,	*2667*
	27:29	Then fearing lest we should have **f** upon	*1601*
	28: 6	have swollen, or **f down** dead suddenly:	*2667*
1Co	15: 6	unto this present, but some are **f asleep**.	*2837*
	15:18	Then they also which are **f asleep** in Christ	*2837*
Gal	5: 4	justified by the law; ye are **f from** grace.	*1601*
Php	1:12	**f out** rather unto the furtherance of	*2064*
Rev	2: 5	therefore from whence thou art **f**,	*1601*
	14: 8	saying, Babylon is **f**, is fallen, *that* great	*4098*
	14: 8	Babylon is fallen, is **f**, *that* great city,	*4098*
	17:10	five are **f**, and one is, *and* the other is not	*4098*
	18: 2	saying, Babylon the great is **f**, is fallen, and	*4098*
	18: 2	is **f**, and is become the habitation of devils,	*4098*

FALLEST (1) [FALL]

Jer	37:13	Thou **f away** to the Chaldeans.	5307

FALLETH (28) [FALL]

Ex	1:10	to pass, that, when there **f out** any war,	7122
Lev	11:33	earthen vessel, whereinto *any* of them **f**,	5307
	11:35	*any part* of their carcase **f** shall be unclean;	5307
Nu	33:54	shall be in the place where his lot **f**;	3318
2Sa	3:29	or that **f** on the sword, or that lacketh bread.	5307
	3:34	as *a man* **f** before wicked men, *so*	5307
	17:12	we *will light* upon him as the dew **f** on	5307
Job	4:13	of the night, when deep sleep **f** on men.	5307
	33:15	of the night, when deep sleep **f** upon men,	5307
Pr	13:17	A wicked messenger **f** into mischief: but	5307
	17:20	he that hath a perverse tongue **f** into	5307
	24:16	For a just *man* **f** seven *times,* and riseth up	5307
	24:17	Rejoice not when thine enemy **f**, and let not	5307
Ecc	4:10	woe to him *that is* alone when he **f**; for *he*	5307
	9:12	an evil time, when it **f** suddenly upon them.	5307
	11: 3	*in* the place where the tree **f**, there it shall	5307
Isa	34: 4	as the leaf **f off** from the vine, and as a	5034
	44:15	it a graven image, and **f down** thereto.	5456
	44:17	he **f down** unto it, and worshippeth *it,* and	5456
Jer	21: 9	**f** to the Chaldeans that besiege you, he shall	5307
Da	3: 6	whoso **f** not **down** and worshippeth shall	5308
	3:11	whoso **f** not **down** and worshippeth, *that* he	5308
Mt	17:15	for ofttimes he **f** into the fire, and oft into	*4098*
Lk	11:17	and a house *divided* against a house **f**.	*4098*
	15:12	give me the portion of goods that **f to** *me.*	*1911*
Ro	14: 4	to his own master he standeth or **f**. Yea,	*4098*
Jas	1:11	and the flower thereof **f**, and the grace of	*1601*
1Pe	1:24	and the flower thereof **f away**:	*1601*

FALLING (15) [FALL]

Nu	24: 4	**f** *into a trance,* but having his eyes open:	5307
	24:16	**f** *into a trance,* but having his eyes open:	5307
Job	4: 4	Thy words have upholden him that was **f**,	3782
	14:18	surely the mountain **f** cometh to nought,	5307
Ps	56:13	*wilt* not *thou deliver* my feet from **f**, that *I*	1762
	116: 8	mine eyes from tears, *and* my feet from **f**.	1762
Pr	25:26	A righteous *man* **f down** before the wicked	4131
Isa	34: 4	the vine, and as a **f** *fig* from the fig tree.	5034
Lk	8:47	came trembling, and **f down before** him,	*4363*
	22:44	great drops of blood **f down** to the ground.	*2597*
Ac	1:18	and **f headlong**, he burst asunder in	*1096+4248*
	27:41	And **f** into a place where two seas met,	*4045*
1Co	14:25	so **f down** on *his* face he will worship God,	*4098*
2Th	2: 3	*not come,* except there come a **f away** first,	*646*
Jude	1:24	unto him that is able to keep you from **f**,	*679*

FALLOW (3)

Dt	14: 5	the **f deer**, and the wild goat, and	3180
Jer	4: 3	Break up your **f ground**, and sow not	5215
Hos	10:12	reap in mercy; break up your **f ground**:	5215

FALLOWDEER (1)

1Ki	4:23	and roebucks, and **f**, and fatted fowl.	3180

FALSE (64) [FALSEHOOD, FALSELY, FALSIFYING]

Ex	20:16	Thou shalt not bear **f** witness against thy	8267
	23: 1	Thou shalt not raise a **f** report: put not thine	7723
	23: 7	Keep thee far from a **f** matter; and	8267
Dt	5:20	Neither shalt thou bear **f** witness against thy	7723
	19:16	If a **f** witness rise up against any man to	2555
	19:18	*if* the witness *be* a **f** witness, *and*	8267
2Ki	9:12	they said, *It is* **f**; tell us now. And he said,	8267
Job	36: 4	For truly my words *shall* not *be* **f**: *he that is*	8267
Ps	27:12	for **f** witnesses are risen up against me, and	8267
	35:11	**F** witnesses did rise up; they laid to my	2555
	119:104	therefore I hate every **f** way.	8267
	119:128	*things* to be right; *and* I hate every **f** way.	8267
	120: 3	shall be done unto thee, thou **f** tongue?	7423
Pr	6:19	A **f** witness *that* speaketh lies, and he that	8267
	11: 1	A **f** balance *is* abomination to the LORD:	4820
	12:17	forth righteousness: but a **f** witness deceit.	8267
	14: 5	will not lie: but a **f** witness will utter lies.	8267
	17: 4	A wicked doer giveth heed to **f** lips; *and*	205

Pr 19: 5 A f witness shall not be unpunished, and 8267
19: 9 A f witness shall not be unpunished, and 8267
20:23 the LORD; and a f balance *is* not good. 4820
21:28 A f witness shall perish: but the man that 3577
25:14 Whoso boasteth himself of a f gift *is like* 8267
25:18 A man that beareth f witness against his 8267
Jer 14:14 they prophesy unto you a f vision and 8267
23:32 I *am* against them that prophesy f dreams, 8267
37:14 said Jeremiah, *It is* f; I fall not away to 8267
La 2:14 have seen for thee f burdens and causes of 7723
Eze 21:23 it shall be unto them as a f divination in 7723
Zec 8:17 against his neighbour; and love no f oath: 8267
10: 2 have seen a lie, and have told f dreams; 7723
Mal 3: 5 against f swearers, and against those that 8267
Mt 7:15 Beware of f **prophets**, which come to you *5578*
15:19 adulteries, fornications, thefts, f **witness**, *5577*
19:18 not steal, Thou shalt not **bear f witness**, *5576*
24:11 And many f **prophets** shall rise, and *5578*
24:24 For there shall arise f **Christs**, and *5580*
24:24 and f **prophets**, and shall shew great signs *5578*
26:59 the council, sought f **witness** against Jesus, *5577*
26:60 yea, though many f **witnesses** came, *5575*
26:60 At the last came two f **witnesses**, *5575*
Mk 10:19 Do not **bear f witness**, Defraud not, *5576*
13:22 For f **Christs** and false prophets shall rise, *5580*
13:22 For false Christs and f **prophets** shall rise, *5578*
14:56 For many **bare f witness** against him, but *5576*
14:57 and **bare f witness** against him, saying, *5576*
Lk 6:26 for so did their fathers to the f **prophets**. *5578*
18:20 Do not steal, Do not **bear f witness**, *5576*
19: 8 **taken** any *thing* from any *man*
by f accusation, *4811*
Ac 6:13 And set up f witnesses, which said, *5571*
13: 6 a f **prophet**, a Jew, whose name *was* *5578*
Ro 13: 9 not steal, Thou shalt not **bear f witness**, *5576*
1Co 15:15 Yea, and we are found f **witnesses** of God; *5575*
2Co 11:13 For such *are* f **apostles**, deceitful workers, *5570*
11:26 in the sea, *in* perils among f **brethren**; *5569*
Gal 2: 4 because of f **brethren** unawares brought in, *5569*
2Ti 3: 3 f **accusers**, incontinent, fierce, *1228*
Tit 2: 3 not f **accusers**, not given to much wine, *1228*
2Pe 2: 1 But there were f **prophets** also among *5578*
2: 1 even as there shall be f **teachers** among *5572*
1Jn 4: 1 many f **prophets** are gone out into *5578*
Rev 16:13 and out of the mouth of the f **prophet**. *5578*
19:20 with him the f **prophet** that wrought *5578*
20:10 where the beast and the f **prophet** *are*, and *5578*

FALSEHOOD (14) [FALSE]

2Sa 18:13 Otherwise I should have wrought f against 8267
Job 21:34 seeing *in* your answers there remaineth f? 4604
Ps 7:14 conceived mischief, and brought forth f. 8267
119:118 err from thy statutes: for their deceit *is* f. 8267
144: 8 and their right hand *is* a right hand of f. 8267
144:11 and their right hand *is* a right hand of f: 8267
Isa 28:15 and under f have we hid ourselves: 8267
57: 4 ye not children of transgression, a seed of f, 8267
59:13 and uttering from the heart words of f. 8267
Jer 10:14 for his molten image *is* f, and *there is* no 8267
13:25 thou hast forgotten me, and trusted in f. 8267
51:17 for his molten image *is* f, and *there is* no 8267
Hos 7: 1 for they commit f; and the thief cometh in, 8267
Mic 2:11 If a man walking *in* the spirit and f do lie, 8267

FALSELY (21) [FALSE]

Ge 21:23 by God that thou wilt not **deal** f with me, 8266
Lev 6: 3 lieth concerning it, and sweareth f; 5921+8267
6: 5 which he hath sworn f; 8267+1886.1+3807.1
19:11 Ye shall not steal, neither **deal** f, neither lie 3584
19:12 not swear by my name f, 8267+1886.1+3807.1
Dt 19:18 *and* hath testified f against his brother; 8267
Ps 44:17 neither have we **dealt** f in thy covenant. 8266
Jer 5: 2 surely they swear f. 8267+1886.1+3807.1
5:31 The prophets prophesy f, 8267+871.1+1886.1
6:13 even unto the priest every one dealeth f. 8267
7: 9 swear f, and burn incense 8267+1886.1+3807.1
8:10 even unto the priest every one dealeth f. 8267
29: 9 For they prophesy f unto you in my name: 8267
40:16 this thing: for thou speakest f of Ishmael. 8267
43: 2 saying unto Jeremiah, Thou speakest f: 8267
Hos 10: 4 swearing f in making a covenant: 7723
Zec 5: 4 into the house of him that sweareth f by my 8267
Mt 5:11 shall say all manner of evil against you f, *5574*
Lk 3:14 violence to no man, neither **accuse** *any* f; *4811*

1Ti 6:20 and oppositions of science f so **called**: *5581*
1Pe 3:16 they may be ashamed that f **accuse** your *1908*

FALSIFYING (1) [FALSE]

Am 8: 5 shekel great, and f the balances by deceit? 5791

FALTERS See PANTED; PANTETH

FAME (24) [FAMOUS]

Ge 45:16 the f *thereof* was heard *in* Pharaoh's house, 6963
Nu 14:15 the nations which have heard the f of thee 8088
Jos 6:27 his f was *noised* throughout all the country. 8089
9: 9 for we have heard the f of him, and all that 8089
1Ki 4:31 and his f was in all nations round about. 8034
10: 1 when the queen of Sheba heard of the f of 8088
10: 7 prosperity exceedeth the f which I heard. 8052
1Ch 14:17 the f of David went out into all lands; and 8034
22: 5 of f and of glory throughout all countries: 8034
2Ch 9: 1 when the queen of Sheba heard of the f of 8088
9: 6 *for* thou exceedest the f that I heard. 8052
Est 9: 4 his f went out throughout all the provinces: 8089
Job 28:22 We have heard the f thereof with our ears. 8088
Isa 66:19 the isles afar off, that have not heard my f, 8088
Jer 6:24 We have heard the f thereof: our hands wax 8089
Zep 3:19 f in every land where they have been put to 8034
Mt 4:24 And his f went throughout all Syria: and *189*
9:26 And the f hereof went abroad into all that *5345*
9:31 **spread abroad** his f in all that country. *1310*
14: 1 At that time Herod the tetrarch heard of the f *189*
Mk 1:28 And immediately his f spread abroad *189*
Lk 4:14 there went out a f of him through all *5345*
4:37 And the f of him went out into every place *2279*
5:15 *much* the more went there a f abroad of *3056*

FAMILIAR (18) [FAMILIARS]

Lev 19:31 Regard not them that have f **spirits**, 178
20: 6 soul that turneth after such as have f **spirits**, 178
20:27 A man also or woman that hath a f **spirit**, or 178
Dt 18:11 or a consulter with f **spirits**, or a wizard, or 178
1Sa 28: 3 Saul had put away those that had f **spirits**, 178
28: 7 Seek me a woman that hath a f **spirit**, that I 178
28: 7 *there is* a woman that hath a f **spirit** at 178
28: 8 divine unto me by the f **spirit**, and bring me 178
28: 9 how he hath cut off those that have f **spirits**, 178
2Ki 21: 6 and dealt with f **spirits** and wizards: 178
23:24 Moreover the *workers with* f **spirits**, and 178
1Ch 10:13 for asking *counsel* of *one that had* a f **spirit**, 178
2Ch 33: 6 and dealt with a f **spirit**, and with wizards: 178
Job 19:14 and my f **friends** have forgotten me. 3045
Ps 41: 9 Yea, mine own f **friend**, in whom I 376+7965
Isa 8:19 Seek unto them that have f **spirits**, and 178
19: 3 to them that have f **spirits**, and to 178
29: 4 as of one that hath a f **spirit**, out of 178

FAMILIARS (1) [FAMILIAR]

Jer 20:10 All my f watched for my halting, 582+7965

FAMILIES (174) [FAMILY]

Ge 10: 5 his tongue, after their f, in their nations. 4940
10:18 afterward were the f of the Canaanites 4940
10:20 after their f, after their tongues, in their 4940
10:31 after their f, after their tongues, in their 4940
10:32 These *are* the f of the sons of Noah, 4940
12: 3 in thee shall all f of the earth be blessed. 4940
28:14 in thy seed shall all the f of the earth be 4940
36:40 according to their f, after their places, 4940
47:12 *with* bread, according to *their* f. 2945
Ex 6:14 and Carmi: these *be* the f of Reuben. 4940
6:15 these *are* the f of Simeon. 4940
6:17 Libni, and Shimi, according to their f. 4940
6:19 these *are* the f of Levi according to their 4940
6:24 Abiasaph: these *are* the f of the Korhites. 4940
6:25 fathers of the Levites according to their f. 4940
12:21 and take you a lamb according to your f, 4940
Lev 25:45 ye buy, and of their f that *are* with you, 4940
Nu 1: 2 after their f, by the house of their fathers, 4940
1:18 they declared their pedigrees after their f, 4940
1:20 *by* their generations, after their f, 4940
1:22 *by* their generations, after their f, 4940
1:24 of Gad, *by* their generations, after their f, 4940
1:26 of Judah, *by* their generations, after their f, 4940
1:28 *by* their generations, after their f, 4940
1:30 *by* their generations, after their f, 4940
1:32 *by* their generations, after their f, by 4940
1:34 *by* their generations, after their f, by 4940

Nu 1:36 *by* their generations, after their f, by 4940
1:38 of Dan, *by* their generations, after their f, 4940
1:40 of Asher, *by* their generations, after their f, 4940
1:42 after their f, by the house of their fathers, 4940
2:34 so they set forward, every one after their f, 4940
3:15 after the house of their fathers, by their f: 4940
3:18 the names of the sons of Gershon by their f; 4940
3:19 the sons of Kohath by their f; Amram, and 4940
3:20 the sons of Merari by their f; Mahli, and 4940
3:20 These *are* the f of the Levites according to 4940
3:21 these *are* the f of the Gershonites. 4940
3:23 The f of the Gershonites shall pitch behind 4940
3:27 these *are* the f of the Kohathites. 4940
3:29 The f of the sons of Kohath shall pitch on 4940
3:30 the chief of the house of the father of the f 4940
3:33 of the Mushites: these *are* the f of Merari. 4940
3:35 the chief of the house of the father of the f 4940
3:39 throughout their f, all the males from a 4940
4: 2 after their f, by the house of their fathers, 4940
4:18 Cut ye not off the tribe of the f of 4940
4:22 the houses of their fathers, by their f; 4940
4:24 This *is* the service of the f of 4940
4:28 This *is* the service of the f of the sons of 4940
4:29 thou shalt number them after their f, 4940
4:33 This *is* the service of the f of the sons of 4940
4:34 the sons of the Kohathites after their f, 4940
4:36 those that were numbered of them by their f 4940
4:37 were numbered of the f of the Kohathites, 4940
4:38 throughout their f, and by the house of their 4940
4:40 throughout their f, by the house of their 4940
4:41 These *are* they that were numbered of the f 4940
4:42 those that were numbered of the f of 4940
4:42 throughout their f, by the house of their 4940
4:44 that were numbered of them after their f, 4940
4:45 These *be* those that were numbered of the f 4940
4:46 after their f, and after the house of their 4940
11:10 heard the people weep throughout their f, 4940
26: 7 These *are* the f of the Reubenites: and 4940
26:12 The sons of Simeon after their f: 4940
26:14 These *are* the f of the Simeonites, twenty 4940
26:15 The children of Gad after their f: 4940
26:18 These *are* the f of the children of Gad 4940
26:20 the sons of Judah after their f were, 4940
26:22 These *are* the f of Judah according to those 4940
26:23 *Of* the sons of Issachar after their f: 4940
26:25 These *are* the f of Issachar according to 4940
26:26 *Of* the sons of Zebulun after their f: 4940
26:27 These *are* the f of the Zebulunites 4940
26:28 The sons of Joseph after their f *were* 4940
26:34 These *are* the f of Manasseh, and those that 4940
26:35 These *are* the sons of Ephraim after their f: 4940
26:37 These *are* the f of the sons of Ephraim 4940
26:37 These *are* the sons of Joseph after their f. 4940
26:38 The sons of Benjamin after their f: of Bela, 4940
26:41 *are* the sons of Benjamin after their f: 4940
26:42 These *are* the sons of Dan after their f: 4940
26:42 These *are* the f of Dan after their families. 4940
26:42 These *are* the families of Dan after their f. 4940
26:43 All the f of the Shuhamites, according to 4940
26:44 *Of* the children of Asher after their f: 4940
26:47 These *are* the f of the sons of Asher 4940
26:48 *Of* the sons of Naphtali after their f: 4940
26:50 These *are* the f of Naphtali according to 4940
26:50 families of Naphtali according to their f: 4940
26:57 were numbered of the Levites after their f: 4940
26:58 These *are* the f of the Levites: the family of 4940
27: 1 of the f of Manasseh the son of Joseph: 4940
33:54 land by lot for an inheritance among your f: 4940
36: 1 the chief fathers of the f of the children of 4940
36: 1 of the f of the sons of Joseph, came near, 4940
36:12 *And* they were married into the f of 4940
Jos 7:14 shall come according to the f *thereof;* 4940
13:15 of Reuben *inheritance* according to their f. 4940
13:23 of the children of Reuben after their f, 4940
13:24 the children of Gad according to their f. 4940
13:28 of the children of Gad after their f, 4940
13:29 tribe of the children of Manasseh by their f. 4940
13:31 half of the children of Machir by their f. 4940
15: 1 the tribe of the children of Judah by their f; 4940
15:12 of Judah round about according to their f. 4940
15:20 the children of Judah according to their f. 4940
16: 5 f was *thus:* even the border of their 4940
16: 8 tribe of the children of Ephraim by their f. 4940
17: 2 rest of the children of Manasseh by their f; 4940
17: 2 of Manasseh the son of Joseph by their f. 4940
18:11 of Benjamin came up according to their f: 4940
18:20 thereof round about, according to their f. 4940
18:21 Benjamin according to their f were Jericho, 4940
18:28 children of Benjamin according to their f. 4940
19: 1 the children of Simeon according to their f: 4940
19: 8 the children of Simeon according to their f. 4940
19:10 the children of Zebulun according to their f: 4940
19:16 the children of Zebulun according to their f, 4940
19:17 the children of Issachar according to their f. 4940
19:23 the children of Issachar according to their f, 4940
19:24 the children of Asher according to their f. 4940
19:31 the children of Asher according to their f, 4940
19:32 children of Naphtali according to their f. 4940
19:39 children of Naphtali according to their f, 4940
19:40 of the children of Dan according to their f. 4940
19:48 of the children of Dan according to their f, 4940
21: 4 the lot came out for the f of the Kohathites: 4940
21: 5 by lot out of the f of the tribe of Ephraim, 4940
21: 6 by lot out of the f of the tribe of Issachar, 4940
21: 7 The children of Merari by their f *had* out of 4940
21:10 of Aaron, *being* of the f of the Kohathites, 4940
21:20 the f of the children of Kohath, the Levites 4940
21:26 f of the children of Kohath that remained. 4940
21:27 children of Gershon, of the f of the Levites, 4940
21:33 f *were* thirteen cities with their suburbs. 4940
21:34 unto the f of the children of Merari, the rest 4940
21:40 cities for the children of Merari by their f, 4940
21:40 which were remaining of the f of 4940
1Sa 9:21 my family the least of all the f of the tribe 4940
10:21 tribe of Benjamin to come near by their f, 4940
1Ch 2:53 the f of Kirjath-jearim; the Ithrites, and 4940
2:55 the f of the scribes which dwelt at Jabez; 4940
4: 2 These *are* the f of the Zorathites. 4940
4: 8 and the f of Aharhel the son of Harum. 4940
4:21 the f of the house of them that wrought fine 4940
4:38 by *their* names *were* princes in their f: 4940
5: 7 his brethren by their f, when the genealogy 4940
6:19 these *are* the f of the Levites according to 4940
6:54 sons of Aaron, of the f of the Kohathites: 4940
6:60 All their cities throughout their f *were* 4940
6:62 to the sons of Gershom throughout their f 4940
6:63 throughout their f, out of the tribe of 4940
6:66 *the residue* of the f of the sons of Kohath 4940
7: 5 their brethren among all the f of Issachar 4940
2Ch 35: 5 f of the fathers of your brethren the people, 1004
35: 5 *after* the division of the f of the Levites. 1+1004
35:12 to the divisions of the f of the people, 1+1004
Ne 4:13 I even set the people after *their* f with their 4940
Job 31:34 or did the contempt of f terrify me, that I 4940
Ps 68: 6 God setteth the solitary in f: he bringeth out 1004
107:41 and maketh *him* f like a flock. 4940
Jer 1:15 I will call all the f of the kingdoms of 4940
2: 4 of Jacob, and all the f of the house of Israel: 4940
10:25 and upon the f that call not on thy name: 4940
25: 9 I will send and take all the f of the north, 4940
31: 1 will I be the God of all the f of Israel, and 4940
33:24 The two f which the LORD hath chosen, 4940
Eze 20:32 as the f of the countries, to serve wood and 4940
Am 3: 2 You only have I known of all the f of 4940
Na 3: 4 and f through her witchcrafts. 4940
Zec 12:14 All the f that remain, every family apart, 4940
14:17 *that* whoso will not come up of *all* the f of 4940

FAMILY (123) [FAMILIES]

Lev 20: 5 against his f, and will cut him off, and all 4940
25:10 and ye shall return every man unto his f. 4940
25:41 shall return unto his own f, and unto 4940
25:47 by thee, or to the stock of the stranger's f: 4940
25:49 *any* that is nigh of kin unto him of his f 4940
Nu 3:21 Of Gershon *was* the f of the Libnites, and 4940
3:21 of the Libnites, and the f of the Shimites: 4940
3:27 of Kohath *was* the f of the Amramites, and 4940
3:27 the f of the Izeharites, and the family of 4940
3:27 the f of the Hebronites, and the family of 4940
3:27 the Hebronites, and the f of the Uzzielites: 4940
3:33 Of Merari *was* the f of the Mahlites, and 4940
3:33 of the Mahlites, and the f of the Mushites: 4940
26: 5 *of whom cometh* the f of the Hanochites: 4940
26: 5 of Pallu, the f of the Palluites: 4940
26: 6 Of Hezron, the f of the Hezronites: 4940
26: 6 of Carmi, the f of the Carmites. 4940
26:12 of Nemuel, the f of the Nemuelites: 4940
26:12 of Jamin, the f of the Jaminites: of Jachin, 4940

Nu 26:12 of Jachin, the f of the Jachinites: 4940
26:13 Of Zerah, the f of the Zarhites: of Shaul, 4940
26:13 of Shaul, the f of the Shaulites. 4940
26:15 of Zephon, the f of the Zephonites: 4940
26:15 of Haggi, the f of the Haggites: of Shuni, 4940
26:15 of Shuni, the f of the Shunites: 4940
26:16 Of Ozni, the f of the Oznites: of Eri, 4940
26:16 of the Oznites: of Eri, the f of the Erites: 4940
26:17 Of Arod, the f of the Arodites: of Areli, 4940
26:17 the Arodites: of Areli, the f of the Arelites. 4940
26:20 of Shelah, the f of the Shelanites: 4940
26:20 of Pharez, the f of the Pharzites: of Zerah, 4940
26:20 of Zerah, the f of the Zarhites. 4940
26:21 of Hezron, the f of the Hezronites: 4940
26:21 of Hamul, the f of the Hamulites. 4940
26:23 *of* Tola, the f of the Tolaites: of Pua, 4940
26:23 of the Tolaites: of Pua, the f of the Punites: 4940
26:24 Of Jashub, the f of the Jashubites: 4940
26:24 of Shimron, the f of the Shimronites. 4940
26:26 of Sered, the f of the Sardites: of Elon, 4940
26:26 of Elon, the f of the Elonites: of Jahleel, 4940
26:26 of Jahleel, the f of the Jahleelites. 4940
26:29 of Machir, the f of the Machirites: and 4940
26:29 of Gilead *come* the f of the Gileadites. 4940
26:30 *of* Jeezer, the f of the Jeezerites: of Helek, 4940
26:30 of Helek, the f of the Helekites: 4940
26:31 *of* Asriel, the f of the Asrielites: and 4940
26:31 and *of* Shechem, the f of the Shechemites: 4940
26:32 *of* Shemida, the f of the Shemidaites: and 4940
26:32 and *of* Hepher, the f of the Hepherites. 4940
26:35 of Shuthelah, the f of the Shuthalhites: 4940
26:35 of Becher, the f of the Bachrites: of Tahan, 4940
26:35 of Tahan, the f of the Tahanites. 4940
26:36 of Shuthelah: of Eran, the f of the Eranites. 4940
26:38 of Bela, the f of the Belaites: of Ashbel, 4940
26:38 of Ashbel, the f of the Ashbelites: 4940
26:38 of Ahiram, the f of the Ahiramites: 4940
26:39 Of Shupham, the f of the Shuphamites: 4940
26:39 of Hupham, the f of the Huphamites. 4940
26:40 *of Ard,* the f of the Ardites: *and* of Naaman, 4940
26:40 *and* of Naaman, the f of the Naamites. 4940
26:42 of Shuham, the f of the Shuhamites. 4940
26:44 of Jimna, the f of the Jimnites: of Jesui, 4940
26:44 of Jesui, the f of the Jesuites: of Beriah, 4940
26:44 the Jesuites: of Beriah, the f of the Beriites. 4940
26:45 of Heber, the f of the Heberites: 4940
26:45 of Malchiel, the f of the Malchielites. 4940
26:48 of Jahzeel, the f of the Jahzeelites: of Guni, 4940
26:48 of Guni, the f of the Gunites: 4940
26:49 Of Jezer, the f of the Jezerites: of Shillem, 4940
26:49 of Shillem, the f of the Shillemites. 4940
26:57 of Gershon, the f of the Gershonites: 4940
26:57 of Kohath, the f of the Kohathites: 4940
26:57 of Merari, the f of the Merarites. 4940
26:58 the f of the Libnites, the family of 4940
26:58 of the Libnites, the f of the Hebronites, 4940
26:58 the f of the Mahlites, the family of 4940
26:58 of the Mahlites, the f of the Mushites, 4940
26:58 of the Mushites, the f of the Korahites. 4940
27: 4 our father be done away from among his f, 4940
27:11 his kinsman that is next to him of his f, 4940
36: 6 only to the f of the tribe of their father shall 4940
36: 8 shall be wife unto one of the f of the tribe 4940
36:12 remained in the tribe of the f of their father. 4940
Dt 29:18 among you man, or woman, or f, or tribe, 4940
Jos 7:14 the f which the LORD shall take shall 4940
7:17 he brought the f of Judah; and he took 4940
7:17 of Judah; and he took the f of the Zarhites: 4940
7:17 he brought the f of the Zarhites man by 4940
Jdg 1:25 but they let go the man and all his f. 4940
6:15 my f *is* poor in Manasseh, and I *am* the least 504
9: 1 with all the f of the house of his mother's 4940
13: 2 of the f of the Danites, whose name *was* 4940
17: 7 out of Beth-lehem-judah of the f of Judah, 4940
18: 2 the children of Dan sent of their f five men 4940
18:11 there went from thence of the f of 4940
18:19 be a priest unto a tribe and a f in Israel? 4940
21:24 every man to his tribe and to his f, and 4940
Ru 2: 1 man of wealth, of the f of Elimelech; 4940
1Sa 9:21 my f the least of all the families of the tribe 4940
10:21 the f of Matri was taken, and Saul the son 4940
18:18 what *is* my life, *or* my father's f in Israel, 4940
20: 6 *there is* a yearly sacrifice there for all the f. 4940
20:29 for our f hath a sacrifice in the city; and 4940
2Sa 14: 7 the whole f is risen against thine handmaid, 4940
16: 5 thence came out a man of the f of the house 4940
1Ch 4:27 neither did all their f multiply, like to 4940
6:61 which were left of the f of *that* tribe, 4940
6:70 for the f of the remnant of the sons of 4940
6:71 out of the f of the half tribe of Manasseh, 4940
13:14 the ark of God remained with the f of 1004
Est 9:28 **every** f, every province, 4940+4940+2050.1
Jer 3:14 and two of a f, and I will bring you *to* Zion: 4940
8: 3 residue of them that remain of this evil f, 4940
Am 3: 1 against the whole f which I brought up 4940
Mic 2: 3 Behold, against this f do I devise an evil, 4940
Zec 12:12 the land shall mourn, **every** f apart; 4940+4940
12:12 the f of the house of David apart, and 4940
12:12 the f of the house of Nathan apart, and 4940
12:13 The f of the house of Levi apart, and 4940
12:13 the f of Shimei apart, and their wives apart; 4940
12:14 **every** f apart, and their wives apart. 4940+4940
14:18 if the f of Egypt go not up, and come not, 4940
Eph 3:15 Of whom the whole f in heaven and earth is *3965*

FAMINE (96) [FAMINES]
Ge 12:10 there was a f in the land: and Abram went 7458
12:10 for the f *was* grievous in the land. 7458
26: 1 there was a f in the land, besides the first 7458
26: 1 besides the first f that was in the days of 7458
41:27 with the east wind shall be seven years of f. 7458
41:30 there shall arise after them seven years of f; 7458
41:30 of Egypt; and the f shall consume the land; 7458
41:31 in the land by reason of that f following; 7458
41:36 to the land against the seven years of f, 7458
41:36 that the land perish not through the f. 7458
41:50 born two sons before the years of f came, 7458
41:56 the f was over all the face of the earth: 7458
41:56 and the f waxed sore in the land of Egypt. 7458
41:57 because that the f was *so* sore in all lands. 7458
42: 5 for the f was in the land of Canaan. 7458
42:19 go ye, carry corn *for* the f of your houses: 7459
42:33 take *food for* the f of your households, and 7459
43: 1 And the f *was* sore in the land. 7458
45: 6 For these two years *hath* the f *been* in 7458
45:11 for yet *there are* five years of f; lest thou, 7458
47: 4 for the f *is* sore in the land of Canaan: 7458
47:13 for the f *was* very sore, so that the land of 7458
47:13 land of Canaan fainted by reason of the f. 7458
47:20 his field, because the f prevailed over them: 7458
Ru 1: 1 judges ruled, that there was a f in the land. 7458
2Sa 21: 1 there was a f in the days of David three 7458
24:13 Shall seven years of f come unto thee in thy 7458
1Ki 8:37 If there be in the land f, if there be 7458
18: 2 And *there was* a sore f in Samaria. 7458
2Ki 6:25 there was a great f in Samaria: and behold, 7458
7: 4 the f *is* in the city, and we shall die there: 7458
8: 1 for the LORD hath called for a f; and 7458
25: 3 on the ninth *day* of the *fourth* month the f 7458
1Ch 21:12 Either three years' f; or three months to be 7458
2Ch 20: 9 *as* the sword, judgment, or pestilence, or f, 7458
32:11 you to give over yourselves to die by f 7458
Job 5:20 In f he shall redeem thee from death: and 7458
5:22 At destruction and f thou shalt laugh: 3720
30: 3 For want and f *they were* solitary; flying 3720
Ps 33:19 from death, and to keep them alive in f. 7458
37:19 and in the days of f they shall be satisfied. 7459
105:16 Moreover, he called *for* a f upon the land: 7458
Isa 14:30 I will kill thy root with f, and he shall slay 7458
51:19 and destruction, and the f, and the sword: 7458
Jer 5:12 upon us; neither shall we see sword nor f: 7458
11:22 their sons and their daughters shall die by f: 7458
14:12 and by the f, and by the pestilence. 7458
14:13 not see the sword, neither shall ye have f; 7458
14:15 Sword and f shall not be in this land; 7458
14:15 and f shall those prophets be consumed. 7458
14:16 because of the f and the sword; 7458
14:18 then behold them that are sick with f: 7458
15: 2 such as *are* for the f, to the famine; and 7458
15: 2 such as *are* for the famine, to the f; and 7458
16: 4 shall be consumed by the sword, and by f; 7458
18:21 Therefore deliver up their children to the f, 7458
21: 7 from the sword, and from the f, 7458
21: 9 and by the f, and by the pestilence: 7458
24:10 the f, and the pestilence, among them, 7458
27: 8 and with the f, and with the pestilence, 7458
27:13 the sword, by the f, and by the pestilence, 7458
29:17 the f, and the pestilence, and will make 7458

F

Jer 29:18 with the f, and with the pestilence, and 7458
32:24 and *of* the f, and *of* the pestilence: 7458
32:36 and by the f, and by the pestilence; 7458
34:17 to the sword, to the pestilence, and to the f; 7458
38: 2 the sword, by the f, and by the pestilence: 7458
42:16 the f, whereof ye were afraid, shall follow 7458
42:17 the sword, by the f, and by the pestilence: 7458
42:22 by the f, and by the pestilence, in the place 7458
44:12 be consumed by the sword, *and* by the f: 7458
44:12 unto the greatest, by the sword and by the f: 7458
44:13 the sword, by the f, and by the pestilence: 7458
44:18 been consumed by the sword and by the f. 7458
44:27 be consumed by the sword and by the f, 7458
52: 6 the f was sore in the city, so that there was 7458
La 5:10 black like an oven because of the terrible f. 7458
Eze 5:12 with f shall they be consumed in the midst 7458
5:16 I shall send upon them the evil arrows of f, 7458
5:16 I *will* increase the f upon you, and 7458
5:17 So will I send upon you f and evil beasts, 7458
6:11 the sword, by the f, and by the pestilence. 7458
6:12 and is besieged shall die by the f: 7458
7:15 and the pestilence and the f within: 7458
7:15 the city, f and pestilence shall devour him. 7458
12:16 from the f, and from the pestilence; 7458
14:13 and will send f upon it, and will cut off man 7458
14:21 the f, and the noisome beast, and 7458
36:29 and will increase it, and lay no f upon you. 7458
36:30 that ye shall receive no more reproach of f 7458
Am 8:11 Lord GOD, that I will send a f in the land, 7458
8:11 not a f of bread, nor a thirst for water, but 7458
Lk 4:25 when great f was throughout all the land; *3042*
15:14 there arose a mighty f in that land; *3042*
Ro 8:35 or f, or nakedness, or peril, or sword? *3042*
Rev 18: 8 in one day, death, and mourning, and f; *3042*

FAMINES (3) [FAMINE]
Mt 24: 7 and there shall be f, and pestilences, and *3042*
Mk 13: 8 and there shall be f and troubles: *3042*
Lk 21:11 be in divers places, and f, and pestilences; *3042*

FAMISH (2) [FAMISHED]
Pr 10: 3 not **suffer** the soul of the righteous **to** f: 7456
Zep 2:11 for he will f all the gods of the earth; and 7329

FAMISHED (2) [FAMISH]
Ge 41:55 when all the land of Egypt was f, 7456
Isa 5:13 their honourable men *are* f, and 7458

FAMOUS (10) [FAME]
Nu 16: 2 f in the congregation, men of renown: 7148
26: 9 Abiram, *which were* f in the congregation, 7148
Ru 4:11 in Ephratah, and be f in Beth-lehem: 7121+8034
4:14 a kinsman, that his name may be f in Israel. 7121
1Ch 5:24 f men, *and* heads of the house of their 8034
12:30 mighty *men* of valour, f throughout 376+8034
Ps 74: 5 *A man* was f according as he had lifted up 3045
136:18 slew f kings: for his mercy *endureth* for 117
Eze 23:10 she became f among women; for they had 8034
32:18 *even* her, and the daughters of the f nations, 117

FAN (8) [FANNERS]
Isa 30:24 winnowed with the shovel and with the f. 4214
41:16 Thou shalt f them, and the wind shall carry 2219
Jer 4:11 of my people, not to f, nor to cleanse, 2219
15: 7 I will f them with a fan in the gates of 2219
15: 7 I will fan them with a f in the gates of 4214
51: 2 that shall f her, and shall empty her land: 2219
Mt 3:12 Whose f *is* in his hand, and he will *4425*
Lk 3:17 Whose f *is* in his hand, and he will *4425*

FANNERS (1) [FAN]
Jer 51: 2 will send unto Babylon f, that shall fan her, 2114

FAR (173) [AFAR, FURTHER] See Index

FARE (3) [FARED, FAREWELL, SEAFARING, WAYFARING]
1Sa 17:18 look how thy brethren f, and take their 7965
Jnh 1: 3 so he paid the f thereof, and went down 7939
Ac 15:29 ye shall do well. **F** ye **well**. *4517*

FARED (1) [FARE]
Lk 16:19 fine linen, and f sumptuously every day: *2165*

FAREWELL (4) [FARE]
Lk 9:61 but let me first go **bid** them f, which are *at* *657*
Ac 18:21 But **bade** them f, saying, I must by all means *657*
23:30 before thee what *they had* against him. F. *4517*
2Co 13:11 Finally, brethren, f. Be perfect, be of good *5463*

FARM (1)
Mt 22: 5 light of *it,* and went their ways, one to his f, *68*

FARMED See TILLAGE

FARMER See HUSBANDMAN

FARTHER (1)
Mk 10: 1 into the coasts of Judea by the f **side** *4008*

FARTHEST See OUTGOINGS; UTTERMOST

FARTHING (3) [FARTHINGS]
Mt 5:26 till thou hast paid the uttermost f. *2835*
10:29 Are not two sparrows sold for a f? and *787*
Mk 12:42 she threw in two mites, which make a f. *2835*

FARTHINGS (1) [FARTHING]
Lk 12: 6 Are not five sparrows sold for two f, and *787*

FASHION (13) [FASHIONED, FASHIONETH, FASHIONING, FASHIONS]
Ge 6:15 this *is the f* which thou shalt make it *of:* NIH
Ex 26:30 f thereof which was shewed thee in 4941
37:19 Three bowls **made after the f of almonds** 8246
1Ki 6:38 and according to all the f of it. 4941
2Ki 16:10 king Ahaz sent to Urijah the priest the f of 1823
Job 31:15 and did not one f us in the womb? 3559
Eze 43:11 the f thereof, and the goings out thereof, 8498
Mk 2:12 saying, We never saw *it* **on this f.** *3779*
Lk 9:29 the f of his countenance was altered, and *1491*
Ac 7:44 that *he* should make it according to the f *5179*
1Co 7:31 as not abusing *it:* for the f of this world *4976*
Php 2: 8 And being found **in** f as a man, he humbled *4976*
Jas 1:11 and the grace of the f of it perisheth: *4383*

FASHIONED (7) [FASHION]
Ex 32: 4 f it with a graving tool, after he had made it 6696
Job 10: 8 made me and f me together round about; 6213
Ps 119:73 Thy hands have made me and f me: 3559
139:16 *which* in continuance were f, when *as yet* 3335
Isa 22:11 neither had respect unto him that f it long 3335
Eze 16: 7 *thy* breasts are f, and thine hair is grown, 3559
Php 3:21 that it may be f **like unto** his glorious body, *4832*

FASHIONETH (3) [FASHION]
Ps 33:15 He f their hearts alike; he considereth all 3335
Isa 44:12 f it with hammers, and worketh it with 3335
45: 9 Shall the clay say to him that f it, 3335

FASHIONING (1) [FASHION]
1Pe 1:14 not f yourselves **according** to the former *4964*

FASHIONS (1) [FASHION]
Eze 42:11 goings out *were* both according to their f, 4941

FAST (85) [FASTED, FASTEST, FASTING, FASTINGS]
Ge 20:18 For the LORD had f **closed up** all 6113+6113
Jdg 4:21 for he was f **asleep** and weary. So he died. 7290
15:13 we will **bind** thee f, and deliver thee 631+631
16:11 If they **bind** me f with new ropes that 631+631
Ru 2: 8 but **abide** here f by my maidens: 1692
2:21 Thou shalt **keep** f by my young men, 1692
2:23 So she **kept** f by the maidens of Boaz to 1692
2Sa 12:21 thou didst f and weep for the child, *while it* 6684
12:23 now he is dead, wherefore should I f? can I 6684
1Ki 21: 9 Proclaim a f, and set Naboth on high 6685
21:12 They proclaimed a f, and set Naboth on 6685
2Ki 6:32 shut the door, and **hold** him f at the door: 3905
2Ch 20: 3 and proclaimed a f throughout all Judah. 6685
Ezr 5: 8 this work goeth f on, and prospereth in their 629
8:21 I proclaimed a f there, at the river Ahava, 6685
Est 4:16 f ye for me, and neither eat nor drink three 6684
4:16 I also and my maidens will f likewise; and 6684
Job 2: 3 still he **holdeth** f his integrity, 2388
8:15 he shall **hold** it f, but it shall not endure. 2388
27: 6 My righteousness I **hold** f, and will not let 2388
38:38 and the clods **cleave** f **together?** 1692
Ps 33: 9 it was *done;* he commanded, and it **stood** f. 5975
38: 2 For thine arrows **stick** f in me, and 5181
41: 8 evil disease, *say they,* **cleaveth** f unto him: 3332
65: 6 Which by his strength **setteth** f 3559

Ps 89:28 and my covenant *shall* **stand** f with him. 539
111: 8 They **stand** f for ever and ever, *and* 5564
Pr 4:13 **Take** f **hold** of instruction; let *her* not go: 2388
Isa 58: 3 in the day of your f you find pleasure, and 6685
58: 4 ye f for strife and debate, and to smite with 6684
58: 4 ye shall not f as *ye do this* day, to make 6684
58: 5 Is it such a f that I have chosen? a day for a 6685
58: 5 and ashes *under him?* wilt thou call this a f, 6685
58: 6 *Is* not this the f that I have chosen? to loose 6685
Jer 8: 5 they **hold** f deceit, they refuse to return. 2388
14:12 When they f, I will not hear their cry; and 6684
36: 9 *that* they proclaimed a f before the LORD 6685
46:14 say ye, **Stand** f, and prepare thee; for 3320
48:16 *is* near to come, and his affliction hasteth f. 3966
50:33 all that took them captives **held** them f; 2388
Joel 1:14 Sanctify ye a f, call a solemn assembly, 6685
2:15 sanctify a f, call a solemn assembly: 6685
Jnh 1: 5 of the ship; and he lay, and was f **asleep**. 7290
3: 5 and proclaimed a f, and put on sackcloth, 6685
Zec 7: 5 did ye **at all** f *unto* me, *even to* me? 6684+6684
8:19 The f of the fourth *month,* and the fast of 6685
8:19 of the fourth *month,* and the f of the fifth, 6685
8:19 the f of the seventh, and the fast of 6685
8:19 fast of the seventh, and the f of the tenth, 6685
Mt 6:16 Moreover when ye f, be not as *3522*
6:16 that they may appear unto men to f. *3522*
6:18 That thou appear not unto men to f, but *3522*
9:14 Why do we and the Pharisees f oft, but *3522*
9:14 Pharisees fast oft, but thy disciples f not? *3522*
9:15 be taken from them, and then shall they f. *3522*
26:48 I shall kiss, that *same* is he: **hold** him f. 2902
Mk 2:18 of John and of the Pharisees used to f: *3522*
2:18 the disciples of John and of the Pharisees f, *3522*
2:18 the Pharisees fast, but thy disciples f not? *3522*
2:19 Can the children of the bridechamber f, *3522*
2:19 the bridegroom with them, they cannot f. *3522*
2:20 and then shall they f in those days. *3522*
Lk 5:33 Why do the disciples of John f often, and *3522*
5:34 ye make the children of the bridechamber f, *3522*
5:35 and then shall they f in those days. *3522*
18:12 I f twice in the week, I give tithes of all that *3522*
Ac 16:24 and **made** their feet f in the stocks. *805*
27: 9 because the f was now already past, Paul *3521*
27:41 and the forepart **stuck** f, and *2043*
1Co 16:13 Watch ye, **stand** f in the faith, quit you like *4739*
Gal 5: 1 **Stand** f therefore in the liberty wherewith *4739*
Php 1:27 of your affairs, that ye **stand** f in one spirit, *4739*
4: 1 my joy and crown, so **stand** f in the Lord, *4739*
1Th 3: 8 For now we live, if ye **stand** f in the Lord. *4739*
5:21 Prove all *things;* **hold** f *that which is* good. *2722*
2Th 2:15 **stand** f, and hold the traditions which ye *4739*
2Ti 1:13 **Hold** f the form of sound words, *2192*
Tit 1: 9 **Holding** f the faithful word as *he* hath been *472*
Heb 3: 6 if we **hold** f the confidence and *2722*
4:14 Son of God, let us **hold** f *our* profession. *2902*
10:23 Let us **hold** f the profession of *our* hope *2722*
Rev 2:13 seat *is:* and thou **holdest** f my name, *2902*
2:25 But *that* which ye have *already* hold f till I *2902*
3: 3 and heard, and **hold** f, and repent. *5083*
3:11 **hold** *that* f which thou hast, that no *man* *2902*

FASTED (15) [FAST]
Jdg 20:26 f that day until even, and offered burnt 6684
1Sa 7: 6 and f on that day, and said there, 6684
31:13 under a tree at Jabesh, and f seven days. 6684
2Sa 1:12 wept, and f until even, for Saul, and 6684
12:16 David f, and went in, and lay all 6684+6685
12:22 While the child *was* yet alive, I f and wept: 6684
1Ki 21:27 and f, and lay in sackcloth, and went softly. 6684
1Ch 10:12 under the oak in Jabesh, and f seven days. 6684
Ezr 8:23 So we f and besought our God for this: and 6684
Ne 1: 4 f, and prayed before the God of heaven, 6684
Isa 58: 3 Wherefore have we f, *say they,* and 6684
Zec 7: 5 When ye f and mourned in the fifth and 6684
Mt 4: 2 And when he had f forty days and *3522*
Ac 13: 2 and f, the Holy Ghost said, Separate me *3522*
13: 3 And when they had f and prayed, and *3522*

FASTEN (5) [FASTENED, FASTENING]
Ex 28:14 and f the wreathen chains to the ouches. 5414
28:25 *chains* thou shalt f in the two ouches, 5414
39:31 lace of blue, to f *it* on high upon the mitre; 5414
Isa 22:23 I will f him *as* a nail in a sure place; and 8628
Jer 10: 4 they f it with nails and with hammers, 2388

FASTENED (18) [FASTEN]
Ex 39:18 wreathen *chains* they f in the two ouches, 5414
40:18 f his sockets, and set up the boards thereof, 5414
Jdg 4:21 into his temples, and f *it* into the ground: 6795
16:14 she f *it* with the pin, and said unto him, 8628
1Sa 31:10 they f his body to the wall of Beth-shan. 8628
2Sa 20: 8 upon it a girdle with a sword f upon his 6775
1Ki 6: 6 that *the beams* should not be f in the walls of 270
1Ch 10:10 and f his head *in* the temple of Dagon. 8628
2Ch 9:18 *which were* f to the throne, and stays on each 270
Est 1: 6 blue *hangings,* f with cords of fine linen and 270
Job 38: 6 Whereupon are the foundations thereof f? 2883
Ecc 12:11 and as nails f *by* the masters of assemblies, 5193
Isa 22:25 shall the nail that is f in the sure place be 8628
41: 7 he f it with nails, *that* it should not be 2388
Eze 40:43 *were* hooks, a hand broad, f round about: 3559
Lk 4:20 *that were* in the synagogue were f on him. *816*
Ac 11: 6 Upon the which when I had f mine **eyes**, *816*
28: 3 a viper out of the heat, and f on his hand. *2510*

FASTENING (1) [FASTEN]
Ac 3: 4 f his **eyes** upon him with John, said, *816*

FASTEST (1) [FAST]
Mt 6:17 But thou, when thou f, anoint thine head, *3522*

FASTING (17) [FAST]
Ne 9: 1 children of Israel were assembled with f, 6685
Est 4: 3 the Jews, and f, and weeping, and wailing; 6685
Ps 35:13 I humbled my soul with f; and my prayer 6685
69:10 I wept, *and chastened* my soul with f, 6685
109:24 My knees are weak through f; and my flesh 6685
Jer 36: 6 *in* the LORD'S house upon the f day: 6685
Da 6:18 went to his palace, and passed the night f: 2908
9: 3 with f, and sackcloth, and ashes: 6685
Joel 2:12 with f, and with weeping, and 6685
Mt 15:32 and I will not send them away f, lest they *3523*
17:21 this kind goeth not out but by prayer and f. *3521*
Mk 8: 3 And if I send them away f to their own *3523*
9:29 come forth by nothing, but by prayer and f. *3521*
Ac 10:30 Four days ago I was f until this hour; *3522*
14:23 and had prayed with f, they commended *3521*
27:33 day that ye have tarried and continued f, *777*
1Co 7: 5 that ye may give yourselves to f and *3521*

FASTINGS (4) [FAST]
Est 9:31 their seed, the matters of the f and their cry. 6685
Lk 2:37 but served *God* with f and prayers night *3521*
2Co 6: 5 in tumults, in labours, in watchings, in f; *3521*
11:27 in hunger and thirst, in f often, in cold and *3521*

FAT (130) [FATFLESHED, FATLING, FATLINGS, FATNESS, FATS, FATTED, FATTER, FATTEST]
Ge 4: 4 firstlings of his flock and of the f thereof. 2459
41: 4 eat up the seven well favoured and f kine. 1277
41:20 kine did eat up the first seven f kine: 1277
45:18 of Egypt, and ye shall eat the f of the land. 2459
49:20 Out of Asher his bread *shall be* f, and 8082
Ex 23:18 neither shall the f of my sacrifice remain 2459
29:13 thou shalt take all the f that covereth 2459
29:13 the f that *is* upon them, and burn *them* upon 2459
29:22 Also thou shalt take of the ram the f and 2459
29:22 the f that covereth the inwards, and the caul 2459
29:22 the f that *is* upon them, and the right 2459
Lev 1: 8 shall lay the parts, the head, and the f, 6309
1:12 it into his pieces, with his head and his f: 6309
3: 3 the f that covereth the inwards, and all 2459
3: 3 and all the f that *is* upon the inwards, 2459
3: 4 the two kidneys, and the f that *is* on them, 2459
3: 9 the f thereof, *and* the whole rump, it shall 2459
3: 9 the f that covereth the inwards, and all 2459
3: 9 and all the f that *is* upon the inwards, 2459
3:10 two kidneys, and the f that *is* upon them, 2459
3:14 the f that covereth the inwards, and all 2459
3:14 and all the f that *is* upon the inwards, 2459
3:15 two kidneys, and the f that *is* upon them, 2459
3:16 a sweet savour: all the f *is* the LORD'S. 2459
3:17 *that* ye eat neither f nor blood. 2459
4: 8 he shall take off from it all the f of 2459
4: 8 the f that covereth the inwards, and all 2459
4: 8 and all the f that *is* upon the inwards, 2459
4: 9 two kidneys, and the f that *is* upon them, 2459
4:19 he shall take all his f from him, and burn *it* 2459
4:26 he shall burn all his f upon the altar, as 2459

Lev 4:26 as the f of the sacrifice of peace offerings: 2459
4:31 he shall take away all the f thereof, as 2459
4:31 as the f is taken away from off the sacrifice 2459
4:35 he shall take away all the f thereof, as 2459
4:35 as the f of the lamb is taken away from 2459
6:12 he shall burn thereon the f of the peace 2459
7: 3 he shall offer of it all the f thereof; 2459
7: 3 and the f that covereth the inwards, 2459
7: 4 the two kidneys, and the f that *is* on them, 2459
7:23 Ye shall eat no *manner* f, of ox, or of sheep, 2459
7:24 the f of the beast that dieth of itself, and 2459
7:24 the f of that which is torn *with beasts,* may 2459
7:25 For whosoever eateth the f of the beast, 2459
7:30 the f with the breast, it shall he bring, 2459
7:31 the priest shall burn the f upon the altar: 2459
7:33 the f, shall have the right shoulder for *his* 2459
8:16 he took all the f that *was* upon the inwards, 2459
8:16 their f, and Moses burned *it* upon the altar. 2459
8:20 burnt the head, and the pieces, and the f. 6309
8:25 he took the f, and the rump, and all the fat 2459
8:25 all the f that *was* upon the inwards, and 2459
8:25 and their f, and the right shoulder: 2459
8:26 put *them* on the f, and upon the right 2459
9:10 the f, and the kidneys, and the caul above 2459
9:19 the f of the bullock and of the ram, 2459
9:20 they put the f upon the breasts, and he burnt 2459
9:20 and he burnt the f upon the altar: 2459
9:24 upon the altar the burnt offering and the f: 2459
10:15 with the offerings made by fire of the f, 2459
16:25 the f of the sin offering shall he burn upon 2459
17: 6 burn the f for a sweet savour unto 2459
Nu 13:20 what the land *is,* whether it *be* f or lean, 8082
18:17 shalt burn their f *for* an offering made by 2459
Dt 31:20 and filled *themselves,* and **waxen** f; 1878
32:14 with f of lambs, and rams of the breed of 2459
32:14 and goats, with the f of kidneys of wheat; 2459
32:15 Jeshurun **waxed** f, and kicked: thou art 8080
32:15 thou art **waxed** f, thou art grown thick, 8080
32:38 Which did eat the f of their sacrifices, *and* 2459
Jdg 3:17 king of Moab: and Eglon *was* a very f man. 1277
3:22 the f closed upon the blade, so that he could 2459
1Sa 2:15 Also before they burnt the f, the priest's 2459
2:16 Let them not fail to burn the f presently, 2459
2:29 to **make** yourselves f with the chiefest of 1254
15:22 *and* to hearken than the f of rams. 2459
28:24 the woman had a f calf in the house; and 4770
2Sa 1:22 blood of the slain, from the f of the mighty, 2459
1Ki 1: 9 oxen and f **cattle** by the stone of Zoheleth, 4806
1:19 and f **cattle** and sheep in abundance, 4806
1:25 hath slain oxen and f **cattle** and sheep in 4806
4:23 Ten f oxen, and twenty oxen out of 1277
8:64 and the f of the peace offerings: 2459
8:64 and the f of the peace offerings. 2459
1Ch 4:40 they found f pasture and good, and the land 8082
2Ch 7: 7 the f of the peace offerings, because 2459
7: 7 and the meat offerings, and the f. 2459
29:35 with the f of the peace offerings, and 2459
35:14 of burnt offerings and the f until night; 2459
Ne 8:10 Go *your way,* eat the f, and drink the sweet, 4924
9:25 a f land, and possessed houses full *of* all 8082
9:25 **became** f, and delighted themselves in thy 8080
9:35 and f land which thou gavest before them, 8082
Job 15:27 and maketh **collops of** f on *his* flanks. 6371
Ps 17:10 They are inclosed *in* their own f: *with* their 2459
22:29 All *they that be* f upon earth shall eat and 1879
37:20 the enemies of the LORD *shall be* as the f 3368
92:14 in old age; they shall be f and flourishing; 1879
119:70 Their heart is as f as grease; *but* I delight *in* 2954
Pr 11:25 The liberal soul shall be **made** f: and 1878
13: 4 but the soul of the diligent shall be **made** f. 1878
15:30 *and* a good report **maketh** the bones f. 1878
28:25 his trust in the LORD shall be **made** f. 1878
Isa 1:11 offerings of rams, and the f of fed beasts; 2459
5:17 the waste places of the f **ones** shall 4220
6:10 **Make** the heart of this people f, and 8080
10:16 of hosts, send among his f **ones** leanness; 4924
25: 6 make unto all people a feast of f **things**, 8081
25: 6 on the lees, of f **things** full of marrow, 8081
28: 1 which *are* on the head of the f valleys of 8081
28: 4 which *is* on the head of the f valley, 8081
30:23 of the earth, and it shall be f and plenteous: 1879
34: 6 it is **made** f with fatness, *and* with 1878
34: 6 goats, with the f of the kidneys of rams: 2459
34: 7 and their dust **made** f with fatness. 1878
43:24 neither hast thou filled me *with* the f of thy 2459
58:11 thy soul in drought, and **make** f thy bones: 2502
Jer 5:28 They are **waxen** f, they shine: yea, 8080
50:11 ye are **grown** f as the heifer at grass, 6335
Eze 34: 3 Ye eat the f, and ye clothe you with 2459
34:14 *in* a f pasture shall they feed upon 8082
34:16 I will destroy the f and the strong; I will 8082
34:20 will judge between the f cattle and 1274
39:19 ye shall eat f till *ye* be full, and drink blood 2459
44: 7 the f and the blood, and they have broken 2459
44:15 shall stand before me to offer unto me the f 2459
45:15 out of the f **pastures** of Israel; 4945
Am 5:22 regard the peace offerings of your f **beasts**. 4806
Hab 1:16 because by them their portion *is* f, and 8082
Zec 11:16 he shall eat the flesh of the f, and tear their 1277

FATAL MISTAKE See DISSEMBLED; DISSIMULATION

FATE See END; EVENT; WAY

FATFLESHED (2) [FAT, FLESH]
Ge 41: 2 river seven well favoured kine and f; 1277+1320
41:18 river seven kine, f and well favoured; 1277+1320

FATHER (979) [FATHER'S, FATHERLESS, FATHERS, FATHERS', FOREFATHERS]
Ge 2:24 Therefore shall a man leave his f and his 1
4:20 he was the f of such as dwell in tents, and 1
4:21 he was the f of all such as handle the harp and 1
9:18 Ham, and Japheth: and Ham *is* the f of Canaan. 1
9:22 Ham, the f of Canaan, saw the nakedness of his 1
9:22 saw the nakedness of his f, and told his two 1
9:23 and covered the nakedness of their f; 1
10:21 Shem also, the f of all the children of Eber, 1
11:28 Haran died before his f Terah in the land of his 1
11:29 the f of Milcah, and the father of Iscah. 1
11:29 the father of Milcah, and the f of Iscah. 1
17: 4 and thou shalt be a f of many nations. 1
17: 5 for a f of many nations have I made thee. 1
19:31 Our f *is* old, and *there is* not a man in the earth 1
19:32 let us make our f drink wine, and we will lie 1
19:32 with him, that we may preserve seed of our f. 1
19:33 And they made their f drink wine that night: 1
19:33 and the firstborn went in, and lay with her f; 1
19:34 Behold, I lay yesternight with my f: 1
19:34 with him, that we may preserve seed of our f. 1
19:35 they made their f drink wine that night also: 1
19:36 both the daughters of Lot with child by their f. 1
19:37 the same *is* the f of the Moabites unto *this* day. 1
19:38 the same *is* the f of the children of Ammon 1
20:12 she *is* the daughter of my f, but not 1
22: 7 And Isaac spake unto Abraham his f, and said, 1
22: 7 spake unto Abraham his father, and said, My f: 1
22:21 Buz his brother, and Kemuel the f of Aram, 1
26: 3 the oath which I sware unto Abraham thy f; 1
26:15 had digged in the days of Abraham his f, 1
26:18 they had digged in the days of Abraham his f; 1
26:18 after the names by which his f had called them. 1
26:24 and said, I *am* the God of Abraham thy f: 1
27: 6 I heard thy f speak unto Esau thy brother, 1
27: 9 and I will make them savoury meat for thy f, 1
27:10 And thou shalt bring *it* to thy f, that he may eat, 1
27:12 My f peradventure will feel me, and I shall 1
27:14 mother made savoury meat, such as his f loved. 1
27:18 And he came unto his f, and said, My father: 1
27:18 And he came unto his father, and said, My f: 1
27:19 Jacob said unto his f, I *am* Esau thy firstborn; 1
27:22 Jacob went near unto Isaac his f; and he felt 1
27:26 And his f Isaac said unto him, Come near now, 1
27:30 gone out from the presence of Isaac his f, 1
27:31 brought *it* unto his f, and said unto his father, 1
27:31 said unto his f, Let my father arise, and eat of 1
27:31 Let my f arise, and eat of his son's venison, 1
27:32 And Isaac his f said unto him, Who *art* thou? 1
27:34 when Esau heard the words of his f, he cried 1
27:34 said unto his f, Bless me, *even* me also, O my 1
27:34 his father, Bless me, *even* me also, O my f. 1
27:38 Esau said unto his f, Hast thou but one 1
27:38 his father, Hast thou but one blessing, my f? 1
27:38 bless me, *even* me also, O my f. And Esau lift 1
27:39 And Isaac his f answered and said unto him, 1
27:41 of the blessing wherewith his f blessed him: 1
27:41 The days of mourning for my f are at hand; 1
28: 2 to the house of Bethuel thy mother's f; 1
28: 7 And that Jacob obeyed his f and his mother, 1

Ge 28: 8 the daughters of Canaan pleased not Isaac his **f**; 1
28:13 I *am* the LORD God of Abraham thy **f**, and 1
29:12 *was* Rebekah's son: and she ran and told her **f**. 1
31: 5 but the God of my **f** hath been with me. 1
31: 6 that with all my power I have served your **f**. 1
31: 7 your **f** hath deceived me, and changed my 1
31: 9 Thus God hath taken away the cattle of your **f**, 1
31:16 all the riches which God hath taken from our **f**, 1
31:18 for to go to Isaac his **f** in the land of Canaan. 1
31:29 the God of your **f** spake unto me yesternight, 1
31:35 she said to her **f**, Let it not displease my lord 1
31:42 Except the God of my **f**, the God of Abraham, 1
31:53 of Nahor, the God of their **f**, judge betwixt us. 1
31:53 And Jacob sware by the fear of his **f** Isaac. 1
32: 9 O God of my **f** Abraham, and God of my father 1
32: 9 of my father Abraham, and God of my **f** Isaac, 1
33:19 Shechem's **f**, for an hundred pieces of money. 1
34: 4 And Shechem spake unto his **f** Hamor, saying, 1
34: 6 Hamor the **f** of Shechem went out unto Jacob 1
34:11 Shechem said unto her **f** and unto her brethren, 1
34:13 and Hamor his **f** deceitfully, 1
34:19 more honourable than all the house of his **f**. 1
35:18 name Ben-oni: but his **f** called him Benjamin. 1
35:27 And Jacob came unto Isaac his **f** unto Mamre, 1
36: 9 these *are* the generations of Esau the **f** of 1
36:24 as he fed the asses of Zibeon his **f**. 1
36:43 he *is* Esau the **f** of the Edomites. 1
37: 1 Jacob dwelt in the land wherein his **f** was a 1
37: 2 and Joseph brought unto his **f** their evil report. 1
37: 4 when his brethren saw that their **f** loved him 1
37:10 And he told *it* to his **f**, and to his brethren: and 1
37:10 his **f** rebuked him, and said unto him, What *is* 1
37:11 envied him; but his **f** observed the saying. 1
37:22 out of their hands, to deliver him to his **f** again. 1
37:32 of many colours, and they brought *it* to their **f**; 1
37:35 my son mourning. Thus his **f** wept for him. 1
38:13 Behold thy **f in law** goeth up to Timnath to 2524
38:25 she sent to her **f in law**, saying, By 2524
42:13 the youngest *is this* day with our **f**, and one *is* 1
42:29 they came unto Jacob their **f** unto the land of 1
42:32 We *be* twelve brethren, sons of our **f**; one *is* 1
42:32 the youngest *is this* day with our **f** in the land 1
42:35 *both* they and their **f** saw the bundles of money, 1
42:36 Jacob their **f** said unto them, Me have ye 1
42:37 Reuben spake unto his **f**, saying, Slay my two 1
43: 2 their **f** said unto them, Go again, buy us a little 1
43: 7 and of our kindred, saying, *Is* your **f** yet alive? 1
43: 8 Judah said unto Israel his **f**, Send the lad with 1
43:11 And their **f** Israel said unto them, If *it must be* 1
43:23 your God, and the God of your **f**, hath given 1
43:27 said, *Is* your **f** well, the old man of whom ye 1
43:28 Thy servant our **f** *is* in good health, he *is* yet 1
44:17 and as for you, get you up in peace unto your **f**. 1
44:19 his servants, saying, Have ye a **f**, or a brother? 1
44:20 We have a **f**, an old man, and a child of *his* old 1
44:20 alone is left of his mother, and his **f** loveth him. 1
44:22 said unto my lord, The lad cannot leave his **f**: 1
44:22 for *if* he should leave his **f**, *his father* would 1
44:22 *if* he should leave his father, *his* ***f*** would die. NIH
44:24 pass when we came up unto thy servant my **f**, 1
44:25 our **f** said, Go again, *and* buy us a little food. 1
44:27 thy servant my **f** said unto us, Ye know that 1
44:30 therefore when I come to thy servant my **f**, 1
44:31 of thy servant our **f** with sorrow to the grave. 1
44:32 servant became surety for the lad unto my **f**, 1
44:32 then I shall bear the blame to my **f** for ever. 1
44:34 For how shall I go up to my **f**, and the lad *be* 1
44:34 I see the evil that shall come on my **f**. 1
45: 3 his brethren, I *am* Joseph; doth my **f** yet live? 1
45: 8 he hath made me a **f** to Pharaoh, and lord of all 1
45: 9 and go up to my **f**, and say unto him, 1
45:13 you shall tell my **f** of all my glory in Egypt, 1
45:13 and ye shall haste and bring down my **f** hither. 1
45:18 take your **f** and your households, and 1
45:19 for your wives, and bring your **f**, and come. 1
45:23 to his **f** he sent after this manner; ten asses 1
45:23 and bread and meat for his **f** by the way. 1
45:25 *into* the land of Canaan unto Jacob their **f**, 1
45:27 to carry him, the spirit of Jacob their **f** revived: 1
46: 1 offered sacrifices unto the God of his **f** Isaac. 1
46: 3 he said, I *am* God, the God of thy **f**: fear not to 1
46: 5 and the sons of Israel carried Jacob their **f**, and 1
46:29 went up to meet Israel his **f**, to Goshen, and 1
47: 1 My **f** and my brethren, and their flocks, and 1
47: 5 Thy **f** and thy brethren are come unto thee: 1
47: 6 in the best of the land make thy **f** and brethren 1
47: 7 Joseph brought in Jacob his **f**, and set him 1
47:11 And Joseph placed his **f** and his brethren, and 1
47:12 And Joseph nourished his **f**, and his brethren, 1
48: 1 that *one* told Joseph, Behold, thy **f** *is* sick: 1
48: 9 And Joseph said unto his **f**, They *are* my sons, 1
48:17 when Joseph saw that his **f** laid his right hand 1
48:18 And Joseph said unto his **f**, Not so, my father: 1
48:18 And Joseph said unto his father, Not so, my **f**: 1
48:19 And his **f** refused, and said, I know *it,* my son, 1
49: 2 sons of Jacob; and hearken unto Israel your **f**. 1
49:25 *Even* by the God of thy **f**, who shall help thee; 1
49:26 The blessings of thy **f** have prevailed above 1
49:28 and this *is it* that their **f** spake unto them, and 1
50: 2 his servants the physicians to embalm his **f**: 1
50: 5 My **f** made me swear, saying, Lo, I die: in my 1
50: 5 and bury my **f**, and I will come again. 1
50: 6 Pharaoh said, Go up, and bury thy **f**, 1
50: 7 Joseph went up to bury his **f**: and with him 1
50:10 and he made a mourning for his **f** seven days. 1
50:14 and all that went up with him to bury his **f**, 1
50:14 him to bury his father, after he had buried his **f**. 1
50:15 when Joseph's brethren saw that their **f** was 1
50:16 Thy **f** did command before he died, saying, 1
50:17 the trespass of the servants of the God of thy **f**. 1
Ex 2:18 And when they came to Reuel their **f**, he said, 1
3: 1 Moses kept the flock of Jethro his **f in law**, 2859
3: 6 Moreover he said, I *am* the God of thy **f**, 1
4:18 and returned to Jethro his **f in law**, 2859
18: 1 the priest of Midian, Moses' **f in law**, 2859
18: 2 Jethro, Moses' **f in law**, took Zipporah, 2859
18: 4 for the God of my **f**, *said he, was* mine help, 1
18: 5 Jethro, Moses' **f in law**, came with his sons 2859
18: 6 I thy **f in law** Jethro am come unto thee, 2859
18: 7 Moses went out to meet his **f in law**, and 2859
18: 8 Moses told his **f in law** all that the LORD 2859
18:12 Jethro, Moses' **f in law**, took a burnt 2859
18:12 to eat bread with Moses' **f in law** before 2859
18:14 when Moses' **f in law** saw all that he did to 2859
18:15 Moses said unto his **f in law**, Because 2859
18:17 Moses' **f in law** said unto him, The thing 2859
18:24 hearkened to the voice of his **f in law**, 2859
18:27 Moses let his **f in law** depart; and he went 2859
20:12 Honour thy **f** and thy mother: that thy days may 1
21:15 he that smiteth his **f**, or his mother, shall be 1
21:17 he that curseth his **f**, or his mother, shall surely 1
22:17 If her **f** utterly refuse to give her unto him, 1
40:15 shalt anoint them, as thou didst anoint their **f**, 1
Lev 18: 7 The nakedness of thy **f**, or the nakedness of thy 1
18: 9 the daughter of thy **f**, or daughter of thy 1
18:11 begotten of thy **f**, she *is* thy sister, thou shalt 1
19: 3 his mother, and his **f**, and keep my sabbaths: 1
20: 9 For every one that curseth his **f** or his mother 1
20: 9 he hath cursed his **f** or his mother; his blood 1
21: 2 for his **f**, and for his son, and for his daughter, 1
21: 9 by playing the whore, she profaneth her **f**: 1
21:11 nor defile himself for his **f**, or for his mother; 1
24:10 whose **f**s *was* an Egyptian, 1121
Nu 3: 4 the priest's office in the sight of Aaron their **f**. 1
3:24 the chief of the house of the **f** of 1
3:30 the chief of the house of the **f** of the families of 1
3:35 the chief of the house of the **f** of the families of 1
6: 7 He shall not make himself unclean for his **f**, 1
10:29 of Raguel the Midianite, Moses' **f in law**, 2859
11:12 as a **nursing f** beareth the sucking child, 539
12:14 unto Moses, If her **f** had but spit in her face, 1
18: 2 the tribe of thy **f**, bring thou with thee, that they 1
27: 3 Our **f** died in the wilderness, and he was not in 1
27: 4 Why should the name of our **f** be done away 1
27: 4 a possession among the brethren of our **f**. 1
27: 7 thou shalt cause the inheritance of their **f** to 1
27:11 if his **f** have no brethren, then ye shall give his 1
30: 4 her **f** hear her vow, and her bond wherewith 1
30: 4 her soul, and her **f** shall hold his peace at her: 1
30: 5 if her **f** disallow her in the day that he heareth; 1
30: 5 shall forgive her, because her **f** disallowed her. 1
30:16 and his wife, between the **f** and his daughter, 1
36: 6 only to the family of the tribe of their **f** shall 1
36: 8 wife unto one of the family of the tribe of her **f**, 1
36:12 remained in the tribe of the family of their **f**. 1
Dt 5:16 Honour thy **f** and thy mother, as the LORD 1
21:13 and bewail her **f** and her mother a full month: 1
21:18 which will not obey the voice of his **f**, or 1

Dt 21:19 shall his f and his mother lay hold on him, 1
22:15 Then shall the f of the damsel, and her mother, 1
22:16 And the damsel's f shall say unto the elders, 1
22:19 and give *them* unto the f of the damsel, because 1
22:29 give unto the damsel's f fifty *shekels* of silver, 1
26: 5 A Syrian ready to perish *was* my f, and he went 1
27:16 Cursed *be* he that setteth light by his f or 1
27:22 the daughter of his f, or the daughter of his 1
32: 6 *is* not he thy f *that* hath bought thee? hath he 1
32: 7 ask thy f, and he will shew thee; thy elders, and 1
33: 9 Who said unto his f and to his mother, I have 1
Jos 2:13 *that* ye will save alive my f, and my mother, 1
2:18 and thou shalt bring thy f, and thy mother, and 1
6:23 her f, and her mother, and her brethren, and 1
15:13 *even* the city of Arba the f of Anak, which *city* 1
15:18 *him,* that she moved him to ask of her f a field: 1
17: 1 the firstborn of Manasseh, the f of Gilead: 1
17: 4 an inheritance among the brethren of their f. 1
19:47 Dan, after the name of Dan their f. 1
21:11 they gave them the city of Arbah the f of Anak, 1
24: 2 the f of Abraham, and the father of Nachor: 1
24: 2 the father of Abraham, and the f of Nachor: 1
24: 3 I took your f Abraham from the *other* side of 1
24:32 f of Shechem for an hundred pieces of silver: 1
Jdg 1:14 *him,* that she moved him to ask of her f a field: 1
1:16 the children of the Kenite, Moses' f **in law**, 2859
4:11 children of Hobab the f **in law** of Moses, 2859
6:25 throw down the altar of Baal that thy f hath, 1
8:32 and was buried in the sepulchre of Joash his f, 1
9: 1 all the family of the house of his mother's f, 1
9:17 (For my f fought for you, and adventured his 1
9:28 serve the men of Hamor the f of Shechem: 1
9:56 which he did unto his f, in slaying his seventy 1
11:36 she said unto him, My f, *if* thou hast opened 1
11:37 she said unto her f, Let this thing be done for 1
11:39 end of two months, that she returned unto her f, 1
14: 2 and told his f and his mother, and said, 1
14: 3 his f and his mother said unto him, *Is there* 1
14: 3 And Samson said unto his f, Get her for me; 1
14: 4 his f and his mother knew not that it *was* of 1
14: 5 his f and his mother, *to* Timnath, and came to 1
14: 6 he told not his f or his mother what he had 1
14: 9 came to his f and mother, and he gave them, 1
14:10 So his f went down unto the woman: and 1
14:16 I have not told *it* my f nor my mother, and shall 1
15: 1 But her f would not suffer him to go in. 1
15: 2 her f said, I verily thought that thou hadst 1
15: 6 came up, and burnt her and her f with fire. 1
16:31 and all the house of his f came down, 1
16:31 Eshtaol in the buryingplace of Manoah his f. 1
17:10 be unto me a f and a priest, and I will give thee 1
18:19 and go with us, and be to us a f and a priest: 1
18:29 after the name of Dan their f, who was born 1
19: 3 when the f of the damsel saw him, he rejoiced 1
19: 4 his f **in law**, the damsel's father, 2859
19: 4 his father in law, the damsel's f, retained him; 1
19: 5 the damsel's f said unto his son in law, 1
19: 6 for the damsel's f had said unto the man, 1
19: 7 rose up to depart, his f **in law** urged him: 2859
19: 8 and the damsel's f said, Comfort thine heart, 1
19: 9 his concubine, and his servant, his f **in law**, 2859
19: 9 the damsel's f, said unto him, Behold now, 1
Ru 2:11 and *how* thou hast left thy f and thy mother, 1
4:17 he *is* the f of Jesse, the father of David. 1
4:17 he *is* the father of Jesse, the f of David. 1
1Sa 2:25 they hearkened not unto the voice of their f, 1
2:27 Did I plainly appear unto the house of thy f, 1
2:28 did I give unto the house of thy f all 1
2:30 indeed *that* thy house, and the house of thy f, 1
4:19 that her f **in law** and her husband were 2524
4:21 because of her f **in law** and her husband. 2524
9: 3 the asses of Kish Saul's f were lost. And Kish 1
9: 5 lest my f leave *caring* for the asses, and 1
10: 2 and lo, thy f hath left the care of the asses, and 1
10:12 place answered and said, But who *is* their f? 1
14: 1 that *is* on the other side. But he told not his f. 1
14:27 Jonathan heard not when his f charged 1
14:28 Thy f straitly charged the people with an oath, 1
14:29 said Jonathan, My f hath troubled the land: 1
14:51 Kish *was* the f of Saul; and Ner the father of 1
14:51 and Ner the f of Abner *was* the son of Abiel. 1
19: 2 saying, Saul my f seeketh to kill thee: 1
19: 3 stand beside my f in the field where thou *art,* 1
19: 3 thou *art,* and I will commune with my f of thee; 1
19: 4 Jonathan spake good of David unto Saul his f, 1
20: 1 what *is* my sin before thy f, that he seeketh my 1
20: 2 my f will do nothing *either* great or small, but 1
20: 2 and why should my f hide this thing from me? 1
20: 3 Thy f certainly knoweth that I have found 1
20: 6 If thy f at all miss me, then say, 1
20: 8 for why shouldest thou bring me to thy f? 1
20: 9 were determined by my f to come upon thee, 1
20:10 tell me? or what *if* thy f answer thee roughly? 1
20:12 when I have sounded my f about to morrow 1
20:13 *but* if it please my f *to do* thee evil, then I will 1
20:13 be with thee, as he hath been with my f. 1
20:32 Jonathan answered Saul his f, and said unto 1
20:33 that it was determined of his f to slay David. 1
20:34 for David, because his f had done him shame. 1
22: 3 Let my f and my mother, I pray thee, 1
22:15 unto his servant, *nor* to all the house of my f: 1
23:17 for the hand of Saul my f shall not find thee; 1
23:17 unto thee; and that also Saul my f knoweth. 1
24:11 Moreover, my f, see, yea see the skirt of thy 1
2Sa 2:32 and buried him in the sepulchre of his f, 1
3: 8 kindness *this* day unto the house of Saul thy f, 1
6:21 which chose me before thy f, and before all his 1
7:14 I will be his f, and he shall be my son. If he 1
9: 7 and will restore thee all the land of Saul thy f; 1
10: 2 of Nahash, as his f shewed kindness unto me. 1
10: 2 him by the hand of his servants for his f. 1
10: 3 Thinkest thou that David doth honour thy f, 1
13: 5 when thy f cometh to see thee, say unto him, 1
16: 3 house of Israel restore me the kingdom of my f. 1
16:21 Israel shall hear that thou art abhorred of thy f: 1
17: 8 thou knowest thy f and his men, that they *be* 1
17: 8 thy f *is* a man of war, and will not lodge with 1
17:10 for all Israel knoweth that thy f *is* a mighty 1
17:23 died, and was buried in the sepulchre of his f. 1
19:37 *and be buried* by the grave of my f and of my 1
21:14 in Zelah, in the sepulchre of Kish his f: 1
1Ki 1: 6 his f had not displeased him at any time in 1
2:12 sat Solomon upon the throne of David his f; 1
2:24 and set me on the throne of David my f, and 1
2:26 the ark of the Lord GOD before David my f, 1
2:26 thou hast been afflicted in all where*in* my f was 1
2:31 from me, and from the house of my f. 1
2:32 my f David not knowing *thereof, to wit,* Abner 1
2:44 heart is privy to, that thou didst to David my f: 1
3: 3 walking in the statutes of David his f: 1
3: 6 Thou hast shewed unto thy servant David my f 1
3: 7 made thy servant king instead of David my f: 1
3:14 as thy f David did walk, then I will lengthen 1
5: 1 had anointed him king in the room of his f: 1
5: 3 Thou knowest how that David my f could not 1
5: 5 as the LORD spake unto David my f, saying, 1
6:12 with thee, which I spake unto David thy f: 1
7:14 and his f *was* a man of Tyre, a worker in brass: 1
7:51 in the *things* which David his f had dedicated; 1
8:15 which spake with his mouth unto David my f, 1
8:17 it was in the heart of David my f to build a 1
8:18 the LORD said unto David my f, Whereas it 1
8:20 and I am risen up in the room of David my f, 1
8:24 Who hast kept with thy servant David my f that 1
8:25 keep with thy servant David my f that thou 1
8:26 thou spakest unto thy servant David my f. 1
9: 4 as David thy f walked, in integrity of heart, and 1
9: 5 as I promised to David thy f, saying, 1
11: 4 his God, as *was* the heart of David his f. 1
11: 6 not fully after the LORD, as *did* David his f. 1
11:27 repaired the breaches of the city of David his f. 1
11:33 and my judgments, as *did* David his f. 1
11:43 and was buried in the city of David his f: 1
12: 4 Thy f made our yoke grievous: now therefore 1
12: 4 make thou the grievous service of thy f, 1
12: 6 that stood before Solomon his f while he *yet* 1
12: 9 Make the yoke which thy f did put upon us 1
12:10 Thy f made our yoke heavy, but make thou *it* 1
12:11 now whereas my f did lade you with a heavy 1
12:11 my f hath chastised you with whips, but I will 1
12:14 My f made your yoke heavy, and I will add to 1
12:14 my f *also* chastised you with whips, but I will 1
13:11 unto the king, them they told also to their f. 1
13:12 And their f said unto them, What way went he? 1
15: 3 he walked in all the sins of his f, which he had 1
15: 3 LORD his God, as the heart of David his f. 1
15:11 in the eyes of the LORD, as *did* David his f. 1
15:15 he brought in *the things* which his f had 1

1Ki 15:19 and thee, *and* between my f and thy father: 1
15:19 and thee, *and* between my father and thy f: 1
15:24 with his fathers in the city of David his f: 1
15:26 walked in the way of his f, and in his sin 1
19:20 kiss my f and my mother, and *then* I will 1
20:34 The cities, which my f took from thy father, 1
20:34 The cities, which my father took from thy f, 1
20:34 thee in Damascus, as my f made in Samaria. 1
22:43 he walked in all the ways of Asa his f; 1
22:46 which remained in the days of his f Asa, 1
22:50 with his fathers in the city of David his f: 1
22:52 walked in the way of his f, and in the way of 1
22:53 of Israel, according unto all that his f had done. 1
2Ki 2:12 Elisha saw *it,* and he cried, My f, my father, 1
2:12 Elisha saw *it,* and he cried, My father, my f, 1
3: 2 but not like his f, and like his mother: 1
3: 2 for he put away the image of Baal that his f had 1
3:13 get thee to the prophets of thy f, and to 1
4:18 a day, that he went out to his f to the reapers. 1
4:19 he said unto his f, My head, my head. And he 1
5:13 came near, and spake unto him, and said, My f, 1
6:21 said unto Elisha, when he saw them, My f, 1
9:25 when I and thou rode together after Ahab his f, 1
13:14 wept over his face, and said, O my f, my father, 1
13:14 wept over his face, and said, O my father, my f, 1
13:25 taken out of the hand of Jehoahaz his f by war. 1
14: 3 sight of the LORD, yet not like David his f: 1
14: 3 he did according to all *things* as Joash his f did. 1
14: 5 slew his servants which had slain the king his f. 1
14:21 and made him king instead of his f Amaziah. 1
15: 3 according to all that his f Amaziah had done; 1
15:34 he did according to all that his f Uzziah had 1
15:38 with his fathers in the city of David his f: 1
16: 2 sight of the LORD his God, like David his f. 1
18: 3 according to all that David his f did. 1
20: 5 Thus saith the LORD, the God of David thy f, 1
21: 3 places which Hezekiah his f had destroyed; 1
21:20 the sight of the LORD, as his f Manasseh did. 1
21:21 he walked in all the way that his f walked *in,* 1
21:21 and served the idols that his f served, 1
22: 2 and walked in all the way of David his f, and 1
23:34 son of Josiah king in the room of Josiah his f, 1
24: 9 according to all that his f had done. 1
1Ch 2:17 and the f of Amasa *was* Jether the Ishmeelite. 1
2:21 in to the daughter of Machir the f of Gilead, 1
2:23 All these *belonged to* the sons of Machir the f 1
2:24 Abiah Hezron's wife bare him Ashur the f of 1
2:42 Mesha his firstborn, which *was* the f of Ziph; 1
2:42 and the sons of Mareshah the f of Hebron. 1
2:44 And Shema begat Raham, the f of Jorkoam: 1
2:45 *was* Maon: and Maon *was* the f of Beth-zur. 1
2:49 She bare also Shaaph the f of Madmannah, 1
2:49 Sheva the f of Machbenah, and the father of 1
2:49 the father of Machbenah, and the f of Gibea: 1
2:50 of Ephratah; Shobal the f of Kirjath-jearim, 1
2:51 Salma the f of Beth-lehem, Hareph the father 1
2:51 of Beth-lehem, Hareph the f of Beth-gader. 1
2:52 And Shobal the f of Kirjath-jearim had sons; 1
2:55 came of Hemath, the f of the house of Rechab. 1
4: 3 And these *were of* the f of Etam; Jezreel, and 1
4: 4 Penuel the f of Gedor, and Ezer the father of 1
4: 4 the father of Gedor, and Ezer the f of Hushah. 1
4: 4 the firstborn of Ephratah, the f of Beth-lehem. 1
4: 5 Ashur the f of Tekoa had two wives, Helah 1
4:11 Shuah begat Mehir, which *was* the f of Eshton. 1
4:12 and Paseah, and Tehinnah the f of Irnahash. 1
4:14 begat Joab, the f of the valley of Charashim; 1
4:17 and Shammai, and Ishbah the f of Eshtemoa. 1
4:18 his wife Jehudijah bare Jered the f of Gedor, 1
4:18 Heber the f of Socho, and Jekuthiel the father 1
4:18 father of Socho, and Jekuthiel the f of Zanoah. 1
4:19 the f of Keilah the Garmite, and Eshtemoa 1
4:21 the son of Judah *were,* Er the f of Lecah, 1
4:21 Laadah the f of Mareshah, and the families of 1
7:14 his concubine the Aramitess bare Machir the f 1
7:22 And Ephraim their f mourned many days, and 1
7:31 Heber, and Malchiel, who *is* the f of Birzavith. 1
8:29 at Gibeon dwelt the f of Gibeon; whose wife's 1
9:19 his brethren, of the house of his f, 1
9:35 And in Gibeon dwelt the f of Gibeon, Jehiel, 1
17:13 I will be his f, and he shall be my son: and 1
19: 2 because his f shewed kindness to me. 1
19: 2 messengers to comfort him concerning his f. 1
19: 3 Thinkest thou that David doth honour thy f, 1
22:10 and he shall be my son, and I *will be* his f; and 1
24: 2 But Nadab and Abihu died before their f, and 1
24:19 according to their manner, under Aaron their f, 1
25: 3 six, under the hands of their f Jeduthun, 1
25: 6 All these *were* under the hands of their f for 1
26: 6 that ruled throughout the house of their f: 1
26:10 not the firstborn, yet his f made him the chief;) 1
28: 4 house of my f to be king over Israel for ever: 1
28: 4 and of the house of Judah, the house of my f; 1
28: 4 among the sons of my f he liked me to make 1
28: 6 chosen him to be my son, and I will be his f. 1
28: 9 know thou the God of thy f, and serve him with 1
29:10 LORD God of Israel our f, for ever and ever. 1
29:23 of the LORD as king instead of David his f, 1
2Ch 1: 8 hast shewed great mercy unto David my f, 1
1: 9 let thy promise unto David my f be established: 1
2: 3 As thou didst deal with David my f, and 1
2: 7 in Jerusalem, whom David my f did provide. 1
2:14 his f *was* a man of Tyre, skilful to work in 1
2:14 with the cunning *men* of my lord David thy f. 1
2:17 after the numbering where*with* David his f had 1
3: 1 where *the LORD* appeared unto David his f, 1
4:16 did Huram his f make to king Solomon for 1
5: 1 in *all the things* that David his f had dedicated; 1
6: 4 which he spake with his mouth to my f David, 1
6: 7 Now it was in the heart of David my f to build 1
6: 8 the LORD said to David my f, Forasmuch as 1
6:10 for I am risen up in the room of David my f, 1
6:15 David my f *that* which thou hast promised him; 1
6:16 keep with thy servant David my f *that* which 1
7:17 as David thy f walked, and do according to all 1
7:18 as I have covenanted with David thy f, 1
8:14 according to the order of David his f, 1
9:31 and he was buried in the city of David his f: 1
10: 4 Thy f made our yoke grievous: now therefore 1
10: 4 thou somewhat the grievous servitude of thy f, 1
10: 6 stood before Solomon his f while he *yet* lived, 1
10: 9 Ease somewhat the yoke that thy f did put upon 1
10:10 Thy f made our yoke heavy, but make thou *it* 1
10:11 For whereas my f put a heavy yoke upon you, 1
10:11 my f chastised you with whips, but I *will* 1
10:14 My f made your yoke heavy, but I will add 1
10:14 my f chastised you with whips, but I *will* 1
15:18 of God *the things* that his f had dedicated, 1
16: 3 thee, as *there was* between my f and thy father: 1
16: 3 thee, as *there was* between my father and thy f: 1
17: 2 cities of Ephraim, which Asa his f had taken. 1
17: 3 he walked in the first ways of his f David, 1
17: 4 sought to the *LORD* God of his f, and 1
20:32 he walked in the way of Asa his f, and 1
21: 3 And their f gave them great gifts of silver, and 1
21: 4 Jehoram was risen up to the kingdom of his f, 1
21:12 Thus saith the LORD God of David thy f, 1
21:12 not walked in the ways of Jehoshaphat thy f, 1
22: 4 after the death of his f to his destruction. 1
24:22 kindness which Jehoiada his f had done to him, 1
25: 3 slew his servants that had killed the king his f. 1
26: 1 made him king in the room of his f Amaziah. 1
26: 4 according to all that his f Amaziah did. 1
27: 2 according to all that his f Uzziah did: 1
28: 1 in the sight of the LORD, like David his f: 1
29: 2 according to all that David his f had done. 1
33: 3 places which Hezekiah his f had broken down, 1
33:22 the sight of the LORD, as did Manasseh his f: 1
33:22 carved images which Manasseh his f had made, 1
33:23 as Manasseh his f had humbled himself; 1
34: 2 walked in the ways of David his f, and 1
34: 3 he began to seek after the God of David his f: 1
Est 2: 7 for she had neither f nor mother, and the maid 1
2: 7 when her f and mother were dead, 1
Job 15:10 and very aged men, much elder than thy f. 1
17:14 I have said to corruption, Thou *art* my f: to 1
29:16 I *was* a f to the poor: and the cause *which* I 1
31:18 as *with* a f, and I have guided her from my 1
38:28 Hath the rain a f? or who hath begotten 1
42:15 their f gave them inheritance among their 1
Ps 27:10 When my f and my mother forsake me, then 1
68: 5 A f of the fatherless, and a judge of 1
89:26 Thou *art* my F, my God, and the rock of my 1
103:13 Like as a f pitieth *his* children, *so* the LORD 1
Pr 1: 8 hear the instruction of thy f, and forsake not 1
3:12 even as a f the son *in whom* he delighteth. 1
4: 1 the instruction of a f, and attend to know 1
10: 1 A wise son maketh a glad f: but a foolish son *is* 1

Pr	15:20	A wise son maketh a glad f: but a foolish man	1
	17:21	*it* to his sorrow: and the f of a fool hath no joy.	1
	17:25	A foolish son *is* a grief to his f, and	1
	19:13	A foolish son *is* the calamity of his f: and	1
	19:26	He that wasteth *his* f, *and* chaseth away *his*	1
	20:20	Whoso curseth his f or his mother, his lamp	1
	23:22	Hearken unto thy f that begat thee, and	1
	23:24	The f of the righteous shall greatly rejoice: and	1
	23:25	Thy f and thy mother shall be glad, and she that	1
	28: 7	is a companion of riotous *men* shameth his f.	1
	28:24	Whoso robbeth his f or his mother, and saith,	1
	29: 3	Whoso loveth wisdom rejoiceth his f: but	1
	30:11	*There is* a generation *that* curseth their f, and	1
	30:17	The eye *that* mocketh at *his* f, and despiseth to	1
Isa	3: 6	take hold of his brother *of* the house of his f,	1
	8: 4	My f, and my mother, the riches of Damascus	1
	9: 6	The mighty God, The everlasting F,	1
	22:21	he shall be a f to the inhabitants of Jerusalem,	1
	38: 5	Thus saith the LORD, the God of David thy f,	1
	38:19	the f to the children shall make known thy	1
	43:27	Thy first f hath sinned, and thy teachers have	1
	45:10	Woe unto him that saith unto *his* f,	1
	51: 2	Look unto Abraham your f, and unto Sarah *that*	1
	58:14	and feed thee with the heritage of Jacob thy f:	1
	63:16	Doubtless thou *art* our f, though Abraham be	1
	63:16	thou, O LORD, *art* our f, our redeemer;	1
	64: 8	now, O LORD, thou *art* our f; we *are* the clay,	1
Jer	2:27	Saying to a stock, Thou *art* my f; and to a	1
	3: 4	unto me, My f, thou *art* the guide of my youth?	1
	3:19	I said, Thou shalt call me, My f; and shalt not	1
	12: 6	For even thy brethren, and the house of thy f,	1
	16: 7	them the cup of consolation to drink for their f	1
	20:15	*be* the man who brought tidings to my f,	1
	22:11	which reigned instead of Josiah his f,	1
	22:15	did not thy f eat and drink, and do judgment	1
	31: 9	for I am a f to Israel, and Ephraim *is* my	1
	35: 6	for Jonadab the son of Rechab our f	1
	35: 8	of Rechab our f in all that he hath charged us,	1
	35:10	done according to all that Jonadab our f	1
	35:16	have performed the commandment of their f,	1
	35:18	obeyed the commandment of Jonadab your f,	1
Eze	16: 3	thy f *was* an Amorite, and thy mother a Hittite.	1
	16:45	mother *was* a Hittite, and your f an Amorite.	1
	18: 4	as the soul of the f, so also the soul of the son	1
	18:17	he shall not die for the iniquity of his f, he shall	1
	18:18	*As for* his f, because he cruelly oppressed,	1
	18:19	doth not the son bear the iniquity of the f?	1
	18:20	The son shall not bear the iniquity of the f,	1
	18:20	neither shall the f bear the iniquity of the son:	1
	22: 7	In thee have they set light by f and mother:	1
	44:25	no dead person to defile *themselves:* but for f,	1
Da	5: 2	silver vessels which his f Nebuchadnezzar had	2
	5:11	and in the days of thy f light and understanding	2
	5:11	whom the king Nebuchadnezzar thy f, the king,	2
	5:11	the king, *I say,* thy f, made master of	2
	5:13	whom the king my f brought out of Jewry?	2
	5:18	the most high God gave Nebuchadnezzar thy f	2
Am	2: 7	a man and his f will go in unto the *same* maid,	1
Mic	7: 6	For the son dishonoureth the f, the daughter	1
Zec	13: 3	his f and his mother that begat him shall say	1
	13: 3	his f and his mother that begat him shall thrust	1
Mal	1: 6	A son honoureth *his* f, and a servant his master:	1
	1: 6	if then I *be* a f, where *is* mine honour? and if I	1
	2:10	Have we not all one f? hath not one God	1
Mt	2:22	reign in Judea in the room of his f Herod,	*3962*
	3: 9	We have Abraham to *our* f:	*3962*
	4:21	his brother, in a ship with Zebedee their f,	*3962*
	4:22	they immediately left the ship and their f,	*3962*
	5:16	and glorify your F which is in heaven.	*3962*
	5:45	That ye may be the children of your F	*3962*
	5:48	even as your F which is in heaven is	*3962*
	6: 1	otherwise ye have no reward of your F	*3962*
	6: 4	thy F which seeth in secret himself shall	*3962*
	6: 6	thy door, pray to thy F which is in secret;	*3962*
	6: 6	thy F which seeth in secret shall reward	*3962*
	6: 8	for your F knoweth what *things* ye have	*3962*
	6: 9	Our F which art in heaven, Hallowed be	*3962*
	6:14	your heavenly F will also forgive you:	*3962*
	6:15	neither will your F forgive your trespasses.	*3962*
	6:18	to fast, but unto thy F which is in secret:	*3962*
	6:18	and thy F, which seeth in secret,	*3962*
	6:26	yet your heavenly F feedeth them.	*3962*
	6:32	for your heavenly F knoweth that ye have	*3962*
	7:11	how much more shall your F which is in	*3962*
	7:21	he that doeth the will of my F which is in	*3962*
	8:21	Lord, suffer me first to go and bury my f.	*3962*
	10:20	the Spirit of your F which speaketh in you.	*3962*
	10:21	up the brother to death, and the f the child:	*3962*
	10:29	shall not fall on the ground without your F.	*3962*
	10:32	him will I confess also before my F which	*3962*
	10:33	him will I also deny before my F which is	*3962*
	10:35	come to set a man at variance against his f,	*3962*
	10:37	He that loveth f or mother more than me is	*3962*
	11:25	Jesus answered and said, I thank thee, O F,	*3962*
	11:26	Even so, F: for so it seemed good in thy	*3962*
	11:27	All *things* are delivered unto me of my F:	*3962*
	11:27	and no *man* knoweth the Son, but the F;	*3962*
	11:27	neither knoweth any *man* the F, save	*3962*
	12:50	For whosoever shall do the will of my F	*3962*
	13:43	forth as the sun in the kingdom of their F.	*3962*
	15: 4	saying, Honour thy f and mother:	*3962*
	15: 4	and, He that curseth f or mother, let him die	*3962*
	15: 5	Whosoever shall say to *his* f or *his* mother,	*3962*
	15: 6	And honour not his f or his mother, *he shall*	*3962*
	15:13	which my heavenly F hath not planted,	*3962*
	16:17	*it* unto thee, but my F which is in heaven.	*3962*
	16:27	come in the glory of his F with his angels:	*3962*
	18:10	behold the face of my F which is in heaven.	*3962*
	18:14	it is not the will of your F which is in	*3962*
	18:19	it shall be done for them of my F which is	*3962*
	18:35	So likewise shall my heavenly F do *also*	*3962*
	19: 5	For this cause shall a man leave f and	*3962*
	19:19	Honour thy f and *thy* mother: and,	*3962*
	19:29	or f, or mother, or wife, or children, or	*3962*
	20:23	*to them* for whom it is prepared of my F.	*3962*
	21:31	Whether of *them* twain did the will of *his* f?	*3962*
	23: 9	And call no *man* your f upon the earth:	*3962*
	23: 9	for one is your F, which is in heaven.	*3962*
	24:36	not the angels of heaven, but my F only.	*3962*
	25:34	his right hand, Come, ye blessed of my F,	*3962*
	26:39	on his face, and prayed, saying, O my F,	*3962*
	26:42	second time, and prayed, saying, O my F,	*3962*
	26:53	thou that I cannot now pray to my F,	*3962*
	28:19	baptizing them in the name of the F, and	*3962*
Mk	1:20	they left their f Zebedee in the ship with	*3962*
	5:40	he taketh the f and the mother of	*3962*
	7:10	Moses said, Honour thy f and thy mother;	*3962*
	7:10	and, Whoso curseth f or mother, let him die	*3962*
	7:11	ye say, If a man shall say to *his* f or mother,	*3962*
	7:12	ye suffer him no more to do ought for his f	*3962*
	8:38	when he cometh in the glory of his F with	*3962*
	9:21	And he asked his f, How long is it ago	*3962*
	9:24	And straightway the f of the child cried out,	*3962*
	10: 7	For this cause shall a man leave his f and	*3962*
	10:19	Defraud not, Honour thy f and mother.	*3962*
	10:29	or f, or mother, or wife, or children, or	*3962*
	11:10	Blessed *be* the kingdom of our f David,	*3962*
	11:25	that your F also which is in heaven may	*3962*
	11:26	neither will your F which is in heaven	*3962*
	13:12	the brother to death, and the f the son;	*3962*
	13:32	are in heaven, neither the Son, but the F.	*3962*
	14:36	And he said, Abba, F, all *things are*	*3962*
	15:21	the f of Alexander and Rufus, to bear his	*3962*
Lk	1:32	give unto him the throne of his f David:	*3962*
	1:59	him Zacharias, after the name of his f.	*3962*
	1:62	And they made signs to his f, how he	*3962*
	1:67	And his f Zacharias was filled with	*3962*
	1:73	The oath which he sware to our f Abraham,	*3962*
	2:48	thy f and I have sought thee sorrowing.	*3962*
	3: 8	We have Abraham to *our* f:	*3962*
	6:36	merciful, as your F also is merciful.	*3962*
	8:51	and the f and the mother of the maiden.	*3962*
	9:42	the child, and delivered him again to his f.	*3962*
	9:59	Lord, suffer me first to go and bury my f.	*3962*
	10:21	and said, I thank thee, O F, Lord of heaven	*3962*
	10:21	even so, F; for so it seemed good in thy	*3962*
	10:22	All *things* are delivered to me of my F: and	*3962*
	10:22	no *man* knoweth who the Son is, but the F;	*3962*
	10:22	and who the F is, but the Son, and *he* to	*3962*
	11: 2	ye pray, say, Our F which art in heaven,	*3962*
	11:11	son shall ask bread of any of you that is a f,	*3962*
	11:13	how much more shall *your* heavenly F give	*3962*
	12:30	your F knoweth that ye have need of these	*3962*
	12:53	The f shall be divided against the son, and	*3962*
	12:53	against the son, and the son against the f;	*3962*
	14:26	and hate not his f, and mother, and wife,	*3962*
	15:12	And the younger of them said to *his* f,	*3962*
	15:12	the younger of them said to *his* father, F,	*3962*

Lk	15:18	I will arise and go to my **f**, and will say	3962
	15:18	go to my father, and will say unto him, **F**,	3962
	15:20	And he arose, and came to his **f**. But when	3962
	15:20	his **f** saw him, and had compassion, and	3962
	15:21	And the son said unto him, **F**, I have sinned	3962
	15:22	But the **f** said to his servants, Bring forth	3962
	15:27	and thy **f** hath killed the fatted calf,	3962
	15:28	therefore came his **f** out and intreated him.	3962
	15:29	And he answering said to *his* **f**, Lo,	3962
	16:24	And he cried and said, **F** Abraham,	3962
	16:27	Then he said, I pray thee therefore, **f**,	3962
	16:30	And he said, Nay, **f** Abraham: but if one	3962
	18:20	false witness, Honour thy **f** and thy mother.	3962
	22:29	as my **F** hath appointed unto me;	3962
	22:42	Saying, **F**, if thou be willing, remove this	3962
	23:34	Then said Jesus, **F**, forgive them; for they	3962
	23:46	he said, **F**, into thy hands I commend my	3962
	24:49	I send the promise of my **F** upon you:	3962
Jn	1:14	the glory as of the only begotten of the **F**,)	3962
	1:18	which is in the bosom of the **F**, he hath	3962
	3:35	The **F** loveth the Son, and hath given all	3962
	4:12	Art thou greater than our **f** Jacob,	3962
	4:21	nor *yet* at Jerusalem, worship the **F**.	3962
	4:23	worshippers shall worship the **F** in spirit	3962
	4:23	for the **F** seeketh such to worship him.	3962
	4:53	So the **f** knew that *it was* at the same hour,	3962
	5:17	answered them, My **F** worketh hitherto,	3962
	5:18	but said also that God was his **F**,	3962
	5:19	of himself, but what he seeth the **F** do:	3962
	5:20	For the **F** loveth the Son, and sheweth him	3962
	5:21	For as the **F** raiseth up the dead, and	3962
	5:22	For the **F** judgeth no *man*, but	3962
	5:23	honour the Son, even as they honour the **F**.	3962
	5:23	honoureth not the **F** which hath sent him.	3962
	5:26	For as the **F** hath life in himself; so hath he	3962
	5:30	but the will of the **F** which hath sent me.	3962
	5:36	for the works which the **F** hath given me to	3962
	5:36	bear witness of me, that the **F** hath sent me.	3962
	5:37	And the **F** himself, which hath sent me,	3962
	5:45	Do not think that I will accuse you to the **F**:	3962
	6:27	unto you: for him hath God the **F** sealed.	3962
	6:32	my **F** giveth you the true bread from	3962
	6:37	All that the **F** giveth me shall come to me;	3962
	6:42	of Joseph, whose **f** and mother we know?	3962
	6:44	except the **F** which hath sent me draw him:	3962
	6:45	that hath heard, and hath learned of the **F**,	3962
	6:46	Not that any *man* hath seen the **F**, save he	3962
	6:46	he which is of God, he hath seen the **F**.	3962
	6:57	As the living **F** hath sent me, and I live by	3962
	6:57	Father hath sent me, and I live by the **F**:	3962
	6:65	except it were given unto him of my **F**.	3962
	8:16	I am not alone, but I and the **F** that sent me.	3962
	8:18	the **F** that sent me beareth witness of me.	3962
	8:19	Then said they unto him, Where is thy **F**?	3962
	8:19	Ye neither know me, nor my **F**:	3962
	8:19	ye should have known my **F** also.	3962
	8:27	not that he spake to them of the **F**.	3962
	8:28	but as my **F** hath taught me, I speak these	3962
	8:29	the **F** hath not left me alone; for I do	3962
	8:38	I speak *that* which I have seen with my **F**:	3962
	8:38	ye do *that* which ye have seen with your **f**.	3962
	8:39	and said unto him, Abraham is our **f**.	3962
	8:41	Ye do the deeds of your **f**. Then said they to	3962
	8:41	of fornication; we have one **F**, *even* God.	3962
	8:42	If God were your **F**, ye would love me:	3962
	8:44	Ye are of *your* **f** the devil, and the lusts of	3962
	8:44	the devil, and the lusts of your **f** ye will do.	3962
	8:44	of his own: for he is a liar, and the **f** of it.	3962
	8:49	but I honour my **F**, and ye do dishonour	3962
	8:53	Art thou greater than our **f** Abraham,	3962
	8:54	it is my **F** that honoureth me; of whom ye	3962
	8:56	Your **f** Abraham rejoiced to see my day:	3962
	10:15	As the **F** knoweth me, *even* so know I	3962
	10:15	Father knoweth me, *even* so know I the **F**:	3962
	10:17	Therefore doth *my* **F** love me, because I lay	3962
	10:18	commandment have I received of my **F**.	3962
	10:29	My **F**, which gave *them* me, is greater than	3962
	10:30	I and *my* **F** are one.	3962
	10:32	good works have I shewed you from my **F**;	3962
	10:36	Say ye *of him*, whom the **F** hath sanctified,	3962
	10:37	If I do not the works of my **F**, believe me	3962
	10:38	believe, that the **F** *is* in me, and I in him.	3962
	11:41	And Jesus lift up *his* eyes, and said, **F**,	3962
	12:26	any *man* serve me, him will *my* **F** honour.	3962
	12:27	**F**, save me from this hour: but for this	3962
	12:28	**F**, glorify thy name. Then came there a	3962
	12:49	but the **F** which sent me, he gave me a	3962
	12:50	even as the **F** said unto me, so I speak.	3962
	13: 1	should depart out of this world unto the **F**,	3962
	13: 3	Jesus knowing that the **F** had given all	3962
	14: 6	no *man* cometh unto the **F**, but by me.	3962
	14: 7	ye should have known my **F** also:	3962
	14: 8	Lord, shew us the **F**, and it sufficeth us.	3962
	14: 9	he that hath seen me hath seen the **F**; and	3962
	14: 9	and how sayest thou *then*, Shew us the **F**?	3962
	14:10	Believest thou not that I am in the **F**, and	3962
	14:10	that I am in the Father, and the **F** in me?	3962
	14:10	but the **F** that dwelleth in me, he doeth	3962
	14:11	Believe me that I *am* in the **F**, and	3962
	14:11	me that I *am* in the Father, and the **F** in me:	3962
	14:12	these shall he do; because I go unto my **F**.	3962
	14:13	I do, that the **F** may be glorified in the Son.	3962
	14:16	And I will pray the **F**, and he shall give you	3962
	14:20	that day ye shall know that I *am* in my **F**,	3962
	14:21	he that loveth me shall be loved of my **F**,	3962
	14:23	and my **F** will love him, and we will come	3962
	14:26	whom the **F** will send in my name,	3962
	14:28	because I said, I go unto the **F**:	3962
	14:28	unto the Father: for my **F** is greater than I.	3962
	14:31	that the world may know that I love the **F**;	3962
	14:31	and as the **F** gave me commandment, *even*	3962
	15: 1	the true vine, and my **F** is the husbandman.	3962
	15: 8	Herein is my **F** glorified, that ye bear much	3962
	15: 9	As the **F** hath loved me, so have I loved	3962
	15:15	for all *things* that I have heard of my **F** I	3962
	15:16	that whatsoever ye shall ask of the **F** in my	3962
	15:23	He that hateth me hateth my **F** also.	3962
	15:24	both seen and hated both me and my **F**.	3962
	15:26	whom I will send unto you from the **F**,	3962
	15:26	which proceedeth from the **F**, he shall	3962
	16: 3	because they have not known the **F**,	3962
	16:10	because I go to my **F**, and ye see me no	3962
	16:15	All *things* that the **F** hath are mine:	3962
	16:16	and ye shall see me, because I go to the **F**.	3962
	16:17	ye shall see me: and, Because I go to the **F**?	3962
	16:23	Whatsoever ye shall ask the **F** in my name,	3962
	16:25	but I shall shew you plainly of the **F**.	3962
	16:26	not unto you, that I will pray the **F** for you:	3962
	16:27	For the **F** himself loveth you, because	3962
	16:28	I came forth from the **F**, and am come into	3962
	16:28	again, I leave the world, and go to the **F**.	3962
	16:32	I am not alone, because the **F** is with me.	3962
	17: 1	to heaven, and said, **F**, the hour is come;	3962
	17: 5	And now, O **F**, glorify thou me with thine	3962
	17:11	Holy **F**, keep through thine own name	3962
	17:21	as thou, **F**, *art* in me, and I in thee, that they	3962
	17:24	**F**, I will that they also, whom thou hast	3962
	17:25	O righteous **F**, the world hath not known	3962
	18:11	the cup which my **F** hath given me, shall I	3962
	18:13	for he was **f in law** to Caiaphas, which was	3995
	20:17	me not; for I am not yet ascended to my **F**:	3962
	20:17	I ascend unto my **F**, and your Father;	3962
	20:17	I ascend unto my Father, and your **F**;	3962
	20:21	as *my* **F** hath sent me, even *so* send I you.	3962
Ac	1: 4	but wait for the promise of the **F**, which,	3962
	1: 7	which the **F** hath put in his own power.	3962
	2:33	having received of the **F** the promise of	3962
	7: 2	The God of glory appeared unto our **f**	3962
	7: 4	and from thence, when his **f** was dead,	3962
	7:14	and called his **f** Jacob to *him*, and all his	3962
	7:16	of the sons of Emmor the ***f*** of Sychem.	NIG
	16: 1	and believed; but his **f** *was* a Greek:	3962
	16: 3	for they knew all that his **f** was a Greek.	3962
	28: 8	that the **f** of Publius lay sick of a fever and	3962
Ro	1: 7	Grace to you and peace from God our **F**,	3962
	4: 1	What shall we say then that Abraham our **f**,	3962
	4:11	that he might be the **f** of all them that	3962
	4:12	And the **f** of circumcision to them who are	3962
	4:12	in the steps of *that* faith of our **F** Abraham,	3962
	4:16	the faith of Abraham; who is the **f** of us all,	3962
	4:17	I have made thee a **f** of many nations,)	3962
	4:18	that he might become the **f** of many	3962
	6: 4	up from the dead by the glory of the **F**,	3962
	8:15	of adoption, whereby we cry, Abba, **F**.	3962
	9:10	had conceived by one, *even* by our **f** Isaac;	3962
	15: 6	even the **F** of our Lord Jesus Christ.	3962
1Co	1: 3	from God our **F**, and *from* the Lord Jesus	3962
	8: 6	But to us *there is but* one God, the **F**,	3962

1Co 15:24 up the kingdom to God, even the **F**; 3962
2Co 1: 2 Grace *be* to you and peace from God our **F**, 3962
1: 3 even the **F** of our Lord Jesus Christ, 3962
1: 3 the **F** of mercies, and the God of all 3962
6:18 And will be a **F** unto you, and ye shall be 3962
11:31 The God and **F** of our Lord Jesus Christ, 3962
Gal 1: 1 by man, but by Jesus Christ, and God the **F**, 3962
1: 3 Grace *be* to you and peace from God the **F**, 3962
1: 4 according to the will of God and our **F**: 3962
4: 2 governors until the time appointed of the **f**. 3962
4: 6 his Son into your hearts, crying, Abba, **F**. 3962
Eph 1: 2 from God our **F**, and *from* the Lord Jesus 3962
1: 3 *be* the God and **F** of our Lord Jesus Christ, 3962
1:17 of our Lord Jesus Christ, the **F** of glory, 3962
2:18 both have access by one Spirit unto the **F**. 3962
3:14 For this cause I bow my knees unto the **F** 3962
4: 6 One God and **F** of all, who *is* above all, and 3962
5:20 the **F** in the name of our Lord Jesus Christ; 3962
5:31 For this cause shall a man leave his **f** and 3962
6: 2 Honour thy **f** and mother; (which is the first 3962
6:23 from God the **F** and the Lord Jesus Christ. 3962
Php 1: 2 from God our **F**, and *from* the Lord Jesus 3962
2:11 Christ *is* Lord, to the glory of God the **F**. 3962
2:22 the proof of him, that, as a son *with the* **f**, 3962
4:20 and our **F** *be* glory for ever and ever. 3962
Col 1: 2 from God our **F** and the Lord Jesus Christ. 3962
1: 3 to God and the **F** of our Lord Jesus Christ, 3962
1:12 Giving thanks unto the **F**, which hath made 3962
1:19 For it pleased *the* **F** that in him should all NIG
2: 2 of the mystery of God and of the **F**, 3962
3:17 giving thanks to God and the **F** by him. 3962
1Th 1: 1 of the Thessalonians *which is* in God the **F** 3962
1: 1 from God our **F**, and the Lord Jesus Christ. 3962
1: 3 Jesus Christ, in the sight of God and our **F**; 3962
2:11 every one of you, as a **f** *doth* his children, 3962
3:11 Now God himself and our **F**, and our Lord 3962
3:13 even our **F**, at the coming of our Lord Jesus 3962
2Th 1: 1 church of the Thessalonians in God our **F** 3962
1: 2 from God our **F** and the Lord Jesus Christ. 3962
2:16 and God, even our **F**, which hath loved us, 3962
1Ti 1: 2 from God our **F** and Jesus Christ our Lord. 3962
5: 1 Rebuke not an elder, but intreat *him* as a **f**; 3962
2Ti 1: 2 from God the **F** and Christ Jesus our Lord. 3962
Tit 1: 4 from God the **F** and the Lord Jesus Christ 3962
Phm 1: 3 from God our **F** and the Lord Jesus Christ. 3962
Heb 1: 5 I will be to him a **F**, and he shall be to me a 3962
7: 3 **Without f**, without mother, without descent, 540
7:10 For he was yet in the loins of his **f**, 3962
12: 7 for what son is *he* whom the **f** chasteneth 3962
12: 9 rather be in subjection unto the **F** of spirits, 3962
Jas 1:17 and cometh down from the **F** of lights, 3962
1:27 and undefiled before God and the **F** is this, 3962
2:21 Was not Abraham our **f** justified by works, 3962
3: 9 Therewith bless we God, even the **F**; and 3962
1Pe 1: 2 to the foreknowledge of God the **F**, 3962
1: 3 *be* the God and **F** of our Lord Jesus Christ, 3962
1:17 And if ye call on the **F**, who without 3962
2Pe 1:17 For he received from God the **F** honour and 3962
1Jn 1: 2 which was with the **F**, and was manifested 3962
1: 3 and truly our fellowship *is* with the **F**, and 3962
2: 1 *man* sin, we have an advocate with the **F**, 3962
2:13 because ye have known the **F**. 3962
2:15 the world, the love of the **F** is not in him. 3962
2:16 of life, is not of the **F**, but is of the world. 3962
2:22 is antichrist, that denieth the **F** and the Son. 3962
2:23 denieth the Son, the same hath not the **F**: 3962
2:23 *he that acknowledgeth the Son hath the* **F** NIG
2:24 also shall continue in the Son, and in the **F**. 3962
3: 1 what manner of love the **F** hath bestowed 3962
4:14 do testify that the **F** sent the Son *to be* 3962
5: 7 the **F**, the Word, and the Holy Ghost: 3962
2Jn 1: 3 from God the **F**, and from the Lord Jesus 3962
1: 3 the Son of the **F**, in truth and love. 3962
1: 4 have received a commandment from the **F**. 3962
1: 9 of Christ, he hath both the **F** and the Son. 3962
Jude 1: 1 to them that are sanctified by God the **F**, 3962
Rev 1: 6 us kings and priests unto God and his **F**; 3962
2:27 to shivers: even as I received of my **F**. 3962
3: 5 but I will confess his name before my **F**, 3962
3:21 and am set down with my **F** in his throne. 3962

FATHER'S (144) [FATHER]

Ge 9:23 and they saw not their **f** nakedness. 1
12: 1 and from thy kindred, and from thy **f** house, 1
20:13 when God caused me to wander from my **f** 1
24: 7 which took me from my **f** house, and from 1
24:23 is there room *in* thy **f** house for us to lodge in? 1
24:38 thou shalt go unto my **f** house, and to my 1
24:40 for my son of my kindred, and of my **f** house: 1
26:15 For all the wells which his **f** servants had 1
28:21 So that I come again to my **f** house in peace; 1
29: 9 Rachel came with her **f** sheep: 1+3807.1
29:12 Jacob told Rachel that he *was* her **f** brother, 1
31: 1 hath taken away all that *was* our **f**; 1+3807.1
31: 1 of *that* which *was* of our **f** hath he 1+3807.1
31: 5 And said unto them, I see your **f** countenance, 1
31:14 or inheritance for us in our **f** house? 1
31:19 had stolen the images that *were* her **f**. 1+3807.1
31:30 because thou sore longedst after thy **f** house, 1
35:22 and lay with Bilhah his **f** concubine: 1
37: 2 and with the sons of Zilpah, his **f** wives: 1
37:12 his brethren went to feed their **f** flock in 1
38:11 Remain a widow *at* thy **f** house, till Shelah my 1
38:11 *did*. And Tamar went and dwelt *in* her **f** house. 1
41:51 made me forget all my toil, and all my **f** house. 1
46:31 unto his **f** house, I will go up, and 1
46:31 say unto him, My brethren, and my **f** house, 1
47:12 and all his **f** household, *with* bread, 1
48:17 he held up his **f** hand, to remove it from 1
49: 4 because thou wentest up to thy **f** bed; then 1
49: 8 thy **f** children shall bow down before thee. 1
50: 1 Joseph fell upon his **f** face, and wept upon him, 1
50: 8 of Joseph, and his brethren, and his **f** house: 1
50:22 And Joseph dwelt in Egypt, he, and his **f** house: 1
Ex 2:16 and filled the troughs to water their **f** flock. 1
6:20 Amram took him Jochebed his **f sister** to 1733
15: 2 a habitation; my **f** God, and I will exalt him. 1
Lev 16:32 to minister in the priest's office in his **f** stead, 1
18: 8 The nakedness of thy **f** wife shalt thou not 1
18: 8 shalt thou not uncover: it *is* thy **f** nakedness. 1
18:11 The nakedness of thy **f** wife's daughter, 1
18:12 Thou shalt not uncover the nakedness of thy **f** 1
18:12 thy father's sister: she *is* thy **f** near kinswoman. 1
18:14 Thou shalt not uncover the nakedness of thy **f** 1
20:11 the man that lieth with his **f** wife hath 1
20:11 father's wife hath uncovered his **f** nakedness: 1
20:17 his **f** daughter, or his mother's daughter, and 1
20:19 of thy mother's sister, nor of thy **f** sister: 1
22:13 have no child, and is returned unto her **f** house, 1
22:13 as *in* her youth, she shall eat of her **f** meat: 1
Nu 2: 2 own standard, with the ensign of their **f** house: 1
18: 1 thy **f** house with thee shall bear the iniquity of 1
27: 7 of an inheritance among their **f** brethren; 1
27:10 ye shall give his inheritance unto his **f** brethren. 1
30: 3 *by* a bond, *being* in her **f** house in her youth; 1
30:16 *being yet* in her youth *in* her **f** house. 1
36:11 were married unto their **f brothers'** sons: 1730
Dt 22:21 bring out the damsel to the door of her **f** house, 1
22:21 folly in Israel, to play the whore *in* her **f** house: 1
22:30 A man shall not take his **f** wife, nor discover 1
22:30 take his father's wife, nor discover his **f** skirt. 1
27:20 Cursed *be* he that lieth with his **f** wife; because 1
27:20 father's wife; because he uncovereth his **f** skirt. 1
Jos 2:12 that ye will also shew kindness unto my **f** 1
2:18 and thy brethren, and all thy **f** household, 1
6:25 and her **f** household, and all that she had; 1
Jdg 6:15 in Manasseh, and I *am* the least in my **f** house. 1
6:25 said unto him, Take thy **f** young bullock, 1
6:27 because he feared his **f** household, and the men 1
9: 5 And he went unto his **f** house at Ophrah, and 1
9:18 ye are risen up against my **f** house *this* day, 1
11: 2 unto him, Thou shalt not inherit in our **f** house; 1
11: 7 ye hate me, and expel me out of my **f** house? 1
14:15 lest we burn thee and thy **f** house with fire: 1
14:19 was kindled, and he went up *to* his **f** house. 1
19: 2 went away from him unto her **f** house to 1
19: 3 she brought him *into* her **f** house: and when 1
1Sa 2:31 cut off thine arm, and the arm of thy **f** house, 1
9:20 *Is it* not on thee, and on all thy **f** house? 1
17:15 returned from Saul to feed his **f** sheep *at* 1
17:25 and make his **f** house free in Israel. 1
17:34 Thy servant kept his **f** sheep, and 1+3807.1
18: 2 would let him go no more home *to* his **f** house. 1
18:18 and what *is* my life, *or* my **f** family in Israel, 1
22: 1 all his **f** house heard *it*, they went down thither 1
22:11 the son of Ahitub, and all his **f** house, 1
22:16 Ahimelech, thou, and all thy **f** house. 1
22:22 *the death* of all the persons of thy **f** house. 1

1Sa 24:21 that thou wilt not destroy my name out of my f 1
2Sa 3: 7 Wherefore hast thou gone in unto my f 1
3:29 rest on the head of Joab, and on all his f house; 1
9: 7 shew thee kindness for Jonathan thy f sake, 1
14: 9 the iniquity *be* on me, and on my f house: 1
15:34 as I *have been* thy f servant hitherto, so *will* I 1
16:19 as I have served in thy f presence, so will I be 1
16:21 unto Absalom, Go in unto thy f concubines, 1
16:22 Absalom went in unto his f concubines in 1
19:28 For all *of* my f house were but dead men before 1
24:17 be against me, and against my f house. 1
1Ki 11:12 in thy days I will not do it for David thy f sake: 1
11:17 certain Edomites of his f servants with him, 1
12:10 My little *finger* shall be thicker than my f loins. 1
18:18 thou, and thy f house, in that ye have forsaken 1
2Ki 10: 3 set *him* on his f throne, and fight for your 1
23:30 anointed him, and made him king in his f stead. 1
24:17 Mattaniah his f **brother** king in his stead, 1730
1Ch 5: 1 but, forasmuch as he defiled his f bed, 1
12:28 and *of* his f house twenty and two captains. 1
21:17 Lord my God, be on me, and on my f house; 1
23:11 in one reckoning, according to *their* f house. 1
2Ch 2:13 endued with understanding, of Huram my f, 1
10:10 My little *finger* shall be thicker than my f loins. 1
21:13 and also hast slain thy brethren of thy f house, 1
36: 1 and made him king in his f stead in Jerusalem. 1
Ne 1: 6 both I and my f house have sinned. 1
Est 4:14 but thou and thy f house shall be destroyed: 1
Ps 45:10 forget also thine own people, and thy f house; 1
Pr 4: 3 For I was my f son, tender and 1+3807.1
6:20 keep thy f commandment, and forsake not 1
13: 1 A wise son *heareth his* f instruction: but 1
15: 5 A fool despiseth his f instruction: but he that 1
27:10 Thine own friend, and thy f friend, forsake not; 1
Isa 7:17 upon thy people, and upon thy f house, 1
22:23 he shall be for a glorious throne to his f house. 1
22:24 they shall hang upon him all the glory of his f 1
Jer 35:14 drink none, but obey their f commandment: 1
Eze 18:14 that seeth all his f sins which he hath done, and 1
22:10 In thee have they discovered their f nakedness: 1
22:11 in thee hath humbled his sister, his f daughter. 1
Mt 26:29 I drink it new with you in my F kingdom. *3962*
Lk 2:49 wist ye not that I must be about my F *3962*
9:26 and *in his* F, and of the holy angels. *3962*
12:32 for it is your F good pleasure to give you *3962*
15:17 How many hired *servants* of my f have *3962*
16:27 that thou wouldest send him to my f house: *3962*
Jn 2:16 make not my F house a house of *3962*
5:43 I am come in my F name, and ye receive *3962*
6:39 And this is the F will which hath sent me, *3962*
10:25 the works that I do in my F name, they bear *3962*
10:29 no *man* is able to pluck *them* out of my F *3962*
14: 2 In my F house are many mansions: if *it* *3962*
14:24 hear is not mine, but the F which sent me. *3962*
15:10 even as I have kept my F commandments, *3962*
Ac 7:20 nourished up in his f house three months: *3962*
1Co 5: 1 that one should have *his* f wife. *3962*
Rev 14: 1 having his F name written in their *3962*

FATHERLESS (43) [FATHER]

Ex 22:22 Ye shall not afflict any widow, or f **child**. 3490
22:24 wives shall be widows, and your children f. 3490
Dt 10:18 He doth execute the judgment of the f and 3490
14:29 the stranger, and the f, and the widow, 3490
16:11 the stranger, and the f, and the widow, 3490
16:14 the stranger, and the f, and the widow, 3490
24:17 the judgment of the stranger, *nor* of the f; 3490
24:19 the stranger, for the f, and for the widow: 3490
24:20 the stranger, for the f, and for the widow. 3490
24:21 the stranger, for the f, and for the widow. 3490
26:12 the stranger, the f, and the widow, 3490
26:13 the stranger, to the f, and to the widow, 3490
27:19 the judgment of the stranger, f, and widow. 3490
Job 6:27 ye overwhelm the f, and you dig *a pit* for 3490
22: 9 and the arms of the f have been broken. 3490
24: 3 They drive away the ass of the f, they take 3490
24: 9 They pluck the f from the breast, and take a 3490
29:12 the f, and *him that had* none to help him. 3490
31:17 and the f hath not eaten thereof; 3490
31:21 If I have lift up my hand against the f, 3490
Ps 10:14 unto thee; thou art the helper of the f. 3490
10:18 To judge the f and the oppressed, that 3490
68: 5 A father of the f, and a judge of 3490
82: 3 Defend the poor and f: do justice to 3490
94: 6 and the stranger, and murder the f. 3490
109: 9 Let his children be f, and his wife a widow. 3490
109:12 let there be any to favour his f **children**. 3490
146: 9 the strangers; he relieveth the f and widow: 3490
Pr 23:10 and enter not into the fields of the f: 3490
Isa 1:17 judge the f, plead for the widow. 3490
1:23 they judge not the f, neither doth the cause 3490
9:17 neither shall have mercy on their f and 3490
10: 2 be their prey, and *that* they may rob the f. 3490
Jer 5:28 the cause of the f, yet they prosper; 3490
7: 6 the f, and the widow, and shed not innocent 3490
22: 3 to the stranger, the f, nor the widow, 3490
49:11 Leave thy f **children**, I will preserve *them* 3490
La 5: 3 We are orphans and f, our mothers *are* as 1+369
Eze 22: 7 in thee have they vexed the f and 3490
Hos 14: 3 our gods: for in thee the f findeth mercy. 3490
Zec 7:10 nor the f, the stranger, nor the poor; 3490
Mal 3: 5 the f, and that turn aside the stranger *from* 3490
Jas 1:27 To visit the f and widows in their affliction, *3737*

FATHERS (538) [FATHER]

Ge 15:15 thou shalt go to thy f in peace; thou shalt be 1
31: 3 Return unto the land of thy f, and to thy 1
46:34 youth even until now, both we, *and* also our f: 1
47: 3 servants *are* shepherds, both we, *and* also our f. 1
47: 9 the life of my f in the days of their pilgrimage. 1
47:30 I will lie with my f, and thou shalt carry me out 1
48:15 before whom my f Abraham and Isaac did 1
48:16 and the name of my f Abraham and Isaac; 1
48:21 and bring you again unto the land of your f. 1
49:29 bury me with my f in the cave that *is* in 1
Ex 3:13 The God of your f hath sent me unto you; 1
3:15 The Lord God of your f, the God of 1
3:16 and say unto them, The Lord God of your f, 1
4: 5 may believe that the Lord God of their f, 1
6:25 these *are* the heads of the f of the Levites 1
10: 6 which neither thy f, nor thy fathers' fathers 1
10: 6 neither thy fathers, nor thy fathers' f have seen, 1
12: 3 according to the house of *their* f, a lamb for a 1
13: 5 which he sware unto thy f to give thee, 1
13:11 as he sware unto thee and to thy f, and 1
20: 5 visiting the iniquity of the f upon the children 1
34: 7 visiting the iniquity of the f upon the children, 1
Lev 25:41 and unto the possession of his f shall he return. 1
26:39 also in the iniquities of their f shall they pine 1
26:40 their iniquity, and the iniquity of their f, 1
Nu 1: 2 after their families, by the house of their f, 1
1: 4 every one head of the house of his f. 1
1:16 princes of the tribes of their f, heads of 1
1:18 by the house of their f, according to the number 1
1:20 after their families, by the house of their f, 1
1:22 after their families, by the house of their f, 1
1:24 after their families, by the house of their f, 1
1:26 after their families, by the house of their f, 1
1:28 after their families, by the house of their f, 1
1:30 after their families, by the house of their f, 1
1:32 after their families, by the house of their f, 1
1:34 after their families, by the house of their f, 1
1:36 after their families, by the house of their f, 1
1:38 after their families, by the house of their f, 1
1:40 after their families, by the house of their f, 1
1:42 after their families, by the house of their f, 1
1:44 each one was for the house of his f. 1
1:45 by the house of their f, from twenty years old 1
1:47 the Levites after the tribe of their f were not 1
2:32 of the children of Israel by the house of their f: 1
2:34 their families, according to the house of their f. 1
3:15 the children of Levi after the house of their f, 1
3:20 of the Levites according to the house of their f. 1
4: 2 after their families, by the house of their f, 1
4:22 throughout the houses of their f, by their 1
4:29 after their families, by the house of their f; 1
4:34 their families, and after the house of their f, 1
4:38 their families, and by the house of their f, 1
4:40 by the house of their f, were two thousand and 1
4:42 their families, by the house of their f, 1
4:46 their families, and after the house of their f, 1
7: 2 princes of Israel, heads of the house of their f, 1
11:12 unto the land which thou swarest unto their f? 1
13: 2 of every tribe of their f shall ye send a man, 1
14:18 of the f upon the children unto the third 1
14:23 not see the land which I sware unto their f, 1
17: 2 of them a rod according to the house of *their* f, 1
17: 2 according to the house of their f twelve rods: 1

F

Nu	17: 3	rod *shall be* for the head of the house of their f.	1
	20:15	How our f went down into Egypt, and we have	1
	20:15	and the Egyptians vexed us, and our f:	1
	26:55	according to the names of the tribes of their f	1
	31:26	the priest, and the chief f of the congregation:	1
	32: 8	Thus did your f, when I sent them from	1
	32:28	the chief f of the tribes of the children of Israel:	1
	33:54	according to the tribes of your f ye shall	1
	34:14	of Reuben according to the house of their f,	1
	34:14	of Gad according to the house of their f,	1
	36: 1	the chief f of the families of the children of	1
	36: 1	the princes, the chief f of the children of Israel:	1
	36: 3	be taken from the inheritance of our f,	1
	36: 4	away from the inheritance of the tribe of our f.	1
	36: 7	himself to the inheritance of the tribe of his f.	1
	36: 8	may enjoy every man the inheritance of his f.	1
Dt	1: 8	the land which the LORD sware unto your f,	1
	1:11	(The LORD God of your f make you a	1
	1:21	possess *it,* as the LORD God of thy f hath said	1
	1:35	good land, which I sware to give unto your f,	1
	4: 1	which the LORD God of your f giveth you.	1
	4:31	nor forget the covenant of thy f which he sware	1
	4:37	because he loved thy f, therefore he chose their	1
	5: 3	The LORD made not this covenant with our f,	1
	5: 9	visiting the iniquity of the f upon the children	1
	6: 3	as the LORD God of thy f hath promised thee,	1
	6:10	thee into the land which he sware unto thy f,	1
	6:18	good land which the LORD sware unto thy f,	1
	6:23	to give us the land which he sware unto our f.	1
	7: 8	keep the oath which he had sworn unto your f,	1
	7:12	and the mercy which he sware unto thy f:	1
	7:13	in the land which he sware unto thy f to give	1
	8: 1	the land which the LORD sware unto your f.	1
	8: 3	thou knewest not, neither did thy f know;	1
	8:16	which thy f knew not, that he might humble	1
	8:18	his covenant which he sware unto thy f,	1
	9: 5	the word which the LORD sware unto thy f,	1
	10:11	which I sware unto their f to give unto them.	1
	10:15	Only the LORD had a delight in thy f to love	1
	10:22	Thy f went down into Egypt with threescore	1
	11: 9	which the LORD sware unto your f to give	1
	11:21	the land which the LORD sware unto your f	1
	12: 1	which the LORD God of thy f giveth thee to	1
	13: 6	which thou hast not known, thou, nor thy f;	1
	13:17	and multiply thee, as he hath sworn unto thy f;	1
	19: 8	as he hath sworn unto thy f, and give thee all	1
	19: 8	the land which he promised to give unto thy f;	1
	24:16	The f shall not be put to death for the children,	1
	24:16	shall the children be put to death for the f:	1
	26: 3	the LORD sware unto our f for to give us.	1
	26: 7	when we cried unto the LORD God of our f,	1
	26:15	as thou swarest unto our f, a land that floweth	1
	27: 3	as the LORD God of thy f hath promised thee.	1
	28:11	in the land which the LORD sware unto thy f	1
	28:36	unto a nation which neither thou nor thy f have	1
	28:64	which neither thou nor thy f have known,	1
	29:13	and as he hath sworn unto thy f, to Abraham,	1
	29:25	the covenant of the LORD God of their f,	1
	30: 5	bring thee into the land which thy f possessed,	1
	30: 5	do thee good, and multiply thee above thy f.	1
	30: 9	over thee for good, as he rejoiced over thy f:	1
	30:20	in the land which the LORD sware unto thy f,	1
	31: 7	LORD hath sworn unto their f to give them;	1
	31:16	Behold, thou shalt sleep with thy f;	1
	31:20	them into the land which I sware unto their f,	1
	32:17	*that* came newly up, whom your f feared not.	1
Jos	1: 6	which I sware unto their f to give them.	1
	4: 6	*that* when your children ask *their f* in time	NIH
	4:21	When your children shall ask their f in time to	1
	5: 6	which the LORD sware unto their f that he	1
	14: 1	the heads of the f of the tribes of the children of	1
	18: 3	which the LORD God of your f hath given	1
	19:51	the heads of the f of the tribes of the children of	1
	21: 1	came near the heads of the f of the Levites unto	1
	21: 1	unto the heads of the f of the tribes of	1
	21:43	all the land which he sware to give unto their f;	1
	21:44	according to all that he sware unto their f:	1
	22:14	each one *was* a head of the house of their f	1
	22:28	which our f made, not for burnt offerings,	1
	24: 2	Your f dwelt on the *other* side of the flood in	1
	24: 6	I brought your f out of Egypt: and you came	1
	24: 6	the Egyptians pursued after your f with chariots	1
	24:14	put away the gods which your f served on	1
	24:15	whether the gods which your f served that *were*	1
	24:17	us up and our f out of the land of Egypt,	1
Jdg	2: 1	you unto the land which I sware unto your f;	1
	2:10	all that generation were gathered unto their f:	1
	2:12	And they forsook the LORD God of their f,	1
	2:17	quickly out of the way which their f walked in,	1
	2:19	and corrupted *themselves* more than their f,	1
	2:20	my covenant which I commanded their f,	1
	2:22	to walk therein, as their f did keep *it,* or not.	1
	3: 4	which he commanded their f by the hand of	1
	6:13	where *be* all his miracles which our f told us of,	1
	21:22	when their f or their brethren come unto us to	1
1Sa	12: 6	that brought your f up out of the land of Egypt.	1
	12: 7	the LORD, which he did to you and to your f.	1
	12: 8	your f cried unto the LORD, then the LORD	1
	12: 8	which brought forth your f out of Egypt, and	1
	12:15	be against you, as *it was* against your f.	1
2Sa	7:12	thou shalt sleep with thy f, I will set up thy	1
1Ki	1:21	when my lord the king shall sleep with his f,	1
	2:10	So David slept with his f, and was buried in	1
	8: 1	the chief of the f of the children of Israel,	1
	8:21	of the LORD, which he made with our f,	1
	8:34	unto the land which thou gavest unto their f.	1
	8:40	live in the land which thou gavest unto our f.	1
	8:48	which thou gavest unto their f, the city which	1
	8:53	when thou broughtest our f out of Egypt,	1
	8:57	our God be with us, as he was with our f:	1
	8:58	and his judgments, which he commanded our f.	1
	9: 9	who brought forth their f out of the land of	1
	11:21	heard in Egypt that David slept with his f,	1
	11:43	Solomon slept with his f, and was buried in	1
	13:22	shall not come unto the sepulchre of thy f.	1
	14:15	which he gave to their f, and shall scatter them	1
	14:20	he slept with his f, and Nadab his son reigned	1
	14:22	had committed, above all that their f had done.	1
	14:31	Rehoboam slept with his f, and was buried with	1
	14:31	and was buried with his f in the city of David.	1
	15: 8	Abijam slept with his f; and they buried him in	1
	15:12	and removed all the idols that his f had made.	1
	15:24	Asa slept with his f, and was buried with his	1
	15:24	was buried with his f in the city of David his	1
	16: 6	So Baasha slept with his f, and was buried in	1
	16:28	So Omri slept with his f, and was buried in	1
	19: 4	away my life; for I *am* not better than my f.	1
	21: 3	that I should give the inheritance of my f unto	1
	21: 4	I will not give thee the inheritance of my f.	1
	22:40	So Ahab slept with his f; and Ahaziah his son	1
	22:50	Jehoshaphat slept with his f, and was buried	1
	22:50	was buried with his f in the city of David his	1
2Ki	8:24	Joram slept with his f, and was buried with his	1
	8:24	and was buried with his f in the city of David:	1
	9:28	buried him in his sepulchre with his f in	1
	10:35	Jehu slept with his f: and they buried him in	1
	12:18	Jehoram, and Ahaziah, his f, kings of Judah,	1
	12:21	they buried him with his f in the city of David:	1
	13: 9	Jehoahaz slept with his f; and they buried him	1
	13:13	Joash slept with his f; and Jeroboam sat upon	1
	14: 6	The f shall not be put to death for the children,	1
	14: 6	nor the children be put to death for the f;	1
	14:16	Jehoash slept with his f, and was buried in	1
	14:20	he was buried at Jerusalem with his f in the city	1
	14:22	it to Judah, after that the king slept with his f.	1
	14:29	Jeroboam slept with his f, *even* with the kings	1
	15: 7	So Azariah slept with his f; and they buried	1
	15: 7	they buried him with his f in the city of David:	1
	15: 9	in the sight of the LORD, as his f had done:	1
	15:22	Menahem slept with his f; and Pekahiah his	1
	15:38	Jotham slept with his f, and was buried with his	1
	15:38	was buried with his f in the city of David his	1
	16:20	Ahaz slept with his f, and was buried with his	1
	16:20	and was buried with his f in the city of David:	1
	17:13	to all the law which I commanded your f,	1
	17:14	hardened their necks, like to the neck of their f,	1
	17:15	and his covenant that he made with their f, and	1
	17:41	as did their f, *so* do they unto this day.	1
	19:12	delivered them which my f have destroyed;	1
	20:17	*that* which thy f have laid up in store unto this	1
	20:21	Hezekiah slept with his f: and Manasseh his	1
	21: 8	any more out of the land which I gave their f;	1
	21:15	since the day their f came forth out of Egypt,	1
	21:18	Manasseh slept with his f, and was buried in	1
	21:22	And he forsook the LORD God of his f, and	1
	22:13	our f have not hearkened unto the words of this	1
	22:20	I will gather thee unto thy f, and thou shalt be	1
	23:32	according to all that his f had done.	1

2Ki 23:37 according to all that his f had done. 1
24: 6 So Jehoiakim slept with his f: and 1
1Ch 4:38 and the house of their f increased greatly. 1
5:13 their brethren of the house of their f *were,* 1
5:15 the son of Guni, chief of the house of their f. 1
5:24 these *were* the heads of the house of their f, 1
5:24 famous men, *and* heads of the house of their f. 1
5:25 they transgressed against the God of their f, 1
6:19 the families of the Levites according to their f. 1
7: 4 by their generations, after the house of their f, 1
7: 7 heads of the house of *their* f, mighty *men* of 1
7: 9 heads of the house of their f, mighty *men* of 1
7:11 by the heads of *their* f, mighty *men* of valour, 1
8: 6 these *are* the heads of the f of the inhabitants of 1
8:10 These *were* his sons, heads of the f. 1
8:13 who *were* heads of the f of the inhabitants of 1
8:28 These *were* heads of the f, by their generations, 1
9: 9 All these men *were* chief of the f in the house 1
9: 9 *were* chief of the fathers in the house of their f. 1
9:13 heads of the house of their f, a thousand and 1
9:19 and their f, *being* over the host of the LORD, 1
9:33 *are* the singers, chief of the f of the Levites, 1
9:34 These chief f of the Levites *were* chief 1
12:17 the God of our f look *thereon,* and rebuke *it.* 1
12:30 famous throughout the house of their f. 1
15:12 Ye *are* the chief of the f of the Levites: 1
17:11 be expired that *thou* must go *to be* with thy f, 1
23: 9 three. These *were* the chief of the f of Laadan. 1
23:24 *were* the sons of Levi after the house of their f; 1
23:24 *even* the chief of the f, as they were counted by 1
24: 4 *were* sixteen chief *men* of the house of *their* f, 1
24: 4 of Ithamar according to the house of their f. 1
24: 6 and *before* the chief of the f of the priests and 1
24:30 sons of the Levites after the house of their f. 1
24:31 and the chief of the f of the priests and Levites, 1
24:31 *even* the principal f over against their younger 1
26:13 according to the house of their f, for every gate. 1
26:21 chief f, *even* of Laadan the Gershonite, 1
26:26 and the chief f, the captains over thousands and 1
26:31 according to the generations of his f. 1
26:32 *were* two thousand and seven hundred chief f, 1
27: 1 *to wit,* the chief f and captains of thousands 1
29: 6 the chief of the f and princes of the tribes of 1
29:15 before thee, and sojourners, as *were* all our f: 1
29:18 God of Abraham, Isaac, and of Israel, our f, 1
29:20 blessed the LORD God of their f, 1
2Ch 1: 2 every governor in all Israel, the chief of the f. 1
5: 2 the chief of the f of the children of Israel, 1
6:25 land which thou gavest to them and to their f. 1
6:31 live in the land which thou gavest unto our f. 1
6:38 which thou gavest unto their f, and *toward* 1
7:22 they forsook the LORD God of their f, 1
9:31 Solomon slept with his f, and he was buried in 1
11:16 to sacrifice unto the LORD God of their f. 1
12:16 Rehoboam slept with his f, and was buried in 1
13:12 fight ye not against the LORD God of your f; 1
13:18 they relied upon the LORD God of their f. 1
14: 1 So Abijah slept with his f, and they buried him 1
14: 4 Judah to seek the LORD God of their f, 1
15:12 the LORD God of their f with all their heart 1
16:13 And Asa slept with his f, and died in the one 1
17:14 of them according to the house of their f: 1
19: 4 them back unto the LORD God of their f. 1
19: 8 *of* the priests, and of the chief of the f of Israel, 1
20: 6 said, O LORD God of our f, *art* not thou God 1
20:33 prepared their hearts unto the God of their f. 1
21: 1 Now Jehoshaphat slept with his f, and 1
21: 1 and was buried with his f in the city of David. 1
21:10 he had forsaken the LORD God of his f. 1
21:19 no burning for him, like the burning of his f. 1
23: 2 the chief of the f of Israel, and they came to 1
24:18 left the house of the LORD God of their f, 1
24:24 they had forsaken the LORD God of their f. 1
25: 4 saying, The f shall not die for the children, 1
25: 4 neither shall the children die for the f, but 1
25: 5 according to the houses of *their* f, 1
25:28 and buried him with his f in the city of Judah. 1
26: 2 it to Judah, after that the king slept with his f. 1
26:12 The whole number of the chief of the f of 1
26:23 So Uzziah slept with his f, and they buried him 1
26:23 they buried him with his f in the field of 1
27: 9 Jotham slept with his f, and they buried him in 1
28: 6 they had forsaken the LORD God of their f. 1
28: 9 the LORD God of your f was wroth with 1
28:25 provoked to anger the LORD God of his f. 1
28:27 Ahaz slept with his f, and they buried him in 1
29: 5 the house of the LORD God of your f, 1
29: 6 For our f have trespassed, and done *that* which 1
29: 9 our f have fallen by the sword, and our sons 1
30: 7 be not ye like your f, and like your brethren, 1
30: 7 trespassed against the LORD God of their f, 1
30: 8 as your f *were, but* yield yourselves unto 1
30:19 his heart to seek God, the LORD God of his f, 1
30:22 confession to the LORD God of their f. 1
31:17 genealogy of the priests by the house of their f, 1
32:13 my f have done unto all the people of *other* 1
32:14 of those nations that my f utterly destroyed, 1
32:15 out of mine hand, and out of the hand of my f: 1
32:33 Hezekiah slept with his f, and they buried him 1
33: 8 of the land which I have appointed for your f; 1
33:12 himself greatly before the God of his f, 1
33:20 So Manasseh slept with his f, and they buried 1
34:21 our f have not kept the word of the LORD, 1
34:28 I will gather thee to thy f, and thou shalt be 1
34:32 to the covenant of God, the God of their f. 1
34:33 from following the LORD, the God of their f. 1
35: 4 prepare *yourselves* by the houses of your f, 1
35: 5 families of the f of your brethren the people, 1
35:24 was buried in *one of the* sepulchres of his f. 1
36:15 the LORD God of their f sent to them by his 1
Ezr 1: 5 rose up the chief of the f of Judah and 1
2:68 *some* of the chief of the f, when they came to 1
3:12 of the priests and Levites and chief of the f, 1
4: 2 and to the chief of the f, and said unto them, 1
4: 3 and the rest of the chief of the f of Israel, 1
4:15 be made in the book of the records of thy f: 2
5:12 after that our f had provoked the God of heaven 2
7:27 Blessed *be* the LORD God of our f, 1
8: 1 These *are* now the chief of their f, and *this is* 1
8:28 offering unto the LORD God of your f. 1
8:29 and the Levites, and chief of the f of Israel, 1
9: 7 Since the days of our f *have* we *been* in a great 1
10:11 confession unto the LORD God of your f, 1
10:16 And Ezra the priest, *with* certain chief of the f, 1
10:16 after the house of their f, and all of them by 1
Ne 7:70 some of the chief of the f gave unto the work. 1
7:71 *some* of the chief of the f gave to the treasure 1
8:13 together the chief of the f of all the people, 1
9: 2 their sins, and the iniquities of their f. 1
9: 9 And didst see the affliction of our f in Egypt, 1
9:16 they and our f dealt proudly, and hardened their 1
9:23 which thou hadst promised to their f, 1
9:32 and on our f, and on all thy people, 1
9:34 our princes, our priests, nor our f, kept thy law, 1
9:36 *for* the land that thou gavest unto our f to eat 1
10:34 after the houses of our f, at times appointed 1
11:13 his brethren, chief of the f, two hundred forty 1
12:12 days of Joiakim were priests, the chief of the f: 1
12:22 and Jaddua, *were* recorded chief of the f: 1
12:23 The sons of Levi, the chief of the f, 1
13:18 Did not your f thus, and *did not* our God bring 1
Job 8: 8 and prepare *thyself* to the search of their f: 1
15:18 Which wise *men* have told from their f, and 1
30: 1 whose f I would have disdained to have set 1
Ps 22: 4 Our f trusted in thee: they trusted, and 1
39:12 with thee, *and* a sojourner, as all my f *were.* 1
44: 1 heard with our ears, O God, our f have told us, 1
45:16 Instead of thy f shall be thy children, 1
49:19 He shall go to the generation of his f; they shall 1
78: 3 have heard and known, and our f have told us. 1
78: 5 a law in Israel, which he commanded our f, 1
78: 8 might not be as their f, a stubborn and 1
78:12 Marvellous things did he in the sight of their f, 1
78:57 turned *back,* and dealt unfaithfully like their f: 1
95: 9 When your f tempted me, proved me, and 1
106: 6 We have sinned with our f, we have committed 1
106: 7 Our f understood not thy wonders in Egypt; 1
109:14 Let the iniquity of his f be remembered with 1
Pr 17: 6 old men; and the glory of children *are* their f. 1
19:14 House and riches *are* the inheritance of f: and 1
22:28 not the ancient landmark, which thy f have set. 1
Isa 14:21 for his children for the iniquity of their f; 1
37:12 delivered them which my f have destroyed, 1
39: 6 *that* which thy f have laid up in store until this 1
49:23 kings shall be thy **nursing** f, and 539
64:11 our beautiful house, where our f praised thee, 1
65: 7 and the iniquities of your f together, 1
Jer 2: 5 What iniquity have your f found in me, 1

Jer 3:18 that I have given for an inheritance unto your f. 1
3:24 For shame hath devoured the labour of our f 1
3:25 we and our f, from our youth even unto this 1
6:21 the f and the sons together shall fall upon them; 1
7: 7 in the land that I gave to your f, for ever and 1
7:14 the place which I gave to you and to your f, 1
7:18 the f kindle the fire, and the women knead *their* 1
7:22 For I spake not unto your f, nor commanded 1
7:25 Since the day that your f came forth out of 1
7:26 their neck: they did worse than their f. 1
9:14 and after Baalim, which their f taught them: 1
9:16 whom neither they nor their f have known: 1
11: 4 Which I commanded your f in the day that I 1
11: 5 the oath which I have sworn unto your f, 1
11: 7 For I earnestly protested unto your f in the day 1
11:10 broken my covenant which I made with their f. 1
13:14 even the f and the sons together, saith 1
14:20 our wickedness, *and* the iniquity of our f: 1
16: 3 concerning their f that begat them in this land; 1
16:11 Because your f have forsaken me, saith 1
16:12 ye have done worse than your f; for behold, 1
16:13 a land that ye know not, *neither* ye nor your f; 1
16:15 again into their land that I gave unto their f. 1
16:19 Surely our f have inherited lies, vanity, and 1
17:22 ye the sabbath day, as I commanded your f. 1
19: 4 whom neither they nor their f have known, nor 1
23:27 as their f have forgotten my name for Baal. 1
23:39 the city that I gave you and your f, *and cast you* 1
24:10 off the land that I gave unto them and to their f. 1
25: 5 given unto you and to your f for ever and ever: 1
30: 3 them to return to the land that I gave to their f, 1
31:29 The f have eaten a sour grape, and 1
31:32 their f in the day *that* I took them by the hand, 1
32:18 recompensest the iniquity of the f into 1
32:22 which thou didst swear to their f to give them, 1
34: 5 with the burnings of thy f, the former kings 1
34:13 I made a covenant with your f in the day that I 1
34:14 your f hearkened not unto me, neither inclined 1
35:15 land which I have given to you and to your f: 1
44: 3 they knew not, *neither* they, you, nor your f. 1
44: 9 Have ye forgotten the wickedness of your f, 1
44:10 that I set before you and before your f. 1
44:17 we, and our f, our kings, and our princes, 1
44:21 ye, and your f, your kings, and your princes, 1
47: 3 the f shall not look back to *their* children for 1
50: 7 of justice, even the LORD, the hope of their f. 1
La 5: 7 Our f have sinned, *and are* not; *and* we have 1
Eze 2: 3 they and their f have transgressed against me, 1
5:10 Therefore the f shall eat the sons in the midst 1
5:10 the midst of thee, and the sons shall eat their f; 1
18: 2 The f have eaten sour grapes, and 1
20: 4 them to know the abominations of their f: 1
20:18 Walk ye not in the statutes of your f, 1
20:27 Yet *in* this your f have blasphemed me, in that 1
20:30 Are ye polluted after the manner of your f? 1
20:36 Like as I pleaded with your f in the wilderness 1
20:42 which I lifted up mine hand to give it to your f. 1
36:28 ye shall dwell in the land that I gave to your f; 1
37:25 Jacob my servant, wherein your f have dwelt; 1
47:14 I lifted up mine hand to give it unto your f: 1
Da 2:23 and praise thee, O thou God of my f, 2
9: 6 and our f, and to all the people of the land. 1
9: 8 to our f, because we have sinned against thee. 1
9:16 and for the iniquities of our f, Jerusalem and 1
11:24 and he shall do *that* which his f have not done, 1
11:24 his fathers have not done, nor his fathers' f; 1
11:37 Neither shall he regard the God of his f, nor 1
11:38 a god whom his f knew not shall he honour 1
Hos 9:10 I saw your f as the firstripe in the fig tree at her 1
Joel 1: 2 in your days, or even in the days of your f? 1
Am 2: 4 to err, after the which their f have walked: 1
Mic 7:20 which thou hast sworn unto our f from the days 1
Zec 1: 2 LORD hath been sore displeased with your f. 1
1: 4 Be ye not as your f, unto whom the former 1
1: 5 Your f, where *are* they? and the prophets, do 1
1: 6 the prophets, did they not take hold of your f? 1
8:14 when your f provoked me to wrath, saith 1
Mal 2:10 his brother, by profaning the covenant of our f? 1
3: 7 Even from the days of your f ye are gone away 1
4: 6 he shall turn the heart of the f to the children, 1
4: 6 the heart of the children to their f, lest I come 1
Mt 23:30 If we had been in the days of our f, *3962*
23:32 Fill ye up then the measure of your f. *3962*
Lk 1:17 to turn the hearts of the f to the children, *3962*
1:55 (As he spake to our f), to Abraham, and *3962*
1:72 To perform the mercy *promised* to our f, *3962*
6:23 for in the like manner did their f unto *3962*
6:26 for so did their f to the false prophets. *3962*
11:47 of the prophets, and your f killed them. *3962*
11:48 witness that ye allow the deeds of your f: *3962*
Jn 4:20 Our f worshipped in this mountain; and *3962*
6:31 Our f did eat manna in the desert; as it is *3962*
6:49 Your f did eat manna in the wilderness, and *3962*
6:58 not as your f did eat manna, and are dead: *3962*
7:22 not because it is of Moses, but of the f; *3962*
Ac 3:13 and of Isaac, and of Jacob, the God of our f, *3962*
3:22 For Moses truly said unto the f, A prophet *3962*
3:25 the covenant which God made with our f, *3962*
5:30 The God of our f raised up Jesus, whom ye *3962*
7: 2 And he said, Men, brethren, and f, hearken; *3962*
7:11 and our f found no sustenance. *3962*
7:12 was corn in Egypt, he sent out our f first. *3962*
7:15 down into Egypt, and died, he, and our f, *3962*
7:19 and evil entreated our f, so that *they* cast *3962*
7:32 *Saying,* I *am* the God of thy f, the God of *3962*
7:38 to him in the mount Sina, and *with* our f: *3962*
7:39 To whom our f would not obey, *3962*
7:44 Our f had the tabernacle of Witness in *3962*
7:45 Which also our f that came after brought in *3962*
7:45 God drave out before the face of our f, *3962*
7:51 the Holy Ghost: as your f *did,* so *do* ye. *3962*
7:52 Which of the prophets have not your f *3962*
13:17 God of this people of Israel chose our f, *3962*
13:32 the promise which was made unto the f, *3962*
13:36 and was laid unto his f, and saw corruption: *3962*
15:10 which neither our f nor we were able to *3962*
22: 1 Men, brethren, and f, hear ye my defence *3962*
22: 3 to the perfect manner of the law of the f, *3971*
22:14 he said, The God of our f hath chosen thee, *3962*
24:14 call heresy, so worship I the God of my f, *3971*
26: 6 of the promise made of God unto *our* f: *3962*
28:17 against the people, or customs of our f, *3971*
28:25 Ghost by Esaias the prophet unto our f, *3962*
Ro 9: 5 Whose *are* the f, and of whom as *3962*
15: 8 to confirm the promises made unto the f: *3962*
1Co 4:15 in Christ, yet *have ye* not many f: *3962*
10: 1 how that all our f were under the cloud, and *3962*
Gal 1:14 zealous of the traditions of my f. *3967*
Eph 6: 4 And, ye f, provoke not your children to *3962*
Col 3:21 F, provoke not your children *to anger,* lest *3962*
1Ti 1: 9 for **murderers of f** and murderers of *3964*
Heb 1: 1 in time past unto the f by the prophets, *3962*
3: 9 When your f tempted me, proved me, and *3962*
8: 9 f in the day when I took them by the hand *3962*
12: 9 Furthermore we have had f of our flesh *3962*
1Pe 1:18 **received by tradition from** your f; *3970*
2Pe 3: 4 for since the f fell asleep, all *things* *3962*
1Jn 2:13 f, because ye have known him that is from *3962*
2:14 f, because ye have known him that is from *3962*

FATHERS' (14) [FATHER]

Ex 6:14 These *be* the heads of their f houses: The sons 1
10: 6 neither thy fathers, nor thy f fathers have seen, 1
Nu 17: 6 according to their f houses, *even* twelve rods: 1
26: 2 years old and upward, throughout their f house, 1
32:14 behold, ye are risen up in your f stead, 1
1Ch 7: 2 Jibsam, and Shemuel, heads of their f house, 1
7:40 heads of *their* f house, choice *and* mighty *men* 1
Ezr 2:59 they could not shew their f house, and 1
Ne 2: 3 the place of my f sepulchres, *lieth* waste, and 1
2: 5 unto the city of my f sepulchres, that I may 1
7:61 they could not shew their f house, nor their 1
Eze 20:24 and their eyes were after their f idols. 1
Da 11:24 his fathers have not done, nor his f fathers; 1
Ro 11:28 *they are* beloved for the f sakes. *3962*

FATHOMS (2)

Ac 27:28 And sounded, and found *it* twenty f: and *3712*
27:28 they sounded again, and found *it* fifteen f. *3712*

FATLING (1) [FAT]

Isa 11: 6 and the young lion and the f together; 4806

FATLINGS (5) [FAT]

1Sa 15: 9 of the f, and the lambs, and all *that was* 4932
2Sa 6:13 gone six paces, he sacrificed oxen and f. 4806
Ps 66:15 I will offer unto thee burnt sacrifices of f, 4220
Eze 39:18 of bullocks, all of them f of Bashan. 4806

Mt 22: 4 my oxen and *my* f *are* killed, and all *things* *4619*

FATNESS (17) [FAT]
Ge 27:28 the f of the earth, and plenty of corn and 4924
27:39 thy dwelling shall be the f of the earth, and 4924
Dt 32:15 thou art covered *with f*; then he forsook NIH
Jdg 9: 9 tree said unto them, Should I leave my f, 1880
Job 15:27 Because he covereth his face with his f, and 2459
36:16 be set on thy table *should be* full *of* f. 1880
Ps 36: 8 abundantly satisfied with the f of thy house; 1880
63: 5 shall be satisfied as *with* marrow and f; 1880
65:11 with thy goodness; and thy paths drop f. 1880
73: 7 Their eyes stand out with f: they have more 2459
109:24 through fasting; and my flesh faileth of f. 8081
Isa 17: 4 and the f of his flesh shall wax lean. 4924
34: 6 it is made fat with f, *and* with the blood of 2459
34: 7 with blood, and their dust made fat with f. 2459
55: 2 *is* good, and let your soul delight itself in f. 1880
Jer 31:14 I will satiate the soul of the priests with f, 1880
Ro 11:17 partakest of the root and f of the olive tree; *4096*

FATS (2) [FAT]
Joel 2:24 and the f shall overflow *with* wine and oil. 3342
3:13 for the press is full, the f overflow; 3342

FATTED (5) [FAT]
1Ki 4:23 and roebucks, and fallowdeer, and f fowl. 75
Jer 46:21 men *are* in the midst of her like f bullocks; 4770
Lk 15:23 And bring hither the f calf, and kill *it;* and *4618*
15:27 and thy father hath killed the f calf, *4618*
15:30 thou hast killed for him the f calf. *4618*

FATTER (1) [FAT]
Da 1:15 f in flesh than all the children which did eat 1277

FATTEST (2) [FAT]
Ps 78:31 slew the f of them, and smote down 4924
Da 11:24 even upon the f **places** of the province; 4924

FAULT (19) [FAULTLESS, FAULTS, FAULTY]
Ex 5:16 *are* beaten; but the f *is* in thine own people. 2398
Dt 25: 2 according to his f, by a *certain* number. 7564
1Sa 29: 3 I have found no *f* in him since he fell *unto* NIH
2Sa 3: 8 that thou chargest me to day with a f 5771
Ps 59: 4 and prepare themselves without *my* f: 5771
Da 6: 4 they could find none occasion nor f; 7844
6: 4 was there any error or f found in him. 7844
Mt 18:15 go and **tell** him his f between thee and *1651*
Mk 7: 2 to say, with unwashen, hands, they **found** f. *3201*
Lk 23: 4 and *to* the people, I find no f in this man. *158*
23:14 have found no f in this man *touching those* *158*
Jn 18:38 and saith unto them, I find in him no f *at all.* *156*
19: 4 that ye may know that I find no f in him. *156*
19: 6 and crucify *him:* for I find no f in him. *156*
Ro 9:19 then unto me, Why doth he yet **find** f? *3201*
1Co 6: 7 therefore there is utterly a f among you, *2275*
Gal 6: 1 Brethren, if a man be overtaken in a f, *3900*
Heb 8: 8 For **finding** f **with** them, *he* saith, Behold, *3201*
Rev 14: 5 for they are **without** f before the throne of *299*

FAULTLESS (2) [FAULT]
Heb 8: 7 For if that first *covenant* had been f, *then* *273*
Jude 1:24 to present *you* f before the presence of his *299*

FAULTS (4) [FAULT]
Ge 41: 9 I do remember my f *this* day: 2399
Ps 19:12 *his* errors? cleanse thou me from secret *f*. NIH
Jas 5:16 Confess *your* f one to another, and pray one *3900*
1Pe 2:20 glory *is it,* if, when ye be buffeted for your f, *264*

FAULTY (2) [FAULT]
2Sa 14:13 king doth speak this thing as one **which is** f, 818
Hos 10: 2 heart is divided; now shall they be **found** f: 816

FAVORITISM See RESPECTER

FAVOUR (70) [FAVOURABLE, FAVOURED, FAVOUREDNESS, FAVOUREST, FAVOURETH, WELLFAVOURED]
Ge 18: 3 My Lord, if now I have found f in thy sight, 2580
30:27 I pray thee, if I have found f in thine eyes, 2580
39:21 gave him f in the sight of the keeper of 2580
Ex 3:21 I will give this people f in the sight of 2580
11: 3 the LORD gave the people f in the sight of 2580
12:36 the LORD gave the people f in the sight of 2580
Nu 11:11 wherefore have I not found f in thy sight, 2580
11:15 out of hand, if I have found f in thy sight; 2580
Dt 24: 1 it come to pass that she find no f in his 2580
28:50 person of the old, nor **shew** f to the young: 2603
33:23 satisfied with f, and full *with* the blessing 7522
Jos 11:20 *and* that they might have no f, but that *he* 8467
Ru 2:13 Let me find f in thy sight, my lord; 2580
1Sa 2:26 was **in** f both with the LORD, and 2896
16:22 before me; for he hath found f in my sight. 2580
20:29 and now, if I have found f in thine eyes, 2580
25: 8 Wherefore let the young men find f in thine 2580
29: 6 the lords f thee not. 2896+5869+871.1
2Sa 15:25 if I shall find f in the eyes of the LORD, 2580
1Ki 11:19 Hadad found great f in the sight of Pharaoh, 2580
Ne 2: 5 and if thy servant have **found** f in thy sight, 3190
Est 2:15 Esther obtained f in the sight of all them 2580
2:17 and f in his sight more than all the virgins; 2617
5: 2 in the court, *that* she obtained f in his sight: 2580
5: 8 If I have found f in the sight of the king, 2580
7: 3 and said, If I have found f in thy sight, 2580
8: 5 if I have found f in his sight, and the thing 2580
Job 10:12 Thou hast granted me life and f, and 2617
Ps 5:12 *with* f wilt thou compass him as *with* a 7522
30: 5 *but* a moment; in his f *is* life: 7522
30: 7 by thy f thou hast made my mountain to 7522
35:27 and be glad, that f my righteous cause: 2655
44: 3 because thou **hadst a** f unto them. 7521
45:12 among the people shall **intreat** thy f. 2470+6440
89:17 and in thy f our horn shall be exalted. 7522
102:13 for the time to f her, yea, the set time, 2603
102:14 in her stones, and f the dust thereof. 2603
106: 4 with the f *that thou bearest* unto thy people: 7522
109:12 neither let there be any to f his fatherless 2603
112: 5 A good man **sheweth** f, and lendeth: 2603
119:58 I intreated thy f with *my* whole heart: 6440
Pr 3: 4 So shalt thou find f and good understanding 2580
8:35 and shall obtain f of the LORD. 7522
11:27 He that diligently seeketh good procureth f: 7522
12: 2 A good *man* obtaineth f of the LORD: but 7522
13:15 Good understanding giveth f: but the way 2580
14: 9 at sin: but among the righteous *there is* f. 7522
14:35 The king's f *is* toward a wise servant: but 7522
16:15 and his f *is* as a cloud of the latter rain. 7522
18:22 good *thing,* and obtaineth f of the LORD. 7522
19: 6 Many will intreat the f of the prince: and 6440
19:12 of a lion; but his f *is* as dew upon the grass. 7522
21:10 his neighbour **findeth** no f in his eyes. 2603
22: 1 *and* loving f rather than silver and gold. 2580
28:23 afterwards shall find more f than he that 2580
29:26 Many seek the ruler's f; but *every* man's 6440
31:30 F *is* deceitful, and beauty *is* vain: *but* 2580
Ecc 9:11 of understanding, nor yet f to men of skill; 2580
SS 8:10 then was I in his eyes as one that found f. 7965
Isa 26:10 Let f be **shewed** to the wicked, *yet* will he 2603
27:11 he that formed them will **shew** them no f. 2603
60:10 but in my f have I had mercy on thee. 7522
Jer 16:13 and night; where I will not shew you f. 2594
Da 1: 9 Now God had brought Daniel into f and 2617
Lk 1:30 Mary: for thou hast found f with God. *5485*
2:52 and stature, and in f with God and man. *5485*
Ac 2:47 and having f with all the people. *5485*
7:10 and gave him f and wisdom in the sight of *5485*
7:46 Who found f before God, and desired to *5485*
25: 3 And desired f against him, that he would *5485*

FAVOURABLE (4) [FAVOUR]
Jdg 21:22 unto them, Be f unto them for our sakes: 2603
Job 33:26 pray unto God, and he will be f unto him: 7521
Ps 77: 7 cast off for ever? and will he be f no more? 7521
85: 1 LORD, thou hast been f unto thy land: 7521

FAVOURED (14) [FAVOUR]
Ge 29:17 but Rachel was beautiful and well f. 4758
39: 6 Joseph was *a* goodly *person,* and well f. 4758
41: 2 there came up out of the river seven well f 4758
41: 3 them out of the river, ill f and leanfleshed; 4758
41: 4 the ill f and leanfleshed kine did eat up 4758
41: 4 leanfleshed kine did eat up the seven well f 4758
41:18 the river seven kine, fatfleshed and well f; 8389
41:19 poor and very ill f and leanfleshed, 8389
41:20 the **ill** f kine did eat up the first seven fat 7451
41:21 but they *were still* ill f, as at the beginning. 4758
41:27 **ill** f kine that came up after them *are* seven 7451
La 4:16 persons of the priests, they f not the elders. 2603
Da 1: 4 well f, and skilful in all wisdom, and 4758

F

Lk 1:28 and said, Hail, *thou that art* **highly f,** 5487

FAVOUREDNESS (1) [FAVOUR]
Dt 17: 1 wherein is blemish, *or* any **evil f:** 1697+7451

FAVOUREST (1) [FAVOUR]
Ps 41:11 By this I know that thou f me, because 2654

FAVOURETH (1) [FAVOUR]
2Sa 20:11 He that f Joab, and he that *is* for David, 2654

FEAR (400) [AFRAID, FEARED, FEAREST, FEARETH, FEARFUL, FEARFULLY, FEARFULNESS, FEARING, FEARS]
Ge 9: 2 the f of you and the dread of you shall be 4172
15: 1 Abram in a vision, saying, F not, Abram: 3372
20:11 Surely the f of God *is* not in this place; 3374
21:17 f not; for God hath heard the voice of 3372
26:24 f not, for I *am* with thee, and will bless 3372
31:42 and the f of Isaac, had been with me, 6343
31:53 Jacob sware by the f of his father Isaac. 6343
32:11 for I f him, lest he will come and smite me, 3373
35:17 that the midwife said unto her, F not; 3372
42:18 the third day, This do, and live; *for* I f God: 3373
43:23 he said, Peace *be* to you, f not: your God, 3372
46: 3 f not to go down into Egypt; for I will there 3372
50:19 Joseph said unto them, F not: for *am* I in 3372
50:21 Now therefore f ye not: I will nourish you 3372
Ex 9:30 I know that ye will not yet f the LORD 3372
14:13 F ye not, stand still, and see the salvation of 3372
15:16 F and dread shall fall upon them; by 367
18:21 such as f God, men of truth, 3373
20:20 Moses said unto the people, F not: for God 3372
20:20 that his f may be before your faces, that ye 3374
23:27 I will send my f before thee, and will destroy 367
Lev 19: 3 Ye shall f every man his mother, and 3372
19:14 before the blind, but shalt f thy God: 3372
19:32 the face of the old man, and f thy God: 3372
25:17 one another; but thou shalt f thy God: 3372
25:36 f thy God; that thy brother may live with 3372
25:43 over him with rigour; but shalt f thy God. 3372
Nu 14: 9 neither f ye the people of the land; 3372
14: 9 and the LORD *is* with us: f them not. 3372
21:34 the LORD said unto Moses, F him not: 3372
Dt 1:21 unto thee; f not, neither be discouraged. 3372
2:25 the f of thee upon the nations *that are* under 3374
3: 2 the LORD said unto me, F him not: for I 3372
3:22 Ye shall not f them: for the LORD your 3372
4:10 that they may learn to f me all the days that 3372
5:29 that they would f me, and keep all my 3372
6: 2 That thou mightest f the LORD thy God, 3372
6:13 Thou shalt f the LORD thy God, and 3372
6:24 to f the LORD our God, for our good 3372
8: 6 thy God, to walk in his ways, and to f him. 3372
10:12 to f the LORD thy God, to walk in all his 3372
10:20 Thou shalt f the LORD thy God; him shalt 3372
11:25 *for* the LORD your God shall lay the f of 6343
13: 4 f him, and keep his commandments, and 3372
13:11 f, and shall do no more any such 3372
14:23 that thou mayest learn to f the LORD thy 3372
17:13 and f, and do no more presumptuously. 3372
17:19 that he may learn to f the LORD his God, 3372
19:20 f, and shall henceforth commit no more any 3372
20: 3 f not, and do not tremble, neither be ye 3372
21:21 among you; and all Israel shall hear, and f. 3372
28:58 that *thou* mayest f this glorious and fearful 3372
28:66 thou shalt f day and night, and shalt have 6342
28:67 for the f of thine heart where*with* thou shalt 6343
28:67 fear of thine heart where*with* thou shalt f, 6342
31: 6 Be strong and of a good courage, f not, 3372
31: 8 forsake thee: f not, neither be dismayed. 3372
31:12 f the LORD your God, and observe to do 3372
31:13 and learn to f the LORD your God, 3372
Jos 4:24 that ye might f the LORD your God for 3372
8: 1 F not, neither be thou dismayed: 3372
10: 8 the LORD said unto Joshua, F them not: 3372
10:25 F not, nor be dismayed, be strong and 3372
22:24 if we have not *rather* done it for f of *this* 1674
24:14 Now therefore f the LORD, and serve him 3372
Jdg 4:18 Turn in, my lord, turn in to me; f not. 3372
6:10 f not the gods of the Amorites, in whose 3372
6:23 said unto him, Peace *be* unto thee; f not: 3372
7:10 if thou f to go down, go thou with Phurah 3373
9:21 **for f of** Abimelech his brother. 4480+6440
Ru 3:11 now, my daughter, f not; I will do to thee 3372
1Sa 4:20 that stood by her said *unto her,* F not; 3372
11: 7 the f of the LORD fell on the people, and 6343
12:14 If ye will f the LORD, and serve him, and 3372
12:20 Samuel said unto the people, F not: ye have 3372
12:24 Only f the LORD, and serve him in truth 3372
21:10 fled that day for f of Saul, and went to 6440
22:23 Abide thou with me, f not: for he that 3372
23:17 he said unto him, F not: for the hand of 3372
23:26 David made haste to get away for f of Saul; 6440
2Sa 9: 7 David said unto him, F not: for I will surely 3372
13:28 Smite Amnon; then kill him, f not: 3372
23: 3 men *must be* just, ruling *in* the f of God. 3374
1Ki 8:40 That they may f thee all the days that they 3372
8:43 thy name, to f thee, as *do* thy people Israel; 3372
17:13 Elijah said unto her, F not; go *and* do as 3372
18:12 *I* thy servant f the LORD from my youth. 3372
2Ki 4: 1 thou knowest that thy servant did f 3373
6:16 he answered, F not: for *they* that *be* with us 3372
17:28 taught them how they should f the LORD. 3372
17:34 they f not the LORD, neither do they after 3373
17:35 saying, Ye shall not f other gods, 3372
17:36 him shall ye f, and him shall ye worship, 3372
17:37 for evermore; and ye shall not f other gods. 3372
17:38 not forget; neither shall ye f other gods. 3372
17:39 the LORD your God ye shall f; and 3372
25:24 F not to be the servants of the Chaldees: 3372
1Ch 14:17 the LORD brought the f of him upon all 6343
16:30 F before him, all the earth: the world also 2342
28:20 and of good courage, and do *it:* f not, 3372
2Ch 6:31 That they may f thee, to walk in thy ways, 3372
6:33 f thee, as *doth* thy people Israel, and may 3372
14:14 for the f of the LORD came upon them: 6343
17:10 the f of the LORD fell upon all 6343
19: 7 Wherefore now let the f of the LORD be 6343
19: 9 Thus shall ye do in the f of the LORD, 3374
20:17 f not, nor be dismayed; to morrow go out 3372
20:29 the f of God was on all the kingdoms of 6343
Ezr 3: 3 for f *was* upon them because of the people of 367
Ne 1:11 of thy servants, who desire to f thy name: 3372
5: 9 ought ye not to walk in the f of our God 3374
5:15 but so did not I, because of the f of God. 3374
6:14 the prophets, that would have **put** me **in** f. 3372
6:19 *And* Tobiah sent letters to **put** me **in** f. 3372
Est 8:17 for the f of the Jews fell upon them. 6343
9: 2 for the f of them fell upon all people. 6343
9: 3 because the f of Mordecai fell upon them. 6343
Job 1: 9 and said, Doth Job f God for nought? 3372
4: 6 *Is* not *this* thy f, thy confidence, thy hope; 3374
4:14 F came upon me, and trembling, 6343
6:14 but he forsaketh the f of the Almighty. 3374
9:34 away from me, and let not his f terrify me: 367
9:35 *Then* would I speak, and not f him; but *it is* 3372
11:15 yea, thou shalt be steadfast, and shalt not f. 3372
15: 4 thou castest off f, and restrainest prayer 3374
21: 9 Their houses *are* safe from f, neither *is* 6343
22: 4 Will he reprove thee for f of thee? will he 3374
22:10 about thee, and sudden f troubleth thee; 6343
25: 2 Dominion and f *are* with him, he maketh 6343
28:28 Behold, the f of *the Lord,* that *is* wisdom; 3374
31:34 Did I f a great multitude, or did 6206
37:24 Men do therefore f him: he respecteth not 3372
39:16 not hers: her labour *is* in vain without f; 6343
39:22 He mocketh at f, and is not affrighted; 6343
41:33 there is not his like, who is made without f. 2844
Ps 2:11 Serve the LORD with f, and rejoice with 3374
5: 7 in thy f will I worship toward thy holy 3374
9:20 Put them in f, O LORD: *that* the nations 4172
14: 5 There were they **in great** f: for God 6342+6343
15: 4 but he honoureth them that f the LORD. 3373
19: 9 The f of the LORD *is* clean, enduring for 3374
22:23 Ye that f the LORD, praise him; all ye 3373
22:23 and f him, all ye the seed of Israel. 1481
22:25 I will pay my vows before them that f him. 3373
23: 4 of the shadow of death, I will f no evil: 3372
25:14 of the LORD *is* with them that f him; 3373
27: 1 my light and my salvation; whom shall I f? 3372
27: 3 encamp against me, my heart shall not f: 3372
31:11 and a f to mine acquaintance: 6343
31:13 f *was* on every side: while they took 4032
31:19 which thou hast laid up for them that f thee; 3373
33: 8 Let all the earth f the LORD: let all 3372
33:18 the eye of the LORD *is* upon them that f him, 3373
34: 7 encampeth round about them that f him, 3373
34: 9 O f the LORD, ye his saints: for *there is* 3372

Ps	34: 9	for *there is* no want to them that f him.	3373
	34:11	I will teach you the f of the LORD.	3374
	36: 1	*that there is* no f of God before his eyes.	6343
	40: 3	many shall see *it,* and f, and shall trust in	3372
	46: 2	Therefore will not we f, though the earth be	3372
	48: 6	F took hold upon them there, *and* pain,	7461
	49: 5	Wherefore should I f in the days of evil,	3372
	52: 6	also shall see, and f, and shall laugh at him:	3372
	53: 5	There were they **in great** f, *where* no	6342+6343
	53: 5	were they in great fear, *where* no f was:	6343
	55:19	have no changes, therefore they f not God.	3372
	56: 4	I will not f what flesh can do unto me.	3372
	60: 4	Thou hast given a banner to them that f	3373
	61: 5	*me* the heritage of those that f thy name.	3373
	64: 1	preserve my life from f of the enemy.	6343
	64: 4	suddenly do they shoot at him, and f not.	3372
	64: 9	all men shall f, and shall declare the work	3372
	66:16	all ye that f God, and I will declare what he	3373
	67: 7	and all the ends of the earth shall f him.	3372
	72: 5	They shall f thee as long as the sun and	3372
	85: 9	Surely his salvation *is* nigh them that f him;	3373
	86:11	in thy truth: unite my heart to f thy name.	3372
	90:11	even according to thy f, *so is* thy wrath.	3374
	96: 9	of holiness: f before him, all the earth.	2342
	102:15	So the heathen shall f the name of	3372
	103:11	great is his mercy toward them that f him.	3373
	103:13	*so* the LORD pitieth them that f him.	3373
	103:17	to everlasting upon them that f him,	3373
	105:38	for the f of them that fell upon them.	6343
	111: 5	He hath given meat unto them that f him:	3373
	111:10	The f of the LORD *is* the beginning of	3374
	115:11	Ye that f the LORD, trust in the LORD:	3373
	115:13	He will bless them that f the LORD, *both*	3373
	118: 4	Let them now that f the LORD say,	3373
	118: 6	The LORD *is* on my side; I will not f:	3372
	119:38	unto thy servant, who *is devoted* to thy f.	3374
	119:39	Turn away my reproach which I f: for thy	3025
	119:63	I *am* a companion of all *them* that f thee,	3372
	119:74	They that f thee will be glad when they see	3373
	119:79	Let those that f thee turn unto me, and	3373
	119:120	My flesh trembleth for f of thee; and I am	6343
	135:20	ye that f the LORD, bless the LORD.	3373
	145:19	He will fulfil the desire of them that f him:	3373
	147:11	The LORD taketh pleasure in them that f	3373
Pr	1: 7	The f of the LORD *is* the beginning of	3374
	1:26	I will mock when your f cometh;	6343
	1:27	When your f cometh as desolation, and	6343
	1:29	and did not choose the f of the LORD:	3374
	1:33	and shall be quiet from f of evil.	6343
	2: 5	shalt thou understand the f of the LORD,	3374
	3: 7	f the LORD, and depart from evil.	3372
	3:25	Be not afraid of sudden f, neither of	6343
	8:13	The f of the LORD *is* to hate evil: pride,	3374
	9:10	The f of the LORD *is* the beginning of	3374
	10:24	The f of the wicked, it shall come *upon*	4034
	10:27	The f of the LORD prolongeth days: but	3374
	14:26	In the f of the LORD *is* strong confidence:	3374
	14:27	The f of the LORD *is* a fountain of life,	3374
	15:16	Better *is* little with the f of the LORD than	3374
	15:33	The f of the LORD *is* the instruction of	3374
	16: 6	by the f of the LORD *men* depart from	3374
	19:23	The f of the LORD *tendeth* to life: and	3374
	20: 2	The f of a king *is* as the roaring of a lion:	367
	22: 4	*and* the f of the LORD *are* riches,	3374
	23:17	*be thou* in the f of the LORD all the day	3374
	24:21	My son, f thou the LORD and the king:	3372
	29:25	The f of man bringeth a snare: but	2731
Ecc	3:14	God doeth *it,* that *men* should f before him.	3372
	5: 7	*are* also *divers* vanities: but f thou God.	3372
	8:12	that it shall be well with them that f God,	3373
	8:12	them that fear God, which f before him:	3372
	12:13	F God, and keep his commandments:	3372
SS	3: 8	upon his thigh because of f in the night.	6343
Isa	2:10	for f of the LORD, and for the glory of his	6343
	2:19	for f of the LORD, and for the glory of his	6343
	2:21	for f of the LORD, and for the glory of his	6343
	7: 4	f not, neither be fainthearted for the two	3372
	7:25	there shall not come thither the f of briers	3374
	8:12	neither f ye their fear, nor be afraid.	3372
	8:12	neither fear ye their f, nor be afraid.	4172
	8:13	*let* him *be* your f, and *let* him *be* your	4172
	11: 2	of knowledge and of the f of the LORD;	3374
	11: 3	quick understanding in the f of the LORD:	3374
	14: 3	from thy f, and from the hard bondage	7267
	19:16	it shall be afraid and f because of	6342
	21: 4	my pleasure hath he turned into f unto me.	2731
	24:17	F, and the pit, and the snare, *are* upon thee,	6343
	24:18	*that* he who fleeth from the noise of the f	6343
	25: 3	the city of the terrible nations shall f thee.	3372
	29:13	their f towards me is taught *by* the precept	3374
	29:23	One of Jacob, and shall f the God of Israel.	6206
	31: 9	he shall pass over *to* his strong hold for f,	4032
	33: 6	the f of the LORD *is* his treasure.	3374
	35: 4	that are of a fearful heart, Be strong, f not:	3372
	41:10	F thou not; for I *am* with thee: be not	3372
	41:13	thy right hand, saying unto thee, F not;	3372
	41:14	F not, thou worm Jacob, *and* ye men of	3372
	43: 1	and he that formed thee, O Israel, F not:	3372
	43: 5	F not: for I *am* with thee: I will bring thy	3372
	44: 2	F not, O Jacob, my servant; and	3372
	44: 8	F ye not, neither be afraid: have not I told	6342
	44:11	let them stand *up; yet* they shall f, *and*	6342
	51: 7	f ye not the reproach of men, neither be ye	3372
	54: 4	F not; for thou shalt not be ashamed:	3372
	54:14	be far from oppression; for thou shalt not f:	3372
	59:19	So shall they f the name of the LORD	3372
	60: 5	flow *together,* and thine heart shall f, and	6342
	63:17	*and* hardened our heart from thy f?	3374
Jer	2:19	*that* my f *is* not in thee, saith the Lord	6345
	5:22	F ye not me? saith the LORD: will ye not	3372
	5:24	Let us now f the LORD our God,	3372
	6:25	sword of the enemy *and* f *is* on every side.	4032
	10: 7	Who would not f thee, O King of nations?	3372
	20:10	the defaming of many, f on every side.	4032
	23: 4	they shall f no more, nor be dismayed,	3372
	26:19	did he not f the LORD, and besought	3373
	30: 5	a voice of trembling, of f, and not of peace.	6343
	30:10	Therefore f thou not, O my servant Jacob,	3372
	32:39	one way, that *they* may f me for ever, for	3372
	32:40	I will put my f in their hearts, that *they*	3374
	33: 9	they shall f and tremble for all the goodness	6342
	35:11	let us go *to* Jerusalem for f of the army of	6440
	35:11	and for f of the army of the Syrians:	6440
	37:11	up from Jerusalem for f of Pharaoh's army,	6440
	40: 9	saying, F not to serve the Chaldeans:	3372
	41: 9	*was* it which Asa the king had made for f of	6440
	46: 5	*for* f *was* round about, saith the LORD.	4032
	46:27	f not thou, O my servant Jacob, and be not	3372
	46:28	F thou not, O Jacob my servant, saith	3372
	48:43	F, and the pit, and the snare, *shall be* upon	6343
	48:44	He that fleeth from the f shall fall into	6343
	49: 5	Behold, I will bring a f upon thee, saith	6343
	49:24	f hath seized on *her:* anguish and	7374
	49:29	they shall cry unto them, F *is* on every side.	4032
	50:16	for f of the oppressing sword they shall turn	6440
	51:46	ye f for the rumour that shall be heard in	3372
La	3:47	F and a snare is come upon us, desolation	6343
	3:57	*that* I called upon thee: thou saidst, F not.	3372
Eze	3: 9	f them not, neither be dismayed at their	3372
	30:13	and I will put a f in the land of Egypt.	3374
Da	1:10	I f my lord the king, who hath appointed	3373
	6:26	and f before the God of Daniel:	1763
	10:12	said he unto me, F not, Daniel: for from	3372
	10:19	said, O man greatly beloved, f not:	3372
Hos	3: 5	shall f the LORD and his goodness in	6342
	10: 5	The inhabitants of Samaria shall f because	1481
Joel	2:21	F not, O land; be glad and rejoice: for	3372
Am	3: 8	The lion hath roared, who will not f?	3372
Jnh	1: 9	I f the LORD, the God of heaven,	3373
Mic	7:17	our God, and shall f because of thee.	3372
Zep	3: 7	I said, Surely thou wilt f me, thou wilt	3372
	3:16	it shall be said to Jerusalem, F thou not:	3372
Hag	1:12	and the people did f before the LORD.	3372
	2: 5	so my spirit remaineth among you: f ye not.	3372
Zec	8:13	f not, *but* let your hands be strong.	3372
	8:15	and to the house of Judah: f ye not.	3372
	9: 5	Ashkelon shall see *it,* and f; Gaza also *shall*	3372
Mal	1: 6	if I *be* a master, where *is* my f? saith	4172
	2: 5	I gave them to him *for* the f wherewith he	4172
	3: 5	the stranger *from his right,* and f not me,	3372
	4: 2	unto you that f my name shall the Sun of	3373
Mt	1:20	f not to take unto *thee* Mary thy wife:	*5399*
	10:26	F them not therefore: for there is nothing	*5399*
	10:28	And f not them which kill the body, but	*5399*
	10:28	rather f him which is able to destroy both	*5399*
	10:31	F ye not therefore, ye are of more value	*5399*
	14:26	It is a spirit; and they cried out for f.	*5401*
	21:26	if we shall say, Of men; we f the people;	*5399*

Mt 28: 4 And for f of him the keepers did shake, *5401*
28: 5 and said unto the women, F not ye: *5399*
28: 8 departed quickly from the sepulchre with f *5401*
Lk 1:12 *him,* he was troubled, and f fell upon him. *5401*
1:13 the angel said unto him, F not, Zacharias: *5399*
1:30 And the angel said unto her, F not, Mary: *5399*
1:50 And his mercy *is* on them that f him from *5399*
1:65 And f came on all that dwelt round about *5401*
1:74 of our enemies might serve him **without** f, *870*
2:10 And the angel said unto them, F not: *5399*
5:10 And Jesus said unto Simon, F not; *5399*
5:26 and were filled with f, saying, *5401*
7:16 And there came a f on all: *5401*
8:37 for they were taken with great f: *5401*
8:50 heard *it,* he answered him, saying, F not: *5399*
12: 5 But I will *fore*warn you whom you shall f: *5399*
12: 5 F him, which after *he* hath killed hath *5399*
12: 5 to cast into hell; yea, I say unto you, F him. *5399*
12: 7 F not therefore: ye are of more value than *5399*
12:32 F not, little flock; for it is your Father's *5399*
18: 4 Though I f not God, nor regard man; *5399*
21:26 Men's hearts failing them for f, and *5401*
23:40 rebuked him, saying, Dost not thou f God, *5399*
Jn 7:13 Howbeit no *man* spake openly of him for f *5401*
12:15 F not, daughter of Sion: behold, thy King *5399*
19:38 of Jesus, but secretly for f of the Jews, *5401*
20:19 disciples were assembled for f of the Jews, *5401*
Ac 2:43 And f came upon every soul: and *5401*
5: 5 great f came on all them that heard these *5401*
5:11 And great f came upon all the church, and *5401*
9:31 and walking in the f of the Lord, and in *5401*
13:16 Men of Israel, and *ye* that f God, *5399*
19:17 and f fell on them all, and the name of *5401*
27:24 Saying, F not, Paul; thou must be brought *5399*
Ro 3:18 There is no f of God before their eyes. *5401*
8:15 received the spirit of bondage again to f; *5401*
11:20 by faith. Be not high-minded, but f: *5399*
13: 7 f to whom fear; honour to whom honour. *5401*
13: 7 fear to whom f; honour to whom honour. *5401*
1Co 2: 3 and in f, and in much trembling. *5401*
16:10 see that he may be with you **without** f: *870*
2Co 7: 1 spirit, perfecting holiness in the f of God. *5401*
7:11 yea, *what* indignation, yea, *what* f, yea, *5401*
7:15 how with f and trembling you received *5401*
11: 3 But I f, lest by any means, as the serpent *5399*
12:20 For I f, lest, when I come, I shall not find *5399*
Eph 5:21 yourselves one to another in the f of God. *5401*
6: 5 with f and trembling, in singleness of your *5401*
Php 1:14 more bold to speak the word **without** f. *870*
2:12 work out your own salvation with f and *5401*
1Ti 5:20 before all, that others also may f. *2192+5401*
2Ti 1: 7 For God hath not given us the spirit of f; *1167*
Heb 2:15 And deliver them who through f of death *5401*
4: 1 Let us therefore f, lest, a promise being left *5399*
11: 7 **moved with** f, prepared an ark to *2125*
12:21 I **exceedingly** f and quake;) *1510+1630*
12:28 God acceptably with reverence and **godly** f: *2124*
13: 6 and I will not f what man shall do unto me. *5399*
1Pe 1:17 pass the time of your sojourning *here* in f: *5401*
2:17 the brotherhood. F God. Honour the king. *5399*
2:18 *be* subject to *your* masters with all f; *5401*
3: 2 your chaste conversation *coupled* with f. *5401*
3:15 the hope that is in you with meekness and f: *5401*
1Jn 4:18 There is no f in love; but perfect love *5401*
4:18 fear in love; but perfect love casteth out f: *5401*
4:18 because f hath torment. He that feareth is *5401*
Jude 1:12 with *you,* feeding themselves **without** f: *870*
1:23 And others save with f, pulling *them* out of *5401*
Rev 1:17 right hand upon me, saying unto me, F not; *5399*
2:10 F none *of those things* which thou shalt *5399*
11:11 and great f fell upon them which saw them. *5401*
11:18 and them that f thy name, small and great; *5399*
14: 7 a loud voice, F God, and give glory to him; *5399*
15: 4 Who shall not f thee, O Lord, and *5399*
18:10 Standing afar off for the f of her torment, *5401*
18:15 shall stand afar off for the f of her torment, *5401*
19: 5 and ye that f him, both small and great. *5399*

FEARED (74) [FEAR]

Ge 19:30 with him; for he f to dwell in Zoar: 3372
26: 7 for he f to say, *She is* my wife; lest, *said he,* 3372
Ex 1:17 the midwives f God, and did not as the king 3372
1:21 came to pass, because the midwives f God, 3372
2:14 Moses f, and said, Surely *this* thing is 3372
9:20 He that f the word of the LORD amongst 3373
14:31 the people f the LORD, and believed 3372
Dt 25:18 *wast* faint and weary; and he f not God. 3373
32:17 came newly up, whom your fathers f not. 8175
32:27 Were it not that I f the wrath of the enemy, 1481
Jos 4:14 they f him, as they feared Moses, all 3372
4:14 they feared him, as they f Moses, all 3372
10: 2 That they f greatly, because Gibeon *was* a 3372
Jdg 6:27 because he f his father's household, and 3372
8:20 for he f, because he *was* yet a youth. 3372
1Sa 3:15 And Samuel f to shew Eli the vision. 3372
12:18 all the people greatly f the LORD and 3372
14:26 hand to his mouth: for the people f the oath. 3372
15:24 because I f the people, and obeyed their 3372
2Sa 3:11 Abner a word again, because he f him. 3372
10:19 So the Syrians f to help the children of 3372
12:18 the servants of David f to tell him that 3372
1Ki 1:50 Adonijah f because of Solomon, and arose, 3372
3:28 the king had judged; and they f the king: 3372
18: 3 (Now Obadiah f the LORD greatly: 3373
2Ki 17: 7 king of Egypt, and had f other gods, 3372
17:25 dwelling there, *that* they f not the LORD: 3372
17:32 So they f the LORD, and made unto 3373
17:33 They f the LORD, and served their own 3373
17:41 So these nations f the LORD, and served 3373
1Ch 16:25 be praised: he also *is* to be f above all gods. 3372
2Ch 20: 3 Jehoshaphat f, and set himself to seek 3372
Ne 7: 2 *was* a faithful man, and f God above many. 3372
Job 1: 1 and **one that** f God, and eschewed evil. 3373
3:25 For the thing which I **greatly** f is come 6343
Ps 76: 7 Thou, *even* thou, *art* to be f: and who may 3372
76: 8 from heaven; the earth f, and was still, 3372
76:11 bring presents unto him that ought to be f. 4172
78:53 he led them on safely, so that they f not: 6342
89: 7 God *is* greatly to be f in the assembly of 6206
96: 4 to be praised: he *is* to be f above all gods. 3372
130: 4 with thee, that thou mayest be f. 3372
Isa 41: 5 The isles saw *it,* and f; the ends of the earth 3372
51:13 hast f continually every day because of 6342
57:11 of whom hast thou been afraid or f, 3372
Jer 3: 8 yet her treacherous sister Judah f not, but 3372
42:16 come to pass, *that* the sword, which ye f, 3373
44:10 neither have they f, nor walked in my law, 3372
Eze 11: 8 Ye have f the sword; and I will bring a 3372
Da 5:19 languages, trembled and f before him: 1763
Hos 10: 3 have no king, because we f not the LORD; 3372
Jnh 1:16 f the LORD **exceedingly,** 1419+3372+3374
Mal 2: 5 them to him *for* the fear wherewith he f me, 3372
3:16 they that f the LORD spake often one to 3373
3:16 before him for them that f the LORD, 3373
Mt 14: 5 he f the multitude, because they counted *5399*
21:46 they f the multitude, because they took him *5399*
27:54 that were done, they f greatly, saying, *5399*
Mk 4:41 And they f exceedingly, and said one *5399+5401*
6:20 For Herod f John, knowing that he *was* a *5399*
11:18 for they f him, because all the people was *5399*
11:32 if we shall say, Of men; they f the people: *5399*
12:12 sought to lay hold on him, but f the people: *5399*
Lk 9:34 and they f as they entered into the cloud. *5399*
9:45 it not: and they f to ask him of that saying. *5399*
18: 2 which f not God, neither regarded man: *5399*
19:21 For I f thee, because thou art an austere *5399*
20:19 to lay hands on him; and they f the people: *5399*
22: 2 they might kill him; for they f the people. *5399*
Jn 9:22 spake his parents, because they f the Jews: *5399*
Ac 5:26 for they f the people, lest they should have *5399*
10: 2 and one that f God with all his house, *5399*
16:38 and they f, when they heard that they were *5399*
Heb 5: 7 him from death, and was heard in that *he* f; *2124*

FEAREST (3) [FEAR]

Ge 22:12 for now I know that thou f God, 3373
Isa 57:11 my peace even of old, and thou f me not? 3372
Jer 22:25 into the hand *of them* whose face thou f, 3016

FEARETH (20) [FEAR]

1Ki 1:51 Behold, Adonijah f king Solomon: 3372
Job 1: 8 **one that** f God, and escheweth evil? 3373
2: 3 **one that** f God, and escheweth evil? 3373
Ps 25:12 What man *is* he that f the LORD? 3373
112: 1 Blessed *is* the man *that* f the LORD, 3372
128: 1 Blessed *is* every one that f the LORD; 3373
128: 4 that thus shall the man be blessed that f 3373
Pr 13:13 he that f the commandment shall be 3373

Pr 14: 2 He that walketh in his uprightness f 3373
14:16 A wise *man* f, and departeth from evil: but 3373
28:14 Happy *is* the man that f alway: but he that 6342
31:30 *but* a woman that f the LORD, she shall 3373
Ecc 7:18 for he that f God shall come forth of them 3373
8:13 as a shadow; because he f not before God. 3373
9: 2 *and* he that sweareth, as he that f an oath. 3373
Isa 50:10 Who *is* among you that f the LORD, 3373
Ac 10:22 and one that f God, and of good report *5399*
10:35 But in every nation he that f him, and *5399*
13:26 and whosoever among you f God, *5399*
1Jn 4:18 He that f is not made perfect in love. *5399*

FEARFUL (11) [FEAR]
Ex 15:11 in holiness, f *in* praises, doing wonders? 3372
Dt 20: 8 What man *is there that is* f and 3373
28:58 *thou* mayest fear this glorious and f name, 3372
Jdg 7: 3 saying, Whosoever *is* f and afraid, let him 3373
Isa 35: 4 Say to them that are of a f heart, Be strong, 4116
Mt 8:26 Why are ye f, O ye of little faith? *1169*
Mk 4:40 And he said unto them, Why are ye so f? *1169*
Lk 21:11 and **f sights** and great signs shall there be *5400*
Heb 10:27 But a certain f looking for of judgment and *5398*
10:31 *It is* a f *thing* to fall into the hands of *5398*
Rev 21: 8 But the f, and unbelieving, and *1169*

FEARFULLY (1) [FEAR]
Ps 139:14 for I am f and wonderfully made: 3372

FEARFULNESS (3) [FEAR]
Ps 55: 5 F and trembling are come upon me, and 3374
Isa 21: 4 My heart panted, f affrighted me: the night 6427
33:14 are afraid; f hath surprised the hypocrites. 7461

FEARING (8) [FEAR]
Jos 22:25 our children cease from f the LORD: 3372
Mk 5:33 But the woman f and trembling, *5399*
Ac 23:10 f lest Paul should have been pulled in *2125*
27:17 f lest they should fall into the quicksands, *5399*
27:29 Then f lest we should have fallen upon *5399*
Gal 2:12 f them which were of the circumcision. *5399*
Col 3:22 but in singleness of heart, f God: *5399*
Heb 11:27 forsook Egypt, not f the wrath of the king: *5399*

FEARS (4) [FEAR]
Ps 34: 4 heard me, and delivered me from all my f. 4035
Ecc 12: 5 f *shall be* in the way, and the almond tree 2849
Isa 66: 4 and will bring their f upon them; 4035
2Co 7: 5 *side;* without *were* fightings, within *were* f. *5401*

FEAST (123) [FEASTED, FEASTING, FEASTS]
Ge 19: 3 he made them a f, and did bake unleavened 4960
21: 8 Abraham made a great f the *same* day that 4960
26:30 he made them a f, and they did eat and 4960
29:22 all the men of the place, and made a f. 4960
40:20 that he made a f unto all his servants: 4960
Ex 5: 1 that they may **hold a** f unto me in 2287
10: 9 for we *must hold* a f unto the LORD. 2282
12:14 you shall keep it a f to the LORD 2282
12:14 you shall **keep** it **a** f by an ordinance for 2287
12:17 ye shall observe the *f of* unleavened bread; NIH
13: 6 in the seventh day *shall be* a f to 2282
23:14 Three times thou shalt **keep** a f unto me in 2287
23:15 Thou shalt keep the f of unleavened bread: 2282
23:16 the f of harvest, the firstfruits of thy 2282
23:16 the f of ingathering, *which is* in the end of 2282
32: 5 and said, To morrow *is* a f to the LORD. 2282
34:18 The f of unleavened bread shalt thou keep: 2282
34:22 thou shalt observe the f of weeks, of 2282
34:22 and the f of ingathering *at* the year's end. 2282
34:25 neither shall the sacrifice of the f of 2282
Lev 23: 6 the f of unleavened bread unto the LORD: 2282
23:34 f of tabernacles *for* seven days unto 2282
23:39 ye shall keep a f unto the LORD seven 2282
23:41 ye shall **keep** it **a** f unto the LORD 2282+2287
Nu 28:17 in the fifteenth day of this month *is* the f: 2282
29:12 ye shall **keep a** f unto the LORD 2282+2287
Dt 16:10 thou shalt keep the f of weeks unto 2282
16:13 Thou shalt observe the f of tabernacles 2282
16:14 thou shalt rejoice in thy f, thou, and 2282
16:15 Seven days shalt thou **keep a solemn** f unto 2287
16:16 in the f of unleavened bread, and in 2282
16:16 in the f of weeks, and in the feast of 2282
16:16 feast of weeks, and in the f of tabernacles: 2282
31:10 the year of release, in the f of tabernacles, 2282
Jdg 14:10 Samson made there a f; for so used 4960
14:12 declare it me *within* the seven days of the f, 4960
14:17 him the seven days, while their f lasted: 4960
21:19 *there is* a f of the LORD in Shiloh yearly 2282
1Sa 25:36 behold, he held a f in his house, like 4960
25:36 a feast in his house, like the f of a king; 4960
2Sa 3:20 and the men that *were* with him a f. 4960
1Ki 3:15 and made a f to all his servants. 4960
8: 2 Solomon at the f in the month Ethanim, 2282
8:65 at that time Solomon held a f, and all Israel 2282
12:32 Jeroboam ordained a f in the eighth month, 2282
12:32 like unto the f that *is* in Judah, and 2282
12:33 and ordained a f unto the children of Israel: 2282
2Ch 5: 3 in the f which *was in* the seventh month. 2282
7: 8 Also at the same time Solomon kept the f 2282
7: 9 the altar seven days, and the f seven days. 2282
8:13 *even* in the f of unleavened bread, and 2282
8:13 in the f of weeks, and in the feast of 2282
8:13 feast of weeks, and in the f of tabernacles. 2282
30:13 f of unleavened bread in the second month, 2282
30:21 f of unleavened bread seven days with great 2282
30:22 they did eat throughout the f seven days, 4150
35:17 the f of unleavened bread seven days. 2282
Ezr 3: 4 They kept also the f of tabernacles, as it is 2282
6:22 kept the f of unleavened bread seven days 2282
Ne 8:14 in booths in the f of the seventh month: 2282
8:18 they kept the f seven days; and on 2282
Est 1: 3 he made a f unto all his princes and 4960
1: 5 the king made a f unto all the people that 4960
1: 9 Also Vashti the queen made a f for 4960
2:18 the king made a great f unto all his princes 4960
2:18 and his servants, *even* Esther's f; 4960
8:17 had joy and gladness, a f and a good day. 4960
Ps 81: 3 in the time appointed, on our **solemn** f day. 2282
Pr 15:15 *that is* of a merry heart *hath* a continual f. 4960
Ecc 10:19 A f is made for laughter, and wine maketh 3899
Isa 25: 6 hosts make unto all people a f of fat things, 4960
25: 6 a f of wines on the lees, of fat things full of 4960
La 2: 7 of the LORD, as *in* the day of a **solemn** f. 4150
Eze 45:21 shall have the passover, a f of seven days; 2282
45:23 seven days of the f he shall prepare a burnt 2282
45:25 shall he do the like in the f *of* the seven 2282
Da 5: 1 Belshazzar the king made a great f to a 3900
Hos 2:11 her f *days,* her new moons, and 2282
9: 5 and in the day of the f of the LORD? 2282
12: 9 as *in* the days of the **solemn** f. 4150
Am 5:21 I despise your f *days,* and I will not smell in 2282
Zec 14:16 of hosts, and to keep the f of tabernacles. 2282
14:18 come not up to keep the f of tabernacles. 2282
14:19 come not up to keep the f of tabernacles. 2282
Mt 26: 2 Ye know that after two days is *the f of* NIG
26: 5 Not on the f *day,* lest there be an uproar *1859*
26:17 Now the first *day* of the *f of* unleavened NIG
27:15 Now at *that* f the governor was wont to *1859*
Mk 14: 1 After two days was *the f of* the passover, NIG
14: 2 Not on the f *day,* lest there be an uproar of *1859*
15: 6 Now at *that* f he released unto them one *1859*
Lk 2:41 every year at the f of the passover. *1859*
2:42 up to Jerusalem after the custom of the f. *1859*
5:29 And Levi made him a great f in his own *1403*
14:13 But when thou makest a f, call the poor, *1403*
22: 1 Now the f of unleavened bread drew nigh, *1859*
23:17 he must release one unto them at the f.) *1859*
Jn 2: 8 and bear unto the **governor of the** f. *755*
2: 9 When the **ruler of the** f had tasted the water *755*
2: 9 the **governor of the** f called the bridegroom, *755*
2:23 in the f *day,* many believed in his name, *1859*
4:45 *the things* that he did at Jerusalem at the f: *1859*
4:45 at the feast: for they also went unto the f. *1859*
5: 1 After this there was a f of the Jews; and *1859*
6: 4 And the passover, a f of the Jews, was nigh. *1859*
7: 2 Now the Jews' f of tabernacles was at hand. *1859*
7: 8 Go ye up unto this f: I go not up yet unto *1859*
7: 8 I go not up yet unto this f; for my time is *1859*
7:10 then went he also up unto the f, not openly, *1859*
7:11 Then the Jews sought him at the f, and said, *1859*
7:14 Now about the midst of the f Jesus went up *1859*
7:37 *that* great *day* of the f, Jesus stood and *1859*
10:22 And it was at Jerusalem *the f of* NIG
11:56 think ye, that he will not come to the f? *1859*
12:12 day much people that were come to the f, *1859*
12:20 them that came up to worship at the f: *1859*
13: 1 Now before the f of the passover, *1859*
13:29 *things* that we have need of against the f; *1859*

Ac 18:21 I must by all means keep *this* f that cometh *1859*
1Co 5: 8 Therefore let us **keep the** f, not with old *1858*
10:27 any of them that believe not bid you *to a f,* NIG
2Pe 2:13 their own deceivings while they f **with** you; *4910*
Jude 1:12 f **with** *you,* feeding themselves without *4910*

FEASTED (1) [FEAST]
Job 1: 4 his sons went and f *in their* houses, 4960+6213

FEASTING (7) [FEAST]
Est 9:17 and made it a day of f and gladness. 4960
9:18 and made it a day of f and gladness. 4960
9:19 of the month Adar *a day of* gladness and f, 4960
9:22 that *they* should make them days of f and 4960
Job 1: 5 when the days of *their* f were gone about, 4960
Ecc 7: 2 of mourning, than to go to the house of f: 4960
Jer 16: 8 Thou shalt not also go *into* the house of f, 4960

FEASTS (32) [FEAST]
Lev 23: 2 unto them, *Concerning* the f of the LORD, 4150
23: 2 *be* holy convocations, *even* these *are* my f. 4150
23: 4 These *are* the f of the LORD, *even* holy 4150
23:37 These *are* the f of the LORD, which ye 4150
23:44 the children of Israel the f of the LORD. 4150
Nu 15: 3 in a freewill offering, or in your **solemn** f, 4150
29:39 ye shall do unto the LORD in your **set** f, 4150
1Ch 23:31 new moons, and on the **set** f, by number, 4150
2Ch 2: 4 on the **solemn** f of the LORD our God. 4150
8:13 on the new moons, and on the **solemn** f, 4150
31: 3 and for the new moons, and for the **set** f, 4150
Ezr 3: 5 of all the **set** f of the LORD that were 4150
Ne 10:33 for the **set** f, and for the holy *things,* and 4150
Ps 35:16 With hypocritical mockers in f, 4580
Isa 1:14 and your **appointed** f my soul hateth: 4150
5:12 the tabret, and pipe, and wine, are *in* their f: 4960
Jer 51:39 In their heat I will make their f, and I will 4960
La 1: 4 because none come to the **solemn** f: 4150
2: 6 the LORD hath caused the **solemn** f and 4150
Eze 36:38 as the flock of Jerusalem in her **solemn** f; 4150
45:17 in the f, and in the new moons, and in 2282
46: 9 come before the LORD in the **solemn** f, 4150
46:11 in the f and in the solemnities the meat 2282
Hos 2:11 and her sabbaths, and all her **solemn** f. 4150
Am 8:10 I will turn your f into mourning, and 2282
Na 1:15 O Judah, keep thy **solemn** f, perform thy 2282
Zec 8:19 of Judah joy and gladness, and cheerful f; 4150
Mal 2: 3 your faces, *even* the dung of your **solemn** f; 2282
Mt 23: 6 And love the uppermost rooms at f, and *1173*
Mk 12:39 and the uppermost rooms at f: *1173*
Lk 20:46 in the synagogues, and the chief rooms at f; *1173*
Jude 1:12 These are spots in your f **of charity** when *26*

FEATHERED (2) [FEATHERS]
Ps 78:27 and f fowls like as the sand of the sea: 3671
Eze 39:17 Speak unto every f fowl, and to every beast 3671

FEATHERS (7) [FEATHERED]
Lev 1:16 he shall pluck away his crop with his f, 5133
Job 39:13 or wings and f *unto* the ostrich? 5133
Ps 68:13 with silver, and her f with yellow gold. 84
91: 4 He shall cover thee with his f, and under his 84
Eze 17: 3 longwinged, full *of* f, which had divers 5133
17: 7 great eagle with great wings and many f: 5133
Da 4:33 till his hairs were grown like eagles' *f,* and NIH

FED (31) [FEED]
Ge 30:36 and Jacob f the rest of Laban's flocks. 7462
36:24 as he f the asses of Zibeon his father. 7462
41: 2 and fatfleshed; and they f in a meadow. 7462
41:18 well favoured; and they f in a meadow: 7462
47:17 he f them with bread for all their cattle for 5095
48:15 the God which f me all my life long unto 7462
Ex 16:32 wherewith I have f you in the wilderness, 398
Dt 8: 3 thee to hunger, and f thee with manna, 398
8:16 Who f thee in the wilderness with manna, 398
2Sa 20: 3 f them, but went not in unto them. 3557
1Ki 18: 4 in a cave, and f them *with* bread and water.) 3557
18:13 in a cave, and f them *with* bread and water? 3557
1Ch 27:29 over the herds that f in Sharon *was* Shitrai 7462
Ps 37: 3 dwell in the land, and verily thou shalt be f. 7462
78:72 So he f them according to the integrity of 7462
81:16 He should have f them also with the finest of 398
Isa 1:11 offerings of rams, and the fat of f **beasts**; 4806
Jer 5: 7 when I had f them **to the full**, they then 7650
5: 8 They were *as* f horses in the morning: 2109
Eze 16:19 and oil, and honey, *wherewith* I f thee, 398
34: 3 you with the wool, ye kill them that are f: 1277
34: 8 the shepherds f themselves, and fed not my 7462
34: 8 fed themselves, and f not my flock; 7462
Da 4:12 the boughs thereof, and all flesh was f of it. 2110
5:21 they f him with grass like oxen, and 2939
Zec 11: 7 the other I called Bands; and I f the flock. 7462
Mt 25:37 and f *thee?* or thirsty, and gave *thee* drink? *5142*
Mk 5:14 And they that f the swine fled, and told *it* in *1006*
Lk 8:34 When they that f *them* saw what was done, *1006*
16:21 And desiring to be f with the crumbs which *5526*
1Co 3: 2 I have f you with milk, and not with meat: *4222*

FEEBLE (20) [FEEBLEMINDED, FEEBLENESS, FEEBLER]
Ge 30:42 when the cattle were f, he put *them* not in: 5848
Dt 25:18 *even* all that were f behind thee, when thou 2826
1Sa 2: 5 and she that hath many children is **waxed** f. 535
2Sa 4: 1 his hands were f, and all the Israelites were 7503
2Ch 28:15 carried all the f of them upon asses, 3782
Ne 4: 2 of Samaria, and said, What do *these* f Jews? 537
Job 4: 4 and thou hast strengthened the f knees. 3766
Ps 38: 8 I am f and sore broken: I have roared by 6313
105:37 *there was* not *one* f *person* among their 3782
Pr 30:26 The conies *are but* a f folk, yet make 3808+6099
Isa 16:14 remnant *shall be* very small *and* f. 3524+3808
35: 3 ye the weak hands, and confirm the f knees. 3782
Jer 6:24 our hands **wax** f: anguish hath taken hold 7503
49:24 Damascus is **waxed** f, *and* turneth herself 7503
50:43 the report of them, and his hands **waxed** f: 7503
Eze 7:17 All hands shall be f, and all knees shall be 7503
21: 7 all hands shall be f, and every spirit shall 7503
Zec 12: 8 he that is f among them at that day shall be 3782
1Co 12:22 which seem to be **more** f, are necessary: *772*
Heb 12:12 hands which hang down, and the f knees; *3886*

FEEBLEMINDED (1) [FEEBLE, MIND]
1Th 5:14 *are* unruly, comfort the f, support the weak, *3642*

FEEBLENESS (1) [FEEBLE]
Jer 47: 3 look back to *their* children for f of hands; 7510

FEEBLER (1) [FEEBLE]
Ge 30:42 so the f were Laban's, and the stronger 5848

FEED (81) [FED, FEEDEST, FEEDETH, FEEDING, FOOD]
Ge 25:30 Esau said to Jacob, F me, I pray thee, 3938
29: 7 water ye the sheep, and go *and* f *them.* 7462
30:31 for me, I will again f *and* keep thy flock: 7462
37:12 his brethren went to f their father's flock in 7462
37:13 Do not thy brethren f *the flock* in 7462
37:16 I pray thee, where they f *their flocks.* 7462
46:32 for their **trade** hath been **to** f **cattle**; 376+4735
Ex 22: 5 his beast, and shall f in another man's field; 1197
34: 3 neither let the flocks nor herds f before that 7462
1Sa 17:15 returned from Saul to f his father's sheep *at* 7462
2Sa 5: 2 Thou shalt f my people Israel, and 7462
7: 7 whom I commanded to f my people Israel, 7462
19:33 and I will f thee with me in Jerusalem. 3557
1Ki 17: 4 I have commanded the ravens to f thee 3557
22:27 f him with bread of affliction and with water 398
1Ch 11: 2 Thou shalt f my people Israel, and 7462
17: 6 whom I commanded to f my people, 7462
2Ch 18:26 f him with bread of affliction and with water 398
Job 24: 2 violently take away flocks, and f *thereof.* 7462
24:20 the worm shall f **sweetly on** him; 4988
Ps 28: 9 f them also, and lift them up for ever. 7462
49:14 death shall f *on* them; and the upright shall 7462
78:71 young he brought him to f Jacob his people, 7462
Pr 10:21 The lips of the righteous f many: but 7462
30: 8 f me with food convenient for me: 2963
SS 1: 8 and f thy kids beside the shepherds' tents. 7462
4: 5 *that are* twins, which f among the lilies. 7462
6: 2 to f in the gardens, and to gather lilies. 7462
Isa 5:17 shall the lambs f after their manner, and 7462
11: 7 the cow and the bear shall f; their young 7462
14:30 the firstborn of the poor shall f, and 7462
27:10 there shall the calf f, and there shall he lie 7462
30:23 in that day shall thy cattle f *in* large 7462
40:11 He shall f his flock like a shepherd: he shall 7462
49: 9 They shall f in the ways, and their pastures 7462
49:26 I will f them that oppress thee with their own 398
58:14 f thee with the heritage of Jacob thy father: 398
61: 5 strangers shall stand and f your flocks, and 7462
65:25 The wolf and the lamb shall f together, and 7462

Jer 3:15 which shall f you with knowledge and 7462
6: 3 they shall f every one *in* his place. 7462
9:15 Behold, I *will* f them, *even* this people, with 398
23: 2 Israel against the pastors that f my people; 7462
23: 4 up shepherds over them which shall f them: 7462
23:15 I will f them with wormwood, and 398
50:19 he shall f on Carmel and Bashan, and 7462
La 4: 5 They that did f delicately are desolate in 398
Eze 34: 2 Woe *be* to the shepherds of Israel that do f 7462
34: 2 should not the shepherds f the flocks? 7462
34: 3 kill them that are fed: *but* ye f not the flock. 7462
34:10 neither shall the shepherds f themselves 7462
34:13 f them upon the mountains of Israel by 7462
34:14 I will f them in a good pasture, and 7462
34:14 *in* a fat pasture shall they f upon 7462
34:15 I will f my flock, and I will cause them to 7462
34:16 and the strong; I will f them with judgment. 7462
34:23 he shall f them, *even* my servant David; 7462
34:23 he shall f them, and he shall be their 7462
Da 11:26 they that f of the portion of his meat shall 398
Hos 4:16 now the LORD will f them as a lamb in a 7462
9: 2 and the winepress shall not f them, 7462
Jnh 3: 7 any thing: let them not f, nor drink water: 7462
Mic 5: 4 and f in the strength of the LORD, 7462
7:14 F thy people with thy rod, the flock of thine 7462
7:14 let them f *in* Bashan and Gilead, as *in* 7462
Zep 2: 7 the house of Judah; they shall f thereupon: 7462
3:13 for they shall f and lie down, and none shall 7462
Zec 11: 4 my God; F the flock of the slaughter; 7462
11: 7 I will f the flock of slaughter, *even* you, 7462
11: 9 said I, I will not f you: that that dieth, let it 7462
11:16 that is broken, nor f that that standeth still: 3557
Lk 15:15 and he sent him into his fields to f swine. *1006*
Jn 21:15 I love thee. He saith unto him, F my lambs. *1006*
21:16 I love thee. He saith unto him, F my sheep. *4165*
21:17 Jesus saith unto him, F my sheep. *1006*
Ac 20:28 to f the church of God, which he hath *4165*
Ro 12:20 Therefore if thine enemy hunger, f him; *5595*
1Co 13: 3 And though I **bestow** all my goods **to f** *5595*
1Pe 5: 2 F the flock of God which is among you, *4165*
Rev 7:17 is in the midst of the throne shall f them, *4165*
12: 6 that they should f her there a thousand two *5142*

FEEDEST (2) [FEED]
Ps 80: 5 Thou f them with the bread of tears; and 398
SS 1: 7 O thou whom my soul loveth, where thou f, 7462

FEEDETH (8) [FEED]
Pr 15:14 but the mouth of fools f **on** foolishness. 7462
SS 2:16 *is* mine, and I *am* his: he f among the lilies. 7462
6: 3 my beloved *is* mine: he f among the lilies. 7462
Isa 44:20 He f **on** ashes: a deceived heart hath turned 7462
Hos 12: 1 Ephraim f **on** wind, and followeth after 7462
Mt 6:26 into barns; yet your heavenly Father f them. *5142*
Lk 12:24 have storehouse nor barn; and God f them: *5142*
1Co 9: 7 or who f a flock, and eateth not of the milk *4165*

FEEDING (9) [FEED]
Ge 37: 2 years old, was f the flock with his brethren; 7462
Job 1:14 were plowing, and the asses f beside them: 7462
Eze 34:10 and cause them to cease from f the flock; 7462
Na 2:11 the f **place** of the young lions, where 4829
Mt 8:30 way off from them a herd of many swine f. *1006*
Mk 5:11 unto the mountains a great herd of swine f. *1006*
Lk 8:32 And there was there a herd of many swine f *1006*
17: 7 having a servant plowing or f **cattle**, *4165*
Jude 1:12 feast with *you,* f themselves without fear: *4165*

FEEL (7) [FEELING, FELT]
Ge 27:12 My father peradventure will f me, and 4959
27:21 I pray thee, that I may f thee, my son, 4184
Jdg 16:26 Suffer me that I may f the pillars 4184
Job 20:20 Surely he shall not f quietness in his belly, 3045
Ps 58: 9 Before your pots can f the thorns, he shall 995
Ecc 8: 5 Whoso keepeth the commandment shall f 3045
Ac 17:27 if haply they might f **after** him, and *5584*

FEELING (2) [FEEL]
Eph 4:19 Who being **past** f have given themselves *524*
Heb 4:15 be **touched with the** f of our infirmities; *4834*

FEET (256) [FOOT]
Ge 18: 4 wash your f, and rest yourselves under 7272
19: 2 wash your f, and ye shall rise up early, and 7272
24:32 water to wash his f, and the men's feet that 7272
24:32 and the men's f that *were* with him. 7272
43:24 gave *them* water, and they washed their f; 7272
49:10 nor a lawgiver from between his f, 7272
49:33 he gathered up his f into the bed, and 7272
Ex 3: 5 put off thy shoes from off thy f, for 7272
4:25 of her son, and cast *it* at his f, and said, 7272
12:11 your shoes on your f, and your staff in your 7272
24:10 *there was* under his f as it were a paved 7272
25:26 four corners that *are* on the four f thereof. 7272
30:19 shall wash their hands and their f thereat: 7272
30:21 So they shall wash their hands and their f, 7272
37:13 four corners that *were* in the four f thereof. 7272
40:31 sons washed their hands and their f thereat: 7272
Lev 8:24 and upon the great toes of their right f: 7272
11:21 which have legs above their f, to leap 7272
11:23 which have four f, *shall be* an abomination 7272
11:42 whatsoever hath more f among all creeping 7272
Nu 20:19 *doing any* thing *else,* go through on my f. 7272
Dt 2:28 only I will pass through on my f; 7272
11:24 Every place whereon the soles of your f 7272
28:57 one that cometh out from between her f, 7272
33: 3 they sat down at thy f; *every one* shall 7272
Jos 3:13 as soon as the soles of the f of the priests 7272
3:15 the f of the priests that bare the ark were 7272
4: 3 out of the place where the priests' f stood 7272
4: 9 in the place where the f of the priests which 7272
4:18 the soles of the priests' f were lift up unto 7272
9: 5 old shoes and clouted upon their f, and 7272
10:24 put your f upon the necks of these kings. 7272
10:24 and put their f upon the necks of them. 7272
14: 9 Surely the land whereon thy f have trodden 7272
Jdg 3:24 Surely he covereth his f in *his* summer 7272
4:10 he went up with ten thousand men at his f: 7272
4:15 off *his* chariot, and fled away on his f. 7272
4:17 Howbeit Sisera fled away on his f to 7272
5:27 At her f he bowed, he fell, he lay down: 7272
5:27 at her f he bowed, he fell: where he bowed, 7272
19:21 they washed their f, and did eat and drink. 7272
Ru 3: 4 go in, and uncover his f, and lay thee down; 4772
3: 7 and uncovered his f, and laid her down. 4772
3: 8 and behold, a woman lay *at* his f. 4772
3:14 she lay *at* his f until the morning: and 4772
1Sa 2: 9 He will keep the f of his saints, and 7272
14:13 climbed up upon his hands and upon his f, 7272
24: 3 *was* a cave; and Saul went in to cover his f: 7272
25:24 fell at his f, and said, Upon me, my lord, 7272
25:41 to wash the f of the servants of my lord. 7272
2Sa 3:34 *were* not bound, nor thy f put into fetters: 7272
4: 4 had a son *that was* lame of *his* f, *and* 7272
4:12 cut off their hands and their f, and 7272
9: 3 hath yet a son, *which is* lame on *his* f. 7272
9:13 king's table; and *was* lame on both his f. 7272
11: 8 Go down to thy house, and wash thy f. 7272
19:24 had neither dressed his f, nor trimmed his 7272
22:10 came down; and darkness *was* under his f. 7272
22:34 He maketh my f like hinds' *feet:* and 7272
22:34 He maketh my feet like hinds' *f:* and NIH
22:37 steps under me; so that my f did not slip. 7166
22:39 not arise: yea, they are fallen under my f. 7272
1Ki 2: 5 and in his shoes that *were* on his f. 7272
5: 3 LORD put them under the soles of his f. 7272
14: 6 *so,* when Ahijah heard the sound of her f, 7272
14:12 *and* when thy f enter into the city, the child 7272
15:23 time of his old age he was diseased in his f. 7272
2Ki 4:27 of God to the hill, she caught him by the f: 7272
4:37 fell at his f, and bowed herself to 7272
6:32 *is* not the sound of his master's f behind 7272
9:35 and the f, and the palms of *her* hands. 7272
13:21 of Elisha, he revived, and stood up on his f. 7272
19:24 with the sole of my f have I dried up all 6471
21: 8 Neither will I make the f of Israel move any 7272
1Ch 28: 2 David the king stood up upon his f, and 7272
2Ch 3:13 they stood on their f, and their faces *were* 7272
16:12 ninth year of his reign was diseased in his f, 7272
Ne 9:21 waxed not old, and their f swelled not. 7272
Est 8: 3 fell down at his f, and besought him with 7272
Job 12: 5 He that is ready to slip with *his* f *is as a* 7272
13:27 Thou puttest my f also in the stocks, and 7272
13:27 thou settest a print upon the heels of my f. 7272
18: 8 For he is cast into a net by his own f, and 7272
18:11 on every side, and shall drive him to his f. 7272
29:15 eyes to the blind, and f *was* I to the lame. 7272
30:12 they push away my f, and they raise up 7272
33:11 He putteth my f in the stocks, he marketh 7272

Ps	8: 6	thou hast put all *things* under his f:	7272
	18: 9	came down: and darkness *was* under his f.	7272
	18:33	He maketh my f like hinds' *feet,* and	7272
	18:33	He maketh my feet like hinds' *f,* and	NIH
	18:36	my steps under me, that my f did not slip.	7166
	18:38	not able to rise: they are fallen under my f.	7272
	22:16	they pierced my hands and my f.	7272
	25:15	for he shall pluck my f out of the net.	7272
	31: 8	thou hast set my f in a large room.	7272
	40: 2	set my f upon a rock, *and* established my	7272
	47: 3	under us, and the nations under our f.	7272
	56:13	*wilt* not *thou deliver* my f from falling,	7272
	58:10	he shall wash his f in the blood of	6471
	66: 9	in life, and suffereth not our f to be moved.	7272
	73: 2	*as for* me, my f were almost gone; my steps	7272
	74: 3	Lift up thy f unto the perpetual desolations;	6471
	91:13	and the dragon shalt thou **trample under** f.	7429
	105:18	Whose f they hurt with fetters: he was laid	7272
	115: 7	f *have* they, but they walk not:	7272
	116: 8	eyes from tears, *and* my f from falling.	7272
	119:59	and turned my f unto thy testimonies.	7272
	119:101	I have refrained my f from every evil way,	7272
	119:105	Thy word *is* a lamp unto my f, and a light	7272
	122: 2	Our f shall stand within thy gates,	7272
Pr	1:16	For their f run to evil, and make haste to	7272
	4:26	Ponder the path of thy f, and let all thy	7272
	5: 5	Her f go down *to* death; her steps take hold	7272
	6:13	with his eyes, he speaketh with his f,	7272
	6:18	f that be swift in running to mischief,	7272
	6:28	go upon hot coals, and his f not be burnt?	7272
	7:11	and stubborn; her f abide not in her house:	7272
	19: 2	and he that hasteth with *his* f, sinneth.	7272
	26: 6	by the hand of a fool cutteth off the f,	7272
	29: 5	his neighbour spreadeth a net for his f.	6471
SS	5: 3	I have washed my f; how shall I defile	7272
	7: 1	How beautiful are thy f with shoes,	6471
Isa	3:16	they go, and making a tinkling with their f:	7272
	3:18	of *their* tinkling ornaments *about their f,*	NIH
	6: 2	with twain he covered his f, and with twain	7272
	7:20	of Assyria, the head, and the hair of the f:	7272
	14:19	of the pit; as a carcase **trodden under** f.	947
	23: 7	her own f shall carry her afar off to sojourn.	7272
	26: 6	*even* the f of the poor, *and* the steps of	7272
	28: 3	of Ephraim, shall be trodden under f:	7272
	32:20	that send forth *thither* the f of the ox and	7272
	37:25	with the sole of my f have I dried up all	6471
	41: 3	*by* the way *that* he had not gone with his f.	7272
	49:23	the earth, and lick up the dust of thy f;	7272
	52: 7	How beautiful upon the mountains are the f	7272
	59: 7	Their f run to evil, and they make haste to	7272
	60:13	and I will make the place of my f glorious.	7272
	60:14	bow themselves down at the soles of thy f;	7272
Jer	13:16	before your f stumble upon the dark	7272
	14:10	they have not refrained their f, therefore	7272
	18:22	a pit to take me, and hid snares for my f.	7272
	38:22	thy f are sunk in the mire, *and* they are	7272
La	1:13	he hath spread a net for my f, he hath	7272
	3:34	To crush under his f all the prisoners of	7272
Eze	1: 7	their f *were* straight feet; and the sole of	7272
	1: 7	their feet *were* straight f; and the sole of	7272
	1: 7	the sole of their f *was* like the sole of a	7272
	2: 1	stand upon thy f, and I will speak unto thee.	7272
	2: 2	set me upon my f, that I heard him that	7272
	3:24	set me upon my f, and spake with me, and	7272
	16:25	hast opened thy f to every one that passed	7272
	24:17	put on thy shoes upon thy f, and cover not	7272
	24:23	your heads, and your shoes upon your f:	7272
	25: 6	stamped with the f, and rejoiced in heart	7272
	32: 2	troubledst the waters with thy f, and	7272
	34:18	ye must tread down with your f the residue	7272
	34:18	but ye must foul the residue with your f?	7272
	34:19	eat that which ye have trodden with your f;	7272
	34:19	that which ye have fouled with your f.	7272
	37:10	they lived, and stood up upon their f,	7272
	43: 7	and the place of the soles of my f,	7272
Da	2:33	of iron, his f part of iron and part of clay.	7271
	2:34	which smote the image upon his f *that were*	7271
	2:41	whereas thou sawest the f and toes, part of	7271
	2:42	*as* the toes of the f *were* part of iron, and	7271
	7: 4	made stand upon the f as a man, and	7271
	7: 7	and stamped the residue with the f of it:	7271
	7:19	and stamped the residue with his f;	7271
	10: 6	and his f like in colour to polished brass,	4772
Na	1: 3	and the clouds *are* the dust of his f.	7272
	1:15	Behold upon the mountains the f of him	7272
Hab	3: 5	and burning coals went forth at his f.	7272
	3:19	he will make my f like hinds' *feet,* and	7272
	3:19	he will make my feet like hinds' *f,* and	NIH
Zec	14: 4	his f shall stand in that day upon the mount	7272
	14:12	away while they stand upon their f,	7272
Mal	4: 3	f in the day that I *shall* do *this,* saith	7272
Mt	7: 6	lest they trample them under their f, and	4228
	10:14	or city, shake off the dust of your f.	4228
	15:30	and cast them *down* at Jesus' f;	4228
	18: 8	or two f to be cast into everlasting fire.	4228
	18:29	And his fellowservant fell down at his f,	4228
	28: 9	And they came and held him by the f, and	4228
Mk	5:22	and when he saw him, he fell at his f,	4228
	6:11	shake off the dust under your f for a	4228
	7:25	heard of him, and came and fell at his f:	4228
	9:45	than having two f to be cast into hell,	4228
Lk	1:79	to guide our f into the way of peace.	4228
	7:38	And stood at his f behind *him* weeping, and	4228
	7:38	and began to wash his f with tears, and	4228
	7:38	and kissed his f, and anointed *them* with	4228
	7:44	thou gavest me no water for my f:	4228
	7:44	but she hath washed my f with tears, and	4228
	7:45	time I came in hath not ceased to kiss my f.	4228
	7:46	this *woman* hath anointed my f with	4228
	8:35	sitting at the f of Jesus, clothed, and in his	4228
	8:41	and he fell down at Jesus' f, and	4228
	9: 5	shake off the very dust from your f for a	4228
	10:39	which also sat at Jesus' f, and heard his	4228
	15:22	put a ring on his hand, and shoes on *his* f:	4228
	17:16	And fell down on *his* face at his f,	4228
	24:39	Behold my hands and my f, that it is I	4228
	24:40	he shewed them *his* hands and *his* f.	4228
Jn	11: 2	and wiped his f with her hair,	4228
	11:32	and saw him, she fell down at his f,	4228
	12: 3	and anointed the f of Jesus, and wiped his	4228
	12: 3	feet of Jesus, and wiped his f with her hair:	4228
	13: 5	and began to wash the disciples' f, and	4228
	13: 6	saith unto him, Lord, dost thou wash my f?	4228
	13: 8	unto him, Thou shalt never wash my f.	4228
	13: 9	not my f only, but also *my* hands and	4228
	13:10	is washed needeth not save to wash *his* f,	4228
	13:12	So after he had washed their f, and	4228
	13:14	*your* Lord and Master, have washed your f;	4228
	13:14	ye also ought to wash one another's f.	4228
	20:12	the one at the head, and the other at the f,	4228
Ac	3: 7	and immediately his f and ankle bones	939
	4:35	And laid *them down* at the apostles' f: and	4228
	4:37	the money, and laid *it* at the apostles' f.	4228
	5: 2	a certain part, and laid *it* at the apostles' f.	4228
	5: 9	the f of them which have buried thy	4228
	5:10	Then fell she down straightway at his f, and	4228
	7:33	Lord to him, Put off *thy* shoes from thy f:	4228
	7:58	laid down their clothes at a young man's f,	4228
	10:25	and fell down at *his* f, and	4228
	13:25	whose shoes of *his* f I am not worthy to	4228
	13:51	But they shook off the dust of their f	4228
	14: 8	a certain man at Lystra, impotent in *his* f,	4228
	14:10	with a loud voice, Stand upright on thy f.	4228
	16:24	and made their f fast in the stocks.	4228
	21:11	and bound his *own* hands and f, and said,	4228
	22: 3	yet brought up in this city at the f of	4228
	26:16	But rise, and stand upon thy f: for I have	4228
Ro	3:15	Their f *are* swift to shed blood:	4228
	10:15	How beautiful *are* the f of them that preach	4228
	16:20	shall bruise Satan under your f shortly.	4228
1Co	12:21	nor again the head to the f, I have no need	4228
	15:25	till he hath put all enemies under his f.	4228
	15:27	For he hath put all *things* under his f.	4228
Eph	1:22	And hath put all *things* under his f, and	4228
	6:15	And *your* f shod with the preparation of	4228
1Ti	5:10	if she have washed the saints' f,	4228
Heb	2: 8	hast put all *things* in subjection under his f.	4228
	12:13	And make straight paths for your f, lest *that*	4228
Rev	1:15	And his f like unto fine brass, as if they	4228
	1:17	And when I saw him, I fell at his f as dead.	4228
	2:18	a flame of fire, and his f *are* like fine brass;	4228
	3: 9	them to come and worship before thy f,	4228
	10: 1	*it were* the sun, and his f as pillars of fire:	4228
	11:11	into them, and they stood upon their f;	4228
	12: 1	and the moon under her f, and upon her	4228
	13: 2	and his f *were* as *the feet* of a bear, and	4228
	13: 2	and his feet *were* as *the f* of a bear, and	NIG
	19:10	And I fell at his f to worship him. And he	4228

F

Rev 22: 8 I fell down to worship before the f of *4228*

FEIGN (3) [FEIGNED, FEIGNEDLY, FEIGNEST, UNFEIGNED]
2Sa 14: 2 f thyself **to be a mourner**, and put on now 56
1Ki 14: 5 that she shall f herself **to be another** 5234
Lk 20:20 which *should* f themselves just *men,* that *5271*

FEIGNED (3) [FEIGN]
1Sa 21:13 f himself **mad** in their hands, and 1984
Ps 17: 1 unto my prayer, *that goeth* not out of f lips. 4820
2Pe 2: 3 And through covetousness shall they with f *4112*

FEIGNEDLY (1) [FEIGN]
Jer 3:10 whole heart, but f, saith the LORD. 8267+871.1

FEIGNEST (2) [FEIGN]
1Ki 14: 6 why f thou thyself **to be another?** 5234
Ne 6: 8 but thou f them out of thine own heart. 908

FELIX (8) [FELIX']
Ac 23:24 and bring *him* safe unto **F** the governor. *5344*
23:26 excellent governor **F** *sendeth* greeting. *5344*
24: 3 *it* always, and in all places, most noble **F**, *5344*
24:22 And when **F** heard these *things,* having *5344*
24:24 when **F** came with his wife Drusilla, *5344*
24:25 and judgment to come, **F** trembled, *5344*
24:27 and **F**, willing to shew the Jews a pleasure, *5344*
25:14 There is a certain man left in bonds by **F**: *5344*

FELIX' (1) [FELIX]
Ac 24:27 two years Porcius Festus came into **F** room: *5344*

FELL (243) [FALL, FELLED, FELLER, FELLEST, FELLING]
Ge 4: 5 was very wroth, and his countenance f. 5307
14:10 of Sodom and Gomorrah fled, and f there; 5307
15:12 going down, a deep sleep f upon Abram; 5307
15:12 lo, a horror of great darkness f upon him. 5307
17: 3 Abram f on his face: and God talked with 5307
17:17 Abraham f upon his face, and laughed, 5307
33: 4 and f on his neck, and kissed him: 5307
44:14 and they f before him on the ground. 5307
45:14 And he f upon his brother Benjamin's neck, 5307
46:29 he f on his neck, and wept on his neck a 5307
50: 1 Joseph f upon his father's face, and 5307
50:18 also went and f **down** before his face; 5307
Ex 32:28 there f of the people that day about three 5307
Lev 9:24 they shouted, and f on their faces. 5307
16: 9 the goat upon which the LORD'S lot f, 5927
16:10 on which the lot f to be the scapegoat, 5927
Nu 11: 4 that *was* among them f **a lusting**: 183+8378
11: 9 when the dew f upon the camp in the night, 3381
11: 9 the camp in the night, the manna f upon it. 3381
14: 5 Aaron f on their faces before all 5307
16: 4 when Moses heard *it,* he f upon his face: 5307
16:22 they f upon their faces, and said, O God, 5307
16:45 in a moment. And they f upon their faces. 5307
20: 6 and they f upon their faces: 5307
22:27 of the LORD, she f **down** under Balaam: 7257
22:31 down his head, and f **flat** on his face. 7812
Dt 9:18 I f **down** before the LORD, as at the first, 5307
9:25 Thus I f **down** before the LORD forty 5307
9:25 as I f **down** *at the first;* because the LORD 5307
Jos 5:14 Joshua f on his face to the earth, and 5307
6:20 that the wall f **down** flat, so that the people 5307
7: 6 f to the earth upon his face before the ark of 5307
8:25 *so* it was, *that* all that f that day, both of 5307
11: 7 of Merom suddenly; and they f upon them. 5307
16: 1 the lot of the children of Joseph f from 3318
17: 5 there f ten portions to Manasseh, beside 5307
22:20 wrath f on all the congregation of Israel? 1961
Jdg 4:16 all the host of Sisera f upon the edge of 5307
5:27 At her feet he bowed, he f, he lay down: 5307
5:27 at her feet he bowed, he f: where he bowed, 5307
5:27 where he bowed, there he f **down** dead. 5307
7:13 and smote it that it f, and overturned it, 5307
8:10 for there f an hundred and twenty thousand 5307
12: 6 there f at that time of the Ephraimites forty 5307
13:20 on *it,* and f on their faces to the ground. 5307
16:30 the house f upon the lords, and upon all 5307
19:26 f **down** *at* the door of the man's house 5307
20:44 there f of Benjamin eighteen thousand men; 5307
20:46 So that all which f that day of Benjamin 5307
Ru 2:10 she f on her face, and bowed herself to 5307
1Sa 4:10 for there f of Israel thirty thousand 5307
4:18 that he f from off the seat backward by 5307
11: 7 And the fear of the LORD f on the people, 5307
14:13 they f before Jonathan; and 5307
17:49 and he f upon his face to the earth. 5307
17:52 the wounded of the Philistines f **down** by 5307
20:41 f on his face to the ground, and 5307
22:18 he f upon the priests, and slew on that day 6293
25:23 f before David on her face, and 5307
25:24 f at his feet, and said, Upon me, my lord, 5307
28:20 Saul f straightway all along on the earth, 5307
29: 3 I have found no *fault* in him since he f *unto* 5307
30:13 left me, because three days agone I f **sick**. 2470
31: 1 and f **down** slain in mount Gilboa. 5307
31: 4 therefore Saul took a sword, and f upon it. 5307
31: 5 he f likewise upon his sword, and died with 5307
2Sa 1: 2 that he f to the earth, and did obeisance. 5307
2:16 his fellow's side; so they f **down** together: 5307
2:23 he f **down** there, and died in the same 5307
2:23 as came to the place where Asahel f **down** 5307
4: 4 haste to flee, that he f, and became lame. 5307
9: 6 he f on his face, and did reverence. 5307
11:17 there f *some* of the people of the servants of 5307
13: 2 *so* vexed, that he f **sick** for his sister Tamar; 2470
14: 4 she f on her face to the ground, and 5307
14:22 Joab f to the ground on his face, and 5307
18:28 he f **down** to the earth upon his face before 7812
19:18 Shimei the son of Gera f **down** before 5307
20: 8 sheath thereof; and as he went forth it f **out**. 5307
21: 9 they f *all* seven together, and were put to 5307
21:22 f by the hand of David, and by the hand of 5307
1Ki 2:25 of Jehoiada; and he f upon him that he died. 6293
2:32 who f **upon** two men more righteous and 6293
2:34 went up, and f upon him, and slew him: 6293
2:46 went out, and f upon him, that he died. 6293
14: 1 that time Abijah the son of Jeroboam f **sick**. 2470
17:17 the mistress of the house, f **sick**; 2470
18: 7 he knew him, and f on his face, and said, 5307
18:38 the fire of the LORD f, and consumed 5307
18:39 when all the people saw *it,* they f on their 5307
20:30 *there* a wall f upon twenty and 5307
2Ki 1: 2 Ahaziah f **down** through a lattice in his 5307
1:13 came and f on his knees before Elijah, and 3766
2:13 He took up also the mantle of Elijah that f 5307
2:14 he took the mantle of Elijah that f from 5307
3:19 shall f every good tree, and stop all wells of 5307
4: 8 it f **on** a day, that Elisha passed to Shunem, 1961
4:11 it f **on** a day, that he came thither, and 1961
4:18 when the child was grown, it f **on** a day, 1961
4:37 f at his feet, and bowed herself to 5307
6: 5 a beam, the axe head f into the water: 5307
6: 6 the man of God said, Where f it? And he 5307
7:20 so it f out unto him: for the people trode 1961
25:11 the fugitives that f **away** to the king of 5307
1Ch 5:10 with the Hagarites, who f by their hand: 5307
5:22 For there f **down** many slain, because 5307
10: 1 and f **down** slain in mount Gilboa. 5307
10: 4 So Saul took a sword, and f upon it. 5307
10: 5 he f likewise on the sword, and died. 5307
12:19 there f *some* of Manasseh to David, 5307
12:20 there f to him of Manasseh, Adnah, and 5307
20: 8 they f by the hand of David, and by 5307
21:14 and there f of Israel seventy thousand men. 5307
21:16 clothed in sackcloth, f upon their faces. 5307
26:14 the lot eastward f to Shelemiah. Then *for* 5307
27:24 because there f wrath for it against Israel; 1961
2Ch 13:17 there f **down** slain of Israel five hundred 5307
15: 9 for they f to him out of Israel in abundance, 5307
17:10 the fear of the LORD f upon all 1961
20:18 the inhabitants of Jerusalem f before 5307
21:19 his bowels f **out** by reason of his sickness: 3318
25:13 f upon the cities of Judah, from Samaria 6584
Ezr 9: 5 I f upon my knees, and spread out my 3766
Est 8: 3 f **down** at his feet, and besought him with 5307
8:17 for the fear of the Jews f upon them. 5307
9: 2 for the fear of them f upon all people. 5307
9: 3 because the fear of Mordecai f upon them. 5307
Job 1:15 the Sabeans f *upon them,* and took them 5307
1:17 f upon the camels, and have carried them 6584
1:19 it f upon the young men, and they are dead; 5307
1:20 f **down** upon the ground, and worshipped, 5307
Ps 27: 2 me to eat up my flesh, they stumbled and f. 5307
78:64 Their priests f by the sword; and 5307
105:38 for the fear of them that f upon them. 5307
107:12 they f **down**, and *there was* none to help. 3782
Jer 39: 9 those that f **away**, that fell to him, with 5307

F

Jer 39: 9 those that fell away, that f to him, with 5307
46:16 made many to fall, yea, one f upon another: 5307
52:15 those that f **away**, that fell to the king of 5307
52:15 that f to the king of Babylon, and the rest of 5307
La 1: 7 when her people f into the hand of 5307
5:13 to grind, and the children f under the wood. 3782
Eze 1:28 when I saw *it*, I f upon my face, and I heard 5307
3:23 by the river of Chebar: and I f on my face. 5307
8: 1 that the hand of the Lord GOD f there 5307
9: 8 that I f upon my face, and cried, and said, 5307
11: 5 the Spirit of the LORD f upon me, and 5307
11:13 f I **down** upon my face, and cried *with* a 5307
39:23 of their enemies: so f they all by the sword. 5307
43: 3 by the river Chebar; and I f upon my face. 5307
44: 4 house of the LORD: and I f upon my face. 5307
Da 2:46 the king Nebuchadnezzar f upon his face, 5308
3: 7 f **down** *and* worshipped the golden image 5308
3:23 f **down** bound into the midst of the burning 5308
4:31 there f a voice from heaven, *saying,* O king 5308
7:20 which came up, and before whom three f; 5308
8:17 he came, I was afraid, and f upon my face: 5307
10: 7 a great quaking f upon them, so that they 5307
Jnh 1: 7 So they cast lots, and the lot f upon Jonah. 5307
Mt 2:11 and f **down**, and worshipped him: 4098
7:25 and beat upon that house; and it f not: 4098
7:27 and beat upon that house; and it f: 4098
13: 4 some *seeds* f by the way side, and the fowls 4098
13: 5 Some f upon stony *places,* where they had 4098
13: 7 And some f among thorns; and the thorns 4098
13: 8 But other f into good ground, and 4098
17: 6 And when the disciples heard *it,* they f on 4098
18:26 The servant therefore f **down**, and 4098
18:29 And his fellowservant f **down** at his feet, 4098
26:39 and f on his face, and prayed, saying, O my 4098
Mk 3:11 f **down before** him, and cried, saying, 4363
4: 4 some f by the way side, and the fowls of 4098
4: 5 And some f on stony ground, where it had 4098
4: 7 And some f among thorns, and the thorns 4098
4: 8 And other f on good ground, and did yield 4098
5:22 and when he saw him, he f at his feet, 4098
5:33 came and f **down before** him, and told him 4363
7:25 heard of him, and came and f at his feet: 4363
9:20 and he f on the ground, and 4098
14:35 and f on the ground, and prayed that, if it 4098
Lk 1:12 was troubled, and fear f **upon** him. 1968
5: 8 When Simon Peter saw *it,* he f **down at** 4363
5:12 who seeing Jesus f on *his* face, and 4098
6:49 did beat vehemently, and immediately it f; 4098
8: 5 and as he sowed, some f by the way side; 4098
8: 6 And some f upon a rock; and as soon as it 4098
8: 7 And some f among thorns; and the thorns 4098
8: 8 And other f on good ground, and sprang up, 4098
8:14 And that which f among thorns are they, 4098
8:23 But as they sailed he f **asleep**: and 879
8:28 and f **down before** him, and with a loud 4363
8:41 and he f **down** at Jesus' feet, and 4098
10:30 and f **among** thieves, which stripped him of 4045
10:36 was neighbour unto him that f among 1706
13: 4 upon whom the tower in Siloam f, and 4098
15:20 and ran, and f on his neck, and kissed him. 1968
16:21 crumbs which f from the rich *man's* table: 4098
17:16 And f **down** on *his* face at his feet, 4098
Jn 11:32 and saw him, she f **down** at his feet, 4098
18: 6 they went backward, and f to the ground. 4098
Ac 1:25 from which Judas **by transgression** f, 3845
1:26 and the lot f upon Matthias; and he was 4098
5: 5 And Ananias hearing these words f **down**, 4098
5:10 Then f she **down** straightway at his feet, 4098
7:60 And when he had said this, he f **asleep**. 2837
9: 4 And he f to the earth, and heard a voice 4098
9:18 And immediately there f from his eyes as it 634
10:10 while they made ready, he f into a trance, 1968
10:25 and f **down** at *his* feet, and 4098
10:44 the Holy Ghost f **on** all them which 1968
11:15 to speak, the Holy Ghost f **on** them, 1968
12: 7 And his chains f **off** from *his* hands. 1601
13:11 And immediately there f **on** him a 1968
13:36 f **on sleep**, and was laid unto his fathers, 2837
16:29 and f **down before** Paul and Silas, 4363
19:17 and fear f **on** them all, and the name 1968
19:35 of the *image* which f **down from Jupiter**? 1356
20: 9 and f down from the third loft, and 4098
20:10 and f **on** him, and embracing *him* said, 1968
20:37 and f on Paul's neck, and kissed him, 1968
22: 7 And I f unto the ground, and heard a voice 4098
Ro 11:22 on them which f, severity; but toward thee, 4098
15: 3 of them that reproached thee f on me. 1968
1Co 10: 8 and f in one day three and twenty thousand. 4098
Heb 3:17 whose carcases f in the wilderness? 4098
11:30 By faith the walls of Jericho f **down**, 4098
2Pe 3: 4 for since the fathers f **asleep**, all *things* 2837
Rev 1:17 And when I saw him, I f at his feet as dead. 4098
5: 8 *and* twenty elders f **down** before the Lamb, 4098
5:14 And the four *and* twenty elders f **down** and 4098
6:13 And the stars of heaven f unto the earth, 4098
7:11 and f before the throne on their faces, and 4098
8:10 and there f a great star from heaven, 4098
8:10 and it f upon the third *part* of the rivers, and 4098
11:11 and great fear f upon them which saw them. 4098
11:13 and the tenth *part* of the city f, and in 4098
11:16 f upon their faces, and worshipped God, 4098
16: 2 and there f a noisome and grievous sore 1096
16:19 three parts, and the cities of the nations f: 4098
16:21 And there f upon men a great hail out of 2597
19: 4 and the four beasts f **down** and 4098
19:10 And I f at his feet to worship him. And he 4098
22: 8 I f **down** to worship before the feet of 4098

FELLED (1) [FELL]

2Ki 3:25 the wells of water, and f all the good trees: 5307

FELLER (1) [FELL]

Isa 14: 8 art laid down, no f is come up against us. 3772

FELLEST (1) [FELL]

2Sa 3:34 *a man* falleth before wicked men, *so* f thou. 5307

FELLING (1) [FELL]

2Ki 6: 5 as one was f a beam, the axe head fell into 5307

FELLOES (1)

1Ki 7:33 their naves, and their f, and their spokes, 2839

FELLOW (27) [FELLOW'S, FELLOW-DISCIPLES, FELLOWCITIZENS, FELLOWHEIRS, FELLOWHELPER, FELLOWHELPERS, FELLOWLABOURER, FELLOWLABOURERS, FELLOWPRISONER, FELLOWPRISONERS, FELLOWS, FELLOWSERVANT, FELLOWSERVANTS, FELLOWSHIP, FELLOWSOLDIER, FELLOWWORKERS, WORKFELLOW, YOKEFELLOW]

Ge 19: 9 they said *again, This* one *f* came in to NIH
Ex 2:13 the wrong, Wherefore smitest thou thy f? 7453
Jdg 7:13 *was* a man that told a dream unto his f, 7453
7:14 his f answered and said, This *is* nothing 7453
7:22 set every man's sword against his f, 7453
1Sa 14:20 every man's sword was against his f, *and* 7453
21:15 that ye have brought this *f* to play the mad NIH
21:15 shall this *f* come into my house? NIH
25:21 Surely in vain have I kept all that this *f* hath NIH
29: 4 Make *this* f return, that he may go again to 376
2Sa 2:16 they caught every one his f by the head, 7453
1Ki 22:27 Put this *f in* the prison, and feed him with NIH
2Ki 9:11 wherefore came this mad *f* to thee? And he NIH
2Ch 18:26 Put this *f in* the prison, and feed him with NIH
Ecc 4:10 For if they fall, the one will lift up his f: but 2270
Isa 34:14 of the island, and the satyr shall cry to his f; 7453
Jnh 1: 7 And they said every one to his f, Come, and 7453
Zec 13: 7 and against the man *that is* my f, 5997
Mt 12:24 This *f* doth not cast out devils, but by NIG
26:61 And said, This *f* said, I am able to destroy NIG
26:71 This *f* was also with Jesus of Nazareth. NIG
Lk 22:59 saying, Of a truth this *f* also was with him: NIG
23: 2 We found this *f* perverting the nation, and NIG
Jn 9:29 *as for* this *f*, we know not from whence he NIG
Ac 18:13 This *f* persuadeth men to worship God NIG
22:22 and said, Away with such *a f* from the earth: NIG
24: 5 For we have found this man a pestilent *f*, NIG

FELLOW'S (1) [FELLOW]

2Sa 2:16 the head, and *thrust* his sword in his f side; 7453

FELLOWCITIZENS (1) [FELLOW, CITIZEN]

Eph 2:19 but f **with** the saints, and of the household 4847

FELLOW-DISCIPLES (1) [DISCIPLE, FELLOW]

Jn 11:16 called Didymus, unto *his* f, Let us also go, 4827

FELLOWHEIRS (1) [FELLOW, HEIR]
Eph 3: 6 That the Gentiles should be f, and of *4789*

FELLOWHELPER (1) [FELLOW, HELP]
2Co 8:23 *he is* my partner and f concerning you: *4904*

FELLOWHELPERS (1) [FELLOW, HELP]
3Jn 1: 8 that we might be f to the truth. *4904*

FELLOWLABOURER (2) [FELLOW, LABOUR]
1Th 3: 2 and our f in the gospel of Christ, *4904*
Phm 1: 1 unto Philemon *our* dearly beloved, and f, *4904*

FELLOWLABOURERS (2) [FELLOW, LABOUR]
Php 4: 3 with Clement also, and *with* other my f, *4904*
Phm 1:24 Marcus, Aristarchus, Demas, Lucas, my f. *4904*

FELLOWPRISONER (2) [FELLOW, PRISON]
Col 4:10 Aristarchus my f saluteth you, and Marcus, *4869*
Phm 1:23 salute thee Epaphras, my f in Christ Jesus; *4869*

FELLOWPRISONERS (1) [FELLOW, PRISON]
Ro 16: 7 and Junia, my kinsmen, and my f, *4869*

FELLOWS (13) [FELLOW]
Jdg 11:37 and bewail my virginity, I and my f. 7464
18:25 lest angry f run upon thee, and thou lose thy 376
2Sa 6:20 as one of the vain *f* shamelessly uncovereth NIH
Ps 45: 7 thee *with* the oil of gladness above thy f. 2270
Isa 44:11 Behold, all his f shall be ashamed: and 2270
Eze 37:19 the tribes of Israel his f, and will put them 2270
Da 2:13 and they sought Daniel and his f to be slain. 2269
2:18 his f should not perish with the rest of 2269
7:20 whose look *was* more stout than his f. 2273
Zec 3: 8 thou, and thy f that sit before thee: 7453
Mt 11:16 in the markets, and calling unto their f, *2083*
Ac 17: 5 took unto *them* certain lewd f of the baser *435*
Heb 1: 9 thee *with* the oil of gladness above thy f. *3353*

FELLOWSERVANT (6) [FELLOW, SERVE]
Mt 18:29 And his f fell down at his feet, and *4889*
18:33 not thou also have had compassion on thy f, *4889*
Col 1: 7 As ye also learned of Epaphras our dear f, *4889*
4: 7 and a faithful minister and f in the Lord: *4889*
Rev 19:10 I am thy f, and of thy brethren that have *4889*
22: 9 for I am thy f, and of thy brethren *4889*

FELLOWSERVANTS (4) [FELLOW, SERVE]
Mt 18:28 servant went out, and found one of his f, *4889*
18:31 So when his f saw what was done, *4889*
24:49 And shall begin to smite *his* f, and to eat *4889*
Rev 6:11 until their f also and their brethren, *4889*

FELLOWSHIP (17) [FELLOW]
Lev 6: 2 or in f, or in a thing taken away by 3027+8667
Ps 94:20 Shall the throne of iniquity have f *with* 2266
Ac 2:42 stedfastly in the apostles' doctrine and f, *2842*
1Co 1: 9 by whom ye were called unto the f of his *2842*
10:20 I would not that ye should have f with *2844*
2Co 6:14 for what f hath righteousness with *3352*
8: 4 *take upon us* the f of the ministering to *2842*
Gal 2: 9 to me and Barnabas the right hands of f; *2842*
Eph 3: 9 And to make all *men* see what *is* the f of *2842*
5:11 And **have** no f **with** the unfruitful works of *4790*
Php 1: 5 For your f in the gospel from the first day *2842*
2: 1 if any f of the Spirit, if any bowels and *2842*
3:10 his resurrection, and the f of his sufferings, *2842*
1Jn 1: 3 unto you, that ye also may have f with us: *2842*
1: 3 and truly our f *is* with the Father, and with *2842*
1: 6 If we say that we have f with him, and *2842*
1: 7 we have f one with another, and the blood *2842*

FELLOWSOLDIER (2) [FELLOW, SOLDIER]
Php 2:25 and f, but your messenger, and he that *4961*
Phm 1: 2 and Archippus our f, and to the church in *4961*

FELLOWWORKERS (1) [FELLOW, WORK]
Col 4:11 These only *are my* f unto the kingdom of *4904*

FELT (5) [FEEL]
Ge 27:22 he f him, and said, The voice *is* Jacob's 4959
Ex 10:21 of Egypt, even darkness *which* may be f. 4959
Pr 23:35 not sick; they have beaten me, *and* I f *it* not: 3045
Mk 5:29 she f in *her* body that she was healed of *that* *1097*
Ac 28: 5 off the beast into the fire, and f no harm. *3958*

FEMALE (24)
Ge 1:27 created he him; male and f created he them. 5347
5: 2 Male and f created he them; and 5347
6:19 alive with thee; they shall be male and f. 5347
7: 2 take to thee by sevens, the male and his f: 802
7: 2 that *are* not clean by two, the male and his f. 802
7: 3 also of the air by sevens, the male and the f; 5347
7: 9 unto Noah into the ark, the male and the f, 5347
7:16 that went in, went in male and f of all flesh, 5347
Lev 3: 1 whether *it be* a male or f, he shall offer it 5347
3: 6 male or f, he shall offer it without blemish. 5347
4:28 a kid of the goats, a f without blemish, 5347
4:32 he shall bring it a f without blemish. 5347
5: 6 a f from the flock, a lamb or a kid of 5347
12: 7 the law for her that hath born a male or a f. 5347
27: 4 if it *be* a f, then thy estimation shall be 5347
27: 5 twenty shekels, and for the f ten shekels. 5347
27: 6 for the f thy estimation *shall be* three 5347
27: 7 be fifteen shekels, and for the f ten shekels. 5347
Nu 5: 3 Both male and f shall ye put out, without 5347
Dt 4:16 of any figure, the likeness of male or f, 5347
7:14 shall not be male or f **barren** among you, 6135
Mt 19: 4 at the beginning made them male and f, *2338*
Mk 10: 6 of the creation God made them male and f. *2338*
Gal 3:28 bond nor free, there is neither male nor f: *2338*

FEMALE SLAVES See WOMENSERVANTS

FENCE (1) [FENCED]
Ps 62: 3 wall *shall ye be, and as* a tottering f. 1447

FENCED (38) [FENCE]
Nu 32:17 our little ones shall dwell in the f cities 4013
32:36 Beth-nimrah, and Beth-haran, f cities: and 4013
Dt 3: 5 All these cities *were* f *with* high walls, 1219
9: 1 than thyself, cities great and f up to heaven, 1219
28:52 until thy high and f walls come down, 1219
Jos 10:20 remained of them entered into f cities. 4013
14:12 and *that* the cities *were* great *and* f: 1219
19:35 the f cities *are* Ziddim, Zer, and Hammath, 4013
1Sa 6:18 *both* of f cities, and of country villages, 4013
2Sa 20: 6 lest he get him f cities, and escape us. 1219
23: 7 the man *that* shall touch them must be f 4390
2Ki 3:19 ye shall smite every f city, and every choice 4013
10: 2 and horses, a f city also, and armour; 4013
17: 9 from the tower of the watchmen to the f 4013
18: 8 from the tower of the watchmen to the f 4013
18:13 come up against all the f cities of Judah, 1219
19:25 that thou shouldest be to lay waste f cities 1219
2Ch 8: 5 f cities, *with* walls, gates, and bars; 4692
11:10 *are* in Judah and in Benjamin, f cities. 4694
11:23 of Judah and Benjamin, unto every f city: 4694
12: 4 he took the f cities which *pertained* to 4694
14: 6 he built f cities in Judah: for the land had 4694
17: 2 he placed forces in all the f cities of Judah, 1219
17:19 besides *those* whom the king put in the f 4013
19: 5 he set judges in the land throughout all the f 1219
21: 3 of precious things, with f cities in Judah: 4694
32: 1 encamped against the f cities, and 1219
33:14 put captains of war in all the f cities of 1219
Job 10:11 flesh, and hast f me with bones and sinews. 7753
19: 8 He hath **f up** my way that I cannot pass, 1443
Isa 2:15 every high tower, and upon every f wall, 1219
5: 2 he f it, and gathered out the stones thereof, 5823
Jer 5:17 they shall impoverish thy f cities, 4013
15:20 I will make thee unto this people a f brasen 1219
Eze 36:35 and desolate and ruined cities *are become* f, 1219
Da 11:15 cast up a mount, and take the **most** f cities: 4013
Hos 8:14 and Judah hath multiplied f cities: 1219
Zep 1:16 the trumpet and alarm against the f cities, 1219

FENS (1)
Job 40:21 shady trees, in the covert of the reed, and f. 1207

FERRET (1)
Lev 11:30 And the f, and the chameleon, and the lizard, 604

FERRY (1)
2Sa 19:18 there went over a f **boat** to carry over 5679

FERVENT (7) [FERVENTLY]
Ac 18:25 and being f in the spirit, he spake and *2204*
Ro 12:11 in business; f in spirit; serving the Lord; *2204*
2Co 7: 7 your mourning, your f **mind** toward me; *2205*
Jas 5:16 The **effectual** f prayer of a righteous *man* *1754*

1Pe 4: 8 And above all *things* have f charity among *1618*
2Pe 3:10 and the elements shall melt with f **heat**, *2741*
3:12 and the elements shall melt with f **heat**? *2741*

FERVENTLY (2) [FERVENT]
Col 4:12 always **labouring** f for you in prayers, *75*
1Pe 1:22 *that ye* love one another with a pure heart f: *1619*

FESTERING See BLAINS; SCAB; SCABBED; SCURVY

FESTIVAL; FESTIVALS See SOLEMNITIES; SOLEMNITY

FESTUS (12) [FESTUS']
Ac 24:27 But after two years Porcius F came into *5347*
25: 1 Now when F was come into the province, *5347*
25: 4 But F answered, that Paul should be kept at *5347*
25: 9 But F, willing to do the Jews a pleasure, *5347*
25:12 Then F, when he had conferred with *5347*
25:13 and Bernice came unto Cesarea to salute F. *5347*
25:14 F declared Paul's cause unto the king, *5347*
25:22 Then Agrippa said unto F, I would also *5347*
25:24 And F said, King Agrippa, and all men *5347*
26:24 F said with a loud voice, Paul, thou art *5347*
26:25 But he said, I am not mad, most noble F; *5347*
26:32 Then said Agrippa unto F, This man might *5347*

FESTUS' (1) [FESTUS]
Ac 25:23 at F commandment Paul was brought *5347*

FET (9) [FETCH]
2Sa 9: 5 f him out of the house of Machir, the son of 3947
11:27 David sent and f her to his house, and 622
1Ki 7:13 king Solomon sent and f Hiram out of Tyre. 3947
9:28 f from thence gold, four hundred and 3947
2Ki 11: 4 and f the rulers over hundreds, 3947
2Ch 12:11 the guard came and f them, and 5375
Jer 26:23 they f **forth** Urijah out of Egypt, and 3318
36:21 So the king sent Jehudi to f the roll: and 3947
Ac 28:13 And from thence we f **a compass**, *4022*

FETCH (30) [FET, FETCHED, FETCHETH, FETCHT]
Ge 18: 5 I will f a morsel of bread, and comfort ye 3947
27: 9 f me from thence two good kids of 3947
27:13 only obey my voice, and go f me *them*. 3947
27:45 I will send, and f thee from thence: why 3947
42:16 let him f your brother, and ye shall be kept 3947
Ex 2: 5 among the flags, she sent her maid to f it. 3947
Nu 20:10 must we f you water out of this rock? 3318
34: 5 the border shall **f a compass** from Azmon 5437
Dt 19:12 of his city shall send and f him thence, 3947
24:10 thou shalt not go into his house to f his 5670
24:19 in the field, thou shalt not go again to f it: 3947
30: 4 gather thee, and from thence will he f thee: 3947
Jdg 11: 5 the elders of Gilead went to f Jephthah out 3947
20:10 to f victual for the people, that *they* may do, 3947
1Sa 4: 3 Let us f the ark of the covenant of 3947
6:21 come ye down, *and* f it **up** to you. 5927
16:11 Samuel said unto Jesse, Send and f him: 3947
20:31 Wherefore now send and f him unto me, 3947
26:22 one of the young men come over and f it. 3947
2Sa 5:23 *but* **f a compass** behind them, and 5437
14:13 in that the king doth not f *home* **again** his 7725
14:20 To f **about** *this* form of speech hath thy 5437
1Ki 17:10 he called to her, and said, F me, I pray thee, 3947
17:11 as she was going to f *it*, he called to her, 3947
2Ki 6:13 spy where he *is*, that I may send and f him. 3947
2Ch 18: 8 said, **F quickly** Micaiah the son of Imla. 4116
Ne 8:15 and f olive branches, and pine branches, and 935
Job 36: 3 I will f my knowledge from afar, and 5375
Isa 56:12 *say they,* I will f wine, and we will fill 3947
Ac 16:37 but let them come themselves and **f us out**. *1806*

FETCHED (7) [FETCH]
Ge 18: 4 be f, and wash your feet, and 3947
27:14 and f, and brought *them* to his mother: 3947
Jos 15: 3 up to Adar, and **f a compass** to Karkaa: 5437
Jdg 18:18 f the carved image, the ephod, and 3947
1Sa 7: 1 f **up** the ark of the LORD, and brought it 5927
10:23 they ran and f him thence: and when he 3947
2Sa 4: 6 *as though* they would have f wheat; 3947

FETCHETH (1) [FETCH]
Dt 19: 5 his hand **f a stroke** with the axe to cut 5080

FETCHT (4) [FETCH]
Ge 18: 7 f a calf tender and good, and gave *it* unto a 3947
2Sa 14: 2 f thence a wise woman, and said unto her, 3947
2Ki 3: 9 they **f a compass** of seven days' journey: 5437
2Ch 1:17 they f **up**, and brought forth out of Egypt a 5927

FETTERS (11)
Jdg 16:21 to Gaza, and bound him with **f of brass**; 5178
2Sa 3:34 *were* not bound, nor thy feet put into f: 5178
2Ki 25: 7 bound him with **f of brass**, and carried him 5178
2Ch 33:11 bound him with f, and carried him to 5178
36: 6 bound him in f, to carry him to Babylon. 5178
Job 36: 8 if *they be* bound in f, *and* be holden in 2131
Ps 105:18 Whose feet they hurt with f: he was laid *in* 3525
149: 8 with chains, and their nobles with f of iron; 3525
Mk 5: 4 that he had been often bound with f *3976*
5: 4 asunder by him, and the f broken in pieces: *3976*
Lk 8:29 and he was kept bound with chains and in f; *3976*

FEVER (9)
Dt 28:22 and with a f, and with an inflammation, and 6920
Mt 8:14 saw his wife's mother laid, and **sick of a f**. *4445*
8:15 And he touched her hand, and the f left her: *4446*
Mk 1:30 But Simon's wife's mother lay **sick of a f**, *4445*
1:31 and immediately the f left her, and *4446*
Lk 4:38 wife's mother was taken with a great f; *4446*
4:39 And he stood over her, and rebuked the f; *4446*
Jn 4:52 Yesterday at the seventh hour the f left him. *4446*
Ac 28: 8 that the father of Publius lay sick of a f and *4446*

FEW (65) [FEWER, FEWEST, FEWNESS]
Ge 24:55 Let the damsel abide with us *a f* days, at NIH
27:44 tarry with him a f days, until thy brother's 259
29:20 they seemed unto him *but* a f days, for 259
34:30 I *being* f in number, they shall gather 4962
47: 9 f and evil have the days of the years of my 4592
Lev 25:52 but f years unto the year of jubile, 4592
26:22 your cattle, and **make** you **f in number**; 4591
Nu 9:20 when the cloud was a f days upon 4557
13:18 whether they *be* strong or weak, f or many; 4592
26:54 to f thou shalt give the less inheritance: 4592
26:56 thereof be divided between many and f. 4592
35: 8 but from *them that have* f ye shall give few: 4592
35: 8 but from *them that have* few ye shall **give** f: 4591
Dt 4:27 ye shall be left f in number among 4962
26: 5 sojourned there with a f, and 4592+4962
28:62 ye shall be left f in number, whereas ye 4592
33: 6 and not die; and let *not* his men be f. 4557
Jos 7: 3 people to labour thither; for they *are but* f. 4592
1Sa 14: 6 to the LORD to save by many or by f. 4592
17:28 with whom hast thou left those f sheep in 4592
2Ki 4: 3 *even* empty vessels; borrow not a f. 4591
1Ch 16:19 When ye were *but* f, even a few, and 4557+4962
16:19 *but* few, even a f, and strangers in it. 4592
2Ch 29:34 the priests were *too* f, so that they could not 4592
Ne 2:12 in the night, I and *some* f men with me; 4592
7: 4 the people *were* f therein, and the houses 4592
Job 10:20 *Are* not my days f? cease then, and let me 4592
14: 1 Man *that is* born of a woman *is* of f days, 7116
16:22 When a f years are come, then I shall go 4557
Ps 105:12 When they were *but a f* men in number; NIH
105:12 in number; yea, *very* f, and strangers in it. 4592
109: 8 Let his days be f; *and* let another take his 4592
Ecc 5: 2 upon earth: therefore let thy words be f. 4592
9:14 *There was* a little city, and f men within it; 4592
12: 3 the grinders cease because they are f, and 4591
Isa 10: 7 heart to destroy and cut off nations not a f. 4592
10:19 the rest of the trees of his forest shall be f, 4557
24: 6 of the earth are burned, and f men left. 4213
Jer 30:19 will multiply them, and they shall not be f; 4591
42: 2 (for we are left *but* a f of many, as thine 4592
Eze 5: 3 Thou shalt also take thereof a f in number, 4592
12:16 I will leave a f men of them from 4557
Da 11:20 within f days he shall be destroyed, 259
Mt 7:14 leadeth unto life, and f there be that find it. *3641*
9:37 truly is plenteous, but the labourers *are* f; *3641*
15:34 And they said, Seven, and a f little fishes. *3641*
20:16 first last: for many be called, but f chosen. *3641*
22:14 For many are called, but f *are* chosen. *3641*
25:21 thou hast been faithful over a f *things,* I *3641*
25:23 thou hast been faithful over a f *things,* I *3641*
Mk 6: 5 save that he laid *his* hands upon a f sick *3641*
8: 7 And they had a f small fishes: and *3641*
Lk 10: 2 truly *is* great, but the labourers *are* f: *3641*
12:48 shall be beaten with f *stripes.* For unto *3641*
13:23 unto him, Lord, are there f that be saved? *3641*

Ac 17: 4 and of the chief women not a f. *3641*
17:12 which were Greeks, and of men, not a f. *3641*
24: 4 hear us of thy clemency a f **words.** *4935*
Eph 3: 3 the mystery; (as I wrote afore in f *words,* *3641*
Heb 12:10 For they verily for a f days chastened *us* *3641*
13:22 for I have written a letter unto you in f *1024*
1Pe 3:20 the ark was a preparing, wherein f, that is, *3641*
Rev 2:14 But I have a f *things* against thee, because *3641*
2:20 Notwithstanding I have a f *things* against *3641*
3: 4 Thou hast a f names even in Sardis, *3641*

FEWER (1) [FEW]
Nu 33:54 to the f ye shall give the less inheritance: 4592

FEWEST (1) [FEW]
Dt 7: 7 any people; for ye *were* the f of all people: 4592

FEWNESS (1) [FEW]
Lev 25:16 according to the f of years thou shalt 4591

FIDELITY (1)
Tit 2:10 Not purloining, but shewing all good f; *4102*

FIELD (290) [FIELDS]
Ge 2: 5 every plant of the f before it was in 7704
2: 5 and every herb of the f before it grew: 7704
2:19 LORD God formed every beast of the f, 7704
2:20 fowl of the air, and to every beast of the f; 7704
3: 1 of the f which the LORD God had made. 7704
3:14 all cattle, and above every beast of the f; 7704
3:18 to thee; and thou shalt eat the herb of the f; 7704
4: 8 it came to pass, when they were in the f, 7704
23: 9 which he hath, which *is* in the end of his f; 7704
23:11 the f give I thee, and the cave that *is* 7704
23:13 I will give *thee* money for the f; take *it* of 7704
23:17 the f of Ephron, which *was* in Machpelah, 7704
23:17 the f, and the cave which *was* therein, 7704
23:17 and all the trees that *were* in the f, 7704
23:19 cave of the f of Machpelah before Mamre: 7704
23:20 the f, and the cave that *is* therein, were 7704
24:63 Isaac went out to meditate in the f at 7704
24:65 What man *is* this that walketh in the f to 7704
25: 9 in the f of Ephron the son of Zohar 7704
25:10 The f which Abraham purchased of 7704
25:27 Esau was a cunning hunter, a man of the f; 7704
25:29 and Esau came from the f, and he *was* faint: 7704
27: 3 go out to the f, and take me *some* venison; 7704
27: 5 Esau went to the f to hunt for venison, *and* 7704
27:27 the smell of my son *is* as the smell of a f 7704
29: 2 and behold a well in the f, and lo, 7704
30:14 found mandrakes in the f, and brought them 7704
30:16 Jacob came out of the f in the evening, and 7704
31: 4 and Leah to the f unto his flock, 7704
33:19 he bought a parcel of a f, where he had 7704
34: 5 now his sons were with his cattle in the f: 7704
34: 7 the sons of Jacob came out of the f when 7704
34:28 *was* in the city, and that which *was* in the f, 7704
36:35 who smote Midian in the f of Moab, 7704
37: 7 we *were* binding sheaves in the f, and lo, 7704
37:15 and behold, *he was* wandering in the f: 7704
39: 5 all that he had in the house, and in the f. 7704
41:48 the food of the f, which *was* round about 7704
47:20 for the Egyptians sold every man his f, 7704
47:24 for seed of the f, and for your food, and 7704
49:29 cave that *is* in the f of Ephron the Hittite, 7704
49:30 In the cave that *is* in the f of Machpelah, 7704
49:30 which Abraham bought with the f of 7704
49:32 The purchase of the f and of the cave that *is* 7704
50:13 buried him in the cave of the f of 7704
50:13 which Abraham bought with the f for a 7704
Ex 1:14 and in all manner of service in the f: 7704
9: 3 LORD is upon thy cattle which *is* in the f, 7704
9:19 thy cattle, and all that thou hast in the f; 7704
9:19 and beast which shall be found in the f, 7704
9:21 left his servants and his cattle in the f. 7704
9:22 upon beast, and upon every herb of the f, 7704
9:25 all the land of Egypt all that *was* in the f, 7704
9:25 the hail smote every herb of the f, and 7704
9:25 of the field, and brake every tree of the f. 7704
10: 5 tree which groweth for you out of the f: 7704
10:15 or in the herbs of the f, through all the land 7704
16:25 to day ye shall not find it in the f. 7704
22: 5 If a man shall cause a f or vineyard to be 7704
22: 5 his beast, and shall feed in another man's f; 7704
22: 5 of the best of his own f, and of the best of 7704
22: 6 of corn, or the standing corn, or the f, 7704
22:31 eat *any* flesh *that is* torn *of beasts* in the f; 7704
23:11 what they leave the beasts of the f shall eat. 7704
23:16 thy labours, which thou hast sown in the f: 7704
23:16 hast gathered in thy labours out of the f. 7704
23:29 and the beast of the f multiply against thee. 7704
Lev 14: 7 let the living bird loose into the open f. 7704
17: 5 which they offer in the open f, even that 7704
19: 9 shalt not wholly reap the corners of thy f, 7704
19:19 thou shalt not sow thy f with mingled seed: 7704
23:22 of the corners of thy f when thou reapest, 7704
25: 3 Six years thou shalt sow thy f, and six years 7704
25: 4 thou shalt neither sow thy f, nor prune thy 7704
25:12 ye shall eat the increase thereof out of the f. 7704
25:34 the f of the suburbs of their cities may not 7704
26: 4 and the trees of the f shall yield their fruit. 7704
27:16 LORD *some part* of a f of his possession, 7704
27:17 If he sanctify his f from the year of jubile, 7704
27:18 if he sanctify his f after the jubile, then 7704
27:19 if he that sanctified the f will in any wise 7704
27:20 if he will not redeem the f, or if he have 7704
27:20 or if he have sold the f to another man, 7704
27:21 the f, when it goeth out in the jubile, 7704
27:21 be holy unto the LORD, as a f devoted; 7704
27:22 if *a man* sanctify unto the LORD a f 7704
27:24 In the year of the jubile the f shall return 7704
27:28 and beast, and of the f of his possession, 7704
Nu 22: 4 as the ox licketh up the grass of the f. 7704
22:23 aside out of the way, and went into the f: 7704
23:14 he brought him *into* the f of Zophim, to 7704
Dt 5:21 his f, or his manservant, or his maidservant, 7704
7:22 lest the beasts of the f increase upon thee. 7704
14:22 that the f bringeth forth year by year. 7704
20:19 down (for the tree of the f *is* man's *life*) 7704
21: 1 lying in the f, *and* it be not known who hath 7704
22:25 if a man find a betrothed damsel in the f, 7704
22:27 For he found her in the f, *and* the betrothed 7704
24:19 thou cuttest down thine harvest in thy f, 7704
24:19 hast forgot a sheaf in the f, thou shalt not 7704
28: 3 the city, and blessed *shalt* thou *be* in the f. 7704
28:16 in the city, and cursed *shalt* thou *be* in the f. 7704
28:38 Thou shalt carry much seed out *into* the f, 7704
Jos 8:24 of slaying all the inhabitants of Ai in the f, 7704
15:18 that she moved him to ask of her father a f: 7704
Jdg 1:14 that she moved him to ask of her father a f: 7704
5: 4 when thou marchedst out of the f of Edom, 7704
5:18 unto the death in the high places of the f. 7704
9:32 that *is* with thee, *and* lie in wait in the f: 7704
9:42 that the people went out *into* the f; 7704
9:43 laid wait in the f, and looked, and behold, 7704
13: 9 again unto the woman as she sat in the f: 7704
19:16 old man from his work out of the f at even, 7704
20:31 the other to Gibeah in the f, about thirty 7704
Ru 2: 2 Let me now go *to* the f, and glean ears of 7704
2: 3 came, and gleaned in the f after the reapers: 7704
2: 3 her hap was to light on a part of the f 7704
2: 8 Go not to glean in another f, neither go 7704
2: 9 *Let* thine eyes *be* on the f that they do reap, 7704
2:17 So she gleaned in the f until even, and 7704
2:22 that they meet thee not in *any* other f. 7704
4: 5 What day thou buyest the f of the hand of 7704
1Sa 4: 2 they slew of the army in the f about four 7704
6:14 the cart came into the f of Joshua, 7704
6:18 *which stone remaineth* unto this day in the f 7704
11: 5 Saul came after the herd out of the f; 7704
14:15 the host, in the f, and among all the people: 7704
17:44 fowls of the air, and to the beasts of the f. 7704
19: 3 stand beside my father in the f where thou 7704
20:11 Come, and let us go out *into* the f. 7704
20:11 And they went out both of them *into* the f. 7704
20:24 So David hid himself in the f: and when 7704
20:35 that Jonathan went out *into* the f at the time 7704
30:11 they found an Egyptian in the f, and 7704
2Sa 10: 8 and Maacah, *were* by themselves in the f. 7704
11:23 came out unto us *into* the f, and we were 7704
14: 6 they two strove together in the f, and 7704
14:30 Joab's f is near mine, and he hath barley 2513
14:30 And Absalom's servants set the f on fire. 2513
14:31 Wherefore have thy servants set my f on 2513
17: 8 as a bear robbed of her whelps in the f: 7704
18: 6 So the people went out *into* the f against 7704
20:12 Amasa out of the highway *into* the f, 7704
21:10 by day, nor the beasts of the f by night. 7704

1Ki 11:29 and they two *were* alone in the f: 7704
14:11 him that dieth in the f shall the fowls of 7704
21:24 him that dieth in the f shall the fowls of 7704
2Ki 4:39 one went out into the f to gather herbs, and 7704
7:12 out of the camp to hide themselves in the f, 7704
8: 6 all the fruits of the f since the day that she 7704
9:25 cast him in the portion of the f of Naboth 7704
9:37 the face of the f in the portion of Jezreel; 7704
18:17 which *is* in the highway of the fuller's f. 7704
19:26 they were *as* the grass of the f, and *as* 7704
1Ch 1:46 which smote Midian in the f of Moab, 7704
19: 9 that were come *were* by themselves in the f. 7704
27:26 over them that did the work of the f for 7704
2Ch 26:23 they buried him with his fathers in the f of 7704
31: 5 and honey, and of all the increase of the f; 7704
Ne 13:10 did the work, were fled every one to his f. 7704
Job 5:23 shalt be in league with the stones of the f: 7704
5:23 the beasts of the f shall be at peace with 7704
24: 6 They reap *every one* his corn in the f: and 7704
40:20 where all the beasts of the f play. 7704
Ps 8: 7 and oxen, yea, and the beasts of the f; 7704
50:11 and the wild beasts of the f *are* mine. 7704
78:12 in the land of Egypt, *in* the f of Zoan. 7704
78:43 in Egypt, and his wonders in the f of Zoan: 7704
80:13 and the wild beast of the f doth devour it. 7704
96:12 Let the f be joyful, and all that *is* therein: 7704
103:15 as a flower of the f, so he flourisheth. 7704
104:11 They give drink to every beast of the f: 7704
Pr 24:27 and make it fit for thyself in the f; 7704
24:30 I went by the f of the slothful, and by 7704
27:26 and the goats *are* the price of the f. 7704
31:16 She considereth a f, and buyeth it: with 7704
Ecc 5: 9 for all: the king *himself* is served by the f. 7704
SS 2: 7 by the roes, and by the hinds of the f, 7704
3: 5 by the roes, and by the hinds of the f, 7704
7:11 my beloved, let us go forth *into* the f; 7704
Isa 5: 8 *that* lay f to field, till *there be* no place, 7704
5: 8 *that* lay field to f, till *there be* no place, 7704
7: 3 upper pool in the highway of the fuller's f; 7704
10:18 and of his **fruitful** f, both soul and body: 3759
16:10 taken away, and joy out of the **plentiful** f; 3759
29:17 Lebanon shall be turned into a **fruitful** f, 3759
29:17 the **fruitful** f shall be esteemed as a forest? 3759
32:15 the wilderness be a **fruitful** f, and 3759
32:15 and the **fruitful** f be counted for a forest. 3759
32:16 and righteousness remain in the **fruitful** f. 3759
36: 2 upper pool in the highway of the fuller's f. 7704
37:27 they were *as* the grass of the f, and *as* 7704
40: 6 goodliness thereof *is* as the flower of the f: 7704
43:20 The beast of the f shall honour me, 7704
55:12 all the trees of the f shall clap *their* hands. 7704
56: 9 All ye beasts of the f, come to devour, 7704
Jer 4:17 As keepers of a f, are they against her 7704
6:25 Go not forth *into* the f, nor walk by 7704
7:20 upon the trees of the f, and upon the fruit of 7704
9:22 of men shall fall as dung upon the open f, 7704
12: 4 and the herbs of every f wither, 7704
12: 9 come ye, assemble all the beasts of the f, 7704
14: 5 the hind also calved in the f, and forsook *it,* 7704
14:18 If I go forth *into* the f, then behold the slain 7704
17: 3 O my mountain in the f, I will give thy 7704
18:14 *which cometh* from the rock of the f? 7704
26:18 Zion shall be plowed *like* a f, and 7704
27: 6 the beasts of the f have I given him also to 7704
28:14 I have given him the beasts of the f also. 7704
32: 7 Buy thee my f that *is* in Anathoth: 7704
32: 8 said unto me, Buy my f, I pray thee, that *is* 7704
32: 9 I bought the f of Hanameel my uncle's son, 7704
32:25 Buy thee the f for money, and 7704
35: 9 neither have we vineyard, nor f, nor seed: 7704
41: 8 for we have treasures in the f, *of* wheat, and 7704
48:33 and gladness is taken from the **plentiful** f, 3759
La 4: 9 through for *want of* the fruits of the f. 7704
Eze 7:15 he that *is* in the f shall die with the sword; 7704
16: 5 thou wast cast out in the open f, to 7704
16: 7 caused thee to multiply as the bud of the f, 7704
17: 5 of the land, and planted it in a fruitful f; 7704
17:24 all the trees of the f shall know that I 7704
20:46 prophesy against the forest of the south f; 7704
26: 6 her daughters which *are* in the f shall be 7704
26: 8 slay with the sword thy daughters in the f: 7704
29: 5 given thee for meat to the beasts of the f 776
31: 4 her little rivers unto all the trees of the f. 7704
31: 5 was exalted above all the trees of the f, 7704
31: 6 under his branches did all the beasts of the f 7704
31:13 all the beasts of the f shall be upon his 7704
31:15 and all the trees of the f fainted for him. 7704
32: 4 I will cast thee forth upon the open f, and 7704
33:27 him that *is* in the open f will I give to 7704
34: 5 they became meat to all the beasts of the f, 7704
34: 8 flock became meat to every beast of the f, 7704
34:27 the tree of the f shall yield her fruit, and 7704
36:30 fruit of the tree, and the increase of the f, 7704
38:20 the beasts of the f, and all creeping things 7704
39: 4 and *to* the beasts of the f to be devoured. 7704
39: 5 Thou shalt fall upon the open f: for I have 7704
39:10 So that they shall take no wood out of the f, 7704
39:17 to every beast of the f, 7704
Da 2:38 the beasts of the f and the fowls of 1251
4:12 the beasts of the f had shadow under it, and 1251
4:15 and brass, in the tender grass of the f; 1251
4:21 under which the beasts of the f dwelt, and 1251
4:23 and brass, in the tender grass of the f; 1251
4:23 *let* his portion *be* with the beasts of the f, 1251
4:25 dwelling shall be with the beasts of the f, 1251
4:32 dwelling *shall be* with the beasts of the f: 1251
Hos 2:12 and the beasts of the f shall eat them. 7704
2:18 a covenant for them with the beasts of the f, 7704
4: 3 with the beasts of the f, and with the fowls 7704
10: 4 up as hemlock in the furrows of the f. 7704
Joel 1:10 The f is wasted, the land mourneth; for 7704
1:11 because the harvest of the f is perished. 7704
1:12 *even* all the trees of the f, are withered: 7704
1:19 the flame hath burnt all the trees of the f. 7704
1:20 The beasts of the f cry also unto thee: 7704
2:22 Be not afraid, ye beasts of the f: for 7704
Mic 1: 6 I will make Samaria as a heap of the f, 7704
3:12 shall Zion for your sake be plowed *as* a f, 7704
4:10 thou shalt dwell in the f, and thou shalt go 7704
Zec 10: 1 showers of rain, to every one grass in the f. 7704
Mal 3:11 vine cast her fruit before the time in the f, 7704
Mt 6:28 Consider the lilies of the f, how they grow; *68*
6:30 Wherefore, if God so clothe the grass of the f, *68*
13:24 unto a man which sowed good seed in his f: *68*
13:27 Sir, didst not thou sow good seed in thy f? *68*
13:31 which a man took, and sowed in his f: *68*
13:36 unto us the parable of the tares of the f. *68*
13:38 The f is the world; the good seed are *68*
13:44 of heaven is like unto treasure hid in a f; *68*
13:44 and selleth all that he hath, and buyeth that f. *68*
24:18 Neither let him which is in the f return back to *68*
24:40 Then shall two be in the f; the one shall be *68*
27: 7 and bought with them the potter's f, to bury *68*
27: 8 Wherefore that f was called, The field of *68*
27: 8 field was called, The f of blood, unto this day. *68*
27:10 And gave them for the potter's f, as the Lord *68*
Mk 13:16 And let him that is in the f not turn back again *68*
Lk 2: 8 same country shepherds abiding in the f, *5561*
12:28 which is to day in the f, and to morrow is cast *68*
15:25 Now his elder son was in the f: and as he *68*
17: 7 when he is come from the f, Go and sit down *68*
17:31 and he that is in the f, let him likewise not *68*
17:36 Two *men* shall be in the f; the one shall be *68*
Ac 1:18 Now this *man* purchased a f with *5564*
1:19 insomuch as that f is called in their proper *5564*
1:19 Aceldama, that is to say, The f of blood. *5564*

FIELD COMMANDER See RABSHAKEH

FIELDS (60) [FIELD]

Ex 8:13 out of the villages, and out of the f. 7704
Lev 14:53 living bird out of the city into the open f, 7704
25:31 shall be counted as the f of the country: 7704
27:22 which *is* not of the f of his possession; 7704
Nu 16:14 or given us inheritance of f and vineyards: 7704
19:16 one that is slain with a sword in the open f, 7704
20:17 we will not pass through the f, or 7704
21:22 we will not turn into the f, or into 7704
Dt 11:15 I will send grass in thy f for thy cattle, 7704
32:13 that he might eat the increase of the f; 7704
32:32 vine of Sodom, and of the f of Gomorrah: 7709
Jos 21:12 the f of the city, and the villages thereof, 7704
Jdg 9:27 they went out *into* the f, and gathered their 7704
9:44 ran upon all *the people* that *were* in the f, 7704
1Sa 8:14 he will take your f, and your vineyards, 7704
20: 5 that I may hide myself in the f unto 7704
22: 7 the son of Jesse give every one of you f 7704
25:15 with them, when we were in the f: 7704

2Sa 1:21 *there be* rain upon you, nor f of offerings: 7704
11:11 of my lord, are encamped in the open f; 7704
1Ki 2:26 Get thee *to* Anathoth, unto thine own f; 7704
16: 4 him that dieth of his in the f shall the fowls 7704
2Ki 23: 4 he burnt them without Jerusalem in the f of 7709
1Ch 6:56 the f of the city, and the villages thereof, 7704
16:32 let the f rejoice, and all that *is* therein. 7704
27:25 over the storehouses in the f, in the cities, 7704
2Ch 31:19 *which were* in the f of the suburbs of their 7704
Ne 11:25 for the villages, with their f, *some* of 7704
11:30 the f thereof, *at* Azekah, and *in* the villages 7704
12:29 and out of the f of Geba and Azmaveth: 7704
12:44 to gather into them out of the f of the cities 7704
Job 5:10 the earth, and sendeth waters upon the f: 2351
Ps 107:37 sow the f, and plant vineyards, which may 7704
132: 6 we found it in the f of the wood. 7704
Pr 8:26 as yet he had not made the earth, nor the f, 2351
23:10 and enter not into the f of the fatherless: 7704
Isa 16: 8 For the f of Heshbon languish, *and* the vine 7709
32:12 for the pleasant f, for the fruitful vine. 7704
Jer 6:12 unto others, *with their* f and wives together: 7704
8:10 their f to them that *shall* inherit *them:* for 7704
13:27 *and* thine abominations on the hills in the f. 7704
31:40 and all the f unto the brook of Kidron, 7709
32:15 Houses and f and vineyards shall be 7704
32:43 f shall be bought in this land, whereof ye 7704
32:44 *Men* shall buy f for money, and 7704
39:10 gave them vineyards and f at the same time. 3010
40: 7 captains of the forces which *were* in the f, 7704
40:13 the captains of the forces that *were* in the f, 7704
Eze 29: 5 thou shalt fall upon the open f; thou shalt 7704
Hos 12:11 altars *are* as heaps in the furrows of the f. 7704
Ob 1:19 and they shall possess the f of Ephraim, and 7704
1:19 the fields of Ephraim, and the f of Samaria: 7704
Mic 2: 2 they covet f, and take *them* by violence; 7704
2: 4 turning away he hath divided our f. 7704
Hab 3:17 shall fail, and the f shall yield no meat; 7709
Mk 2:23 that he went through the **corn** f on *4702*
Lk 6: 1 the first, that he went through the **corn** f; *4702*
15:15 and he sent him into his f to feed swine. *68*
Jn 4:35 Lift up your eyes, and look on the f; *5561*
Jas 5: 4 labourers which have reaped *down* your f, *5561*

FIERCE (41) [FIERCENESS, FIERCER, FIERY]
Ge 49: 7 Cursed *be* their anger, for *it was* f; and 5794
Ex 32:12 Turn from thy f wrath, and repent of *this* 2740
Nu 25: 4 that the f anger of the LORD may be 2740
32:14 to augment yet the f anger of the LORD 2740
Dt 28:50 A nation of f countenance, which shall not 5794
1Sa 20:34 So Jonathan arose from the table in f anger, 2750
28:18 nor executedst his f wrath upon Amalek, 2740
2Ch 28:11 for the f wrath of the LORD *is* upon you. 2740
28:13 is great, and *there is* f wrath against Israel. 2740
29:10 that his f wrath may turn away from us. 2740
Ezr 10:14 until the f wrath of our God for this matter 2740
Job 4:10 the voice of the f **lion**, and the teeth of 7826
10:16 Thou huntest me as a f **lion**: and again thou 7826
28: 8 not trodden it, nor the f **lion** passed by it. 7826
41:10 None *is so* f that dare stir him up: who then 393
Ps 88:16 Thy f **wrath** goeth over me; thy terrors 2740
Isa 7: 4 for the f anger of Rezin with Syria, and 2750
13: 9 cruel both *with* wrath and f anger, to lay 2740
13:13 of hosts, and in the day of his f anger. 2740
19: 4 a f king shall rule over them, saith the Lord, 5794
33:19 Thou shalt not see a f people, a people of a 3267
Jer 4: 8 for the f anger of the LORD is not turned 2740
4:26 presence of the LORD, *and* by his f anger. 2740
12:13 because of the f anger of the LORD. 2740
25:37 because of the f anger of the LORD. 2740
25:38 the oppressor, and because of his f anger. 2740
30:24 The f anger of the LORD shall not return, 2740
49:37 *even* my f anger, saith the LORD; 2740
51:45 deliver ye every man his soul from the f 2740
La 1:12 hath afflicted *me* in the day of his f anger. 2740
2: 3 He hath cut off in *his* f anger all the horn of 2750
4:11 he hath poured out his f anger, and 2740
Da 8:23 a king of f countenance, and 5794
Jnh 3: 9 and repent, and turn away from his f anger, 2740
Hab 1: 8 and are more f than the evening wolves: 2300
Zep 2: 2 before the f anger of the LORD come 2740
3: 8 them mine indignation, *even* all my f anger: 2740
Mt 8:28 exceeding f, so that no *man* might pass by *5467*
Lk 23: 5 And they were the **more** f, saying, He *2001*
2Ti 3: 3 trucebreakers, false accusers, incontinent, f, *434*
Jas 3: 4 they be so great, and are driven of f winds, *4642*

FIERCENESS (12) [FIERCE]
Dt 13:17 that the LORD may turn from the f of his 2740
Jos 7:26 So the LORD turned from the f of his 2740
2Ki 23:26 turned not from the f of his great wrath, 2740
2Ch 30: 8 that the f of his wrath may turn away from 2740
Job 39:24 He swalloweth the ground with f and rage: 7494
Ps 78:49 He cast upon them the f of his anger, wrath, 2740
85: 3 thou hast turned *thyself* from the f of thine 2740
Jer 25:38 because of the f of the oppressor, 2740
Hos 11: 9 I will not execute the f of mine anger, I will 2740
Na 1: 6 who can abide in the f of his anger? 2740
Rev 16:19 to give unto her the cup of the wine of the f *2372*
19:15 and he treadeth the winepress of the f and *2372*

FIERCER (1) [FIERCE]
2Sa 19:43 the words of the men of Judah were f than 7185

F

FIERY (20) [FIERCE]
Nu 21: 6 the LORD sent f serpents among 8314
21: 8 Make thee a f *serpent,* and set it upon a 8314
Dt 8:15 *wherein were* f serpents, and scorpions, and 8314
33: 2 from his right hand *went* a f law for them. 784
Ps 21: 9 Thou shalt make them as a f oven in the time 784
Isa 14:29 and his fruit *shall be* a f flying **serpent**. 8314
30: 6 and old lion, the viper and f flying **serpent**, 8314
Da 3: 6 cast into the midst of a burning f furnace. 5135
3:11 cast into the midst of a burning f furnace. 5135
3:15 hour into the midst of a burning f furnace; 5135
3:17 to deliver us from the burning f furnace, 5135
3:20 *and* to cast *them* into the burning f furnace. 5135
3:21 were cast into the midst of the burning f 5135
3:23 into the midst of the burning f furnace. 5135
3:26 near to the mouth of the burning f furnace, 5135
7: 9 his throne *was like* the f flame, *and* 5135
7:10 A f stream issued and came forth from 5135
Eph 6:16 able to quench all the f darts of the wicked. *4448*
Heb 10:27 looking for of judgment and f indignation, *4442*
1Pe 4:12 think it not strange concerning the f **trial** *4451*

FIFTEEN (24) [FIFTEENTH]
Ge 5:10 Cainan eight hundred and f years, 2568+6240
7:20 F cubits upward did the waters 2568+6240
25: 7 **threescore and** f years. 2568+7657+2050.1
Ex 27:14 *one side of the gate shall be* f cubits: 2568+6240
27:15 f *cubits:* their pillars three, and 2568+6240
38:14 the *one* side *of the gate were* f cubits; 2568+6240
38:15 that hand, *were* hangings of f cubits; 2568+6240
38:25 **threescore and** f 2568+7657+2050.1+2050.1
Lev 27: 7 thy estimation shall be f shekels, and 2568+6240
Nu 31:37 *and* **threescore and** f. 2568+7657+2050.1
Jdg 8:10 about f thousand *men,* all that were 2568+6240
2Sa 9:10 Ziba had f sons and twenty servants. 2568+6240
19:17 his f sons and his twenty servants 2568+6240
1Ki 7: 3 *lay* on forty five pillars, f *in* a row. 2568+6240
2Ki 14:17 of Jehoahaz king of Israel f years. 2568+6240
20: 6 I will add unto thy days f years; and 2568+6240
2Ch 25:25 of Jehoahaz king of Israel f years. 2568+6240
Isa 38: 5 I will add unto thy days f years. 2568+6240
Eze 45:12 twenty shekels, f shekels, 2568+6235+2050.1
Hos 3: 2 So I bought her to me for f *pieces* of 2568+6240
Jn 11:18 nigh unto Jerusalem, about f furlongs off: *1178*
Ac 7:14 his kindred, **threescore and** f souls. *1440+4002*
27:28 they sounded again, and found *it* f fathoms. *1178*
Gal 1:18 to see Peter, and abode with him f days. *1178*

FIFTEENTH (18) [FIFTEEN]
Ex 16: 1 on the f day of the second month 2568+6240
Lev 23: 6 on the f day of the same month *is* 2568+6240
23:34 The f day of this seventh month *shall* 2568+6240
23:39 Also in the f day of the seventh 2568+6240
Nu 28:17 in the f day of this month *is* the feast: 2568+6240
29:12 on the f day of the seventh month ye 2568+6240
33: 3 on the f day of the first month; 2568+6240
1Ki 12:32 on the f day of the month, like unto 2568+6240
12:33 the f day of the eighth month, 2568+6240
2Ki 14:23 In the f year of Amaziah the son of 2568+6240
1Ch 24:14 The f to Bilgah, the sixteenth to 2568+6240
25:22 The f to Jeremoth, *he,* his sons, and 2568+6240
2Ch 15:10 in the f year of the reign of Asa. 2568+6240
Est 9:18 on the f *day* of the same they rested, 2568+6240
9:21 and the f day of the same, yearly, 2568+6240
Eze 32:17 in the f *day* of the month, 2568+6240

Eze 45:25 In the seventh *month,* in the f day of 2568+6240
Lk 3: 1 Now in the f year of the reign of Tiberius *4003*

FIFTH (61) [FIVE]

Ge 1:23 and the morning were the f day. 2549
30:17 she conceived, and bare Jacob the f son. 2549
41:34 **take up the f** *part* of the land of Egypt in 2567
47:24 that you shall give the f *part* unto Pharaoh, 2549
47:26 *that* Pharaoh should have the f *part;* except 2569
Lev 5:16 holy *thing,* and shall add the f *part* thereto, 2549
6: 5 shall add the f *part* more thereto, *and* give it 2549
19:25 in the f year shall ye eat of the fruit thereof, 2549
22:14 he shall put the f *part* thereof unto it, and 2549
27:13 he shall add a f *part* thereof unto thy 2549
27:15 he shall add the f *part* of the money of thy 2549
27:19 he shall add the f *part* of the money of thy 2549
27:27 and shall add a f *part* of it thereto: 2549
27:31 he shall add thereto the f *part* thereof. 2549
Nu 5: 7 add unto it the f *part* thereof, and give *it* 2549
7:36 On the f day Shelumiel the son of 2549
29:26 on the f day nine bullocks, two rams, *and* 2549
33:38 of Egypt, in the first *day* of the f month. 2549
Jos 19:24 the f lot came out for the tribe of 2549
Jdg 19: 8 he arose early in the morning on the f day 2549
2Sa 2:23 f *rib,* that the spear came out behind him; 2570
3: 4 and the f, Shephatiah the son of Abital; 2549
3:27 smote him there *under* the f *rib,* that he 2570
4: 6 they smote him under the f *rib:* and Rechab 2570
20:10 so he smote him therewith in the f *rib,* and 2570
1Ki 6:31 *and* side posts *were* a f *part of the wall.* 2549
14:25 it came to pass in the f year of king 2549
2Ki 8:16 in the f year of Joram the son of Ahab king 2568
25: 8 in the f month, on the seventh *day* of 2549
1Ch 2:14 Nethaneel the fourth, Raddai the f, 2549
3: 3 The f, Shephatiah of Abital: the sixth, 2549
8: 2 Nohah the fourth, and Rapha the f. 2549
12:10 Mishmannah the fourth, Jeremiah the f, 2549
24: 9 The f to Malchijah, the sixth to Mijamin, 2549
25:12 The f *to* Nethaniah, *he,* his sons, and 2549
26: 3 Elam the f, Jehohanan the sixth, 2549
26: 4 and Sacar the fourth, and Nethaneel the f, 2549
27: 8 The f captain for the fifth month *was* 2549
27: 8 The fifth captain for the f month *was* 2549
2Ch 12: 2 *that* in the f year of king Rehoboam 2549
Ezr 7: 8 he came *to* Jerusalem in the f month, 2549
7: 9 on the first *day* of the f month came he to 2549
Ne 6: 5 the f time with an open letter in his hand; 2549
6:15 in the twenty and f *day of the month* Elul, 2568
Jer 1: 3 away of Jerusalem captive in the f month. 2549
28: 1 in the fourth year, *and* in the f month, 2549
36: 9 it came to pass in the f year of Jehoiakim 2549
52:12 Now in the f month, in the tenth *day* of 2549
Eze 1: 1 in the fourth *month,* in the f *day* of 2568
1: 2 In the f *day* of the month, which *was* 2568
1: 2 which *was* the f year of king Jehoiachin's 2549
8: 1 in the sixth *month,* in the f *day* of 2568
20: 1 in the f *month,* the tenth *day* of the month, 2549
33:21 in the tenth *month,* in the f *day* of 2568
Zec 7: 3 Should I weep in the f month, 2549
7: 5 When ye fasted and mourned in the f and 2549
8:19 of the fourth *month,* and the fast of the f, 2549
Rev 6: 9 And when he had opened the f seal, I saw *3991*
9: 1 And the f angel sounded, and I saw a star *3991*
16:10 And the f angel poured out his vial upon *3991*
21:20 The f, sardonyx; the sixth, sardius; *3991*

FIFTIES (8) [FIFTY]

Ex 18:21 of hundreds, rulers of f, and rulers of tens: 2572
18:25 of hundreds, rulers of f, and rulers of tens. 2572
Dt 1:15 captains over f, and captains over tens, and 2572
1Sa 8:12 over thousands, and captains over f; 2572
2Ki 1:14 burnt up the two captains of the former f 2572
1:14 captains of the former fifties with their f: 2572
Mk 6:40 sat down in ranks, by hundreds, and by f. *4004*
Lk 9:14 Make them sit down by f in a company. *4004*

FIFTIETH (4) [FIFTY]

Lev 25:10 ye shall hallow the f year, and 2572
25:11 A jubile shall that f year be unto you: 2572
2Ki 15:23 In the f year of Azariah king of Judah 2572
15:27 f year of Azariah king of Judah Pekah 2572

FIFTY (157) [FIFTIES, FIFTIETH]

Ge 6:15 the breadth of it f cubits, and the height of 2572
7:24 upon the earth an hundred and f days. 2572
8: 3 and f days the waters were abated. 2572
9:28 after the flood three hundred and f years. 2572
9:29 of Noah were nine hundred and f years: 2572
18:24 Peradventure there be f righteous within 2572
18:24 not spare the place for the f righteous that 2572
18:26 If I find in Sodom f righteous within 2572
18:28 Peradventure there shall lack five of the f 2572
Ex 26: 5 F loops shalt thou make in the one curtain, 2572
26: 5 f loops shalt thou make in the edge of 2572
26: 6 thou shalt make f taches of gold, and 2572
26:10 thou shalt make f loops on the edge of 2572
26:10 f loops in the edge of the curtain which 2572
26:11 thou shalt make f taches of brass, and 2572
27:12 the west side *shall be* hangings of f cubits: 2572
27:13 on the east side eastward *shall be* f cubits. 2572
27:18 **f every where,** 2572+2572+871.1+1886.1
30:23 *even* two hundred and f *shekels,* and 2572
30:23 sweet calamus two hundred and f *shekels,* 2572
36:12 F loops made he in one curtain, and 2572
36:12 f loops made he in the edge of the curtain 2572
36:13 he made f taches of gold, and coupled 2572
36:17 he made f loops upon the uttermost edge of 2572
36:17 f loops made he upon the edge of 2572
36:18 he made f taches of brass to couple the tent 2572
38:12 for the west side *were* hangings of f cubits, 2572
38:13 And for the east side eastward f cubits. 2572
38:26 and five hundred and f *men.* 2572
Lev 23:16 the seventh sabbath shall ye number f days; 2572
27: 3 even thy estimation shall be f shekels of 2572
27:16 a homer of barley seed *shall be valued* at f 2572
Nu 1:23 *were* f and nine thousand and 2572
1:25 and five thousand six hundred and f. 2572
1:29 *were* f and four thousand and four hundred. 2572
1:31 *were* f and seven thousand and 2572
1:43 *were* f and three thousand and 2572
1:46 and three thousand and five hundred and f. 2572
2: 6 *were* f and four thousand and four hundred. 2572
2: 8 *were* f and seven thousand and 2572
2:13 *were* f and nine thousand and 2572
2:15 and five thousand and six hundred and f. 2572
2:16 f and one thousand and four hundred and 2572
2:16 and one thousand and four hundred and f, 2572
2:30 *were* f and three thousand and 2572
2:31 and f and seven thousand and six hundred. 2572
2:32 and three thousand and five hundred and f. 2572
4: 3 years old and upward even until f years old, 2572
4:23 upward until f years old shalt thou number 2572
4:30 upward even unto f years old shalt thou 2572
4:35 years old and upward even unto f years old, 2572
4:36 were two thousand seven hundred and f. 2572
4:39 years old and upward even unto f years old, 2572
4:43 years old and upward even unto f years old, 2572
4:47 years old and upward even unto f years old, 2572
8:25 from the age of f years they shall cease 2572
16: 2 two hundred and f princes of the assembly, 2572
16:17 man his censer, two hundred and f censers; 2572
16:35 and f men that offered incense. 2572
26:10 the fire devoured two hundred and f men: 2572
26:34 f and two thousand and seven hundred. 2572
26:47 *who were* f and three thousand and 2572
31:30 thou shalt take one portion of f, of 2572
31:47 Moses took one portion of f, *both* of man 2572
31:52 thousand seven hundred and f shekels. 2572
Dt 22:29 unto the damsel's father f *shekels* of silver, 2572
Jos 7:21 a wedge of gold of f shekels weight, then 2572
1Sa 6:19 even he smote of the people f thousand 2572
2Sa 15: 1 and horses, and f men to run before him. 2572
24:24 and the oxen for f shekels of silver. 2572
1Ki 1: 5 and horsemen, and f men to run before him. 2572
7: 2 the breadth thereof f cubits, and the height 2572
7: 6 the length thereof *was* f cubits, and 2572
9:23 five hundred and f, which bare rule over 2572
10:29 of silver, and a horse for an hundred and f: 2572
18: 4 hid them *by* f in a cave, and fed them *with* 2572
18:13 LORD'S prophets **by f** in a cave, 2572+2572
18:19 the prophets of Baal four hundred and f, 2572
18:22 prophets *are* four hundred and f men. 2572
2Ki 1: 9 the king sent unto him a captain of f with 2572
1: 9 sent unto him a captain of fifty with his f. 2572
1:10 Elijah answered and said to the captain of f, 2572
1:10 from heaven, and consume thee and thy f. 2572
1:10 from heaven, and consumed him and his f. 2572
1:11 unto him another captain of f with his fifty. 2572

2Ki 1:11 unto him another captain of fifty with his f. 2572
1:12 from heaven, and consume thee and thy f. 2572
1:12 from heaven, and consumed him and his f. 2572
1:13 he sent again a captain of the third f with 2572
1:13 again a captain of the third fifty with his f. 2572
1:13 the third captain of f went up, and came 2572
1:13 my life, and the life of these f thy servants, 2572
2: 7 And f men of the sons of the prophets went, 2572
2:16 there be with thy servants f strong men; 2572
2:17 They sent therefore f men; and they sought 2572
13: 7 *of* the people to Jehoahaz but f horsemen, 2572
15: 2 he reigned two and f years in Jerusalem. 2572
15:20 of each man f shekels *of* silver, to give to 2572
15:25 and with him f men of the Gileadites: 2572
21: 1 and reigned f and five years in Jerusalem. 2572
1Ch 5:21 *of* their camels f thousand, and *of* sheep 2572
5:21 *of* sheep two hundred and f thousand, and 2572
8:40 and sons' sons, an hundred and f. 2572
9: 9 nine hundred and f and six. 2572
12:33 of war, f thousand, which could keep rank: 2572
2Ch 1:17 of silver, and a horse for an hundred and f: 2572
2:17 f thousand and three thousand and 2572
3: 9 the weight of the nails *was* f shekels of 2572
8:10 *even* two hundred and f, that bare rule over 2572
8:18 thence four hundred and f talents of gold, 2572
26: 3 he reigned f and two years in Jerusalem. 2572
33: 1 he reigned f and five years in Jerusalem: 2572
Ezr 2: 7 a thousand two hundred f and four. 2572
2:14 children of Bigvai, two thousand f and six. 2572
2:15 children of Adin, four hundred f and four. 2572
2:22 The men of Netophah, f and six. 2572
2:29 The children of Nebo, f and two. 2572
2:30 children of Magbish, an hundred f and six. 2572
2:31 a thousand two hundred f and four. 2572
2:37 children of Immer, a thousand f and two. 2572
2:60 children of Nekoda, six hundred f and two. 2572
8: 3 genealogy of the males an hundred and f. 2572
8: 6 the son of Jonathan, and with him f males. 2572
8:26 hand six hundred and f talents *of* silver, 2572
Ne 5:17 an hundred and f of the Jews and rulers, 2572
6:15 *day* of *the month* Elul, in f and two days. 2572
7:10 children of Arah, six hundred f and two. 2572
7:12 a thousand two hundred f and four. 2572
7:20 children of Adin, six hundred f and five. 2572
7:33 The men of the other Nebo, f and two. 2572
7:34 a thousand two hundred f and four. 2572
7:40 children of Immer, a thousand f and two. 2572
7:70 f basons, five hundred and thirty priests' 2572
Est 5:14 Let a gallows be made of f cubits high, and 2572
7: 9 Behold also, the gallows f cubits high, 2572
Isa 3: 3 The captain of f, and the honourable *man,* 2572
Eze 40:15 of the porch of the inner gate *were* f cubits. 2572
40:21 the length thereof *was* f cubits, and 2572
40:25 the length *was* f cubits, and the breadth five 2572
40:29 *it was* f cubits long, and five and 2572
40:33 *it was* f cubits long, and five and 2572
40:36 the length *was* f cubits, and the breadth five 2572
42: 2 north door, and the breadth *was* f cubits. 2572
42: 7 the length thereof *was* f cubits. 2572
42: 8 that *were* in the utter court *was* f cubits: 2572
45: 2 f cubits round about *for* the suburbs 2572
48:17 be toward the north two hundred and f, 2572
48:17 toward the south two hundred and f, and 2572
48:17 toward the east two hundred and f, and 2572
48:17 and toward the west two hundred and f. 2572
Hag 2:16 for to draw out f *vessels out of* the press, 2572
Lk 7:41 ought five hundred pence, and the other f. *4004*
16: 6 thy bill, and sit down quickly, and write f. *4004*
Jn 8:57 Thou art not yet f years old, and hast thou *4004*
21:11 of great fishes, an hundred and f *and* three: *4004*
Ac 13:20 about *the space of* four hundred and f years, *4004*
19:19 found *it* f **thousand** *pieces* of silver. *3461+4002*

FIG (41) [FIGS]

Ge 3: 7 they sewed f leaves together, and 8384
Dt 8: 8 and vines, and f **trees**, and pomegranates; 8384
Jdg 9:10 the trees said to the f **tree**, Come thou, *and* 8384
9:11 the f **tree** said unto them, Should I forsake 8384
1Ki 4:25 man under his vine and under his f **tree**, 8384
2Ki 18:31 every one of his f **tree**, and drink ye every 8384
Ps 105:33 He smote their vines also and their f **trees**; 8384
Pr 27:18 Whoso keepeth the f **tree** shall eat the fruit 8384
SS 2:13 The f **tree** putteth forth her green figs, and 8384
Isa 34: 4 the vine, and as a falling *f* from the fig tree. NIH
34: 4 the vine, and as a falling *fig* from the f **tree**. 8384
36:16 every one *of* his f **tree**, and drink ye every 8384
Jer 5:17 they shall eat up thy vines and thy f **trees**: 8384
8:13 nor figs on the f **tree**, and the leaf shall 8384
Hos 2:12 And I will destroy her vines and her f **trees**, 8384
9:10 as the firstripe in the f **tree** at her first time: 8384
Joel 1: 7 laid my vine waste, and barked my f **tree**: 8384
1:12 vine is dried up, and the f **tree** languisheth; 8384
2:22 the f **tree** and the vine do yield their 8384
Am 4: 9 and your vineyards and your f **trees** and 8384
Mic 4: 4 man under his vine and under his f **tree**; 8384
Na 3:12 All thy strong holds *shall be like* f **trees** 8384
Hab 3:17 Although the f **tree** shall not blossom, 8384
Hag 2:19 the f **tree**, and the pomegranate, and 8384
Zec 3:10 under the vine and under the f **tree**. 8384
Mt 21:19 And when he saw a f **tree** in the way, *4808*
21:19 And presently the f **tree** withered away. *4808*
21:20 How soon is the f **tree** withered away! *4808*
21:21 not only do this which is done to the f **tree**, *4808*
24:32 Now learn a parable of the f **tree**; When his *4808*
Mk 11:13 And seeing a f **tree** afar off having leaves, *4808*
11:20 they saw the f **tree** dried up from the roots. *4808*
11:21 the f **tree** which thou cursedst is withered *4808*
13:28 Now learn a parable of the f **tree**; When her *4808*
Lk 13: 6 A certain *man* had a f **tree** planted in his *4808*
13: 7 years I come seeking fruit on this f **tree**, *4808*
21:29 Behold the f **tree**, and all the trees; *4808*
Jn 1:48 when thou wast under the f **tree**, I saw thee. *4808*
1:50 I saw thee under the f **tree**, believest thou? *4808*
Jas 3:12 Can the f **tree**, my brethren, bear olive *4808*
Rev 6:13 *even* as a f **tree** casteth her untimely figs, *4808*

FIGHT (107) [FIGHTETH, FIGHTING, FIGHTINGS, FOUGHT]

Ex 1:10 f against us, and *so* get them up out of 3898
14:14 The LORD shall f for you, and ye shall 3898
17: 9 us out men, and go out, f with Amalek: 3898
Dt 1:30 which goeth before you, he shall f for you, 3898
1:41 against the LORD, we will go up and f, 3898
1:42 Say unto them, Go not up, neither f; 3898
2:32 he and all his people, to f *at* Jahaz. 4421
3:22 for the LORD your God he shall f for you. 3898
20: 4 to f for you against your enemies, to save 3898
20:10 When thou comest nigh unto a city to f 3898
Jos 9: 2 to f with Joshua and with Israel, *with* one 3898
10:25 do to all your enemies against whom ye f. 3898
11: 5 at the waters of Merom, to f against Israel. 3898
19:47 the children of Dan went up to f against 3898
Jdg 1: 1 the Canaanites first, to f against them? 3898
1: 3 that we may f against the Canaanites; 3898
1: 9 went down to f against the Canaanites, 3898
8: 1 when thou wentest to f with the Midianites? 3898
9:38 go out, I pray now, and f with them. 3898
10: 9 passed over Jordan to f also against Judah, 3898
10:18 What man *is he* that will begin to f against 3898
11: 6 that we may f with the children of Ammon. 3898
11: 8 f against the children of Ammon, and 3898
11: 9 If ye bring me *home* again to f against 3898
11:12 that thou art come against me to f in my 3898
11:25 or did he **ever** f against them, 3898+3898
11:32 the children of Ammon to f against them; 3898
12: 1 Wherefore passedst thou over to f against 3898
12: 3 come up unto me this day, to f against me? 3898
20:20 in array to f against them at Gibeah. 4421
1Sa 4: 9 to you: quit yourselves like men, and f. 3898
8:20 and go out before us, and f our battles. 3898
13: 5 themselves together to f with Israel, 3898
15:18 and f against them until they be consumed. 3898
17: 9 If he be able to f with me, and *to* kill me, 3898
17:10 give me a man, that we may f together. 3898
17:20 as the host was going forth to the f, and 4634
17:32 servant will go and f with this Philistine. 3898
17:33 to go against this Philistine to f with him: 3898
18:17 valiant for me, and f the LORD'S battles. 3898
23: 1 the Philistines f against Keilah, and 3898
28: 1 armies together for warfare, to f with Israel. 3898
29: 8 that I may not go f against the enemies of 3898
2Sa 11:20 *so* nigh unto the city when *ye* did f? 3898
1Ki 12:21 to f against the house of Israel, 3898
12:24 nor f against your brethren the children of 3898
20:23 let us f against them in the plain, and 3898
20:25 we will f against them in the plain, *and* 3898
20:26 and went up to Aphek, to f against Israel. 4421
22:31 saying, F neither with small nor great, 3898
22:32 they turned aside to f against him: and 3898

2Ki 3:21 the kings were come up to f against them, 3898
10: 3 and f for your master's house. 3898
19: 9 Behold, he is come out to f against thee: 3898
2Ch 11: 1 to f against Israel, that *he* might bring 3898
11: 4 shall not go up, nor f against your brethren: 3898
13:12 f ye not against the LORD God of your 3898
18:30 saying, F ye not with small or great, 3898
18:31 Therefore they compassed about him to f: 3898
20:17 Ye shall not need to f in this *battle:* set 3898
32: 2 that he was purposed to f against 4421
32: 8 our God to help us, and to f our battles. 3898
35:20 Necho king of Egypt came up to f against 3898
35:22 that *he* might f with him, and hearkened not 3898
35:22 and came to f in the valley of Megiddo. 3898
Ne 4: 8 to come *and* to f against Jerusalem, 3898
4:14 and terrible, and f for your brethren, 3898
4:20 ye thither unto us: our God shall f for us. 3898
Ps 35: 1 f against them that fight against me. 3898
35: 1 fight against them that f against me. 3898
56: 2 for *they be* many that f against me, O thou 3898
144: 1 my hands to war, *and* my fingers to f: 4421
Isa 19: 2 they shall f every one against his brother, 3898
29: 7 the multitude of all the nations that f 6633
29: 7 even all that f against her and her munition, 6638
29: 8 the nations be, that f against mount Zion. 6633
30:32 and in battles of shaking will he f with it. 3898
31: 4 shall the LORD of hosts come down to f 6633
Jer 1:19 they shall f against thee; but they shall not 3898
15:20 they shall f against thee, but they shall not 3898
21: 4 wherewith ye f against the king of Babylon, 3898
21: 5 I myself will f against you with an 3898
32: 5 though ye f with the Chaldeans, ye shall not 3898
32:24 that f against it, because of the sword, and 3898
32:29 that f against this city, shall come and 3898
33: 5 They come to f with the Chaldeans, but *it is* 3898
34:22 they shall f against it, and take it, and 3898
37: 8 f against this city, and take it, and burn it 3898
37:10 army of the Chaldeans that f against you, 3898
41:12 went to f with Ishmael the son of 3898
51:30 mighty *men* of Babylon have forborn to f, 3898
Da 10:20 now will I return to f with the prince of 3898
11:11 shall come forth and f with him, *even* with 3898
Zec 10: 5 they shall f, because the LORD *is* with 3898
14: 3 go forth, and f against those nations, 3898
14:14 Judah also shall f at Jerusalem; and 3898
Jn 18:36 were of this world, then would my servants f, *75*
Ac 5:39 haply ye be found even to f **against God**. *2314*
23: 9 spoken to him, let us not f **against God**. *2313*
1Co 9:26 so f I, not as one that beateth the air: *4438*
1Ti 6:12 F the good fight of faith, lay hold on eternal *75*
6:12 Fight the good f of faith, lay hold on eternal *73*
2Ti 4: 7 I have fought a good f, I have finished *my* *73*
Heb 10:32 ye endured a great f of afflictions; *119*
11:34 were made strong, waxed valiant in f, *4171*
Jas 4: 2 ye f and war, yet ye have not, because ye *3164*
Rev 2:16 will f against them with the sword of my *4170*

FIGHTETH (3) [FIGHT]
Ex 14:25 for the LORD f for them against 3898
Jos 23:10 he *it is* that f for you, as he hath promised 3898
1Sa 25:28 my lord f the battles of the LORD, 3898

FIGHTING (3) [FIGHT]
1Sa 17:19 in the valley of Elah, f with the Philistines. 3898
2Ch 26:11 Moreover Uzziah had a host of f 4421+6213
Ps 56: 1 swallow me up; he f daily oppresseth me. 3898

FIGHTINGS (2) [FIGHT]
2Co 7: 5 troubled on every *side;* without *were* f, *3163*
Jas 4: 1 From whence *come* wars and f among you? *3163*

FIGS (25) [FIG]
Nu 13:23 *brought* of the pomegranates, and of the f. 8384
20: 5 or of f, or vines, or of pomegranates; 8384
1Sa 25:18 two hundred cakes *of f*, and laid *them* on NIH
30:12 they gave him a piece of a cake *of f*, and NIH
2Ki 20: 7 Isaiah said, Take a lump of f. And they 8384
1Ch 12:40 cakes *of f*, and bunches of raisins, and wine, NIH
Ne 13:15 grapes, and f, and all *manner of* burdens, 8384
SS 2:13 The fig tree putteth forth her **green** f, and 6291
Isa 38:21 Let them take a lump of f, and lay *it* for a 8384
Jer 8:13 nor f on the fig tree, and the leaf shall fade; 8384
24: 1 two baskets of f *were* set before the temple 8384
24: 2 One basket *had* very good f, *even* like 8384
24: 2 good figs, *even* like the f *that are* first ripe: 8384
24: 2 the other basket *had* very naughty f, 8384
24: 3 And I said, F; the good figs, very good; and 8384
24: 3 the good f, very good; and the evil, 8384
24: 5 Like these good f, so will I acknowledge 8384
24: 8 as the evil f, which cannot be eaten, 8384
29:17 and will make them like vile f, 8384
Na 3:12 *shall be like* fig trees with the **firstripe** f: 1061
Mt 7:16 gather grapes of thorns, or f of thistles? *4810*
Mk 11:13 but leaves; for the time of f was not *yet.* *4810*
Lk 6:44 For of thorns *men* do not gather f, nor of a *4810*
Jas 3:12 either a vine, f? so *can* no fountain *both* *4810*
Rev 6:13 *even* as a fig tree casteth her **untimely** f, *3653*

FIGURE (7) [FIGURES]
Dt 4:16 the similitude of any f, the likeness of male 5566
Isa 44:13 maketh it after the f of a man, according to 8403
Ro 5:14 who is the f of *him* that was to come. *5179*
1Co 4: 6 I have **in a f transferred** to myself and *3345*
Heb 9: 9 Which *was* a f for the time *then* present, *3850*
11:19 from whence also he received him in a f. *3850*
1Pe 3:21 The **like** f whereunto *even* baptism doth also *499*

FIGURES (3) [FIGURE]
1Ki 6:29 about *with* **carved** f of cherubims 4734+6603
Ac 7:43 f which ye made to worship them: *5179*
Heb 9:24 made with hands, *which are* the f of the true; *499*

FILE (1)
1Sa 13:21 Yet they had a f for the mattocks, 6310+6477

FILIGREE See OUCHES

FILL (49) [FILLED, FILLEDST, FILLEST, FILLING, FULL, FULLY, FULNESS]
Ge 1:22 f the waters in the seas, and let fowl 4390
42:25 Joseph commanded to f their sacks *with* 4390
44: 1 saying, F the men's sacks *with* food, 4390
Ex 10: 6 they shall f thy houses, and the houses of 4390
16:32 F an omer of it to be kept for your 4393
Lev 25:19 ye shall eat *your* f, and dwell therein in 7648
Dt 23:24 thou mayest eat grapes thy f at thine own 7648
1Sa 16: 1 f thine horn *with* oil, and go, I will send 4390
1Ki 18:33 F four barrels *with* water, and pour *it* on 4390
Job 8:21 Till he f thy mouth *with* laughing, and 4390
15: 2 and f his belly *with* the east wind? 4390
20:23 *When* he is about to f his belly, *God* shall 4390
23: 4 and f my mouth *with* arguments. 4390
38:39 or f the appetite of the young lions, 4390
41: 7 Canst thou f his skin with barbed irons? or 4390
Ps 81:10 open thy mouth wide, and I will f it. 4390
83:16 F their faces *with* shame; that they may 4390
110: 6 he shall f *the places with* the dead bodies; 4390
Pr 1:13 we shall f our houses *with* spoil: 4390
7:18 let us **take** our f of love until the morning: 7301
8:21 and I will f their treasures. 4390
Isa 8: 8 the stretching out of his wings shall f 4393
14:21 nor f the face of the world *with* cities. 4390
27: 6 bud, and f the face of the world *with* fruit. 4390
56:12 and we will f ourselves with strong drink; 5433
Jer 13:13 I *will* f all the inhabitants of this land, 4390
23:24 Do not I f heaven and earth? saith 4392
33: 5 *it is* to f them with the dead bodies of men, 4390
51:14 *saying,* Surely I will f thee *with* men, 4390
Eze 3: 3 f thy bowels with this roll that I give thee. 4390
7:19 satisfy their souls, neither f their bowels: 4390
9: 7 the house, and f the courts *with* the slain: 4390
10: 2 f thine hand *with* coals of fire from 4390
24: 4 and the shoulder; f *it with* the choice bones. 4390
30:11 against Egypt, and f the land *with* the slain. 4390
32: 4 I will f the beasts of the whole earth with 7646
32: 5 and f the valleys *with* thy height. 4390
35: 8 I will f his mountains *with* his slain *men:* in 4390
Zep 1: 9 which f their masters' houses *with* violence 4390
Hag 2: 7 I will f this house *with* glory, saith 4390
Mt 9:16 for that which is **put in to** f **it up** taketh *4138*
15:33 the wilderness, as to f so great a multitude? *5526*
23:32 F ye **up** then the measure of your fathers. *4137*
Jn 2: 7 unto them, F the waterpots with water. *1072*
Ro 15:13 Now the God of hope f you **with** all joy *4137*
Eph 4:10 all heavens, that he might f all *things.*) *4137*
Col 1:24 f **up** that which is behind of the afflictions of *466*
1Th 2:16 they might be saved, to f **up** their sins alway: *378*
Rev 18: 6 in the cup which she hath filled f to her *2767*

FILLED (159) [FILL]

Ge 6:11 and the earth was f *with* violence. 4390
6:13 for the earth is f *with* violence through 4390
21:19 f the bottle *with* water, and gave the lad 4390
24:16 to the well, and f her pitcher, and came up. 4390
26:15 had stopped them, and f them *with* earth. 4390
Ex 1: 7 and the land was f with them. 4390
2:16 f the troughs to water their father's flock. 4390
16:12 and in the morning ye shall be f *with* bread; 7646
28: 3 whom I have f with the spirit of wisdom, 4390
31: 3 I have f him *with* the spirit of God, 4390
35:31 he hath f him *with* the spirit of God, 4390
35:35 Them hath he f *with* wisdom of heart, 4390
40:34 the glory of the LORD f the tabernacle. 4390
40:35 the glory of the LORD f the tabernacle. 4390
Nu 14:21 all the earth shall be f *with* the glory of 4390
Dt 26:12 that they may eat within thy gates, and be f; 7646
31:20 and f *themselves*, and waxen fat; 7646
Jos 9:13 bottles of wine, which we f, *were* new; 4390
1Ki 7:14 he was f *with* wisdom, and understanding, 4390
8:10 that the cloud f the house of the LORD, 4390
8:11 for the glory of the LORD had f the house 4390
18:35 and he f the trench also *with* water. 4390
20:27 flocks of kids; but the Syrians f the country. 4390
2Ki 3:17 yet that valley shall be f *with* water, that ye 4390
3:20 of Edom, and the country was f with water. 4390
3:25 of land cast every man his stone, and f it; 4390
21:16 till he had f Jerusalem from one end to 4390
23:14 and f their places *with* the bones of men. 4390
24: 4 for he f Jerusalem *with* innocent blood; 4390
2Ch 5:13 that *then* the house was f *with* a cloud, 4390
5:14 for the glory of the LORD had f the house 4390
7: 1 and the glory of the LORD f the house. 4390
7: 2 the glory of the LORD had f 4390
16:14 laid him in the bed which was f *with* sweet 4390
Ezr 9:11 which have f it from one end to another 4390
Ne 9:25 were f, and became fat, and 7646
Job 3:15 had gold, who f their houses *with* silver: 4390
16: 8 thou hast f me **with wrinkles**, *which* is a 7059
22:18 Yet he f their houses *with* good *things:* but 4390
Ps 38: 7 For my loins are f *with* a loathsome 4390
71: 8 Let my mouth be f *with* thy praise *and* 4390
72:19 let the whole earth be f *with* his glory; 4390
78:29 So they did eat, and were well f: for he 7646
80: 9 cause it to take deep root, and it f the land. 4390
104:28 openest thine hand, they are f *with* good. 7646
123: 3 for we are exceedingly f *with* contempt. 7646
123: 4 Our soul is exceedingly f *with* the scorning 7646
126: 2 was our mouth f *with* laughter, and 4390
Pr 1:31 own way, and be f with their own devices. 7646
3:10 So shall thy barns be f *with* plenty, and 4390
5:10 Lest strangers be f *with* thy wealth; and 7646
12:21 but the wicked shall be f *with* mischief. 4390
14:14 The backslider in heart shall be f with his 7646
18:20 *with* the increase of his lips shall he be f. 7646
20:17 afterwards his mouth shall be f *with* gravel. 4390
24: 4 by knowledge shall the chambers be f *with* 4390
25:16 lest thou be f there*with*, and vomit it. 7646
30:16 the earth *that* is not f *with* water; and 7646
30:22 and a fool when he is f *with* meat; 7646
Ecc 1: 8 with seeing, nor the ear f with hearing. 4390
6: 3 his soul be not f with good, and also *that* he 7646
6: 7 for his mouth, and yet the appetite is not f. 4390
SS 5: 2 for my head is f *with* dew, *and* my locks 4390
Isa 6: 1 and lifted up, and his train f the temple. 4392
6: 4 that cried, and the house was f *with* smoke. 4390
21: 3 Therefore are my loins f *with* pain: 4390
33: 5 he hath f Zion *with* judgment and 4390
34: 6 The sword of the LORD is f *with* blood, 4390
43:24 neither hast thou f me *with* the fat of thy 7301
65:20 nor an old man that hath not f his days: 4390
Jer 13:12 of Israel, Every bottle shall be f *with* wine: 4390
13:12 know that every bottle shall be f *with* wine? 4390
15:17 for thou hast f me *with* indignation. 4390
16:18 they have f mine inheritance with 4390
19: 4 have f this place *with* the blood of 4390
41: 9 Ishmael the son of Nethaniah f it *with them* 4390
46:12 *of* thy shame, and thy cry hath f the land: 4390
51: 5 though their land was f *with* sin against 4390
51:34 he hath f his belly with my delicates, 4390
La 3:15 He hath f me with bitterness, he hath made 7646
3:30 that smiteth him: he is f **full** with reproach. 7646
Eze 8:17 for they have f the land *with* violence, and 4390
10: 3 went in; and the cloud f the inner court. 4390
10: 4 the house was f with the cloud, and 4390
11: 6 ye have f the streets thereof *with* the slain. 4390
23:33 Thou shalt be f *with* drunkenness and 4390
28:16 they have f the midst of thee *with* violence, 4390
36:38 shall the waste cities be f *with* flocks of 4392
39:20 Thus ye shall be f at my table *with* horses 7646
43: 5 the glory of the LORD f the house. 4390
44: 4 the glory of the LORD f the house of 4390
Da 2:35 a great mountain, and f the whole earth. 4391
Hos 13: 6 According to their pasture, so were they f; 7646
13: 6 they were f, and their heart was exalted; 7646
Na 2:12 f his holes *with* prey, and his dens *with* 4390
Hab 2:14 For the earth shall be f with the knowledge 4390
2:16 Thou art f *with* shame for glory: drink thou 7646
Hag 1: 6 *ye* drink, but ye are not f **with drink**; 7937
Zec 9:13 f the bow *with* Ephraim, and raised up thy 4390
9:15 they shall be f like bowls, *and* as 4390
Mt 5: 6 after righteousness: for they shall be f. *5526*
14:20 And they did all eat, and were f: and *5526*
15:37 And they did all eat, and were f: and *5526*
27:48 and f *it* with vinegar, and put *it* on a reed, *4130*
Mk 2:21 else the new **piece that** f **it up** taketh away *4138*
6:42 And they did all eat, and were f. *5526*
7:27 said unto her, Let the children first be f: *5526*
8: 8 So they did eat, and were f: and they took *5526*
15:36 And one ran and f a spunge *full* of vinegar, *1072*
Lk 1:15 and he shall be f with the Holy Ghost, *4130*
1:41 and Elisabeth was f with the Holy Ghost: *4130*
1:53 He hath f the hungry with good *things;* and *1705*
1:67 And his father Zacharias was f with *4130*
2:40 and waxed strong in spirit, f with wisdom: *4137*
3: 5 Every valley shall be f, and every mountain *4137*
4:28 when they heard these *things,* were f with *4130*
5: 7 and f both the ships, so that they began to *4130*
5:26 glorified God, and were f with fear, saying, *4130*
6:11 And they were f with madness; and *4130*
6:21 for ye shall be f. Blessed *are ye* that weep *5526*
8:23 and they were f *with water,* and were in *4845*
9:17 And they did eat, and were all f: and *5526*
14:23 *them* to come in, that my house may be f. *1072*
15:16 And he would fain have f his belly with *1072*
Jn 2: 7 with water. And they f them up to the brim. *1072*
6:12 When they were f, he said unto his *1705*
6:13 f twelve baskets with the fragments of *1072*
6:26 ye did eat of the loaves, and were f. *5526*
12: 3 the house was f with the odour of *4137*
16: 6 *things* unto you, sorrow hath f your heart. *4137*
19:29 and they f a spunge with vinegar, and put *it* *4130*
Ac 2: 2 it f all the house where they were sitting. *4137*
2: 4 And they were all f with the Holy Ghost, *4130*
3:10 and they were f with wonder and *4130*
4: 8 Then Peter, f with the Holy Ghost, *4130*
4:31 and they were all f with the Holy Ghost, *4130*
5: 3 why hath Satan f thine heart to lie to *4137*
5:17 and were f with indignation, *4130*
5:28 ye have f Jerusalem with your doctrine, and *4137*
9:17 thy sight, and be f with the Holy Ghost. *4130*
13: 9 f with the Holy Ghost, set his eyes on him, *4130*
13:45 they were f with envy, and spake against *4130*
13:52 And the disciples were f with joy, and *4137*
19:29 And the whole city was f with confusion: *4130*
Ro 1:29 Being f **with** all unrighteousness, *4137*
15:14 are full of goodness, f with all knowledge, *4137*
15:24 if first I be somewhat f with your *1705*
2Co 7: 4 I am f with comfort, I am exceeding joyful *4137*
Eph 3:19 that ye might be f with all the fulness of *4137*
5:18 wherein is excess; but be f with the Spirit; *4137*
Php 1:11 Being f with the fruits of righteousness, *4137*
Col 1: 9 to desire that ye might be f *with* *4137*
2Ti 1: 4 of thy tears, that I may be f with joy; *4137*
Jas 2:16 Depart in peace, be you warmed and f; *5526*
Rev 8: 5 and f it with fire of the altar, and cast *it* into *1072*
15: 1 for in them is f **up** the wrath of God. *5055*
15: 8 And the temple was f with smoke from *1072*
18: 6 in the cup which she hath f fill to her *2767*
19:21 and all the fowls were f with their flesh. *5526*

FILLEDST (2) [FILL]

Dt 6:11 houses full *of* all good *things,* which thou f 4390
Eze 27:33 forth out of the seas, thou f many people; 7646

FILLEST (1) [FILL]

Ps 17:14 whose belly thou f *with* thy hid *treasure:* 4390

FILLET (1) [FILLETED, FILLETH, FILLETS]
Jer 52:21 a f of twelve cubits did compass it; and 2339

FILLETED (3) [FILLET]
Ex 27:17 round about the court *shall be* f *with* silver; 2836
38:17 all the pillars of the court *were* f *with* 2836
38:28 and overlaid their chapiters, and f them. 2836

FILLETH (6) [FILLET]
Job 9:18 to take my breath, but f me *with* bitterness. 7646
Ps 84: 6 make it a well; the rain also f the pools. 5844
107: 9 and f the hungry soul *with* goodness. 4390
129: 7 Where*with* the mower f not his hand; 4390
147:14 *and* f thee *with* the finest of the wheat. 7646
Eph 1:23 his body, the fulness of him that f all in all. *4137*

FILLETS (8) [FILLET]
Ex 27:10 of the pillars and their f *shall be of* silver. 2838
27:11 the hooks of the pillars and their f *of* silver. 2838
36:38 their chapiters and their f with gold: 2838
38:10 of the pillars and their f *were of* silver. 2838
38:11 the hooks of the pillars and their f *of* silver. 2838
38:12 the hooks of the pillars and their f *of* silver. 2838
38:17 the hooks of the pillars and their f *of* silver; 2838
38:19 of their chapiters and their f *of* silver. 2838

FILLING (1) [FILL]
Ac 14:17 f our hearts **with** food and gladness. *1705*

FILTH (4) [FILTHINESS, FILTHY]
Isa 4: 4 washed away the f of the daughters of Zion, 6675
Na 3: 6 I will cast **abominable** f upon thee, and 8251
1Co 4:13 we are made as the f of the world, *and* *4027*
1Pe 3:21 (not the putting away of the f of the flesh, *4509*

FILTHINESS (16) [FILTH]
2Ch 29: 5 and carry forth the f out of the holy *place.* 5079
Ezr 6:21 them from the f of the heathen of the land, 2932
9:11 *is* an unclean land with the f of the people 5079
Pr 30:12 and *yet* is not washed from their f. 6675
Isa 28: 8 For all tables are full *of* vomit *and* f, *so* 6675
La 1: 9 Her f *is* in her skirts; she remembereth not 2932
Eze 16:36 Because thy f was poured out, and 5178
22:15 and will consume thy f out of thee. 2932
24:11 and *that* the f of it may be molten in it, 2932
24:13 In thy f *is* lewdness: because I have purged 2932
24:13 thou shalt not be purged from thy f any 2932
36:25 from all your f, and from all your idols, 2932
2Co 7: 1 let us cleanse ourselves from all f of *3436*
Eph 5: 4 Neither f, nor foolish talking, nor jesting, *151*
Jas 1:21 Wherefore lay apart all f and superfluity of *4507*
Rev 17: 4 full of abominations and f of her fornication: *168*

FILTHY (17) [FILTH]
Job 15:16 How much more abominable and f *is* man, 444
Ps 14: 3 gone aside, they are *all* together become f: 444
53: 3 is gone back, they are altogether become f; 444
Isa 64: 6 and all our righteousnesses *are* as f rags; 5708
Zep 3: 1 Woe to her that is f and polluted, to 4754
Zec 3: 3 Now Joshua was clothed with f garments, 6674
3: 4 Take away the f garments from him. 6674
Col 3: 8 **f communication** out of your mouth. *148*
1Ti 3: 3 to wine, no striker, not **greedy of f lucre**; *146*
3: 8 given to much wine, not **greedy of f lucre**; *146*
Tit 1: 7 to wine, no striker, not **given to f lucre**; *146*
1:11 which *they* ought not, for f lucre's sake. *150*
1Pe 5: 2 not **for f lucre**, but of a ready mind; *147*
2Pe 2: 7 vexed with the f conversation of the wicked: *766*
Jude 1: 8 Likewise also these *f* dreamers defile NIG
Rev 22:11 and he which is f, let him be filthy still: and *4510*
22:11 and he which is filthy, let him be f still: and *4510*

FINALLY (6)
2Co 13:11 **F**, brethren, farewell. Be perfect, be of *3062*
Eph 6:10 **F**, my brethren, be strong in *3062+3588*
Php 3: 1 **F**, my brethren, rejoice in the Lord. *3062+3588*
4: 8 **F**, brethren, whatsoever *things* are *3062+3588*
2Th 3: 1 **F**, brethren, pray for us, that *3062+3588*
1Pe 3: 8 **F**, *be ye* all of one mind, *3588+5056*

FIND (156) [FINDEST, FINDETH, FINDING, FOUND]
Ge 18:26 If I f in Sodom fifty righteous within 4672
18:28 he said, If I f there forty and five, I will not 4672
18:30 he said, I will not do *it,* if I f thirty there. 4672
19:11 that they wearied themselves to f the door. 4672
32: 5 tell my lord, that I may f grace in thy sight. 4672
32:19 shall you speak unto Esau, when you f him. 4672
33: 8 *These are* to f grace in the sight of my lord. 4672
33:15 let me f grace in the sight of my lord. 4672
34:11 Let me f grace in your eyes, and what ye 4672
38:22 returned to Judah, and said, I cannot f her; 4672
41:38 Can we f *such a one* as this *is,* a man in 4672
47:25 let us f grace in the sight of my lord, and 4672
Ex 5:11 get you straw where you can f *it:* yet not 4672
16:25 to day ye shall not f it in the field. 4672
33:13 know thee, that I may f grace in thy sight: 4672
Nu 32:23 and be sure your sin will f you **out**. 4672
35:27 the revenger of blood f him without 4672
Dt 4:29 thou shalt f *him,* if thou seek him with all 4672
22:23 and a man f her in the city, and lie with her; 4672
22:25 if a man f a betrothed damsel in the field, 4672
22:28 If a man f a damsel *that is* a virgin, which is 4672
24: 1 it come to pass that she f no favour in his 4672
28:65 among these nations shalt thou f no **ease**, 7280
Jdg 9:33 thou do to them as thou shalt f **occasion**. 4672
14:12 f *it* **out**, then I will give you thirty sheets 4672
17: 8 to sojourn where he could f *a place:* 4672
17: 9 I go to sojourn where I may f *a place.* 4672
Ru 1: 9 The LORD grant you that you may f rest, 4672
2: 2 after *him* in whose sight I shall f grace. 4672
2:13 Let me f favour in thy sight, my lord; 4672
1Sa 1:18 Let thine handmaid f grace in thy sight. 4672
9:13 *into* the city, ye shall straightway f him, 4672
9:13 you up; for about *this* time ye shall f him. 4672
10: 2 thou shalt f two men by Rachel's sepulchre 4672
20:21 send a lad, *saying,* Go, f **out** the arrows. 4672
20:36 Run, f **out** now the arrows which I shoot. 4672
23:17 for the hand of Saul my father shall not f 4672
24:19 For if a man f his enemy, will he let him go 4672
25: 8 Wherefore let the young men f favour in 4672
2Sa 15:25 if I shall f favour in the eyes of the LORD, 4672
16: 4 I humbly beseech thee *that* I may f grace in 4672
17:20 could not f *them,* they returned *to* 4672
1Ki 18: 5 peradventure we may f grass to save 4672
18:12 I come and tell Ahab, and he cannot f thee, 4672
2Ch 2:14 to f **out** every device which shall be put to 2803
20:16 ye shall f them at the end of the brook, 4672
30: 9 your children *shall f* compassion before NIH
32: 4 kings of Assyria come, and f much water? 4672
Ezr 4:15 so shalt thou f in the book of the records, 7912
7:16 gold that thou canst f in all the province of 7912
Job 3:22 are glad, when they can f the grave? 4672
11: 7 Canst thou *by* searching f **out** God? 4672
11: 7 canst thou f **out** the Almighty unto 4672
17:10 for I cannot f *one* wise *man* among you. 4672
23: 3 O that I knew where I might f him! *that* I 4672
34:11 **cause** every man **to** f according to *his* 4672
37:23 the Almighty, we cannot f him **out**: 4672
Ps 10:15 seek out his wickedness *till* thou f none. 4672
17: 3 thou hast tried me, *and* shalt f nothing; 4672
21: 8 Thine hand shall f **out** all thine enemies: 4672
21: 8 thy right hand shall f **out** those that hate 4672
132: 5 Until I f **out** a place for the LORD, 4672
Pr 1:13 We shall f all precious substance, we shall 4672
1:28 shall seek me early, but they shall not f me: 4672
2: 5 the LORD, and f the knowledge of God. 4672
3: 4 So shalt thou f favour and 4672
4:22 For they *are* life unto those that f them, and 4672
8: 9 and right to them that f knowledge. 4672
8:12 and f **out** knowledge of witty inventions. 4672
8:17 and those that seek me early shall f me. 4672
16:20 He that handleth a matter wisely shall f 4672
19: 8 he that keepeth understanding shall f good. 4672
20: 6 but a faithful man who can f? 4672
28:23 afterwards shall f more favour than he that 4672
31:10 Who can f a virtuous woman? for her price 4672
Ecc 3:11 that no man can f **out** the work that God 4672
7:14 to the end that man should f nothing after 4672
7:24 and exceeding deep, who can f it **out**? 4672
7:26 I f more bitter than death the woman, 4672
7:27 *counting* one by one, to f **out** the account: 4672
7:28 Which yet my soul seeketh, but I f not: 4672
8:17 that a man cannot f **out** the work that is 4672
8:17 seek *it* out, yet he shall not f *it;* yea further, 4672
8:17 to know *it,* yet shall he not be able to f *it.* 4672
11: 1 for thou shalt f it after many days. 4672
12:10 The Preacher sought to f **out** acceptable 4672
SS 5: 6 I sought him, but I could not f him; I called 4672
5: 8 if ye f my beloved, that ye tell him, that I 4672

F

SS 8: 1 *when* I should f thee without, I would kiss 4672
Isa 34:14 rest there, and f for herself a place of rest. 4672
41:12 Thou shalt seek them, and shalt not f them, 4672
58: 3 in the day of your fast you f pleasure, and 4672
Jer 2:24 in her month they shall f her. 4672
5: 1 the broad places thereof, if ye can f a man, 4672
6:16 and ye shall f rest for your souls. 4672
10:18 and will distress them, that they may f *it so.* 4672
29:13 f *me,* when ye shall search for me with all 4672
45: 3 I fainted in my sighing, and I f no rest. 4672
La 1: 6 her princes are become like harts *that* f no 4672
2: 9 the law *is* no *more;* her prophets also f no 4672
Da 6: 4 princes sought to f occasion against Daniel 7912
6: 4 they could f none occasion nor fault; 7912
6: 5 We shall not f any occasion against this 7912
6: 5 except we f *it* against him concerning 7912
Hos 2: 6 make a wall, that she shall not f her paths. 4672
2: 7 shall not f *them:* then shall she say, I will 4672
5: 6 they shall not f *him;* he hath withdrawn 4672
12: 8 *in* all my labours they shall f none iniquity 4672
Am 8:12 the word of the LORD, and shall not f *it.* 4672
Mt 7: 7 seek, and ye shall f; knock, and it shall be *2147*
7:14 leadeth unto life, and few there be that f it. *2147*
10:39 he that loseth his life for my sake shall f it. *2147*
11:29 in heart: and ye shall f rest unto your souls. *2147*
16:25 will lose his life for my sake shall f it. *2147*
17:27 his mouth, thou shalt f a piece of money: *2147*
18:13 And if so be that he f it, verily I say unto *2147*
21: 2 and straightway ye shall f an ass tied, and *2147*
22: 9 the highways, and as many as ye shall f, *2147*
24:46 whom his lord when he cometh shall f so *2147*
Mk 11: 2 ye shall f a colt tied, whereon never man *2147*
11:13 if haply he might f any *thing* thereon: *2147*
13:36 Lest coming suddenly he f you sleeping. *2147*
Lk 2:12 Ye shall f *the* babe wrapped in swaddling *2147*
5:19 And when they could not f by what *way* *2147*
6: 7 that they might f an accusation against him. *2147*
11: 9 seek, and ye shall f; knock, and it shall be *2147*
12:37 whom the lord when he cometh shall f *2147*
12:38 or come in the third watch, and f *them* so, *2147*
12:43 whom his lord when he cometh shall f so *2147*
13: 7 seeking fruit on this fig tree, and f none: *2147*
15: 4 and go after that which is lost, until he f it? *2147*
15: 8 the house, and seek diligently till she f *it?* *2147*
18: 8 man cometh, shall he f faith on the earth? *2147*
19:30 which at your entering ye shall f a colt tied, *2147*
19:48 And could not f what they might do: for all *2147*
23: 4 and *to* the people, I f no fault in this man. *2147*
Jn 7:34 and shall not f *me:* and where I am, *2147*
7:35 Whither will he go, that we shall not f him? *2147*
7:36 and shall not f *me:* and where I am, *2147*
10: 9 and shall go in and out, and f pasture. *2147*
18:38 saith unto them, I f in him no fault *at all.* *2147*
19: 4 that ye may know that I f no fault in him. *2147*
19: 6 and crucify *him:* for I f no fault in him. *2147*
21: 6 on the right side of the ship, and ye shall f. *2147*
Ac 7:46 desired to f a tabernacle for the God of *2147*
17:27 f *him,* though he be not far from every one *2147*
23: 9 strove, saying, We f no evil in this man: *2147*
Ro 7:18 *how* to perform that which is good I f not. *2147*
7:21 I f then a law, that, when I would do good, *2147*
9:19 then unto me, Why doth he yet f **fault**? *3201*
2Co 9: 4 and f you unprepared, we (that we say not, *2147*
12:20 I shall not f you such as I would, and *that* I *2147*
2Ti 1:18 The Lord grant unto him that *he* may f *2147*
Heb 4:16 and f grace to help in time of need. *2147*
Rev 9: 6 shall men seek death, and shall not f it; *2147*
18:14 and thou shalt f them no more at all. *2147*

FINDEST (2) [FIND]

Ge 31:32 With whomsoever thou f thy gods, let him 4672
Eze 3: 1 said unto me, Son of man, eat that thou f; 4672

FINDETH (27) [FIND]

Ge 4:14 *that* every one that f me shall slay me. 4672
Job 33:10 Behold, he f occasions against me, 4672
Ps119:162 rejoice at thy word, as one that f great spoil. 4672
Pr 3:13 Happy *is* the man *that* f wisdom, and 4672
8:35 For whoso f me findeth life, and 4672
8:35 For whoso findeth me f life, and 4672
14: 6 A scorner seeketh wisdom, and *f it* not: but NIH
17:20 He that hath a froward heart f no good: and 4672
18:22 *Whoso* f a wife findeth a good *thing,* and 4672
18:22 *Whoso* findeth a wife f a good *thing,* and 4672
21:10 his neighbour f no **favour** in his eyes. 2603
21:21 after righteousness and mercy f life, 4672
Ecc 9:10 Whatsoever thy hand f to do, do *it* with thy 4672
La 1: 3 dwelleth among the heathen, she f no rest: 4672
Hos 14: 3 our gods: for in thee the fatherless f **mercy**. 7355
Mt 7: 8 that asketh receiveth; and he that seeketh f: *2147*
10:39 He that f his life shall lose it: and he that *2147*
12:43 dry places, seeking rest, and f none. *2147*
12:44 he f *it* empty, swept, and garnished. *2147*
26:40 and f them asleep, and saith unto Peter, *2147*
Mk 14:37 and f them sleeping, and saith unto Peter, *2147*
Lk 11:10 and he that seeketh f; and to him that *2147*
11:25 he cometh, he f *it* swept and garnished. *2147*
Jn 1:41 He first f his own brother Simon, and *2147*
1:43 and f Philip, and saith unto him, *2147*
1:45 Philip f Nathanael, and saith unto him, *2147*
5:14 Afterward Jesus f him in the temple, and *2147*

FINDING (10) [FIND]

Ge 4:15 upon Cain, lest any f him should kill him. 4672
Job 9:10 Which doeth great *things* past f **out**; yea, 2714
Isa 58:13 thine own ways, nor f thine own pleasure, 4672
Lk 11:24 and f none, he saith, I will return unto my *2147*
Ac 4:21 f nothing how they might punish them, *2147*
19: 1 came to Ephesus: and f certain disciples, *2147*
21: 2 And f a ship sailing over unto Phenicia, *2147*
21: 4 And f disciples, we tarried there seven days: *429*
Ro 11:33 *are* his judgments, and his ways **past** f **out**! *421*
Heb 8: 8 For f **fault with** them, *he* saith, Behold, *3201*

FINE (113) [FINER, FINEST, FINING]

Ge 18: 6 Make ready quickly three measures of f 5560
41:42 arrayed him in vestures of f **linen**, and put a 8336
Ex 25: 4 and scarlet, and f **linen**, and goats' *hair,* 8336
26: 1 *with* ten curtains *of* f twined **linen**, 8336
26:31 f twined **linen** *of* cunning work: 8336
26:36 and purple, and scarlet, and f twined **linen**, 8336
27: 9 f twined **linen** of an hundred cubits long for 8336
27:16 and purple, and scarlet, and f twined **linen**, 8336
27:18 the height five cubits *of* f twined **linen**, and 8336
28: 5 and purple, and scarlet, and f **linen**. 8336
28: 6 *of* purple, *of* scarlet, and f twined **linen**, 8336
28: 8 and purple, and scarlet, and f twined **linen**. 8336
28:15 and *of* scarlet, and *of* f twined **linen**, 8336
28:39 thou shalt embroider the coat of f **linen**, 8336
28:39 thou shalt make the mitre *of* f **linen**, and 8336
35: 6 and scarlet, and f **linen**, and goats' *hair,* 8336
35:23 f **linen**, and goats' *hair,* and red skins of 8336
35:25 and of purple, *and* of scarlet, and of f **linen**. 8336
35:35 in scarlet, and in f **linen**, and of the weaver, 8336
36: 8 made ten curtains *of* f twined **linen**, 8336
36:35 and purple, and scarlet, and f twined **linen**: 8336
36:37 purple, and scarlet, and f twined **linen**, 8336
38: 9 of the court *were of* f twined **linen**, 8336
38:16 court round about *were of* f twined **linen**. 8336
38:18 and purple, and scarlet, and f twined **linen**: 8336
38:23 and in purple, and in scarlet, and f **linen**. 8336
39: 2 and purple, and scarlet, and f twined **linen**. 8336
39: 3 and in the scarlet, and in the f **linen**, 8336
39: 5 and purple, and scarlet, and f twined **linen**; 8336
39: 8 and purple, and scarlet, and f twined **linen**. 8336
39:27 they made coats *of* f **linen** *of* woven work 8336
39:28 a mitre *of* f **linen**, and goodly bonnets *of* 8336
39:28 goodly bonnets *of* f **linen**, and linen 8336
39:28 and linen breeches *of* f twined **linen**, 8336
39:29 a girdle *of* f twined **linen**, and blue, and 8336
Lev 2: 1 the LORD, his offering shall be *of* f **flour**; 5560
2: 4 *it shall be* unleavened cakes of f **flour** 5560
2: 5 it shall be *of* f **flour** unleavened, 5560
2: 7 it shall be made *of* f **flour** with oil. 5560
5:11 of an ephah of f **flour** for a sin offering; 5560
6:20 the tenth *part* of an ephah of f **flour** *for* a 5560
7:12 cakes mingled with oil, of f **flour**, fried. 5560
14:10 three tenth deals of f **flour** *for* a meat 5560
14:21 one tenth deal of f **flour** mingled with oil 5560
23:13 two tenth deals *of* f **flour** mingled with oil, 5560
23:17 they shall be *of* f **flour**; they shall be baken 5560
24: 5 thou shalt take f **flour**, and bake twelve 5560
Nu 6:15 cakes *of* f **flour** mingled with oil, and 5560
7:13 both of them *were* full *of* f **flour** mingled 5560
7:19 both of them full *of* f **flour** mingled with 5560
7:25 both of them full *of* f **flour** mingled with 5560
7:31 both of them full *of* f **flour** mingled with 5560
7:37 both of them full *of* f **flour** mingled with 5560

Nu	7:43	both of them full *of* f **flour** mingled with	5560
	7:49	both of them full *of* f **flour** mingled with	5560
	7:55	both of them full *of* f **flour** mingled with	5560
	7:61	both of them full *of* f **flour** mingled with	5560
	7:67	both of them full *of* f **flour** mingled with	5560
	7:73	both of them full *of* f **flour** mingled with	5560
	7:79	both of them full *of* f **flour** mingled with	5560
	8: 8	*even* f **flour** mingled with oil, and	5560
1Ki	4:22	for one day was thirty measures of f **flour**,	5560
2Ki	7: 1	a measure of f **flour** *be sold* for a shekel,	5560
	7:16	So a measure of f **flour** was *sold* for a	5560
	7:18	and a measure of f **flour** for a shekel,	5560
1Ch	4:21	of the house of them that wrought f **linen**,	948
	9:29	the f **flour**, and the wine, and the oil, and	5560
	15:27	David *was* clothed with a robe of f **linen**,	948
	23:29	for the f **flour** for meat offering, and for	5560
2Ch	2:14	in blue, and in f **linen**, and in crimson;	948
	3: 5	which he overlaid with f gold, and	2896
	3: 8	he overlaid it with f gold, *amounting* to six	2896
	3:14	and f **linen**, and wrought cherubims thereon.	948
Ezr	8:27	two vessels of f copper, precious as	2896+6668
Est	1: 6	blue *hangings,* fastened with cords of f **linen**	948
	8:15	and *with* a garment of f **linen** and purple:	948
Job	28: 1	and a place for gold *where* they f *it.*	2212
	28:17	of it *shall not be for* jewels of f **gold**.	6337
	31:24	or have said to the f **gold**, *Thou art* my	3800
Ps	19:10	*are they* than gold, yea, than much f **gold**:	6337
	119:127	above gold; yea, above f **gold**.	6337
Pr	3:14	of silver, and the gain thereof than f **gold**.	2742
	7:16	*with* carved *works, with* f **linen** of Egypt.	330
	8:19	fruit *is* better than gold, yea, than f **gold**;	6337
	25:12	an ornament of f **gold**, *so is* a wise reprover	3800
	31:24	She maketh f **linen**, and selleth *it;* and	5466
SS	5:11	His head *is as* the most f **gold**, his locks *are*	6337
	5:15	of marble, set upon sockets of f **gold**:	6337
Isa	3:23	the f **linen**, and the hoods, and the vails.	5466
	13:12	will make a man more precious than f **gold**;	6337
	19: 9	Moreover they that work in f flax, and	8305
La	4: 1	*how* is the most f **gold** changed! the stones	3800
	4: 2	sons of Zion, comparable to f **gold**,	6337
Eze	16:10	and I girded thee about with f **linen**,	8336
	16:13	thy raiment *was of* f **linen**, and silk, and	8336
	16:13	thou didst eat f **flour**, and honey, and oil:	5560
	16:19	f **flour**, and oil, and honey, *wherewith* I fed	5560
	27: 7	F **linen** with broidered work from Egypt	8336
	27:16	and f **linen**, and coral, and agate.	948
	46:14	of a hin of oil, to temper with the f **flour**;	5560
Da	2:32	This image's head *was* of f gold, his breast	2869
	10: 5	whose loins *were* girded with f **gold** of	3800
Zec	9: 3	and f **gold** as the mire of the streets.	2742
Mk	15:46	And he bought f **linen**, and took him down,	*4616*
Lk	16:19	which was clothed in purple and f **linen**,	*1040*
Rev	1:15	And his feet like unto f **brass**, as if they	*5474*
	2:18	a flame of fire, and his feet *are* like f **brass**;	*5474*
	18:12	and f **linen**, and purple, and silk, and	*1040*
	18:13	and oil, and f **flour**, and wheat, and beasts,	*4585*
	18:16	that was clothed in f **linen**, and purple, and	*1039*
	19: 8	that she should be arrayed in f **linen**,	*1039*
	19: 8	for the f **linen** is the righteousness of saints.	*1039*
	19:14	clothed in f **linen**, white and clean.	*1039*

FINER (1) [FINE]

Pr	25: 4	and there shall come forth a vessel for the f.	6884

FINERY See BRAVERY

FINEST (2) [FINE]

Ps	81:16	He should have fed them also with the f of	2459
	147:14	*and* filleth thee *with* the f of the wheat.	2459

FINGER (26) [FINGERS]

Ex	8:19	said unto Pharaoh, This *is* the f of God:	676
	29:12	put *it* upon the horns of the altar with thy f,	676
	31:18	tables of stone, written with the f of God.	676
Lev	4: 6	the priest shall dip his f in the blood, and	676
	4:17	the priest shall dip his f *in some* of the blood,	676
	4:25	of the blood of the sin offering with his f,	676
	4:30	shall take of the blood thereof with his f,	676
	4:34	of the blood of the sin offering with his f,	676
	8:15	the horns of the altar round about with his f,	676
	9: 9	he dipt his f in the blood, and put *it* upon	676
	14:16	the priest shall dip his right f in the oil that *is*	676
	14:16	shall sprinkle of the oil with his f seven	676
	14:27	the priest shall sprinkle with his right f *some*	676
	16:14	sprinkle *it* with his f upon the mercy seat	676
	16:14	sprinkle of the blood with his f seven times.	676
	16:19	of the blood upon it with his f seven times,	676
Nu	19: 4	the priest shall take of her blood with his f,	676
Dt	9:10	two tables of stone written with the f of God;	676
1Ki	12:10	My little *f* shall be thicker than my father's	NIH
2Ch	10:10	My little *f* shall be thicker than my father's	NIH
Isa	58: 9	the putting forth of the f, and	676
Lk	11:20	But if I with the f of God cast out devils,	*1147*
	16:24	that he may dip the tip of his f in water, and	*1147*
Jn	8: 6	and with *his* f wrote on the ground,	*1147*
	20:25	and put my f into the print of the nails, and	*1147*
	20:27	Reach hither thy f, and behold my hands;	*1147*

FINGERS (15) [FINGER]

2Sa	21:20	that had on every hand six f, and on every	676
1Ch	20: 6	whose f **and toes** *were* four and twenty,	676
Ps	8: 3	the work of thy f, the moon and the stars,	676
	144: 1	teacheth my hands to war, *and* my f to fight:	676
Pr	6:13	speaketh with his feet, he teacheth with his f;	676
	7: 3	Bind them upon thy f, write them upon	676
SS	5: 5	my f *with* sweet smelling myrrh, upon	676
Isa	2: 8	*that* which their own f have made:	676
	17: 8	neither shall respect *that* which his f have	676
	59: 3	defiled with blood, and your f with iniquity;	676
Jer	52:21	and the thickness thereof *was* four f:	676
Da	5: 5	In the same hour came forth f of a man's	677
Mt	23: 4	will not move them with *one of* their f.	*1147*
Mk	7:33	and put his f into his ears, and he spit, and	*1147*
Lk	11:46	touch not the burdens with one of your f.	*1147*

FINING (2) [FINE]

Pr	17: 3	The f **pot** *is* for silver, and the furnace for	4715
	27:21	*As* the f **pot** for silver, and the furnace for	4715

FINISH (11) [FINISHED, FINISHER]

Ge	6:16	the ark, and in a cubit shalt thou f it above;	3615
Da	9:24	to f the transgression, and to make an end	3607
Zec	4: 9	his hands shall also f *it;* and thou shalt	1214
Lk	14:28	the cost, whether he have sufficient to f it?	*535*
	14:29	is not able to f *it,* all that behold *it* begin to	*1615*
	14:30	man began to build, and was not able to f.	*1615*
Jn	4:34	will of him that sent me, and to f his work.	*5048*
	5:36	works which the Father hath given me to f,	*5048*
Ac	20:24	so that *I* might f my course with joy, and	*5048*
Ro	9:28	For he will f the work, and cut *it* short in	*4931*
2Co	8: 6	he would also f in you the same grace also.	*2005*

FINISHED (42) [FINISH]

Ge	2: 1	Thus the heavens and the earth were f, and	3615
Ex	39:32	tabernacle of the tent of the congregation f:	3615
	40:33	of the court gate. So Moses f the work.	3615
Dt	31:24	of this law in a book, until they were f,	8552
Jos	4:10	until every thing was f that the LORD	8552
Ru	3:18	be in rest, until he have f the thing *this* day.	3615
1Ki	6: 9	So he built the house, and f it; and	3615
	6:14	So Solomon built the house, and f it.	3615
	6:22	with gold, until *he* had f all the house:	8552
	6:38	was the house f throughout all the parts	3615
	7: 1	house thirteen years, and he f all his house.	3615
	7:22	lily work: so was the work of the pillars f.	8552
	9: 1	when Solomon had f the building of	3615
	9:25	*was* before the LORD. So he f the house.	7999
1Ch	27:24	he f not, because there fell wrath for it	3615
	28:20	until *thou* hast f all the work for the service	3615
2Ch	4:11	Huram f the work that he was to make for	3615
	5: 1	made for the house of the LORD was f:	7999
	7:11	Thus Solomon f the house of the LORD,	3615
	8:16	the house of the LORD, and until it was f.	3615
	24:14	when they had f *it,* they brought the rest of	3615
	29:28	*continued* until the burnt offering was f.	3615
	31: 1	Now when all this was f, all Israel that	3615
	31: 7	the heaps, and f *them* in the seventh month.	3615
Ezr	5:16	*hath it been* in building, and *yet it is* not f.	8000
	6:14	f *it,* according to the commandment of	3635
	6:15	this house was f on the third day of	3319
Ne	6:15	So the wall was f in the twenty and	7999
Da	5:26	God hath numbered thy kingdom, and f it.	8000
	12: 7	the holy people, all these *things* shall be f.	3615
Mt	13:53	*that* when Jesus had f these parables,	*5055*
	19: 1	*that* when Jesus had f these sayings,	*5055*
	26: 1	to pass, when Jesus had f all these sayings,	*5055*
Jn	17: 4	I have f the work which thou gavest me to	*5048*
	19:30	had received the vinegar, he said, It is f:	*5055*

Ac 21: 7 And when we had f *our* course from Tyre, *1274*
2Ti 4: 7 I have f *my* course, I have kept the faith: *5055*
Heb 4: 3 although the works were f from *1096*
Jas 1:15 and sin, when it is f, bringeth forth death. *658*
Rev 10: 7 to sound, the mystery of God should be f, *5055*
11: 7 And when they shall have f their testimony, *5055*
20: 5 not again until the thousand years were f. *5055*

FINISHER (1) [FINISH]
Heb 12: 2 unto Jesus the author and f of *our* faith; *5051*

FINS (5)
Lev 11: 9 whatsoever hath f and scales in the waters, 5579
11:10 all that have not f nor scales in the seas, 5579
11:12 Whatsoever hath no f nor scales in 5579
Dt 14: 9 all that have f and scales shall ye eat: 5579
14:10 whatsoever hath not f and scales ye may 5579

FIR (21)
2Sa 6: 5 all *manner of instruments made of* f wood, 1265
1Ki 5: 8 timber of cedar, and concerning timber of f. 1265
5:10 and f trees *according to* all his desire. 1265
6:15 the floor of the house with planks of f. 1265
6:34 the two doors *were* of f tree: the two leaves 1265
9:11 Solomon with cedar trees and f trees, 1265
2Ki 19:23 trees thereof, *and* the choice f **trees** thereof: 1265
2Ch 2: 8 f **trees**, and algum trees, out of Lebanon: 1265
3: 5 the greater house he cieled with f tree, 1265
Ps 104:17 *as for* the stork, the f **trees** *are* her house. 1265
SS 1:17 of our house *are* cedar, *and* our rafters of f. 1266
Isa 14: 8 the f **trees** rejoice at thee, *and* the cedars of 1265
37:24 *and* the choice f **trees** thereof: 1265
41:19 I will set in the desert the f **tree**, *and* 1265
55:13 of the thorn shall come up the f **tree**, 1265
60:13 the f **tree**, the pine tree, and the box 1265
Eze 27: 5 made all thy *ship* boards of f **trees** of Senir: 1265
31: 8 the f **trees** were not like his boughs, and 1265
Hos 14: 8 I *am* like a green f **tree**. From me is thy 1265
Na 2: 3 and the f **trees** shall be terribly shaken. 1265
Zec 11: 2 Howl, f **tree**; for the cedar is fallen; 1265

FIRE (549) [FIREBRAND, FIREBRANDS, FIREPANS, FIRES]
Ge 19:24 and f from the LORD out of heaven; 784
22: 6 he took the f in his hand, and a knife; and 784
22: 7 And he said, Behold the f and the wood: but 784
Ex 3: 2 in a flame of f out of the midst of a bush: 784
3: 2 the bush burned with f, and the bush was not 784
9:23 hail, and the f ran along upon the ground; 784
9:24 and f mingled with the hail, very grievous, 784
12: 8 roast with f, and unleavened bread; 784
12: 9 nor sodden at all with water, but roast with f; 784
12:10 of it until the morning ye shall burn with f. 784
13:21 by night in a pillar of f, to give them light; 784
13:22 nor the pillar of f by night, *from* before 784
14:24 host of the Egyptians through the pillar of f 784
19:18 the LORD descended upon it in f: 784
22: 6 If f break out, and catch in thorns, so that 784
22: 6 kindled the f shall surely make restitution. 1200
24:17 f on the top of the mount in the eyes of 784
29:14 shalt thou burn with f without the camp: 784
29:18 an **offering made by** f unto the LORD. 801
29:25 it *is* an **offering made by** f unto the LORD. 801
29:34 then thou shalt burn the remainder with f: 784
29:41 an **offering made by** f unto the LORD. 801
30:20 to burn **offering made by** f unto 801
32:20 and burnt *it* in the f, and ground *it* to powder, 784
32:24 I cast it into the f, and there came out this 784
35: 3 Ye shall kindle no f throughout your 784
40:38 f was on it by night, in the sight of all 784
Lev 1: 7 the sons of Aaron the priest shall put f upon 784
1: 7 and lay the wood in order upon the f: 784
1: 8 in order upon the wood that *is* on the f which 784
1: 9 *be* a burnt sacrifice, an **offering made by** f, 801
1:12 wood that *is* on the f which *is* upon the altar: 784
1:13 it *is* a burnt sacrifice, an **offering made by** f, 801
1:17 the altar, upon the wood that *is* upon the f: 784
1:17 it *is* a burnt sacrifice, an **offering made by** f, 801
2: 2 *to be* an **offering made by** f, of a sweet 801
2: 3 of the **offerings** of the LORD **made by** f. 801
2: 9 *it is* an **offering made by** f, of a sweet 801
2:10 of the **offerings** of the LORD **made by** f. 801
2:11 *in* any **offering** of the LORD **made by** f. 801
2:14 firstfruits green ears of corn dried by the f, 784
2:16 *it is* an **offering made by** f unto the LORD. 801
3: 3 an **offering made by** f unto the LORD; 801
3: 5 which *is* upon the wood that *is* on the f: 784
3: 5 *it is* an **offering made by** f, of a sweet 801
3: 9 an **offering made by** f unto the LORD; 801
3:11 *it is* the food of the **offering made by** f unto 801
3:14 *even* an **offering made by** f unto 801
3:16 *it is* the food of the **offering made by** f for a 801
4:12 and burn him on the wood with f: 784
4:35 according to the **offerings made by** f unto 801
5:12 according to the **offerings made by** f unto 801
6: 9 and the f of the altar shall be burning in it. 784
6:10 take up the ashes which the f hath consumed 784
6:12 the f upon the altar shall be burning in it; 784
6:13 The f shall ever be burning upon the altar; 784
6:17 *for* their portion of my **offerings made by** f; 801
6:18 the **offerings** of the LORD **made by** f: 801
6:30 shall be eaten: it shall be burnt in the f. 784
7: 5 *for* an **offering made by** f unto the LORD: 801
7:17 on the third day shall be burnt with f. 784
7:19 shall not be eaten; it shall be burnt with f: 784
7:25 of which *men* offer an **offering made by** f 801
7:30 the **offerings** of the LORD **made by** f, 801
7:35 of the **offerings** of the LORD **made by** f, 801
8:17 his dung, he burnt with f without the camp; 784
8:21 *and* an **offering made by** f unto the LORD; 801
8:28 it *is* an **offering made by** f unto the LORD. 801
8:32 and of the bread shall ye burn with f. 784
9:11 the hide he burnt with f without the camp. 784
9:24 there came a f out from before the LORD, 784
10: 1 put f therein, and put incense thereon, 784
10: 1 offered strange f before the LORD, 784
10: 2 there went out f from the LORD, and 784
10:12 of the **offerings** of the LORD **made by** f, 801
10:13 of the **sacrifices** of the LORD **made by** f: 801
10:15 with the **offerings made by** f of the fat, 801
13:52 *is* a fretting leprosy; it shall be burnt in the f. 784
13:55 it *is* unclean; thou shalt burn it in the f; it *is* 784
13:57 shalt burn that wherein the plague *is* with f. 784
16:12 shall take a censer full of burning coals of f 784
16:13 he shall put the incense upon the f before 784
16:27 they shall burn in the f their skins, and their 784
18:21 of thy seed pass through *the f* to Molech, NIH
19: 6 until the third day, it shall be burnt in the f. 784
20:14 they shall be burnt with f, both he and they; 784
21: 6 for the **offerings** of the LORD **made by** f, 801
21: 9 her father: she shall be burnt with f. 784
21:21 the **offerings** of the LORD **made by** f: 801
22:22 nor make an **offering by** f of them upon 801
22:27 **offering made by** f unto the LORD. 801+7133
23: 8 ye shall offer an **offering made by** f unto 801
23:13 an **offering made by** f unto the LORD *for* 801
23:18 drink offerings, *even* an **offering made by** f, 801
23:25 ye shall offer an **offering made by** f unto 801
23:27 offer an **offering made by** f unto 801
23:36 an **offering made by** f unto the LORD: 801
23:36 ye shall offer an **offering made by** f unto 801
23:37 to offer an **offering made by** f unto 801
24: 7 *even* an **offering made by** f unto 801
24: 9 of the **offerings** of the LORD **made by** f, 801
Nu 3: 4 when they offered strange f before 784
6:18 put *it* in the f which *is* under the sacrifice of 784
9:15 the tabernacle as it were the appearance of f, 784
9:16 it *by day*, and the appearance of f by night. 784
11: 1 the f of the LORD burnt among them, and 784
11: 2 unto the LORD, the f was quenched. 784
11: 3 the f of the LORD burnt among them. 784
14:14 pillar of a cloud, and in a pillar of f by night. 784
15: 3 will make an **offering by** f unto the LORD, 801
15:10 *for* an **offering made by** f, of a sweet savour 801
15:13 in offering an **offering made by** f, of a 801
15:14 will offer an **offering made by** f, of a sweet 801
15:25 a **sacrifice made by** f unto the LORD, and 801
16: 7 put f therein, and put incense in them before 784
16:18 put f in them, and laid incense thereon, 784
16:35 there came out a f from the LORD, and 784
16:37 of the burning, and scatter thou the f yonder; 784
16:46 put f therein from off the altar, and put on 784
18: 9 of the most holy *things, reserved* from the f: 784
18:17 burn their fat *for* an **offering made by** f, 801
21:28 For there is a f gone out of Heshbon, a flame 784
26:10 what time the f devoured two hundred and 784
26:61 when they offered strange f before 784
28: 2 *and* my bread for my **sacrifices made by** f, 801
28: 3 This *is* the **offering made by** f which ye 801

31:10 and all their goodly castles, with f.	784
	31:23 Every thing that may abide the f, ye shall	784
	31:23 ye shall make *it* go through the f, and it shall	784
	31:23 all that abideth not the f ye shall make go	784
Dt	1:33 a place to pitch your tents *in*, in f by night,	784
	4:11 the mountain burnt with f unto the midst of	784
	4:12 spake unto you out of the midst of the f:	784
	4:15 unto you in Horeb out of the midst of the f:	784
	4:24 For the LORD thy God *is* a consuming f,	784
	4:33 of God speaking out of the midst of the f,	784
	4:36 upon earth he shewed thee his great f; and	784
	4:36 heardest his words out of the midst of the f.	784
	5: 4 to face in the mount out of the midst of the f,	784
	5: 5 for ye were afraid by reason of the f, and	784
	5:22 in the mount out of the midst of the f,	784
	5:23 (for the mountain did burn with f,)	784
	5:24 heard his voice out of the midst of the f:	784
	5:25 for this great f will consume us: if we hear	784
	5:26 living God speaking out of the midst of the f,	784
	7: 5 and burn their graven images with f.	784
	7:25 images of their gods shall ye burn with f:	784
	9: 3 *as* a consuming f he shall destroy them, and	784
	9:10 the midst of the f in the day of the assembly.	784
	9:15 the mount, and the mount burned with f:	784
	9:21 burnt it with f, and stamped it, *and* ground *it*	784
	10: 4 the midst of the f in the day of the assembly:	784
	12: 3 their pillars, and burn their groves with f;	784
	12:31 their daughters they have burnt in the f to	784
	13:16 shalt burn with f the city, and all the spoil	784
	18: 1 eat the **offerings** of the LORD **made by** f,	801
	18:10 his son or his daughter to pass through the f,	784
	18:16 neither let me see this great f any more,	784
	32:22 For a f is kindled in my anger, and shall burn	784
	32:22 **set on** f the foundations of the mountains.	3857
Jos	6:24 they burnt the city with f, and all that *was*	784
	7:15 with the accursed thing shall be burnt with f,	784
	7:25 him *with* stones, and burned them with f,	784
	8: 8 taken the city, *that* ye shall set the city on f:	784
	8:19 and took it, and hasted and set the city on f.	784
	11: 6 their horses, and burn their chariots with f.	784
	11: 9 their horses, and burnt their chariots with f.	784
	11:11 left to breathe: and he burnt Hazor with f.	784
	13:14 **sacrifices** of the LORD God of Israel	
	made by f	801
Jdg	1: 8 the edge of the sword, and set the city on f.	784
	6:21 and there rose up f out of the rock,	784
	9:15 let f come out of the bramble, and devour	784
	9:20 let f come out from Abimelech, and	784
	9:20 let f come out from the men of Shechem,	784
	9:49 to the hold, and set the hold on f upon them;	784
	9:52 unto the door of the tower to burn it with f.	784
	12: 1 we will burn thine house upon thee with f.	784
	14:15 we burn thee and thy father's house with f:	784
	15: 5 when he had set the brands on f, he let *them*	784
	15: 6 came up, and burnt her and her father with f.	784
	15:14 arms became as flax that was burnt with f,	784
	16: 9 of tow is broken when it toucheth the f.	784
	18:27 edge of the sword, and burnt the city with f.	784
	20:48 also they set on f all the cities that they came	784
1Sa	2:28 **offerings made by** f of the children of	801
	30: 1 and smitten Ziklag, and burnt it with f;	784
	30: 3 to the city, and behold, *it was* burnt with f;	784
	30:14 south of Caleb; and we burnt Ziklag with f.	784
2Sa	14:30 and he hath barley there; go and set it on f.	784
	14:30 And Absalom's servants set the field on f.	784
	14:31 have thy servants set my field on f?	784
	22: 9 his nostrils, and f out of his mouth devoured:	784
	22:13 before him were coals of f kindled.	784
	23: 7 they shall be utterly burnt with f in the same	784
1Ki	9:16 burnt it with f, and slain the Canaanites that	784
	16:18 burnt the king's house over him with f, and	784
	18:23 put no f *under:* and I will dress the other	784
	18:23 and lay *it* on wood, and put no f *under:*	784
	18:24 the God that answereth by f, let him be God.	784
	18:25 the name of your gods, but put no f *under.*	784
	18:38 the f of the LORD fell, and consumed	784

	19:12 after the earthquake a f; *but* the LORD *was*	784
	19:12 a fire; *but* the LORD *was* not in the f:	784
	19:12 in the fire: and after the f a still small voice.	784
2Ki	1:10 let f come down from heaven, and	784
	1:10 there came down f from heaven, and	784
	1:12 let f come down from heaven, and	784
	1:12 the f of God came down from heaven, and	784
	1:14 there came f down from heaven, and	784
	2:11 *there appeared* a chariot of f, and horses of	784
	2:11 horses of f, and parted them both asunder;	784
	6:17 and chariots of f round about Elisha.	784
	8:12 their strong holds wilt thou set on f, and	784
	16: 3 yea, and made his son to pass through the f,	784
	17:17 and their daughters to pass through the f,	784
	17:31 the Sepharvites burnt their children in f to	784
	19:18 have cast their gods into the f: for they *were*	784
	21: 6 And he made his son pass through the f, and	784
	23:10 his daughter to pass through the f to Molech.	784
	23:11 and burnt the chariots of the sun with f.	784
	25: 9 and every great *man's* house burnt he with f.	784
1Ch	14:12 a commandment, and they were burnt with f.	784
	21:26 he answered him from heaven by f upon	784
2Ch	7: 1 the f came down from heaven, and	784
	7: 3 when all the children of Israel saw how the f	784
	28: 3 burnt his children in the f after	784
	33: 6 he caused his children to pass through the f	784
	35:13 they roasted the passover with f according to	784
	36:19 burnt all the palaces thereof with f, and	784
Ne	1: 3 and the gates thereof are burnt with f.	784
	2: 3 and the gates thereof are consumed with f?	784
	2:13 and the gates thereof were consumed with f.	784
	2:17 and the gates thereof are burnt with f:	784
	9:12 in the night by a pillar of f, to give them	784
	9:19 neither the pillar of f by night, to shew them	784
Job	1:16 The f of God is fallen from heaven, and	784
	15:34 f shall consume the tabernacles of bribery.	784
	18: 5 put out, and the spark of his f shall not shine.	784
	20:26 a f not blown shall consume him; it shall go	784
	22:20 but the remnant of them the f consumeth.	784
	28: 5 and under it is turned up as it were f.	784
	31:12 For it *is* a f *that* consumeth to destruction,	784
	41:19 go burning lamps, *and* sparks of f leap out.	784
Ps	11: 6 f and brimstone, and a horrible tempest:	784
	18: 8 his nostrils, and f out of his mouth devoured:	784
	18:12 clouds passed, hail-*stones* and coals of f.	784
	18:13 gave his voice; hail-*stones* and coals of f.	784
	21: 9 up in his wrath, and the f shall devour them.	784
	29: 7 voice of the LORD divideth the flames of f.	784
	39: 3 within me, while I was musing the f burned:	784
	46: 9 in sunder; he burneth the chariot in the f.	784
	50: 3 a f shall devour before him, and it shall be	784
	57: 4 *and* I lie *even among* them that are **set on** f,	3857
	66:12 we went through f and through water:	784
	68: 2 as wax melteth before the f, *so* let	784
	74: 7 They have cast f into thy sanctuary,	784
	78:14 a cloud, and all the night with a light of f.	784
	78:21 so a f was kindled against Jacob, and	784
	78:63 The f consumed their young men; and	784
	79: 5 for ever? shall thy jealousy burn like f?	784
	80:16 *It is* burnt with f, *it is* cut down: they perish	784
	83:14 As the f burneth a wood, and as the flame	784
	83:14 as the flame **setteth** the mountains **on** f;	3857
	89:46 for ever? shall thy wrath burn like f?	784
	97: 3 A f goeth before him, and burneth up his	784
	104: 4 his angels spirits; his ministers a flaming f:	784
	105:32 hail *for* rain, *and* flaming f in their land.	784
	105:39 a covering; and f to give light in the night.	784
	106:18 a f was kindled in their company; the flame	784
	118:12 they are quenched as the f of thorns:	784
	140:10 let them be cast into the f; into deep pits,	784
	148: 8 F, and hail; snow, and vapour; stormy wind	784
Pr	6:27 Can a man take f in his bosom, and	784
	16:27 up evil: and in his lips *there is* as a burning f.	784
	25:22 For thou shalt heap **coals of** f upon his	1513
	26:20 Where no wood is, *there* the f goeth out: so	784
	26:21 *As* coals *are* to burning coals, and wood to f;	784
	30:16 and the f *that* saith not, It is enough.	784
SS	8: 6 the coals thereof *are* coals of f, *which hath* a	784
Isa	1: 7 *is* desolate, your cities *are* burnt with f:	784
	4: 5 and the shining of a flaming f by night:	784
	5:24 Therefore as the f devoureth	784+3956
	9: 5 but *this* shall be with burning *and* fuel of f.	784
	9:18 For wickedness burneth as the f: it shall	784
	9:19 and the people shall be as the fuel of the f:	784

Isa	10:16	shall kindle a burning like the burning of a f.	784
	10:17	the light of Israel shall be for a f, and	784
	26:11	the f of thine enemies shall devour them.	784
	27:11	the women come, *and* **set** them **on** f: for it *is*	215
	29: 6	and tempest, and the flame of devouring f.	784
	30:14	of it a sheard to take f from the hearth,	784
	30:27	and his tongue as a devouring f:	784
	30:30	*with* the flame of a devouring f,	784
	30:33	the pile thereof *is* f and much wood;	784
	31: 9	whose f *is* in Zion, and his furnace in	217
	33:11	your breath, *as* f, shall devour you.	784
	33:12	*as* thorns cut up shall they be burnt in the f.	784
	33:14	among us shall dwell *with* the devouring f?	784
	37:19	have cast their gods into the f: for they *were*	784
	42:25	it hath **set** him **on** f round about, yet he	3857
	43: 2	when thou walkest through the f, thou shalt	784
	44:16	He burneth part thereof in the f; with part	784
	44:16	and saith, Aha, I am warm, I have seen the f:	217
	44:19	to say, I have burnt part of it in the f;	784
	47:14	shall be as stubble; the f shall burn them;	784
	47:14	*be* a coal to warm at, *nor* f to sit before it.	217
	50:11	Behold, all ye that kindle a f, that compass	784
	50:11	walk in the light of your f, and in the sparks	784
	54:16	the smith that bloweth the coals in the f,	784
	64: 2	As *when* the melting f burneth, the fire	784
	64: 2	fire burneth, the f causeth the waters to boil,	784
	64:11	our fathers praised thee, is burnt up with f:	784
	65: 5	in my nose, a f that burneth all the day.	784
	66:15	the LORD will come with f, and with his	784
	66:15	with fury, and his rebuke with flames of f.	784
	66:16	For by f and by his sword will the LORD	784
	66:24	not die, neither shall their f be quenched;	784
Jer	4: 4	lest my fury come forth like f, and burn that	784
	5:14	I will make my words in thy mouth f, and	784
	6: 1	and set up a **sign of** f in Beth-haccerem:	4864
	6:29	are burnt, the lead is consumed of the f;	784
	7:18	the fathers kindle the f, and the women	784
	7:31	burn their sons and their daughters in the f;	784
	11:16	of a great tumult he hath kindled f upon it,	784
	15:14	for a f is kindled in mine anger, *which* shall	784
	17: 4	for ye have kindled a f in mine anger,	784
	17:27	then will I kindle a f in the gates thereof, and	784
	19: 5	to burn their sons with f *for* burnt offerings	784
	20: 9	*his word* was in mine heart as a burning f	784
	21:10	king of Babylon, and he shall burn it with f.	784
	21:12	lest my fury go out like f, and burn that none	784
	21:14	and I will kindle a f in the forest thereof, and	784
	22: 7	thy choice cedars, and cast *them* into the f.	784
	23:29	*Is* not my word like as a f? saith the LORD;	784
	29:22	whom the king of Babylon roasted in the f;	784
	32:29	shall come and set f on this city, and burn it	784
	32:35	their daughters to pass through *the f* unto	NIH
	34: 2	king of Babylon, and he shall burn it with f:	784
	34:22	against it, and take it, and burn it with f:	784
	36:22	*there was a f on* the hearth burning before	NIH
	36:23	cast *it* into the f that *was* on the hearth,	784
	36:23	until all the roll was consumed in the f that	784
	36:32	Jehoiakim king of Judah had burnt in the f:	784
	37: 8	this city, and take it, and burn it with f.	784
	37:10	man in his tent, and burn this city with f.	784
	38:17	and this city shall not be burnt with f;	784
	38:18	they shall burn it with f, and thou shalt not	784
	38:23	thou shalt cause this city to be burnt with f.	784
	39: 8	with f, and brake down the walls of	784
	43:12	I will kindle a f in the houses of the gods of	784
	43:13	gods of the Egyptians shall he burn with f.	784
	48:45	but a f shall come forth out of Heshbon, and	784
	49: 2	and her daughters shall be burnt with f:	784
	49:27	I will kindle a f in the wall of Damascus,	784
	50:32	I will kindle a f in his cities, and it shall	784
	51:32	the reeds they have burnt with f, and the men	784
	51:58	her high gates shall be burnt with f;	784
	51:58	and the folk in the f, and they shall be weary.	784
	52:13	the houses of the great *men,* burnt he with f:	784
La	1:13	From above hath he sent f into my bones,	784
	2: 3	and he burned against Jacob like a flaming f,	784
	2: 4	of Zion: he poured out his fury like f.	784
	4:11	hath kindled a f in Zion, and it hath	784
Eze	1: 4	a f infolding itself, and a brightness *was*	784
	1: 4	the colour of amber, out of the midst of the f.	784
	1:13	their appearance *was* like burning coals of f,	784
	1:13	the f was bright, and out of the fire went	784
	1:13	and out of the f went forth lightning.	784
	1:27	as the appearance of f round about within it,	784
	1:27	I saw as it were the appearance of f, and	784
	5: 2	Thou shalt burn with f a third *part* in	217
	5: 4	cast them into the midst of the f, and	784
	5: 4	the midst of the fire, and burn them in the f;	784
	5: 4	*for* thereof shall a f come forth into all	784
	8: 2	and lo, a likeness as the appearance of f:	784
	8: 2	appearance of his loins even downward, f;	784
	10: 2	fill thine hand *with* coals of f from between	784
	10: 6	saying, Take f from between the wheels,	784
	10: 7	unto the f that *was* between the cherubims,	784
	15: 4	Behold, it is cast into the f for fuel; the fire	784
	15: 4	the f devoureth both the ends of it, and	784
	15: 5	when the f hath devoured it, and it is	784
	15: 6	which I have given to the f for fuel, so will I	784
	15: 7	they shall go out from *one* f, and *another* fire	784
	15: 7	*one* fire, and *another* f shall devour them;	784
	16:21	cause them to pass through *the f* for them?	NIH
	16:41	And they shall burn thine houses with f, and	784
	19:12	and withered; the f consumed them.	784
	19:14	f is gone out of a rod of her branches,	784
	20:26	in that they caused to pass through *the f* all	NIH
	20:31	*ye* make your sons to pass through the f,	784
	20:47	I *will* kindle a f in thee, and it shall devour	784
	21:31	I will blow against thee in the f of my wrath,	784
	21:32	Thou shalt be for fuel to the f; thy blood	784
	22:20	to blow the f upon it, to melt *it;* so will I	784
	22:21	and blow upon you in the f of my wrath, and	784
	22:31	I have consumed them with the f of my	784
	23:25	and thy residue shall be devoured by the f.	784
	23:37	to pass for them through *the f,* to devour	NIH
	23:47	and burn up their houses with f.	784
	24: 9	I will even make the **pile for** f great.	4071
	24:10	Heap on wood, kindle the f, consume	784
	24:12	forth out of her: her scum *shall be* in the f.	784
	28:14	and down in the midst of the stones of f.	784
	28:16	from the midst of the stones of f.	784
	28:18	will I bring forth a f from the midst of thee,	784
	30: 8	when I have set a f in Egypt, and *when* all	784
	30:14	will set f in Zoan, and will execute	784
	30:16	I will set f in Egypt: Sin shall have great	784
	36: 5	Surely in the f of my jealousy have I spoken	784
	38:19	*and* in the f of my wrath have I spoken,	784
	38:22	and great hailstones, f, and brimstone.	784
	39: 6	I will send a f on Magog, and among them	784
	39: 9	shall **set on** f and burn the weapons,	1197
	39: 9	and they shall burn them with f seven years:	784
	39:10	for they shall burn the weapons with f:	784
Da	3:22	the flame of the f slew those men that took	5135
	3:24	three men bound into the midst of the f?	5135
	3:25	walking in the midst of the f, and they have	5135
	3:26	came forth of the midst of the f.	5135
	3:27	upon whose bodies the f had no power,	5135
	3:27	nor the smell of f had passed on them.	5135
	7: 9	the fiery flame, *and* his wheels *as* burning f.	5135
	10: 6	and his eyes as lamps of f, and his arms and	784
Hos	7: 6	*in* the morning it burneth as a flaming f.	784
	8:14	I will send a f upon his cities, and it shall	784
Joel	1:19	for the f hath devoured the pastures of	784
	1:20	the f hath devoured the pastures of	784
	2: 3	A f devoureth before them; and behind them	784
	2: 5	like the noise of a flame of f that devoureth	784
	2:30	the earth, blood, and f, and pillars of smoke.	784
Am	1: 4	I will send a f into the house of Hazael,	784
	1: 7	I will send a f on the wall of Gaza,	784
	1:10	I will send a f on the wall of Tyrus,	784
	1:12	I will send a f upon the Teman, which shall	784
	1:14	I will kindle a f in the wall of Rabbah, and	784
	2: 2	I will send a f upon Moab, and it shall	784
	2: 5	I will send a f upon Judah, and it shall	784
	5: 6	lest he break out like f *in* the house of	784
	7: 4	the Lord GOD called to contend by f, and	784
Ob	1:18	the house of Jacob shall be a f, and the house	784
Mic	1: 4	as wax before the f, *and* as the waters *that*	784
	1: 7	all the hires thereof shall be burnt with the f,	784
Na	1: 6	his fury is poured out like f, and the rocks	784
	3:13	thine enemies: the f shall devour thy bars.	784
	3:15	There shall the f devour thee; the sword shall	784
Hab	2:13	that the people shall labour in the very f,	784
Zep	1:18	the whole land shall be devoured by the f of	784
	3: 8	for all the earth shall be devoured with the f	784
Zec	2: 5	will be unto her a wall of f round about, and	784
	3: 2	*is* not this a brand pluckt out of the f?	784
	9: 4	in the sea; and she shall be devoured with f.	784
	11: 1	that the f may devour thy cedars.	784

Zec 12: 6 of Judah like a hearth of f among the wood, 784
12: 6 the wood, and like a torch of f in a sheaf; 784
13: 9 And I will bring the third *part* through the f, 784
Mal 1:10 do ye kindle *f on* mine altar for nought. NIH
3: 2 for he *is* like a refiner's f, and like fullers' 784
Mt 3:10 fruit is hewn down, and cast into the f. *4442*
3:11 you with the Holy Ghost, and *with* f: *4442*
3:12 will burn up the chaff with unquenchable f. *4442*
5:22 *Thou* fool, shall be in danger of hell f. *4442*
7:19 fruit is hewn down, and cast into the f. *4442*
13:40 the tares are gathered and burnt in the f; *4442*
13:42 And shall cast them into a furnace of f: *4442*
13:50 And shall cast them into the furnace of f: *4442*
17:15 for ofttimes he falleth into the f, and *4442*
18: 8 or two feet to be cast into everlasting f. *4442*
18: 9 than having two eyes to be cast into hell f. *4442*
25:41 from me, ye cursed, into everlasting f, *4442*
Mk 9:22 And ofttimes it hath cast him into the f, and *4442*
9:43 into the f that never shall be quenched: *4442*
9:44 worm dieth not, and the f is not quenched. *4442*
9:45 into the f that never shall be quenched: *4442*
9:46 worm dieth not, and the f is not quenched. *4442*
9:47 than having two eyes to be cast into hell f: *4442*
9:48 worm dieth not, and the f is not quenched. *4442*
9:49 For every one shall be salted with f, and *4442*
14:54 the servants, and warmed himself at the f. *5457*
Lk 3: 9 fruit is hewn down, and cast into the f. *4442*
3:16 you with the Holy Ghost and *with* f: *4442*
3:17 the chaff he will burn with f unquenchable. *4442*
9:54 wilt thou *that* we command f to come down *4442*
12:49 I am come to send f on the earth; and *4442*
17:29 day that Lot went out of Sodom it rained f *4442*
22:55 And when they had kindled a f in the midst *4442*
22:56 a certain maid beheld him as he sat by the f, *5457*
Jn 15: 6 and cast *them* into the f, and they are *4442*
18:18 stood *there,* who had made a **f of coals**; *439*
21: 9 they saw a **f of coals** there, and fish laid *439*
Ac 2: 3 unto them cloven tongues like as of f, *4442*
2:19 blood, and f, and vapour of smoke: *4442*
7:30 angel of the Lord in a flame of f in a bush. *4442*
28: 2 for they kindled a f, and received us every *4443*
28: 3 and laid *them* on the f, there came a viper *4443*
28: 5 And he shook off the beast into the f, and *4442*
Ro 12:20 doing thou shalt heap coals of f on his *4442*
1Co 3:13 declare *it,* because it shall be revealed by f; *4442*
3:13 the f shall try every man's work of what *4442*
3:15 he himself shall be saved; yet so as by f. *4442*
2Th 1: 8 In flaming f, taking vengeance on them that *4442*
Heb 1: 7 and his ministers a flame of f. *4442*
11:34 Quenched the violence of f, escaped *4442*
12:18 and that burned with f, nor unto blackness, *4442*
12:29 For our God *is* a consuming f. *4442*
Jas 3: 5 how great a matter a little f kindleth. *4442*
3: 6 And the tongue *is* a f, a world of iniquity: *4442*
3: 6 and **setteth on** f the course of nature; *5394*
3: 6 course of nature; and it is **set on** f of hell. *5394*
5: 3 and shall eat your flesh as *it were* f: *4442*
1Pe 1: 7 though it be tried with f, might be found *4442*
2Pe 3: 7 reserved unto f against the day of judgment *4442*
3:12 wherein the heavens being **on** f shall be *4448*
Jude 1: 7 suffering the vengeance of eternal f. *4442*
1:23 save with fear, pulling *them* out of the f; *4442*
Rev 1:14 as snow; and his eyes *were* as a flame of f; *4442*
2:18 who hath his eyes like unto a flame of f, *4442*
3:18 thee to buy of me gold tried in the f, *4442*
4: 5 *there were* seven lamps of f burning before *4442*
8: 5 and filled it with f of the altar, and cast *it* *4442*
8: 7 followed hail and f mingled with blood, *4442*
8: 8 as *it were* a great mountain burning with f *4442*
9:17 having breastplates of f, and of jacinth, and *4447*
9:17 and out of their mouths issued f and smoke *4442*
9:18 by the f, and by the smoke, and by *4442*
10: 1 *it were* the sun, and his feet as pillars of f: *4442*
11: 5 f proceedeth out of their mouth, and *4442*
13:13 that he maketh f come down from heaven *4442*
14:10 and he shall be tormented with f and *4442*
14:18 out from the altar, which had power over f; *4442*
15: 2 as *it were* a sea of glass mingled with f: *4442*
16: 8 was given unto him to scorch men with f. *4442*
17:16 and shall eat her flesh, and burn her with f. *4442*
18: 8 and she shall be utterly burnt with f: *4442*
19:12 His eyes *were* as a flame of f, and on his *4442*
19:20 *These* both were cast alive into a lake of f *4442*
20: 9 and f came down from God out of heaven, *4442*
20:10 deceived them was cast into the lake of f *4442*
20:14 and hell were cast into the lake of f. *4442*
20:15 the book of life was cast into the lake of f. *4442*
21: 8 their part in the lake which burneth with f *4442*

FIREBRAND (2) [FIRE, BRAND]

Jdg 15: 4 and put a f in the midst between two tails. 3940
Am 4:11 and ye were as a f pluckt out of the burning: 181

FIREBRANDS (3) [FIRE, BRAND]

Jdg 15: 4 took f, and turned tail to tail, and put a 3940
Pr 26:18 As a mad *man* who casteth f, arrows, and 2131
Isa 7: 4 for the two tails of these smoking f, 181

FIREPANS (4) [FIRE, PAN]

Ex 27: 3 his basons, and his fleshhooks, and his f: 4289
38: 3 the basons, *and* the fleshhooks, and the f: 4289
2Ki 25:15 the f, and the bowls, *and* such *things* as 4289
Jer 52:19 the f, and the bowls, and the caldrons, and 4289

FIRES (1) [FIRE]

Isa 24:15 Wherefore glorify ye the LORD in the f, 217

FIRKINS (1)

Jn 2: 6 the Jews, containing two or three f apiece. *3355*

FIRM (7)

Jos 3:17 f on dry *ground* in the midst of Jordan, 3559
4: 3 of the place where the priests' feet stood f, 3559
Job 41:23 they are f in themselves; they cannot be 3332
41:24 His heart is as f as a stone; yea, as hard as 3332
Ps 73: 4 bands in their death: but their strength *is* f. 1277
Da 6: 7 to **make** a f decree, that whosoever shall 8631
Heb 3: 6 and the rejoicing of the hope f unto the end. *949*

FIRMAMENT (17)

Ge 1: 6 Let there be a f in the midst of the waters, 7549
1: 7 God made the f, and divided the waters 7549
1: 7 divided the waters which *were* under the f 7549
1: 7 from the waters which *were* above the f: 7549
1: 8 God called the f Heaven. And the evening 7549
1:14 Let there be lights in the f of the heaven to 7549
1:15 let them be for lights in the f of the heaven 7549
1:17 God set them in the f of the heaven to give 7549
1:20 fly above the earth in the open f of heaven. 7549
Ps 19: 1 of God; and the f sheweth his handywork. 7549
150: 1 praise him in the f of his power. 7549
Eze 1:22 the likeness of the f upon the heads of 7549
1:23 under the f *were* their wings straight, 7549
1:25 there was a voice from the f that *was* over 7549
1:26 above the f that *was* over their heads *was* 7549
10: 1 in the f that *was* above the head of 7549
Da 12: 3 wise shall shine as the brightness of the f; 7549

FIRST (436) [FIRSTBEGOTTEN, FIRSTBORN, FIRSTFRUIT, FIRSTFRUITS, FIRSTLING, FIRSTLINGS, FIRSTRIPE]

Ge 1: 5 the evening and the morning were the f day. 259
2:11 The name of the f *is* Pison: that *is it* which 259
8: 5 in the tenth *month,* on the f *day* of 259
8:13 came to pass in the six hundredth and f year, 259
8:13 in the f *month,* the first *day* of the month, 7223
8:13 in the first *month,* the f *day* of the month, 259
13: 4 the altar, which he had made there at the f: 7223
25:25 the f came out red, all over like a hairy 7223
26: 1 besides the f famine that was in the days of 7223
28:19 name of *that* city *was called* Luz at the f. 7223
38:28 a scarlet thread, saying, This came out f. 7223
41:20 the ill favoured kine did eat up the f seven 7223
43:18 in our sacks at the f **time** *are* we brought in; 8462
43:20 we came indeed down at the f **time** to buy 8462
Ex 4: 8 neither hearken to the voice of the f sign, 7223
12: 2 it *shall be* the f month of the year to you. 7223
12: 5 be without blemish, a male of the f year: 1121
12:15 even the f day ye shall put away leaven out 7223
12:15 bread from the f day until the seventh day, 7223
12:16 in the f day *there shall be* a holy 7223
12:18 In the f *month,* on the fourteenth day of 7223
22:29 Thou shalt not delay *to offer the f of* thy NIH
23:19 The f of the firstfruits of thy land thou shalt 7225
28:17 *the f* row *shall be* a sardius, a topaz, and NIH
28:17 and a carbuncle: this *shall be* the f row. 259
29:38 two lambs of the f year day by day 1121
34: 1 thee two tables of stone like unto the f: 7223
34: 1 tables the words that were in the f tables, 7223
34: 4 hewed two tables of stone like unto the f; 7223

Ex	34:26	The f of the firstfruits of thy land thou shalt	7225
	39:10	*the f* row *was* a sardius, a topaz, and	NIH
	39:10	a topaz, and a carbuncle: *this was* the f row.	259
	40: 2	On the f day of the first month shalt thou	7223
	40: 2	On the first day of the f month shalt thou set	259
	40:17	it came to pass in the f month in the second	7223
	40:17	on the f *day* of the month, *that* the tabernacle	259
Lev	4:21	and burn him as he burned the f bullock:	7223
	5: 8	offer *that* which *is* for the sin offering f,	7223
	9: 3	a calf and a lamb, both of the f year,	1121
	9:15	and slew it, and offered it for sin, as the f.	7223
	12: 6	she shall bring a lamb of the f year for a	1121
	14:10	one ewe lamb of the f year without	1323
	23: 5	In the fourteenth *day* of the f month at even	7223
	23: 7	In the f day ye shall have a holy	7223
	23:12	f year for a burnt offering unto the LORD.	1121
	23:18	seven lambs without blemish of the f year,	1121
	23:19	two lambs of the f year for a sacrifice of	1121
	23:24	the seventh month, in the f *day* of the month,	259
	23:35	On the f day *shall be* a holy convocation:	7223
	23:39	on the f day *shall be* a sabbath, and on	7223
	23:40	ye shall take you on the f day the boughs of	7223
Nu	1: 1	on the f *day* of the second month,	259
	1:18	together on the f *day* of the second month,	259
	2: 9	their armies. *These* shall f set forth.	7223
	6:12	shall bring a lamb of the f **year** for a	1121+8141
	6:14	one he lamb of the f **year** without	1121+8141
	6:14	one ewe lamb of the f **year** without	1323+8141
	7:12	he that offered his offering the f day was	7223
	7:15	one ram, one lamb of the f **year**,	1121+8141
	7:17	he goats, five lambs of the f **year**:	1121+8141
	7:21	one ram, one lamb of the f **year**,	1121+8141
	7:23	he goats, five lambs of the f **year**:	1121+8141
	7:27	one ram, one lamb of the f **year**,	1121+8141
	7:29	he goats, five lambs of the f **year**:	1121+8141
	7:33	one ram, one lamb of the f **year**,	1121+8141
	7:35	he goats, five lambs of the f **year**:	1121+8141
	7:39	one ram, one lamb of the f **year**,	1121+8141
	7:41	he goats, five lambs of the f **year**:	1121+8141
	7:45	one ram, one lamb of the f **year**,	1121+8141
	7:47	he goats, five lambs of the f **year**:	1121+8141
	7:51	one ram, one lamb of the f **year**,	1121+8141
	7:53	he goats, five lambs of the f **year**:	1121+8141
	7:57	one ram, one lamb of the f **year**,	1121+8141
	7:59	he goats, five lambs of the f **year**:	1121+8141
	7:63	one ram, one lamb of the f **year**,	1121+8141
	7:65	he goats, five lambs of the f **year**:	1121+8141
	7:69	one ram, one lamb of the f **year**,	1121+8141
	7:71	he goats, five lambs of the f **year**:	1121+8141
	7:75	one ram, one lamb of the f **year**,	1121+8141
	7:77	he goats, five lambs of the f **year**:	1121+8141
	7:81	one ram, one lamb of the f **year**,	1121+8141
	7:83	he goats, five lambs of the f **year**:	1121+8141
	7:87	the lambs of the f **year** twelve,	1121+8141
	7:88	the lambs of the f **year** sixty.	1121+8141
	9: 1	in the f month of the second year after they	7223
	9: 5	f month at even in the wilderness of Sinai:	7223
	10:13	they f took their journey according to	7223
	10:14	In the f *place* went the standard of the camp	7223
	13:20	Now the time *was* the time of the f **ripe**	1061
	15:20	Ye shall offer up a cake *of* the f of your	7225
	15:21	Of the f of your dough ye shall give unto	7225
	15:27	he shall bring a she goat of the f year for a	1323
	18:13	*And* whatsoever is f **ripe** in the land,	1061
	20: 1	*into* the desert of Zin in the f month:	7223
	24:20	and said, Amalek *was* the f of the nations;	7225
	28: 3	two lambs of the f **year** without spot	1121+8141
	28: 9	on the sabbath day two lambs of the f year	1121
	28:11	lambs of the f **year** without spot;	1121+8141
	28:16	in the fourteenth day of the f month *is*	7223
	28:18	In the f day *shall be* a holy convocation;	7223
	28:19	and seven lambs of the f **year**:	1121+8141
	28:27	one ram, seven lambs of the f **year**;	1121+8141
	29: 1	seventh month, on the f *day* of the month,	259
	29: 2	lambs of the f **year** without blemish:	1121+8141
	29: 8	*and* seven lambs of the f **year**;	1121+8141
	29:13	*and* fourteen lambs of the f **year**;	1121+8141
	29:17	lambs of the f **year** without spot:	1121+8141
	29:20	fourteen lambs of the f **year** without	1121+8141
	29:23	fourteen lambs of the f **year** without	1121+8141
	29:26	lambs of the f **year** without spot:	1121+8141
	29:29	fourteen lambs of the f **year** without	1121+8141
	29:32	fourteen lambs of the f **year** without	1121+8141
	29:36	lambs of the f **year** without blemish:	1121+8141
	33: 3	they departed from Rameses in the f month,	7223
	33: 3	on the fifteenth day of the f month;	7223
	33:38	land of Egypt, in the f *day* of the fifth month.	259
Dt	1: 3	eleventh month, on the f *day* of the month,	259
	9:18	as at the f, forty days and forty nights:	7223
	9:25	as I fell down *at the f*; because the LORD	NIH
	10: 1	thee two tables of stone like unto the f,	7223
	10: 2	that were in the f tables which thou brakest,	7223
	10: 3	hewed two tables of stone like unto the f,	7223
	10: 4	according to the f writing, the ten	7223
	10:10	according to the f time, forty days and	7223
	11:14	the f **rain** and the latter rain, that thou	3138
	13: 9	thine hand shall be f upon him to put him to	7223
	16: 4	which thou sacrificedst the f day at even,	7223
	17: 7	The hands of the witnesses shall be f upon	7223
	18: 4	thy oil, and the f of the fleece of thy sheep,	7225
	26: 2	That thou shalt take of the f of all the fruit	7225
	33:21	he provided the f *part* for himself, because	7225
Jos	4:19	of Jordan on the tenth *day* of the f month,	7223
	8: 5	as at the f, that we will flee before them,	7223
	8: 6	will say, *They* flee before us, as at the f:	7223
	21:10	of Levi, had: for theirs was the f lot.	7223
Jdg	1: 1	shall go up for us against the Canaanites f,	8462
	18:29	the name of the city *was* Laish at the f.	7223
	20:18	Which of us shall go up f to	8462+871.1+1886.1
	20:18	Judah *shall go up* f.	8462+871.1+1886.1
	20:22	they put *themselves* in array the f day.	7223
	20:32	*are* smitten down before us, as at the f.	7223
	20:39	smitten down before us, as *in* the f battle.	7223
1Sa	14:14	*that* f slaughter, which Jonathan and	7223
	14:35	the same was the f altar that he built unto	2490
2Sa	3:13	f bring Michal Saul's daughter,	6440+3807.1
	17: 9	when *some* of them be overthrown at the f,	8462
	19:20	I am come the f *this* day of all the house of	7223
	19:43	that our advice should not be f had in	7223
	21: 9	in the f *days*, in the beginning of barley	7223
	23:19	howbeit he attained not unto the *f* three.	NIH
	23:23	the thirty, but he attained not to the *f* three.	NIH
1Ki	16:23	f year of Asa king of Judah *began* Omri to	259
	17:13	me thereof a little cake f,	7223+871.1+1886.1
	18:25	one bullock for yourselves, and dress *it* f;	7223
	20: 9	send for to thy servant at the f I will do:	7223
	20:17	of the princes of the provinces went out f;	7223
1Ch	9: 2	Now the f inhabitants that *dwelt* in their	7223
	11: 6	Whosoever smiteth the Jebusites f shall be	7223
	11: 6	So Joab the son of Zeruiah went f up, and	7223
	11:21	howbeit he attained not to the *f* three.	NIH
	11:25	the thirty, but attained not to the *f* three:	NIH
	12: 9	Ezer the f, Obadiah the second, Eliab	7218
	12:15	they that went over Jordan in the f month,	7223
	15:13	For because ye *did it* not at the f,	7223
	16: 7	on that day David delivered f *this psalm* to	7218
	23:19	Jeriah the f, Amariah the second,	7218
	23:20	Michah the f, and Jesiah the second.	7218
	24: 7	Now the f lot came forth to Jehoiarib,	7223
	24:21	of the sons of Rehabiah, the f *was* Isshiah.	7218
	24:23	the sons *of Hebron;* Jeriah *the f*, Amariah	NIH
	25: 9	Now the f lot came forth for Asaph to	7223
	27: 2	Over the f course for the first month *was*	7223
	27: 2	Over the first course for the f month *was*	7223
	27: 3	all the captains of the host for the f month.	7223
	29:29	acts of David the king, f and last, behold,	7223
2Ch	3: 3	The length *by* cubits after the f measure	7223
	9:29	the rest of the acts of Solomon, f and last,	7223
	12:15	Now the acts of Rehoboam, f and last, *are*	7223
	16:11	behold, the acts of Asa, f and last, lo,	7223
	17: 3	he walked in the f ways of his father David,	7223
	20:34	rest of the acts of Jehoshaphat, f and last,	7223
	25:26	of the acts of Amaziah, f and last, behold,	7223
	26:22	f and last, did Isaiah the prophet, the son of	7223
	28:26	and of all his ways, f and last, behold,	7223
	29: 3	He in the f year of his reign, in the first	7223
	29: 3	in the first year of his reign, in the f month,	7223
	29:17	Now they began on the f *day* of the first	259
	29:17	Now they began on the first *day* of the f	7223
	29:17	in the sixteenth day of the f month they	7223
	35: 1	on the fourteenth *day* of the f month.	7223
	35:27	his deeds, f and last, behold, they *are*	7223
	36:22	Now in the f year of Cyrus king of Persia,	259
Ezr	1: 1	Now in the f year of Cyrus king of Persia,	259
	3: 6	From the f day of the seventh month began	259
	3:12	*who were* ancient men that had seen the f	7223
	5:13	in the f year of Cyrus the king of Babylon	2298
	6: 3	In the f year of Cyrus the king *the same*	2298

Ezr	6:19	upon the fourteenth *day* of the f month.	7223
	7: 9	For upon the f *day* of the first month began	259
	7: 9	For upon the first *day* of the f month began	7223
	7: 9	on the f *day* of the fifth month came he to	259
	8:31	of Ahava on the twelfth *day* of the f month,	7223
	10:16	sat down in the f day of the tenth month to	259
	10:17	strange wives by the f day of the first month.	259
	10:17	wives by the first day of the f month.	7223
Ne	7: 5	genealogy of them which came up at the f,	7223
	8: 2	upon the f day of the seventh month.	259
	8:18	by day, from the f day unto the last day,	7223
Est	1:14	*and* which sat the f in the kingdom;)	7223
	3: 7	In the f month, that *is,* the month Nisan,	7223
	3:12	called on the thirteenth day of the f month,	7223
Job	15: 7	*Art* thou the f man *that* was born? or	7223
	42:14	he called the name of the f, Jemima; and	259
Pr	18:17	*He that is* f in his own cause *seemeth* just;	7223
Isa	1:26	And I will restore thy judges as at the f, and	7223
	9: 1	when at the f he lightly afflicted the land of	7223
	41: 4	I the LORD, the f, and with the last; I *am*	7223
	41:27	The f *shall say* to Zion, Behold,	7223
	43:27	Thy f father hath sinned, and thy teachers	7223
	44: 6	I *am* the f, and I *am* the last; and besides	7223
	48:12	I *am* he; I *am* the f, I also *am* the last.	7223
	60: 9	the ships of Tarshish f, to bring thy sons	7223
Jer	4:31	as of her that **bringeth forth** her f **child**,	1069
	7:12	where I set my name at the f, and see what	7223
	16:18	f I will recompense their iniquity and	7223
	24: 2	good figs, *even* like the figs *that are* f **ripe**:	1073
	25: 1	that *was* the f year of Nebuchadrezzar king	7224
	33: 7	to return, and will build them, as at the f.	7223
	33:11	to return the captivity of the land as at the f,	7223
	36:28	all the former words that were in the f roll,	7223
	50:17	f the king of Assyria hath devoured him;	7223
	52:31	*that* Evil-merodach king of Babylon in the *f*	NIH
Eze	10:14	the f face *was* the face of a cherub, and	259
	26: 1	the eleventh year, in the f *day* of the month,	259
	29:17	in the f *month,* in the first *day* of the month,	7223
	29:17	in the first *month,* in the f *day* of the month,	259
	30:20	in the f *month,* in the seventh *day* of	7223
	31: 1	in the third *month,* in the f *day* of the month,	259
	32: 1	the twelfth *month,* in the f *day* of the month,	259
	40:21	thereof were after the measure of the f gate:	7223
	44:30	the f of all the firstfruits of all *things,* and	7225
	44:30	ye shall also give unto the priest the f of	7225
	45:18	In the f *month,* in the first *day* of	7223
	45:18	In the first *month,* in the f *day* of the month,	259
	45:21	In the f *month,* in the fourteenth day of	7223
	46:13	*of* a lamb of the f year without blemish:	1121
Da	1:21	Daniel continued *even* unto the f year of	259
	6: 2	three presidents; of whom Daniel *was* f:	2298
	7: 1	In the f year of Belshazzar king of Babylon	2298
	7: 4	The f *was* like a lion, and had eagle's	6933
	7: 8	before whom there were three of the f	6933
	7:24	he shall be diverse from the f, and he shall	6933
	8: 1	after that which appeared unto me at the f.	8462
	8:21	horn that *is* between his eyes *is* the f king.	7223
	9: 1	In the f year of Darius the son of Ahasuerus,	259
	9: 2	In the f year of his reign I Daniel understood	259
	10: 4	the four and twentieth day of the f month,	7223
	10:12	for from the f day that thou didst set thine	7223
	11: 1	Also I in the f year of Darius the Mede,	259
Hos	2: 7	I will go and return to my f husband;	7223
	9:10	as the firstripe in the fig tree at her f **time**:	7225
Joel	2:23	and the latter rain in the f *month.*	7223
Am	6: 7	they go captive with the f that go captive,	7218
Mic	4: 8	thee shall it come, even the f dominion;	7223
Hag	1: 1	in the sixth month, in the f day of the month,	259
	2: 3	you that saw this house in her f glory?	7223
Zec	6: 2	In the f chariot *were* red horses; and in	7223
	12: 7	LORD also shall save the tents of Judah f,	7223
	14:10	gate unto the place of the f gate,	7223
Mt	5:24	f be reconciled to thy brother, and then	*4412*
	6:33	But seek ye f the kingdom of God, and	*4412*
	7: 5	f cast out the beam out of thine own eye;	*4412*
	8:21	Lord, suffer me f to go and bury my father.	*4412*
	10: 2	The f, Simon, who is called Peter, and	*4413*
	12:29	except he f bind the strong *man?* and then	*4412*
	12:45	the last *state* of that man is worse than the f.	*4413*
	13:30	Gather ye together f the tares, and	*4412*
	17:10	then say the scribes that Elias must f come?	*4412*
	17:11	Elias truly shall f come, and restore all	*4412*
	17:27	and take up the fish that f cometh up;	*4412*
	19:30	But many *that are* f shall be last; and	*4413*
	19:30	*are* first shall be last; and *the* last *shall be* f.	*4413*
	20: 8	beginning from the last unto the f.	*4413*
	20:10	But when the f came, they supposed that	*4413*
	20:16	So the last shall be f, and the first last:	*4413*
	20:16	So the last shall be first, and the f last:	*4413*
	21:28	and he came to the f, and said, Son,	*4413*
	21:31	They say unto him, The f. Jesus saith unto	*4413*
	21:36	he sent other servants moe than the f:	*4413*
	22:25	and the f, when he had married *a wife,*	*4413*
	22:38	This is the f and great commandment.	*4413*
	23:26	cleanse f that *which is* within the cup and	*4412*
	26:17	Now the f *day* of the *feast of* unleavened	*4413*
	27:64	so the last error shall be worse than the f.	*4413*
	28: 1	as it began to dawn towards the f *day* of	*1520*
Mk	3:27	except he will f bind the strong *man;* and	*4412*
	4:28	f the blade, then the ear, after that the full	*4412*
	7:27	said unto her, Let the children f be filled:	*4412*
	9:11	Why say the scribes that Elias must f	*4412*
	9:12	Elias verily cometh f, and restoreth all	*4412*
	9:35	saith unto them, If any *man* desire to be f,	*4413*
	10:31	But many *that are* f shall be last; and	*4413*
	10:31	*that are* first shall be last; and the last f.	*4413*
	12:20	and the f took a wife, and dying left no	*4413*
	12:28	Which is the f commandment of all?	*4413*
	12:29	The f of all the commandments *is,* Hear,	*4413*
	12:30	all thy strength: this *is* the f commandment.	*4413*
	13:10	And the gospel must f be published among	*4412*
	14:12	And the f day of unleavened bread,	*4413*
	16: 2	And very early in the morning the f *day* of	*1520*
	16: 9	Now when *Jesus* was risen early the f *day*	*4413*
	16: 9	he appeared f to Mary Magdalene, out of	*4412*
Lk	1: 3	understanding of all *things* **from the very** f,	*509*
	2: 2	(*And* this taxing was f made when Cyrenius	*4413*
	6: 1	to pass on the **second** sabbath **after the** f,	*1207*
	6:42	cast out f the beam out of thine own eye,	*4412*
	9:59	Lord, suffer me f to go and bury my father.	*4412*
	9:61	but let me f go bid them farewell, which are	*4412*
	10: 5	ye enter, f say, Peace *be* to this house.	*4412*
	11:26	the last *state* of that man is worse than the f.	*4413*
	11:38	that he had not f washed before dinner.	*4412*
	12: 1	he began to say unto his disciples f *of all,*	*4412*
	13:30	there are last which shall be f, and there are	*4413*
	13:30	be first, and there are f which shall be last.	*4413*
	14:18	The f said unto him, I have bought a piece	*4413*
	14:28	sitteth not down f, and counteth the cost,	*4412*
	14:31	sitteth not down f, and consulteth whether	*4412*
	16: 5	lord's debtors unto *him,* and said unto the f,	*4413*
	17:25	But f must he suffer many *things,* and	*4412*
	19:16	Then came the f, saying, Lord, thy pound	*4413*
	20:29	and the f took a wife, and died without	*4413*
	21: 9	for these *things* must f come to pass; but	*4412*
	24: 1	Now upon the f *day* of the week, very early	*1520*
Jn	1:41	He f findeth his own brother Simon, and	*4413*
	5: 4	f after the troubling of the water stepped in,	*4413*
	8: 7	sin among you, let him f cast a stone at her.	*4413*
	10:40	into the place where John **at** f baptized;	*4412*
	12:16	*things* understood not his disciples **at** the f:	*4412*
	18:13	And led him away to Annas f; for he was	*4412*
	19:32	and brake the legs of the f, and of the other	*4413*
	19:39	which at the f came to Jesus by night, and	*4412*
	20: 1	The f *day* of the week cometh Mary	*1520*
	20: 4	outrun Peter, and came f to the sepulchre.	*4413*
	20: 8	which came f to the sepulchre, and he saw,	*4413*
	20:19	day at evening, being the f *day* of the week,	*1520*
Ac	3:26	Unto you f God, having raised up his Son	*4412*
	7:12	was corn in Egypt, he sent out our fathers f.	*4412*
	11:26	the disciples were called Christians f in	*4412*
	12:10	When they were past the f and the second	*4413*
	13:24	When John had f **preached** before his	*4296*
	13:46	of God should f have been spoken to you:	*4412*
	15:14	Simeon hath declared how God at the f did	*4412*
	20: 7	And upon the f *day* of the week, when	*1520*
	20:18	from the f day that I came into Asia,	*4413*
	26: 4	which was at the f among mine own nation	*746*
	26:20	But shewed f unto them of Damascus,	*4412*
	26:23	that he *should be* the f *that* should rise from	*4413*
	27:43	swim should cast *themselves* f into the sea,	*4413*
Ro	1: 8	F, I thank my God through Jesus Christ for	*4412*
	1:16	to the Jew f, and *also* to the Greek.	*4412*
	2: 9	of the Jew f, and *also* of the Gentile;	*4412*
	2:10	to the Jew f, and *also* to the Gentile:	*4412*
	10:19	F Moses saith, I will provoke you to	*4413*
	11:35	Or who hath f **given** to him, and it shall be	*4272*
	15:24	if f I be somewhat filled with your	*4412*

1Co 11:18 For f **of all**, when ye come together in 4412
12:28 f apostles, secondarily prophets, 4412
14:30 that sitteth *by,* let the f hold his peace. 4413
15: 3 For I delivered unto you f *of all* that *1722+4413*
15:45 The f man Adam was made a living soul; 4413
15:46 Howbeit *that was* not f *which is* spiritual, 4412
15:47 The f man *is* of the earth, earthy: 4413
16: 2 Upon the f *day* of the week let every one of 1520
16: S The f *epistle* to the Corinthians was written 4413
2Co 8: 5 but f gave their own selves to the Lord, and 4412
8:12 For if there be f a willing mind, *it is* 4295
Gal 4:13 I preached the gospel unto you **at** the f. 4387
Eph 1:12 praise of his glory, who f **trusted** in Christ: 4276
4: 9 that he also descended f into the lower parts 4412
6: 2 (which is the f commandment with 4413
Php 1: 5 For your fellowship in the gospel from the f 4413
1Th 4:16 of God: and the dead in Christ shall rise f: 4412
5: S The f *epistle* unto the Thessalonians was 4413
2Th 2: 3 *come,* except there come a falling away f, 4412
1Ti 1:16 that in me f Jesus Christ might shew forth 4413
2: 1 I exhort therefore that, f of all, 4412
2:13 For Adam was f formed, then Eve. 4413
3:10 And let these also f be proved; then 4412
5: 4 let them learn f to shew piety at home, and 4412
5:12 because they have cast off *their* f faith. 4413
6: S The f to Timothy was written from 4413
2Ti 1: 5 which dwelt f in thy grandmother Lois, and 4412
2: 6 The husbandman that laboureth must be f 4413
4:16 At my f answer no *man* stood with me, but 4413
4: S ordained the f bishop of the church of 4413
Tit 3:10 A man *that is* a heretick after the f and 1520
3: S ordained the f bishop of the church of 4413
Heb 2: 3 which at the f began to be spoken by 746
4: 6 they to whom it was f preached entered not 4387
5:12 *be* the f principles of the oracles of God; 746
7: 2 f being by interpretation King of 4412
7:27 f for his own sins, *and* then for 4387
8: 7 For if that f *covenant* had been faultless, 4413
8:13 A new *covenant,* he hath made the f old. 4413
9: 1 Then verily the f *covenant* had also 4413
9: 2 the f, wherein *was* the candlestick, and 4413
9: 6 the priests went always into the f 4413
9: 8 while as the f tabernacle was yet standing: 4413
9:15 that were under the f testament, 4413
9:18 Whereupon neither the f *testament* was 4413
10: 9 He taketh away the f, that he may establish 4413
Jas 3:17 But the wisdom that is from above is f 4412
1Pe 4:17 and if *it* f *begin* at us, what *shall* the end *be* 4412
2Pe 1:20 Knowing this f, that no prophecy of 4412
3: 3 Knowing this f, that there shall come in 4412
1Jn 4:19 We love him, because he f loved us. 4413
Jude 1: 6 And the angels which kept not their f **estate**, 746
Rev 1: 5 *and* the f **begotten** of the dead, and 4416
1:11 I am Alpha and Omega, the f and the last: 4413
1:17 unto me, Fear not; I am the f and the last: 4413
2: 4 because thou hast left thy f love. 4413
2: 5 art fallen, and repent, and do the f works; 4413
2: 8 These *things* saith the f and the last, 4413
2:19 and the last *to be* more than the f. 4413
4: 1 the f voice which I heard *was* as *it were* of 4413
4: 7 And the f beast *was* like a lion, and 4413
8: 7 The f angel sounded, and there followed 4413
13:12 And he exerciseth all the power of the f 4413
13:12 them which dwell therein to worship the f 4413
16: 2 And the f went, and poured out his vial 4413
20: 5 were finished. This *is* the f resurrection. 4413
20: 6 holy *is* he that hath part in the f 4413
21: 1 for the f heaven and the first earth were 4413
21: 1 and the f earth were passed away; 4413
21:19 The f foundation *was* jasper; the second, 4413
22:13 and the end, the f and the last. 4413

FIRSTBEGOTTEN (1) [FIRST, BEGET]

Heb 1: 6 when he bringeth in the f into the world, 4416

FIRSTBORN (117) [FIRST, BEAR]

Ge 10:15 And Canaan begat Sidon his f, and Heth, 1060
19:31 the f said unto the younger, Our father *is* 1067
19:33 the f went in, and lay with her father; and 1067
19:34 that the f said unto the younger, Behold, 1067
19:37 the f bare a son, and called his name Moab: 1067
22:21 Huz his f, and Buz his brother, and Kemuel 1060
25:13 the f of Ishmael, Nebajoth; and Kedar, and 1060
27:19 Jacob said unto his father, I *am* Esau thy f; 1060
27:32 And he said, I *am* thy son, thy f Esau. 1060
29:26 to give the younger before the f. 1067
35:23 Jacob's f, and Simeon, and Levi, and 1060
36:15 the sons of Eliphaz the f *son* of Esau; 1060
38: 6 Judah took a wife for Er his f, whose name 1060
38: 7 Er, Judah's f, was wicked in the sight of 1060
41:51 Joseph called the name of the f Manasseh: 1060
43:33 the f according to his birthright, and 1060
46: 8 Jacob and his sons: Reuben, Jacob's f. 1060
48:14 hands wittingly; for Manasseh *was* the f. 1060
48:18 for this *is* the f; put thy right hand upon his 1060
49: 3 Reuben, thou *art* my f, my might, and 1060
Ex 4:22 the LORD, Israel *is* my son, *even* my f: 1060
4:23 behold, I will slay thy son, *even* thy f. 1060
6:14 The sons of Reuben the f of Israel; Hanoch, 1060
11: 5 all the f in the land of Egypt shall die, 1060
11: 5 from the f of Pharaoh that sitteth upon his 1060
11: 5 *even* unto the f of the maidservant that *is* 1060
11: 5 *is* behind the mill; and all the f of beasts. 1060
12:12 will smite all the f in the land of Egypt, 1060
12:29 that at midnight the LORD smote all the f 1060
12:29 from the f of Pharaoh that sat on his throne 1060
12:29 the f of the captive that *was* in the dungeon; 1060
12:29 *was* in the dungeon; and all the f of cattle. 1060
13: 2 Sanctify unto me all the f, 1060
13:13 all the f of man amongst thy children shalt 1060
13:15 that the LORD slew all the f in the land of 1060
13:15 both the f of man, and the firstborn of 1060
13:15 the firstborn of man, and the f of beast: 1060
13:15 but all the f of my children I redeem. 1060
22:29 the f of thy sons shalt thou give unto me. 1060
34:20 All the f of thy sons thou shalt redeem: and 1060
Nu 3: 2 Nadab the f, and Abihu, Eleazar, and 1060
3:12 f that openeth the matrix among 1060
3:13 Because all the f *are* mine; *for* on the day 1060
3:13 *for* on the day that I smote all the f in 1060
3:13 Egypt I hallowed unto me all the f in Israel, 1060
3:40 Number all the f of the males of 1060
3:41 instead of all the f among the children of 1060
3:42 all the f among the children of Israel. 1060
3:43 all the f males by the number of names, 1060
3:45 Take the Levites instead of all the f among 1060
3:46 thirteen of the f of the children of Israel, 1060
3:50 Of the f of the children of Israel took he 1060
8:16 *even instead of* the f of all the children of 1060
8:17 For all the f of the children of Israel *are* 1060
8:17 on the day that I smote every f in the land 1060
8:18 I have taken the Levites for all the f of 1060
18:15 nevertheless the f of man shalt thou surely 1060
33: 4 For the Egyptians buried all *their* f, which 1060
Dt 21:15 and *if* the f son be hers that was hated: 1060
21:16 **make** the son of the beloved f before 1069
21:16 the son of the hated, *which is indeed* the f: 1060
21:17 acknowledge the son of the hated *for* the f, 1060
21:17 of his strength; the right of the f *is* his. 1062
25: 6 *that* the f which she beareth shall succeed 1060
Jos 6:26 he shall lay the foundation thereof in his f, 1060
17: 1 for he *was* the f of Joseph; *to wit,* for 1060
17: 1 *to wit,* for Machir the f of Manasseh, 1060
Jdg 8:20 he said unto Jether his f, Up, *and* slay them. 1060
1Sa 8: 2 Now the name of his f was Joel; and 1060
14:49 *were these;* the name of the f Merab, 1067
17:13 sons that went to the battle *were* Eliab the f, 1060
2Sa 3: 2 his f was Amnon, of Ahinoam 1060
1Ki 16:34 laid the foundation thereof in Abiram his f, 1060
1Ch 1:13 And Canaan begat Zidon his f, and Heth, 1060
1:29 The f of Ishmael, Nebajoth; then Kedar, 1060
2: 3 Er, the f of Judah, was evil in the sight of 1060
2:13 Jesse begat his f Eliab, and Abinadab 1060
2:25 the sons of Jerahmeel the f of Hezron were, 1060
2:25 Ram the f, and Bunah, and Oren, and 1060
2:27 the sons of Ram the f of Jerahmeel were, 1060
2:42 the brother of Jerahmeel *were,* Mesha his f, 1060
2:50 of Caleb the son of Hur, the f of Ephratah; 1060
3: 1 the f Amnon, of Ahinoam the Jezreelitess; 1060
3:15 the sons of Josiah *were,* the f Johanan, 1060
4: 4 the f of Ephratah, the father of Beth-lehem. 1060
5: 1 Now the sons of Reuben the f of Israel, 1060
5: 1 the firstborn of Israel, (for he *was* the f; 1060
5: 3 *I say,* of Reuben the f of Israel *were,* 1060
6:28 sons of Samuel; the f Vashni, and Abiah. 1060
8: 1 Now Benjamin begat Bela his f, Ashbel 1060
8:30 his f son Abdon, and Zur, and Kish, and 1060
8:39 sons of Eshek his brother *were,* Ulam his f, 1060

1Ch 9: 5 of the Shilonites; Asaiah the f, and his sons. 1060
9:31 who *was* the f of Shallum the Korahite, 1060
9:36 his f son Abdon, then Zur, and Kish, and 1060
26: 2 sons of Meshelemiah *were,* Zechariah the f, 1060
26: 4 sons of Obed-edom *were,* Shemaiah the f, 1060
26:10 the chief, (for *though* he was not the f, 1060
2Ch 21: 3 gave he to Jehoram; because he *was* the f. 1060
Ne 10:36 Also the f of our sons, and of our cattle, 1060
Job 18:13 *even* the f of death shall devour his 1060
Ps 78:51 smote all the f in Egypt; the chief of *their* 1060
89:27 Also I will make him *my* f, higher than 1060
105:36 He smote also all the f in their land, 1060
135: 8 Who smote the f of Egypt, both of man and 1060
136:10 To him that smote Egypt in their f: for his 1060
Isa 14:30 the f of the poor shall feed, and the needy 1060
Jer 31: 9 I am a father to Israel, and Ephraim *is* my f. 1060
Mic 6: 7 shall I give my f *for* my transgression, 1060
Zec 12:10 for him, as one that is in bitterness for *his* f. 1060
Mt 1:25 her not till she had brought forth her f son: *4416*
Lk 2: 7 And she brought forth her f son, and *4416*
Ro 8:29 that he might be the f amongst many *4416*
Col 1:15 of the invisible God, the f of every creature: *4416*
1:18 who is the beginning, the f from the dead; *4416*
Heb 11:28 lest he that destroyed the f should touch *4416*
12:23 the general assembly, and church of the f, *4416*

FIRSTFRUIT (2) [FIRST, FRUIT]
Dt 18: 4 The f *also* of thy corn, of thy wine, and 7225
Ro 11:16 For if the f *be* holy, the lump *is* also *holy:* *536*

FIRSTFRUITS (32) [FIRST, FRUIT]
Ex 23:16 the feast of harvest, the f of thy labours, 1061
23:19 The first of the f of thy land thou shalt 1061
34:22 of the f of wheat harvest, and the feast of 1061
34:26 The first of the f of thy land thou shalt 1061
Lev 2:12 *As for* the oblation of the f, ye shall offer 7225
2:14 if thou offer a meat offering of *thy* f unto 1061
2:14 of thy f green ears of corn dried by the fire, 1061
23:10 ye shall bring a sheaf of the f of your 7225
23:17 *they are* the f unto the LORD. 1061
23:20 f *for* a wave offering before the LORD, 1061
Nu 18:12 the f of them which they shall offer unto 7225
28:26 Also in the day of the f, when ye bring a 1061
Dt 26:10 I have brought the f of the land, 6529+7225
2Ki 4:42 brought the man of God bread of the f, 1061
2Ch 31: 5 Israel brought in abundance the f of corn, 7225
Ne 10:35 to bring the f of our ground, and 1061
10:35 the f of all fruit of all trees, year by year, 1061
10:37 *that* we should bring the f of our dough, 7225
12:44 the offerings, for the f, and for the tithes, 7225
13:31 at times appointed, and for the f. 1061
Pr 3: 9 and with the f of all thine increase: 7225
Jer 2: 3 unto the LORD, *and* the f of his increase: 7225
Eze 20:40 the f of your oblations, with all your holy 7225
44:30 the first of all the f of all *things,* and 1061
48:14 nor alienate the f of the land: 7225
Ro 8:23 ourselves also, which have the f of the Spirit, *536*
16: 5 who is the f of Achaia unto Christ. *536*
1Co 15:20 *and* become the f of them that slept. *536*
15:23 Christ the f; afterward they that are Christ's *536*
16:15 that it is the f of Achaia, and *that* they have *536*
Jas 1:18 that we should be a kind of f of his creatures. *536*
Rev 14: 4 *being* the f unto God and to the Lamb. *536*

FIRSTLING (14) [FIRST]
Ex 13:12 every f that cometh of a beast which thou 6363
13:13 every f of an ass thou shalt redeem with a 6363
34:19 every f amongst thy cattle, *whether* ox or 6363
34:20 the f of an ass thou shalt redeem with a 6363
Lev 27:26 Only the f of the beasts, which should be 1060
27:26 which should be the LORD'S f, no man 1069
Nu 18:15 the f of unclean beasts shalt thou redeem. 1060
18:17 the f of a cow, or the firstling of a sheep, 1060
18:17 or the f of a sheep, or the firstling of a goat, 1060
18:17 or the f of a goat, thou shalt not redeem; 1060
Dt 15:19 All the f males that come of thy herd and 1060
15:19 thou shalt do no work with the f of thy 1060
15:19 of thy bullock, nor shear the f of thy sheep. 1060
33:17 His glory *is like* the f of his bullock, and 1060

FIRSTLINGS (6) [FIRST]
Ge 4: 4 he also brought of the f of his flock and 1062
Nu 3:41 the cattle of the Levites instead of all the f 1060
Dt 12: 6 and the f of your herds and of your flocks: 1062
12:17 thy oil, or the f of thy herds or of thy flock, 1062
14:23 and the f of thy herds and of thy flocks; 1062
Ne 10:36 and the f of our herds and of our flocks, 1062

FIRSTRIPE (3) [FIRST, RIPE]
Hos 9:10 I saw your fathers as the f in the fig tree at 1063
Mic 7: 1 cluster to eat: my soul desired the f **fruit**. 1063
Na 3:12 holds *shall be like* fig trees with the f **figs**: 1061

FISH (35) [FISH'S, FISHER'S, FISHERMEN, FISHERS, FISHES, FISHHOOKS, FISHING, FISHPOOLS]
Ge 1:26 let them have dominion over the f of 1710
1:28 have dominion over the f of the sea, and 1710
Ex 7:18 the f that *is* in the river shall die, and 1710
7:21 the f that *was* in the river died; and the river 1710
Nu 11: 5 We remember the f, which we did eat in 1710
11:22 shall all the f of the sea be gathered 1709
Dt 4:18 the likeness of any f that *is* in the waters 1710
2Ch 33:14 even to the entering in at the f gate, and 1709
Ne 3: 3 the f gate did the sons of Hassenaah build, 1709
12:39 above the f gate, and the tower of 1709
13:16 which brought f, and all *manner of* ware, 1709
Job 41: 7 barbed irons? or his head with f spears? 1709
Ps 8: 8 the f of the sea, *and whatsoever* passeth 1709
105:29 their waters into blood, and slew their f. 1710
Isa 19:10 all that make sluces *and* ponds for f. 5315
50: 2 their f stinketh, because *there is* no water, 1710
Jer 16:16 saith the LORD, and they shall f them; 1770
Eze 29: 4 I will cause the f of thy rivers to stick unto 1710
29: 4 all the f of thy rivers shall stick unto thy 1710
29: 5 thee and all the f of thy rivers: 1710
47: 9 there shall be a very great multitude of f, 1710
47:10 their f shall be according to their kinds, 1710
47:10 as the f of the great sea, exceeding many. 1710
Jnh 1:17 Now the LORD had prepared a great f to 1709
1:17 Jonah was in the belly of the f three days 1709
2:10 the LORD spake unto the f, and 1709
Zep 1:10 *shall be* the noise of a cry from the f gate, 1709
Mt 7:10 Or if he ask a f, will he give him a serpent? *2486*
17:27 and take up the f that first cometh up; *2486*
Lk 11:11 or if *he ask* a f, will he for a fish give him a *2486*
11:11 a fish, will he for a f give him a serpent? *2486*
24:42 And they gave him a piece of a broiled f, *2486*
Jn 21: 9 of coals there, and f laid thereon, and bread. *3795*
21:10 Bring of the f which ye have now caught. *3795*
21:13 and giveth them, and f likewise. *3795*

FISH'S (1) [FISH]
Jnh 2: 1 unto the LORD his God out of the f belly, 1710

FISHER'S (1) [FISH]
Jn 21: 7 he girt *his* f **coat** unto him, (for he was *1903*

FISHERMEN (1) [FISH, MAN]
Lk 5: 2 but the f were gone out of them, and *231*

FISHERS (7) [FISH]
Isa 19: 8 The f also shall mourn, and all they that 1771
Jer 16:16 Behold, I will send for many f, saith 1771
Eze 47:10 *that* the f shall stand upon it from En-gedi 1728
Mt 4:18 casting a net into the sea: for they were f. *231*
4:19 Follow me, and I will make you f of men. *231*
Mk 1:16 casting a net into the sea: for they were f. *231*
1:17 and I will make you to become f of men. *231*

FISHES (27) [FISH]
Ge 9: 2 *upon* the earth, and upon all the f of the sea; 1709
1Ki 4:33 of fowl, and of creeping things, and of f. 1709
Job 12: 8 and the f of the sea shall declare unto thee. 1709
Ecc 9:12 as the f that are taken in an evil net, and 1709
Eze 38:20 So that the f of the sea, and the fowls of 1709
Hos 4: 3 the f of the sea also shall be taken away. 1709
Hab 1:14 makest men as the f of the sea, as 1709
Zep 1: 3 the f of the sea, and the stumblingblocks 1709
Mt 14:17 We have here but five loaves, and two f. *2486*
14:19 and the two f, and looking up to heaven, *2486*
15:34 And they said, Seven, and a few **little** f. *2485*
15:36 And he took the seven loaves and the f, and *2486*
Mk 6:38 when they knew, they say, Five, and two f. *2486*
6:41 he had taken the five loaves and the two f, *2486*
6:41 and the two f divided he among *them* all. *2486*
6:43 baskets full of the fragments, and of the f. *2486*
8: 7 And they had a few **small** f: and he blessed, *2485*
Lk 5: 6 they inclosed a great multitude of f: *2486*
5: 9 at the draught of the f which they had *2486*

Lk 9:13 We have no more but five loaves and two f; *2486*
9:16 Then he took the five loaves and the two f, *2486*
Jn 6: 9 hath five barley loaves, and two **small** f: *3795*
6:11 likewise of the f as much as they would. *3795*
21: 6 not able to draw it for the multitude of f. *2486*
21: 8 hundred cubits,) dragging the net with f. *2486*
21:11 and drew the net to land full of great f, *2486*
1Co 15:39 of beasts, another of f, *and* another of birds. *2486*

FISHHOOKS (1) [FISH, HOOK]
Am 4: 2 and your posterity with f. 1729+5518

FISHING (1) [FISH]
Jn 21: 3 Simon Peter saith unto them, I go a f. *232*

FISHPOOLS (1) [FISH, POOL]
SS 7: 4 thine eyes *like* the f in Heshbon, 1295

FIST (2)
Ex 21:18 or with *his* f, and he die not, but keepeth *his* 106
Isa 58: 4 and to smite with the f of wickedness: 106

FISTS (1) [HOOK]
Pr 30: 4 who hath gathered the wind in his f? 2651

FIT (9) [FITLY, FITTED, FITTETH]
Lev 16:21 shall send *him* away by the hand of a f man 6261
1Ch 7:11 two hundred *soldiers, f* to go out *for* war NIH
12: 8 *and* men of war *f* for the battle, that could NIH
Job 34:18 *Is it f* to say to a king, *Thou art* wicked? *and* NIH
Pr 24:27 and **make** it f for thyself in the field; 6257
Lk 9:62 looking back, is f for the kingdom of God. *2111*
14:35 It is neither f for the land, nor yet for *2111*
Ac 22:22 the earth: for it is not f that he should live. *2520*
Col 3:18 your own husbands, as it is f in the Lord. *433*

FITCHES (4)
Isa 28:25 doth he not cast abroad the f, and 7100
28:27 For the f are not threshed with a threshing 7100
28:27 the f are beaten out with a staff, and 7100
Eze 4: 9 f, and put them in one vessel, and 3698

FITLY (4) [FIT]
Pr 25:11 A word f spoken *is like* apples of gold 212+5921
SS 5:12 of waters, washed with milk, *and* f set. 4402
Eph 2:21 f **framed together** groweth unto a holy *4883*
4:16 whom the whole body f **joined together** *4883*

FITTED (3) [FIT]
1Ki 6:35 covered *them* with gold f upon the carved 3474
Pr 22:18 they shall withal be f in thy lips. 3559
Ro 9:22 *the* vessels of wrath f to destruction: *2675*

FITTETH (1) [FIT]
Isa 44:13 he f it with planes, and he marketh it out 6213

FITTING See SEEMLY

FIVE (345) [FIFTH]
Ge 5: 6 Seth lived an hundred and f years, and 2568
5:11 of Enos were nine hundred and f years: 2568
5:15 Mahalaleel lived sixty and f years, 2568
5:17 were eight hundred ninety and f years: 2568
5:21 Enoch lived sixty and f years, and 2568
5:23 were three hundred sixty and f years: 2568
5:30 Lamech lived after he begat Noah f 2568
5:30 begat Noah five hundred ninety and f years, 2568
5:32 Noah was f hundred years old: and 2568
11:11 Shem lived after he begat Arphaxad f 2568
11:12 Arphaxad lived f and thirty years, and 2568
11:32 of Terah were two hundred and f years: 2568
12: 4 f years old when he departed out of Haran. 2568
14: 9 Arioch king of Ellasar; four kings with f. 2568
18:28 Peradventure there shall lack f of the fifty 2568
18:28 wilt thou destroy all the city for *lack of* f? 2568
18:28 he said, If I find there forty and f, I will not 2568
43:34 Benjamin's mess was f times so much as 2568
45: 6 yet *there are* f years, *in* the which *there* 2568
45:11 for yet *there are* f years of famine; 2568
45:22 *pieces* of silver, and f changes of raiment. 2568
47: 2 *even* f men, and presented them unto 2568
Ex 22: 1 he shall restore f oxen for an ox, and 2568
26: 3 The f curtains shall be coupled together one 2568
26: 3 *other* f curtains *shall be* coupled one to 2568
26: 9 thou shalt couple f curtains by themselves, 2568
26:26 f for the boards of the one side of 2568
26:27 f bars for the boards of the other side of 2568
26:27 f bars for the boards of the side of 2568
26:37 thou shalt make for the hanging f pillars of 2568
26:37 thou shalt cast f sockets of brass for them. 2568
27: 1 f cubits long, and five cubits broad; 2568
27: 1 five cubits long, and f cubits broad; 2568
27:18 the height f cubits *of* fine twined linen, and 2568
30:23 of pure myrrh f hundred *shekels,* and 2568
30:24 of cassia f hundred *shekels,* after the shekel 2568
36:10 he coupled the f curtains one unto another: 2568
36:10 *the other* f curtains he coupled one unto 2568
36:16 he coupled f curtains by themselves, and 2568
36:31 f for the boards of the one side of 2568
36:32 f bars for the boards of the other side of 2568
36:32 f bars for the boards of the tabernacle for 2568
36:38 the f pillars of it with their hooks: and 2568
36:38 with gold: but their f sockets *were of* brass. 2568
38: 1 f cubits *was* the length thereof, and 2568
38: 1 and f cubits the breadth thereof; 2568
38:18 and the height in the breadth *was* f cubits, 2568
38:26 and f hundred and fifty *men.* 2568
38:28 and f *shekels* he made hooks for the pillars, 2568
Lev 26: 8 f of you shall chase an hundred, and 2568
27: 5 if *it be* from f years old even unto twenty 2568
27: 6 if *it be* from a month old even unto f years 2568
27: 6 thy estimation shall be of the male f shekels 2568
Nu 1:21 *were* forty and six thousand and f hundred. 2568
1:25 and f thousand six hundred and fifty. 2568
1:33 *were* forty thousand and f hundred. 2568
1:37 *were* thirty and f thousand and 2568
1:41 *were* forty and one thousand and f hundred. 2568
1:46 and three thousand and f hundred and fifty. 2568
2:11 *were* forty and six thousand and f hundred. 2568
2:15 *were* forty and f thousand and six hundred 2568
2:19 *were* forty thousand and f hundred. 2568
2:23 *were* thirty and f thousand and 2568
2:28 *were* forty and one thousand and f hundred. 2568
2:32 and three thousand and f hundred and fifty. 2568
3:22 them *were* seven thousand and f hundred. 2568
3:47 Thou shalt even take f shekels **apiece** 2568+2568
3:50 f *shekels,* after the shekel of the sanctuary: 2568
4:48 and f hundred and fourscore. 2568
7:17 two oxen, f rams, five he goats, five lambs 2568
7:17 two oxen, five rams, f he goats, five lambs 2568
7:17 five he goats, f lambs of the first year: 2568
7:23 two oxen, f rams, five he goats, five lambs 2568
7:23 two oxen, five rams, f he goats, five lambs 2568
7:23 five he goats, f lambs of the first year: 2568
7:29 two oxen, f rams, five he goats, five lambs 2568
7:29 two oxen, five rams, f he goats, five lambs 2568
7:29 five he goats, f lambs of the first year: 2568
7:35 two oxen, f rams, five he goats, five lambs 2568
7:35 two oxen, five rams, f he goats, five lambs 2568
7:35 five he goats, f lambs of the first year: 2568
7:41 two oxen, f rams, five he goats, five lambs 2568
7:41 two oxen, five rams, f he goats, five lambs 2568
7:41 five he goats, f lambs of the first year: 2568
7:47 two oxen, f rams, five he goats, five lambs 2568
7:47 two oxen, five rams, f he goats, five lambs 2568
7:47 five he goats, f lambs of the first year: 2568
7:53 two oxen, f rams, five he goats, five lambs 2568
7:53 two oxen, five rams, f he goats, five lambs 2568
7:53 five he goats, f lambs of the first year: 2568
7:59 two oxen, f rams, five he goats, five lambs 2568
7:59 two oxen, five rams, f he goats, five lambs 2568
7:59 five he goats, f lambs of the first year: 2568
7:65 two oxen, f rams, five he goats, five lambs 2568
7:65 two oxen, five rams, f he goats, five lambs 2568
7:65 five he goats, f lambs of the first year: 2568
7:71 two oxen, f rams, five he goats, five lambs 2568
7:71 two oxen, five rams, f he goats, five lambs 2568
7:71 five he goats, f lambs of the first year: 2568
7:77 two oxen, f rams, five he goats, five lambs 2568
7:77 two oxen, five rams, f he goats, five lambs 2568
7:77 five he goats, f lambs of the first year: 2568
7:83 two oxen, f rams, five he goats, five lambs 2568
7:83 two oxen, five rams, f he goats, five lambs 2568
7:83 five he goats, f lambs of the first year: 2568
8:24 from twenty and f years old and 2568
11:19 nor two days, nor f days, neither ten days, 2568
18:16 *for* the money of f shekels, 2568
26:18 of them, forty thousand and f hundred. 2568
26:22 and sixteen thousand and f hundred. 2568
26:27 threescore thousand and f hundred. 2568

Nu	26:37	thirty and two thousand and f hundred.	2568
	26:41	*were* forty and f thousand and six hundred.	2568
	26:50	and f thousand and four hundred.	2568
	31: 8	and Hur, and Reba, f kings of Midian:	2568
	31:28	one soul of f hundred, *both* of the persons,	2568
	31:32	and seventy thousand and f thousand sheep,	2568
	31:36	and thirty thousand and f hundred sheep:	2568
	31:39	asses *were* thirty thousand and f hundred;	2568
	31:43	*and* seven thousand and f hundred sheep,	2568
	31:45	And thirty thousand asses and f hundred,	2568
Jos	8:12	he took about f thousand men, and set them	2568
	10: 5	Therefore the f kings of the Amorites,	2568
	10:16	these f kings fled, and hid themselves in a	2568
	10:17	The f kings are found hid in a cave at	2568
	10:22	bring out those f kings unto me out of	2568
	10:23	brought forth those f kings unto him out of	2568
	10:26	and slew them, and hanged them on f trees:	2568
	13: 3	f lords of the Philistines; the Gazathites,	2568
	14:10	me alive, as he said, these forty and f years,	2568
	14:10	I *am this* day fourscore and f years old.	2568
Jdg	3: 3	*Namely,* f lords of the Philistines, and	2568
	18: 2	the children of Dan sent of their family f	2568
	18: 7	the f men departed, and came to Laish,	2568
	18:14	answered the f men that went to spy out	2568
	18:17	the f men that went to spy out the land went	2568
	20:35	and f thousand and an hundred men:	2568
	20:45	they gleaned of them in the highways f	2568
	20:46	and f thousand men that drew the sword;	2568
1Sa	6: 4	F golden emerods, and five golden mice,	2568
	6: 4	Five golden emerods, and f golden mice,	2568
	6:16	when the f lords of the Philistines had seen	2568
	6:18	of the Philistines *belonging* to the f lords,	2568
	17: 5	the weight of the coat *was* f thousand	2568
	17:40	chose him f smooth stones out of the brook,	2568
	21: 3	give *me* f *loaves of* bread in mine hand, or	2568
	22:18	and f persons that did wear a linen ephod.	2568
	25:18	f sheep ready dressed, and five measures of	2568
	25:18	f measures of parched *corn,* and an hundred	2568
	25:42	with f damsels of hers that went after her;	2568
2Sa	4: 4	was f years old when the tidings came of	2568
	21: 8	the f sons of Michal the daughter of Saul,	2568
	24: 9	the men of Judah *were* f hundred thousand	2568
1Ki	4:32	and his songs were a thousand and f.	2568
	6: 6	The nethermost chamber *was* f cubits	2568
	6:10	against all the house, f cubits high:	2568
	6:24	f cubits *was* the one wing of the cherub,	2568
	6:24	and f cubits the other wing of the cherub:	2568
	7: 3	that *lay* on forty f pillars, fifteen *in* a row.	2568
	7:16	the height of the one chapiter *was* f cubits,	2568
	7:16	the height of the other chapiter *was* f	2568
	7:23	round all about, and his height *was* f cubits:	2568
	7:39	he put f bases on the right side of the house,	2568
	7:39	and f on the left side of the house:	2568
	7:49	f on the right side, and five on the left,	2568
	7:49	f on the left, before the oracle, with	2568
	9:23	f hundred and fifty, which bare rule over	2568
	22:42	and f years old when he *began* to reign;	2568
	22:42	he reigned twenty and f years in Jerusalem.	2568
2Ki	6:25	the fourth part of a kab of dove's dung for f	2568
	7:13	I pray thee, f of the horses that remain,	2568
	13:19	*Thou* shouldest have smitten f or six times;	2568
	14: 2	and f years old when he *began* to reign,	2568
	15:33	F and twenty years old was he when he	2568
	18: 2	f years old was he when he *began* to reign;	2568
	19:35	an hundred fourscore and f thousand:	2568
	21: 1	and reigned fifty and f years in Jerusalem.	2568
	23:36	and f year old when he *began* to reign;	2568
	25:19	f men of them that were in the king's	2568
1Ch	2: 4	and Zerah. All the sons of Judah *were* f.	2568
	2: 6	and Calcol, and Dara: f of them in all.	2568
	3:20	Berechiah, and Hasadiah, Jushabhesed, f.	2568
	4:32	Rimmon, and Tochen, and Ashan, f cities:	2568
	4:42	f hundred men, went to mount Seir,	2568
	7: 3	Michael, and Obadiah, and Joel, Ishiah, f:	2568
	7: 7	Uzzi, and Uzziel, and Jerimoth, and Iri, f;	2568
	11:23	f cubits *high;* and in the Egyptian's hand	2568
	29: 7	the house of God *of* gold f thousand talents	2568
2Ch	3:11	*one* wing of the one *cherub was* f cubits,	2568
	3:11	the other wing *was likewise* f cubits,	2568
	3:12	*one* wing of the other cherub *was* f cubits,	2568
	3:12	the other wing *was* f cubits *also,* joining to	2568
	3:15	house two pillars of thirty and f cubits high,	2568
	3:15	*was* on the top *of each* of them *was* f cubits.	2568
	4: 2	in compass, and f cubits the height thereof;	2568
	4: 6	put f on the right hand, and five on the left,	2568
	4: 6	and f on the left, to wash in them:	2568
	4: 7	f on the right hand, and five on the left.	2568
	4: 7	five on the right hand, and f on the left.	2568
	4: 8	f on the right side, and five on the left.	2568
	4: 8	five on the right side, and f on the left.	2568
	6:13	of f cubits long, and five cubits broad,	2568
	6:13	f cubits broad, and three cubits high,	2568
	13:17	there fell down slain of Israel f hundred	2568
	15:19	there was no *more* war unto the f and	2568
	20:31	and f years old when he *began* to reign,	2568
	20:31	he reigned twenty and f years in Jerusalem.	2568
	25: 1	and f years old *when* he *began* to reign,	2568
	26:13	and seven thousand and f hundred,	2568
	27: 1	and f years old when he *began* to reign,	2568
	27: 8	He was f and twenty years old when he	2568
	29: 1	Hezekiah *began* to reign *when he was* f and	2568
	33: 1	he reigned fifty and f years in Jerusalem:	2568
	35: 9	passover *offerings* f thousand *small cattle,*	2568
	35: 9	thousand *small cattle,* and f hundred oxen.	2568
	36: 5	and f years old when he *began* to reign,	2568
Ezr	1:11	of silver *were* f thousand and four hundred.	2568
	2: 5	of Arah, seven hundred seventy and f.	2568
	2: 8	children of Zattu, nine hundred forty and f.	2568
	2:20	The children of Gibbar, ninety and f.	2568
	2:33	and Ono, seven hundred twenty and f.	2568
	2:34	of Jericho, three hundred forty and f.	2568
	2:66	six; their mules, two hundred forty and f;	2568
	2:67	Their camels, four hundred thirty and f;	2568
	2:69	f thousand pound *of* silver, and	2568
Ne	7:13	children of Zattu, eight hundred forty and f.	2568
	7:20	children of Adin, six hundred fifty and f.	2568
	7:25	The children of Gibeon, ninety and f.	2568
	7:36	of Jericho, three hundred forty and f.	2568
	7:67	and f singing *men* and singing *women.*	2568
	7:68	six: their mules, two hundred forty and f:	2568
	7:69	*Their* camels, four hundred thirty and f:	2568
	7:70	f hundred and thirty priests' garments.	2568
Est	9: 6	Jews slew and destroyed f hundred men.	2568
	9:12	destroyed f hundred men in Shushan	2568
	9:16	slew of their foes seventy and f thousand,	2568
Job	1: 3	f hundred yoke of oxen, and five hundred	2568
	1: 3	f hundred she asses, and a very great	2568
Isa	7: 8	and f years shall Ephraim be broken,	2568
	17: 6	f in the outmost fruitful branches thereof,	2568
	19:18	In that day shall f cities in the land of Egypt	2568
	30:17	of one; at the rebuke of f shall ye flee:	2568
	37:36	an hundred and fourscore and f thousand:	2568
Jer	52:22	the height of one chapiter *was* f cubits,	2568
	52:30	the Jews seven hundred forty and f persons:	2568
	52:31	in the f and twentieth *day* of the month,	2568
Eze	8:16	and the altar, *were* about f and twenty men,	2568
	11: 1	behold at the door of the gate f and	2568
	40: 1	In the f and twentieth year of our captivity,	2568
	40: 7	between the little chambers *were* f cubits;	2568
	40:13	the breadth *was* f and twenty cubits,	2568
	40:21	and the breadth f and twenty cubits.	2568
	40:25	and the breadth f and twenty cubits.	2568
	40:29	cubits long, and f and twenty cubits broad.	2568
	40:30	the arches round about *were* f and	2568
	40:30	and twenty cubits long, and f cubits broad.	2568
	40:33	cubits long, and f and twenty cubits broad.	2568
	40:36	and the breadth f and twenty cubits.	2568
	40:48	f cubits on this side, and five cubits on that	2568
	40:48	cubits on this side, and f cubits on that side:	2568
	41: 2	the sides of the door *were* f cubits on	2568
	41: 2	the one side, and f cubits on the other side:	2568
	41: 9	for the side chamber without, *was* f cubits:	2568
	41:11	the breadth of the place that was left *was* f	2568
	41:12	the wall of the building *was* f cubits thick	2568
	42:16	f hundred reeds, with the measuring reed	2568
	42:17	measured the north side, f hundred reeds,	2568
	42:18	f hundred reeds, with the measuring reed.	2568
	42:19	measured f hundred reeds with	2568
	42:20	f hundred *reeds* long, and five hundred	2568
	42:20	hundred *reeds* long, and f hundred broad,	2568
	45: 1	the length *shall be* the length *of* f and	2568
	45: 2	Of this there shall be for the sanctuary f	2568
	45: 2	f hundred *in breadth,* square round about;	2568
	45: 3	measure shalt thou measure the length of f	2568
	45: 5	*the* f and twenty thousand of length, and	2568
	45: 6	ye shall appoint the possession of the city f	2568
	45: 6	and f and twenty thousand long,	2568
	45:12	f and twenty shekels, fifteen shekels,	2568

Eze 48: 8 be the offering which ye shall offer *of* f 2568
48: 9 ye shall offer unto the LORD *shall be of* f 2568
48:10 toward the north f and twenty thousand *in* 2568
48:10 toward the south f and twenty thousand *in* 2568
48:13 the Levites *shall have* f and 2568
48:13 all the length *shall be* f and 2568
48:15 the f thousand, that are left in the breadth 2568
48:15 that are left in the breadth over against the f 2568
48:16 the north side four thousand and f hundred, 2568
48:16 the south side four thousand and f hundred, 2568
48:16 the east side four thousand and f hundred, 2568
48:16 the west side four thousand and f hundred. 2568
48:20 All the oblation *shall be* f and 2568
48:20 twenty thousand by f and twenty thousand: 2568
48:21 over against the f and twenty thousand of 2568
48:21 westward over against the f and 2568
48:30 four thousand and f hundred measures. 2568
48:32 the east side four thousand and f hundred: 2568
48:33 side four thousand and f hundred measures: 2568
48:34 the west side four thousand and f hundred, 2568
Da 12:12 three hundred *and* f and thirty days. 2568
Mt 14:17 We have here but f loaves, and two fishes. *4002*
14:19 and took the f loaves, and the two fishes, *4002*
14:21 that had eaten were about f **thousand** men, *4000*
16: 9 neither remember the f loaves of the five *4002*
16: 9 the five loaves of the f **thousand**, *4000*
25: 2 And f of them were wise, and five *were* *4002*
25: 2 five of them were wise, and f *were* foolish. *4002*
25:15 And unto one he gave f talents, to another *4002*
25:16 Then he that had received the f talents *4002*
25:16 the same, and made *them* other f talents. *4002*
25:20 *so* he that had received f talents came and *4002*
25:20 talents came and brought other f talents, *4002*
25:20 Lord, thou deliveredst unto me f talents: *4002*
25:20 I have gained besides them f talents moe. *4002*
Mk 6:38 they knew, they say, F, and two fishes. *4002*
6:41 And when he had taken the f loaves and *4002*
6:44 *of* the loaves were about f **thousand** men. *4000*
8:19 When I brake the f loaves among five *4002*
8:19 I brake the five loaves among f **thousand**, *4000*
Lk 1:24 and hid herself f months, saying, *4002*
7:41 the one ought f **hundred** pence, and *4001*
9:13 have no more but f loaves and two fishes; *4002*
9:14 For they were about f **thousand** men. *4000*
9:16 Then he took the f loaves and the two *4002*
12: 6 Are not f sparrows sold for two farthings, *4002*
12:52 For from henceforth there shall be f in one *4002*
14:19 I have bought f yoke of oxen, and I go to *4002*
16:28 For I have f brethren; that he may testify *4002*
19:18 Lord, thy pound hath gained f pounds. *4002*
19:19 likewise to him, Be thou also over f cities. *4002*
Jn 4:18 For thou hast had f husbands; and he whom *4002*
5: 2 Hebrew tongue Bethesda, having f porches. *4002*
6: 9 which hath f barley loaves, and two small *4002*
6:10 sat down, *in* number about f **thousand**. *4000*
6:13 with the fragments of the f barley loaves, *4002*
6:19 So when they had rowed about f and *4002*
Ac 4: 4 the number of the men was about f *4002*
20: 6 and came unto them to Troas in f days; *4002*
24: 1 And after f days Ananias the high priest *4002*
1Co 14:19 Yet in the church I had rather speak f words *4002*
15: 6 he was seen of above f **hundred** brethren at *4001*
2Co 11:24 Of the Jews f **times** received I forty *stripes* *3999*
Rev 9: 5 but that they should be tormented f months: *4002*
9:10 and their power *was* to hurt men f months. *4002*
17:10 f are fallen, and one is, *and* the other is not *4002*

FIXED (5)
Ps 57: 7 My heart is f, O God, my heart is fixed: 3559
57: 7 My heart is fixed, O God, my heart is f: 3559
108: 1 O God, my heart is f; I will sing and 3559
112: 7 his heart is f, trusting in the LORD. 3559
Lk 16:26 between us and you there is a great gulf f: *4741*

FLAG (1) [FLAGS]
Job 8:11 without mire? can the f grow without water? 260

FLAGON (2) [FLAGONS]
2Sa 6:19 a f *of wine*. So all the people departed every 809
1Ch 16: 3 and a good piece *of flesh*, and a f *of wine*. 809

FLAGONS (3) [FLAGON]
SS 2: 5 Stay me with f, comfort me with apples: 809
Isa 22:24 vessels of cups, even to all the vessels of f. 5035
Hos 3: 1 who look to other gods, and love f of wine. 809

FLAGS (3) [FLAG]
Ex 2: 3 she laid *it* in the f by the river's brink. 5488
2: 5 when she saw the ark among the f, she sent 5488
Isa 19: 6 and dried up: the reeds and f shall wither. 5488

FLAGSTAFF See BEACON

FLAKES (1)
Job 41:23 The f of his flesh are joined together: 4651

FLAME (34) [FLAMES, FLAMING]
Ex 3: 2 him in a f of fire out of the midst of a bush: 3827
Nu 21:28 out of Heshbon, a f from the city of Sihon: 3852
Jdg 13:20 when the f went up toward heaven from off 3851
13:20 the LORD ascended in the f of the altar. 3851
20:38 that they should make a great f with smoke 4864
20:40 when the f began to arise up out of the city 4864
20:40 the f of the city ascended up to heaven. 3632
Job 15:30 the f shall dry up his branches, and by 7957
41:21 and a f goeth out of his mouth. 3851
Ps 83:14 and as the f setteth the mountains on fire; 3852
106:18 in their company; the f burnt up the wicked. 3852
SS 8: 6 of fire, *which hath* a **most vehement** f. 7957
Isa 5:24 the f consumeth the chaff, *so* their root 3852
10:17 shall be for a fire, and his Holy One for a f: 3852
29: 6 and tempest, and the f of devouring fire. 3851
30:30 *with* the f of a devouring fire, 3851
43: 2 neither shall the f kindle upon thee. 3852
47:14 deliver themselves from the power of the f: 3852
Jer 48:45 a f from the midst of Sihon, and 3852
Eze 20:47 the flaming f shall not be quenched, and 7957
Da 3:22 the f of the fire slew those men that took up 7631
7: 9 his throne *was like* the fiery f, *and* 7631
7:11 body destroyed, and given to the burning f. 785
11:33 by f, by captivity, and by spoil, *many* days. 3852
Joel 1:19 and the f hath burnt all the trees of the field. 3852
2: 3 before them; and behind them a f burneth: 3852
2: 5 like the noise of a f of fire that devoureth 3851
Ob 1:18 the house of Joseph a f, and the house of 3852
Lk 16:24 my tongue; for I am tormented in this f. *5395*
Ac 7:30 an angel of the Lord in a f of fire in a bush. *5395*
Heb 1: 7 angels spirits, and his ministers a f of fire. *5395*
Rev 1:14 as snow; and his eyes *were* as a f of fire; *5395*
2:18 who hath his eyes like unto a f of fire, and *5395*
19:12 His eyes *were* as a f of fire, and on his head *5395*

FLAMES (3) [FLAME]
Ps 29: 7 The voice of the LORD divideth the f of 3852
Isa 13: 8 one at another; their faces *shall be as* f. 3851
66:15 with fury, and his rebuke with f of fire. 3851

FLAMING (9) [FLAME]
Ge 3:24 a f sword which turned every way, to keep 3858
Ps 104: 4 his angels spirits; his ministers a f fire: 3857
105:32 them hail *for* rain, *and* f fire in their land. 3852
Isa 4: 5 by day, and the shining of a f fire by night: 3852
La 2: 3 he burned against Jacob like a f fire, 3852
Eze 20:47 the f flame shall not be quenched, and 3852
Hos 7: 6 *in* the morning it burneth as a f fire. 3852
Na 2: 3 the chariots *shall be* with f torches in the day 784
2Th 1: 8 In f fire, taking vengeance on them that *5395*

FLANKS (6)
Lev 3: 4 which *is* by the f, and the caul above 3689
3:10 which *is* by the f, and the caul above 3689
3:15 which *is* by the f, and the caul above 3689
4: 9 which *is* by the f, and the caul above 3689
7: 4 which *is* by the f, and the caul *that is* above 3689
Job 15:27 and maketh collops of fat on *his* f. 3689

FLASH (1)
Eze 1:14 as the appearance of a f **of lightning**. 965

FLASK See BOX; VIAL; VIALS

FLAT (4)
Lev 21:18 or he that hath a f **nose**, or any thing 2763
Nu 22:31 down his head, and **fell** f on his face. 7812
Jos 6: 5 the wall of the city shall fall down f, 8478
6:20 that the wall fell down f, so that the people 8478

FLATTER (2) [FLATTERETH, FLATTERIES, FLATTERING, FLATTERY]
Ps 5: 9 an open sepulchre; they f with their tongue. 2505

Ps 78:36 Nevertheless they did f him with their 6601

FLATTERETH (6) [FLATTER]

Ps 36: 2 For he f himself in his own eyes, until his 2505
Pr 2:16 *even* from the stranger *which* f with her 2505
7: 5 from the stranger *which* f with her words. 2505
20:19 meddle not with him that f *with* his lips. 6601
28:23 more favour than he that f with the tongue. 2505
29: 5 A man that f his neighbour spreadeth a net 2505

FLATTERIES (3) [FLATTER]

Da 11:21 in peaceably, and obtain the kingdom by f. 2519
11:32 against the covenant shall he corrupt by f: 2514
11:34 but many shall cleave to them with f. 2519

FLATTERING (8) [FLATTER]

Job 32:21 neither let me **give f titles** unto man. 3655
32:22 For I know not to **give f titles**; *in so* 3655
Ps 12: 2 *with* f lips *and* with a double heart do they 2513
12: 3 The LORD shall cut off all f lips, *and* 2513
Pr 7:21 with the f of her lips she forced him. 2506
26:28 afflicted by it; and a f mouth worketh ruin. 2509
Eze 12:24 nor f divination within the house of Israel. 2509
1Th 2: 5 For neither at any time used we f words, *2850*

FLATTERY (2) [FLATTER]

Job 17: 5 He *that* speaketh f to *his* friends, 2506+3807.1
Pr 6:24 from the f of the tongue of a strange 2513

FLAWLESS See UNDEFILED

FLAX (11)

Ex 9:31 the f and the barley was smitten: for 6594
9:31 barley *was* in the ear, and the f *was* bolled. 6594
Jos 2: 6 hid them with the stalks of f, which she had 6593
Jdg 15:14 arms became as f that was burnt with fire, 6593
Pr 31:13 f, and worketh willingly with her hands. 6593
Isa 19: 9 Moreover they that work in fine f, and 6593
42: 3 and the smoking f shall he not quench: 6594
Eze 40: 3 with a line of f in his hand, and a measuring 6593
Hos 2: 5 my wool and my f, mine oil and my drink. 6593
2: 9 and my f *given* to cover her nakedness. 6593
Mt 12:20 and smoking f shall he not quench, *3043*

FLAY (3) [FLAYED]

Lev 1: 6 he shall f the burnt offering, and cut it into 6584
2Ch 29:34 that they could not f all the burnt offerings: 6584
Mic 3: 3 my people, and f their skin from off them; 6584

FLAYED (1) [FLAY]

2Ch 35:11 from their hands, and the Levites f *them.* 6584

FLEA (2)

1Sa 24:14 dost thou pursue? after a dead dog, after a f. 6550
26:20 the king of Israel is come out to seek a f, 6550

FLED (148) [FLEE]

Ge 14:10 the kings of Sodom and Gomorrah f, and 5127
14:10 they that remained f to the mountain. 5127
16: 6 dealt hardly with her, she f from her face. 1272
31:20 the Syrian, in that he told him not that he f. 1272
31:21 So he f with all that he had; and he rose up, 1272
31:22 Laban on the third day that Jacob was f. 1272
35: 7 when he f from the face of his brother. 1272
39:12 in her hand, and f, and got him out. 5127
39:13 his garment in her hand, and was f forth, 5127
39:15 garment with me, and f, and got him out. 5127
39:18 that he left his garment with me, and f out. 5127
Ex 2:15 Moses f from the face of Pharaoh, and 1272
4: 3 a serpent; and Moses f from before it. 5127
14: 5 was told the king of Egypt that the people f: 1272
14:27 the Egyptians f against it; and the LORD 5127
Nu 16:34 all Israel that *were* round about them f at 5127
35:25 to the city of his refuge, whither he was f: 5127
35:26 of the city of his refuge, whither he was f; 5127
35:32 ye shall take no satisfaction for him that is f 5127
Jos 7: 4 and they f before the men of Ai. 5127
8:15 and f *by* the way of the wilderness. 5127
8:20 the people that f *to* the wilderness turned 5127
10:11 as they f from before Israel, *and* were in 5127
10:16 these five kings f, and hid themselves in a 5127
20: 6 own house, unto the city from whence he f. 5127
Jdg 1: 6 Adoni-bezek f; and they pursued after him, 5127
4:15 off *his* chariot, and f **away** on his feet. 5127
4:17 Howbeit Sisera f **away** on his feet to 5127
7:21 and all the host ran, and cried, and f. 5127
7:22 the host f to Beth-shittah in Zererath, *and* 5127
8:12 when Zebah and Zalmunna f, he pursued 5127
9:21 and f, and went to Beer, and dwelt there, 1272
9:40 he f before him, and many were 5127
9:51 thither f all the men and women, and 5127
11: 3 Jephthah f from his brethren, and dwelt in 1272
20:45 f toward the wilderness unto the rock of 5127
20:47 f to the wilderness unto the rock Rimmon, 5127
1Sa 4:10 and they f every man into his tent: 5127
4:16 of the army, and I f to day out of the army. 5127
4:17 Israel is f before the Philistines, and 5127
14:22 *when* they heard that the Philistines f, 5127
17:24 the man, f from him, and were sore afraid. 5127
17:51 saw their champion was dead, they f. 5127
19: 8 *with* a great slaughter; and they f from him. 5127
19:10 and David f, and escaped that night. 5127
19:12 a window: and he went, and f, and escaped. 1272
19:18 So David f, and escaped, and came to 1272
20: 1 David f from Naioth in Ramah, and came 1272
21:10 f that day for fear of Saul, and went to 1272
22:17 because they knew when he f, and did not 1272
22:20 escaped, and f after David. 1272
23: 6 when Abiathar the son of Ahimelech f to 1272
27: 4 it was told Saul that David was f *to* Gath: 1272
30:17 young men, which rode upon camels, and f. 5127
31: 1 the men of Israel f from before 5127
31: 7 saw that the men of Israel f, and that Saul 5127
31: 7 were dead, they forsook the cities, and f; 5127
2Sa 1: 4 That the people are f from the battle, and 5127
4: 3 the Beerothites f to Gittaim, and 1272
4: 4 of Jezreel, and his nurse took him up, and f: 5127
10:13 against the Syrians: and they f before him. 5127
10:14 of Ammon saw that the Syrians were f, 5127
10:14 *then* f they *also* before Abishai, and 5127
10:18 the Syrians f before Israel; and David slew 5127
13:29 every man gat him up upon his mule, and f. 5127
13:34 Absalom f. And the young man that kept 1272
13:37 Absalom f, and went to Talmai, the son of 1272
13:38 So Absalom f, and went to Geshur, and 1272
18:17 and all Israel f every one to his tent. 5127
19: 8 for Israel had f every man to his tent. 5127
19: 9 now he is f out of the land for Absalom. 1272
23:11 and the people f from the Philistines. 5127
1Ki 2: 7 for so they came to me when I f because of 1272
2:28 Joab f unto the tabernacle of the LORD, 5127
2:29 it was told king Solomon that Joab was f 5127
11:17 That Hadad f, he and certain Edomites of 1272
11:23 which f from his lord Hadadezer king of 1272
11:40 Jeroboam arose, and f *into* Egypt, 1272
12: 2 heard *of it,* (for he was f from the presence 1272
20:20 the Syrians f; and Israel pursued them: and 5127
20:30 the rest f to Aphek, into the city; and 5127
20:30 Ben-hadad f, and came into the city, into an 5127
2Ki 3:24 the Moabites, so that they f before them: 5127
7: 7 Wherefore they arose and f in the twilight, 5127
7: 7 *even* the camp as it *was,* and f for their life. 5127
8:21 and the people f into their tents. 5127
9:10 to bury *her.* And he opened the door, and f. 5127
9:23 f, and said to Ahaziah, *There is* treachery, 5127
9:27 *this,* he f *by* the way of the garden house. 5127
9:27 And he f *to* Megiddo, and died there. 5127
14:12 and they f every man to their tents. 5127
14:19 he f to Lachish; but they sent after him to 5127
25: 4 all the men of war *f* by night *by* the way of NIH
1Ch 10: 1 the men of Israel f from before 5127
10: 7 that *were* in the valley saw that they f, 5127
10: 7 then they forsook their cities, and f: 5127
11:13 and the people f from before the Philistines. 5127
19:14 unto the battle; and they f before him. 5127
19:15 of Ammon saw that the Syrians were f, 5127
19:15 they likewise f before Abishai his brother, 5127
19:18 the Syrians f before Israel; and David slew 5127
2Ch 10: 2 whither he had f from the presence of 1272
13:16 the children of Israel f before Judah: and 5127
14:12 and before Judah; and the Ethiopians f. 5127
25:22 and they f every man to his tent. 5127
25:27 him in Jerusalem; and he f to Lachish: 5127
Ne 13:10 did the work, were f every one to his field. 1272
Ps 3: T of David, when he f from Absalom his son. 1272
31:11 they that did see me without f from me. 5074
57: T of David, when he f from Saul in the cave. 1272
104: 7 At thy rebuke they f; at the voice of thy 5127
114: 3 The sea saw *it,* and f: Jordan was driven 5127

Isa 10:29 Ramah is afraid; Gibeah of Saul is f. 5127
21:14 they prevented with their bread him that f. 5074
21:15 For they f from the swords, from the drawn 5074
22: 3 All thy rulers are f together, they are bound 5074
22: 3 are bound together, *which* have f from far. 1272
33: 3 At the noise of the tumult the people f; 5074
Jer 4:25 and all the birds of the heavens were f. 5074
9:10 the fowl of the heavens and the beast are f; 5074
26:21 he was afraid, and f, and went *into* Egypt; 1272
39: 4 they f, and went forth out of the city by 1272
46: 5 and are f **apace**, and look not back: 4498+5127
46:21 are turned back, *and* are f **away** together; 5127
48:45 They that f stood under the shadow of 5127
52: 7 all the men of war f, and went forth out of 1272
La 4:15 touch not, when they f **away** and wandered: 5132
Da 10: 7 so that they f to hide themselves. 1272
Hos 7:13 for they have f from me: destruction unto 5074
12:12 Jacob f *into* the country of Syria, and 1272
Jnh 1:10 For the men knew that he f from 1272
4: 2 Therefore I f before unto Tarshish: for I 1272
Zec 14: 5 like as ye f from before the earthquake in 5127
Mt 8:33 And they that kept *them* f, and went their *5343*
26:56 Then all the disciples forsook him, and f. *5343*
Mk 5:14 And they that fed the swine f, and told *it* in *5343*
14:50 And they all forsook him, and f. *5343*
14:52 left the linen cloth, and f from them naked. *5343*
16: 8 went out quickly, and f from the sepulchre; *5343*
Lk 8:34 they f, and went and told *it* in the city and *5343*
Ac 7:29 Then f Moses at this saying, and was a *5343*
14: 6 ware of *it,* and f unto Lystra and Derbe, *2703*
16:27 supposing that the prisoners had been f. *1628*
19:16 so that *they* f **out** of that house naked and *1628*
Heb 6:18 who have f **for refuge** to lay hold upon *2703*
Rev 12: 6 And the woman f into the wilderness, *5343*
16:20 And every island f *away,* and *5343*
20:11 face the earth and the heaven f *away;* and *5343*

FLEDDEST (2) [FLEE]
Ge 35: 1 that appeared unto thee when thou f from 1272
Ps 114: 5 What ailed thee, O thou sea, that thou f? 5127

FLEE (105) [FLED, FLEDDEST, FLEEING, FLEETH]
Ge 16: 8 I f from the face of my mistress Sarai. 1272
19:20 this city *is* near to f unto, and it *is* a little 5127
27:43 arise, f thou to Laban my brother to Haran; 1272
31:27 Wherefore didst thou f **away** secretly, 1272
Ex 9:20 Pharaoh **made** his servants and his cattle f 5127
14:25 Let us f from the face of Israel; 5127
21:13 will appoint thee a place whither he shall f. 5127
Lev 26:17 and ye shall f when none pursueth you. 5127
26:36 they shall f, as fleeing from a sword; and 5127
Nu 10:35 and let them that hate thee f before thee. 5127
24:11 Therefore now f thou to thy place: 1272
35: 6 for the manslayer, that he may f thither: 5127
35:11 that the slayer may f thither, which killeth 5127
35:15 killeth *any* person unawares may f thither. 5127
Dt 4:42 That the slayer might f thither, which 5127
19: 3 three parts, that every slayer may f thither. 5127
19: 4 which shall f thither, that he may live: 5127
19: 5 he shall f unto one of those cities, and live: 5127
28: 7 one way, and f before thee seven ways. 5127
28:25 and f seven ways before them: 5127
Jos 8: 5 as at the first, that we will f before them, 5127
8: 6 will say, *They* f before us, as at the first: 5127
8: 6 at the first: therefore we will f before them. 5127
8:20 they had no power to f this way or 5127
20: 3 *and* unwittingly may f thither: 5127
20: 4 when he that doth f unto one of those cities 5127
20: 9 *any* person at unawares might f thither, 5127
Jdg 20:32 Let us f, and draw them from the city unto 5127
2Sa 4: 4 as she made haste to f, that he fell, and 5127
15:14 with him at Jerusalem, Arise, and let us f; 1272
17: 2 all the people that *are* with him shall f; and 5127
18: 3 for if we f **away**, they will not care 5127+5127
19: 3 ashamed steal away when they f in battle. 5127
24:13 wilt thou f three months before thine 5127
1Ki 12:18 get *him* up to *his* chariot, to f *to* Jerusalem. 5127
2Ki 9: 3 Then open the door, and f, and tarry not. 5127
2Ch 10:18 get *him* up to *his* chariot, to f *to* Jerusalem. 5127
Ne 6:11 I said, Should such a man as I f? and who *is* 1272
Job 9:25 than a post: they f **away**, they see no good. 1272
20:24 He shall f from the iron weapon, *and* 1272
27:22 he **would fain** f out of his hand. 1272+1272
30:10 they f **far** from me, and spare not to spit in 7368
41:28 The arrow cannot **make** him f: 1272
Ps 11: 1 to my soul, F *as* a bird *to* your mountain? 5110
64: 8 all that see them shall f **away**. 5074
68: 1 let them also that hate him f before him. 5127
68:12 Kings of armies did f **apace**: and 5074+5074
139: 7 or whither shall I f from thy presence? 1272
143: 9 mine enemies: I f unto thee **to hide** me. 3680
Pr 28: 1 The wicked f when no man pursueth: but 5127
28:17 to the blood of *any* person shall f to the pit; 5127
SS 2:17 the shadows f **away**, turn, my beloved, and 5127
4: 6 the day break, and the shadows f **away**, 5127
Isa 10: 3 to whom will ye f for help? and where will 5127
10:31 of Gebim **gather** themselves **to f**. 5756
13:14 and f every one into his own land. 5127
15: 5 his fugitives *shall f* unto Zoar, a heifer of NIH
17:13 they shall f far off, and shall be chased as 5127
20: 6 whither we f for help to be delivered from 5127
30:16 ye said, No; for we will f upon horses; 5127
30:16 will flee upon horses; therefore shall ye f: 5127
30:17 One thousand *shall f* at the rebuke of one; NIH
30:17 of one; at the rebuke of five shall ye f: 5127
31: 8 he shall f from the sword, and his young 5127
35:10 and sorrow and sighing shall f **away**. 5127
48:20 forth of Babylon, f ye from the Chaldeans, 1272
51:11 joy; *and* sorrow and mourning shall f **away**. 5127
Jer 4:29 The whole city shall f for the noise of 1272
6: 1 **gather** yourselves **to** f out of the midst of 5756
25:35 the shepherds shall have no **way to** f, 4498
46: 6 Let not the swift f **away**, nor the mighty 5127
48: 6 F, save your lives, and be like the heath in 5127
48: 9 unto Moab, that it may f and get away: 5323
49: 8 F ye, turn back, dwell deep, O inhabitants 5127
49:24 *and* turneth herself to f, and fear hath seized 5127
49:30 F, get you far off, dwell deep, O ye 5127
50:16 and they shall f every one to his own land. 5127
50:28 The voice of them that f and escape out of 5127
51: 6 F out of the midst of Babylon, and 5127
Am 2:16 the mighty shall f **away** naked in that day, 5127
5:19 As if a man did f from a lion, and a bear 5127
7:12 go, f thee **away** into the land of Judah, and 1272
9: 1 he that fleeth of them shall not f **away**, and 5127
Jnh 1: 3 Jonah rose up to f unto Tarshish from 1272
Na 2: 8 yet they *shall* f **away**. Stand, stand, 5127
3: 7 *that* all they that look upon thee shall f from 5074
3:17 *but* when the sun ariseth they f **away**, and 5074
Zec 2: 6 and f from the land of the north, 5127
14: 5 ye shall f *to* the valley of the mountains; 5127
14: 5 yea, ye shall f, like as ye fled from before 5127
Mt 2:13 and f into Egypt, and be thou there until I *5343*
3: 7 who hath warned you to f from the wrath to *5343*
10:23 persecute you in this city, f ye into another: *5343*
24:16 Then let them which be in Judea f into *5343*
Mk 13:14 let them that be in Judea f to the mountains: *5343*
Lk 3: 7 who hath warned you to f from the wrath to *5343*
21:21 Then let them which are in Judea f to *5343*
Jn 10: 5 will they not follow, but will f from him: *5343*
Ac 27:30 And as the shipmen were about to f out of *5343*
1Co 6:18 F fornication. Every sin that a man doeth is *5343*
10:14 my dearly beloved, f from idolatry. *5343*
1Ti 6:11 f these *things;* and follow *after* *5343*
2Ti 2:22 F also youthful lusts: but *5343*
Jas 4: 7 Resist the devil, and he will f from you. *5343*
Rev 9: 6 desire to die, and death shall f from them. *5343*

FLEECE (9)
Dt 18: 4 of thy oil, and the first of the f of thy sheep, 1488
Jdg 6:37 Behold, I will put a f of wool in the floor; 1492
6:37 *and* if the dew be on the f only, and *it be* 1492
6:38 thrust the f together, and wringed the dew 1492
6:38 wringed the dew out of the f, a bowl full *of* 1492
6:39 I pray thee, but *this* once with the f; 1492
6:39 let it now be dry only upon the f, and 1492
6:40 for it was dry upon the f only, and 1492
Job 31:20 *if* he were *not* warmed with the f of my 1488

FLEEING (2) [FLEE]
Lev 26:36 they shall flee, as f from a sword; and 4499
Dt 4:42 that f unto one of these cities he might live: 5127

FLEET See NAVY

FLEETH (8) [FLEE]
Dt 19:11 that he die, and f into one of these cities: 5127
Job 14: 2 he f also as a shadow, and continueth not. 1272

Isa 24:18 *that* he who f from the noise of the fear 5127
Jer 48:19 ask him that f, and her that escapeth, *and* 5127
48:44 He that f from the fear shall fall into the pit; 5127
Am 9: 1 he that f of them shall not flee away, and 5127
Jn 10:12 wolf coming, and leaveth the sheep, and f: *5343*
10:13 The hireling f, because he is a hireling, and *5343*

FLEETING See FLEE; FLEETH; FRAIL; VANITIES; VANITY

FLESH (420) [FATFLESHED, FLESHHOOK, FLESHHOOKS, FLESHLY, FLESHY, LEANFLESHED]

Ge 2:21 his ribs, and closed up the f instead thereof; 1320
2:23 now bone of my bones, and f of my flesh: 1320
2:23 now bone of my bones, and flesh of my f: 1320
2:24 unto his wife: and they shall be one f. 1320
6: 3 always strive with man, for that he also *is* f: 1320
6:12 for all f had corrupted his way upon 1320
6:13 The end of all f is come before me; 1320
6:17 to destroy all f, wherein *is* the breath of life, 1320
6:19 of every living *thing* of all f, two of every 1320
7:15 two and two of all f, wherein *is* the breath 1320
7:16 went in, went in male and female of all f, 1320
7:21 all f died that moved upon the earth, 1320
8:17 of all f, *both* of fowl, and of cattle, and 1320
9: 4 f with the life thereof, *which is* the blood 1320
9:11 neither shall all f be cut off any more by 1320
9:15 and you and every living creature of all f; 1320
9:15 no more become a flood to destroy all f. 1320
9:16 every living creature of all f that *is* upon 1320
9:17 between me and all f that *is* upon the earth. 1320
17:11 ye shall circumcise the f of your foreskin; 1320
17:13 my covenant shall be in your f for an 1320
17:14 the uncircumcised man *child* whose f of his 1320
17:23 circumcised the f of their foreskin in 1320
17:24 when he was circumcised *in* the f of his 1320
17:25 when he was circumcised in the f of his 1320
29:14 to him, Surely thou *art* my bone and my f. 1320
37:27 upon him; for he *is* our brother *and* our f. 1320
40:19 and the birds shall eat thy f from off thee. 1320
Ex 4: 7 behold, it was turned again as his *other* f. 1320
12: 8 they shall eat the f in that night, roast with 1320
12:46 thou shalt not carry forth *ought* of the f 1320
16: 3 when we sat by the f pots, *and* when we did 1320
16: 8 shall give you in the evening f to eat, 1320
16:12 At even ye shall eat f, and in the morning 1320
21:28 surely stoned, and his f shall not be eaten; 1320
22:31 neither shall ye eat *any* f *that is* torn *of* 1320
29:14 the f of the bullock, and his skin, and his 1320
29:31 and seethe his f in the holy place. 1320
29:32 and his sons shall eat the f of the ram, 1320
29:34 if *ought* of the f of the consecrations, or 1320
30:32 Upon man's f shall it not be poured, 1320
Lev 4:11 all his f, with his head, and with his legs, 1320
6:10 *his* linen breeches shall he put upon his f, 1320
6:27 Whatsoever shall touch the f thereof shall 1320
7:15 the f of the sacrifice of his peace offerings 1320
7:17 the remainder of the f of the sacrifice on 1320
7:18 if *any* of the f of the sacrifice of his peace 1320
7:19 the f that toucheth any unclean *thing* shall 1320
7:19 *as for* the f, all that be clean shall eat 1320
7:20 the soul that eateth *of* the f of the sacrifice 1320
7:21 eat of the f of the sacrifice of peace 1320
8:17 and his hide, his f, and his dung, 1320
8:31 Boil the f *at* the door of the tabernacle of 1320
8:32 that which remaineth of the f and of 1320
9:11 the f and the hide he burnt with fire without 1320
11: 8 Of their f shall ye not eat, and their carcase 1320
11:11 ye shall not eat of their f, but you shall have 1320
12: 3 in the eighth day the f of his foreskin shall 1320
13: 2 When a man shall have in the skin of his f a 1320
13: 2 it be in the skin of his f like the plague of 1320
13: 3 shall look on the plague in the skin of the f: 1320
13: 3 in sight *be* deeper than the skin of his f, 1320
13: 4 the bright spot *be* white in the skin of his f, 1320
13:10 and *there be* quick raw f in the rising; 1320
13:11 It *is* an old leprosy in the skin of his f, and 1320
13:13 behold, *if* the leprosy have covered all his f, 1320
13:14 when raw f appeareth in him, he shall be 1320
13:15 the priest shall see the raw f, and 1320
13:15 *for* the raw f *is* unclean: it *is* a leprosy. 1320
13:16 Or if the raw f turn again, and be changed 1320
13:18 The f also, in which, *even* in the skin 1320
13:24 Or if there be *any* f, in the skin whereof 1320
13:24 the quick *f* that burneth have a white bright NIH
13:38 a woman have in the skin of their f bright 1320
13:39 *if* the bright spots in the skin of their f *be* 1320
13:43 as the leprosy appeareth in the skin of the f; 1320
14: 9 also he shall wash his f in water, and 1320
15: 2 any man hath a running issue out of his f, 1320
15: 3 *whether* his f run with his issue, or his flesh 1320
15: 3 or his f be stopped from his issue, it *is* his 1320
15: 7 he that toucheth the f of him that hath 1320
15:13 bathe his f in running water, and shall be 1320
15:16 he shall wash all his f in water, and 1320
15:19 an issue, *and* her issue in her f be blood, 1320
16: 4 he shall have the linen breeches upon his f, 1320
16: 4 therefore shall he wash his f in water, and 1320
16:24 he shall wash his f with water in the holy 1320
16:26 bathe his f in water, and afterward come 1320
16:27 fire their skins, and their f, and their dung. 1320
16:28 bathe his f in water, and afterward he shall 1320
17:11 For the life of the f *is* in the blood: and 1320
17:14 For *it is* the life of all f; the blood of it *is* for 1320
17:14 Ye shall eat the blood of no *manner of* f: 1320
17:14 for the life of all f *is* the blood thereof: 1320
17:16 if he wash *them* not, nor bathe his f; then 1320
19:28 Ye shall not make any cuttings in your f for 1320
21: 5 nor make any cuttings in their f. 1320
22: 6 *things,* unless he wash his f with water. 1320
26:29 ye shall eat the f of your sons, and the flesh 1320
26:29 and the f of your daughters shall ye eat. 1320
Nu 8: 7 let them shave all their f, and let them wash 1320
11: 4 and said, Who shall give us f to eat? 1320
11:13 Whence should I have f to give unto all this 1320
11:13 unto me, saying, Give us f, that we may eat. 1320
11:18 against to morrow, and ye shall eat f: 1320
11:18 saying, Who shall give us f to eat? 1320
11:18 therefore the LORD will give you f, and 1320
11:21 thou hast said, I will give them f, that they 1320
11:33 while the f *was* yet between their teeth, 1320
12:12 of whom the f is half consumed when he 1320
16:22 said, O God, the God of the spirits of all f, 1320
18:15 Every thing that openeth the matrix in all f, 1320
18:18 the f of them shall be thine, as the wave 1320
19: 5 her skin, and her f, and her blood, with her 1320
19: 7 he shall bathe his f in water, and 1320
19: 8 bathe his f in water, and shall be unclean 1320
27:16 the LORD, the God of the spirits of all f, 1320
Dt 5:26 For who *is there of* all f, that hath heard 1320
12:15 thou mayest kill and eat f in all thy gates, 1320
12:20 I will eat f, because thy soul longeth to eat 1320
12:20 eat flesh, because thy soul longeth to eat f; 1320
12:20 thou mayest eat f, whatsoever thy soul 1320
12:23 and thou mayest not eat the life with the f. 1320
12:27 the f and the blood, upon the altar of 1320
12:27 LORD thy God, and thou shalt eat the f. 1320
14: 8 ye shall not eat of their f, nor touch their 1320
16: 4 neither shall there *any thing* of the f, 1320
28:53 the f of thy sons and of thy daughters, 1320
28:55 of the f of his children whom he shall eat: 1320
32:42 with blood, and my sword shall devour f; 1320
Jdg 6:19 the f he put in a basket, and he put the broth 1320
6:20 Take the f and the unleavened *cakes,* and 1320
6:21 touched the f and the unleavened *cakes;* 1320
6:21 consumed the f and the unleavened *cakes.* 1320
8: 7 I will tear your f with the thorns of 1320
9: 2 also that I *am* your bone and your f. 1320
1Sa 2:13 servant came, while the f was in seething, 1320
2:15 that sacrificed, Give f to roast for the priest; 1320
2:15 for he will not have sodden f of thee, but 1320
17:44 I will give thy f unto the fowls of the air, 1320
25:11 my f that I have killed for my shearers, and 2878
2Sa 5: 1 Behold, we *are* thy bone and thy f. 1320
6:19 a good piece *of f,* and a flagon *of wine.* So NIH
19:12 *are* my brethren, ye *are* my bones and my f: 1320
19:13 *Art* thou not *of* my bone, and *of* my f? 1320
1Ki 17: 6 brought him bread and f in the morning, 1320
17: 6 and bread and f in the evening; 1320
19:21 boiled their f with the instruments of 1320
21:27 put sackcloth upon his f, and fasted, and 1320
2Ki 4:34 and the f of the child waxed warm. 1320
5:10 thy f shall come again to thee, and 1320
5:14 his f came again like unto the flesh of a 1320
5:14 his flesh came again like unto the f of a 1320
6:30 behold, *he had* sackcloth within upon his f. 1320
9:36 In the portion of Jezreel shall dogs eat the f 1320
1Ch 11: 1 Behold, we *are* thy bone and thy f. 1320
16: 3 and a good piece *of f,* and a flagon *of wine.* NIH

2Ch	32: 8	With him *is* an arm of f; but with us *is*	1320
Ne	5: 5	Yet now our f *is* as the flesh of our	1320
	5: 5	Yet now our flesh *is* as the f of our	1320
Job	2: 5	touch his bone and his f, and he will curse	1320
	4:15	before my face; the hair of my f stood up:	1320
	6:12	the strength of stones? or *is* my f of brass?	1320
	7: 5	My f is clothed with worms and clods of	1320
	10: 4	Hast thou eyes of f? or seest thou as man	1320
	10:11	Thou hast clothed me with skin and f, and	1320
	13:14	Wherefore do I take my f in my teeth, and	1320
	14:22	his f upon him shall have pain, and his soul	1320
	19:20	My bone cleaveth to my skin and to my f,	1320
	19:22	me as God, and are not satisfied with my f?	1320
	19:26	this *body,* yet in my f shall I see God:	1320
	21: 6	and trembling taketh hold on my f.	1320
	31:31	tabernacle said not, O that we had of his f!	1320
	33:21	His f is consumed away, that it cannot be	1320
	33:25	His f shall be fresher than a child's: he shall	1320
	34:15	All f shall perish together, and man shall	1320
	41:23	The flakes of his f are joined together:	1320
Ps	16: 9	glory rejoiceth: my f also shall rest in hope.	1320
	27: 2	and my foes, came upon me to eat up my f,	1320
	38: 3	*There is* no soundness in my f because	1320
	38: 7	and *there is* no soundness in my f.	1320
	50:13	Will I eat the f of bulls, or drink the blood	1320
	56: 4	I will not fear what f can do unto me.	1320
	63: 1	my f longeth for thee, in a dry and	1320
	65: 2	hearest prayer, unto thee shall all f come.	1320
	73:26	My f and my heart faileth: *but* God *is*	7607
	78:20	bread also? can he provide f for his people?	7607
	78:27	He rained f also upon them as dust, and	7607
	78:39	For he remembered that they *were but* f;	1320
	79: 2	the f of thy saints unto the beasts of	1320
	84: 2	and my f crieth out for the living God.	1320
	109:24	through fasting; and my f faileth of fatness.	1320
	119:120	My f trembleth for fear of thee; and I am	1320
	136:25	Who giveth food to all f: for his mercy	1320
	145:21	let all f bless his holy name for ever and	1320
Pr	4:22	that find them, and health to all their f.	1320
	5:11	when thy f and thy body are consumed,	1320
	11:17	but *he that is* cruel troubleth his own f.	7607
	14:30	A sound heart *is* the life of the f: but	1320
	23:20	amongst riotous eaters of f:	1320
Ecc	4: 5	his hands together, and eateth his own f.	1320
	5: 6	Suffer not thy mouth to cause thy f to sin;	1320
	11:10	thy heart, and put away evil from thy f:	1320
	12:12	and much study *is* a weariness of the f.	1320
Isa	9:20	they shall eat every man the f of his own	1320
	17: 4	and the fatness of his f shall wax lean.	1320
	22:13	killing sheep, eating f, and drinking wine:	1320
	31: 3	not God; and their horses f, and not spirit.	1320
	40: 5	be revealed, and all f shall see *it* together:	1320
	40: 6	All f *is* grass, and all the goodliness thereof	1320
	44:16	with part thereof he eateth f; he roasteth	1320
	44:19	I have roasted f, and eaten *it:* and shall I	1320
	49:26	them that oppress thee with their own f;	1320
	49:26	all f shall know that I the LORD *am* thy	1320
	58: 7	that thou hide not thyself from thine own f?	1320
	65: 4	which eat swine's f, and broth of	1320
	66:16	his sword will the LORD plead with all f:	1320
	66:17	eating swine's f, and the abomination, and	1320
	66:23	shall all f come to worship before me,	1320
	66:24	and they shall be an abhorring unto all f.	1320
Jer	7:21	offerings unto your sacrifices, and eat f.	1320
	11:15	and the holy f is passed from thee?	1320
	12:12	*other* end of the land: no f *shall* have peace.	1320
	17: 5	maketh f his arm, and whose heart	1320
	19: 9	I will cause them to eat the f of their sons	1320
	19: 9	of their sons and the f of their daughters,	1320
	19: 9	they shall eat every one the f of his friend	1320
	25:31	with the nations, he *will* plead with all f;	1320
	32:27	Behold, I *am* the LORD, the God of all f:	1320
	45: 5	for behold, I *will* bring evil upon all f,	1320
	51:35	done to me and *to* my f *be* upon Babylon,	7607
La	3: 4	My f and my skin hath he made old;	1320
Eze	4:14	neither came there abominable f into my	1320
	11: 3	this *city is* the caldron, and we *be* the f.	1320
	11: 7	they *are* the f, and this *city is* the caldron:	1320
	11:11	neither shall ye be the f in the midst	1320
	11:19	I will take the stony heart out of their f, and	1320
	11:19	their flesh, and will give them a heart of f:	1320
	16:26	the Egyptians thy neighbours, great of f;	1320
	20:48	all f shall see that I the LORD have	1320
	21: 4	against all f from the south *to* the north:	1320
	21: 5	That all f may know that I the LORD have	1320
	23:20	whose f *is as* the flesh of asses, and	1320
	23:20	whose flesh *is as* the f of asses, and	1320
	24:10	consume the f, and spice it well, and let	1320
	32: 5	I will lay thy f upon the mountains, and	1320
	36:26	will take away the stony heart out of your f,	1320
	36:26	your flesh, and I will give you a heart of f.	1320
	37: 6	will bring up f upon you, and cover you	1320
	37: 8	lo, the sinews and the f came up upon them,	1320
	39:17	of Israel, that ye may eat f, and drink blood.	1320
	39:18	Ye shall eat the f of the mighty, and	1320
	40:43	upon the tables *was* the f of the offering.	1320
	44: 7	uncircumcised in f, to be in my sanctuary,	1320
	44: 9	in heart, nor uncircumcised in f,	1320
Da	1:15	fatter in f than all the children which did eat	1320
	2:11	the gods, whose dwelling is not with f.	1321
	4:12	the boughs thereof, and all f was fed of it.	1321
	7: 5	they said thus unto it, Arise, devour much f.	1321
	10: 3	neither came f nor wine in my mouth,	1320
Hos	8:13	They sacrifice f *for* the sacrifices of mine	1320
Joel	2:28	that I will pour out my spirit upon all f;	1320
Mic	3: 2	off them, and their f from off their bones;	7607
	3: 3	Who also eat the f of my people, and	7607
	3: 3	as for the pot, and as f within the caldron.	1320
Zep	1:17	poured out as dust, and their f as the dung.	3894
Hag	2:12	If one bear holy f in the skirt of his	1320
Zec	2:13	Be silent, O all f, before the LORD: for he	1320
	11: 9	let the rest eat every one the f of another.	1320
	11:16	he shall eat the f of the fat, and tear their	1320
	14:12	Their f *shall* consume away while they	1320
Mt	16:17	for f and blood hath not revealed *it* unto	*4561*
	19: 5	to his wife: and they twain shall be one f?	*4561*
	19: 6	they are no more twain, but one f.	*4561*
	24:22	be shortened, there should no f be saved:	*4561*
	26:41	spirit indeed *is* willing, but the f *is* weak.	*4561*
Mk	10: 8	And they twain shall be one f: so then	*4561*
	10: 8	so then they are no more twain, but one f.	*4561*
	13:20	shortened *those* days, no f should be saved:	*4561*
	14:38	The spirit truly *is* ready, but the f *is* weak.	*4561*
Lk	3: 6	And all f shall see the salvation of God.	*4561*
	24:39	for a spirit hath not f and bones, as ye see	*4561*
Jn	1:13	not of blood, nor of the will of the f,	*4561*
	1:14	And the Word was made f, and	*4561*
	3: 6	That which is born of the f is flesh; and	*4561*
	3: 6	That which is born of the flesh is f; and	*4561*
	6:51	and the bread that I will give is my f,	*4561*
	6:52	How can this *man* give us *his* f to eat?	*4561*
	6:53	Except ye eat the f of the Son of man, and	*4561*
	6:54	Whoso eateth my f, and drinketh my blood,	*4561*
	6:55	For my f is meat indeed,	*4561*
	6:56	He that eateth my f, and drinketh my blood,	*4561*
	6:63	that quickeneth; the f profiteth nothing:	*4561*
	8:15	Ye judge after the f; I judge no *man.*	*4561*
	17: 2	As thou hast given him power over all f,	*4561*
Ac	2:17	I will pour out of my Spirit upon all f:	*4561*
	2:26	moreover also my f shall rest in hope:	*4561*
	2:30	of the fruit of his loins, according to the f,	*4561*
	2:31	left in hell, neither his f did see corruption.	*4561*
Ro	1: 3	of the seed of David according to the f;	*4561*
	2:28	which is outward in the f:	*4561*
	3:20	law there shall no f be justified in his sight:	*4561*
	4: 1	as pertaining to the f, hath found?	*4561*
	6:19	of men because of the infirmity of your f:	*4561*
	7: 5	For when we were in the f, the motions of	*4561*
	7:18	For I know that in me (that is, in my f,)	*4561*
	7:25	law of God; but with the f the law of sin.	*4561*
	8: 1	*are* in Christ Jesus who walk not after the f,	*4561*
	8: 3	not do, in that it was weak through the f,	*4561*
	8: 3	his own Son in the likeness of sinful f,	*4561*
	8: 3	and for sin, condemned sin in the f:	*4561*
	8: 4	who walk not after the f, but after	*4561*
	8: 5	For they that are after the f do mind	*4561*
	8: 5	after the flesh do mind the *things* of the f;	*4561*
	8: 8	they that are in the f cannot please God.	*4561*
	8: 9	But ye are not in the f, but in the Spirit, if	*4561*
	8:12	we are debtors, not to the f,	*4561*
	8:12	not to the flesh, to live after the f.	*4561*
	8:13	For if ye live after the f, ye shall die: but	*4561*
	9: 3	my kinsmen according to the f:	*4561*
	9: 5	of whom as concerning the f Christ *came,*	*4561*
	9: 8	*They which are* the children of the f,	*4561*
	11:14	provoke to emulation *them which are* my f,	*4561*
	13:14	and make not provision for the f, to *fulfil*	*4561*
	14:21	*It is* good neither to eat f, nor to drink wine,	*2907*

1Co 1:26 how that not many wise *men* after the f, *4561*
1:29 That no f should glory in his presence. *4561*
5: 5 one unto Satan for the destruction of the f, *4561*
6:16 one body? for two, saith *he,* shall be one f. *4561*
7:28 such shall have trouble in the f: *4561*
8:13 I will eat no f while the world standeth, *2907*
10:18 Behold Israel after the f: are not they which *4561*
15:39 All f *is* not the same flesh: but *there is* one *4561*
15:39 All flesh *is* not the same f: but *there is* one *4561*
15:39 but *there is* one *kind of* f of men, *4561*
15:39 another f of beasts, another of fishes, *and* *4561*
15:50 that f and blood cannot inherit the kingdom *4561*
2Co 1:17 I purpose, do I purpose according to the f, *4561*
4:11 might be made manifest in our mortal f. *4561*
5:16 henceforth know we no *man* after the f: *4561*
5:16 though we have known Christ after the f, *4561*
7: 1 cleanse ourselves from all filthiness of the f *4561*
7: 5 our f had no rest, but *we were* troubled on *4561*
10: 2 of us as if we walked according to the f. *4561*
10: 3 For though we walk in the f, we do not war *4561*
10: 3 walk in the flesh, we do not war after the f: *4561*
11:18 Seeing that many glory after the f, I will *4561*
12: 7 there was given to me a thorn in the f, *4561*
Gal 1:16 immediately I conferred not with f and *4561*
2:16 for by the works of the law shall no f be *4561*
2:20 *the life* which I now live in the f I live by *4561*
3: 3 are ye now made perfect by the f? *4561*
4:13 Ye know how through infirmity of the f I *4561*
4:14 And my temptation which was in my f ye *4561*
4:23 of the bondwoman was born after the f; *4561*
4:29 he that was born after the f persecuted him *4561*
5:13 only *use* not liberty for an occasion to the f, *4561*
5:16 and ye shall not fulfil the lust of the f. *4561*
5:17 For the f lusteth against the Spirit, and *4561*
5:17 the Spirit, and the Spirit against the f: *4561*
5:19 Now the works of the f are manifest, *4561*
5:24 have crucified the f with the affections *4561*
6: 8 For he that soweth to his f shall of the flesh *4561*
6: 8 For he that soweth to his flesh shall of the f *4561*
6:12 many as desire to make a fair shew in the f, *4561*
6:13 that they may glory in your f. *4561*
Eph 2: 3 in times past in the lusts of our f, *4561*
2: 3 fulfilling the desires of the f and of *4561*
2:11 ye *being* in time passed Gentiles in the f, *4561*
2:11 the Circumcision in the f made by hands; *4561*
2:15 Having abolished in his f the enmity, *4561*
5:29 For no *man* ever yet hated his own f; but *4561*
5:30 of his body, of his f, and of his bones. *4561*
5:31 unto his wife, and they two shall be one f. *4561*
6: 5 *that are your* masters according to the f, *4561*
6:12 For we wrestle not against f and blood, but *4561*
Php 1:22 But if *I* live in the f, this *is* the fruit of my *4561*
1:24 Nevertheless to abide in the f *is* more *4561*
3: 3 and have no confidence in the f. *4561*
3: 4 I *might* also have confidence in the f. *4561*
3: 4 that *he hath whereof he* might trust in the f, *4561*
Col 1:22 In the body of his f through death, *4561*
1:24 of Christ in my f for his body's sake, *4561*
2: 1 as many as have not seen my face in the f; *4561*
2: 5 For though I be absent in the f, yet am I *4561*
2:11 in putting off the body of the sins of the f, *4561*
2:13 *your* sins and the uncircumcision of your f, *4561*
2:23 not in any honour to the satisfying of the f. *4561*
3:22 all *things your* masters according to the f; *4561*
1Ti 3:16 God was manifest in the f, justified in *4561*
Phm 1:16 unto thee, both in the f, and in the Lord? *4561*
Heb 2:14 then as the children are partakers of f and *4561*
5: 7 Who in the days of his f, when he had *4561*
9:13 sanctifieth to the purifying of the f: *4561*
10:20 for us, through the vail, that is to say, his f; *4561*
12: 9 Furthermore we have had fathers of our f *4561*
Jas 5: 3 and shall eat your f as *it were* fire: *4561*
1Pe 1:24 For all f *is* as grass, and all the glory of *4561*
3:18 being put to death in the f, but *4561*
3:21 us (not the putting away of the filth of the f, *4561*
4: 1 then as Christ hath suffered for us in the f, *4561*
4: 1 for he that hath suffered in the f hath ceased *4561*
4: 2 rest of *his* time in the f to the lusts of men, *4561*
4: 6 might be judged according to men in the f, *4561*
2Pe 2:10 But chiefly them that walk after the f in *4561*
2:18 they allure through the lusts of the f, *4561*
1Jn 2:16 the lust of the f, and the lust of the eyes, *4561*
4: 2 that Jesus Christ is come in the f is of God: *4561*
4: 3 Jesus Christ is come in the f is not of God: *4561*
2Jn 1: 7 not that Jesus Christ is come in the f. *4561*
Jude 1: 7 and going after strange f, are set forth for *4561*
1: 8 also these *filthy* dreamers defile the f, *4561*
1:23 hating even the garment spotted by the f. *4561*
Rev 17:16 and shall eat her f, and burn her with fire. *4561*
19:18 That ye may eat the f of kings, and the flesh *4561*
19:18 and the f of captains, and the flesh of *4561*
19:18 and the f of mighty *men,* and the flesh of *4561*
19:18 flesh of mighty *men,* and the f of horses, *4561*
19:18 and the f of all *men,* both free and bond, *4561*
19:21 and all the fowls were filled with their f. *4561*

FLESHHOOK (2) [FLESH, HOOK]
1Sa 2:13 with a f of three teeth in his hand; 4207
2:14 all that the f brought up the priest took for 4207

FLESHHOOKS (5) [FLESH, HOOK]
Ex 27: 3 and his basons, and his f, and his firepans: 4207
38: 3 and the basons, *and* the f, and the firepans: 4207
Nu 4:14 the f, and the shovels, and the basons, 4207
1Ch 28:17 Also pure gold *for* the f, and the bowls, and 4207
2Ch 4:16 and the f, and all their instruments, 4207

FLESHLY (3) [FLESH]
2Co 1:12 not with f wisdom, but by the grace of God, *4559*
Col 2:18 hath not seen, vainly puft up by his f mind, *4561*
1Pe 2:11 and pilgrims, abstain from f lusts, *4559*

FLESHY (1) [FLESH]
2Co 3: 3 tables of stone, but in f tables of the heart. *4560*

FLEW (2) [FLY]
1Sa 14:32 the people f upon the spoil, and took sheep, 5860
Isa 6: 6 f one of the seraphims unto me, having a 5774

FLIES (10) [FLY]
Ex 8:21 I will send swarms *of f* upon thee, and NIH
8:21 the Egyptians shall be full of swarms *of f,* NIH
8:22 that no swarms *of f* shall be there; NIH
8:24 there came a grievous swarm *of f* into NIH
8:24 was corrupted by reason of the swarm *of f.* NIH
8:29 the swarms *of f* may depart from Pharaoh, NIH
8:31 he removed the swarms *of f* from Pharaoh, NIH
Ps 78:45 He sent divers sorts *of f* among them, NIH
105:31 there came divers sorts *of f, and* lice in all NIH
Ecc 10: 1 Dead f cause the ointment of 2070

FLIETH (5) [FLY]
Dt 4:17 the likeness of any winged fowl that f in 5774
14:19 every creeping thing that f *is* unclean unto 5775
28:49 the end of the earth, *as swift* as the eagle f; 1675
Ps 91: 5 by night; *nor* for the arrow *that* f by day; 5774
Na 3:16 the cankerworm spoileth, and f **away**. 5774

FLIGHT (8) [FLY]
Lev 26: 8 hundred of you shall **put** ten thousand **to** f: 7291
Dt 32:30 two **put** ten thousand **to** f, except their 5127
1Ch 12:15 they **put to** f all *them of* the valleys, 1272
Isa 52:12 ye shall not go out with haste, nor go by f: 4499
Am 2:14 Therefore the f shall perish from the swift, 4498
Mt 24:20 But pray ye that your f be not in the winter, *5437*
Mk 13:18 And pray ye that your f be not in *5437*
Heb 11:34 **turned to** f the armies of the aliens. *2827*

FLINT (5) [FLINTY]
Dt 8:15 thee forth water out of the rock of f; 2496
Ps 114: 8 the f into a fountain of waters. 2496
Isa 5:28 their horses' hoofs shall be counted like f, 6864
50: 7 therefore have I set my face like a f, and 2496
Eze 3: 9 As an adamant harder than f have I made 6864

FLINTY (1) [FLINT]
Dt 32:13 out of the rock, and oil out of the f rock; 2496

FLIXE (1)
Ac 28: 8 lay sick of a fever and of a **bloody** f: *1420*

FLOAT See FLOTES; SWIM

FLOCK (111) [FLOCKS]
Ge 4: 4 he also brought of the firstlings of his f and 6629
21:28 Abraham set seven ewe lambs of the f by 6629
27: 9 Go now to the f, and fetch me from thence 6629
29:10 watered the f of Laban his mother's 6629
30:31 for me, I will again feed *and* keep thy f: 6629
30:32 I will pass through all thy f to day, 6629

Ge 30:40 and all the brown in the f of Laban; 6629
31: 4 and Leah to the field unto his f, 6629
31:38 and the rams of thy f have I not eaten. 6629
33:13 overdrive them one day, all the f will die. 6629
37: 2 was feeding the f with his brethren; 6629
37:12 his brethren went to feed their father's f in 6629
37:13 Do not thy brethren feed *the f* in Shechem? NIH
38:17 he said, I will send *thee* a kid from the f. 6629
Ex 2:16 filled the troughs to water their father's f. 6629
2:17 and helped them, and watered their f. 6629
2:19 water enough for us, and watered the f. 6629
3: 1 Now Moses kept the f of Jethro his father 6629
3: 1 he led the f to the backside of the desert, 6629
Lev 1: 2 of the cattle, *even* of the herd, and of the f. 6629
3: 6 peace offering unto the LORD *be* of the f, 6629
5: 6 a female from the f, a lamb or a kid of 6629
5:18 bring a ram without blemish out of the f, 6629
6: 6 a ram without blemish out of the f, with thy 6629
27:32 *concerning* the tithe of the herd, or of the f, 6629
Nu 15: 3 unto the LORD, of the herd, or of the f: 6629
Dt 12:17 or the firstlings of thy herds or of thy f, 6629
12:21 thou shalt kill of thy herd and of thy f, 6629
15:14 shalt furnish him liberally out of thy f, 6629
15:19 of thy f thou shalt sanctify unto the LORD 6629
16: 2 the LORD thy God, *of* the f and the herd, 6629
1Sa 17:34 and a bear, and took a lamb out of the f: 5739
2Sa 12: 4 he spared to take of his own f and of his 6629
2Ch 35: 7 gave to the people, *of* the f, lambs and kids, 6629
Ezr 10:19 *they offered* a ram of the f for their 6629
Job 21:11 They send forth their little ones like a f, and 6629
30: 1 disdained to have set with the dogs of my f. 6629
Ps 77:20 Thou leddest thy people like a f by the hand 6629
78:52 and guided them in the wilderness like a f. 5739
80: 1 of Israel, thou that leadest Joseph like a f; 6629
107:41 and maketh *him* families like a f. 6629
SS 1: 7 where thou makest *thy f* to rest at noon: NIH
1: 8 go thy way forth by the footsteps of the f, 6629
4: 1 thy hair *is* as a f of goats, that appear from 5739
4: 2 Thy teeth *are* like a f of *sheep that are* even 5739
6: 5 thy hair *is* as a f of goats that appear from 5739
6: 6 Thy teeth *are* as a f of sheep which go up 5739
Isa 40:11 He shall feed his f like a shepherd: he shall 5739
63:11 up out of the sea with the shepherd of his f? 6629
Jer 13:17 the LORD'S f is carried away captive. 5739
13:20 where *is* the f *that* was given thee, 5739
13:20 flock *that* was given thee, thy beautiful f? 6629
23: 2 Ye have scattered my f, and driven them 6629
23: 3 I will gather the remnant of my f out of all 6629
25:34 *in the ashes,* ye principal of the f: 6629
25:35 to flee, nor the principal of the f to escape. 6629
25:36 and a howling of the principal of the f, 6629
31:10 and keep him as a shepherd *doth* his f. 5739
31:12 and for the young of the f and of the herd: 6629
49:20 Surely the least of the f shall draw them 6629
50:45 Surely the least of the f shall draw them 6629
51:23 in pieces with thee the shepherd and his f; 5739
Eze 24: 5 Take the choice of the f, and burn also 6629
34: 3 kill them that are fed: *but* ye feed not the f. 6629
34: 6 my f was scattered upon all the face of 6629
34: 8 surely because my f became a prey, and 6629
34: 8 my f became meat to every beast of 6629
34: 8 neither did my shepherds search for my f, 6629
34: 8 fed themselves, and fed not my f; 6629
34:10 I will require my f at their hand, and 6629
34:10 and cause them to cease from feeding the f; 6629
34:10 for I will deliver my f from their mouth, 6629
34:12 As a shepherd seeketh out his f in the day 5739
34:15 I will feed my f, and I will cause them to lie 6629
34:17 *as for* you, O my f, thus saith the Lord 6629
34:19 *as for* my f, they eat that which ye have 6629
34:22 Therefore will I save my f, and they shall 6629
34:31 ye my f, the flock of my pasture, *are* men, 6629
34:31 the f of my pasture, *are* men, *and* I *am* your 6629
36:37 I will increase them *with* men like a f. 6629
36:38 As the holy f, as the flock of Jerusalem in 6629
36:38 as the f of Jerusalem in her solemn feasts; 6629
43:23 and a ram out of the f without blemish. 6629
43:25 and a ram out of the f, without blemish. 6629
45:15 one lamb out of the f, out of two hundred, 6629
Am 6: 4 eat the lambs out of the f, and the calves 6629
7:15 the LORD took me as I followed the f, 6629
Jnh 3: 7 man nor beast, herd nor f, taste any thing: 6629
Mic 2:12 as the f in the midst of their fold: 5739
4: 8 thou, O tower of the f, the strong hold of 5739
7:14 people with thy rod, the f of thine heritage, 6629
Hab 3:17 the f shall be cut off from the fold, and 6629
Zec 9:16 save them in that day as the f of his people: 6629
10: 2 therefore they went their way as a f, 6629
10: 3 for the LORD of hosts hath visited his f 5739
11: 4 my God; Feed the f of the slaughter; 6629
11: 7 And I will feed the f of slaughter, *even* you, 6629
11: 7 of slaughter, *even* you, O poor of the f. 6629
11: 7 and the other I called Bands; and I fed the f. 6629
11:11 the poor of the f that waited upon me knew 6629
11:17 Woe to the idol shepherd that leaveth the f! 6629
Mal 1:14 which hath in his f a male, and voweth, and 5739
Mt 26:31 the sheep of the f shall be scattered abroad. *4167*
Lk 2: 8 keeping watch over their f by night. *4167*
12:32 Fear not, little f; for it is your Father's good *4168*
Ac 20:28 therefore unto yourselves, and to all the f, *4168*
20:29 enter in among you, not sparing the f. *4168*
1Co 9: 7 or who feedeth a f, and eateth not of *4167*
9: 7 a flock, and eateth not of the milk of the f? *4167*
1Pe 5: 2 Feed the f of God which is among you, *4168*
5: 3 but being ensamples to the f. *4168*

FLOCKS (80) [FLOCK]

Ge 13: 5 with Abram, had f, and herds, and tents. 6629
24:35 he hath given him f, and herds, and silver, 6629
26:14 For he had possession of f, and 6629
29: 2 lo, there *were* three f of sheep lying by it; 5739
29: 2 by it; for out of that well they watered the f: 5739
29: 3 thither were all the f gathered: and 5739
29: 8 until all the f be gathered together, and 5739
30:36 and Jacob fed the rest of Laban's f. 6629
30:38 f in the gutters in the watering troughs 6629
30:38 watering troughs when the f came to drink, 6629
30:39 the f conceived before the rods, and 6629
30:40 set the faces of the f toward the ringstraked, 6629
30:40 he put his own f by themselves, and 5739
32: 5 f, and menservants, and womenservants: 6629
32: 7 the f, and herds, and the camels, into two 6629
33:13 the f and herds with young *are* with me: 6629
37:14 well with thy brethren, and well with the f; 6629
37:16 tell me, I pray thee, where they feed *their f.* NIH
45:10 thy f, and thy herds, and all that thou hast: 6629
46:32 they have brought their f, and their herds, 6629
47: 1 their f, and their herds, and all that they 6629
47: 4 for thy servants have no pasture for their f; 6629
47:17 for the f, and for the cattle of 4735+6629
50: 8 their little ones, and their f, and their herds, 6629
Ex 10: 9 with our f and with our herds will we go; 6629
10:24 only let your f and your herds be stayed: 6629
12:32 Also take your f and your herds, as ye have 6629
12:38 and f, and herds, *even* very much cattle. 6629
34: 3 neither let the f nor herds feed before that 6629
Lev 1:10 if his offering *be* of the f, *namely,* of 6629
5:15 LORD a ram without blemish out of the f, 6629
Nu 11:22 Shall the f and the herds be slain for them, 6629
31: 9 and all their f, and all their goods. 4735
31:30 of the beeves, of the asses, and of the f, 6629
32:26 our wives, our f, and all our cattle, 4735
Dt 7:13 increase of thy kine, and the f of thy sheep, 6251
8:13 *when* thy herds and thy f multiply, and thy 6629
12: 6 the firstlings of your herds and of your f: 6629
14:23 and the firstlings of thy herds and of thy f; 6629
28: 4 increase of thy kine, and the f of thy sheep. 6251
28:18 increase of thy kine, and the f of thy sheep. 6251
28:51 the increase of thy kine, or f of thy sheep, 6251
Jdg 5:16 to hear the bleatings of the f? 5739
1Sa 30:20 David took all the f and the herds, 6629
2Sa 12: 2 The rich *man* had exceeding many f and 6629
1Ki 20:27 pitched before them like two **little** f of kids; 2835
1Ch 4:39 of the valley, to seek pasture for their f. 6629
4:41 because *there was* pasture there for their f. 6629
27:31 over the f *was* Jaziz the Hagerite. All these 6629
2Ch 17:11 the Arabians brought him f, seven thousand 6629
32:28 for all *manner of* beasts, and cotes for f. 5739
32:29 possessions of f and herds in abundance: 6629
Ne 10:36 and the firstlings of our herds and of our f, 6629
Job 24: 2 they violently take away f, and 5739
Ps 65:13 The pastures are clothed with f; the valleys 6629
78:48 to the hail, and their f to hot thunderbolts. 4735
Pr 27:23 Be thou diligent to know the state of thy f, 6629
SS 1: 7 turneth aside by the f of thy companions? 5739
Isa 17: 2 they shall be for f, which shall lie down, 5739
32:14 for ever, a joy of wild asses, a pasture of f; 5739
60: 7 All the f of Kedar shall be gathered 6629

F

Isa 61: 5 strangers shall stand and feed your f, and 6629
65:10 Sharon shall be a fold of f, and the valley of 6629
Jer 3:24 their f and their herds, their sons and their 6629
5:17 they shall eat up thy f and thine herds: 6629
6: 3 The shepherds with their f shall come unto 5739
10:21 and all their f shall be scattered. 4830
31:24 husbandmen, and they *that* go forth with f. 5739
33:12 of shepherds causing *their* f to lie down. 6629
33:13 shall the f pass again under the hands of 6629
49:29 their f shall they take *away:* they shall take 6629
50: 8 and be as the he goats before the f. 6629
Eze 25: 5 and the Ammonites a couching place for f: 6629
34: 2 should not the shepherds feed the f? 6629
36:38 shall the waste cities be filled *with* f of 6629
Hos 5: 6 They shall go with their f and with their 6629
Joel 1:18 yea, the f of sheep are made desolate. 5739
Mic 5: 8 as a young lion among the f of sheep: 5739
Zep 2: 6 *and* cottages for shepherds, and folds for f. 6629
2:14 f shall lie down in the midst of her, all 5739

F

FLOG; FLOGGED; FLOGGING; FLOGGINGS See SCOURGES; SCOURGETH; SCOURGING; SCOURGINGS; STRIPE; STRIPES

FLOOD (43) [FLOODS, WATERFLOOD]
Ge 6:17 do bring a f of waters upon the earth, 3999
7: 6 Noah *was* six hundred years old when the f 3999
7: 7 into the ark, because of the waters of the f. 3999
7:10 that the waters of the f were upon the earth. 3999
7:17 the f was forty days upon the earth; and 3999
9:11 be cut off any more by the waters of a f; 3999
9:11 neither shall there any more be a f to 3999
9:15 the waters shall no more become a f to 3999
9:28 Noah lived after the f three hundred and 3999
10: 1 and unto them were sons born after the f. 3999
10:32 the nations divided in the earth after the f. 3999
11:10 and begat Arphaxad two years after the f: 3999
Jos 24: 2 Your fathers dwelt on the *other* side of the f 5104
24: 3 father Abraham from the *other* side of the f, 5104
24:14 fathers served on the *other* side of the f, 5104
24:15 served that *were* on the *other* side of the f, 5104
Job 14:11 the sea, and the f decayeth and drieth up: 5104
22:16 whose foundation was overflown *with* a f: 5104
28: 4 The f breaketh out from the inhabitant; 5158
Ps 29:10 The Lord sitteth upon the f; yea, 3999
66: 6 dry *land:* they went through the f on foot: 5104
74:15 Thou didst cleave the fountain and the f: 5158
90: 5 Thou **carriest** them **away as with a f;** 2229
Isa 28: 2 as a f of mighty waters overflowing, 2230
59:19 When the enemy shall come in like a f, 5104
Jer 46: 7 Who *is* this *that* cometh up as a f, 2975
46: 8 Egypt riseth up like a f, and *his* waters are 2975
47: 2 shall be an overflowing f, and 5158
Da 9:26 the end thereof *shall be* with a f, and 7858
11:22 *with* the arms of a f shall they be overflown 7858
Am 8: 8 it shall rise up wholly as a f; and it shall be 2975
8: 8 cast out and drowned, as *by* the f of Egypt. 2975
9: 5 it shall rise up wholly like a f; and shall be 2975
9: 5 and shall be drowned, as *by* the f of Egypt. 2975
Na 1: 8 with an overrunning f he will make an utter 7858
Mt 24:38 For as in the days that were before the f *2627*
24:39 And knew not until the f came, and *2627*
Lk 6:48 and when the f arose, the stream beat *4132*
17:27 and the f came, and destroyed *them* all. *2627*
2Pe 2: 5 bringing in the f upon the world of *2627*
Rev 12:15 of his mouth water as a f after the woman, *4215*
12:15 cause her to be **carried away of the f.** *4216*
12:16 swallowed up the f which the dragon cast *4215*

FLOODS (19) [FLOOD]
Ex 15: 8 the f stood upright as a heap, *and* the depths 5140
2Sa 22: 5 the f of ungodly men made me afraid; 5158
Job 20:17 the f, the brooks of honey and butter. 5104
28:11 He bindeth the f from overflowing; and 5104
Ps 18: 4 and the f of ungodly men made me afraid. 5158
24: 2 upon the seas, and established it upon the f. 5104
32: 6 surely in the f of great waters they shall not 7858
69: 2 into deep waters, where the f overflow me. 7641
78:44 and their f, *that* they could not drink. 5140
93: 3 The f have lifted up, O Lord, the floods 5104
93: 3 O Lord, the f have lifted up their voice; 5104
93: 3 up their voice; the f lift up their waves. 5104
98: 8 Let the f clap *their* hands: let the hills be 5104
SS 8: 7 quench love, neither can the f drown it: 5104
Isa 44: 3 f upon the dry *ground:* I will pour my spirit 5140
Eze 31:15 I restrained the f thereof, and the great 5104
Jnh 2: 3 of the seas; and the f compassed me about: 5104
Mt 7:25 and the f came, and the winds blew, and *4215*
7:27 and the f came, and the winds blew, and *4215*

FLOODWATERS See WATERFLOOD

FLOOR (19) [BARNFLOOR, CORNFLOOR, FLOORS, THRESHINGFLOOR, THRESHINGFLOORS]
Ge 50:11 saw the mourning in the f of Atad, they 1637
Nu 5:17 of the dust that is in the f of the tabernacle 7172
Dt 15:14 and out of thy f, and out of thy winepress: 1637
Jdg 6:37 Behold, I will put a fleece of wool in the f; 1637
Ru 3: 3 upon thee, and get thee down *to* the f: 1637
3: 6 she went down *unto* the f, and 1637
3:14 not be known that a woman came *into* the f. 1637
1Ki 6:15 both the f of the house, and the walls of 7172
6:15 covered the f of the house with planks of 7172
6:16 both the f and the walls with boards of 7172
6:30 the f of the house he overlaid with gold, 7172
7: 7 cedar from one side of the f to the other. 7172
2Ch 34:11 to f the houses which the kings of Judah 7136
Isa 21:10 O my threshing, and the corn of my f: 1637
Hos 9: 2 The f and the winepress shall not feed 1637
13: 3 *that* is driven with a whirlwind out of the f, 1637
Mic 4:12 shall gather them as the sheaves into the f. 1637
Mt 3:12 and he will throughly purge his f, and *257*
Lk 3:17 and he will throughly purge his f, and *257*

FLOORS (1) [FLOOR]
Joel 2:24 the f shall be full *of* wheat, and the fats 1637

FLOTES (2)
1Ki 5: 9 I will convey them by sea *in* f unto 1702
2Ch 2:16 we will bring it to thee *in* f by sea *to* Joppa; 7513

FLOUR (58)
Ex 29: 2 *of* wheaten f shalt thou make them. 5560
29:40 with the one lamb a tenth deal of f mingled 5560
Lev 2: 1 the Lord, his offering shall be *of* **fine** f; 5560
2: 2 he shall take thereout his handful of the f 5560
2: 4 *it shall be* unleavened cakes of **fine** f 5560
2: 5 it shall be *of* **fine** f unleavened, 5560
2: 7 it shall be made *of* **fine** f with oil. 5560
5:11 *part* of an ephah of **fine** f for a sin offering; 5560
6:15 of the f of the meat offering, and of the oil 5560
6:20 the tenth *part* of an ephah of **fine** f *for* a 5560
7:12 and cakes mingled with oil, of **fine** f, fried. 5560
14:10 three tenth deals of **fine** f *for* a meat 5560
14:21 one tenth deal of **fine** f mingled with oil for 5560
23:13 two tenth deals *of* **fine** f mingled with oil, 5560
23:17 they shall be *of* **fine** f; they shall be baken 5560
24: 5 thou shalt take **fine** f, and bake twelve 5560
Nu 6:15 cakes *of* **fine** f mingled with oil, and 5560
7:13 both of them *were* full *of* **fine** f mingled 5560
7:19 both of them full *of* **fine** f mingled with oil 5560
7:25 both of them full *of* **fine** f mingled with oil 5560
7:31 both of them full *of* **fine** f mingled with oil 5560
7:37 both of them full *of* **fine** f mingled with oil 5560
7:43 both of them full *of* **fine** f mingled with oil 5560
7:49 both of them full *of* **fine** f mingled with oil 5560
7:55 both of them full *of* **fine** f mingled with oil 5560
7:61 both of them full *of* **fine** f mingled with oil 5560
7:67 both of them full *of* **fine** f mingled with oil 5560
7:73 both of them full *of* **fine** f mingled with oil 5560
7:79 both of them full *of* **fine** f mingled with oil 5560
8: 8 *even* **fine** f mingled with oil, and 5560
15: 4 f mingled with the fourth *part* of a hin of 5560
15: 6 f mingled with the third *part* of a hin of oil. 5560
15: 9 deals *of* f mingled with half a hin of oil. 5560
28: 5 a tenth *part* of an ephah *of* f for a meat 5560
28: 9 two tenth deals *of* f *for* a meat offering, 5560
28:12 three tenth deals *of* f *for* a meat offering, 5560
28:12 two tenth deals *of* f *for* a meat offering, 5560
28:13 a several tenth deal of f mingled with oil 5560
28:20 their meat offering *shall be of* f mingled 5560
28:28 their meat offering *of* f mingled with oil, 5560
29: 3 their meat offering *shall be of* f mingled 5560
29: 9 their meat offering *shall be of* f mingled 5560
29:14 their meat offering *shall be of* f mingled 5560
Jdg 6:19 and unleavened *cakes of* an ephah of f: 7058
1Sa 1:24 one ephah of f, and a bottle of wine, and 7058
28:24 took f, and kneaded *it,* and did bake 7058

2Sa 13: 8 she took f, and kneaded *it,* and made cakes 1217
17:28 **f,** and parched *corn,* and beans, and lentiles, 7058
1Ki 4:22 for one day was thirty measures of **fine f,** 5560
2Ki 7: 1 a measure of **fine f** *be sold* for a shekel, 5560
7:16 So a measure of **fine f** was *sold* for a 5560
7:18 and a measure of **fine f** for a shekel, 5560
1Ch 9:29 the **fine f,** and the wine, and the oil, and 5560
23:29 for the **fine f** for meat offering, and for 5560
Eze 16:13 thou didst eat **fine f,** and honey, and oil: 5560
16:19 **fine f,** and oil, and honey, *wherewith* I fed 5560
46:14 of a hin of oil, to temper with the **fine f;** 5560
Rev 18:13 and oil, and **fine f,** and wheat, and beasts, *4585*

FLOURISH (13) [FLOURISHED, FLOURISHETH, FLOURISHING]
Ps 72: 7 In his days shall the righteous f; and 6524
72:16 *they* of the city shall f like grass of 6692
92: 7 and when all the workers of iniquity do f; 6692
92:12 The righteous shall f like the palm tree: 6524
92:13 the LORD shall f in the courts of our God. 6524
132:18 but upon himself shall his crown f. 6692
Pr 11:28 but the righteous shall f as a branch. 6524
14:11 but the tabernacle of the upright shall f. 6524
Ecc 12: 5 the almond tree shall f, and the grasshopper 5340
SS 7:12 let us see if the vine f, *whether* the tender 6524
Isa 17:11 the morning shalt thou **make** thy seed **to f:** 6524
66:14 and your bones shall f like an herb: 6524
Eze 17:24 green tree, and have **made** the dry tree **to f:** 6524

FLOURISHED (2) [FLOURISH]
SS 6:11 *and* to see whether the vine f, *and* 6524
Php 4:10 now at the last your care of me hath f **again;** *330*

FLOURISHETH (2) [FLOURISH]
Ps 90: 6 In the morning it f, and groweth up; in 6692
103:15 *are* as grass: as a flower of the field, so he f. 6692

FLOURISHING (2) [FLOURISH]
Ps 92:14 forth fruit in old age; they shall be fat and f; 7488
Da 4: 4 at rest in mine house, and f in my palace: 7487

FLOW (13) [FLOWED, FLOWETH, FLOWING, OVERFLOW]
Job 20:28 *his goods shall* **f away** in the day of his 5064
Ps 147:18 causeth his wind to blow, *and* the waters f. 5140
SS 4:16 *that* the spices thereof may f **out.** 5140
Isa 2: 2 the hills; and all nations shall f unto it. 5102
48:21 he **caused** the waters **to f** out of the rock 5140
60: 5 f *together,* and thine heart shall fear, and 5102
64: 1 that the mountains might f **down** at thy 2151
Jer 31:12 shall f *together* to the goodness of 5102
51:44 the nations shall not f *together* any more 5102
Joel 3:18 the hills shall f *with* milk, and all the rivers 1980
3:18 all the rivers of Judah shall f *with* waters, 1980
Mic 4: 1 above the hills; and people shall f unto it. 5102
Jn 7:38 out of his belly shall f rivers of living *4482*

FLOWED (3) [FLOW]
Jos 4:18 and f over all his banks, as *they did* before. 1980
Isa 64: 3 the mountains f **down** at thy presence. 2151
La 3:54 Waters f over mine head; *then* I said, I am 6687

FLOWER (20) [FLOWERS]
Ex 25:33 *with* a knop and a f in one branch; 6525
25:33 in the other branch, *with* a knop and a f: 6525
37:19 of almonds in one branch, a knop and a f; 6525
37:19 almonds in another branch, a knop and a f: 6525
1Sa 2:33 of thine house shall die **in the f of** their **age.** 376
Job 14: 2 He cometh forth like a f, and is cut down: 6731
15:33 the vine, and shall cast off his f as the olive. 5328
Ps 103:15 as a f of the field, so he flourisheth. 6731
Isa 18: 5 and the sour grape is ripening in the f, 5328
28: 1 whose glorious beauty *is* a fading f, 6731
28: 4 shall be a fading f, *and* as the hasty fruit 6733
40: 6 all the goodliness thereof *is* as the f of 6731
40: 7 The grass withereth, the f fadeth: because 6731
40: 8 The grass withereth, the f fadeth: but 6731
Na 1: 4 Carmel, and the f of Lebanon languisheth. 6525
1Co 7:36 if she **pass the f of** *her* **age,** *1510+5230*
Jas 1:10 as the f of the grass he shall pass away. *438*
1:11 and the f thereof falleth, and the grace of *438*
1Pe 1:24 and all the glory of man as the f of grass. *438*
1:24 and the f thereof falleth away: *438*

FLOWERS (17) [FLOWER]
Ex 25:31 his bowls, his knops, and his f, 6525
25:34 unto almonds, *with* their knops and their f. 6525
37:17 his branch, his bowls, his knops, and his f, 6525
37:20 made like almonds, his knops, and his f: 6525
Lev 15:24 her f be upon him, he shall be unclean 5079
15:33 of her that is sick of her f, and of him that 5079
Nu 8: 4 unto the f thereof, *was* beaten work: 6525
1Ki 6:18 within *was* carved with knops and open f: 6731
6:29 of cherubims and palm trees and open f, 6731
6:32 of cherubims and palm trees and open f, 6731
6:35 and palm trees and open f: 6731
7:26 like the brim of a cup, *with* f of lilies: 6525
7:49 with the f, and the lamps, and the tongs *of* 6525
2Ch 4: 5 work of the brim of a cup, *with* f of lilies; 6525
4:21 the f, and the lamps, and the tongs, *made he* 6525
SS 2:12 The f appear on the earth; the time of 5339
5:13 cheeks *are* as a bed of spices, *as* sweet f: 4026

FLOWETH (12) [FLOW]
Lev 20:24 a land that f with milk and honey: 2100
Nu 13:27 and surely it f with milk and honey; 2100
14: 8 it us; a land which f with milk and honey. 2100
16:13 brought us up out of a land that f with milk 2100
16:14 not brought us into a land that f with milk 2100
Dt 6: 3 *in* the land that f with milk and honey. 2100
11: 9 a land that f with milk and honey. 2100
26: 9 *even* a land that f with milk and honey. 2100
26:15 a land that f with milk and honey. 2100
27: 3 a land that f with milk and honey; 2100
31:20 their fathers, that f with milk and honey; 2100
Jos 5: 6 give us, a land that f with milk and honey. 2100

FLOWING (12) [FLOW]
Ex 3: 8 a large, unto a land f with milk and honey; 2100
3:17 unto a land f with milk and honey. 2100
13: 5 to give thee, a land f with milk and honey, 2100
33: 3 Unto a land f with milk and honey: for I 2100
Pr 18: 4 *and* the wellspring of wisdom *as* a f brook. 5042
Isa 66:12 the glory of the Gentiles like a f stream: 7857
Jer 11: 5 to give them a land f with milk and honey, 2100
18:14 shall the cold f waters that come from 5140
32:22 to give them, a land f with milk and honey; 2100
49: 4 thy f valley, O backsliding daughter? 2100
Eze 20: 6 f with milk and honey, which *is* the glory 2100
20:15 land which I had given *them,* f with milk 2100

FLUTE (4)
Da 3: 5 f, harp, sackbut, psaltery, dulcimer, and 4953
3: 7 f, harp, sackbut, psaltery, and all kinds of 4953
3:10 f, harp, sackbut, psaltery, and dulcimer, and 4953
3:15 f, harp, sackbut, psaltery, and dulcimer, and 4953

FLUTTERETH (1)
Dt 32:11 f over her young, spreadeth abroad her 7363

FLY (25) [FLEW, FLIES, FLIETH, FLIGHT, FLYING]
Ge 1:20 fowl *that* may f above the earth in the open 5774
1Sa 15:19 didst f upon the spoil, and didst evil in 5860
2Sa 22:11 he rode upon a cherub, and did f: and 5774
Job 5: 7 is born unto trouble, as the sparks f upward. 5774
20: 8 He shall f **away** as a dream, and shall not 5774
39:26 Doth the hawk f by thy wisdom, *and* 82
Ps 18:10 he rode upon a cherub, and did f: yea, 5774
18:10 yea, he did f upon the wings of the wind. 1675
55: 6 *for then* would I f **away,** and be at rest. 5774
90:10 for it is soon cut off, and we f **away.** 5774
Pr 23: 5 they f **away** as an eagle *toward* heaven. 5774
Isa 6: 2 he covered his feet, and with twain he did f. 5774
7:18 *that* the LORD shall hiss for the f that *is* in 2070
11:14 they shall f upon the shoulders of 5774
60: 8 Who *are* these *that* f as a cloud, and as 5774
Jer 48:40 he shall f as an eagle, and shall spread his 1675
49:22 he shall come up and f as the eagle, and 1675
Eze 13:20 ye there hunt the souls to **make** *them* f, 6524
13:20 *even* the souls that ye hunt to **make** *them* f. 6524
Da 9:21 at the beginning, being **caused to f** swiftly, 3286
Hos 9:11 their glory shall f **away** like a bird, 5774
Hab 1: 8 they shall f as the eagle *that* hasteth to eat. 5774
Rev 12:14 that she might f into the wilderness, *4072*
14: 6 And I saw another angel f in the midst of *4072*
19:17 saying to all the fowls that f in the midst of *4072*

FLYING (12) [FLY]
Lev 11:21 Yet these may ye eat of every f creeping 5775
11:23 all *other* f creeping things, which have four 5775
Job 30: 3 f *into* the wilderness in former time 6207

F

Ps 148:10 all cattle; creeping things, and f fowl: 3671
Pr 26: 2 as the swallow by f, so the curse causeless 5774
Isa 14:29 and his fruit *shall be* a fiery f serpent. 5774
30: 6 and old lion, the viper and fiery f serpent, 5774
31: 5 As birds f, so will the LORD of hosts 5774
Zec 5: 1 mine eyes, and looked, and behold, a f roll. 5774
5: 2 I answered, I see a f roll; the length thereof 5774
Rev 4: 7 and the fourth beast *was* like a f eagle. *4072*
8:13 heard an angel f through the midst of *4072*

FOAL (3) [FOALS]
Ge 49:11 Binding his f unto the vine, and his ass's 5895
Zec 9: 9 upon an ass, and upon a colt the f of an ass. 1121
Mt 21: 5 upon an ass, and a colt the f of an ass. *5207*

FOALS (1) [FOAL]
Ge 32:15 and ten bulls, twenty she asses, and ten f. 5895

FOAM (1) [FOAMETH, FOAMING]
Hos 10: 7 her king is cut off as the f upon the water. 7110

FOAMETH (2) [FOAM]
Mk 9:18 and he f, and gnasheth with his teeth, and *875*
Lk 9:39 and it teareth him that he f again, and *876+3326*

FOAMING (2) [FOAM]
Mk 9:20 and he fell on the ground, and wallowed f. *875*
Jude 1:13 waves of the sea, f **out** their own shame; *1890*

FODDER (1)
Job 6: 5 he hath grass? or loweth the ox over his f? 1098

FOES (7)
1Ch 21:12 three months to be destroyed before thy f, 6862
Est 9:16 slew of their f seventy and five thousand, 8130
Ps 27: 2 the wicked, *even* mine enemies and my f, 341
30: 1 and hast not made my f to rejoice over me. 341
89:23 I will beat down his f before his face, and 6862
Mt 10:36 And a man's f *shall be* they of his own *2190*
Ac 2:35 Until I make thy f thy footstool. *2190*

FOLD (9) [FOLDEN, FOLDETH, FOLDING, FOLDS, SHEEPFOLD, SHEEPFOLDS]
Isa 13:20 neither shall the shepherds **make** their f 7257
65:10 Sharon shall be a f of flocks, and the valley 5116
Eze 34:14 the high mountains of Israel shall their f be: 5116
34:14 there shall they lie in a good f, and *in* a fat 5116
Mic 2:12 as the flock in the midst of their f: 1699
Hab 3:17 the flock shall be cut off from the f, and 4356
Jn 10:16 other sheep I have, which are not of this f: *833*
10:16 and there shall be one f, *and* one shepherd. *4167*
Heb 1:12 And as a vesture shalt thou f them **up**, and *1667*

FOLDEN (1) [FOLD]
Na 1:10 For while *they be* f **together** *as* thorns, and 5440

FOLDETH (1) [FOLD]
Ecc 4: 5 The fool f his hands **together**, and 2263

FOLDING (4) [FOLD]
1Ki 6:34 the two leaves of the one door *were* f, and 1550
6:34 and the two leaves of the other door *were* f. 1550
Pr 6:10 a little f of the hands to sleep: 2264
24:33 a little f of the hands to sleep: 2264

FOLDS (5) [FOLD]
Nu 32:24 for your little ones, and f for your sheep; 1448
32:36 fenced cities: and f for sheep. 1448
Ps 50: 9 out of thy house, *nor* he goats out of thy f. 4356
Jer 23: 3 and will bring them again to their f; 5116
Zep 2: 6 *and* cottages for shepherds, and f for flocks. 1448

FOLK (5) [FOLKS, KINSFOLK, KINSFOLKS]
Ge 33:15 Let me now leave with thee *some* of the f 5971
Pr 30:26 The conies *are but* a feeble f, yet make they 5971
Jer 51:58 the f in the fire, and they shall be weary. 3816
Mk 6: 5 that he laid *his* hands upon a few sick *f*, NIG
Jn 5: 3 In these lay a great multitude of impotent *f*, NIG

FOLKS (1) [FOLK]
Ac 5:16 bringing sick *f*, and *them which were* vexed NIG

FOLLOW (86) [FOLLOWED, FOLLOWEDST, FOLLOWERS, FOLLOWETH, FOLLOWING]
Ge 24: 5 not be willing to f me unto this land: 310+1980
24: 8 if the woman will not be willing to f 310+1980
24:39 the woman will not f me. 310+1980
44: 4 said unto his steward, Up, f after the men; 7291
Ex 11: 8 and all the people that f thee: 7272+871.1
14: 4 Pharaoh's heart, that he shall f after them; 7291
14:17 of the Egyptians, and they shall f them: 310+935
21:22 fruit depart *from her*, and yet no mischief f: 1961
21:23 if *any* mischief f, then thou shalt give life 1961
23: 2 Thou shalt not f a multitude to *do* 310+1961
Dt 16:20 That which is altogether just shalt thou f, 7291
18:22 if the thing f not, nor come to pass, that *is* 1961
Jdg 3:28 he said unto them, F after me: for 7291
8: 5 of bread unto the people that f me; 7272+871.1
9: 3 their hearts inclined to f Abimelech; for they 310
1Sa 25:27 the young men that f my lord. 1980+7272+871.1
30:21 so faint that they could not f David, 310+1980
2Sa 17: 9 There is a slaughter among the people that f 310
1Ki 18:21 if the LORD *be* God, f him: but 310+1980
18:21 if Baal, *then* f him. And the people 310+1980
19:20 and my mother, and *then* I will f thee. 310+1980
20:10 handfuls for all the people that f me. 7272+871.1
2Ki 6:19 f me, and I will bring you to the man 310+1980
Ps 23: 6 mercy shall f me all the days of my life: 7291
38:20 because I f *the thing that* good *is*. 7291
45:14 the virgins her companions that f her *shall be* 310
94:15 and all the upright in heart shall f it. 310
119:150 They draw nigh that f **after** mischief: 7291
Isa 5:11 the morning, *that* they may f strong drink; 7291
51: 1 to me, ye that f **after** righteousness, 7291
Jer 17:16 I have not hastened from *being* a pastor to f 310
42:16 shall f **close** after you there *in* Egypt; 1692
Eze 13: 3 that f their own spirit, and have seen 310+1980
Hos 2: 7 she shall f **after** her lovers, but she shall 7291
6: 3 we know, *if* we f on to know the LORD: 7291
Mt 4:19 **F** me, and I will make you fishers of *1205+3694*
8:19 I will f thee whithersoever thou goest. *190*
8:22 But Jesus said unto him, **F** me; and let *190*
9: 9 and he saith unto him, **F** me. And he arose, *190*
16:24 and take up his cross, and f me. *190*
19:21 have treasure in heaven: and come *and* f me. *190*
Mk 2:14 receipt of custom, and said unto him, **F** me. *190*
5:37 And he suffered no *man* to f him, *4870*
6: 1 into his own country; and his disciples f him. *190*
8:34 and take up his cross, and f me. *190*
10:21 and come, take up the cross, and f me. *190*
14:13 you a man bearing a pitcher of water: f him. *190*
16:17 And these signs shall f them that believe; *3877*
Lk 5:27 of custom: and he said unto him, **F** me. *190*
9:23 and take up his cross daily, and f me. *190*
9:57 Lord, I will f thee whithersoever thou goest. *190*
9:59 And he said unto another, **F** me. But he said, *190*
9:61 And another also said, Lord, I will f thee; but *190*
17:23 or, see there: go not after *them*, nor f *them*. *1377*
18:22 have treasure in heaven: and come, f me. *190*
22:10 f him into the house where he entereth in. *190*
22:49 which were about him saw what would f, *1510*
Jn 1:43 and findeth Philip, and saith unto him, **F** me. *190*
10: 4 he goeth before them, and the sheep f him: *190*
10: 5 And a stranger will they not f, but will flee *190*
10:27 my voice, and I know them, and they f me: *190*
12:26 If any *man* serve me, let him f me; and *190*
13:36 Whither I go, thou canst not f me now; *190*
13:36 me now; but thou shalt f me afterwards. *190*
13:37 unto him, Lord, why cannot I f thee now? *190*
21:19 he had spoken this, he saith unto him, **F** me. *190*
21:22 till I come, what *is that* to thee? f thou me. *190*
Ac 3:24 from Samuel and those that f **after**, *2517*
12: 8 Cast thy garment about thee, and f me. *190*
Ro 14:19 f *after* the *things* which make for peace, *1377*
1Co 14: 1 **F after** charity, and desire spiritual *gifts*, *1377*
Php 3:12 I f *after*, if that I may apprehend *that* for *1377*
1Th 5:15 any *man*; but ever f *that which is* good, *1377*
2Th 3: 7 For yourselves know how *ye* ought to f us: *3401*
3: 9 ourselves an ensample unto you to f us. *3401*
1Ti 5:24 to judgment; and some *men* they f **after**. *1872*
6:11 flee these *things;* and f *after* righteousness, *1377*
2Ti 2:22 but f righteousness, faith, charity, peace, *1377*
Heb 12:14 **F** peace with all *men*, and holiness, *1377*
13: 7 whose faith f, considering the end of *their* *3401*
1Pe 1:11 and the glory **that should** f. *3326+3778*
2:21 us an example, that ye should f his steps: *1872*
2Pe 2: 2 And many shall f their pernicious ways; *1811*
3Jn 1:11 f not *that which is* evil, but *that which is* *3401*
Rev 14: 4 These are they which f the Lamb *190*
14:13 their labours; and their works do f them. *190*

FOLLOWED (108) [FOLLOW]

Ge	24:61	rode upon the camels, and f the man:	310+1980
	32:19	and all that f the droves, saying,	310+1980
Nu	14:24	another spirit with him, and hath f me fully,	310
	16:25	Abiram; and the elders of Israel f him.	310+1980
	32:11	because they have not wholly f me:	310
	32:12	of Nun: for they have wholly f the LORD.	310
Dt	1:36	because he hath wholly f the LORD.	310
	4: 3	for all the men that f Baal-peor,	310+1980
Jos	6: 8	of the covenant of the LORD f them.	310+1980
	14: 8	but I wholly f the LORD my God.	310
	14: 9	thou hast wholly f the LORD my God.	310
	14:14	that he wholly f the LORD God of Israel.	310
Jdg	2:12	of the land of Egypt, and f other gods,	310+1980
	9: 4	and light persons, which f him.	310+1980
	9:49	f Abimelech, and put *them* to the hold,	310+1980
1Sa	13: 7	in Gilgal, and all the people f him trembling.	310
	14:22	even they also f **hard** after them in	1692
	17:13	of Jesse went *and* f Saul to the battle:	310+1980
	17:14	and the three eldest f Saul.	310+1980
	31: 2	the Philistines f **hard** upon Saul and upon	1692
2Sa	1: 6	and horsemen f **hard after** him.	1692
	2:10	But the house of Judah f David.	310+1961
	3:31	And king David *himself* f the bier.	310+1980
	11: 8	f him a mess *of meat* from the king.	310+3318
	17:23	Ahithophel saw that his counsel was not f,	6213
	20: 2	after David, *and* f Sheba the son of Bichri:	310
1Ki	12:20	there was none that f the house of David, but	310
	14: 8	and who f me with all his heart,	310+1980
	16:21	half of the people f Tibni the son of	310+1961
	16:21	to make him king; and half f Omri.	310
	16:22	the people that f Omri prevailed against	310
	16:22	the people that f Tibni the son of Ginath:	310
	18:18	the LORD, and thou hast f Baalim.	310+1980
	20:19	out of the city, and the army which f them.	310
2Ki	3: 9	and for the cattle that f them.	7272+871.1
	4:30	leave thee. And he arose, and f her.	310+1980
	5:21	So Gehazi f after Naaman. And when	7291
	9:27	Jehu f after him, and said, Smite him also	7291
	13: 2	f the sins of Jeroboam the son of	310+1980
	17:15	they f vanity, and became vain, and	310+1980
1Ch	10: 2	the Philistines f **hard** after Saul, and	1692
Ne	4:23	nor the men of the guard which f me,	310
Ps	68:25	the players on instruments *f* after;	NIH
Eze	10:11	*to* the place whither the head looked they f	1980
Am	7:15	the LORD took me as I f the flock, and	310
Mt	4:20	they straightway left *their* nets, and f him.	*190*
	4:22	left the ship and their father, and f him.	*190*
	4:25	And there f him great multitudes *of people*	*190*
	8: 1	from the mountain, great multitudes f him.	*190*
	8:10	and said to them that f, Verily I say unto	*190*
	8:23	was entered into a ship, his disciples f him.	*190*
	9: 9	Follow me. And he arose, and f him.	*190*
	9:19	and f him, and *so did* his disciples.	*190*
	9:27	two blind men f him, crying, and saying,	*190*
	12:15	and great multitudes f him, and he healed	*190*
	14:13	when the people had heard *thereof,* they f	*190*
	19: 2	And great multitudes f him; and he healed	*190*
	19:27	Behold, we have forsaken all, and f thee;	*190*
	19:28	That ye which have f me, in	*190*
	20:29	from Jericho, a great multitude f him.	*190*
	20:34	their eyes received sight, and they f him.	*190*
	21: 9	and that f, cried, saying, Hosanna to the Son	*190*
	26:58	But Peter f him afar off unto the high priest's	*190*
	27:55	which f Jesus from Galilee, ministering unto	*190*
	27:62	that f the *day of the* preparation,	*1510+3326*
Mk	1:18	they forsook their nets, and f him.	*190*
	1:36	and they that were with him f **after** him.	*2614*
	2:14	Follow me. And he arose and f him.	*190*
	2:15	for there were many, and they f him.	*190*
	3: 7	and a great multitude from Galilee f him,	*190*
	5:24	and much people f him, and thronged him.	*190*
	10:28	Lo, we have left all, and have f thee.	*190*
	10:32	and as they f, they were afraid.	*190*
	10:52	he received his sight, and f Jesus in the way.	*190*
	11: 9	and they that f, cried, saying, Hosanna;	*190*
	14:51	And there f him a certain young man,	*190*
	14:54	And Peter f him afar off, even into	*190*
	15:41	in Galilee, f him, and ministered unto him;)	*190*
Lk	5:11	ships to land, they forsook all, and f him.	*190*
	5:28	And he left all, rose up, and f him.	*190*
	7: 9	and said unto the people that f him,	*190*
	9:11	And the people, when they knew *it,* f him:	*190*
	18:28	Peter said, Lo, we have left all, and f thee.	*190*
	18:43	received his sight, and f him, glorifying God:	*190*
	22:39	of Olives; and his disciples also f him.	*190*
	22:54	the high priest's house. And Peter f afar off.	*190*
	23:27	And there f him a great company of people,	*190*
	23:49	and the women that f him from Galilee,	*4870*
	23:55	f **after**, and beheld the sepulchre, and	*2628*
Jn	1:37	disciples heard him speak, and they f Jesus.	*190*
	1:40	and f him, was Andrew, Simon Peter's	*190*
	6: 2	And a great multitude f him, because	*190*
	11:31	rose up hastily and went out, f her, saying,	*190*
	18:15	And Simon Peter f Jesus, and *so did* another	*190*
Ac	12: 9	And he went out, and f him; and wist not	*190*
	13:43	and religious proselytes f Paul and Barnabas:	*190*
	16:17	The same f Paul and us, and cried, saying,	*2628*
	21:36	For the multitude of the people f *after,*	*190*
Ro	9:30	which f not *after* righteousness,	*1377*
	9:31	which f *after* the law of righteousness,	*1377*
1Co	10: 4	for they drank of *that* spiritual Rock that f	*190*
1Ti	5:10	if she have **diligently** f every good work.	*1872*
2Pe	1:16	For we have not f cunningly devised fables,	*1811*
Rev	6: 8	sat on him *was* Death, and Hell f with him.	*190*
	8: 7	and there f hail and fire mingled with	*1096*
	14: 8	And there f another angel, saying,	*190*
	14: 9	And *the* third angel f them, saying with a	*190*
	19:14	And the armies which were in heaven f him	*190*

FOLLOWEDST (1) [FOLLOW]

Ru	3:10	inasmuch as *thou* f not young men,	310+1980

FOLLOWERS (8) [FOLLOW]

1Co	4:16	Wherefore I beseech you, be ye f of me.	*3402*
	11: 1	Be ye f of me, even as I also *am* of Christ.	*3402*
Eph	5: 1	Be ye therefore f of God, as dear children;	*3402*
Php	3:17	be f **together** of me, and mark them which	*4831*
1Th	1: 6	And ye became f of us, and of the Lord,	*3402*
	2:14	became f of the churches of God which in	*3402*
Heb	6:12	but f of them who through faith and	*3402*
1Pe	3:13	harm you, if ye be f of *that which is* good?	*3402*

FOLLOWETH (15) [FOLLOW]

2Ki	11:15	him that f her kill with the sword.	310+935
2Ch	23:14	whoso f her, let him be slain with	310+935
Ps	63: 8	My soul f **hard** after thee: thy right hand	1692
Pr	12:11	he that f vain *persons is* void of	7291
	15: 9	he loveth him that f **after** righteousness.	7291
	21:21	He that f **after** righteousness and	7291
	28:19	he that f **after** vain *persons* shall have	7291
Isa	1:23	every one loveth gifts, and f **after** rewards:	7291
Eze	16:34	whereas none f thee to commit whoredoms:	310
Hos	12: 1	feedeth on wind, and f **after** the east wind:	7291
Mt	10:38	and f after me, is not worthy of me.	*190*
Mk	9:38	out devils in thy name, and he f not us:	*190*
	9:38	and we forbad him, because he f not us.	*190*
Lk	9:49	and we forbad him, because he f not with us.	*190*
Jn	8:12	he that f me shall not walk in darkness, but	*190*

FOLLOWING (43) [FOLLOW]

Ge	41:31	in the land by reason of that famine f;	310+3651
Dt	7: 4	For they will turn away thy son from f me,	310
	12:30	to thyself that thou be not snared by f them,	310
Jos	22:16	to turn away *this* day from f the LORD,	310
	22:18	that ye must turn away *this* day from f	310
	22:23	That we have built us an altar to turn from f	310
	22:29	turn *this* day from f the LORD, to build an	310
Jdg	2:19	in f other gods to serve them, and	310+1980
Ru	1:16	to leave thee, *or* to return from f **after** thee:	310
1Sa	12:14	over you continue f the LORD your God:	310
	12:20	yet turn not aside from f the LORD, but	310
	14:46	Saul went up from f the Philistines: and	310
	15:11	for he is turned back from f me, and hath not	310
	24: 1	when Saul was returned from f	310
2Sa	2:19	to the right hand nor to the left from f Abner.	310
	2:21	Asahel would not turn aside from f of him.	310
	2:22	again to Asahel, Turn thee aside from f me:	310
	2:26	ere thou bid the people return from f their	310
	2:27	had gone up every one from f his brother.	310
	2:30	Joab returned from f Abner: and when he	310
	7: 8	from f the sheep, to be ruler over my people,	310
1Ki	1: 7	the priest: and they f Adonijah helped *him.*	310
	9: 6	*But* if you shall at all turn from f me, you or	310
	21:26	he did very abominably in f idols,	310+1980
2Ki	17:21	Jeroboam drave Israel from f the LORD,	310
	18: 6	*and* departed not from f him, but kept his	310

1Ch 17: 7 from the sheepcote, *even* from f the sheep, 310
2Ch 25:27 f the LORD they made a conspiracy against 310
34:33 *And* all his days they departed not from f 310
Ps 48:13 that ye may tell *it* to the generation f. 314
78:71 From f the *ewes* great with young he brought 310
109:13 in the generation f let their name be blotted 312
Mk 16:20 and confirming the word with signs f. *1872*
Lk 13:33 walk to day, and to morrow, and the *day* f: *2192*
Jn 1:38 and saw them f, and saith unto them, *190*
1:43 The **day** f Jesus would go forth into *1887*
6:22 The **day** f, when the people which stood on *1887*
20: 6 Then cometh Simon Peter f him, and *190*
21:20 seeth the disciple whom Jesus loved f; *190*
Ac 21: 1 and the *day* f unto Rhodes, and from thence *1836*
21:18 And the *day* f Paul went in with us unto *1966*
23:11 And the night f the Lord stood by him, and *1966*
2Pe 2:15 f the way of Balaam *the son* of Bosor, *1811*

F

FOLLY (37) [FOOL]

Ge 34: 7 he had wrought f in Israel in lying with 5039
Dt 22:21 because she hath wrought f in Israel, 5039
Jos 7:15 and because he hath wrought f in Israel. 5039
Jdg 19:23 man is come into mine house, do not this f. 5039
20: 6 have committed lewdness and f in Israel. 5039
20:10 according to all the f that they have 5039
1Sa 25:25 *is* he; Nabal *is* his name, and f *is* with him: 5039
2Sa 13:12 to be done in Israel: do not thou this f. 5039
Job 4:18 and his angels he charged with f: 8417
24:12 crieth out: yet God layeth not f *to them.* 8604
42: 8 lest *I* deal with you *after your* f, in that ye 5039
Ps 49:13 This their way *is* their f: yet their posterity 3689
85: 8 his saints: but let them not turn *again* to f. 3690
Pr 5:23 in the greatness of his f he shall go astray. 200
13:16 with knowledge: but a fool layeth open *his* f. 200
14: 8 his way: but the f of fools *is* deceit. 200
14:18 The simple inherit f: but the prudent are 200
14:24 their riches: *but* the foolishness of fools *is* f. 200
14:29 but *he that is* hasty of spirit exalteth f. 200
15:21 F *is* joy to *him that is* destitute of wisdom: 200
16:22 that hath it: but the instruction of fools *is* f. 200
17:12 meet a man, rather than a fool in his f. 200
18:13 a matter before he heareth *it*, it *is* f 200
26: 4 Answer not a fool according to his f, 200
26: 5 Answer a fool according to his f, lest he be 200
26:11 to his vomit, *so* a fool returneth to his f. 200
Ecc 1:17 know wisdom, and to know madness and f: 5531
2: 3 to lay hold on f, till I might see what *was* 5531
2:12 to behold wisdom, and madness, and f: 5531
2:13 I saw that wisdom excelleth f, as far as 5531
7:25 *of things,* and to know the wickedness of f, 3689
10: 1 *doth* a little f *him that is* in reputation for 5531
10: 6 F is set in great dignity, and the rich sit in 5529
Isa 9:17 an evildoer, and every mouth speaketh f. 5039
Jer 23:13 I have seen f in the prophets of Samaria; 8604
2Co 11: 1 *God* you could bear with me a little in *my* f: *877*
2Ti 3: 9 for their f shall be manifest unto all *men,* as *454*

FOOD (55) [FEED]

Ge 2: 9 that is pleasant to the sight, and good for f; 3978
3: 6 the woman saw that the tree *was* good for f, 3978
6:21 take thou unto thee of all f that is eaten, 3978
6:21 and it shall be for f for thee, and for them. 402
41:35 let them gather all the f of those good years 400
41:35 of Pharaoh, and let them keep f in the cities. 400
41:36 *that* f shall be for store to the land against 400
41:48 he gathered up all the f of the seven years, 400
41:48 land of Egypt, and laid up the f in the cities: 400
41:48 the f of the field, which *was* round about 400
42: 7 they said, From the land of Canaan to buy f. 400
42:10 my lord, but to buy f are thy servants come. 400
42:33 take *f for* the famine of your households, NIH
43: 2 said unto them, Go again, buy us a little f. 400
43: 4 with us, we will go down and buy thee f: 400
43:20 came indeed down at the first time to buy f: 400
43:22 have we brought down in our hands to buy f: 400
44: 1 saying, Fill the men's sacks *with* f, as much 400
44:25 father said, Go again, *and* buy us a little f. 400
47:24 for your f, and for them of your households, 400
47:24 and for f for your little ones. 398
Ex 21:10 If he take him another *wife;* her f, 7607
Lev 3:11 *it is* the f of the offering made by fire unto 3899
3:16 *it is* the f of the offering made by fire for a 3899
19:23 shall have planted all *manner of* trees for f, 3978
22: 7 eat of the holy *things;* because it *is* his f. 3899
Dt 10:18 the stranger, in giving him f and raiment. 3899
1Sa 14:24 Cursed *be* the man that eateth *any* f until 3899
14:24 So none of the people tasted *any* f. 3899
14:28 Cursed *be* the man that eateth *any* f *this* 3899
2Sa 9:10 that thy master's son may have f to eat: 3899
1Ki 5: 9 my desire, in giving f for my household. 3899
5:11 measures of wheat *for* f to his household, 4361
Job 23:12 of his mouth more than my necessary *f.* NIH
24: 5 the wilderness *yieldeth* f for them *and* 3899
38:41 Who provideth for the raven his f? 6718
40:20 Surely the mountains bring him forth f, 944
Ps 78:25 Man did eat angels' f: he sent them meat to 3899
104:14 that *he* may bring forth f out of the earth; 3899
136:25 Who giveth f to all flesh: for his mercy 3899
146: 7 which giveth f to the hungry. The LORD 3899
147: 9 He giveth to the beast his f, *and* to 3899
Pr 6: 8 *and* gathereth her f in the harvest. 3978
13:23 Much f *is in* the tillage of the poor: but 400
27:27 *shalt have* goats' milk enough for thy f, 3899
27:27 for the f of thy household, and *for* 3899
28: 3 *is like* a sweeping rain which leaveth no f. 3899
30: 8 feed me with f convenient for me: 3899
31:14 she bringeth her f from afar. 3899
Eze 16:27 have diminished thine ordinary *f,* and NIH
48:18 the increase thereof shall be for f unto them 3899
Ac 14:17 filling our hearts with f and gladness. *5160*
2Co 9:10 to the sower both minister bread for *your* f, *1035*
1Ti 6: 8 And having f and raiment let us be *1305*
Jas 2:15 or sister be naked, and destitute of daily f, *5160*

FOOL (66) [FOLLY, FOOL'S, FOOLISH, FOOLISHLY, FOOLISHNESS, FOOLS, FOOLS']

1Sa 26:21 I have **played the** f, and have erred 5528
2Sa 3:33 and said, Died Abner as a f dieth? 5036
Ps 14: 1 The f hath said in his heart, *There is* no 5036
49:10 likewise the f and the brutish person perish, 3684
53: 1 The f hath said in his heart, *There is* no 5036
92: 6 neither doth a f understand this. 3684
Pr 7:22 or as a f to the correction of the stocks; 191
10: 8 but a prating f shall fall. 191
10:10 eye causeth sorrow: but a prating f shall fall. 191
10:18 and he that uttereth a slander, *is* a f. 3684
10:23 *It is* as sport to a f to do mischief: but a 3684
11:29 the f *shall be* servant to the wise of heart. 191
12:15 The way of a f *is* right in his own eyes: but 191
13:16 but a f layeth open *his* folly. 3684
14:16 from evil: but the f rageth, and *is* confident. 3684
15: 5 A f despiseth his father's instruction: but 191
17: 7 Excellent speech becometh not a f: 5036
17:10 a wise *man* than an hundred stripes into a f. 3684
17:12 meet a man, rather than a f in his folly. 3684
17:16 Wherefore *is there* a price in the hand of a f 3684
17:21 He that begetteth a f *doeth it* to his sorrow: 3684
17:21 his sorrow: and the father of a f hath no joy. 5036
17:24 the eyes of a f *are* in the ends of the earth. 3684
17:28 Even a f, when he holdeth his peace, 191
18: 2 A f hath no delight in understanding, but 3684
19: 1 *he that is* perverse in his lips, and *is* a f. 3684
19:10 Delight *is* not seemly for a f; much less for 3684
20: 3 from strife: but every f will be meddling. 191
23: 9 Speak not in the ears of a f: for he will 3684
24: 7 Wisdom *is too* high for a f: he openeth not 191
26: 1 in harvest, so honour *is* not seemly for a f. 3684
26: 4 Answer not a f according to his folly, 3684
26: 5 Answer a f according to his folly, lest he be 3684
26: 6 by the hand of a f cutteth off the feet, 3684
26: 8 in a sling, so *is* he that giveth honour to a f. 3684
26:10 that formed all *things* both rewardeth the f, 3684
26:11 to his vomit, *so* a f returneth to his folly. 3684
26:12 *there is* more hope of a f than of him. 3684
27:22 Though thou shouldest bray a f in a mortar 191
28:26 He that trusteth in his own heart *is* a f: but 3684
29:11 A f uttereth all his mind: but a wise *man* 3684
29:20 *there is* more hope of a f than of him. 3684
30:22 and a f when he is filled *with* meat; 5036
Ecc 2:14 in his head; but the f walketh in darkness: 3684
2:15 As it happeneth to the f, so it happeneth 3684
2:16 of the wise more than of the f for ever; 3684
2:16 And how dieth the wise *man?* as the f. 3684
2:19 whether he shall be a wise *man* or a f? 5530
4: 5 The f foldeth his hands together, and 3684
6: 8 For what hath the wise more than the f? 3684
7: 6 under a pot, so *is* the laughter of the f: 3684
10: 3 when he that is a f walketh by the way, 5530

Ecc 10: 3 and he saith to every one *that* he *is* a f. 5530
10:12 but the lips of a f will swallow up himself. 3684
10:14 A f also is full of words: a man cannot tell 5530
Jer 17:11 of his days, and at his end shall be a f. 5036
Hos 9: 7 Israel shall know *it:* the prophet *is* a f, 191
Mt 5:22 but whosoever shall say, *Thou* f, shall be in *3474*
Lk 12:20 But God said unto him, *Thou* f, this night *878*
1Co 3:18 let him become a f, that he may be wise. *3474*
15:36 *Thou* f, *that* which thou sowest is not *878*
2Co 11:16 I say again, Let no *man* think me a f; *878*
11:16 if otherwise, yet as a f receive me, that I may *878*
11:23 (I speak as a f) I *am* more; in labours more *3912*
12: 6 I would desire to glory, I shall not be a f; *878*
12:11 I am become a f in glorying; ye have *878*

FOOL'S (6) [FOOL]

Pr 12:16 A f wrath is presently known: but a prudent 191
18: 6 A f lips enter into contention, and 3684
18: 7 A f mouth *is* his destruction, and his lips 3684
27: 3 but a f wrath *is* heavier than them both. 191
Ecc 5: 3 a f voice *is known* by multitude of words. 3684
10: 2 *is* at his right hand; but a f heart at his left. 3684

FOOLISH (52) [FOOL]

Dt 32: 6 the LORD, O f people and unwise? 5036
32:21 I will provoke them to anger with a f 5036
Job 2:10 Thou speakest as one of the f *women* 5036
5: 2 For wrath killeth the f **man**, and 191
5: 3 I have seen the f taking root: but suddenly I 191
Ps 5: 5 The f shall not stand in thy sight: 1984
39: 8 make me not the reproach of the f. 5036
73: 3 For I was envious at the f, *when* I saw 1984
73:22 So f *was* I, and ignorant: I was *as* a beast 1198
74:18 *that* the f people have blasphemed thy 5036
74:22 remember how the f *man* reproacheth thee 5036
Pr 9: 6 Forsake the f, and live; and go in the way 6612
9:13 A f woman *is* clamorous: *she is* simple, and 3687
10: 1 but a f son *is* the heaviness of his mother. 3684
10:14 but the mouth of the f *is* near destruction. 191
14: 1 but the f plucketh it down with her hands. 200
14: 3 In the mouth of the f *is* a rod of pride: but 191
14: 7 Go from the presence of a f man, 3684
15: 7 but the heart of the f *doeth* not so. 3684
15:20 but a f man despiseth his mother. 3684
17:25 A f son *is* a grief to his father, and 3684
19:13 A f son *is* the calamity of his father: and 3684
21:20 of the wise; but a f man spendeth it up. 3684
29: 9 If a wise man contendeth with a f man, 191
Ecc 4:13 and a wise child than an old and f king, 3684
7:17 not over much wicked, neither be thou f: 5530
10:15 The labour of the f wearieth every one of 3684
Isa 44:25 and **maketh** their knowledge f; 5528
Jer 4:22 For my people *is* f, they have not known me; 191
5: 4 I said, Surely these *are* poor; they are f: 2973
5:21 O f people, and without understanding; 5530
10: 8 they are altogether brutish and f: the stock 3688
La 2:14 have seen vain and f **things** for thee: 8602
Eze 13: 3 Woe unto the f prophets, that follow their 5036
Zec 11:15 Take unto thee yet the instruments of a f 196
Mt 7:26 them not, shall be likened unto a f man, *3474*
25: 2 five of them were wise, and five *were* f. *3474*
25: 3 They that *were* f took their lamps, and *3474*
25: 8 And the f said unto the wise, Give us of *3474*
Ro 1:21 and their f heart was darkened. *801*
2:20 An instructor of the f, a teacher of babes, *878*
10:19 no people, *and* by a f nation I will anger you. *801*
1Co 1:20 hath not God **made** f the wisdom of this *3471*
1:27 But God hath chosen the f *things* of *3474*
Gal 3: 1 O f Galatians, who hath bewitched you, *453*
3: 3 Are ye so f? having begun in the Spirit, *453*
Eph 5: 4 Neither filthiness, nor f **talking**, nor jesting, *3473*
1Ti 6: 9 a snare, and *into* many f and hurtful lusts, *453*
2Ti 2:23 But f and unlearned questions avoid, *3474*
Tit 3: 3 For we ourselves also were sometimes f, *453*
3: 9 But avoid f questions, and genealogies, and *3474*
1Pe 2:15 *ye* may put to silence the ignorance of f men: *878*

FOOLISHLY (12) [FOOL]

Ge 31:28 thou hast now **done** f in *so* doing. 5528
Nu 12:11 wherein we have **done** f, and wherein we 2973
1Sa 13:13 And Samuel said to Saul, Thou hast **done** f: 5528
2Sa 24:10 of thy servant; for I have **done** very f. 5528
1Ch 21: 8 of thy servant; for I have **done** very f. 5528
2Ch 16: 9 Herein thou hast **done** f: therefore 5528
Job 1:22 all this Job sinned not, nor charged God f. 8604
Ps 75: 4 I said unto the fools, **Deal** not f: and to 1984
Pr 14:17 *He that is* soon angry dealeth f: and a man of 200
30:32 If thou hast **done** f in lifting up thyself, or 5034
2Co 11:17 *it* not after the Lord, but as *it were* f, *877+1722*
11:21 whereinsoever any is bold, (I speak f,) *877+1722*

FOOLISHNESS (20) [FOOL]

2Sa 15:31 **turn** the counsel of Ahithophel **into** f. 5528
Ps 38: 5 *and* are corrupt because of my f. 200
69: 5 O God, thou knowest my f; and my sins are 200
Pr 12:23 but the heart of fools proclaimeth f. 200
14:24 wise *is* their riches: *but* the f of fools *is* folly. 200
15: 2 but the mouth of fools poureth out f. 200
15:14 but the mouth of fools feedeth on f. 200
19: 3 The f of man perverteth his way: and 200
22:15 F *is* bound in the heart of a child; *but* the rod 200
24: 9 The thought of f *is* sin: and the scorner *is* an 200
27:22 a pestle, *yet* will not his f depart from him. 200
Ecc 7:25 wickedness of folly, even of f *and* madness: 5531
10:13 beginning of the words of his mouth *is* f: 5531
Mk 7:22 an evil eye, blasphemy, pride, f: *877*
1Co 1:18 of the cross is to them that perish f; *3472*
1:21 it pleased God by the f of preaching to save *3472*
1:23 a stumblingblock, and unto the Greeks f; *3472*
1:25 Because the f of God is wiser than men; *3474*
2:14 for they are f unto him: neither can he *3472*
3:19 For the wisdom of this world is f with God. *3472*

FOOLS (42) [FOOL]

2Sa 13:13 thou shalt be as one of the f in Israel. 5036
Job 12:17 away spoiled, and **maketh** the judges f. 1984
30: 8 *They were* children of f, yea, children of 5036
Ps 75: 4 I said unto the f, Deal not foolishly: and 1984
94: 8 the people: and ye f, when will ye be wise? 3684
107:17 F because of their transgression, and because 191
Pr 1: 7 *but* f despise wisdom and instruction. 191
1:22 in their scorning, and f hate knowledge? 3684
1:32 and the prosperity of f shall destroy them. 3684
3:35 but shame shall be the promotion of f. 3684
8: 5 and, ye f, be ye of an understanding heart. 3684
10:21 feed many: but f die for want of wisdom. 191
12:23 but the heart of f proclaimeth foolishness. 3684
13:19 *it is* abomination to f to depart from evil. 3684
13:20 but a companion of f shall be destroyed. 3684
14: 8 his way: but the folly of f *is* deceit. 3684
14: 9 F make a mock at sin: but among 191
14:24 their riches: *but* the foolishness of f *is* folly. 3684
14:33 *that which is* in the midst of f is made 3684
15: 2 but the mouth of f poureth out foolishness. 3684
15:14 but the mouth of f feedeth on foolishness. 3684
16:22 that hath it: but the instruction of f *is* folly. 191
19:29 for scorners, and stripes for the back of f. 3684
26: 7 not equal: so *is* a parable in the mouth of f. 3684
26: 9 so *is* a parable in the mouth of f. 3684
Ecc 5: 1 ready to hear, than to give the sacrifice of f: 3684
5: 4 not to pay it; for *he hath* no pleasure in f: 3684
7: 4 but the heart of f *is* in the house of mirth. 3684
7: 5 than for a man to hear the song of f. 3684
7: 9 for anger resteth in the bosom of f. 3684
9:17 than the cry of him that ruleth among f. 3684
Isa 19:11 Surely the princes of Zoan *are* f, the counsel 191
19:13 The princes of Zoan are become f, 2973
35: 8 the wayfaring men, though f, shall not err 191
Mt 23:17 *Ye* f and blind: for whether is greater, *3474*
23:19 *Ye* f and blind: for whether *is* greater, *3474*
Lk 11:40 *Ye* f, did not he that made that *which is* *878*
24:25 O f, and slow of heart to believe all that *453*
Ro 1:22 *themselves* to be wise, they became f, *3471*
1Co 4:10 We *are* f for Christ's sake, but ye *are* wise *3474*
2Co 11:19 For ye suffer f gladly, seeing ye *yourselves* *878*
Eph 5:15 ye walk circumspectly, not as f, but as wise, *781*

FOOLS' (1) [FOOL]

Pr 26: 3 a bridle for the ass, and a rod for the f back. 3684

FOOT (95) [AFOOT, BAREFOOT, BROKENFOOTED, CLOVENFOOTED, FEET, FOOTMEN, FOOTSTEPS, FOOTSTOOL, FOURFOOTED]

Ge 8: 9 the dove found no rest for the sole of her f, 7272
41:44 lift up his hand or f in all the land of Egypt. 7272
Ex 12:37 about six hundred thousand **on** f *that were* 7273
21:24 tooth for tooth, hand for hand, f for foot, 7272
21:24 tooth for tooth, hand for hand, foot for f, 7272

Ex 29:20 upon the great toe of their right f, and 7272
30:18 his f *also of* brass, to wash *withal:* and 3653
30:28 with all his vessels, and the laver and his f. 3653
31: 9 all his furniture, and the laver and his f, 3653
35:16 and all his vessels, the laver and his f, 3653
38: 8 the laver *of* brass, and the f of it *of* brass, 3653
39:39 and all his vessels, the laver and his f, 3653
40:11 thou shalt anoint the laver and his f, and 3653
Lev 8:11 and all his vessels, both the laver and his f, 3653
8:23 and upon the great toe of his right f. 7272
13:12 *hath* the plague from his head even to his f, 7272
14:14 and upon the great toe of his right f: 7272
14:17 and upon the great toe of his right f, 7272
14:25 and upon the great toe of his right f: 7272
14:28 and upon the great toe of his right f: 7272
Nu 22:25 and crusht Balaam's f against the wall: 7272
Dt 2: 5 no, not so much as a f breadth; 3709+7272
8: 4 neither did thy f swell, these forty years. 7272
11:10 wateredst *it* with thy f, as a garden of herbs: 7272
19:21 tooth for tooth, hand for hand, f for foot. 7272
19:21 tooth for tooth, hand for hand, foot for f. 7272
25: 9 loose his shoe from off his f, and spit in his 7272
28:35 from the sole of thy f unto the top of thy 7272
28:56 of her f upon the ground for delicateness 7272
28:65 neither shall the sole of thy f have rest: 7272
29: 5 and thy shoe is not waxen old upon thy f. 7272
32:35 recompence; their f shall slide in *due* time: 7272
33:24 to his brethren, and let him dip his f in oil. 7272
Jos 1: 3 Every place that the sole of your f shall 7272
5:15 unto Joshua, Loose thy shoe from off thy f; 7272
Jdg 5:15 he was sent on f into the valley. For 7272
2Sa 2:18 and Asahel *was as* light of f as a wild roe. 7272
14:25 from the sole of his f even to the crown of 7272
21:20 on every f six toes, four and twenty *in* 7272
2Ki 9:33 on the horses: and he **trode** her **under** f. 7429
1Ch 20: 6 six *on each hand,* and six *on each f:* and NIH
2Ch 33: 8 Neither will I any more remove the f of 7272
Job 2: 7 boils from the sole of his f unto his crown. 7272
23:11 My f hath held his steps, his way have I 7272
28: 4 *even the waters* forgotten of the f: 7272
31: 5 with vanity, or *if* my f hath hasted to deceit; 7272
39:15 forgetteth that the f may crush them, or 7272
Ps 9:15 in the net which they hid is their own f 7272
26:12 My f standeth in an even place: in 7272
36:11 Let not the f of pride come against me, and 7272
38:16 when my f slippeth, they magnify 7272
66: 6 dry *land:* they went through the flood on f: 7272
68:23 That thy f may be dipped in the blood of 7272
91:12 lest thou dash thy f against a stone. 7272
94:18 When I said, My f slippeth; thy mercy, 7272
121: 3 He will not suffer thy f to be moved: 7272
Pr 1:15 with them; refrain thy f from their path: 7272
3:23 thy way safely, and thy f shall not stumble. 7272
3:26 and shall keep thy f from being taken. 7272
4:27 hand nor *to* the left: remove thy f from evil. 7272
25:17 Withdraw thy f from thy neighbour's 7272
25:19 *is like* a broken tooth, and a f out of joint. 7272
Ecc 5: 1 Keep thy f when thou goest to the house of 7272
Isa 1: 6 From the sole of the f even unto the head 7272
14:25 and upon my mountains **tread** him **under** f: 947
18: 7 a nation meted out and **trodden under** f, 4001
20: 2 thy loins, and put off thy shoe from thy f. 7272
26: 6 The f shall tread it down, *even* the feet of 7272
41: 2 called him to his f, gave the nations before 7272
58:13 If thou turn away thy f from the sabbath, 7272
Jer 2:25 Withhold thy f from being unshod, and 7272
12:10 they have **trodden** my portion **under** f, 947
La 1:15 The Lord hath **trodden under** f all my 5541
Eze 1: 7 of their feet *was* like the sole of a calf's f: 7272
6:11 thine hand, and stamp with thy f, and say, 7272
29:11 No f of man shall pass through it, nor foot 7272
29:11 nor f of beast shall pass through it, 7272
32:13 neither shall the f of man trouble them any 7272
Da 8:13 and the host to be **trodden under** f? 4823
Am 2:15 *he that is* swift of f shall not deliver 7272
Mt 4: 6 lest at any time thou dash thy f against a *4228*
5:13 cast out, and to be **trodden under** f of men. *2662*
14:13 they followed him **on** f out of the cities. *3979*
18: 8 Wherefore if thy hand or thy f offend thee, *4228*
22:13 Bind him hand and f, and take him away, *4228*
Mk 9:45 And if thy f offend thee, cut it off: it is *4228*
Lk 4:11 lest at any time thou dash thy f against a *4228*
Jn 11:44 bound hand and f with graveclothes: *4228*
Ac 7: 5 in it, no, not so much as to set his f on: *4228*
1Co 12:15 If the f shall say, Because I am not *4228*
Heb 10:29 who hath **trodden under** f the Son of God, *2662*
Rev 1:13 clothed with a garment **down to the** f, and *4158*
10: 2 and he set his right f upon the sea, and *4228*
10: 2 foot upon the sea, and *his* left *f* on the earth, NIG
11: 2 the holy city shall they **tread under** f forty *3961*

FOOTHILLS See VALE

FOOTMEN (12) [FOOT, MAN]
Nu 11:21 whom I *am, are* six hundred thousand f; 7273
Jdg 20: 2 hundred thousand f that drew sword. 376+7273
1Sa 4:10 for there fell of Israel thirty thousand f. 7273
15: 4 two hundred thousand f, and ten thousand 7273
22:17 the king said unto the f that stood about 7323
2Sa 8: 4 and twenty thousand f: 376+7273
10: 6 twenty thousand f, and of king Maacah a 7273
1Ki 20:29 Syrians an hundred thousand f in one day. 7273
2Ki 13: 7 and ten chariots, and ten thousand f; 7273
1Ch 18: 4 and twenty thousand f: 376+7273
19:18 forty thousand f, and killed Shophach 376+7273
Jer 12: 5 If thou hast run with the f, and they have 7273

FOOTSTEPS (4) [FOOT, STEP]
Ps 17: 5 my goings in thy paths, *that* my f slip not. 6471
77:19 the great waters, and thy f are not known. 6119
89:51 wherewith they have reproached the f of 6119
SS 1: 8 go thy way forth by the f of the flock, and 6119

FOOTSTOOL (16) [FOOT, STOOL]
1Ch 28: 2 for the f of our God, and had made 1916+7272
2Ch 9:18 with a f of gold, *which were* fastened to 3534
Ps 99: 5 our God, and worship at his f; 1916+7272
110: 1 I make thine enemies thy f. 1916+7272+3807.1
132: 7 we will worship at his f. 1916+7272
Isa 66: 1 *is* my throne, and the earth *is* my f: 1916+7272
La 2: 1 remembered not his f in the day of 1916+7272
Mt 5:35 Nor by the earth; for it is his f: neither by *5286*
22:44 right hand, till I make thine enemies thy f? *5286*
Mk 12:36 right hand, till I make thine enemies thy f. *5286*
Lk 20:43 Till I make thine enemies thy f. *5286*
Ac 2:35 Until I make thy foes thy f. *5286*
7:49 Heaven *is* my throne, and earth *is* my f: *5286*
Heb 1:13 until I make thine enemies thy f? *5286*
10:13 expecting till his enemies be made his f. *5286*
Jas 2: 3 Stand thou there, or sit here under my f: *5286*

FOR (8985) [FORASMUCH, FORSOMUCH] See Index

FORAGING See BETIMES

FORASMUCH (42) [AS, FOR, MUCH] See Index

FORBAD (5) [FORBID]
Dt 2:37 nor *unto* whatsoever the LORD our God f 6680
Mt 3:14 But John f him, saying, I have need to be *1254*
Mk 9:38 and we f him, because he followeth not us. *2967*
Lk 9:49 and we f him, because he followeth not *2967*
2Pe 2:16 the dumb ass speaking with man's voice f *2967*

FORBARE (3) [FORBEAR]
1Sa 23:13 escaped from Keilah; and he f to go forth. 2308
2Ch 25:16 the prophet f, and said, I know that God 2308
Jer 41: 8 So he f, and slew them not among their 2308

FORBEAR (22) [FORBARE, FORBEARANCE, FORBEARETH, FORBEARING, FORBORN]
Ex 23: 5 wouldest f to help him, thou shalt surely 2308
Dt 23:22 if thou shalt f to vow, it shall be no sin in 2308
1Ki 22: 6 Ramoth-gilead to battle, or shall I f? 2308
22:15 Ramoth-gilead to battle, or shall we f? 2308
2Ch 18: 5 go to Ramoth-gilead to battle, or shall I f? 2308
18:14 go to Ramoth-gilead to battle, or shall I f? 2308
25:16 f; why shouldest thou be smitten? Then 2308
35:21 f thee from meddling with God, who *is* 2308
Ne 9:30 Yet many years didst thou f them, 4900+5921
Job 16: 6 and *though* I f, what am I eased? 2308
Pr 24:11 If thou f to deliver *them that are* drawn unto 2820
Jer 40: 4 unto thee to come with me *into* Babylon, f: 2308
Eze 2: 5 they will hear, or whether they will f, 2308
2: 7 they will hear, or whether they will f: 2308
3:11 they will hear, or whether they will f. 2308
3:27 him hear; and he that forbeareth, let him f: 2308
24:17 F to cry, make no mourning *for* the dead, 1826
Zec 11:12 think good, give *me* my price; and if not, f. 2308
1Co 9: 6 Barnabas, have not we power to f working? *3361*

2Co 12: 6 but *now* I f, lest any *man* should think of *5339*
1Th 3: 1 Wherefore when we could no longer f, *4722*
3: 5 For this cause, when I could no longer f, *4722*

FORBEARANCE (2) [FORBEAR]
Ro 2: 4 of his goodness and f and longsuffering; *463*
3:25 of sins that are past, through the f of God; *463*

FORBEARETH (2) [FORBEAR]
Nu 9:13 not in a journey, and f to keep the passover, 2308
Eze 3:27 let him hear; and he that f, let him forbear: 2310

FORBEARING (5) [FORBEAR]
Pr 25:15 By long f is a prince persuaded, and a soft 639
Jer 20: 9 I was weary with f, and I could not stay. 3557
Eph 4: 2 with longsuffering, f one another in love; *430*
6: 9 do the same *things* unto them, f threatening: *447*
Col 3:13 F one another, and forgiving one another, *430*

FORBID (37) [FORBAD, FORBIDDEN, FORBIDDETH, FORBIDDING]
Ge 44: 7 **God** f that thy servants should do according 2486
44:17 he said, **God** f that I should do so: *but* 2486
Nu 11:28 answered and said, My lord Moses, f them. 3607
Jos 22:29 **God** f that we should rebel against 2486
24:16 **God** f that we should forsake the LORD, 2486
1Sa 12:23 **God** f that I should sin against the LORD 2486
14:45 **God** f: *as* the LORD liveth, there shall not 2486
20: 2 he said unto him, **God** f; thou shalt not die: 2486
24: 6 The LORD f that I should do this thing 2486
26:11 The LORD f that *I* should stretch forth 2486
1Ki 21: 3 Naboth said to Ahab, The LORD **f it** me, 2486
1Ch 11:19 said, My God **f it** me, that *I* should do this 2486
Job 27: 5 **God** f that I should justify you: till I die I 2486
Mt 19:14 and f them not, to come unto me: *2967*
Mk 9:39 But Jesus said, F him not: for there is no *2967*
10:14 children to come unto me, and f them not: *2967*
Lk 6:29 him that taketh away thy cloke f not *to take* *2967*
9:50 And Jesus said unto him, F *him* not: for he *2967*
18:16 children to come unto me, and f them not: *2967*
20:16 when they heard *it,* they said, **God** f. *1096+3361*
Ac 10:47 Can any *man* f water, that these should not *2967*
24:23 that *he* should f none of his acquaintance to *2967*
Ro 3: 4 **God** f: yea, let God be true, but *1096+3361*
3: 6 **God** f: for then how shall God judge *1096+3361*
3:31 **God** f: yea, we establish the law. *1096+3361*
6: 2 **God** f. How shall we, that are dead *1096+3361*
6:15 the law, but under grace? **God** f. *1096+3361*
7: 7 **God** f. Nay, I had not known sin, but *1096+3361*
7:13 **God** f. But sin, that it might appear *1096+3361*
9:14 unrighteousness with God? **God** f. *1096+3361*
11: 1 **God** f. For I also am an Israelite, *1096+3361*
11:11 that they should fall? **God** f: *1096+3361*
1Co 6:15 the members of a harlot? **God** f. *1096+3361*
14:39 and f not to speak with tongues. *2967*
Gal 2:17 Christ the minister of sin? **God** f. *1096+3361*
3:21 **God** f: for if there had been a law *1096+3361*
6:14 But **God** f that I should glory, *1096+3361*

FORBIDDEN (3) [FORBID]
Lev 5:17 commit any *of these things* which are f to 3808
Dt 4:23 which the LORD thy God hath f thee. 6680
Ac 16: 6 were f of the Holy Ghost to preach *2967*

FORBIDDETH (1) [FORBID]
3Jn 1:10 and f them that would, and casteth *them* out *2967*

FORBIDDING (4) [FORBID]
Lk 23: 2 and f to give tribute to Cesar, saying that he *2967*
Ac 28:31 with all confidence, **no** man f him. *209*
1Th 2:16 F us to speak to the Gentiles that they *2967*
1Ti 4: 3 F to marry, *and commanding* to abstain *2967*

FORBORN (1) [FORBEAR]
Jer 51:30 The mighty *men* of Babylon have f to fight, 2308

FORCE (19) [FORCED, FORCES, FORCIBLE, FORCING]
Ge 31:31 Peradventure thou wouldest **take by** f thy 1497
Dt 22:25 and the man f her, and lie with her: 2388
34: 7 eye was not dim, nor his **natural** f abated. 3893
1Sa 2:16 *it me* now: and if not, I will take *it* by f. 2394
2Sa 13:12 Nay, my brother, do not f me; 6031
Ezr 4:23 and made them to cease by f and power. 153
Est 7: 8 Will he f the queen also before me in 3533
Job 30:18 By the great f *of my disease* is my garment 3581
40:16 and his f *is* in the navel of his belly. 202
Jer 18:21 pour out their *blood* by the f of the sword; 3027
23:10 their course is evil, and their f *is* not right. 1369
48:45 the shadow of Heshbon because of the f: 3581
Eze 34: 4 with f and with cruelty have ye ruled them. 2394
35: 5 f of the sword in the time of their calamity, 3027
Am 2:14 the strong shall not strengthen his f, 3581
Mt 11:12 and the violent **take** it **by** f. *726*
Jn 6:15 that they would come and **take** him **by** f, *726*
Ac 23:10 and to **take** him **by** f from among them, and *726*
Heb 9:17 For a testament *is* of f after *men* are dead: *949*

FORCED (7) [FORCE]
Jdg 1:34 the Amorites f the children of Dan into 3905
20: 5 my concubine have they f, that she is dead. 6031
1Sa 13:12 I f myself therefore, and offered a burnt 662
2Sa 13:14 stronger than she, f her, and lay with her. 6031
13:22 because he had f his sister Tamar. 6031
13:32 from the day that he f his sister Tamar. 6031
Pr 7:21 with the flattering of her lips she f him. 5080

FORCES (16) [FORCE]
2Ch 17: 2 he placed f in all the fenced cities of Judah, 2428
Job 36:19 *no,* not gold, nor all the f of strength. 3981
Isa 60: 5 the f of the Gentiles shall come unto thee. 2428
60:11 that *men* may bring unto thee the f of 2428
Jer 40: 7 *Now* when all the captains of the f which 2428
40:13 all the captains of the f that *were* in 2428
41:11 all the captains of the f that *were* with him, 2428
41:13 all the captains of the f that *were* with him, 2428
41:16 all the captains of the f that *were* with him, 2428
42: 1 all the captains of the f, and Johanan 2428
42: 8 all the captains of the f which *were* with 2428
43: 4 all the captains of the f, and all the people, 2428
43: 5 all the captains of the f, took all 2428
Da 11:10 and shall assemble a multitude of great f: 2428
11:38 in his estate shall he honour the God of f: 4581
Ob 1:11 the strangers carried away captive his f, 2428

FORCIBLE (1) [FORCE]
Job 6:25 How f are right words! but what doth your 4834

FORCING (2) [FORCE]
Dt 20:19 thou shalt not destroy the trees thereof by f 5080
Pr 30:33 so the f of wrath bringeth forth strife. 4330

FORD (1) [FORDS]
Ge 32:22 eleven sons, and passed over the f Jabbok. 4569

FORDS (3) [FORD]
Jos 2: 7 after them the way to Jordan unto the f: 4569
Jdg 3:28 took the f of Jordan toward Moab, and 4569
Isa 16: 2 the daughters of Moab shall be *at* the f of 4569

FORECAST (2)
Da 11:24 he shall f his devices **against** the strong 2803
11:25 for they shall f devices against him. 2803

FOREFATHERS (2) [FATHER]
Jer 11:10 turned back to the iniquities of their f, 1+7223
2Ti 1: 3 whom I serve from *my* f with pure *4269*

FOREFRONT (10) [FRONT]
Ex 26: 9 shalt double the sixth curtain in the f 4136+6440
28:37 upon the f of the mitre it shall be. 4136+6440
Lev 8: 9 also upon the mitre, *even* upon his f, did he 6440
1Sa 14: 5 The f of the one *was* situate northward over 8127
2Sa 11:15 Set ye Uriah in the f of the hottest 4136+6440
2Ki 16:14 from the f of the house, from between 6440
2Ch 20:27 and Jehoshaphat in the f of them, 7218
Eze 40:19 he measured the breadth from the f 6440+3807.1
40:19 gate unto the f of the inner court without, 6440
47: 1 for the f of the house *stood toward* the east, 6440

FOREHEAD (16) [HEAD]
Ex 28:38 it shall be upon Aaron's f, that Aaron may 4696
28:38 it shall be always upon his f, that they may 4696
Lev 13:41 of *his head toward* his face, he *is* f **bald**: 1371
13:42 bald head, or **bald** f, a white reddish sore; 1372
13:42 sprung up in his bald head, or his **bald** f. 1372
13:43 or in his **bald** f, as the leprosy appeareth in 1372
1Sa 17:49 slang *it,* and smote the Philistine in his f, 4696
17:49 his forehead, that the stone sunk into his f; 4696
2Ch 26:19 the leprosy even rose up in his f before 4696
26:20 he *was* leprous in his f, and they thrust him 4696

F

Jer 3: 3 thou hadst a whore's f, thou refusedst to be 4696
Eze 3: 8 and thy f strong against their foreheads. 4696
3: 9 harder than flint have I made thy f: 4696
16:12 I put a jewel on thy f, and earrings in thine 639
Rev 14: 9 and receive *his* mark in his f, or in his hand, *3359*
17: 5 And upon her f *was* a name written, *3359*

FOREHEADS (8) [HEAD]
Eze 3: 8 and thy forehead strong against their f. 4696
9: 4 set a mark upon the f of the men that sigh 4696
Rev 7: 3 sealed the servants of our God in their f. *3359*
9: 4 which have not the seal of God in their f. *3359*
13:16 a mark in their right hand, or in their f: *3359*
14: 1 having his Father's name written in their f. *3359*
20: 4 neither had received *his* mark upon their f, *3359*
22: 4 his face; and his name *shall be* in their f. *3359*

FOREIGN See OUTLANDISH; STRANGE

FOREIGNER (2) [FOREIGNERS]
Ex 12:45 A f and a hired servant shall not eat thereof. 8453
Dt 15: 3 Of a f thou mayest exact *it again:* but 5237

FOREIGNERS (2) [FOREIGNER]
Ob 1:11 f entered *into* his gates, and cast lots upon 5237
Eph 2:19 therefore ye are no more strangers and f, *3941*

FOREKNEW (1) [KNOW]
Ro 11: 2 hath not cast away his people which he f. *4267*

FOREKNOW (1) [KNOW]
Ro 8:29 For whom he did f, he also did predestinate *4267*

FOREKNOWLEDGE (2) [KNOW]
Ac 2:23 by the determinate counsel and f of God, *4268*
1Pe 1: 2 Elect according to the f of God the Father, *4268*

FOREMOST (3)
Ge 32:17 he commanded the f, saying, When Esau 7223
33: 2 he put the handmaids and their children f, 7223
2Sa 18:27 Me thinketh the running of the f *is* like 7223

FOREORDAINED (1) [ORDAIN]
1Pe 1:20 Who verily was f before the foundation of *4267*

FOREPART (5) [PART]
Ex 28:27 towards the f thereof, over against *the other* 6440
39:20 toward the f of it, over against 4136+6440
1Ki 6:20 the oracle in the f *was* twenty cubits in 6440
Eze 42: 7 towards the utter court on the f of 6440
Ac 27:41 and the f stuck fast, and *4408*

FORERUNNER (1) [RUN]
Heb 6:20 Whither the f is for us entered, *even* Jesus, *4274*

FORESAIL See MAINSAIL

FORESAW (1) [SEE]
Ac 2:25 I f the Lord always before my face, for he *4308*

FORESEEING (1) [SEE]
Gal 3: 8 f that God would justify the heathen *4275*

FORESEETH (2) [SEE]
Pr 22: 3 A prudent *man* f the evil, and 7200
27:12 A prudent *man* f the evil, *and* 7200

FORESHIP (1) [SHIP]
Ac 27:30 they would have cast anchors out of the f, *4408*

FORESKIN (9) [SKIN]
Ge 17:11 ye shall circumcise the flesh of your f; and 6190
17:14 whose flesh of his f is not circumcised, 6190
17:23 circumcised the flesh of their f in 6190
17:24 he was circumcised *in* the flesh of his f. 6190
17:25 he was circumcised in the flesh of his f. 6190
Ex 4:25 cut off the f of her son, and cast *it* at his 6190
Lev 12: 3 in the eighth day the flesh of his f shall be 6190
Dt 10:16 Circumcise therefore the f of your heart, 6190
Hab 2:16 drink thou also, and let thy f be **uncovered**: 6188

FORESKINS (5) [SKIN]
Jos 5: 3 the children of Israel at the hill of the f. 6190
1Sa 18:25 but an hundred f of the Philistines, 6190
18:27 David brought their f, and they gave them 6190
2Sa 3:14 which I espoused to me for an hundred f of 6190
Jer 4: 4 take away the f of your heart, ye men of 6190

FOREST (38) [FORESTS]
1Sa 22: 5 and came *into* the f of Hareth. 3293
1Ki 7: 2 He built also the house of the f of Lebanon; 3293
10:17 the king put them *in* the house of the f of 3293
10:21 all the vessels of the house of the f of 3293
2Ki 19:23 of his borders, *and into* the f of his Carmel. 3293
2Ch 9:16 the king put them in the house of the f of 3293
9:20 all the vessels of the house of the f of 3293
Ne 2: 8 letter unto Asaph the keeper of the king's f, 6508
Ps 50:10 For every beast of the f *is* mine, *and* 3293
104:20 wherein all the beasts of the f do creep 3293
Isa 9:18 shall kindle in the thickets of the f, and 3293
10:18 shall consume the glory of his f, and of his 3293
10:19 the rest of the trees of his f shall be few, 3293
10:34 he shall cut down the thickets of the f with 3293
21:13 In the f in Arabia shall ye lodge, O ye 3293
22: 8 that day to the armour of the house of the f. 3293
29:17 the fruitful field shall be esteemed as a f? 3293
32:15 and the fruitful field be counted for a f. 3293
32:19 When it shall hail, coming down *on* the f; 3293
37:24 of his border, *and* the f of his Carmel. 3293
44:14 for himself among the trees of the f: 3293
44:23 ye mountains, O f, and every tree therein: 3293
56: 9 come to devour, *yea,* all ye beasts in the f. 3293
Jer 5: 6 Wherefore a lion out of the f shall slay 3293
10: 3 for *one* cutteth a tree out of the f, the work 3293
12: 8 Mine heritage is unto me as a lion in the f; 3293
21:14 I will kindle a fire in the f thereof, and 3293
26:18 of the house as the high places of a f. 3293
46:23 They shall cut down her f, saith 3293
Eze 15: 2 a branch which is among the trees of the f? 3293
15: 6 As the vine tree among the trees of the f, 3293
20:46 prophesy against the f of the south field; 3293
20:47 say to the f of the south, Hear the word of 3293
Hos 2:12 I will make them a f, and the beasts of 3293
Am 3: 4 Will a lion roar in the f, when he hath no 3293
Mic 3:12 of the house as the high places of the f. 3293
5: 8 people as a lion among the beasts of the f, 3293
Zec 11: 2 for the f of the vintage is come down. 3293

FORESTS (3) [FOREST]
2Ch 27: 4 and in the f he built castles and towers. 2793
Ps 29: 9 the hinds to calve, and discovereth the f: 3295
Eze 39:10 the field, neither cut down *any* out of the f; 3293

FORETELL (1) [TELL]
2Co 13: 2 f *you,* as if I were present the second *time;* *4302*

FORETOLD (2) [TELL]
Mk 13:23 ye heed: behold, I have f you all *things.* *4302*
Ac 3:24 have spoken, have likewise f of these days. *4293*

FOREWARN (1) [WARN]
Lk 12: 5 But I will f you whom you shall fear: *5263*

FOREWARNED (1) [WARN]
1Th 4: 6 all such, as we also have f you and testified. *4302*

FORFEITED (1)
Ezr 10: 8 all his substance should be f, and 2763

FORGAT (8) [FORGET]
Ge 40:23 chief butler remember Joseph, but f him. 7911
Jdg 3: 7 f the LORD their God, and served Baalim 7911
1Sa 12: 9 when they f the LORD their God, he sold 7911
Ps 78:11 f his works, and his wonders that he had 7911
106:13 They soon f his works; they waited not for 7911
106:21 They f God their saviour, which had done 7911
La 3:17 my soul far off from peace: I f prosperity. 5382
Hos 2:13 her lovers, and f me, saith the LORD. 7911

FORGAVE (9) [FORGIVE]
Ps 78:38 f *their* iniquity, and destroyed *them* not: 3722
Mt 18:27 and loosed him, and f him the debt. *863*
18:32 I f thee all that debt, because thou desiredst *863*
Lk 7:42 had nothing to pay, he **frankly** f *them* both. *5483*
7:43 said, I suppose that *he,* to whom he f most. *5483*
2Co 2:10 for if I f any *thing,* to whom I forgave *it,* for *5483*
2:10 for if I forgave any *thing,* to whom I f *it,* for *5483*
2:10 for your sakes *f I it* in the person of Christ; NIG
Col 3:13 even as Christ f you, so also *do* ye. *5483*

FORGAVEST (2) [FORGIVE]
Ps 32: 5 and thou f the iniquity of my sin. 5375
99: 8 thou wast a God that f them, though thou 5375

FORGED (1) [FORGERS]
Ps 119:69 The proud have f a lie against me: *but* I will 2950

FORGERS (1) [FORGED]
Job 13: 4 ye *are* f of lies, ye *are* all physicians of no 2950

FORGET (54) [FORGAT, FORGETFUL, FORGETFULNESS, FORGETTEST, FORGETTETH, FORGETTING]
Ge 27:45 and he f *that* which thou hast done to him: 7911
41:51 *said he,* hath **made** me f all my toil, and all 5382
Dt 4: 9 lest thou f the things which thine eyes have 7911
4:23 lest ye f the covenant of the LORD your 7911
4:31 nor f the covenant of thy fathers which he 7911
6:12 *Then* beware lest thou f the LORD, 7911
8:11 Beware that thou f not the LORD thy 7911
8:14 lifted up, and thou f the LORD thy God, 7911
8:19 if thou **do at all** f the LORD thy 7911+7911
9: 7 Remember, *and* f not, how thou provokedst 7911
25:19 from under heaven; thou shalt not f *it.* 7911
1Sa 1:11 not f thine handmaid, but wilt give unto 7911
2Ki 17:38 that I have made with you ye shall not f; 7911
Job 8:13 So *are* the paths of all that f God; and 7911
9:27 If I say, I will f my complaint, I will leave 7911
11:16 Because thou shalt f *thy* misery, *and* 7911
24:20 The womb shall f him; the worm shall feed 7911
Ps 9:17 into hell, *and* all the nations that f God. 7913
10:12 O God, lift up thine hand: f not the humble. 7911
13: 1 How long wilt thou f me, O LORD? 7911
45:10 f also thine own people, and thy father's 7911
50:22 Now consider this, ye that f God, lest I tear 7911
59:11 Slay them not, lest my people f: 7911
74:19 f not the congregation of thy poor for ever. 7911
74:23 F not the voice of thine enemies: the tumult 7911
78: 7 not f the works of God, but keep his 7911
102: 4 like grass; so that I f to eat my bread. 7911
103: 2 O my soul, and f not all his benefits: 7911
119:16 myself in thy statutes: I will not f thy word. 7911
119:83 in the smoke; *yet* do I not f thy statutes. 7911
119:93 I will never f thy precepts: for with them 7911
119:109 in my hand: yet do I not f thy law. 7911
119:141 and despised: *yet* do not I f thy precepts. 7911
119:153 and deliver me: for I do not f thy law. 7911
119:176 for I do not f thy commandments. 7911
137: 5 If I f thee, O Jerusalem, let my right hand 7911
137: 5 let my right hand f *her cunning.* 7911
Pr 3: 1 My son, f not my law; but let thine heart 7911
4: 5 f *it* not; neither decline from the words of 7911
31: 5 f the law, and pervert the judgment of any 7911
31: 7 f his poverty, and remember his misery no 7911
Isa 49:15 Can a woman f her sucking child, that *she* 7911
49:15 yea, they may f, yet will I not forget thee. 7911
49:15 yea, they may forget, yet will I not f thee. 7911
54: 4 for thou shalt f the shame of thy youth, and 7911
65:11 that f my holy mountain, that prepare a 7913
Jer 2:32 Can a maid f her ornaments, *or* a bride her 7911
23:27 Which think to **cause** my people **to** f my 7911
23:39 will **utterly** f you, and I will forsake 5377+5382
La 5:20 Wherefore dost thou f us for ever, *and* 7911
Hos 4: 6 law of thy God, I will also f thy children. 7911
Am 8: 7 Surely I will never f any of their works. 7911
Heb 6:10 For God *is* not unrighteous to f your work *1950*
13:16 But to do good and to communicate f not: *1950*

FORGETFUL (2) [FORGET]
Heb 13: 2 Be not f to entertain strangers: for thereby *1950*
Jas 1:25 continueth *therein,* he being not a f hearer, *1953*

FORGETFULNESS (1) [FORGET]
Ps 88:12 and thy righteousness in the land of f? 5388

FORGETTEST (2) [FORGET]
Ps 44:24 *and* f our affliction and our oppression? 7911
Isa 51:13 f the LORD thy Maker, that hath stretched 7911

FORGETTETH (4) [FORGET]
Job 39:15 f that the foot may crush them, or *that* 7911
Ps 9:12 he f not the cry of the humble. 7911
Pr 2:17 of her youth, and f the covenant of her God. 7911
Jas 1:24 straightway f what manner of *man* he was. *1950*

FORGETTING (1) [FORGET]
Php 3:13 *this one thing I do,* f those *things which are* *1950*

FORGIVE (56) [FORGAVE, FORGAVEST, FORGIVEN, FORGIVENESS, FORGIVENESSES, FORGIVETH, FORGIVING, FORGOT, FORGOTTEN]
Ge 50:17 F, I pray thee now, the trespass of thy 5375
50:17 f the trespass of the servants of the God of 5375
Ex 10:17 Now therefore f, I pray thee, my sin only 5375
32:32 Yet now, if thou wilt f their sin; and if not, 5375
Nu 30: 5 the LORD shall f her, because her father 5545
30: 8 of none effect: and the LORD shall f her. 5545
30:12 them void; and the LORD shall f her. 5545
Jos 24:19 he will not f your transgressions nor your 5375
1Sa 25:28 pray thee, f the trespass of thine handmaid: 5375
1Ki 8:30 dwelling place: and when thou hearest, f. 5545
8:34 f the sin of thy people Israel, and 5545
8:36 f the sin of thy servants, and of thy people 5545
8:39 f, and do, and give to every man according 5545
8:50 f thy people that have sinned against thee, 5545
2Ch 6:21 from heaven; and when thou hearest, f. 5545
6:25 f the sin of thy people Israel, and 5545
6:27 f the sin of thy servants, and of thy people 5545
6:30 f, and render unto every man according 5545
6:39 f thy people which have sinned against 5545
7:14 and will f their sin, and will heal their land. 5545
Ps 25:18 and my pain; and f all my sins. 5375
86: 5 For thou, Lord, *art* good, and **ready to** f; 5546
Isa 2: 9 humbleth himself; therefore f them not. 5375
Jer 18:23 against me to slay *me:* f not their iniquity, 3722
31:34 for I will f their iniquity, and I will 5545
36: 3 that I may f their iniquity and their sin. 5545
Da 9:19 O Lord, hear; O Lord, f; O Lord, hearken 5545
Am 7: 2 I said, O Lord GOD, f, I beseech thee: 5545
Mt 6:12 And f us our debts, as we forgive our *863*
6:12 forgive us our debts, as we f our debtors. *863*
6:14 For if ye f men their trespasses, *863*
6:14 your heavenly Father will also f you: *863*
6:15 But if ye f not men their trespasses, *863*
6:15 neither will your Father f your trespasses. *863*
9: 6 the Son of man hath power on earth to f sins, *863*
18:21 shall my brother sin against me, and I f him? *863*
18:35 if ye from your hearts f not every one his *863*
Mk 2: 7 who can f sins but God only? *863*
2:10 the Son of man hath power on earth to f sins, *863*
11:25 And when ye stand praying, f, if ye have *863*
11:25 is in heaven may f you your trespasses. *863*
11:26 But if ye do not f, neither will your Father *863*
11:26 neither will your Father which is in heaven f *863*
Lk 5:21 Who can f sins, but God alone? *863*
5:24 Son of man hath power upon earth to f sins, *863*
6:37 be condemned: f, and ye shall be forgiven: *630*
11: 4 And f us our sins; for we also forgive every *863*
11: 4 for we also f every one *that is* indebted to us. *863*
17: 3 rebuke him; and if he repent, f him. *863*
17: 4 to thee, saying, I repent; thou shalt f him. *863*
23:34 Then said Jesus, Father, f them; for they *863*
2Co 2: 7 So that contrariwise ye *ought* rather to f *5483*
2:10 To whom ye f any *thing,* I *forgive* also: for *5483*
2:10 To whom ye forgive any *thing,* I *f* also: for NIG
12:13 not burdensome to you? f me this wrong. *5483*
1Jn 1: 9 he is faithful and just to f us *our* sins, and *863*

FORGIVEN (42) [FORGIVE]
Lev 4:20 atonement for them, and it shall be f them. 5545
4:26 as concerning his sin, and it shall be f him. 5545
4:31 an atonement for him, and it shall be f him. 5545
4:35 he hath committed, and it shall be f him. 5545
5:10 which he had sinned, and it shall be f him. 5545
5:13 sinned in one of these, and it shall be f him: 5545
5:16 the trespass offering, and it shall be f him. 5545
5:18 and wist *it* not, and it shall be f him. 5545
6: 7 it shall be f him for any *thing* of all that he 5545
19:22 the sin which he hath done shall be f him. 5545
Nu 14:19 as thou hast f this people, from Egypt even 5375
15:25 the children of Israel, and it shall be f them; 5545
15:26 it shall be f all the congregation of 5545
15:28 an atonement for him; and it shall be f him. 5545
Dt 21: 8 And the blood shall be f them. 3722
Ps 32: 1 Blessed *is he* whose transgression *is* f, 5375
85: 2 Thou hast f the iniquity of thy people, 5375
Isa 33:24 the people that dwell therein *shall be* f *their* 5375
Mt 9: 2 Son, be of good cheer; thy sins be f thee. *863*
9: 5 whether is easier, to say, *Thy* sins be f thee; *863*
12:31 *of* sin and blasphemy shall be f unto men: *863*
12:31 the *Holy* Ghost shall not be f unto men. *863*

Mt 12:32 against the Son of man, it shall be f him: *863*
12:32 it shall not be f him, neither in this world, *863*
Mk 2: 5 the sick of the palsy, Son, thy sins be f thee. *863*
2: 9 to the sick of the palsy, *Thy* sins be f thee; *863*
3:28 All sins shall be f unto the sons of men, and *863*
4:12 and *their* sins should be f them. *863*
Lk 5:20 he said unto him, Man, thy sins are f thee. *863*
5:23 Whether is easier, to say, Thy sins be f thee; *863*
6:37 not be condemned: forgive, and ye shall be f: *630*
7:47 unto thee, Her sins, which are many, are f; *863*
7:47 but to whom little is f, *the same* loveth little. *863*
7:48 And he said unto her, Thy sins are f. *863*
12:10 against the Son of man, it shall be f him: *863*
12:10 against the Holy Ghost it shall not be f. *863*
Ac 8:22 if perhaps the thought of thine heart may be f *863*
Ro 4: 7 Blessed *are they* whose iniquities are f, *863*
Eph 4:32 even as God for Christ's sake hath f you. *5483*
Col 2:13 with him, having f you all trespasses; *5483*
Jas 5:15 he have committed sins, they shall be f him. *863*
1Jn 2:12 *your* sins are f you for his name's sake. *863*

FORGIVENESS (7) [FORGIVE]
Ps 130: 4 *there is* f with thee, that thou mayest be 5547
Mk 3:29 against the Holy Ghost hath never f, *859*
Ac 5:31 for to give repentance to Israel, and f of sins. *859*
13:38 this *man* is preached unto you the f of sins: *859*
26:18 that they may receive f of sins, and *859*
Eph 1: 7 the f of sins, according to the riches of his *859*
Col 1:14 through his blood, *even* the f of sins: *859*

FORGIVENESSES (1) [FORGIVE]
Da 9: 9 To the Lord our God *belong* mercies and f, 5547

FORGIVETH (2) [FORGIVE]
Ps 103: 3 Who f all thine iniquities; who healeth all 5545
Lk 7:49 Who is this that f sins also? *863*

FORGIVING (4) [FORGIVE]
Ex 34: 7 f iniquity and transgression and sin, and 5375
Nu 14:18 f iniquity and transgression, and by no 5375
Eph 4:32 to another, tenderhearted, f one another, *5483*
Col 3:13 Forbearing one another, and f one another, *5483*

FORGOT (1) [FORGIVE]
Dt 24:19 hast f a sheaf in the field, thou shalt not go 7911

FORGOTTEN (46) [FORGIVE]
Ge 41:30 all the plenty shall be f in the land of 7911
Dt 26:13 thy commandments, neither have I f *them:* 7911
31:21 for it shall not be f out of the mouths of 7911
32:18 and hast f God that formed thee. 7911
Job 19:14 and my familiar friends have f me. 7911
28: 4 the inhabitant; *even the waters* f of the foot: 7911
Ps 9:18 For the needy shall not alway be f: 7911
10:11 He hath said in his heart, God hath f: 7911
31:12 I am f as a dead man out of mind: I am like 7911
42: 9 unto God my rock, Why hast thou f me? 7911
44:17 yet have we not f thee, neither have we 7911
44:20 If we have f the name of our God, or 7911
77: 9 Hath God f to be gracious? hath he in anger 7911
119:61 have robbed me: *but* I have not f thy law. 7911
119:139 because mine enemies have f thy words. 7911
Ecc 2:16 now *is, in* the days to come shall all be f. 7911
8:10 they were f in the city where they had so 7911
9: 5 a reward; for the memory of them is f. 7911
Isa 17:10 Because thou hast f the God of thy 7911
23:15 that Tyre shall be f seventy years, 7911
23:16 about the city, thou harlot that hast been f; 7911
44:21 O Israel, thou shalt not be f of me. 5382
49:14 hath forsaken me, and my Lord hath f me. 7911
65:16 because the former troubles are f, and 7911
Jer 2:32 yet my people have f me days without 7911
3:21 *and* they have f the LORD their God. 7911
13:25 because thou hast f me, and trusted in 7911
18:15 Because my people hath f me, they have 7911
20:11 *their* everlasting confusion shall never be f. 7911
23:27 as their fathers have f my name for Baal. 7911
23:40 and a perpetual shame, which shall not be f. 7911
30:14 All thy lovers have f thee; they seek thee 7911
44: 9 Have ye f the wickedness of your fathers, 7911
50: 5 *in* a perpetual covenant *that* shall not be f. 7911
50: 6 to hill, they have f their resting place. 7911
La 2: 6 **caused** the solemn feasts and sabbaths **to be f** 7911
Eze 22:12 and hast f me, saith the Lord GOD. 7911
23:35 Because thou hast f me, and cast me behind 7911

Hos 4: 6 seeing thou hast f the law of thy God, I will 7911
8:14 For Israel hath f his Maker, and 7911
13: 6 heart was exalted; therefore have they f me. 7911
Mt 16: 5 to the other side, they had f to take bread. *1950*
Mk 8:14 Now *the disciples* had f to take bread, *1950*
Lk 12: 6 and not one of them is f before God? *1950*
Heb 12: 5 And ye have f the exhortation which *1585*
2Pe 1: 9 f that *he* was purged from his old *2983+3024*

FORKS (1)
1Sa 13:21 for the f, and for the axes, and 7053+7969

FORM (24) [FORMED, FORMER, FORMETH, FORMS]
Ge 1: 2 the earth was **without** f, and void; and 8414
1Sa 28:14 he said unto her, What f is he of? And she 8389
2Sa 14:20 To fetch about *this* f of speech hath thy 6440
2Ch 4: 7 candlesticks of gold according to their f, 4941
Job 4:16 but I could not discern the f thereof: 4758
Isa 45: 7 I f the light, and create darkness: I make 3335
52:14 and his f more than the sons of men: 8389
53: 2 he hath no f nor comeliness; and when we 8389
Jer 4:23 and lo, *it was* **without** f, and void; 8414
Eze 8: 3 he put forth the f of a hand, and took me by 8403
8:10 behold every f of creeping things, and 8403
10: 8 there appeared in the cherubims the f of a 8403
43:11 shew them the f of the house, and 6699
43:11 that they may keep the whole f thereof, and 6699
Da 2:31 before thee; and the f thereof *was* terrible. 7299
3:19 the f of his visage was changed against 6755
3:25 the f of the fourth *is* like the Son of God. 7299
Mk 16:12 After that he appeared in another f unto two *3444*
Ro 2:20 which hast the f of knowledge and of *3446*
6:17 ye have obeyed from the heart *that* f of *5179*
Php 2: 6 Who, being in the f of God, thought it not *3444*
2: 7 and took *upon him* the f of a servant, and *3444*
2Ti 1:13 Hold fast the f of sound words, which thou *5296*
3: 5 Having a f of godliness, but denying *3446*

FORMED (33) [FORM]
Ge 2: 7 the LORD God f man *of* the dust of 3335
2: 8 and there he put the man whom he had f. 3335
2:19 out of the ground the LORD God f every 3335
Dt 32:18 and hast forgotten God that f thee. 2342
2Ki 19:25 *and* of ancient times that I have f it? 3335
Job 26: 5 Dead *things* are f from under the waters, 2342
26:13 his hand hath f the crooked serpent. 2342
33: 6 in God's stead: I also am f out of the clay. 7169
Ps 90: 2 or ever thou hadst f the earth and the world, 2342
94: 9 not hear? he that f the eye, shall he not see? 3335
95: 5 he made it: and his hands f the dry *land.* 3335
Pr 26:10 The great *God* that f all *things* both 2342
Isa 27:11 he that f them will shew them no favour. 3335
37:26 *and* of ancient times, that I have f it? 3335
43: 1 O Jacob, and he that f thee, O Israel, 3335
43: 7 created him for my glory, I have f him; 3335
43:10 before me there was no God f, neither shall 3335
43:21 This people have I f for myself; they shall 3335
44: 2 f thee from the womb, *which* will help thee; 3335
44:10 Who hath f a god, or molten a graven 3335
44:21 I have f thee; thou *art* my servant: O Israel, 3335
44:24 and he that f thee from the womb, 3335
45:18 God himself that f the earth and made it; 3335
45:18 created it not in vain, he f it to be inhabited: 3335
49: 5 saith the LORD that f me from the womb 3335
54:17 No weapon *that* is f against thee shall 3335
Jer 1: 5 Before I f thee in the belly I knew thee; and 3335
33: 2 the LORD that f it, to establish it; 3335
Am 7: 1 he f grasshoppers in the beginning of 3335
Ro 9:20 Shall the thing f say to him that formed *it,* *4110*
9:20 Shall the thing formed say to him that f *it,* *4111*
Gal 4:19 in birth again until Christ be f in you, *3445*
1Ti 2:13 For Adam was first f, then Eve. *4111*

FORMER (50) [FORM]
Ge 40:13 after the f manner when thou wast his 7223
Nu 21:26 who had fought against the f king of Moab, 7223
Dt 24: 4 Her f husband, which sent her away, 7223
Ru 4: 7 Now this *was the manner* **in f time** 6440+3807.1
1Sa 17:30 the people answered him again after the f 7223
2Ki 1:14 burnt up the two captains of the f fifties 7223
17:34 Unto this day they do after the f manners: 7223
17:40 but they did after their f manner. 7223
Ne 5:15 the f governors that *had been* before me 7223
Job 8: 8 of the f age, and prepare *thyself* to 7223

Job 30: 3 flying *into* the wilderness **in f time** desolate 570
Ps 79: 8 O remember not against us f iniquities: 7223
89:49 Lord, where *are* thy f lovingkindnesses, 7223
Ecc 1:11 *There is* no remembrance of f *things;* 7223
7:10 What is *the cause* that the f days were 7223
Isa 41:22 let them shew the f *things,* what they *be,* 7223
42: 9 the f *things* are come to pass, and 7223
43: 9 shew us f *things?* let them bring forth their 7223
43:18 Remember ye not the f *things,* neither 7223
46: 9 Remember the f *things* of old: for I *am* 7223
48: 3 I have declared the f *things* from 7223
61: 4 they shall raise up the f desolations, and 7223
65: 7 will I measure their f work into their 7223
65:16 because the f troubles are forgotten, and 7223
65:17 the f shall not be remembered, nor come 7223
Jer 5:24 both the f and the latter, in his season: 3138
10:16 for he *is* the f of all *things;* and Israel *is* 3335
34: 5 the f kings which were before thee, so 7223
36:28 write in it all the f words that were in 7223
51:19 for he *is* the f of all *things:* and *Israel is* 3335
Eze 16:55 shall return to their f **estate**, and Samaria 6927
16:55 her daughters shall return to their f **estate**, 6927
16:55 thy daughters shall return to your f **estate**. 6927
Da 11:13 shall set forth a multitude greater than the f, 7223
11:29 but it shall not be as the f, or as the latter. 7223
Hos 6: 3 as the latter *and* f **rain** *unto* the earth. 3384
Joel 2:23 for he hath given you the f **rain** 4175
2:23 the f **rain**, and the latter rain in the first 4175
Hag 2: 9 latter house shall be greater than of the f, 7223
Zec 1: 4 unto whom the f prophets have cried, 7223
7: 7 the LORD hath cried by the f prophets, 7223
7:12 hath sent in his spirit by the f prophets: 7223
8:11 the residue of this people as *in* the f days, 7223
14: 8 half of them toward the f sea, and half of 6931
Mal 3: 4 as *in* the days of old, and as *in* f years. 6931
Ac 1: 1 The f treatise have I made, O Theophilus, *4413*
Eph 4:22 That ye put off concerning the f *4387*
Heb 10:32 But call to remembrance the f days, *4387*
1Pe 1:14 not fashioning yourselves according to the f *4387*
Rev 21: 4 more pain: for the f *things* are passed away. *4413*

FORMETH (2) [FORM]
Am 4:13 he that f the mountains, and createth 3335
Zec 12: 1 and f the spirit of man within him. 3335

FORMS (2) [FORM]
Eze 43:11 all the f thereof, and all the ordinances 6699
43:11 all the f thereof, and all the laws thereof: 6699

FORNICATION (36) [FORNICATIONS, FORNICATOR, FORNICATORS]
2Ch 21:11 **caused** the inhabitants of Jerusalem **to commit f**, 2181
Isa 23:17 shall **commit** f with all the kingdoms of 2181
Eze 16:26 Thou hast also **committed** f with 2181
16:29 Thou hast moreover multiplied thy f in 8457
Mt 5:32 saving for the cause of f, causeth her to *4202*
19: 9 except *it be* for f, and shall marry another, *4202*
Jn 8:41 Then said they to him, We be not born of f; *4202*
Ac 15:20 and *from* f, and *from* things strangled, and *4202*
15:29 and from things strangled, and from f: *4202*
21:25 from blood, and from strangled, and from f. *4202*
Ro 1:29 f, wickedness, covetousness, *4202*
1Co 5: 1 It is reported commonly *that there is* f *4202*
5: 1 and such f as is not so much as named *4202*
6:13 Now the body *is* not for f, but for the Lord; *4202*
6:18 Flee f. Every sin that a man doeth is *4202*
6:18 he that **committeth** f sinneth against his *4203*
7: 2 Nevertheless, to avoid f, let every man have *4202*
10: 8 Neither let us **commit** f, as some of them *4203*
2Co 12:21 not repented of the uncleanness and f and *4202*
Gal 5:19 f, uncleanness, lasciviousness, *4202*
Eph 5: 3 But f, and all uncleanness, or covetousness, *4202*
Col 3: 5 f, uncleanness, inordinate affection, *4202*
1Th 4: 3 that ye should abstain from f: *4202*
Jude 1: 7 in like manner **giving** themselves **over to** f, *1608*
Rev 2:14 sacrificed unto idols, and to **commit** f. *4203*
2:20 and to seduce my servants to **commit** f, *4203*
2:21 And I gave her space to repent of her f; and *4202*
9:21 nor of their f, nor of their thefts. *4202*
14: 8 drink of the wine of the wrath of her f. *4202*
17: 2 the kings of the earth have **committed** f, *4203*
17: 2 been made drunk with the wine of her f. *4202*
17: 4 full of abominations and filthiness of her f: *4202*
18: 3 drunk of the wine of the wrath of her f, *4202*
18: 3 the kings of the earth have **committed** f *4203*
18: 9 who have **committed** f and *4203*
19: 2 which did corrupt the earth with her f, and *4202*

FORNICATIONS (3) [FORNICATION]
Eze 16:15 pouredst out thy f on every one that passed 8457
Mt 15:19 murders, adulteries, f, thefts, false witness, *4202*
Mk 7:21 evil thoughts, adulteries, f, murders, *4202*

FORNICATOR (2) [FORNICATION]
1Co 5:11 if any *man that is* called a brother be a f, or *4205*
Heb 12:16 Lest there *be* any f, or profane *person,* as *4205*

FORNICATORS (3) [FORNICATION]
1Co 5: 9 you in an epistle not to company with f: *4205*
5:10 Yet not altogether with the f of this world, *4205*
6: 9 neither f, nor idolaters, nor adulterers, *4205*

FORSAKE (58) [FORSAKEN, FORSAKETH, FORSAKING, FORSOOK, FORSOOKEST]
Dt 4:31 he will not f thee, neither destroy thee, 7503
12:19 Take heed to thyself that thou f not 5800
14:27 *is* within thy gates; thou shalt not f him; 5800
31: 6 with thee; he will not fail thee, nor f thee. 5800
31: 8 he will not fail thee, neither f thee: 5800
31:16 will f me, and break my covenant which I 5800
31:17 I will f them, and I will hide my face from 5800
Jos 1: 5 be with thee: I will not fail thee, nor f thee. 5800
24:16 God forbid that we should f the LORD, 5800
24:20 If ye f the LORD, and serve strange gods, 5800
Jdg 9:11 Should I f my sweetness, and my good 2308
1Sa 12:22 For the LORD will not f his people for his 5203
1Ki 6:13 of Israel, and will not f my people Israel. 5800
8:57 our fathers: let him not leave us, nor f us: 5203
2Ki 21:14 I will f the remnant of mine inheritance, 5203
1Ch 28: 9 if thou f him, he will cast thee off for ever. 5800
28:20 he will not fail thee, nor f thee, until *thou* 5800
2Ch 7:19 and f my statutes and my commandments, 5800
15: 2 of you; but if ye f him, he will forsake you. 5800
15: 2 of you; but if ye forsake him, he will f you. 5800
Ezr 8:22 and his wrath *is* against all them that f him. 5800
Ne 9:31 didst not utterly consume them, nor f them; 5800
10:39 and we will not f the house of our God. 5800
Job 20:13 *Though* he spare it, and f it not; but keep it 5800
Ps 27: 9 leave me not, neither f me, O God of my 5800
27:10 When my father and my mother f me, then 5800
37: 8 Cease from anger, and f wrath: fret not 5800
38:21 F me not, O LORD: O my God, be not far 5800
71: 9 old age; f me not when my strength faileth. 5800
71:18 I am old and grayheaded, O God, f me not; 5800
89:30 If his children f my law, and walk not in 5800
94:14 his people, neither will he f his inheritance. 5800
119: 8 I will keep thy statutes: O f me not utterly. 5800
119:53 because of the wicked that f thy law. 5800
138: 8 f not the works of thine own hands. 7503
Pr 1: 8 thy father, and f not the law of thy mother: 5203
3: 3 Let not mercy and truth f thee: bind them 5800
4: 2 I give you good doctrine, f you not my law. 5800
4: 6 F her not, and she shall preserve thee: 5800
6:20 and f not the law of thy mother: 5203
9: 6 F the foolish, and live; and go in the way of 5800
27:10 own friend, and thy father's friend, f not; 5800
28: 4 They that f the law praise the wicked: but 5800
Isa 1:28 they that f the LORD shall be consumed. 5800
41:17 *I* the God of Israel will not f them. 5800
42:16 things will I do unto them, and not f them. 5800
55: 7 Let the wicked f his way, and 5800
65:11 ye *are* they that f the LORD, that forget 5800
Jer 17:13 all that f thee shall be ashamed, and 5800
23:33 I will even f you, saith the LORD. 5203
23:39 and I will f you, and the city that I gave you 5203
51: 9 f her, and let us go every one into his own 5800
La 5:20 forget us for ever, *and* f us so long time? 5800
Eze 20: 8 neither did they f the idols of Egypt: 5800
Da 11:30 have intelligence with them that f the holy 5800
Jnh 2: 8 They that observe lying vanities f their own 5800
Ac 21:21 are among the Gentiles to f Moses, *575+646*
Heb 13: 5 hath said, I will never leave thee, nor f thee. *1459*

FORSAKEN (76) [FORSAKE]
Dt 28:20 of thy doings, where*by* thou hast f me. 5800
29:25 Because they have f the covenant of 5800
Jdg 6:13 now the LORD hath f us, and delivered us 5203

Jdg 10:10 both because we have f our God, and 5800
10:13 Yet ye have f me, and served other gods: 5800
1Sa 8: 8 wherewith they have f me, and served other 5800
12:10 because we have f the LORD, and 5800
1Ki 11:33 Because that they have f me, and 5800
18:18 in that ye have f the commandments of 5800
19:10 for the children of Israel have f thy 5800
19:14 the children of Israel have f thy covenant, 5800
2Ki 22:17 Because they have f me, and have burnt 5800
2Ch 12: 5 Ye have f me, and *therefore* have I also left 5800
13:10 LORD *is* our God, and we have not f him; 5800
13:11 of the LORD our God; but ye have f him. 5800
21:10 he had f the LORD God of his fathers. 5800
24:20 because ye have f the LORD, he hath also 5800
24:20 forsaken the LORD, he hath also f you. 5800
24:24 they had f the LORD God of their fathers. 5800
28: 6 they had f the LORD God of their fathers. 5800
29: 6 have f him, and have turned away their 5800
34:25 Because they have f me, and have burned 5800
Ezr 9: 9 yet our God hath not f us in our bondage, 5800
9:10 for we have f thy commandments, 5800
Ne 13:11 and said, Why is the house of God f? 5800
Job 18: 4 shall the earth be f for thee? and shall 5800
20:19 he hath oppressed *and* hath f the poor; 5800
Ps 9:10 LORD, hast not f them that seek thee. 5800
22: 1 My God, my God, why hast thou f me? 5800
37:25 yet have I not seen the righteous f, nor his 5800
71:11 Saying, God hath f him: persecute and 5800
Isa 1: 4 they have f the LORD, they have 5800
2: 6 Therefore thou hast f thy people the house 5203
7:16 the land that thou abhorrest shall be f of 5800
17: 2 The cities of Aroer *are* f: they shall be for 5800
17: 9 In that day shall his strong cities be as a f 5800
27:10 *and* the habitation f, and left like a 7971
32:14 Because the palaces shall be f; 5203
49:14 The LORD hath f me, and my Lord hath 5800
54: 6 the LORD hath called thee as a woman f 5800
54: 7 For a small moment have I f thee; but 5800
60:15 Whereas thou hast been f and hated, so 5800
62: 4 Thou shalt no more be termed F; 5800
62:12 shalt be called, Sought out, A city not f. 5800
Jer 1:16 who have f me, and have burnt incense 5800
2:13 they have f me the fountain of living 5800
2:17 in that thou hast f the LORD thy God, 5800
2:19 that thou hast f the LORD thy God, and 5800
4:29 every city *shall be* f, and not a man dwell 5800
5: 7 thy children have f me, and sworn by *them* 5800
5:19 Like as ye have f me, and served strange 5800
7:29 and f the generation of his wrath. 5203
9:13 Because they have f my law which I set 5800
9:19 because we have f the land, because 5800
12: 7 I have f mine house, I have left mine 5800
15: 6 Thou hast f me, saith the LORD, thou art 5203
16:11 Because your fathers have f me, saith 5800
16:11 and have f me, and have not kept my law; 5800
17:13 because they have f the LORD, 5800
18:14 waters that come from another place be f? 5428
19: 4 Because they have f me, and 5800
22: 9 Because they have f the covenant of 5800
25:38 He hath f his covert, as the lion: for their 5800
51: 5 For Israel *hath* not *been* f, nor Judah of his 488
Eze 8:12 seeth us not; the LORD hath f the earth. 5800
9: 9 The LORD hath f the earth, and 5800
36: 4 to the cities that are f, which became a prey 5800
Am 5: 2 she is f upon her land; *there is* none to raise 5203
Zep 2: 4 For Gaza shall be f, and Ashkelon a 5800
Mt 19:27 Behold, we have f all, and followed thee; *863*
19:29 And every one that hath f houses, or *863*
27:46 My God, my God, why hast thou f me? *1459*
Mk 15:34 My God, my God, why hast thou f me? *1459*
2Co 4: 9 Persecuted, but not f; cast down, but *1459*
2Ti 4:10 For Demas hath f me, having loved *this* *1459*
2Pe 2:15 Which have f the right way, and are gone *2641*

FORSAKETH (6) [FORSAKE]

Job 6:14 his friend; but he f the fear of the Almighty. 5800
Ps 37:28 loveth judgment, and f not his saints; 5800
Pr 2:17 Which f the guide of her youth, and 5800
15:10 Correction *is* grievous unto him that f 5800
28:13 and f *them* shall have mercy. 5800
Lk 14:33 whosoever *he be* of you that f not all that he *657*

FORSAKING (2) [FORSAKE]

Isa 6:12 *there be* a great f in the midst of the land. 5805
Heb 10:25 Not f the assembling of ourselves together, *1459*

FORSOMUCH (2) [FOR, MUCH, SO] See Index

FORSOOK (24) [FORSAKE]

Dt 32:15 then he f God *which* made him, 5203
Jdg 2:12 And they f the LORD God of their fathers, 5800
2:13 they f the LORD, and served Baal and 5800
10: 6 and f the LORD, and served not him. 5800
1Sa 31: 7 sons were dead, they f the cities, and fled; 5800
1Ki 9: 9 Because they f the LORD their God, 5800
12: 8 he f the counsel of the old men, which they 5800
12:13 f the old men's counsel that they gave him; 5800
2Ki 21:22 he f the LORD God of his fathers, and 5800
1Ch 10: 7 were dead, then they f their cities, and fled: 5800
2Ch 7:22 Because they f the LORD God of their 5800
10: 8 he f the counsel which the old men gave 5800
10:13 king Rehoboam f the counsel of the old 5800
12: 1 he f the law of the LORD, and all Israel 5800
Ps 78:60 So that he f the tabernacle of Shiloh, 5203
119:87 me upon earth; but I f not thy precepts. 5800
Isa 58: 2 and f not the ordinance of their God: 5800
Jer 14: 5 and f *it,* because there was no grass. 5800
Mt 26:56 Then all the disciples f him, and fled. *863*
Mk 1:18 And straightway they f their nets, and *863*
14:50 And they all f him, and fled. *863*
Lk 5:11 had brought *their* ships to land, they f all, *863*
2Ti 4:16 no *man* stood with me, but all *men* f me: *1459*
Heb 11:27 By faith he f Egypt, not fearing the wrath *2641*

FORSOOKEST (2) [FORSAKE]

Ne 9:17 and of great kindness, and f them not. 5800
9:19 Yet thou in thy manifold mercies f them 5800

FORSWEAR (1) [SWEAR]

Mt 5:33 Thou shalt not f thyself, but shalt perform *1964*

FORT (6) [FORTIFIED, FORTIFY, FORTRESS, FORTRESSES, FORTS]

2Sa 5: 9 So David dwelt in the f, and called it 4686
Isa 25:12 the fortress of the **high** f of thy walls shall 4869
Eze 4: 2 build a f against it, and cast a mount against 1785
21:22 the gates, to cast a mount, *and* to build a f. 1785
26: 8 he shall make a f against thee, and cast a 1785
Da 11:19 he shall turn his face towards the f of his 4581

FORTH (888) [HENCEFORTH] See Index

FORTHWITH (10)

Ezr 6: 8 f expences be given unto these men, 629
Mt 13: 5 and f they sprung up, because *they* had no *2112*
26:49 And f he came to Jesus, and said, Hail, *2112*
Mk 1:29 And f, when they were come out of *2112*
1:43 straitly charged him, and f sent him away; *2112*
5:13 And f Jesus gave them leave. And *2112*
Jn 19:34 and f came there out blood and water. *2112*
Ac 9:18 and he received sight f, and arose, and *3916*
12:10 and f the angel departed from him. *2112*
21:30 of the temple: and f the doors were shut. *2112*

FORTIETH (4) [FORTY]

Nu 33:38 in the f year after the children of Israel were 705
Dt 1: 3 it came to pass in the f year, in the eleventh 705
1Ch 26:31 In the f year of the reign of David they were 705
2Ch 16:13 and died in the one and f year of his reign. 705

FORTIFIED (4) [FORT]

2Ch 11:11 he f the strong holds, and put captains in 2388
26: 9 and at the turning *of the wall,* and f them. 2388
Ne 3: 8 and they f Jerusalem unto the broad wall. 5800
Mic 7:12 *from* the f cities, and from the fortress even 4693

FORTIFY (6) [FORT]

Jdg 9:31 and behold, they f the city against thee. 6696
Ne 4: 2 will they f themselves? will they sacrifice? 5800
Isa 22:10 the houses have ye broken down to f 1219
Jer 51:53 though she should f the height of her 1219
Na 2: 1 make *thy* loins strong, f *thy* power mightily. 553
3:14 thee waters for the siege, f thy strong holds: 2388

FORTRESS (15) [FORT]

2Sa 22: 2 *is* my rock, and my f, and my deliverer; 4686
Ps 18: 2 *is* my rock, and my f, and my deliverer; 4686
31: 3 For thou *art* my rock and my f; therefore 4686
71: 3 to save me; for thou *art* my rock and my f. 4686
91: 2 of the LORD, *He is* my refuge and my f: 4686

Ps 144: 2 My goodness, and my f; my high tower, 4686
Isa 17: 3 The f also shall cease from Ephraim, and 4013
25:12 the f of the high fort of thy walls shall he 4013
Jer 6:27 thee *for* a tower *and* a f among my people, 4013
10:17 wares out of the land, O inhabitant of the f. 4692
16:19 my f, and my refuge in the day of affliction, 4581
Da 11: 7 shall enter into the f of the king of 4581
11:10 he return, and be stirred up, *even* to his f. 4581
Am 5: 9 so that the spoiled shall come against the f. 4013
Mic 7:12 from the f even to the river, and from sea *to* 4693

FORTRESSES (2) [FORT]
Isa 34:13 nettles and brambles in the f thereof: 4013
Hos 10:14 thy people, and all thy f shall be spoiled, 4013

FORTS (6) [FORT]
2Ki 25: 1 and they built f against it round about. 1785
Isa 29: 3 *with* a mount, and I will raise f against thee. 4694
32:14 the f and towers shall be for dens for ever, 6076
Jer 52: 4 against it, and built f against it round about. 1785
Eze 17:17 by casting up mounts, and building f, to cut 1785
33:27 *they* that *be* in the f and in the caves shall 4679

FORTUNATUS (2)
1Co 16:17 coming of Stephanas and F and Achaicus: *5415*
16: S and F, and Achaicus, and Timotheus. *5415*

FORTY (157) [FORTIETH, FORTY'S]
Ge 5:13 begat Mahalaleel eight hundred and f years, 705
7: 4 I will cause it to rain upon the earth f days 705
7: 4 to rain upon the earth forty days and f nights; 705
7:12 the rain was upon the earth f days and 705
7:12 was upon the earth forty days and f nights. 705
7:17 And the flood was f days upon the earth; and 705
8: 6 it came to pass at the end of f days, 705
18:28 he said, If I find there f and five, I will not 705
18:29 Peradventure there shall be f found there. 705
25:20 Isaac was f years old when he took Rebekah 705
26:34 Esau was f years old when he took to wife 705
32:15 f kine, and ten bulls, twenty she asses, and 705
47:28 so the whole age of Jacob was an hundred f 705
50: 3 f days were fulfilled for him; for so 705
Ex 16:35 the children of Israel did eat manna f years, 705
24:18 Moses was in the mount f days and 705
24:18 was in the mount forty days and f nights. 705
26:19 thou shalt make f sockets of silver under 705
26:21 their f sockets *of* silver; two sockets under 705
34:28 he was there with the LORD f days and 705
34:28 with the LORD forty days and f nights; 705
36:24 f sockets of silver he made under the twenty 705
36:26 their f sockets *of* silver; two sockets under 705
Lev 25: 8 seven sabbaths of years shall be unto thee f 705
Nu 1:21 *were* f and six thousand and five hundred. 705
1:25 *were* f and five thousand six hundred and 705
1:33 *were* f thousand and five hundred. 705
1:41 *were* f and one thousand and five hundred. 705
2:11 *were* f and six thousand and five hundred. 705
2:15 *were* f and five thousand and six hundred 705
2:19 of them, *were* f thousand and five hundred. 705
2:28 *were* f and one thousand and five hundred. 705
13:25 from searching of the land after f days. 705
14:33 shall wander in the wilderness f years, 705
14:34 *even* f days, each day for a year, shall ye 705
14:34 *even* f years, and ye shall know my breach 705
26: 7 they that were numbered of them were f and 705
26:18 of them, f thousand and five hundred. 705
26:41 they that were numbered of them *were* f and 705
26:50 they that were numbered of them *were* f and 705
32:13 he made them wander in the wilderness f 705
35: 6 to them ye shall add f and two cities. 705
35: 7 which ye shall give to the Levites *shall be* f 705
Dt 2: 7 these f years the LORD thy God *hath been* 705
8: 2 God led thee these f years in the wilderness, 705
8: 4 neither did thy foot swell, these f years. 705
9: 9 I abode in the mount f days and forty nights, 705
9: 9 I abode in the mount forty days and f nights, 705
9:11 it came to pass at the end of f days and 705
9:11 to pass at the end of forty days and f nights, 705
9:18 as at the first, f days and forty nights: 705
9:18 as at the first, forty days and f nights: 705
9:25 Thus I fell down before the LORD f days 705
9:25 before the LORD forty days and f nights, 705
10:10 to the first time, f days and forty nights; 705
10:10 to the first time, forty days and f nights; 705
25: 3 F stripes he may give him, *and* not exceed: 705
29: 5 And I have led you f years in the wilderness: 705
Jos 4:13 About f thousand prepared for war passed 705
5: 6 For the children of Israel walked f years in 705
14: 7 F years old *was* I when Moses the servant of 705
14:10 me alive, as he said, these f and five years, 705
21:41 possession of the children of Israel *were* f 705
Jdg 3:11 the land had rest f years. And Othniel 705
5: 8 or spear seen among f thousand in Israel? 705
5:31 in his might. And the land had rest f years. 705
8:28 the country was in quietness f years in 705
12: 6 there fell at that time of the Ephraimites f 705
12:14 he had f sons and thirty nephews, that rode 705
13: 1 them into the hand of the Philistines f years. 705
1Sa 4:18 and heavy. And he had judged Israel f years. 705
17:16 and evening, and presented himself f days. 705
2Sa 2:10 Ish-bosheth Saul's son *was* f years old when 705
5: 4 he *began* to reign, *and* he reigned f years. 705
10:18 f thousand horsemen, and smote Shobach 705
15: 7 it came to pass after f years, that Absalom 705
1Ki 2:11 that David reigned over Israel *were* f years: 705
4:26 Solomon had f thousand stalls of horses for 705
6:17 *is,* the temple before it, was f cubits *long.* 705
7: 3 that *lay* on f five pillars, fifteen *in* a row. 705
7:38 one laver contained f baths: *and* every laver 705
11:42 in Jerusalem over all Israel *was* f years. 705
14:21 Rehoboam *was* f and one years old when he 705
15:10 And f and one years reigned he in Jerusalem. 705
19: 8 went in the strength of that meat f days and 705
19: 8 and f nights unto Horeb the mount of God. 705
2Ki 2:24 and tare f and two children of them. 705
8: 9 f camels' burden, and came and stood before 705
10:14 of the shearing house, *even* two and f men; 705
12: 1 to reign; and f years reigned he in Jerusalem. 705
14:23 in Samaria, *and reigned* f and one years. 705
1Ch 5:18 *were* four and f thousand seven hundred and 705
12:36 forth to battle, expert in war, f thousand. 705
19:18 f thousand footmen, and killed Shophach 705
29:27 the time that he reigned over Israel *was* f 705
2Ch 9:30 reigned in Jerusalem over all Israel f years. 705
12:13 and f years old when he *began* to reign, 705
22: 2 F and two years old *was* Ahaziah when he 705
24: 1 to reign, and he reigned f years in Jerusalem. 705
Ezr 2: 8 children of Zattu, nine hundred f and five. 705
2:10 The children of Bani, six hundred f and two. 705
2:24 The children of Azmaveth, f and two. 705
2:25 and Beeroth, seven hundred and f and three. 705
2:34 children of Jericho, three hundred f and five. 705
2:38 a thousand two hundred f and seven. 705
2:64 together *was* f *and* **two thousand** 505+702+7239
2:66 and six; their mules, two hundred f and five; 705
Ne 5:15 and wine, beside f shekels of silver; 705
7:13 children of Zattu, eight hundred f and five. 705
7:15 children of Binnui, six hundred f and eight. 705
7:28 The men of Beth-azmaveth, f and two. 705
7:29 and Beeroth, seven hundred f and three. 705
7:36 children of Jericho, three hundred f and five. 705
7:41 a thousand two hundred f and seven. 705
7:44 children of Asaph, an hundred f and eight. 705
7:62 children of Nekoda, six hundred f and two. 705
7:66 together *was* f *and* **two thousand** 505+702+7239
7:67 they had two hundred f and five singing *men* 705
7:68 and six: their mules, two hundred f and five: 705
9:21 f years didst thou sustain them in 705
11:13 chief of the fathers, two hundred f and two: 705
Job 42:16 After this lived Job an hundred and f years, 705
Ps 95:10 F years long was I grieved with *this* 705
Jer 52:30 away captive *of* the Jews seven hundred f 705
Eze 4: 6 the iniquity of the house of Judah f days: 705
29:11 neither shall it be inhabited f years. 705
29:12 *that are* laid waste shall be desolate f years: 705
29:13 At the end of f years will I gather 705
41: 2 and he measured the length thereof, f cubits: 705
46:22 *there were* courts joined *of* f *cubits* long 705
Am 2:10 led you f years through the wilderness, 705
5:25 and offerings in the wilderness f years, 705
Jnh 3: 4 Yet f days, and Nineveh *shall be* 705
Mt 4: 2 And when he had fasted f days and *5062*
4: 2 when he had fasted forty days and f nights, *5062*
Mk 1:13 And he was there in the wilderness f days, *5062*
Lk 4: 2 Being f days tempted of the devil. And in *5062*
Jn 2:20 F and six years was this temple in building, *5062*
Ac 1: 3 being seen of them f days, and speaking of *5062*
4:22 For the man was above f years old, *5062*

Ac 7:23 And when he was full f **years** old, it came *5063*
7:30 And when f years were expired, *5062*
7:36 the Red sea, and in the wilderness f years. *5062*
7:42 sacrifices *by the space of* f years in *5062*
13:18 And about the time of f **years** suffered he *5063*
13:21 tribe of Benjamin, *by the space of* f years. *5062*
23:13 And they were more *than* f which had made *5062*
23:21 lie in wait for him of them moe *than* f men, *5062*
2Co 11:24 Of the Jews five times received I f *stripes* *5062*
Heb 3: 9 proved me, and saw my works f years. *5062*
3:17 But with whom was he grieved f years? *5062*
Rev 7: 4 *and there were* sealed an hundred *and* f *and* *5062*
11: 2 the holy city shall they tread under foot f *5062*
13: 5 power was given unto him to continue f *5062*
14: 1 and with him an hundred f *and* *5062*
14: 3 but the hundred *and* f *and* four thousand, *5062*
21:17 an hundred *and* f *and* four cubits, *5062*

FORTY'S (1) [FORTY]
Ge 18:29 And he said, I will not do *it* for f sake. 705

FORUM (1)
Ac 28:15 they came to meet us as far as Appii f, and *5410*

FORWARD (47) [FORWARDNESS, HENCEFORWARD]
Ge 26:13 **went** f, and grew until he became very 1980
Ex 14:15 unto the children of Israel, that they **go** f: 5265
Nu 1:51 when the tabernacle **setteth** f, the Levites 5265
2:17 **set** f *with* the camp of the Levites in 5265
2:17 as they encamp, so shall they **set** f, 5265
2:24 And they shall **go** f in the third rank. 5265
2:34 so they **set** f, every one after their families, 5265
4: 5 when the camp **setteth** f, Aaron shall come, 5265
4:15 of the sanctuary, as the camp is to **set** f; 5265
10: 5 camps that lie on the east parts shall **go** f. 5265
10:17 of Gershon and the sons of Merari **set** f, 5265
10:18 the standard of the camp of Reuben **set** f 5265
10:21 the Kohathites **set** f, bearing the sanctuary: 5265
10:22 of Ephraim **set** f according to their armies: 5265
10:25 of the camp of the children of Dan **set** f, 5265
10:28 according to their armies, when they **set** f. 5265
10:35 when the ark **set** f, that Moses said, 5265
21:10 the children of Israel **set** f, and pitched in 5265
22: 1 the children of Israel **set** f, and pitched in 5265
32:19 with them on *yonder* side Jordan, or f; 1973
Jdg 9:44 **rushed** f, and stood *in* the entering of 6584
1Sa 10: 3 shalt thou go on f from thence, and 1973
16:13 came upon David from that day f. 4605+1886.5
18: 9 And Saul eyed David from that day and f. 1973
30:25 it was *so* from that day f, that he 4605+1886.5
2Ki 3:24 they **went** f smiting the Moabites, even in 935
4:24 Drive, and go *f;* slack not *thy* riding for me, NIH
20: 9 shall the shadow **go** f ten degrees, or 1980
1Ch 23: 4 four thousand *were* to **set** f the work of 5329
2Ch 34:12 of the sons of the Kohathites, to **set** *it* f; 5329
Ezr 3: 8 to **set** f the work of the house of 5329
3: 9 to **set** f the workmen in the house of God: 5329
Job 23: 8 I go f, but he *is* not *there;* and backward, 6924
30:13 They mar my path, they **set** f my calamity, 3276
Jer 7:24 and went backward, and not f. 6440+3807.1
Eze 1: 9 they went every one **straight** f. 413+5676+6440
1:12 they went every one **straight** f: 413+5676+6440
10:22 they went every one **straight** f. 413+5676+6440
39:22 the LORD their God from that day and f. 1973
43:27 it shall be, *that* upon the eight day, and *so* f, 1973
Zec 1:15 and they **helped** f the affliction. 5826
Mk 14:35 And he **went** f a little, and fell on *4281*
Ac 19:33 of the multitude, the Jews **putting** him f. *4261*
2Co 8:10 not only to do, but also to be f a year ago. *2309*
8:17 but being **more** f, of his own accord he *4707*
Gal 2:10 the poor; the same which I also was f to do. *4704*
3Jn 1: 6 whom if thou **bring** f **on** their **journey** *4311*

FORWARDNESS (2) [FORWARD]
2Co 8: 8 but by occasion of the f of others, and *4710*
9: 2 For I know the **f of** your **mind**, for which I *4288*

FOUGHT (64) [FIGHT]
Ex 17: 8 and f with Israel in Rephidim. 3898
17:10 Moses had said to him, and f with Amalek: 3898
Nu 21: 1 he f against Israel, and took *some* of them 3898
21:23 and he came *to* Jahaz, and f against Israel. 3898
21:26 who had f against the former king of Moab, 3898
Jos 10:14 voice of a man: for the LORD f for Israel. 3898
10:29 *unto* Libnah, and f against Libnah: 3898
10:31 and encamped against it, and f against it: 3898
10:34 they encamped against it, and f against it: 3898
10:36 unto Hebron; and they f against it: 3898
10:38 Israel with him, to Debir; and f against it: 3898
10:42 the LORD God of Israel f for Israel. 3898
23: 3 for the LORD your God *is* he that hath f 3898
24: 8 the *other* side Jordan; and they f with you: 3898
24:11 the men of Jericho f against you, 3898
Jdg 1: 5 they f against him, and they slew 3898
1: 8 Now the children of Judah had f against 3898
5:19 The kings came *and* f, then fought the kings 3898
5:19 f the kings of Canaan in Taanach by 3898
5:20 They f from heaven; the stars in their 3898
5:20 the stars in their courses f against Sisera. 3898
9:17 (For my father f for you, and 3898
9:39 men of Shechem, and f with Abimelech. 3898
9:45 Abimelech f against the city all that day; 3898
9:52 f against it, and went hard unto the door of 3898
11:20 and pitched in Jahaz, and f against Israel. 3898
12: 4 all the men of Gilead, and f with Ephraim: 3898
1Sa 4:10 the Philistines f, and Israel was smitten, 3898
12: 9 the king of Moab, and they f against them. 3898
14:47 f against all his enemies on every side, 3898
19: 8 f with the Philistines, and slew them *with* a 3898
23: 5 f with the Philistines, and brought away 3898
31: 1 Now the Philistines f against Israel: and 3898
2Sa 2:28 Israel no more, neither f they any more. 3898
8:10 because he had f against Hadadezer, and 3898
10:17 in array against David, and f with him. 3898
11:17 men of the city went out, and f with Joab: 3898
12:26 Joab f against Rabbah of the children of 3898
12:27 I have f against Rabbah, and have taken 3898
12:29 to Rabbah, and f against it, and took it. 3898
21:15 with him, and f **against** the Philistines: 3898
2Ki 8:29 when he f against Hazael king of Syria. 3898
9:15 when he f with Hazael king of Syria.) 3898
12:17 went up, and f against Gath, and took it: 3898
13:12 his might where*with* he f against Amaziah 3898
14:15 and how he f with Amaziah king of Judah, 3898
1Ch 10: 1 Now the Philistines f against Israel; and 3898
18:10 because he had f against Hadarezer, and 3898
19:17 array against the Syrians, they f with him. 3898
19:18 seven thousand *men which f in* chariots, NIH
2Ch 20:29 when they had heard that the LORD f 3898
22: 6 when he f with Hazael king of Syria. 3898
27: 5 He f also with the king of the Ammonites, 3898
Ps 109: 3 of hatred; and f against me without a cause. 3898
Isa 20: 1 and f against Ashdod, and took it; 3898
63:10 to be their enemy, *and* he f against them. 3898
Jer 34: 1 f against Jerusalem, and against all 3898
34: 7 When the king of Babylon's army f against 3898
Zec 14: 3 as when he f in the day of battle. 3898
14:12 all the people that have f against Jerusalem; 6633
1Co 15:32 of men I have **f with beasts** at Ephesus, *2341*
2Ti 4: 7 I have f a good fight, I have finished *my* *75*
Rev 12: 7 and his angels f against the dragon; *4170*
12: 7 the dragon; and the dragon f and his angels, *4170*

FOUL (5) [FOULED, FOULEDST]
Job 16:16 My face is f with weeping, and on mine 2560
Eze 34:18 but ye must f the residue with your feet? 7515
Mt 16: 3 in the morning, *It will be* **f weather** to day: *5494*
Mk 9:25 he rebuked the f spirit, saying unto him, *169*
Rev 18: 2 and the hold of every f spirit, and a cage of *169*

FOULED (1) [FOUL]
Eze 34:19 they drink **that which** ye have f with your 4833

FOULEDST (1) [FOUL]
Eze 32: 2 the waters with thy feet, and f their rivers. 7515

FOUND (403) [FIND, FOUNDATION, FOUNDATIONS, FOUNDED, FOUNDER, FOUNDEST]
Ge 2:20 for Adam there was not f a help meet for 4672
6: 8 Noah f grace in the eyes of the LORD. 4672
8: 9 the dove f no rest for the sole of her foot, 4672
11: 2 that they f a plain in the land of Shinar; 4672
16: 7 the angel of the LORD f her by a fountain 4672
18: 3 if now I have f favour in thy sight, 4672
18:29 Peradventure there shall be forty f there. 4672
18:30 Peradventure there shall thirty be f there. 4672
18:31 Peradventure there shall be twenty f there. 4672
18:32 Peradventure ten shall be f there. And he 4672

Ge 19:19 thy servant hath f grace in thy sight, and 4672
26:19 and f there a well of springing water. 4672
26:32 and said unto him, We have f water. 4672
27:20 How *is it that* thou hast f *it so* quickly, my 4672
30:14 f mandrakes in the field, and brought them 4672
30:27 I pray thee, if I have f favour in thine eyes, 4672
31:33 two maidservants' tents; but he f *them* not. 4672
31:34 Laban searched all the tent, but f *them* not. 4672
31:35 And he searched, but f not the images. 4672
31:37 what hast thou f of all thy household stuff? 4672
33:10 if now I have f grace in thy sight, then 4672
36:24 this *was that* Anah that f the mules in 4672
37:15 a *certain* man f him, and behold, *he was* 4672
37:17 after his brethren, and f them in Dothan. 4672
37:32 *it* to their father; and said, This have we f: 4672
38:20 from the woman's hand: but he f her not. 4672
38:23 I sent this kid, and thou hast not f her. 4672
39: 4 Joseph f grace in his sight, and he served 4672
44: 8 which we f in our sacks' mouths, 4672
44: 9 With whom*soever* of thy servants it be f, 4672
44:10 he with whom it is f shall be my servant; 4672
44:12 and the cup was f in Benjamin's sack. 4672
44:16 God hath f **out** the iniquity of thy servants: 4672
44:16 and *he* also with whom the cup is f. 4672
44:17 *but* the man in whose hand the cup is f, 4672
47:14 Joseph gathered up all the money that was f 4672
47:29 If now I have f grace in thy sight, put, 4672
50: 4 If now I have f grace in your eyes, speak, 4672
Ex 9:19 and beast which shall be f in the field, 4672
12:19 Seven days shall there be no leaven f in 4672
15:22 days in the wilderness, and f no water. 4672
16:27 seventh day for to gather, and they f none. 4672
21:16 and selleth him, or if he be f in his hand, 4672
22: 2 If a thief be f breaking up, and be smitten 4672
22: 4 If the theft be **certainly** f in his hand 4672+4672
22: 7 if the thief be f, let him pay double. 4672
22: 8 If the thief be not f, then the master of 4672
33:12 and thou hast also f grace in my sight. 4672
33:13 I pray thee, if I have f grace in thy sight, 4672
33:16 and thy people have f grace in thy sight? 4672
33:17 for thou hast f grace in my sight, and 4672
34: 9 If now I have f grace in thy sight, O Lord, 4672
35:23 with whom was f blue, and purple, and 4672
35:24 with whom was f shittim wood for any 4672
Lev 6: 3 Or have f that which was lost, and 4672
6: 4 him to keep, or the lost *thing* which he f, 4672
Nu 11:11 wherefore have I not f favour in thy sight, 4672
11:15 out of hand, if I have f favour in thy sight; 4672
15:32 they f a man that gathered sticks upon 4672
15:33 they that f him gathering sticks brought him 4672
32: 5 said they, if we have f grace in thy sight, 4672
Dt 17: 2 If there be f among you, within any of thy 4672
18:10 There shall not be f among you *any one* 4672
20:11 *that* all the people that is f therein shall be 4672
21: 1 If *one* be f slain in the land which 4672
22: 3 which he hath lost, and thou hast f, shalt 4672
22:14 when I came to her, I f her not a maid: 4672
22:17 *her,* saying, I f not thy daughter a maid; 4672
22:20 *the tokens of* virginity be not f for 4672
22:22 If a man be f lying with a woman married 4672
22:27 For he f her in the field, *and* the betrothed 4672
22:28 hold on her, and lie with her, and they be f; 4672
24: 1 because he hath f some uncleanness in her: 4672
24: 7 If a man be f stealing any of his brethren of 4672
32:10 He f him in a desert land, and in the waste 4672
33:29 and thine enemies shall be f **liars** unto thee; 3584
Jos 2:22 throughout all the way, but f *them* not. 4672
10:17 The five kings are f hid in a cave at 4672
Jdg 1: 5 they f Adoni-bezek in Bezek: and 4672
6:17 If now I have f grace in thy sight, then 4672
14:18 with my heifer, ye had not f **out** my riddle. 4672
15:15 he f a new jawbone of an ass, and put forth 4672
21:12 they f among the inhabitants of 4672
Ru 2:10 unto him, Why have I f grace in thine eyes, 4672
1Sa 9: 4 the land of Shalisha, but they f *them* not: 4672
9: 4 land of the Benjamites, but they f *them* not. 4672
9:11 they f young maidens going out to draw 4672
9:20 set not thy mind on them; for they are f. 4672
10: 2 The asses which thou wentest to seek are f: 4672
10:16 He told us plainly that the asses were f. 4672
10:21 when they sought him, he could not be f. 4672
12: 5 that ye have not f ought in my hand. 4672
13:19 Now there was no smith f throughout all 4672
13:22 that there was neither sword nor spear f in 4672
13:22 and with Jonathan his son was there f. 4672
14:30 of the spoil of their enemies which they f? 4672
16:22 before me; for he hath f favour in my sight. 4672
20: 3 Thy father certainly knoweth that I have f 4672
20:29 and now, if I have f favour in thine eyes, 4672
25:28 and evil hath not been f in thee *all* thy days. 4672
27: 5 If I have now f grace in thine eyes, 4672
29: 3 I have f no *fault* in him since he fell *unto* 4672
29: 6 for I have not f evil in thee since the day of 4672
29: 8 what hast thou f in thy servant so long as I 4672
30:11 they f an Egyptian in the field, and 4672
31: 8 that they f Saul and his three sons fallen in 4672
2Sa 7:27 hath thy servant f in his heart to pray this 4672
14:22 To day thy servant knoweth that I have f 4672
17:12 him in some place where he shall be f, 4672
17:13 until there be not one small stone f there. 4672
1Ki 1: 3 f Abishag a Shunammite, and brought her 4672
1:52 if wickedness shall be f in him, he shall die. 4672
7:47 neither was the weight of the brass f **out**. 2713
11:19 Hadad f great favour in the sight of 4672
11:29 that the prophet Ahijah the Shilonite f him 4672
13:14 man of God, and f him sitting under an oak: 4672
13:28 he went and f his carcase cast in the way, 4672
14:13 in him there is f *some* good thing toward 4672
18:10 and nation, that they f thee not. 4672
19:19 and f Elisha the son of Shaphat, 4672
20:36 from him, a lion f him, and slew him. 4672
20:37 he f another man, and said, Smite me, 4672
21:20 to Elijah, Hast thou f me, O mine enemy? 4672
21:20 I have f *thee:* because thou hast sold thyself 4672
2Ki 2:17 and they sought three days, but f him not. 4672
4:39 f a wild vine, and gathered thereof wild 4672
9:35 but they f no more of her than the skull, and 4672
12: 5 wheresoever any breach shall be f. 4672
12:10 told the money that was f *in* the house of 4672
12:18 all the gold that was f in the treasures of 4672
14:14 all the vessels that were f *in* the house of 4672
16: 8 gold that was f *in* the house of the Lord, 4672
17: 4 the king of Assyria f conspiracy in Hoshea: 4672
18:15 Hezekiah gave *him* all the silver that was f 4672
19: 8 f the king of Assyria warring against 4672
20:13 and all that was f in his treasures: 4672
22: 8 I have f the book of the law in the house of 4672
22: 9 gathered the money that was f in the house, 4672
22:13 concerning the words of this book that is f: 4672
23: 2 which was f in the house of the Lord. 4672
23:24 the priest f *in* the house of the Lord. 4672
25:19 which were f in the city, and the principal 4672
25:19 people of the land that were f in the city: 4672
1Ch 4:40 they f fat pasture and good, and the land 4672
4:41 the habitations that were f there, 4672
10: 8 that they f Saul and his sons fallen in mount 4672
17:25 thy servant hath f *in his heart* to pray before 4672
20: 2 f it to weigh a talent of gold, and *there were* 4672
24: 4 there were moe chief men f of the sons of 4672
26:31 there were f among them mighty *men* of 4672
28: 9 if thou seek him, he will be f of thee; but 4672
29: 8 they with whom *precious* stones were f 4672
2Ch 2:17 they were f an hundred and fifty thousand 4672
4:18 the weight of the brass could not be f **out**. 2713
15: 2 if ye seek him, he will be f of you; but if ye 4672
15: 4 of Israel, and sought him, he was f of them. 4672
15:15 their whole desire; and he was f of them: 4672
19: 3 Nevertheless there are good things f in 4672
20:25 they f among them in abundance both 4672
21:17 carried away all the substance that was f in 4672
22: 8 f the princes of Judah, and the sons of 4672
25: 5 f them three hundred thousand choice *men,* 4672
25:24 all the vessels that were f in the house of 4672
29:16 brought out all the uncleanness that they f 4672
34:14 Hilkiah the priest f a book of the law of 4672
34:15 I have f the book of the law in the house of 4672
34:17 that was f in the house of the Lord, 4672
34:21 concerning the words of the book that is f: 4672
34:30 that was f *in* the house of the Lord. 4672
36: 8 he did, and that which was f in him, behold, 4672
Ezr 2:62 by genealogy, but they were not f: 4672
4:19 it is f that this city of old time *hath* made 7912
6: 2 there was f at Achmetha, in the palace that 7912
8:15 and f there none of the sons of Levi. 4672
10:18 among the sons of the priests there were f 4672
Ne 2: 5 if thy servant have f **favour** in thy sight, 3190
5: 8 they their peace, and f nothing *to answer.* 4672
7: 5 I f a register of the genealogy of them 4672

F

Ne	7: 5	came up at the first, and f written therein,	4672
	7:64	reckoned by genealogy, but it was not f:	4672
	8:14	they f written in the law which the LORD	4672
	13: 1	therein was f written, that the Ammonite	4672
Est	2:23	was made of the matter, it was f **out**;	4672
	5: 8	If I have f favour in the sight of the king,	4672
	6: 2	it was f written, that Mordecai had told of	4672
	7: 3	and said, If I have f favour in thy sight,	4672
	8: 5	if I have f favour in his sight, and the thing	4672
Job	19:28	seeing the root of the matter is f in me;	4672
	20: 8	fly away as a dream, and shall not be f:	4672
	28:12	where shall wisdom be f? and where *is*	4672
	28:13	neither is it f in the land of the living.	4672
	31:29	hated me, or lift up myself when evil f him:	4672
	32: 3	because they had f no answer, and *yet* had	4672
	32:13	Lest ye should say, We have f **out** wisdom:	4672
	33:24	going down *to* the pit: I have f a ransom.	4672
	42:15	in all the land were no women f *so* fair as	4672
Ps	32: 6	unto thee in a time when thou mayest be f:	4672
	36: 2	until his iniquity be f to be hateful.	4672
	37:36	yea, I sought him, but he could not be f.	4672
	69:20	*was* none; and for comforters, but I f none.	4672
	76: 5	none of the men of might have f their	4672
	84: 3	the sparrow hath f a house, and the swallow	4672
	89:20	I have f David my servant; with my holy oil	4672
	107: 4	in a solitary way; they f no city to dwell in.	4672
	116: 3	gat hold upon me: I f trouble and sorrow.	4672
	132: 6	we f it in the fields of the wood.	4672
Pr	6:31	*if* he be f, he shall restore sevenfold; he	4672
	7:15	to seek thy face, and I have f thee.	4672
	10:13	of him that hath understanding wisdom is f:	4672
	16:31	*if* it be f in the way of righteousness.	4672
	24:14	when thou hast f *it,* then there shall be a	4672
	25:16	Hast thou f honey? eat so much as is	4672
	30: 6	lest he reprove thee, and thou be **f a liar**.	3576
	30:10	lest he curse thee, and thou be f **guilty**.	816
Ecc	7:27	Behold, this have I f, saith the Preacher,	4672
	7:28	one man among a thousand have I f; but	4672
	7:28	but a woman among all those have I not f.	4672
	7:29	Lo, this only have I f, that God hath made	4672
	9:15	Now there was f in it a poor wise man, and	4672
SS	3: 1	soul loveth: I sought him, but I f him not.	4672
	3: 2	soul loveth: I sought him, but I f him not.	4672
	3: 3	The watchmen that go about the city f me:	4672
	3: 4	but I f *him* whom my soul loveth:	4672
	5: 7	The watchmen that went about the city f	4672
	8:10	then was I in his eyes as one that f favour.	4672
Isa	10:10	As my hand hath f the kingdoms of	4672
	10:14	my hand hath f as a nest the riches of	4672
	13:15	Every one that is f shall be thrust through;	4672
	22: 3	all that are f in thee are bound together,	4672
	30:14	that there shall not be f in the bursting of it	4672
	35: 9	shall go up thereon, it shall not be f there;	4672
	37: 8	f the king of Assyria warring against	4672
	39: 2	and all that was f in his treasures:	4672
	51: 3	joy and gladness shall be f therein,	4672
	55: 6	Seek ye the LORD while he may be f,	4672
	57:10	thou hast f the life of thine hand; therefore	4672
	65: 1	*for me:* I am f of *them that* sought me not:	4672
	65: 8	As the new wine is f in the cluster, and	4672
Jer	2: 5	What iniquity have your fathers f in me,	4672
	2:26	As the thief is ashamed when he is f, so	4672
	2:34	Also in thy skirts is f the blood of the souls	4672
	2:34	I have not f it by secret search, but upon all	4672
	5:26	For among my people are f wicked *men:*	4672
	11: 9	A conspiracy is f among the men of Judah,	4672
	14: 3	they came to the pits, *and* f no water;	4672
	15:16	Thy words were f, and I did eat them; and	4672
	23:11	yea, in my house have I f their wickedness,	4672
	29:14	I will be f of you, saith the LORD: and	4672
	31: 2	The people which were left of the sword f	4672
	41: 3	the Chaldeans that were f there, *and*	4672
	41: 8	ten men were f among them that said unto	4672
	41:12	f him by the great waters that *are* in	4672
	48:27	was he f among thieves? for since thou	4672
	50: 7	All that f them have devoured them: and	4672
	50:20	the sins of Judah, and they shall not be f:	4672
	50:24	thou art f, and also caught, because	4672
	52:25	the king's person, which were f in the city;	4672
	52:25	the land, that were f in the midst of the city.	4672
La	2:16	we looked for; we have f, we have seen it.	4672
Eze	22:30	that *I* should not destroy it: but I f none.	4672
	26:21	yet shalt thou never be f again, saith	4672
	28:15	thou wast created, till iniquity was f in thee.	4672
Da	1:19	among them all was f none like Daniel,	4672
	1:20	he f them ten times better than all	4672
	2:25	I have f a man of the captives of Judah,	7912
	2:35	them away, that no place was f for them:	7912
	5:11	like the wisdom of the gods, was f in him;	7912
	5:12	of doubts, were f in the same Daniel,	7912
	5:14	and excellent wisdom is f in thee.	7912
	5:27	weighed in the balances, and art f wanting.	7912
	6: 4	neither was there any error or fault f in him.	7912
	6:11	f Daniel praying and making supplication	7912
	6:22	forasmuch as before him innocency was f	7912
	6:23	no manner of hurt was f upon him, because	7912
	11:19	but he shall stumble and fall, and not be f.	4672
	12: 1	every one that *shall* be f written in	4672
Hos	9:10	I f Israel like grapes in the wilderness;	4672
	10: 2	heart is divided; now shall they be f **faulty**:	816
	12: 4	he f him *in* Beth-el, and there he spake with	4672
	12: 8	am become rich, I have f me **out** substance:	4672
	14: 8	like a green fir tree. From me is thy fruit f.	4672
Jnh	1: 3	*to* Joppa; and he f a ship going *to* Tarshish:	4672
Mic	1:13	for the transgressions of Israel were f in	4672
Zep	3:13	neither shall a deceitful tongue be f in their	4672
Zec	10:10	Lebanon; and *place* shall not be f for them.	4672
Mal	2: 6	and iniquity was not f in his lips:	4672
Mt	1:18	she was f with child of the Holy Ghost.	*2147*
	2: 8	when ye have f *him,* bring me word again,	*2147*
	8:10	I have not f so great faith, no not in Israel.	*2147*
	13:44	the which when a man hath f, he hideth,	*2147*
	13:46	when he had f one pearl of great price,	*2147*
	18:28	went out, and f one of his fellowservants,	*2147*
	20: 6	and f others standing idle, and saith unto	*2147*
	21:19	he came to it, and f nothing thereon,	*2147*
	22:10	and gathered together all as many as they f,	*2147*
	26:43	And he came and f them asleep again:	*2147*
	26:60	But f none: yea, though many false	*2147*
	26:60	many false witnesses came, *yet* f they none.	*2147*
	27:32	they f a man of Cyrene, Simon by name:	*2147*
Mk	1:37	And when they had f him, they said unto	*2147*
	7: 2	to say, with unwashen, hands, they f **fault**.	*3201*
	7:30	she f the devil gone out, and *her* daughter	*2147*
	11: 4	f the colt tied by the door without in a place	*2147*
	11:13	when he came to it, he f nothing but leaves;	*2147*
	14:16	the city, and f as he had said unto them:	*2147*
	14:40	when he returned, he f them asleep again,	*2147*
	14:55	Jesus to put him to death; and f none.	*2147*
Lk	1:30	Mary: for thou hast f favour with God.	*2147*
	2:16	and f Mary, and Joseph, and the babe lying	*429*
	2:45	And when they f him not, they turned back	*2147*
	2:46	*that* after three days they f him in	*2147*
	4:17	he f the place where it was written,	*2147*
	7: 9	I have not f so great faith, no, not in Israel.	*2147*
	7:10	f the servant whole that had been sick.	*2147*
	8:35	and came to Jesus, and f the man, out of	*2147*
	9:36	when the voice was past, Jesus was f alone.	*2147*
	13: 6	and sought fruit thereon, and f none.	*2147*
	15: 5	And when he hath f *it,* he layeth *it* on his	*2147*
	15: 6	for I have f my sheep which was lost.	*2147*
	15: 9	And when she hath f *it,* she calleth *her*	*2147*
	15: 9	for I have f the piece which I had lost.	*2147*
	15:24	and is alive again; he was lost, and is f.	*2147*
	15:32	and is alive again; and was lost, and is f.	*2147*
	17:18	There are not f that returned to give glory	*2147*
	19:32	and f even as he had said unto them.	*2147*
	22:13	they went, and f as he had said unto them:	*2147*
	22:45	his disciples, he f them sleeping for sorrow,	*2147*
	23: 2	We f this *fellow* perverting the nation, and	*2147*
	23:14	have f no fault in this man *touching those*	*2147*
	23:22	I have f no cause of death in him: I will	*2147*
	24: 2	And they f the stone rolled away from	*2147*
	24: 3	and f not the body of the Lord Jesus.	*2147*
	24:23	And when they f not his body, they came,	*2147*
	24:24	and f *it* even so as the women had said:	*2147*
	24:33	and f the eleven gathered together, and	*2147*
Jn	1:41	unto him, We have f the Messias, which is,	*2147*
	1:45	and saith unto him, We have f him,	*2147*
	2:14	And f in the temple those that sold oxen	*2147*
	6:25	And when they had f him on the other side	*2147*
	9:35	and when he had f him, he said unto him,	*2147*
	11:17	he f that he had *lien* in the grave four days	*2147*
	12:14	And Jesus, when he had f a young ass,	*2147*
Ac	5:10	and f her dead, and, carrying *her* forth,	*2147*
	5:22	and f them not in the prison, they returned,	*2147*
	5:23	The prison truly f we shut with all safety,	*2147*
	5:23	when we had opened, we f no *man* within.	*2147*

Ac 5:39 lest haply ye be f even to fight against God. 2147
7:11 and our fathers f no sustenance. 2147
7:46 Who f favour before God, and desired to 2147
8:40 But Philip was f at Azotus: and 2147
9: 2 that if he f any of *this* way, whether they 2147
9:33 And there he f a certain man named 2147
10:27 and f many *that were* come together. 2147
11:26 And when he had f him, he brought him 2147
12:19 and f *him* not, he examined the keepers, 2147
13: 6 they f a certain sorcerer, a false prophet, 2147
13:22 and said, I have f David the *son* of Jesse, 2147
13:28 And though they f no cause of death *in* 2147
17: 6 And when they f them not, they drew Jason 2147
17:23 I f an altar with this inscription, 2147
18: 2 And f a certain Jew named Aquila, born in 2147
19:19 and f *it* fifty thousand *pieces* of silver. 2147
24: 5 For we have f this man a pestilent *fellow,* 2147
24:12 And they neither f me in the temple 2147
24:18 Whereupon certain Jews from Asia f me 2147
24:20 if they have f any evil doing in me, 2147
25:25 But when I f that he had committed nothing 2638
27: 6 And there the centurion f a ship of 2147
27:28 And sounded, and f *it* twenty fathoms: and 2147
27:28 sounded again, and f *it* fifteen fathoms. 2147
28:14 Where we f brethren, and were desired to 2147
Ro 4: 1 our father, as pertaining to the flesh, hath f? 2147
7:10 was *ordained* to life, I f *to be* unto death. 2147
10:20 saith, I was f of them that sought me not; 2147
1Co 4: 2 in stewards, that a man be f faithful. 2147
15:15 Yea, and we are f false witnesses of God; 2147
2Co 2:13 my spirit, because I f not Titus my brother: 2147
5: 3 be that being clothed we shall not be f 2147
7:14 which *I made* before Titus, is f a truth. 1096
11:12 they glory, they may be f even as we. 2147
12:20 *that* I shall be f unto you such as ye would 2147
Gal 2:17 we ourselves also are f sinners, *is* therefore 2147
Php 2: 8 And being f in fashion as a man, 2147
3: 9 And be f in him, not having mine own 2147
1Ti 3:10 the office of a deacon, being *f* blameless. NIG
2Ti 1:17 sought me out very diligently, and f *me.* 2147
Heb 11: 5 and was not f, because God had translated 2147
12:17 for he f no place of repentance, though he 2147
1Pe 1: 7 might be f unto praise and honour and 2147
2:22 did no sin, neither was guile f in his mouth: 2147
2Pe 3:14 diligent that ye may be f of him in peace, 2147
2Jn 1: 4 I rejoiced greatly that I f of thy children 2147
Rev 2: 2 and are not, and hast f them liars: 2147
3: 2 for I have not f thy works perfect before 2147
5: 4 because no *man* was f worthy to open and 2147
12: 8 neither was their place f any more in 2147
14: 5 And in their mouth was f no guile: for they 2147
16:20 fled *away,* and the mountains were not f. 2147
18:21 thrown down, and shall be f no more at all. 2147
18:22 of whatsoever craft *he be,* shall be f any 2147
18:24 And in her was f the blood of prophets, and 2147
20:11 and there was f no place for them. 2147
20:15 And whosoever was not f written in 2147

FOUNDATION (54) [FOUND]

Ex 9:18 such as hath not been in Egypt since the f 3245
Jos 6:26 he shall **lay** the f thereof in his firstborn, 3245
1Ki 5:17 *and* hewed stones, to **lay the** f of the house. 3245
6:37 was the f of the house of the LORD **laid**, 3245
7: 9 even from the f unto the coping, and *so* 4527
7:10 the f *was of* costly stones, *even* great 3245
16:34 he **laid** the f thereof in Abiram his 3245
2Ch 8:16 the day of the f of the house of the LORD, 4143
23: 5 and a third *part* at the gate of the f: 3247
31: 7 In the third month they began to **lay** the f of 3245
Ezr 3: 6 f of the temple of the LORD was not *yet* **laid**. 3245
3:10 when the builders **laid** the f of the temple 3245
3:11 the f of the house of the LORD was **laid**. 3245
3:12 when the f of this house was **laid** before 3245
5:16 laid the f of the house of God which *is* in 787
Job 4:19 whose f *is* in the dust, which are crushed 3247
22:16 whose f was overflown *with* a flood: 3247
Ps 87: 1 His f *is* in the holy mountains. 3248
102:25 Of old hast thou **laid** the f of the earth: and 3245
137: 7 Rase *it,* rase *it, even* to the f thereof. 3247
Pr 10:25 but the righteous *is* an everlasting f. 3247
Isa 28:16 Behold, I **lay** in Zion **for a** f a stone, a tried 3245
28:16 a precious corner *stone,* a **sure** f: 3245+4143
44:28 and *to* the temple, Thy f shall be **laid**. 3245
48:13 Mine hand also hath **laid** the f of the earth, 3245
Eze 13:14 so that the f thereof shall be discovered, 3247
Hab 3:13 by discovering the f unto the neck. 3247
Hag 2:18 that the f of the LORD'S temple was **laid**, 3245
Zec 4: 9 The hands of Zerubbabel have **laid** the f of 3245
8: 9 f of the house of the LORD of hosts was **laid**, 3245
12: 1 **layeth** the f of the earth, and formeth 3245
Mt 13:35 *been* kept secret from the f of the world. 2602
25:34 prepared for you from the f of the world: 2602
Lk 6:48 and digged deep, and laid the f on a rock: 2310
6:49 is like a man that without a f built a house 2310
11:50 which was shed from the f of the world, 2602
14:29 after he hath laid the f, and is not able to 2310
Jn 17:24 for thou lovedst me before the f of 2602
Ro 15:20 lest I should build upon another *man's* f: 2310
1Co 3:10 I have laid the f, and another buildeth 2310
3:11 For other f can no *man* lay than that is laid, 2310
3:12 Now if any *man* build upon this f gold, 2310
Eph 1: 4 chosen us in him before the f of the world, 2602
2:20 And are built upon the f of the apostles and 2310
1Ti 6:19 Laying up in store for themselves a good f 2310
2Ti 2:19 Nevertheless the f of God standeth sure, 2310
Heb 1:10 in the beginning hast **laid the** f of the earth; 2311
4: 3 although the works were finished from the f 2602
6: 1 not laying again the f of repentance from 2310
9:26 must he often have suffered since the f of 2602
1Pe 1:20 Who verily was foreordained before the f 2602
Rev 13: 8 of the Lamb slain from the f of the world. 2602
17: 8 in the book of life from the f of the world, 2602
21:19 The first f *was* jasper; the second, sapphire; 2310

FOUNDATIONS (32) [FOUND]

Dt 32:22 and set on fire the f of the mountains. 4144
2Sa 22: 8 the f of heaven moved and shook, because 4146
22:16 the f of the world were discovered, at 4146
Ezr 4:12 set up the walls *thereof,* and joined the f. 787
6: 3 and *let* the f thereof *be* strongly laid; 787
Job 38: 4 Where wast thou when I **laid** the f of 3245
38: 6 Whereupon are the f thereof fastened? or 134
Ps 11: 3 If the f be destroyed, what can the righteous 8356
18: 7 the f also of the hills moved and 4146
18:15 the f of the world were discovered at thy 4146
82: 5 all the f of the earth are out of course. 4144
104: 5 *Who* laid the f of the earth, *that* it should 4349
Pr 8:29 when he appointed the f of the earth: 4144
Isa 16: 7 for the f of Kir-hareseth shall ye mourn; 808
24:18 are open, and the f of the earth do shake. 4146
40:21 have ye not understood *from* the f of 4146
51:13 the heavens, and **laid** the f of the earth; 3245
51:16 **lay** the f of the earth, and say unto Zion, 3245
54:11 fair colours, and **lay** thy f with sapphires. 3245
58:12 thou shalt raise up the f of many 4146
Jer 31:37 and the f of the earth searched out beneath, 4146
50:15 her f are fallen, her walls are thrown down: 803
51:26 thee a stone for a corner, nor a stone for f; 4146
La 4:11 in Zion, and it hath devoured the f thereof. 3247
Eze 30: 4 and her f shall be broken down. 3247
41: 8 the f of the side chambers *were* a full reed 4155
Mic 1: 6 the valley, and I will discover the f thereof. 3247
6: 2 and ye strong f of the earth: 4146
Ac 16:26 so that the f of the prison were shaken: 2310
Heb 11:10 For he looked for a city which hath f, 2310
Rev 21:14 And the wall of the city had twelve f, and 2310
21:19 And the f of the wall of the city *were* 2310

FOUNDED (10) [FOUND]

Ps 24: 2 For he hath f it upon the seas, and 3245
89:11 and the fulness thereof, thou hast f them. 3245
104: 8 unto the place which thou hast f for them. 3245
119:152 I have known of old that thou hast f them 3245
Pr 3:19 The LORD by wisdom hath f the earth; 3245
Isa 14:32 That the LORD hath f Zion, and the poor 3245
23:13 *till* the Assyrian f it for them that dwell in 3245
Am 9: 6 and hath f his troop in the earth; 3245
Mt 7:25 and it fell not: for it was f upon a rock. 2311
Lk 6:48 could not shake it: for it was f upon a rock. 2311

FOUNDER (5) [FOUND]

Jdg 17: 4 gave them to the f, who made thereof a 6884
Jer 6:29 consumed of the fire; the f melteth in vain: 6884
10: 9 of the workman, and of the hands of the f: 6884
10:14 every f is confounded by the graven image: 6884
51:17 every f is confounded by the graven image: 6884

FOUNDEST (1) [FOUND]
Ne 9: 8 f his heart faithful before thee, and 4672

FOUNTAIN (33) [FOUNTAINS]
Ge 16: 7 the angel of the LORD found her by a f of 5869
16: 7 the wilderness, by the f in the way to Shur. 5869
Lev 11:36 Nevertheless a f or pit, *wherein there is* 4599
20:18 he hath discovered her f, and she hath 4726
20:18 and she hath uncovered the f of her blood: 4726
Dt 33:28 the f of Jacob *shall be* upon a land of corn 5869
Jos 15: 9 the hill unto the f of the water of Nephtoah, 4599
1Sa 29: 1 the Israelites pitched by a f which *is* in 5869
Ne 2:14 I went on to the gate of the f, and to 5869
3:15 the gate of the f repaired Shallun the son of 5869
12:37 at the f gate, which *was* over against them, 5869
Ps 36: 9 For with thee *is* the f of life: in thy light 4726
68:26 *even* the Lord, from the f of Israel. 4726
74:15 Thou didst cleave the f and the flood: 4599
114: 8 a standing water, the flint into a f of waters. 4599
Pr 5:18 Let thy f be blessed: and rejoice with 4726
13:14 The law of the wise *is* a f of life, to depart 4726
14:27 The fear of the LORD *is* a f of life, 4726
25:26 down before the wicked *is as* a troubled f, 4599
Ecc 12: 6 or the pitcher be broken at the f, or 4002
SS 4:12 *my* spouse; a spring shut up, a f sealed. 4599
4:15 A f of gardens, a well of living waters, and 4599
Jer 2:13 they have forsaken me the f of living 4726
6: 7 As a f casteth out her waters, so she casteth 953
9: 1 mine eyes a f of tears, that I might weep 4726
17:13 forsaken the LORD, the f of living waters. 4726
Hos 13:15 become dry, and his f shall be dried up: 4599
Joel 3:18 a f shall come forth of the house of 4599
Zec 13: 1 In that day there shall be a f opened to 4726
Mk 5:29 And straightway the f of her blood was *4077*
Jas 3:11 Doth a f send forth at the same place sweet *4077*
3:12 so *can* no f *both* yield salt water and fresh. *4077*
Rev 21: 6 I will give unto him that is athirst of the f of *4077*

FOUNTAINS (15) [FOUNTAIN]
Ge 7:11 the same day were all the f of the great 4599
8: 2 The f also of the deep and the windows of 4599
Nu 33: 9 in Elim *were* twelve f of water, and 5869
Dt 8: 7 of f and depths that spring out of 5869
1Ki 18: 5 unto all f of water, and unto all brooks: 4599
2Ch 32: 3 his mighty *men* to stop the waters of the f 5869
32: 4 who stopt all the f, and the brook that ran 4599
Pr 5:16 Let thy f be dispersed abroad, *and* rivers of 4599
8:24 when *there were* no f abounding with 4599
8:28 when *he* strengthened the f of the deep: 5869
Isa 41:18 and f in the midst of the valleys: 4599
Rev 7:17 and shall lead them unto living f of waters: *4077*
8:10 *part* of the rivers, and upon the f of waters; *4077*
14: 7 and earth, and the sea, and the f of waters. *4077*
16: 4 out his vial upon the rivers and f of waters; *4077*

FOUR (328) [FOURFOLD, FOURFOOTED, FOURSCORE, FOURSQUARE, FOURTH]
Ge 2:10 it was parted, and became into f heads. 702
11:13 Arphaxad lived after he begat Salah f 702
11:15 Salah lived after he begat Eber f hundred 702
11:16 Eber lived f and thirty years, and 702
11:17 Eber lived after he begat Peleg f hundred 702
14: 9 and Arioch king of Ellasar; f kings with five. 702
15:13 and they shall afflict them f hundred years; 702
23:15 the land *is worth* f hundred shekels of silver; 702
23:16 f hundred shekels of silver, current *money* 702
32: 6 to meet thee, and f hundred men with him. 702
33: 1 Esau came, and with him f hundred men. 702
47:24 f parts shall be your own, for seed of 702
Ex 12:40 in Egypt, *was* f hundred and thirty years. 702
12:41 it came to pass at the end of the f hundred 702
22: 1 five oxen for an ox, and f sheep for a sheep. 702
25:12 And thou shalt cast f rings of gold for it, and 702
25:12 for it, and put *them* in the f corners thereof; 702
25:26 thou shalt make for it f rings of gold, and 702
25:26 put the rings in the f corners that *are* on 702
25:26 the four corners that *are* on the f feet thereof. 702
25:34 in the candlestick *shall be* f bowls made like 702
26: 2 and the breadth of one curtain f cubits: 702
26: 8 and the breadth of one curtain f cubits: 702
26:32 thou shalt hang it upon f pillars of shittim 702
26:32 *shall be of* gold, upon the f sockets of silver. 702
27: 2 thou shalt make the horns of it upon the f 702
27: 4 upon the net shalt thou make f brasen rings 702
27: 4 four brasen rings in the f corners thereof. 702
27:16 *and* their pillars *shall be* f, and their sockets 702
27:16 their pillars *shall be* four, and their sockets f. 702
28:17 in it settings of stones, *even* f rows of stones: 702
36: 9 the breadth of one curtain f cubits: 702
36:15 and f cubits *was* the breadth of one curtain: 702
36:36 he made thereunto f pillars of shittim *wood,* 702
36:36 and he cast for them f sockets of silver. 702
37: 3 he cast for it f rings of gold, *to be set* by 702
37: 3 rings of gold, *to be set* by the f corners of it; 702
37:13 he cast for it f rings of gold, and put 702
37:13 put the rings upon the f corners that *were* in 702
37:13 four corners that *were* in the f feet thereof. 702
37:20 in the candlestick *were* f bowls made like 702
38: 2 he made the horns thereof on the f corners of 702
38: 5 he cast f rings for the four ends of the grate 702
38: 5 he cast four rings for the f ends of the grate 702
38:19 their pillars *were* f, and their sockets *of* brass 702
38:19 pillars *were* four, and their sockets *of* brass f; 702
38:29 and two thousand and f hundred shekels. 702
39:10 they set in it f rows of stones: *the first* row 702
Lev 11:20 All fowls that creep, going upon *all* f, 702
11:21 flying creeping thing that goeth upon *all* f, 702
11:23 which have f feet, *shall be* an abomination 702
11:27 among all *manner of* beasts that go on *all* f, 702
11:42 whatsoever goeth upon *all* f, or 702
Nu 1:29 *were* fifty and f thousand and four hundred. 702
1:29 *were* fifty and four thousand and f hundred. 702
1:31 *were* fifty and seven thousand and f hundred. 702
1:37 *were* thirty and five thousand and f hundred. 702
1:43 *were* fifty and three thousand and f hundred. 702
2: 6 *were* fifty and f thousand and four hundred. 702
2: 6 *were* fifty and four thousand and f hundred. 702
2: 8 *were* fifty and seven thousand and f hundred. 702
2: 9 and six thousand and f hundred, 702
2:16 and one thousand and f hundred and fifty, 702
2:23 *were* thirty and five thousand and f hundred. 702
2:30 *were* fifty and three thousand and f hundred. 702
7: 7 and f oxen he gave unto the sons of Gershon, 702
7: 8 f wagons and eight oxen he gave unto 702
7:85 f hundred *shekels,* after the shekel of 702
7:88 peace offerings *were* twenty and f bullocks, 702
25: 9 in the plague were twenty and f thousand. 702
26:25 threescore and f thousand and three hundred. 702
26:43 and f thousand and four hundred. 702
26:43 and four thousand and f hundred. 702
26:47 *were* fifty and three thousand and f hundred. 702
26:50 *were* forty and five thousand and f hundred. 702
Dt 3:11 f cubits the breadth of it, after the cubit of a 702
22:12 Thou shalt make thee fringes upon the f 702
Jos 19: 7 Ether, and Ashan; f cities and their villages: 702
21:18 and Almon with her suburbs; f cities. 702
21:22 and Beth-horon with her suburbs; f cities. 702
21:24 Gath-rimmon with her suburbs; f cities. 702
21:29 En-gannim with her suburbs; f cities. 702
21:31 and Rehob with her suburbs; f cities. 702
21:35 Nahalal with her suburbs; f cities. 702
21:37 and Mephaath with her suburbs; f cities. 702
21:39 Jazer with her suburbs; f cities in all. 702
Jdg 9:34 they laid wait against Shechem *in* f 702
11:40 of Jephthah the Gileadite f days in a year. 702
19: 2 was there f whole months. 702
20: 2 f hundred thousand footmen that drew 702
20:17 were numbered f hundred thousand men that 702
20:47 and abode in the rock Rimmon f months. 702
21:12 of Jabesh-gilead f hundred young virgins, 702
1Sa 4: 2 they slew of the army in the field about f 702
22: 2 there were with him about f hundred men. 702
25:13 there went up after David about f hundred 702
27: 7 the Philistines was a full year and f months. 702
30:10 David pursued, he and f hundred men: 702
30:17 save f hundred young men, which rode upon 702
2Sa 21:20 every foot six toes, f and twenty *in* number; 702
21:22 These f were born to the giant in Gath, and 702
1Ki 6: 1 it came to pass in the f hundred and 702
7: 2 thirty cubits, upon f rows of cedar pillars, 702
7:19 *were* of lily work in the porch, f cubits). 702
7:27 f cubits *was* the length of one base, and 702
7:27 f cubits the breadth thereof, and three cubits 702
7:30 every base had f brasen wheels, and plates of 702
7:30 the f corners thereof had undersetters: under 702
7:32 under the borders *were* f wheels; and 702
7:34 *there were* f undersetters to the four corners 702
7:34 *there were* four undersetters to the f corners 702

1Ki 7:38 *and* every laver was f cubits: *and* upon every 702
7:42 f hundred pomegranates for the two 702
9:28 f hundred and twenty talents, and brought *it* 702
10:26 he had a thousand and f hundred chariots, 702
15:33 over all Israel in Tirzah, twenty and f years. 702
18:19 and the prophets of Baal f hundred and fifty, 702
18:19 and the prophets of the groves f hundred, 702
18:22 Baal's prophets *are* f hundred and fifty men. 702
18:33 Fill f barrels *with* water, and pour *it* on 702
22: 6 about f hundred men, and said unto them, 702
2Ki 7: 3 there were f leprous men *at* the entering in of 702
14:13 unto the corner gate, f hundred cubits. 702
1Ch 3: 5 and Shobab, and Nathan, and Solomon, f, 702
5:18 *were* f and forty thousand seven hundred and 702
7: 1 and Puah, Jashub, and Shimron, f. 702
7: 7 and two thousand and thirty and f. 702
9:24 In f quarters were the porters, toward 702
9:26 For these Levites, the f chief porters, *were* in 702
12:26 Of the children of Levi f thousand and 702
20: 6 whose fingers and toes *were* f and twenty, 702
21: 5 Judah *was* f hundred threescore and 702
21:20 and his f sons with him hid themselves. 702
23: 4 f thousand *were* to set forward the work of 702
23: 5 Moreover f thousand *were* porters; and 702
23: 5 f thousand praised the LORD with 702
23:10 and Beriah. These f *were* the sons of Shimei. 702
23:12 Amram, Izhar, Hebron, and Uzziel, f. 702
24:18 to Delaiah, the f and twentieth to Maaziah. 702
25:31 The f and twentieth to Romamti-ezer, *he,* his 702
26:17 northward f a day, southward four a day, and 702
26:17 southward f a day, and toward Asuppim two 702
26:18 f at the causeway, *and* two at Parbar. 702
27: 1 *of* every course *were* twenty and f thousand. 702
27: 2 in his course *were* twenty and f thousand. 702
27: 4 course likewise *were* twenty and f thousand. 702
27: 5 in his course *were* twenty and f thousand. 702
27: 7 in his course *were* twenty and f thousand. 702
27: 8 in his course *were* twenty and f thousand. 702
27: 9 in his course *were* twenty and f thousand. 702
27:10 in his course *were* twenty and f thousand. 702
27:11 in his course *were* twenty and f thousand. 702
27:12 in his course *were* twenty and f thousand. 702
27:13 in his course *were* twenty and f thousand. 702
27:14 in his course *were* twenty and f thousand. 702
27:15 in his course *were* twenty and f thousand. 702
2Ch 1:14 he had a thousand and f hundred chariots, 702
4:13 f hundred pomegranates on the two wreaths; 702
8:18 took thence f hundred and fifty talents of 702
9:25 Solomon had f thousand stalls for horses 702
13: 3 *even* f hundred thousand chosen men: 702
18: 5 gathered together *of* prophets f hundred men, 702
25:23 Ephraim to the corner gate, f hundred cubits. 702
Ezr 1:10 silver basons of a second sort f hundred and 702
1:11 of silver *were* five thousand and f hundred. 702
2: 7 of Elam, a thousand two hundred fifty and f. 702
2:15 children of Adin, f hundred fifty and four. 702
2:15 children of Adin, four hundred fifty and f. 702
2:31 a thousand two hundred fifty and f. 702
2:40 of the children of Hodaviah, seventy and f. 702
2:67 Their camels, f hundred thirty and five; 702
6:17 two hundred rams, f hundred lambs; 703
Ne 6: 4 Yet they sent unto me f times after this sort; 702
7:12 of Elam, a thousand two hundred fifty and f. 702
7:23 of Bezai, three hundred twenty and f. 702
7:34 a thousand two hundred fifty and f. 702
7:43 of the children of Hodevah, seventy and f. 702
7:69 *Their* camels, f hundred thirty and five: 702
11: 6 at Jerusalem *were* f hundred threescore 702
11:18 holy city *were* two hundred fourscore and f. 702
Job 1:19 smote the f corners of the house, and it fell 702
42:16 and his sons' sons, *even* f generations. 702
Pr 30:15 *yea,* f *things* say not, *It is* enough: 702
30:18 wonderful for me, yea, f which I know not: 702
30:21 is disquieted, and for f *which* it cannot bear: 702
30:24 There be f *things which are* little upon 702
30:29 which go well, yea, f are comely in going: 702
Isa 11:12 of Judah from the f corners of the earth. 702
17: 6 f *or* five in the outmost fruitful branches 702
Jer 15: 3 I will appoint over them f kinds, saith 702
36:23 *that* when Jehudi had read three or f leaves, 702
49:36 upon Elam will I bring the f winds from 702
49:36 the four winds from the f quarters of heaven, 702
52:21 and the thickness thereof *was* f fingers: 702
52:30 all the persons *were* f thousand and 702
Eze 1: 5 *came* the likeness of f living creatures. 702
1: 6 *every* one had f faces, and every one had 702
1: 6 had four faces, and every one had f wings. 702
1: 8 of a man under their wings on their f sides; 702
1: 8 and they f had their faces and their wings. 702
1:10 they f had the face of a man, and the face of 702
1:10 they f had the face of an ox on the left side; 702
1:10 left side; they f also had the face of an eagle. 702
1:15 earth by the living creatures, with his f faces. 702
1:16 they f had one likeness: and their appearance 702
1:17 they went, they went upon their f sides: 702
1:18 rings *were* full *of* eyes round about them f. 702
7: 2 the end is come upon the f corners of 702
10: 9 behold the f wheels by the cherubims, 702
10:10 their appearances, they f had one likeness, 702
10:11 they went, they went upon their f sides; 702
10:12 round about, *even* the wheels that they f had. 702
10:14 *every* one had f faces: the first face *was* 702
10:21 Every one had f faces **apiece**, and every 702+702
10:21 had four faces apiece, and every one f wings; 702
14:21 How much more when I send my f sore 702
37: 9 Come from the f winds, O breath, and 702
40:41 F tables *were* on this side, and four tables on 702
40:41 f tables on that side, by the side of the gate; 702
40:42 the f tables *were* of hewn stone for the burnt 702
41: 5 the breadth of *every* side chamber, f cubits, 702
42:20 He measured it by the f sides: it had a wall 702
43:14 *even* to the greater settle *shall be* f cubits, 702
43:15 So the altar *shall be* f cubits; and from 702
43:15 from the altar and upward *shall be* f horns. 702
43:16 twelve broad, square in the f squares thereof. 702
43:17 and fourteen broad in the f squares thereof; 702
43:20 put *it* on the f horns of it, and on the four 702
43:20 on the f corners of the settle, and upon 702
45:19 upon the f corners of the settle of the altar, 702
46:21 caused me to pass by the f corners of 702
46:22 In the f corners of the court *there were* courts 702
46:22 these f corners *were* of one measure. 702
46:23 round about them f, and *it was* made *with* 702
48:16 the north side f thousand and five hundred, 702
48:16 the south side f thousand and five hundred, 505
48:16 on the east side f thousand and five hundred, 702
48:16 the west side f thousand and five hundred. 702
48:30 f thousand and five hundred measures. 702
48:32 at the east side f thousand and five hundred: 702
48:33 *at* the south side f thousand and five hundred 702
48:34 *At* the west side f thousand and 702
Da 1:17 As for these f children, God gave them 702
3:25 He answered and said, Lo, I see f men loose, 703
7: 2 the f winds of the heaven strove upon 703
7: 3 f great beasts came up from the sea, 703
7: 6 which had upon the back of it f wings of a 703
7: 6 the beast had also f heads; and dominion *was* 703
7:17 great beasts, which *are* f, *are* four kings, 703
7:17 great beasts, which *are* four, *are* f kings, 703
8: 8 for it came up f notable ones toward the four 702
8: 8 for it came up four notable ones toward the f 702
8:22 that being broken, whereas f stood up for it, 702
8:22 f kingdoms shall stand up out of the nation, 702
10: 4 in the f and twentieth day of the first month, 702
11: 4 shall be divided toward the f winds of 702
Am 1: 3 three transgressions of Damascus, and for f, 702
1: 6 For three transgressions of Gaza, and for f, 702
1: 9 For three transgressions of Tyrus, and for f, 702
1:11 For three transgressions of Edom, and for f, 702
1:13 for f, I will not turn away *the punishment* 702
2: 1 For three transgressions of Moab, and for f, 702
2: 4 For three transgressions of Judah, and for f, 702
2: 6 For three transgressions of Israel, and for f, 702
Hag 1:15 In the f and twentieth day of the sixth month, 702
2:10 In the f and twentieth *day* of the ninth 702
2:18 from the f and twentieth day of the ninth 702
2:20 of the LORD came unto Haggai in the f 702
Zec 1: 7 Upon the f and twentieth day of the eleventh 702
1:18 I up mine eyes, and saw, and behold f horns. 702
1:20 And the LORD shewed me f carpenters. 702
2: 6 for I have spread you abroad as the f winds 702
6: 1 there came f chariots out from between two 702
6: 5 These *are* the f spirits of the heavens, 702
Mt 15:38 And they that did eat were f **thousand** men, *5070*
16:10 Neither the seven loaves of the f **thousand**, *5070*
24:31 gather together his elect from the f winds, *5064*
Mk 2: 3 one sick of the palsy, *which was* borne of f. *5064*
8: 9 they that had eaten were about f **thousand**: *5070*

F

Mk	8:20	And when the seven among f **thousand,**	*5070*
	13:27	shall gather together his elect from the f	*5064*
Lk	2:37	a widow of about fourscore and f years,	*5064*
Jn	4:35	There are yet f **months**, and *then* cometh	*5072*
	11:17	he found that he had *lien* in the grave f days	*5064*
	11:39	he stinketh: for he hath been *dead* f **days**.	*5066*
	19:23	took his garments, and made f parts,	*5064*
Ac	5:36	about f **hundred**, joined themselves:	*5071*
	7: 6	and entreat *them* evil f **hundred** years.	*5071*
	10:11	as *it had been* a great sheet knit at the f	*5064*
	10:30	F days ago I was fasting until this hour;	*5067*
	11: 5	let down from heaven by f corners;	*5064*
	12: 4	delivered *him* to f quaternions of soldiers to	*5064*
	13:20	*them* judges about *the space of* f **hundred**	*5071*
	21: 9	And the same *man* had f daughters, virgins,	*5064*
	21:23	We have f men which have a vow on them;	*5064*
	21:38	leddest out into the wilderness f **thousand**	*5070*
	27:29	they cast f anchors out of the stern, and	*5064*
Gal	3:17	which was f **hundred** and thirty years	*5071*
Rev	4: 4	And round about the throne *were* f and	*5064*
	4: 4	and upon the seats I saw f and	*5064*
	4: 6	*were* f beasts full of eyes before and	*5064*
	4: 8	And the f beasts had each of them six	*5064*
	4:10	The f and twenty elders fall down before	*5064*
	5: 6	the midst of the throne and of the f beasts,	*5064*
	5: 8	the f beasts and four *and* twenty elders fell	*5064*
	5: 8	the four beasts and f *and* twenty elders fell	*5064*
	5:14	And the f beasts said, Amen. And the four	*5064*
	5:14	And the f *and* twenty elders fell down and	*5064*
	6: 1	one of the f beasts saying, Come and see.	*5064*
	6: 6	And I heard a voice in the midst of the f	*5064*
	7: 1	And after these *things* I saw f angels	*5064*
	7: 1	standing on the f corners of the earth,	*5064*
	7: 1	holding the f winds of the earth, that	*5064*
	7: 2	he cried with a loud voice to the f angels,	*5064*
	7: 4	f thousand of all the tribes of the children	*5064*
	7:11	and *about* the elders and the f beasts, and	*5064*
	9:13	I heard a voice from the f horns of	*5064*
	9:14	Loose the f angels which are bound in	*5064*
	9:15	And the f angels were loosed, which were	*5064*
	11:16	And the f and twenty elders, which sat	*5064*
	14: 1	with him an hundred forty *and* f thousand,	*5064*
	14: 3	and before the f beasts, and the elders:	*5064*
	14: 3	but the hundred *and* forty *and* f thousand,	*5064*
	15: 7	And one of the f beasts gave unto the seven	*5064*
	19: 4	And the f and twenty elders and the four	*5064*
	19: 4	twenty elders and the f beasts fell down and	*5064*
	20: 8	which are in the f quarters of the earth,	*5064*
	21:17	an hundred *and* forty *and* f cubits,	*5064*

FOURFOLD (2) [FOUR]

2Sa	12: 6	he shall restore the lamb f, because he did	702
Lk	19: 8	*man* by false accusation, I restore *him* f.	*5073*

FOURFOOTED (3) [FOUR, FOOT]

Ac	10:12	Wherein were all *manner of* f **beasts** of	*5074*
	11: 6	and saw f **beasts** of the earth, and	*5074*
Ro	1:23	to birds, and f **beasts**, and creeping things.	*5074*

FOURSCORE (36) [EIGHTY, FOUR]

Ge	16:16	Abram *was* f and six years old, when Hagar	8084
	35:28	days of Isaac were an hundred and f years.	8084
Ex	7: 7	Moses *was* f years old, and	8084
	7: 7	Aaron f and three years old, when they	8084
Nu	2: 9	f thousand and six thousand and	8084
	4:48	eight thousand and five hundred and f.	8084
Jos	14:10	now lo, I *am this* day f and five years old.	8084
Jdg	3:30	of Israel. And the land had rest f years.	8084
1Sa	22:18	slew on that day f and five persons that did	8084
2Sa	19:32	was a very aged man, *even* f years old:	8084
	19:35	I *am this* day f years old: *and* can I discern	8084
1Ki	5:15	and f thousand hewers in the mountains;	8084
	12:21	f thousand chosen *men,* which were	8084
2Ki	6:25	until an ass's head was *sold* for f *pieces* of	8084
	10:24	Jehu appointed f men without, and said,	8084
	19:35	in the camp of the Assyrians an hundred f	8084
1Ch	7: 5	reckoned in all by their genealogies f and	8084
	15: 9	Eliel the chief, and his brethren f:	8084
	25: 7	were cunning, was two hundred f and eight.	8084
2Ch	2: 2	f thousand to hew in the mountain, and	8084
	2:18	f thousand *to be* hewers in the mountain,	8084
	11: 1	f thousand chosen *men,* which were	8084
	14: 8	drew bows, two hundred and f thousand:	8084
	17:15	and with him two hundred and f thousand.	8084
	17:18	and f thousand ready prepared for the war.	8084
	26:17	with him f priests of the LORD, *that were*	8084
Ezr	8: 8	the son of Michael, and with him f males.	8084
Ne	7:26	and Netophah, an hundred f and eight.	8084
	11:18	Levites in the holy city *were* two hundred f	8084
Est	1: 4	many days, *even* an hundred and f days.	8084
Ps	90:10	if by reason of strength *they be* f years,	8084
SS	6: 8	f concubines, and virgins without number.	8084
Isa	37:36	an hundred and f and five thousand:	8084
Jer	41: 5	and from Samaria, *even* f men,	8084
Lk	2:37	And she *was* a widow of about f and	*3589*
	16: 7	he said unto him, Take thy bill, and write f.	*3589*

FOURSQUARE (10) [FOUR, SQUARE]

Ex	27: 1	and five cubits broad; the altar shall be f:	7251
	28:16	F it shall be *being* doubled; a span *shall be*	7251
	30: 2	and a cubit the breadth thereof; f shall it be:	7251
	37:25	*it was* f; and two cubits *was* the height of it;	7251
	38: 1	*it was* f; and three cubits the height thereof.	7251
	39: 9	It was f; they made the breastplate double:	7251
1Ki	7:31	gravings with their borders, f, not round.	7251
Eze	40:47	cubits long, and an hundred cubits broad, f;	7251
	48:20	ye shall offer the holy oblation f, with	7243
Rev	21:16	And the city lieth f, and the length is as	*5068*

FOURTEEN (26) [FOURTEENTH]

Ge	31:41	I served thee f years for thy two	702+6240
	46:22	born to Jacob: all the souls *were* f.	702+6240
Nu	1:27	*were* **threescore and f**	702+7657+2050.1
	2: 4	*were* **threescore and f**	702+7657+2050.1
	16:49	died in the plague were f thousand	702+6240
	29:13	*and* f lambs of the first year;	702+6240
	29:15	tenth deal to each lamb of the f lambs:	702+6240
	29:17	f lambs of the first year without spot:	702+6240
	29:20	f lambs of the first year without	702+6240
	29:23	f lambs of the first year without	702+6240
	29:26	f lambs of the first year without spot:	702+6240
	29:29	f lambs of the first year without	702+6240
	29:32	f lambs of the first year without	702+6240
Jos	15:36	f cities with their villages.	702+6240
	18:28	*and* Kirjath; f cities with their villages.	702+6240
1Ki	8:65	and seven days, *even* f days.	702+6240
1Ch	25: 5	God gave to Heman f sons and	702+6240
2Ch	13:21	married f wives, and begat twenty and	702+6240
Job	42:12	for he had f thousand sheep, and	702+6240
Eze	43:17	the settle *shall be* f *cubits* long and	702+6240
	43:17	f broad in the four squares thereof;	702+6240
Mt	1:17	from Abraham to David *are* f generations;	*1180*
	1:17	away into Babylon *are* f generations;	*1180*
	1:17	into Babylon unto Christ *are* f generations.	*1180*
2Co	12: 2	I knew a man in Christ above f years ago,	*1180*
Gal	2: 1	Then f years after I went up again to	*1180*

FOURTEENTH (25) [FOURTEEN]

Ge	14: 5	in the f year came Chedorlaomer, and	702+6240
Ex	12: 6	ye shall keep it *up* until the f day of	702+6240
	12:18	In the first *month,* on the f day of	702+6240
Lev	23: 5	In the f *day* of the first month at even	702+6240
Nu	9: 3	In the f day of this month, at even,	702+6240
	9: 5	they kept the passover on the f day of	702+6240
	9:11	The f day of the second month at even	702+6240
	28:16	in the f day of the first month *is*	702+6240
Jos	5:10	kept the passover on the f day of	702+6240
2Ki	18:13	Now in the f year of king Hezekiah	702+6240
1Ch	24:13	to Huppah, the f to Jeshebeab,	702+6240
	25:21	The f *to* Mattithiah, *he,* his sons, and	702+6240
2Ch	30:15	they killed the passover on the f *day*	702+6240
	35: 1	they killed the passover on the f *day*	702+6240
Ezr	6:19	upon the f *day* of the first month.	702+6240
Est	9:15	on the f day also of the month Adar,	702+6240
	9:17	on the f day of the same rested they,	702+6240
	9:18	*day* thereof, and on the f thereof;	702+6240
	9:19	made the f day of the month Adar *a*	702+6240
	9:21	that they should keep the f day of	702+6240
Isa	36: 1	Now it came to pass in the f year of	702+6240
Eze	40: 1	f year after that the city was smitten,	702+6240
	45:21	In the first *month,* in the f day of	702+6240
Ac	27:27	But when the f night was come, as we were	*5065*
	27:33	This day is the f day that ye have tarried	*5065*

FOURTH (84) [FOUR]

Ge	1:19	and the morning were the f day.	7243
	2:14	of Assyria. And the f river *is* Euphrates.	7243
	15:16	*in* the f generation they shall come hither	7243

Ex 20: 5 and f *generation* of them that hate me; 7256
28:20 the f row a beryl, and an onyx, and a jasper: 7243
29:40 with the f **part** of a hin of beaten oil; 7253
29:40 the f *part* of a hin of wine *for* a drink 7243
34: 7 unto the third and to the f *generation.* 7256
39:13 the f row, a beryl, an onyx, and a jasper: 7243
Lev 19:24 in the f year all the fruit thereof shall be 7243
23:13 thereof *shall be of* wine, the f *part* of a hin. 7243
Nu 7:30 On the f day Elizur the son of Shedeur, 7243
14:18 children unto the third and f *generation.* 7256
15: 4 flour mingled with the f *part* of a hin of oil. 7243
15: 5 the f *part* of a hin *of* wine for a drink 7243
23:10 and the number *of* the f **part** of Israel? 7255
28: 5 mingled with the f *part* of a hin of beaten 7243
28: 7 the drink offering thereof *shall be* the f *part* 7243
28:14 a ram, and a f *part* of a hin unto a lamb: 7243
29:23 on the f day ten bullocks, two rams, *and* 7243
Dt 5: 9 and f *generation* of them that hate me, 7256
Jos 19:17 *And* the f lot came out to Issachar, for 7243
Jdg 19: 5 it came to pass on the f day, when they 7243
1Sa 9: 8 I have here at hand the f **part** of a shekel of 7253
2Sa 3: 4 the f, Adonijah the son of Haggith; and 7243
1Ki 6: 1 in the f year of Solomon's reign over Israel, 7243
6:33 posts of olive tree, a f *part of the wall.* 7243
6:37 In the f year was the foundation of 7243
22:41 Judah in the f year of Ahab king of Israel. 702
2Ki 6:25 the f **part** of a kab of dove's dung for five 7255
10:30 thy children of the f *generation* shall sit on 7243
15:12 throne of Israel unto the f *generation.* And 7243
18: 9 it came to pass in the f year of king 7243
25: 3 on the ninth *day* of the *f* month the famine NIH
1Ch 2:14 Nethaneel the f, Raddai the fifth, 7243
3: 2 the f, Adonijah the son of Haggith: 7243
3:15 the third Zedekiah, the f Shallum. 7243
8: 2 Nohah the f, and Rapha the fifth. 7243
12:10 Mishmannah the f, Jeremiah the fifth, 7243
23:19 Jahaziel the third, and Jekameam the f. 7243
24: 8 The third to Harim, the f to Seorim, 7243
24:23 Jahaziel the third, Jekameam the f. 7243
25:11 The f to Izri, *he,* his sons, and his brethren, 7243
26: 2 Zebadiah the third, Jathniel the f, 7243
26: 4 and Sacar the f, and Nethaneel the fifth, 7243
26:11 Tebaliah the third, Zechariah the f: 7243
27: 7 The f *captain* for the fourth month *was* 7243
27: 7 The fourth *captain* for the f month *was* 7243
2Ch 3: 2 the second month, in the f year of his reign. 702
20:26 on the f day they assembled themselves in 7243
Ezr 8:33 Now on the f day was the silver and 7243
Ne 9: 1 f day of this month the children of Israel 702
9: 3 the LORD their God *one* f *part* of the day; 7243
9: 3 *another* f *part* they confessed, and 7243
Jer 25: 1 f year of Jehoiakim the son of Josiah king 7243
28: 1 in the f year, *and* in the fifth month, 7243
36: 1 it came to pass in the f year of Jehoiakim 7243
39: 2 in the f month, the ninth *day* of the month, 7243
45: 1 in the f year of Jehoiakim the son of Josiah 7243
46: 2 f year of Jehoiakim the son of Josiah king 7243
51:59 *into* Babylon in the f year of his reign. 7243
52: 6 in the f month, in the ninth *day* of 7243
Eze 1: 1 in the f *month,* in the fifth *day* of 7243
10:14 face of a lion, and the f the face of an eagle. 7243
Da 2:40 the f kingdom shall be strong as iron: 7244
3:25 and the form of the f *is* like the Son of God. 7244
7: 7 behold, a f beast, dreadful and terrible, and 7244
7:19 I would know the truth of the f beast, 7244
7:23 The f beast shall be the fourth kingdom 7244
7:23 The fourth beast shall be the f kingdom 7244
11: 2 and the f shall be far richer than *they* all: 7243
Zec 6: 3 and in the f chariot grisled *and* bay horses. 7243
Eze 7: 1 it came to pass in the f year of king Darius, 702
7: 1 Zechariah in the f *day* of the ninth month, 702
8:19 The fast of the f *month,* and the fast of 7243
Mt 14:25 And in the f watch of the night Jesus went *5067*
Mk 6:48 about the f watch of the night he cometh *5067*
Rev 4: 7 and the f beast *was* like a flying eagle. *5067*
6: 7 And when he had opened the f seal, I heard *5067*
6: 7 I heard the voice of the f beast say, Come *5067*
6: 8 And power was given unto them over the f *5067*
8:12 And the f angel sounded, and the third *part* *5067*
16: 8 And the f angel poured out his vial upon *5067*
21:19 the third, a chalcedony; the f, an emerald; *5067*

FOWL (31) [FOWLER, FOWLERS, FOWLS]

Ge 1:20 f *that* may fly above the earth in the open 5775
1:21 and every winged f after his kind: 5775
1:22 in the seas, and let f multiply in the earth. 5775
1:26 over the f of the air, and over the cattle, and 5775
1:28 over the f of the air, and over every living 5775
1:30 to every f of the air, and to every *thing* that 5775
2:19 beast of the field, and every f of the air; 5775
2:20 to the f of the air, and to every beast of 5775
7:14 every f after his kind, every bird of every 5775
7:21 *both* of f, and of cattle, and of beast, and 5775
7:23 the creeping things, and the f of the heaven; 5775
8:17 *both* of f, and of cattle, and of every 5775
8:19 every f, *and* whatsoever creepeth upon 5775
8:20 of every clean f, and offered burnt offerings 5775
9: 2 upon every f of the air, upon all that 5775
9:10 of the f, of the cattle, and of every beast of 5775
Lev 7:26 *whether it be* of f or of beast, in any of your 5775
11:46 of the f, and of every living creature that 5775
17:13 catcheth *any* beast or f that may be eaten; 5775
20:25 or by f, or by any *manner of living thing* 5775
Dt 4:17 the likeness of any winged f that flieth in 6833
1Ki 4:23 and roebucks, and fallowdeer, and fatted f. 1257
4:33 of f, and of creeping things, and of fishes. 5775
Job 28: 7 *There is* a path which no f knoweth, and 5861
Ps 8: 8 The f of the air, and the fish of the sea, *and* 6833
148:10 all cattle; creeping things, and flying f: 6833
Jer 9:10 both the f of the heavens and the beast are 5775
Eze 17:23 under it shall dwell all f of every wing; 6833
39:17 Speak unto every feathered f, and to every 6833
44:31 of itself, or torn, whether it be f or beast. 5775
Da 7: 6 had upon the back of it four wings of a f; 5776

FOWLER (3) [FOWL]

Ps 91: 3 he shall deliver thee from the snare of the f, 3353
Pr 6: 5 and as a bird from the hand of the f. 3353
Hos 9: 8 the prophet *is* a snare of a f in all his ways, 3352

FOWLERS (1) [FOWL]

Ps 124: 7 is escaped as a bird out of the snare of the f: 3369

FOWLS (55) [FOWL]

Ge 6: 7 and the creeping thing, and the f of the air; 5775
6:20 Of f after their kind, and of cattle after their 5775
7: 3 Of f also of the air by sevens, the male and 5775
7: 8 of f, and of every *thing* that creepeth upon 5775
15:11 when the f came down upon the carcases, 5861
Lev 1:14 for his offering to the LORD *be* of f, 5775
11:13 ye shall have in abomination among the f; 5775
11:20 All f that creep, going upon *all* four, 5775
20:25 and between unclean f and clean: 5775
Dt 14:20 *But* of all clean f ye may eat. 5775
28:26 thy carcase shall be meat unto all f of 5775
1Sa 17:44 I will give thy flesh unto the f of the air, 5775
17:46 the Philistines this day unto the f of the air, 5775
1Ki 14:11 him that dieth in the field shall the f of 5775
16: 4 him that dieth of his in the fields shall the f 5775
21:24 him that dieth in the field shall the f of 5775
Ne 5:18 also f were prepared for me, and once in 6833
Job 12: 7 and the f of the air, and they shall tell thee: 5775
28:21 and kept close from the f of the air. 5775
35:11 and maketh us wiser than the f of heaven? 5775
Ps 50:11 I know all the f of the mountains: and 5775
78:27 and feathered f like as the sand of the sea: 5775
79: 2 given *to be* meat unto the f of the heaven, 5775
104:12 By them shall the f of the heaven have their 5775
Isa 18: 6 They shall be left together unto the f of 5861
18: 6 the f shall summer upon them, and all 5861
Jer 7:33 people shall be meat for the f of the heaven, 5775
15: 3 the f of the heaven, and the beasts of 5775
16: 4 their carcases shall be meat for the f of 5775
19: 7 I give to be meat for the f of the heaven, 5775
34:20 shall be for meat unto the f of the heaven, 5775
Eze 29: 5 of the field and to the f of the heaven. 5775
31: 6 All the f of heaven made their nests in his 5775
31:13 Upon his ruin shall all the f of the heaven 5775
32: 4 will cause all the f of the heaven to remain 5775
38:20 the f of the heaven, and the beasts of 5775
Da 2:38 the f of the heaven hath he given into thine 5776
4:12 the f of the heaven dwelt in the boughs 6853
4:14 from under it, and the f from his branches: 6853
4:21 upon whose branches the f of the heaven 6853
Hos 2:18 with the f of heaven, and *with* the creeping 5775
4: 3 beasts of the field, and with the f of heaven; 5775
7:12 I will bring them down as the f of 5775
Zep 1: 3 I will consume the f of the heaven, and 5775

Mt 6:26 Behold the f of the air: for they sow not, *4071*
13: 4 and the f came and devoured them up: *4071*
Mk 4: 4 and the f of the air came and devoured it *4071*
4:32 that the f of the air may lodge under *4071*
Lk 8: 5 and the f of the air devoured it. *4071*
12:24 how much more are ye better than the f? *4071*
13:19 the f of the air lodged in the branches of it. *4071*
Ac 10:12 and creeping things, and f of the air. *4071*
11: 6 and creeping things, and f of the air. *4071*
Rev 19:17 saying to all the f that fly in the midst of *3732*
19:21 and all the f were filled with their flesh. *3732*

FOX (2) [FOXES]
Ne 4: 3 Even *that* which they build, if a f go up, 7776
Lk 13:32 Go ye, and tell that f, Behold, I cast out *258*

FOXES (8) [FOX]
Jdg 15: 4 Samson went and caught three hundred f, 7776
Ps 63:10 by the sword: they shall be a portion for f. 7776
SS 2:15 Take us the f, the little foxes, that spoil 7776
2:15 Take us the foxes, the little f, that spoil 7776
La 5:18 which is desolate, the f walk upon it. 7776
Eze 13: 4 thy prophets are like the f in the deserts. 7776
Mt 8:20 The f have holes, and the birds of the air *258*
Lk 9:58 F have holes, and birds of the air *have* nests; *258*

FRAGMENT See SHERD; SHERDS

FRAGMENTS (7)
Mt 14:20 they took up of the f that remained twelve *2801*
Mk 6:43 they took up twelve baskets full of the f, *2801*
8:19 how many baskets full of f took ye up? *2801*
8:20 how many baskets full of f took ye up? *2801*
Lk 9:17 there was taken up of f that remained to *2801*
Jn 6:12 Gather up the f that remain, that nothing be *2801*
6:13 filled twelve baskets with the f of the five *2801*

FRAGRANT See SWEETSMELLING

FRAIL (1)
Ps 39: 4 what it *is; that* I may know how f I *am*. 2310

FRAME (5) [FRAMED, FRAMETH]
Jdg 12: 6 for he **could** not f to pronounce *it* right. 3559
Ps 103:14 For he knoweth our f; he remembereth that 3336
Jer 18:11 I f evil against you, and devise a device 3335
Eze 40: 2 by which *was* as the f of a city on the south. 4011
Hos 5: 4 They will not f their doings to turn unto 5414

FRAMED (4) [FRAME]
Isa 29:16 shall the **thing** f say of him that framed it, 3336
29:16 shall the thing framed say of him that f it, 3335
Eph 2:21 In whom all the building **fitly** f **together** *4883*
Heb 11: 3 that the worlds were f by the word of God, *2675*

FRAMETH (2) [FRAME]
Ps 50:19 thy mouth to evil, and thy tongue f deceit. 6775
94:20 *with* thee, which f mischief by a law? 3335

FRANKINCENSE (17) [INCENSE]
Ex 30:34 galbanum; *these* sweet spices with pure f: 3828
Lev 2: 1 he shall pour oil upon it, and put f thereon: 3828
2: 2 and of the oil thereof, with all the f thereof; 3828
2:15 thou shalt put oil upon it, and lay f thereon: 3828
2:16 *part* of the oil thereof, with all the f thereof: 3828
5:11 upon it, neither shall he put *any* f thereon: 3828
6:15 all the f which *is* upon the meat offering, 3828
24: 7 thou shalt put pure f upon *each* row, that it 3828
Nu 5:15 shall pour no oil upon it, nor put f thereon; 3828
1Ch 9:29 and the oil, and the f, and the spices. 3828
Ne 13: 5 the f, and the vessels, and the tithes of 3828
13: 9 of God, with the meat offering and the f. 3828
SS 3: 6 perfumed *with* myrrh and f, with all 3828
4: 6 the mountain of myrrh, and to the hill of f. 3828
4:14 calamus and cinnamon, with all trees of f; 3828
Mt 2:11 unto him gifts; gold, and f, and myrrh. *3030*
Rev 18:13 and f, and wine, and oil, and fine flour, and *3030*

FRANKLY (1)
Lk 7:42 had nothing to pay, he f **forgave** *them* both. *5483*

FRAUD (2)
Ps 10: 7 mouth is full *of* cursing and deceit and f: 8496
Jas 5: 4 which is of you **kept back by** f, crieth: *650*

FRAY (3)
Dt 28:26 of the earth, and no man shall f *them* **away**. 2729
Jer 7:33 of the earth; and none shall f *them* **away**. 2729
Zec 1:21 these are come to f them, to cast out 2729

FRECKLED (1)
Lev 13:39 it *is* a f **spot** *that* groweth in the skin: 933

FREE (59) [FREED, FREEDOM, FREELY, FREEMAN, FREEWILL, FREEWOMAN]
Ex 21: 2 in the seventh he shall go out f for nothing. 2670
21: 5 and my children; I will not go out f: 2670
21:11 then shall she go out f without money. 2600
21:26 he shall let him go f for his eye's sake. 2670
21:27 he shall let him go f for his tooth's sake. 2670
36: 3 yet unto him f **offerings** every morning. 5071
Lev 19:20 not be put to death, because she was not f. 2666
Nu 5:19 be thou f from this bitter water that causeth 5352
5:28 then she shall be f, and shall conceive seed. 5352
Dt 15:12 in the seventh year thou shalt let him go f 2670
15:13 when thou sendest him out f from thee, 2670
15:18 when thou sendest him away f from thee; 2670
24: 5 *but* he shall be f at home one year, and 5355
1Sa 17:25 and make his father's house f in Israel. 2670
1Ch 9:33 *who remaining* in the chambers *were* f: 6362
2Ch 29:31 as many as were of a f heart burnt 5081
Job 3:19 and the servant *is* f from his master. 2670
39: 5 Who hath sent out the wild ass f? or 2670
Ps 51:12 and uphold me *with thy* f spirit. 5081
88: 5 F among the dead, like the slain that lie in 2670
105:20 the ruler of the people, and let him **go** f. 6605
Isa 58: 6 to let the oppressed go f, and *that* ye break 2670
Jer 34: 9 *being* a Hebrew or a Hebrewess, go f; 2670
34:10 and every one his maidservant, go f, 2670
34:11 whom they had let go f, to return, and 2670
34:14 six years, thou shalt let him go f from thee: 2670
Am 4: 5 and proclaim *and* publish the f **offerings**: 5071
Mt 15: 6 *he shall be f.* Thus have ye made NIG
17:26 saith unto him, Then are the children f. *1658*
Mk 7:11 mightest be profited by me; *he shall be f.* NIG
Jn 8:32 the truth, and the truth shall **make** you f. *1659*
8:33 *man:* how sayest thou, Ye shall be made f? *1658*
8:36 If the Son therefore shall **make** you f, *1659*
8:36 shall make you free, ye shall be f indeed. *1658*
Ac 22:28 And Paul said, But I was *f* born. NIG
Ro 5:15 But not as the offence, so also *is* the f **gift**. *5486*
5:16 the f **gift** *is* of many offences unto *5486*
5:18 by the righteousness of one *the f gift came* NIG
6:18 Being then **made** f from sin, ye became *1659*
6:20 of sin, ye were f from righteousness. *1658*
6:22 But now being **made** f from sin, and *1659*
7: 3 *her* husband be dead, she is f from *that* law; *1658*
8: 2 Jesus hath **made** me f from the law of sin *1659*
1Co 7:21 but if thou mayest be made f, use *it* rather. *1658*
7:22 he that is called, *being* f, is Christ's servant. *1658*
9: 1 am I not f? have I not seen Jesus Christ our *1658*
9:19 For though I be f from all *men,* yet have I *1658*
12:13 or Gentiles, whether *we be* bond or f; *1658*
Gal 3:28 Jew nor Greek, there is neither bond nor f, *1658*
4:26 But Jerusalem which is above is f, which is *1658*
4:31 children of *the* bondwoman, but of the f. *1658*
5: 1 liberty wherewith Christ hath **made us** f, *1659*
Eph 6: 8 of the Lord, whether *he be* bond or f. *1658*
Col 3:11 barbarian, Scythian, bond *nor* f: *1658*
2Th 3: 1 that the word of the Lord may have *f* NIG
1Pe 2:16 As f, and not using *your* liberty for a cloke *1658*
Rev 6:15 every f *man,* hid themselves in the dens and *1658*
13:16 and great, rich and poor, f and bond, *1658*
19:18 and the flesh of all *men,* both f and bond, *1658*

FREED (2) [FREE]
Jos 9:23 there shall none of you be f from being 3772
Ro 6: 7 For he that is dead is f from sin. *1344*

FREEDMEN See LIBERTINES

FREEDOM (2) [FREE]
Lev 19:20 and not at all redeemed, nor f given her; 2668
Ac 22:28 With a great sum obtained I this f. *4174*

FREELY (17) [FREE]
Ge 2:16 tree of the garden thou mayest f **eat**: 398+398
Nu 11: 5 the fish, which we did eat in Egypt f; 2600
1Sa 14:30 if haply the people had **eaten** f to day 398+398

Ezr 2:68 **offered** f for the house of God to set it up 5068
7:15 his counsellers have f **offered** unto the God 5069
Ps 54: 6 I will f sacrifice unto thee: I will 5071+871.1
Hos 14: 4 heal their backsliding, I will love them f: 5071
Mt 10: 8 out devils: f ye have received, freely give. *1432*
10: 8 out devils: freely ye have received, f give. *1432*
Ac 2:29 let *me* f speak unto you of *3326+3954*
26:26 of these *things,* before whom also I speak f: *3955*
Ro 3:24 Being justified f by his grace through *1432*
8:32 how shall he not with him also f **give** us all *5483*
1Co 2:12 the *things* that are f **given** to us of God. *5483*
2Co 11: 7 I have preached to you the gospel of God f? *1432*
Rev 21: 6 athirst of the fountain of the water of life f. *1432*
22:17 let him take the water of life f. *1432*

FREEMAN (1) [FREE, MAN]
1Co 7:22 in the Lord, *being* a servant, is the Lord's f: *558*

FREEWILL (17) [FREE, WILL]
Lev 22:18 for all his vows, and for all his f **offerings,** 5071
22:21 or a f **offering** in beeves or sheep, it shall 5071
22:23 that mayest thou offer *for* a f **offering**; 5071
23:38 your vows, and beside all your f **offerings,** 5071
Nu 15: 3 or in a f **offering**, or in your solemn feasts, 5071
29:39 besides your vows, and your f **offerings,** 5071
Dt 12: 6 your f **offerings**, and the firstlings of your 5071
12:17 nor thy f **offerings**, or heave offering of 5071
16:10 *with* a tribute of a f **offering** of thine hand, 5071
23:23 *even* a f **offering**, according as thou hast 5071
2Ch 31:14 the east, *was* over the f **offerings** of God, 5071
Ezr 1: 4 besides the f **offering** for the house of God 5071
3: 5 offered a f **offering** unto the LORD. 5071
7:13 *which are* **minded of** their **own** f to go *up* 5069
7:16 with the f **offering** of the people, and of 5069
8:28 the gold *are* a f **offering** unto the LORD 5071
Ps119:108 the f **offerings** of my mouth, O LORD, 5071

FREEWOMAN (3) [FREE, WOMAN]
Gal 4:22 the one by a bondmaid, the other by a f. *1658*
4:23 the flesh; but he of the f *was* by promise. *1658*
4:30 shall not be heir with the son of the f. *1658*

FREQUENT (1)
2Co 11:23 in prisons **more** f, in deaths oft. *4056*

FRESH (4) [AFRESH, FRESHER]
Nu 11: 8 and the taste of it was as the taste of f oil. 3955
Job 29:20 My glory *was* f in me, and my bow was 2319
Ps 92:10 *of* an unicorn: I shall be anointed with f oil. 7488
Jas 3:12 *can* no fountain *both* yield salt water and f. *1099*

FRESHER (1) [FRESH]
Job 33:25 His flesh shall be f than a child's: he shall 7375

FRET (7) [FRETTED, FRETTETH, FRETTING]
Lev 13:55 it *is* f inward, *whether* it *be* bare within or 6356
1Sa 1: 6 for to **make** her f, because the LORD had 7481
Ps 37: 1 F not thyself because of evildoers, 2734
37: 7 f not thyself because of him who prospereth 2734
37: 8 f not thyself in any wise to do evil. 2734
Pr 24:19 F not thyself because of evil *men,* neither 2734
Isa 8:21 they shall f themselves, and curse their king 7107

FRETTED (1) [FRET]
Eze 16:43 hast f me in all these *things;* behold 7264

FRETTETH (1) [FRET]
Pr 19: 3 his way: and his heart f against the LORD. 2196

FRETTING (3) [FRET]
Lev 13:51 the plague *is* a f leprosy; it *is* unclean. 3992
13:52 for it *is* a f leprosy; it shall be burnt in 3992
14:44 in the house, it *is* a f leprosy in the house: 3992

FRIED (2) [FRYINGPAN]
Lev 7:12 and cakes mingled with oil, of fine flour, f. 7246
1Ch 23:29 for that which is f, and for all *manner of* 7246

FRIEND (53) [FRIENDLY, FRIENDS, FRIENDSHIP]
Ge 38:12 he and his f Hirah the Adullamite. 7453
38:20 Judah sent the kid by the hand of his f 7453
Ex 33:11 face to face, as a man speaketh unto his f. 7453
Dt 13: 6 or the wife of thy bosom, or thy f, 7453
Jdg 14:20 his companion, whom he had used as his f. 7462
2Sa 13: 3 Amnon had a f, whose name *was* Jonadab, 7453
15:37 So Hushai David's f came *into* the city, and 7463
16:16 David's f, was come unto Absalom, 7463
16:17 said to Hushai, *Is* this thy kindness to thy f? 7453
16:17 why wentest thou not with thy f? 7453
1Ki 4: 5 *was* principal officer, *and* the king's f: 7463
2Ch 20: 7 gavest it to the seed of Abraham thy f for 157
Job 6:14 afflicted pity *should be shewed* from his f; 7453
6:27 the fatherless, and you dig *a pit* for your f. 7453
Ps 35:14 behaved myself as though *he had been* my f 7453
41: 9 Yea, mine own **familiar** f, in whom I 376+7965
88:18 Lover and f hast thou put far from me, *and* 7453
Pr 6: 1 My son, if thou be surety for thy f, *if* thou 7453
6: 3 when thou art come into the hand of thy f; 7453
6: 3 go, humble thyself, and make sure thy f. 7453
17:17 A f loveth at all times, and a brother is born 7453
17:18 becometh surety in the presence of his f. 7453
18:24 there is a f *that* sticketh closer than a brother. 157
19: 6 every *man is* a f to him that giveth gifts. 7453
22:11 the grace of his lips the king *shall be* his f. 7453
27: 6 Faithful *are* the wounds of a f; but the kisses 157
27: 9 *doth* the sweetness of a man's f by hearty 7453
27:10 Thine own f, and thy father's friend, 7453
27:10 own friend, and thy father's f, forsake not; 7453
27:14 He that blesseth his f with a loud voice, 7453
27:17 a man sharpeneth the countenance of his f. 7453
SS 5:16 This *is* my beloved, and this *is* my f, 7453
Isa 41: 8 I have chosen, the seed of Abraham my f. 157
Jer 6:21 the neighbour and his f shall perish. 7453
19: 9 they shall eat every one the flesh of his f in 7453
Hos 3: 1 Go yet, love a woman beloved of *her* f, 7453
Mic 7: 5 Trust ye not in a f, put ye not confidence in 7453
Mt 11:19 a winebibber, a f of publicans and sinners. *5384*
20:13 of them, and said, F, I do thee no wrong: *2083*
22:12 And he saith unto him, F, how camest thou *2083*
26:50 And Jesus said unto him, F, wherefore art *2083*
Lk 7:34 a winebibber, a f of publicans and sinners. *5384*
11: 5 Which of you shall have a f, and shall go *5384*
11: 5 and say unto him, F, lend me three loaves; *5384*
11: 6 For a f of mine in *his* journey is come to *5384*
11: 8 because *he* is his f, yet because of his *5384*
14:10 he may say unto thee, F, go up higher: *5384*
Jn 3:29 but the f of the bridegroom, which standeth *5384*
11:11 he saith unto them, Our f Lazarus sleepeth; *5384*
19:12 thou let this *man* go, thou art not Cesar's f: *5384*
Ac 12:20 **made** Blastus the king's chamberlain their f, *3982*
Jas 2:23 and he was called the F of God. *5384*
4: 4 will be a f of the world is the enemy of *5384*

FRIENDLY (3) [FRIEND]
Jdg 19: 3 f unto her, *and* to bring her again, 3820+5921
Ru 2:13 for that thou hast spoken f unto thine 3820+5921
Pr 18:24 man that hath friends must **shew** himself f: 7462

FRIENDS (49) [FRIEND]
Ge 26:26 Ahuzzath *one* of his f, and Phichol the chief 4828
1Sa 30:26 the elders of Judah, *even* to his f, saying, 7453
2Sa 3: 8 to his f, and have not delivered thee into 4828
19: 6 thou lovest thine enemies, and hatest thy f: 157
1Ki 16:11 a wall, neither *of* his kinsfolks, nor *of* his f. 7453
Est 5:10 he sent and called for his f, and Zeresh his 157
5:14 said Zeresh his wife and all his f unto him, 157
6:13 all his f every *thing* that had befallen him. 157
Job 2:11 Now when Job's three f heard of all this 7453
16:20 My f scorn me: *but* mine eye poureth out 7453
17: 5 He *that* speaketh flattery to *his* f, even 7453
19:14 and my **familiar** f have forgotten me. 3045
19:19 All my inward f abhorred me: and 4962
19:21 upon me, have pity upon me, O ye my f; 7453
32: 3 Also against his three f was his wrath 7453
42: 7 kindled against thee, and against thy two f: 7453
42:10 captivity of Job, when he prayed for his f: 7453
Ps 38:11 and my f stand aloof from my sore; 7453
Pr 14:20 his own neighbour: but the rich *hath* many f. 157
16:28 and a whisperer separateth **chief** f. 441
17: 9 he that repeateth a matter separateth **very** f. 441
18:24 A man that hath f must shew himself 7453
19: 4 Wealth maketh many f; but the poor is 7453
19: 7 how much more do his f go far from him! 4828
SS 5: 1 eat, O f; drink, yea, drink abundantly, 7453
Jer 20: 4 make thee a terror to thyself, and to all thy f: 157
20: 6 and shalt be buried there, thou, and all thy f, 157
38:22 Thy f have set thee on, and 376+7965
La 1: 2 all her f have dealt treacherously with her, 7453
Zec 13: 6 which I was wounded *in* the house of my f. 157

Mk 3:21 And when his f heard *of it,* they went 3588+3844
5:19 Go home to thy *f,* and tell them how great NIG
Lk 7: 6 the centurion sent f to him, saying unto 5384
12: 4 And I say unto you my f, Be not afraid of 5384
14:12 makest a dinner or a supper, call not thy f, 5384
15: 6 he calleth together *his* f and neighbours, 5384
15: 9 when she hath found *it,* she calleth *her* f 5384
15:29 a kid, that I might make merry with my f: 5384
16: 9 Make to yourselves f of the mammon of 5384
21:16 and brethren, and kinsfolks, and f; 5384
23:12 Pilate and Herod were made f together: 5384
Jn 15:13 that a man lay down his life for his f. 5384
15:14 Ye are my f, if ye do whatsoever I 5384
15:15 but I have called you f; for all *things* that I 5384
Ac 10:24 had called together his kinsmen and near f. 5384
19:31 of Asia, which were his f, sent unto him, 5384
27: 3 gave *him* liberty to go unto *his* f to refresh 5384
3Jn 1:14 *Our* f salute thee. Greet the friends by 5384
1:14 friends salute thee. Greet the f by name. 5384

FRIENDSHIP (2) [FRIEND]
Pr 22:24 **Make** no f with an angry man; and with a 7462
Jas 4: 4 know ye not that the f of the world is 5373

FRIGHTENED See ABASE; ABASED; ABASING

FRINGE (2) [FRINGES]
Nu 15:38 that they put upon the f of the borders a 6734
15:39 it shall be unto you for a f, that ye may look 6734

FRINGES (2) [FRINGE]
Nu 15:38 bid them that they make them f in 6734
Dt 22:12 Thou shalt make thee f upon the four 1434

FRO (25) See Index

FROGS (14)
Ex 8: 2 behold, I will smite all thy borders with f: 6854
8: 3 And the river shall bring forth f abundantly, 6854
8: 4 the f shall come up *both* on thee, and 6854
8: 5 cause f to come up upon the land of Egypt. 6854
8: 6 the f came up, and covered the land of 6854
8: 7 and brought up f upon the land of Egypt. 6854
8: 8 that he may take away the f from me, and 6854
8: 9 to destroy the f from thee and thy houses, 6854
8:11 the f shall depart from thee, and from thy 6854
8:12 of the f which he had brought against 6854
8:13 the f died out of the houses, out of 6854
Ps 78:45 and f, which destroyed them. 6854
105:30 Their land brought forth f in abundance, 6854
Rev 16:13 And I saw three unclean spirits like f *come* 944

FROM (3660) [THEREFROM] See Index

FRONT (2) [FOREFRONT]
2Sa 10: 9 When Joab saw that the f of the battle was 6440
2Ch 3: 4 the porch that *was* **in** the f *of* 5921+6440

FRONTIERS (1)
Eze 25: 9 from his cities *which are* on his f, the glory 7097

FRONTLETS (3)
Ex 13:16 thine hand, and for f between thine eyes: 2903
Dt 6: 8 and they shall be as f between thine eyes. 2903
11:18 that they may be as f between your eyes. 2903

FROST (6) [HOARFROST]
Ge 31:40 drought consumed me, and the f by night; 7140
Ex 16:14 *as* small as the **hoar** f on the ground. 3713
Job 37:10 By the breath of God f is given: and 7140
38:29 the **hoary** f of heaven, who hath gendered 3713
Ps 78:47 with hail, and their sycomore trees with f. 2602
Jer 36:30 the day to the heat, and in the night to the f. 7140

FROWARD (21) [FROWARDLY, FROWARDNESS]
Dt 32:20 *shall be:* for they *are* a **very** f generation, 8419
2Sa 22:27 with the f thou wilt shew thyself 6141
Job 5:13 and the counsel of the f is carried headlong. 6617
Ps 18:26 with the f thou wilt shew thyself froward. 6141
18:26 with the froward thou wilt **shew** thyself f. 6617
101: 4 A f heart shall depart from me: I will not 6141
Pr 2:12 *man,* from the man that speaketh f **things**; 8419
2:15 ways *are* crooked, and *they* f in their paths: 3868
3:32 For the f *is* abomination to the LORD: but 3868
4:24 Put away from thee a f mouth, and 6143
6:12 a wicked man, walketh *with* a f mouth. 6143
8: 8 *there is* nothing f or perverse in them. 6617
8:13 the evil way, and the f mouth, do I hate. 8419
10:31 but the f tongue shall be cut out. 8419
11:20 *They that are* of a f heart *are* abomination 6141
16:28 A f man soweth strife: and a whisperer 8419
16:30 He shutteth his eyes to devise f **things**: 8419
17:20 He that hath a f heart findeth no good: and 6141
21: 8 The way of man *is* f and strange: but *as for* 2019
22: 5 Thorns *and* snares *are* in the way of the f: 6141
1Pe 2:18 to the good and gentle, but also to the f. 4646

FROWARDLY (1) [FROWARD]
Isa 57:17 and he went on f in the way of his heart. 7726

FROWARDNESS (3) [FROWARD]
Pr 2:14 do evil, *and* delight in the f of the wicked; 8419
6:14 F *is* in his heart, he deviseth mischief 8419
10:32 but the mouth of the wicked *speaketh* f. 8419

FROZEN (1)
Job 38:30 *with* a stone, and the face of the deep is f. 3920

FRUIT (208) [FIRSTFRUIT, FIRSTFRUITS, FRUITFUL, FRUITS, UNFRUITFUL]
Ge 1:11 *and* the f tree yielding fruit after his kind, 6529
1:11 *and* the fruit tree yielding f after his kind, 6529
1:12 the tree yielding f, whose seed *was* in itself, 6529
1:29 in the which *is* the f of a tree yielding seed; 6529
3: 2 We may eat of the f of the trees of 6529
3: 3 of the f of the tree which *is* in the midst of 6529
3: 6 she took of the f thereof, and did eat, and 6529
4: 3 that Cain brought of the f of the ground an 6529
30: 2 who hath withheld from thee the f of 6529
Ex 10:15 all the f of the trees which the hail had left: 6529
21:22 so that her f depart *from her,* and yet no 3206
Lev 19:23 ye shall count the f thereof as 6529
19:24 in the fourth year all the f thereof shall be 6529
19:25 in the fifth year shall ye eat of the f thereof, 6529
23:39 when ye have gathered in the f of the land, 8393
25: 3 thy vineyard, and gather in the f thereof; 8393
25:19 the land shall yield her f, and ye shall eat 6529
25:21 it shall bring forth f for three years. 8393
25:22 and eat *yet* of old f until the ninth year; 8393
26: 4 and the trees of the field shall yield their f. 6529
27:30 *or* of the f of the tree, *is* the LORD'S: 6529
Nu 13:20 and bring of the f of the land. 6529
13:26 and shewed them the f of the land. 6529
13:27 with milk and honey; and this *is* the f of it. 6529
Dt 1:25 they took of the f of the land in their hands, 6529
7:13 he will also bless the f of thy womb, and 6529
7:13 the f of thy land, thy corn, and thy wine, 6529
11:17 be no rain, and *that* the land yield not her f; 2981
22: 9 lest the f of *thy* seed which thou hast sown, 4395
22: 9 and the f of thy vineyard, be defiled. 8393
26: 2 That thou shalt take of the first of all the f 6529
28: 4 Blessed *shall be* the f of thy body, and 6529
28: 4 the f of thy ground, and the fruit of thy 6529
28: 4 fruit of thy ground, and the f of thy cattle, 6529
28:11 in the f of thy body, and in the fruit of thy 6529
28:11 in the f of thy cattle, and in the fruit of thy 6529
28:11 of thy cattle, and in the f of thy ground, 6529
28:18 Cursed *shall be* the f of thy body, and 6529
28:18 the f of thy land, the increase of thy kine, 6529
28:33 The f of thy land, and all thy labours, 6529
28:40 *with* the oil; for thine olive shall cast *his f.* NIH
28:42 and f of thy land shall the locust consume. 6529
28:51 he shall eat the f of thy cattle, and the fruit 6529
28:51 the f of thy land, until thou be destroyed: 6529
28:53 thou shalt eat the f of thine own body, 6529
30: 9 in the f of thy body, and in the fruit of thy 6529
30: 9 in the f of thy cattle, and in the fruit of thy 6529
30: 9 thy cattle, and in the f of thy land, for good: 6529
Jos 5:12 they did eat of the f of the land of Canaan 8393
Jdg 9:11 my good f, and go to be promoted over 8570
2Sa 16: 2 and **summer** f for the young men to eat; 7019
2Ki 19:30 take root downward, and bear f upward. 6529
Ne 9:25 and oliveyards, and f trees in abundance: 3978
9:36 gavest unto our fathers to eat the f thereof 6529
10:35 the firstfruits of all f of all trees, year by 6529
10:37 and the f of all *manner of* trees, of wine and 6529
Ps 1: 3 that bringeth forth his f in his season; 6529
21:10 Their f shalt thou destroy from the earth, 6529
72:16 the f thereof shall shake like Lebanon: 6529
92:14 They shall still **bring forth** f in old age; 5107

Ps 104:13 the earth is satisfied with the f of thy 6529
105:35 and devoured the f of their ground. 6529
127: 3 *and* the f of the womb *is his* reward. 6529
132:11 Of the f of thy body will I set upon thy 6529
Pr 1:31 Therefore shall they eat of the f of their 6529
8:19 My f *is* better than gold, yea, than fine 6529
10:16 *tendeth* to life: the f of the wicked to sin. 8393
11:30 The f of the righteous *is* a tree of life; and 6529
12:12 but the root of the righteous yieldeth *f.* NIH
12:14 A man shall be satisfied *with* good by the f 6529
13: 2 A man shall eat good by the f of *his* mouth: 6529
18:20 A man's belly shall be satisfied with the f 6529
18:21 and they that love it shall eat the f thereof. 6529
27:18 Whoso keepeth the fig tree shall eat the f 6529
31:16 with the f of her hands she planteth a 6529
31:31 Give her of the f of her hands; and let her 6529
SS 2: 3 and his f *was* sweet to my taste. 6529
8:11 every one for the f thereof was to bring a 6529
8:12 those that keep the f thereof two hundred. 6529
Isa 3:10 *him:* for they shall eat the f of their doings. 6529
4: 2 the f of the earth *shall be* excellent and 6529
10:12 I will punish the f of the stout heart of 6529
13:18 they shall have no pity on the f of 6529
14:29 and his f *shall be* a fiery flying serpent. 6529
27: 6 bud, and fill the face of the world *with* f. 8570
27: 9 and this *is* all the f to take away his sin; 6529
28: 4 *and* as the **hasty** f before the summer; 1061
37:30 and plant vineyards, and eat the f thereof. 6529
37:31 take root downward, and bear f upward. 6529
57:19 I create the f of the lips; Peace, peace to 5108
65:21 shall plant vineyards, and eat the f of them. 6529
Jer 2: 7 to eat the f thereof and the goodness 6529
6:19 *even* the f of their thoughts, because 6529
7:20 of the field, and upon the f of the ground; 6529
11:16 A green olive tree, fair, *and* of goodly f: 6529
11:19 *saying,* Let us destroy the tree with the f 3899
12: 2 they grow, yea, they bring forth f: thou *art* 6529
17: 8 neither shall cease from yielding f. 6529
17:10 *and* according to the f of his doings. 6529
21:14 I will punish you according to the f of your 6529
29: 5 and plant gardens, and eat the f of them; 6529
29:28 and plant gardens, and eat the f of them. 6529
32:19 and according to the f of his doings: 6529
La 2:20 Shall the women eat their f, *and* children of 6529
Eze 17: 8 that *it* might bear f, that *it* might be a 6529
17: 9 and cut off the f thereof, that it wither? 6529
17:23 and bear f, and be a goodly cedar: 6529
19:12 and the east wind dried up her f: 6529
19:14 *which* hath devoured her f, so that she hath 6529
25: 4 they shall eat thy f, and they shall drink thy 6529
34:27 the tree of the field shall yield her f, and 6529
36: 8 and yield your f to my people of Israel; 6529
36:11 beast; and they shall increase and **bring** f: 6509
36:30 I will multiply the f of the tree, and 6529
47:12 neither shall the f thereof be consumed: 6529
47:12 it shall **bring forth new** f according to his 1069
47:12 the f thereof shall be for meat, and the leaf 6529
Da 4:12 the f thereof much, and in it *was* meat for all: 4
4:14 shake off his leaves, and scatter his f: 4
4:21 the f thereof much, and in it *was* meat for all; 4
Hos 9:16 their root is dried up, they shall bear no f: 6529
9:16 yet will I slay *even* the beloved *f* of their NIH
10: 1 he bringeth forth f unto himself: 6529
10: 1 according to the multitude of his f he hath 6529
10:13 reaped iniquity; ye have eaten the f of lies: 6529
14: 8 a green fir tree. From me is thy f found. 6529
Joel 2:22 for the tree beareth her f, the fig tree and 6529
Am 2: 9 yet I destroyed his f from above, and 6529
6:12 and the f of righteousness into hemlock: 6529
7:14 a herdman, and a gatherer of **sycomore** f: 8256
8: 1 and behold, a basket of **summer** f. 7019
8: 2 I said, A basket of **summer** f. Then said 7019
9:14 also make gardens, and eat the f of them. 6529
Mic 6: 7 the f of my body *for* the sin of my soul? 6529
7: 1 to eat: my soul desired the **firstripe** f. 1063
7:13 that dwell therein, for the f of their doings. 6529
Hab 3:17 not blossom, neither *shall* f *be* in the vines; 2981
Hag 1:10 and the earth is stayed *from* her f. 2981
Zec 8:12 the vine shall give her f, and the ground 6529
Mal 1:12 the f thereof, *even* his meat, 5108
3:11 vine **cast** her f **before the time** in the field, 7921
Mt 3:10 every tree which bringeth not forth good f *2590*
7:17 so every good tree bringeth forth good f; *2590*
7:17 but a corrupt tree bringeth forth evil f. *2590*
7:18 A good tree cannot bring forth evil f, *2590*
7:18 *can* a corrupt tree bring forth good f. *2590*
7:19 Every tree that bringeth not forth good f is *2590*
12:33 Either make the tree good, and his f good; *2590*
12:33 make the tree corrupt, and his f corrupt: *2590*
12:33 fruit corrupt: for the tree is known by *his* f. *2590*
13: 8 fell into good ground, and brought forth f, *2590*
13:23 and understandeth *it;* which also **beareth** f, *2592*
13:26 and brought forth f, then appeared the tares *2590*
21:19 Let no f grow on thee henceforward for *2590*
21:34 And when the time of the f drew near, *2590*
26:29 I will not drink henceforth of this f of *1081*
Mk 4: 7 grew up, and choked it, and it yielded no f. *2590*
4: 8 and did yield f that sprang up and *2590*
4:20 the word, and receive *it,* and **bring forth** f, *2592*
4:28 For the earth **bringeth forth** f of herself; *2592*
4:29 But when the f is brought forth, *2590*
11:14 No *man* eat f of thee hereafter for ever. *2590*
12: 2 the husbandmen of the f of the vineyard. *2590*
14:25 I will drink no more of the f of the vine, *1081*
Lk 1:42 and blessed *is* the f of thy womb. *2590*
3: 9 which bringeth not forth good f is hewn *2590*
6:43 For a good tree bringeth not forth corrupt f; *2590*
6:43 doth a corrupt tree bring forth good f. *2590*
6:44 For every tree is known by his own f. *2590*
8: 8 and sprang up, and bare f an hundredfold. *2590*
8:14 of *this* life, and bring no f to perfection. NIG
8:15 keep *it,* and **bring forth** f with patience. *2592*
13: 6 and he came and sought f thereon, *2590*
13: 7 *these* three years I come seeking f on this *2590*
13: 9 And if it bear f, *well:* and if not, *then* *2590*
20:10 that they should give him of the f of *2590*
22:18 I will not drink of the f of the vine, *1081*
Jn 4:36 and gathereth f unto life eternal: *2590*
12:24 but if it die, it bringeth forth much f. *2590*
15: 2 Every branch in me that beareth not f he *2590*
15: 2 and every *branch* that beareth f, he purgeth *2590*
15: 2 he purgeth it, that it may bring forth more f. *2590*
15: 4 As the branch cannot bear f of itself, *2590*
15: 5 I in him, the same bringeth forth much f: *2590*
15: 8 is my Father glorified, that ye bear much f; *2590*
15:16 that you should go and bring forth f, and *2590*
15:16 forth fruit, and *that* your f should remain: *2590*
Ac 2:30 that of the f of his loins, according to *2590*
Ro 1:13 that I might have some f among you also, *2590*
6:21 What f had ye then *in those things* whereof *2590*
6:22 ye have your f unto holiness, and the end *2590*
7: 4 that we should **bring forth** f unto God. *2592*
7: 5 did work in our members to **bring forth** f *2592*
15:28 and have sealed to them this f, *2590*
1Co 9: 7 a vineyard, and eateth not of the f thereof? *2590*
Gal 5:22 But the f of the Spirit is love, joy, peace, *2590*
Eph 5: 9 (For the f of the Spirit *is* in all goodness *2590*
Php 1:22 *I* live in the flesh, this *is* the f of my labour: *2590*
4:17 I desire f that *may* abound to your account. *2590*
Col 1: 6 and **bringeth forth** f, as *it doth* also in you, *2592*
Heb 12:11 f of righteousness unto them which are *2590*
13:15 the f of *our* lips giving thanks to his name. *2590*
Jas 3:18 And the f of righteousness is sown in peace *2590*
5: 7 the husbandman waiteth for the precious f *2590*
5:18 gave rain, and the earth brought forth her f. *2590*
Jude 1:12 trees whose f **withereth**, without fruit, *5352*
1:12 **without** f, twice dead, plucked up by *175*
Rev 22: 2 *of* fruits, *and* yielded her f every month: *2590*

FRUITFUL (35) [FRUIT]

Ge 1:22 Be f, and multiply, and fill the waters in 6509
1:28 Be f, and multiply, and replenish the earth, 6509
8:17 and be f, and multiply upon the earth. 6509
9: 1 Be f, and multiply, and replenish the earth. 6509
9: 7 you, be ye f, and multiply; bring forth 6509
17: 6 I will **make** thee exceeding f, and I will 6509
17:20 will **make** him f, and will multiply him 6509
26:22 room for us, and we shall be f in the land. 6509
28: 3 and **make** thee f, and multiply thee, 6509
35:11 be f and multiply; a nation and a company 6509
41:52 For God hath **caused** me **to be** f in the land 6509
48: 4 I will **make** thee f, and multiply thee, and 6509
49:22 Joseph *is* a f **bough**, *even* a fruitful 1121+6509
49:22 *even* a f **bough** by a well; 1121+6509
Ex 1: 7 the children of Israel were f, and 6509
Lev 26: 9 **make** you f, and multiply you, and 6509
Ps 107:34 A f land into barrenness, for 6529
128: 3 Thy wife *shall be* as a f vine by the sides of 6509

F

Ps 148: 9 all hills; f trees, and all cedars: 6529
Isa 5: 1 hath a vineyard in a **very** f hill: 1121+8081
10:18 and of his f **field**, both soul and body: 3759
17: 6 *or* five in the outmost f branches thereof, 6509
29:17 Lebanon shall be turned into a f **field**, and 3759
29:17 the f **field** shall be esteemed as a forest? 3759
32:12 for the pleasant fields, for the f vine. 6509
32:15 the wilderness be a f **field**, and the fruitful 3759
32:15 and the f **field** be counted for a forest. 3759
32:16 and righteousness remain in the f **field**. 3759
Jer 4:26 lo, the f **place** *was* a wilderness, and all 3759
23: 3 their folds; and they shall be f and increase. 6509
Eze 17: 5 seed of the land, and planted it in a f field; 2233
19:10 she was f and full of branches by reason of 6509
Hos 13:15 Though he be f among *his* brethren, an east 6500
Ac 14:17 gave us rain from heaven, and f seasons, *2593*
Col 1:10 being f in every good work, and *2592*

F

FRUITS (42) [FRUIT]
Ge 43:11 take of the **best** f in the land in your 2173
Ex 22:29 not delay *to offer the first of* thy **ripe** f, 4395
23:10 thy land, and shalt gather in the f thereof: 8393
Lev 25:15 according unto the number of years of the f 8393
25:16 *of the years* of the f doth he sell unto thee. 8393
25:22 until her f come in ye shall eat *of* the old 8393
26:20 shall the trees of the land yield their f. 6529
Dt 33:14 for the precious f brought forth by the sun, 8393
2Sa 9:10 thou shalt bring in *the f,* that thy master's NIH
16: 1 an hundred of **summer** f, and a bottle of 7019
2Ki 8: 6 all the f of the field since the day that she 8393
19:29 and plant vineyards, and eat the f thereof. 6529
Job 31:39 If I have eaten the f thereof without money, 3581
Ps 107:37 which may yield f of increase. 6529
Ecc 2: 5 and I planted trees in them of all *kind of* f: 6529
SS 4:13 orchard of pomegranates, with pleasant f; 6529
4:16 come into his garden, and eat his pleasant f. 6529
6:11 I went down into the garden of nuts to see the f 3
7:13 at our gates *are* all *manner of* pleasant *f,* NIH
Isa 16: 9 for the shouting for thy **summer** f and 7019
33: 9 and Bashan and Carmel shake off *their f.* NIH
Jer 40:10 **summer** f, and oil, and put *them* in your 7019
40:12 gathered wine and **summer** f very much. 7019
48:32 the spoiler is fallen upon thy **summer** f and 7019
La 4: 9 stricken through for *want of* the f of 8570
Mic 7: 1 as when they have gathered the **summer** f, 7019
Mal 3:11 he shall not destroy the f of your ground; 6529
Mt 3: 8 Bring forth therefore f meet for repentance: *2590*
7:16 Ye shall know them by their f. Do *men* *2590*
7:20 Wherefore by their f ye shall know them. *2590*
21:34 that *they* might receive the f of it. *2590*
21:41 which shall render him the f in their *2590*
21:43 given to a nation bringing forth the f *2590*
Lk 3: 8 therefore f worthy of repentance, *2590*
12:17 I have no room where to bestow my f? *2590*
12:18 and there will I bestow all my f and *1081*
2Co 9:10 and increase the f of your righteousness;) *1081*
Php 1:11 Being filled with the f of righteousness, *2590*
2Ti 2: 6 laboureth must be first partaker of the f. *2590*
Jas 3:17 full of mercy and good f, without partiality, *2590*
Rev 18:14 And the f that thy soul lusted after are *3703*
22: 2 which bare twelve *manner of* f, and *2590*

FRUSTRATE (2) [FRUSTRATETH]
Ezr 4: 5 to f their purpose, all the days of Cyrus 6565
Gal 2:21 I do not f the grace of God: for if *114*

FRUSTRATED See NOUGHT; VEX; VEXATION; VEXED

FRUSTRATETH (1) [FRUSTRATE]
Isa 44:25 That f the tokens of the liars, and 6565

FRUSTRATION See VANITIES; VANITY

FRYINGPAN (2) [FRIED, PAN]
Lev 2: 7 oblation *be* a meat offering *baken* in the f, 4802
7: 9 all *that* is dressed in the f, and in the pan, 4802

FUEL (5)
Isa 9: 5 but *this* shall be with burning *and* f of fire. 3980
9:19 and the people shall be as the f of the fire: 3980
Eze 15: 4 Behold, it is cast into the fire for f; the fire 402
15: 6 which I have given to the fire for f, so will I 402
21:32 Thou shalt be for f to the fire; thy blood shall 402

FUGITIVE (2) [FUGITIVES]
Ge 4:12 a f and a vagabond shalt thou be in 5128
4:14 I shall be a f and a vagabond in the earth; 5128

FUGITIVES (4) [FUGITIVE]
Jdg 12: 4 Ye Gileadites *are* f of Ephraim among 6412
2Ki 25:11 the f that fell away to the king of Babylon, 5307
Isa 15: 5 his f *shall flee* unto Zoar, a heifer of three 1280
Eze 17:21 all his f with all his bands shall fall by 4015

FULFIL (24) [FULFILLED, FULFILLING]
Ge 29:27 F her week, and we will give thee this also 4390
Ex 5:13 F your works, *your* daily tasks, as when 3615
23:26 in thy land: the number of thy days I will f. 4390
1Ki 2:27 that *he* might f the word of the LORD, 4390
1Ch 22:13 if thou takest heed to f the statutes and 6213
2Ch 36:21 To f the word of the LORD by the mouth 4390
36:21 kept sabbath, to f threescore and ten years. 4390
Job 39: 2 Canst thou number the months *that* they f? 4390
Ps 20: 4 to thine own heart, and f all thy counsel. 4390
20: 5 *our* banners: the LORD f all thy petitions. 4390
145:19 He will f the desire of them that fear him: 6213
Mt 3:15 for thus it becometh us to f all *4137*
5:17 I am not come to destroy, but to f. *4137*
Ac 13:22 mine own heart, which shall f all my will. *4160*
Ro 2:27 if it f the law, judge thee, who by the letter *5055*
13:14 for the flesh, to *f* the lusts *thereof.* NIG
Gal 5:16 and ye shall not f the lust of the flesh. *5055*
6: 2 another's burdens, and so f the law of Christ. *378*
Php 2: 2 F ye my joy, that ye be likeminded, having *4137*
Col 1:25 given to me for you, to f the word of God; *4137*
4:17 hast received in the Lord, that thou f it. *4137*
2Th 1:11 and f all the good pleasure of *his* goodness, *4137*
Jas 2: 8 If ye f the royal law according to *5055*
Rev 17:17 For God hath put in their hearts to f his *4160*

FULFILLED (82) [FULFIL]
Ge 25:24 when her days to be delivered were f, 4390
29:21 Give *me* my wife, for my days are f, that I 4390
29:28 Jacob did so, and f her week: and he gave 4390
50: 3 forty days were f for him; for so 4390
50: 3 are f the days of those which are 4390
Ex 5:14 Wherefore have ye not f your task in 3615
7:25 seven days were f, after *that* the LORD 4390
Lev 12: 4 until the days of her purifying be f. 4390
12: 6 when the days of her purifying are f, for a 4390
Nu 6: 5 until the days be f, *in* the which he 4390
6:13 when the days of his separation are f: 4390
2Sa 7:12 when thy days be f, and thou shalt sleep 4390
14:22 in that the king hath f the request of his 6213
1Ki 8:15 and hath with his hand f *it,* saying, 4390
8:24 hast f *it* with thine hand, as *it is* this day. 4390
2Ch 6: 4 who hath with his hands f *that* which he 4390
6:15 hast f *it* with thine hand, as *it is* this day. 4390
Ezr 1: 1 by the mouth of Jeremiah might be f, 3615
Job 36:17 thou hast f the judgment of the wicked: 4390
Jer 44:25 your mouths, and f with your hand, saying, 4390
La 2:17 he hath f his word that he had commanded 1214
4:18 our end is near, our days are f; for our end 4390
Eze 5: 2 of the city, when the days of the siege are f: 4390
Da 4:33 The same hour was the thing f upon 5487
10: 3 myself at all, till three whole weeks were f. 4390
Mt 1:22 that it might be f which was spoken of *4137*
2:15 that it might be f which was spoken of *4137*
2:17 Then was f that which was spoken by *4137*
2:23 that it might be f which was spoken by *4137*
4:14 That it might be f which was spoken by *4137*
5:18 in no wise pass from the law, till all be f. *1096*
8:17 That it might be f which was spoken by *4137*
12:17 That it might be f which was spoken by *4137*
13:14 And in them is f the prophecy of Esaias, *378*
13:35 That it might be f which was spoken by *4137*
21: 4 that it might be f which was spoken by *4137*
24:34 shall not pass, till all these *things* be f. *1096*
26:54 *But* how then shall the scriptures be f, *4137*
26:56 the scriptures of the prophets might be f. *4137*
27: 9 Then was f that which was spoken by *4137*
27:35 that it might be f which was spoken by *4137*
Mk 1:15 And saying, The time is f, *4137*
13: 4 *be* the sign when all these *things* shall be f? *4931*
14:49 took me not: but the scriptures must be f. *4137*
15:28 And the scripture was f, which saith, *4137*
Lk 1:20 my words, which shall be f in their season. *4137*
2:43 And when they had f the days, as they *5048*

Lk 4:21 This day is this scripture f in your ears. *4137*
21:22 that all *things* which are written may be f. *4137*
21:24 until the times of the Gentiles be f. *4137*
21:32 generation shall not pass away, till all be f. *1096*
22:16 until it be f in the kingdom of God. *4137*
24:44 I was yet with you, that all *things* must be f, *4137*
Jn 3:29 this my joy therefore is f. *4137*
12:38 the saying of Esaias the prophet might be f, *4137*
13:18 but that the scripture may be f, He that *4137*
15:25 word might be f that is written in their law, *4137*
17:12 of perdition; that the scripture might be f. *4137*
17:13 that they might have my joy f in *4137*
18: 9 That the saying might be f, which he spake, *4137*
18:32 That the saying of Jesus might be f, *4137*
19:24 that the scripture might be f, which saith, *4137*
19:28 that the scripture might be f, saith, I thirst. *5048*
19:36 were done, that the scripture should be f, *4137*
Ac 1:16 this scripture must needs have been f, *4137*
3:18 that Christ should suffer, he hath so f. *4137*
9:23 And after that many days were f, the Jews *4137*
12:25 when they had f *their* ministry, and *4137*
13:25 And as John f *his* course, he said, *4137*
13:27 they have f *them* in condemning *him*. *4137*
13:29 And when they had f all that was written of *5055*
13:33 God hath f the same unto us their children, *1603*
14:26 the grace of God for the work which they f. *4137*
Ro 8: 4 righteousness of the law might be f in us, *4137*
13: 8 for he that loveth another hath f the law. *4137*
2Co 10: 6 all disobedience, when your obedience is f. *4137*
Gal 5:14 For all the law is f in one word, *even* in *4137*
Jas 2:23 And the scripture was f which saith, *4137*
Rev 6:11 should be killed as they *were*, should be f. *4137*
15: 8 seven plagues of the seven angels were f. *5055*
17:17 the beast, until the words of God shall be f. *5055*
20: 3 no more, till the thousand years should be f: *5055*

FULFILLING (3) [FULFIL]

Ps 148: 8 snow, and vapour; stormy wind f his word: 6213
Ro 13:10 therefore love *is* the f of the law. *4138*
Eph 2: 3 f the desires of the flesh and of the mind; *4160*

FULL (260) [FILL]

Ge 14:10 of Siddim *was* f **of slimepits**; 875+875+2564
15:16 for the iniquity of the Amorites *is* not yet f. 8003
25: 8 f *of years;* and was gathered to his people. 7649
35:29 unto his people, *being* old and f of days: 7649
41: 1 to pass at the end of **two f years**, 3117+8141
41: 7 ears devoured the seven rank and f ears. 4392
41:22 ears came up in one stalk, f and good: 4392
43:21 mouth of his sack, our money in f **weight**: 4948
Ex 8:21 the houses of the Egyptians shall be f of 4390
16: 3 *and* when we did eat bread to the f; 7648
16: 8 to eat, and in the morning bread to the f; 7646
16:33 put an omer f of manna therein, and lay it 4393
22: 3 *for* he should **make f restitution**; if 7999+7999
Lev 2:14 by the fire, *even* **corn** beaten out **of f ears**. 3759
16:12 he shall take a censer f of burning coals of 4393
16:12 his hands f of sweet incense beaten small, 4393
19:29 and the land **become** f of wickedness. 4390
25:29 it is sold; *within* a **f year** may he redeem it. 3117
25:30 if it be not redeemed within the space of a f 8549
26: 5 ye shall eat your bread to the f, and dwell in 7648
Nu 7:13 both of them *were* f *of* fine flour mingled 4392
7:14 spoon of ten *shekels* of gold, f *of* incense: 4392
7:19 both of them f *of* fine flour mingled with 4392
7:20 One spoon of gold of ten *shekels*, f *of* 4392
7:25 both of them f *of* fine flour mingled with 4392
7:26 One golden spoon of ten *shekels*, f *of* 4392
7:31 both of them f *of* fine flour mingled with 4392
7:32 One golden spoon *of* ten *shekels*, f *of* 4392
7:37 both of them f *of* fine flour mingled with 4392
7:38 One golden spoon of ten *shekels*, f *of* 4392
7:43 both of them f *of* fine flour mingled with 4392
7:44 One golden spoon of ten *shekels*, f *of* 4392
7:49 both of them f *of* fine flour mingled with 4392
7:50 One golden spoon of ten *shekels*, f *of* 4392
7:55 both of them f *of* fine flour mingled with 4392
7:56 One golden spoon of ten *shekels*, f *of* 4392
7:61 both of them f *of* fine flour mingled with 4392
7:62 One golden spoon of ten *shekels*, f *of* 4392
7:67 both of them f *of* fine flour mingled with 4392
7:68 One golden spoon of ten *shekels*, f *of* 4392
7:73 both of them f *of* fine flour mingled with 4392
7:74 One golden spoon of ten *shekels*, f *of* 4392
7:79 both of them f *of* fine flour mingled with 4392
7:80 One golden spoon of ten *shekels*, f *of* 4392
7:86 f *of* incense, *weighing* ten *shekels* apiece, 4392
22:18 If Balak would give me his house f *of* silver 4393
24:13 If Balak would give me his house f *of* silver 4393
Dt 6:11 houses f *of* all good *things*, which thou 4392
6:11 when thou shalt have eaten and be f; 7646
8:10 When thou hast eaten and art f, then 7646
8:12 Lest *when* thou hast eaten and art f, and 7646
11:15 for thy cattle, that thou mayest eat and be f. 7646
21:13 her father and her mother a **f month**: 3117+3391
33:23 and f *with* the blessing of the LORD: 4392
34: 9 Joshua the son of Nun was f *of* the spirit of 4392
Jdg 6:38 the dew out of the fleece, a bowl f *of* water. 4393
16:27 Now the house was f *of* men and women; 4390
Ru 1:21 I went out f, and the LORD hath brought 4392
2:12 a f reward be given thee of the LORD 8003
1Sa 2: 5 *They that were* f have hired out themselves 7649
18:27 and they **gave** them **in f tale** to the king, 4390
27: 7 the country of the Philistines was a **f year** 3117
2Sa 8: 2 to death, and *with* one f line to keep alive. 4393
13:23 it came to pass after **two f years**, 3117+8141
14:28 So Absalom dwelt **two f years** in 3117+8141
23:11 where was a piece of ground f *of* lentiles: 4392
2Ki 3:16 Make this valley f **of ditches**. 1356+1356
4: 4 and thou shalt set aside *that* which *is* f. 4392
4: 6 it came to pass, when the vessels were f, 4390
4:39 gathered thereof wild gourds his lap f, and 4393
4:42 and f **ears of corn** in the husk thereof. 3759
6:17 the mountain was f *of* horses and 4390
7:15 all the way *was* f *of* garments and vessels, 4392
9:24 **drew** a bow **with** his f **strength**, 3027+4390+871.1
10:21 the house of Baal was f from one end to 4390
15:13 and he reigned a f **month** in Samaria. 3117+3391
1Ch 11:13 where was a parcel of ground f *of* barley; 4392
21:22 thou shalt grant it me for the f price: 4392
21:24 Nay; but I will verily buy *it* for the f price: 4392
23: 1 So when David was old and f *of* days, 7646
29:28 good old age, f of days, riches, and honour: 7649
2Ch 24:15 waxed old, and was f *of* days when he died; 7646
Ne 9:25 and possessed houses f *of* all goods, 4392
Est 3: 5 him reverence, *then* was Haman f *of* wrath. 4390
5: 9 he was f *of* indignation against Mordecai. 4390
Job 5:26 Thou shalt come to *thy* grave in a **f age**, 3624
7: 4 I am f *of* tossings to and fro unto 7646
10:15 *I am* f of confusion; therefore see thou 7649
11: 2 and should a man **f of talk** be justified? 8193
14: 1 of a woman *is* of few days, and f of trouble. 7649
20:11 His bones are f *of the sin of* his youth, 4390
21:23 One dieth in his f strength, *being* wholly at 8537
21:24 His breasts are f *of* milk, and his bones are 4390
32:18 For I am f *of* matter, the spirit within me 4390
36:16 be set on thy table *should be* f *of* fatness. 4390
42:17 So Job died, *being* old and f of days. 7649
Ps 10: 7 His mouth is f *of* cursing and deceit and 4390
17:14 *with* thy hid *treasure:* they are f *of* children, 7646
26:10 and their right hand is f *of* bribes. 4390
29: 4 the voice of the LORD *is* f **of majesty**. 1926
33: 5 the earth is f *of* the goodness of 4390
48:10 thy right hand is f *of* righteousness. 4390
65: 9 it *with* the river of God, *which* is f *of* water: 4390
69:20 broken my heart; and I am **f of heaviness**: 5136
73:10 waters of a f *cup* are wrung out to them. 4392
74:20 for the dark places of the earth are f *of* 4390
75: 8 it is f *of* mixture; and he poureth out of 4392
78:25 eat angels' food: he sent them meat to the f. 7648
78:38 he, *being* **f of compassion**, forgave *their* 7349
86:15 *art* a God **f of compassion**, and gracious, 7349
88: 3 For my soul is f of troubles: and my life 7646
104:16 The trees of the LORD are f *of sap;* 7646
104:24 made them all: the earth is f *of* thy riches. 4390
111: 4 LORD *is* gracious and **f of compassion**. 7349
112: 4 and **f of compassion**, and righteous. 7349
119:64 The earth, O LORD, is f *of* thy mercy: 4390
127: 5 Happy *is* the man that hath his quiver f of 4390
144:13 *That* our garners *may be* f, affording all 4392
145: 8 LORD *is* gracious, and **f of compassion**; 7349
Pr 17: 1 than a house f *of* sacrifices with strife. 4392
27: 7 The f soul loatheth a honeycomb; but *to* 7649
27:20 Hell and destruction are never f; so the eyes 7646
30: 9 Lest I be f, and deny *thee,* and say, Who *is* 7646
Ecc 1: 7 rivers run into the sea; yet the sea *is* not f; 4392
1: 8 All things *are* **f of labour**; man cannot utter 3023

F

Ecc 4: 6 than both the hands f *with* travail and 4393
9: 3 also the heart of the sons of men is f *of* evil, 4390
10:14 A fool also is f of words: a man cannot tell 7235
11: 3 If the clouds be f *of* rain, they empty 4390
Isa 1:11 I am f *of* the burnt offerings of rams, and 7646
1:15 I will not hear: your hands are f *of* blood. 4390
1:21 *it was* f of judgment; righteousness lodged 4392
2: 7 Their land also is f *of* silver and gold, 4390
2: 7 their land is also f *of* horses, neither *is there* 4390
2: 8 Their land also is f *of* idols; they worship 4390
6: 3 of hosts: the whole earth *is* f of his glory. 4393
11: 9 for the earth shall be f *of* the knowledge of 4390
13:21 their houses shall be f *of* doleful creatures; 4390
15: 9 For the waters of Dimon shall be f *of* 4390
22: 2 Thou *that art* f *of* stirs, a tumultuous city, 4392
22: 7 *that* thy choicest valleys shall be f *of* 4390
25: 6 on the lees, of fat things **f of marrow**, 4229
28: 8 For all tables are f *of* vomit *and* filthiness, 4390
30:27 his lips are f *of* indignation, and his tongue 4390
51:20 *they are* f *of* the fury of the LORD, 4392
Jer 4:12 *Even* a f wind from those *places* shall come 4392
4:27 be desolate; yet will I not make a **f end**. 3617
5: 7 when I had **fed** them **to the f**, they then 7650
5:10 and destroy; but make not a **f end**: 3617
5:18 I will not make a **f end** with you. 3617
5:27 As a cage *is* f *of* birds, so *are* their houses 4392
5:27 full *of* birds, so *are* their houses f *of* deceit: 4392
6:11 Therefore I am f *of* the fury of the LORD; 4390
6:11 the aged with *him that is* f of days. 4392
23:10 For the land is f *of* adulterers; for because 4390
28: 3 Within **two f years** *will* I bring again 3117+8141
28:11 within the space of **two f years**. 3117+8141
30:11 though I make a **f end** of all nations 3617
30:11 yet will I not make a **f end** of thee: 3617
35: 5 the house of the Rechabites pots f *of* wine, 4392
46:28 for I will make a **f end** of all the nations 3617
46:28 I will not make a **f end** of thee, but 3617
La 1: 1 the city sit solitary, *that was* f of people! 7227
3:30 smiteth him: he is **filled** f with reproach. 7646
Eze 1:18 their rings *were* f *of* eyes round about them 4392
7:23 for the land is f *of* bloody crimes, and 4390
7:23 bloody crimes, and the city is f *of* violence. 4390
9: 9 the land is f *of* blood, and the city full *of* 4390
9: 9 full *of* blood, and the city f *of* perverseness: 4390
10: 4 the court was f of the brightness of 4390
10:12 and the wheels, *were* f *of* eyes round about, 4392
11:13 *wilt* thou make a **f end** of the remnant of 3617
17: 3 longwinged, f *of* feathers, which had divers 4392
19:10 **f of branches** by reason of many waters. 6058
28:12 f *of* wisdom, and perfect in beauty. 4392
32: 6 and the rivers shall be f of thee. 4390
32:15 shall be destitute of that whereof it was f, 4393
37: 1 midst of the valley which *was* f *of* bones, 4392
39:19 ye shall eat fat till *ye* be f, and drink blood 7654
41: 8 chambers *were* a f reed of six great cubits. 4393
Da 3:19 was Nebuchadnezzar f *of* fury, and 4391
8:23 when the transgressors are **come to the f**, 8552
10: 2 Daniel was mourning three **f weeks**. 3117+7620
Joel 2:24 the floors shall be f *of* wheat, and the fats 4390
3:13 for the press is f, the fats overflow; 4390
Am 2:13 as a cart is pressed *that is* f *of* sheaves. 4392
Mic 3: 8 truly I am f *of* power by the spirit of 4390
6:12 For the rich *men* thereof are f *of* violence, 4390
Na 3: 1 it *is* all f *of* lies *and* robbery; the prey 4392
Hab 3: 3 and the earth was f *of* his praise. 4390
Zec 8: 5 the streets of the city shall be f *of* boys and 4390
Mt 6:22 thy whole body shall be **f of light**. *5460*
6:23 thy whole body shall be **f of darkness**. *4652*
13:48 Which, when it was f, they drew to shore, *4137*
14:20 fragments that remained twelve baskets f. *4134*
15:37 broken *meat* that was left seven baskets f. *4134*
23:25 but within they are f of extortion and *1073*
23:27 but are within f of dead *men's* bones, and *1073*
23:28 but within ye are f of hypocrisy and *3324*
Mk 4:28 then the ear, after that the f corn in the ear. *4134*
4:37 beat into the ship, so that it was now f. *1072*
6:43 And they took up twelve baskets f of *4134*
7: 9 **F well** ye reject the commandment of God, *2573*
8:19 how many baskets f of fragments took ye *4134*
8:20 how many baskets f of fragments took ye *4138*
15:36 one ran and filled a spunge *f* of vinegar, NIG
Lk 1:57 Now Elisabeth's f time **came** that she *4130*
4: 1 And Jesus being f of the Holy Ghost *4134*
5:12 in a certain city, behold a man f of leprosy: *4134*
6:25 Woe unto you that are f: for ye shall *1705*
11:34 is single, thy whole body also is **f of light**; *5460*
11:34 *eye* is evil, thy body also *is* **f of darkness**. *4652*
11:36 If thy whole body therefore *be* **f of light**, *5460*
11:36 no part dark, the whole shall be **f of light**, *5460*
11:39 but your inward part is f of ravening and *1073*
16:20 which was laid at his gate, **f of sores**, *1669*
Jn 1:14 begotten of the Father,) f of grace and truth. *4134*
7: 8 this feast; for my time is not yet **f come**. *4137*
15:11 remain in you, and *that* your joy might be f. *4137*
16:24 and ye shall receive, that your joy may be f. *4137*
19:29 Now there was set a vessel f of vinegar: *3324*
21:11 and drew the net to land f of great fishes, *3324*
Ac 2:13 *These men* are f of new wine. *3325*
2:28 thou shalt **make** me f of joy with thy *4137*
6: 3 f of the Holy Ghost and wisdom, whom we *4134*
6: 5 a man f of faith and of the Holy Ghost, and *4134*
6: 8 And Stephen, f of faith and power, *4134*
7:23 And when he was f forty years old, it came *4137*
7:55 But he, being f of the Holy Ghost, *4134*
9:36 this *woman* was f of good works and *4134*
11:24 and f of the Holy Ghost and of faith: *4134*
13:10 O f of all subtilty and all mischief, *4134*
19:28 heard *these sayings*, they were f of wrath, *4134*
Ro 1:29 f of envy, murder, debate, deceit, *3324*
3:14 Whose mouth is f of cursing and bitterness: *1073*
15:14 my brethren, that ye also are f of goodness, *3324*
1Co 4: 8 Now ye are f, now ye are rich, ye have *2880*
Php 2:26 and *was* **f of heaviness**, because that ye had *85*
4:12 in all *things* I am instructed both to be f and *5526*
4:18 I am f, having received of Epaphroditus *4137*
Col 2: 2 unto all riches of the f **assurance** of *4136*
2Ti 4: 5 **make f proof** of thy ministry. *4135*
Heb 5:14 meat belongeth to *them that are* of **f age**, *5046*
6:11 to the f **assurance** of hope unto the end: *4136*
10:22 with a true heart in f **assurance** of faith, *4136*
Jas 3: 8 *it is* an unruly evil, f of deadly poison. *3324*
3:17 f of mercy and good fruits, *3324*
1Pe 1: 8 rejoice with joy unspeakable and **f of glory**: *1392*
2Pe 2:14 Having eyes f of adultery and that cannot *3324*
1Jn 1: 4 write we unto you, that your joy may be f. *4137*
2Jn 1: 8 but *that* we receive a f reward. *4134*
1:12 speak face to face, that our joy may be f. *4137*
Rev 4: 6 *were* four beasts f of eyes before and *1073*
4: 8 about *him;* and *they were* f of eyes within: *1073*
5: 8 and golden vials f of odours, which are *1073*
15: 7 seven golden vials f of the wrath of God, *1073*
16:10 and his kingdom was **f of darkness**; and *4656*
17: 3 **f of** names of blasphemy, having seven *1073*
17: 4 having a golden cup in her hand **f of** *1073*
21: 9 the seven vials f of the seven last plagues, *1073*

FULLER (1) [FULLER'S, FULLERS']

Mk 9: 3 so as no f on earth can white *them.* *1102*

FULLER'S (3) [FULLER]

2Ki 18:17 which *is* in the highway of the f field. 3526
Isa 7: 3 the upper pool in the highway of the f field; 3526
36: 2 the upper pool in the highway of the f field. 3526

FULLERS' (1) [FULLER]

Mal 3: 2 he *is* like a refiner's fire, and like f sope: 3526

FULLY (13) [FILL]

Nu 7: 1 it came to pass on the day that Moses had f 3615
14:24 spirit with him, and hath followed me f, 4390
Ru 2:11 unto her, It hath f **been shewed** me, 5046+5046
1Ki 11: 6 **went** not f after the LORD, as *did* David 4390
Ecc 8:11 the heart of the sons of men is f **set** in them 4390
Na 1:10 they shall be devoured as stubble f dry. 4392
Ac 2: 1 And when the day of Pentecost was f **come**, *4845*
Ro 4:21 And being f **persuaded** that, what he had *4135*
14: 5 man be f **persuaded** in his own mind. *4135*
15:19 I have f preached the gospel of Christ. *4137*
2Ti 3:10 But thou hast f **known** my doctrine, *3877*
4:17 by me the preaching might be f **known**, *4135*
Rev 14:18 vine of the earth; for her grapes are **f ripe**. *187*

FULNESS (25) [FILL]

Nu 18:27 and as the f of the winepress. 4395
Dt 33:16 precious things of the earth and f thereof, 4393
1Ch 16:32 Let the sea roar, and the f thereof: let 4393
Job 20:22 In the f of his sufficiency he shall be in 4390
Ps 16:11 in thy presence *is* f of joy; at thy right hand 7648

Ps 24: 1 earth *is* the LORD'S, and the f thereof; 4393
50:12 for the world *is* mine, and the f thereof. 4393
89:11 *as for* the world and the f thereof, thou hast 4393
96:11 be glad; let the sea roar, and the f thereof. 4393
98: 7 Let the sea roar, and the f thereof; 4393
Eze 16:49 f of bread, and abundance of idleness was 7653
19: 7 and the land was desolate, and the f thereof, 4393
Jn 1:16 And of his f have all we received, and *4138*
Ro 11:12 of the Gentiles; how much more their f? *4138*
11:25 until the f of the Gentiles be come in. *4138*
15:29 I shall come in the f of the blessing of *4138*
1Co 10:26 the earth *is* the Lord's, and the f thereof. *4138*
10:28 for the earth *is* the Lord's, and the f thereof: *4138*
Gal 4: 4 But when the f of the time was come, *4138*
Eph 1:10 That in the dispensation of the f of times *he* *4138*
1:23 his body, the f of him that filleth all in all. *4138*
3:19 that ye might be filled with all the f of God. *4138*
4:13 unto the measure of the stature of the f of *4138*
Col 1:19 *the Father* that in him should all f dwell; *4138*
2: 9 For in him dwelleth all the f of *4138*

FURBISH (1) [FURBISHED]
Jer 46: 4 f the spears, *and* put on the brigandines. 4838

FURBISHED (5) [FURBISH]
Eze 21: 9 A sword, a sword is sharpened, and also f: 4803
21:10 a sore slaughter; *it is* f that it may glitter: 4803
21:11 he hath given it to be f, that *it* may be 4803
21:11 this sword is sharpened, and it *is* f, to give 4803
21:28 for the slaughter *it is* f, to consume because 4803

FURIOUS (6) [FURY]
Pr 22:24 and with a f man thou shalt not go: 2534
29:22 and a f man aboundeth in transgression. 2534
Eze 5:15 thee in anger and in fury and in f rebukes. 2534
25:17 great vengeance upon them with f rebukes, 2534
Da 2:12 this cause the king was angry and very f, 7108
Na 1: 2 the LORD revengeth, and *is* f; 1167+2534

FURIOUSLY (2) [FURY]
2Ki 9:20 the son of Nimshi; for he driveth f. 7697+871.1
Eze 23:25 and they shall deal f with thee: 2534+871.1

FURLONGS (5)
Lk 24:13 was from Jerusalem *about* threescore f. *4712*
Jn 6:19 had rowed about five and twenty or thirty f, *4712*
11:18 nigh unto Jerusalem, about fifteen f off: *4712*
Rev 14:20 the space of a thousand *and* six hundred f. *4712*
21:16 the city with the reed, twelve thousand f. *4712*

FURNACE (30) [FURNACES]
Ge 15:17 behold a smoking f, and a burning lamp 8574
19:28 of the country went up as the smoke of a f. 3536
Ex 9: 8 Take to you handfuls of ashes of the f, and 3536
9:10 they took ashes of the f, and stood before 3536
19:18 thereof ascended as the smoke of a f, 3536
Dt 4:20 brought you forth out of the iron f, *even* out 3564
1Ki 8:51 of Egypt, from the midst of the f of iron: 3564
Ps 12: 6 *as* silver tried in a f of earth, purified seven 5948
Pr 17: 3 fining pot *is* for silver, and the f for gold: 3564
27:21 the fining pot for silver, and the f for gold; 3564
Isa 31: 9 fire *is* in Zion, and his f in Jerusalem. 8574
48:10 I have chosen thee in the f of affliction. 3564
Jer 11: 4 from the iron f, saying, Obey my voice, and 3564
Eze 22:18 tin, and iron, and lead, in the midst of the f; 3564
22:20 and lead, and tin, into the midst of the f, 3564
22:22 As silver is melted in the midst of the f, so 3564
Da 3: 6 be cast into the midst of a burning fiery f. 861
3:11 be cast into the midst of a burning fiery f. 861
3:15 same hour into the midst of a burning fiery f; 861
3:17 *is* able to deliver us from the burning fiery f, 861
3:19 commanded that *they* should heat the f one 861
3:20 *and* to cast *them* into the burning fiery f. 861
3:21 cast into the midst of the burning fiery f. 861
3:22 *was* urgent, and the f exceeding hot, 861
3:23 bound into the midst of the burning fiery f. 861
3:26 near to the mouth of the burning fiery f, 861
Mt 13:42 And shall cast them into a f of fire: *2575*
13:50 And shall cast them into the f of fire: *2575*
Rev 1:15 like unto fine brass, as if they burned in a f; *2575*
9: 2 out of the pit, as the smoke of a great f; *2575*

FURNACES (2) [FURNACE]
Ne 3:11 the other piece, and the tower of the f. 8574
12:38 from beyond the tower of the f even unto 8574

FURNISH (4) [FURNISHED, FURNITURE]
Dt 15:14 Thou shalt f him **liberally** out of thy 6059+6059
Ps 78:19 Can God f a table in the wilderness? 6186
Isa 65:11 that f the drink offering **unto** *that* number. 4390
Jer 46:19 f thyself to go into captivity: 3627+6213

FURNISHED (6) [FURNISH]
1Ki 9:11 (*Now* Hiram the king of Tyre had f 5375
Pr 9: 2 mingled her wine; she hath also f her table. 6186
Mt 22:10 good: and the wedding was f with guests. *4130*
Mk 14:15 And he will shew you a large upper room f *4766*
Lk 22:12 he shall shew you a large upper room f: *4766*
2Ti 3:17 **throughly** f unto all good works. *1822*

FURNISHINGS See FURNITURE

FURNITURE (8) [FURNISH]
Ge 31:34 put them in the camel's f, and sat upon 3733
Ex 31: 7 *is* thereupon, and all the f of the tabernacle, 3627
31: 8 the table and his f, and the pure candlestick 3627
31: 8 the pure candlestick with all his f, and 3627
31: 9 the altar of burnt offering with all his f, 3627
35:14 his f, and his lamps, with the oil for 3627
39:33 the tent, and all his f, his taches, his boards, 3627
Na 2: 9 the store *and* glory out of all the pleasant f. 3627

FURROW (1) [FURROWS]
Job 39:10 bind the unicorn *with* his band in the f? 8525

FURROWS (8) [FURROW]
Job 31:38 or that the f likewise thereof complain; 8525
Ps 65:10 *thou* settlest the f thereof: thou makest it 1418
129: 3 upon my back: they made long their f. 4618
Eze 17: 7 that *he* might water it by the f of her 6170
17:10 it shall wither in the f where it grew. 6170
Hos 10: 4 up as hemlock in the f of the field. 8525
10:10 *they* shall bind themselves in their two f. 5772
12:11 their altars *are* as heaps in the f of 8525

FURTHER (24) [FAR, FURTHERANCE, FURTHERED, FURTHERMORE] See Index

FURTHERANCE (2) [FURTHER]
Php 1:12 fallen out rather unto the f of the gospel; *4297*
1:25 and continue with you all for your f and *4297*

FURTHERED (1) [FURTHER] See Index

FURTHERMORE (14) [FURTHER] See Index

FURY (70) [FURIOUS, FURIOUSLY]
Ge 27:44 a few days, until thy brother's f turn away; 2534
Lev 26:28 I will walk contrary unto you also in f; 2534
Job 20:23 *God* shall cast the f of his wrath upon him, 2740
Isa 27: 4 F *is* not in me: who would set the briers 2534
34: 2 all nations, and *his* f upon all their armies: 2534
42:25 Therefore he hath poured upon him the f of 2534
51:13 every day because of the f of the oppressor, 2534
51:13 and where *is* the f of the oppressor? 2534
51:17 at the hand of the LORD the cup of his f; 2534
51:20 *they are* full *of* the f of the LORD, 2534
51:22 *even* the dregs of the cup of my f; 2534
59:18 he will repay, f to his adversaries, 2534
63: 3 in mine anger, and trample them in my f; 2534
63: 5 salvation unto me; and my f, it upheld me. 2534
63: 6 make them drunk in my f, and I will bring 2534
66:15 to render his anger with f, and his rebuke 2534
Jer 4: 4 lest my f come forth like fire, and burn that 2534
6:11 Therefore I am full *of* the f of the LORD; 2534
7:20 my f *shall be* poured out upon this place, 2534
10:25 Pour out thy f upon the heathen that know 2534
21: 5 even in anger, and in f, and in great wrath. 2534
21:12 lest my f go out like fire, and burn that 2534
23:19 whirlwind of the LORD is gone forth *in* f, 2534
25:15 Take the wine cup of this f at mine hand, 2534
30:23 of the LORD goeth forth *with* f, 2534
32:31 of my f from the day that they built it even 2534
32:37 mine anger, and in my f, and in great wrath; 2534
33: 5 I have slain in mine anger and in my f, 2534
36: 7 the f that the LORD hath pronounced 2534
42:18 my f hath been poured forth upon 2534
42:18 so shall my f be poured forth upon you, 2534
44: 6 Wherefore my f and mine anger was 2534
La 2: 4 of Zion: he poured out his f like fire. 2534
4:11 The LORD hath accomplished his f; 2534
Eze 5:13 and I will cause my f to rest upon them, and 2534

Eze 5:13 when I have accomplished my **f** in them. 2534
5:15 in anger and in **f** and in furious rebukes. 2534
6:12 thus will I accomplish my **f** upon them. 2534
7: 8 Now will I shortly pour out my **f** upon thee, 2534
8:18 Therefore will I also deal in **f**: mine eye 2534
9: 8 in thy pouring out of thy **f** upon Jerusalem? 2534
13:13 even rent *it with* a stormy wind in my **f**; 2534
13:13 and great hailstones in *my* **f** to consume *it.* 2534
14:19 pour out my **f** upon it in blood, to cut off 2534
16:38 and I will give thee blood in **f** and jealousy. 2534
16:42 So will I make my **f** towards thee to rest, 2534
19:12 she was plucked up in **f**, she was cast down 2534
20: 8 I said, *I* will pour out my **f** upon them, 2534
20:13 *I* would pour out my **f** upon them in 2534
20:21 I said, *I* would pour out my **f** upon them, 2534
20:33 and with **f** poured out, will I rule over you: 2534
20:34 a stretched out arm, and with **f** poured out. 2534
21:17 and I will cause my **f** to rest: 2534
22:20 will I gather *you* in mine anger and in my **f**, 2534
22:22 LORD have poured out my **f** upon you. 2534
24: 8 That *it* might cause **f** to come up to take 2534
24:13 till I have caused my **f** to rest upon thee. 2534
25:14 to mine anger and according to my **f**; 2534
30:15 I will pour my **f** upon Sin, the strength of 2534
36: 6 I have spoken in my jealousy and in my **f**, 2534
36:18 Wherefore I poured my **f** upon them for 2534
38:18 *that* my **f** shall come up in my face. 2534
Da 3:13 and **f** commanded to bring Shadrach, 2528
3:19 was Nebuchadnezzar full *of* **f**, and the form 2528
8: 6 and ran unto him in the **f** of his power. 2534
9:16 thy **f** be turned away from thy city 2534
11:44 he shall go forth with great **f** to destroy, 2534
Mic 5:15 vengeance in anger and **f** upon the heathen, 2534
Na 1: 6 his **f** is poured out like fire, and the rocks 2534
Zec 8: 2 and I was jealous for her *with* great **f**. 2534

FUTILE See VANITIES; VANITY

FUTILITY See VANITIES; VANITY

FUTURE See HEREAFTER

G

GAAL (9)
Jdg 9:26 **G** the son of Ebed came with his brethren, 1603
9:28 **G** the son of Ebed said, Who *is* Abimelech, 1603
9:30 city heard the words of **G** the son of Ebed, 1603
9:31 **G** the son of Ebed and his brethren be come 1603
9:35 **G** the son of Ebed went out, and stood *in* 1603
9:36 when **G** saw the people, he said to Zebul, 1603
9:37 **G** spake again and said, See there come 1603
9:39 **G** went out before the men of Shechem, 1603
9:41 Zebul thrust out **G** and his brethren, 1603

GAASH (4)
Jos 24:30 on the north side of the hill of **G**. 1608
Jdg 2: 9 of Ephraim, on the north side of the hill **G**. 1608
2Sa 23:30 the Pirathonite, Hiddai of the brooks of **G**, 1608
1Ch 11:32 Hurai of the brooks of **G**, Abiel 1608

GABA (2)
Jos 18:24 and Ophni, and **G**; 1387
Ezr 2:26 The children of Ramah and **G**, six hundred 1387

GABBAI (1)
Ne 11: 8 after him **G**, Sallai, nine hundred twenty 1373

GABBATHA (1)
Jn 19:13 called the Pavement, but in the Hebrew, **G**. *1042*

GABRIEL (4)
Da 8:16 which called, and said, **G**, make this *man* to 1403
9:21 I *was* speaking in prayer, even the man **G**, 1403
Lk 1:19 I am **G**, that stand in the presence of God; *1043*
1:26 And in the sixth month the angel **G** was *1043*

GAD (72) [BAAL-GAD, DIBON-GAD, GADITE, GADITES]
Ge 30:11 A troop cometh: and she called his name **G**. 1410
35:26 of Zilpah, Leah's handmaid; **G**, and Asher: 1410
46:16 the sons of **G**; Ziphion, and Haggi, Shuni, 1410
49:19 **G**, a troop shall overcome him: but he shall 1410
Ex 1: 4 Dan, and Naphtali, **G**, and Asher. 1410
Nu 1:14 Of **G**; Eliasaph the son of Deuel. 1410
1:24 Of the children of **G**, *by* their generations, 1410
1:25 *even* of the tribe of **G**, *were* forty and 1410
2:14 the tribe of **G**: and the captain of the sons 1410
2:14 the captain of the sons of **G** *shall be* 1410
7:42 prince of the children of **G**, *offered:* 1410
10:20 of **G** *was* Eliasaph the son of Deuel. 1410
13:15 Of the tribe of **G**, Geuel the son of Machi. 1410
26:15 The children of **G** after their families: 1410
26:18 These *are* the families of the children of **G** 1410
32: 1 the children of **G** had a very great 1410
32: 2 The children of **G** and the children of 1410
32: 6 Moses said unto the children of **G** and 1410
32:25 the children of **G** and the children of 1410
32:29 If the children of **G** and the children of 1410
32:31 the children of **G** and the children of 1410
32:33 *even* to the children of **G**, and to 1410
32:34 the children of **G** built Dibon, and Ataroth, 1410
34:14 the tribe of the children of **G** according to 1425
Dt 27:13 **G**, and Asher, and Zebulun, Dan, and 1410
33:20 of **G** he said, Blessed *be* he that enlargeth 1410
33:20 he said, Blessed *be* he that enlargeth **G**: 1410
Jos 4:12 the children of **G**, and half the tribe of 1410
13:24 Moses gave *inheritance* unto the tribe of **G**, 1410
13:24 *even* unto the children of **G** according to 1410
13:28 This *is* the inheritance of the children of **G** 1410
18: 7 **G**, and Reuben, and half the tribe of 1410
20: 8 Ramoth in Gilead out of the tribe of **G**, and 1410
21: 7 out of the tribe of **G**, and out of the tribe of 1410
21:38 out of the tribe of **G**, Ramoth in Gilead 1410
22: 9 of Reuben and the children of **G** and 1410
22:10 of Reuben and the children of **G** and 1410
22:11 of Reuben and the children of **G** and 1410
22:13 to the children of **G**, and to the half tribe of 1410
22:15 to the children of **G**, and to the half tribe of 1410
22:21 of Reuben and the children of **G** and 1410
22:25 ye children of Reuben and children of **G**; 1410
22:30 the children of **G** and the children of 1410
22:31 to the children of **G**, and to the children of 1410
22:32 from the children of **G**, out of the land of 1410
22:33 the children of Reuben and **G** dwelt. 1410
22:34 the children of **G** called the altar *Ed:* for it 1410
1Sa 13: 7 Hebrews went over Jordan *to* the land of **G** 1410
22: 5 the prophet **G** said unto David, Abide not 1410
2Sa 24: 5 city that *lieth* in the midst of the river of **G**, 1410
24:11 of the LORD came unto the prophet **G**, 1410
24:13 So **G** came to David, and told him, and 1410
24:14 David said unto **G**, I am in a great strait: 1410
24:18 **G** came that day to David, and said unto 1410
24:19 David, according to the saying of **G**, 1410
1Ch 2: 2 and Benjamin, Naphtali, **G**, and Asher. 1410
5:11 the children of **G** dwelt over against them, 1410
6:63 out of the tribe of **G**, and out of the tribe of 1410
6:80 out of the tribe of **G**; Ramoth in Gilead 1410
12:14 These *were* of the sons of **G**, captains of 1410
21: 9 the LORD spake unto **G**, David's seer, 1410
21:11 So **G** came to David, and said unto him, 1410
21:13 David said unto **G**, I am in a great strait: 1410
21:18 the angel of the LORD commanded **G** to 1410
21:19 David went up at the saying of **G**, which he 1410
29:29 the prophet, and in the book of **G** the seer, 1410
2Ch 29:25 of **G** the king's seer, and Nathan 1410
Jer 49: 1 why *then* doth their king inherit **G**, and 1410
Eze 48:27 east side unto the west side, **G** a *portion.* 1410
48:28 by the border of **G**, at the south side 1410
48:34 one gate of **G**, one gate of Asher, one gate 1410
Rev 7: 5 Of the tribe of **G** *were* sealed twelve *1045*

GADARENES (3)
Mk 5: 1 side of the sea, into the country of the **G**. *1046*
Lk 8:26 And they arrived at the country of the **G**, *1046*
8:37 **G** round about besought him to depart from *1046*

GADDEST (1)
Jer 2:36 Why **g** thou **about** *so* much to change thy 235

GADDI (1)
Nu 13:11 of the tribe of Manasseh, **G** the son of Susi. 1426

GADDIEL (1)
Nu 13:10 Of the tribe of Zebulun, **G** the son of Sodi. 1427

GADI (2)
2Ki 15:14 For Menahem the son of **G** went up from 1424
15:17 Menahem the son of **G** to reign over Israel, 1424

GADITE (1) [GAD]
2Sa 23:36 the son of Nathan of Zobah, Bani the **G**, 1425

GADITES (14) [GAD]
Dt 3:12 gave I unto the Reubenites and to the **G**. 1425
3:16 unto the **G** I gave from Gilead even unto 1425
4:43 Ramoth in Gilead, of the **G**; and Golan in 1425
29: 8 to the **G**, and to the half tribe of Manasseh. 1425
Jos 1:12 to the **G**, and to half the tribe of Manasseh, 1425
12: 6 and the **G**, and the half tribe of Manasseh. 1425
13: 8 and the **G** have received their inheritance, 1425
22: 1 and the **G**, and the half tribe of Manasseh, 1425
2Ki 10:33 the **G**, and the Reubenites, and 1425
1Ch 5:18 the **G**, and half the tribe of Manasseh, 1425
5:26 the **G**, and the half tribe of Manasseh, and 1425
12: 8 of the **G** there separated themselves unto 1425
12:37 the **G**, and of the half tribe of Manasseh, 1425
26:32 the **G**, and the half tribe of Manasseh, 1425

GAHAM (1)
Ge 22:24 and **G**, and Thahash, and Maachah. 1514

GAHAR (2)
Ezr 2:47 the children of **G**, the children of Reaiah, 1515
Ne 7:49 the children of Giddel, the children of **G**, 1515

GAIN (30) [GAINED, GAINS]
Jdg 5:19 of Megiddo; they took no **g** of money. 1215
Job 22: 3 *is it* **g** *to him*, that thou makest thy ways 1215
Pr 1:19 of every one that is **greedy of g**; 1214+1215
3:14 of silver, and the **g** thereof than fine gold. 8393
15:27 He that is **greedy of g** troubleth his 1214+1215
28: 8 and **unjust g** increaseth his substance, 8636
Isa 33:15 he that despiseth the **g** of oppressions, 1215
56:11 every one for his **g**, from his quarter. 1215
Eze 22:13 at thy **dishonest g** which thou hast made, 1215
22:27 to destroy souls, to **get dishonest g**. 1214+1215
Da 2: 8 I know of certainty that ye would **g** 2084
11:39 over many, and shall divide the land for **g**. 4242
Mic 4:13 I will consecrate their **g** unto the LORD, 1215
Mt 16:26 if he shall **g** the whole world, and lose his *2770*
Mk 8:36 if he shall **g** the whole world, and lose his *2770*
Lk 9:25 if he **g** the whole world, and lose himself, *2770*
Ac 16:16 which brought her masters much **g** by *2039*
19:24 brought no small **g** unto the craftsmen; *2039*
1Co 9:19 servant unto all, that I might **g** the more. *2770*
9:20 I became as a Jew, that I might **g** *the* Jews; *2770*
9:20 that I might **g** them that are under the law; *2770*
9:21 that I might **g** them *that are* without law. *2770*
9:22 became I as weak, that I might **g** the weak: *2770*
2Co 12:17 Did I **make a g** of you by any of them *4122*
12:18 Did Titus **make a g** of you? walked we not *4122*
Php 1:21 For to me to live *is* Christ, and to die *is* **g**. *2771*
3: 7 But what *things* were **g** to me, those I *2771*
1Ti 6: 5 of the truth, supposing that **g** is godliness: *4200*
6: 6 But godliness with contentment is great **g**. *4200*
Jas 4:13 there a year, and buy and sell, and **get g**: *2770*

GAINED (10) [GAIN]
Job 27: 8 though he hath **g**, when God taketh away 1214
Eze 22:12 thou hast **greedily g** of thy neighbours by 1214
Mt 18:15 he shall hear thee, thou hast **g** thy brother. *2770*
25:17 that *had received* two, he also **g** other two. *2770*
25:20 I have **g** besides them five talents moe. *2770*
25:22 I have **g** two other talents besides them. *2770*
Lk 19:15 how much every *man* had **g by trading**. *1281*
19:16 saying, Lord, thy pound hath **g** ten pounds. *4333*
19:18 saying, Lord, thy pound hath **g** five pounds. *4160*
Ac 27:21 and to have **g** this harm and loss. *2770*

GAINS (1) [GAIN]
Ac 16:19 saw that the hope of their **g** was gone, *2039*

GAINSAY (1) [GAINSAYERS, GAINSAYING, SAY]
Lk 21:15 adversaries shall not be able to **g** nor resist. *471*

GAINSAYERS (1) [GAINSAY]
Tit 1: 9 both to exhort and to convince the **g**. *483*

GAINSAYING (3) [GAINSAY]
Ac 10:29 Therefore came I *unto you* **without g**, *369*
Ro 10:21 my hands unto a disobedient and **g** people. *483*
Jude 1:11 for reward, and perished in the **g** of Core. *485*

GAIUS (5)
Ac 19:29 and having caught **G** and Aristarchus, *1050*
20: 4 and **G** of Derbe, and Timotheus; and *1050*
Ro 16:23 **G** mine host, and of the whole church, *1050*
1Co 1:14 I baptized none of you, but Crispus and **G**; *1050*
3Jn 1: 1 The elder unto the wellbeloved **G**, whom I *1050*

GALAL (3)
1Ch 9:15 and **G**, and Mattaniah the son of Micah, 1559
9:16 the son of **G**, the son of Jeduthun, and 1559
Ne 11:17 the son of **G**, the son of Jeduthun. 1559

GALATIA (6) [GALATIANS]
Ac 16: 6 throughout Phrygia and the region **of G**, *1054*
18:23 and went over *all* the country **of G** and *1054*
1Co 16: 1 as I have given order to the churches of **G**, *1053*
Gal 1: 2 which are with me, unto the churches of **G**: *1053*
2Ti 4:10 Crescens to **G**, Titus unto Dalmatia. *1053*
1Pe 1: 1 **G**, Cappadocia, Asia, and Bithynia, *1053*

GALATIANS (2) [GALATIA]
Gal 3: 1 O foolish **G**, who hath bewitched you, *1052*
6: S Unto the **G** written from Rome. *1052*

GALBANUM (1)
Ex 30:34 sweet spices, stacte, and onycha, and **g**; 2464

GALEED (2)
Ge 31:47 it Jegar-sahadutha: but Jacob called it **G**. 1567
31:48 Therefore was the name of it called **G**; 1567

GALILEAN (3) [GALILEE]
Mk 14:70 for thou art a **G**, and thy speech agreeth *1057*
Lk 22:59 this *fellow* also was with him: for he is a **G**. *1057*
23: 6 he asked whether the man were a **G**. *1057*

GALILEANS (5) [GALILEE]
Lk 13: 1 at that season some that told him of the **G**, *1057*
13: 2 Suppose ye that these **G** were sinners above *1057*
13: 2 Galileans were sinners above all the **G**, *1057*
Jn 4:45 was come into Galilee, the **G** received him, *1057*
Ac 2: 7 Behold, are not all these which speak **G**? *1057*

GALILEE (72) [GALILEAN, GALILEANS]
Jos 20: 7 they appointed Kedesh in **G** in mount 1551
21:32 of Naphtali, Kedesh in **G** with her suburbs, 1551
1Ki 9:11 gave Hiram twenty cities in the land of **G**. 1551
2Ki 15:29 and Kedesh, and Hazor, and Gilead, and **G**, 1551
1Ch 6:76 Kedesh in **G** with her suburbs, and 1551
Isa 9: 1 the sea, beyond Jordan, in **G** of the nations. 1551
Mt 2:22 he turned aside into the parts of **G**: *1056*
3:13 Then cometh Jesus from **G** to Jordan unto *1056*
4:12 was cast into prison, he departed into **G**; *1056*
4:15 the sea, beyond Jordan, **G** of the Gentiles; *1056*
4:18 And Jesus, walking by the sea of **G**, *1056*
4:23 And Jesus went about all **G**, teaching in *1056*
4:25 him great multitudes *of people* from **G**, *1056*
15:29 and came nigh unto the sea of **G**; *1056*
17:22 And while they abode in **G**, Jesus said unto *1056*
19: 1 he departed from **G**, and came into *1056*
21:11 This is Jesus the prophet of Nazareth of **G**. *1056*
26:32 am risen *again*, I will go before you into **G**. *1056*
26:69 saying, Thou also wast with Jesus **of G**. *1057*
27:55 which followed Jesus from **G**, *1056*
28: 7 and behold, he goeth before you into **G**; *1056*
28:10 go tell my brethren that they go into **G**, and *1056*
28:16 the eleven disciples went *away* into **G**, *1056*
Mk 1: 9 *that* Jesus came from Nazareth of **G**, and *1056*
1:14 John was put in prison, Jesus came into **G**, *1056*
1:16 Now as he walked by the sea of **G**, he saw *1056*
1:28 throughout all the region round about **G**. *1056*
1:39 in their synagogues throughout all **G**, *1056*
3: 7 and a great multitude from **G** followed him, *1056*
6:21 high captains, and chief *estates* of **G**; *1056*
7:31 and Sidon, he came unto the sea of **G**, *1056*
9:30 departed thence, and passed through **G**; *1056*
14:28 that I am risen, I will go before you into **G**. *1056*
15:41 (Who also, when he was in **G**, *1056*
16: 7 and Peter that he goeth before you into **G**: *1056*
Lk 1:26 was sent from God unto a city of **G**, *1056*

G

Lk 2: 4 And Joseph also went up from G, out of 1056
2:39 they returned into G, to their own city 1056
3: 1 and Herod being tetrarch of G, and 1056
4:14 returned in the power of the Spirit into G: 1056
4:31 a city of G, and taught them on the sabbath 1056
4:44 And he preached in the synagogues of G. 1056
5:17 which were come out of every town of G, 1056
8:26 of the Gadarenes, which is over against G. 1056
17:11 passed through the midst of Samaria and G. 1056
23: 5 all Jewry, beginning from G to this place. 1056
23: 6 When Pilate heard of G, he asked whether 1056
23:49 and the women that followed him from G, 1056
23:55 which came with him from G, 1056
24: 6 he spake unto you when he was yet in G, 1056
Jn 1:43 day following Jesus would go forth into G, 1056
2: 1 day there was a marriage in Cana of G; 1056
2:11 of miracles did Jesus in Cana of G, 1056
4: 3 He left Judea, and departed again into G. 1056
4:43 days he departed thence, and went into G. 1056
4:45 Then when he was come into G, 1056
4:46 So Jesus came again into Cana of G, 1056
4:47 that Jesus was come out of Judea into G, 1056
4:54 when he was come out of Judea into G. 1056
6: 1 these *things* Jesus went over the sea of G, 1056
7: 1 After these *things* Jesus walked in G: for he 1056
7: 9 these *words* unto them, he abode *still* in G. 1056
7:41 But some said, Shall Christ come out of G? 1056
7:52 and said unto him, Art thou also of G? 1056
7:52 and look: for out of G ariseth no prophet. 1056
12:21 which was of Bethsaida of G, and 1056
21: 2 and Nathanael of Cana in G, and the *sons* 1056
Ac 1:11 Which also said, Ye men of G, why stand 1057
5:37 After this *man* rose up Judas of G 1057
9:31 throughout all Judea and G and Samaria, 1056
10:37 and began from G, after the baptism which 1056
13:31 came up with him from G to Jerusalem, 1056

GALL (14)
Dt 29:18 should be among you a root that beareth g 7219
32:32 their grapes *are* grapes of g, their clusters 7219
Job 16:13 he poureth out my g upon the ground. 4845
20:14 is turned, *it is* the g of asps within him. 4846
20:25 the glistering sword cometh out of his g: 4846
Ps 69:21 They gave me also g for my meat; and 7219
Jer 8:14 given us water of g to drink, because 7219
9:15 and give them water of g to drink. 7219
23:15 and make them drink the water of g: 7219
La 3: 5 and compassed *me* with g and travail. 7219
3:19 and my misery, the wormwood and the g. 7219
Am 6:12 for ye have turned judgment into g, and 7219
Mt 27:34 gave him vinegar to drink mingled with g: 5521
Ac 8:23 For I perceive that thou art in the g of 5521

GALLANT (1)
Isa 33:21 with oars, neither shall g ship pass thereby. 117

GALLERIES (4) [GALLERY]
SS 7: 5 head like purple; the king *is* held in the g. 7298
Eze 41:15 the g thereof on the one side and on the other 862
41:16 the g round about on their three *stories,* over 862
42: 5 for the g were higher than these, than 862

GALLERY (2) [GALLERIES]
Eze 42: 3 *was* g against gallery in three *stories.* 862
42: 3 *was* gallery against g in three *stories.* 862

GALLEY (1)
Isa 33:21 wherein shall go no g with oars, neither shall 590

GALLIM (2)
1Sa 25:44 to Phalti the son of Laish, which *was* of G. 1554
Isa 10:30 Lift up thy voice, O daughter of G: cause *it* 1530

GALLIO (3)
Ac 18:12 And when G was the deputy of Achaia, 1058
18:14 G said unto the Jews, If it were a matter of 1058
18:17 And G cared for none of those *things.* 1058

GALLONS See FIRKINS

GALLOWS (8)
Est 5:14 Let a g be made of fifty cubits high, and to 6086
5:14 and he caused the g to be made. 6086
6: 4 on the g that he had prepared for him. 6086
7: 9 Behold also, the g fifty cubits high, 6086
7:10 So they hanged Haman on the g that he had 6086
8: 7 him they have hanged upon the g, because 6086
9:13 let Haman's ten sons be hanged upon the g. 6086
9:25 and his sons should be hanged on the g. 6086

GAMALIEL (7)
Nu 1:10 of Manasseh; G the son of Pedahzur. 1583
2:20 Manasseh *shall be* G the son of Pedahzur. 1583
7:54 On the eighth day *offered* G the son of 1583
7:59 this *was* the offering of G the son of 1583
10:23 of Manasseh *was* G the son of Pedahzur. 1583
Ac 5:34 a Pharisee, named G, a doctor of law, 1059
22: 3 yet brought up in this city at the feet of G, 1059

GAME See VENISON

GAMMAD See GAMMADIMS

GAMMADIMS (1)
Eze 27:11 round about, and the G were in thy towers: 1575

GAMUL (1) [BETH-GAMUL]
1Ch 24:17 to Jachin, the two and twentieth to G, 1577

GANGRENE See CANKER

GAP (1) [GAPS]
Eze 22:30 stand in the g before me for the land, that *I* 6556

GAPED (2)
Job 16:10 They have g upon me with their mouth; 6473
Ps 22:13 They g upon me *with* their mouths, *as* a 6475

GAPS (1) [GAP]
Eze 13: 5 Ye have not gone up into the g, 6556

GARDEN (52) [GARDENER, GARDENS]
Ge 2: 8 the LORD God planted a g eastward in 1588
2: 9 the tree of life also in the midst of the g, 1588
2:10 a river went out of Eden to water the g; 1588
2:15 put him into the g of Eden to dress it and 1588
2:16 Of every tree of the g thou mayest freely 1588
3: 1 Ye shall not eat of every tree of the g? 1588
3: 2 We may eat of the fruit of the trees of the g: 1588
3: 3 of the tree which *is* in the midst of the g, 1588
3: 8 God walking in the g in the cool of the day: 1588
3: 8 the LORD God amongst the trees of the g. 1588
3:10 I heard thy voice in the g, and I was afraid, 1588
3:23 God sent him forth from the g of Eden, 1588
3:24 he placed at the east of the g of Eden 1588
13:10 *even* as the g of the LORD, 1588
Dt 11:10 wateredst *it* with thy foot, as a g of herbs: 1588
1Ki 21: 2 that I may have it for a g of herbs, because 1588
2Ki 9:27 saw *this,* he fled *by* the way of the g house. 1588
21:18 was buried in the g of his own house, in 1588
21:18 garden of his own house, in the g of Uzza: 1588
21:26 he was buried in his sepulchre in the g of 1588
25: 4 two walls, which *is* by the king's g: 1588
Ne 3:15 wall of the pool of Siloah by the king's g, 1588
Est 1: 5 in the court of the g of the king's palace; 1594
7: 7 of wine in his wrath *went* into the palace g: 1594
7: 8 the king returned out of the palace g into 1594
Job 8:16 and his branch shooteth forth in his g, 1593
SS 4:12 A g inclosed *is* my sister, *my* spouse; 1588
4:16 blow upon my g, *that* the spices thereof 1588
4:16 Let my beloved come into his g, and eat his 1588
5: 1 I am come into my g, my sister, *my* spouse: 1588
6: 2 My beloved is gone down into his g, to 1588
6:11 I went down into the g of nuts to see 1594
Isa 1: 8 as a lodge in a g of cucumbers, as a 4750
1:30 leaf fadeth, and as a g that hath no water. 1593
51: 3 and her desert like the g of the LORD; 1588
58:11 thou shalt be like a watered g, and like a 1588
61:11 as the g causeth the things that are sown in 1593
Jer 31:12 their soul shall be as a watered g; and 1588
39: 4 *by* the way of the king's g, by the gate 1588
52: 7 the two walls, which *was* by the king's g; 1588
La 2: 6 away his tabernacle, as *if it were of* a g: 1588
Eze 28:13 Thou hast been in Eden the g of God; 1588
31: 8 The cedars in the g of God could not hide 1588
31: 8 nor any tree in the g of God was like unto 1588
31: 9 that *were* in the g of God, envied him. 1588
36:35 was desolate is become like the g of Eden; 1588
Joel 2: 3 the land *is* as the g of Eden before them, 1588
Lk 13:19 which a man took, and cast into his g; 2779
Jn 18: 1 where was a g, into the which he entered, 2779

Jn 18:26 saith, Did not I see thee in the **g** with him? *2779*
19:41 place where he was crucified there was a **g**; *2779*
19:41 and in the **g** a new sepulchre, wherein was *2779*

GARDENER (1) [GARDEN]
Jn 20:15 She, supposing him to be the **g**, saith unto *2780*

GARDENS (12) [GARDEN]
Nu 24: 6 are they spread forth, as **g** by the river side, 1593
Ecc 2: 5 I made me **g** and orchards, and I planted 1593
SS 4:15 A fountain of **g**, a well of living waters, and 1588
6: 2 to feed in the **g**, and to gather lilies. 1588
8:13 Thou that dwellest in the **g**, the companions 1588
Isa 1:29 ye shall be confounded for the **g** that ye 1593
65: 3 that sacrificeth in **g**, and burneth incense 1593
66:17 purify themselves in the **g** behind one *tree* 1593
Jer 29: 5 dwell *in them;* and plant **g**, and eat the fruit 1593
29:28 dwell *in them;* and plant **g**, and eat the fruit 1593
Am 4: 9 when your **g** and your vineyards and 1593
9:14 they shall also make **g**, and eat the fruit of 1593

GAREB (3)
2Sa 23:38 Ira an Ithrite, **G** an Ithrite, 1619
1Ch 11:40 Ira the Ithrite, **G** the Ithrite, 1619
Jer 31:39 yet go forth over against it upon the hill **G**, 1619

GARLANDS (1)
Ac 14:13 brought oxen and **g** unto the gates, and *4725*

GARLICK (1)
Nu 11: 5 and the leeks, and the onions, and the **g**: 7762

GARMENT (86) [GARMENTS]
Ge 9:23 Shem and Japheth took a **g**, and laid *it* upon 8071
25:25 the first came out red, all over like a hairy **g**; 155
39:12 she caught him by his **g**, saying, Lie with 899
39:12 he left his **g** in her hand, and fled, and 899
39:13 when she saw that he had left his **g** in her 899
39:15 that he left his **g** with me, and fled, and 899
39:16 she laid up his **g** by her, until his lord came 899
39:18 cried, that he left his **g** with me, and fled out. 899
Lev 6:10 the priest shall put on his linen **g**, and 4055
6:27 is sprinkled of the blood thereof upon *any* **g**, 899
13:47 The **g** also that the plague of leprosy is in, 899
13:47 *whether it be* a woollen **g**, or a linen 899
13:47 *it be* a woollen garment, or a linen **g**; 899
13:49 *if* the plague be greenish or reddish in the **g**, 899
13:51 if the plague be spread in the **g**, either in 899
13:52 He shall therefore burn *that* **g**, whether warp 899
13:53 behold, the plague be not spread in the **g**, 899
13:56 he shall rend it out of the **g**, or out of 899
13:57 if it appear still in the **g**, either in the warp, 899
13:58 the **g**, either warp, or woof, or 899
13:59 This *is* the law of the plague of leprosy in a **g** 899
14:55 And for the leprosy of a **g**, and of a house, 899
15:17 every **g**, and every skin, whereon is the seed 899
19:19 neither shall a **g** mingled of linen and 899
Dt 22: 5 neither shall a man put on a woman's **g**: 8071
22:11 Thou shalt not wear a **g of divers sorts**, 8162
Jos 7:21 among the spoils a goodly Babylonish **g**, 155
7:24 the **g**, and the wedge of gold, and his sons, 155
Jdg 8:25 willingly give *them.* And they spread a **g**, 8071
2Sa 13:18 *she had* a **g** of divers colours upon her: 3801
13:19 rent her **g** of divers colours that *was* on her, 3801
20: 8 Joab's **g** that he had put on *was* girded unto 4055
1Ki 11:29 he had clad himself with a new **g**; and 8008
11:30 Ahijah caught the new **g** that *was* on him, 8008
2Ki 9:13 took every man his **g**, and put *it* under him 899
Ezr 9: 3 I rent my **g** and my mantle, and pluckt off 899
9: 5 having rent my **g** and my mantle, I fell upon 899
Est 8:15 and *with* a **g** of fine linen and purple: 8509
Job 13:28 consumeth, as a **g** that is moth-eaten. 899
30:18 By the great force *of my disease* is my **g** 3830
38: 9 When I made the cloud the **g** thereof, and 3830
38:14 as clay *to* the seal; and they stand as a **g**. 3830
41:13 Who can discover the face of his **g**? *or* 3830
Ps 69:11 I made sackcloth also my **g**; and I became a 3830
73: 6 as a chain; violence covereth them *as* a **g**. 7897
102:26 yea, all of them shall wax old like a **g**; as a 899
104: 2 Who coverest *thyself with* light as *with* a **g**: 8008
104: 6 Thou coveredst it *with* the deep as *with* a **g**: 3830
109:18 himself with cursing like as with his **g**, 4055
109:19 Let it be unto him as the **g** *which* covereth 899
Pr 20:16 Take his **g** that is surety *for* a stranger: and 899
25:20 *As* he that taketh away a **g** in cold weather, 899
27:13 Take his **g** that is surety *for* a stranger, and 899
30: 4 who hath bound the waters in a **g**? 8071
Isa 50: 9 lo, they all shall wax old as a **g**; the moth 899
51: 6 the earth shall wax old like a **g**, and they that 899
51: 8 For the moth shall eat them up like a **g**, and 899
61: 3 the **g** of praise for the spirit of heaviness; 4594
Jer 43:12 land of Egypt, as a shepherd putteth on his **g**; 899
Eze 18: 7 and hath covered the naked with a **g**; 899
18:16 and hath covered the naked with a **g**, 899
Da 7: 9 whose **g** *was* white as snow, and the hair of 3831
Mic 2: 8 ye pull off the robe with the **g** from them 8008
Hag 2:12 If one bear holy flesh in the skirt of his **g**, 899
Zec 13: 4 neither shall they wear a rough **g** to deceive: 155
Mal 2:16 for *one* covereth violence with his **g**, 3830
Mt 9:16 putteth a piece of new cloth unto an old **g**; *2440*
9:16 is put in to fill it up taketh from the **g**, *2440*
9:20 behind *him,* and touched the hem of his **g**: *2440*
9:21 If I may but touch his **g**, I shall be whole. *2440*
14:36 that they might only touch the hem of his **g**: *2440*
22:11 there a man which had not on a wedding **g**: *1742*
22:12 thou in hither not having a wedding **g**? *1742*
Mk 2:21 seweth a piece of new cloth on an old **g**: *2440*
5:27 in the press behind, and touched his **g**. *2440*
6:56 touch if it were but the border of his **g**: *2440*
10:50 casting away his **g**, rose, and came to Jesus. *2440*
13:16 not turn back again for to take up his **g**. *2440*
16: 5 on the right side, clothed in a **long** white **g**; *4749*
Lk 5:36 No *man* putteth a piece of a new **g** upon an *2440*
8:44 and touched the border of his **g**: *2440*
22:36 no sword, let him sell his **g**, and buy one. *2440*
Ac 12: 8 Cast thy **g** about thee, and follow me. *2440*
Heb 1:11 and they all shall wax old as *doth* a **g**; *2440*
Jude 1:23 hating even the **g** spotted by the flesh. *5509*
Rev 1:13 **clothed with a g** down to the foot, and *1746*

GARMENTS (103) [GARMENT]
Ge 35: 2 and be clean, and change your **g**: 8071
38:14 And she put her widow's **g** off from her, and 899
38:19 and put on the **g** of her widowhood. 899
49:11 he washed his **g** in wine, and his clothes in 3830
Ex 28: 2 thou shalt make holy **g** for Aaron thy 899
28: 3 that they may make Aaron's **g** to consecrate 899
28: 4 these *are* the **g** which they shall make; 899
28: 4 they shall make holy **g** for Aaron thy 899
29: 5 thou shalt take the **g**, and put upon Aaron 899
29:21 upon his **g**, and upon his sons, and upon 899
29:21 and upon the **g** of his sons with him: 899
29:21 his **g**, and his sons, and his sons' garments 899
29:21 and his sons, and his sons' **g** with him. 899
29:29 the holy **g** of Aaron shall be his sons' after 899
31:10 the holy **g** for Aaron the priest, and 899
31:10 the **g** of his sons, to minister in the priest's 899
35:19 to do service in the holy *place,* the holy **g** for 899
35:19 the **g** of his sons, to minister in the priest's 899
35:21 and for all his service, and for the holy **g**. 899
39: 1 holy *place,* and made the holy **g** for Aaron; 899
39:41 and the holy **g** for Aaron the priest, 899
39:41 his sons' **g**, to minister in the priest's office. 899
40:13 thou shalt put upon Aaron the holy **g**, and 899
Lev 6:11 he shall put off his **g**, and put on other 899
6:11 put on other **g**, and carry forth the ashes 899
8: 2 the **g**, and the anointing oil, and a bullock *for* 899
8:30 *and* upon his **g**, and upon his sons, and 899
8:30 his sons, and upon his sons' **g** with him; 899
8:30 *and* his **g**, and his sons, and his sons' 899
8:30 and his sons, and his sons' **g** with him. 899
16: 4 these *are* holy **g**; therefore shall he wash his 899
16:23 shall put off the linen **g**, which he put on 899
16:24 put on his **g**, and come forth, and offer his 899
16:32 put on the linen clothes, *even* the holy **g**: 899
21:10 that is consecrated to put on the **g**, shall not 899
Nu 15:38 of their **g** throughout their generations, 899
20:26 strip Aaron of his **g**, and put them upon 899
20:28 Moses stripped Aaron of his **g**, and put them 899
Jos 9: 5 upon their feet, and old **g** upon them; 8008
9:13 these our **g** and our shoes are become old 8008
Jdg 14:12 give you thirty sheets and thirty change of **g**: 899
14:13 give me thirty sheets and thirty change of **g**. 899
14:19 gave change *of* **g** unto them which NIH
1Sa 18: 4 gave it to David, and his **g**, even to his 4055
2Sa 10: 4 cut off their **g** in the middle, *even* to their 4063
13:31 and tare his **g**, and lay on the earth; 899
1Ki 10:25 **g**, and armour, and spices, horses, and 8008
2Ki 5:22 a talent of silver, and two changes of **g**. 899

2Ki 5:23 with two changes of g, and laid *them* upon 899
5:26 to receive g, and oliveyards, and vineyards, 899
7:15 and lo, all the way *was* full *of* g and vessels, 899
25:29 changed his prison g: and he did eat bread 899
1Ch 19: 4 cut off their g in the midst hard by *their* 4063
Ezr 2:69 pound *of* silver, and one hundred priests' g. 3801
Ne 7:70 five hundred and thirty priests' g. 3801
7:72 and threescore and seven priests' g. 3801
Job 37:17 How thy g *are* warm, when he quieteth 899
Ps 22:18 They part my g among them, and cast lots 899
45: 8 All thy g *smell of* myrrh, and aloes, *and* 899
133: 2 that went down to the skirts of his g; 4060
Ecc 9: 8 Let thy g be always white; and let thy head 899
SS 4:11 the smell of thy g *is* like the smell of 8008
Isa 9: 5 with confused noise, and g rolled in blood; 8071
52: 1 put on thy beautiful g, O Jerusalem, the holy 899
59: 6 Their webs shall not become g, neither shall 899
59:17 he put on the g of vengeance *for* clothing, 899
61:10 for he hath clothed me with the g of 899
63: 1 from Edom, with dyed g from Bozrah? 899
63: 2 thy g like him that treadeth in the winefat? 899
63: 3 their blood shall be sprinkled upon my g, 899
Jer 36:24 not afraid, nor rent their g, *neither* the king, 899
52:33 changed his prison g: and he did continually 899
La 4:14 so that *men* could not touch their g. 3830
Eze 16:16 of thy g thou didst take, and deckedst thy 899
16:18 tookest thy broidered g, and coveredst them: 899
26:16 their robes, and put off their broidered g: 899
42:14 there they shall lay their g wherein they 899
42:14 shall put on other g, and shall approach to 899
44:17 they shall be clothed with linen g; 899
44:19 they shall put off their g wherein they 899
44:19 holy chambers, and they shall put on other g; 899
44:19 shall not sanctify the people with their g. 899
Da 3:21 their *other* g, and were cast into the midst 3831
Joel 2:13 not your g, and turn unto the LORD your 899
Zec 3: 3 Now Joshua was clothed with filthy g, and 899
3: 4 Take away the filthy g from him. 899
3: 5 mitre upon his head, and clothed him with g. 899
Mt 21: 8 And a very great multitude spread their g in *2440*
23: 5 and enlarge the borders of their g, *2440*
27:35 crucified him, and parted his g, casting lots: *2440*
27:35 They parted my g among them, and *2440*
Mk 11: 7 the colt to Jesus, and cast their g on him; *2440*
11: 8 And many spread their g in the way: and *2440*
15:24 they parted his g, casting lots upon them, *2440*
Lk 19:35 and they cast their g upon the colt, and *2440*
24: 4 two men stood by them in shining g: *2067*
Jn 13: 4 He riseth from supper, and laid aside *his* g; *2440*
13:12 and had taken his g, and was set down *2440*
19:23 took his g, and made four parts, to every *2440*
Ac 9:39 the coats and g which Dorcas made, *2440*
Jas 5: 2 are corrupted, and your g are motheaten. *2440*
Rev 3: 4 in Sardis, which have not defiled their g; *2440*
16:15 and keepeth his g, lest he walk naked, and *2440*

GARMITE (1)
1Ch 4:19 the father of Keilah the G, and 1636

GARNER (2) [GARNERS]
Mt 3:12 his floor, and gather his wheat into the g; *596*
Lk 3:17 and will gather the wheat into his g; *596*

GARNERS (2) [GARNER]
Ps 144:13 *That* our g *may be* full, affording all 4200
Joel 1:17 the g are laid desolate, the barns are broken 214

GARNISH (1) [GARNISHED]
Mt 23:29 and g the sepulchres of the righteous, *2885*

GARNISHED (5) [GARNISH]
2Ch 3: 6 he g the house with precious stones for 6823
Job 26:13 By his spirit he hath g the heavens; 8235
Mt 12:44 is come, he findeth *it* empty, swept, and g. *2885*
Lk 11:25 when he cometh, he findeth *it* swept and g. *2885*
Rev 21:19 *were* g with all *manner of* precious stones. *2885*

GARRISON (13) [GARRISONS]
1Sa 10: 5 of God, where *is* the g of the Philistines: 5333
13: 3 Jonathan smote the g of the Philistines that 5333
13: 4 *that* Saul had smitten a g of the Philistines, 5333
13:23 the g of the Philistines went out to 4673
14: 1 and let us go over to the Philistines' g, 4673
14: 4 sought to go over unto the Philistines' g, 4673
14: 6 let us go over unto the g of these 4673
14:11 themselves unto the g of the Philistines: 4673
14:12 the men of the g answered Jonathan and 4675
14:15 the g, and the spoilers, they also trembled, 4673
2Sa 23:14 the g of the Philistines *was* then 4673
1Ch 11:16 the Philistines' g *was* then at Beth-lehem. 5333
2Co 11:32 *with a* g, desirous to apprehend me: NIG

GARRISONS (7) [GARRISON]
2Sa 8: 6 David put g in Syria of Damascus: and 5333
8:14 he put g in Edom; throughout all Edom put 5333
8:14 throughout all Edom put he g, and all they 5333
1Ch 18: 6 David put *g* in Syria-damascus; and NIH
18:13 he put g in Edom; and all the Edomites 5333
2Ch 17: 2 set g in the land of Judah, and in the cities 5333
Eze 26:11 thy strong g shall go down to the ground. 4676

GASHMU (1) [GESHEM]
Ne 6: 6 G saith *it, that* thou and the Jews think to 1654

GAT (20) [GET]
Ge 19:27 Abraham **g up early** in the morning to 7925
Ex 24:18 of the cloud, and g him **up** into the mount: 5927
Nu 11:30 Moses g him into the camp, he and 622
14:40 g them **up** into the top of the mountain, 5927
16:27 So they g **up** from the tabernacle of Korah, 5927
Jdg 9:48 Abimelech g him **up** *to* mount Zalmon, 5927
9:51 g them **up** to the top of the tower. 5927
19:28 the man rose up, and g him unto his place. 1980
1Sa 13:15 g him **up** from Gilgal *unto* Gibeah of 5927
24:22 and his men g them **up** unto the hold. 5927
26:12 they g them **away**, and no man saw *it*, nor 1980
2Sa 4: 7 g them **away** through the plain all night. 1980
8:13 David g *him* a name when he returned from 6213
13:29 every man g him **up** upon his mule, and 7392
17:23 arose, and g him *home* to his house, to his 1980
19: 3 the people g them by stealth that day *into* 935
1Ki 1: 1 covered him with clothes, but he g **no heat**. 3179
Ps 116: 3 and the pains of hell g **hold upon** me: 4672
Ecc 2: 8 I g me *men* singers and *women* singers, and 6213
La 5: 9 We g our bread with *the peril of* our lives 935

GATAM (3)
Ge 36:11 Omar, Zepho, and G, and Kenaz. 1609
36:16 Duke Korah, duke G, *and* duke Amalek: 1609
1Ch 1:36 Omar, Zephi, and G, Kenaz, and Timna, 1609

GATE (275) [GATES]
Ge 19: 1 at even; and Lot sat in the g of Sodom: 8179
22:17 thy seed shall possess the g of his enemies; 8179
23:10 *even* of all that went in *at* the g of his city, 8179
23:18 before all that went in *at* the g of his city. 8179
24:60 let thy seed possess the g of those which 8179
28:17 house of God, and this *is* the g of heaven. 8179
34:20 Shechem his son came unto the g of their 8179
34:24 all that went out of the g of his city; 8179
34:24 all that went out of the g of his city. 8179
Ex 27:14 The hangings of *one* side *of the g shall be* NIH
27:16 for the g of the court *shall be* a hanging of 8179
32:26 Then Moses stood in the g of the camp, and 8179
32:27 out from g to gate throughout the camp, 8179
32:27 out from gate to g throughout the camp, 8179
38:14 The hangings of the *one* side *of the g were* NIH
38:15 for the other side of the court g, on this 8179
38:18 the hanging for the g of the court *was* 8179
38:31 the sockets of the court g, and all the pins 8179
39:40 the hanging for the court g, his cords, and 8179
40: 8 and hang up the hanging at the court g. 8179
40:33 and set up the hanging of the court g. 8179
Nu 4:26 the hanging for the door of the g of 8179
Dt 21:19 of his city, and unto the g of his place; 8179
22:15 virginity unto the elders of the city in the g: 8179
22:24 ye shall bring them both out unto the g of 8179
25: 7 let his brother's wife go up to the g unto 8179
Jos 2: 5 to pass *about the time* of shutting of the g, 8179
2: 7 after them were gone out, they shut the g. 8179
7: 5 for they chased them *from* before the g 8179
8:29 cast it at the entering of the g of the city, 8179
20: 4 stand *at* the entering of the g of the city, 8179
Jdg 9:35 stood *in* the entering of the g of the city: 8179
9:40 wounded, *even* unto the entering of the g. 8179
9:44 stood *in* the entering of the g of the city: 8179
16: 2 laid wait for him all night in the g of 8179
16: 3 took the doors of the g of the city, and 8179
18:16 of Dan, stood *by* the entering of the g. 8179

Jdg 18:17 the priest stood *in* the entering of the **g** with 8179
Ru 4: 1 went Boaz up *to* the **g**, and sat him down 8179
4:10 his brethren, and from the **g** of his place: 8179
4:11 all the people that *were* in the **g**, and 8179
1Sa 4:18 off the seat backward by the side of the **g**, 8179
9:18 Saul drew near to Samuel in the **g**, and 8179
21:13 scrabled on the doors of the **g**, and let his 8179
2Sa 3:27 Joab took him aside in the **g** to speak with 8179
10: 8 battle in array *at* the entering in of the **g**: 8179
11:23 upon them *even* unto the entering of the **g**. 8179
15: 2 up early, and stood beside the way of the **g**: 8179
18: 4 the king stood by the **g** side, and all 8179
18:24 went *up* to the roof over the **g** unto the wall, 8179
18:33 went up to the chamber over the **g**, and 8179
19: 8 the king rose, and sat in the **g**. And they 8179
19: 8 Behold, the king doth sit in the **g**. 8179
23:15 the well of Beth-lehem, which *is* by the **g**. 8179
23:16 that *was* by the **g**, and took *it*, and 8179
1Ki 17:10 when he came to the **g** of the city, behold, 6607
22:10 in a void place *in* the entrance of the **g** of 8179
2Ki 7: 1 of barley for a shekel, in the **g** of Samaria. 8179
7: 3 four leprous men *at* the entering in of the **g**: 8179
7:17 hand he leaned to have the charge of the **g**: 8179
7:17 the people trode upon him in the **g**, and 8179
7:18 shall be to morrow about *this* time in the **g** 8179
7:20 for the people trode upon him in the **g**, and 8179
9:31 as Jehu entered in at the **g**, she said, *Had* 8179
10: 8 *at* the entering in of the **g** until the morning. 8179
11: 6 And a third *part shall be* at the **g** of Sur; and 8179
11: 6 and a third *part* at the **g** behind the guard: 8179
11:19 came *by* the way of the **g** of the guard *to* 8179
14:13 from the **g** of Ephraim unto the corner gate, 8179
14:13 from the gate of Ephraim unto the corner **g**, 8179
15:35 He built the higher **g** of the house of 8179
23: 8 of the **g** of Joshua the governor of the city, 8179
23: 8 which *were* on a man's left hand at the **g** of 8179
25: 4 *by* the way of the **g** between two walls, 8179
1Ch 9:18 Who hitherto *waited* in the king's **g** 8179
11:17 of the well of Beth-lehem, that *is* at the **g**. 8179
11:18 that *was* by the **g**, and took *it*, and 8179
19: 9 put the battle in array *before* the **g** of 6607
26:13 of their fathers, for **every g**. 8179+8179+2050.1
26:16 with the **g** Shallecheth, by the causeway of 8179
2Ch 8:14 by their courses at **every g**: 8179+8179+2050.1
18: 9 place *at* the entering in of the **g** of Samaria; 8179
23: 5 and a third *part* at the **g** of the foundation: 8179
23:15 entering of the horse **g** *by* the king's house, 8179
23:20 they came through the high **g** *into* 8179
24: 8 set it without at the **g** of the house of 8179
25:23 from the **g** of Ephraim to the corner gate, 8179
25:23 from the gate of Ephraim to the corner **g**, 8179
26: 9 built towers in Jerusalem at the corner **g**, 8179
26: 9 at the valley **g**, and at the turning *of* 8179
27: 3 He built the high **g** of the house of 8179
32: 6 to him in the street of the **g** of the city, 8179
33:14 even to the entering in at the fish **g**, and 8179
35:15 porters *waited* at **every g**; 8179+8179+2050.1
Ne 2:13 I went out by night by the **g** of the valley, 8179
2:14 I went on to the **g** of the fountain, and 8179
2:15 entered by the **g** of the valley, and *so* 8179
3: 1 the priests, and they built the sheep **g**; 8179
3: 3 the fish **g** did the sons of Hassenaah build, 8179
3: 6 Moreover the old **g** repaired Jehoiada 8179
3:13 The valley **g** repaired Hanun, and 8179
3:13 cubits on the wall unto the dung **g**. 8179
3:14 the dung **g** repaired Malchiah the son of 8179
3:15 the **g** of the fountain repaired Shallun 8179
3:26 unto *the place* over against the water **g** 8179
3:28 From above the horse **g** repaired the priests, 8179
3:29 son of Shechaniah, the keeper of the east **g**. 8179
3:31 over against the **g** Miphkad, and to 8179
3:32 unto the sheep **g** repaired the goldsmiths 8179
8: 1 into the street that *was* before the water **g**; 8179
8: 3 the water **g** from the morning until midday, 8179
8:16 in the street of the water **g**, and in the street 8179
8:16 and in the street of the **g** of Ephraim. 8179
12:31 right hand upon the wall toward the dung **g**: 8179
12:37 at the fountain **g**, which *was* over against 8179
12:37 of David, even unto the water **g** east*ward*. 8179
12:39 from above the **g** of Ephraim, and 8179
12:39 above the old **g**, and above the fish gate, 8179
12:39 above the fish **g**, and the tower of 8179
12:39 the tower of Meah, even unto the sheep **g**: 8179
12:39 and they stood still in the prison **g**. 8179
Est 2:19 then Mordecai sat in the king's **g**. 8179
2:21 while Mordecai sat in the king's **g**, 8179
3: 2 that *were* in the king's **g**, bowed, and 8179
3: 3 which *were* in the king's **g**, said unto 8179
4: 2 came even before the king's **g**: for none 8179
4: 2 for none might enter into the king's **g** 8179
4: 6 of the city, which *was* before the king's **g**. 8179
5: 1 over against the **g** of the house. 6607
5: 9 when Haman saw Mordecai in the king's **g**, 8179
5:13 see Mordecai the Jew sitting at the king's **g**. 8179
6:10 the Jew, that sitteth at the king's **g**: 8179
6:12 Mordecai came again to the king's **g**. 8179
Job 5: 4 from safety, and they are crushed in the **g**, 8179
29: 7 When I went out *to* the **g** through the city, 8179
31:21 the fatherless, when I saw my help in the **g**: 8179
Ps 69:12 They that sit in the **g** speak against me; and 8179
118:20 This **g** of the LORD, into which 8179
127: 5 they shall speak with the enemies in the **g**. 8179
Pr 17:19 he that exalteth his **g** seeketh destruction. 6607
22:22 neither oppress the afflicted in the **g**: 8179
24: 7 a fool: he openeth not his mouth in the **g**. 8179
SS 7: 4 in Heshbon, by the **g** of Bath-rabbim: 8179
Isa 14:31 Howl, O **g**; cry, O city; thou, 8179
22: 7 shall set themselves in array at the **g**. 8179
24:12 and the **g** is smitten *with* destruction. 8179
28: 6 strength to them that turn the battle to the **g**. 8179
29:21 lay a snare for him that reproveth in the **g**, 8179
Jer 7: 2 Stand in the **g** of the LORD's house, and 8179
17:19 stand in the **g** of the children of the people, 8179
19: 2 which *is by* the entry of the east **g**, and 8179
20: 2 put him in the stocks that *were* in the high **g** 8179
26:10 sat down in the entry of the new **g** of 8179
31:38 tower of Hananeel unto the **g** of the corner. 8179
31:40 unto the corner of the horse **g** towards 8179
36:10 in the higher court *at* the entry of the new **g** 8179
37:13 when he was in the **g** of Benjamin, 8179
38: 7 the king then sitting in the **g** of Benjamin; 8179
39: 3 sat in the middle **g**, *even* Nergal-sharezer, 8179
39: 4 by the **g** betwixt the two walls: 8179
52: 7 *by* the way of the **g** between the two walls, 8179
La 5:14 The elders have ceased from the **g**, 8179
Eze 8: 3 to the door of the inner **g** that looketh 8179
8: 5 northward at the **g** of the altar this image of 8179
8:14 he brought me to the door of the **g** of 8179
9: 2 six men came from the way of the higher **g**, 8179
10:19 *every one* stood *at* the door of the east **g** of 8179
11: 1 brought me unto the east **g** of the LORD'S 8179
11: 1 behold at the door of the **g** five and 8179
40: 3 a measuring reed; and he stood in the **g**. 8179
40: 6 came he unto the **g** which looketh toward 8179
40: 6 and measured the threshold of the **g**, 8179
40: 6 the other threshold *of the* **g**, *which was* one NIH
40: 7 the threshold of the **g** by the porch of 8179
40: 7 by the porch of the **g** within *was* one reed. 8179
40: 8 He measured also the porch of the **g** within, 8179
40: 9 measured he the porch of the **g**, 8179
40: 9 and the porch of the **g** *was* inward. 8179
40:10 the little chambers of the **g** eastward *were* 8179
40:11 measured the breadth of the entry of the **g**, 8179
40:11 *and* the length of the **g**, thirteen cubits. 8179
40:13 the **g** from the roof of *one* little chamber to 8179
40:14 unto the post of the court round about the **g**. 8179
40:15 from the face of the **g** of the entrance unto 8179
40:15 of the porch of the inner **g** *were* fifty cubits. 8179
40:16 to their posts within the **g** round about, 8179
40:19 **g** unto the forefront of the inner court 8179
40:20 the **g** of the outward court that looked 8179
40:21 were after the measure of the first **g**: 8179
40:22 *were* after the measure of the **g** that looketh 8179
40:23 the **g** of the inner court *was* over against 8179
40:23 *was* over against the **g** toward the north, 8179
40:23 he measured from **g** to gate an hundred 8179
40:23 he measured from gate to **g** an hundred 8179
40:24 the south, and behold a **g** toward the south: 8179
40:27 *there was* a **g** in the inner court toward 8179
40:27 he measured from **g** to gate toward 8179
40:27 he measured from gate to **g** toward 8179
40:28 me to the inner court by the south **g**: 8179
40:28 he measured the south **g** according to these 8179
40:32 he measured the **g** according to these 8179
40:35 he brought me to the north **g**, and 8179
40:39 in the porch of the **g** *were* two tables on this 8179
40:40 as one goeth up to the entry of the north **g**, 8179
40:40 which *was* at the porch of the **g**, *were* two 8179

Eze	40:41	four tables on that side, by the side of the **g**;	8179
	40:44	without the inner **g** *were* the chambers of	8179
	40:44	which *was* at the side of the north **g**;	8179
	40:44	one at the side of the east **g** *having*	8179
	40:48	the breadth of the **g** *was* three cubits on this	8179
	42:15	he brought me forth toward the **g** whose	8179
	43: 1	Afterward he brought me to the **g**, *even*	8179
	43: 1	*even* the **g** that looketh toward the east:	8179
	43: 4	of the **g** whose prospect *is* toward the east.	8179
	44: 1	he brought me back the way of the **g** of	8179
	44: 2	This **g** shall be shut, it shall not be opened,	8179
	44: 3	enter by the way of the porch of *that* **g**,	8179
	44: 4	brought he me the way of the north **g**	8179
	45:19	upon the posts of the **g** of the inner court.	8179
	46: 1	The **g** of the inner court that looketh *toward*	8179
	46: 2	by the way of the porch of *that* **g** without,	8179
	46: 2	shall stand by the post of the **g**, and	8179
	46: 2	he shall worship at the threshold of the **g**:	8179
	46: 2	but the **g** shall not be shut until the evening.	8179
	46: 3	of this **g** before the LORD in the sabbaths	8179
	46: 8	go in *by* the way of the porch of *that* **g**,	8179
	46: 9	he that entereth in *by* the way of the north **g**	8179
	46: 9	shall go out *by* the way of the south **g**;	8179
	46: 9	he that entereth *by* the way of the south **g**	8179
	46: 9	shall go forth *by* the way of the north **g**:	8179
	46: 9	he shall not return *by* the way of the **g**	8179
	46:12	open him the **g** that looketh *toward* the east,	8179
	46:12	after his going forth *one* shall shut the **g**.	8179
	46:19	the entry, which *was* at the side of the **g**,	8179
	47: 2	brought he me out *of* the way of the **g**	8179
	47: 2	utter **g** *by* the way that looketh eastward;	8179
	48:31	one **g** of Reuben, one gate of Judah,	8179
	48:31	one **g** of Judah, one gate of Levi.	8179
	48:31	one gate of Judah, one **g** of Levi.	8179
	48:32	one **g** of Joseph, one gate of Benjamin,	8179
	48:32	one **g** of Benjamin, one gate of Dan.	8179
	48:32	one gate of Benjamin, one **g** of Dan.	8179
	48:33	one **g** of Simeon, one gate of Issachar,	8179
	48:33	one gate of Simeon, one **g** of Issachar,	8179
	48:33	one gate of Issachar, one **g** of Zebulun.	8179
	48:34	one **g** of Gad, one gate of Asher, one gate	8179
	48:34	one gate of Gad, one **g** of Asher, one gate	8179
	48:34	one gate of Asher, one **g** of Naphtali.	8179
Da	2:49	but Daniel *sat* in the **g** of the king.	8651
Am	5:10	They hate him that rebuketh in the **g**, and	8179
	5:12	they turn aside the poor in the **g** *from their*	8179
	5:15	the good, and establish judgment in the **g**:	8179
Ob	1:13	Thou shouldest not have entered into the **g**	8179
Mic	1: 9	he is come unto the **g** of my people, *even* to	8179
	1:12	from the LORD unto the **g** of Jerusalem.	8179
	2:13	have passed through the **g**, and are gone out	8179
Zep	1:10	*shall be* the noise of a cry from the fish **g**,	8179
Zec	14:10	from Benjamin's **g** unto the place of	8179
	14:10	gate unto the place of the first **g**,	8179
	14:10	unto the corner **g**, and *from* the tower of	8179
Mt	7:13	Enter ye in at the strait **g**: for wide *is*	*4439*
	7:13	for wide *is* the **g**, and broad *is* the way,	*4439*
	7:14	Because strait *is* the **g**, and narrow *is*	*4439*
Lk	7:12	Now when he came nigh to the **g** of	*4439*
	13:24	Strive to enter in at the strait **g**: for many,	*4439*
	16:20	which was laid at his **g**, full of sores,	*4440*
Ac	3: 2	whom they laid daily at the **g** of the temple	*2374*
	3:10	for alms at the Beautiful **g** of the temple:	*4439*
	10:17	for Simon's house, and stood before the **g**,	*4440*
	12:10	they came unto the iron **g** that leadeth unto	*4439*
	12:13	And as Peter knocked at the door of the **g**,	*4440*
	12:14	she opened not the **g** for gladness, but	*4440*
	12:14	and told how Peter stood before the **g**.	*4440*
Heb	13:12	with his own blood, suffered without the **g**.	*4439*
Rev	21:21	every several **g** was of one pearl:	*4440*

GATES (144) [GATE]

Ex	20:10	nor thy stranger that *is* within thy **g**:	8179
Dt	3: 5	*were* fenced *with* high walls, **g**, and bars;	1817
	5:14	nor thy stranger that *is* within thy **g**;	8179
	6: 9	upon the posts of thy house, and on thy **g**.	8179
	11:20	door posts of thine house, and upon thy **g**:	8179
	12:12	and the Levite that *is* within your **g**;	8179
	12:15	thou mayest kill and eat flesh in all thy **g**,	8179
	12:17	Thou mayest not eat within thy **g** the tithe	8179
	12:18	and the Levite that *is* within thy **g**:	8179
	12:21	thou shalt eat in thy **g** whatsoever thy soul	8179
	14:21	give it unto the stranger that *is* in thy **g**,	8179
	14:27	the Levite that *is* within thy **g**; thou shalt	8179
	14:28	same year, and shalt lay *it* up within thy **g**:	8179
	14:29	the widow, which *are* within thy **g**,	8179
	15: 7	**g** in thy land which the LORD thy God	8179
	15:22	Thou shalt eat it within thy **g**: the unclean	8179
	16: 5	sacrifice the passover within any of thy **g**,	8179
	16:11	the Levite that *is* within thy **g**, and	8179
	16:14	and the widow, that *are* within thy **g**.	8179
	16:18	officers shalt thou make thee in all thy **g**,	8179
	17: 2	within any of thy **g** which the LORD thy	8179
	17: 5	unto thy **g**, *even that* man or *that* woman,	8179
	17: 8	*being* matters of controversy within thy **g**:	8179
	18: 6	if a Levite come from any of thy **g** out of	8179
	23:16	place which he shall choose in one of thy **g**,	8179
	24:14	strangers that *are* in thy land within thy **g**:	8179
	26:12	that they may eat within thy **g**, and	8179
	28:52	he shall besiege thee in all thy **g**, until thy	8179
	28:52	he shall besiege thee in all thy **g** throughout	8179
	28:55	enemies shall distress thee in all thy **g**.	8179
	28:57	thine enemy shall distress thee in thy **g**.	8179
	31:12	and thy stranger that *is* within thy **g**,	8179
Jos	6:26	in his youngest *son* shall he set up the **g** of	1817
Jdg	5: 8	chose new gods; then *was* war in the **g**:	8179
	5:11	the people of the LORD go down to the **g**.	8179
1Sa	17:52	come *to* the valley, and to the **g** of Ekron.	8179
	23: 7	by entering into a town that hath **g** and	1817
2Sa	18:24	David sat between the two **g**: and	8179
1Ki	16:34	set up the **g** thereof in his youngest *son*	1817
2Ki	23: 8	brake down the high places of the **g** that	8179
1Ch	9:19	keepers of the **g** of the tabernacle:	5592
	9:22	to be porters in the **g** *were* two hundred	5592
	9:23	their children had the oversight of the **g** of	8179
	22: 3	for the nails for the doors of the **g**,	8179
2Ch	8: 5	fenced cities, *with* walls, **g**, and bars;	1817
	14: 7	about *them* walls, and towers, **g**, and bars,	1817
	23:19	he set the porters at the **g** of the house of	8179
	31: 2	to praise in the **g** of the tents of	8179
Ne	1: 3	and the **g** thereof are burnt with fire.	8179
	2: 3	and the **g** thereof are consumed with fire?	8179
	2: 8	**g** of the palace which *appertained* to	8179
	2:13	and the **g** thereof were consumed with fire.	8179
	2:17	and the **g** thereof are burnt with fire:	8179
	6: 1	time I had not set up the doors upon the **g**;)	8179
	7: 3	Let not the **g** of Jerusalem be opened until	8179
	11:19	Talmon, and their brethren that kept the **g**,	8179
	12:25	keeping the ward at the thresholds of the **g**.	8179
	12:30	purified the people, and the **g**, and the wall.	8179
	13:19	that when the **g** of Jerusalem began to be	8179
	13:19	I commanded that the **g** should be shut, and	1817
	13:19	*some* of my servants set I at the **g**,	8179
	13:22	*that* they should come *and* keep the **g**,	8179
Job	38:17	Have the **g** of death been opened unto thee?	8179
Ps	9:13	thou that liftest me up from the **g** of death:	8179
	9:14	That I may shew forth all thy praise in the **g**	8179
	24: 7	Lift up your heads, O ye **g**; and be ye lift	8179
	24: 9	Lift up your heads, O ye **g**; even lift *them*	8179
	87: 2	The LORD loveth the **g** of Zion more than	8179
	100: 4	Enter *into* his **g** with thanksgiving, *and*	8179
	107:16	For he hath broken the **g** of brass, and	1817
	107:18	and they draw near unto the **g** of death.	8179
	118:19	Open to me the **g** of righteousness: I will go	8179
	122: 2	Our feet shall stand within thy **g**,	8179
	147:13	For he hath strengthened the bars of thy **g**;	8179
Pr	1:21	of concourse, in the openings of the **g**:	8179
	8: 3	She crieth at the **g**, at the entry of the city,	8179
	8:34	watching daily at my **g**, waiting at the posts	1817
	14:19	and the wicked at the **g** of the righteous.	8179
	31:23	Her husband is known in the **g**, when he	8179
	31:31	and let her own works praise her in the **g**.	8179
SS	7:13	at our **g** *are* all *manner of* pleasant *fruits,*	6607
Isa	3:26	her **g** shall lament and mourn; and	6607
	13: 2	that they may go *into* the **g** of the nobles.	6607
	26: 2	Open ye the **g**, that the righteous nation	8179
	38:10	of my days, I shall go to the **g** of the grave:	8179
	45: 1	to open before him the **two leaved g**;	1817
	45: 1	leaved gates; and the **g** shall not be shut;	8179
	45: 2	I will break in pieces the **g** of brass, and	1817
	54:12	thy **g** of carbuncles, and all thy borders of	8179
	60:11	Therefore thy **g** shall be open continually;	8179
	60:18	call thy walls Salvation, and thy **g** Praise.	8179
	62:10	Go through, go through the **g**; prepare you	8179
Jer	1:15	throne *at* the entering of the **g** of Jerusalem,	8179
	7: 2	that enter in at these **g** to worship	8179
	14: 2	Judah mourneth, and the **g** thereof languish;	8179
	15: 7	I will fan them with a fan in the **g** of	8179

Jer 17:19 they go out, and in all the **g** of Jerusalem; 8179
17:20 of Jerusalem, that enter in by these **g**: 8179
17:21 nor bring *it* in by the **g** of Jerusalem; 8179
17:24 to bring in no burden through the **g** of this 8179
17:25 shall there enter into the **g** of this city kings 8179
17:27 even entering in at the **g** of Jerusalem on 8179
17:27 will I kindle a fire in the **g** thereof, and 8179
22: 2 and thy people that enter in by these **g**: 8179
22: 4 shall there enter in by the **g** of this house 8179
22:19 and cast forth beyond the **g** of Jerusalem. 8179
49:31 the LORD, which have neither **g** nor bars, 1817
51:58 her high **g** shall be burnt with fire; 8179
La 1: 4 all her **g** are desolate: her priests sigh: 8179
2: 9 Her **g** are sunk into the ground; he hath 8179
4:12 the enemy should have entered into the **g** of 8179
Eze 21:15 set the point of the sword against all their **g**, 8179
21:22 to appoint *battering* rams against the **g**, 8179
26: 2 she is broken *that was* the **g** of the people: 1817
26:10 the chariots, when he shall enter into thy **g**, 8179
38:11 and having neither bars nor **g**, 1817
40:18 the pavement by the side of the **g** over 8179
40:18 the length of the **g** *was* the lower pavement. 8179
40:38 entries thereof *were* by the posts of the **g**, 8179
44:11 *having* charge at the **g** of the house, and 8179
44:17 *that* when they enter in at the **g** of the inner 8179
44:17 whiles they minister in the **g** of the inner 8179
48:31 the **g** of the city *shall be* after the names of 8179
48:31 three **g** northward; one gate of Reuben, 8179
48:32 three **g**; and one gate of Joseph, one gate of 8179
48:33 three **g**; one gate of Simeon, one gate of 8179
48:34 and five hundred, *with* their three **g**; 8179
Ob 1:11 foreigners entered *into* his **g**, and cast lots 8179
Na 2: 6 The **g** of the rivers shall be opened, and 8179
3:13 the **g** of thy land shall be set wide open 8179
Zec 8:16 the judgment of truth and peace in your **g**: 8179
Mt 16:18 and the **g** of hell shall not prevail against it. *4439*
Ac 9:24 And they watched the **g** day and night to *4439*
14:13 brought oxen and garlands unto the **g**, and *4440*
Rev 21:12 and had twelve **g**, and at the gates twelve *4440*
21:12 and at the **g** twelve angels, and *4440*
21:13 On the east three **g**; on the north three *4440*
21:13 the east three gates; on the north three **g**; *4440*
21:13 on the south three **g**; and on the west three *4440*
21:13 south three gates; and on the west three **g**. *4440*
21:15 and the **g** thereof, and the wall thereof. *4440*
21:21 And the twelve **g** *were* twelve pearls; *4440*
21:25 And the **g** of it shall not be shut at all by *4440*
22:14 and may enter in through the **g** into the city. *4440*

GATH (33) [GATH-HEPHER, GATH-RIMMON, GITTITE, GITTITES, MORESHETH-GATH]

Jos 11:22 only in Gaza, in **G**, and in Ashdod, 1661
1Sa 5: 8 the God of Israel be carried about *unto* **G**. 1661
6:17 for Askelon one, for **G** one, for Ekron one; 1661
7:14 restored to Israel, from Ekron even unto **G**; 1661
17: 4 named Goliath, of **G**, whose height *was* six 1661
17:23 the Philistine of **G**, Goliath by name, 1661
17:52 to Shaaraim, even unto **G**, and unto Ekron. 1661
21:10 of Saul, and went to Achish the king of **G**. 1661
21:12 was sore afraid of Achish the king of **G**. 1661
27: 2 unto Achish, the son of Maoch, king of **G**. 1661
27: 3 David dwelt with Achish at **G**, he and 1661
27: 4 it was told Saul that David was fled *to* **G**: 1661
27:11 to bring *tidings to* **G**, saying, Lest they 1661
2Sa 1:20 Tell *it* not in **G**, publish *it* not in the streets 1661
15:18 men which came after him from **G**, 1661
21:20 there was yet a battle in **G**, where was a 1661
21:22 These four were born to the giant in **G**, and 1661
1Ki 2:39 unto Achish son of Maachah king of **G**. 1661
2:39 Behold, thy servants *be* in **G**. 1661
2:40 went to **G** to Achish to seek his servants: 1661
2:40 and brought his servants from **G**. 1661
2:41 that Shimei had gone from Jerusalem *to* **G**, 1661
2Ki 12:17 went up, and fought against **G**, and took it: 1661
1Ch 7:21 whom the men of **G** that were born in *that* 1661
8:13 who drove away the inhabitants of **G**: 1661
18: 1 took **G** and her towns out of the hand of 1661
20: 6 yet again there was war at **G**, where was a 1661
20: 8 These were born unto the giant in **G**; and 1661
2Ch 11: 8 And **G**, and Mareshah, and Ziph, 1661
26: 6 brake down the wall of **G**, and the wall of 1661
Ps 56: T when the Philistines took him in **G**. 1661
Am 6: 2 go down *to* **G** of the Philistines: *be they* 1661
Mic 1:10 Declare ye *it* not at **G**, weep ye not at all: 1661

GATHER (165) [GATHERED, GATHERER, GATHEREST, GATHERETH, GATHERING, GATHERINGS, GRAPEGATHERER, GRAPEGATHERERS, GRAPE-GATHERERS, INGATHERING]

Ge 6:21 food that is eaten, and thou shalt **g** *it* to thee; 622
31:46 Jacob said unto his brethren, **G** stones; and 3950
34:30 they shall **g** themselves **together** against me, 622
41:35 let them **g** all the food of those good years 6908
49: 1 his sons, and said, **G** yourselves **together**, 622
49: 2 **G** yourselves **together**, and hear, ye sons of 6908
Ex 3:16 **g** the elders of Israel **together**, and say unto 622
5: 7 let them go and **g** straw for themselves. 7197
5:12 Egypt to **g stubble** instead of straw. 7179+7197
9:19 *and* **g** thy cattle, and all that thou hast in 5756
16: 4 shall go out and **g** a certain rate every day, 3950
16: 5 it shall be twice as much as they **g** daily. 3950
16:16 **G** of it every man according to his eating, 3950
16:26 Six days ye shall **g** it; but on the seventh 3950
16:27 of the people on the seventh day for to **g**, 3950
23:10 thy land, and shalt **g** in the fruits thereof: 622
Lev 8: 3 **g** thou all the congregation **together** unto 6950
19: 9 neither shalt thou **g** the gleanings of thy 3950
19:10 neither shalt thou **g** *every* grape of thy 3950
23:22 neither shalt thou **g** *any* gleaning of thy 3950
25: 3 prune thy vineyard, and **g** in the fruit thereof; 622
25: 5 neither **g** the grapes of thy vine undressed: 1219
25:11 nor **g** *the grapes* in it of thy vine undressed. 1219
25:20 we shall not sow, nor **g in** our increase: 622
Nu 8: 9 **g** the whole assembly of the children of Israel **together**: 6950
10: 4 of Israel, shall **g** themselves unto thee. 3259
11:16 **G** unto me seventy men of the elders of 622
19: 9 a man *that is* clean shall **g up** the ashes of 622
20: 8 **g** thou the assembly **together**, thou, and 6950
21:16 **G** the people **together**, and I will give them 622
Dt 4:10 **G** me the people **together**, and I will make 6950
11:14 that thou mayest **g in** thy corn, and thy wine, 622
13:16 thou shalt **g** all the spoil of it into the midst 6908
28:30 and shalt not **g the grapes** thereof. 2490
28:38 out *into* the field, and shalt **g** *but* little **in**; 622
28:39 nor **g** *the grapes;* for the worms shall eat 103
30: 3 will return and **g** thee from all the nations, 6908
30: 4 from thence will the LORD thy God **g** 6908
31:12 **G** the people **together**, men, and women, 6950
31:28 **G** unto me all the elders of your tribes, and 6950
Ru 2: 7 and **g** after the reapers amongst the sheaves: 622
1Sa 7: 5 **G** all Israel to Mizpeh, and I will pray for 6908
2Sa 3:21 and will **g** all Israel unto my lord the king, 6908
12:28 therefore **g** the rest of the people **together**, 622
1Ki 18:19 *and* **g** to me all Israel unto mount Carmel, 6908
2Ki 4:39 one went out into the field to **g** herbs, and 3950
22:20 I will **g** thee unto thy fathers, and thou shalt 622
1Ch 13: 2 that they may **g** themselves unto us: 6908
16:35 **g** us **together**, and deliver us from 6908
22: 2 David commanded to **g together** 3664
2Ch 24: 5 **g** of all Israel money to repair the house of 6908
34:28 I will **g** thee to thy fathers, and thou shalt be 622
Ezr 10: 7 that *they* should **g** themselves **together** 6908
Ne 1: 9 *yet* will I **g** them from thence, and 6908
7: 5 my God put into mine heart to **g together** 6908
12:44 to **g** into them out of the fields of the cities 3664
Est 2: 3 that they may **g together** all the fair young 6908
4:16 **g together** all the Jews that are present in 3664
8:11 in every city to **g** themselves **together**, 6950
Job 11:10 or **g together**, then who can hinder him? 6950
24: 6 and they **g** the vintage of the wicked. 3953
34:14 If he set his heart upon *man, if* he **g** unto 622
39:12 bring home thy seed, and **g** *it into* thy barn? 622
Ps 26: 9 **G** not my soul with sinners, nor my life with 622
39: 6 and knoweth not who shall **g** them. 622
50: 5 **G** my saints together unto me; those that 622
56: 6 They **g** themselves **together**, they hide 1481
94:21 They **g** themselves **together** against 1413
104:22 they **g** themselves **together**, and lay them 622
104:28 *That* thou givest them they **g**: thou openest 3950
106:47 our God, and **g** us from among the heathen, 6908
Pr 28: 8 he shall **g** it for him that will pity the poor. 6908
Ecc 2:26 sinner he giveth travail, to **g** and to heap up, 622
3: 5 and a time to **g** stones **together**; 3664
SS 6: 2 to feed in the gardens, and to **g** lilies. 3950
Isa 10:31 inhabitants of Gebim **g** themselves **to flee**. 5756
11:12 **g together** the dispersed of Judah from 6908
34:15 lay, and hatch, and **g** under her shadow: 1716

G

Isa 40:11 he shall **g** the lambs with his arm, and 6908
43: 5 from the east, and **g** thee from the west; 6908
49:18 all these **g** themselves **together**, *and* 6908
54: 7 but with great mercies will I **g** thee. 6908
54:15 they shall **surely g together**, *but* 1481+1481
54:15 whosoever shall **g together** against thee 1481
56: 8 Yet will I **g** *others* to him, besides those 6908
60: 4 all they **g** themselves **together**, they come 6908
62:10 cast up the highway; **g** out the stones; 5619
66:18 that *I* will **g** all nations and tongues; 6908
Jer 4: 5 cry, **g together**, and say, 4390
6: 1 **g** yourselves **to flee** out of the midst of 5756
7:18 The children **g** wood, and the fathers kindle 3950
9:22 after the harvestman, and none shall **g** *them.* 622
10:17 **G up** thy wares out of the land, O inhabitant 622
23: 3 I will **g** the remnant of my flock out of all 6908
29:14 I will **g** you from all the nations, and 6908
31: 8 and **g** them from the coasts of the earth, *and* 6908
31:10 He that scattered Israel will **g** him, and 6908
32:37 Behold, I *will* **g** them out of all countries, 6908
40:10 ye, **g** ye wine, and summer fruits, and oil, 622
49: 5 none shall **g up** him that wandereth. 6908
49:14 *saying,* **G** ye **together**, and come against 6908
51:11 **g** the shields: the LORD hath raised up 4390
Eze 11:17 I will even **g** you from the people, and 6908
16:37 Behold therefore, I will **g** all thy lovers, 6908
16:37 I will even **g** them round about against thee, 6908
20:34 will **g** you out of the countries wherein ye 6908
20:41 **g** you out of the countries wherein ye have 6908
22:19 I will **g** you into the midst of Jerusalem. 6908
22:20 *As they* **g** silver, and brass, and iron, and 6910
22:20 to melt *it;* so will I **g** *you* in mine anger and 6908
22:21 I will **g** you, and blow upon you in the fire 3664
24: 4 **G** the pieces thereof into it, *even* every good 622
29:13 At the end of forty years will I **g** 6908
34:13 **g** them from the countries, and will bring 6908
36:24 **g** you out of all countries, and will bring 6908
37:21 will **g** them on every side, and bring them 6908
39:17 **g** yourselves on every side to my sacrifice 622
Da 3: 2 the king sent to **g together** 3673
Hos 8:10 now will I **g** them, and they shall sorrow a 6908
9: 6 Egypt shall **g** them **up**, Memphis shall bury 6908
Joel 1:14 **g** the elders *and* all the inhabitants of 622
2: 6 be much pained: all faces shall **g** blackness. 6908
2:16 **G** the people, sanctify the congregation, 622
2:16 **g** the children, and those that suck 622
3: 2 I will also **g** all nations, and will bring them 6908
3:11 and **g** yourselves **together** round about: 6908
Mic 2:12 I will **surely g** the remnant of Israel; 6908+6908
4: 6 I will **g** her that is driven out, and *her* that I 6908
4:12 for he shall **g** them as the sheaves into 6908
5: 1 Now **g** thyself **in troops**, O daughter of 1413
Na 2:10 and the faces of them all **g** blackness. 6908
Hab 1: 9 and they shall **g** the captivity as the sand. 622
1:15 them in their net, and **g** them in their drag: 622
Zep 2: 1 **G** yourselves **together**, yea, 7197
2: 1 yea, **g together**, O nation not desired; 7197
3: 8 for my determination *is* to **g** the nations, 622
3:18 I will **g** *them that are* sorrowful for 622
3:19 that halteth, and **g** her that was driven out; 6908
3:20 you *again,* even in the time that I **g** you: 6908
Zec 10: 8 I will hiss for them, and **g** them; for I have 6908
10:10 land of Egypt, and **g** them out of Assyria; 6908
14: 2 For I will **g** all nations against Jerusalem to 622
Mt 3:12 his floor, and **g** his wheat into the garner; *4863*
6:26 neither do they reap, nor **g** into barns; *4863*
7:16 Do *men* **g** grapes of thorns, or figs of *4816*
13:28 Wilt thou then *that* we go and **g** them **up**? *4816*
13:29 lest while ye **g up** the tares, ye root up also *4816*
13:30 **G** ye **together** first the tares, and bind them *4816*
13:30 to burn them: but **g** the wheat into my barn. *4863*
13:41 they shall **g** out of his kingdom all things *4816*
24:31 they shall **g together** his elect from the four *1996*
25:26 sowed not, and **g** where I have not strawed: *4863*
Mk 13:27 shall **g together** his elect from the four *1996*
Lk 3:17 and will **g** the wheat into his garner; *4863*
6:44 For of thorns *men* do not **g** figs, nor of a *4816*
6:44 nor of a bramble bush **g** they grapes. *5166*
13:34 as a hen *doth* **g** her brood under *her* wings, NIG
Jn 6:12 **G up** the fragments that remain, *4863*
11:52 that also he should **g together** in one *4863*
15: 6 and *men* **g** them, and cast *them* into the fire, *4863*
Eph 1:10 might **g together in one** all *things* in Christ, *346*
Rev 14:18 and **g** the clusters of the vine of the earth; *5166*
16:14 to **g** them to the battle of that great day of *4863*
19:17 **g** yourselves **together** unto the supper of *4863*
20: 8 and Magog, to **g** them **together** to battle: *4863*

GATHERED (267) [GATHER]

Ge 1: 9 the heaven be **g together** unto one place, 6960
12: 5 all their substance that they had **g**, and 7408
25: 8 and full *of years;* and was **g** to his people. 622
25:17 and died; and was **g** unto his people. 622
29: 3 thither were all the flocks **g**: and they rolled 622
29: 7 *is it* time that the cattle should be **g together**: 622
29: 8 until all the flocks be **g together**, and 622
29:22 Laban **g together** all the men of the place, 622
35:29 died, and was **g** unto his people, *being* old 622
41:48 And he **g up** all the food of the seven years, 6908
41:49 Joseph **g** corn as the sand of the sea, 6651
47:14 Joseph **g up** all the money that was found 3950
49:29 said unto them, I *am to be* **g** unto my people: 622
49:33 he **g up** his feet into the bed, and yielded up 622
49:33 up the ghost, and was **g** unto his people. 622
Ex 4:29 **g together** all the elders of the children of 622
8:14 they **g** them **together** upon heaps: and 6651
15: 8 of thy nostrils the waters were **g together**, 6192
16:17 Israel did so, and **g**, some more, some less. 3950
16:18 he that **g much** had nothing over, and 7235
16:18 and he that **g little** had no lack; 4591
16:18 they **g** every man according to his eating. 3950
16:21 they **g** it every morning, every man 3950
16:22 *that* on the sixth day they **g** twice as much 3950
23:16 when thou hast **g in** thy labours out of 622
32: 1 the people **g** themselves **together** unto 6950
32:26 all the sons of Levi **g** themselves **together** 622
35: 1 **g** all the congregation of the children of Israel **together**, 6950
Lev 8: 4 the assembly was **g together** unto the door 6950
23:39 when ye have **g in** the fruit of the land, 622
26:25 when ye are **g together** within your cities, 622
Nu 10: 7 when the congregation is to be **g together**, 6950
11: 8 **g** *it,* and ground *it* in mills, or beat *it* in a 3950
11:22 shall all the fish of the sea be **g together** for 622
11:24 **g** the seventy men of the elders of 622
11:32 and all the next day, and they **g** the quails: 622
11:32 he that **g least** gathered ten homers: and 4591
11:32 he that gathered least **g** ten homers: and 622
14:35 that are **g together** against me: 3259
15:32 they found a man that **g** sticks upon 7197
16: 3 they **g** themselves **together** against Moses 6950
16:11 all thy company *are* **g together** against 3259
16:19 Korah **g** all the congregation against them 6950
16:42 when the congregation was **g** against 6950
20: 2 they **g** themselves **together** against Moses 6950
20:10 Aaron **g** the congregation **together** before 6950
20:24 Aaron shall be **g** unto his people: for he shall 622
20:26 Aaron shall be **g** *unto his people,* and 622
21:23 Sihon **g** all his people **together**, and 622
27: 3 **g** themselves **together** against the LORD 3259
27:13 seen it, thou also shalt be **g** unto thy people, 622
27:13 unto thy people, as Aaron thy brother was **g**. 622
31: 2 afterward shalt thou be **g** unto thy people. 622
Dt 16:13 after that thou hast **g** in thy corn and thy 622
32:50 thou goest up, and be **g** unto thy people; 622
32:50 in mount Hor, and was **g** unto his people: 622
33: 5 *and* the tribes of Israel were **g** together. 622
Jos 9: 2 That they **g** themselves together, to fight 6908
10: 5 **g** themselves **together**, and went up, they 622
10: 6 in the mountains are **g together** against us. 6908
22:12 of Israel **g** themselves **together** *at* Shiloh, 6950
24: 1 Joshua **g** all the tribes of Israel to Shechem, 622
Jdg 1: 7 toes cut off, **g** *their meat* under my table: 3950
2:10 also all that generation were **g** unto their 622
3:13 he **g** unto him the children of Ammon and 622
4:13 Sisera **g together** all his chariots, *even* nine 2199
6:33 and the children of the east were **g** together, 622
6:34 a trumpet; and Abi-ezer was **g** after him. 2199
6:35 all Manasseh; who also was **g** after him: 2199
7:23 the men of Israel **g** themselves **together** out 6817
7:24 the men of Ephraim **g** themselves **together**, 6817
9: 6 And all the men of Shechem **g together**, and 622
9:27 **g** their vineyards, and trode *the grapes,* and 1219
9:47 of the tower of Shechem were **g together**. 6908
10:17 the children of Ammon were **g together**, 6817
11: 3 there were **g** vain men to Jephthah, and 3950
11:20 Sihon **g** all his people **together**, and 622
12: 1 men of Ephraim **g themselves together**, 6817

Jdg 12: 4 Jephthah **g together** all the men of Gilead, 6908
16:23 the lords of the Philistines **g** them **together** 622
18:22 near to Micah's house were **g together**, 2199
20: 1 the congregation was **g together** as one 6950
20:11 So all the men of Israel were **g** against 622
20:14 **g** themselves **together** out of the cities unto 622
1Sa 5: 8 **g** all the lords of the Philistines unto them, 622
5:11 **g together** all the lords of the Philistines, 622
7: 6 they **g together** to Mizpeh, and drew water, 6908
7: 7 of Israel were **g together** to Mizpeh, 6908
8: 4 the elders of Israel **g** themselves **together**, 6908
13: 5 the Philistines **g** themselves **together** to fight 622
13:11 *that* the Philistines **g** themselves **together** *at* 622
14:48 he **g** a host, and smote the Amalekites, and 6213
15: 4 Saul **g** the people **together**, and 8085
17: 1 Now the Philistines **g together** their armies 622
17: 1 were **g together** *at* Shochoh, 622
17: 2 and the men of Israel were **g together**, 622
20:38 Jonathan's lad **g up** the arrows, and 3950
22: 2 *was* discontented, **g** themselves unto him; 6908
25: 1 all the Israelites were **g together**, and 6908
28: 1 that the Philistines **g** their armies **together** 6908
28: 4 the Philistines **g** themselves **together**, and 6908
28: 4 Saul **g** all Israel **together**, and they pitched 6908
29: 1 Now the Philistines **g together** all their 6908
2Sa 2:25 **g** themselves **together** after Abner, 6908
2:30 when he had **g** all the people **together**, 6908
6: 1 David **g together** all the chosen *men* of 622
10:15 before Israel, they **g** themselves together. 622
10:17 he **g** all Israel **together**, and passed over 622
12:29 David **g** all the people **together**, and went to 622
14:14 which cannot be **g up** *again;* neither doth 622
17:11 *that* all Israel be **generally g** unto thee, 622+622
20:14 they were **g together**, and went also after 6950
21:13 they **g** the bones of them that were hanged. 622
23: 9 *that* were there **g together** to battle, 622
23:11 the Philistines were **g together** into a troop, 622
1Ki 10:26 Solomon **g together** chariots and horsemen: 622
11:24 he **g** men unto him, and became captain 6908
18:20 **g** the prophets **together** unto mount 6908
20: 1 the king of Syria **g** all his host **together**: 6908
22: 6 the king of Israel **g** the prophets **together**, 6908
2Ki 3:21 they **g** all that *were able to* put on armour, 6817
4:39 **g** thereof wild gourds his lap full, and came 3950
6:24 that Ben-hadad king of Syria **g** all his host, 6908
10:18 Jehu **g** all the people **together**, and 6908
22: 4 which the keepers of the door have **g** of 622
22: 9 Thy servants have **g** the money that was 5413
22:20 and thou shalt be **g** into thy grave in peace; 622
23: 1 they **g** unto him all the elders of Judah and 622
1Ch 11: 1 all Israel **g** themselves to David unto 6908
11:13 there the Philistines were **g together** to 622
13: 5 So David **g** all Israel **together**, from Shihor 6950
15: 3 David **g** all Israel **together** to Jerusalem, 6950
19: 7 **g** themselves **together** from their cities, 622
19:17 he **g** all Israel, and passed over Jordan, and 622
23: 2 he **g together** all the princes of Israel, 622
2Ch 1:14 And Solomon **g** chariots and horsemen: and 622
11: 1 he **g** *of* the house of Judah and Benjamin an 6950
12: 5 that were **g together** to Jerusalem because 622
13: 7 there are **g** unto him vain men, the children 6908
15: 9 he **g** all Judah and Benjamin, and 6908
15:10 So they **g** themselves **together** *at* Jerusalem 6908
18: 5 Therefore the king of Israel **g together** *of* 6908
20: 4 Judah **g** themselves **together**, to ask *help* of 6908
23: 2 **g** the Levites out of all the cities of Judah, 6908
24: 5 he **g together** the priests and the Levites, 6908
24:11 did day by day, and **g** money in abundance. 622
25: 5 Moreover Amaziah **g** Judah **together**, and 6908
28:24 Ahaz **g together** the vessels of the house of 622
29: 4 and **g** them **together** into the east street, 622
29:15 they **g** their brethren, and 622
29:20 **g** the rulers of the city, and went up *to* 622
30: 3 people **g** themselves **together** to Jerusalem. 622
32: 4 So there was **g** much people **together**, 6908
32: 6 **g** them **together** to him in the street of 6908
34: 9 which the Levites that kept the doors had **g** 622
34:17 they have **g together** the money that was 5413
34:28 and thou shalt be **g** to thy grave in peace, 622
34:29 **g together** all the elders of Judah and 622
Ezr 3: 1 the people **g** themselves **together** as one 622
7:28 I **g together** out of Israel chief *men* to go 6908
8:15 I **g** them **together** to the river that runneth 6908
10: 9 Benjamin **g** themselves **together** *unto* 6908

Ne 5:16 all my servants *were* **g** thither unto 6908
8: 1 all the people **g** themselves **together** as one 622
8:13 on the second day were **g together** the chief 622
12:28 sons of the singers **g** themselves **together**, 622
13:11 I **g** them **together**, and set them in their 6908
Est 2: 8 when many maidens were **g together** unto 6908
2:19 when the virgins were **g together** 6908
9: 2 The Jews **g** themselves **together** in their 6950
9:15 **g** themselves **together** on the fourteenth 6950
9:16 king's provinces **g** themselves **together**, 6950
Job 16:10 they have **g** themselves together against 4390
27:19 *man* shall lie down, but he shall not be **g**: 622
30: 7 under the nettles they were **g together**. 5596
Ps 35:15 they rejoiced, and **g** themselves **together**: 622
35:15 *yea,* the abjects **g** themselves **together** 622
47: 9 The princes of the people are **g together**, 622
59: 3 the mighty are **g** against me; not *for* my 1481
102:22 When the people are **g** together, and 6908
107: 3 **g** them out of the lands, from the east, and 6908
140: 2 continually are they **g together** *for* war. 1481
Pr 27:25 and herbs of the mountains are **g**. 622
30: 4 who hath **g** the wind in his fists? who hath 622
Ecc 2: 8 I **g** me also silver and gold, and the peculiar 3664
SS 5: 1 I have **g** my myrrh with my spice; I have 717
Isa 5: 2 **g out** the **stones** thereof, and planted it *with* 5619
10:14 eggs *that are* left, have I **g** all the earth; 622
13: 4 noise of the kingdoms of nations **g together**: 622
22: 9 ye **g together** the waters of the lower pool. 6908
24:22 they shall be **g together**, *as* prisoners 622+626
24:22 *as* prisoners are **g** in the pit, and shall be NIH
27:12 ye shall be **g** one by one, O ye children of 3950
33: 4 your spoil shall be **g** *like* the gathering of 622
34:15 there shall the vultures also be **g**, every one 6908
34:16 and his spirit it hath **g** them. 6908
43: 9 Let all the nations be **g** together, and let 6908
44:11 let them all be **g together**, let them stand 6908
49: 5 Jacob again to him, Though Israel be not **g**, 622
56: 8 to him, besides those that are **g** unto him. 6908
60: 7 All the flocks of Kedar shall be **g together** 6908
62: 9 they that have **g** it shall eat it, and praise 622
Jer 3:17 all the nations shall be **g** unto it, to 6960
8: 2 they shall not be **g**, nor be buried; they shall 622
25:33 shall not be lamented, neither **g**, nor buried; 622
26: 9 all the people were **g** against Jeremiah in 6950
40:12 and **g** wine and summer fruits very much. 622
40:15 that all the Jews which are **g** unto thee 6908
Eze 28:25 When I shall have **g** the house of Israel 6908
29: 5 thou shalt not be brought together, nor **g**: 6908
38: 8 *and is* **g** out of many people, against 6908
38:12 upon the people *that are* **g** out of the nations, 622
38:13 hast thou **g** thy company to take a prey? to 6950
39:27 **g** them out of their enemies' lands, and 6908
39:28 I have **g** them unto their own land, and 3664
Da 3: 3 were **g together** unto the dedication of 3673
3:27 being **g together**, saw these men, 3673
Hos 1:11 and the children of Israel be **g** together, 6908
10:10 *the* people shall be **g** against them, 622
Mic 1: 7 for she **g** *it* of the hire of a harlot, and 6908
4:11 Now also many nations are **g** against thee, 622
7: 1 for I am as when they have **g** the summer 625
Zec 12: 3 people of the earth be **g together** against it. 622
14:14 the heathen round about shall be **g together**, 622
Mt 2: 4 **g** all the chief priests and scribes of the people **together**, *4863*
13: 2 And great multitudes were **g together** unto *4863*
13:40 As therefore the tares are **g** and burnt in *4816*
13:47 *was* cast into the sea, and **g** of every kind: *4863*
13:48 and **g** the good into vessels, but cast the bad *4816*
18:20 or three are **g together** in my name, *4863*
22:10 and **g together** all as many as they found, *4863*
22:34 Sadducees to silence, they were **g** together. *4863*
22:41 While the Pharisees were **g together**, Jesus *4863*
23:37 often would I have **g** thy children **together**, *1996*
24:28 there will the eagles be **g together**. *4863*
25:32 And before him shall be **g** all nations: and *4863*
27:17 Therefore when they were **g together**, *4863*
27:27 and **g** unto him the whole band *of soldiers.* *4863*
Mk 1:33 And all the city was **g together** at the door. *1996*
2: 2 And straightway many were **g together**, *4863*
4: 1 and there was **g** unto him a great multitude, *4863*
5:21 the other side, much people **g** unto him: *4863*
6:30 And the apostles **g** themselves **together** *4863*
Lk 8: 4 And when much people were **g together**, *4896*
11:29 when the people were **g thick together**, *1865*

Lk 12: 1 when there were g **together** an *1996*
13:34 often would I have g thy children **together**, *1996*
15:13 days after the younger son g all **together**, *4863*
17:37 *is,* thither will the eagles be g **together**. *4863*
24:33 and found the eleven g **together**, and *4867*
Jn 6:13 Therefore they g *them* **together**, and *4863*
11:47 Then g the chief priests and the Pharisees a *4863*
Ac 4: 6 high priest, were g **together** at Jerusalem. *4863*
4:26 the rulers were g together against the Lord, *4863*
4:27 and the people of Israel, were g **together**, *4863*
12:12 where many were g **together** praying. *4867*
14:27 were come, and had g the church **together**, *4863*
15:30 when they had g the multitude **together**, *4863*
17: 5 and g **a company**, and set all the city on an *3792*
20: 8 where they were g **together**. *4863*
28: 3 And when Paul had g a bundle of sticks, *4962*
1Co 5: 4 when ye are g **together**, and my spirit, *4863*
2Co 8:15 He that *had* g much had nothing over; NIG
8:15 and he that *had* g little had no lack. NIG
Rev 14:19 and g the vine of the earth, and cast *it* into *5166*
16:16 And he g them **together** into a place called *4863*
19:19 g **together** to make war against him that sat *4863*

G

GATHERER (1) [GATHER]
Am 7:14 I *was* a herdman, and a g of sycomore fruit: 1103

GATHEREST (1) [GATHER]
Dt 24:21 When thou g the **grapes** of thy vineyard, 1219

GATHERETH (17) [GATHER]
Nu 19:10 he that g the ashes of the heifer shall wash 622
Ps 33: 7 He g the waters of the sea **together** as a 3664
41: 6 his heart g iniquity to itself; *when* he goeth 6908
147: 2 he g **together** the outcasts of Israel. 3664
Pr 6: 8 in the summer, *and* g her food in the harvest. 103
10: 5 He that g in summer *is* a wise son: *but* 103
13:11 but he that g by labour shall increase. 6908
Isa 10:14 as *one* g eggs *that are* left, have I gathered all 622
17: 5 it shall be as when the harvestman g 622
17: 5 it shall be as he that g ears in the valley of 3950
56: 8 The Lord GOD which g the outcasts of 6908
Na 3:18 upon the mountains, and no man g *them.* 6908
Hab 2: 5 g unto him all nations, and heapeth unto him 622
Mt 12:30 and he that g not with me scattereth abroad. *4863*
23:37 even as a hen g her chickens under *her* *1996*
Lk 11:23 and he that g not with me scattereth. *4863*
Jn 4:36 and g fruit unto life eternal: *4863*

GATHERING (11) [GATHER]
Ge 1:10 the g **together** of the waters called he Seas: 4723
49:10 and unto him *shall* the g of the people *be.* 3349
Nu 15:33 they that found him g sticks brought him 7197
1Ki 17:10 the widow woman *was* there g of sticks: 7197
17:12 behold, I *am* g two sticks, that I may go in 7197
2Ch 20:25 they were three days in g of the spoil, it was 962
Isa 32:10 the vintage shall fail, the g shall not come. 625
33: 4 your spoil shall be gathered *like* the g of 625
Mt 25:24 and g where thou hast not strawed: *4863*
Ac 16:10 **assuredly** g that the Lord had called us for *4822*
2Th 2: 1 and *by* our g **together** unto him, *1997*

GATHERINGS (1) [GATHER]
1Co 16: 2 that there be no g when I come. *3048*

GATH-HEPHER (1) [GATH, GITTAH-HEPHER, HEPHER]
2Ki 14:25 of Amittai, the prophet, which *was* of G. 1661

GATH-RIMMON (4) [GATH, RIMMON]
Jos 19:45 And Jehud, and Bene-berak, and G, 1667
21:24 with her suburbs, G with her suburbs; 1667
21:25 with her suburbs, and G with her suburbs; 1667
1Ch 6:69 with her suburbs, and G with her suburbs: 1667

GAVE (465) [GIVE]
Ge 2:20 Adam g names to all cattle, and to the fowl 7121
3: 6 and g also unto her husband with her; 5414
3:12 with me, she g me of the tree, and I did eat. 5414
14:20 into thy hand. And he g him tithes of all. 5414
16: 3 g her to her husband Abram to be his wife. 5414
18: 7 and good, and g *it* unto a young man; 5414
20:14 g *them* unto Abraham, and restored him 5414
21:14 and a bottle of water, and g *it* unto Hagar, 5414
21:19 the bottle *with* water, and g the lad **drink**. 8248
21:27 and oxen, and g *them* unto Abimelech; 5414
24:18 pitcher upon her hand, and g him **drink**. 8248
24:32 g straw and provender for the camels, and 5414
24:53 and raiment, and g *them* to Rebekah: 5414
24:53 he g also to her brother and to her mother 5414
25: 5 And Abraham g all that he had unto Isaac. 5414
25: 6 Abraham g gifts, and sent them away from 5414
25: 8 Abraham g **up the ghost**, and died in a 1478
25:17 he g **up the ghost** and died; and 1478
25:34 Jacob g Esau bread and pottage of lentiles; 5414
27:17 she g the savoury meat and the bread, 5414
28: 4 art a stranger, which God g unto Abraham. 5414
28: 6 that as he blessed him he g him **a charge**, 6680
29:24 Laban g unto his daughter Leah Zilpah his 5414
29:28 he g him Rachel his daughter to wife *also.* 5414
29:29 Laban g to Rachel his daughter Bilhah his 5414
30: 4 she g him Bilhah her handmaid to wife: 5414
30: 9 Zilpah her maid, and g her Jacob to wife. 5414
30:35 and g *them* into the hand of his sons. 5414
35: 4 they g unto Jacob all the strange gods 5414
35:12 the land which I g Abraham and Isaac, 5414
35:29 Isaac g **up the ghost**, and died, and 1478
38:18 he g *it* her, and came in unto her, and 5414
38:26 because that I g her not to Shelah my son. 5414
39:21 g him favour in the sight of the keeper of 5414
40:11 and I g the cup into Pharaoh's hand. 5414
40:21 and he g the cup into Pharaoh's hand: 5414
41:45 he g him to wife Asenath the daughter of 5414
43:24 g *them* water, and they washed their feet; 5414
43:24 their feet; and he g their asses provender. 5414
45:21 Joseph g them wagons, according to 5414
45:21 and g them provision for the way. 5414
45:22 To all of them he g each man changes of 5414
45:22 to Benjamin he g three hundred *pieces* of 5414
46:18 whom Laban g to Leah his daughter, and 5414
46:25 which Laban g unto Rachel his daughter, 5414
47:11 g them a possession in the land of Egypt, 5414
47:17 Joseph g them bread *in exchange* for 5414
47:22 did eat their portion which Pharaoh g them: 5414
Ex 2:21 and he g Moses Zipporah his daughter. 5414
6:13 g them **a charge** unto the children of Israel, 6680
11: 3 the LORD g the people favour in the sight 5414
12:36 the LORD g the people favour in the sight 5414
14:20 *to them,* but it g **light** by night *to these:* so 215
31:18 he g unto Moses, when he had made an end 5414
32:24 So they g *it* me: then I cast it into the fire, 5414
34:32 he g them **in commandment** all that 6680
36: 6 Moses g **commandment**, and they caused 6680
Nu 3:51 Moses g the money of them that were 5414
7: 6 and the oxen, and g them unto the Levites. 5414
7: 7 four oxen he g unto the sons of Gershon, 5414
7: 8 eight oxen he g unto the sons of Merari, 5414
7: 9 upon the sons of Kohath he g none: because 5414
11:25 upon him, and g *it* unto the seventy elders: 5414
17: 6 every one of their princes g him a rod 5414
27:23 his hands upon him, and g him **a charge**, 6680
31:41 Moses g the tribute, *which was* 5414
31:47 and of beast, and g them unto the Levites, 5414
32:33 Moses g unto them, *even* to the children of 5414
32:38 g other names unto the cities which they 7121
32:40 Moses g Gilead unto Machir the son of 5414
Dt 2:12 which the LORD g unto them.) 5414
3:12 g I unto the Reubenites and to the Gadites. 5414
3:13 of Og, g I unto the half tribe of Manasseh; 5414
3:15 And I g Gilead unto Machir. 5414
3:16 unto the Gadites I g from Gilead even unto 5414
9:11 *that* the LORD g me the two tables of 5414
10: 4 and the LORD g them unto me. 5414
22:16 I g my daughter unto this man to wife, and 5414
29: 8 g it for an inheritance unto the Reubenites, 5414
31:23 he g Joshua the son of Nun **a charge**, 6680
Jos 1:14 shall remain in the land which Moses g you 5414
1:15 which Moses the LORD'S servant g you 5414
11:23 Joshua g it for an inheritance unto Israel 5414
12: 6 Moses the servant of the LORD g it *for* a 5414
12: 7 which Joshua g unto the tribes of Israel *for* 5414
13: 8 which Moses g them, beyond Jordan 5414
13: 8 *even* as Moses the servant of the LORD g 5414
13:14 Only unto the tribe of Levi he g none 5414
13:15 Moses g unto the tribe of the children of 5414
13:24 Moses g *inheritance* unto the tribe of Gad, 5414
13:29 Moses g *inheritance* unto the half tribe of 5414
13:33 unto the tribe of Levi Moses g not *any* 5414
14: 3 unto the Levites he g none inheritance 5414
14: 4 they g no part unto the Levites in the land, 5414
14:13 g unto Caleb the son of Jephunneh Hebron 5414

Jos	15:13	unto Caleb the son of Jephunneh he **g** a part	5414
	15:17	and he **g** him Achsah his daughter to wife.	5414
	15:19	he **g** her the upper springs, and the nether	5414
	17: 4	**g** them an inheritance among the brethren	5414
	18: 7	which Moses the servant of the LORD **g**	5414
	19:49	the children of Israel **g** an inheritance to	5414
	19:50	to the word of the LORD they **g**	5414
	21: 3	the children of Israel **g** unto the Levites out	5414
	21: 8	the children of Israel **g** by lot unto	5414
	21: 9	they **g** out of the tribe of the children of	5414
	21:11	they **g** them the city of Arbah the father of	5414
	21:12	**g** they to Caleb the son of Jephunneh for	5414
	21:13	Thus they **g** to the children of Aaron	5414
	21:21	For they **g** them Shechem with her suburbs	5414
	21:27	of the *other* half tribe of Manasseh *they g*	NIH
	21:43	the LORD **g** unto Israel all the land which	5414
	21:44	the LORD **g** them **rest** round about,	5117
	22: 4	which Moses the servant of the LORD **g**	5414
	22: 7	unto the *other* half thereof **g** Joshua among	5414
	24: 3	and multiplied his seed, and **g** him Isaac.	5414
	24: 4	I **g** unto Isaac Jacob and Esau: and I gave	5414
	24: 4	I **g** unto Esau mount Seir, to possess it;	5414
	24: 8	I **g** them into your hand, that ye might	5414
Jdg	1:13	and he **g** him Achsah his daughter to wife.	5414
	1:15	Caleb **g** her the upper springs and	5414
	1:20	they **g** Hebron unto Caleb, as Moses said:	5414
	3: 6	**g** their daughters to their sons, and	5414
	4:19	of milk, and **g** him **drink**, and covered him.	8248
	5:25	He asked water, *and* she **g** *him* milk;	5414
	6: 9	out from before you, and **g** you their land;	5414
	9: 4	they **g** him threescore and ten *pieces* of	5414
	14: 9	and he **g** them, and they did eat:	5414
	14:19	**g** change *of garments* unto them which	5414
	15: 2	therefore I **g** her to thy companion:	5414
	17: 4	**g** them to the founder, who made thereof a	5414
	19:21	his house, and **g provender** unto the asses:	1101
	20:36	for the men of Israel **g** place to	5414
	21:14	they **g** them wives which they had saved	5414
Ru	2:18	**g** to her that she had reserved after she was	5414
	3:17	These six *measures* of barley **g** he me;	5414
	4: 7	off his shoe, and **g** *it* to his neighbour:	5414
	4:13	the LORD **g** her conception, and she bare	5414
	4:17	And the *women her* neighbours **g** it a name,	7121
1Sa	1: 4	he **g** to Peninnah his wife, and to all her	5414
	1: 5	unto Hannah he **g** a worthy portion; for he	5414
	1:23	and **g** her son **suck** until she weaned him.	3243
	9:23	Bring the portion which I **g** thee, of which I	5414
	10: 9	go from Samuel, God **g** him another heart:	2015
	18: 4	**g** it to David, and his garments, even to his	5414
	18:27	and they **g** them **in full tale** to the king,	4390
	18:27	Saul **g** him Michal his daughter to wife.	5414
	20:40	Jonathan **g** his artillery unto his lad, and	5414
	21: 6	So the priest **g** him hallowed *bread:* for	5414
	22:10	**g** him victuals, and gave him the sword of	5414
	22:10	**g** him the sword of Goliath the Philistine.	5414
	27: 6	Achish **g** him Ziklag that day: wherefore	5414
	30:11	to David, and **g** him bread, and he did eat;	5414
	30:12	they **g** him a piece of a cake *of figs,* and	5414
2Sa	12: 8	I **g** thee thy master's house, and thy	5414
	12: 8	and **g** thee the house of Israel and of Judah;	5414
	18: 5	**g** all the captains **charge** concerning	6680
	24: 9	Joab **g** *up* the sum of the number of	5414
1Ki	4:29	God **g** Solomon wisdom and	5414
	5:10	So Hiram **g** Solomon cedar trees and	5414
	5:11	Solomon **g** Hiram twenty thousand	5414
	5:11	thus **g** Solomon to Hiram year by year.	5414
	5:12	the LORD **g** Solomon wisdom, as he	5414
	9:11	king Solomon **g** Hiram twenty cities in	5414
	10:10	she **g** the king an hundred and	5414
	10:10	the queen of Sheba **g** to king Solomon.	5414
	10:13	king Solomon **g** unto the queen of Sheba all	5414
	10:13	besides *that* which Solomon **g** her of his	5414
	11:18	which **g** him a house, and appointed him	5414
	11:18	and appointed him victuals, and **g** him land.	5414
	11:19	that he **g** him *to* wife the sister of his own	5414
	12:13	old men's **counsel** that they **g** him;	3289+6098
	13: 3	he **g** a sign the same day, saying, This *is*	5414
	14: 8	from the house of David, and **g** it thee:	5414
	14:15	which he **g** to their fathers, and shall scatter	5414
	19:21	and **g** unto the people, and they did eat.	5414
2Ki	10:15	he **g** *him* his hand; and he took him up to	5414
	11:12	crown upon him, and *g him* the Testimony;	NIH
	12:11	they **g** the money, being told, into the hands	5414
	12:14	they **g** that to the workmen, and	5414
	13: 5	(And the LORD **g** Israel a saviour, so	5414
	15:19	Menahem **g** Pul a thousand talents of silver,	5414
	17: 3	became his servant, and **g** him presents.	7725
	18:15	Hezekiah **g** *him* all the silver that was	5414
	18:16	and **g** it to the king of Assyria.	5414
	21: 8	more out of the land which I **g** their fathers;	5414
	22: 8	Hilkiah **g** the book to Shaphan, and he read	5414
	23:35	Jehoiakim **g** the silver and the gold to	5414
	25: 6	to Riblah; and they **g** judgment upon him.	1696
1Ch	2:35	Sheshan **g** his daughter to Jarha his servant	5414
	6:55	they **g** them Hebron in the land of Judah,	5414
	6:56	they **g** to Caleb the son of Jephunneh.	5414
	6:57	to the sons of Aaron they **g** the cities of	5414
	6:64	the children of Israel **g** to the Levites *these*	5414
	6:65	they **g** by lot out of the tribe of the children	5414
	6:67	they **g** unto them, *of* the cities of refuge,	5414
	6:67	*they g* also Gezer with her suburbs,	NIH
	14:12	David **g a commandment**, and they were	559
	21: 5	Joab **g** the sum of the number of the people	5414
	21:25	So David **g** to Ornan for the place six	5414
	25: 5	God **g** to Heman fourteen sons and	5414
	28:11	David **g** to Solomon his son the pattern of	5414
	28:14	*He g* of gold by weight for *things of* gold,	NIH
	28:16	*by* weight *he g* gold for the tables of	NIH
	28:17	for the golden basons *he g gold* by weight	NIH
	29: 7	**g** for the service of the house of God *of*	5414
	29: 8	**g** *them* to the treasure of the house of	5414
2Ch	9: 9	she **g** the king an hundred and	5414
	9: 9	as the queen of Sheba **g** king Solomon.	5414
	9:12	king Solomon **g** to the queen of Sheba all	5414
	10: 8	**counsel** which the old men **g** him,	3289+6098
	11:23	he **g** them victual in abundance. And he	5414
	13: 5	**g** the kingdom over Israel to David for	5414
	13:15	the men of Judah **g a shout**: and as the men	7321
	15:15	and the LORD **g** them **rest** round about.	5117
	20:30	for his God **g** him **rest** round about.	5117
	21: 3	their father **g** them great gifts of silver, and	5414
	21: 3	the kingdom **g** he to Jehoram; because	5414
	23:11	*g him* the Testimony, and made him king.	NIH
	24:12	Jehoiada **g** it to such as did the work of	5414
	26: 8	the Ammonites **g** gifts to Uzziah: and	5414
	27: 5	the children of Ammon **g** him the same	5414
	28:15	**g** them **to eat** and to drink, and	398
	28:21	and **g** *it* unto the king of Assyria:	5414
	30: 7	*who* therefore **g** them **up** to desolation,	5414
	30:24	the princes **g** to the congregation a	7311
	32:24	and he spake unto him, and he **g** him a sign.	5414
	34:10	they **g** it *to* the workmen that wrought in	5414
	34:11	and builders **g** they *it,* to buy hewn stone,	5414
	35: 7	Josiah **g** to the people, *of* the flock, lambs	7311
	35: 8	And his princes **g** willingly unto the people,	7311
	35: 8	**g** unto the priests for the passover *offerings*	5414
	35: 9	**g** unto the Levites for passover *offerings*	7311
	36:17	stooped for age: he **g** *them* all into his hand.	5414
Ezr	2:69	They **g** after their ability unto the treasure	5414
	3: 7	They **g** money also unto the masons, and	5414
	5:12	he **g** them into the hand of Nebuchadnezzar	3052
	7:11	the king Artaxerxes **g** unto Ezra the priest,	5414
	10:19	they **g** their hands that *they* would put away	5414
Ne	2: 1	I took up the wine, and **g** *it* unto the king.	5414
	2: 9	the river, and **g** them the king's letters.	5414
	7: 2	**g** my brother Hanani, and Hananiah the ruler of the palace, **charge**	6680
	7:70	some of the chief of the fathers **g** unto	5414
	7:70	The Tirshatha **g** to the treasure a thousand	5414
	7:71	*some* of the chief of the fathers **g** to	5414
	7:72	*that* which the rest of the people **g** *was*	5414
	8: 8	**g** the sense, and caused *them* to understand	7760
	12:31	two great *companies of them that g* thanks,	NIH
	12:38	the other *company of them that g* thanks	NIH
	12:40	So stood the two *companies of them that g*	NIH
	12:47	**g** the portions of the singers and the porters,	5414
Est	1: 7	*they g them* **drink** in vessels of gold,	8248
	2: 9	he speedily **g** her her things for	5414
	2:18	**g** gifts, according to the state of the king.	5414
	3:10	**g** it unto Haman the son of Hammedatha	5414
	4: 5	**g** him **a commandment** to Mordecai,	6680
	4: 8	Also he **g** him the copy of the writing of	5414
	4:10	and **g** him **commandment** unto Mordecai:	6680
	8: 2	taken from Haman, and **g** it unto Mordecai.	5414
Job	1:21	the LORD **g**, and the LORD hath taken	5414
	19:16	called my servant, and he **g** *me* no **answer**;	6030
	29:11	when the eye saw *me,* it **g witness to** me:	5749
	29:21	Unto me *men* **g ear**, and waited, and	8085

Job	32:11	I **g** **ear** to your reasons, whilst you searched	238
	42:10	also the LORD **g** Job twice as much as he	3254
	42:11	every man also **g** him a piece of money,	5414
	42:15	their father **g** them inheritance among their	5414
Ps	18:13	in the heavens, and the Highest **g** his voice;	5414
	68:11	The Lord **g** the word: great *was*	5414
	69:21	They **g** me also gall for my meat; and in my	5414
	69:21	in my thirst they **g** me vinegar **to drink**.	8248
	77: 1	God *with* my voice; and he **g** **ear** unto me.	238
	78:15	**g** *them* **drink** as *out of* the great depths.	8248
	78:29	well filled: for he **g** them their own desire;	935
	78:46	He **g** also their increase unto the caterpillar,	5414
	78:48	He **g** **up** their cattle also to the hail, and	5462
	78:50	but **g** their life **over** to the pestilence;	5462
	78:62	He **g** his people **over** also unto the sword;	5462
	81:12	So I **g** them **up** unto their own heart's lust:	7971
	99: 7	and the ordinance *that* he **g** them.	5414
	105:32	He **g** them hail *for* rain, *and* flaming fire in	5414
	105:44	**g** them the lands of the heathen: and	5414
	106:15	he **g** them their request; but sent leanness	5414
	106:41	And he **g** them into the hand of the heathen;	5414
	135:12	**g** their land *for* an heritage, an heritage unto	5414
	136:21	**g** their land for an heritage: for his mercy	5414
Pr	8:29	When he **g** to the sea his decree, that	7760
Ecc	1:13	I **g** my heart to seek and search out by	5414
	1:17	I **g** my heart to know wisdom, and to know	5414
	12: 7	the spirit shall return unto God who **g** it.	5414
	12: 9	he **g** **good heed**, and sought out, *and* set in	239
SS	5: 6	I called him, but he **g** me no **answer**.	6030
Isa	41: 2	**g** the nations before him, and made *him*	5414
	41: 2	he **g** *them* as the dust *to* his sword, *and*	5414
	42:24	Who **g** Jacob for a spoil, and Israel to	5414
	43: 3	I **g** Egypt *for* thy ransom, Ethiopia and	5414
	50: 6	I **g** my back to the smiters, and my cheeks	5414
Jer	7: 7	in the land that I **g** to your fathers, for ever	5414
	7:14	unto the place which I **g** to you and to your	5414
	16:15	into their land that I **g** unto their fathers.	5414
	17: 4	discontinue from thine heritage that I **g**	5414
	23:39	the city that I **g** you and your fathers, *and*	5414
	24:10	from off the land that I **g** unto them	5414
	30: 3	to return to the land that I **g** to their fathers,	5414
	32:12	I **g** the evidence of the purchase unto	5414
	36:32	**g** it to Baruch the scribe, the son of Neriah;	5414
	39: 5	of Hamath, where he **g** judgment upon him.	1696
	39:10	**g** them vineyards and fields at the same	5414
	39:11	**g** **charge** concerning Jeremiah to	6680
	40: 5	So the captain of the guard **g** him victuals	5414
	44:30	as I **g** Zedekiah king of Judah into the hand	5414
	52: 9	of Hamath; where he **g** judgment upon him.	1696
La	1:19	and mine elders **g** **up the ghost** in the city,	1478
Eze	16:19	My meat also which I **g** thee, fine flour, and	5414
	20:11	I **g** them my statutes, and shewed them my	5414
	20:12	Moreover also I **g** them my sabbaths, to be	5414
	20:25	Wherefore I **g** them also statutes *that were*	5414
	36:28	ye shall dwell in the land that I **g** to your	5414
	39:23	and **g** them into the hand of their enemies:	5414
Da	1: 2	the Lord **g** Jehoiakim king of Judah into his	5414
	1: 7	Unto whom the prince of the eunuchs **g**	7760
	1: 7	for he **g** unto Daniel *the name of*	7760
	1:16	that they should drink; and **g** them pulse.	5414
	1:17	God **g** them knowledge and skill in all	5414
	2:48	**g** him many great gifts, and made him ruler	3052
	5:18	the most high God **g** Nebuchadnezzar thy	3052
	5:19	for the majesty that he **g** him, all people,	3052
	6:10	prayed, and **g** **thanks** before his God, as he	3029
Hos	2: 8	For she did not know that I **g** her corn, and	5414
	13:11	I **g** thee a king in mine anger, and took *him*	5414
Am	2:12	ye **g** the Nazarites wine **to drink**;	8248
Mal	2: 5	I **g** them to him *for* the fear wherewith he	5414
Mt	8:18	he **g** **commandment** to depart unto	*2753*
	10: 1	he **g** them power against unclean spirits,	*1325*
	14:19	and **g** the loaves to *his* disciples, and	*1325*
	15:36	and **g** **thanks**, and brake *them,* and gave to	*2168*
	15:36	and brake *them,* and **g** to his disciples, and	*1325*
	21:23	these *things?* and who **g** thee this authority?	*1325*
	25:15	And unto one he **g** five talents, to another	*1325*
	25:35	For I was a hungred, and ye **g** me meat:	*1325*
	25:35	I was thirsty, and ye **g** me **drink**: I was a	*4222*
	25:37	and fed *thee?* or thirsty, and **g** *thee* **drink**?	*4222*
	25:42	For I was a hungred, and ye **g** me no meat:	*1325*
	25:42	I was thirsty, and ye **g** me no **drink**:	*4222*
	26:26	and brake *it,* and **g** *it* to the disciples,	*1325*
	26:27	and **g** **thanks**, and gave *it* to them, saying,	*2168*
	26:27	and gave thanks, and **g** *it* to them, saying,	*1325*
	26:48	Now he that betrayed him **g** them a sign,	*1325*
	27:10	And **g** them for the potter's field, as	*1325*
	27:34	They **g** him vinegar to drink mingled with	*1325*
	27:48	and put *it* on a reed, and **g** him **to drink**.	*4222*
	28:12	they **g** large money unto the soldiers,	*1325*
Mk	2:26	and **g** also to them which were with him?	*1325*
	5:13	And forthwith Jesus **g** them **leave**. And	*2010*
	6: 7	two; and **g** them power over unclean spirits;	*1325*
	6:28	head in a charger, and **g** it to the damsel:	*1325*
	6:28	and the damsel **g** it to her mother.	*1325*
	6:41	**g** *them* to his disciples to set before them;	*1325*
	8: 6	and **g** **thanks**, and brake, and gave to his	*2168*
	8: 6	**g** to his disciples to set before *them;* and	*1325*
	11:28	who **g** thee this authority to do these	*1325*
	13:34	and **g** authority to his servants, and to every	*1325*
	14:22	and brake *it,* and **g** to them, and said, Take,	*1325*
	14:23	when he had given thanks, he **g** *it* to them:	*1325*
	15:23	And they **g** him to drink wine mingled with	*1325*
	15:36	and **g** him **to drink**, saying, Let alone;	*4222*
	15:37	cried with a loud voice, and **g** **up the ghost**.	*1606*
	15:39	so cried out, and **g** **up the ghost**, he said,	*1606*
	15:45	*it* of the centurion, he **g** the body to Joseph.	*1433*
Lk	2:38	that instant **g** **thanks** *likewise* **unto** the Lord,	*437*
	4:20	and he **g** *it* **again** to the minister, and	*591*
	6: 4	and **g** also to them that were with him;	*1325*
	7:21	and unto many *that were* blind he **g** sight.	*5483*
	9: 1	and **g** them power and authority over all	*1325*
	9:16	**g** to the disciples to set before	*1325*
	10:35	and **g** *them* to the host, and said unto him,	*1325*
	15:16	the swine did eat: and no *man* **g** unto him.	*1325*
	18:43	when they saw *it,* **g** praise unto God.	*1325*
	20: 2	or who is he that **g** thee this authority?	*1325*
	22:17	and **g** **thanks**, and said, Take this, and	*2168*
	22:19	and **g** **thanks**, and brake *it,* and gave unto	*2168*
	22:19	and brake *it,* and **g** unto them, saying,	*1325*
	23:24	And Pilate **g** **sentence** that it should be as	*1948*
	23:29	and the paps which never **g** **suck**.	*2337*
	23:46	and having said thus, he **g** **up the ghost**.	*1606*
	24:30	and blessed *it,* and brake, and **g** to them.	*1929*
	24:42	And they **g** him a piece of a broiled fish,	*1929*
Jn	1:12	to them **g** he power to become the sons of	*1325*
	3:16	the world, that he **g** his only begotten Son,	*1325*
	4: 5	near to the parcel of ground that Jacob **g** to	*1325*
	4:12	which **g** us the well, and drank thereof	*1325*
	6:31	He **g** them bread from heaven to eat.	*1325*
	6:32	Moses **g** you not *that* bread from heaven;	*1325*
	7:22	Moses therefore **g** unto you circumcision,	*1325*
	10:29	My Father, which **g** *them* me, is greater	*1325*
	12:49	he **g** me a commandment, what I should	*1325*
	13:26	he **g** *it* to Judas Iscariot, *the son* of Simon.	*1325*
	14:31	and as the Father **g** me **commandment**,	*1781*
	18:14	was he, which **g** **counsel** to the Jews,	*4823*
	19: 9	art thou? But Jesus **g** him no answer.	*1325*
	19:30	and he bowed *his* head, and **g** **up** the ghost.	*3860*
	19:38	and Pilate **g** *him* **leave**. He came therefore,	*2010*
Ac	1:26	And they **g** **forth** their lots; and the lot fell	*1325*
	2: 4	as the Spirit **g** them utterance.	*1325*
	3: 5	And he **g** heed unto them, expecting to	NIG
	4:33	And with great power **g** the apostles witness	*591*
	5: 5	these words fell down, and **g** **up the ghost**:	*1634*
	7: 5	And he **g** him none inheritance in it, no, not	*1325*
	7: 8	And he **g** him the covenant of circumcision:	*1325*
	7:10	and **g** him favour and wisdom in the sight	*1325*
	7:42	**g** them **up** to worship the host of heaven;	*3860*
	8: 6	And the people with one accord **g** **heed**	*4337*
	8:10	To whom they all **g** **heed**, from the least to	*4337*
	9:41	And he **g** her *his* hand, and lift her up, and	*1325*
	10: 2	which **g** much alms to the people, and	*4160*
	11:17	as God **g** them the like gift as *he did* unto	*1325*
	12:22	And the people **g** **a shout**, *saying, It is*	*2019*
	12:23	smote him, because he **g** not God the glory:	*1325*
	12:23	he was eaten of worms, and **g** **up the ghost**.	*1634*
	13:20	And after that he **g** *unto them* judges about	*1325*
	13:21	and God **g** unto them Saul the son of Cis,	*1325*
	13:22	to whom also he **g** **testimony**, and said,	*3140*
	14: 3	which **g** **testimony** unto the word of his	*3140*
	14:17	and **g** us rain from heaven, and	*1325*
	15:12	and **g** **audience** to Barnabas and Paul,	*191*
	15:24	to whom we **g** no *such* **commandment**:	*1291*
	22:22	And they **g** him **audience** unto this word,	*191*
	23:30	**g** **commandment** to *his* accusers also to	*3853*
	26:10	put to death, I **g** my voice against *them.*	*2702*
	27: 3	**g** *him* **liberty** to go unto *his* friends to	*2010*
	27:35	**g** **thanks** to God in presence of *them* all:	*2168*

Ro 1:24 Wherefore God also g them up to 3860
1:26 For this cause God g them up unto vile 3860
1:28 God g them over to a reprobate mind, to do 3860
1Co 3: 5 even as the Lord g to every man? 1325
3: 6 Apollos watered; but God g the increase. 837
2Co 8: 5 but first g their own selves to the Lord, and 1325
Gal 1: 4 Who g himself for our sins, that he might 1325
2: 5 To whom we g place by subjection, no, 1502
2: 9 they g to me and Barnabas the right hands 1325
2:20 who loved me, and g himself for me. 3860
3:18 but God g *it* to Abraham by promise. 5483
Eph 1:22 g him *to be* the head over all *things* to 1325
4: 8 led captivity captive, and g gifts unto men. 1325
4:11 And he g some, apostles; and some, 1325
5:25 also loved the church, and g himself for it; 3860
1Th 4: 2 For ye know what commandments we g 1325
1Ti 2: 6 Who g himself a ransom for all, to be 1325
Tit 2:14 Who g himself for us, that he might redeem 1325
Heb 7: 2 To whom also Abraham g a tenth *part* of 3307
7: 4 patriarch Abraham g the tenth of the spoils. 1325
7:13 of which no *man* g attendance at the altar. 4337
11:22 g commandment concerning his bones. 1781
12: 9 corrected *us,* and we g *them* reverence: 1788
Jas 5:18 and the heaven g rain, and the earth brought 1325
1Pe 1:21 him up from the dead, and g him glory; 1325
1Jn 3:23 love one another, as he g us commandment. 1325
5:10 he believeth not the record that God g of 3140
Jude 1: 3 when I g all diligence to write unto you of 4160
Rev 1: 1 of Jesus Christ, which God g unto him, 1325
2:21 And I g her space to repent of her 1325
11:13 and g glory to the God of heaven. 1325
13: 2 and the dragon g him his power, and 1325
13: 4 And they worshipped the dragon which g 1325
15: 7 And one of the four beasts g unto the seven 1325
20:13 And the sea g up the dead which were in it; 1325

GAVEST (34) [GIVE]
Ge 3:12 The woman whom thou g *to be* with me, 5414
1Ki 8:34 the land which thou g unto their fathers. 5414
8:40 in the land which thou g unto our fathers. 5414
8:48 which thou g unto their fathers, the city 5414
2Ch 6:25 again unto the land which thou g to them 5414
6:31 long as they live in the land which thou g 5414
6:38 which thou g unto their fathers, and 5414
20: 7 g it to the seed of Abraham thy friend for 5414
Ne 9: 7 and g him the name of Abraham; 7760
9:13 g them right judgments, and true laws, 5414
9:15 g them bread from heaven for their hunger, 5414
9:20 Thou g also thy good spirit to instruct them, 5414
9:20 and g them water for their thirst. 5414
9:22 Moreover thou g them kingdoms and 5414
9:24 the Canaanites, and g them into their hands, 5414
9:27 according to thy manifold mercies thou g 5414
9:30 g thou them into the hand of the people of 5414
9:35 in thy great goodness that thou g them, and 5414
9:35 and fat land which thou g before them, 5414
9:36 *for* the land that thou g unto our fathers to 5414
Job 39:13 G *thou* the goodly wings unto the peacocks? NIH
Ps 21: 4 He asked life of thee, *and* thou g *it* him, 5414
74:14 g him *to be* meat to the people inhabiting 5414
Lk 7:44 thou g me no water for my feet: 1325
7:45 Thou g me no kiss: but this *woman* since 1325
15:29 and yet thou never g me a kid, that I might 1325
19:23 then g not thou my money into the bank, 1325
Jn 17: 4 I have finished the work which thou g me 1325
17: 6 the men which thou g me out of the world: 1325
17: 6 thine they were, and thou g them me; and 1325
17: 8 unto them the words which thou g me; 1325
17:12 *those* that thou g me I have kept, and 1325
17:22 And the glory which thou g me I have 1325
18: 9 Of them which thou g me have I lost none. 1325

GAY (1)
Jas 2: 3 respect to him that weareth the g clothing, 2986

GAZA (19) [GAZATHITES, GAZITES]
Ge 10:19 as thou comest to Gerar, unto G; 5804
Jos 10:41 them from Kadesh-barnea even unto G, 5804
11:22 only in G, in Gath, and in Ashdod, 5804
15:47 G *with* her towns and her villages, 5804
Jdg 1:18 Also Judah took G with the coast thereof, 5804
6: 4 till thou come *unto* G, and left no 5804
16: 1 went Samson to G, and saw there a harlot, 5804
16:21 brought him down to G, and bound him 5804
1Sa 6:17 for Ashdod one, for G one, for Askelon 5804
2Ki 18: 8 *even* unto G, and the borders thereof, 5804
1Ch 7:28 unto G and the towns thereof: 5804
Jer 47: 1 before that Pharaoh smote G. 5804
47: 5 Baldness is come upon G; Ashkelon is cut 5804
Am 1: 6 For three transgressions of G, and for four, 5804
1: 7 I will send a fire on the wall of G, 5804
Zep 2: 4 For G shall be forsaken, and Ashkelon a 5804
Zec 9: 5 G also *shall see it,* and be very sorrowful, 5804
9: 5 the king shall perish from G, and 5804
Ac 8:26 that goeth down from Jerusalem unto G, 1048

GAZATHITES (1) [GAZA]
Jos 13: 3 the G, and the Ashdothites, 5841

GAZE (1) [GAZING, GAZING-STOCK, GAZINGSTOCK, STARGAZERS]
Ex 19:21 they break through unto the LORD to g, 7200

GAZELLE See ROEBUCK; ROES

GAZER (2)
2Sa 5:25 Philistines from Geba until thou come *to* G. 1507
1Ch 14:16 of the Philistines from Gibeon even to G. 1507

GAZEZ (2)
1Ch 2:46 bare Haran, and Moza, and G: 1495
2:46 and Moza, and Gazez: and Haran begat G. 1495

GAZING (1) [GAZE]
Ac 1:11 of Galilee, why stand ye g up into heaven? 1689

GAZINGSTOCK, GAZING-STOCK (2) [GAZE]
Na 3: 6 and make thee vile, and will set thee as a g. 7210
Heb 10:33 whilst ye were made a g both by 2301

GAZITES (1) [GAZA]
Jdg 16: 2 *And it was told* the G, saying, Samson is 5841

GAZZAM (2)
Ezr 2:48 the children of Nekoda, the children of G, 1502
Ne 7:51 The children of G, the children of Uzza, 1502

GE HARASHIM See CHARASHIM

GEBA (13)
Jos 21:17 with her suburbs, G with her suburbs, 1387
1Sa 13: 3 the garrison of the Philistines that *was* in G, 1387
2Sa 5:25 smote the Philistines from G until thou 1387
1Ki 15:22 king Asa built with them G of Benjamin, 1387
2Ki 23: 8 from G to Beer-sheba, and brake down 1387
1Ch 6:60 G with her suburbs, and Alemeth with her 1387
8: 6 heads of the fathers of the inhabitants of G, 1387
2Ch 16: 6 and he built therewith G and Mizpah. 1387
Ne 7:30 The men of Ramah and G, six hundred 1387
11:31 The children also of Benjamin from G 1387
12:29 and out of the fields of G and Azmaveth: 1387
Isa 10:29 they have taken up their lodging at G; 1387
Zec 14:10 from G to Rimmon south of Jerusalem: 1387

GEBAL (2) [GIBLITES]
Ps 83: 7 G, and Ammon, and Amalek; 1381
Eze 27: 9 The ancients of G and the wise *men* thereof 1380

GEBALITES See GIBLITES

GEBER (2)
1Ki 4:13 The son of G, in Ramoth-gilead; to him 1398
4:19 G the son of Uri *was* in the country of 1398

GEBIM (1)
Isa 10:31 the inhabitants of G gather themselves to 1374

GEDALIAH (32)
2Ki 25:22 even over them he made G the son of 1436
25:23 heard that the king of Babylon had made G 1436
25:23 there came to G *to* Mizpah, even Ishmael 1436
25:24 And G sware to them, and to their men, and 1436
25:25 and smote G, that he died, and the Jews and 1436
1Ch 25: 3 G, and Zeri, and Jeshaiah, Hashabiah, and 1436
25: 9 the second *to* G, who with his brethren and 1436
Ezr 10:18 Maaseiah, and Eliezer, and Jarib, and G. 1436
Jer 38: 1 G the son of Pashur, and Jucal the son of 1436
39:14 committed him unto G the son of Ahikam 1436
40: 5 *he said,* Go back also to G the son of 1436
40: 6 went Jeremiah unto G the son of Ahikam to 1436
40: 7 heard that the king of Babylon had made G 1436

G

Jer 40: 8 they came to **G** to Mizpah, even Ishmael 1436
40: 9 **G** the son of Ahikam the son of Shaphan 1436
40:11 that he had set over them **G** the son of 1436
40:12 to **G**, unto Mizpah, and gathered wine and 1436
40:13 *were* in the fields, came to **G** to Mizpah, 1436
40:14 **G** the son of Ahikam believed them not. 1436
40:15 Johanan the son of Kareah spake to **G** in 1436
40:16 **G** the son of Ahikam said unto Johanan 1436
41: 1 came unto **G** the son of Ahikam to Mizpah; 1436
41: 2 smote **G** the son of Ahikam the son of 1436
41: 3 *even* with **G** at Mizpah, and the Chaldeans 1436
41: 4 to pass the second day after *he* had slain **G**, 1436
41: 6 unto them, Come to **G** the son of Ahikam. 1436
41: 9 the men, whom he had slain because of **G**, 1436
41:10 had committed to **G** the son of Ahikam: 1436
41:16 after *that* he had slain **G** the son of Ahikam, 1436
41:18 Ishmael the son of Nethaniah had slain **G** 1436
43: 6 **G** the son of Ahikam the son of Shaphan, 1436
Zep 1: 1 the son of **G**, the son of Amariah, the son 1436

GEDEON (1) [GIDEON]
Heb 11:32 for the time would fail me to tell of **G**, and *1066*

GEDER (1)
Jos 12:13 The king of Debir, one; the king of **G**, one; 1445

GEDERAH (1)
Jos 15:36 and Adithaim, and **G**, and Gederothaim; 1449

GEDERATHITE (1)
1Ch 12: 4 Jahaziel, and Johanan, and Josabad the **G**, 1452

GEDERITE (1)
1Ch 27:28 in the low plains *was* Baal-hanan the **G**: 1451

GEDEROTH (2)
Jos 15:41 **G**, Beth-dagon, and Naamah, and 1450
2Ch 28:18 **G**, and Shocho with the villages thereof, 1450

GEDEROTHAIM (1)
Jos 15:36 and Adithaim, and Gederah, and **G**; 1453

GEDOR (7)
Jos 15:58 Halhul, Beth-zur, and **G**, 1446
1Ch 4: 4 Penuel the father of **G**, and Ezer the father 1446
4:18 wife Jehudijah bare Jered the father of **G**, 1446
4:39 they went to the entrance of **G**, *even* unto 1446
8:31 And **G**, and Ahio, and Zacher. 1446
9:37 **G**, and Ahio, and Zechariah, and Mikloth. 1446
12: 7 and Zebadiah, the sons of Jeroham of **G**. 1446

GEHAZI (12)
2Ki 4:12 he said to **G** his servant, Call this 1522
4:14 **G** answered, Verily she hath no child, and 1522
4:25 that he said to **G** his servant, Behold, 1522
4:27 **G** came near to thrust her away. And 1522
4:29 he said to **G**, Gird up thy loins, and take my 1522
4:31 **G** passed on before them, and laid the staff 1522
4:36 he called **G**, and said, Call this 1522
5:20 **G**, the servant of Elisha the man of God, 1522
5:21 So **G** followed after Naaman. And when 1522
5:25 said unto him, Whence *comest thou*, **G**? 1522
8: 4 the king talked with **G** the servant of 1522
8: 5 **G** said, My lord, O king, this *is* the woman, 1522

GELILOTH (1)
Jos 18:17 *to* En-shemesh, and went forth toward **G**, 1553

GEMALLI (1)
Nu 13:12 Of the tribe of Dan, Ammiel the son of **G**. 1582

GEMARIAH (5)
Jer 29: 3 son of Shaphan, and **G** the son of Hilkiah, 1587
36:10 in the chamber of **G** the son of Shaphan 1587
36:11 When Michaiah the son of **G**, the son of 1587
36:12 **G** the son of Shaphan, and Zedekiah 1587
36:25 **G** had made intercession to the king that *he* 1587

GENDER (2) [GENDERED, GENDERETH]
Lev 19:19 Thou shalt not let thy cattle **g with** a 7250
2Ti 2:23 knowing that they do **g** strifes. *1080*

GENDERED (1) [GENDER]
Job 38:29 the hoary frost of heaven, who hath **g** it? 3205

GENDERETH (2) [GENDER]
Job 21:10 Their bull **g**, and faileth not; their cow 5674
Gal 4:24 which **g** to bondage, which is Agar. *1080*

GENEALOGIES (8) [GENEALOGY]
1Ch 5:17 All these were **reckoned by g** in the days 3187
7: 5 **reckoned** in all **by** their **g** fourscore and 3187
7: 7 were **reckoned by** their **g** twenty and 3187
9: 1 So all Israel were **reckoned by g**; and 3187
2Ch 12:15 and of Iddo the seer concerning **g**? 3187
31:19 to all that were **reckoned by g** among 3187
1Ti 1: 4 Neither give heed to fables and endless **g**, *1076*
Tit 3: 9 and **g**, and contentions, and strivings about *1076*

GENEALOGY (15) [GENEALOGIES]
1Ch 4:33 These *were* their habitations, and their **g**. 3187
5: 1 the **g** is not to be **reckoned** after 3187
5: 7 the **g** of their generations was **reckoned**, 3187
7: 9 the **number** of them, **after** their **g** by their 3187
7:40 the number **throughout** the **g** of them *that* 3187
9:22 These were **reckoned by** their **g** in their 3187
2Ch 31:16 Beside their **g** of males, from three years 3187
31:17 Both *to* the **g** of the priests by the house of 3187
31:18 to the **g** of all their little ones, their wives, 3187
Ezr 2:62 *among* those that were **reckoned by g**, 3187
8: 1 *this is* the **g** of them that went up with me 3187
8: 3 with him were **reckoned by g** of the males 3187
Ne 7: 5 that *they* might be **reckoned by g**. 3187
7: 5 I found a register of the **g** of them which 3188
7:64 *among* those that were **reckoned by g**, 3187

GENERAL (2) [GENERALLY]
1Ch 27:34 and the **g** of the king's army *was* Joab. 8269
Heb 12:23 To the **g assembly**, and church of *3831*

GENERALLY (2) [GENERAL]
2Sa 17:11 *that* all Israel be **g gathered** unto thee, 622+622
Jer 48:38 *There shall be* lamentation **g** upon all 3605

GENERATION (107) [GENERATIONS]
Ge 7: 1 have I seen righteous before me in this **g**. 1755
15:16 *in* the fourth **g** they shall come hither again: 1755
50:23 *g*: the children also of Machir the son of NIH
Ex 1: 6 and all his brethren, and all that **g**. 1755
17:16 war with Amalek from **g** *to* generation. 1755
17:16 war with Amalek from generation *to* **g**. 1755
20: 5 the third and fourth *g* of them that hate me; NIH
34: 7 unto the third and to the fourth *g*. NIH
Nu 14:18 the children unto the third and fourth *g*. NIH
32:13 until all the **g**, that had done evil in 1755
Dt 1:35 these men of this evil **g** see that good land, 1755
2:14 until all the **g** of the men of war were 1755
5: 9 the third and fourth *g* of them that hate me, NIH
23: 2 even *to* his tenth **g** shall he not enter into 1755
23: 3 even *to* their tenth **g** shall they not enter 1755
23: 8 congregation of the LORD *in* their third **g**. 1755
29:22 So that the **g** to come of your children that 1755
32: 5 *they are* a perverse and crooked **g**. 1755
32:20 end *shall be*: for they *are* a very froward **g**, 1755
Jdg 2:10 also all that **g** were gathered unto their 1755
2:10 there arose another **g** after them, 1755
2Ki 10:30 thy children of the fourth *g* shall sit on NIH
15:12 the throne of Israel unto the fourth *g*. And NIH
Est 9:28 throughout **every g**, 1755+1755+3605+2050.1
Ps 12: 7 thou shalt preserve them from this **g** for 1755
14: 5 for God *is* in the **g** of the righteous. 1755
22:30 it shall be accounted to the Lord for a **g**. 1755
24: 6 This *is* the **g** of them that seek him, 1755
48:13 that ye may tell *it* to the **g** following. 1755
49:19 He shall go to the **g** of his fathers; 1755
71:18 until I have shewed thy strength unto *this* **g**, 1755
73:15 I should offend *against* the **g** of thy 1755
78: 4 shewing to the **g** to come the praises of 1755
78: 6 That the **g** to come might know *them, even* 1755
78: 8 as their fathers, a stubborn and rebellious **g**; 1755
78: 8 a **g** *that* set not their heart aright, and 1755
95:10 Forty years long was I grieved with *this* **g**, 1755
102:18 This shall be written for the **g** to come: and 1755
109:13 in the **g** following let their name be blotted 1755
112: 2 the **g** of the upright shall be blessed. 1755
145: 4 One **g** shall praise thy works to another, 1755
Pr 27:24 crown *endure* to **every g**? 1755+1755+2050.1
30:11 *There is* a **g** *that* curseth their father, and 1755
30:12 *There is* a **g** *that are* pure in their own eyes, 1755

Pr 30:13 *There is* a **g**, O how lofty are their eyes! 1755
30:14 *There is* a **g**, whose teeth *are as* swords, and 1755
Ecc 1: 4 *One* **g** passeth away, and 1755
1: 4 passeth away, and *another* **g** cometh: 1755
Isa 13:20 neither shall it be dwelt in from **g** to 1755
13:20 shall it be dwelt in from generation to **g**: 1755
34:10 from **g** to generation it shall lie waste; 1755
34:10 from generation to **g** it shall lie waste; 1755
34:17 from **g** to generation shall they dwell 1755
34:17 from generation to **g** shall they dwell 1755
51: 8 and my salvation from **g** to generation. 1755
51: 8 and my salvation from generation to **g**. 1755
53: 8 who shall declare his **g**? for he was cut off 1755
Jer 2:31 O **g**, see ye the word of the LORD. Have I 1755
7:29 and forsaken the **g** of his wrath. 1755
50:39 neither shall it be dwelt in from **g** to 1755
50:39 shall it be dwelt in from generation to **g**. 1755
La 5:19 for ever; thy throne from **g** to generation. 1755
5:19 for ever; thy throne from generation to **g**. 1755
Da 4: 3 and his dominion *is* from **g** to generation. 1859
4: 3 and his dominion *is* from generation to **g**. 1859
4:34 and his kingdom *is* from **g** to generation: 1859
4:34 and his kingdom *is* from generation to **g**: 1859
Joel 1: 3 their children, and their children another **g**. 1755
3:20 and Jerusalem from **g** to generation. 1755
3:20 and Jerusalem from generation to **g**. 1755
Mt 1: 1 The book of the **g** of Jesus Christ, the son *1078*
3: 7 he said unto them, O **g** of vipers, *1081*
11:16 But whereunto shall I liken this **g**? It is like *1074*
12:34 O **g** of vipers, how can ye, being evil, *1081*
12:39 and adulterous **g** seeketh after a sign; *1074*
12:41 Nineveh shall rise in judgment with this **g**, *1074*
12:42 shall rise up in the judgment with this **g**, *1074*
12:45 *Even* so shall it be also unto this wicked **g**. *1074*
16: 4 and adulterous **g** seeketh after a sign; *1074*
17:17 and said, O faithless and perverse **g**, *1074*
23:33 *Ye* serpents, *ye* **g** of vipers, how can ye *1081*
23:36 All these *things* shall come upon this **g**. *1074*
24:34 Verily I say unto you, This **g** shall not pass, *1074*
Mk 8:12 saith, Why doth this **g** seek after a sign? *1074*
8:12 There shall no sign be given unto this **g**. *1074*
8:38 of my words in this adulterous and sinful **g**; *1074*
9:19 He answereth him, and saith, O faithless **g**, *1074*
13:30 I say unto you, that this **g** shall not pass, *1074*
Lk 1:50 on them that fear him from **g** to generation. *1074*
1:50 on them that fear him from generation to **g**. *1074*
3: 7 O **g** of vipers, who hath warned you to flee *1081*
7:31 then shall I liken the men of this **g**? *1074*
9:41 answering said, O faithless and perverse **g**, *1074*
11:29 he began to say, This is an evil **g**: *1074*
11:30 so shall also the Son of man be to this **g**. *1074*
11:31 up in the judgment with the men of this **g**, *1074*
11:32 shall rise up in the judgment with this **g**, *1074*
11:50 of the world, may be required of this **g**; *1074*
11:51 I say unto you, It shall be required of this **g**. *1074*
16: 8 for the children of this world are in their **g** *1074*
17:25 many *things*, and be rejected of this **g**. *1074*
21:32 This **g** shall not pass away, till all be *1074*
Ac 2:40 Save yourselves from this untoward **g**. *1074*
8:33 and who shall declare his **g**? for his life is *1074*
13:36 after he had served his own **g** by the will of *1074*
Heb 3:10 Wherefore I was grieved with that **g**, and *1074*
1Pe 2: 9 But ye *are* a chosen **g**, a royal priesthood, *1085*

GENERATIONS (118) [GENERATION]

Ge 2: 4 These *are* the **g** of the heavens and of 8435
5: 1 This *is* the book of the **g** of Adam. In 8435
6: 9 These *are* the **g** of Noah: Noah was a just 8435
6: 9 Noah was a just man *and* perfect in his **g**, 1755
9:12 creature that *is* with you, for perpetual **g**: 1755
10: 1 Now these *are* the **g** of the sons of Noah, 8435
10:32 sons of Noah, after their **g**, in their nations: 8435
11:10 These *are* the **g** of Shem: Shem *was* an 8435
11:27 Now these *are* the **g** of Terah: Terah begat 8435
17: 7 thy seed after thee in their **g** for an 1755
17: 9 thou, and thy seed after thee in their **g**. 1755
17:12 every man *child* in your **g**, he that is born in 1755
25:12 Now these *are* the **g** of Ishmael, 8435
25:13 by their names, according to their **g**: 8435
25:19 these *are* the **g** of Isaac, Abraham's son: 8435
36: 1 Now these *are* the **g** of Esau, who *is* Edom. 8435
36: 9 these *are* the **g** of Esau the father of 8435
37: 2 These *are* the **g** of Jacob. Joseph, 8435
Ex 3:15 and this *is* my memorial unto **all g**. 1755+1755
6:16 of the sons of Levi according to their **g**; 8435
6:19 the families of Levi according to their **g**. 8435
12:14 it a feast to the LORD throughout your **g**; 1755
12:17 shall ye observe this day in your **g** by an 1755
12:42 of all the children of Israel in their **g**. 1755
16:32 Fill an omer of it to be kept for your **g**; 1755
16:33 before the LORD, to be kept for your **g**. 1755
27:21 *it shall be* a statute for ever unto their **g** on 1755
29:42 **g** *at* the door of the tabernacle of 1755
30: 8 before the LORD throughout your **g**. 1755
30:10 make atonement upon it throughout your **g**: 1755
30:21 to him and to his seed throughout their **g**. 1755
30:31 anointing oil unto me throughout your **g**. 1755
31:13 between me and you throughout your **g**; 1755
31:16 to observe the sabbath throughout their **g**, 1755
40:15 everlasting priesthood throughout their **g**. 1755
Lev 3:17 *It shall be* a perpetual statute for your **g** 1755
6:18 *It shall be* a statute for ever in your **g** 1755
7:36 *by* a statute for ever throughout their **g**. 1755
10: 9 *be* a statute for ever throughout your **g**: 1755
17: 7 for ever unto them throughout their **g**. 1755
21:17 Whosoever *he be* of thy seed in their **g** that 1755
22: 3 *he be* of all your seed among your **g**, 1755
23:14 throughout your **g** in all your dwellings. 1755
23:21 in all your dwellings throughout your **g**. 1755
23:31 throughout your **g** in all your dwellings. 1755
23:41 *It shall be* a statute for ever in your **g**: 1755
23:43 That your **g** may know that I made 1755
24: 3 *it shall be* a statute for ever in your **g**. 1755
25:30 ever to him that bought it throughout his **g**: 1755
Nu 1:20 Israel's eldest son, *by* their **g**, after their 8435
1:22 of Simeon, *by* their **g**, after their families, 8435
1:24 of Gad, *by* their **g**, after their families, 8435
1:26 of Judah, *by* their **g**, after their families, 8435
1:28 of Issachar, *by* their **g**, after their families, 8435
1:30 of Zebulun, *by* their **g**, after their families, 8435
1:32 *by* their **g**, after their families, by the house 8435
1:34 *by* their **g**, after their families, by the house 8435
1:36 *by* their **g**, after their families, by the house 8435
1:38 of Dan, *by* their **g**, after their families, 8435
1:40 of Asher, *by* their **g**, after their families, 8435
1:42 *throughout* their **g**, after their families, 8435
3: 1 These also *are* the **g** of Aaron and Moses in 8435
10: 8 an ordinance for ever throughout your **g**. 1755
15:14 or whosoever *be* among you in your **g**, and 1755
15:15 *with you*, an ordinance for ever in your **g**: 1755
15:21 unto the LORD a heave offering in your **g**. 1755
15:23 and henceforward among your **g**; 1755
15:38 of their garments throughout their **g**, 1755
18:23 *be* a statute for ever throughout your **g**, 1755
35:29 throughout your **g** in all your dwellings. 1755
Dt 7: 9 keep his commandments to a thousand **g**; 1755
32: 7 the years of **many g**: 1755+1755+2050.1
Jos 22:27 between us, and you, and our **g** after us, 1755
22:28 *so* say to us or to our **g** in time to come, 1755
Jdg 3: 2 Only that the **g** of the children of Israel 1755
Ru 4:18 Now these *are* the **g** of Pharez: 8435
1Ch 1:29 These *are* their **g**: The firstborn of Ishmael, 8435
5: 7 when the genealogy of their **g** was 8435
7: 2 *they were* valiant *men* of might in their **g**; 8435
7: 4 with them, by their **g**, after the house of 8435
7: 9 of them, after their genealogy by their **g**, 8435
8:28 These *were* heads of the fathers, by their **g**, 8435
9: 9 according to their **g**, nine hundred and fifty 8435
9:34 the Levites *were* chief throughout their **g**; 8435
16:15 *which* he commanded to a thousand **g**; 1755
26:31 according to the **g** of his fathers. 8435
Job 42:16 his sons, and his sons' sons, *even* four **g**. 1755
Ps 33:11 thoughts of his heart to **all g**. 1755+1755+2050.1
45:17 remembered in **all g**: 1755+1755+3605+2050.1
49:11 their dwelling places to **all g**; 1755+1755+2050.1
61: 6 *and* his years as **many g**. 1755+1755+2050.1
72: 5 and moon endure, **throughout all g**. 1755+1755
79:13 forth thy praise to **all g**. 1755+1755+2050.1
85: 5 out thine anger to **all g**? 1755+1755+2050.1
89: 1 thy faithfulness to **all g**. 1755+1755+2050.1
89: 4 build up thy throne to **all g**. 1755+1755+2050.1
90: 1 our dwelling place in **all g**. 1755+1755+2050.1
100: 5 his truth *endureth* to **all g**. 1755+1755+2050.1
102:12 thy remembrance unto **all g**. 1755+1755+2050.1
102:24 thy years *are* throughout **all g**. 1755+1755
105: 8 *which* he commanded to a thousand **g**. 1755
106:31 unto **all g** for evermore. 1755+1755+2050.1
119:90 faithfulness *is* unto **all g**: 1755+1755+2050.1

Ps 135:13 O LORD, throughout **all g**. 1755+1755+2050.1
145:13 *endureth* throughout all **g**. 1755+1755+2050.1
146:10 thy God, O Zion, unto **all g**. 1755+1755+2050.1
Isa 41: 4 done *it,* calling the **g** from the beginning? 1755
51: 9 as *in* the ancient days, *in* the **g** of old. 1755
58:12 the foundations of **many g**; 1755+1755+2050.1
60:15 a joy of **many g**. 1755+1755+2050.1
61: 4 the desolations of **many g**. 1755+1755+2050.1
Joel 2: 2 *even* to the years of **many g**. 1755+1755+2050.1
Mt 1:17 So all the **g** from Abraham to David *are* *1074*
1:17 from Abraham to David *are* fourteen **g**; *1074*
1:17 carrying away into Babylon *are* fourteen **g**; *1074*
1:17 into Babylon unto Christ *are* fourteen **g**. *1074*
Lk 1:48 from henceforth all **g** shall call me blessed. *1074*
Col 1:26 which hath been hid from ages and from **g**, *1074*

GENESARET (1) [GENNESARET]
Mk 6:53 they came into the land of **G**, and drew to *1082*

GENNESARET (2) [GENESARET]
Mt 14:34 gone over, they came into the land of **G**. *1082*
Lk 5: 1 the word of God, he stood by the lake of **G**, *1082*

GENTILE (2) [GENTILES]
Ro 2: 9 of the Jew first, and *also* of the **G**; *1672*
2:10 to the Jew first, and *also* to the **G**: *1672*

GENTILES (129) [GENTILE]
Ge 10: 5 By these were the isles of the **G** divided in 1471
Jdg 4: 2 which dwelt in Harosheth of the **G**. 1471
4:13 from Harosheth of the **G** unto the river of 1471
4:16 and after the host, unto Harosheth of the **G**: 1471
Isa 11:10 ensign of the people; to it shall the **G** seek: 1471
42: 1 he shall bring forth judgment to the **G**. 1471
42: 6 covenant of the people, for a light of the **G**; 1471
49: 6 I will also give thee for a light to the **G**, 1471
49:22 I will lift up mine hand to the **G**, and set up 1471
54: 3 thy seed shall inherit the **G**, and make 1471
60: 3 the **G** shall come to thy light, and kings to 1471
60: 5 the forces of the **G** shall come unto thee. 1471
60:11 may bring unto thee the forces of the **G**, 1471
60:16 Thou shalt also suck the milk of the **G**, and 1471
61: 6 ye shall eat the riches of the **G**, and in their 1471
61: 9 their seed shall be known among the **G**, 1471
62: 2 the **G** shall see thy righteousness, and 1471
66:12 the glory of the **G** like a flowing stream: 1471
66:19 they shall declare my glory among the **G**. 1471
Jer 4: 7 and the destroyer of the **G** is on his way; 1471
14:22 Are there *any* among the vanities of the **G** 1471
16:19 the **G** shall come unto thee from the ends of 1471
46: 1 to Jeremiah the prophet against the **G**; 1471
La 2: 9 her king and her princes *are* among the **G**: 1471
Eze 4:13 Israel eat their defiled bread among the **G**, 1471
Hos 8: 8 now shall they be among the **G** as a vessel 1471
Joel 3: 9 Proclaim ye this among the **G**; Prepare war, 1471
Mic 5: 8 the remnant of Jacob shall be among the **G** 1471
Zec 1:21 to fray them, to cast out the horns of the **G**, 1471
Mal 1:11 same my name *shall be* great among the **G**; 1471
Mt 4:15 of the sea, beyond Jordan, Galilee of the **G**; *1484*
6:32 (For after all these *things* do the **G** seek): *1484*
10: 5 Go not into the way of the **G**, and into *any* *1484*
10:18 for a testimony against them and the **G**. *1484*
12:18 and he shall shew judgment to the **G**. *1484*
12:21 And in his name shall the **G** trust. *1484*
20:19 And shall deliver him to the **G** to mock, *1484*
20:25 Ye know that the princes of the **G** exercise *1484*
Mk 10:33 to death, and shall deliver him to the **G**: *1484*
10:42 over the **G** exercise lordship over them; *1484*
Lk 2:32 A light to lighten the **G**, and the glory of *1484*
18:32 For he shall be delivered unto the **G**, and *1484*
21:24 Jerusalem shall be trodden down of the **G**, *1484*
21:24 until the times of the **G** be fulfilled. *1484*
22:25 The kings of the **G** exercise lordship over *1484*
Jn 7:35 will he go unto the dispersed among the **G**, *1672*
7:35 among the Gentiles, and teach the **G**? *1672*
Ac 4:27 with the **G**, and the people of Israel, *1484*
7:45 in with Jesus into the possession of the **G**, *1484*
9:15 to bear my name before the **G**, and kings, *1484*
10:45 that on the **G** also was poured out the gift *1484*
11: 1 brethren that were in Judea heard that the **G** *1484*
11:18 Then hath God also to the **G** granted *1484*
13:42 the **G** besought that these words might be *1484*
13:46 of everlasting life, lo, we turn to the **G**. *1484*
13:47 I have set thee to be a light of the **G**, *1484*
13:48 And when the **G** heard *this,* they were glad, *1484*
14: 2 But the unbelieving Jews stirred up the **G**, *1484*
14: 5 there was an assault made both of the **G**, *1484*
14:27 he had opened *the* door of faith unto the **G**. *1484*
15: 3 Samaria, declaring the conversion of the **G**: *1484*
15: 7 that the **G** by my mouth should hear *1484*
15:12 wonders God had wrought among the **G** by *1484*
15:14 how God at the first did visit the **G**, *1484*
15:17 and all the **G**, upon whom my name is *1484*
15:19 which from among the **G** are turned to *1484*
15:23 the brethren which are of the **G** in Antioch *1484*
18: 6 from henceforth I will go unto the **G**. *1484*
21:11 shall deliver *him* into the hands of the **G**. *1484*
21:19 had wrought among the **G** by his ministry. *1484*
21:21 which are among the **G** to forsake Moses, *1484*
21:25 As touching the **G** which believe, we have *1484*
22:21 for I will send thee far hence unto the **G**. *1484*
26:17 and *from* the **G**, unto whom now I send *1484*
26:20 and *then* to the **G**, that *they* should repent *1484*
26:23 shew light unto the people, and to the **G**. *1484*
28:28 that the salvation of God is sent unto the **G**, *1484*
Ro 1:13 among you also, even as among other **G**. *1484*
2:14 For when *the* **G**, which have not the law, *1484*
2:24 is blasphemed among the **G** through you, *1484*
3: 9 we have before proved both Jews and **G**, *1672*
3:29 *is he* not also of the **G**? Yes, of the Gentiles *1484*
3:29 not also of the Gentiles? Yes, of the **G** also: *1484*
9:24 not of the Jews only, but also of the **G**? *1484*
9:30 That the **G**, which followed not *after* *1484*
11:11 their fall salvation *is come* unto the **G**, *1484*
11:12 the diminishing of them the riches of the **G**; *1484*
11:13 For I speak to you **G**, inasmuch as I am *1484*
11:13 inasmuch as I am the apostle of the **G**, *1484*
11:25 until the fulness of the **G** be come in. *1484*
15: 9 And that the **G** might glorify God for *his* *1484*
15: 9 cause I will confess to thee among the **G**, *1484*
15:10 *he* saith, Rejoice, *ye* **G**, with his people. *1484*
15:11 And again, Praise the Lord, all ye **G**; and *1484*
15:12 and he that *shall* rise to reign over the **G**; *1484*
15:12 over the Gentiles; in him shall the **G** trust. *1484*
15:16 be the minister of Jesus Christ to the **G**, *1484*
15:16 that the offering up of the **G** might be *1484*
15:18 to make the **G** obedient, by word and deed, *1484*
15:27 For if the **G** have been made partakers of *1484*
16: 4 but also all the churches of the **G**. *1484*
1Co 5: 1 as is not so much as named amongst the **G**, *1484*
10:20 But *I say,* that *the things* which the **G** *1484*
10:32 neither to the Jews, nor to the **G**, *1672*
12: 2 Ye know that ye were **G**, carried away unto *1484*
12:13 whether *we be* Jews or **G**, whether *we be* *1672*
Gal 2: 2 *that* gospel which I preach among the **G**, *1484*
2: 8 *the same* was mighty in me towards the **G**:) *1484*
2:12 came from James, he did eat with the **G**: *1484*
2:14 livest **after the manner of G**, and not as do *1483*
2:14 why compellest thou the **G** to live as do *1484*
2:15 Jews by nature, and not sinners of the **G**, *1484*
3:14 might come on the **G** through Jesus Christ; *1484*
Eph 2:11 that ye *being* in time passed **G** in the flesh, *1484*
3: 1 the prisoner of Jesus Christ for you **G**, *1484*
3: 6 That the **G** should be fellowheirs, and *1484*
3: 8 that *I* should preach among the **G** *1484*
4:17 that ye henceforth walk not as other **G** *1484*
Col 1:27 of the glory of this mystery among the **G**; *1484*
1Th 2:16 Forbidding us to speak to the **G** that they *1484*
4: 5 even as the **G** which know not God: *1484*
1Ti 2: 7 a teacher of the **G** in faith and verity. *1484*
3:16 seen of angels, preached unto the **G**, *1484*
2Ti 1:11 and an apostle, and a teacher of the **G**. *1484*
4:17 fully known, and *that* all the **G** might hear: *1484*
1Pe 2:12 your conversation honest among the **G**: *1484*
4: 3 us to have wrought the will of the **G**, *1484*
3Jn 1: 7 they went forth, taking nothing of the **G**. *1484*
Rev 11: 2 measure it not; for it is given unto the **G**: *1484*

GENTLE (5) [GENTLENESS, GENTLY]
1Th 2: 7 But we were **g** among you, *even* as a nurse *2261*
2Ti 2:24 but be **g** unto all *men,* apt to teach, patient, *2261*
Tit 3: 2 *but* **g**, shewing all meekness unto all men. *1933*
Jas 3:17 then peaceable, **g**, *and* easy to be intreated, *1933*
1Pe 2:18 not only to the good and **g**, but also to *1933*

GENTLENESS (4) [GENTLE]
2Sa 22:36 and thy **g** hath made me great. 6031
Ps 18:35 me up, and thy **g** hath made me great. 6037

2Co 10: 1 you by the meekness and **g** of Christ, *1932*
Gal 5:22 peace, longsuffering, **g**, goodness, faith, *5544*

GENTLY (2) [GENTLE]
2Sa 18: 5 saying, *Deal* **g** for my sake with 328+3807.1
Isa 40:11 *and* shall **g lead** those that are with young. 5095

GENUBATH (2)
1Ki 11:20 the sister of Tahpenes bare him **G** his son, 1592
11:20 **G** was *in* Pharaoh's household among 1592

GERA (9)
Ge 46:21 Ashbel, **G**, and Naaman, Ehi, and Rosh, 1617
Jdg 3:15 Ehud the son of **G**, a Benjamite, a man 1617
2Sa 16: 5 whose name *was* Shimei, the son of **G**: 1617
19:16 Shimei the son of **G**, a Benjamite, 1617
19:18 Shimei the son of **G** fell down before 1617
1Ki 2: 8 *thou hast* with thee Shimei the son of **G**, 1617
1Ch 8: 3 of Bela were, Addar, and **G**, and Abihud, 1617
8: 5 And **G**, and Shephuphan, and Huram. 1617
8: 7 Naaman, and Ahiah, and **G**, he removed 1617

GERAHS (5)
Ex 30:13 (a shekel *is* twenty **g**:) a half shekel *shall be* 1626
Lev 27:25 the sanctuary: twenty **g** shall be the shekel. 1626
Nu 3:47 thou take *them:* (the shekel *is* twenty **g**:) 1626
18:16 shekel of the sanctuary, which *is* twenty **g**. 1626
Eze 45:12 the shekel *shall be* twenty **g**: 1626

GERAR (10)
Ge 10:19 as thou comest to **G**, unto Gaza; 1642
20: 1 and Shur, and sojourned in **G**. 1642
20: 2 Abimelech king of **G** sent, and took Sarah. 1642
26: 1 Abimelech king of the Philistims unto **G**. 1642
26: 6 And Isaac dwelt in **G**: 1642
26:17 pitched his tent in the valley of **G**, and 1642
26:20 the herdmen of **G** did strive with Isaac's 1642
26:26 Abimelech went to him from **G**, and 1642
2Ch 14:13 that *were* with him pursued them unto **G**: 1642
14:14 they smote all the cities round about **G**; 1642

GERGESENES (1)
Mt 8:28 to the other side into the country of the **G**, *1086*

GERIZIM (3) [GERIZZIM]
Dt 11:29 thou shalt put the blessing upon mount **G**, 1630
Jos 8:33 half of them over against mount **G**, and half 1630
Jdg 9: 7 he went and stood in the top of mount **G**, 1630

GERIZZIM (1) [GERIZIM]
Dt 27:12 These shall stand upon mount **G** to bless 1630

GERSHOM (14)
Ex 2:22 bare *him* a son, and he called his name **G**: 1647
18: 3 of which the name of the one *was* **G**; for he 1647
Jdg 18:30 Jonathan, the son of **G**, the son of 1647
1Ch 6:16 The sons of Levi; **G**, Kohath, and Merari. 1647
6:17 these *be* the names of the sons of **G**; Libni, 1647
6:20 Of **G**; Libni his son, Jahath his son, 1647
6:43 son of Jahath, the son of **G**, the son of Levi. 1647
6:62 to the sons of **G** throughout their families 1647
6:71 Unto the sons of **G** *were given* out of 1647
15: 7 Of the sons of **G**; Joel the chief, and 1647
23:15 The sons of Moses *were,* **G**, and Eliezer. 1647
23:16 *Of* the sons of **G**, Shebuel *was* the chief. 1647
26:24 Shebuel the son of **G**, the son of Moses, 1647
Ezr 8: 2 Of the sons of Phinehas; **G**: of the sons of 1647

GERSHON (18) [GERSHONITE, GERSHONITES]
Ge 46:11 the sons of Levi; **G**, Kohath, and Merari. 1648
Ex 6:16 **G**, and Kohath, and Merari: 1648
6:17 The sons of **G**; Libni, and Shimi, 1648
Nu 3:17 by their names; **G**, and Kohath, and Merari. 1648
3:18 these *are* the names of the sons of **G** by 1648
3:21 Of **G** *was* the family of the Libnites, and 1648
3:25 the charge of the sons of **G** in 1648
4:22 Take also the sum of the sons of **G**, 1648
4:28 of **G** in the tabernacle of the congregation: 1649
4:38 those that were numbered of the sons of **G**, 1648
4:41 numbered of the families of the sons of **G**, 1648
7: 7 and four oxen he gave unto the sons of **G**, 1648
10:17 the sons of **G** and the sons of Merari set 1648
26:57 of **G**, the family of the Gershonites: 1648
Jos 21: 6 the children of **G** *had* by lot out of 1648
21:27 unto the children of **G**, of the families of 1648
1Ch 6: 1 The sons of Levi; **G**, Kohath, and Merari. 1648
23: 6 of Levi, *namely,* **G**, Kohath, and Merari. 1648

GERSHONITE (3) [GERSHON]
1Ch 26:21 the sons of the **G** Laadan, chief fathers, 1649
26:21 *even* of Laadan the **G**, *were* Jehieli. 1649
29: 8 of the LORD, by the hand of Jehiel the **G**. 1649

GERSHONITES (9) [GERSHON]
Nu 3:21 these *are* the families of the **G**. 1649
3:23 The families of the **G** shall pitch behind 1649
3:24 the chief of the house of the father of the **G** 1649
4:24 This *is* the service of the families of the **G**, 1649
4:27 shall be all the service of the sons of the **G**, 1649
26:57 of Gershon, the family of the **G**: of Kohath, 1649
Jos 21:33 All the cities of the **G** according to their 1649
1Ch 23: 7 Of the **G** *were,* Laadan, and Shimei. 1649
2Ch 29:12 of the **G**; Joah the son of Zimmah, and 1649

GESHAN (1)
1Ch 2:47 and **G**, and Pelet, and Ephah, and Shaaph. 1529

GESHEM (3) [GASHMU]
Ne 2:19 the Ammonite, and **G** the Arabian, 1654
6: 1 **G** the Arabian, and the rest of our enemies, 1654
6: 2 That Sanballat and **G** sent unto me, saying, 1654

GESHUR (8) [GESHURI, GESHURITES]
2Sa 3: 3 Maacah the daughter of Talmai king of **G**; 1650
13:37 to Talmai, the son of Ammihud, king of **G**. 1650
13:38 and went to **G**, and was there three years. 1650
14:23 So Joab arose and went to **G**, and 1650
14:32 to say, Wherefore am I come from **G**? 1650
15: 8 vowed a vow while I abode at **G** in Syria, 1650
1Ch 2:23 he took **G**, and Aram, with the towns of 1650
3: 2 Maachah the daughter of Talmai king of **G**: 1650

GESHURI (2) [GESHUR]
Dt 3:14 the country of Argob unto the coasts of **G** 1651
Jos 13: 2 all the borders of the Philistines, and all **G**, 1651

GESHURITES (5) [GESHUR]
Jos 12: 5 unto the border of the **G** and 1651
13:11 the border of the **G** and Maachathites, and 1651
13:13 the children of Israel expelled not the **G**, 1651
13:13 the **G** and the Maachathites dwell among 1650
1Sa 27: 8 invaded the **G**, and the Gezrites, and 1651

GET (118) [GAT, GETTETH, GETTING, GOT, GOTTEN]
Ge 12: 1 **G** thee out of thy country, and from thy 1980
19:14 and said, Up, **g** ye **out** of this place; 3318
22: 2 and **g** thee into the land of Moriah; 1980
31:13 **g** thee **out** from this land, and return unto 3318
34: 4 saying, **G** me this damsel to wife. 3947
34:10 you therein, and **g** you **possessions** therein. 270
42: 2 **g** you **down** thither, and buy for us from 3381
44:17 for you, **g** you **up** in peace unto your father. 5927
45:17 and go, **g** you unto the land of Canaan; 935
Ex 1:10 and *so* **g** them **up** out of the land. 5927
5: 4 from their works? **g** you unto your burdens. 1980
5:11 **g** you straw where you can find *it:* yet not 3947
7:15 **G** thee unto Pharaoh in the morning; lo, 1980
10:28 **G** thee from me, take heed to thyself, 1980
11: 8 **G** thee **out**, and all the people that follow 3318
12:31 *and* **g** you **forth** from amongst my people, 3318
14:17 I will **g** me **honour** upon Pharaoh, and 3513
19:24 **g** thee **down**, and thou shalt come up, thou, 3381
32: 7 LORD said unto Moses, Go, **g** thee **down**; 3381
Lev 14:21 cannot **g** *so much;* then he shall take 3027+5381
14:22 such as he is **able to g**; 3027+5381
14:30 the young pigeons, such as he **can g**; 3027+5381
14:31 *Even* such as he is **able to g**, the one 3027+5381
14:32 whose **hand is not able to g** *that* 3027+5381
Nu 6:21 besides *that* that his hand shall **g**: 5381
13:17 **G** you **up** this *way* southward, and go up 5927
14:25 **g** you *into* the wilderness *by* the way of 5265
16:24 **G** you **up** from about the tabernacle of 5927
16:45 **G** you **up** from among this congregation, 7426
22:13 the princes of Balak, **G** you into your land: 1980
22:34 if it displease thee, I will **g** me **back again**. 7725
27:12 **G** thee **up** into this mount Abarim, and 5927
Dt 2:13 *said I,* and **g** you **over** the brook Zered. 5674
3:27 **G** thee **up** *into* the top of Pisgah, and lift up 5927

Dt 5:30 say to them, **G** you into your tents **again**. 7725
8:18 for *it is* he that giveth thee power to **g** 6213
9:12 Arise, **g** thee **down** quickly from hence; 3381
17: 8 **g** thee **up** into the place which the LORD 5927
28:43 The stranger that *is* within thee shall **g up** 5927
32:49 **G** thee **up** into this mountain Abarim, 5927
Jos 2:16 she said unto them, **G** you to the mountain, 1980
7:10 the LORD said unto Joshua, **G** thee **up**; 6965
17:15 *then* **g** thee **up** to the wood *country,* and 5927
22: 4 **g** ye unto your tents, *and* unto the land of 1980
Jdg 7: 9 unto him, Arise, **g** thee **down** unto the host; 3381
14: 2 therefore **g** her for me to wife. 3947
14: 3 Samson said unto his father, **G** her for me; 3947
19: 9 to morrow **g** you **early** on your way, that 7925
Ru 3: 3 upon thee, and **g** thee **down** *to* the floor: 3381
1Sa 9:13 Now therefore **g** you **up**; for about *this* time 5927
15: 6 **g** you **down** from among the Amalekites, 3381
20:29 let me **g away**, I pray thee, and see my 4422
22: 5 depart, and **g** thee *into* the land of Judah. 935
23:26 David made haste to **g away** for fear of 1980
25: 5 **G** you **up** to Carmel, and go to Nabal, and 5927
2Sa 20: 6 lest he **g** him fenced cities, and escape us. 4672
1Ki 1: 2 that my lord the king may **g heat**. 2552
1:13 Go and **g** thee **in** unto king David, and 935
2:26 **G** thee *to* Anathoth, unto thine own fields; 1980
12:18 made speed to **g** *him* **up** to *his* chariot, 5927
14: 2 the wife of Jeroboam; and **g** thee *to* Shiloh: 1980
14:12 thou therefore, **g** thee to thine own house: 1980
17: 3 **G** thee hence, and turn thee eastward, 1980
17: 9 Arise, **g** thee to Zarephath, which *belongeth* 1980
18:41 said unto Ahab, **G** thee **up**, eat and drink; 5927
18:44 Prepare *thy chariot,* and **g** thee **down**, 3381
2Ki 3:13 **g** thee to the prophets of thy father, and 1980
7:12 we shall catch them alive, and **g** into the city. 935
2Ch 10:18 king Rehoboam made speed to **g** *him* **up** to 5927
Ne 9:10 So didst thou **g** thee a name, as *it is* this 6213
Ps119:104 Through thy precepts I **g** understanding: NIH
Pr 4: 5 **G** wisdom, get understanding: forget *it* not; 7069
4: 5 Get wisdom, **g** understanding: forget *it* not; 7069
4: 7 *is* the principal thing; *therefore* **g** wisdom: 7069
4: 7 and with all thy getting **g** understanding. 7069
6:33 A wound and dishonour shall he **g**; and 4672
16:16 How much better *is it* to **g** wisdom than 7069
16:16 to **g** understanding rather to be chosen than 7069
17:16 a price in the hand of a fool to **g** wisdom, 7069
22:25 learn his ways, and **g** a snare to thy soul. 3947
Ecc 3: 6 A time to **g**, and a time to lose; a time to 1245
SS 4: 6 I will **g** me to the mountain of myrrh, and 1980
7:12 Let us **g up early** to the vineyards; let us 7925
Isa 22:15 Go, **g** thee unto this treasurer, *even* unto 935
30:11 **G** ye **out** of the way, turn aside out of 5493
30:22 thou shalt say unto it, **G** thee **hence**. 3318
40: 9 **g** thee **up** into the high mountain; 5927
47: 5 Sit thou silent, and **g** thee into darkness, 935
Jer 5: 5 I will **g** me unto the great men, and 1980
13: 1 Go and **g** thee a linen girdle, and put it 7069
19: 1 Go and **g** a potter's earthen bottle, and 7069
46: 4 **g up**, ye horsemen, and stand forth with 5927
48: 9 unto Moab, that it may flee and **g away**: 3318
49:30 Flee, **g** you far off, dwell deep, O ye 5110
49:31 Arise, **g** you **up** unto the wealthy nation, 5927
La 3: 7 hath hedged me about, that I cannot **g out**: 3318
Eze 3: 4 go, **g** thee unto the house of Israel, and 935
3:11 go, **g** thee to them of the captivity, unto 935
11:15 have said, **G** ye far from the LORD: NIH
22:27 to destroy souls, to **g dishonest gain**. 1214+1215
Da 4:14 let the beasts **g away** from under it, and 5111
Joel 3:13 come, **g** you **down**; for the press is full, 3381
Zep 3:19 I will **g** them praise and fame in every land 7760
Zec 6: 7 **G** ye *hence,* walk to and fro through 1980
Mt 4:10 saith Jesus unto him, **G** thee **hence**, Satan: *5217*
14:22 constrained his disciples to **g** into a ship, *1684*
16:23 said unto Peter, **G** thee behind me, Satan: *5217*
Mk 6:45 constrained his disciples to **g** into the ship, *1684*
8:33 saying, **G** thee behind me, Satan: *5217*
Lk 4: 8 said unto him, **G** thee behind me, Satan: *5217*
9:12 round about, and lodge, and **g** victuals: *2147*
13:31 unto him, **G** *thee* **out**, and depart hence: *1831*
Ac 7: 3 **G** thee **out** of thy country, and *1831*
10:20 and **g** *thee* **down**, and go with them, *2597*
22:18 and **g** *thee* quickly **out** of Jerusalem: *1831*
27:43 *themselves* first into *the sea,* and **g** to land: *1826*
2Co 2:11 Lest Satan should **g an advantage** of us: *4122*
Jas 4:13 there a year, and buy and sell, and **g gain**: *2770*

GETHER (2)
Ge 10:23 of Aram; Uz, and Hul, and **G**, and Mash. 1666
1Ch 1:17 and Uz, and Hul, and **G**, and Meshech. 1666

GETHSEMANE (2)
Mt 26:36 Jesus with them unto a place called **G**, *1068*
Mk 14:32 they came to a place which was named **G**: *1068*

GETTETH (9) [GET]
2Sa 5: 8 Whosoever **g up** to the gutter, and 5060
Pr 3:13 and the man *that* **g** understanding. 6329
9: 7 He that reproveth a scorner **g** to himself 3947
9: 7 he that rebuketh a wicked *man* **g** himself a NIH
15:32 but he that heareth reproof **g** understanding. 7069
18:15 The heart of the prudent **g** knowledge; and 7069
19: 8 He that **g** wisdom loveth his own soul: 7069
Jer 17:11 *so* he that **g** riches, and not by right, 6213
48:44 he that **g up** out of the pit shall be taken in 5927

GETTING (3) [GET]
Ge 31:18 which he had gotten, the cattle of his **g**, 7075
Pr 4: 7 and with all thy **g** get understanding. 7075
21: 6 The **g** of treasures by a lying tongue *is* a 6467

GEUEL (1)
Nu 13:15 Of the tribe of Gad, **G** the son of Machi. 1345

GEZER (13) [GEZRITES]
Jos 10:33 Horam king of **G** came up to help Lachish; 1507
12:12 The king of Eglon, one; the king of **G**, one; 1507
16: 3 coast of Beth-horon the nether, and to **G**: 1507
16:10 not out the Canaanites that dwelt in **G**: 1507
21:21 for the slayer; and **G** with her suburbs, 1507
Jdg 1:29 drive out the Canaanites that dwelt in **G**; 1507
1:29 but the Canaanites dwelt in **G** among them. 1507
1Ki 9:15 and Hazor, and Megiddo, and **G**. 1507
9:16 taken **G**, and burnt it with fire, and slain 1507
9:17 Solomon built **G**, and Beth-horon 1507
1Ch 6:67 *they gave* also **G** with her suburbs, 1507
7:28 and eastward Naaran, and westward **G**, 1507
20: 4 that there arose war at **G** with 1507

GEZRITES (1) [GEZER]
1Sa 27: 8 and the **G**, and the Amalekites: 1511

GHOST (109)
Ge 25: 8 Abraham **gave up the g**, and died in a good 1478
25:17 he **gave up the g** and died; and 1478
35:29 Isaac **gave up the g**, and died, and 1478
49:33 **yielded up the g**, and was gathered unto 1478
Job 3:11 *why* did I *not* **give up the g** when I came 1478
10:18 *Oh that* I had **given up the g**, and no eye 1478
11:20 *shall be as* the **giving up of the g**. 4646+5315
13:19 if I hold my tongue, I shall **give up the g**. 1478
14:10 yea, man **giveth up the g**, and where *is* he? 1478
Jer 15: 9 she hath **given up the g**; her sun is 5301+5315
La 1:19 and mine elders **gave up the g** in the city, 1478
Mt 1:18 she was found with child of the Holy **G**. *4151*
1:20 which is conceived in her is of the Holy **G**. *4151*
3:11 he shall baptize you with the Holy **G**, and *4151*
12:31 the blasphemy against the *Holy* **G** shall not *4151*
12:32 whosoever speaketh against the Holy **G**, *4151*
27:50 again with a loud voice, yielded up the **g**. *4151*
28:19 and of the Son, and of the Holy **G**: *4151*
Mk 1: 8 but he shall baptize you with the Holy **G**. *4151*
3:29 against the Holy **G** hath never forgiveness, *4151*
12:36 For David himself said by the Holy **G**, *4151*
13:11 for it is not ye that speak, but the Holy **G**. *4151*
15:37 cried with a loud voice, and **gave up the g**. *1606*
15:39 so cried out, and **gave up the g**, he said, *1606*
Lk 1:15 and he shall be filled with the Holy **G**, *4151*
1:35 The Holy **G** shall come upon thee, and *4151*
1:41 and Elisabeth was filled with the Holy **G**: *4151*
1:67 Zacharias was filled with the Holy **G**, *4151*
2:25 of Israel: and the Holy **G** was upon him. *4151*
2:26 it was revealed unto him by the Holy **G**, *4151*
3:16 he shall baptize you with the Holy **G** and *4151*
3:22 And the Holy **G** descended in a bodily *4151*
4: 1 And Jesus being full of the Holy **G** *4151*
12:10 against the Holy **G** it shall not be forgiven. *4151*
12:12 For the Holy **G** shall teach you in the same *4151*
23:46 and having said thus, he **gave up the g**. *1606*
Jn 1:33 is he which baptizeth with the Holy **G**. *4151*
7:39 for the Holy **G** was not yet *given;* because *4151*

Jn 14:26 But the Comforter, *which is* the Holy **G**, *4151*
19:30 and he bowed *his* head, and gave up the **g**. *4151*
20:22 saith unto them, Receive ye the Holy **G**: *4151*
Ac 1: 2 after that he through the Holy **G** had given *4151*
1: 5 ye shall be baptized with the Holy **G** not *4151*
1: 8 after that the Holy **G** is come upon you: *4151*
1:16 which the Holy **G** by the mouth of David *4151*
2: 4 And they were all filled with the Holy **G**, *4151*
2:33 of the Father the promise of the Holy **G**, *4151*
2:38 and ye shall receive the gift of the Holy **G**. *4151*
4: 8 Then Peter, filled with the Holy **G**, *4151*
4:31 and they were all filled with the Holy **G**, *4151*
5: 3 Satan filled thine heart to lie to the Holy **G**, *4151*
5: 5 these words fell down, and **gave up the g**: *1634*
5:10 at his feet, and **yielded up the g**: *1634*
5:32 and *so is* also the Holy **G**, whom God hath *4151*
6: 3 full of the Holy **G** and wisdom, whom we *4151*
6: 5 a man full of faith and of the Holy **G**, and *4151*
7:51 and ears, ye do always resist the Holy **G**: *4151*
7:55 But he, being full of the Holy **G**, looked up *4151*
8:15 that they might receive the Holy **G**: *4151*
8:17 on them, and they received the Holy **G**. *4151*
8:18 the apostles' hands the Holy **G** was given, *4151*
8:19 I lay hands, he may receive the Holy **G**. *4151*
9:17 thy sight, and be filled with the Holy **G**. *4151*
9:31 and in the comfort of the Holy **G**, *4151*
10:38 anointed Jesus of Nazareth with the Holy **G** *4151*
10:44 the Holy **G** fell on all them which heard *4151*
10:45 also was poured out the gift of the Holy **G**. *4151*
10:47 which have received the Holy **G** as well as *4151*
11:15 I began to speak, the Holy **G** fell on them, *4151*
11:16 but ye shall be baptized with the Holy **G**. *4151*
11:24 and full of the Holy **G** and of faith: *4151*
12:23 he was eaten of worms, and **gave up the g**. *1634*
13: 2 and fasted, the Holy **G** said, Separate me *4151*
13: 4 So they, being sent forth by the Holy **G**, *4151*
13: 9 filled with the Holy **G**, set his eyes on him, *4151*
13:52 were filled with joy, and with the Holy **G**. *4151*
15: 8 bare them witness, giving them the Holy **G**, *4151*
15:28 For it seemed good to the Holy **G**, and *4151*
16: 6 were forbidden of the Holy **G** to preach *4151*
19: 2 Have ye received the Holy **G** since ye *4151*
19: 2 as heard whether there be *any* Holy **G**. *4151*
19: 6 upon them, the Holy **G** came on them; *4151*
20:23 Save that the Holy **G** witnesseth in every *4151*
20:28 over the which the Holy **G** hath made you *4151*
21:11 and feet, and said, Thus saith the Holy **G**, *4151*
28:25 Well spake the Holy **G** by Esaias *4151*
Ro 5: 5 by the Holy **G** which is given unto us. *4151*
9: 1 also bearing me witness in the Holy **G**, *4151*
14:17 and peace, and joy in the Holy **G**. *4151*
15:13 in hope, through the power of the Holy **G**. *4151*
15:16 being sanctified by the Holy **G**. *4151*
1Co 2:13 but which the Holy **G** teacheth; *4151*
6:19 is the temple of the Holy **G** which is in you, *4151*
12: 3 that Jesus is the Lord, but by the Holy **G**. *4151*
2Co 6: 6 by kindness, by the Holy **G**, *4151*
13:14 and the communion of the Holy **G**, *be* with *4151*
1Th 1: 5 and in the Holy **G**, and in much assurance; *4151*
1: 6 in much affliction, with joy of the Holy **G**: *4151*
2Ti 1:14 keep by the Holy **G** which dwelleth in us. *4151*
Tit 3: 5 and renewing of the Holy **G**; *4151*
Heb 2: 4 divers miracles, and gifts of the Holy **G**, *4151*
3: 7 Wherefore, as the Holy **G** saith, To day if *4151*
6: 4 and were made partakers of the Holy **G**, *4151*
9: 8 The Holy **G** this signifying, that the way *4151*
10:15 *Whereof* the Holy **G** also is a witness to us: *4151*
1Pe 1:12 with the Holy **G** sent *down* from heaven; *4151*
2Pe 1:21 spake *as they were* moved by the Holy **G**. *4151*
1Jn 5: 7 the Father, the Word, and the Holy **G**: *4151*
Jude 1:20 most holy faith, praying in the Holy **G**, *4151*

GIAH (1)
2Sa 2:24 that *lieth* before **G** *by* the way of 1520

GIANT (8) [GIANTS]
2Sa 21:16 which *was* of the sons of the **g**, 7497
21:18 slew Saph, which *was* of the sons of the **g**. 7497
21:20 *in* number; and he also was born to the **g**. 7497
21:22 These four were born to the **g** in Gath, and 7497
1Ch 20: 4 *that was* of the children of the **g**: 7497
20: 6 *each foot:* and he also was the son of the **g**. 7497
20: 8 These were born unto the **g** in Gath; and 7497
Job 16:14 upon breach, he runneth upon me like a **g**. 1368

GIANTS (13) [GIANT]
Ge 6: 4 There were **g** in the earth in those days; 5303
Nu 13:33 there we saw the **g**, the sons of Anak, 5303
13:33 the sons of Anak, *which come* of the **g**: 5303
Dt 2:11 Which also were accounted **g**, as 7497
2:20 (That also was accounted a land of **g**: 7497
2:20 **g** dwelt therein in old time; and 7497
3:11 of Bashan remained of the remnant of **g**; 7497
3:13 all Bashan, which was called the land of **g**. 7497
Jos 12: 4 *which was* of the remnant of the **g**, 7497
13:12 who remained of the remnant of the **g**: 7497
15: 8 which *is* at the end of the valley of the **g** 7497
17:15 in the land of the Perizzites and of the **g**, 7497
18:16 which *is* in the valley of the **g** on the north, 7497

GIBBAR (1)
Ezr 2:20 The children of **G**, ninety and five. 1402

GIBBETHON (6)
Jos 19:44 And Eltekeh, and **G**, and Baalath, 1405
21:23 with her suburbs, **G** with her suburbs, 1405
1Ki 15:27 Baasha smote him at **G**, which *belongeth* to 1405
15:27 for Nadab and all Israel laid siege to **G**. 1405
16:15 the people *were* encamped against **G**, 1405
16:17 Omri went up from **G**, and all Israel with 1405

GIBEA (1)
1Ch 2:49 father of Machbenah, and the father of **G**: 1388

GIBEAH (48) [GIBEATH, GIBEATHITE]
Jos 15:57 Cain, **G**, and Timnah; ten cities with their 1390
Jdg 19:12 children of Israel; we will pass over to **G**. 1390
19:13 places to lodge all night, in **G**, or in Ramah. 1390
19:14 down upon them *when they were* by **G**, 1390
19:15 aside thither, to go in *and* to lodge in **G**: 1390
19:16 of mount Ephraim; and he sojourned in **G**: 1390
20: 4 I came into **G** that *belongeth* to Benjamin, I 1390
20: 5 the men of **G** rose against me, and beset 1390
20: 9 *shall be* the thing which we will do to **G**; 1390
20:10 may do, when they come to **G** of Benjamin, 1387
20:13 the children of Belial, which *are* in **G**, 1390
20:14 together out of the cities unto **G**, 1390
20:15 drew sword, beside the inhabitants of **G**, 1390
20:19 in the morning, and encamped against **G**. 1390
20:20 in array to fight against them at **G**. 1390
20:21 children of Benjamin came forth out of **G**, 1390
20:25 Benjamin went forth against them out of **G** 1390
20:29 And Israel set liers in wait round about **G**. 1390
20:30 put *themselves* in array against **G**, as at 1390
20:31 the other to **G** in the field, about thirty men 1390
20:33 their places, *even* out of the meadows of **G**. 1387
20:34 there came against **G** ten thousand chosen 1390
20:36 liers in wait which they had set beside **G**. 1390
20:37 the liers in wait hasted, and rushed upon **G**; 1390
20:43 trode them down with ease over against **G** 1390
1Sa 10:26 Saul also went home to **G**; and there went 1390
11: 4 came the messengers *to* **G** of Saul, and 1390
13: 2 a thousand were with Jonathan in **G** of 1390
13:15 gat him up from Gilgal *unto* **G** of 1390
13:16 with them, abode in **G** of Benjamin: 1387
14: 2 Saul tarried in the uttermost part of **G** 1390
14: 5 and the other southward over against **G**. 1387
14:16 the watchmen of Saul in **G** of Benjamin 1390
15:34 and Saul went up to his house *to* **G** of Saul. 1390
22: 6 (now Saul abode in **G** under a tree in 1390
23:19 came up the Ziphites to Saul to **G**, saying, 1390
26: 1 the Ziphites came unto Saul to **G**, saying, 1390
2Sa 6: 3 out of the house of Abinadab that *was* in **G**: 1390
6: 4 of the house of Abinadab which *was* at **G**, 1390
21: 6 them up unto the LORD in **G** of Saul, 1390
23:29 Ittai the son of Ribai out of **G** of 1390
1Ch 11:31 Ithai the son of Ribai of **G**, that pertained to 1390
2Ch 13: 2 *was* Michaiah the daughter of Uriel of **G**. 1390
Isa 10:29 at Geba; Ramah is afraid; **G** of Saul is fled. 1390
Hos 5: 8 Blow ye the cornet in **G**, *and* the trumpet in 1390
9: 9 corrupted *themselves*, as *in* the days of **G**: 1390
10: 9 thou hast sinned from the days of **G**: 1390
10: 9 the battle in **G** against the children of 1390

GIBEATH (1) [GIBEAH]
Jos 18:28 which *is* Jerusalem, **G**, *and* Kirjath; 1390

GIBEATHITE (1) [GIBEAH]
1Ch 12: 3 then Joash, the sons of Shemaah the **G**; 1395

GIBEON (37) [GIBEONITE, GIBEONITES]
Jos 9: 3 when the inhabitants of **G** heard what 1391
9:17 Now their cities *were* **G**, and Chephirah, 1391
10: 1 how the inhabitants of **G** had made peace 1391
10: 2 feared greatly, because **G** *was* a great city, 1391
10: 4 and help me, that we may smite **G**: 1391
10: 5 encamped before **G**, and made war against 1391
10: 6 the men of **G** sent unto Joshua to the camp 1391
10:10 slew them *with* a great slaughter at **G**, and 1391
10:12 sight of Israel, Sun, stand thou still upon **G**; 1391
10:41 and all the country of Goshen, even unto **G**. 1391
11:19 save the Hivites the inhabitants of **G**: 1391
18:25 **G**, and Ramah, and Beeroth, 1391
21:17 **G** with her suburbs, Geba with her suburbs, 1391
2Sa 2:12 son of Saul, went out from Mahanaim to **G**. 1391
2:13 and met together by the pool of **G**: 1391
2:16 called Helkath-hazzurim, which *is* in **G**. 1391
2:24 Giah *by* the way of the wilderness of **G**. 1391
3:30 he had slain their brother Asahel at **G** in 1391
20: 8 they *were* at the great stone which *is* in **G**, 1391
1Ki 3: 4 the king went to **G** to sacrifice there; 1391
3: 5 In **G** the LORD appeared to Solomon in a 1391
9: 2 as he had appeared unto him at **G**. 1391
1Ch 8:29 at **G** dwelt the father of Gibeon; 1391
8:29 at Gibeon dwelt the father of **G**; 1391
9:35 in **G** dwelt the father of Gibeon, Jehiel, 1391
9:35 in Gibeon dwelt the father of **G**, Jehiel, 1391
14:16 of the Philistines from **G** even to Gazer. 1391
16:39 the LORD in the high place that *was* at **G**, 1391
21:29 *were* at that season in the high place at **G**. 1391
2Ch 1: 3 went to the high place that *was* at **G**; 1391
1:13 the high place that *was* at **G** *to* Jerusalem, 1391
Ne 3: 7 the men of **G**, and of Mizpah, 1391
7:25 The children of **G**, ninety and five. 1391
Isa 28:21 he shall be wroth as *in* the valley of **G**, 1391
Jer 28: 1 son of Azur the prophet, which *was* of **G**, 1391
41:12 found him by the great waters that *are* in **G**. 1391
41:16 whom he had brought again from **G**: 1391

GIBEONITE (2) [GIBEON]
1Ch 12: 4 Ismaiah the **G**, a mighty *man* among 1393
Ne 3: 7 next unto them repaired Melatiah the **G**, 1393

GIBEONITES (6) [GIBEON]
2Sa 21: 1 *his* bloody house, because he slew the **G**. 1393
21: 2 the king called the **G**, and said unto them; 1393
21: 2 (now the **G** *were* not of the children of 1393
21: 3 Wherefore David said unto the **G**, 1393
21: 4 the **G** said unto him, We will have no silver 1393
21: 9 he delivered them into the hands of the **G**, 1393

GIBLITES (1) [GEBAL]
Jos 13: 5 the land of the **G**, and all Lebanon, 1382

GIDDALTI (2)
1Ch 25: 4 Hanani, Eliathah, **G**, and Romamti-ezer, 1437
25:29 The two and twentieth to **G**, *he*, his sons, 1437

GIDDEL (4)
Ezr 2:47 The children of **G**, the children of Gahar, 1435
2:56 the children of Darkon, the children of **G**, 1435
Ne 7:49 the children of **G**, the children of Gahar, 1435
7:58 the children of Darkon, the children of **G**, 1435

GIDEON (39) [GEDEON, JERUBBAAL]
Jdg 6:11 his son **G** threshed wheat by the winepress, 1439
6:13 **G** said unto him, O my lord, if the LORD 1439
6:19 **G** went in, and made ready a kid, and 1439
6:22 when **G** perceived that he *was* an angel of 1439
6:22 the LORD, **G** said, Alas, O Lord GOD! 1439
6:24 **G** built an altar there unto the LORD, 1439
6:27 **G** took ten men of his servants, and did as 1439
6:29 **G** the son of Joash hath done this thing. 1439
6:34 the spirit of the LORD came upon **G**, and 1439
6:36 **G** said unto God, If thou wilt save Israel by 1439
6:39 **G** said unto God, Let not thine anger be hot 1439
7: 1 who *is* **G**, and all the people that *were* with 1439
7: 2 the LORD said unto **G**, The people that 1439
7: 4 the LORD said unto **G**, The people *are* yet 1439
7: 5 the LORD said unto **G**, Every one that 1439
7: 7 the LORD said unto **G**, By the three 1439
7:13 when **G** was come, behold, *there was* a 1439
7:14 This *is* nothing else save the sword of **G** 1439
7:15 *so,* when **G** heard the telling of the dream, 1439
7:18 say, *The sword* of the LORD, and of **G**. 1439
7:19 So **G**, and the hundred men that *were* with 1439
7:20 The sword of the LORD, and of **G**. 1439
7:24 **G** sent messengers throughout all mount 1439
7:25 and Zeeb to **G** on the *other* side Jordan. 1439
8: 4 **G** came to Jordan, *and* passed over, he, 1439
8: 7 **G** said, Therefore when the LORD hath 1439
8:11 **G** went up *by* the way of them that dwelt in 1439
8:13 **G** the son of Joash returned from battle 1439
8:21 **G** arose, and slew Zebah and Zalmunna, 1439
8:22 the men of Israel said unto **G**, Rule thou 1439
8:23 **G** said unto them, I will not rule over you, 1439
8:24 **G** said unto them, I would desire a request 1439
8:27 **G** made an ephod thereof, and put it in his 1439
8:27 which *thing* became a snare unto **G**, and 1439
8:28 in quietness forty years in the days of **G**. 1439
8:30 **G** had threescore and ten sons of his body 1439
8:32 **G** the son of Joash died in a good old age, 1439
8:33 it came to pass, as soon as **G** was dead, 1439
8:35 to the house of Jerubbaal, *namely,* **G**, 1439

GIDEONI (5)
Nu 1:11 Of Benjamin; Abidan the son of **G**. 1441
2:22 of Benjamin *shall be* Abidan the son of **G**. 1441
7:60 On the ninth day Abidan the son of **G**, 1441
7:65 *was* the offering of Abidan the son of **G**. 1441
10:24 of Benjamin *was* Abidan the son of **G**. 1441

GIDOM (1)
Jdg 20:45 pursued hard after them unto **G**, and 1440

GIER (2)
Lev 11:18 the swan, and the pelican, and the **g eagle**, 7360
Dt 14:17 and the **g eagle**, and the cormorant, 7360

GIFT (59) [GIVE]
Ge 34:12 Ask me never so much dowry and **g**, and 4976
Ex 23: 8 thou shalt take no **g**: for the gift blindeth 7810
23: 8 for the **g** blindeth the wise, and 7810
Nu 8:19 I have given the Levites *as* a **g** to Aaron 5414
18: 6 to you *they are* given *as* a **g** for the LORD, 4979
18: 7 priest's office *unto you as* a service of **g**: 4979
18:11 the heave offering of their **g**, with all 4976
Dt 16:19 shalt not respect persons, neither take a **g**: 7810
16:19 for a **g** doth blind the eyes of the wise, and 7810
2Sa 19:42 the king's *cost?* or hath he given us *any* **g**? 5375
Ps 45:12 the daughter of Tyre *shall be there* with a **g**; 4503
Pr 17: 8 A **g** *is as* a precious stone in the eyes of him 7810
17:23 A wicked *man* taketh a **g** out of the bosom 7810
18:16 A man's **g** maketh room for him, and 4976
21:14 A **g** in secret pacifieth anger: and a reward 4976
25:14 Whoso boasteth himself of a false **g** *is like* 4991
Ecc 3:13 the good of all his labour, it *is* the **g** of God. 4991
5:19 to rejoice in his labour; this *is* the **g** of God. 4991
7: 7 wise *man* mad; and a **g** destroyeth the heart. 4979
Eze 46:16 If the prince give a **g** unto any of his sons, 4979
46:17 if he give a **g** of his inheritance to one of 4979
Mt 5:23 Therefore if thou bring thy **g** to the altar, *1435*
5:24 Leave there thy **g** before the altar, and *1435*
5:24 thy brother, and then come and offer thy **g**. *1435*
8: 4 offer the **g** that Moses commanded for a *1435*
15: 5 say to *his* father or *his* mother, *It is* a **g**, *1435*
23:18 whosoever sweareth by the **g** that is upon it, *1435*
23:19 the **g**, or the altar that sanctifieth the gift? *1435*
23:19 the gift, or the altar that sanctifieth the **g**? *1435*
Mk 7:11 or mother, *It is* Corban, that is to say, a **g**, *1435*
Jn 4:10 If thou knewest the **g** of God, and who it is *1431*
Ac 2:38 ye shall receive the **g** of the Holy Ghost. *1431*
8:20 thou hast thought that the **g** of God may be *1431*
10:45 was poured out the **g** of the Holy Ghost. *1431*
11:17 as God gave them the like **g** as *he did* unto *1431*
Ro 1:11 that I may impart unto you some spiritual **g**, *5486*
5:15 But not as the offence, so also *is* the **free g**. *5486*
5:15 and the **g** by grace, which is by one man, *1431*
5:16 not as *it was* by one that sinned, *so is* the **g**: *1434*
5:16 the **free g** *is* of many offences unto *5486*
5:17 of the **g** of righteousness shall reign in life *1431*
5:18 by the righteousness of one *the free g came* NIG
6:23 the **g** of God *is* eternal life through Jesus *5486*
1Co 1: 7 So that ye come behind in no **g**; waiting for *5486*
7: 7 But every man hath his proper **g** of God, *5486*
13: 2 And though I have *the* **g** *of* prophecy, and NIG
2Co 1:11 that for the **g** *bestowed* upon us by *5486*
8: 4 much intreaty that we would receive the **g**, *5485*

2Co 9:15 Thanks *be* unto God for his unspeakable **g**. *1431*
Eph 2: 8 that not of yourselves: *it is* the **g** of God: *1435*
3: 7 according to the **g** of the grace of God *1431*
4: 7 according to the measure of the **g** of Christ. *1431*
Php 4:17 Not because I desire a **g**: but I desire fruit *1390*
1Ti 4:14 Neglect not the **g** that is in thee, which was *5486*
2Ti 1: 6 remembrance that *thou* stir up the **g** of God, *5486*
Heb 6: 4 and have tasted of the heavenly **g**, and *1431*
Jas 1:17 Every good **g** and every perfect gift is from *1394*
1:17 good gift and every perfect **g** is from above, *1434*
1Pe 4:10 As every man hath received *the* **g**, *even so* *5486*

GIFTS (53) [GIVE]

Ge 25: 6 Abraham gave **g**, and sent them away from 4979
Ex 28:38 of Israel shall hallow in all their holy **g**; 4979
Lev 23:38 beside your **g**, and beside all your vows, 4979
Nu 18:29 Out of all your **g** ye shall offer every heave 4979
2Sa 8: 2 became David's servants, and brought **g**. 4503
8: 6 became servants to David, and brought **g**. 4503
1Ch 18: 2 became David's servants, and brought **g**. 4503
18: 6 became David's servants, and brought **g**. 4503
2Ch 19: 7 nor respect of persons, nor taking of **g**. 7810
21: 3 And their father gave them great **g** of silver, 4979
26: 8 the Ammonites gave **g** to Uzziah: and 4503
32:23 many brought **g** unto the LORD to 4503
Est 2:18 gave **g**, according to the state of the king. 4864
9:22 portions one to another, and **g** to the poor. 4979
Ps 68:18 thou hast received **g** for men; yea, *for* 4979
72:10 the kings of Sheba and Seba shall offer **g**. 814
Pr 6:35 he rest content, though thou givest many **g**. 7810
15:27 own house; but he that hateth **g** shall live. 4979
19: 6 every *man is* a friend to him that **giveth g**. 4976
29: 4 but he that receiveth **g** overthroweth it. 8641
Isa 1:23 every one loveth **g**, and followeth after 7810
Eze 16:33 They give **g** to all whores: but thou givest 5078
16:33 thou givest thy **g** to all thy lovers, and 5083
20:26 I polluted them in their own **g**, in that they 4979
20:31 For when *ye* offer your **g**, when *ye* make 4979
20:39 ye my holy name no more with your **g**, 4979
22:12 In thee have they taken **g** to shed blood; 7810
Da 2: 6 ye shall receive of me **g** and rewards and 4978
2:48 gave him many great **g**, and made him ruler 4978
5:17 Let thy **g** be to thyself, and give thy 4978
Mt 2:11 their treasures, they presented unto him **g**; *1435*
7:11 know how to give good **g** unto your *1390*
Lk 11:13 know how to give good **g** unto your *1390*
21: 1 saw the rich *men* casting their **g** into *1435*
21: 5 it was adorned with goodly stones and **g**, *334*
Ro 11:29 For the **g** and calling of God *are* without *5486*
12: 6 **g** differing according to the grace that is *5486*
1Co 12: 1 Now concerning spiritual **g**, brethren, NIG
12: 4 Now there are diversities of **g**, but the same *5486*
12: 9 to another the **g** of healing by the same *5486*
12:28 then **g** of healings, helps, governments, *5486*
12:30 Have all the **g** of healing? do all speak with *5486*
12:31 But covet earnestly the best **g**: and yet shew *5486*
14: 1 and desire spiritual *g*, but rather that ye may NIG
14:12 forasmuch as ye are zealous of spiritual *g*, NIG
Eph 4: 8 led captivity captive, and gave **g** unto men. *1390*
Heb 2: 4 divers miracles, and **g** of the Holy Ghost, *3311*
5: 1 that he may offer both **g** and sacrifices for *1435*
8: 3 For every high priest is ordained to offer **g** *1435*
8: 4 seeing that there are priests that offer **g** *1435*
9: 9 in which were offered both **g** and sacrifices, *1435*
11: 4 he was righteous, God testifying of his **g**: *1435*
Rev 11:10 and shall send **g** one to another; *1435*

GIHON (6)

Ge 2:13 the name of the second river *is* **G**: the same 1521
1Ki 1:33 mine own mule, and bring him down to **G**: 1521
1:38 king David's mule, and brought him to **G**. 1521
1:45 the prophet have anointed him king in **G**: 1521
2Ch 32:30 also stopped the upper watercourse of **G**, 1521
33:14 on the west *side* of **G**, in the valley, even to 1521

GILALAI (1)

Ne 12:36 Shemaiah, and Azarael, Milalai, **G**, Maai, 1562

GILBOA (8)

1Sa 28: 4 all Israel together, and they pitched in **G**. 1533
31: 1 and fell down slain in mount **G**. 1533
31: 8 and his three sons fallen in mount **G**. 1533
2Sa 1: 6 As I happened by chance upon mount **G**, 1533
1:21 Ye mountains of **G**, *let there be* no dew, 1533
21:12 when the Philistines had slain Saul in **G**: 1533
1Ch 10: 1 and fell down slain in mount **G**. 1533
10: 8 found Saul and his sons fallen in mount **G**. 1533

GILEAD (100) [GILEAD'S, GILEADITE, GILEADITES, JABESH-GILEAD, RAMOTH-GILEAD]

Ge 31:21 and set his face *toward* the mount **G**. 1568
31:23 and they overtook him in the mount **G**. 1568
31:25 his brethren pitched in the mount of **G**. 1568
37:25 a company of Ishmeelites came from **G** 1568
Nu 26:29 Machir begat **G**: of Gilead *come* the family 1568
26:29 of **G** *come* the family of the Gileadites. 1568
26:30 These *are* the sons of **G**: *of* Jeezer, 1568
27: 1 of Hepher, the son of **G**, the son of Machir, 1568
32: 1 the land of **G**, that behold, the place *was* a 1568
32:26 our cattle, shall be there in the cities of **G**: 1568
32:29 ye shall give them the land of **G** for a 1568
32:39 of Machir the son of Manasseh went to **G**, 1568
32:40 Moses gave **G** unto Machir the son of 1568
36: 1 fathers of the families of the children of **G**, 1568
Dt 2:36 the city that *is* by the river, even unto **G**, 1568
3:10 and all **G**, and all Bashan, unto Salchah and 1568
3:12 half mount **G**, and the cities thereof, gave I 1568
3:13 the rest of **G**, and all Bashan, *being* 1568
3:15 And I gave **G** unto Machir. 1568
3:16 unto the Gadites I gave from **G** even unto 1568
4:43 Ramoth in **G**, of the Gadites; and Golan in 1568
34: 1 the LORD shewed him all the land of **G**, 1568
Jos 12: 2 *from* half **G**, even unto the river Jabbok, 1568
12: 5 and the Maachathites, and half **G**, 1568
13:11 **G**, and the border of the Geshurites and 1568
13:25 all the cities of **G**, and half the land of 1568
13:31 half **G**, and Ashtaroth, and Edrei, cities of 1568
17: 1 the firstborn of Manasseh, the father of **G**: 1568
17: 1 of war, therefore he had **G** and Bashan. 1568
17: 3 of Hepher, the son of **G**, the son of Machir, 1568
17: 5 beside the land of **G** and Bashan, 1568
17: 6 rest of Manasseh's sons had the land of **G**. 1568
20: 8 Ramoth in **G** out of the tribe of Gad, and 1568
21:38 of Gad, Ramoth in **G** with her suburbs, 1568
22: 9 to go unto the country of **G**, to the land of 1568
22:13 half tribe of Manasseh, into the land of **G**, 1568
22:15 unto the land of **G**, and they spake with 1568
22:32 out of the land of **G**, unto the land of 1568
Jdg 5:17 **G** abode beyond Jordan: and why did Dan 1568
7: 3 him return and depart early from mount **G**. 1568
10: 4 unto this day, which *are* in the land of **G**. 1568
10: 8 in the land of the Amorites, which *is* in **G**. 1568
10:17 gathered together, and encamped in **G**. 1568
10:18 *and* princes of **G** said one to another, 1568
10:18 shall be head over all the inhabitants of **G**. 1568
11: 1 the son of a harlot: and **G** begat Jephthah. 1568
11: 5 the elders of **G** went to fetch Jephthah out 1568
11: 7 Jephthah said unto the elders of **G**, Did not 1568
11: 8 the elders of **G** said unto Jephthah, 1568
11: 8 be our head over all the inhabitants of **G**. 1568
11: 9 Jephthah said unto the elders of **G**, If ye 1568
11:10 the elders of **G** said unto Jephthah, 1568
11:11 Jephthah went with the elders of **G**, and 1568
11:29 he passed over **G** and Manasseh, and 1568
11:29 passed over Mizpeh of **G**, and from Mizpeh 1568
11:29 from Mizpeh of **G** he passed over *unto* 1568
12: 4 gathered together all the men of **G**, 1568
12: 4 the men of **G** smote Ephraim, because 1568
12: 5 that the men of **G** said unto him, *Art* thou 1568
12: 7 and was buried in *one of* the cities of **G**. 1568
20: 1 with the land of **G**, unto the LORD *in* 1568
1Sa 13: 7 went over Jordan *to* the land of Gad and **G**. 1568
2Sa 2: 9 he made him king over **G**, and over 1568
17:26 and Absalom pitched *in* the land of **G**. 1568
24: 6 they came to **G**, and to the land of 1568
1Ki 4:13 Jair the son of Manasseh, which *are* in **G**; 1568
4:19 the son of Uri *was* in the country of **G**, 1568
17: 1 *who was* of the inhabitants of **G**, said unto 1568
22: 3 Know ye that Ramoth in **G** *is* ours, and 1568
2Ki 10:33 all the land of **G**, the Gadites, and 1568
10:33 *is* by the river Arnon, even **G** and Bashan. 1568
15:29 and Hazor, and **G**, and Galilee, 1568
1Ch 2:21 to the daughter of Machir the father of **G**, 1568
2:22 had three and twenty cities in the land of **G**. 1568
2:23 *to* the sons of Machir the father of **G**. 1568
5: 9 cattle were multiplied in the land of **G**. 1568
5:10 their tents throughout all the east *land* of **G**. 1568
5:14 the son of Jaroah, the son of **G**, the son of 1568

G

1Ch 5:16 they dwelt in G in Bashan, and in her 1568
6:80 Ramoth in G with her suburbs, and 1568
7:14 the Aramitess bare Machir the father of G: 1568
7:17 These *were* the sons of G, the son of 1568
26:31 them mighty *men* of valour at Jazer of G. 1568
27:21 Of the half *tribe* of Manasseh in G, 1568
Ps 60: 7 G *is* mine, and Manasseh *is* mine; 1568
108: 8 G *is* mine; Manasseh *is* mine; Ephraim also 1568
SS 4: 1 a flock of goats, that appear from mount G. 1568
6: 5 *is* as a flock of goats that appear from G. 1568
Jer 8:22 *Is there* no balm in G; *is there* no physician 1568
22: 6 Thou *art* G unto me, *and* the head of 1568
46:11 Go up *into* G, and take balm, O virgin, 1568
50:19 be satisfied upon mount Ephraim and G. 1568
Eze 47:18 from G, and from the land of Israel *by* 1568
Hos 6: 8 G *is* a city of them that work iniquity, *and* 1568
12:11 *Is there* iniquity *in* G? surely they are 1568
Am 1: 3 they have threshed G with threshing 1568
1:13 have ript up the women with child at G, 1568
Ob 1:19 of Samaria: and Benjamin *shall possess* G. 1568
Mic 7:14 let them feed *in* Bashan and G, as *in* 1568
Zec 10:10 and I will bring them into the land of G and 1568

GILEAD'S (1) [GILEAD]
Jdg 11: 2 G wife bare him sons; and *his* wife's sons 1568

GILEADITE (9) [GILEAD]
Jdg 10: 3 a G, and judged Israel twenty and 1569
11: 1 Now Jephthah the G was a mighty *man* of 1569
11:40 of Jephthah the G four days in a year. 1569
12: 7 died Jephthah the G, and was buried in *one* 1569
2Sa 17:27 and Barzillai the G of Rogelim, 1569
19:31 Barzillai the G came down from Rogelim, 1569
1Ki 2: 7 kindness unto the sons of Barzillai the G, 1569
Ezr 2:61 a wife of the daughters of Barzillai the G, 1569
Ne 7:63 of the daughters of Barzillai the G *to* wife, 1569

GILEADITES (4) [GILEAD]
Nu 26:29 of Gilead *come* the family of the G. 1569
Jdg 12: 4 Ye G *are* fugitives of Ephraim among 1568
12: 5 the G took the passages of Jordan before 1568
2Ki 15:25 and with him fifty men of the G: 1121+1569

GILGAL (41)
Dt 11:30 dwell in the champaign over against G, 1537
Jos 4:19 encamped in G, in the east border of 1537
4:20 took out of Jordan, did Joshua pitch in G. 1537
5: 9 the name of the place is called G 1537
5:10 the children of Israel encamped in G, and 1537
9: 6 they went to Joshua unto the camp *at* G, 1537
10: 6 Gibeon sent unto Joshua to the camp to G, 1537
10: 7 So Joshua ascended from G, he, and all 1537
10: 9 *and* went up from G all night. 1537
10:15 and all Israel with him, unto the camp to G. 1537
10:43 and all Israel with him, unto the camp to G. 1537
12:23 one; the king of the nations of G, one; 1537
14: 6 children of Judah came unto Joshua in G: 1537
15: 7 *so* northward, looking toward G, that *is* 1537
Jdg 2: 1 an angel of the LORD came up from G to 1537
3:19 again from the quarries that *were* by G, 1537
1Sa 7:16 G, and Mizpeh, and judged Israel in all 1537
10: 8 thou shalt go down before me *to* G; and 1537
11:14 let us go *to* G, and renew the kingdom 1537
11:15 all the people went *to* G; and there they 1537
11:15 made Saul king before the LORD in G; 1537
13: 4 people were called together after Saul *to* G. 1537
13: 7 he *was* yet in G, and all the people 1537
13: 8 *had appointed:* but Samuel came not *to* G; 1537
13:12 will come down now upon me *to* G, 1537
13:15 gat him up from G *unto* Gibeah of 1537
15:12 and passed on, and gone down *to* G. 1537
15:21 to sacrifice unto the LORD thy God in G. 1537
15:33 Agag in pieces before the LORD in G. 1537
2Sa 19:15 Judah came to G, to go to meet the king, 1537
19:40 the king went on to G, and Chimham went 1537
2Ki 2: 1 that Elijah went with Elisha from G. 1537
4:38 Elisha came again to G: and *there was* a 1537
Ne 12:29 Also from the house of G, and out of 1537
Hos 4:15 come not ye *unto* G, neither go ye up *to* 1537
9:15 All their wickedness *is* in G, for there I 1537
12:11 they sacrifice bullocks in G; yea, 1537
Am 4: 4 *at* G multiply transgression; and bring your 1537
5: 5 nor enter *into* G, and pass not *to* 1537
5: 5 for G shall surely go into captivity, 1537
Mic 6: 5 Beor answered him; from Shittim unto G; 1537

GILOH (2) [GILONITE]
Jos 15:51 Goshen, and Holon, and G; eleven cities 1542
2Sa 15:12 from his city, *even* from G, 1542

GILONITE (2) [GILOH]
2Sa 15:12 Absalom sent *for* Ahithophel the G, 1526
23:34 Eliam the son of Ahithophel the G, 1526

GIMZO (1)
2Ch 28:18 G also and the villages thereof: 1579

GIN (2) [see also GRIN, GRINS]
Isa 8:14 for a g and for a snare to the inhabitants of 6341
Am 3: 5 upon the earth, where no g *is* for him? 4170

GINATH (2)
1Ki 16:21 of the people followed Tibni the son of G, 1527
16:22 people that followed Tibni the son of G: 1527

GINNETHO (1) [GINNETHON]
Ne 12: 4 Iddo, G, Abijah, 1599

GINNETHON (2) [GINNETHO]
Ne 10: 6 Daniel, G, Baruch, 1599
12:16 Of Iddo, Zechariah; of G, Meshullam; 1599

GIRD (27) [GIRDED, GIRDEDST, GIRDETH, GIRDING, GIRDLE, GIRDLES, GIRT, UNDERGIRDING, UNGIRDED]
Ex 29: 5 g him with the curious girdle of the ephod: 640
29: 9 thou shalt g them *with* girdles, Aaron and 2296
Jdg 3:16 he did g it under his raiment upon his right 2296
1Sa 25:13 his men, G you **on** every man his sword. 2296
2Sa 3:31 g you with sackcloth, and mourn before 2296
2Ki 4:29 G **up** thy loins, and take my staff in thine 2296
9: 1 G **up** thy loins, and take this box of oil in 2296
Job 38: 3 G **up** now thy loins like a man; for I will 247
40: 7 G **up** thy loins now like a man: I will 247
Ps 45: 3 G thy sword upon *thy* thigh, O *most* 2296
Isa 8: 9 g yourselves, and ye shall be broken in 247
8: 9 g yourselves, and ye shall be broken in 247
15: 3 In their streets they shall g themselves **with** 2296
32:11 ye bare, and g *sackcloth* upon *your* loins. 2290
Jer 1:17 Thou therefore g **up** thy loins, and arise, and 247
4: 8 For this g you **with** sackcloth, lament and 2296
6:26 g *thee* **with** sackcloth, and wallow thyself 2296
49: 3 daughters of Rabbah, g ye **with** sackcloth; 2296
Eze 7:18 They shall also g *themselves* **with** 2296
27:31 g them **with** sackcloth, and they shall weep 2296
44:18 they shall not g *themselves* **with** any thing 2296
Joel 1:13 G yourselves, and lament, ye priests: howl, 2296
Lk 12:37 that he shall g himself, and make them to *4024*
17: 8 and g thyself, and serve me, till I have *4024*
Jn 21:18 and another shall g thee, and carry *thee* *2224*
Ac 12: 8 G thyself, and bind on thy sandals. *4024*
1Pe 1:13 Wherefore g **up** the loins of your mind, *328*

GIRDED (32) [GIRD]
Ex 12:11 *with* your loins g, your shoes on your feet, 2296
Lev 8: 7 g him with the girdle, and clothed him with 2296
8: 7 he g him with the curious girdle of 2296
8:13 g them *with* girdles, and put bonnets upon 2296
16: 4 shall be g with a linen girdle, and with 2296
Dt 1:41 when ye had g **on** every man his weapons 2296
1Sa 2:18 *being* a child, g *with* a linen ephod. 2296
17:39 David g his sword upon his armour, and 2296
25:13 they g **on** every man his sword; and 2296
25:13 his sword; and David also g **on** his sword: 2296
2Sa 6:14 and David *was* g *with* a linen ephod. 2296
20: 8 Joab's garment that he had put on *was* g 2296
21:16 he being g *with* a new *sword,* thought to 2296
22:40 For thou hast g me with strength to battle: 247
1Ki 18:46 he g **up** his loins, and ran before Ahab to 8151
20:32 So they g sackcloth on their loins, and 2296
Ne 4:18 every one had his sword g by his side, and *so* 631
Ps 18:39 For thou hast g me *with* strength unto 247
30:11 off my sackcloth, and g me *with* gladness; 247
65: 6 fast the mountains; *being* g with power: 247
93: 1 with strength, *wherewith* he hath g himself: 247
109:19 for a girdle where*with* he is g continually. 2296
Isa 45: 5 I g thee though thou hast not known me: 247
La 2:10 they have g themselves **with** sackcloth: 2296
Eze 16:10 and I g thee **about** with fine linen, 2280
23:15 G **with** girdles upon their loins, 2289

Da 10: 5 whose loins *were* **g** with fine gold of 2296
Joel 1: 8 Lament like a virgin **g with** sackcloth for 2296
Lk 12:35 Let your loins be **g about**, and *your* lights *4024*
Jn 13: 4 and took a towel, and **g** himself. *1241*
13: 5 *them* with the towel wherewith he was **g**. *1241*
Rev 15: 6 having their breasts **g** with golden girdles. *4024*

GIRDEDST (1) [GIRD]
Jn 21:18 thou **g** thyself, and walkedst whither thou *2224*

GIRDETH (4) [GIRD]
1Ki 20:11 Tell *him,* Let not him that **g on** *his harness* 2296
Job 12:18 bond of kings, and **g** their loins with a girdle. 631
Ps 18:32 *It is* God that **g** me *with* strength, and 247
Pr 31:17 She **g** her loins with strength, and 2296

GIRDING (2) [GIRD]
Isa 3:24 and instead of a stomacher a **g** of sackcloth; 4228
22:12 and to baldness, and to **g with** sackcloth: 2296

GIRDLE (38) [GIRD]
Ex 28: 4 a robe, and a broidered coat, a mitre, and a **g**: 73
28: 8 the **curious g** of the ephod, which *is* upon 2805
28:27 above the **curious g** of the ephod. 2805
28:28 that *it* may be above the **curious g** of 2805
28:39 and thou shalt make the **g** *of* needlework. 73
29: 5 gird him with the **curious g** of the ephod: 2805
39: 5 the **curious g** of his ephod, that *was* upon 2805
39:20 above the **curious g** of the ephod. 2805
39:21 that *it* might be above the **curious g** of 2805
39:29 a **g** *of* fine twined linen, and blue, and purple, 73
Lev 8: 7 girded him with the **g**, and clothed him with 73
8: 7 he girded him with the **curious g** of 2805
16: 4 and shall be girded with a linen **g**, 73
1Sa 18: 4 to his sword, and to his bow, and to his **g**. 2289
2Sa 18:11 given thee ten *shekels of* silver, and a **g**. 2290
20: 8 upon it a **g** with a sword fastened upon his 2289
1Ki 2: 5 put the blood of war upon his **g** that *was* 2290
2Ki 1: 8 girt *with* a **g** of leather about his loins. 232
Job 12:18 of kings, and girdeth their loins with a **g**. 232
Ps 109:19 for a **g** where*with* he is girded continually. 4206
Isa 3:24 instead of a **g** a rent; and instead of well set 2290
5:27 neither shall the **g** of their loins be loosed, 232
11: 5 And righteousness shall be the **g** of his loins, 232
11: 5 his loins, and faithfulness the **g** of his reins. 232
22:21 strengthen him *with* thy **g**, and I will commit 73
Jer 13: 1 Go and get thee a linen **g**, and put it upon thy 232
13: 2 So I got a **g**, according to the word of 232
13: 4 Take the **g** that thou hast got, which *is* upon 232
13: 6 go to Euphrates, and take the **g** from thence, 232
13: 7 took the **g** from the place where I had hid it: 232
13: 7 behold, the **g** was marred, it was profitable 232
13:10 and to worship them, shall even be as this **g**, 232
13:11 For as the **g** cleaveth to the loins of a man, 232
Mt 3: 4 and a leathern **g** about his loins; *2223*
Mk 1: 6 and with a **g** of a skin about his loins; *2223*
Ac 21:11 he took Paul's **g**, and bound his *own* hands *2223*
21:11 at Jerusalem bind the man that oweth this **g**, *2223*
Rev 1:13 and girt about the paps with a golden **g**. *2223*

GIRDLES (6) [GIRD]
Ex 28:40 thou shalt make for them **g**, and bonnets shalt 73
29: 9 thou shalt gird them *with* **g**, Aaron and 73
Lev 8:13 girded them *with* **g**, and put bonnets upon 73
Pr 31:24 and delivereth **g** unto the merchant. 2289
Eze 23:15 Girded with **g** upon their loins, exceeding in 232
Rev 15: 6 having their breasts girded with golden **g**. *2223*

GIRGASHITE (2) [GIRGASHITES]
Ge 10:16 the Jebusite, and the Amorite, and the **G**, 1622
1Ch 1:14 Jebusite also, and the Amorite, and the **G**, 1622

GIRGASHITES (5) [GIRGASHITE]
Ge 15:21 and the **G**, and the Jebusites. 1622
Dt 7: 1 the **G**, and the Amorites, and 1622
Jos 3:10 the **G**, and the Amorites, and the Jebusites. 1622
24:11 and the **G**, the Hivites, and the Jebusites; 1622
Ne 9: 8 the Perizzites, and the Jebusites, and the **G**, 1622

GIRL (1) [GIRLS]
Joel 3: 3 and sold a **g** for wine, that they might drink. 3207

GIRLS (1) [GIRL]
Zec 8: 5 *of* boys and **g** playing in the streets thereof. 3207

GIRT (5) [GIRD]
1Sa 2: 4 and they that stumbled are **g** with strength. 247
2Ki 1: 8 and **g** *with* a girdle of leather about his loins. 247
Jn 21: 7 he **g** *his* fisher's coat unto him, (for he was *1241*
Eph 6:14 having your loins **g about** with truth, and *4024*
Rev 1:13 and **g** about the paps with a golden girdle. *4024*

GIRZITES See GEZRITES

GISHPA See GISPA

GISPA (1)
Ne 11:21 and Ziha and **G** *were* over the Nethinims. 1658

GITTAH-HEPHER (1) [GATH-HEPHER]
Jos 19:13 thence passeth on along on the east to **G**, 1661

GITTAIM (2)
2Sa 4: 3 the Beerothites fled to **G**, and 1664
Ne 11:33 Hazor, Ramah, **G**, 1664

GITTITE (8) [GATH]
2Sa 6:10 it aside *into* the house of Obed-edom the **G**. 1663
6:11 house of Obed-edom the **G** three months: 1663
15:19 said the king to Ittai the **G**, Wherefore 1663
15:22 Ittai the **G** passed over, and all his men, 1663
18: 2 a third part under the hand of Ittai the **G**. 1663
21:19 slew *the brother of* Goliath the **G**, 1663
1Ch 13:13 it aside into the house of Obed-edom the **G**. 1663
20: 5 slew Lahmi the brother of Goliath the **G**, 1663

GITTITES (2) [GATH]
Jos 13: 3 the Eshkalonites, the **G**, and the Ekronites; 1663
2Sa 15:18 and all the Pelethites, and all the **G**, 1663

GITTITH (3)
Ps 8: T To the chief Musician upon **G**, A Psalm of 1665
81: T To the chief Musician upon **G**, *A Psalm* of 1665
84: T To the chief Musician upon **G**, A Psalm for 1665

GIVE (880) [GAVE, GAVEST, GIFT, GIFTS, GIVEN, GIVER, GIVEST, GIVETH, GIVING, LAWGIVER, THANKSGIVING, THANKSGIVINGS]
Ge 1:15 of the heaven to **g light** upon the earth: 215
1:17 of the heaven to **g light** upon the earth, 215
12: 7 and said, Unto thy seed will I **g** this land: 5414
13:15 to thee will I **g** it, and to thy seed for ever. 5414
13:17 in the breadth of it; for I will **g** it unto thee. 5414
14:21 **G** me the persons, and take the goods to 5414
15: 2 Lord God, what wilt thou **g** me, 5414
15: 7 to **g** thee this land to inherit it. 5414
17: 8 I will **g** unto thee, and to thy seed after 5414
17:16 will bless her, and **g** thee a son also of her: 5414
23: 4 **g** me a possession of a buryingplace with 5414
23: 9 That he may **g** me the cave of Machpelah, 5414
23: 9 for as much money as it is worth he shall **g** 5414
23:11 the field **g** I thee, and the cave that *is* 5414
23:11 and the cave that *is* therein, I **g** it thee; 5414
23:11 in the presence of the sons of my people **g** I 5414
23:13 saying, But if thou *wilt g it,* I pray thee, NIH
23:13 I will **g** *thee* money for the field; take *it* of 5414
24: 7 saying, Unto thy seed will I **g** this land; 5414
24:14 Drink, and I will **g** thy camels **drink** also: 8248
24:41 if they **g** not thee *one,* thou shalt be clear 5414
24:43 **G** me, I pray thee, a little water of thy pitcher **to drink**; 8248
24:46 Drink, and I will **g** thy camels **drink** also: 8248
26: 3 I will **g** all these countries, and I will 5414
26: 4 and will **g** unto thy seed all these countries; 5414
27:28 Therefore God **g** thee of the dew of heaven, 5414
28: 4 **g** thee the blessing of Abraham, to thee, 5414
28:13 to thee will I **g** it, and to thy seed; 5414
28:20 will **g** me bread to eat, and raiment to put 5414
28:22 of all that thou shalt **g** me I will surely give 5414
28:22 I will **surely g the tenth** unto thee. 6237+6237
29:19 Laban said, *It is* better that I **g** her to thee, 5414
29:19 than that I should **g** her to another man: 5414
29:21 **G** *me* my wife, for my days are fulfilled, 3051
29:26 to **g** the younger before the firstborn. 5414
29:27 we will **g** thee this also for the service 5414
30: 1 unto Jacob, **G** me children, or else I die. 3051
30:14 **G** me, I pray thee, of thy son's mandrakes. 5414
30:26 **G** *me* my wives and my children, for whom 5414
30:28 Appoint me thy wages, and I will **g** *it.* 5414
30:31 he said, What shall I **g** thee? And Jacob 5414

Ge 30:31 Jacob said, Thou shalt not **g** me any thing: 5414
34: 8 I pray you **g** her him to wife. 5414
34: 9 *and* **g** your daughters unto us, and take our 5414
34:11 and what ye shall say unto me I will **g**. 5414
34:12 I will **g** according as ye shall say unto me: 5414
34:12 say unto me: but **g** me the damsel to wife. 5414
34:14 to **g** our sister to one that is uncircumcised; 5414
34:16 will we **g** our daughters unto you, and we 5414
34:21 for wives, and let us **g** them our daughters. 5414
35:12 to thee I will **g** it, and to thy seed after thee 5414
35:12 and to thy seed after thee will I **g** the land. 5414
38: 9 lest that he should **g** seed to his brother. 5414
38:16 she said, What wilt thou **g** me, that thou 5414
38:17 she said, Wilt thou **g** *me* a pledge, till thou 5414
38:18 he said, What pledge shall I **g** thee? 5414
41:16 God shall **g** Pharaoh **an answer** of peace. 6030
42:25 and to **g** them provision for the way: 5414
42:27 as one *of them* opened his sack to **g** his ass 5414
43:14 God Almighty **g** you mercy before the man, 5414
45:18 I will **g** you the good of the land of Egypt, 5414
47:15 came unto Joseph, and said, **G** us bread: 3051
47:16 Joseph said, **G** your cattle; and I will give 3051
47:16 I will **g** you for your cattle, if money fail. 5414
47:19 **g** *us* seed, that we may live, and not die, 5414
47:24 that you shall **g** the fifth *part* unto Pharaoh, 5414
48: 4 will **g** this land to thy seed after thee *for* an 5414
Ex 2: 9 nurse it for me, and I will **g** *thee* thy wages. 5414
3:21 I will **g** this people favour in the sight of 5414
5: 7 Ye shall no more **g** the people straw to 5414
5:10 Thus saith Pharaoh, I will not **g** you straw. 5414
6: 4 to **g** them the land of Canaan, the land of 5414
6: 8 *concerning* the which I did swear to **g** it to 5414
6: 8 to Jacob; and I will **g** it you *for* an heritage: 5414
10:25 Thou must **g** us also sacrifices 3027+5414+871.1
12:25 to the land which the LORD will **g** you, 5414
13: 5 which he sware unto thy fathers to **g** thee, 5414
13:11 and to thy fathers, and shall **g** it thee, 5414
13:21 by night in a pillar of fire, to **g** them **light**; 215
15:26 wilt **g** **ear** to his commandments, and 238
16: 8 *This shall be,* when the LORD shall **g** you 5414
17: 2 and said, **G** us water that we may drink. 5414
18:19 I will **g** thee **counsel**, and God shall be with 3289
21:23 then thou shalt **g** life for life, 5414
21:30 he shall **g** *for* the ransom of his life 5414
21:32 he shall **g** unto their master thirty shekels *of* 5414
21:34 *and* **g** money unto the owner of them; 7725
22:17 If her father utterly refuse to **g** her unto 5414
22:29 the firstborn of thy sons shalt thou **g** unto 5414
22:30 on the eighth day thou shalt **g** it me. 5414
24:12 I will **g** thee tables of stone, and a law, and 5414
25:16 the ark the Testimony which I shall **g** thee. 5414
25:21 shalt put the Testimony that I shall **g** thee. 5414
25:22 **g** thee **in commandment** unto the children 6680
25:37 that they may **g** **light** over against it. 215
30:12 shall they **g** every man a ransom for his 5414
30:13 This they shall **g**, every one that passeth 5414
30:14 above, shall **g** an offering unto the LORD. 5414
30:15 The rich shall not **g** **more**, and the poor 7235
30:15 the poor shall not **g** **less** than half a shekel, 4591
30:15 when *they* **g** an offering unto the LORD, 5414
32:13 all this land that I have spoken of will I **g** 5414
33: 1 to Jacob, saying, Unto thy seed will I **g** it: 5414
33:14 shall go *with thee,* and I will **g** thee **rest**. 5117
Lev 5:16 fifth *part* thereto, and **g** it unto the priest: 5414
6: 5 *and* **g** it unto him to whom it appertaineth, 5414
7:32 the right shoulder shall ye **g** unto the priest 5414
14:34 which I **g** to you for a possession, and I put 5414
15:14 and **g** them unto the priest: 5414
20:24 and I will **g** it unto you to possess it, 5414
22:14 shall **g** *it* unto the priest with the holy 5414
23:10 When ye be come into the land which I **g** 5414
23:38 which ye **g** unto the LORD. 5414
25: 2 When ye come into the land which I **g** you, 5414
25:37 Thou shalt not **g** him thy money upon 5414
25:38 to **g** you the land of Canaan, *and* to be your 5414
25:51 **g** **again** the price of his redemption out of 7725
25:52 he **g** *him* **again** the price of his redemption. 7725
26: 4 I will **g** you rain in due season, and the land 5414
26: 6 I will **g** peace in the land, and ye shall lie 5414
27:23 he shall **g** thine estimation in that day, *as* a 5414
Nu 3: 9 thou shalt **g** the Levites unto Aaron and 5414
3:48 thou shalt **g** the money, wherewith the odd 5414
5: 7 **g** *it* unto *him* against whom he hath 5414
6:26 countenance upon thee, and **g** thee peace. 7760
7: 5 thou shalt **g** them unto the Levites, to every 5414
8: 2 the seven lamps shall **g** **light** over against 215
10:29 of which the LORD said, I will **g** it you: 5414
11: 4 and said, Who shall **g** us flesh **to eat**? 398
11:13 Whence should I have flesh to **g** unto all 5414
11:13 saying, **G** us flesh, that we may eat. 5414
11:18 saying, Who shall **g** us flesh **to eat**? 398
11:18 therefore the LORD will **g** you flesh, and 5414
11:21 thou hast said, I will **g** them flesh, that they 5414
13: 2 which I **g** unto the children of Israel: 5414
14: 8 he will bring us into this land, and **g** it us; 5414
15: 2 of your habitations, which I **g** unto you, 5414
15:21 Of the first of your dough ye shall **g** unto 5414
18:28 ye shall **g** thereof the LORD'S heave 5414
19: 3 ye shall **g** her unto Eleazar the priest, 5414
20: 8 it shall **g** **forth** his water, and thou shalt 5414
20: 8 **g** the congregation and their beasts **drink**. 8248
20:21 Thus Edom refused to **g** Israel passage 5414
21:16 people together, and I will **g** them water. 5414
22:13 for the LORD refuseth to **g** me **leave** to go 5414
22:18 If Balak would **g** me his house full *of* silver 5414
24:13 If Balak would **g** me his house full *of* silver 5414
25:12 Behold, I **g** unto him my covenant of peace: 5414
26:54 To many thou shalt **g** the **more** inheritance, 7235
26:54 to few thou shalt **g** the **less** inheritance: 4591
27: 4 **G** unto us *therefore* a possession among 5414
27: 7 thou shalt **surely** **g** them a possession 5414+5414
27: 9 ye shall **g** his inheritance unto his brethren. 5414
27:10 ye shall **g** his inheritance unto his father's 5414
27:11 ye shall **g** his inheritance unto his kinsman 5414
27:19 and **g** him **a charge** in their sight. 6680
31:29 their half, and **g** *it* unto Eleazar the priest, 5414
31:30 *of* beasts, and **g** them unto the Levites, 5414
32:29 ye shall **g** them the land of Gilead for a 5414
33:54 to the moe ye shall **g** the **more** inheritance, 7235
33:54 to the fewer ye shall **g** the **less** inheritance: 4591
34:13 which the LORD commanded to **g** unto 5414
35: 2 that they **g** unto the Levites of 5414
35: 2 ye shall **g** *also* unto the Levites suburbs for 5414
35: 4 the cities, which ye shall **g** unto the Levites, 5414
35: 6 *among* the cities which ye shall **g** unto 5414
35: 7 *So* all the cities which ye shall **g** to 5414
35: 7 them *shall ye* **g** with their suburbs. NIH
35: 8 the cities which ye shall **g** *shall be* of 5414
35: 8 from *them that have* many ye shall **g** **many**; 7235
35: 8 but from *them that have* few ye shall **g** **few**: 4591
35: 8 every one shall **g** of his cities unto 5414
35:13 *of these* cities which ye shall **g** six cities 5414
35:14 Ye shall **g** three cities on *this* side Jordan, 5414
35:14 three cities shall ye **g** in the land of Canaan, 5414
36: 2 The LORD commanded my lord to **g** 5414
36: 2 **g** the inheritance of Zelophehad our brother 5414
Dt 1: 8 to **g** unto them and to their seed after them. 5414
1:20 which the LORD our God doth **g** unto us. 5414
1:25 land which the LORD our God doth **g** us. 5414
1:35 which I sware to **g** unto your fathers, 5414
1:36 to him will I **g** the land that he hath trodden 5414
1:39 unto them will I **g** it, and they shall possess 5414
1:45 hearken to your voice, nor **g** **ear** unto you. 238
2: 5 for I will not **g** you of their land, no, not so 5414
2: 9 for I will not **g** thee of their land *for* a 5414
2:19 for I will not **g** thee of the land of 5414
2:28 **g** me water for money, that I may drink: 5414
2:31 I have begun to **g** Sihon and his land before 5414
4:38 to **g** thee their land *for* an inheritance, as *it* 5414
5:31 that they may do *them* in the land which I **g** 5414
6:10 to Jacob, to **g** thee great and goodly cities, 5414
6:23 to **g** us the land which he sware unto our 5414
7: 3 thy daughter thou shalt not **g** unto his son, 5414
7:13 which he sware unto thy fathers to **g** thee. 5414
10:11 which I sware unto their fathers to **g** unto 5414
11: 9 sware unto your fathers to **g** unto them 5414
11:14 That I will **g** *you* the rain of your land in his 5414
11:21 LORD sware unto your fathers to **g** them, 5414
14:21 thou shalt **g** it unto the stranger that *is* in 5414
15:10 Thou shalt **surely** **g** him, and 5414+5414
15:14 hath blessed thee thou shalt **g** unto him. 5414
16:10 which thou shalt **g** *unto the LORD thy* 5414
16:17 Every man *shall* **g** as he is able, according NIH
18: 3 they shall **g** unto the priest the shoulder, 5414
18: 4 of the fleece of thy sheep, shalt thou **g** him. 5414
19: 8 **g** thee all the land which he promised to 5414
19: 8 which he promised to **g** unto thy fathers; 5414
20:16 which the LORD thy God doth **g** thee *for* 5414

Dt 22:14 **g** occasions of speech against her, and 7760
22:19 **g** *them* unto the father of the damsel, 5414
22:29 the man that lay with her shall **g** unto 5414
23:14 and to **g up** thine enemies before thee; 5414
24: 1 **g** *it* in her hand, and send her out of his 5414
24:15 At his day thou shalt **g** *him* his hire, 5414
25: 3 Forty **stripes** he may **g** him, *and* 5221
26: 3 LORD sware unto our fathers for to **g** us. 5414
28:11 LORD sware unto thy fathers to **g** thee. 5414
28:12 the heaven to **g** the rain unto thy land in his 5414
28:55 So that *he* will not **g** to any of them of 5414
28:65 the LORD shall **g** thee there a trembling 5414
30:20 to Isaac, and to Jacob, to **g** them. 5414
31: 5 the LORD shall **g** them **up** before your 5414
31: 7 hath sworn unto their fathers to **g** them; 5414
31:14 that I may **g** him **a charge**. 6680
32: 1 **G ear**, O ye heavens, and I will speak; and 238
32:49 which I **g** unto the children of Israel for a 5414
32:52 the land which I **g** the children of Israel. 5414
34: 4 unto Jacob, saying, I will **g** it unto thy seed: 5414
Jos 1: 2 unto the land which I do **g** to them, 5414
1: 6 which I sware unto their fathers to **g** them. 5414
2:12 my father's house, and **g** me a true token: 5414
5: 6 sware unto their fathers that he would **g** us, 5414
7:19 said unto Achan, My son, **g**, I pray thee, 7760
8:18 toward Ai; for I will **g** it into thine hand. 5414
9:24 his servant Moses to **g** you all the land, 5414
14:12 Now therefore **g** me this mountain, 5414
15:16 to him will I **g** Achsah my daughter to wife. 5414
15:19 Who answered, **G** me a blessing; for thou 5414
15:19 a south land; **g** me also springs of water. 5414
17: 4 The LORD commanded Moses to **g** us an 5414
18: 4 **G** out from among you three men for *each* 3051
20: 4 **g** him a place, that he may dwell among 5414
21: 2 the hand of Moses to **g** us cities to dwell in, 5414
21:43 land which he sware to **g** unto their fathers; 5414
Jdg 1:12 to him will I **g** Achsah my daughter to wife. 5414
1:15 she said unto him, **G** me a blessing: 3051
1:15 a south land; **g** me also springs of water. 5414
4:19 **G** me, I pray thee, a little water **to drink**; 8248
5: 3 **g ear**, O ye princes; I, *even* I, will sing unto 238
7: 2 for me to **g** the Midianites into their hands, 5414
8: 5 unto the men of Succoth, **G**, I pray you, 5414
8: 6 that we should **g** bread unto thine army? 5414
8:15 that we should **g** bread unto thy men *that* 5414
8:24 that you would **g** me every man 5414
8:25 We will **willingly g** *them*. And they 5414+5414
14:12 I will **g** you thirty sheets and thirty change 5414
14:13 shall ye **g** me thirty sheets and 5414
16: 5 we will **g** thee every one *of us* eleven 5414
17:10 I will **g** thee ten *shekels* of silver by 5414
20: 7 of Israel; **g** here your advice and counsel. 3051
21: 1 There shall not any of us **g** his daughter 5414
21: 7 will not **g** them of our daughters to wives? 5414
21:18 Howbeit we may not **g** them wives of our 5414
21:22 for ye did not **g** unto them at *this* time, 5414
Ru 4:12 of the seed which the LORD shall **g** thee 5414
1Sa 1:11 wilt **g** unto thine handmaid a man child, 5414
1:11 I will **g** him unto the LORD all the days of 5414
2:10 he shall **g** strength unto his king, and 5414
2:15 **G** flesh to roast for the priest; 5414
2:16 *Nay;* but thou shalt **g** *it me* now: 5414
2:20 The LORD **g** thee seed of this woman for 7760
2:28 did I **g** unto the house of thy father all 5414
2:32 in all *the wealth* which *God* shall **g** Israel: 3190
6: 5 and ye shall **g** glory unto the God of Israel: 5414
8: 6 when they said, **G** us a king to judge us. 5414
8:14 the best *of them,* and **g** *them* to his servants. 5414
8:15 and **g** to his officers, and to his servants. 5414
9: 8 *that* will I **g** to the man of God, to tell us 5414
10: 4 salute thee, and **g** thee two *loaves* of bread; 5414
11: 3 said unto him, **G** us seven days' **respite**, 7503
14:41 **G** a perfect *lot*. And Saul and 3051
17:10 **g** me a man, that we may fight together. 5414
17:25 will **g** him his daughter, and make his 5414
17:44 I will **g** thy flesh unto the fowls of the air, 5414
17:46 I will **g** the carcases of the host of 5414
17:47 and he will **g** you into our hands. 5414
18:17 daughter Merab, her will I **g** thee to wife: 5414
18:21 Saul said, I will **g** him her, that she may be 5414
21: 3 **g** *me* five *loaves of* bread in mine hand, or 5414
21: 9 David said, *There is* none like that; **g** it me. 5414
22: 7 will the son of Jesse **g** every one of you 5414
25: 8 **g**, I pray thee, whatsoever cometh to thine 5414
25:11 **g** *it* unto men, whom I know not whence 5414
27: 5 let them **g** me a place in some town in 5414
30:22 we will not **g** them *ought* of the spoil that 5414
2Sa 12:11 **g** *them* unto thy neighbour, and he shall lie 5414
13: 5 **g** me meat, and dress the meat in my sight, 1262
14: 8 and I will **g charge** concerning thee. 6680
16:20 **G** counsel among you what we shall do. 3051
21: 6 And the king said, I will **g** *them*. 5414
22:50 Therefore I will **g thanks** unto thee, 3034
23:15 Oh that one would **g** me **drink** *of* the water 8248
24:23 did Araunah, *as* a king, **g** unto the king. 5414
1Ki 1:12 let me, I pray thee, **g** thee **counsel**, 3289+6098
2:17 that he **g** me Abishag the Shunammite to 5414
3: 5 and God said, Ask what I shall **g** thee. 5414
3: 9 **G** therefore thy servant an understanding 5414
3:21 I rose in the morning to **g** my child **suck**, 3243
3:25 and **g** half to the one, and half to the other. 5414
3:26 **g** her the living child, and in no wise slay it. 5414
3:27 **G** her the living child, and in no wise slay 5414
5: 6 unto thee will I **g** hire for thy servants 5414
8:32 to **g** him according to his righteousness. 5414
8:36 **g** rain upon thy land, which thou hast given 5414
8:39 and **g** to every man according to his ways, 5414
8:50 **g** them compassion before them who 5414
11:11 from thee, and will **g** it to thy servant. 5414
11:13 will **g** one tribe to thy son for David my 5414
11:31 of Solomon, and will **g** ten tribes to thee: 5414
11:35 and will **g** it unto thee, *even* ten tribes. 5414
11:36 unto his son will I **g** one tribe, that David 5414
11:38 built for David, and will **g** Israel unto thee. 5414
12: 9 What **counsel g** ye that we may answer this 3289
13: 7 refresh *thyself,* and I will **g** thee a reward. 5414
13: 8 If thou wilt **g** me half thine house, I will not 5414
14:16 he shall **g** Israel **up** because of the sins of 5414
15: 4 his God **g** him a lamp in Jerusalem, 5414
17:19 he said unto her, **G** me thy son. And he 5414
18:23 Let them therefore **g** us two bullocks; and 5414
21: 2 unto Naboth, saying, **G** me thy vineyard, 5414
21: 2 I will **g** thee for it a better vineyard than it; 5414
21: 2 I will **g** thee the worth of it *in* money. 5414
21: 3 that I should **g** the inheritance of my fathers 5414
21: 4 I will not **g** thee the inheritance of my 5414
21: 6 unto him, **G** me thy vineyard for money; 5414
21: 6 I will **g** thee *another* vineyard for it: 5414
21: 6 he answered, I will not **g** thee my vineyard. 5414
21: 7 I will **g** thee the vineyard of Naboth 5414
21:15 which he refused to **g** thee for money: 5414
2Ki 4:42 he said, **G** unto the people, that they may 5414
4:43 He said again, **G** the people, that they may 5414
5:22 **g** them, I pray thee, a talent of silver, and 5414
6:28 This woman said unto me, **G** thy son, 5414
6:29 next day, **G** thy son, that we may eat him: 5414
8:19 as he promised him to **g** to him alway a 5414
10:15 If it be, **g** *me* thine hand. And he gave *him* 5414
11:10 the captains over hundreds did the priest **g** 5414
14: 9 **G** thy daughter to my son to wife: 5414
15:20 *of* silver, to **g** to the king of Assyria. 5414
18:23 **g pledges** to my lord the king of Assyria, 6148
22: 5 let them **g** it to the doers of the work which 5414
23:35 he taxed the land to **g** the money according 5414
23:35 to his taxation, to **g** *it* unto Pharaoh-nechoh. 5414
1Ch 11:17 Oh that one would **g** me **drink** *of* the water 8248
16: 8 **G thanks** unto the LORD, call upon his 3034
16:18 Unto thee will I **g** the land of Canaan, 5414
16:28 **G** unto the LORD, ye kindreds of 3051
16:28 **g** unto the LORD glory and strength. 3051
16:29 **G** unto the LORD the glory due unto his 3051
16:34 O **g thanks** unto the LORD; for *he is* 3034
16:35 that *we* may **g thanks** to thy holy name, 3034
16:41 to **g thanks** to the LORD, because 3034
21:23 I **g** *thee* the oxen *also* for burnt offerings, 5414
21:23 the wheat for the meat offering; I **g** *it* all. 5414
22: 9 I will **g** him **rest** from all his enemies round 5117
22: 9 I will **g** peace and quietness unto Israel in 5414
22:12 Only the LORD **g** thee wisdom and 5414
22:12 and **g** thee **charge** concerning Israel, 6680
25: 3 to **g thanks** and to praise the LORD. 3034
29:12 *is* to make great, and to **g strength** unto all. 2388
29:19 **g** unto Solomon my son a perfect heart, 5414
2Ch 1: 7 and said unto him, Ask what I shall **g** thee. 5414
1:10 **G** me now wisdom and knowledge, that I 5414
1:12 I will **g** thee riches, and wealth, and honour, 5414
2:10 behold, I will **g** to thy servants, the hewers 5414
10: 6 What **counsel g** ye *me* to return answer to 3289

2Ch	10: 9	What **advice** **g** ye that we may return	3289
	21: 7	as he promised to **g** a light to him and to his	5414
	24:19	against them: but they would not **g** **ear**.	238
	25: 9	The LORD is able to **g** thee much more	5414
	25:18	**G** thy daughter to my son to wife:	5414
	30:12	Also in Judah the hand of God was to **g**	5414
	30:24	For Hezekiah king of Judah did **g** to	7311
	31: 2	to **g** **thanks**, and to praise in the gates of	3034
	31: 4	in Jerusalem to **g** the portion of the priests	5414
	31:15	set office, to **g** to their brethren by courses,	5414
	31:19	to **g** portions to all the males among	5414
	32:11	Doth not Hezekiah persuade you to **g** **over**	5414
	35:12	that they might **g** according to the divisions	5414
Ezr	4:21	**G** ye now commandment to cause these	7761
	9: 8	and to **g** us a nail in his holy place,	5414
	9: 8	and **g** us a little reviving in our bondage.	5414
	9: 9	to **g** us a reviving, to set up the house of our	5414
	9: 9	to **g** us a wall in Judah and in Jerusalem.	5414
	9:12	**g** not your daughters unto their sons,	5414
Ne	2: 8	that he may **g** me timber to make beams for	5414
	4: 4	**g** them for a prey in the land of captivity:	5414
	9: 8	madest a covenant with him to **g** the land of	5414
	9: 8	to **g** *it, I say,* to his seed, and	5414
	9:12	to **g** them **light** in the way wherein they	215
	9:15	the land which thou hadst sworn to **g** them.	5414
	9:30	yet would they not **g** **ear**: therefore	238
	10:30	that we would not **g** our daughters unto	5414
	12:24	against them, to praise *and* to **g** **thanks**,	3034
	13:25	*saying,* Ye shall not **g** your daughters unto	5414
Est	1:19	let the king **g** her royal estate unto another	5414
	1:20	all the wives shall **g** to their husbands	5414
	8: 1	On that day did the king Ahasuerus **g**	5414
Job	2: 4	all that a man hath will he **g** for his life.	5414
	3:11	*why* did I *not* **g** **up the ghost** when I came	1478
	6:22	or, **G** **a reward** for me of your substance?	7809
	13:19	if I hold my tongue, I shall **g** **up the ghost**.	1478
	32:21	neither let me **g** **flattering titles** unto man.	3655
	32:22	For I know not to **g** **flattering titles**; *in so*	3655
	34: 2	ye wise *men;* and **g** **ear** unto me,	238
Ps	2: 8	I shall **g** *thee* the heathen *for* thine	5414
	5: 1	**G** **ear** to my words, O LORD, consider my	238
	6: 5	in the grave who shall **g** thee **thanks**?	3034
	17: 1	attend unto my cry, **g** **ear** unto my prayer,	238
	18:49	Therefore will I **g** **thanks** unto thee,	3034
	28: 4	**G** them according to their deeds, and	5414
	28: 4	**g** them after the work of their hands;	5414
	29: 1	**G** unto the LORD, O ye mighty, give unto	3051
	29: 1	**g** unto the LORD glory and strength.	3051
	29: 2	**G** unto the LORD the glory due unto his	3051
	29:11	The LORD will **g** strength unto his	5414
	30: 4	**g** **thanks** at the remembrance of his	3034
	30:12	my God, I will **g** **thanks** unto thee for ever.	3034
	35:18	I will **g** thee **thanks** in the great	3034
	37: 4	he shall **g** thee the desires of thine heart.	5414
	39:12	O LORD, and **g** **ear** unto my cry;	238
	49: 1	**g** **ear**, all ye inhabitants of the world:	238
	49: 7	*his* brother, nor **g** to God a ransom for him:	5414
	51:16	else would I **g** *it:* thou delightest not in	5414
	54: 2	O God; **g** **ear** to the words of my mouth.	238
	55: 1	**G** **ear** to my prayer, O God; and hide not	238
	57: 7	my heart is fixed: I will sing and **g** **praise**.	2167
	60:11	**G** us help from trouble: for vain *is* the help	3051
	72: 1	**G** the king thy judgments, O God, and	5414
	75: 1	Unto thee, O God, do we **g** **thanks**,	3034
	75: 1	we give thanks, *unto thee* do we **g** **thanks**:	3034
	78: 1	**G** **ear**, O my people, to my law: incline your	238
	78:20	streams overflowed; can he **g** bread also?	5414
	79:13	sheep of thy pasture will **g** thee **thanks** for	3034
	80: 1	**G** **ear**, O Shepherd of Israel, thou that	238
	84: 8	my prayer: **g** **ear**, O God of Jacob. Selah.	238
	84:11	the LORD will **g** grace and glory: no good	5414
	85:12	Yea, the LORD shall **g** *that which is* good;	5414
	86: 6	**G** **ear**, O LORD, unto my prayer; and	238
	86:16	**g** thy strength unto thy servant, and	5414
	91:11	For he shall **g** his angels **charge** over thee,	6680
	92: 1	*It is a* good *thing* to **g** **thanks** unto	3034
	94:13	That *thou* mayest **g** him **rest** from the days	8252
	96: 7	**G** unto the LORD, O ye kindreds of	3051
	96: 7	**g** unto the LORD glory and strength.	3051
	96: 8	**G** unto the LORD the glory due unto his	3051
	97:12	**g** **thanks** at the remembrance of his	3034
	104:11	They **g** **drink** to every beast of the field:	8248
	104:27	that *thou* mayest **g** *them* their meat in due	5414
	105: 1	O **g** **thanks** unto the LORD; call upon his	3034
	105:11	Unto thee will I **g** the land of Canaan,	5414
	105:39	a covering; and fire to **g** **light** in the night.	215
	106: 1	O **g** **thanks** unto the LORD; for *he is*	3034
	106:47	to **g** **thanks** unto thy holy name, *and*	3034
	107: 1	O **g** **thanks** unto the LORD, for *he is*	3034
	108: 1	I will sing and **g** **praise**, even *with* my	2167
	108:12	**G** us help from trouble: for vain *is* the help	3051
	109: 4	my adversaries: but I *g myself unto* prayer.	NIH
	111: 6	that *he* may **g** them the heritage of	5414
	115: 1	not unto us, but unto thy name **g** glory,	5414
	118: 1	O **g** **thanks** unto the LORD; for *he is*	3034
	118:29	O **g** **thanks** unto the LORD; for *he is*	3034
	119:34	**G** me **understanding**, and I shall keep thy	995
	119:62	At midnight I will rise to **g** **thanks** unto	3034
	119:73	**g** me **understanding**, that I may learn thy	995
	119:125	**g** me **understanding**, that I may know thy	995
	119:144	**g** me **understanding**, and I shall live.	995
	119:169	**g** me **understanding** according to thy word.	995
	122: 4	to **g** **thanks** unto the name of the LORD.	3034
	132: 4	I will not **g** sleep to mine eyes, *or*	5414
	136: 1	O **g** **thanks** unto the LORD; for *he is*	3034
	136: 2	O **g** **thanks** unto the God of gods: for his	3034
	136: 3	O **g** **thanks** to the Lord of lords: for his	3034
	136:26	O **g** **thanks** unto the God of heaven: for his	3034
	140:13	Surely the righteous shall **g** **thanks** unto	3034
	141: 1	**g** **ear** unto my voice, when I cry unto thee.	238
	143: 1	O LORD, **g** **ear** to my supplications:	238
Pr	1: 4	To **g** subtilty to the simple, to the young	5414
	3:28	and come again, and to morrow I will **g**;	5414
	4: 2	For I **g** you good doctrine, forsake you not	5414
	4: 9	She shall **g** to thine head an ornament of	5414
	5: 9	Lest thou **g** thine honour unto others, and	5414
	6: 4	**G** not sleep to thine eyes, nor slumber to	5414
	6:31	he shall **g** all the substance of his house.	5414
	9: 9	**G** *instruction* to a wise *man,* and he will be	5414
	23:26	**g** me thine heart, and let thine eyes observe	5414
	25:21	thine enemy *be* hungry, **g** him bread **to eat**;	398
	25:21	and if he *be* thirsty, **g** him water **to drink**:	8248
	29:15	The rod and reproof **g** wisdom: but a child	5414
	29:17	Correct thy son, and he shall **g** thee **rest**;	5117
	29:17	yea, he shall **g** delight unto thy soul.	5414
	30: 8	**g** me neither poverty nor riches; feed me	5414
	30:15	hath two daughters, *crying,* **G**, give.	3051
	30:15	hath two daughters, *crying,* Give, **g**.	3051
	31: 3	**G** not thy strength unto women, nor thy	5414
	31: 6	**G** strong drink unto him that is ready to	5414
	31:31	**G** her of the fruit of her hands; and let her	5414
Ecc	2: 3	I sought in mine heart to **g** myself unto	4900
	2:26	that *he* may **g** to *him that is* good before	5414
	5: 1	to hear, than to **g** the sacrifice of fools:	5414
	11: 2	**G** a portion to seven, and also to eight;	5414
SS	2:13	the vines *with* the tender grape **g** a *good*	5414
	7:12	bud forth: there will I **g** thee my loves.	5414
	7:13	The mandrakes **g** a smell, and at our gates	5414
	8: 7	if a man would **g** all the substance of his	5414
Isa	1: 2	Hear, O heavens, and **g** **ear**, O earth: for	238
	1:10	**g** **ear** unto the law of our God, ye people of	238
	3: 4	I will **g** children *to be* their princes, and	5414
	7:14	Therefore the Lord himself shall **g** you a	5414
	7:22	for the abundance of milk *that they* shall **g**	6213
	8: 9	in pieces; and **g** **ear**, all ye of far countries:	238
	10: 6	people of my wrath will I **g** him **a charge**,	6680
	13:10	the constellations thereof shall not **g** their	1984
	14: 3	LORD shall **g** thee **rest** from thy sorrow,	5117
	19: 4	the Egyptians will I **g** **over** into the hand of	5534
	28:23	**G** ye **ear**, and hear my voice; hearken, and	238
	30:20	*though* the Lord **g** you the bread of	5414
	30:23	shall he **g** the rain of thy seed, that thou	5414
	32: 9	ye careless daughters, **g** **ear** unto my speech.	238
	36: 8	Now therefore **g** **pledges**, I pray thee, to my	6148
	36: 8	and I will **g** thee two thousand horses,	5414
	41:27	I will **g** to Jerusalem one that bringeth good	5414
	42: 6	and **g** thee for a covenant of the people,	5414
	42: 8	my glory will I not **g** to another, neither my	5414
	42:12	Let them **g** glory unto the LORD, and	7760
	42:23	Who among you will **g** **ear** to this? *who* will	238
	43: 4	therefore will I **g** men for thee, and	5414
	43: 6	**G** *up;* and to the south, Keep not back:	5414
	43:20	because I **g** waters in the wilderness, *and*	5414
	43:20	to **g** **drink** to my people, my chosen.	8248
	45: 3	I will **g** thee the treasures of darkness, and	5414
	48:11	and I will not **g** my glory unto another.	5414
	49: 6	I will also **g** thee for a light to the Gentiles,	5414
	49: 8	and **g** thee for a covenant of the people,	5414

Isa	49:20	for me: **g place** to me that I may dwell.	5066
	51: 4	my people; and **g ear** unto me, O my nation:	238
	55:10	that it may **g** seed to the sower, and	5414
	56: 5	Even unto them will I **g** in mine house and	5414
	56: 5	I will **g** them an everlasting name, that shall	5414
	60:19	neither for brightness shall the moon **g light**	215
	61: 3	to **g** unto them beauty for ashes, the oil of	5414
	62: 7	**g** him no rest, till he establish, and till he	5414
	62: 8	Surely I will no more **g** thy corn *to be* meat	5414
Jer	3:15	I will **g** you pastors according to mine	5414
	3:19	the children, and **g** thee a pleasant land,	5414
	4:12	now also will I **g** sentence against them.	1696
	4:16	**g out** their voice against the cities of Judah.	5414
	6:10	and **g warning**, that they may hear?	5749
	8:10	Therefore will I **g** their wives unto others,	5414
	9:15	and **g** them water of gall **to drink**.	8248
	11: 5	to **g** them a land flowing with milk and	5414
	13:15	Hear ye, and **g ear**; be not proud: for	238
	13:16	**G** glory to the LORD your God, before he	5414
	14:13	but I will **g** you assured peace in this place.	5414
	14:22	or can the heavens **g** showers? *art* not thou	5414
	15:13	thy treasures will I **g** to the spoil without	5414
	16: 7	**g** them the cup of consolation **to drink** for	8248
	17: 3	I will **g** thy substance *and* all thy treasures	5414
	17:10	even to **g** every man according to his ways,	5414
	18:18	and let us not **g heed** to any of his words.	7181
	18:19	**G heed** to me, O LORD, and hearken to	7181
	19: 7	their carcases will I **g** to be meat for	5414
	20: 4	I will **g** all Judah into the hand of the king	5414
	20: 5	will I **g** into the hand of their enemies,	5414
	22:25	I will **g** thee into the hand of them that seek	5414
	24: 7	I will **g** them a heart to know me, that I *am*	5414
	24: 8	So will I **g** Zedekiah the king of Judah, and	5414
	25:30	he shall **g a shout**, as they that tread	1959+6030
	25:31	he will **g** them *that are* wicked to the sword,	5414
	26:24	that *they* should not **g** him into the hand of	5414
	29: 6	**g** your daughters to husbands, that they	5414
	29:11	and not of evil, to **g** you an expected end.	5414
	30:16	all that prey upon thee will I **g** for a prey.	5414
	32: 3	I *will* **g** this city into the hand of the king of	5414
	32:19	to **g** every one according to his ways, and	5414
	32:22	which thou didst swear to their fathers to **g**	5414
	32:28	I *will* **g** this city into the hand of	5414
	32:39	I will **g** them one heart, and one way,	5414
	34: 2	I *will* **g** this city into the hand of the king of	5414
	34:18	I will **g** the men that have transgressed my	5414
	34:20	I will even **g** them into the hand of their	5414
	34:21	his princes will I **g** into the hand of their	5414
	35: 2	of the chambers, and **g** them wine **to drink**.	8248
	37:21	that *they* should **g** him daily a piece of	5414
	38:15	if I **g** thee **counsel**, wilt thou not hearken	3289
	38:16	neither will I **g** thee into the hand of these	5414
	44:30	I *will* **g** Pharaoh-hophra king of Egypt into	5414
	45: 5	thy life will I **g** unto thee for a prey in all	5414
	48: 9	**G** wings unto Moab, that it may flee and	5414
	50:34	that he may **g rest** to the land, and	7280
La	2:18	**g** thyself no rest; let not the apple of thine	5414
	3:65	**G** them sorrow of heart, thy curse unto	5414
	4: 3	the breast, they **g suck** to their young ones:	3243
Eze	2: 8	open thy mouth, and eat that I **g** thee.	5414
	3: 3	fill thy bowels with this roll that I **g** thee.	5414
	3:17	my mouth, and **g** them **warning** from me.	2094
	7:21	I will **g** it into the hands of the strangers for	5414
	11: 2	and **g** wicked **counsel** in this city:	3289+6098
	11:17	and I will **g** you the land of Israel.	5414
	11:19	I will **g** them one heart, and I will put a new	5414
	11:19	their flesh, and will **g** them a heart of flesh:	5414
	15: 6	so will I **g** the inhabitants of Jerusalem.	5414
	16:33	They **g** gifts to all whores: but thou givest	5414
	16:36	thy children, which thou didst **g** unto them;	5414
	16:38	and I will **g** thee blood in fury and jealousy.	5414
	16:39	I will also **g** thee into their hand, and	5414
	16:41	and thou also shalt **g** no hire any more.	5414
	16:61	I will **g** them unto thee for daughters, but	5414
	17:15	that *they* might **g** him horses and	5414
	20:28	*for* the which I lifted up mine hand to **g** it to	5414
	20:42	I lifted up mine hand to **g** it to your fathers.	5414
	21:11	to **g** it into the hand of the slayer.	5414
	21:27	come whose right it is; and I will **g** it *him.*	5414
	23:31	therefore will I **g** her cup into thine hand.	5414
	23:46	and *will* **g** them to be removed and spoiled.	5414
	25:10	and will **g** them in possession,	5414
	29:19	I *will* **g** the land of Egypt unto	5414
	29:21	I will **g** thee the opening of the mouth in	5414
	32: 7	and the moon shall not **g** her **light**.	215+216
	33:15	**g again** that he had robbed, walk in	7999
	33:27	him that *is* in the open field will I **g** to	5414
	36:26	A new heart also will I **g** you, and a new	5414
	36:26	your flesh, and I will **g** you a heart of flesh.	5414
	39: 4	I will **g** thee unto the ravenous birds of	5414
	39:11	*that* I will **g** unto Gog a place there of	5414
	43:19	thou shalt **g** to the priests the Levites that	5414
	44:28	ye shall **g** them no possession in Israel:	5414
	44:30	ye shall also **g** unto the priest the first of	5414
	45: 8	*the rest of* the land shall they **g** to the house	5414
	45:13	ye shall **g the sixth part** of an ephah of a	8341
	45:16	All the people of the land shall **g** this	413+1961
	45:17	it shall be the prince's part *to* **g** burnt	NIH
	46: 5	for the lambs as he shall be able to **g**,	4991
	46:11	to the lambs as he is able to **g**, and a hin of	4991
	46:16	If the prince **g** a gift unto any of his sons,	5414
	46:17	if he **g** a gift of his inheritance to one of his	5414
	46:18	he shall **g** his sons **inheritance** out of his	5157
	47:14	up mine hand to **g** it unto your fathers:	5414
	47:23	there shall ye **g** *him* his inheritance,	5414
Da	1:12	let them **g** us pulse to eat, and water to	5414
	2:16	desired of the king that he would **g** him	5415
	5:17	be to thyself, and **g** thy rewards to another;	3052
	6: 2	that the princes might **g** accounts unto	3052
	8:13	to **g** both the sanctuary and the host to be	5414
	9:22	I am now come forth to **g** thee **skill** and	7919
	11:17	he shall **g** him the daughter of women,	5414
	11:21	to whom they shall not **g** the honour of	5414
Hos	2: 5	that **g** *me* my bread and my water, my wool	5414
	2:15	I will **g** her her vineyards from thence, and	5414
	4:18	her rulers *with* shame do love, **G** ye.	3051
	5: 1	of Israel; and **g** ye **ear**, O house of the king;	238
	9:14	**G** them, O LORD: what wilt thou give?	5414
	9:14	what wilt thou **g**? give them a miscarrying	5414
	9:14	**g** them a miscarrying womb and	5414
	11: 8	How shall I **g** thee **up**, Ephraim? *how* shall	5414
	13:10	thou saidst, **G** me a king and princes?	5414
Joel	1: 2	Hear this, ye old men, and **g ear**, all ye	238
	2:17	and **g** not thine heritage to reproach,	5414
Mic	1:14	Therefore shalt thou **g** presents to	5414
	5: 3	Therefore will he **g** them **up**, until the time	5414
	6: 7	shall I **g** my firstborn *for* my transgression,	5414
	6:14	*that* which thou deliverest will I **g up** to	5414
Hag	2: 9	in this place will I **g** peace, saith	5414
Zec	3: 7	I will **g** thee places to walk among these	5414
	8:12	the vine shall **g** her fruit, and the ground	5414
	8:12	the ground shall **g** her increase, and	5414
	8:12	and the heavens shall **g** their dew;	5414
	10: 1	**g** them showers of rain, to every one grass	5414
	11:12	unto them, If ye think good, **g** *me* my price;	3051
Mal	2: 2	to **g** glory unto my name, saith the LORD	5414
Mt	4: 6	He shall **g** his angels **charge** concerning	*1781*
	4: 9	unto him, All these *things* will I **g** thee,	*1325*
	5:31	let him **g** her a writing of divorcement:	*1325*
	5:42	**G** to him that asketh thee, and from him	*1325*
	6:11	**G** us this day our daily bread.	*1325*
	7: 6	**G** not that which is holy unto the dogs,	*1325*
	7: 9	if his son ask bread, will he **g** him a stone?	*1929*
	7:10	Or if he ask a fish, will he **g** him a serpent?	*1929*
	7:11	know how to **g** good gifts unto your	*1325*
	7:11	heaven **g** good *things* to them that ask him?	*1325*
	9:24	He said unto them, **G place**: for the maid is	*402*
	10: 8	out devils: freely ye have received, freely **g**.	*1325*
	10:42	And whosoever shall **g to drink** unto one	*4222*
	11:28	and are heavy laden, and I will **g** you **rest**.	*373*
	12:36	they shall **g** account thereof in the day of	*591*
	14: 7	Whereupon he promised with an oath to **g**	*1325*
	14: 8	**G** me here John Baptist's head in a charger.	*1325*
	14:16	They need not depart; **g** ye them to eat.	*1325*
	16:19	And I will **g** unto thee the keys of	*1325*
	16:26	what shall a man **g** in exchange for his	*1325*
	17:27	that take, and **g** unto them for me and thee.	*1325*
	19: 7	command to **g** a writing of divorcement,	*1325*
	19:21	and **g** to the poor, and thou shalt have	*1325*
	20: 4	and whatsoever is right I will **g** you.	*1325*
	20: 8	Call the labourers, and **g** them *their* hire,	*591*
	20:14	I will **g** unto this last, even as unto thee.	*1325*
	20:23	is not mine to **g**, but *it shall be given to*	*1325*
	20:28	and to **g** his life a ransom for many.	*1325*
	22:17	Is it lawful to **g** tribute unto Cesar, or not?	*1325*
	24:19	and to them that **g suck** in those days.	*2337*
	24:29	and the moon shall not **g** her light, and	*1325*
	24:45	to **g** them meat in due season?	*1325*

Mt 25: 8 foolish said unto the wise, **G** us of your oil; *1325*
25:28 and **g** *it* unto him which hath ten talents. *1325*
26:15 And said *unto them,* What will ye **g** me, *1325*
26:53 he shall presently **g** me more than twelve *3936*
Mk 6:22 whatsoever thou wilt, and I will **g** *it* thee. *1325*
6:23 I will **g** *it* thee, unto the half of my *1325*
6:25 I will that thou **g** me by and by in a charger *1325*
6:37 and said unto them, **G** ye them to eat. *1325*
6:37 pennyworth of bread, and **g** them to eat? *1325*
8:37 Or what shall a man **g** in exchange for his *1325*
9:41 **g** you a cup of water **to drink** in my name, *4222*
10:21 and **g** to the poor, and thou shalt have *1325*
10:40 and on my left hand is not mine to **g**; *1325*
10:45 and to **g** his life a ransom for many. *1325*
12: 9 and will **g** the vineyard unto others. *1325*
12:14 Is it lawful to **g** tribute to Cesar, or not? *1325*
12:15 Shall we **g**, or shall we not give? But he, *1325*
12:15 Shall we give, or shall we not **g**? But he, *1325*
13:17 and to them that **g suck** in those days. *2337*
13:24 and the moon shall not **g** her light, *1325*
14:11 were glad, and promised to **g** him money. *1325*
Lk 1:32 the Lord God shall **g** unto him the throne of *1325*
1:77 To **g** knowledge of salvation unto his *1325*
1:79 To **g light** to them that sit in darkness and *2014*
4: 6 All this power will I **g** thee, and the glory *1325*
4: 6 unto me; and to whomsoever I will I **g** it. *1325*
4:10 He shall **g** his angels **charge** over thee, to *1781*
6:30 **G** to every man that asketh of thee; and *1325*
6:38 **G**, and it shall be given unto you; *1325*
6:38 running over, shall *men* **g** into your bosom. *1325*
8:55 and he commanded to **g** her meat. *1325*
9:13 But he said unto them, **G** ye them to eat. *1325*
10: 7 and drinking **such** *things* **as** they **g**: *3588+3844*
10:19 I **g** unto you power to tread on serpents and *1325*
11: 3 **G** us day by day our daily bread. *1325*
11: 7 with me in bed; I cannot rise and **g** thee? *1325*
11: 8 Though he will not rise and **g** him, because *1325*
11: 8 will rise and **g** him as many as he needeth. *1325*
11:11 you that is a father, will he **g** him a stone? *1929*
11:11 a fish, will he for a fish **g** him a serpent? *1929*
11:13 know how to **g** good gifts unto your *1325*
11:13 **g** the Holy Spirit to them that ask him? *1325*
11:36 bright shining of a candle doth **g** thee **light**. *5461*
11:41 But rather **g** alms *of* such *things* as *you* *1325*
12:32 for it is your Father's good pleasure to **g** *1325*
12:33 Sell that ye have, and **g** alms; *1325*
12:42 to **g** *them their* portion of meat in due *1325*
12:51 Suppose ye that I am come to **g** peace on *1325*
12:58 **g** diligence that *thou* mayest be delivered *1325*
14: 9 and say to thee, **G** this *man* place; *1325*
15:12 **g** me the portion of goods that falleth to *1325*
16: 2 **g** an account of thy stewardship; for thou *591*
16:12 who shall **g** you that which is your own? *1325*
17:18 There are not found that returned to **g** glory *1325*
18:12 in the week, I **g tithes** of all that I possess. *586*
19: 8 Lord, the half of my goods I **g** to the poor; *1325*
19:24 and **g** *it* to him that hath ten pounds. *1325*
20:10 that they should **g** him of the fruit of *1325*
20:16 and shall **g** the vineyard to others. *1325*
20:22 Is it lawful for us to **g** tribute unto Cesar, or *1325*
21:15 For I will **g** you a mouth and wisdom, *1325*
21:23 and to them that **g suck**, in those days, *2337*
22: 5 were glad, and covenanted to **g** him money. *1325*
23: 2 and forbidding to **g** tribute to Cesar, saying *1325*
Jn 1:22 that we may **g** an answer to them that sent *1325*
4: 7 Jesus saith unto her, **G** me to drink. *1325*
4:10 who it is that saith to thee, **G** me to drink; *1325*
4:14 water that I shall **g** him shall never thirst; *1325*
4:14 the water that I shall **g** him shall be in him a *1325*
4:15 Sir, **g** me this water, that I thirst not, *1325*
6:27 which the Son of man shall **g** unto you: *1325*
6:34 unto him, Lord, evermore **g** us this bread. *1325*
6:51 and the bread that I will **g** is my flesh, *1325*
6:51 which I will **g** for the life of the world. *1325*
6:52 How can this *man* **g** us *his* flesh to eat? *1325*
7:19 Did not Moses **g** you the law, and *yet* none *1325*
9:24 and said unto him, **G** God the praise: *1325*
10:28 And I **g** unto them eternal life; and *1325*
11:22 thou wilt ask of God, God will **g** *it* thee. *1325*
13:26 He it is, to whom I shall **g** a sop, *1929*
13:29 or that he should **g** something to the poor. *1325*
13:34 A new commandment I **g** unto you, That ye *1325*
14:16 and he shall **g** you another Comforter, *1325*
14:27 I leave with you, my peace I **g** unto you: *1325*
14:27 not as the world giveth, **g** I unto you. *1325*
15:16 of the Father in my name, he may **g** it you. *1325*
16:23 ask the Father in my name, he will **g** *it* you. *1325*
17: 2 that he should **g** eternal life to as many as *1325*
Ac 3: 6 have I none; but such as I have **g** I thee: *1325*
5:31 for to **g** repentance to Israel, and *1325*
6: 4 But we will **g** ourselves **continually to** *4342*
7: 5 yet he promised that *he* would **g** it to him *1325*
7:38 who received *the* lively oracles to **g** unto *1325*
8:19 Saying, **G** me also this power, that on *1325*
10:43 To him **g** all the prophets **witness**, *3140*
13:16 of Israel, and *ye* that fear God, **g audience**. *191*
13:34 I will **g** you the sure mercies of David. *1325*
19:40 there being no cause whereby we may **g** an *591*
20:32 to **g** you an inheritance among all them *1325*
20:35 It is more blessed to **g** than to receive. *1325*
Ro 8:32 how shall he not with him also **freely g** us *5483*
12:19 but *rather* **g** place unto wrath: *1325*
12:20 feed him; if he thirst, **g** him **drink**: *4222*
14:12 every one of us shall **g** account of himself *1325*
16: 4 unto whom not only I **g thanks**, but also all *2168*
1Co 7: 5 that ye may **g** yourselves to fasting and *4980*
7:25 yet I **g** *my* judgment, as one that hath *1325*
10:30 spoken of for *that for* which I **g thanks**? *2168*
10:32 **G** none offence, neither to the Jews, nor to *1096*
12: 3 Wherefore I **g** you **to understand**, that no *1107*
13: 3 and though I **g** my body to be burned, *3860*
14: 7 except they **g** a distinction in the sounds, *1325*
14: 8 For if the trumpet **g** an uncertain sound, *1325*
2Co 4: 6 to **g** the light of the knowledge of the glory NIG
5:12 but **g** you occasion to glory on our behalf, *1325*
8:10 And herein I **g** *my* advice: for this is *1325*
9: 7 in *his* heart, *so let him g*; not grudgingly, NIG
Eph 1:16 Cease not to **g thanks** for you, *2168*
1:17 may **g** unto you the spirit of wisdom and *1325*
4:27 Neither **g** place to the devil. *1325*
4:28 that he may have to **g** to him that needeth. *3330*
5:14 from the dead, and Christ shall **g** thee **light**. *2017*
Col 1: 3 We **g thanks** to God and the Father of our *2168*
4: 1 **g unto** *your* servants that which is just and *3930*
1Th 1: 2 We **g thanks** to God always for you all, *2168*
5:18 In every *thing* **g thanks**: for this *is* the will *2168*
2Th 2:13 But we are bound to **g thanks** alway to *2168*
3:16 Now the Lord of peace himself **g** you peace *1325*
1Ti 1: 4 Neither **g heed** to fables and *4337*
4:13 Till I come, **g attendance** to reading, *4337*
4:15 Meditate upon these *things;* **g** thyself *1510*
5: 7 And these *things* **g in charge**, that they *3853*
5:14 **g** none occasion to the adversary to speak *1325*
6:13 I **g** thee **charge** in the sight of God, *3853*
2Ti 1:16 The Lord **g** mercy unto the house of *1325*
2: 7 the Lord **g** thee understanding in all *things.* *1325*
2:25 if God peradventure will **g** them repentance *1325*
4: 8 the righteous judge, shall **g** me at that day: *591*
Heb 2: 1 **g** the more earnest **heed to** the *things* which *4337*
13:17 as they that must **g** account, that they may do *591*
Jas 2:16 notwithstanding ye **g** them not those *things* *1325*
1Pe 3:15 *be* ready always to *g* an answer to every NIG
4: 5 Who shall **g** account to him that is ready to *591*
2Pe 1:10 **g diligence** to make your calling and *4704*
1Jn 5:16 he shall **g** him life for them that sin not *1325*
Rev 2: 7 To him that overcometh will I **g** to eat of *1325*
2:10 unto death, and I will **g** thee a crown of life. *1325*
2:17 To him that overcometh will I **g** to eat of *1325*
2:17 and will **g** him a white stone, and in *1325*
2:23 I will **g** unto every one of you according to *1325*
2:26 to him will I **g** power over the nations: *1325*
2:28 And I will **g** him the morning star. *1325*
4: 9 And when *those* beasts **g** glory and honour *1325*
10: 9 and said unto him, **G** me the little book. *1325*
11: 3 And I will **g** *power* unto my two witnesses, *1325*
11:17 Saying, We **g** thee **thanks**, O Lord God *2168*
11:18 that *thou* shouldest **g** reward unto thy *1325*
13:15 And he had power to **g** life unto the image *1325*
14: 7 a loud voice, Fear God, and **g** glory to him; *1325*
16: 9 and they repented not to **g** him glory. *1325*
16:19 to **g** unto her the cup of the wine of *1325*
17:13 and shall **g** their power and strength unto *1239*
17:17 and **g** their kingdom unto the beast, *1325*
18: 7 so much torment and sorrow **g** her: *1325*
19: 7 be glad and rejoice, and **g** honour to him: *1325*
21: 6 I will **g** unto him that is athirst of *1325*
22:12 to **g** every man according as his work shall *591*

GIVE LIFE See QUICKEN

GIVE TO NEEDY See ALMS

GIVEN (498) [GIVE]

Ge 1:29 I have **g** you every herb bearing seed, 5414
1:30 *is* life, *I have* **g** every green herb for meat: NIH
9: 3 *even* as the green herb have I **g** you all 5414
15: 3 Behold, to me thou hast **g** no seed: 5414
15:18 saying, Unto thy seed have I **g** this land, 5414
16: 5 I have **g** my maid into thy bosom; and 5414
20:16 I have **g** thy brother a thousand *pieces* of 5414
21: 7 that Sarah should have **g** children **suck**? 3243
24:35 he hath **g** him flocks, and herds, and silver, 5414
24:36 and unto him hath he **g** all that he hath. 5414
27:37 all his brethren have I **g** to him for servants; 5414
29:33 he hath therefore **g** me this *son* also: 5414
30: 6 also heard my voice, and hath **g** me a son: 5414
30:18 God hath **g** *me* my hire, because I have 5414
30:18 I have **g** my maiden to my husband: 5414
31: 9 the cattle of your father, and **g** *them* to me. 5414
33: 5 The children which God hath **graciously g** 2603
38:14 and she was not **g** unto him to wife. 5414
43:23 hath **g** you treasure in your sacks: 5414
48: 9 whom God hath **g** me in this *place.* And he 5414
48:22 Moreover I have **g** to thee one portion 5414
Ex 5:16 *There is* no straw **g** unto thy servants, and 5414
5:18 for there shall no straw be **g** you, yet shall 5414
16:15 This *is* the bread which the LORD hath **g** 5414
16:29 for that the LORD hath **g** you the sabbath, 5414
21: 4 If his master have **g** him a wife, and 5414
31: 6 I, behold, I have **g** with him Aholiab, 5414
Lev 6:17 I have **g** it *unto them for* their portion of my 5414
7:34 have **g** them unto Aaron the priest and 5414
7:36 Which the LORD commanded to be **g** 5414
10:14 *which* are **g** out of the sacrifices of peace 5414
10:17 *God* hath **g** it you to bear the iniquity of 5414
17:11 I have **g** it to you upon the altar to make an 5414
19:20 and not at all redeemed, nor freedom **g** her; 5414
20: 3 because he hath **g** of his seed unto Molech, 5414
Nu 3: 9 they *are* **wholly g** unto him out of 5414+5414
8:16 For they *are* **wholly g** unto me from 5414+5414
8:19 I have **g** the Levites *as* a gift to Aaron and 5414
16:14 or **g** us inheritance of fields and vineyards: 5414
18: 6 to you *they are* **g** *as* a gift for the LORD, 5414
18: 7 I have **g** your priest's office *unto you as* a 5414
18: 8 I also have **g** thee the charge of mine heave 5414
18: 8 unto thee have I **g** them by reason of 5414
18:11 I have **g** them unto thee, and to thy sons 5414
18:12 offer unto the LORD, them have I **g** thee. 5414
18:19 have I **g** thee, and thy sons and thy 5414
18:21 I have **g** the children of Levi all the tenth in 5414
18:24 I have **g** to the Levites to inherit: 5414
18:26 have **g** you from them for your inheritance, 5414
20:12 into the land which I have **g** them. 5414
20:24 which I have **g** unto the children of Israel, 5414
21:29 he hath **g** his sons that escaped, and 5414
26:54 *to* every one shall his inheritance be **g** 5414
26:62 there was no inheritance **g** them among 5414
27:12 see the land which I have **g** unto 5414
32: 5 let this land be **g** unto thy servants for a 5414
32: 7 the land which the LORD hath **g** them? 5414
32: 9 into the land which the LORD had **g** them. 5414
33:53 for I have **g** you the land to possess it. 5414
Dt 1: 3 had **g** him **in commandment** unto them; 6680
2: 5 I have **g** mount Seir unto Esau *for* a 5414
2: 9 I have **g** Ar unto the children of Lot *for* a 5414
2:19 I have **g** it unto the children of Lot *for* a 5414
2:24 I have **g** into thy hand Sihon the Amorite, 5414
3:18 The LORD your God hath **g** you this land 5414
3:19 shall abide in your cities which I have **g** 5414
3:20 Until the LORD have **g rest** unto your 5117
3:20 your God hath **g** them beyond Jordan: 5414
3:20 unto his possession, which I have **g** you. 5414
8:10 for the good land which he hath **g** thee. 5414
9:23 and possess the land which I have **g** you; 5414
12:15 the LORD thy God which he hath **g** thee: 5414
12:21 of thy flock, which the LORD hath **g** thee, 5414
13:12 which the LORD thy God hath **g** thee to 5414
16:17 the LORD thy God which he hath **g** thee. 5414
20:14 which the LORD thy God hath **g** thee. 5414
22:17 he hath **g** occasions of speech *against her,* 7760
25:19 when the LORD thy God hath **g** thee **rest** 5117
26: 9 hath **g** us this land, *even* a land that floweth 5414
26:10 the land, which thou, O LORD, hast **g** me. 5414
26:11 the LORD thy God hath **g** unto thee, 5414
26:12 hast **g** *it* unto the Levite, the stranger, 5414
26:13 also have **g** them unto the Levite, and 5414
26:14 *use,* nor **g** *ought* thereof for the dead: 5414
26:15 and the land which thou hast **g** us, 5414
28:31 thy sheep *shall be* **g** unto thine enemies, 5414
28:32 thy daughters *shall be* **g** unto another 5414
28:52 which the LORD thy God hath **g** thee. 5414
28:53 which the LORD thy God hath **g** thee, 5414
29: 4 Yet the LORD hath not **g** you a heart to 5414
29:26 and *whom* he had not **g** unto them: 2505
Jos 1: 3 that have I **g** unto you, as I said unto 5414
1:13 The LORD your God hath **g** you **rest**, and 5117
1:13 given you rest, and hath **g** you this land. 5414
1:15 the LORD have **g** your brethren **rest**, 5117
1:15 as *he hath* **g** you, and they also have NIH
2: 9 I know that the LORD hath **g** you 5414
2:14 when the LORD hath **g** us the land, 5414
6: 2 I have **g** into thine hand Jericho, and 5414
6:16 Shout; for the LORD hath **g** you the city. 5414
8: 1 I have **g** into thy hand the king of Ai, and 5414
14: 3 For Moses had **g** the inheritance of two 5414
15:19 a blessing; for thou hast **g** me a south land; 5414
17:14 Why hast thou **g** me *but* one lot and 5414
18: 3 LORD God of your fathers hath **g** you? 5414
22: 4 now the LORD your God hath **g rest** unto 5117
22: 7 Moses had **g** *possession* in Bashan: 5414
23: 1 **g rest** unto Israel from all their enemies 5117
23:13 which the LORD your God hath **g** you. 5414
23:15 which the LORD your God hath **g** you. 5414
23:16 off the good land which he hath **g** unto you. 5414
24:13 I have **g** you a land for which ye did not 5414
24:33 which was **g** him in mount Ephraim. 5414
Jdg 1:15 for thou hast **g** me a south land; give me 5414
14:20 But Samson's wife was *g* to his companion, NIH
15: 6 taken his wife, and **g** her to his companion. 5414
15:18 Thou hast **g** this great deliverance into 5414
18:10 for God hath **g** it into your hands; a place 5414
Ru 2:12 a full reward be **g** thee **of** the LORD 4480+5973
1Sa 1:27 the LORD hath **g** me my petition which I 5414
15:28 hath **g** it to a neighbour of thine, *that is* 5414
18:19 daughter should have been **g** to David, 5414
18:19 that she was **g** unto Adriel the Meholathite 5414
22:13 in that thou hast **g** him bread and a sword, 5414
25:27 let it even be **g** unto the young men that 5414
25:44 Saul had **g** Michal his daughter, 5414
28:17 and **g** it to thy neighbour, *even* to David: 5414
30:23 with *that* which the LORD hath **g** us, 5414
2Sa 4:10 who *thought* that I would have **g** him a 5414
7: 1 the LORD had **g** him **rest** round about 5117
9: 9 I have **g** unto thy master's son all that 5414
12: 8 I would **moreover** have **g** unto thee such 3254
12:14 **g great occasion** to the enemies of the
LORD **to blaspheme**, 5006+5006
17: 7 The **counsel** that Ahithophel hath **g** 3289+6098
18:11 I would have **g** thee ten *shekels of* silver, 5414
19:42 of the king's *cost?* or hath he **g** us *any* gift? 5375
22:36 Thou hast also **g** me the shield of thy 5414
22:41 Thou hast also **g** me the necks of mine 5414
1Ki 1:48 which hath **g** *one* to sit on my throne *this* 5414
2:21 Let Abishag the Shunammite be **g** to 5414
3: 6 that thou hast **g** him a son to sit on his 5414
3:12 I have **g** thee a wise and an understanding 5414
3:13 I have also **g** thee *that* which thou hast not 5414
5: 4 now the LORD my God hath **g** me **rest** on 5117
5: 7 which hath **g** unto David a wise son over 5414
8:36 which thou hast **g** to thy people for an 5414
8:56 that hath **g** rest unto his people Israel, 5414
9: 7 Israel out of the land which I have **g** them; 5414
9:12 to see the cities which Solomon had **g** him; 5414
9:13 What cities *are* these which thou hast **g** me, 5414
9:16 **g** it *for* a present unto his daughter, 5414
12: 8 **counsel** of the old men, which they
had **g** 3289+6098
13: 5 of God had **g** by the word of the LORD. 5414
18:26 they took the bullock which was **g** them, 5414
2Ki 5: 1 by him the LORD had **g** deliverance unto 5414
5:17 be **g** to thy servant two mules' burden of 5414
8:29 which the Syrians had **g** him at Ramah, 5221
9:15 of the wounds which the Syrians had **g** him, 5221
23:11 that the kings of Judah had **g** to the sun, 5414
25:30 his allowance was a continual allowance **g** 5414
1Ch 5: 1 his birthright was **g** unto the sons of Joseph 5414

G

1Ch 6:61 *were cities* **g** out of the half tribe, NIH
6:63 Unto the sons of Merari *were* **g** by lot, NIH
6:71 Unto the sons of Gershom *were* **g** out of NIH
6:77 Merari *were* **g** out of the tribe of Zebulun, NIH
6:78 *were* **g** *them* out of the tribe of Reuben, NIH
22:18 hath he *not* **g** you **rest** on every side? for he 5117
22:18 for he hath **g** the inhabitants of the land into 5414
23:25 The LORD God of Israel hath **g rest** unto 5117
28: 5 (for the LORD hath **g** me many sons,) 5414
29: 3 *which* I have **g** to the house of my God, 5414
29:14 of thee, and of thine own have we **g** thee. 5414
2Ch 2:12 who hath **g** to David the king a wise son, 5414
6:27 which thou hast **g** unto thy people for an 5414
7:20 roots out of my land which I have **g** them; 5414
14: 6 because the LORD had **g** him **rest**. 5117
14: 7 and he hath **g** us **rest** on every side. 5117
20:11 which thou hast **g** us **to inherit**. 3423
22: 6 of the wounds which were **g** him at Ramah, 5221
25: 9 talents which I have **g** to the army of Israel? 5414
32:29 for God had **g** him substance very much. 5414
34:14 book of the law of the LORD *g* by Moses. NIH
34:18 Hilkiah the priest hath **g** me a book. 5414
36:23 earth hath the LORD God of heaven **g** me; 5414
Ezr 1: 2 The LORD God of heaven hath **g** me all 5414
4:21 until *another* commandment shall be **g** from 7761
6: 4 let the expences be **g** out of the king's 3052
6: 8 forthwith expences be **g** unto these men, 3052
6: 9 let *it* be **g** them day by day without fail: 3052
7: 6 which the LORD God of Israel had **g**: 5414
7:19 The vessels also that *are* **g** thee for 3052
9:13 and hast **g** us *such* deliverance as this; 5414
Ne 2: 7 let letters be **g** me to the governors beyond 5414
10:29 which was **g** by Moses the servant of God, 5414
13: 5 which was commanded *to be g* to NIH
13:10 had not been **g** *them:* for the Levites 5414
Est 2: 3 let their things for purification be **g** *them:* 5414
2: 9 *which were* meet to be **g** her, 5414
2:13 whatsoever she desired was **g** her to go 5414
3:11 The silver *is* **g** to thee, the people also, 5414
3:14 **g** in every province *was* published unto all 5414
3:15 and the decree was **g** in Shushan the palace. 5414
4: 8 that was **g** at Shushan to destroy them, 5414
5: 3 it shall be even **g** thee to the half of 5414
7: 3 let my life be **g** me at my petition, and 5414
8: 7 I have **g** Esther the house of Haman, and 5414
8:13 **g** in every province *was* published unto all 5414
8:14 and the decree was **g** at Shushan the palace. 5414
9:14 the decree was **g** at Shushan; and they 5414
Job 3:20 Wherefore is light **g** to him that is in 5414
3:23 *Why is light* **g** to a man whose way is hid, NIH
9:24 The earth is **g** into the hand of the wicked: 5414
10:18 *Oh that* I had **g up the ghost**, and no eye 1478
15:19 Unto whom alone the earth was **g**, and 5414
22: 7 hast not **g** water to the weary **to drink**, 8248
24:23 *Though* it be **g** him *to be* in safety, 5414
33: 4 the breath of the Almighty hath **g** me **life**. 2421
34:13 Who hath **g** him **a charge** over the earth? 6485
37:10 By the breath of God frost is **g**: and 5414
38:36 or who hath **g** understanding to the heart? 5414
39:19 Hast thou **g** the horse strength? hast thou 5414
Ps 16: 7 bless the LORD, who hath **g** me **counsel**: 3289
18:35 Thou hast also **g** me the shield of thy 5414
18:40 Thou hast also **g** me the necks of mine 5414
21: 2 Thou hast **g** him his heart's desire, and 5414
44:11 Thou hast **g** us like sheep appointed for 5414
60: 4 Thou hast **g** a banner to them that fear thee, 5414
61: 5 thou hast **g** *me* the heritage of those that 5414
71: 3 thou hast **g commandment** to save me; 6680
72:15 and to him shall be **g** of the gold of Sheba: 5414
78:24 and had **g** them *of* the corn of heaven. 5414
78:63 and their maidens were not **g to marriage**. 1984
79: 2 The dead bodies of thy servants have they **g** 5414
111: 5 He hath **g** meat unto them that fear him: 5414
112: 9 He hath dispersed, he hath **g** to the poor; 5414
115:16 the earth hath he **g** to the children of men. 5414
118:18 but he hath not **g** me **over** unto death. 5414
120: 3 What shall be **g** unto thee? or what shall be 5414
124: 6 who hath not **g** us *as* a prey to their teeth. 5414
Pr 19:17 that which he hath **g** will he pay him again. 1576
23: 2 thy throat, if thou *be* a man **g to appetite**. 5315
24:21 meddle not with them that are **g to change**: 8138
Ecc 1:13 this sore travail hath God **g** to the sons of 5414
3:10 which God hath **g** to the sons of men to be 5414
5:19 Every man also to whom God hath **g** riches 5414
5:19 hath **g** him **power** to eat thereof, and 7980
6: 2 A man to whom God hath **g** riches, wealth, 5414
8: 8 wickedness deliver **those that are g to** it. 1167
9: 9 which he hath **g** thee under the sun, all 5414
12:11 *which* are **g** from one shepherd. 5414
Isa 3:11 for the reward of his hands shall be **g** him. 6213
8:18 the children whom the LORD hath **g** me 5414
9: 6 unto us a child is born, unto us a Son is **g**: 5414
23:11 the LORD hath **g a commandment** 6680
33:16 bread *shall be* **g** him; his waters *shall be* 5414
35: 2 the glory of Lebanon shall be **g** unto it, 5414
37:10 Jerusalem shall not be **g** into the hand of 5414
43:28 have **g** Jacob to the curse, and Israel to 5414
47: 6 and **g** them into thine hand: 5414
47: 8 *thou that art* **g to pleasures**, that dwellest 5719
50: 4 The Lord GOD hath **g** me the tongue of 5414
55: 4 I have **g** him *for* a witness to the people, 5414
Jer 3: 8 put her away, and **g** her a bill of divorce; 5414
3:18 **g for an inheritance** unto your fathers. 5157
6:13 them every one *is* **g to covetousness**; 1214+1215
8:10 even unto the greatest is **g** to covetousness, 1214
8:13 *the things that* I have **g** them shall pass 5414
8:14 **g** us water of gall **to drink**, because 8248
11:18 the LORD hath **g** me **knowledge** *of it,* 3045
12: 7 I have **g** the dearly beloved of my soul into 5414
13:20 where *is* the flock *that* was **g** thee, 5414
15: 9 she hath **g up the ghost**; her sun is 5301+5315
21:10 it shall be **g** into the hand of the king of 5414
25: 5 dwell in the land that the LORD hath **g** 5414
27: 5 have **g** it unto whom it seemed meet unto 5414
27: 6 now have I **g** all these lands into the hand 5414
27: 6 the beasts of the field have I **g** him also to 5414
28:14 I have **g** him the beasts of the field also. 5414
32:22 hast **g** them this land, which thou didst 5414
32:24 the city is **g** into the hand of the Chaldeans, 5414
32:25 for the city is **g** into the hand of 5414
32:43 beast; it is **g** into the hand of the Chaldeans. 5414
35:15 ye shall dwell in the land which I have **g** to 5414
38: 3 This city shall **surely** be **g** into 5414+5414
38:18 shall this city be **g** into the hand of 5414
39:17 thou shalt not be **g** into the hand of the men 5414
44:20 the people which had **g** him *that* **answer**, 6030
47: 7 seeing the LORD hath **g** it **a charge** 6680
50:15 she hath **g** her hand: her foundations are 5414
52:34 there was a continual diet **g** him of the king 5414
La 1:11 they have **g** their pleasant things for meat to 5414
2: 7 he hath **g up** into the hand of the enemy 5462
5: 6 We have **g** the hand *to* the Egyptians, *and* 5414
Eze 3:20 because thou hast not **g** him **warning**, 2094
4:15 I have **g** thee cow's dung for man's dung, 5414
11:15 unto us is this land **g** in possession. 5414
15: 6 which I have **g** to the fire for fuel, so will I 5414
16:17 which I had **g** thee, and madest to thyself 5414
16:34 no reward is **g** unto thee, therefore thou art 5414
17:18 he had **g** his hand, and hath done all these 5414
18: 7 hath **g** his bread to the hungry, and 5414
18: 8 He *that* hath not **g forth** upon usury, 5414
18:13 Hath **g forth** upon usury, and hath taken 5414
18:16 *but* hath **g** his bread to the hungry, and 5414
20:15 land which I had **g** *them,* flowing with milk 5414
21:11 he hath **g** it to be furbished, that *it* may be 5414
28:25 shall they dwell in their land that I have **g** 5414
29: 5 I have **g** thee for meat to the beasts of 5414
29:20 I have **g** him the land of Egypt *for* his 5414
33:24 *are* many; the land is **g** us for inheritance. 5414
35:12 are laid desolate, they are **g** us to consume. 5414
37:25 they shall dwell in the land that I have **g** 5414
47:11 shall not be healed; they shall be **g** to salt. 5414
Da 2:23 who hast **g** me wisdom and might, and 3052
2:37 for the God of heaven hath **g** thee a 3052
2:38 the fowls of the heaven hath he **g** into thine 3052
4:16 let a beast's heart be **g** unto him; 3052
5:28 is divided, and **g** to the Medes and Persians. 3052
7: 4 feet as a man, and a man's heart was **g** to it. 3052
7: 6 also four heads; and dominion *was* **g** to it. 3052
7:11 body destroyed, and **g** to the burning flame. 3052
7:14 there *was* **g** him dominion, and glory, and 3052
7:22 judgment *was* **g** to the saints of the most 3052
7:25 they shall be **g** into his hand until a time 3052
7:27 *shall be* **g** to the people of the saints of 3052
8:12 a host was **g** *him* against the daily *sacrifice* 5414
11: 6 she shall be **g up**, and they that brought her, 5414
11:11 but the multitude shall be **g** into his hand. 5414
Hos 2: 9 and my flax *g* to cover her nakedness. NIH

Hos	2:12	*are* my rewards that my lovers have **g**	5414
Joel	2:23	for he hath **g** you the former rain	5414
	3: 3	have **g** a boy for a harlot, and sold a girl for	5414
Am	4: 6	I also have **g** you cleanness of teeth in all	5414
	9:15	up out of their land which I have **g** them,	5414
Na	1:14	the LORD hath **g a commandment**	6680
Mt	7: 7	Ask, and it shall be **g** you; seek, and	*1325*
	9: 8	which had **g** such power unto men.	*1325*
	10:19	for it shall be **g** you in that *same* hour what	*1325*
	12:39	and there shall no sign be **g** to it, but	*1325*
	13:11	Because it is **g** unto you to know	*1325*
	13:11	kingdom of heaven, but to them it is not **g**.	*1325*
	13:12	to him shall be **g**, and he shall have *more*	*1325*
	14: 9	him at meat, he commanded *it* to be **g** *her.*	*1325*
	14:11	brought in a charger, and **g** to the damsel:	*1325*
	16: 4	and there shall no sign be **g** unto it, but	*1325*
	19:11	this saying, save *they* to whom it is **g**.	*1325*
	20:23	*it shall be* **g** *to them* for whom it is prepared	NIG
	21:43	**g** to a nation bringing forth the fruits	*1325*
	22:30	they neither marry, nor are **g in marriage**,	*1547*
	25:29	For unto every one that hath shall be **g**, and	*1325*
	26: 9	have been sold for much, and **g** to the poor.	*1325*
	28:18	All power is **g** unto me in heaven and	*1325*
Mk	4:11	Unto you it is **g** to know the mystery of	*1325*
	4:24	and unto you that hear shall **more** be **g**.	*4369*
	4:25	For he that hath, to him shall be **g**: and	*1325*
	5:43	commanded that *something* should be **g** her	*1325*
	6: 2	what wisdom *is this* which is **g** unto him,	*1325*
	8:12	There shall no sign be **g** unto this	*1325*
	10:40	*it shall be* **g** *to them* for whom it is prepared.	NIG
	12:25	they neither marry, nor are **g in marriage**;	*1061*
	13:11	but whatsoever shall be **g** you in that hour,	*1325*
	14: 5	and have been **g** to the poor.	*1325*
	14:23	and when he had **g thanks**, he gave *it* to	*2168*
	14:44	And he that betrayed him had **g** them a	*1325*
Lk	6:38	Give, and it shall be **g** unto you;	*1325*
	8:10	Unto you it is **g** to know the mysteries of	*1325*
	8:18	for whosoever hath, to him shall be **g**; and	*1325*
	11: 9	I say unto you, Ask, and it shall be **g** you;	*1325*
	11:29	and there shall no sign be **g** it, but the sign	*1325*
	12:48	*stripes.* For unto whomsoever much is **g**,	*1325*
	17:27	married *wives,* they were **g in marriage**,	*1547*
	19:15	unto him, to whom he had **g** the money,	*1325*
	19:26	That unto every one which hath shall be **g**;	*1325*
	20:34	of this world marry, and are **g in marriage**:	*1548*
	20:35	neither marry, nor are **g in marriage**:	*1548*
	22:19	saying, This is my body which is **g** for you:	*1325*
Jn	1:17	For the law was **g** by Moses, *but* grace and	*1325*
	3:27	except it be **g** him from heaven.	*1325*
	3:35	the Son, and hath **g** all *things* into his hand.	*1325*
	4:10	and he would have **g** thee living water.	*1325*
	5:26	hath he **g** to the Son to have life in himself;	*1325*
	5:27	And hath **g** him authority to execute	*1325*
	5:36	for the works which the Father hath **g** me to	*1325*
	6:11	and when he had **g thanks**, he distributed	*2168*
	6:23	eat bread, after that the Lord had **g thanks**:)	*2168*
	6:39	that of all which he hath **g** me I should lose	*1325*
	6:65	except it were **g** unto him of my Father.	*1325*
	7:39	for the Holy Ghost was not yet *g*; because	NIG
	11:57	and the Pharisees had **g** a commandment,	*1325*
	12: 5	for three hundred pence, and **g** to the poor?	*1325*
	13: 3	Jesus knowing that the Father had **g** all	*1325*
	13:15	For I have **g** you an example, that ye should	*1325*
	17: 2	As thou hast **g** him power over all flesh,	*1325*
	17: 2	eternal life to as many as thou hast **g** him.	*1325*
	17: 7	whatsoever thou hast **g** me are of thee.	*1325*
	17: 8	For I have **g** unto them the words which	*1325*
	17: 9	but for *them* which thou hast **g** me;	*1325*
	17:11	own name those whom thou hast **g** me,	*1325*
	17:14	I have **g** them thy word; and the world hath	*1325*
	17:22	glory which thou gavest me I have **g** them;	*1325*
	17:24	I will that they also, whom thou hast **g** me,	*1325*
	17:24	behold my glory, which thou hast **g** me:	*1325*
	18:11	the cup which my Father hath **g** me, shall I	*1325*
	19:11	except it were **g** thee from above:	*1325*
Ac	1: 2	**g commandments** unto the Apostles whom	*1781*
	3:16	the faith which is by him hath **g** him this	*1325*
	4:12	other name under heaven **g** among men,	*1325*
	5:32	whom God hath **g** to them that obey him.	*1325*
	8:18	the apostles' hands the Holy Ghost was **g**,	*1325*
	17:16	he saw the city **wholly g to idolatry**.	*1510+2712*
	17:31	*whereof* he hath **g** assurance unto all *men,*	*3930*
	20: 2	and had **g** them much **exhortation**,	*3056+3870*
	21:40	And when he had **g** *him* **licence**, Paul stood	*2010*
	24:26	that money should have been **g** him of Paul,	*1325*
	27:24	God hath **g** thee all them that sail with thee.	*5483*
Ro	5: 5	by the Holy Ghost which is **g** unto us.	*1325*
	11: 8	God hath **g** them the spirit of slumber,	*1325*
	11:35	Or who hath **first g** to him, and it shall be	*4272*
	12: 3	For I say, through the grace **g** unto me,	*1325*
	12: 6	according to the grace that is **g** to us,	*1325*
	12:13	to the necessity of saints; **g to** hospitality.	*1377*
	15:15	because of the grace that is **g** to me of God,	*1325*
1Co	1: 4	for the grace of God which is **g** you by	*1325*
	2:12	the *things* that are **freely g** to us of God.	*5483*
	3:10	According to the grace of God which is **g**	*1325*
	11:15	to her: for *her* hair is **g** her for a covering.	*1325*
	11:24	And when he had **g thanks**, he brake *it,* and	*2168*
	12: 7	But the manifestation of the Spirit is **g** to	*1325*
	12: 8	For to one is **g** by the Spirit the word of	*1325*
	12:24	having **g** more abundant honour to that *part*	*1325*
	16: 1	as I have **g order** to the churches of	*1299*
2Co	1:11	**thanks** may be **g** by many on our behalf.	*2168*
	1:22	and **g** the earnest of the Spirit in our hearts.	*1325*
	5: 5	who also hath **g** unto us the earnest of	*1325*
	5:18	hath **g** to us the ministry of reconciliation;	*1325*
	9: 9	dispersed abroad; he hath **g** to the poor:	*1325*
	10: 8	which the Lord hath **g** us for edification,	*1325*
	12: 7	there was **g** to me a thorn in the flesh,	*1325*
	13:10	which the Lord hath **g** me to edification,	*1325*
Gal	2: 9	perceived the grace that was **g** unto me,	*1325*
	3:21	for if there had been a law **g** which could	*1325*
	3:21	a law given which could have **g life,**	*2227*
	3:22	Christ might be **g** to them that believe.	*1325*
	4:15	out your own eyes, and have **g** *them* to me.	*1325*
Eph	3: 2	grace of God which is **g** me to you-ward:	*1325*
	3: 7	according to the gift of the grace of God **g**	*1325*
	3: 8	than the least of all saints, is this grace **g**,	*1325*
	4: 7	But unto every one of us is **g** grace	*1325*
	4:19	**g** themselves **over** unto lasciviousness,	*3860*
	5: 2	and hath **g** himself for us an offering and	*3860*
	6:19	for me, that utterance may be **g** unto me,	*1325*
Php	1:29	For unto you it is **g** in the behalf of Christ,	*5483*
	2: 9	**g** him a name which is above every name:	*5483*
Col	1:25	of God which is **g** to me for you,	*1325*
1Th	4: 8	who hath also **g** unto us his holy Spirit.	*1325*
2Th	2:16	and hath **g** *us* everlasting consolation and	*1325*
1Ti	3: 2	**g to hospitality**, apt to teach;	*5382*
	3: 3	Not **g to wine**, no striker, not greedy of	*3943*
	3: 8	not doubletongued, not **g to** much wine,	*4337*
	4:14	is in thee, which was **g** thee by prophecy,	*1325*
2Ti	1: 7	For God hath not **g** us the spirit of fear; but	*1325*
	1: 9	which was **g** us in Christ Jesus before	*1325*
	3:16	All scripture *is* **g by inspiration of God**,	*2315*
Tit	1: 7	not soon angry, not **g to wine**, no striker,	*3943*
	1: 7	to wine, no striker, not **g to filthy lucre**;	*146*
	2: 3	not false accusers, not **g** to much wine,	*1402*
Phm	1:22	through your prayers I shall be **g** unto you.	*5483*
Heb	2:13	I, and the children which God hath **g** me.	*1325*
	4: 8	For if Jesus had **g** them **rest**, *then* would he	*2664*
Jas	1: 5	and upbraideth not; and it shall be **g** him.	*1325*
2Pe	1: 3	According as his divine power hath **g** unto	*1433*
	1: 4	Whereby are **g** unto us exceeding great and	*1433*
	3:15	wisdom **g** unto him hath written unto you;	*1325*
1Jn	3:24	in us, by the Spirit which he hath **g** us.	*1325*
	4:13	he in us, because he hath **g** us of his Spirit.	*1325*
	5:11	that God hath **g** to us eternal life, and	*1325*
	5:20	and hath **g** us an understanding, that we	*1325*
Rev	6: 2	had a bow; and a crown was **g** unto him:	*1325*
	6: 4	*power* was **g** to him that sat thereon to take	*1325*
	6: 4	and there was **g** unto him a great sword.	*1325*
	6: 8	And power was **g** unto them over the fourth	*1325*
	6:11	And white robes were **g** unto every one of	*1325*
	7: 2	to whom it was **g** to hurt the earth and	*1325*
	8: 2	and to them were **g** seven trumpets.	*1325*
	8: 3	and there was **g** unto him much incense,	*1325*
	9: 1	to him was **g** the key of the bottomless pit.	*1325*
	9: 3	and unto them was **g** power, as	*1325*
	9: 5	And to them it was **g** that they should not	*1325*
	11: 1	And there was **g** me a reed like unto a rod:	*1325*
	11: 2	measure it not; for it is **g** unto the Gentiles:	*1325*
	12:14	And to the woman were **g** two wings of a	*1325*
	13: 5	And there was **g** unto him a mouth	*1325*
	13: 5	power was **g** unto him to continue forty *and*	*1325*
	13: 7	And it was **g** unto him to make war with	*1325*
	13: 7	and power was **g** him over all kindreds, and	*1325*
	16: 6	and thou hast **g** them blood to drink;	*1325*
	16: 8	*power* was **g** unto him to scorch men with	*1325*

Rev 20: 4 upon them, and judgment was **g** unto them: *1325*

GIVER (2) [GIVE]

Isa 24: 2 of usury, so *with* the **g of usury** to him. 5383
2Co 9: 7 of necessity: for God loveth a cheerful **g**. *1395*

GIVEST (12) [GIVE]

Dt 15: 9 thy poor brother, and thou **g** him nought; 5414
15:10 thine heart shall not be grieved when thou **g** 5414
Job 35: 7 If thou be righteous, what **g** thou him? or 5414
Ps 50:19 Thou **g** thy mouth to evil, and thy tongue 7971
80: 5 and **g** them tears **to drink** *in great* measure. 8248
104:28 *That* thou **g** them they gather: thou openest 5414
145:15 and thou **g** them their meat in due season. 5414
Pr 6:35 he rest content, though thou **g many** gifts. 7235
Eze 3:18 thou **g** him not **warning**, nor speakest to 2094
16:33 thou **g** thy gifts to all thy lovers, and 5414
16:34 in that thou **g** a reward, and no reward is 5414
1Co 14:17 For thou verily **g thanks** well, but the other *2168*

GIVETH (126) [GIVE]

Ge 49:21 *is* a hind let loose: he **g** goodly words. 5414
Ex 16:29 he **g** you on the sixth day the bread of two 5414
20:12 the land which the LORD thy God **g** thee. 5414
25: 2 of every man that **g** it **willingly** with his 5068
Lev 20: 2 that **g** *any* of his seed unto Molech; 5414
20: 4 when he **g** of his seed unto Molech, and 5414
27: 9 all that *any man* **g** of such unto the LORD 5414
Nu 5:10 whatsoever any man **g** the priest, it shall be 5414
Dt 2:29 the land which the LORD our God **g** us. 5414
4: 1 the LORD God of your fathers **g** you. 5414
4:21 which the LORD thy God **g** thee *for* an 5414
4:40 which the LORD thy God **g** thee, for ever. 5414
5:16 in the land which the LORD thy God **g** 5414
8:18 for *it is* he that **g** thee power to get wealth, 5414
9: 6 that the LORD thy God **g** thee not this 5414
11:17 off the good land which the LORD **g** you. 5414
11:31 land which the LORD your God **g** you, 5414
12: 1 which the LORD God of thy fathers **g** 5414
12: 9 which the LORD your God **g** you. 5414
12:10 the LORD your God **g** you **to inherit**, 5157
12:10 *when* he **g** you **rest** from all your enemies 5117
13: 1 of dreams, and **g** thee a sign or a wonder, 5414
15: 4 God **g** thee *for* an inheritance to possess it: 5414
15: 7 thy land which the LORD thy God **g** thee, 5414
16: 5 which the LORD thy God **g** thee: 5414
16:18 which the LORD thy God **g** thee, 5414
16:20 the land which the LORD thy God **g** thee. 5414
17: 2 gates which the LORD thy God **g** thee, 5414
17:14 the land which the LORD thy God **g** thee, 5414
18: 9 the land which the LORD thy God **g** thee, 5414
19: 1 whose land the LORD thy God **g** thee, and 5414
19: 2 which the LORD thy God **g** thee to 5414
19: 3 the LORD thy God **g** thee **to inherit**, 5157
19:10 which the LORD thy God **g** thee *for* an 5414
19:14 the LORD thy God **g** thee to possess it. 5414
21: 1 the LORD thy God **g** thee to possess it, 5414
21:23 which the LORD thy God **g** thee *for* an 5414
24: 3 **g** *it* in her hand, and sendeth her out of his 5414
24: 4 which the LORD thy God **g** thee *for* an 5414
25:15 the land which the LORD thy God **g** thee. 5414
25:19 in the land which the LORD thy God **g** 5414
26: 1 LORD thy God **g** thee *for* an inheritance, 5414
26: 2 of thy land that the LORD thy God **g** thee, 5414
27: 2 the land which the LORD thy God **g** thee, 5414
27: 3 the land which the LORD thy God **g** thee, 5414
28: 8 the land which the LORD thy God **g** thee. 5414
Jos 1:11 which the LORD your God **g** you to 5414
1:15 land which the LORD your God **g** them: 5414
Jdg 11:24 which Chemosh thy god **g** thee **to possess**? 3423
21:18 Cursed *be* he that **g** a wife to Benjamin. 5414
Job 5:10 Who **g** rain upon the earth, and 5414
14:10 yea, man **g up the ghost**, and where *is* he? 1478
32: 8 of the Almighty **g** them **understanding**. 995
33:13 for he **g** not **account** of any of his matters. 6030
34:29 When he **g quietness**, who then can make 8252
35:10 God my Maker, who **g** songs in the night; 5414
35:12 none **g answer**, because of the pride of evil 6030
36: 6 life of the wicked: but **g** right to the poor. 5414
36:31 he the people; he **g** meat in abundance. 5414
Ps 18:50 **Great** deliverance **g** he to his king; and 1431
37:21 but the righteous sheweth mercy, and **g**. 5414
68:35 the God of Israel *is* he that **g** strength and 5414
119:130 The entrance of thy words **g light**; it giveth 215
119:130 it **g understanding** unto the simple. 995
127: 2 of sorrows: *for* so he **g** his beloved sleep. 5414
136:25 Who **g** food to all flesh: for his mercy 5414
144:10 *It is he* that **g** salvation unto kings: 5414
146: 7 which **g** food to the hungry. The LORD 5414
147: 9 He **g** to the beast his food, *and* to the young 5414
147:16 He **g** snow like wool: he scattereth 5414
Pr 2: 6 For the LORD **g** wisdom: out of his 5414
3:34 the scorners: but he **g** grace unto the lowly. 5414
13:15 Good understanding **g** favour: but the way 5414
17: 4 A wicked doer **g heed** to false lips; *and* 7181
17: 4 *and* a liar **g ear** to a naughty tongue. 238
19: 6 every *man is* a friend to him that **g gifts**. 4976
21:26 but the righteous **g** and spareth not. 5414
22: 9 be blessed; for he **g** of his bread to the poor. 5414
22:16 increase his *riches, and* he that **g** to the rich, 5414
23:31 when it **g** his colour in the cup, *when* it 5414
24:26 *Every man* shall kiss *his* lips that **g** a right 7725
26: 8 in a sling, so *is* he that **g** honour to a fool. 5414
28:27 He that **g** unto the poor *shall* not lack: but 5414
31:15 **g** meat to her household, and a portion to 5414
Ecc 2:26 For *God* **g** to a man that *is* good in his sight 5414
2:26 to the sinner he **g** travail, to gather and 5414
5:18 all the days of his life, which God **g** him: 5414
6: 2 yet God **g** him not **power** to eat thereof, but 7980
7:12 *is, that* wisdom **g life** to them that have it. 2421
8:15 of his life, which God **g** him under the sun. 5414
Isa 40:29 He **g** power to the faint; and to *them that* 5414
42: 5 he that **g** breath unto the people upon it, 5414
Jer 5:24 that **g** rain, both the former and the latter, 5414
22:13 without wages, and **g** him not *for* his work; 5414
31:35 which **g** the sun for a light by day, *and* 5414
La 3:30 He **g** *his* cheek to him that smiteth him: 5414
Da 2:21 he **g** wisdom unto the wise, and 3052
4:17 **g** it to whomsoever he will, and setteth up 5415
4:25 of men, and **g** it to whomsoever he will. 5415
4:32 of men, and **g** it to whomsoever he will. 5415
Hab 2:15 Woe unto him that **g** his neighbour **drink**, 8248
Mt 5:15 and it **g light** unto all that are in the house. *2989*
Jn 3:34 for God **g** not the Spirit by measure *unto* *1325*
6:32 my Father **g** you the true bread from *1325*
6:33 from heaven, and **g** life unto the world. *1325*
6:37 All that the Father **g** me shall come to me; *1325*
10:11 the good shepherd **g** his life for the sheep. *5087*
14:27 not as the world **g**, give I unto you. Let not *1325*
21:13 taketh bread, and **g** them, and fish likewise. *1325*
Ac 17:25 as though he needed any *thing,* seeing he **g** *1325*
Ro 12: 8 he that **g**, *let him do it* with simplicity; *3330*
14: 6 eateth to the Lord, for he **g** God **thanks**; *2168*
14: 6 the Lord he eateth not, and **g** God **thanks**. *2168*
1Co 3: 7 that watereth; but God that **g** the **increase**. *837*
7:38 then he that **g** *her* **in marriage** doeth well; *1547*
7:38 he that **g** *her* not **in marriage** doeth better. *1547*
15:38 But God **g** it a body as it hath pleased him, *1325*
15:57 which **g** us the victory through our Lord *1325*
2Co 3: 6 for the letter killeth, but the spirit **g life**. *2227*
1Ti 6:17 who **g** us richly all *things* to enjoy; *3930*
Jas 1: 5 that **g** to all *men* liberally, and *1325*
4: 6 But he **g** more grace. Wherefore *he* saith, *1325*
4: 6 the proud, but **g** grace unto the humble. *1325*
1Pe 4:11 *let him do it* as of the ability which God **g**: *5524*
5: 5 the proud, and **g** grace to the humble. *1325*
Rev 22: 5 of the sun; for the Lord God **g** them **light**: *5461*

GIVING (29) [GIVE]

Ge 24:19 when she had done **g** him **drink**, she said, 8248
Dt 10:18 the stranger, in **g** him food and raiment. 5414
21:17 by **g** him a double portion of all that he 5414
Ru 1: 6 had visited his people in **g** them bread. 5414
1Ki 5: 9 my desire, in **g** food for my household. 5414
2Ch 6:23 by **g** him according to his righteousness. 5414
Ezr 3:11 in praising and **g thanks** unto the LORD; 3034
Job 11:20 *shall be as* the **g up of the ghost**. 4646+5315
Mt 24:38 and drinking, marrying and **g in marriage**, *1547*
Lk 17:16 down on *his* face at his feet, **g** him **thanks**: *2168*
Ac 8: 9 **g out** that himself was some great one: *3004*
15: 8 bare them witness, **g** them the Holy Ghost, *1325*
Ro 4:20 but was strong in faith, **g** glory to God; *1325*
9: 4 and the **g of the law**, and the service *of* *3548*
1Co 14: 7 *And* even *things* without life **g** sound, *1325*
14:16 the unlearned say Amen at thy **g of thanks**, *2169*
2Co 6: 3 **G** no offence in any *thing,* that the ministry *1325*
Eph 5: 4 are not convenient: but rather **g** of **thanks**. *2169*
5:20 **G thanks** always for all *things* unto God *2168*

Php 4:15 communicated with me as concerning **g** *1394*
Col 1:12 **G thanks** unto the Father, which hath made *2168*
3:17 **g thanks** to God and the Father by him. *2168*
1Ti 2: 1 prayers, intercessions, *and* **g** of **thanks**, *2169*
4: 1 **g heed** to seducing spirits, and doctrines of *4337*
Tit 1:14 Not **g heed** to Jewish fables, and *4337*
Heb 13:15 the fruit of *our* lips **g thanks** to his name. *3670*
1Pe 3: 7 **g** honour unto the wife, as unto the weaker *632*
2Pe 1: 5 And beside this, **g** all diligence, add to your *3923*
Jude 1: 7 manner **g** themselves **over to fornication**, *1608*

GIZONITE (1)
1Ch 11:34 The sons of Hashem the **G**, Jonathan 1493

GLAD (89) [GLADLY, GLADNESS]
Ex 4:14 he seeth thee, he will be **g** in his heart. 8055
Jdg 18:20 the priest's heart was **g**, and he took 3190
1Sa 11: 9 *it* to the men of Jabesh; and they were **g**. 8055
1Ki 8:66 **g** of heart for all the goodness that 2896
1Ch 16:31 Let the heavens be **g**, and let the earth 8055
2Ch 7:10 **g** and merry in heart for the goodness that 8056
Est 5: 9 forth that day joyful and with a **g** heart: 2896
8:15 and the city of Shushan rejoiced and was **g**. 8056
Job 3:22 Which rejoice exceedingly, *and* are **g**, 7797
22:19 The righteous see *it,* and are **g**: and 8055
Ps 9: 2 I will be **g** and rejoice in thee: I will sing 8055
14: 7 Jacob shall rejoice, *and* Israel shall be **g**. 8055
16: 9 Therefore my heart is **g**, and my glory 8055
21: 6 thou hast made him exceeding **g** with thy 8057
31: 7 I will be **g** and rejoice in thy mercy: 1523
32:11 Be **g** in the LORD, and rejoice, 8055
34: 2 the humble shall hear *thereof,* and be **g**. 8055
35:27 Let them shout for joy, and be **g**, 8055
40:16 that seek thee rejoice and be **g** in thee: 8055
45: 8 *where*by they have **made** thee **g**. 8055
46: 4 the streams whereof shall **make g** the city 8055
48:11 let the daughters of Judah be **g**, because 1523
53: 6 Jacob shall rejoice, *and* Israel shall be **g**. 8055
64:10 The righteous shall be **g** in the LORD, and 8055
67: 4 O let the nations be **g** and sing for joy: 8055
68: 3 let the righteous be **g**; let them rejoice 8055
69:32 The humble shall see *this, and* be **g**: and 8055
70: 4 that seek thee rejoice and be **g** in thee: 8055
90:14 that we may rejoice and be **g** all our days. 8055
90:15 **Make** us **g** according to the days *wherein* 8055
92: 4 hast **made** me **g** through thy work: 8055
96:11 the heavens rejoice, and let the earth be **g**; 1523
97: 1 let the multitude of isles be **g** *thereof.* 8055
97: 8 was **g**, and the daughters of Judah rejoiced, 8055
104:15 wine *that* **maketh g** the heart of man, 8055
104:34 shall be sweet: I will be **g** in the LORD. 8055
105:38 Egypt was **g** when they departed: for 8055
107:30 are they **g** because they be quiet; so 8055
118:24 hath made; we will rejoice and be **g** in it. 8055
119:74 They that fear thee will be **g** when they see 8055
122: 1 I was **g** when they said unto me, Let us go 8055
126: 3 done great things for us; *whereof* we are **g**. 8056
Pr 10: 1 A wise son **maketh** a **g** father: but a foolish 8055
12:25 it stoop: but a good word **maketh** it **g**. 8055
15:20 A wise son **maketh** a **g** father: but a foolish 8055
17: 5 he that is **g** at calamities shall not be 8056
23:25 Thy father and thy mother shall be **g**, and 8055
24:17 let not thine heart be **g** when he stumbleth: 1523
27:11 My son, be wise, and **make** my heart **g**, 8055
SS 1: 4 we will be **g** and rejoice in thee, we will 1523
Isa 25: 9 we will be **g** and rejoice in his salvation. 1523
35: 1 and the solitary place shall be **g** *for* them; 7797
39: 2 Hezekiah was **g** of them, and shewed them 8055
65:18 be you **g** and rejoice for ever *in that* which I 7797
66:10 and be **g** with her, all ye that love her: 1523
Jer 20:15 born unto thee; **making** him **very g**. 8055+8055
41:13 that *were* with him, then they were **g**. 8055
50:11 Because ye were **g**, because ye rejoiced, 8055
La 1:21 they are **g** that thou hast done *it:* thou wilt 7797
4:21 Rejoice and be **g**, O daughter of Edom, 8055
Da 6:23 Then was the king exceeding **g** for him, and 2868
Hos 7: 3 They **make** the king **g** with their 8055
Joel 2:21 Fear not, O land; be **g** and rejoice: for 1523
2:23 Be **g** then, ye children of Zion, and 1523
Jnh 4: 6 was **exceeding g** of the gourd. 1419+8055+8057
Hab 1:15 their drag: therefore they rejoice and are **g**. 1523
Zep 3:14 be **g** and rejoice with all the heart, 8055
Zec 10: 7 yea, their children shall see *it,* and be **g**; 8055
Mt 5:12 Rejoice, and be **exceeding g**: for great *is* your *21*
Mk 14:11 And when they heard *it,* they were **g**, and *5463*
Lk 1:19 unto thee, and to **shew** thee these **g tidings**. *2097*
8: 1 **shewing the g tidings** of the kingdom of *2097*
15:32 meet that *we* should make merry, and be **g**: *5463*
22: 5 And they were **g**, and covenanted to give *5463*
23: 8 Herod saw Jesus, he was exceeding **g**: *5463*
Jn 8:56 to see my day: and he saw *it,* and was **g**. *5463*
11:15 And I am **g** for your sakes that I was not *5463*
20:20 Then were the disciples **g**, when they saw *5463*
Ac 2:26 did my heart rejoice, and my tongue was **g**; *21*
11:23 grace of God, was **g**, and exhorted *them* all, *5463*
13:32 And we **declare** unto you **g tidings**, *2097*
13:48 when the Gentiles heard *this,* they were **g**, *5463*
Ro 10:15 and **bring g tidings** of good *things!* *2097*
16:19 is come abroad unto all *men.* I am **g** *5463*
1Co 16:17 I am **g** of the coming of Stephanas and *5463*
2Co 2: 2 who is he then that **maketh** me **g**, but *2165*
13: 9 For we are **g**, when we are weak, and ye are *5463*
1Pe 4:13 ye may be **g** also with exceeding joy. *5463*
Rev 19: 7 Let us be **g** and rejoice, and give honour to *5463*

GLADLY (8) [GLAD]
Mk 6:20 he did many *things,* and heard him **g**. *2234*
12:37 And the common people heard him **g**. *2234*
Lk 8:40 was returned, the people **g received** him: *588*
Ac 2:41 Then they that **g** received his word were *780*
21:17 to Jerusalem, the brethren received us **g**. *780*
2Co 11:19 For ye suffer fools **g**, seeing ye *yourselves* *2234*
12: 9 **Most g** therefore will I rather glory in my *2236*
12:15 And I will **very g** spend and be spent for *2236*

GLADNESS (47) [GLAD]
Nu 10:10 Also in the day of your **g**, and in your 8057
Dt 28:47 with **g** of heart, for the abundance of all 2898
2Sa 6:12 Obed-edom *into* the city of David with **g**. 8057
1Ch 16:27 strength and **g** *are* in his place. 2304
29:22 before the LORD on that day with great **g**. 8057
2Ch 29:30 they *sang* praises with **g**, and they bowed 8057
30:21 unleavened bread seven days with great **g**: 8057
30:23 and they kept *other* seven days *with* **g**. 8057
Ne 8:17 Israel done so. And there was very great **g**. 8057
12:27 to keep the dedication with **g**, both with 8057
Est 8:16 Jews had light, and **g**, and joy, and honour. 8057
8:17 the Jews had joy and **g**, a feast and a good 8342
9:17 and made it a day of feasting and **g**. 8057
9:18 and made it a day of feasting and **g**. 8057
9:19 day of the month Adar *a day of* **g** 8057
Ps 4: 7 Thou hast put **g** in my heart, more than *in* 8057
30:11 put off my sackcloth, and girded me *with* **g**; 8057
45: 7 hath anointed thee *with* the oil of **g** above 8342
45:15 With **g** and rejoicing shall they be brought: 8057
51: 8 Make me to hear joy and **g**; *that* the bones 8057
97:11 the righteous, and **g** for the upright in heart. 8057
100: 2 Serve the LORD with **g**: come before his 8057
105:43 his people with joy, *and* his chosen with **g**: 7440
106: 5 that *I* may rejoice in the **g** of thy nation, 8057
Pr 10:28 The hope of the righteous *shall be* **g**: but 8057
SS 3:11 and in the day of the **g** of his heart. 8057
Isa 16:10 **g** is taken away, and joy out of the plentiful 8057
22:13 behold joy and **g**, slaying oxen, and 8057
30:29 **g** of heart, as when one goeth with a pipe to 8057
35:10 they shall obtain joy and **g**, and sorrow and 8057
51: 3 joy and **g** shall be found therein, 8057
51:11 they shall obtain **g** and joy; *and* sorrow and 8342
Jer 7:34 the voice of mirth, and the voice of **g**, 8057
16: 9 the voice of mirth, and the voice of **g**, 8057
25:10 the voice of **g**, the voice of the bridegroom, 8057
31: 7 Sing with **g** for Jacob, and shout among 8057
33:11 The voice of joy, and the voice of **g**, 8057
48:33 and **g** is taken from the plentiful field, 1524
Joel 1:16 *yea,* joy and **g** from the house of our God? 1524
Zec 8:19 shall be to the house of Judah joy and **g**, 8057
Mk 4:16 the word, immediately receive it with **g**; *5479*
Lk 1:14 And thou shalt have joy and **g**; and many shall *20*
Ac 2:46 did eat *their* meat with **g** and singleness of *20*
12:14 she opened not the gate for **g**, but ran in, *5479*
14:17 filling our hearts with food and **g**. *2167*
Php 2:29 therefore in the Lord with all **g**; *5479*
Heb 1: 9 hath anointed thee *with* the oil of **g** above thy *20*

GLASS (9) [GLASSES, LOOKING-GLASSES]
Job 37:18 *which is* strong, *and* as a molten **looking g**? 7209
1Co 13:12 For now we see through a **g**, darkly; *2072*
2Co 3:18 with open face **beholding as in a g** *2734*

G

Jas 1:23 a man beholding his natural face in a **g**: *2072*
Rev 4: 6 And before the throne *there was* a sea **of g** *5193*
15: 2 And I saw as *it were* a sea **of g** mingled *5193*
15: 2 stand on the sea **of g**, having *the* harps of *5193*
21:18 the city *was* pure gold, like unto clear **g**. *5194*
21:21 city *was* pure gold, as *it were* transparent **g**. *5194*

GLASSES (1) [GLASS]
Isa 3:23 The **g**, and the fine linen, and the hoods, 1549

GLEAN (10) [GLEANED, GLEANING, GLEANINGS, GRAPEGLEANINGS]
Lev 19:10 thou shalt not **g** thy vineyard, neither shalt 5953
Dt 24:21 thy vineyard, thou shalt not **g** *it* afterward: 5953
Ru 2: 2 **g** ears of corn after *him* in whose sight I 3950
2: 7 let me **g** and gather after the reapers 3950
2: 8 Go not to **g** in another field, neither go 3950
2:15 when she was risen up to **g**, Boaz 3950
2:15 Let her **g** even among the sheaves, and 3950
2:16 leave *them,* that she may **g** *them,* and 3950
2:23 she kept fast by the maidens of Boaz to **g** 3950
Jer 6: 9 They shall **throughly g** the remnant 5953+5953

GLEANED (6) [GLEAN]
Jdg 20:45 they **g** of them in the highways five 5953
Ru 2: 3 came, and **g** in the field after the reapers: 3950
2:17 So she **g** in the field until even, and beat out 3950
2:17 field until even, and beat out that she had **g**: 3950
2:18 her mother in law saw what she had **g**: and 3950
2:19 said unto her, Where hast thou **g** to day? 3950

GLEANING (5) [GLEAN]
Lev 23:22 neither shalt thou gather *any* **g** of thy 3951
Jdg 8: 2 *Is* not the **g of** the **grapes** of Ephraim better 5955
Isa 17: 6 Yet **g grapes** shall be left in it, as 5955
24:13 as the **g grapes** when the vintage is done. 5955
Jer 49: 9 would they not leave *some* **g grapes**? 5955

GLEANINGS (1) [GLEAN]
Lev 19: 9 neither shalt thou gather the **g** of thy 3951

GLEDE (1)
Dt 14:13 the **g**, and the kite, and the vulture after his 7201

GLISTERING (3)
1Ch 29: 2 **g** stones, and of divers colours, and 6320
Job 20:25 yea, the **g sword** cometh out of his gall: 1300
Lk 9:29 and his raiment *was* white *and* **g**. *1823*

GLITTER (1) [GLITTERING]
Eze 21:10 sore slaughter; *it is* furbished that it may **g**: 1300

GLITTERING (5) [GLITTER]
Dt 32:41 If I whet my **g** sword, and mine hand take 1300
Job 39:23 against him, the **g** spear and the shield. 3851
Eze 21:28 *it is* furbished, to consume because of the **g**: 1300
Na 3: 3 up both the bright sword and the **g** spear: 1300
Hab 3:11 they went, *and* at the shining of thy **g** spear. 1300

GLOOMINESS (2)
Joel 2: 2 A day of darkness and of **g**, a day of clouds 653
Zep 1:15 and desolation, a day of darkness and **g**, 653

GLORIEST (1) [GLORY]
Jer 49: 4 Wherefore **g** thou in the valleys, 1984

GLORIETH (3) [GLORY]
Jer 9:24 let him that **g** glory in this, that *he* 1984
1Co 1:31 That, according as it is written, He that **g**, *2744*
2Co 10:17 But he that **g**, let him glory in the Lord. *2744*

GLORIFIED (50) [GLORY]
Lev 10: 3 and before all the people I will be **g**. 3513
Isa 26:15 thou art **g**: thou hadst removed *it* far *unto* 3513
44:23 redeemed Jacob, and **g** himself in Israel. 6286
49: 3 my servant, O Israel, in whom I will be **g**. 6286
55: 5 the Holy One of Israel; for he hath **g** thee. 6286
60: 9 Holy One of Israel, because he hath **g** thee. 6286
60:21 the work of my hands, that *I* may be **g**. 6286
61: 3 planting of the LORD, that *he* might be **g**. 6286
66: 5 my name's sake, said, Let the LORD be **g**: 3513
Eze 28:22 and I will be **g** in the midst of thee: 3513
39:13 to them a renown the day that I shall be **g**, 3513
Da 5:23 and whose *are* all thy ways, hast thou not **g**: 1922
Hag 1: 8 in it, and I will be **g**, saith the LORD. 3513
Mt 9: 8 and **g** God, which had given such power *1392*
15:31 blind to see: and they **g** the God of Israel. *1392*
Mk 2:12 and **g** God, saying, We never saw *it* on this *1392*
Lk 4:15 taught in their synagogues, being **g** of all. *1392*
5:26 and they **g** God, and were filled with fear, *1392*
7:16 and they **g** God, saying, That a great *1392*
13:13 she was made straight, and **g** God. *1392*
17:15 turned back, and with a loud voice **g** God, *1392*
23:47 he **g** God, saying, Certainly this was a *1392*
Jn 7:39 *given;* because that Jesus was not yet **g**.) *1392*
11: 4 that the Son of God might be **g** thereby. *1392*
12:16 but when Jesus was **g**, then *1392*
12:23 is come, that the Son of man should be **g**. *1392*
12:28 *saying,* I have both **g** *it,* and will glorify *it* *1392*
13:31 Now is the Son of man **g**, and God is *1392*
13:31 Son of man glorified, and God is **g** in him. *1392*
13:32 If God be **g** in him, God shall also glorify *1392*
14:13 I do, that the Father may be **g** in the Son. *1392*
15: 8 Herein is my Father **g**, that ye bear much *1392*
17: 4 I have **g** thee on the earth: I have finished *1392*
17:10 and thine are mine; and I am **g** in them. *1392*
Ac 3:13 God of our fathers, hath **g** his Son Jesus; *1392*
4:21 for all *men* **g** God for that which was done. *1392*
11:18 they held their peace, and **g** God, saying, *1392*
13:48 they were glad, and **g** the word of the Lord: *1392*
21:20 And when they heard *it,* they **g** the Lord, *1392*
Ro 1:21 they knew God, they **g** *him* not as God, *1392*
8:17 with *him,* that we may be also **g together**. *4888*
8:30 and whom he justified, them he also **g**. *1392*
Gal 1:24 And they **g** God in me. *1392*
2Th 1:10 When he shall come to be **g** in his saints, *1740*
1:12 of our Lord Jesus Christ may be **g** in you, *1740*
3: 1 *free* course, and be **g**, even as *it is* with you: *1392*
Heb 5: 5 So also Christ **g** not himself to be made a *1392*
1Pe 4:11 that God in all *things* may be **g** through *1392*
4:14 is evil spoken of, but on your part he is **g**. *1392*
Rev 18: 7 How much she hath **g** herself, and *1392*

GLORIFIETH (1) [GLORY]
Ps 50:23 Whoso offereth praise **g** me: and to him 3513

GLORIFY (25) [GLORY]
Ps 22:23 all ye the seed of Jacob, **g** him; and 3513
50:15 I will deliver thee, and thou shalt **g** me. 3513
86: 9 before thee, O Lord; and shall **g** thy name. 3513
86:12 and I will **g** thy name for evermore. 3513
Isa 24:15 Wherefore **g** ye the LORD in the fires, 3513
25: 3 Therefore shall the strong people **g** thee, 3513
60: 7 and I will **g** the house of my glory. 6286
Jer 30:19 I will also **g** them, and they shall not be 3513
Mt 5:16 and **g** your Father which is in heaven. *1392*
Jn 12:28 Father, **g** thy name. Then came there a *1392*
12:28 I have both glorified *it,* and will **g** *it* again. *1392*
13:32 in him, God shall also **g** him in himself, *1392*
13:32 in himself, and shall straightway **g** him. *1392*
16:14 He shall **g** me: for he shall receive of mine, *1392*
17: 1 **g** thy Son, that thy Son also may glorify *1392*
17: 1 thy Son, that thy Son also may **g** thee: *1392*
17: 5 **g** thou me with thine own self with *1392*
21:19 signifying by what death he should **g** God. *1392*
Ro 15: 6 may with one mind *and* one mouth **g** God, *1392*
15: 9 And that the Gentiles might **g** God for *his* *1392*
1Co 6:20 therefore **g** God in your body, and in your *1392*
2Co 9:13 **g** God for your professed subjection unto *1392*
1Pe 2:12 shall behold, **g** God in the day of visitation. *1392*
4:16 but let him **g** God on this behalf. *1392*
Rev 15: 4 not fear thee, O Lord, and **g** thy name? *1392*

GLORIFYING (3) [GLORY]
Lk 2:20 **g** and praising God for all *the things* that *1392*
5:25 and departed to his own house, **g** God. *1392*
18:43 his sight, and followed him, **g** God: *1392*

GLORIOUS (45) [GLORY]
Ex 15: 6 O LORD, is **become g** in power: 142
15:11 who *is* like thee, **g** in holiness, fearful *in* 142
Dt 28:58 that *thou* mayest fear this **g** and fearful 3513
2Sa 6:20 said, How **g** was the king of Israel to day, 3513
1Ch 29:13 we thank thee, and praise thy **g** name. 8597
Ne 9: 5 blessed be thy **g** name, which *is* exalted 3519
Est 1: 4 When he shewed the riches of his **g** 3519
Ps 45:13 The king's daughter *is* all **g** within: 3520
66: 2 the honour of his name: make his praise **g**. 3519
72:19 blessed *be* his **g** name for ever: and let 3519
76: 4 Thou *art* more **g** *and* excellent than 215

Ps	87: 3	**G** *things* are spoken of thee, O city of God.	3513
	111: 3	His work *is* honourable and **g**: and	1926
	145: 5	I will speak of the **g** honour of thy majesty,	3519
	145:12	and the **g** majesty of his kingdom.	3519
Isa	4: 2	branch of the LORD be beautiful and **g**,	3519
	11:10	the Gentiles seek: and his rest shall be **g**.	3519
	22:23	he shall be for a **g** throne to his father's	3519
	28: 1	whose **g** beauty *is* a fading flower,	6643
	28: 4	the **g** beauty, which *is* on the head of the fat	6643
	30:30	the LORD shall cause his **g** voice to be	1935
	33:21	there the **g** LORD *will be* unto us a place of	117
	49: 5	yet shall I be **g** in the eyes of the LORD,	3513
	60:13	and I will **make** the place of my feet **g**.	3513
	63: 1	this *that is* **g** in his apparel, travelling in	1921
	63:12	by the right hand of Moses *with* his **g** arm,	8597
	63:14	lead thy people, to make thyself a **g** name.	8597
Jer	17:12	A **g** high throne from the beginning *is*	3519
Eze	27:25	and **made** very **g** in the midst of the seas.	3513
Da	11:16	he shall stand in the **g** land, which by his	6643
	11:41	He shall enter also into the **g** land, and	6643
	11:45	between the seas in the **g** holy mountain;	6643
Lk	13:17	all the people rejoiced for all the **g** *things*	*1741*
Ro	8:21	into the **g** liberty of the children of God.	*1391*
2Co	3: 7	*and* engraven in stones, was **g**,	*1391+1722*
	3: 8	ministration of the spirit be rather **g**?	*1391+1722*
	3:10	For even that which was **made g** had no	*1392*
	3:11	For if that which is done away *was* **g**,	*1223+1391*
	3:11	more that which remaineth *is* **g**.	*1391+1722*
	4: 4	lest the light of the **g** gospel of Christ,	*1391*
Eph	5:27	That he might present it to himself a **g**	*1741*
Php	3:21	that it may be fashioned like unto his **g**	*1391*
Col	1:11	according to his **g** power, unto all patience	*1391*
1Ti	1:11	According to the **g** gospel of the blessed	*1391*
Tit	2:13	and the **g** appearing of the great God and	*1391*

GLORIOUSLY (3) [GLORY]

Ex	15: 1	for he hath **triumphed g**:	1342+1342
	15:21	for he hath **triumphed g**;	1342+1342
Isa	24:23	and in Jerusalem, and before his ancients **g**.	3519

GLORY (402) [GLORIEST, GLORIETH, GLORIFIED, GLORIFIETH, GLORIFY, GLORIFYING, GLORIOUS, GLORIOUSLY, GLORYING, VAINGLORY]

Ge	31: 1	*was* of our father's hath he gotten all this **g**.	3519
	45:13	you shall tell my father of all my **g** in	3519
Ex	8: 9	Moses said unto Pharaoh, **G** over me: when	6286
	16: 7	then ye shall see the **g** of the LORD;	3519
	16:10	the **g** of the LORD appeared in the cloud.	3519
	24:16	the **g** of the LORD abode upon mount	3519
	24:17	the sight of the **g** of the LORD *was* like	3519
	28: 2	for Aaron thy brother, for **g** and for beauty.	3519
	28:40	thou make for them, for **g** and for beauty.	3519
	29:43	*the tabernacle* shall be sanctified by my **g**.	3519
	33:18	And he said, I beseech thee, shew me thy **g**.	3519
	33:22	shall come to pass, while my **g** passeth by,	3519
	40:34	the **g** of the LORD filled the tabernacle.	3519
	40:35	the **g** of the LORD filled the tabernacle.	3519
Lev	9: 6	the **g** of the LORD shall appear unto you.	3519
	9:23	the **g** of the LORD appeared unto all	3519
Nu	14:10	the **g** of the LORD appeared in	3519
	14:21	all the earth shall be filled *with* the **g** of	3519
	14:22	all *those* men which have seen my **g**,	3519
	16:19	the **g** of the LORD appeared unto all	3519
	16:42	and the **g** of the LORD appeared.	3519
	20: 6	the **g** of the LORD appeared unto them.	3519
Dt	5:24	the LORD our God hath shewed us his **g**	3519
	33:17	His **g** *is like* the firstling of his bullock, and	1926
Jos	7:19	**g** to the LORD God of Israel, and	3519
1Sa	2: 8	and to make them inherit the throne of **g**:	3519
	4:21	The **g** is departed from Israel:	3519
	4:22	And she said, The **g** is departed from Israel:	3519
	6: 5	and ye shall give **g** unto the God of Israel:	3519
1Ki	8:11	for the **g** of the LORD had filled the house	3519
2Ki	14:10	**g** *of this*, and tarry at home: for why	3513
1Ch	16:10	**G** ye in his holy name: let the heart of them	1984
	16:24	Declare his **g** among the heathen;	3519
	16:27	**G** and honour *are* in his presence; strength	1935
	16:28	give unto the LORD **g** and strength.	3519
	16:29	Give unto the LORD the **g** due unto his	3519
	16:35	to thy holy name, *and* **g** in thy praise.	7623
	22: 5	of fame and of **g** throughout all countries:	8597
	29:11	and the **g**, and the victory, and the majesty:	8597
2Ch	5:14	for the **g** of the LORD had filled the house	3519
	7: 1	and the **g** of the LORD filled the house.	3519
	7: 2	the **g** of the LORD had filled	3519
	7: 3	and the **g** of the LORD upon the house,	3519
Est	5:11	Haman told them of the **g** of his riches,	3519
Job	19: 9	He hath stript me of my **g**, and taken	3519
	29:20	My **g** *was* fresh in me, and my bow was	3519
	39:20	the **g** of his nostrils *is* terrible.	1935
	40:10	and array thyself with **g** and beauty.	1935
Ps	3: 3	my **g**, and the lifter up of mine head.	3519
	4: 2	how long *will ye turn* my **g** into shame?	3519
	8: 1	who hast set thy **g** above the heavens.	1935
	8: 5	and hast crowned him *with* **g** and honour.	3519
	16: 9	my heart is glad, and my **g** rejoiceth:	3519
	19: 1	The heavens declare the **g** of God; and	3519
	21: 5	His **g** *is* great in thy salvation: honour and	3519
	24: 7	and the King of **g** shall come in.	3519
	24: 8	Who *is* this King of **g**? the LORD strong	3519
	24: 9	and the King of **g** shall come in.	3519
	24:10	Who is this King of **g**? The LORD of	3519
	24:10	The LORD of hosts, he *is* the King of **g**.	3519
	29: 1	give unto the LORD **g** and strength.	3519
	29: 2	Give unto the LORD the **g** due unto his	3519
	29: 3	the God of **g** thundereth: the LORD *is*	3519
	29: 9	in his temple doth every one speak of *his* **g**.	3519
	30:12	To the end that *my* **g** may sing *praise* to	3519
	45: 3	O *most* mighty, *with* thy **g** and thy majesty.	1935
	49:16	when the **g** of his house is increased;	3519
	49:17	his **g** shall not descend after him.	3519
	57: 5	the heavens; *let* thy **g** *be* above all the earth.	3519
	57: 8	Awake up, my **g**; awake, psaltery and harp:	3519
	57:11	the heavens: *let* thy **g** *be* above all the earth.	3519
	62: 7	In God *is* my salvation and my **g**: the rock	3519
	63: 2	To see thy power and thy **g**, so *as* I have	3519
	63:11	every one that sweareth by him shall **g**:	1984
	64:10	in him; and all the upright in heart shall **g**.	1984
	72:19	let the whole earth be filled *with* his **g**;	3519
	73:24	thy counsel, and afterward receive me *to* **g**.	3519
	78:61	and his **g** into the enemy's hand.	8597
	79: 9	God of our salvation, for the **g** of thy name:	3519
	84:11	the LORD will give grace and **g**: no good	3519
	85: 9	that fear him; that **g** may dwell in our land.	3519
	89:17	For thou *art* the **g** of their strength: and	8597
	89:44	Thou hast made his **g** to cease, and cast his	2892
	90:16	thy servants, and thy **g** unto their children.	1926
	96: 3	Declare his **g** among the heathen,	3519
	96: 7	give unto the LORD **g** and strength.	3519
	96: 8	Give unto the LORD the **g** due unto his	3519
	97: 6	and all the people see his **g**.	3519
	102:15	and all the kings of the earth thy **g**.	3519
	102:16	shall build up Zion, he shall appear in his **g**.	3519
	104:31	The **g** of the LORD shall endure for ever:	3519
	105: 3	**G** ye in his holy name: let the heart of them	1984
	106: 5	that *I* may **g** with thine inheritance.	1984
	106:20	Thus they changed their **g** into	3519
	108: 1	I will sing and give praise, even *with* my **g**.	3519
	108: 5	the heavens: and thy **g** above all the earth.	3519
	113: 4	all nations, *and* his **g** above the heavens.	3519
	115: 1	not unto us, but unto thy name give **g**,	3519
	138: 5	for great *is* the **g** of the LORD.	3519
	145:11	They shall speak of the **g** of thy kingdom,	3519
	148:13	his **g** *is* above the earth and heaven.	1935
	149: 5	Let the saints be joyful in **g**: let them sing	3519
Pr	3:35	The wise shall inherit **g**: but shame shall be	3519
	4: 9	a crown of **g** shall she deliver *to* thee.	8597
	16:31	The hoary head *is* a crown of **g**, *if* it be	8597
	17: 6	and the **g** of children *are* their fathers.	8597
	19:11	and *it is* his **g** to pass over a transgression.	8597
	20:29	The **g** of young men *is* their strength: and	8597
	25: 2	*It is* the **g** of God to conceal a thing: but	3519
	25:27	*for men* to search their own **g** *is not* glory.	3519
	25:27	*for men* to search their own glory *is not* **g**.	3519
	28:12	righteous *men* do rejoice, *there is* great **g**:	8597
Isa	2:10	of the LORD, and for the **g** of his majesty.	1926
	2:19	of the LORD, and for the **g** of his majesty,	1926
	2:21	of the LORD, and for the **g** of his majesty,	1926
	3: 8	the LORD, to provoke the eyes of his **g**.	3519
	4: 5	for upon all the **g** *shall be* a defence.	3519
	5:14	their **g**, and their multitude, and their pomp,	1926
	6: 3	of hosts: the whole earth *is* full of his **g**.	3519
	8: 7	*even* the king of Assyria, and all his **g**:	3519
	10: 3	for help? and where will ye leave your **g**?	3519
	10:12	king of Assyria, and the **g** of his high looks.	8597
	10:16	under his **g** he shall kindle a burning like	3519
	10:18	shall consume the **g** of his forest, and of his	3519
	13:19	Babylon, the **g** of kingdoms, the beauty of	6643

Isa	14:18	of the nations, *even* all of them, lie in **g**,	3519
	16:14	and the **g** of Moab shall be contemned,	3519
	17: 3	they shall be as the **g** of the children of	3519
	17: 4	*that* the **g** of Jacob shall be made thin, and	3519
	20: 5	their expectation, and of Egypt their **g**.	8597
	21:16	a hireling, and all the **g** of Kedar shall fail:	3519
	22:18	there the chariots of thy **g** *shall be*	3519
	22:24	they shall hang upon him all the **g** of his	3519
	23: 9	to stain the pride of all **g**, *and* to bring into	6643
	24:16	we heard songs, *even* **g** to the righteous.	6643
	28: 5	the LORD of hosts be for a crown of **g**,	6643
	35: 2	the **g** of Lebanon shall be given unto it,	3519
	35: 2	they shall see the **g** of the LORD, *and*	3519
	40: 5	the **g** of the LORD shall be revealed, and	3519
	41:16	*and* shalt **g** in the Holy One of Israel.	1984
	42: 8	my **g** will I not give to another, neither my	3519
	42:12	Let them give **g** unto the LORD, and	3519
	43: 7	for I have created him for my **g**, I have	3519
	45:25	the seed of Israel be justified, and shall **g**.	1984
	46:13	will place salvation in Zion for Israel my **g**.	8597
	48:11	and I will not give my **g** unto another.	3519
	58: 8	the **g** of the LORD shall be thy rereward.	3519
	59:19	and his **g** from the rising of the sun.	3519
	60: 1	and the **g** of the LORD is risen upon thee.	3519
	60: 2	and his **g** shall be seen upon thee.	3519
	60: 7	and I will glorify the house of my **g**.	8597
	60:13	The **g** of Lebanon shall come unto thee,	3519
	60:19	thee an everlasting light, and thy God thy **g**.	8597
	61: 6	and in their **g** shall you boast yourselves.	3519
	62: 2	see thy righteousness, and all kings thy **g**:	3519
	62: 3	Thou shalt also be a crown of **g** in the hand	8597
	63:15	the habitation of thy holiness and of thy **g**:	8597
	66:11	be delighted with the abundance of her **g**.	3519
	66:12	the **g** of the Gentiles like a flowing stream:	3519
	66:18	and they shall come, and see my **g**.	3519
	66:19	not heard my fame, neither have seen my **g**;	3519
	66:19	they shall declare my **g** among the Gentiles.	3519
Jer	2:11	my people have changed their **g** for *that*	3519
	4: 2	themselves in him, and in him shall they **g**.	1984
	9:23	Let not the wise *man* **g** in his wisdom,	1984
	9:23	neither let the mighty *man* **g** in his might,	1984
	9:23	let not the rich *man* **g** in his riches:	1984
	9:24	let him that glorieth **g** in this, that *he*	1984
	13:11	for a name, and for a praise, and for a **g**:	8597
	13:16	Give **g** to the LORD your God, before he	3519
	13:18	shall come down, *even* the crown of your **g**.	8597
	14:21	do not disgrace the throne of thy **g**:	3519
	22:18	for him, *saying,* Ah lord! or, Ah his **g**.	1935
	48:18	come down from *thy* **g**, and sit in thirst;	3519
Eze	1:28	of the likeness of the **g** of the LORD.	3519
	3:12	*saying,* Blessed *be* the **g** of the LORD	3519
	3:23	behold, the **g** of the LORD stood there,	3519
	3:23	as the **g** which I saw by the river of Chebar:	3519
	8: 4	the **g** of the God of Israel *was* there,	3519
	9: 3	the **g** of the God of Israel was gone up from	3519
	10: 4	the **g** of the LORD went up from	3519
	10: 4	full of the brightness of the LORD'S **g**.	3519
	10:18	the **g** of the LORD departed from off	3519
	10:19	the **g** of the God of Israel *was* over them	3519
	11:22	the **g** of the God of Israel *was* over them	3519
	11:23	the **g** of the LORD went up from the midst	3519
	20: 6	and honey, which *is* the **g** of all lands:	6643
	20:15	and honey, which *is* the **g** of all lands;	6643
	24:25	the joy of their **g**, the desire of their eyes,	8597
	25: 9	the **g** of the country, Beth-jeshimoth,	6643
	26:20	and I shall set **g** in the land of the living;	6643
	31:18	To whom art thou thus like in **g** and	3519
	39:21	And I will set my **g** among the heathen, and	3519
	43: 2	the **g** of the God of Israel came from	3519
	43: 2	and the earth shined with his **g**.	3519
	43: 4	the **g** of the LORD came into the house by	3519
	43: 5	the **g** of the LORD filled the house.	3519
	44: 4	the **g** of the LORD filled the house of	3519
Da	2:37	thee a kingdom, power, and strength, and **g**.	3367
	4:36	for the **g** of my kingdom, mine honour and	3367
	5:18	a kingdom, and majesty, and **g**, and honour:	3367
	5:20	and they took *his* **g** from him:	3367
	7:14	**g**, and a kingdom, that all people, nations,	3367
	11:20	a raiser of taxes *in* the **g** of the kingdom:	1925
	11:39	he shall acknowledge *and* increase *with* **g**:	3519
Hos	4: 7	*therefore* will I change their **g** into shame.	3519
	9:11	their **g** shall fly away like a bird, from	3519
	10: 5	for the **g** thereof, because it is departed	3519
Mic	1:15	he shall come unto Adullam the **g** of Israel.	3519
	2: 9	children have ye taken *away* my **g** for ever.	1926
Na	2: 9	*and* **g** out of all the pleasant furniture.	3519
Hab	2:14	with the knowledge of the **g** of the LORD,	3519
	2:16	Thou art filled *with* shame for **g**: drink thou	3519
	2:16	and shameful spuing *shall be* on thy **g**.	3519
	3: 3	His **g** covered the heavens, and the earth	1935
Hag	2: 3	you that saw this house in her first **g**?	3519
	2: 7	I will fill this house *with* **g**, saith	3519
	2: 9	The **g** of this latter house shall be greater	3519
Zec	2: 5	and will be the **g** in the midst of her.	3519
	2: 8	After the **g** hath he sent me unto the nations	3519
	6:13	he shall bear the **g**, and shall sit and	1935
	11: 3	of the shepherds; for their **g** is spoiled:	155
	12: 7	that the **g** of the house of David and	8597
	12: 7	the **g** of the inhabitants of Jerusalem do not	8597
Mal	2: 2	to give **g** unto my name, saith the LORD	3519
Mt	4: 8	kingdoms of the world, and the **g** of them;	*1391*
	6: 2	in the streets, that they may **have g** of men.	*1392*
	6:13	and the power, and the **g**, for ever.	*1391*
	6:29	That even Solomon in all his **g** was not	*1391*
	16:27	For the Son of man shall come in the **g** of	*1391*
	19:28	Son of man shall sit in the throne of his **g**,	*1391*
	24:30	clouds of heaven with power and great **g**.	*1391*
	25:31	When the Son of man shall come in his **g**,	*1391*
	25:31	then shall he sit upon the throne of his **g**:	*1391*
Mk	8:38	when he cometh in the **g** of his Father with	*1391*
	10:37	and the other on thy left hand, in thy **g**.	*1391*
	13:26	in *the* clouds with great power and **g**.	*1391*
Lk	2: 9	the **g** of the Lord shone round about them:	*1391*
	2:14	**G** to God in the highest, and on earth	*1391*
	2:32	the Gentiles, and the **g** of thy people Israel.	*1391*
	4: 6	power will I give thee, and the **g** of them:	*1391*
	9:26	when he shall come in his own **g**, and *in his*	*1391*
	9:31	Who appeared in **g**, and spake of his	*1391*
	9:32	they saw his **g**, and the two men that stood	*1391*
	12:27	*that* Solomon in all his **g** was not arrayed	*1391*
	17:18	There are not found that returned to give **g**	*1391*
	19:38	peace in heaven, and **g** in the highest.	*1391*
	21:27	coming in a cloud with power and great **g**.	*1391*
	24:26	these *things,* and to enter into his **g**?	*1391*
Jn	1:14	and dwelt among us, (and we beheld his **g**,	*1391*
	1:14	the **g** as of the only begotten of the Father,)	*1391*
	2:11	Cana of Galilee, and manifested forth his **g**;	*1391*
	7:18	that speaketh of himself seeketh his own **g**:	*1391*
	7:18	but he that seeketh his **g** that sent him,	*1391*
	8:50	And I seek not mine own **g**: there is *one*	*1391*
	11: 4	is not unto death, but for the **g** of God,	*1391*
	11:40	thou shouldest see the **g** of God?	*1391*
	12:41	when he saw his **g**, and spake of him.	*1391*
	17: 5	**g** which I had with thee before the world	*1391*
	17:22	And the **g** which thou gavest me I have	*1391*
	17:24	that they may behold my **g**, which thou hast	*1391*
Ac	7: 2	The God of **g** appeared unto our father	*1391*
	7:55	and saw the **g** of God, and Jesus standing	*1391*
	12:23	smote him, because he gave not God the **g**:	*1391*
	22:11	And when I could not see for the **g** of that	*1391*
Ro	1:23	And changed the **g** of the uncorruptible	*1391*
	2: 7	patient continuance in well doing seek for **g**	*1391*
	2:10	But **g**, honour, and peace, to every *man* that	*1391*
	3: 7	*more* abounded through my lie unto his **g**;	*1391*
	3:23	and come short of the **g** of God;	*1391*
	4: 2	justified by works, he hath whereof to **g**;	*2745*
	4:20	but was strong in faith, giving **g** to God;	*1391*
	5: 2	and rejoice in hope of the **g** of God.	*1391*
	5: 3	not only *so,* but we **g** in tribulations also:	*2744*
	6: 4	up from the dead by the **g** of the Father,	*1391*
	8:18	with the **g** which shall be revealed in us.	*1391*
	9: 4	and the **g**, and the covenants, and the giving	*1391*
	9:23	the riches of his **g** on the vessels of mercy,	*1391*
	9:23	which he had afore prepared unto **g**,	*1391*
	11:36	*are* all *things:* to whom *be* **g** for ever.	*1391*
	15: 7	as Christ also received us, to the **g** of God.	*1391*
	15:17	whereof *I* may **g** through Jesus Christ *in*	*2746*
	16:27	*be* **g** through Jesus Christ for ever.	*1391*
1Co	1:29	That no flesh should **g** in his presence.	*2744*
	1:31	He that glorieth, let him **g** in the Lord.	*2744*
	2: 7	God ordained before the world unto our **g**:	*1391*
	2: 8	would not have crucified the Lord of **g**.	*1391*
	3:21	Therefore let no *man* **g** in men. For all	*2744*
	4: 7	if thou didst receive *it,* why dost thou **g**,	*2744*
	9:16	I preach the gospel, I have nothing to **g** of:	*2745*
	10:31	or whatsoever ye do, do all to the **g** of God.	*1391*
	11: 7	forasmuch as he is the image and **g** of God:	*1391*
	11: 7	of God: but the woman is the **g** of the man.	*1391*

1Co 11:15 if a woman have long hair, it is a **g** to her: *1391*
15:40 but the **g** of the celestial *is* one, and *1391*
15:40 *is* one, and the **g** of the terrestrial *is* another. NIG
15:41 *There is* one **g** of the sun, and another glory *1391*
15:41 and another **g** of the moon, and *1391*
15:41 of the moon, and another **g** of the stars: *1391*
15:41 for *one* star differeth from *another* star in **g**. *1391*
15:43 It is sown in dishonour; it is raised in **g**: *1391*
2Co 1:20 and in him Amen, unto the **g** of God by us. *1391*
3: 7 face of Moses for the **g** of his countenance; *1391*
3: 7 which **g** was to be done away: NIG
3: 9 if the ministration of condemnation *be* **g**, *1391*
3: 9 ministration of righteousness exceed in **g**. *1391*
3:10 was made glorious **had** no **g** in this respect, *1392*
3:10 by reason of the **g** that excelleth. *1391*
3:18 with open face beholding as in a glass the **g** *1391*
3:18 are changed *into* the same image from **g** to *1391*
3:18 *into* the same image from glory to **g**, *1391*
4: 6 to give the light of the knowledge of the **g** *1391*
4:15 of many redound to the **g** of God. *1391*
4:17 far more exceeding *and* eternal weight of **g**; *1391*
5:12 but give you occasion to **g** on our behalf, *2745*
5:12 to *answer* them which **g** in appearance, *2744*
8:19 which is administered by us to the **g** of *1391*
8:23 of the churches, *and* the **g** of Christ. *1391*
10:17 But he that glorieth, let him **g** in the Lord. *2744*
11:12 that wherein they **g**, they may be found *2744*
11:18 Seeing that many **g** after the flesh, I will *2744*
11:18 that many glory after the flesh, I will **g** also. *2744*
11:30 If I must needs **g**, I will glory of the *things* *2744*
11:30 I will **g** of the *things* which concern mine *2744*
12: 1 It is not expedient for me doubtless to **g**. I *2744*
12: 5 Of such a one will I **g**: yet of myself I will *2744*
12: 5 yet of myself I will not **g**, but in mine *2744*
12: 6 For though I would desire to **g**, I shall not *2744*
12: 9 therefore will I rather **g** in my infirmities, *2744*
Gal 1: 5 To whom *be* **g** for ever and ever. Amen. *1391*
5:26 Let us not be desirous of **vain g**, *2755*
6:13 that they may **g** in your flesh. *2744*
6:14 But God forbid that I should **g**, save in *2744*
Eph 1: 6 To the praise of the **g** of his grace, *1391*
1:12 That we should be to the praise of his **g**, *1391*
1:14 unto the praise of his **g**. *1391*
1:17 of our Lord Jesus Christ, the Father of **g**, *1391*
1:18 what the riches of the **g** of his inheritance in *1391*
3:13 at my tribulations for you, which is your **g**. *1391*
3:16 grant you, according to the riches of his **g**, *1391*
3:21 Unto him *be* **g** in the church by Christ Jesus *1391*
Php 1:11 which are by Jesus Christ unto the **g** and *1391*
2:11 Christ *is* Lord, to the **g** of God the Father. *1391*
3:19 *is their* belly, and *whose* **g** *is* in their shame, *1391*
4:19 according to his riches in **g** by Christ Jesus. *1391*
4:20 and our Father *be* **g** for ever and ever. *1391*
Col 1:27 the **g** of this mystery among the Gentiles; *1391*
1:27 which is Christ in you, the hope of **g**: *1391*
3: 4 then shall ye also appear with him in **g**. *1391*
1Th 2: 6 Nor of men sought we **g**, neither of you, *1391*
2:12 hath called you unto his kingdom and **g**. *1391*
2:20 For ye are our **g** and joy. *1391*
2Th 1: 4 So that we ourselves **g** in you in *2744*
1: 9 of the Lord, and from the **g** of his power; *1391*
2:14 to the obtaining of the **g** of our Lord Jesus *1391*
1Ti 1:17 *be* honour and **g** for ever and ever. *1391*
3:16 on in the world, received up into **g**. *1391*
2Ti 2:10 which is in Christ Jesus with eternal **g**. *1391*
4:18 to whom *be* **g** for ever and ever. Amen. *1391*
Heb 1: 3 Who being the brightness of *his* **g**, and *1391*
2: 7 thou crownedst him with **g** and honour, and *1391*
2: 9 of death, crowned with **g** and honour; *1391*
2:10 all *things,* in bringing many sons unto **g**, *1391*
3: 3 For this *man* was counted worthy of more **g** *1391*
9: 5 And over it the cherubims of **g** shadowing *1391*
13:21 to whom *be* **g** for ever and ever. *1391*
Jas 2: 1 *the Lord* of **g**, with respect of persons. *1391*
3:14 **g** not, and lie *not* against the truth. *2620*
1Pe 1: 7 and **g** at the appearing of Jesus Christ: *1391*
1: 8 rejoice with joy unspeakable and **full of g**: *1392*
1:11 of Christ, and the **g** that should follow. *1391*
1:21 him up from the dead, and gave him **g**; *1391*
1:24 and all the **g** of man as the flower of grass. *1391*
2:20 For what **g** *is it,* if, when ye be buffeted for *2811*
4:13 that, when his **g** shall be revealed, ye may *1391*
4:14 happy *are ye;* for the spirit of **g** and of God *1391*
5: 1 also a partaker of the **g** that shall be *1391*
5: 4 ye shall receive a crown of **g** that fadeth not *1391*
5:10 who hath called us into his eternal **g** by *1391*
5:11 To him *be* **g** and dominion for ever and *1391*
2Pe 1: 3 knowledge of him that hath called us to **g** *1391*
1:17 from God the Father honour and **g**, *1391*
1:17 such a voice to him from the excellent **g**, *1391*
3:18 To him *be* **g** both now and for ever. Amen. *1391*
Jude 1:24 the presence of his **g** with exceeding joy, *1391*
1:25 *be* **g** and majesty, dominion and power, *1391*
Rev 1: 6 to him *be* **g** and dominion for ever and *1391*
4: 9 And when *those* beasts give **g** and honour *1391*
4:11 to receive **g** and honour and power: *1391*
5:12 strength, and honour, and **g**, and blessing. *1391*
5:13 Blessing, and honour, and **g**, and power, *1391*
7:12 and **g**, and wisdom, and thanksgiving, and *1391*
11:13 and gave **g** to the God of heaven. *1391*
14: 7 a loud voice, Fear God, and give **g** to him; *1391*
15: 8 was filled with smoke from the **g** of God, *1391*
16: 9 and they repented not to give him **g**. *1391*
18: 1 and the earth was lightened with his **g**. *1391*
19: 1 Alleluia; Salvation, and **g**, and honour, *1391*
21:11 Having the **g** of God: and her light *was* like *1391*
21:23 for the **g** of God did lighten it, and *1391*
21:24 the kings of the earth do bring their **g** and *1391*
21:26 And they shall bring the **g** and honour of *1391*

GLORYING (4) [GLORY]
1Co 5: 6 Your **g** *is* not good. Know ye not that a *2745*
9:15 than that any *man* should make my **g** void. *2745*
2Co 7: 4 of speech toward you, great *is* my **g** of you: *2746*
12:11 I am become a fool in **g**; ye have compelled *2744*

GLOWING METAL See AMBER

GLUTTON (2) [GLUTTONOUS]
Dt 21:20 obey our voice; *he is* a **g**, and a drunkard. 2151
Pr 23:21 and the **g** shall come to poverty: 2151

GLUTTONOUS (2) [GLUTTON]
Mt 11:19 Behold a man **g**, and a winebibber, *5314*
Lk 7:34 ye say, Behold a **g** man, and a winebibber, *5314*

GNASH (2) [GNASHED, GNASHETH, GNASHING]
Ps 112:10 he shall **g** *with* his teeth, and melt away: 2786
La 2:16 they hiss and **g** the teeth: they say, We have 2786

GNASHED (2) [GNASH]
Ps 35:16 in feasts, *they* **g** upon me *with* their teeth. 2786
Ac 7:54 and they **g** on him *with their* teeth. *1031*

GNASHETH (3) [GNASH]
Job 16: 9 he **g** upon me with his teeth; mine enemy 2786
Ps 37:12 the just, and **g** upon him *with* his teeth. 2786
Mk 9:18 and **g** with his teeth, and pineth away: *5149*

GNASHING (7) [GNASH]
Mt 8:12 there shall be weeping and **g** of teeth. *1030*
13:42 of fire: there shall be wailing and **g** of teeth. *1030*
13:50 of fire: there shall be wailing and **g** of teeth. *1030*
22:13 there shall be weeping and **g** of teeth. *1030*
24:51 there shall be weeping and **g** of teeth. *1030*
25:30 there shall be weeping and **g** of teeth. *1030*
Lk 13:28 There shall be weeping and **g** of teeth, *1030*

GNAT (1)
Mt 23:24 which strain out a **g**, and swallow a camel. *2971*

GNAW (1) [GNAWED]
Zep 3: 3 they **g** not the **bones** till the morrow. 1633

GNAWED (1) [GNAW]
Rev 16:10 and they **g** their tongues for pain, *3145*

GO (1492) [GOEST, GOETH, GOING, GOINGS, GONE, OUTGOINGS, OUTWENT, WENT, WENTEST] See Index

GOAD (1) [GOADS]
Jdg 3:31 Philistines six hundred men with an ox **g**: 4451

GOADS (2) [GOAD]
1Sa 13:21 for the axes, and to sharpen the **g**. 1861
Ecc 12:11 The words of the wise *are* as **g**, and as nails 1861

GOAH See GOATH

GOAT (35) [GOATS, GOATS', GOATSKINS, SCAPEGOAT]
Ge 15: 9 a **she g** of three years old, and a ram of 5795

Lev 3:12 if his offering *be* a **g**, then he shall offer it 5795
4:24 he shall lay his hand upon the head of the **g**, 8163
7:23 no *manner* fat, of ox, or of sheep, or of **g**. 5795
9:15 the people's offering, and took the **g**, 8163
10:16 Moses diligently sought the **g** of the sin 8163
16: 9 Aaron shall bring the **g** upon which 8163
16:10 the **g**, on which the lot fell to be 8163
16:15 shall he kill the **g** of the sin offering, that *is* 8163
16:18 of the blood of the **g**, and put *it* upon 8163
16:20 and the altar, he shall bring the live **g**: 8163
16:21 both his hands upon the head of the live **g**, 8163
16:21 putting them upon the head of the **g**, and 8163
16:22 the **g** shall bear upon him all their iniquities 8163
16:22 and he shall let go the **g** in the wilderness. 8163
16:26 he that let go the **g** for the scapegoat shall 8163
16:27 sin offering, and the **g** for the sin offering, 8163
17: 3 or lamb, or **g**, in the camp, or that killeth *it* 5795
22:27 or a sheep, or a **g**, is brought forth, then 5795
Nu 15:27 he shall bring a **she g** of the first year for a 5795
18:17 or the firstling of a **g**, thou shalt not 5795
28:22 one **g** for a sin offering, to make an 8163
29:22 one **g** for a sin offering; beside 8163
29:28 one **g** for a sin offering; beside 8163
29:31 one **g** for a sin offering; beside 8163
29:34 one **g** for a sin offering; beside 8163
29:38 one **g** for a sin offering; beside 8163
Dt 14: 4 shall eat: the ox, the sheep, and the **g**, 5795+7716
14: 5 the **wild g**, and the pygarg, and the wild ox, 689
Pr 30:31 a **he g** also; and a king, against whom *there* 8495
Eze 43:25 Seven days shalt thou prepare every day a **g** 8163
Da 8: 5 a **he g** came from the west on 5795+6842
8: 5 the **g** *had* a notable horn between his eyes. 6842
8: 8 Therefore the **he g** waxed very great: 5795+6842
8:21 the rough **g** *is* the king of Grecia: and 6842

GOAT IDOLS See DEVILS

GOATH (1)
Jer 31:39 hill Gareb, and shall compass about to **G**. 1601

GOATS (87) [GOAT]
Ge 27: 9 me from thence two good kids of the **g**; 5795
27:16 she put the skins of the kids of the **g** upon 5795
30:32 and the spotted and speckled among the **g**: 5795
30:33 *is* not speckled and spotted amongst the **g**, 5795
30:35 he removed that day the **he g** that were 8495
30:35 all the **she g** that were speckled and 5795
31:38 and thy **she g** have not cast their young, 5795
32:14 Two hundred **she g**, and twenty he goats, 5795
32:14 twenty **he g**, two hundred ewes, and 8495
37:31 killed a kid of the **g**, and dipped the coat in 5795
Ex 12: 5 take *it* out from the sheep, or from the **g**: 5795
Lev 1:10 the sheep, or of the **g**, for a burnt sacrifice; 5795
4:23 a kid of the **g**, a male without blemish; 5795
4:28 a kid of the **g**, a female without blemish, 5795
5: 6 a lamb or a kid of the **g**, for a sin offering; 5795
9: 3 Take ye a kid of the **g** for a sin offering; 5795
16: 5 of Israel two kids of the **g** for a sin offering, 5795
16: 7 he shall take the two **g**, and present them 8163
16: 8 Aaron shall cast lots upon the two **g**; 8163
22:19 of the beeves, of the sheep, or of the **g**. 5795
23:19 ye shall sacrifice one kid of the **g** for a sin 5795
Nu 7:16 One kid of the **g** for a sin offering: 5795
7:17 two oxen, five rams, five **he g**, five lambs 6260
7:22 One kid of the **g** for a sin offering: 5795
7:23 two oxen, five rams, five **he g**, five lambs 6260
7:28 One kid of the **g** for a sin offering: 5795
7:29 two oxen, five rams, five **he g**, five lambs 6260
7:34 One kid of the **g** for a sin offering: 5795
7:35 two oxen, five rams, five **he g**, five lambs 6260
7:40 One kid of the **g** for a sin offering: 5795
7:41 two oxen, five rams, five **he g**, five lambs 6260
7:46 One kid of the **g** for a sin offering: 5795
7:47 two oxen, five rams, five **he g**, five lambs 6260
7:52 One kid of the **g** for a sin offering: 5795
7:53 two oxen, five rams, five **he g**, five lambs 6260
7:58 One kid of the **g** for a sin offering: 5795
7:59 two oxen, five rams, five **he g**, five lambs 6260
7:64 One kid of the **g** for a sin offering: 5795
7:65 two oxen, five rams, five **he g**, five lambs 6260
7:70 One kid of the **g** for a sin offering: 5795
7:71 two oxen, five rams, five **he g**, five lambs 6260
7:76 One kid of the **g** for a sin offering: 5795
7:77 two oxen, five rams, five **he g**, five lambs 6260
7:82 One kid of the **g** for a sin offering: 5795
7:83 two oxen, five rams, five **he g**, five lambs 6260
7:87 the kids of the **g** for sin offering twelve. 5795
7:88 four bullocks, the rams sixty, the **he g** sixty, 6260
15:24 and one kid of the **g** for a sin offering. 5795
28:15 one kid of the **g** for a sin offering unto 5795
28:30 *And* one kid of the **g**, to make an atonement 5795
29: 5 one kid of the **g** for a sin offering, to make 5795
29:11 One kid of the **g** *for* a sin offering; beside 5795
29:16 one kid of the **g** *for* a sin offering; beside 5795
29:19 one kid of the **g** *for* a sin offering; beside 5795
29:25 one kid of the **g** *for* a sin offering; beside 5795
Dt 32:14 and rams of the breed of Bashan, and **g**, 6260
1Sa 24: 2 and his men upon the rocks of the **wild g**. 3277
25: 2 three thousand sheep, and a thousand **g**: 5795
2Ch 17:11 seven thousand and seven hundred **he g**. 8495
29:21 seven lambs, and seven **he g**, 5795+6842
29:23 they brought forth the **he g** for the sin 8163
Ezr 6:17 offering for all Israel, twelve **he g**, 5796+6841
8:35 seven lambs, twelve **he g** *for* a sin offering: 6842
Job 39: 1 Knowest thou the time when the **wild g** of 3277
Ps 50: 9 out of thy house, *nor* **he g** out of thy folds. 6260
50:13 the flesh of bulls, or drink the blood of **g**? 6260
66:15 of rams; I will offer bullocks with **g**. 6260
104:18 The high hills *are* a refuge for the **wild g**; 3277
Pr 27:26 and the **g** *are* the price of the field. 6260
SS 4: 1 thy hair *is* as a flock of **g**, that appear from 5795
6: 5 thy hair *is* as a flock of **g** that appear from 5795
Isa 1:11 blood of bullocks, or of lambs, or of **he g**. 6260
34: 6 *and* with the blood of lambs and **g**, 6260
Jer 50: 8 and be as the **he g** before the flocks. 6260
51:40 lambs to the slaughter, like rams with **he g**. 6260
Eze 27:21 with thee in lambs, and rams, and **g**: 6260
34:17 and cattle, between the rams and the **he g**. 6260
39:18 of rams, of lambs, and of **g**, of bullocks, 6260
43:22 of the **g** without blemish for a sin offering; 5795
45:23 and a kid of the **g** daily *for* a sin offering. 5795
Zec 10: 3 against the shepherds, and I punished the **g**: 6260
Mt 25:32 as a shepherd divideth *his* sheep from the **g**: *2056*
25:33 on his right hand, but the **g** on the left. *2055*
Heb 9:12 Neither by the blood of **g** and calves, *5131*
9:13 For if the blood of bulls and of **g**, and *5131*
9:19 he took the blood of calves and of **g**, *5131*
10: 4 of bulls and of **g** should take away sins. *5131*

GOATS' (10) [GOAT]
Ex 25: 4 and scarlet, and fine linen, and **g** *hair,* 5795
26: 7 thou shalt make curtains *of* **g** *hair* to be a 5795
35: 6 and scarlet, and fine linen, and **g** *hair,* 5795
35:23 **g** *hair,* and red skins of rams, and 5795
35:26 stirred them up in wisdom spun **g** *hair.* 5795
36:14 he made curtains *of* **g** *hair* for the tent over 5795
Nu 31:20 all work of **g** *hair,* and all things made of 5795
1Sa 19:13 put a pillow of **g** *hair for* his bolster, and 5795
19:16 with a pillow of **g** *hair for* his bolster. 5795
Pr 27:27 *thou shalt have* **g** milk enough for thy food, 5795

GOATSKINS (1) [GOAT, SKIN]
Heb 11:37 wandered about in sheepskins and **g**; *122+1192*

GOB (2)
2Sa 21:18 was again a battle with the Philistines at **G**: 1359
21:19 there was again a battle in **G** with 1359

GOBLET (1)
SS 7: 2 Thy navel *is like* a round **g**, *which* wanteth 101

GOD (4135) [BETH-EL, GOD'S, GOD-WARD, GODDESS, GODHEAD, GODLINESS, GODLY, GODS, UNGODLINESS; See also GOD*]
Ge 1: 1 In the beginning **G** created the heaven and 430
1: 2 the Spirit of **G** moved upon the face of 430
1: 3 **G** said, Let there be light: and there was 430
1: 4 **G** saw the light, that *it was* good: and 430
1: 4 and **G** divided the light from the darkness. 430
1: 5 **G** called the light Day, and the darkness he 430
1: 6 **G** said, Let there be a firmament in the midst 430
1: 7 **G** made the firmament, and divided 430
1: 8 **G** called the firmament Heaven. And 430
1: 9 **G** said, Let the waters under the heaven be 430
1:10 **G** called the dry *land* Earth; and 430
1:10 called he Seas: and **G** saw that *it was* good. 430
1:11 **G** said, Let the earth bring forth grass, 430
1:12 after his kind: and **G** saw that *it was* good. 430

Ge 1:14 **G** said, Let there be lights in the firmament 430
1:16 **G** made two great lights; the greater light to 430
1:17 **G** set them in the firmament of the heaven to 430
1:18 the darkness: and **G** saw that *it was* good. 430
1:20 **G** said, Let the waters bring forth abundantly 430
1:21 **G** created great whales, and every living 430
1:21 after his kind: and **G** saw that *it was* good. 430
1:22 And **G** blessed them, saying, Be fruitful, and 430
1:24 **G** said, Let the earth bring forth the living 430
1:25 **G** made the beast of the earth after his kind, 430
1:25 after his kind: and **G** saw that *it was* good. 430
1:26 And **G** said, Let us make man in our image, 430
1:27 So **G** created man in his own image, in 430
1:27 in the image of **G** created he him; 430
1:28 **G** blessed them, and God said unto them, 430
1:28 **G** said unto them, Be fruitful, and multiply, 430
1:29 **G** said, Behold, I have given you every herb 430
1:31 **G** saw every thing that he had made, and 430
2: 2 on the seventh day **G** ended his work which 430
2: 3 **G** blessed the seventh day, and sanctified it: 430
2: 3 rested from all his work which **G** created 430
2: 4 in the day that the LORD **G** made the earth 430
2: 5 for the LORD **G** had not caused it to rain 430
2: 7 the LORD **G** formed man *of* the dust of 430
2: 8 the LORD **G** planted a garden eastward in 430
2: 9 out of the ground made the LORD **G** to 430
2:15 the LORD **G** took the man, and put him 430
2:16 the LORD **G** commanded the man, saying, 430
2:18 the LORD **G** said, *It is* not good that 430
2:19 out of the ground the LORD **G** formed 430
2:21 the LORD **G** caused a deep sleep to fall 430
2:22 which the LORD **G** had taken from man, 430
3: 1 of the field which the LORD **G** had made. 430
3: 1 he said unto the woman, Yea, hath **G** said, 430
3: 3 **G** hath said, Ye shall not eat of it, 430
3: 5 For **G** doth know that in the day ye eat 430
3: 8 they heard the voice of the LORD **G** 430
3: 8 LORD **G** amongst the trees of the garden. 430
3: 9 the LORD **G** called unto Adam, and 430
3:13 the LORD **G** said unto the woman, What *is* 430
3:14 the LORD **G** said unto the serpent, 430
3:21 to his wife did the LORD **G** make coats of 430
3:22 the LORD **G** said, Behold, the man is 430
3:23 Therefore the LORD **G** sent him forth from 430
4:25 For **G**, *said she,* hath appointed me another 430
5: 1 In the day that **G** created man, in 430
5: 1 in the likeness of **G** made he him; 430
5:22 Enoch walked with **G** after he begat 430
5:24 And Enoch walked with **G**: and he *was* not; 430
5:24 with God: and he *was* not; for **G** took him. 430
6: 2 That the sons of **G** saw the daughters of men 430
6: 4 when the sons of **G** came in unto 430
6: 9 in his generations, *and* Noah walked with **G**. 430
6:11 The earth also was corrupt before **G**, and 430
6:12 **G** looked upon the earth, and behold, it was 430
6:13 **G** said unto Noah, The end of all flesh is 430
6:22 according to all that **G** commanded him, so 430
7: 9 and the female, as **G** had commanded Noah. 430
7:16 of all flesh, as **G** had commanded him: 430
8: 1 **G** remembered Noah, and every living thing, 430
8: 1 **G** made a wind to pass over the earth, and 430
8:15 And **G** spake unto Noah, saying, 430
9: 1 **G** blessed Noah and his sons, and said unto 430
9: 6 be shed: for in the image of **G** made he man. 430
9: 8 **G** spake unto Noah, and to his sons with 430
9:12 **G** said, This *is* the token of the covenant 430
9:16 the everlasting covenant between **G** 430
9:17 **G** said unto Noah, This *is* the token of 430
9:26 he said, Blessed *be* the LORD **G** of Shem; 430
9:27 **G** shall enlarge Japheth, and he shall dwell 430
14:18 and he *was* the priest of the most high **G**. 410
14:19 said, Blessed *be* Abram of the most high **G**, 410
14:20 blessed *be* the most high **G**, which hath 410
14:22 the most high **G**, the possessor of heaven 410
16:13 that spake unto her, Thou **G** seest me: 410
17: 1 and said unto him, I *am* the Almighty **G**; 410
17: 3 on his face: and **G** talked with him, saying, 430
17: 7 to be a **G** unto thee, and to thy seed after 430
17: 8 everlasting possession; and I will be their **G**. 430
17: 9 **G** said unto Abraham, Thou shalt keep my 430
17:15 **G** said unto Abraham, *As for* Sarai thy wife, 430
17:18 Abraham said unto **G**, O that Ishmael might 430
17:19 **G** said, Sarah thy wife shall bear thee a son 430
17:22 with him, and **G** went up from Abraham. 430
17:23 in the selfsame day, as **G** had said unto him. 430
19:29 when **G** destroyed the cities of the plain, 430
19:29 that **G** remembered Abraham, and sent Lot 430
20: 3 **G** came to Abimelech in a dream by night, 430
20: 6 **G** said unto him in a dream, Yea, I know 430
20:11 Surely the fear of **G** *is* not in this place; 430
20:13 when **G** caused me to wander from my 430
20:17 So Abraham prayed unto **G**: and God healed 430
20:17 **G** healed Abimelech, and his wife, and 430
21: 2 at the set time of which **G** had spoken to 430
21: 4 eight days old, as **G** had commanded him. 430
21: 6 **G** hath made me to laugh, *so that* all that 430
21:12 **G** said unto Abraham, Let it not be grievous 430
21:17 **G** heard the voice of the lad; and the angel 430
21:17 the angel of **G** called to Hagar out of heaven, 430
21:17 for **G** hath heard the voice of the lad where 430
21:19 **G** opened her eyes, and she saw a well of 430
21:20 **G** was with the lad; and he grew, and 430
21:22 **G** *is* with thee in all that thou doest: 430
21:23 swear unto me here by **G** that thou wilt not 430
21:33 the name of the LORD, the everlasting **G**. 410
22: 1 that **G** did tempt Abraham, and said unto 430
22: 3 went unto the place of which **G** had told 430
22: 8 **G** will provide himself a lamb for a burnt 430
22: 9 they came to the place which **G** had told him 430
22:12 for now I know that thou fearest **G**, 430
24: 3 the **G** of heaven, and the God of the earth, 430
24: 3 the God of heaven, and the **G** of the earth, 430
24: 7 The LORD **G** of heaven, which took me 430
24:12 O LORD **G** of my master Abraham, I pray 430
24:27 Blessed *be* the LORD **G** of my master 430
24:42 said, O LORD **G** of my master Abraham, 430
24:48 blessed the LORD **G** of my master 430
25:11 of Abraham, that **G** blessed his son Isaac; 430
26:24 and said, I *am* the **G** of Abraham thy father: 430
27:20 Because the LORD thy **G** brought *it* to me. 430
27:28 Therefore **G** give thee of the dew of heaven, 430
28: 3 **G** Almighty bless thee, and make thee 410
28: 4 art a stranger, which **G** gave unto Abraham. 430
28:12 behold the angels of **G** ascending and 430
28:13 I *am* the LORD **G** of Abraham thy father, 430
28:13 of Abraham thy father, and the **G** of Isaac: 430
28:17 this *is* none other but the house of **G**, and 430
28:20 If **G** will be with me, and will keep me in 430
28:21 in peace; then shall the LORD be my **G**: 430
30: 6 **G** hath judged me, and hath also heard my 430
30:17 **G** hearkened unto Leah, and she conceived, 430
30:18 **G** hath given *me* my hire, because I have 430
30:20 **G** hath endued me with a good dowry; 430
30:22 **G** remembered Rachel, and God hearkened 430
30:22 **G** hearkened to her, and opened her womb. 430
30:23 and said, **G** hath taken away my reproach: 430
31: 5 the **G** of my father hath been with me. 430
31: 7 ten times; but **G** suffered him not to hurt me. 430
31: 9 Thus **G** hath taken away the cattle of your 430
31:11 the angel of **G** spake unto me in a dream, 430
31:13 I *am* the **G** of Beth-el, where thou anointedst 410
31:16 For all the riches which **G** hath taken from 430
31:16 whatsoever **G** hath said unto thee, do. 430
31:24 **G** came to Laban the Syrian in a dream by 430
31:29 the **G** of your father spake unto me 430
31:42 Except the **G** of my father, the God of 430
31:42 the **G** of Abraham, and the fear of Isaac, 430
31:42 **G** hath seen mine affliction and the labour of 430
31:50 see, **G** *is* witness betwixt me and thee. 430
31:53 The **G** of Abraham, and the God of Nahor, 430
31:53 The God of Abraham, and the **G** of Nahor, 430
31:53 the **G** of their father, judge betwixt us. 430
32: 1 on his way, and the angels of **G** met him. 430
32: 9 O **G** of my father Abraham, and God of my 430
32: 9 father Abraham, and **G** of my father Isaac, 430
32:28 for as a prince hast thou power with **G** and 430
32:30 for I have seen **G** face to face, and my life is 430
33: 5 The children which **G** hath graciously given 430
33:10 as though I had seen the face of **G**, and 430
33:11 because **G** hath dealt graciously with me, 430
35: 1 **G** said unto Jacob, Arise, go up to Beth-el, 430
35: 1 make there an altar unto **G**, that appeared 410
35: 3 I will make there an altar unto **G**, 410
35: 5 the terror of **G** was upon the cities that *were* 430
35: 7 because there **G** appeared unto him, when he 430
35: 9 **G** appeared unto Jacob again, when he came 430
35:10 **G** said unto him, Thy name *is* Jacob: 430
35:11 **G** said unto him, I *am* God Almighty: 430

Ge	35:11	God said unto him, I *am* **G** Almighty:	410
	35:13	**G** went up from him in the place where he	430
	35:15	Jacob called the name of the place where **G**	430
	39: 9	do this great wickedness, and sin against **G**?	430
	40: 8	*Do* not interpretations *belong* to **G**?	430
	41:16	**G** shall give Pharaoh an answer of peace.	430
	41:25	**G** hath shewed Pharaoh what he *is* about to	430
	41:28	What **G** *is* about to do he sheweth unto	430
	41:32	*it is* because the thing *is* established by **G**,	430
	41:32	by God, and **G** will shortly bring it to pass.	430
	41:38	as this *is,* a man in whom the spirit of **G** *is?*	430
	41:39	Forasmuch as **G** hath shewed thee all this,	430
	41:51	For **G**, *said he,* hath made me forget all my	430
	41:52	For **G** hath caused me to be fruitful in	430
	42:18	the third day, This do, and live; *for* I fear **G**:	430
	42:28	What *is* this *that* **G** hath done unto us?	430
	43:14	**G** Almighty give you mercy before the man,	410
	43:23	your **G**, and the God of your father,	430
	43:23	your God, and the **G** of your father,	430
	43:29	he said, **G** be gracious unto thee, my son.	430
	44: 7	**G forbid** that thy servants should do	2486
	44:16	**G** hath found out the iniquity of thy	430
	44:17	he said, **G forbid** that I should do so: *but*	2486
	45: 5	for **G** did send me before you to preserve	430
	45: 7	**G** sent me before you to preserve you a	430
	45: 8	*it was* not you *that* sent me hither, but **G**:	430
	45: 9	**G** hath made me lord of all Egypt:	430
	46: 1	offered sacrifices unto the **G** of his father	430
	46: 2	**G** spake unto Israel in the visions of	430
	46: 3	he said, I *am* **G**, the God of thy father:	410
	46: 3	he said, I *am* God, the **G** of thy father:	430
	48: 3	**G** Almighty appeared unto me at Luz in	410
	48: 9	whom **G** hath given me in this *place.* And he	430
	48:11	and lo, **G** hath shewed me also thy seed.	430
	48:15	he blessed Joseph, and said, **G**, before whom	430
	48:15	the **G** which fed me all my life long unto this	430
	48:20	**G** make thee as Ephraim and as Manasseh:	430
	48:21	**G** shall be with you, and bring you again	430
	49:24	by the hands of the mighty **G** of Jacob;	NIH
	49:25	*Even* by the **G** of thy father, who shall help	410
	50:17	forgive the trespass of the servants of the **G**	430
	50:19	Fear not: for *am* I in the place of **G**?	430
	50:20	*but* **G** meant it unto good, to bring to pass,	430
	50:24	**G** will surely visit you, and bring you out of	430
	50:25	**G** will surely visit you, and ye shall carry up	430
Ex	1:17	the midwives feared **G**, and did not as	430
	1:20	Therefore **G** dealt well with the midwives:	430
	1:21	to pass, because the midwives feared **G**,	430
	2:23	their cry came up unto **G** by reason of	430
	2:24	**G** heard their groaning, and	430
	2:24	**G** remembered his covenant with Abraham,	430
	2:25	**G** looked upon the children of Israel, and	430
	2:25	of Israel, and **G** had respect unto *them.*	430
	3: 1	came to the mountain of **G**, *even* to Horeb.	430
	3: 4	**G** called unto him out of the midst of	430
	3: 6	Moreover he said, I *am* the **G** of thy father,	430
	3: 6	the **G** of Abraham, the God of Isaac, and	430
	3: 6	the **G** of Isaac, and the God of Jacob.	430
	3: 6	the God of Isaac, and the **G** of Jacob.	430
	3: 6	his face; for he was afraid to look upon **G**.	430
	3:11	Moses said unto **G**, Who *am* I, that I should	430
	3:12	ye shall serve **G** upon this mountain.	430
	3:13	Moses said unto **G**, Behold, *when* I come	430
	3:13	The **G** of your fathers hath sent me unto you;	430
	3:14	And **G** said unto Moses, I AM THAT I AM:	430
	3:15	**G** said moreover unto Moses, Thus shalt	430
	3:15	The LORD **G** of your fathers, the God of	430
	3:15	the **G** of Abraham, the God of Isaac, and	430
	3:15	the **G** of Isaac, and the God of Jacob,	430
	3:15	the God of Isaac, and the **G** of Jacob,	430
	3:16	unto them, The LORD **G** of your fathers,	430
	3:16	the **G** of Abraham, of Isaac, and of Jacob,	430
	3:18	The LORD **G** of the Hebrews hath met	430
	3:18	that we may sacrifice to the LORD our **G**.	430
	4: 5	That they may believe that the LORD **G** of	430
	4: 5	the **G** of Abraham, the God of Isaac, and	430
	4: 5	the **G** of Isaac, and the God of Jacob,	430
	4: 5	the God of Isaac, and the **G** of Jacob,	430
	4:16	and thou shalt be to him instead of **G**.	430
	4:20	and Moses took the rod of **G** in his hand.	430
	4:27	met him in the mount of **G**, and kissed him.	430
	5: 1	Thus saith the LORD **G** of Israel,	430
	5: 3	The **G** of the Hebrews hath met with us:	430
	5: 3	and sacrifice unto the LORD our **G**;	430
	5: 8	saying, Let us go *and* sacrifice to our **G**.	430
	6: 2	And **G** spake unto Moses, and said unto him,	430
	6: 3	by *the name of* **G** Almighty, but *by* my name	410
	6: 7	to me for a people, and I will be to you a **G**:	430
	6: 7	ye shall know that I *am* the LORD your **G**,	430
	7: 1	See, I have made thee a **g** to Pharaoh:	430
	7:16	The LORD **G** of the Hebrews hath sent me	430
	8:10	*there is* none like unto the LORD our **G**.	430
	8:19	said unto Pharaoh, This *is* the finger of **G**:	430
	8:25	said, Go ye, sacrifice to your **G** in the land.	430
	8:26	of the Egyptians to the LORD our **G**:	430
	8:27	sacrifice to the LORD our **G**, as he shall	430
	8:28	that ye may sacrifice to the LORD your **G**	430
	9: 1	Thus saith the LORD **G** of the Hebrews,	430
	9:13	Thus saith the LORD **G** of the Hebrews,	430
	9:30	know that ye will not yet fear the LORD **G**.	430
	10: 3	Thus saith the LORD **G** of the Hebrews,	430
	10: 7	that they may serve the LORD their **G**:	430
	10: 8	unto them, Go, serve the LORD your **G**:	430
	10:16	I have sinned against the LORD your **G**,	430
	10:17	*this* once, and intreat the LORD your **G**,	430
	10:25	we may sacrifice unto the LORD our **G**.	430
	10:26	must we take to serve the LORD our **G**;	430
	13:17	that **G** led them not *through* the way of	430
	13:17	for **G** said, Lest peradventure the people	430
	13:18	**G** led the people about, *through* the way of	430
	13:19	of Israel, saying, **G** will surely visit you;	430
	14:19	the angel of **G**, which went before the camp	430
	15: 2	he *is* my **G**, and I will prepare him a	410
	15: 2	my father's **G**, and I will exalt him.	430
	15:26	hearken to the voice of the LORD thy **G**,	430
	16: 3	**Would to G** we had died by the hand	4310+5414
	16:12	ye shall know that I *am* the LORD your **G**.	430
	17: 9	of the hill with the rod of **G** in mine hand.	430
	18: 1	heard of all that **G** had done for Moses, and	430
	18: 4	for the **G** of my father, *said he, was* mine	430
	18: 5	where he encamped *at* the mount of **G**:	430
	18:12	took a burnt offering and sacrifices for **G**:	430
	18:12	bread with Moses' father in law before **G**.	430
	18:15	the people come unto me to inquire of **G**:	430
	18:16	and I do make *them* know the statutes of **G**,	430
	18:19	give thee counsel, and **G** shall be with thee:	430
	18:19	that thou mayest bring the causes unto **G**:	430
	18:21	such as fear **G**, men of truth,	430
	18:23	**G** command thee *so,* then thou shalt be able	430
	19: 3	Moses went up unto **G**, and the LORD	430
	19:17	the people out of the camp to meet with **G**;	430
	19:19	and **G** answered him by a voice.	430
	20: 1	And **G** spake all these words, saying,	430
	20: 2	I *am* the LORD thy **G**, which have brought	430
	20: 5	for I the LORD thy **G** *am* a jealous God,	430
	20: 5	for I the LORD thy God *am* a jealous **G**,	410
	20: 7	take the name of the LORD thy **G** in vain;	430
	20:10	day *is* the sabbath of the LORD thy **G**:	430
	20:12	land which the LORD thy **G** giveth thee.	430
	20:19	but let not **G** speak with us, lest we die.	430
	20:20	for **G** is come to prove you, and that his fear	430
	20:21	near unto the thick darkness where **G** *was.*	430
	21:13	not in wait, but **G** deliver *him* into his hand;	430
	22:20	He that sacrificeth unto *any* **g**, save unto	430
	23:19	bring *into* the house of the LORD thy **G**.	430
	23:25	ye shall serve the LORD your **G**, and	430
	24:10	they saw the **G** of Israel: and *there was*	430
	24:11	also they saw **G**, and did eat and drink.	430
	24:13	and Moses went up into the mount of **G**.	430
	29:45	the children of Israel, and will be their **G**.	430
	29:46	shall know that I *am* the LORD their **G**,	430
	29:46	amongst them: I *am* the LORD their **G**.	430
	31: 3	I have filled him *with* the spirit of **G**,	430
	31:18	tables of stone, written with the finger of **G**.	430
	32:11	And Moses besought the LORD his **G**, and	430
	32:16	the tables *were* the work of **G**, and	430
	32:16	the writing *was* the writing of **G**, graven	430
	32:27	Thus saith the LORD **G** of Israel,	430
	34: 6	The LORD **G**, merciful and gracious,	410
	34:14	For thou shalt worship no other **g**: for	410
	34:14	whose name *is* Jealous, *is* a jealous **G**:	410
	34:23	before the Lord GOD, the **G** of Israel.	430
	34:24	before the LORD thy **G** thrice in the year.	430
	34:26	bring *unto* the house of the LORD thy **G**.	430
	35:31	he hath filled him *with* the spirit of **G**,	430
Lev	2:13	thy **G** to be lacking from thy meat offering:	430
	4:22	**G** *concerning things* which should not be	430
	10:17	**G** hath given it you to bear the iniquity of	NIH

Lev 11:44 For I *am* the LORD your **G**: ye shall 430
11:45 up out of the land of Egypt, to be your **G**: 430
18: 2 and say unto them, I *am* the LORD your **G**. 430
18: 4 to walk therein: I *am* the LORD your **G**. 430
18:21 neither shalt thou profane the name of thy **G**: 430
18:30 yourselves therein: I *am* the LORD your **G**. 430
19: 2 be holy: for I the LORD your **G** *am* holy. 430
19: 3 keep my sabbaths: I *am* the LORD your **G**. 430
19: 4 molten gods: I *am* the LORD your **G**. 430
19:10 and stranger: I *am* the LORD your **G**. 430
19:12 neither shalt thou profane the name of thy **G**: 430
19:14 before the blind, but shalt fear thy **G**: 430
19:25 increase thereof: I *am* the LORD your **G**. 430
19:31 defiled by them: I *am* the LORD your **G**. 430
19:32 the face of the old man, and fear thy **G**: 430
19:34 the land of Egypt: I *am* the LORD your **G**. 430
19:36 I *am* the LORD your **G**, which brought you 430
20: 7 and be ye holy: for I *am* the LORD your **G**. 430
20:24 I *am* the LORD your **G**, which have 430
21: 6 They shall be holy unto their **G**, and 430
21: 6 and not profane the name of their **G**: 430
21: 6 *and* the bread of their **G**, they do offer: 430
21: 7 from her husband: for he *is* holy unto his **G**. 430
21: 8 for he offereth the bread of thy **G**: 430
21:12 nor profane the sanctuary of his **G**; 430
21:12 for the crown of the anointing oil of his **G** *is* 430
21:17 him not approach to offer the bread of his **G**. 430
21:21 not come nigh to offer the bread of his **G**. 430
21:22 He shall eat the bread of his **G**, *both* of 430
22:25 ye offer the bread of your **G** of any of these; 430
22:33 you out of the land of Egypt, to be your **G**: 430
23:14 ye have brought an offering unto your **G**: 430
23:22 and to the stranger: I *am* the LORD your **G**. 430
23:28 for you before the LORD your **G**. 430
23:40 ye shall rejoice before the LORD your **G** 430
23:43 the land of Egypt: I *am* the LORD your **G**. 430
24:15 Whosoever curseth his **G** shall bear his sin. 430
24:22 own country: for I *am* the LORD your **G**. 430
25:17 one another; but thou shalt fear thy **G**: 430
25:17 fear thy God: for I *am* the LORD your **G**. 430
25:36 fear thy **G**; that thy brother may live with 430
25:38 I *am* the LORD your **G**, which brought you 430
25:38 you the land of Canaan, *and* to be your **G**. 430
25:43 over him with rigour; but shalt fear thy **G**. 430
25:55 the land of Egypt: I *am* the LORD your **G**. 430
26: 1 down unto it: for I *am* the LORD your **G**. 430
26:12 will be your **G**, and ye shall be my people. 430
26:13 I *am* the LORD your **G**, which brought you 430
26:44 with them: for I *am* the LORD their **G**. 430
26:45 sight of the heathen, that *I* might be their **G**: 430
Nu 6: 7 the consecration of his **G** *is* upon his head. 430
10: 9 be remembered before the LORD your **G**, 430
10:10 may be to you for a memorial before your **G**: 430
10:10 before your God: I *am* the LORD your **G**. 430
11:29 **would G that** all the LORD's 4310+5414
12:13 Heal her now, O **G**, I beseech thee. 410
14: 2 **Would G that** we had died in the land of 3863
14: 2 or **would G** we had died in this wilderness! 3863
15:40 and be holy unto your **G**. 430
15:41 I *am* the LORD your **G**, which brought you 430
15:41 you out of the land of Egypt, to be your **G**: 430
15:41 to be your God: I *am* the LORD your **G**. 430
16: 9 that the **G** of Israel hath separated you from 430
16:22 they fell upon their faces, and said, O **G**, 410
16:22 said, O God, the **G** of the spirits of all flesh, 430
20: 3 **Would G** that we had died when our 3863
21: 5 the people spake against **G**, and 430
22: 9 **G** came unto Balaam, and said, What men 430
22:10 Balaam said unto **G**, Balak the son of 430
22:12 **G** said unto Balaam, Thou shalt not go with 430
22:18 go beyond the word of the LORD my **G**, 430
22:20 **G** came unto Balaam at night, and said unto 430
22:38 the word that **G** putteth in my mouth, that 430
23: 4 **G** met Balaam: and he said unto him, I have 430
23: 8 How shall I curse, whom **G** hath not cursed? 410
23:19 **G** *is* not a man, that he should lie; neither 410
23:21 the LORD his **G** *is* with him, and the shout 430
23:22 **G** brought them out of Egypt; he hath as it 410
23:23 and of Israel, What hath **G** wrought! 410
23:27 peradventure it will please **G** that thou 430
24: 2 and the spirit of **G** came upon him. 430
24: 4 He hath said, which heard the words of **G**, 410
24: 8 **G** brought him forth out of Egypt; he hath as 410
24:16 which heard the words of **G**, and knew 410
24:23 said, Alas, who shall live when **G** doeth this! 410
25:13 because he was zealous for his **G**, and 430
27:16 the LORD, the **G** of the spirits of all flesh, 430
Dt 1: 6 The LORD our **G** spake unto us in Horeb, 430
1:10 The LORD your **G** hath multiplied you, 430
1:11 (The LORD **G** of your fathers make you a 430
1:19 as the LORD our **G** commanded us; 430
1:20 which the LORD our **G** doth give unto us. 430
1:21 the LORD thy **G** hath set the land before 430
1:21 possess *it*, as the LORD **G** of thy fathers 430
1:25 *It is* a good land which the LORD our **G** 430
1:26 the commandment of the LORD your **G**: 430
1:30 The LORD your **G** which goeth before 430
1:31 seen how that the LORD thy **G** bare thee, 430
1:32 thing ye did not believe the LORD your **G**, 430
1:41 according to all that the LORD our **G** 430
2: 7 For the LORD thy **G** hath blessed thee in 430
2: 7 these forty years the LORD thy **G** *hath* 430
2:29 the land which the LORD our **G** giveth us. 430
2:30 for the LORD thy **G** hardened his spirit, 430
2:33 the LORD our **G** delivered him before us; 430
2:36 the LORD our **G** delivered all unto us: 430
2:37 nor *unto* whatsoever the LORD our **G** 430
3: 3 So the LORD our **G** delivered into our 430
3:18 The LORD your **G** hath given you this land 430
3:20 your **G** hath given them beyond Jordan: 430
3:21 your **G** hath done unto these two kings: 430
3:22 for the LORD your **G** he shall fight for 430
3:24 for what **G** *is there* in heaven or in earth, 410
4: 1 possess the land which the LORD **G** of 430
4: 2 the LORD your **G** which I command you. 430
4: 3 the LORD thy **G** hath destroyed them from 430
4: 4 ye that did cleave unto the LORD your **G** 430
4: 5 even as the LORD my **G** commanded me, 430
4: 7 *so* great, who hath **G** *so* nigh unto them, 430
4: 7 as the LORD our **G** *is* in all *things that* we 430
4:10 stoodest before the LORD thy **G** in Horeb, 430
4:19 which the LORD thy **G** hath divided unto 430
4:21 which the LORD thy **G** giveth thee *for* an 430
4:23 forget the covenant of the LORD your **G**, 430
4:23 the LORD thy **G** hath forbidden thee. 430
4:24 For the LORD thy **G** *is* a consuming fire, 430
4:24 God *is* a consuming fire, *even* a jealous **G**. 410
4:25 do evil in the sight of the LORD thy **G**, 430
4:29 thence thou shalt seek the LORD thy **G**, 430
4:30 if thou turn to the LORD thy **G**, and 430
4:31 (For the LORD thy **G** *is* a merciful God;) 430
4:31 (For the LORD thy God *is* a merciful **G**;) 410
4:32 since the day that **G** created man upon 430
4:33 Did *ever* people hear the voice of **G** 430
4:34 Or hath **G** assayed to go *and* take him a 430
4:34 according to all that the LORD your **G** did 430
4:35 thou mightest know that the LORD he *is* **G**; 430
4:39 that the LORD he *is* **G** in heaven above, 430
4:40 which the LORD thy **G** giveth thee, 430
5: 2 The LORD our **G** made a covenant with us 430
5: 6 I *am* the LORD thy **G**, which brought thee 430
5: 9 for I the LORD thy **G** *am* a jealous God, 430
5: 9 for I the LORD thy God *am* a jealous **G**, 410
5:11 take the name of the LORD thy **G** in vain: 430
5:12 as the LORD thy **G** hath commanded thee. 430
5:14 day *is* the sabbath of the LORD thy **G**: 430
5:15 *that* the LORD thy **G** brought thee out 430
5:15 the LORD thy **G** commanded thee to keep 430
5:16 as the LORD thy **G** hath commanded thee; 430
5:16 in the land which the LORD thy **G** giveth 430
5:24 the LORD our **G** hath shewed us his glory 430
5:24 we have seen this day that **G** doth talk with 430
5:25 if we hear the voice of the LORD our **G** 430
5:26 that hath heard the voice of the living **G** 430
5:27 and hear all that the LORD our **G** shall say: 430
5:27 speak thou unto us all that the LORD our **G** 430
5:32 as the LORD your **G** hath commanded you: 430
5:33 the LORD your **G** hath commanded you, 430
6: 1 which the LORD your **G** commanded to 430
6: 2 That thou mightest fear the LORD thy **G**, 430
6: 3 as the LORD **G** of thy fathers hath 430
6: 4 O Israel: The LORD our **G** *is* one LORD: 430
6: 5 thou shalt love the LORD thy **G** with all 430
6:10 when the LORD thy **G** shall have brought 430
6:13 Thou shalt fear the LORD thy **G**, and 430
6:15 (For the LORD thy **G** *is* a jealous God 430
6:15 (For the LORD thy God *is* a jealous **G** 410
6:15 lest the anger of the LORD thy **G** be 430

G

Dt	6:16	Ye shall not tempt the LORD your **G**, as ye	430
	6:17	the commandments of the LORD your **G**,	430
	6:20	which the LORD our **G** hath commanded	430
	6:24	to fear the LORD our **G**, for our good	430
	6:25	commandments before the LORD our **G**,	430
	7: 1	When the LORD thy **G** shall bring thee	430
	7: 2	when the LORD thy **G** shall deliver them	430
	7: 6	*art* a holy people unto the LORD thy **G**:	430
	7: 6	the LORD thy **G** hath chosen thee to be a	430
	7: 9	Know therefore that the LORD thy **G**, he *is*	430
	7: 9	he *is* **G**, the faithful God, which keepeth	430
	7: 9	he *is* God, the faithful **G**, which keepeth	410
	7:12	that the LORD thy **G** shall keep unto thee	430
	7:16	which the LORD thy **G** shall deliver thee;	430
	7:18	shalt well remember what the LORD thy **G**	430
	7:19	where*by* the LORD thy **G** brought thee out:	430
	7:19	shall the LORD thy **G** do unto all	430
	7:20	Moreover the LORD thy **G** will send	430
	7:21	for the LORD thy **G** *is* among you,	430
	7:21	God *is* among you, a mighty **G** and terrible.	410
	7:22	the LORD thy **G** will put out those nations	430
	7:23	the LORD thy **G** shall deliver them unto	430
	7:25	it *is* an abomination to the LORD thy **G**.	430
	8: 2	**G** led thee these forty years in	430
	8: 5	*so* the LORD thy **G** chasteneth thee.	430
	8: 6	the commandments of the LORD thy **G**,	430
	8: 7	For the LORD thy **G** bringeth thee into a	430
	8:10	thou shalt bless the LORD thy **G** for	430
	8:11	that thou forget not the LORD thy **G**,	430
	8:14	lifted up, and thou forget the LORD thy **G**,	430
	8:18	But thou shalt remember the LORD thy **G**:	430
	8:19	if thou do at all forget the LORD thy **G**,	430
	8:20	unto the voice of the LORD your **G**.	430
	9: 3	that the LORD thy **G** *is* he which goeth	430
	9: 4	after that the LORD thy **G** hath cast them	430
	9: 5	thy **G** doth drive them out from before thee,	430
	9: 6	that the LORD thy **G** giveth thee not this	430
	9: 7	how thou provokedst the LORD thy **G** to	430
	9:10	tables of stone written with the finger of **G**;	430
	9:16	ye had sinned against the LORD your **G**,	430
	9:23	the commandment of the LORD your **G**,	430
	10: 9	according as the LORD thy **G** promised	430
	10:12	what doth the LORD thy **G** require of thee,	430
	10:12	to fear the LORD thy **G**, to walk in all his	430
	10:12	to serve the LORD thy **G** with all thy heart	430
	10:14	heaven of heavens *is* the LORD'S thy **G**,	430
	10:17	For the LORD your **G** *is* God of gods, and	430
	10:17	For the LORD your God *is* **G** of gods, and	430
	10:17	of lords, a great **G**, a mighty, and a terrible,	410
	10:20	Thou shalt fear the LORD thy **G**; him shalt	430
	10:21	He *is* thy praise, and he *is* thy **G**, that hath	430
	10:22	now the LORD thy **G** hath made thee as	430
	11: 1	Therefore thou shalt love the LORD thy **G**,	430
	11: 2	seen the chastisement of the LORD your **G**,	430
	11:12	A land which the LORD thy **G** careth for:	430
	11:12	the eyes of the LORD thy **G** *are* always	430
	11:13	to love the LORD your **G**, and to serve him	430
	11:22	to do them, to love the LORD your **G**,	430
	11:25	*for* the LORD your **G** shall lay the fear of	430
	11:27	the commandments of the LORD your **G**,	430
	11:28	the commandments of the LORD your **G**,	430
	11:29	when the LORD thy **G** hath brought thee in	430
	11:31	land which the LORD your **G** giveth you,	430
	12: 1	which the LORD **G** of thy fathers giveth	430
	12: 4	Ye shall not do so unto the LORD your **G**.	430
	12: 5	unto the place which the LORD your **G**	430
	12: 7	there ye shall eat before the LORD your **G**,	430
	12: 7	where*in* the LORD thy **G** hath blessed thee.	430
	12: 9	which the LORD your **G** giveth you.	430
	12:10	dwell in the land which the LORD your **G**	430
	12:11	**G** shall choose to cause his name to dwell	430
	12:12	ye shall rejoice before the LORD your **G**,	430
	12:15	the LORD thy **G** which he hath given thee:	430
	12:18	thou must eat them before the LORD thy **G**	430
	12:18	place which the LORD thy **G** shall choose,	430
	12:18	thou shalt rejoice before the LORD thy **G**	430
	12:20	When the LORD thy **G** shall enlarge thy	430
	12:21	If the place which the LORD thy **G** hath	430
	12:27	upon the altar of the LORD thy **G**:	430
	12:27	out upon the altar of the LORD thy **G**,	430
	12:28	and right in the sight of the LORD thy **G**.	430
	12:29	When the LORD thy **G** shall cut off	430
	12:31	Thou shalt not do so unto the LORD thy **G**:	430
	13: 3	for the LORD your **G** proveth you, to know	430

13: 3	love the LORD your **G** with all your heart	430
13: 4	Ye shall walk after the LORD your **G**, and	430
13: 5	to turn *you* away from the LORD your **G**,	430
13: 5	LORD thy **G** commanded thee to walk in.	430
13:10	to thrust thee away from the LORD thy **G**,	430
13:12	which the LORD thy **G** hath given thee to	430
13:16	thereof every whit, for the LORD thy **G**:	430
13:18	hearken to the voice of the LORD thy **G**,	430
13:18	*is* right in the eyes of the LORD thy **G**.	430
14: 1	Ye *are* the children of the LORD your **G**:	430
14: 2	*art* a holy people unto the LORD thy **G**,	430
14:21	*art* a holy people unto the LORD thy **G**.	430
14:23	And thou shalt eat before the LORD thy **G**,	430
14:23	learn to fear the LORD thy **G** always.	430
14:24	which the LORD thy **G** shall choose to set	430
14:24	when the LORD thy **G** hath blessed thee:	430
14:25	place which the LORD thy **G** shall choose:	430
14:26	shalt eat there before the LORD thy **G**,	430
14:29	that the LORD thy **G** may bless thee in all	430
15: 4	**G** giveth thee *for* an inheritance to possess	430
15: 5	hearken unto the voice of the LORD thy **G**,	430
15: 6	For the LORD thy **G** blesseth thee, as he	430
15: 7	land which the LORD thy **G** giveth thee,	430
15:10	that for this thing the LORD thy **G** shall	430
15:14	*of that* where*with* the LORD thy **G** hath	430
15:15	and the LORD thy **G** redeemed thee:	430
15:18	the LORD thy **G** shall bless thee in all that	430
15:19	thou shalt sanctify unto the LORD thy **G**:	430
15:20	Thou shalt eat it before the LORD thy **G**	430
15:21	shalt not sacrifice it unto the LORD thy **G**.	430
16: 1	keep the passover unto the LORD thy **G**:	430
16: 1	for in the month of Abib the LORD thy **G**	430
16: 2	the passover unto the LORD thy **G**,	430
16: 5	which the LORD thy **G** giveth thee:	430
16: 6	at the place which the LORD thy **G** shall	430
16: 7	eat *it* in the place which the LORD thy **G**	430
16: 8	*be* a solemn assembly to the LORD thy **G**:	430
16:10	**G** *with* a tribute of a freewill offering of	430
16:10	**G**, according as the LORD thy God hath	NIH
16:10	as the LORD thy **G** hath blessed thee:	430
16:11	thou shalt rejoice before the LORD thy **G**,	430
16:11	in the place which the LORD thy **G** hath	430
16:15	**G** in the place which the LORD shall	430
16:15	the LORD thy **G** shall bless thee in all thy	430
16:16	thy **G** in the place which he shall choose;	430
16:17	the LORD thy **G** which he hath given thee.	430
16:18	which the LORD thy **G** giveth thee,	430
16:20	inherit the land which the LORD thy **G**	430
16:21	near unto the altar of the LORD thy **G**,	430
16:22	*any* image; which the LORD thy **G** hateth.	430
17: 1	unto the LORD thy **G** *any* bullock,	430
17: 1	*is* an abomination unto the LORD thy **G**.	430
17: 2	gates which the LORD thy **G** giveth thee,	430
17: 2	in the sight of the LORD thy **G**,	430
17: 8	place which the LORD thy **G** shall choose;	430
17:12	to minister there before the LORD thy **G**,	430
17:14	land which the LORD thy **G** giveth thee,	430
17:15	whom the LORD thy **G** shall choose:	430
17:19	that he may learn to fear the LORD his **G**,	430
18: 5	For the LORD thy **G** hath chosen him out	430
18: 7	minister in the name of the LORD his **G**,	430
18: 9	land which the LORD thy **G** giveth thee,	430
18:12	of these abominations the LORD thy **G**	430
18:13	shalt be perfect with the LORD thy **G**.	430
18:14	the LORD thy **G** hath not suffered thee so	430
18:15	The LORD thy **G** will raise up unto thee a	430
18:16	thy **G** in Horeb in the day of the assembly,	430
18:16	hear again the voice of the LORD my **G**,	430
19: 1	When the LORD thy **G** hath cut off	430
19: 1	whose land the LORD thy **G** giveth thee,	430
19: 2	which the LORD thy **G** giveth thee to	430
19: 3	which the LORD thy **G** giveth thee to	430
19: 8	if the LORD thy **G** enlarge thy coast, as he	430
19: 9	to love the LORD thy **G**, and to walk ever	430
19:10	which the LORD thy **G** giveth thee *for* an	430
19:14	the LORD thy **G** giveth thee to possess it.	430
20: 1	for the LORD thy **G** *is* with thee,	430
20: 4	For the LORD your **G** *is* he that goeth with	430
20:13	when the LORD thy **G** hath delivered it	430
20:14	which the LORD thy **G** hath given thee.	430
20:16	which the LORD thy **G** doth give thee *for*	430
20:17	as the LORD thy **G** hath commanded thee:	430
20:18	so should ye sin against the LORD your **G**.	430
21: 1	the LORD thy **G** giveth thee to possess it,	430

Dt	21: 5	for them the LORD thy **G** hath chosen to	430
	21:10	the LORD thy **G** hath delivered them into	430
	21:23	(for he that is hanged *is* accursed of **G**;)	430
	21:23	which the LORD thy **G** giveth thee *for* an	430
	22: 5	so *are* abomination unto the LORD thy **G**.	430
	23: 5	Nevertheless the LORD thy **G** would not	430
	23: 5	the LORD thy **G** turned the curse into a	430
	23: 5	because the LORD thy **G** loved thee.	430
	23:14	For the LORD thy **G** walketh in the midst	430
	23:18	*into* the house of the LORD thy **G** for any	430
	23:18	*are* abomination unto the LORD thy **G**.	430
	23:20	that the LORD thy **G** may bless thee in all	430
	23:21	shalt vow a vow unto the LORD thy **G**,	430
	23:21	for the LORD thy **G** will surely require it	430
	23:23	as thou hast vowed unto the LORD thy **G**,	430
	24: 4	which the LORD thy **G** giveth thee *for* an	430
	24: 9	Remember what the LORD thy **G** did unto	430
	24:13	unto thee before the LORD thy **G**.	430
	24:18	the LORD thy **G** redeemed thee thence:	430
	24:19	that the LORD thy **G** may bless thee in all	430
	25:15	land which the LORD thy **G** giveth thee.	430
	25:16	*are* an abomination unto the LORD thy **G**.	430
	25:18	*wast* faint and weary; and he feared not **G**.	430
	25:19	when the LORD thy **G** hath given thee rest	430
	25:19	in the land which the LORD thy **G** giveth	430
	26: 1	LORD thy **G** giveth thee *for* an inheritance,	430
	26: 2	thy land that the LORD thy **G** giveth thee,	430
	26: 2	thy **G** shall choose to place his name there.	430
	26: 3	I profess *this* day unto the LORD thy **G**,	430
	26: 4	down before the altar of the LORD thy **G**.	430
	26: 5	and say before the LORD thy **G**,	430
	26: 7	when we cried unto the LORD **G** of our	430
	26:10	thou shalt set it before the LORD thy **G**,	430
	26:10	and worship before the LORD thy **G**:	430
	26:11	the LORD thy **G** hath given unto thee,	430
	26:13	thou shalt say before the LORD thy **G**,	430
	26:14	hearkened to the voice of the LORD my **G**,	430
	26:16	This day the LORD thy **G** hath commanded	430
	26:17	avouched the LORD *this* day to be thy **G**,	430
	26:19	be a holy people unto the LORD thy **G**,	430
	27: 2	land which the LORD thy **G** giveth thee,	430
	27: 3	land which the LORD thy **G** giveth thee,	430
	27: 3	as the LORD **G** of thy fathers hath	430
	27: 5	thou build an altar unto the LORD thy **G**,	430
	27: 6	altar of the LORD thy **G** *of* whole stones:	430
	27: 6	offerings thereon unto the LORD thy **G**:	430
	27: 7	and rejoice before the LORD thy **G**.	430
	27: 9	art become the people of the LORD thy **G**.	430
	27:10	obey the voice of the LORD thy **G**,	430
	28: 1	unto the voice of the LORD thy **G**,	430
	28: 1	that the LORD thy **G** will set thee on high	430
	28: 2	hearken unto the voice of the LORD thy **G**.	430
	28: 8	land which the LORD thy **G** giveth thee.	430
	28: 9	the commandments of the LORD thy **G**,	430
	28:13	the commandments of the LORD thy **G**,	430
	28:15	hearken unto the voice of the LORD thy **G**,	430
	28:45	not unto the voice of the LORD thy **G**,	430
	28:47	Because thou servedst not the LORD thy **G**	430
	28:52	which the LORD thy **G** hath given thee.	430
	28:53	which the LORD thy **G** hath given thee,	430
	28:58	and fearful name, THE LORD THY **G**;	430
	28:62	not obey the voice of the LORD thy **G**.	430
	28:67	shalt say, **Would G** it were even!	4310+5414
	28:67	shalt say, **Would G** it were morning!	4310+5414
	29: 6	might know that I *am* the LORD your **G**.	430
	29:10	day all of you before the LORD your **G**;	430
	29:12	enter into covenant with the LORD thy **G**,	430
	29:12	which the LORD thy **G** maketh with thee	430
	29:13	*that* he may be unto thee a **G**, as he hath said	430
	29:15	with us *this* day before the LORD our **G**,	430
	29:18	away *this* day from the LORD our **G**,	430
	29:25	covenant of the LORD **G** of their fathers,	430
	29:29	secret *things belong* unto the LORD our **G**:	430
	30: 1	whither the LORD thy **G** hath driven thee,	430
	30: 2	And shalt return unto the LORD thy **G**, and	430
	30: 3	the LORD thy **G** will turn thy captivity,	430
	30: 3	whither the LORD thy **G** hath scattered	430
	30: 4	from thence will the LORD thy **G** gather	430
	30: 5	the LORD thy **G** will bring thee into	430
	30: 6	the LORD thy **G** will circumcise thine	430
	30: 6	to love the LORD thy **G** with all thine	430
	30: 7	the LORD thy **G** will put all these curses	430
	30: 9	the LORD thy **G** will make thee plenteous	430
	30:10	hearken unto the voice of the LORD thy **G**,	430
	30:10	if thou turn unto the LORD thy **G** with all	430
	30:16	thee *this* day to love the LORD thy **G**,	430
	30:16	the LORD thy **G** shall bless thee in the land	430
	30:20	That thou mayest love the LORD thy **G**,	430
	31: 3	The LORD thy **G**, he will go over before	430
	31: 6	for the LORD thy **G**, he *it is* that doth go	430
	31:11	thy **G** in the place which he shall choose,	430
	31:12	fear the LORD your **G**, and observe to do	430
	31:13	and learn to fear the LORD your **G**,	430
	31:17	upon us, because our **G** *is* not amongst us?	430
	31:26	ark of the covenant of the LORD your **G**,	430
	32: 3	ascribe ye greatness unto our **G**.	430
	32: 4	a **G** of truth and without iniquity, just and	410
	32:12	and *there was* no strange **g** with him.	410
	32:15	then he forsook **G** *which* made him,	433
	32:17	They sacrificed unto devils, not *to* **G**;	433
	32:18	and hast forgotten **G** that formed thee.	410
	32:21	me to jealousy with *that which is* not **G**;	410
	32:39	*even* I, *am* he, and *there is* no **g** with me:	430
	33: 1	wherewith Moses the man of **G** blessed	430
	33:26	*There is* none like unto the **G** of Jeshurun,	410
	33:27	The eternal **G** *is thy* refuge, and underneath	430
Jos	1: 9	for the LORD thy **G** *is* with thee	430
	1:11	which the LORD your **G** giveth you to	430
	1:13	The LORD your **G** hath given you rest, and	430
	1:15	land which the LORD your **G** giveth them:	430
	1:17	only the LORD thy **G** be with thee, as he	430
	2:11	for the LORD your **G**, he *is* God in heaven	430
	2:11	he *is* **G** in heaven above, and in earth	430
	3: 3	ark of the covenant of the LORD your **G**,	430
	3: 9	and hear the words of the LORD your **G**.	430
	3:10	Hereby ye shall know that the living **G** *is*	410
	4: 5	the LORD your **G** into the midst of Jordan,	430
	4:23	For the LORD your **G** dried up the waters	430
	4:23	as the LORD your **G** did to the Red sea,	430
	4:24	that ye might fear the LORD your **G** for	430
	7: 7	**would to G** we had been content,	3863+2050.1
	7:13	for thus saith the LORD **G** of Israel,	430
	7:19	glory to the LORD **G** of Israel, and	430
	7:20	Indeed I have sinned against the LORD **G**	430
	8: 7	for the LORD your **G** will deliver it into	430
	8:30	Joshua built an altar unto the LORD **G** of	430
	9: 9	because of the name of the LORD thy **G**:	430
	9:18	sworn unto them by the LORD **G** of Israel.	430
	9:19	We have sworn unto them by the LORD **G**	430
	9:23	and drawers of water for the house of my **G**.	430
	9:24	how that the LORD thy **G** commanded his	430
	10:19	for the LORD your **G** hath delivered them	430
	10:40	as the LORD **G** of Israel commanded.	430
	10:42	the LORD **G** of Israel fought for Israel.	430
	13:14	the sacrifices of the LORD **G** of Israel	430
	13:33	the LORD **G** of Israel *was* their	430
	14: 6	unto Moses the man of **G** concerning me	430
	14: 8	I wholly followed the LORD my **G**.	430
	14: 9	hast wholly followed the LORD my **G**.	430
	14:14	that he wholly followed the LORD **G** of	430
	18: 3	which the LORD **G** of your fathers hath	430
	18: 6	lots for you here before the LORD our **G**.	430
	22: 3	of the commandment of the LORD your **G**.	430
	22: 4	now the LORD your **G** hath given rest unto	430
	22: 5	to love the LORD your **G**, and to walk in	430
	22:16	ye have committed against the **G** of Israel,	430
	22:19	altar beside the altar of the LORD our **G**.	430
	22:22	The LORD **G** of gods, the LORD God of	410
	22:22	the LORD **G** of gods, he knoweth, and	410
	22:24	What have you to do with the LORD **G** of	430
	22:29	**G forbid** that we should rebel against	2486
	22:29	besides the altar of the LORD our **G** that *is*	430
	22:33	the children of Israel blessed **G**, and did not	430
	22:34	a witness between us that the LORD *is* **G**.	430
	23: 3	ye have seen all that the LORD your **G**	430
	23: 3	for the LORD your **G** *is* he that hath fought	430
	23: 5	the LORD your **G**, he shall expel them	430
	23: 5	as the LORD your **G** hath promised unto	430
	23: 8	cleave unto the LORD your **G**, as ye have	430
	23:10	for the LORD your **G**, he *it is* that fighteth	430
	23:11	that ye love the LORD your **G**.	430
	23:13	for a certainty that the LORD your **G**	430
	23:13	which the LORD your **G** hath given you.	430
	23:14	the LORD your **G** spake concerning you;	430
	23:15	which the LORD your **G** promised you;	430
	23:15	which the LORD your **G** hath given you.	430
	23:16	the covenant of the LORD your **G**,	430
	24: 1	and they presented themselves before **G**.	430

G

Jos 24: 2 Thus saith the LORD **G** of Israel, 430
24:16 **G forbid** that we should forsake 2486
24:17 For the LORD our **G**, he *it is* that brought 430
24:18 we also serve the LORD; for he *is* our **G**. 430
24:19 for he *is* a holy **G**; he *is* a jealous God; 430
24:19 for he *is* a holy God; he *is* a jealous **G**; 410
24:23 incline your heart unto the LORD **G** of 430
24:24 The LORD our **G** will we serve, and his 430
24:26 these words in the book of the law of **G**, 430
24:27 a witness unto you, lest ye deny your **G**. 430
Jdg 1: 7 as I have done, so **G** hath requited me. 430
2:12 they forsook the LORD **G** of their fathers, 430
3: 7 forgat the LORD their **G**, and 430
3:20 I have a message from **G** unto thee. 430
4: 6 Hath not the LORD **G** of Israel 430
4:23 So **G** subdued on that day Jabin the king of 430
5: 3 I will sing *praise* to the LORD **G** of Israel. 430
5: 5 *even* that Sinai from before the LORD **G** of 430
6: 8 Thus saith the LORD **G** of Israel, 430
6:10 I said unto you, I *am* the LORD your **G**; 430
6:20 the angel of **G** said unto him, Take the flesh 430
6:26 build an altar unto the LORD thy **G** upon 430
6:31 if he *be* a **g**, let him plead for himself, 430
6:36 Gideon said unto **G**, If thou wilt save Israel 430
6:39 Gideon said unto **G**, Let not thine anger be 430
6:40 **G** did so that night: for it was dry upon 430
7:14 *for* into his hand hath **G** delivered Midian, 430
8: 3 **G** hath delivered into your hands the princes 430
8:33 after Baalim, and made Baal-berith their **g**. 430
8:34 Israel remembered not the LORD their **G**, 430
9: 7 of Shechem, that **G** may hearken unto you. 430
9: 9 wherewith by me they honour **G** and man, 430
9:13 which cheereth **G** and man, and go to be 430
9:23 **G** sent an evil spirit between Abimelech 430
9:27 went *into* the house of their **g**, and did eat 430
9:29 **would to G** this people were under 4310+5414
9:46 into a hold of the house of the **g** Berith. 410
9:56 Thus **G** rendered the wickedness of 430
9:57 all the evil of the men of Shechem did **G** 430
10:10 both because we have forsaken our **G**, and 430
11:21 And the LORD **G** of Israel delivered Sihon 430
11:23 So now the LORD **G** of Israel hath 430
11:24 Chemosh thy **g** giveth thee to possess? 430
11:24 So whomsoever the LORD our **G** shall 430
13: 5 for the child shall be a Nazarite unto **G** from 430
13: 6 A man of **G** came unto me, and 430
13: 6 *was* like the countenance of an angel of **G**, 430
13: 7 to **G** from the womb to the day of his death. 430
13: 8 let the man of **G** which thou didst send come 430
13: 9 **G** hearkened to the voice of Manoah; and 430
13: 9 the angel of **G** came again unto the woman 430
13:22 shall surely die, because we have seen **G**. 430
15:19 **G** clave a hollow place that *was* in the jaw, 430
16:17 for I *have been* a Nazarite unto **G** from my 430
16:23 to offer a great sacrifice unto Dagon their **g**, 430
16:23 Our **g** hath delivered Samson our enemy into 430
16:24 the people saw him, they praised their **g**: 430
16:24 Our **g** hath delivered into our hands our 430
16:28 I pray thee, only this once, O **G**, 430
18: 5 unto him, Ask *counsel*, we pray thee, of **G**, 430
18:10 for **G** hath given it into your hands; a place 430
18:31 all the time that the house of **G** was in 430
20: 2 in the assembly of the people of **G**, 430
20:18 went up *to* the house of **G**, and 410
20:18 of God, and asked *counsel* of **G**, and said, 430
20:26 and came *unto* the house of **G**, and wept, and 410
20:27 (for the ark of the covenant of **G** *was* there 430
20:31 *of* which one goeth up *to* the house of **G**, and 410
21: 2 And the people came *to* the house of **G**, and 410
21: 2 abode there till even before **G**, and lift up 430
21: 3 said, O LORD **G** of Israel, why is this 430
Ru 1:16 *shall be* my people, and thy **G** my God: 430
1:16 *shall be* my people, and thy God my **G**: 430
2:12 a full reward be given thee of the LORD **G** 430
1Sa 1:17 the **G** of Israel grant *thee* thy petition that 430
2: 2 neither *is there* any rock like our **G**. 430
2: 3 for the LORD *is* a **G** of knowledge, and 410
2:27 there came a man of **G** unto Eli, and 430
2:30 Wherefore the LORD **G** of Israel saith, 430
2:32 in all *the wealth* which **G** shall give Israel: NIH
3: 3 ere the lamp of **G** went out in the temple of 430
3: 3 where the ark of **G** *was*, and Samuel was 430
3:17 **G** do so to thee, and more also, if thou hide 430
4: 4 *were* there with the ark of the covenant of **G**. 430
4: 7 for they said, **G** is come into the camp. 430
4:11 the ark of **G** was taken; and the two sons of 430
4:13 for his heart trembled for the ark of **G**. 430
4:17 are dead, and the ark of **G** is taken. 430
4:18 when he made mention of the ark of **G**, 430
4:19 when she heard the tidings that the ark of **G** 430
4:21 because the ark of **G** was taken, and because 430
4:22 from Israel: for the ark of **G** is taken. 430
5: 1 the Philistines took the ark of **G**, and 430
5: 2 When the Philistines took the ark of **G**, they 430
5: 7 The ark of the **G** of Israel shall not abide 430
5: 7 hand is sore upon us, and upon Dagon our **g**. 430
5: 8 What shall we do with the ark of the **G** of 430
5: 8 Let the ark of the **G** of Israel be carried 430
5: 8 they carried the ark of the **G** of Israel about 430
5:10 Therefore they sent the ark of **G** *to* Ekron, 430
5:10 came to pass, as the ark of **G** came *to* Ekron, 430
5:10 They have brought about the ark of the **G** of 430
5:11 Send away the ark of the **G** of Israel, and 430
5:11 the city; the hand of **G** was very heavy there. 430
6: 3 If ye send away the ark of the **G** of Israel, 430
6: 5 and ye shall give glory unto the **G** of Israel: 430
6:20 is able to stand before this holy LORD **G**? 430
7: 8 Cease not to cry unto the LORD our **G** for 430
9: 6 *there is* in this city a man of **G**, and *he is* an 430
9: 7 *is* not a present to bring to the man of **G**: 430
9: 8 *that* will I give to the man of **G**, to tell us our 430
9: 9 when a man went to inquire of **G**, thus he 430
9:10 went unto the city where the man of **G** *was*. 430
9:27 a while, that I may shew thee the word of **G**. 430
10: 3 thee three men going up to **G** *to* Beth-el, 430
10: 5 After that thou shalt come to the hill of **G**, 430
10: 7 do as occasion serve thee; for **G** *is* with thee. 430
10: 9 go from Samuel, **G** gave him another heart: 430
10:10 the spirit of **G** came upon him, and 430
10:18 Thus saith the LORD **G** of Israel, I brought 430
10:19 ye have *this* day rejected your **G**, 430
10:24 people shouted, and said, **G save** the king. 2421
10:26 a band of men, whose hearts **G** had touched. 430
11: 6 the spirit of **G** came upon Saul when he 430
12: 9 when they forgat the LORD their **G**, he 430
12:12 when the LORD your **G** *was* your king. 430
12:14 you continue following the LORD your **G**: 430
12:19 Pray for thy servants unto the LORD thy **G**, 430
12:23 **G forbid** that I should sin against 2486
13:13 the commandment of the LORD thy **G**, 430
14:18 said unto Ahiah, Bring hither the ark of **G**. 430
14:18 For the ark of **G** was at that time with 430
14:36 the priest, Let us draw near hither unto **G**. 430
14:37 Saul asked *counsel* of **G**, Shall I go down 430
14:41 Therefore Saul said unto the LORD **G** of 430
14:44 And Saul answered, **G** do so and more also: 430
14:45 **G forbid**: *as* the LORD liveth, there shall 2486
14:45 for he hath wrought with **G** this day. 430
15:15 to sacrifice unto the LORD thy **G**; 430
15:21 to sacrifice unto the LORD thy **G** in Gilgal. 430
15:30 that I may worship the LORD thy **G**. 430
16:15 an evil spirit from **G** troubleth thee. 430
16:16 when the evil spirit from **G** is upon thee, 430
16:23 when the *evil* spirit from **G** was upon Saul, 430
17:26 he should defy the armies of the living **G**? 430
17:36 he hath defied the armies of the living **G**. 430
17:45 the **G** of the armies of Israel, whom thou 430
17:46 that all the earth may know that there is a **G** 430
18:10 that the evil spirit from **G** came upon Saul, 430
19:20 the spirit of **G** was upon the messengers of 430
19:23 the spirit of **G** was upon him also, and 430
20: 2 he said unto him, **G forbid**; thou shalt not 2486
20:12 said unto David, O LORD **G** of Israel, 430
22: 3 with you, till I know what **G** will do for me. 430
22:13 and a sword, and hast inquired of **G** for him, 430
22:15 Did I then begin to inquire of **G** for him? 430
23: 7 **G** hath delivered him into mine hand; 430
23:10 said David, O LORD **G** of Israel, 430
23:11 O LORD **G** of Israel, I beseech thee, 430
23:14 but **G** delivered him not into his hand. 430
23:16 the wood, and strengthened his hand in **G**. 430
25:22 more also do **G** unto the enemies of David, 430
25:29 in the bundle of life with the LORD thy **G**; 430
25:32 Blessed *be* the LORD **G** of Israel, 430
25:34 very deed, *as* the LORD **G** of Israel liveth, 430
26: 8 **G** hath delivered thine enemy into thine 430
28:15 **G** is departed from me, and answereth me no 430
29: 9 thou *art* good in my sight, as an angel of **G**: 430

1Sa 30: 6	encouraged himself in the LORD his **G**.	430
30:15	he said, Swear unto me by **G**, that thou wilt	430
2Sa 2:27	Joab said, *As* **G** liveth, unless thou hadst	430
3: 9	So do **G** to Abner, and more also, except,	430
3:35	So do **G** to me, and more also, if	430
5:10	and the LORD **G** of hosts *was* with him.	430
6: 2	to bring up from thence the ark of **G**,	430
6: 3	they set the ark of **G** upon a new cart, and	430
6: 4	*was* at Gibeah, accompanying the ark of **G**:	430
6: 6	Uzzah put forth *his hand* to the ark of **G**, and	430
6: 7	**G** smote him there for *his* error; and there he	430
6: 7	*his* error; and there he died by the ark of **G**.	430
6:12	*pertaineth* unto him, because of the ark of **G**.	430
6:12	brought up the ark of **G** from the house of	430
7: 2	but the ark of **G** dwelleth within curtains.	430
7:22	Wherefore thou art great, O LORD **G**:	136
7:22	like thee, neither *is there any* **G** beside thee,	430
7:23	whom **G** went to redeem for a people to	430
7:24	and thou, LORD, art become their **G**.	430
7:25	now, O LORD **G**, the word that thou hast	430
7:26	The LORD of hosts *is* the **G** over Israel:	430
7:27	For thou, O LORD of hosts, **G** of Israel,	430
7:28	thou *art* that **G**, and thy words be true, and	430
9: 3	that I may shew the kindness of **G** unto him?	430
10:12	for our people, and for the cities of our **G**:	430
12: 7	Thus saith the LORD **G** of Israel,	430
12:16	David therefore besought **G** for the child;	430
14:11	let the king remember the LORD thy **G**,	430
14:13	such a thing against the people of **G**?	430
14:14	up *again;* neither doth **G** respect *any* person:	430
14:16	my son together out of the inheritance of **G**.	430
14:17	for as an angel of **G**, so *is* my lord the king	430
14:17	the LORD thy **G** will be with thee.	430
14:20	according to the wisdom of an angel of **G**,	430
15:24	bearing the ark of the covenant of **G**:	430
15:24	they set down the ark of **G**; and	430
15:25	Carry back the ark of **G** *into* the city:	430
15:29	Abiathar carried the ark of **G** again *to*	430
15:32	top *of the mount,* where he worshipped **G**,	430
16:16	**G save** the king, God save the king.	2421
16:16	God save the king, **G save** the king.	2421
16:23	as if a man had inquired at the oracle of **G**:	430
18:28	and said, Blessed *be* the LORD thy **G**,	430
18:33	would **G** I had died for thee, O Absalom,	5414
19:13	**G** do so to me, and more also, if thou be not	430
19:27	but my lord the king *is* as an angel of **G**:	430
21:14	And after that **G** was intreated for the land.	430
22: 3	The **G** of my rock; in him will I trust: *he is*	430
22: 7	called upon the LORD, and cried to my **G**:	430
22:22	and have not wickedly departed from my **G**.	430
22:30	a troop: by my **G** have I leaped over a wall.	430
22:31	*As for* **G**, his way *is* perfect; the word of	410
22:32	For who *is* **G**, save the LORD? and who *is*	410
22:32	the LORD? and who *is* a rock, save our **G**?	430
22:33	**G** *is* my strength *and* power: and he maketh	410
22:47	exalted be the **G** of the rock of my salvation.	430
22:48	*It is* **G** that avengeth me, and that bringeth	410
23: 1	the anointed of the **G** of Jacob, and the sweet	430
23: 3	The **G** of Israel said, the Rock of Israel	430
23: 3	men *must be* just, ruling *in* the fear of **G**.	430
23: 5	Although my house *be* not so with **G**; yet he	410
24: 3	Now the LORD thy **G** add unto the people,	430
24:23	the king, The LORD thy **G** accept thee.	430
24:24	my **G** of that which doth cost me nothing.	430
1Ki 1:17	thou swarest by the LORD thy **G** unto thine	430
1:25	before him, and say, **G save** king Adonijah.	2421
1:30	Even as I sware unto thee by the LORD **G**	430
1:34	and say, **G save** king Solomon.	2421
1:36	the LORD **G** of my lord the king say so	430
1:39	all the people said, **G save** king Solomon.	2421
1:47	**G** make the name of Solomon better than thy	430
1:48	the king, Blessed *be* the LORD **G** of Israel,	430
2: 3	keep the charge of the LORD thy **G**,	430
2:23	**G** do so to me, and more also,	430
3: 5	and **G** said, Ask what I shall give thee.	430
3: 7	now, O LORD my **G**, thou hast made thy	430
3:11	**G** said unto him, Because thou hast asked	430
3:28	for they saw that the wisdom of **G** *was* in	430
4:29	**G** gave Solomon wisdom and	430
5: 3	**G** for the wars which were about him on	430
5: 4	now the LORD my **G** hath given me rest on	430
5: 5	a house unto the name of the LORD my **G**,	430
8:15	he said, Blessed *be* the LORD **G** of Israel,	430
8:17	for the name of the LORD **G** of Israel.	430

8:20	for the name of the LORD **G** of Israel.	430
8:23	he said, LORD **G** of Israel, *there is* no God	430
8:23	*there is* no **G** like thee, in heaven above, or	430
8:25	Therefore now, LORD **G** of Israel,	430
8:26	now, O **G** of Israel, let thy word, I pray thee,	430
8:27	will **G** indeed dwell on the earth? behold,	430
8:28	to his supplication, O LORD my **G**,	430
8:57	The LORD our **G** be with us, as he was	430
8:59	be nigh unto the LORD our **G** day and	430
8:60	of the earth may know that the LORD *is* **G**,	430
8:61	therefore be perfect with the LORD our **G**,	430
8:65	before the LORD our **G**, seven days and	430
9: 9	Because they forsook the LORD their **G**,	430
10: 9	Blessed be the LORD thy **G**,	430
10:24	his wisdom, which **G** had put in his heart.	430
11: 4	heart was not perfect with the LORD his **G**,	430
11: 9	his heart was turned from the LORD **G** of	430
11:23	**G** stirred him up *another* adversary, Rezon	430
11:31	saith the LORD, the **G** of Israel, Behold,	430
11:33	Chemosh the **g** of the Moabites, and Milcom	430
11:33	and Milcom the **g** of the children of Ammon,	430
12:22	the word of **G** came unto Shemaiah the man	430
12:22	of God came unto Shemaiah the man of **G**,	430
13: 1	there came a man of **G** out of Judah by	430
13: 4	Jeroboam heard the saying of the man of **G**,	430
13: 5	according to the sign which the man of **G**	430
13: 6	king answered and said unto the man of **G**,	430
13: 6	Intreat now the face of the LORD thy **G**,	430
13: 6	And the man of **G** besought the LORD, and	430
13: 7	the king said unto the man of **G**, Come home	430
13: 8	the man of **G** said unto the king, If thou wilt	430
13:11	told him all the works that the man of **G** had	430
13:12	sons had seen what way the man of **G** went,	430
13:14	went after the man of **G**, and found him	430
13:14	*Art* thou the man of **G** that camest from	430
13:21	he cried unto the man of **G** that came from	430
13:21	which the LORD thy **G** commanded thee,	430
13:26	It *is* the man of **G**, who was disobedient unto	430
13:29	prophet took up the carcase of the man of **G**,	430
13:31	sepulchre wherein the man of **G** *is* buried;	430
14: 7	Thus saith the LORD **G** of Israel,	430
14:13	**G** of Israel in the house of Jeroboam.	430
15: 3	heart was not perfect with the LORD his **G**,	430
15: 4	LORD his **G** give him a lamp in Jerusalem,	430
15:30	provoked the LORD **G** of Israel to anger.	430
16:13	in provoking the LORD **G** of Israel to	430
16:26	to provoke the LORD **G** of Israel to anger	430
16:33	Ahab did more to provoke the LORD **G** of	430
17: 1	*As* the LORD **G** of Israel liveth,	430
17:12	she said, *As* the LORD thy **G** liveth, I have	430
17:14	For thus saith the LORD **G** of Israel,	430
17:18	have I to do with thee, O thou man of **G**?	430
17:20	unto the LORD, and said, O LORD my **G**,	430
17:21	and said, O LORD my **G**, I pray thee,	430
17:24	Now *by* this I know that thou *art* a man of **G**,	430
18:10	*As* the LORD thy **G** liveth, there is no	430
18:21	if the LORD *be* **G**, follow him: but if Baal,	430
18:24	the **G** that answereth by fire, let him be God.	430
18:24	the God that answereth by fire, let him be **G**.	430
18:27	for he *is* a **g**; either he is talking, or he is	430
18:36	and said, LORD **G** of Abraham, Isaac, and	430
18:36	let it be known *this* day that thou *art* **G** in	430
18:37	may know that thou *art* the LORD **G**,	430
18:39	they said, The LORD, he *is* the **G**;	430
18:39	he *is* the God; the LORD, he *is* the **G**.	430
19: 8	and forty nights unto Horeb the mount of **G**.	430
19:10	I have been very jealous for the LORD **G**	430
19:14	I have been very jealous for the LORD **G**	430
20:28	there came a man of **G**, and spake unto	430
20:28	The LORD *is* **G** of the hills, but he *is* not	430
20:28	he *is* not **G** of the valleys, therefore will I	430
21:10	Thou didst blaspheme **G** and the king.	430
21:13	Naboth did blaspheme **G** and the king.	430
22:53	provoked to anger the LORD **G** of Israel,	430
2Ki 1: 2	inquire of Baal-zebub the **g** of Ekron	430
1: 3	*Is it* not because *there is* not a **G** in Israel,	430
1: 3	*that* ye go to inquire of Baal-zebub the **g** of	430
1: 6	*Is it* not because *there is* not a **G** in Israel,	430
1: 6	to inquire of Baal-zebub the **g** of Ekron?	430
1: 9	Thou man of **G**, the king hath said,	430
1:10	If I *be* a man of **G**, then let fire come down	430
1:11	he answered and said unto him, O man of **G**,	430
1:12	and said unto them, If I *be* a man of **G**,	430
1:12	the fire of **G** came down from heaven, and	430

2Ki	1:13	O man of **G**, I pray thee, let my life, and	430
	1:16	to inquire of Baal-zebub the **g** of Ekron,	430
	1:16	*there is* no **G** in Israel to inquire of his word?	430
	2:14	and said, Where *is* the LORD **G** of Elijah?	430
	4: 7	she came and told the man of **G**. And he	430
	4: 9	I perceive that this *is* a holy man of **G**,	430
	4:16	And she said, Nay, my lord, thou man of **G**,	430
	4:21	and laid him on the bed of the man of **G**, and	430
	4:22	that I may run to the man of **G**, and	430
	4:25	came unto the man of **G** to mount Carmel.	430
	4:25	to pass, when the man of **G** saw her afar off,	430
	4:27	when she came to the man of **G** to the hill,	430
	4:27	the man of **G** said, Let her alone; for her soul	430
	4:40	they cried out, and said, O thou man of **G**,	430
	4:42	brought the man of **G** bread of the firstfruits,	430
	5: 3	**Would G** my lord *were* with the prophet that	305
	5: 7	and said, *Am* I **G**, to kill and to make alive,	430
	5: 8	when Elisha the man of **G** had heard that	430
	5:11	call on the name of the LORD his **G**, and	430
	5:14	according to the saying of the man of **G**:	430
	5:15	he returned to the man of **G**, he and all his	430
	5:15	now I know that *there is* no **G** in all	430
	5:20	the servant of Elisha the man of **G**, said,	430
	6: 6	the man of **G** said, Where fell it? And he	430
	6: 9	the man of **G** sent unto the king of Israel,	430
	6:10	to the place which the man of **G** told him	430
	6:15	when the servant of the man of **G** was risen	430
	6:31	he said, **G** do so and more also to me, if	430
	7: 2	the king leaned answered the man of **G**,	430
	7:17	and he died, as the man of **G** had said,	430
	7:18	it came to pass as the man of **G** had spoken	430
	7:19	*that* lord answered the man of **G**, and said,	430
	8: 2	and did after the saying of the man of **G**:	430
	8: 4	with Gehazi the servant of the man of **G**,	430
	8: 7	saying, The man of **G** is come hither.	430
	8: 8	go, meet the man of **G**, and inquire of	430
	8:11	*he* was ashamed: and the man of **G** wept.	430
	9: 6	unto him, Thus saith the LORD **G** of Israel,	430
	10:31	of the LORD **G** of Israel with all his heart:	430
	11:12	clapt their hands, and said, **G save** the king.	2421
	13:19	the man of **G** was wroth with him, and said,	430
	14:25	according to the word of the LORD **G** of	430
	16: 2	*was* right in the sight of the LORD his **G**,	430
	17: 7	had sinned against the LORD their **G**,	430
	17: 9	*were* not right against the LORD their **G**,	430
	17:14	that did not believe in the LORD their **G**.	430
	17:16	the commandments of the LORD their **G**,	430
	17:19	the commandments of the LORD their **G**,	430
	17:26	know not the manner of the **G** of the land:	430
	17:26	they know not the manner of the **G** of	430
	17:27	let him teach them the manner of the **G** of	430
	17:39	the LORD your **G** ye shall fear; and	430
	18: 5	He trusted in the LORD **G** of Israel; so	430
	18:12	obeyed not the voice of the LORD their **G**,	430
	18:22	say unto me, We trust in the LORD our **G**:	430
	19: 4	It may be the LORD thy **G** will hear all	430
	19: 4	his master hath sent to reproach the living **G**;	430
	19: 4	words which the LORD thy **G** hath heard:	430
	19:10	Let not thy **G** in whom thou trustest deceive	430
	19:15	said, O LORD **G** of Israel, which dwellest	430
	19:15	thou *art* the **G**, *even* thou alone, of all	430
	19:16	hath sent him to reproach the living **G**.	430
	19:19	O LORD our **G**, I beseech thee,	430
	19:19	earth may know that thou *art* the LORD **G**,	430
	19:20	Thus saith the LORD **G** of Israel,	430
	19:37	worshipping *in* the house of Nisroch his **g**,	430
	20: 5	saith the LORD, the **G** of David thy father,	430
	21:12	Therefore thus saith the LORD **G** of Israel,	430
	21:22	And he forsook the LORD **G** of his fathers,	430
	22:15	Thus saith the LORD **G** of Israel,	430
	22:18	to him, Thus saith the LORD **G** of Israel,	430
	23:16	the LORD which the man of **G** proclaimed,	430
	23:17	*It is* the sepulchre of the man of **G**,	430
	23:21	Keep the passover unto the LORD your **G**,	430
1Ch	4:10	And Jabez called on the **G** of Israel, saying,	430
	4:10	And **G** granted *him that* which he requested.	430
	5:20	for they cried to **G** in the battle, and he was	430
	5:22	down many slain, because the war *was* of **G**.	430
	5:25	they transgressed against the **G** of their	430
	5:25	of the land, whom **G** destroyed before them.	430
	5:26	the **G** of Israel stirred up the spirit of Pul	430
	6:48	service of the tabernacle of the house of **G**.	430
	6:49	according to all that Moses the servant of **G**	430
	9:11	son of Ahitub, the ruler of the house of **G**;	430
	9:13	*for* the work of the service of the house of **G**.	430
	9:26	and treasuries of the house of **G**.	430
	9:27	they lodged round about the house of **G**,	430
	11: 2	the LORD thy **G** said unto thee, Thou shalt	430
	11:19	said, My **G** forbid it me, that *I* should do this	430
	12:17	the **G** of our fathers look *thereon,* and	430
	12:18	*be* to thine helpers; for thy **G** helpeth thee.	430
	12:22	until it was a great host, like the host of **G**.	430
	13: 2	and *that it be* of the LORD our **G**,	430
	13: 3	And let us bring again the ark of our **G** to us:	430
	13: 5	to bring the ark of **G** from Kirjath-jearim.	430
	13: 6	to bring up thence the ark of **G** the LORD,	430
	13: 7	they carried the ark of **G** in a new cart out of	430
	13: 8	all Israel played before **G** with all *their*	430
	13:10	hand to the ark: and there he died before **G**.	430
	13:12	And David was afraid of **G** that day, saying,	430
	13:12	How shall I bring the ark of **G** *home* to me?	430
	13:14	the ark of **G** remained with the family of	430
	14:10	David inquired of **G**, saying, Shall I go up	430
	14:11	**G** hath broken in upon mine enemies by	430
	14:14	Therefore David inquired again of **G**; and	430
	14:14	**G** said unto him, Go not up after them;	430
	14:15	for **G** is gone forth before thee to smite	430
	14:16	David therefore did as **G** commanded him:	430
	15: 1	prepared a place for the ark of **G**, and	430
	15: 2	None ought to carry the ark of **G** but	430
	15: 2	the LORD chosen to carry the ark of **G**,	430
	15:12	**G** of Israel unto *the place that* I have	430
	15:13	the LORD our **G** made a breach upon us,	430
	15:14	bring up the ark of the LORD **G** of Israel.	430
	15:15	the children of the Levites bare the ark of **G**	430
	15:24	blow with the trumpets before the ark of **G**:	430
	15:26	when **G** helped the Levites that bare the ark	430
	16: 1	So they brought the ark of **G**, and set it in	430
	16: 1	and peace offerings before **G**.	430
	16: 4	to thank and praise the LORD **G** of Israel:	430
	16: 6	before the ark of the covenant of **G**.	430
	16:14	He *is* the LORD our **G**; his judgments *are*	430
	16:35	O **G** of our salvation, and gather us together,	430
	16:36	Blessed *be* the LORD **G** of Israel for ever	430
	16:42	a sound, and with musical instruments of **G**.	430
	17: 2	all that *is* in thine heart; for **G** *is* with thee.	430
	17: 3	that the word of **G** came to Nathan, saying,	430
	17:16	*am* I, O LORD **G**, and what *is* mine house,	430
	17:17	*yet* this was a small thing *in* thine eyes, O **G**;	430
	17:17	estate of a man of high degree, O LORD **G**.	430
	17:20	like thee, neither *is there any* **G** besides thee,	430
	17:21	whom **G** went to redeem *to be* his own	430
	17:22	and thou, LORD, becamest their **G**.	430
	17:24	The LORD of hosts *is* the **G** of Israel,	430
	17:24	hosts *is* the God of Israel, *even* a **G** to Israel:	430
	17:25	For thou, O my **G**, hast told thy servant that	430
	17:26	thou *art* **G**, and hast promised this goodness	430
	19:13	for our people, and for the cities of our **G**:	430
	21: 7	**G** was displeased with this thing; therefore	430
	21: 8	David said unto **G**, I have sinned greatly,	430
	21:15	**G** sent an angel unto Jerusalem to destroy it:	430
	21:17	David said unto **G**, *Is it* not I *that*	430
	21:17	O LORD my **G**, be on me, and on my	430
	21:30	David could not go before it to inquire of **G**:	430
	22: 1	This *is* the house of the LORD **G**, and	430
	22: 2	hew wrought stones to build the house of **G**.	430
	22: 6	to build a house for the LORD **G** of Israel.	430
	22: 7	a house unto the name of the LORD my **G**:	430
	22:11	and build the house of the LORD thy **G**,	430
	22:12	mayest keep the law of the LORD thy **G**.	430
	22:18	*Is* not the LORD your **G** with you? and	430
	22:19	and your soul to seek the LORD your **G**;	430
	22:19	and build ye the sanctuary of the LORD **G**,	430
	22:19	of the LORD, and the holy vessels of **G**,	430
	23:14	Now *concerning* Moses the man of **G**,	430
	23:25	The LORD **G** of Israel hath given rest unto	430
	23:28	the work of the service of the house of **G**;	430
	24: 5	governors *of the house* of **G**, were of	430
	24:19	as the LORD **G** of Israel had commanded	430
	25: 5	of Heman the king's seer in the words of **G**,	430
	25: 5	**G** gave to Heman fourteen sons and	430
	25: 6	and harps, for the service of the house of **G**,	430
	26: 5	Peulthai the eighth: for **G** blessed him.	430
	26:20	*was* over the treasures of the house of **G**,	430
	26:32	for every matter pertaining to **G**, and	430
	28: 2	for the footstool of our **G**, and had made	430
	28: 3	**G** said unto me, Thou shalt not build a house	430
	28: 4	Howbeit the LORD **G** of Israel chose me	430

1Ch 28: 8	in the audience of our **G**, keep and seek for	430
28: 8	the commandments of the LORD your **G**:	430
28: 9	know thou the **G** of thy father, and serve him	430
28:12	of the treasuries of the house of **G**, and	430
28:20	for the LORD **G**, *even* my God, *will be*	430
28:20	LORD God, *even* my **G**, *will be* with thee;	430
28:21	*thee* for all the service of the house of **G**:	430
29: 1	whom alone **G** hath chosen, *is yet* young and	430
29: 1	palace *is* not for man, but for the LORD **G**.	430
29: 2	my **G** the gold for *things to be made of* gold,	430
29: 3	have set my affection to the house of my **G**,	430
29: 3	*which* I have given to the house of my **G**,	430
29: 7	gave for the service of the house of **G** *of*	430
29:10	LORD **G** of Israel our father, for ever and	430
29:13	our **G**, we thank thee, and praise thy glorious	430
29:16	O LORD our **G**, all this store that we have	430
29:17	I know also, my **G**, that thou triest the heart,	430
29:18	O LORD **G** of Abraham, Isaac, and	430
29:20	Now bless the LORD your **G**.	430
29:20	all the congregation blessed the LORD **G**	430
2Ch 1: 1	the LORD his **G** *was* with him, and	430
1: 3	was the tabernacle of the congregation of **G**,	430
1: 4	the ark of **G** had David brought up from	430
1: 7	In that night did **G** appear unto Solomon,	430
1: 8	Solomon said unto **G**, Thou hast shewed	430
1: 9	Now, O LORD **G**, let thy promise unto	430
1:11	**G** said to Solomon, Because this was in	430
2: 4	a house to the name of the LORD my **G**,	430
2: 4	on the solemn feasts of the LORD our **G**.	430
2: 5	*is* great: for great *is* our **G** above all gods.	430
2:12	Blessed *be* the LORD **G** of Israel,	430
3: 3	instructed for the building of the house of **G**.	430
4:11	make for king Solomon for the house of **G**;	430
4:19	all the vessels that *were for* the house of **G**,	430
5: 1	he among the treasures of the house of **G**.	430
5:14	of the LORD had filled the house of **G**.	430
6: 4	he said, Blessed *be* the LORD **G** of Israel,	430
6: 7	for the name of the LORD **G** of Israel.	430
6:10	for the name of the LORD **G** of Israel.	430
6:14	said, O LORD **G** of Israel, *there is* no God	430
6:14	*there is* no **G** like thee in the heaven, nor in	430
6:16	Now therefore, O LORD **G** of Israel,	430
6:17	Now then, O LORD **G** of Israel, let thy	430
6:18	will **G** in very deed dwell with men on	430
6:19	to his supplication, O LORD my **G**,	430
6:40	Now, my **G**, let, I beseech thee, thine eyes	430
6:41	Now therefore arise, O LORD **G**, into thy	430
6:41	let thy priests, O LORD **G**, be clothed *with*	430
6:42	O LORD **G**, turn not away the face of thine	430
7: 5	and all the people dedicated the house of **G**.	430
7:22	Because they forsook the LORD **G** of their	430
8:14	for so had David the man of **G** commanded.	430
9: 8	Blessed be the LORD thy **G**,	430
9: 8	his throne, to be king for the LORD thy **G**:	430
9: 8	because thy **G** loved Israel, to establish them	430
9:23	hear his wisdom, that **G** had put in his heart.	430
10:15	for the cause was of **G**, that the LORD	430
11: 2	the LORD came to Shemaiah the man of **G**,	430
11:16	the LORD **G** of Israel came *to* Jerusalem,	430
11:16	to sacrifice unto the LORD **G** of their	430
13: 5	Ought you not to know that the LORD **G** of	430
13:10	the LORD *is* our **G**, and we have not	430
13:11	for we keep the charge of the LORD our **G**;	430
13:12	**G** *himself is* with us for *our* captain, and	430
13:12	fight ye not against the LORD **G** of your	430
13:15	that **G** smote Jeroboam and all Israel before	430
13:16	and **G** delivered them into their hand.	430
13:18	they relied upon the LORD **G** of their	430
14: 2	and right in the eyes of the LORD his **G**:	430
14: 4	commanded Judah to seek the LORD **G** of	430
14: 7	because we have sought the LORD our **G**,	430
14:11	Asa cried unto the LORD his **G**, and said,	430
14:11	help us, O LORD our **G**; for we rest on	430
14:11	O LORD, thou *art* our **G**; let not man	430
15: 1	the spirit of **G** came upon Azariah the son of	430
15: 3	season Israel *hath been* without the true **G**,	430
15: 4	trouble did turn unto the LORD **G** of Israel,	430
15: 6	for **G** did vex them with all adversity.	430
15: 9	when they saw that the LORD his **G** *was*	430
15:12	LORD **G** of their fathers with all their heart	430
15:13	LORD **G** of Israel should be put to death,	430
15:18	he brought *into* the house of **G** *the things*	430
16: 7	not relied on the LORD thy **G**, therefore	430
17: 4	sought to the *LORD* **G** of his father, and	430
18: 5	for **G** will deliver *it* into the king's hand.	430
18:13	even what my **G** saith, that will I speak.	430
18:31	and **G** moved them *to depart* from him.	430
19: 3	and hast prepared thine heart to seek **G**.	430
19: 4	brought them back unto the LORD **G** of	430
19: 7	*there is* no iniquity with the LORD our **G**,	430
20: 6	said, O LORD **G** of our fathers, *art* not thou	430
20: 6	God of our fathers, *art* not thou **G** in heaven?	430
20: 7	*Art* not thou our **G**, who didst drive out	430
20:12	O our **G**, wilt thou not judge them? for we	430
20:19	stood up to praise the LORD **G** of Israel	430
20:20	Believe in the LORD your **G**, so shall you	430
20:29	the fear of **G** was on all the kingdoms of	430
20:30	for his **G** gave him rest round about.	430
20:33	their hearts unto the **G** of their fathers.	430
21:10	he had forsaken the LORD **G** of his fathers.	430
21:12	Thus saith the LORD **G** of David thy	430
22: 7	the destruction of Ahaziah was of **G** by	430
22:12	he was with them hid in the house of **G** six	430
23: 3	a covenant with the king in the house of **G**.	430
23: 9	king David's, which *were in* the house of **G**.	430
23:11	anointed him, and said, **G save** the king.	2421
24: 5	repair the house of your **G** from year to year,	430
24: 7	had broken up the house of **G**;	430
24: 9	of **G** laid upon Israel in the wilderness.	430
24:13	they set the house of **G** in his state, and	430
24:16	both towards **G**, and *towards* his house.	430
24:18	they left the house of the LORD **G** of their	430
24:20	the spirit of **G** came upon Zechariah the son	430
24:20	and said unto them, Thus saith **G**,	430
24:24	they had forsaken the LORD **G** of their	430
24:27	and the repairing of the house of **G**,	430
25: 7	there came a man of **G** to him, saying,	430
25: 8	**G** shall make thee fall before the enemy:	430
25: 8	for **G** hath power to help, and to cast down.	430
25: 9	Amaziah said to the man of **G**, But what	430
25: 9	the man of **G** answered, The LORD is able	430
25:16	I know that **G** hath determined to destroy	430
25:20	for it *came* of **G**, that *he* might deliver them	430
25:24	found in the house of **G** with Obed-edom,	430
26: 5	he sought **G** in the days of Zechariah,	430
26: 5	who had understanding in the visions of **G**:	430
26: 5	sought the LORD, **G** made him to prosper.	430
26: 7	**G** helped him against the Philistines, and	430
26:16	he transgressed against the LORD his **G**,	430
26:18	*it be* for thine honour from the LORD **G**.	430
27: 6	prepared his ways before the LORD his **G**.	430
28: 5	Wherefore the LORD his **G** delivered him	430
28: 6	they had forsaken the LORD **G** of their	430
28: 9	the LORD **G** of your fathers was wroth	430
28:10	with you, sins against the LORD your **G**?	430
28:24	together the vessels of the house of **G**,	430
28:24	cut in pieces the vessels of the house of **G**,	430
28:25	provoked to anger the LORD **G** of his	430
29: 5	sanctify the house of the LORD **G** of your	430
29: 6	*was* evil in the eyes of the LORD our **G**,	430
29: 7	in the holy *place* unto the **G** of Israel.	430
29:10	a covenant with the LORD **G** of Israel,	430
29:36	the people, that **G** had prepared the people:	430
30: 1	to keep the passover unto the LORD **G** of	430
30: 5	unto the LORD **G** of Israel at Jerusalem:	430
30: 6	turn again unto the LORD **G** of Abraham,	430
30: 7	which trespassed against the LORD **G** of	430
30: 8	serve the LORD your **G**, that the fierceness	430
30: 9	for the LORD your **G** *is* gracious and	430
30:12	Also in Judah the hand of **G** was to give	430
30:16	according to the law of Moses the man of **G**:	430
30:19	*That* prepareth his heart to seek **G**,	430
30:19	to seek God, the LORD **G** of his fathers,	430
30:22	making confession to the LORD **G** of their	430
31: 6	were consecrated unto the LORD their **G**,	430
31:13	and Azariah the ruler of the house of **G**.	430
31:14	*was* over the freewill offerings of **G**,	430
31:20	and right and truth before the LORD his **G**.	430
31:21	he began in the service of the house of **G**,	430
31:21	and in the commandments, to seek his **G**,	430
32: 8	with us *is* the LORD our **G** to help us, and	430
32:11	The LORD our **G** shall deliver us out of	430
32:14	that your **G** should be able to deliver you out	430
32:15	for no **g** of any nation or kingdom was able	433
32:15	how much less shall your **G** deliver you out	430
32:16	spake yet *more* against the LORD **G**,	430
32:17	He wrote also letters to rail on the LORD **G**	430
32:17	shall not the **G** of Hezekiah deliver his	430

G

1Ch	32:19	they spake against the **G** of Jerusalem,	430
	32:21	when he was come *into* the house of his **g**,	430
	32:29	for **G** had given him substance very much.	430
	32:31	**G** left him, to try him, that *he* might know	430
	33: 7	idol which he had made, in the house of **G**,	430
	33: 7	of which **G** had said to David and	430
	33:12	he besought the LORD his **G**, and	430
	33:12	humbled himself greatly before the **G** of his	430
	33:13	Manasseh knew that the LORD he *was* **G**.	430
	33:16	commanded Judah to serve the LORD **G** of	430
	33:17	*yet* unto the LORD their **G** only.	430
	33:18	his prayer unto his **G**, and the words of	430
	33:18	him in the name of the LORD **G** of Israel,	430
	33:19	*how* **G** was intreated of him, and all his sin,	NIH
	34: 3	he began to seek after the **G** of David his	430
	34: 8	to repair the house of the LORD his **G**.	430
	34: 9	money that was brought *into* the house of **G**,	430
	34:23	Thus saith the LORD **G** of Israel,	430
	34:26	Thus saith the LORD **G** of Israel	430
	34:27	and thou didst humble thyself before **G**,	430
	34:32	did according to the covenant of **G**,	430
	34:32	the covenant of God, the **G** of their fathers.	430
	34:33	to serve, *even* to serve the LORD their **G**.	430
	34:33	following the LORD, the **G** of their fathers.	430
	35: 3	serve now the LORD your **G**, and his	430
	35: 8	and Jehiel, rulers of the house of **G**,	430
	35:21	for **G** commanded me to make haste:	430
	35:21	forbear thee from meddling with **G**, who *is*	430
	35:22	the words of Necho from the mouth of **G**,	430
	36: 5	*was* evil in the sight of the LORD his **G**.	430
	36:12	*was* evil in the sight of the LORD his **G**,	430
	36:13	who had made him swear by **G**:	430
	36:13	from turning unto the LORD **G** of Israel.	430
	36:15	the LORD **G** of their fathers sent to them	430
	36:16	they mocked the messengers of **G**, and	430
	36:18	all the vessels of the house of **G**, great and	430
	36:19	they burnt the house of **G**, and brake down	430
	36:23	hath the LORD **G** of heaven given me;	430
	36:23	The LORD his **G** *be* with him, and let him	430
Ezr	1: 2	The LORD **G** of heaven hath given me all	430
	1: 3	his **G** be with him, and let him go up to	430
	1: 3	build the house of the LORD **G** of Israel,	430
	1: 3	of the LORD God of Israel, (he *is* the **G**,)	430
	1: 4	for the house of **G** that *is* in Jerusalem.	430
	1: 5	with all *them* whose spirit **G** had raised,	430
	2:68	offered freely for the house of **G** to set it up	430
	3: 2	and builded the altar of the **G** of Israel,	430
	3: 2	is written in the law of Moses the man of **G**.	430
	3: 8	coming unto the house of **G** at Jerusalem,	430
	3: 9	set forward the workmen in the house of **G**:	430
	4: 1	the temple unto the LORD **G** of Israel;	430
	4: 2	for we seek your **G**, as ye *do;* and we do	430
	4: 3	to do with us to build a house unto our **G**;	430
	4: 3	will build unto the LORD **G** of Israel,	430
	4:24	ceased the work of the house of the **G** which	426
	5: 1	and Jerusalem in the name of the **G** of Israel,	426
	5: 2	began to build the house of **G** which *is* at	426
	5: 2	with them *were* the prophets of **G** helping	426
	5: 5	the eye of their **G** was upon the elders of	426
	5: 8	to the house of the great **G**, which *is* builded	426
	5:11	We are the servants of the **G** of heaven and	426
	5:12	after that our fathers had provoked the **G** of	426
	5:13	made a decree to build this house of **G**.	426
	5:14	also of gold and silver of the house of **G**,	426
	5:15	let the house of **G** be builded in his place.	426
	5:16	laid the foundation of the house of **G** which	426
	5:17	king to build this house of **G** at Jerusalem,	426
	6: 3	*concerning* the house of **G** at Jerusalem,	426
	6: 5	and silver vessels of the house of **G**,	426
	6: 5	his place, and place *them* in the house of **G**.	426
	6: 7	Let the work of this house of **G** alone; let	426
	6: 7	the elders of the Jews build this house of **G**	426
	6: 8	Jews for the building of this house of **G**:	426
	6: 9	for the burnt offerings of the **G** of heaven,	426
	6:10	of sweet savours unto the **G** of heaven,	426
	6:12	the **G** that hath caused his name to dwell	426
	6:12	to destroy this house of **G** which *is* at	426
	6:14	to the commandment of the **G** of Israel,	426
	6:16	kept the dedication of this house of **G** with	426
	6:17	offered at the dedication of this house of **G**	426
	6:18	for the service of **G**, which *is* at Jerusalem;	426
	6:21	to seek the LORD **G** of Israel, did eat,	430
	6:22	their hands in the work of the house of **G**,	430
	6:22	work of the house of God, the **G** of Israel.	430
	7: 6	which the LORD **G** of Israel had given:	430
	7: 6	according to the hand of the LORD his **G**	430
	7: 9	according to the good hand of his **G** upon	430
	7:12	a scribe of the law of the **G** of heaven,	426
	7:14	according to the law of thy **G** which *is* in	426
	7:15	have freely offered unto the **G** of Israel,	426
	7:16	offering willingly for the house of their **G**	426
	7:17	the house of your **G** which *is* in Jerusalem.	426
	7:18	and gold, *that* do after the will of your **G**.	426
	7:19	thee for the service of the house of thy **G**,	426
	7:19	*those* deliver thou before the **G** of Jerusalem.	426
	7:20	more *shall be* needful for the house of thy **G**,	426
	7:21	the scribe of the law of the **G** of heaven,	426
	7:23	Whatsoever *is* commanded by the **G** of	426
	7:23	it be diligently done for the house of the **G**	426
	7:24	or ministers of this house of **G**,	426
	7:25	thou, Ezra, after the wisdom of thy **G**, that *is*	426
	7:25	the river, all such as know the laws of thy **G**;	426
	7:26	And whosoever will not do the law of thy **G**,	426
	7:27	Blessed *be* the LORD **G** of our fathers,	430
	7:28	the hand of the LORD my **G** *was* upon me,	430
	8:17	unto us ministers for the house of our **G**.	430
	8:18	by the good hand of our **G** upon us they	430
	8:21	that *we* might afflict ourselves before our **G**,	430
	8:22	The hand of our **G** *is* upon all them for good	430
	8:23	So we fasted and besought our **G** for this:	430
	8:25	*even* the offering of the house of our **G**,	430
	8:28	offering unto the LORD **G** of your fathers.	430
	8:30	*them* to Jerusalem unto the house of our **G**.	430
	8:31	the hand of our **G** was upon us, and	430
	8:33	the vessels weighed in the house of our **G** by	430
	8:35	offered burnt offerings unto the **G** of Israel,	430
	8:36	furthered the people, and the house of **G**.	430
	9: 4	that trembled at the words of the **G** of Israel,	430
	9: 5	spread out my hands unto the LORD my **G**,	430
	9: 6	said, O my **G**, I am ashamed and blush to lift	430
	9: 6	and blush to lift up my face to thee, my **G**:	430
	9: 8	hath been *shewed* from the LORD our **G**,	430
	9: 8	that our **G** may lighten our eyes, and give us	430
	9: 9	yet our **G** hath not forsaken us in our	430
	9: 9	to set up the house of our **G**, and to repair	430
	9:10	now, O our **G**, what shall we say after this?	430
	9:13	seeing that thou our **G** hast punished us less	430
	9:15	O LORD **G** of Israel, thou *art* righteous:	430
	10: 1	casting himself down before the house of **G**,	430
	10: 2	We have trespassed against our **G**, and	430
	10: 3	let us make a covenant with our **G** to put	430
	10: 3	that tremble at the commandment of our **G**;	430
	10: 6	Ezra rose up from before the house of **G**,	430
	10: 9	the people sat in the street of the house of **G**,	430
	10:11	make confession unto the LORD **G** of your	430
	10:14	until the fierce wrath of our **G** for this matter	430
Ne	1: 4	and prayed before the **G** of heaven,	430
	1: 5	O LORD **G** of heaven, the great and	430
	1: 5	the great and terrible **G**, that keepeth	410
	2: 4	So I prayed to the **G** of heaven.	430
	2: 8	according to the good hand of my **G** upon	430
	2:12	neither told I *any* man what my **G** had put in	430
	2:18	I told them of the hand of my **G** which was	430
	2:20	said unto them, The **G** of heaven, he will	430
	4: 4	Hear, O our **G**; for we are despised: and	430
	4: 9	we made our prayer unto our **G**,	430
	4:15	**G** had brought their counsel to nought,	430
	4:20	ye thither unto us: our **G** shall fight for us.	430
	5: 9	ought ye not to walk in the fear of our **G**	430
	5:13	So **G** shake out every man from his house,	430
	5:15	but so did not I, because of the fear of **G**.	430
	5:19	Think upon me, my **G**, for good,	430
	6: 9	Now therefore, *O* **G**, strengthen my hands.	NIH
	6:10	Let us meet together in the house of **G**,	430
	6:12	And lo, I perceived that **G** had not sent him;	430
	6:14	My **G**, think thou upon Tobiah and Sanballat	430
	6:16	that this work was wrought of our **G**.	430
	7: 2	a faithful man, and feared **G** above many.	430
	7: 5	my **G** put into mine heart to gather together	430
	8: 6	Ezra blessed the LORD, the great **G**.	430
	8: 8	So they read in the book in the law of **G**	430
	8: 9	*This* day *is* holy unto the LORD your **G**;	430
	8:16	in the courts of the house of **G**, and in	430
	8:18	last day, he read in the book of the law of **G**.	430
	9: 3	LORD their **G** *one* fourth *part* of the day;	430
	9: 3	and worshipped the LORD their **G**.	430
	9: 4	with a loud voice unto the LORD their **G**.	430
	9: 5	*and* bless the LORD your **G** for ever and	430

Ne 9: 7 Thou *art* the LORD the **G**, who didst 430
9:17 thou *art* a **G** ready to pardon, gracious and 433
9:18 This *is* thy **G** that brought thee up out of 430
9:31 for thou *art* a gracious and merciful **G**. 410
9:32 our **G**, the great, the mighty, and the terrible 430
9:32 the great, the mighty, and the terrible **G**, 410
10:28 the people of the lands unto the law of **G**, 430
10:29 which was given by Moses the servant of **G**, 430
10:32 shekel for the service of the house of our **G**; 430
10:33 and *for* all the work of the house of our **G**. 430
10:34 to bring *it* into the house of our **G**, 430
10:34 to burn upon the altar of the LORD our **G**, 430
10:36 of our flocks, to bring to the house of our **G**, 430
10:36 priests that minister in the house of our **G**: 430
10:37 to the chambers of the house of our **G**; 430
10:38 tithe of the tithes unto the house of our **G**, 430
10:39 and we will not forsake the house of our **G**. 430
11:11 of Ahitub, *was* the ruler of the house of **G**. 430
11:16 of the outward business of the house of **G**. 430
11:22 *were* over the business of the house of **G**. 430
12:24 to the commandment of David the man of **G**, 430
12:36 musical instruments of David the man of **G**, 430
12:40 *of them that gave* thanks in the house of **G**, 430
12:43 for **G** had made them rejoice *with* great joy: 430
12:45 and the porters kept the ward of their **G**, 430
12:46 songs of praise and thanksgiving unto **G**. 430
13: 1 come into the congregation of **G** for ever; 430
13: 2 howbeit our **G** turned the curse into a 430
13: 4 of the chamber of the house of our **G**, 430
13: 7 a chamber in the courts of the house of **G**. 430
13: 9 I again the vessels of the house of **G**, 430
13:11 and said, Why is the house of **G** forsaken? 430
13:14 Remember me, O my **G**, concerning this, 430
13:14 that I have done for the house of my **G**, 430
13:18 and *did not* our **G** bring all this evil upon us, 430
13:22 Remember me, O my **G**, *concerning* this 430
13:25 off their hair, and made them swear by **G**, 430
13:26 who was beloved of his **G**, and God made 430
13:26 and **G** made him king over all Israel: 430
13:27 to transgress against our **G** in marrying 430
13:29 O my **G**, because they have defiled 430
13:31 Remember me, O my **G**, for good. 430
Job 1: 1 and one that feared **G**, and eschewed evil. 430
1: 5 have sinned, and cursed **G** in their hearts. 430
1: 6 Now there was a day when the sons of **G** 430
1: 8 one that feareth **G**, and escheweth evil? 430
1: 9 and said, Doth Job fear **G** for nought? 430
1:16 The fire of **G** is fallen from heaven, and 430
1:22 this Job sinned not, nor charged **G** foolishly. 430
2: 1 Again there was a day when the sons of **G** 430
2: 3 one that feareth **G**, and escheweth evil? 430
2: 9 still retain thine integrity? curse **G**, and die. 430
2:10 shall we receive good at the hand of **G**, and 430
3: 4 let not **G** regard it from above, neither let 433
3:23 way is hid, and whom **G** hath hedged in? 433
4: 9 By the blast of **G** they perish, and by 433
4:17 Shall mortal man be more just than **G**? 433
5: 8 I would seek unto **G**, and unto God would I 410
5: 8 and unto **G** would I commit my cause: 430
5:17 happy *is* the man whom **G** correcteth: 433
6: 4 the terrors of **G** do set *themselves* in array 433
6: 8 *that* **G** would grant *me* the thing that I long 433
6: 9 Even *that* it would please **G** to destroy me: 433
8: 3 Doth **G** pervert judgment? or doth 410
8: 5 If thou wouldest seek unto **G** betimes, and 410
8:13 So *are* the paths of all that forget **G**; and 410
8:20 **G** will not cast away a perfect *man,* neither 410
9: 2 a truth: but how should man be just with **G**? 410
9:13 *If* **G** will not withdraw his anger, the proud 433
10: 2 I will say unto **G**, Do not condemn me; 433
11: 5 O that **G** would speak, and open his lips 433
11: 6 that **G** exacteth of thee *less* than thine 433
11: 7 Canst thou *by* searching find out **G**? 433
12: 4 who calleth upon **G**, and he answereth him: 433
12: 6 and they that provoke **G** are secure; 410
12: 6 into whose hand **G** bringeth *abundantly.* 433
13: 3 the Almighty, and I desire to reason with **G**. 410
13: 7 Will you speak wickedly for **G**? and 410
13: 8 ye accept his person? will ye contend for **G**? 410
15: 4 off fear, and restrainest prayer before **G**. 410
15: 8 Hast thou heard the secret of **G**? and 433
15:11 *Are* the consolations of **G** small with thee? 410
15:13 That thou turnest thy spirit against **G**, and 410
15:25 For he stretcheth out his hand against **G**, and 410
16:11 **G** hath delivered me to the ungodly, and 410
16:20 *but* mine eye poureth out *tears* unto **G**. 433
16:21 O that *one* might plead for a man with **G**, 433
18:21 this *is* the place *of him that* knoweth not **G**. 410
19: 6 Know now that **G** hath overthrown me, and 433
19:21 for the hand of **G** hath touched me. 433
19:22 Why do ye persecute me as **G**, and are not 410
19:26 this *body,* yet in my flesh shall I see **G**: 433
20:15 up again: **G** shall cast them out of his belly. 410
20:23 **G** shall cast the fury of his wrath upon him, NIH
20:29 This *is* the portion of a wicked man from **G**, 430
20:29 and the heritage appointed unto him by **G**. 410
21: 9 from fear, neither *is* the rod of **G** upon them. 433
21:14 Therefore they say unto **G**, Depart from us; 410
21:17 **G** distributeth sorrows in his anger. NIH
21:19 **G** layeth up his iniquity for his children: 433
21:22 Shall *any* teach **G** knowledge? seeing he 410
22: 2 Can a man be profitable unto **G**, as he that is 410
22:12 *Is* not **G** *in* the height of heaven? and 433
22:13 thou sayest, How doth **G** know? can he 410
22:17 Which said unto **G**, Depart from us: and 410
22:26 and shalt lift up thy face unto **G**. 433
23:16 For **G** maketh my heart soft, and 410
24:12 crieth out: yet **G** layeth not folly *to them.* 433
25: 4 How then can man be justified with **G**? or 410
27: 2 *As* **G** liveth, *who* hath taken away my 410
27: 3 *is* in me, and the spirit of **G** *is* in my nostrils; 433
27: 5 **G forbid** that I should justify you: till I die 2486
27: 8 hath gained, when **G** taketh away his soul? 433
27: 9 Will **G** hear his cry when trouble cometh 410
27:10 the Almighty? will he always call upon **G**? 433
27:11 I will teach you by the hand of **G**: *that* which 410
27:13 This *is* the portion of a wicked man with **G**, 410
27:22 For **G** shall cast upon him, and not spare: NIH
28:23 **G** understandeth the way thereof, and 430
29: 2 as *in* the days *when* **G** preserved me; 433
29: 4 when the secret of **G** *was* upon my 433
31: 2 For what portion of **G** *is there* from above? 433
31: 6 that **G** may know mine integrity. 433
31:14 What then shall I do when **G** riseth up? and 410
31:23 For destruction from **G** *was* a terror to me, 410
31:28 for I should have denied the **G** *that is* above. 410
32: 2 because he justified himself rather than **G**. 430
32:13 out wisdom: **G** thrusteth him down, not man. 410
33: 4 The Spirit of **G** hath made me, and 410
33:12 will answer thee, that **G** is greater than man. 433
33:14 For **G** speaketh once, yea twice, *yet man* 410
33:26 He shall pray unto **G**, and he will be 433
33:29 all these *things* worketh **G** oftentimes with 410
34: 5 and **G** hath taken away my judgment. 410
34: 9 that he should delight himself with **G**. 430
34:10 far be it from **G**, *that he should do* 410
34:12 Yea, surely **G** will not do wickedly, 410
34:23 that *he* should enter into judgment with **G**. 410
34:31 Surely it is *meet to be* said unto **G**, I have 410
34:37 and multiplieth his words against **G**. 410
35:10 none saith, Where *is* **G** my Maker, 433
35:13 Surely **G** will not hear vanity, neither will 410
36: 5 **G** *is* mighty, and despiseth not *any: he is* 410
36:22 Behold, **G** exalteth by his power: 410
36:26 Behold, **G** *is* great, and we know *him* not, 410
37: 5 **G** thundereth marvellously with his voice; 410
37:10 By the breath of **G** frost is given: and 410
37:14 and consider the wondrous works of **G**. 410
37:15 Dost thou know when **G** disposed them, and 433
37:22 out of the north: with **G** *is* terrible majesty. 433
38: 7 and all the sons of **G** shouted for joy? 430
38:41 when his young ones cry unto **G**, 410
39:17 Because **G** hath deprived her of wisdom, 433
40: 2 Almighty instruct *him?* he that reproveth **G**, 433
40: 9 Hast thou an arm like **G**? or, canst thou 410
40:19 He *is* the chief of the ways of **G**: he that 410
Ps 3: 2 of my soul, *There is* no help for him in **G**. 430
3: 7 Arise, O LORD; save me, O my **G**: 430
4: 1 me when I call, O **G** of my righteousness: 430
5: 2 the voice of my cry, my King, and my **G**: 430
5: 4 For thou *art* not a **G** that hath pleasure in 410
5:10 Destroy thou them, O **G**; let them fall by 430
7: 1 O LORD my **G**, in thee do I put my trust: 430
7: 3 O LORD my **G**, if I have done this; if there 430
7: 9 for the righteous **G** trieth the hearts and 430
7:10 My defence *is* of **G**, which saveth 430
7:11 **G** judgeth the righteous, and God is angry 430
7:11 and **G** is angry *with the wicked* every day. 410

G

G

Ps 9:17 into hell, *and* all the nations that forget **G**. 430
10: 4 will not seek *after* **G**: God *is* not *in* all his NIH
10: 4 will not seek *after God:* **G** *is* not *in* all his 430
10:11 He hath said in his heart, **G** hath forgotten: 410
10:12 Arise, O LORD; O **G**, lift up thine hand: 410
10:13 Wherefore doth the wicked contemn **G**? 430
13: 3 Consider *and* hear me, O LORD my **G**: 430
14: 1 fool hath said in his heart, *There is* no **G**. 430
14: 2 were *any* that did understand, *and* seek **G**. 430
14: 5 for **G** *is* in the generation of the righteous. 430
16: 1 Preserve me, O **G**: for in thee do I put my 410
16: 4 **g**: their drink offerings of blood will I not NIH
17: 6 called upon thee, for thou wilt hear me, O **G**: 410
18: 2 my **G**, my strength, in whom I will trust; 410
18: 6 upon the LORD, and cried unto my **G**: 430
18:21 and have not wickedly departed from my **G**. 430
18:28 the LORD my **G** will enlighten my 430
18:29 and by my **G** have I leaped over a wall. 430
18:30 *As for* **G**, his way *is* perfect: the word of 410
18:31 For who *is* **G** save the LORD? or who *is* a 433
18:31 the LORD? or who *is* a rock save our **G**? 430
18:32 *It is* **G** that girdeth me *with* strength, and 410
18:46 and let the **G** of my salvation be exalted. 430
18:47 *It is* **G** that avengeth me, and subdueth 410
19: 1 The heavens declare the glory of **G**; and 410
20: 1 the name of the **G** of Jacob defend thee; 430
20: 5 in the name of our **G** we will set up *our* 430
20: 7 remember the name of the LORD our **G**. 430
22: 1 My **G**, my God, why hast thou forsaken me? 410
22: 1 My God, my **G**, why hast thou forsaken me? 410
22: 2 O my **G**, I cry in the daytime, but 430
22:10 thou *art* my **G** from my mother's belly. 410
24: 5 righteousness from the **G** of his salvation. 430
25: 2 O my **G**, I trust in thee: let me not be 430
25: 5 for thou *art* the **G** of my salvation; on thee 430
25:22 Redeem Israel, O **G**, out of all his troubles. 430
27: 9 neither forsake me, O **G** of my salvation. 430
29: 3 the **G** of glory thundereth: the LORD *is* 410
30: 2 O LORD my **G**, I cried unto thee, and 430
30:12 O LORD my **G**, I will give thanks unto 430
31: 5 hast redeemed me, O LORD **G** of truth. 410
31:14 in thee, O LORD: I said, Thou *art* my **G**. 430
33:12 Blessed *is* the nation whose **G** *is* 430
35:23 *even* unto my cause, my **G** and my Lord. 430
35:24 Judge me, O LORD my **G**, according to thy 430
36: 1 *that there is* no fear of **G** before his eyes. 430
36: 7 How excellent *is* thy lovingkindness, O **G**! 430
37:31 The law of his **G** *is* in his heart; none of his 430
38:15 do I hope: thou wilt hear, O Lord my **G**. 430
38:21 O LORD: O my **G**, be not far from me. 430
40: 3 song in my mouth, *even* praise unto our **G**: 430
40: 5 Many, O LORD my **G**, *are* thy wonderful 430
40: 8 I delight to do thy will, O my **G**: yea, 430
40:17 my deliverer; make no tarrying, O my **G**. 430
41:13 Blessed *be* the LORD **G** of Israel from 430
42: 1 so panteth my soul after thee, O **G**. 430
42: 2 My soul thirsteth for **G**, for the living God: 430
42: 2 My soul thirsteth for God, for the living **G**: 410
42: 2 when shall I come and appear before **G**? 430
42: 3 continually say unto me, Where *is* thy **G**? 430
42: 4 I went with them to the house of **G**, with 430
42: 5 hope thou in **G**: for I shall yet praise him *for* 430
42: 6 O my **G**, my soul is cast down within me: 430
42: 8 *and my* prayer unto the **G** of my life. 410
42: 9 I will say unto **G** my rock, Why hast thou 410
42:10 they say daily unto me, Where *is* thy **G**? 430
42:11 hope thou in **G**: for I shall yet praise him, 430
42:11 *is* the health of my countenance, and my **G**. 430
43: 1 O **G**, and plead my cause against an ungodly 430
43: 2 For thou *art* the **G** of my strength: why dost 430
43: 4 will I go unto the altar of **G**, unto God my 430
43: 4 the altar of God, unto **G** my exceeding joy: 410
43: 4 the harp will I praise thee, O **G** my God. 430
43: 4 the harp will I praise thee, O God my **G**. 430
43: 5 hope in **G**: for I shall yet praise him, *who is* 430
43: 5 *is* the health of my countenance, and my **G**. 430
44: 1 with our ears, O **G**, our fathers have told us, 430
44: 4 Thou *art* my King, O **G**: 430
44: 8 In **G** we boast all the day long, and 430
44:20 If we have forgotten the name of our **G**, or 430
44:20 or stretched out our hands to a strange **g**; 410
44:21 Shall not **G** search this out? for he knoweth 430
45: 2 therefore **G** hath blessed thee for ever. 430
45: 6 Thy throne, O **G**, *is* for ever and ever: 430
45: 7 therefore **G**, thy God, hath anointed thee 430
45: 7 therefore God, thy **G**, hath anointed thee 430
46: 1 **G** *is* our refuge and strength, a very present 430
46: 4 whereof shall make glad the city of **G**, 430
46: 5 **G** *is* in the midst of her; she shall not be 430
46: 5 **G** shall help her, *and that* right early. 430
46: 7 hosts *is* with us; the **G** of Jacob *is* our refuge. 430
46:10 Be still, and know that I *am* **G**: I will be 430
46:11 hosts *is* with us; the **G** of Jacob *is* our refuge. 430
47: 1 shout unto **G** with the voice of triumph. 430
47: 5 **G** is gone up with a shout, the LORD with 430
47: 6 Sing *praises* to **G**, sing *praises:* sing *praises* 430
47: 7 For **G** *is* the King of all the earth: sing ye 430
47: 8 **G** reigneth over the heathen: God sitteth 430
47: 8 **G** sitteth upon the throne of his holiness. 430
47: 9 *even* the people of the **G** of Abraham: 430
47: 9 for the shields of the earth *belong* unto **G**: 430
48: 1 and greatly to be praised in the city of our **G**, 430
48: 3 **G** is known in her palaces for a refuge. 430
48: 8 of the LORD of hosts, in the city of our **G**: 430
48: 8 our God: **G** will establish it for ever. Selah. 430
48: 9 O **G**, in the midst of thy temple. 430
48:10 O **G**, so *is* thy praise unto the ends of 430
48:14 For this **G** *is* our God for ever and ever: 430
48:14 For this God *is* our **G** for ever and ever: 430
49: 7 *his* brother, nor give to **G** a ransom for him: 430
49:15 **G** will redeem my soul from the power of 430
50: 1 The mighty **G**, *even* the LORD, 430
50: 2 the perfection of beauty, **G** hath shined. 430
50: 3 Our **G** shall come, and shall not keep 430
50: 6 for **G** *is* judge himself. Selah. 430
50: 7 testify against thee: I *am* **G**, *even* thy God. 430
50: 7 testify against thee: I *am* God, *even* thy **G**. 430
50:14 Offer unto **G** thanksgiving; and pay thy 430
50:16 unto the wicked **G** saith, What hast thou to 430
50:22 Now consider this, ye that forget **G**, lest I 433
50:23 *aright* will I shew the salvation of **G**. 430
51: 1 Have mercy upon me, O **G**, according to thy 430
51:10 Create in me a clean heart, O **G**; and renew a 430
51:14 O **G**, thou God of my salvation: 430
51:14 O God, thou **G** of my salvation: 430
51:17 The sacrifices of **G** *are* a broken spirit: 430
51:17 a broken and a contrite heart, O **G**, thou wilt 430
52: 1 O mighty *man?* the goodness of **G** *endureth* 410
52: 5 **G** shall likewise destroy thee for ever, 410
52: 7 *this is* the man *that* made not **G** his strength; 430
52: 8 *am* like a green olive tree in the house of **G**: 430
52: 8 I trust in the mercy of **G** for ever and ever. 430
53: 1 fool hath said in his heart, *There is* no **G**. 430
53: 2 **G** looked down from heaven upon 430
53: 2 *any* that did understand, that did seek **G**. 430
53: 4 they eat bread: they have not called upon **G**. 430
53: 5 for **G** hath scattered the bones of him that 430
53: 5 to shame, because **G** hath despised them. 430
53: 6 When **G** bringeth back the captivity of his 430
54: 1 Save me, O **G**, by thy name, and judge me 430
54: 2 Hear my prayer, O **G**; give ear to the words 430
54: 3 they have not set **G** before them. Selah. 430
54: 4 Behold, **G** *is* mine helper: the Lord *is* with 430
55: 1 Give ear to my prayer, O **G**; and hide not 430
55:14 *and* walked unto the house of **G** in company. 430
55:16 *As for* me, I will call upon **G**; and 430
55:19 **G** shall hear, and afflict them, even he that 410
55:19 have no changes, therefore they fear not **G**. 430
55:23 thou, O **G**, shalt bring them down into the pit 430
56: 1 Be merciful unto me, O **G**: for man would 430
56: 4 In **G** I will praise his word, in God I have 430
56: 4 praise his word, in **G** I have put my trust; 430
56: 7 in *thine* anger cast down the people, O **G**. 430
56: 9 turn back: this I know; for **G** *is* for me. 430
56:10 In **G** will I praise *his* word: in the LORD 430
56:11 In **G** have I put my trust: I will not be afraid 430
56:12 Thy vows *are* upon me, O **G**: I will render 430
56:13 that *I* may walk before **G** in the light of 430
57: 1 merciful unto me, O **G**, be merciful unto me: 430
57: 2 I will cry unto **G** most High; unto God that 430
57: 2 unto **G** that performeth *all things* for me. 410
57: 3 **G** shall send forth his mercy and his truth. 430
57: 5 Be thou exalted, O **G**, above the heavens; 430
57: 7 My heart is fixed, O **G**, my heart is fixed: 430
57:11 Be thou exalted, O **G**, above the heavens: 430
58: 6 Break their teeth, O **G**, in their mouth: 430
58:11 verily he is a **G** that judgeth in the earth. 430
59: 1 Deliver me from mine enemies, O my **G**: 430

Ps 59: 5 Thou therefore, O LORD **G** *of* hosts, 430
59: 5 O LORD God *of* hosts, the **G** of Israel, 430
59: 9 will I wait upon thee: for **G** *is* my defence. 430
59:10 The **G** of my mercy shall prevent me: 430
59:10 **G** shall let me see *my desire* upon mine 430
59:13 let them know that **G** ruleth in Jacob unto 430
59:17 for **G** *is* my defence, *and* the God of my 430
59:17 God *is* my defence, *and* the **G** of my mercy. 430
60: 1 O **G**, thou hast cast us off, thou hast 430
60: 6 **G** hath spoken in his holiness; I will rejoice, 430
60:10 *Wilt* not thou, O **G**, *which* hadst cast us off? 430
60:10 *thou,* O **G**, *which* didst not go out with our 430
60:12 Through **G** we shall do valiantly: for he *it is* 430
61: 1 Hear my cry, O **G**; attend unto my prayer. 430
61: 5 For thou, O **G**, hast heard my vows: 430
61: 7 He shall abide before **G** for ever: O prepare 430
62: 1 Truly my soul waiteth upon **G**: from him 430
62: 5 My soul, wait thou only upon **G**; for my 430
62: 7 In **G** *is* my salvation and my glory: the rock 430
62: 7 rock of my strength, *and* my refuge, *is* in **G**. 430
62: 8 heart before him: **G** *is* a refuge for us. Selah. 430
62:11 **G** hath spoken once; twice have I heard this; 430
62:11 I heard this; that power *belongeth* unto **G**. 430
63: 1 O **G**, thou *art* my God; early will I seek thee: 430
63: 1 O God, thou *art* my **G**; early will I seek thee: 410
63:11 the king shall rejoice in **G**; every one that 430
64: 1 Hear my voice, O **G**, in my prayer: 430
64: 7 **G** shall shoot at them *with* an arrow; 430
64: 9 shall fear, and shall declare the work of **G**; 430
65: 1 Praise waiteth for thee, O **G**, in Zion: and 430
65: 5 wilt thou answer us, O **G** of our salvation; 430
65: 9 thou greatly enrichest it *with* the river of **G**, 430
66: 1 Make a joyful noise unto **G**, all ye lands: 430
66: 3 Say unto **G**, How terrible *art thou in* thy 430
66: 5 Come and see the works of **G**: *he is* terrible 430
66: 8 O bless our **G**, ye people, and make 430
66:10 For thou, O **G**, hast proved us: thou hast 430
66:16 all ye that fear **G**, and I will declare what he 430
66:19 *But* verily **G** hath heard *me;* he hath attended 430
66:20 Blessed *be* **G**, which hath not turned away 430
67: 1 **G** be merciful unto us, and bless us; *and* 430
67: 3 Let the people praise thee, O **G**; let all 430
67: 5 Let the people praise thee, O **G**; let all 430
67: 6 *and* **G**, *even* our own God, shall bless us. 430
67: 6 *and* God, *even* our own **G**, shall bless us. 430
67: 7 **G** shall bless us; and all the ends of the earth 430
68: 1 Let **G** arise, let his enemies be scattered: 430
68: 2 *so* let the wicked perish at the presence of **G**. 430
68: 3 righteous be glad; let them rejoice before **G**: 430
68: 4 Sing unto **G**, sing *praises to* his name: 430
68: 5 of the widows, *is* **G** in his holy habitation. 430
68: 6 **G** setteth the solitary in families: he bringeth 430
68: 7 O **G**, when thou wentest forth before thy 430
68: 8 heavens also dropped at the presence of **G**: 430
68: 8 Sinai itself *was moved* at the presence of **G**, 430
68: 8 at the presence of God, the **G** of Israel. 430
68: 9 Thou, O **G**, didst send a plentiful rain, 430
68:10 thou, O **G**, hast prepared of thy goodness for 430
68:15 The hill of **G** *is as* the hill of Bashan; a high 430
68:16 *this is* the hill *which* **G** desireth to dwell in; 430
68:17 The chariots of **G** *are* twenty thousand, 430
68:18 that the LORD **G** might dwell *among* 430
68:19 us *with benefits, even* the **G** of our salvation. 410
68:20 *He that is* our **G** *is* the God of salvation; and 410
68:20 *He that is* our God *is* the **G** of salvation; and 410
68:21 **G** shall wound the head of his enemies, *and* 430
68:24 They have seen thy goings, O **G**; *even* 430
68:24 *even* the goings of my **G**, my King, in 410
68:26 Bless ye **G** in the congregations, *even* 430
68:28 Thy **G** hath commanded thy strength: 430
68:28 strengthen, O **G**, that which thou hast 430
68:31 shall soon stretch out her hands unto **G**. 430
68:32 Sing unto **G**, ye kingdoms of the earth; 430
68:34 Ascribe ye strength unto **G**: his excellency *is* 430
68:35 O **G**, *thou art* terrible out of thy holy places: 430
68:35 the **G** of Israel *is* he that giveth strength and 410
68:35 and power unto *his* people. Blessed *be* **G**. 430
69: 1 Save me, O **G**; for the waters are come in 430
69: 3 mine eyes fail while *I* wait for my **G**. 430
69: 5 O **G**, thou knowest my foolishness; and 430
69: 6 be confounded for my sake, O **G** of Israel. 430
69:13 O **G**, in the multitude of thy mercy hear me, 430
69:29 let thy salvation, O **G**, set me up on high. 430
69:30 I will praise the name of **G** with a song; and 430
69:32 and your heart shall live that seek **G**. 430
69:35 For **G** will save Zion, and will build 430
70: 1 *Make haste,* O **G**, to deliver me; make haste 430
70: 4 say continually, Let **G** be magnified. 430
70: 5 make haste unto me, O **G**: thou *art* my help 430
71: 4 Deliver me, O my **G**, out of the hand of 430
71:11 Saying, **G** hath forsaken him: persecute and 430
71:12 O **G**, be not far from me: O my God, 430
71:12 from me: O my **G**, make haste for my help. 430
71:17 O **G**, thou hast taught me from my youth: 430
71:18 also when I am old and grayheaded, O **G**, 430
71:19 Thy righteousness also, O **G**, *is* very high, 430
71:19 very high, who hast done great *things:* O **G**, 430
71:22 with the psaltery, *even* thy truth, O my **G**: 430
72: 1 O **G**, and thy righteousness unto the king's 430
72:18 Blessed *be* the LORD **G**, the God of Israel, 430
72:18 Blessed *be* the LORD God, the **G** of Israel, 430
73: 1 Truly **G** *is* good to Israel, *even* to such as are 430
73:11 they say, How doth **G** know? and is there 410
73:17 Until I went into the sanctuary of **G**; *then* 410
73:26 *but* **G** *is* the strength of my heart, and 430
73:28 *it is* good for me to draw near to **G**: I have 430
74: 1 O **G**, why hast thou cast *us* off for ever? 430
74: 8 they have burnt up all the synagogues of **G** 410
74:10 O **G**, how long shall the adversary reproach? 430
74:12 For **G** *is* my King of old, working salvation 430
74:22 Arise, O **G**, plead thine own cause: 430
75: 1 Unto thee, O **G**, do we give thanks, 430
75: 7 But **G** *is* the judge: he putteth down one, and 430
75: 9 I will sing *praises* to the **G** of Jacob. 430
76: 1 In Judah *is* **G** known: his name *is* great in 430
76: 6 At thy rebuke, O **G** of Jacob, both 430
76: 9 When **G** arose to judgment, to save all 430
76:11 Vow, and pay unto the LORD your **G**: 430
77: 1 I cried unto **G** *with* my voice, *even* unto God 430
77: 1 *with* my voice, *even* unto **G** *with* my voice; 430
77: 3 I remembered **G**, and was troubled: 430
77: 9 Hath **G** forgotten to be gracious? hath he in 410
77:13 Thy way, O **G**, *is* in the sanctuary: who *is so* 430
77:13 who *is so* great a **G** as *our* God? 410
77:13 who *is so* great a God as *our* **G**? 430
77:14 Thou *art* the **G** that doest wonders: thou hast 410
77:16 waters saw thee, O **G**, the waters saw thee; 430
78: 7 That they might set their hope in **G**, and 430
78: 7 not forget the works of **G**, but keep his 410
78: 8 and whose spirit was not stedfast with **G**. 410
78:10 They kept not the covenant of **G**, and 430
78:18 they tempted **G** in their heart by asking meat 410
78:19 Yea, they spake against **G**; they said, Can 430
78:19 Can **G** furnish a table in the wilderness? 410
78:22 Because they believed not in **G**, and 430
78:31 The wrath of **G** came upon them, and 430
78:34 and they returned and inquired early after **G**. 410
78:35 And they remembered that **G** *was* their rock, 430
78:35 their rock, and the high **G** their redeemer. 410
78:41 they turned *back* and tempted **G**, and 410
78:56 they tempted and provoked the most high **G**, 430
78:59 When **G** heard *this,* he was wroth, and 430
79: 1 O **G**, the heathen are come into thine 430
79: 9 Help us, O **G** of our salvation, for the glory 430
79:10 should the heathen say, Where *is* their **G**? 430
80: 3 us again, O **G**, and cause thy face to shine; 430
80: 4 O LORD **G** *of* hosts, how long wilt thou be 430
80: 7 O **G** *of* hosts, and cause thy face to shine; 430
80:14 Return, we beseech thee, O **G** *of* hosts: 430
80:19 Turn us again, O LORD **G** *of* hosts, 430
81: 1 Sing aloud unto **G** our strength: make a 430
81: 1 make a joyful noise unto the **G** of Jacob. 430
81: 4 for Israel, *and* a law of the **G** of Jacob. 430
81: 9 There shall no strange **g** be in thee; 410
81: 9 neither shall thou worship *any* strange **g**. 410
81:10 I *am* the LORD thy **G**, which brought thee 430
82: 1 **G** standeth in the congregation of 430
82: 8 Arise, O **G**, judge the earth: for thou shalt 430
83: 1 Keep not thou silence, O **G**: hold not thy 430
83: 1 hold not thy peace, and be not still, O **G**. 410
83:12 Let us take to ourselves the houses of **G** in 430
83:13 O my **G**, make them like a wheel; as 430
84: 2 and my flesh crieth out for the living **G**. 410
84: 3 O LORD of hosts, my King, and my **G**. 430
84: 7 *one of them* in Zion appeareth before **G**. 430
84: 8 O LORD **G** *of* hosts, hear my prayer: 430
84: 8 my prayer: give ear, O **G** of Jacob. Selah. 430
84: 9 O **G** our shield, and look upon the face of 430

Ps	84:10	rather be a doorkeeper in the house of my **G**,	430
	84:11	For the LORD **G** *is* a sun and shield:	430
	85: 4	O **G** of our salvation, and cause thine anger	430
	85: 8	I will hear what **G** the LORD will speak:	410
	86: 2	O thou my **G**, save thy servant that trusteth	430
	86:10	and doest wondrous *things:* thou *art* **G** alone.	430
	86:12	I will praise thee, O Lord my **G**, with all my	430
	86:14	O **G**, the proud are risen against me, and	430
	86:15	*art* a **G** full of compassion, and gracious,	410
	87: 3	*things* are spoken of thee, O city of **G**.	430
	88: 1	O LORD **G** of my salvation, I have cried	430
	89: 7	**G** *is* greatly to be feared in the assembly of	410
	89: 8	O LORD **G** of hosts, who *is* a strong	430
	89:26	my **G**, and the rock of my salvation.	410
	90: T	A Prayer of Moses the man of **G**.	430
	90: 2	from everlasting to everlasting, thou *art* **G**.	410
	90:17	let the beauty of the LORD our **G** be upon	430
	91: 2	and my fortress: my **G**; in him will I trust.	430
	92:13	LORD shall flourish in the courts of our **G**.	430
	94: 1	O LORD **G**, to whom vengeance	410
	94: 1	O **G**, to whom vengeance belongeth,	410
	94: 7	neither shall the **G** of Jacob regard *it.*	430
	94:22	and my **G** *is* the rock of my refuge.	430
	94:23	*yea,* the LORD our **G** shall cut them off.	430
	95: 3	For the LORD *is* a great **G**, and a great	410
	95: 7	For he *is* our **G**; and we *are* the people of his	430
	98: 3	of the earth have seen the salvation of our **G**.	430
	99: 5	Exalt ye the LORD our **G**, and worship at	430
	99: 8	Thou answeredst them, O LORD our **G**:	430
	99: 8	thou wast a **G** that forgavest them,	410
	99: 9	Exalt the LORD our **G**, and worship at his	430
	99: 9	his holy hill; for the LORD our **G** *is* holy.	430
	100: 3	Know ye that the LORD he *is* **G**: *it is* he	430
	102:24	I said, O my **G**, take me not away in	410
	104: 1	O LORD my **G**, thou art very great;	430
	104:21	after *their* prey, and seek their meat from **G**.	410
	104:33	I will sing *praise* to my **G** while I have my	430
	105: 7	He *is* the LORD our **G**: his judgments *are*	430
	106:14	the wilderness, and tempted **G** in the desert.	410
	106:21	They forgat **G** their saviour, which had done	410
	106:47	O LORD our **G**, and gather us from among	430
	106:48	Blessed *be* the LORD **G** of Israel from	430
	107:11	they rebelled against the words of **G**,	410
	108: 1	O **G**, my heart is fixed; I will sing and	430
	108: 5	Be thou exalted, O **G**, above the heavens:	430
	108: 7	**G** hath spoken in his holiness; I will rejoice,	430
	108:11	*Wilt* not *thou,* O **G**, *who* hast cast us off?	430
	108:11	wilt not thou, O **G**, go forth with our hosts?	430
	108:13	Through **G** we shall do valiantly: for he *it is*	430
	109: 1	Hold not thy peace, O **G** of my praise;	430
	109:26	Help me, O LORD my **G**: O save me	430
	113: 5	Who *is* like unto the LORD our **G**, who	430
	114: 7	the Lord, at the presence of the **G** of Jacob;	433
	115: 2	the heathen say, Where *is* now their **G**?	430
	115: 3	our **G** *is* in the heavens: he hath done	430
	116: 5	and righteous; yea, our **G** *is* merciful.	430
	118:27	**G** *is* the LORD, which hath shewed us	410
	118:28	Thou *art* my **G**, and I will praise thee:	410
	118:28	praise thee: *thou art* my **G**, I will exalt thee.	430
	119:115	for I will keep the commandments of my **G**.	430
	122: 9	Because of the house of the LORD our **G** I	430
	123: 2	so our eyes *wait* upon the LORD our **G**,	430
	132: 2	*and* vowed unto the mighty **G** of Jacob;	NIH
	132: 5	a habitation for the mighty **G** of Jacob.	NIH
	135: 2	in the courts of the house of our **G**,	430
	136: 2	O give thanks unto the **G** of gods: for his	430
	136:26	O give thanks unto the **G** of heaven: for his	410
	139:17	precious also are thy thoughts unto me, O **G**:	410
	139:19	Surely thou wilt slay the wicked, O **G**:	433
	139:23	Search me, O **G**, and know my heart: try me,	410
	140: 6	I said unto the LORD, Thou *art* my **G**:	410
	143:10	Teach me to do thy will; for thou *art* my **G**:	430
	144: 9	I will sing a new song unto thee, O **G**:	430
	144:15	*is that* people, whose **G** *is* the LORD.	430
	145: 1	I will extol thee, my **G**, O king; and I will	430
	146: 2	I will sing *praises* unto my **G** while I have	430
	146: 5	Happy *is he* that *hath* the **G** of Jacob for his	410
	146: 5	his help, whose hope *is* in the LORD his **G**:	430
	146:10	*even* thy **G**, O Zion, unto all generations.	430
	147: 1	for *it is* good to sing *praises* unto our **G**;	430
	147: 7	sing *praise* upon the harp unto our **G**:	430
	147:12	O Jerusalem; praise thy **G**, O Zion.	430
	149: 6	*Let* the high *praises* of **G** *be* in their mouth,	410
	150: 1	Praise **G** in his sanctuary: praise him in	410
Pr	2: 5	of the LORD, and find the knowledge of **G**.	430
	2:17	and forgetteth the covenant of her **G**.	430
	3: 4	good understanding in the sight of **G** and	430
	21:12	**G** overthroweth the wicked for *their*	NIH
	25: 2	*It is* the glory of **G** to conceal a thing: but	430
	26:10	The great **G** that formed all *things* both	NIH
	30: 5	Every word of **G** *is* pure: he *is* a shield unto	433
	30: 9	steal, and take the name of my **G** *in vain.*	430
Ecc	1:13	this sore travail hath **G** given to the sons of	430
	2:24	also I saw, that it *was* from the hand of **G**.	430
	2:26	For **G** giveth to a man that *is* good in his	NIH
	2:26	*he* may give to *him that is* good before **G**.	430
	3:10	which **G** hath given to the sons of men to be	430
	3:11	that no man can find out the work that **G**	430
	3:13	the good of all his labour, it *is* the gift of **G**.	430
	3:14	I know that, whatsoever **G** doeth, it shall be	430
	3:14	**G** doeth *it,* that *men* should fear before him.	430
	3:15	and **G** requireth that which is past.	430
	3:17	**G** shall judge the righteous and the wicked:	430
	3:18	that **G** might manifest them, and that *they*	430
	5: 1	thy foot when thou goest to the house of **G**,	430
	5: 2	heart be hasty to utter *any* thing before **G**:	430
	5: 2	for **G** *is* in heaven, and thou upon earth:	430
	5: 4	When thou vowest a vow unto **G**, defer not	430
	5: 6	wherefore should **G** be angry at thy voice,	430
	5: 7	*are* also *divers* vanities: but fear thou **G**.	430
	5:18	all the days of his life, which **G** giveth him:	430
	5:19	Every man also to whom **G** hath given	430
	5:19	to rejoice in his labour; this *is* the gift of **G**.	430
	5:20	**G** answereth *him* in the joy of his heart.	430
	6: 2	A man to whom **G** hath given riches, wealth,	430
	6: 2	yet **G** giveth him not power to eat thereof,	430
	7:13	Consider the work of **G**: for who can make	430
	7:14	**G** also hath set the one over against	430
	7:18	for he that feareth **G** shall come forth of	430
	7:26	whoso pleaseth **G** shall escape from her; but	430
	7:29	have I found, that **G** hath made man upright;	430
	8: 2	and *that* in regard of the oath of **G**.	430
	8:12	that it shall be well with them that fear **G**,	430
	8:13	a shadow; because he feareth not before **G**.	430
	8:15	his life, which **G** giveth him under the sun.	430
	8:17	I beheld all the work of **G**, that a man cannot	430
	9: 1	and their works, *are* in the hand of **G**:	430
	9: 7	merry heart; for **G** now accepteth thy works.	430
Ecc	11: 5	thou knowest not the works of **G** who	430
	11: 9	that for all these *things* **G** will bring thee into	430
	12: 7	the spirit shall return unto **G** who gave it.	430
	12:13	Fear **G**, and keep his commandments:	430
	12:14	For **G** shall bring every work into judgment,	430
Isa	1:10	give ear unto the law of our **G**, ye people of	430
	2: 3	the LORD, to the house of the **G** of Jacob;	430
	5:16	**G** that is holy shall be sanctified in	410
	7:11	Ask thee a sign of the LORD thy **G**; ask it	430
	7:13	to weary men, but will ye weary my **G** also?	430
	8:10	and it shall not stand: for **G** *is* with us.	410
	8:19	should not a people seek unto their **G**?	430
	8:21	curse their king and their **G**, and	430
	9: 6	Counseller, The mighty **G**, The everlasting	410
	10:21	the remnant of Jacob, unto the mighty **G**.	410
	12: 2	Behold, **G** *is* my salvation; I will trust, and	410
	13:19	shall be as when **G** overthrew Sodom and	430
	14:13	I will exalt my throne above the stars of **G**:	410
	17: 6	saith the LORD **G** of Israel.	430
	17:10	Because thou hast forgotten the **G** of thy	430
	17:13	**G** shall rebuke them, and they shall flee far	NIH
	21:10	the **G** of Israel, have I declared unto you.	430
	21:17	for the LORD **G** of Israel hath spoken *it.*	430
	24:15	*even* the name of the LORD **G** of Israel in	430
	25: 1	O LORD, thou *art* my **G**; I will exalt thee,	430
	25: 9	it shall be said in that day, Lo, this *is* our **G**;	430
	26: 1	salvation will **G** appoint *for* walls and	NIH
	26:13	O LORD our **G**, *other* lords besides thee	430
	28:26	For his **G** doth instruct him to discretion, *and*	430
	29:23	One of Jacob, and shall fear the **G** of Israel.	430
	30:18	for the LORD *is* a **G** of judgment:	430
	31: 3	Now the Egyptians *are* men, and not **G**; and	410
	35: 2	of the LORD, *and* the excellency of our **G**.	430
	35: 4	behold, your **G** will come *with* vengeance,	430
	35: 4	*with* vengeance, *even* **G** *with* a recompence;	430
	36: 7	say to me, We trust in the LORD our **G**:	430
	37: 4	It may be the LORD thy **G** will hear	430
	37: 4	his master hath sent to reproach the living **G**,	430
	37: 4	words which the LORD thy **G** hath heard:	430
	37:10	saying, Let not thy **G**, in whom thou trustest,	430

Isa	37:16	O LORD of hosts, **G** of Israel, that dwellest	430
	37:16	thou *art* the **G**, *even* thou alone, of all	430
	37:17	which hath sent to reproach the living **G**.	430
	37:20	Now therefore, O LORD our **G**, save us	430
	37:21	Thus saith the LORD **G** of Israel,	430
	37:38	worshipping *in* the house of Nisroch his **g**,	430
	38: 5	saith the LORD, the **G** of David thy father,	430
	40: 1	comfort ye my people, saith your **G**.	430
	40: 3	straight in the desert a highway for our **G**.	430
	40: 8	but the word of our **G** shall stand for ever.	430
	40: 9	say unto the cities of Judah, Behold your **G**.	430
	40:18	To whom then will ye liken **G**? or	410
	40:27	and my judgment is passed over from my **G**?	430
	40:28	*that* the everlasting **G**, the LORD,	430
	41:10	be not dismayed; for I *am* thy **G**: I will	430
	41:13	For I the LORD thy **G** will hold thy right	430
	41:17	*I* the **G** of Israel will not forsake them.	430
	42: 5	Thus saith **G** the LORD, he that created	410
	43: 3	For I *am* the LORD thy **G**, the Holy One of	430
	43:10	before me there was no **G** formed,	410
	43:12	when *there was* no strange **g** among you:	NIH
	43:12	my witnesses, saith the LORD, that I *am* **G**.	410
	44: 6	I *am* the last; and besides me *there is* no **G**.	430
	44: 8	Is there a **G** besides me? yea, *there is* no	433
	44: 8	yea, *there is* no **G**; I know not *any*.	6697
	44:10	Who hath formed a **g**, or molten a graven	410
	44:15	he maketh a **g**, and worshippeth *it;* he	410
	44:17	the residue thereof he maketh a **g**, *even* his	410
	44:17	and saith, Deliver me; for thou *art* my **g**.	410
	45: 3	call *thee* by thy name, *am* the **G** of Israel.	430
	45: 5	*there is* none else, *there is* no **G** besides me:	430
	45:14	unto thee, *saying,* Surely **G** *is* in thee;	410
	45:14	in thee; and *there is* none else, *there is* no **G**.	430
	45:15	Verily thou *art* a **G** that hidest thyself,	410
	45:15	that hidest thyself, O **G** of Israel, the saviour.	430
	45:18	**G** himself that formed the earth and made it;	430
	45:20	and pray unto a **g** *that* cannot save.	410
	45:21	and *there is* no **G** else beside me; a just God	430
	45:21	a just **G** and a saviour; *there is* none beside	410
	45:22	the earth: for I *am* **G**, and *there is* none else.	410
	46: 6	*and* hire a goldsmith; and he maketh it a **g**:	410
	46: 9	for I *am* **G**, and *there is* none else; *I am* God,	410
	46: 9	none else; *I am* **G**, and *there is* none like me,	430
	48: 1	make mention of the **G** of Israel, *but* not in	430
	48: 2	and stay themselves upon the **G** of Israel;	430
	48:17	*I am* the LORD thy **G** which teacheth thee	430
	49: 4	with the LORD, and my work with my **G**.	430
	49: 5	the LORD, and my **G** shall be my strength.	430
	50:10	name of the LORD, and stay upon his **G**.	430
	51:15	*I am* the LORD thy **G**, that divided the sea,	430
	51:20	the fury of the LORD, the rebuke of thy **G**.	430
	51:22	thy **G** *that* pleadeth the cause of his people,	430
	52: 7	that saith unto Zion, Thy **G** reigneth!	430
	52:10	of the earth shall see the salvation of our **G**.	430
	52:12	and the **G** of Israel *will be* your rereward.	430
	53: 4	him stricken, smitten of **G**, and afflicted.	430
	54: 5	The **G** of the whole earth shall he be called.	430
	54: 6	when thou wast refused, saith thy **G**.	430
	55: 5	run unto thee because of the LORD thy **G**,	430
	55: 7	and to our **G**, for he will abundantly pardon.	430
	57:21	*is* no peace, saith my **G**, to the wicked.	430
	58: 2	and forsook not the ordinance of their **G**:	430
	58: 2	they take delight in approaching to **G**.	430
	59: 2	have separated between you and your **G**,	430
	59:13	departing away from our **G**,	430
	60: 9	unto the name of the LORD thy **G**, and	430
	60:19	an everlasting light, and thy **G** thy glory.	430
	61: 2	and the day of vengeance of our **G**;	430
	61: 6	*men* shall call you the Ministers of our **G**:	430
	61:10	my soul shall be joyful in my **G**;	430
	62: 3	and a royal diadem in the hand of thy **G**.	430
	62: 5	the bride, *so* shall thy **G** rejoice over thee.	430
	64: 4	neither hath the eye seen, O **G**, besides thee,	430
	65:16	earth shall bless himself in the **G** of truth;	430
	65:16	in the earth shall swear by the **G** of truth;	430
	66: 9	bring forth, and shut *the womb?* saith thy **G**.	430
Jer	2:17	in that thou hast forsaken the LORD thy **G**,	430
	2:19	that thou hast forsaken the LORD thy **G**,	430
	3:13	hast transgressed against the LORD thy **G**,	430
	3:21	*and* they have forgotten the LORD their **G**.	430
	3:22	unto thee; for thou *art* the LORD our **G**.	430
	3:23	truly in the LORD our **G** *is* the salvation of	430
	3:25	we have sinned against the LORD our **G**,	430
	3:25	not obeyed the voice of the LORD our **G**.	430
	5: 4	of the LORD, *nor* the judgment of their **G**.	430
	5: 5	of the LORD, *and* the judgment of their **G**:	430
	5:14	Wherefore thus saith the LORD **G** of hosts,	430
	5:19	Wherefore doth the LORD our **G** all these	430
	5:24	Let us now fear the LORD our **G**,	430
	7: 3	the **G** of Israel, Amend your ways and	430
	7:21	saith the LORD of hosts, the **G** of Israel;	430
	7:23	I will be your **G**, and ye shall be my people:	430
	7:28	obeyeth not the voice of the LORD their **G**,	430
	8:14	for the LORD our **G** hath put us to silence,	430
	9:15	saith the LORD of hosts, the **G** of Israel;	430
	10:10	the LORD *is* the true **G**, he *is* the living	430
	10:10	he *is* the living **G**, and an everlasting king:	430
	11: 3	Thus saith the LORD **G** of Israel;	430
	11: 4	shall ye be my people, and I will be your **G**:	430
	13:12	Thus saith the LORD **G** of Israel,	430
	13:16	Give glory to the LORD your **G**, before he	430
	14:22	*art* not thou he, O LORD our **G**? therefore	430
	15:16	called by thy name, O LORD **G** of hosts.	430
	16: 9	saith the LORD of hosts, the **G** of Israel;	430
	16:10	have committed against the LORD our **G**?	430
	19: 3	saith the LORD of hosts, the **G** of Israel;	430
	19:15	saith the LORD of hosts, the **G** of Israel;	430
	21: 4	Thus saith the LORD **G** of Israel; Behold,	430
	22: 9	the covenant of the LORD their **G**,	430
	23: 2	Therefore thus saith the LORD **G** of Israel	430
	23:23	*Am* I a **G** at hand, saith the LORD, and	430
	23:23	saith the LORD, and not a **G** afar off?	430
	23:36	ye have perverted the words of the living **G**,	430
	23:36	living God, of the LORD of hosts our **G**.	430
	24: 5	Thus saith the LORD, the **G** of Israel;	430
	24: 7	shall be my people, and I will be their **G**:	430
	25:15	For thus saith the LORD **G** of Israel unto	430
	25:27	saith the LORD of hosts, the **G** of Israel;	430
	26:13	and obey the voice of the LORD your **G**;	430
	26:16	to us in the name of the LORD our **G**.	430
	27: 4	saith the LORD of hosts, the **G** of Israel;	430
	27:21	saith the LORD of hosts, the **G** of Israel,	430
	28: 2	the LORD of hosts, the **G** of Israel, saying,	430
	28:14	saith the LORD of hosts, the **G** of Israel;	430
	29: 4	saith the LORD of hosts, the **G** of Israel,	430
	29: 8	saith the LORD of hosts, the **G** of Israel;	430
	29:21	the **G** of Israel, of Ahab the son of Kolaiah,	430
	29:25	the LORD of hosts, the **G** of Israel, saying,	430
	30: 2	Thus speaketh the LORD **G** of Israel,	430
	30: 9	But they shall serve the LORD their **G**, and	430
	30:22	ye shall be my people, and I will be your **G**.	430
	31: 1	will I be the **G** of all the families of Israel,	430
	31: 6	let us go up *to* Zion unto the LORD our **G**.	430
	31:18	be turned; for thou *art* the LORD my **G**.	430
	31:23	saith the LORD of hosts, the **G** of Israel;	430
	31:33	will be their **G**, and they shall be my people.	430
	32:14	saith the LORD of hosts, the **G** of Israel;	430
	32:15	saith the LORD of hosts, the **G** of Israel;	430
	32:18	the Great, the Mighty **G**, the LORD of	410
	32:27	Behold, I *am* the LORD, the **G** of all flesh:	430
	32:36	the **G** of Israel, concerning this city,	430
	32:38	shall be my people, and I will be their **G**:	430
	33: 4	For thus saith the LORD, the **G** of Israel,	430
	34: 2	Thus saith the LORD, the **G** of Israel; Go	430
	34:13	Thus saith the LORD, the **G** of Israel;	430
	35: 4	of Hanan, the son of Igdaliah, a man of **G**,	430
	35:13	saith the LORD of hosts, the **G** of Israel;	430
	35:17	Therefore thus saith the LORD **G** of hosts,	430
	35:17	the LORD God of hosts, the **G** of Israel;	430
	35:18	saith the LORD of hosts, the **G** of Israel;	430
	35:19	saith the LORD of hosts, the **G** of Israel;	430
	37: 3	Pray now unto the LORD our **G** for us.	430
	37: 7	Thus saith the LORD, the **G** of Israel;	430
	38:17	the **G** of hosts, the God of Israel;	430
	38:17	the God of hosts, the **G** of Israel;	430
	39:16	saith the LORD of hosts, the **G** of Israel;	430
	40: 2	The LORD thy **G** hath pronounced this evil	430
	42: 2	pray for us unto the LORD thy **G**, *even* for	430
	42: 3	That the LORD thy **G** may shew us	430
	42: 4	I *will* pray unto the LORD your **G**	430
	42: 5	the LORD thy **G** shall send thee to us.	430
	42: 6	we will obey the voice of the LORD our **G**,	430
	42: 6	we obey the voice of the LORD our **G**.	430
	42: 9	Thus saith the LORD, the **G** of Israel,	430
	42:13	obey the voice of the LORD your **G**,	430
	42:15	saith the LORD of hosts, the **G** of Israel;	430
	42:18	saith the LORD of hosts, the **G** of Israel;	430
	42:20	when ye sent me unto the LORD your **G**,	430

Jer	42:20	Pray for us unto the LORD our **G**;	430
	42:20	according unto all that the LORD our **G**	430
	42:21	not obeyed the voice of the LORD your **G**,	430
	43: 1	people all the words of the LORD their **G**,	430
	43: 1	*for* which the LORD their **G** had sent him	430
	43: 2	the LORD our **G** hath not sent thee to say,	430
	43:10	saith the LORD of hosts, the **G** of Israel;	430
	44: 2	saith the LORD of hosts, the **G** of Israel;	430
	44: 7	the **G** of hosts, the God of Israel;	430
	44: 7	the God of hosts, the **G** of Israel;	430
	44:11	saith the LORD of hosts, the **G** of Israel;	430
	44:25	the LORD of hosts, the **G** of Israel, saying;	430
	45: 2	the **G** of Israel, unto thee, O Baruch;	430
	46:25	The LORD of hosts, the **G** of Israel, saith;	430
	48: 1	saith the LORD of hosts, the **G** of Israel;	430
	50: 4	they shall go, and seek the LORD their **G**.	430
	50:18	saith the LORD of hosts, the **G** of Israel;	430
	50:28	in Zion the vengeance of the LORD our **G**,	430
	50:40	As **G** overthrew Sodom and Gomorrah and	430
	51: 5	nor Judah of his **G**, of the LORD of hosts;	430
	51:10	in Zion the work of the LORD our **G**.	430
	51:33	saith the LORD of hosts, the **G** of Israel;	430
	51:56	for the LORD **G** of recompences shall	410
La	3:41	heart with *our* hands unto **G** in the heavens.	410
Eze	1: 1	were opened, and I saw visions of **G**.	430
	8: 3	brought me in the visions of **G** to Jerusalem,	430
	8: 4	the glory of the **G** of Israel *was* there,	430
	9: 3	the glory of the **G** of Israel was gone up	430
	10: 5	as the voice of the Almighty **G** when he	410
	10:19	the glory of the **G** of Israel *was* over them	430
	10:20	under the **G** of Israel by the river of Chebar;	430
	11:20	shall be my people, and I will be their **G**.	430
	11:22	the glory of the **G** of Israel *was* over them	430
	11:24	brought me in vision by the Spirit of **G** into	430
	14:11	and I may be their **G**, saith the Lord GOD.	430
	20: 5	unto them, saying, I *am* the LORD your **G**;	430
	20: 7	the idols of Egypt: I *am* the LORD your **G**.	430
	20:19	I *am* the LORD your **G**; walk in my	430
	20:20	*ye* may know that I *am* the LORD your **G**.	430
	28: 2	thou hast said, I *am* a **G**, I sit *in* the seat of	410
	28: 2	hast said, I *am* a God, I sit *in* the seat of **G**,	430
	28: 2	yet thou *art* a man, and not **G**, though thou	410
	28: 2	though thou set thine heart as the heart of **G**:	430
	28: 6	thou hast set thine heart as the heart of **G**;	430
	28: 9	yet say before him that slayeth thee, I *am* **G**?	430
	28: 9	thou *shalt be* a man, and no **G**, in the hand of	410
	28:13	Thou hast been in Eden the garden of **G**;	430
	28:14	*so:* thou wast upon the holy mountain of **G**;	430
	28:16	thee as profane out of the mountain of **G**:	430
	28:26	shall know that I *am* the LORD their **G**.	430
	31: 8	The cedars in the garden of **G** could not hide	430
	31: 8	nor any tree in the garden of **G** was like unto	430
	31: 9	that *were* in the garden of **G**, envied him.	430
	34:24	I the LORD will be their **G**, and my servant	430
	34:30	that I the LORD their **G** *am* with them,	430
	34:31	*are* men, *and* I *am* your **G**, saith the Lord	430
	36:28	ye shall be my people, and I will be your **G**.	430
	37:23	they be my people, and I will be their **G**.	430
	37:27	I will be their **G**, and they shall be my	430
	39:22	that I *am* the LORD their **G** from that day	430
	39:28	they know that I *am* the LORD their **G**,	430
	40: 2	In the visions of **G** brought he me into	430
	43: 2	the glory of the **G** of Israel came from	430
	44: 2	because the LORD, the **G** of Israel,	430
Da	1: 2	with part of the vessels of the house of **G**:	430
	1: 2	*into* the land of Shinar *to* the house of his **g**;	430
	1: 2	the vessels *into* the treasure house of his **g**.	430
	1: 9	Now **G** had brought Daniel into favour and	430
	1:17	**G** gave them knowledge and skill in all	430
	2:18	That *they* would desire mercies of the **G** of	426
	2:19	Then Daniel blessed the **G** of heaven.	426
	2:20	Blessed be the name of **G** for ever and ever:	426
	2:23	and praise thee, O thou **G** of my fathers,	426
	2:28	there is a **G** in heaven that revealeth secrets,	426
	2:37	for the **G** of heaven hath given thee a	426
	2:44	in the days of these kings shall the **G** of	426
	2:45	the great **G** hath made known to the king	426
	2:47	Of a truth *it is,* that your **G** *is* a God of gods,	426
	2:47	Of a truth *it is,* that your God *is* a **G** of gods,	426
	3:15	who *is* that **G** that shall deliver you out of	426
	3:17	our **G** whom we serve *is* able to deliver us	426
	3:25	the form of the fourth *is* like the Son of **G**.	426
	3:26	ye servants of the most high **G**, come forth,	426
	3:28	said, Blessed *be* the **G** of Shadrach,	426
	3:28	that they might not serve nor worship any **g**,	426
	3:28	nor worship any god, except their own **G**.	426
	3:29	which speak any thing amiss against the **G**	426
	3:29	there is no other **G** that can deliver after this	426
	4: 2	wonders that the high **G** hath wrought	426
	4: 8	according to the name of my **g**, and in whom	426
	5: 3	of the house of **G** which *was* at Jerusalem;	426
	5:18	the most high **G** gave Nebuchadnezzar thy	426
	5:21	till he knew that the most high **G** ruled in	426
	5:23	the **G** in whose hand thy breath *is,* and	426
	5:26	**G** hath numbered thy kingdom, and	426
	6: 5	*it* against him concerning the law of his **G**.	426
	6: 7	that whosoever shall ask a petition of any **G**	426
	6:10	prayed, and gave thanks before his **G**, as he	426
	6:11	and making supplication before his **G**.	426
	6:12	every man that shall ask *a petition* of any **G**	426
	6:16	Thy **G** whom thou servest continually,	426
	6:20	O Daniel, servant of the living **G**, is thy	426
	6:20	servant of the living God, is thy **G**,	426
	6:22	My **G** hath sent his angel, and hath shut	426
	6:23	upon him, because he believed in his **G**.	426
	6:26	and fear before the **G** of Daniel:	426
	6:26	for he *is* the living **G**, and stedfast for ever,	426
	9: 3	I set my face unto the Lord **G**, to seek *by*	430
	9: 4	I prayed unto the LORD my **G**, and	430
	9: 4	and said, O Lord, the great and dreadful **G**,	410
	9: 9	To the Lord our **G** *belong* mercies and	430
	9:10	we obeyed the voice of the LORD our **G**,	430
	9:11	written in the law of Moses the servant of **G**,	430
	9:13	we not our prayer before the LORD our **G**,	430
	9:14	for the LORD our **G** *is* righteous in all his	430
	9:15	now, O Lord our **G**, that hast brought thy	430
	9:17	Now therefore, O our **G**, hear the prayer of	430
	9:18	O my **G**, incline thine ear, and hear;	430
	9:19	do; defer not, for thine own sake, O my **G**:	430
	9:20	my **G** for the holy mountain of my God;	430
	9:20	my God for the holy mountain of my **G**;	430
	10:12	to chasten thyself before thy **G**, thy words	430
	11:32	the people that do know their **G** shall be	430
	11:36	magnify himself above every **g**, and	410
	11:36	shall speak marvellous *things* against the **G**	410
	11:37	Neither shall he regard the **G** of his fathers,	430
	11:37	nor the desire of women, nor regard any **g**:	433
	11:38	in his estate shall he honour the **G** of forces:	433
	11:38	a **g** whom his fathers knew not shall he	433
	11:39	do in the most strong holds with a strange **g**,	433
Hos	1: 6	**G** said unto him, Call her name	NIH
	1: 7	will save them by the LORD their **G**, and	430
	1: 9	said **G**, Call his name Lo-ammi: for ye *are*	NIH
	1: 9	not my people, and I will not be your **G**.	NIH
	1:10	unto them, *Ye are* the sons of the living **G**.	410
	2:23	and they shall say, *Thou art* my **G**.	430
	3: 5	seek the LORD their **G**, and David their	430
	4: 1	nor mercy, nor knowledge of **G** in the land.	430
	4: 6	seeing thou hast forgotten the law of thy **G**,	430
	4:12	have gone a whoring from under their **G**.	430
	5: 4	not frame their doings to turn unto their **G**:	430
	6: 6	the knowledge of **G** more than burnt	430
	7:10	they do not return to the LORD their **G**,	430
	8: 2	shall cry unto me, My **G**, we know thee.	430
	8: 6	the workman made it; therefore it *is* not **G**:	430
	9: 1	for thou hast gone a whoring from thy **G**,	430
	9: 8	The watchman of Ephraim *was* with my **G**:	430
	9: 8	his ways, *and* hatred in the house of his **G**.	430
	9:17	My **G** will cast them away, because they did	430
	11: 9	for I *am* **G**, and not man; the Holy One in	410
	11:12	Judah yet ruleth with **G**, and is faithful with	410
	12: 3	and by his strength he had power with **G**:	430
	12: 5	Even the LORD **G** of hosts; the LORD *is*	430
	12: 6	Therefore turn thou to thy **G**: keep mercy	430
	12: 6	judgment, and wait on thy **G** continually.	430
	12: 9	I *that am* the LORD thy **G** from the land of	430
	13: 4	Yet I *am* the LORD thy **G** from the land of	430
	13: 4	of Egypt, and thou shalt know no **g** but me:	430
	13:16	for she hath rebelled against her **G**:	430
	14: 1	O Israel, return unto the LORD thy **G**;	430
Joel	1:13	all night in sackcloth, ye ministers of my **G**;	430
	1:13	is withholden from the house of your **G**.	430
	1:14	land *into* the house of the LORD your **G**,	430
	1:16	and gladness from the house of our **G**?	430
	2:13	and turn unto the LORD your **G**:	430
	2:14	a drink offering unto the LORD your **G**?	430
	2:17	say among the people, Where *is* their **G**?	430
	2:23	of Zion, and rejoice in the LORD your **G**:	430

Joel	2:26	and praise the name of the LORD your **G**,	430
	2:27	*that* I *am* the LORD your **G**, and none else:	430
	3:17	I *am* the LORD your **G** dwelling in Zion,	430
Am	2: 8	of the condemned *in* the house of their **g**.	430
	3:13	saith the Lord GOD, the **G** of hosts,	430
	4:11	as **G** overthrew Sodom and Gomorrah, and	430
	4:12	unto thee, prepare to meet thy **G**, O Israel.	430
	4:13	The LORD, The **G** of hosts, *is* his name.	430
	5:14	so the LORD, the **G** of hosts, shall be with	430
	5:15	it may be that the LORD **G** of hosts will be	430
	5:16	the **G** of hosts, the Lord, saith thus;	430
	5:26	and Chiun your images, the star of your **g**,	430
	5:27	the LORD, whose name *is* The **G** of hosts.	430
	6: 8	saith the LORD the **G** of hosts, I abhor	430
	6:14	of Israel, saith the LORD the **G** of hosts;	430
	8:14	of Samaria, and say, Thy **g**, O Dan, liveth;	430
	9:15	I have given them, saith the LORD thy **G**.	430
Jnh	1: 5	cried every man unto his **g**, and cast forth	430
	1: 6	call upon thy **G**, if so be that God will think	430
	1: 6	if so be that **G** will think upon us, that we	430
	1: 9	I fear the LORD, the **G** of heaven,	430
	2: 1	Jonah prayed unto the LORD his **G** out of	430
	2: 6	my life from corruption, O LORD my **G**.	430
	3: 5	So the people of Nineveh believed **G**, and	430
	3: 8	with sackcloth, and cry mightily unto **G**:	430
	3: 9	Who can tell *if* **G** will turn and repent, and	430
	3:10	**G** saw their works, that they turned from	430
	3:10	**G** repented of the evil, that he had said that	430
	4: 2	for I knew that thou *art* a gracious **G**, and	410
	4: 6	the LORD **G** prepared a gourd, and made *it*	430
	4: 7	**G** prepared a worm when the morning rose	430
	4: 8	that **G** prepared a vehement east wind;	430
	4: 9	**G** said to Jonah, Doest thou well to be angry	430
Mic	3: 7	cover their lips; for *there is* no answer of **G**.	430
	4: 2	and to the house of the **G** of Jacob;	430
	4: 5	will walk every one in the name of his **g**,	430
	4: 5	in the name of the LORD our **G** for ever	430
	5: 4	majesty of the name of the LORD his **G**;	430
	6: 6	*and* bow myself before the high **G**?	430
	6: 8	love mercy, and to walk humbly with thy **G**?	430
	7: 7	I will wait for the **G** of my salvation:	430
	7: 7	the God of my salvation: my **G** will hear me.	430
	7:10	said unto me, Where is the LORD thy **G**?	430
	7:17	they shall be afraid of the LORD our **G**,	430
	7:18	Who *is* a **G** like unto thee, that pardoneth	410
Na	1: 2	**G** *is* jealous, and the LORD revengeth;	410
Hab	1:11	offend, *imputing* this his power unto his **g**.	433
	1:12	O LORD my **G**, mine Holy One?	430
	1:12	and, O **mighty G**, thou hast established	6697
	3: 3	**G** came from Teman, and the Holy One	433
	3:18	I will joy in the **G** of my salvation.	430
Zep	2: 7	for the LORD their **G** shall visit them, and	430
	2: 9	saith the LORD of hosts, the **G** of Israel,	430
	3: 2	in the LORD; she drew not near to her **G**.	430
	3:17	The LORD thy **G** in the midst of thee *is*	430
Hag	1:12	obeyed the voice of the LORD their **G**, and	430
	1:12	as the LORD their **G** had sent him, and	430
	1:14	in the house of the LORD of hosts, their **G**,	430
Zec	6:15	obey the voice of the LORD your **G**.	430
	7: 2	When they had sent *unto* the house of **G**	410
	8: 8	I will be their **G**, in truth and	430
	8:23	for we have heard *that* **G** *is* with you.	430
	9: 7	*shall be* for our **G**, and he shall be as a	430
	9:16	the LORD their **G** shall save them in that	430
	10: 6	for I *am* the LORD their **G**, and will hear	430
	11: 4	Thus saith the LORD my **G**; Feed the flock	430
	12: 5	my strength in the LORD of hosts their **G**.	430
	12: 8	the house of David *shall be* as **G**, as	430
	13: 9	and they shall say, The LORD *is* my **G**.	430
	14: 5	the LORD my **G** shall come, *and* all	430
Mal	1: 9	beseech **G** that he will be gracious unto us:	410
	2:10	hath not one **G** created us? why do we deal	410
	2:11	and hath married the daughter of a strange **g**.	410
	2:16	*For* the LORD, the **G** of Israel, saith that he	430
	2:17	in them; or, Where *is* the **G** of judgment?	430
	3: 8	Will a man rob **G**? Yet ye *have* robbed me.	430
	3:14	Ye have said, It *is* vain to serve **G**: and	430
	3:15	yea, *they that* tempt **G** are even delivered.	430
	3:18	between him that serveth **G** and *him* that	430
Mt	1:23	which being interpreted is, **G** with us.	2316
	2:12	And being **warned of G** in a dream that	5537
	2:22	being **warned of G** in a dream,	5537
	3: 9	that **G** is able of these stones to raise up	2316
	3:16	he saw the Spirit of **G** descending like a	2316
	4: 3	to him, he said, If thou be the Son of **G**,	2316
	4: 4	that proceedeth out of the mouth of **G**.	2316
	4: 6	If thou be the Son of **G**, cast thyself down:	2316
	4: 7	Thou shalt not tempt the Lord thy **G**.	2316
	4:10	Thou shalt worship the Lord thy **G**, and	2316
	5: 8	*are* the pure in heart: for they shall see **G**.	2316
	5: 9	for they shall be called the children of **G**.	2316
	6:24	the other. Ye cannot serve **G** and mammon.	2316
	6:30	if **G** so clothe the grass of the field,	2316
	6:33	But seek ye first the kingdom of **G**, and	2316
	8:29	we to do with thee, Jesus, *thou* Son of **G**?	2316
	9: 8	and glorified **G**, which had given such	2316
	12: 4	How he entered into the house of **G**, and	2316
	12:28	But if I cast out devils by the Spirit of **G**,	2316
	12:28	then the kingdom of **G** is come unto you.	2316
	14:33	saying, Of a truth thou art the Son of **G**.	2316
	15: 3	the commandment of **G** by your tradition?	2316
	15: 4	For **G** commanded, saying, Honour thy	2316
	15: 6	of **G** of none effect by your tradition.	2316
	15:31	to see: and they glorified the **G** of Israel.	2316
	16:16	Thou art the Christ, the Son of the living **G**.	2316
	16:23	thou savourest not the *things* that be of **G**,	2316
	19: 6	What therefore **G** hath joined together,	2316
	19:17	*there is* none good but one, *that is,* **G**: but	2316
	19:24	a rich *man* to enter into the kingdom of **G**.	2316
	19:26	but with **G** all *things* are possible.	2316
	21:12	And Jesus went into the temple of **G**, and	2316
	21:31	the harlots go into the kingdom of **G** before	2316
	21:43	The kingdom of **G** shall be taken from you,	2316
	22:16	art true, and teachest the way of **G** in truth,	2316
	22:21	and unto **G** the *things* that are God's.	2316
	22:29	knowing the scriptures, nor the power of **G**.	2316
	22:30	but are as *the* angels of **G** in heaven.	2316
	22:31	read that which was spoken unto you by **G**,	2316
	22:32	I am the **G** of Abraham, and the God of	2316
	22:32	and the **G** of Isaac, and the God of Jacob?	2316
	22:32	and the God of Isaac, and the **G** of Jacob?	2316
	22:32	**G** is not the God of the dead, but of	2316
	22:32	God is not the **G** of the dead, but of	2316
	22:37	Thou shalt love the Lord thy **G** with all thy	2316
	23:22	sweareth by the throne of **G**, and by him	2316
	26:61	I am able to destroy the temple of **G**, and	2316
	26:63	said unto him, I adjure thee by the living **G**,	2316
	26:63	whether thou be the Christ, the Son of **G**.	2316
	27:40	If thou be the Son of **G**, come down from	2316
	27:43	He trusted in **G**; let him deliver him now,	2316
	27:43	have him: for he said, I am the Son of **G**.	2316
	27:46	that is to say, My **G**, my God, why hast	2316
	27:46	that is to say, My God, my **G**, why hast	2316
	27:54	saying, Truly this was the Son of **G**.	2316
Mk	1: 1	of the gospel of Jesus Christ, the Son of **G**;	2316
	1:14	preaching the gospel of the kingdom of **G**,	2316
	1:15	and the kingdom of **G** is at hand:	2316
	1:24	thee who thou art, the Holy One of **G**.	2316
	2: 7	who can forgive sins but **G** only?	2316
	2:12	and glorified **G**, saying, We never saw *it* on	2316
	2:26	How he went into the house of **G** in	2316
	3:11	and cried, saying, Thou art the Son of **G**.	2316
	3:35	For whosoever shall do the will of **G**,	2316
	4:11	to know the mystery of the kingdom of **G**:	2316
	4:26	And he said, So is the kingdom of **G**, as if a	2316
	4:30	shall we liken the kingdom of **G**?	2316
	5: 7	Jesus, *thou* Son of the most high **G**?	2316
	5: 7	I adjure thee by **G**, that thou torment me	2316
	7: 8	For laying aside the commandment of **G**,	2316
	7: 9	Full well ye reject the commandment of **G**,	2316
	7:13	Making the word of **G** of none effect	2316
	8:33	thou savourest not the *things* that be of **G**,	2316
	9: 1	till they have seen the kingdom of **G** come	2316
	9:47	enter into the kingdom of **G** with one eye,	2316
	10: 6	But from the beginning of the creation **G**	2316
	10: 9	What therefore **G** hath joined together,	2316
	10:14	them not: for of such is the kingdom of **G**.	2316
	10:15	receive the kingdom of **G** as a little child,	2316
	10:18	*there is* none good but one, *that is,* **G**.	2316
	10:23	have riches enter into the kingdom of **G**!	2316
	10:24	in riches to enter into the kingdom of **G**!	2316
	10:25	a rich *man* to enter into the kingdom of **G**.	2316
	10:27	With men *it is* impossible, but not with **G**:	2316
	10:27	for with **G** all *things* are possible.	2316
	11:22	answering saith unto them, Have faith in **G**.	2316
	12:14	of men, but teachest the way of **G** in truth:	2316
	12:17	and to **G** the *things* that are God's.	2316
	12:24	not the scriptures, neither the power of **G**?	2316

G

Mk	12:26	how in the bush **G** spake unto him, saying,	*2316*
	12:26	I *am* the **G** of Abraham, and the God of	*2316*
	12:26	and the **G** of Isaac, and the God of Jacob?	*2316*
	12:26	and the God of Isaac, and the **G** of Jacob?	*2316*
	12:27	He is not the **G** of the dead, but the God of	*2316*
	12:27	the God of the dead, but the **G** of the living:	*2316*
	12:29	O Israel; The Lord our **G** is one Lord:	*2316*
	12:30	And thou shalt love the Lord thy **G** with all	*2316*
	12:32	for there is one **G**; and there is none other	*2316*
	12:34	Thou art not far from the kingdom of **G**.	*2316*
	13:19	the creation which **G** created unto this time,	*2316*
	14:25	day that I drink it new in the kingdom of **G**.	*2316*
	15:34	which is, being interpreted, My **G**, my God,	*2316*
	15:34	which is, being interpreted, My God, my **G**,	*2316*
	15:39	he said, Truly this man was the Son of **G**.	*2316*
	15:43	which also waited for the kingdom of **G**,	*2316*
	16:19	into heaven, and sat on the right hand of **G**.	*2316*
Lk	1: 6	And they were both righteous before **G**,	*2316*
	1: 8	office before **G** in the order of his course,	*2316*
	1:16	of Israel shall he turn to the Lord their **G**.	*2316*
	1:19	am Gabriel, that stand in the presence of **G**;	*2316*
	1:26	was sent from **G** unto a city of Galilee,	*2316*
	1:30	Mary: for thou hast found favour with **G**.	*2316*
	1:32	the Lord **G** shall give unto him the throne	*2316*
	1:35	born of thee shall be called the Son of **G**.	*2316*
	1:37	For with **G** nothing shall be unpossible.	*2316*
	1:47	And my spirit hath rejoiced in **G** my	*2316*
	1:64	and he spake, and praised **G**.	*2316*
	1:68	Blessed *be* the Lord **G** of Israel; for he hath	*2316*
	1:78	Through the tender mercy of our **G**;	*2316*
	2:13	multitude of the heavenly host praising **G**,	*2316*
	2:14	Glory to **G** in the highest, and on earth	*2316*
	2:20	praising **G** for all *the things* that they had	*2316*
	2:28	*up* in his arms, and blessed **G**, and said,	*2316*
	2:37	but served **G** with fastings and prayers night	NIG
	2:40	and the grace of **G** was upon him.	*2316*
	2:52	and stature, and in favour with **G** and man.	*2316*
	3: 2	the word of **G** came unto John the son of	*2316*
	3: 6	And all flesh shall see the salvation of **G**.	*2316*
	3: 8	That **G** is able of these stones to raise up	*2316*
	3:38	*the son* of Adam, which was *the son* of **G**.	*2316*
	4: 3	said unto him, If thou be the Son of **G**,	*2316*
	4: 4	by bread alone, but by every word of **G**.	*2316*
	4: 8	Thou shalt worship the Lord thy **G**, and	*2316*
	4: 9	and said unto him, If thou be the Son of **G**,	*2316*
	4:12	Thou shalt not tempt the Lord thy **G**.	*2316*
	4:34	thee who thou art, the Holy One of **G**.	*2316*
	4:41	and saying, Thou art Christ the Son of **G**.	*2316*
	4:43	I must preach the kingdom of **G** to other	*2316*
	5: 1	pressed upon him to hear the word of **G**,	*2316*
	5:21	Who can forgive sins, but **G** alone?	*2316*
	5:25	departed to his own house, glorifying **G**.	*2316*
	5:26	and they glorified **G**, and were filled with	*2316*
	6: 4	How he went into the house of **G**, and	*2316*
	6:12	and continued all night in prayer to **G**.	*2316*
	6:20	*be ye* poor: for yours is the kingdom of **G**.	*2316*
	7:16	and they glorified **G**, saying, That a great	*2316*
	7:16	and, That **G** hath visited his people.	*2316*
	7:28	he that is least in the kingdom of **G** is	*2316*
	7:29	heard *him,* and the publicans, justified **G**,	*2316*
	7:30	lawyers rejected the counsel of **G** against	*2316*
	8: 1	the glad tidings of the kingdom of **G**:	*2316*
	8:10	to know the mysteries of the kingdom of **G**:	*2316*
	8:11	parable is this: The seed is the word of **G**.	*2316*
	8:21	are these which hear the word of **G**,	*2316*
	8:28	with thee, Jesus, *thou* Son of **G** most high?	*2316*
	8:39	shew how great *things* **G** hath done unto	*2316*
	9: 2	he sent them to preach the kingdom of **G**,	*2316*
	9:11	and spake unto them of the kingdom of **G**,	*2316*
	9:20	Peter answering said, The Christ of **G**.	*2316*
	9:27	of death, till they see the kingdom of **G**.	*2316*
	9:43	were all amazed at the mighty power of **G**.	*2316*
	9:60	but go thou and preach the kingdom of **G**.	*2316*
	9:62	looking back, is fit for the kingdom of **G**.	*2316*
	10: 9	The kingdom of **G** is come nigh unto you.	*2316*
	10:11	that the kingdom of **G** is come nigh unto	*2316*
	10:27	Thou shalt love the Lord thy **G** with all thy	*2316*
	11:20	But if I with the finger of **G** cast out devils,	*2316*
	11:20	no doubt the kingdom of **G** is come upon	*2316*
	11:28	blessed *are* they that hear the word of **G**,	*2316*
	11:42	and pass over judgment and the love of **G**:	*2316*
	11:49	Therefore also said the wisdom of **G**, I will	*2316*
	12: 6	and not one of them is forgotten before **G**?	*2316*
	12: 8	of man also confess before the angels of **G**:	*2316*
	12: 9	men shall be denied before the angels of **G**.	*2316*
	12:20	But **G** said unto him, *Thou* fool, this night	*2316*
	12:21	for himself, and is not rich towards **G**.	*2316*
	12:24	storehouse nor barn; and **G** feedeth them:	*2316*
	12:28	If then **G** so clothe the grass, which is to	*2316*
	12:31	But rather seek ye the kingdom of **G**;	*2316*
	13:13	she was made straight, and glorified **G**.	*2316*
	13:18	Unto what is the kingdom of **G** like?	*2316*
	13:20	Whereunto shall I liken the kingdom of **G**?	*2316*
	13:28	in the kingdom of **G**, and you yourselves	*2316*
	13:29	and shall sit down in the kingdom of **G**.	*2316*
	14:15	*he* that shall eat bread in the kingdom of **G**.	*2316*
	15:10	angels of **G** over one sinner that repenteth.	*2316*
	16:13	the other. Ye cannot serve **G** and mammon.	*2316*
	16:15	before men; but **G** knoweth your hearts:	*2316*
	16:15	men is abomination in the sight of **G**.	*2316*
	16:16	since that time the kingdom of **G** is	*2316*
	17:15	and with a loud voice glorified **G**,	*2316*
	17:18	not found that returned to give glory to **G**,	*2316*
	17:20	when the kingdom of **G** should come,	*2316*
	17:20	The kingdom of **G** cometh not with	*2316*
	17:21	for behold, the kingdom of **G** is within you.	*2316*
	18: 2	which feared not **G**, neither regarded man:	*2316*
	18: 4	Though I fear not **G**, nor regard man;	*2316*
	18: 7	And shall not **G** avenge his own elect,	*2316*
	18:11	prayed thus with himself, **G**, I thank thee,	*2316*
	18:13	saying, **G** be merciful to me a sinner.	*2316*
	18:16	them not: for of such is the kingdom of **G**.	*2316*
	18:17	**G** as a little child shall in no wise enter	*2316*
	18:19	none *is* good, save one, *that is,* **G**.	*2316*
	18:24	have riches enter into the kingdom of **G**!	*2316*
	18:25	a rich *man* to enter into the kingdom of **G**.	*2316*
	18:27	unpossible with men are possible with **G**.	*2316*
	18:43	his sight, and followed him, glorifying **G**:	*2316*
	18:43	when they saw *it,* gave praise unto **G**.	*2316*
	19:11	they thought that the kingdom of **G** should	*2316*
	19:37	praise **G** with a loud voice for all	*2316*
	20:16	they heard *it,* they said, **G forbid**.	*1096+3361*
	20:21	*of any,* but teachest the way of **G** truly:	*2316*
	20:25	and unto **G** the *things* which be God's.	*2316*
	20:36	and are the children of **G**, being	*2316*
	20:37	when he calleth the Lord the **G** of	*2316*
	20:37	and the **G** of Isaac, and the God of Jacob.	*2316*
	20:37	and the God of Isaac, and the **G** of Jacob.	*2316*
	20:38	For he is not a **G** of the dead, but of	*2316*
	21: 4	abundance cast in unto the offerings of **G**:	*2316*
	21:31	know ye that the kingdom of **G** is nigh at	*2316*
	22:16	until it be fulfilled in the kingdom of **G**.	*2316*
	22:18	until the kingdom of **G** shall come.	*2316*
	22:69	sit on the right hand of the power of **G**.	*2316*
	22:70	said they all, Art thou then the Son of **G**?	*2316*
	23:35	if he be Christ, the chosen of **G**.	*2316*
	23:40	rebuked him, saying, Dost not thou fear **G**,	*2316*
	23:47	he glorified **G**, saying, Certainly this was a	*2316*
	23:51	also himself waited for the kingdom of **G**.	*2316*
	24:19	and word before **G** and all the people:	*2316*
	24:53	in the temple, praising and blessing **G**.	*2316*
Jn	1: 1	and the Word was with **G**, and the Word	*2316*
	1: 1	Word was with God, and the Word was **G**.	*2316*
	1: 2	The same was in the beginning with **G**.	*2316*
	1: 6	There was a man sent from **G**, whose name	*2316*
	1:12	gave he power to become the sons of **G**,	*2316*
	1:13	the flesh, nor of the will of man, but of **G**.	*2316*
	1:18	No *man* hath seen **G** at any time; the only	*2316*
	1:29	and saith, Behold the Lamb of **G**,	*2316*
	1:34	and bare record that this is the Son of **G**.	*2316*
	1:36	he walked, he saith, Behold the Lamb of **G**.	*2316*
	1:49	unto him, Rabbi, thou art the Son of **G**;	*2316*
	1:51	and the angels of **G** ascending and	*2316*
	3: 2	know that thou art a teacher come from **G**:	*2316*
	3: 2	that thou doest, except **G** be with him.	*2316*
	3: 3	he cannot see the kingdom of **G**.	*2316*
	3: 5	he cannot enter into the kingdom of **G**.	*2316*
	3:16	For **G** so loved the world, that he gave his	*2316*
	3:17	For **G** sent not his Son into the world to	*2316*
	3:18	in the name of the only begotten Son of **G**.	*2316*
	3:21	made manifest, that they are wrought in **G**.	*2316*
	3:33	testimony hath set to *his* seal that **G** is true.	*2316*
	3:34	For he whom **G** hath sent speaketh	*2316*
	3:34	God hath sent speaketh the words of **G**:	*2316*
	3:34	for **G** giveth not the Spirit by measure *unto*	*2316*
	3:36	see life; but the wrath of **G** abideth on him.	*2316*
	4:10	If thou knewest the gift of **G**, and who it is	*2316*
	4:24	**G** *is* a Spirit: and they that worship him	*2316*

Jn	5:18	but said also that **G** was his Father,	*2316*
	5:18	his Father, making himself equal with **G**.	*2316*
	5:25	dead shall hear the voice of the Son of **G**:	*2316*
	5:42	that ye have not the love of **G** in you.	*2316*
	5:44	seek not the honour that *cometh* from **G**	*2316*
	6:27	unto you: for him hath **G** the Father sealed.	*2316*
	6:28	we do, that we might work the works of **G**?	*2316*
	6:29	and said unto them, This is the work of **G**,	*2316*
	6:33	For the bread of **G** is he which cometh	*2316*
	6:45	And they shall be all taught of **G**.	*2316*
	6:46	save he which is of **G**, he hath seen	*2316*
	6:69	thou art *that* Christ, the Son of the living **G**.	*2316*
	7:17	whether it be of **G**, or *whether* I speak of	*2316*
	8:40	told you the truth, which I have heard of **G**:	*2316*
	8:41	of fornication; we have one Father, *even* **G**.	*2316*
	8:42	If **G** were your Father, ye would love me:	*2316*
	8:42	for I proceeded forth and came from **G**;	*2316*
	8:47	He that is of **G** heareth God's words: ye	*2316*
	8:47	hear *them* not, because ye are not of **G**.	*2316*
	8:54	of whom ye say, that he is your **G**:	*2316*
	9: 3	that the works of **G** should be made	*2316*
	9:16	This man is not of **G**, because he keepeth	*2316*
	9:24	and said unto him, Give **G** the praise:	*2316*
	9:29	We know that **G** spake unto Moses: *as for*	*2316*
	9:31	Now we know that **G** heareth not sinners:	*2316*
	9:31	but if any *man* be a **worshipper of G**, and	*2318*
	9:33	If this *man* were not of **G**, he could do	*2316*
	9:35	Dost thou believe on the Son of **G**?	*2316*
	10:33	that thou, being a man, makest thyself **G**.	*2316*
	10:35	unto whom the word of **G** came, and	*2316*
	10:36	because I said, I am the Son of **G**?	*2316*
	11: 4	is not unto death, but for the glory of **G**,	*2316*
	11: 4	that the Son of **G** might be glorified	*2316*
	11:22	even now, whatsoever thou wilt ask of **G**,	*2316*
	11:22	thou wilt ask of God, **G** will give *it* thee.	*2316*
	11:27	that thou art the Christ, the Son of **G**,	*2316*
	11:40	thou shouldest see the glory of **G**?	*2316*
	11:52	children of **G** that were scattered abroad.	*2316*
	12:43	praise of men more than the praise of **G**.	*2316*
	13: 3	and that he was come from **G**, and went to	*2316*
	13: 3	that he was come from God, and went to **G**;	*2316*
	13:31	of man glorified, and **G** is glorified in him.	*2316*
	13:32	If **G** be glorified in him, God shall also	*2316*
	13:32	in him, **G** shall also glorify him in himself,	*2316*
	14: 1	ye believe in **G**, believe also in me.	*2316*
	16: 2	you will think that he doeth **G** service.	*2316*
	16:27	and have believed that I came out from **G**.	*2316*
	16:30	we believe that thou camest forth from **G**.	*2316*
	17: 3	that they might know thee the only true **G**,	*2316*
	19: 7	because he made himself the Son of **G**.	*2316*
	20:17	your Father; and *to* my **G**, and your God.	*2316*
	20:17	your Father; and *to* my God, and your **G**.	*2316*
	20:28	and said unto him, My Lord and my **G**.	*2316*
	20:31	that Jesus is the Christ, the Son of **G**;	*2316*
	21:19	by what death he should glorify **G**.	*2316*
Ac	1: 3	the *things* pertaining to the kingdom of **G**:	*2316*
	2:11	in our tongues the wonderful works of **G**.	*2316*
	2:17	shall come to pass in the last days, saith **G**,	*2316*
	2:22	a man approved of **G** among you by	*2316*
	2:22	which **G** did by him in the midst of you,	*2316*
	2:23	and foreknowledge of **G**,	*2316*
	2:24	Whom **G** hath raised up, having loosed	*2316*
	2:30	knowing that **G** had sworn with an oath to	*2316*
	2:32	This Jesus hath **G** raised up, whereof we all	*2316*
	2:33	Therefore being by the right hand of **G**	*2316*
	2:36	that **G** hath made that same Jesus, whom ye	*2316*
	2:39	*even* as many as the Lord our **G** shall call.	*2316*
	2:47	Praising **G**, and having favour with all	*2316*
	3: 8	walking, and leaping, and praising **G**.	*2316*
	3: 9	people saw him walking and praising **G**:	*2316*
	3:13	The **G** of Abraham, and of Isaac, and	*2316*
	3:13	of Isaac, and of Jacob, the **G** of our fathers,	*2316*
	3:15	of life, whom **G** hath raised from the dead;	*2316*
	3:18	But *those things,* which **G** before had	*2316*
	3:21	**G** hath spoken by the mouth of all his holy	*2316*
	3:22	A prophet shall the Lord your **G** raise up	*2316*
	3:25	of the covenant which **G** made with our	*2316*
	3:26	Unto you first **G**, having raised up his Son	*2316*
	4:10	ye crucified, whom **G** raised from the dead,	*2316*
	4:19	Whether it be right in the sight of **G** to	*2316*
	4:19	God to hearken unto you more than unto **G**,	*2316*
	4:21	for all *men* glorified **G** for that which was	*2316*
	4:24	lift up their voice to **G** with one accord,	*2316*
	4:24	and said, Lord, thou *art* **G**, which hast made	*2316*
	4:31	they spake the word of **G** with boldness.	*2316*
	5: 4	thou hast not lied unto men, but unto **G**.	*2316*
	5:29	said, We ought to obey **G** rather than men.	*2316*
	5:30	The **G** of our fathers raised up Jesus,	*2316*
	5:31	Him hath **G** exalted with his right hand *to*	*2316*
	5:32	whom **G** hath given to them that obey him.	*2316*
	5:39	But if it be of **G**, ye cannot overthrow it;	*2316*
	5:39	haply ye be found even to **fight against G**.	*2314*
	6: 2	reason that we should leave the word of **G**,	*2316*
	6: 7	And the word of **G** increased; and	*2316*
	6:11	words against Moses, and *against* **G**.	*2316*
	7: 2	The **G** of glory appeared unto our father	*2316*
	7: 6	And **G** spake on this wise, That his seed	*2316*
	7: 7	shall be in bondage will I judge, said **G**:	*2316*
	7: 9	Joseph into Egypt: but **G** was with him,	*2316*
	7:17	which **G** had sworn to Abraham, the people	*2316*
	7:25	that **G** by his hand would deliver them:	*2316*
	7:32	*Saying,* I *am* the **G** of thy fathers, the God	*2316*
	7:32	the **G** of Abraham, and the God of Isaac,	*2316*
	7:32	and the **G** of Isaac, and the God of Jacob.	*2316*
	7:32	and the God of Isaac, and the **G** of Jacob.	*2316*
	7:35	the same did **G** send *to be* a ruler and	*2316*
	7:37	A prophet shall the Lord your **G** raise up	*2316*
	7:42	Then **G** turned, and gave them up to	*2316*
	7:43	of Moloch, and the star of your **g** Remphan,	*2316*
	7:45	whom **G** drave out before the face of our	*2316*
	7:46	Who found favour before **G**, and desired to	*2316*
	7:46	desired to find a tabernacle for the **G** of	*2316*
	7:55	and saw the glory of **G**, and Jesus standing	*2316*
	7:55	and Jesus standing on the right hand of **G**,	*2316*
	7:56	of man standing on the right hand of **G**.	*2316*
	7:59	calling upon **G**, and saying, Lord Jesus,	NIG
	8:10	saying, This *man* is the great power of **G**.	*2316*
	8:12	the *things* concerning the kingdom of **G**,	*2316*
	8:14	that Samaria had received the word of **G**,	*2316*
	8:20	thou hast thought that the gift of **G** may be	*2316*
	8:21	for thy heart is not right in the sight of **G**.	*2316*
	8:22	of this thy wickedness, and pray **G**,	*2316*
	8:37	I believe that Jesus Christ is the Son of **G**.	*2316*
	9:20	in the synagogues, that he is the Son of **G**.	*2316*
	10: 2	and one that feared **G** with all his house,	*2316*
	10: 2	alms to the people, and prayed to **G** alway.	*2316*
	10: 3	an angel of **G** coming in to him, and	*2316*
	10: 4	alms are come up for a memorial before **G**.	*2316*
	10:15	What **G** hath cleansed, *that* call not thou	*2316*
	10:22	and one that feareth **G**, and of good report	*2316*
	10:22	was **warned from G** by a holy angel to	*5537*
	10:28	**G** hath shewed me that *I* should not call	*2316*
	10:31	are had in remembrance in the sight of **G**.	*2316*
	10:33	therefore are we all here present before **G**,	*2316*
	10:33	all *things* that are commanded thee of **G**.	*2316*
	10:34	Of a truth I perceive that **G** is no respecter	*2316*
	10:36	The word which **G** sent unto the children of	NIG
	10:38	How **G** anointed Jesus of Nazareth with	*2316*
	10:38	oppressed of the devil; for **G** was with him.	*2316*
	10:40	Him **G** raised up the third day, and	*2316*
	10:41	but unto witnesses chosen before of **G**,	*2316*
	10:42	was ordained of **G** *to be* the Judge of quick	*2316*
	10:46	them speak with tongues, and magnify **G**.	*2316*
	11: 1	Gentiles had also received the word of **G**.	*2316*
	11: 9	What **G** hath cleansed, *that* call not thou	*2316*
	11:17	as **G** gave them the like gift as *he did* unto	*2316*
	11:17	what was I, that I could withstand **G**?	*2316*
	11:18	held their peace, and glorified **G**, saying,	*2316*
	11:18	Then hath **G** also to the Gentiles granted	*2316*
	11:23	and had seen the grace of **G**, was glad, and	*2316*
	12: 5	ceasing of the church unto **G** for him.	*2316*
	12:22	*saying, It is* the voice of a **g**, and not of a	*2316*
	12:23	because he gave not **G** the glory:	*2316*
	12:24	But the word of **G** grew and multiplied.	*2316*
	13: 5	they preached the word of **G** in	*2316*
	13: 7	Saul, and desired to hear the word of **G**.	*2316*
	13:16	Men of Israel, and *ye* that fear **G**,	*2316*
	13:17	The **G** of this people of Israel chose our	*2316*
	13:21	and **G** gave unto them Saul the son of Cis,	*2316*
	13:23	Of this *man's* seed hath **G** according to *his*	*2316*
	13:26	and whosoever among you feareth **G**,	*2316*
	13:30	But **G** raised him from the dead:	*2316*
	13:33	**G** hath fulfilled the same unto us their	*2316*
	13:36	served his own generation by the will of **G**,	*2316*
	13:37	whom **G** raised *again,* saw no corruption.	*2316*
	13:43	them to continue in the grace of **G**.	*2316*
	13:44	whole city together to hear the word of **G**.	*2316*
	13:46	It was necessary that the word of **G** should	*2316*

Ac 14:15 turn from these vanities unto the living **G**, 2316
14:22 tribulation enter into the kingdom of **G**. 2316
14:26 of **G** for the work which they fulfilled. 2316
14:27 they rehearsed all that **G** had done with 2316
15: 4 they declared all *things* that **G** had done 2316
15: 7 ye know how that a good while ago **G** 2316
15: 8 And **G**, which knoweth the hearts, 2316
15:10 Now therefore why tempt ye **G**, to put a 2316
15:12 wonders **G** had wrought among 2316
15:14 Simeon hath declared how **G** at the first did 2316
15:18 Known unto **G** are all his works from 2316
15:19 from among the Gentiles are turned to **G**: 2316
15:40 by the brethren unto the grace of **G**. 2316
16:14 the city of Thyatira, which worshipped **G**, 2316
16:17 men are the servants of the most high **G**, 2316
16:25 and Silas prayed, and sang praises unto **G**: 2316
16:34 rejoiced, believing in **G** with all his house. 2316
17:13 word of **G** was preached of Paul at Berea, 2316
17:23 this inscription, TO *THE* UNKNOWN **G**. 2316
17:24 **G** that made the world and all *things* 2316
17:29 then as we are the offspring of **G**, 2316
17:30 And the times of *this* ignorance **G** winked 2316
18: 7 named Justus, one that worshipped **G**, 2316
18:11 teaching the word of **G** among them. 2316
18:13 This *fellow* persuadeth men to worship **G** 2316
18:21 but I will return again unto you, if **G** will. 2316
18:26 expounded unto him the way of **G** more 2316
19: 8 the *things* concerning the kingdom of **G**. 2316
19:11 And **G** wrought special miracles by 2316
19:20 So mightily grew the word of **G** and 2962
20:21 repentance toward **G**, and faith toward our 2316
20:24 to testify the gospel of the grace of **G**. 2316
20:25 I have gone preaching the kingdom of **G**, 2316
20:27 to declare unto you all the counsel of **G**. 2316
20:28 to feed the church of **G**, which he hath 2316
20:32 I commend you to **G**, and to the word of his 2316
21:19 he declared particularly what *things* **G** had 2316
22: 3 and was zealous towards **G**, as ye all are 2316
22:14 The **G** of our fathers hath chosen thee, 2316
23: 1 have lived in all good conscience before **G** 2316
23: 3 **G** shall smite thee, *thou* whited wall: 2316
23: 9 spoken to him, let us not **fight against G**. 2313
24:14 so worship I the **G** of my fathers, 2316
24:15 And have hope towards **G**, which they 2316
24:16 a conscience void of offence toward **G**, 2316
26: 6 of the promise made of **G** unto *our* fathers: 2316
26: 7 instantly serving **G** day and night, hope to NIG
26: 8 with you, that **G** should raise the dead? 2316
26:18 and *from* the power of Satan unto **G**, 2316
26:20 that *they* should repent and turn to **G**, and 2316
26:22 Having therefore obtained help of **G**, 2316
26:29 And Paul said, I would to **G**, that not only 2316
27:23 there stood by me this night *the* angel of **G**, 2316
27:24 **G** hath given thee all them that sail with 2316
27:25 for I believe **G**, that it shall be even as it 2316
27:35 gave thanks to **G** in presence of *them* all: 2316
28: 6 *their minds,* and said that he was a **g**. 2316
28:15 Paul saw, he thanked **G**, and took courage. 2316
28:23 and testified the kingdom of **G**, 2316
28:28 that the salvation of **G** is sent unto 2316
28:31 Preaching the kingdom of **G**, and 2316
Ro 1: 1 an apostle, separated unto the gospel of **G**, 2316
1: 4 *And* declared *to be* the Son of **G** with 2316
1: 7 in Rome, beloved of **G**, called *to be* saints: 2316
1: 7 Grace to you and peace from **G** our Father, 2316
1: 8 I thank my **G** through Jesus Christ for you 2316
1: 9 For **G** is my witness, whom I serve with 2316
1:10 journey by the will of **G** to come unto you. 2316
1:16 for it is the power of **G** unto salvation to 2316
1:17 For therein is the righteousness of **G** 2316
1:18 For the wrath of **G** is revealed from heaven 2316
1:19 Because that which may be known of **G** is 2316
1:19 in them; for **G** hath shewed *it* unto them. 2316
1:21 Because that, when they knew **G**, 2316
1:21 knew God, they glorified *him* not as **G**, 2316
1:23 **G** into an image made like to corruptible 2316
1:24 Wherefore **G** also gave them up to 2316
1:25 Who changed the truth of **G** into a lie, and 2316
1:26 For this cause **G** gave them up unto vile 2316
1:28 And even as they did not like to retain **G** in 2316
1:28 **G** gave them over to a reprobate mind, 2316
1:30 **haters of G**, despiteful, proud, boasters, 2319
1:32 Who knowing the judgment of **G**, that they 2316
2: 2 But we are sure that the judgment of **G** is 2316
2: 3 that thou shalt escape the judgment of **G**? 2316
2: 4 not knowing that the goodness of **G** leadeth 2316
2: 5 revelation of the righteous judgment of **G**; 2316
2:11 For there is no respect of persons with **G**. 2316
2:13 not the hearers of the law *are* just before **G**, 2316
2:16 In the day when **G** shall judge the secrets of 2316
2:17 in the law, and makest thy boast of **G**, 2316
2:23 breaking the law dishonourest thou **G**? 2316
2:24 For the name of **G** is blasphemed among 2316
2:29 whose praise *is* not of men, but of **G**. 2316
3: 2 them were committed the oracles of **G**. 2316
3: 3 shall their unbelief make the faith of **G** 2316
3: 4 **G forbid**: yea, let God be true, but 1096+3361
3: 4 yea, let **G** be true, but every man a liar; as it 2316
3: 5 commend the righteousness of **G**, 2316
3: 5 *Is* **G** unrighteous who taketh vengeance? 2316
3: 6 **G forbid**: for then how shall God 1096+3361
3: 6 then how shall **G** judge the world? 2316
3: 7 For if the truth of **G** hath *more* abounded 2316
3:11 there is none that seeketh after **G**. 2316
3:18 There is no fear of **G** before their eyes. 2316
3:19 all the world may become guilty before **G**. 2316
3:21 But now the righteousness of **G** without 2316
3:22 Even the righteousness of **G** *which is* by 2316
3:23 and come short of the glory of **G**; 2316
3:25 Whom **G** hath set forth *to be* a propitiation 2316
3:25 that are past, through the forbearance of **G**; 2316
3:29 *Is he* the **G** of the Jews only? *is he* not also 2316
3:30 Seeing *it is* one **G**, which shall justify 2316
3:31 **G forbid**: yea, we establish the law. 1096+3361
4: 2 he hath whereof to glory; but not before **G**. 2316
4: 3 Abraham believed **G**, and it was counted 2316
4: 6 unto whom **G** imputeth righteousness 2316
4:17 *even* **G**, who quickeneth the dead, and 2316
4:20 He staggered not at the promise of **G** 2316
4:20 but was strong in faith, giving glory to **G**; 2316
5: 1 we have peace with **G** through our Lord 2316
5: 2 and rejoice in hope of the glory of **G**. 2316
5: 5 the love of **G** is shed abroad in our hearts 2316
5: 8 But **G** commendeth his love toward us, 2316
5:10 we were reconciled to **G** by the death of his 2316
5:11 we also joy in **G** through our Lord Jesus 2316
5:15 much more the grace of **G**, and the gift by 2316
6: 2 **G forbid**. How shall we, that are 1096+3361
6:10 but in that he liveth, he liveth unto **G**. 2316
6:11 alive unto **G** through Jesus Christ our Lord. 2316
6:13 but yield yourselves unto **G**, as *those that* 2316
6:13 *as* instruments of righteousness unto **G**. 2316
6:15 the law, but under grace? **G forbid**. 1096+3361
6:17 But **G** be thanked, that ye were the servants 2316
6:22 and become servants to **G**, ye have your 2316
6:23 the gift of **G** *is* eternal life through Jesus 2316
7: 4 that we should bring forth fruit unto **G**. 2316
7: 7 **G forbid**. Nay, I had not known sin, 1096+3361
7:13 **G forbid**. But sin, that it might 1096+3361
7:22 For I delight in the law of **G** after 2316
7:25 I thank **G** through Jesus Christ our Lord. So 2316
7:25 with the mind I myself serve the law of **G**; 2316
8: 3 **G** sending his own Son in the likeness of 2316
8: 7 the carnal mind *is* enmity against **G**: 2316
8: 7 for it is not subject to the law of **G**, 2316
8: 8 they that are in the flesh cannot please **G**. 2316
8: 9 if so be that the Spirit of **G** dwell in you. 2316
8:14 For as many as are led by the Spirit of **G**, 2316
8:14 by the Spirit of God, they are the sons of **G**. 2316
8:16 our spirit, that we are the children of **G**: 2316
8:17 heirs of **G**, and joint-heirs with Christ; if so 2316
8:19 for the manifestation of the sons of **G**. 2316
8:21 the glorious liberty of the children of **G**. 2316
8:27 for the saints according to *the will of* **G**. 2316
8:28 work together for good to them that love **G**, 2316
8:31 then say to these *things?* If **G** *be* for us, 2316
8:33 of God's elect? *It is* **G** that justifieth: 2316
8:34 *again,* who is even at the right hand of **G**, 2316
8:39 be able to separate us from the love of **G**, 2316
9: 4 and the service *of* **G**, and the promises; NIG
9: 5 *came,* who is over all, **G** blessed for ever. 2316
9: 6 Not as though the word of **G** hath taken 2316
9: 8 of the flesh, these *are* not the children of **G**: 2316
9:11 that the purpose of **G** according to election 2316
9:14 *Is there* unrighteousness with **G**? 2316
9:14 with God? **G forbid**. 1096+3361
9:16 that runneth, but of **G** that sheweth mercy. 2316
9:20 who art thou that repliest against **G**? 2316

Ro 9:22 What if **G**, willing to shew *his* wrath, and 2316
9:26 they be called the children of the living **G**. 2316
10: 1 heart's desire and prayer to **G** for Israel is, 2316
10: 2 bear them record that they have a zeal of **G**, 2316
10: 3 themselves unto the righteousness of **G**. 2316
10: 9 shalt believe in thine heart that **G** hath 2316
10:17 by hearing, and hearing by the word of **G**. 2316
11: 1 I say then, Hath **G** cast away his people? 2316
11: 1 **G forbid**. For I also am an Israelite, 1096+3361
11: 2 **G** hath not cast away his people which he 2316
11: 2 how he maketh intercession to **G** against 2316
11: 4 But what saith the **answer of G** unto him? 5538
11: 8 **G** hath given them the spirit of slumber, 2316
11:11 that they should fall? **G forbid**: 1096+3361
11:21 For if **G** spared not the natural branches, 2316
11:22 therefore the goodness and severity of **G**: 2316
11:23 for **G** is able to graff them in again. 2316
11:29 and calling of **G** *are* without repentance. 2316
11:30 For as ye in times past have not believed **G**, 2316
11:32 For **G** hath concluded *them* all in unbelief, 2316
11:33 both of the wisdom and knowledge of **G**! 2316
12: 1 brethren, by the mercies of **G**, 2316
12: 1 holy, acceptable unto **G**, *which is* your 2316
12: 2 and acceptable, and perfect, will of **G**. 2316
12: 3 according as **G** hath dealt to every man 2316
13: 1 For there is no power but of **G**: the powers 2316
13: 1 the powers that be are ordained of **G**. 2316
13: 2 the power, resisteth the ordinance of **G**: 2316
13: 4 For he is the minister of **G** to thee for good. 2316
13: 4 for he is the minister of **G**, a revenger to 2316
14: 3 him that eateth: for **G** hath received him. 2316
14: 4 holden up: for **G** is able to make him stand. 2316
14: 6 eateth to the Lord, for he giveth **G** thanks; 2316
14: 6 Lord he eateth not, and giveth **G** thanks. 2316
14:11 to me, and every tongue shall confess to **G**. 2316
14:12 of us shall give account of himself to **G**. 2316
14:17 For the kingdom of **G** is not meat and 2316
14:18 *things* serveth Christ *is* acceptable to **G**, 2316
14:20 For meat destroy not the work of **G**. 2316
14:22 have *it* to thyself before **G**. Happy *is* he that 2316
15: 5 Now the **G** of patience and consolation 2316
15: 6 with one mind *and* one mouth glorify **G**, 2316
15: 7 Christ also received us, to the glory of **G**. 2316
15: 8 of the circumcision for the truth of **G**, 2316
15: 9 And that the Gentiles might glorify **G** for 2316
15:13 Now the **G** of hope fill you with all joy and 2316
15:15 of the grace that is given to me of **G**, 2316
15:16 ministering the gospel of **G**, that 2316
15:17 Christ *in those things* which pertain to **G**. 2316
15:19 wonders, by the power of the Spirit of **G**; 2316
15:30 with me in *your* prayers to **G** for me; 2316
15:32 come unto you with joy by the will of **G**, 2316
15:33 Now the **G** of peace *be* with you all. Amen. 2316
16:20 And the **G** of peace shall bruise Satan 2316
16:26 to the commandment of the everlasting **G**, 2316
16:27 To **G** only wise, *be* glory through Jesus 2316
1Co 1: 1 of Jesus Christ through the will of **G**, 2316
1: 2 Unto the church of **G** which is at Corinth, 2316
1: 3 from **G** our Father, and *from* the Lord Jesus 2316
1: 4 I thank my **G** always on your behalf, 2316
1: 4 for the grace of **G** which is given you by 2316
1: 9 **G** *is* faithful, by whom ye were called unto 2316
1:14 I thank **G** that I baptized none of you, but 2316
1:18 us which are saved it is the power of **G**. 2316
1:20 hath not **G** made foolish the wisdom of this 2316
1:21 For after that in the wisdom of **G** the world 2316
1:21 of God the world by wisdom knew not **G**, 2316
1:21 it pleased **G** by the foolishness of preaching 2316
1:24 Christ the power of **G**, and the wisdom of 2316
1:24 the power of God, and the wisdom of **G**. 2316
1:25 Because the foolishness of **G** is wiser than 2316
1:25 the weakness of **G** is stronger than men. 2316
1:27 But **G** hath chosen the foolish *things* of 2316
1:27 **G** hath chosen the weak *things* of the world 2316
1:28 hath **G** chosen, *yea,* and *things* which are 2316
1:30 who of **G** is made unto us wisdom, and 2316
2: 1 declaring unto you the testimony of **G**. 2316
2: 5 the wisdom of men, but in the power of **G**. 2316
2: 7 But we speak the wisdom of **G** in a 2316
2: 7 *even* the hidden *wisdom,* which **G** ordained 2316
2: 9 *the things* which **G** hath prepared for them 2316
2:10 But **G** hath revealed *them* unto us by his 2316
2:10 all *things,* yea, the deep things of **G**. 2316
2:11 so the *things* of **G** knoweth no *man,* but 2316
2:11 God knoweth no *man,* but the Spirit of **G**. 2316
2:12 of the world, but the Spirit which is of **G**; 2316
2:12 the *things* that are freely given to us of **G**. 2316
2:14 receiveth not the *things* of the Spirit of **G**: 2316
3: 6 Apollos watered; but **G** gave the increase. 2316
3: 7 but **G** that giveth the increase. 2316
3: 9 For we are labourers together with **G**: 2316
3:10 According to the grace of **G** which is given 2316
3:16 Know ye not that ye are the temple of **G**, 2316
3:16 and *that* the Spirit of **G** dwelleth in you? 2316
3:17 If any *man* defile the temple of **G**, 2316
3:17 the temple of God, him shall **G** destroy; 2316
3:17 for the temple of **G** is holy, which *temple* 2316
3:19 wisdom of this world is foolishness with **G**. 2316
4: 1 and stewards of the mysteries of **G**. 2316
4: 5 and then shall every man have praise of **G**. 2316
4: 8 and I would *to* **G** ye did reign, that we also NIG
4: 9 For I think that **G** hath set forth us 2316
4:20 For the kingdom of **G** *is* not in word, but 2316
5:13 But them that are without **G** judgeth. 2316
6: 9 shall not inherit the kingdom of **G**? 2316
6:10 shall inherit the kingdom of **G**. 2316
6:11 the Lord Jesus, and by the Spirit of our **G**. 2316
6:13 but **G** shall destroy both it and them. 2316
6:14 And **G** hath both raised up the Lord, and 2316
6:15 the members of a harlot? **G forbid**. 1096+3361
6:19 which ye have of **G**, and ye are not your 2316
6:20 therefore glorify **G** in your body, and 2316
7: 7 But every man hath his proper gift of **G**, 2316
7:15 such *cases:* but **G** hath called us to peace. 2316
7:17 But as **G** hath distributed to every man, 2316
7:19 the keeping of the commandments of **G**. 2316
7:24 wherein he is called, therein abide with **G**. 2316
7:40 and I think also that *I* have the Spirit of **G**. 2316
8: 3 But if any *man* love **G**, the same is known 2316
8: 4 and that *there is* none other **G** but one. 2316
8: 6 But to us *there is but* one **G**, the Father, 2316
8: 8 But meat commendeth us not to **G**: 2316
9: 9 out the corn. Doth **G** take care for oxen? 2316
9:21 (being not without law to **G**, but under 2316
10: 5 But with many of them **G** was not well 2316
10:13 but **G** *is* faithful, who will not suffer you to 2316
10:20 they sacrifice to devils, and not to **G**: 2316
10:31 whatsoever ye do, do all to the glory of **G**. 2316
10:32 nor to the Gentiles, nor to the church of **G**: 2316
11: 3 *is* the man; and the head of Christ *is* **G**. 2316
11: 7 as he is the image and glory of **G**: 2316
11:12 also by the woman; but all *things* of **G**. 2316
11:13 is it comely that a woman pray unto **G** 2316
11:16 no such custom, neither the churches of **G**. 2316
11:22 to drink *in?* or despise ye the church of **G**, 2316
12: 3 that no *man* speaking by the Spirit of **G** 2316
12: 6 it is the same **G** which worketh all in all. 2316
12:18 But now hath **G** set the members every one 2316
12:24 but **G** hath tempered the body together, 2316
12:28 And **G** hath set some in the church, 2316
14: 2 tongue speaketh not unto men, but unto **G**: 2316
14:18 I thank my **G**, I speak with tongues more 2316
14:25 falling down on *his* face he will worship **G**, 2316
14:25 and report that **G** is in you of a truth. 2316
14:28 and let him speak to himself, and to **G**. 2316
14:33 For **G** is not *the author* of confusion, but 2316
14:36 came the word of **G** out from you? or 2316
15: 9 because I persecuted the church of **G**. 2316
15:10 But by the grace of **G** I am what I am: and 2316
15:10 but the grace of **G** which was with me. 2316
15:15 and we are found false witnesses of **G**; 2316
15:15 we have testified of **G** that he raised up 2316
15:24 shall have delivered up the kingdom to **G**, 2316
15:28 *things* under him, that **G** may be all in all. 2316
15:34 for some have not the knowledge of **G**: 2316
15:38 But **G** giveth it a body as it hath pleased 2316
15:50 and blood cannot inherit the kingdom of **G**; 2316
15:57 But thanks *be* to **G**, which giveth us 2316
16: 2 as **G** hath prospered him, that there be no NIG
2Co 1: 1 an apostle of Jesus Christ by the will of **G**, 2316
1: 1 unto the church of **G** which is at Corinth, 2316
1: 2 *be* to you and peace from **G** our Father, 2316
1: 3 Blessed *be* **G**, even the Father of our Lord 2316
1: 3 Father of mercies, and the **G** of all comfort; 2316
1: 4 we ourselves are comforted of **G**. 2316
1: 9 but in **G** which raiseth the dead: 2316
1:12 with fleshly wisdom, but by the grace of **G**, 2316
1:18 But *as* **G** *is* true, our word toward you was 2316

2Co 1:19 For the Son of **G**, Jesus Christ, who was *2316*
1:20 For all the promises of **G** in him *are* yea, *2316*
1:20 in him Amen, unto the glory of **G** by us. *2316*
1:21 you in Christ, and hath anointed us, *is* **G**; *2316*
1:23 Moreover I call **G** for a record upon my *2316*
2:14 Now thanks *be* unto **G**, which always *2316*
2:15 For we are unto **G** a sweet savour of Christ, *2316*
2:17 not as many, which corrupt the word of **G**: *2316*
2:17 but as of sincerity, but as of **G**, in the sight *2316*
2:17 in the sight of **G** speak we in Christ. *2316*
3: 3 with ink, but with the Spirit of the living **G**; *2316*
3: 5 as of ourselves; but our sufficiency *is* of **G**; *2316*
4: 2 nor handling the word of **G** deceitfully; *2316*
4: 2 every man's conscience in the sight of **G**. *2316*
4: 4 In whom the **g** of this world hath blinded *2316*
4: 4 who is the image of **G**, should shine unto *2316*
4: 6 For **G**, who commanded the light to shine *2316*
4: 6 of the glory of **G** in the face of Jesus Christ. *2316*
4: 7 the excellency of the power may be of **G**, *2316*
4:15 of many redound to the glory of **G**. *2316*
5: 1 we have a building of **G**, a house not made *2316*
5: 5 hath wrought us for the selfsame *thing is* **G**, *2316*
5:11 but we are made manifest unto **G**; and *2316*
5:13 whether we be besides ourselves, *it is* to **G**: *2316*
5:18 And all *things are* of **G**, who hath *2316*
5:19 that **G** was in Christ reconciling the world *2316*
5:20 as though **G** did beseech *you* by us: *2316*
5:20 in Christ's stead, be ye reconciled to **G**. *2316*
5:21 be made the righteousness of **G** in him. *2316*
6: 1 that ye receive not the grace of **G** in vain. *2316*
6: 4 approving ourselves as the ministers of **G**, *2316*
6: 7 By the word of truth, by the power of **G**, *2316*
6:16 And what agreement hath the temple of **G** *2316*
6:16 for ye are the temple of the living **G**; *2316*
6:16 as **G** hath said, I will dwell in them, and *2316*
6:16 and walk in *them;* and I will be their **G**, and *2316*
7: 1 spirit, perfecting holiness in the fear of **G**. *2316*
7: 6 Nevertheless **G**, that comforteth *those that* *2316*
7:12 that our care for you in the sight of **G** might *2316*
8: 1 we do you to wit of the grace of **G** *2316*
8: 5 to the Lord, and unto us by the will of **G**. *2316*
8:16 But thanks *be* to **G**, which put the same *2316*
9: 7 of necessity: for **G** loveth a cheerful giver. *2316*
9: 8 And **G** *is* able to make all grace abound *2316*
9:11 causeth through us thanksgiving to **G**. *2316*
9:12 also by many thanksgivings unto **G**; *2316*
9:13 **G** for your professed subjection unto *2316*
9:14 you for the exceeding grace of **G** in you. *2316*
9:15 Thanks *be* unto **G** for his unspeakable gift. *2316*
10: 4 mighty through **G** to the pulling down of *2316*
10: 5 exalteth itself against the knowledge of **G**, *2316*
10:13 of the rule which **G** hath distributed to us, *2316*
11: 1 Would *to* **G** you could bear with me a little NIG
11: 7 I have preached to you the gospel of **G** *2316*
11:11 because I love you not? **G** knoweth. *2316*
11:31 The **G** and Father of our Lord Jesus Christ, *2316*
12: 2 **G** knoweth;) such a one caught up to *2316*
12: 3 out of the body, I cannot tell: **G** knoweth;) *2316*
12:19 we speak before **G** in Christ: but *we do* all *2316*
12:21 my **G** will humble *me* among you, and *2316*
13: 4 yet he liveth by the power of **G**. *2316*
13: 4 we shall live with him by the power of **G** *2316*
13: 7 Now I pray to **G** that ye do no evil; not that *2316*
13:11 and the **G** of love and peace shall be with *2316*
13:14 and the love of **G**, and the communion of *2316*
Gal 1: 1 but by Jesus Christ, and **G** the Father, *2316*
1: 3 *be* to you and peace from **G** the Father, *2316*
1: 4 according to the will of **G** and our Father: *2316*
1:10 For do I now persuade men, or **G**? or do I *2316*
1:13 measure I persecuted the church of **G**, *2316*
1:15 But when it pleased **G**, who separated me *2316*
1:20 I write unto you, behold, before **G**, I lie not. *2316*
1:24 And they glorified **G** in me. *2316*
2: 6 **G** accepteth no man's person:) for they *2316*
2:17 Christ the minister of sin? **G forbid**. *1096+3361*
2:19 dead to the law, that I might live unto **G**. *2316*
2:20 the flesh I live by the faith of the Son of **G**, *2316*
2:21 I do not frustrate the grace of **G**: for if *2316*
3: 6 Even as Abraham believed **G**, and it was *2316*
3: 8 foreseeing that **G** would justify the heathen *2316*
3:11 is justified by the law in the sight of **G**, *2316*
3:17 that was confirmed before of **G** in Christ, *2316*
3:18 but **G** gave *it* to Abraham by promise. *2316*
3:20 is not *a mediator* of one, but **G** is one. *2316*
3:21 *Is* the law then against the promises of **G**? *2316*
3:21 **G forbid**: for if there had been a law *1096+3361*
3:26 For ye are all the children of **G** by faith in *2316*
4: 4 **G** sent forth his Son, made of a woman, *2316*
4: 6 **G** hath sent forth the Spirit of his Son into *2316*
4: 7 if a son, then an heir of **G** through Christ. *2316*
4: 8 Howbeit then, when ye knew not **G**, ye did *2316*
4: 9 after that ye have known **G**, or rather are *2316*
4: 9 or rather are known of **G**, how turn ye *2316*
4:14 but received me as an angel of **G**, *even* as *2316*
5:21 *things* shall not inherit the kingdom of **G**. *2316*
6: 7 Be not deceived; **G** is not mocked: *2316*
6:14 But **G forbid** that I should glory, *1096+3361*
6:16 and mercy, and upon the Israel of **G**. *2316*
Eph 1: 1 an apostle of Jesus Christ by the will of **G**, *2316*
1: 2 from **G** our Father, and *from* the Lord Jesus *2316*
1: 3 Blessed *be* the **G** and Father of our Lord *2316*
1:17 That the **G** of our Lord Jesus Christ, *2316*
2: 4 But **G**, who is rich in mercy, for his great *2316*
2: 8 that not of yourselves: *it is* the gift of **G**: *2316*
2:10 which **G** hath before ordained that we *2316*
2:12 having no hope, and **without G** in the world: *112*
2:16 And *that* he might reconcile both unto **G** in *2316*
2:19 with the saints, and of the household of **G**; *2316*
2:22 for a habitation of **G** through the Spirit. *2316*
3: 2 grace of **G** which is given me to you-ward: *2316*
3: 7 according to the gift of the grace of **G** *2316*
3: 9 beginning of the world hath been hid in **G**, *2316*
3:10 by the church the manifold wisdom of **G**, *2316*
3:19 ye might be filled with all the fulness of **G**. *2316*
4: 6 One **G** and Father of all, who *is* above all, *2316*
4:13 and of the knowledge of the Son of **G**, *2316*
4:18 being alienated from the life of **G** through *2316*
4:24 which after **G** is created in righteousness *2316*
4:30 And grieve not the holy Spirit of **G**, *2316*
4:32 even as **G** for Christ's sake hath forgiven *2316*
5: 1 Be ye therefore followers of **G**, as dear *2316*
5: 2 a sacrifice to **G** for a sweetsmelling savour. *2316*
5: 5 in the kingdom of Christ and of **G**. *2316*
5: 6 of these *things* cometh the wrath of **G** upon *2316*
5:20 Giving thanks always for all *things* unto **G** *2316*
5:21 yourselves one to another in the fear of **G**. *2316*
6: 6 doing the will of **G** from the heart; *2316*
6:11 Put on the whole armour of **G**, that ye may *2316*
6:13 take unto *you* the whole armour of **G**, *2316*
6:17 sword of the Spirit, which is the word of **G**: *2316*
6:23 from **G** the Father and the Lord Jesus *2316*
Php 1: 2 from **G** our Father, and *from* the Lord Jesus *2316*
1: 3 I thank my **G** upon every remembrance of *2316*
1: 8 For **G** is my record, how *greatly* I long *2316*
1:11 Jesus Christ unto the glory and praise of **G**. *2316*
1:28 but to you of salvation, and that of **G**. *2316*
2: 6 Who, being in the form of **G**, thought it not *2316*
2: 6 thought it not robbery to be equal with **G**: *2316*
2: 9 Wherefore **G** also hath highly exalted him, *2316*
2:11 Christ *is* Lord, to the glory of **G** the Father. *2316*
2:13 For it is **G** which worketh in you both to *2316*
2:15 harmless, the sons of **G** without rebuke, *2316*
2:27 but **G** had mercy on him; and not on him *2316*
3: 3 which worship **G** in the spirit, and *2316*
3: 9 the righteousness which is of **G** by faith: *2316*
3:14 of the high calling of **G** in Christ Jesus. *2316*
3:15 **G** shall reveal even this unto you. *2316*
3:19 whose **G** *is their* belly, and *whose* glory *is* *2316*
4: 6 let your requests be made known unto **G**. *2316*
4: 7 And the peace of **G**, which passeth all *2316*
4: 9 do: and the **G** of peace shall be with you. *2316*
4:18 a sacrifice acceptable, well pleasing to **G**. *2316*
4:19 But my **G** shall supply all your need *2316*
4:20 Now unto **G** and our Father *be* glory for *2316*
Col 1: 1 an apostle of Jesus Christ by the will of **G**, *2316*
1: 2 from **G** our Father and the Lord Jesus *2316*
1: 3 We give thanks to **G** and the Father of our *2316*
1: 6 of *it,* and knew the grace of **G** in truth: *2316*
1:10 and increasing in the knowledge of **G**; *2316*
1:15 Who is the image of the invisible **G**, *2316*
1:25 according to the dispensation of **G** which is *2316*
1:25 given to me for you, to fulfil the word of **G**; *2316*
1:27 To whom **G** would make known what *is* *2316*
2: 2 the acknowledgement of the mystery of **G** *2316*
2:12 *him* through the faith of the operation of **G**, *2316*
2:19 increaseth *with* the increase of **G**. *2316*
3: 1 where Christ sitteth on the right hand of **G**. *2316*
3: 3 and your life is hid with Christ in **G**. *2316*

Col 3: 6 For which *things'* sake the wrath of **G** *2316*
3:12 as the elect of **G**, holy and beloved, *2316*
3:15 And let the peace of **G** rule in your hearts, *2316*
3:17 giving thanks to **G** and the Father by him. *2316*
3:22 but in singleness of heart, fearing **G**: *2316*
4: 3 that **G** would open unto us a door of *2316*
4:11 *my* fellowworkers unto the kingdom of **G**, *2316*
4:12 and complete in all the will of **G**. *2316*
1Th 1: 1 the Thessalonians *which is* in **G** the Father *2316*
1: 1 from **G** our Father, and the Lord Jesus *2316*
1: 2 We give thanks to **G** always for you all, *2316*
1: 3 in the sight of **G** and our Father; *2316*
1: 4 brethren beloved, your election of **G**. *2316*
1: 9 how ye turned to **G** from idols to serve *2316*
1: 9 from idols to serve the living and true **G**, *2316*
2: 2 we were bold in our **G** to speak unto you *2316*
2: 2 you the gospel of **G** with much contention. *2316*
2: 4 But as we were allowed of **G** to be put in *2316*
2: 4 not as pleasing men, but **G**, which trieth *2316*
2: 5 nor a cloke of covetousness; **G** *is* witness: *2316*
2: 8 not the gospel of **G** only, but also our own *2316*
2: 9 we preached unto you the gospel of **G**. *2316*
2:10 and **G** *also,* how holily and justly and *2316*
2:12 That ye would walk worthy of **G**, who hath *2316*
2:13 For this cause also thank we **G** without *2316*
2:13 when ye received the word of **G** which *ye* *2316*
2:13 of men, but as it is in truth, the word of **G**, *2316*
2:14 became followers of the churches of **G** *2316*
2:15 and they please not **G**, and are contrary to *2316*
3: 2 and minister of **G**, and our fellowlabourer *2316*
3: 9 For what thanks can we render to **G** again *2316*
3: 9 we joy for your sakes before our **G**; *2316*
3:11 Now **G** himself and our Father, and *2316*
3:13 hearts unblameable in holiness before **G**, *2316*
4: 1 us how ye ought to walk and to please **G**, *2316*
4: 3 For this is the will of **G**, *even* your *2316*
4: 5 even as the Gentiles which know not **G**: *2316*
4: 7 For **G** hath not called us unto uncleanness, *2316*
4: 8 that despiseth, despiseth not man, but **G**, *2316*
4: 9 for ye yourselves are **taught of G** to love *2312*
4:14 them also which sleep in Jesus will **G** bring *2316*
4:16 of the archangel, and with the trump of **G**: *2316*
5: 9 For **G** hath not appointed us to wrath, but *2316*
5:18 for this *is* the will of **G** in Christ Jesus *2316*
5:23 And the very **G** of peace sanctify you *2316*
5:23 and *I pray* **G** your whole spirit and soul and NIG
2Th 1: 1 unto the church of the Thessalonians in **G** *2316*
1: 2 from **G** our Father and the Lord Jesus *2316*
1: 3 We are bound to thank **G** always for you, *2316*
1: 4 you in the churches of **G** for your patience *2316*
1: 5 token of the righteous judgment of **G**, *2316*
1: 5 be counted worthy of the kingdom of **G**, *2316*
1: 6 Seeing *it is* a righteous *thing* with **G** to *2316*
1: 8 taking vengeance on them that know not **G**, *2316*
1:11 that our **G** would count you worthy of *this* *2316*
1:12 according to the grace of our **G** and *2316*
2: 4 exalteth himself above all that is called **G**, *2316*
2: 4 so that he as **G** sitteth in the temple of God, NIG
2: 4 so that he as God sitteth in the temple of **G**, *2316*
2: 4 of God, shewing himself that he is **G**. *2316*
2:11 And for this cause **G** shall send them strong *2316*
2:13 bound to give thanks alway to **G** for you, *2316*
2:13 **G** hath from the beginning chosen you to *2316*
2:16 and **G**, even our Father, which hath loved *2316*
3: 5 Lord direct your hearts into the love of **G**, *2316*
1Ti 1: 1 by the commandment of **G** our Saviour, *2316*
1: 2 from **G** our Father and Jesus Christ our *2316*
1:11 to the glorious gospel of the blessed **G**, *2316*
1:17 immortal, invisible, the only wise **G**, *2316*
2: 3 acceptable in the sight of **G** our Saviour; *2316*
2: 5 For *there is* one **G**, and one mediator *2316*
2: 5 and one mediator between **G** and men, *2316*
3: 5 how shall he take care of the church of **G**?) *2316*
3:15 to behave thyself in the house of **G**, *2316*
3:15 which is the church of the living **G**, *2316*
3:16 **G** was manifest in the flesh, justified in *2316*
4: 3 which **G** hath created to be received with *2316*
4: 4 For every creature of **G** *is* good, and *2316*
4: 5 For it is sanctified by the word of **G** and *2316*
4:10 because we trust in the living **G**, *2316*
5: 4 for that is good and acceptable before **G**. *2316*
5: 5 trusteth in **G**, and continueth in *2316*
5:21 I charge *thee* before **G**, and the Lord Jesus *2316*
6: 1 that the name of **G** and *his* doctrine be not *2316*
6:11 But thou, O man of **G**, flee these *things;* *2316*
6:13 I give thee charge in the sight of **G**, *2316*
6:17 trust in uncertain riches, but in the living **G**, *2316*
2Ti 1: 1 an apostle of Jesus Christ by the will of **G**, *2316*
1: 2 from **G** the Father and Christ Jesus our *2316*
1: 3 I thank **G**, whom I serve from *my* *2316*
1: 6 remembrance that *thou* stir up the gift of **G**, *2316*
1: 7 For **G** hath not given us the spirit of fear; *2316*
1: 8 of the gospel according to the power of **G**; *2316*
2: 9 unto bonds; but the word of **G** is not bound. *2316*
2:15 Study to shew thyself approved unto **G**, *2316*
2:19 Nevertheless the foundation of **G** standeth *2316*
2:25 if **G** peradventure will give them *2316*
3: 4 lovers of pleasures more than **lovers of G**; *5377*
3:16 All scripture *is* **given by inspiration of G**, *2315*
3:17 That the man of **G** may be perfect, *2316*
4: 1 I charge *thee* therefore before **G**, and *2316*
4:16 *I pray* **G** that it may not be laid to their NIG
Tit 1: 1 a servant of **G**, and an apostle of Jesus *2316*
1: 2 of eternal life, which **G**, that cannot lie, *2316*
1: 3 to the commandment of **G** our Saviour; *2316*
1: 4 from **G** the Father and the Lord Jesus *2316*
1: 7 must be blameless, as the steward of **G**; *2316*
1:16 They profess that *they* know **G**; but *2316*
2: 5 that the word of **G** be not blasphemed. *2316*
2:10 that they may adorn the doctrine of **G** our *2316*
2:11 For the grace of **G** that bringeth salvation *2316*
2:13 the glorious appearing of the great **G** and *2316*
3: 4 love of **G** our Saviour toward man *2316*
3: 8 that they which have believed in **G** might *2316*
Phm 1: 3 from **G** our Father and the Lord Jesus *2316*
1: 4 I thank my **G**, making mention of thee *2316*
Heb 1: 1 **G**, who at sundry times and in divers *2316*
1: 6 And let all the angels of **G** worship him. *2316*
1: 8 *saith,* Thy throne, O **G**, *is* for ever and ever: *2316*
1: 9 therefore **G**, *even* thy God, hath anointed *2316*
1: 9 therefore God, *even* thy **G**, hath anointed *2316*
2: 4 **G** also bearing *them* witness, both with *2316*
2: 9 that he by the grace of **G** should taste *2316*
2:13 I, and the children which **G** hath given me. *2316*
2:17 high priest *in things* pertaining to **G**, *2316*
3: 4 some *man;* but he that built all *things is* **G**. *2316*
3:12 of unbelief, in departing from the living **G**. *2316*
4: 4 And **G** did rest the seventh day from all his *2316*
4: 9 therefore a rest to the people of **G**. *2316*
4:10 from his own works, as **G** *did* from his. *2316*
4:12 For the word of **G** *is* quick, and powerful, *2316*
4:14 Jesus the Son of **G**, let us hold fast *our* *2316*
5: 1 ordained for men *in things* pertaining to **G**, *2316*
5: 4 but he that is called of **G**, as *was* Aaron. *2316*
5:10 Called of **G** a high priest after the order of *2316*
5:12 *be* the first principles of the oracles of **G**; *2316*
6: 1 from dead works, and of faith towards **G**, *2316*
6: 3 And this will we do, if **G** permit. *2316*
6: 5 And have tasted the good word of **G**, and *2316*
6: 6 crucify to themselves the Son of **G** afresh, *2316*
6: 7 it is dressed, receiveth blessing from **G**: *2316*
6:10 For **G** *is* not unrighteous to forget your *2316*
6:13 For when **G** made promise to Abraham, *2316*
6:17 Wherein **G**, willing more abundantly to *2316*
6:18 in which *it was* impossible for **G** to lie, *2316*
7: 1 king of Salem, priest of the most high **G**, *2316*
7: 3 of life; but made like unto the Son of **G**; *2316*
7:19 *did;* by the which we draw nigh unto **G**. *2316*
7:25 to the uttermost that come unto **G** by him, *2316*
8: 5 **admonished of G** when he was about to *5537*
8:10 and I will be to them a **G**, and they shall be *2316*
9: 6 accomplishing the service *of* **G**. NIG
9:14 Spirit offered himself without spot to **G**, *2316*
9:14 from dead works to serve the living **G**? *2316*
9:20 This *is* the blood of the testament which **G** *2316*
9:24 now to appear in the presence of **G** for us: *2316*
10: 7 it is written of me,) to do thy will, O **G**. *2316*
10: 9 said he, Lo, I come to do thy will, O **G**. *2316*
10:12 for ever, sat down on the right hand of **G**; *2316*
10:21 *having* a high priest over the house of **G**; *2316*
10:29 who hath trodden under foot the Son of **G**, *2316*
10:31 *thing* to fall into the hands of the living **G**. *2316*
10:36 that, after ye have done the will of **G**, *2316*
11: 3 the worlds were framed by the word of **G**, *2316*
11: 4 By faith Abel offered unto **G** a more *2316*
11: 4 he was righteous, **G** testifying of his gifts: *2316*
11: 5 not found, because **G** had translated him: *2316*
11: 5 he had this testimony, that *he* pleased **G**. *2316*

Heb 11: 6 he that cometh to **G** must believe that he is, *2316*
11: 7 being **warned of G** of *things* not seen as *5537*
11:10 whose builder and maker *is* **G**. *2316*
11:16 wherefore **G** is not ashamed to be called *2316*
11:16 God is not ashamed to be called their **G**: *2316*
11:19 Accounting that **G** *was* able to raise *him* *2316*
11:25 to suffer affliction with the people of **G**, *2316*
11:40 **G** having provided some better *thing* for us, *2316*
12: 2 down at the right hand of the throne of **G**. *2316*
12: 7 **G** dealeth with you as with sons; *2316*
12:15 lest any *man* fail of the grace of **G**; *2316*
12:22 and unto the city of the living **G**, *2316*
12:23 and to **G** the Judge of all, and to the spirits *2316*
12:28 whereby we may serve **G** acceptably with *2316*
12:29 For our **G** *is* a consuming fire. *2316*
13: 4 and adulterers **G** will judge. *2316*
13: 7 who have spoken unto you the word of **G**: *2316*
13:15 let us offer the sacrifice of praise to **G** *2316*
13:16 for with such sacrifices **G** is well pleased. *2316*
13:20 Now the **G** of peace, that brought again *2316*
Jas 1: 1 a servant of **G** and of the Lord Jesus Christ, *2316*
1: 5 any of you lack wisdom, let him ask of **G**, *2316*
1:13 say when he is tempted, I am tempted of **G**: *2316*
1:13 for **G** cannot be tempted with evil, *2316*
1:20 of man worketh not the righteousness of **G**. *2316*
1:27 Pure religion and undefiled before **G** and *2316*
2: 5 Hath not **G** chosen the poor of this world *2316*
2:19 Thou believest that there is one **G**; *2316*
2:23 Abraham believed **G**, and it was imputed *2316*
2:23 and he was called the Friend of **G**. *2316*
3: 9 Therewith bless we **G**, even the Father; and *2316*
3: 9 which are made after the similitude of **G**. *2316*
4: 4 friendship of the world is enmity with **G**? *2316*
4: 4 be a friend of the world is the enemy of **G**. *2316*
4: 6 **G** resisteth the proud, but giveth grace unto *2316*
4: 7 Submit yourselves therefore to **G**. Resist *2316*
4: 8 Draw nigh to **G**, and he will draw nigh to *2316*
1Pe 1: 2 Elect according to the foreknowledge of **G** *2316*
1: 3 Blessed *be* the **G** and Father of our Lord *2316*
1: 5 Who are kept by the power of **G** through *2316*
1:21 Who by him do believe in **G**, that raised *2316*
1:21 that your faith and hope might be in **G**. *2316*
1:23 by the word of **G**, which liveth and *2316*
2: 4 of men, but chosen of **G**, *and* precious, *2316*
2: 5 acceptable to **G** by Jesus Christ. *2316*
2:10 not a people, but *are* now the people of **G**: *2316*
2:12 glorify **G** in the day of visitation. *2316*
2:15 For so is the will of **G**, that with well doing *2316*
2:16 of maliciousness, but as the servants of **G**. *2316*
2:17 the brotherhood. Fear **G**. Honour the king. *2316*
2:19 if a man for conscience toward **G** endure *2316*
2:20 take it patiently, this *is* acceptable with **G**. *2316*
3: 4 which is in the sight of **G** of great price. *2316*
3: 5 who trusted in **G**, adorned themselves, *2316*
3:15 But sanctify the Lord **G** in your hearts: and *2316*
3:17 For *it is* better, if the will of **G** be so, *2316*
3:18 for the unjust, that he might bring us to **G**, *2316*
3:20 when once the longsuffering of **G** waited in *2316*
3:21 answer of a good conscience toward **G**,) *2316*
3:22 into heaven, and is on the right hand of **G**; *2316*
4: 2 to the lusts of men, but to the will of **G**. *2316*
4: 6 but live according to **G** in the spirit. *2316*
4:10 good stewards of the manifold grace of **G**. *2316*
4:11 *let him speak* as the oracles of **G**; *2316*
4:11 *let him do it* as of the ability which **G** *2316*
4:11 that **G** in all *things* may be glorified *2316*
4:14 spirit of glory and of **G** resteth upon you: *2316*
4:16 but let him glorify **G** on this behalf. *2316*
4:17 judgment must begin at the house of **G**: *2316*
4:17 *be* of them that obey not the gospel of **G**? *2316*
4:19 **G** commit the keeping of their souls *to him* *2316*
5: 2 Feed the flock of **G** which is among you, *2316*
5: 5 for **G** resisteth the proud, and giveth grace *2316*
5: 6 therefore under the mighty hand of **G**, *2316*
5:10 But the **G** of all grace, who hath called us *2316*
5:12 testifying that this is the true grace of **G** *2316*
2Pe 1: 1 with us through the righteousness of **G** *2316*
1: 2 unto you through the knowledge of **G**, *2316*
1:17 For he received from **G** the Father honour *2316*
1:21 holy men of **G** spake *as they were* moved *2316*
2: 4 For if **G** spared not the angels that sinned, *2316*
3: 5 that by the word of **G** the heavens were of *2316*
3:12 hasting *unto* the coming of the day of **G**, *2316*
1Jn 1: 5 that **G** is light, and in him is no darkness at *2316*
2: 5 in him verily is the love of **G** perfected: *2316*
2:14 and the word of **G** abideth in you, and *2316*
2:17 he that doeth the will of **G** abideth for ever. *2316*
3: 1 that we should be called the sons of **G**: *2316*
3: 2 now are we the sons of **G**, and it doth not *2316*
3: 8 For this purpose the Son of **G** was *2316*
3: 9 Whosoever is born of **G** doth not commit *2316*
3: 9 and he cannot sin, because he is born of **G**. *2316*
3:10 In this the children of **G** are manifest, and *2316*
3:10 doeth not righteousness is not of **G**, *2316*
3:16 Hereby perceive we the love *of* **G**, because NIG
3:17 how dwelleth the love of **G** in him? *2316*
3:20 **G** is greater than our heart, and *2316*
3:21 us not, *then* have we confidence towards **G**. *2316*
4: 1 but try the spirits whether they are of **G**: *2316*
4: 2 Hereby know ye the Spirit of **G**: *2316*
4: 2 Jesus Christ is come in the flesh is of **G**: *2316*
4: 3 Christ is come in the flesh is not of **G**: *2316*
4: 4 Ye are of **G**, little children, and *2316*
4: 6 We are of **G**: he that knoweth God heareth *2316*
4: 6 he that knoweth **G** heareth us; *he* that is not *2316*
4: 6 *he* that is not of **G** heareth not us. *2316*
4: 7 for love is of **G**; and every one that loveth *2316*
4: 7 and every one that loveth is born of **G**, and *2316*
4: 7 that loveth is born of God, and knoweth **G**. *2316*
4: 8 He that loveth not, knoweth not **G**; for God *2316*
4: 8 loveth not, knoweth not God; for **G** is love. *2316*
4: 9 In this was manifested the love of **G** *2316*
4: 9 that **G** sent his only begotten Son into *2316*
4:10 not that we loved **G**, but that he loved us, *2316*
4:11 Beloved, if **G** so loved us, we ought also to *2316*
4:12 No *man* hath seen **G** at any time. If we love *2316*
4:12 **G** dwelleth in us, and his love is perfected *2316*
4:15 shall confess that Jesus is the Son of **G**, *2316*
4:15 of God, **G** dwelleth in him, and he in God. *2316*
4:15 of God, God dwelleth in him, and he in **G**. *2316*
4:16 and believed the love that **G** hath to us. *2316*
4:16 **G** is love; and he that dwelleth in love *2316*
4:16 and he that dwelleth in love dwelleth in **G**, *2316*
4:16 in love dwelleth in God, and **G** in him. *2316*
4:20 I love **G**, and hateth his brother, he is a liar: *2316*
4:20 how can he love **G** whom he hath not seen? *2316*
4:21 That he who loveth **G** love his brother also. *2316*
5: 1 that Jesus is the Christ is born of **G**: *2316*
5: 2 we know that we love the children of **G**, *2316*
5: 2 when we love **G**, and keep his *2316*
5: 3 For this is the love of **G**, that we keep his *2316*
5: 4 For whatsoever is born of **G** overcometh *2316*
5: 5 he that believeth that Jesus is the Son of **G**? *2316*
5: 9 witness of men, the witness of **G** is greater: *2316*
5: 9 for this is the witness of **G** which he hath *2316*
5:10 He that believeth on the Son of **G** hath *2316*
5:10 he that believeth not **G** hath made him a *2316*
5:10 he believeth not the record that **G** gave of *2316*
5:11 that **G** hath given to us eternal life, and *2316*
5:12 he that hath not the Son of **G** hath not life. *2316*
5:13 that believe on the name of the Son of **G**; *2316*
5:13 may believe on the name of the Son of **G**. *2316*
5:18 We know that whosoever is born of **G** *2316*
5:18 he that is begotten of **G** keepeth himself, *2316*
5:19 *And* we know that we are of **G**, and *2316*
5:20 And we know that the Son of **G** is come, *2316*
5:20 This is the true **G**, and eternal life. *2316*
2Jn 1: 3 from **G** the Father, and from the Lord Jesus *2316*
1: 9 not in the doctrine of Christ, hath not **G**. *2316*
1:10 into *your* house, neither bid him **G speed**: *5463*
1:11 For he that biddeth him **G speed** is partaker *5463*
3Jn 1:11 He that doeth good is of **G**: but he that *2316*
1:11 but he that doeth evil hath not seen **G**. *2316*
Jude 1: 1 to them that are sanctified by **G** the Father, *2316*
1: 4 ungodly *men,* turning the grace of our **G** *2316*
1: 4 and denying the only Lord **G**, and our Lord *2316*
1:21 Keep yourselves in the love of **G**, *2316*
1:25 To the only wise **G** our Saviour, *be* glory *2316*
Rev 1: 1 of Jesus Christ, which **G** gave unto him, *2316*
1: 2 Who bare record of the word of **G**, and *2316*
1: 6 us kings and priests unto **G** and his Father; *2316*
1: 9 for the word of **G**, and for the testimony of *2316*
2: 7 which is in the midst of the paradise of **G**. *2316*
2:18 These *things* saith the Son of **G**, who hath *2316*
3: 1 saith he that hath the seven spirits of **G**, *2316*
3: 2 have not found thy works perfect before **G**. *2316*
3:12 will I make a pillar in the temple of my **G**, *2316*
3:12 I will write upon him the name of my **G**, *2316*

Rev	3:12	and the name of the city of my **G**, *which is*	*2316*
	3:12	cometh down out of heaven from my **G**:	*2316*
	3:14	the beginning of the creation of **G**;	*2316*
	4: 5	the throne, which are the seven spirits of **G**.	*2316*
	4: 8	saying, Holy, holy, holy, Lord **G** Almighty,	*2316*
	5: 6	which are the seven spirits of **G** sent forth	*2316*
	5: 9	hast redeemed us to **G** by thy blood out of	*2316*
	5:10	And hast made us unto our **G** kings and	*2316*
	6: 9	of them that were slain for the word of **G**,	*2316*
	7: 2	the east, having the seal of the living **G**:	*2316*
	7: 3	till we have sealed the servants of our **G** in	*2316*
	7:10	Salvation to our **G** which sitteth upon	*2316*
	7:11	throne on their faces, and worshipped **G**,	*2316*
	7:12	and might, *be* unto our **G** for ever and ever.	*2316*
	7:15	Therefore are they before the throne of **G**,	*2316*
	7:17	**G** shall wipe away all tears from their eyes.	*2316*
	8: 2	saw the seven angels which stood before **G**;	*2316*
	8: 4	ascended up before **G** out of the angel's	*2316*
	9: 4	have not the seal of **G** in their foreheads.	*2316*
	9:13	horns of the golden altar which is before **G**,	*2316*
	10: 7	the mystery of **G** should be finished,	*2316*
	11: 1	and measure the temple of **G**, and the altar,	*2316*
	11: 4	the two candlesticks standing before the **G**	*2316*
	11:11	a half the spirit of life from **G** entered into	*2316*
	11:13	and gave glory to the **G** of heaven.	*2316*
	11:16	which sat before **G** on their seats,	*2316*
	11:16	fell upon their faces, and worshipped **G**,	*2316*
	11:17	O Lord **G** Almighty, which art, and wast,	*2316*
	11:19	And the temple of **G** was opened in heaven,	*2316*
	12: 5	and her child was caught up unto **G**, and	*2316*
	12: 6	where she hath a place prepared of **G**,	*2316*
	12:10	and the kingdom of our **G**, and the power	*2316*
	12:10	which accused them before our **G** day and	*2316*
	12:17	which keep the commandments of **G**, and	*2316*
	13: 6	opened his mouth in blasphemy against **G**,	*2316*
	14: 4	*being* the firstfruits unto **G** and to	*2316*
	14: 5	are without fault before the throne of **G**.	*2316*
	14: 7	a loud voice, Fear **G**, and give glory to him;	*2316*
	14:10	shall drink of the wine of the wrath of **G**,	*2316*
	14:12	*are* they that keep the commandments of **G**,	*2316*
	14:19	into the great winepress of the wrath of **G**.	*2316*
	15: 1	for in them is filled up the wrath of **G**.	*2316*
	15: 2	on the sea of glass, having *the* harps of **G**.	*2316*
	15: 3	sing the song of Moses the servant of **G**,	*2316*
	15: 3	*are* thy works, Lord **G** Almighty;	*2316*
	15: 7	seven golden vials full of the wrath of **G**,	*2316*
	15: 8	was filled with smoke from the glory of **G**,	*2316*
	16: 1	pour out the vials of the wrath of **G** upon	*2316*
	16: 7	Lord **G** Almighty, true and righteous *are*	*2316*
	16: 9	and blasphemed the name of **G**, which hath	*2316*
	16:11	And blasphemed the **G** of heaven because	*2316*
	16:14	the battle of that great day of **G** Almighty.	*2316*
	16:19	Babylon came in remembrance before **G**,	*2316*
	16:21	and men blasphemed **G** because of	*2316*
	17:17	For **G** hath put in their hearts to fulfil his	*2316*
	17:17	until the words of **G** shall be fulfilled.	*2316*
	18: 5	and **G** hath remembered her iniquities.	*2316*
	18: 8	for strong *is* the Lord **G** who judgeth her.	*2316*
	18:20	for **G** hath avenged you on her.	*2316*
	19: 1	honour, and power, unto the Lord our **G**:	*2316*
	19: 4	and worshipped **G** that sat on the throne,	*2316*
	19: 5	saying, Praise our **G**, all ye his servants,	*2316*
	19: 6	for the Lord **G** Omnipotent reigneth.	*2316*
	19: 9	unto me, These are the true sayings of **G**.	*2316*
	19:10	worship **G**: for the testimony of Jesus is	*2316*
	19:13	and his name is called The Word of **G**.	*2316*
	19:15	of the fierceness and wrath of Almighty **G**.	*2316*
	19:17	together unto the supper of the great **G**;	*2316*
	20: 4	and for the word of **G**, and which had not	*2316*
	20: 6	but they shall be priests of **G** and of Christ,	*2316*
	20: 9	and fire came down from **G** out of heaven,	*2316*
	20:12	the dead, small and great, stand before **G**;	*2316*
	21: 2	coming down from **G** out of heaven,	*2316*
	21: 3	the tabernacle of **G** *is* with men, and he will	*2316*
	21: 3	and **G** himself shall be with them, *and*	*2316*
	21: 3	himself shall be with them, *and be* their **G**.	*2316*
	21: 4	And **G** shall wipe away all tears from their	*2316*
	21: 7	shall inherit all *things;* and I will be his **G**,	*2316*
	21:10	descending out of heaven from **G**,	*2316*
	21:11	Having the glory of **G**: and her light *was*	*2316*
	21:22	for the Lord **G** Almighty and the Lamb are	*2316*
	21:23	for the glory of **G** did lighten it, and	*2316*
	22: 1	proceeding out of the throne of **G** and	*2316*
	22: 3	but the throne of **G** and of the Lamb shall	*2316*
	22: 5	the sun; for the Lord **G** giveth them light:	*2316*
	22: 6	the Lord **G** of the holy prophets sent his	*2316*
	22: 9	keep the sayings of this book: worship **G**.	*2316*
	22:18	If any *man* shall add unto these *things*, **G**	*2316*
	22:19	**G** shall take away his part out of the book	*2316*

GOD* (309) [LORD*; this is the proper name of God, *Yahweh* or *Jehovah*, used in the phrase Lord GOD]

Ge	6: 5	**G** saw that the wickedness of man *was*	3068
	15: 2	Abram said, Lord **G**, what wilt thou give	3068
	15: 8	he said, Lord **G**, whereby shall I know that	3068
Ex	23:17	thy males shall appear before the Lord **G**.	3068
	34:23	men children appear before the Lord **G**,	3068
Dt	3:24	O Lord **G**, thou hast begun to shew thy	3068
	9:26	unto the LORD, and said, O Lord **G**,	3068
Jos	7: 7	Joshua said, Alas, O Lord **G**,	3068
Jdg	6:22	the LORD, Gideon said, Alas, O Lord **G**!	3068
	16:28	said, O Lord **G**, remember me, I pray thee,	3068
2Sa	7:18	and he said, Who *am* I, O Lord **G**?	3068
	7:19	yet a small thing in thy sight, O Lord **G**;	3068
	7:19	And *is* this the manner of man, O Lord **G**?	3068
	7:20	for thou, Lord **G**, knowest thy servant.	3068
	7:28	now, O Lord **G**, thou *art* that God, and	3068
	7:29	for thou, O Lord **G**, hast spoken *it:* and	3068
	12:22	Who can tell *whether* **G** will be gracious to	3068
1Ki	2:26	thou barest the ark of the Lord **G** before	3068
	8:53	our fathers out of Egypt, O Lord **G**.	3068
Ps	68:20	unto **G** the Lord *belong* the issues from	3068
	69: 6	O Lord **G** of hosts, be ashamed for my	3068
	71: 5	For thou *art* my hope, O Lord **G**: *thou art*	3068
	71:16	I will go in the strength of the Lord **G**:	3068
	73:28	I have put my trust in the Lord **G**, that *I*	3068
	109:21	do thou for me, O **G** the Lord, for thy	3068
	140: 7	O **G** the Lord, the strength of my salvation,	3068
	141: 8	mine eyes *are* unto thee, O **G** the Lord:	3068
Isa	3:15	of the poor? saith the Lord **G** of hosts.	3068
	7: 7	Thus saith the Lord **G**, It shall not stand,	3068
	10:23	For the Lord **G** of hosts shall make a	3068
	10:24	Therefore thus saith the Lord **G** of hosts,	3068
	22: 5	of perplexity by the Lord **G** of hosts in	3068
	22:12	in that day did the Lord **G** of hosts call to	3068
	22:14	you till ye die, saith the Lord **G** of hosts.	3068
	22:15	Thus saith the Lord **G** of hosts, Go, get thee	3068
	25: 8	the Lord **G** will wipe away tears from off	3068
	28:16	Therefore thus saith the Lord **G**, Behold,	3068
	28:22	for I have heard from the Lord **G** of hosts a	3068
	30:15	For thus saith the Lord **G**, the Holy One of	3068
	40:10	the Lord **G** will come with strong *hand,* and	3068
	48:16	now the Lord **G**, and his Spirit, hath sent	3068
	49:22	Thus saith the Lord **G**, Behold, I will lift up	3068
	50: 4	The Lord **G** hath given me the tongue of	3068
	50: 5	The Lord **G** hath opened mine ear, and	3068
	50: 7	For the Lord **G** will help me; therefore	3068
	50: 9	Behold, the Lord **G** will help me; who *is* he	3068
	52: 4	For thus saith the Lord **G**, My people went	3068
	56: 8	The Lord **G** which gathereth the outcasts of	3068
	61: 1	The Spirit of the Lord **G** *is* upon me;	3068
	61:11	so the Lord **G** will cause righteousness and	3068
	65:13	Therefore thus saith the Lord **G**, Behold,	3068
	65:15	for the Lord **G** shall slay thee, and call his	3068
Jer	1: 6	said I, Ah, Lord **G**, behold, I cannot speak:	3068
	2:19	*is* not in thee, saith the Lord **G** of hosts.	3068
	2:22	*is* marked before me, saith the Lord **G**.	3068
	4:10	(Then said I, Ah, Lord **G**! surely thou hast	3068
	7:20	Therefore thus saith the Lord **G**; Behold,	3068
	14:13	said I, Ah Lord **G**! behold, the prophets say	3068
	32:17	Ah Lord **G**! behold, thou hast made	3068
	32:25	thou hast said unto me, O Lord **G**, Buy thee	3068
	44:26	land of Egypt, saying, The Lord **G** liveth.	3068
	46:10	For this *is* the day of the Lord **G** of hosts,	3068
	46:10	for the Lord **G** of hosts hath a sacrifice in	3068
	49: 5	a fear upon thee, saith the Lord **G** of hosts,	3068
	50:25	for this *is* the work of the Lord **G** of hosts	3068
	50:31	*thou* most proud, saith the Lord **G** of hosts:	3068
Eze	2: 4	shalt say unto them, Thus saith the Lord **G**.	3068
	3:11	and tell them, Thus saith the Lord **G**;	3068
	3:27	shalt say unto them, Thus saith the Lord **G**;	3068
	4:14	said I, Ah Lord **G**, behold, my soul *hath* not	3068
	5: 5	Thus saith the Lord **G**; This *is* Jerusalem:	3068
	5: 7	Therefore thus saith the Lord **G**;	3068
	5: 8	Therefore thus saith the Lord **G**; Behold, I,	3068
	5:11	Wherefore, *as* I live, saith the Lord **G**;	3068
	6: 3	of Israel, hear the word of the Lord **G**;	3068
	6: 3	Thus saith the Lord **G** to the mountains,	3068

Eze 6:11	Thus saith the Lord **G**; Smite with thine	3068
7: 2	thus saith the Lord **G** unto the land of	3068
7: 5	Thus saith the Lord **G**; An evil, an only	3068
8: 1	that the hand of the Lord **G** fell there upon	3068
9: 8	my face, and cried, and said, Ah Lord **G**,	3068
11: 7	Therefore thus saith the Lord **G**; Your slain	3068
11: 8	bring a sword upon you, saith the Lord **G**.	3068
11:13	*with* a loud voice, and said, Ah Lord **G**,	3068
11:16	Therefore say, Thus saith the Lord **G**;	3068
11:17	Therefore say, Thus saith the Lord **G**; I will	3068
11:21	upon their own heads, saith the Lord **G**.	3068
12:10	Say thou unto them, Thus saith the Lord **G**;	3068
12:19	Thus saith the Lord **G**, of the inhabitants of	3068
12:23	Tell them therefore, Thus saith the Lord **G**;	3068
12:25	and will perform it, saith the Lord **G**.	3068
12:28	say unto them, Thus saith the Lord **G**;	3068
12:28	spoken shall be done, saith the Lord **G**.	3068
13: 3	Thus saith the Lord **G**; Woe unto	3068
13: 8	Therefore thus saith the Lord **G**;	3068
13: 8	I *am* against you, saith the Lord **G**.	3068
13: 9	and ye shall know that I *am* the Lord **G**.	3068
13:13	Therefore thus saith the Lord **G**; I will even	3068
13:16	and *there is* no peace, saith the Lord **G**.	3068
13:18	say, Thus saith the Lord **G**; Woe to	3068
13:20	Wherefore thus saith the Lord **G**; Behold,	3068
14: 4	and say unto them, Thus saith the Lord **G**;	3068
14: 6	the house of Israel, Thus saith the Lord **G**;	3068
14:11	and I may be their God, saith the Lord **G**.	3068
14:14	by their righteousness, saith the Lord **G**.	3068
14:16	men *were* in it, *as* I live, saith the Lord **G**,	3068
14:18	men *were* in it, *as* I live, saith the Lord **G**,	3068
14:20	Job, *were* in it, *as* I live, saith the Lord **G**,	3068
14:21	For thus saith the Lord **G**; How much more	3068
14:23	all that I have done in it, saith the Lord **G**.	3068
15: 6	Therefore thus saith the Lord **G**; As	3068
15: 8	committed a trespass, saith the Lord **G**.	3068
16: 3	Thus saith the Lord **G** unto Jerusalem;	3068
16: 8	saith the Lord **G**, and thou becamest mine.	3068
16:14	I had put upon thee, saith the Lord **G**.	3068
16:19	and *thus* it was, saith the Lord **G**.	3068
16:23	(woe, woe unto thee! saith the Lord **G**;)	3068
16:30	How weak is thine heart, saith the Lord **G**,	3068
16:36	Thus saith the Lord **G**; Because thy	3068
16:43	thy way upon *thine* head, saith the Lord **G**:	3068
16:48	*As* I live, saith the Lord **G**, Sodom thy	3068
16:59	For thus saith the Lord **G**; I will even deal	3068
16:63	for all that thou hast done, saith the Lord **G**.	3068
17: 3	say, Thus saith the Lord **G**; A great eagle	3068
17: 9	Say thou, Thus saith the Lord **G**; Shall it	3068
17:16	*As* I live, saith the Lord **G**, surely in	3068
17:19	Therefore thus saith the Lord **G**; *As* I live,	3068
17:22	Thus saith the Lord **G**; I will also take of	3068
18: 3	*As* I live, saith the Lord **G**, ye shall not	3068
18: 9	he shall surely live, saith the Lord **G**.	3068
18:23	saith the Lord **G**: *and* not that he should	3068
18:30	according to his ways, saith the Lord **G**.	3068
18:32	death of him that dieth, saith the Lord **G**:	3068
20: 3	and say unto them, Thus saith the Lord **G**;	3068
20: 3	*As* I live, saith the Lord **G**, I will not be	3068
20: 5	say unto them, Thus saith the Lord **G**;	3068
20:27	and say unto them, Thus saith the Lord **G**;	3068
20:30	the house of Israel, Thus saith the Lord **G**;	3068
20:31	*As* I live, saith the Lord **G**, I will not be	3068
20:33	*As* I live, saith the Lord **G**, surely with a	3068
20:36	so will I plead with you, saith the Lord **G**.	3068
20:39	O house of Israel, thus saith the Lord **G**;	3068
20:40	saith the Lord **G**, there shall all the house	3068
20:44	O ye house of Israel, saith the Lord **G**.	3068
20:47	Thus saith the Lord **G**; Behold, I *will*	3068
20:49	said I, Ah Lord **G**, they say of me, Doth he	3068
21: 7	shall be brought to pass, saith the Lord **G**.	3068
21:13	it shall be no *more,* saith the Lord **G**.	3068
21:24	Therefore thus saith the Lord **G**;	3068
21:26	Thus saith the Lord **G**; Remove	3068
21:28	Thus saith the Lord **G** concerning	3068
22: 3	say thou, Thus saith the Lord **G**, The city	3068
22:12	and hast forgotten me, saith the Lord **G**.	3068
22:19	Therefore thus saith the Lord **G**;	3068
22:28	unto them, saying, Thus saith the Lord **G**,	3068
22:31	upon their heads, saith the Lord **G**.	3068
23:22	O Aholibah, thus saith the Lord **G**;	3068
23:28	For thus saith the Lord **G**; Behold, I *will*	3068
23:32	Thus saith the Lord **G**; Thou shalt drink *of*	3068
23:34	for I have spoken *it,* saith the Lord **G**.	3068
23:35	Therefore thus saith the Lord **G**;	3068
23:46	For thus saith the Lord **G**; *I will* bring up a	3068
23:49	and ye shall know that I *am* the Lord **G**.	3068
24: 3	and say unto them, Thus saith the Lord **G**;	3068
24: 6	Wherefore thus saith the Lord **G**; Woe to	3068
24: 9	Therefore thus saith the Lord **G**; Woe to	3068
24:14	shall they judge thee, saith the Lord **G**.	3068
24:21	the house of Israel, Thus saith the Lord **G**;	3068
24:24	ye shall know that I *am* the Lord **G**.	3068
25: 3	Hear the word of the Lord **G**;	3068
25: 3	Thus saith the Lord **G**; Because thou saidst,	3068
25: 6	For thus saith the Lord **G**; Because thou	3068
25: 8	Thus saith the Lord **G**; Because that Moab	3068
25:12	Thus saith the Lord **G**; Because that Edom	3068
25:13	Therefore thus saith the Lord **G**; I will also	3068
25:14	know my vengeance, saith the Lord **G**.	3068
25:15	Thus saith the Lord **G**; Because	3068
25:16	Therefore thus saith the Lord **G**; Behold,	3068
26: 3	Therefore thus saith the Lord **G**; Behold,	3068
26: 5	for I have spoken *it,* saith the Lord **G**: and	3068
26: 7	For thus saith the Lord **G**; Behold, I *will*	3068
26:14	LORD have spoken *it,* saith the Lord **G**.	3068
26:15	Thus saith the Lord **G** to Tyrus; Shall not	3068
26:19	For thus saith the Lord **G**; When I shall	3068
26:21	never be found again, saith the Lord **G**.	3068
27: 3	for many isles, Thus saith the Lord **G**;	3068
28: 2	the prince of Tyrus, Thus saith the Lord **G**;	3068
28: 6	Therefore thus saith the Lord **G**;	3068
28:10	for I have spoken *it,* saith the Lord **G**.	3068
28:12	and say unto him, Thus saith the Lord **G**;	3068
28:22	say, Thus saith the Lord **G**; Behold, I *am*	3068
28:24	and they shall know that I *am* the Lord **G**.	3068
28:25	Thus saith the Lord **G**; When I shall have	3068
29: 3	Speak, and say, Thus saith the Lord **G**;	3068
29: 8	Therefore thus saith the Lord **G**; Behold,	3068
29:13	Yet thus saith the Lord **G**; At the end of	3068
29:16	but they shall know that I *am* the Lord **G**.	3068
29:19	Therefore thus saith the Lord **G**; Behold,	3068
29:20	they wrought for me, saith the Lord **G**.	3068
30: 2	prophesy and say, Thus saith the Lord **G**;	3068
30: 6	fall in it by the sword, saith the Lord **G**.	3068
30:10	Thus saith the Lord **G**; I will also make	3068
30:13	Thus saith the Lord **G**; I will also destroy	3068
30:22	Therefore thus saith the Lord **G**; Behold,	3068
31:10	Therefore thus saith the Lord **G**;	3068
31:15	Thus saith the Lord **G**; In the day when he	3068
31:18	and all his multitude, saith the Lord **G**.	3068
32: 3	Thus saith the Lord **G**; I will therefore	3068
32: 8	darkness upon thy land, saith the Lord **G**.	3068
32:11	For thus saith the Lord **G**; The sword of	3068
32:14	their rivers to run like oil, saith the Lord **G**.	3068
32:16	and for all her multitude, saith the Lord **G**.	3068
32:31	army slain by the sword, saith the Lord **G**.	3068
32:32	and all his multitude, saith the Lord **G**.	3068
33:11	Say unto them, *As* I live, saith the Lord **G**,	3068
33:25	say unto them, Thus saith the Lord **G**;	3068
33:27	thou thus unto them, Thus saith the Lord **G**;	3068
34: 2	Thus saith the Lord **G** unto the shepherds;	3068
34: 8	saith the Lord **G**, surely because my flock	3068
34:10	Thus saith the Lord **G**; Behold, I *am*	3068
34:11	For thus saith the Lord **G**; Behold, I,	3068
34:15	cause them to lie down, saith the Lord **G**.	3068
34:17	*for* you, O my flock, thus saith the Lord **G**;	3068
34:20	Therefore thus saith the Lord **G** unto them;	3068
34:30	of Israel, *are* my people, saith the Lord **G**.	3068
34:31	*and* I *am* your God, saith the Lord **G**.	3068
35: 3	say unto it, Thus saith the Lord **G**; Behold,	3068
35: 6	Therefore, *as* I live, saith the Lord **G**, I will	3068
35:11	Therefore, *as* I live, saith the Lord **G**, I will	3068
35:14	Thus saith the Lord **G**; When the whole	3068
36: 2	Thus saith the Lord **G**; Because the enemy	3068
36: 3	and say, Thus saith the Lord **G**;	3068
36: 4	of Israel, hear the word of the Lord **G**;	3068
36: 4	Thus saith the Lord **G** to the mountains,	3068
36: 5	Therefore thus saith the Lord **G**; Surely in	3068
36: 6	and to the valleys, Thus saith the Lord **G**;	3068
36: 7	Therefore thus saith the Lord **G**; I have	3068
36:13	Thus saith the Lord **G**; Because they say	3068
36:14	thy nations any more, saith the Lord **G**.	3068
36:15	nations to fall any more, saith the Lord **G**.	3068
36:22	the house of Israel, Thus saith the Lord **G**;	3068
36:23	that I *am* the LORD, saith the Lord **G**,	3068
36:32	for your sakes do I *this,* saith the Lord **G**,	3068
36:33	Thus saith the Lord **G**; In the day that I	3068

Eze 36:37 Thus saith the Lord **G**; I will yet *for* this be 3068
37: 3 And I answered, O Lord **G**, thou knowest. 3068
37: 5 Thus saith the Lord **G** unto these bones; 3068
37: 9 and say to the wind, Thus saith the Lord **G**; 3068
37:12 and say unto them, Thus saith the Lord **G**; 3068
37:19 Say unto them, Thus saith the Lord **G**; 3068
37:21 say unto them, Thus saith the Lord **G**; 3068
38: 3 say, Thus saith the Lord **G**; Behold, I *am* 3068
38:10 Thus saith the Lord **G**; It shall also come to 3068
38:14 and say unto Gog, Thus saith the Lord **G**; 3068
38:17 Thus saith the Lord **G**; *Art* thou he of 3068
38:18 saith the Lord **G**, *that* my fury shall come 3068
38:21 all my mountains, saith the Lord **G**: 3068
39: 1 and say, Thus saith the Lord **G**; 3068
39: 5 for I have spoken *it,* saith the Lord **G**. 3068
39: 8 it is come, and it is done, saith the Lord **G**; 3068
39:10 those that robbed them, saith the Lord **G**. 3068
39:13 that I shall be glorified, saith the Lord **G**. 3068
39:17 thou son of man, thus saith the Lord **G**; 3068
39:20 and *with* all men of war, saith the Lord **G**. 3068
39:25 Therefore thus saith the Lord **G**; Now will I 3068
39:29 upon the house of Israel, saith the Lord **G**. 3068
43:18 Son of man, thus saith the Lord **G**; 3068
43:19 to minister unto me, saith the Lord **G**, 3068
43:27 and I will accept you, saith the Lord **G**. 3068
44: 6 the house of Israel, Thus saith the Lord **G**; 3068
44: 9 Thus saith the Lord **G**; No stranger, 3068
44:12 saith the Lord **G**, and they shall bear their 3068
44:15 me the fat and the blood, saith the Lord **G**: 3068
44:27 offer his sin offering, saith the Lord **G**. 3068
45: 9 Thus saith the Lord **G**; Let it suffice you, 3068
45: 9 from my people, saith the Lord **G**. 3068
45:15 reconciliation for them, saith the Lord **G**. 3068
45:18 Thus saith the Lord **G**; In the first *month,* 3068
46: 1 Thus saith the Lord **G**; The gate of 3068
46:16 Thus saith the Lord **G**; If the prince give a 3068
47:13 Thus saith the Lord **G**; This *shall be* 3068
47:23 give *him* his inheritance, saith the Lord **G**. 3068
48:29 these *are* their portions, saith the Lord **G**. 3068
Am 1: 8 Philistines shall perish, saith the Lord **G**. 3068
3: 7 Surely the Lord **G** will do nothing, but he 3068
3: 8 the Lord **G** hath spoken, who can but 3068
3:11 Therefore thus saith the Lord **G**; 3068
3:13 saith the Lord **G**, the God of hosts, 3068
4: 2 The Lord **G** hath sworn by his holiness, 3068
4: 5 O ye children of Israel, saith the Lord **G**. 3068
5: 3 For thus saith the Lord **G**; The city that 3068
6: 8 The Lord **G** hath sworn by himself, saith 3068
7: 1 Thus hath the Lord **G** shewed unto me; and 3068
7: 2 I said, O Lord **G**, forgive, I beseech thee: 3068
7: 4 Thus hath the Lord **G** shewed unto me: and 3068
7: 4 the Lord **G** called to contend by fire, and 3068
7: 5 said I, O Lord **G**, cease, I beseech thee: 3068
7: 6 This also shall not be, saith the Lord **G**. 3068
8: 1 Thus hath the Lord **G** shewed unto me: and 3068
8: 3 be howlings in that day, saith the Lord **G**: 3068
8: 9 come to pass in that day, saith the Lord **G**, 3068
8:11 Behold, the days come, saith the Lord **G**, 3068
9: 5 the Lord **G** of hosts *is* he that toucheth 3068
9: 8 the eyes of the Lord **G** *are* upon the sinful 3068
Ob 1: 1 Thus saith the Lord **G** concerning Edom; 3068
Mic 1: 2 let the Lord **G** be witness against you, 3068
Hab 3:19 The Lord **G** *is* my strength, and he will 3068
Zep 1: 7 thy peace at the presence of the Lord **G**: 3068
Zec 9:14 the Lord **G** shall blow the trumpet, and 3068

GOD'S (26) [GOD]
Ge 28:22 I have set *for* a pillar, shall be **G** house: 430
30: 2 he said, *Am* I in **G** stead, who hath withheld 430
32: 2 Jacob saw them, he said, This *is* **G** host: 430
Nu 22:22 **G** anger was kindled because he went: and 430
Dt 1:17 of the face of man; for the judgment *is* **G**: 430
2Ch 20:15 for the battle *is* not yours, but **G**. 430+3807.1
Ne 10:29 a curse, and into an oath, to walk in **G** law, 430
Job 33: 6 I *am* according to thy wish in **G** stead: 410
35: 2 My righteousness *is* more than **G**? 410
36: 2 thee that *I have* yet to speak on **G** behalf. 433
Mt 5:34 at all; neither by heaven; for it is **G** throne: *2316*
22:21 and unto God the *things* that are **G**. *2316*
Mk 12:17 and to God the *things* that are **G**. *2316*
Lk 18:29 or children, for the kingdom of **G** sake, *2316*
20:25 and unto God the *things* which be **G**. *2316*
Jn 8:47 He that is of God heareth **G** words: ye *2316*
Ac 23: 4 stood by said, Revilest thou **G** high priest? *2316*
Ro 8:33 Who shall lay any thing to the charge of **G** *2316*
10: 3 For they being ignorant of **G** righteousness, *2316*
13: 6 for they are **G** ministers, *2316*
1Co 3: 9 ye are **G** husbandry, *ye are* God's building. *2316*
3: 9 ye are God's husbandry, *ye are* **G** building. *2316*
3:23 And ye *are* Christ's; and Christ *is* **G**. *2316*
6:20 your body, and in your spirit, which are **G**. *2316*
Tit 1: 1 according to the faith of **G** elect, and *2316*
1Pe 5: 3 Neither as being lords over **G** heritage, but NIG

GODDESS (5) [GOD]
1Ki 11: 5 For Solomon went after Ashtoreth the **g** of 430
11:33 have worshipped Ashtoreth the **g** of 430
Ac 19:27 also that the temple of the great **g** Diana *2299*
19:35 is a worshipper of the great **g** Diana, *2299*
19:37 of churches, nor yet blasphemers of your **g**. *2299*

GODHEAD (3) [GOD]
Ac 17:29 we ought not to think that the **G** is like unto *2304*
Ro 1:20 are made, *even* his eternal power and **G**; *2305*
Col 2: 9 For in him dwelleth all the fulness of the **G** *2320*

G

GODLINESS (15) [GOD]
1Ti 2: 2 and peaceable life in all **g** and honesty. *2150*
2:10 But (which becometh women professing **g**) *2317*
3:16 controversy great is the mystery of **g**: *2150*
4: 7 and exercise thyself *rather* unto **g**. *2150*
4: 8 **g** is profitable unto all *things,* having *2150*
6: 3 and to the doctrine which is according to **g**; *2150*
6: 5 of the truth, supposing that gain is **g**: *2150*
6: 6 But **g** with contentment is great gain. *2150*
6:11 **g**, faith, love, patience, meekness. *2150*
2Ti 3: 5 Having a form of **g**, but denying the power *2150*
Tit 1: 1 acknowledging of the truth which is after **g**, *2150*
2Pe 1: 3 us all *things* that *pertain* unto life and **g**, *2150*
1: 6 to temperance patience; and to patience **g**; *2150*
1: 7 And to **g** brotherly kindness; and *2150*
3:11 ye to be in all holy conversation and **g**, *2150*

GODLY (15) [GOD]
Ps 4: 3 hath set apart *him that is* **g** for himself: 2623
12: 1 Help, LORD; for the **g** *man* ceaseth; 2623
32: 6 For this shall every one *that is* **g** pray unto 2623
Mal 2:15 That he might seek a **g** seed. Therefore take 430
2Co 1:12 that in simplicity and **g** sincerity, not with *2316*
7: 9 for ye were made sorry after a **g** manner, *2316*
7:10 For **g** sorrow worketh repentance to *2316+2596*
7:11 *thing,* that ye sorrowed after a **g** sort, *2316*
11: 2 For I am jealous over you with **g** jealousy: *2316*
1Ti 1: 4 rather than **g** edifying which is in faith: *2316*
2Ti 3:12 all that will live **g** in Christ Jesus shall *2153*
Tit 2:12 and **g**, in *this* present world; *2153*
Heb 12:28 God acceptably with reverence and **g fear**: *2124*
2Pe 2: 9 The Lord knoweth *how* to deliver the **g** out *2152*
3Jn 1: 6 forward on their journey after a **g** sort, *2316*

GODS (244) [GOD]
Ge 3: 5 and ye shall be as **g**, knowing good and evil. 430
31:30 *yet* wherefore hast thou stolen my **g**? 430
31:32 With whomsoever thou findest thy **g**, let him 430
35: 2 Put away the strange **g** that *are* among you, 430
35: 4 they gave unto Jacob all the strange **g** which 430
Ex 12:12 against all the **g** of Egypt I will execute 430
15:11 *is* like unto thee, O LORD, among the **g**? 410
18:11 I know that the LORD *is* greater than all **g**: 430
20: 3 Thou shalt have no other **g** before me. 430
20:23 Ye shall not make with me **g** of silver, 430
20:23 neither shall ye make unto you **g** of gold. 430
22:28 Thou shalt not revile the **g**, nor curse 430
23:13 and make no mention of the name of other **g**, 430
23:24 Thou shalt not bow down to their **g**, 430
23:32 no covenant with them, nor with their **g**. 430
23:33 for if thou serve their **g**, it will surely be a 430
32: 1 said unto him, Up, make us **g**, which shall go 430
32: 4 they said, These *be* thy **g**, O Israel, 430
32: 8 and said, These *be* thy **g**, O Israel, 430
32:23 For they said unto me, Make us **g**, 430
32:31 a great sin, and have made them **g** of gold. 430
34:15 they go a whoring after their **g**, and 430
34:15 do sacrifice unto their **g**, and *one* call thee, 430
34:16 their daughters go a whoring after their **g**, 430
34:16 make thy sons go a whoring after their **g**. 430
34:17 Thou shalt make thee no molten **g**. 430
Lev 19: 4 unto idols, nor make to yourselves molten **g**: 430

Nu	25: 2	the people unto the sacrifices of their **g**:	430
	25: 2	people did eat, and bowed down to their **g**.	430
	33: 4	upon their **g** also the LORD executed	430
Dt	4:28	there ye shall serve **g**, the work of men's	430
	5: 7	Thou shalt have none other **g** before me.	430
	6:14	Ye shall not go after other **g**, of the gods of	430
	6:14	of the **g** of the people which *are* round about	430
	7: 4	following me, that they may serve other **g**:	430
	7:16	neither shalt thou serve their **g**; for that *will*	430
	7:25	The graven images of their **g** shall ye burn	430
	8:19	walk after other **g**, and serve them, and	430
	10:17	For the LORD your God *is* God of **g**, and	430
	11:16	and serve other **g**, and worship them;	430
	11:28	to go after other **g**, which ye have not	430
	12: 2	which ye shall possess served their **g**,	430
	12: 3	shall hew down the graven images of their **g**,	430
	12:30	that thou inquire not after their **g**, saying,	430
	12:30	saying, How did these nations serve their **g**?	430
	12:31	which he hateth, have they done unto their **g**;	430
	12:31	they have burnt in the fire to their **g**.	430
	13: 2	saying, Let us go after other **g**, which thou	430
	13: 6	saying, Let us go and serve other **g**,	430
	13: 7	*Namely,* of the **g** of the people which *are*	430
	13:13	saying, Let us go and serve other **g**, which ye	430
	17: 3	hath gone and served other **g**, and	430
	18:20	or that shall speak in the name of other **g**,	430
	20:18	which they have done unto their **g**;	430
	28:14	*to* the left, to go after other **g** to serve them.	430
	28:36	and there shalt thou serve other **g**, wood and	430
	28:64	there thou shalt serve other **g**, which neither	430
	29:18	to go *and* serve the **g** of these nations;	430
	29:26	For they went and served other **g**, and	430
	29:26	**g** whom they knew not, and *whom* he had	430
	30:17	and worship other **g**, and serve them;	430
	31:16	go a whoring after the **g** of the strangers of	430
	31:18	in that they are turned unto other **g**.	430
	31:20	will they turn unto other **g**, and serve them,	430
	32:16	**g**, with abominations provoked they him to	NIH
	32:17	*to* **g** whom they knew not, *to* new *gods that*	430
	32:17	knew not, *to* new **g** *that* came newly up,	NIH
	32:37	he shall say, Where *are* their **g**, *their* rock in	430
Jos	22:22	The LORD God of **g**, the LORD God of	430
	22:22	the LORD God of **g**, he knoweth, and	430
	23: 7	neither make mention of the name of their **g**,	430
	23:16	have gone and served other **g**, and	430
	24: 2	father of Nachor: and they served other **g**.	430
	24:14	put away the **g** which your fathers served on	430
	24:15	whether the **g** which your fathers served that	430
	24:15	or the **g** of the Amorites, in whose land ye	430
	24:16	should forsake the LORD, to serve other **g**;	430
	24:20	serve strange **g**, then he will turn and do you	430
	24:23	*said he,* the strange **g** which *are* among you,	430
Jdg	2: 3	and their **g** shall be a snare unto you.	430
	2:12	of the land of Egypt, and followed other **g**,	430
	2:12	of the **g** of the people that *were* round about	430
	2:17	they went a whoring after other **g**, and	430
	2:19	in following other **g** to serve them, and	430
	3:6	daughters to their sons, and served their **g**.	430
	5: 8	They chose new **g**; then *was* war in	430
	6:10	fear not the **g** of the Amorites, in whose land	430
	10: 6	the **g** of Syria, and the gods of Zidon, and	430
	10: 6	the **g** of Zidon, and the gods of Moab, and	430
	10: 6	the **g** of Moab, and the gods of the children	430
	10: 6	the **g** of the children of Ammon, and	430
	10: 6	the **g** of the Philistines, and forsook	430
	10:13	Yet ye have forsaken me, and served other **g**:	430
	10:14	Go and cry unto the **g** which ye have chosen;	430
	10:16	they put away the strange **g** from among	430
	17: 5	the man Micah had a house of **g**, and	430
	18:24	Ye have taken away my **g** which I made, and	430
Ru	1:15	is gone back unto her people, and unto her **g**:	430
1Sa	4: 8	us out of the hand of these mighty **G**?	430
	4: 8	these *are* the **G** that smote the Egyptians	430
	6: 5	and from off your **g**, and from off your land.	430
	7: 3	*then* put away the strange **g** and Ashtaroth	430
	8: 8	and served other **g**, so do they also unto thee.	430
	17:43	And the Philistine cursed David by his **g**.	430
	26:19	of the LORD, saying, Go, serve other **g**.	430
	28:13	unto Saul, I saw **g** ascending out of the earth.	430
2Sa	7:23	from Egypt, *from* the nations and their **g**?	430
1Ki	9: 6	but go and serve other **g**, and worship them:	430
	9: 9	have taken hold upon other **g**, and	430
	11: 2	they will turn away your heart after their **g**:	430
	11: 4	his wives turned away his heart after other **g**:	430
	11: 8	burnt incense and sacrificed unto their **g**.	430
	11:10	this thing, that *he* should not go after other **g**:	430
	12:28	behold thy **g**, O Israel, which brought thee	430
	14: 9	for thou hast gone and made thee other **g**,	430
	18:24	call ye on the name of your **g**, and I will call	430
	18:25	call on the name of your **g**, but put no fire	430
	19: 2	saying, So let the **g** do *to me,* and more also,	430
	20:10	said, The **g** do so unto me, and more also,	430
	20:23	said unto him, Their **g** *are* gods of the hills;	430
	20:23	said unto him, Their gods *are* **g** of the hills;	430
2Ki	5:17	burnt offering nor sacrifice unto other **g**,	430
	17: 7	king of Egypt, and had feared other **g**,	430
	17:29	Howbeit every nation made **g** of their own,	430
	17:31	and Anammelech, the **g** of Sepharvaim.	430
	17:33	feared the LORD, and served their own **g**,	430
	17:35	saying, Ye shall not fear other **g**,	430
	17:37	for evermore; and ye shall not fear other **g**.	430
	17:38	shall not forget; neither shall ye fear other **g**.	430
	18:33	Hath any of the **g** of the nations delivered at	430
	18:34	Where *are* the **g** of Hamath, and of Arpad?	430
	18:34	where *are* the **g** of Sepharvaim, Hena, and	430
	18:35	Who *are they* among all the **g** of	430
	19:12	Have the **g** of the nations delivered them	430
	19:18	have cast their **g** into the fire: for they *were*	430
	19:18	for they *were* no **g**, but the work of men's	430
	22:17	and have burnt incense unto other **g**,	430
1Ch	5:25	went a whoring after the **g** of the people of	430
	10:10	they put his armour *in* the house of their **g**,	430
	14:12	when they had left their **g** there, David gave	430
	16:25	he also *is* to be feared above all **g**.	430
	16:26	For all the **g** of the people *are* idols: but	430
2Ch	2: 5	*is* great: for great *is* our God above all **g**.	430
	7:19	shall go and serve other **g**, and	430
	7:22	laid hold on other **g**, and worshipped them,	430
	13: 8	which Jeroboam made you for **g**.	430
	13: 9	*same* may be a priest of *them that are* no **g**.	430
	14: 3	For he took away the altars of the strange **g**,	NIH
	25:14	that he brought the **g** of the children of Seir,	430
	25:14	set them up to be his **g**, and bowed down	430
	25:15	Why hast thou sought after the **g** of	430
	25:20	because they sought after the **g** of Edom.	430
	28:23	For he sacrificed unto the **g** of Damascus,	430
	28:23	Because the **g** of the kings of Syria help	430
	28:25	high places to burn incense unto other **g**,	430
	32:13	were the **g** of the nations of *those* lands any	430
	32:14	Who *was there* among all the **g** of those	430
	32:17	As the **g** of the nations of *other* lands have	430
	32:19	as against the **g** of the people of the earth,	430
	33:15	he took away the strange **g**, and the idol out	430
	34:25	and have burned incense unto other **g**,	430
Ezr	1: 7	and had put them in the house of his **g**;	430
Ps	82: 1	of the mighty; he judgeth among the **g**.	430
	82: 6	I have said, Ye *are* **g**; and all of you *are*	430
	86: 8	Among the **g** *there is* none like unto thee,	430
	95: 3	*is* a great God, and a great King above all **g**.	430
	96: 4	to be praised: he *is* to be feared above all **g**.	430
	96: 5	For all the **g** of the nations *are* idols: but	430
	97: 7	themselves of idols: worship him, all ye **g**.	430
	97: 9	all the earth: thou art exalted far above all **g**.	430
	135: 5	*is* great, and *that* our Lord *is* above all **g**.	430
	136: 2	O give thanks unto the God of **g**: for his	430
	138: 1	before the **g** will I sing *praise* unto thee.	430
Isa	21: 9	all the graven images of her **g** he hath broken	430
	36:18	Hath any of the **g** of the nations delivered his	430
	36:19	Where *are* the **g** of Hamath and Arphad?	430
	36:19	where *are* the **g** of Sepharvaim? and have	430
	36:20	Who *are they* amongst all the **g** of these	430
	37:12	Have the **g** of the nations delivered them	430
	37:19	have cast their **g** into the fire: for they *were*	430
	37:19	for they *were* no **g**, but the work of men's	430
	41:23	that we may know that ye *are* **g**:	430
	42:17	that say to the molten images, Ye *are* our **g**.	430
Jer	1:16	have burnt incense unto other **g**, and	430
	2:11	Hath a nation changed *their* **g**, which *are* yet	430
	2:11	changed *their* gods, which *are* yet no **g**?	430
	2:28	where *are* thy **g** that thou hast made thee?	430
	2:28	to the number of thy cities are thy **g**,	430
	5: 7	and sworn by *them that are* no **g**:	430
	5:19	served strange **g** in your land, so shall ye	430
	7: 6	neither walk after other **g** to your hurt:	430
	7: 9	and walk after other **g** whom ye know not;	430
	7:18	and to pour out drink offerings unto other **g**,	430
	10:11	The **g** that have not made the heavens and	426
	11:10	and they went after other **g** to serve them:	430

Jer 11:12 cry unto the g unto whom they offer incense: 430
11:13 *to* the number of thy cities were thy g, 430
13:10 walk after other g, to serve them, and 430
16:11 have walked after other g, and have served 430
16:13 there shall ye serve other g day and night; 430
16:20 Shall a man make g unto himself, and 430
16:20 make gods unto himself, and they *are* no g? 430
19: 4 and have burnt incense in it unto other g, 430
19:13 have poured out drink offerings unto other g. 430
22: 9 and worshipped other g, and served them. 430
25: 6 go not after other g to serve them, and 430
32:29 and poured out drink offerings unto other g, 430
35:15 go not after other g to serve them, and 430
43:12 I will kindle a fire in the houses of the g of 430
43:13 the houses of the g of the Egyptians shall he 430
44: 3 *and* to serve other g, whom they knew not, 430
44: 5 to burn no incense unto other g. 430
44: 8 burning incense unto other g in the land of 430
44:15 their wives had burnt incense unto other g, 430
46:25 and Egypt, with their g, and their kings; 430
48:35 and him that burneth incense to his g. 430
Da 2:11 except the g, whose dwelling is not with 426
2:47 Of a truth *it is,* that your God *is* a God of g, 426
3:12 they serve not thy g, nor worship the golden 426
3:14 and Abed-nego, do not ye serve my g, 426
3:18 O king, that we will not serve thy g, 426
4: 8 and in whom *is* the spirit of the holy g: 426
4: 9 I know that the spirit of the holy g *is* in thee, 426
4:18 *art* able; for the spirit of the holy g *is* in thee. 426
5: 4 praised the g of gold, and of silver, of brass, 426
5:11 in whom *is* the spirit of the holy g; 426
5:11 and wisdom, like the wisdom of the g, 426
5:14 that the spirit of the g *is* in thee, and 426
5:23 thou hast praised the g of silver, and gold, 426
11: 8 shall also carry captives *into* Egypt their g, 430
11:36 marvellous *things* against the God of g, 410
Hos 3: 1 who look to other g, and love flagons of 430
14: 3 more to the work of our hands, *Ye are* our g: 430
Na 1:14 out of the house of thy g will I cut off 430
Zep 2:11 for he will famish all the g of the earth; and 430
Jn 10:34 it not written in your law, I said, Ye are g? *2316*
10:35 If he called them g, unto whom the word of *2316*
Ac 7:40 unto Aaron, Make us g to go before us: *2316*
14:11 The g are come down to us in the likeness *2316*
17:18 He seemeth to be a setter forth of strange g: *1140*
19:26 much people, saying that they be no g, *2316*
1Co 8: 5 For though there be that are called g, *2316*
8: 5 (as there be g many, and lords many,) *2316*
Gal 4: 8 service unto them which by nature are no g. *2316*

GOD-WARD (3) [GOD]
Ex 18:19 be thou for the people to G, 430+4136+1886.1
2Co 3: 4 such trust have we through Christ to G: *2316*
1Th 1: 8 also in every place your faith to G is spread *2316*

GOEST (46) [GO] See Index

GOETH (135) [GO] See Index

GOG (11) [HAMON-GOG]
1Ch 5: 4 his son, G his son, Shimei his son, 1463
Eze 38: 2 Son of man, set thy face against G, the land 1463
38: 3 Behold, I *am* against thee, O G, the chief 1463
38:14 son of man, prophesy and say unto G, 1463
38:16 sanctified in thee, O G, before their eyes. 1463
38:18 G shall come against the land of Israel, 1463
39: 1 son of man, prophesy against G, and say, 1463
39: 1 Behold, I *am* against thee, O G, the chief 1463
39:11 *that* I will give unto G a place there of 1463
39:11 there shall they bury G and all his 1463
Rev 20: 8 G and Magog, to gather them together to *1136*

GOING (92) [GO] See Index

GOINGS (26) [GO] See Index

GOLAN (4)
Dt 4:43 and G in Bashan, of the Manassites. 1474
Jos 20: 8 G in Bashan out of the tribe of Manasseh. 1474
21:27 *they gave* G in Bashan with her suburbs, 1474
1Ch 6:71 G in Bashan with her suburbs, and 1474

GOLD (417) [GOLDEN, GOLDSMITH, GOLDSMITH'S, GOLDSMITHS]
Ge 2:11 the whole land of Havilah, where *there is* g; 2091
2:12 the g of that land *is* good: there *is* bdellium 2091
13: 2 *was* very rich in cattle, in silver, and in g. 2091
24:22 for her hands of ten *shekels* weight of g; 2091
24:35 g, and menservants, and maidservants, and 2091
24:53 jewels of g, and raiment, and gave *them* to 2091
41:42 fine linen, and put a g chain about his neck; 2091
44: 8 we steal out of thy lord's house silver or g? 2091
Ex 3:22 of silver, and jewels of g, and raiment: 2091
11: 2 jewels of silver, and jewels of g. 2091
12:35 of silver, and jewels of g, and raiment: 2091
20:23 neither shall ye make unto you gods of g. 2091
25: 3 shall take of them; g, and silver, and brass, 2091
25:11 thou shalt overlay it with pure g, within 2091
25:11 shalt make upon it a crown *of* g round 2091
25:12 thou shalt cast four rings of g for it, and 2091
25:13 of shittim wood, and overlay them with g. 2091
25:17 thou shalt make a mercy seat *of* pure g: 2091
25:18 thou shalt make two cherubims *of* g, 2091
25:24 thou shalt overlay it with pure g, and 2091
25:24 and make thereto a crown *of* g round about. 2091
25:26 thou shalt make for it four rings of g, and 2091
25:28 overlay them with g, that the table may be 2091
25:29 *of* pure g shalt thou make them. 2091
25:31 thou shalt make a candlestick of pure g: 2091
25:36 all it *shall be* one beaten work *of* pure g. 2091
25:38 the snuffdishes thereof, *shall be of* pure g. 2091
25:39 *Of* a talent of pure g shall he make it, 2091
26: 6 thou shalt make fifty taches of g, and 2091
26:29 thou shalt overlay the boards with g, and 2091
26:29 make their rings *of* g *for* places for the bars: 2091
26:29 and thou shalt overlay the bars with g. 2091
26:32 four pillars of shittim *wood* overlaid with g: 2091
26:32 their hooks *shall be of* g, upon the four 2091
26:37 of shittim *wood,* and overlay them with g, 2091
26:37 with gold, *and* their hooks *shall be of* g: 2091
28: 5 they shall take g, and blue, and purple, and 2091
28: 6 they shall make the ephod *of* g, *of* blue, 2091
28: 8 *even of* g, *of* blue, and purple, and scarlet, 2091
28:11 shalt make them to be set *in* ouches *of* g. 2091
28:13 And thou shalt make ouches *of* g; 2091
28:14 two chains *of* pure g at the ends; 2091
28:15 *of* g, *of* blue, and *of* purple, and *of* scarlet, 2091
28:20 they shall be set in g in their inclosings. 2091
28:22 at the ends *of* wreathen work *of* pure g. 2091
28:23 make upon the breastplate two rings of g, 2091
28:24 thou shalt put the two wreathen *chains of* g 2091
28:26 thou shalt make two rings of g, and 2091
28:27 two *other* rings of g thou shalt make, and 2091
28:33 and bells of g between them round about: 2091
28:36 thou shalt make a plate *of* pure g, and 2091
30: 3 thou shalt overlay it with pure g, the top 2091
30: 3 thou shalt make unto it a crown *of* g round 2091
30: 5 *of* shittim wood, and overlay them with g. 2091
31: 4 to work in g, and in silver, and in brass, 2091
32:24 Whosoever hath *any* g, let them break *it* 2091
32:31 a great sin, and have made them gods of g. 2091
35: 5 of the LORD; g, and silver, and brass, 2091
35:22 and rings, and tablets, all jewels of g: 2091
35:22 *offered* an offering of g unto the LORD. 2091
35:32 to work in g, and in silver, and in brass, 2091
36:13 he made fifty taches of g, and coupled 2091
36:34 he overlaid the boards with g, and made 2091
36:34 made their rings *of* g *to be* places for 2091
36:34 for the bars, and overlaid the bars with g. 2091
36:36 of shittim *wood,* and overlaid them with g: 2091
36:36 their hooks *were of* g; and he cast for them 2091
36:38 their chapiters and their fillets with g: 2091
37: 2 he overlaid it with pure g within 2091
37: 2 and made a crown *of* g to it round about. 2091
37: 3 he cast for it four rings of g, *to be set* by 2091
37: 4 of shittim wood, and overlaid them with g. 2091
37: 6 he made the mercy seat *of* pure g: 2091
37: 7 he made two cherubims *of* g, beaten out of 2091
37:11 he overlaid it with pure g, and 2091
37:11 made thereunto a crown *of* g round about. 2091
37:12 made a crown of g for the border thereof 2091
37:13 he cast for it four rings of g, and put 2091
37:15 and overlaid them with g, to bear the table. 2091
37:16 and *his* covers to cover withal, *of* pure g. 2091
37:17 he made the candlestick *of* pure g: 2091
37:22 all of it *was* one beaten work *of* pure g. 2091
37:23 his snuffers, and his snuffdishes, *of* pure g. 2091
37:24 *Of* a talent *of* pure g made he it, and all 2091
37:26 he overlaid it with pure g, *both* the top of it, 2091
37:26 also he made unto it a crown *of* g round 2091

Ex	37:27	he made two rings of **g** for it under	2091
	37:28	*of* shittim wood, and overlaid them with **g**.	2091
	38:24	All the **g** that was occupied for the work in	2091
	38:24	of the holy *place,* even the **g** of the offering,	2091
	39: 2	he made the ephod *of* **g**, blue, and purple,	2091
	39: 3	And they did beat the **g** into thin plates, and	2091
	39: 5	*of* **g**, blue, and purple, and scarlet, and	2091
	39: 6	onyx stones inclosed *in* ouches *of* **g**,	2091
	39: 8	*of* **g**, blue, and purple, and scarlet, and	2091
	39:13	*they were* inclosed *in* ouches *of* **g** in their	2091
	39:15	at the ends, *of* wreathen work *of* pure **g**.	2091
	39:16	they made two ouches *of* **g**, and two gold	2091
	39:16	made two ouches *of* gold, and two **g** rings;	2091
	39:17	they put the two wreathen *chains of* **g** in	2091
	39:19	they made two rings of **g**, and put *them* on	2091
	39:25	they made bells of pure **g**, and put the bells	2091
	39:30	made the plate of the holy crown *of* pure **g**,	2091
	40: 5	thou shalt set the altar of **g** for the incense	2091
Nu	7:14	One spoon of ten *shekels* of **g**, full *of*	2091
	7:20	One spoon of **g** of ten *shekels,* full *of*	2091
	7:84	twelve silver bowls, twelve spoons of **g**:	2091
	7:86	all the **g** of the spoons *was* an hundred and	2091
	8: 4	work of the candlestick *was of* beaten **g**,	2091
	22:18	give me his house full *of* silver and **g**,	2091
	24:13	give me his house full *of* silver and **g**,	2091
	31:22	Only the **g**, and the silver, the brass,	2091
	31:50	*of* jewels of **g**, chains, and bracelets, rings,	2091
	31:51	and Eleazar the priest took the **g** of them,	2091
	31:52	all the **g** of the offering that they offered up	2091
	31:54	Eleazar the priest took the **g** of the captains	2091
Dt	7:25	not desire the silver or **g** *that is* on them,	2091
	8:13	thy silver and thy **g** is multiplied, and	2091
	17:17	he greatly multiply to himself silver and **g**.	2091
	29:17	their idols, wood and stone, silver and **g**,	2091
Jos	6:19	and **g**, and vessels of brass and iron,	2091
	6:24	the **g**, and the vessels of brass and of iron,	2091
	7:21	a wedge of **g** of fifty shekels weight, then	2091
	7:24	the wedge of **g**, and his sons, and his	2091
	22: 8	with **g**, and with brass, and with iron, and	2091
Jdg	8:26	a thousand and seven hundred *shekels* of **g**;	2091
1Sa	6: 8	put the jewels of **g**, which ye return him *for*	2091
	6:11	the coffer with the mice of **g** and	2091
	6:15	wherein the jewels of **g** *were,* and put *them*	2091
2Sa	1:24	who put on ornaments of **g** upon your	2091
	8: 7	David took the shields of **g** that were on	2091
	8:10	and vessels of **g**, and vessels of brass:	2091
	8:11	**g** that he had dedicated of all nations which	2091
	12:30	the weight whereof *was* a talent of **g** with	2091
	21: 4	We will have no silver nor **g** of Saul, nor of	2091
1Ki	6:20	he overlaid it with pure **g**; and *so*	2091
	6:21	overlaid the house within with pure **g**:	2091
	6:21	he made a partition by the chains of **g**	2091
	6:21	before the oracle; and he overlaid it with **g**.	2091
	6:22	the whole house he overlaid with **g**, until *he*	2091
	6:22	that *was* by the oracle he overlaid with **g**.	2091
	6:28	And he overlaid the cherubims with **g**.	2091
	6:30	the floor of the house he overlaid with **g**,	2091
	6:32	overlaid *them* with **g**, and spread gold upon	2091
	6:32	spread **g** upon the cherubims, and upon	2091
	6:35	covered *them* with **g** fitted upon the carved	2091
	7:48	the altar of **g**, and the table *of* gold,	2091
	7:48	the altar of gold, and the table *of* **g**,	2091
	7:49	the candlesticks *of* pure **g**, five on the right	2091
	7:49	and the lamps, and the tongs *of* **g**,	2091
	7:50	and the spoons, and the censers *of* pure **g**;	2091
	7:50	the hinges *of* **g**, *both* for the doors of	2091
	7:51	*even* the silver, and the **g**, and the vessels,	2091
	9:11	with cedar trees and fir trees, and with **g**,	2091
	9:14	Hiram sent to the king sixscore talents of **g**.	2091
	9:28	fet from thence **g**, four hundred and	2091
	10: 2	and very much **g**, and precious stones:	2091
	10:10	the king an hundred and twenty talents of **g**,	2091
	10:11	also of Hiram, that brought **g** from Ophir,	2091
	10:14	Now the weight of **g** that came to Solomon	2091
	10:14	six hundred threescore and six talents of **g**,	2091
	10:16	made two hundred targets *of* beaten **g**:	2091
	10:16	six hundred *shekels* of **g** went to one target.	2091
	10:17	*he made* three hundred shields *of* beaten **g**;	2091
	10:17	three pound *of* **g** went to one shield:	2091
	10:18	of ivory, and overlaid it with the best **g**.	2091
	10:21	king Solomon's drinking vessels *were of* **g**,	2091
	10:21	of the forest of Lebanon *were of* pure **g**:	2091
	10:22	bringing **g**, and silver, ivory, and apes, and	2091
	10:25	and vessels of **g**, and garments, and armour,	2091
	12:28	made two calves of **g**, and said unto them,	2091
	14:26	he took away all the shields of **g** which	2091
	15:15	of the LORD, silver, and **g**, and vessels.	2091
	15:18	the **g** that were left in the treasures of	2091
	15:19	sent unto thee a present of silver and **g**;	2091
	20: 3	Thy silver and thy **g** *is* mine; thy wives also	2091
	20: 5	and thy **g**, and thy wives, and thy children;	2091
	20: 7	and for my silver, and for my **g**;	2091
	22:48	ships of Tharshish to go to Ophir for **g**:	2091
2Ki	5: 5	six thousand *pieces* of **g**, and ten changes of	2091
	7: 8	and **g**, and raiment, and went and hid *it;* and	2091
	12:13	any vessels of **g**, or vessels of silver,	2091
	12:18	all the **g** that was found in the treasures of	2091
	14:14	he took all the **g** and silver, and all	2091
	16: 8	**g** that was found *in* the house of	2091
	18:14	talents of silver and thirty talents of **g**.	2091
	18:16	At that time did Hezekiah cut off *the* **g** *from*	NIH
	20:13	the **g**, and the spices, and the precious	2091
	23:33	hundred talents of silver, and a talent of **g**.	2091
	23:35	gave the silver and the **g** to Pharaoh;	2091
	23:35	and the **g** of the people of the land,	2091
	24:13	cut in pieces all the vessels of **g** which	2091
	25:15	*and* such *things* as *were* of **g**, *in* gold, and	2091
	25:15	*were of* gold, *in* **g**, and *of* silver, *in* silver,	2091
1Ch	18: 7	David took the shields of **g** that were on	2091
	18:10	*with him* all *manner of* vessels of **g** and	2091
	18:11	the **g** that he brought from all *these* nations;	2091
	20: 2	found it to weigh a talent of **g**, and	2091
	21:25	place six hundred shekels of **g** *by* weight.	2091
	22:14	LORD an hundred thousand talents *of* **g**,	2091
	22:16	Of the **g**, the silver, and the brass, and	2091
	28:14	*He gave* of **g** by weight for *things of* gold,	2091
	28:14	*He gave* of gold by weight for *things of* **g**,	2091
	28:15	Even the weight for the candlesticks of **g**,	2091
	28:15	*for* their lamps of **g**, by weight for every	2091
	28:16	*by* weight *he gave* **g** for the tables of	2091
	28:17	Also pure **g** *for* the fleshhooks, and	2091
	28:17	for the golden basons *he gave* **g** by weight	NIH
	28:18	for the altar of incense refined **g** by weight;	2091
	28:18	**g** for the pattern of the chariot of	2091
	29: 2	my God the **g** for *things to be made of* gold,	2091
	29: 2	my God the gold for *things to be made of* **g**,	2091
	29: 3	of mine own proper good, *of* **g** and silver,	2091
	29: 4	*Even* three thousand talents of **g**, of	2091
	29: 4	of the **g** of Ophir, and seven thousand	2091
	29: 5	The **g** for *things of* gold, and the silver for	2091
	29: 5	The gold for *things of* **g**, and the silver for	2091
	29: 7	the house of God *of* **g** five thousand talents	2091
2Ch	1:15	and **g** at Jerusalem *as plenteous* as stones,	2091
	2: 7	therefore a man cunning to work in **g**,	2091
	2:14	skilful to work in **g**, and in silver, in brass,	2091
	3: 4	and he overlaid it within with pure **g**.	2091
	3: 5	which he overlaid with fine **g**, and	2091
	3: 6	for beauty: and the **g** *was* gold of Parvaim.	2091
	3: 6	for beauty: and the gold *was* **g** of Parvaim.	2091
	3: 7	walls thereof, and the doors thereof, with **g**;	2091
	3: 8	he overlaid it with fine **g**, *amounting* to six	2091
	3: 9	weight of the nails *was* fifty shekels of **g**.	2091
	3: 9	And he overlaid the upper chambers with **g**.	2091
	3:10	of image work, and overlaid them with **g**.	2091
	4: 7	he made ten candlesticks of **g** according to	2091
	4: 8	And he made an hundred basons of **g**.	2091
	4:20	the manner before the oracle, *of* pure **g**;	2091
	4:21	*made he of* **g**, *and* that perfect gold;	2091
	4:21	*made he of* gold, *and* that perfect **g**;	2091
	4:22	and the spoons, and the censers, of pure **g**:	2091
	4:22	doors of the house of the temple, *were of* **g**.	2091
	5: 1	and the **g**, and all the instruments,	2091
	8:18	thence four hundred and fifty talents of **g**,	2091
	9: 1	and **g** in abundance, and precious stones:	2091
	9: 9	the king an hundred and twenty talents of **g**,	2091
	9:10	which brought **g** from Ophir,	2091
	9:13	Now the weight of **g** that came to Solomon	2091
	9:13	and threescore and six talents of **g**;	2091
	9:14	governors of the country brought **g** and	2091
	9:15	made two hundred targets *of* beaten **g**:	2091
	9:15	six hundred *shekels* of beaten **g** went to one	2091
	9:16	three hundred shields *made he of* beaten **g**:	2091
	9:16	three hundred *shekels* of **g** went to one	2091
	9:17	throne of ivory, and overlaid it with pure **g**.	2091
	9:18	with a footstool of **g**, *which were* fastened	2091
	9:20	vessels of king Solomon *were of* **g**,	2091
	9:20	of the forest of Lebanon *were of* pure **g**:	2091
	9:21	once came the ships of Tarshish bringing **g**,	2091

2Ch 9:24 vessels of **g**, and raiment, harness, and 2091
12: 9 he carried away also the shields of **g** which 2091
13:11 the candlestick of **g** with the lamps thereof, 2091
15:18 had dedicated, silver, and **g**, and vessels. 2091
16: 2 **g** out of the treasures of the house of 2091
16: 3 behold, I have sent thee silver and **g**; go, 2091
21: 3 of **g**, and of precious things, with fenced 2091
24:14 and spoons, and vessels of **g** and silver. 2091
25:24 *he took* all the **g** and the silver, and all 2091
32:27 for **g**, and for precious stones, and 2091
36: 3 hundred talents of silver and a talent of **g**. 2091
Ezr 1: 4 with **g**, and with goods, and with beasts, 2091
1: 6 with **g**, with goods, and with beasts, and 2091
1: 9 thirty chargers of **g**, a thousand chargers of 2091
1:10 Thirty basons of **g**, silver basons of a 2091
1:11 All the vessels of **g** and of silver *were* five 2091
2:69 and one thousand drams *of* **g**, 2091
5:14 the vessels also of **g** and silver of the house 1722
7:15 to carry the silver and **g**, which the king 1722
7:16 **g** that thou canst find in all the province of 1722
7:18 to do with the rest of the silver and **g**, 1722
8:25 them the silver, and the **g**, and the vessels, 2091
8:26 *and of* **g** an hundred talents; 2091
8:27 Also twenty basons of **g**, of a thousand 2091
8:27 two vessels of fine copper, precious as **g**. 2091
8:28 the **g** *are* a freewill offering unto 2091
8:30 of the silver, and the **g**, and the vessels, 2091
8:33 the fourth day was the silver and the **g** and 2091
Ne 7:70 gave to the treasure a thousand drams *of* **g**, 2091
7:71 of the work twenty thousand drams *of* **g**, 2091
7:72 gave *was* twenty thousand drams *of* **g**, 2091
Est 1: 6 the beds *were of* **g** and silver, upon a 2091
1: 7 *they* gave *them* drink in vessels of **g**, 2091
8:15 *with* a great crown of **g**, and *with* a garment 2091
Job 3:15 Or with princes that had **g**, who filled their 2091
22:24 shalt thou lay up **g** as dust, and *the gold of* 1220
22:24 *the* **g** *of* Ophir as the stones of the brooks. NIH
23:10 he hath tried me, I shall come forth as **g**. 2091
28: 1 and a place for **g** *where* they fine *it*. 2091
28: 6 the place of sapphires: and it hath dust of **g**. 2091
28:15 It cannot be gotten for **g**, neither shall silver 5458
28:16 It cannot be valued with the **g** of Ophir, 3800
28:17 The **g** and the crystal cannot equal it: and 2091
28:17 of it *shall not be for* jewels of **fine g**. 6337
28:19 neither shall it be valued with pure **g**. 3800
31:24 If I have made **g** my hope, or have said to 2091
31:24 or have said to the **fine g**, *Thou art* my 3800
36:19 *no*, not **g**, nor all the forces of strength. 1222
42:11 of money, and every one an earring of **g**. 2091
Ps 19:10 More to be desired *are they* than **g**, yea, 2091
19:10 *are they* than gold, yea, than much **fine g**: 6337
21: 3 thou settest a crown of **pure g** on his head. 6337
45: 9 hand did stand the queen in **g** of Ophir. 3800
45:13 her clothing *is* of wrought **g**. 2091
68:13 with silver, and her feathers with yellow **g**. 2742
72:15 and to him shall be given of the **g** of Sheba: 2091
105:37 brought them forth also with silver and **g**: 2091
115: 4 Their idols *are* silver and **g**, the work of 2091
119:72 mouth *is* better unto me than thousands of **g** 2091
119:127 I love thy commandments above **g**; 2091
119:127 above gold; yea, above **fine g**. 6337
135:15 The idols of the heathen *are* silver and **g**, 2091
Pr 3:14 of silver, and the gain thereof than **fine g**. 2742
8:10 and knowledge rather than choice **g**. 2742
8:19 My fruit *is* better than **g**, yea, than fine 2742
8:19 fruit *is* better than gold, yea, than **fine g**; 6337
11:22 *As* a jewel of **g** in a swine's snout, *so is* a 2091
16:16 much better *is it* to get wisdom than **g**! 2742
17: 3 pot *is* for silver, and the furnace for **g**: 2091
20:15 There is **g**, and a multitude of rubies: but 2091
22: 1 *and* loving favour rather than silver and **g**. 2091
25:11 A word fitly spoken *is like* apples of **g** in 2091
25:12 *As* an earring of **g**, and an ornament of fine 2091
25:12 an ornament of **fine g**, *so is* a wise reprover 3800
27:21 fining pot for silver, and the furnace for **g**; 2091
Ecc 2: 8 I gathered me also silver and **g**, and 2091
SS 1:10 rows *of jewels*, thy neck with chains *of* **g**. NIH
1:11 We will make thee borders of **g** with studs 2091
3:10 the bottom thereof *of* **g**, the covering of it 2091
5:11 His head *is as* the most **fine g**, his locks *are* 6337
5:14 His hands *are as* **g** rings set with the beryl: 2091
5:15 of marble, set upon sockets of **fine g**: 6337
Isa 2: 7 Their land also is full *of* silver and **g**, 2091
2:20 cast his idols of silver, and his idols of **g**, 2091
13:12 will make a man more precious than **fine g**; 6337
13:17 and *as for* **g**, they shall not delight in it. 2091
30:22 the ornament of thy molten images of **g**: 2091
31: 7 his idols of **g**, which your own hands have 2091
39: 2 the **g**, and the spices, and the precious 2091
40:19 the goldsmith spreadeth it over with **g**, and 2091
46: 6 They lavish **g** out of the bag, and 2091
60: 6 they shall bring **g** and incense; and 2091
60: 9 from far, their silver and their **g** with them, 2091
60:17 For brass I will bring **g**, and for iron I will 2091
Jer 4:30 thou deckest thee with ornaments of **g**, 2091
10: 4 They deck it with silver and with **g**; 2091
10: 9 **g** from Uphaz, the work of the workman, 2091
52:19 *that* which *was of* **g** *in* gold, and *that* which 2091
52:19 *that* which *was of* gold *in* **g**, and *that* which 2091
La 4: 1 How is the **g** become dim! *how* is the most 2091
4: 1 *how* is the most **fine g** changed! the stones 3800
4: 2 sons of Zion, comparable to **fine g**, 6337
Eze 7:19 in the streets, and their **g** shall be removed: 2091
7:19 their **g** shall not be able to deliver them in 2091
16:13 Thus wast thou decked *with* **g** and silver; 2091
16:17 Thou hast also taken thy fair jewels of my **g** 2091
27:22 and with all precious stones, and **g**. 2091
28: 4 hast gotten **g** and silver into thy treasures: 2091
28:13 the emerald, and the carbuncle, and **g**: 2091
38:13 to carry away silver and **g**, to take *away* 2091
Da 2:32 This image's head *was* of fine **g**, his breast 1722
2:35 the clay, the brass, the silver, and the **g**, 1722
2:38 ruler over them all. Thou *art* this head of **g**. 1722
2:45 the brass, the clay, the silver, and the **g**; 1722
3: 1 the king made an image of **g**, 1722
5: 4 praised the gods of **g**, and of silver, of 1722
5: 7 *have* a chain of **g** about his neck, and 1722
5:16 *have* a chain of **g** about thy neck, and 1722
5:23 **g**, of brass, iron, wood, and stone, which 1722
5:29 *put* a chain of **g** about his neck, and made a 1722
10: 5 whose loins *were* girded with **fine g** of 3800
11: 8 their precious vessels *of* silver and *of* **g**; 2091
11:38 his fathers knew not shall he honour with **g**, 2091
11:43 he shall have power over the treasures of **g** 2091
Hos 2: 8 and oil, and multiplied her silver and **g**, 2091
8: 4 and their **g** have they made them idols, 2091
Joel 3: 5 Because ye have taken my silver and my **g**, 2091
Na 2: 9 ye the spoil of silver, take the spoil of **g**: 2091
Hab 2:19 it *is* laid over *with* **g** and silver, and *there is* 2091
Zep 1:18 Neither their silver nor their **g** shall be able 2091
Hag 2: 8 The silver *is* mine, and the **g** *is* mine, 2091
Zec 4: 2 and behold, a candlestick all of **g**, 2091
6:11 take silver and **g**, and make crowns, and 2091
9: 3 and **fine g** as the mire of the streets. 2742
13: 9 is refined, and will try them as **g** is tried: 2091
14:14 **g**, and silver, and apparel, in great 2091
Mal 3: 3 of Levi, and purge them as **g** and silver, 2091
Mt 2:11 him gifts; **g**, and frankincense, and myrrh. *5557*
10: 9 Provide neither **g**, nor silver, nor brass in *5557*
23:16 whosoever shall swear by the **g** of *5557*
23:17 the **g**, or the temple that sanctifieth *5557*
23:17 or the temple that sanctifieth the **g**? *5557*
Ac 3: 6 Then Peter said, Silver and **g** have I none; *5553*
17:29 not to think that the Godhead is like unto **g**, *5557*
20:33 coveted no *man's* silver, or **g**, or apparel. *5553*
1Co 3:12 if any *man* build upon this foundation **g**, *5557*
1Ti 2: 9 or **g**, or pearls, or costly array; *5557*
2Ti 2:20 a great house there are not only vessels **of g** *5552*
Heb 9: 4 the covenant overlaid round about with **g**, *5553*
Jas 2: 2 unto your assembly a man **with a g ring**, *5554*
5: 3 Your **g** and silver is cankered; and the rust *5557*
1Pe 1: 7 *being* much more precious than of **g** that *5553*
1:18 with corruptible *things, as* silver and **g**, *5553*
3: 3 and of wearing of **g**, or of putting on of *5553*
Rev 3:18 I counsel thee to buy of me **g** tried in *5553*
4: 4 and they had on their heads crowns of **g**. *5552*
9: 7 their heads *were* as *it were* crowns like **g**, *5557*
9:20 should not worship devils, and idols of **g**, *5552*
17: 4 and **decked with g** and *5557+5558*
18:12 The merchandise of **g**, and silver, and *5557*
18:16 and decked with **g**, and precious stones, and *5557*
21:18 and the city *was* pure **g**, like unto clear *5553*
21:21 and the street of the city *was* pure **g**, as *it* *5553*

GOLDEN (66) [GOLD]

Ge 24:22 that the man took a **g** earring of half a 2091
Ex 25:25 thou shalt make a **g** crown to the border 2091
28:34 A **g** bell and a pomegranate, a golden bell 2091

Ex 28:34 a pomegranate, a g bell and a pomegranate, 2091
30: 4 two g rings shalt thou make to it under 2091
32: 2 said unto them, Break off the g earrings, 2091
32: 3 all the people brake off the g earrings 2091
39:20 they made two *other* g rings, and put them 2091
39:38 the g altar, and the anointing oil, and 2091
40:26 he put the g altar in the tent of 2091
Lev 8: 9 did he put the g plate, the holy crown; 2091
Nu 4:11 upon the g altar they shall spread a cloth of 2091
7:26 One g spoon of ten *shekels,* full *of* incense: 2091
7:32 One g spoon *of* ten *shekels,* full *of* incense: 2091
7:38 One g spoon of ten *shekels,* full *of* incense: 2091
7:44 One g spoon of ten *shekels,* full *of* incense: 2091
7:50 One g spoon of ten *shekels,* full *of* incense: 2091
7:56 One g spoon of ten *shekels,* full *of* incense: 2091
7:62 One g spoon of ten *shekels,* full *of* incense: 2091
7:68 One g spoon of ten *shekels,* full *of* incense: 2091
7:74 One g spoon of ten *shekels,* full *of* incense: 2091
7:80 One g spoon of ten *shekels,* full *of* incense: 2091
7:86 The g spoons *were* twelve, full *of* incense, 2091
Jdg 8:24 (For they had g earrings, because they *were* 2091
8:26 the weight of the g earrings that he 2091
1Sa 6: 4 Five g emerods, and five golden mice, 2091
6: 4 Five golden emerods, and five g mice, 2091
6:17 these *are* the g emerods which 2091
6:18 the g mice, *according to* the number of all 2091
2Ki 10:29 *to wit,* the g calves that *were in* Beth-el, 2091
1Ch 28:17 for the g basons *he gave gold* by weight for 2091
2Ch 4:19 the g altar also, and the tables whereon 2091
13: 8 and *there are* with you g calves, 2091
Ezr 6: 5 also let the g and silver vessels of the house 1722
Est 4:11 whom the king shall hold out the g sceptre, 2091
5: 2 the king held out to Esther the g sceptre 2091
8: 4 the king held out the g sceptre toward 2091
Ecc 12: 6 or the g bowl be broken, or the pitcher be 2091
Isa 13:12 even a man than the g **wedge** of Ophir. 3800
14: 4 the oppressor ceased! the g **city** ceased! 4062
Jer 51: 7 Babylon *hath been* a g cup in the LORD'S 2091
Da 3: 5 worship the g image that Nebuchadnezzar 1722
3: 7 worshipped the g image that 1722
3:10 shall fall down and worship the g image: 1722
3:12 nor worship the g image which thou hast 1722
3:14 nor worship the g image which I have set 1722
3:18 nor worship the g image which thou hast 1722
5: 2 commanded to bring the g and 1722
5: 3 they brought the g vessels that were taken 1722
Zec 4:12 g pipes empty the golden *oil* out of 2091
4:12 pipes empty the g *oil* out of themselves? 2091
Heb 9: 4 Which had the g censer, and the ark of *5552*
9: 4 wherein *was* the g pot that had manna, and *5552*
Rev 1:12 being turned, I saw seven g candlesticks; *5552*
1:13 and girt about the paps with a g girdle. *5552*
1:20 right hand, and the seven g candlesticks. *5552*
2: 1 who walketh in the midst of the seven g *5552*
5: 8 and g vials full of odours, which are *5552*
8: 3 and stood at the altar, having a g censer; *5552*
8: 3 the g altar which was before the throne. *5552*
9:13 I heard a voice from the four horns of the g *5552*
14:14 having on his head a g crown, and in his *5552*
15: 6 having their breasts girded with g girdles. *5552*
15: 7 seven g vials full of the wrath of God, *5552*
17: 4 having a g cup in her hand full of *5552*
21:15 And he that talked with me had a g reed to *5552*

GOLDSMITH (3) [GOLD]
Isa 40:19 the g spreadeth it over with gold, and 6884
41: 7 So the carpenter encouraged the g, *and* 6884
46: 6 weigh silver in the balance, *and* hire a g; 6884

GOLDSMITH'S (1) [GOLD]
Ne 3:31 After him repaired Malchiah the g son unto 6885

GOLDSMITHS (2) [GOLD]
Ne 3: 8 Uzziel the son of Harhaiah, *of* the g. 6884
3:32 corner unto the sheep gate repaired the g 6884

GOLGOTHA (3) [CALVARY]
Mt 27:33 they were come unto a place called G, *1115*
Mk 15:22 And they bring him unto the place G, *1115*
Jn 19:17 of a skull, which is called in the Hebrew G: *1115*

GOLIATH (6)
1Sa 17: 4 named G, of Gath, whose height *was* six 1555
17:23 the Philistine of Gath, G by name, 1555
21: 9 priest said, The sword of G the Philistine, 1555
22:10 and gave him the sword of G the Philistine. 1555
2Sa 21:19 slew *the brother of* G the Gittite, 1555
1Ch 20: 5 slew Lahmi the brother of G the Gittite, 1555

GOMER (6)
Ge 10: 2 G, and Magog, and Madai, and Javan, and 1586
10: 3 the sons of G; Ashkenaz, and Riphath, and 1586
1Ch 1: 5 G, and Magog, and Madai, and Javan, and 1586
1: 6 the sons of G; Ashchenaz, and Riphath, 1586
Eze 38: 6 G, and all his bands; the house of 1586
Hos 1: 3 and took G the daughter of Diblaim; 1586

GOMORRAH (19) [GOMORRHA]
Ge 10:19 G, and Admah, and Zeboim, even unto 6017
13:10 the LORD destroyed Sodom and G, 6017
14: 2 with Birsha king of G, Shinab king of 6017
14: 8 the king of G, and the king of Admah, and 6017
14:10 the kings of Sodom and G fled, and 6017
14:11 they took all the goods of Sodom and G, 6017
18:20 Because the cry of Sodom and G is great, 6017
19:24 upon G brimstone and fire from 6017
19:28 he looked toward Sodom and G, and 6017
Dt 29:23 of Sodom, and G, Admah, and Zeboim, 6017
32:32 the vine of Sodom, and of the fields of G: 6017
Isa 1: 9 *and* we should have been like unto G. 6017
1:10 unto the law of our God, ye people of G. 6017
13:19 be as when God overthrew Sodom and G. 6017
Jer 23:14 as Sodom, and the inhabitants thereof as G. 6017
49:18 and G and the neighbour *cities* thereof, 6017
50:40 As God overthrew Sodom and G and 6017
Am 4:11 as God overthrew Sodom and G, and 6017
Zep 2: 9 the children of Ammon as G, *even* 6017

GOMORRHA (5) [GOMORRAH]
Mt 10:15 of Sodom and G in the day of judgment, *1116*
Mk 6:11 for Sodom and G in the day of judgment, *1116*
Ro 9:29 as Sodoma, and been made like unto G. *1116*
2Pe 2: 6 G into ashes condemned *them* with an *1116*
Jude 1: 7 *Even* as Sodom and G, and the cities about *1116*

GONE (214) [GO] See Index

GOOD (720) [BEST, BETTER, BETTERED, GOODLIER, GOODLIEST, GOODLINESS, GOODLY, GOODMAN, GOODNESS, GOODNESS', GOODS]
Ge 1: 4 God saw the light, that *it was* g: and 2896
1:10 called he Seas: and God saw that *it was* g. 2896
1:12 after his kind: and God saw that *it was* g. 2896
1:18 the darkness: and God saw that *it was* g. 2896
1:21 after his kind: and God saw that *it was* g. 2896
1:25 after his kind: and God saw that *it was* g. 2896
1:31 he had made, and behold, *it was* very g. 2896
2: 9 that is pleasant to the sight, and g for food; 2896
2: 9 and the tree of knowledge of g and evil. 2896
2:12 the gold of that land *is* g: there *is* bdellium 2896
2:17 of the tree of the knowledge of g and evil, 2896
2:18 *It is* not g that the man should be alone; 2896
3: 5 ye shall be as gods, knowing g and evil. 2896
3: 6 when the woman saw that the tree *was* g for 2896
3:22 is become as one of us, to know g and evil: 2896
15:15 thou shalt be buried in a g old age. 2896
18: 7 fetcht a calf tender and g, and gave *it* unto a 2896
19: 8 and do ye to them as *is* g in your eyes: 2896
21:16 sat her down over against *him* a g **way off**, 7368
24:12 **send** me g **speed** *this* day, 6440+7136+3807.1
24:50 we cannot speak unto thee bad or g. 2896
25: 8 died in a g old age, an old man, and full *of* 2896
26:29 as we have done unto thee nothing but g, 2896
27: 9 fetch me from thence two g kids of 2896
27:46 the daughters of the land, **what** g 4100+3807.1
30:20 God hath endued me with a g dowry; 2896
31:24 heed that thou speak not to Jacob either g 2896
31:29 heed that thou speak not to Jacob either g 2896
32:12 I will **surely do** thee g, and make thy 3190+3190
40:16 baker saw that the interpretation was g, 2896
41: 5 of corn came up upon one stalk, rank and g. 2896
41:22 seven ears came up in one stalk, full and g: 2896
41:24 the thin ears devoured the seven g ears: 2896
41:26 The seven g kine *are* seven years; and 2896
41:26 and the seven g ears *are* seven years: 2896
41:35 let them gather all the food of those g years 2896
41:37 the thing was g in the eyes of Pharaoh, and 3190
43:28 Thy servant our father *is* **in** g **health**, he *is* 7965

Ge	44: 4	Wherefore have ye rewarded evil for **g**?	2896
	45:18	I will give you the **g** of the land of Egypt,	2898
	45:20	for the **g** of all the land of Egypt *is* yours.	2898
	45:23	ten asses laden with the **g things** of Egypt,	2898
	46:29	his neck, and wept on his neck a **g while**.	5750
	49:15	he saw that rest *was* **g**, and the land that *it*	2896
	50:20	*but* God meant it unto **g**, to bring to pass,	2896
Ex	3: 8	to bring them up out of that land unto a **g**	2896
	18:17	unto him, The thing that thou doest *is* not **g**.	2896
	21:34	The owner of the pit shall **make** *it* **g**, *and*	7999
	22:11	accept *thereof,* and he shall not **make** *it* **g**.	7999
	22:13	he shall not **make g** that which was torn.	7999
	22:14	not with it, he shall **surely make** *it* **g**.	7999+7999
	22:15	thereof *be* with it, he shall not **make** *it* **g**:	7999
Lev	5: 4	with *his* lips to do evil, or to **do g**,	3190
	24:18	he that killeth a beast shall **make** it **g**;	7999
	27:10	change it, a **g** for a bad, or a bad for a good:	2896
	27:10	change it, a good for a bad, or a bad for a **g**:	2896
	27:12	priest shall value it, whether it be **g** or bad:	2896
	27:14	shall estimate it, whether it be **g** or bad:	2896
	27:33	He shall not search whether it be **g** or bad,	2896
Nu	10:29	come thou with us, and we will **do** thee **g**:	2895
	10:29	for the LORD hath spoken **g** concerning	2896
	13:19	*is* that they dwell in, whether it *be* **g** or bad;	2896
	13:20	be ye **of g courage**, and bring of the fruit of	2388
	14: 7	through to search it, *is* an exceeding **g** land.	2896
	23:19	hath he spoken, and shall he not **make** it **g**?	6965
	24:13	to do *either* **g** or bad of mine own mind;	2896
Dt	1:14	The thing which thou hast spoken *is* **g** *for*	2896
	1:25	*It is* a **g** land which the LORD our God	2896
	1:35	men of this evil generation see that **g** land,	2896
	1:39	*in that* day had no knowledge between **g**	2896
	2: 4	take ye **g** heed unto yourselves therefore:	3966
	3:25	and see the **g** land that *is* beyond Jordan,	2896
	4:15	Take ye therefore **g** heed unto yourselves;	3966
	4:21	and that *I* should not go in unto *that* **g** land,	2896
	4:22	ye *shall* go over, and possess that **g** land.	2896
	6:11	houses full *of* all **g** *things,* which thou	2898
	6:18	*is* right and **g** in the sight of the LORD:	2896
	6:18	possess the **g** land which the LORD sware	2896
	6:24	fear the LORD our God, for our **g** always,	2896
	8: 7	thy God bringeth thee into a **g** land,	2896
	8:10	for the **g** land which he hath given thee.	2896
	8:16	prove thee, to **do** thee **g** at thy latter end;	3190
	9: 6	**g** land to possess it for thy righteousness;	2896
	10:13	which I command thee *this* day for thy **g**?	2896
	11:17	*lest* ye perish quickly from off the **g** land	2896
	12:28	when thou doest *that which is* **g** and right in	2896
	26:11	thou shalt rejoice in every **g** *thing* which	2896
	28:12	The LORD shall open unto thee his **g**	2896
	28:63	the LORD rejoiced over you to **do** you **g**,	3190
	30: 5	he will **do** thee **g**, and multiply thee above	3190
	30: 9	thy cattle, and in the fruit of thy land, for **g**:	2896
	30: 9	LORD will again rejoice over thee for **g**,	2896
	30:15	I have set before thee *this* day life and **g**,	2896
	31: 6	Be strong and **of a g courage**, fear not,	553
	31: 7	of all Israel, Be strong and **of a g courage**:	553
	31:23	said, Be strong and **of a g courage**:	553
	33:16	*for* the **g will** of him that dwelt in the bush:	7522
Jos	1: 6	Be strong and **of a g courage**: for unto this	553
	1: 8	and then thou shalt **have g success**.	7919
	1: 9	Be strong and **of a g courage**; be not afraid,	553
	1:18	to death: only be strong and **of a g courage**.	553
	9:25	as it seemeth **g** and right unto thee to do	2896
	10:25	be dismayed, be strong and **of g courage**:	553
	21:45	There failed not ought of any **g** thing which	2896
	23:11	Take **g** heed therefore unto yourselves, that	3966
	23:13	until ye perish from off this **g** land which	2896
	23:14	that not one thing hath failed of all the **g**	2896
	23:15	*that* as all **g** things are come upon you,	2896
	23:15	until he have destroyed you from off this **g**	2896
	23:16	ye shall perish quickly from off the **g** land	2896
	24:20	after that he hath **done** you **g**.	3190
Jdg	8:32	Gideon the son of Joash died in a **g** old age,	2896
	9:11	my **g** fruit, and go to be promoted over	2896
	10:15	do thou unto us whatsoever seemeth **g** unto	2896
	17:13	Now know I that the LORD will **do** me **g**,	3190
	18: 9	have seen the land, and behold, it *is* very **g**:	2896
	18:22	*And* when they were a **g way** from	7368
	19:24	and do with them what seemeth **g** unto you:	2896
Ru	2:22	*It is* **g**, my daughter, that thou go out with	2896
1Sa	1:23	said unto her, Do what seemeth thee **g**;	2896
	2:24	my sons; for *it is* no **g** report that I hear:	2896
	3:18	let him do what seemeth him **g**.	2896
	11:10	ye shall do with us all that seemeth **g** unto	2896
	12:23	but I will teach you the **g** and the right way:	2896
	14:36	Do whatsoever seemeth **g** unto thee.	2896
	14:40	unto Saul, Do what seemeth **g** unto thee.	2896
	15: 9	all *that was* **g**, and would not utterly destroy	2896
	19: 4	Jonathan spake **g** of David unto Saul his	2896
	19: 4	his works *have been* to thee-ward very **g**:	2896
	20:12	*if there be* **g** toward David, and I then	2895
	24: 4	do to him as it shall seem **g** unto thee.	3190
	24:17	for thou hast rewarded me **g**, whereas I	2896
	24:19	wherefore the LORD reward thee **g** for	2896
	25: 3	*she was* a woman of **g** understanding, and	2896
	25: 8	for we come in a **g** day: give, I pray thee,	2896
	25:15	the men *were* very **g** unto us, and we were	2896
	25:21	and he hath requited me evil for **g**.	2896
	25:30	the **g** that he hath spoken concerning thee,	2896
	26:16	This thing *is* not **g** that thou hast done.	2896
	29: 6	thy coming in with me in the host *is* **g** in	2896
	29: 9	I know that thou *art* **g** in my sight,	2896
2Sa	3:19	David in Hebron all that seemed **g** to Israel,	2896
	3:19	that seemed **g** to the whole house of	NIH
	4:10	thinking to have **brought g tidings**,	1319
	6:19	a **g piece** *of flesh,* and a flagon *of wine.* So	829
	10:12	Be **of g courage**, and let us play the men	2388
	10:12	the LORD do that which seemeth him **g**.	2896
	13:22	unto his brother Amnon neither **g** nor bad:	2896
	14:17	so *is* my lord the king to discern **g** and bad:	2896
	14:32	*it had been* **g** for me *to have been* there	2896
	15: 3	unto him, See, thy matters *are* **g** and right;	2896
	15:26	let him do to me as seemeth **g** unto him.	2896
	16:12	that the LORD will requite me **g** for his	2896
	17: 7	Ahithophel hath given *is* not **g** at this time.	2896
	17:14	to defeat the **g** counsel of Ahithophel,	2896
	18:27	He *is* a **g** man, and cometh with good	2896
	18:27	*is* a good man, and cometh with **g** tidings.	2896
	19:18	and to do what he thought **g**.	2896
	19:27	do therefore what *is* **g** in thine eyes.	2896
	19:35	*and* can I discern between **g** and evil? can	2896
	19:37	and do to him what shall seem **g** unto thee.	2896
	19:38	I will do to him *that* which shall seem **g**	2896
	24:22	and offer up what seemeth **g** unto him:	2896
1Ki	1:42	*art* a valiant man, and bringest **g** tidings.	2896
	2:38	Shimei said unto the king, The saying *is* **g**:	2896
	2:42	unto me, The word *that* I have heard *is* **g**.	2896
	3: 9	that *I* may discern between **g** and bad:	2896
	8:36	that thou teach them the **g** way wherein	2896
	8:56	there hath not failed one word of all his **g**	2896
	12: 7	speak **g** words to them, then they will be	2896
	14:13	in him there is found *some* **g** thing toward	2896
	14:15	he shall root up Israel out of this **g** land,	2896
	21: 2	*or, if it seem* **g** to thee, I will give thee	2896
	22: 8	for he doth not prophesy **g** concerning me,	2896
	22:13	the words of the prophets *declare* **g** unto	2896
	22:13	of one of them, and speak *that which is* **g**.	2896
	22:18	he would prophesy no **g** concerning me,	2896
2Ki	3:19	shall fell every **g** tree, and stop all wells of	2896
	3:19	and mar every **g** piece of land with stones.	2896
	3:25	*on* every **g** piece of land cast every man his	2896
	3:25	the wells of water, and felled all the **g** trees:	2896
	7: 9	this day *is* a day of **g tidings**, and we hold	1309
	8: 9	even *of* every **g thing** of Damascus,	2898
	10: 5	do thou *that* which *is* **g** in thine eyes.	2896
	20: 3	and have done *that* which *is* **g** in thy sight.	2896
	20:19	**G** *is* the word of the LORD which thou	2896
	20:19	*Is it* not **g**, if peace and truth be in my days?	NIH
1Ch	4:40	they found fat pasture and **g**, and the land	2896
	13: 2	If *it seem* **g** unto you, and *that it be* of	2895
	16: 3	and a **g piece** *of flesh,* and a flagon *of wine.*	829
	16:34	for *he is* **g**; for his mercy *endureth* for ever.	2896
	19:13	Be **of g courage**, and let us behave	2388
	19:13	let the LORD do *that* which *is* **g** in his	2896
	21:23	let my lord the king do *that* which *is* **g** in	2896
	22:13	be strong, and **of g courage**; dread not,	553
	28: 8	that ye may possess *this* **g** land, and leave *it*	2896
	28:20	Be strong and **of g courage**, and do *it:* fear	553
	29: 3	I have of mine own **proper g**, *of* gold and	5459
	29:28	he died in a **g** old age, full of days, riches,	2896
2Ch	5:13	praised the LORD, *saying,* For *he is* **g**;	2896
	6:27	when thou hast taught them the **g** way,	2896
	7: 3	praised the LORD, *saying,* For *he is* **g**;	2896
	10: 7	please them, and speak **g** words to them,	2896
	14: 2	Asa did *that* which *was* **g** and right in	2896
	18: 7	for he never prophesied **g** unto me,	2896
	18:12	the words of the prophets *declare* **g** to	2896

2Ch	18:12	be like one of theirs, and speak thou **g**.	2896
	18:17	thee *that* he would not prophesy **g** unto me,	2896
	19: 3	Nevertheless there are **g** things found in	2896
	19:11	and the LORD shall be with the **g**.	2896
	24:16	because he had done **g** in Israel,	2896
	30:18	The **g** LORD pardon every one	2896
	30:22	that taught the **g** knowledge of the LORD:	2896
	31:20	and wrought *that* which *was* **g** and right and	2896
Ezr	3:11	because *he is* **g**, for his mercy *endureth* for	2896
	5:17	Now therefore, if *it seem* **g** to the king,	2869
	7: 9	according to the **g** hand of his God upon	2896
	7:18	whatsoever shall **seem g** to thee, and to thy	3191
	8:18	by the **g** hand of our God upon us they	2896
	8:22	The hand of our God *is* upon all them for **g**	2896
	9:12	eat the **g** of the land, and leave *it* for an	2898
	10: 4	*be* with thee: be **of g courage**, and do *it*.	2388
Ne	2: 8	according to the **g** hand of my God upon	2896
	2:18	the hand of my God which was **g** upon me;	2896
	2:18	So they strengthened their hands for *this* **g**	2896
	5: 9	Also I said, It *is* not **g** that ye do: ought ye	2896
	5:19	Think upon me, my God, for **g**,	2896
	6:19	Also they reported his **g deeds** before me,	2896
	9:13	true laws, **g** statutes and commandments:	2896
	9:20	Thou gavest also thy **g** spirit to instruct	2896
	9:36	to eat the fruit thereof and the **g** thereof,	2898
	13:14	wipe not out my **g deeds** that I have done	2617
	13:31	Remember me, O my God, for **g**.	2896
Est	3:11	to do with them as it seemeth **g** to thee.	2896
	5: 4	If *it seem* **g** unto the king, let the king and	2895
	7: 9	who had spoken **g** for the king, standeth in	2896
	8:17	had joy and gladness, a feast and a **g** day.	2896
	9:19	a **g** day, and *of* sending portions one to	2896
	9:22	to joy, and from mourning into a **g** day:	2896
Job	2:10	shall we receive **g** at the hand of God, and	2896
	5:27	it *is;* hear it, and know thou *it* **for** thy **g**.	3807.1
	7: 7	life *is* wind: mine eye shall no more see **g**.	2896
	9:25	than a post: they flee away, they see no **g**.	2896
	10: 3	*Is it* **g** unto thee that thou shouldest oppress,	2895
	13: 9	*Is it* **g** that he should search you out? or	2895
	15: 3	*with* speeches wherewith he can **do** no **g**?	3276
	21:16	Lo, their **g** *is* not in their hand: the counsel	2898
	22:18	Yet he filled their houses *with* **g** *things:* but	2896
	22:21	be at peace: thereby **g** shall come *unto* thee.	2896
	24:21	beareth not: and **doeth** not **g** to the widow.	3190
	30:26	When I looked for **g**, then evil came *unto*	2896
	34: 4	let us know among ourselves what *is* **g**.	2896
	39: 4	Their young ones are **in g liking**, they grow	2492
Ps	4: 6	*be* many that say, Who will shew us *any* **g**?	2896
	14: 1	*there is* none that doeth **g**.	2896
	14: 3	*there is* none that doeth **g**, no, not one.	2896
	25: 8	**G** and upright *is* the LORD: therefore	2896
	27:14	be **of g courage**, and he shall strengthen	2388
	31:24	Be **of g courage**, and he shall strengthen	2388
	34: 8	O taste and see that the LORD *is* **g**:	2896
	34:10	the LORD shall not want any **g** *thing*.	2896
	34:12	*and* loveth *many* days, that *he* may see **g**?	2896
	34:14	Depart from evil, and do **g**; seek peace, and	2896
	35:12	They rewarded me evil for **g** *to* the spoiling	2896
	36: 3	he hath left off to be wise, *and* to **do g**.	3190
	36: 4	he setteth himself in a way *that is* not **g**;	2896
	37: 3	Trust in the LORD, and do **g**; *so*	2896
	37:23	The steps of a *g* man are ordered by	NIH
	37:27	Depart from evil, and do **g**; and dwell for	2896
	38:20	They also that render evil for **g** are mine	2896
	38:20	because I follow *the thing that* **g** *is*.	2896
	39: 2	*with* silence, I held my peace, *even* from **g**;	2896
	45: 1	My heart is inditing a **g** matter: I speak of	2896
	51:18	**Do g** in thy good pleasure unto Zion:	3190
	51:18	Do good in thy **g pleasure** unto Zion:	7522
	52: 3	Thou lovest evil more than **g**; *and*	2896
	52: 9	on thy name; for *it is* **g** before thy saints.	2896
	53: 1	*there is* none that doeth **g**.	2896
	53: 3	*there is* none that doeth **g**, no, not one.	2896
	54: 6	will praise thy name, O LORD; for *it is* **g**.	2896
	69:16	O LORD; for thy lovingkindness *is* **g**:	2896
	73: 1	Truly God *is* **g** to Israel, *even* to such as are	2896
	73:28	*it is* **g** for me to draw near to God: I have	2896
	84:11	no **g** *thing* will he withhold from them that	2896
	85:12	Yea, the LORD shall give *that which is* **g**;	2896
	86: 5	For thou, Lord, *art* **g**, and ready to forgive;	2896
	86:17	Shew me a token for **g**; that they which	2896
	92: 1	*It is a* **g** *thing* to give thanks unto	2896
	100: 5	For the LORD *is* **g**; his mercy *is*	2896
	103: 5	Who satisfieth thy mouth with **g** *things; so*	2896
	104:28	openest thine hand, they are filled *with* **g**.	2896
	106: 1	O give thanks unto the LORD; for *he is* **g**:	2896
	106: 5	That *I* may see the **g** of thy chosen, that *I*	2896
	107: 1	O give thanks unto the LORD, for *he is* **g**:	2896
	109: 5	they have rewarded me evil for **g**, and	2896
	109:21	because thy mercy *is* **g**, deliver thou me.	2896
	111:10	a **g** understanding have all they that do *his*	2896
	112: 5	A **g** man sheweth favour, and lendeth:	2896
	118: 1	O give thanks unto the LORD; for *he is* **g**:	2896
	118:29	O give thanks unto the LORD; for *he is* **g**:	2896
	119:39	which I fear: for thy judgments *are* **g**.	2896
	119:66	Teach me **g** judgment and knowledge: for I	2898
	119:68	Thou *art* **g**, and doest good; teach me thy	2896
	119:68	Thou *art* good, and **doest g**; teach me thy	2895
	119:71	*It is* **g** for me that I have been afflicted; that	2896
	119:122	Be surety for thy servant for **g**: let not	2896
	122: 9	of the LORD our God I will seek thy **g**.	2896
	125: 4	**Do g**, O LORD, unto *those that be* good,	2895
	125: 4	unto *those that be* **g**, and to *them that are*	2896
	128: 5	thou shalt see the **g** of Jerusalem all	2898
	133: 1	how **g** and how pleasant *it is* for brethren to	2896
	135: 3	Praise the LORD; for the LORD *is* **g**:	2896
	136: 1	O give thanks unto the LORD; for *he is* **g**:	2896
	143:10	thy spirit *is* **g**; lead me into the land of	2896
	145: 9	The LORD *is* **g** to all: and his tender	2896
	147: 1	for *it is* **g** to sing *praises* unto our God;	2896
Pr	2: 9	judgment, and equity; *yea,* every **g** path.	2896
	2:20	That thou mayest walk in the way of **g**	2896
	3: 4	and **g** understanding in the sight of God and	2896
	3:27	Withhold not **g** from them to whom it is	2896
	4: 2	For I give you **g** doctrine, forsake you not	2896
	11:17	The merciful man **doeth g** to his own soul:	1580
	11:23	The desire of the righteous *is* only **g**: *but*	2896
	11:27	He that diligently seeketh **g** procureth	2896
	12: 2	A **g** *man* obtaineth favour of the LORD:	2896
	12:14	A man shall be satisfied *with* **g** by the fruit	2896
	12:25	it stoop: but a **g** word maketh it glad.	2896
	13: 2	A man shall eat **g** by the fruit of *his* mouth:	2896
	13:15	**G** understanding giveth favour: but the way	2896
	13:21	but to the righteous **g** shall be repayed.	2896
	13:22	A **g** *man* leaveth an inheritance to *his*	2896
	14:14	and a **g** man *shall be satisfied* from himself.	2896
	14:19	The evil bow before the **g**; and the wicked	2896
	14:22	and truth *shall be to* them that devise **g**.	2896
	15: 3	in every place, beholding the evil and the **g**.	2896
	15:23	a word *spoken* in due season, how **g** *is it!*	2896
	15:30	*and* a **g** report maketh the bones fat.	2896
	16:20	that handleth a matter wisely shall find **g**:	2896
	16:29	and leadeth him into the way *that is* not **g**.	2896
	17:13	Whoso rewardeth evil for **g**, evil shall not	2896
	17:20	He that hath a froward heart findeth no **g**:	2896
	17:22	A merry heart **doeth g** *like* a medicine: but	3190
	17:26	Also to punish the just *is* not **g**, *nor* to strike	2896
	18: 5	*It is* not **g** to accept the person of	2896
	18:22	*Whoso* findeth a wife findeth a **g** *thing,* and	2896
	19: 2	the soul *be* without knowledge, *it is* not **g**;	2896
	19: 8	he that keepeth understanding shall find **g**.	2896
	20:18	by counsel: and with **g advice** make war.	8458
	20:23	the LORD; and a false balance *is* not **g**.	2896
	22: 1	A *g* name *is* rather to be chosen than great	NIH
	24:13	My son, eat thou honey, because *it is* **g**; and	2896
	24:23	*It is* not **g** to have respect of persons in	2896
	24:25	and a **g** blessing shall come upon them.	2896
	25:25	so *is* **g** news from a far country.	2896
	25:27	*It is* not **g** to eat much honey: so *for men* to	2896
	28:10	the upright shall have **g** *things* in	2896
	28:21	To have respect of persons *is* not **g**: for for	2896
	31:12	She will do him **g** and not evil all the days	2896
	31:18	She perceiveth that her merchandise *is* **g**:	2896
Ecc	2: 3	till I might see what *was* that **g** for the sons	2896
	2:24	*that* he should make his soul enjoy **g** in his	2896
	2:26	For *God* giveth to a man that *is* **g** in his	2896
	2:26	that *he* may give to *him that is* **g** before	2896
	3:12	I know that *there is* no **g** in them, but for *a*	2896
	3:12	for *a man* to rejoice, and to do **g** in his life.	2896
	3:13	and drink, and enjoy the **g** of all his labour,	2896
	4: 8	do I labour, and bereave my soul of **g**?	2896
	4: 9	they have a **g** reward for their labour.	2896
	5:11	what **g** *is there* to the owners thereof,	3788
	5:18	*it is* **g** and comely *for one* to eat and	2896
	5:18	to enjoy the **g** of all his labour that he	2896
	6: 3	his soul be not filled with **g**, and also *that*	2896
	6: 6	years twice *told,* yet hath he seen no **g**:	2896
	6:12	For who knoweth what *is* **g** for man in *this*	2896

Ecc	7: 1	A *g* name *is* better than precious ointment;	NIH
	7:11	Wisdom *is* **g** with an inheritance: and *by it*	2896
	7:18	*It is* **g** that thou shouldest take hold of this;	2896
	7:20	upon earth, that doeth **g**, and sinneth not.	2896
	9: 2	to the **g** and to the clean, and to	2896
	9: 2	as *is* the **g**, so *is* the sinner; *and* he that	2896
	9:18	of war: but one sinner destroyeth much **g**.	2896
	11: 6	that, or whether they both *shall be* alike **g**.	2896
	12: 9	he **gave g heed**, and sought out, *and* set in	239
	12:14	with every secret *thing,* whether *it be* **g**, or	2896
SS	1: 3	Because of the savour of thy **g** ointments	2896
	2:13	the vines *with* the tender grape give a **g**	NIH
Isa	1:19	and obedient, ye shall eat the **g** of the land:	2898
	5:20	Woe unto them that call evil **g**, and good	2896
	5:20	unto them that call evil good, and **g** evil;	2896
	7:15	know to refuse the evil, and choose the **g**.	2896
	7:16	know to refuse the evil, and choose the **g**,	2896
	38: 3	and have done *that* which *is* **g** in thy sight.	2896
	39: 8	**G** *is* the word of the LORD which thou	2896
	40: 9	O Zion, that **bringest g tidings**, get thee up	1319
	40: 9	O Jerusalem, that **bringest g tidings**, lift up	1319
	41: 6	*one* said to his brother, Be of **g courage**.	2388
	41:23	yea, **do g**, or do evil, that we may be	3190
	41:27	to Jerusalem one that **bringeth g tidings**.	1319
	52: 7	are the feet of him that **bringeth g tidings**,	1319
	52: 7	that **bringeth g tidings** of good,	1319
	52: 7	that bringeth good tidings of **g**,	2896
	55: 2	eat ye *that which is* **g**, and let your soul	2896
	61: 1	me to **preach g tidings unto** the meek;	1319
	65: 2	which walketh *in* a way *that was* not **g**,	2896
Jer	4:22	but to **do g** they have no knowledge.	3190
	5:25	your sins have withholden **g** *things* from	2896
	6:16	where *is* the **g** way, and walk therein,	2896
	8:15	no **g** *came; and* for a time of health, and	2896
	10: 5	do evil, neither also *is it* in them to **do g**.	3190
	13:10	be as this girdle, which is **g** for nothing.	6743
	13:23	*then* may ye also **do g**, that are accustomed	3190
	14:11	Pray not for this people for *their* **g**.	2896
	14:19	*we* looked for peace, and *there is* no **g**; and	2896
	17: 6	and shall not see when **g** cometh;	2896
	18: 4	as seemed **g** to the potter to make *it*.	3474
	18:10	not my voice, then I will repent of the **g**,	2896
	18:11	and **make** your ways and your doings **g**.	3190
	18:20	Shall evil be recompensed for **g**? for they	2896
	18:20	that I stood before thee to speak **g** for them,	2896
	21:10	for evil, and not for **g**, saith the LORD:	2896
	24: 2	One basket *had* very **g** figs, *even* like	2896
	24: 3	the **g** figs, very good; and the evil,	2896
	24: 3	the good figs, very **g**; and the evil,	2896
	24: 5	Like these **g** figs, so will I acknowledge	2896
	24: 5	*into* the land of the Chaldeans for *their* **g**.	2896
	24: 6	For I will set mine eyes upon them for **g**,	2896
	26:14	do with me as seemeth **g** and meet unto	2896
	29:10	perform my **g** word towards you, in causing	2896
	29:32	neither shall he behold the **g** that I will do	2896
	32:39	for the **g** of them, and of their children after	2896
	32:40	not turn away from them, to **do** them **g**;	3190
	32:41	I will rejoice over them to **do** them **g**, and	2895
	32:42	will I bring upon them all the **g** that I have	2896
	33: 9	which shall hear all the **g** that I do unto	2896
	33:11	for the LORD *is* **g**; for his mercy *endureth*	2896
	33:14	that I will perform *that* **g** thing which I have	2896
	39:16	words upon this city for evil, and not for **g**;	2896
	40: 4	If it seem **g** unto thee to come with me *into*	2896
	40: 4	whither it seemeth **g** and convenient for	2896
	42: 6	Whether *it be* **g**, or whether *it be* evil,	2896
	44:27	*will* watch over them for evil, and not for **g**:	2896
La	3:25	The LORD *is* **g** unto them that wait for	2896
	3:26	*It is* **g** *that a man should* both hope and	2896
	3:27	*It is* **g** for a man that he bear the yoke in his	2896
	3:38	of the most High proceedeth not evil and **g**.	2896
Eze	16:50	therefore I took them away as I saw *g*.	NIH
	17: 8	It *was* planted in a **g** soil by great waters,	2896
	18:18	did *that* which *is* not **g** among his people,	2896
	20:25	I gave them also statutes *that were* not **g**,	2896
	24: 4	*even* every **g** piece, the thigh, and	2896
	34:14	I will feed them in a **g** pasture, and	2896
	34:14	there shall they lie in a **g** fold, and *in* a fat	2896
	34:18	unto you to have eaten up the **g** pasture,	2896
	36:31	your doings that *were* not **g**, and shall lothe	2896
Da	4: 2	I thought it **g** to shew the signs and	8232
Hos	4:13	and elms, because the shadow thereof *is* **g**:	2896
	8: 3	Israel hath cast off *the thing that is* **g**:	2896
Am	5:14	Seek **g**, and not evil, that ye may live: and	2896

	5:15	love the **g**, and establish judgment in	2896
	9: 4	mine eyes upon them for evil, and not for **g**.	2896
Mic	1:12	inhabitant of Maroth waited carefully for **g**:	2896
	2: 7	do not my words **do g** to him that walketh	3190
	3: 2	Who hate the **g**, and love the evil;	2896
	6: 8	He hath shewed thee, O man, what *is* **g**; and	2896
	7: 2	The **g** *man* is perished out of the earth: and	2623
Na	1: 7	The LORD *is* **g**, a strong hold in the day	2896
	1:15	the feet of him that **bringeth g tidings**,	1319
Zep	1:12	in their heart, The LORD will not **do g**,	3190
Zec	1:13	the angel that talked with me *with* **g** words	2896
	11:12	unto them, If ye think **g**, give *me* my price;	2896
Mal	2:13	or receiveth *it with* **g will** at your hand.	7522
	2:17	Every one that doeth evil *is* **g** in the sight of	2896
Mt	3:10	every tree which bringeth not forth **g** fruit	*2570*
	5:13	it is thenceforth **g** for nothing, but to be cast	*2480*
	5:16	that they may see your **g** works, and	*2570*
	5:44	do **g** to them that hate you, and pray for	*2573*
	5:45	his sun to rise on the evil and *on* the **g**,	*18*
	7:11	know how to give **g** gifts unto your children,	*18*
	7:11	in heaven give **g** *things* to them that ask him?	*18*
	7:17	*Even* so every **g** tree bringeth forth good fruit;	*18*
	7:17	so every good tree bringeth forth **g** fruit;	*2570*
	7:18	A **g** tree cannot bring forth evil fruit,	*18*
	7:18	neither *can* a corrupt tree bring forth **g** fruit.	*2570*
	7:19	Every tree that bringeth not forth **g** fruit is	*2570*
	8:30	And there was a **g way off** from them a	*3112*
	9: 2	Son, **be of g cheer**; thy sins be forgiven	*2293*
	9:22	he said, Daughter, **be of g comfort**;	*2293*
	11:26	Father: for so it seemed **g** in thy sight.	*2107*
	12:33	Either make the tree **g**, and his fruit good;	*2570*
	12:33	Either make the tree good, and his fruit **g**;	*2570*
	12:34	speak **g** *things?* for out of the abundance of	*18*
	12:35	A **g** man out of the good treasure of the heart	*18*
	12:35	A good man out of the **g** treasure of the heart	*18*
	12:35	treasure of the heart bringeth forth **g** *things:*	*18*
	13: 8	But other fell into **g** ground, and	*2570*
	13:23	But he that received seed into the **g** ground	*2570*
	13:24	unto a man which sowed **g** seed in his field:	*2570*
	13:27	Sir, didst not thou sow **g** seed in thy field?	*2570*
	13:37	He that soweth the **g** seed is the Son of	*2570*
	13:38	the **g** seed are the children of the kingdom;	*2570*
	13:48	and gathered the **g** into vessels, but cast	*2570*
	14:27	spake unto them, saying, **Be of g cheer**;	*2293*
	17: 4	unto Jesus, Lord, it is **g** for us to be here:	*2570*
	19:10	so with *his* wife, it is not **g** to marry.	*4851*
	19:16	one came and said unto him, **G** Master,	*18*
	19:16	Good Master, what **g** *thing* shall I do,	*18*
	19:17	And he said unto him, Why callest thou me **g**?	*18*
	19:17	*there is* none **g** but one, *that is,* God: but	*18*
	20:15	mine own? Is thine eye evil, because I am **g**?	*18*
	22:10	all as many as they found, both bad and **g**:	*18*
	25:21	Well *done, thou* **g** and faithful servant:	*18*
	25:23	unto him, Well *done,* **g** and faithful servant;	*18*
	26:10	for she hath wrought a **g** work upon me.	*2570*
	26:24	it had been **g** for that man if he had not	*2570*
Mk	3: 4	Is it lawful to **do g** on the sabbath days, or	*15*
	4: 8	And other fell on **g** ground, and did yield	*2570*
	4:20	And these are they which are sown on **g**	*2570*
	6:50	and saith unto them, **Be of g cheer**:	*2293*
	9: 5	to Jesus, Master, it is **g** for us to be here:	*2570*
	9:50	Salt *is* **g**: but if the salt have lost his	*2570*
	10:17	and kneeled to him, and asked him, **G** Master,	*18*
	10:18	Jesus said unto him, Why callest thou me **g**?	*18*
	10:18	*there is* none **g** but one, *that is,* God.	*18*
	10:49	saying unto him, **Be of g comfort**, rise;	*2293*
	14: 6	you her? she hath wrought a **g** work on me.	*2570*
	14: 7	and whensoever ye will ye may do them **g**:	*2095*
	14:21	**g** were it for that man if he had never been	*2570*
Lk	1: 3	It **seemed g** to me also, having had perfect	*1380*
	1:53	He hath filled the hungry with **g** *things;* and	*18*
	2:10	I **bring** you **g tidings** of great joy,	*2097*
	2:14	and on earth peace, **g will** towards men.	*2107*
	3: 9	which bringeth not forth **g** fruit is hewn	*2570*
	6: 9	*thing;* Is it lawful on the sabbath days to **do g**,	*15*
	6:27	your enemies, do **g** to them which hate you,	*2573*
	6:33	And if ye **do g** to them which do good to you,	*15*
	6:33	And if ye do good to them which **do g** to you,	*15*
	6:35	and **do g**, and lend, hoping for nothing again;	*15*
	6:38	**g** measure, pressed down, and	*2570*
	6:43	For a **g** tree bringeth not forth corrupt fruit;	*2570*
	6:43	neither doth a corrupt tree bring forth **g**	*2570*
	6:45	A **g** man out of the good treasure of his heart	*18*
	6:45	A good man out of the **g** treasure of his heart	*18*

Lk 6:45 of his heart bringeth forth that which is **g**; *18*
8: 8 And other fell on **g** ground, and sprang up, *18*
8:15 But that on the **g** ground are they, which in *2570*
8:15 which in an honest and **g** heart, having heard *18*
8:48 said unto her, Daughter, **be of g comfort**: *2293*
9:33 unto Jesus, Master, it is **g** for us to be here: *2570*
10:21 Father; for so it seemed **g** in thy sight. *2107*
10:42 and Mary hath chosen *that* **g** part, which shall *18*
11:13 know how to give **g** gifts unto your children: *18*
12:32 for it is your Father's **g pleasure** to give *2106*
14:34 Salt *is* **g**: but if the salt have lost his savour, *2570*
16:25 thou in thy lifetime receivedst thy **g** *things,* *18*
18:18 a certain ruler asked him, saying, **G** Master, *18*
18:19 Jesus said unto him, Why callest thou me **g**? *18*
18:19 me good? none *is* **g**, save one, *that is,* God. *18*
19:17 And he said unto him, Well, *thou* **g** servant: *18*
23:50 a counseller; *and he was* a **g** man, and a just: *18*
Jn 1:46 Can there any **g** *thing* come out of Nazareth? *18*
2:10 Every man at the beginning doth set forth **g** *2570*
2:10 *but* thou hast kept the **g** wine until now. *2570*
5:29 they that have done **g**, unto the resurrection of *18*
7:12 some said, He is a **g** *man:* others said, Nay; *18*
10:11 I am the **g** shepherd: the good shepherd *2570*
10:11 the **g** shepherd giveth his life for the sheep. *2570*
10:14 I am the **g** shepherd, and know my *sheep,* *2570*
10:32 Many **g** works have I shewed you from my *2570*
10:33 saying, For a **g** work we stone thee not; *2570*
16:33 but **be of g cheer**; I have overcome *2293*
Ac 4: 9 If we this day be examined of the **g deed** *2108*
9:36 this *woman* was full of **g** works and *18*
10:22 of **g report** among all the nation of *3140*
10:38 who went about **doing g**, and healing all *2109*
11:24 For he was a **g** man, and full of the Holy *18*
14:17 not himself without witness, in that he **did g**, *15*
15: 7 ye know how that **a g while ago** *575+744+2250*
15:25 It **seemed g** unto us, being assembled with *1380*
15:28 For it **seemed g** to the Holy Ghost, and *1380*
15:38 But Paul **thought** not **g** to take him with *515*
18:18 *after this* tarried *there* yet a **g while**, *2250+2425*
22:12 **having a g report** of all the Jews which *3140*
23: 1 I have lived in all **g** conscience before God *18*
23:11 by him, and said, **Be of g cheer**, Paul: *2293*
27:22 And now I exhort you to **be of g cheer**: *2114*
27:25 Wherefore, sirs, **be of g cheer**: for I believe *2114*
27:36 Then were they all **of g cheer**, and *2115*
Ro 2:10 and peace, to every *man* that worketh **g**, *18*
3: 8 that we say,) Let us do evil, that **g** may come? *18*
3:12 there is none that doeth **g**, no, not one. *5544*
5: 7 yet peradventure for a **g** *man* some would *18*
7:12 and the commandment holy, and just, and **g**. *18*
7:13 then that which is **g** made death unto me? *18*
7:13 working death in me by that which is **g**; *18*
7:16 I consent unto the law that *it is* **g**. *2570*
7:18 dwelleth no **g** *thing:* for to will is present with *18*
7:18 *how* to perform that which is **g** I find not. *2570*
7:19 For the **g** that I would I do not: but the evil *18*
7:21 I find then a law, that, when I would do **g**, *2570*
8:28 work together for **g** to them that love God, *18*
9:11 yet born, neither having done any **g** or evil, *18*
10:15 of peace, and bring glad tidings of **g** *things!* *18*
11:24 contrary to nature into a **g olive tree**: *2565*
12: 2 that ye may prove what *is that* **g**, and *18*
12: 9 *that which is* evil; cleave to *that which is* **g**. *18*
12:21 overcome of evil, but overcome evil with **g**. *18*
13: 3 For rulers are not a terror to **g** works, but *18*
13: 3 do *that which is* **g**, and thou shalt have praise *18*
13: 4 For he is the minister of God to thee for **g**. *18*
14:16 Let not then your **g** be evil spoken of: *18*
14:21 *It is* **g** neither to eat flesh, nor to drink *2570*
15: 2 please *his* neighbour for *his* **g** to edification. *18*
16:18 and by **g words** and fair speeches deceive *5542*
16:19 I would have you wise unto *that which is* **g**, *18*
1Co 5: 6 Your glorying *is* not **g**. Know ye not that a *2570*
7: 1 *It is* **g** for a man not to touch a woman. *2570*
7: 8 It is **g** for them if they abide even as I. *2570*
7:26 that this is **g** for the present distress, *2570*
7:26 *I say,* that *it is* **g** for a man so to be. *2570*
15:33 evil communications corrupt **g** manners. *5543*
2Co 5:10 to that he hath done, whether *it be* **g** or bad. *18*
6: 8 and dishonour, by evil report and **g report**: *2162*
9: 8 in all *things,* may abound to every **g** work: *18*
13:11 Be perfect, be **of g comfort**, be of one *3870*
Gal 4:18 But *it is* **g** to be zealously affected always *2570*
4:18 to be zealously affected always in a **g** *thing,* *2570*
6: 6 unto him that teacheth in all **g** *things.* *18*
6:10 let us do **g** unto all *men,* especially unto them *18*
Eph 1: 5 according to the **g pleasure** of his will, *2107*
1: 9 according to his **g pleasure** which he had *2107*
2:10 created in Christ Jesus unto **g** works, *18*
4:28 working with *his* hands the *thing which is* **g**, *18*
4:29 but that which *is* **g** to the use of edifying, *18*
6: 7 With **g will** doing service, as to the Lord, *2133*
6: 8 Knowing that whatsoever **g** *thing* any man *18*
Php 1: 6 **g** work in you will perform *it* until the day of *18*
1:15 of envy and strife; and some also of **g will**: *2107*
2:13 both to will and to do of *his* **g pleasure**. *2107*
2:19 that I also may be **of g comfort**, when I *2174*
4: 8 whatsoever *things are* of **g report**; *2163*
Col 1:10 being fruitful in every **g** work, and *18*
1Th 3: 1 we **thought** it **g** to be left at Athens alone; *2106*
3: 6 and **brought** us **g tidings** of your faith and *2097*
3: 6 and that ye have **g** remembrance of us always, *18*
5:15 unto any *man;* but ever follow *that which is* **g**, *18*
5:21 Prove all *things;* hold fast *that which is* **g**. *2570*
2Th 1:11 fulfil all the **g pleasure** of *his* goodness, *2107*
2:16 and **g** hope through grace, *18*
2:17 and stablish you in every **g** word and work. *18*
1Ti 1: 5 and *of* a **g** conscience, and *of* faith unfeigned: *18*
1: 8 But we know that the law *is* **g**, if a man use *2570*
1:18 that thou by them mightest war a **g** warfare; *2570*
1:19 Holding faith, and a **g** conscience; *18*
2: 3 For this *is* **g** and acceptable in the sight of *2570*
2:10 women professing godliness) with **g** works. *18*
3: 1 the office of a bishop, he desireth a **g** work. *2570*
3: 2 vigilant, sober, of **g behaviour**, given to *2887*
3: 7 Moreover he must have a **g** report of them *2570*
3:13 well purchase to themselves a **g** degree, *2570*
4: 4 For every creature of God *is* **g**, and *2570*
4: 6 thou shalt be a **g** minister of Jesus Christ, *2570*
4: 6 up in the words of faith and of **g** doctrine, *2570*
5: 4 for that is **g** and acceptable before God. *2570*
5:10 Well reported of for **g** works; if she have *2570*
5:10 if she have diligently followed every **g** work. *18*
5:25 Likewise also the **g** works *of some* are *2570*
6:12 Fight the **g** fight of faith, lay hold on *2570*
6:12 hast professed a **g** profession before many *2570*
6:13 who before Pontius Pilate witnessed a **g** *2570*
6:18 That *they* **do g**, that *they* be rich in good *14*
6:18 that *they* be rich in **g** works, ready to *2570*
6:19 Laying up in store for themselves a **g** *2570*
2Ti 1:14 *That* **g thing** which was committed unto *2570*
2: 3 as a **g** soldier of Jesus Christ. *2570*
2:21 master's use, *and* prepared unto every **g** work. *18*
3: 3 fierce, **despisers of** *those that are* **g**, *865*
3:17 throughly furnished unto all **g** works. *18*
4: 7 I have fought a **g** fight, I have finished *my* *2570*
Tit 1: 8 a **lover of g** *men,* sober, just, holy, *5358*
1:16 disobedient, and unto every **g** work reprobate. *18*
2: 3 given to much wine, **teachers of g things**; *2567*
2: 5 *To be* discreet, chaste, keepers at home, **g**, *18*
2: 7 In all *things* shewing thyself a pattern of **g** *2570*
2:10 Not purloining, but shewing all **g** fidelity; *18*
2:14 a peculiar people, zealous of **g** works. *2570*
3: 1 obey magistrates, to be ready to every **g** work, *18*
3: 8 God might be careful to maintain **g** works. *2570*
3: 8 These *things* are **g** and profitable unto men. *2570*
3:14 And let ours also learn to maintain **g** works *2570*
Phm 1: 6 every **g** *thing* which is in you in Christ Jesus. *18*
Heb 5:14 their senses exercised to discern both **g** *2570*
6: 5 And have tasted the **g** word of God, and *2570*
9:11 But Christ being come a high priest of **g** *18*
10: 1 For the law having a shadow of **g** *things* to *18*
10:24 to provoke unto love and to **g** works: *2570*
11: 2 For by it the elders **obtained a g report**. *3140*
11:12 and him **as g as dead**, *so many* as the stars *3499*
11:39 having **obtained a g report** through faith, *3140*
13: 9 For *it is* a **g** *thing* that the heart be *2570*
13:16 But to **do g** and to communicate forget not: *2140*
13:18 for we trust we have a **g** conscience, in all *2570*
13:21 Make you perfect in every **g** work to do his *18*
Jas 1:17 Every **g** gift and every perfect gift is from *18*
2: 3 and say unto him, Sit thou here in a **g place**; *2573*
3:13 let him shew out of a **g** conversation his *2570*
3:17 full of mercy and **g** fruits, without partiality, *18*
4:17 Therefore to him that knoweth to do **g**, and *2570*
1Pe 2:12 they may by *your* **g** works, *which* they shall *2570*
2:18 not only to the **g** and gentle, but also to *18*
3:10 For he that will love life, and see **g** days, *18*

1Pe 3:11 Let him eschew evil, and do **g**; let him seek *18*
3:13 if ye be followers of *that which is* **g**? *18*
3:16 Having a **g** conscience; that, whereas they *18*
3:16 falsely accuse your **g** conversation in Christ. *18*
3:21 but the answer of a **g** conscience toward God,) *18*
4:10 as **g** stewards of the manifold grace of God. *2570*
1Jn 3:17 But whoso hath *this* world's **g**, and seeth his *979*
3Jn 1:11 not *that which is* evil, but *that which is* **g**. *18*
1:11 He that **doeth g** is of God: but he that doeth *15*
1:12 Demetrius **hath g report** of all *men*, and *3140*

GOODLIER (1) [GOOD]
1Sa 9: 2 the children of Israel a **g** person than he: 2896

GOODLIEST (2) [GOOD]
1Sa 8:16 your **g** young men, and your asses, and put 2896
1Ki 20: 3 and thy children, *even* the **g**, *are* mine. 2896

GOODLINESS (1) [GOOD]
Isa 40: 6 all the **g** thereof *is* as the flower of the field: 2617

GOODLY (33) [GOOD]
Ge 27:15 Rebekah took **g** raiment of her eldest son 2532
39: 6 Joseph was *a* **g** *person*, and 3303+8389
49:21 *is* a hind let loose: he giveth **g** words. 8233
Ex 2: 2 when she saw him that he *was a* **g** *child*, 2896
39:28 **g** bonnets *of* fine linen, and linen breeches 6287
Lev 23:40 you on the first day the boughs of **g** trees, 1926
Nu 24: 5 How **g** are thy tents, O Jacob, *and* 2895
31:10 they dwelt, and all their **g castles**, with fire. 2918
Dt 3:25 that **g** mountain, and Lebanon. 2896
6:10 and to Jacob, to give thee great and **g** cities, 2896
8:12 and hast built **g** houses, and dwelt *therein*; 2896
Jos 7:21 When I saw among the spoils a **g** 2896
1Sa 9: 2 *was* Saul, a choice *young man*, and a **g**: 2896
16:12 a beautiful countenance, and **g** to look to. 2896
2Sa 23:21 he slew an Egyptian, a **g** man: and 4758
1Ki 1: 6 he also *was* a very **g** *man*; and 2896+8389
2Ch 36:10 with the **g** vessels of the house of 2532
36:19 and destroyed all the **g** vessels thereof. 4261
Job 39:13 *Gavest thou* the **g** wings unto the peacocks? 7443
Ps 16: 6 in pleasant *places*; yea, I have a **g** heritage. 8231
80:10 the boughs thereof *were like* the **g** cedars. 410
Jer 3:19 a **g** heritage of the hosts of nations? 6643
11:16 A green olive tree, fair, *and* of **g** fruit: 8389
Eze 17: 8 *it* might bear fruit, that *it* might be a **g** vine. 155
17:23 and bear fruit, and be a **g** cedar: 117
Hos 10: 1 of his land they have **made g** images. 2895
Joel 3: 5 have carried into your temples my **g** 2896
Zec 10: 3 hath made them as his **g** horse in the battle. 1935
11:13 a **g** price that I was prised at of them. And I 145
Mt 13:45 like unto a merchant man, seeking **g** pearls: *2570*
Lk 21: 5 how it was adorned with **g** stones and gifts, *2570*
Jas 2: 2 in **g** apparel, and there come in also a poor *2986*
Rev 18:14 *were* dainty and **g** are departed from thee, *2986*

GOODMAN (6) [GOOD, MAN]
Pr 7:19 For the **g** *is* not at home, he is gone a long 376
Mt 20:11 they murmured against the **g of the house**, *3617*
24:43 that if the **g of the house** had known in *3617*
Mk 14:14 say ye to the **g of the house**, The Master *3617*
Lk 12:39 that if the **g of the house** had known what *3617*
22:11 And ye shall say unto the **g** of the house, *3617*

GOODNESS (50) [GOOD]
Ex 18: 9 Jethro rejoiced for all the **g** which 2896
33:19 I will make all my **g** pass before thee, and 2898
34: 6 longsuffering, and abundant in **g** and truth, 2617
Nu 10:32 *that* what **g** the LORD shall do unto us, 2896
Jdg 8:35 according to all the **g** which he had shewed 2896
2Sa 7:28 thou hast promised this **g** unto thy servant: 2896
1Ki 8:66 glad of heart for all the **g** that the LORD 2896
1Ch 17:26 and hast promised this **g** unto thy servant: 2896
2Ch 6:41 and let thy saints rejoice in **g**. 2896
7:10 merry in heart for the **g** that the LORD 2896
32:32 of the acts of Hezekiah, and his **g**, behold, 2617
35:26 the rest of the acts of Josiah, and his **g**, 2617
Ne 9:25 and delighted themselves in thy great **g**. 2898
9:35 in thy great **g** that thou gavest them, and 2898
Ps 16: 2 *art* my Lord: my **g** *extendeth* not to thee; 2896
21: 3 thou preventest him *with* the blessings of **g**: 2896
23: 6 Surely **g** and mercy shall follow me all 2896
27:13 **g** of the LORD in the land of the living. 2898
31:19 O how great *is* thy **g**, which thou hast laid 2898
33: 5 the earth is full *of* the **g** of the LORD. 2617
52: 1 O mighty *man*? the **g** of God *endureth* 2617
65: 4 we shall be satisfied with the **g** of thy 2898
65:11 Thou crownest the year with thy **g**; and 2896
68:10 O God, hast prepared of thy **g** for the poor. 2896
107: 8 *men* would praise the LORD *for* his **g**, 2617
107: 9 and filleth the hungry soul *with* **g**. 2896
107:15 *men* would praise the LORD *for* his **g**, 2617
107:21 *men* would praise the LORD *for* his **g**, 2617
107:31 *men* would praise the LORD *for* his **g**, 2617
144: 2 My **g**, and my fortress; my high tower, and 2617
145: 7 abundantly utter the memory of thy great **g**, 2898
Pr 20: 6 men will proclaim every one his own **g**: 2617
Isa 63: 7 and the great **g** towards the house of Israel, 2898
Jer 2: 7 to eat the fruit thereof and the **g** thereof; 2898
31:12 shall flow *together* to the **g** of the LORD, 2898
31:14 my people shall be satisfied with my **g**, 2898
33: 9 they shall fear and tremble for all the **g** and 2896
Hos 3: 5 fear the LORD and his **g** in the latter days. 2898
6: 4 for your **g** *is* as a morning cloud, and as 2617
10: 1 according to the **g** of his land they have 2896
Zec 9:17 For how great *is* his **g**, and how great *is* his 2898
Ro 2: 4 Or despisest thou the riches of his **g** and *5544*
2: 4 not knowing that the **g** of God leadeth thee *5543*
11:22 Behold therefore the **g** and severity of God: *5544*
11:22 but toward thee, **g**, if thou continue in *his* *5544*
11:22 goodness, if thou continue in *his* **g**: *5544*
15:14 my brethren, that ye also are full of **g**, *19*
Gal 5:22 joy, peace, longsuffering, gentleness, **g**, faith, *19*
Eph 5: 9 (For the fruit of the Spirit *is* in all **g** and *19*
2Th 1:11 and fulfil all the good pleasure of *his* **g**, and *19*

GOODNESS' (1) [GOOD]
Ps 25: 7 mercy remember thou me for thy **g** sake, 2898

GOODS (42) [GOOD]
Ge 14:11 they took all the **g** of Sodom and 7399
14:12 dwelt in Sodom, and his **g**, and departed. 7399
14:16 he brought back all the **g**, and also brought 7399
14:16 his **g**, and the women also, and the people. 7399
14:21 me the persons, and take the **g** to thyself. 7399
24:10 for all the **g** of his master *were* in his hand: 2898
31:18 all his **g** which he had gotten, the cattle of 7399
46: 6 they took their cattle, and their **g**, 7399
Ex 22: 8 have put his hand unto his neighbour's **g**. 4399
22:11 not put his hand unto his neighbour's **g**; 4399
Nu 16:32 that *appertained* unto Korah, and all *their* **g**. 7399
31: 9 and all their flocks, and all their **g**. 2428
35: 3 and for their **g**, and for all their beasts. 7399
Dt 28:11 the LORD shall make thee plenteous in **g**, 2896
2Ch 21:14 thy children, and thy wives, and all thy **g**: 7399
Ezr 1: 4 and with gold, and with **g**, and with beasts, 7399
1: 6 with **g**, and with beasts, and with precious 7399
6: 8 that of the king's **g**, *even* of the tribute 5232
7:26 or to confiscation of **g**, or to imprisonment. 5232
Ne 9:25 fat land, and possessed houses full *of* all **g**, 2898
Job 20:10 the poor, and his hands shall restore their **g**. 202
20:21 therefore shall no *man* look for his **g**. 2898
20:28 *his* **g** *shall* flow away in the day of his NIH
Ecc 5:11 When **g** increase, they are increased that eat 2896
Eze 38:12 which have gotten cattle and **g**, that dwell 7075
38:13 and gold, to take *away* cattle and **g**, 7075
Zep 1:13 Therefore their **g** shall become a booty, and 2428
Mt 12:29 and spoil his **g**, except he first bind *4632*
24:47 That he shall make him ruler over all his **g**. *5225*
25:14 and delivered unto them his **g**. *5225*
Mk 3:27 and spoil his **g**, except he will first bind *4632*
Lk 6:30 of him that taketh away thy **g** ask *them* not NIG
11:21 keepeth his palace, his **g** are in peace: *5225*
12:18 there will I bestow all my fruits and my **g**. *18*
12:19 thou hast much **g** laid up for many years; *18*
15:12 give me the portion of **g** that falleth to *me*. *3776*
16: 1 accused unto him that he had wasted his **g**. *5225*
19: 8 Lord, the half of my **g** I give to the poor; *5225*
Ac 2:45 And sold their possessions and **g**, and *5223*
1Co 13: 3 And though I bestow all my **g** to feed *5225*
Heb 10:34 and took joyfully the spoiling of your **g**, *5225*
Rev 3:17 and **increased with g**, and have need of *4147*

GOPHER (1)
Ge 6:14 Make thee an ark of **g** wood; rooms shalt 1613

GORE (1) [GORED]
Ex 21:28 If an ox **g** a man or a woman, that they die: 5055

GORED (2) [GORE]
Ex 21:31 Whether he have **g** a son, or have gored a 5055
21:31 he have gored a son, or have **g** a daughter, 5055

GORGEOUS (1) [GORGEOUSLY]
Lk 23:11 mocked *him,* and arrayed him in a **g** robe, *2986*

GORGEOUSLY (2) [GORGEOUS]
Eze 23:12 captains and rulers clothed **most g**, 4358
Lk 7:25 they which are **g** apparelled, and *1722+1741*

GOSHEN (15)
Ge 45:10 thou shalt dwell in the land of **G**, and 1657
46:28 him unto Joseph, to direct his face unto **G**; 1657
46:28 and they came into the land of **G**. 1657
46:29 to **G**, and presented himself unto him; 1657
46:34 that ye may dwell in the land of **G**; 1657
47: 1 and behold, they *are* in the land of **G**. 1657
47: 4 let thy servants dwell in the land of **G**. 1657
47: 6 to dwell; in the land of **G** let them dwell: 1657
47:27 in the land of Egypt, in the country of **G**; 1657
50: 8 and their herds, they left in the land of **G**. 1657
Ex 8:22 I will sever in that day the land of **G**, 1657
9:26 Only in the land of **G**, where the children 1657
Jos 10:41 and all the country of **G**, even unto Gibeon. 1657
11:16 all the south *country,* and all the land of **G**, 1657
15:51 **G**, and Holon, and Giloh; eleven cities with 1657

GOSPEL (101) [GOSPEL'S]
Mt 4:23 and preaching the **g** of the kingdom, *2098*
9:35 and preaching the **g** of the kingdom, and *2098*
11: 5 and the poor have **the g preached** to them. *2097*
24:14 And this **g** of the kingdom shall be *2098*
26:13 Wheresoever this **g** shall be preached in *2098*
Mk 1: 1 The beginning of the **g** of Jesus Christ, *2098*
1:14 preaching the **g** of the kingdom of God, *2098*
1:15 God is at hand: repent ye, and believe the **g**. *2098*
13:10 And the **g** must first be published among all *2098*
14: 9 Wheresoever this **g** shall be preached *2098*
16:15 and preach the **g** to every creature. *2098*
Lk 4:18 he hath anointed me to **preach the g** to *2097*
7:22 are raised, to the poor **the g** is **preached**. *2097*
9: 6 **preaching the g**, and healing every where. *2097*
20: 1 and **preached the g**, the chief priests and *2097*
Ac 8:25 **preached the g** in many villages of *2097*
14: 7 And there they **preached the g**. *2097*
14:21 And when they had **preached the g** to that *2097*
15: 7 by my mouth should hear the word of the **g**, *2098*
16:10 called us for to **preach the g** unto them. *2097*
20:24 to testify the **g** of the grace of God. *2098*
Ro 1: 1 *be* an apostle, separated unto the **g** of God, *2098*
1: 9 whom I serve with my spirit in the **g** of his *2098*
1:15 I am ready to **preach the g** to you that are *2097*
1:16 For I am not ashamed of the **g** of Christ: *2098*
2:16 of men by Jesus Christ according to my **g**. *2098*
10:15 the feet of them that **preach the g** of peace, *2097*
10:16 But they have not all obeyed the **g**. *2098*
11:28 As concerning the **g**, *they are* enemies for *2098*
15:16 ministering the **g** of God, that the offering *2098*
15:19 I have fully preached the **g** of Christ. *2098*
15:20 Yea, so have I strived to **preach the g**, *2097*
15:29 fulness of the blessing of the **g** of Christ. *2098*
16:25 of power to stablish you according to my **g**, *2098*
1Co 1:17 sent me not to baptize, but to **preach the g**: *2097*
4:15 Jesus I have begotten you through the **g**. *2098*
9:12 suffer all *things,* lest we should hinder the **g** *2098*
9:14 preach the **g** should live of the gospel. *2098*
9:14 preach the gospel should live of the **g**. *2098*
9:16 For though I **preach the g**, I have nothing *2097*
9:16 yea, woe is unto me, if I **preach** not **the g**! *2097*
9:17 a dispensation *of the g* is committed unto NIG
9:18 *Verily* that, when I **preach the g**, I may *2097*
9:18 I may make the **g** of Christ without charge, *2098*
9:18 that *I* abuse not my power in the **g**. *2098*
15: 1 I declare unto you the **g** which I preached *2098*
2Co 2:12 when I came to Troas to *preach* Christ's **g**, *2098*
4: 3 But if our **g** be hid, it is hid to them that are *2098*
4: 4 lest the light of the glorious **g** of Christ, *2098*
8:18 whose praise *is* in the **g** throughout all *2098*
9:13 professed subjection unto the **g** of Christ, *2098*
10:14 as to you also in *preaching* the **g** of Christ: *2098*
10:16 To **preach the g** in the *regions* beyond you, *2097*
11: 4 which ye have not received, or another **g**, *2098*
11: 7 I have preached to you the **g** of God freely? *2098*
Gal 1: 6 you into the grace of Christ unto another **g**: *2098*
1: 7 and would pervert the **g** of Christ. *2098*
1: 8 **preach** any other **g** unto you than *that* *2097*
1: 9 If any *man* **preach** any other **g** unto you *2097*
1:11 that the **g** which was preached of me is not *2098*
2: 2 communicated unto them *that* **g** which I *2098*
2: 5 that the truth of the **g** might continue with *2098*
2: 7 when they saw that the **g** of *2098*
2: 7 as *the g* of the circumcision *was* unto Peter; NIG
2:14 not uprightly according to the truth of the **g**, *2098*
3: 8 **preached before the g** unto Abraham, *4283*
4:13 flesh I **preached the g** unto you at the first. *2097*
Eph 1:13 the word of truth, the **g** of your salvation: *2098*
3: 6 partakers of his promise in Christ by the **g**: *2098*
6:15 shod with the preparation of the **g** of peace; *2098*
6:19 to make known the mystery of the **g**, *2098*
Php 1: 5 For your fellowship in the **g** from the first *2098*
1: 7 *in* the defence and confirmation of the **g**, *2098*
1:12 out rather unto the furtherance of the **g**; *2098*
1:17 that I am set for the defence of the **g**. *2098*
1:27 be as it becometh the **g** of Christ: *2098*
1:27 mind striving together for the faith of the **g**; *2098*
2:22 *the* father, he hath served with me in the **g**. *2098*
4: 3 *women* which laboured with me in the **g**, *2098*
4:15 know also, that in the beginning of the **g**, *2098*
Col 1: 5 before in the word of the truth of the **g**; *2098*
1:23 *be* not moved away from the hope of the **g**, *2098*
1Th 1: 5 For our **g** came not unto you in word only, *2098*
2: 2 you the **g** of God with much contention. *2098*
2: 4 allowed of God to be put in trust with the **g**, *2098*
2: 8 not the **g** of God only, but also our own *2098*
2: 9 of you, we preached unto you the **g** of God. *2098*
3: 2 and our fellowlabourer in the **g** of Christ, *2098*
2Th 1: 8 that obey not the **g** of our Lord Jesus *2098*
2:14 Whereunto he called you by our **g**, to *2098*
1Ti 1:11 According to the glorious **g** of the blessed *2098*
2Ti 1: 8 be thou partaker of the afflictions of the **g** *2098*
1:10 and immortality to light through the **g**: *2098*
2: 8 raised from the dead according to my **g**: *2098*
Phm 1:13 ministered unto me in the bonds of the **g**: *2098*
Heb 4: 2 For unto us was **the g preached**, as well as *2097*
1Pe 1:12 **preached the g** unto you with the Holy *2097*
1:25 word which by the **g** is **preached** unto you. *2097*
4: 6 For for this cause was the **g preached** also *2097*
4:17 end *be* of them that obey not the **g** of God? *2098*
Rev 14: 6 having the everlasting **g** to preach unto *2098*

GOSPEL'S (3) [GOSPEL]
Mk 8:35 shall lose his life for my sake and the **g**, *2098*
10:29 children, or lands, for my sake, and the **g**, *2098*
1Co 9:23 And this I do for the **g** sake, that I might be *2098*

GOSSIP See TALEBEARER

GOSSIPS See TATTLERS

GOT (7) [GET]
Ge 36: 6 which he had **g** in the land of Canaan; 7408
39:12 in her hand, and fled, and **g** him out. 3318
39:15 garment with me, and fled, and **g** him out. 3318
Ps 44: 3 For they **g** not the land **in possession** by 3423
Ecc 2: 7 I **g** *me* servants and maidens, and 7069
Jer 13: 2 So I **g** a girdle, according to the word of 7069
13: 4 Take the girdle that thou hast **g**, which *is* 7069

GOTTEN (25) [GET]
Ge 4: 1 and said, I have **g** a man from the LORD. 7069
12: 5 and the souls that they had **g** in Haran; 6213
31: 1 of *that* which *was* of our father's hath he **g** 6213
31:18 all his goods which he had **g**, the cattle of 7408
31:18 his getting, which he had **g** in Padan-aram, 7408
46: 6 which they had **g** in the land of Canaan, 7408
Ex 14:18 when I have **g** me **honour** upon Pharaoh, 3513
Lev 6: 4 thing which he hath **deceitfully g**, 6231+6233
Nu 31:50 what every man hath **g**, *of* jewels of gold, 4672
Dt 8:17 the might of mine hand hath **g** me this 6213
2Sa 17:13 if he be **g** into a city, then shall all Israel 622
Job 28:15 It cannot be **g** for gold, neither shall silver 5414
31:25 and because mine hand had **g** much; 4672
Ps 98: 1 and his holy arm, hath **g** him the **victory**. 3467
Pr 13:11 Wealth **g** by vanity shall be diminished: but NIH
20:21 An inheritance *may be* **g hastily** at 926
Ecc 1:16 have **g more** wisdom than all *they* that 3254
Isa 15: 7 Therefore the abundance they have **g**, and 6213
Jer 48:36 the riches *that* he hath **g** are perished. 6213

Eze 28: 4 with thine understanding thou hast g thee 6213
28: 4 hast g gold and silver into thy treasures: 6213
38:12 which have g cattle and goods, that dwell in 6213
Da 9:15 and hast g thee renown, as *at* this day; 6213
Ac 21: 1 that after we were **g from** them, and *645*
Rev 15: 2 them that had **g the victory** over the beast, *3528*

GOURD (5) [GOURDS]
Jnh 4: 6 the LORD God prepared a g, and made *it* 7021
4: 6 So Jonah was exceeding glad of the g. 7021
4: 7 and it smote the g, that it withered. 7021
4: 9 Doest thou well to be angry for the g? 7021
4:10 the LORD, Thou hast had pity on the g, 7021

GOURDS (1) [GOURD]
2Ki 4:39 gathered thereof wild g his lap full, and 6498

GOVERN (3) [GOVERNMENT, GOVERNMENTS, GOVERNOR, GOVERNOR'S, GOVERNORS]
1Ki 21: 7 Dost thou now g the kingdom of Israel? 6213
Job 34:17 Shall even he that hateth right g? and wilt 2280
Ps 67: 4 and g the nations upon earth. 5148

GOVERNMENT (4) [GOVERN]
Isa 9: 6 the g shall be upon his shoulder: and 4951
9: 7 Of the increase of *his* g and peace *there* 4951
22:21 and I will commit thy g into his hand: 4475
2Pe 2:10 in the lust of uncleanness, and despise g. *2963*

GOVERNMENTS (1) [GOVERN]
1Co 12:28 then gifts of healings, helps, g, *2941*

GOVERNOR (59) [GOVERN]
Ge 42: 6 Joseph *was* the g over the land, *and* he *it* 7989
45:26 and he *is* g over all the land of Egypt. 4910
1Ki 18: 3 which *was* the g^s **of** *his* house. 5921
22:26 carry him back unto Amon the g of the city, 8269
2Ki 23: 8 in of the gate of Joshua the g of the city, 8269
25:23 the king of Babylon had **made** Gedaliah g, 6485
1Ch 29:22 *him* unto the LORD to be the **chief** g, 5057
2Ch 1: 2 to the judges, and to every g in all Israel, 5387
18:25 carry him back to Amon the g of the city, 8269
28: 7 Azrikam the g of the house, and Elkanah 5057
34: 8 Maaseiah the g of the city, and Joah the son 8269
Ezr 5: 3 g on *this* side the river, and Shethar-boznai, 6347
5: 6 g on *this* side the river, and Shethar-boznai, 6347
5:14 *was* Sheshbazzar, whom he had made g; 6347
6: 6 Now *therefore,* Tatnai, g beyond the river, 6347
6: 7 let the g of the Jews and the elders of 6347
6:13 Tatnai, g on *this* side the river, 6347
Ne 3: 7 unto the throne of the g on *this* side 6346
5:14 appointed to be their g in the land of Judah, 6346
5:14 brethren have not eaten the bread of the g. 6346
5:18 for *all* this required not I the bread of the g, 6346
12:26 in the days of Nehemiah the g, and of Ezra 6346
Ps 22:28 and *he is* the g among the nations. 4910
Jer 20: 1 who *was* also chief g in the house of 6496
30:21 their g shall proceed from the midst of 4910
40: 5 whom the king of Babylon hath **made** g 6485
40: 7 **made** Gedaliah the son of Ahikam g in 6485
41: 2 whom the king of Babylon had **made** g 6485
41:18 whom the king of Babylon **made** g in 6485
Hag 1: 1 g of Judah, and to Joshua the son of 6346
1:14 g of Judah, and the spirit of Joshua the son 6346
2: 2 g of Judah, and to Joshua the son of 6346
2:21 Speak to Zerubbabel, g of Judah, saying, 6346
Zec 9: 7 he shall be as a g in Judah, and Ekron as a 441
Mal 1: 8 offer it now unto thy g; will he be pleased 6346
Mt 2: 6 for out of thee shall come a G, that shall 2233
27: 2 and delivered him to Pontius Pilate the g. *2232*
27:11 And Jesus stood before the g: and *2232*
27:11 and the g asked him, saying, Art thou *2232*
27:14 insomuch that the g marvelled greatly. *2232*
27:15 Now at *that* feast the g was wont to release *2232*
27:21 The g answered and said unto them, *2232*
27:23 And the g said, Why, what evil hath he *2232*
27:27 Then the soldiers of the g took Jesus into *2232*
Lk 2: 2 first made when Cyrenius was g of Syria.) *2230*
3: 1 Pontius Pilate being g of Judea, and *2230*
20:20 him unto the power and authority of the g. *2232*
Jn 2: 8 out now, and bear unto the **g of the feast**. *755*
2: 9 the **g of the feast** called the bridegroom, *755*
Ac 7:10 and he made him g over Egypt and all his *2232*
23:24 and bring *him* safe unto Felix the g. *2232*
23:26 Claudius Lysias unto the most excellent g *2232*
23:33 and delivered the epistle to the g, *2232*
23:34 And when the g had read *the letter,* he *2232*
24: 1 who informed the g against Paul. *2232*
24:10 after that the g had beckoned unto him to *2232*
26:30 thus spoken, the king rose up, and the g, *2232*
2Co 11:32 In Damascus the g under Aretas the king *1481*
Jas 3: 4 small helm, whithersoever the g listeth. *3730*

GOVERNOR'S (1) [GOVERN]
Mt 28:14 And if this come to the g ears, we will *2232*

GOVERNORS (22) [GOVERN]
Jdg 5: 9 My heart *is* toward the g of Israel, 2710
5:14 out of Machir came down g, and out of 2710
1Ki 10:15 kings of Arabia, and *of* the g of the country. 6346
1Ch 24: 5 for the g of the sanctuary, and governors *of* 8269
24: 5 g *of the house* of God, were of the sons of 8269
2Ch 9:14 g of the country brought gold and silver to 6346
23:20 the g of the people, and all the people of 4910
Ezr 8:36 and *to* the g on *this* side the river: 6346
Ne 2: 7 let letters be given me to the g beyond 6346
2: 9 I came to the g beyond the river, and 6346
5:15 the former g that *had been* before me were 6346
Est 3:12 to the g that *were* over every province, 6346
Da 2:48 chief of the g over all the wise *men* of 5460
3: 2 the g, and the captains, the judges, 5460
3: 3 the g and captains, the judges, 5460
3:27 g, and captains, and the king's counsellers, 5460
6: 7 the g, and the princes, the counsellers and 5460
Zec 12: 5 the g of Judah shall say in their heart, 441
12: 6 In that day will I make the g of Judah like a 441
Mt 10:18 And ye shall be brought before g and kings *2232*
Gal 4: 2 and g until the time appointed of the father. *3623*
1Pe 2:14 Or unto g, as unto them that are sent by him *2232*

GOZAN (5)
2Ki 17: 6 in Halah and in Habor *by* the river of G, 1470
18:11 in Halah and in Habor *by* the river of G, 1470
19:12 *as* G, and Haran, and Rezeph, and 1470
1Ch 5:26 Habor, and Hara, and to the river G, 1470
Isa 37:12 *as* G, and Haran, and Rezeph, and 1470

GRACE (170) [GRACIOUS, GRACIOUSLY]
Ge 6: 8 Noah found g in the eyes of the LORD. 2580
19:19 thy servant hath found g in thy sight, and 2580
32: 5 tell my lord, that I may find g in thy sight. 2580
33: 8 *These are* to find g in the sight of my lord. 2580
33:10 if now I have found g in thy sight, then 2580
33:15 let me find g in the sight of my lord. 2580
34:11 Let me find g in your eyes, and what ye 2580
39: 4 Joseph found g in his sight, and he served 2580
47:25 let us find g in the sight of my lord, and 2580
47:29 If now I have found g in thy sight, put, 2580
50: 4 If now I have found g in your eyes, speak, 2580
Ex 33:12 and thou hast also found g in my sight. 2580
33:13 I pray thee, if I have found g in thy sight, 2580
33:13 know thee, that I may find g in thy sight: 2580
33:16 and thy people have found g in thy sight? 2580
33:17 for thou hast found g in my sight, and 2580
34: 9 If now I have found g in thy sight, O Lord, 2580
Nu 32: 5 said they, if we have found g in thy sight, 2580
Jdg 6:17 If now I have found g in thy sight, then 2580
Ru 2: 2 corn after *him* in whose sight I shall find g. 2580
2:10 Why have I found g in thine eyes, 2580
1Sa 1:18 Let thine handmaid find g in thy sight. 2580
20: 3 knoweth that I have found g in thine eyes; 2580
27: 5 If I have now found g in thine eyes, 2580
2Sa 14:22 knoweth that I have found g in thy sight, 2580
16: 4 I humbly beseech thee *that* I may find g in 2580
Ezr 9: 8 now for a little space g hath been *shewed* 8467
Est 2:17 she obtained g and favour in his sight more 2580
Ps 45: 2 g is poured into thy lips: therefore God hath 2580
84:11 the LORD will give g and glory: no good 2580
Pr 1: 9 For they *shall be* an ornament of g unto thy 2580
3:22 be life unto thy soul, and g to thy neck. 2580
3:34 the scorners: but he giveth g unto the lowly. 2580
4: 9 shall give to thine head an ornament of g: 2580
22:11 *for* the g of his lips the king *shall be* his 2580
Jer 31: 2 left of the sword found g in the wilderness; 2580
Zec 4: 7 *with* shoutings, *crying,* G, grace unto it. 2580
4: 7 *with* shoutings, *crying,* Grace, g unto it. 2580
12:10 the spirit of g and of supplications: 2580
Lk 2:40 and the g of God was upon him. *5485*

Jn	1:14	begotten of the Father,) full of **g** and truth.	*5485*
	1:16	have all we received, and **g** for grace.	*5485*
	1:16	have all we received, and grace for **g**.	*5485*
	1:17	*but* **g** and truth came by Jesus Christ.	*5485*
Ac	4:33	Lord Jesus: and great **g** was upon them all.	*5485*
	11:23	and had seen the **g** of God, was glad, and	*5485*
	13:43	persuaded them to continue in the **g** of God.	*5485*
	14: 3	gave testimony unto the word of his **g**,	*5485*
	14:26	**g** of God for the work which they fulfilled.	*5485*
	15:11	But we believe that through the **g** of	*5485*
	15:40	by the brethren unto the **g** of God.	*5485*
	18:27	them much which had believed through **g**:	*5485*
	20:24	to testify the gospel of the **g** of God.	*5485*
	20:32	you to God, and to the word of his **g**,	*5485*
Ro	1: 5	By whom we have received **g** and	*5485*
	1: 7	**G** to you and peace from God our Father,	*5485*
	3:24	Being justified freely by his **g** through	*5485*
	4: 4	worketh is the reward not reckoned of **g**,	*5485*
	4:16	*it is* of faith, that *it might be* by **g**;	*5485*
	5: 2	by faith into this **g** wherein we stand,	*5485*
	5:15	much more the **g** of God, and the gift by	*5485*
	5:15	and the gift by **g**, which is by one man,	*5485*
	5:17	more they which receive abundance of **g**	*5485*
	5:20	sin abounded, **g** did much more abound:	*5485*
	5:21	might **g** reign through righteousness unto	*5485*
	6: 1	we continue in sin, that **g** may abound?	*5485*
	6:14	for ye are not under the law, but under **g**.	*5485*
	6:15	we are not under the law, but under **g**?	*5485*
	11: 5	is a remnant according to the election of **g**.	*5485*
	11: 6	And if by **g**, *then is it* no more of works:	*5485*
	11: 6	otherwise **g** is no more grace. But if *it be* of	*5485*
	11: 6	otherwise grace is no more **g**. But if *it be* of	*5485*
	11: 6	But if *it be* of works, *then* is it no more **g**:	*5485*
	12: 3	For I say, through the **g** given unto me,	*5485*
	12: 6	gifts differing according to the **g** that is	*5485*
	15:15	because of the **g** that is given to me of God,	*5485*
	16:20	The **g** of our Lord Jesus Christ *be* with you.	*5485*
	16:24	The **g** of our Lord Jesus Christ *be* with you	*5485*
1Co	1: 3	**G** *be* unto you, and peace, from God our	*5485*
	1: 4	for the **g** of God which is given you by	*5485*
	3:10	According to the **g** of God which is given	*5485*
	10:30	For if I by **g** be a partaker, why am I evil	*5485*
	15:10	But by the **g** of God I am what I am: and	*5485*
	15:10	his **g** which was *bestowed* upon me was not	*5485*
	15:10	not I, but the **g** of God which was with me.	*5485*
	16:23	The **g** of *our* Lord Jesus Christ *be* with you.	*5485*
2Co	1: 2	**G** *be* to you and peace from God our	*5485*
	1:12	with fleshly wisdom, but by the **g** of God,	*5485*
	4:15	that the abundant **g** might through	*5485*
	6: 1	that ye receive not the **g** of God in vain.	*5485*
	8: 1	we do you to wit of the **g** of God bestowed	*5485*
	8: 6	he would also finish in you the same **g** also.	*5485*
	8: 7	love to us, *see* that ye abound in this **g** also.	*5485*
	8: 9	For ye know the **g** of our Lord Jesus Christ,	*5485*
	8:19	of the churches to travel with us with this **g**,	*5485*
	9: 8	And God *is* able to make all **g** abound	*5485*
	9:14	which long after you for the exceeding **g** of	*5485*
	12: 9	he said unto me, My **g** is sufficient for thee:	*5485*
	13:14	The **g** of the Lord Jesus Christ, and the love	*5485*
Gal	1: 3	**G** *be* to you and peace from God	*5485*
	1: 6	into the **g** of Christ unto another gospel:	*5485*
	1:15	my mother's womb, and called *me* by his **g**,	*5485*
	2: 9	perceived the **g** that was given unto me,	*5485*
	2:21	I do not frustrate the **g** of God: for if	*5485*
	5: 4	justified by the law; ye are fallen from **g**.	*5485*
	6:18	the **g** of our Lord Jesus Christ *be* with your	*5485*
Eph	1: 2	**G** *be* to you, and peace, from God our	*5485*
	1: 6	To the praise of the glory of his **g**,	*5485*
	1: 7	of sins, according to the riches of his **g**;	*5485*
	2: 5	*us* together with Christ, (by **g** ye are saved;)	*5485*
	2: 7	**g** in *his* kindness towards us through Christ	*5485*
	2: 8	For by **g** are ye saved through faith; and	*5485*
	3: 2	If ye have heard of the dispensation of the **g**	*5485*
	3: 7	according to the gift of the **g** of God given	*5485*
	3: 8	than the least of all saints, is this **g** given,	*5485*
	4: 7	But unto every one of us is given **g**	*5485*
	4:29	that it may minister **g** unto the hearers.	*5485*
	6:24	**G** *be* with all them that love our Lord Jesus	*5485*
Php	1: 2	**G** *be* unto you, and peace, from God our	*5485*
	1: 7	of the gospel, ye all are partakers of my **g**.	*5485*
	4:23	The **g** of our Lord Jesus Christ *be* with you	*5485*
Col	1: 2	**G** *be* unto you, and peace, from God our	*5485*
	1: 6	heard of *it*, and knew the **g** of God in truth:	*5485*
	3:16	singing with **g** in your hearts to the Lord.	*5485*
	4: 6	Let your speech *be* alway with **g**,	*5485*
	4:18	my bonds. **G** *be* with you. Amen.	*5485*
1Th	1: 1	**G** *be* unto you, and peace, from God our	*5485*
	5:28	The **g** of our Lord Jesus Christ *be* with you.	*5485*
2Th	1: 2	**G** unto you, and peace, from God our	*5485*
	1:12	according to the **g** of our God and the Lord	*5485*
	2:16	and good hope through **g**,	*5485*
	3:18	The **g** of our Lord Jesus Christ *be* with you	*5485*
1Ti	1: 2	**G**, mercy, *and* peace, from God our Father	*5485*
	1:14	And the **g** of our Lord was exceeding	*5485*
	6:21	the faith. **G** *be* with thee. Amen.	*5485*
2Ti	1: 2	**G**, mercy, *and* peace, from God the Father	*5485*
	1: 9	but according to his own purpose and **g**,	*5485*
	2: 1	be strong in the **g** that is in Christ Jesus.	*5485*
	4:22	*be* with thy spirit. **G** *be* with you. Amen.	*5485*
Tit	1: 4	**G**, mercy, *and* peace, from God the Father	*5485*
	2:11	For the **g** of God that bringeth salvation	*5485*
	3: 7	That being justified by his **g**, we should be	*5485*
	3:15	us in the faith. **G** *be* with you all. Amen.	*5485*
Phm	1: 3	**G** to you, and peace, from God our Father	*5485*
	1:25	The **g** of our Lord Jesus Christ *be* with your	*5485*
Heb	2: 9	that he by the **g** of God should taste death	*5485*
	4:16	therefore come boldly unto the throne of **g**,	*5485*
	4:16	and find **g** to help in time of need.	*5485*
	10:29	and hath done despite unto the Spirit of **g**?	*5485*
	12:15	diligently lest any *man* fail of the **g**	*5485*
	12:28	let us have **g**, whereby we may serve God	*5485*
	13: 9	*thing* that the heart be established with **g**;	*5485*
	13:25	**G** *be* with you all. Amen.	*5485*
Jas	1:11	and the **g** of the fashion of it perisheth:	*2143*
	4: 6	But he giveth more **g**. Wherefore *he* saith,	*5485*
	4: 6	the proud, but giveth **g** unto the humble.	*5485*
1Pe	1: 2	**G** unto you, and peace, be multiplied.	*5485*
	1:10	who prophesied of the **g** *that should come*	*5485*
	1:13	hope to the end for the **g** that is *to be*	*5485*
	3: 7	and as *being* heirs together of the **g** of life;	*5485*
	4:10	as good stewards of the manifold **g** of God.	*5485*
	5: 5	the proud, and giveth **g** to the humble.	*5485*
	5:10	But the God of all **g**, who hath called us	*5485*
	5:12	testifying that this is the true **g** of God	*5485*
2Pe	1: 2	**G** and peace be multiplied unto you	*5485*
	3:18	But grow in **g**, and *in* the knowledge of our	*5485*
2Jn	1: 3	**G** be with you, mercy, *and* peace,	*5485*
Jude	1: 4	ungodly *men*, turning the **g** of our God into	*5485*
Rev	1: 4	**G** *be* unto you, and peace, from him which	*5485*
	22:21	The **g** of our Lord Jesus Christ *be* with you	*5485*

GRACIOUS (31) [GRACE]

Ge	43:29	And he said, God be **g** unto thee, my son.	2603
Ex	22:27	crieth unto me, that I will hear; for I *am* **g**.	2587
	33:19	will be **g** to whom I will be gracious, and	2603
	33:19	will be gracious to whom I will be **g**, and	2603
	34: 6	merciful and **g**, longsuffering, and	2587
Nu	6:25	face shine upon thee, and be **g** unto thee:	2603
2Sa	12:22	Who can tell *whether* GOD will be **g** to	2603
2Ki	13:23	the LORD was **g** unto them, and	2603
2Ch	30: 9	for the LORD your God *is* **g** and merciful,	2587
Ne	9:17	**g** and merciful, slow to anger, and of great	2587
	9:31	for thou *art* a **g** and merciful God.	2587
Job	33:24	he is **g** unto him, and saith, Deliver him	2603
Ps	77: 9	Hath God forgotten to be **g**? hath he in	2589
	86:15	**g**, longsuffering, and plenteous in mercy	2587
	103: 8	The LORD *is* merciful and **g**, slow to	2587
	111: 4	the LORD *is* **g** and full of compassion.	2587
	112: 4	*he is* **g**, and full of compassion, and	2587
	116: 5	**G** *is* the LORD, and righteous; yea,	2587
	145: 8	The LORD *is* **g**, and full of compassion;	2587
Pr	11:16	A **g** woman retaineth honour: and	2580
Ecc	10:12	The words of a wise *man's* mouth *are* **g**;	2580
Isa	30:18	that *he* may be **g** unto you, and therefore	2603
	30:19	he will be **very g** unto thee at	2603+2603
	33: 2	O LORD, be **g** unto us; we have waited	2603
Jer	22:23	how **g** shalt thou be when pangs come upon	2603
Joel	2:13	for he *is* **g** and merciful, slow to anger, and	2587
Am	5:15	hosts will be **g** unto the remnant of Joseph.	2603
Jnh	4: 2	for I knew that thou *art* a **g** God, and	2587
Mal	1: 9	beseech God that he will be **g** unto us:	2603
Lk	4:22	wondered at the **g** words which proceeded	*5485*
1Pe	2: 3	If so be ye have tasted that the Lord *is* **g**.	*5543*

GRACIOUSLY (4) [GRACE]

Ge	33: 5	The children which God hath **g given** thy	2603
	33:11	because God hath **dealt g** with me, and	2603
Ps	119:29	the way of lying: and **grant** me thy law **g**.	2603

Hos 14: 2 Take away all iniquity, and receive *us* **g**: 2896

GRAFF (1) [GRAFFED]
Ro 11:23 for God is able to **g** them **in** again. *1461*

GRAFFED (5) [GRAFF]
Ro 11:17 wert **g in** amongst them, and with *them* *1461*
11:19 were broken off, that I might be **g in**. *1461*
11:23 they bide not still in unbelief, shall be **g in**: *1461*
11:24 wert **g** contrary to nature into a good olive *1461*
11:24 which be the natural *branches,* be **g into** *1461*

GRAFT; GRAFTED See GRAFF; GRAFFED

GRAIN (8)
Am 9: 9 yet shall not the **least g** fall *upon* the earth. 6872
Mt 13:31 of heaven is like unto a **g of** mustard **seed**, *2848*
17:20 If ye have faith as a **g of** mustard **seed**, *2848*
Mk 4:31 *It is* like a **g of** mustard **seed**, which, *2848*
Lk 13:19 It is like a **g of** mustard **seed**, which a man *2848*
17: 6 If ye had faith as a **g of** mustard **seed**, *2848*
1Co 15:37 but bare **g**, it may chance of wheat, or *2848*
15:37 it may chance of wheat, or of some other **g**: NIG

GRANDMOTHER (1) [MOTHER]
2Ti 1: 5 which dwelt first in thy **g** Lois, and *3125*

GRANT (22) [GRANTED]
Lev 25:24 in all the land of your possession ye shall **g** 5414
Ru 1: 9 The LORD **g** you that you may find rest, 5414
1Sa 1:17 the God of Israel **g** *thee* thy petition that 5414
1Ch 21:22 **G** me the place of *this* threshingfloor, 5414
21:22 thou shalt **g** it me for the full price: that 5414
2Ch 12: 7 but I will **g** them some deliverance; 5414
Ezr 3: 7 according to the **g** that they had of Cyrus 7558
Ne 1:11 and **g** him mercy in the sight of this man. 5414
Est 5: 8 if it please the king to **g** my petition, and 5414
Job 6: 8 *that* God would **g** *me* the thing that I long 5414
Ps 20: 4 **G** thee according to thine own heart, and 5414
85: 7 O LORD, and **g** us thy salvation. 5414
119:29 way of lying: and **g** me thy law **graciously**. 2603
140: 8 **G** not, O LORD, the desires of 5414
Mt 20:21 **G** that these my two sons may sit, *3004*
Mk 10:37 said unto him, **G** unto us that we may sit, *1325*
Lk 1:74 That *he* would **g** unto us, that *we* being *1325*
Ac 4:29 and **g** unto thy servants, that with all *1325*
Ro 15: 5 consolation **g** you to be likeminded one *1325*
Eph 3:16 That he would **g** you, according to *1325*
2Ti 1:18 The Lord **g** unto him that *he* may find *1325*
Rev 3:21 To him that overcometh will I **g** to sit with *1325*

GRANTED (15) [GRANT]
1Ch 4:10 And God **g** *him that* which he requested. 935
2Ch 1:12 Wisdom and knowledge *is* **g** unto thee; and 5414
Ezr 7: 6 the king **g** him all his request, according to 5414
Ne 2: 8 the king **g** me, according to the good hand 5414
Est 5: 6 it shall be **g** thee: and what *is* thy request? 5414
7: 2 it shall be **g** thee: and what *is* thy request? 5414
8:11 Where*in* the king **g** the Jews which *were* in 5414
9:12 it shall be **g** thee: or what *is* thy request 5414
9:13 let it be **g** to the Jews which *are* in Shushan 5414
Job 10:12 Thou hast **g** me life and favour, and 6213
Pr 10:24 but the desire of the righteous shall be **g**. 5414
Ac 3:14 and desired a murderer to be **g** unto you; *5483*
11:18 Then hath God also to the Gentiles **g** *1325*
14: 3 and **g** signs and wonders to be done by their *1325*
Rev 19: 8 And to her was **g** that she should be arrayed *1325*

GRAPE (8) [GRAPEGATHERER, GRAPEGATHERERS, GRAPE-GATHERERS, GRAPEGLEANINGS, GRAPES]
Lev 19:10 neither shalt thou gather *every* **g** of thy 6528
Dt 32:14 thou didst drink the pure blood of the **g**. 6025
Job 15:33 He shall shake off his **unripe g** as the vine, 1154
SS 2:13 the vines *with* the **tender g** give a *good* 5563
7:12 *whether* the **tender g** appear, *and* 5563
Isa 18: 5 and the **sour g** is ripening in the flower, 1155
Jer 31:29 The fathers have eaten a **sour g**, and 1155
31:30 every man that eateth the **sour g**, his teeth 1155

GRAPEGATHERER (1) [GRAPE, GATHER]
Jer 6: 9 turn back thine hand as a **g** into the baskets. 1219

GRAPEGATHERERS, GRAPE-GATHERERS (2) [GRAPE, GATHER]
Jer 49: 9 If **g** come to thee, would they not leave 1219
Ob 1: 5 if the **g** came to thee, would they not leave 1219

GRAPEGLEANINGS (1) [GRAPE, GLEAN]
Mic 7: 1 the summer fruits, as the **g** of the vintage: 5955

GRAPES (37) [GRAPE]
Ge 40:10 the clusters thereof brought forth ripe **g**: 6025
40:11 I took the **g**, and pressed them into 6025
49:11 in wine, and his clothes in the blood of **g**: 6025
Lev 25: 5 neither gather the **g** of thy vine undressed: 6025
25:11 nor gather *the* **g** in it of thy vine undressed. NIH
Nu 6: 3 neither shall he drink any liquor of **g**, 6025
6: 3 liquor of grapes, nor eat moist **g**, or dried. 6025
13:20 the time *was* the time of the first ripe **g**. 6025
13:23 from thence a branch with one cluster of **g**, 6025
13:24 of the **cluster of g** which the children of 811
Dt 23:24 thou mayest eat **g** thy fill at thine own 6025
24:21 When thou **gatherest** the **g** of thy vineyard, 1219
28:30 and shalt not **gather the g** thereof. 2490
28:39 nor gather *the* **g**; for the worms shall eat NIH
32:32 their **g** *are* grapes of gall, their clusters *are* 6025
32:32 their grapes *are* **g** of gall, their clusters *are* 6025
Jdg 8: 2 *Is* not the **gleaning of** the **g** of Ephraim 5955
9:27 trode *the* **g**, and made merry, and went *into* NIH
Ne 13:15 **g**, and figs, and all *manner of* burdens, 6025
SS 2:15 spoil the vines: for our vines *have* **tender g**. 5563
7: 7 a palm tree, and thy breasts to clusters *of* **g**. NIH
Isa 5: 2 he looked that *it* should bring forth **g**, and 6025
5: 2 forth grapes, and it brought forth **wild g**. 891
5: 4 when I looked that *it* should bring forth **g**, 6025
5: 4 bring forth grapes, brought it forth **wild g**? 891
17: 6 Yet **gleaning g** shall be left in it, as 5955
24:13 as the **gleaning g** when the vintage is done. 5955
Jer 8:13 *there shall be* no **g** on the vine, nor figs on 6025
25:30 as they that tread *the* **g**, against all NIH
49: 9 would they not leave *some* **gleaning g**? 5955
Eze 18: 2 The fathers have eaten **sour g**, and 1155
Hos 9:10 I found Israel like **g** in the wilderness; I saw 6025
Am 9:13 and the treader of **g** him that soweth seed; 6025
Ob 1: 5 came to thee, would they not leave *some* **g**? 5955
Mt 7:16 Do *men* gather **g** of thorns, or figs of *4718*
Lk 6:44 nor of a bramble bush gather they **g**. *4718*
Rev 14:18 vine of the earth; for her **g** are fully ripe. *4718*

GRASS (62)
Ge 1:11 God said, Let the earth bring forth **g**, 1877
1:12 the earth brought forth **g**, *and* herb yielding 1877
Nu 22: 4 as the ox licketh up the **g** of the field. 3418
Dt 11:15 And I will send **g** in thy fields for thy cattle, 6212
29:23 nor beareth, nor any **g** groweth therein, 6212
32: 2 tender herb, and as the showers upon the **g**: 6212
2Sa 23: 4 *as* the **tender g** *springing* out of the earth 1877
1Ki 18: 5 peradventure we may find **g** to save 2682
2Ki 19:26 they were *as* the **g** of the field, and *as* 6212
19:26 *as* the **g** on the housetops, and *as* corn 2682
Job 5:25 and thine offspring as the **g** of the earth. 6212
6: 5 Doth the wild ass bray when he hath **g**? or 1877
40:15 I made with thee; he eateth **g** as an ox. 2682
Ps 37: 2 For they shall soon be cut down like the **g**, 2682
72: 6 come down like rain upon the **mown g**: 1488
72:16 *they* of the city shall flourish like **g** of 6212
90: 5 in the morning *they are* like **g** *which* 2682
92: 7 When the wicked spring as the **g**, and 6212
102: 4 My heart is smitten, and withered like **g**; so 6212
102:11 that declineth; and I am withered like **g**. 6212
103:15 *As for* man, his days *are* as **g**: as a flower of 2682
104:14 He causeth the **g** to grow for the cattle, and 2682
106:20 into the similitude of an ox that eateth **g**. 6212
129: 6 Let them be as the **g** upon the housetops, 2682
147: 8 who maketh **g** to grow *upon* the mountains. 2682
Pr 19:12 a lion; but his favour *is* as dew upon the **g**. 6212
27:25 the **tender g** sheweth itself, and herbs of 1877
Isa 15: 6 the **g** faileth, there is no green thing. 1877
35: 7 each lay, *shall be* **g** with reeds and rushes. 2682
37:27 they were *as* the **g** of the field, and *as* 6212
37:27 *as* the **g** on the housetops, and *as* corn 2682
40: 6 All flesh *is* **g**, and all the goodliness thereof 2682
40: 7 The **g** withereth, the flower fadeth: because 2682
40: 7 bloweth upon it: surely the people *is* **g**. 2682
40: 8 The **g** withereth, the flower fadeth: but 2682
44: 4 they shall spring up *as* among the **g**, 2682
51:12 of the son of man *which* shall be made *as* **g**; 2682
Jer 14: 5 and forsook *it,* because there was no **g**. 1877
14: 6 their eyes did fail, because *there was* no **g**. 6212

Jer 50:11 because ye are grown fat as the heifer at g, 1877
Da 4:15 and brass, in the tender g of the field; 1883
4:15 *let* his portion *be* with the beasts in the g of 6211'
4:23 and brass, in the tender g of the field; 1883
4:25 they shall make thee to eat g as oxen, 6211'
4:32 they shall make thee to eat g as oxen, and 6211'
4:33 did eat g as oxen, and his body was wet 6211'
5:21 they fed him with g like oxen, and his body 6211'
Am 7: 2 had made an end of eating the g of the land, 6212
Mic 5: 7 as the showers upon the g, that tarrieth not 6212
Zec 10: 1 showers of rain, to every one g in the field. 6212
Mt 6:30 if God so clothe the g of the field, *5528*
14:19 the multitude to sit down on the g, *5528*
Mk 6:39 sit down by companies upon the green g. *5528*
Lk 12:28 If then God so clothe the g, which is to day *5528*
Jn 6:10 Now there was much g in the place. So *5528*
Jas 1:10 as the flower of the g he shall pass away. *5528*
1:11 but it withereth the g, and the flower *5528*
1Pe 1:24 For all flesh *is* as g, and all the glory of *5528*
1:24 and all the glory of man as the flower of g. *5528*
1:24 The g withereth, and the flower thereof *5528*
Rev 8: 7 was burnt up, and all green g was burnt up. *5528*
9: 4 that they should not hurt the g of the earth, *5528*

GRASSHOPPER (3) [GRASSHOPPERS]
Lev 11:22 after his kind, and the g after his kind. 2284
Job 39:20 Canst thou make him afraid as a g? the glory 697
Ecc 12: 5 the g shall be a burden, and desire shall 2284

GRASSHOPPERS (7) [GRASSHOPPER]
Nu 13:33 we were in our own sight as g, and so 2284
Jdg 6: 5 their tents, and they came as g for multitude; 697
7:12 lay along in the valley like g for multitude; 697
Isa 40:22 and the inhabitants thereof *are* as g; 2284
Jer 46:23 because they are more than the g, and 697
Am 7: 1 he formed g in the beginning of 1462
Na 3:17 and thy captains as the great g, 1462+1462

GRATE (6) [GRAVE, GRAVE'S, GRAVECLOTHES, GRAVED, GRAVEN, GRAVES, GRAVETH, GRAVING, GRAVINGS]
Ex 27: 4 thou shalt make for it a g of network *of* 4345
35:16 altar of burnt offering with his brasen g, 4345
38: 4 he made for the altar a brasen g of network 4345
38: 5 he cast four rings for the four ends of the g 4345
38:30 the brasen g for it, and all the vessels of 4345
39:39 his g of brass, his staves, and all his 4345

GRATING See NETWORKS

GRAVE (67) [GRATE]
Ge 35:20 Jacob set a pillar upon her g: that *is* 6900
35:20 that *is* the pillar of Rachel's g unto *this* day. 6900
37:35 For I will go down into the g unto my son 7585
42:38 down my gray hairs with sorrow to the g. 7585
44:29 down my gray hairs with sorrow to the g. 7585
44:31 thy servant our father with sorrow to the g. 7585
50: 5 in my g which I have digged for me in 6913
Ex 28: 9 g on them the names of the children of 6605
28:36 g upon it, *like* the engravings of a signet, 6605
Nu 19:16 or a dead *body,* or a bone of a man, or a g, 6913
19:18 a bone, or one slain, or one dead, or a g: 6913
1Sa 2: 6 he bringeth down *to* the g, and bringeth up. 7585
2Sa 3:32 up his voice, and wept at the g of Abner; 6913
19:37 *and be buried* by the g of my father and 6913
1Ki 2: 6 let not his hoar head go down *to* the g in 7585
2: 9 his hoar head bring thou down *to* the g with 7585
13:30 he laid his carcase in his own g; and 6913
14:13 he only of Jeroboam shall come to the g, 6913
2Ki 22:20 thou shalt be gathered into thy g in peace; 6913
2Ch 2: 7 that can skill to g with the cunning 6603+3807.1
2:14 also to g any *manner of* graving, and to find 6605
34:28 thou shalt be gathered to thy g in peace, 6913
Job 3:22 are glad, when they can find the g? 6913
5:26 Thou shalt come to *thy* g in a full age, 6913
7: 9 he that goeth down *to* the g shall come up 7585
10:19 have been carried from the womb to the g. 6913
14:13 O that thou wouldest hide me in the g, 7585
17:13 If I wait, the g *is* mine house: I have made 7585
21:13 and in a moment go down *to* the g. 7585
21:32 Yet shall he be brought to the g, and 6913
24:19 *so doth* the g *those which* have sinned. 7585
30:24 he will not stretch out *his* hand to the g, 5856
33:22 his soul draweth near unto the g, and 7845
Ps 6: 5 of thee: in the g who shall give thee thanks? 7585
30: 3 thou hast brought up my soul from the g: 7585
31:17 be ashamed, *and* let them be silent in the g. 7585
49:14 Like sheep they are laid in the g; 7585
49:14 their beauty shall consume *in* the g from 7585
49:15 redeem my soul from the power of the g: 7585
88: 3 and my life draweth nigh unto the g. 7585
88: 5 the dead, like the slain that lie in the g, 6913
88:11 thy lovingkindness be declared in the g? 6913
89:48 he deliver his soul from the hand of the g? 7585
Pr 1:12 Let us swallow them up alive as the g; and 7585
30:16 The g; and the barren womb; the earth *that* 7585
Ecc 9:10 nor knowledge, nor wisdom, in the g, 7585
SS 8: 6 *is* strong as death; jealousy *is* cruel as the g: 7585
Isa 14:11 Thy pomp is brought down *to* the g, *and* 7585
14:19 thou art cast out of thy g like an 6913
38:10 of my days, I shall go to the gates of the g: 7585
38:18 For the g cannot praise thee, death can *not* 7585
53: 9 he made his g with the wicked, and 6913
Jer 20:17 or that my mother might have been my g, 6913
Eze 31:15 In the day when he went down to the g I 7585
32:23 and her company is round about her g: 6900
32:24 and all her multitude round about her g, 6900
Hos 13:14 I will ransom them from the power of the g; 7585
13:14 thy plagues; O g, I will be thy destruction: 7585
Na 1:14 I will make thy g; for thou art vile. 6913
Jn 11:17 he found that he had *lien* in the g four days *3419*
11:31 saying, She goeth unto the g to weep there. *3419*
11:38 again groaning in himself cometh to the g. *3419*
12:17 him when he called Lazarus out of *his* g, *3419*
1Co 15:55 where *is* thy sting? O g, where *is* thy victory? *86*
1Ti 3: 8 Likewise *must* the deacons *be* g, *4586*
3:11 Even so *must their* wives *be* g, *4586*
Tit 2: 2 g, temperate, sound in faith, in charity, *4586*

GRAVE'S (1) [GRATE]
Ps 141: 7 Our bones are scattered at the g mouth, 7585

GRAVECLOTHES (1) [CLOTHE, GRATE]
Jn 11:44 came forth, bound hand and foot with g: *2750*

GRAVED (2) [GRATE]
1Ki 7:36 he g cherubims, lions, and palm trees, 6605
2Ch 3: 7 with gold; and g cherubims on the walls. 6605

GRAVEL (3)
Pr 20:17 afterwards his mouth shall be filled *with* g. 2687
Isa 48:19 the offspring of thy bowels like the g 4579
La 3:16 hath also broken my teeth with g stones, 2687

GRAVEN (55) [GRATE]
Ex 20: 4 shalt not make unto thee *any* g image, 6459
32:16 *was* the writing of God, g upon the tables. 2801
39: 6 g *as* signets are graven, with the names of 6603
39: 6 graven *as* signets are g, with the names of 6605
Lev 26: 1 Ye shall make you no idols nor g image, 6459
Dt 4:16 and make you a g image, 6459
4:23 make you a g image, *or* the likeness of any 6459
4:25 corrupt *yourselves,* and make a g image, 6459
5: 8 Thou shalt not make thee *any* g image, *or* 6459
7: 5 and burn their g images with fire. 6456
7:25 The g images of their gods shall ye burn 6456
12: 3 you shall hew down the g images of their 6456
27:15 Cursed *be* the man that maketh *any* g or 6459
Jdg 17: 3 to make a g image and a molten image: 6459
17: 4 who made thereof a g image and a molten 6459
18:14 and a g image, and a molten image? 6459
18:17 *and* took the g image, and the ephod, and 6459
18:20 the g image, and went in the midst of 6459
18:30 the children of Dan set up the g image: 6459
18:31 they set them up Micah's g image, 6459
2Ki 17:41 served their g images, both their children, 6456
21: 7 he set a g image of the grove that he had 6459
2Ch 33:19 set up groves and g images, before he was 6456
34: 7 had beaten the g images into powder, and 6456
Job 19:24 That they were g with an iron pen and 2672
Ps 78:58 moved him to jealousy with their g images. 6456
97: 7 be all they that serve g images, 6459
Isa 10:10 whose g images did excel *them of* 6456
21: 9 all the g images of her gods he hath broken 6456
30:22 also the covering of thy g images of silver, 6456
40:19 The workman melteth a g image, and 6459
40:20 a cunning workman to prepare a g image, 6459
42: 8 to another, neither my praise to g images. 6456
42:17 that trust in g images, that say to 6459

Isa 44: 9 They that make a **g image** *are* all of them 6459
44:10 molten a **g image** *that* is profitable for 6459
44:15 worshippeth *it;* he maketh it a **g image**, and 6459
44:17 thereof he maketh a god, *even* his **g image**: 6459
45:20 that set up the wood of their **g image**, 6459
48: 5 my **g image**, and my molten image, 6459
49:16 I have **g** thee upon the palms of *my* hands; 2710
Jer 8:19 provoked me to anger with their **g images**, 6456
10:14 founder is confounded by the **g image**: 6459
17: 1 *it is* **g** upon the table of their heart, and 2790
50:38 for it *is* the land of **g images**, and they are 6456
51:17 founder is confounded by the **g image**: 6459
51:47 that I will do judgment upon the **g images** 6456
51:52 that I will do judgment upon her **g images**: 6456
Hos 11: 2 and burned incense to **g images**. 6456
Mic 1: 7 all the **g images** thereof shall be beaten to 6456
5:13 Thy **g images** also will I cut off, and 6456
Na 1:14 house of thy gods will I cut off the **g image** 6459
Hab 2:18 What profiteth the **g image** that the maker 6459
2:18 image that the maker thereof hath **g** it; 6458
Ac 17:29 silver, or stone, **g** by art and man's device. *5480*

GRAVES (21) [GRATE]
Ex 14:11 Because *there were* no **g** in Egypt, 6913
2Ki 23: 6 cast the powder thereof upon the **g** of 6913
2Ch 34: 4 strowed *it* upon the **g** of them that had 6913
Job 17: 1 my days are extinct, the **g** *are ready* for me. 6913
Isa 65: 4 Which remain among the **g**, and lodge in 6913
Jer 8: 1 the inhabitants of Jerusalem, out of their **g**: 6913
26:23 cast his dead body into the **g** of 6913
Eze 32:22 his **g** *are* about him: all of them slain, fallen 6913
32:23 Whose **g** are set in the sides of the pit, and 6913
32:25 her **g** *are* round about him: all of them 6913
32:26 her **g** *are* round about him: all of them 6913
37:12 I *will* open your **g**, and cause you to come 6913
37:12 cause you to come up out of your **g**, and 6913
37:13 when I have opened your **g**, O my people, 6913
37:13 and brought you up out of your **g**, 6913
39:11 *that* I will give unto Gog a place there of **g** 6913
Mt 27:52 And the **g** were opened; and many bodies *3419*
27:53 And came out of the **g** after his *3419*
Lk 11:44 for ye are as **g** which appear not, and *3419*
Jn 5:28 in the which all that are in the **g** shall hear *3419*
Rev 11: 9 not suffer their dead bodies to be put in **g**. *3418*

GRAVETH (1) [GRATE]
Isa 22:16 that **g** a habitation for himself in a rock? 2710

GRAVING (3) [GRATE]
Ex 32: 4 fashioned it with a **g tool**, after he had 2747
2Ch 2:14 also to grave any *manner of* **g**, and to find 6603
Zec 3: 9 behold, I *will* engrave the **g** thereof, 6603

GRAVINGS (1) [GRATE]
1Ki 7:31 also upon the mouth of it *were* **g** with their 4734

GRAVITY (2)
1Ti 3: 4 having *his* children in subjection with all **g**; *4587*
Tit 2: 7 *shewing* uncorruptness, **g**, sincerity, *4587*

GRAY (6) [GRAYHEADED]
Ge 42:38 shall ye bring down my **g hairs** with 7872
44:29 ye shall bring down my **g hairs** with 7872
44:31 thy servants shall bring down the **g hairs** of 7872
Dt 32:25 the suckling *also* with the man of **g hairs**. 7872
Pr 20:29 and the beauty of old men *is* the **g head**. 7872
Hos 7: 9 yea, **g hairs** are here and there upon him, 7872

GRAYHEADED (3) [GRAY, HEAD]
1Sa 12: 2 I am old and **g**; and behold, my sons *are* 7867
Job 15:10 With us *are* both the **g** and very aged men, 7867
Ps 71:18 Now also when I am old and **g**, O God, 7872

GREASE (1)
Ps 119:70 Their heart is as fat as **g**; *but* I delight *in* thy 2459

GREAT (962) [GREATER, GREATEST, GREATLY, GREATNESS]
Ge 1:16 God made two **g** lights; the greater light to 1419
1:21 God created **g** whales, and every living 1419
6: 5 the wickedness of man *was* **g** in the earth, 7227
7:11 the same day were all the fountains of the **g** 7227
10:12 and Calah: the same *is* a **g** city. 1419
12: 2 I will make of thee a **g** nation, and I will 1419
12: 2 and I will bless thee, and **make** thy name **g**; 1431
12:17 his house with **g** plagues because of Sarai 1419
13: 6 for their substance was **g**, so that they could 7227
15: 1 *am* thy shield, *and* thy exceeding **g** reward. 7235
15:12 lo, a horror of **g** darkness fell upon him. 1419
15:14 afterward shall they come out with **g** 1419
15:18 from the river of Egypt unto the **g** river, 1419
17:20 he beget, and I will make him a **g** nation. 1419
18:18 that Abraham shall surely become a **g** 1419
18:20 the cry of Sodom and Gomorrah is **g**, 7227
19:11 the house with blindness, both small and **g**; 1419
19:13 the cry of them is **waxen g** before the face 1431
20: 9 brought on me and on my kingdom a **g** sin? 1419
21: 8 Abraham made a **g** feast the *same* day that 1419
21:18 thine hand; for I will make him a **g** nation. 1419
24:35 my master greatly; and he is become **g**: 1431
26:13 the man **waxed g**, and went forward, 1431
26:13 and grew until he **became** very **g**: 1431
26:14 of herds, and **g store** of servants: 7227
27:34 he cried with a **g** and exceeding bitter cry, 1419
29: 2 and a **g** stone *was* upon the well's mouth. 1419
30: 8 With **g** wrestlings have I wrestled with my 430
39: 9 how then can I do this **g** wickedness, and 1419
41:29 there come seven years of **g** plenty 1419
45: 7 and to save your lives by a **g** deliverance. 1419
46: 3 for I will there make of thee a **g** nation. 1419
48:19 become a people, and he also shall be **g**: 1431
50: 9 horsemen: and it was a very **g** company. 3515
50:10 there they mourned with a **g** and very sore 1419
Ex 3: 3 I will now turn aside, and see this **g** sight, 1419
6: 6 a stretched out arm, and with **g** judgments: 1419
7: 4 out of the land of Egypt by **g** judgments. 1419
11: 3 Moreover the man Moses *was* very **g** in 1419
11: 6 there shall be a **g** cry throughout all 1419
11: 8 And he went out from Pharaoh in a **g** anger. 2750
12:30 and there was a **g** cry in Egypt; 1419
14:31 Israel saw *that* **g** work which the LORD 1419
18:22 *that* every **g** matter they shall bring unto 1419
29:20 upon the **g toe** of their right foot, and 931
32:10 and I will make of thee a **g** nation. 1419
32:11 forth out of the land of Egypt with **g** power, 1419
32:21 thou hast brought *so* **g** a sin upon them? 1419
32:30 unto the people, Ye have sinned a **g** sin: 1419
32:31 this people have sinned a **g** sin, and 1419
Lev 8:23 and upon the **g toe** of his right foot. 931
8:24 and upon the **g toes** of their right feet: 931
11:17 little owl, and the cormorant, and the **g owl**, 3244
14:14 and upon the **g toe** of his right foot: 931
14:17 and upon the **g toe** of his right foot, 931
14:25 and upon the **g toe** of his right foot: 931
14:28 and upon the **g toe** of his right foot, 931
Nu 11:33 the LORD smote the people *with* a very **g** 7227
13:28 and the cities *are* walled, *and* very **g**: 1419
13:32 that we saw in it *are* men of a **g stature**. 4060
14:17 let the power of my Lord be **g**, 1431
14:18 of **g** mercy, forgiving iniquity and 7227
22:17 For I will promote thee unto **very g** honour, 3966
23:24 the people shall rise up as a **g lion**, and 3833
24: 9 he lay down as a lion, and as a **g lion**: 3833
24:11 to **promote** thee **unto g honour**; 3513+3513
32: 1 the children of Gad had a very **g** multitude 6099
34: 6 you shall even have the **g** sea for a border: 1419
34: 7 from the **g** sea you shall point out for you 1419
Dt 1: 7 *unto* Lebanon, unto the **g** river, the river 1419
1:17 you shall hear the small as well as the **g**; 1419
1:19 we went *through* all that **g** and terrible 1419
1:28 the cities *are* **g** and walled up to heaven; 1419
2: 7 he knoweth thy walking *through* this **g** 1419
2:10 a people **g**, and many, and tall, as 1419
2:21 A people **g**, and many, and tall, as 1419
3: 5 and bars; beside unwalled towns a **g** many. 3966
4: 6 Surely this **g** nation *is* a wise and 1419
4: 7 For what nation *is there so* **g**, who hath God 1419
4: 8 what nation *is there so* **g**, that hath statutes 1419
4:32 hath been *any such thing* as this **g** thing *is,* 1419
4:34 by a stretched out arm, and by **g** terrors, 1419
4:36 upon earth he shewed thee his **g** fire; and 1419
5:22 and of the thick darkness, *with* a **g** voice: 1419
5:25 for this **g** fire will consume us: if we hear 1419
6:10 to Jacob, to give thee **g** and goodly cities, 1419
6:22 shewed signs and wonders, **g** and sore, 1419
7:19 The **g** temptations which thine eyes saw, 1419
8:15 Who led thee through *that* **g** and terrible 1419
9: 1 cities **g** and fenced up to heaven, 1419
9: 2 A people **g** and tall, the children of 1419
10:17 of lords, a **g** God, a mighty, and a terrible, 1419

G

Dt 10:21 that hath done for thee these **g** and terrible 1419
11: 7 your eyes have seen all the **g** acts of 1419
14:16 The little owl, and the **g owl**, and the swan, 3244
18:16 neither let me see this **g** fire any more, 1419
25:13 in thy bag divers weights, a **g** and a small. 1419
25:14 house divers measures, a **g** and a small. 1419
26: 5 there a nation, **g**, mighty, and populous: 1419
26: 8 with **g** terribleness, and with signs, and 1419
27: 2 that thou shalt set thee up **g** stones, and 1419
28:59 *even* **g** plagues, and of long continuance, 1419
29: 3 The **g** temptations which thine eyes have 1419
29: 3 have seen, the signs, and those **g** miracles: 1419
29:24 what *meaneth* the heat of this **g** anger? 1419
29:28 in **g** indignation, and cast them into another 1419
34:12 in all the **g** terror which Moses shewed in 1419
Jos 1: 4 and this Lebanon even unto the **g** river, 1419
1: 4 unto the **g** sea *toward* the going down of 1419
6: 5 all the people shall shout *with* a **g** shout; 1419
6:20 the people shouted *with* a **g** shout, that 1419
7: 9 and what wilt thou do unto thy **g** name? 1419
7:26 they raised over him a **g** heap of stones 1419
8:29 raise thereon a **g** heap of stones, 1419
9: 1 in all the coasts of the **g** sea over against 1419
10: 2 because Gibeon *was* a **g** city, 1419
10:10 and slew them *with* a **g** slaughter at Gibeon, 1419
10:11 that the LORD cast down **g** stones from 1419
10:18 Roll **g** stones upon the mouth of the cave, 1419
10:20 end of slaying them *with* a very **g** slaughter, 1419
10:27 laid **g** stones in the cave's mouth, 1419
11: 8 chased them unto **g** Zidon, and 7227
14:12 and *that* the cities *were* **g** *and* fenced: 1419
14:15 which *Arba was* a **g** man among 1419
15:12 the west border *was* to the **g** sea, and 1419
15:47 and the **g** sea, and the border *thereof.* 1419
17:14 portion to inherit, seeing I *am* a **g** people, 7227
17:15 If thou *be* a **g** people, *then* get thee up to 7227
17:17 Thou *art* a **g** people, and hast great power: 7227
17:17 Thou *art* a great people, and hast **g** power: 1419
19:28 Hammon, and Kanah, *even* unto **g** Zidon; 7227
22:10 there an altar by Jordan, a **g** altar to see to. 1419
23: 4 have cut off, even *unto* the **g** sea westward. 1419
23: 9 hath driven out from before you **g** nations 1419
24:17 which did those **g** signs in our sight, and 1419
24:26 took a **g** stone, and set it up there under an 1419
Jdg 1: 6 and cut off his thumbs and his **g toes**. 7272
1: 7 having their thumbs and their **g toes** cut off, 7272
2: 7 who had seen all the **g** works of 1419
5:15 For the divisions of Reuben *there were* **g** 1419
5:16 For the divisions of Reuben *there were* **g** 1419
11:33 of the vineyards, *with* a very **g** slaughter. 1419
12: 2 my people were at **g** strife with the children 3966
15: 8 them hip and thigh *with* a **g** slaughter: 1419
15:18 Thou hast given this **g** deliverance into 1419
16: 5 see wherein his **g** strength *lieth,* and 1419
16: 6 wherein thy **g** strength *lieth,* and 1419
16:15 hast not told me wherein thy **g** strength 1419
16:23 to offer a **g** sacrifice unto Dagon their god, 1419
20:38 that they should make a **g** flame with 7235
21: 5 For *they* had made a **g** oath concerning *him* 1419
1Sa 2:17 young men was very **g** before the LORD: 1419
4: 5 all Israel shouted *with* a **g** shout, so that 1419
4: 6 What *meaneth* the noise of this **g** shout in 1419
4:10 there was a very **g** slaughter; for there fell 1419
4:17 there hath been also a **g** slaughter among 1419
5: 9 against the city *with* a very **g** destruction: 1419
5: 9 both small and **g**, and they had emerods in 1419
6: 9 *then* he hath done us this **g** evil: 1419
6:14 stood there, where *there was* a **g** stone: 1419
6:15 of gold *were,* and put *them* on the **g** stone: 1419
6:18 even unto the **g** *stone of* Abel, 1419
6:19 *many* of the people *with* a **g** slaughter. 1419
7:10 the LORD thundered with a **g** thunder on 1419
12:16 Now therefore stand and see this **g** thing, 1419
12:17 and see that your wickedness *is* **g**, 7227
12:22 forsake his people for his **g** name's sake: 1419
12:24 for consider how **g things** he hath **done** for 1431
14:15 earth quaked: so it was a **very g** trembling. 430
14:20 *and there was* a very **g** discomfiture. 1419
14:33 roll a **g** stone unto me *this* day. 1419
14:45 who hath wrought this **g** salvation in Israel? 1419
15:22 Hath the LORD *as* **g** delight in burnt NIH
17:25 the king will enrich him *with* **g** riches, and 1419
19: 5 the LORD wrought a **g** salvation for all 1419
19: 8 and slew them *with* a **g** slaughter; 1419
19:22 and came to a **g** well that *is* in Sechu: 1419
20: 2 my father will do nothing *either* **g** or small, 1419
23: 5 and smote them *with* a **g** slaughter. 1419
25: 2 the man *was* very **g**, and he had three 1419
26:13 hill afar off; a **g** space *being* between them: 7227
26:25 thou shalt both **do g things**, and 6213+6213
30: 2 either **g** or small, but carried *them* away, 1419
30:16 of all the **g** spoil that they had taken out of 1419
30:19 neither small nor **g**, neither sons nor 1419
2Sa 3:22 a troop, and brought in a **g** spoil with them: 7227
3:38 and a **g** *man* fallen this day in Israel? 1419
5:10 **grew g**, and the LORD God of hosts *was* 1419
7: 9 of thy sight, and have made thee a **g** name, 1419
7: 9 like unto the name of the **g** *men* that *are* in 1419
7:19 house for a **g while to come.** 4480+7350
7:21 hast thou done all these **g things**, 1420
7:22 Wherefore thou art **g**, O LORD God: 1431
7:23 to do for you **g things** and terrible, for thy 1420
12:14 **given g occasion** to the enemies of the LORD **to blaspheme**, 5006+5006
12:30 he brought forth the spoil of the city in **g** 3966
18: 7 there was there a **g** slaughter that day *of* 1419
18: 9 the mule went under the thick boughs of a **g** 1419
18:17 cast him into a **g** pit in the wood, and laid a 1419
18:17 and laid a very **g** heap of stones upon him: 1419
18:29 I saw a **g** tumult, but I knew not what *it* 1419
19:32 lay at Mahanaim; for he *was* a very **g** man. 1419
20: 8 When they *were* at the **g** stone which *is* in 1419
21:20 where was a man of **g** stature, that had on NIH
22:36 and thy gentleness hath **made** me **g**. 7235
23:10 the LORD wrought a **g** victory that day; 1419
23:12 and the LORD wrought a **g** victory. 1419
24:14 And David said unto Gad, I am in a **g** strait: 3966
24:14 hand of the LORD; for his mercies *are* **g**: 7227
1Ki 1:40 rejoiced *with* **g** joy, so that the earth rent 1419
3: 4 for that *was* the **g** high place: 1419
3: 6 unto thy servant David my father **g** mercy, 1419
3: 6 thou hast kept for him this **g** kindness, that 1419
3: 8 a **g** people, that cannot be numbered nor 7227
3: 9 who is able to judge this thy *so* **g** a people? 3515
4:13 threescore **g** cities *with* walls and 1419
5: 7 unto David a wise son over this **g** people. 7227
5:17 they brought **g** stones, costly stones, *and* 1419
7: 9 and *so* on the outside toward the **g** court. 1419
7:10 *even* **g** stones, stones of ten cubits, and 1419
7:12 the **g** court round about *was with* three 1419
8:42 (For they shall hear of thy **g** name, and of 1419
8:65 and all Israel with him, a **g** congregation, 1419
10: 2 she came to Jerusalem with a very **g** train, 3515
10:10 of spices very **g store**, and precious stones: 7235
10:11 brought in from Ophir **g** plenty of almug 3966
10:18 Moreover the king made a **g** throne of 1419
11:19 Hadad found **g** favour in the sight of 3966
18:32 **as g as** would contain two measures of 3509.1
18:45 and wind, and there was a **g** rain. 1419
19: 7 eat; because the journey *is* too **g** for thee. 7227
19:11 and a **g** and strong wind rent the mountains, 1419
20:13 Hast thou seen all this **g** multitude? 1419
20:21 and slew the Syrians with a **g** slaughter. 1419
20:28 will I deliver all this **g** multitude into thine 1419
22:31 saying, Fight neither with small nor **g**, 1419
2Ki 3:27 there was **g** indignation against Israel: and 1419
4: 8 passed to Shunem, where *was* a **g** woman; 1419
4:38 Set on the **g** pot, and seethe pottage for 1419
5: 1 was a **g** man with his master, and 1419
5:13 *if* the prophet had bid thee *do some* **g** thing, 1419
6:14 he thither horses, and chariots, and a **g** host: 3515
6:23 he prepared **g** provision for them: and 1419
6:25 there was a **g** famine in Samaria: and 1419
7: 6 noise of horses, *even* the noise of a **g** host: 1419
8: 4 all the **g** *things* that Elisha hath done. 1419
8:13 a dog, that he should do this **g** thing? 1419
10: 6 *were* with the **g** *men* of the city, 1419
10:11 all his **g** *men*, and his kinsfolks, and 1419
10:19 for I have a **g** sacrifice *to do* to Baal; 1419
16:15 Upon the **g** altar burn the morning burnt 1419
17:21 the LORD, and made them sin a **g** sin. 1419
17:36 up out of the land of Egypt with **g** power 1419
18:17 Hezekiah with a **g** host *against* Jerusalem. 3515
18:19 Thus saith the **g** king, the king of Assyria, 1419
18:28 spake, saying, Hear the word of the **g** king, 1419
22:13 for **g** *is* the wrath of the LORD that is 1419
23: 2 and all the people, both small and **g**: 1419
23:26 not from the fierceness of his **g** wrath, 1419

2Ki	25: 9	and every **g** *man's* house burnt he with fire.	1419
	25:26	both small and **g**, and the captains of	1419
1Ch	11:14	the LORD saved *them by* a **g** deliverance.	1419
	11:23	a man of *g* stature, five cubits *high;* and	NIH
	12:22	until it was a **g** host, like the host of God.	1419
	16:25	For **g** *is* the LORD, and greatly to be	1419
	17: 8	the name of the **g** *men* that *are* in the earth.	1419
	17:17	house for a **g while to come**,	4480+7350
	17:19	in making known all *these* **g things**.	1420
	20: 6	where was a man of *g* stature, whose fingers	NIH
	21:13	And David said unto Gad, I am in a **g** strait:	3966
	21:13	of the LORD; for very **g** *are* his mercies:	7227
	22: 8	blood abundantly, and hast made **g** wars:	1419
	25: 8	against *ward,* as well the small as the **g**,	1419
	26:13	they cast lots, as well the small as the **g**,	1419
	29: 1	*is yet* young and tender, and the work *is* **g**:	1419
	29: 9	and David the king also rejoiced *with* **g** joy.	1419
	29:12	in thine hand *it is* to **make g**, and to give	1431
	29:22	drink before the LORD on that day with **g**	1419
2Ch	1: 8	Thou hast shewed **g** mercy unto David my	1419
	1:10	who can judge this thy people, *that is so* **g**?	1419
	2: 5	the house which I build *is* **g**: for great *is* our	1419
	2: 5	*is* great: for **g** *is* our God above all gods.	1419
	2: 9	I am about to build *shall be* wonderful **g**.	1419
	4: 9	and the **g** court, and doors for the court, and	1419
	4:18	Thus Solomon made all these vessels in **g**	3966
	6:32	is come from a far country for thy **g** name's	1419
	7: 8	all Israel with him, a very **g** congregation,	1419
	9: 1	with a very **g** company, and camels that	3515
	9: 9	of spices **g** abundance, and precious stones:	3966
	9:17	Moreover the king made a **g** throne of	1419
	13: 8	ye *be* a **g** multitude, and *there are* with you	7227
	13:17	his people slew them *with* a **g** slaughter:	7227
	15: 5	**g** vexations *were* upon all the inhabitants of	7227
	15:13	whether small or **g**, whether man or	1419
	16:12	until his disease *was* exceeding *g*: yet in his	NIH
	16:14	and they made a very **g** burning for him.	1419
	17:12	And Jehoshaphat waxed **g** exceedingly; and	1432
	18:30	saying, Fight ye not with small or **g**,	1419
	20: 2	There cometh a **g** multitude against thee	7227
	20:12	for we have no might against this **g**	7227
	20:15	nor dismayed by reason of this **g** multitude;	7227
	21: 3	their father gave them **g** gifts of silver, and	7227
	21:14	*with* a **g** plague will the LORD smite thy	1419
	21:15	thou *shalt* have **g** sickness by disease of thy	7227
	24:24	the LORD delivered a very **g** host into	7230
	24:25	from him, (for they left him in **g** diseases,)	7227
	25:10	and they returned home in **g** anger.	2750
	26:15	to shoot arrows and **g** stones withal.	1419
	28: 5	carried away a **g multitude** of them	1419
	28: 5	who smote him *with* a **g** slaughter.	1419
	28:13	for our trespass is **g**, and *there is* fierce	7227
	30:13	in the second month, a very **g** congregation.	7230
	30:21	bread seven days with **g** gladness:	1419
	30:24	a **g number** of priests sanctified	7230+3807.1
	30:26	So there was **g** joy in Jerusalem: for since	1419
	31:10	and that which is left *is* this **g store**.	1995
	31:15	by courses, as well *to* the **g** as *to* the small:	1419
	33:14	**raised** it **up a** very **g height**, and	1361
	34:21	for **g** *is* the wrath of the LORD that is	1419
	34:30	the Levites, and all the people, **g** and small:	1419
	36:18	**g** and small, and the treasures of the house	1419
Ezr	3:11	all the people shouted *with* a **g** shout,	1419
	4:10	the rest of the nations whom the **g** and	7229
	5: 8	to the house of the **g** God, which *is* builded	7229
	5: 8	which *is* builded *with* **g** stones, and	1560
	5:11	which a **g** king of Israel builded and set up.	7229
	6: 4	*With* three rows of **g** stones, and a row of	1560
	9: 7	*have we been* in a **g** trespass unto this day;	1419
	9:13	us for our evil deeds, and for our **g** trespass,	1419
	10: 1	out of Israel a very **g** congregation *of* men	7227
	10: 9	because of *this* matter, and for the **g rain**.	1653
Ne	1: 3	there in the province *are* in **g** affliction	1419
	1: 5	the **g** and terrible God, that keepeth	1419
	1:10	whom thou hast redeemed by thy **g** power,	1419
	3:27	over against the **g** tower that lieth out,	1419
	4: 1	took **g** indignation, and mocked the Jews.	7235
	4:14	*which is* **g** and terrible, and fight for your	1419
	4:19	The work *is* **g** and large, and we *are*	7235
	5: 1	there was a **g** cry of the people and of their	1419
	5: 7	And I set a **g** assembly against them.	1419
	6: 3	I *am* doing a **g** work, so that I cannot come	1419
	7: 4	Now the city *was* large and **g**: but	1419
	8: 6	Ezra blessed the LORD, the **g** God.	1419
	8:12	to make **g** mirth, because they had	1419
	8:17	done so. And there was very **g** gladness.	1419
	9:17	and of **g** kindness, and forsookest them not.	7227
	9:18	of Egypt, and had wrought **g** provocations;	1419
	9:25	delighted themselves in thy **g** goodness.	1419
	9:26	to thee, and they wrought **g** provocations.	1419
	9:31	Nevertheless for thy **g** mercies' sake thou	7227
	9:32	our God, the **g**, the mighty, and the terrible	1419
	9:35	in thy **g** goodness that thou gavest them,	7227
	9:37	at their pleasure, and we *are* in **g** distress.	1419
	11:14	*was* Zabdiel, the son of *one of* the **g** *men*.	1419
	12:31	appointed two **g** *companies of them that*	1419
	12:43	Also that day they offered **g** sacrifices, and	1419
	12:43	for God had made them rejoice *with* **g** joy:	1419
	13: 5	he had prepared for him a **g** chamber,	1419
	13:27	then hearken unto you to do all this **g** evil,	1419
Est	1: 5	both unto **g** and small, seven days, in	1419
	1:20	throughout all his empire, (for it *is* **g**,)	7227
	1:20	their husbands honour, both to **g** and small.	1419
	2:18	the king made a **g** feast unto all his princes	1419
	4: 3	*there was* **g** mourning among the Jews, and	1419
	8:15	*with* a **g** crown of gold, and *with* a garment	1419
	9: 4	For Mordecai *was* **g** in the king's house,	1419
	10: 3	**g** among the Jews, and accepted of	1419
Job	1: 3	hundred she asses, and a very **g** household;	7227
	1:19	there came a **g** wind from the wilderness,	1419
	2:13	for they saw that *his* grief was very **g**.	1431
	3:19	The small and **g** *are* there; and the servant	1419
	5: 9	Which doeth **g** *things* and unsearchable;	1419
	5:25	shalt know also that thy seed *shall be* **g**,	7227
	9:10	Which doeth **g** *things* past finding out; yea,	1419
	22: 5	*Is* not thy wickedness **g**? and	7227
	23: 6	Will he plead against me with *his* **g** power?	7230
	30:18	By the **g** force *of my disease* is my garment	7230
	31:25	If I rejoiced because my wealth *was* **g**, and	7227
	31:34	Did I fear a **g** multitude, or did	7227
	32: 9	**G men** are not *always* wise: neither do	7227
	35:15	yet he knoweth *it* not in **g** extremity:	3966
	36:18	then a **g** ransom cannot deliver thee.	7230
	36:26	Behold, God *is* **g**, and we know *him* not,	7689
	37: 5	**g** *things* doeth he, which we cannot	1419
	37: 6	small rain, and *to* the **g** rain of his strength.	4306
	38:21	or *because* the number of thy days *is* **g**?	7227
	39:11	thou trust him, because his strength *is* **g**?	7227
Ps	14: 5	There were they **in g fear**: for God *is*	6342+6343
	18:35	me up, and thy gentleness hath **made** me **g**.	7235
	18:50	**G** deliverance **giveth** he to his king; and	1431
	19:11	*and* in keeping of them *there is* **g** reward.	7227
	19:13	I shall be innocent from *the* **g** transgression.	7227
	21: 5	His glory *is* **g** in thy salvation: honour and	1419
	22:25	My praise *shall be* of thee in the **g**	7227
	25:11	O LORD, pardon mine iniquity; for it *is* **g**.	7227
	31:19	O how **g** *is* thy goodness, which thou hast	7227
	32: 6	surely in the floods of **g** waters they shall	7227
	33:17	neither shall he deliver *any* by his **g**	7230
	35:18	I will give thee thanks in the **g**	7227
	36: 6	Thy righteousness *is* like the **g** mountains;	410
	36: 6	thy judgments *are* a **g** deep:	7227
	37:35	I have seen the wicked in **g power**, and	6184
	40: 9	I have preached righteousness in the **g**	7227
	40:10	and thy truth from the **g** congregation.	7227
	47: 2	*is* terrible; *he is* a **g** King over all the earth.	1419
	48: 1	**G** *is* the LORD, and greatly to be praised	1419
	48: 2	sides of the north, the city of the **g** King.	7227
	53: 5	There were they **in g fear**, *where* no	6342+6343
	57:10	For thy mercy *is* **g** unto the heavens, and	1419
	58: 6	break out the **g teeth** of the young lions,	4459
	68:11	**g** *was* the company of those that published	7227
	71:19	very high, who hast done **g** *things:* O God,	1419
	71:20	*Thou,* which hast shewed me **g** and	7227
	76: 1	*is* God known: his name *is* **g** in Israel.	1419
	77:13	who *is so* **g** a God as *our* God?	1419
	77:19	thy path in the **g** waters, and thy footsteps	7227
	78:15	and gave *them* drink as *out of* the **g** depths.	7227
	78:71	From following the *ewes* **g with young** he	5763
	80: 5	and givest them tears to drink *in g* measure.	NIH
	86:10	For thou *art* **g**, and doest wondrous *things:*	1419
	86:13	For **g** *is* thy mercy toward me: and	1419
	92: 5	O LORD, how **g** are thy works! *and*	1431
	95: 3	For the LORD *is* a **g** God, and a great	1419
	95: 3	*is* a great God, and a **g** King above all gods.	1419
	96: 4	For the LORD *is* **g**, and greatly to be	1419
	99: 2	The LORD *is* **g** in Zion; and he *is* high	1419
	99: 3	Let them praise thy **g** and terrible name;	1419

Ps 103:11 **g** is his mercy toward them that fear him. 1396
104: 1 O LORD my God, thou art very **g**; 1431
104:25 *So is* this **g** and wide sea, wherein *are* 1419
104:25 both small and **g** beasts. 1419
106:21 which had done **g** *things* in Egypt; 1419
107:23 sea in ships, that do business in **g** waters; 7227
108: 4 For thy mercy *is* **g** above the heavens: and 1419
111: 2 The works of the LORD *are* **g**, sought out 1419
115:13 that fear the LORD, *both* small and **g**. 1419
117: 2 For his merciful kindness is **g** toward us: 1396
119:156 **G** *are* thy tender mercies, O LORD: 7227
119:162 at thy word, as one that findeth **g** spoil. 7227
119:165 **G** peace have they which love thy law: and 7227
126: 2 The LORD hath done **g** things for them. 1431
126: 3 The LORD hath done **g** things for us; 1431
131: 1 neither do I exercise myself in **g** *matters,* or 1419
135: 5 For I know that the LORD *is* **g**, and 1419
135:10 Who smote **g** nations, and slew mighty 7227
136: 4 To him who alone doeth **g** wonders: for his 1419
136: 7 To him that made **g** lights: for his mercy 1419
136:17 To him which smote **g** kings: for his mercy 1419
138: 5 for **g** *is* the glory of the LORD. 1419
139:17 unto me, O God: how **g** is the sum of them! 6105
144: 7 rid me, and deliver me out of **g** waters, 7227
145: 3 **G** *is* the LORD, and greatly to be praised; 1419
145: 7 utter the memory of thy **g** goodness, 7227
145: 8 slow to anger, and of **g** mercy. 1419
147: 5 **G** *is* our Lord, and of great power: 1419
147: 5 Great *is* our Lord, and of **g** power: 7227
Pr 13: 7 that maketh himself poor, yet *hath* **g** riches. 7227
14:29 *He that is* slow to wrath *is* of **g** 7227
15:16 with the fear of the LORD than **g** treasure 7227
16: 8 Better *is* a little with righteousness than **g** 7230
18: 9 work *is* brother to **him that is** a **g** waster. 1167
18:16 for him, and bringeth him before **g** *men.* 1419
19:19 *A man* of **g** wrath *shall* suffer punishment: 1419
22: 1 A *good* name *is* rather to be chosen than **g** 7227
25: 6 and stand not in the place of **g** *men:* 1419
26:10 The **g** *God* that formed all *things* both 7227
28:12 righteous *men* do rejoice, *there is* **g** glory: 7227
28:16 understanding *is* also a **g** oppressor: 7227
Ecc 1:16 Lo, I am **come to g estate**, and have gotten 1431
1:16 my heart had **g** experience of wisdom and 7235
2: 4 I **made** me **g** works; I builded me houses; 1431
2: 7 also I had **g** possessions of great and 7235
2: 7 had great possessions of **g** and small **cattle** 1241
2: 9 So I was **g**, and increased more than all that 1431
2:21 his portion. This also *is* vanity and a **g** evil. 7227
8: 6 therefore the misery of man *is* **g** upon him. 7227
9:13 under the sun, and it *seemed* **g** unto me: 1419
9:14 there came a **g** king against it, and 1419
9:14 besieged it, and built **g** bulwarks against it: 1419
10: 4 thy place; for yielding pacifieth **g** offences. 1419
10: 6 Folly is set in **g** dignity, and the rich sit in 7227
SS 2: 3 sat down under his shadow **with g delight**, 2530
Isa 2: 9 and the **g** man humbleth himself; NIH
5: 9 *even* **g** and fair, without inhabitant. 1419
6:12 *there be* a **g** forsaking in the midst of 7227
8: 1 Take thee a **g** roll, and write in it with a 1419
9: 2 that walked in darkness have seen a **g** light: 1419
12: 6 for **g** *is* the Holy One of Israel in the midst 1419
13: 4 in the mountains, like as of a **g** people; 7227
16:14 be contemned, with all *that* **g** multitude; 7227
19:20 and a **g one**, and he shall deliver them. 7227
23: 3 by **g** waters the seed of Sihor, the harvest of 7227
27: 1 day the LORD with his sore and **g** and 1419
27:13 *that* the **g** trumpet shall be blown, and 1419
29: 6 **g** noise, *with* storm and tempest, and 1419
30:25 streams of waters in the day of the **g** 7227
32: 2 as the shadow of a **g** rock in a weary land. 3515
33:23 is the prey of a **g** spoil divided; the lame 4766
34: 6 and a **g** slaughter in the land of Idumea. 1419
34:15 There shall the **g owl** make her nest, and 7091
36: 2 unto king Hezekiah with a **g** army. 3515
36: 4 Thus saith the **g** king, the king of Assyria, 1419
36:13 said, Hear ye the words of the **g** king, 1419
38:17 Behold, for peace I had **g bitterness**: 4751+4843
47: 9 for the **g** abundance of thine enchantments. 3966
51:10 hath dried the sea, the waters of the **g** deep; 7227
53:12 will I divide him *a portion* with the **g**, 7227
54: 7 but with **g** mercies will I gather thee. 1419
54:13 and **g** *shall be* the peace of thy children. 7227
63: 7 the **g** goodness towards the house of Israel, 7227
Jer 4: 6 evil from the north, and a **g** destruction. 1419
5: 5 I will get me unto the **g men**, and 1419
5:27 therefore they are become **g**, and 1431
6: 1 out of the north, and **g** destruction. 1419
6:22 a **g** nation shall be raised from the sides of 1419
10: 6 thou *art* **g**, and thy name *is* great in might. 1419
10: 6 thou *art* great, and thy name *is* **g** in might. 1419
10:22 a **g** commotion out of the north country, 1419
11:16 with the noise of a **g** tumult he hath kindled 1419
13: 9 of Judah, and the **g** pride of Jerusalem. 7227
14:17 of my people is broken *with* a **g** breach, 1419
16: 6 Both the **g** and the small shall die in this 1419
16:10 pronounced all this **g** evil against us? 1419
20:17 and her womb *to be* always **g** *with me.* 2030
21: 5 even in anger, and in fury, and in **g** wrath. 1419
21: 6 and beast: they shall die of a **g** pestilence. 1419
22: 8 hath the LORD done thus unto this **g** city? 1419
25:14 **g** kings shall serve themselves of them also: 1419
25:32 a **g** whirlwind shall be raised up from 1419
26:19 Thus *might* we procure **g** evil against our 1419
27: 5 by my **g** power and by my outstretched 1419
27: 7 and **g** kings shall serve themselves of him. 1419
28: 8 and against **g** kingdoms, of war, and of evil, 1419
30: 7 for that day *is* **g**, so that none *is* like it: it *is* 1419
31: 8 a **g** company shall return thither. 1419
32:17 the earth by thy **g** power and stretched out 1419
32:18 the **G**, the Mighty God, the LORD of 1419
32:19 **G** in counsel, and mighty in work: for thine 1419
32:21 with a stretched out arm, and with **g** terror; 1419
32:37 mine anger, and in my fury, and in **g** wrath; 1419
32:42 Like as I have brought all this **g** evil upon 1419
33: 3 shew thee **g** and mighty *things,* which thou 1419
36: 7 for **g** *is* the anger and the fury that 1419
41:12 found him by the **g** waters that *are* in 7227
43: 9 Take **g** stones in thine hand, and hide them 1419
44: 7 Wherefore commit ye *this* **g** evil against 1419
44:15 all the women that stood *by,* a **g** multitude, 1419
44:26 Behold, I have sworn by my **g** name, 1419
45: 5 seekest thou **g** *things* for thyself? seek *them* 1419
48: 3 from Horonaim, spoiling and **g** destruction. 1419
50: 9 of **g** nations from the north country: 1419
50:22 of battle *is* in the land, and of **g** destruction. 1419
50:41 a **g** nation, and many kings shall be raised 1419
51:54 **g** destruction from the land of 1419
51:55 and destroyed out of her the **g** voice; 1419
51:55 when her waves do roar like **g** waters, 7227
52:13 all the houses of the **g** *men,* burnt he with 1419
La 1: 1 she *that was* **g** among the nations, *and* 7227
1: 3 of affliction, and because of **g** servitude: 7230
2:13 for thy breach *is* **g** like the sea: who can 1419
3:23 new every morning: **g** *is* thy faithfulness. 7227
Eze 1: 4 a **g** cloud, and a fire infolding itself, and 1419
1:24 like the noise of **g** waters, as the voice of 7227
3:12 I heard behind me a voice of a **g** rushing, 1419
3:13 against them, and a noise of a **g** rushing. 1419
8: 6 *even* the **g** abominations that the house of 1419
9: 9 house of Israel and Judah *is* exceeding **g**, 1419
13:11 ye, O **g hailstones**, shall fall; and 68+417
13:13 **g hailstones** in *my* fury to consume *it.* 68+417
16: 7 thou hast increased and **waxen g**, and 1431
16:26 the Egyptians thy neighbours, **g** of flesh; 1432
17: 3 A **g** eagle with great wings, longwinged, 1419
17: 3 A great eagle with **g** wings, longwinged, 1419
17: 5 he placed *it* by **g** waters, *and* set it *as* a 7227
17: 7 There was also another **g** eagle with great 1419
17: 7 There was also another great eagle with **g** 1419
17: 8 It *was* planted in a good soil by **g** waters, 7227
17: 9 even without **g** power or many people to 1419
17:17 and **g** company make for him in the war, 7227
21:14 it *is* the sword of the **g** *men that are* slain, 1419
23:23 captains and rulers, **g lords** and renowned, 7991
24: 9 I will even **make** the pile for fire **g**. 1431
24:12 and her **g** scum went not forth out of her: 7227
25:17 I will execute **g** vengeance upon them with 1419
26:19 upon thee, and **g** waters shall cover thee; 7227
27:26 Thy rowers have brought thee into **g** 7227
28: 5 By thy **g** wisdom *and* by thy traffick hast 7230
29: 3 the **g** dragon that lieth in the midst of his 1419
29:18 his army to serve a **g** service against Tyrus: 1419
30: 4 **g pain** shall be in Ethiopia, when the slain 2479
30: 9 **g pain** shall come upon them, as *in* the day 2479
30:16 Sin shall **have g pain**, and No shall 2342+2342
31: 4 The waters **made** him **g**, the deep set him 1431
31: 6 and under his shadow dwelt all **g** nations. 7227
31: 7 his branches: for his root was by **g** waters. 7227

Eze 31:15 and the **g** waters were stayed: 7227
32:13 beasts thereof from besides the **g** waters; 7227
36:23 I will sanctify my **g** name, which was 1419
37:10 up upon their feet, an exceeding **g** army. 1419
38: 4 *of armour, even* a **g** company *with* bucklers 7227
38:13 *away* cattle and goods, to take a **g** spoil? 1419
38:15 a **g** company, and a mighty army: 1419
38:19 Surely in that day there shall be a **g** shaking 1419
38:22 and **g hailstones**, fire, and brimstone. 68+417
39:17 *even* a **g** sacrifice upon the mountains of 1419
41: 8 chambers *were* a full reed of six **g** cubits. 679
47: 9 there shall be a very **g multitude** of fish, 7227
47:10 as the fish of the **g** sea, exceeding many. 1419
47:15 from the **g** sea, the way of Hethlon, as *men* 1419
47:19 of strife *in* Kadesh, *the* river to the **g** sea. 1419
47:20 The west side also *shall be* the **g** sea from 1419
48:28 *and to the* river toward the **g** sea. 1419
Da 2: 6 of me gifts and rewards and **g** honour: 7690
2:31 O king, sawest, and behold a **g** image. 7690
2:31 This **g** image, whose brightness *was* 7229
2:35 the stone that smote the image became a **g** 7229
2:45 the **g** God hath made known to the king 7229
2:48 the king **made** Daniel a **g** man, and 7236
2:48 gave him many **g** gifts, and made him ruler 7260
4: 3 How **g** *are* his signs! and how mighty *are* 7260
4:10 of the earth, and the height thereof *was* **g**. 7690
4:30 king spake, and said, *Is* not this **g** Babylon, 7229
5: 1 Belshazzar the king made a **g** feast to a 7229
7: 2 winds of the heaven strove upon the **g** sea. 7229
7: 3 four **g** beasts came up from the sea, 7260
7: 7 strong exceedingly; and it had **g** iron teeth: 7260
7: 8 of man, and a mouth speaking **g** *things*. 7260
7:11 of the voice of the **g** words which the horn 7260
7:17 These **g** beasts, which *are* four, *are* four 7260
7:20 a mouth that spake **very g** *things*, whose 7229
7:25 he shall speak *g* words against the most NIH
8: 4 he did according to his will, and became **g**. 1431
8: 8 Therefore the he goat **waxed** very **g**: and 1431
8: 8 when he was strong, the **g** horn was broken; 1419
8: 9 which waxed exceeding **g**, toward 1431
8:10 And it **waxed g**, *even* to the host of heaven; 1431
8:21 the **g** horn that *is* between his eyes *is* 1419
9: 4 and said, O Lord, the **g** and dreadful God, 1419
9:12 judged us, by bringing upon us a **g** evil: 1419
9:18 our righteousnesses, but for thy **g** mercies. 7227
10: 4 as I was by the side of the **g** river, which *is* 1419
10: 7 a **g** quaking fell upon them, so that they 1419
10: 8 saw this **g** vision, and there remained no 1419
11: 3 that shall rule *with* **g** dominion, and 7227
11: 5 his dominion *shall be* a **g** dominion. 7227
11:10 and shall assemble a multitude of **g** forces: 7227
11:11 he shall set forth a **g** multitude; but 7227
11:13 come after certain years with a **g** army 1419
11:25 against the king of the south with a **g** army; 1419
11:25 shall be stirred up to battle with a very **g** 1419
11:28 shall he return *into* his land with **g** riches; 1419
11:44 he shall go forth with **g** fury to destroy, 1419
12: 1 the **g** prince which standeth for the children 1419
Hos 1: 2 land hath **committed g whoredom**, 2181+2181
1:11 of the land: for **g** *shall be* the day of Jezreel. 1419
8:12 I have written to him the **g things** of my 7230
9: 7 of thine iniquity, and the **g** hatred. 7227
10:15 because of your **g wickedness**; 7451+7465
13: 5 in the wilderness, in the land of **g drought**. 8514
Joel 1: 6 and he hath the cheek-teeth of a **g lion**. 3833
2: 2 a **g** people and a strong; there hath not been 7227
2:11 for his camp *is* very **g**: for *he is* strong that 7227
2:11 for the day of the LORD *is* **g** and 1419
2:13 of **g** kindness, and repenteth him of 7227
2:20 come up, because he hath done **g things**. 1431
2:21 rejoice: for the LORD will do **g things**. 1431
2:25 my **g** army which I sent among you. 1419
2:31 before the **g** and the terrible day of 1419
3:13 the fats overflow; for their wickedness *is* **g**. 7227
Am 3: 9 behold the **g** tumults in the midst thereof, 7227
3:15 the **g** houses shall have an end, saith 7227
6: 2 and from thence go ye *to* Hamath the **g**: 7227
6:11 he will smite the **g** house *with* breaches, 1419
7: 4 it devoured the **g** deep, and did eat up a 7227
8: 5 the shekel **g**, and falsifying the balances by 1431
Jnh 1: 2 to Nineveh, *that* **g** city, and cry against it; 1419
1: 4 the LORD sent out a **g** wind into the sea, 1419
1:12 for I know that for my sake this **g** tempest 1419
1:17 Now the LORD had prepared a **g** fish to 1419
3: 2 *that* **g** city, and preach unto it the preaching 1419
3: 3 Now Nineveh was an exceeding **g** city of 1419
4: 2 of **g** kindness, and repentest thee of 7227
4:11 And should not I spare Nineveh, *that* **g** city, 1419
Mic 2:12 they shall **make** a **g noise** by reason of 1949
5: 4 for now shall he be **g** unto the ends of 1431
7: 3 the **g** *man*, he uttereth his mischievous 1419
Na 1: 3 **g** in power, and will not at all acquit 1419
3: 3 of slain, and a **g number** of carcases; 3514
3:10 and all her **g** *men* were bound in chains. 1419
3:17 thy captains as the **g grasshoppers**, 1462+1462
Hab 3:15 thine horses, *through* the heap of **g** waters. 7227
Zep 1:10 the second, and a **g** crashing from the hills. 1419
1:14 The **g** day of the LORD *is* near, *it is* near, 1419
Zec 1:14 and for Zion *with* a **g** jealousy. 1419
4: 7 Who *art* thou, O **g** mountain? 1419
7:12 came a **g** wrath from the LORD of hosts. 1419
8: 2 I was jealous for Zion *with* **g** jealousy, and 1419
8: 2 and I was jealous for her *with* **g** fury. 1419
9:17 For **how g** *is* his goodness, and how great *is* 4100
9:17 *is* his goodness, and **how g** *is* his beauty! 4100
12:11 In that day shall there be a **g** mourning in 1431
14: 4 the west, *and there shall be* a very **g** valley; 1419
14:13 *that* a **g** tumult from the LORD shall be 7227
14:14 and silver, and apparel, in **g** abundance. 3966
Mal 1:11 my name *shall be* **g** among the Gentiles; 1419
1:11 for my name *shall be* **g** among the heathen, 1419
1:14 the Lord a corrupt *thing*: for I *am* a **g** King, 1419
4: 5 the prophet before the coming of the **g** 1419
Mt 2:10 the star, they rejoiced *with* exceeding **g** joy. *3173*
2:18 lamentation, and weeping, and **g** mourning, *4183*
4:16 The people which sat in darkness saw **g** *3173*
4:25 And there followed him **g** multitudes *of* *4183*
5:12 for **g** *is* your reward in heaven: for so *4183*
5:19 teach *them*, the same shall be called **g** in *3173*
5:35 for it is the city of the **g** King. *3173*
6:23 in thee be darkness, **how g** *is* that darkness? *4214*
7:27 and it fell: and **g** was the fall of it. *3173*
8: 1 the mountain, **g** multitudes followed him. *4183*
8:10 I have not found **so g** faith, no not in Israel. *5118*
8:18 Now when Jesus saw **g** multitudes about *4183*
8:24 there arose a **g** tempest in the sea, *3173*
8:26 and the sea; and there was a **g** calm. *3173*
12:15 and **g** multitudes followed him, and *4183*
13: 2 And **g** multitudes were gathered together *4183*
13:46 when he had found one pearl of **g price**, *4186*
14:14 and saw a **g** multitude, and was moved with *4183*
15:28 and said unto her, O woman, **g** *is* thy faith: *3173*
15:30 And **g** multitudes came unto him, *4183*
15:33 the wilderness, as to fill **so g** a multitude? *5118*
19: 2 And **g** multitudes followed him; and *4183*
19:22 away sorrowful: for he had **g** possessions. *4183*
20:25 they *that are* **g** exercise authority upon *3173*
20:26 but whosoever will be **g** among you, *3173*
20:29 from Jericho, a **g** multitude followed him. *4183*
21: 8 And a **very g** multitude spread their *4183*
22:36 which *is* the **g** commandment in the law? *3173*
22:38 This is the first and **g** commandment. *3173*
24:21 For then shall be **g** tribulation, such as was *3173*
24:24 and shall shew **g** signs and wonders; *3173*
24:30 clouds of heaven with power and **g** glory. *4183*
24:31 And he shall send his angels with a **g** sound *3173*
26:47 with him a **g** multitude with swords and *4183*
27:60 he rolled a **g** stone to the door of *3173*
28: 2 And behold, there was a **g** earthquake: *3173*
28: 8 from the sepulchre with fear and **g** joy; *3173*
Mk 1:35 rising up a **g while** before day, he went out, *3029*
3: 7 a **g** multitude from Galilee followed him, *4183*
3: 8 they about Tyre and Sidon, a **g** multitude, *4183*
3: 8 when they had heard **what g** *things* he did, *3745*
4: 1 there was gathered unto him a **g** multitude, *4183*
4:32 than all herbs, and shooteth out **g** branches; *3173*
4:37 And there arose a **g** storm of wind, and *3173*
4:39 the wind ceased, and there was a **g** calm. *3173*
5:11 the mountains a **g** herd of swine feeding. *3173*
5:19 tell them **how g** *things* the Lord hath done *3745*
5:20 began to publish in Decapolis **how g** *things* *3745*
5:42 And they were astonished with a **g** *3173*
7:36 much the more a **g deal** they published *it*; *4054*
8: 1 In those days the multitude being **very g**, *3827*
9:14 he saw a **g** multitude about them, and *4183*
10:22 away grieved: for he had **g** possessions. *4183*
10:42 their **g ones** exercise authority upon them. *3173*
10:43 but whosoever will be **g** among you, *3173*

Mk	10:46	his disciples and a **g number** of people,	*2425*
	10:48	but he cried the more a **g deal**, *Thou* Son of	*4183*
	13: 2	said unto him, Seest thou these **g** buildings?	*3173*
	13:26	of man coming in *the* clouds with **g** power	*4183*
	14:43	with him a **g** multitude with swords and	*4183*
	16: 4	stone was rolled away: for it was very **g**.	*3173*
Lk	1:15	For he shall be **g** in the sight of the Lord,	*3173*
	1:32	He shall be **g**, and shall be called the Son of	*3173*
	1:49	he *that is* mighty hath done to me **g things**;	*3167*
	1:58	the Lord had **shewed g** mercy upon her;	*3170*
	2: 5	his espoused wife, being **g with child**.	*1471*
	2:10	I bring you good tidings of **g** joy,	*3173*
	2:36	of the tribe of Aser: she was of a **g** age,	*4183*
	4:25	when **g** famine was throughout all the land;	*3173*
	4:38	wife's mother was taken with a **g** fever;	*3173*
	5: 6	they inclosed a **g** multitude of fishes:	*4183*
	5:15	and **g** multitudes came together to hear, and	*4183*
	5:29	And Levi made him a **g** feast in his own	*3173*
	5:29	there was a **g** company of publicans and	*4183*
	6:17	a **g** multitude of people out of all Judea and	*4183*
	6:23	*joy:* for behold, your reward *is* **g** in heaven:	*4183*
	6:35	and your reward shall be **g**, and ye shall be	*4183*
	6:49	it fell; and the ruin of that house was **g**.	*3173*
	7: 9	I have not found **so g** faith, no, not in Israel.	*5118*
	7:16	That a **g** prophet is risen up among us;	*3173*
	8:37	from them; for they were taken with **g** fear:	*3173*
	8:39	shew **how g** *things* God hath done unto	*3745*
	8:39	published throughout the whole city **how g**	*3745*
	9:48	is least among you all, the same shall be **g**.	*3173*
	10: 2	The harvest truly *is* **g**, but the labourers *are*	*4183*
	10:13	they had a **g while ago** repented, sitting in	*3819*
	13:19	and it grew, and waxed a **g** tree; and	*3173*
	14:16	A certain man made a **g** supper, and	*3173*
	14:25	And there went **g** multitudes with him: and	*4183*
	14:32	Or else, while the other is yet a **g way off**,	*4206*
	15:20	But when he was yet a **g way** off, his father	*3112*
	16:26	between us and you there is a **g** gulf fixed:	*3173*
	21:11	And **g** earthquakes shall be in divers places,	*3173*
	21:11	and **g** signs shall there be from heaven.	*3173*
	21:23	for there shall be **g** distress in the land, and	*3173*
	21:27	coming in a cloud with power and **g** glory.	*4183*
	22:44	his sweat was as it were **g** drops of blood	NIG
	23:27	And there followed him a **g** company of	*4183*
	24:52	and returned to Jerusalem with **g** joy:	*3173*
Jn	5: 3	In these lay a **g** multitude of impotent *folk*,	*4183*
	6: 2	And a **g** multitude followed him, because	*4183*
	6: 5	and saw a **g** company come unto him,	*4183*
	6:18	And the sea arose by reason of a **g** wind	*3173*
	7:37	*that* **g** *day* of the feast, Jesus stood and	*3173*
	21:11	and drew the net to land full of **g** fishes,	*3173*
Ac	2:20	before *that* **g** and notable day of the Lord	*3173*
	4:33	And with **g** power gave the apostles witness	*3173*
	4:33	Lord Jesus: and **g** grace was upon them all.	*3173*
	5: 5	**g** fear came on all them that heard these	*3173*
	5:11	And **g** fear came upon all the church, and	*3173*
	6: 7	a **g** company of the priests were obedient to	*4183*
	6: 8	did **g** wonders and miracles among	*3173*
	7:11	land of Egypt and Canaan, and **g** affliction:	*3173*
	8: 1	And at that time there was a **g** persecution	*3173*
	8: 2	and made **g** lamentation over him.	*3173*
	8: 8	And there was **g** joy in that city.	*3173*
	8: 9	giving out that himself was some **g one**:	*3173*
	8:10	saying, This *man* is the **g** power of God.	*3173*
	8:27	an eunuch **of g authority** under Candace	*1413*
	9:16	For I will shew him **how g** *things* he must	*3745*
	10:11	as *it had been* a **g** sheet knit at the four	*3173*
	11: 5	vessel descend, as *it had been* a **g** sheet,	*3173*
	11:21	and a **g** number believed, and turned unto	*4183*
	11:28	signified by the Spirit that there should be **g**	*3173*
	14: 1	that a **g** multitude both of the Jews and	*4183*
	15: 3	and they caused **g** joy unto all the brethren.	*3173*
	16:26	And suddenly there was a **g** earthquake, so	*3173*
	17: 4	and of the devout Greeks a **g** multitude, and	*4183*
	19:27	also that the temple of the **g** goddess Diana	*3173*
	19:28	saying, **G** *is* Diana of the Ephesians.	*3173*
	19:34	cried out, **G** *is* Diana of the Ephesians.	*3173*
	19:35	is a worshipper of the **g** goddess Diana,	*3173*
	21:40	And when there was made a **g** silence,	*4183*
	22: 6	suddenly there shone from heaven a **g** light	*2425*
	22:28	With a **g** sum obtained I this freedom.	*4183*
	23: 9	And there arose a **g** cry: and the scribes *that*	*3173*
	23:10	And when there arose a **g** dissension,	*4183*
	23:14	have **bound** ourselves **under a g curse**,	*331+332*
	24: 2	Seeing that by thee we enjoy **g** quietness,	*4183*
	24: 7	with **g** violence took *him* away out of our	*4183*
	25:23	with **g** pomp, and were entered into	*4183*
	26:22	this day, witnessing both to small and **g**,	*3173*
	28: 6	but after they had looked **a g while**,	*1909+4183*
	28:29	and had **g** reasoning among themselves.	*4183*
Ro	9: 2	That I have **g** heaviness and	*3173*
	15:23	having a **g desire** these many years to come	*1974*
1Co	9:11	**g** *thing* if we shall reap your carnal *things?*	*3173*
	16: 9	For a **g** door and effectual is opened unto	*3173*
2Co	1:10	Who delivered us from **so g** a death, and	*5082*
	3:12	such hope, we use **g** plainness of speech:	*4183*
	7: 4	**G** *is* my boldness of speech toward you,	*4183*
	7: 4	toward you, **g** *is* my glorying of you:	*4183*
	8: 2	How that in a **g** trial of affliction	*4183*
	8:22	upon the **g** confidence which *I have* in you.	*4183*
	11:15	Therefore *it is* no **g** *thing* if his ministers	*3173*
Eph	2: 4	for his **g** love wherewith he loved us,	*4183*
	5:32	This is a **g** mystery: but I speak concerning	*3173*
Col	2: 1	For I would that ye knew **what g** conflict I	*2245*
	4:13	that he hath a **g** zeal for you, and them that	*4183*
1Th	2:17	abundantly to see your face with **g** desire.	*4183*
1Ti	3:13	**g** boldness in the faith which is in Christ	*4183*
	3:16	And without controversy **g** is the mystery	*3173*
	6: 6	But godliness with contentment is **g** gain.	*3173*
2Ti	2:20	But in a **g** house there are not only vessels	*3173*
Tit	2:13	the glorious appearing of the **g** God and	*3173*
Phm	1: 7	For we have **g** joy and consolation in thy	*4183*
Heb	2: 3	we escape, if we neglect so **g** salvation;	*5082*
	4:14	Seeing then that we have a **g** high priest,	*3173*
	7: 4	Now consider **how g** this *man was,* unto	*4080*
	10:32	ye endured a **g** fight of afflictions;	*4183*
	10:35	which hath **g** recompence of reward.	*3173*
	12: 1	about with **so g** a cloud of witnesses,	*5118*
	13:20	*that* **g** shepherd of the sheep, through	*3173*
Jas	3: 4	which though they be **so g**, and are driven	*5082*
	3: 5	is a little member, and boasteth **g things**.	*3173*
	3: 5	**how g** a matter a little fire kindleth.	*2245*
1Pe	3: 4	which is in the sight of God of **g price**.	*4185*
2Pe	1: 4	Whereby are given unto us **exceeding g**	*3176*
	2:18	For when they speak **g swelling** *words* of	*5246*
	3:10	the heavens shall pass away with a **g noise**,	*4500*
Jude	1: 6	darkness unto the judgment of the **g** day.	*3173*
	1:16	their mouth speaketh **g swelling** *words,*	*5246*
Rev	1:10	and heard behind me a **g** voice, as of a	*3173*
	2:22	them that commit adultery with her into **g**	*3173*
	6: 4	and there was given unto him a **g** sword.	*3173*
	6:12	sixth seal, and lo, there was a **g** earthquake;	*3173*
	6:15	and the **g men**, and the rich *men,* and	*3175*
	6:17	For the **g** day of his wrath is come; and	*3173*
	7: 9	After this I beheld, and lo, a **g** multitude,	*4183*
	7:14	These are they which came out of **g**	*3173*
	8: 8	as *it were* a **g** mountain burning with fire	*3173*
	8:10	and there fell a **g** star from heaven,	*3173*
	9: 2	out of the pit, as the smoke of a **g** furnace;	*3173*
	9:14	which are bound in the **g** river Euphrates.	*3173*
	11: 8	bodies *shall lie* in the street of the **g** city,	*3173*
	11:11	and **g** fear fell upon them which saw them.	*3173*
	11:12	And they heard a **g** voice from heaven	*3173*
	11:13	And the same hour was there a **g**	*3173*
	11:15	and there were **g** voices in heaven, saying,	*3173*
	11:17	thou hast taken *to thee* thy **g** power,	*3173*
	11:18	and them that fear thy name, small and **g**;	*3173*
	11:19	thunderings, and an earthquake, and **g** hail.	*3173*
	12: 1	And there appeared a **g** wonder in heaven;	*3173*
	12: 3	and behold a **g** red dragon, having seven	*3173*
	12: 9	And the **g** dragon was cast *out, that* old	*3173*
	12:12	having **g** wrath, because he knoweth that he	*3173*
	12:14	woman were given two wings of a **g** eagle,	*3173*
	13: 2	his power, and his seat, and **g** authority.	*3173*
	13: 5	given unto him a mouth speaking **g** *things*	*3173*
	13:13	And he doeth **g** wonders, so that he maketh	*3173*
	13:16	*both* small and **g**, rich and poor, free and	*3173*
	14: 2	and as the voice of a **g** thunder:	*3173*
	14: 8	Babylon is fallen, is fallen, *that* **g** city,	*3173*
	14:19	cast *it* into the **g** winepress of the wrath of	*3173*
	15: 1	another sign in heaven, **g** and marvellous,	*3173*
	15: 3	saying, **G** and marvellous *are* thy works,	*3173*
	16: 1	And I heard a **g** voice out of the temple	*3173*
	16: 9	And men were scorched *with* **g** heat, and	*3173*
	16:12	out his vial upon the **g** river Euphrates;	*3173*
	16:14	to gather them to the battle of that **g** day of	*3173*
	16:17	there came a **g** voice out of the temple of	*3173*
	16:18	and there was a **g** earthquake, such as was	*3173*
	16:18	so mighty an earthquake, *and* so **g**.	*3173*

Rev 16:19 And the **g** city was *divided* into three parts, *3173*
16:19 **g** Babylon came in remembrance before *3173*
16:21 And there fell upon men a **g** hail out of *3173*
16:21 for the plague thereof was exceeding **g**. *3173*
17: 1 I will shew unto thee the judgment of the **g** *3173*
17: 5 MYSTERY, BABYLON THE **G**, *3173*
17: 6 I saw her, I wondered *with* **g** admiration. *3173*
17:18 And the woman which thou sawest is *that* **g** *3173*
18: 1 come down from heaven, having **g** power; *3173*
18: 2 saying, Babylon the **g** is fallen, is fallen, *3173*
18:10 saying, Alas, alas, *that* **g** city Babylon, *3173*
18:16 And saying, Alas, alas, *that* **g** city, that was *3173*
18:17 in one hour **so g** riches is come to nought. *5118*
18:18 saying, What *city is* like unto *this* **g** city? *3173*
18:19 and wailing, saying, Alas, alas, *that* **g** city, *3173*
18:21 And a mighty angel took up a stone like a **g** *3173*
18:21 Thus with violence shall *that* **g** city *3173*
18:23 for thy merchants were the **g men** of *3175*
19: 1 And after these *things* I heard a **g** voice of *3173*
19: 2 for he hath judged the **g** whore, which did *3173*
19: 5 and ye that fear him, both small and **g**. *3173*
19: 6 And I heard as *it were* the voice of a **g** *4183*
19:17 together unto the supper of the **g** God; *3173*
19:18 *men,* both free and bond, both small and **g**. *3173*
20: 1 the bottomless *pit* and a **g** chain in his hand. *3173*
20:11 And I saw a **g** white throne, and him that *3173*
20:12 the dead, small and **g**, stand before God; *3173*
21: 3 And I heard a **g** voice out of heaven saying, *3173*
21:10 And he carried me away in the spirit to a **g** *3173*
21:10 high mountain, and shewed me *that* **g** city, *3173*
21:12 And had a wall **g** and high, and had twelve *3173*

GREATER (77) [GREAT]

Ge 1:16 the **g** light to rule the day, and the lesser 1419
4:13 My punishment *is* **g** than *I* can bear. 1419
39: 9 *There is* none **g** in this house than I; neither 1419
41:40 only *in* the throne will I be **g** than thou. 1431
48:19 truly his younger brother shall be **g** than he, 1431
Ex 18:11 Now I know that the LORD *is* **g** than all 1419
Nu 14:12 will make of thee a **g** nation and 1419
Dt 1:28 The people *is* **g** and taller than we; 1419
4:38 To drive out nations from before thee **g** and 1419
7: 1 seven nations **g** and mightier than thou; 7227
9: 1 to go in to possess nations **g** and 1419
9:14 of thee a nation mightier and **g** than they. 7227
11:23 ye shall possess **g** nations and mightier than 1419
Jos 10: 2 because it *was* **g** than Ai, and all the men 1419
1Sa 14:30 for had there not been now a **much g** 7235
2Sa 13:15 **g** than the love wherewith he had loved her. 1419
13:16 this evil in sending me away *is* **g** than 1419
1Ki 1:37 **make** his throne **g** than the throne of my 1431
1:47 and **make** his throne **g** than thy throne. 1431
1Ch 11: 9 So David **waxed g** and greater: 1980+1980
11: 9 So David waxed greater and **g**: for 1419
2Ch 3: 5 the **g** house he cieled with fir tree, which he 1419
Est 9: 4 for *this* man Mordecai **waxed g** and 1980
9: 4 for *this* man Mordecai waxed greater and **g**. 1419
Job 33:12 I will answer thee, that God is **g** than man. 7235
La 4: 6 **g** than the punishment of the sin of Sodom, 1431
Eze 8: 6 *and* thou shalt see **g** abominations. 1419
8:13 thou shalt see **g** abominations that they 1419
8:15 thou shalt see **g** abominations than these. 1419
43:14 from the lesser settle *even* to the **g** settle 1419
Da 11:13 shall set forth a multitude **g** than 7227
Am 6: 2 or their border **g** than your border? 7227
Hag 2: 9 The glory of this latter house shall be **g** 1419
Mt 11:11 hath not risen a **g than** John the Baptist: *3187*
11:11 in the kingdom of heaven is **g than** he. *3187*
12: 6 That in this place is *one* **g than** the temple. *3187*
12:41 and behold, a **g than** Jonas *is* here. *4183*
12:42 and behold, a **g than** Solomon *is* here. *4183*
23:14 therefore ye shall receive the **g** damnation. *4053*
23:17 for whether is **g**, the gold, or the temple that *3187*
23:19 for whether *is* **g**, the gift, or the altar that *3187*
Mk 4:32 and becometh **g than** all herbs, and *3187*
12:31 There is none other commandment **g than** *3187*
12:40 these shall receive **g** damnation. *4053*
Lk 7:28 is not a **g** prophet **than** John the Baptist: *3187*
7:28 is least in the kingdom of God is **g than** he. *3187*
11:31 and behold, a **g than** Solomon *is* here. *4183*
11:32 and behold, a **g than** Jonas *is* here. *4183*
12:18 I will pull down my barns, and build **g**; and *3187*
20:47 the same shall receive **g** damnation. *4054*
22:27 For whether *is* **g**, he that sitteth at meat, or *3187*
Jn 1:50 thou shalt see **g** *things* **than** these. *3187*
4:12 Art thou **g than** our father Jacob, *3187*
5:20 and he will shew him **g** works **than** these, *3187*
5:36 But I have **g** witness **than** *that of* John: *3187*
8:53 Art thou **g than** our father Abraham, *3187*
10:29 which gave *them* me, is **g than** all; *3187*
13:16 The servant is not **g than** his lord; *3187*
13:16 neither he that is sent **g than** he that sent *3187*
14:12 and **g** *works* **than** these shall he do; *3187*
14:28 unto the Father: for my Father is **g than** I. *3187*
15:13 **G** love hath no *man* **than** this, that a man *3187*
15:20 The servant is not **g than** his lord. *3187*
19:11 he that delivered me unto thee hath the **g** *3187*
Ac 15:28 to lay upon you no **g** burden than these *4183*
1Co 14: 5 for **g** *is* he that prophesieth than he that *3187*
15: 6 of whom the **g part** remain unto this *4183*
Heb 6:13 because he could swear by no **g**, he sware *3187*
6:16 For men verily swear by the **g**: and an oath *3187*
9:11 by a **g** and more perfect tabernacle, *3187*
11:26 Christ **g** riches **than** the treasures in Egypt: *3187*
Jas 3: 1 knowing that we shall receive the **g** *3187*
2Pe 2:11 which are **g** in power and might, *3187*
1Jn 3:20 God is **g than** our heart, and knoweth all *3187*
4: 4 because **g** is he that is in you, than he that is *3187*
5: 9 the witness of men, the witness of God is **g**: *3187*
3Jn 1: 4 I have no **g** joy **than** to hear that my *3186*

GREATEST (21) [GREAT]

1Ch 12:14 over an hundred, and the **g** over a thousand. 1419
12:29 for hitherto the **g part** of them had kept 4768
Job 1: 3 that this man was the **g** of all the men of 1419
Jer 6:13 For from the least of them even unto the **g** 1419
8:10 even unto the **g** is given to covetousness, 1419
31:34 from the least of them unto the **g** of them, 1419
42: 1 the people from the least even unto the **g**, 1419
42: 8 all the people from the least even to the **g**, 1419
44:12 from the least even unto the **g**, by the sword 1419
Jnh 3: 5 from the **g** of them even to the least of 1419
Mt 13:32 it is the **g** among herbs, and becometh a *3187*
18: 1 Who is the **g** in the kingdom of heaven? *3187*
18: 4 the same is **g** in the kingdom of heaven. *3187*
23:11 But he that is **g** among you shall be your *3187*
Mk 9:34 among themselves, who *should be* the **g**. *3187*
Lk 9:46 among them, which of them should be **g**. *3187*
22:24 which of them should be accounted the **g**. *3187*
22:26 but he that is **g** among you, let him be as *3187*
Ac 8:10 gave heed, from the least to the **g**, saying, *3173*
1Co 13:13 these three; but the **g** of these *is* charity. *3187*
Heb 8:11 all shall know me, from the least to the **g**. *3173*

GREATLY (87) [GREAT]

Ge 3:16 I will **g multiply** thy sorrow and 7235+7235
7:18 and were increased **g** upon the earth; 3966
19: 3 he pressed upon them **g**; and they turned in 3966
24:35 the LORD hath blessed my master **g**; and 3966
32: 7 Then Jacob was **g** afraid and distressed: and 3966
Ex 19:18 a furnace, and the whole mount quaked **g**. 3966
Nu 11:10 and the anger of the LORD was kindled **g**; 3966
14:39 of Israel: and the people mourned **g**. 3966
Dt 15: 4 for the LORD shall **g bless** thee in 1288+1288
17:17 neither shall he **g** multiply to himself silver 3966
Jos 10: 2 That they feared **g**, because Gibeon *was* a 3966
Jdg 2:15 unto them: and they were **g** distressed. 3966
6: 6 Israel was **g** impoverished because of 3966
1Sa 11: 6 those tidings, and his anger was kindled **g**. 3966
11:15 and all the men of Israel rejoiced **g**. 3966
12:18 all the people **g** feared the LORD and 3966
16:21 he loved him **g**; and he became his 3966
17:11 they were dismayed, and **g** afraid. 3966
28: 5 he was afraid, and his heart **g** trembled. 3966
30: 6 David was **g** distressed; for the people 3966
2Sa 10: 5 because the men were **g** ashamed: 3966
12: 5 David's anger was **g** kindled against 3966
24:10 I have sinned **g** *in* that I have done: 3966
1Ki 2:12 and his kingdom was established **g**. 3966
5: 7 that he rejoiced **g**, and said, Blessed *be* 3966
18: 3 (Now Obadiah feared the LORD **g**: 3966
1Ch 4:38 house of their fathers increased **g**. 7230+3807.1
16:25 great *is* the LORD, and **g** to be praised: 3966
19: 5 for the men were **g** ashamed. And the king 3966
21: 8 I have sinned **g**, because I have done this 3966
2Ch 25:10 their anger was **g** kindled against Judah, 3966
33:12 humbled himself **g** before the God of his 3966
Job 3:25 For the thing which I **g feared** is come 6343

G

Job 8: 7 yet thy latter end should **g** increase. 3966
Ps 21: 1 and in thy salvation how **g** shall he rejoice! 3966
28: 7 therefore my heart **g rejoiceth**; and 5937
38: 6 I am troubled; I am bowed down **g**; 3966+5704
45:11 So shall the king **g desire** thy beauty: for he 183
47: 9 the earth *belong* unto God: he is **g** exalted. 3966
48: 1 and **g** to be praised in the city of our God, 3966
62: 2 *he is* my defence; I shall not be **g** moved. 7227
65: 9 thou **g** enrichest it *with* the river of God, 7227
71:23 My lips shall **g rejoice** when I sing unto 7442
78:59 *this,* he was wroth, and **g** abhorred Israel: 3966
89: 7 God *is* **g** to be feared in the assembly of 7227
96: 4 the LORD *is* great, and **g** to be praised: 3966
105:24 he increased his people **g**; and made them 3966
107:38 them also, so that they are multiplied **g**; 3966
109:30 I will **g** praise the LORD with my mouth; 3966
112: 1 *that* delighteth **g** in his commandments. 3966
116:10 therefore have I spoken: I was **g** afflicted: 3966
119:51 The proud have had me **g** in derision: 3966+5704
145: 3 Great *is* the LORD, and **g** to be praised; 3966
Pr 23:24 of the righteous shall **g rejoice**: 1523+1524
Isa 42:17 turned back, they shall be **g ashamed**, 954+1322
61:10 I will **g rejoice** in the LORD, 7797+7797
Jer 3: 1 shall not that land be **g polluted**? 2610+2610
4:10 surely thou hast **g deceived** this 5377+5377
9:19 we are **g** confounded, because we have 3966
20:11 they shall be **g** ashamed: for they shall not 3966
Eze 20:13 in them; and my sabbaths they **g** polluted: 3966
25:12 hath **g offended**, and revenged himself 816+816
Da 5: 9 *was* king Belshazzar **g** troubled, and 7690
9:23 come to shew *thee;* for thou *art* **g beloved**: 2532
10:11 said unto me, O Daniel, a man **g beloved**, 2532
10:19 said, O man **g beloved**, fear not: peace *be* 2532
Ob 1: 2 among the heathen: thou *art* **g** despised. 3966
Zep 1:14 the LORD *is* near, *it is* near, and hasteth **g**, 3966
Zec 9: 9 Rejoice **g**, O daughter of Zion; shout, 3966
Mt 27:14 insomuch that the governor marvelled **g**. *3029*
27:54 that were done, they feared **g**, saying, *4970*
Mk 5:23 And besought him **g**, saying, My little *4183*
5:38 and them that wept and wailed **g**. *4183*
9:15 were **g amazed**, and running to *him* saluted *1568*
12:27 the God of the living: ye therefore do **g** err. *4183*
Jn 3:29 **rejoiceth g** because of *5463+5479*
Ac 3:11 that is called Solomon's, **g wondering**. *1569*
6: 7 of the disciples multiplied in Jerusalem **g**; *4970*
1Co 16:12 I **g** desired him to come unto you with *4183*
Php 1: 8 how *g* I long after you all in the bowels of NIG
4:10 But I rejoiced in the Lord **g**, that now at *3171*
1Th 3: 6 **desiring g** to see us, as we also *to see* you: *1971*
2Ti 1: 4 **G desiring** to see thee, being mindful of *1971*
4:15 for he hath **g** withstood our words. *3029*
1Pe 1: 6 Wherein ye **g rejoice**, though now for a *21*
2Jn 1: 4 I rejoiced **g** that I found of thy children *3029*
3Jn 1: 3 For I rejoiced **g**, when *the* brethren came *3029*

GREATNESS (32) [GREAT]
Ex 15: 7 in the **g** of thine excellency thou hast 7230
15:16 by the **g** of thine arm they shall be *as* still as 1419
Nu 14:19 people according unto the **g** of thy mercy, 1433
Dt 3:24 thou hast begun to shew thy servant thy **g**, 1433
5:24 our God hath shewed us his glory and his **g**, 1433
9:26 which thou hast redeemed through thy **g**, 1433
11: 2 his **g**, his mighty hand, and his stretched 1433
32: 3 of the LORD: ascribe ye **g** unto our God. 1433
1Ch 17:19 to thine own heart, hast thou done all this **g**, 1420
17:21 to make thee a name of **g** and terribleness, 1420
29:11 *is* the **g**, and the power, and the glory, and 1420
2Ch 9: 6 *the one* half of the **g** of thy wisdom was not 4768
24:27 the **g** of the burdens *laid* upon him, and 7230
Ne 13:22 spare me according to the **g** of thy mercy. 7230
Est 10: 2 and the declaration of the **g** of Mordecai, 1420
Ps 66: 3 through the **g** of thy power shall thine 7230
71:21 Thou shalt increase my **g**, and comfort me 1420
79:11 according to the **g** of thy power: 1433
145: 3 to be praised; and his **g** *is* unsearchable. 1420
145: 6 of thy terrible acts: and I will declare thy **g**. 1420
150: 2 praise him according to his excellent **g**. 1433
Pr 5:23 and in the **g** of his folly he shall go astray. 7230
Isa 40:26 he calleth them all by names by the **g** of *his* 7230
57:10 Thou art wearied in the **g** of thy way; 7230
63: 1 travelling in the **g** of his strength? 7230
Jer 13:22 For the **g** of thine iniquity are thy skirts 7230
Eze 31: 2 his multitude; Whom art thou like in thy **g**? 1433
31: 7 Thus was he fair in his **g**, in the length of 1433
31:18 in glory and in **g** among the trees of Eden? 1433
Da 4:22 for thy **g** is grown, and reacheth unto 7238
7:27 the **g** of the kingdom under the whole 7238
Eph 1:19 And what *is* the exceeding **g** of his power *3174*

GREAVES (1)
1Sa 17: 6 *he had* **g** of brass upon his legs, and a target 4697

GRECIA (3) [GREECE]
Da 8:21 the rough goat *is* the king of **G**: and 3120
10:20 gone forth, lo, the prince of **G** shall come. 3120
11: 2 he shall stir up all against the realm of **G**. 3120

GRECIANS (4) [GREECE]
Joel 3: 6 Jerusalem have ye sold unto the **G**, 1121+3125
Ac 6: 1 there arose a murmuring of the **G** against *1675*
9:29 the Lord Jesus, and disputed against the **G**: *1675*
11:20 spake unto the **G**, preaching the Lord Jesus. *1675*

GREECE (2) [GRECIA, GRECIANS, GREEK, GREEKS]
Zec 9:13 O **G**, and made thee as the sword of a 3120
Ac 20: 2 them much exhortation, he came into **G**, *1671*

GREEDILY (3) [GREEDINESS]
Pr 21:26 He **coveteth g** all the day long: but 183+8378
Eze 22:12 thou hast **g gained** of thy neighbours by 1214
Jude 1:11 **ran g after** the error of Balaam for reward, *1632*

GREEDINESS (1) [GREEDILY, GREEDY]
Eph 4:19 to work all uncleanness with **g**. *4124*

GREEDY (6) [GREEDINESS]
Ps 17:12 Like as a lion *that* is **g** of his prey, and as it 3700
Pr 1:19 ways of every one that is **g of gain**; 1214+1215
15:27 He that is **g of gain** troubleth his own 1214+1215
Isa 56:11 *they are* **g** dogs *which* can never 5315+5794
1Ti 3: 3 to wine, no striker, not **g of filthy lucre**; *146*
3: 8 given to much wine, not **g of filthy lucre**; *146*

GREEK (12) [GREECE]
Mk 7:26 The woman was a **G**, a Syrophenician by *1674*
Lk 23:38 also was written over him in letters of **G**, *1673*
Jn 19:20 it was written in Hebrew, *and* **G**, *and* Latin. *1676*
Ac 16: 1 and believed; but his father *was* a **G**: *1672*
16: 3 for they knew all that his father was a **G**. *1672*
21:37 unto thee? Who said, Canst thou speak **G**? *1676*
Ro 1:16 to the Jew first, and *also* to the **G**. *1672*
10:12 is no difference between the Jew and the **G**: *1672*
Gal 2: 3 neither Titus, who was with me, being a **G**, *1672*
3:28 There is neither Jew nor **G**, there is neither *1672*
Col 3:11 Where there is neither **G** nor Jew, *1672*
Rev 9:11 in the **G** *tongue* hath *his* name Apollyon. *1673*

GREEKS (14) [GREECE]
Jn 12:20 And there were certain **G** among them that *1672*
Ac 14: 1 both of the Jews and *also* of the **G** believed. *1672*
17: 4 and of the devout **G** a great multitude, and *1672*
17:12 also of honourable women which were **G**, *1674*
18: 4 and persuaded *the* Jews and *the* **G**. *1672*
18:17 Then all the **G** took Sosthenes, the *chief* *1672*
19:10 word of the Lord Jesus, both Jews and **G**. *1672*
19:17 the Jews and **G** also dwelling at Ephesus; *1672*
20:21 and *also* to the **G**, repentance toward God, *1672*
21:28 and further brought **G** also into the temple, *1672*
Ro 1:14 I am debtor both to the **G**, and to *1672*
1Co 1:22 a sign, and the **G** seek after wisdom: *1672*
1:23 and unto the **G** foolishness; *1672*
1:24 both Jews and **G**, Christ the power of God, *1672*

GREEN (41) [GREENISH, GREENNESS]
Ge 1:30 *is* life, *I have given* every **g** herb for meat: 3418
9: 3 *even* as the **g** herb have I given you all 3418
30:37 Jacob took him rods of **g** poplar, and of 3892
Ex 10:15 there remained not any **g thing** in the trees, 3418
Lev 2:14 thy firstfruits **g ears of corn** dried by the fire, 24
23:14 neither bread, nor parched *corn,* nor **g ears**, 3759
Dt 12: 2 and upon the hills, and under every **g** tree: 7488
Jdg 16: 7 If they bind me with seven **g** withs that 3892
16: 8 her seven **g** withs which had not been dried, 3892
1Ki 14:23 on every high hill, and under every **g** tree. 7488
2Ki 16: 4 and on the hills, and under every **g** tree. 7488
17:10 in every high hill, and under every **g** tree: 7488
19:26 *as* the **g** herb, *as* the grass on the housetops, 3419
2Ch 28: 4 and on the hills, and under every **g** tree. 7488
Est 1: 6 **g**, and blue *hangings,* fastened with cords 3768

Job 8:16 He *is* **g** before the sun, and his branch 7373
15:32 his time, and his branch shall not be **g**. 7488
39: 8 and he searcheth after every **g thing**. 3387
Ps 23: 2 He maketh me to lie down in **g** pastures: 1877
37: 2 like the grass, and wither as the **g** herb. 3418
37:35 and spreading himself like a **g** bay tree. 7488
52: 8 I *am* like a **g** olive tree in the house of God: 7488
SS 1:16 yea, pleasant: also our bed *is* **g**. 7488
2:13 The fig tree putteth forth her **g figs**, and 6291
Isa 15: 6 the grass faileth, there is no **g thing**. 3418
37:27 *as* the **g** herb, *as* the grass on the housetops, 3419
57: 5 yourselves with idols under every **g** tree, 7488
Jer 2:20 and under every **g** tree thou wanderest, 7488
3: 6 high mountain and under every **g** tree, 7488
3:13 ways to the strangers under every **g** tree, 7488
11:16 A **g** olive tree, fair, *and* of goodly fruit: 7488
17: 2 their groves by the **g** trees upon the high 7488
17: 8 when heat cometh, but her leaf shall be **g**; 7488
Eze 6:13 under every **g** tree, and under every thick 7488
17:24 have dried up the **g** tree, and have made 3892
20:47 it shall devour every **g** tree in thee, and 3892
Hos 14: 8 I *am* like a **g** fir tree. From me is thy fruit 7488
Mk 6:39 all sit down by companies upon the **g** grass. *5515*
Lk 23:31 For if they do these *things* in a **g** tree, *5200*
Rev 8: 7 was burnt up, and all **g** grass was burnt up. *5515*
9: 4 neither any **g** *thing,* neither any tree; *5515*

GREENISH (2) [GREEN]
Lev 13:49 *if* the plague be **g** or reddish in the garment, 3422
14:37 **g** or reddish, which in sight *are* lower than 3422

GREENNESS (1) [GREEN]
Job 8:12 Whilst it *is* yet in his **g**, *and* not cut down, it 3

GREET (16) [GREETETH, GREETING, GREETINGS]
1Sa 25: 5 and **g** him in my name: 7592+7965+3807.1
Ro 16: 3 **G** Priscilla and Aquila my helpers in Christ *782*
16: 5 Likewise *g* the church that is in their house. NIG
16: 6 **G** Mary, who bestowed much labour on us. *782*
16: 8 **G** Amplias my beloved in the Lord. *782*
16:11 **G** them that be of the *household* of *782*
1Co 16:20 All the brethren **g** you. Greet ye one another *782*
16:20 greet you. **G** ye one another with a holy kiss. *782*
2Co 13:12 **G** one another with a holy kiss. *782*
Php 4:21 The brethren which are with me **g** you. *782*
Col 4:14 the beloved physician, and Demas, **g** you. *782*
1Th 5:26 **G** all the brethren with a holy kiss. *782*
Tit 3:15 **G** them that love us in the faith. Grace *be* *782*
1Pe 5:14 **G** ye one another with a kiss of charity. *782*
2Jn 1:13 The children of thy elect sister **g** thee. Amen. *782*
3Jn 1:14 friends salute thee. **G** the friends by name. *782*

GREETETH (1) [GREET]
2Ti 4:21 Eubulus **g** thee, and Pudens, and Linus, and *782*

GREETING (3) [GREET]
Ac 15:23 brethren *send* **g** unto the brethren which are *5463*
23:26 most excellent governor Felix *sendeth* **g**. *5463*
Jas 1: 1 twelve tribes which are scattered abroad, **g**. *5463*

GREETINGS (3) [GREET]
Mt 23: 7 And **g** in the markets, and to be called of *783*
Lk 11:43 in the synagogues, and **g** in the markets. *783*
20:46 and love **g** in the markets, and the highest *783*

GREW (28) [GROW]
Ge 2: 5 and every herb of the field before it **g**: 6779
19:25 and **that which g** upon the ground. 6780
21: 8 the child **g**, and was weaned: and 1431
21:20 he **g**, and dwelt in the wilderness, and 1431
25:27 the boys **g**: and Esau was a cunning hunter, 1431
26:13 and **g** until he became very great: 1432
47:27 and **g**, and multiplied exceedingly. 6509
Ex 1:12 the more they multiplied and **g**. 6555
2:10 the child **g**, and she brought him unto 1431
Jdg 11: 2 *his* wife's sons **g up**, and they thrust out 1431
13:24 the child **g**, and the LORD blessed him. 1431
1Sa 2:21 And the child Samuel **g** before the LORD. 1431
2:26 the child Samuel **g** on, and was in favour 1432
3:19 Samuel **g**, and the LORD was with him, 1431
2Sa 5:10 **g great**, and the LORD God of hosts *was* 1419
12: 3 it **g up** together with him, and with his 1431
Eze 17: 6 it **g**, and became a spreading vine of low 6779
17:10 it shall wither in the furrows where it **g**. 6780
Da 4:11 The tree **g**, and was strong, and the height 7236
4:20 that thou sawest, which **g**, and was strong, 7236
Mk 4: 7 and the thorns **g up**, and choked it, and *305*
5:26 nothing bettered, but rather **g** worse, *1519+2064*
Lk 1:80 And the child **g**, and waxed strong in spirit, *837*
2:40 And the child **g**, and waxed strong in spirit, *837*
13:19 and it **g**, and waxed a great tree; and *837*
Ac 7:17 the people **g** and multiplied in Egypt, *837*
12:24 But the word of God **g** and multiplied. *837*
19:20 So mightily **g** the word of God and *837*

GREYHOUND (1)
Pr 30:31 A **g**; a he goat also; and a king, 2223+4975

GRIEF (26) [GRIEFS, GRIEVANCE, GRIEVE, GRIEVED, GRIEVETH, GRIEVING, GRIEVOUS, GRIEVOUSLY, GRIEVOUSNESS]
Ge 26:35 Which were a **g** of mind unto Isaac and 4786
1Sa 1:16 my complaint and **g** have I spoken hitherto. 3708
25:31 That this shall be no **g** unto thee, 6330
2Ch 6:29 one shall know his own sore and his own **g**, 4341
Job 2:13 for they saw that *his* **g** was very great. 3511
6: 2 Oh that my **g** were throughly weighed, 3708
16: 5 moving of my lips should asswage *your g*. NIH
16: 6 Though I speak, my **g** is not asswaged: and 3511
Ps 6: 7 Mine eye is consumed because of **g**; 3708
31: 9 mine eye is consumed with **g**, *yea,* my soul 3708
31:10 For my life is spent with **g**, and my years 3015
69:26 they talk to the **g** of those whom thou hast 4341
Pr 17:25 A foolish son *is* a **g** to his father, and 3708
Ecc 1:18 For in much wisdom *is* much **g**: and he that 3708
2:23 all his days *are* sorrows, and his travail **g**; 3708
Isa 17:11 the harvest *shall be* a heap in the day of **g** 2470
53: 3 a man of sorrows, and acquainted with **g**: 2483
53:10 to bruise him; he hath **put** *him* **to g**: 2470
Jer 6: 7 before me continually *is* **g** and wounds. 2483
10:19 I said, Truly this *is* a **g**, and I must bear it. 2483
45: 3 for the LORD hath added **g** to my sorrow; 3015
La 3:32 though he **cause g**, yet will he have 3013
Jnh 4: 6 over his head, to deliver him from his **g**. 7451
2Co 2: 5 But if any have **caused g**, he hath not *3076*
Heb 13:17 that they may do it with joy, and not with **g**: *4727*
1Pe 2:19 a man for conscience toward God endure **g**, *3077*

GRIEFS (1) [GRIEF]
Isa 53: 4 Surely he hath borne our **g**, and carried our 2483

GRIEVANCE (1) [GRIEF]
Hab 1: 3 me iniquity, and cause *me* to behold **g**? 5999

GRIEVE (5) [GRIEF]
1Sa 2:33 to consume thine eyes, and to **g** thine heart: 109
1Ch 4:10 keep *me* from evil, that it may not **g** me. 6087
Ps 78:40 in the wilderness, *and* **g** him in the desert! 6087
La 3:33 For he doth not afflict willingly nor **g** 3013
Eph 4:30 And **g** not the holy Spirit of God, *3076*

GRIEVED (40) [GRIEF]
Ge 6: 6 man on the earth, and it **g** him at his heart. 6087
34: 7 when they heard *it:* and the men were **g**, 6087
45: 5 Now therefore be not **g**, nor angry with 6087
49:23 The archers have **sorely g** him, and shot *at* 4843
Ex 1:12 they were **g** because of the children of 6973
Dt 15:10 thine heart shall not be **g** when thou givest 3415
Jdg 10:16 and his soul was **g** for the misery of Israel. 7114
1Sa 1: 8 why is thy heart **g**? *am* not I better to thee 3415
15:11 it **g** Samuel; and he cried unto the LORD 2734
20: 3 Let not Jonathan know this, lest he be **g**: 6087
20:34 for he was **g** for David, because his father 6087
30: 6 because the soul of all the people was **g**, 4843
2Sa 19: 2 say that day *how* the king was **g** for his son. 6087
Ne 2:10 **g** them **exceedingly** that there 1419+7451+7489
8:11 for the day *is* holy; neither be ye **g**. 6087
13: 8 it **g** me sore: therefore I cast forth all 3415
Est 4: 4 was the queen exceedingly **g**; and she sent 2342
Job 4: 2 to commune with thee, wilt thou be **g**? 3811
30:25 in trouble? was *not* my soul **g** for the poor? 5701
Ps 73:21 Thus my heart was **g**, and I was pricked *in* 2556
95:10 Forty years long was I **g** with *this* 6962
112:10 The wicked shall see *it,* and be **g**; he shall 3707
119:158 I beheld the transgressors, and was **g**; 6962
139:21 am not I **g** with those that rise up against 6962
Isa 54: 6 thee as a woman forsaken and **g** in spirit, 6087
57:10 of thine hand; therefore thou wast not **g**. 2470
Jer 5: 3 hast stricken them, but they have not **g**; 2342

Da 7:15 I Daniel was **g** in my spirit in the midst of 3735
11:30 therefore he shall be **g**, and return, and 3512
Am 6: 6 they are not **g** for the affliction of Joseph. 2470
Mk 3: 5 being **g** for the hardness of their hearts, *4818*
10:22 he was sad at *that* saying, and went away **g**: *3076*
Jn 21:17 Peter was **g** because he said unto him *3076*
Ac 4: 2 Being **g** that they taught the people, and *1278*
16:18 being **g**, turned and said to the spirit, *1278*
Ro 14:15 But if thy brother be **g** with *thy* meat, *3076*
2Co 2: 4 not that you should be **g**, but that ye might *3076*
2: 5 caused grief, he hath not **g** me, but in part: *3076*
Heb 3:10 Wherefore I was **g** with that generation, *4360*
3:17 But with whom was he **g** forty years? *was it* *4360*

GRIEVETH (2) [GRIEF]
Ru 1:13 for it **g** me much for your sakes that 4843
Pr 26:15 it **g** him to bring it again to his mouth. 3811

GRIEVING (1) [GRIEF]
Eze 28:24 nor *any* **g** thorn of all *that are* round about 3510

GRIEVOUS (38) [GRIEF]
Ge 12:10 for the famine *was* **g** in the land. 3515
18:20 is great, and because their sin is very **g**; 3513
21:11 the thing was very **g** in Abraham's sight 3415
21:12 Let it not be **g** in thy sight because of 3415
41:31 that famine following; for it *shall be* very **g**. 3515
50:11 This *is* a **g** mourning to the Egyptians: 3515
Ex 8:24 there came a **g** swarm *of flies* into 3515
9: 3 the sheep: *there shall be* a very **g** murrain. 3515
9:18 *this* time I will cause it to rain a very **g** hail, 3515
9:24 and fire mingled with the hail, very **g**, 3515
10:14 very **g** *were they;* before them there were 3515
1Ki 2: 8 which cursed me *with* a **g** curse in the day 4834
12: 4 Thy father **made** our yoke **g**: now therefore 7185
12: 4 make thou the **g** service of thy father, 7186
2Ch 10: 4 Thy father **made** our yoke **g**: now therefore 7185
10: 4 ease thou somewhat the **g** servitude of thy 7186
Ps 10: 5 His ways are always **g**; thy judgments *are* 2342
31:18 which speak **g things** proudly and 6277
Pr 15: 1 away wrath: but **g** words stir up anger. 6089
15:10 Correction *is* **g** unto him that forsaketh 7451
Ecc 2:17 the work that is wrought under the sun *is* **g** 7451
Isa 15: 4 shall cry out; his life shall be **g** unto him. 3415
21: 2 A **g** vision is declared unto me; 7186
Jer 6:28 They *are* all **g** revolters, walking with 5493
10:19 my wound *is* **g**: but I said, Truly this *is* a 2470
14:17 *with* a great breach, *with* a very **g** blow. 2470
16: 4 They shall die of **g** deaths; they shall not be 8463
23:19 is gone forth *in* fury, even a **g** whirlwind: 2342
30:12 Thy bruise *is* incurable, *and* thy wound *is* **g**. 2470
Na 3:19 *is* no healing of thy bruise; thy wound *is* **g**: 2470
Mt 23: 4 they bind heavy burdens and **g to be borne**, *1419*
Lk 11:46 ye lade men *with* burdens **g to be borne**, *1419*
Ac 20:29 that after my departing shall **g** wolves enter *926*
25: 7 laid many and **g** complaints against Paul, *926*
Php 3: 1 to me indeed *is* not **g**, but for you *it is* safe. *3636*
Heb 12:11 for the present seemeth to be joyous, but **g**: *3077*
1Jn 5: 3 and his commandments are not **g**. *926*
Rev 16: 2 **g** sore upon the men which had the mark of *4190*

GRIEVOUSLY (7) [GRIEF]
Isa 9: 1 afterward did **more g afflict** *her by* the way 3513
Jer 23:19 it shall **fall g** upon the head of the wicked. 2342
La 1: 8 Jerusalem hath **g sinned**; therefore 2398+2399
1:20 within me; for I have **g rebelled**: 4784+4784
Eze 14:13 sinneth against me by **trespassing g**, 4603+4604
Mt 8: 6 lieth at home sick of the palsy, **g** tormented. *1171*
15:22 my daughter is **g** vexed with a devil. *2560*

GRIEVOUSNESS (2) [GRIEF]
Isa 10: 1 that write **g** *which* they have prescribed; 5999
21:15 from the bent bow, and from the **g** of war. 3514

GRIN (1) [GRINS; see also GIN]
Job 18: 9 The **g** shall take *him* by the heel, *and* 6341

GRIND (7) [GRINDERS, GRINDING]
Jdg 16:21 of brass; and he did **g** in the prison house. 2912
Job 31:10 *Then* let my wife **g** unto another, and 2912
Isa 3:15 to pieces, and **g** the faces of the poor? 2912
47: 2 Take the millstones, and **g** meal: 2912
La 5:13 They took the young men to **g**, and 2911
Mt 21:44 it shall fall, it will **g** him **to powder**. *3039*
Lk 20:18 it shall fall, it will **g** him **to powder**. *3039*

GRINDERS (1) [GRIND]
Ecc 12: 3 the **g** cease because they are few, and 2912

GRINDING (3) [GRIND]
Ecc 12: 4 when the sound of the **g** is low, and he shall 2913
Mt 24:41 Two *women shall be* **g** at the mill; *the* one *229*
Lk 17:35 Two *women* shall be **g** together; the one *229*

GRINS (2) [GRIN; see also GIN]
Ps 140: 5 net by the way side; they have set **g** for me. 4170
141: 9 for me, and the **g** of the workers of iniquity. 4170

GRISLED (4)
Ge 31:10 the cattle *were* ringstraked, speckled, and **g**. 1261
31:12 the cattle *are* ringstraked, speckled, and **g**: 1261
Zec 6: 3 and in the fourth chariot **g** *and* bay horses. 1261
6: 6 and the **g** go forth toward the south country. 1261

GROAN (7) [GROANED, GROANETH, GROANING, GROANINGS]
Job 24:12 Men **g** from out of the city, and the soul of 5008
Jer 51:52 and through all her land the wounded shall **g**. 602
Eze 30:24 he shall **g** before him *with* the groanings of 5008
Joel 1:18 How do the beasts **g**! the herds of cattle are 584
Ro 8:23 even we ourselves **g** within ourselves, *4727*
2Co 5: 2 For in this we **g**, earnestly desiring to be *4727*
5: 4 For we that are in *this* tabernacle do **g**, *4727*

GROANED (1) [GROAN]
Jn 11:33 he **g** in the spirit, and was troubled, *1690*

GROANETH (1) [GROAN]
Ro 8:22 For we know that the whole creation **g** and *4959*

GROANING (9) [GROAN]
Ex 2:24 God heard their **g**, and God remembered 5009
6: 5 I have also heard the **g** of the children of 5009
Job 23: 2 my stroke is heavier than my **g**. 585
Ps 6: 6 I am weary with my **g**; all the night make I 585
38: 9 *is* before thee; and my **g** is not hid from thee. 585
102: 5 By reason of the voice of my **g** my bones 585
102:20 To hear the **g** of the prisoner; to loose those 603
Jn 11:38 again **g** in himself cometh to the grave. *1690*
Ac 7:34 and I have heard their **g**, and am come *4726*

GROANINGS (3) [GROAN]
Jdg 2:18 of their **g** by reason of them that oppressed 5009
Eze 30:24 he shall groan before him *with* the **g** of a 5009
Ro 8:26 for us with **g** which cannot be uttered. *4726*

GROPE (5) [GROPETH]
Dt 28:29 thou shalt **g** at noondays, as the blind 4959
Job 5:14 and **g** in the noonday as in the night. 4959
12:25 They **g** *in* the dark without light, and 4959
Isa 59:10 We **g** for the wall like the blind, and 1659
59:10 the blind, and we **g** as if *we had* no eyes: 1659

GROPETH (1) [GROPE]
Dt 28:29 as the blind **g** in darkness, and thou shalt 4959

GROSS (4)
Isa 60: 2 cover the earth, and **g darkness** the people: 6205
Jer 13:16 shadow of death, *and* make *it* **g darkness**. 6205
Mt 13:15 For this people's heart is **waxed g**, and *3975*
Ac 28:27 For the heart of this people is **waxed g**, and *3975*

GROUND (192) [AGROUND, GROUNDED]
Ge 2: 5 and *there was* not a man to till the **g**. 127
2: 6 and watered the whole face of the **g**. 127
2: 7 God formed man *of* the dust of the **g**, 127
2: 9 out of the **g** made the LORD God to grow 127
2:19 out of the **g** the LORD God formed every 127
3:17 cursed *is* the **g** for thy sake; in sorrow shalt 127
3:19 thou eat bread, till thou return unto the **g**; 127
3:23 to till the **g** from whence he was taken. 127
4: 2 of sheep, but Cain was a tiller of the **g**. 127
4: 3 that Cain brought of the fruit of the **g** an 127
4:10 brother's blood crieth unto me from the **g**. 127
4:12 When thou tillest the **g**, it shall not 127
5:29 of the **g** which the LORD hath cursed. 127
7:23 destroyed which *was* upon the face of the **g**, 127
8: 8 were abated from off the face of the **g**; 127
8:13 and behold, the face of the **g** was dry. 127
8:21 I will not again curse the **g** any more for 127
18: 2 tent door, and bowed himself toward the **g**, 776

Ge 19: 1 he bowed himself with his face toward the **g**; 776
19:25 of the cities, and that which grew upon the **g**. 127
33: 3 and bowed himself to the **g** seven times, 776
38: 9 his brother's wife, that he spilled *it* on the **g**, 776
44:11 took down every man his sack to the **g**, 776
44:14 yet there: and they fell before him on the **g**. 776
Ex 3: 5 the place whereon thou standest *is* holy **g**. 127
4: 3 he said, Cast it on the **g**. And he cast it on 776
4: 3 he cast it on the **g**, and it became a serpent; 776
8:21 *of flies,* and also the **g** whereon they *are.* 127
9:23 and hail, and the fire ran along upon the **g**; 776
14:16 the children of Israel shall go on dry ***g*** NIH
14:22 into the midst of the sea upon the dry ***g***: NIH
16:14 *as* small as the hoar frost on the **g**. 776
32:20 **g** *it* to powder, and strawed *it* upon 2912
Lev 20:25 *manner of living thing* that creepeth *on* the **g**, 127
Nu 11: 8 gathered *it,* and **g** *it* in mills, or beat *it* in a 2912
16:31 that the **g** clave asunder that *was* under them: 127
Dt 4:18 likeness of any *thing* that creepeth on the **g**, 127
9:21 and stamped it, *and* **g** *it* **very small**, 2912
15:23 thou shalt pour it upon the **g** as water. 776
22: 6 or on the **g**, *whether they be* young ones, or 776
28: 4 the fruit of thy **g**, and the fruit of thy cattle, 127
28:11 fruit of thy cattle, and in the fruit of thy **g**, 127
28:56 sole of her foot upon the **g** for delicateness 776
Jos 3:17 stood firm on dry ***g*** in the midst of Jordan, NIH
3:17 all the Israelites passed over on dry ***g***, until NIH
24:32 in a parcel of **g** which Jacob bought of 7704
Jdg 4:21 into his temples, and fastened *it* into the **g**: 776
6:39 and upon all the **g** let there be dew. 776
6:40 fleece only, and there was dew on all the **g**. 776
13:20 looked on *it,* and fell on their faces to the **g**. 776
20:21 destroyed *down* to the **g** of the Israelites that 776
20:25 destroyed *down* to the **g** of the children of 776
Ru 2:10 bowed herself to the **g**, and said unto him, 776
1Sa 3:19 and did let none of his words fall to the **g**. 776
5: 4 Dagon *was* fallen upon his face to the **g** 776
8:12 *will set them* to ear his **g**, and to reap his 2758
14:25 to a wood; and there was honey upon the **g**. 7704
14:32 oxen, and calves, and slew *them* on the **g**: 776
14:45 shall not one hair of his head fall to the **g**; 776
20:31 as long as the son of Jesse liveth upon the **g**, 127
20:41 fell on his face to the **g**, and bowed himself 776
25:23 on her face, and bowed herself *to* the **g**, 776
26: 7 and his spear stuck in the **g** *at* his bolster: 776
28:14 he stooped *with his* face to the **g**, and 776
2Sa 2:22 wherefore should I smite thee to the **g**? how 776
8: 2 them with a line, casting them down to the **g**; 776
14: 4 she fell on her face to the **g**, and 776
14:14 needs die, and *are* as water spilt on the **g**, 776
14:22 Joab fell to the **g** on his face, and 776
14:33 bowed himself on his face to the **g** before 776
17:12 *light* upon him as the dew falleth on the **g**: 127
17:19 well's mouth, and spread **g corn** thereon; 7383
18:11 why didst thou not smite him there to the **g**? 776
20:10 fifth *rib,* and shed out his bowels to the **g**, 776
23:11 where was a piece of **g** full *of* lentiles: 7704
23:12 he stood in the midst of the **g**, and 2513
24:20 before the king *on* his face upon the **g**. 776
1Ki 1:23 before the king with his face to the **g**. 776
7:46 in the clay **g** between Succoth and Zarthan. 127
2Ki 2: 8 thither, so that they two went over on dry ***g***. NIH
2:15 and bowed themselves to the **g** before him. 776
2:19 but the water *is* naught, and the **g** barren. 776
4:37 bowed herself to the **g**, and took up her son, 776
9:26 cast him into the plat *of* **g**, according to NIH
13:18 unto the king of Israel, Smite upon the **g**. 776
1Ch 11:13 where was a parcel of **g** full *of* barley; 7704
21:21 himself to David *with his* face to the **g**. 776
27:26 tillage of the **g** *was* Ezri the son of Chelub: 127
2Ch 4:17 in the clay **g** between Succoth and 127
7: 3 *with their* faces to the **g** upon the pavement, 776
20:18 bowed his head *with his* face to the **g**: 776
Ne 8: 6 the LORD *with their* faces to the **g**. 776
10:35 to bring the firstfruits of our **g**, and 127
10:37 the tithes of our **g** unto the Levites, that 127
Job 1:20 and fell down upon the **g**, and worshipped, 776
2:13 So they sat down with him upon the **g** seven 776
5: 6 neither doth trouble spring out of the **g**; 127
14: 8 the earth, and the stock thereof die in the **g**; 6083
16:13 not spare; he poureth out my gall upon the **g**. 776
18:10 The snare *is* laid for him in the **g**, and a trap 776
38:27 To satisfy the desolate and waste ***g***; and NIH
39:24 He swalloweth the **g** with fierceness and 776
Ps 74: 7 the dwelling place of thy name to the **g**. 776
89:39 profaned his crown *by casting it* to the **g**. 776
89:44 to cease, and cast his throne down to the **g**. 776
105:35 their land, and devoured the fruit of their **g**. 127
107:33 and the watersprings into **dry g**; 6774
107:35 standing water, and dry **g** into watersprings; 776
143: 3 he hath smitten my life down to the **g**; 776
147: 6 he casteth the wicked down to the **g**. 776
Isa 3:26 and she *being* desolate shall sit upon the **g**. 776
14:12 *how* art thou cut down to the **g**, which didst 776
21: 9 of her gods he hath broken unto the **g**. 776
25:12 lay low, *and* bring to the **g**, *even* to the dust. 776
26: 5 layeth it low; he layeth it low, *even* to the **g**; 776
28:24 doth he open and break the clods of his **g**? 127
29: 4 *and* shalt speak out of the **g**, and thy speech 776
29: 4 out of the **g**, and thy speech shall whisper 776
30:23 of thy seed, that thou shalt sow the **g** withal; 127
30:24 the young asses that ear the **g** shall eat clean 127
35: 7 the **parched g** shall become a pool, and 8273
44: 3 floods upon the dry ***g***: I will pour my spirit NIH
47: 1 O virgin daughter of Babylon, sit on the **g**: 776
51:23 thou hast laid thy body as the **g**, and as 776
53: 2 as a tender plant, and as a root out of a dry **g**: 776
Jer 4: 3 Break up your **fallow g**, and sow not 5215
7:20 trees of the field, and upon the fruit of the **g**; 127
14: 2 they are black unto the **g**; and the cry of 776
14: 4 Because the **g** is chapt, for there was no rain 127
25:33 nor buried; they shall be dung upon the **g**. 127
27: 5 the man and the beast that *are* upon the **g**, 776
La 2: 2 he hath brought *them* down to the **g**: 776
2: 9 Her gates are sunk into the **g**; he hath 776
2:10 elders of the daughter of Zion sit upon the **g**, 776
2:10 of Jerusalem hang down their heads to the **g**. 776
2:21 and the old lie on the **g** in the streets: 776
Eze 12: 6 shalt cover thy face, that thou see not the **g**: 776
12:12 his face, that he see not the **g** with *his* eyes. 776
13:14 and bring it down to the **g**, 776
19:12 she was cast down to the **g**, and the east 776
19:13 in the wilderness, in a dry and thirsty **g**. 776
24: 7 she poured it not upon the **g**, to cover it with 776
26:11 thy strong garrisons shall go down to the **g**. 776
26:16 they shall sit upon the **g**, and shall tremble at 776
28:17 I will cast thee to the **g**, I will lay thee before 776
38:20 shall fall, and every wall shall fall to the **g**. 776
41:16 *from* the **g** up to the windows, and 776
41:20 From the **g** unto above the door *were* 776
42: 6 the lowest and the middlemost from the **g**. 776
43:14 from the bottom *upon* the **g** *even* to 776
Da 8: 5 of the whole earth, and touched not the **g**: 776
8: 7 he cast him down to the **g**, and stamped upon 776
8:10 *some* of the host and of the stars to the **g**, 776
8:12 and it cast down the truth to the **g**; 776
8:18 was in a deep sleep on my face toward the **g**: 776
10: 9 sleep on my face, and my face toward the **g**: 776
10:15 I set my face toward the **g**, and I became 776
Hos 2:18 and *with* the creeping things of the **g**: 127
10:12 reap in mercy; break up your **fallow g**: 5215
Am 3:14 of the altar shall be cut off, and fall to the **g**. 776
Ob 1: 3 his heart, Who shall bring me down *to* the **g**? 776
Hag 1:11 and upon *that* which the **g** bringeth forth, and 127
Zec 8:12 the **g** shall give her increase, and the heavens 776
Mal 3:11 and he shall not destroy the fruits of your **g**; 127
Mt 10:29 one of them shall not fall on the **g** without *1093*
13: 8 But other fell into good **g**, and *1093*
13:23 But he that received seed into the good **g** is *1093*
15:35 the multitude to sit down on the **g**. *1093*
Mk 4: 5 And some fell on **stony g**, where it had not *4075*
4: 8 And other fell on good **g**, and did yield fruit *1093*
4:16 they likewise which are sown on **stony g**; *4075*
4:20 these are they which are sown on good **g**; *1093*
4:26 as if a man should cast seed into the **g**, *1093*
8: 6 the people to sit down on the **g**: *1093*
9:20 and he fell on the **g**, and *1093*
14:35 and fell on the **g**, and prayed that, if it were *1093*
Lk 8: 8 And other fell on good **g**, and sprang up, *1093*
8:15 But that on the good **g** are they, which in an *1093*
12:16 The **g** of a certain rich man brought forth *5561*
13: 7 cut it down; why cumbereth it the **g**? *1093*
14:18 I have bought a **piece of g**, and I must needs *68*
19:44 And shall **lay thee even with the g**, and thy *1474*
22:44 great drops of blood falling down to the **g**. *1093*
Jn 4: 5 near to the **parcel of g** that Jacob gave to *5564*
8: 6 and with *his* finger wrote on the **g**, *1093*
8: 8 again he stooped down, and wrote on the **g**. *1093*

Jn 9: 6 he spat **on the g**, and made clay of 5476
12:24 Except a corn of wheat fall into the g and 1093
18: 6 *he,* they went backward, and fell **to the g**. 5476
Ac 7:33 for the place where thou standest is holy **g**. 1093
22: 7 And I fell unto the **g**, and heard a voice 1475
1Ti 3:15 the living God, the pillar and **g** of the truth. 1477

GROUNDED (3) [GROUND]
Isa 30:32 *in* every *place* where the **g** staff shall pass, 4145
Eph 3:17 by faith; that ye, being rooted and **g** in love, 2311
Col 1:23 If ye continue in the faith **g** and settled, and 2311

GROVE (17) [GROVES]
Ge 21:33 And *Abraham* planted a **g** in Beer-sheba, and 815
Dt 16:21 Thou shalt not plant thee a **g** *of* any trees 842
Jdg 6:25 father hath, and cut down the **g** that *is* by it: 842
6:26 offer a burnt sacrifice with the wood of the **g** 842
6:28 the **g** was cut down that *was* by it, and 842
6:30 he hath cut down the **g** that *was* by it. 842
1Ki 15:13 because she had made an idol in a **g**; 842
16:33 Ahab made a **g**; and Ahab did more to 842
2Ki 13: 6 there remained the **g** also in Samaria.) 842
17:16 made a **g**, and worshipped all the host of 842
21: 3 and made a **g**, as did Ahab king of Israel; 842
21: 7 he set a graven image of the **g** that he had 842
23: 4 and for the **g**, and for all the host of heaven: 842
23: 6 he brought out the **g** from the house of 842
23: 7 where the women wove hangings for the **g**. 842
23:15 stampt *it* small to powder, and burnt the **g**. 842
2Ch 15:16 because she had made an idol in a **g**: 842

GROVES (24) [GROVE]
Ex 34:13 break their images, and cut down their **g**: 842
Dt 7: 5 cut down their **g**, and burn their graven 842
12: 3 break their pillars, and burn their **g** with fire; 842
Jdg 3: 7 their God, and served Baalim and the **g**. 842
1Ki 14:15 because they have made their **g**, 842
14:23 images, and **g**, on every high hill, and 842
18:19 fifty, and the prophets of the **g** four hundred, 842
2Ki 17:10 set them up images and **g** in every high hill, 842
18: 4 cut down the **g**, and brake in pieces 842
23:14 cut down the **g**, and filled their places *with* 842
2Ch 14: 3 brake down the images, and cut down the **g**: 842
17: 6 away the high places and **g** out of Judah. 842
19: 3 in that thou hast taken away the **g** out of 842
24:18 God of their fathers, and served **g** and idols: 842
31: 1 the images *in pieces,* and cut down the **g**, 842
33: 3 made **g**, and worshipped all the host of 842
33:19 set up **g** and graven images, before he was 842
34: 3 the **g**, and the carved images, and the molten 842
34: 4 the **g**, and the carved images, and the molten 842
34: 7 he had broken down the altars and the **g**, 842
Isa 17: 8 have made, either the **g**, or the images. 842
27: 9 the **g** and images shall not stand up. 842
Jer 17: 2 their **g** by the green trees upon the high hills. 842
Mic 5:14 I will pluck up thy **g** out of the midst of thee: 842

GROW (38) [GREW, GROWETH, GROWN, GROWTH]
Ge 2: 9 **made** the LORD God **to g** every tree that 6779
48:16 let them **g** into a multitude in the midst of 1711
Nu 6: 5 shall let the locks of the hair of his head **g**. 1431
Jdg 16:22 Howbeit the hair of his head began to **g** 6779
2Sa 23: 5 all *my* desire, although he **make** *it* **not** to **g**. 6779
2Ki 19:29 *this* year **such things as g of themselves**, 5599
Ezr 4:22 why should damage **g** to the hurt of 7680
Job 8:11 Can the rush **g up** without mire? can 1342
8:11 without mire? can the flag **g** without water? 7685
8:19 his way, and out of the earth shall others **g**. 6779
14:19 thou washest away the **things which g** out 5599
31:40 Let thistles **g** instead of wheat, and 3318
39: 4 are in good liking, they **g up** with corn; 7235
Ps 92:12 he shall **g** like a cedar in Lebanon. 7685
104:14 He **causeth** the grass **to g** for the cattle, and 6779
147: 8 who **maketh** grass **to g** *upon* 6779
Ecc 11: 5 *nor* how the bones *do* **g** in the womb of her NIH
Isa 11: 1 and a Branch shall **g** out of his roots: 6509
17:11 In the day shalt thou **make** thy plant **to g**, 7735
53: 2 For he shall **g up** before him as a tender 5927
Jer 12: 2 they **g**, yea, they bring forth fruit: thou *art* 1980
33:15 **cause** the Branch of righteousness **to g up** 6779
Eze 44:20 their heads, nor **suffer** *their* locks **to g long**; 7971
47:12 and on that side, shall **g** all trees for meat, 5927
Hos 14: 5 he shall **g** as the lily, and cast forth his roots 6524
14: 7 shall revive *as* the corn, and **g** as the vine: 6524
Jnh 4:10 thou hast not laboured, neither **madest** it **g**; 1431
Zec 6:12 he shall **g up** out of his place, and he shall 6779
Mal 4: 2 go forth, and **g up** as calves of the stall. 6335
Mt 6:28 Consider the lilies of the field, how they **g**; 837
13:30 Let both **g together** until the harvest: and 4885
21:19 Let no fruit **g** on thee henceforward for 1096
Mk 4:27 day, and the seed should spring and **g up**, 3373
Lk 12:27 Consider the lilies how they **g**: they toil not, 837
Ac 5:24 doubted of them whereunto this would **g**. 1096
Eph 4:15 may **g** *up* into him *in* all *things,* which is 837
1Pe 2: 2 milk of the word, that ye may **g** thereby: 837
2Pe 3:18 But **g** in grace, and *in* the knowledge of our 837

GROWETH (14) [GROW]
Ex 10: 5 shall eat every tree which **g** for you out of 6779
Lev 13:39 it *is* a freckled spot *that* **g** in the skin: 6524
25: 5 **That which g of it own accord** of thy 5599
25:11 neither reap **that which g of itself** in it, 5599
Dt 29:23 nor beareth, nor any grass **g** therein, 5927
Jdg 19: 9 behold, the day **g to an end**, lodge here, 2583
Job 38:38 When the dust **g** into hardness, and 3332
Ps 90: 5 the morning *they are* like grass *which* **g up**. 2498
90: 6 In the morning it flourisheth, and **g up**; 2498
129: 6 which withereth afore it **g up**: 8025
Isa 37:30 Ye shall eat *this* year **such as g of itself**; 5599
Mk 4:32 it **g up**, and becometh greater than all herbs, 305
Eph 2:21 together **g** unto a holy temple in the Lord: 837
2Th 1: 3 because that your faith **g exceedingly**, and 5232

GROWN (23) [GROW]
Ge 38:11 thy father's house, till Shelah my son be **g**: 1431
38:14 for she saw that Shelah was **g**, and she was 1431
Ex 2:11 to pass in those days, when Moses was **g**, 1431
9:32 rye were not smitten: for they *were* **not g up**. 648
Lev 13:37 and *that* there is black hair **g up** therein; 6779
Dt 32:15 thou art waxed fat, thou art **g thick**, thou art 5666
Ru 1:13 Would ye tarry for them till they were **g**? 1431
2Sa 10: 5 Tarry at Jericho until your beards be **g**, and 6779
1Ki 12: 8 the young men that were **g up** with him, 1431
12:10 the young men that were **g up** with him 1431
2Ki 4:18 when the child was **g**, it fell on a day, 1431
19:26 and *as* corn blasted before it be **g up**. 7054
1Ch 19: 5 Tarry at Jericho until your beards be **g**, and 6779
Ezr 9: 6 and our trespass is **g up** unto the heavens. 1431
Ps 144:12 That our sons *may be* as plants **g up** in their 1431
Pr 24:31 it was all **g over** *with* thorns, *and* 5927
Isa 37:27 and *as* corn blasted before it be **g up**. 7054
Jer 50:11 because ye are **g fat** as the heifer at grass, 6335
Eze 16: 7 thine hair is **g**, whereas thou *wast* naked 6779
Da 4:22 O king, that art **g** and become strong: 7236
4:22 for thy greatness is **g**, and reacheth unto 7236
4:33 till his hairs were **g** like eagles' *feathers,* 7236
Mt 13:32 but when it is **g**, it is the greatest among 837

GROWTH (2) [GROW]
Am 7: 1 of the shooting up of the **latter g**; 3954
7: 1 *it was* the **latter g** after the king's 3954

GRUDGE (3) [GRUDGING, GRUDGINGLY]
Lev 19:18 nor **bear any g against** the children of thy 5201
Ps 59:15 for meat, and **g** if they be not satisfied. 3885
Jas 5: 9 **G** not one against another, brethren, lest ye 4727

GRUDGING (1) [GRUDGE]
1Pe 4: 9 Use hospitality one to another without **g**. 1112

GRUDGINGLY (1) [GRUDGE]
2Co 9: 7 in *his* heart, *so let him give;* not **g**, 1537+3077

GRUMBLE; GRUMBLED; GRUMBLERS; GRUMBLING See MURMUR MURMURED; MURMURERS; MURMURING; MURMURINGS

GUARANTEE; GUARANTEED See SURETY

GUARD (50) [GUARD'S, SAFEGUARD]
Ge 37:36 officer of Pharaoh's, *and* captain of the **g**. 2876
39: 1 of Pharaoh, captain of the **g**, an Egyptian, 2876
40: 3 in ward *in* the house of the captain of the **g**, 2876
40: 4 the captain of the **g** charged Joseph with 2876
41:12 a Hebrew, servant to the captain of the **g**; 2876
2Sa 23:23 *first* three. And David set him over his **g**. 4928
1Ki 14:27 *them* unto the hands of the chief of the **g**, 7323
14:28 *that* the **g** bare them, and brought them 7323
14:28 and brought them back into the **g** chamber. 7323

2Ki 10:25 that Jehu said to the g and to the captains, 7323
10:25 the g and the captains cast them out, and 7323
11: 4 with the captains and the g, and 7323
11: 6 and a third part at the gate behind the g: 7323
11:11 the g stood, every man with his weapons in 7323
11:13 when Athaliah heard the noise of the g and 7323
11:19 and the g, and all the people of the land; 7323
11:19 came by the way of the gate of the g to 7323
25: 8 came Nebuzar-adan, captain of the g, 2876
25:10 that were with the captain of the g, 2876
25:11 did Nebuzar-adan the captain of the g carry 2876
25:12 the captain of the g left of the poor of 2876
25:15 in silver, the captain of the g took away. 2876
25:18 the captain of the g took Seraiah the chief 2876
25:20 Nebuzar-adan captain of the g took these, 2876
1Ch 11:25 first three: and David set him over his g. 4928
2Ch 12:10 them to the hands of the chief of the g, 7323
12:11 the g came and fet them, and brought them 7323
12:11 and brought them again into the g chamber. 7323
Ne 4:22 that in the night they may be a g to us, and 4929
4:23 nor the men of the g which followed me, 4929
Jer 39: 9 Nebuzar-adan the captain of the g carried 2876
39:10 Nebuzar-adan the captain of the g left of 2876
39:11 to Nebuzar-adan the captain of the g, 2876
39:13 So Nebuzar-adan the captain of the g sent, 2876
40: 1 after that Nebuzar-adan the captain of the g 2876
40: 2 the captain of the g took Jeremiah, and 2876
40: 5 So the captain of the g gave him victuals 2876
41:10 whom Nebuzar-adan the captain of the g 2876
43: 6 g had left with Gedaliah the son of Ahikam 2876
52:12 came Nebuzar-adan, captain of the g, 2876
52:14 that were with the captain of the g, 2876
52:15 Nebuzar-adan the captain of the g carried 2876
52:16 Nebuzar-adan the captain of the g left 2876
52:19 in silver, took the captain of the g away. 2876
52:24 the captain of the g took Seraiah the chief 2876
52:26 So Nebuzar-adan the captain of the g took 2876
52:30 g carried away captive of the Jews seven 2876
Eze 38: 7 unto thee, and be thou a g unto them. 4929
Da 2:14 to Arioch the captain of the king's g, 2877
Ac 28:16 the prisoners to the captain of the g: 4759

GUARD'S (1) [GUARD]
Ge 41:10 put me in ward in the captain of the g 2876

GUARDIANS See TUTORS

GUDGODAH (2)
Dt 10: 7 From thence they journeyed unto G; and 1412
10: 7 from G to Jotbath, a land of rivers of 1412

GUEST (1) [GUESTCHAMBER, GUESTS]
Lk 19: 7 That he was gone to be g with a man that is 2647

GUEST ROOM See GUESTCHAMBER

GUESTCHAMBER (2) [CHAMBER, GUEST]
Mk 14:14 the house, The Master saith, Where is the g, 2646
Lk 22:11 The Master saith unto thee, Where is the g, 2646

GUESTS (6) [GUEST]
1Ki 1:41 all the g that were with him heard it as they 7121
1:49 all the g that were with Adonijah were 7121
Pr 9:18 and that her g are in the depths of hell. 7121
Zep 1: 7 hath prepared a sacrifice, he hath bid his g. 7121
Mt 22:10 good: and the wedding was furnished with g. 345
22:11 And when the king came in to see the g, 345

GUIDE (23) [GUIDED, GUIDES, GUIDING]
Job 38:32 or canst thou g Arcturus with his sons? 5148
Ps 25: 9 The meek will he g in judgment: and 1869
31: 3 for thy name's sake lead me, and g me. 5095
32: 8 thou shalt go: I will g thee with mine eye. 3289
48:14 and ever: he will be our g even unto death. 5090
55:13 mine equal, my g, and mine acquaintance. 441
73:24 Thou shalt g me with thy counsel, and 5148
112: 5 he will g his affairs with discretion. 3557
Pr 2:17 Which forsaketh the g of her youth, and 441
6: 7 Which having no g, overseer, or ruler, 7101
11: 3 The integrity of the upright shall g them: 5148
23:19 and be wise, and g thine heart in the way. 833
Isa 49:10 even by the springs of water shall he g 5095
51:18 There is none to g her among all the sons 5095
58:11 the LORD shall g thee continually, and 5148
Jer 3: 4 My father, thou art the g of my youth? 441
Mic 7: 5 not in a friend, put ye not confidence in a g: 441
Lk 1:79 to g our feet into the way of peace. 2720
Jn 16:13 is come, he will g you into all truth: 3594
Ac 1:16 which was g to them that took Jesus. 3595
8:31 How can I, except some man should g me? 3594
Ro 2:19 And art confident that thou thyself art a g 3595
1Ti 5:14 women marry, bear children, g the house, 3616

GUIDED (5) [GUIDE]
Ex 15:13 thou hast g them in thy strength unto thy 5095
2Ch 32:22 hand of all other, and g them on every side. 5095
Job 31:18 and I have g her from my mother's womb;) 5148
Ps 78:52 and g them in the wilderness like a flock. 5090
78:72 and g them by the skilfulness of his hands. 5148

GUIDES (2) [GUIDE]
Mt 23:16 Woe unto you, ye blind g, which say, 3595
23:24 Ye blind g, which strain out a gnat, and 3595

GUIDING (1) [GUIDE]
Ge 48:14 Manasseh's head, g his hands wittingly; 7919

GUILE (11)
Ex 21:14 upon his neighbour, to slay him with g; 6195
Ps 32: 2 and in whose spirit there is no g. 7423
34:13 from evil, and thy lips from speaking g. 4820
55:11 and g depart not from her streets. 4820
Jn 1:47 an Israelite indeed, in whom is no g. 1388
2Co 12:16 being crafty, I caught you with g. 1388
1Th 2: 3 not of deceit, nor of uncleanness, nor in g: 1388
1Pe 2: 1 and all g, and hypocrisies, and envies, and 1388
2:22 no sin, neither was g found in his mouth: 1388
3:10 from evil, and his lips that they speak no g: 1388
Rev 14: 5 And in their mouth was found no g: 1388

GUILT (2) [BLOODGUILTINESS, GUILTINESS, GUILTLESS, GUILTY]
Dt 19:13 thou shalt put away the g of innocent blood NIH
21: 9 So shalt thou put away the g of innocent NIH

GUILTINESS (1) [GUILT]
Ge 26:10 and thou shouldest have brought g upon us. 817

GUILTLESS (10) [GUILT]
Ex 20: 7 for the LORD will not hold him g that 5352
Nu 5:31 shall the man be g from iniquity, and this 5352
32:22 be g before the LORD, and before Israel; 5355
Dt 5:11 for the LORD will not hold him g that 5352
Jos 2:19 shall be upon his head, and we will be g: 5355
1Sa 26: 9 against the LORD'S anointed, and be g? 5352
2Sa 3:28 my kingdom are g before the LORD for 5355
14: 9 and the king and his throne be g. 5355
1Ki 2: 9 Now therefore hold him not g: for thou art 5352
Mt 12: 7 ye would not have condemned the g. 338

GUILTY (26) [GUILT]
Ge 42:21 We are verily g concerning our brother, 818
Ex 34: 7 that will by no means clear the g; visiting NIH
Lev 4:13 things which should not be done, and are g; 816
4:22 things which should not be done, and is g; 816
4:27 things which ought not to be done, and be g; 816
5: 2 from him; he also shall be unclean, and g. 816
5: 3 when he knoweth of it, then he shall be g. 816
5: 4 of it, then he shall be g in one of these. 816
5: 5 when he shall be g in one of these things, 816
5:17 it not, yet is he g, and shall bear his iniquity. 816
6: 4 it shall be, because he hath sinned, and is g, 816
Nu 5: 6 against the LORD, and that person be g; 816
14:18 by no means clearing the g, visiting NIH
35:27 kill the slayer; he shall not be g of blood: 3807.1
35:31 the life of a murderer, which is g of death: 7563
Jdg 21:22 unto them at this time, that you should be g. 816
Ezr 10:19 being g, they offered a ram of the flock for 818
Pr 30:10 lest he curse thee, and thou be found g. 816
Eze 22: 4 Thou art become g in thy blood that thou 816
Zec 11: 5 slay them, and hold themselves not g: 816
Mt 23:18 sweareth by the gift that is upon it, he is g. 3784
26:66 They answered and said, He is g of death. 1777
Mk 14:64 And they all condemned him to be g of 1777
Ro 3:19 all the world may become g before God. 5267
1Co 11:27 shall be g of the body and blood of 1777
Jas 2:10 and yet offend in one point, he is g of all. 1777

GULF (1)
Lk 16:26 between us and you there is a great g fixed: 5490

G

GULL See CUCKOW

GUM RESIN See STACTE

GUNI (4) [GUNITES]
Ge 46:24 Jahzeel, and **G**, and Jezer, and Shillem. 1476
Nu 26:48 of **G**, the family of the Gunites: 1476
1Ch 5:15 Ahi the son of Abdiel, the son of **G**, 1476
7:13 Jahziel, and **G**, and Jezer, and Shallum, 1476

GUNITES (1) [GUNI]
Nu 26:48 of Guni, the family of the **G**: 1477

GUR (1)
2Ki 9:27 *And they did so* at the going up to **G**, 1483

GUR-BAAL (1) [BAAL]
2Ch 26: 7 against the Arabians that dwelt in **G**, and 1485

GUSH (1) [GUSHED]
Jer 9:18 and our eyelids **g out** with waters. 5140

GUSHED (5) [GUSH]
1Ki 18:28 and lancets, till the blood **g out** upon them. 8210
Ps 78:20 that the waters **g out**, and the streams 2100
105:41 He opened the rock, and the waters **g out**; 2100
Isa 48:21 he clave the rock also, and the waters **g out**. 2100
Ac 1:18 in the midst, and all his bowels **g out**. *1632*

GUTTER (1) [GUTTERS]
2Sa 5: 8 Whosoever getteth up to the **g**, and 6794

GUTTERS (2) [GUTTER]
Ge 30:38 **g** in the watering troughs when the flocks 7298
30:41 rods before the eyes of the cattle in the **g**, 7298

H

HA (2) [AHA]
Job 39:25 He saith among the trumpets, **H**, ha; and 1889
39:25 He saith among the trumpets, Ha, **h**; and NIH

HAAHASHTARI (1)
1Ch 4: 6 and Hepher, and Temeni, and **H**. 326

HABAIAH (2)
Ezr 2:61 the children of **H**, the children of Koz, 2252
Ne 7:63 the children of **H**, the children of Koz, 2252

HABAKKUK (2)
Hab 1: 1 The burden which **H** the prophet did see. 2265
3: 1 A prayer of **H** the prophet upon Shigionoth. 2265

HABAZINIAH (1)
Jer 35: 3 the son of **H**, and his brethren, and all his 2262

HABAZZINIAH See HABAZINIAH

HABERGEON (3) [HABERGEONS]
Ex 28:32 as it were the hole of an **h**, *that* it be not 8473
39:23 as the hole of an **h**, *with* a band round about 8473
Job 41:26 cannot hold: the spear, the dart, nor the **h**. 8302

HABERGEONS (2) [HABERGEON]
2Ch 26:14 and **h**, and bows, and slings to cast stones. 8302
Ne 4:16 the shields, and the bows, and the **h**; 8302

HABIT See WONT

HABITABLE (1) [INHABIT]
Pr 8:31 Rejoicing in the **h part** of his earth; and 8398

HABITATION (58) [INHABIT]
Ex 15: 2 he *is* my God, and I will **prepare him a h**; 5115
15:13 *them* in thy strength unto thy holy **h**. 5116
Lev 13:46 without the camp *shall* his **h** *be*. 4186
Dt 12: 5 *even* unto his **h** shall ye seek, and 7931
26:15 Look down from thy holy **h**, from heaven, 4583
1Sa 2:29 which I have commanded *in my* **h**; 4583
2:32 thou shalt see an enemy *in my* **h**, in all 4583
2Sa 15:25 me again, and shew me *both* it, and his **h**: 5116
2Ch 6: 2 I have built a house of **h** for thee, and 2073
29: 6 have turned away their faces from the **h** of 4908
Ezr 7:15 the God of Israel, whose **h** *is* in Jerusalem, 4907
Job 5: 3 taking root: but suddenly I cursed his **h**. 5116
5:24 and thou shalt visit thy **h**, and shalt not sin. 5116
8: 6 make the **h** of thy righteousness 5116
18:15 brimstone shall be scattered upon his **h**. 5116
Ps 26: 8 I have loved the **h** of thy house, and 4583
33:14 From the place of his **h** he looketh upon all 3427
68: 5 a judge of the widows, *is* God in his holy **h**. 4583
69:25 Let their **h** be desolate; *and* let none dwell 2918
71: 3 Be thou my strong **h**, whereunto *I* may 4583
89:14 and judgment *are* the **h** of thy throne: 4349
91: 9 *is* my refuge, *even* the most High, thy **h**; 4583
97: 2 and judgment *are* the **h** of his throne. 4349
104:12 shall the fowls of the heaven have their **h**, 7931
107: 7 right way, that *they* might go to a city of **h**. 4186
107:36 to dwell, that they may prepare a city for **h**; 4186
132: 5 a **h** for the mighty *God* of Jacob. 4908
132:13 chosen Zion; he hath desired *it* for his **h**. 4186
Pr 3:33 but he blesseth the **h** of the just. 5116
Isa 22:16 *and* that graveth a **h** for himself in a rock? 4908
27:10 *and* the **h** forsaken, and left like a 5116
32:18 my people shall dwell in a peaceable **h**, 5116
33:20 thine eyes shall see Jerusalem a quiet **h**, 5116
34:13 it shall be a **h** of dragons, *and* a court for 5116
35: 7 in the **h** of dragons, where each lay, 5116
63:15 behold from the **h** of thy holiness and 2073
Jer 9: 6 Thine **h** *is* in the midst of deceit; 3427
10:25 and have made his **h** desolate. 5116
25:30 and utter his voice from his holy **h**; 4583
25:30 he shall mightily roar upon his **h**; he shall 5116
31:23 O **h** of justice, *and* mountain of holiness. 5116
33:12 shall be a **h** of shepherds causing *their* 5116
41:17 and dwelt in the **h** of Chimham, 1628
49:19 of Jordan against the **h** of the strong: 5116
50: 7 the **h** of justice, even the LORD, the hope 5116
50:19 I will bring Israel again to his **h**, and 5116
50:44 swelling of Jordan unto the **h** of the strong: 5116
50:45 surely he shall make *their* **h** desolate with 5116
Eze 29:14 the land of Pathros, into the land of their **h**; 4351
Da 4:21 the fowls of the heaven had their **h**: 7932
Ob 1: 3 in the clefts of the rock, whose **h** *is* high; 7675
Hab 3:11 The sun *and* moon stood still in *their* **h**: 2073
Zec 2:13 for he is raised up out of his holy **h**. 4583
Ac 1:20 Let his **h** be desolate, and let no man dwell *1886*
17:26 before appointed, and the bounds of their **h**; *2733*
Eph 2:22 together for a **h** of God through the Spirit. *2732*
Jude 1: 6 not their first estate, but left their own **h**, *3613*
Rev 18: 2 is fallen, and is become the **h** of devils, *2732*

HABITATIONS (20) [INHABIT]
Ge 36:43 according to their **h** in the land of their 4186
49: 5 instruments of cruelty *are in* their **h**. 4380
Ex 12:20 in all your **h** shall ye eat unleavened bread. 4186
35: 3 Ye shall kindle no fire throughout your **h** 4186
Lev 23:17 Ye shall bring out of your **h** two wave 4186
Nu 15: 2 When ye be come into the land of your **h**, 4186
1Ch 4:33 These *were* their **h**, and their genealogy. 4186
4:41 the **h** that were found there, and 4583
7:28 and **h** *were*, Beth-el and the towns thereof, 4186
Ps 74:20 of the earth are full *of* the **h** of cruelty. 4999
78:28 midst of their camp, round about their **h**. 4908
Isa 54: 2 them stretch forth the curtains of thine **h**: 4908
Jer 9:10 for the **h** of the wilderness a lamentation, 4999
21:13 against us? or who shall enter into our **h**? 4585
25:37 the peaceable **h** are cut down because of 4999
49:20 surely he shall make their **h** desolate with 5116
La 2: 2 The Lord hath swallowed up all the **h** of 4999
Eze 6:14 wilderness toward Diblath, in all their **h**: 4186
Am 1: 2 the **h** of the shepherds shall mourn, and 4999
Lk 16: 9 they may receive you into everlasting **h**. *4633*

HABOR (3)
2Ki 17: 6 in Halah and in **H** *by* the river of Gozan, 2249
18:11 in Halah and in **H** *by* the river of Gozan, 2249
1Ch 5:26 **H**, and Hara, and to the river Gozan, 2249

HACHALIAH (2)
Ne 1: 1 The words of Nehemiah the son of **H**. 2446
10: 1 the Tirshatha, the son of **H**, and Zidkijah, 2446

HACHILAH (3)
1Sa 23:19 in the hill of **H**, which *is* on the south of 2444
26: 1 not David hide himself in the hill of **H**, 2444
26: 3 Saul pitched in the hill of **H**, which *is* 2444

HACHMONI (1) [HACHMONITE]
1Ch 27:32 Jehiel the son of **H** *was* with the king's 2453

HACHMONITE (1) [HACHMONI]
1Ch 11:11 a **H**, the chief of the captains: 1121+2453

HACMONI See HACHMONI

HACMONITE See HACHMONITE

HAD (2030) [HAVE] See Index

HADAD (14) [HADADEZER, HADADRIMMON]
Ge 36:35 And Husham died, and **H** the son of Bedad, 1908
36:36 **H** died, and Samlah of Masrekah reigned in 1908
1Ki 11:14 adversary unto Solomon, **H** the Edomite: 1908
11:17 That **H** fled, he and certain Edomites of his 111
11:17 to go *into* Egypt; **H** *being yet* a little child. 1908
11:19 **H** found great favour in the sight of 1908
11:21 when **H** heard in Egypt that David slept 1908
11:21 **H** said to Pharaoh, Let me depart, that I 1908
11:25 beside the mischief that **H** *did:* and 1908
1Ch 1:30 Mishma, and Dumah, Massa, **H**, and Tema, 2301
1:46 Husham was dead, **H** the son of Bedad, 1908
1:47 when **H** was dead, Samlah of Masrekah 1908
1:50 was dead, **H** reigned in his stead: 1908
1:51 **H** died also. And the dukes of Edom were; 1908

HADADEZER (9) [HADAD, HADAREZER]
2Sa 8: 3 David smote also **H**, the son of Rehob, 1909
8: 5 came to succour **H** king of Zobah, 1909
8: 7 of gold that were on the servants of **H**, 1909
8: 8 from Betah, and from Berothai, cities of **H**, 1909
8: 9 that David had smitten all the host of **H**, 1909
8:10 because he had fought against **H**, and 1909
8:10 for **H** had wars with Toi. And *Joram* 1909
8:12 of Amalek, and of the spoil of **H**, son of 1909
1Ki 11:23 which fled from his lord **H** king of Zobah: 1909

HADADRIMMON (1) [HADAD, RIMMON]
Zec 12:11 as the mourning of **H** in the valley of 1910

HADAR (2) [HADAREZER]
Ge 25:15 **H**, and Tema, Jetur, Naphish, and 2316
36:39 of Achbor died, and **H** reigned in his stead: 1924

HADAREZER (12) [HADADEZER, HADAR]
2Sa 10:16 **H** sent, and brought out the Syrians that 1928
10:16 Shobach the captain of the host of **H** *went* 1928
10:19 when all the kings *that were* servants to **H** 1928
1Ch 18: 3 David smote **H** king of Zobah unto 1928
18: 5 Damascus came to help **H** king of Zobah, 1928
18: 7 of gold that were on the servants of **H**, 1928
18: 8 from Tibhath, and from Chun, cities of **H**, 1928
18: 9 had smitten all the host of **H** king of Zobah; 1928
18:10 because he had fought against **H**, and 1928
18:10 (for **H** had war with Tou;) and *with him* all 1928
19:16 Shophach the captain of the host of **H** *went* 1928
19:19 when the servants of **H** saw that they were 1928

HADASHAH (1)
Jos 15:37 Zenan, and **H**, and Migdal-gad, 2322

HADASSAH (1) [ESTHER]
Est 2: 7 he brought up **H**, that *is*, Esther, his uncle's 1919

HADATTAH See HAZOR HADATTAH

HADID (3)
Ezr 2:33 The children of Lod, **H**, and Ono, 2307
Ne 7:37 The children of Lod, **H**, and Ono, 2307
11:34 **H**, Zeboim, Neballat, 2307

HADLAI (1)
2Ch 28:12 son of Shallum, and Amasa the son of **H**, 2311

HADORAM (4)
Ge 10:27 And **H**, and Uzal, and Diklah, 1913
1Ch 1:21 **H** also, and Uzal, and Diklah, 1913
18:10 He sent **H** his son to king David, to inquire 1913
2Ch 10:18 king Rehoboam sent **H** that *was* over 1913

HADRACH (1)
Zec 9: 1 of the word of the LORD in the land of **H**, 2317

HADST (22) [HAVE] See Index

HAELEPH See ELEPH

HAFT (1)
Jdg 3:22 the **h** also went in after the blade; and 5325

HAGAB (1) [HAGABA, HAGABAH]
Ezr 2:46 The children of **H**, the children of Shalmai, 2285

HAGABA (1) [HAGAB]
Ne 7:48 The children of Lebana, the children of **H**, 2286

HAGABAH (1) [HAGAB]
Ezr 2:45 the children of **H**, the children of Akkub, 2286

HAGAR (12) [AGAR]
Ge 16: 1 an Egyptian, whose name *was* **H**. 1904
16: 3 Sarai Abram's wife took **H** her maid 1904
16: 4 he went in unto **H**, and she conceived: and 1904
16: 8 he said, **H**, Sarai's maid, whence camest 1904
16:15 **H** bare Abram a son: and Abram called his 1904
16:15 his son's name, which **H** bare, Ishmael. 1904
16:16 years old, when **H** bare Ishmael to Abram. 1904
21: 9 Sarah saw the son of **H** the Egyptian, 1904
21:14 and a bottle of water, and gave *it* unto **H**, 1904
21:17 the angel of God called to **H** out of heaven, 1904
21:17 and said unto her, What aileth thee, **H**? 1904
25:12 Abraham's son, whom **H** the Egyptian, 1904

HAGARENES (1) [HAGARITES]
Ps 83: 6 and the Ishmaelites; of Moab, and the **H**; 1905

HAGARITES (3) [HAGARENES, HAGERITE]
1Ch 5:10 the days of Saul they made war with the **H**, 1905
5:19 they made war with the **H**, with Jetur, and 1905
5:20 the **H** were delivered into their hand, and 1905

HAGERITE (1) [HAGARITES]
1Ch 27:31 over the flocks *was* Jaziz the **H**. All these 1905

HAGGAI (11)
Ezr 5: 1 **H** the prophet, and Zechariah the son of 2292
6:14 through the prophesying of **H** the prophet 2292
Hag 1: 1 came the word of the LORD by **H** 2292
1: 3 came the word of the LORD by **H** 2292
1:12 the words of **H** the prophet, as the LORD 2292
1:13 spake **H** the LORD'S messenger in 2292
2: 1 the word of the LORD by the prophet **H**, 2292
2:10 came the word of the LORD by **H** 2292
2:13 said **H**, If *one that is* unclean *by* a dead 2292
2:14 answered **H**, and said, So *is* this people, 2292
2:20 again the word of the LORD came unto **H** 2292

HAGGERI (1)
1Ch 11:38 the brother of Nathan, Mibhar the son of **H**, 1905

HAGGI (2) [HAGGITES]
Ge 46:16 **H**, Shuni, and Ezbon, Eri, and Arodi, and 2291
Nu 26:15 of **H**, the family of the Haggites: of Shuni, 2291

HAGGIAH (1)
1Ch 6:30 Shimea his son, **H** his son, Asaiah his son. 2293

HAGGITES (1) [HAGGI]
Nu 26:15 of Haggi, the family of the **H**: of Shuni, 2291

HAGGITH (5)
2Sa 3: 4 the fourth, Adonijah the son of **H**; 2294
1Ki 1: 5 Adonijah the son of **H** exalted himself, 2294
1:11 that Adonijah the son of **H** doth reign, 2294
2:13 Adonijah the son of **H** came to Bath-sheba 2294
1Ch 3: 2 the fourth, Adonijah the son of **H**: 2294

HAGRI See HAGGERI

HAGRITE See HAGARITES; HAGERITE

HAI (2) [AI]
Ge 12: 8 Beth-el on the west, and **H** on the east: 5857
13: 3 at the beginning, between Beth-el and **H**; 5857

HAIL (36) [HAILSTONES, HAIL-STONES]
Ex 9:18 I will cause it to rain a very grievous **h**, 1259

H

Ex 9:19 the **h** shall come down upon them, and 1259
9:22 that there may be **h** in all the land of Egypt, 1259
9:23 the LORD sent thunder and **h**, and the fire 1259
9:23 the LORD rained **h** upon the land of 1259
9:24 So there was **h**, and fire mingled with 1259
9:24 and fire mingled with the **h**, very grievous, 1259
9:25 the **h** smote throughout all the land of 1259
9:25 the **h** smote every herb of the field, and 1259
9:26 the children of Israel *were*, was there no **h**. 1259
9:28 there be no *more* mighty thunderings and **h**; 1259
9:29 neither shall there be any more **h**; 1259
9:33 the thunders and **h** ceased, and the rain was 1259
9:34 and the **h** and the thunders were ceased, 1259
10: 5 which remaineth unto you from the **h**, 1259
10:12 of the land, *even* all that the **h** hath left. 1259
10:15 all the fruit of the trees which the **h** had 1259
Job 38:22 or hast thou seen the treasures of the **h**, 1259
Ps 78:47 He destroyed their vines with **h**, and 1259
78:48 He gave up their cattle also to the **h**, and 1259
105:32 He gave them **h** *for* rain, *and* flaming fire in 1259
148: 8 Fire, and **h**; snow, and vapour; stormy wind 1259
Isa 28: 2 *which* as a tempest of **h** *and* a destroying 1259
28:17 the **h** shall sweep away the refuge of lies, 1259
32:19 When it shall **h**, coming down *on* 1258
Hag 2:17 and with **h** *in* all the labours of your hands; 1259
Mt 26:49 he came to Jesus, and said, **H**, master; *5463*
27:29 and mocked him, saying, **H**, King of *5463*
28: 9 behold, Jesus met them, saying, *All* **h**. *5463*
Mk 15:18 began to salute him, **H**, King of the Jews. *5463*
Lk 1:28 and said, **H**, *thou that art* highly favoured, *5463*
Jn 19: 3 And said, **H**, King of the Jews: and *5463*
Rev 8: 7 and there followed **h** and fire mingled with *5464*
11:19 and an earthquake, and great **h**. *5464*
16:21 And there fell upon men a great **h** out of *5464*
16:21 because of the plague of the **h**; *5464*

HAILSTONES, HAIL-STONES (7) [HAIL, STONE]

Jos 10:11 **h** than *they* whom the children 68+1259+1886.1
Ps 18:12 clouds passed, **h** and coals of fire. 1259
18:13 gave his voice; **h** and coals of fire. 1259
Isa 30:30 *with* scattering, and tempest, and **h**. 68+1259
Eze 13:11 ye, O **great h**, shall fall; and a stormy 68+417
13:13 and **great h** in *my* fury to consume *it*. 68+417
38:22 and **great h**, fire, and brimstone. 68+417

HAIR (64) [HAIRS, HAIRY]

Ex 25: 4 and scarlet, and fine linen, and goats' *h*, NIH
26: 7 thou shalt make curtains *of* goats' *h* to be a NIH
35: 6 and scarlet, and fine linen, and goats' *h*, NIH
35:23 goats' *h*, and red skins of rams, and NIH
35:26 stirred them up in wisdom spun goats' *h*. NIH
36:14 he made curtains *of* goats' *h* for the tent NIH
Lev 13: 3 *when* the **h** in the plague is turned white, 8181
13: 4 and the **h** thereof be not turned white; 8181
13:10 it have turned the **h** white, and *there be* 8181
13:20 the skin, and the **h** thereof be turned white; 8181
13:25 *if* the **h** in the bright spot be turned white, 8181
13:26 *there be* no white **h** in the bright spot, and 8181
13:30 *there be* in it a yellow thin **h**; then the priest 8181
13:31 the skin, and *that there is* no black **h** in it; 8181
13:32 there be in it no yellow **h**, and the scall *be* 8181
13:36 the priest shall not seek for yellow **h**: 8181
13:37 and *that* there is black **h** grown up therein; 8181
13:40 And the man whose **h** is **fallen off** his head, 4803
13:41 he that hath his **h fallen off** from the part of 4803
14: 8 shave off all his **h**, and wash *himself* in 8181
14: 9 *that* he shall shave all his **h** off his head and 8181
14: 9 even all his **h** he shall shave off: 8181
Nu 6: 5 shall let the locks of the **h** of his head grow. 8181
6:18 shall take the **h** of the head of his 8181
6:19 after *the* **h** *of* his separation is shaven: NIH
31:20 all work of goats' *h*, and all things made of NIH
Jdg 16:22 Howbeit the **h** of his head began to grow 8181
20:16 every one could sling stones at a **h** *breadth*, 8185
1Sa 14:45 there shall not one **h** of his head fall to 8185
19:13 put a pillow of goats' *h for* his bolster, and NIH
19:16 with a pillow of goats' *h for* his bolster. NIH
2Sa 14:11 there shall not one **h** of thy son fall to 8185
14:26 polled *it:* because *the* **h** was heavy on him, NIH
14:26 he weighed the **h** of his head *at* two 8181
1Ki 1:52 there shall not a **h** of him fall to the earth: 8185
Ezr 9: 3 pluckt off the **h** of my head and of my 8181
Ne 13:25 **pluckt off** their **h**, and made them swear by 4803
Job 4:15 before my face; the **h** of my flesh stood up: 8185

SS 4: 1 thy **h** *is* as a flock of goats, that appear 8181
6: 5 thy **h** *is* as a flock of goats that appear from 8181
7: 5 and the **h** of thine head like purple; 1803
Isa 3:24 instead of **well set h** baldness; and 4639+4748
7:20 of Assyria, the head, and the **h** of the feet: 8181
50: 6 my cheeks to them that **plucked off** the **h**: 4803
Jer 7:29 Cut off thine **h**, *O Jerusalem*, and cast *it* 5145
Eze 5: 1 thee balances to weigh, and divide *the h*. NIH
16: 7 thine **h** is grown, whereas thou *wast* naked 8181
Da 3:27 nor was a **h** of their head singed, 8177
7: 9 and the **h** of his head like the pure wool: 8177
Mt 3: 4 the same John had his raiment of camel's **h**, *2359*
5:36 thou canst not make one **h** white or black. *2359*
Mk 1: 6 And John was clothed with camel's **h**, and *2359*
Lk 21:18 But there shall not a **h** of your head perish. *2359*
Jn 11: 2 and wiped his feet with her **h**, *2359*
12: 3 feet of Jesus, and wiped his feet with her **h**: *2359*
Ac 27:34 for there shall not a **h** fall from the head of *2359*
1Co 11:14 that, if a man **have long h**, it is a shame *2863*
11:15 But if a woman **have long h**, it is a glory to *2863*
11:15 to her: for *her* **h** is given her for a covering. *2864*
1Ti 2: 9 and sobriety; not with **broided h**, *4117*
1Pe 3: 3 be that outward *adorning* of plaiting the **h**, *2359*
Rev 6:12 and the sun became black as sackcloth **of h**, *5155*
9: 8 And they had **h** as the hair of women, and *2359*
9: 8 And they had hair as the **h** of women, and *2359*

HAIRS (15) [HAIR]

Ge 42:38 shall ye bring down my **gray h** with sorrow 7872
44:29 ye shall bring down my **gray h** with sorrow 7872
44:31 thy servants shall bring down the **gray h** of 7872
Lev 13:21 *there be* no white **h** therein, and *if* it *be* not 8181
Dt 32:25 the suckling *also* with the man of **gray h**. 7872
Ps 40:12 *up;* they are moe than the **h** of mine head: 8185
69: 4 a cause are moe than the **h** of mine head: 8185
Isa 46: 4 *even* to **hoar h** will I carry *you:* I have 7872
Da 4:33 till his **h** were grown like eagles' *feathers,* 8177
Hos 7: 9 yea, **gray h** are here and there upon him, 7872
Mt 10:30 But the very **h** of your head are all *2359*
Lk 7:38 and did wipe *them* with the **h** of her head, *2359*
7:44 and wiped *them* with the **h** of her head. *2359*
12: 7 But even the *very* **h** of your head are all *2359*
Rev 1:14 His head and *his* **h** *were* white like wool, *2359*

HAIRY (5) [HAIR]

Ge 25:25 came out red, all over like a **h** garment; 8181
27:11 Esau my brother *is* a **h** man, and I *am* a 8163
27:23 him not, because his hands were **h**, 8163
2Ki 1: 8 *He was* a **h** man, and girt *with* a girdle of 8181
Ps 68:21 the **h** scalp of such a one as goeth on still in 8181

HAKILAH See HACHILAH

HAKKATAN (1)

Ezr 8:12 Johanan the son of **H**, and with him an 6997

HAKKOZ (1)

1Ch 24:10 The seventh to **H**, the eighth to Abijah, 6976

HAKUPHA (2)

Ezr 2:51 the children of **H**, the children of Harhur, 2709
Ne 7:53 the children of **H**, the children of Harhur, 2709

HALAH (3)

2Ki 17: 6 placed them in **H** and in Habor *by* the river 2477
18:11 put them in **H** and in Habor *by* the river of 2477
1Ch 5:26 brought them unto **H**, and Habor, and Hara, 2477

HALAK (2)

Jos 11:17 *Even* from the mount **H**, that goeth up *to* 2510
12: 7 valley of Lebanon even unto the mount **H**, 2510

HALE (1) [HALING]

Lk 12:58 lest he **h** thee to the judge, and the judge *2694*

HALF (136)

Ge 24:22 took a golden earring of **h a shekel** weight, 1235
Ex 24: 6 Moses took **h** of the blood, and put *it* in 2677
24: 6 and **h** of the blood he sprinkled on the altar. 2677
25:10 and a **h** *shall be* the length thereof, 2677
25:10 a cubit and a **h** the breadth thereof, and 2677
25:10 and a cubit and a **h** the height thereof. 2677
25:17 and a **h** *shall be* the length thereof, 2677
25:17 and a cubit and a **h** the breadth thereof. 2677
25:23 and a cubit and a **h** the height thereof. 2677

Ex 26:12 the **h** curtain that remaineth, shall hang 2677
26:16 and a **h** *shall be* the breadth of one board. 2677
30:13 **h** a shekel after the shekel of the sanctuary: 4276
30:13 a **h** shekel *shall be* the offering of 4276
30:15 the poor shall not give less than **h** a shekel, 4276
30:23 and of sweet cinnamon **h so much**, 4276
36:21 the breadth of a board one cubit and a **h**. 2677
37: 1 two cubits and a **h** *was* the length of it, and 2677
37: 1 a cubit and a **h** the breadth of it, and a cubit 2677
37: 1 of it, and a cubit and a **h** the height of it: 2677
37: 6 two cubits and a **h** *was* the length thereof, 2677
37: 6 and one cubit and a **h** the breadth thereof. 2677
37:10 and a cubit and a **h** the height thereof: 2677
38:26 A bekah for every man, *that is*, **h** a shekel, 4276
Lev 6:20 **h** of it in the morning, and half thereof at 4276
6:20 of it in the morning, and **h** thereof at night. 4276
Nu 12:12 of whom the flesh is **h** consumed when he 2677
15: 9 deals *of* flour mingled with **h** a hin of oil. 2677
15:10 thou shalt bring for a drink offering **h** a hin 2677
28:14 their drink offerings shall be **h** a hin of 2677
31:29 Take *it* of their **h**, and give *it* unto Eleazar 4276
31:30 of the children of Israel's **h**, thou shalt take 4276
31:36 the **h**, *which was* the portion of them that 4275
31:42 of the children of Israel's **h**, which Moses 4276
31:43 (Now the **h** that pertained unto 4275
31:47 Even of the children of Israel's **h**, 4276
32:33 unto **h** the tribe of Manasseh the son of 2677
34:13 give unto the nine tribes, and *to* the **h** tribe: 2677
34:14 **h** the tribe of Manasseh have received their 2677
34:15 the **h** tribe have received their inheritance 2677
Dt 3:12 **h** mount Gilead, and the cities thereof, 2677
3:13 of Og, gave I unto the **h** tribe of Manasseh; 2677
3:16 **h** the valley, and the border, even unto 8432
29: 8 the Gadites, and to the **h** tribe of Manasseh. 2677
Jos 1:12 to **h** the tribe of Manasseh, spake Joshua, 2677
4:12 of Gad, and **h** the tribe of Manasseh, 2677
8:33 **h** of them over against mount Gerizim, and 2677
8:33 and **h** of them over against mount Ebal; 2677
12: 2 *from* **h** Gilead, even unto the river Jabbok, 2677
12: 5 and the Maachathites, and **h** Gilead, 2677
12: 6 the Gadites, and the **h** tribe of Manasseh. 2677
13: 7 the nine tribes, and the **h** tribe of Manasseh, 2677
13:25 and **h** the land of the children of Ammon, 2677
13:29 Moses gave *inheritance* unto the **h** tribe of 2677
13:29 *this was the possession* of the **h** tribe of 2677
13:31 **h** Gilead, and Ashtaroth, and Edrei, 2677
13:31 *even* to the **one h** of the children of Machir 2677
14: 2 for the nine tribes, and *for* the **h** tribe. 2677
14: 3 and a **h** tribe on the *other* side Jordan: 2677
18: 7 and Reuben, and **h** the tribe of Manasseh, 2677
21: 5 out of the **h** tribe of Manasseh, ten cities. 2677
21: 6 out of the **h** tribe of Manasseh in Bashan, 2677
21:25 out of the **h** tribe of Manasseh, Tanach with 4276
21:27 out of the *other* **h** tribe of Manasseh *they* 2677
22: 1 the Gadites, and the **h** tribe of Manasseh, 2677
22: 7 Now to the *one* **h** of the tribe of Manasseh 2677
22: 7 unto the *other* **h** thereof gave Joshua among 2677
22: 9 and the **h** tribe of Manasseh returned, 2677
22:10 the **h** tribe of Manasseh built there an altar 2677
22:11 the **h** tribe of Manasseh have built an altar 2677
22:13 of Gad, and to the **h** tribe of Manasseh, 2677
22:15 of Gad, and to the **h** tribe of Manasseh, 2677
22:21 and the **h** tribe of Manasseh answered, 2677
1Sa 14:14 within as it were a **h** acre of land, 2677
2Sa 10: 4 shaved off the *one* **h** of their beards, and 2677
18: 3 neither if **h** of us die, will they care for us: 2677
19:40 the king, and also **h** the people of Israel. 2677
1Ki 3:25 and give **h** to the one, and half to the other. 2677
3:25 and give half to the one, and **h** to the other. 2677
7:31 *after* the work of the base, a cubit and a **h**: 2677
7:32 height of a wheel *was* a cubit and **h** a cubit. 2677
7:35 *there* a round compass of **h** a cubit high: 2677
10: 7 seen *it*: and behold, the **h** was not told me: 2677
13: 8 If thou wilt give me **h** thine house, I will 2677
16: 9 captain of **h** *his* chariots, conspired against 4276
16:21 **h** of the people followed Tibni the son of 2677
16:21 to make him king; and **h** followed Omri. 2677
1Ch 2:52 Haroeh, *and* **h** of the Manahethites. 2677
2:54 and **h** of the Manahethites, the Zorites. 2677
5:18 the Gadites, and **h** the tribe of Manasseh, 2677
5:23 the children of the **h** tribe of Manasseh 2677
5:26 the **h** tribe of Manasseh, and brought them 2677
6:61 *were cities given* out of the **h** tribe, 2677
6:61 *namely, out of* the **h** *tribe* of Manasseh, 4276
6:70 out of the **h** tribe of Manasseh; Aner with 4276
6:71 of the family of the **h** tribe of Manasseh, 2677
12:31 of the **h** tribe of Manasseh eighteen 2677
12:37 the Gadites, and of the **h** tribe of Manasseh, 2677
26:32 the Gadites, and the **h** tribe of Manasseh, 2677
27:20 of the **h** tribe of Manasseh, Joel the son of 2677
27:21 Of the **h** *tribe* of Manasseh in Gilead, 2677
2Ch 9: 6 *the one* **h** of the greatness of thy wisdom 2677
Ne 3: 9 of Hur, the ruler of the **h** part of Jerusalem. 2677
3:12 the ruler of the **h** part of Jerusalem, he and 2677
3:16 the ruler of the **h** part of Beth-zur, 2677
3:17 the ruler of the **h** part of Keilah, in his part. 2677
3:18 the ruler of the **h** part of Keilah. 2677
4: 6 all the wall was joined together unto the **h** 2677
4:16 *that* the **h** of my servants wrought in 2677
4:16 the *other* **h** of them held both the spears, 2677
4:21 **h** of them held the spears from the rising of 2677
12:32 and **h** of the princes of Judah, 2677
12:38 and the **h** of the people upon the wall, 2677
12:40 and I, and the **h** of the rulers with me: 2677
13:24 their children spake **h** in the speech of 2677
Est 5: 3 it shall be even given thee to the **h** of 2677
5: 6 even to the **h** of the kingdom it shall be 2677
7: 2 *even* to the **h** of the kingdom. 2677
Ps 55:23 deceitful men shall not **live out h** their 2673
Eze 16:51 Neither hath Samaria committed **h** of thy 2677
40:42 of a cubit and a **h** long, and a cubit and 2677
40:42 a cubit and a **h** broad, and one cubit high: 2677
43:17 the border about it *shall be* **h** a cubit; and 2677
Da 12: 7 that *it shall be* for a time, times, and a **h**; 2677
Hos 3: 2 homer of barley, and a **h homer** of barley: 3963
Zec 14: 2 **h** of the city shall go forth into captivity, 2677
14: 4 **h** of the mountain shall remove toward 2677
14: 4 the north, and **h** of it toward the south. 2677
14: 8 **h** of them toward the former sea, and 2677
14: 8 and **h** of them toward the hinder sea: 2677
Mk 6:23 will give *it* thee, unto the **h** of my kingdom. *2255*
Lk 10:30 and departed, leaving *him* **h dead**. *2253*
19: 8 Lord, the **h** of my goods I give to the poor; *2255*
Rev 8: 1 in heaven about the space of **h an hour**. *2256*
11: 9 see their dead bodies three days and a **h**, *2255*
11:11 a **h** the spirit of life from God entered into *2255*
12:14 and times, and **h** a time, from the face of *2255*

HALHUL (1)
Jos 15:58 **H**, Beth-zur, and Gedor, 2478

HALI (1)
Jos 19:25 and **H**, and Beten, and Achshaph, 2482

HALING (1) [HALE]
Ac 8: 3 and **h** men and women committed *them* to *4951*

HALL (8)
Mt 27:27 governor took Jesus into the **common h**, *4232*
Mk 15:16 And the soldiers led him away into the **h**, *833*
Lk 22:55 they had kindled a fire in the midst of the **h**, *833*
Jn 18:28 from Caiaphas unto the **h of judgment**: *4232*
18:28 themselves went not into the **judgment h**, *4232*
18:33 Then Pilate entered into the **judgment h** *4232*
19: 9 And went again into the **judgment h**, and *4232*
Ac 23:35 him to be kept in Herod's **judgment h**. *4232*

HALLELUIA See ALLELUIA

HALLOHESH (2)
Ne 3:12 unto him repaired Shallum the son of **H**, 3873
10:24 **H**, Pileha, Shobek, 3873

HALLOW (15) [HALLOWED]
Ex 28:38 of Israel shall **h** in all their holy gifts; 6942
29: 1 that thou shalt do unto them to **h** them, 6942
40: 9 shalt **h** it, and all the vessels thereof: 6942
Lev 16:19 **h** it from the uncleanness of the children of 6942
22: 2 name *in those things* which they **h** unto me: 6942
22: 3 the children of Israel **h** unto the LORD, 6942
22:32 of Israel: I *am* the LORD which **h** you, 6942
25:10 ye shall **h** the fiftieth year, and 6942
Nu 6:11 and shall **h** his head that *same* day. 6942
1Ki 8:64 The same day did the king **h** the middle of 6942
Jer 17:22 do ye any work, but **h** ye the sabbath day, 6942
17:24 **h** the sabbath day, to do no work therein; 6942
17:27 if you will not hearken unto me to **h** 6942
Eze 20:20 **h** my sabbaths; and they shall be a sign 6942
44:24 and they shall **h** my sabbaths. 6942

H

HALLOWED (22) [HALLOW]
Ex 20:11 LORD blessed the sabbath day, and **h** it. 6942
29:21 he shall be **h**, and his garments, and 6942
Lev 12: 4 she shall touch no **h** *thing*, nor come into 6944
19: 8 he hath profaned the **h** *thing* of 6944
22:32 but I will be **h** among the children of Israel: 6942
Nu 3:13 Egypt I **h** unto me all the firstborn in Israel, 6942
5:10 every man's **h** *things* shall be his: 6944
16:37 scatter thou the fire yonder; for they are **h**. 6942
16:38 before the LORD, therefore they are **h**: 6942
18: 8 of all the **h** *things* of the children of Israel; 6944
18:29 *even* the **h** *part* thereof out of it. 4720
Dt 26:13 I have brought away the **h** *things* out of 6944
1Sa 21: 4 under mine hand, but there is **h** bread; 6944
21: 6 So the priest gave him **h** *bread*: for there 6944
1Ki 9: 3 I have **h** this house, which thou hast built, 6942
9: 7 *this* house, which I have **h** for my name, 6942
2Ki 12:18 Jehoash king of Judah took all the **h** *things* 6944
12:18 his own **h** *things*, and all the gold that was 6944
2Ch 7: 7 Moreover Solomon **h** the middle of 6942
36:14 the LORD which he had **h** in Jerusalem. 6942
Mt 6: 9 Father which art in heaven, **H** be thy name. *37*
Lk 11: 2 Father which art in heaven, **H** be thy name. *37*

HALT (6) [HALTED, HALTETH, HALTING]
1Ki 18:21 said, How long **h** ye between two opinions? 6452
Ps 38:17 For I *am* ready to **h**, and my sorrow *is* 6761
Mt 18: 8 it is better for thee to enter into life **h** or *5560*
Mk 9:45 it is better for thee to enter **h** into life, *5560*
Lk 14:21 and the maimed, and the **h**, and the blind. *5560*
Jn 5: 3 **h**, withered, waiting for the moving of *5560*

HALTED (2) [HALT]
Ge 32:31 sun rose upon him, and he **h** upon his thigh. 6760
Mic 4: 7 I will make her that **h** a remnant, and 6760

HALTETH (2) [HALT]
Mic 4: 6 will I assemble her that **h**, and I will gather 6760
Zep 3:19 I will save her that **h**, and gather her that 6760

HALTING (1) [HALT]
Jer 20:10 All my familiars watched for my **h**, 6763

HAM (17)
Ge 5:32 and Noah begat Shem, **H**, and Japheth. 2526
6:10 begat three sons, Shem, **H**, and Japheth. 2526
7:13 Shem, and **H**, and Japheth, the sons of 2526
9:18 of the ark, were Shem, and **H**, and Japheth: 2526
9:18 and Japheth: and **H** *is* the father of Canaan. 2526
9:22 **H**, the father of Canaan, saw the nakedness 2526
10: 1 of the sons of Noah, Shem, **H**, and Japheth: 2526
10: 6 And the sons of **H**; Cush, and Mizraim, and 2526
10:20 These *are* the sons of **H**, after their 2526
14: 5 the Zuzims in **H**, and the Emims in Shaveh 1990
1Ch 1: 4 Noah, Shem, **H**, and Japheth. 2526
1: 8 The sons of **H**; Cush, and Mizraim, Put, 2526
4:40 for *they* of **H** had dwelt there of old. 2526
Ps 78:51 of *their* strength in the tabernacles of **H**: 2526
105:23 and Jacob sojourned in the land of **H**. 2526
105:27 among them, and wonders in the land of **H**. 2526
106:22 Wondrous works in the land of **H**, *and* 2526

HAMAN (50) [HAMAN'S]
Est 3: 1 **H** the son of Hammedatha the Agagite, 2001
3: 2 the king's gate, bowed, and reverenced **H**: 2001
3: 4 hearkened not unto them, that they told **H**, 2001
3: 5 And when **H** saw that Mordecai bowed not, 2001
3: 5 him reverence, *then* was **H** full *of* wrath. 2001
3: 6 wherefore **H** sought to destroy all the Jews 2001
3: 7 before **H** from day to day, and from month 2001
3: 8 **H** said unto king Ahasuerus, There is a 2001
3:10 gave it unto **H** the son of Hammedatha 2001
3:11 the king said unto **H**, The silver *is* given to 2001
3:12 there was written according to all that **H** 2001
3:15 the king and **H** sat down to drink; but 2001
4: 7 of the sum of the money that **H** had 2001
5: 4 **H** come *this* day unto the banquet that I 2001
5: 5 the king said, Cause **H** to make haste, that 2001
5: 5 **H** came to the banquet that Esther had 2001
5: 8 **H** come to the banquet that I shall prepare 2001
5: 9 went **H** forth that day joyful and with a 2001
5: 9 when **H** saw Mordecai in the king's gate, 2001
5:10 Nevertheless **H** refrained himself: and 2001
5:11 **H** told them of the glory of his riches, and 2001
5:12 **H** said moreover, Yea, Esther the queen did 2001
5:14 the thing pleased **H**; and he caused 2001
6: 4 Now **H** was come into the outward court of 2001
6: 5 unto him, Behold, **H** standeth in the court. 2001
6: 6 So **H** came in. And the king said unto him, 2001
6: 6 Now **H** thought in his heart, To whom 2001
6: 7 **H** answered the king, *For* the man whom 2001
6:10 the king said to **H**, Make haste, *and* take 2001
6:11 took **H** the apparel and the horse, and 2001
6:12 **H** hasted to his house mourning, and 2001
6:13 **H** told Zeresh his wife and all his friends 2001
6:14 hasted to bring **H** unto the banquet that 2001
7: 1 **H** came to banquet with Esther the queen. 2001
7: 6 The adversary and enemy *is* this wicked **H**. 2001
7: 6 **H** was afraid before the king and the queen. 2001
7: 7 **H** stood *up* to make request for his life to 2001
7: 8 **H** was fallen upon the bed whereon Esther 2001
7: 9 which **H** had made for Mordecai, 2001
7: 9 for the king, standeth in the house of **H**. 2001
7:10 So they hanged **H** on the gallows that he 2001
8: 1 **H** the Jews' enemy unto Esther the queen. 2001
8: 2 which he had taken from **H**, and gave it 2001
8: 2 Esther set Mordecai over the house of **H**. 2001
8: 3 to put away the mischief of **H** the Agagite, 2001
8: 5 by **H** the son of Hammedatha the Agagite, 2001
8: 7 I have given Esther the house of **H**, and 2001
9:10 The ten sons of **H** the son of Hammedatha, 2001
9:12 Shushan the palace, and the ten sons of **H**; 2001
9:24 Because **H** the son of Hammedatha, 2001

HAMAN'S (3) [HAMAN]
Est 7: 8 of the king's mouth, they covered **H** face. 2001
9:13 let **H** ten sons be hanged upon the gallows. 2001
9:14 at Shushan; and they hanged **H** ten sons. 2001

HAMATH (34) [HAMATH-ZOBAH, HAMATHITE]
Nu 13:21 of Zin unto Rehob, as *men* come to **H**. 2574
34: 8 out *your border* unto the entrance of **H**; 2574
Jos 13: 5 mount Hermon unto the entering into **H**. 2574
Jdg 3: 3 Baal-hermon unto the entering in of **H**. 2574
2Sa 8: 9 When Toi king of **H** heard that David had 2574
1Ki 8:65 from the entering in of **H** unto the river of 2574
2Ki 14:25 the entering of **H** unto the sea of the plain, 2574
14:28 and **H**, *which belonged* to Judah, for Israel, 2574
17:24 from **H**, and from Sepharvaim, and 2574
17:30 and the men of **H** made Ashima, 2574
18:34 Where *are* the gods of **H**, and of Arpad? 2574
19:13 Where *is* the king of **H**, and the king of 2574
23:33 put him in bands at Riblah in the land of **H**, 2574
25:21 and slew them at Riblah in the land of **H**. 2574
1Ch 18: 3 smote Hadarezer king of Zobah unto **H**, 2574
18: 9 Now when Tou king of **H** heard how David 2574
2Ch 7: 8 from the entering in of **H** unto the river of 2574
8: 4 and all the store cities, which he built in **H**. 2574
Isa 10: 9 *is* not **H** as Arpad? *is* not Samaria as 2574
11:11 from **H**, and from the islands of the sea. 2574
36:19 Where *are* the gods of **H** and Arphad? 2574
37:13 Where *is* the king of **H**, and the king of 2574
Jer 39: 5 king of Babylon to Riblah in the land of **H**, 2574
49:23 **H** is confounded, and Arpad: for they have 2574
52: 9 king of Babylon to Riblah in the land of **H**; 2574
52:27 them to death in Riblah in the land of **H**. 2574
Eze 47:16 **H**, Berothah, Sibraim, which *is* between 2574
47:16 border of Damascus and the border of **H**; 2574
47:17 the north northward, and the border of **H**. 2574
47:20 the border, till *a man* come over against **H**. 2574
48: 1 as *one* goeth to **H**, Hazar-enan, the border 2574
48: 1 of Damascus northward, to the coast of **H**; 2574
Am 6: 2 see; and from thence go ye *to* **H** the great: 2574
Zec 9: 2 **H** also shall border thereby; Tyrus, and 2574

HAMATHITE (2) [HAMATH]
Ge 10:18 the Arvadite, and the Zemarite, and the **H**: 2577
1Ch 1:16 the Arvadite, and the Zemarite, and the **H**. 2577

HAMATH-ZOBAH (1) [HAMATH, ZOBAH]
2Ch 8: 3 Solomon went *to* **H**, and prevailed against 2574

HAMMATH (1)
Jos 19:35 Zer, and **H**, Rakkath, and Chinnereth, 2575

HAMMEDATHA (5)
Est 3: 1 promote Haman the son of **H** the Agagite, 4099
3:10 gave it unto Haman the son of **H** 4099
8: 5 by Haman the son of **H** the Agagite, 4099

Est 9:10 The ten sons of Haman the son of **H**, 4099
9:24 Because Haman the son of **H**, the Agagite, 4099

HAMMELECH (2)
Jer 36:26 king commanded Jerahmeel the son of **H**, 4429
38: 6 into the dungeon of Malchiah the son of **H**, 4429

HAMMER (7) [HAMMERS]
Jdg 4:21 took a **h** in her hand, and went softly unto 4717
5:26 and her right hand to the workmen's **h**; 1989
5:26 with the **h** she smote Sisera, she smote off NIH
1Ki 6: 7 that there was neither **h** nor axe *nor* any 4717
Isa 41: 7 he that smootheth *with* the **h** him that 6360
Jer 23:29 like a **h** *that* breaketh the rock in pieces? 6360
50:23 How is the **h** of the whole earth cut asunder 6360

HAMMERS (3) [HAMMER]
Ps 74: 6 work thereof at once with axes and **h**. 3597
Isa 44:12 fashioneth it with **h**, and worketh it with 4717
Jer 10: 4 they fasten it with nails and with **h**, that it 4717

HAMMOLEKETH (1)
1Ch 7:18 his sister **H** bare Ishod, and Abiezer, and 4447

HAMMON (2)
Jos 19:28 and Rehob, and **H**, and Kanah, 2540
1Ch 6:76 **H** with her suburbs, and Kirjathaim with 2540

HAMMOTH-DOR (1) [DOR]
Jos 21:32 **H** with her suburbs, and Kartan with her 2576

HAMMUEL See HAMUEL

HAMONAH (1)
Eze 39:16 also the name of the city *shall be* **H**. 1997

HAMON-GOG (2) [GOG]
Eze 39:11 and they shall call *it* The valley of **H**. 1995
39:15 the buriers have buried it in the valley of **H**. 1995

HAMOR (12) [EMMOR, HAMOR'S]
Ge 33:19 at the hand of the children of **H**, 2544
34: 2 when Shechem the son of **H** the Hivite, 2544
34: 4 Shechem spake unto his father **H**, saying, 2544
34: 6 **H** the father of Shechem went out unto 2544
34: 8 **H** communed with them, saying, The soul 2544
34:13 and **H** his father deceitfully, 2544
34:18 their words pleased **H**, and Shechem 2544
34:20 **H** and Shechem his son came unto the gate 2544
34:24 unto **H** and unto Shechem his son 2544
34:26 they slew **H** and Shechem his son with 2544
Jos 24:32 **H** the father of Shechem for an hundred 2544
Jdg 9:28 serve the men of **H** the father of Shechem: 2544

HAMOR'S (1) [HAMOR]
Ge 34:18 words pleased Hamor, and Shechem **H** son. 2544

HAMSTRING See HOUGH

HAMUEL (1)
1Ch 4:26 **H** his son, Zacchur his son, Shimei his son. 2536

HAMUL (3) [HAMULITES]
Ge 46:12 the sons of Pharez were Hezron and **H**. 2538
Nu 26:21 of **H**, the family of the Hamulites. 2538
1Ch 2: 5 The sons of Pharez; Hezron, and **H**. 2538

HAMULITES (1) [HAMUL]
Nu 26:21 of Hamul, the family of the **H**. 2539

HAMUTAL (3)
2Ki 23:31 his mother's name *was* **H**, the daughter of 2537
24:18 his mother's name *was* **H**, the daughter of 2537
Jer 52: 1 his mother's name *was* **H** the daughter of 2537

HANAMEEL (4)
Jer 32: 7 **H** the son of Shallum thine uncle *shall* 2601
32: 8 So **H** mine uncle's son came to me in 2601
32: 9 And I bought the field of **H** my uncle's son, 2601
32:12 in the sight of **H** mine uncle's *son,* and 2601

HANAMEL See HANAMEEL

HANAN (12) [BAAL-HANAN, ELON-BETH-HANAN]
1Ch 8:23 And Abdon, and Zichri, and **H**, 2605
8:38 and Sheariah, and Obadiah, and **H**. 2605
9:44 and Sheariah, and Obadiah, and **H**: 2605
11:43 **H** the son of Maachah, and Joshaphat 2605
Ezr 2:46 the children of Shalmai, the children of **H**, 2605
Ne 7:49 The children of **H**, the children of Giddel, 2605
8: 7 Jozabad, **H**, Pelaiah, and the Levites, 2605
10:10 Shebaniah, Hodijah, Kelita, Pelaiah, **H**, 2605
10:22 Pelatiah, **H**, Anaiah, 2605
10:26 And Ahijah, **H**, Anan, 2605
13:13 next to them *was* **H** the son of Zaccur, 2605
Jer 35: 4 into the chamber of the sons of **H**, the son 2605

HANANEEL (4)
Ne 3: 1 they sanctified it, unto the tower of **H**. 2606
12:39 and the tower of **H**, and the tower of Meah, 2606
Jer 31:38 the tower of **H** unto the gate of the corner. 2606
Zec 14:10 *from* the tower of **H** unto the king's 2606

HANANEL See HANANEEL

HANANI (11)
1Ki 16: 1 came to Jehu the son of **H** against Baasha, 2607
16: 7 **H** came the word of the LORD against 2607
1Ch 25: 4 **H**, Eliathah, Giddalti, and Romamti-ezer, 2607
25:25 The eighteenth to **H**, *he,* his sons, and 2607
2Ch 16: 7 at that time **H** the seer came to Asa king of 2607
19: 2 Jehu the son of **H** the seer went out to meet 2607
20:34 written in the book of Jehu the son of **H**, 2607
Ezr 10:20 of the sons of Immer; **H**, and Zebadiah. 2607
Ne 1: 2 That **H**, one of my brethren, came, he and 2607
7: 2 That I gave my brother **H**, and Hananiah 2607
12:36 Gilalai, Maai, Nethaneel, and Judah, **H**, 2607

HANANIAH (29)
1Ch 3:19 and **H**, and Shelomith their sister: 2608
3:21 the sons of **H**; Pelatiah, and Jesaiah: 2608
8:24 And **H**, and Elam, and Antothijah, 2608
25: 4 **H**, Hanani, Eliathah, Giddalti, and 2608
25:23 The sixteenth to **H**, *he,* his sons, and 2608
2Ch 26:11 Maaseiah the ruler, under the hand of **H**, 2608
Ezr 10:28 Jehohanan, **H**, Zabbai, *and* Athlai. 2608
Ne 3: 8 Next unto him also repaired **H** the son of 2608
3:30 After him repaired **H** the son of Shelemiah, 2608
7: 2 **H** the ruler of the palace, charge over 2608
10:23 Hoshea, **H**, Hashub, 2608
12:12 of Seraiah, Meraiah; of Jeremiah, **H**; 2608
12:41 Michaiah, Elioenai, Zechariah, *and* **H**, 2608
Jer 28: 1 *that* **H** the son of Azur the prophet, 2608
28: 5 the prophet **H** in the presence of the priests, 2608
28:10 **H** the prophet took the yoke from off 2608
28:11 **H** spake in the presence of all the people, 2608
28:12 **H** the prophet had broken the yoke from off 2608
28:13 Go and tell **H**, saying, Thus saith 2608
28:15 said the prophet Jeremiah unto **H** 2608
28:15 unto Hananiah the prophet, Hear now, **H**; 2608
28:17 So **H** the prophet died the same year in 2608
36:12 Zedekiah the son of **H**, and all the princes. 2608
37:13 the son of Shelemiah, the son of **H**; 2608
Da 1: 6 of Judah, Daniel, **H**, Mishael, and Azariah: 2608
1: 7 to **H**, of Shadrach; and to Mishael, 2608
1:11 set over Daniel, **H**, Mishael, and Azariah, 2608
1:19 none like Daniel, **H**, Mishael, and Azariah: 2608
2:17 made the thing known to **H**, Mishael, and 2608

HAND (1470) [BROKENHANDED, HANDBREADTH, HANDED, HANDFUL, HANDFULS, HANDS, HANDSTAVES, HANDWRITING, HANDYWORK, LEFTHANDED]
Ge 3:22 lest he put forth his **h**, and take also of 3027
4:11 to receive thy brother's blood from thy **h**. 3027
8: 9 he put forth his **h**, and took her, and 3027
9: 2 of the sea; into your **h** are they delivered. 3027
9: 5 at the **h** of every beast will I require it, and 3027
9: 5 beast will I require it, and at the **h** of man; 3027
9: 5 at the **h** of every man's brother will I 3027
13: 9 if *thou wilt take* the **left h**, then I will go to 8040
13: 9 or if *thou depart to* the **right h**, then I will 3225
14:15 which *is* on the **left h** of Damascus. 8040
14:20 hath delivered thine enemies into thy **h**. 3027
14:22 I have lift up mine **h** unto the LORD, 3027
16: 6 unto Sarai, Behold, thy maid *is* in thy **h**; 3027
16:12 his **h** *will be* against every man, and 3027
16:12 every man, and every man's **h** against him; 3027
19:10 the men put forth their **h**, and pulled Lot 3027
19:16 the men laid hold upon his **h**, and upon 3027
19:16 upon the **h** of his wife, and upon the hand 3027
19:16 and upon the **h** of his two daughters; 3027

Ge 21:18 lift up the lad, and hold him in thine **h**; 3027
21:30 seven ewe lambs shalt thou take of my **h**, 3027
22: 6 he took the fire in his **h**, and a knife; and 3027
22:10 Abraham stretched forth his **h**, and took 3027
22:12 he said, Lay not thine **h** upon the lad, 3027
24: 2 Put, I pray thee, thy **h** under my thigh: 3027
24: 9 the servant put his **h** under the thigh of 3027
24:10 all the goods of his master *were* in his **h**: 3027
24:18 let down her pitcher upon her **h**, and 3027
24:49 that I may turn to the **right h**, or to the left. 3225
25:26 and his **h** took hold on Esau's heel; 3027
27:17 had prepared, into the **h** of her son Jacob. 3027
27:41 days of mourning for my father are **at h**; 7126
30:35 and gave *them* into the **h** of his sons. 3027
31:29 It is in the power of my **h** to do you hurt: 3027
31:39 of my **h** didst thou require it, 3027
32:11 I pray thee, from the **h** of my brother, 3027
32:11 the hand of my brother, from the **h** of Esau: 3027
32:13 took of that which came to his **h** a present 3027
32:16 he delivered *them* into the **h** of his servants, 3027
33:10 thy sight, then receive my present at my **h**: 3027
33:19 at the **h** of the children of Hamor, 3027
35: 4 all the strange gods which *were* in their **h**, 3027
37:22 lay no **h** upon him, that he might rid him 3027
37:27 and let not our **h** be upon him; 3027
38:18 thy bracelets, and thy staff that *is* in thine **h**. 3027
38:20 Judah sent the kid by the **h** of his friend 3027
38:20 to receive *his* pledge from the woman's **h**: 3027
38:28 she travailed, that *the one* put out *his* **h**: 3027
38:28 and bound upon his **h** a scarlet thread, 3027
38:29 to pass, as he drew back his **h**, that, behold, 3027
38:30 that had the scarlet thread upon his **h**: 3027
39: 1 bought him of the **h** of the Ishmeelites, 3027
39: 3 made all that he did to prosper in his **h**. 3027
39: 4 and all *that* he had he put into his **h**. 3027
39: 6 he left all that he had in Joseph's **h**; and 3027
39: 8 he hath committed all that he hath to my **h**; 3027
39:12 he left his garment in her **h**, and fled, and 3027
39:13 saw that he had left his garment in her **h**, 3027
39:22 **h** all the prisoners that *were* in the prison; 3027
39:23 not to any thing *that was* under his **h**; 3027
40:11 Pharaoh's cup *was* in my **h**: and I took 3027
40:11 and I gave the cup into Pharaoh's **h**. 3709
40:13 thou shalt deliver Pharaoh's cup into his **h**, 3027
40:21 and he gave the cup into Pharaoh's **h**: 3709
41:35 and lay up corn under the **h** of Pharaoh, and 3027
41:42 Pharaoh took off his ring from his **h**, and 3027
41:42 put it upon Joseph's **h**, and arrayed him in 3027
41:44 without thee shall no man lift up his **h** or 3027
42:37 deliver him into my **h**, and I will bring him 3027
43: 9 for him; of my **h** shalt thou require him: 3027
43:12 take double money in your **h**; and 3027
43:12 of your sacks, carry *it* again in your **h**; 3027
43:15 they took double money in their **h**, and 3027
43:21 we have brought it again in our **h**. 3027
43:26 present which *was* in their **h** into the house, 3027
44:17 *but* the man in whose **h** the cup is found, 3027
46: 4 and Joseph shall put his **h** upon thine eyes. 3027
47:29 thy **h** under my thigh, and deal kindly and 3027
48:13 Ephraim in his **right h** toward Israel's left 3225
48:13 in his right hand toward Israel's **left h**, 8040
48:13 Manasseh in his **left h** towards Israel's 8040
48:13 in his left hand towards Israel's **right h**, 3225
48:14 Israel stretched out his **right h**, and laid *it* 3225
48:14 and his **left h** upon Manasseh's head, 8040
48:17 laid his right **h** upon the head of Ephraim, 3027
48:17 he held up his father's **h**, to remove it from 3027
48:18 the firstborn; put thy **right h** upon his head. 3225
48:22 which I took out of the **h** of the Amorite 3027
49: 8 thy **h** *shall be* in the neck of thine enemies; 3027
Ex 2:19 An Egyptian delivered us out of the **h** of 3027
3: 8 deliver them out of the **h** of the Egyptians, 3027
3:19 will not let you go, no, not by a mighty **h**. 3027
3:20 I will stretch out my **h**, and smite Egypt 3027
4: 2 said unto him, What *is* that in thine **h**? 3027
4: 4 Put forth thine **h**, and take it by the tail. 3027
4: 4 he put forth his **h**, and caught it, and 3027
4: 4 and caught it, and it became a rod in his **h**: 3709
4: 6 unto him, Put now thine **h** into thy bosom. 3027
4: 6 he put his **h** into his bosom: and when he 3027
4: 6 it out, behold, his **h** *was* leprous as snow. 3027
4: 7 he said, Put thine **h** into thy bosom again. 3027
4: 7 he put his **h** into his bosom again; and 3027
4:13 by the **h** *of him whom* thou wilt send. 3027
4:17 thou shalt take this rod in thine **h**, 3027
4:20 and Moses took the rod of God in his **h**. 3027
4:21 which I have put in thine **h**: 3027
5:21 to put a sword in their **h** to slay us. 3027
6: 1 for with a strong **h** shall he let them go, and 3027
6: 1 with a strong **h** shall he drive them out of 3027
7: 4 that I may lay my **h** upon Egypt, and 3027
7: 5 when I stretch forth mine **h** upon Egypt, 3027
7:15 to a serpent shalt thou take in thine **h**. 3027
7:17 I will smite with the rod that *is* in mine **h** 3027
7:19 stretch out thine **h** upon the waters of 3027
8: 5 Stretch forth thine **h** with thy rod over 3027
8: 6 Aaron stretched out his **h** over the waters of 3027
8:17 for Aaron stretched out his **h** with his rod, 3027
9: 3 the **h** of the LORD is upon thy cattle 3027
9:15 For now I will stretch out my **h**, that I may 3027
9:22 Stretch forth thine **h** toward heaven, 3027
10:12 Stretch out thine **h** over the land of Egypt 3027
10:21 Stretch out thine **h** toward heaven, 3027
10:22 Moses stretched forth his **h** toward heaven; 3027
12:11 shoes on your feet, and your staff in your **h**; 3027
13: 3 for by strength of **h** the LORD brought 3027
13: 9 it shall be for a sign unto thee upon thine **h**, 3027
13: 9 for with a strong **h** hath the LORD 3027
13:14 By strength of **h** the LORD brought us out 3027
13:16 it shall be for a token upon thine **h**, and 3027
13:16 for by strength of **h** the LORD brought us 3027
14: 8 children of Israel went out with a high **h**. 3027
14:16 stretch out thine **h** over the sea, and 3027
14:21 And Moses stretched out his **h** over the sea; 3027
14:22 *were* a wall unto them on their **right h**, 3225
14:26 Stretch out thine **h** over the sea, 3027
14:27 Moses stretched forth his **h** over the sea, 3027
14:29 *were* a wall unto them on their **right h**, 3225
14:30 that day out of the **h** of the Egyptians; 3027
15: 6 Thy **right h**, O LORD, is become glorious 3225
15: 6 thy **right h**, O LORD, hath dashed in 3225
15: 9 draw my sword, my **h** shall destroy them. 3027
15:12 Thou stretchedst out thy **right h**, the earth 3225
15:20 the sister of Aaron, took a timbrel in her **h**; 3027
16: 3 Would to God we had died by the **h** of 3027
17: 5 smotest the river, take in thine **h**, and go. 3027
17: 9 of the hill with the rod of God in mine **h**. 3027
17:11 it came to pass, when Moses held up his **h**, 3027
17:11 when he let down his **h**, Amalek prevailed. 3027
18: 9 whom he had delivered out of the **h** of 3027
18:10 who hath delivered you out of the **h** of 3027
18:10 the Egyptians, and out of the **h** of Pharaoh, 3027
18:10 people from under the **h** of the Egyptians. 3027
19:13 There shall not a **h** touch it, but he shall 3027
21:13 not in wait, but God deliver *him* into his **h**; 3027
21:16 and selleth him, or if he be found in his **h**, 3027
21:20 with a rod, and he die under his **h**; 3027
21:24 tooth for tooth, **h** for hand, foot for foot, 3027
21:24 tooth for tooth, hand for **h**, foot for foot, 3027
22: 4 If the theft be certainly found in his **h** alive, 3027
22: 8 *to see* whether he have put his **h** unto his 3027
22:11 that he hath not put his **h** unto his 3027
23: 1 put not thine **h** with the wicked to be an 3027
23:31 the inhabitants of the land into your **h**; 3027
24:11 of the children of Israel he laid not his **h**: 3027
29:20 upon the thumb of their right **h**, and 3027
32: 4 he received *them* at their **h**, and fashioned it 3027
32:11 with great power, and with a mighty **h**? 3027
32:15 two tables of the Testimony *were* in his **h**: 3027
33:22 will cover thee with my **h** while I pass by: 3709
33:23 I will take away mine **h**, and thou shalt see 3709
34: 4 and took in his **h** the two tables of stone. 3027
34:29 the two tables of Testimony in Moses' **h**, 3027
35:29 commanded to be made by the **h** of Moses. 3027
38:15 on **this h** and that hand, *were* hangings of 2088
38:15 on this hand and **that h**, *were* hangings of 2088
38:21 by the **h** of Ithamar, son to Aaron the priest. 3027
Lev 1: 4 he shall put his **h** upon the head of 3027
3: 2 he shall lay his **h** upon the head of his 3027
3: 8 he shall lay his **h** upon the head of his 3027
3:13 he shall lay his **h** upon the head of it, and 3027
4: 4 shall lay his **h** upon the bullock's head, and 3027
4:24 he shall lay his **h** upon the head of the goat, 3027
4:29 he shall lay his **h** upon the head of the sin 3027
4:33 he shall lay his **h** upon the head of the sin 3027
8:23 upon the thumb of his right **h**, and upon 3027
8:36 the LORD commanded by the **h** of Moses. 3027
9:22 Aaron lift up his **h** towards the people, and 3027

Lev 10:11 hath spoken unto them by the **h** of Moses. 3027
14:14 upon the thumb of his right **h**, and upon 3027
14:15 and pour *it* into the **palm of** his own left **h**: 3709
14:16 his right finger in the oil that *is* in his left **h**, 3709
14:17 of the rest of the oil that *is* in his **h** shall 3709
14:17 upon the thumb of his right **h**, and upon 3027
14:18 **h** he shall pour upon the head of him that is 3709
14:25 upon the thumb of his right **h**, and upon 3027
14:26 of the oil into the **palm of** his own left **h**: 3709
14:27 in his left **h** seven times before the LORD: 3709
14:28 the priest shall put of the oil that *is* in his **h** 3709
14:28 upon the thumb of his right **h**, and upon 3027
14:29 the rest of the oil that *is* in the priest's **h** he 3709
14:32 whose **h is** not **able to get** *that which* 3027+5381
16:21 shall send *him* away by the **h** of a fit man 3027
22:25 Neither from a stranger's **h** shall ye offer 3027
25:14 or buyest *ought* of thy neighbour's **h**, 3027
25:28 that which is sold shall remain in the **h** of 3027
26:25 ye shall be delivered into the **h** of 3027
26:46 of Israel in mount Sinai by the **h** of Moses. 3027
Nu 4:28 their charge *shall be* under the **h** of Ithamar 3027
4:33 under the **h** of Ithamar the son of Aaron 3027
4:37 of the LORD by the **h** of Moses. 3027
4:45 the word of the LORD by the **h** of Moses. 3027
4:49 they were numbered by the **h** of Moses, 3027
5:18 the priest shall have in his **h** the bitter water 3027
5:25 the jealousy offering out of the woman's **h**, 3027
6:21 besides *that* that his **h** shall get: 3027
7: 8 under the **h** of Ithamar the son of Aaron 3027
9:23 of the LORD by the **h** of Moses. 3027
10:13 of the LORD by the **h** of Moses. 3027
11:15 **kill** me, I pray thee, **out of h**, 2026+2026
11:23 Is the LORD's **h** waxed short? 3027
15:23 hath commanded you by the **h** of Moses, 3027
16:40 as the LORD said to him by the **h** of 3027
20:11 Moses lift up his **h**, and with his rod he 3027
20:17 we will not turn *to* the **right h** nor *to* 3225
20:20 him with much people, and with a strong **h**. 3027
21: 2 wilt indeed deliver this people into my **h**, 3027
21:26 taken all his land out of his **h**, *even* unto 3027
21:34 for I have delivered him into thy **h**, and all 3027
22: 7 with the rewards of divination in their **h**; 3027
22:23 in the way, and his sword drawn in his **h**: 3027
22:26 *was* no way to turn *either to* the **right h** 3225
22:29 I would there were a sword in mine **h**, 3027
22:31 in the way, and his sword drawn in his **h**: 3027
25: 7 and took a javelin in his **h**; 3027
27:18 *is* the spirit, and lay thine **h** upon him; 3027
27:23 as the LORD commanded by the **h** of 3027
31: 6 and the trumpets to blow in his **h**. 3027
33: 1 with their armies under the **h** of Moses 3027
33: 3 a high **h** in the sight of all the Egyptians. 3027
35:18 Or *if* he smite him with a **h** weapon of 3027
35:21 Or in enmity smite him with his **h**, that he 3027
35:25 slayer out of the **h** of the revenger of blood, 3027
36:13 which the LORD commanded by the **h** of 3027
Dt 1:27 to deliver us into the **h** of the Amorites, 3027
2: 7 hath blessed thee in all the works of thy **h**: 3027
2:15 For indeed the **h** of the LORD was against 3027
2:24 I have given into thy **h** Sihon the Amorite, 3027
2:27 I will neither turn *unto* the **right h** nor *to* 3225
2:30 that he might deliver him into thy **h**, 3027
3: 2 and all his people, and his land, into thy **h**; 3027
3: 8 we took at that time out of the **h** of the two 3027
3:24 thy servant thy greatness, and thy mighty **h**: 3027
4:34 by a mighty **h**, and by a stretched out arm, 3027
5:15 brought thee out thence through a mighty **h** 3027
5:32 ye shall not turn aside *to* the **right h** or *to* 3225
6: 8 shalt bind them for a sign upon thine **h**, 3027
6:21 brought us out of Egypt with a mighty **h**: 3027
7: 8 LORD brought you out with a mighty **h**, 3027
7: 8 from the **h** of Pharaoh king of Egypt. 3027
7:19 the mighty **h**, and the stretched out arm, 3027
7:24 he shall deliver their kings into thine **h**, 3027
8:17 the might of mine **h** hath gotten me this 3027
9:26 brought forth out of Egypt with a mighty **h**. 3027
10: 3 the mount, having the two tables in mine **h**. 3027
11: 2 his mighty **h**, and his stretched out arm, 3027
11:18 and bind them for a sign upon your **h**, 3027
12: 6 heave offerings of your **h**, and your vows, 3027
12: 7 ye shall rejoice in all that you put your **h** 3027
12:11 the heave offering of your **h**, and all your 3027
12:17 or heave offering of thine **h**: 3027
13: 9 thine **h** shall be first upon him to put him to 3027
13: 9 and afterwards the **h** of all the people. 3027
13:17 nought of the cursed thing to thine **h**: 3027
14:25 bind up the money in thine **h**, and shalt go 3027
14:29 in all the work of thine **h** which thou doest. 3027
15: 3 *that* which is thine with thy brother thine **h** 3027
15: 7 nor shut thine **h** from thy poor brother: 3027
15: 8 thou shalt open thine **h** wide unto him, and 3027
15: 9 seventh year, the year of release, is **at h**; 7126
15:10 and in all that thou puttest thine **h** unto. 3027
15:11 Thou shalt open thine **h** wide unto thy 3027
16:10 a tribute of a freewill offering of thine **h**, 3027
17:11 shew thee, *to* the **right h**, nor *to* the left. 3225
17:20 *to* the **right h**, or *to* the left: 3225
19: 5 his **h** fetcheth a stroke with the axe to cut 3027
19:12 deliver him into the **h** of the avenger of 3027
19:21 tooth for tooth, **h** for hand, foot for foot. 3027
19:21 tooth for tooth, hand for **h**, foot for foot. 3027
23:20 **h** to in the land whither thou goest to 3027
23:25 thou mayest pluck the ears with thine **h**; 3027
24: 1 give *it* in her **h**, and send her out of his 3027
24: 3 giveth *it* in her **h**, and sendeth her out of his 3027
25:11 out of the **h** of him that smiteth him, 3027
25:11 putteth forth her **h**, and taketh him by 3027
25:12 thou shalt cut off her **h**, thine eye shall not 3709
26: 4 priest shall take the basket out of thine **h**, 3027
26: 8 us forth out of Egypt with a mighty **h**, 3027
28: 8 and in all that thou settest thine **h** unto; 3027
28:12 and to bless all the work of thine **h**: 3027
28:14 *to* the **right h**, or *to* the left, to go after 3225
28:20 in all that thou settest thine **h** unto for to do, 3027
28:32 and *there shall be* no might in thine **h**. 3027
30: 9 thee plenteous in every work of thine **h**, 3027
32:27 Our **h** is high, and the LORD hath not 3027
32:35 for the day of their calamity *is* **at h**, and 7138
32:39 *is there any* that can deliver out of my **h**. 3027
32:40 For I lift up my **h** to heaven, and say, I live 3027
32:41 and mine **h** take hold on judgment; 3027
33: 2 from his **right h** *went* a fiery law for them. 3225
33: 3 loved the people; all his saints *are* in thy **h**: 3027
34:12 in all *that* mighty **h**, and in all the great 3027
Jos 1: 7 turn not from it *to* the **right h** or *to* the left, 3225
2:19 *shall be* on our head, if *any* **h** be upon him. 3027
4:24 the earth might know the **h** of the LORD, 3027
5:13 against him with his sword drawn in his **h**: 3027
6: 2 I have given into thine **h** Jericho, and 3027
7: 7 to deliver us into the **h** of the Amorites, 3027
8: 1 I have given into thy **h** the king of Ai, and 3027
8: 7 your God will deliver it into your **h**. 3027
8:18 Stretch out the spear that *is* in thy **h** toward 3027
8:18 toward Ai; for I will give it into thine **h**. 3027
8:18 spear that *he had* in his **h** toward the city. 3027
8:19 ran as soon as *he* had stretched out his **h**: 3027
8:26 For Joshua drew not his **h** back, 3027
9:25 now, behold, we *are* in thine **h**: as it 3027
9:26 delivered them out of the **h** of the children 3027
10: 6 Slack not thy **h** from thy servants; 3027
10: 8 for I have delivered them into thine **h**; 3027
10:19 your God hath delivered them into your **h**. 3027
10:30 the king thereof, into the **h** of Israel; 3027
10:32 the LORD delivered Lachish into the **h** of 3027
11: 8 the LORD delivered them into the **h** of 3027
14: 2 as the LORD commanded by the **h** of 3027
17: 7 the border went *along* on the **right h** unto 3225
19:27 Neiel, and goeth out to Cabul on the **left h**, 8040
20: 2 whereof I spake unto you by the **h** of 3027
20: 5 shall not deliver the slayer up into his **h**; 3027
20: 9 not die by the **h** of the avenger of blood, 3027
21: 2 The LORD commanded by the **h** of 3027
21: 8 as the LORD commanded by the **h** of 3027
21:44 delivered all their enemies into their **h**. 3027
22: 9 the word of the LORD by the **h** of Moses. 3027
22:31 of Israel out of the **h** of the LORD. 3027
23: 6 *ye* turn not aside therefrom *to* the **right h** 3225
24: 8 I gave them into your **h**, that ye might 3027
24:10 you still: so I delivered you out of his **h**. 3027
24:11 and I delivered them into your **h**. 3027
Jdg 1: 2 behold, I have delivered the land into his **h**. 3027
1: 4 and the Perizzites into their **h**: 3027
1:35 yet the **h** of the house of Joseph prevailed, 3027
2:15 the **h** of the LORD was against them for 3027
2:16 which delivered them out of the **h** of those 3027
2:18 delivered them out of the **h** of their enemies 3027
2:23 neither delivered he them into the **h** of 3027
3: 4 which he commanded their fathers by the **h** 3027

Jdg 3: 8 he sold them into the **h** of 3027
3:10 king of Mesopotamia into his **h**; 3027
3:10 his **h** prevailed against Chushan-rishathaim. 3027
3:21 Ehud put forth his left **h**, and took 3027
3:28 your enemies the Moabites into your **h**. 3027
3:30 So Moab was subdued that day under the **h** 3027
4: 2 the LORD sold them into the **h** of Jabin 3027
4: 7 and I will deliver him into thine **h**. 3027
4: 9 for the LORD shall sell Sisera into the **h** 3027
4:14 LORD hath delivered Sisera into thine **h**: 3027
4:21 took a hammer in her **h**, and went softly 3027
4:24 the **h** of the children of Israel prospered, 3027
5:26 She put her **h** to the nail, and her right hand 3027
5:26 and her **right h** to the workmen's hammer; 3225
6: 1 the LORD delivered them into the **h** of 3027
6: 2 the **h** of Midian prevailed against Israel: 3027
6: 9 I delivered you out of the **h** of 3027
6: 9 out of the **h** of all that oppressed you, and 3027
6:14 thou shalt save Israel from the **h** of 3709
6:21 forth the end of the staff that *was* in his **h**, 3027
6:36 If thou wilt save Israel by mine **h**, as thou 3027
6:37 I know that thou wilt save Israel by mine **h**, 3027
7: 2 saying, Mine own **h** hath saved me. 3027
7: 6 putting their **h** to their mouth, were three 3027
7: 7 and deliver the Midianites into thine **h**: 3027
7: 8 So the people took victuals in their **h**, and 3027
7: 9 the host; for I have delivered it into thine **h**. 3027
7:14 *for* into his **h** hath God delivered Midian, 3027
7:15 for the LORD hath delivered into your **h** 3027
7:16 he put a trumpet in every man's **h**, 3027
8: 6 of Zebah and Zalmunna now in thine **h**, 3027
8: 7 delivered Zebah and Zalmunna into mine **h**, 3027
8:15 of Zebah and Zalmunna now in thine **h**, 3027
8:22 for thou hast delivered us from the **h** of 3027
9:17 and delivered you out of the **h** of Midian: 3027
9:29 would to God this people were under my **h**; 3027
9:48 Abimelech took an axe in his **h**, and 3027
10:12 to me, and I delivered you out of their **h**. 3027
11:21 and all his people into the **h** of Israel, 3027
12: 3 and the LORD delivered them into my **h**: 3027
13: 1 the LORD delivered them into the **h** of 3027
13: 5 he shall begin to deliver Israel out of the **h** 3027
14: 6 have rent a kid, and *he had* nothing in his **h**: 3027
15:12 that we may deliver thee into the **h** of 3027
15:13 bind thee fast, and deliver thee into their **h**: 3027
15:15 put forth his **h**, and took it, and slew a 3027
15:17 that he cast away the jawbone out of his **h**, 3027
15:18 great deliverance into the **h** of thy servant: 3027
15:18 and fall into the **h** of the uncircumcised? 3027
16:18 up unto her, and brought money in their **h**. 3027
16:23 delivered Samson our enemy into our **h**. 3027
16:26 said unto the lad that held him by the **h**, 3027
16:29 of the one with his **right h**, and of the other 3225
17: 3 unto the LORD from my **h** for my son, 3027
18:19 lay thine **h** upon thy mouth, and go with us, 3027
20:28 to morrow I will deliver them into thine **h**. 3027
20:48 as the beast, and all that **came to h**: 4672
Ru 1:13 the **h** of the LORD is gone out against me. 3027
4: 5 What day thou buyest the field of the **h** of 3027
4: 9 and Mahlon's, of the **h** of Naomi. 3027
1Sa 2:13 with a fleshhook of three teeth in his **h**; 3027
4: 3 it may save us out of the **h** of our enemies. 3709
4: 8 who shall deliver us out of the **h** of these 3027
5: 6 the **h** of the LORD was heavy upon them 3027
5: 7 for his **h** is sore upon us, and upon Dagon 3027
5: 9 the **h** of the LORD was against the city 3027
5:11 the city; the **h** of God was very heavy there. 3027
6: 3 it shall be known to you why his **h** is not 3027
6: 5 peradventure he will lighten his **h** from off 3027
6: 9 we shall know that *it is* not his **h** *that* smote 3027
6:12 turned not aside *to* the **right h** or *to* the left; 3225
7: 3 he will deliver you out of the **h** of 3027
7: 8 that he will save us out of the **h** of 3027
7:13 the **h** of the LORD was against 3027
9: 8 I have here at **h** the fourth part of a shekel 3027
9:16 that *he* may save my people out of the **h** of 3027
10:18 delivered you out of the **h** of the Egyptians, 3027
10:18 out of the **h** of all kingdoms, *and* of them 3027
12: 3 of whose **h** have I received *any* bribe to 3027
12: 4 hast thou taken ought of any man's **h**. 3027
12: 5 that ye have not found ought in my **h**. 3027
12: 9 he sold them into the **h** of Sisera, captain of 3027
12: 9 into the **h** of the Philistines, and into 3027
12: 9 into the **h** of the king of Moab, and 3027
12:10 now deliver us out of the **h** of our enemies, 3027
12:11 delivered you out of the **h** of your enemies 3027
12:15 shall the **h** of the LORD be against you, 3027
13:22 **h** of any of the people that *were* with Saul 3027
14:10 the LORD hath delivered them into our **h**: 3027
14:12 hath delivered them into the **h** of Israel. 3027
14:19 Saul said unto the priest, Withdraw thine **h**. 3027
14:26 but no man put his **h** to his mouth: 3027
14:27 forth the end of the rod that *was* in his **h**, 3027
14:27 a honeycomb, and put his **h** to his mouth; 3027
14:37 wilt thou deliver them into the **h** of Israel? 3027
14:43 with the end of the rod that *was* in mine **h**, 3027
16:16 that he shall play with his **h**, and thou shalt 3027
16:23 David took a harp, and played with his **h**: 3027
17:22 David left his carriage in the **h** of 3027
17:37 he will deliver me out of the **h** of this 3027
17:40 he took his staff in his **h**, and chose him 3027
17:40 even in a scrip; and his sling *was* in his **h**: 3027
17:46 will the LORD deliver thee into mine **h**; 3027
17:49 David put his **h** in *his* bag, and took thence 3027
17:50 but *there was* no sword in the **h** of David. 3027
17:57 Saul with the head of the Philistine in his **h**. 3027
18:10 David played with his **h**, as at other times: 3027
18:10 and *there was* a javelin in Saul's **h**. 3027
18:17 Let not mine **h** be upon him, but let 3027
18:17 but let the **h** of the Philistines be upon him. 3027
18:21 that the **h** of the Philistines may be against 3027
18:25 Saul thought to make David fall by the **h** of 3027
19: 5 For he did put his life in his **h**, and slew 3709
19: 9 he sat in his house with his javelin in his **h**: 3027
19: 9 in his hand: and David played with *his* **h**. 3027
20:16 even require *it* at the **h** of David's enemies. 3027
20:19 hide thyself when the business was *in* **h**, NIH
21: 3 Now therefore what is under thine **h**? 3027
21: 3 give *me* five *loaves of* bread in mine **h**, or 3027
21: 4 *There is* no common bread under mine **h**, 3027
21: 8 is there not here under thine **h** spear or 3027
22: 6 having his spear in his **h**, and all his 3027
22:17 because their **h** also *is* with David, and 3027
22:17 **h** to fall upon the priests of the LORD. 3027
23: 4 for I will deliver the Philistines into thine **h**. 3027
23: 6 *that* he came down *with* an ephod in his **h**. 3027
23: 7 God hath delivered him into mine **h**; 3027
23:11 the men of Keilah deliver me up into his **h**? 3027
23:12 deliver me and my men into the **h** of Saul? 3027
23:14 but God delivered him not into his **h**. 3027
23:16 the wood, and strengthened his **h** in God. 3027
23:17 for the **h** of Saul my father shall not find 3027
23:20 *shall be* to deliver him into the king's **h**. 3027
24: 4 I will deliver thine enemy into thine **h**, 3027
24: 6 to stretch forth mine **h** against him, 3027
24:10 thee to day into mine **h** in the cave: 3027
24:10 I will not put forth mine **h** against my lord; 3027
24:11 see, yea see the skirt of thy robe in my **h**: 3027
24:11 *is* neither evil nor transgression in mine **h**, 3027
24:12 of thee: but mine **h** shall not be upon thee. 3027
24:13 but mine **h** shall not be upon thee. 3027
24:15 my cause, and deliver me out of thine **h**. 3027
24:18 the LORD had delivered me into thine **h**, 3027
24:20 of Israel shall be established in thine **h**. 3027
25: 8 whatsoever cometh to thine **h** unto thy 3027
25:26 *from* avenging thyself with thine own **h**, 3027
25:33 *from* avenging myself with mine own **h**. 3027
25:35 So David received of her **h** *that* which she 3027
25:39 cause of my reproach from the **h** of Nabal, 3027
26: 8 hath delivered thine enemy into thine **h** 3027
26: 9 for who can stretch forth his **h** against 3027
26:11 mine **h** against the LORD'S anointed: 3027
26:18 have I done? or what evil *is* in mine **h**? 3027
26:23 for the LORD delivered thee into *my* **h** to 3027
26:23 I would not stretch forth mine **h** against 3027
27: 1 I shall now perish one day by the **h** of Saul: 3027
27: 1 of Israel: so shall I escape out of his **h**. 3027
28:17 hath rent the kingdom out of thine **h**, 3027
28:19 Israel with thee into the **h** of the Philistines: 3027
28:19 host of Israel into the **h** of the Philistines. 3027
28:21 I have put my life in my **h**, and 3709
30:23 company that came against us into our **h**. 3027
2Sa 1:14 thine **h** to destroy the LORD'S anointed? 3027
2:19 in going he turned not to the **right h** nor to 3225
2:21 Turn thee aside to thy **right h** or to thy left, 3225
3: 8 have not delivered thee into the **h** of David, 3027
3:12 behold, my **h** *shall be* with thee, to bring 3027
3:18 By the **h** of my servant David I will save 3027

2Sa 3:18 people Israel out of the **h** of the Philistines, 3027
3:18 and out of the **h** of all their enemies. 3027
4:11 therefore now require his blood of your **h**, 3027
5:19 wilt thou deliver them into mine **h**? 3027
5:19 deliver the Philistines into thine **h**. 3027
6: 6 Uzzah put forth *his* **h** to the ark of God, and NIH
8: 1 David took Metheg-ammah out of the **h** of 3027
10: 2 David sent to comfort him by the **h** of his 3027
10:10 delivered into the **h** of Abishai his brother, 3027
11:14 letter to Joab, and sent *it* by the **h** of Uriah. 3027
12: 7 and I delivered thee out of the **h** of Saul; 3027
12:25 And he sent by the **h** of Nathan the prophet; 3027
13: 5 that I may see *it,* and eat *it* at her **h**. 3027
13: 6 of cakes in my sight, that I may eat at her **h**. 3027
13:10 *into* the chamber, that I may eat of thine **h**. 3027
13:19 laid her **h** on her head, and went on crying. 3027
14:16 to deliver his handmaid out of the **h** of 3709
14:19 *Is not* the **h** of Joab with thee in all this? 3027
14:19 none can **turn to the right h** or to the left 3231
15: 5 he put forth his **h**, and took him, and 3027
16: 6 all the mighty *men were* on his **right h** and 3225
16: 8 the kingdom into the **h** of Absalom thy son: 3027
18: 2 third part of the people under the **h** of Joab, 3027
18: 2 a third part under the **h** of Abishai the son 3027
18: 2 a third part under the **h** of Ittai the Gittite. 3027
18:12 a thousand *shekels of* silver in mine **h**, 3709
18:12 *yet* would I not put forth mine **h** against 3027
18:14 he took three darts in his **h**, and thrust them 3709
18:28 that lift up their **h** against my lord the king. 3027
19: 9 The king saved us out of the **h** of our 3709
19: 9 he delivered us out of the **h** of 3709
20: 9 by the beard with the right **h** to kiss him. 3027
20:10 no heed to the sword that *was* in Joab's **h**: 3027
20:21 hath lift up his **h** against the king, 3027
21:20 that had on every **h** six fingers, and 3027
21:22 fell by the **h** of David, and by the hand of 3027
21:22 hand of David, and by the **h** of his servants. 3027
22: 1 him out of the **h** of all his enemies, 3709
22: 1 of all his enemies, and out of the **h** of Saul: 3709
23:10 smote the Philistines until his **h** was weary, 3027
23:10 was weary, and his **h** clave unto the sword: 3027
23:21 the Egyptian had a spear in his **h**; but 3027
23:21 plucked the spear out of the Egyptian's **h**, 3027
24:14 let us fall now into the **h** of the LORD; 3027
24:14 and let me not fall into the **h** of man. 3027
24:16 when the angel stretched out his **h** *upon* 3027
24:16 stay now thine **h**. And the angel of 3027
24:17 let thine **h**, I pray thee, be against me, and 3027
1Ki 2:19 king's mother; and she sat on his **right h**. 3225
2:25 king Solomon sent by the **h** of Benaiah 3027
2:46 the kingdom was established in the **h** of 3027
8:15 and hath with his **h** fulfilled *it,* saying, 3027
8:24 hast fulfilled *it* with thine **h**, as *it is* this 3027
8:42 of thy strong **h**, and of thy stretched out 3027
8:53 as thou spakest by the **h** of Moses thy 3027
8:56 which he promised by the **h** of Moses his 3027
11:12 *but* I will rend it out of the **h** of thy son. 3027
11:26 even he lift up *his* **h** against the king. 3027
11:27 this *was* the cause that he lift up *his* **h** 3027
11:31 I will rent the kingdom out of the **h** of 3027
11:34 not take the whole kingdom out of his **h**: 3027
11:35 I will take the kingdom out of his son's **h**, 3027
13: 4 that he put forth his **h** from the altar, 3027
13: 4 his **h**, which he put forth against him, 3027
13: 6 that my **h** may be restored me again. 3027
13: 6 the king's **h** was restored him again, and 3027
14:18 which he spake by the **h** of his servant 3027
15:18 delivered them into the **h** of his servants: 3027
16: 7 also by the **h** of the prophet Jehu the son of 3027
17:11 I pray thee, a morsel of bread in thine **h**. 3027
18: 9 deliver thy servant into the **h** of Ahab, 3027
18:44 a little cloud out of the sea, like a man's **h**. 3709
18:46 the **h** of the LORD was on Elijah; and 3027
20: 6 they shall put *it* in their **h**, and take *it* away. 3027
20:13 I will deliver it into thine **h** *this* day; 3027
20:28 deliver all this great multitude into thine **h**, 3027
20:42 Because thou hast let go out of *thy* **h** a man 3027
22: 3 take it not out of the **h** of the king of Syria? 3027
22: 6 for the Lord shall deliver *it* into the **h** of 3027
22:12 LORD shall deliver *it* into the king's **h**. 3027
22:15 for the LORD shall deliver *it* into the **h** of 3027
22:19 of heaven standing by him on his **right h** 3225
22:34 Turn thine **h**, and carry me out of the host; 3027
2Ki 3:10 to deliver them into the **h** of Moab. 3027
3:13 to deliver them into the **h** of Moab. 3027
3:15 that the **h** of the LORD came upon him. 3027
3:18 will deliver the Moabites also into your **h**. 3027
4:29 take my staff in thine **h**, and go *thy way:* if 3027
5:11 strike his **h** over the place, and recover 3027
5:18 he leaneth on my **h**, and I bow myself *in* 3027
5:24 he took *them* from their **h**, and 3027
6: 7 to thee. And he put out his **h**, and took it. 3027
7: 2 a lord on whose **h** the king leaned answered 3027
7:17 the king appointed the lord on whose **h** he 3027
8: 8 Take a present in thine **h**, and go, meet 3027
8:20 In his days Edom revolted from under the **h** 3027
8:22 Yet Edom revolted from under the **h** of 3027
9: 1 take this box of oil in thine **h**, and go *to* 3027
9: 7 servants of the LORD, at the **h** of Jezebel. 3027
10:15 If it be, give *me* thine **h**. And he gave *him* 3027
10:15 he gave *him* his **h**; and he took him up to 3027
11: 8 every man with his weapons in his **h**: 3027
11:11 every man with his weapons in his **h**, 3027
12:15 into whose **h** they delivered the money to 3027
13: 3 he delivered them into the **h** of Hazael king 3027
13: 3 into the **h** of Ben-hadad the son of Hazael, 3027
13: 5 that they went out from under the **h** of 3027
13:16 king of Israel, Put thine **h** upon the bow. 3027
13:16 he put his **h** *upon it:* and Elisha put his 3027
13:25 **h** of Ben-hadad the son of Hazael the cities, 3027
13:25 which he had taken out of the **h** of 3027
14: 5 as the kingdom was confirmed in his **h**, 3027
14:25 which he spake by the **h** of his servant 3027
14:27 he saved them by the **h** of Jeroboam the son 3027
15:19 that his **h** might be with him to confirm 3027
15:19 with him to confirm the kingdom in his **h**. 3027
16: 7 save me out of the **h** of the king of Syria, 3709
16: 7 out of the **h** of the king of Israel, which rise 3709
17: 7 from under the **h** of Pharaoh king of Egypt, 3027
17:20 and delivered them into the **h** of spoilers, 3027
17:39 he shall deliver you out of the **h** of all your 3027
18:21 man lean, it will go into his **h**, and pierce it: 3709
18:29 shall not be able to deliver you out of his **h**: 3027
18:30 this city shall not be delivered into the **h** of 3027
18:33 his land out of the **h** of the king of Assyria? 3027
18:34 have they delivered Samaria out of mine **h**? 3027
18:35 have delivered their country out of mine **h**, 3027
18:35 should deliver Jerusalem out of mine **h**? 3027
19:10 Jerusalem shall not be delivered into the **h** 3027
19:14 Hezekiah received the letter of the **h** of 3027
19:19 I beseech thee, save *thou* us out of his **h**, 3027
20: 6 this city out of the **h** of the king of Assyria; 3709
21:14 deliver them into the **h** of their enemies; 3027
22: 2 turned not aside *to* the **right h** or *to* the left. 3225
22: 5 let them deliver it into the **h** of the doers of 3027
22: 7 the money that was delivered into their **h**, 3027
22: 9 have delivered it into the **h** of them that do 3027
23: 8 which *were* on a man's **left h** at the gate of 8040
23:13 which *were* on the **right h** of the mount of 3225
1Ch 4:10 that thine **h** might be with me, and that thou 3027
5:10 war with the Hagarites, who fell by their **h**: 3027
5:20 the Hagarites were delivered into their **h**, 3027
6:15 and Jerusalem by the **h** of Nebuchadnezzar. 3027
6:39 brother Asaph, who stood on his **right h**, 3225
6:44 the sons of Merari *stood* on the **left h**: 8040
11:23 in the Egyptian's **h** *was* a spear like a 3027
11:23 pluckt the spear out of the Egyptian's **h**, 3027
12: 2 could **use** both **the right h** and the left in 3231
13: 9 Uzza put forth his **h** to hold the ark; 3027
13:10 smote him, because he put his **h** to the ark: 3027
14:10 wilt thou deliver them into mine **h**? 3027
14:10 Go up; for I will deliver them into thine **h**. 3027
14:11 by mine **h** like the breaking forth of waters: 3027
16: 7 to thank the LORD into the **h** of Asaph 3027
18: 1 her towns out of the **h** of the Philistines. 3027
19:11 delivered unto the **h** of Abishai his brother, 3027
20: 6 six *on each* **h**, and six *on each foot:* and NIH
20: 8 they fell by the **h** of David, and by the hand 3027
20: 8 hand of David, and by the **h** of his servants. 3027
21:13 let me fall now into the **h** of the LORD; 3027
21:13 but let me not fall into the **h** of man. 3027
21:15 *It is* enough, stay now thine **h**. 3027
21:16 having a drawn sword in his **h** stretched out 3027
21:17 let thine **h**, I pray thee, O LORD my God, 3027
22:18 the inhabitants of the land into mine **h**; 3027
26:28 *anything, it was* under the **h** of Shelomith, 3027
28:19 me understand in writing by *his* **h** upon me, 3027
29: 8 by the **h** of Jehiel the Gershonite. 3027

1Ch	29:12	in thine **h** *is* power and might; and in thine	3027
	29:12	in thine **h** *it is* to make great, and to give	3027
	29:16	for thine holy name *cometh* of thine **h**,	3027
2Ch	3:17	one on the **right h**, and the other on	3225
	3:17	called the name of *that on* the **right h**	3233
	4: 6	put five on the **right h**, and five on the left,	3225
	4: 7	five on the **right h**, and five on the left.	3225
	6:15	hast fulfilled *it* with thine **h**, as *it is* this	3027
	6:32	thy mighty **h**, and thy stretched out arm;	3027
	10:15	which he spake by the **h** of Ahijah	3027
	12: 5	have I also left you in the **h** of Shishak.	3027
	12: 7	out upon Jerusalem by the **h** of Shishak.	3027
	13: 8	the LORD in the **h** of the sons of David;	3027
	13:16	and God delivered them into their **h**.	3027
	16: 7	of the king of Syria escaped out of thine **h**.	3027
	16: 8	the LORD, he delivered them into thine **h**.	3027
	17: 5	LORD stablished the kingdom in his **h**;	3027
	18: 5	for God will deliver *it* into the king's **h**.	3027
	18:11	for the LORD shall deliver *it* into the **h** of	3027
	18:14	and they shall be delivered into your **h**.	3027
	18:18	the host of heaven standing on his **right h**	3225
	18:33	he said to *his* chariot man, Turn thine **h**,	3027
	20: 6	and in thine **h** *is there not* power and might,	3027
	21:10	So the Edomites revolted from under the **h**	3027
	21:10	also did Libnah revolt from under his **h**;	3027
	23: 7	every man with his weapons in his **h**;	3027
	23:10	every man having his weapon in his **h**,	3027
	23:18	LORD by the **h** of the priests the Levites,	3027
	24:11	the king's office by the **h** of the Levites,	3027
	24:24	delivered a very great host into their **h**,	3027
	25:15	not deliver their own people out of thine **h**?	3027
	25:20	that *he* might deliver them into the **h** *of*	3027
	26:11	of their account by the **h** of Jeiel the scribe	3027
	26:11	the ruler, under the **h** of Hananiah,	3027
	26:13	under their **h** *was* an army, three hundred	3027
	26:19	and *had* a censer in his **h** to burn incense:	3027
	28: 5	him into the **h** of the king of Syria;	3027
	28: 5	he was also delivered into the **h** of the king	3027
	28: 9	he hath delivered them into your **h**, and	3027
	30: 6	that are escaped out of the **h** of the kings of	3709
	30:12	Also in Judah the **h** of God was to give	3027
	30:16	*which they received* of the **h** of the Levites.	3027
	31:13	*were* overseers under the **h** of Cononiah	3027
	32:11	us out of the **h** of the king of Assyria?	3709
	32:13	able to deliver their lands out of mine **h**?	3027
	32:14	that could deliver his people out of mine **h**,	3027
	32:14	be able to deliver you out of mine **h**?	3027
	32:15	able to deliver his people out of mine **h**,	3027
	32:15	mine hand, and out of the **h** of my fathers:	3027
	32:15	shall your God deliver you out of mine **h**?	3027
	32:17	not delivered their people out of mine **h**,	3027
	32:17	Hezekiah deliver his people out of mine **h**.	3027
	32:22	the inhabitants of Jerusalem from the **h** of	3027
	32:22	from the **h** of all *other*, and guided them on	3027
	33: 8	and the ordinances by the **h** of Moses.	3027
	34: 2	declined neither *to* the **right h**, nor *to*	3225
	34: 9	doors had gathered of the **h** of Manasseh	3027
	34:10	they put *it* in the **h** of the workmen that had	3027
	34:17	have delivered it into the **h** of the overseers,	3027
	34:17	the overseers, and to the **h** of the workmen.	3027
	35: 6	the word of the LORD by the **h** of Moses.	3027
	36:17	stooped for age: he gave *them* all into his **h**.	3027
Ezr	1: 8	forth by the **h** of Mithredath the treasurer,	3027
	5:12	he gave them into the **h** of Nebuchadnezzar	3028
	6:12	that shall put to their **h** to alter *and*	3028
	7: 6	according to the **h** of the LORD his God	3027
	7: 9	according to the good **h** of his God upon	3027
	7:14	to the law of thy God which *is* in thine **h**;	3028
	7:25	that *is* in thine **h**, set magistrates and	3028
	7:28	I was strengthened as the **h** of the LORD	3027
	8:18	by the good **h** of our God upon us they	3027
	8:22	The **h** of our God *is* upon all them for good	3027
	8:26	I even weighed unto their **h** six hundred	3027
	8:31	the **h** of our God was upon us, and	3027
	8:31	he delivered us from the **h** of the enemy,	3709
	8:33	**h** of Meremoth the son of Uriah the priest;	3027
	9: 2	the **h** of the princes and rulers hath been	3027
	9: 7	been delivered into the **h** of the kings of	3027
Ne	1:10	by thy great power, and by thy strong **h**.	3027
	2: 8	according to the good **h** of my God upon	3027
	2:18	I told them of the **h** of my God which was	3027
	4:17	and with the other *h* held a weapon.	NIH
	6: 5	the fifth time with an open letter in his **h**;	3027
	8: 4	and Hilkiah, and Maaseiah, on his **right h**;	3225
	8: 4	and on his **left h**, Pedaiah, and Mishael, and	8040
	9:14	and laws, by the **h** of Moses thy servant:	3027
	9:27	Therefore thou deliveredst them into the **h**	3027
	9:27	who saved them out of the **h** of their	3027
	9:28	leftest thou them in the **h** of their enemies,	3027
	9:30	gavest thou them into the **h** of the people of	3027
	11:24	*was* at the king's **h** in all matters	3027
	12:31	whereof *one* went on the **right h** upon	3225
Est	2:21	and sought to lay **h** on the king Ahasuerus.	3027
	3:10	the king took his ring from his **h**, and	3027
	5: 2	Esther the golden sceptre that *was* in his **h**.	3027
	6: 2	who sought to lay **h** on the king Ahasuerus.	3027
	6: 9	horse be delivered to the **h** of one of	3027
	8: 7	because he laid his **h** upon the Jews.	3027
	9: 2	to lay **h** on such as sought their hurt:	3027
	9:10	but on the spoil laid they not their **h**.	3027
	9:15	but on the prey they laid not their **h**.	3027
Job	1:11	put forth thine **h** now, and touch all that he	3027
	1:12	only upon himself put not forth thine **h**.	3027
	2: 5	put forth thine **h** now, and touch his bone	3027
	2: 6	said unto Satan, Behold, he *is* in thine **h**;	3027
	2:10	shall we receive good **at the h of** God,	854+4480
	5:15	their mouth, and from the **h** of the mighty.	3027
	6: 9	*that* he would let loose his **h**, and cut me	3027
	6:23	Or, Deliver me from the enemy's **h**? or,	3027
	6:23	or, Redeem me from the **h** of the mighty?	3027
	9:24	The earth is given into the **h** of the wicked:	3027
	9:33	*that* might lay his **h** upon us both.	3027
	10: 7	*there is* none that can deliver out of thine **h**.	3027
	11:14	If iniquity *be* in thine **h**, put it far away, and	3027
	12: 6	into whose **h** God bringeth *abundantly*.	3027
	12: 9	Who knoweth not in all these that the **h** of	3027
	12:10	In whose **h** *is* the soul of every living *thing*,	3027
	13:14	in my teeth, and put my life in mine **h**?	3709
	13:21	Withdraw thine **h** far from me: and let not	3709
	15:23	that the day of darkness is ready at his **h**.	3027
	15:25	For he stretcheth out his **h** against God, and	3027
	19:21	for the **h** of God hath touched me.	3027
	20:22	every **h** of the wicked shall come *upon* him.	3027
	21: 5	and lay *your* **h** upon *your* mouth.	3027
	21:16	Lo, their good *is* not in their **h**: the counsel	3027
	23: 9	*On* the **left h**, where he doth work, but	8040
	23: 9	*him*: he hideth *himself* on the **right h**,	3225
	26:13	his **h** hath formed the crooked serpent.	3027
	27:11	I will teach you by the **h** of God: *that* which	3027
	27:22	not spare: he would fain flee out of his **h**.	3027
	28: 9	He putteth forth his **h** upon the rock;	3027
	29: 9	and laid *their* **h** on their mouth.	3709
	29:20	in me, and my bow was renewed in my **h**.	3027
	30:12	Upon *my* **right h** rise the youth; they push	3225
	30:21	with thy strong **h** thou opposest thyself	3027
	30:24	Howbeit *he* will not stretch out *his* **h** to	3027
	31:21	If I have lift up my **h** against the fatherless,	3027
	31:25	and because mine **h** had gotten much;	3027
	31:27	or my mouth hath kissed my **h**:	3027
	33: 7	neither shall my **h** be heavy upon thee.	405
	34:20	the mighty shall be taken away without **h**.	3027
	35: 7	thou him? or what receiveth he of thine **h**?	3027
	37: 7	He sealeth up the **h** of every man; that all	3027
	40: 4	I will lay my **h** upon my mouth.	3027
	40:14	thee that thine own **right h** can save thee.	3225
	41: 8	Lay thine **h** upon him, remember the battle,	3709
Ps	10:12	Arise, O LORD; O God, lift up thine **h**:	3027
	10:14	and spite, to requite *it* with thy **h**:	3027
	16: 8	because *he is* at my **right h**, I shall not be	3225
	16:11	at thy **right h** *there are* pleasures for	3225
	17: 7	O thou that savest by thy **right h** them	3225
	17:14	From men *which are* thy **h**, O LORD,	3027
	18: T	delivered him from the **h** of all his enemies,	3709
	18: T	of all his enemies, and from the **h** of Saul:	3027
	18:35	thy **right h** hath holden me up, and	3225
	20: 6	with the saving strength of his **right h**.	3225
	21: 8	Thine **h** shall find out all thine enemies:	3027
	21: 8	thy **right h** shall find out those that hate	3225
	26:10	and their **right h** is full *of* bribes.	3225
	31: 5	Into thine **h** I commit my spirit: thou hast	3027
	31: 8	hast not shut me up into the **h** of	3027
	31:15	My times *are* in thy **h**: deliver me from	3027
	31:15	deliver me from the **h** of mine enemies, and	3027
	32: 4	and night thy **h** was heavy upon me:	3027
	36:11	and let not the **h** of the wicked remove me.	3027
	37:24	for the LORD upholdeth *him with* his **h**.	3027
	37:33	The LORD will not leave him in his **h**,	3027
	38: 2	stick fast in me, and thy **h** presseth me sore.	3027

Ps	39:10	I am consumed by the blow of thine **h**.	3027
	44: 2	thou didst drive out the heathen *with* thy **h**,	3027
	44: 3	thy **right h**, and thine arm, and the light of	3225
	45: 4	thy **right h** shall teach thee terrible *things.*	3225
	45: 9	**right h** did stand the queen in gold of	3225
	48:10	thy **right h** is full *of* righteousness.	3225
	60: 5	save *with* thy **right h**, and hear me.	3225
	63: 8	hard after thee: thy **right h** upholdeth me.	3225
	71: 4	O my God, out of the **h** of the wicked,	3027
	71: 4	out of the **h** of the unrighteous and	3709
	73:23	thou hast holden *me* by my right **h**.	3027
	74:11	Why withdrawest thou thy **h**, even thy right	3027
	74:11	thou thy hand, even thy **right h**?	3225
	75: 8	For in the **h** of the LORD *there is* a cup,	3027
	77:10	*I will remember* the years of the **right h** of	3225
	77:20	thy people like a flock by the **h** of Moses	3027
	78:42	They remembered not his **h**: *nor* the day	3027
	78:54	*which* his **right h** had purchased.	3225
	78:61	and his glory into the enemy's **h**.	3027
	80:15	the vineyard which thy **right h** hath	3225
	80:17	Let thy **h** be upon the man of thy right	3027
	80:17	thy hand be upon the man of thy **right h**,	3225
	81:14	and turned my **h** against their adversaries.	3027
	82: 4	needy: rid *them* out of the **h** of the wicked.	3027
	88: 5	no more: and they are cut off from thy **h**.	3027
	89:13	strong is thy **h**, *and* high is thy right hand.	3027
	89:13	strong is thy hand, *and* high is thy **right h**.	3225
	89:21	With whom my **h** shall be established:	3027
	89:25	I will set his **h** also in the sea, and his right	3027
	89:25	also in the sea, and his **right h** in the rivers.	3225
	89:42	Thou hast set up the **right h** of his	3225
	89:48	shall he deliver his soul from the **h** of	3027
	91: 7	at thy side, and ten thousand at thy **right h**;	3225
	95: 4	In his **h** *are* the deep places of the earth:	3027
	95: 7	of his pasture, and the sheep of his **h**.	3027
	97:10	he delivereth them out of the **h** of	3027
	98: 1	hath done marvellous *things:* his **right h**,	3225
	104:28	thou openest thine **h**, they are filled *with*	3027
	106:10	he saved them from the **h** of him that hated	3027
	106:10	redeemed them from the **h** of the enemy.	3027
	106:26	Therefore he lifted up his **h** against them,	3027
	106:41	And he gave them into the **h** of the heathen;	3027
	106:42	were brought into subjection under their **h**.	3027
	107: 2	whom he hath redeemed from the **h** of	3027
	108: 6	save *with* thy **right h**, and answer me.	3225
	109: 6	over him: and let Satan stand at his **right h**.	3225
	109:27	That they may know that this *is* thy **h**;	3027
	109:31	For he shall stand at the **right h** of the poor,	3225
	110: 1	said unto my Lord, Sit thou at my **right h**,	3225
	110: 5	The Lord at thy **right h** shall strike through	3225
	118:15	the **right h** of the LORD doeth valiantly.	3225
	118:16	The **right h** of the LORD is exalted:	3225
	118:16	the **right h** of the LORD doeth valiantly.	3225
	119:109	My soul *is* continually in my **h**: yet do I not	3709
	119:173	Let thine **h** help me; for I have chosen thy	3027
	121: 5	the LORD *is* thy shade upon thy right **h**.	3027
	123: 2	as the eyes of servants *look* unto the **h** of	3027
	123: 2	as the eyes of a maiden unto the **h** of her	3027
	127: 4	As arrows *are* in the **h** of a mighty *man;* so	3027
	129: 7	Where*with* the mower filleth not his **h**;	3709
	136:12	With a strong **h**, and with a stretched out	3027
	137: 5	let my **right h** forget *her cunning.*	3225
	138: 7	thou shalt stretch forth thine **h** against	3027
	138: 7	and thy **right h** shall save me.	3225
	139: 5	and before, and laid thine **h** upon me.	3709
	139:10	Even there shall thy **h** lead me, and	3027
	139:10	lead me, and thy **right h** shall hold me.	3225
	142: 4	I looked *on my* **right h**, and beheld, but	3225
	144: 7	Send thine **h** from above; rid me, and	3027
	144: 7	from the **h** of strange children;	3027
	144: 8	their **right h** *is* a right hand of falsehood.	3225
	144: 8	their right hand *is* a **right h** of falsehood.	3225
	144:11	deliver me from the **h** of strange children,	3027
	144:11	their **right h** *is* a right hand of falsehood:	3225
	144:11	their right hand *is* a **right h** of falsehood:	3225
	145:16	Thou openest thine **h**, and satisfiest	3027
	149: 6	and a twoedged sword in their **h**;	3027
Pr	1:24	I have stretched out my **h**, and no man	3027
	3:16	Length of days *is* in her **right h**; and in her	3225
	3:16	and in her **left h** riches and honour.	8040
	3:27	when it is in the power of thine **h** to do *it.*	3027
	4:27	Turn not *to* the **right h** nor *to* the left:	3225
	6: 1	*if* thou hast stricken thy **h** with a stranger,	3709
	6: 3	when thou art come into the **h** of thy friend;	3709
	6: 5	Deliver thyself as a roe from the **h** *of*	3027
	6: 5	and as a bird from the **h** of the fowler.	3027
	10: 4	*becometh* poor that dealeth *with* a slack **h**:	3709
	10: 4	but the **h** of the diligent maketh rich.	3027
	11:21	*Though* **h** *join* in hand, the wicked shall not	3027
	11:21	*Though* hand *join* in **h**, the wicked shall not	3027
	12:24	The **h** of the diligent shall bear rule: but	3027
	16: 5	*though* **h** *join* in hand, he shall not be	3027
	16: 5	*though* hand *join* in **h**, he shall not be	3027
	17:16	Wherefore *is there* a price in the **h** of a fool	3027
	19:24	A slothful *man* hideth his **h** in *his* bosom,	3027
	21: 1	The king's heart *is* in the **h** of the LORD,	3027
	26: 6	He that sendeth a message by the **h** of a	3027
	26: 9	*As* a thorn goeth up into the **h** of a	3027
	26:15	The slothful hideth his **h** in *his* bosom;	3027
	27:16	the wind, and the ointment of his **right h**,	3225
	30:32	thought evil, *lay thine* **h** upon thy mouth.	3027
	31:20	She stretcheth out her **h** to the poor; yea,	3709
Ecc	2:24	also I saw, that it *was* from the **h** of God.	3027
	5:14	a son, and *there is* nothing in his **h**.	3027
	5:15	which he may carry away in his **h**.	3027
	7:18	yea, also from this withdraw not thine **h**:	3027
	9: 1	and their works, *are* in the **h** of God:	3027
	9:10	Whatsoever thy **h** findeth to do, do *it* with	3027
	10: 2	A wise *man's* heart *is* at his **right h**; but	3225
	11: 6	and in the evening withhold not thine **h**:	3027
SS	2: 6	His **left h** *is* under my head, and his right	8040
	2: 6	my head, and his **right h** doth embrace me.	3225
	5: 4	My beloved put in his **h** by the hole *of*	3027
	8: 3	His **left h** *should be* under my head, and	8040
	8: 3	and his **right h** should embrace me.	3225
Isa	1:12	who hath required this at your **h**, to tread	3027
	1:25	I will turn my **h** upon thee, and purely	3027
	3: 6	our ruler, and *let* this ruin *be* under thy **h**:	3027
	5:25	he hath stretched forth his **h** against them,	3027
	5:25	turned away, but his **h** *is* stretched out still.	3027
	6: 6	unto me, having a live coal in his **h**,	3027
	8:11	LORD spake thus to me with a strong **h**,	3027
	9:12	turned away, but his **h** *is* stretched out still.	3027
	9:17	turned away, but his **h** *is* stretched out still.	3027
	9:20	he shall snatch on the **right h**, and	3225
	9:20	he shall eat on the **left h**, and they shall not	8040
	9:21	turned away, but his **h** *is* stretched out still.	3027
	10: 4	turned away, but his **h** *is* stretched out still.	3027
	10: 5	and the staff in their **h** *is* mine indignation.	3027
	10:10	As my **h** hath found the kingdoms of	3027
	10:13	By the strength of my **h** I have done *it,* and	3027
	10:14	my **h** hath found as a nest the riches of	3027
	10:32	he shall shake his **h** *against* the mount of	3027
	11: 8	the weaned child shall put his **h** on	3027
	11:11	*that* the Lord shall set his **h** again	3027
	11:14	they shall lay their **h** upon Edom and	3027
	11:15	with his mighty wind shall he shake his **h**	3027
	13: 2	exalt the voice unto them, shake the **h**,	3027
	13: 6	Howl ye; for the day of the LORD *is* **at h**;	7138
	14:26	this *is* the **h** that is stretched out upon all	3027
	14:27	shall disannul *it?* and his **h** *is* stretched out,	3027
	19: 4	the Egyptians will I give over into the **h** of	3027
	19:16	of the shaking of the **h** of the LORD of	3027
	22:21	I will commit thy government into his **h**:	3027
	23:11	He stretched out his **h** over the sea,	3027
	25:10	For in this mountain shall the **h** of	3027
	26:11	LORD, *when* thy **h** is lifted up, they will	3027
	28: 2	shall cast down to the earth with the **h**.	3027
	28: 4	while it is yet in his **h** he eateth it up.	3709
	30:21	when ye **turn to the right h**, and when ye	541
	31: 3	When the LORD shall stretch out his **h**,	3027
	34:17	and his **h** hath divided it unto them by line:	3027
	36: 6	man lean, it will go into his **h**, and pierce it:	3709
	36:15	this city shall not be delivered into the **h** of	3027
	36:18	his land out of the **h** of the king of Assyria?	3027
	36:19	have they delivered Samaria out of my **h**?	3027
	36:20	that have delivered their land out of my **h**,	3027
	36:20	should deliver Jerusalem out of my **h**?	3027
	37:10	Jerusalem shall not be given into the **h** of	3027
	37:14	Hezekiah received the letter from the **h** of	3027
	37:20	O LORD our God, save us from his **h**,	3027
	38: 6	this city out of the **h** of the king of Assyria:	3709
	40: 2	for she hath received of the LORD'S **h**	3027
	40:10	the Lord GOD will come with strong *h*,	NIH
	40:12	measured the waters in the **hollow of** his **h**,	8168
	41:10	I will uphold thee with the **right h** of my	3225
	41:13	I the LORD thy God will hold thy **right h**,	3225
	41:20	that the **h** of the LORD hath done this,	3027

Isa	42: 6	will hold thine **h**, and will keep thee, and	3027
	43:13	*there is* none that can deliver out of my **h**:	3027
	44: 5	another shall subscribe *with* his **h** unto	3027
	44:20	nor say, *Is there* not a lie in my **right h**?	3225
	45: 1	to Cyrus, whose **right h** I have holden, to	3225
	47: 6	and given them into thine **h**:	3027
	48:13	Mine **h** also hath laid the foundation of	3027
	48:13	and my **right h** hath spanned the heavens:	3225
	49: 2	in the shadow of his **h** hath he hid me, and	3027
	49:22	I will lift up mine **h** to the Gentiles, and	3027
	50: 2	Is my **h** shortened at all, that *it* cannot	3027
	50:11	This shall ye have of mine **h**; ye shall lie	3027
	51:16	have covered thee in the shadow of mine **h**,	3027
	51:17	which hast drunk at the **h** of the LORD	3027
	51:18	neither *is there any* that taketh her by the **h**	3027
	51:22	I have taken out of thine **h** the cup of	3027
	51:23	I will put it into the **h** of them that afflict	3027
	53:10	of the LORD shall prosper in his **h**.	3027
	54: 3	For thou shalt break forth *on* the **right h**	3225
	56: 2	and keepeth his **h** from doing any evil.	3027
	57:10	thou hast found the life of thine **h**; therefore	3027
	59: 1	Behold, the LORD'S **h** is not shortened,	3027
	62: 3	Thou shalt also be a crown of glory in the **h**	3027
	62: 3	and a royal diadem in the **h** of thy God.	3709
	62: 8	The LORD hath sworn by his **right h**, and	3225
	63:12	That led *them* by the **right h** of Moses *with*	3225
	64: 8	and we all *are* the work of thine **h**.	3027
	66: 2	For all those *things* hath mine **h** made, and	3027
	66:14	the **h** of the LORD shall be known	3027
Jer	1: 9	the LORD put forth his **h**, and touched my	3027
	6: 9	turn back thine **h** as a grapegatherer into	3027
	6:12	for I will stretch out my **h** upon	3027
	11:21	of the LORD, that thou die not by our **h**:	3027
	12: 7	of my soul into the **h** of her enemies.	3709
	15: 6	will I stretch out my **h** against thee,	3027
	15:17	nor rejoiced; I sat alone because of thy **h**:	3027
	15:21	I will deliver thee out of the **h** of	3027
	15:21	I will redeem thee out of the **h** of	3709
	16:21	I will cause them to know mine **h** and my	3027
	18: 4	of clay was marred in the **h** of the potter:	3027
	18: 6	as the clay *is* in the potter's **h**, so *are* ye in	3027
	18: 6	so *are* ye in mine **h**, O house of Israel.	3027
	20: 4	I will give all Judah into the **h** of the king	3027
	20: 5	will I give into the **h** of their enemies,	3027
	20:13	the soul of the poor from the **h** of evildoers.	3027
	21: 5	fight against you with an outstretched **h**	3027
	21: 7	into the **h** of Nebuchadrezzar king of	3027
	21: 7	into the **h** of their enemies, and into	3027
	21: 7	and into the **h** of those that seek their life:	3027
	21:10	it shall be given into the **h** of the king of	3027
	21:12	deliver *him that is* spoiled out of the **h** of	3027
	22: 3	deliver the spoiled out of the **h** of	3027
	22:24	of Judah were the signet upon my right **h**,	3027
	22:25	I will give thee into the **h** of them that seek	3027
	22:25	into the **h** *of them* whose face thou fearest,	3027
	22:25	even into the **h** of Nebuchadrezzar king of	3027
	22:25	and into the **h** of the Chaldeans.	3027
	23:23	*Am* I a God at **h**, saith the LORD, and	7138
	25:15	Take the wine cup of this fury at mine **h**,	3027
	25:17	took I the cup at the LORD'S **h**, and	3027
	25:28	if they refuse to take the cup at thine **h** to	3027
	26:14	As for me, behold, I *am* in your **h**: do with	3027
	26:24	Nevertheless the **h** of Ahikam the son of	3027
	26:24	that *they* should not give him into the **h** of	3027
	27: 3	by the **h** of the messengers which come *to*	3027
	27: 6	now have I given all these lands into the **h**	3027
	27: 8	until I have consumed them by his **h**.	3027
	29: 3	By the **h** of Elasah the son of Shaphan, and	3027
	29:21	I will deliver them into the **h** of	3027
	31:11	ransomed him from the **h** of *him that was*	3027
	31:32	fathers in the day *that* I took them by the **h**,	3027
	32: 3	I *will* give this city into the **h** of the king of	3027
	32: 4	not escape out of the **h** of the Chaldeans,	3027
	32: 4	shall surely be delivered into the **h** of	3027
	32:21	with a strong **h**, and with a stretched out	3027
	32:24	the city is given into the **h** of	3027
	32:25	for the city is given into the **h** of	3027
	32:28	I *will* give this city into the **h** of	3027
	32:28	into the **h** of Nebuchadrezzar king of	3027
	32:36	It shall be delivered into the **h** of the king	3027
	32:43	it is given into the **h** of the Chaldeans.	3027
	34: 2	I *will* give this city into the **h** of the king of	3027
	34: 3	thou shalt not escape out of his **h**, but	3027
	34: 3	surely be taken, and delivered into his **h**;	3027
	34:20	I will even give them into the **h** of their	3027
	34:20	and into the **h** of them that seek their life:	3027
	34:21	his princes will I give into the **h** of their	3027
	34:21	into the **h** of them that seek their life, and	3027
	34:21	into the **h** of the king of Babylon's army,	3027
	36:14	Take in thine **h** the roll wherein thou hast	3027
	36:14	the son of Neriah took the roll in his **h**,	3027
	37:17	thou shalt be delivered into the **h** of	3027
	38: 3	This city shall surely be given into the **h** of	3027
	38: 5	the king said, Behold, he *is* in your **h**:	3027
	38:16	neither will I give thee into the **h** of these	3027
	38:18	shall this city be given into the **h** of	3027
	38:18	and thou shalt not escape out of their **h**.	3027
	38:19	lest they deliver me into their **h**, and	3027
	38:23	thou shalt not escape out of their **h**, but	3027
	38:23	shalt be taken by the **h** of the king of	3027
	39:17	thou shalt not be given into the **h** of	3027
	40: 4	from the chains which *were* upon thine **h**.	3027
	41: 5	with offerings and incense in their **h**,	3027
	42:11	to save you, and to deliver you from his **h**.	3027
	43: 3	for to deliver us into the **h** of	3027
	43: 9	Take great stones in thine **h**, and hide them	3027
	44:25	and fulfilled with your **h**, saying,	3027
	44:30	king of Egypt into the **h** of his enemies,	3027
	44:30	and into the **h** of them that seek his life;	3027
	44:30	as I gave Zedekiah king of Judah into the **h**	3027
	46:24	she shall be delivered into the **h** of	3027
	46:26	I will deliver them into the **h** of those that	3027
	46:26	into the **h** of Nebuchadrezzar king of	3027
	46:26	of Babylon, and into the **h** of his servants:	3027
	50:15	she hath given her **h**: her foundations are	3027
	51: 7	*hath been* a golden cup in the LORD'S **h**,	3027
	51:25	I will stretch out mine **h** upon thee, and	3027
La	1: 7	when her people fell into the **h** of	3027
	1:10	The adversary hath spread out his **h** upon	3027
	1:14	of my transgressions is bound by his **h**:	3027
	2: 3	he hath drawn back his **right h** from before	3225
	2: 4	*he* stood *with* his **right h** as an adversary,	3225
	2: 7	he hath given up into the **h** of the enemy	3027
	2: 8	he hath not withdrawn his **h** from	3027
	3: 3	he turneth his **h** *against me* all the day.	3027
	5: 6	We have given the **h** *to* the Egyptians, *and*	3027
	5: 8	*is* none that doth deliver *us* out of their **h**.	3027
	5:12	Princes are hanged up by their **h**: the faces	3027
Eze	1: 3	the **h** of the LORD was there upon him.	3027
	2: 9	I looked, behold, a **h** *was* sent unto me;	3027
	3:14	the **h** of the LORD was strong upon me.	3027
	3:18	but his blood will I require at thine **h**.	3027
	3:20	but his blood will I require at thine **h**.	3027
	3:22	the **h** of the LORD was there upon me;	3027
	6:11	Smite with thine **h**, and stamp with thy	3709
	6:14	So will I stretch out mine **h** upon them, and	3027
	8: 1	that the **h** of the Lord GOD fell there upon	3027
	8: 3	he put forth the form of a **h**, and took me	3027
	8:11	with every man his censer in his **h**;	3027
	9: 1	man *with* his destroying weapon in his **h**.	3027
	9: 2	and every man a slaughter weapon in his **h**;	3027
	10: 2	fill thine **h** *with* coals of fire from between	2651
	10: 7	*one* cherub stretched forth his **h** from	3027
	10: 8	the form of a man's **h** under their wings.	3027
	12: 7	I digged through the wall with mine **h**;	3027
	12:23	The days are **at h**, and the effect of every	7126
	13: 9	mine **h** shall be upon the prophets that see	3027
	13:21	deliver my people out of your **h**, and	3027
	13:21	they shall be no more in your **h** to be	3027
	13:23	for I will deliver my people out of your **h**:	3027
	14: 9	I will stretch out my **h** upon him, and	3027
	14:13	will I stretch out mine **h** upon it, and	3027
	16:27	I have stretched out my **h** over thee, and	3027
	16:39	I will also give thee into their **h**, and	3027
	16:46	and her daughters that dwell at thy **left h**:	8040
	16:46	that dwelleth at thy **right h**, *is* Sodom and	3225
	16:49	neither did she strengthen the **h** of the poor	3027
	17:18	he had given his **h**, and hath done all these	3027
	18: 8	*that* hath withdrawn his **h** from iniquity,	3027
	18:17	*That* hath taken off his **h** from the poor,	3027
	20: 5	lifted up mine **h** unto the seed of the house	3027
	20: 5	when I lifted up mine **h** unto them, saying,	3027
	20: 6	In the day *that* I lifted up mine **h** unto them,	3027
	20:15	Yet also I lifted up my **h** unto them in	3027
	20:22	Nevertheless I withdrew mine **h**, and	3027
	20:23	I lifted up mine **h** unto them also in	3027
	20:28	*for* the which I lifted up mine **h** to give it to	3027
	20:33	surely with a mighty **h**, and with a stretched	3027

Eze 20:34 with a mighty **h**, and with a stretched out 3027
20:42 I lifted up mine **h** to give it to your fathers. 3027
21:11 to give it into the **h** of the slayer. 3027
21:16 other, *either* **on the right h**, *or* on the left, 3231
21:22 At his **right h** was the divination for 3225
21:24 ye shall be taken with the **h**. 3709
21:31 deliver thee into the **h** of brutish men, *and* 3027
22:13 I have smitten mine **h** at thy dishonest gain 3709
23: 9 Wherefore I have delivered her into the **h** 3027
23: 9 into the **h** of the Assyrians, upon whom she 3027
23:28 I *will* deliver thee into the **h** *of them* whom 3027
23:28 into the **h** *of them* from whom thy mind is 3027
23:31 therefore will I give her cup into thine **h**. 3027
25: 7 I will stretch out mine **h** upon thee, and 3027
25:13 I will also stretch out mine **h** upon Edom, 3027
25:14 upon Edom by the **h** of my people Israel: 3027
25:16 I *will* stretch out mine **h** upon 3027
27:15 isles *were* the merchandise of thine **h**: 3027
28: 9 no God, in the **h** of him that slayeth thee. 3027
28:10 of the uncircumcised by the **h** of strangers: 3027
29: 7 When they took hold of thee by thy **h**, 3709
30:10 the **h** of Nebuchadrezzar king of Babylon. 3027
30:12 and sell the land into the **h** of the wicked: 3027
30:12 and all that is therein, by the **h** of strangers: 3027
30:22 I will cause the sword to fall out of his **h**. 3027
30:24 of Babylon, and put my sword in his **h**: 3027
30:25 when I shall put my sword into the **h** of 3027
31:11 delivered him into the **h** of the mighty one 3027
33: 6 blood will I require at the watchman's **h**. 3027
33: 8 but his blood will I require at thine **h**. 3027
33:22 Now the **h** of the LORD was upon me in 3027
34:10 I will require my flock at their **h**, and 3027
34:27 delivered them out of the **h** of those that 3027
35: 3 I will stretch out mine **h** against thee, and 3027
36: 7 I have lifted up mine **h**, Surely the heathen 3027
36: 8 people of Israel; for they are **at h** to come. 7126
37: 1 The **h** of the LORD was upon me, and 3027
37:17 and they shall become one in thine **h**. 3027
37:19 which *is* in the **h** of Ephraim, and the tribes 3027
37:19 one stick, and they shall be one in mine **h**. 3027
37:20 writest shall be in thine **h** before their eyes. 3027
38:12 to turn thine **h** upon the desolate places *that* 3027
39: 3 I will smite thy bow out of thy left **h**, and 3027
39: 3 cause thine arrows to fall out of thy right **h**. 3027
39:21 and my **h** that I have laid upon them. 3027
39:23 and gave them into the **h** of their enemies: 3027
40: 1 in the selfsame day the **h** of the LORD 3027
40: 3 with a line of flax in his **h**, and a measuring 3027
40: 5 in the man's **h** a measuring reed of six 3027
40: 5 cubits *long* by the cubit and a **h breadth**: 2948
40:43 a **h broad**, fastened round about: 2948
43:13 The cubit *is* a cubit and a **h breadth**; 2948
44:12 have I lift up mine **h** against them, 3027
46: 7 for the lambs according as his **h** shall attain 3027
47: 3 when the man that had the line in his **h** 3027
47:14 *concerning* the which I lifted up mine **h** to 3027
Da 1: 2 gave Jehoiakim king of Judah into his **h**, 3027
2:38 of the heaven hath he given into thine **h**, 3028
3:17 he will deliver *us* out of thine **h**, O king. 3028
4:35 none can stay his **h**, or say unto him, 3028
5: 5 same hour came forth fingers of a man's **h**, 3028
5: 5 the king saw the part of the **h** that wrote. 3028
5:23 the God in whose **h** thy breath *is,* and 3028
5:24 *was* the part of the **h** sent from him; and 3028
7:25 they shall be given into his **h** until a time 3028
8: 4 *there any* that could deliver out of his **h**; 3027
8: 7 none that could deliver the ram out of his **h**. 3027
8:25 also he shall cause craft to prosper in his **h**; 3027
8:25 but he shall be broken without **h**. 3027
9:15 out of the land of Egypt with a mighty **h**, 3027
10:10 behold, a **h** touched me, which set me upon 3027
11:11 but the multitude shall be given into his **h**. 3027
11:16 which by his **h** shall be consumed. 3027
11:41 these shall escape out of his **h**, *even* Edom, 3027
11:42 He shall stretch forth his **h** also upon 3027
12: 7 when he held up his **right h** and his left 3225
12: 7 his right hand and his **left h** unto heaven, 8040
Hos 2:10 and none shall deliver her out of mine **h**, 3027
7: 5 he stretched out his **h** with scorners. 3027
12: 7 the balances of deceit *are* in his **h**: 3027
Joel 1:15 for the day of the LORD *is* **at h**, and as a 7138
2: 1 of the LORD cometh, for *it is* **nigh at h**; 7138
3: 8 your daughters into the **h** of the children of 3027
Am 1: 8 and I will turn mine **h** against Ekron: 3027
5:19 leaned his **h** on the wall, and a serpent bit 3027
7: 7 by a plumbline, with a plumbline in his **h**. 3027
9: 2 dig into hell, thence shall mine **h** take them; 3027
Jnh 4:11 that cannot discern between their **right h** 3225
4:11 between their right hand and their **left h**; 8040
Mic 2: 1 because it is in the power of their **h**. 3027
4:10 redeem thee from the **h** of thine enemies. 3709
5: 9 Thine **h** shall be lift up upon thine 3027
5:12 I will cut off witchcrafts out of thine **h**; 3027
7:16 they shall lay *their* **h** upon *their* mouth, 3027
Hab 2:16 the cup of the LORD'S **right h** shall be 3225
3: 4 the light; he had horns *coming* out of his **h**: 3027
Zep 1: 4 I will also stretch out mine **h** upon Judah, 3027
1: 7 for the day of the LORD *is* **at h**: for 7138
2:13 he will stretch out his **h** against the north, 3027
2:15 passeth by her shall hiss, *and* wag his **h**. 3027
Zec 2: 1 a man with a measuring line in his **h**. 3027
2: 9 I *will* shake mine **h** upon them, and 3027
3: 1 Satan standing at his **right h** to resist him. 3225
4:10 shall see the plummet in the **h** of 3027
8: 4 every man with his staff in his **h** for very 3027
11: 6 the men every one into his neighbour's **h**, 3027
11: 6 and into the **h** of his king: 3027
11: 6 and out of their **h** I will not deliver *them.* 3027
12: 6 round about, on the **right h** and on the left: 3225
13: 7 and I will turn mine **h** upon the little ones. 3027
14:13 they shall lay hold every one on the **h** of his 3027
14:13 his **h** shall rise up against the hand of his 3027
14:13 his hand shall rise up against the **h** of his 3027
Mal 1:10 neither will I accept an offering at your **h**. 3027
1:13 should I accept this of your **h**? saith 3027
2:13 or receiveth *it with* good will at your **h**. 3027
Mt 3: 2 for the kingdom of heaven is **at h**. *1448*
3:12 Whose fan *is* in his **h**, and he will throughly *5495*
4:17 Repent: for the kingdom of heaven is **at h**. *1448*
5:30 And if thy right **h** offend thee, cut it off, *5495*
6: 3 let not thy **left h** know what thy right hand *710*
6: 3 let not thy left hand know what thy **right h** *1188*
8: 3 And Jesus put forth *his* **h**, and touched him, *5495*
8:15 And he touched her **h**, and the fever left *5495*
9:18 but come and lay thy **h** upon her, and *5495*
9:25 and took her by the **h**, and the maid arose. *5495*
10: 7 saying, The kingdom of heaven is **at h**. *1448*
12:10 there was a man which had *his* **h** withered. *5495*
12:13 saith he to the man, Stretch forth thine **h**. *5495*
12:49 And he stretched forth his **h** toward his *5495*
14:31 immediately Jesus stretched forth *his* **h**, *5495*
18: 8 Wherefore if thy **h** or thy foot offend thee, *5495*
20:21 the one on thy **right h**, and the other on *1188*
20:23 am baptized *with:* but to sit on my **right h**, *1188*
22:13 Bind him **h** and foot, and take him away, *5495*
22:44 said unto my Lord, Sit thou on my **right h**, *1188*
25:33 And he shall set the sheep on his **right h**, *1188*
25:34 shall the King say unto them on his **right h**, *1188*
25:41 shall he say also unto them on the **left h**, *2176*
26:18 The Master saith, My time is **at h**; *1451*
26:23 He that dippeth *his* **h** with me in the dish, *5495*
26:45 the hour is **at h**, and the Son of man is *1448*
26:46 behold, he is **at h** that doth betray me. *1448*
26:51 which were with Jesus stretched out *his* **h**, *5495*
26:64 Son of man sitting on the **right h** of power, *1188*
27:29 *it* upon his head, and a reed in his **right h**: *1188*
27:38 one on the **right h**, and another on the left. *1188*
Mk 1:15 and the kingdom of God is **at h**: *1448*
1:31 And he came and took her by the **h**, and *5495*
1:41 put forth *his* **h**, and touched him, and *5495*
3: 1 was a man there which had a withered **h**. *5495*
3: 3 unto the man which had the withered **h**, *5495*
3: 5 he saith unto the man, Stretch forth thine **h**. *5495*
3: 5 and his **h** was restored whole as the other. *5495*
5:41 And he took the damsel by the **h**, and *5495*
7:32 they beseech him to put *his* **h** upon him. *5495*
8:23 And he took the blind man by the **h**, and *5495*
9:27 But Jesus took him by the **h**, and lifted him *5495*
9:43 And if thy **h** offend thee, cut it off: it is *5495*
10:37 one on thy **right h**, and the other on thy left *1188*
10:37 and the other on thy **left h**, in thy glory. *2176*
10:40 But to sit on my **right h** and on my left *1188*
10:40 and on my **left h** is not mine to give; *2176*
12:36 said to my Lord, Sit thou on my **right h**, *1188*
14:42 let us go; lo, he that betrayeth me is **at h**. *1448*
14:62 Son of man sitting on the **right h** of power, *1188*
15:27 the one on *his* **right h**, and the other on his *1188*
16:19 into heaven, and sat on the **right h** of God. *1188*

H

Lk 1: 1 Forasmuch as many have **taken in h** to set *2021*
1:66 And the **h** of the Lord was with him. *5495*
1:71 and from the **h** of all that hate us; *5495*
1:74 that *we* being delivered out of the **h** of our *5495*
3:17 Whose fan *is* in his **h**, and he will throughly *5495*
5:13 And he put forth *his* **h**, and touched him, *5495*
6: 6 there was a man whose right **h** was *5495*
6: 8 said to the man which had the withered **h**, *5495*
6:10 he said unto the man, Stretch forth thy **h**. *5495*
6:10 and his **h** was restored whole as the other. *5495*
8:54 and took her by the **h**, and called, saying, *5495*
9:62 No *man* having put his **h** to the plough, and *5495*
15:22 and put *it* on him; and put a ring on his **h**, *5495*
20:42 said to my Lord, Sit thou on my **right h**, *1188*
21:30 own selves that summer is now **nigh at h**. *1451*
21:31 ye that the kingdom of God is **nigh at h**. *1451*
22:21 the **h** of him that betrayeth me *is* with me *5495*
22:69 man sit on the **right h** of the power of God. *1188*
23:33 one on the **right h**, and the other on *1188*
Jn 2:13 And the Jews' passover was **at h**, and *1451*
3:35 and hath given all *things* into his **h**. *5495*
7: 2 the Jews' feast of tabernacles was **at h**. *1451*
10:28 shall any *man* pluck them out of my **h**. *5495*
10:29 is able to pluck *them* out of my Father's **h**. *5495*
10:39 to take him: but he escaped out of their **h**, *5495*
11:44 bound **h** and foot with graveclothes: *5495*
11:55 And the Jews' passover was **nigh at h**: and *1451*
18:22 **stroke** Jesus **with the palm of** his **h**, *1325+4475*
19:42 *day;* for the sepulchre was **nigh at h**. *1451*
20:25 and thrust my **h** into his side, I will not *5495*
20:27 and reach *hither* thy **h**, and thrust *it* into my *5495*
Ac 2:25 for he is on my **right h**, that I should not be *1188*
2:33 Therefore being by the **right h** of God *1188*
2:34 said unto my Lord, Sit thou on my **right h**, *1188*
3: 7 And he took him by the right **h**, and lift *him* *5495*
4:28 For to do whatsoever thy **h** and thy counsel *5495*
4:30 By stretching forth thine **h** to heal; and *5495*
5:31 Him hath God exalted with his **right h** *to* *1188*
7:25 how that God by his **h** would deliver them: *5495*
7:35 a deliverer by the **h** of the angel which *5495*
7:50 Hath not my **h** made all these *things?* *5495*
7:55 and Jesus standing on the **right h** of God, *1188*
7:56 the Son of man standing on the **right h** of *1188*
9: 8 he saw no *man:* but they **led** him **by the h**, *5496*
9:12 and putting *his* **h** on him, that he might *5495*
9:41 And he gave her *his* **h**, and lift her up, and *5495*
11:21 And the **h** of the Lord was with them: and *5495*
12:11 hath delivered me out of the **h** of Herod, *5495*
12:17 beckoning unto them with the **h** to hold *5495*
13:11 the **h** of the Lord *is* upon thee, and *5495*
13:11 about seeking *some* to **lead** him **by the h**. *5497*
13:16 and beckoning with *his* **h** said, Men of *5495*
19:33 And Alexander beckoned with the **h**, and *5495*
21: 3 we left it on the **left h**, and sailed into *2176*
21:40 and beckoned with the **h** unto the people. *5495*
22:11 being **led by the h** of them that were with *5496*
23:19 Then the chief captain took him by the **h**, *5495*
26: 1 Then Paul stretched forth the **h**, and *5495*
28: 3 viper out of the heat, and fastened on his **h**. *5495*
28: 4 saw the *venomous* beast hang on his **h**, *5495*
Ro 8:34 *again,* who is even at the **right h** of God, *1188*
13:12 The night is far spent, the day is **at h**: let us *1448*
1Co 12:15 the foot shall say, Because I am not the **h**, *5495*
12:21 And the eye cannot say unto the **h**, I have *5495*
16:21 The salutation of *me* Paul with mine own **h**. *5495*
2Co 5: 1 a house **not made with h**, eternal in *886*
6: 7 the armour of righteousness on the **right h** *1188*
10:16 line of *things* **made ready to** our **h**. *1519+2092*
Gal 3:19 *it was* ordained by angels in the **h** of a *5495*
6:11 I have written unto you with mine own **h**. *5495*
Eph 1:20 set *him* at his own **right h** in the heavenly *1188*
Php 4: 5 be known unto all men. The Lord *is* **at h**. *1451*
Col 3: 1 where Christ sitteth on the **right h** of God. *1188*
4:18 The salutation by the **h** of me Paul. *5495*
2Th 2: 2 as from us, as that the day of Christ is **at h**. *1764*
3:17 The salutation of Paul with mine own **h**, *5495*
2Ti 4: 6 and the time of my departure is **at h**. *2186*
Phm 1:19 I Paul have written *it* with mine own **h**, *5495*
Heb 1: 3 sat down on the **right h** of the Majesty on *1188*
1:13 Sit on my **right h**, until I make thine *1188*
8: 1 who is set on the **right h** of the throne of *1188*
8: 9 the **h** to lead them out of the land of Egypt; *5495*
10:12 for ever, sat down on the **right h** of God; *1188*
12: 2 is set down at the **right h** of the throne of *1188*
1Pe 3:22 into heaven, and is on the **right h** of God; *1188*
4: 7 But the end of all *things* is **at h**: be ye *1448*
5: 6 therefore under the mighty **h** of God, *5495*
Rev 1: 3 are written therein: for the time *is* **at h**. *1451*
1:16 And he had in his right **h** seven stars: and *5495*
1:17 And he laid his right **h** upon me, *5495*
1:20 stars which thou sawest in my **right h**, *1188*
2: 1 that holdeth the seven stars in his **right h**, *1188*
5: 1 And I saw in the **right h** of him that sat on *1188*
5: 7 took the book out of the **right h** of him that *1188*
6: 5 sat on him had a pair of balances in his **h**. *5495*
8: 4 up before God out of the angel's **h**. *5495*
10: 2 And he had in his **h** a little book open: and *5495*
10: 5 upon the earth lifted up his **h** to heaven, *5495*
10: 8 take the little book which is open in the **h** *5495*
10:10 I took the little book out of the angel's **h**, *5495*
13:16 to receive a mark in their right **h**, or in their *5495*
14: 9 *his* mark in his forehead, or in his **h**, *5495*
14:14 a golden crown, and in his **h** a sharp sickle. *5495*
17: 4 having a golden cup in her **h** full of *5495*
19: 2 avenged the blood of his servants at her **h**. *5495*
20: 1 bottomless *pit* and a great chain in his **h**. *5495*
22:10 prophecy of this book: for the time is **at h**. *1451*

HANDBREADTH (5) [BREADTH, HAND]
Ex 25:25 thou shalt make unto it a border of a **h** 2948
37:12 Also he made thereunto a border of a **h** 2948
1Ki 7:26 it *was* a **h** thick, and the brim thereof was 2947
2Ch 4: 5 the thickness of it *was* a **h**, and the brim of 2947
Ps 39: 5 Behold, thou hast made my days *as* a **h**; 2947

HANDED (1) [HAND]
2Sa 17: 2 upon him while he *is* weary and weak **h**, 3027

HANDFUL (9) [HAND]
Lev 2: 2 he shall **take** thereout his **h** of 4393+7061+7062
5:12 the priest shall **take** his **h** of it, 4393+7061+7062
6:15 he shall take of it his **h**, of the flour of 7062
9:17 **took a h** thereof, and burnt *it* upon 3709+4390
Nu 5:26 the priest shall **take a h** of the offering, 7061
1Ki 17:12 a **h** of meal in a barrel, and a little oil 3709+4393
Ps 72:16 There shall be a **h** of corn in the earth upon 6451
Ecc 4: 6 Better *is* a **h** *with* quietness, 3709+4393
Jer 9:22 as the **h** after the harvestman, and 5995

HANDFULS (5) [HAND]
Ge 41:47 years the earth brought forth by **h**. 7062
Ex 9: 8 Take to you **h** of ashes of 2651+4393
Ru 2:16 let fall also *some* of the **h** of purpose for 6653
1Ki 20:10 if the dust of Samaria shall suffice for **h** for 8168
Eze 13:19 will ye pollute me among my people for **h** 8168

HANDKERCHIEFS (1) [KERCHIEFS]
Ac 19:12 from his body were brought unto the sick **h** *4676*

HANDLE (11) [HANDLED, HANDLES, HANDLETH, HANDLING]
Ge 4:21 he was the father of all such as **h** the harp 8610
Jdg 5:14 out of Zebulun they that **h** the pen of 4900
1Ch 12: 8 the battle, that could **h** shield and buckler, 6186
2Ch 25: 5 forth *to* war, that could **h** spear and shield. 270
Ps 115: 7 They *have* hands, but they **h** not: feet *have* 4184
Jer 2: 8 they that **h** the law knew me not: 8610
46: 9 and the Libyans, that **h** the shield; 8610
46: 9 and the Lydians, that **h** *and* bend the bow. 8610
Eze 27:29 all that **h** the oar, the mariners, *and* all 8610
Lk 24:39 **h** me, and see; for a spirit hath not flesh and *5584*
Col 2:21 (Touch not; taste not; **h** not; *2345*

HANDLED (3) [HANDLE]
Eze 21:11 that *it* may be **h**: 3709+8610+871.1+1886.1
Mk 12: 4 the head, and sent *him* away **shamefully h**. *821*
1Jn 1: 1 and our hands have **h**, of the Word of life; *5584*

HANDLES (1) [HANDLE]
SS 5: 5 smelling myrrh, upon the **h** of the lock. 3709

HANDLETH (3) [HANDLE]
Pr 16:20 He that **h** a matter **wisely** shall find good: 7919
Jer 50:16 him that **h** the sickle in the time of harvest; 8610
Am 2:15 Neither shall he stand that **h** the bow; and 8610

HANDLING (2) [HANDLE]
Eze 38: 4 and shields, all of them **h** swords: 8610
2Co 4: 2 nor **h** the word of God **deceitfully**; *1389*

HANDMAID (45) [MAID]

Ge 16: 1 wife bare him no *children:* and she had a **h**, 8198
25:12 Sarah's **h**, bare unto Abraham: 8198
29:24 his daughter Leah Zilpah his maid *for* a **h**. 8198
29:29 his daughter Bilhah his **h** to be her maid. 8198
30: 4 And she gave him Bilhah her **h** to wife: and 8198
35:25 the sons of Bilhah, Rachel's **h**; Dan, and 8198
35:26 the sons of Zilpah, Leah's **h**; Gad, and 8198
Ex 23:12 the son of thy **h**, and the stranger, may be 519
Jdg 19:19 for thy **h**, and for the young man *which is* 519
Ru 2:13 that thou hast spoken friendly unto thine **h**, 8198
3: 9 And she answered, I *am* Ruth thine **h**: spread 519
3: 9 spread therefore thy skirt over thine **h**; 519
1Sa 1:11 wilt indeed look on the affliction of thine **h**, 519
1:11 not forget thine **h**, but wilt give unto thine 519
1:11 wilt give unto thine **h** a man child, then 519
1:16 Count not thine **h** for a daughter of Belial: 519
1:18 she said, Let thine **h** find grace in thy sight. 8198
25:24 *upon* me *let this* iniquity *be:* and let thine **h**, 519
25:24 and hear the words of thine **h**. 519
25:25 I thine **h** saw not the young men of my lord, 519
25:27 now this blessing which thine **h** hath 8198
25:28 I pray thee, forgive the trespass of thine **h**: 519
25:31 well with my lord, then remember thine **h**. 519
25:41 *let* thine **h** *be* a servant to wash the feet of 519
28:21 thine **h** hath obeyed thy voice, and I have 8198
28:22 hearken thou also unto the voice of thine **h**, 8198
2Sa 14: 6 thy **h** had two sons, and they two strove 8198
14: 7 the whole family is risen against thine **h**, 8198
14:12 the woman said, Let thine **h**, I pray thee, 8198
14:15 thy **h** said, I will now speak unto the king; 8198
14:15 the king will perform the request of his **h**. 519
14:16 to deliver his **h** out of the hand of the man 519
14:17 thine **h** said, The word of my lord the king 8198
14:19 put all these words in the mouth of thine **h**: 8198
20:17 she said unto him, Hear the words of thine **h**. 519
1Ki 1:13 my lord O king, swear unto thine **h**, saying, 519
1:17 swarest by the LORD thy God unto thine **h**, 519
3:20 while thine **h** slept, and laid it in her bosom, 519
2Ki 4: 2 Thine **h** hath not any thing in the house, 8198
4:16 thou man of God, do not lie unto thine **h**. 8198
Ps 86:16 unto thy servant, and save the son of thine **h**. 519
116:16 I *am* thy servant, *and* the son of thy **h**: 519
Pr 30:23 and a **h** that is heir to her mistress. 8198
Jer 34:16 man his servant, and every man his **h**, 8198
Lk 1:38 And Mary said, Behold the **h** of the Lord; *1399*

HANDMAIDEN (1) [MAID]

Lk 1:48 he hath regarded the low estate of his **h**: *1399*

HANDMAIDENS (3) [MAID]

Ge 33: 6 the **h** came near, they and their children, 8198
Ru 2:13 though I be not like unto one of thy **h**. 8198
Ac 2:18 on my **h** I will pour out in those days of my *1399*

HANDMAIDS (8) [MAID]

Ge 33: 1 and unto Rachel, and unto the two **h**. 8198
33: 2 he put the **h** and their children foremost, 8198
2Sa 6:20 to day in the eyes of the **h** of his servants, 519
Isa 14: 2 the land of the LORD for servants and **h**: 8198
Jer 34:11 caused the servants and the **h**, whom they 8198
34:11 them into subjection for servants and for **h**. 8198
34:16 to be unto you for servants and for **h**. 8198
Joel 2:29 upon the **h** in those days will I pour out my 8198

HANDS (459) [HAND]

Ge 5:29 us concerning our work and toil of our **h**, 3027
16: 9 and submit thyself under her **h**. 3027
20: 5 and innocency of my **h** have I done this. 3709
24:22 two bracelets for her **h** of ten *shekels* 3027
24:30 and bracelets upon his sister's **h**, 3027
24:47 upon her face, and the bracelets upon her **h**. 3027
27:16 skins of the kids of the goats upon his **h**, 3027
27:22 but the **h** *are* the hands of Esau. 3027
27:22 but the hands *are* the **h** of Esau. 3027
27:23 him not, because his **h** were hairy, 3027
27:23 hands were hairy, as his brother Esau's **h**: 3027
31:42 seen mine affliction and the labour of my **h**, 3709
37:21 and he delivered him out of their **h**; 3027
37:22 that he might rid him out of their **h**, 3027
43:22 we brought down in our **h** to buy food: 3027
48:14 Manasseh's head, guiding his **h** wittingly; 3027
49:24 the arms of his **h** were made strong by 3027
49:24 strong by the **h** of the mighty *God* of Jacob; 3027
Ex 9:29 I will spread abroad my **h** unto the LORD; 3709
9:33 spread abroad his **h** unto the LORD: 3709
15:17 O Lord, *which* thy **h** have established. 3027
17:12 Moses' **h** *were* heavy; and they took a 3027
17:12 Aaron and Hur stayed up his **h**, the one on 3027
17:12 his **h** were steady until the going down of 3027
29:10 his sons shall put their **h** upon the head of 3027
29:15 his sons shall put their **h** upon the head of 3027
29:19 his sons shall put their **h** upon the head of 3027
29:24 thou shalt put all in the **h** of Aaron, and 3709
29:24 hands of Aaron, and in the **h** of his sons; 3709
29:25 thou shalt receive them of their **h**, and 3027
30:19 and his sons shall wash their **h** and 3027
30:21 So they shall wash their **h** and their feet, 3027
32:19 he cast the tables out of his **h**, and 3027
35:25 that were wise hearted did spin with their **h**, 3027
40:31 and Aaron and his sons washed their **h** and 3027
Lev 4:15 **h** upon the head of the bullock before 3027
7:30 His own **h** shall bring the offerings of 3027
8:14 his sons laid their **h** upon the head of 3027
8:18 his sons laid their **h** upon the head of 3027
8:22 his sons laid their **h** upon the head of 3027
8:24 upon the thumbs of their right **h**, and 3027
8:27 he put all upon Aaron's **h**, and upon his 3709
8:27 upon his sons' **h**, and waved them *for* a 3709
8:28 Moses took them from off their **h**, and 3709
15:11 hath not rinsed his **h** in water, he shall wash 3027
16:12 his **h** full of sweet incense beaten small, 2651
16:21 Aaron shall lay both his **h** upon the head of 3027
24:14 let all that heard *him* lay their **h** upon his 3027
Nu 5:18 and put the offering of memorial in her **h**, 3709
6:19 shall put *them* upon the **h** of the Nazarite, 3709
8:10 the children of Israel shall put their **h** upon 3027
8:12 the Levites shall lay their **h** upon the heads 3027
24:10 and he smote his **h** together: 3709
27:23 he laid his **h** upon him, and gave him a 3027
Dt 1:25 they took of the fruit of the land in their **h**, 3027
3: 3 our God delivered into our **h** Og also, 3027
4:28 the work of men's **h**, wood and stone, 3027
9:15 tables of the covenant *were* in my two **h**. 3027
9:17 cast them out of my two **h**, and brake them 3027
12:18 thy God in all that thou puttest thine **h** unto. 3027
16:15 in all the works of thine **h**, therefore 3027
17: 7 The **h** of the witnesses shall be first upon 3027
17: 7 and afterward the **h** of all the people. 3027
20:13 thy God hath delivered it into thine **h**, 3027
21: 6 **h** over the heifer that is beheaded in 3027
21: 7 and say, Our **h** have not shed this blood, 3027
21:10 thy God hath delivered them into thine **h**, 3027
24:19 may bless thee in all the work of thine **h**. 3027
27:15 the work of the **h** of the craftsman, and 3027
31:29 him to anger through the work of your **h**. 3027
33: 7 let his **h** *be* sufficient for him; and be thou a 3027
33:11 his substance, and accept the work of his **h**: 3027
34: 9 for Moses had laid his **h** upon him: 3027
Jos 2:24 Truly the LORD hath delivered into our **h** 3027
Jdg 2:14 he delivered them into the **h** of spoilers that 3027
2:14 he sold them into the **h** of their enemies 3027
6:13 delivered us into the **h** of the Midianites. 3709
7: 2 for me to give the Midianites into their **h**, 3027
7:11 afterward shall thine **h** be strengthened to 3027
7:19 and brake the pitchers that *were* in their **h**. 3027
7:20 held the lamps in their left **h**, and 3027
7:20 the trumpets in their right **h** to blow *withal:* 3027
8: 3 God hath delivered into your **h** the princes 3027
8: 6 *Are* the **h** of Zebah and Zalmunna now in 3709
8:15 *Are* the **h** of Zebah and Zalmunna now in 3709
8:34 who had delivered them out of the **h** of all 3027
9:16 him according to the deserving of his **h**; 3027
10: 7 he sold them into the **h** of the Philistines, 3027
10: 7 and into the **h** of the children of Ammon. 3027
11:30 deliver the children of Ammon into mine **h**, 3027
11:32 and the LORD delivered them into his **h**. 3027
12: 2 ye delivered me not out of their **h**. 3027
12: 3 I put my life in my **h**, and passed over 3709
13:23 burnt offering and a meat offering at our **h**, 3027
14: 9 he took thereof in his **h**, and went on 3709
15:14 and his bands loosed from off his **h**. 3027
16:24 Our god hath delivered into our **h** our 3027
18:10 for God hath given it into your **h**; a place 3027
19:27 and her **h** *were* upon the threshold. 3027
1Sa 5: 4 both the palms of his **h** *were* cut off upon 3027
7:14 Israel deliver out of the **h** of the Philistines. 3027
10: 4 which thou shalt receive of their **h**. 3027

1Sa 11: 7 the coasts of Israel by the **h** of messengers, 3027
14:13 Jonathan climbed up upon his **h** and 3027
14:48 delivered Israel out of the **h** of them that 3027
17:47 and he will give you into our **h**. 3027
21:13 feigned himself mad in their **h**, and 3027
30:15 nor deliver me into the **h** of my master, and 3027
2Sa 2: 7 Therefore now let your **h** be strengthened, 3027
3:34 Thy **h** *were* not bound, nor thy feet put into 3027
4: 1 his **h** were feeble, and all the Israelites were 3027
4:12 cut off their **h** and their feet, and 3027
16:21 shall the **h** of all that *are* with thee be 3027
21: 9 he delivered them into the **h** of 3027
22:21 according to the cleanness of my **h** hath he 3027
22:35 He teacheth my **h** to war; so that a bow of 3027
23: 6 because they cannot be taken with **h**: 3027
1Ki 8:22 and spread forth his **h** *toward* heaven: 3709
8:38 and spread forth his **h** towards this house: 3709
8:54 from kneeling on his knees with his **h** 3709
14:27 committed *them* unto the **h** of the chief of 3027
16: 7 him to anger with the work of his **h**, 3027
2Ki 3:11 which poured water on the **h** of Elijah. 3027
4:34 upon his eyes, and his **h** upon his hands: 3709
4:34 upon his eyes, and his hands upon his **h**: 3709
5:20 in not receiving at his **h** *that* which he 3027
9:23 Joram turned his **h**, and fled, and said to 3027
9:35 and the feet, and the palms of *her* **h**. 3027
10:24 whom I *have* brought into your **h** escape, 3027
11:12 they clapt their **h**, and said, God save 3709
11:16 they laid **h** on her; and she went *by* the way 3027
12:11 into the **h** of *them* that did the work, 3027
13:16 and Elisha put his **h** upon the king's hands. 3027
13:16 and Elisha put his hands upon the king's **h**. 3027
19:18 but the work of men's **h**, wood and stone: 3027
22:17 me to anger with all the works of their **h**; 3027
1Ch 12:17 seeing *there is* no wrong in mine **h**, the God 3709
25: 2 the sons of Asaph under the **h** of Asaph, 3027
25: 3 six, under the **h** of their father Jeduthun, 3027
25: 6 All these *were* under the **h** of their father 3027
29: 5 for all *manner of* work *to be made* by the **h** 3027
2Ch 6: 4 who hath with his **h** fulfilled *that* which he 3027
6:12 of Israel, and spread forth his **h**: 3709
6:13 and spread forth his **h** towards heaven, 3709
6:29 and shall spread forth his **h** in this house: 3709
8:18 Huram sent him by the **h** of his servants 3027
12:10 committed *them* to the **h** of the chief of 3027
15: 7 and let not your **h** be weak: 3027
23:15 So they laid **h** on her; and when she was 3027
29:23 and laid their **h** upon them: 3027
32:19 *which were* the work of the **h** of man. 3027
34:25 me to anger with all the works of their **h**; 3027
35:11 the priests sprinkled *the blood* from their **h**, 3027
Ezr 1: 6 strengthened their **h** with vessels of silver, 3027
4: 4 the people of the land weakened the **h** of 3027
5: 8 goeth fast on, and prospereth in their **h**. 3028
6:22 to strengthen their **h** in the work of 3027
9: 5 spread out my **h** unto the LORD my God, 3709
10:19 they gave their **h** that *they* would put away 3027
Ne 2:18 So they strengthened their **h** for *this* good 3027
4:17 *every one* with one of his **h** wrought in 3027
6: 9 Their **h** shall be weakened from the work, 3027
6: 9 Now therefore, *O God,* strengthen my **h**. 3027
8: 6 Amen, Amen, with lifting up their **h**: 3027
9:24 and gavest them into their **h**, 3027
13:21 if ye do *so* again, I will lay **h** on you. 3027
Est 3: 6 he thought scorn to lay **h** on Mordecai 3027
3: 9 **h** of those that have the charge of 3027
9:16 but they laid not their **h** on the prey, 3027
Job 1:10 thou hast blessed the work of his **h**, and 3027
4: 3 and thou hast strengthened the weak **h**. 3027
5:12 that their **h** cannot perform *their* enterprise. 3027
5:18 he woundeth, and his **h** make whole. 3027
9:30 snow water, and make my **h** never so clean; 3709
10: 3 thou shouldest despise the work of thine **h**, 3709
10: 8 Thine **h** have made me and fashioned me 3027
11:13 and stretch out thine **h** toward him; 3709
14:15 wilt have a desire to the work of thine **h**. 3027
16:11 turned me over into the **h** of the wicked. 3027
16:17 Not for *any* injustice in mine **h**: also my 3709
17: 3 who *is* he *that* will strike **h** with me? 3027
17: 9 he that hath clean **h** shall be stronger and 3027
20:10 the poor, and his **h** shall restore their goods. 3027
22:30 it is delivered by the pureness of thine **h**. 3709
27:23 *Men* shall clap their **h** at him, and shall hiss 3709
30: 2 whereto *might* the strength of their **h** profit 3027
31: 7 and *if any* blot hath cleaved to my **h**; 3709
34:19 the poor? for they all *are* the work of his **h**. 3027
34:37 he clappeth *his* **h** amongst us, and NIH
Ps 7: 3 have done this; if there be iniquity in my **h**; 3709
8: 6 to have dominion over the works of thy **h**; 3027
9:16 wicked is snared in the work of his own **h**. 3709
18:20 according to the cleanness of my **h** hath he 3027
18:24 according to the cleanness of my **h** in his 3027
18:34 He teacheth my **h** to war, so that a bow of 3027
22:16 they pierced my **h** and my feet. 3027
24: 4 He that hath clean **h**, and a pure heart; 3709
26: 6 I will wash mine **h** in innocency: so will I 3709
26:10 In whose **h** *is* mischief, and their right hand 3027
28: 2 when I lift up my **h** toward thy holy oracle. 3027
28: 4 give them after the work of their **h**; 3027
28: 5 nor the operation of his **h**, he shall destroy 3027
44:20 or stretched out our **h** to a strange god; 3709
47: 1 O clap *your* **h**, all ye people; shout unto 3709
55:20 He hath put forth his **h** against such as be at 3027
58: 2 you weigh the violence of your **h** in 3027
63: 4 while I live: I will lift up my **h** in thy name. 3709
68:31 Ethiopia shall soon stretch out her **h** unto 3027
73:13 *in* vain, and washed my **h** in innocency. 3709
76: 5 of the men of might have found their **h**. 3027
78:72 and guided them by the skilfulness of his **h**. 3709
81: 6 his **h** were delivered from the pots. 3709
88: 9 I have stretched out my **h** unto thee. 3709
90:17 establish thou the work of our **h** upon us; 3027
90:17 yea, the work of our **h** establish thou it. 3027
91:12 They shall bear thee up in *their* **h**, lest thou 3709
92: 4 I will triumph in the works of thy **h**. 3027
95: 5 he made it: and his **h** formed the dry *land*. 3027
98: 8 Let the floods clap *their* **h**: let the hills be 3709
102:25 and the heavens *are* the work of thy **h**. 3027
111: 7 The works of his **h** *are* verity and 3027
115: 4 *are* silver and gold, the work of men's **h**. 3027
115: 7 They *have* **h**, but they handle not: feet *have* 3027
119:48 My **h** also will I lift up unto thy 3709
119:73 Thy **h** have made me and fashioned me: 3027
125: 3 lest the righteous put forth their **h** unto 3027
128: 2 For thou shalt eat the labour of thine **h**: 3709
134: 2 Lift up your **h** *in* the sanctuary, and 3027
135:15 *are* silver and gold, the work of men's **h**. 3027
138: 8 forsake not the works of thine own **h**. 3027
140: 4 O LORD, from the **h** of the wicked; 3027
141: 2 the lifting up of my **h** *as* the evening 3709
143: 5 all thy works; I muse on the work of thy **h**. 3027
143: 6 I stretch forth my **h** unto thee: my soul 3027
144: 1 which teacheth my **h** to war, *and* 3027
Pr 6:10 a little folding of the **h** to sleep: 3027
6:17 and **h** that shed innocent blood, 3027
12:14 the recompence of a man's **h** shall be 3027
14: 1 but the foolish plucketh it down with her **h**. 3027
17:18 A man void of understanding striketh **h**, 3709
21:25 killeth him; for his **h** refuse to labour. 3027
22:26 Be not thou *one* of them that strike **h**, *or* 3709
24:33 a little folding of the **h** to sleep: 3027
30:28 The spider taketh hold with her **h**, and *is* in 3027
31:13 and flax, and worketh willingly with her **h**. 3709
31:16 with the fruit of her **h** she planteth a 3709
31:19 She layeth her **h** to the spindle, and 3027
31:19 to the spindle, and her **h** hold the distaff. 3709
31:20 yea, she reacheth forth her **h** to the needy. 3027
31:31 Give her of the fruit of her **h**; and let her 3027
Ecc 2:11 I looked on all the works that my **h** had 3027
4: 5 The fool foldeth his **h** together, and 3027
4: 6 than **both** the **h** full *with* travail and 2651
5: 6 thy voice, and destroy the work of thine **h**? 3027
7:26 heart *is* snares and nets, *and* her **h** *as* bands: 3027
10:18 through idleness of the **h** the house 3027
SS 5: 5 my **h** dropped *with* myrrh, and my fingers 3027
5:14 His **h** *are as* gold rings set with the beryl: 3027
7: 1 the work of the **h** of a cunning workman. 3027
Isa 1:15 when ye spread forth your **h**, I will hide 3709
1:15 I will not hear: your **h** are full *of* blood. 3027
2: 8 they worship the work of their own **h**, 3027
3:11 for the reward of his **h** shall be given him. 3027
5:12 neither consider the operation of his **h**. 3027
13: 7 Therefore shall all **h** be faint, and 3027
17: 8 not look to the altars, the work of his **h**, 3027
19:25 Assyria the work of my **h**, and Israel mine 3027
25:11 he shall spread forth his **h** in the midst of 3027
25:11 as he that swimmeth spreadeth forth *his* **h** to NIH
25:11 pride together with the spoils of their **h**. 3027

Isa 29:23 the work of mine **h**, in the midst of him, 3027
31: 7 which your own **h** have made unto you *for* 3027
33:15 that shaketh his **h** from holding of bribes, 3709
35: 3 Strengthen ye the weak **h**, and confirm 3027
37:19 but the work of men's **h**, wood and stone: 3027
45: 9 makest thou? or thy work, He hath no **h**? 3027
45:11 concerning the work of my **h** command ye 3027
45:12 I, *even* my **h**, have stretched out 3027
49:16 I have graven thee upon the **palms of** *my* **h**; 3709
55:12 all the trees of the field shall clap *their* **h**. 3709
59: 3 For your **h** are defiled with blood, and 3709
59: 6 and the act of violence *is* in their **h**. 3709
60:21 the work of my **h**, that *I* may be glorified. 3027
65: 2 I have spread out mine **h** all the day unto a 3027
65:22 elect shall long enjoy the work of their **h**. 3027
Jer 1:16 and worshipped the works of their own **h**. 3027
2:37 from him, and thine **h** upon thine head: 3027
4:31 *that* bewaileth herself, *that* spreadeth her **h**, 3709
6:24 our **h** wax feeble: anguish hath taken hold 3027
10: 3 the work of the **h** of the workman, with 3027
10: 9 the workman, and of the **h** of the founder: 3027
19: 7 and by the **h** of them that seek their lives: 3027
21: 4 back the weapons of war that *are* in your **h**, 3027
23:14 they strengthen also the **h** of evildoers, 3027
25: 6 me not to anger with the works of your **h**; 3027
25: 7 with the works of your **h** to your own hurt. 3027
25:14 and according to the works of their own **h**. 3027
30: 6 wherefore do I see every man *with* his **h** on 3027
32:30 me to anger with the work of their **h**, 3027
33:13 shall the flocks pass again under the **h** of 3027
38: 4 for thus he weakeneth the **h** of the men of 3027
38: 4 the **h** of all the people, in speaking such 3027
44: 8 me unto wrath with the works of your **h**, 3027
47: 3 back to *their* children for feebleness of **h**; 3027
48:37 upon all the **h** *shall be* cuttings, and 3027
50:43 the report of them, and his **h** waxed feeble: 3027
La 1:14 the Lord hath delivered me into *their* **h**, 3027
1:17 Zion spreadeth forth her **h**, *and there is* 3027
2:15 All that pass by clap *their* **h** at thee; 3709
2:19 lift up thy **h** toward him for the life of thy 3709
3:41 Let us lift up our heart with *our* **h** unto God 3709
3:64 according to the work of their **h**. 3027
4: 2 the work of the **h** of the potter! 3027
4: 6 as in a moment, and no **h** stayed on her. 3027
4:10 The **h** of the pitiful women have sodden 3027
Eze 1: 8 *they had* the **h** of a man under their wings 3027
7:17 All **h** shall be feeble, and all knees shall be 3027
7:21 I will give it into the **h** of the strangers for a 3027
7:27 the **h** of the people of the land shall be 3027
10: 7 put *it* into the **h** of *him that was* clothed 2651
10:12 their **h**, and their wings, and the wheels, 3027
10:21 the likeness of the **h** of a man *was* under 3027
11: 9 deliver you into the **h** of strangers, and 3027
13:22 strengthened the **h** of the wicked, that *he* 3027
16:11 I put bracelets upon thine **h**, and a chain on 3027
21: 7 all **h** shall be feeble, and every spirit shall 3027
21:14 smite *thine* **h together**, and 413+3709+3709
21:17 will also smite mine **h together**, 413+3709+3709
22:14 thine heart endure, or can thine **h** be strong, 3027
23:37 blood *is* in their **h**, and with their idols have 3027
23:42 which put bracelets upon their **h**, and 3027
23:45 *are* adulteresses, and blood *is* in their **h**. 3027
25: 6 Because thou hast clapped *thine* **h**, and 3027
Da 2:34 till that a stone was cut out without **h**, 3028
2:45 was cut out of the mountain without **h**, 3028
3:15 that God that shall deliver you out of my **h**? 3028
10:10 my knees and *upon* the palms of my **h**. 3027
Hos 14: 3 will we say any more to the work of our **h**, 3027
Ob 1:13 nor have laid *h* on their substance in the day NIH
Jnh 3: 8 and from the violence that *is* in their **h**. 3709
Mic 5:13 shalt no more worship the work of thine **h**. 3027
7: 3 That *they* may do evil with both **h** 3709
Na 3:19 the bruit of thee shall clap the **h** over thee: 3709
Hab 3:10 uttered his voice, *and* lift up his **h** on high. 3027
Zep 3:16 *and to* Zion, Let not thine **h** be slack. 3027
Hag 1:11 and upon all the labour of the **h**. 3709
2:14 so *is* every work of their **h**; and *that* which 3027
2:17 and with hail *in* all the labours of your **h**; 3027
Zec 4: 9 The **h** of Zerubbabel have laid 3027
4: 9 his **h** shall also finish *it*; and thou shalt 3027
8: 9 Let your **h** be strong, ye that hear in these 3027
8:13 fear not, *but* let your **h** be strong. 3027
13: 6 What *are* these wounds in thine **h**? 3027
Mt 4: 6 and in *their* **h** they shall bear thee up, lest at *5495*
15: 2 for they wash not their **h** when they eat *5495*
15:20 to eat with unwashen **h** defileth not a man. *5495*
17:22 The Son of man shall be betrayed into the **h** *5495*
18: 8 rather than having two **h** or two feet to be *5495*
18:28 and he **laid h on** him, and took *him* by *2902*
19:13 that he should put *his* **h** on them, and pray: *5495*
19:15 And he laid *his* **h** on them, and *5495*
21:46 But when they sought to **lay h on** him, *2902*
26:45 the Son of man is betrayed into the **h** of *5495*
26:50 and laid **h** on Jesus, and took him. *5495*
26:67 **smote** *him* **with the palms of** their **h**, *4474*
27:24 and washed *his* **h** before the multitude, *5495*
Mk 5:23 *I pray thee,* come and lay *thy* **h** on her, *5495*
6: 2 such mighty works are wrought by his **h**? *5495*
6: 5 save that he laid *his* **h** upon a few sick *folk*, *5495*
7: 2 that is to say, with unwashen, **h**, they found *5495*
7: 3 except they wash *their* **h** oft, eat not, *5495*
7: 5 the elders, but eat bread with unwashen **h**? *5495*
8:23 spit on his eyes, and put *his* **h** upon him, *5495*
8:25 After that he put *his* **h** again upon his eyes, *5495*
9:31 The Son of man is delivered into the **h** of *5495*
9:43 than having two **h** to go into hell, into *5495*
10:16 put *his* **h** upon them, and blessed them. *5495*
14:41 the Son of man is betrayed into the **h** of *5495*
14:46 And they laid their **h** on him, and took him. *5495*
14:58 destroy this temple that is **made with h**, *5499*
14:58 days I will build another **made without h**. *886*
14:65 **strike** him **with the palms of** their **h**. *906+4475*
16:18 they shall lay **h** on the sick, and they shall *5495*
Lk 4:11 And in *their* **h** they shall bear thee up, *5495*
4:40 and he laid *his* **h** on every one of them, and *5495*
6: 1 and did eat, rubbing *them* in *their* **h**. *5495*
9:44 of man shall be delivered into the **h** of men. *5495*
13:13 And he laid *his* **h** on her: and *5495*
20:19 the scribes the same hour sought to lay **h** on *5495*
21:12 they shall lay their **h** on you, and *5495*
22:53 ye stretched forth no **h** against me: *5495*
23:46 Father, into thy **h** I commend my spirit: *5495*
24: 7 must be delivered into the **h** of sinful men, *5495*
24:39 Behold my **h** and my feet, that it is I *5495*
24:40 he shewed them *his* **h** and *his* feet. *5495*
24:50 and he lift up his **h**, and blessed them. *5495*
Jn 7:30 but no *man* laid **h** on him, because his hour *5495*
7:44 have taken him; but no *man* laid **h** on him. *5495*
8:20 and no *man* **laid h on** him; for his hour was *4084*
13: 3 the Father had given all *things* into his **h**, *5495*
13: 9 my feet only, but also *my* **h** and *my* head. *5495*
19: 3 and they **smote** him **with** their **h**. *1325+4475*
20:20 he shewed unto them *his* **h** and his side. *5495*
20:25 Except I shall see in his **h** the print of *5495*
20:27 Reach hither thy finger, and behold my **h**; *5495*
21:18 thou shalt stretch forth thy **h**, and *5495*
Ac 2:23 and by wicked **h** have crucified and slain: *5495*
4: 3 And they laid **h** on them, and put *them* in *5495*
5:12 And by the **h** of the apostles were many *5495*
5:18 And laid their **h** on the apostles, and *5495*
6: 6 they had prayed, they laid *their* **h** on them. *5495*
7:41 and rejoiced in the works of their own **h**. *5495*
7:48 High dwelleth not in temples **made with h**; *5499*
8:17 Then laid they *their* **h** on them, and *5495*
8:18 the apostles' **h** the Holy Ghost was given, *5495*
8:19 this power, that on whomsoever I lay **h**, *5495*
9:17 and putting his **h** on him said, Brother Saul, *5495*
11:30 sent it to the elders by the **h** of Barnabas *5495*
12: 1 forth *his* **h** to vex certain of the church. *5495*
12: 7 And his chains fell off from *his* **h**. *5495*
13: 3 and prayed, and laid *their* **h** on them, *5495*
14: 3 and wonders to be done by their **h**. *5495*
17:24 dwelleth not in temples **made with h**; *5499*
17:25 Neither is worshipped with men's **h**, *5495*
19: 6 And when Paul had laid *his* **h** upon them, *5495*
19:11 And God wrought special miracles by the **h** *5495*
19:26 they be no gods, which are made with **h**: *5495*
20:34 that these **h** have ministered unto my *5495*
21:11 and bound his *own* **h** and feet, and said, *5495*
21:11 shall deliver *him* into the **h** of the Gentiles. *5495*
21:27 stirred up all the people, and laid **h** on him, *5495*
24: 7 great violence took *him* away out of our **h**, *5495*
27:19 *out* **with our own h** the tackling of the ship. *849*
28: 8 and laid *his* **h** on him, and healed him. *5495*
28:17 from Jerusalem into the **h** of the Romans. *5495*
Ro 10:21 All day long have I stretched forth my **h** *5495*
1Co 4:12 And labour, working with our own **h**: *5495*
2Co 11:33 I let down by the wall, and escaped his **h**. *5495*

Gal 2: 9 and Barnabas the **right h** of fellowship; *1188*
Eph 2:11 the Circumcision in the flesh **made by h**; *5499*
4:28 working with *his* **h** the *thing which is* good, *5495*
Col 2:11 with the circumcision **made without h**, *886*
1Th 4:11 and to work with your own **h**, *5495*
1Ti 2: 8 lifting up holy **h**, without wrath and *5495*
4:14 with the laying on of the **h** of *5495*
5:22 Lay **h** suddenly on no *man*, neither be *5495*
2Ti 1: 6 which is in thee by the putting on of my **h**. *5495*
Heb 1:10 and the heavens are the works of thine **h**: *5495*
2: 7 and didst set him over the works of thy **h**: *5495*
6: 2 and of laying on of **h**, and of resurrection of *5495*
9:11 not **made with h**, that is to say, not of this *5499*
9:24 entered into the holy *places* **made with h**, *5499*
10:31 *It is* a fearful *thing* to fall into the **h** of *5495*
12:12 Wherefore lift up the **h** which hang down, *5495*
Jas 4: 8 Cleanse *your* **h**, *ye* sinners; and purify *your* *5495*
1Jn 1: 1 and our **h** have handled, of the Word of *5495*
Rev 7: 9 with white robes, and palms in their **h**; *5495*
9:20 *yet* repented not of the works of their **h**, *5495*
20: 4 *his* mark upon their foreheads, or in their **h**; *5495*

HANDSOME See GOODLIER; GOODLIEST; GOODLY

HANDSTAVES (1) [HAND, STAFF]
Eze 39: 9 the **h**, and the spears, and they shall 3027+4731

HANDWRITING (1) [HAND, WRITE]
Col 2:14 Blotting out the **h** of ordinances that was *5498*

HANDYWORK (1) [HAND, WORK]
Ps 19: 1 and the firmament sheweth his **h**. 3027+4639

HANES (1)
Isa 30: 4 at Zoan, and his ambassadors came to **H**. 2609

HANG (19) [HANGED, HANGETH, HANGING, HANGINGS]
Ge 40:19 from off thee, and shall **h** thee on a tree; 8518
Ex 26:12 shall **h** over the backside of the tabernacle. 5628
26:13 it shall **h** over the sides of the tabernacle on 5628
26:32 thou shalt **h** it upon four pillars of shittim 5414
26:33 thou shalt **h up** the vail under the taches, 5414
40: 8 and **h up** the hanging at the court gate. 5414
Nu 25: 4 **h** them **up** before the LORD against 3363
Dt 21:22 *to be* put to death, and thou **h** him on a tree: 8518
28:66 thy life shall **h in doubt** before thee; and 8511
2Sa 21: 6 we will **h** them **up** unto the LORD in 3363
Est 6: 4 to speak unto the king to **h** Mordecai on 8518
7: 9 Then the king said, **H** him thereon. 8518
SS 4: 4 whereon there **h** a thousand bucklers, 8518
Isa 22:24 they shall **h** upon him all the glory of his 8518
La 2:10 the virgins of Jerusalem **h down** their heads 3381
Eze 15: 3 will *men* take a pin of it to **h** any vessel 8518
Mt 22:40 On these two commandments **h** all the law *2910*
Ac 28: 4 saw the *venomous* beast **h** on his hand, *2910*
Heb 12:12 Wherefore lift up the hands which **h down**, *3935*

HANGED (30) [HANG]
Ge 40:22 he **h** the chief baker: as Joseph had 8518
41:13 he restored unto mine office, and him he **h**. 8518
Dt 21:23 (for he that is **h** *is* accursed of God;) 8518
Jos 8:29 the king of Ai he **h** on a tree until eventide: 8518
10:26 and slew them, and **h** them on five trees: 8518
2Sa 4:12 and **h** *them* **up** over the pool in Hebron. 8518
17:23 **h** himself, and died, and was buried in 2614
18:10 said, Behold, I saw Absalom **h** in an oak. 8518
21: 9 they **h** them in the hill before the LORD: 3363
21:12 where the Philistines had **h** them, when 8511
21:13 gathered the bones of them that were **h**. 3363
Ezr 6:11 and being set up, let him be **h** thereon; 4223
Est 2:23 therefore they were both **h** on a tree: 8518
5:14 the king that Mordecai may be **h** thereon: 8518
7:10 So they **h** Haman on the gallows that he 8518
8: 7 him they have **h** upon the gallows, because 8518
9:13 let Haman's ten sons be **h** upon 8518
9:14 at Shushan; and they **h** Haman's ten sons. 8518
9:25 and his sons should be **h** on the gallows. 8518
Ps 137: 2 We **h** our harps upon the willows in 8518
La 5:12 Princes are **h up** by their hand: the faces of 8518
Eze 27:10 they **h** the shield and helmet in thee; 8518
27:11 they **h** their shields upon thy walls round 8518
Mt 18: 6 were better for him that a millstone were **h** *2910*
27: 5 and departed, and went and **h** himself. *519*
Mk 9:42 it is better for him that a millstone were **h** *4029*
Lk 17: 2 a millstone were **h about** his neck, *4029*
23:39 And one of the malefactors which were **h** *2910*
Ac 5:30 up Jesus, whom ye slew and **h** on a tree. *2910*
10:39 whom they slew and **h** on a tree: *2910*

HANGETH (2) [HANG]
Job 26: 7 empty place, *and* **h** the earth upon nothing. 8518
Gal 3:13 Cursed *is* every one that **h** on a tree: *2910*

HANGING (18) [HANG]
Ex 26:36 thou shalt make a **h** for the door of the tent, 4539
26:37 thou shalt make for the **h** five pillars of 4539
27:16 for the gate of the court *shall be* a **h** of 4539
35:15 the **h** for the door at the entering in of 4539
35:17 and the **h** for the door of the court, 4539
36:37 he made a **h** for the tabernacle door *of* blue, 4539
38:18 the **h** for the gate of the court *was* 4539
39:38 and the **h** for the tabernacle door, 4539
39:40 the **h** for the court gate, his cords, and 4539
40: 5 and put the **h** of the door to the tabernacle. 4539
40: 8 and hang up the **h** at the court gate. 4539
40:28 he set up the **h** at the door of the tabernacle. 4539
40:33 the altar, and set up the **h** of the court gate. 4539
Nu 3:25 the **h** for the door of the tabernacle of 4539
3:31 and the **h**, and all the service thereof. 4539
4:25 the **h** for the door of the tabernacle of 4539
4:26 the **h** for the door of the gate of the court, 4539
Jos 10:26 they were **h** upon the trees until 8518

HANGINGS (18) [HANG]
Ex 27: 9 the south side southward *there shall be* **h** 7050
27:11 *there shall be* **h** of an hundred *cubits* long, 7050
27:12 on the west side *shall be* **h** of fifty cubits: 7050
27:14 The **h** of *one* side *of the gate shall be* 7050
27:15 on the other side *shall be* **h**, fifteen *cubits*: 7050
35:17 The **h** of the court, his pillars, and 7050
38: 9 on the south side southward the **h** of 7050
38:11 for the north side *the* **h** *were* an hundred NIH
38:12 And for the west side *were* **h** of fifty cubits, 7050
38:14 The **h** of the *one* side *of the gate were* 7050
38:15 and that hand, *were* **h** of fifteen cubits; 7050
38:16 All the **h** of the court round about *were of* 7050
38:18 answerable to the **h** of the court. 7050
39:40 The **h** of the court, his pillars, and his 7050
Nu 3:26 the **h** of the court, and the curtain for 7050
4:26 the **h** of the court, and the hanging for 7050
2Ki 23: 7 where the women wove **h** for the grove. 1004
Est 1: 6 blue *h*, fastened with cords of fine linen and NIH

HANIEL (1)
1Ch 7:39 the sons of Ulla; Arah, and **H**, and Rezia. 2592

HANNAH (13)
1Sa 1: 2 the name of the one *was* **H**, and the name 2584
1: 2 had children, but **H** had no children. 2584
1: 5 unto **H** he gave a worthy portion; for he 2584
1: 5 he gave a worthy portion; for he loved **H**: 2584
1: 8 her husband to her, **H**, why weepest thou? 2584
1: 9 So **H** rose up after *they* had eaten in Shiloh, 2584
1:13 Now **H**, she spake in her heart; only her 2584
1:15 **H** answered and said, No, my lord, I *am* a 2584
1:19 Elkanah knew **H** his wife; and the LORD 2584
1:20 when the time was come about after **H** had 2584
1:22 **H** went not up; for she said unto her 2584
2: 1 **H** prayed, and said, My heart rejoiceth in 2584
2:21 the LORD visited **H**, so that she 2584

HANNATHON (1)
Jos 19:14 compasseth it on the north side *to* **H**: 2615

HANNIEL (1)
Nu 34:23 children of Manasseh, **H** the son of Ephod. 2592

HANOCH (5) [HANOCHITES]
Ge 25: 4 and Epher, and **H**, and Abidah, and Eldaah. 2585
46: 9 **H**, and Phallu, and Hezron, and Carmi. 2585
Ex 6:14 of Israel; **H**, and Pallu, Hezron, and Carmi: 2585
Nu 26: 5 **H**, *of whom cometh* the family of 2585
1Ch 5: 3 of Reuben the firstborn of Israel *were*, **H**, 2585

HANOCHITES (1) [HANOCH]
Nu 26: 5 *of whom cometh* the family of the **H**: 2599

HANUN (11)
2Sa 10: 1 and **H** his son reigned in his stead. 2586
10: 2 I will shew kindness unto **H** the son of 2586

2Sa 10: 3 children of Ammon said unto **H** their lord, 2586
10: 4 Wherefore **H** took David's servants, and 2586
1Ch 19: 2 I will shew kindness unto **H** the son of 2586
19: 2 the land of the children of Ammon to **H**, 2586
19: 3 of the children of Ammon said to **H**, 2586
19: 4 Wherefore **H** took David's servants, and 2586
19: 6 **H** and the children of Ammon sent a 2586
Ne 3:13 The valley gate repaired **H**, and 2586
3:30 **H** the sixth son of Zalaph, another piece. 2586

HAP (1) [HAPPEN]
Ru 2: 3 her **h** was to light on a part of the field 4745

HAPHARAIM (1)
Jos 19:19 And **H**, and Shion, and Anaharath, 2663

HAPLY (6) [HAPPEN]
1Sa 14:30 **if h** the people had eaten freely to day of 3863
Mk 11:13 if **h** he might find any *thing* thereon: *686*
Lk 14:29 **Lest h**, after he hath laid the foundation, *3379*
Ac 5:39 **lest h** ye be found even to fight against *3379*
17:27 if **h** they might feel after him, and *686+1065*
2Co 9: 4 **Lest h** if they of Macedonia come with me, *3381*

HAPPEN (4) [HAP, HAPLY, HAPPENED, HAPPENETH]
1Sa 28:10 there shall no punishment **h** to thee for this 7136
Pr 12:21 There shall no evil **h** to the just: but 579
Isa 41:22 bring *them* forth, and shew us what shall **h**: 7136
Mk 10:32 began to tell them what *things* should **h** *4819*

HAPPENED (12) [HAPPEN]
1Sa 6: 9 *that* smote us; it *was* a chance *that* **h** to us. 1961
2Sa 1: 6 As I **h by chance** upon mount Gilboa, 7122
20: 1 there **h to be** there a man of Belial, whose 7122
Est 4: 7 Mordecai told him of all that had **h** unto 7136
Jer 44:23 therefore this evil is **h unto** you, as *at* this 7122
Lk 24:14 together of all these *things* which had **h**. *4819*
Ac 3:10 amazement at that which had **h** unto him. *4819*
Ro 11:25 that blindness in part is **h** to Israel, until *1096*
1Co 10:11 Now all these *things* **h** unto them for *4819*
Php 1:12 that the *things which* **h** unto me have fallen NIG
1Pe 4:12 as though *some* strange *thing* **h** unto you: *4819*
2Pe 2:22 But it is **h** unto them according to the true *4819*

HAPPENETH (6) [HAPPEN]
Ecc 2:14 I myself perceived also that one event **h** to 7136
2:15 As it **h** to the fool, so it happeneth even to 4745
2:15 it happeneth to the fool, so it **h** even to me; 7136
8:14 that there be just *men,* unto whom it **h** 5060
8:14 there be wicked *men,* to whom it **h** 5060
9:11 of skill; but time and chance **h** to them all. 7136

HAPPIER (1) [HAPPY]
1Co 7:40 But she is **h** if she so abide, after my *3107*

HAPPIZZEZ See APHSES

HAPPY (28) [HAPPIER]
Ge 30:13 Leah said, **H** am I, for the daughters will call 837
Dt 33:29 **H** *art* thou, O Israel: who *is* like unto thee, 835
1Ki 10: 8 **H** *are* thy men, happy *are* these thy servants, 835
10: 8 Happy *are* thy men, **h** *are* these thy servants, 835
2Ch 9: 7 **H** *are* thy men, and happy *are* these thy 835
9: 7 *are* thy men, and **h** *are* these thy servants, 835
Job 5:17 Behold, **h** *is* the man whom God correcteth: 835
Ps 127: 5 **H** *is* the man that hath his quiver full of 835
128: 2 **h** *shalt* thou *be,* and *it shall be* well with 835
137: 8 **h** *shall he be,* that rewardeth thee as thou 835
137: 9 **H** *shall he be* that taketh and dasheth thy 835
144:15 **H** *is that* people, that is in such a case: *yea,* 835
144:15 *yea,* **h** *is that* people, whose God *is* 835
146: 5 **H** *is he* that *hath* the God of Jacob for his 835
Pr 3:13 **H** *is* the man *that* findeth wisdom, and 835
3:18 and **h** *is* every one that retaineth her. 833
14:21 but he that hath mercy on the poor, **h** *is* he. 835
16:20 and whoso trusteth in the LORD, **h** *is* he. 835
28:14 **H** *is* the man that feareth alway: but he that 835
29:18 but he that keepeth the law, **h** *is* he. 835
Jer 12: 1 *wherefore* are all they **h** that deal very 7951
Mal 3:15 now we **call** the proud **h**; yea, they that work 833
Jn 13:17 If ye know these *things,* **h** are ye if ye do *3107*
Ac 26: 2 I think myself **h**, king Agrippa, because *3107*
Ro 14:22 **H** *is* he that condemneth not himself in *that* *3107*
Jas 5:11 Behold, we **count** them **h** which endure. *3106*
1Pe 3:14 **h** *are ye:* and be not afraid of their terror, *3107*
4:14 **h** *are ye;* for the spirit of glory and of God *3107*

HARA (1)
1Ch 5:26 Habor, and **H**, and to the river Gozan, 2024

HARADAH (2)
Nu 33:24 from mount Shapher, and encamped in **H**. 2732
33:25 they removed from **H**, and pitched in 2732

HARAN (19) [BETH-HARAN, CHARRAN]
Ge 11:26 and begat Abram, Nahor, and **H**. 2039
11:27 Terah begat Abram, Nahor, and **H**; and 2039
11:27 and Haran; and **H** begat Lot. 2039
11:28 **H** died before his father Terah in the land 2039
11:29 Milcah, the daughter of **H**, the father of 2039
11:31 Lot the son of **H** his son's son, and Sarai 2039
11:31 and they came unto **H**, and dwelt there. 2771
11:32 five years: and Terah died in **H**. 2771
12: 4 five years old when he departed out of **H**. 2771
12: 5 and the souls that they had gotten in **H**; 2771
27:43 arise, flee thou to Laban my brother to **H**; 2771
28:10 out from Beer-sheba, and went toward **H**. 2771
29: 4 whence *be* ye? And they said, Of **H** *are* we. 2771
2Ki 19:12 **H**, and Rezeph, and the children of Eden 2771
1Ch 2:46 bare **H**, and Moza, and Gazez: 2771
2:46 and Moza, and Gazez: and **H** begat Gazez. 2771
23: 9 Shelomith, and Haziel, and **H**, three. 2039
Isa 37:12 **H**, and Rezeph, and the children of Eden 2771
Eze 27:23 **H**, and Canneh, and Eden, the merchants of 2771

HARARITE (5)
2Sa 23:11 him *was* Shammah the son of Agee the **H**. 2043
23:33 Shammah the **H**, Ahiam the son of Sharar 2043
23:33 Ahiam the son of Sharar the **H**, 2043
1Ch 11:34 Jonathan the son of Shage the **H**, 2043
11:35 Ahiam the son of Sacar the **H**, Eliphal 2043

HARBONA (1) [HARBONAH]
Est 1:10 Biztha, **H**, Bigtha, and Abagtha, Zethar, 2726

HARBONAH (1) [HARBONA]
Est 7: 9 **H**, one of the chamberlains, said before 2726

HARD (45) [HARDEN, HARDENED, HARDENETH, HARDER, HARDHEARTED, HARDLY, HARDNESS]
Ge 18:14 Is any thing too **h** for the LORD? At 6381
35:16 and Rachel travailed, and she had **h** labour. 7185
35:17 it came to pass, when she was in **h** labour, 7185
Ex 1:14 they made their lives bitter with **h** bondage, 7186
18:26 the **h** causes they brought unto Moses, but 7186
Lev 3: 9 he take off **h by** the back bone; 5980+3807.1
Dt 1:17 the cause that is too **h** for you, bring *it* unto 7185
15:18 It shall not seem **h** unto thee, when thou 7185
17: 8 If there arise a matter too **h** for thee in 6381
26: 6 afflicted us, and laid upon us **h** bondage: 7186
Jdg 9:52 **went h** unto the door of the tower to burn it 5066
20:45 **pursued h** after them unto Gidom, and 1692
1Sa 14:22 even they also **followed h** after them in 1692
31: 2 the Philistines **followed h** upon Saul and 1692
2Sa 1: 6 and horsemen **followed h after** him. 1692
3:39 these men the sons of Zeruiah *be* too **h** for 7186
13: 2 Amnon thought it **h** for him to do any thing 6381
1Ki 10: 1 she came to prove him with **h questions**. 2420
21: 1 **h by** the palace of Ahab king of Samaria. 681
2Ki 2:10 he said, Thou hast asked a **h thing**: 7185
1Ch 10: 2 the Philistines **followed h** after Saul, and 1692
19: 4 cut off their garments in the midst **h by** 5704
2Ch 9: 1 Solomon with **h questions** at Jerusalem, 2420
Job 41:24 yea, as **h** as a piece of the nether *millstone.* 3332
Ps 60: 3 Thou hast shewed thy people **h** *things:* thou 7186
63: 8 My soul **followeth h** after thee: thy right 1692
88: 7 Thy wrath **lieth h** upon me, and thou hast 5564
94: 4 shall they utter *and* speak **h** *things? and* 6277
Pr 13:15 but the way of transgressors *is* **h**. 386
Isa 14: 3 from the **h** bondage wherein thou wast 7186
Jer 32:17 out arm, *and* there is nothing too **h** for thee: 6381
32:27 of all flesh: is there any thing too **h** for me? 6381
Eze 3: 5 of a strange speech and of a **h** language, 3515
3: 6 of a strange speech and of a **h** language, 3515
Da 5:12 shewing of **h sentences**, and dissolving of 280
Jnh 1:13 Nevertheless the men **rowed h** to bring *it* to 2864
Mt 25:24 Lord, I knew thee that thou art a **h** man, *4642*
Mk 10:24 how **h** is it for them that trust in riches to *1422*
Jn 6:60 they had heard *this,* said, This is a **h** saying; *4642*
Ac 9: 5 *it is* **h** for thee to kick against the pricks. *4642*

H

Ac 18: 7 whose house **joined h to** the synagogue. *4927*
26:14 *it is* **h** for thee to kick against the pricks. *4642*
Heb 5:11 and **h** to be uttered, seeing ye are dull of *1421*
2Pe 3:16 which are some *things* **h to be understood**, *1425*
Jude 1:15 of all *their* **h** *speeches* which ungodly *4642*

HARDEN (12) [HARD]
Ex 4:21 I will **h** his heart, that he shall not let 2388
7: 3 I will **h** Pharaoh's heart, and multiply my 7185
14: 4 I will **h** Pharaoh's heart, that he shall 2388
14:17 I will **h** the hearts of the Egyptians, and 2388
Dt 15: 7 thou shalt not **h** thy heart, nor shut thine 553
Jos 11:20 For it was of the LORD to **h** their hearts, 2388
1Sa 6: 6 Wherefore then do ye **h** your hearts, as 3513
Job 6:10 yea, I would **h** myself in sorrow; let him 5539
Ps 95: 8 **H** not your heart, as *in* the provocation, *and* 7185
Heb 3: 8 **H** not your hearts, as in the provocation, *4645*
3:15 **h** not your hearts, as in the provocation. *4645*
4: 7 if ye will hear his voice, **h** not your hearts. *4645*

HARDENED (33) [HARD]
Ex 7:13 he **h** Pharaoh's heart, that he hearkened not 2388
7:14 Pharaoh's heart *is* **h**, he refuseth to let 3515
7:22 Pharaoh's heart was **h**, neither did he 2388
8:15 he **h** his heart, and hearkened not unto 3513
8:19 Pharaoh's heart was **h**, and he hearkened 2388
8:32 Pharaoh **h** his heart at this time also, 3513
9: 7 the heart of Pharaoh was **h**, and he did not 3513
9:12 the LORD **h** the heart of Pharaoh, and 2388
9:34 and **h** his heart, he and his servants. 3513
9:35 the heart of Pharaoh was **h**, neither would 2388
10: 1 for I have **h** his heart, and the heart of his 3513
10:20 the LORD **h** Pharaoh's heart, so that he 2388
10:27 the LORD **h** Pharaoh's heart, and 2388
11:10 the LORD **h** Pharaoh's heart, so that he 2388
14: 8 the LORD **h** the heart of Pharaoh king of 2388
Dt 2:30 for the LORD thy God **h** his spirit, and 7185
1Sa 6: 6 the Egyptians and Pharaoh **h** their hearts? 3513
2Ki 17:14 **h** their necks, like to the neck of their 7185
2Ch 36:13 **h** his heart from turning unto the LORD 553
Ne 9:16 **h** their necks, and hearkened not to thy 7185
9:17 **h** their necks, and in their rebellion 7185
9:29 and **h** their neck, and would not hear. 7185
Job 9: 4 who hath **h** *himself* against him, and 7185
39:16 She is **h against** her young ones, as though 7188
Isa 63:17 thy ways, *and* **h** our heart from thy fear? 7188
Jer 7:26 nor inclined their ear, but **h** their neck: 7185
19:15 because they have **h** their necks, that *they* 7185
Da 5:20 heart was lifted up, and his mind **h** in pride, 8631
Mk 6:52 *miracle* of the loaves: for their heart was **h**. *4456*
8:17 have ye your heart yet **h**? *4456*
Jn 12:40 hath blinded their eyes, and **h** their heart; *4456*
Ac 19: 9 But when divers were **h**, and believed not, *4645*
Heb 3:13 lest any of you be **h** through *4645*

HARDENETH (4) [HARD]
Pr 21:29 A wicked man **h** his face: but *as for* 5810
28:14 he that **h** his heart shall fall into mischief. 7185
29: 1 He, that being often reproved **h** *his* neck, 7185
Ro 9:18 he will *have mercy,* and whom he will he **h**. *4645*

HARDER (3) [HARD]
Pr 18:19 A brother offended *is* **h** *to be won* than a NIH
Jer 5: 3 they have **made** their faces **h** than a rock; 2388
Eze 3: 9 As an adamant **h** than flint have I made thy 2389

HARDHEARTED (1) [HARD, HEART]
Eze 3: 7 house of Israel *are* impudent and **h**. 3820+7186

HARDLY (8) [HARD]
Ge 16: 6 when Sarai **dealt h with** her, she fled from 6031
Ex 13:15 to pass, when Pharaoh would **h** let us go, 7185
Isa 8:21 pass through it, **h bestead** and hungry: 7185
Mt 19:23 That a rich *man* shall **h** enter into *1423*
Mk 10:23 How **h** shall they that have riches enter into *1423*
Lk 9:39 and bruising him **h** departeth from him. *3425*
18:24 How **h** shall they that have riches enter into *1423*
Ac 27: 8 And **h** passing it, came unto a place *which* *3433*

HARDNESS (7) [HARD]
Job 38:38 When the dust groweth into **h**, and 4165
Mt 19: 8 of the **h of** your **hearts** suffered you to put *4641*
Mk 3: 5 being grieved for the **h** of their hearts, *4457*
10: 5 For the **h of** your **heart** he wrote you this *4641*
16:14 them with their unbelief and **h of heart**, *4641*
Ro 2: 5 But after thy **h** and impenitent heart *4643*
2Ti 2: 3 Thou therefore **endure h**, as a good soldier *2553*

HARDSHIP; HARDSHIPS See TRAVAIL; TRAVAILED; TRAVAILEST; TRAVAILETH

HARE (2)
Lev 11: 6 the **h**, because he cheweth the cud, but 768
Dt 14: 7 *as* the camel, and the **h**, and the coney: 768

HAREPH (1)
1Ch 2:51 of Beth-lehem, **H** the father of Beth-gader. 2780

HARETH (1)
1Sa 22: 5 and came *into* the forest of **H**. 2802

HARHAIAH (1)
Ne 3: 8 unto him repaired Uzziel the son of **H**, 2736

HARHAS (1)
2Ki 22:14 the son of **H**, keeper of the wardrobe; 2745

HARHUR (2)
Ezr 2:51 the children of Hakupha, the children of **H**, 2744
Ne 7:53 the children of Hakupha, the children of **H**, 2744

HARIM (11)
1Ch 24: 8 The third to **H**, the fourth to Seorim, 2766
Ezr 2:32 The children of **H**, three hundred and 2766
2:39 The children of **H**, a thousand and 2766
10:21 of the sons of **H**; Maaseiah, and Elijah, 2766
10:31 *of* the sons of **H**; Eliezer, Ishijah, Malchiah, 2766
Ne 3:11 Malchijah the son of **H**, and Hashub 2766
7:35 The children of **H**, three hundred and 2766
7:42 The children of **H**, a thousand *and* 2766
10: 5 **H**, Meremoth, Obadiah, 2766
10:27 Malluch, **H**, Baanah. 2766
12:15 Of **H**, Adna; of Meraioth, Helkai; 2766

HARIPH (2)
Ne 7:24 The children of **H**, an hundred *and* twelve. 2756
10:19 **H**, Anathoth, Nebai, 2756

HARLOT (40) [HARLOT'S, HARLOTS, HARLOTS']
Ge 34:31 Should he deal with our sister as with a **h**? 2181
38:15 Judah saw her, he thought her to be a **h**; 2181
38:21 saying, Where *is* the **h**, that *was* openly by 6948
38:21 they said, There was no **h** in this *place.* 6948
38:22 *that* there was no **h** in this *place.* 6948
38:24 thy daughter in law hath **played the h**; 2181
Lev 21:14 or a divorced *woman,* or profane, *or* a **h**, 2181
Jos 6:17 only Rahab the **h** shall live, she and all that 2181
6:25 Joshua saved Rahab the **h** alive, and her 2181
Jdg 11: 1 *man* of valour, and he *was* the son of a **h**: 2181
16: 1 and saw there a **h**, and went in unto her. 2181
Pr 7:10 met him a woman *with* the attire of a **h**, 2181
Isa 1:21 How is the faithful city become a **h**! *it was* 2181
23:15 end of seventy years shall Tyre sing as a **h**. 2181
23:16 the city, thou **h** that hast been forgotten; 2181
Jer 2:20 green tree thou wanderest, **playing the h**. 2181
3: 1 thou hast **played the h** with many lovers; 2181
3: 6 green tree, and there hath **played the h**. 2181
3: 8 feared not, but went and **played the h** also. 2181
Eze 16:15 **playedst the h** because of thy renown, and 2181
16:16 and **playedst the h** thereupon: 2181
16:28 thou hast **played the h** with them, and 2181
16:31 hast not been as a **h**, in that *thou* scornest 2181
16:35 Wherefore, O **h**, hear the word of 2181
16:41 cause thee to cease from **playing the h**, 2181
23: 5 Aholah **played the h** when she was mine; 2181
23:19 wherein she had **played the h** in the land of 2181
23:44 go in unto a woman that **playeth the h**: 2181
Hos 2: 5 For their mother hath **played the h**: 2181
3: 3 thou shalt not **play the h**, and thou shalt not 2181
4:15 Though thou, Israel, **play the h**, *yet* let not 2181
Joel 3: 3 have given a boy for a **h**, and sold a girl for 2181
Am 7:17 Thy wife shall be a **h** in the city, and 2181
Mic 1: 7 for she gathered *it* of the hire of a **h**, and 2181
1: 7 and they shall return to the hire of a **h**. 2181
Na 3: 4 of the whoredoms of the wellfavoured **h**, 2181
1Co 6:15 and make *them* the members of a **h**? *4204*
6:16 know ye not that he which is joined to a **h** *4204*
Heb 11:31 By faith the **h** Rahab perished not with *4204*
Jas 2:25 Likewise also was not Rahab the **h** justified *4204*

HARLOT'S (2) [HARLOT]
Jos 2: 1 came *into* a **h** house, named Rahab, and 2181
6:22 Go *into* the **h** house, and bring out thence 2181

HARLOTS (7) [HARLOT]
1Ki 3:16 *that were* **h**, unto the king, and stood before 2181
Pr 29: 3 he that keepeth company with **h** spendeth 2181
Hos 4:14 with whores, and they sacrifice with **h**: 6948
Mt 21:31 the **h** go into the kingdom of God before *4204*
21:32 but the publicans and the **h** believed him: *4204*
Lk 15:30 which hath devoured thy living with **h**, *4204*
Rev 17: 5 THE MOTHER OF **H** AND *4204*

HARLOTS' (1) [HARLOT]
Jer 5: 7 assembled themselves by troops *in* the **h** 2181

HARM (16) [HARMLESS]
Ge 31:52 over this heap and this pillar unto me, for **h**. 7451
Lev 5:16 the **h** that he hath **done** in the holy *thing,* 2398
Nu 35:23 *was* not his enemy, neither sought his **h**: 7451
1Sa 26:21 for I will no more **do** thee **h**, because my 7489
2Sa 20: 6 of Bichri **do** us more **h** than *did* Absalom: 3415
2Ki 4:41 may eat. And there was no **h** in the pot. 7451
1Ch 16:22 mine anointed, and **do** my prophets no **h**. 7489
Ps 105:15 mine anointed, and **do** my prophets no **h**. 7489
Pr 3:30 without cause, if he have done thee no **h**. 7451
Jer 39:12 and look well to him, and do him no **h**; 7451
Ac 16:28 with a loud voice, saying, Do thyself no **h**: *2556*
27:21 and to have gained this **h** and loss. *5196*
28: 5 off the beast into the fire, and felt no **h**. *2556*
28: 6 and saw no **h** come to him, they changed *824*
28:21 that came shewed or spake any **h** of thee. *4190*
1Pe 3:13 And who *is* he that will **h** you, if ye be *2559*

HARMLESS (3) [HARM]
Mt 10:16 therefore wise as serpents, and **h** as doves. *185*
Php 2:15 That ye may be blameless and **h**, the sons of *185*
Heb 7:26 *who is* holy, **h**, undefiled, separate from *172*

HARMONY See CONCORD

HARNEPHER (1)
1Ch 7:36 and **H**, and Shual, and Beri, and Imrah, 2774

HARNESS (5) [HARNESSED]
1Ki 20:11 Tell *him,* Let not him that girdeth on *his* **h** NIH
22:34 king of Israel between the joints of the **h**: 8302
2Ch 9:24 raiment, **h**, and spices, horses, and mules, 5402
18:33 king of Israel between the joints of the **h**: 8302
Jer 46: 4 **H** the horses; and get up, ye horsemen, and 631

HARNESSED (1) [HARNESS]
Ex 13:18 the children of Israel went up **h** out of 2571

HAROD (1) [HARODITE]
Jdg 7: 1 up early, and pitched beside the well of **H**: 5878

HARODITE (2) [HAROD]
2Sa 23:25 Shammah the **H**, Elika the Harodite, 2733
23:25 Shammah the Harodite, Elika the **H**, 2733

HAROEH (1)
1Ch 2:52 had sons; **H**, *and* half of the Manahethites. 7204

HARORITE (1)
1Ch 11:27 Shammoth the **H**, Helez the Pelonite, 2033

HAROSHETH (3)
Jdg 4: 2 which dwelt in **H** of the Gentiles. 2800
4:13 from **H** of the Gentiles unto the river of 2800
4:16 and after the host, unto **H** of the Gentiles: 2800

HARP (30) [HARPED, HARPERS, HARPING, HARPS]
Ge 4:21 he was the father of all such as handle the **h** 3658
31:27 and with songs, with tabret, and with **h**? 3658
1Sa 10: 5 a tabret, and a pipe, and a **h**, before them; 3658
16:16 out a man, *who is* a cunning player on a **h**: 3658
16:23 that David took a **h**, and played with his 3658
1Ch 25: 3 who prophesied with a **h**, to give thanks 3658
Job 21:12 They take the timbrel and **h**, and rejoice at 3658
30:31 My **h** also is *turned* to mourning, and 3658
Ps 33: 2 Praise the LORD with **h**: sing unto him 3658
43: 4 yea, upon the **h** will I praise thee, O God 3658
49: 4 I will open my dark saying upon the **h**. 3658
57: 8 my glory; awake, psaltery and **h**: 3658
71:22 unto thee will I sing with the **h**, O thou 3658
81: 2 the timbrel, the pleasant **h** with the psaltery. 3658
92: 3 upon the **h** with a solemn sound. 3658
98: 5 Sing unto the LORD with the **h**; with 3658
98: 5 with the **h**, and the voice of a psalm. 3658
108: 2 Awake, psaltery and **h**: I *myself* will awake 3658
147: 7 sing *praise* upon the **h** unto our God: 3658
149: 3 *praises* unto him with the timbrel and **h**. 3658
150: 3 praise him with the psaltery and **h**. 3658
Isa 5:12 the **h**, and the viol, the tabret, and pipe, 3658
16:11 Wherefore my bowels shall sound like a **h** 3658
23:16 Take a **h**, go about the city, thou harlot that 3658
24: 8 that rejoice endeth, the joy of the **h** ceaseth. 3658
Da 3: 5 flute, **h**, sackbut, psaltery, dulcimer, and 7030
3: 7 flute, **h**, sackbut, psaltery, and all kinds of 7030
3:10 flute, **h**, sackbut, psaltery, and dulcimer, 7030
3:15 flute, **h**, sackbut, psaltery, and dulcimer, 7030
1Co 14: 7 life giving sound, whether pipe or **h**, *2788*

HARPED (1) [HARP]
1Co 14: 7 how shall it be known what is piped or **h**? *2789*

HARPERS (2) [HARP]
Rev 14: 2 I heard the voice of **h** harping with their *2790*
18:22 And the voice of **h**, and musicians, and *2790*

HARPING (1) [HARP]
Rev 14: 2 I heard the voice of harpers **h** with their *2789*

HARPIST See MINSTREL

HARPS (20) [HARP]
2Sa 6: 5 even on **h**, and on psalteries, and 3658
1Ki 10:12 **h** also and psalteries for singers: 3658
1Ch 13: 8 with **h**, and with psalteries, and 3658
15:16 psalteries and **h** and cymbals, sounding, 3658
15:21 Azaziah, with **h** on the Sheminith to excel. 3658
15:28 making a noise with psalteries and **h**. 3658
16: 5 Jeiel with psalteries and with **h**; but 3658
25: 1 of Jeduthun, who should prophesy with **h**, 3658
25: 6 with cymbals, psalteries, and **h**, for 3658
2Ch 5:12 having cymbals and psalteries and **h**, 3658
9:11 and **h** and psalteries for singers: 3658
20:28 **h** and trumpets unto the house of 3658
29:25 with psalteries, and with **h**, according to 3658
Ne 12:27 *with* cymbals, psalteries, and with **h**. 3658
Ps 137: 2 We hanged our **h** upon the willows in 3658
Isa 30:32 lay upon him, *it* shall be with tabrets and **h**: 3658
Eze 26:13 the sound of thy **h** shall be no more heard. 3658
Rev 5: 8 having every one *of them* **h**, and *2788*
14: 2 the voice of harpers harping with their **h**: *2788*
15: 2 on the sea of glass, having *the* **h** of God. *2788*

HARROW (1) [HARROWS]
Job 39:10 or will he **h** the valleys after thee? 7702

HARROWS (2) [HARROW]
2Sa 12:31 under **h** of iron, and under axes of iron, and 2757
1Ch 20: 3 and with **h** of iron, and with axes. 2757

HARSH See FROWARD; SHARPNESS; STOUT

HARSHA (2)
Ezr 2:52 the children of Mehida, the children of **H**, 2797
Ne 7:54 the children of Mehida, the children of **H**, 2797

HART (9) [HARTS]
Dt 12:15 as of the roebuck, and as of the **h**. 354
12:22 Even as the roebuck and the **h** is eaten, so 354
14: 5 The **h**, and the roebuck, and the fallow deer, 354
15:22 *eat it* alike, as the roebuck, and as the **h**. 354
Ps 42: 1 As the **h** panteth after the water brooks, so 354
SS 2: 9 My beloved *is* like a roe or a young **h**: 354
2:17 or a young **h** upon the mountains of Bether. 354
8:14 to a young **h** upon the mountains of spices. 354
Isa 35: 6 shall the lame *man* leap as a **h**, and 354

HARTS (2) [HART]
1Ki 4:23 beside **h**, and roebucks, and fallowdeer, and 354
La 1: 6 her princes are become like **h** *that* find no 354

HARUM (1)
1Ch 4: 8 and the families of Aharhel the son of **H**. 2037

HARUMAPH (1)
Ne 3:10 unto them repaired Jedaiah the son of **H**, 2739

HARUPHITE (1)
1Ch 12: 5 and Shemariah, and Shephatiah the **H**, 2741

HARUZ (1)
2Ki 21:19 the daughter of **H** of Jotbah. 2743

HARVEST (61) [HARVESTMAN]
Ge 8:22 seedtime and **h**, and cold and heat, and 7105
30:14 Reuben went in the days of wheat **h**, and 7105
45: 6 which *there shall* neither *be* earing nor **h**. 7105
Ex 23:16 the feast of **h**, the firstfruits of thy labours, 7105
34:21 in earing time and in **h** thou shalt rest. 7105
34:22 of the firstfruits of wheat **h**, and the feast of 7105
Lev 19: 9 when ye reap the **h** of your land, thou shalt 7105
19: 9 shalt thou gather the gleanings of thy **h**. 7105
23:10 shall reap the **h** thereof, then ye shall bring 7105
23:10 of the firstfruits of your **h** unto the priest: 7105
23:22 when ye reap the **h** of your land, thou shalt 7105
23:22 shalt thou gather *any* gleaning of thy **h**: 7105
25: 5 it own accord of thy **h** thou shalt not reap, 7105
Dt 24:19 When thou **cuttest down** thine **h** in 7105+7114
Jos 3:15 overfloweth all his banks all the time of **h**,) 7105
Jdg 15: 1 in the time of wheat **h**, that Samson visited 7105
Ru 1:22 *to* Beth-lehem in the beginning of barley **h**. 7105
2:21 young men, until they have ended all my **h**. 7105
2:23 of Boaz to glean unto the end of barley **h** 7105
2:23 the end of barley harvest and of wheat **h**; 7105
1Sa 6:13 *were* reaping *their* wheat **h** in the valley: 7105
8:12 to reap his **h**, and to make his instruments 7105
12:17 *Is it* not wheat **h** to day? I will call unto 7105
2Sa 21: 9 and were put to death in the days of **h**, 7105
21: 9 the first *days*, in the beginning of barley **h**. 7105
21:10 from the beginning of **h** until water 7105
23:13 came to David in the **h time** unto the cave 7105
Job 5: 5 Whose **h** the hungry eateth up, and taketh it 7105
Pr 6: 8 *and* gathereth her food in the **h**. 7105
10: 5 he that sleepeth in **h** *is* a son that causeth 7105
20: 4 therefore shall he beg in **h**, and 7105
25:13 As the cold of snow in the time of **h**, *so is* a 7105
26: 1 as rain in **h**, so honour *is* not seemly for a 7105
Isa 9: 3 joy before thee according to the joy in **h**, 7105
16: 9 thy summer fruits and for thy **h** is fallen. 7105
17:11 *but* the **h** *shall be* a heap in the day of grief 7105
18: 4 *and* like a cloud of dew in the heat of **h**. 7105
18: 5 For afore the **h**, when the bud is perfect, 7105
23: 3 of Sihor, the **h** of the river, *is* her revenue; 7105
Jer 5:17 they shall eat up thine **h**, and thy bread, 7105
5:24 unto us the appointed weeks of the **h**. 7105
8:20 The **h** is past, the summer is ended, and 7105
50:16 that handleth the sickle in the time of **h**; 7105
51:33 and the time of her **h** shall come. 7105
Hos 6:11 Also, O Judah, he hath set a **h** for thee, 7105
Joel 1:11 because the **h** of the field is perished. 7105
3:13 Put ye in the sickle, for the **h** is ripe: come, 7105
Am 4: 7 when *there were* yet three months to the **h**: 7105
Mt 9:37 The **h** truly is plenteous, but the labourers *2326*
9:38 Pray ye therefore the Lord of the **h**, that he *2326*
9:38 that he will send forth labourers into his **h**. *2326*
13:30 Let both grow together until the **h**: and *2326*
13:30 in the time of **h** I will say to the reapers, *2326*
13:39 the **h** is the end of the world; and *2326*
Mk 4:29 putteth in the sickle, because the **h** is come. *2326*
Lk 10: 2 The **h** truly *is* great, but the labourers *are* *2326*
10: 2 pray ye therefore the Lord of the **h**, that he *2326*
10: 2 he would send forth labourers into his **h**. *2326*
Jn 4:35 are yet four months, and *then* cometh **h**? *2326*
4:35 the fields; for they are white already to **h**. *2326*
Rev 14:15 thee to reap; for the **h** of the earth is ripe. *2326*

HARVESTMAN (2) [HARVEST, MAN]
Isa 17: 5 it shall be as when the **h** gathereth the corn, 7105
Jer 9:22 as the handful after the **h**, and none shall 7114

HASADIAH (1)
1Ch 3:20 Ohel, and Berechiah, and **H**, Jushabhesed, 2619

HASENUAH (1)
1Ch 9: 7 the son of Hodaviah, the son of **H**, 5574

HASHABIAH (15)
1Ch 6:45 The son of **H**, the son of Amaziah, the son 2811
9:14 the son of Azrikam, the son of **H**, of 2811
25: 3 Zeri, and Jeshaiah, **H**, and Mattithiah, six, 2811
25:19 The twelfth to **H**, *he*, his sons, and 2811
26:30 **H** and his brethren, men of valour, 2811
27:17 Of the Levites, **H** the son of Kemuel: of 2811
2Ch 35: 9 his brethren, and **H** and Jeiel and Jozabad, 2811
Ezr 8:19 **H**, and with him Jeshaiah of the sons of 2811
8:24 **H**, and ten of their brethren with them, 2811
Ne 3:17 Next unto him repaired **H**, the ruler of 2811
10:11 Micha, Rehob, **H**, 2811
11:15 of Azrikam, the son of **H**, the son of Bunni; 2811
11:22 the son of **H**, the son of Mattaniah, the son 2811
12:21 Of Hilkiah, **H**; of Jedaiah, Nethaneel. 2811
12:24 **H**, Sherebiah, and Jeshua the son of 2811

HASHABNAH (1)
Ne 10:25 Rehum, **H**, Maaseiah, 2812

HASHABNEIAH See HASHABNIAH

HASHABNIAH (2)
Ne 3:10 unto him repaired Hattush the son of **H**. 2813
9: 5 Jeshua and Kadmiel, Bani, **H**, Sherebiah, 2813

HASHBADANA (1)
Ne 8: 4 and Malchiah, and Hashum, and **H**, 2806

HASHBADDANA See HASHBADANA

HASHEM (1)
1Ch 11:34 The sons of **H** the Gizonite, Jonathan 2044

HASHMONAH (2)
Nu 33:29 they went from Mithcah, and pitched in **H**. 2832
33:30 they departed from **H**, and encamped at 2832

HASHUB (4)
Ne 3:11 **H** the son of Pahath-moab, repaired 2815
3:23 and **H** over against their house. 2815
10:23 Hoshea, Hananiah, **H**, 2815
11:15 Shemaiah the son of **H**, the son of 2815

HASHUBAH (1)
1Ch 3:20 **H**, and Ohel, and Berechiah, and Hasadiah, 2807

HASHUM (5)
Ezr 2:19 The children of **H**, two hundred twenty and 2828
10:33 Of the sons of **H**; Mattenai, Mattathah, 2828
Ne 7:22 The children of **H**, three hundred twenty 2828
8: 4 and Malchiah, and **H**, and Hashbadana, 2828
10:18 Hodijah, **H**, Bezai, 2828

HASHUPHA (1) [HASUPHA]
Ne 7:46 the children of Ziha, the children of **H**, 2817

HASRAH (1)
2Ch 34:22 the son of **H**, keeper of the wardrobe; 2641

HASSENAAH (1)
Ne 3: 3 the fish gate did the sons of **H** build, 5570

HASSENUAH See HASENUAH; SENUAH

HASSHUB (1)
1Ch 9:14 Shemaiah the son of **H**, the son of 2815

HAST (1071) [HAVE] See Index

HASTE (56) [HASTED, HASTEN, HASTENED, HASTENETH, HASTETH, HASTILY, HASTING, HASTY]
Ge 19:22 **H** thee, escape thither; for I cannot do any 4116
24:46 she **made h**, and let down her pitcher from 4116
43:30 Joseph **made h**; for his bowels did yern 4116
45: 9 **H** you, and go up to my father, and 4116
45:13 ye shall **h** and bring down my father hither. 4116
Ex 10:16 Pharaoh called for Moses and Aaron **in h**; 4116
12:11 staff in your hand; and ye shall eat it in **h**: 2649
12:33 they might send them out of the land **in h**; 4116
34: 8 Moses **made h**, and bowed his head toward 4116
Dt 16: 3 camest forth out of the land of Egypt in **h**: 2649
32:35 things that shall come upon them **make h**. 2363
Jdg 9:48 me do, **make h**, *and* do as I *have done*. 4116
13:10 the woman **made h**, and ran, and 4116
1Sa 9:12 **make h** now, for he came to day to the city; 4116
20:38 cried after the lad, Make speed, **h**, stay not. 2363
21: 8 because the king's business required **h**. 5169
23:26 David **made h** to get away for fear of Saul; 2648
23:27 unto Saul, saying, **H** thee, and come; 4116
25:18 Abigail **made h**, and took two hundred 4116
2Sa 4: 4 as she **made h** to flee, that he fell, and 2648

H

2Ki 7:15 which the Syrians had cast away in their **h**. 2648
2Ch 24: 5 year to year, and *see that* ye **h** the matter. 4116
35:21 for God commanded me to **make h**: 926
Ezr 4:23 they went up in **h** to Jerusalem unto 924
Est 5: 5 the king said, **Cause** Haman **to make h**, 4116
6:10 **Make h**, *and* take the apparel and 4116
Job 20: 2 cause me to answer, and for *this* I **make h**. 2363
Ps 22:19 O my strength, **h** thee to help me. 2363
31:22 For I said in my **h**, I am cut off from before 2648
38:22 **Make h** to help me, O Lord my salvation. 2363
40:13 deliver me: O LORD, **make h** to help me. 2363
70: 1 *Make h*, O God, to deliver me; make haste NIH
70: 1 deliver me; **make h** to help me, O LORD. 2363
70: 5 **make h** unto me, O God: thou *art* my help 2363
71:12 from me: O my God, **make h** for my help. 2363
116:11 I said in my **h**, All men *are* liars. 2648
119:60 I **made h**, and delayed not to keep thy 2363
141: 1 **make h** unto me; give ear unto my voice, 2363
Pr 1:16 feet run to evil, and **make h** to shed blood. 4116
28:20 he that **maketh h** to be rich shall not be 213
SS 8:14 **Make h**, my beloved, and be thou like to a 1272
Isa 28:16 he that believeth shall not **make h**. 2363
49:17 Thy children shall **make h**; thy destroyers 4116
52:12 For ye shall not go out with **h**, nor go by 2649
59: 7 and they **make h** to shed innocent blood: 4116
Jer 9:18 let them **make h**, and take up a wailing for 4116
Da 2:25 brought in Daniel before the king in **h**, 927
3:24 rose up in **h**, *and* spake, and said unto his 927
6:19 and went in **h** unto the den of lions. 927
Na 2: 5 they shall **make h** *to* the wall thereof, and 4116
Mk 6:25 And she came in straightway with **h** unto *4710*
Lk 1:39 and went into the hill country with **h**, into a *4710*
2:16 And they came **with h**, and found Mary, *4692*
19: 5 Zaccheus, **make h**, and come down; *4692*
19: 6 And he **made h**, and came down, and *4692*
Ac 22:18 **Make h**, and get *thee* quickly out of *4692*

HASTED (24) [HASTE]
Ge 18: 7 *it* unto a young man; and he **h** to dress it. 4116
24:18 she **h**, and let down her pitcher upon her 4116
24:20 she **h**, and emptied her pitcher into 4116
Ex 5:13 the taskmasters **h** *them*, saying, Fulfil your 213
Jos 4:10 and the people **h** and passed over. 4116
8:14 when the king of Ai saw *it*, that they **h** and 4116
8:19 and took it, and **h** and set the city on fire. 4116
10:13 and **h** not to go down about a whole day. 213
Jdg 20:37 the liers in wait **h**, and rushed upon Gibeah; 2363
1Sa 17:48 that David **h**, and ran *toward* the army to 4116
25:23 she **h**, and lighted off the ass, and 4116
25:34 except thou hadst **h** and come to meet me, 4116
25:42 Abigail **h**, and rose, and rode upon an ass, 4116
28:24 she **h**, and killed it, and took flour, and 4116
2Sa 19:16 **h** and came down with the men of Judah to 4116
1Ki 20:41 he **h**, and took the ashes away from his 4116
2Ki 9:13 they **h**, and took every man his garment, 4116
2Ch 26:20 yea, himself **h** also to go out, because 1765
Est 6:12 Haman **h** to his house mourning, and 1765
6:14 **h** to bring Haman unto the banquet that 926
Job 31: 5 with vanity, or *if* my foot hath **h** to deceit; 2363
Ps 48: 5 they were troubled, *and* **h away**. 2648
104: 7 at the voice of thy thunder they **h away**. 2648
Ac 20:16 for he **h**, if it were possible for him, to be at *4692*

HASTEN (7) [HASTE]
1Ki 22: 9 said, **H** *hither* Micaiah the son of Imlah. 4116
Ps 16: 4 Their sorrows shall be multiplied *that* **h** 4116
55: 8 I would **h** my escape from the windy storm 2363
Ecc 2:25 or who else can **h** *hereunto*, more than I? 2363
Isa 5:19 *and* **h** his work, that we may see *it*: and 2363
60:22 I the LORD will **h** it in his time. 2363
Jer 1:12 for I will **h** my word to perform it. 8245

HASTENED (6) [HASTE]
Ge 18: 6 Abraham **h** into the tent unto Sarah, and 4116
19:15 the angels **h** Lot, saying, Arise, take thy 213
2Ch 24: 5 the matter. Howbeit the Levites **h** *it* not. 4116
Est 3:15 being **h** by the king's commandment, and 1765
8:14 being **h** and pressed on by the king's 926
Jer 17:16 I have not **h** from *being* a pastor to follow 213

HASTENETH (1) [HASTE]
Isa 51:14 The captive exile **h** that *he* may be loosed, 4116

HASTETH (9) [HASTE]
Job 9:26 swift ships: as the eagle *that* **h** to the prey. 2907
40:23 Behold, he drinketh up a river, *and* **h** not: 2648
Pr 7:23 as a bird **h** to the snare, and knoweth not 4116
19: 2 not good; and he that **h** with *his* feet, sinneth. 213
28:22 He that **h** to be rich *hath* an evil eye, and 926
Ecc 1: 5 and **h** to his place where he arose. 7602
Jer 48:16 *is* near to come, and his affliction **h** fast. 4116
Hab 1: 8 they shall fly as the eagle *that* **h** to eat. 2363
Zep 1:14 the LORD *is* near, *it is* near, and **h** greatly, 4118

HASTILY (8) [HASTE]
Ge 41:14 they **brought** him **h** out of the dungeon: 7323
Jdg 2:23 those nations, without driving them out **h**; 4118
9:54 he called **h** unto the young man his 4120
1Sa 4:14 And the man came in **h**, and told Eli. 4116
1Ki 20:33 did **h** catch *it*: and they said, Thy brother 4116
Pr 20:21 An inheritance *may be* **gotten h** at 926
25: 8 Go not forth **h** to strive, lest *thou know not* 4118
Jn 11:31 that she rose up **h** and went out, *5030*

HASTING (2) [HASTE]
Isa 16: 5 and seeking judgment, and **h** righteousness. 4106
2Pe 3:12 and **h** *unto* the coming of the day of God, *4692*

HASTY (9) [HASTE]
Pr 14:29 but *he that is* **h** of spirit exalteth folly. 7116
21: 5 but *of* every one that is **h** only to want. 213
29:20 Seest thou a man that is **h** in his words? 213
Ecc 5: 2 let not thine heart be **h** to utter *any* thing 4116
7: 9 Be not **h** in thy spirit to be angry: for anger 926
8: 3 Be not **h** to go out of his sight: stand not in 926
Isa 28: 4 *and* as the **h fruit** before the summer; 1061
Da 2:15 Why *is* the decree *so* **h** from the king? 2685
Hab 1: 6 up the Chaldeans, *that* bitter and **h** nation, 4116

HASUPHA (1) [HASHUPHA]
Ezr 2:43 the children of Ziha, the children of **H**, 2817

HATACH (4)
Est 4: 5 called Esther for **H**, *one* of the king's 2047
4: 6 So **H** went forth to Mordecai unto the street 2047
4: 9 **H** came and told Esther the words of 2047
4:10 Again Esther spake unto **H**, and gave him 2047

HATCH (2) [HATCHETH]
Isa 34:15 lay, and **h**, and gather under her shadow: 1234
59: 5 They **h** cockatrice' eggs, and weave 1234

HATCHETH (1) [HATCH]
Jer 17:11 partridge sitteth *on eggs*, and **h** *them* not; 3205

HATE (87) [HATED, HATEFUL, HATEFULLY, HATERS, HATEST, HATETH, HATING, HATRED]
Ge 24:60 possess the gate of those which **h** them. 8130
26:27 seeing ye **h** me, and have sent me away 8130
50:15 Joseph will peradventure **h** us, and 7852
Ex 20: 5 and fourth *generation* of them that **h** me; 8130
Lev 19:17 Thou shalt not **h** thy brother in thine heart: 8130
26:17 they that **h** you shall reign over you; and 8130
Nu 10:35 and let them that **h** thee flee before thee. 8130
Dt 5: 9 and fourth *generation* of them that **h** me, 8130
7:10 repayeth them that **h** him to their face, 8130
7:15 but will lay them upon all *them* that **h** thee. 8130
19:11 if any man **h** his neighbour, and lie in wait 8130
22:13 take a wife, and go in unto her, and **h** her, 8130
24: 3 *if* the latter husband **h** her, and write her a 8130
30: 7 on them that **h** thee, which persecuted thee. 8130
32:41 and will reward them that **h** me. 8130
33:11 of them that **h** him, that they rise not again. 8130
Jdg 11: 7 Did not ye **h** me, and expel me out of my 8130
14:16 Thou dost but **h** me, and lovest me not: 8130
2Sa 22:41 that I might destroy them that **h** me. 8130
1Ki 22: 8 I **h** him; for he doth not prophesy good 8130
2Ch 18: 7 I **h** him; for he never prophesied good unto 8130
19: 2 and love them that **h** the LORD? 8130
Job 8:22 They that **h** thee shall be clothed with 8130
Ps 9:13 trouble *which I suffer* of them that **h** me, 8130
18:40 that I might destroy them that **h** me. 8130
21: 8 thy right hand shall find out those that **h** 8130
25:19 are many; and they **h** me *with* cruel hatred. 8130
34:21 they that **h** the righteous shall be desolate. 8130
35:19 *neither* let them wink *with* the eye that **h** 8130
38:19 they that **h** me wrongfully are multiplied. 8130

H

Ps 41: 7 All that **h** me whisper together against me: 8130
44:10 and they which **h** us spoil for themselves. 8130
55: 3 iniquity upon me, and in wrath they **h** me. 7852
68: 1 let them also that **h** him flee before him. 8130
69: 4 They that **h** me without a cause are moe 8130
69:14 let me be delivered from them that **h** me, 8130
83: 2 and they that **h** thee have lift up the head. 8130
86:17 that they which **h** me may see *it,* and 8130
89:23 his face, and plague them that **h** him. 8130
97:10 Ye that love the LORD, **h** evil: 8130
101: 3 I **h** the work of them that turn aside; *it* shall 8130
105:25 He turned their heart to **h** his people, 8130
118: 7 shall I see *my desire* upon them that **h** me. 8130
119:104 I **h** every false way. 8130
119:113 I **h** *vain* thoughts: but thy law do I love. 8130
119:128 *things* to be right; *and* I **h** every false way. 8130
119:163 I **h** and abhor lying: *but* thy law do I love. 8130
129: 5 be confounded and turned back that **h** Zion. 8130
139:21 Do not I **h** them, O LORD, that hate thee? 8130
139:21 Do not I hate them, O LORD, that **h** thee? 8130
139:22 I **h** them *with* perfect hatred: I count them 8130
Pr 1:22 in their scorning, and fools **h** knowledge? 8130
6:16 These six *things* doth the LORD **h**: yea, 8130
8:13 The fear of the LORD *is* to **h** evil: pride, 8130
8:13 evil way, and the froward mouth, do I **h**. 8130
8:36 his own soul: all they that **h** me love death. 8130
9: 8 Reprove not a scorner, lest he **h** thee: 8130
19: 7 All the brethren of the poor do **h** him: 8130
25:17 lest he be weary *of* thee, and *so* **h** thee. 8130
29:10 The bloodthirsty **h** the upright: but the just 8130
Ecc 3: 8 A time to love, and a time to **h**; a time of 8130
Isa 61: 8 I **h** robbery for burnt offering; 8130
Jer 44: 4 Oh, do not this abominable thing that I **h**. 8130
Eze 16:27 delivered thee unto the will of them that **h** 8130
Da 4:19 the dream *be* to them that **h** thee, and 8131
Am 5:10 They **h** him that rebuketh in the gate, and 8130
5:15 **H** the evil, and love the good, and 8130
5:21 I **h**, I despise your feast *days,* and I will not 8130
6: 8 the excellency of Jacob, and **h** his palaces: 8130
Mic 3: 2 Who **h** the good, and love the evil; 8130
Zec 8:17 for all these *are things* that I **h**, saith 8130
Mt 5:43 love thy neighbour, and **h** thine enemy. *3404*
5:44 do good to them that **h** you, and pray for *3404*
6:24 for either he will **h** the one, and love *3404*
24:10 betray one another, and shall **h** one another. *3404*
Lk 1:71 and from the hand of all that **h** us; *3404*
6:22 when men shall **h** you, and when they shall *3404*
6:27 do good to them which **h** you, *3404*
14:26 and **h** not his father, and mother, and wife, *3404*
16:13 for either he will **h** the one, and love *3404*
Jn 7: 7 The world cannot **h** you; but me it hateth, *3404*
15:18 If the world **h** you, ye know that it hated *3404*
Ro 7:15 that do I not; but what I **h**, that do I. *3404*
1Jn 3:13 my brethren, if the world **h** you. *3404*
Rev 2: 6 the deeds of the Nicolaitans, which I also **h**. *3404*
2:15 doctrine of the Nicolaitans, which *thing* I **h**. *3404*
17:16 these shall **h** the whore, and shall make her *3404*

HATED (60) [HATE]

Ge 27:41 Esau **h** Jacob because of the blessing 7852
29:31 when the LORD saw that Leah *was* **h**, 8130
29:33 the LORD hath heard that I *was* **h**, 8130
37: 4 they **h** him, and could not speak peaceably 8130
37: 5 his brethren: and they **h** him yet the more. 8130
37: 8 they **h** him yet the more for his dreams, 8130
49:23 grieved him, and shot *at him,* and **h** him: 7852
Dt 1:27 and said, Because the LORD **h** us, 8135
4:42 and **h** him not in times past; 8130
9:28 because he **h** them, he hath brought them 8135
19: 4 whom he **h** not in time past; 8130
19: 6 inasmuch as he **h** him not in time past. 8130
21:15 another **h**, and they have born him children, 8130
21:15 him children, *both* the beloved and the **h**; 8130
21:15 and *if* the firstborn son be hers that was **h**: 8146
21:16 beloved firstborn before the son of the **h**, 8130
21:17 he shall acknowledge the son of the **h** *for* 8130
Jos 20: 5 and **h** him not beforetime. 8130
Jdg 15: 2 thought that thou hadst **utterly h** her; 8130+8130
2Sa 5: 8 and the blind, *that are* **h** of David's soul, 8130
13:15 **h** her **exceedingly**; 1419+3966+8130+8135
13:15 that the hatred wherewith he **h** her *was* 8130
13:22 for Absalom **h** Amnon, because he had 8130
22:18 strong enemy, *and* from them that **h** me: 8130
Est 9: 1 the Jews had rule over them that **h** them;) 8130
9: 5 did what they would unto those that **h** 8130
Job 31:29 If I rejoiced at the destruction of him that **h** 8130
Ps 18:17 strong enemy, and from them which **h** me: 8130
26: 5 I have **h** the congregation of evildoers; and 8130
31: 6 I have **h** them that regard lying vanities: but 8130
44: 7 and hast put them to shame that **h** us. 8130
55:12 **h** me *that* did magnify *himself* against me; 8130
106:10 he saved them from the hand of him that **h** 8130
106:41 and they that **h** them ruled over them. 8130
Pr 1:29 For that they **h** knowledge, and did not 8130
5:12 How have I **h** instruction, and my heart 8130
14:17 and a man of wicked devices is **h**. 8130
14:20 The poor is **h** even of his own neighbour: 8130
Ecc 2:17 Therefore I **h** life; because the work that is 8130
2:18 I **h** all my labour which I *had* taken under 8130
Isa 60:15 Whereas thou hast been forsaken and **h**, so 8130
66: 5 Your brethren that **h** you, that cast you out 8130
Jer 12: 8 crieth out against me: therefore have I **h** it. 8130
Eze 16:37 hast loved, with all *them* that thou hast **h**; 8130
35: 6 sith thou hast not **h** blood, even blood shall 8130
Hos 9:15 wickedness *is* in Gilgal, for there I **h** them: 8130
Mal 1: 3 I **h** Esau, and laid his mountains and his 8130
Mt 10:22 And ye shall be **h** of all *men* for my name's *3404*
24: 9 ye shall be **h** of all nations for my name's *3404*
Mk 13:13 And ye shall be **h** of all *men* for my name's *3404*
Lk 19:14 But his citizens **h** him, and sent a message *3404*
21:17 And ye shall be **h** of all *men* for my name's *3404*
Jn 15:18 ye know that it **h** me before *it hated* you. *3404*
15:18 ye know that it hated me before *it* **h** you. NIG
15:24 both seen and **h** both me and my Father. *3404*
15:25 in their law, They **h** me without a cause. *3404*
17:14 and the world hath **h** them, because *3404*
Ro 9:13 Jacob have I loved, but Esau have I **h**. *3404*
Eph 5:29 For no *man* ever yet **h** his own flesh; but *3404*
Heb 1: 9 hast loved righteousness, and **h** iniquity; *3404*

HATEFUL (3) [HATE]

Ps 36: 2 until his iniquity be found to be **h**. 8130
Tit 3: 3 and envy, **h**, *and* hating one another. *4767*
Rev 18: 2 and a cage of every unclean and **h** bird. *3404*

HATEFULLY (1) [HATE]

Eze 23:29 they shall deal with thee **h**, and 8135+871.1

HATERS (2) [HATE]

Ps 81:15 The **h** of the LORD should have 8130
Ro 1:30 **h of God**, despiteful, proud, boasters, *2319*

HATEST (6) [HATE]

2Sa 19: 6 lovest thine enemies, and **h** thy friends: 8130
Ps 5: 5 in thy sight: thou **h** all workers of iniquity. 8130
45: 7 lovest righteousness, and **h** wickedness: 8130
50:17 Seeing thou **h** instruction, and castest my 8130
Eze 23:28 thee into the hand *of them* whom thou **h**, 8130
Rev 2: 6 that thou **h** the deeds of the Nicolaitans, *3404*

HATETH (31) [HATE]

Ex 23: 5 If thou see the ass of him that **h** thee lying 8130
Dt 7:10 he will not be slack to him that **h** him, 8130
12:31 which he **h**, have they done unto their gods; 8130
16:22 *any* image; which the LORD thy God **h**. 8130
22:16 unto this man to wife, and he **h** her; 8130
Job 16: 9 He teareth *me in* his wrath, who **h** me: 7852
34:17 Shall even he that **h** right govern? and wilt 8130
Ps 11: 5 and him that loveth violence his soul **h**. 8130
120: 6 My soul hath long dwelt with him that **h** 8130
Pr 11:15 smart *for it:* and he that **h** suretiship *is* sure. 8130
12: 1 but he that **h** reproof *is* brutish. 8130
13: 5 A righteous *man* **h** lying: but a wicked *man* 8130
13:24 He that spareth his rod **h** his son: but 8130
15:10 the way: *and* he that **h** reproof shall die. 8130
15:27 his own house; but he that **h** gifts shall live. 8130
26:24 He that **h** dissembleth with his lips, and 8130
26:28 A lying tongue **h** *those that are* afflicted by 8130
28:16 he that **h** covetousness shall prolong *his* 8130
29:24 Whoso is partner with a thief **h** his own 8130
Isa 1:14 and your appointed feasts my soul **h**: 8130
Mal 2:16 God of Israel, saith that he **h** putting away: 8130
Jn 3:20 For every one that doeth evil **h** the light, *3404*
7: 7 but me it **h**, because I testify of it, that *3404*
12:25 he that **h** his life in this world shall keep it *3404*
15:19 out of the world, therefore the world **h** you. *3404*
15:23 He that **h** me hateth my Father also. *3404*
15:23 He that hateth me **h** my Father also. *3404*

1Jn 2: 9 and **h** his brother, is in darkness *even* until 3404
2:11 But he that **h** his brother is in darkness, and 3404
3:15 Whosoever **h** his brother is a murderer: and 3404
4:20 I love God, and **h** his brother, he is a liar: 3404

HATH (2262) [HAVE] See Index

HATHACH See HATACH

HATHATH (1)
1Ch 4:13 and Seraiah: and the sons of Othniel; **H.** 2867

HATING (3) [HATE]
Ex 18:21 as fear God, men of truth, **h** covetousness; 8130
Tit 3: 3 and envy, hateful, *and* **h** one another. 3404
Jude 1:23 **h** even the garment spotted by the flesh. 3404

HATIPHA (2)
Ezr 2:54 The children of Neziah, the children of **H.** 2412
Ne 7:56 The children of Neziah, the children of **H.** 2412

HATITA (2)
Ezr 2:42 the children of Akkub, the children of **H,** 2410
Ne 7:45 the children of Akkub, the children of **H,** 2410

HATRED (18) [HATE]
Nu 35:20 if he thrust him of **h**, or hurl at him by 8135
2Sa 13:15 that the **h** wherewith he hated her *was* 8135
Ps 25:19 and they hate me *with* **cruel h.** 2555+8135
109: 3 compassed me about also *with* words of **h**; 8135
109: 5 me evil for good, and **h** for my love. 8135
139:22 I hate them *with* perfect **h**: I count them 8135
Pr 10:12 **H** stirreth up strifes: but love covereth all 8135
10:18 He that hideth **h** *with* lying lips, and he that 8135
15:17 love is, than a stalled ox and **h** therewith. 8135
26:26 *Whose* **h** is covered by deceit, 8135
Ecc 9: 1 either love or **h** *by* all *that is* before them. 8135
9: 6 Also their love, and their **h**, and their envy, 8135
Eze 25:15 a despiteful heart, to destroy *it for* the old **h**; 342
35: 5 Because thou hast had a perpetual **h**, and 342
35:11 thou hast used out of thy **h** against them; 8135
Hos 9: 7 multitude of thine iniquity, and the great **h.** 4895
9: 8 all his ways, *and* **h** in the house of his God. 4895
Gal 5:20 Idolatry, witchcraft, **h**, variance, 2189

HATS (1)
Da 3:21 their **h**, and their *other* garments, and 3737

HATTIL (2)
Ezr 2:57 children of Shephatiah, the children of **H,** 2411
Ne 7:59 children of Shephatiah, the children of **H,** 2411

HATTUSH (5)
1Ch 3:22 **H**, and Igeal, and Bariah, and Neariah, and 2407
Ezr 8: 2 of Ithamar; Daniel: of the sons of David; **H.** 2407
Ne 3:10 next unto him repaired **H** the son of 2407
10: 4 **H**, Shebaniah, Malluch, 2407
12: 2 Amariah, Malluch, **H,** 2407

HAUGHTILY (1) [HAUGHTY]
Mic 2: 3 remove your necks; neither shall ye go **h**: 7317

HAUGHTINESS (5) [HAUGHTY]
Isa 2:11 the **h** of men shall be bowed down, and 7312
2:17 and the **h** of men shall be made low: 7312
13:11 and will lay low the **h** of the terrible. 1346
16: 6 *even* of his **h**, and his pride, and his wrath: 1346
Jer 48:29 and his pride, and the **h** of his heart. 7312

HAUGHTY (10) [HAUGHTINESS]
2Sa 22:28 thine eyes *are* upon the **h**, *that* thou mayest 7311
Ps 131: 1 LORD, my heart is not **h**, nor mine eyes 1361
Pr 16:18 and a **h** spirit before a fall. 1363
18:12 Before destruction the heart of man is **h**, 1361
21:24 Proud *and* **h** scorner *is* his name, 3093
Isa 3:16 Because the daughters of Zion are **h**, and 1361
10:33 *be* hewn down, and the **h** shall be humbled. 1364
24: 4 the **h** people of the earth do languish. 4791
Eze 16:50 they were **h**, and committed abomination 1361
Zep 3:11 thou shalt no more be **h** because of my holy 1361

HAUNT (3)
1Sa 23:22 know and see his place where his **h** is, *and* 7272
30:31 David himself and his men were **wont to h.** 1980
Eze 26:17 which cause their terror *to be* on all that **h** 3427

HAURAN (2)
Eze 47:16 Hazar-hatticon, which *is* by the coast of **H.** 2362
47:18 the east side ye shall measure from **H**, and 2362

HAVE (3902) [HAD, HADST, HAST, HATH, HAVING] See Index

HAVEN (5) [HAVENS]
Ge 49:13 Zebulun shall dwell at the **h** of the sea; and 2348
49:13 he *shall be* for a **h** of ships; and his border 2348
Ps 107:30 so he bringeth them unto their desired **h.** 4231
Ac 27:12 the **h** was not commodious to winter in, 3040
27:12 *which is* a **h** of Crete, and lieth toward 3040

HAVENS (1) [HAVEN]
Ac 27: 8 unto a place *which is* called The **fair h**; 2568

HAVILAH (7)
Ge 2:11 *is it* which compasseth the whole land of **H,** 2341
10: 7 **H**, and Sabtah, and Raamah, and Sabtecha: 2341
10:29 Ophir, and **H**, and Jobab: all these *were* 2341
25:18 they dwelt from **H** unto Shur, that *is* before 2341
1Sa 15: 7 Saul smote the Amalekites from **H** *until* 2341
1Ch 1: 9 **H**, and Sabta, and Raamah, and Sabtecha. 2341
1:23 Ophir, and **H**, and Jobab. All these *were* 2341

HAVING (193) [HAVE] See Index

HAVOCK (1)
Ac 8: 3 As for Saul, he **made h** of the church, 3075

HAVOTH-JAIR (2) [BASHAN-HAVOTH-JAIR]
Nu 32:41 the small towns thereof, and called them **H.** 2334
Jdg 10: 4 which are called **H** unto this day, 2334

HAVVOTH JAIR See BASHAN-HAVOTH-JAIR; HAVOTH-JAIR

HAWK (5)
Lev 11:16 the **night h**, and the cuckow, and the hawk 8464
11:16 and the cuckow, and the **h** after his kind, 5322
Dt 14:15 the **night h**, and the cuckow, and the hawk 8464
14:15 and the cuckow, and the **h** after his kind, 5322
Job 39:26 Doth the **h** fly by thy wisdom, *and* 5322

HAY (3)
Pr 27:25 The **h** appeareth, and the tender grass 2682
Isa 15: 6 for the **h** is withered away, the grass faileth, 2682
1Co 3:12 silver, precious stones, wood, **h**, stubble; 5528

HAZAEL (23)
1Ki 19:15 anoint **H** to be king over Syria: 2371
19:17 *that* him that escapeth the sword of **H** shall 2371
2Ki 8: 8 the king said unto **H**, Take a present in 2371
8: 9 So **H** went to meet him, and took a present 2371
8:12 **H** said, Why weepeth my lord? And he 2371
8:13 **H** said, But what, *is* thy servant a dog, 2371
8:15 so that he died: and **H** reigned in his stead. 2371
8:28 against **H** king of Syria in Ramoth-gilead; 2371
8:29 when he fought against **H** king of Syria. 2371
9:14 and all Israel, because of **H** king of Syria. 2371
9:15 when he fought with **H** king of Syria.) 2371
10:32 **H** smote them in all the coasts of Israel; 2371
12:17 **H** king of Syria went up, and fought against 2371
12:17 and **H** set his face to go up to Jerusalem. 2371
12:18 king's house, and sent *it* to **H** king of Syria: 2371
13: 3 he delivered them into the hand of **H** king 2371
13: 3 into the hand of Ben-hadad the son of **H,** 2371
13:22 **H** king of Syria oppressed Israel all 2371
13:24 So **H** king of Syria died; and Ben-hadad his 2371
13:25 hand of Ben-hadad the son of **H** the cities, 2371
2Ch 22: 5 against **H** king of Syria at Ramoth-gilead: 2371
22: 6 when he fought with **H** king of Syria. 2371
Am 1: 4 I will send a fire into the house of **H,** 2371

HAZAIAH (1)
Ne 11: 5 the son of **H**, the son of Adaiah, the son of 2382

HAZAR-ADDAR (1) [ADDAR]
Nu 34: 4 shall go on *to* **H**, and pass on to Azmon: 2692

HAZARDED (1)
Ac 15:26 Men that have **h** their lives for the name of 3860

HAZAR-ENAN (4) [ENAN]
Nu 34: 9 and the goings out of it shall be at **H**: 2704
34:10 ye shall point out your east border from **H** 2704

Eze 47:17 the border from the sea shall be **H**, 2703
48: 1 as *one* goeth to Hamath, **H**, the border of 2704

HAZAR-GADDAH (1)
Jos 15:27 And **H**, and Heshmon, and Beth-palet, 2693

HAZAR-HATTICON (1)
Eze 47:16 **H**, which *is* by the coast of Hauran. 2691

HAZARMAVETH (2)
Ge 10:26 and Sheleph, and **H**, and Jerah, 2700
1Ch 1:20 and Sheleph, and **H**, and Jerah, 2700

HAZAR-SHUAL (4) [SHUAL]
Jos 15:28 And **H**, and Beer-sheba, and Bizjothjah, 2705
19: 3 And **H**, and Balah, and Azem, 2705
1Ch 4:28 dwelt at Beer-sheba, and Moladah, and **H**, 2705
Ne 11:27 at **H**, and at Beer-sheba, and *in* the villages 2705

HAZAR-SUSAH (1) [HAZAR-SUSIM]
Jos 19: 5 And Ziklag, and Beth-marcaboth, and **H**, 2701

HAZAR-SUSIM (1) [HAZAR-SUSAH]
1Ch 4:31 and **H**, and at Beth-birei, and at Shaaraim. 2702

HAZAZON-TAMAR (1) [HAZEZON-TAMAR, TAMAR]
2Ch 20: 2 and behold, they *be* in **H**, which *is* En-gedi. 2688

HAZEL (1)
Ge 30:37 green poplar, and of the **h** and chesnut tree; 3869

HAZELELPONI (1)
1Ch 4: 3 Idbash: and the name of their sister *was* **H**: 6753

HAZER HATTICON See HAZAR-HATTICON

HAZERIM (1)
Dt 2:23 the Avims which dwelt in **H**, *even* unto 2699

HAZEROTH (6)
Nu 11:35 journeyed from Kibroth-hattaavah *unto* **H**; 2698
11:35 *unto* Hazeroth; and abode at **H**. 2698
12:16 afterward the people removed from **H**, and 2698
33:17 and encamped at **H**. 2698
33:18 they departed from **H**, and pitched in 2698
Dt 1: 1 and Laban, and **H**, and Dizahab. 2698

HAZEZON-TAMAR (1) [HAZAZON-TAMAR, TAMAR]
Ge 14: 7 and also the Amorites, that dwelt in **H**. 2688

HAZIEL (1)
1Ch 23: 9 Shelomith, and **H**, and Haran, three. 2381

HAZO (1)
Ge 22:22 **H**, and Pildash, and Jidlaph, and Bethuel. 2375

HAZOR (18) [BAAL-HAZOR, HAZOR HADATTAH]
Jos 11: 1 when Jabin king of **H** had heard *those* 2674
11:10 took **H**, and smote the king thereof with 2674
11:10 for **H** beforetime *was* the head of all those 2674
11:11 left to breathe: and he burnt **H** with fire. 2674
11:13 Israel burned none of them, save **H** only; 2674
12:19 king of Madon, one; the king of **H**, one; 2674
15:23 And Kedesh, and **H**, and Ithnan, 2674
15:25 and Kerioth, *and* Hezron, which *is* **H**, 2674
19:36 And Adamah, and Ramah, and **H**, 2674
Jdg 4: 2 of Jabin king of Canaan, that reigned in **H**; 2674
4:17 *was* peace between Jabin the king of **H** 2674
1Sa 12: 9 captain of the host of **H**, and into the hand 2674
1Ki 9:15 and **H**, and Megiddo, and Gezer. 2674
2Ki 15:29 and **H**, and Gilead, and Galilee, 2674
Ne 11:33 **H**, Ramah, Gittaim, 2674
Jer 49:28 and concerning the kingdoms of **H**, 2674
49:30 far off, dwell deep, O ye inhabitants of **H**, 2674
49:33 **H** shall be a dwelling for dragons, *and* 2674

HAZOR HADATTAH (1) [HAZOR]
Jos 15:25 **H**, and Kerioth, *and* Hezron, 2675

HAZZELELPONI See HAZELELPONI

HAZZOBEBAH See ZOBEBAH

HE (10430) [HIM, HIMSELF, HIS] See Index

HEAD (364) [FOREHEAD, FOREHEADS, GRAYHEADED, HEADBANDS, HEADLONG, HEADS, HEADSTONE, HEADY]
Ge 3:15 it shall bruise thy **h**, and thou shalt bruise 7218
24:26 the man **bowed down** his **h**, and 6915
24:48 I **bowed down** my **h**, and worshipped 6915
40:13 three days shall Pharaoh lift up thine **h**, 7218
40:16 behold, *I had* three white baskets on my **h**: 7218
40:17 did eat them out of the basket upon my **h**. 7218
40:19 shall Pharaoh lift up thy **h** from off thee, 7218
40:20 he lifted up the **h** of the chief butler and 7218
47:31 And Israel bowed himself upon the bed's **h**. 7218
48:14 laid *it* upon Ephraim's **h**, who *was* 7218
48:14 and his left hand upon Manasseh's **h**, 7218
48:17 laid his right hand upon the **h** of Ephraim, 7218
48:17 to remove it from Ephraim's **h** unto 7218
48:17 it from Ephraim's head unto Manasseh's **h**. 7218
48:18 the firstborn; put thy right hand upon his **h**. 7218
49:26 they shall be on the **h** of Joseph, and on 7218
49:26 on the **crown of the h** of him *that was* 6936
Ex 12: 9 his **h** with his legs, and with the purtenance 7218
12:27 the people **bowed the h** and worshipped. 6915
26:24 they shall be coupled together above the **h** 7218
29: 6 thou shalt put the mitre upon his **h**, and 7218
29: 7 and pour *it* upon his **h**, and anoint him. 7218
29:10 his sons shall put their hands upon the **h** of 7218
29:15 his sons shall put their hands upon the **h** of 7218
29:17 put *them* unto his pieces, and unto his **h**. 7218
29:19 his sons shall put their hands upon the **h** of 7218
34: 8 **bowed** his **h** toward the earth, and 6915
36:29 coupled together at the **h** thereof, to one 7218
Lev 1: 4 he shall put his hand upon the **h** of 7218
1: 8 shall lay the parts, the **h**, and the fat, 7218
1:12 cut it into his pieces, with his **h** and his fat: 7218
1:15 and wring off his **h**, and burn *it* on the altar; 7218
3: 2 he shall lay his hand upon the **h** of his 7218
3: 8 he shall lay his hand upon the **h** of his 7218
3:13 he shall lay his hand upon the **h** of it, and 7218
4: 4 shall lay his hand upon the bullock's **h**, and 7218
4:11 with his **h**, and with his legs, and 7218
4:15 the **h** of the bullock before the LORD: 7218
4:24 he shall lay his hand upon the **h** of the goat, 7218
4:29 he shall lay his hand upon the **h** of the sin 7218
4:33 he shall lay his hand upon the **h** of the sin 7218
5: 8 wring off his **h** from his neck, but shall not 7218
8: 9 he put the mitre upon his **h**; also upon 7218
8:12 poured of the anointing oil upon Aaron's **h**, 7218
8:14 his sons laid their hands upon the **h** of 7218
8:18 his sons laid their hands upon the **h** of 7218
8:20 Moses burnt the **h**, and the pieces, and 7218
8:22 his sons laid their hands upon the **h** of 7218
9:13 with the pieces thereof, and the **h**: 7218
13:12 *hath* the plague from his **h** even to his foot, 7218
13:29 or woman hath a plague upon the **h** or 7218
13:30 *even* a leprosy upon the **h** or beard. 7218
13:40 the man whose hair is fallen off his **h**, he *is* 7218
13:41 off from the part of *his h toward* his face, NIH
13:42 if there be in the **bald h**, or bald forehead, 7146
13:42 it *is* a leprosy sprung up in his **bald h**, or 7146
13:43 of the sore *be* white reddish in his **bald h**, 7146
13:44 him utterly unclean, his plague *is* in his **h**. 7218
13:45 his **h** bare, and he shall put a covering upon 7218
14: 9 *that* he shall shave all his hair off his **h** and 7218
14:18 upon the **h** of him that is to be cleansed: 7218
14:29 put upon the **h** of him that is to be cleansed, 7218
16:21 Aaron shall lay both his hands upon the **h** 7218
16:21 putting them upon the **h** of the goat, and 7218
19:32 Thou shalt rise up before the **hoary h**, and 7872
21: 5 They shall not make baldness upon their **h**, 7218
21:10 upon whose **h** the anointing oil was poured, 7218
21:10 shall not uncover his **h**, nor rend his 7218
24:14 that heard *him* lay their hands upon his **h**, 7218
Nu 1: 4 every one **h** of the house of his fathers. 7218
5:18 uncover the woman's **h**, and put 7218
6: 5 there shall no rasor come upon his **h**: 7218
6: 5 shall let the locks of the hair of his **h** grow. 7218
6: 7 the consecration of his God *is* upon his **h**. 7218
6: 9 he hath defiled the **h** of his consecration; 7218
6: 9 he shall shave his **h** in the day of his 7218
6:11 and shall hallow his **h** that *same* day. 7218
6:18 the Nazarite shall shave the **h** of his 7218
6:18 shall take the hair of the **h** of his separation, 7218
17: 3 for one rod *shall be* for the **h** of the house 7218
22:31 he **bowed down** his **h**, and fell flat on his 6915
25:15 he *was* **h** over a people, *and* of a chief 7218
Dt 19: 5 the **h** slippeth from the helve, and 1270
21:12 she shall shave her **h**, and pare her nails; 7218
28:13 the LORD shall make thee the **h**, and 7218

Dt 28:23 thy heaven that *is* over thy **h** shall be brass, 7218
28:35 the sole of thy foot unto the **top of** thy **h**. 6936
28:44 he shall be the **h**, and thou shalt be the tail. 7218
33:16 let *the blessing* come upon the **h** of Joseph, 7218
33:16 upon the **top of the h** of him *that was* 6936
33:20 teareth the arm with the **crown of the h**. 6936
Jos 2:19 his blood *shall be* upon his **h**, and we *will* 7218
2:19 his blood *shall be* on our **h**, if *any* hand be 7218
11:10 for Hazor beforetime *was* the **h** of all those 7218
22:14 each one *was* a **h** of the house of their 7218
Jdg 5:26 she smote off his **h**, when she had pierced 7218
9:53 a piece of a millstone upon Abimelech's **h**, 7218
10:18 he shall be **h** over all the inhabitants of 7218
11: 8 be our **h** over all the inhabitants of Gilead. 7218
11: 9 deliver them before me, shall I be your **h**? 7218
11:11 the people made him **h** and captain over 7218
13: 5 a son; and no rasor shall come on his **h**: 7218
16:13 If thou weavest the seven locks of my **h** 7218
16:17 There hath not come a rasor upon mine **h**; 7218
16:19 *him* to shave off the seven locks of his **h**; 7218
16:22 Howbeit the hair of his **h** began to grow 7218
1Sa 1:11 and there shall no rasor come upon his **h**. 7218
4:12 his clothes rent, and *with* earth upon his **h**. 7218
5: 4 the **h** of Dagon and both the palms of his 7218
10: 1 poured *it* upon his **h**, and kissed him, and 7218
14:45 there shall not one hair of his **h** fall to 7218
15:17 *wast* thou not *made* the **h** of the tribes of 7218
17: 5 *he had* a helmet of brass upon his **h**, and 7218
17: 7 his spear's **h** *weighed* six hundred shekels 3852
17:38 and he put a helmet of brass upon his **h**; 7218
17:46 will smite thee, and take thine **h** from thee; 7218
17:51 and slew him, and cut off his **h** therewith. 7218
17:54 David took the **h** of the Philistine, and 7218
17:57 brought him before Saul with the **h** of 7218
25:39 the wickedness of Nabal upon his own **h**. 7218
28: 2 will I make thee keeper of mine **h** for ever. 7218
31: 9 they cut off his **h**, and stripped off his 7218
2Sa 1: 2 with his clothes rent, and earth upon his **h**: 7218
1:10 I took the crown that *was* upon his **h**, and 7218
1:16 said unto him, Thy blood *be* upon thy **h**; 7218
2:16 they caught every one his fellow by the **h**, 7218
3: 8 of Ish-bosheth, and said, *Am* I a dog's **h**, 7218
3:29 Let it rest on the **h** of Joab, and on all his 7218
4: 7 took his **h**, and gat them away through 7218
4: 8 they brought the **h** of Ish-bosheth unto 7218
4: 8 Behold the **h** of Ish-bosheth the son of Saul 7218
4:12 they took the **h** of Ish-bosheth, and buried *it* 7218
12:30 he took their king's crown from off his **h**, 7218
12:30 it was *set* on David's **h**. And he brought 7218
13:19 Tamar put ashes on her **h**, and rent her 7218
13:19 laid her hand on her **h**, and went on crying. 7218
14:25 **crown of** his **h** there was no blemish in 6936
14:26 when he polled his **h**, (for it was at every 7218
14:26 he weighed the hair of his **h** *at* two hundred 7218
15:30 had his **h** covered, and he went barefoot: 7218
15:30 that *was* with him covered every man his **h**, 7218
15:32 with his coat rent, and earth upon his **h**: 7218
16: 9 me go over, I pray thee, and take off his **h**. 7218
18: 9 his **h** caught hold of the oak, and he was 7218
20:21 his **h** *shall be* thrown to thee over the wall. 7218
20:22 they cut off the **h** of Sheba the son of 7218
22:44 thou hast kept me to be **h** of the heathen: 7218
1Ki 2: 6 let not his **hoar h** go down *to* the grave in 7872
2: 9 his **hoar h** bring thou down *to* the grave 7872
2:32 shall return his blood upon his own **h**, 7218
2:33 therefore return upon the **h** of Joab, 7218
2:33 of Joab, and upon the **h** of his seed for ever: 7218
2:37 thy blood shall be upon thine own **h**. 7218
2:44 return thy wickedness upon thine own **h**; 7218
8:32 the wicked, to bring his way upon his **h**; 7218
19: 6 on the coals, and a cruse of water *at* his **h**. 4763
2Ki 2: 3 take away thy master from thy **h** to day? 7218
2: 5 take away thy master from thy **h** to day? 7218
2:23 and said unto him, Go up, thou **bald h**; 7142
2:23 Go up, thou bald head; go up, thou **bald h**. 7142
4:19 he said unto his father, My **h**, my head. 7218
4:19 he said unto his father, My head, my **h**. 7218
6: 5 felling a beam, the **axe h** fell into the water: 1270
6:25 until an ass's **h** was *sold* for fourscore 7218
6:31 if the **h** of Elisha the son of Shaphat shall 7218
6:32 a murderer hath sent to take away mine **h**? 7218
9: 3 pour *it* on his **h**, and say, Thus saith 7218
9: 6 he poured the oil on his **h**, and said unto 7218
9:30 tired her **h**, and looked out at a window. 7218
19:21 of Jerusalem hath shaken her **h** at thee. 7218
25:27 did lift up the **h** of Jehoiachin king of Judah 7218
1Ch 10: 9 they took his **h**, and his armour, and 7218
10:10 and fastened his **h** *in* the temple of Dagon. 1538
20: 2 took the crown of their king from off his **h**, 7218
20: 2 stones in it; and it was *set* upon David's **h**: 7218
29:11 and *thou* art exalted as **h** above all. 7218
2Ch 6:23 by recompensing his way upon his own **h**; 7218
20:18 Jehoshaphat **bowed** his **h** *with his* face to 6915
Ezr 9: 3 pluckt off the hair of my **h** and of my 7218
9: 6 for our iniquities are increased over *our* **h**, 7218
Ne 4: 4 turn their reproach upon their own **h**, and 7218
Est 2:17 so that he set the royal crown upon her **h**, 7218
6: 8 the crown royal which is set upon his **h**: 7218
6:12 house mourning, and having his **h** covered. 7218
9:25 should return upon his own **h**, and that he 7218
Job 1:20 shaved his **h**, and fell down upon 7218
10:15 *if* I be righteous, *yet* will I not lift up my **h**. 7218
16: 4 against you, and shake mine **h** at you. 7218
19: 9 my glory, and taken the crown *from* my **h**. 7218
20: 6 and his **h** reach unto the clouds; 7218
29: 3 When his candle shined upon my **h**, *and* 7218
41: 7 barbed irons? or his **h** with fish spears? 7218
Ps 3: 3 my glory, and the lifter up of mine **h**. 7218
7:16 His mischief shall return upon his own **h**, 7218
18:43 thou hast made me the **h** of the heathen: 7218
21: 3 thou settest a crown of pure gold on his **h**. 7218
22: 7 shoot out the lip, they shake the **h**, *saying,* 7218
23: 5 thou anointest my **h** with oil; my cup 7218
27: 6 now shall mine **h** be lifted up above mine 7218
38: 4 For mine iniquities are gone *over* mine **h**: 7218
40:12 *up;* they are moe than the hairs of mine **h**: 7218
44:14 a shaking of the **h** among the people. 7218
60: 7 Ephraim also *is* the strength of mine **h**; 7218
68:21 God shall wound the **h** of his enemies, *and* 7218
69: 4 a cause are moe than the hairs of mine **h**: 7218
83: 2 and they that hate thee have lift up the **h**. 7218
108: 8 Ephraim also *is* the strength of mine **h**; 7218
110: 7 in the way: therefore shall he lift up the **h**. 7218
118:22 refused is become the **h** *stone* of the corner. 7218
133: 2 *It is* like the precious ointment upon the **h**, 7218
140: 7 thou hast covered my **h** in the day of battle. 7218
140: 9 *As for* the **h** of those that compass me 7218
141: 5 excellent oil, *which* shall not break my **h**: 7218
Pr 1: 9 *shall be* an ornament of grace unto thy **h**, 7218
4: 9 She shall give to thine **h** an ornament of 7218
10: 6 Blessings *are* upon the **h** of the just: but 7218
11:26 blessing *shall be* upon the **h** of him that 7218
16:31 The **hoary h** *is* a crown of glory, *if* it be 7872
20:29 and the beauty of old men *is* the **gray h**. 7872
25:22 For thou shalt heap coals of fire upon his **h**, 7218
Ecc 2:14 The wise *man's* eyes *are* in his **h**; but 7218
9: 8 and let thy **h** lack no ointment. 7218
SS 2: 6 His left hand *is* under my **h**, and his right 7218
5: 2 for my **h** is filled *with* dew, *and* my locks 7218
5:11 His **h** *is as* the most fine gold, his locks *are* 7218
7: 5 Thine **h** upon thee *is* like Carmel, and 7218
7: 5 and the hair of thine **h** like purple; 7218
8: 3 His left hand *should be* under my **h**, and 7218
Isa 1: 5 the whole **h** *is* sick, and the whole heart 7218
1: 6 From the sole of the foot even unto the **h** 7218
3:17 **crown of the h** of the daughters of Zion, 6936
7: 8 For the **h** of Syria *is* Damascus, and 7218
7: 8 and the **h** of Damascus *is* Rezin; 7218
7: 9 the **h** of Ephraim *is* Samaria, and the head 7218
7: 9 and the **h** of Samaria *is* Remaliah's son. 7218
7:20 of Assyria, the **h**, and the hair of the feet: 7218
9:14 the LORD will cut off from Israel **h** 7218
9:15 The ancient and honourable, he *is* the **h**; 7218
19:15 which the **h** or tail, branch or rush, may do. 7218
28: 1 which *are* on the **h** of the fat valleys of 7218
28: 4 which *is* on the **h** of the fat valley, shall be 7218
37:22 of Jerusalem hath shaken her **h** at thee. 7218
51:11 and everlasting joy *shall be* upon their **h**: 7218
51:20 they lie at the **h** of all the streets, as a wild 7218
58: 5 *is it* to bow down his **h** as a bulrush, and 7218
59:17 and a helmet of salvation upon his **h**; 7218
Jer 2:16 Tahapanes have broken the **crown of** thy **h**. 6936
2:37 from him, and thine hands upon thine **h**: 7218
9: 1 O that my **h** were waters, and mine eyes a 7218
18:16 thereby shall be astonished, and wag his **h**. 7218
22: 6 *art* Gilead unto me, *and* the **h** of Lebanon: 7218
23:19 it shall fall grievously upon the **h** of 7218
30:23 it shall fall with pain upon the **h** of 7218

Jer 48:37 For every **h** *shall be* bald, and every beard 7218
48:45 the **crown of the h** of the tumultuous ones. 6936
52:31 lifted up the **h** of Jehoiachin king of Judah, 7218
La 2:15 wag their **h** at the daughter of Jerusalem, 7218
3:54 Waters flowed over mine **h**; *then* I said, 7218
5:16 The crown is fallen *from* our **h**: woe unto 7218
Eze 5: 1 cause *it* to pass upon thine **h** and upon thy 7218
8: 3 of a hand, and took me by a lock of mine **h**; 7218
9:10 I will recompense their way upon their **h**. 7218
10: 1 in the firmament that *was* above the **h** of 7218
10:11 *to* the place whither the **h** looked they 7218
13:18 make kerchiefs upon the **h** of every stature 7218
16:12 and a beautiful crown upon thine **h**. 7218
16:25 Thou hast built thy high place at every **h** of 7218
16:31 thine eminent place in the **h** of every way, 7218
16:43 also will recompense thy way upon *thine* **h**, 7218
17:19 even it will I recompense upon his own **h**. 7218
21:19 choose *it,* at the **h** of the way to the city. 7218
21:21 at the **h** of the two ways, to use divination: 7218
24:17 bind the **tire of** thine **h** upon thee, and 6287
29:18 every **h** *was* made bald, and every shoulder 7218
33: 4 his blood shall be upon his own **h**. 7218
42:12 the south *was* a door in the **h** of the way, 7218
Da 1:10 shall ye make *me* endanger my **h** to 7218
2:28 the visions of thy **h** upon thy bed, *are* these; 7217
2:32 This image's **h** *was* of fine gold, his breast 7217
2:38 ruler over them all. Thou *art* this **h** of gold. 7217
3:27 nor was a hair of their **h** singed, 7217
4: 5 and the visions of my **h** troubled me. 7217
4:10 Thus *were* the visions of mine **h** in my bed; 7217
4:13 I saw in the visions of my **h** upon my bed, 7217
7: 1 a dream and visions of his **h** upon his bed: 7217
7: 9 and the hair of his **h** like the pure wool: 7217
7:15 and the visions of my **h** troubled me. 7217
7:20 of the ten horns that *were* in his **h**, and 7217
Hos 1:11 appoint themselves one **h**, and they shall 7218
Joel 3: 4 I return your recompence upon your own **h**; 7218
3: 7 return your recompence upon your own **h**: 7218
Am 2: 7 the dust of the earth on the **h** of the poor, 7218
8:10 upon all loins, and baldness upon every **h**; 7218
9: 1 cut them in the **h**, all of them; and I will 7218
Ob 1:15 thy reward shall return upon thine own **h**. 7218
Jnh 2: 5 the weeds *were* wrapt about my **h**. 7218
4: 6 that *it* might be a shadow over his **h**, 7218
4: 8 the sun beat upon the **h** of Jonah, that he 7218
Mic 2:13 and the LORD on the **h** of them. 7218
Hab 3:13 thou woundedst the **h** out of the house of 7218
3:14 with his staves the **h** of his villages: 7218
Zec 1:21 so that no man did lift up his **h**: 7218
3: 5 I said, Let them set a fair mitre upon his **h**. 7218
3: 5 So they set a fair mitre upon his **h**, and 7218
6:11 set *them* upon the **h** of Joshua the son of 7218
Mt 5:36 Neither shalt thou swear by thy **h**, because *2776*
6:17 anoint thine **h**, and wash thy face; *2776*
8:20 the Son of man hath not where to lay *his* **h**. *2776*
10:30 But the very hairs of your **h** are all *2776*
14: 8 Give me here John Baptist's **h** in a charger. *2776*
14:11 And his **h** was brought in a charger, and *2776*
21:42 the same is become the **h** of the corner: *2776*
26: 7 and poured *it* on his **h**, as he sat at meat. *2776*
27:29 they put *it* upon his **h**, and a reed in his *2776*
27:30 and took the reed, and smote him on the **h**. *2776*
27:37 And set up over his **h** his accusation *2776*
Mk 6:24 And she said, The **h** of John the Baptist. *2776*
6:25 by in a charger the **h** of John the Baptist. *2776*
6:27 and commanded his **h** to be brought: *2776*
6:28 And brought his **h** in a charger, and gave it *2776*
12: 4 and **wounded** *him* **in the h**, and sent *him* *2775*
12:10 rejected is become the **h** of the corner: *2776*
14: 3 she brake the box, and poured *it* on his **h**. *2776*
15:17 a crown of thorns, and put *it* about his **h**, NIG
15:19 And they smote him on the **h** with a reed, *2776*
Lk 7:38 and did wipe *them* with the hairs of her **h**, *2776*
7:44 and wiped *them* with the hairs of her **h**. *2776*
7:46 Mine **h** with oil thou didst not anoint: but *2776*
9:58 the Son of man hath not where to lay *his* **h**. *2776*
12: 7 But even the *very* hairs of your **h** are all *2776*
20:17 the same is become the **h** of the corner? *2776*
21:18 But there shall not a hair of your **h** perish. *2776*
Jn 13: 9 my feet only, but also *my* hands and *my* **h**. *2776*
19: 2 and put *it* on his **h**, and they put on him a *2776*
19:30 and he bowed *his* **h**, and gave up the ghost. *2776*
20: 7 And the napkin, that was about his **h**, *2776*
20:12 the one at the **h**, and the other at the feet, *2776*
Ac 4:11 which is become the **h** of the corner. *2776*
18:18 having shorn *his* **h** in Cenchrea: for he had *2776*
27:34 for there shall not a hair fall from the **h** of *2776*
Ro 12:20 doing thou shalt heap coals of fire on his **h**. *2776*
1Co 11: 3 that the **h** of every man is Christ; *2776*
11: 3 and the **h** of the woman *is* the man; and *2776*
11: 3 *is* the man; and the **h** of Christ *is* God. *2776*
11: 4 or prophesying, having *his* **h** covered, *2776*
11: 4 *his* head covered, dishonoureth his **h**. *2776*
11: 5 prophesieth with *her* **h** uncovered *2776*
11: 5 *her* head uncovered dishonoureth her **h**: *2776*
11: 7 For a man indeed ought not to cover *his* **h**, *2776*
11:10 ought the woman to have power on *her* **h** *2776*
12:21 nor again the **h** to the feet, I have no need *2776*
Eph 1:22 gave him *to be* the **h** over all *things* to *2776*
4:15 *up* into him *in* all *things,* which is the **h**, *2776*
5:23 For the husband is the **h** of the wife, *2776*
5:23 even as Christ *is* the **h** of the church: *2776*
Col 1:18 And he is the **h** of the body, the church: *2776*
2:10 which is the **h** of all principality and power: *2776*
2:19 And not holding the **h**, from which all *2776*
1Pe 2: 7 the same is made the **h** of the corner, *2776*
Rev 1:14 His **h** and *his* hairs *were* white like wool, *2776*
10: 1 and a rainbow *was* upon *his* **h**, and his face *2776*
12: 1 and upon her **h** a crown of twelve stars: *2776*
14:14 having on his **h** a golden crown, and in his *2776*
19:12 of fire, and on his **h** *were* many crowns; *2776*

HEADBANDS (1) [BAND, HEAD]

Isa 3:20 and the **h**, and the tablets, and the earrings, 7196

HEADDRESSES See BONNETS

HEADLONG (3) [HEAD]

Job 5:13 and the counsel of the froward is **carried h**. 4116
Lk 4:29 was built, that *they* might **cast** him **down h**. *2630*
Ac 1:18 and **falling h**, he burst asunder in *1096+4248*

HEADS (110) [HEAD]

Ge 2:10 it was parted, and became into four **h**. 7218
43:28 they **bowed down** their **h**, and 6915
Ex 4:31 then they **bowed** their **h** and worshipped. 6915
6:14 These *be* the **h** of their fathers' houses: 7218
6:25 these *are* the **h** of the fathers of the Levites 7218
18:25 made them **h** over the people, rulers of 7218
Lev 10: 6 unto Ithamar his sons, Uncover not your **h**, 7218
19:27 Ye shall not round the corners of your **h**, 7218
Nu 1:16 of their fathers, **h** of thousands in Israel. 7218
7: 2 of Israel, **h** of the house of their fathers, 7218
8:12 the Levites shall lay their hands upon the **h** 7218
10: 4 *which are* **h** of the thousands of Israel, 7218
13: 3 all those men *were* **h** of the children of 7218
25: 4 Take all the **h** of the people, and hang them 7218
30: 1 Moses spake unto the **h** of the tribes 7218
Dt 1:15 and known, and made them **h** over you, 7218
5:23 *even* all the **h** of your tribes, and 7218
33: 5 when the **h** of the people *and* the tribes of 7218
33:21 he came *with* the **h** of the people, 7218
Jos 7: 6 elders of Israel, and put dust upon their **h**. 7218
14: 1 the **h** of the fathers of the tribes of 7218
19:51 the **h** of the fathers of the tribes of 7218
21: 1 came near the **h** of the fathers of 7218
21: 1 unto the **h** of the fathers of the tribes of 7218
22:21 said unto the **h** of the thousands of Israel, 7218
22:30 **h** of the thousands of Israel which *were* 7218
23: 2 for their **h**, and for their judges, and 7218
24: 1 for their **h**, and for their judges, and 7218
Jdg 7:25 brought the **h** of Oreb and Zeeb to Gideon 7218
8:28 so that they lifted up their **h** no more. 7218
9:57 of Shechem did God render upon their **h**: 7218
1Sa 29: 4 *should it* not *be* with the **h** of these men? 7218
1Ki 8: 1 elders of Israel, and all the **h** of the tribes, 7218
20:31 ropes upon our **h**, and go out to the king of 7218
20:32 *put* ropes on their **h**, and came to the king 7218
2Ki 10: 6 take ye the **h** of the men your master's 7218
10: 7 put their **h** in baskets, and sent him *them* to 7218
10: 8 They have brought the **h** of the king's sons. 7218
1Ch 5:24 these *were* the **h** of the house of their 7218
5:24 *and* **h** of the house of their fathers. 7218
7: 2 and Shemuel, **h** of their fathers' house, 7218
7: 7 **h** of the house of *their* fathers, mighty *men* 7218
7: 9 **h** of the house of their fathers, mighty *men* 7218
7:11 by the **h** of *their* fathers, mighty *men* of 7218
7:40 **h** of *their* fathers' house, choice *and* 7218

1Ch 8: 6 these *are* the **h** of the fathers of 7218
8:10 These *were* his sons, **h** of the fathers. 7218
8:13 who *were* **h** of the fathers of the inhabitants 7218
8:28 These *were* **h** of the fathers, by their 7218
9:13 **h** of the house of their fathers, a thousand 7218
12:19 to his master Saul to *the jeopardy of* our **h**. 7218
12:32 the **h** of them *were* two hundred; and 7218
29:20 **bowed down** their **h**, and worshipped 6915
2Ch 3:16 and put *them* on the **h** of the pillars; 7218
5: 2 elders of Israel, and all the **h** of the tribes, 7218
28:12 certain of the **h** of the children of Ephraim, 7218
29:30 and they **bowed** their **h** and worshipped. 6915
Ne 8: 6 they **bowed** their **h**, and worshipped 6915
Job 2:12 sprinkled dust upon their **h** toward heaven. 7218
Ps 24: 7 Lift up your **h**, O ye gates; and be ye lift 7218
24: 9 Lift up your **h**, O ye gates; even lift *them* 7218
66:12 Thou hast caused men to ride over our **h**; 7218
74:13 thou brakest the **h** of the dragons in 7218
74:14 Thou brakest the **h** of leviathan in pieces, 7218
109:25 they looked upon me they shaked their **h**. 7218
110: 6 he shall wound the **h** over many countries. 7218
Isa 15: 2 on all their **h** *shall be* baldness, *and* 7218
35:10 with songs and everlasting joy upon their **h**: 7218
Jer 14: 3 and confounded, and covered their **h**. 7218
14: 4 were ashamed, they covered their **h**. 7218
La 2:10 they have cast up dust upon their **h**; 7218
2:10 the virgins of Jerusalem hang down their **h** 7218
Eze 1:22 the likeness of the firmament upon the **h** of 7218
1:22 stretched forth over their **h** above. 7218
1:25 from the firmament that *was* over their **h**, 7218
1:26 above the firmament that *was* over their **h** 7218
7:18 all faces, and baldness upon all their **h**. 7218
11:21 recompense their way upon their own **h**, 7218
22:31 own way have I recompensed upon their **h**, 7218
23:15 exceeding in dyed attire upon their **h**, all of 7218
23:42 and beautiful crowns upon their **h**. 7218
24:23 your tires *shall be* upon your **h**, and 7218
27:30 and shall cast up dust upon their **h**, 7218
32:27 they have laid their swords under their **h**, 7218
44:18 They shall have linen bonnets upon their **h**, 7218
44:20 Neither shall they shave their **h**, nor suffer 7218
44:20 to grow long; they shall only poll their **h**. 7218
Da 7: 6 the beast had also four **h**; and 7217
Mic 3: 1 O **h** of Jacob, and ye princes of the house 7218
3: 9 ye **h** of the house of Jacob, and princes of 7218
3:11 The **h** thereof judge for reward, and 7218
Mt 27:39 passed by, reviled him, wagging their **h**, *2776*
Mk 15:29 wagging their **h**, and saying, Ah, *thou* that *2776*
Lk 21:28 to pass, *then* look up, and lift up your **h**; *2776*
Ac 18: 6 Your blood *be* upon your own **h**; *2776*
21:24 with them, that they may shave *their* **h**: *2776*
Rev 4: 4 and they had on their **h** crowns of gold. *2776*
9: 7 on their **h** *were* as *it were* crowns like gold, *2776*
9:17 the **h** of the horses *were* as the heads of *2776*
9:17 the heads of the horses *were* as the **h** of *2776*
9:19 and had **h**, and with them they do hurt. *2776*
12: 3 having seven **h** and ten horns, and *2776*
12: 3 ten horns, and seven crowns upon his **h**. *2776*
13: 1 having seven **h** and ten horns, and upon his *2776*
13: 1 and upon his **h** the name of blasphemy. *2776*
13: 3 And I saw one of his **h** as *it were* wounded *2776*
17: 3 having seven **h** and ten horns. *2776*
17: 7 which hath the seven **h** and ten horns. *2776*
17: 9 The seven **h** are seven mountains, on which *2776*
18:19 And they cast dust on their **h**, and cried, *2776*

HEADSTONE (1) [HEAD, STONE]
Zec 4: 7 he shall bring forth the **h** *thereof with* 68+7222

HEADY (1) [HEAD]
2Ti 3: 4 Traitors, **h**, highminded, lovers of pleasures *4312*

HEAL (40) [HEALED, HEALER, HEALETH, HEALING, HEALINGS, HEALTH]
Nu 12:13 **H** her now, O God, I beseech thee. 7495
Dt 32:39 I kill, and I make alive; I wound, and I **h**: 7495
2Ki 20: 5 behold, I will **h** thee: on the third day thou 7495
20: 8 *shall be* the sign that the LORD will **h** me, 7495
2Ch 7:14 will forgive their sin, and will **h** their land. 7495
Ps 6: 2 O LORD, **h** me; for my bones are vexed. 7495
41: 4 **h** my soul; for I have sinned against thee. 7495
60: 2 **h** the breaches thereof; for it shaketh. 7495
Ecc 3: 3 A time to kill, and a time to **h**; a time to 7495
Isa 19:22 *he* shall smite and **h** *it:* and they shall return 7495
19:22 shall be intreated of them, and shall **h** them. 7495
57:18 I have seen his ways, and will **h** him: I will 7495
57:19 *is* near, saith the LORD; and I will **h** him. 7495
Jer 3:22 *and* I will **h** your backslidings. 7495
17:14 **H** me, O LORD, and I shall be healed; 7495
30:17 I will **h** thee of thy wounds, saith 7495
La 2:13 *is* great like the sea: who can **h** thee? 7495
Hos 5:13 yet could he not **h** you nor cure you of your 7495
6: 1 for he hath torn, and he will **h** us; he hath 7495
14: 4 I will **h** their backsliding, I will love them 7495
Zec 11:16 nor **h** that that is broken, nor feed that that 7495
Mt 8: 7 saith unto him, I will come and **h** him. *2323*
10: 1 and to **h** all *manner of* sickness and *2323*
10: 8 **H** the sick, cleanse the lepers, raise *2323*
12:10 Is it lawful to **h** on the sabbath days? *2323*
13:15 should be converted, and I should **h** them. *2390*
Mk 3: 2 whether he would **h** him on the sabbath *2323*
3:15 And to have power to **h** sicknesses, and to *2323*
Lk 4:18 he hath sent me to **h** the broken-hearted, *2390*
4:23 unto me this proverb, Physician, **h** thyself: *2323*
5:17 the power of the Lord was *present* to **h** *2390*
6: 7 whether he would **h** on the sabbath day; *2323*
7: 3 him that he would come and **h** his servant. *1295*
9: 2 the kingdom of God, and to **h** the sick. *2390*
10: 9 And **h** the sick that are therein, *2323*
14: 3 saying, Is it lawful to **h** on the sabbath day? *2323*
Jn 4:47 that he would come down, and **h** his son: *2390*
12:40 and be converted, and I should **h** them. *2390*
Ac 4:30 By stretching forth thine hand to **h**; and *2392*
28:27 should be converted, and I should **h** them. *2390*

HEALED (79) [HEAL]
Ge 20:17 God **h** Abimelech, and his wife, and 7495
Ex 21:19 shall **cause** *him* **to be thoroughly h**. 7495+7495
Lev 13:18 in the skin thereof, was a boil, and is **h**, 7495
13:37 grown up therein; the scall is **h**, he *is* clean: 7495
14: 3 *if* the plague of leprosy be **h** in the leper; 7495
14:48 the house clean, because the plague is **h**. 7495
Dt 28:27 with the itch, where*of* thou canst not be **h**. 7495
28:35 the legs, with a sore botch that cannot be **h**, 7495
1Sa 6: 3 ye shall be **h**, and it shall be known to you 7495
2Ki 2:21 saith the LORD, I have **h** these waters; 7495
2:22 So the waters were **h** unto this day, 7495
8:29 king Joram went back to be **h** in Jezreel of 7495
9:15 king Joram was returned to be **h** in Jezreel 7495
2Ch 22: 6 he returned to be **h** in Jezreel because of 7495
30:20 hearkened to Hezekiah, and **h** the people. 7495
Ps 30: 2 I cried unto thee, and thou hast **h** me. 7495
107:20 **h** them, and delivered *them* from their 7495
Isa 6:10 *with* their heart, and convert, and be **h**. 7495
53: 5 upon him; and with his stripes we are **h**. 7495
Jer 6:14 They have **h** also the hurt of *the daughter of* 7495
8:11 For they have **h** the hurt of the daughter of 7495
15:18 wound incurable, *which* refuseth to be **h**? 7495
17:14 Heal me, O LORD, and I shall be **h**; 7495
51: 8 balm for her pain, if so be she may be **h**. 7495
51: 9 We would have **h** Babylon, but she is not 7495
51: 9 have healed Babylon, but she is not **h**: 7495
Eze 30:21 lo, it shall not be bound up to be **h**, to put a 7499
34: 4 neither have ye **h** that which was sick, 7495
47: 8 forth into the sea, the waters shall be **h**. 7495
47: 9 for they shall be **h**; and every *thing* shall 7495
47:11 and the marishes thereof shall not be **h**; 7495
Hos 7: 1 When I *would have* **h** Israel, then 7495
11: 3 their arms; but they knew not that I **h** them. 7495
Mt 4:24 and those that had the palsy; and he **h** them. *2323*
8: 8 the word only, and my servant shall be **h**. *2390*
8:13 And his servant was **h** in the selfsame hour. *2390*
8:16 with *his* word, and **h** all that were sick: *2323*
12:15 multitudes followed him, and he **h** them all, *2323*
12:22 and he **h** him, insomuch that the blind and *2323*
14:14 toward them, and he **h** their sick. *2323*
15:30 them *down* at Jesus' feet; and he **h** them: *2323*
19: 2 followed him; and he **h** them there. *2323*
21:14 came to him in the temple; and he **h** them. *2323*
Mk 1:34 And he **h** many *that were* sick of divers *2323*
3:10 For he had **h** many; insomuch that *they* *2323*
5:23 lay *thy* hands on her, that she may be **h**; *4982*
5:29 she felt in *her* body that she was **h** of *that* *2390*
6: 5 hands upon a few sick *folk*, and **h** *them*. *2323*
6:13 with oil many *that were* sick, and **h** *them*. *2323*
Lk 4:40 hands on every one of them, and **h** them. *2323*
5:15 and to be **h** by him of their infirmities. *2323*
6:17 to hear him, and to be **h** of their diseases; *2390*

Lk 6:18 with unclean spirits: and they were **h**. *2323*
6:19 went virtue out of him, and **h** *them* all. *2390*
7: 7 say in a word, and my servant shall be **h**. *2390*
8: 2 which had been **h** of evil spirits and *2323*
8:36 he that was possessed of the devils was **h**. *4982*
8:43 upon physicians, neither could be **h** of any, *2323*
8:47 and how she was **h** immediately. *2390*
9:11 and **h** them that had need of healing. *2390*
9:42 and **h** the child, and delivered him again to *2390*
13:14 that Jesus had **h** on the sabbath day, *2323*
13:14 in them therefore come and be **h**, and *2323*
14: 4 And he took *him,* and **h** him, and let *him* *2390*
17:15 when he saw that he was **h**, turned back, *2390*
22:51 thus far. And he touched his ear, and **h** him. *2390*
Jn 5:13 And he that was **h** wist not who it was: *2390*
Ac 3:11 And as the lame *man* which was **h** held *2390*
4:14 And beholding the man which was **h** *2323*
5:16 unclean spirits: and they were **h** every one. *2323*
8: 7 with palsies, and *that were* lame, were **h**. *2323*
14: 9 and perceiving that he had faith to be **h**, *4982*
28: 8 and laid *his* hands on him, and **h** him. *2390*
28: 9 diseases in the island, came, and were **h**: *2323*
Heb 12:13 turned out of the way; but let it rather be **h**. *2390*
Jas 5:16 and pray one for another, that ye may be **h**. *2390*
1Pe 2:24 by whose stripes ye were **h**. *2390*
Rev 13: 3 to death; and his deadly wound was **h**: *2323*
13:12 the first beast, whose deadly wound was **h**. *2323*

HEALER (1) [HEAL]
Isa 3: 7 shall he swear, saying, I will not be a **h**; 2280

HEALETH (4) [HEAL]
Ex 15:26 for I *am* the LORD that **h** thee. 7495
Ps 103: 3 all thine iniquities; who **h** all thy diseases; 7495
147: 3 He **h** the broken in heart, and bindeth up 7495
Isa 30:26 his people, and **h** the stroke of their wound. 7495

HEALING (14) [HEAL]
Jer 14:19 thou smitten us, and *there is* no **h** for us? 4832
14:19 and for the time of **h**, and behold trouble. 4832
30:13 be bound up: thou hast no **h** medicines. 8585
Na 3:19 *There is* no **h** of thy bruise; thy wound *is* 3545
Mal 4: 2 of righteousness arise with **h** in his wings; 4832
Mt 4:23 and **h** all *manner of* sickness and *2323*
9:35 and **h** every sickness and every disease *2323*
Lk 9: 6 preaching the gospel, and **h** every where. *2323*
9:11 of God, and healed them that had need of **h**. *2322*
Ac 4:22 on whom this miracle of **h** was shewed. *2392*
10:38 and **h** all that were oppressed of the devil; *2390*
1Co 12: 9 to another the gifts of **h** by the same Spirit; *2386*
12:30 Have all the gifts of **h**? do all speak with *2386*
Rev 22: 2 the leaves of the tree *were* for the **h** of *2322*

HEALINGS (1) [HEAL]
1Co 12:28 then gifts of **h**, helps, governments, *2386*

HEALTH (17) [HEAL]
Ge 43:28 Thy servant our father *is* **in good h**, he *is* 7965
2Sa 20: 9 said to Amasa, *Art* thou **in h**, my brother? 7965
Ps 42:11 *who is* the **h** of my countenance, and 3444
43: 5 *who is* the **h** of my countenance, and 3444
67: 2 upon earth, thy **saving h** among all nations. 3444
Pr 3: 8 It shall be **h** to thy navel, and marrow to thy 7500
4:22 those that find them, and **h** to all their flesh. 4832
12:18 of a sword: but the tongue of the wise *is* **h**. 4832
13:17 but a faithful ambassador *is* **h**. 4832
16:24 sweet to the soul, and **h** to the bones. 4832
Isa 58: 8 and thine **h** shall spring forth speedily: 724
Jer 8:15 no good *came; and* for a time of **h**, and 4832
8:22 is not the **h** of the daughter of my people 724
30:17 For I will restore **h** unto thee, and I will heal 724
33: 6 I *will* bring it **h** and cure, and I will cure 724
Ac 27:34 for this is for your **h**: for there shall not a *4991*
3Jn 1: 2 *things* that thou mayest prosper and be in **h**, *5198*

HEAP (38) [HEAPED, HEAPETH, HEAPS]
Ge 31:46 and they took stones, and made a **h**: 1530
31:46 a heap: and they did eat there upon the **h**. 1530
31:48 This **h** *is* a witness between me and thee 1530
31:51 Behold this **h**, and behold *this* pillar, 1530
31:52 This **h** *be* witness, and *this* pillar *be* 1530
31:52 that I will not pass over this **h** to thee, and 1530
31:52 that thou shalt not pass over this **h** and 1530
Ex 15: 8 the floods stood upright as a **h**, *and* 5067
Dt 13:16 it shall be a **h** for ever; it shall not be built 8510
32:23 I will **h** mischiefs upon them; I will spend 5595
Jos 3:13 from above; and they shall stand *upon* a **h**. 5067
3:16 above stood *and* rose up *upon* a **h** very far, 5067
7:26 they raised over him a great **h** of stones 1530
8:28 Joshua burnt Ai, and made it a **h** for ever, 8510
8:29 raise thereon a great **h** of stones, 1530
Ru 3: 7 he went to lie down at the end of the **h** *of* 6194
2Sa 18:17 and laid a very great **h** of stones upon him: 1530
Job 8:17 His roots are wrapped about the **h**, *and* 1530
16: 4 I could **h up** words against you, and 2266
27:16 Though he **h up** silver as the dust, and 6651
36:13 the hypocrites in heart **h up** wrath: they cry 7760
Ps 33: 7 the waters of the sea together as a **h**: 5067
78:13 and he made the waters to stand as a **h**. 5067
Pr 25:22 For thou shalt **h** coals of fire upon his head, 2846
Ecc 2:26 he giveth travail, to gather and to **h up**, 3664
SS 7: 2 thy belly *is like* a **h** of wheat set about with 6194
Isa 17: 1 *being* a city, and it shall be a ruinous **h**. 4596
17:11 the harvest *shall be* a **h** in the day of grief 5067
25: 2 For thou hast made of a city a **h**; *of* a 1530
Jer 30:18 the city shall be builded upon her own **h**, 8510
49: 2 it shall be a desolate **h**, and her daughters 8510
Eze 24:10 **H** on wood, kindle the fire, consume 7235
Mic 1: 6 Therefore I will make Samaria as a **h** of 5856
Hab 1:10 for they shall **h** dust, and take it. 6651
3:15 thine horses, *through* the **h** of great waters. 2563
Hag 2:16 when *one* came to a **h** of twenty *measures,* 6194
Ro 12:20 doing thou shalt **h** coals of fire on his head. *4987*
2Ti 4: 3 after their own lusts shall they **h** to *2002*

HEAPED (2) [HEAP]
Zec 9: 3 **h up** silver as the dust, and fine gold as 6651
Jas 5: 3 ye have **h treasure together** for the last *2343*

HEAPETH (2) [HEAP]
Ps 39: 6 he **h up** *riches,* and knoweth not who shall 6651
Hab 2: 5 him all nations, and **h** unto him all people: 6908

HEAPS (20) [HEAP]
Ex 8:14 they gathered them together **upon h**: 2563+2563
Jdg 15:16 With the jawbone of an ass, **h** upon heaps, 2565
15:16 With the jawbone of an ass, heaps upon **h**, 2565
2Ki 10: 8 Lay ye them *in* two **h** *at* the entering in of 6652
19:25 be to lay waste fenced cities *into* ruinous **h**. 1530
2Ch 31: 6 their God, and laid *them* **by h**. 6194+6194
31: 7 they began to lay the foundation of the **h**, 6194
31: 8 and the princes came and saw the **h**, 6194
31: 9 and the Levites concerning the **h**. 6194
Ne 4: 2 will they revive the stones out of the **h** of 6194
Job 15:28 which are ready to become **h**. 1530
Ps 79: 1 they defiled; they have laid Jerusalem on **h**. 5856
Isa 37:26 to lay waste defenced cities *into* ruinous **h**. 1530
Jer 9:11 I will make Jerusalem **h**, *and* a den of 1530
26:18 Jerusalem shall become **h**, and 5856
31:21 Set thee up waymarks, make thee **high h**: 8564
50:26 cast her up as **h**, and destroy her utterly: 6194
51:37 Babylon shall become **h**, a dwelling place 1530
Hos 12:11 their altars *are* as **h** in the furrows of 1530
Mic 3:12 Jerusalem shall become **h**, and 5856

HEAR (550) [HEARD, HEARDEST, HEARER, HEARERS, HEAREST, HEARETH, HEARING]
Ge 4:23 his wives, Adah and Zillah, **H** my voice; 8085
21: 6 *so that* all that **h** will laugh with me. 8085
23: 6 **H** us, my lord: thou *art* a mighty prince 8085
23: 8 **h** me, and intreat for me to Ephron the son 8085
23:11 Nay, my lord, **h** me: the field give I thee, 8085
23:13 But if thou *wilt give it,* I pray thee, **h** me: 8085
37: 6 he said unto them, **H**, I pray you, this 8085
42:21 when he besought us, and we would not **h**; 8085
42:22 sin against the child; and ye would not **h**? 8085
49: 2 and **h**, ye sons of Jacob; 8085
Ex 6:12 how then shall Pharaoh **h** me, who *am* of 8085
7:16 and behold, hitherto thou wouldest not **h**. 8085
15:14 The people shall **h**, *and* be afraid: 8085
19: 9 that the people may **h** when I speak with 8085
20:19 Speak thou with us, and we will **h**: 8085
22:23 all unto me, I will **surely h** their cry; 8085+8085
22:27 when he crieth unto me, that I will **h**; 8085
32:18 *but* the noise of *them that* sing do I **h**. 8085
Lev 5: 1 **h** the voice of swearing, and *is* a witness, 8085
Nu 9: 8 I will **h** what the LORD will command 8085
12: 6 he said, **H** now my words: If there be a 8085
14:13 the Egyptians shall **h** *it,* (for thou 8085

Nu 16: 8 unto Korah, **H**, I pray you, ye sons of Levi: 8085
20:10 and he said unto them, **H** now, ye rebels; 8085
23:18 his parable, and said, Rise up, Balak, and **h**; 8085
30: 4 her father **h** her vow, and her bond 8085
Dt 1:16 **H** *the causes* between your brethren, and 8085
1:17 you shall **h** the small as well as the great; 8085
1:17 for you, bring *it* unto me, and I will **h** it. 8085
1:43 you would not **h**, but rebelled against 8085
2:25 who shall **h** report of thee, and 8085
3:26 me for your sakes, and would not **h** me: 8085
4: 6 which shall **h** all these statutes, and say, 8085
4:10 and I will **make** them **h** my words, 8085
4:28 which neither see, nor **h**, nor eat, nor smell. 8085
4:33 Did *ever* people **h** the voice of God 8085
4:36 Out of heaven he **made** thee **to h** his voice, 8085
5: 1 **H**, O Israel, the statutes and judgments 8085
5:25 if we **h** the voice of the LORD our God 8085
5:27 **h** all that the LORD our God shall say: 8085
5:27 speak unto thee; and we will **h** *it*, and do *it*. 8085
6: 3 **H** therefore, O Israel, and observe to do *it*; 8085
6: 4 **H**, O Israel: The LORD our God *is* one 8085
9: 1 **H**, O Israel: Thou art to pass over Jordan 8085
12:28 **h** all these words which I command thee, 8085
13:11 all Israel shall **h**, and fear, and shall do no 8085
13:12 If thou shalt **h** *say* in one of thy cities, 8085
17:13 all the people shall **h**, and fear, and do no 8085
18:16 Let me not **h** again the voice of the LORD 8085
19:20 those which remain shall **h**, and fear, and 8085
20: 3 shall say unto them, **H**, O Israel, 8085
21:21 among you; and all Israel shall **h**, and fear. 8085
29: 4 and eyes to see, and ears to **h**, unto this day. 8085
30:12 bring it unto us, that we may **h** it, and do it? 8085
30:13 bring it unto us, that we may **h** it, and do it? 8085
30:17 so that thou wilt not **h**, but shalt be drawn 8085
31:12 that they may **h**, and that they may learn, 8085
31:13 which have not known *any thing*, may **h**, 8085
32: 1 and **h**, O earth, the words of my mouth. 8085
33: 7 and he said, **H**, LORD, the voice of Judah, 8085
Jos 3: 9 and **h** the words of the LORD your God. 8085
6: 5 *and* when ye **h** the sound of the trumpet, 8085
7: 9 all the inhabitants of the land shall **h** *of it*, 8085
Jdg 5: 3 **H**, O ye kings; give ear, O ye princes; I, 8085
5:16 to **h** the bleatings of the flocks? 8085
7:11 thou shalt **h** what they say; and 8085
14:13 Put forth thy riddle, that we may **h** it. 8085
1Sa 2:23 for I **h** of your evil dealings by all this 8085
2:24 my sons; for *it is* no good report that I **h**: 8085
8:18 and the LORD will not **h** you in that day. 6030
13: 3 all the land, saying, Let the Hebrews **h**. 8085
15:14 and the lowing of the oxen which I **h**? 8085
16: 2 if Saul **h** *it*, he will kill me. And 8085
22: 7 stood about him, **H** now, ye Benjamites; 8085
22:12 Saul said, **H** now, thou son of Ahitub. 8085
25:24 and **h** the words of thine handmaid. 8085
26:19 let my lord the king **h** the words of his 8085
2Sa 14:16 For the king will **h**, to deliver his handmaid 8085
15: 3 *there is* no man *deputed* of the king to **h** 8085
15:10 As soon as ye **h** the sound of the trumpet, 8085
15:35 *that* what thing soever thou shalt **h** out of 8085
15:36 send unto me every thing that ye can **h**. 8085
16:21 all Israel shall **h** that thou art abhorred of 8085
17: 5 and let us **h** likewise what he saith. 8085
19:35 can I **h** any more the voice of singing *men* 8085
20:16 cried a wise woman out of the city, **H**, hear; 8085
20:16 cried a wise woman out of the city, Hear, **h**; 8085
20:17 unto him, **H** the words of thine handmaid. 8085
20:17 thine handmaid. And he answered, I do **h**. 8085
22: 7 he did **h** my voice out of his temple, and 8085
22:45 as soon as they **h**, they shall be 241+8085
1Ki 4:34 there came of all people to **h** the wisdom of 8085
8:30 **h** thou in heaven thy dwelling place: and 8085
8:32 **h** thou *in* heaven, and do, and judge thy 8085
8:34 **h** thou *in* heaven, and forgive the sin of thy 8085
8:36 **h** thou *in* heaven, and forgive the sin of thy 8085
8:39 **h** thou *in* heaven thy dwelling place, and 8085
8:42 (For they shall **h** of thy great name, and of 8085
8:43 **H** thou *in* heaven thy dwelling place, and 8085
8:45 **h** thou *in* heaven their prayer and their 8085
8:49 **h** thou their prayer and their supplication *in* 8085
10: 8 before thee, *and* that **h** thy wisdom. 8085
10:24 to **h** his wisdom, which God had put in his 8085
18:26 even until noon, saying, O Baal, **h** us. 6030
18:37 **H** me, O LORD, hear me, that this people 6030
18:37 Hear me, O LORD, **h** me, that this people 6030
22:19 **H** thou therefore the word of the LORD: 8085
2Ki 7: 1 Elisha said, **H** ye the word of the LORD; 8085
7: 6 **made** the host of the Syrians **to h** a noise of 8085
14:11 Amaziah would not **h**. Therefore Jehoash 8085
17:14 Notwithstanding they would not **h**, but 8085
18:12 and would not **h** *them*, nor do *them*. 8085
18:28 spake, saying, **H** the word of the great king, 8085
19: 4 It may be the LORD thy God will **h** all 8085
19: 7 he shall **h** a rumour, and shall return to his 8085
19:16 LORD, bow down thine ear, and **h**: open, 8085
19:16 **h** the words of Sennacherib, which hath 8085
20:16 unto Hezekiah, **H** the word of the LORD. 8085
1Ch 14:15 when thou shalt **h** a sound of going in 8085
28: 2 said, **H** me, my brethren, and my people: 8085
2Ch 6:21 **h** thou from thy dwelling place, *even* from 8085
6:23 **h** thou from heaven, and do, and judge thy 8085
6:25 **h** thou from the heavens, and forgive 8085
6:27 **h** thou *from* heaven, and forgive the sin of 8085
6:30 **h** thou from heaven thy dwelling place, 8085
6:33 **h** thou from the heavens, *even* from thy 8085
6:35 **h** thou from the heavens their prayer and 8085
6:39 **h** thou from the heavens, *even* from thy 8085
7:14 will I **h** from heaven, and will forgive their 8085
9: 7 continually before thee, and **h** thy wisdom. 8085
9:23 to **h** his wisdom, that God had put in his 8085
13: 4 said, **H** me, *thou* Jeroboam, and all Israel; 8085
15: 2 **H** ye me, Asa, and all Judah and Benjamin; 8085
18:18 Therefore **h** the word of the LORD; 8085
20: 9 in our affliction, then thou wilt **h** and help. 8085
20:20 Jehoshaphat stood and said, **H** me, 8085
25:20 Amaziah would not **h**; for it *came* of God, 8085
28:11 Now **h** me therefore, and deliver 8085
29: 5 said unto them, **H** me, ye Levites, 8085
Ne 1: 6 that *thou* mayest **h** the prayer of thy 8085
4: 4 **H**, O our God; for we are despised: and 8085
4:20 *therefore* ye **h** the sound of the trumpet, 8085
8: 2 and all that could **h** with understanding, 8085
9:29 and hardened their neck, and would not **h**. 8085
Job 3:18 they **h** not the voice of the oppressor. 8085
5:27 so it *is*; **h** it, and know thou *it* for thy good. 8085
13: 6 **H** now my reasoning, and hearken to 8085
13:17 **H diligently** my speech, and 8085+8085
15:17 I will shew thee, **h** me; and that which I 8085
21: 2 **H diligently** my speech, and let this 8085+8085
22:27 he shall **h** thee, and thou shalt pay thy 8085
27: 9 Will God **h** his cry when trouble cometh 8085
30:20 I cry unto thee, and thou dost not **h** me: 6030
31:35 O that one would **h** me! behold, my desire 8085
33: 1 **h** my speeches, and hearken to all my 8085
34: 2 **H** my words, O ye wise *men*; and give ear 8085
34:16 If now *thou hast* understanding, **h** this: 8085
35:13 Surely God will not **h** vanity, neither will 8085
37: 2 **H attentively** the noise of his voice, and 8085
42: 4 **H**, I beseech thee, and I will speak: I will 8085
Ps 4: 1 **H** me when I call, O God of my 6030
4: 1 have mercy upon me, and **h** my prayer. 8085
4: 3 the LORD will **h** when I call unto him. 8085
5: 3 My voice shalt thou **h** *in* the morning, 8085
10:17 their heart, thou wilt **cause** thine ear **to h**: 7181
13: 3 Consider *and* **h** me, O LORD my God: 6030
17: 1 **H** the right, O LORD, attend unto my cry, 8085
17: 6 upon thee, for thou wilt **h** me, O God: 6030
17: 6 incline thine ear unto me, *and* **h** my speech. 8085
18:44 As soon as they **h** *of me*, they shall obey 8088
20: 1 The LORD **h** thee in the day of trouble; 6030
20: 6 he will **h** him from his holy heaven with 6030
20: 9 LORD: let the king **h** us when we call. 6030
27: 7 **H**, O LORD, *when* I cry *with* my voice: 8085
28: 2 **H** the voice of my supplications, when I cry 8085
30:10 **H**, O LORD, and have mercy upon me: 8085
34: 2 the humble shall **h** *thereof*, and be glad. 8085
38:15 do I hope: thou wilt **h**, O Lord my God. 6030
38:16 *H me*, lest *otherwise* they should rejoice NIH
39:12 **H** my prayer, O LORD, and give ear unto 8085
49: 1 **H** this, all ye people; give ear, all ye 8085
50: 7 **H**, O my people, and I will speak; O Israel, 8085
51: 8 **Make** me **to h** joy and gladness; *that* 8085
54: 2 **H** my prayer, O God; give ear to the words 8085
55: 2 Attend unto me, and **h** me: I mourn in my 6030
55:17 and cry aloud: and he shall **h** my voice. 8085
55:19 God shall **h**, and afflict them, even he that 8085
59: 7 *are* in their lips: for who, *say they*, doth **h**? 8085
60: 5 save *with* thy right hand, and **h** me. 6030
61: 1 **H** my cry, O God; attend unto my prayer. 8085

H

Ps	64: 1	**H** my voice, O God, in my prayer:	8085
	66:16	Come *and* **h**, all ye that fear God, and I will	8085
	66:18	in my heart, the Lord will not **h** *me:*	8085
	69:13	O God, in the multitude of thy mercy **h** me,	6030
	69:16	**H** me, O LORD; for thy lovingkindness *is*	6030
	69:17	for I am in trouble: **h** me speedily.	6030
	81: 8	**H**, O my people, and I will testify unto	8085
	84: 8	O LORD God *of* hosts, **h** my prayer:	8085
	85: 8	I will **h** what God the LORD will speak:	8085
	86: 1	Bow down thine ear, O LORD, **h** me: for I	6030
	92:11	mine ears shall **h** *my desire* of the wicked	8085
	94: 9	He that planted the ear, shall he not **h**? he	8085
	95: 7	of his hand. To day if ye will **h** his voice,	8085
	102: 1	**H** my prayer, O LORD, and let my cry	8085
	102:20	To **h** the groaning of the prisoner; to loose	8085
	115: 6	They have ears, but they **h** not: noses have	8085
	119:145	with *my* whole heart; **h** me, O LORD:	6030
	119:149	**H** my voice according unto thy	8085
	130: 2	Lord, **h** my voice: let thine ears be attentive	8085
	135:17	They have ears, but they **h** not; neither is	238
	138: 4	when they **h** the words of thy mouth.	8085
	140: 6	**h** the voice of my supplications, O LORD.	238
	141: 6	in stony places, they shall **h** my words;	8085
	143: 1	**H** my prayer, O LORD, give ear to my	8085
	143: 7	**H** me speedily, O LORD: my spirit	6030
	143: 8	**Cause** me **to h** thy lovingkindness in	8085
	145:19	he also will **h** their cry, and will save them.	8085
Pr	1: 5	A wise *man* will **h**, and will increase	8085
	1: 8	**h** the instruction of thy father, and	8085
	4: 1	**H**, ye children, the instruction of a father,	8085
	4:10	**H**, O my son, and receive my sayings; and	8085
	5: 7	**H** me now therefore, O ye children, and	8085
	8: 6	**H**, for I will speak of excellent things; and	8085
	8:33	**H** instruction, and be wise, and refuse *it*	8085
	19:20	**H** counsel, and receive instruction,	8085
	19:27	to **h** the instruction *that causeth* to err from	8085
	22:17	**h** the words of the wise, and apply thine	8085
	23:19	**H** thou, my son, and be wise, and	8085
Ecc	5: 1	*be* more ready to **h**, than to give	8085
	7: 5	*It is* better to **h** the rebuke of the wise,	8085
	7: 5	than for a man to **h** the song of fools.	8085
	7:21	lest thou **h** thy servant curse thee:	8085
	12:13	Let us **h** the conclusion of the whole	8085
SS	2:14	me see thy countenance, let me **h** thy voice;	8085
	8:13	hearken to thy voice: **cause** me **to h** *it.*	8085
Isa	1: 2	**H**, O heavens, and give ear, O earth: for	8085
	1:10	**H** the word of the LORD, ye rulers of	8085
	1:15	when ye make many prayers, I will not **h**:	8085
	6: 9	**H** ye **indeed**, but understand not;	8085+8085
	6:10	**h** with their ears, and understand *with* their	8085
	7:13	he said, **H** ye now, O house of David; *Is it* a	8085
	18: 3	and when *he* bloweth a trumpet, **h** ye.	8085
	28:12	this *is* the refreshing: yet they would not **h**.	8085
	28:14	Wherefore **h** the word of the LORD,	8085
	28:23	Give ye ear, and **h** my voice; hearken, and	8085
	28:23	hear my voice; hearken, and **h** my speech.	8085
	29:18	in that day shall the deaf **h** the words of	8085
	30: 9	children *that* will not **h** the law of	8085
	30:19	when *he* shall **h** it, he will answer thee.	8085
	30:21	thine ears shall **h** a word behind thee,	8085
	32: 3	and the ears of them that **h** shall hearken.	8085
	32: 9	ye women that are at ease, **h** my voice;	8085
	33:13	**H**, ye *that are* far off, what I have done; and	8085
	34: 1	Come near, ye nations, to **h**; and hearken,	8085
	34: 1	let the earth **h**, and all that is therein;	8085
	36:13	said, **H** ye the words of the great king,	8085
	37: 4	It may be the LORD thy God will **h**	8085
	37: 7	he shall **h** a rumour, and return to his own	8085
	37:17	Incline thine ear, O LORD, and **h**;	8085
	37:17	**h** all the words of Sennacherib, which hath	8085
	39: 5	**H** the word of the LORD of hosts:	8085
	41:17	faileth for thirst, I the LORD will **h** them,	6030
	42:18	**H**, ye deaf; and look, ye blind, that *ye* may	8085
	42:23	will hearken and **h** for the time to come?	8085
	43: 9	or let them **h**, and say, *It is* truth.	8085
	44: 1	Yet now **h**, O Jacob my servant; and Israel,	8085
	47: 8	Therefore **h** now this, *thou that art* given to	8085
	48: 1	**H** ye this, O house of Jacob, which are	8085
	48:14	All ye, assemble yourselves, and **h**;	8085
	48:16	Come ye near unto me, **h** ye this; I have not	8085
	50: 4	he wakeneth mine ear to **h** as the learned.	8085
	51:21	Therefore **h** now this, thou afflicted, and	8085
	55: 3	**h**, and your soul shall live; and I will make	8085
	59: 1	neither his ear heavy, that *it* cannot **h**:	8085
	59: 2	hid *his* face from you, that *he* will not **h**.	8085
	65:12	when I spake, ye did not **h**; but did evil	8085
	65:24	and whiles they are yet speaking, I will **h**.	8085
	66: 4	did answer; when I spake, they did not **h**:	8085
	66: 5	**H** the word of the LORD, ye that tremble	8085
Jer	2: 4	**H** ye the word of the LORD, O house of	8085
	4:21	*and* **h** the sound of the trumpet?	8085
	5:21	**H** now this, O foolish people, and	8085
	5:21	and see not; which have ears, and **h** not:	8085
	6:10	I speak, and give warning, that they may **h**?	8085
	6:18	Therefore **h**, ye nations, and know,	8085
	6:19	**H**, O earth: behold, I will bring evil upon	8085
	7: 2	say, **H** the word of the LORD, all *ye of*	8085
	7:16	intercession to me: for I *will* not **h** thee.	8085
	9:10	neither can *men* **h** the voice of the cattle;	8085
	9:20	Yet **h** the word of the LORD, O ye	8085
	10: 1	**H** ye the word which the LORD speaketh	8085
	11: 2	**H** ye the words of this covenant, and	8085
	11: 6	**H** ye the words of this covenant, and	8085
	11:10	which refused to **h** my words;	8085
	11:14	for I will not **h** *them* in the time that they	8085
	13:10	evil people, which refuse to **h** my words,	8085
	13:11	and for a glory: but they would not **h**.	8085
	13:15	**H** ye, and give ear; be not proud: for	8085
	13:17	if ye will not **h** it, my soul shall weep in	8085
	14:12	When they fast, I will not **h** their cry; and	8085
	17:20	**H** ye the word of the LORD, ye kings of	8085
	17:23	made their neck stiff, that *they* might not **h**,	8085
	18: 2	and there I will **cause** thee **to h** my words.	8085
	19: 3	say, **H** ye the word of the LORD, O kings	8085
	19:15	that *they* might not **h** my words.	8085
	20:16	let him **h** the cry in the morning, and	8085
	21:11	*say,* **H** ye the word of the LORD.	8085
	22: 2	say, **H** the word of the LORD, O king of	8085
	22: 5	if ye will not **h** these words, I swear by	8085
	22:21	thy prosperity; *but* thou saidst, I will not **h**.	8085
	22:29	earth, earth, **h** the word of the LORD.	8085
	23:22	had **caused** my people **to h** my words, then	8085
	25: 4	not hearkened, nor inclined your ear to **h**.	8085
	28: 7	Nevertheless **h** thou now this word that I	8085
	28:15	Hananiah the prophet, **H** now, Hananiah;	8085
	29:19	and sending *them;* but ye would not **h**,	8085
	29:20	**H** ye therefore the word of the LORD,	8085
	31:10	**H** the word of the LORD, O ye nations,	8085
	33: 9	which shall **h** all the good that I do unto	8085
	34: 4	Yet **h** the word of the LORD, O Zedekiah	8085
	36: 3	It may be that the house of Judah will **h** all	8085
	36:25	not burn the roll: but he would not **h** them.	8085
	37:20	Therefore **h** now, I pray thee, O my lord	8085
	38:25	if the princes **h** that I have talked with thee,	8085
	42:14	nor **h** the sound of the trumpet, nor have	8085
	42:15	therefore **h** the word of the LORD,	8085
	44:24	all the women, **H** the word of the LORD,	8085
	44:26	Therefore **h** ye the word of the LORD,	8085
	49:20	Therefore **h** the counsel of the LORD,	8085
	50:45	Therefore **h** ye the counsel of the LORD,	8085
La	1:18	**h**, I pray you, all people, and behold my	8085
Eze	2: 5	whether they will **h**, or whether they will	8085
	2: 7	whether they will **h**, or whether they will	8085
	2: 8	son of man, **h** what I say unto thee;	8085
	3:10	receive in thine heart, and **h** with thine ears.	8085
	3:11	whether they will **h**, or whether they will	8085
	3:17	therefore **h** the word at my mouth, and	8085
	3:27	He that heareth, let him **h**; and he that	8085
	6: 3	of Israel, **h** the word of the Lord GOD;	8085
	8:18	*with* a loud voice, *yet* will I not **h** them.	8085
	12: 2	see not; they have ears to **h**, and hear not:	8085
	12: 2	see not; they have ears to hear, and **h** not:	8085
	13: 2	own hearts, **H** ye the word of the LORD;	8085
	13:19	by your lying to my people that **h** *your* lies?	8085
	16:35	O harlot, **h** the word of the LORD:	8085
	18:25	**H** now, O house of Israel; Is not my way	8085
	20:47	of the south, **H** the word of the LORD;	8085
	24:26	to **cause** *thee* **to h** *it* with *thine* ears?	2045
	25: 3	**H** the word of the Lord GOD;	8085
	33: 7	thou shalt **h** the word at my mouth,	8085
	33:30	**h** what *is* the word that cometh forth from	8085
	33:31	they **h** thy words, but they will not do	8085
	33:32	for they **h** thy words, but they do them not.	8085
	34: 7	ye shepherds, **h** the word of the LORD;	8085
	34: 9	O ye shepherds, **h** the word of the LORD;	8085
	36: 1	of Israel, **h** the word of the LORD:	8085
	36: 4	of Israel, **h** the word of the Lord GOD;	8085
	36:15	Neither will I **cause** *men* **to h** in thee	8085

Eze	37: 4	O ye dry bones, **h** the word of the LORD.	8085
	40: 4	**h** with thine ears, and set thine heart upon	8085
	44: 5	**h** with thine ears all that I say unto thee	8085
Da	3: 5	*That* at what time ye **h** the sound of	8086
	3:10	that every man that shall **h** the sound of	8086
	3:15	Now if ye be ready that at what time ye **h**	8086
	5:23	stone, which see not, nor **h**, nor know:	8086
	9:17	**h** the prayer of thy servant, and	8085
	9:18	O my God, incline thine ear, and **h**;	8085
	9:19	O Lord, **h**; O Lord, forgive; O Lord,	8085
Hos	2:21	I will **h**, saith the LORD, I will hear	6030
	2:21	I will **h** the heavens, and they shall hear	6030
	2:21	hear the heavens, and they shall **h** the earth;	6030
	2:22	the earth shall **h** the corn, and the wine,	6030
	2:22	and the oil; and they shall **h** Jezreel.	6030
	4: 1	**H** the word of the LORD, ye children of	8085
	5: 1	**H** ye this, O priests; and hearken, ye house	8085
Joel	1: 2	**H** this, ye old men, and give ear, all ye	8085
Am	3: 1	**H** this word that the LORD hath spoken	8085
	3:13	**H** ye, and testify in the house of Jacob,	8085
	4: 1	**H** this word, ye kine of Bashan, that *are* in	8085
	5: 1	**H** ye this word which I take up against you,	8085
	5:23	for I will not **h** the melody of thy viols.	8085
	7:16	therefore **h** thou the word of the LORD:	8085
	8: 4	**H** this, O ye that swallow up the needy,	8085
Mic	1: 2	**H**, all ye people; hearken, O earth, and	8085
	3: 1	I said, **H**, I pray you, O heads of Jacob,	8085
	3: 4	unto the LORD, but he will not **h** them:	6030
	3: 9	**H** this, I pray you, ye heads of the house of	8085
	6: 1	**H** ye now what the LORD saith; Arise,	8085
	6: 1	the mountains, and let the hills **h** thy voice.	8085
	6: 2	**H** ye, O mountains, the LORD'S	8085
	6: 9	**h** ye the rod, and who hath appointed it.	8085
	7: 7	God of my salvation: my God will **h** me.	8085
Na	3:19	all that **h** the bruit of thee shall clap	8085
Hab	1: 2	how long shall I cry, and thou wilt not **h**?	8085
Zec	1: 4	they did not **h**, nor hearken unto me,	8085
	3: 8	**H** now, O Joshua the high priest, thou, and	8085
	7: 7	*Should* ye not **h** the words which	NIH
	7:11	stopped their ears, that *they* should not **h**.	8085
	7:12	lest *they* should **h** the law, and the words	8085
	7:13	*that* as he cried, and they would not **h**;	8085
	7:13	so they cried, and I would not **h**, saith	8085
	8: 9	ye that **h** in these days these words by	8085
	10: 6	*am* the LORD their God, and will **h** them.	6030
	13: 9	shall call on my name, and I will **h** them:	6030
Mal	2: 2	If ye will not **h**, and if ye will not lay *it* to	8085
Mt	10:14	nor **h** your words, when ye depart out of that	*191*
	10:27	and what ye **h** in the ear, *that* preach ye upon	*191*
	11: 4	shew John again *those things* which ye do **h**	*191*
	11: 5	and the deaf **h**, the dead are raised up, and	*191*
	11:15	He that hath ears to **h**, let him hear.	*191*
	11:15	He that hath ears to hear, let him **h**.	*191*
	12:19	neither shall any *man* **h** his voice in	*191*
	12:42	of the earth to **h** the wisdom of Solomon;	*191*
	13: 9	Who hath ears to **h**, let him hear.	*191*
	13: 9	Who hath ears to hear, let him **h**.	*191*
	13:13	and hearing they **h** not, neither do they	*191*
	13:14	By hearing ye shall **h**, and shall not	*191*
	13:15	see with *their* eyes, and **h** with *their* ears,	*191*
	13:16	for they see: and your ears, for they **h**.	*191*
	13:17	and to **h** *those things* which ye hear,	*191*
	13:17	and to hear *those things* which ye **h**,	*191*
	13:18	**H** ye therefore the parable of the sower.	*191*
	13:43	Who hath ears to **h**, let him hear.	*191*
	13:43	Who hath ears to hear, let him **h**.	*191*
	15:10	and said unto them, **H**, and understand:	*191*
	17: 5	in whom I am well pleased; **h** ye him.	*191*
	18:15	if he shall **h** thee, thou hast gained thy	*191*
	18:16	But if he will not **h** *thee, then* take with thee	*191*
	18:17	And if he shall **neglect to h** them, tell *it*	*3878*
	18:17	but if he **neglect to h** the church, let him be	*3878*
	21:33	**H** another parable: There was a certain	*191*
	24: 6	And ye shall **h** of wars and rumours of wars:	*191*
Mk	4: 9	He that hath ears to **h**, let him hear.	*191*
	4: 9	He that hath ears to hear, let him **h**.	*191*
	4:12	and hearing they may **h**, and not understand;	*191*
	4:18	are sown among thorns; such as **h** the word,	*191*
	4:20	such as **h** the word, and receive *it*, and	*191*
	4:23	If any *man* have ears to **h**, let him hear.	*191*
	4:23	If any *man* have ears to hear, let him **h**.	*191*
	4:24	he said unto them, Take heed what you **h**:	*191*
	4:24	and unto you that **h** shall more be given.	*191*
	4:33	word unto them, as they were able to **h** *it*.	*191*
	6:11	nor **h** you, when ye depart thence,	*191*
	7:16	If any *man* have ears to **h**, let him hear.	*191*
	7:16	If any *man* have ears to hear, let him **h**.	*191*
	7:37	he maketh both the deaf to **h**, and the dumb	*191*
	8:18	and having ears, **h** ye not? and do ye not	*191*
	9: 7	saying, This is my beloved Son: **h** him.	*191*
	12:29	The first of all the commandments *is*, **H**,	*191*
	13: 7	And when ye shall **h** of wars and rumours of	*191*
Lk	5: 1	as the people pressed upon him to **h**	*191*
	5:15	and great multitudes came together to **h**, and	*191*
	6:17	which came to **h** him, and to be healed of	*191*
	6:27	But I say unto you which **h**, Love your	*191*
	7:22	are cleansed, the deaf **h**, the dead are raised,	*191*
	8: 8	he cried, He that hath ears to **h**, let him hear.	*191*
	8: 8	he cried, He that hath ears to hear, let him **h**.	*191*
	8:12	Those by the way side are they that **h**; then	*191*
	8:13	when they **h**, receive the word with joy;	*191*
	8:18	Take heed therefore how ye **h**:	*191*
	8:21	my brethren are these which **h** the word of	*191*
	9: 9	of whom I **h** such *things?* And he desired to	*191*
	9:35	saying, This is my beloved Son: **h** him.	*191*
	10:24	and to **h** *those things* which ye hear,	*191*
	10:24	and to hear *those things* which ye **h**,	*191*
	11:28	blessed *are* they that **h** the word of God, and	*191*
	11:31	of the earth to **h** the wisdom of Solomon;	*191*
	14:35	it out. He that hath ears to **h**, let him hear.	*191*
	14:35	it out. He that hath ears to hear, let him **h**.	*191*
	15: 1	all the publicans and sinners for to **h** him.	*191*
	16: 2	said unto him, How *is* it *that* I **h** this of thee?	*191*
	16:29	and the prophets; let them **h** them.	*191*
	16:31	If they **h** not Moses and the prophets,	*191*
	18: 6	the Lord said, **H** what the unjust judge saith.	*191*
	19:48	for all the people were very attentive to **h**	*191*
	21: 9	But when ye shall **h** of wars and	*191*
	21:38	morning to him in the temple, for to **h** him.	*191*
Jn	5:25	when the dead shall **h** the voice of the Son of	*191*
	5:25	of the Son of God: and they that **h** shall live.	*191*
	5:28	in the which all that are in the graves shall **h**	*191*
	5:30	as I **h**, I judge: and my judgment is just;	*191*
	6:60	This is a hard saying; who can **h** it?	*191*
	7:51	before it **h** him, and know what he doeth?	*191*
	8:43	*even* because ye cannot **h** my word.	*191*
	8:47	ye therefore **h** *them* not, because ye are not	*191*
	9:27	I have told you already, and ye did not **h**:	*191*
	9:27	wherefore would you **h** *it* again? will ye also	*191*
	10: 3	porter openeth; and the sheep **h** his voice:	*191*
	10: 8	and robbers: but the sheep did not **h** them.	*191*
	10:16	also I must bring, and they shall **h** my voice;	*191*
	10:20	He hath a devil, and is mad; why **h** ye him?	*191*
	10:27	My sheep **h** my voice, and I know them, and	*191*
	12:47	And if any *man* **h** my words, and	*191*
	14:24	and the word which you **h** is not mine, but	*191*
	16:13	but whatsoever he shall **h**, *that* shall he	*191*
Ac	2: 8	And how **h** we every man in our own	*191*
	2:11	we do **h** them speak in our tongues	*191*
	2:22	Ye men of Israel, **h** these words; Jesus of	*191*
	2:33	hath shed forth this, which ye now see and **h**.	*191*
	3:22	him shall ye **h** in all *things* whatsoever he	*191*
	3:23	every soul, which will not **h** that prophet,	*191*
	7:37	your brethren, like unto me; him shall ye **h**.	*191*
	10:22	thee into his house, and to **h** words of thee.	*191*
	10:33	to **h** all *things* that are commanded thee of	*191*
	13: 7	and Saul, and desired to **h** the word of God.	*191*
	13:44	whole city together to **h** the word of God.	*191*
	15: 7	that the Gentiles by my mouth should **h**	*191*
	17:21	but *either* to tell, or to **h** some new *thing*.)	*191*
	17:32	We will **h** thee again of this *matter*.	*191*
	19:26	Moreover ye see and **h**, that not alone at	*191*
	21:22	for they will **h** that thou art come.	*191*
	22: 1	**h** ye my defence *which I make* now unto	*191*
	22:14	and shouldest **h** the voice of his mouth.	*191*
	23:35	I will **h** thee, said he, when thine accusers	*1251*
	24: 4	I pray *thee* that thou wouldest **h** us of thy	*191*
	25:22	unto Festus, I would also **h** the man myself.	*191*
	25:22	To morrow, said he, thou shalt **h** him.	*191*
	26: 3	wherefore I beseech thee to **h** me patiently.	*191*
	26:29	but also all that **h** me this day, were both	*191*
	28:22	But we desire to **h** of thee what thou	*191*
	28:26	Hearing ye shall **h**, and shall not understand;	*191*
	28:27	and **h** with *their* ears, and understand with	*191*
	28:28	sent unto the Gentiles, and *that* they will **h** it.	*191*
Ro	10:14	and how shall they **h** without a preacher?	*191*
	11: 8	not see, and ears that *they* should not **h**;)	*191*
1Co	11:18	I **h** that there be divisions among you;	*191*

1Co	14:21	and yet for all that will they not **h** me,	*1522*
Gal	4:21	to be under the law, do ye not **h** the law?	*191*
Php	1:27	or *else* be absent, I may **h** of your affairs,	*191*
	1:30	which ye saw in me, and now **h** *to be* in me.	*191*
2Th	3:11	For we **h** that *there are* some which walk	*191*
1Ti	4:16	shalt both save thyself, and them that **h** thee.	*191*
2Ti	4:17	and *that* all the Gentiles might **h**:	*191*
Heb	3: 7	Ghost saith, To day if ye will **h** his voice,	*191*
	3:15	it is said, To day if ye will **h** his voice,	*191*
	4: 7	as it is said, To day if ye will **h** his voice,	*191*
Jas	1:19	let every man be swift to **h**, slow to speak,	*191*
1Jn	5:15	And if we know that he **h** us, whatsoever we	*191*
3Jn	1: 4	I have no greater joy than to **h** that my	*191*
Rev	1: 3	and they that **h** the words of *this* prophecy,	*191*
	2: 7	let him **h** what the Spirit saith unto	*191*
	2:11	let him **h** what the Spirit saith unto	*191*
	2:17	let him **h** what the Spirit saith unto	*191*
	2:29	let him **h** what the Spirit saith unto	*191*
	3: 6	let him **h** what the Spirit saith unto	*191*
	3:13	let him **h** what the Spirit saith unto	*191*
	3:20	if any *man* **h** my voice, and open the door, I	*191*
	3:22	let him **h** what the Spirit saith unto	*191*
	9:20	which neither can see, nor **h**, nor walk:	*191*
	13: 9	If any *man* have an ear, let him **h**.	*191*

HEARD (641) [HEAR]

Ge	3: 8	they **h** the voice of the LORD God	8085
	3:10	I **h** thy voice in the garden, and I was	8085
	14:14	when Abram **h** that his brother was taken	8085
	16:11	because the LORD hath **h** thy affliction.	8085
	17:20	as for Ishmael, I have **h** thee: Behold,	8085
	18:10	Sarah **h** *it in* the tent door, which *was*	8085
	21:17	God **h** the voice of the lad; and the angel of	8085
	21:17	for God hath **h** the voice of the lad where	8085
	21:26	thou tell me, neither yet **h** I *of it,* but to day.	8085
	24:30	when he **h** the words of Rebekah his sister,	8085
	24:52	when Abraham's servant **h** their words,	8085
	27: 5	Rebekah **h** when Isaac spake to Esau his	8085
	27: 6	I **h** thy father speak unto Esau thy brother,	8085
	27:34	when Esau **h** the words of his father, he	8085
	29:13	when Laban **h** the tidings of Jacob his	8085
	29:33	Because the LORD hath **h** that I *was*	8085
	30: 6	hath also **h** my voice, and hath given me a	8085
	31: 1	he **h** the words of Laban's sons, saying,	8085
	34: 5	Jacob **h** that he had defiled Dinah his	8085
	34: 7	Jacob came out of the field when they **h** *it:*	8085
	35:22	Israel **h** *it.* Now the sons of Jacob were	8085
	37:17	for I **h** *them* say, Let us go to Dothan.	8085
	37:21	Reuben **h** *it,* and he delivered him out of	8085
	39:15	when he **h** that I lifted up my voice and	8085
	39:19	when his master **h** the words of his wife,	8085
	41:15	I have **h** say of thee, *that* thou canst	8085
	42: 2	Behold, I have **h** that there is corn in Egypt:	8085
	43:25	for they **h** that they should eat bread there.	8085
	45: 2	the Egyptians and the house of Pharaoh **h**.	8085
	45:16	the fame *thereof* was **h** *in* Pharaoh's house,	8085
Ex	2:15	Now when Pharaoh **h** this thing, he sought	8085
	2:24	God **h** their groaning, and God remembered	8085
	3: 7	have **h** their cry by reason of their	8085
	4:31	when they **h** that the LORD had visited	8085
	6: 5	I have also **h** the groaning of the children of	8085
	16: 9	for he hath **h** your murmurings.	8085
	16:12	I have **h** the murmurings of the children of	8085
	18: 1	**h** of all that God had done for Moses, and	8085
	23:13	neither let it be **h** out of thy mouth.	8085
	28:35	his sound shall be **h** when he goeth in unto	8085
	32:17	when Joshua **h** the noise of the people as	8085
	33: 4	when the people **h** these evil tidings, they	8085
Lev	10:20	And when Moses **h** *that,* he was content.	8085
	24:14	let all that **h** *him* lay their hands upon his	8085
Nu	7:89	he **h** the voice of one speaking unto him	8085
	11: 1	the LORD **h** *it;* and his anger was kindled;	8085
	11:10	Moses **h** the people weep throughout their	8085
	12: 2	spoken also by us? And the LORD **h** *it.*	8085
	14:14	*for* they have **h** that thou LORD *art*	8085
	14:15	the nations which have **h** the fame of thee	8085
	14:27	I have **h** the murmurings of the children of	8085
	16: 4	And when Moses **h** *it,* he fell upon his face:	8085
	20:16	he **h** our voice, and sent an angel, and	8085
	21: 1	**h** *tell* that Israel came *by* the way of	8085
	22:36	when Balak **h** that Balaam was come, he	8085
	24: 4	He hath said, which **h** the words of God,	8085
	24:16	which **h** the words of God, and knew	8085
	30: 7	her husband **h** *it,* and held his peace at her	8085
	30: 7	held his peace at her in the day that he **h** *it:*	8085
	30: 8	disallow her on the day that he **h** *it;*	8085
	30:11	her husband **h** *it,* and held his peace at her,	8085
	30:12	made them void on the day he **h** *them;*	8085
	30:14	he held his peace at her in the day that he **h**	8085
	30:15	make them void after *that* he hath **h** *them;*	8085
	33:40	**h** of the coming of the children of Israel.	8085
Dt	1:34	the LORD **h** the voice of your words, and	8085
	4:12	ye **h** the voice of the words, but saw no	8085
	4:12	but saw no similitude; only *ye* **h** a voice.	NIH
	4:32	as this great thing *is,* or hath been **h** like it?	8085
	4:33	midst of the fire, as thou hast **h**, and live?	8085
	5:23	when ye **h** the voice out of the midst of	8085
	5:24	we have **h** his voice out of the midst of	8085
	5:26	that hath **h** the voice of the living God	8085
	5:28	the LORD **h** the voice of your words,	8085
	5:28	I have **h** the voice of the words of this	8085
	9: 2	*of whom* thou hast **h** *say,* Who can stand	8085
	17: 4	thou hast **h** *of it,* and inquired diligently,	8085
	26: 7	the LORD **h** our voice, and looked on our	8085
Jos	2:10	For we have **h** how the LORD dried up	8085
	2:11	as soon as we had **h** *these things,* our hearts	8085
	5: 1	**h** that the LORD had dried up the waters	8085
	6:20	when the people **h** the sound of	8085
	9: 1	the Hivite, and the Jebusite, **h** *thereof;*	8085
	9: 3	when the inhabitants of Gibeon **h** what	8085
	9: 9	for we have **h** the fame of him, and all that	8085
	9:16	that they **h** that they *were* their neighbours,	8085
	10: 1	when Adoni-zedek king of Jerusalem had **h**	8085
	11: 1	when Jabin king of Hazor had **h** *those*	8085
	22:11	the children of Israel **h** say, Behold,	8085
	22:12	when the children of Israel **h** *of it,*	8085
	22:30	**h** the words that the children of Reuben and	8085
	24:27	for it hath **h** all the words of the LORD	8085
Jdg	7:15	*so,* when Gideon **h** the telling of the dream,	8085
	9:30	when Zebul the ruler of the city **h**	8085
	9:46	**h** *that,* they entered into a hold of the house	8085
	18:25	Let not thy voice be **h** among us, lest angry	8085
	20: 3	(Now the children of Benjamin **h** that	8085
Ru	1: 6	for she had **h** in the country of Moab how	8085
1Sa	1:13	her lips moved, but her voice was not **h**:	8085
	2:22	and **h** all that his sons did unto all Israel;	8085
	4: 6	when the Philistines **h** the noise of	8085
	4:14	when Eli **h** the noise of the crying, he said,	8085
	4:19	when she **h** the tidings that the ark of God	8085
	7: 7	when the Philistines **h** that the children of	8085
	7: 7	when the children of Israel **h** *it,* they were	8085
	7: 9	LORD for Israel; and the LORD **h** him.	6030
	8:21	Samuel **h** all the words of the people, and	8085
	11: 6	spirit of God came upon Saul when he **h**	8085
	13: 3	the Philistines **h** *of it.* And Saul blew	8085
	13: 4	all Israel **h** say *that* Saul had smitten a	8085
	14:22	*when* they **h** that the Philistines fled,	8085
	14:27	Jonathan **h** not when his father charged	8085
	17:11	all Israel **h** those words of the Philistine,	8085
	17:23	to the same words: and David **h** *them.*	8085
	17:28	Eliab his eldest brother **h** when he spake	8085
	17:31	when the words were **h** which David spake,	8085
	22: 1	all his father's house **h** *it,* they went down	8085
	22: 6	When Saul **h** that David was discovered,	8085
	23:10	thy servant hath **certainly h** that Saul	8085+8085
	23:11	Saul come down, as thy servant hath **h**?	8085
	23:25	when Saul **h** *that,* he pursued after David *in*	8085
	25: 4	David **h** in the wilderness that Nabal did	8085
	25: 7	now I have **h** that thou hast shearers:	8085
	25:39	when David **h** that Nabal was dead, he said,	8085
	31:11	when the inhabitants of Jabesh-gilead **h** of	8085
2Sa	3:28	afterward when David **h** *it,* he said, I and	8085
	4: 1	when Saul's son **h** that Abner was dead in	8085
	5:17	when the Philistines **h** that they had	8085
	5:17	David **h** *of it,* and went down to the hold.	8085
	7:22	according to all that we have **h** with our	8085
	8: 9	When Toi king of Hamath **h** that David had	8085
	10: 7	when David **h** *of it,* he sent Joab, and all	8085
	11:26	when the wife of Uriah **h** that Uriah her	8085
	13:21	when king David **h** of all these things, he	8085
	18: 5	all the people **h** when the king gave all	8085
	19: 2	for the people **h** say that day *how* the king	8085
1Ki	1:11	Hast thou not **h** that Adonijah the son of	8085
	1:41	all the guests that *were* with him **h** *it* as	8085
	1:41	when Joab **h** the sound of the trumpet, he	8085
	1:45	rang again. This *is* the noise that ye have **h**.	8085
	2:42	unto me, The word *that* I have **h** *is* good.	8085
	3:28	all Israel **h** of the judgment which the king	8085

1Ki	4:34	of the earth, which had **h** of his wisdom.	8085
	5: 1	for he had **h** that they had anointed him	8085
	5: 7	when Hiram **h** the words of Solomon,	8085
	6: 7	nor axe *nor* any tool of iron **h** in the house,	8085
	9: 3	I have **h** thy prayer and thy supplication,	8085
	10: 1	when the queen of Sheba **h** of the fame of	8085
	10: 6	It was a true report that I **h** in mine own	8085
	10: 7	prosperity exceedeth the fame which I **h**.	8085
	11:21	when Hadad **h** in Egypt that David slept	8085
	12: 2	**h** *of it,* (for he was fled from the presence	8085
	12:20	when all Israel **h** that Jeroboam was come	8085
	13: 4	when king Jeroboam **h** the saying of	8085
	13:26	him back from the way **h** *thereof,* he said,	8085
	14: 6	*so,* when Ahijah **h** the sound of her feet,	8085
	15:21	when Baasha **h** *thereof,* that he left off	8085
	16:16	the people that *were* encamped **h** say,	8085
	17:22	the LORD **h** the voice of Elijah; and	8085
	19:13	when Elijah **h** *it,* that he wrapped his face	8085
	20:12	when *Ben-hadad* **h** this message, as he *was*	8085
	20:31	we have **h** that the kings of the house of	8085
	21:15	when Jezebel **h** that Naboth was stoned,	8085
	21:16	when Ahab **h** that Naboth was dead,	8085
	21:27	it came to pass, when Ahab **h** those words,	8085
2Ki	3:21	when all the Moabites **h** that the kings were	8085
	5: 8	when Elisha the man of God had **h** that	8085
	6:30	when the king **h** the words of the woman,	8085
	9:30	Jezebel **h** *of it;* and she painted her face,	8085
	11:13	And when Athaliah **h** the noise of the guard	8085
	19: 1	when king Hezekiah **h** *it,* that he rent his	8085
	19: 4	words which the LORD thy God hath **h**:	8085
	19: 6	not afraid of the words which thou hast **h**,	8085
	19: 8	for he had **h** that he was departed from	8085
	19: 9	when he **h** say of Tirhakah king of	8085
	19:11	thou hast **h** what the kings of Assyria have	8085
	19:20	Sennacherib king of Assyria I have **h**.	8085
	19:25	Hast thou not **h** long ago *how* I have done	8085
	20: 5	I have **h** thy prayer, I have seen thy tears:	8085
	20:12	for he had **h** that Hezekiah had been sick.	8085
	22:11	when the king had **h** the words of the book	8085
	22:18	*As touching* the words which thou hast **h**;	8085
	22:19	I also have **h** *thee,* saith the LORD.	8085
	25:23	**h** that the king of Babylon had made	8085
1Ch	10:11	when all Jabesh-gilead **h** all that	8085
	14: 8	when the Philistines **h** that David was	8085
	14: 8	David **h** *of it,* and went out against them.	8085
	17:20	according to all that we have **h** with our	8085
	18: 9	Now when Tou king of Hamath **h** how	8085
	19: 8	when David **h** *of it,* he sent Joab, and all	8085
2Ch	5:13	to **make** one sound **to be h** in praising and	8085
	7:12	I have **h** thy prayer, and have chosen this	8085
	9: 1	when the queen of Sheba **h** of the fame of	8085
	9: 5	*It was* a true report which I **h** in mine own	8085
	9: 6	*for* thou exceedest the fame that I **h**.	8085
	10: 2	**h** *it,* that Jeroboam returned out of Egypt.	8085
	15: 8	when Asa **h** these words, and the prophecy	8085
	16: 5	when Baasha **h** *it,* that he left off building	8085
	20:29	when they had **h** that the LORD fought	8085
	23:12	Now when Athaliah **h** the noise of	8085
	30:27	their voice was **h**, and their prayer came *up*	8085
	33:13	**h** his supplication, and brought him again	8085
	34:19	when the king had **h** the words of the law,	8085
	34:26	*concerning* the words which thou hast **h**;	8085
	34:27	I have even **h** *thee* also, saith the LORD.	8085
Ezr	3:13	a loud shout, and the noise was **h** afar off.	8085
	4: 1	Benjamin **h** that the children of	8085
	9: 3	when I **h** this thing, I rent my garment and	8085
Ne	1: 4	when I **h** these words, *that* I sat down and	8085
	2:10	**h** *of it,* it grieved them exceedingly that	8085
	2:19	**h** *it,* they laughed us to scorn, and	8085
	4: 1	that when Sanballat **h** that we builded	8085
	4: 7	**h** that the walls of Jerusalem were made up,	8085
	4:15	when our enemies **h** that it was known unto	8085
	5: 6	I was very angry when I **h** their cry and	8085
	6: 1	**h** that I had builded the wall, and *that* there	8085
	6:16	that when all our enemies **h** *thereof,* and	8085
	8: 9	when they **h** the words of the law.	8085
	12:43	that the joy of Jerusalem was **h** even afar	8085
	13: 3	it came to pass, when they had **h** the law,	8085
Est	1:18	which have **h** of the deed of the queen.	8085
	2: 8	king's commandment and his decree was **h**,	8085
Job	2:11	Now when Job's three friends **h** of all this	8085
	4:16	*there was* silence, and I **h** a voice, *saying,*	8085
	13: 1	mine eye hath seen all *this,* mine ear hath **h**	8085
	15: 8	Hast thou **h** the secret of God? and	8085
	16: 2	I have **h** many such *things:* miserable	8085
	19: 7	Behold, I cry out *of* wrong, but I am not **h**:	6030
	20: 3	I have **h** the check of my reproach, and	8085
	26:14	how little a portion is **h** of him? but	8085
	28:22	We have **h** the fame thereof with our ears.	8085
	29:11	When the ear **h** *me,* then it blessed me; and	8085
	33: 8	I have **h** the voice of *thy* words,	8085
	37: 4	he will not stay them when his voice is **h**.	8085
	42: 5	I have **h** of thee by the hearing of the ear:	8085
Ps	3: 4	my voice, and he **h** me out of his holy hill.	6030
	6: 8	for the LORD hath **h** the voice of my	8085
	6: 9	The LORD hath **h** my supplication;	8085
	10:17	thou hast **h** the desire of the humble:	8085
	18: 6	he **h** my voice out of his temple, and	8085
	19: 3	nor language, *where* their voice is not **h**.	8085
	22:21	for thou hast **h** me from the horns of	6030
	22:24	but when he cried unto him, he **h**.	8085
	28: 6	he hath **h** the voice of my supplications.	8085
	31:13	For I have **h** the slander of many: fear *was*	8085
	34: 4	he **h** me, and delivered me from all my	6030
	34: 6	the LORD **h** *him,* and saved him out of all	8085
	38:13	I, as a deaf *man,* **h** not; and *I was* as a dumb	8085
	40: 1	and he inclined unto me, and **h** my cry.	8085
	44: 1	We have **h** with our ears, O God,	8085
	48: 8	As we have **h**, so have we seen in the city	8085
	61: 5	For thou, O God, hast **h** my vows: thou hast	8085
	62:11	God hath spoken once; twice have I **h** this;	8085
	66: 8	and **make** the voice of his praise **to be h**:	8085
	66:19	*But* verily God hath **h** *me;* he hath attended	8085
	76: 8	Thou didst **cause** judgment **to be h** from	8085
	78: 3	Which we have **h** and known, and	8085
	78:21	Therefore the LORD **h** *this,* and	8085
	78:59	When God **h** *this,* he was wroth, and	8085
	81: 5	*where* I **h** a language *that* I understood not.	8085
	97: 8	Zion **h**, and was glad, and the daughters of	8085
	106:44	their affliction, when he **h** their cry:	8085
	116: 1	because he hath **h** my voice *and*	8085
	118:21	for thou hast **h** me, and art become my	6030
	120: 1	I cried unto the LORD, and he **h** me.	6030
	132: 6	Lo, we **h** *of* it at Ephratah: we found it in	8085
Pr	21:13	he also shall cry himself, but shall not be **h**.	6030
Ecc	9:16	*is* despised, and his words *are* not **h**.	8085
	9:17	The words of wise *men are* **h** in quiet,	8085
SS	2:12	and the voice of the turtle is **h** in our land;	8085
Isa	6: 8	Also I **h** the voice of the Lord, saying,	8085
	10:30	**cause** *it* **to be h** unto Laish, O poor	7181
	15: 4	their voice shall be **h** *even* unto Jahaz:	8085
	16: 6	We have **h** of the pride of Moab; *he is* very	8085
	21:10	that which I have **h** of the LORD of hosts,	8085
	24:16	uttermost part of the earth have we **h** songs,	8085
	28:22	for I have **h** from the Lord GOD of hosts a	8085
	30:30	shall **cause** his glorious voice **to be h**,	8085
	37: 1	when king Hezekiah **h** *it,* that he rent his	8085
	37: 4	words which the LORD thy God hath **h**:	8085
	37: 6	Be not afraid of the words that thou hast **h**,	8085
	37: 8	for he had **h** that he was departed from	8085
	37: 9	he **h** say concerning Tirhakah king of	8085
	37: 9	when he **h** *it,* he sent messengers to	8085
	37:11	thou hast **h** what the kings of Assyria have	8085
	37:26	Hast thou not **h** long ago, *how* I have done	8085
	38: 5	I have **h** thy prayer, I have seen thy tears:	8085
	39: 1	for he had **h** that he had been sick, and	8085
	40:21	have ye not **h**? hath it not been told you	8085
	40:28	hast thou not **h**, *that* the everlasting God,	8085
	42: 2	nor **cause** his voice **to be h** in the street.	8085
	48: 6	Thou hast **h**, see all this; and will not ye	8085
	49: 8	In an acceptable time have I **h** thee, and	6030
	52:15	*that* which they had not **h** shall they	8085
	58: 4	to **make** your voice **to be h** on high.	8085
	60:18	Violence shall no more be **h** in thy land,	8085
	64: 4	the beginning of the world *men* have not **h**,	8085
	65:19	the voice of weeping shall be no more **h** in	8085
	66: 8	Who hath **h** such *a thing?* who hath seen	8085
	66:19	the isles afar off, that have not **h** my fame,	8085
Jer	3:21	A voice was **h** upon the high places,	8085
	4:19	my peace, because thou hast **h**, O my soul,	8085
	4:31	For I have **h** a voice as of a woman in	8085
	6: 7	violence and spoil is **h** in her; before me	8085
	6:24	We have **h** the fame thereof: our hands wax	8085
	7:13	rising up early and speaking, but ye **h** not;	8085
	8: 6	I hearkened and **h**, *but* they spake not	8085
	8:16	The snorting of his horses was **h** from Dan:	8085
	9:19	For a voice of wailing is **h** out of Zion,	8085
	18:13	who hath **h** such *things:* the virgin of Israel	8085

Jer	18:22	Let a cry be **h** from their houses, when thou	8085
	20: 1	**h** *that* Jeremiah prophesied these things.	8085
	20:10	For I **h** the defaming of many, fear on	8085
	23:18	and hath perceived and **h** his word?	8085
	23:18	who hath marked his word, and **h** *it?*	8085
	23:25	I have **h** what the prophets said,	8085
	25: 8	of hosts; Because ye have not **h** my words,	8085
	25:36	*shall be* **h**: for the LORD *hath* spoiled their	NIH
	26: 7	all the people **h** Jeremiah speaking these	8085
	26:10	When the princes of Judah **h** these things,	8085
	26:11	this city, as ye have **h** with your ears.	8085
	26:12	this city all the words that ye have **h**.	8085
	26:21	and all the princes, **h** his words,	8085
	26:21	when Urijah **h** *it,* he was afraid, and fled,	8085
	30: 5	We have **h** a voice of trembling, of fear,	8085
	31:15	A voice was **h** in Ramah, lamentation, *and*	8085
	31:18	I have **surely h** Ephraim bemoaning	8085+8085
	33:10	Again there shall be **h** in this place, which	8085
	34:10	**h** that every one should let his manservant,	8085
	35:17	spoken unto them, but they have not **h**;	8085
	36:11	had **h** out of the book all the words of	8085
	36:13	unto them all the words that he had **h**,	8085
	36:16	Now it came to pass when they had **h** all	8085
	36:24	nor any of his servants that **h** all these	8085
	37: 5	that besieged Jerusalem **h** tidings of them,	8085
	38: 1	**h** the words that Jeremiah had spoken unto	8085
	38: 7	**h** that they had put Jeremiah in	8085
	40: 7	**h** that the king of Babylon had made	8085
	40:11	**h** that the king of Babylon had left a	8085
	41:11	**h** of all the evil that Ishmael the son of	8085
	42: 4	said unto them, I have **h** *you;* behold,	8085
	46:12	The nations have **h** *of* thy shame, and	8085
	48: 4	her little ones have **caused** a cry **to be h**.	8085
	48: 5	the enemies have **h** a cry of destruction.	8085
	48:29	We have **h** the pride of Moab; *he is*	8085
	49: 2	that I will **cause** an alarm of war **to be h** in	8085
	49:14	I have **h** a rumour from the LORD, and	8085
	49:21	the noise thereof was **h** in the Red sea.	8085
	49:23	for they have **h** evil tidings: they are	8085
	50:43	The king of Babylon hath **h** the report of	8085
	50:46	and the cry is **h** among the nations.	8085
	51:46	ye fear for the rumour that shall be **h** in	8085
	51:51	because we have **h** reproach:	8085
La	1:21	They have **h** that I sigh; *there is* none to	8085
	1:21	all mine enemies have **h** of my trouble;	8085
	3:56	Thou hast **h** my voice: hide not thine ear at	8085
	3:61	Thou hast **h** their reproach, O LORD, *and*	8085
Eze	1:24	they went, I **h** the noise of their wings,	8085
	1:28	my face, and I **h** a voice of one that spake.	8085
	2: 2	my feet, that I **h** him that spake unto me.	8085
	3:12	I **h** behind me a voice of a great rushing,	8085
	3:13	*I h* also the noise of the wings of the living	NIH
	10: 5	the sound of the cherubims' wings was **h**	8085
	19: 4	The nations also **h** of him; he was taken in	8085
	19: 9	that his voice should no more be **h** upon	8085
	26:13	the sound of thy harps shall be no more **h**.	8085
	27:30	shall **cause** their voice **to be h** against thee,	8085
	33: 5	He **h** the sound of the trumpet, and took not	8085
	35:12	*that* I have **h** all thy blasphemies which	8085
	35:13	your words against me: I have **h** *them.*	8085
	43: 6	I **h** *him* speaking unto me out of the house;	8085
Da	3: 7	when all the people **h** the sound of	8086
	5:14	I have even **h** of thee, that the spirit of	8086
	5:16	I have **h** of thee, that thou canst make	8086
	6:14	the king, when he **h** *these* words, was sore	8086
	8:13	I **h** one saint speaking, and another saint	8085
	8:16	I **h** a man's voice between *the banks of*	8085
	10: 9	Yet **h** I the voice of his words: and when I	8085
	10: 9	when I **h** the voice of his words, then was I	8085
	10:12	thy words were **h**, and I am come for thy	8085
	12: 7	I **h** the man clothed in linen, which *was*	8085
	12: 8	I **h**, but I understood not: then said I, O my	8085
Hos	7:12	chastise them, as their congregation hath **h**.	8088
	14: 8	I have **h** *him,* and observed him: I *am* like a	6030
Ob	1: 1	We have **h** a rumour from the LORD, and	8085
Jnh	2: 2	affliction unto the LORD, and he **h** me;	6030
Mic	5:15	upon the heathen, such as they have not **h**.	8085
Na	2:13	voice of thy messengers shall no more be **h**.	8085
Hab	3: 2	I have **h** thy speech, *and* was afraid:	8085
	3:16	When I **h**, my belly trembled; my lips	8085
Zep	2: 8	I have **h** the reproach of Moab, and	8085
Zec	8:23	for we have **h** *that* God *is* with you.	8085
Mal	3:16	**h** *it,* and a book of remembrance was	8085
Mt	2: 3	When Herod the king had **h** *these things,* he	*191*
	2: 9	When they had **h** the king, they departed;	*191*
	2:18	In Rama was there a voice **h**, lamentation,	*191*
	2:22	But when he **h** that Archelaus did reign in	*191*
	4:12	Now when Jesus had **h** that John was cast	*191*
	5:21	Ye have **h** that it was said by them of old	*191*
	5:27	Ye have **h** that it was said by them of old	*191*
	5:33	ye have **h** that it hath been said by them of	*191*
	5:38	Ye have **h** that it hath been said, An eye for	*191*
	5:43	Ye have **h** that it hath been said, Thou shalt	*191*
	6: 7	they shall be **h** for their much speaking.	*1522*
	8:10	When Jesus **h** *it,* he marvelled, and said to	*191*
	9:12	But when Jesus **h** *that,* he said unto them,	*191*
	11: 2	Now when John had **h** in the prison	*191*
	12:24	But when the Pharisees **h** *it,* they said,	*191*
	13:17	*things* which ye hear, and have not **h** *them.*	*191*
	14: 1	At that time Herod the tetrarch **h** of the fame	*191*
	14:13	When Jesus **h** *of it,* he departed thence by	*191*
	14:13	when the people had **h** *thereof,* they	*191*
	15:12	were offended, after they **h** *this* saying?	*191*
	17: 6	And when the disciples **h** *it,* they fell on	*191*
	19:22	But when the young man **h** *that* saying,	*191*
	19:25	When his disciples **h** *it,* they were	*191*
	20:24	And when the ten **h** *it,* they were moved	*191*
	20:30	when they **h** that Jesus passed by, cried out,	*191*
	21:45	and Pharisees had **h** his parables,	*191*
	22: 7	But when the king **h** *thereof,* he was wroth:	*191*
	22:22	When they had **h** *these words,* they	*191*
	22:33	And when the multitude **h** *this,* they were	*191*
	22:34	But when the Pharisees had **h** that he had put	*191*
	26:65	behold, now ye have **h** his blasphemy.	*191*
	27:47	when they **h** *that,* said, This *man* calleth for	*191*
Mk	2:17	When Jesus **h** *it,* he saith unto them, They	*191*
	3: 8	when they had **h** what great *things* he did,	*191*
	3:21	And when his friends **h** *of it,* they went out	*191*
	4:15	but when they have **h**, Satan cometh	*191*
	4:16	who, when they have **h** the word,	*191*
	5:27	When she had **h** of Jesus, came in the press	*191*
	5:36	As soon as Jesus **h** the word *that was*	*191*
	6:14	And king Herod **h** *of him;* (for his name was	*191*
	6:16	But when Herod **h** *thereof,* he said, It is	*191*
	6:20	and when he **h** him, he did many *things,* and	*191*
	6:20	he did many *things,* and **h** him gladly.	*191*
	6:29	And when his disciples **h** *of it,* they came	*191*
	6:55	those that were sick, where they **h** he was.	*191*
	7:25	daughter had an unclean spirit, **h** of him,	*191*
	10:41	And when the ten **h** *it,* they began to be	*191*
	10:47	And when he **h** that it was Jesus of Nazareth,	*191*
	11:14	hereafter for ever. And his disciples **h** *it.*	*191*
	11:18	And the scribes and chief priests **h** *it,* and	*191*
	12:28	and having **h** them reasoning together, and	*191*
	12:37	And the common people **h** him gladly.	*191*
	14:11	And when they **h** *it,* they were glad, and	*191*
	14:58	We **h** him say, I will destroy this temple that	*191*
	14:64	Ye have **h** the blasphemy: what think ye?	*191*
	15:35	when they **h** *it,* said, Behold, he calleth	*191*
	16:11	when they had **h** that he was alive, and	*191*
Lk	1:13	for thy prayer is **h**; and thy wife Elisabeth	*1522*
	1:41	And it came to pass *that,* when Elisabeth **h**	*191*
	1:58	her cousins **h** how the Lord had shewed	*191*
	1:66	And all they that **h** *them* laid *them* up in	*191*
	2:18	And all they that **h** *it* wondered at those	*191*
	2:20	God for all *the things* that they had **h**	*191*
	2:47	And all that **h** him were astonished at his	*191*
	4:23	whatsoever we have **h** done in Capernaum,	*191*
	4:28	when they **h** these *things,* were filled with	*191*
	7: 3	And when he **h** of Jesus, he sent unto him	*191*
	7: 9	When Jesus **h** these *things,* he marvelled at	*191*
	7:22	tell John what *things* ye have seen and **h**;	*191*
	7:29	And all the people that **h** *him,* and	*191*
	8:14	which, when they have **h**, go *forth,* and	*191*
	8:15	having **h** the word, keep *it,* and bring forth	*191*
	8:50	But when Jesus **h** *it,* he answered him,	*191*
	9: 7	Now Herod the tetrarch **h** of all that was	*191*
	10:24	*things* which ye hear, and have not **h** *them.*	*191*
	10:39	which also sat at Jesus' feet, and **h** his word.	*191*
	12: 3	spoken in darkness shall be **h** in the light;	*191*
	14:15	with *him* **h** these *things,* he said unto him,	*191*
	15:25	nigh to the house, he **h** musick and dancing.	*191*
	16:14	**h** all these *things:* and they derided him.	*191*
	18:22	Now when Jesus **h** these *things,* he said unto	*191*
	18:23	And when he **h** this, he was very sorrowful:	*191*
	18:26	And they that **h** *it* said, Who then can be	*191*
	19:11	And as they **h** these *things,* he added and	*191*
	20:16	And when they **h** *it,* they said, God forbid.	*191*

Lk 22:71 for we ourselves have **h** of his own mouth. *191*
23: 6 When Pilate **h** of Galilee, he asked whether *191*
23: 8 because *he* had **h** many *things* of him; *191*
Jn 1:37 And the two disciples **h** him speak, and *191*
1:40 One of the two which **h** John speak, and *191*
3:32 And what he hath seen and **h**, that he *191*
4: 1 the Lord knew how the Pharisees had **h** that *191*
4:42 for we have **h** *him* ourselves, and know that *191*
4:47 When he **h** that Jesus was come out of Judea *191*
5:37 Ye have neither **h** his voice at any time, *191*
6:45 Every *man* therefore that hath **h**, and *191*
6:60 of his disciples, when they had **h** *this,* said, *191*
7:32 The Pharisees **h** that the people murmured *191*
7:40 when they **h** *this* saying, said, Of a truth this *191*
8: 6 on the ground, *as though he **h** them not.* NIG
8: 9 And they which **h** *it,* being convicted by *191*
8:26 world those *things* which I have **h** of him. *191*
8:40 told you the truth, which I have **h** of God: *191*
9:32 Since the world began was it not **h** that any *191*
9:35 Jesus **h** that they had cast him out; *191*
9:40 which were with him **h** these *words,* *191*
11: 4 When Jesus **h** *that,* he said, This sickness is *191*
11: 6 When he had **h** therefore that he was sick, he *191*
11:20 as soon as she **h** that Jesus was coming, went *191*
11:29 As soon as she **h** *that,* she arose quickly, and *191*
11:41 said, Father, I thank thee that thou hast **h** me. *191*
12:12 when they **h** that Jesus was coming to *191*
12:18 for that they **h** that he had done this miracle. *191*
12:29 that stood *by,* and **h** *it,* said that it thundered: *191*
12:34 We have **h** out of the law that Christ abideth *191*
14:28 Ye have **h** how I said unto you, I go away, *191*
15:15 for all *things* that I have **h** of my Father I *191*
18:21 ask them which **h** *me,* what I have said unto *191*
19: 8 When Pilate therefore **h** that saying, he was *191*
19:13 When Pilate therefore **h** that saying, *191*
21: 7 Now when Simon Peter **h** that it was *191*
Ac 1: 4 the Father, which, *saith he,* ye have **h** of me. *191*
2: 6 that every man **h** them speak in his own *191*
2:37 Now when they **h** *this,* they were pricked in *191*
4: 4 Howbeit many of them which **h** the word *191*
4:20 speak *the things* which we have seen and **h**. *191*
4:24 And when they **h** *that,* they lift up their voice *191*
5: 5 great fear came on all them that **h** these *191*
5:11 and upon as many as **h** these *things.* *191*
5:21 And when they **h** *that,* they entered into *191*
5:24 and the chief priests **h** these things, *191*
5:33 When they **h** *that,* they were cut *to the heart,* *191*
6:11 We have **h** him speak blasphemous words *191*
6:14 For we have **h** him say, that this Jesus of *191*
7:12 But when Jacob **h** that there was corn in *191*
7:34 and I have **h** their groaning, and am come *191*
7:54 When they **h** these *things,* they were cut to *191*
8:14 **h** that Samaria had received the word of *191*
8:30 to *him,* and **h** him read the prophet Esaias, *191*
9: 4 and **h** a voice saying unto him, Saul, Saul, *191*
9:13 Lord, I have **h** by many of this man, *191*
9:21 But all that **h** *him* were amazed, and said; *191*
9:38 and the disciples had **h** that Peter was there, *191*
10:31 thy prayer is **h**, and thine alms are had in *1522*
10:44 the Holy Ghost fell on all them which **h** *191*
10:46 For they **h** them speak with tongues, and *191*
11: 1 brethren that were in Judea **h** that *191*
11: 7 And I **h** a voice saying unto me, Arise, Peter; *191*
11:18 When they **h** these *things,* they held their *191*
13:48 And when the Gentiles **h** *this,* they were *191*
14: 9 The same **h** Paul speak: who stedfastly *191*
14:14 **h** *of,* they rent their clothes, and ran in *191*
15:24 Forasmuch as we have **h**, that certain which *191*
16:14 **h** *us:* whose heart the Lord opened, *191*
16:25 praises unto God: and the prisoners **h** them. *1874*
16:38 when they **h** that they were Romans, *191*
17: 8 rulers of the city, when they **h** these *things.* *191*
17:32 And when they **h** of the resurrection of *191*
18:26 whom when Aquila and Priscilla had **h**, *191*
19: 2 much as **h** whether there be *any* Holy Ghost. *191*
19: 5 When they **h** *this,* they were baptized in *191*
19:10 that all they which dwelt in Asia **h** the word *191*
19:28 And when they **h** *these sayings,* they were *191*
21:12 And when we **h** these *things,* both we, and *191*
21:20 And when they **h** *it,* they glorified the Lord, *191*
22: 2 (And when they **h** that he spake in *191*
22: 7 and **h** a voice saying unto me, Saul, Saul, *191*
22: 9 they **h** not the voice of him that spake to me. *191*
22:15 unto all men of what thou hast seen and **h**. *191*
22:26 When the centurion **h** *that,* he went and *191*
23:16 And when Paul's sister's son **h** of *their* lying *191*
24:22 And when Felix **h** these *things,* having more *191*
24:24 and **h** him concerning the faith in Christ. *191*
26:14 I **h** a voice speaking unto me, and saying in *191*
28:15 And from thence, when the brethren **h** of us, *191*
Ro 10:14 believe *in him* of whom they have not **h**? *191*
10:18 But I say, Have they not **h**? Yes verily, *191*
15:21 and they that have not **h** shall understand. *191*
1Co 2: 9 as it is written, Eye hath not seen, nor ear **h**, *191*
2Co 6: 2 I have **h** thee in a time accepted, and in *1873*
12: 4 and **h** unspeakable words, which *it is* not *191*
Gal 1:13 For ye have **h** of my conversation in time *191*
1:23 But they had **h** only, That he which *191*
Eph 1:13 In whom ye also *trusted,* after that ye **h** *191*
1:15 after I **h** of your faith in the Lord Jesus, and *191*
3: 2 If ye have **h** of the dispensation of the grace *191*
4:21 If so be that ye have **h** him, and have been *191*
Php 2:26 because that ye had **h** that he had been sick. *191*
4: 9 and received, and **h**, and seen in me, do: *191*
Col 1: 4 Since we **h** of your faith in Christ Jesus, and *191*
1: 5 whereof ye **h** **before** in the word of *4257*
1: 6 since the day ye **h** of *it,* and knew the grace *191*
1: 9 since the day we **h** *it,* do not cease to pray *191*
1:23 which ye have **h**, *and* which was preached to *191*
1Th 2:13 received the word of God which *ye* **h** of us, *189*
2Ti 1:13 which thou hast **h** of me, in faith and *191*
2: 2 And *the things* that thou hast **h** of me among *191*
Heb 2: 1 earnest heed to the *things* which we have **h**, *191*
2: 3 was confirmed unto us by them that **h** *him;* *191*
3:16 For some, when they had **h**, did provoke: *191*
4: 2 not being mixed with faith in them that **h** *it.* *191*
5: 7 from death, and was **h** in that *he* feared; *1522*
12:19 which *voice* they that **h** intreated that *191*
Jas 5:11 Ye have **h** of the patience of Job, and *191*
2Pe 1:18 this voice which came from heaven we **h**, *191*
1Jn 1: 1 which we have **h**, which we have seen with *191*
1: 3 we have seen and **h** declare we unto you, *191*
1: 5 then is the message which we have **h** of him, *191*
2: 7 word which ye have **h** from the beginning. *191*
2:18 and as ye have **h** that antichrist shall come, *191*
2:24 in you, which ye have **h** from the beginning. *191*
2:24 If *that* which ye have **h** from the beginning *191*
3:11 For this is the message that ye **h** from *191*
4: 3 whereof you have **h** that it should come; *191*
2Jn 1: 6 That, as ye have **h** from the beginning, *191*
Rev 1:10 and **h** behind me a great voice, as of a *191*
3: 3 therefore how thou hast received and **h**, *191*
4: 1 the first voice which I **h** *was* as *it were* of a *191*
5:11 I **h** the voice of many angels round about *191*
5:13 **h** I saying, Blessing, and honour, and glory, *191*
6: 1 and I **h**, as *it were* the noise of thunder, *191*
6: 3 I **h** the second beast say, Come and see. *191*
6: 5 I **h** the third beast say, Come and see. *191*
6: 6 And I **h** a voice in the midst of the four *191*
6: 7 I **h** the voice of the fourth beast say, Come *191*
7: 4 And I **h** the number of them which were *191*
8:13 **h** an angel flying through the midst of *191*
9:13 I **h** a voice from the four horns of the golden *191*
9:16 and I **h** the number of them. *191*
10: 4 and I **h** a voice from heaven saying unto me, *191*
10: 8 And the voice which I **h** from heaven spake *191*
11:12 And they **h** a great voice from heaven saying *191*
12:10 And I **h** a loud voice saying in heaven, *191*
14: 2 And I **h** a voice from heaven, as the voice of *191*
14: 2 I **h** the voice of harpers harping with their *191*
14:13 And I **h** a voice from heaven saying unto *191*
16: 1 And I **h** a great voice out of the temple *191*
16: 5 And I **h** the angel of the waters say, Thou art *191*
16: 7 And I **h** another out of the altar say, Even so, *191*
18: 4 And I **h** another voice from heaven, saying, *191*
18:22 trumpeters, shall be **h** no more at all in thee; *191*
18:22 the sound of a millstone shall be **h** no more *191*
18:23 of the bride shall be **h** no more at all in thee: *191*
19: 1 And after these *things* I **h** a great voice of *191*
19: 6 And I **h** as *it were* the voice of a great *191*
21: 3 And I **h** a great voice out of heaven saying, *191*
22: 8 and **h** *them.* And when I had heard and seen, *191*
22: 8 and heard *them.* And when I had **h** and seen, *191*

HEARDEST (12) [HEAR]

Dt 4:36 thou **h** his words out of the midst of 8085
Jos 14:12 for thou **h** in that day how the Anakims 8085
2Ki 22:19 when thou **h** what I spake against this 8085

2Ch 34:27 when thou **h** his words against this place, 8085
Ne 9: 9 in Egypt, and **h** their cry by the Red sea; 8085
9:27 cried unto thee, thou **h** *them* from heaven; 8085
9:28 cried unto thee, thou **h** *them* from heaven; 8085
Ps 31:22 nevertheless thou **h** the voice of my 8085
119:26 I have declared my ways, and thou **h** me: 6030
Isa 48: 7 even before the day when thou **h** them not; 8085
48: 8 Yea, thou **h** not; yea, thou knewest not; 8085
Jnh 2: 2 belly of hell cried I, *and* thou **h** my voice. 8085

HEARER (2) [HEAR]
Jas 1:23 For if any be a **h** of the word, and not a doer, *202*
1:25 *therein,* he being not a forgetful **h**, *202*

HEARERS (4) [HEAR]
Ro 2:13 (For not the **h** of the law *are* just before God, *202*
Eph 4:29 that it may minister grace unto the **h**. *191*
2Ti 2:14 to no profit, *but* to the subverting of the **h**. *191*
Jas 1:22 and not **h** only, deceiving your own selves. *202*

HEAREST (11) [HEAR]
Ru 2: 8 Boaz unto Ruth, **H** thou not, my daughter? 8085
1Sa 24: 9 Wherefore **h** thou men's words, saying, 8085
2Sa 5:24 when thou **h** the sound of a going in 8085
1Ki 8:30 dwelling place: and when thou **h**, forgive. 8085
2Ch 6:21 from heaven; and when thou **h**, forgive. 8085
Ps 22: 2 I cry in the daytime, but thou **h** not; 6030
65: 2 O thou that **h** prayer, unto thee shall all 8085
Mt 21:16 And said unto him, **H** thou what these say? *191*
27:13 **H** thou not how many *things* they witness *191*
Jn 3: 8 and thou **h** the sound thereof, but canst not *191*
11:42 And I knew that thou **h** me always: but *191*

HEARETH (52) [HEAR]
Ex 16: 7 for that he **h** your murmurings against 8085
16: 8 for that the LORD **h** your murmurings 8085
Nu 30: 5 her father disallow her in the day that he **h**; 8085
Dt 29:19 to pass, when he **h** the words of this curse, 8085
1Sa 3: 9 shalt say, Speak, LORD; for thy servant **h**. 8085
3:10 Samuel answered, Speak; for thy servant **h**. 8085
3:11 *at* which both the ears of every one that **h** it 8085
2Sa 17: 9 the first, that whosoever **h** *it* will say, 8085+8085
2Ki 21:12 and Judah, that whosoever **h** of it, 8085
Job 34:28 unto him, and he **h** the cry of the afflicted. 8085
Ps 34:17 the LORD **h**, and delivereth them out of 8085
38:14 Thus I was as a man that **h** not, and 8085
69:33 For the LORD **h** the poor, and despiseth 8085
Pr 8:34 Blessed *is* the man that **h** me, watching 8085
13: 1 A wise son ***h*** *his* father's instruction: but NIH
13: 1 but a scorner **h** not rebuke. 8085
13: 8 *are* his riches: but the poor **h** not rebuke. 8085
15:29 but he **h** the prayer of the righteous. 8085
15:31 The ear that **h** the reproof of life abideth 8085
15:32 but he that **h** reproof getteth understanding. 8085
18:13 He that answereth a matter before he **h** *it,* it 8085
21:28 but the man that **h**, speaketh constantly. 8085
25:10 Lest he that **h** *it* put thee to shame, and 8085
29:24 he **h** cursing, and bewrayeth *it* not. 8085
Isa 41:26 yea, *there is* none that **h** your words. 8085
42:20 opening the ears, but he **h** not. 8085
Jer 19: 3 the which whosoever **h**, his ears shall 8085
Eze 3:27 He that **h**, let him hear; and he that 8085
33: 4 whosoever **h** the sound of 8085+8085
Mt 7:24 Therefore whosoever **h** these sayings of *191*
7:26 And every one that **h** these sayings of mine, *191*
13:19 When any one **h** the word of the kingdom, *191*
13:20 stony *places,* the same is he that **h** the word, *191*
13:22 seed among the thorns is he that **h** the word; *191*
13:23 into the good ground is he that **h** the word, *191*
Lk 6:47 to me, and **h** my sayings, and doeth them, *191*
6:49 But he that **h**, and doeth not, is like a man *191*
10:16 He that **h** you heareth me; and he that *191*
10:16 He that heareth you **h** me; and he that *191*
Jn 3:29 which standeth and **h** him, rejoiceth greatly *191*
5:24 He that **h** my word, and believeth on him *191*
8:47 He that is of God **h** God's words: ye *191*
9:31 Now we know that God **h** not sinners: but *191*
9:31 of God, and doeth his will, him he **h**. *191*
18:37 Every one that is of the truth **h** my voice. *191*
2Co 12: 6 which he seeth me *to be,* or that he **h** of me. *191*
1Jn 4: 5 they of the world, and the world **h** them. *191*
4: 6 he that knoweth God **h** us; *he* that is not of *191*
4: 6 heareth us; *he* that is not of God **h** not us. *191*
5:14 ask any *thing* according to his will, he **h** us: *191*

Rev 22:17 And let him that **h** say, Come. And let him *191*
22:18 For I testify unto every *man* that **h** the words *191*

HEARING (39) [HEAR]
Dt 31:11 shalt read this law before all Israel in their **h**. 241
2Sa 18:12 for in our **h** the king charged thee and 241
2Ki 4:31 but *there was* neither voice, nor **h**. 7182
Job 33: 8 Surely thou hast spoken in mine **h**, and 241
42: 5 I have heard of thee by the **h** of the ear: but 8088
Pr 20:12 The **h** ear, and the seeing eye, the LORD 8085
28: 9 He that turneth away his ear from **h** 8085
Ecc 1: 8 with seeing, nor the ear filled with **h**. 8085
Isa 11: 3 neither reprove after the **h** of his ears: 4926
21: 3 I was bowed down at the **h** *of it;* I was 8085
33:15 that stoppeth his ears from **h** of blood, and 8085
Eze 9: 5 to the others he said in mine **h**, Go ye after 241
10:13 it was cried unto them in my **h**, O wheel. 241
Am 8:11 but of **h** the words of the LORD: 8085
Mt 13:13 and **h** they hear not, neither do they *191*
13:14 By **h** ye shall hear, and shall not understand; *189*
13:15 and *their* ears are dull of **h**, and their eyes *191*
Mk 4:12 and **h** they may hear, and not understand; *191*
6: 2 and many **h** *him* were astonished, saying, *191*
Lk 2:46 both **h** them, and asking them *questions.* *191*
8:10 not see, and **h** they might not understand. *191*
18:36 And **h** the multitude pass by, he asked what *191*
Ac 5: 5 And Ananias **h** these words fell down, and *191*
8: 6 **h** and seeing the miracles which he did. *191*
9: 7 **h** a voice, but seeing no *man.* *191*
18: 8 and many of the Corinthians **h** believed, and *191*
25:21 to be reserved unto the **h** of Augustus, *1233*
25:23 and were entered into the **place of h**, *201*
28:26 **H** ye shall hear, and shall not understand; *189*
28:27 and *their* ears are dull of **h**, and their eyes *191*
Ro 10:17 So then faith *cometh* by **h**, *189*
10:17 by hearing, and **h** by the word of God. *189*
1Co 12:17 whole body *were* an eye, where *were* the **h**? *189*
12:17 If the whole *were* **h**, where *were* *189*
Gal 3: 2 by the works of the law, or by the **h** of faith? *189*
3: 5 by the works of the law, or by the **h** of faith? *189*
Phm 1: 5 **H** of thy love and faith, which thou hast *191*
Heb 5:11 hard to be uttered, seeing ye are dull of **h**. *189*
2Pe 2: 8 *man* dwelling among them, in seeing and **h**, *189*

HEARKEN (153) [HEARKENED, HEARKENEDST, HEARKENETH, HEARKENING]
Ge 4:23 ye wives of Lamech, **h** unto my speech: 238
21:12 Sarah hath said unto thee, **h** unto her voice; 8085
23:15 My lord, **h** unto me: the land *is worth* four 8085
34:17 if ye will not **h** unto us, to be circumcised; 8085
49: 2 sons of Jacob; and **h** unto Israel your father. 8085
Ex 3:18 they shall **h** to thy voice: and thou shalt 8085
4: 1 will not believe me, nor **h** unto my voice: 8085
4: 8 neither **h** to the voice of the first sign, 8085
4: 9 these two signs, neither **h** unto thy voice, 8085
6:30 and how shall Pharaoh **h** unto me? 8085
7: 4 Pharaoh shall not **h** unto you, that I may lay 8085
7:22 was hardened, neither did he **h** unto them; 8085
11: 9 unto Moses, Pharaoh shall not **h** unto you; 8085
15:26 If thou wilt **diligently h** to the voice 8085+8085
18:19 **H** now unto my voice, I will give thee 8085
Lev 26:14 if ye will not **h** unto me, and will not do all 8085
26:18 And if ye will not yet for *all* this **h** unto me, 8085
26:21 contrary unto me, and will not **h** unto me; 8085
26:27 And if ye will not for *all* this **h** unto me, but 8085
Nu 23:18 and hear; **h** unto me, thou son of Zippor: 238
Dt 1:45 the LORD would not **h** to your voice, 8085
4: 1 Now therefore **h**, O Israel, unto the statutes 8085
7:12 if ye **h** to these judgments, and keep, and 8085
11:13 if you shall **h diligently** unto my 8085+8085
13: 3 Thou shalt not **h** unto the words of that 8085
13: 8 shalt not consent unto him, nor **h** unto him; 8085
13:18 When thou shalt **h** to the voice of 8085
15: 5 Only if thou **carefully h** unto 8085+8085
17:12 will not **h** unto the priest that standeth to 8085
18:15 like unto me; unto him ye shall **h**; 8085
18:19 *that* whosoever will not **h** unto my words 8085
21:18 have chastened him, will not **h** unto them: 8085
23: 5 LORD thy God would not **h** unto Balaam; 8085
26:17 and his judgments, and to **h** unto his voice: 8085
27: 9 saying, Take heed, and **h**, O Israel; 8085
28: 1 if thou shalt **h diligently** unto 8085+8085
28: 2 if thou shalt **h** unto the voice of the LORD 8085
28:13 if that thou **h** unto the commandments of 8085

Dt 28:15 if thou wilt not **h** unto the voice of 8085
30:10 If thou shalt **h** unto the voice of the LORD 8085
Jos 1:17 Moses in all *things,* so will we **h** unto thee: 8085
1:18 will not **h** unto thy words in all that thou 8085
24:10 I would not **h** unto Balaam; therefore 8085
Jdg 2:17 yet they would not **h** unto their judges, but 8085
3: 4 to know whether they would **h unto** 8085
9: 7 and cried, and said unto them, **H** unto me, 8085
9: 7 men of Shechem, that God may **h** unto you. 8085
11:17 the king of Edom would not **h** *thereto.* And 8085
19:25 the men would not **h** to him: so the man 8085
20:13 the children of Benjamin would not **h** to 8085
1Sa 8: 7 **H** unto the voice of the people in all that 8085
8: 9 Now therefore **h** unto their voice: 8085
8:22 **H** unto their voice, and make them a king. 8085
15: 1 **h** thou unto the voice of the words of 8085
15:22 than sacrifice, *and* to **h** than the fat of rams. 7181
28:22 **h** thou also unto the voice of thine 8085
30:24 For who will **h** unto you in this matter? but 8085
2Sa 12:18 and he would not **h** unto our voice: 8085
13:14 Howbeit he would not **h** unto her voice: 8085
13:16 didst unto me. But he would not **h** unto her. 8085
1Ki 8:28 to **h** unto the cry and to the prayer, 8085
8:29 that *thou* mayest **h** unto the prayer which 8085
8:30 **h** thou to the supplication of thy servant, 8085
8:52 to **h** unto them in all that they call for unto 8085
11:38 if thou wilt **h** unto all that I command thee, 8085
20: 8 said unto him, **H** not *unto him,* nor consent. 8085
22:28 he said, **H**, O people, every one of you. 8085
2Ki 10: 6 ye *be* mine, and *if* ye will **h** unto my voice, 8085
17:40 Howbeit they did not **h**, but they did after 8085
18:31 **H** not to Hezekiah: for thus saith the king 8085
18:32 **h** not unto Hezekiah, when he persuadeth 8085
2Ch 6:19 to **h** unto the cry and the prayer which thy 8085
6:20 to **h** unto the prayer which thy servant 8085
6:21 **H** therefore unto the supplications of thy 8085
10:16 saw that the king would not **h** unto them, 8085
18:27 by me. And he said, **H**, all ye people. 8085
20:15 **H** ye, all Judah, and ye inhabitants of 7181
33:10 and to his people: but they would not **h**. 7181
Ne 13:27 then **h** unto you to do all this great evil, 8085
Job 13: 6 and **h** to the pleadings of my lips. 7181
32:10 Therefore I said, **H** to me; I also will shew 8085
33: 1 hear my speeches, and **h** to all my words. 238
33:31 Mark well, O Job, **h** unto me: hold thy 8085
33:33 If not, **h** unto me: hold thy peace, and 8085
34:10 Therefore **h** unto me, ye men of 8085
34:16 hear this: **h** to the voice of my words. 238
34:34 tell me, and let a wise man **h** unto me. 8085
37:14 **H** unto this, O Job: stand still, and 238
Ps 5: 2 **H** unto the voice of my cry, my King, and 7181
34:11 Come, ye children, **h** unto me: I will teach 8085
45:10 **H**, O daughter, and consider, and 8085
58: 5 Which will not **h** to the voice of charmers, 8085
81: 8 unto thee: O Israel, if thou wilt **h** unto me; 8085
81:11 my people would not **h** to my voice; and 8085
Pr 7:24 **H** unto me now therefore, O ye children, 8085
8:32 Now therefore **h** unto me, O ye children: 8085
23:22 **H** unto thy father that begat thee, and 8085
29:12 If a ruler **h** to lies, all his servants *are* 7181
SS 8:13 the gardens, the companions **h** to thy voice: 7181
Isa 28:23 and hear my voice; **h**, and hear my speech. 7181
32: 3 and the ears of them that hear shall **h**. 7181
34: 1 ye nations, to hear; and **h**, ye people: 7181
36:16 **H** not to Hezekiah: for thus saith the king 8085
42:23 *who* will **h** and hear for the time to come? 7181
46: 3 **H** unto me, O house of Jacob, and all 8085
46:12 **H** unto me, ye stouthearted, that *are* far 8085
48:12 **H** unto me, O Jacob, and Israel my called; 8085
49: 1 unto me; and **h**, ye people, from afar; 7181
51: 1 **H** to me, ye that follow after righteousness, 8085
51: 4 **H** unto me, my people; and give ear unto 7181
51: 7 **H** unto me, ye that know righteousness, 8085
55: 2 **h diligently** unto me, and eat ye *that which* 8085
Jer 6:10 ear *is* uncircumcised, and they cannot **h**: 7181
6:17 *saying,* **H** to the sound of the trumpet. 7181
6:17 the trumpet. But they said, We will not **h**. 7181
7:27 unto them; but they will not **h** to thee: 8085
11:11 shall cry unto me, I will not **h** unto them. 8085
16:12 his evil heart, that *they* may not **h** unto me: 8085
17:24 if ye **diligently h** unto me, saith 8085+8085
17:27 if you will not **h** unto me to hallow 8085
18:19 **h** to the voice of them that contend with 8085
23:16 **H** not unto the words of the prophets that 8085
26: 3 If so be they will **h**, and turn every man 8085
26: 4 If ye will not **h** to me, to walk in my law, 8085
26: 5 To **h** to the words of my servants 8085
27: 9 Therefore **h** not ye to your prophets, nor to 8085
27:14 Therefore **h** not unto the words of 8085
27:16 **H** not to the words of your prophets that 8085
27:17 **H** not unto them; serve the king of 8085
29: 8 neither **h** to your dreams which ye cause to 8085
29:12 and pray unto me, and I will **h** unto you. 8085
35:13 Will ye not receive instruction to **h** to my 8085
37: 2 did **h** unto the words of the LORD, 8085
38:15 give thee counsel, wilt thou not **h** unto me? 8085
44:16 of the LORD, we will not **h** unto thee. 8085
Eze 3: 7 the house of Israel will not **h** unto thee; 8085
3: 7 unto thee; for they will not **h** unto me: 8085
20: 8 against me, and would not **h** unto me: 8085
20:39 and hereafter *also,* if ye will not **h** unto me: 8085
Da 9:19 hear; O Lord, forgive; O Lord, **h** and do; 7181
Hos 5: 1 **h**, ye house of Israel; and give ye ear, 7181
9:17 because they did not **h** unto him: 8085
Mic 1: 2 ye people; **h**, O earth, and all that therein is: 7181
Zec 1: 4 they did not hear, nor **h** unto me, saith 7181
7:11 they refused to **h**, and pulled away 7181
Mk 4: 3 **H**; Behold, there went out a sower to sow: *191*
7:14 **H** unto me every one of you, and *191*
Ac 2:14 this known unto you, and **h** to my words: *1801*
4:19 Whether it be right in the sight of God to **h** *191*
7: 2 And he said, Men, brethren, and fathers, **h**; *191*
12:13 a damsel came to **h**, named Rhoda. *5219*
15:13 saying, Men *and* brethren, **h** unto me: *191*
Jas 2: 5 **H**, my beloved brethren, Hath not God *191*

HEARKENED (81) [HEARKEN]

Ge 3:17 Because thou hast **h** unto the voice of thy 8085
16: 2 by her. And Abram **h** to the voice of Sarai. 8085
23:16 Abraham **h** unto Ephron; and 8085
30:17 God **h** unto Leah, and she conceived, and 8085
30:22 and God **h** to her, and opened her womb. 8085
34:24 unto Shechem his son **h** all that went out of 8085
39:10 that he **h** not unto her, to lie by her, *or* to be 8085
Ex 6: 9 they **h** not unto Moses for anguish of spirit, 8085
6:12 the children of Israel have not **h** unto me; 8085
7:13 Pharaoh's heart, that he **h** not unto them; 8085
8:15 he hardened his heart, and **h** not unto them; 8085
8:19 was hardened, and he **h** not unto them; 8085
9:12 heart of Pharaoh, and he **h** not unto them; 8085
16:20 Notwithstanding they **h** not unto Moses; 8085
18:24 So Moses **h** to the voice of his father in 8085
Nu 14:22 ten times, and have not **h** to my voice; 8085
21: 3 the LORD **h** to the voice of Israel, and 8085
Dt 9:19 But the LORD **h** unto me at that time also. 8085
9:23 and ye believed him not, nor **h** to his voice. 8085
10:10 and the LORD **h** unto me at that time also, 8085
18:14 **h** unto observers of times, and 8085
26:14 I have **h** to the voice of the LORD my 8085
34: 9 the children of Israel **h** unto him, and did as 8085
Jos 1:17 According as we **h** unto Moses in all 8085
10:14 that the LORD **h** unto the voice of a man: 8085
Jdg 2:20 their fathers, and have not **h** unto my voice; 8085
11:28 **h** not unto the words of Jephthah which he 8085
13: 9 God **h** to the voice of Manoah; and 8085
1Sa 2:25 Notwithstanding they **h** not unto the voice 8085
12: 1 I have **h** unto your voice in all that ye said 8085
19: 6 Saul **h** unto the voice of Jonathan: and 8085
25:35 I have **h** to thy voice, and have accepted 8085
28:21 have **h** unto thy words which thou spakest 8085
28:23 compelled him; and he **h** unto their voice. 8085
1Ki 12:15 Wherefore the king **h** not unto the people; 8085
12:16 So when all Israel saw that the king **h** not 8085
12:24 They **h** therefore to the word of 8085
15:20 So Ben-hadad **h** unto king Asa, and sent 8085
20:25 And he **h** unto their voice, and did so. 8085
2Ki 13: 4 the LORD, and the LORD **h** unto him: 8085
16: 9 the king of Assyria **h** unto him: for the king 8085
20:13 Hezekiah **h** unto them, and shewed them all 8085
21: 9 they **h** not: and Manasseh seduced them to 8085
22:13 our fathers have not **h** unto the words of 8085
2Ch 10:15 So the king **h** not unto the people: for 8085
16: 4 Ben-hadad **h** unto king Asa, and sent 8085
24:17 to the king. Then the king **h** unto them. 8085
25:16 done this, and hast not **h** unto my counsel. 8085
30:20 the LORD **h** to Hezekiah, and healed 8085
35:22 **h** not unto the words of Necho from 8085
Ne 9:16 and **h** not to thy commandments, 8085

Ne 9:29 **h** not unto thy commandments, but 8085
9:34 nor **h** unto thy commandments and thy 7181
Est 3: 4 he **h** not unto them, that they told Haman, 8085
Job 9:16 *yet* would I not believe that he had **h** unto 238
Ps 81:13 O that my people had **h** unto me, *and* 8085
106:25 *and* **h** not unto the voice of the LORD. 8085
Isa 21: 7 and he **h** **diligently** *with* much heed: 7181+7182
48:18 O that thou hadst **h** to my commandments! 7181
Jer 6:19 because they have not **h** unto my words, 7181
7:24 they **h** not, nor inclined their ear, but 8085
7:26 Yet they **h** not unto me, nor inclined their 8085
8: 6 I **h** and heard, *but* they spake not aright: 7181
25: 3 and speaking; but ye have not **h**. 8085
25: 4 and sending *them;* but ye have not **h**, 8085
25: 7 Yet ye have not **h** unto me, saith 8085
26: 5 and sending *them,* but ye have not **h**; 8085
29:19 Because they have not **h** to my words, 8085
32:33 teaching *them,* yet they have not **h** to 8085
34:14 your fathers **h** not unto me, neither inclined 8085
34:17 Ye have not **h** unto me, in proclaiming 8085
35:14 and speaking; but ye **h** not unto me. 8085
35:15 have not inclined your ear, nor **h** unto me. 8085
35:16 but this people hath not **h** unto me: 8085
36:31 pronounced against them; but they **h** not. 8085
37:14 he **h** not to him: so Irijah took Jeremiah, 8085
44: 5 they **h** not, nor inclined their ear to turn 8085
Eze 3: 6 thee to them, they would have **h** unto thee. 8085
Da 9: 6 Neither have we **h** unto thy servants 8085
Mal 3:16 the LORD **h**, and heard *it,* and a book of 7181
Ac 27:21 *ye* should have **h** unto me, and not have *3980*

HEARKENEDST (1) [HEARKEN]
Dt 28:45 thou **h** not unto the voice of the LORD thy 8085

HEARKENETH (2) [HEARKEN]
Pr 1:33 whoso **h** unto me shall dwell safely, and 8085
12:15 but he that **h** unto counsel *is* wise. 8085

HEARKENING (1) [HEARKEN]
Ps 103:20 **h** unto the voice of his word. 8085

HEART (830) [BROKEN-HEARTED, FAINTHEARTED, HARDHEARTED, HEART'S, HEARTED, HEARTS, MERRYHEARTED, STOUTHEARTED, TENDERHEARTED]
Ge 6: 5 thoughts of his **h** *was* only evil continually. 3820
6: 6 on the earth, and it grieved him at his **h**. 3820
8:21 the LORD said in his **h**, I will not again 3820
8:21 for the imagination of man's **h** *is* evil from 3820
17:17 his face, and laughed, and said in his **h**, 3820
20: 5 in the integrity of my **h** and innocency of 3824
20: 6 that thou didst this in the integrity of thy **h**; 3824
24:45 before I had done speaking in mine **h**, 3820
27:41 Esau said in his **h**, The days of mourning 3820
42:28 their **h** failed *them,* and they were afraid, 3820
45:26 *Jacob's* **h** fainted, for he believed them not. 3820
Ex 4:14 when he seeth thee, he will be glad in his **h**. 3820
4:21 I will harden his **h**, that he shall not let 3820
7: 3 I will harden Pharaoh's **h**, and multiply my 3820
7:13 he hardened Pharaoh's **h**, that he hearkened 3820
7:14 Pharaoh's **h** *is* hardened, he refuseth to let 3820
7:22 Pharaoh's **h** was hardened, neither did he 3820
7:23 neither did he set his **h** to this also. 3820
8:15 he hardened his **h**, and hearkened not unto 3820
8:19 Pharaoh's **h** was hardened, and 3820
8:32 Pharaoh hardened his **h** at this time also, 3820
9: 7 the **h** of Pharaoh was hardened, and he did 3820
9:12 the LORD hardened the **h** of Pharaoh, 3820
9:14 this time send all my plagues upon thine **h**, 3820
9:34 and hardened his **h**, he and his servants. 3820
9:35 the **h** of Pharaoh was hardened, 3820
10: 1 for I have hardened his **h**, and the heart of 3820
10: 1 his heart, and the **h** of his servants, 3820
10:20 the LORD hardened Pharaoh's **h**, so 3820
10:27 the LORD hardened Pharaoh's **h**, and 3820
11:10 the LORD hardened Pharaoh's **h**, so 3820
14: 4 I will harden Pharaoh's **h**, that he shall 3820
14: 5 the **h** of Pharaoh and of his servants was 3824
14: 8 the LORD hardened the **h** of Pharaoh king 3820
15: 8 the depths were congealed in the **h** of 3820
23: 9 for ye know the **h** of a stranger, seeing ye 5315
25: 2 with his **h** ye shall take my offering. 3820
28:29 in the breastplate of judgment upon his **h**, 3820
28:30 they shall be upon Aaron's **h**, when he 3820
28:30 upon his **h** before the LORD continually. 3820
35: 5 whosoever *is* of a willing **h**, let him bring 3820
35:21 every one whose **h** stirred him up, and 3820
35:26 all the women whose **h** stirred them up in 3820
35:29 whose **h** made them willing to bring for all 3820
35:34 he hath put in his **h** that *he* may teach, 3820
35:35 Them hath he filled *with* wisdom of **h**, 3820
36: 2 in whose **h** the LORD had put wisdom, 3820
36: 2 *even* every one whose **h** stirred him up to 3820
Lev 19:17 Thou shalt not hate thy brother in thine **h**: 3824
26:16 consume the eyes, and cause sorrow of **h**: 5315
Nu 15:39 that ye seek not after your own **h** and 3824
32: 7 wherefore discourage ye the **h** of 3820
32: 9 they discouraged the **h** of the children of 3820
Dt 1:28 our brethren have discouraged our **h**, 3824
2:30 made his **h** obstinate, that he might deliver 3824
4: 9 lest they depart from thy **h** all the days of 3824
4:29 find *him,* if thou seek him with all thy **h** 3824
4:39 *this* day, and consider *it* in thine **h**, 3824
5:29 O that there were such a **h** in them, 3824
6: 5 love the LORD thy God with all thine **h**, 3824
6: 6 command thee *this* day, shall be in thine **h**: 3824
7:17 If thou shalt say in thine **h**, These nations 3824
8: 2 to prove thee, to know what *was* in thine **h**, 3824
8: 5 Thou shalt also consider in thine **h**, that, 3824
8:14 thine **h** be lifted up, and thou forget 3824
8:17 thou say in thine **h**, My power and 3824
9: 4 Speak not thou in thine **h**, after that 3824
9: 5 or for the uprightness of thine **h**, 3824
10:12 to serve the LORD thy God with all thy **h** 3824
10:16 therefore the foreskin of your **h**, 3824
11:13 to serve him with all your **h** and with all 3824
11:16 that your **h** be not deceived, and ye turn 3824
11:18 shall ye lay up these my words in your **h** 3824
13: 3 love the LORD your God with all your **h** 3824
15: 7 thou shalt not harden thy **h**, nor shut thine 3824
15: 9 that there be not a thought in thy wicked **h**, 3824
15:10 thine **h** shall not be grieved when thou 3824
17:17 wives to himself, that his **h** turn not away: 3824
17:20 That his **h** be not lifted up above his 3824
18:21 if thou say in thine **h**, How shall we know 3824
19: 6 while his **h** is hot, and overtake him, 3824
20: 8 lest his brethren's **h** faint as well as his 3824
20: 8 his brethren's heart faint as well as his **h**. 3824
24:15 for he *is* poor, and setteth his **h** upon it: 5315
26:16 therefore keep and do them with all thine **h**, 3824
28:28 and blindness, and astonishment of **h**: 3824
28:47 with gladness of **h**, for the abundance of 3824
28:65 LORD shall give thee there a trembling **h**, 3820
28:67 for the fear of thine **h** where*with* thou shalt 3824
29: 4 Yet the LORD hath not given you a **h** to 3820
29:18 whose **h** turneth away *this* day from 3824
29:19 that he bless himself in his **h**, saying, I shall 3824
29:19 though I walk in the imagination of mine **h**, 3820
30: 2 with all thine **h**, and with all thy soul; 3824
30: 6 LORD thy God will circumcise thine **h**, 3824
30: 6 the **h** of thy seed, to love the LORD thy 3824
30: 6 love the LORD thy God with all thine **h**, 3824
30:10 unto the LORD thy God with all thine **h**, 3824
30:14 in thy mouth, and in thy **h**, that *thou* mayest 3824
30:17 if thine **h** turn away, so that thou wilt not 3824
Jos 5: 1 we were passed over, that their **h** melted, 3824
14: 7 him word again as *it was* in mine **h**. 3824
14: 8 up with me made the **h** of the people melt: 3820
22: 5 to serve him with all your **h** and with all 3824
24:23 incline your **h** unto the LORD God of 3824
Jdg 5: 9 My **h** *is* toward the governors of Israel, 3820
5:15 of Reuben *there were* great thoughts of **h**. 3820
5:16 of Reuben *there were* great searchings of **h**. 3820
16:15 I love thee, when thine **h** *is* not with me? 3820
16:17 That he told her all his **h**, and said unto her, 3820
16:18 Delilah saw that he had told her all his **h**, 3820
16:18 *this* once, for he hath shewed me all his **h**. 3820
18:20 the priest's **h** was glad, and he took 3820
19: 5 Comfort thine **h** *with* a morsel of bread, 3820
19: 6 and tarry all night, and let thine **h** be merry. 3820
19: 8 father said, Comfort thine **h**, I pray thee. 3824
19: 9 lodge here, that thine **h** may be merry; 3824
Ru 3: 7 had eaten and drunk, and his **h** was merry, 3820
1Sa 1: 8 why is thy **h** grieved? *am* not I better to 3824
1:13 Now Hannah, she spake in her **h**; only her 3820
2: 1 and said, My **h** rejoiceth in the LORD, 3820
2:33 consume thine eyes, and to grieve thine **h**: 5315
2:35 shall do according to *that* which *is* in my **h** 3824
4:13 for his **h** trembled for the ark of God. 3820

1Sa	9:19	and will tell thee all that *is* in thine **h**.	3824
	10: 9	go from Samuel, God gave him another **h**:	3820
	12:20	but serve the LORD with all your **h**;	3824
	12:24	and serve him in truth with all your **h**:	3824
	13:14	hath sought him a man after his own **h**,	3824
	14: 7	said unto him, Do all that *is* in thine **h**:	3824
	14: 7	behold, I *am* with thee according to thy **h**.	3824
	16: 7	but the LORD looketh on the **h**.	3824
	17:28	thy pride, and the naughtiness of thine **h**;	3824
	17:32	to Saul, Let no man's **h** fail because of him;	3820
	21:12	David laid up these words in his **h**, and	3824
	24: 5	that David's **h** smote him, because he had	3820
	25:31	unto thee, nor offence of **h** unto my lord,	3820
	25:36	Nabal's **h** *was* merry within him, for he	3820
	25:37	that his **h** died within him, and he became	3820
	27: 1	David said in his **h**, I shall now perish one	3820
	28: 5	he was afraid, and his **h** greatly trembled.	3820
2Sa	3:21	that thou mayest reign over all that thine **h**	5315
	6:16	the LORD; and she despised him in her **h**.	3820
	7: 3	to the king, Go, do all that *is* in thine **h**;	3824
	7:21	word's sake, and according to thine own **h**,	3820
	7:27	hath thy servant found in his **h** to pray this	3820
	13:28	Mark ye now when Amnon's **h** is merry	3820
	13:33	not my lord the king take the thing to his **h**,	3820
	14: 1	that the king's **h** *was* toward Absalom.	3820
	17:10	whose **h** *is* as the heart of a lion,	3820
	17:10	whose heart *is* as the **h** of a lion,	3820
	18:14	and thrust them through the **h** of Absalom,	3820
	19:14	he bowed the **h** of all the men of Judah,	3824
	19:14	the men of Judah, *even* as *the* **h** *of* one man;	NIH
	19:19	that the king should take *it* to his **h**.	3820
	24:10	David's **h** smote him after that he had	3820
1Ki	2: 4	to walk before me in truth with all their **h**	3824
	2:44	the wickedness which thine **h** is privy to,	3824
	3: 6	and in uprightness of **h** with thee;	3824
	3: 9	thy servant an understanding **h** to judge thy	3820
	3:12	given thee a wise and an understanding **h**;	3820
	4:29	exceeding much, and largeness of **h**,	3820
	8:17	it was in the **h** of David my father to build a	3824
	8:18	Whereas it was in thine **h** to build a house	3824
	8:18	thou didst well that it was in thine **h**.	3824
	8:23	that walk before thee with all their **h**:	3820
	8:38	know every man the plague of his own **h**,	3824
	8:39	to his ways, whose **h** thou knowest;	3824
	8:48	And *so* return unto thee with all their **h**, and	3824
	8:61	Let your **h** therefore be perfect with	3824
	8:66	glad of **h** for all the goodness that	3820
	9: 3	and mine **h** shall be there perpetually.	3820
	9: 4	in integrity of **h**, and in uprightness,	3824
	10: 2	with him of all that was in her **h**.	3824
	10:24	his wisdom, which God had put in his **h**.	3820
	11: 2	*for* surely they will turn away your **h** after	3824
	11: 3	and his wives turned away his **h**.	3820
	11: 4	*that* his wives turned away his **h** after other	3824
	11: 4	his **h** was not perfect with the LORD his	3824
	11: 4	his God, as *was* the **h** of David his father.	3824
	11: 9	his **h** was turned from the LORD God of	3824
	12:26	Jeroboam said in his **h**, Now shall	3820
	12:27	shall the **h** of this people turn again unto	3820
	12:33	month which he had devised of his own **h**;	3820
	14: 8	and who followed me with all his **h**,	3824
	15: 3	his **h** was not perfect with the LORD his	3824
	15: 3	his God, as the **h** of David his father.	3824
	15:14	nevertheless Asa's **h** was perfect with	3824
	18:37	and *that* thou hast turned their **h** back again.	3820
	21: 7	*and* eat bread, and let thine **h** be merry:	3820
2Ki	5:26	Went not mine **h** *with thee,* when the man	3820
	6:11	Therefore the **h** of the king of Syria was	3820
	9:24	the arrow went out at his **h**, and he sunk	3820
	10:15	and said to him, Is thine **h** right,	3824
	10:15	thine heart right, as my **h** *is* with thy heart?	3824
	10:15	thine heart right, as my heart *is* with thy **h**?	3824
	10:30	Ahab according to all that *was* in mine **h**,	3824
	10:31	of the LORD God of Israel with all his **h**:	3824
	12: 4	all the money that cometh into any man's **h**	3820
	14:10	and thine **h** hath lifted thee up:	3820
	20: 3	before thee in truth and with a perfect **h**,	3824
	22:19	Because thine **h** was tender, and thou hast	3824
	23: 3	his statutes with all *their* **h** and all *their*	3820
	23:25	that turned to the LORD with all his **h**,	3824
1Ch	12:17	to help me, mine **h** shall be knit unto you:	3824
	12:33	*they were* not of **double h**.	3820+3820+2050.1
	12:38	came with a perfect **h** to Hebron,	3824
	12:38	all the rest also of Israel *were of* one **h** to	3820
	15:29	and playing: and she despised him in her **h**.	3820
	16:10	let the **h** of them rejoice that seek	3820
	17: 2	said unto David, Do all that *is* in thine **h**;	3824
	17:19	and according to thine own **h**,	3820
	17:25	thy servant hath found *in his* **h** to pray	NIH
	22:19	Now set your **h** and your soul to seek	3824
	28: 2	*As for me,* I *had* in mine **h** to build a house	3824
	28: 9	serve him with a perfect **h** and with a	3820
	29: 9	with perfect **h** they offered willingly to	3820
	29:17	that thou triest the **h**, and hast pleasure in	3824
	29:17	in the uprightness of mine **h** I have	3824
	29:18	of the thoughts of the **h** of thy people,	3824
	29:18	of thy people, and prepare their **h** unto thee:	3824
	29:19	And give unto Solomon my son a perfect **h**,	3824
2Ch	1:11	Because this was in thine **h**, and thou hast	3824
	6: 7	Now it was in the **h** of David my father to	3824
	6: 8	Forasmuch as it was in thine **h** to build a	3824
	6: 8	thou didst well *in* that it was in thine **h**:	3824
	6:30	unto all his ways, whose **h** thou knowest;	3824
	6:38	If they return to thee with all their **h** and	3820
	7:10	merry in **h** for the goodness that	3820
	7:11	all that came into Solomon's **h** to make in	3820
	7:16	and mine **h** shall be there perpetually.	3820
	9: 1	with him of all that was in her **h**.	3824
	9:23	hear his wisdom, that God had put in his **h**.	3820
	12:14	he prepared not his **h** to seek the LORD.	3820
	15:12	LORD God of their fathers with all their **h**	3824
	15:15	for they had sworn with all their **h**, and	3824
	15:17	nevertheless the **h** of Asa was perfect all	3824
	16: 9	of *them* whose **h** *is* perfect towards him.	3824
	17: 6	his **h** was lift up in the ways of the LORD:	3820
	19: 3	and hast prepared thine **h** to seek God.	3824
	19: 9	faithfully, and with a perfect **h**.	3824
	22: 9	who sought the LORD with all his **h**.	3824
	25: 2	of the LORD, but not with a perfect **h**.	3824
	25:19	and thine **h** lifteth thee up to boast:	3820
	26:16	his **h** was lifted up to *his* destruction:	3820
	29:10	Now *it is* in mine **h** to make a covenant	3824
	29:31	as many as were of a free **h** burnt offerings.	3820
	29:34	for the Levites *were* more upright in **h** to	3824
	30:12	one **h** to do the commandment of the king	3820
	30:19	*That* prepareth his **h** to seek God,	3824
	31:21	he did *it* with all his **h**, and prospered.	3824
	32:25	*done* unto him; for his **h** was lifted up:	3820
	32:26	humbled himself for the pride of his **h**,	3820
	32:31	that *he* might know all *that was* in his **h**.	3824
	34:27	Because thine **h** was tender, and thou didst	3824
	34:31	with all his **h**, and with all his soul,	3824
	36:13	hardened his **h** from turning unto	3824
Ezr	6:22	turned the **h** of the king of Assyria unto	3820
	7:10	For Ezra had prepared his **h** to seek the law	3824
	7:27	hath put *such a thing* as this in the king's **h**,	3820
Ne	2: 2	this *is* nothing *else* but sorrow of **h**. Then I	3820
	2:12	God had put in my **h** to do at Jerusalem:	3820
	6: 8	but thou feignest them out of thine own **h**.	3820
	7: 5	my God put into mine **h** to gather together	3820
	9: 8	And foundest his **h** faithful before thee, and	3824
Est	1:10	when the **h** of the king was merry with	3820
	5: 9	forth that day joyful and with a glad **h**:	3820
	6: 6	Now Haman thought in his **h**, To whom	3820
	7: 5	*is* he, that durst presume in his **h** to do so?	3820
Job	7:17	that thou shouldest set thine **h** upon him?	3820
	8:10	*and* tell thee, and utter words out of their **h**?	3820
	9: 4	*He is* wise in **h**, and mighty in strength:	3824
	10:13	these *things* hast thou hid in thine **h**: I know	3824
	11:13	If thou prepare thine **h**, and stretch out	3820
	12:24	He taketh away the **h** of the chief of	3820
	15:12	Why doth thine **h** carry thee away? and	3820
	17: 4	For thou hast hid their **h** from	3820
	17:11	are broken off, *even* the thoughts of my **h**.	3824
	22:22	his mouth, and lay up his words in thine **h**.	3824
	23:16	For God maketh my **h** soft, and	3820
	27: 6	my **h** shall not reproach *me* so long as I	3824
	29:13	and I caused the widow's **h** to sing for joy.	3820
	31: 7	mine **h** walked after mine eyes, and *if any*	3820
	31: 9	If mine **h** have been deceived by a woman,	3820
	31:27	my **h** hath been secretly enticed, or	3820
	33: 3	words *shall be of* the uprightness of my **h**:	3820
	34:14	If he set his **h** upon *man, if* he gather unto	3820
	36:13	the hypocrites in **h** heap up wrath: they cry	3820
	37: 1	At this also my **h** trembleth, and is moved	3820
	37:24	he respecteth not any *that are* wise of **h**.	3820
	38:36	or who hath given understanding to the **h**?	7907
	41:24	His **h** is as firm as a stone; yea, as hard as	3820

H

Ps 4: 4 commune with your own **h** upon your bed, 3824
4: 7 Thou hast put gladness in my **h**, more than 3820
7:10 *is* of God, which saveth the upright in **h**. 3820
9: 1 praise *thee,* O LORD, with my whole **h**; 3820
10: 6 He hath said in his **h**, I shall not be moved: 3820
10:11 He hath said in his **h**, God hath forgotten: 3820
10:13 he hath said in his **h**, Thou wilt not require 3820
10:17 thou wilt prepare their **h**, thou wilt cause 3820
11: 2 *they* may privily shoot at the upright in **h**. 3820
12: 2 a **double h** do they speak. 3820+3820+2050.1
13: 2 in my soul, *having* sorrow in my **h** daily? 3824
13: 5 my **h** shall rejoice in thy salvation. 3820
14: 1 The fool hath said in his **h**, *There is* no 3820
15: 2 and speaketh the truth in his **h**. 3824
16: 9 Therefore my **h** is glad, and my glory 3820
17: 3 Thou hast proved mine **h**; thou hast visited 3820
19: 8 of the LORD *are* right, rejoicing the **h**: 3820
19:14 the meditation of my **h**, be acceptable in 3820
20: 4 Grant thee according to thine own **h**, and 3824
22:14 my **h** is like wax; it is melted in the midst 3820
22:26 that seek him: your **h** shall live for ever. 3824
24: 4 He that hath clean hands, and a pure **h**; 3824
25:17 The troubles of my **h** are enlarged: O bring 3824
26: 2 and prove me; try my reins and my **h**. 3820
27: 3 encamp against me, my **h** shall not fear: 3820
27: 8 my **h** said unto thee, Thy face, LORD, 3820
27:14 and he shall strengthen thine **h**: 3820
28: 7 my **h** trusted in him, and I am helped: 3820
28: 7 therefore my **h** greatly rejoiceth; and 3820
31:24 and he shall strengthen your **h**, 3824
32:11 shout for joy, all *ye that are* upright in **h**. 3820
33:11 the thoughts of his **h** to all generations. 3820
33:21 For our **h** shall rejoice in him, because 3820
34:18 *is* nigh unto them that are of a broken **h**; 3820
36: 1 of the wicked saith within my **h**, 3820
36:10 and thy righteousness to the upright in **h**. 3820
37: 4 and he shall give thee the desires of thine **h**. 3820
37:15 Their sword shall enter into their own **h**, 3820
37:31 The law of his God *is* in his **h**; none of his 3820
38: 8 by reason of the disquietness of my **h**. 3820
38:10 My **h** panteth, my strength faileth me: 3820
39: 3 My **h** was hot within me, while I was 3820
40: 8 O my God: yea, thy law *is* within my **h**. 4578
40:10 have not hid thy righteousness within my **h**; 3820
40:12 of mine head: therefore my **h** faileth me. 3820
41: 6 his **h** gathereth iniquity to itself; *when* he 3820
44:18 Our **h** is not turned back, neither have our 3820
44:21 for he knoweth the secrets of the **h**. 3820
45: 1 My **h** is inditing a good matter: I speak of 3820
45: 5 Thine arrows *are* sharp in the **h** of 3820
49: 3 the meditation of my **h** *shall be of* 3820
51:10 Create in me a clean **h**, O God; and renew a 3820
51:17 a broken and a contrite **h**, O God, thou wilt 3820
53: 1 The fool hath said in his **h**, *There is* no 3820
55: 4 My **h** is sore pained within me: and 3820
55:21 smoother than butter, but war *was* in his **h**: 3820
57: 7 My **h** is fixed, O God, my heart is fixed: 3820
57: 7 My heart is fixed, O God, my **h** is fixed: 3820
58: 2 Yea, in **h** you work wickedness; you weigh 3820
61: 2 cry unto thee, when my **h** is overwhelmed: 3820
62: 8 ye people, pour out your **h** before him: 3824
62:10 riches increase, set not *your* **h** *upon them.* 3820
64: 6 *thought* of every one *of them,* and the **h**, 3820
64:10 in him; and all the upright in **h** shall glory. 3820
66:18 If I regard iniquity in my **h**, the Lord will 3820
69:20 Reproach hath broken my **h**; and I am full 3820
69:32 and your **h** shall live that seek God. 3824
73: 1 to Israel, *even* to such as are of a clean **h**. 3824
73: 7 they have more than **h** could wish. 3824
73:13 Verily I have cleansed my **h** *in* vain, and 3824
73:21 Thus my **h** was grieved, and I was pricked 3824
73:26 My flesh and my **h** faileth: *but* God *is* 3824
73:26 *but* God *is* the strength of my **h**, and 3824
77: 6 I commune with mine own **h**: and my spirit 3824
78: 8 a generation *that* set not their **h** aright, and 3820
78:18 they tempted God in their **h** by asking meat 3824
78:37 For their **h** was not right with him, 3820
78:72 fed them according to the integrity of his **h**; 3824
84: 2 my **h** and my flesh crieth out for the living 3820
84: 5 in thee; in whose **h** *are* the ways *of them.* 3824
86:11 in thy truth: unite my **h** to fear thy name. 3824
86:12 praise thee, O Lord my God, with all my **h**: 3824
94:15 and all the upright in **h** shall follow it. 3820
95: 8 Harden not your **h**, as *in* the provocation, 3824
95:10 It *is* a people that do err in *their* **h**, and 3824
97:11 and gladness for the upright in **h**. 3820
101: 2 will walk within my house with a perfect **h**. 3824
101: 4 A froward **h** shall depart from me: I will 3824
101: 5 a high look and a proud **h** will not I suffer. 3824
102: 4 My **h** is smitten, and withered like grass; so 3820
104:15 wine *that* maketh glad the **h** of man, 3824
104:15 and bread *which* strengtheneth man's **h**. 3824
105: 3 let the **h** of them rejoice that seek 3820
105:25 He turned their **h** to hate his people, to deal 3820
107:12 Therefore he brought down their **h** with 3820
108: 1 O God, my **h** is fixed; I will sing and 3820
109:16 that *he* might even slay the broken in **h**. 3824
109:22 needy, and my **h** is wounded within me. 3820
111: 1 I will praise the LORD with *my* whole **h**, 3824
112: 7 his **h** is fixed, trusting in the LORD. 3820
112: 8 His **h** *is* established, he shall not be afraid, 3820
119: 2 *and that* seek him with the whole **h**. 3820
119: 7 I will praise thee with uprightness of **h**, 3824
119:10 With my whole **h** have I sought thee: O let 3820
119:11 Thy word have I hid in mine **h**, that I might 3820
119:32 when thou shalt enlarge my **h**. 3820
119:34 yea, I shall observe it with *my* whole **h**. 3820
119:36 Incline my **h** unto thy testimonies, and 3820
119:58 I intreated thy favour with *my* whole **h**: 3820
119:69 I will keep thy precepts with *my* whole **h**. 3820
119:70 Their **h** is as fat as grease; *but* I delight *in* 3820
119:80 Let my **h** be sound in thy statutes; that I be 3820
119:111 for ever: for they *are* the rejoicing of my **h**. 3820
119:112 I have inclined mine **h** to perform thy 3820
119:145 I cried with *my* whole **h**; hear me, 3820
119:161 but my **h** standeth in awe of thy word. 3820
131: 1 LORD, my **h** is not haughty, nor mine 3820
138: 1 I will praise thee with my whole **h**: 3820
139:23 Search me, O God, and know my **h**: try me, 3824
140: 2 Which imagine mischiefs in *their* **h**; 3820
141: 4 Incline not my **h** to *any* evil thing, 3820
143: 4 within me; my **h** within me is desolate. 3820
147: 3 He healeth the broken in **h**, and bindeth up 3820
Pr 2: 2 *and* apply thine **h** to understanding; 3820
2:10 When wisdom entereth into thine **h**, and 3820
3: 1 but let thine **h** keep my commandments: 3820
3: 3 write them upon the table of thine **h**: 3820
3: 5 Trust in the LORD with all thine **h**; and 3820
4: 4 said unto me, Let thine **h** retain my words: 3820
4:21 keep them in the midst of thine **h**. 3824
4:23 Keep thy **h** with all diligence; for out of it 3820
5:12 and my **h** despised reproof; 3820
6:14 Frowardness *is* in his **h**, he deviseth 3820
6:18 A **h** that deviseth wicked imaginations, 3820
6:21 Bind them continually upon thine **h**, *and* 3820
6:25 Lust not after her beauty in thine **h**; 3824
7: 3 write them upon the table of thine **h**. 3820
7:10 *with* the attire of a harlot, and subtil of **h**. 3820
7:25 Let not thine **h** decline to her ways, go not 3820
8: 5 and, ye fools, be ye of an understanding **h**. 3820
10: 8 The wise in **h** will receive commandments: 3820
10:20 the **h** of the wicked *is* little worth. 3820
11:20 *They that are* of a froward **h** *are* 3820
11:29 the fool *shall be* servant to the wise of **h**. 3820
12: 8 he that is of a perverse **h** shall be despised. 3820
12:20 Deceit *is* in the **h** of them that imagine evil: 3820
12:23 but the **h** of fools proclaimeth foolishness. 3820
12:25 Heaviness in the **h** of man maketh it stoop: 3820
13:12 Hope deferred maketh the **h** sick: but 3820
14:10 The **h** knoweth his own bitterness; and 3820
14:13 Even in laughter the **h** is sorrowful; and 3820
14:14 The backslider in **h** shall be filled with his 3820
14:30 A sound **h** *is* the life of the flesh: but 3820
14:33 Wisdom resteth in the **h** of him that hath 3820
15: 7 but the **h** of the foolish *doeth* not so. 3820
15:13 A merry **h** maketh a cheerful countenance: 3820
15:13 but by sorrow of the **h** the spirit *is* broken. 3820
15:14 The **h** of him that hath understanding 3820
15:15 *he that is* of a merry **h** *hath* a continual 3820
15:28 The **h** of the righteous studieth to answer: 3820
15:30 The light of the eyes rejoiceth the **h**: *and* 3820
16: 1 The preparations of the **h** in man, and 3820
16: 5 Every one *that is* proud in **h** *is* an 3820
16: 9 A man's **h** deviseth his way: but 3820
16:21 The wise in **h** shall be called prudent: and 3820
16:23 The **h** of the wise teacheth his mouth, and 3820
17:16 to get wisdom, seeing *he hath* no **h** *to it?* 3820
17:20 He that hath a froward **h** findeth no good: 3820

Pr 17:22 A merry **h** doeth good *like* a medicine: but 3820
18: 2 but that his **h** may discover itself. 3820
18:12 Before destruction the **h** of man is haughty, 3820
18:15 The **h** of the prudent getteth knowledge; 3820
19: 3 and his **h** fretteth against the LORD. 3820
19:21 *There are* many devices in a man's **h**; 3820
20: 5 Counsel in the **h** of man *is like* deep water; 3820
20: 9 Who can say, I have made my **h** clean, I am 3820
21: 1 The king's **h** *is* in the hand of the LORD, 3820
21: 4 a proud **h**, *and* the plowing of the wicked, 3820
22:11 He that loveth pureness of **h**, *for* the grace 3820
22:15 Foolishness *is* bound in the **h** of a child; *but* 3820
22:17 and apply thine **h** unto my knowledge. 3820
23: 7 For as he thinketh in his **h**, so *is* he: Eat and 5315
23: 7 saith he to thee; but his **h** *is* not with thee. 3820
23:12 Apply thine **h** unto instruction, and 3820
23:15 My son, if thine **h** be wise, my heart shall 3820
23:15 be wise, my **h** shall rejoice, even mine. 3820
23:17 Let not thine **h** envy sinners: but *be thou* in 3820
23:19 and be wise, and guide thine **h** in the way. 3820
23:26 give me thine **h**, and let thine eyes observe 3820
23:33 and thine **h** shall utter perverse things. 3820
24: 2 For their **h** studieth destruction, and 3820
24:12 doth not he that pondereth the **h** consider 3826
24:17 let not thine **h** be glad when he stumbleth: 3820
25: 3 and the **h** of kings *is* unsearchable. 3820
25:20 so *is* he that singeth songs to a heavy **h**. 3820
26:23 a wicked **h** *are like* a potsherd covered with 3820
26:25 for *there are* seven abominations in his **h**. 3820
27: 9 Ointment and perfume rejoice the **h**: so 3820
27:11 My son, be wise, and make my **h** glad, 3820
27:19 *answereth* to face, so the **h** of man to man. 3820
28:14 he that hardeneth his **h** shall fall into 3820
28:25 He that is of a proud **h** stirreth up strife: but 5315
28:26 He that trusteth in his own **h** *is* a fool: but 3820
31:11 The **h** of her husband doth *safely* trust in 3820
Ecc 1:13 I gave my **h** to seek and search out by 3820
1:16 I communed with mine own **h**, saying, Lo, 3820
1:16 my **h** had great experience of wisdom and 3820
1:17 I gave my **h** to know wisdom, and to know 3820
2: 1 I said in mine **h**, Go to now, I will prove 3820
2: 3 I sought in mine **h** to give myself unto 3820
2: 3 (yet acquainting mine **h** with wisdom) 3820
2:10 I withheld not my **h** from any joy; 3820
2:10 any joy; for my **h** rejoiced in all my labour: 3820
2:15 said I in my **h**, As it happeneth to the fool, 3820
2:15 Then I said in my **h**, that this also *is* vanity. 3820
2:20 Therefore I went about to cause my **h** to 3820
2:22 all his labour, and of the vexation of his **h**, 3820
2:23 yea, his **h** taketh not rest in the night. 3820
3:11 also he hath set the world in their **h**, so that 3820
3:17 I said in mine **h**, God shall judge 3820
3:18 I said in my **h** concerning the estate of 3820
5: 2 let not thine **h** be hasty to utter *any* thing 3820
5:20 God answereth *him* in the joy of his **h**. 3820
7: 2 all men; and the living will lay *it* to his **h**. 3820
7: 3 for by the sadness of the countenance the **h** 3820
7: 4 The **h** of the wise *is* in the house of 3820
7: 4 but the **h** of fools *is* in the house of mirth. 3820
7: 7 wise *man* mad; and a gift destroyeth the **h**. 3820
7:22 For oftentimes also thine own **h** knoweth 3820
7:25 I applied mine **h** to know, and to search, 3820
7:26 whose **h** *is* snares and nets, *and* her hands 3820
8: 5 a wise *man's* **h** discerneth *both* time and 3820
8: 9 applied my **h** unto every work that is done 3820
8:11 the **h** of the sons of men is fully set in them 3820
8:16 When I applied mine **h** to know wisdom, 3820
9: 1 For all this I considered in my **h** even to 3820
9: 3 also the **h** of the sons of men is full *of* evil, 3820
9: 3 madness *is* in their **h** while they live, and 3824
9: 7 and drink thy wine with a merry **h**; 3820
10: 2 A wise *man's* **h** *is* at his right hand; but 3820
10: 2 *is* at his right hand; but a fool's **h** at his left. 3820
11: 9 let thy **h** cheer thee in the days of thy 3820
11: 9 walk in the ways of thine **h**, and in the sight 3820
11:10 Therefore remove sorrow from thy **h**, and 3820
SS 3:11 and in the day of the gladness of his **h**. 3820
4: 9 Thou hast **ravished** my **h**, my sister, 3823
4: 9 thou hast **ravished** my **h** with one of thine 3823
5: 2 I sleep, but my **h** waketh: *it is* the voice of 3820
8: 6 Set me as a seal upon thine **h**, as a seal 3820
Isa 1: 5 whole head *is* sick, and the whole **h** faint. 3824
6:10 Make the **h** of this people fat, and 3820
6:10 understand *with* their **h**, and convert, and 3824
7: 2 his **h** was moved, and the heart of his 3824
7: 2 heart was moved, and the **h** of his people, 3824
9: 9 that say in the pride and stoutness of **h**, 3824
10: 7 meaneth not so, neither doth his **h** think so; 3824
10: 7 *it is* in his **h** to destroy and cut off nations 3824
10:12 I will punish the fruit of the stout **h** of 3824
13: 7 be faint, and every man's **h** shall melt: 3824
14:13 For thou hast said in thine **h**, I will ascend 3824
15: 5 My **h** shall cry out for Moab; his fugitives 3820
19: 1 the **h** of Egypt shall melt in the midst of it. 3824
21: 4 My **h** panted, fearfulness affrighted me: 3824
29:13 have removed their **h** far from me, and 3820
30:29 gladness of **h**, as when one goeth with a 3824
32: 4 The **h** also of the rash shall understand 3824
32: 6 his **h** will work iniquity, to practise 3820
33:18 Thine **h** shall meditate terror. Where *is* 3820
35: 4 Say to them that are of a fearful **h**, 3820
38: 3 before thee in truth and with a perfect **h**, 3820
42:25 and it burned him, yet he laid *it* not to **h**. 3820
44:19 none considereth in his **h**, neither *is there* 3820
44:20 a deceived **h** hath turned him aside, that he 3820
47: 7 that thou didst not lay these *things* to thy **h**, 3820
47: 8 that sayest in thine **h**, I *am*, and none else 3824
47:10 thou hast said in thine **h**, I *am*, and 3820
49:21 shalt thou say in thine **h**, Who hath 3824
51: 7 the people in whose **h** *is* my law; 3820
57: 1 and no man layeth *it* to **h**: 3820
57:11 not remembered me, nor laid *it* to thy **h**? 3820
57:15 and to revive the **h** of the contrite ones. 3820
57:17 he went on frowardly in the way of his **h**. 3820
59:13 and uttering from the **h** words of falsehood. 3820
60: 5 flow *together*, and thine **h** shall fear, and 3824
63: 4 For the day of vengeance *is* in mine **h**, and 3820
63:17 *and* hardened our **h** from thy fear? 3820
65:14 my servants shall sing for joy of **h**, but 3820
65:14 ye shall cry for sorrow of **h**, and shall howl 3820
66:14 when ye see *this*, your **h** shall rejoice, and 3820
Jer 3:10 hath not turned unto me with her whole **h**, 3820
3:15 I will give you pastors according to mine **h**, 3820
3:17 more after the imagination of their evil **h**. 3820
4: 4 take away the foreskins of your **h**, ye men 3824
4: 9 *that* the **h** of the king shall perish, and 3820
4: 9 king shall perish, and the **h** of the princes; 3820
4:14 wash thine **h** from wickedness, 3820
4:18 *it is* bitter, because it reacheth unto thine **h**. 3820
4:19 I am pained *at* my **very h**; my heart 3820+7023
4:19 my **h** maketh a noise in me; I cannot hold 3820
5:23 people hath a revolting and a rebellious **h**; 3820
5:24 Neither say they in their **h**, Let us now fear 3824
7:24 *and* in the imagination of their evil **h**, 3820
7:31 *them* not, neither came it into my **h**. 3820
8:18 myself against sorrow, my **h** *is* faint in me. 3820
9: 8 with his mouth, but in **h** he layeth his wait. 7130
9:14 after the imagination of their own **h**, 3820
9:26 house of Israel *are* uncircumcised in the **h**. 3820
11: 8 every one in the imagination of their evil **h**: 3820
11:20 that triest the reins and the **h**, 3820
12: 3 seen me, and tried mine **h** towards thee: 3820
12:11 because no man layeth *it* to **h**. 3820
13:10 which walk in the imagination of their **h**, 3820
13:22 if thou say in thine **h**, Wherefore come 3824
14:14 a thing of nought, and the deceit of their **h**. 3820
15:16 unto me the joy and rejoicing of mine **h**: 3824
16:12 one after the imagination of his evil **h**, 3820
17: 1 *it is* graven upon the table of their **h**, and 3820
17: 5 and whose **h** departeth from the LORD. 3820
17: 9 The **h** *is* deceitful above all *things*, and 3820
17:10 I the LORD search the **h**, *I* try the reins, 3820
18:12 every one do the imagination of his evil **h**. 3820
20: 9 *his word* was in mine **h** as a burning fire 3820
20:12 the righteous, *and* seest the reins and the **h**, 3820
22:17 thine eyes and thine **h** *are* not but for thy 3820
23: 9 Mine **h** within me is broken because of 3820
23:16 they speak a vision of their own **h**, *and* 3820
23:17 walketh after the imagination of his own **h**, 3820
23:20 he have performed the thoughts of his **h**: 3820
23:26 How long shall *this* be in the **h** of 3820
23:26 *are* prophets of the deceit of their own **h**; 3820
24: 7 I will give them a **h** to know me, that I *am* 3820
24: 7 shall return unto me with their whole **h**. 3820
29:13 ye shall search for me with all your **h**. 3824
30:21 for who *is* this that engaged his **h** to 3820
30:24 until he have performed the intents of his **h**: 3820
31:21 set thine **h** toward the highway, *even* 3820

Jer	32:39	I will give them one **h**, and one way,	3820
	32:41	in this land assuredly with my whole **h**	3820
	48:29	and his pride, and the haughtiness of his **h**.	3820
	48:31	*mine h* shall mourn for the men of	NIH
	48:36	Therefore mine **h** shall sound for Moab like	3820
	48:36	mine **h** shall sound like pipes for the men	3820
	48:41	shall be as the **h** of a woman in her pangs.	3820
	49:16	hath deceived thee, *and* the pride of thine **h**,	3820
	49:22	at that day shall the **h** of the mighty *men* of	3820
	49:22	Edom be as the **h** of a woman in her pangs.	3820
	51:46	lest your **h** faint, and ye fear for the rumour	3824
La	1:20	are troubled; mine **h** is turned within me;	3820
	1:22	for my sighs *are* many, and my **h** *is* faint.	3820
	2:18	Their **h** cried unto the Lord, O wall of	3820
	2:19	pour out thine **h** like water before the face	3820
	3:41	Let us lift up our **h** with *our* hands unto	3824
	3:51	Mine eye affecteth mine **h** because of all	5315
	3:65	Give them sorrow of **h**, thy curse unto	3820
	5:15	The joy of our **h** is ceased; our dance is	3820
	5:17	For this our **h** is faint; for these *things* our	3820
Eze	3:10	I shall speak unto thee receive in thine **h**,	3824
	6: 9	because I am broken with their whorish **h**,	3820
	11:19	I will give them one **h**, and I will put a new	3820
	11:19	and I will take the stony **h** out of their flesh,	3820
	11:19	their flesh, and will give them a **h** of flesh:	3820
	11:21	*as for them* whose **h** walketh after the heart	3820
	11:21	*as for them* whose heart walketh after the **h**	3820
	13:17	which prophesy out of their own **h**;	3820
	13:22	Because *with* lies *ye* have made the **h** of	3820
	14: 3	these men have set up their idols in their **h**,	3820
	14: 4	of Israel that setteth up his idols in his **h**,	3820
	14: 5	may take the house of Israel in their own **h**,	3820
	14: 7	setteth up his idols in his **h**, and putteth	3820
	16:30	How weak is thine **h**, saith the Lord God,	3826
	18:31	and make you a new **h** and a new spirit:	3820
	20:16	for their **h** went after their idols.	3820
	21: 7	every **h** shall melt, and all hands shall be	3820
	21:15	that *their* **h** may faint, and *their* ruins be	3820
	22:14	Can thine **h** endure, or can thine hands be	3820
	25: 6	rejoiced in **h** with all thy despite against	5315
	25:15	have taken vengeance with a despiteful **h**,	5315
	27:31	they shall weep for thee with bitterness of **h**	5315
	28: 2	Because thine **h** *is* lifted up, and thou hast	3820
	28: 2	though thou set thine **h** as the heart of God:	3820
	28: 2	though thou set thine heart as the **h** of God:	3820
	28: 5	thine **h** is lifted up because of thy riches:	3824
	28: 6	Because thou hast set thine **h** as the heart of	3824
	28: 6	Because thou hast set thine heart as the **h** of	3820
	28:17	Thine **h** was lifted up because of thy	3820
	31:10	and his **h** is lifted up in his height;	3824
	33:31	*but* their **h** goeth after their covetousness.	3820
	36: 5	their possession with the joy of all *their* **h**,	3824
	36:26	A new **h** also will I give you, and a new	3820
	36:26	I will take away the stony **h** out of your	3820
	36:26	your flesh, and I will give you a **h** of flesh.	3820
	40: 4	set thine **h** upon all that I shall shew thee;	3820
	44: 7	uncircumcised in **h**, and uncircumcised in	3820
	44: 9	No stranger, uncircumcised in **h**,	3820
Da	1: 8	Daniel purposed in his **h** that he would not	3820
	2:30	thou mightest know the thoughts of thy **h**.	3825
	4:16	Let his **h** be changed from man's, and let a	3825
	4:16	let a beast's **h** be given unto him;	3825
	5:20	when his **h** was lifted up, and his mind	3825
	5:21	his **h** was made like the beasts, and	3825
	5:22	O Belshazzar, hast not humbled thine **h**,	3825
	6:14	and set *his* **h** on Daniel to deliver him:	1079
	7: 4	as a man, and a man's **h** was given to it.	3825
	7:28	in me: but I kept the matter in my **h**.	3821
	8:25	he shall magnify *himself* in his **h**, and	3824
	10:12	that thou didst set thine **h** to understand,	3820
	11:12	away the multitude, his **h** shall be lifted up;	3824
	11:28	his **h** *shall be* against the holy covenant;	3824
Hos	4: 8	and they set their **h** on their iniquity.	5315
	4:11	and wine and new wine take *away* the **h**.	3820
	7: 6	For they have made ready their **h** like an	3820
	7:11	Ephraim also is like a silly dove, without **h**:	3820
	7:14	they have not cried unto me with their **h**,	3820
	10: 2	Their **h** is divided; now shall they be found	3820
	11: 8	mine **h** is turned within me, my repentings	3820
	13: 6	they were filled, and their **h** was exalted;	3820
	13: 8	will rent the caul of their **h**, and there will I	3820
Joel	2:12	turn ye *even* to me with all your **h**, and	3824
	2:13	rent your **h**, and not your garments, and	3824
Ob	1: 3	The pride of thine **h** hath deceived thee,	3820
	1: 3	that saith in his **h**, Who shall bring me	3820
Na	2:10	the **h** melteth, and the knees smite together,	3820
Zep	1:12	that say in their **h**, The Lord will not do	3824
	2:15	that said in her **h**, I *am*, and *there is* none	3824
	3:14	be glad and rejoice with all the **h**,	3820
Zec	7:10	imagine evil against his brother in your **h**.	3824
	10: 7	and their **h** shall rejoice as *through* wine:	3820
	10: 7	be glad; their **h** shall rejoice in the Lord.	3820
	12: 5	the governors of Judah shall say in their **h**,	3820
Mal	2: 2	will not hear, and if ye will not lay *it* to **h**,	3820
	2: 2	them already, because ye do not lay *it* to **h**.	3820
	4: 6	he shall turn the **h** of the fathers to	3820
	4: 6	the **h** of the children to their fathers, lest I	3820
Mt	5: 8	Blessed *are* the pure in **h**: for they shall see	*2588*
	5:28	adultery with her already in his **h**.	*2588*
	6:21	your treasure is, there will your **h** be also.	*2588*
	11:29	learn of me; for I am meek and lowly in **h**:	*2588*
	12:34	the abundance of the **h** the mouth speaketh.	*2588*
	12:35	treasure of the **h** bringeth forth good *things:*	*2588*
	12:40	and three nights in the **h** of the earth.	*2588*
	13:15	For this people's **h** is waxed gross, and	*2588*
	13:15	and should understand with *their* **h**, and	*2588*
	13:19	away that which was sown in his **h**.	*2588*
	15: 8	with *their* lips; but their **h** is far from me.	*2588*
	15:18	out of the mouth come forth from the **h**;	*2588*
	15:19	For out of the **h** proceed evil thoughts,	*2588*
	22:37	shalt love the Lord thy God with all thy **h**,	*2588*
	24:48	*and* if that evil servant shall say in his **h**,	*2588*
Mk	6:52	of the loaves: for their **h** was hardened.	*2588*
	7: 6	with *their* lips, but their **h** is far from me.	*2588*
	7:19	Because it entereth not into his **h**, but	*2588*
	7:21	For from within, out of the **h** of men,	*2588*
	8:17	have ye your **h** yet hardened?	*2588*
	10: 5	For the **hardness of** your **h** he wrote you	*4641*
	11:23	and shall not doubt in his **h**, but	*2588*
	12:30	shalt love the Lord thy God with all thy **h**,	*2588*
	12:33	And to love him with all the **h**, and with all	*2588*
	16:14	them with their unbelief and **hardness of h**,	*4641*
Lk	2:19	these things, and pondered *them* in her **h**.	*2588*
	2:51	his mother kept all these sayings in her **h**.	*2588*
	6:45	of his **h** bringeth forth that which is good;	*2588*
	6:45	an evil man out of the evil treasure of his **h**	*2588*
	6:45	for of the abundance of the **h** his mouth	*2588*
	8:15	which in an honest and good **h**,	*2588*
	9:47	perceiving the thought of their **h**,	*2588*
	10:27	shalt love the Lord thy God with all thy **h**,	*2588*
	12:34	your treasure is, there will your **h** be also.	*2588*
	12:45	But and if that servant say in his **h**, My lord	*2588*
	24:25	slow of **h** to believe all that the prophets	*2588*
	24:32	to another, Did not our **h** burn within us,	*2588*
Jn	12:40	blinded their eyes, and hardened their **h**;	*2588*
	12:40	nor understand with *their* **h**, and	*2588*
	13: 2	the devil having now put into the **h** of Judas	*2588*
	14: 1	Let not your **h** be troubled: ye believe in	*2588*
	14:27	Let not your **h** be troubled, neither let it be	*2588*
	16: 6	*things* unto you, sorrow hath filled your **h**.	*2588*
	16:22	and your **h** shall rejoice, and your joy no	*2588*
Ac	2:26	Therefore did my **h** rejoice, and my tongue	*2588*
	2:37	heard *this,* they were pricked in *their* **h**,	*2588*
	2:46	meat with gladness and singleness of **h**,	*2588*
	4:32	of them that believed were of one **h**	*2588*
	5: 3	why hath Satan filled thine **h** to lie to	*2588*
	5: 4	hast thou conceived this thing in thine **h**?	*2588*
	5:33	they heard *that,* they were cut *to the h*,	NIG
	7:23	it came into his **h** to visit his brethren	*2588*
	7:51	and uncircumcised in **h** and ears,	*2588*
	7:54	heard these *things,* they were cut to the **h**,	*2588*
	8:21	for thy **h** is not right in the sight of God.	*2588*
	8:22	if perhaps the thought of thine **h** may be	*2588*
	8:37	If thou believest with all *thine* **h**,	*2588*
	11:23	that with purpose of **h** *they* would cleave	*2588*
	13:22	a man after mine own **h**, which shall fulfil	*2588*
	16:14	heard *us:* whose **h** the Lord opened,	*2588*
	21:13	mean ye to weep and to break mine **h**?	*2588*
	28:27	For the **h** of this people is waxed gross, and	*2588*
	28:27	and understand with *their* **h**, and should be	*2588*
Ro	1:21	and their foolish **h** was darkened.	*2588*
	2: 5	impenitent **h** treasurest up unto thyself	*2588*
	2:29	and circumcision *is that* of the **h**, in	*2588*
	6:17	ye have obeyed from the **h** *that* form of	*2588*
	9: 2	and continual sorrow in my **h**.	*2588*
	10: 6	Say not in thine **h**, Who shall ascend into	*2588*
	10: 8	nigh thee, *even* in thy mouth, and in thy **h**:	*2588*
	10: 9	shalt believe in thine **h** that God hath raised	*2588*

Ro 10:10 For with the **h** *man* believeth unto 2588
1Co 2: 9 neither have entered into the **h** of man, 2588
7:37 he that standeth stedfast in *his* **h**, 2588
7:37 decreed in his **h** that *he* will keep his virgin, 2588
14:25 And thus are the secrets of his **h** made 2588
2Co 2: 4 anguish of **h** I wrote unto you with many 2588
3: 3 tables of stone, but in fleshy tables of the **h**. 2588
3:15 Moses is read, the vail is upon their **h**. 2588
5:12 which glory in appearance, and not in **h**. 2588
6:11 mouth is open unto you, our **h** is enlarged. 2588
8:16 which put the same earnest care into the **h** 2588
9: 7 man according as he purposeth in *his* **h**, 2588
Eph 4:18 in them, because of the blindness of their **h**: 2588
5:19 and making melody in your **h** to the Lord; 2588
6: 5 and trembling, in singleness of your **h**, 2588
6: 6 of Christ, doing the will of God from the **h**; *5590*
Php 1: 7 this of you all, because I have you in *my* **h**; 2588
Col 3:22 but in singleness of **h**, fearing God: 2588
1Th 2:17 you for a short time in presence, not in **h**, 2588
1Ti 1: 5 commandment is charity out of a pure **h**, 2588
2Ti 2:22 them that call on the Lord out of a pure **h**. 2588
Heb 3:10 and said, They do alway err in *their* **h**; 2588
3:12 lest there be in any of you an evil **h** of 2588
4:12 of the thoughts and intents of the **h**. 2588
10:22 Let us draw near with a true **h** in full 2588
13: 9 For *it is* a good *thing* that the **h** be 2588
Jas 1:26 not his tongue, but deceiveth his own **h**, 2588
1Pe 1:22 *see that ye* love one another with a pure **h** 2588
3: 4 But *let it be* the hidden man of the **h**, in *that* 2588
2Pe 2:14 a **h** they have exercised with covetous 2588
1Jn 3:20 For if *our* **h** condemn us, God is greater 2588
3:20 God is greater than our **h**, and knoweth all 2588
3:21 if our **h** condemn us not, *then* have we 2588
Rev 18: 7 for she saith in her **h**, I sit a queen, and 2588

HEART'S (4) [HEART]
Ps 10: 3 For the wicked boasteth of his **h** desire, and 5315
21: 2 Thou hast given him his **h** desire, and 3820
81:12 So I gave them up unto their own **h** lust: 3820
Ro 10: 1 my **h** desire and prayer to God for Israel is, 2588

HEARTED (10) [HEART]
Ex 28: 3 thou shalt speak unto all *that are* wise **h**, 3820
31: 6 in the hearts of all that are wise **h** I have put 3820
35:10 every wise **h** among you shall come, and 3820
35:22 as many as were willing **h**, *and* 3820
35:25 all the women that were wise **h** did spin 3820
36: 1 and Aholiab, and every wise **h** man, 3820
36: 2 and Aholiab, and every wise **h** man, 3820
36: 8 every wise **h** *man* among them that 3820
2Ch 13: 7 when Rehoboam was young and tender **h**, 3824
Eze 2: 4 For *they are* impudent children and stiff **h**. 3820

HEARTH (7)
Ge 18: 6 knead *it*, and make cakes upon the **h**. NIH
Ps 102: 3 like smoke, and my bones are burnt as a **h**. 4168
Isa 30:14 of it a sheard to take fire from the **h**, 3344
Jer 36:22 *there was a fire on* the **h** burning before him. 254
36:23 cast *it* into the fire that *was* on the **h**, 254
36:23 was consumed in the fire that *was* on the **h**. 254
Zec 12: 6 of Judah like a **h** of fire among the wood, 3595

HEARTILY (1) [HEARTY]
Col 3:23 **h**, as to the Lord, and not unto men; *1537+5590*

HEARTS (112) [HEART]
Ge 18: 5 a morsel of bread, and comfort ye your **h**; 3820
Ex 14:17 I will harden the **h** of the Egyptians, and 3820
31: 6 in the **h** of all that are wise hearted I have 3820
Lev 26:36 into their **h** in the lands of their enemies; 3824
26:41 if then their uncircumcised **h** be humbled, 3824
Dt 20: 3 let not your **h** faint, fear not, and do not 3824
32:46 Set your **h** unto all the words which I 3824
Jos 2:11 as soon as we had heard *these things,* our **h** 3824
7: 5 wherefore the **h** of the people melted, and 3824
11:20 For it was of the LORD to harden their **h**, 3820
23:14 ye know in all your **h** and in all your souls, 3824
Jdg 9: 3 their **h** inclined to follow Abimelech; 3820
16:25 when their **h** were merry, that they said, 3820
19:22 *Now* as they were making their **h** merry, 3820
1Sa 6: 6 Wherefore then do ye harden your **h**, as 3824
6: 6 and Pharaoh hardened their **h**? 3820
7: 3 do return unto the LORD with all your **h**, 3824
7: 3 prepare your **h** unto the LORD, and 3824
10:26 a band of men, whose **h** God had touched. 3820
2Sa 15: 6 so Absalom stole the **h** of the men of Israel. 3820
15:13 The **h** of the men of Israel are after 3820
1Ki 8:39 knowest the **h** of all the children of men;) 3824
8:58 That *he* may incline our **h** unto him, 3824
1Ch 28: 9 for the LORD searcheth all **h**, and 3824
2Ch 6:14 that walk before thee with all their **h**: 3820
6:30 (for thou only knowest the **h** of the children 3824
11:16 **h** to seek the LORD God of Israel came *to* 3824
20:33 their **h** unto the God of their fathers. 3824
Job 1: 5 have sinned, and cursed God in their **h**. 3824
Ps 7: 9 for the righteous God trieth the **h** and reins. 3826
28: 3 their neighbours, but mischief *is* in their **h**. 3824
33:15 He fashioneth their **h** alike; he considereth 3820
35:25 Let them not say in their **h**, Ah, so 3820
74: 8 They said in their **h**, Let us destroy them 3820
90:12 that we may apply *our* **h** *unto* wisdom. 3824
125: 4 and to *them that are* upright in their **h**. 3826
Pr 15:11 then the **h** of the children of men? 3826
17: 3 for gold: but the LORD trieth the **h**. 3826
21: 2 own eyes: but the LORD pondereth the **h**. 3826
31: 6 and wine unto those that be of heavy **h**. 5315
Isa 44:18 *and* their **h**, that *they* cannot understand. 3826
Jer 31:33 in their inward parts, and write it in their **h**; 3820
32:40 I will put my fear in their **h**, that *they* shall 3824
42:20 For ye dissembled in your **h**, when ye sent 5315
48:41 the mighty *men's* **h** in Moab at that day 3820
Eze 13: 2 unto them that prophesy out of their own **h**, 3820
32: 9 I will also vex the **h** of many people, 3820
Da 11:27 both these kings' **h** *shall be* to do mischief, 3824
Hos 7: 2 they consider not in their **h** *that* I remember 3824
Zec 7:12 they made their **h** *as* an adamant stone, 3820
8:17 let none of you imagine evil in your **h** 3824
Mt 9: 4 Wherefore think ye evil in your **h**? *2588*
18:35 if ye from your **h** forgive not every one his *2588*
19: 8 of the **hardness of** your **h** suffered you to *4641*
Mk 2: 6 sitting there, and reasoning in their **h**, *2588*
2: 8 Why reason ye these *things* in your **h**? *2588*
3: 5 being grieved for the hardness of their **h**, *2588*
4:15 away the word that was sown in their **h**. *2588*
Lk 1:17 to turn the **h** of the fathers to the children, *2588*
1:51 the proud in the imagination of their **h**. *2588*
1:66 that heard *them* laid *them* up in their **h**, *2588*
2:35 that the thoughts of many **h** may be *2588*
3:15 and all *men* mused in their **h** of John, *2588*
5:22 said unto them, What reason ye in your **h**? *2588*
8:12 and taketh away the word out of their **h**, *2588*
16:15 before men; but God knoweth your **h**: *2588*
21:14 Settle *it* therefore in your **h**, not to meditate *2588*
21:26 Men's **h failing** them for fear, and *674*
21:34 lest at any time your **h** be overcharged with *2588*
24:38 and why do thoughts arise in your **h**? *2588*
Ac 1:24 which **knowest** the **h** of all *men,* shew *2589*
7:39 and in their **h** turned *back again* into Egypt, *2588*
14:17 filling our **h** with food and gladness. *2588*
15: 8 And God, which **knoweth** the **h**, bare them *2589*
15: 9 and them, purifying their **h** by faith. *2588*
Ro 1:24 through the lusts of their own **h**, *2588*
2:15 shew the work of the law written in their **h**, *2588*
5: 5 the love of God is shed abroad in our **h** by *2588*
8:27 And he that searcheth the **h** knoweth what *2588*
16:18 fair speeches deceive the **h** of the simple. *2588*
1Co 4: 5 will make manifest the counsels of the **h**: *2588*
2Co 1:22 and given the earnest of the Spirit in our **h**. *2588*
3: 2 Ye are our epistle written in our **h**, known *2588*
4: 6 shine out of darkness, hath shined in our **h**, *2588*
7: 3 that you are in our **h** to die and live with *2588*
Gal 4: 6 sent forth the Spirit of his Son into your **h**, *2588*
Eph 3:17 That Christ may dwell in your **h** by faith; *2588*
6:22 and *that* he might comfort your **h**. *2588*
Php 4: 7 shall keep your **h** and minds through Christ *2588*
Col 2: 2 That their **h** might be comforted, being knit *2588*
3:15 And let the peace of God rule in your **h**, *2588*
3:16 singing with grace in your **h** to the Lord. *2588*
4: 8 know your estate, and comfort your **h**; *2588*
1Th 2: 4 pleasing men, but God, which trieth our **h**. *2588*
3:13 To the end *he* may stablish your **h** *2588*
2Th 2:17 Comfort your **h**, and stablish you in every *2588*
3: 5 And the Lord direct your **h** into the love of *2588*
Heb 3: 8 Harden not your **h**, as in the provocation, *2588*
3:15 harden not your **h**, as in the provocation. *2588*
4: 7 if ye will hear his voice, harden not your **h**. *2588*
8:10 into their mind, and write them in their **h**: *2588*
10:16 I will put my laws into their **h**, and in their *2588*

Heb 10:22 having *our* **h** sprinkled from an evil 2588
Jas 3:14 ye have bitter envying and strife in your **h**, 2588
4: 8 and purify *your* **h**, *ye* double minded. 2588
5: 5 ye have nourished your **h**, as in a day of 2588
5: 8 Be ye also patient; stablish your **h**: for 2588
1Pe 3:15 But sanctify the Lord God in your **h**: and 2588
2Pe 1:19 day dawn, and the day star arise in your **h**: 2588
1Jn 3:19 the truth, and shall assure our **h** before him. 2588
Rev 2:23 I am he which searcheth the reins and **h**: 2588
17:17 For God hath put in their **h** to fulfil his will, 2588

HEARTY (1) [HEARTILY]
Pr 27: 9 *doth* the sweetness of a man's friend by **h** 5315

HEAT (33) [HEATED]
Ge 8:22 cold and **h**, and summer and winter, and 2527
18: 1 he sat *in* the tent door in the **h** of the day; 2527
Dt 29:24 what *meaneth* the **h** of this great anger? 2750
32:24 devoured with **burning h**, and with bitter 7565
1Sa 11:11 slew the Ammonites until the **h** of the day: 2527
2Sa 4: 5 came about the **h** of the day to the house of 2527
1Ki 1: 1 covered him with clothes, but he **gat** no **h**. 3179
1: 2 that my lord the king may **get h**. 2552
Job 24:19 Drought and **h** consume the snow waters: 2527
30:30 upon me, and my bones are burnt with **h**. 2721
Ps 19: 6 and there is nothing hid from the **h** thereof. 2535
Ecc 4:11 if two lie together, then they **have h**: 2552
Isa 4: 6 for a shadow in the daytime from the **h**, 2721
18: 4 dwelling place like a clear **h** upon herbs, 2527
18: 4 *and* like a cloud of dew in the **h** of harvest. 2527
25: 4 from the storm, a shadow from the **h**, 2721
25: 5 noise of strangers, as the **h** in a dry place; 2721
25: 5 *even* the **h** with the shadow of a cloud: 2721
49:10 neither shall the **h** nor sun smite them: 8273
Jer 17: 8 shall not see when **h** cometh, but her leaf 2527
36:30 body shall be cast out in the day to the **h**, 2721
51:39 In their **h** I will make their feasts, and I will 2527
Eze 3:14 I went in bitterness, in the **h** of my spirit; 2534
Da 3:19 commanded that *they* should **h** the furnace 228
3:19 seven *times* more than *it was* wont to be **h**. 228
Mt 20:12 have borne the burden and **h** of the day. 2742
Lk 12:55 south wind blow, ye say, There will be **h**; 2742
Ac 28: 3 there came a viper out of the **h**, and 2329
Jas 1:11 sun is no sooner risen with a **burning h**, 2742
2Pe 3:10 and the elements shall melt with **fervent h**, 2741
3:12 and the elements shall melt with **fervent h**? 2741
Rev 7:16 shall the sun light on them, nor any **h**. 2738
16: 9 And men were scorched *with* great **h**, and 2738

HEATED (1) [HEAT]
Hos 7: 4 all adulterers, as an oven **h** by the baker, 1197

HEATH (2)
Jer 17: 6 For he shall be like the **h** in the desert, and 6199
48: 6 and be like the **h** in the wilderness. 6176

HEATHEN (150)
Lev 25:44 *shall be* of the **h** that *are* round about you; 1471
26:33 I will scatter you among the **h**, and 1471
26:38 ye shall perish among the **h**, and the land of 1471
26:45 of the land of Egypt in the sight of the **h**, 1471
Dt 4:27 ye shall be left few in number among the **h**, 1471
2Sa 22:44 thou hast kept me to be head of the **h**: 1471
22:50 among the **h**, and I will sing praises unto 1471
2Ki 16: 3 according to the abominations of the **h**, 1471
17: 8 walked in the statutes of the **h**, whom 1471
17:11 as *did* the **h** whom the LORD carried 1471
17:15 *went* after the **h** that *were* round about 1471
21: 2 after the abominations of the **h**, whom 1471
1Ch 16:24 Declare his glory among the **h**; 1471
16:35 us together, and deliver us from the **h**, 1471
2Ch 20: 6 *not* thou over all the kingdoms of the **h**? 1471
28: 3 **h** whom the LORD had cast out before 1471
33: 2 like unto the abominations of the **h**, 1471
33: 9 to err, *and* to do worse than the **h**, 1471
36:14 much after all the abominations of the **h**; 1471
Ezr 6:21 from the filthiness of the **h** of the land, 1471
Ne 5: 8 the Jews, which were sold unto the **h**; 1471
5: 9 of the reproach of the **h** our enemies? 1471
5:17 unto us from among the **h** that *are* about us. 1471
6: 6 *It is* reported among the **h**, and 1471
6:16 all the **h** that *were* about us saw *these* 1471
Ps 2: 1 Why do the **h** rage, and the people imagine 1471
2: 8 I shall give *thee* the **h** *for* thine inheritance, 1471
9: 5 Thou hast rebuked the **h**, thou hast 1471
9:15 The **h** are sunk down in the pit *that* they 1471
9:19 let the **h** be judged in thy sight. 1471
10:16 and ever: the **h** are perished out of his land. 1471
18:43 *and* thou hast made me the head of the **h**: 1471
18:49 among the **h**, and sing *praises* unto thy 1471
33:10 The LORD bringeth the counsel of the **h** 1471
44: 2 *How* thou didst drive out the **h** *with* thy 1471
44:11 and hast scattered us among the **h**. 1471
44:14 Thou makest us a byword among the **h**, 1471
46: 6 The **h** raged, the kingdoms were moved: 1471
46:10 I will be exalted among the **h**, I will be 1471
47: 8 God reigneth over the **h**: God sitteth upon 1471
59: 5 the God of Israel, awake to visit all the **h**: 1471
59: 8 thou shalt have all the **h** in derision. 1471
78:55 He cast out the **h** also before them, and 1471
79: 1 the **h** are come into thine inheritance; 1471
79: 6 Pour out thy wrath upon the **h** that have not 1471
79:10 Wherefore should the **h** say, Where *is* their 1471
79:10 let him be known among the **h** in our sight 1471
80: 8 thou hast cast out the **h**, and planted it. 1471
94:10 He that chastiseth the **h**, shall not he 1471
96: 3 Declare his glory among the **h**, his wonders 1471
96:10 Say among the **h** *that* the LORD reigneth: 1471
98: 2 hath he openly shewed in the sight of the **h**. 1471
102:15 So the **h** shall fear the name of the LORD, 1471
105:44 gave them the lands of the **h**: and 1471
106:35 were mingled among the **h**, and 1471
106:41 he gave them into the hand of the **h**; and 1471
106:47 our God, and gather us from among the **h**, 1471
110: 6 He shall judge among the **h**, he shall fill 1471
111: 6 that *he* may give them the heritage of the **h**. 1471
115: 2 Wherefore should the **h** say, Where *is* now 1471
126: 2 said they among the **h**, The LORD hath 1471
135:15 The idols of the **h** *are* silver and gold, 1471
149: 7 To execute vengeance upon the **h**, *and* 1471
Isa 16: 8 the lords of the **h** have broken down 1471
Jer 9:16 I will scatter them also among the **h**, 1471
10: 2 Learn not the way of the **h**, and be not 1471
10: 2 of heaven; for the **h** are dismayed at them. 1471
10:25 Pour out thy fury upon the **h** that know thee 1471
18:13 Ask ye now among the **h**, who hath heard 1471
49:14 an ambassador *is* sent unto the **h**, 1471
49:15 I will make thee small among the **h**, *and* 1471
La 1: 3 she dwelleth among the **h**, she findeth no 1471
1:10 for she hath seen *that* the **h** entered into her 1471
4:15 they said among the **h**, They shall no more 1471
4:20 his shadow we shall live among the **h**. 1471
Eze 7:24 Wherefore I will bring the worst of the **h**, 1471
11:12 have done after the manners of the **h** that 1471
11:16 I have cast them far off among the **h**, 1471
12:16 among the **h** whither they come; 1471
16:14 thy renown went forth among the **h** for thy 1471
20: 9 that *it* should not be polluted before the **h**, 1471
20:14 that *it* should not be polluted before the **h**, 1471
20:22 should not be polluted in the sight of the **h**, 1471
20:23 that *I* would scatter them among the **h**, and 1471
20:32 that ye say, We will be as the **h**, as 1471
20:41 and I will be sanctified in you before the **h**. 1471
22: 4 have I made thee a reproach unto the **h**, 1471
22:15 I will scatter thee among the **h**, and 1471
22:16 inheritance in thyself in the sight of the **h**, 1471
23:30 thou hast gone a whoring after the **h**, 1471
25: 7 and will deliver thee for a spoil to the **h**; 1471
25: 8 the house of Judah *is* like unto all the **h**; 1471
28:25 be sanctified in them in the sight of the **h**, 1471
30: 3 a cloudy day; it shall be the time of the **h**. 1471
31:11 into the hand of the mighty one of the **h**; 1471
31:17 under his shadow in the midst of the **h**. 1471
34:28 they shall no more be a prey to the **h**, 1471
34:29 neither bear the shame of the **h** any more. 1471
36: 3 be a possession unto the residue of the **h**, 1471
36: 4 derision to the residue of the **h** that *are* 1471
36: 5 have I spoken against the residue of the **h**, 1471
36: 6 because ye have borne the shame of the **h**: 1471
36: 7 mine hand, Surely the **h** that *are* about you, 1471
36:15 to hear in thee the shame of the **h** any more, 1471
36:19 I scattered them among the **h**, and 1471
36:20 when they entered unto the **h**, whither they 1471
36:21 house of Israel had profaned among the **h**, 1471
36:22 which ye have profaned among the **h**, 1471
36:23 which was profaned among the **h**, 1471
36:23 the **h** shall know that I *am* the LORD, 1471
36:24 For I will take you from among the **h**, and 1471

Eze 36:30 no more reproach of famine among the **h**. 1471
36:36 the **h** that are left round about you shall 1471
37:21 the children of Israel from among the **h**, 1471
37:28 the **h** shall know that I the LORD do 1471
38:16 against my land, that the **h** may know me, 1471
39: 7 the **h** shall know that I *am* the LORD, 1471
39:21 I will set my glory among the **h**, and all 1471
39:21 all the **h** shall see my judgment that I have 1471
39:23 the **h** shall know that the house of Israel 1471
39:28 them to be led into captivity among the **h**: 1471
Joel 2:17 that the **h** should rule over them: 1471
2:19 no more make you a reproach among the **h**: 1471
3:11 all ye **h**, and gather yourselves together 1471
3:12 Let the **h** be wakened, and come up to 1471
3:12 for there will I sit to judge all the **h** round 1471
Am 9:12 of all the **h**, which are called by my name, 1471
Ob 1: 1 an ambassador is sent among the **h**, 1471
1: 2 I have made thee small among the **h**: 1471
1:15 day of the LORD *is* near upon all the **h**: 1471
1:16 *so* shall all the **h** drink continually, yea, 1471
Mic 5:15 vengeance in anger and fury upon the **h**, 1471
Hab 1: 5 Behold ye among the **h**, and regard, and 1471
3:12 thou didst thresh the **h** in anger. 1471
Zep 2:11 from his place, *even* all the isles of the **h**. 1471
Hag 2:22 the strength of the kingdoms of the **h**; 1471
Zec 1:15 I am very sore displeased with the **h** *that* 1471
8:13 *that* as ye were a curse among the **h**, 1471
9:10 he shall speak peace unto the **h**: and 1471
14:14 the wealth of all the **h** round about shall be 1471
14:18 where*with* the LORD will smite the **h** that 1471
Mal 1:11 for my name *shall be* great among the **h**, 1471
1:14 and my name *is* dreadful among the **h**. 1471
Mt 6: 7 as the **h** *do*: for they think that they shall be *1482*
18:17 let him be unto thee as a **h** *man* and *1482*
Ac 4:25 Why did the **h** rage, and the people *1484*
2Co 11:26 *in* perils by the **h**, *in* perils in the city, *1484*
Gal 1:16 that I might preach him among the **h**; *1484*
2: 9 that we *should go* unto the **h**, and they unto *1484*
3: 8 foreseeing that God would justify the **h** *1484*

HEAVE (29) [HEAVED]

Ex 29:27 the shoulder of the **h offering**, which is 8641
29:28 for it *is* a **h offering**: and it shall be a heave 8641
29:28 it shall be a **h offering** from the children of 8641
29:28 *even* their **h offering** unto the LORD. 8641
Lev 7:14 oblation *for* a **h offering** unto the LORD, 8641
7:32 **h offering** of the sacrifices of your peace 8641
7:34 the **h** shoulder have I taken of the children 8641
10:14 and **h** shoulder shall ye eat in a clean place; 8641
10:15 The **h** shoulder and the wave breast shall 8641
Nu 6:20 with the wave breast and **h** shoulder: 8641
15:19 ye shall offer up a **h offering** unto 8641
15:20 *of* the first of your dough *for* a **h offering**: 8641
15:20 as *ye do* the **h offering** of 8641
15:20 of the threshingfloor, so shall ye **h** it. 7311
15:21 LORD a **h offering** in your generations. 8641
18: 8 **h offerings** of all the hallowed *things* of 8641
18:11 the **h offering** of their gift, with all 8641
18:19 All the **h offerings** of the holy *things*, 8641
18:24 which they offer *as* a **h offering** unto 8641
18:26 ye shall offer up a **h offering** of it for 8641
18:27 *this* your **h offering** shall be reckoned unto 8641
18:28 Thus you also shall offer a **h offering** unto 8641
18:28 LORD'S **h offering** to Aaron the priest. 8641
18:29 shall offer every **h offering** of the LORD, 8641
31:29 the priest, *for* a **h offering** of the LORD. 8641
31:41 *which was* the LORD'S **h offering**, 8641
Dt 12: 6 **h offerings** of your hand, and your vows, 8641
12:11 the **h offering** of your hand, and all your 8641
12:17 or **h offering** of thine hand: 8641

HEAVED (3) [HEAVE]

Ex 29:27 which is waved, and which is **h up**, of 7311
Nu 18:30 When ye have **h** the best thereof from it, 7311
18:32 of it, when ye have **h** from it the best of it: 7311

HEAVEN (582) [HEAVEN'S, HEAVENLY, HEAVENS]

Ge 1: 1 In the beginning God created the **h** and 8064
1: 8 God called the firmament **H**. And 8064
1: 9 Let the waters under the **h** be gathered 8064
1:14 Let there be lights in the firmament of the **h** 8064
1:15 of the **h** to give light upon the earth: 8064
1:17 God set them in the firmament of the **h** to 8064
1:20 above the earth in the open firmament of **h**. 8064
6:17 wherein *is* the breath of life, from under **h**; 8064
7:11 and the windows of **h** were opened. 8064
7:19 that *were* under the whole **h**, were covered. 8064
7:23 the creeping things, and the fowl of the **h**; 8064
8: 2 and the windows of **h** were stopped, 8064
8: 2 and the rain from **h** was restrained; 8064
11: 4 and a tower, whose top *may reach* unto **h**; 8064
14:19 most high God, possessor of **h** and earth: 8064
14:22 high God, the possessor of **h** and earth, 8064
15: 5 Look now towards **h**, and tell the stars, 8064
19:24 and fire from the LORD out of **h**; 8064
21:17 the angel of God called to Hagar out of **h**, 8064
22:11 of the LORD called unto him out of **h**, 8064
22:15 unto Abraham out of **h** the second time, 8064
22:17 I will multiply thy seed as the stars of the **h**, 8064
24: 3 the God of **h**, and the God of the earth, 8064
24: 7 The LORD God of **h**, which took me from 8064
26: 4 make thy seed to multiply as the stars of **h**, 8064
27:28 Therefore God give thee of the dew of **h**, 8064
27:39 the earth, and of the dew of **h** from above; 8064
28:12 on the earth, and the top of it reached to **h**: 8064
28:17 the house of God, and this *is* the gate of **h**. 8064
49:25 who shall bless thee *with* blessings of **h** 8064
Ex 9: 8 let Moses sprinkle it towards the **h** in 8064
9:10 Moses sprinkled it *up* toward **h**; and 8064
9:22 Stretch forth thine hand toward **h**, 8064
9:23 Moses stretched forth his rod toward **h**: 8064
10:21 Stretch out thine hand toward **h**, 8064
10:22 Moses stretched forth his hand toward **h**; 8064
16: 4 Behold, I will rain bread from **h** for you; 8064
17:14 the remembrance of Amalek from under **h**. 8064
20: 4 any likeness *of any thing* that *is* in **h** above, 8064
20:11 For *in* six days the LORD made **h** and 8064
20:22 seen that I have talked with you from **h**. 8064
24:10 as it were the body of **h** in *his* clearness. 8064
31:17 for *in* six days the LORD made **h** and 8064
32:13 I will multiply your seed as the stars of **h**, 8064
Lev 26:19 I will make your **h** as iron, and your earth 8064
Dt 1:10 you *are this* day as the stars of **h** for 8064
1:28 the cities *are* great and walled up to **h**; and 8064
2:25 upon the nations *that are* under the whole **h**, 8064
3:24 for what God *is there* in **h** or in earth, 8064
4:11 burnt with fire unto the midst of **h**, 8064
4:19 lest thou lift up thine eyes unto **h**, and 8064
4:19 and the stars, *even* all the host of **h**, 8064
4:19 divided unto all nations under the whole **h**. 8064
4:26 I call **h** and earth to witness against you *this* 8064
4:32 *ask* from the one side of **h** unto the other, 8064
4:36 Out of **h** he made thee to hear his voice, 8064
4:39 that the LORD he *is* God in **h** above, and 8064
5: 8 any likeness *of any thing* that *is* in **h** above, 8064
7:24 thou shalt destroy their name from under **h**: 8064
9: 1 than thyself, cities great and fenced up to **h**, 8064
9:14 and blot out their name from under **h**: 8064
10:14 the **h** and the heaven of heavens *is* 8064
10:14 the **h** of heavens *is* the LORD'S thy God, 8064
10:22 made thee as the stars of **h** for multitude. 8064
11:11 valleys, *and* drinketh water of the rain of **h**: 8064
11:17 he shut up the **h**, that there be no rain, and 8064
11:21 give them, as the days of **h** upon the earth. 8064
17: 3 the sun, or moon, or any of the host of **h**, 8064
25:19 the remembrance of Amalek from under **h**; 8064
26:15 from **h**, and bless thy people Israel, and 8064
28:12 the **h** to give the rain unto thy land in his 8064
28:23 thy **h** that *is* over thy head shall be brass, 8064
28:24 from **h** shall it come down upon thee, 8064
28:62 whereas ye were as the stars of **h** for 8064
29:20 shall blot out his name from under **h**. 8064
30: 4 be driven out unto the outmost parts of **h**, 8064
30:12 It *is* not in **h**, that *thou* shouldest say, 8064
30:12 Who shall go up for us to **h**, and bring it 8064
30:19 I call **h** and earth to record *this* day against 8064
31:28 call **h** and earth to record against them. 8064
32:40 For I lift up my hand to **h**, and say, I live 8064
33:13 for the precious things of **h**, for the dew, 8064
33:26 *who* rideth *upon* the **h** in thy help, and 8064
Jos 2:11 he *is* God in **h** above, and in earth beneath. 8064
8:20 the smoke of the city ascended up to **h**, and 8064
10:11 stones from **h** upon them unto Azekah, 8064
10:13 So the sun stood still in the midst of **h**, and 8064
Jdg 5:20 They fought from **h**; the stars in their 8064
13:20 when the flame went up toward **h** from off 8064
20:40 the flame of the city ascended up to **h**. 8064
1Sa 2:10 out of **h** shall he thunder upon them: 8064

1Sa 5:12 and the cry of the city went up *to* **h**. 8064
2Sa 18: 9 he was taken up between the **h** and 8064
21:10 until water dropped upon them out of **h**, 8064
22: 8 the foundations of **h** moved and shook, 8064
22:14 The LORD thundered from **h**, and 8064
1Ki 8:22 and spread forth his hands *toward* **h**: 8064
8:23 in **h** above, or on earth beneath, 8064
8:27 the **h** and heaven of heavens cannot contain 8064
8:27 and **h** of heavens cannot contain thee; 8064
8:30 hear thou in **h** thy dwelling place: and 8064
8:32 hear thou *in* **h**, and do, and judge thy 8064
8:34 hear thou *in* **h**, and forgive the sin of thy 8064
8:35 When **h** is shut up, and there is no rain, 8064
8:36 hear thou *in* **h**, and forgive the sin of thy 8064
8:39 hear thou *in* **h** thy dwelling place, and 8064
8:43 Hear thou *in* **h** thy dwelling place, and 8064
8:45 hear thou *in* **h** their prayer and their 8064
8:49 their supplication *in* **h** thy dwelling place, 8064
8:54 on his knees with his hands spread *up to* **h**. 8064
18:45 that the **h** was black *with* clouds and wind, 8064
22:19 all the host of **h** standing by him on his 8064
2Ki 1:10 let fire come down from **h**, and 8064
1:10 there came down fire from **h**, and 8064
1:12 let fire come down from **h**, and 8064
1:12 the fire of God came down from **h**, and 8064
1:14 there came fire down from **h**, and burnt up 8064
2: 1 would take up Elijah *into* **h** by a whirlwind, 8064
2:11 and Elijah went up by a whirlwind *into* **h**. 8064
7: 2 *if* the LORD would make windows in **h**, 8064
7:19 *if* the LORD should make windows in **h**, 8064
14:27 blot out the name of Israel from under **h**: 8064
17:16 worshipped all the host of **h**, and 8064
19:15 of the earth; thou hast made **h** and earth. 8064
21: 3 worshipped all the host of **h**, and 8064
21: 5 he built altars for all the host of **h** in 8064
23: 4 and for the grove, and for all the host of **h**: 8064
23: 5 and to the planets, and to all the host of **h**. 8064
1Ch 21:16 LORD stand between the earth and the **h**, 8064
21:26 he answered him from **h** by fire upon 8064
29:11 for all *that is* in the **h** and in the earth *is* 8064
2Ch 2: 6 seeing the **h** and heaven of heavens cannot 8064
2: 6 and **h** of heavens cannot contain him? 8064
2:12 God of Israel, that made **h** and earth, 8064
6:13 and spread forth his hands towards **h**, 8064
6:14 *there is* no God like thee in the **h**, nor in 8064
6:18 **h** and the heaven of heavens cannot contain 8064
6:18 and the **h** of heavens cannot contain thee; 8064
6:21 thou from thy dwelling place, *even* from **h**; 8064
6:23 hear thou from **h**, and do, and judge thy 8064
6:26 When the **h** is shut up, and there is no rain, 8064
6:27 hear thou *from* **h**, and forgive the sin of thy 8064
6:30 hear thou from **h** thy dwelling place, and 8064
7: 1 the fire came down from **h**, and 8064
7:13 If I shut up **h** that there be no rain, or if I 8064
7:14 will I hear from **h**, and will forgive their 8064
18:18 all the host of **h** standing on his right hand 8064
20: 6 God of our fathers, *art* not thou God in **h**? 8064
28: 9 slain them in a rage *that* reacheth up unto **h**. 8064
30:27 *up* to his holy dwelling place, *even* unto **h**. 8064
32:20 the son of Amoz, prayed and cried *to* **h**. 8064
33: 3 worshipped all the host of **h**, and 8064
33: 5 he built altars for all the host of **h** in 8064
36:23 earth hath the LORD God of **h** given me; 8064
Ezr 1: 2 The LORD God of **h** hath given me all 8064
5:11 We are the servants of the God of **h** and 8065
5:12 had provoked the God of **h** unto wrath, 8065
6: 9 for the burnt offerings of the God of **h**, 8065
6:10 of sweet savours unto the God of **h**, 8065
7:12 a scribe of the law of the God of **h**, 8065
7:21 the scribe of the law of the God of **h**, 8065
7:23 *is* commanded by the God of **h**, 8065
7:23 done for the house of the God of **h**: 8065
Ne 1: 4 and fasted, and prayed before the God of **h**, 8064
1: 5 O LORD God of **h**, the great and terrible 8064
1: 9 cast out unto the uttermost part of the **h**, 8064
2: 4 make request? So I prayed to the God of **h**. 8064
2:20 said unto them, The God of **h**, he will 8064
9: 6 thou hast made **h**, the heaven of heavens, 8064
9: 6 the **h** of heavens, with all their host, 8064
9: 6 and the host of **h** worshippeth thee. 8064
9:13 spakest with them from **h**, and gavest them 8064
9:15 gavest them bread from **h** for their hunger, 8064
9:23 also multipliedst thou as the stars of **h**, 8064
9:27 cried unto thee, thou heardest *them* from **h**; 8064
9:28 cried unto thee, thou heardest *them* from **h**; 8064
Job 1:16 The fire of God is fallen from **h**, and 8064
2:12 sprinkled dust upon their heads toward **h**. 8064
11: 8 *It is* as high as **h**; what canst thou do? 8064
16:19 behold my witness *is* in **h**, and my record *is* 8064
20:27 The **h** shall reveal his iniquity; and 8064
22:12 *Is* not God *in* the height of **h**? and 8064
22:14 and he walketh *in* the circuit of **h**. 8064
26:11 The pillars of **h** tremble and are astonished 8064
28:24 of the earth, *and* seeth under the whole **h**; 8064
35:11 and maketh us wiser than the fowls of **h**? 8064
37: 3 He directeth it under the whole **h**, and 8064
38:29 the hoary frost of **h**, who hath gendered it? 8064
38:33 Knowest thou the ordinances of **h**? canst 8064
38:37 or who can stay the bottles of **h**, 8064
41:11 *whatsoever is* under the whole **h** *is* mine. 8064
Ps 11: 4 holy temple, the LORD'S throne *is* in **h**: 8064
14: 2 The LORD looked down from **h** upon 8064
19: 6 His going forth *is* from the end of the **h**, 8064
20: 6 he will hear him from his holy **h** with 8064
33:13 The LORD looketh from **h**; he beholdeth 8064
53: 2 God looked down from **h** upon the children 8064
57: 3 He shall send from **h**, and save me *from* 8064
69:34 Let the **h** and earth praise him, the seas, and 8064
73:25 Whom have I in **h** *but thee?* and *there is* 8064
76: 8 didst cause judgment to be heard from **h**; 8064
77:18 The voice of thy thunder *was* in the **h**: 1534
78:23 from above, and opened the doors of **h**, 8064
78:24 to eat, and had given them *of* the corn of **h**. 8064
78:26 He caused an east wind to blow in the **h**: 8064
79: 2 given *to be* meat unto the fowls of the **h**, 8064
80:14 look down from **h**, and behold, and 8064
85:11 and righteousness shall look down from **h**. 8064
89: 6 For who in the **h** can be compared unto 7834
89:29 for ever, and his throne as the days of **h**. 8064
89:37 as the moon, and *as* a faithful witness in **h**. 7834
102:19 from **h** did the LORD behold the earth; 8064
103:11 For as the **h** is high above the earth, *so* 8064
104:12 By them shall the fowls of the **h** have their 8064
105:40 and satisfied them *with* the bread of **h**. 8064
107:26 They mount up *to* the **h**, they go down 8064
113: 6 *himself* to behold *the things that are* in **h**, 8064
115:15 *are* blessed of the LORD which made **h** 8064
115:16 The **h**, *even* the heavens, *are* the LORD'S: 8064
119:89 O LORD, thy word *is* settled in **h**. 8064
121: 2 from the LORD, which made **h** and earth. 8064
124: 8 of the LORD, who made **h** and earth. 8064
134: 3 The LORD that made **h** and earth bless 8064
135: 6 *that* did he in **h**, and in earth, in the seas, 8064
136:26 O give thanks unto the God of **h**: for his 8064
139: 8 If I ascend up *into* **h**, thou *art* there: if I 8064
146: 6 Which made **h**, and earth, the sea, and all 8064
147: 8 Who covereth the **h** with clouds, 8064
148:13 his glory *is* above the earth and **h**. 8064
Pr 23: 5 they fly away as an eagle *toward* **h**. 8064
25: 3 The **h** for height, and the earth for depth, 8064
30: 4 Who hath ascended up *into* **h**, or 8064
Ecc 1:13 concerning all *things* that are done under **h**: 8064
2: 3 which they should do under the **h** all 8064
3: 1 and a time to every purpose under the **h**: 8064
5: 2 for God *is* in **h**, and thou upon earth: 8064
Isa 13: 5 from the end of the **h**, *even* the LORD, 8064
13:10 For the stars of **h** and the constellations 8064
14:12 How art thou fallen from **h**, O Lucifer, 8064
14:13 hast said in thine heart, I will ascend *into* **h**, 8064
34: 4 And all the host of **h** shall be dissolved, and 8064
34: 5 For my sword shall be bathed in **h**: behold, 8064
37:16 of the earth: thou hast made **h** and earth. 8064
40:12 meted out **h** with the span, and 8064
55:10 the snow from **h**, and returneth not thither, 8064
63:15 Look down from **h**, and behold from 8064
66: 1 The **h** *is* my throne, and the earth *is* my 8064
Jer 7:18 to make cakes to the queen of **h**, and 8064
7:33 people shall be meat for the fowls of the **h**, 8064
8: 2 the moon, and all the host of **h**, whom they 8064
8: 7 the stork in the **h** knoweth her appointed 8064
10: 2 and be not dismayed at the signs of **h**; 8064
15: 3 the fowls of the **h**, and the beasts of 8064
16: 4 carcases shall be meat for the fowls of **h**, 8064
19: 7 will I give to be meat for the fowls of the **h**, 8064
19:13 have burnt incense unto all the host of **h**, 8064
23:24 Do not I fill **h** and earth? saith the LORD. 8064
31:37 If **h** above can be measured, and 8064
32:17 thou hast made the **h** and the earth by thy 8064

Jer 33:22 As the host of **h** cannot be numbered, 8064
33:25 *if* I have not appointed the ordinances of **h** 8064
34:20 shall be for meat unto the fowls of the **h**, 8064
44:17 to burn incense unto the queen of **h**, and 8064
44:18 left off to burn incense to the queen of **h**, 8064
44:19 when we burnt incense to the queen of **h**, 8064
44:25 to burn incense to the queen of **h**, and 8064
49:36 the four winds from the four quarters of **h**, 8064
51: 9 for her judgment reacheth unto **h**, and 8064
51:15 hath stretched out the **h** by his 8064
51:48 the **h** and the earth, and all that *is* therein, 8064
51:53 Though Babylon should mount up *to* **h**, and 8064
La 2: 1 cast down from **h** *unto* the earth the beauty 8064
3:50 the LORD look down, and behold from **h**. 8064
4:19 are swifter than the eagles of the **h**: 8064
Eze 8: 3 lift me up between the earth and the **h**, 8064
29: 5 beasts of the field and to the fowls of the **h**. 8064
31: 6 All the fowls of **h** made their nests in his 8064
31:13 Upon his ruin shall all the fowls of the **h** 8064
32: 4 will cause all the fowls of the **h** to remain 8064
32: 7 I will cover the **h**, and make the stars 8064
32: 8 All the bright lights of **h** will I make dark 8064
38:20 the fowls of the **h**, and the beasts of 8064
Da 2:18 of the God of **h** concerning this secret; 8065
2:19 Then Daniel blessed the God of **h**. 8065
2:28 there is a God in **h** that revealeth secrets, 8065
2:37 for the God of **h** hath given thee a 8065
2:38 the fowls of the **h** hath he given into thine 8065
2:44 the days of these kings shall the God of **h** 8065
4:11 the height thereof reached unto **h**, and 8065
4:12 the fowls of the **h** dwelt in the boughs 8065
4:13 and a holy one came down from **h**; 8065
4:15 let it be wet with the dew of **h**, and *let* his 8065
4:20 whose height reached unto the **h**, and 8065
4:21 upon whose branches the fowls of the **h** 8065
4:22 reacheth unto **h**, and thy dominion to 8065
4:23 and a holy one coming down from **h**, 8065
4:23 let it be wet with the dew of **h**, and *let* his 8065
4:25 they *shall* wet thee with the dew of **h**, 8065
4:31 there fell a voice from **h**, *saying,* O king 8065
4:33 and his body was wet with the dew of **h**, 8065
4:34 I Nebuchadnezzar lift up mine eyes unto **h**, 8065
4:35 according to his will in the army of **h**, 8065
4:37 and extol and honour the King of **h**, 8065
5:21 and his body was wet with the dew of **h**; 8065
5:23 hast lifted up thyself against the Lord of **h**; 8065
6:27 and wonders in **h** and in earth, 8065
7: 2 the four winds of the **h** strove upon 8065
7:13 the Son of man came with the clouds of **h**, 8065
7:27 of the kingdom under the whole **h**, 8065
8: 8 notable ones toward the four winds of **h**. 8064
8:10 it waxed great, *even* to the host of **h**; and 8064
9:12 for under the whole **h** hath not been done as 8064
11: 4 shall be divided toward the four winds of **h**; 8064
12: 7 up his right hand and his left hand unto **h**, 8064
Hos 2:18 with the fowls of **h**, and *with* the creeping 8064
4: 3 beasts of the field, and with the fowls of **h**; 8064
7:12 will bring them down as the fowls of the **h**; 8064
Am 9: 2 though they climb up *to* **h**, thence will I 8064
9: 6 *It is* he that buildeth his stories in the **h**, and 8064
Jnh 1: 9 I fear the LORD, the God of **h**, which hath 8064
Na 3:16 thy merchants above the stars of **h**: 8064
Zep 1: 3 I will consume the fowls of the **h**, and 8064
1: 5 them that worship the host of **h** upon 8064
Hag 1:10 Therefore the **h** over you is stayed from 8064
Zec 2: 6 you abroad as the four winds of the **h**, 8064
5: 9 up the ephah between the earth and the **h**. 8064
Mal 3:10 if I will not open you the windows of **h**, 8064
Mt 3: 2 Repent ye: for the kingdom of **h** is at hand. *3772*
3:17 And lo a voice from **h**, saying, This is my *3772*
4:17 Repent: for the kingdom of **h** is at hand. *3772*
5: 3 in spirit: for theirs is the kingdom of **h**. *3772*
5:10 for theirs is the kingdom of **h**. *3772*
5:12 for great *is* your reward in **h**: for so *3772*
5:16 and glorify your Father which is in **h**. *3772*
5:18 Till **h** and earth pass, one jot or one tittle *3772*
5:19 be called the least in the kingdom of **h**: *3772*
5:19 shall be called great in the kingdom of **h**. *3772*
5:20 in no case enter into the kingdom of **h**. *3772*
5:34 say unto you, Swear not at all; neither by **h**; *3772*
5:45 the children of your Father which is in **h**: *3772*
5:48 even as your Father which is in **h** is perfect. *3772*
6: 1 no reward of your Father which is in **h**. *3772*
6: 9 Our Father which art in **h**, Hallowed be thy *3772*
6:10 Thy will be done in earth, as *it is* in **h**. *3772*
6:20 But lay up for yourselves treasures in **h**, *3772*
7:11 in **h** give good *things* to them that ask him? *3772*
7:21 Lord, shall enter into the kingdom of **h**; *3772*
7:21 doeth the will of my Father which is in **h**. *3772*
8:11 and Isaac, and Jacob, in the kingdom of **h**. *3772*
10: 7 saying, The kingdom of **h** is at hand. *3772*
10:32 also before my Father which is in **h**. *3772*
10:33 I also deny before my Father which is in **h**. *3772*
11:11 least in the kingdom of **h** is greater than he. *3772*
11:12 now the kingdom of **h** suffereth violence, *3772*
11:23 Capernaum, which art exalted unto **h**, *3772*
11:25 Lord of **h** and earth, because thou hast hid *3772*
12:50 shall do the will of my Father which is in **h**, *3772*
13:11 to know the mysteries of the kingdom of **h**, *3772*
13:24 The kingdom of **h** is likened unto a man *3772*
13:31 The kingdom of **h** is like unto a grain of *3772*
13:33 The kingdom of **h** is like unto leaven, *3772*
13:44 the kingdom of **h** is like unto treasure hid in *3772*
13:45 the kingdom of **h** is like unto a merchant *3772*
13:47 Again, the kingdom of **h** is like unto a net, *3772*
13:52 **h** is like unto a man *that is* a householder, *3772*
14:19 and looking up to **h**, he blessed, and brake, *3772*
16: 1 that *he* would shew them a sign from **h**. *3772*
16:17 *it* unto thee, but my Father which is in **h**. *3772*
16:19 unto thee the keys of the kingdom of **h**: *3772*
16:19 shalt bind on earth shall be bound in **h**: *3772*
16:19 shalt loose on earth shall be loosed in **h**. *3772*
18: 1 Who is the greatest in the kingdom of **h**? *3772*
18: 3 ye shall not enter into the kingdom of **h**. *3772*
18: 4 the same is greatest in the kingdom of **h**. *3772*
18:10 That in **h** their angels do always behold *3772*
18:10 behold the face of my Father which is in **h**. *3772*
18:14 is not the will of your Father which is in **h**, *3772*
18:18 ye shall bind on earth shall be bound in **h**: *3772*
18:18 ye shall loose on earth shall be loosed in **h**. *3772*
18:19 done for them of my Father which is in **h**. *3772*
18:23 Therefore is the kingdom of **h** likened unto *3772*
19:14 unto me: for of such is the kingdom of **h**. *3772*
19:21 the poor, and thou shalt have treasure in **h**: *3772*
19:23 shall hardly enter into the kingdom of **h**. *3772*
20: 1 For the kingdom of **h** is like unto a man *3772*
21:25 from **h**, or of men? And they reasoned with *3772*
21:25 saying, If we shall say, From **h**; *3772*
22: 2 The kingdom of **h** is like unto a certain *3772*
22:30 but are as *the* angels of God in **h**. *3772*
23: 9 for one is your Father, which is in **h**. *3772*
23:13 for ye shut up the kingdom of **h** against *3772*
23:22 And he that shall swear by **h**, sweareth by *3772*
24:29 and the stars shall fall from **h**, and *3772*
24:30 appear the sign of the Son of man in **h**: *3772*
24:30 man coming in the clouds of **h** with power *3772*
24:31 four winds, from one end of **h** to the other. *3772*
24:35 **H** and earth shall pass away, but my words *3772*
24:36 not the angels of **h**, but my Father only. *3772*
25: 1 Then shall the kingdom of **h** be likened *3772*
25:14 For *the kingdom of* **h** *is* as a man travelling NIG
26:64 of power, and coming in the clouds of **h**. *3772*
28: 2 for *the* angel of the Lord descended from **h**, *3772*
28:18 All power is given unto me in **h** and *3772*
Mk 1:11 And there came a voice from **h**, *3772*
6:41 he looked up to **h**, and blessed, and *3772*
7:34 And looking up to **h**, he sighed, and *3772*
8:11 seeking of him a sign from **h**, *3772*
10:21 the poor, and thou shalt have treasure in **h**: *3772*
11:25 that your Father also which is in **h** may *3772*
11:26 neither will your Father which is in **h** *3772*
11:30 baptism of John, was *it* from **h**, or of men? *3772*
11:31 saying, If we shall say, From **h**; *3772*
12:25 but are as *the* angels which are in **h**. *3772*
13:25 And the stars of **h** shall fall, *3772*
13:25 the powers that are in **h** shall be shaken. *3772*
13:27 part of the earth to the uttermost part of **h**. *3772*
13:31 **H** and earth shall pass away: but my words *3772*
13:32 not the angels which are in **h**, neither *3772*
14:62 of power, and coming in the clouds of **h**. *3772*
16:19 he was received up into **h**, and sat on *3772*
Lk 2:15 angels were gone away from them into **h**, *3772*
3:21 and praying, the **h** was opened, *3772*
3:22 and a voice came from **h**, which said, *3772*
4:25 when the **h** was shut up three years and *3772*
6:23 *joy:* for behold, your reward *is* great in **h**: *3772*
9:16 and the two fishes, and looking up to **h**, *3772*
9:54 we command fire to come down from **h**, *3772*

Lk	10:15	Capernaum, which art exalted to **h**,	*3772*
	10:18	I beheld Satan as lightning fall from **h**.	*3772*
	10:20	because your names are written in **h**.	*3772*
	10:21	I thank thee, O Father, Lord of **h** and earth,	*3772*
	11: 2	ye pray, say, Our Father which art in **h**,	*3772*
	11: 2	Thy will be done, as in **h**, so in earth.	*3772*
	11:16	tempting *him,* sought of him a sign from **h**.	*3772*
	15: 7	that likewise joy shall be in **h** over one	*3772*
	15:18	I have sinned against **h**, and before thee,	*3772*
	15:21	I have sinned against **h**, and in thy sight,	*3772*
	16:17	And it is easier for **h** and earth to pass,	*3772*
	17:24	that lighteneth out of the one *part* under **h**,	*3772*
	17:24	shineth unto the other *part* under **h**;	*3772*
	17:29	Sodom it rained fire and brimstone from **h**,	*3772*
	18:13	not lift up so much as *his* eyes unto **h**,	*3772*
	18:22	the poor, and thou shalt have treasure in **h**:	*3772*
	19:38	peace in **h**, and glory in the highest.	*3772*
	20: 4	baptism of John, was it from **h**, or of men?	*3772*
	20: 5	saying, If we shall say, From **h**;	*3772*
	21:11	and great signs shall there be from **h**.	*3772*
	21:26	for the powers of **h** shall be shaken.	*3772*
	21:33	**H** and earth shall pass away: but my words	*3772*
	22:43	there appeared an angel unto him from **h**,	*3772*
	24:51	parted from them, and carried up into **h**.	*3772*
Jn	1:32	I saw the Spirit descending from **h** like a	*3772*
	1:51	Hereafter ye shall see **h** open, and	*3772*
	3:13	And no *man* hath ascended up to **h**, but he	*3772*
	3:13	but he that came down from **h**, *even*	*3772*
	3:13	*even* the Son of man which is in **h**.	*3772*
	3:27	except it be given him from **h**.	*3772*
	3:31	he that cometh from **h** is above all.	*3772*
	6:31	He gave them bread from **h** to eat.	*3772*
	6:32	Moses gave you not *that* bread from **h**;	*3772*
	6:32	my Father giveth you the true bread from **h**.	*3772*
	6:33	of God is he which cometh down from **h**,	*3772*
	6:38	For I came down from **h**, not to do mine	*3772*
	6:41	I am the bread which came down from **h**.	*3772*
	6:42	then *that* he saith, I came down from **h**?	*3772*
	6:50	is the bread which cometh down from **h**,	*3772*
	6:51	the living bread which came down from **h**:	*3772*
	6:58	is *that* bread which came down from **h**:	*3772*
	12:28	Then came there a voice from **h**, *saying,* I	*3772*
	17: 1	and lift up his eyes to **h**, and said, Father,	*3772*
Ac	1:10	And while they looked stedfastly toward **h**	*3772*
	1:11	of Galilee, why stand ye gazing up into **h**?	*3772*
	1:11	which is taken up from you into **h**, shall so	*3772*
	1:11	like manner as ye have seen him go into **h**.	*3772*
	2: 2	And suddenly there came a sound from **h**	*3772*
	2: 5	devout men, out of every nation under **h**.	*3772*
	2:19	And I will shew wonders in **h** above, and	*3772*
	3:21	Whom the **h** must receive until the times of	*3772*
	4:12	for there is none other name under **h** given	*3772*
	4:24	which hast made **h**, and earth, and the sea,	*3772*
	7:42	and gave them up to worship the host of **h**;	*3772*
	7:49	**H** *is* my throne, and earth *is* my footstool:	*3772*
	7:55	looked up stedfastly into **h**, and saw	*3772*
	9: 3	shined round about him a light from **h**:	*3772*
	10:11	And saw **h** opened, and a certain vessel	*3772*
	10:16	and the vessel was received up again into **h**.	*3772*
	11: 5	let down from **h** by four corners;	*3772*
	11: 9	But *the* voice answered me again from **h**,	*3772*
	11:10	and all were drawn up again into **h**.	*3772*
	14:15	which made **h**, and earth, and the sea, and	*3772*
	14:17	and gave us rain **from h**, and	*3771*
	17:24	seeing that he is Lord of **h** and earth,	*3772*
	22: 6	suddenly there shone from **h** a great light	*3772*
	26:13	O king, I saw in the way a light **from h**,	*3771*
Ro	1:18	For the wrath of God is revealed from **h**	*3772*
	10: 6	not in thine heart, Who shall ascend into **h**?	*3772*
1Co	8: 5	whether in **h** or in earth, (as there be gods	*3772*
	15:47	earthy: the second man *is* the Lord from **h**.	*3772*
2Co	5: 2	upon with our house which is from **h**:	*3772*
	12: 2	such a one caught up to the third **h**.	*3772*
Gal	1: 8	But though we, or an angel from **h**,	*3772*
Eph	1:10	both which are in **h**, and which are on	*3772*
	3:15	Of whom the whole family in **h** and earth is	*3772*
	6: 9	knowing that your Master also is in **h**;	*3772*
Php	2:10	of *things* **in h**, and *things* in earth, and	*2032*
	3:20	For our conversation is in **h**; from whence	*3772*
Col	1: 5	For the hope which is laid up for you in **h**,	*3772*
	1:16	that are in **h**, and that are in earth, visible	*3772*
	1:20	*they be things* in earth, or *things* in **h**.	*3772*
	1:23	to every creature which is under **h**;	*3772*
	4: 1	knowing that ye also have a Master in **h**.	*3772*
1Th	1:10	And to wait for his Son from **h**, whom he	*3772*
	4:16	For the Lord himself shall descend from **h**	*3772*
2Th	1: 7	be revealed from **h** with his mighty angels,	*3772*
Heb	9:24	but into **h** itself, now to appear in	*3772*
	10:34	knowing in yourselves that *ye* have in **h** a	*3772*
	12:23	which are written in **h**, and to God	*3772*
	12:25	turn away from him that *speaketh* from **h**:	*3772*
	12:26	*more* I shake not the earth only, but also **h**.	*3772*
Jas	5:12	swear not, neither by **h**, neither by	*3772*
	5:18	and the **h** gave rain, and the earth brought	*3772*
1Pe	1: 4	that fadeth not away, reserved in **h** for you,	*3772*
	1:12	you with the Holy Ghost sent *down* from **h**;	*3772*
	3:22	Who is gone into **h**, and is on the right hand	*3772*
2Pe	1:18	And this voice which came from **h** we	*3772*
1Jn	5: 7	For there are three that bear record in **h**,	*3772*
Rev	3:12	which cometh down out of **h** from my God:	*3772*
	4: 1	and behold, a door *was* opened in **h**:	*3772*
	4: 2	a throne was set in **h**, and one sat on	*3772*
	5: 3	And no *man* in **h**, nor in earth,	*3772*
	5:13	And every creature which is in **h**, and	*3772*
	6:13	And the stars of **h** fell unto the earth,	*3772*
	6:14	And the **h** departed as a scrole when it is	*3772*
	8: 1	there was silence in **h** about the space of	*3772*
	8:10	and there fell a great star from **h**,	*3772*
	8:13	an angel flying through the **midst of h**,	*3321*
	9: 1	and I saw a star fall from **h** unto the earth:	*3772*
	10: 1	another mighty angel come down from **h**,	*3772*
	10: 4	and I heard a voice from **h** saying unto me,	*3772*
	10: 5	and upon the earth lifted up his hand to **h**,	*3772*
	10: 6	who created **h**, and the *things* that therein	*3772*
	10: 8	And the voice which I heard from **h** spake	*3772*
	11: 6	These have power to shut **h**, that it rain not	*3772*
	11:12	And they heard a great voice from **h** saying	*3772*
	11:12	And they ascended up to **h** in a cloud; and	*3772*
	11:13	and gave glory to the God of **h**.	*3772*
	11:15	and there were great voices in **h**, saying,	*3772*
	11:19	And the temple of God was opened in **h**,	*3772*
	12: 1	And there appeared a great wonder in **h**;	*3772*
	12: 3	And there appeared another wonder in **h**;	*3772*
	12: 4	his tail drew the third *part* of the stars of **h**,	*3772*
	12: 7	And there was war in **h**: Michael and	*3772*
	12: 8	was their place found any more in **h**.	*3772*
	12:10	And I heard a loud voice saying in **h**,	*3772*
	13: 6	his tabernacle, and them that dwell in **h**.	*3772*
	13:13	that he maketh fire come down from **h** on	*3772*
	14: 2	And I heard a voice from **h**, as the voice of	*3772*
	14: 6	I saw another angel fly in the **midst of h**,	*3321*
	14: 7	and worship him that made **h**, and earth,	*3772*
	14:13	And I heard a voice from **h** saying unto me,	*3772*
	14:17	angel came out of the temple which is in **h**,	*3772*
	15: 1	And I saw another sign in **h**, great and	*3772*
	15: 5	of the testimony in **h** was opened:	*3772*
	16:11	And blasphemed the God of **h** because	*3772*
	16:17	came a great voice out of the temple of **h**,	*3772*
	16:21	there fell upon men a great hail out of **h**,	*3772*
	18: 1	I saw another angel come down from **h**,	*3772*
	18: 4	And I heard another voice from **h**, saying,	*3772*
	18: 5	For her sins have reached unto **h**, and God	*3772*
	18:20	*thou* **h**, and ye holy apostles and prophets;	*3772*
	19: 1	I heard a great voice of much people in **h**,	*3772*
	19:11	And I saw **h** opened, and behold a white	*3772*
	19:14	And the armies which were in **h** followed	*3772*
	19:17	to all the fowls that fly in the **midst of h**,	*3321*
	20: 1	And I saw an angel come down from **h**,	*3772*
	20: 9	and fire came down from God out of **h**,	*3772*
	20:11	face the earth and the **h** fled *away;* and	*3772*
	21: 1	And I saw a new **h** and a new earth: for	*3772*
	21: 1	for the first **h** and the first earth were	*3772*
	21: 2	coming down from God out of **h**,	*3772*
	21: 3	And I heard a great voice out of **h** saying,	*3772*
	21:10	descending out of **h** from God,	*3772*

HEAVEN'S (1) [HEAVEN]

Mt	19:12	eunuchs for the kingdom of **h** sake.	*3772*

HEAVENLY (23) [HEAVEN]

Mt	6:14	your **h** Father will also forgive you:	*3770*
	6:26	into barns; yet your **h** Father feedeth them.	*3770*
	6:32	for your **h** Father knoweth that ye have	*3770*
	15:13	which my **h** Father hath not planted,	*3770*
	18:35	So likewise shall my **h** Father do *also* unto	*2032*
Lk	2:13	a multitude of the **h** host praising God,	*3770*
	11:13	how much more shall *your* **h** Father	*1537+3772*
Jn	3:12	shall ye believe, if I tell you *of* **h** *things?*	*2032*

Ac 26:19 I was not disobedient unto the **h** vision: *3770*
1Co 15:48 and as *is* the **h**, such *are they* also *that are* *2032*
15:48 the heavenly, such *are they* also *that are* **h**. *2032*
15:49 we shall also bear the image of the **h**. *2032*
Eph 1: 3 all spiritual blessings in **h** *places* in Christ: *2032*
1:20 set *him* at his own right hand in the **h** *2032*
2: 6 made *us* sit together in **h** *places* in Christ *2032*
3:10 powers in **h** *places* might be known by *2032*
2Ti 4:18 and will preserve *me* unto his **h** kingdom: *2032*
Heb 3: 1 holy brethren, partakers of the **h** calling, *2032*
6: 4 and have tasted of the **h** gift, and *2032*
8: 5 shadow of **h** *things,* as Moses was *2032*
9:23 the **h** *things* themselves with better *2032*
11:16 they desire a better *country,* that is, a **h**: *2032*
12:22 the **h** Jerusalem, and to an innumerable *2032*

HEAVENS (133) [HEAVEN]

Ge 2: 1 Thus the **h** and the earth were finished, and 8064
2: 4 These *are* the generations of the **h** and 8064
2: 4 the LORD God made the earth and the **h**, 8064
Dt 10:14 the heaven of **h** *is* the LORD'S thy God, 8064
32: 1 Give ear, O ye **h**, and I will speak; and 8064
33:28 and wine; also his **h** shall drop down dew. 8064
Jdg 5: 4 the earth trembled, and the **h** dropped, 8064
2Sa 22:10 He bowed the **h** also, and came down; and 8064
1Ki 8:27 and heaven of **h** cannot contain thee; 8064
1Ch 16:26 *are* idols: but the LORD made the **h**. 8064
16:31 Let the **h** be glad, and let the earth rejoice: 8064
27:23 increase Israel like to the stars of the **h**. 8064
2Ch 2: 6 and heaven of **h** cannot contain him? 8064
6:18 and the heaven of **h** cannot contain thee; 8064
6:25 hear thou from the **h**, and forgive the sin of 8064
6:33 hear thou from the **h**, *even* from thy 8064
6:35 hear thou from the **h** their prayer and their 8064
6:39 hear thou from the **h**, *even* from thy 8064
Ezr 9: 6 and our trespass is grown up unto the **h**. 8064
Ne 9: 6 the heaven of **h**, with all their host, 8064
Job 9: 8 Which alone spreadeth out the **h**, and 8064
14:12 till the **h** *be* no more, they shall not awake, 8064
15:15 yea, the **h** are not clean in his sight. 8064
20: 6 Though his excellency mount up to the **h**, 8064
26:13 By his spirit he hath garnished the **h**; 8064
35: 5 Look unto the **h**, and see; and behold 8064
Ps 2: 4 He that sitteth in the **h** shall laugh: 8064
8: 1 who hast set thy glory above the **h**. 8064
8: 3 When I consider thy **h**, the work of thy 8064
18: 9 He bowed the **h** also, and came down: and 8064
18:13 The LORD also thundered in the **h**, and 8064
19: 1 The **h** declare the glory of God; and 8064
33: 6 By the word of the LORD were the **h** 8064
36: 5 Thy mercy, O LORD, *is* in the **h**; *and* 8064
50: 4 He shall call to the **h** from above, and to 8064
50: 6 the **h** shall declare his righteousness: 8064
57: 5 Be thou exalted, O God, above the **h**; 8064
57:10 For thy mercy *is* great unto the **h**, and 8064
57:11 Be thou exalted, O God, above the **h**: 8064
68: 4 extol him that rideth upon the **h** by his 6160
68: 8 the **h** also dropped at the presence of God: 8064
68:33 To him that rideth upon the **h** of heavens, 8064
68:33 To him that rideth upon the heavens of **h**, 8064
73: 9 They set their mouth against the **h**, and 8064
89: 2 shalt thou establish in the very **h**. 8064
89: 5 the **h** shall praise thy wonders, O LORD: 8064
89:11 The **h** *are* thine, the earth also *is* thine: 8064
96: 5 *are* idols: but the LORD made the **h**. 8064
96:11 Let the **h** rejoice, and let the earth be glad; 8064
97: 6 The **h** declare his righteousness, and all 8064
102:25 and the **h** *are* the work of thy hands. 8064
103:19 LORD hath prepared his throne in the **h**; 8064
104: 2 who stretchest out the **h** like a curtain: 8064
108: 4 For thy mercy *is* great above the **h**: and 8064
108: 5 Be thou exalted, O God, above the **h**: and 8064
113: 4 all nations, *and* his glory above the **h**. 8064
115: 3 our God *is* in the **h**: he hath done 8064
115:16 The heaven, *even* the **h**, *are* the LORD'S: 8064
123: 1 up mine eyes, O thou that dwellest in the **h**. 8064
136: 5 To him that by wisdom made the **h**: for his 8064
144: 5 Bow thy **h**, O LORD, and come down: 8064
148: 1 Praise ye the LORD from the **h**: 8064
148: 4 ye **h** of heavens, and ye waters that *be* 8064
148: 4 ye heavens of **h**, and ye waters that *be* 8064
148: 4 and ye waters that *be* above the **h**. 8064
Pr 3:19 by understanding hath he established the **h**. 8064
8:27 When he prepared the **h**, I *was* there: 8064
Isa 1: 2 Hear, O **h**, and give ear, O earth: for 8064
5:30 and the light is darkened in the **h** thereof. 6183
13:13 Therefore I will shake the **h**, and the earth 8064
34: 4 the **h** shall be rolled together as a scrole: 8064
40:22 that stretcheth out the **h** as a curtain, and 8064
42: 5 he that created the **h**, and stretched them 8064
44:23 Sing, O ye **h**; for the LORD hath done *it:* 8064
44:24 all *things;* that stretcheth forth the **h** alone; 8064
45: 8 Drop down, ye **h**, from above, and let 8064
45:12 have stretched out the **h**, and all their host 8064
45:18 thus saith the LORD that created the **h**; 8064
48:13 and my right hand hath spanned the **h**: 8064
49:13 Sing, O **h**; and be joyful, O earth; and 8064
50: 3 I clothe the **h** with blackness, and I make 8064
51: 6 Lift up your eyes to the **h**, and look upon 8064
51: 6 for the **h** shall vanish away like smoke, and 8064
51:13 that hath stretched forth the **h**, and laid 8064
51:16 that I may plant the **h**, and lay 8064
55: 9 For *as* the **h** are higher than the earth, so 8064
64: 1 O that thou wouldest rend the **h**, that thou 8064
65:17 behold, I create new **h** and a new earth: 8064
66:22 For as the new **h** and the new earth, which I 8064
Jer 2:12 O ye **h**, at this, and be horribly afraid, 8064
4:23 and void; and the **h**, and they *had* no light. 8064
4:25 no man, and all the birds of the **h** were fled. 8064
4:28 the earth mourn, and the **h** above be black: 8064
9:10 both the fowl of the **h** and the beast are 8064
10:11 The gods that have not made the **h** and 8065
10:11 from the earth, and from under these **h**. 8065
10:12 hath stretched out the **h** by his discretion. 8064
10:13 *there is* a multitude of waters in the **h**, and 8064
14:22 or can the **h** give showers? *art* not thou he, 8064
51:16 *there is* a multitude of waters in the **h**; 8064
La 3:41 our heart with *our* hands unto God in the **h**. 8064
3:66 destroy them in anger from under the **h** of 8064
Eze 1: 1 *that* the **h** were opened, and I saw visions 8064
Da 4:26 after that thou shalt have known that the **h** 8065
Hos 2:21 I will hear the **h**, and they shall hear 8064
Joel 2:10 quake before them; the **h** shall tremble: 8064
2:30 I will shew wonders in the **h** and in 8064
3:16 and the **h** and the earth shall shake: 8064
Hab 3: 3 His glory covered the **h**, and the earth was 8064
Hag 2: 6 I *will* shake the **h**, and the earth, and 8064
2:21 I *will* shake the **h** and the earth; 8064
Zec 6: 5 unto me, These *are* the four spirits of the **h**, 8064
8:12 her increase, and the **h** shall give their dew; 8064
12: 1 which stretcheth forth the **h**, and layeth 8064
Mt 3:16 and lo, the **h** were opened unto him, and *3772*
24:29 and the powers of the **h** shall be shaken: *3772*
Mk 1:10 he saw the **h** opened, and the Spirit like a *3772*
Lk 12:33 a treasure in the **h** that faileth not, where no *3772*
Ac 2:34 For David is not ascended into the **h**: but *3772*
7:56 And said, Behold, I see the **h** opened, *3772*
2Co 5: 1 house not made with hand, eternal in the **h**. *3772*
Eph 4:10 same also that ascended up far above all **h**, *3772*
Heb 1:10 and the **h** are the works of thine hands: *3772*
4:14 that is passed into the **h**, Jesus the Son of *3772*
7:26 from sinners, and made higher than the **h**; *3772*
8: 1 hand of the throne of the Majesty in the **h**; *3772*
9:23 in the **h** should be purified with these; *3772*
2Pe 3: 5 that by the word of God the **h** were of old, *3772*
3: 7 But the **h** and the earth, which are now, *3772*
3:10 in the which the **h** shall pass away with a *3772*
3:12 wherein the **h** being on fire shall be *3772*
3:13 look for new **h** and a new earth, *3772*
Rev 12:12 ye **h**, and ye that dwell in them. *3772*

HEAVIER (3) [HEAVY]

Job 6: 3 For now it would be **h** than the sand of 3513
23: 2 my stroke is **h** than my groaning. 3513
Pr 27: 3 but a fool's wrath *is* **h** than them both. 3515

HEAVILY (3) [HEAVY]

Ex 14:25 that they drave them **h**: 3517+871.1
Ps 35:14 I bowed down **h**, as one that mourneth for 6937
Isa 47: 6 upon the ancient hast thou very **h laid** thy 3513

HEAVINESS (14) [HEAVY]

Ezr 9: 5 the evening sacrifice I arose up from my **h**; 8589
Job 9:27 I will leave off my **h**, and comfort myself: 6440
Ps 69:20 hath broken my heart; and I am **full of h**: 5136
119:28 My soul melteth for **h**: strengthen thou me 8424
Pr 10: 1 but a foolish son *is* the **h** of his mother. 8424
12:25 **H** in the heart of man maketh it stoop: but 1674

Pr 14:13 is sorrowful; and the end of that mirth *is* **h**. 8424
Isa 29: 2 and there shall be **h** and sorrow: 8386
61: 3 the garment of praise for the spirit of **h**; 3544
Ro 9: 2 That I have great **h** and continual sorrow in *3077*
2Co 2: 1 that *I* would not come again to you in **h**. *3077*
Php 2:26 and *was* **full of h**, because that ye had heard *85*
Jas 4: 9 be turned to mourning, and *your* joy to **h**. *2726*
1Pe 1: 6 ye are in **h** through manifold temptations: *3076*

HEAVY (40) [HEAVIER, HEAVILY, HEAVINESS]
Ex 17:12 Moses' hands *were* **h**; and they took a 3515
18:18 for *this* thing *is* too **h** for thee; thou art not 3515
Nu 11:14 people alone, because *it is* too **h** for me. 3515
1Sa 4:18 for he was an old man, and **h**. And he had 3515
5: 6 the hand of the LORD was **h** upon them 3513
5:11 the city; the hand of God was very **h** there. 3513
2Sa 14:26 he polled *it:* because *the hair* was **h** on him, 3513
1Ki 12: 4 his **h** yoke which he put upon us, lighter, 3515
12:10 Thy father **made** our yoke **h**, but make thou 3513
12:11 my father did lade you with a **h** yoke, 3515
12:14 My father **made** your yoke **h**, and I will 3513
14: 6 for I *am* sent to thee *with* **h** *tidings.* 7186
20:43 the king of Israel went to his house **h** and 5620
21: 4 Ahab came into his house **h** and displeased 5620
2Ch 10: 4 his **h** yoke that he put upon us, and we will 3515
10:10 Thy father **made** our yoke **h**, but make thou 3513
10:11 For whereas my father put a **h** yoke upon 3515
10:14 My father **made** your yoke **h**, but I will add 3513
Ne 5:18 the bondage was **h** upon this people. 3513
Job 33: 7 neither shall my hand be **h** upon thee. 3513
Ps 32: 4 For day and night thy hand was **h** upon me: 3513
38: 4 as a **h** burden they are too heavy for me. 3515
38: 4 as a heavy burden they are too **h** for me. 3513
Pr 25:20 so *is* he that singeth songs to a **h** heart. 7451
27: 3 A stone *is* **h**, and the sand weighty; but 3514
31: 6 and wine unto those that be of **h** hearts. 4751
Isa 6:10 and **make** their ears **h**, and shut their eyes; 3513
24:20 the transgression thereof shall be **h** upon it; 3513
30:27 *with* his anger, and the burden *thereof is* **h**: 3514
46: 1 your carriages *were* **h loaden**; *they are* a 6006
58: 6 to undo the **h** burdens, and to let 4133
59: 1 neither his ear **h**, that *it* cannot hear: 3513
La 3: 7 I cannot get out: he hath **made** my chain **h**. 3513
Mt 11:28 all *ye* that labour and are **h laden**, and I *5412*
23: 4 For they bind **h** burdens and grievous to be *926*
26:37 and began to be sorrowful and **very h**. *85*
26:43 them asleep again: for their eyes were **h**. *916*
Mk 14:33 began to be sore amazed, and to be **very h**; *85*
14:40 them asleep again, (for their eyes were **h**,) *916*
Lk 9:32 they that were with him were **h** with sleep: *916*

HEBER (13) [EBER, HEBER'S, HEBERITES]
Ge 46:17 and the sons of Beriah; **H**, and Malchiel. 2268
Nu 26:45 of **H**, the family of the Heberites: 2268
Jdg 4:11 Now **H** the Kenite, *which was* of 2268
4:17 to the tent of Jael the wife of **H** the Kenite: 2268
4:17 of Hazor and the house of **H** the Kenite. 2268
5:24 shall Jael the wife of **H** the Kenite be, 2268
1Ch 4:18 **H** the father of Socho, and Jekuthiel 2268
5:13 Jorai, and Jachan, and Zia, and **H**, seven. 5677
7:31 **H**, and Malchiel, who *is* the father of 2268
7:32 **H** begat Japhlet, and Shomer, and Hotham, 2268
8:17 and Meshullam, and Hezeki, and **H**, 2268
8:22 And Ishpan, and **H**, and Eliel, 5677
Lk 3:35 which was *the son* of **H**, which was *the son* *1443*

HEBER'S (1) [HEBER]
Jdg 4:21 Jael **H** wife took a nail of the tent, and 2268

HEBERITES (1) [HEBER]
Nu 26:45 of Heber, the family of the **H**: of Malchiel, 2277

HEBREW (26) [HEBREWESS, HEBREWS, HEBREWS']
Ge 14:13 that had escaped, and told Abram the **H**; 5680
39:14 he hath brought in a **H** unto us to mock us; 5680
39:17 saying, The **H** servant, which thou hast 5680
41:12 a **H**, servant to the captain of the guard; 5680
Ex 1:15 the king of Egypt spake to the **H** midwives, 5680
1:16 do the office of a midwife to the **H women**, 5680
1:19 Because the **H women** *are* not as 5680
2: 7 and call to thee a nurse of the **H** women, 5680
2:11 he spied an Egyptian smiting a **H**, *one* of 5680
21: 2 If thou buy a **H** servant, six years he shall 5680
Dt 15:12 a **H man**, or a Hebrew woman, be sold 5680
15:12 a Hebrew man, or a **H woman**, be sold 5680
Jer 34: 9 *being* a **H** or a Hebrewess, go free; 5680
34:14 years let ye go every man his brother a **H**, 5680
Jnh 1: 9 he said unto them, I *am* a **H**; and I fear 5680
Lk 23:38 and Latin, and **H**, THIS IS THE KING OF *1444*
Jn 5: 2 which is called **in the H tongue** Bethesda, *1447*
19:13 the Pavement, but **in the H**, Gabbatha. *1447*
19:17 a skull, which is called **in the H** Golgotha: *1447*
19:20 and it was written **in H**, *and* Greek, *and* *1447*
Ac 21:40 he spake unto *them* **in the H** tongue, *1446*
22: 2 that he spake **in the H** tongue to them, *1446*
26:14 and saying **in the H** tongue, Saul, Saul, *1446*
Php 3: 5 the tribe of Benjamin, a **H** of the Hebrews; *1445*
Rev 9:11 whose name **in the H tongue** *is* Abaddon, *1447*
16:16 place called **in the H tongue** Armageddon. *1447*

HEBREWESS (1) [HEBREW]
Jer 34: 9 *being* a Hebrew or a **H**, go free; 5680

HEBREWS (21) [HEBREW]
Ge 40:15 I was stolen away out of the land of the **H**: 5680
43:32 Egyptians might not eat bread with the **H**; 5680
Ex 2:13 two men of the **H** strove together: 5680
3:18 The LORD God of the **H** hath met with 5680
5: 3 The God of the **H** hath met with us: 5680
7:16 The LORD God of the **H** hath sent me 5680
9: 1 Thus saith the LORD God of the **H**, 5680
9:13 Thus saith the LORD God of the **H**, 5680
10: 3 Thus saith the LORD God of the **H**, 5680
1Sa 4: 6 of this great shout in the camp of the **H**? 5680
4: 9 that ye be not servants unto the **H**, 5680
13: 3 all the land, saying, Let the **H** hear. 5680
13: 7 *some of the* **H** went over Jordan *to* the land 5680
13:19 Lest the **H** make *them* swords or spears: 5680
14:11 the **H** come forth out of the holes where 5680
14:21 Moreover the **H** *that* were with 5680
29: 3 What *do* these **H** *here?* And Achish said 5680
Ac 6: 1 a murmuring of the Grecians against the **H**, *1445*
2Co 11:22 Are they **H**? so *am* I. Are they Israelites? so *1445*
Php 3: 5 the tribe of Benjamin, a Hebrew of the **H**; *1445*
Heb 13: S Written to the **H** from Italy by Timothy. *1445*

HEBREWS' (1) [HEBREW]
Ex 2: 6 and said, This *is one* of the **H** children. 5680

HEBRON (73) [HEBRONITES]
Ge 13:18 which *is* in **H**, and built there an altar unto 2275
23: 2 the same *is* **H** in the land of Canaan: 2275
23:19 the same *is* **H** in the land of Canaan. 2275
35:27 which *is* **H**, where Abraham and 2275
37:14 So he sent him out of the vale of **H**, and 2275
Ex 6:18 Amram, and Izhar, and **H**, and Uzziel: 2275
Nu 3:19 Amram, and Izehar, **H**, and Uzziel. 2275
13:22 ascended by the south, and came unto **H**; 2275
13:22 *were.* (Now **H** was built seven years before 2275
Jos 10: 3 of Jerusalem sent unto Hoham king of **H**, 2275
10: 5 the king of **H**, the king of Jarmuth, the king 2275
10:23 the king of **H**, the king of Jarmuth, the king 2275
10:36 and all Israel with him, unto **H**; 2275
10:39 as he had done to **H**, so he did to Debir, and 2275
11:21 from **H**, from Debir, from Anab, and 2275
12:10 king of Jerusalem, one; the king of **H**, one; 2275
14:13 gave unto Caleb the son of Jephunneh **H** 2275
14:14 **H** therefore became the inheritance of 2275
14:15 the name of **H** before *was* Kirjath-arba; 2275
15:13 of Arba the father of Anak, which *city is* **H**. 2275
15:54 and Kirjath-arba, which *is* **H**, and Zior; 2275
19:28 **H**, and Rehob, and Hammon, and Kanah, 5683
20: 7 Kirjath-arba, which *is* **H**, in the mountain 2275
21:11 which *city is* **H**, in the hill *country* of 2275
21:13 of Aaron the priest **H** with her suburbs, 2275
Jdg 1:10 against the Canaanites that dwelt in **H**: 2275
1:10 (now the name of **H** before *was* 2275
1:20 they gave **H** unto Caleb, as Moses said: 2275
16: 3 them up to the top of a hill that *is* before **H**. 2275
1Sa 30:31 to *them* which *were* in **H**, and to all 2275
2Sa 2: 1 shall I go up? And he said, Unto **H**. 2275
2: 3 and they dwelt in the cities of **H**. 2275
2:11 the time that David was king in **H** over 2275
2:32 and they came to **H** at break of day. 2275
3: 2 unto David were sons born in **H**: and 2275
3: 5 These were born to David in **H**. 2275
3:19 David in **H** all that seemed good to Israel, 2275
3:20 So Abner came to David *to* **H**, and 2275

2Sa 3:22 Abner *was* not with David in **H**; for he had 2275
3:27 when Abner was returned *to* **H**, Joab took 2275
3:32 they buried Abner in **H**: and the king lift up 2275
4: 1 Saul's son heard that Abner was dead in **H**, 2275
4: 8 the head of Ish-bosheth unto David *to* **H**, 2275
4:12 and hanged *them* up over the pool in **H**. 2275
4:12 buried *it* in the sepulchre of Abner in **H**. 2275
5: 1 all the tribes of Israel to David unto **H**, 2275
5: 3 the elders of Israel came to the king to **H**; 2275
5: 3 king David made a league with them in **H** 2275
5: 5 In **H** he reigned over Judah seven years and 2275
5:13 of Jerusalem, after he was come from **H**: 2275
15: 7 I have vowed unto the LORD, in **H**. 2275
15: 9 Go in peace. So he arose, and went to **H**. 2275
15:10 then ye shall say, Absalom reigneth in **H**. 2275
1Ki 2:11 seven years reigned he in **H**, and thirty and 2275
1Ch 2:42 and the sons of Mareshah the father of **H**. 2275
2:43 the sons of **H**; Korah, and Tappuah, and 2275
3: 1 of David, which were born unto him in **H**; 2275
3: 4 *These* six were born unto him in **H**; and 2275
6: 2 Amram, Izhar, and **H**, and Uzziel. 2275
6:18 and Izhar, and **H**, and Uzziel. 2275
6:55 And they gave them **H** in the land of Judah, 2275
6:57 *namely,* **H**, *the city* of refuge, and Libnah 2275
11: 1 gathered themselves to David unto **H**, 2275
11: 3 all the elders of Israel to the king to **H**; 2275
11: 3 David made a covenant with them in **H** 2275
12:23 *and* came to David to **H**, to turn 2275
12:38 keep rank, came with a perfect heart to **H**, 2275
15: 9 Of the sons of **H**; Eliel the chief, and 2275
23:12 Amram, Izhar, **H**, and Uzziel, four. 2275
23:19 *Of* the sons of **H**; Jeriah the first, 2275
24:23 the sons *of* **H**; Jeriah *the first,* Amariah NIH
29:27 seven years reigned he in **H**, and thirty and 2275
2Ch 11:10 Zorah, and Aijalon, and **H**, which *are* in 2275

HEBRONITES (6) [HEBRON]

Nu 3:27 the family of the **H**, and the family of 2276
26:58 family of the Libnites, the family of the **H**, 2276
1Ch 26:23 the Izharites, the **H**, *and* the Uzzielites: 2276
26:30 *And* of the **H**, Hashabiah and his brethren, 2276
26:31 Among the **H** *was* Jerijah the chief, 2276
26:31 *even* among the **H**, according to 2276

HEDGE (9) [HEDGED, HEDGES]

Job 1:10 Hast not thou **made a h** about him, and 7753
Pr 15:19 The way of the slothful *man is* as a **h** of 4881
Ecc 10: 8 whoso breaketh a **h**, a serpent shall bite 1447
Isa 5: 5 I *will* take away the **h** thereof, and it shall 4881
Eze 13: 5 neither **made up the h** for the house 1443+1447
22:30 that *should* **make up the h**, 1443+1447
Hos 2: 6 I will **h up** thy way with thorns, and make a 7753
Mic 7: 4 the *most* upright *is sharper* than a **thorn h**: 4534
Mk 12: 1 and set a **h** about *it,* and digged *a place for* *5418*

HEDGED (3) [HEDGE]

Job 3:23 way is hid, and whom God hath **h in**? 5526
La 3: 7 He hath **h** me about, that I cannot get out: 1443
Mt 21:33 and **h** it round about, and digged a *5418*

HEDGES (6) [HEDGE]

1Ch 4:23 and those that dwelt amongst plants and **h**: 1448
Ps 80:12 Why hast thou *then* broken down her **h**, so 1447
89:40 Thou hast broken down all his **h**; thou hast 1448
Jer 49: 3 lament, and run to and fro by the **h**; 1448
Na 3:17 which camp in the **h** in the cold day, *but* 1448
Lk 14:23 Go out into the *high*ways and **h**, and *5418*

HEED (80)

Ge 31:24 **Take h** that thou speak not to Jacob either 8104
31:29 **Take** thou **h** that thou speak not to Jacob 8104
Ex 10:28 Get thee from me, **take h** to thyself, see my 8104
19:12 saying, **Take h** to yourselves, *that ye* go 8104
34:12 **Take h** to thyself, lest thou make a 8104
Nu 23:12 Must I not **take h** to speak that which 8104
Dt 2: 4 **take** ye good **h** unto yourselves therefore: 8104
4: 9 Only **take h** to thyself, and keep thy soul 8104
4:15 **Take** ye therefore good **h** unto yourselves; 8104
4:23 **Take h** unto yourselves, lest ye forget 8104
11:16 **Take h** to yourselves, that your heart be not 8104
12:13 **Take h** to thyself that thou offer not thy 8104
12:19 **Take h** to thyself that thou forsake not 8104
12:30 **Take h** to thyself that thou be not snared by 8104
24: 8 **Take h** in the plague of leprosy, that *thou* 8104
27: 9 **Take h**, and hearken, O Israel; 5535
Jos 22: 5 But **take** diligent **h** to do the commandment 8104
23:11 **Take** good **h** therefore unto yourselves, 8104
1Sa 19: 2 **take h** to thyself until the morning, and 8104
2Sa 20:10 Amasa **took** no **h** to the sword that *was* in 8104
1Ki 2: 4 saying, If thy children **take h** to their way, 8104
8:25 so that thy children **take h** to their way, 8104
2Ki 10:31 Jehu **took** no **h** to walk in the law of 8104
1Ch 22:13 if thou **takest h** to fulfil the statutes and 8104
28:10 **Take h** now; for the LORD hath chosen 7200
2Ch 6:16 that thy children **take h** to their way to 8104
19: 6 said to the judges, **Take h** what ye do: 7200
19: 7 **take h** and do *it:* for *there is* no iniquity 8104
33: 8 that they will **take h** to do all that I have 8104
Ezr 4:22 **Take h** now that ye fail not to do this: why 2095
Job 36:21 **Take h**, regard not iniquity: for this hast 8104
Ps 39: 1 I said, I will **take h** to my ways, that *I* sin 8104
119: 9 by **taking h** *thereto* according to thy word. 8104
Pr 17: 4 A wicked doer **giveth h** to false lips; *and* 7181
Ecc 7:21 Also **take** no **h** unto all words that 3820+5414
12: 9 he **gave good h**, and sought out, *and* set in 239
Isa 7: 4 say unto him, **Take h**, and be quiet; 8104
21: 7 and he hearkened diligently *with* much **h**: 7182
Jer 9: 4 **Take** ye **h** every one of his neighbour, and 8104
17:21 **Take h** to yourselves, and bear no burden 8104
18:18 and let us not **give h** to any of his words. 7181
18:19 **Give h** to me, O LORD, and hearken to 7181
Hos 4:10 they have left off to **take h** to the LORD. 8104
Mal 2:15 Therefore **take h** to your spirit, and 8104
2:16 therefore **take h** to your spirit, that ye deal 8104
Mt 6: 1 **Take h** that *ye* do not your alms before *4337*
16: 6 **Take h** and beware of the leaven of *3708*
18:10 **Take h** that ye despise not one of these *3708*
24: 4 unto them, **Take h** that no *man* deceive you. *991*
Mk 4:24 he said unto them, **Take h** what you hear: *991*
8:15 And he charged them, saying, **Take h**, *3708*
13: 5 to say, **Take h** lest any *man* deceive you: *991*
13: 9 But **take h** to yourselves: for they shall *991*
13:23 But **take** ye **h**: behold, I have foretold you *991*
13:33 **Take** ye **h**, watch and pray: for ye know not *991*
Lk 8:18 **Take h** therefore how ye hear: *991*
11:35 **Take h** therefore that the light which is in *4648*
12:15 **Take h**, and beware of covetousness: *3708*
17: 3 **Take h** to yourselves: If thy brother *4337*
21: 8 And he said, **Take h** that ye be not deceived: *991*
21:34 And **take h** to yourselves, lest at any time *4337*
Ac 3: 5 And he gave **h** unto them, expecting to *1907*
5:35 **take h** to yourselves what ye intend to do *4337*
8: 6 And the people with one accord **gave h** *4337*
8:10 To whom they all **gave h**, from the least to *4337*
20:28 **Take h** therefore unto yourselves, and *4337*
22:26 saying, **Take h** what thou doest: *3708*
Ro 11:21 *take h* lest he also spare not thee. NIG
1Co 3:10 But let every man **take h** how he buildeth *991*
8: 9 But **take h** lest by any means this liberty of *991*
10:12 that thinketh he standeth **take h** lest he fall. *991*
Gal 5:15 **take h** ye be not consumed one of another. *991*
Col 4:17 **Take h** to the ministry which thou hast *991*
1Ti 1: 4 Neither **give h** to fables and *4337*
4: 1 **giving h** to seducing spirits, and *4337*
4:16 **Take h** unto thyself, and unto the doctrine; *1907*
Tit 1:14 Not **giving h** to Jewish fables, and *4337*
Heb 2: 1 **give** the more earnest **h to** the *things* which *4337*
3:12 **Take h**, brethren, lest there be in any of you *991*
2Pe 1:19 whereunto ye do well that ye **take h**, *4337*

HEEL (6) [HEELS]

Ge 3:15 bruise thy head, and thou shalt bruise his **h**. 6119
25:26 and his hand took hold on Esau's **h**; 6119
Job 18: 9 The grin shall take *him* by the **h**, *and* 6119
Ps 41: 9 *of* my bread, hath lift up *his* **h** against me. 6119
Hos 12: 3 He **took** his brother **by the h** in the womb, 6117
Jn 13:18 bread with me hath lift up his **h** against me. *4418*

HEELS (4) [HEEL]

Ge 49:17 that biteth the horse **h**, so that his rider shall 6119
Job 13:27 thou settest a print upon the **h** of my feet. 8328
Ps 49: 5 *when* the iniquity of my **h** shall compass 6120
Jer 13:22 thy skirts discovered, *and* thy **h** made bare. 6119

HEGAI (3) [HEGE]

Est 2: 8 to the custody of **H**, that Esther was 1896
2: 8 to the custody of **H**, keeper of the women. 1896
2:15 but what **H** the king's chamberlain, 1896

HEGE (1) [HEGAI]
Est 2: 3 unto the custody of **H** the king's 1896

HEIFER (19) [HEIFER'S]
Ge 15: 9 Take me a **h** of three years old, and a she 5697
Nu 19: 2 that they bring thee a red **h** without spot, 6510
19: 5 *one* shall burn the **h** in his sight; her skin, 6510
19: 6 *it* into the midst of the burning of the **h**. 6510
19: 9 *is* clean shall gather up the ashes of the **h**, 6510
19:10 he that gathereth the ashes of the **h** shall 6510
19:17 ashes of the burnt *h* of purification for sin, NIH
Dt 21: 3 the elders of that city shall take a **h**, 1241+5697
21: 4 shall bring down the **h** unto a rough valley, 5697
21: 6 over the **h** that is beheaded in the valley: 5697
Jdg 14:18 unto them, If ye had not plowed with my **h**, 5697
1Sa 16: 2 Take a **h** with thee, and say, 1241+5697
Isa 15: 5 *shall flee* unto Zoar, a **h** of three years old: 5697
Jer 46:20 Egypt *is like* a very fair **h**, *but* 5697
48:34 unto Horonaim, *as* a **h** of three years old: 5697
50:11 because ye are grown fat as the **h** at grass, 5697
Hos 4:16 For Israel slideth back as a backsliding **h**: 6510
10:11 Ephraim *is as* a **h** *that is* taught, *and* 5697
Heb 9:13 and the ashes of a **h** sprinkling the unclean, *1151*

H

HEIFER'S (1) [HEIFER]
Dt 21: 4 shall strike off the **h** neck there in 5697

HEIGHT (62) [HIGH]
Ge 6:15 it fifty cubits, and the **h** of it thirty cubits. 6967
Ex 25:10 and a cubit and a half the **h** thereof. 6967
25:23 and a cubit and a half the **h** thereof. 6967
27: 1 and the **h** thereof *shall be* three cubits. 6967
27:18 the **h** five cubits *of* fine twined linen, and 6967
30: 2 two cubits *shall be* the **h** thereof: the horns 6967
37: 1 of it, and a cubit and a half the **h** of it: 6967
37:10 and a cubit and a half the **h** thereof: 6967
37:25 and two cubits *was* the **h** of it; 6967
38: 1 and three cubits the **h** thereof. 6967
38:18 and the **h** in the breadth *was* five cubits, 6967
1Sa 16: 7 his countenance, or on the **h** of his stature; 1364
17: 4 of Gath, whose **h** *was* six cubits and a span. 1363
1Ki 6: 2 and the **h** thereof thirty cubits. 6967
6:20 and twenty cubits in the **h** thereof: 6967
6:26 The **h** of the one cherub *was* ten cubits, and 6967
7: 2 fifty cubits, and the **h** thereof thirty cubits, 6967
7:16 the **h** of the one chapiter *was* five cubits, 6967
7:16 the **h** of the other chapiter *was* five cubits: 6967
7:23 round all about, and his **h** *was* five cubits: 6967
7:27 breadth thereof, and three cubits the **h** of it. 6967
7:32 the **h** of a wheel *was* a cubit and half a 6967
2Ki 19:23 I am come up *to* the **h** of the mountains, 4791
25:17 The **h** of the one pillar *was* eighteen cubits, 6967
25:17 the **h** of the chapiter three cubits; and 6967
2Ch 3: 4 and the **h** *was* an hundred and twenty: 1363
4: 1 and ten cubits the **h** thereof. 6967
4: 2 in compass, and five cubits the **h** thereof; 6967
33:14 **raised** it **up a** very **great h**, and 1361
Ezr 6: 3 the **h** thereof threescore cubits, *and* 7314
Job 22:12 *Is* not God *in* the **h** of heaven? and 1470
22:12 behold the **h** of the stars, how high they are. 7218
Ps 102:19 For he hath looked down from the **h** of his 4791
Pr 25: 3 The heaven for **h**, and the earth for depth, 7312
Isa 7:11 ask it either in the depth, or in the **h** above. 1361
37:24 am I come up *to* the **h** of the mountains, 4791
37:24 I will enter *into* the **h** of his border, *and* 4791
Jer 31:12 they shall come and sing in the **h** of Zion, 4791
49:16 of the rock, that holdest the **h** of the hill: 4791
51:53 though she should fortify the **h** of her 4791
52:21 the **h** of one pillar *was* eighteen cubits; 6967
52:22 the **h** of one chapiter *was* five cubits, 6967
Eze 17:23 In the mountain of the **h** of Israel will I 4791
19:11 she appeared in her **h** with the multitude of 1363
20:40 in the mountain of the **h** of Israel, saith 4791
31: 5 Therefore his **h** was exalted above all 6967
31:10 Because thou hast lifted up thyself in **h**, and 6967
31:10 and his heart is lifted up in his **h**; 1363
31:14 by the waters exalt themselves for their **h**, 6967
31:14 neither their trees stand up in their **h**, 1363
32: 5 and fill the valleys *with* thy **h**. 7419
40: 5 the building, one reed; and the **h**, one reed. 6967
41: 8 I saw also the **h** of the house round about: 1363
Da 3: 1 whose **h** *was* threescore cubits, *and* 7314
4:10 of the earth, and the **h** thereof *was* great. 7314
4:11 the **h** thereof reached unto heaven, and 7314
4:20 whose **h** reached unto the heaven, and 7314
Am 2: 9 whose **h** *was* like the height of the cedars, 1363
2: 9 whose height *was* like the **h** of the cedars, 1363
Ro 8:39 Nor **h**, nor depth, nor any other creature, *5313*
Eph 3:18 *is* the breadth, and length, and depth, and **h**; *5311*
Rev 21:16 and the breadth and the **h** of it are equal. *5311*

HEIGHTS (2) [HIGH]
Ps 148: 1 from the heavens: praise him in the **h**. 4791
Isa 14:14 I will ascend above the **h** of the clouds; 1116

HEINOUS (1)
Job 31:11 For this *is* a **h crime**; yea, it *is* an iniquity 2154

HEIR (18) [FELLOWHEIRS, HEIRS, JOINT-HEIRS]
Ge 15: 3 and lo, one born in my house is mine **h**. 3423
15: 4 unto him, saying, This shall not be thine **h**; 3423
15: 4 out of thine own bowels shall be thine **h**. 3423
21:10 bondwoman shall not be **h** with my son, 3423
2Sa 14: 7 he slew; and we will destroy the **h** also: 3423
Pr 30:23 and a handmaid that is **h** to her mistress. 3423
Jer 49: 1 Hath he no **h**? why *then* doth their king 3423
49: 2 shall Israel be **h** unto them that were his 3423
Mic 1:15 Yet will I bring an **h** unto thee, 3423
Mt 21:38 they said among themselves, This is the **h**; *2818*
Mk 12: 7 said amongst themselves, This is the **h**; *2818*
Lk 20:14 among themselves, saying, This is the **h**: *2818*
Ro 4:13 that he should be the **h** of the world, *2818*
Gal 4: 1 Now I say, *That* the **h**, as long as he is a *2818*
4: 7 if a son, then an **h** of God through Christ. *2818*
4:30 not be **h** with the son of the freewoman. *2816*
Heb 1: 2 whom he hath appointed **h** of all *things*, by *2818*
11: 7 became **h** of the righteousness which is by *2818*

HEIRS (11) [HEIR]
Jer 49: 2 Israel be heir unto them that were his **h**, 3423
Ro 4:14 For if they which are of the law *be* **h**, faith *2818*
8:17 And if children, then **h**; heirs of God, and *2818*
8:17 **h** of God, and joint-heirs with Christ; if so *2818*
Gal 3:29 and **h** according to the promise. *2818*
Tit 3: 7 we should be made **h** according to the hope *2818*
Heb 1:14 for them who shall be **h** of salvation? *2816*
6:17 willing more abundantly to shew unto the **h** *2818*
11: 9 Jacob, the **h with** *him* of the same promise: *4789*
Jas 2: 5 **h** of the kingdom which he hath promised *2818*
1Pe 3: 7 and as *being* **h together** of the grace of life; *4789*

HELAH (2)
1Ch 4: 5 of Tekoa had two wives, **H** and Naarah. 2458
4: 7 the sons of **H** *were*, Zereth, and Jezoar, 2458

HELAM (2)
2Sa 10:16 they came *to* **H**; and Shobach the captain of 2431
10:17 and passed over Jordan, and came to **H**. 2431

HELBAH (1)
Jdg 1:31 nor of **H**, nor of Aphik, nor of Rehob: 2462

HELBON (1)
Eze 27:18 in the wine of **H**, and white wool. 2463

HELD (52) [HOLD]
Ge 24:21 the man wondering at her **h** his **peace**, 2790
34: 5 Jacob **h** his **peace** until they were come. 2790
48:17 he **h up** his father's hand, to remove it from 8551
Ex 17:11 it came to pass, when Moses **h up** his hand, 7311
36:12 the loops **h** one *curtain* to another. 6901
Lev 10: 3 I will be glorified. And Aaron **h** his **peace**. 1826
Nu 30: 7 **h** his **peace** at her in the day that he heard 2790
30:11 husband heard *it*, and **h** his **peace** at her, 2790
30:14 he **h** his **peace** at her in the day that he 2790
Jdg 7:20 **h** the lamps in their left hands, and 2388
16:26 Samson said unto the lad that **h** him by 2388
Ru 3:15 when she **h** it, he measured six *measures* of 270
1Sa 10:27 no presents. But he **h** his **peace**. 2790+3509.1
25:36 behold, he **h** a feast in his house, like 3807.1
2Sa 18:16 after Israel: for Joab **h back** the people. 2820
1Ki 8:65 at that time Solomon **h** a feast, and 6213
2Ki 18:36 the people **h** their **peace**, and answered him 2790
2Ch 4: 5 *and* it received and **h** three thousand baths. 3557
Ne 4:16 the *other* half of them **h** both the spears, 2388
4:17 and with the other *hand* **h** a weapon. 2388
4:21 half of them **h** the spears from the rising of 2388
5: 8 **h** they their **peace**, and found nothing *to* 2790
Est 5: 2 the king **h out** to Esther the golden sceptre 3447

Est 7: 4 and bondwomen, I had **h** my **tongue**, 2790
8: 4 the king **h out** the golden sceptre toward 3447
Job 23:11 My foot hath **h** his steps, his way have I 270
29:10 The nobles **h** their **peace**, and 2244+6963
Ps 32: 9 whose mouth must be **h in** with bit and 1102
39: 2 I **h** my **peace**, *even* from good; 2814
94:18 thy mercy, O LORD, **h** me **up**. 5582
SS 3: 4 I **h** him, and would not let him go, until I had 270
7: 5 like purple; the king *is* **h** in the galleries. 631
Isa 36:21 they **h** their **peace**, and answered him not a 2790
57:11 have not I **h** my **peace** even of old, and 2814
Jer 50:33 all that took them captives **h** them **fast**; 2388
Da 12: 7 when he **h up** his right hand and his left 7311
Mt 12:14 went out, and **h** a council against him, *2983*
26:63 But Jesus **h** his **peace**. And the high priest *4623*
28: 9 And they came and **h** him by the feet, and *2902*
Mk 3: 4 save life, or to kill? But they **h** their **peace**. *4623*
9:34 But they **h** their **peace**: for by the way they *4623*
14:61 But he **h** his **peace**, and answered nothing. *4623*
15: 1 priests **h** a consultation with the elders *4160*
Lk 14: 4 And they **h** their **peace**. And he took *him*, *2270*
20:26 marvelled at his answer, and **h** their **peace**. *4601*
22:63 And the men that **h** Jesus mocked him, and *4912*
Ac 3:11 And as the lame *man* which was healed **h** *2902*
11:18 they heard these *things*, they **h** their **peace**, *2270*
14: 4 and part **h** with the Jews, and part with *1510*
15:13 And after they had **h** their **peace**, *4601*
Ro 7: 6 *that* being dead wherein we were **h**; *2722*
Rev 6: 9 of God, and for the testimony which they **h**: *2192*

HELD FAST See CLEAVE; CLEAVED; CLEAVETH

HELDAI (2)
1Ch 27:15 the twelfth month *was* **H** the Netophathite, 2469
Zec 6:10 *even* of **H**, of Tobijah, and of Jedaiah, 2469

HELEB (1)
2Sa 23:29 **H** the son of Baanah, a Netophathite, 2460

HELED (1)
1Ch 11:30 **H** the son of Baanah the Netophathite, 2466

HELEK (2) [HELEKITES]
Nu 26:30 of **H**, the family of the Helekites: 2507
Jos 17: 2 for the children of **H**, and for the children 2507

HELEKITES (1) [HELEK]
Nu 26:30 of Helek, the family of the **H**: 2516

HELEM (2)
1Ch 7:35 the son of his brother **H**; Zophah, and 1987
Zec 6:14 the crowns shall be to **H**, and to Tobijah, 2494

HELEPH (1)
Jos 19:33 their coast was from **H**, from Allon to 2501

HELEZ (5)
2Sa 23:26 **H** the Paltite, Ira the son of Ikkesh 2503
1Ch 2:39 Azariah begat **H**, and Helez begat Eleasah, 2503
2:39 Azariah begat Helez, and **H** begat Eleasah, 2503
11:27 Shammoth the Harorite, **H** the Pelonite, 2503
27:10 for the seventh month *was* **H** the Pelonite, 2503

HELI (1)
Lk 3:23 the son of Joseph, which was *the son* of **H**, *2242*

HELKAI (1)
Ne 12:15 Of Harim, Adna; of Meraioth, **H**; 2517

HELKATH (2) [HELKATH-HAZZURIM]
Jos 19:25 their border was **H**, and Hali, and Beten, 2520
21:31 **H** with her suburbs, and Rehob with her 2520

HELKATH-HAZZURIM (1) [HELKATH]
2Sa 2:16 wherefore that place was called **H**, which *is* 2521

HELL (54)
Dt 32:22 shall burn unto the lowest **h**, and 7585
2Sa 22: 6 The sorrows of **h** compassed me about; 7585
Job 11: 8 deeper than **h**; what canst thou know? 7585
26: 6 **H** *is* naked before him, and destruction hath 7585
Ps 9:17 The wicked shall be turned into **h**, *and* 7585
16:10 For thou wilt not leave my soul in **h**; 7585
18: 5 The sorrows of **h** compassed me about: 7585
55:15 *and* let them go down quick *into* **h**: 7585
86:13 hast delivered my soul from the lowest **h**. 7585
116: 3 and the pains of **h** gat hold upon me: 7585
139: 8 if I make my bed in **h**, behold, thou *art* 7585
Pr 5: 5 go down *to* death; her steps take hold on **h**. 7585
7:27 Her house *is* the way to **h**, going down to 7585
9:18 *and that* her guests *are* in the depths of **h**. 7585
15:11 **H** and destruction *are* before the LORD: 7585
15:24 that *he* may depart from **h** beneath. 7585
23:14 the rod, and shalt deliver his soul from **h**. 7585
27:20 **H** and destruction are never full; so 7585
Isa 5:14 Therefore **h** hath enlarged herself, 7585
14: 9 **H** from beneath is moved for thee to meet 7585
14:15 Yet thou shalt be brought down to **h**, to 7585
28:15 with death, and with **h** are we at agreement; 7585
28:18 and your agreement with **h** shall not stand; 7585
57: 9 and didst debase *thyself even* unto **h**. 7585
Eze 31:16 when I cast him down to **h** with them that 7585
31:17 They also went down into **h** with him unto 7585
32:21 of the midst of **h** with them that help him: 7585
32:27 which are gone down *to* **h** with their 7585
Am 9: 2 Though they dig into **h**, thence shall mine 7585
Jnh 2: 2 out of the belly of **h** cried I, *and* 7585
Hab 2: 5 who enlargeth his desire as **h**, and *is* as 7585
Mt 5:22 *Thou* fool, shall be in danger of **h** fire. *1067*
5:29 *that* thy whole body should be cast into **h**. *1067*
5:30 *that* thy whole body should be cast into **h**. *1067*
10:28 is able to destroy both soul and body in **h**. *1067*
11:23 unto heaven, shalt be brought down to **h**: *86*
16:18 and the gates of **h** shall not prevail against it. *86*
18: 9 than having two eyes to be cast into **h** *1067*
23:15 ye make him twofold more *the* child of **h** *1067*
23:33 how can ye escape the damnation of **h**? *1067*
Mk 9:43 than having two hands to go into **h**, into *1067*
9:45 than having two feet to be cast into **h**, *1067*
9:47 than having two eyes to be cast into **h** fire: *1067*
Lk 10:15 exalted to heaven, shalt be thrust down to **h**. *86*
12: 5 *he* hath killed hath power to cast into **h**; *1067*
16:23 And in **h** he lift up his eyes, being in *86*
Ac 2:27 Because thou wilt not leave my soul in **h**, *86*
2:31 of Christ, that his soul was not left in **h**, *86*
Jas 3: 6 course of nature; and it is set on fire of **h**. *1067*
2Pe 2: 4 but **cast** *them* **down to h**, and *5020*
Rev 1:18 Amen; and have the keys of **h** and of death. *86*
6: 8 on him *was* Death, and **H** followed with him. *86*
20:13 **h** delivered up the dead which were in them: *86*
20:14 and **h** were cast into the lake of fire. *86*

HELM (1)
Jas 3: 4 are they turned about with a very small **h**, *4079*

HELMET (8) [HELMETS]
1Sa 17: 5 *he had* a **h** of brass upon his head, and 3553
17:38 and he put a **h** of brass upon his head; 6959
Isa 59:17 and a **h** of salvation upon his head; 3553
Eze 23:24 thee buckler and shield and **h** round about: 6959
27:10 they hanged the shield and **h** in thee; 3553
38: 5 with them; all of them *with* shield and **h**: 3553
Eph 6:17 And take the **h** of salvation, and the sword *4030*
1Th 5: 8 and love; and for a **h**, the hope of salvation. *4030*

HELMETS (2) [HELMET]
2Ch 26:14 **h**, and habergeons, and bows, and slings to 3553
Jer 46: 4 ye horsemen, and stand forth with *your* **h**; 3553

HELON (5)
Nu 1: 9 Of Zebulun; Eliab the son of **H**. 2497
2: 7 Eliab the son of **H** *shall be* captain of 2497
7:24 On the third day Eliab the son of **H**, 2497
7:29 this *was* the offering of Eliab the son of **H**. 2497
10:16 children of Zebulun *was* Eliab the son of **H**. 2497

HELP (126) [FELLOWHELPER, FELLOWHELPERS, HELPED, HELPER, HELPERS, HELPETH, HELPING, HELPS, HOLPEN]
Ge 2:18 be alone; I will make him a **h** meet for him. 5828
2:20 for Adam there was not found a **h** meet for 5828
49:25 by the God of thy father, who shall **h** thee; 5826
Ex 18: 4 *said he, was* mine **h**, and delivered me from 5828
23: 5 wouldest forbear to **h** him, thou shalt surely 5800
23: 5 thou shalt **surely h** with him. 5800+5800
Dt 22: 4 thou shalt surely **h** him to lift *them* up 5973
32:38 let them rise up and **h** you, *and* be your 5826
33: 7 and be thou a **h** *to him* from his enemies. 5828
33:26 *who* rideth *upon* the heaven in thy **h**, and 5828
33:29 the shield of thy **h**, and who *is* the sword of 5828
Jos 1:14 all the mighty *men* of valour, and **h** them; 5826

Jos 10: 4 Come up unto me, and **h** me, that we may 5826
10: 6 up to us quickly, and save us, and **h** us: 5826
10:33 Horam king of Gezer came up to **h** 5826
Jdg 5:23 they came not to the **h** of the LORD, 5833
5:23 to the **h** of the LORD against the mighty. 5833
1Sa 11: 9 by *that time* the sun be hot, ye shall have **h**. 8668
2Sa 10:11 strong for me, then thou shalt **h** me: 1961+3444
10:11 strong for thee, then I will come and **h** thee. 3467
10:19 So the Syrians feared to **h** the children of 3467
14: 4 and did obeisance, and said, **H**, O king. 3467
2Ki 6:26 unto him, saying, **H**, my lord, O king. 3467
6:27 he said, *If* the LORD do not **h** thee, 3467
6:27 do not help thee, whence shall I **h** thee? 3467
1Ch 12:17 If ye be come peaceably unto me to **h** me, 5826
12:22 day by day there came to David to **h** him, 5826
18: 5 when the Syrians of Damascus came to **h** 5826
19:12 strong for me, then thou shalt **h** me: 1961+8668
19:12 be too strong for thee, then I will **h** thee. 3467
19:19 neither would the Syrians **h** the children of 3467
22:17 the princes of Israel to **h** Solomon his son, 5826
2Ch 14:11 said, LORD, *it is* nothing with thee to **h**, 5826
14:11 **h** us, O LORD our God; for we rest on 5826
19: 2 Shouldest thou **h** the ungodly, and 5826
20: 4 to ask *h* of the LORD: NIH
20: 9 in our affliction, then thou wilt hear and **h**. 3467
25: 8 for God hath power to **h**, and to cast down. 5826
26:13 to **h** the king against the enemy. 5826
28:16 send unto the kings of Assyria to **h** him. 5826
28:23 Because the gods of the kings of Syria **h** 5826
28:23 will I sacrifice to them, that they may **h** me. 5826
29:34 wherefore their brethren the Levites did **h** 2388
32: 3 *were* without the city: and they did **h** him. 5826
32: 8 with us *is* the LORD our God to **h** us, and 5826
Ezr 1: 4 let the men of his place **h** him with silver, 5375
8:22 horsemen to **h** us against the enemy in 5826
Job 6:13 *Is* not my **h** in me? and is wisdom driven 5833
8:20 will he **h** the evil doers: 2388+3027+871.1
29:12 and *him that had* none to **h** him. 5826
31:21 the fatherless, when I saw my **h** in the gate: 5833
Ps 3: 2 of my soul, *There is* no **h** for him in God. 3444
12: 1 **H**, LORD; for the godly *man* ceaseth; 3467
20: 2 Send thee **h** from the sanctuary, and 5828
22:11 for trouble *is* near; for *there is* none to **h**. 5826
22:19 O my strength, haste thee to **h** me. 5833
27: 9 thou hast been my **h**; leave me not, 5833
33:20 for the LORD: he *is* our **h** and our shield. 5828
35: 2 and buckler, and stand up for mine **h**. 5833
37:40 the LORD shall **h** them, and deliver them: 5826
38:22 Make haste to **h** me, O Lord my salvation. 5833
40:13 deliver me: O LORD, make haste to **h** me. 5833
40:17 thou *art* my **h** and my deliverer; make no 5833
42: 5 for I shall yet praise him *for* the **h** of his 3444
44:26 Arise for our **h**, and redeem us for thy 5833
46: 1 and strength, a very present **h** in trouble. 5833
46: 5 God shall **h** her, *and that* right early. 5826
59: 4 *my* fault: awake to **h** me, and behold. 7125
60:11 Give us **h** from trouble: for vain *is* the help 5833
60:11 help from trouble: for vain *is* the **h** of man. 8668
63: 7 Because thou hast been my **h**, therefore 5833
70: 1 deliver me; make haste to **h** me, O LORD. 5833
70: 5 thou *art* my **h** and my deliverer; O LORD, 5828
71:12 from me: O my God, make haste for my **h**. 5833
79: 9 **H** us, O God of our salvation, for the glory 5826
89:19 I have laid **h** upon *one that is* mighty; 5828
94:17 Unless the LORD *had been* my **h**, my soul 5833
107:12 they fell down, and *there was* none to **h**. 5826
108:12 Give us **h** from trouble: for vain *is* the help 5833
108:12 help from trouble: for vain *is* the **h** of man. 8668
109:26 **H** me, O LORD my God: O save me 5826
115: 9 the LORD: he *is* their **h** and their shield. 5828
115:10 the LORD: he *is* their **h** and their shield. 5828
115:11 the LORD: he *is* their **h** and their shield. 5828
118: 7 taketh my part with them that **h** me: 5826
119:86 they persecute me wrongfully; **h** thou me. 5826
119:173 Let thine hand **h** me; for I have chosen thy 5826
119:175 praise thee; and let thy judgments **h** me. 5826
121: 1 unto the hills, from whence cometh my **h**. 5828
121: 2 My **h** *cometh* from the LORD, 5828
124: 8 Our **h** *is* in the name of the LORD, 5828
146: 3 in the son of man, in whom *there is* no **h**. 8668
146: 5 *is he* that *hath* the God of Jacob for his **h**, 5828
Ecc 4:10 for *he hath* not another to **h** him **up**. 6965
Isa 10: 3 to whom will ye flee for **h**? and where will 5833
20: 6 whither we flee for **h** to be delivered from 5833
30: 5 nor be a **h** nor profit, but a shame, and 5828
30: 7 For the Egyptians shall **h** in vain, and to no 5826
31: 1 Woe to them that go down *to* Egypt for **h**; 5833
31: 2 against the **h** of them that work iniquity. 5833
41:10 yea, I will **h** thee; yea, I will uphold thee 5826
41:13 saying unto thee, Fear not; I will **h** thee. 5826
41:14 I will **h** thee, saith the LORD, and 5826
44: 2 thee from the womb, *which* will **h** thee; 5826
50: 7 For the Lord GOD will **h** me; therefore 5826
50: 9 Behold, the Lord GOD will **h** me; who *is* 5826
63: 5 I looked, and *there was* none to **h**; and 5826
Jer 37: 7 which is come forth to **h** you, 5833
La 1: 7 the hand of the enemy, and none did **h** her: 5826
4:17 for us, our eyes as yet failed for our vain **h**: 5833
Eze 12:14 every wind all that *are* about him to **h** him, 5828
32:21 of the midst of hell with them that **h** him: 5826
Da 10:13 one of the chief princes, came to **h** me; 5826
11:34 they shall be holpen *with* a little **h**: 5828
11:45 shall come to his end, and none shall **h** him. 5826
Hos 13: 9 hast destroyed thyself; but in me *is* thine **h**. 5828
Mt 15:25 and worshipped him, saying, Lord, **h** me. *997*
Mk 9:22 any *thing,* have compassion on us, and **h** us. *997*
9:24 Lord, I believe; **h** thou mine unbelief. *997*
Lk 5: 7 that *they* should come and **h** them. *4815*
10:40 bid her therefore that she **h** me. *4878*
Ac 16: 9 Come over into Macedonia, and **h** us. *997*
21:28 Crying out, Men of Israel, **h**: This is *997*
26:22 Having therefore obtained **h** of God, *1947*
Php 4: 3 **h** those *women* which laboured with me in *4815*
Heb 4:16 and find grace to **h** in time of need. *996*

HELPED (24) [HELP]

Ex 2:17 Moses stood up and **h** them, and 3467
1Sa 7:12 Hitherto hath the LORD **h** us. 5826
1Ki 1: 7 and they following Adonijah **h** *him.* 5826
20:16 the thirty and two kings that **h** him. 5826
1Ch 5:20 they were **h** against them, and the Hagarites 5826
12:19 they **h** them not: for the lords of 5826
12:21 they **h** David against the band *of the rovers:* 5826
15:26 when God **h** the Levites that bare the ark of 5826
2Ch 18:31 cried out, and the LORD **h** him; 5826
20:23 of Seir, every one **h** to destroy another. 5826
26: 7 God **h** him against the Philistines, and 5826
26:15 for he was marvellously **h**, till he was 5826
28:21 unto the king of Assyria: but he **h** him not. 5833
Ezr 10:15 and Shabbethai the Levite **h** them. 5826
Est 9: 3 and officers of the king, **h** the Jews; 5375
Job 26: 2 How hast thou **h** *him that is* without 5826
Ps 28: 7 my heart trusted in him, and I am **h**: 5826
116: 6 the simple: I was brought low, and he **h** me. 3467
118:13 me that *I* might fall: but the LORD **h** me. 5826
Isa 41: 6 They **h** every one his neighbour; and 5826
49: 8 and in a day of salvation have I **h** thee: 5826
Zec 1:15 and they **h** **forward** the affliction. 5826
Ac 18:27 **h** them much which had believed through *4820*
Rev 12:16 And the earth **h** the woman, and the earth *997*

HELPER (9) [HELP]

2Ki 14:26 shut up, nor any left, nor any **h** for Israel. 5826
Job 30:13 set forward my calamity, they have no **h**. 5826
Ps 10:14 unto thee; thou art the **h** of the fatherless. 5826
30:10 mercy upon me: LORD, be thou my **h**. 5826
54: 4 Behold, God *is* mine **h**: the Lord *is* with 5826
72:12 the poor also, and *him* that hath no **h**. 5826
Jer 47: 4 and Zidon every **h** that remaineth: 5826
Ro 16: 9 Salute Urban our **h** in Christ, and *4904*
Heb 13: 6 The Lord *is* my **h**, and I will not fear what *998*

HELPERS (7) [HELP]

1Ch 12: 1 they *were* among the mighty *men,* **h** of 5826
12:18 peace *be* unto thee, and peace *be* to thine **h**; 5826
Job 9:13 his anger, the proud **h** do stoop under him. 5826
Eze 30: 8 and *when* all her **h** shall be destroyed. 5826
Na 3: 9 *it was* infinite; Put and Lubim were thy **h**. 5833
Ro 16: 3 and Aquila my **h** in Christ Jesus: *4904*
2Co 1:24 over your faith, but are **h** of your joy: *4904*

HELPETH (4) [HELP]

1Ch 12:18 *be* to thine helpers; for thy God **h** thee. 5826
Isa 31: 3 both he that **h** shall fall, and he that is 5826
Ro 8:26 Likewise the Spirit also **h** our infirmities: *4878*
1Co 16:16 and to every one that **h** **with** *us,* and *4903*

HELPING (3) [HELP]
Ezr 5: 2 with them *were* the prophets of God **h** 5583
Ps 22: 1 *why art thou so* far from **h** me, *and* 3444
2Co 1:11 You also **h together** by prayer for us, *4943*

HELPING THE POOR See ALMSDEEDS

HELPS (2) [HELP]
Ac 27:17 taken up, they used **h**, undergirding the ship; *996*
1Co 12:28 then gifts of healings, **h**, governments, *484*

HELVE (1)
Dt 19: 5 the head slippeth from the **h**, and 6086

HEM (7) [HEMS]
Ex 28:33 *beneath* upon the **h** of it thou shalt make 7757
28:33 and of scarlet, round about the **h** thereof; 7757
28:34 upon the **h** of the robe round about. 7757
39:25 the pomegranates upon the **h** of the robe, 7757
39:26 round about the **h** of the robe to minister *in;* 7757
Mt 9:20 and touched the **h** of his garment: *2899*
14:36 they might only touch the **h** of his garment: *2899*

HEMAM (1)
Ge 36:22 the children of Lotan were Hori and **H**; 1967

HEMAN (17)
1Ki 4:31 **H**, and Chalcol, and Darda, the sons of 1968
1Ch 2: 6 and Ethan, and **H**, and Calcol, and Dara: 1968
6:33 **H** a singer, the son of Joel, the son of 1968
15:17 So the Levites appointed **H** the son of Joel; 1968
15:19 So the singers, **H**, Asaph, and Ethan, 1968
16:41 with them **H** and Jeduthun, and the rest that 1968
16:42 with them **H** and Jeduthun *with* trumpets 1968
25: 1 of **H**, and of Jeduthun, who should 1968
25: 4 Of **H**: the sons of Heman; Bukkiah, 1968
25: 4 the sons of **H**; Bukkiah, Mattaniah, Uzziel, 1968
25: 5 All these *were* the sons of **H** the king's seer 1968
25: 5 God gave to **H** fourteen sons and 1968
25: 6 the king's order *to* Asaph, Jeduthun, and **H**. 1968
2Ch 5:12 of **H**, of Jeduthun, with their sons and 1968
29:14 of the sons of **H**; Jehiel, and Shimei: and 1968
35:15 and **H**, and Jeduthun the king's seer; 1968
Ps 88: T Maschil of **H** the Ezrahite. 1968

HEMATH (3)
1Ch 2:55 These *are* the Kenites that came of **H**, 2575
13: 5 of Egypt even unto the entering of **H**, 2574
Am 6:14 in of **H** unto the river of the wilderness. 2574

HEMDAN (1)
Ge 36:26 **H**, and Eshban, and Ithran, and Cheran. 2533

HEMLOCK (2)
Hos 10: 4 thus judgment springeth up as **h** in 7219
Am 6:12 and the fruit of righteousness into **h**: 3939

HEMS (1) [HEM]
Ex 39:24 they made upon the **h** of the robe 7757

HEN (3)
Zec 6:14 to Jedaiah, and to **H** the son of Zephaniah, 2581
Mt 23:37 even as a **h** gathereth her chickens under *3733*
Lk 13:34 as a **h** *doth gather* her brood under *her* *3733*

HENA (3)
2Ki 18:34 *are* the gods of Sepharvaim, **H**, and Ivah? 2012
19:13 of the city of Sepharvaim, *of* **H**, and Ivah? 2012
Isa 37:13 of the city of Sepharvaim, **H**, and Ivah? 2012

HENADAD (4)
Ezr 3: 9 the sons of **H**, *with* their sons and 2582
Ne 3:18 repaired their brethren, Bavai the son of **H**, 2582
3:24 After him repaired Binnui the son of **H** 2582
10: 9 Binnui of the sons of **H**, Kadmiel; 2582

HENCE (30) [HENCEFORTH, HENCEFORWARD]
Ge 37:17 the man said, They are departed **h**; 2088+4480
42:15 of Pharaoh ye shall not go forth **h**, 2088+4480
50:25 and ye shall carry up my bones from **h**. 2088
Ex 11: 1 afterwards he will let you go **h**: 2088+4480
11: 1 surely thrust you out **h** altogether. 2088+4480
13:19 ye shall carry up my bones away **h** with 2088
33: 1 *and* go up **h**, thou and the people which 2088
33:15 go not *with me,* carry us not up **h**. 2088+4480
Dt 9:12 Arise, get thee down quickly from **h**; 2088
Jos 4: 3 Take you **h** out of the midst of Jordan, NIH
Jdg 6:18 Depart not **h**, I pray thee, until I 2088+4480
Ru 2: 8 neither go from **h**, but abide here fast by 2088
1Ki 17: 3 Get thee **h**, and turn thee eastward, 2088+4480
Ps 39:13 before I go **h**, and be no more. NIH
Isa 30:22 thou shalt say unto it, **Get** thee **h**. 3318
Jer 38:10 Take from **h** thirty men with thee, and 2088
Zec 6: 7 Get ye *h*, walk to and fro through the earth. NIH
Mt 4:10 saith Jesus unto him, **Get** thee **h**, Satan: *5217*
17:20 this mountain, Remove **h** to yonder place; *1782*
Lk 4: 9 the Son of God, cast thyself down **from h**: *1782*
13:31 unto him, Get *thee* out, and depart **h**: *1782*
16:26 that they which would pass **from h** to you *1782*
Jn 2:16 them that sold doves, Take these *things* **h**; *1782*
7: 3 said unto him, Depart **h**, and go into Judea, *1782*
14:31 *even* so I do. Arise, let us go **h**. *1782*
18:36 but now is my kingdom not **from h**. *1782*
20:15 if thou have borne him *h*, tell me where NIG
Ac 1: 5 the Holy Ghost not many days **h**. *3326+3778*
22:21 for I will send thee **far h** unto the Gentiles. *3112*
Jas 4: 1 *come they* not **h**, *even* of your lusts that *1782*

HENCEFORTH (33) [FORTH, HENCE]
Ge 4:12 it shall not **h** yield unto thee her strength; 3254
Nu 18:22 Neither must the children of Israel **h** come 5750
Dt 17:16 Ye shall **h** return no more that way. 3254
19:20 shall **h** commit no more any such evil 3254
Jdg 2:21 I also will not **h** drive out any from before 3254
2Ki 5:17 for thy servant will **h** offer neither burnt 5750
2Ch 16: 9 therefore from **h** thou shalt have wars. 6258
Ps 125: 2 about his people from **h** even for ever. 6258
131: 3 Let Israel hope in the LORD from **h** and 6258
Isa 9: 7 and with justice from **h** even for ever. 6258
52: 1 for **h** there shall no more come into thee 3254
59:21 saith the LORD, from **h** and for ever. 6258
Eze 36:12 thou shalt no more **h** bereave them of men. 3254
Mic 4: 7 reign over them in mount Zion from **h**, 6258
Mt 23:39 Ye shall not see me **h**, till ye shall say, *575+737*
26:29 will not drink **h** of this fruit of the vine, *575+737*
Lk 1:48 from **h** all generations shall call me *3568+3588*
5:10 from **h** thou shalt catch men. *3568+3588*
12:52 For from **h** there shall be five in one *3568+3588*
Jn 14: 7 and from **h** ye know him, and have seen him. *737*
15:15 **H** I call you **not** servants; for the servant *3765*
Ac 4:17 that *they* speak **h** to no man in this name. *3371*
18: 6 from **h** I will go unto the Gentiles. *3568*
Ro 6: 6 that **h** we should **not** serve sin. *3371*
2Co 5:15 that they which live should **not h** live unto *3371*
5:16 Wherefore **h** know we no *man* *575+3568+3588*
5:16 the flesh, yet **now h** know we *him* no more. *3568*
Gal 6:17 **From h** let no *man* trouble me: for I *3062+3588*
Eph 4:14 That we *h* be no more children, tossed to NIG
4:17 that ye **h** walk **not** as other Gentiles walk, *3371*
2Ti 4: 8 **H** there is laid up for me a crown of *3062*
Heb 10:13 From **h** expecting till his enemies be *3062+3588*
Rev 14:13 *are* the dead which die in the Lord from **h**: *534*

HENCEFORWARD (2) [FORWARD, HENCE]
Nu 15:23 and **h** among your generations; 1973
Mt 21:19 Let **no** fruit grow on thee **h** for ever. *3371*

HENNA See CAMPHIRE

HENOCH (2) [ENOCH]
1Ch 1: 3 **H**, Methuselah, Lamech, 2585
1:33 and Epher, and **H**, and Abida, and Eldaah. 2585

HEPHER (9) [GATH-HEPHER, HEPHERITES]
Nu 26:32 and *of* **H**, the family of the Hepherites. 2660
26:33 Zelophehad the son of **H** had no sons, but 2660
27: 1 the son of **H**, the son of Gilead, the son of 2660
Jos 12:17 king of Tappuah, one; the king of **H**, one; 2660
17: 2 for the children of **H**, and for the children 2660
17: 3 Zelophehad, the son of **H**, the son of 2660
1Ki 4:10 *pertained* Sochoh, and all the land of **H**: 2660
1Ch 4: 6 and **H**, and Temeni, and Haahashtari. 2660
11:36 **H** the Mecherathite, Ahijah the Pelonite, 2660

HEPHERITES (1) [HEPHER]
Nu 26:32 and *of* Hepher, the family of the **H**. 2662

HEPHZI-BAH (2)
2Ki 21: 1 And his mother's name *was* **H**. 2657
Isa 62: 4 thou shalt be called **H**, and thy land Beulah: 2657

HER (1993) [SHE] See Index

HERALD (1)
Da 3: 4 a **h** cried aloud, To you it is commanded, 3744

HERB (19) [HERBS]
Ge 1:11 the **h** yielding seed, *and* the fruit tree 6212
1:12 *and* **h** yielding seed after his kind, and 6212
1:29 I have given you every **h** bearing seed, 6212
1:30 *is* life, *I have given* every green **h** for meat: 6212
2: 5 and every **h** of the field before it grew: 6212
3:18 to thee; and thou shalt eat the **h** of the field; 6212
9: 3 *even* as the green **h** have I given you all 6212
Ex 9:22 upon beast, and upon every **h** of the field, 6212
9:25 the hail smote every **h** of the field, and 6212
10:12 eat every **h** of the land, *even* all that the hail 6212
10:15 they did eat every **h** of the land, and all 6212
Dt 32: 2 as the small rain upon the **tender h**, and 1877
2Ki 19:26 *as* the green **h**, *as* the grass on 1877
Job 8:12 cut down, it withereth before any *other* **h**. 2682
38:27 to cause the bud of the **tender h** to spring 1877
Ps 37: 2 like the grass, and wither as the green **h**. 1877
104:14 for the cattle, and **h** for the service of man: 6212
Isa 37:27 *as* the green **h**, *as* the grass on 1877
66:14 and your bones shall flourish like an **h**: 1877

HERBS (18) [HERB]
Ex 10:15 or in the **h** of the field, through all the land 6212
12: 8 *and* with bitter *h* they shall eat it. NIH
Nu 9:11 eat it with unleavened bread and bitter *h*. NIH
Dt 11:10 wateredst *it* with thy foot, as a garden of **h**: 3419
1Ki 21: 2 that I may have it for a garden of **h**, 3419
2Ki 4:39 one went out into the field to gather **h**, and 219
Ps 105:35 did eat up all the **h** in their land, and 6212
Pr 15:17 Better *is* a dinner of **h** where love is, than a 3419
27:25 and **h** of the mountains are gathered. 6212
Isa 18: 4 my dwelling place like a clear heat upon **h**, 216
26:19 for thy dew *is as* the dew of **h**, and the earth 219
42:15 and hills, and dry up all their **h**; 6212
Jer 12: 4 land mourn, and the **h** of every field wither, 6212
Mt 13:32 it is the greatest among **h**, and becometh a *3001*
Mk 4:32 and becometh greater than all **h**, and *3001*
Lk 11:42 ye tithe mint and rue and all *manner of* **h**, *3001*
Ro 14: 2 all *things:* another, who is weak, eateth **h**. *3001*
Heb 6: 7 bringeth forth **h** meet for them by whom it *1008*

HERD (22) [HERDMAN, HERDMEN, HERDS, SHEPHERD, SHEPHERD'S, SHEPHERDS, SHEPHERDS']
Ge 18: 7 Abraham ran unto the **h**, and fetcht a calf 1241
Lev 1: 2 of the cattle, *even* of the **h**, and of the flock. 1241
1: 3 If his offering *be* a burnt sacrifice of the **h**, 1241
3: 1 of peace offering, if he offer *it* of the **h**; 1241
27:32 *concerning* the tithe of the **h**, or of 1241
Nu 15: 3 unto the LORD, of the **h**, or of the flock: 1241
Dt 12:21 thou shalt kill of thy **h** and of thy flock, 1241
15:19 All the firstling males that come of thy **h** 1241
16: 2 the LORD thy God, *of* the flock and the **h**, 1241
1Sa 11: 5 Saul came after the **h** out of the field; 1241
2Sa 12: 4 to take of his own flock and of his own **h**, 1241
Jer 31:12 and for the young of the flock and of the **h**: 1241
Jnh 3: 7 man nor beast, **h** nor flock, taste any thing: 1241
Hab 3:17 and *there shall be* no **h** in the stalls: 1241
Mt 8:30 And there was a good way off from them a **h** *34*
8:31 suffer us to go away into the **h** of swine. *34*
8:32 were come out, they went into the **h** of swine: *34*
8:32 the whole **h** of swine ran violently down a *34*
Mk 5:11 unto the mountains a great **h** of swine feeding. *34*
5:13 the **h** ran violently down a steep place into *34*
Lk 8:32 And there was there a **h** of many swine *34*
8:33 the **h** ran violently down a steep place into *34*

HERDMAN (1) [HERD, MAN]
Am 7:14 I *was* a **h**, and a gatherer of sycomore fruit: 951

HERDMEN (8) [HERD, MAN]
Ge 13: 7 there was a strife between the **h** of Abram's 7462
13: 7 of Abram's cattle and the **h** of Lot's cattle: 7462
13: 8 and between my **h** and thy herdmen; 7462
13: 8 and between my herdmen and thy **h**; 7462
26:20 the **h** of Gerar did strive with Isaac's 7462
26:20 herdmen of Gerar did strive with Isaac's **h**, 7462
1Sa 21: 7 the chiefest of the **h** that *belonged* to Saul. 7462
Am 1: 1 of Amos, who was among the **h** of Tekoa, 5349

HERDS (33) [HERD]
Ge 13: 5 with Abram, had flocks, and **h**, and tents. 1241
24:35 **h**, and silver, and gold, and menservants, 1241
26:14 possession of **h**, and great store of servants: 1241
32: 7 the flocks, and **h**, and the camels, into two 1241
33:13 the flocks and **h** with young *are* with me: 1241
45:10 thy flocks, and thy **h**, and all that thou hast: 1241
46:32 and their **h**, and all that they have. 1241
47: 1 and their **h**, and all that they have, 1241
47:17 and for the cattle of the **h**, and for the asses: 1241
47:18 is spent; my lord also had our **h** of cattle; 4735
50: 8 little ones, and their flocks, and their **h**, 1241
Ex 10: 9 with our flocks and with our **h** will we go; 1241
10:24 only let your flocks and your **h** be stayed: 1241
12:32 Also take your flocks and your **h**, as ye 1241
12:38 and flocks, and **h**, *even* very much cattle. 1241
34: 3 neither let the flocks nor **h** feed before that 1241
Nu 11:22 Shall the flocks and the **h** be slain for them, 1241
Dt 8:13 *when* thy **h** and thy flocks multiply, and 1241
12: 6 the firstlings of your **h** and of your flocks: 1241
12:17 or the firstlings of thy **h** or of thy flock, 1241
14:23 and the firstlings of thy **h** and of thy flocks; 1241
1Sa 30:20 David took all the flocks and the **h**, 1241
2Sa 12: 2 rich *man* had exceeding many flocks and **h**: 1241
1Ch 27:29 over the **h** that fed in Sharon *was* Shitrai 1241
27:29 over the **h** *that were* in the valleys *was* 1241
2Ch 32:29 possessions of flocks and **h** in abundance: 1241
Ne 10:36 and the firstlings of our **h** and of our flocks, 1241
Pr 27:23 state of thy flocks, *and* look well to thy **h**. 5739
Isa 65:10 the valley of Achor a place for the **h** to lie 1241
Jer 3:24 their flocks and their **h**, their sons and their 1241
5:17 they shall eat up thy flocks and thine **h**: 1241
Hos 5: 6 and with their **h** to seek the LORD; 1241
Joel 1:18 the **h** of cattle are perplexed, because 5739

HERE (162) [HEREAFTER, HEREBY, HEREIN, HEREOF, HERETOFORE, HEREUNTO, HEREWITH] See Index

HEREAFTER (14) [AFTER, HERE] See Index

HEREBY (13) [BY, HERE] See Index

HEREIN (9) [HERE, IN] See Index

HEREOF (2) [HERE, OF]
Mt 9:26 And the fame **h** went abroad into all that *3778*
Heb 5: 3 And **by reason h** he ought, as for *1223+3778*

HERES (1)
Jdg 1:35 the Amorites would dwell in mount **H** in 2776

HERESH (1)
1Ch 9:15 **H**, and Galal, and Mattaniah the son of 2792

HERESIES (3) [HERESY]
1Co 11:19 For there must be also **h** among you, *139*
Gal 5:20 emulations, wrath, strife, seditions, **h**, *139*
2Pe 2: 1 who privily shall bring in damnable **h**, *139*

HERESY (1) [HERESIES, HERETICK]
Ac 24:14 that after the way which they call **h**, so *139*

HERETICK (1) [HERESY]
Tit 3:10 A man *that is* a **h** after the first and *141*

HERETOFORE (8) [HERE, TO] See Index

HEREUNTO (2) [HERE, UNTO]
Ecc 2:25 or who else can hasten *h*, more than I? NIH
1Pe 2:21 For *even* **h** were ye called: because *1519+3778*

HEREWITH (2) [HERE, WITH]
Eze 16:29 and yet thou wast not satisfied **h**. 2063+871.1
Mal 3:10 prove me now **h**, saith the LORD 2063+871.1

HERITAGE (30) [HERITAGES]
Ex 6: 8 and to Jacob; and I will give it you *for* an **h**: 4181
Job 20:29 and the **h** appointed unto him by God. 5159
27:13 the **h** of oppressors, *which* they shall 5159
Ps 16: 6 in pleasant *places;* yea, I have a goodly **h**. 5159
61: 5 thou hast given *me* the **h** of those that fear 3425
94: 5 thy people, O LORD, and afflict thine **h**. 5159
111: 6 that *he* may give them the **h** of the heathen. 5159
119:111 Thy testimonies have I **taken as an h** for 5157
127: 3 Lo, children *are* an **h** of the LORD: *and* 5159
135:12 gave their land *for* an **h**, an heritage unto 5159

Ps 135:12 *for* an heritage, an **h** unto Israel his people. 5159
136:21 gave their land for an **h**: for his mercy 5159
136:22 *Even* an **h** unto Israel his servant: for his 5159
Isa 54:17 This *is* the **h** of the servants of the LORD, 5159
58:14 feed thee with the **h** of Jacob thy father: 5159
Jer 2: 7 my land, and made mine **h** an abomination. 5159
3:19 a goodly **h** of the hosts of nations? 5159
12: 7 forsaken mine house, I have left mine **h**; 5159
12: 8 Mine **h** is unto me as a lion in the forest; 5159
12: 9 Mine **h** *is* unto me *as* a speckled bird, 5159
12:15 every man to his **h**, and every man to his 5159
17: 4 shalt discontinue from thine **h** that I gave 5159
50:11 O ye destroyers of mine **h**, because ye are 5159
Joel 2:17 and give not thine **h** to reproach, 5159
3: 2 there for my people and *for* my **h** Israel, 5159
Mic 2: 2 a man and his house, even a man and his **h**. 5159
7:14 people with thy rod, the flock of thine **h**, 5159
7:18 the transgression of the remnant of his **h**? 5159
Mal 1: 3 his **h** waste for the dragons of 5159
1Pe 5: 3 Neither as being lords over *God's* **h**, but *2819*

HERITAGES (1) [HERITAGE]
Isa 49: 8 the earth, to cause to inherit the desolate **h**; 5159

HERMAS (1)
Ro 16:14 Phlegon, **H**, Patrobas, Hermes, and *2057*

HERMES (1)
Ro 16:14 **H**, and the brethren which are with them. *2060*

HERMOGENES (1)
2Ti 1:15 from me; of whom are Phygellus and **H**. *2061*

HERMON (13) [BAAL-HERMON, HERMONITES]
Dt 3: 8 from the river of Arnon unto mount **H**; 2768
3: 9 (*Which* **H** the Sidonians call Sirion; and 2768
4:48 even unto mount Sion, which *is* **H**, 2768
Jos 11: 3 *to* the Hivite under **H** in the land of 2768
11:17 in the valley of Lebanon under mount **H**: 2768
12: 1 from the river Arnon unto mount **H**, and 2768
12: 5 reigned in mount **H**, and in Salcah, and 2768
13: 5 from Baal-gad under mount **H** unto 2768
13:11 all mount **H**, and all Bashan unto Salcah; 2768
1Ch 5:23 and Senir, and *unto* mount **H**. 2768
Ps 89:12 Tabor and **H** shall rejoice in thy name. 2768
133: 3 As the dew of **H**, *and as the dew* that 2768
SS 4: 8 from the top of Shenir and **H**, from 2768

HERMONITES (1) [HERMON]
Ps 42: 6 and of the **H**, from the hill Mizar. 2769

HEROD (40) [HEROD'S, HERODIANS]
Mt 2: 1 of Judea in the days of **H** the king, *2264*
2: 3 When **H** the king had heard *these things,* he *2264*
2: 7 Then **H**, when he had privily called *2264*
2:12 in a dream that *they* should not return to **H**, *2264*
2:13 for **H** will seek the young child to destroy *2264*
2:15 And was there until the death of **H**: that it *2264*
2:16 Then **H**, when he saw that he was mocked *2264*
2:19 But when **H** was dead, behold, an angel of *2264*
2:22 reign in Judea in the room of his father **H**, *2264*
14: 1 At that time **H** the tetrarch heard of *2264*
14: 3 For **H** had laid hold on John, and *2264*
14: 6 danced before them, and pleased **H**. *2264*
Mk 6:14 And king **H** heard *of him;* (for his name *2264*
6:16 But when **H** heard *thereof,* he said, It is *2264*
6:17 For **H** himself had sent forth and laid hold *2264*
6:18 For John had said unto **H**, It is not lawful *2264*
6:20 For **H** feared John, knowing that he *was* a *2264*
6:21 that **H** on his birthday made a supper to his *2264*
6:22 and pleased **H** and them that sat with *him,* *2264*
8:15 of the Pharisees, and *of* the leaven of **H**. *2264*
Lk 1: 5 There was in the days of **H**, the king of *2264*
3: 1 and **H** being tetrarch of Galilee, and *2264*
3:19 But **H** the tetrarch, being reproved by him *2264*
3:19 and for all the evils which **H** had done, *2264*
9: 7 Now **H** the tetrarch heard of all that was *2264*
9: 9 And **H** said, John have I beheaded: but *2264*
13:31 and depart hence: for **H** will kill thee. *2264*
23: 7 he sent him to **H**, who himself also was at *2264*
23: 8 And when **H** saw Jesus, he was exceeding *2264*
23:11 And **H** with his men of war set him at *2264*
23:12 Pilate and **H** were made friends together: *2264*
23:15 No, nor yet **H**: for I sent you to him; *2264*
Ac 4:27 both **H**, and Pontius Pilate, with *2264*
12: 1 Now about that time **H** the king stretched *2264*
12: 6 And when **H** would have brought him *2264*
12:11 and hath delivered me out of the hand of **H**, *2264*
12:19 And when **H** had sought for him, and *2264*
12:20 And **H** was highly displeased with them of *2264*
12:21 And upon a set day **H**, arrayed in royal *2264*
13: 1 which had been brought up with **H** *2264*

HEROD'S (4) [HEROD]
Mt 14: 6 But when **H** birthday was kept, *2264*
Lk 8: 3 And Joanna the wife of Chuza **H** steward, *2264*
23: 7 knew that he belonged unto **H** jurisdiction, *2264*
Ac 23:35 And he commanded him to be kept in **H** *2264*

HERODIANS (3) [HEROD]
Mt 22:16 sent out unto him their disciples with the **H**, *2265*
Mk 3: 6 straightway took counsel with the **H** *2265*
12:13 him certain of the Pharisees and of the **H**, *2265*

HERODIAS (4) [HERODIAS']
Mt 14: 6 the daughter of **H** danced before them, and *2266*
Mk 6:19 Therefore **H** had a quarrel against him, and *2266*
6:22 And when the daughter of the said **H** came *2266*
Lk 3:19 being reproved by him for **H** his brother *2266*

HERODIAS' (2) [HERODIAS]
Mt 14: 3 and put *him* in prison for **H** sake, *2266*
Mk 6:17 and bound him in prison for **H** sake, *2266*

HERODION (1)
Ro 16:11 Salute **H** my kinsman. Greet them that be *2267*

HERON (2)
Lev 11:19 the **h** after her kind, and the lapwing, and 601
Dt 14:18 the **h** after her kind, and the lapwing, and 601

HERS (4) [SHE] See Index

HERSELF (42) [SELF, SHE] See Index

HESED (1)
1Ki 4:10 The son of **H**, in Aruboth; to him *pertained* 2618

HESHBON (38)
Nu 21:25 in **H**, and in all the villages thereof. 2809
21:26 For **H** *was* the city of Sihon the king of 2809
21:27 Come *into* **H**, let the city of Sihon be built 2809
21:28 For there is a fire gone out of **H**, a flame 2809
21:30 **H** is perished even unto Dibon, and 2809
21:34 king of the Amorites, which dwelt at **H**. 2809
32: 3 **H**, and Elealeh, and Shebam, and Nebo, 2809
32:37 the children of Reuben built **H**, and 2809
Dt 1: 4 which dwelt in **H**, and Og the king of 2809
2:24 Sihon the Amorite, king of **H**, and his land: 2809
2:26 unto Sihon king of **H** *with* words of peace, 2809
2:30 Sihon king of **H** would not let us pass by 2809
3: 2 king of the Amorites, which dwelt at **H**. 2809
3: 6 as we did unto Sihon king of **H**, 2809
4:46 who dwelt at **H**, whom Moses and 2809
29: 7 Sihon the king of **H**, and Og the king of 2809
Jos 9:10 to Sihon king of **H**, and to Og king of 2809
12: 2 who dwelt in **H**, *and* ruled from Aroer, 2809
12: 5 half Gilead, the border of Sihon king of **H**. 2809
13:10 which reigned in **H**, unto the border of 2809
13:17 **H**, and all her cities that *are* in the plain; 2809
13:21 king of the Amorites, which reigned in **H**, 2809
13:26 from **H** unto Ramath-mizpeh, and Betonim; 2809
13:27 the rest of the kingdom of Sihon king of **H**, 2809
21:39 **H** with her suburbs, Jazer with her suburbs; 2809
Jdg 11:19 Sihon king of the Amorites, the king of **H**; 2809
11:26 While Israel dwelt in **H** and her towns, and 2809
1Ch 6:81 **H** with her suburbs, and Jazer with her 2809
Ne 9:22 the land of the king of **H**, and the land of 2809
SS 7: 4 thine eyes *like* the *fish*pools in **H**, by 2809
Isa 15: 4 **H** shall cry, and Elealeh: their voice shall 2809
16: 8 For the fields of **H** languish, *and* the vine of 2809
16: 9 water thee *with* my tears, O **H**, and Elealeh: 2809
Jer 48: 2 in **H** they have devised evil against it; 2809
48:34 From the cry of **H** *even* unto Elealeh, *and* 2809
48:45 They that fled stood under the shadow of **H** 2809
48:45 a fire shall come forth out of **H**, and 2809
49: 3 Howl, O **H**, for Ai is spoiled: cry, 2809

HESHMON (1)
Jos 15:27 And Hazar-gaddah, and **H**, and Beth-palet, 2829

HETH (14)
Ge 10:15 Canaan begat Sidon his firstborn, and **H**, 2845
23: 3 and spake unto the sons of **H**, saying, 2845
23: 5 the children of **H** answered Abraham, 2845
23: 7 of the land, *even* to the children of **H**. 2845
23:10 Ephron dwelt amongst the children of **H**: 2845
23:10 in the audience of the children of **H**, 2845
23:16 named in the audience of the sons of **H**, 2845
23:18 in the presence of the children of **H**, 2845
23:20 of a buryingplace by the sons of **H**. 2845
25:10 Abraham purchased of the sons of **H**: 2845
27:46 of my life because of the daughters of **H**: 2845
27:46 if Jacob take a wife of the daughters of **H**, 2845
49:32 that *is* therein *was* from the children of **H**. 2845
1Ch 1:13 Canaan begat Zidon his firstborn, and **H**, 2845

HETHLON (2)
Eze 47:15 from the great sea, the way of **H**, as *men* go 2855
48: 1 the north end to the coast of the way of **H**, 2855

HEW (12) [HEWED, HEWER, HEWERS, HEWETH, HEWN]
Ex 34: 1 **H** thee two tables of stone like unto 6458
Dt 10: 1 **H** thee two tables of stone like unto 6458
12: 3 you shall **h down** the graven images of 1438
19: 5 the wood with his neighbour to **h** wood, 2404
1Ki 5: 6 command thou that they **h** me cedar trees 3772
5: 6 skill to **h** timber like unto the Sidonians. 3772
5:18 Hiram's builders did **h** *them,* and 6458
1Ch 22: 2 he set masons to **h** wrought stones to build 2672
2Ch 2: 2 fourscore thousand to **h** in the mountain, 2672
Jer 6: 6 **H** ye **down** trees, and cast a mount against 3772
Da 4:14 **H down** the tree, and cut off his branches, 1414
4:23 saying, **H** the tree **down**, and destroy it; 1414

HEWED (13) [HEW]
Ex 34: 4 he **h** two tables of stone like unto the first; 6458
Dt 10: 3 **h** two tables of stone like unto the first, and 6458
1Sa 11: 7 **h** them **in pieces**, and sent *them* throughout 5408
15:33 Samuel **h** Agag **in pieces** before 8158
1Ki 5:17 great stones, costly stones, *and* **h** stones, 1496
6:36 the inner court *with* three rows of **h stone**, 1496
7: 9 according to the measures of **h stones**, 1496
7:11 after the measures of **h stones**, and cedars. 1496
7:12 about *was with* three rows *of* **h stones**, 1496
2Ki 12:12 **h** stone to repair the breaches of the house 4274
Isa 22:16 that thou hast **h** thee **out** a sepulchre here, 2672
Jer 2:13 **h** them **out** cisterns, broken cisterns, 2672
Hos 6: 5 Therefore have I **h** *them* by the prophets; 2672

HEWER (1) [HEW]
Dt 29:11 from the **h** of thy wood unto the drawer of 2404

HEWERS (9) [HEW]
Jos 9:21 let them be **h** of wood and drawers of water 2404
9:23 **h** of wood and drawers of water for 2404
9:27 Joshua made them that day **h** of wood and 2404
1Ki 5:15 and fourscore thousand **h** in the mountains; 2672
2Ki 12:12 **h** of stone, and to buy timber and 2672
1Ch 22:15 **h** and workers of stone and timber, and 2672
2Ch 2:10 give to thy servants, the **h** that cut timber, 2404
2:18 fourscore thousand *to be* **h** in the mountain, 2672
Jer 46:22 come against her with axes, as **h** of wood. 2404

HEWETH (3) [HEW]
Isa 10:15 Shall the axe boast itself against him that **h** 2672
22:16 *as* he that **h** him **out** a sepulchre on high, 2672
44:14 *He* **h** him **down** cedars, and taketh 3772

HEWN (17) [HEW]
Ex 20:25 of stone, thou shalt not build it *of* **h stone**: 1496
2Ki 22: 6 buy timber and **h** stone to repair the house. 4274
2Ch 34:11 and builders gave they *it,* to buy **h** stone, 4274
Pr 9: 1 her house, she hath **h out** her seven pillars: 2672
Isa 9:10 but we will build *with* **h stones**: 1496
10:33 the high ones of stature *shall be* **h down**, 1438
33: 9 Lebanon is ashamed *and* **h down**: Sharon is 7060
51: 1 look unto the rock *whence* ye are **h**, and 2672
La 3: 9 He hath inclosed my ways with **h stone**, 1496
Eze 40:42 the four tables *were* of **h** stone for the burnt 1496
Am 5:11 ye have built houses of **h stone**, but 1496
Mt 3:10 bringeth not forth good fruit is **h down**, *1581*
7:19 that bringeth not forth good fruit is **h down**, *1581*
27:60 new tomb, which he had **h out** in the rock: *2998*
Mk 15:46 laid him in a sepulchre which was **h** out of *2998*
Lk 3: 9 bringeth not forth good fruit is **h down**, *1581*
23:53 laid it in a sepulchre *that was* **h in stone**, *2991*

HEZEKI (1)
1Ch 8:17 and Meshullam, and **H**, and Heber, 2395

HEZEKIAH (128) [EZEKIAS]
2Ki 16:20 and **H** his son reigned in his stead. 2396
18: 1 *that* **H** the son of Ahaz king of Judah *began* 2396
18: 9 it came to pass in the fourth year of king **H**, 2396
18:10 *even* in the sixth year of **H**, that *is* the ninth 2396
18:13 Now in the fourteenth year of king **H** did 2396
18:14 **H** king of Judah sent to the king of Assyria 2396
18:14 the king of Assyria appointed unto **H** king 2396
18:15 **H** gave *him* all the silver that was found *in* 2396
18:16 At that time did **H** cut off *the gold from* 2396
18:16 *from* the pillars which **H** king of Judah had 2396
18:17 Rab-shakeh from Lachish to king **H** with a 2396
18:19 Speak ye now to **H**, Thus saith the great 2396
18:22 and whose altars **H** hath taken away, 2396
18:29 Thus saith the king, Let not **H** deceive you: 2396
18:30 Neither let **H** make you trust in 2396
18:31 Hearken not to **H**: for thus saith the king of 2396
18:32 hearken not unto **H**, when he persuadeth 2396
18:37 to **H** with *their* clothes rent, and told him 2396
19: 1 when king **H** heard *it,* that he rent his 2396
19: 3 they said unto him, Thus saith **H**, This day 2396
19: 5 So the servants of king **H** came to Isaiah. 2396
19: 9 he sent messengers again unto **H**, saying, 2396
19:10 Thus shall ye speak to **H** king of Judah, 2396
19:14 **H** received the letter of the hand of 2396
19:14 **H** went up *into* the house of the LORD, 2396
19:15 And **H** prayed before the LORD, and said, 2396
19:20 Isaiah the son of Amoz sent to **H**, saying, 2396
20: 1 In those days was **H** sick unto death. 2396
20: 3 *is* good in thy sight. And **H** wept sore. 2396
20: 5 and tell **H** the captain of my people, 2396
20: 8 **H** said unto Isaiah, What *shall be* the sign 2396
20:10 **H** answered, It is a light thing for 3169
20:12 sent letters and a present unto **H**: 2396
20:12 for he had heard that **H** had been sick. 2396
20:13 **H** hearkened unto them, and shewed them 2396
20:13 all his dominion, that **H** shewed them not. 2396
20:14 came Isaiah the prophet unto king **H**, and 2396
20:14 **H** said, They are come from a far country, 2396
20:15 **H** answered, All *the things* that *are* in mine 2396
20:16 Isaiah said unto **H**, Hear the word of 2396
20:19 said **H** unto Isaiah, Good *is* the word of 2396
20:20 the rest of the acts of **H**, and all his might, 2396
20:21 **H** slept with his fathers: and Manasseh his 2396
21: 3 places which **H** his father had destroyed; 2396
1Ch 3:13 Ahaz his son, **H** his son, Manasseh his son, 2396
3:23 Elioenai, and **H**, and Azrikam, three. 2396
4:41 name came in the days of **H** king of Judah, 3169
2Ch 28:27 and **H** his son reigned in his stead. 3169
29: 1 **H** *began* to reign *when he was* five and 3169
29:18 they went in to **H** the king, and said, 2396
29:20 **H** the king rose early, and gathered 3169
29:27 **H** commanded to offer the burnt offering 2396
29:30 Moreover **H** the king and the princes 3169
29:31 **H** answered and said, Now ye have 3169
29:36 **H** rejoiced, and all the people, that God had 3169
30: 1 **H** sent to all Israel and Judah, and 3169
30:18 **H** prayed for them, saying, The good 3169
30:20 the LORD hearkened to **H**, and healed 3169
30:22 **H** spake comfortably unto all the Levites 3169
30:24 For **H** king of Judah did give to 2396
31: 2 **H** appointed the courses of the priests and 3169
31: 8 when **H** and the princes came and saw 3169
31: 9 **H** questioned with the priests and 3169
31:11 **H** commanded to prepare chambers in 3169
31:13 at the commandment of **H** the king, and 3169
31:20 thus did **H** throughout all Judah, and 3169
32: 2 when **H** saw that Sennacherib was come, 3169
32: 8 upon the words of **H** king of Judah. 3169
32: 9 unto **H** king of Judah, and unto all Judah 3169
32:11 Doth not **H** persuade you to give over 3169
32:12 Hath not the same **H** taken away his high 3169
32:15 Now therefore let not **H** deceive you, 2396
32:16 the LORD God, and against his servant **H**. 3169
32:17 shall not the God of **H** deliver his people 3169
32:20 for this *cause* **H** the king, and the prophet 3169
32:22 Thus the LORD saved **H** and 3169
32:23 and presents to **H** king of Judah: 3169

2Ch 32:24 In those days **H** was sick to the death, and 3169
32:25 **H** rendered not again according to 3169
32:26 Notwithstanding **H** humbled himself for 3169
32:26 came not upon them in the days of **H**. 3169
32:27 **H** had exceeding much riches and honour: 3169
32:30 This same **H** also stopped the upper 3169
32:30 And **H** prospered in all his works. 3169
32:32 Now the rest of the acts of **H**, and 3169
32:33 **H** slept with his fathers, and they buried 3169
33: 3 For he built again the high places which **H** 3169
Ezr 2:16 The children of Ater of **H**, ninety and eight. 3169
Ne 7:21 The children of Ater of **H**, ninety and eight. 2396
Pr 25: 1 which the men of **H** king of Judah copied 2396
Isa 1: 1 Jotham, Ahaz, *and* **H**, kings of Judah. 3169
36: 1 to pass in the fourteenth year of king **H**, 2396
36: 2 Jerusalem unto king **H** with a great army. 2396
36: 4 Say ye now to **H**, Thus saith the great king, 2396
36: 7 and whose altars **H** hath taken away, 2396
36:14 Thus saith the king, Let not **H** deceive you: 2396
36:15 Neither let **H** make you trust in 2396
36:16 Hearken not to **H**: for thus saith the king of 2396
36:18 *Beware* lest **H** persuade you, saying, 2396
36:22 to **H** with *their* clothes rent, and told him 2396
37: 1 when king **H** heard *it,* that he rent his 2396
37: 3 they said unto him, Thus saith **H**, This day 2396
37: 5 So the servants of king **H** came to Isaiah. 2396
37: 9 when he heard *it,* he sent messengers to **H**, 2396
37:10 Thus shall ye speak to **H** king of Judah, 2396
37:14 **H** received the letter from the hand of 2396
37:14 **H** went up *unto* the house of the LORD, 2396
37:15 And **H** prayed unto the LORD, saying, 2396
37:21 Isaiah the son of Amoz sent unto **H**, saying, 2396
38: 1 In those days was **H** sick unto death. 2396
38: 2 **H** turned his face toward the wall, and 2396
38: 3 *is* good in thy sight. And **H** wept sore. 2396
38: 5 Go and say to **H**, Thus saith the LORD, 2396
38: 9 The writing of **H**, king of Judah, when he 2396
38:22 **H** also had said, What *is* the sign that I 2396
39: 1 of Babylon, sent letters and a present to **H**: 2396
39: 2 **H** was glad of them, and shewed them 2396
39: 2 all his dominion, that **H** shewed them not. 2396
39: 3 came Isaiah the prophet unto king **H**, and 2396
39: 3 **H** said, They are come from a far country 2396
39: 4 **H** answered, All that *is* in mine house have 2396
39: 5 said Isaiah to **H**, Hear the word of 2396
39: 8 said **H** to Isaiah, Good *is* the word of 2396
Jer 15: 4 of Manasseh the son of **H** king of Judah, 3169
26:18 prophesied in the days of **H** king of Judah, 2396
26:19 Did **H** king of Judah and all Judah put him 2396
Hos 1: 1 Jotham, Ahaz, *and* **H**, kings of Judah, and 3169
Mic 1: 1 Ahaz, *and* **H**, kings of Judah, which he saw 3169

HEZION (1)
1Ki 15:18 of Tabrimon, the son of **H**, king of Syria, 2383

HEZIR (2)
1Ch 24:15 The seventeenth to **H**, the eighteenth to 2387
Ne 10:20 Magpiash, Meshullam, **H**, 2387

HEZRAI (1)
2Sa 23:35 **H** the Carmelite, Paarai the Arbite, 2695

HEZRO (1)
1Ch 11:37 **H** the Carmelite, Naarai the son of Ezbai, 2695

HEZRON (17) [ESROM, HEZRON'S, HEZRONITES]
Ge 46: 9 Hanoch, and Phallu, and **H**, and Carmi. 2696
46:12 And the sons of Pharez were **H** and Hamul. 2696
Ex 6:14 of Israel; Hanoch, and Pallu, **H**, and Carmi: 2696
Nu 26: 6 Of **H**, the family of the Hezronites: 2696
26:21 of **H**, the family of the Hezronites: 2696
Jos 15: 3 passed along *to* **H**, and went up to Adar, 2696
15:25 Hazor, Hadattah, and Kerioth, *and* **H**, 2696
Ru 4:18 the generations of Pharez: Pharez begat **H**, 2696
4:19 **H** begat Ram, and Ram begat Amminadab, 2696
1Ch 2: 5 The sons of Pharez; **H**, and Hamul. 2696
2: 9 The sons also of **H**, that were born unto 2696
2:18 Caleb the son of **H** begat *children* of 2696
2:21 afterward **H** went in to the daughter of 2696
2:24 after that **H** was dead in Caleb-ephratah, 2696
2:25 the sons of Jerahmeel the firstborn of **H** 2696
4: 1 **H**, and Carmi, and Hur, and Shobal. 2696
5: 3 *were,* Hanoch, and Pallu, **H**, and Carmi. 2696

HEZRON'S (1) [HEZRON]
1Ch 2:24 Abiah **H** wife bare him Ashur the father of 2696

HEZRONITES (2) [HEZRON]
Nu 26: 6 Of Hezron, the family of the **H**: of Carmi, 2697
26:21 of Hezron, the family of the **H**: 2697

HID (130) [HIDE]
Ge 3: 8 his wife **h** themselves from the presence of 2244
3:10 because I *was* naked; and I **h** myself. 2244
4:14 from thy face shall I be **h**; and I shall be a 5641
35: 4 Jacob **h** them under the oak which *was* by 2934
Ex 2: 2 *a* goodly *child,* she **h** him three months. 6845
2:12 slew the Egyptian, and **h** him in the sand. 2934
3: 6 Moses **h** his face; for he was afraid to look 5641
Lev 4:13 the thing be **h** from the eyes of 5956
5: 3 be defiled withal, and it be **h** from him; 5956
5: 4 with an oath, and it be **h** from him; 5956
Nu 5:13 it be **h** from the eyes of her husband, and 5956
Dt 33:19 of the seas, and *of* treasures **h** in the sand. 2934
Jos 2: 4 **h** them, and said thus, There came men 6845
2: 6 **h** them with the stalks of flax, which she 2934
6:17 because she **h** the messengers that we sent. 2244
6:25 because she **h** the messengers, 2244
7:21 they *are* **h** in the earth in the midst of my 2934
7:22 *it was* **h** in his tent, and the silver under it. 2934
10:16 and **h** themselves in a cave at Makkedah. 2244
10:17 The five kings are found **h** in a cave at 2244
10:27 into the cave wherein they had been **h**, 2244
Jdg 9: 5 son of Jerubbaal was left; for he **h** himself. 2244
1Sa 3:18 him every whit, and **h** nothing from him. 3582
10:22 Behold, he hath **h** himself among the stuff. 2244
14:11 of the holes where they had **h** themselves. 2244
14:22 Likewise all the men of Israel which had **h** 2244
20:24 So David **h** himself in the field: and 5641
2Sa 17: 9 he is **h** now in some pit, or in some *other* 2244
18:13 for there is no matter **h** from the king, and 3582
1Ki 10: 3 there was not *any* thing **h** from the king, 5956
18: 4 **h** them *by* fifty in a cave, and fed them *with* 2244
18:13 how I **h** an hundred men of the LORD'S 2244
2Ki 4:27 the LORD hath **h** *it* from me, and hath not 5956
6:29 we may eat him: and she hath **h** her son. 2244
7: 8 went and **h** *it;* and came again, and 2934
7: 8 and carried thence *also,* and went and **h** *it.* 2934
11: 2 they **h** him, *even* him and his nurse, in 5641
11: 3 he was with her **h** *in* the house of 2244
1Ch 21:20 and his four sons with him **h** themselves. 2244
2Ch 9: 2 there was nothing **h** from Solomon which 5956
22: 9 they caught him, (for he *was* **h** in Samaria,) 2244
22:11 **h** him from Athaliah, so that she slew him 5641
22:12 he was with them **h** in the house of God six 2244
Job 3:10 nor **h** sorrow from mine eyes. 5641
3:21 and dig for it more than for **h** **treasures**; 4301
3:23 *is light given* to a man whose way is **h**, 5641
5:21 Thou shalt be **h** from the scourge of 2244
6:16 of the ice, *and* wherein the snow is **h**: 5956
10:13 these *things* hast thou **h** in thine heart: 6845
15:18 told from their fathers, and have not **h** *it:* 3582
17: 4 For thou hast **h** their heart from 6845
20:26 All darkness *shall be* **h** in his secret places: 2934
28:11 the **thing that is h** bringeth he forth *to* 8587
28:21 Seeing it is **h** from the eyes of all living, 5956
29: 8 The young men saw me, and **h** themselves: 2244
38:30 The waters are **h** as *with* a stone, and 2244
Ps 9:15 in the net which they **h** is their own foot 2934
17:14 whose belly thou fillest *with* thy **h** *treasure:* 6845
19: 6 there is nothing **h** from the heat thereof. 5641
22:24 neither hath he **h** his face from him; but 5641
32: 5 unto thee, and mine iniquity have I not **h**. 3680
35: 7 For without cause have they **h** for me their 2934
35: 8 and let his net that he hath **h** catch himself: 2934
38: 9 and my groaning is not **h** from thee. 5641
40:10 I have not **h** thy righteousness within my 3680
55:12 then I would have **h** myself from him: 5641
69: 5 and my sins are not **h** from thee. 3582
119:11 Thy word have I **h** in mine heart, that I 6845
139:15 My substance was not **h** from thee, when I 3582
140: 5 The proud have **h** a snare for me, and 2934
Pr 2: 4 and searchest for her as *for* **h** **treasures**; 4301
Isa 28:15 and under falsehood have we **h** ourselves: 5641
29:14 of their prudent *men* shall be **h**. 5641
40:27 My way is **h** from the LORD, and 5641
42:22 in holes, and they are **h** in prison houses: 2244
49: 2 in the shadow of his hand hath he **h** me, 2244

H

Isa 49: 2 a polished shaft; in his quiver hath he **h** me; 5641
50: 6 I **h** not my face from shame and spitting. 5641
53: 3 we **h** as it were *our* faces from him; he was 4564
54: 8 In a little wrath I **h** my face from thee for a 5641
57:17 I **h** me, and was wroth, and he went on 5641
59: 2 and your sins have **h** *his* face from you, 5641
64: 7 for thou hast **h** thy face from us, and 5641
65:16 and because they are **h** from mine eyes. 5641
Jer 13: 5 So I went, and **h** it by Euphrates, as 2934
13: 7 the girdle from the place where I had **h** it: 2934
16:17 they are not **h** from my face, neither is their 5641
16:17 neither is their iniquity **h** from mine eyes. 6845
18:22 a pit to take me, and **h** snares for my feet. 2934
33: 5 for all whose wickedness I have **h** my face 5641
36:26 the prophet: but the LORD **h** them. 5641
43:10 his throne upon these stones that I have **h**; 2934
Eze 22:26 have **h** their eyes from my sabbaths, and 5956
39:23 therefore **h** I my face from them, and 5641
39:24 done unto them, and **h** my face from them. 5641
Hos 5: 3 know Ephraim, and Israel is not **h** from me: 3582
13:12 of Ephraim *is* bound up; his sin *is* **h**. 6845
13:14 repentance shall be **h** from mine eyes. 5641
Am 9: 3 though they be **h** from my sight in 5641
Ob 1: 6 *how* are his **h things** sought up! 4710
Na 3:11 thou shalt be **h**, thou also shalt seek 5956
Zep 2: 3 it may be ye shall be **h** in the day of 5641
Mt 5:14 A city that is set on a hill cannot be **h**. *2928*
10:26 be revealed; and **h**, that shall not be known. *2927*
11:25 thou hast **h** these *things* from the wise and *613*
13:33 and **h** in three measures of meal, *1470*
13:44 of heaven is like unto treasure **h** in a field; *2928*
25:18 digged in the earth, and **h** his lord's money. *613*
25:25 and went and **h** thy talent in the earth: *2928*
Mk 4:22 For there is nothing **h**, which shall not be *2927*
7:24 no *man* know *it:* but he could not be **h**. *2990*
Lk 1:24 and **h** herself five months, saying, *4032*
8:17 neither *any thing* **h**, that shall not be known *614*
8:47 when the woman saw that she was not **h**, *2990*
9:45 and it was **h** from them, that they perceived *3871*
10:21 that thou hast **h** these *things* **from** *613*
12: 2 neither **h**, that shall not be known. *2927*
13:21 and **h** in three measures of meal, *1470*
18:34 and this saying was **h** from them, *2928*
19:42 but now they are **h** from thine eyes. *2928*
Jn 8:59 but Jesus **h** himself, and went out of *2928*
2Co 4: 3 But if our gospel be **h**, it is hid to them that *2572*
4: 3 gospel be hid, it is **h** to them that are lost: *2572*
Eph 3: 9 beginning of the world hath been **h** in God, *613*
Col 1:26 mystery which hath been **h from** ages *613*
Col 2: 3 In whom are **h** all the treasures of wisdom *614*
3: 3 and your life is **h** with Christ in God. *2928*
1Ti 5:25 and they that are otherwise cannot be **h**. *2928*
Heb 11:23 was **h** three months of his parents, because *2928*
Rev 6:15 every free *man,* **h** themselves in the dens *2928*

HIDDAI (1)
2Sa 23:30 the Pirathonite, **H** of the brooks of Gaash, 1914

HIDDEKEL (2)
Ge 2:14 the name of the third river *is* **H**: that *is it* 2313
Da 10: 4 by the side of the great river, which *is* **H**; 2313

HIDDEN (16) [HIDE]
Lev 5: 2 creeping things, and *if* it be **h** from him; 5956
Dt 30:11 it *is* not **h** from thee, neither *is* it far off. 6381
Job 3:16 Or as a **h** untimely birth I had not been; 2934
15:20 the number of years is **h** to the oppressor. 6845
24: 1 seeing times are not **h** from the Almighty, 6845
Ps 51: 6 in the **h** *part* thou shalt make me to know 5640
83: 3 and consulted against thy **h ones**. 6845
Pr 28:12 but when the wicked rise, a man is **h**. 2664
Isa 45: 3 **h riches** of secret places, that thou mayest 4301
48: 6 even **h** *things,* and thou didst not know 5341
Ac 26:26 that none of these *things* are **h** from him; *2990*
1Co 2: 7 *even* the **h** *wisdom,* which God ordained *613*
4: 5 who both will bring to light the **h** *things* of *2927*
2Co 4: 2 But have renounced the **h** *things* of *2927*
1Pe 3: 4 But *let it be* the **h** man of the heart, in *that* *2927*
Rev 2:17 will I give to eat of the **h** manna, *2928*

HIDE (83) [HID, HIDDEN, HIDEST, HIDETH, HIDING]
Ge 18:17 Shall I **h** from Abraham *that thing* which I 3680
47:18 unto him, We will not **h** *it* from my lord, 3582
Ex 2: 3 when she could not longer **h** him, she took 6845
Lev 8:17 and his **h**, his flesh, and his dung, 5785
9:11 the **h** he burnt with fire without the camp. 5785
20: 4 **any ways h** their eyes from the man, 5956+5956
Dt 7:20 and **h** themselves from thee, be destroyed. 5641
22: 1 sheep go astray, and **h** thyself from them: 5956
22: 3 thou do likewise: thou mayest not **h** thyself. 5956
22: 4 down by the way, and **h** thyself from them: 5956
31:17 I will **h** my face from them, and they shall 5641
31:18 I will **surely h** my face in that day 5641+5641
32:20 he said, I will **h** my face from them, I will 5641
Jos 2:16 **h** yourselves there three days, until 2244
7:19 now what thou hast done; **h** *it* not from me. 3582
Jdg 6:11 the winepress, to **h** *it* from the Midianites. 5127
1Sa 3:17 I pray thee **h** *it* not from me: God do so 3582
3:17 if thou **h** *any* thing from me of all 3582
13: 6 the people did **h** themselves in caves, and 2244
19: 2 and abide in a secret place, and **h** thyself: 2244
20: 2 why should my father **h** this thing from 5641
20: 5 that I may **h** myself in the fields unto 5641
20:19 come to the place where thou didst **h** 5641
23:19 Doth not David **h** himself with us in strong 5641
26: 1 Doth not David **h** himself in the hill of 5641
2Sa 14:18 the woman, **H** not from me, I pray thee, 3582
1Ki 17: 3 **h** thyself by the brook Cherith, 5641
22:25 shalt go into an inner chamber to **h** thyself. 2247
2Ki 7:12 are they gone out of the camp to **h** 2247
2Ch 18:24 shalt go into an inner chamber to **h** thyself. 2244
Job 13:20 unto me: then will I not **h** myself from thee. 5641
14:13 O that thou wouldest **h** me in the grave, 6845
20:12 his mouth, *though* he **h** it under his tongue; 3582
24: 4 the poor of the earth **h** themselves together. 2244
33:17 *from his* purpose, and **h** pride from man. 3680
34:22 where the workers of iniquity may **h** 5641
40:13 **H** them in the dust together; *and* bind their 2934
Ps 13: 1 how long wilt thou **h** thy face from me? 5641
17: 8 **h** me under the shadow of thy wings, 5641
27: 5 For in the time of trouble he shall **h** me in 6845
27: 5 in the secret of his tabernacle shall he **h** me; 5641
27: 9 **H** not thy face *far* from me; put not thy 5641
30: 7 thou didst **h** thy face, *and* I was troubled. 5641
31:20 Thou shalt **h** them in the secret of thy 5641
51: 9 **H** thy face from my sins, and blot out all 5641
54: T to Saul, Doth not David **h** himself with us? 5641
55: 1 and **h** not thyself from my supplication. 5956
56: 6 they **h** themselves, they mark my steps, 6845
64: 2 **H** me from the secret counsel of 5641
69:17 **h** not thy face from thy servant; for I am in 5641
78: 4 We will not **h** *them* from their children, 3582
89:46 wilt thou **h** thyself, for ever? shall thy 5641
102: 2 **H** not thy face from me in the day *when* I 5641
119:19 **h** not thy commandments from me. 5641
143: 7 **h** not thy face from me, lest I be like unto 5641
143: 9 mine enemies: I **flee** unto thee **to h** me. 3680
Pr 2: 1 and **h** my commandments with thee; 6845
28:28 When the wicked rise, men **h** themselves: 5641
Isa 1:15 your hands, I will **h** mine eyes from you: 5956
2:10 Enter into the rock, and **h** thee in the dust, 2934
3: 9 declare their sin as Sodom, they **h** *it* not. 3582
16: 3 **h** the outcasts; bewray not him that 5641
26:20 **h** thyself as it were for a little moment, 2247
29:15 Woe unto them that seek deep to **h** *their* 5641
58: 7 that thou **h** not thyself from thine own 5956
Jer 13: 4 and **h** it there in a hole of the rock. 2934
13: 6 which I commanded thee to **h** there. 2934
23:24 Can any **h** himself in secret places that I 5641
36:19 Go, **h** thee, thou and Jeremiah; 5641
38:14 I *will* ask thee a thing; **h** nothing from me. 3582
38:25 **h** *it* not from us, and we will not put thee to 3582
43: 9 and **h** them in the clay in the brickkiln, 2934
49:10 and he shall not be able to **h** himself: 2247
La 3:56 **h** not thine ear at my breathing, at my cry. 5956
Eze 28: 3 *there is* no secret *that* they can **h** *from* thee: 6004
31: 8 in the garden of God could not **h** him: 6004
39:29 Neither will I **h** my face any more from 5641
Da 10: 7 so that they fled to **h** themselves. 2244
Am 9: 3 though they **h** themselves in the top of 2244
Mic 3: 4 he will even **h** his face from them at that 5641
Jn 12:36 and departed, and did **h** himself from them. *2928*
Jas 5:20 from death, and shall **h** a multitude of sins. *2572*
Rev 6:16 **h** us from the face of him that sitteth on *2928*

HIDEST (6) [HIDE]
Job 13:24 Wherefore **h** thou thy face, and holdest me 5641
Ps 10: 1 *why* **h** thou *thyself* in times of trouble? 5956

Ps 44:24 Wherefore **h** thou thy face, *and* 5641
88:14 off my soul? *why* **h** thou thy face from me? 5641
104:29 Thou **h** thy face, they are troubled: 5641
Isa 45:15 Verily thou *art* a God that **h** thyself, O God 5641

HIDETH (16) [HIDE]
1Sa 23:23 all the lurking places where he **h** himself, 2244
Job 23: 9 I cannot behold *him:* he **h** *himself* on 5848
34:29 when he **h** *his* face, who then can behold 5641
42: 3 Who *is* he that **h** counsel without 5956
Ps 10:11 he **h** his face; he will never see *it.* 5641
139:12 Yea, the darkness **h** not from thee; but 2821
Pr 10:18 He that **h** hatred *with* lying lips, and he that 3680
19:24 A slothful *man* **h** his hand in *his* bosom, 2934
22: 3 *man* foreseeth the evil, and **h** himself: 5641
26:15 The slothful **h** his hand in *his* bosom; 2934
27:12 *man* foreseeth the evil, *and* **h** himself; 5641
27:16 Whosoever **h** her, hideth the wind, and 6845
27:16 **h** the wind, and the ointment of his right 6845
28:27 he that **h** his eyes shall have many a curse. 5956
Isa 8:17 that **h** his face from the house of Jacob, and 5641
Mt 13:44 he **h**, and for joy thereof goeth and *2928*

HIDING (6) [HIDE]
Job 31:33 as Adam, by **h** mine iniquity in my bosom: 2934
Ps 32: 7 Thou *art* my **h place**; thou shalt preserve 5643
119:114 Thou *art* my **h place** and my shield: I hope 5643
Isa 28:17 and the waters shall overflow the **h place**. 5643
32: 2 a man shall be as a **h place** from the wind, 4224
Hab 3: 4 his hand: and there *was* the **h** of his power. 2253

HIEL (1)
1Ki 16:34 In his days did **H** the Bethelite build 2419

HIERAPOLIS (1)
Col 4:13 them that are in Laodicea, and them in **H**. *2404*

HIGGAION (1)
Ps 9:16 in the work of his own hands. **H**. Selah. 1902

HIGH (416) [HEIGHT, HEIGHTS, HIGHER, HIGHEST, HIGHLY, HIGHMINDED, HIGH-MINDED, HIGHNESS, HIGHWAY, HIGHWAYS]
Ge 7:19 all the **h** hills, that *were* under the whole 1364
14:18 and he *was* the priest of the **most h** God. 5945
14:19 said, Blessed *be* Abram of the **most h** God, 5945
14:20 blessed *be* the **most h** God, which hath 5945
14:22 the **most h** God, the possessor of heaven 5945
29: 7 he said, Lo, *it is* yet **h** day, neither *is it* time 1419
Ex 14: 8 the children of Israel went out with a **h** 7311
25:20 forth *their* wings **on h**, 4605+1886.5+3807.1
37: 9 out *their* wings **on h**, 4605+1886.5+3807.1
39:31 **on h** upon the mitre; 4480+4605+1886.5+3807.1
Lev 21:10 *he that is* the **h** priest among his brethren, 1419
26:22 and your *h* ways shall be desolate. NIH
26:30 I will destroy your **h places**, and cut down 1116
Nu 11:31 as it were two cubits *h* upon the face of NIH
20:17 we will go *by* the king's *h* way, we will not NIH
20:19 said unto him, We will go by the **h way**: 4546
21:22 *but* we will go along by the king's *h* way, NIH
21:28 *and* the lords of the **h places** of Arnon. 1116
22:41 brought him up *into* the **h places** of Baal, 1116
23: 3 I will tell thee. And he went to a **h place**. 8205
24:16 and knew the knowledge of the **most H**, 5945
33: 3 a **h** hand in the sight of all the Egyptians. 7311
33:52 and quite pluck down all their **h places**: 1116
35:25 he shall abide in it unto the death of the **h** 1419
35:28 of his refuge until the death of the **h** priest: 1419
35:28 after the death of the **h** priest the slayer 1419
Dt 2:27 I will go along by the **h way**, I will neither 1870
3: 5 All these cities *were* fenced *with* **h** walls, 1364
12: 2 upon the **h** mountains, and upon the hills, 7311
26:19 to make thee **h** above all nations which he 5945
28: 1 that the LORD thy God will set thee **on h** 5945
28:43 above thee **very h**; 4605+4605+1886.5+1886.5
28:52 until thy **h** and fenced walls come down, 1364
32: 8 When the **most H** divided to the nations 5945
32:13 He made him ride on the **h places** of 1116
32:27 Our hand is **h**, and the LORD hath not 7311
33:29 and thou shalt tread upon their **h places**. 1116
Jos 20: 6 until the death of the **h** priest that shall be 1419
Jdg 5:18 unto the death in the **h places** of the field. 4791
1Sa 9:12 of the people to day in the **h place**: 1116
9:13 before he go up to the **h place** to eat: 1116
9:14 against them, for to go up *to* the **h place**. 1116
9:19 go up before me *unto* the **h place**; for ye 1116
9:25 come down from the **h place** *into* the city, 1116
10: 5 down from the **h place** with a psaltery, 1116
10:13 end of prophesying, he came *to* the **h place**. 1116
13: 6 and in rocks, and in **h places**, and in pits. 6877
2Sa 1:19 beauty of Israel *is* slain upon thy **h places**: 1116
1:25 *thou wast* slain in thine **h places**. 1116
22: 3 my **h tower**, and my refuge, my saviour; 4869
22:14 and the **most H** uttered his voice. 5945
22:34 and setteth me upon my **h places**. 1116
22:49 thou also hast **lifted** me **up on h** above 7311
23: 1 and the man *who* was raised up **on h**, 5920
1Ki 3: 2 Only the people sacrificed in **h places**, 1116
3: 3 he sacrificed and burnt incense in **h places**. 1116
3: 4 for that *was* the great **h place**: 1116
6:10 against all the house, five cubits **h**: 6967
6:23 cherubims *of* olive tree, each ten cubits **h**. 6967
7:15 pillars *of* brass, of eighteen cubits **h** apiece: 6967
7:35 *there* a round compass of half a cubit **h**: 6967
9: 8 *at* this house, *which* is **h**, every one that 5945
11: 7 did Solomon build a **h place** for Chemosh, 1116
12:31 he made a house of **h places**, and 1116
12:32 priests of the **h places** which he had made. 1116
13: 2 of the **h places** that burn incense upon thee, 1116
13:32 against all the houses of the **h places** which 1116
13:33 lowest of the people priests of the **h places**: 1116
13:33 became *one of* the priests of the **h places**. 1116
14:23 For they also built them **h places**, and 1116
14:23 on every **h** hill, and under every green tree. 1364
15:14 the **h places** were not removed: 1116
21: 9 and set Naboth on **h** among the people: 7218
21:12 and set Naboth on **h** among the people. 7218
22:43 the **h places** were not taken away; 1116
22:43 and burnt incense yet in the **h places**. 1116
2Ki 12: 3 the **h places** were not taken away: 1116
12: 3 and burnt incense in the **h places**. 1116
12:10 the king's scribe and the **h** priest came up, 1419
14: 4 Howbeit the **h places** were not taken away: 1116
14: 4 and burnt incense on the **h places**. 1116
15: 4 Save that the **h places** were not removed: 1116
15: 4 and burnt incense still on the **h places**. 1116
15:35 Howbeit the **h places** were not removed: 1116
15:35 and burnt incense still in the **h places**. 1116
16: 4 and burnt incense in the **h places**, 1116
17: 9 they built them **h places** in all their cities, 1116
17:10 them up images and groves in every **h** hill, 1364
17:11 there they burnt incense in all the **h places**, 1116
17:29 put *them* in the houses of the **h places** 1116
17:32 the lowest of them priests of the **h places**, 1116
17:32 for them in the houses of the **h places**. 1116
18: 4 He removed the **h places**, and brake 1116
18:22 whose **h places** and whose altars Hezekiah 1116
19:22 *thy* voice, and lift up thine eyes **on h**? 4791
21: 3 For he built *up* again the **h places** which 1116
22: 4 Go up to Hilkiah the **h** priest, that he may 1419
22: 8 Hilkiah the **h** priest said unto Shaphan 1419
23: 4 the king commanded Hilkiah the **h** priest, 1419
23: 5 in the **h places** in the cities of Judah, 1116
23: 8 defiled the **h places** where the priests had 1116
23: 8 brake down the **h places** of the gates that 1116
23: 9 Nevertheless the priests of the **h places** 1116
23:13 the **h places** that *were* before Jerusalem, 1116
23:15 the **h place** which Jeroboam the son of 1116
23:15 that altar and the **h place** he brake down, 1116
23:15 burnt the **h place**, *and* stampt *it* small to 1116
23:19 all the houses also of the **h places** that *were* 1116
23:20 he slew all the priests of the **h places** that 1116
1Ch 11:23 five cubits *h*; and in the Egyptian's hand NIH
14: 2 kingdom *was* lift up **on h**, 4605+1886.5+3807.1
16:39 LORD in the **h place** that *was* at Gibeon, 1116
17:17 to the estate of a man of **h degree**, 4609
21:29 *were* at that season in the **h place** at 1116
2Ch 1: 3 went to the **h place** that *was* at Gibeon; 1116
1:13 **h place** that *was* at Gibeon *to* Jerusalem, 1116
3:15 house two pillars of thirty and five cubits **h**, 753
6:13 three cubits **h**, and had set it in the midst of 6967
7:21 this house, which is **h**, shall be an 5945
11:15 he ordained him priests for the **h places**, 1116
14: 3 altars of the strange *gods*, and the **h places**, 1116
14: 5 out of all the cities of Judah the **h places** 1116
15:17 the **h places** were not taken away out of 1116
17: 6 moreover he took away the **h places** and 1116
20:19 with a loud voice **on h**. 4605+1886.5+3807.1

2Ch 20:33 Howbeit the **h places** were not taken away: 1116
21:11 Moreover he made **h places** in 1116
23:20 they came through the **h** gate *into* 5945
24:11 and the **h** priest's officer came and 7218
27: 3 He built the **h** gate of the house of 5945
28: 4 and burnt incense in the **h places**, 1116
28:25 **h places** to burn incense unto other gods, 1116
31: 1 threw down the **h places** and the altars out 1116
32:12 the same Hezekiah taken away his **h places** 1116
33: 3 For he built again the **h places** which 1116
33:17 the people did sacrifice still in the **h places**, 1116
33:19 the places wherein he built **h places**, and 1116
34: 3 and Jerusalem from the **h places**, 1116
34: 4 the images, that *were* **on h** 4605+1886.5+3807.1
34: 9 when they came to Hilkiah the **h** priest, 1419
Ne 3: 1 Eliashib the **h** priest rose up with his 1419
3:20 door of the house of Eliashib the **h** priest. 1419
3:25 the tower which lieth out from the king's **h** 5945
13:28 of Joiada, the son of Eliashib the **h** priest, 1419
Est 5:14 Let a gallows be made of fifty cubits **h**, and 1364
7: 9 Behold also, the gallows fifty cubits **h**, 1364
Job 5:11 To set up **on h** those that be low; that those 4791
11: 8 *It is* as **h** as heaven; what canst thou do? 1363
16:19 witness *is* in heaven, and my record *is* **on h**. 4791
21:22 seeing he judgeth those that are **h**. 7311
22:12 the height of the stars, how **h** they are. 7311
25: 2 with him, he maketh peace in his **h places**. 4791
31: 2 inheritance of the Almighty from **on h**? 4791
38:15 and the **h** arm shall be broken. 7311
39:18 What time she lifteth up herself on **h**, 4791
39:27 at thy command, and **make** her nest **on h**? 7311
41:34 He beholdeth all **h** *things:* he *is* a king over 1364
Ps 7: 7 for their sakes therefore return thou on **h**. 4791
7:17 *praise* to the name of the LORD **most H**. 5945
9: 2 sing *praise* to thy name, O thou **most H**. 5945
18: 2 the horn of my salvation, *and* my **h tower**. 4869
18:27 but wilt bring down **h** looks. 7311
18:33 and setteth me upon my **h places**. 1116
21: 7 through the mercy of the **most H** he shall 5945
46: 4 holy *place* of the tabernacles of the **most H**. 5945
47: 2 For the LORD **most H** *is* terrible; *he is* a 5945
49: 2 Both low and **h**s, rich and poor, 376+1121
50:14 and pay thy vows unto the **most H**: 5945
56: 2 many that fight against me, O thou *most* **H**. 4791
57: 2 I will cry unto God **most H**; unto God that 5945
62: 9 *and* **men of h degree** *are* a lie: 376+1121
68:15 of Bashan; a **h** hill *as* the hill of Bashan. 1386
68:16 Why leap ye, ye **h** hills? *this is* the hill 1386
68:18 Thou hast ascended on **h**, thou hast led 4791
69:29 let thy salvation, O God, **set me up on h**. 7682
71:19 righteousness also, O God, *is* **very h**, 4791+5704
73:11 and is there knowledge in the **most H**? 5945
75: 5 Lift not up your horn on **h**: speak *not* with a 4791
77:10 the years of the right hand of the **most H**. 5945
78:17 by provoking the **most H** in the wilderness. 5945
78:35 their rock, and the **h** God their redeemer. 5945
78:56 and provoked the **most h** God, 5945
78:58 provoked him to anger with their **h places**, 1116
78:69 he built his sanctuary like **h** *palaces,* like 7311
82: 6 and all of you *are* children of the **most H**. 5945
83:18 *art* the **most H** over all the earth. 5945
89:13 strong is thy hand, *and* **h** is thy right hand. 7311
91: 1 **most H** shall abide under the shadow of 5945
91: 9 my refuge, *even* the **most H**, thy habitation; 5945
91:14 I will **set** him **on h**, because he hath known 7682
92: 1 to sing *praises* unto thy name, O **most H**: 5945
92: 8 But thou, LORD, *art most* **h** for evermore. 4791
93: 4 The LORD **on h** *is* 4791+871.1+1886.1
97: 9 LORD, *art* **H** above all the earth: 5945
99: 2 in Zion; and he *is* **h** above all the people. 7311
101: 5 him that hath a **h** look and a proud heart 1362
103:11 For as the heaven is **h** above the earth, *so* 1361
104:18 The **h** hills *are* a refuge for the wild goats; 1364
107:11 and contemned the counsel of the **most H**: 5945
107:41 Yet **setteth** he the poor **on h** from 7682
113: 4 The LORD *is* **h** above all nations, *and* 7311
113: 5 the LORD our God, who dwelleth **on h**, 1361
131: 1 in great *matters,* or in *things* too **h** for me. 6381
138: 6 Though the LORD *be* **h**, yet hath he 7311
139: 6 for me; it is **h**, I cannot attain unto it. 7682
144: 2 my **h tower**, and my deliverer; my shield, 4869
149: 6 *Let* the **h** *praises* of God *be* in their mouth, 7319
150: 5 praise him upon the **h sounding** cymbals. 8643
Pr 8: 2 She standeth in the top of **h places** by 4791
9:14 on a seat in the **h places** of the city, 4791
18:11 and as a **h** wall in his own conceit. 7682
21: 4 A **h** look, and a proud heart, *and* 7312
24: 7 Wisdom *is too* **h** for a fool: he openeth not 7311
Ecc 12: 5 *when* they shall be afraid of *that which is* **h**, 1364
Isa 2:13 that are **h** and lifted up, and upon all 7311
2:14 upon all the **h** mountains, and upon all 7311
2:15 upon every **h** tower, and upon every fenced 1364
6: 1 **h** and lifted up, and his train filled 7311
10:12 of Assyria, and the glory of his **h** looks. 7312
10:33 the **h ones** of stature *shall be* hewn down, 7311
13: 2 Lift ye up a banner upon the **h** mountain, 8192
14:14 of the clouds; I will be like the **most H**. 5945
15: 2 and *to* Dibon, the **h places**, to weep: 1116
16:12 is seen that Moab is weary on the **h place**, 1116
22:16 *as* he that heweth him out a sepulchre **on h**, 4791
24:18 for the windows from **on h** are open, and 4791
24:21 the host of the **h ones** *that are* on high, 4791
24:21 the host of the high ones *that are* on **h**, 4791
25:12 the fortress of the **h fort** of thy walls shall 4869
26: 5 For he bringeth down them that dwell **on h**; 4791
30:13 swelling out in a **h** wall, whose breaking 7682
30:25 there shall be upon every **h** mountain, and 1364
30:25 upon every **h** hill, rivers *and* streams of 5375
32:15 the spirit be poured upon us from **on h**, 4791
33: 5 LORD *is* exalted; for he dwelleth **on h**: 4791
33:16 He shall dwell **on h**: his place of defence 4791
36: 7 whose **h places** and whose altars Hezekiah 1116
37:23 *thy* voice, and lifted up thine eyes **on h**? 4791
40: 9 get thee up into the **h** mountain; 1364
40:26 Lift up your eyes **on h**, and behold who 4791
41:18 I will open rivers in **h places**, and 8205
49: 9 and their pastures *shall be* in all **h places**. 8205
52:13 be exalted and extolled, and be very **h**. 1361
57: 7 and **h** mountain hast thou set thy bed: 5375
57:15 For thus saith the **h** and lofty One that 7311
57:15 I dwell *in* the **h** and holy *place,* with him 4791
58: 4 to make your voice to be heard on **h**. 4791
58:14 I will cause thee to ride upon the **h places** 1116
Jer 2:20 when upon every **h** hill and under every 1364
3: 2 Lift up thine eyes unto the **h places**, and 8205
3: 6 she is gone up upon every **h** mountain and 1364
3:21 A voice was heard upon the **h places**, 8205
4:11 A dry wind of the **h places** in 8205
7:29 and take up a lamentation on **h places**; 8205
7:31 they have built the **h places** of Tophet, 1116
12:12 The spoilers are come upon all **h places** 8205
14: 6 the wild asses did stand in the **h places**, 8205
17: 2 their groves by the green trees upon the **h** 1364
17: 3 *and* thy **h places** for sin, throughout all thy 1116
17:12 A glorious **h** throne from the beginning *is* 4791
19: 5 They have built also the **h places** of Baal, 1116
20: 2 put him in the stocks that *were* in the **h** gate 5945
25:30 The LORD shall roar from **on h**, and 4791
26:18 the mountain of the house as the **h places** 1116
31:21 Set thee up waymarks, make thee **h heaps**: 8564
32:35 they built the **h places** of Baal, which *are* in 1116
48:35 him that offereth *in* the **h places**, and 1116
49:16 though thou shouldest **make** thy nest as **h** 1361
51:58 her **h** gates shall be burnt with fire; 1364
La 3:35 of a man before the face of the **most H**, 5945
3:38 Out of the mouth of the **most H** proceedeth 5945
Eze 1:18 they were so **h** that they were dreadful; 1363
6: 3 upon you, and I will destroy your **h places**. 1116
6: 6 and the **h places** shall be desolate; 1116
6:13 upon every **h** hill, in all the tops of 7311
16:16 deckedst thy **h places** with divers colours, 1116
16:24 hast made thee a **h place** in every street. 7413
16:25 Thou hast built thy **h place** at every head of 7413
16:31 and makest thine **h place** in every street; 7413
16:39 and shall break down thy **h places**: 7413
17:22 take of the highest branch of the **h** cedar, 7311
17:22 will plant *it* upon a **h** mountain and 1364
17:24 I the LORD have brought down the **h** tree, 1364
20:28 they saw every **h** hill, and all the thick 7311
20:29 What *is* the **h place** whereunto ye go? 1116
21:26 *him that is* low, and abase *him that is* **h**. 1364
31: 3 a shadowing shrowd, and of a **h** stature; 1362
31: 4 the deep **set** him **up on h** with her rivers 7311
34: 6 all the mountains, and upon every **h** hill: 7311
34:14 upon the **h** mountains of Israel shall their 4791
36: 2 even the ancient **h places** are ours in 1116
40: 2 set me upon a very **h** mountain, by which 1364
40:42 a cubit and a half broad, and one cubit **h**: 1363

H

Eze 41:22 The altar *of* wood *was* three cubits **h**, and 1364
43: 7 the carcases of their kings *in* their **h places**. 1116
Da 3:26 ye servants of the **most h** God, come forth, 5943
4: 2 wonders that the **h** God hath wrought 5943
4:17 the **most H** ruleth in the kingdom of men, 5943
4:24 and this *is* the decree of the **most H**, 5943
4:25 till thou know that the **most H** ruleth in 5943
4:32 until thou know that the **most H** ruleth in 5943
4:34 I blessed the **most H**, and I praised and 5943
5:18 the **most h** God gave Nebuchadnezzar thy 5943
5:21 till he knew that the **most h** God ruled in 5943
7:18 the saints of the **most H** shall take 5946
7:22 *was* given to the saints of the **most H**; 5946
7:25 shall speak *great* words against the **most H**, 5943
7:25 shall wear out the saints of the **most H**, and 5946
7:27 to the people of the saints of the **most H**, 5946
8: 3 the two horns *were* **h**; but one *was* higher 1364
Hos 7:16 They return, *but* not *to* the **most H**: they are 5920
10: 8 The **h places** also of Aven, the sin of Israel, 1116
11: 7 though they called them to the **most H**, 5920
Am 4:13 treadeth upon the **h places** of the earth, 1116
7: 9 the **h places** of Isaac shall be desolate, and 1116
Ob 1: 3 the clefts of the rock, whose habitation *is* **h**; 4791
Mic 1: 3 and tread upon the **h places** of the earth. 1116
1: 5 what *are* the **h places** of Judah? *are they* 1116
3:12 the mountain of the house as the **h places** 1116
6: 6 *and* bow myself before the **h** God? 4791
Hab 2: 9 that *he* may set his nest on **h**, that *he* may 4791
3:10 uttered his voice, *and* lift up his hands **on h**. 7315
3:19 will make me to walk upon mine **h places**. 1116
Zep 1:16 the fenced cities, and against the **h** towers. 1364
Hag 1: 1 to Joshua the son of Josedech the **h** priest, 1419
1:12 Joshua the son of Josedech the **h** priest, 1419
1:14 of Joshua the son of Josedech the **h** priest, 1419
2: 2 to Joshua the son of Josedech the **h** priest 1419
2: 4 O Joshua, son of Josedech, the **h** priest; 1419
Zec 3: 1 he shewed me Joshua the **h** priest standing 1419
3: 8 O Joshua the **h** priest, thou, and thy fellows 1419
6:11 of Joshua the son of Josedech the **h** priest; 1419
Mt 4: 8 the devil taketh him *up* into an exceeding **h** *5308*
17: 1 bringeth them up into a **h** mountain apart, *5308*
26: 3 of the people, unto the palace of the **h priest**, *749*
26:51 and stroke a servant of the **h priest's**, and *749*
26:57 Jesus led *him* away to Caiaphas the **h priest**, *749*
26:58 him afar off unto the **h priest's** palace, *749*
26:62 And the **h priest** arose, and said unto him, *749*
26:63 And the **h priest** answered and said unto *749*
26:65 Then the **h priest** rent his clothes, saying, *749*
Mk 2:26 of God in the days of Abiathar the **h priest**, *749*
5: 7 Jesus, *thou* Son of the **most h** God? *5310*
6:21 **h captains**, and chief *estates* of Galilee; *5506*
9: 2 leadeth them up into a **h** mountain apart by *5308*
14:47 and smote a servant of the **h priest**, and *749*
14:53 And they led Jesus away to the **h priest**: and *749*
14:54 afar off, even into the palace of the **h priest**: *749*
14:60 And the **h priest** stood up in the midst, and *749*
14:61 Again the **h priest** asked him, and said unto *749*
14:63 Then the **h priest** rent his clothes, and saith, *749*
14:66 cometh one of the maids of the **h priest**: *749*
Lk 1:78 whereby the dayspring from **on h** hath *5311*
3: 2 Annas and Caiaphas being the **h priests**, *749*
4: 5 the devil, taking him up into a **h** mountain, *5308*
8:28 with thee, Jesus, *thou* Son of God **most h**? *5310*
22:50 of them smote the servant of the **h priest**, *749*
22:54 and brought him into the **h priest's** house. *749*
24:49 until ye be endued with power from **on h**. *5311*
Jn 11:49 being the **h priest** that *same* year, said unto *749*
11:51 but being **h priest** that year, he prophesied *749*
18:10 and smote the **h priest's** servant, and cut off *749*
18:13 which was the **h priest** that *same* year. *749*
18:15 that disciple was known unto the **h priest**, *749*
18:15 in with Jesus into the palace of the **h priest**. *749*
18:16 which was known unto the **h priest**, and *749*
18:19 The **h priest** then asked Jesus of his *749*
18:22 saying, Answerest thou the **h priest** so? *749*
18:24 sent him bound unto Caiaphas the **h priest**. *749*
18:26 One of the servants of the **h priest**, being *his* *749*
19:31 (for that sabbath day was a **h** day,) *3173*
Ac 4: 6 And Annas the **h priest**, and Caiaphas, and *749*
4: 6 many as were of the kindred of the **h priest**, *748*
5:17 Then the **h priest** rose up, and all they that *749*
5:21 But the **h priest** came, and they that were *749*
5:24 Now when the *h* priest and the captain of NIG
5:27 the council: and the **h priest** asked them, *749*
7: 1 Then said the **h priest**, Are these *things* so? *749*
7:48 Howbeit the **most H** dwelleth not in *5310*
9: 1 disciples of the Lord, went unto the **h priest**, *749*
13:17 and with a **h** arm brought he them out of it. *5308*
16:17 These men are the servants of the **most h** *5310*
22: 5 As also the **h priest** doth bear me witness, *749*
23: 2 And the **h priest** Ananias commanded them *749*
23: 4 stood by said, Revilest thou God's **h priest**? *749*
23: 5 I wist not, brethren, that he was the **h priest**: *749*
24: 1 And after five days Ananias the **h priest** *749*
25: 2 Then the **h priest** and the chief of the Jews *749*
Ro 12:16 Mind not **h** *things*, but condescend to *men* *5308*
13:11 **now** *it is* **h time** to awake out of *2235+5610*
2Co 10: 5 every **h** thing that exalteth itself against *5313*
Eph 4: 8 *he* saith, When he ascended up on **h**, *5311*
6:12 against spiritual wickedness in **h** *places*. *2032*
Php 3:14 I press toward the mark for the prize of the **h** *507*
Heb 1: 3 on the right hand of the Majesty on **h**; *5308*
2:17 faithful **h priest** *in things* pertaining to God, *749*
3: 1 the Apostle and **H Priest** of our profession, *749*
4:14 Seeing then that we have a great **h priest**, *749*
4:15 For we have not a **h priest** which cannot be *749*
5: 1 For every **h priest** taken from among men is *749*
5: 5 glorified not himself to be made a **h priest**; *749*
5:10 Called of God a **h priest** after the order of *749*
6:20 made a **h priest** for ever after the order of *749*
7: 1 king of Salem, priest of the **most h** God, *5310*
7:26 For such a **h priest** became us, *who is* holy, *749*
7:27 as *those* **h priests**, to offer up sacrifice, *749*
7:28 For the law maketh men **h priests** which *749*
8: 1 We have such a **h priest**, who is set on *749*
8: 3 For every **h priest** is ordained to offer gifts *749*
9: 7 But into the second *went* the **h priest** alone *749*
9:11 But Christ being come a **h priest** of good *749*
9:25 as the **h priest** entereth into the holy *place* *749*
10:21 And *having* a **h** priest over the house of *3173*
13:11 into the sanctuary by the **h priest** for sin, *749*
Rev 21:10 in the spirit to a great and **h** mountain, *5308*
21:12 And had a wall great and **h**, and had twelve *5308*

HIGHER (21) [HIGH]

Nu 24: 7 his king shall be **h** than Agag, and 7311
1Sa 9: 2 upward *he was* **h** than any of the people. 1364
10:23 he was **h** than any of the people from his 1361
2Ki 15:35 He built the **h** gate of the house of 5945
Ne 4:13 places behind the wall, *and* on the **h places**, 6706
Job 35: 5 behold the clouds *which* are **h** than thou. 1361
Ps 61: 2 lead me to the rock *that* is **h** than I. 7311
89:27 *my* firstborn, **h** than the kings of the earth. 5945
Ecc 5: 8 for *he that is* **h** than the highest regardeth; 1364
5: 8 highest regardeth; and *there be* **h** than they. 1364
Isa 55: 9 For *as* the heavens are **h** than the earth, so 1361
55: 9 so are my ways **h** than your ways, and 1361
Jer 36:10 in the **h** court *at* the entry of the new gate of 5945
Eze 9: 2 six men came from the way of the **h** gate, 5945
42: 5 for the galleries were **h** than these, than 398
43:13 and this *shall be* the **h place** of the altar. 1354
Da 8: 3 one *was* **h** than the other, and the higher 1364
8: 3 than the other, and the **h** came up last. 1364
Lk 14:10 he may say unto thee, Friend, go up **h**: *511*
Ro 13: 1 Let every soul be subject unto the **h** *5242*
Heb 7:26 and made **h than** the heavens; *5308*

HIGHEST (18) [HIGH]

Ps 18:13 in the heavens, and the **H** gave his voice; 5945
87: 5 and the **H** himself shall establish her. 5945
Pr 8:26 nor the **h part** of the dust of the world. 7218
9: 3 crieth upon the **h places** of the city, 1610+4791
Ecc 5: 8 for *he that is* higher than the **h** regardeth; 1364
Eze 17: 3 and took the **h branch** of the cedar: 6788
17:22 I will also take of the **h branch** of the high 6788
41: 7 increased *from* the lowest *chamber* to the **h** 5945
Mt 21: 9 in the name of the Lord; Hosanna in the **h**. *5310*
Mk 11:10 in the name of the Lord: Hosanna in the **h**. *5310*
Lk 1:32 and shall be called the Son of the **H**: *5310*
1:35 the power of the **H** shall overshadow thee: *5310*
1:76 child, shalt be called the prophet of the **H**: *5310*
2:14 Glory to God in the **h**, and on earth peace, *5310*
6:35 and ye shall be the children of the **H**: *5310*
14: 8 to a wedding, sit not down in the **h room**; *4411*
19:38 peace in heaven, and glory in the **h**. *5310*
20:46 and the **h seats** in the synagogues, and *4410*

HIGHLY (6) [HIGH]
Lk 1:28 and said, Hail, *thou that art* **h favoured,** *5487*
16:15 for that which is **h esteemed** amongst men *5308*
Ac 12:20 And Herod was **h displeased** with them of *2371*
Ro 12: 3 not to **think** *of himself* more **h** than he *5252*
Php 2: 9 Wherefore God also hath **h exalted** him, *5251*
1Th 5:13 And to esteem them very **h** in love *1537+4053*

HIGHMINDED, HIGH-MINDED (3) [HIGH, MIND]
Ro 11:20 thou standest by faith. Be not **h**, but fear: *5309*
1Ti 6:17 that *they* be not **h**, nor trust in uncertain *5309*
2Ti 3: 4 Traitors, heady, **h**, lovers of pleasures more *5187*

HIGHNESS (2) [HIGH]
Job 31:23 and by reason of his **h** I could not endure. 7613
Isa 13: 3 mine anger, *even* them that rejoice in my **h**. 1346

HIGHWAY (16) [HIGH, WAY]
Jdg 21:19 on the east side of the **h** that goeth up from 4546
1Sa 6:12 *and* went along the **h**, lowing as they went, 4546
2Sa 20:12 wallowed in blood in the midst of the **h**. 4546
20:12 he removed Amasa out of the **h** *into* 4546
20:13 When he was removed out of the **h**, all 4546
2Ki 18:17 which *is* in the **h** of the fuller's field. 4546
Pr 16:17 The **h** of the upright *is* to depart from evil: 4546
Isa 7: 3 the upper pool in the **h** of the fuller's field; 4546
11:16 there shall be a **h** for the remnant of his 4546
19:23 In that day shall there be a **h** out of Egypt 4546
35: 8 a **h** shall be there, and a way, and it shall be 4547
36: 2 the upper pool in the **h** of the fuller's field. 4546
40: 3 make straight in the desert a **h** for our God. 4546
62:10 cast up, cast up the **h**; gather out the stones; 4546
Jer 31:21 set thine heart toward the **h**, *even* the way 4546
Mk 10:46 of Timeus, sat by the ***h*****way side** begging. *3598*

HIGHWAYS (10) [HIGH, WAY]
Jdg 5: 6 the **h** were unoccupied, and the travellers 734
20:31 *and* kill, as at other times, in the **h**, 4546
20:32 and draw them from the city unto the **h**. 4546
20:45 they gleaned of them in the **h** five thousand 4546
Isa 33: 8 The **h** lie waste, the wayfaring man 4546
49:11 a way, and my **h** shall be exalted. 4546
Am 5:16 and they shall say in all the **h**, Alas! 2351
Mt 22: 9 Go ye therefore into the **h**, *1327+3588+3598*
22:10 So those servants went out into the ***h*****ways**, *3598*
Lk 14:23 Go out into the ***h*****ways** and hedges, and *3598*

HILEN (1)
1Ch 6:58 **H** with her suburbs, Debir with her 2432

HILKIAH (33) [HILKIAH'S]
2Ki 18:18 came out to them Eliakim the son of **H**, 2518
18:26 said Eliakim the son of **H**, and Shebna, 2518
18:37 came Eliakim the son of **H**, which *was* over 2518
22: 4 Go up to **H** the high priest, that he may sum 2518
22: 8 **H** the high priest said unto Shaphan 2518
22: 8 **H** gave the book to Shaphan, and he read it. 2518
22:10 **H** the priest hath delivered me a book. 2518
22:12 the king commanded **H** the priest, and 2518
22:14 So **H** the priest, and Ahikam, and Achbor, 2518
23: 4 the king commanded **H** the high priest, 2518
23:24 **H** the priest found *in* the house of 2518
1Ch 6:13 Shallum begat **H**, and Hilkiah begat 2518
6:13 begat Hilkiah, and **H** begat Azariah, 2518
6:45 the son of Amaziah, the son of **H**, 2518
9:11 Azariah the son of **H**, the son of 2518
26:11 **H** the second, Tebaliah the third, 2518
2Ch 34: 9 when they came to **H** the high priest, 2518
34:14 **H** the priest found a book of the law of 2518
34:15 **H** answered and said to Shaphan the scribe, 2518
34:15 And **H** delivered the book to Shaphan. 2518
34:18 **H** the priest hath given me a book. 2518
34:20 the king commanded **H**, and Ahikam 2518
34:22 **H**, and *they* that the king *had appointed,* 2518
35: 8 **H** and Zechariah and Jehiel, rulers of 2518
Ezr 7: 1 the son of Azariah, the son of **H**, 2518
Ne 8: 4 Anaiah, and Urijah, and **H**, and Maaseiah, 2518
11:11 Seraiah the son of **H**, the son of 2518
12: 7 Sallu, Amok, **H**, Jedaiah. These *were* 2518
12:21 Of **H**, Hashabiah; of Jedaiah, Nethaneel. 2518
Isa 22:20 I will call my servant Eliakim the son of **H**: 2518
36:22 came Eliakim, the son of **H**, that *was* over 2518
Jer 1: 1 The words of Jeremiah the son of **H**, of 2518
29: 3 of Shaphan, and Gemariah the son of **H**, 2518

HILKIAH'S (1) [HILKIAH]
Isa 36: 3 **H** son, which *was* over the house, and 2518

HILL (75) [AREOPAGUS, DUNGHILL, DUNGHILLS, HILL'S, HILLS, MARS' HILL]
Ex 17: 9 to morrow I will stand on the top of the **h** 1389
17:10 Aaron, and Hur went up *to* the top of the **h**. 1389
24: 4 builded an altar under the **h**, and 2022
Nu 14:44 they presumed to go up unto the **h** top: 2022
14:45 the Canaanites which dwelt in that **h**, 2022
Dt 1:41 of war, ye were ready to go up into the **h**. 2022
1:43 and went presumptuously up into the **h**. 2022
Jos 5: 3 circumcised the children of Israel at the **h** 1389
13: 6 All the inhabitants of the **h country** from 2022
15: 9 the border was drawn from the top of the **h** 2022
17:16 of Joseph said, The **h** is not enough for us: 2022
18:13 near the **h** that *lieth* on the south side of 2022
18:14 from the **h** that *lieth* before Beth-horon 2022
21:11 *city is* Hebron, in the **h** *country* of Judah, 2022
24:30 on the north side of the **h** of Gaash. 2022
24:33 they buried him in a **h** that pertained to 1389
Jdg 2: 9 on the north side of the **h** Gaash. 2022
7: 1 of them, by the **h** of Moreh, in the valley. 1389
16: 3 carried them up to the top of a **h** that *is* 2022
1Sa 7: 1 it into the house of Abinadab in the **h**, 1389
9:11 *And* as they went up the **h** to the city, they 4608
10: 5 After that thou shalt come to the **h** of God, 1389
10:10 when they came thither to the **h**, behold, 1389
23:19 in the **h** of Hachilah, which *is* on the south 1389
25:20 that she came down by the covert of the **h**, 2022
26: 1 Doth not David hide himself in the **h** of 1389
26: 3 Saul pitched in the **h** of Hachilah, which *is* 1389
26:13 and stood on the top of a **h** afar off; 2022
2Sa 2:24 when they were come to the **h** of Ammah, 1389
2:25 one troop, and stood on the top of a **h**. 1389
13:34 people by the way of the **h** side behind him. 2022
16: 1 was a little past the top *of the* **h**, behold, NIH
21: 9 they hanged them in the **h** before 2022
1Ki 11: 7 in the **h** that *is* before Jerusalem, and 2022
14:23 on every high **h**, and under every green 1389
16:24 he bought the **h** Samaria of Shemer for two 2022
16:24 built *on* the **h**, and called the name of 2022
16:24 name of Shemer, owner of the **h**, Samaria. 2022
2Ki 1: 9 behold, he sat on the top of a **h**. And he 2022
4:27 when she came to the man of God to the **h**, 2022
17:10 them up images and groves in every high **h**, 1389
Ps 2: 6 Yet have I set my king upon my holy **h** of 2022
3: 4 and he heard me out of his holy **h**. 2022
15: 1 who shall dwell in thy holy **h**? 2022
24: 3 Who shall ascend into the **h** of 2022
42: 6 and of the Hermonites, from the **h** Mizar. 2022
43: 3 let them bring me unto thy holy **h**, and 2022
68:15 The **h** of God *is as* the hill of Bashan; 2022
68:15 The hill of God *is as* the **h** of Bashan; 2022
68:15 of Bashan; a high **h** *as* the hill of Bashan. 2022
68:15 of Bashan; a high hill *as* the **h** of Bashan. 2022
68:16 *this is* the **h** *which* God desireth to dwell in; 2022
99: 9 our God, and worship at his holy **h**; 2022
SS 4: 6 of myrrh, and to the **h** of frankincense. 1389
Isa 5: 1 hath a vineyard in a very fruitful **h**: 7161
10:32 of the daughter of Zion, the **h** of Jerusalem. 1389
30:17 top of a mountain, and as an ensign on a **h**. 1389
30:25 upon every high **h**, rivers *and* streams of 1389
31: 4 fight for mount Zion, and for the **h** thereof. 1389
40: 4 every mountain and **h** shall be made low: 1389
Jer 2:20 when upon every high **h** and under every 1389
16:16 from every **h**, and out of the holes of 1389
31:39 go forth over against it upon the **h** Gareb, 1389
49:16 of the rock, that holdest the height of the **h**: 1389
50: 6 they have gone from mountain to **h**, 1389
Eze 6:13 upon every high **h**, in all the tops of 1389
20:28 they saw every high **h**, and all the thick 1389
34: 6 all the mountains, and upon every high **h**: 1389
34:26 and the places round about my **h** a blessing; 1389
Mt 5:14 A city that is set on a **h** cannot be hid. *3735*
Lk 1:39 and went into the **h country** with haste, *3714*
1:65 throughout all the **h country** of Judea. *3714*
3: 5 every mountain and **h** shall be brought low; *1015*
4:29 led him unto the brow of the **h** whereon *3735*
9:37 when they were come down from the **h**, *3735*

HILL'S (1) [HILL]
2Sa 16:13 Shimei went along on the **h** side over 2022

HILLEL (2)
Jdg 12:13 after him Abdon the son of **H**, 1985
12:15 Abdon the son of **H** the Pirathonite died, 1985

HILLS (65) [HILL]
Ge 7:19 all the high **h**, that *were* under the whole 2022
49:26 unto the utmost bound of the everlasting **h**: 1389
Nu 23: 9 I see him, and from the **h** I behold him: 1389
Dt 1: 7 in the **h**, and in the vale, and in the south, 2022
8: 7 depths that spring out of the valleys and **h**; 2022
8: 9 and out of whose **h** thou mayest dig brass. 2042
11:11 *is* a land of **h** and valleys, *and* 2022
12: 2 and upon the **h**, and under every green tree: 1389
33:15 and for the precious things of the lasting **h**, 1389
Jos 9: 1 in the **h**, and in the valleys, and in all 2022
10:40 So Joshua smote all the country of the **h**, 2022
11:16 the **h**, and all the south *country*, and all 2022
1Ki 20:23 said unto him, Their gods *are* gods of the **h**; 2022
20:28 The LORD *is* God of the **h**, but he *is* not 2022
22:17 I saw all Israel scattered upon the **h**, 2022
2Ki 16: 4 and on the **h**, and under every green tree. 1389
2Ch 28: 4 and on the **h**, and under every green tree. 1389
Job 15: 7 was born? or wast thou made before the **h**? 1389
Ps 18: 7 the foundations also of the **h** moved and 2022
50:10 *is* mine, *and* the cattle upon a thousand **h**. 2042
65:12 and the **little h** rejoice on every side. 1389
68:16 Why leap ye, ye high **h**? *this is* the hill 2022
72: 3 and the **little h**, by righteousness. 1389
80:10 The **h** were covered *with* the shadow of it, 2022
95: 4 of the earth: the strength of the **h** *is* his also. 2022
97: 5 The **h** melted like wax at the presence of 2022
98: 8 *their* hands: let the **h** be joyful together 2022
104:10 into the valleys, *which* run among the **h**. 2022
104:13 He watereth the **h** from his chambers: 2022
104:18 The high **h** *are* a refuge for the wild goats; 2022
104:32 he toucheth the **h**, and they smoke. 2022
114: 4 like rams, *and* the **little h** like lambs. 1389
114: 6 like rams; *and* ye **little h**, like lambs? 1389
121: 1 I will lift up mine eyes unto the **h**, 2022
148: 9 Mountains, and all **h**; fruitful trees, and 1389
Pr 8:25 before the **h** was I brought forth: 1389
SS 2: 8 upon the mountains, skipping upon the **h**. 1389
Isa 2: 2 and *shall be* exalted above the **h**; 1389
2:14 upon all the **h** that are lifted up, 1389
5:25 the **h** did tremble, and their carcases were 2022
7:25 *on* all **h** that shall be digged with 2022
40:12 mountains in scales, and the **h** in a balance? 1389
41:15 *them* small, and shalt make the **h** as chaff. 1389
42:15 I will make waste mountains and **h**, and 1389
54:10 shall depart, and the **h** be removed; 1389
55:12 the **h** shall break forth before you *into* 1389
65: 7 and blasphemed me upon the **h**: 1389
Jer 3:23 in vain *is salvation hoped for* from the **h**, 1389
4:24 they trembled, and all the **h** moved lightly. 1389
13:27 thine abominations on the **h** in the fields. 1389
17: 2 groves by the green trees upon the high **h**. 1389
Eze 6: 3 to the **h**, to the rivers, and to the valleys; 1389
35: 8 his mountains *with* his slain *men*: in thy **h**, 1389
36: 4 to the **h**, to the rivers, and to the valleys, 1389
36: 6 to the **h**, to the rivers, and to the valleys, 1389
Hos 4:13 burn incense upon the **h**, under oaks and 1389
10: 8 Cover us; and to the **h**, Fall on us. 1389
Joel 3:18 the **h** shall flow *with* milk, and all the rivers 1389
Am 9:13 drop sweet wine, and all the **h** shall melt. 1389
Mic 4: 1 and *it shall be* exalted above the **h**; 1389
6: 1 the mountains, and let the **h** hear thy voice. 1389
Na 1: 5 the **h** melt, and the earth is burnt at his 1389
Hab 3: 6 were scattered, the perpetual **h** did bow: 1389
Zep 1:10 the second, and a great crashing from the **h**. 1389
Lk 23:30 Fall on us; and to the **h**, Cover us. *1015*

HIM (6667) [HE] See Index

HIMSELF (528) [HE, SELF] See Index

HIN (22)
Ex 29:40 with the fourth part of a **h** of beaten oil; 1969
29:40 the fourth *part* of a **h** of wine *for* a drink 1969
30:24 shekel of the sanctuary, and of oil olive a **h**: 1969
Lev 19:36 just weights, a just ephah, and a just **h**, 1969
23:13 *shall be of* wine, the fourth *part* of a **h**. 1969
Nu 15: 4 mingled with the fourth *part* of a **h** of oil. 1969
15: 5 the fourth *part* of a **h** *of* wine for a drink 1969
15: 6 mingled with the third *part* of a **h** of oil. 1969
15: 7 shalt offer the third *part* of a **h** *of* wine, 1969
15: 9 deals *of* flour mingled with half a **h** of oil. 1969
15:10 thou shalt bring for a drink offering half a **h** 1969
28: 5 mingled with the fourth *part* of a **h** of 1969
28: 7 *be* the fourth *part* of a **h** for the one lamb: 1969
28:14 their drink offerings shall be half a **h** of 1969
28:14 the third *part* of a **h** unto a ram, and 1969
28:14 a ram, and a fourth *part* of a **h** unto a lamb: 1969
Eze 4:11 also water by measure, the sixth *part* of a **h**: 1969
45:24 for a ram, and a **h** of oil for an ephah. 1969
46: 5 be able to give, and a **h** of oil to an ephah. 1969
46: 7 shall attain unto, and a **h** of oil to an ephah. 1969
46:11 is able to give, and a **h** of oil to an ephah. 1969
46:14 of an ephah, and the third *part* of a **h** of oil, 1969

HIND (3) [HINDS, HINDS']
Ge 49:21 Naphtali *is* a **h** let loose: he giveth goodly 355
Pr 5:19 *Let her be as* the loving **h** and pleasant roe; 365
Jer 14: 5 the **h** also calved in the field, and forsook *it*, 365

HINDER (16) [HINDERED, HINDERETH, HINDERMOST, HINDMOST]
Ge 24:56 he said unto them, **H** me not, seeing 309
Nu 22:16 I pray thee, **h** thee from coming unto me: 4513
2Sa 2:23 wherefore Abner with the **h end** of the spear 310
1Ki 7:25 and all their **h parts** *were* inward. 268
2Ch 4: 4 and all their **h parts** *were* inward. 268
Ne 4: 8 fight against Jerusalem, and to **h** it. 6213+8442
Job 9:12 Behold, he taketh away, who can **h** him? 7725
11:10 or gather together, then who can **h** him? 7725
Ps 78:66 he smote his enemies in the **h parts**: he put 268
Joel 2:20 his **h part** towards the utmost sea, and 5490
Zec 14: 8 and half of them toward the **h** sea: 314
Mk 4:38 And he was in the **h part of** the **ship**, *4403*
Ac 8:36 *is* water; what doth **h** me to be baptized? *2967*
27:41 the **h part** was broken with the violence of *4403*
1Co 9:12 suffer all *things*, lest we should **h** *1325+1464*
Gal 5: 7 who did **h** you that *ye* should not obey *348*

HINDERED (5) [HINDER]
Ezr 6: 8 be given unto these men, that *they* be not **h**. 989
Lk 11:52 and them that were entering in ye **h**. *2967*
Ro 15:22 I have been much **h from** coming to you. *1465*
1Th 2:18 even I Paul, once and again; but Satan **h** us. *1465*
1Pe 3: 7 the grace of life; that your prayers be not **h**. *1581*

HINDERETH (1) [HINDER]
Isa 14: 6 nations in anger, *is* persecuted, *and* none **h**. 2820

HINDERMOST (2) [HINDER]
Ge 33: 2 her children after, and Rachel and Joseph **h**. 314
Jer 50:12 the **h** of the nations *shall be* a wilderness, 319

HINDMOST (3) [HINDER]
Nu 2:31 They shall go **h** with their standards. 314
Dt 25:18 thee by the way, and **smote the h** of thee, 2179
Jos 10:19 your enemies, and **smite the h** of them; 2179

HINDS (4) [HIND]
Job 39: 1 *or* canst thou mark when the **h** do calve? 355
Ps 29: 9 The voice of the LORD maketh the **h** to 355
SS 2: 7 by the roes, and by the **h** of the field, that ye 355
3: 5 by the roes, and by the **h** of the field, that ye 355

HINDS' (3) [HIND]
2Sa 22:34 He maketh my feet like **h** *feet*: and 355
Ps 18:33 He maketh my feet like **h** *feet*, and 355
Hab 3:19 he will make my feet like **h** *feet*, and he will 355

HINGES (2)
1Ki 7:50 the **h** *of* gold, *both* for the doors of 6596
Pr 26:14 *As* the door turneth upon his **h**, so *doth* 6735

HINNOM (13)
Jos 15: 8 son of **H** unto the south side of the Jebusite; 2011
15: 8 that *lieth* before the valley of **H** westward, 2011
18:16 that *lieth* before the valley of the son of **H**, 2011
18:16 descended *to* the valley of **H**, to the side of 2011
2Ki 23:10 which *is* in the valley of the children of **H**, 2011
2Ch 28: 3 burnt incense in the valley of the son of **H**, 2011
33: 6 the fire in the valley of the son of **H**: 2011
Ne 11:30 from Beer-sheba unto the valley of **H**. 2011
Jer 7:31 which *is* in the valley of the son of **H**, 2011
7:32 nor the valley of the son of **H**, but 2011
19: 2 go forth unto the valley of the son of **H**, 2011

Jer 19: 6 nor The valley of the son of **H**, but The 2011
32:35 which *are* in the valley of the son of **H**, 2011

HIP (1)
Jdg 15: 8 he smote them **h** and thigh *with* a great 7785

HIRAH (2)
Ge 38: 1 a certain Adullamite, whose name *was* **H**. 2437
38:12 he and his friend **H** the Adullamite. 2437

HIRAM (22) [HIRAM'S]
2Sa 5:11 **H** king of Tyre sent messengers to David, 2438
1Ki 5: 1 **H** king of Tyre sent his servants unto 2438
5: 1 his father: for **H** was ever a lover of David. 2438
5: 2 And Solomon sent to **H**, saying, 2438
5: 7 when **H** heard the words of Solomon, 2438
5: 8 **H** sent to Solomon, saying, I have 2438
5:10 So **H** gave Solomon cedar trees and 2438
5:11 Solomon gave **H** twenty thousand measures 2438
5:11 thus gave Solomon to **H** year by year. 2438
5:12 there was peace between **H** and Solomon; 2438
7:13 king Solomon sent and fet **H** out of Tyre. 2438
7:40 **H** made the lavers, and the shovels, and 2438
7:40 So **H** made an end of doing all the work 2438
7:45 which **H** made to king Solomon *for* 2438
9:11 (*Now* **H** the king of Tyre had furnished 2438
9:11 king Solomon gave **H** twenty cities in 2438
9:12 **H** came out from Tyre to see the cities 2438
9:14 **H** sent to the king sixscore talents of gold. 2438
9:27 **H** sent in the navy his servants, 2438
10:11 the navy also of **H**, that brought gold from 2438
10:22 sea a navy of Tharshish with the navy of **H**: 2438
1Ch 14: 1 Now **H** king of Tyre sent messengers to 2438

HIRAM'S (1) [HIRAM]
1Ki 5:18 **H** builders did hew *them*, and 2438

HIRE (23) [HIRED, HIRELING, HIRES, HIREST]
Ge 30:18 God hath given *me* my **h**, because I have 7939
30:32 the goats: and *of such* shall be my **h**. 7939
30:33 when it shall come for my **h** before thy 7939
31: 8 he said thus, The ringstraked shall be thy **h**; 7939
Ex 22:15 if it *be* a hired *thing*, it came for his **h**. 7939
Dt 23:18 Thou shalt not bring the **h** of a whore, or 868
24:15 At his day thou shalt give *him* his **h**, 7939
1Ki 5: 6 unto thee will I give **h** for thy servants 7939
1Ch 19: 6 thousand talents of silver to **h** them chariots 7936
Isa 23:17 she shall turn to her **h**, and shall commit 868
23:18 and her **h** shall be holiness to the LORD: 868
46: 6 silver in the balance, *and* **h** a goldsmith; 7936
Eze 16:31 not been as a harlot, in that *thou* scornest **h**; 868
16:41 and thou also shalt give no **h** any more. 868
Mic 1: 7 for she gathered *it* of the **h** of a harlot, and 868
1: 7 and they shall return to the **h** of a harlot. 868
3:11 the priests thereof teach for **h**, and 4242
Zec 8:10 For before these days there was no **h** for 7939
8:10 was no hire for man, nor any **h** for beast; 7939
Mt 20: 1 which went out early in the morning to **h** *3409*
20: 8 Call the labourers, and give them *their* **h**, *3408*
Lk 10: 7 for the labourer is worthy of his **h**. Go not *3408*
Jas 5: 4 the **h** of the labourers which have reaped *3408*

HIRED (34) [HIRE]
Ge 30:16 for **surely** I have **h** thee with my 7936+7936
Ex 12:45 and a **h servant** shall not eat thereof. 7916
22:15 if it *be* a **h** *thing*, it came for his hire. 7916
Lev 19:13 neither rob *him*: the wages of **him that is h** 7916
22:10 or a **h servant**, shall not eat *of* the holy 7916
25: 6 for thy **h servant**, and for thy stranger that 7916
25:40 *But* as a **h servant**, *and* as a sojourner, 7916
25:50 according to the time of a **h servant** shall it 7916
25:53 *And* as a yearly **h servant** shall he be with 7916
Dt 15:18 for he hath been worth a double **h servant** 7916
23: 4 they **h** against thee Balaam the son of Beor 7936
24:14 Thou shalt not oppress a **h servant** *that is* 7916
Jdg 9: 4 wherewith Abimelech **h** vain and 7936
18: 4 with me, and hath **h** me, and I am his priest. 7936
1Sa 2: 5 *They that were* full have **h out** themselves 7936
2Sa 10: 6 and **h** the Syrians of Beth-rehob, 7936
2Ki 7: 6 the king of Israel hath **h** against us 7936
1Ch 19: 7 So they **h** thirty and two thousand chariots, 7936
2Ch 24:12 **h** masons and carpenters to repair the house 7936
25: 6 He **h** also an hundred thousand mighty *men* 7936
Ezr 4: 5 **h** counsellers against them, to frustrate their 7936
Ne 6:12 for Tobiah and Sanballat had **h** him. 7936
6:13 Therefore *was* he **h**, that I should be afraid, 7936
13: 2 and with water, but **h** Balaam against them, 7936
Isa 7:20 shall the Lord shave with a rasor that is **h**, 7917
Jer 46:21 Also her **h men** *are* in the midst of her like 7916
Hos 8: 9 alone by himself: Ephraim hath **h** lovers. 8566
8:10 though they have **h** among the nations, 8566
Mt 20: 7 say unto him, Because no *man* hath **h** us. *3409*
20: 9 And when they came that *were* **h** about NIG
Mk 1:20 Zebedee in the ship with the **h servants**, *3411*
Lk 15:17 How many **h** *servants* of my father's have *3407*
15:19 thy son: make me as one of thy **h** *servants*. *3407*
Ac 28:30 dwelt two whole years in his own **h house**, *3410*

HIRED HAND; HIRED MAN See HIRELING

HIRELING (9) [HIRE]
Job 7: 1 *are not* his days also like the days of a **h**? 7916
7: 2 as a **h** looketh for the reward of his work: 7916
14: 6 till he shall accomplish, as a **h**, his day. 7916
Isa 16:14 as the years of a **h**, and the glory of Moab 7916
21:16 according to the years of a **h**, and all 7916
Mal 3: 5 against those that oppress the **h** in *his* 7916
Jn 10:12 But *he that is* a **h**, and not the shepherd, *3411*
10:13 The **h** fleeth, because he is a hireling, and *3411*
10:13 because he is a **h**, and careth not for *3411*

HIRES (1) [HIRE]
Mic 1: 7 all the **h** thereof shall be burnt with the fire, 868

HIREST (1) [HIRE]
Eze 16:33 thy gifts to all thy lovers, and **h** them, 7809

HIS (8478) [HE] See Index

HISS (12) [HISSING]
1Ki 9: 8 by it shall be astonished, and shall **h**; 8319
Job 27:23 at him, and shall **h** him out of his place. 8319
Isa 5:26 will **h** unto them from the end of the earth: 8319
7:18 *that* the LORD shall **h** for the fly that *is* in 8319
Jer 19: 8 and **h** because of all the plagues thereof. 8319
49:17 and shall **h** at all the plagues thereof. 8319
50:13 be astonished, and **h** at all her plagues. 8319
La 2:15 they **h** and wag their head at the daughter 8319
2:16 they **h** and gnash the teeth: they say, 8319
Eze 27:36 The merchants among the people shall **h** at 8319
Zep 2:15 every one that passeth by her shall **h**, *and* 8319
Zec 10: 8 I will **h** for them, and gather them; for I 8319

HISSING (8) [HISS]
2Ch 29: 8 to astonishment, and to **h**, as ye see with 8322
Jer 18:16 make their land desolate, *and* a perpetual **h**; 8292
19: 8 I will make this city desolate, and a **h**; 8322
25: 9 and a **h**, and perpetual desolations. 8322
25:18 an astonishment, a **h**, and a curse; 8322
29:18 an astonishment, and a **h**, and a reproach, 8322
51:37 an astonishment, and a **h**, without an 8322
Mic 6:16 and the inhabitants thereof a **h**: 8322

HIT (2)
1Sa 31: 3 sore against Saul, and the archers **h** him; 4672
1Ch 10: 3 the archers **h** him, and he was wounded of 4672

HITHER (67) [HITHERTO] See Index

HITHERTO (19) [HITHER, TO] See Index

HITTITE (26) [HITTITES]
Ge 23:10 Ephron the **H** answered Abraham in 2850
25: 9 the field of Ephron the son of Zohar the **H**, 2850
26:34 to wife Judith the daughter of Beeri the **H**, 2850
26:34 and Bashemath the daughter of Elon the **H**: 2850
36: 2 Adah the daughter of Elon the **H**, and 2850
49:29 the cave that *is* in the field of Ephron the **H**, 2850
49:30 the **H** for a possession of a buryingplace. 2850
50:13 of a buryingplace of Ephron the **H**, 2850
Ex 23:28 the Canaanite, and the **H**, from before thee. 2850
33: 2 and the **H**, and the Perizzite, the Hivite, and 2850
34:11 and the **H**, and the Perizzite, and the Hivite, 2850
Jos 9: 1 the **H**, and the Amorite, the Canaanite, 2850
11: 3 the **H**, and the Perizzite, and the Jebusite in 2850
1Sa 26: 6 and said to Ahimelech the **H**, 2850
2Sa 11: 3 daughter of Eliam, the wife of Uriah the **H**? 2850
11: 6 sent to Joab, *saying*, Send me Uriah the **H**. 2850
11:17 of David; and Uriah the **H** died also. 2850
11:21 Thy servant Uriah the **H** is dead also. 2850
11:24 and thy servant Uriah the **H** is dead also. 2850

2Sa 12: 9 thou hast killed Uriah the **H** with 2850
12:10 hast taken the wife of Uriah the **H** to be thy 2850
23:39 Uriah the **H**: thirty and seven *in* all. 2850
1Ki 15: 5 save only in the matter of Urijah the **H**. 2850
1Ch 11:41 Uriah the **H**, Zabad the son of Ahlai, 2850
Eze 16: 3 father *was* an Amorite, and thy mother a **H**. 2850
16:45 your mother *was* a **H**, and your father an 2850

HITTITES (22) [HITTITE]
Ge 15:20 the **H**, and the Perizzites, and 2850
Ex 3: 8 the **H**, and the Amorites, and the Perizzites, 2850
3:17 the **H**, and the Amorites, and the Perizzites, 2850
13: 5 the **H**, and the Amorites, and the Hivites, 2850
23:23 the **H**, and the Perizzites, and 2850
Nu 13:29 the **H**, and the Jebusites, and the Amorites, 2850
Dt 7: 1 the **H**, and the Girgashites, and 2850
20:17 *namely,* the **H**, and the Amorites, 2850
Jos 1: 4 all the land of the **H**, and unto the great sea 2850
3:10 the **H**, and the Hivites, and the Perizzites, 2850
12: 8 in the south *country;* the **H**, the Amorites, 2850
24:11 the **H**, and the Girgashites, the Hivites, and 2850
Jdg 1:26 the man went *into* the land of the **H**, and 2850
3: 5 **H**, and Amorites, and Perizzites, 2850
1Ki 9:20 **H**, Perizzites, Hivites, and Jebusites, 2850
10:29 so for all the kings of the **H**, and for 2850
11: 1 Ammonites, Edomites, Zidonians, *and* **H**; 2850
2Ki 7: 6 hath hired against us the kings of the **H**, 2850
2Ch 1:17 they out *horses* for all the kings of the **H**, 2850
8: 7 *As for* all the people that were left of the **H**, 2850
Ezr 9: 1 the **H**, the Perizzites, the Jebusites, 2850
Ne 9: 8 the **H**, the Amorites, and the Perizzites, and 2850

HIVITE (9) [HIVITES]
Ge 10:17 And the **H**, and the Arkite, and the Sinite, 2340
34: 2 when Shechem the son of Hamor the **H**, 2340
36: 2 of Anah the daughter of Zibeon the **H**; 2340
Ex 23:28 which shall drive out the **H**, the Canaanite, 2340
33: 2 and the Perizzite, the **H**, and the Jebusite: 2340
34:11 the Perizzite, and the **H**, and the Jebusite. 2340
Jos 9: 1 the Perizzite, the **H**, and the Jebusite, 2340
11: 3 *to* the **H** under Hermon in the land of 2340
1Ch 1:15 And the **H**, and the Arkite, and the Sinite, 2340

HIVITES (16) [HIVITE]
Ex 3: 8 the Perizzites, and the **H**, and the Jebusites. 2340
3:17 the Perizzites, and the **H**, and the Jebusites, 2340
13: 5 the Amorites, and the **H**, and the Jebusites, 2340
23:23 the Canaanites, the **H**, and the Jebusites: 2340
Dt 7: 1 the Perizzites, and the **H**, and the Jebusites, 2340
20:17 and the Perizzites, the **H**, and the Jebusites; 2340
Jos 3:10 the **H**, and the Perizzites, and 2340
9: 7 the men of Israel said unto the **H**, 2340
11:19 save the **H** the inhabitants of Gibeon: 2340
12: 8 the Perizzites, the **H**, and the Jebusites: 2340
24:11 the Girgashites, the **H**, and the Jebusites; 2340
Jdg 3: 3 and the **H** that dwelt in mount Lebanon, 2340
3: 5 and Perizzites, and **H**, and Jebusites: 2340
2Sa 24: 7 *to* all the cities of the **H**, and of 2340
1Ki 9:20 Hittites, Perizzites, **H**, and Jebusites, 2340
2Ch 8: 7 the Perizzites, and the **H**, and the Jebusites, 2340

HIZKI See HEZEKI

HIZKIAH (1)
Zep 1: 1 the son of Amariah, the son of **H**, 2396

HIZKIJAH (1)
Ne 10:17 Ater, **H**, Azzur, 2396

HO (4)
Ru 4: 1 *H*, such a one, turn aside, sit down here. NIH
Isa 55: 1 **H**, every one that thirsteth, come ye to 1945
Zec 2: 6 **H**, ho, *come forth,* and flee from the land of 1945
2: 6 Ho, **h**, *come forth,* and flee from the land of 1945

HOAR (4) [HOARFROST, HOARY]
Ex 16:14 *as* small as the **h frost** on the ground. 3713
1Ki 2: 6 let not his **h head** go down *to* the grave in 7872
2: 9 his **h head** bring thou down *to* the grave 7872
Isa 46: 4 *even* to **h hairs** will I carry *you:* I have 7872

HOARFROST (1) [FROST, HOAR]
Ps 147:16 like wool: he scattereth the **h** like ashes. 3713

HOARY (4) [HOAR]
Lev 19:32 Thou shalt rise up before the **h head**, and 7872
Job 38:29 the **h frost** of heaven, who hath gendered 3713
41:32 after him; *one* would think the deep to be **h**. 7872
Pr 16:31 The **h head** *is* a crown of glory, *if* it be 7872

HOBAB (2)
Nu 10:29 Moses said unto **H**, the son of Raguel 2246
Jdg 4:11 *which was* of the children of **H** the father in 2246

HOBAH (1)
Ge 14:15 and smote them, and pursued them unto **H**, 2327

HOBAIAH See HABAIAH

HOD (1)
1Ch 7:37 **H**, and Shamma, and Shilshah, and Ithran, 1936

HODAIAH (1)
1Ch 3:24 the sons of Elioenai *were,* **H**, and Eliashib, 1939

HODAVIAH (3)
1Ch 5:24 Azriel, and Jeremiah, and **H**, and Jahdiel, 1938
9: 7 the son of **H**, the son of Hasenuah, 1938
Ezr 2:40 of the children of **H**, seventy and four. 1938

HODESH (1)
1Ch 8: 9 he begat of **H** his wife, Jobab, and Zibia, 2321

HODEVAH (1)
Ne 7:43 *and* of the children of **H**, seventy and four. 1937

HODIAH (1)
1Ch 4:19 the sons of *his* wife **H** the sister of Naham, 1940

HODIJAH (5)
Ne 8: 7 **H**, Maaseiah, Kelita, Azariah, Jozabad, 1941
9: 5 Sherebiah, **H**, Shebaniah, *and* Pethahiah, 1941
10:10 Shebaniah, **H**, Kelita, Pelaiah, Hanan, 1941
10:13 **H**, Bani, Beninu. 1941
10:18 **H**, Hashum, Bezai, 1941

HOGLAH (4)
Nu 26:33 and Noah, **H**, Milcah, and Tirzah. 2295
27: 1 Noah, and **H**, and Milcah, and Tirzah. 2295
36:11 Tirzah, and **H**, and Milcah, and Noah, 2295
Jos 17: 3 Mahlah, and Noah, **H**, Milcah, and Tirzah. 2295

HOHAM (1)
Jos 10: 3 of Jerusalem sent unto **H** king of Hebron, 1944

HOISED (1)
Ac 27:40 and **h up** the mainsail to the wind, and *1869*

HOLD (185) [HELD, HOLDEN, HOLDEST, HOLDETH, HOLDING, HOLDS]
Ge 19:16 the men **laid h** upon his hand, and upon 2388
21:18 lift up the lad, and **h** him in thine hand; 2388
25:26 and his hand **took h** on Esau's heel; 270
Ex 5: 1 that they may **h a feast** unto me in 2287
9: 2 refuse to let *them* go, and wilt **h** them still, 2388
10: 9 for we *must* **h** a feast unto the LORD. NIH
14:14 fight for you, and ye shall **h** your **peace**. 2790
15:14 sorrow shall **take h** on the inhabitants of 270
15:15 of Moab, trembling shall **take h** upon them; 270
20: 7 for the LORD will not **h** him **guiltless** that 5352
26: 5 that the loops may **take h** one of another. 6901
Nu 30: 4 and her father shall **h** his **peace** at her: 2790
30:14 **altogether h** his **peace** at her from 2790+2790
Dt 5:11 for the LORD will not **h** *him* **guiltless** that 5352
21:19 his father and his mother **lay h** on him, 8610
22:28 **lay h on** her, and lie with her, and they be 8610
32:41 and mine hand **take h** on judgment; 270
Jdg 9:46 into a **h** of the house of the god Berith. 6877
9:49 put *them* to the **h**, and set the hold on fire 6877
9:49 to the hold, and set the **h** on fire upon them; 6877
16:29 Samson **took h** of the two middle pillars 3943
18:19 they said unto him, **H** thy **peace**, lay thine 2790
19:29 **laid h** on his concubine, and divided her, 2388
Ru 3:15 the vail that *thou hast* upon thee, and **h** it. 270
1Sa 15:27 he **laid h** upon the skirt of his mantle, and 2388
22: 4 him all the while that David was in the **h**. 4686
22: 5 Gad said unto David, Abide not in the **h**; 4686
24:22 David and his men gat them up unto the **h**. 4686
2Sa 1:11 David **took h** on his clothes, and rent them; 2388
2:21 and **lay** thee **h on** one of the young men, and 270

2Sa 2:22 should I **h up** my face to Joab thy brother? 5375
4:10 I **took h** of him, and slew him in Ziklag, 270
5: 7 Nevertheless David took the **strong h** of 4686
5:17 David heard *of it,* and went down to the **h**. 4686
6: 6 *his hand* to the ark of God, and **took h** of it; 270
13:11 he **took h** of her, and said unto her, 2388
13:20 **h** now thy **peace**, my sister: he *is* thy 2790
18: 9 his head **caught h** of the oak, and he was 2388
23:14 David *was* then in a **h**, and the garrison of 4686
24: 7 came *to* the **strong h** of Tyre, and *to* all 4013
1Ki 1:50 and **caught h** on the horns of the altar. 2388
1:51 he hath **caught h** on the horns of the altar, 270
2: 9 Now therefore **h** him not **guiltless**: for thou 5352
2:28 and **caught h** on the horns of the altar. 2388
9: 9 have **taken h** upon other gods, and 2388
13: 4 hand from the altar, saying, **Lay h on** him. 8610
2Ki 2: 3 he said, Yea, I know *it;* **h** you your **peace**. 2814
2: 5 Yea, I know *it;* **h** you your **peace**. 2814
2:12 he **took h** of his own clothes, and rent them 2388
6:32 shut the door, and **h** him **fast** at the door: 3905
7: 9 a day of good tidings, and we **h** our **peace**: 2814
1Ch 11:16 David *was* then in the **h**, and 4686
12: 8 into the **h** to the wilderness men of might, 4679
12:16 of Benjamin and Judah to the **h** unto David. 4679
13: 9 Uzza put forth his hand to **h** the ark; 270
2Ch 7:22 **laid h** on other gods, and worshipped them, 2388
Ne 8:11 **H** your **peace**, for the day *is* holy; 2013
Est 4:11 except such to whom the king shall **h out** 3447
Job 6:24 Teach me, and I will **h** my **tongue**: and 2790
8:15 he shall **h** it **fast**, but it shall not endure. 2388
9:28 I know that thou wilt not **h** me **innocent**. 5352
11: 3 Should thy lies **make** men **h** their **peace**? 2790
13: 5 you would **altogether h** your **peace**, 2790+2790
13:13 **H** your **peace**, let me alone, that I may 2790
13:19 for now, if I **h** my **tongue**, I shall give up 2790
17: 9 The righteous also shall **h on** his way, and 270
21: 6 and trembling **taketh h on** my flesh. 270
27: 6 My righteousness I **h fast**, and will not let 2388
27:20 Terrors **take h on** him as waters, a tempest 5381
30:16 the days of affliction have **taken h upon** me. 270
33:31 unto me: **h** thy **peace**, and I will speak. 2790
33:33 **h** thy **peace**, and I shall teach thee wisdom. 2790
36:17 judgment and justice **take h on** *thee.* 8551
38:13 That *it* might **take h** of the ends of the earth, 270
41:26 sword of him that layeth at him cannot **h**: 6965
Ps 17: 5 **H up** my goings in thy paths, *that* my 8551
35: 2 **Take h** of shield and buckler, and stand up 2388
39:12 unto my cry; **h** not thy **peace** at my tears: 2790
40:12 mine iniquities have **taken h upon** me, so 5381
48: 6 Fear **took h upon** them there, *and* pain, as of 270
69:24 and let thy wrathful anger **take h** of them. 5381
83: 1 **h** not thy **peace**, and be not still, O God. 2790
109: 1 **H** not thy **peace**, O God of my praise; 2790
116: 3 and the pains of hell **gat h upon** me: 4672
119:53 Horror hath **taken h upon** me because of 270
119:117 **H** thou me **up**, and I shall be safe: and 5582
119:143 Trouble and anguish have **taken h on** me: 4672
139:10 hand lead me, and thy right hand shall **h** me. 270
Pr 2:19 neither **take** they **h** of the paths of life. 5381
3:18 She *is* a tree of life to them that **lay h** upon 2388
4:13 **Take fast h** of instruction; let *her* not go: 2388
5: 5 go down *to* death; her steps **take h** on hell. 8551
30:28 The spider **taketh h** with her hands, and 8610
31:19 to the spindle, and her hands **h** the distaff. 8551
Ecc 2: 3 to **lay h** on folly, till I might see what *was* 270
7:18 *It is* good that thou shouldest **take h** of this; 270
SS 3: 8 They all **h** swords, *being* expert in war: 270
7: 8 I will **take h** of the boughs thereof: 270
Isa 3: 6 When a man shall **take h** of his brother *of* 8610
4: 1 in that day seven women shall **take h** of 2388
5:29 **lay h** of the prey, and shall carry *it* away 270
13: 8 sorrows shall **take h** of *them;* they shall be 270
21: 3 pangs have **taken h upon** me, as the pangs 270
27: 5 Or let him **take h** of my strength, *that* he 2388
31: 9 he shall pass over *to* his **strong h** for fear, 5553
41:13 For I the LORD thy God will **h** thy right 2388
42: 6 will **h** thine hand, and will keep thee, and 2388
56: 2 and the son of man *that* **layeth h** on it; 2388
56: 4 that please me, and **take h** of my covenant; 2388
56: 6 polluting it, and **taketh h** of my covenant; 2388
62: 1 For Zion's sake will I not **h my peace**, and 2814
62: 6 *which* shall never **h** their **peace** day nor 2814
64: 7 that stirreth up himself to **take h** of thee: 2388
64:12 wilt thou **h** thy **peace**, and afflict us very 2814

Jer 2:13 broken cisterns, that can **h** no water. 3557
4:19 I cannot **h** my **peace**, because thou hast 2790
6:23 They shall **lay h on** bow and spear; they *are* 2388
6:24 anguish hath **taken h** of us, *and* pain, as of 2388
8: 5 they **h fast** deceit, they refuse to return. 2388
8:21 astonishment hath **taken h on** me. 2388
50:42 They shall **h** the bow and the lance: 2388
50:43 anguish **took h** of him, *and* pangs as of a 2388
Eze 29: 7 When they **took h** of thee by thy hand, 8610
30:21 to bind it, to make it strong to **h** the sword. 8610
41: 6 that *they* might have **h**, but they had not hold 270
41: 6 but they had not **h** in the wall of the house. 270
Am 6:10 shall he say, **H** thy **tongue**: for *we may* not 2013
Mic 4: 8 the **strong h** of the daughter of Zion, 6077
6:14 thou shalt **take h**, but shalt not deliver; and 5253
Na 1: 7 *is* good, a **strong h** in the day of trouble; 4581
Hab 1:10 they shall deride every **strong h**; for they 4013
Zep 1: 7 **H** thy **peace** at the presence of the Lord 2013
Zec 1: 6 did they not **take h** of your fathers? 5381
8:23 **take h** out of all languages of the nations, 2388
8:23 even shall **take h** of the skirt of him that is 2388
9: 3 And Tyrus did build herself a **strong h**, and 4692
9:12 Turn ye to the **strong h**, ye prisoners of 1225
11: 5 slay them, and **h** themselves not **guilty**: 816
14:13 they shall **lay h** every one on the hand of 2388
Mt 6:24 or else he will **h to** the one, and despise *472*
12:11 will he not **lay h on** it, and lift *it* out? *2902*
14: 3 For Herod had **laid h on** John, and *2902*
20:31 because they should **h** their **peace**: *4623*
21:26 fear the people; for all **h** John as a prophet. *2192*
26:48 I shall kiss, that *same* is he: **h** him **fast**. *2902*
26:55 in the temple, and ye **laid** no **h** on me. *2902*
26:57 And they that had **laid h** on Jesus led *him* *2902*
Mk 1:25 saying, **H** thy **peace**, and come out of him. *5392*
3:21 heard *of it,* they went out to **lay h on** him: *2902*
6:17 had sent forth and **laid h upon** John, *2902*
7: 4 which they have received to **h**, *as* *2902*
7: 8 ye **h** the tradition of men, *as* the washing of *2902*
10:48 charged him that he should **h** his **peace**: *4623*
12:12 And they sought to **lay h on** him, but *2902*
14:51 and the young men **laid h on** him: *2902*
Lk 4:35 saying, **H** thy **peace**, and come out of him. *5392*
16:13 or else he will **h to** the one, and despise *472*
18:39 rebuked him, that he should **h** his **peace**: *4623*
19:40 I tell you that, if these should **h** their **peace**, *4623*
20:20 *men,* that they might **take h** of his words, *1949*
20:26 And they could not **take h** of his words *1949*
23:26 they **laid h upon** one Simon, a Cyrenian, *1949*
Ac 4: 3 and put *them* in **h** unto the next day: *5084*
12:17 unto them with the hand to **h** their **peace**, *4601*
18: 9 not afraid, but speak, and **h** not thy **peace**: *4623*
Ro 1:18 of men, who **h** the truth in unrighteousness; *2722*
1Co 14:30 that sitteth *by,* let the first **h** his **peace**. *4601*
Php 2:29 with all gladness; and **h** such in reputation: *2192*
1Th 5:21 Prove all *things;* **h fast** *that which is* good. *2722*
2Th 2:15 **h** the traditions which ye have been taught, *2902*
1Ti 6:12 the good fight of faith, **lay h on** eternal life, *1949*
6:19 to come, that they may **lay h on** eternal life. *1949*
2Ti 1:13 **H fast** the form of sound words, *2192*
Heb 3: 6 if we **h fast** the confidence and *2722*
3:14 if we **h** the beginning of *our* confidence *2722*
4:14 the Son of God, let us **h fast** *our* profession. *2902*
6:18 who have fled for refuge to **lay h upon** *2902*
10:23 Let us **h fast** the profession of *our* hope *2722*
Rev 2:14 thou hast there them that **h** the doctrine of *2902*
2:15 So hast thou also them that **h** the doctrine *2902*
2:25 But *that* which ye have *already* **h** fast till I NIG
3: 3 and heard, and **h fast**, and repent. *5083*
3:11 **h** *that* **fast** which thou hast, that no *man* *2902*
18: 2 and the **h** of every foul spirit, and a cage of *5438*
20: 2 And he **laid h on** the dragon, *that* old *2902*

HOLD FAST See CLEAVE; CLEAVED; CLEAVETH

HOLD GUILTY See IMPUTE; IMPUTED; IMPUTETH; IMPUTING

HOLDEN (12) [HOLD]

2Ki 23:22 Surely there was not **h** such a passover 6213
23:23 *wherein* this passover was **h** to the LORD 6213
Job 36: 8 in fetters, *and* be **h** in cords of affliction; 3920
Ps 18:35 thy right hand hath **h** me **up**, and 5582
71: 6 By thee have I been **h up** from the womb: 5564
73:23 with thee: thou hast **h** *me* by my right hand. 270
Pr 5:22 he shall be **h** with the cords of his sins. 8551

Isa 42:14 I have long time **h** my **peace**; I have been 2814
45: 1 to Cyrus, whose right hand I have **h**, to 2388
Lk 24:16 But their eyes were **h** that *they* should not *2902*
Ac 2:24 it was not possible that he should be **h** of it. *2902*
Ro 14: 4 Yea, he shall be **h up**: for God is able to *2476*

HOLDEST (6) [HOLD]
Est 4:14 For if thou **altogether h** thy **peace** at 2790+2790
Job 13:24 thou thy face, and **h** me for thine enemy? 2803
Ps 77: 4 Thou **h** mine eyes waking: I am *so* 270
Jer 49:16 of the rock, that **h** the height of the hill: 8610
Hab 1:13 **h** thy **tongue** when the wicked devoureth 2790
Rev 2:13 Satan's seat *is:* and thou **h fast** my name, *2902*

HOLDETH (9) [HOLD]
Job 2: 3 still he **h fast** his integrity, although thou 2388
26: 9 He **h back** the face of *his* throne, *and* 270
Ps 66: 9 Which **h** our soul in life, and suffereth not 7760
Pr 11:12 but a man of understanding **h** his **peace**. 2790
17:28 Even a fool, when he **h** his **peace**, 2790
Da 10:21 *there is* none that **h** with me in these *things,* 2388
Am 1: 5 him that **h** the sceptre from the house of 8551
1: 8 him that **h** the sceptre from Ashkelon, and 8551
Rev 2: 1 These *things* saith he that **h** the seven stars *2902*

HOLDING (9) [HOLD]
Isa 33:15 that shaketh his hands from **h** of bribes, 8551
Jer 6:11 fury of the LORD; I am weary with **h in**: 3557
Mk 7: 3 eat not, **h** the tradition of the elders. *2902*
Php 2:16 **H forth** the word of life; that I may rejoice *1907*
Col 2:19 And not **h** the head, from which all *2902*
1Ti 1:19 **H** faith, and a good conscience; *2192*
3: 9 **H** the mystery of the faith in a pure *2192*
Tit 1: 9 **H fast** the faithful word as *he* hath been *472*
Rev 7: 1 **h** the four winds of the earth, that the wind *2902*

HOLDS (21) [HOLD]
Nu 13:19 dwell in, whether in tents, or in **strong h**; 4013
Jdg 6: 2 in the mountains, and caves, and **strong h**. 4679
1Sa 23:14 David abode in the wilderness in **strong h**, 4679
23:19 himself with us in **strong h** in the wood, 4679
23:29 and dwelt in **strong h** at En-gedi. 4679
2Ki 8:12 their **strong h** wilt thou set on fire, and 4013
2Ch 11:11 he fortified the **strong h**, and put captains 4694
Ps 89:40 thou hast brought his **strong h** to ruin. 4013
Isa 23:11 *city,* to destroy the **strong h** thereof. 4581
Jer 48:18 *and* he shall destroy thy **strong h**. 4013
48:41 the **strong h** are surprised, and the mighty 4679
51:30 to fight, they have remained in *their* **h**: 4679
La 2: 2 the **strong h** of the daughter of Judah; 4013
2: 5 he hath destroyed his **strong h**, and 4013
Eze 19: 9 they brought him into **h**, that his voice 4685
Da 11:24 forecast his devices against the **strong h**, 4013
11:39 Thus shall he do in the most strong **h** with a 4013
Mic 5:11 thy land, and throw down all thy **strong h**: 4013
Na 3:12 All thy **strong h** *shall be like* fig trees with 4013
3:14 waters for the siege, fortify thy **strong h**: 4013
2Co 10: 4 God to the pulling down of **strong h**;) *3794*

HOLE (12) [ARMHOLES, HOLE'S, HOLES]
Ex 28:32 there shall be a **h** in the top of it, in 6310
28:32 of woven work round about the **h** of it, 6310
28:32 as it were the **h** of an habergeon, *that* it be 6310
39:23 *there was* a **h** in the midst of the robe, 6310
39:23 as the **h** of an habergeon, *with* a band round 6310
39:23 *with* a band round about the **h**, *that* it 6310
2Ki 12: 9 bored a **h** in the lid of it, and set it beside 2356
SS 5: 4 My beloved put in his hand by the **h** *of* 2356
Isa 11: 8 the sucking child shall play on the **h** of 2352
51: 1 to the **h** of the pit *whence* ye are digged. 4718
Jer 13: 4 and hide it there in a **h** of the rock. 5357
Eze 8: 7 and when I looked, behold a **h** in the wall. 2356

HOLE'S (1) [HOLE]
Jer 48:28 maketh her nest in the sides of the **h** mouth. 6354

HOLES (11) [HOLE]
1Sa 14:11 the Hebrews come forth out of the **h** where 2356
Isa 2:19 they shall go into the **h** of the rocks, and 4631
7:19 in the **h** of the rocks, and upon all thorns, 5357
42:22 *they are* all of them snared in **h**, and 2352
Jer 16:16 every hill, and out of the **h** of the rocks. 5357
Mic 7:17 they shall move out of their **h** like worms 4526
Na 2:12 filled his **h** *with* prey, and his dens *with* 2356
Hag 1: 6 earneth wages *to put it* into a bag with **h**. 5344
Zec 14:12 their eyes shall consume away in their **h**, 2356
Mt 8:20 The foxes have **h**, and the birds of the air *5454*
Lk 9:58 Foxes have **h**, and birds of the air *have* *5454*

HOLIER (1) [HOLY]
Isa 65: 5 come not near to me; for I am **h** than thou. 6942

HOLIEST (3) [HOLY]
Heb 9: 3 the tabernacle which is called the **h of all**; *40+40*
9: 8 that the way into the **h** *of all* was not yet made *40*
10:19 boldness to enter into the **h** by the blood of *40*

HOLILY (1) [HOLY]
1Th 2:10 and God *also,* how **h** and justly and *3743*

HOLINESS (43) [HOLY]
Ex 15:11 who *is* like thee, glorious in **h**, fearful *in* 6944
28:36 engravings of a signet, **H TO THE LORD**. 6944
39:30 engravings of a signet, **H TO THE LORD**. 6944
1Ch 16:29 worship the LORD in the beauty of **h**. 6944
2Ch 20:21 that should praise the beauty of **h**, as *they* 6944
31:18 set office they sanctified themselves *in* **h**: 6944
Ps 29: 2 worship the LORD in the beauty of **h**. 6944
30: 4 give thanks at the remembrance of his **h**. 6944
47: 8 God sitteth upon the throne of his **h**. 6944
48: 1 city of our God, *in* the mountain of his **h**. 6944
60: 6 God hath spoken in his **h**; I will rejoice, 6944
89:35 Once have I sworn by my **h** that I will not 6944
93: 5 **h** becometh thine house, O LORD, 6944
96: 9 O worship the LORD in the beauty of **h**: 6944
97:12 give thanks at the remembrance of his **h**. 6944
108: 7 God hath spoken in his **h**; I will rejoice, 6944
110: 3 in the beauties of **h** from the womb of 6944
Isa 23:18 and her hire shall be **h** to the LORD: 6944
35: 8 a way, and it shall be called The way of **h**; 6944
62: 9 together shall drink it in the courts of my **h**. 6944
63:15 behold from the habitation of thy **h** and 6944
63:18 The people of thy **h** have possessed *it* but 6944
Jer 2: 3 Israel *was* **h** unto the LORD, *and* 6944
23: 9 and because of the words of his **h**. 6944
31:23 O habitation of justice, *and* mountain of **h**. 6944
Am 4: 2 The Lord GOD hath sworn by his **h**, 6944
Ob 1:17 shall be deliverance, and there shall be **h**; 6944
Zec 14:20 bells of the horses, **H UNTO THE LORD**; 6944
14:21 in Judah shall be **h** unto the LORD of 6944
Mal 2:11 for Judah hath profaned the **h** of 6944
Lk 1:75 In **h** and righteousness before him, all *3742*
Ac 3:12 or **h** we had made this *man* to walk? *2150*
Ro 1: 4 according to the Spirit of **h**, by *42*
6:19 members servants to righteousness unto **h**. *38*
6:22 ye have your fruit unto **h**, and the end *38*
2Co 7: 1 and spirit, perfecting **h** in the fear of God. *42*
Eph 4:24 God is created in righteousness and true **h**. *3742*
1Th 3:13 your hearts unblameable in **h** before God, *42*
4: 7 not called us unto uncleanness, but unto **h**. *38*
1Ti 2:15 in faith and charity and **h** with sobriety. *38*
Tit 2: 3 *that they be* in behaviour **as becometh h**, *2412*
Heb 12:10 *our* profit, that *we* might be partakers of his **h**. *41*
12:14 Follow peace with all *men,* and **h**, *38*

HOLLOW (10)
Ge 32:25 against him, he touched the **h** of his thigh; 3709
32:25 the **h** of Jacob's thigh was out of joint, 3709
32:32 which *is* upon the **h** of the thigh, unto this 3709
32:32 he touched the **h** of Jacob's thigh in 3709
Ex 27: 8 **H** with boards shalt thou make it: as it was 5014
38: 7 it withal; he made *the altar* **h** with boards. 5014
Lev 14:37 *be* in the walls of the house with **h strakes**, 8258
Jdg 15:19 God clave a **h place** that *was* in the jaw, 4388
Isa 40:12 measured the waters in the **h of his hand**, 8168
Jer 52:21 thickness thereof *was* four fingers: *it was* **h**. 5014

HOLON (3)
Jos 15:51 Goshen, and **H**, and Giloh; eleven cities 2473
21:15 **H** with her suburbs, and Debir with her 2473
Jer 48:21 upon **H**, and upon Jahazah, and 2473

HOLPEN (5) [HELP]
Ps 83: 8 they have **h** the children of Lot. Selah. 2220
86:17 LORD, hast **h** me, and comforted me. 5826
Isa 31: 3 he that is **h** shall fall down, and they all 5826
Da 11:34 shall fall, they shall be **h** *with* a little help: 5826
Lk 1:54 He hath **h** his servant Israel, in remembrance *482*

HOLY (611) [HOLIER, HOLIEST, HOLILY, HOLINESS, HOLYDAY, UNHOLY]

Ex 3: 5 for the place whereon thou standest *is* **h** 6944
12:16 in the first day *there shall be* a **h** 6944
12:16 in the seventh day there shall be a **h** 6944
15:13 *them* in thy strength unto thy **h** habitation. 6944
16:23 To morrow *is* the rest of the **h** sabbath unto 6944
19: 6 me a kingdom of priests, and a **h** nation. 6918
20: 8 Remember the sabbath day, to **keep** it **h**. 6942
22:31 ye shall be **h** men unto me: neither shall ye 6944
26:33 the vail shall divide unto you between the **h** 6944
26:33 the holy *place* and the **most h**. 6944+6944
26:34 the Testimony in the **most h** *place.* 6944+6944
28: 2 thou shalt make **h** garments for Aaron thy 6944
28: 4 they shall make **h** garments for Aaron thy 6944
28:29 when he goeth in unto the **h** *place,* for a 6944
28:35 in unto the **h** *place* before the LORD, 6944
28:38 that Aaron may bear the iniquity of the **h** 6944
28:38 of Israel shall hallow in all their **h** gifts; 6944
28:43 in the **h** *place;* that they bear not iniquity, 6944
29: 6 and put the **h** crown upon the mitre. 6944
29:29 the **h** garments of Aaron shall be his sons' 6944
29:30 the congregation to minister in the **h** *place.* 6944
29:31 and seethe his flesh in the **h** place. 6918
29:33 shall not eat *thereof,* because they *are* **h**. 6944
29:34 it shall not be eaten, because it *is* **h**. 6944
29:37 and it shall be an altar **most h**: 6944+6944
29:37 whatsoever toucheth the altar shall be **h**. 6942
30:10 it *is* **most h** unto the LORD. 6944+6944
30:25 And thou shalt make it an oil of **h** ointment, 6944
30:25 the apothecary: it shall be a **h** anointing oil. 6944
30:29 that they may be **most h**: 6944+6944
30:29 whatsoever toucheth them shall be **h**. 6942
30:31 This shall be a **h** anointing oil unto me 6944
30:32 of it: it *is* **h**, *and* it shall be holy unto you. 6944
30:32 of it: it *is* holy, *and* it shall be **h** unto you. 6944
30:35 tempered together, pure *and* **h**: 6944
30:36 it shall be unto you **most h**. 6944+6944
30:37 it shall be unto thee **h** for the LORD. 6944
31:10 the **h** garments for Aaron the priest, and 6944
31:11 sweet incense for the **h** *place:* according to 6944
31:14 the sabbath therefore; for it *is* **h** unto you: 6944
31:15 *is* the sabbath of rest, **h** to the LORD: 6944
35: 2 on the seventh day there shall be to you a **h** 6944
35:19 to do service in the **h** *place,* the holy 6944
35:19 to do service in the holy *place,* the **h** 6944
35:21 for all his service, and for the **h** garments. 6944
37:29 he made the **h** anointing oil, and the pure 6944
38:24 the **h** *place,* even the gold of the offering, 6944
39: 1 to do service in the **h** *place,* and made 6944
39: 1 and made the **h** garments for Aaron; 6944
39:30 they made the plate of the **h** crown *of* pure 6944
39:41 The clothes of service to do service in the **h** 6944
39:41 and the **h** garments for Aaron the priest, 6944
40: 9 and all the vessels thereof: and it shall be **h**. 6944
40:10 and it shall be an altar **most h**. 6944+6944
40:13 thou shalt put upon Aaron the **h** garments, 6944

Lev 2: 3 *it is a thing* **most h** of the offerings 6944+6944
2:10 *it is* a **thing most h** of the offerings 6944+6944
5:15 in the **h** *things* of the LORD; 6944
5:16 the harm that he hath done in the **h** *thing,* 6944
6:16 bread shall it be eaten in the **h** place; 6918
6:17 it *is* **most h**, as *is* the sin offering, 6944+6944
6:18 every one that toucheth them shall be **h**. 6942
6:25 before the LORD: it *is* **most h**. 6944+6944
6:26 in the **h** place shall it be eaten, in the court 6918
6:27 shall touch the flesh thereof shall be **h**: 6942
6:27 whereon it was sprinkled in the **h** place. 6918
6:29 priests shall eat thereof: it *is* **most h**. 6944+6944
6:30 *withal* in the **h** *place,* shall be eaten: 6944
7: 1 of the trespass offering: it *is* **most h**. 6944+6944
7: 6 it shall be eaten in the **h** place: it *is* most 6918
7: 6 eaten in the holy place: it *is* **most h**. 6944+6944
8: 9 did he put the golden plate, the **h** crown; 6944
10:10 that *ye* may put difference between **h** and 6944
10:12 beside the altar: for it *is* **most h**: 6944+6944
10:13 ye shall eat it in the **h** place, because it *is* 6918
10:17 ye not eaten the sin offering in the **h** place, 6944
10:17 seeing it *is* **most h**, and *God* hath 6944+6944
10:18 **h** *place:* ye should indeed have eaten it in 6944
10:18 eaten it in the **h** *place,* as I commanded. 6944
11:44 sanctify yourselves, and ye shall be **h**; 6918
11:44 and ye shall be holy; for I *am* **h**: 6918
11:45 ye shall therefore be **h**, for I *am* holy. 6918
11:45 ye shall therefore be holy, for I *am* **h**. 6918
14:13 and the burnt offering, in the **h** place: 6944
14:13 *is* the trespass offering: it *is* **most h**: 6944+6944
16: 2 that he come not at all times into the **h** 6944
16: 3 Thus shall Aaron come into the **h** *place:* 6944
16: 4 He shall put on the **h** linen coat, and 6944
16: 4 these *are* **h** garments; therefore shall he 6944
16:16 he shall make an atonement for the **h** *place,* 6944
16:17 atonement in the **h** *place,* until he come out, 6944
16:20 made an end of reconciling the **h** *place,* 6944
16:23 which he put on when he went into the **h** 6944
16:24 he shall wash his flesh with water in the **h** 6918
16:27 **h** *place,* shall *one* carry forth without 6944
16:32 on the linen clothes, *even* the **h** garments: 6944
16:33 he shall make an atonement for the **h** 6944
19: 2 of Israel, and say unto them, Ye shall be **h**: 6918
19: 2 be holy: for I the LORD your God *am* **h**. 6918
19:24 shall be **h** to praise the LORD *withal.* 6944
20: 3 my sanctuary, and to profane my **h** name. 6944
20: 7 Sanctify yourselves therefore, and be ye **h**: 6918
20:26 ye shall be **h** unto me: for I the LORD *am* 6918
20:26 for I the LORD *am* **h**, and have severed 6918
21: 6 They shall be **h** unto their God, and 6944
21: 6 they do offer: therefore they shall be **h**. 6918
21: 7 from her husband: for he *is* **h** unto his God. 6918
21: 8 he shall be **h** unto thee: for I the LORD, 6918
21: 8 for I the LORD, which sanctify you, *am* **h**. 6918
21:22 *both* of the **most h**, and of the holy. 6944+6944
21:22 *both* of the most holy, and of the **h**. 6944
22: 2 that they separate themselves from the **h** 6944
22: 2 that they profane not my **h** name *in those* 6944
22: 3 that goeth unto the **h** *things* which 6944
22: 4 he shall not eat of the **h** *things,* until he be 6944
22: 6 shall not eat of the **h** *things,* unless he wash 6944
22: 7 shall afterward eat of the **h** *things;* because 6944
22:10 There shall no stranger eat *of* the **h** *thing:* a 6944
22:10 a hired servant, shall not eat *of* the **h** *thing.* 6944
22:12 she may not eat of an offering of the **h** 6944
22:14 if a man eat *of* the **h** *thing* unwittingly, then 6944
22:14 shall give *it* unto the priest with the **h** 6944
22:15 they shall not profane the **h** *things* of 6944
22:16 when they eat their **h** *things:* for I 6944
22:32 Neither shall ye profane my **h** name; but 6944
23: 2 which ye shall proclaim *to be* **h** 6944
23: 3 day *is* the sabbath of rest, a **h** convocation; 6944
23: 4 feasts of the LORD, *even* **h** convocations, 6944
23: 7 In the first day ye shall have a **h** 6944
23: 8 in the seventh day *is* a **h** convocation: 6944
23:20 they shall be **h** to the LORD for the priest. 6944
23:21 *that* it may be a **h** convocation unto you: 6944
23:24 of blowing of trumpets, a **h** convocation. 6944
23:27 it shall be a **h** convocation unto you; and 6944
23:35 On the first day *shall be* a **h** convocation: 6944
23:36 on the eighth day shall be a **h** convocation 6944
23:37 which ye shall proclaim *to be* **h** 6944
24: 9 and they shall eat it in the **h** place: 6918
24: 9 for it *is* **most h** unto him of 6944+6944
25:12 For it *is* the jubile; it shall be **h** unto you: 6944
27: 9 giveth of such unto the LORD shall be **h**. 6944
27:10 then it and the exchange thereof shall be **h**. 6944
27:14 when a man shall sanctify his house *to be* **h** 6944
27:21 shall be **h** unto the LORD, as a field 6944
27:23 in that day, *as* a **h** *thing* unto the LORD. 6944
27:28 every devoted thing *is* **most h** unto 6944+6944
27:30 *is* the LORD'S: *it is* **h** unto the LORD. 6944
27:32 the tenth shall be **h** unto the LORD. 6944
27:33 both it and the change thereof shall be **h**; 6944

Nu 4: 4 *about* the **most h** *things:* 6944+6944
4:15 they shall not touch *any* **h** *thing,* lest they 6944
4:19 unto the **most h** *things:* Aaron 6944+6944
4:20 they shall not go in to see when the **h** 6944
5: 9 every offering of all the **h** *things* of 6944
5:17 the priest shall take **h** water in an earthen 6918
6: 5 he shall be **h**, *and* shall let the locks of 6918
6: 8 All the days of his separation he *is* **h** unto 6918
6:20 this *is* **h** for the priest, with the wave breast 6944
15:40 and be **h** unto your God. 6918
16: 3 seeing all the congregation *are* **h**, every one 6918
16: 5 will shew who *are* his, and *who is* **h**; 6918
16: 7 the LORD doth choose, he *shall be* **h**: 6918
18: 9 This shall be thine of the **most h** 6944+6944
18: 9 *be* **most h** for thee and for thy sons. 6944+6944
18:10 In the **most h** *place* shalt thou eat it; 6944+6944

Nu 18:10 male shall eat it: it shall be **h** unto thee. 6944
18:17 of a goat, thou shalt not redeem; they *are* **h**: 6944
18:19 All the heave offerings of the **h** *things,* 6944
18:32 neither shall ye pollute the **h** *things* of 6944
28: 7 in the **h** *place* shalt thou cause the strong 6944
28:18 In the first day *shall be* a **h** convocation; 6944
28:25 on the seventh day ye shall have a **h** 6944
28:26 after your weeks *be out,* ye shall have a **h** 6944
29: 1 the month, ye shall have a **h** convocation; 6944
29: 7 *day* of this seventh month a **h** convocation; 6944
29:12 month ye shall have a **h** convocation; 6944
31: 6 with the **h** instruments, and the trumpets to 6944
35:25 which was anointed with the **h** oil. 6944
Dt 7: 6 For thou *art* a **h** people unto the LORD 6918
12:26 Only thy **h** *things* which thou hast, and 6944
14: 2 For thou *art* a **h** people unto the LORD 6918
14:21 for thou *art* a **h** people unto the LORD thy 6918
23:14 before thee; therefore shall thy camp be **h**: 6918
26:15 Look down from thy **h** habitation, 6944
26:19 that thou mayest be a **h** people unto 6918
28: 9 The LORD shall establish thee a **h** people 6918
33: 8 and thy Urim *be* with thy **h** one, 2623
Jos 5:15 for the place whereon thou standest *is* **h**. 6944
24:19 for he *is* a **h** God; he *is* a jealous God; 6918
1Sa 2: 2 *There is* none **h** as the LORD: for *there is* 6918
6:20 Who is able to stand before this **h** LORD 6918
21: 5 and the vessels of the young men are **h**, and 6944
1Ki 6:16 *even* for the **most h** *place.* 6944+6944
7:50 the **most h** *place, and* for the doors 6944+6944
8: 4 all the **h** vessels that *were* in the tabernacle, 6944
8: 6 to the **most h** *place,* even under 6944+6944
8: 8 seen out in the **h** *place* before the oracle, 6944
8:10 when the priests were come out of the **h** 6944
2Ki 4: 9 I perceive that this *is* a **h** man of God, 6918
19:22 on high? *even* against the **H One** of Israel. 6918
1Ch 6:49 for all the work of the *place* **most h,** 6944+6944
16:10 Glory ye in his **h** name: let the heart of 6944
16:35 that *we* may give thanks to thy **h** name, 6944
22:19 of the LORD, and the **h** vessels of God, 6944
23:13 should sanctify the **most h** *things,* he 6944+6944
23:28 in the purifying of all **h** *things,* and 6944
23:32 the charge of the **h** *place,* and the charge of 6944
29: 3 above all *that* I have prepared for the **h** 6944
29:16 for thine **h** name *cometh* of thine hand, 6944
2Ch 3: 8 he made the **most h** house, the length 6944+6944
3:10 in the **most h** house he made two 6944+6944
4:22 doors thereof for the **most h** *place,* 6944+6944
5: 5 all the **h** vessels that *were* in the tabernacle, 6944
5: 7 into the **most h** *place,* even under 6944+6944
5:11 when the priests were come out of the **h** 6944
8:11 because *the places are* **h**, whereunto the ark 6944
23: 6 the Levites; they shall go in, for they *are* **h**: 6944
29: 5 carry forth the filthiness out of the **h** *place.* 6944
29: 7 in the **h** *place* unto the God of Israel. 6944
30:27 their prayer came *up* to his **h dwelling** 6944
31: 6 the tithe of **h** *things* which were 6944
31:14 the LORD, and the **most h** *things.* 6944+6944
35: 3 all Israel, which were **h** unto the LORD, 6918
35: 3 Put the **h** ark in the house which Solomon 6944
35: 5 stand in the **h** *place* according to 6944
35:13 the *other* **h** *offerings* sod they in pots, and 6944
Ezr 2:63 **most h** *things* till there stood *up* a 6944+6944
8:28 said unto them, Ye *are* **h** unto the LORD; 6944
8:28 the vessels *are* **h** also; and the silver and 6944
9: 2 that the **h** seed have mingled themselves 6944
9: 8 and to give us a nail in his **h** place, 6944
Ne 7:65 **most h** *things,* till there stood *up* a 6944+6944
8: 9 *This* day *is* **h** unto the LORD your God; 6918
8:10 for *this* day *is* **h** unto our Lord: neither be 6918
8:11 Hold your peace, for the day *is* **h**; 6918
9:14 madest known unto them thy **h** sabbath, 6944
10:31 *it* of them on the sabbath, or on the **h** day: 6944
10:33 for the **h** *things,* and for the sin offerings to 6944
11: 1 one of ten to dwell in Jerusalem the **h** city, 6944
11:18 All the Levites in the **h** city *were* two 6944
12:47 they sanctified *h things* unto the Levites; NIH
Job 6:10 not concealed the words of the **H One.** 6918
Ps 2: 6 Yet have I set my king upon my **h** hill of 6944
3: 4 my voice, and he heard me out of his **h** hill. 6944
5: 7 in thy fear will I worship toward thy **h** 6944
11: 4 The LORD *is* in his **h** temple, 6944
15: 1 who shall dwell in thy **h** hill? 6944
16:10 neither wilt thou suffer thine **H One** to see 2623
20: 6 he will hear him from his **h** heaven with 6944
22: 3 thou *art* **h**, O thou that inhabitest the praises 6918
24: 3 and who shall stand in his **h** place? 6944
28: 2 when I lift up my hands toward thy **h** 6944
33:21 because we have trusted in his **h** name. 6944
43: 3 let them bring me unto thy **h** hill, and to thy 6944
46: 4 the **h** *place* of the tabernacles of the most 6918
51:11 and take not thy **h** Spirit from me. 6944
65: 4 of thy house, *even* of thy **h** temple. 6918
68: 5 of the widows, *is* God in his **h** habitation. 6944
68:17 *is* among them, *as in* Sinai, in the **h** *place.* 6944
68:35 O God, *thou art* terrible out of thy **h places**: 4720
71:22 sing with the harp, O thou **H One** of Israel. 6918
78:41 and limited the **H One** of Israel. 6918
79: 1 thy **h** temple have they defiled; they have 6944
86: 2 Preserve my soul; for I *am* **h**: O thou my 2623
87: 1 His foundation *is* in the **h** mountains. 6944
89:18 and the **H One** of Israel *is* our king. 6918
89:19 thou spakest in vision to thy **h one**, and 2623
89:20 with my **h** oil have I anointed him: 6944
98: 1 and his **h** arm, hath gotten him the victory. 6944
99: 3 thy great and terrible name; *for* it *is* **h**. 6918
99: 5 and worship at his footstool; *for* he *is* **h**. 6918
99: 9 LORD our God, and worship at his **h** hill; 6944
99: 9 his holy hill; for the LORD our God *is* **h**. 6918
103: 1 and all that is within me, *bless* his **h** name. 6944
105: 3 Glory ye in his **h** name: let the heart of 6944
105:42 For he remembered his **h** promise, 6944
106:47 to give thanks unto thy **h** name, *and* 6944
111: 9 for ever: **h** and reverend *is* his name. 6918
138: 2 I will worship toward thy **h** temple, and 6944
145:17 in all his ways, and **h** in all his works. 2623
145:21 let all flesh bless his **h** name for ever and 6944
Pr 9:10 the knowledge of the **h** *is* understanding. 6918
20:25 to the man *who* devoureth *that which is* **h**, 6944
30: 3 nor have the knowledge of the **h**. 6918
Ecc 8:10 had come and gone from the place of the **h**, 6918
Isa 1: 4 they have provoked the **H One** of Israel 6918
4: 3 remaineth in Jerusalem, shall be called **h**, 6918
5:16 God that is **h** shall be sanctified in 6918
5:19 let the counsel of the **H One** of Israel draw 6918
5:24 despised the word of the **H One** of Israel. 6918
6: 3 said, **H**, holy, holy, *is* the LORD of hosts: 6918
6: 3 said, Holy, **h**, holy, *is* the LORD of hosts: 6918
6: 3 said, Holy, holy, **h**, *is* the LORD of hosts: 6918
6:13 *so* the **h** seed *shall be* the substance thereof. 6944
10:17 be for a fire, and his **H One** for a flame: 6918
10:20 the LORD, the **H One** of Israel, in truth. 6918
11: 9 They shall not hurt nor destroy in all my **h** 6944
12: 6 for great *is* the **H One** of Israel in the midst 6918
17: 7 his eyes shall have respect to the **H One** of 6918
27:13 shall worship the LORD in the **h** mount at 6944
29:19 men shall rejoice in the **H One** of Israel. 6918
29:23 sanctify the **H One** of Jacob, and shall fear 6918
30:11 cause the **H One** of Israel to cease from 6918
30:12 Wherefore thus saith the **H One** of Israel, 6918
30:15 saith the Lord GOD, the **H One** of Israel; 6918
30:29 as *in* the night when a **h** solemnity is **kept**; 6942
31: 1 they look not unto the **H One** of Israel, 6918
37:23 on high? *even* against the **H One** of Israel. 6918
40:25 or shall I be equal? saith the **H One.** 6918
41:14 and thy redeemer, the **H One** of Israel. 6918
41:16 *and* shalt glory in the **H One** of Israel. 6918
41:20 and the **H One** of Israel hath created it. 6918
43: 3 thy God, the **H One** of Israel, thy Saviour: 6918
43:14 your redeemer, the **H One** of Israel; 6918
43:15 I *am* the LORD, your **H One**, the creator 6918
45:11 the **H One** of Israel, and his maker, 6918
47: 4 of hosts *is* his name, the **H One** of Israel. 6918
48: 2 For they call themselves of the **h** city, and 6944
48:17 thy redeemer, the **H One** of Israel; 6918
49: 7 the redeemer of Israel, *and* his **H One**, 6918
49: 7 *and* the **H One** of Israel, and he shall 6918
52: 1 beautiful garments, O Jerusalem, the **h** city: 6944
52:10 The LORD hath made bare his **h** arm in 6944
54: 5 and thy redeemer the **H One** of Israel; 6918
55: 5 thy God, and for the **H One** of Israel; 6918
56: 7 Even them will I bring to my **h** mountain, 6944
57:13 the land, and shall inherit my **h** mountain; 6944
57:15 that inhabiteth eternity, whose name *is* **H**; 6918
57:15 **h** *place,* with him also *that is* of a contrite 6918
58:13 *from* doing thy pleasure on my **h** day; 6944
58:13 a delight, the **h** of the LORD, honourable; 6918
60: 9 to the **H One** of Israel, because he hath 6918
60:14 The Zion of the **H One** of Israel. 6918

Isa	62:12	they shall call them, The **h** people,	6944
	63:10	they rebelled, and vexed his **h** Spirit:	6944
	63:11	where *is* he that put his **h** Spirit within him?	6944
	64:10	Thy **h** cities are a wilderness, Zion is a	6944
	64:11	Our **h** and our beautiful house, where our	6944
	65:11	that forget my **h** mountain, that prepare a	6944
	65:25	They shall not hurt nor destroy in all my **h**	6944
	66:20	to my **h** mountain Jerusalem, saith	6944
Jer	11:15	and the **h** flesh is passed from thee?	6944
	25:30	and utter his voice from his **h** habitation;	6944
	31:40	the east, *shall be* **h** unto the LORD;	6944
	50:29	the LORD, against the **H One** of Israel.	6918
	51: 5	filled *with* sin against the **H One** of Israel.	6918
Eze	7:24	to cease; and their **h places** shall be defiled.	6942
	20:39	pollute ye my **h** name no more with your	6944
	20:40	For in mine **h** mountain, in the mountain of	6944
	20:40	of your oblations, with all your **h** *things.*	6944
	21: 2	drop *thy word* toward the **h places**, and	4720
	22: 8	Thou hast despised mine **h** *things,* and hast	6944
	22:26	have profaned mine **h** *things:* they have put	6944
	22:26	they have put no difference between the **h**	6944
	28:14	*so:* thou wast upon the **h** mountain of God;	6944
	36:20	they went, they profaned my **h** name,	6944
	36:21	I had pity for mine **h** name, which	6944
	36:22	house of Israel, but for mine **h** name's sake,	6944
	36:38	As the **h** flock, as the flock of Jerusalem in	6944
	39: 7	So will I make my **h** name known in	6944
	39: 7	I will not let *them* pollute my **h** name any	6944
	39: 7	that I *am* the LORD, the **H One** in Israel.	6918
	39:25	and will be jealous for my **h** name;	6944
	41: 4	unto me, This *is* the **most h** *place.*	6944+6944
	42:13	the separate place, they *be* **h** chambers,	6944
	42:13	**most h** *things:* there shall they lay	6944+6944
	42:13	shall they lay the **most h** *things,*	6944+6944
	42:13	and the trespass offering; for the place *is* **h**.	6918
	42:14	shall they not go out of the **h** *place* into	6944
	42:14	for they *are* **h**; and shall put on other	6944
	43: 7	my **h** name, shall the house of Israel no	6944
	43: 8	they have even defiled my **h** name by their	6944
	43:12	thereof round about *shall be* **most h**.	6944+6944
	44: 8	ye have not kept the charge of mine **h**	6944
	44:13	nor to come near to any of my **h** *things,* in	6944
	44:13	my holy *things,* in the **most h** *place:*	6944+6944
	44:19	lay them in the **h** chambers, and they shall	6944
	44:23	my people *the difference* between the **h**	6944
	45: 1	unto the LORD, a **h** *portion* of the land:	6944
	45: 1	This *shall be* **h** in all the borders thereof	6944
	45: 3	the sanctuary *and* the **most h** *place.*	6944+6944
	45: 4	The **h** *portion* of the land shall be for	6944
	45: 4	and a **h place** for the sanctuary.	4720
	45: 6	over against the oblation of the **h** *portion:* it	6944
	45: 7	on the other side of the oblation of the **h**	6944
	45: 7	before the oblation of the **h** *portion,* and	6944
	46:19	into the **h** chambers of the priests,	6944
	48:10	*even* for the priests, shall be *this* **h** oblation;	6944
	48:12	**most h** by the border of the Levites.	6944+6944
	48:14	of the land: for *it is* **h** unto the LORD.	6944
	48:18	**h** *portion shall be* ten thousand eastward,	6944
	48:18	it shall be over against the oblation of the **h**	6944
	48:20	ye shall offer the **h** oblation foursquare,	6944
	48:21	one side and on the other of the **h** oblation,	6944
	48:21	it shall be the **h** oblation; and the sanctuary	6944
Da	4: 8	and in whom *is* the spirit of the **h** gods:	6922
	4: 9	I know that the spirit of the **h** gods *is* in	6922
	4:13	and a **h one** came down from heaven;	6922
	4:17	and the demand *by* the word of the **h ones**:	6922
	4:18	for the spirit of the **h** gods *is* in thee.	6922
	4:23	and a **h one** coming down from heaven,	6922
	5:11	in whom *is* the spirit of the **h** gods;	6922
	8:24	shall destroy the mighty and the **h** people.	6918
	9:16	from thy city Jerusalem, thy **h** mountain:	6944
	9:20	my God for the **h** mountain of my God;	6944
	9:24	upon thy people and upon thy **h** city,	6944
	9:24	prophecy, and to anoint the **most H**.	6944+6944
	11:28	his heart *shall be* against the **h** covenant;	6944
	11:30	have indignation against the **h** covenant:	6944
	11:30	with them that forsake the **h** covenant.	6944
	11:45	the seas in the glorious **h** mountain;	6944
	12: 7	to scatter the power of the **h** people,	6944
Hos	11: 9	not man; the **H One** in the midst of thee:	6918
Joel	2: 1	and sound an alarm in my **h** mountain:	6944
	3:17	God dwelling in Zion, my **h** mountain:	6944
	3:17	shall Jerusalem be **h**, and there shall no	6944
Am	2: 7	unto the *same* maid, to profane my **h** name:	6944
Ob	1:16	For as ye have drunk upon my **h** mountain,	6944
Jnh	2: 4	yet I will look again toward thy **h** temple.	6944
	2: 7	came in unto thee, into thine **h** temple.	6944
Mic	1: 2	against you, the Lord from his **h** temple.	6944
Hab	1:12	O LORD my God, mine **H One**?	6918
	2:20	the LORD *is* in his **h** temple: let all	6944
	3: 3	and the **H One** from mount Paran.	6918
Zep	3:11	be haughty because of my **h** mountain.	6944
Hag	2:12	If one bear **h** flesh in the skirt of his	6944
	2:12	or wine, or oil, or any meat, shall it be **h**?	6942
Zec	2:12	shall inherit Judah his portion in the **h** land,	6944
	2:13	for he is raised up out of his **h** habitation.	6944
	8: 3	the mountain of the LORD of hosts the **h**	6944
Mt	1:18	she was found with child of the **H** Ghost.	*40*
	1:20	for that which is conceived in her is of the **H**	*40*
	3:11	he shall baptize you with the **H** Ghost, and	*40*
	4: 5	Then the devil taketh him *up* into the **h** city,	*40*
	7: 6	Give not that which is **h** unto the dogs,	*40*
	12:31	the blasphemy against the ***H*** Ghost shall not	NIG
	12:32	but whosoever speaketh against the **H** Ghost,	*40*
	24:15	stand in the **h** place, (whoso readeth, let him	*40*
	25:31	and all the **h** angels with him, then shall he sit	*40*
	27:53	and went into the **h** city, and appeared unto	*40*
	28:19	and of the Son, and of the **H** Ghost:	*40*
Mk	1: 8	but he shall baptize you with the **H** Ghost.	*40*
	1:24	I know thee who thou art, the **H One** of God.	*40*
	3:29	But he that shall blaspheme against the **H**	*40*
	6:20	knowing that he *was* a just man and a **h**, and	*40*
	8:38	in the glory of his Father with the **h** angels.	*40*
	12:36	For David himself said by the **H** Ghost,	*40*
	13:11	for it is not ye that speak, but the **H** Ghost.	*40*
Lk	1:15	and he shall be filled with the **H** Ghost,	*40*
	1:35	The **H** Ghost shall come upon thee, and	*40*
	1:35	also *that* **h thing** which shall be born of thee	*40*
	1:41	and Elisabeth was filled with the **H** Ghost:	*40*
	1:49	done to me great things; and **h** *is* his name.	*40*
	1:67	And his father Zacharias was filled with the **H**	*40*
	1:70	(As he spake by the mouth of his **h** prophets,	*40*
	1:72	our fathers, and to remember his **h** covenant;	*40*
	2:23	the womb shall be called **h** to the Lord;)	*40*
	2:25	of Israel: and the **H** Ghost was upon him.	*40*
	2:26	And it was revealed unto him by the **H** Ghost,	*40*
	3:16	he shall baptize you with the **H** Ghost and	*40*
	3:22	And the **H** Ghost descended in a bodily shape	*40*
	4: 1	And Jesus being full of the **H** Ghost returned	*40*
	4:34	I know thee who thou art, the **H One** of God.	*40*
	9:26	and *in his* Father's, and of the **h** angels.	*40*
	11:13	Father give the **H** Spirit to them that ask him?	*40*
	12:10	unto him that blasphemeth against the **H**	*40*
	12:12	For the **H** Ghost shall teach you in the same	*40*
Jn	1:33	the same is he which baptizeth with the **H**	*40*
	7:39	for the **H** Ghost was not yet *given;* because	*40*
	14:26	But the Comforter, *which is* the **H** Ghost,	*40*
	17:11	**H** Father, keep through thine own name those	*40*
	20:22	and saith unto them, Receive ye the **H** Ghost:	*40*
Ac	1: 2	after that he through the **H** Ghost had given	*40*
	1: 5	ye shall be baptized with the **H** Ghost not	*40*
	1: 8	after that the **H** Ghost is come upon you:	*40*
	1:16	which the **H** Ghost by the mouth of David	*40*
	2: 4	And they were all filled with the **H** Ghost,	*40*
	2:27	neither wilt thou suffer thine **H One** to see	*3741*
	2:33	of the Father the promise of the **H** Ghost,	*40*
	2:38	and ye shall receive the gift of the **H** Ghost.	*40*
	3:14	But ye denied the **H One** and the Just, and	*40*
	3:21	of all his **h** prophets since the world began.	*40*
	4: 8	Then Peter, filled with the **H** Ghost, said unto	*40*
	4:27	For of a truth against thy **h** child Jesus,	*40*
	4:30	wonders may be done by the name of thy **h**	*40*
	4:31	and they were all filled with the **H** Ghost, and	*40*
	5: 3	hath Satan filled thine heart to lie to the **H**	*40*
	5:32	and *so is* also the **H** Ghost, whom God hath	*40*
	6: 3	full of the **H** Ghost and wisdom, whom we	*40*
	6: 5	a man full of faith and of the **H** Ghost, and	*40*
	6:13	blasphemous words against this **h** place,	*40*
	7:33	for the place where thou standest is **h** ground.	*40*
	7:51	and ears, ye do always resist the **H** Ghost:	*40*
	7:55	But he, being full of the **H** Ghost, looked up	*40*
	8:15	for them, that they might receive the **H** Ghost:	*40*
	8:17	on them, and they received the **H** Ghost.	*40*
	8:18	of the apostles' hands the **H** Ghost was given,	*40*
	8:19	I lay hands, he may receive the **H** Ghost.	*40*
	9:17	thy sight, and be filled with the **H** Ghost.	*40*
	9:31	and in the comfort of the **H** Ghost,	*40*
	10:22	was warned from God by a **h** angel to send	*40*

Ac 10:38 anointed Jesus of Nazareth with the **H** Ghost 40
10:44 the **H** Ghost fell on all them which heard 40
10:45 also was poured out the gift of the **H** Ghost. 40
10:47 which have received the **H** Ghost as well as 40
11:15 as I began to speak, the **H** Ghost fell on them, 40
11:16 but ye shall be baptized with the **H** Ghost. 40
11:24 and full of the **H** Ghost and of faith: 40
13: 2 and fasted, the **H** Ghost said, Separate me 40
13: 4 So they, being sent forth by the **H** Ghost, 40
13: 9 filled with the **H** Ghost, set his eyes on him, 40
13:35 not suffer thine **H One** to see corruption. *3741*
13:52 were filled with joy, and with the **H** Ghost. 40
15: 8 bare them witness, giving them the **H** Ghost, 40
15:28 For it seemed good to the **H** Ghost, and to us, 40
16: 6 were forbidden of the **H** Ghost to preach 40
19: 2 Have ye received the **H** Ghost since ye 40
19: 2 much as heard whether there be *any* **H** Ghost. 40
19: 6 hands upon them, the **H** Ghost came on them; 40
20:23 Save that the **H** Ghost witnesseth in every 40
20:28 over the which the **H** Ghost hath made you 40
21:11 and feet, and said, Thus saith the **H** Ghost, 40
21:28 into the temple, and hath polluted this **h** place. 40
28:25 Well spake the **H** Ghost by Esaias the prophet 40
Ro 1: 2 afore by his prophets in the **h** scriptures,) 40
5: 5 hearts by the **H** Ghost which is given unto us. 40
7:12 Wherefore the law *is* **h**, and 40
7:12 and the commandment **h**, and just, and good. 40
9: 1 also bearing me witness in the **H** Ghost, 40
11:16 For if the firstfruit *be* **h**, the lump *is* also *holy:* 40
11:16 the lump *is* also *h:* and if the root *be* holy, NIG
11:16 the lump *is* also *holy:* and if the root *be* **h**, so 40
12: 1 **h**, acceptable unto God, *which is* your 40
14:17 and peace, and joy in the **H** Ghost. 40
15:13 in hope, through the power of the **H** Ghost. 40
15:16 being sanctified by the **H** Ghost. 40
16:16 Salute one another with a **h** kiss. The 40
1Co 2:13 but which the **H** Ghost teacheth; 40
3:17 for the temple of God is **h**, which *temple* ye 40
6:19 is the temple of the **H** Ghost which is in you, 40
7:14 your children unclean; but now are they **h**. 40
7:34 that she may be **h** both in body and in spirit: 40
9:13 **h** *things* live of *the things of* the temple? *2413*
12: 3 say that Jesus is the Lord, but by the **H** Ghost. 40
16:20 greet you. Greet ye one another with a **h** kiss. 40
2Co 6: 6 by kindness, by the **H** Ghost, 40
13:12 Greet one another with a **h** kiss. 40
13:14 and the communion of the **H** Ghost, *be* with 40
Eph 1: 4 that we should be **h** and without blame before 40
1:13 ye were sealed with *that* **h** Spirit of promise, 40
2:21 together groweth unto a **h** temple in the Lord: 40
3: 5 as it is now revealed unto his **h** apostles and 40
4:30 And grieve not the **h** Spirit of God, 40
5:27 or any such *thing;* but that it should be **h** and 40
Col 1:22 to present you **h** and unblameable and 40
3:12 **h** and beloved, bowels of mercies, kindness, 40
1Th 1: 5 and in the **H** Ghost, and in much assurance; 40
1: 6 in much affliction, with joy of the **H** Ghost: 40
4: 8 God, who hath also given unto us his **h** Spirit. 40
5:26 Greet all the brethren with a **h** kiss. 40
5:27 *this* epistle be read unto all the **h** brethren. 40
1Ti 2: 8 lifting up **h** hands, without wrath and *3741*
2Ti 1: 9 hath saved us, and called *us* with a **h** calling, 40
1:14 keep by the **H** Ghost which dwelleth in us. 40
3:15 a child thou hast known the **h** scriptures, *2413*
Tit 1: 8 of good *men,* sober, just, **h**, temperate; *3741*
3: 5 of regeneration, and renewing of the **H** Ghost; 40
Heb 2: 4 with divers miracles, and gifts of the **H** Ghost, 40
3: 1 Wherefore, **h** brethren, partakers of 40
3: 7 Wherefore, as the **H** Ghost saith, To day if ye 40
6: 4 and were made partakers of the **H** Ghost, 40
7:26 *who is* **h**, harmless, undefiled, *3741*
9: 8 The **H** Ghost this signifying, that the way into 40
9:12 **h** *place,* having obtained eternal redemption 40
9:24 For Christ is not entered into the **h** *places* 40
9:25 as the high priest entereth into the **h** *place* 40
10:15 *Whereof* the **H** Ghost also is a witness to us: 40
1Pe 1:12 you with the **H** Ghost sent *down* from heaven; 40
1:15 But as he which hath called you is **h**, so be ye 40
1:15 so be ye **h** in all *manner of* conversation; 40
1:16 Because it is written, Be ye **h**; for I am holy. 40
1:16 Because it is written, Be ye holy; for I am **h**. 40
2: 5 are built *up* a spiritual house, a **h** priesthood, 40
2: 9 a **h** nation, a peculiar people; 40
3: 5 For after this manner in the old time the **h** 40
2Pe 1:18 when we were with him in the **h** mount. 40
1:21 **h** men of God spake *as they were* moved by NIG
1:21 spake *as they were* moved by the **H** Ghost. 40
2:21 after they have known *it,* to turn from the **h** 40
3: 2 which were spoken before by the **h** prophets, 40
3:11 *of persons* ought ye to be in all **h** conversation 40
1Jn 2:20 But ye have an unction from the **H One**, and 40
5: 7 the Father, the Word, and the **H** Ghost: 40
Jude 1:20 building up yourselves on your **most h** faith, 40
1:20 your most holy faith, praying in the **H** Ghost, 40
Rev 3: 7 These *things* saith he *that is* **h**, he *that is* true, 40
4: 8 rest not day and night, saying, **H**, holy, holy, 40
4: 8 rest not day and night, saying, Holy, **h**, holy, 40
4: 8 rest not day and night, saying, Holy, holy, **h**, 40
6:10 saying, How long, O Lord, **h** and true, 40
11: 2 the **h** city shall they tread under foot forty *and* 40
14:10 and brimstone in the presence of the **h** angels, 40
15: 4 for *thou* only *art* **h**: for all nations shall *3741*
18:20 *thou* heaven, and ye **h** apostles and prophets; 40
20: 6 **h** *is* he that hath part in the first resurrection: 40
21: 2 And I John saw the **h** city, new Jerusalem, 40
21:10 shewed me *that* great city, the **h** Jerusalem, 40
22: 6 the Lord God of the **h** prophets sent his angel 40
22:11 and *he that is* **h**, let him be holy still. 40
22:11 and *he that is* holy, let him be **h** still. 37
22:19 and out of the **h** city, and *from* the *things* 40

HOLY SPIRIT See also HOLY GHOST

HOLYDAY (2) [DAY, HOLY]
Ps 42: 4 and praise, *with* a multitude that **kept h**. 2287
Col 2:16 or in respect of a **h**, or of the new moon, or *1859*

HOMAM (1)
1Ch 1:39 the sons of Lotan; Hori, and **H**: and 1950

HOME (51) [HOMEBORN]
Ge 39:16 his garment by her, until his lord came **h**. 1004
43:16 Bring *these* men **h**, and slay, and 1004
43:26 when Joseph came **h**, they brought him 1004
Ex 9:19 shall not be brought **h**, the hail shall come 1004
Lev 18: 9 *whether she be* born at **h**, or born abroad, 1004
Dt 21:12 thou shalt bring her **h** to thine house; and NIH
24: 5 *but* he shall be free at **h** one year, and 1004
Jos 2:18 and all thy father's household, **h** unto thee. 1004
Jdg 11: 9 If ye bring me *h* again to fight against NIH
19: 9 early on your way, that thou mayest go **h**. 168
Ru 1:21 the LORD hath brought me *h* again empty: NIH
1Sa 2:20 And they went unto their own **h**. 4725
6: 7 and bring their calves **h** from them: 1004
6:10 to the cart, and shut up their calves at **h**: 1004
10:26 Saul also went **h** to Gibeah; and there went 1004
18: 2 would let him **go** no more **h** *to* his father's 7725
24:22 Saul went **h**; but David and his men gat 1004
2Sa 13: 7 David sent **h** to Tamar, saying, Go now *to* 1004
14:13 in that the king doth not fetch *h* again his NIH
17:23 arose, and gat him *h* to his house, to his NIH
1Ki 5:14 were in Lebanon, *and* two months at **h**: 1004
13: 7 Come **h** with me, and refresh *thyself,* and 1004
13:15 unto him, Come **h** with me, and eat bread. 1004
2Ki 14:10 glory *of this,* and tarry at **h**: for why 1004
1Ch 13:12 How shall I bring the ark of God *h* to me? NIH
13:13 So David brought not the ark *h* to himself to NIH
2Ch 25:10 to go **h** *again:* wherefore their anger was 4725
25:10 and they returned **h** in great anger. 4725
25:19 abide now at **h**; why shouldest thou meddle 1004
Est 5:10 when he came **h**, he sent and called for his 1004
Job 39:12 that he will **bring h** thy seed, and gather *it* 7725
Ps 68:12 she that tarried at **h** divided the spoil. 1004
Pr 7:19 For the goodman *is* not at **h**, he is gone a 1004
7:20 *and* will come **h** at the day appointed. 1004
Ecc 12: 5 because man goeth to his long **h**, and 1004
Jer 39:14 son of Shaphan, that *he* should carry him **h**: 1004
La 1:20 the sword bereaveth, at **h** *there is* as death. 1004
Hab 2: 5 *he is* a proud man, neither **keepeth at h**, 5115
Hag 1: 9 when ye brought *it* **h**, I did blow upon it. 1004
Mt 8: 6 my servant lieth at **h** sick of the palsy, *3614*
Mk 5:19 Go **h** to thy *friends,* and tell them how great *3624*
Lk 9:61 them farewell, which are *at h* in my house. NIG
15: 6 And when he cometh **h**, he calleth together *3624*
Jn 19:27 hour *that* disciple took her unto his own *h*. NIG
20:10 went away again unto **their own h**. *1438*
Ac 21: 6 and they returned **h** *again.* *1519+2398+3588*
1Co 11:34 And if any *man* hunger, let him eat at **h**; *3624*

1Co 14:35 any *thing,* let them ask their husbands at **h**: *3624*
2Co 5: 6 whilst we are **at h** in the body, *1736*
1Ti 5: 4 let them learn first to shew piety at **h**, and *3624*
Tit 2: 5 *To be* discreet, chaste, **keepers at h**, good, *3626*

HOMEBORN (2) [BEAR, HOME]
Ex 12:49 One law shall be to him that is **h**, and 249
Jer 2:14 *is* he a **h** *slave?* why is he spoiled? 1004+3211

HOMELAND See HABITATION; NATIVITY

HOMER (11) [HOMERS]
Lev 27:16 a **h** of barley seed *shall be valued* at fifty 2563
Isa 5:10 and the seed of a **h** shall yield an ephah. 2563
Eze 45:11 the bath may contain the tenth part of a **h**, 2563
45:11 and the ephah the tenth *part* of a **h**: 2563
45:11 the measure thereof shall be after the **h**. 2563
45:13 the sixth *part* of an ephah of a **h** of wheat, 2563
45:13 the sixth part of an ephah of a **h** of barley: 2563
45:14 out of the cor, *which is* a **h** of ten baths; 2563
45:14 a homer of ten baths; for ten baths *are* a **h**: 2563
Hos 3: 2 *for* a **h** of barley, and a half homer of 2563
3: 2 a homer of barley, and a **half h** of barley: 3963

HOMERS (1) [HOMER]
Nu 11:32 he that gathered least gathered ten **h**: and 2563

HONEST (7) [HONESTLY, HONESTY]
Lk 8:15 which in an **h** and good heart, having heard *2570*
Ac 6: 3 ye out among you seven men **of h report**, *3140*
Ro 12:17 Provide *things* **h** in the sight of all men. *2570*
2Co 8:21 Providing *for* **h** *things,* not only in the sight *2570*
13: 7 but that ye should do *that which is* **h**, *2570*
Php 4: 8 whatsoever *things are* **h**, whatsoever *things* *4586*
1Pe 2:12 Having your conversation **h** among *2570*

HONESTLY (3) [HONEST]
Ro 13:13 Let us walk **h**, as in the day; not in rioting *2156*
1Th 4:12 That ye may walk **h** toward them that are *2156*
Heb 13:18 in all *things* willing to live **h**. *2573*

HONESTY (1) [HONEST]
1Ti 2: 2 and peaceable life in all godliness and **h**. *4587*

HONEY (56) [HONEYCOMB]
Ge 43:11 a little **h**, spices, and myrrh, nuts, and 1706
Ex 3: 8 unto a land flowing with milk and **h**; 1706
3:17 unto a land flowing with milk and **h**. 1706
13: 5 give thee, a land flowing with milk and **h**, 1706
16:31 the taste of it *was* like wafers *made* with **h**. 1706
33: 3 Unto a land flowing with milk and **h**: for I 1706
Lev 2:11 for ye shall burn no leaven, nor any **h**, 1706
20:24 a land that floweth with milk and **h**: 1706
Nu 13:27 and surely it floweth with milk and **h**; 1706
14: 8 it us; a land which floweth with milk and **h**. 1706
16:13 out of a land that floweth with milk and **h**, 1706
16:14 us into a land that floweth with milk and **h**, 1706
Dt 6: 3 *in* the land that floweth with milk and **h**. 1706
8: 8 pomegranates; a land of oil olive, and **h**; 1706
11: 9 a land that floweth with milk and **h**. 1706
26: 9 *even* a land that floweth with milk and **h**. 1706
26:15 a land that floweth with milk and **h**. 1706
27: 3 a land that floweth with milk and **h**; 1706
31:20 their fathers, that floweth with milk and **h**; 1706
32:13 he made him to suck **h** out of the rock, and 1706
Jos 5: 6 a land that floweth with milk and **h**. 1706
Jdg 14: 8 of bees and **h** in the carcase of the lion. 1706
14: 9 he told not them that he had taken the **h** out 1706
14:18 sun went down, What *is* sweeter than **h**? 1706
1Sa 14:25 a wood; and there was **h** upon the ground. 1706
14:26 come into the wood, behold the **h** dropped; 1706
14:29 because I tasted a little of this **h**. 1706
14:43 taste a little **h** with the end of the rod that 1706
2Sa 17:29 **h**, and butter, and sheep, and cheese of 1706
1Ki 14: 3 cracknels, and a cruse of **h**, and go to him: 1706
2Ki 18:32 and vineyards, a land of oil olive and of **h**, 1706
2Ch 31: 5 oil, and **h**, and of all the increase of 1706
Job 20:17 the floods, the brooks of **h** and butter. 1706
Ps 19:10 sweeter also than **h** and the honeycomb. 1706
81:16 *with* **h** out of the rock should I have 1706
119:103 my taste! *yea, sweeter* than **h** to my mouth! 1706
Pr 24:13 My son, eat thou **h**, because *it is* good; and 1706
25:16 Hast thou found **h**? eat so much as is 1706
25:27 *It is* not good to eat much **h**: so *for men* to 1706
SS 4:11 **h** and milk *are* under thy tongue; and 1706
5: 1 I have eaten my honeycomb with my **h**; 1706
Isa 7:15 Butter and **h** shall he eat, that he may know 1706
7:22 **h** shall every one eat that is left in the land. 1706
Jer 11: 5 give them a land flowing with milk and **h**, 1706
32:22 give them, a land flowing with milk and **h**; 1706
41: 8 and *of* barley, and *of* oil, and *of* **h**. 1706
Eze 3: 3 and it was in my mouth as **h** for sweetness. 1706
16:13 thou didst eat fine flour, and **h**, and oil: 1706
16:19 fine flour, and oil, and **h**, *wherewith* I fed 1706
20: 6 flowing with milk and **h**, which *is* the glory 1706
20:15 I had given *them,* flowing with milk and **h**, 1706
27:17 and Pannag, and **h**, and oil, and balm. 1706
Mt 3: 4 and his meat was locusts and wild **h**. *3192*
Mk 1: 6 his loins; and he did eat locusts and wild **h**; *3192*
Rev 10: 9 but it shall be in thy mouth sweet as **h**. *3192*
10:10 it up; and it was in my mouth sweet as **h**: *3192*

HONEYCOMB (9) [HONEY]
1Sa 14:27 dipt it in a **h**, and put his 1706+3295+1886.1
Ps 19:10 sweeter also than honey and the **h**. 5317+6688
Pr 5: 3 For the lips of a strange *woman* drop *as* a **h**, 5317
16:24 Pleasant words *are as* a **h**, sweet to 1706+6688
24:13 and the **h**, *which is* sweet to thy taste: 5317
27: 7 The full soul loatheth a **h**; but *to* the hungry 5317
SS 4:11 Thy lips, O *my* spouse, drop *as* the **h**: 5317
5: 1 I have eaten my **h** with my honey; I have 3293
Lk 24:42 him a piece of a broiled fish, and of a **h**. *3193*

HONOR See UPPERMOST

HONOUR (146) [HONOURABLE, HONOURED, HONOUREST, HONOURETH, HONOURS]
Ge 49: 6 their assembly, mine **h**, be not thou united: 3519
Ex 14:17 I will **get** me **h** upon Pharaoh, and upon all 3513
14:18 when I have **gotten** me **h** upon Pharaoh, 3513
20:12 **H** thy father and thy mother: that thy days 3513
Lev 19:15 of the poor, nor **h** the person of the mighty: 1921
19:32 **h** the face of the old man, and fear thy God: 1921
Nu 22:17 will **promote** thee **unto** very great **h**, 3513+3513
22:37 am I not able indeed to **promote** thee **to h**? 3513
24:11 to **promote** thee **unto great h**; 3513+3513
24:11 lo, the LORD hath kept thee back from **h**. 3519
27:20 thou shalt put *some* of thine **h** upon him, 1935
Dt 5:16 **H** thy father and thy mother, as the LORD 3513
26:19 hath made, in praise, and in name, and in **h**; 8597
Jdg 4: 9 that thou takest shall not be for thine **h**; 8597
9: 9 wherewith by me they **h** God and man, and 3513
13:17 sayings come to pass we may **do** thee **h**? 3513
1Sa 2:30 for them that **h** me I will honour, and 3513
2:30 for them that honour me I will **h**, and 3513
15:30 *yet* **h** me now, I pray thee, before the elders 3513
2Sa 6:22 hast spoken of, of them shall I be **had in h**. 3513
10: 3 Thinkest thou that David doth **h** thy father, 3513
1Ki 3:13 thou hast not asked, both riches, and **h**: 3519
1Ch 16:27 Glory and **h** *are* in his presence; strength 1926
17:18 *speak* more to thee for the **h** of thy servant? 3519
19: 3 Thinkest thou that David doth **h** thy father, 3513
29:12 Both riches and **h** *come* of thee, and 3519
29:28 a good old age, full of days, riches, and **h**: 3519
2Ch 1:11 and thou hast not asked riches, wealth, or **h**, 3519
1:12 I will give thee riches, and wealth, and **h**, 3519
17: 5 and he had riches and **h** in abundance. 3519
18: 1 Jehoshaphat had riches and **h** in abundance, 3519
26:18 neither *shall it be* for thine **h** from 3519
32:27 had exceeding much riches and **h**: 3519
32:33 the inhabitants of Jerusalem did him **h** at 3519
Est 1: 4 the **h** of his excellent majesty many days, 3366
1:20 all the wives shall give to their husbands **h**, 3366
6: 3 What **h** and dignity hath been done to 3366
6: 6 the man whom the king delighteth to **h**? 3366
6: 6 To whom would the king delight to do **h** 3366
6: 7 *For* the man whom the king delighteth to **h**, 3366
6: 9 man *withal* whom the king delighteth to **h**, 3366
6: 9 to the man whom the king delighteth to **h**. 3366
6:11 the man whom the king delighteth to **h**. 3366
8:16 had light, and gladness, and joy, and **h**. 3366
Job 14:21 His sons **come to h**, and he knoweth *it* not; 3513
Ps 7: 5 upon the earth, and lay mine **h** in the dust. 3519
8: 5 and hast crowned him *with* glory and **h**. 1926
21: 5 **h** and majesty hast thou laid upon him. 1935
26: 8 and the place where thine **h** dwelleth. 3519
49:12 Nevertheless man *being* in **h** abideth not: 3366
49:20 Man *that is* in **h**, and understandeth not, 3366
66: 2 Sing forth the **h** of his name: make his 3519

Ps 71: 8 *with* thy praise *and with* thy **h** all the day. 8597
91:15 in trouble; I will deliver him, and **h** him. 3513
96: 6 **H** and majesty *are* before him: strength and 1935
104: 1 thou art clothed with **h** and majesty. 1935
112: 9 for ever; his horn shall be exalted with **h**. 3519
145: 5 I will speak of the glorious **h** of thy 1926
149: 9 this **h** have all his saints. Praise ye 1926
Pr 3: 9 **H** the LORD with thy substance, and 3513
3:16 and in her left hand riches and **h**. 3519
4: 8 she shall **bring** thee **to h**, when thou dost 3513
5: 9 Lest thou give thine **h** unto others, and 1935
8:18 Riches and **h** *are* with me; *yea,* durable 3519
11:16 A gracious woman retaineth **h**: and 3519
14:28 In the multitude of people *is* the king's **h**: 1927
15:33 of wisdom; and before **h** *is* humility. 3519
18:12 of man is haughty, and before **h** *is* humility. 3519
20: 3 *It is* an **h** for a man to cease from strife: but 3519
21:21 mercy findeth life, righteousness, and **h**. 3519
22: 4 of the LORD *are* riches, and **h**, and life. 3519
25: 2 but the **h** of kings *is* to search out a matter. 3519
26: 1 in harvest, so **h** *is* not seemly for a fool. 3519
26: 8 in a sling, so *is* he that giveth **h** to a fool. 3519
29:23 but **h** shall uphold the humble in spirit. 3519
31:25 Strength and **h** *are* her clothing; and 1926
Ecc 6: 2 **h**, so that he wanteth nothing for his soul of 3519
10: 1 *him that is* in reputation for wisdom *and* **h**. 3519
Isa 29:13 with their lips do **h** me, but have removed 3513
43:20 The beast of the field shall **h** me, 3513
58:13 shalt **h** him, not doing thine own ways, 3513
Jer 33: 9 and an **h** before all the nations of the earth, 8597
Da 2: 6 of me gifts and rewards and great **h**: 3367
4:30 of my power, and for the **h** of my majesty? 3367
4:36 mine **h** and brightness returned unto me; 1923
4:37 and extol and **h** the King of heaven, 1922
5:18 a kingdom, and majesty, and glory, and **h**: 1923
11:21 to whom they shall not give the **h** of 1935
11:38 in his estate shall he **h** the God of forces: 3513
11:38 a god whom his fathers knew not shall he **h** 3513
Mal 1: 6 if then I *be* a father, where *is* mine **h**? and 3519
Mt 13:57 A prophet is not **without h**, save in his own *820*
15: 4 saying, **H** thy father and mother: *5091*
15: 6 And **h** not his father or his mother, *he shall* *5091*
19:19 **H** thy father and *thy* mother: and, *5091*
Mk 6: 4 A prophet is not **without h**, but in his own *820*
7:10 Moses said, **H** thy father and thy mother; *5091*
10:19 Defraud not, **H** thy father and mother. *5091*
Lk 18:20 false witness, **H** thy father and thy mother. *5091*
Jn 4:44 that a prophet hath no **h** in his own country. *5092*
5:23 That all *men* should **h** the Son, even as they *5091*
5:23 honour the Son, even as they **h** the Father. *5091*
5:41 I receive not **h** from men. *1391*
5:44 which receive **h** one of another, and *1391*
5:44 seek not the **h** that *cometh* from God only? *1391*
8:49 but I **h** my Father, and ye do dishonour me. *5091*
8:54 Jesus answered, If I **h** myself, my honour is *1392*
8:54 If I honour myself, my **h** is nothing: *1391*
12:26 if any *man* serve me, him will *my* Father **h**. *5091*
Ro 2: 7 doing seek for glory and **h** and immortality, *5092*
2:10 But glory, **h**, and peace, to every *man* that *5092*
9:21 the same lump to make one vessel unto **h**, *5092*
12:10 brotherly love; in **h** preferring one another; *5092*
13: 7 fear to whom fear; **h** to whom honour. *5092*
13: 7 fear to whom fear; honour to whom **h**. *5092*
1Co 12:23 upon these we bestow more abundant **h**; *5092*
12:24 having given more abundant **h** to that *part* *5092*
2Co 6: 8 By **h** and dishonour, by evil report and *1391*
Eph 6: 2 **H** thy father and mother; (which is the first *5091*
Col 2:23 not in any **h** to the satisfying of the flesh. *5092*
1Th 4: 4 to possess his vessel in sanctification and **h**; *5092*
1Ti 1:17 wise God, *be* **h** and glory for ever and ever. *5092*
5: 3 **H** widows that are widows indeed. *5091*
5:17 rule well be counted worthy of double **h**, *5092*
6: 1 count their own masters worthy of all **h**, *5092*
6:16 to whom *be* **h** and power everlasting. *5092*
2Ti 2:20 and some to **h**, and some to dishonour. *5092*
2:21 he shall be a vessel unto **h**, sanctified, and *5092*
Heb 2: 7 thou crownedst him with glory and **h**, and *5092*
2: 9 of death, crowned with glory and **h**; *5092*
3: 3 the house hath more **h** than the house. *5092*
5: 4 And no *man* taketh *this* **h** unto himself, but *5092*
1Pe 1: 7 might be found unto praise and **h** and *5092*
2:17 **H** all *men.* Love the brotherhood. *5091*
2:17 the brotherhood. Fear God. **H** the king. *5091*
3: 7 giving **h** unto the wife, as unto the weaker *5092*
2Pe 1:17 For he received from God the Father **h** and *5092*
Rev 4: 9 when *those* beasts give glory and **h** and *5092*
4:11 O Lord, to receive glory and **h** and power: *5092*
5:12 strength, and **h**, and glory, and blessing. *5092*
5:13 Blessing, and **h**, and glory, and power, *5092*
7:12 and **h**, and power, and might, *5092*
19: 1 Alleluia; Salvation, and glory, and **h**, *5092*
19: 7 us be glad and rejoice, and give **h** to him: *1391*
21:24 the earth do bring their glory and **h** into it. *5092*
21:26 bring the glory and **h** of the nations into it. *5092*

HONOURABLE (30) [HONOUR]

Ge 34:19 he *was* more **h** than all the house of his 3513
Nu 22:15 again princes, more, and more **h** than they. 3513
1Sa 9: 6 this city a man of God, and *he is* an **h** man; 3513
22:14 at thy bidding, and *is* **h** in thine house? 3513
2Sa 23:19 Was he not most **h** of three? therefore 3513
23:23 He was more **h** than the thirty, but 3513
2Ki 5: 1 **h**, because by him the LORD had 5375+6440
1Ch 4: 9 Jabez was more **h** than his brethren: and 3513
11:21 Of the three, he was more **h** than the two; 3513
11:25 he was **h** among the thirty, but attained not 3513
Job 22: 8 the earth; and the **h** *man* dwelt in it. 5375+6440
Ps 45: 9 Kings' daughters *were* among thy **h** 3368
111: 3 His work *is* **h** and glorious: and 1935
Isa 3: 3 the **h** *man,* and the counseller, and 5375+6440
3: 5 the ancient, and the base against the **h**. 3513
5:13 their **h** men *are* famished, and 3519
9:15 The ancient and **h**, he *is* the head; 5375+6440
23: 8 whose traffickers *are* the **h** of the earth? 3513
23: 9 to bring into contempt all the **h** of the earth. 3513
42:21 he will magnify the law, and **make** *it* **h**. 142
43: 4 thou hast been **h**, and I have loved thee: 3513
58:13 a delight, the holy of the LORD, **h**; 3513
Na 3:10 they cast lots for her **h** *men,* and all her 3513
Mk 15:43 Joseph of Arimathea, an **h** counseller, *2158*
Lk 14: 8 lest a **more h** *man* **than** thou be bidden of *1784*
Ac 13:50 Jews stirred up the devout and **h** women, *2158*
17:12 also of **h** women which were Greeks, and *2158*
1Co 4:10 ye *are* strong; ye *are* **h**, but we *are* despised. *1741*
12:23 of the body, which we think to be **less h**, *820*
Heb 13: 4 Marriage *is* **h** in all, and the bed undefiled: *5093*

HONOURED (9) [HONOUR]

Ex 14: 4 I will be **h** upon Pharaoh, and upon all his 3513
Pr 13:18 but he that regardeth reproof shall be **h**. 3513
27:18 so he that waiteth on his master shall be **h**. 3513
Isa 43:23 neither hast thou **h** me *with* thy sacrifices. 3513
La 1: 8 all that **h** her despise her, because they have 3513
5:12 their hand: the faces of elders were not **h**. 1921
Da 4:34 and I praised and **h** him that liveth for ever, 1922
Ac 28:10 Who also **h** us with many honours; and *5091*
1Co 12:26 suffer with *it;* or one member be **h**, *1392*

HONOUREST (1) [HONOUR]

1Sa 2:29 **h** thy sons above me, to make yourselves 3513

HONOURETH (9) [HONOUR]

Ps 15: 4 but he **h** them that fear the LORD. 3513
Pr 12: 9 *is* better than he that **h** himself, and 3513
14:31 but he that **h** him hath mercy on the poor. 3513
Mal 1: 6 A son **h** *his* father, and a servant his master: 3513
Mt 15: 8 with their mouth, and **h** me with *their* lips; *5091*
Mk 7: 6 This people **h** me with *their* lips, but *5091*
Jn 5:23 He that **h** not the Son honoureth not *5091*
5:23 He that honoureth not the Son **h** not *5091*
8:54 it is my Father that **h** me; of whom ye say, *1392*

HONOURS (1) [HONOUR]

Ac 28:10 Who also honoured us with many **h**; and *5092*

HOODS (1)

Isa 3:23 and the fine linen, and the **h**, and the vails. 6797

HOOF (12) [HOOFS, HORSEHOOFS]

Ex 10:26 with us; there shall not a **h** be left behind; 6541
Lev 11: 3 Whatsoever parteth the **h**, and 6541
11: 4 chew the cud, or of them that divide the **h**: 6541
11: 4 he cheweth the cud, but divideth not the **h**; 6541
11: 5 he cheweth the cud, but divideth not the **h**; 6541
11: 6 he cheweth the cud, but divideth not the **h**; 6541
11: 7 though he divide the **h**, and 6541
11:26 of every beast which divideth the **h**, 6541
Dt 14: 6 every beast that parteth the **h**, and 6541
14: 7 the cud, or of them that divide the cloven **h**; 6541

H

Dt 14: 7 for they chew the cud, but divide not the **h**; 6541
14: 8 the swine, because it divideth the **h**, 6541

HOOFS (6) [HOOF]

Ps 69:31 than an ox *or* bullock that hath horns *and* **h**. 6536
Isa 5:28 their horses' **h** shall be counted like flint, 6541
Jer 47: 3 At the noise of the stamping of the **h** of his 6541
Eze 26:11 With the **h** of his horses shall he tread 6541
32:13 any more, nor the **h** of beasts trouble them. 6541
Mic 4:13 horn iron, and I will make thy **h** brass: 6541

HOOK (5) [FISHHOOKS, FLESHHOOK, FLESHHOOKS, HOOKS, PRUNINGHOOKS]

2Ki 19:28 therefore I will put my **h** in thy nose, and 2397
Job 41: 1 Canst thou draw out leviathan with a **h**? or 2443
41: 2 Canst thou put a **h** into his nose? or bore his 100
Isa 37:29 therefore will I put my **h** in thy nose, and 2397
Mt 17:27 and cast a **h**, and take up the fish that first *44*

HOOKS (18) [HOOK]

Ex 26:32 their **h** *shall be of* gold, upon the four 2053
26:37 with gold, *and* their **h** *shall be of* gold: 2053
27:10 the **h** of the pillars and their fillets *shall be* 2053
27:11 the **h** of the pillars and their fillets *of* silver. 2053
27:17 their **h** *shall be of* silver, and their sockets 2053
36:36 their **h** *were of* gold; and he cast for them 2053
36:38 the five pillars of it with their **h**: and 2053
38:10 the **h** of the pillars and their fillets *were of* 2053
38:11 the **h** of the pillars and their fillets *of* silver. 2053
38:12 the **h** of the pillars and their fillets *of* silver. 2053
38:17 the **h** of the pillars and their fillets *of* silver; 2053
38:19 their **h** *of* silver, and the overlaying of their 2053
38:28 and five *shekels* he made **h** for the pillars, 2053
Isa 18: 5 both cut off the sprigs with **pruning h**, 4211
Eze 29: 4 I will put **h** in thy jaws, and I will cause 2397
38: 4 put **h** into thy jaws, and I will bring thee 2397
40:43 within *were* **h**, a hand broad, 8240
Am 4: 2 that he will take you away with **h**, and 6793

HOOPOE See LAPWING

HOPE (130) [HOPE'S, HOPED, HOPETH, HOPING]

Ru 1:12 If I should say, I have **h**, *if* I should have a 8615
Ezr 10: 2 yet now there is **h** in Israel concerning this 4723
Job 4: 6 *Is* not *this* thy fear, thy confidence, thy **h**; 8615
5:16 So the poor hath **h**, and iniquity stoppeth 8615
6:11 What *is* my strength, that I should **h**? and 3176
7: 6 a weaver's shuttle, and are spent without **h**. 8615
8:13 and the hypocrite's **h** shall perish: 8615
8:14 Whose **h** shall be cut off, and whose trust 3689
11:18 thou shalt be secure, because there is **h**; 8615
11:20 their **h** *shall be as* the giving up of 8615
14: 7 For there is **h** of a tree, if it be cut down, 8615
14:19 the earth; and thou destroyest the **h** of man. 8615
17:15 where *is* now my **h**? as for my hope, 8615
17:15 my hope? as for my **h**, who shall see it? 8615
19:10 and mine **h** hath he removed like a tree. 8615
27: 8 For what *is* the **h** of the hypocrite, 8615
31:24 If I have made gold my **h**, or have said to 3689
41: 9 Behold, the **h** of him is in vain: shall *not* 8431
Ps 16: 9 glory rejoiceth: my flesh also shall rest in **h**. 983
22: 9 thou didst **make** me **h** *when I was* upon my 982
31:24 your heart, all ye that **h** in the LORD. 3176
33:18 fear him, upon them that **h** in his mercy; 3176
33:22 be upon us, according as we **h** in thee. 3176
38:15 For in thee, O LORD, do I **h**: thou wilt 3176
39: 7 Lord, what wait I for? my **h** *is* in thee. 8431
42: 5 **h** thou in God: for I shall yet praise him *for* 3176
42:11 **h** thou in God: for I shall yet praise him, 3176
43: 5 **h** in God: for I shall yet praise him, *who is* 3176
71: 5 For thou *art* my **h**, O Lord GOD: *thou art* 8615
71:14 I will **h** continually, and will yet praise thee 3176
78: 7 That they might set their **h** in God, and 3689
119:49 upon which thou hast **caused** me **to h**. 3176
119:81 for thy salvation: *but* I **h** in thy word. 3176
119:114 hiding place and my shield: I **h** in thy word. 3176
119:116 and let me not be ashamed of my **h**. 7664
130: 5 my soul doth wait, and in his word do I **h**. 3176
130: 7 Let Israel **h** in the LORD: for with 3176
131: 3 Let Israel **h** in the LORD from henceforth 3176
146: 5 his help, whose **h** *is* in the LORD his God: 7664
147:11 that fear him, in those that **h** in his mercy. 3176
Pr 10:28 The **h** of the righteous *shall be* gladness: 8431
11: 7 and the **h** of unjust *men* perisheth. 8431
13:12 **H** deferred maketh the heart sick: but 8431
14:32 but the righteous hath **h** in his death. 2620
19:18 Chasten thy son while there is **h**, and let not 8615
26:12 *there is* more **h** of a fool than of him. 8615
29:20 *there is* more **h** of a fool than of him. 8615
Ecc 9: 4 him that is joined to all the living there is **h**: 986
Isa 38:18 they that go down into the pit cannot **h** for 7663
57:10 thy way; *yet* saidst thou not, There is **no h**: 2976
Jer 2:25 thou saidst, There is **no h**: no; for I have 2976
14: 8 O the **h** of Israel, the saviour thereof in 4723
17: 7 in the LORD, and whose **h** the LORD is. 4009
17:13 O LORD, the **h** of Israel, all that forsake 4723
17:17 unto me: thou *art* my **h** in the day of evil. 4268
18:12 they said, There is **no h**: but we will walk 2976
31:17 there is **h** in thine end, saith the LORD, 8615
50: 7 even the LORD, the **h** of their fathers. 4723
La 3:18 and my **h** is perished from the LORD: 8431
3:21 This I recall to my mind, therefore have I **h**. 3176
3:24 saith my soul; therefore will I **h** in him. 3176
3:26 *It is* good *that a man should* both **h** and 3175
3:29 mouth in the dust; if so be there may be **h**. 8615
Eze 13: 6 they have **made** *others* **to h** that *they* would 3176
19: 5 *and* her **h** was lost, then she took another of 8615
37:11 Our bones are dried, and our **h** is lost: 8615
Hos 2:15 and the valley of Achor for a door of **h**: 8615
Joel 3:16 the LORD *will be* the **h** of his people, and 4268
Zec 9:12 ye to the strong hold, ye prisoners of **h**: 8615
Lk 6:34 And if ye lend *to them* of whom ye **h** to *1679*
Ac 2:26 moreover also my flesh shall rest in **h**: *1680*
16:19 And when her masters saw that the **h** of *1680*
23: 6 of the **h** and resurrection of the dead I am *1680*
24:15 And have **h** towards God, which they *1680*
26: 6 am judged for the **h** of the promise made of *1680*
26: 7 serving *God* day and night, **h** to come. *1679*
27:20 no small tempest lay on *us*, all **h** that we *1680*
28:20 that for the **h** of Israel I am bound with this *1680*
Ro 4:18 Who against **h** believed in hope, that he *1680*
4:18 Who against hope believed in **h**, that he *1680*
5: 2 and rejoice in **h** of the glory of God. *1680*
5: 4 experience; and experience, **h**: *1680*
5: 5 And **h** maketh not ashamed; because *1680*
8:20 of him who hath subjected *the same,* in **h**, *1680*
8:24 For we are saved by **h**: but hope that is seen *1680*
8:24 but **h** that is seen is not hope: for what a *1680*
8:24 but hope that is seen is not **h**: for what a *1680*
8:24 what a man seeth, why doth he yet **h for**? *1679*
8:25 But if we **h for** that we see not, *then* do we *1679*
12:12 Rejoicing in **h**; patient in tribulation; *1680*
15: 4 and comfort of the scriptures might have **h**. *1680*
15:13 Now the God of **h** fill you with all joy and *1680*
15:13 in believing, that ye may abound in **h**, *1680*
1Co 9:10 that he that ploweth should plow in **h**; and *1680*
9:10 that he that thresheth in **h** should be *1680*
9:10 in hope should be partaker of his **h**. *1680*
13:13 now abideth faith, **h**, charity, these three; *1680*
15:19 If in this life only we have **h** in Christ, *1679*
2Co 1: 7 And our **h** of you *is* stedfast, knowing, *1680*
3:12 Seeing then that we have such **h**, we use *1680*
10:15 but having **h**, when your faith is increased, *1680*
Gal 5: 5 For we through the Spirit wait for the **h** of *1680*
Eph 1:18 that ye may know what is the **h** of his *1680*
2:12 having no **h**, and without God in the world: *1680*
4: 4 even as ye are called in one **h** of your *1680*
Php 1:20 to my earnest expectation and *my* **h**, *1680*
2:23 Him therefore I **h** to send presently, so *1679*
Col 1: 5 For the **h** which is laid up for you in *1680*
1:23 *be* not moved away from the **h** of *1680*
1:27 which is Christ in you, the **h** of glory: *1680*
1Th 1: 3 and patience of **h** in our Lord Jesus Christ, *1680*
2:19 For what *is* our **h**, or joy, or crown of *1680*
4:13 even as others which have no **h**. *1680*
5: 8 love; and for a helmet, the **h** of salvation. *1680*
2Th 2:16 and good **h** through grace, *1680*
1Ti 1: 1 and Lord Jesus Christ, *which is* our **h**; *1680*
Tit 1: 2 In **h** of eternal life, which God, that cannot *1680*
2:13 Looking for *that* blessed **h**, and the glorious *1680*
3: 7 we should be made heirs according to the **h** *1680*
Heb 3: 6 and the rejoicing of the **h** firm unto the end. *1680*
6:11 to the full assurance of **h** unto the end: *1680*
6:18 refuge to lay hold upon the **h** set before *us*: *1680*
6:19 Which *h* we have as an anchor of the soul, NIG
7:19 the bringing in of a better **h** *did;* by *1680*
10:23 Let us hold fast the profession of *our* **h** *1680*
1Pe 1: 3 **h** by the resurrection of Jesus Christ from *1680*

1Pe 1:13 **h** to the end for the grace that is *to be* 1679
1:21 that your faith and **h** might be in God. *1680*
3:15 reason of the **h** that is in you with meekness *1680*
1Jn 3: 3 And every *man* that hath this **h** in him *1680*

HOPE'S (1) [HOPE]
Ac 26: 7 For which **h** sake, king Agrippa, I am *1680*

HOPED (11) [HOPE]
Est 9: 1 in the day that the enemies of the Jews **h** to 7663
Job 6:20 They were confounded because they had **h**; 982
Ps 119:43 my mouth; for I have **h** in thy judgments. 3176
119:74 they see me; because I have **h** in thy word. 3176
119:147 of the morning, and cried: I **h** in thy word. 3176
119:166 I have **h** for thy salvation, and done thy 7663
Jer 3:23 Truly in vain *is salvation* **h** *for* from NIH
Lk 23: 8 he **h** to have seen some miracle done by *1679*
Ac 24:26 He **h** also that money should have been *1679*
2Co 8: 5 And *this they did,* not as we **h**, but *1679*
Heb 11: 1 Now faith is the substance of *things* **h for**, *1679*

HOPETH (1) [HOPE]
1Co 13: 7 Beareth all *things*, believeth all *things*, **h** *1679*

HOPHNI (5)
1Sa 1: 3 the two sons of Eli, **H** and Phinehas, 2652
2:34 upon thy two sons, on **H** and Phinehas; 2652
4: 4 the two sons of Eli, **H** and Phinehas, 2652
4:11 sons of Eli, **H** and Phinehas, were slain. 2652
4:17 **H** and Phinehas, are dead, and the ark of 2652

HOPING (2) [HOPE]
Lk 6:35 and do good, and lend, **h for nothing again**; *560*
1Ti 3:14 I unto thee, **h** to come unto thee shortly: *1679*

HOR (12)
Nu 20:22 from Kadesh, and came *unto* mount **H**. 2023
20:23 spake unto Moses and Aaron in mount **H**, 2023
20:25 his son, and bring them up *unto* mount **H**: 2023
20:27 they went up into mount **H** in the sight of 2023
21: 4 they journeyed from mount **H** *by* the way 2023
33:37 pitched in mount **H**, in the edge of the land 2023
33:38 Aaron the priest went up into mount **H** at 2023
33:39 three years old when he died in mount **H**. 2023
33:41 they departed from mount **H**, and 2023
34: 7 sea you shall point out for you mount **H**: 2023
34: 8 From mount **H** ye shall point out *your* 2023
Dt 32:50 as Aaron thy brother died in mount **H**, 2023

HOR HAGGIDGAD See HOR-HAGIDGAD

HORAM (1)
Jos 10:33 **H** king of Gezer came up to help Lachish; 2036

HOREB (17) [SINAI]
Ex 3: 1 came to the mountain of God, *even* to **H**. 2722
17: 6 stand before thee there upon the rock in **H**; 2722
33: 6 of their ornaments by the mount **H**. 2722
Dt 1: 2 (*There are* eleven days' *journey* from **H** *by* 2722
1: 6 The LORD our God spake unto us in **H**, 2722
1:19 when we departed from **H**, we went 2722
4:10 stoodest before the LORD thy God in **H**, 2722
4:15 unto you in **H** out of the midst of the fire: 2722
5: 2 our God made a covenant with us in **H**. 2722
9: 8 Also in **H** ye provoked the LORD to 2722
18:16 thy God in **H** in the day of the assembly, 2722
29: 1 covenant which he made with them in **H**. 2722
1Ki 8: 9 of stone, which Moses put there at **H**, 2722
19: 8 and forty nights unto **H** the mount of God. 2722
2Ch 5:10 two tables which Moses put *therein* at **H**, 2722
Ps 106:19 They made a calf in **H**, and worshipped 2722
Mal 4: 4 which I commanded unto him in **H** for all 2722

HOREM (1)
Jos 19:38 **H**, and Beth-anath, and Beth-shemesh; 2765

HOR-HAGIDGAD (2)
Nu 33:32 from Bene-jaakan, and encamped at **H**. 2735
33:33 they went from **H**, and pitched in 2735

HORI (4) [HORIMS, HORITE, HORITES]
Ge 36:22 the children of Lotan were **H** and Hemam; 2753
36:30 these *are* the dukes *that came* of **H**, 2753
Nu 13: 5 the tribe of Simeon, Shaphat the son of **H**. 2753
1Ch 1:39 And the sons of Lotan; **H**, and Homam: and 2753

HORIMS (2) [HORI]
Dt 2:12 The **H** also dwelt in Seir beforetime; but 2752
2:22 when he destroyed the **H** from before them; 2752

HORITE (1) [HORI]
Ge 36:20 These *are* the sons of Seir the **H**, 2752

HORITES (3) [HORI]
Ge 14: 6 the **H** in their mount Seir, unto El-paran, 2752
36:21 these *are* the dukes of the **H**, the children of 2752
36:29 These *are* the dukes *that came* of the **H**; 2752

HORMAH (9)
Nu 14:45 and discomfited them, *even* unto **H**. 2767
21: 3 and he called the name of the place **H**. 2767
Dt 1:44 and destroyed you in Seir, *even* unto **H**. 2767
Jos 12:14 The king of **H**, one; the king of Arad, one; 2767
15:30 And Eltolad, and Chesil, and **H**, 2767
19: 4 And Eltolad, and Bethul, and **H**, 2767
Jdg 1:17 and the name of the city was called **H**. 2767
1Sa 30:30 to *them* which *were* in **H**, and to *them* 2767
1Ch 4:30 And at Bethuel, and at **H**, and at Ziklag, 2767

HORN (36) [HORNS, INKHORN]
Ex 21:29 if the ox *were* **wont to push with his h** in 5056
Jos 6: 5 *they* make a long blast with the ram's **h**, 7161
1Sa 2: 1 mine **h** is exalted in the LORD: 7161
2:10 his king, and exalt the **h** of his anointed. 7161
16: 1 fill thine **h** *with* oil, and go, I will send thee 7161
16:13 Samuel took the **h** of oil, and anointed him 7161
2Sa 22: 3 the **h** of my salvation, my high tower, and 7161
1Ki 1:39 Zadok the priest took a **h** of oil out of 7161
1Ch 25: 5 seer in the words of God, to lift up the **h**. 7161
Job 16:15 upon my skin, and defiled my **h** in the dust. 7161
Ps 18: 2 the **h** of my salvation, *and* my high tower. 7161
75: 4 and to the wicked, Lift not up the **h**: 7161
75: 5 Lift not up your **h** on high: speak *not* with a 7161
89:17 and in thy favour our **h** shall be exalted. 7161
89:24 and in my name shall his **h** be exalted. 7161
92:10 my **h** shalt thou exalt like *the horn of* an 7161
92:10 my horn shalt thou exalt like *the* **h** *of* an NIH
112: 9 for ever; his **h** shall be exalted with honour. 7161
132:17 There will I make the **h** of David to bud: 7161
148:14 He also exalteth the **h** of his people, 7161
Jer 48:25 The **h** of Moab is cut off, and his arm is 7161
La 2: 3 He hath cut off in *his* fierce anger all the **h** 7161
2:17 he hath set up the **h** of thine adversaries. 7161
Eze 29:21 In that day will I cause the **h** of the house 7161
Da 7: 8 there came up among them another little **h**, 7162
7: 8 in this **h** *were* eyes like the eyes of man, 7162
7:11 of the voice of the great words which the **h** 7162
7:20 even *of* that **h** that had eyes, and a mouth 7162
7:21 the same **h** made war with the saints, and 7162
8: 5 the goat *had* a notable **h** between his eyes. 7161
8: 8 he was strong, the great **h** was broken; 7161
8: 9 out of one of them came forth a little **h**, 7161
8:21 the great **h** that *is* between his eyes *is* 7161
Mic 4:13 for I will make thine **h** iron, and I will 7161
Zec 1:21 which lift up *their* **h** over the land of Judah 7161
Lk 1:69 And hath raised up a **h** of salvation for us *2768*

HORNET (2) [HORNETS]
Dt 7:20 thy God will send the **h** among them, 6880
Jos 24:12 I sent the **h** before you, which drave them 6880

HORNETS (1) [HORNET]
Ex 23:28 I will send **h** before thee, which shall drive 6880

HORNS (67) [HORN]
Ge 22:13 *him* a ram caught in a thicket by his **h**: 7161
Ex 27: 2 thou shalt make the **h** of it upon the four 7161
27: 2 his **h** shall be of the same: and thou shalt 7161
29:12 put *it* upon the **h** of the altar with thy 7161
30: 2 the **h** thereof *shall be* of the same. 7161
30: 3 thereof round about, and the **h** thereof; 7161
30:10 Aaron shall make an atonement upon the **h** 7161
37:25 height of it; the **h** thereof were of the same. 7161
37:26 sides thereof round about, and the **h** of it: 7161
38: 2 he made the **h** thereof on the four corners 7161
38: 2 of it; the **h** thereof were of the same: 7161
Lev 4: 7 **h** of the altar of sweet incense before 7161
4:18 he shall put *some* of the blood upon the **h** 7161
4:25 put *it* upon the **h** of the altar of burnt 7161
4:30 put *it* upon the **h** of the altar of burnt 7161

Lev 4:34 put *it* upon the **h** of the altar of burnt 7161
8:15 put *it* upon the **h** of the altar round about 7161
9: 9 put *it* upon the **h** of the altar, and poured 7161
16:18 put *it* upon the **h** of the altar round about. 7161
Dt 33:17 and his **h** *are like* the horns of unicorns: 7161
33:17 and his horns *are like* the **h** of unicorns: 7161
Jos 6: 4 before the ark seven trumpets of **rams' h**: 3104
6: 6 of **rams' h** before the ark of the LORD. 3104
6: 8 of **rams' h** passed on before the LORD, 3104
6:13 **rams' h** before the ark of the LORD went 3104
1Ki 1:50 went, and caught hold on the **h** of the altar. 7161
1:51 he hath caught hold on the **h** of the altar, 7161
2:28 and caught hold on the **h** of the altar. 7161
22:11 the son of Chenaanah made him **h** of iron: 7161
2Ch 18:10 son of Chenaanah had made him **h** of iron, 7161
Ps 22:21 for thou hast heard me from the **h** of 7161
69:31 than an ox *or* bullock that hath **h** *and* hoofs. 7160
75:10 All the **h** of the wicked also will I cut off; 7161
75:10 *but* the **h** of the righteous shall be exalted. 7161
118:27 with cords, *even* unto the **h** of the altar. 7161
Jer 17: 1 of their heart, and upon the **h** of your altars; 7161
Eze 27:15 they brought thee *for* a present **h** of ivory 7161
34:21 and pusht all the diseased with your **h**, 7161
43:15 from the altar and upward *shall be* four **h**. 7161
43:20 put *it* on the four **h** of it, and on the four 7161
Da 7: 7 beasts that *were* before it; and it had ten **h**. 7162
7: 8 I considered the **h**, and behold, there came 7162
7: 8 before whom there were three of the first **h** 7162
7:20 of the ten **h** that *were* in his head, and 7162
7:24 the ten **h** out of this kingdom *are* ten kings 7162
8: 3 before the river a ram which had **two h**: 7161
8: 3 the **two h** *were* high; but one *was* higher 7161
8: 6 he came to the ram that had **two h**, which I 7161
8: 7 and smote the ram, and brake his two **h**: 7161
8:20 The ram which thou sawest having **two h** 7161
Am 3:14 the **h** of the altar shall be cut off, and fall to 7161
6:13 Have we not taken to us **h** by our own 7161
Hab 3: 4 the light; he had **h** *coming* out of his hand: 7161
Zec 1:18 I up mine eyes, and saw, and behold four **h**. 7161
1:19 These *are* the **h** which have scattered 7161
1:21 These *are* the **h** which have scattered 7161
1:21 fray them, to cast out the **h** of the Gentiles, 7161
Rev 5: 6 *been* slain, having seven **h** and seven eyes, *2768*
9:13 I heard a voice from the four **h** of *2768*
12: 3 having seven heads and ten **h**, and *2768*
13: 1 having seven heads and ten **h**, and upon his *2768*
13: 1 and upon his **h** ten crowns, and upon his *2768*
13:11 and he had two **h** like a lamb, and he spake *2768*
17: 3 having seven heads and ten **h**. *2768*
17: 7 which hath the seven heads and ten **h**. *2768*
17:12 And the ten **h** which thou sawest are ten *2768*
17:16 And the ten **h** which thou sawest upon *2768*

HORONAIM (4)

Isa 15: 5 for *in* the way of **H** they shall raise up a cry 2773
Jer 48: 3 A voice of crying *shall be* from **H**, spoiling 2773
48: 5 for in the going down of **H** the enemies 2773
48:34 from Zoar *even* unto **H**, *as* a heifer of three 2773

HORONITE (3)

Ne 2:10 When Sanballat the **H**, and Tobiah 2772
2:19 when Sanballat the **H**, and Tobiah 2772
13:28 *was* son in law to Sanballat the **H**: 2772

HORRIBLE (6) [HORROR]

Ps 11: 6 fire and brimstone, and a **h** tempest: 2152
40: 2 He brought me up also out of a **h** pit, out of 7588
Jer 5:30 and **h thing** is committed in the land; 8186
18:13 virgin of Israel hath done a very **h thing**. 8186
23:14 also in the prophets of Jerusalem a **h thing**: 8186
Hos 6:10 I have seen a **h thing** in the house of Israel: 8186

HORRIBLY (2) [HORROR]

Jer 2:12 O ye heavens, at this, and be **h afraid**, 8175
Eze 32:10 and their kings shall be **h** afraid for thee, 8178

HORROR (4) [HORRIBLE, HORRIBLY]

Ge 15:12 and, lo, a **h** of great darkness fell upon him. 367
Ps 55: 5 upon me, and **h** hath overwhelmed me. 6427
119:53 **H** hath taken hold upon me because of 2152
Eze 7:18 with sackcloth, and **h** shall cover them; 6427

HORSE (43) [HORSEBACK, HORSEHOOFS, HORSELEACH, HORSEMAN, HORSEMEN, HORSES, HORSES']

Ge 49:17 that biteth the **h** heels, so that his rider shall 5483
Ex 15: 1 the **h** and his rider hath he thrown into 5483
15:19 For the **h** of Pharaoh went in with his 5483
15:21 the **h** and his rider hath he thrown into 5483
1Ki 10:29 of silver, and a **h** for an hundred and fifty: 5483
20:20 Ben-hadad the king of Syria escaped on a **h** 5483
20:25 **h** for horse, and chariot for chariot: 5483
20:25 horse for **h**, and chariot for chariot: 5483
2Ch 1:17 of silver, and a **h** for an hundred and fifty: 5483
23:15 when she was come to the entering of the **h** 5483
Ne 3:28 From above the **h** gate repaired the priests, 5483
Est 6: 8 the **h** that the king rideth upon, and 5483
6: 9 **h** be delivered to the hand of one of 5483
6:10 Make haste, *and* take the apparel and the **h**, 5483
6:11 took Haman the apparel and the **h**, and 5483
Job 39:18 on high, she scorneth the **h** and his rider. 5483
39:19 Hast thou given the **h** strength? hast thou 5483
Ps 32: 9 Be ye not as the **h**, *or* as the mule, 5483
33:17 A **h** *is* a vain thing for safety: neither shall 5483
76: 6 the chariot and **h** *are* cast into a dead sleep. 5483
147:10 He delighteth not in the strength of the **h**: 5483
Pr 21:31 The **h** *is* prepared against the day of battle: 5483
26: 3 A whip for the **h**, a bridle for the ass, and 5483
Isa 43:17 Which bringeth forth the chariot and **h**, 5483
63:13 as a **h** in the wilderness, *that* they should 5483
Jer 8: 6 his course, as the **h** rusheth into the battle. 5483
31:40 unto the corner of the **h** gate towards 5483
51:21 with thee will I break in pieces the **h** and 5483
Am 2:15 shall he that rideth the **h** deliver himself. 5483
Zec 1: 8 behold a man riding upon a red **h**, and 5483
9:10 the **h** from Jerusalem, and the battle bow 5483
10: 3 hath made them as his goodly **h** in 5483
12: 4 I will smite every **h** with astonishment, and 5483
12: 4 will smite every **h** of the people with 5483
14:15 so shall be the plague of the **h**, of the mule, 5483
Rev 6: 2 And I saw, and behold a white **h**: and *2462*
6: 4 And there went out another **h** *that was* red: *2462*
6: 5 And I beheld, and lo a black **h**; and he that *2462*
6: 8 And I looked, and behold a pale **h**: and *2462*
14:20 *even* unto the **h** bridles, by the space of a *2462*
19:11 I saw heaven opened, and behold a white **h**; *2462*
19:19 to make war against him that sat on the **h**, *2462*
19:21 with the sword of him that sat upon the **h**, *2462*

HORSEBACK (5) [BACK, HORSE]

2Ki 9:18 So there went one **on h** to meet him, 5483+7392
9:19 he sent *out* a second **on h**, which 5483+7392
Est 6: 9 bring him on **h** through the street of 5483
6:11 **brought** him **on h** through the street of 7392
8:10 sent letters by posts on **h**, *and* riders on 5483

HORSEHOOFS (1) [HOOF, HORSE]

Jdg 5:22 were the **h** broken by the means of 5483+6119

HORSELEACH (1) [HORSE]

Pr 30:15 The **h** hath two daughters, *crying*, Give, 5936

HORSEMAN (2) [HORSE, MAN]

2Ki 9:17 Take a **h**, and send to meet them, and 7395
Na 3: 3 The **h** lifteth up both the bright sword and 6571

HORSEMEN (59) [HORSE, MAN]

Ge 50: 9 there went up with him both chariots and **h**: 6571
Ex 14: 9 of Pharaoh, and his **h**, and his army) 6571
14:17 his host, upon his chariots, and upon his **h**. 6571
14:18 upon his chariots, and upon his **h**. 6571
14:23 all Pharaoh's horses, his chariots, and his **h**. 6571
14:26 upon their chariots, and upon their **h**. 6571
14:28 the **h**, and all the host of Pharaoh that came 6571
15:19 his chariots and with his **h** into the sea, 6571
Jos 24: 6 with chariots and **h** *unto* the Red sea. 6571
1Sa 8:11 for himself, for his chariots, and to be his **h**; 6571
13: 5 six thousand **h**, and people as the sand 6571
2Sa 1: 6 and **h** followed hard after him. 1167+6571
8: 4 a thousand *chariots*, and seven hundred **h**, 6571
10:18 forty thousand **h**, and smote Shobach 6571
1Ki 1: 5 he prepared him chariots and **h**, and 6571
4:26 for his chariots, and twelve thousand **h**. 6571
9:19 cities for his **h**, and that which Solomon 6571
9:22 and rulers of his chariots, and his **h**. 6571
10:26 Solomon gathered together chariots and **h**: 6571
10:26 hundred chariots, and twelve thousand **h**, 6571

1Ki 20:20 king of Syria escaped on a horse with the **h**. 6571
2Ki 2:12 the chariot of Israel, and the **h** thereof. 6571
13: 7 leave *of* the people to Jehoahaz but fifty **h**, 6571
13:14 the chariot of Israel, and the **h** thereof. 6571
18:24 thy trust on Egypt for chariots and for **h**? 6571
1Ch 18: 4 seven thousand **h**, and twenty thousand 6571
19: 6 them chariots and **h** out of Mesopotamia, 6571
2Ch 1:14 Solomon gathered chariots and **h**: and 6571
1:14 hundred chariots, and twelve thousand **h**, 6571
8: 6 the cities of the **h**, and all that Solomon 6571
8: 9 and captains of his chariots and **h**. 6571
9:25 and chariots, and twelve thousand **h**; 6571
12: 3 and threescore thousand **h**: 6571
16: 8 huge host, with very many chariots and **h**? 6571
Ezr 8:22 **h** to help us against the enemy in the way: 6571
Ne 2: 9 sent captains of the army and **h** with me. 6571
Isa 21: 7 he saw a chariot *with* a couple of **h**, 6571
21: 9 a chariot of men, *with* a couple of **h**. 6571
22: 6 bare the quiver with chariots of men *and* **h**, 6571
22: 7 the **h** shall set themselves in array at 6571
28:28 wheel of his cart, nor bruise it *with* his **h**. 6571
31: 1 in **h**, because they are very strong; but 6571
36: 9 thy trust on Egypt for chariots and for **h**? 6571
Jer 4:29 whole city shall flee for the noise of the **h** 6571
46: 4 ye **h**, and stand forth with *your* helmets; 6571
Eze 23: 6 desirable young men, **h** riding upon horses. 6571
23:12 most gorgeously, **h** riding upon horses, 6571
26: 7 with **h**, and companies, and much people. 6571
26:10 thy walls shall shake at the noise of the **h**, 6571
27:14 in thy fairs with horses and **h** and mules. 6571
38: 4 thee forth, and all thine army, horses and **h**, 6571
Da 11:40 and with **h**, and with many ships; 6571
Hos 1: 7 nor by battle, by horses, nor by **h**. 6571
Joel 2: 4 of horses; and as **h**, so shall they run. 6571
Hab 1: 8 their **h** shall spread themselves, and 6571
1: 8 and their **h** shall come from far; 6571
Ac 23:23 and **h** threescore *and* ten, and spearmen two *2460*
23:32 On the morrow they left the **h** to go with *2460*
Rev 9:16 And the number of the army of the **h** *were* *2461*

HORSES (109) [HORSE]

Ge 47:17 Joseph gave them bread *in exchange* for **h**, 5483
Ex 9: 3 upon the **h**, upon the asses, upon 5483
14: 9 the Egyptians pursued after them (all the **h** 5483
14:23 *even* all Pharaoh's **h**, his chariots, and 5483
Dt 11: 4 of Egypt, unto their **h**, and to their chariots; 5483
17:16 he shall not multiply **h** to himself, 5483
17:16 to the end that he should multiply **h**: 5483
20: 1 seest **h**, and chariots, *and* a people more 5483
Jos 11: 4 with **h** and chariots very many. 5483
11: 6 thou shalt hough their **h**, and burn their 5483
11: 9 he houghed their **h**, and burnt their chariots 5483
2Sa 8: 4 David houghed all the chariot *h*, but NIH
15: 1 that Absalom prepared him chariots and **h**, 5483
1Ki 4:26 Solomon had forty thousand stalls of **h** for 5483
4:28 Barley also and straw for the **h** and 5483
10:25 and armour, and spices, **h**, and mules, 5483
10:28 Solomon had **h** brought out of Egypt, and 5483
18: 5 we may find grass to save the **h** 5483
20: 1 two kings with him, and **h**, and chariots: 5483
20:21 smote the **h** and chariots, and slew 5483
22: 4 people as thy people, my **h** as thy horses. 5483
22: 4 people as thy people, my horses as thy **h**. 5483
2Ki 2:11 and **h** of fire, and parted them both asunder; 5483
3: 7 as thy people, *and* my **h** as thy horses. 5483
3: 7 as thy people, *and* my horses as thy **h**. 5483
5: 9 So Naaman came with his **h** and with his 5483
6:14 Therefore sent he thither **h**, and chariots, 5483
6:15 a host compassed the city both with **h** and 5483
6:17 the mountain was full *of* **h** and chariots of 5483
7: 6 a noise of **h**, *even* the noise of a great host: 5483
7: 7 left their tents, and their **h**, and their asses, 5483
7:10 **h** tied, and asses tied, and the tents as they 5483
7:13 I pray thee, five of the **h** that remain, 5483
7:14 They took therefore two chariot **h**; and 5483
9:33 was sprinkled on the wall, and on the **h**: 5483
10: 2 *there are* with you chariots and **h**, a fenced 5483
11:16 she went *by* the way by the which the **h** 5483
14:20 they brought him on **h**: and he was buried 5483
18:23 and I will deliver thee two thousand **h**, 5483
23:11 he took away the **h** that the kings of Judah 5483
1Ch 18: 4 David also houghed all the chariot *h*, but NIH
2Ch 1:16 Solomon had **h** brought out of Egypt, and 5483
1:17 brought they out *h* for all the kings of NIH
9:24 raiment, harness, and spices, **h**, and mules, 5483
9:25 And Solomon had four thousand stalls for **h** 5483
9:28 they brought unto Solomon **h** out of Egypt, 5483
25:28 they brought him upon **h**, and buried him 5483
Ezr 2:66 Their **h** *were* seven hundred thirty and six; 5483
Ne 7:68 Their **h**, seven hundred thirty and six: 5483
Ps 20: 7 Some *trust* in chariots, and some in **h**: but 5483
Ecc 10: 7 I have seen servants upon **h**, and 5483
SS 1: 9 to a **company of h** in Pharaoh's chariots. 5484
Isa 2: 7 their land is also full *of* **h**, neither *is there* 5483
30:16 ye said, No; for we will flee upon **h**; 5483
31: 1 stay on **h**, and trust in chariots, because 5483
31: 3 not God; and their **h** flesh, and not spirit. 5483
36: 8 and I will give thee two thousand **h**, 5483
66:20 unto the LORD out of all nations upon **h**, 5483
Jer 4:13 his **h** are swifter than eagles. Woe unto us! 5483
5: 8 They were *as* fed **h** in the morning: 5483
6:23 they ride upon **h**, set in array as men for 5483
8:16 The snorting of his **h** was heard from Dan: 5483
12: 5 then how canst thou contend with **h**? 5483
17:25 riding in chariots and on **h**, they, and 5483
22: 4 riding in chariots and on **h**, he, and 5483
46: 4 Harness the **h**; and get up, ye horsemen, 5483
46: 9 Come up, ye **h**; and rage, ye chariots; and 5483
47: 3 his strong *h*, at the rushing of his chariots, NIH
50:37 A sword *is* upon their **h**, and upon their 5483
50:42 they shall ride upon **h**, *every one* put in 5483
51:27 cause the **h** to come up as the rough 5483
Eze 17:15 that *they* might give him **h** and 5483
23: 6 young men, horsemen riding upon **h**. 5483
23:12 most gorgeously, horsemen riding upon **h**, 5483
23:20 and whose issue *is like* the issue of **h**. 5483
23:23 and renowned, all of them riding upon **h**. 5483
26: 7 with **h**, and with chariots, and 5483
26:10 By reason of the abundance of his **h** their 5483
26:11 With the hoofs of his **h** shall he tread down 5483
27:14 of Togarmah traded in thy fairs with **h** 5483
38: 4 and all thine army, **h** and horsemen, 5483
38:15 all of them riding upon **h**, a great company, 5483
39:20 Thus ye shall be filled at my table *with* **h** 5483
Hos 1: 7 nor by sword, nor by battle, by **h**, nor by 5483
14: 3 we will not ride upon **h**: neither will we say 5483
Joel 2: 4 of them *is* as the appearance of **h**; 5483
Am 4:10 the sword, and have taken away your **h**; 5483
6:12 Shall **h** run upon the rock? will *one* plow 5483
Mic 5:10 that I will cut off thy **h** out of the midst of 5483
Na 3: 2 of the pransing **h**, and of the jumping 5483
Hab 1: 8 Their **h** also are swifter than the leopards, 5483
3: 8 that thou didst ride upon thine **h** *and* 5483
3:15 didst walk through the sea *with* thine **h**, 5483
Hag 2:22 the **h** and their riders shall come down, 5483
Zec 1: 8 behind him *were there* red **h**, speckled, and 5483
6: 2 In the first chariot *were* red **h**; and in 5483
6: 2 and in the second chariot black **h**; 5483
6: 3 in the third chariot white **h**; and in 5483
6: 3 and in the fourth chariot grisled *and* bay **h**. 5483
6: 6 The black **h** which *are* therein go forth into 5483
10: 5 and the riders on **h** shall be confounded. 5483
14:20 day shall there be upon the bells of the **h**, 5483
Rev 9: 7 *were* like unto **h** prepared unto battle; *2462*
9: 9 of chariots of many **h** running to battle. *2462*
9:17 And thus I saw the **h** in the vision, and *2462*
9:17 the heads of the **h** *were* as the heads of *2462*
18:13 and **h**, and chariots, and slaves, and souls of *2462*
19:14 were in heaven followed him upon white **h**, *2462*
19:18 the flesh of mighty *men,* and the flesh of **h**, *2462*

HORSES' (2) [HORSE]

Isa 5:28 their **h** hoofs shall be counted like flint, and 5483
Jas 3: 3 Behold, we put bits in the **h** mouths, *2462*

HOSAH (5)

Jos 19:29 the coast turneth *to* **H**; and the outgoings 2621
1Ch 16:38 the son of Jeduthun and **H** to be porters: 2621
26:10 Also **H**, of the children of Merari, had sons; 2621
26:11 the sons and brethren of **H** *were* thirteen. 2621
26:16 and **H** *the lot came forth* westward, 2621

HOSANNA (6)

Mt 21: 9 cried, saying, **H** to the Son of David: *5614*
21: 9 in the name of the Lord; **H** in the highest. *5614*
21:15 and saying, **H** to the Son of David; *5614*
Mk 11: 9 and they that followed, cried, saying, **H**; *5614*
11:10 in the name of the Lord: **H** in the highest. *5614*

Jn 12:13 and went forth to meet him, and cried, **H**: *5614*

HOSEA (3) [OSEE]
Hos 1: 1 The word of the LORD that came unto **H**, 1954
1: 2 beginning of the word of the LORD by **H**. 1954
1: 2 the LORD said to **H**, Go, take unto thee a 1954

HOSEN (1)
Da 3:21 their **h**, and their hats, and their *other* 6361

HOSHAIAH (3)
Ne 12:32 after them went **H**, and half of the princes 1955
Jer 42: 1 Jezaniah the son of **H**, and all the people 1955
43: 2 spake Azariah the son of **H**, and 1955

HOSHAMA (1)
1Ch 3:18 and Shenazar, Jecamiah, **H**, and Nedabiah. 1953

HOSHEA (11) [JOSHUA]
Dt 32:44 of the people, he and **H** the son of Nun. 1954
2Ki 15:30 **H** the son of Elah made a conspiracy 1954
17: 1 **H** the son of Elah to reign in Samaria over 1954
17: 3 **H** became his servant, and gave him 1954
17: 4 the king of Assyria found conspiracy in **H**: 1954
17: 6 In the ninth year of **H**, the king of Assyria 1954
18: 1 Now it came to pass in the third year of **H** 1954
18: 9 which *was* the seventh year of **H** son of 1954
18:10 that *is* the ninth year of **H** king of Israel, 1954
1Ch 27:20 children of Ephraim, **H** the son of Azaziah: 1954
Ne 10:23 **H**, Hananiah, Hashub, 1954

HOSPITALITY (4)
Ro 12:13 to the necessity of saints; given to **h**. *5381*
1Ti 3: 2 of good behaviour, **given to h**, apt to teach; *5382*
Tit 1: 8 But a **lover of h**, a lover of good *men*, *5382*
1Pe 4: 9 Use **h** one to another without grudging. *5382*

HOST (192) [HOSTS]
Ge 2: 1 earth were finished, and all the **h** of them. 6635
21:22 Phichol the chief captain of his **h** spake 6635
21:32 Phichol the chief captain of his **h**, and 6635
32: 2 Jacob saw them, he said, This *is* God's **h**: 4264
Ex 14: 4 honoured upon Pharaoh, and upon all his **h**; 2428
14:17 upon all his **h**, upon his chariots, and 2428
14:24 **h** of the Egyptians through the pillar of fire 4264
14:24 and troubled the **h** of the Egyptians, 4264
14:28 all the **h** of Pharaoh that came into the sea 2428
15: 4 and his **h** hath he cast into the sea: 2428
16:13 the morning the dew lay round about the **h**. 4264
Nu 2: 4 his **h**, and those that were numbered of 6635
2: 6 his **h**, and those that were numbered 6635
2: 8 his **h**, and those that were numbered 6635
2:11 his **h**, and those that were numbered 6635
2:13 his **h**, and those that were numbered of 6635
2:15 his **h**, and those that were numbered of 6635
2:19 his **h**, and those that were numbered of 6635
2:21 his **h**, and those that were numbered of 6635
2:23 his **h**, and those that were numbered of 6635
2:26 his **h**, and those that were numbered 6635
2:28 his **h**, and those that were numbered of 6635
2:30 his **h**, and those that were numbered of 6635
4: 3 until fifty years old, all that enter into the **h**, 6635
10:14 over his **h** *was* Nahshon the son of 6635
10:15 over the **h** of the tribe of the children of 6635
10:16 over the **h** of the tribe of the children of 6635
10:18 over his **h** *was* Elizur the son of Shedeur. 6635
10:19 over the **h** of the tribe of the children of 6635
10:20 over the **h** of the tribe of the children of 6635
10:22 over his **h** *was* Elishama the son of 6635
10:23 over the **h** of the tribe of the children of 6635
10:24 over the **h** of the tribe of the children of 6635
10:25 over his **h** *was* Ahiezer the son of 6635
10:26 over the **h** of the tribe of the children of 6635
10:27 over the **h** of the tribe of the children of 6635
31:14 Moses was wroth with the officers of the **h**, 2428
31:48 which *were* over thousands of the **h**, 6635
Dt 2:14 of war were wasted out from among the **h**, 4264
2:15 to destroy them from among the **h**, 4264
4:19 and the stars, *even* all the **h** of heaven, 6635
17: 3 the sun, or moon, or any of the **h** of heaven, 6635
23: 9 When the **h** goeth forth against thine 4264
Jos 1:11 Pass through the **h**, and command 4264
3: 2 that the officers went through the **h**; 4264
5:14 *as* captain of the **h** of the LORD am I now 6635
5:15 the captain of the LORD's **h** said unto 6635
8:13 *even* all the **h** that *was* on the north of 4264
18: 9 came *again* to Joshua to the **h** *at* Shiloh. 4264
Jdg 4: 2 the captain of whose **h** *was* Sisera, which 6635
4:15 and all *his* chariots, and all *his* **h**, 4264
4:16 after the **h**, unto Harosheth of the Gentiles: 4264
4:16 all the **h** of Sisera fell upon the edge of 4264
7: 1 that the **h** of the Midianites were on 4264
7: 8 the **h** of Midian was beneath him in 4264
7: 9 unto him, Arise, get thee down unto the **h**; 4264
7:10 with Phurah thy servant down to the **h**: 4264
7:11 be strengthened to go down unto the **h**. 4264
7:11 of the armed *men* that *were* in the **h**. 4264
7:13 a cake of barley bread tumbled into the **h** of 4264
7:14 hath God delivered Midian, and all the **h**. 4264
7:15 returned into the **h** of Israel, and said, 4264
7:15 delivered into your hand the **h** of Midian. 4264
7:21 and all the **h** ran, and cried, and fled. 4264
7:22 his fellow, even throughout all the **h**: 4264
7:22 the **h** fled to Beth-shittah in Zererath, *and* 4264
8:11 of Nobah and Jogbehah, and smote the **h**: 4264
8:11 and smote the host: for the **h** was secure. 4264
8:12 and Zalmunna, and discomfited all the **h**. 4264
1Sa 11:11 they came into the midst of the **h** in 4264
12: 9 captain of the **h** of Hazor, and into the hand 6635
14:15 there was trembling in the **h**, in the field, 4264
14:19 that the noise that *was* in the **h** of 4264
14:48 he gathered a **h**, and smote the Amalekites, 2428
14:50 the name of the captain of his **h** *was* Abner, 6635
17:20 as the **h** was going forth to the fight, and 2428
17:46 I will give the carcases of the **h** of 4264
17:55 unto Abner, the captain of the **h**, Abner, 6635
26: 5 Abner the son of Ner, the captain of his **h**: 6635
28: 5 when Saul saw the **h** of the Philistines, he 4264
28:19 the LORD also shall deliver the **h** of Israel 4264
29: 6 thy coming in with me in the **h** *is* good in 4264
2Sa 2: 8 Abner the son of Ner, captain of Saul's **h**, 6635
3:23 and all the **h** that *was* with him were come, 6635
5:24 to smite the **h** of the Philistines. 4264
8: 9 David had smitten all the **h** of Hadadezer, 2428
8:16 Joab the son of Zeruiah *was* over the **h**; 6635
10: 7 sent Joab, and all the **h** *of* the mighty *men*. 6635
10:16 Shobach the captain of the **h** of Hadarezer 6635
10:18 smote Shobach the captain of their **h**, 6635
17:25 Absalom made Amasa captain of the **h** 6635
19:13 if thou be not captain of the **h** before me 6635
20:23 Now Joab *was* over all the **h** of Israel: and 6635
23:16 the three mighty *men* brake through the **h** 4264
24: 2 the king said to Joab the captain of the **h**, 2428
24: 4 and against the captains of the **h**. 2428
24: 4 the captains of the **h** went out from 2428
1Ki 1:19 the priest, and Joab the captain of the **h**: 6635
1:25 the captains of the **h**, and Abiathar 6635
2:32 captain of the **h** of Israel, and Amasa 6635
2:32 the son of Jether, captain of the **h** of Judah. 6635
2:35 the son of Jehoiada in his room over the **h**: 6635
4: 4 the son of Jehoiada *was* over the **h**: 6635
11:15 Joab the captain of the **h** was gone up to 6635
11:21 that Joab the captain of the **h** was dead, 6635
16:16 all Israel made Omri, the captain of the **h**, 6635
20: 1 king of Syria gathered all his **h** together: 2428
22:19 all the **h** of heaven standing by him on his 6635
22:34 Turn thine hand, and carry me out of the **h**; 4264
22:36 there went a proclamation throughout the **h** 4264
2Ki 3: 9 there was no water for the **h**, and for 4264
4:13 for to the king, or to the captain of the **h**? 6635
5: 1 captain of the **h** of the king of Syria, 6635
6:14 thither horses, and chariots, and a great **h**: 2428
6:15 a **h** compassed the city both with horses 2428
6:24 Ben-hadad king of Syria gathered all his **h**, 4264
7: 4 and let us fall unto the **h** of the Syrians: 4264
7: 6 For the Lord had made the **h** of the Syrians 4264
7: 6 noise of horses, *even* the noise of a great **h**: 2428
7:14 the king sent after the **h** of the Syrians, 4264
9: 5 the captains of the **h** *were* sitting; 2428
11:15 the officers of the **h**, and said unto them, 2428
17:16 worshipped all the **h** of heaven, and 6635
18:17 Hezekiah with a great **h** *against* Jerusalem. 2426
21: 3 worshipped all the **h** of heaven, and 6635
21: 5 he built altars for all the **h** of heaven in 6635
23: 4 for the grove, and for all the **h** of heaven: 6635
23: 5 to the planets, and to all the **h** of heaven. 6635
25: 1 he, and all his **h**, against Jerusalem, and 2428
25:19 in the city, and the principal scribe of the **h**, 6635
1Ch 9:19 *being* over the **h** of the LORD, 4264

1Ch 11:15 the **h** of the Philistines encamped in 4264
11:18 the three brake through the **h** of 4264
12:14 *were* of the sons of Gad, captains of the **h**: 6635
12:21 *men* of valour, and were captains in the **h**. 6635
12:22 until it was a great **h**, like the host of God. 4264
12:22 until it was a great host, like the **h** of God. 4264
14:15 before thee to smite the **h** of the Philistines. 4264
14:16 they smote the **h** of the Philistines from 4264
18: 9 all the **h** of Hadarezer king of Zobah; 2428
18:15 Joab the son of Zeruiah *was* over the **h**; 6635
19: 8 sent Joab, and all the **h** *of* the mighty *men*. 6635
19:16 Shophach the captain of the **h** of Hadarezer 6635
19:18 killed Shophach the captain of the **h**. 6635
25: 1 the captains of the **h** separated to 6635
26:26 and hundreds, and the captains of the **h**, 6635
27: 3 all the captains of the **h** for the first month. 6635
27: 5 The third captain of the **h** for the third 6635
2Ch 14: 9 Ethiopian with a **h** of a thousand thousand, 2428
14:13 before the LORD, and before his **h**; 4264
16: 7 is the **h** of the king of Syria escaped out of 2428
16: 8 the Ethiopians and the Lubims a huge **h**, 2428
18:18 all the **h** of heaven standing on his right 6635
18:33 that thou mayest carry me out of the **h**; 4264
23:14 of hundreds that were set over the **h**, 2428
24:23 *that* the **h** of Syria came up against him: 2428
24:24 the LORD delivered a very great **h** into 2428
26:11 Moreover Uzziah had a **h** of fighting *men*, 2428
26:14 for them throughout all the **h** shields, 6635
28: 9 he went out before the **h** that came to 6635
33: 3 worshipped all the **h** of heaven, and 6635
33: 5 he built altars for all the **h** of heaven in 6635
33:11 the captains of the **h** of the king of Assyria, 6635
Ne 9: 6 with all their **h**, the earth, and all *things* that 6635
9: 6 and the **h** of heaven worshippeth thee. 6635
Ps 27: 3 Though a **h** should encamp against me, 4264
33: 6 all the **h** of them by the breath of his 6635
33:16 is no king saved by the multitude of a **h**: 2428
136:15 and his **h** in the Red sea: 2428
Isa 13: 4 the LORD of hosts mustereth the **h** of 6635
24:21 *that* the LORD shall punish the **h** of 6635
34: 4 all the **h** of heaven shall be dissolved, and 6635
34: 4 all their **h** shall fall down, as the leaf falleth 6635
40:26 *things*, that bringeth out their **h** by number: 6635
45:12 and all their **h** have I commanded. 6635
Jer 8: 2 the moon, and all the **h** of heaven, 6635
19:13 have burnt incense unto all the **h** of heaven, 6635
33:22 As the **h** of heaven cannot be numbered, 6635
51: 3 her young men; destroy ye utterly all her **h**. 6635
52:25 the principal scribe of the **h**, who mustered 6635
Eze 1:24 the voice of speech, as the noise of a **h**: 4264
Da 8:10 it waxed great, *even* to the **h** of heaven; 6635
8:10 it cast down *some* of the **h** and of the stars 6635
8:11 *himself even* to the prince of the **h**, 6635
8:12 a **h** was given *him* against the daily 6635
8:13 and the **h** to be trodden under foot? 6635
Ob 1:20 the captivity of this **h** of the children of 2426
Zep 1: 5 them that worship the **h** of heaven upon 6635
Lk 2:13 a multitude of the heavenly **h** praising God, *4756*
10:35 and gave *them* to the **h**, and said unto him, *3830*
Ac 7:42 gave them up to worship the **h** of heaven; *4756*
Ro 16:23 Gaius mine **h**, and of the whole church, *3581*

HOSTAGES (2)
2Ki 14:14 and **h**, and returned to Samaria. 1121+8594
2Ch 25:24 the **h** also, and returned *to* Samaria. 1121+8594

HOSTILE See VEX; VEXATION; VEXED

HOSTS (299) [HOST]
Ex 12:41 *that* all the **h** of the LORD went out from 6635
Nu 1:52 by his own standard, throughout their **h**. 6635
2:32 their **h** *were* six hundred thousand 6635
10:25 of all the camps throughout their **h**: 6635
Jos 10: 5 they and all their **h**, and encamped before 4264
11: 4 they and all their **h** with them, 4264
Jdg 8:10 *were* in Karkor, and their **h** with them, 4264
8:10 left of all the **h** of the children of the east: 4264
1Sa 1: 3 to sacrifice unto the LORD of **h** in Shiloh. 6635
1:11 she vowed a vow, and said, O LORD of **h**, 6635
4: 4 the ark of the covenant of the LORD of **h**, 6635
15: 2 Thus saith the LORD of **h**, I remember 6635
17:45 to thee in the name of the LORD of **h**, 6635
2Sa 5:10 and the LORD God of **h** *was* with him. 6635
6: 2 of **h** that dwelleth *between* the cherubims. 6635
6:18 the people in the name of the LORD of **h**. 6635
7: 8 Thus saith the LORD of **h**, I took thee 6635
7:26 The LORD of **h** *is* the God over Israel: 6635
7:27 For thou, O LORD of **h**, God of Israel, 6635
1Ki 2: 5 what he did to the two captains of the **h** of 6635
15:20 sent the captains of the **h** which he had 2428
18:15 Elijah said, *As* the LORD of **h** liveth, 6635
19:10 been very jealous for the LORD God of **h**: 6635
19:14 been very jealous for the LORD God of **h**: 6635
2Ki 3:14 And Elisha said, *As* the LORD of **h** liveth, 6635
19:31 the zeal of the LORD *of* **h** shall do this. NIH
1Ch 11: 9 greater: for the LORD of **h** *was* with him. 6635
17: 7 Thus saith the LORD of **h**, I took thee 6635
17:24 The LORD of **h** *is* the God of Israel, 6635
Ps 24:10 The LORD of **h**, he *is* the King of glory. 6635
46: 7 The LORD of **h** *is* with us; the God of 6635
46:11 The LORD of **h** *is* with us; the God of 6635
48: 8 we seen in the city of the LORD of **h**, 6635
59: 5 Thou therefore, O LORD God *of* **h**, 6635
69: 6 O Lord GOD of **h**, be ashamed for my 6635
80: 4 O LORD God *of* **h**, how long wilt thou be 6635
80: 7 O God *of* **h**, and cause thy face to shine; 6635
80:14 Return, we beseech thee, O God *of* **h**: 6635
80:19 Turn us again, O LORD God *of* **h**, 6635
84: 1 *are* thy tabernacles, O LORD of **h**! 6635
84: 3 O LORD of **h**, my King, and my God. 6635
84: 8 O LORD God *of* **h**, hear my prayer: 6635
84:12 O LORD of **h**, blessed *is* the man that 6635
89: 8 O LORD God of **h**, who *is* a strong 6635
103:21 Bless ye the LORD, all ye his **h**; 6635
108:11 wilt not thou, O God, go forth with our **h**? 6635
148: 2 all his angels: praise ye him, all his **h**. 6635
Isa 1: 9 Except the LORD of **h** had left unto us a 6635
1:24 Therefore saith the Lord, the LORD of **h**, 6635
2:12 For the day of the LORD of **h** *shall be* 6635
3: 1 For behold, the Lord, the LORD of **h**, 6635
3:15 of the poor? saith the Lord GOD of **h**. 6635
5: 7 For the vineyard of the LORD of **h** *is* 6635
5: 9 In mine ears *said* the LORD of **h**, Of a 6635
5:16 the LORD of **h** shall be exalted in 6635
5:24 have cast away the law of the LORD of **h**, 6635
6: 3 said, Holy, holy, holy, *is* the LORD of **h**: 6635
6: 5 eyes have seen the King, the LORD of **h**. 6635
8:13 Sanctify the LORD of **h** himself; and 6635
8:18 for wonders in Israel from the LORD of **h**, 6635
9: 7 The zeal of the LORD of **h** will perform 6635
9:13 neither do they seek the LORD of **h**. 6635
9:19 Through the wrath of the LORD of **h** is 6635
10:16 Therefore shall the Lord, the Lord of **h**, 6635
10:23 For the Lord GOD of **h** shall make a 6635
10:24 Therefore thus saith the Lord GOD of **h**, 6635
10:26 the LORD of **h** shall stir up a scourge for 6635
10:33 Behold, the Lord, the LORD of **h**, 6635
13: 4 the LORD of **h** mustereth the host of 6635
13:13 in the wrath of the LORD of **h**, and in 6635
14:22 saith the LORD of **h**, and cut off from 6635
14:23 of destruction, saith the LORD of **h**. 6635
14:24 The LORD of **h** hath sworn, saying, 6635
14:27 For the LORD of **h** hath purposed, and 6635
17: 3 children of Israel, saith the LORD of **h**. 6635
18: 7 unto the LORD of **h** *of* a people scattered 6635
18: 7 the place of the name of the LORD of **h**, 6635
19: 4 over them, saith the Lord, the LORD of **h**. 6635
19:12 let them know what the LORD of **h** hath 6635
19:16 the shaking of the hand of the LORD of **h**, 6635
19:17 because of the counsel of the LORD of **h**, 6635
19:18 of Canaan, and swear to the LORD of **h**: 6635
19:20 for a witness unto the LORD of **h** in 6635
19:25 Whom the LORD of **h** shall bless, saying, 6635
21:10 that which I have heard of the LORD of **h**, 6635
22: 5 of perplexity by the Lord GOD of **h** in 6635
22:12 in that day did the Lord GOD of **h** call to 6635
22:14 revealed in mine ears *by* the LORD of **h**, 6635
22:14 you till ye die, saith the Lord GOD of **h**. 6635
22:15 Thus saith the Lord GOD of **h**, Go, 6635
22:25 In that day, saith the LORD of **h**, shall 6635
23: 9 The LORD of **h** hath purposed it, to stain 6635
24:23 when the LORD of **h** shall reign in mount 6635
25: 6 in this mountain shall the LORD of **h** 6635
28: 5 In that day shall the LORD of **h** be for a 6635
28:22 for I have heard from the Lord GOD of **h** 6635
28:29 also cometh forth from the LORD of **h**, 6635
29: 6 Thou shalt be visited of the LORD of **h** 6635
31: 4 shall the LORD of **h** come down to fight 6635

Isa	31: 5	so will the LORD of **h** defend Jerusalem;	6635
	37:16	O LORD of **h**, God of Israel, that dwellest	6635
	37:32	the zeal of the LORD of **h** shall do this.	6635
	39: 5	Hear the word of the LORD of **h**:	6635
	44: 6	and his redeemer the LORD of **h**;	6635
	45:13	for price nor reward, saith the LORD of **h**.	6635
	47: 4	our redeemer, the LORD of **h** *is* his name,	6635
	48: 2	of Israel; The LORD of **h** *is* his name.	6635
	51:15	The LORD of **h** *is* his name.	6635
	54: 5	the LORD of **h** *is* his name; and	6635
Jer	2:19	*is* not in thee, saith the Lord GOD of **h**.	6635
	3:19	a goodly heritage of the **h** of nations?	6635
	5:14	Wherefore thus saith the LORD God of **h**,	6635
	6: 6	For thus hath the LORD of **h** said, Hew ye	6635
	6: 9	Thus saith the LORD of **h**, They shall	6635
	7: 3	Thus saith the LORD of **h**, the God of	6635
	7:21	Thus saith the LORD of **h**, the God of	6635
	8: 3	I have driven them, saith the LORD of **h**.	6635
	9: 7	Therefore thus saith the LORD of **h**,	6635
	9:15	Therefore thus saith the LORD of **h**,	6635
	9:17	Thus saith the LORD of **h**, Consider ye,	6635
	10:16	The LORD of **h** *is* his name.	6635
	11:17	For the LORD of **h**, that planted thee,	6635
	11:20	But, O LORD of **h**, that judgest	6635
	11:22	Therefore thus saith the LORD of **h**,	6635
	15:16	called by thy name, O LORD God of **h**.	6635
	16: 9	For thus saith the LORD of **h**, the God of	6635
	19: 3	Thus saith the LORD of **h**, the God of	6635
	19:11	say unto them, Thus saith the LORD of **h**;	6635
	19:15	Thus saith the LORD of **h**, the God of	6635
	20:12	But, O LORD of **h**, that triest	6635
	23:15	Therefore thus saith the LORD of **h**	6635
	23:16	Thus saith the LORD of **h**, Hearken not	6635
	23:36	living God, of the LORD of **h** our God.	6635
	25: 8	Therefore thus saith the LORD of **h**;	6635
	25:27	Thus saith the LORD of **h**, the God of	6635
	25:28	say unto them, Thus saith the LORD of **h**;	6635
	25:29	of the earth, saith the LORD of **h**.	6635
	25:32	Thus saith the LORD of **h**, Behold,	6635
	26:18	saying, Thus saith the LORD of **h**;	6635
	27: 4	Thus saith the LORD of **h**, the God of	6635
	27:18	now make intercession to the LORD of **h**,	6635
	27:19	For thus saith the LORD of **h** concerning	6635
	27:21	Yea, thus saith the LORD of **h**, the God of	6635
	28: 2	Thus speaketh the LORD of **h**, the God of	6635
	28:14	For thus saith the LORD of **h**, the God of	6635
	29: 4	Thus saith the LORD of **h**, the God of	6635
	29: 8	For thus saith the LORD of **h**, the God of	6635
	29:17	Thus saith the LORD of **h**; Behold, I will	6635
	29:21	Thus saith the LORD of **h**, the God of	6635
	29:25	Thus speaketh the LORD of **h**, the God of	6635
	30: 8	to pass in that day, saith the LORD of **h**,	6635
	31:23	Thus saith the LORD of **h**, the God of	6635
	31:35	thereof roar; The LORD of **h** *is* his name:	6635
	32:14	Thus saith the LORD of **h**, the God of	6635
	32:15	For thus saith the LORD of **h**, the God of	6635
	32:18	Mighty God, the LORD of **h**, *is* his name,	6635
	33:11	them that shall say, Praise the LORD of **h**:	6635
	33:12	Thus saith the LORD of **h**; Again in this	6635
	35:13	Thus saith the LORD of **h**, the God of	6635
	35:17	Therefore thus saith the LORD God of **h**,	6635
	35:18	Thus saith the LORD of **h**, the God of	6635
	35:19	Therefore thus saith the LORD of **h**,	6635
	38:17	the God of **h**, the God of Israel;	6635
	39:16	saying, Thus saith the LORD of **h**,	6635
	42:15	Thus saith the LORD of **h**, the God of	6635
	42:18	For thus saith the LORD of **h**, the God of	6635
	43:10	Thus saith the LORD of **h**, the God of	6635
	44: 2	Thus saith the LORD of **h**, the God of	6635
	44: 7	the God of **h**, the God of Israel;	6635
	44:11	Therefore thus saith the LORD of **h**,	6635
	44:25	Thus saith the LORD of **h**, the God of	6635
	46:10	For this *is* the day of the Lord GOD of **h**,	6635
	46:10	for the Lord GOD of **h** hath a sacrifice in	6635
	46:18	the King, whose name *is* the LORD of **h**,	6635
	46:25	The LORD of **h**, the God of Israel, saith;	6635
	48: 1	Against Moab thus saith the LORD of **h**,	6635
	48:15	the King, whose name *is* the LORD of **h**.	6635
	49: 5	a fear upon thee, saith the Lord GOD of **h**,	6635
	49: 7	thus saith the LORD of **h**;	6635
	49:26	cut off in that day, saith the LORD of **h**.	6635
	49:35	Thus saith the LORD of **h**; Behold, I *will*	6635
	50:18	Therefore thus saith the LORD of **h**,	6635
	50:25	for this *is* the work of the Lord GOD of **h**	6635
	50:31	most proud, saith the Lord GOD of **h**:	6635
	50:33	Thus saith the LORD of **h**; The children	6635
	50:34	*is* strong; the LORD of **h** *is* his name:	6635
	51: 5	nor Judah of his God, of the LORD of **h**;	6635
	51:14	The LORD of **h** hath sworn by himself,	6635
	51:19	the LORD of **h** *is* his name.	6635
	51:33	For thus saith the LORD of **h**, the God of	6635
	51:57	the King, whose name *is* the LORD of **h**.	6635
	51:58	Thus saith the LORD of **h**; The broad	6635
Hos	12: 5	Even the LORD God of **h**; the LORD *is*	6635
Am	3:13	saith the Lord GOD, the God of **h**,	6635
	4:13	The LORD, The God of **h**, *is* his name.	6635
	5:14	so the LORD, the God of **h**, shall be with	6635
	5:15	it may be that the LORD God of **h** will be	6635
	5:16	the God of **h**, the Lord, saith thus;	6635
	5:27	the LORD, whose name *is* The God of **h**.	6635
	6: 8	saith the LORD the God of **h**, I abhor	6635
	6:14	of Israel, saith the LORD the God of **h**;	6635
	9: 5	the Lord GOD of **h** *is* he that toucheth	6635
Mic	4: 4	for the mouth of the LORD of **h** hath	6635
Na	2:13	saith the LORD of **h**, and I will burn her	6635
	3: 5	I *am* against thee, saith the LORD of **h**;	6635
Hab	2:13	*is it* not of the LORD of **h** that the people	6635
Zep	2: 9	saith the LORD of **h**, the God of Israel,	6635
	2:10	against the people of the LORD of **h**.	6635
Hag	1: 2	Thus speaketh the LORD of **h**, saying,	6635
	1: 5	Now therefore thus saith the LORD of **h**;	6635
	1: 7	Thus saith the LORD of **h**; Consider your	6635
	1: 9	saith the LORD of **h**. Because of mine	6635
	1:14	did work in the house of the LORD of **h**,	6635
	2: 4	for I *am* with you, saith the LORD of **h**:	6635
	2: 6	For thus saith the LORD of **h**; Yet once,	6635
	2: 7	house *with* glory, saith the LORD of **h**.	6635
	2: 8	and the gold *is* mine, saith the LORD of **h**.	6635
	2: 9	than of the former, saith the LORD of **h**:	6635
	2: 9	will I give peace, saith the LORD of **h**.	6635
	2:11	Thus saith the LORD of **h**; Ask now	6635
	2:23	In that day, saith the LORD of **h**, will I	6635
	2:23	I have chosen thee, saith the LORD of **h**.	6635
Zec	1: 3	unto them, Thus saith the LORD of **h**;	6635
	1: 3	saith the LORD of **h**, and I will turn unto	6635
	1: 3	I will turn unto you, saith the LORD of **h**.	6635
	1: 4	saying, Thus saith the LORD of **h**;	6635
	1: 6	Like as the LORD of **h** thought to do unto	6635
	1:12	and said, O LORD of **h**,	6635
	1:14	saying, Thus saith the LORD of **h**;	6635
	1:16	saith the LORD of **h**, and a line shall be	6635
	1:17	saying, Thus saith the LORD of **h**;	6635
	2: 8	For thus saith the LORD of **h**; After	6635
	2: 9	ye shall know that the LORD of **h** hath	6635
	2:11	thou shalt know that the LORD of **h** hath	6635
	3: 7	Thus saith the LORD of **h**; If thou wilt	6635
	3: 9	saith the LORD of **h**, and I will remove	6635
	3:10	In that day, saith the LORD of **h**, shall ye	6635
	4: 6	but by my spirit, saith the LORD of **h**.	6635
	4: 9	thou shalt know that the LORD of **h** hath	6635
	5: 4	saith the LORD of **h**, and it shall enter	6635
	6:12	Thus speaketh the LORD of **h**, saying,	6635
	6:15	ye shall know that the LORD of **h** hath	6635
	7: 3	*were* in the house of the LORD of **h**,	6635
	7: 4	came the word of the LORD of **h** unto me,	6635
	7: 9	Thus speaketh the LORD of **h**, saying,	6635
	7:12	the words which the LORD of **h** hath sent	6635
	7:12	came a great wrath from the LORD of **h**.	6635
	7:13	I would not hear, saith the LORD of **h**:	6635
	8: 1	Again the word of the LORD of **h** came *to*	6635
	8: 2	Thus saith the LORD of **h**; I was jealous	6635
	8: 3	the mountain of the LORD of **h** the holy	6635
	8: 4	Thus saith the LORD of **h**; There shall yet	6635
	8: 6	Thus saith the LORD of **h**; If it be	6635
	8: 6	in my eyes? saith the LORD of **h**.	6635
	8: 7	Thus saith the LORD of **h**; Behold, I *will*	6635
	8: 9	Thus saith the LORD of **h**; Let your hands	6635
	8: 9	of the house of the LORD of **h** was laid,	6635
	8:11	*in* the former days, saith the LORD of **h**.	6635
	8:14	For thus saith the LORD of **h**; As I	6635
	8:14	saith the LORD of **h**, and I repented not:	6635
	8:18	the word of the LORD of **h** came unto me,	6635
	8:19	Thus saith the LORD of **h**; The fast of	6635
	8:20	Thus saith the LORD of **h**; *It shall* yet	6635
	8:21	the LORD, and to seek the LORD of **h**:	6635
	8:22	come to seek the LORD of **h** in Jerusalem,	6635
	8:23	Thus saith the LORD of **h**; In those days *it*	6635
	9:15	The LORD of **h** shall defend them; and	6635

Zec 10: 3 for the LORD of **h** hath visited his flock 6635
12: 5 my strength in the LORD of **h** their God. 6635
13: 2 to pass in that day, saith the LORD of **h**, 6635
13: 7 *that is* my fellow, saith the LORD of **h**: 6635
14:16 the LORD of **h**, and to keep the feast of 6635
14:17 the LORD of **h**, even upon them shall be 6635
14:21 shall be holiness unto the LORD of **h**: 6635
14:21 Canaanite in the house of the LORD of **h**. 6635
Mal 1: 4 thus saith the LORD of **h**, They shall 6635
1: 6 saith the LORD of **h** unto you, O priests, 6635
1: 8 accept thy person? saith the LORD of **h**. 6635
1: 9 your persons? saith the LORD of **h**. 6635
1:10 no pleasure in you, saith the LORD of **h**, 6635
1:11 among the heathen, saith the LORD of **h**. 6635
1:13 have snuffed at it, saith the LORD of **h**; 6635
1:14 saith the LORD of **h**, and my name *is* 6635
2: 2 glory unto my name, saith the LORD of **h**, 6635
2: 4 might be with Levi, saith the LORD of **h**. 6635
2: 7 for he *is* the messenger of the LORD of **h**. 6635
2: 8 covenant of Levi, saith the LORD of **h**. 6635
2:12 offereth an offering unto the LORD of **h**. 6635
2:16 with his garment, saith the LORD of **h**: 6635
3: 1 he *shall* come, saith the LORD of **h**. 6635
3: 5 and fear not me, saith the LORD of **h**. 6635
3: 7 will return unto you, saith the LORD of **h**. 6635
3:10 me now herewith, saith the LORD of **h**, 6635
3:11 the time in the field, saith the LORD of **h**. 6635
3:12 a delightsome land, saith the LORD of **h**. 6635
3:14 mournfully before the LORD of **h**? 6635
3:17 they shall be mine, saith the LORD of **h**, 6635
4: 1 shall burn them up, saith the LORD of **h**, 6635
4: 3 that I *shall* do *this,* saith the LORD of **h**. 6635

HOT (31) [HOTLY, HOTTEST]

Ex 16:21 and when the sun **waxed h**, it melted. 2552
22:24 my wrath shall **wax h**, and I will kill you 2734
32:10 that my wrath may **wax h** against them, and 2734
32:11 why doth thy wrath **wax h** against thy 2734
32:19 Moses' anger **waxed h**, and he cast 2734
32:22 Let not the anger of my lord **wax h**: 2734
Lev 13:24 in the skin whereof *there is* a **h** burning, and 784
Dt 9:19 I was afraid of the anger and **h displeasure**, 2534
19: 6 while his heart is **h**, and overtake him, 3179
Jos 9:12 This our bread we took **h** for our provision 2525
Jdg 2:14 the anger of the LORD was **h** against 2734
2:20 the anger of the LORD was **h** against 2734
3: 8 Therefore the anger of the LORD was **h** 2734
6:39 Let not thine anger be **h** against me, and 2734
10: 7 the anger of the LORD was **h** against 2734
1Sa 11: 9 To morrow, by *that time* the sun be **h**, 2527
21: 6 to put **h** bread in the day when it was taken 2527
Ne 7: 3 of Jerusalem be opened until the sun be **h**; 2527
Job 6:17 when it is **h**, they are consumed out of their 2527
Ps 6: 1 neither chasten me in thy **h displeasure**. 2534
38: 1 neither chasten me in thy **h displeasure**. 2534
39: 3 My heart was **h** within me, while I was 2552
78:48 the hail, and their flocks to **h thunderbolts**. 7565
Pr 6:28 Can one go upon **h coals**, and his feet not 1513
Eze 24:11 that the brass of it may be **h**, and may burn, 3179
Da 3:22 *was* urgent, and the furnace exceeding **h**, 228
Hos 7: 7 They are all **h** as an oven, and 2552
1Ti 4: 2 their conscience **seared with a h iron**; *2743*
Rev 3:15 thy works, that thou art neither cold nor **h**: *2200*
3:15 cold nor hot: I would thou wert cold or **h**. *2200*
3:16 thou art lukewarm, and neither cold nor **h**, *2200*

HOTHAM (1)

1Ch 7:32 and Shomer, and **H**, and Shua their sister. 2369

HOTHAN (1)

1Ch 11:44 and Jehiel the sons of **H** the Aroerite, 2369

HOTHIR (2)

1Ch 25: 4 Joshbekashah, Mallothi, **H**, *and* Mahazioth: 1956
25:28 The one and twentieth to **H**, *he,* his sons, 1956

HOTLY (1) [HOT]

Ge 31:36 that thou hast *so* **h pursued** after me? 1814

HOTTEST (1) [HOT]

2Sa 11:15 Set ye Uriah in the forefront of the **h** battle, 2389

HOUGH (1) [HOUGHED]

Jos 11: 6 thou shalt **h** their horses, and burn their 6131

HOUGHED (3) [HOUGH]

Jos 11: 9 he **h** their horses, and burnt their chariots 6131
2Sa 8: 4 David **h** all the chariot *horses,* but 6131
1Ch 18: 4 David also **h** all the chariot *horses,* but 6131

HOUR (94) [HOURS]

Da 3: 6 worshippeth shall the same **h** be cast into 8160
3:15 ye shall be cast the same **h** into the midst of 8160
4:19 was astonied for one **h**, and his thoughts 8160
4:33 The same **h** was the thing fulfilled upon 8160
5: 5 In the same **h** came forth fingers of a man's 8160
Mt 8:13 his servant was healed in the selfsame **h**. *5610*
9:22 the woman was made whole from that **h**.) *5610*
10:19 for it shall be given you in that *same* **h** *5610*
15:28 daughter was made whole from that *very* **h**. *5610*
17:18 and the child was cured from that *very* **h**. *5610*
20: 3 And he went out about the third **h**, and *5610*
20: 5 he went out about the sixth and ninth **h**, *5610*
20: 6 And about the eleventh **h** he went out, and *5610*
20: 9 came that *were hired* about the eleventh **h**, *5610*
20:12 These last have wrought *but* one **h**, and *5610*
24:36 But of that day and **h** knoweth no *man,* no, *5610*
24:42 for ye know not what **h** your Lord doth *5610*
24:44 for in such an **h** as you think not the Son of *5610*
24:50 for *him,* and in an **h** that he is not ware of, *5610*
25:13 for ye know neither the day nor the **h** *5610*
26:40 What, could ye not watch with me one **h**? *5610*
26:45 the **h** is at hand, and the Son of man is *5610*
26:55 In that *same* **h** said Jesus to the multitudes, *5610*
27:45 Now from the sixth **h** there was darkness *5610*
27:45 darkness over all the land unto the ninth **h**. *5610*
27:46 And about the ninth **h** Jesus cried with a *5610*
Mk 13:11 but whatsoever shall be given you in that **h**, *5610*
13:32 of that day and *that* **h** knoweth no *man,* no, *5610*
14:35 were possible, the **h** might pass from him. *5610*
14:37 couldest not thou watch one **h**? *5610*
14:41 it is enough, the **h** is come; behold, the Son *5610*
15:25 And it was the third **h**, and they crucified *5610*
15:33 And when the sixth **h** was come, there was *5610*
15:33 over the whole land until the ninth **h**. *5610*
15:34 And at the ninth **h** Jesus cried with a loud *5610*
Lk 7:21 And in that *same* **h** he cured many of *their* *5610*
10:21 In that **h** Jesus rejoiced in spirit, and said, *5610*
12:12 you in the same **h** what ye ought to say. *5610*
12:39 had known what **h** the thief would come, *5610*
12:40 for the Son of man cometh at an **h** when ye *5610*
12:46 for *him,* and at an **h** when he is not ware, *5610*
20:19 the scribes the same **h** sought to lay hands *5610*
22:14 And when the **h** was come, he sat down, *5610*
22:53 but this is your **h**, and the power of *5610*
22:59 And about the space of one **h** after another *5610*
23:44 And it was about the sixth **h**, and there was *5610*
23:44 darkness over all the earth until the ninth **h**. *5610*
24:33 And they rose up the same **h**, and *5610*
Jn 1:39 him that day: for it was about the tenth **h**. *5610*
2: 4 I to do with thee? mine **h** is not yet come. *5610*
4: 6 on the well: *and* it was about the sixth **h**. *5610*
4:21 Woman, believe me, the **h** cometh, *5610*
4:23 But the **h** cometh, and now is, when *5610*
4:52 Then inquired he of them the **h** when he *5610*
4:52 Yesterday at the seventh **h** the fever left *5610*
4:53 the father knew that *it was* at the same **h**, *5610*
5:25 say unto you, The **h** is coming, and now is, *5610*
5:28 for the **h** is coming, in the which all that are *5610*
7:30 on him, because his **h** was not yet come. *5610*
8:20 hands on him; for his **h** was not yet come. *5610*
12:23 answered them, saying, The **h** is come, *5610*
12:27 Father, save me from this **h**: but for this *5610*
12:27 but for this cause came I unto this **h**. *5610*
13: 1 when Jesus knew that his **h** was come that *5610*
16:21 travail hath sorrow, because her **h** is come: *5610*
16:32 Behold, the **h** cometh, yea, is now come, *5610*
17: 1 to heaven, and said, Father, the **h** is come; *5610*
19:14 of the passover, and about the sixth **h**: *5610*
19:27 And from that **h** *that* disciple took her unto *5610*
Ac 2:15 seeing it is *but* the third **h** of the day. *5610*
3: 1 together into the temple at the **h** of prayer, *5610*
3: 1 at the hour of prayer, *being* the ninth **h**. NIG
10: 3 about the ninth **h** of the day, *5610*
10: 9 up upon the house to pray about the sixth **h**: *5610*
10:30 Four days ago I was fasting until this **h**; *5610*
10:30 and at the ninth **h** I prayed in my house, *5610*
16:18 out of her. And he came out the same **h**. *5610*

Ac 16:33 And he took them the same **h** of the night, *5610*
22:13 And the same **h** I looked up upon him. *5610*
23:23 two hundred, at the third **h** of the night; *5610*
1Co 4:11 Even unto this present **h** we both hunger, *5610*
8: 7 some with conscience of the idol unto **this h**, *737*
15:30 And why stand we in jeopardy every **h**? *5610*
Gal 2: 5 gave place by subjection, no, not for an **h**; *5610*
Rev 3: 3 thou shalt not know what **h** I will come *5610*
3:10 I also will keep thee from the **h** of *5610*
8: 1 in heaven about the space of **half an h**. *2256*
9:15 which were prepared for an **h**, and a day, *5610*
11:13 And the same **h** was there a great *5610*
14: 7 to him; for the **h** of his judgment is come: *5610*
17:12 receive power as kings one **h** with *5610*
18:10 for in one **h** is thy judgment come. *5610*
18:17 For in one **h** so great riches is come to *5610*
18:19 for in one **h** is she made desolate. *5610*

HOURS (3) [HOUR]
Jn 11: 9 Are there not twelve **h** in the day? *5610*
Ac 5: 7 And it was about the space of three **h** after, *5610*
19:34 all with one voice about the space of two **h** *5610*

HOUSE (2025) [HOUSE OF APHRAH, HOUSEHOLD, HOUSEHOLDER, HOUSEHOLDS, HOUSES, HOUSETOP, HOUSETOPS, STOREHOUSE, STOREHOUSES, WINTERHOUSE]
Ge 7: 1 Come thou and all thy **h** into the ark; 1004
12: 1 from thy kindred, and from thy father's **h**, 1004
12:15 and the woman was taken into Pharaoh's **h**. 1004
12:17 his **h** with great plagues because of Sarai 1004
14:14 his trained *servants,* born in his own **h**, 1004
15: 2 the steward of my **h** *is* this Eliezer of 1004
15: 3 and lo, one born in my **h** is mine heir. 1004
17:12 he that is born in the **h**, or bought with 1004
17:13 He that is born in thy **h**, and he that is 1004
17:23 all that were born in his **h**, and all that were 1004
17:23 male among the men of Abraham's **h**; 1004
17:27 all the men of his **h**, born in the house, and 1004
17:27 born in the **h**, and bought with money of 1004
19: 2 into your servant's **h**, and tarry all night, 1004
19: 3 turned in unto him, and entered into his **h**; 1004
19: 4 compassed the **h** round, both old and 1004
19:10 pulled Lot into the **h** to them, and shut to 1004
19:11 *were at* the door of the **h** with blindness, 1004
20:13 caused me to wander from my father's **h**, 1004
20:18 up all the wombs of the **h** of Abimelech, 1004
24: 2 of his **h** that ruled over all that he had, 1004
24: 7 which took me from my father's **h**, and 1004
24:23 is there room *in* thy father's **h** for us to 1004
24:27 the LORD led me to the **h** of my master's 1004
24:28 told *them of* her mother's **h** these things. 1004
24:31 for I have prepared the **h**, and room for 1004
24:32 the man came into the **h**: and he ungirded 1004
24:38 thou shalt go unto my father's **h**, and to my 1004
24:40 son of my kindred, and of my father's **h**: 1004
27:15 which *were* with her in the **h**, and put them 1004
28: 2 to the **h** of Bethuel thy mother's father; 1004
28:17 this *is* none other but the **h** of God, and 1004
28:21 So that I come again to my father's **h** in 1004
28:22 I have set *for* a pillar, shall be God's **h**: 1004
29:13 and kissed him, and brought him to his **h**. 1004
30:30 now when shall I provide for mine own **h** 1004
31:14 or inheritance for us in our father's **h**? 1004
31:30 thou sore longedst after thy father's **h**, 1004
31:41 Thus have I been twenty years in thy **h**; 1004
33:17 built him a **h**, and made booths for his 1004
34:19 he *was* more honourable than all the **h** of 1004
34:26 took Dinah out of Shechem's **h**, and 1004
34:29 and spoiled even all that *was* in the **h**. 1004
34:30 and I shall be destroyed, I and my **h**. 1004
36: 6 all the persons of his **h**, and his cattle, and 1004
38:11 Remain a widow *at* thy father's **h**, 1004
38:11 Tamar went and dwelt *in* her father's **h**. 1004
39: 2 he was in the **h** of his master the Egyptian. 1004
39: 4 he made him overseer over his **h**, and 1004
39: 5 *that* he had made him overseer in his **h**, 1004
39: 5 that the LORD blessed the Egyptian's **h** 1004
39: 5 LORD was upon all that he had in the **h**, 1004
39: 8 wotteth not what *is* with me in the **h**, 1004
39: 9 *There is* none greater in this **h** than I; 1004
39:11 that *Joseph* went into the **h** to do his 1004
39:11 *there was* none of the men of the **h** there 1004
39:14 That she called unto the men of her **h**, and 1004
40: 3 he put them in ward *in* the **h** of the captain 1004
40: 7 *were* with him in the ward of his lord's **h**, 1004
40:14 unto Pharaoh, and bring me out of this **h**: 1004
41:10 me in ward *in* the captain of the guard's **h**, 1004
41:40 Thou shalt be over my **h**, and 1004
41:51 me forget all my toil, and all my father's **h**. 1004
42:19 brethren be bound in the **h** of your prison: 1004
43:16 he said to the ruler of his **h**, Bring *these* 1004
43:17 the man brought the men into Joseph's **h**. 1004
43:18 because they were brought into Joseph's **h**; 1004
43:19 came near to the steward of Joseph's **h**, 1004
43:19 communed with him *at* the door of the **h**, 1004
43:24 the man brought the men into Joseph's **h**, 1004
43:26 present which *was* in their hand into the **h**, 1004
44: 1 he commanded the steward of his **h**, saying, 1004
44: 8 should we steal out of thy lord's **h** silver or 1004
44:14 and his brethren came to Joseph's **h**; 1004
45: 2 the Egyptians and the **h** of Pharaoh heard. 1004
45: 8 lord of all his **h**, and a ruler throughout all 1004
45:16 the fame *thereof* was heard *in* Pharaoh's **h**, 1004
46:27 all the souls of the **h** of Jacob, which came 1004
46:31 unto his father's **h**, I will go up, and 1004
46:31 unto him, My brethren, and my father's **h**, 1004
47:14 brought the money into Pharaoh's **h**. 1004
50: 4 Joseph spake unto the **h** of Pharaoh, saying, 1004
50: 7 the elders of his **h**, and all the elders of 1004
50: 8 all the **h** of Joseph, and his brethren, and 1004
50: 8 and his brethren, and his father's **h**: 1004
50:22 dwelt in Egypt, he, and his father's **h**: 1004
Ex 2: 1 there went a man of the **h** of Levi, and 1004
3:22 of her that sojourneth in her **h**, jewels of 1004
7:23 Pharaoh turned and went into his **h**, 1004
8: 3 which shall go up and come into thine **h**, 1004
8: 3 into the **h** of thy servants, and upon thy 1004
8:24 swarm *of flies* into the **h** of Pharaoh, 1004
12: 3 according to the **h** of *their* fathers, a lamb 1004
12: 3 to the house of *their* fathers, a lamb for a **h**: 1004
12: 4 his neighbour next unto his **h** take *it* 1004
12:22 none of you shall go out at the door of his **h** 1004
12:30 for *there was* not a **h** where *there was* not 1004
12:46 In one **h** shall it be eaten; thou shalt not 1004
12:46 forth *ought* of the flesh abroad out of the **h**; 1004
13: 3 out from Egypt, out of the **h** of bondage; 1004
13:14 us out from Egypt, from the **h** of bondage: 1004
16:31 the **h** of Israel called the name thereof 1004
19: 3 Thus shalt thou say to the **h** of Jacob, and 1004
20: 2 the land of Egypt, out of the **h** of bondage. 1004
20:17 Thou shalt not covet thy neighbour's **h**, 1004
22: 7 to keep, and it be stolen out of the man's **h**; 1004
22: 8 the master of the **h** shall be brought unto 1004
23:19 bring *into* the **h** of the LORD thy God. 1004
34:26 bring *unto* the **h** of the LORD thy God. 1004
40:38 it by night, in the sight of all the **h** of Israel, 1004
Lev 10: 6 let your brethren, the whole **h** of Israel, 1004
14:34 I put the plague of leprosy in a **h** of the land 1004
14:35 he that owneth the **h** shall come and tell 1004
14:35 to me *there is* as it were a plague in the **h**: 1004
14:36 priest shall command that they empty the **h**, 1004
14:36 that all that *is* in the **h** be not *made* unclean: 1004
14:36 afterward the priest shall go in to see the **h**: 1004
14:37 *if* the plague *be* in the walls of the **h** with 1004
14:38 the priest shall go out of the **h** to the door 1004
14:38 go out of the house to the door of the **h**, 1004
14:38 of the house, and shut up the **h** seven days: 1004
14:39 *if* the plague be spread in the walls of the **h**; 1004
14:41 he shall cause the **h** to be scraped within 1004
14:42 take other morter, and shall plaister the **h**. 1004
14:43 plague come again, and break out in the **h**, 1004
14:43 after he hath scraped the **h**, and after it is 1004
14:44 and behold, *if* the plague be spread in the **h**, 1004
14:44 in the house, it *is* a fretting leprosy in the **h**: 1004
14:45 he shall break down the **h**, the stones of it, 1004
14:45 timber thereof, and all the morter of the **h**; 1004
14:46 Moreover he that goeth into the **h** all 1004
14:47 he that lieth in the **h** shall wash his clothes; 1004
14:47 he that eateth in the **h** shall wash his 1004
14:48 behold, the plague hath not spread in the **h**, 1004
14:48 in the house, after the **h** was plaistered: 1004
14:48 the priest shall pronounce the **h** clean, 1004
14:49 he shall take to cleanse the **h** two birds, 1004
14:51 and sprinkle the **h** seven times: 1004
14:52 he shall cleanse the **h** with the blood of 1004
14:53 and make an atonement for the **h**: 1004
14:55 for the leprosy of a garment, and of a **h**, 1004

Lev 16: 6 an atonement for himself, and for his **h**. 1004
16:11 for his **h**, and shall kill the bullock of 1004
17: 3 What man soever *there be* of the **h** of 1004
17: 8 Whatsoever man *there be* of the **h** of Israel, 1004
17:10 whatsoever man *there be* of the **h** of Israel, 1004
22:11 shall eat of it, and he that is born in his **h**: 1004
22:13 and is returned unto her father's **h**, 1004
22:18 Whatsoever *he be* of the **h** of Israel, or 1004
25:29 if a man sell a dwelling **h** in a walled city, 1004
25:30 the **h** that *is* in the walled city shall be 1004
25:33 the **h** that was sold, and the city of his 1004
27:14 when a man shall sanctify his **h** *to be* holy 1004
27:15 if he that sanctified *it* will redeem his **h**, 1004
Nu 1: 2 after their families, by the **h** of their fathers, 1004
1: 4 every one head of the **h** of his fathers. 1004
1:18 by the **h** of their fathers, according to 1004
1:20 after their families, by the **h** of their fathers, 1004
1:22 after their families, by the **h** of their fathers, 1004
1:24 after their families, by the **h** of their fathers, 1004
1:26 after their families, by the **h** of their fathers, 1004
1:28 after their families, by the **h** of their fathers, 1004
1:30 after their families, by the **h** of their fathers, 1004
1:32 after their families, by the **h** of their fathers, 1004
1:34 after their families, by the **h** of their fathers, 1004
1:36 after their families, by the **h** of their fathers, 1004
1:38 after their families, by the **h** of their fathers, 1004
1:40 after their families, by the **h** of their fathers, 1004
1:42 after their families, by the **h** of their fathers, 1004
1:44 each one was for the **h** of his fathers. 1004
1:45 by the **h** of their fathers, from twenty years 1004
2: 2 with the ensign of their father's **h**: 1004
2:32 children of Israel by the **h** of their fathers: 1004
2:34 according to the **h** of their fathers. 1004
3:15 Number the children of Levi after the **h** of 1004
3:20 Levites according to the **h** of their fathers. 1004
3:24 the chief of the **h** of the father of 1004
3:30 the chief of the **h** of the father of 1004
3:35 the chief of the **h** of the father of 1004
4: 2 after their families, by the **h** of their fathers, 1004
4:29 after their families, by the **h** of their fathers; 1004
4:34 and after the **h** of their fathers, 1004
4:38 their families, and by the **h** of their fathers, 1004
4:40 by the **h** of their fathers, were two thousand 1004
4:42 their families, by the **h** of their fathers, 1004
4:46 and after the **h** of their fathers, 1004
7: 2 of Israel, heads of the **h** of their fathers, 1004
12: 7 *is* not so, who *is* faithful in all mine **h**. 1004
17: 2 a rod according to the **h** of *their* fathers, 1004
17: 2 of all their princes according to the **h** of 1004
17: 3 for one rod *shall be* for the head of the **h** of 1004
17: 8 the rod of Aaron for the **h** of Levi was 1004
18: 1 thy father's **h** with thee shall bear 1004
18:11 every one *that is* clean in thy **h** shall eat of 1004
18:13 every one *that is* clean in thine **h** shall eat 1004
20:29 Aaron thirty days, *even* all the **h** of Israel. 1004
22:18 If Balak would give me his **h** full *of* silver 1004
24:13 If Balak would give me his **h** full *of* silver 1004
25:14 a prince of a chief **h** among the Simeonites. 1004
25:15 over a people, *and* of a chief **h** in Midian. 1004
26: 2 and upward, throughout their fathers' **h**, 1004
30: 3 a bond, *being* in her father's **h** in her youth; 1004
30:10 if she vowed *in* her husband's **h**, or 1004
30:16 *being yet* in her youth *in* her father's **h**. 1004
34:14 Reuben according to the **h** of their fathers, 1004
34:14 of Gad according to the **h** of their fathers, 1004
Dt 5: 6 the land of Egypt, from the **h** of bondage. 1004
5:21 neither shalt thou covet thy neighbour's **h**, 1004
6: 7 talk of them when thou sittest in thine **h**, 1004
6: 9 shalt write them upon the posts of thy **h**, 1004
6:12 the land of Egypt, from the **h** of bondage. 1004
7: 8 and redeemed you out of the **h** of bondmen, 1004
7:26 thou bring an abomination into thine **h**, 1004
8:14 the land of Egypt, from the **h** of bondage; 1004
11:19 of them when thou sittest in thine **h**, 1004
11:20 write them upon the door posts of thine **h**, 1004
13: 5 and redeemed you out of the **h** of bondage, 1004
13:10 the land of Egypt, from the **h** of bondage. 1004
15:16 because he loveth thee and thine **h**, because 1004
20: 5 What man *is there* that hath built a new **h**, 1004
20: 5 let him go and return to his **h**, lest he die in 1004
20: 6 let him *also* go and return unto his **h**, lest he 1004
20: 7 let him go and return unto his **h**, lest he die 1004
20: 8 let him go and return unto his **h**, lest his 1004
21:12 thou shalt bring her home to thine **h**; and 1004
21:13 shall remain in thine **h**, and bewail her 1004
22: 2 thou shalt bring it unto thine own **h**, and 1004
22: 8 When thou buildest a new **h**, then 1004
22: 8 that thou bring not blood upon thine **h**, 1004
22:21 out the damsel to the door of her father's **h**, 1004
22:21 to play the whore *in* her father's **h**: 1004
23:18 *into* the **h** of the LORD thy God for any 1004
24: 1 *it* in her hand, and send her out of his **h**. 1004
24: 2 when she is departed out of his **h**, she may 1004
24: 3 *it* in her hand, and sendeth her out of his **h**; 1004
24:10 thou shalt not go into his **h** to fetch his 1004
25: 9 man that will not build up his brother's **h**. 1004
25:10 The **h** of him that hath his shoe loosed. 1004
25:14 Thou shalt not have in thine **h** divers 1004
26:11 unto thine **h**, thou, and the Levite, and 1004
26:13 away the hallowed *things* out of *mine* **h**, 1004
28:30 thou shalt build a **h**, and thou shalt not 1004
Jos 2: 1 came *into* a harlot's **h**, named Rahab, and 1004
2: 3 to thee, which are entered into thine **h**: 1004
2: 6 had brought them up to the **roof of the h**, 1406
2:12 will also shew kindness unto my father's **h**, 1004
2:15 for her **h** *was* upon the town wall, and 1004
2:19 go out of the doors of thy **h** into the street, 1004
2:19 whosoever shall be with thee in the **h**, 1004
6:17 she and all that *are* with her in the **h**, 1004
6:22 Go *into* the harlot's **h**, and bring out thence 1004
6:24 they put *into* the treasury of the **h** of 1004
9:23 and drawers of water for the **h** of my God. 1004
17:17 Joshua spake unto the **h** of Joseph, *even* to 1004
18: 5 the **h** of Joseph shall abide in their coasts 1004
20: 6 unto his own city, and unto his own **h**, 1004
21:45 LORD had spoken unto the **h** of Israel; 1004
22:14 of each chief **h** a prince throughout all 1004
22:14 each one *was* a head of the **h** of their 1004
24:15 as for me and my **h**, we will serve 1004
24:17 from the **h** of bondage, and which did those 1004
Jdg 1:22 the **h** of Joseph, they also went up *against* 1004
1:23 the **h** of Joseph sent to descry Beth-el. 1004
1:35 yet the hand of the **h** of Joseph prevailed, 1004
4:17 of Hazor and the **h** of Heber the Kenite. 1004
6: 8 brought you forth out of the **h** of bondage; 1004
6:15 and I *am* the least in my father's **h**. 1004
8:27 became a snare unto Gideon, and to his **h**. 1004
8:29 son of Joash went and dwelt in his own **h**. 1004
8:35 Neither shewed they kindness to the **h** of 1004
9: 1 with all the family of the **h** of his mother's 1004
9: 4 ten *pieces* of silver out of the **h** of 1004
9: 5 he went unto his father's **h** at Ophrah, and 1004
9: 6 all the **h** of Millo, and went, and 1004
9:16 ye have dealt well with Jerubbaal and his **h**, 1004
9:18 ye are risen up against my father's **h** *this* 1004
9:19 with Jerubbaal and with his **h** this day, 1004
9:20 the men of Shechem, and the **h** of Millo; 1004
9:20 from the **h** of Millo, and 1004
9:27 and went *into* the **h** of their god, and did eat 1004
9:46 into a hold of the **h** of the god Berith. 1004
10: 9 and against the **h** of Ephraim; 1004
11: 2 Thou shalt not inherit in our father's **h**; 1004
11: 7 and expel me out of my father's **h**? 1004
11:31 forth of the doors of my **h** to meet me, 1004
11:34 Jephthah came *to* Mizpeh unto his **h**, and 1004
12: 1 we will burn thine **h** upon thee with fire. 1004
14:15 we burn thee and thy father's **h** with fire: 1004
14:19 and he went up *to* his father's **h**. 1004
16:21 of brass; and he did grind in the prison **h**. 1004
16:25 they called for Samson out of the prison **h**; 1004
16:26 feel the pillars whereupon the **h** standeth, 1004
16:27 Now the **h** was full *of* men and women; and 1004
16:29 two middle pillars upon which the **h** stood, 1004
16:30 the **h** fell upon the lords, and upon all 1004
16:31 and all the **h** of his father came down, 1004
17: 4 and they were in the **h** of Micah. 1004
17: 5 the man Micah had a **h** of gods, and 1004
17: 8 he came *to* mount Ephraim to the **h** of 1004
17:12 his priest, and was in the **h** of Micah. 1004
18: 2 to the **h** of Micah, they lodged there. 1004
18: 3 When they *were* by the **h** of Micah, they 1004
18:13 and came unto the **h** of Micah. 1004
18:15 came to the **h** of the young man the Levite, 1004
18:15 *even unto* the **h** of Micah, and saluted him. 1004
18:18 these went *into* Micah's **h**, and fetched 1004
18:19 *is it* better for thee to be a priest unto the **h** 1004
18:22 they were a good way from the **h** of Micah, 1004
18:22 near to Micah's **h** were gathered together, 1004

Jdg 18:26 he turned and went back unto his **h**. 1004
18:31 all the time that the **h** of God was in Shiloh. 1004
19: 2 went away from him unto her father's **h** to 1004
19: 3 she brought him *into* her father's **h**: and 1004
19:15 man that took them into *his* **h** to lodging. 1004
19:18 I am *now* going *to* the **h** of the LORD; 1004
19:18 and there *is* no man that receiveth me to **h**. 1004
19:21 So he brought him into his **h**, and 1004
19:22 beset the **h** round about, *and* beat at 1004
19:22 spake to the master of the **h**, the old man, 1004
19:22 Bring forth the man that came into thine **h**, 1004
19:23 the man, the master of the **h**, went out unto 1004
19:23 seeing that this man is come into mine **h**, 1004
19:26 fell down *at* the door of the man's **h** where 1004
19:27 opened the doors of the **h**, and went out to 1004
19:27 *was* fallen down *at* the door of the **h**, 1004
19:29 when he was come into his **h**, he took a 1004
20: 5 beset the **h** round about upon me by night, 1004
20: 8 neither will we any *of us* turn into his **h**. 1004
20:18 went up *to* the **h** of God, and asked *counsel* 1004
20:26 came *unto* the **h** of God, and wept, and 1004
20:31 *of* which one goeth up *to* the **h** of God, and 1004
21: 2 the people came *to* the **h** of God, and 1004
Ru 1: 8 in law, Go, return each to her mother's **h**: 1004
1: 9 each *of you in* the **h** of her husband. 1004
2: 7 until now, that she tarried a little in the **h**. 1004
4:11 that is come into thine **h** like Rachel 1004
4:11 which two did build the **h** of Israel: 1004
4:12 let thy **h** be like the house of Pharez, 1004
4:12 let thy house be like the **h** of Pharez, 1004
1Sa 1: 7 when she went up to the **h** of the LORD, 1004
1:19 returned, and came to their **h** to Ramah: 1004
1:21 the man Elkanah, and all his **h**, went up to 1004
1:24 brought him *unto* the **h** of the LORD *in* 1004
2:11 Elkanah went to Ramah to his **h**. And 1004
2:27 Did I plainly appear unto the **h** of thy 1004
2:27 when they were in Egypt in Pharaoh's **h**? 1004
2:28 did I give unto the **h** of thy father all 1004
2:30 I said indeed *that* thy **h**, and the house of 1004
2:30 *that* thy house, and the **h** of thy father, 1004
2:31 off thine arm, and the arm of thy father's **h**, 1004
2:31 there shall not be an old man in thine **h**. 1004
2:32 there shall not be an old man in thine **h** for 1004
2:33 all the increase of thine **h** shall die in 1004
2:35 I will build him a sure **h**; and he shall walk 1004
2:36 *that* every one that is left in thine **h** shall 1004
3:12 which I have spoken concerning his **h**: 1004
3:13 For I have told him that I will judge his **h** 1004
3:14 I have sworn unto the **h** of Eli, 1004
3:14 that the iniquity of Eli's **h** shall not be 1004
3:15 opened the doors of the **h** of the LORD. 1004
5: 2 they brought it *into* the **h** of Dagon, and 1004
5: 5 nor any that come *into* Dagon's **h**, 1004
7: 1 brought it into the **h** of Abinadab in the hill, 1004
7: 2 all the **h** of Israel lamented after 1004
7: 3 Samuel spake unto all the **h** of Israel, 1004
7:17 for there *was* his **h**; and there he judged 1004
9:18 Tell me, I pray thee, where the seer's **h** *is*. 1004
9:20 *Is it* not on thee, and on all thy father's **h**? 1004
9:25 communed with Saul upon the **top of** the **h**. 1406
9:26 that Samuel called Saul to the **top of** the **h**, 1406
10:25 all the people away, every man to his **h**. 1004
15:34 Saul went up to his **h** *to* Gibeah of Saul. 1004
17:25 and make his father's **h** free in Israel. 1004
18: 2 let him go no more home *to* his father's **h**. 1004
18:10 and he prophesied in the midst of the **h**: 1004
19: 9 as he sat in his **h** with his javelin in his 1004
19:11 Saul also sent messengers unto David's **h**, 1004
20:15 cut off thy kindness from my **h** for ever: 1004
20:16 So Jonathan made *a covenant* with the **h** of 1004
21:15 shall this *fellow* come into my **h**? 1004
22: 1 all his father's **h** heard *it*, they went down 1004
22:11 the son of Ahitub, and all his father's **h**, 1004
22:14 thy bidding, and *is* honourable in thine **h**? 1004
22:15 his servant, *nor* to all the **h** of my father: 1004
22:16 Ahimelech, thou, and all thy father's **h**. 1004
22:22 *death* of all the persons of thy father's **h**. 1004
23:18 in the wood, and Jonathan went to his **h**. 1004
24:21 not destroy my name out of my father's **h**. 1004
25: 1 and buried him in his **h** at Ramah. 1004
25: 3 his doings; and he *was* **of the h of Caleb**. 3614
25: 6 peace *be to* thine **h**, and peace *be unto* all 1004
25:28 will certainly make my lord a sure **h**; 1004
25:35 said unto her, Go up in peace to thine **h**; 1004
25:36 behold, he held a feast in his **h**, like 1004
28:24 the woman had a fat calf in the **h**; and 1004
31: 9 to publish *it in* the **h** of their idols, and 1004
31:10 they put his armour *in* the **h** of Ashtaroth: 1004
2Sa 1:12 of the LORD, and for the **h** of Israel; 1004
2: 4 there they anointed David king over the **h** 1004
2: 7 also the **h** of Judah have anointed me king 1004
2:10 But the **h** of Judah followed David. 1004
2:11 over the **h** of Judah was seven years 1004
3: 1 Now there was long war between the **h** of 1004
3: 1 the house of Saul and the **h** of David: 1004
3: 1 the **h** of Saul waxed weaker and weaker. 1004
3: 6 while there was war between the **h** of Saul 1004
3: 6 the house of Saul and the **h** of David, 1004
3: 6 that Abner made himself strong for the **h** of 1004
3: 8 *this* day unto the **h** of Saul thy father, 1004
3:10 To translate the kingdom from the **h** of 1004
3:19 that seemed *good* to the whole **h** of 1004
3:29 the head of Joab, and on all his father's **h**; 1004
3:29 let there not fail from the **h** of Joab one that 1004
4: 5 came about the heat of the day to the **h** of 1004
4: 6 they came thither into the midst of the **h**, 1004
4: 7 For when they came *into* the **h**, he lay on 1004
4:11 person in his own **h** upon his bed? 1004
5: 8 and the lame shall not come into the **h**. 1004
5:11 masons: and they built David a **h**. 1004
6: 3 brought it out of the **h** of Abinadab that *was* 1004
6: 4 they brought it out of the **h** of Abinadab 1004
6: 5 all the **h** of Israel played before the LORD 1004
6:10 David carried it aside *into* the **h** of 1004
6:11 the ark of the LORD continued *in* the **h** of 1004
6:12 The LORD hath blessed the **h** of 1004
6:12 brought up the ark of God from the **h** of 1004
6:15 all the **h** of Israel brought up the ark of 1004
6:19 all the people departed every one to his **h**. 1004
6:21 me before thy father, and before all his **h**, 1004
7: 1 when the king sat in his **h**, and the LORD 1004
7: 2 I dwell in a **h** of cedar, but the ark of God 1004
7: 5 Shalt thou build me a **h** for me to dwell in? 1004
7: 6 Whereas I have not dwelt in *any* **h** since 1004
7: 7 Why build ye not me a **h** of cedar? 1004
7:11 telleth thee that he will make thee a **h**. 1004
7:13 He shall build a **h** for my name, and I will 1004
7:16 thine **h** and thy kingdom shall be stablished 1004
7:18 what *is* my **h**, that thou hast brought me 1004
7:19 thou hast spoken also of thy servant's **h** for 1004
7:25 concerning his **h**, establish *it* for ever, and 1004
7:26 let the **h** of thy servant David be 1004
7:27 to thy servant, saying, I will build thee a **h**: 1004
7:29 it please thee to bless the **h** of thy servant, 1004
7:29 with thy blessing let the **h** of thy servant be 1004
9: 1 Is there yet *any* that is left of the **h** of Saul, 1004
9: 2 *there was* of the **h** of Saul a servant whose 1004
9: 3 *Is there* not yet any of the **h** of Saul, 1004
9: 4 Behold, he *is in* the **h** of Machir, the son of 1004
9: 5 fet him out of the **h** of Machir, the son of 1004
9: 9 all that pertained to Saul and to all his **h**. 1004
9:12 all that dwelt in the **h** of Ziba *were* servants 1004
11: 2 and walked upon the roof of the king's **h**: 1004
11: 4 and she returned unto her **h**. 1004
11: 8 Go down to thy **h**, and wash thy feet. 1004
11: 8 And Uriah departed out of the king's **h**, and 1004
11: 9 Uriah slept *at* the door of the king's **h** with 1004
11: 9 of his lord, and went not down to his **h**. 1004
11:10 saying, Uriah went not down unto his **h**, 1004
11:10 *then* didst thou not go down unto thine **h**? 1004
11:11 shall I then go into mine **h**, to eat and 1004
11:13 of his lord, but went not down to his **h**. 1004
11:27 David sent and fet her to his **h**, and 1004
12: 8 I gave thee thy master's **h**, and thy master's 1004
12: 8 and gave thee the **h** of Israel and of Judah; 1004
12:10 the sword shall never depart from thine **h**, 1004
12:11 up evil against thee out of thine own **h**, 1004
12:15 Nathan departed unto his **h**. And 1004
12:17 the elders of his **h** arose, *and went* to him, 1004
12:20 came *into* the **h** of the LORD, and 1004
12:20 he came to his own **h**; and when he 1004
13: 7 Go now *to* thy brother Amnon's **h**, and 1004
13: 8 So Tamar went *to* her brother Amnon's **h**; 1004
13:20 desolate *in* her brother Absalom's **h**. 1004
14: 8 Go to thine **h**, and I will give charge 1004
14: 9 iniquity *be* on me, and on my father's **h**: 1004
14:24 Let him turn to his own **h**, and let him not 1004
14:24 So Absalom returned to his own **h**, and 1004

2Sa 14:31	came to Absalom unto *his* **h**, and said unto	1004
15:16	*which were* concubines, to keep the **h**.	1004
15:35	soever thou shalt hear out of the king's **h**,	1004
16: 3	To day shall the **h** of Israel restore me	1004
16: 5	out a man of the family of the **h** of Saul,	1004
16: 8	upon thee all the blood of the **h** of Saul,	1004
16:21	which he hath left to keep the **h**;	1004
16:22	Absalom a tent upon the **top of** the **h**;	1406
17:18	came to a man's **h** in Bahurim, which had a	1004
17:20	servants came to the woman to the **h**,	1004
17:23	arose, and gat him *home* to his **h**, to his	1004
19: 5	Joab came *into* the **h** to the king, and said,	1004
19:11	ye the last to bring the king back to his **h**?	1004
19:11	all Israel is come to the king, *even* to his **h**.	1004
19:17	Ziba the servant of the **h** of Saul, and	1004
19:20	I am come the first *this* day of all the **h** of	1004
19:28	For all *of* my father's **h** were but dead men	1004
19:30	king is come *again* in peace unto his own **h**.	1004
20: 3	David came to his **h** *at* Jerusalem; and	1004
20: 3	whom he had left to keep the **h**, and	1004
21: 1	for *his* bloody **h**, because he slew	1004
21: 4	no silver nor gold of Saul, nor of his **h**;	1004
23: 5	Although my **h** *be* not so with God; yet he	1004
24:17	be against me, and against my father's **h**.	1004
1Ki 1:53	and Solomon said unto him, Go to thine **h**.	1004
2:24	and who hath made me a **h**, as he promised,	1004
2:27	which he spake concerning the **h** of Eli in	1004
2:31	from me, and from the **h** of my father.	1004
2:33	and upon his **h**, and upon his throne,	1004
2:34	he was buried in his own **h** in	1004
2:36	Build thee a **h** in Jerusalem, and	1004
3: 1	he had made an end of building his own **h**,	1004
3: 1	the **h** of the LORD, and the wall of	1004
3: 2	there was no **h** built unto the name of	1004
3:17	my lord, I and this woman dwell in one **h**;	1004
3:17	I was delivered of a child with her in the **h**.	1004
3:18	*there was* no stranger with us in the **h**,	1004
3:18	with us in the house, save we two in the **h**.	1004
5: 3	**h** unto the name of the LORD his God for	1004
5: 5	I purpose to build a **h** unto the name of	1004
5: 5	thy room, he shall build a **h** unto my name.	1004
5:17	to lay the foundation of the **h**.	1004
5:18	prepared timber and stones to build the **h**.	1004
6: 1	that he *began* to build the **h** of the LORD.	1004
6: 2	the **h** which king Solomon built for	1004
6: 3	the porch before the temple of the **h**,	1004
6: 3	according to the breadth of the **h**;	1004
6: 3	cubits *was* the breadth thereof before the **h**.	1004
6: 4	for the **h** he made windows of narrow	1004
6: 5	against the wall of the **h** he built chambers	1004
6: 5	*against* the walls of the **h** round about,	1004
6: 6	for without *in the wall* of the **h** he made	1004
6: 6	should not be fastened in the walls of the **h**.	1004
6: 7	the **h**, when it was in building, was built *of*	1004
6: 7	nor axe *nor* any tool of iron heard in the **h**,	1004
6: 8	chamber *was* in the right side of the **h**:	1004
6: 9	So he built the **h**, and finished it; and	1004
6: 9	covered the **h** with beams and boards of	1004
6:10	*then* he built chambers against all the **h**,	1004
6:10	they rested on the **h** with timber of cedar.	1004
6:12	*Concerning* this **h** which thou art in	1004
6:14	So Solomon built the **h**, and finished it.	1004
6:15	he built the walls of the **h** within with	1004
6:15	both the floor of the **h**, and the walls of	1004
6:15	covered the floor of the **h** with planks of	1004
6:16	he built twenty cubits on the sides of the **h**,	1004
6:17	the **h**, that *is*, the temple before it,	1004
6:18	the cedar of the **h** within *was* carved with	1004
6:19	the oracle he prepared in the **h** within, to	1004
6:21	So Solomon overlaid the **h** within with pure	1004
6:22	the whole **h** he overlaid with gold, until *he*	1004
6:22	with gold, until *he* had finished all the **h**:	1004
6:27	he set the cherubims within the inner **h**:	1004
6:27	touched one another in the midst of the **h**.	1004
6:29	he carved all the walls of the **h** round about	1004
6:30	the floor of the **h** he overlaid with gold,	1004
6:37	the foundation of the **h** of the LORD laid,	1004
6:38	was the **h** finished throughout all the parts	1004
7: 1	Solomon was building his own **h** thirteen	1004
7: 1	thirteen years, and he finished all his **h**.	1004
7: 2	He built also the **h** of the forest of Lebanon;	1004
7: 8	his **h** where he dwelt *had* another court	1004
7: 8	Solomon made also a **h** for Pharaoh's	1004
7:12	both for the inner court of the **h** of	1004
7:12	of the LORD, and for the porch of the **h**.	1004
7:39	he put five bases on the right side of the **h**,	1004
7:39	the house, and five on the left side of the **h**:	1004
7:39	he set the sea on the right side of the **h**	1004
7:40	king Solomon *for* the **h** of the LORD:	1004
7:45	to king Solomon *for* the **h** of the LORD,	1004
7:48	that *pertained unto* the **h** of the LORD:	1004
7:50	*of* gold, *both* for the doors of the inner **h**,	1004
7:50	most holy *place, and* for the doors of the **h**,	1004
7:51	Solomon made *for* the **h** of the LORD.	1004
7:51	did he put among the treasures of the **h** of	1004
8: 6	into the oracle of the **h**, to the most holy	1004
8:10	that the cloud filled the **h** of the LORD,	1004
8:11	for the glory of the LORD had filled the **h**	1004
8:13	I have surely built thee a **h** to dwell in,	1004
8:16	out of all the tribes of Israel to build a **h**,	1004
8:17	**h** for the name of the LORD God of	1004
8:18	Whereas it was in thine heart to build a **h**	1004
8:19	Nevertheless thou shalt not build the **h**; but	1004
8:19	he shall build the **h** unto my name.	1004
8:20	have built a **h** for the name of the LORD	1004
8:27	how much less this **h** that I have builded?	1004
8:29	That thine eyes may be open toward this **h**	1004
8:31	the oath come before thine altar in this **h**:	1004
8:33	and make supplication unto thee in this **h**:	1004
8:38	and spread forth his hands towards this **h**:	1004
8:42	he shall come and pray towards this **h**;	1004
8:43	that *they* may know that this **h**, which I	1004
8:44	*toward* the **h** that I have built for thy name:	1004
8:48	and the **h** which I have built for thy name:	1004
8:63	all the children of Israel dedicated the **h** of	1004
8:64	court that *was* before the **h** of the LORD:	1004
9: 1	the building of the **h** of the LORD,	1004
9: 1	the king's **h**, and all Solomon's desire	1004
9: 3	I have hallowed this **h**, which thou hast	1004
9: 7	*this* **h**, which I have hallowed for my name,	1004
9: 8	*at* this **h**, *which* is high, every one that	1004
9: 8	done thus unto this land, and to this **h**?	1004
9:10	the **h** of the LORD, and the king's house,	1004
9:10	the house of the LORD, and the king's **h**,	1004
9:15	for to build the **h** of the LORD, and his	1004
9:15	his own **h**, and Millo, and the wall of	1004
9:24	her **h** which *Solomon* had built for her:	1004
9:25	before the LORD. So he finished the **h**.	1004
10: 4	and the **h** that he had built,	1004
10: 5	his ascent *by* which he went up *unto* the **h**	1004
10:12	almug trees pillars for the **h** of the LORD,	1004
10:12	for the king's **h**, harps also and	1004
10:17	the king put them *in* the **h** of the forest of	1004
10:21	all the vessels of the **h** of the forest of	1004
11:18	which gave him a **h**, and appointed him	1004
11:20	whom Tahpenes weaned in Pharaoh's **h**:	1004
11:28	ruler over all the charge of the **h** of Joseph.	1004
11:38	build thee a sure **h**, as I built for David, and	1004
12:16	now see to thine own **h**, David. So Israel	1004
12:19	So Israel rebelled against the **h** of David	1004
12:20	there was none that followed the **h** of	1004
12:21	he assembled all the **h** of Judah, with	1004
12:21	to fight against the **h** of Israel,	1004
12:23	unto all the **h** of Judah and Benjamin, and	1004
12:24	return every man to his **h**; for this thing is	1004
12:26	Now shall the kingdom return to the **h** of	1004
12:27	If this people go up to do sacrifice in the **h**	1004
12:31	he made a **h** of high places, and	1004
13: 2	a child *shall be* born unto the **h** of David,	1004
13: 8	If thou wilt give me half thine **h**, I will not	1004
13:18	Bring him back with thee into thine **h**,	1004
13:19	and did eat bread in his **h**, and drank water.	1004
13:34	this thing became sin unto the **h** of	1004
14: 4	*to* Shiloh, and came *to* the **h** of Ahijah.	1004
14: 8	rent the kingdom away from the **h** of	1004
14:10	I will bring evil upon the **h** of Jeroboam,	1004
14:10	will take away the remnant of the **h** of	1004
14:12	thou therefore, get thee to thine own **h**:	1004
14:13	LORD God of Israel in the **h** of Jeroboam.	1004
14:14	who shall cut off the **h** of Jeroboam that	1004
14:26	he took away the treasures of the **h** of	1004
14:26	and the treasures of the king's **h**;	1004
14:27	which kept the door of the king's **h**.	1004
14:28	when the king went *into* the **h** of	1004
15:15	*into* the **h** of the LORD, silver, and gold,	1004
15:18	left in the treasures of the **h** of the LORD,	1004
15:18	the treasures of the king's **h**, and	1004
15:27	of the **h** of Issachar, conspired against him;	1004

1Ki 15:29 *that* he smote all the **h** of Jeroboam; 1004
16: 3 of Baasha, and the posterity of his **h**; 1004
16: 3 will make thy **h** like the house of Jeroboam 1004
16: 3 will make thy house like the **h** of Jeroboam 1004
16: 7 against his **h**, even for all the evil that he 1004
16: 7 his hands, in being like the **h** of Jeroboam; 1004
16: 9 drinking *himself* drunk *in* the **h** of Arza 1004
16: 9 house of Arza steward of *his* **h** in Tirzah. 1004
16:11 his throne, *that* he slew all the **h** of Baasha: 1004
16:12 Thus did Zimri destroy all the **h** of Baasha, 1004
16:18 that he went into the palace of the king's **h**, 1004
16:18 burnt the king's **h** over him with fire, and 1004
16:32 he reared up an altar for Baal *in* the **h** of 1004
17:15 she, and he, and her **h**, did eat *many* days. 1004
17:17 the woman, the mistress of the **h**, fell sick; 1004
17:23 him down out of the chamber into the **h**, 1004
18: 3 which *was* the governor of *his* **h**. 1004
18:18 thou, and thy father's **h**, in that ye have 1004
20: 6 they shall search thine **h**, and the houses of 1004
20:31 we have heard that the kings of the **h** of 1004
20:43 the king of Israel went to his **h** heavy and 1004
21: 2 of herbs, because it *is* near unto my **h**: 1004
21: 4 Ahab came into his **h** heavy and displeased 1004
21:22 will make thine **h** like the house of 1004
21:22 will make thine house like the **h** of 1004
21:22 like the **h** of Baasha the son of Ahijah, 1004
21:29 son's days will I bring the evil upon his **h**. 1004
22:17 let them return every man to his **h** in peace. 1004
22:39 the ivory **h** which he made, and all 1004
2Ki 4: 2 tell me, what hast thou in the **h**? And she 1004
4: 2 Thine handmaid hath not any thing in the **h**, 1004
4:32 when Elisha was come into the **h**, behold, 1004
4:35 he returned, and walked in the **h** to and fro; 1004
5: 9 and stood *at* the door of the **h** of Elisha. 1004
5:18 *that* when my master goeth *into* the **h** of 1004
5:18 and I bow myself *in* the **h** of Rimmon: 1004
5:18 when I bow down myself *in* the **h** of 1004
5:24 their hand, and bestowed *them* in the **h**: 1004
6:32 Elisha sat in his **h**, and the elders sat with 1004
7:11 and they told *it to* the king's **h** within. 1004
8: 3 she went forth to cry unto the king for her **h** 1004
8: 5 cried to the king for her **h** and for her land. 1004
8:18 of the kings of Israel, as did the **h** of Ahab: 1004
8:27 And he walked in the way of the **h** of Ahab, 1004
8:27 sight of the LORD, as *did* the **h** of Ahab: 1004
8:27 for he *was* the son in law of the **h** of Ahab. 1004
9: 6 he arose, and went into the **h**; and 1004
9: 7 thou shalt smite the **h** of Ahab thy master, 1004
9: 8 For the whole **h** of Ahab shall perish: and 1004
9: 9 I will make the **h** of Ahab like the house of 1004
9: 9 I will make the house of Ahab like the **h** of 1004
9: 9 and like the **h** of Baasha the son of Ahijah: 1004
9:27 *this,* he fled *by* the way of the garden **h**. 1004
10: 3 and fight for your master's **h**. 1004
10: 5 *he* that *was* over the **h**, and *he* that *was* over 1004
10:10 which the LORD spake concerning the **h** 1004
10:11 So Jehu slew all that remained of the **h** of 1004
10:12 *And* as he *was at* the shearing **h** in the way, 1004
10:14 slew them at the pit of the shearing **h**, 1004
10:21 they came *into* the **h** of Baal; and the house 1004
10:21 the **h** of Baal was full from one end to 1004
10:23 *into* the **h** of Baal, and said unto 1004
10:25 and went to the city of the **h** of Baal. 1004
10:26 they brought forth the images out of the **h** 1004
10:27 brake down the **h** of Baal, and made it a 1004
10:27 and made it a **draught h** unto *this* day. 4280
10:30 hast done unto the **h** of Ahab according to 1004
11: 3 he was with her hid *in* the **h** of the LORD 1004
11: 4 brought them to him *into* the **h** of 1004
11: 4 took an oath of them in the **h** of 1004
11: 5 be keepers of the watch of the king's **h**; 1004
11: 6 so shall ye keep the watch of the **h**, that it 1004
11: 7 even they shall keep the watch of the **h** of 1004
11:15 Let her not be slain *in* the **h** of the LORD. 1004
11:16 which the horses came *into* the king's **h**: 1004
11:18 all the people of the land went *into* the **h** of 1004
11:18 the priest appointed officers over the **h** of 1004
11:19 they brought down the king from the **h** of 1004
11:19 way of the gate of the guard *to* the king's **h**. 1004
11:20 with the sword *beside* the king's **h**. 1004
12: 4 that is brought *into* the **h** of the LORD, 1004
12: 4 heart to bring *into* the **h** of the LORD, 1004
12: 5 let them repair the breaches of the **h**, 1004
12: 6 had not repaired the breaches of the **h**. 1004
12: 7 Why repair ye not the breaches of the **h**? 1004
12: 7 but deliver it for the breaches of the **h**. 1004
12: 8 neither to repair the breaches of the **h**. 1004
12: 9 on the right side as one cometh *into* the **h** 1004
12: 9 that was brought *into* the **h** of the LORD. 1004
12:10 told the money that was found *in* the **h** of 1004
12:11 that had the oversight *of* the **h** of 1004
12:11 that wrought upon the **h** of the LORD, 1004
12:12 hewed stone to repair the breaches of the **h** 1004
12:12 for all that was laid out for the **h** to repair 1004
12:13 Howbeit there were not made *for* the **h** of 1004
12:13 of the money that was brought *into* the **h** of 1004
12:14 and repaired therewith the **h** of the LORD. 1004
12:16 sin money was not brought *into* the **h** of 1004
12:18 in the treasures of the **h** of the LORD, 1004
12:18 *in* the king's **h**, and sent *it* to Hazael king of 1004
12:20 slew Joash *in* the **h** of Millo, 1004
13: 6 not from the sins of the **h** of Jeroboam, 1004
14:14 all the vessels that were found *in* the **h** of 1004
14:14 in the treasures of the king's **h**, and 1004
15: 5 day of his death, and dwelt in a several **h**. 1004
15: 5 Jotham the king's son *was* over the **h**, 1004
15:25 in the palace of the king's **h**, with Argob 1004
15:35 He built the higher gate of the **h** of 1004
16: 8 gold that was found *in* the **h** of the LORD, 1004
16: 8 in the treasures of the king's **h**, and sent *it* 1004
16:14 from the forefront of the **h**, from between 1004
16:14 between the altar and the **h** of the LORD, 1004
16:18 for the sabbath that they had built in the **h**, 1004
16:18 turned he *from* the **h** of the LORD for 1004
17:21 For he rent Israel from the **h** of David; and 1004
18:15 that was found *in* the **h** of the LORD, 1004
18:15 and in the treasures of the king's **h**. 1004
19: 1 and went *into* the **h** of the LORD. 1004
19:14 Hezekiah went up *into* the **h** of the LORD, 1004
19:30 the remnant that is escaped of the **h** of 1004
19:37 as he was worshipping *in* the **h** of Nisroch 1004
20: 1 Thus saith the LORD, Set thine **h** in order; 1004
20: 5 on the third day thou shalt go up *unto* the **h** 1004
20: 8 *that* I shall go up *into* the **h** of the LORD 1004
20:13 shewed them all the **h** of his precious 1004
20:13 all the **h** of his armour, and all that was 1004
20:13 there was nothing in his **h**, nor in all his 1004
20:15 he said, What have they seen in thine **h**? 1004
20:15 All *the things* that *are* in mine **h** have they 1004
20:17 that all that *is* in thine **h**, and *that* which thy 1004
21: 4 he built altars in the **h** of the LORD, 1004
21: 5 in the two courts of the **h** of the LORD. 1004
21: 7 of the grove that he had made in the **h**, 1004
21: 7 his son, In this **h**, and in Jerusalem, 1004
21:13 and the plummet of the **h** of Ahab: 1004
21:18 was buried in the garden of his own **h**, 1004
21:23 and slew the king in his own **h**. 1004
22: 3 the scribe, *to* the **h** of the LORD, saying, 1004
22: 4 which is brought *into* the **h** of the LORD, 1004
22: 5 that have the oversight of the **h** of 1004
22: 5 the work which *is* in the **h** of the LORD, 1004
22: 5 the LORD, to repair the breaches of the **h**, 1004
22: 6 buy timber and hewn stone to repair the **h**. 1004
22: 8 I have found the book of the law in the **h** of 1004
22: 9 gathered the money that was found in the **h**, 1004
22: 9 that have the oversight *of* the **h** of 1004
23: 2 the king went up *into* the **h** of the LORD, 1004
23: 2 which was found in the **h** of the LORD. 1004
23: 6 he brought out the grove from the **h** of 1004
23: 7 that *were* by the **h** of the LORD, 1004
23:11 at the entering in of the **h** of the LORD, 1004
23:12 in the two courts of the **h** of the LORD, 1004
23:24 the priest found *in* the **h** of the LORD. 1004
23:27 the **h** of which I said, My name shall be 1004
24:13 all the treasures of the **h** of the LORD, 1004
24:13 the treasures of the king's **h**, and cut in 1004
25: 9 he burnt the **h** of the LORD, and 1004
25: 9 the king's **h**, and all the houses of 1004
25: 9 and every great *man's* **h** burnt he with fire. 1004
25:13 the pillars of brass that *were in* the **h** of 1004
25:13 the brasen sea that *was* in the **h** of 1004
25:16 had made for the **h** of the LORD; 1004
1Ch 2:54 the **h** of Joab, and half of the Manahethites, 1004
2:55 of Hemath, the father of the **h** of Rechab. 1004
4:21 the families of the **h** of them that wrought 1004
4:21 that wrought fine linen, of the **h** of Ashbea, 1004
4:38 and the **h** of their fathers increased greatly. 1004
5:13 their brethren of the **h** of their fathers *were,* 1004

1Ch 5:15 son of Guni, chief of the **h** of their fathers. 1004
5:24 these *were* the heads of the **h** of their 1004
5:24 *and* heads of the **h** of their fathers. 1004
6:31 the service of song *in* the **h** of the LORD, 1004
6:32 until Solomon had built the **h** of 1004
6:48 *of* service of the tabernacle of the **h** of God. 1004
7: 2 and Shemuel, heads of their fathers' **h**, 1004
7: 4 after the **h** of their fathers, 1004
7: 7 heads of the **h** of *their* fathers, mighty *men* 1004
7: 9 heads of the **h** of their fathers, mighty *men* 1004
7:23 because it went evil with his **h**. 1004
7:40 heads of *their* fathers' **h**, choice *and* 1004
9: 9 chief of the fathers in the **h** of their fathers. 1004
9:11 the son of Ahitub, the ruler of the **h** of God; 1004
9:13 heads of the **h** of their fathers, a thousand 1004
9:13 *for* the work of the service of the **h** of God. 1004
9:19 his brethren, of the **h** of his father, 1004
9:23 of the gates of the **h** of the LORD, 1004
9:23 *namely,* the **h** of the tabernacle, by wards. 1004
9:26 and treasuries of the **h** of God. 1004
9:27 they lodged round about the **h** of God, 1004
10: 6 his three sons, and all his **h** died together. 1004
10:10 they put his armour *in* the **h** of their gods, 1004
12:28 *of* his father's **h** twenty and two captains. 1004
12:29 of them had kept the ward of the **h** of Saul. 1004
12:30 famous throughout the **h** of their fathers. 1004
13: 7 God in a new cart out of the **h** of Abinadab: 1004
13:13 carried it aside into the **h** of Obed-edom 1004
13:14 of Obed-edom in his **h** three months. 1004
13:14 the LORD blessed the **h** of Obed-edom, 1004
14: 1 and carpenters, to build him a **h**. 1004
15:25 out of the **h** of Obed-edom with joy. 1004
16:43 all the people departed every man to his **h**: 1004
16:43 and David returned to bless his **h**. 1004
17: 1 Now it came to pass, as David sat in his **h**, 1004
17: 1 I dwell in a **h** of cedars, but the ark of 1004
17: 4 Thou shalt not build me a **h** to dwell in: 1004
17: 5 For I have not dwelt in a **h** since the day 1004
17: 6 Why have ye not built me a **h** of cedars? 1004
17:10 thee that the LORD will build thee a **h**. 1004
17:12 He shall build me a **h**, and I will stablish 1004
17:14 I will settle him in mine **h** and in my 1004
17:16 *am* I, O LORD God, and what *is* mine **h**, 1004
17:17 for thou hast *also* spoken of thy servant's **h** 1004
17:23 concerning his **h** be established for ever, 1004
17:24 *let* the **h** of David thy servant *be* 1004
17:25 thy servant that *thou* wilt build him a **h**: 1004
17:27 let it please thee to bless the **h** of thy 1004
21:17 my God, be on me, and on my father's **h**; 1004
22: 1 This *is* the **h** of the LORD God, and this *is* 1004
22: 2 hew wrought stones to build the **h** of God. 1004
22: 5 the **h** *that is* to be builded for the LORD 1004
22: 6 charged him to build a **h** for the LORD 1004
22: 7 it was in my mind to build a **h** unto 1004
22: 8 thou shalt not build a **h** unto my name, 1004
22:10 He shall build a **h** for my name; and 1004
22:11 and build the **h** of the LORD thy God, 1004
22:14 in my trouble I have prepared for the **h** of 1004
22:19 into the **h** that is *to be* built to the name of 1004
23: 4 forward the work of the **h** of the LORD; 1004
23:11 according to *their* father's **h**. 1004
23:24 These *were* the sons of Levi after the **h** of 1004
23:24 that did the work for the service of the **h** of 1004
23:28 for the service of the **h** of the LORD, 1004
23:28 and the work of the service of the **h** of God; 1004
23:32 in the service of the **h** of the LORD. 1004
24: 4 sixteen chief *men* of the **h** of *their* fathers, 1004
24: 4 Ithamar according to the **h** of their fathers. 1004
24: 5 governors *of the* **h** of God, were of the sons NIH
24:19 service to come into the **h** of the LORD, 1004
24:30 of the Levites after the **h** of their fathers. 1004
25: 6 their father for song *in* the **h** of the LORD, 1004
25: 6 and harps, for the service of the **h** of God, 1004
26: 6 that ruled throughout the **h** of their father: 1004
26:12 to minister in the **h** of the LORD. 1004
26:13 according to the **h** of their fathers, for every 1004
26:15 to his sons the **h** of Asuppim. 1004
26:20 Ahijah *was* over the treasures of the **h** of 1004
26:22 *which were* over the treasures of the **h** of 1004
26:27 dedicate to maintain the **h** of the LORD. 1004
28: 2 *As for me,* I *had* in mine heart to build a **h** 1004
28: 3 Thou shalt not build a **h** for my name, 1004
28: 4 **h** of my father to be king over Israel for 1004
28: 4 of the **h** of Judah, the house of my father; 1004
28: 4 of the house of Judah, the **h** of my father; 1004
28: 6 thy son, he shall build my **h** and my courts: 1004
28:10 chosen thee to build a **h** for the sanctuary: 1004
28:12 of the courts of the **h** of the LORD, and 1004
28:12 of the treasuries of the **h** of God, and of 1004
28:13 for all the work of the service of the **h** of 1004
28:13 for all the vessels of service in the **h** of 1004
28:20 for the service of the **h** of the LORD. 1004
28:21 *thee* for all the service of the **h** of God: 1004
29: 2 **h** of my God the gold for *things to be made* 1004
29: 3 I have set my affection to the **h** of my God, 1004
29: 3 *which* I have given to the **h** of my God, 1004
29: 3 all *that* I have prepared for the holy **h**, 1004
29: 7 gave for the service of the **h** of God *of* gold 1004
29: 8 *them* to the treasure of the **h** of the LORD, 1004
29:16 **h** for thine holy name *cometh* of thine 1004
2Ch 2: 1 Solomon determined to build a **h** for 1004
2: 1 of the LORD, and a **h** for his kingdom. 1004
2: 3 didst send him cedars to build him a **h** to 1004
2: 4 I build a **h** to the name of the LORD my 1004
2: 5 the **h** which I build *is* great: for great *is* our 1004
2: 6 who is able to build him a **h**, seeing 1004
2: 6 who *am* I then, that I should build him a **h**, 1004
2: 9 for the **h** which I am about to build *shall be* 1004
2:12 that might build a **h** for the LORD, and 1004
2:12 for the LORD, and a **h** for his kingdom. 1004
3: 1 Solomon began to build the **h** of 1004
3: 3 instructed for the building of the **h** of God. 1004
3: 4 the porch that *was* in the front *of the* **h**, NIH
3: 4 *of it was* according to the breadth of the **h**, 1004
3: 5 the greater **h** he cieled with fir tree, 1004
3: 6 he garnished the **h** with precious stones for 1004
3: 7 He overlaid also the **h**, the beams, 1004
3: 8 he made the most holy **h**, the length 1004
3: 8 *was* according to the breadth of the **h**, 1004
3:10 in the most holy **h** he made two cherubims 1004
3:11 five cubits, reaching to the wall of the **h**: 1004
3:12 five cubits, reaching to the wall of the **h**: 1004
3:15 Also he made before the **h** two pillars of 1004
4:11 to make for king Solomon for the **h** of God; 1004
4:16 for the **h** of the LORD *of* bright brass. 1004
4:19 all the vessels that *were for* the **h** of God, 1004
4:22 the entry of the **h**, the inner doors thereof 1004
4:22 and the doors of the **h** of the temple, 1004
5: 1 made for the **h** of the LORD was finished: 1004
5: 1 put he among the treasures of the **h** of God. 1004
5: 7 to the oracle of the **h**, into the most holy 1004
5:13 that *then* the **h** was filled *with* a cloud, 1004
5:13 *with* a cloud, *even* the **h** of the LORD; 1004
5:14 for the glory of the LORD had filled the **h** 1004
6: 2 I have built a **h** of habitation for thee, and 1004
6: 5 build a **h** *in,* that my name might be there; 1004
6: 7 **h** for the name of the LORD God of 1004
6: 8 was in thine heart to build a **h** for my name, 1004
6: 9 Notwithstanding thou shalt not build the **h**; 1004
6: 9 thy loins, he shall build the **h** for my name. 1004
6:10 have built the **h** for the name of the LORD 1004
6:18 how much less this **h** which I have built? 1004
6:20 That thine eyes may be open upon this **h** 1004
6:22 the oath come before thine altar in this **h**; 1004
6:24 and make supplication before thee in this **h**; 1004
6:29 and shall spread forth his hands in this **h**: 1004
6:32 out arm; if they come and pray in this **h**; 1004
6:33 may know that this **h** which I have built is 1004
6:34 the **h** which I have built for thy name; 1004
6:38 toward the **h** which I have built for thy 1004
7: 1 and the glory of the LORD filled the **h**. 1004
7: 2 the priests could not enter into the **h** of 1004
7: 2 of the LORD had filled the LORD'S **h**. 1004
7: 3 and the glory of the LORD upon the **h**, 1004
7: 5 and all the people dedicated the **h** of God. 1004
7: 7 court that *was* before the **h** of the LORD: 1004
7:11 Thus Solomon finished the **h** of 1004
7:11 the house of the LORD, and the king's **h**: 1004
7:11 heart to make in the **h** of the LORD, 1004
7:11 and in his own **h**, he prosperously effected. 1004
7:12 have chosen this place to myself for a **h** of 1004
7:16 now have I chosen and sanctified this **h**, 1004
7:20 this **h**, which I have sanctified for my 1004
7:21 this **h**, which is high, shall be an 1004
7:21 done thus unto this land, and unto this **h**? 1004
8: 1 wherein Solomon had built the **h** of 1004
8: 1 the house of the LORD, and his own **h**, 1004
8:11 David unto the **h** that he had built for her: 1004

2Ch	8:11	My wife shall not dwell in the **h** of David	1004
	8:16	of the foundation of the **h** of the LORD,	1004
	8:16	*So* the **h** of the LORD was perfected.	1004
	9: 3	of Solomon, and the **h** that he had built,	1004
	9: 4	his ascent *by* which he went up *into* the **h**	1004
	9:11	algum trees terraces to the **h** of the LORD,	1004
	9:16	the king put them in the **h** of the forest of	1004
	9:20	all the vessels of the **h** of the forest of	1004
	10:16	*and* now, David, see to thine own **h**. So all	1004
	10:19	Israel rebelled against the **h** of David unto	1004
	11: 1	he gathered *of* the **h** of Judah and	1004
	11: 4	return every man to his **h**, for this thing is	1004
	12: 9	took away the treasures of the **h** of	1004
	12: 9	and the treasures of the king's **h**;	1004
	12:10	that kept the entrance of the king's **h**.	1004
	12:11	when the king entered *into* the **h** of	1004
	15:18	he brought *into* the **h** of God *the things* that	1004
	16: 2	gold out of the treasures of the **h** of	1004
	16: 2	house of the LORD and of the king's **h**,	1004
	16:10	with the seer, and put him *in* a prison **h**;	1004
	17:14	of them according to the **h** of their fathers:	1004
	18:16	*therefore* every man to his **h** in peace.	1004
	19: 1	returned to his **h** in peace to Jerusalem.	1004
	19:11	the ruler of the **h** of Judah, for all the king's	1004
	20: 5	and Jerusalem, in the **h** of the LORD,	1004
	20: 9	we stand before this **h**, and in thy presence,	1004
	20: 9	in thy presence, (for thy name *is* in this **h**,)	1004
	20:28	and trumpets unto the **h** of the LORD.	1004
	21: 6	kings of Israel, like as did the **h** of Ahab:	1004
	21: 7	LORD would not destroy the **h** of David,	1004
	21:13	like to the whoredoms of the **h** of Ahab,	1004
	21:13	hast slain thy brethren of thy father's **h**,	1004
	21:17	substance that was found in the king's **h**,	1004
	22: 3	He also walked in the ways of the **h** of	1004
	22: 4	the sight of the LORD, like the **h** of Ahab:	1004
	22: 7	had anointed to cut off the **h** of Ahab.	1004
	22: 8	executing judgment upon the **h** of Ahab,	1004
	22: 9	So the **h** of Ahaziah had no power to keep	1004
	22:10	destroyed all the seed royal of the **h** of	1004
	22:12	he was with them hid in the **h** of God six	1004
	23: 3	a covenant with the king in the **h** of God.	1004
	23: 5	a third *part shall be* at the king's **h**; and	1004
	23: 5	all the people *shall be* in the courts of the **h**	1004
	23: 6	let none come *into* the **h** of the LORD,	1004
	23: 7	whosoever *else* cometh into the **h**, he shall	1004
	23: 9	king David's, which *were in* the **h** of God.	1004
	23:12	she came to the people *into* the **h** of	1004
	23:14	Slay her not *in* the **h** of the LORD.	1004
	23:15	entering of the horse gate *by* the king's **h**,	1004
	23:17	all the people went *to* the **h** of Baal, and	1004
	23:18	**h** of the LORD by the hand of the priests	1004
	23:18	whom David had distributed in the **h** of	1004
	23:19	he set the porters at the gates of the **h** of	1004
	23:20	brought down the king from the **h** of	1004
	23:20	through the high gate *into* the king's **h**,	1004
	24: 4	*that* Joash was minded to repair the **h** of	1004
	24: 5	gather of all Israel money to repair the **h** of	1004
	24: 7	had broken up the **h** of God;	1004
	24: 7	also all the dedicate *things* of the **h** of	1004
	24: 8	set it without at the gate of the **h** of	1004
	24:12	work of the service of the **h** of the LORD,	1004
	24:12	carpenters to repair the **h** of the LORD,	1004
	24:12	and brass to mend the **h** of the LORD.	1004
	24:13	they set the **h** of God in his state, and	1004
	24:14	whereof were made vessels for the **h** of	1004
	24:14	they offered burnt offerings in the **h** of	1004
	24:16	both towards God, and *towards* his **h**.	1004
	24:18	they left the **h** of the LORD God of their	1004
	24:21	king in the court of the **h** of the LORD.	1004
	24:27	and the repairing of the **h** of God,	1004
	25:24	all the vessels that were found in the **h** of	1004
	25:24	the treasures of the king's **h**, the hostages	1004
	26:19	before the priests in the **h** of the LORD,	1004
	26:21	and dwelt *in* a several **h**, *being* a leper;	1004
	26:21	for he was cut off from the **h** of	1004
	26:21	Jotham his son *was* over the king's **h**,	1004
	27: 3	He built the high gate of the **h** of	1004
	28: 7	Azrikam the governor of the **h**, and	1004
	28:21	For Ahaz took away a portion *out* of the **h**	1004
	28:21	*out* of the **h** of the king, and of the princes,	1004
	28:24	Ahaz gathered together the vessels of the **h**	1004
	28:24	cut in pieces the vessels of the **h** of God,	1004
	28:24	shut up the doors of the **h** of the LORD,	1004
	29: 3	opened the doors of the **h** of the LORD,	1004
	29: 5	sanctify the **h** of the LORD God of your	1004
	29:15	to cleanse the **h** of the LORD.	1004
	29:16	the priests went into the inner part *of* the **h**	1004
	29:16	into the court of the **h** of the LORD.	1004
	29:17	they sanctified the **h** of the LORD in eight	1004
	29:18	We have cleansed all the **h** of the LORD,	1004
	29:20	and went up *to* the **h** of the LORD.	1004
	29:25	he set the Levites *in* the **h** of the LORD	1004
	29:31	thank offerings into the **h** of the LORD.	1004
	29:35	So the service of the **h** of the LORD was	1004
	30: 1	that *they* should come to the **h** of	1004
	30:15	brought in the burnt offerings *into* the **h** of	1004
	31:10	Azariah the chief priest of the **h** of Zadok	1004
	31:10	the offerings *into* the **h** of the LORD,	1004
	31:11	prepare chambers in the **h** of the LORD;	1004
	31:13	and Azariah the ruler of the **h** of God.	1004
	31:16	*even* unto every one that entereth into the **h**	1004
	31:17	of the priests by the **h** of their fathers,	1004
	31:21	that he began in the service of the **h** of God,	1004
	32:21	when he was come *into* the **h** of his god,	1004
	33: 4	Also he built altars in the **h** of the LORD,	1004
	33: 5	in the two courts of the **h** of the LORD.	1004
	33: 7	idol which he had made, in the **h** of God,	1004
	33: 7	his son, In this **h**, and in Jerusalem,	1004
	33:15	and the idol out of the **h** of the LORD, and	1004
	33:15	built in the mount of the **h** of the LORD,	1004
	33:20	and they buried him *in* his own **h**:	1004
	33:24	against him, and slew him in his own **h**.	1004
	34: 8	when he had purged the land, and the **h**,	1004
	34: 8	to repair the **h** of the LORD his God.	1004
	34: 9	money that was brought *into* the **h** of God,	1004
	34:10	had the oversight of the **h** of the LORD,	1004
	34:10	that wrought in the **h** of the LORD,	1004
	34:10	of the LORD, to repair and mend the **h**:	1004
	34:14	that was brought *into* the **h** of the LORD,	1004
	34:15	I have found the book of the law in the **h** of	1004
	34:17	that was found in the **h** of the LORD,	1004
	34:30	the king went up *into* the **h** of the LORD,	1004
	34:30	that was found *in* the **h** of the LORD.	1004
	35: 2	encouraged them to the service of the **h** of	1004
	35: 3	Put the holy ark in the **h** which Solomon	1004
	35: 8	and Jehiel, rulers of the **h** of God,	1004
	35:21	but against the **h** wherewith I have war:	1004
	36: 7	vessels of the **h** of the LORD to Babylon,	1004
	36:10	with the goodly vessels of the **h** of	1004
	36:14	polluted the **h** of the LORD which he had	1004
	36:17	with the sword in the **h** of their sanctuary,	1004
	36:18	all the vessels of the **h** of God, great and	1004
	36:18	the treasures of the **h** of the LORD, and	1004
	36:19	they burnt the **h** of God, and brake down	1004
	36:23	he hath charged me to build him a **h** in	1004
Ezr	1: 2	he hath charged me to build him a **h** at	1004
	1: 3	build the **h** of the LORD God of Israel,	1004
	1: 4	besides the freewill offering for the **h** of	1004
	1: 5	to go up to build the **h** of the LORD	1004
	1: 7	forth the vessels of the **h** of the LORD,	1004
	1: 7	and had put them in the **h** of his gods;	1004
	2:36	of the **h** of Jeshua, nine hundred seventy	1004
	2:59	they could not shew their fathers' **h**, and	1004
	2:68	when they came to the **h** of the LORD	1004
	2:68	offered freely for the **h** of God to set it up	1004
	3: 8	coming unto the **h** of God at Jerusalem,	1004
	3: 8	to set forward the work of the **h** of	1004
	3: 9	to set forward the workmen in the **h** of	1004
	3:11	the foundation of the **h** of the LORD was	1004
	3:12	*were* ancient men that had seen the first **h**,	1004
	3:12	when the foundation of this **h** was laid	1004
	4: 3	You have nothing to do with us to build a **h**	1004
	4:24	ceased the work of the **h** of the God which	1005
	5: 2	began to build the **h** of God which *is* at	1005
	5: 3	Who hath commanded you to build this **h**,	1005
	5: 8	to the **h** of the great God, which *is* builded	1005
	5: 9	Who commanded you to build this **h**, and	1005
	5:11	build the **h** that was builded these many	1005
	5:12	who destroyed this **h**, and carried	1005
	5:13	Cyrus made a decree to build this **h** of God.	1005
	5:14	also of gold and silver of the **h** of God,	1005
	5:15	and let the **h** of God be builded in his place.	1005
	5:16	laid the foundation of the **h** of God which *is*	1005
	5:17	be search made in the king's treasure **h**,	1005
	5:17	king to build this **h** of God at Jerusalem,	1005
	6: 1	and search was made in the **h** of the rolls,	1005
	6: 3	*concerning* the **h** of God at Jerusalem,	1005
	6: 3	Let the **h** be builded, the place where they	1005

Ezr 6: 4 the expences be given out of the king's **h**: 1005
6: 5 and silver vessels of the **h** of God, 1005
6: 5 his place, and place *them* in the **h** of God. 1005
6: 7 Let the work of this **h** of God alone; let 1005
6: 7 the elders of the Jews build this **h** of God in 1005
6: 8 Jews for the building of this **h** of God: 1005
6:11 let timber be pulled down from his **h**, and 1005
6:11 let his **h** be made a dunghill for this. 1005
6:12 to destroy this **h** of God which *is* at 1005
6:15 this **h** was finished on the third day of 1005
6:16 kept the dedication of this **h** of God with 1005
6:17 offered at the dedication of this **h** of God an 1005
6:22 their hands in the work of the **h** of God, 1004
7:16 offering willingly for the **h** of their God 1005
7:17 offer them upon the altar of the **h** of your 1005
7:19 thee for the service of the **h** of thy God, 1005
7:20 whatsoever more *shall be* needful for the **h** 1005
7:20 bestow *it* out of the king's treasure **h**. 1005
7:23 let it be diligently done for the **h** of the God 1005
7:24 or ministers of this **h** of God, 1005
7:27 to beautify the **h** of the LORD which *is* in 1004
8:17 unto us ministers for the **h** of our God. 1004
8:25 *even* the offering of the **h** of our God, 1004
8:29 *in* the chambers of the **h** of the LORD. 1004
8:30 to bring *them* to Jerusalem unto the **h** of 1004
8:33 the vessels weighed in the **h** of our God by 1004
8:36 they furthered the people, and the **h** of God. 1004
9: 9 to set up the **h** of our God, and to repair 1004
10: 1 casting himself down before the **h** of God, 1004
10: 6 Ezra rose up from before the **h** of God, 1004
10: 9 all the people sat in the street of the **h** of 1004
10:16 after the **h** of their fathers, and all of them 1004
Ne 1: 6 both I and my father's **h** have sinned. 1004
2: 8 of the palace which *appertained* to the **h**, 1004
2: 8 the city, and for the **h** that I shall enter into. 1004
3:10 son of Harumaph, even over against his **h**. 1004
3:16 was made, and unto the **h** of the mighty. 1004
3:20 the door of the **h** of Eliashib the high priest. 1004
3:21 from the door of the **h** of Eliashib even to 1004
3:21 even to the end of the **h** of Eliashib. 1004
3:23 and Hashub over against their **h**. 1004
3:23 of Maaseiah the son of Ananiah by his **h**. 1004
3:24 from the **h** of Azariah unto the turning *of* 1004
3:25 which lieth out from the king's high **h**, 1004
3:28 the priests, every one over against his **h**. 1004
3:29 Zadok the son of Immer over against his **h**. 1004
4:16 the rulers *were* behind all the **h** of Judah. 1004
5:13 So God shake out every man from his **h**, 1004
6:10 Afterward I came *unto* the **h** of Shemaiah 1004
6:10 Let us meet together in the **h** of God, 1004
7: 3 and every one *to be* over against his **h**. 1004
7:39 of the **h** of Jeshua, nine hundred seventy 1004
7:61 they could not shew their fathers' **h**, 1004
8:16 every one upon the **roof of** his **h**, and 1406
8:16 in the courts of the **h** of God, and in 1004
10:32 a shekel for the service of the **h** of our God; 1004
10:33 and *for* all the work of the **h** of our God. 1004
10:34 to bring *it* into the **h** of our God, 1004
10:35 year by year, unto the **h** of the LORD: 1004
10:36 of our flocks, to bring to the **h** of our God, 1004
10:36 unto the priests that minister in the **h** of our 1004
10:37 to the chambers of the **h** of our God; 1004
10:38 the tithe of the tithes unto the **h** of our God, 1004
10:38 to the chambers, into the treasure **h**. 1004
10:39 and we will not forsake the **h** of our God. 1004
11:11 of Ahitub, *was* the ruler of the **h** of God. 1004
11:12 their brethren that did the work of the **h** 1004
11:16 of the outward business of the **h** of God. 1004
11:22 the singers *were* over the business of the **h** 1004
12:29 Also from the **h** of Gilgal, and out of 1004
12:37 going up of the wall, above the **h** of David, 1004
12:40 *of them that gave* thanks in the **h** of God, 1004
13: 4 of the chamber of the **h** of our God, 1004
13: 7 a chamber in the courts of the **h** of God. 1004
13: 9 thither brought I again the vessels of the **h** 1004
13:11 and said, Why is the **h** of God forsaken? 1004
13:14 deeds that I have done for the **h** of my God, 1004
Est 1: 8 had appointed to all the officers of his **h**, 1004
1: 9 royal **h** which *belonged* to king Ahasuerus. 1004
1:22 every man should bear rule in his own **h**, 1004
2: 3 to the **h** of the women, unto the custody of 1004
2: 8 Esther was brought *also* unto the king's **h**, 1004
2: 9 meet to be given her, out of the king's **h**: 1004
2: 9 her maids unto the best *place* of the **h** of 1004
2:11 day before the court of the women's **h**, 1004
2:13 the **h** of the women unto the king's house. 1004
2:13 the house of the women unto the king's **h**. 1004
2:14 returned into the second **h** of the women, 1004
2:16 into his **h** royal in the tenth month, 1004
4:13 that *thou* shalt escape *in* the king's **h**, 1004
4:14 thou and thy father's **h** shall be destroyed: 1004
5: 1 and stood in the inner court of the king's **h**, 1004
5: 1 the king's house, over against the king's **h**: 1004
5: 1 sat upon his royal throne in the royal **h**, 1004
5: 1 royal house, over against the gate of the **h**. 1004
6: 4 into the outward court of the king's **h**, 1004
6:12 Haman hasted to his **h** mourning, and 1004
7: 8 he force the queen also before me in the **h**? 1004
7: 9 for the king, standeth in the **h** of Haman. 1004
8: 1 **h** of Haman the Jews' enemy unto Esther 1004
8: 2 Esther set Mordecai over the **h** of Haman. 1004
8: 7 I have given Esther the **h** of Haman, and 1004
9: 4 For Mordecai *was* great in the king's **h**, and 1004
Job 1:10 about his **h**, and about all that he hath on 1004
1:13 drinking wine in their eldest brother's **h**: 1004
1:18 drinking wine in their eldest brother's **h**: 1004
1:19 smote the four corners of the **h**, and it fell 1004
7:10 He shall return no more to his **h**, 1004
8:15 He shall lean upon his **h**, but it shall not 1004
17:13 If I wait, the grave *is* mine **h**: I have made 1004
19:15 They that dwell in mine **h**, and 1004
20:19 he hath violently taken away a **h** which he 1004
20:28 The increase of his **h** shall depart, *and* 1004
21:21 For what pleasure hath he in his **h** after 1004
21:28 For ye say, Where *is* the **h** of the prince? 1004
27:18 He buildeth his **h** as a moth, and as a booth 1004
30:23 and *to* the **h** appointed for all living. 1004
38:20 that thou shouldest know the paths to the **h** 1004
39: 6 Whose **h** I have made the wilderness, and 1004
42:11 and did eat bread with him in his **h**: 1004
Ps 5: 7 I will come *into* thy **h** in the multitude of 1004
23: 6 I will dwell in the **h** of the LORD for ever. 1004
26: 8 I have loved the habitation of thy **h**, and 1004
27: 4 that I may dwell in the **h** of the LORD all 1004
30: T Song *at* the dedication of the **h** of David. 1004
31: 2 strong rock, for a **h** of defence to save me. 1004
36: 8 satisfied with the fatness of thy **h**; 1004
42: 4 I went with them to the **h** of God, with 1004
45:10 also thine own people, and thy father's **h**; 1004
49:16 when the glory of his **h** is increased; 1004
50: 9 I will take no bullock out of thy **h**, *nor* he 1004
52: T David is come to the **h** of Ahimelech. 1004
52: 8 I *am* like a green olive tree in the **h** of God: 1004
55:14 *and* walked unto the **h** of God in company. 1004
59: T Saul sent, and they watcht the **h** to kill him. 1004
65: 4 be satisfied with the goodness of thy **h**, 1004
66:13 I will go *into* thy **h** with burnt offerings: 1004
69: 9 For the zeal of thine **h** hath eaten me up; 1004
84: 3 the sparrow hath found a **h**, and 1004
84: 4 Blessed *are* they that dwell in thy **h**: 1004
84:10 I had rather be a doorkeeper in the **h** of my 1004
92:13 Those that be planted in the **h** of 1004
93: 5 holiness becometh thine **h**, O LORD, 1004
98: 3 and his truth toward the **h** of Israel: 1004
101: 2 I will walk within my **h** with a perfect 1004
101: 7 worketh deceit shall not dwell within my **h**: 1004
104:17 *as for* the stork, the fir trees *are* her **h**. 1004
105:21 He made him lord of his **h**, and ruler of all 1004
112: 3 Wealth and riches *shall be* in his **h**: and 1004
113: 9 He maketh the barren *woman* to keep **h**, 1004
114: 1 the **h** of Jacob from a people of strange 1004
115:10 O **h** of Aaron, trust in the LORD: he *is* 1004
115:12 he will bless *us;* he will bless the **h** of 1004
115:12 of Israel; he will bless the **h** of Aaron. 1004
116:19 In the courts of the LORD'S **h**, in 1004
118: 3 Let the **h** of Aaron now say, that his mercy 1004
118:26 we have blessed you out of the **h** of 1004
119:54 Thy statutes have been my songs in the **h** of 1004
122: 1 Let us go *into* the **h** of the LORD. 1004
122: 5 of judgment, the thrones of the **h** of David. 1004
122: 9 Because of the **h** of the LORD our God I 1004
127: 1 Except the LORD build the **h**, they labour 1004
128: 3 *be* as a fruitful vine by the sides of thine **h**: 1004
132: 3 I will not come into the tabernacle of my **h**, 1004
134: 1 which by night stand in the **h** of 1004
135: 2 Ye that stand in the **h** of the LORD, in 1004
135: 2 in the courts of the **h** of our God, 1004
135:19 Bless the LORD, O **h** of Israel: bless 1004

Ps 135:19 of Israel: bless the LORD, O **h** of Aaron: 1004
135:20 Bless the LORD, O **h** of Levi: ye that fear 1004
Pr 2:18 For her **h** inclineth unto death, and 1004
3:33 The curse of the LORD *is* in the **h** of 1004
5: 8 and come not nigh the door of her **h**: 1004
5:10 and thy labours *be* in the **h** of a stranger; 1004
6:31 he shall give all the substance of his **h**. 1004
7: 6 For at the window of my **h** I looked 1004
7: 8 her corner; and he went the way to her **h**, 1004
7:11 and stubborn; her feet abide not in her **h**: 1004
7:27 Her **h** *is* the way to hell, going down to 1004
9: 1 Wisdom hath builded her **h**, she hath hewn 1004
9:14 For she sitteth at the door of her **h**, on a 1004
11:29 He that troubleth his own **h** shall inherit 1004
12: 7 but the **h** of the righteous shall stand. 1004
14: 1 Every wise woman buildeth her **h**: but 1004
14:11 The **h** of the wicked shall be overthrown: 1004
15: 6 *In* the **h** of the righteous *is* much treasure: 1004
15:25 The LORD will destroy the **h** of 1004
15:27 that is greedy of gain troubleth his own **h**; 1004
17: 1 than a **h** full *of* sacrifices with strife. 1004
17:13 for good, evil shall not depart from his **h**. 1004
19:14 **H** and riches *are* the inheritance of fathers: 1004
21: 9 than with a brawling woman in a wide **h**. 1004
21:12 The righteous *man* wisely considereth the **h** 1004
24: 3 Through wisdom is a **h** builded; and 1004
24:27 in the field; and afterwards build thine **h**. 1004
25:17 Withdraw thy foot from thy neighbour's **h**; 1004
25:24 with a brawling woman and in a wide **h**. 1004
27:10 neither go *into* thy brother's **h** in the day of 1004
Ecc 2: 7 maidens, and had servants born in *my* **h**; 1004
5: 1 Keep thy foot when thou goest to the **h** of 1004
7: 2 *It is* better to go to the **h** of mourning, 1004
7: 2 of mourning, than to go to the **h** of feasting: 1004
7: 4 The heart of the wise *is* in the **h** of 1004
7: 4 but the heart of fools *is* in the **h** of mirth. 1004
10:18 through idleness of the hands the **h** 1004
12: 3 In the day when the keepers of the **h** shall 1004
SS 1:17 The beams of our **h** *are* cedar, *and* 1004
2: 4 He brought me to the banqueting **h**, and 1004
3: 4 until I had brought him into my mother's **h**, 1004
8: 2 *and* bring thee into my mother's **h**, 1004
8: 7 give all the substance of his **h** for love, 1004
Isa 2: 2 *that* the mountain of the LORD'S **h** shall 1004
2: 3 the LORD, to the **h** of the God of Jacob; 1004
2: 5 O **h** of Jacob, come ye, and let us walk in 1004
2: 6 hast forsaken thy people the **h** of Jacob, 1004
3: 6 hold of his brother *of* the **h** of his father, 1004
3: 7 for in my **h** *is* neither bread nor clothing: 1004
5: 7 of the LORD of hosts *is* the **h** of Israel, 1004
5: 8 Woe unto them that join **h** to house, 1004
5: 8 Woe unto them that join house to **h**, 1004
6: 4 that cried, and the **h** was filled *with* smoke. 1004
7: 2 it was told the **h** of David, saying, Syria is 1004
7:13 he said, Hear ye now, O **h** of David; *Is it* a 1004
7:17 upon thy people, and upon thy father's **h**, 1004
8:17 that hideth his face from the **h** of Jacob, 1004
10:20 and such as are escaped of the **h** of Jacob, 1004
14: 1 and they shall cleave to the **h** of Jacob. 1004
14: 2 the **h** of Israel shall possess them in 1004
14:17 *that* opened not the **h** of his prisoners? 1004
14:18 lie in glory, every one in his own **h**. 1004
22: 8 that day to the armour of the **h** of the forest. 1004
22:15 unto Shebna, which *is* over the **h**, *and say,* 1004
22:18 thy glory *shall be* the shame of thy lord's **h**. 1004
22:21 of Jerusalem, and to the **h** of Judah. 1004
22:22 the key of the **h** of David will I lay upon his 1004
22:23 be for a glorious throne to his father's **h**. 1004
22:24 upon him all the glory of his father's **h**, 1004
23: 1 so that *there is* no **h**, no entering in: 1004
24:10 every **h** is shut up, that no *man may* come 1004
29:22 concerning the **h** of Jacob, 1004
31: 2 will arise against the **h** of the evildoers, and 1004
36: 3 which *was* over the **h**, and Shebna 1004
37: 1 and went *into* the **h** of the LORD. 1004
37:14 Hezekiah went up *unto* the **h** of 1004
37:31 the remnant that is escaped of the **h** of 1004
37:38 as he was worshipping *in* the **h** of Nisroch 1004
38: 1 Thus saith the LORD, Set thine **h** in order: 1004
38:20 the days of our life in the **h** of the LORD. 1004
38:22 What *is* the sign that I shall go up *to* the **h** 1004
39: 2 shewed them the **h** of his precious things, 1004
39: 2 all the **h** of his armour, and all that was 1004
39: 2 there was nothing in his **h**, nor in all his 1004
39: 4 said he, What have they seen in thine **h**? 1004
39: 4 All that *is* in mine **h** have they seen: 1004
39: 6 that all that *is* in thine **h**, and *that* which thy 1004
42: 7 that sit in darkness out of the prison **h**. 1004
44:13 of a man; that it may remain *in* the **h**. 1004
46: 3 O **h** of Jacob, and all the remnant of 1004
46: 3 and all the remnant of the **h** of Israel, 1004
48: 1 Hear ye this, O **h** of Jacob, which are called 1004
56: 5 Even unto them will I give in mine **h** and 1004
56: 7 and make them joyful in my **h** of prayer: 1004
56: 7 for mine **h** shall be called a house of prayer 1004
56: 7 for mine house shall be called a **h** of prayer 1004
58: 1 and the **h** of Jacob their sins. 1004
58: 7 bring the poor that are cast out *to thy* **h**? 1004
60: 7 and I will glorify the **h** of my glory. 1004
63: 7 the great goodness towards the **h** of Israel, 1004
64:11 Our holy and our beautiful **h**, where our 1004
66: 1 where *is* the **h** that ye build unto me? 1004
66:20 in a clean vessel *into* the **h** of the LORD. 1004
Jer 2: 4 O **h** of Jacob, and all the families of 1004
2: 4 and all the families of the **h** of Israel: 1004
2:26 he is found, so is the **h** of Israel ashamed; 1004
3:18 In those days the **h** of Judah shall walk with 1004
3:18 of Judah shall walk with the **h** of Israel, 1004
3:20 with me, O **h** of Israel, saith the LORD. 1004
5:11 For the **h** of Israel and the house of Judah 1004
5:11 the **h** of Judah have dealt very 1004
5:15 from far, O **h** of Israel, saith the LORD: 1004
5:20 Declare this in the **h** of Jacob, and 1004
7: 2 Stand in the gate of the LORD'S **h**, and 1004
7:10 come and stand before me in this **h**, which 1004
7:11 Is this **h**, which is called by my name, 1004
7:14 Therefore will I do unto *this* **h**, which is 1004
7:30 they have set their abominations in the **h** 1004
9:26 all the **h** of Israel *are* uncircumcised in 1004
10: 1 LORD speaketh unto you, O **h** of Israel: 1004
11:10 the **h** of Israel and the house of Judah have 1004
11:10 the **h** of Judah have broken my covenant 1004
11:15 What hath my beloved to do in mine **h**, 1004
11:17 for the evil of the **h** of Israel and of 1004
11:17 of the house of Israel and of the **h** of Judah, 1004
12: 6 even thy brethren, and the **h** of thy father, 1004
12: 7 I have forsaken mine **h**, I have left mine 1004
12:14 pluck out the **h** of Judah from among them. 1004
13:11 to cleave unto me the whole **h** of Israel 1004
13:11 house of Israel and the whole **h** of Judah, 1004
16: 5 Enter not *into* the **h** of mourning, 1004
16: 8 Thou shalt not also go *into* the **h** of 1004
17:26 *of* praise, *unto* the **h** of the LORD. 1004
18: 2 go down *to* the potter's **h**, and there I will 1004
18: 3 I went down *to* the potter's **h**, and behold, 1004
18: 6 O **h** of Israel, cannot I do with you as this 1004
18: 6 so *are* ye in mine hand, O **h** of Israel. 1004
19:14 he stood in the court of the LORD'S **h**; 1004
20: 1 who *was* also chief governor in the **h** of 1004
20: 2 which *was* by the **h** of the LORD. 1004
20: 6 all that dwell in thine **h** shall go into 1004
21:11 touching the **h** of the king of Judah, 1004
21:12 O **h** of David, thus saith the LORD; 1004
22: 1 Go down *to* the **h** of the king of Judah, and 1004
22: 4 shall there enter in by the gates of this **h** 1004
22: 5 that this **h** shall become a desolation. 1004
22: 6 For thus saith the LORD unto the king's **h** 1004
22:13 Woe unto him that buildeth his **h** by 1004
22:14 I will build me a wide **h** and 1004
23: 8 which led the seed of the **h** of Israel out of 1004
23:11 yea, in my **h** have I found their wickedness, 1004
23:34 I will even punish that man and his **h**. 1004
26: 2 Stand in the court of the LORD'S **h**, and 1004
26: 2 which come to worship *in* the LORD'S **h**, 1004
26: 6 will I make this **h** like Shiloh, and will 1004
26: 7 these words in the **h** of the LORD. 1004
26: 9 This **h** shall be like Shiloh, and this city 1004
26: 9 against Jeremiah in the **h** of the LORD. 1004
26:10 they came up from the king's **h** *unto* 1004
26:10 the king's house *unto* the **h** of the LORD, 1004
26:10 entry of the new gate of the LORD'S *h*. NIH
26:12 LORD sent me to prophesy against this **h** 1004
26:18 the mountain of the **h** as the high places of 1004
27:16 the vessels of the LORD'S **h** *shall* now 1004
27:18 that the vessels which are left in the **h** of 1004
27:18 *in* the **h** of the king of Judah, and 1004
27:21 concerning the vessels that remain *in* the **h** 1004
27:21 *in* the **h** of the king of Judah and 1004

Jer	28: 1	spake unto me in the **h** of the LORD,	1004
	28: 3	this place all the vessels of the LORD'S **h**,	1004
	28: 5	people that stood in the **h** of the LORD,	1004
	28: 6	bring again the vessels of the LORD'S **h**,	1004
	29:26	that *ye* should be officers in the **h** of	1004
	31:27	that I will sow the **h** of Israel and the house	1004
	31:27	and the **h** of Judah *with* the seed of man,	1004
	31:31	that I will make a new covenant with the **h**	1004
	31:31	the house of Israel, and with the **h** of Judah:	1004
	31:33	that I will make with the **h** of Israel;	1004
	32: 2	which *was in* the king of Judah's **h**.	1004
	32:34	they set their abominations in the **h**,	1004
	33:11	sacrifice of praise *into* the **h** of the LORD.	1004
	33:14	which I have promised unto the **h** of Israel	1004
	33:14	the house of Israel and to the **h** of Judah.	1004
	33:17	to sit upon the throne of the **h** of Israel;	1004
	34:13	of Egypt, out of the **h** of bondmen, saying,	1004
	34:15	ye had made a covenant before me in the **h**	1004
	35: 2	Go unto the **h** of the Rechabites, and	1004
	35: 2	and bring them *into* the **h** of the LORD,	1004
	35: 3	his sons, and the whole **h** of the Rechabites;	1004
	35: 4	I brought them *into* the **h** of the LORD,	1004
	35: 5	I set before the sons of the **h** of	1004
	35: 7	Neither shall ye build **h**, nor sow seed,	1004
	35:18	Jeremiah said unto the **h** of the Rechabites,	1004
	36: 3	It may be that the **h** of Judah will hear all	1004
	36: 5	I cannot go *into* the **h** of the LORD:	1004
	36: 6	*in* the LORD'S **h** upon the fasting day:	1004
	36: 8	words of the LORD *in* the LORD'S **h**.	1004
	36:10	words of Jeremiah *in* the **h** of the LORD,	1004
	36:10	entry of the new gate of the LORD'S **h**,	1004
	36:12	he went down *into* the king's **h**, into	1004
	37:15	put him *in* prison *in* the **h** of Jonathan	1004
	37:17	and the king asked him secretly in his **h**,	1004
	37:20	that thou cause me not to return *to* the **h** of	1004
	38: 7	of the eunuchs which *was* in the king's **h**,	1004
	38: 8	Ebed-melech went forth out of the king's **h**,	1004
	38:11	went *into* the **h** of the king under	1004
	38:14	third entry that *is* in the **h** of the LORD:	1004
	38:17	with fire; and thou shalt live, and thine **h**:	1004
	38:22	**h** *shall be* brought forth to the king of	1004
	38:26	not cause me to return *to* Jonathan's **h**,	1004
	39: 8	the Chaldeans burnt the king's **h**, and	1004
	41: 5	to bring *them to* the **h** of the LORD.	1004
	43: 9	which *is* at the entry of Pharaoh's **h** in	1004
	48:13	as the **h** of Israel was ashamed of Beth-el	1004
	51:51	into the sanctuaries of the LORD'S **h**.	1004
	52:13	burnt the **h** of the LORD, and the king's	1004
	52:13	the house of the LORD, and the king's **h**;	1004
	52:17	Also the pillars of brass that *were* in the **h**	1004
	52:17	the brasen sea that *was* in the **h** of	1004
	52:20	which king Solomon had made in the **h** of	1004
La	2: 7	they have made a noise in the **h** of	1004
Eze	2: 5	will forbear, (for they *are* a rebellious **h**,)	1004
	2: 6	their looks, though they *be* a rebellious **h**.	1004
	2: 8	not thou rebellious like *that* rebellious **h**:	1004
	3: 1	this roll, and go speak unto the **h** of Israel.	1004
	3: 4	go, get thee unto the **h** of Israel, and	1004
	3: 5	of a hard language, *but* to the **h** of Israel;	1004
	3: 7	the **h** of Israel will not hearken unto thee;	1004
	3: 7	for all the **h** of Israel *are* impudent	1004
	3: 9	their looks, though they *be* a rebellious **h**.	1004
	3:17	I have made thee a watchman unto the **h** of	1004
	3:24	unto me, Go, shut thyself within thine **h**.	1004
	3:26	them a reprover: for they *are* a rebellious **h**.	1004
	3:27	let him forbear: for they *are* a rebellious **h**.	1004
	4: 3	This *shall be* a sign to the **h** of Israel.	1004
	4: 4	lay the iniquity of the **h** of Israel upon it:	1004
	4: 5	shalt thou bear the iniquity of the **h** of	1004
	4: 6	thou shalt bear the iniquity of the **h** of	1004
	5: 4	a fire come forth into all the **h** of Israel.	1004
	6:11	Alas for all the evil abominations of the **h**	1004
	8: 1	as I sat in mine **h**, and the elders of Judah	1004
	8: 6	*even* the great abominations that the **h** of	1004
	8:10	and all the idols of the **h** of Israel,	1004
	8:11	men of the ancients of the **h** of Israel,	1004
	8:12	hast thou seen what the ancients of the **h** of	1004
	8:14	LORD'S **h** which *was* towards the north;	1004
	8:16	me into the inner court of the LORD'S **h**,	1004
	8:17	Is it a light thing to the **h** of Judah that *they*	1004
	9: 3	he was, to the threshold of the **h**.	1004
	9: 6	at the ancient men which *were* before the **h**.	1004
	9: 7	Defile the **h**, and fill the courts *with*	1004
	9: 9	The iniquity of the **h** of Israel and Judah *is*	1004
	10: 3	cherubims stood on the right side of the **h**,	1004
	10: 4	*and stood* over the threshold of the **h**;	1004
	10: 4	the **h** was filled with the cloud, and	1004
	10:18	departed from off the threshold of the **h**,	1004
	10:19	the door of the east gate of the LORD'S **h**;	1004
	11: 1	me unto the east gate of the LORD'S **h**,	1004
	11: 5	Thus have ye said, O **h** of Israel:	1004
	11:15	thy kindred, and all the **h** of Israel wholly,	1004
	12: 2	thou dwellest in the midst of a rebellious **h**,	1004
	12: 2	and hear not: for they *are* a rebellious **h**.	1004
	12: 3	will consider, though they *be* a rebellious **h**.	1004
	12: 6	for I have set thee *for* a sign unto the **h** of	1004
	12: 9	Son of man, hath not the **h** of Israel,	1004
	12: 9	the rebellious **h**, said unto thee, What doest	1004
	12:10	and all the **h** of Israel that *are* among them.	1004
	12:24	flattering divination within the **h** of Israel.	1004
	12:25	for in your days, O rebellious **h**, will I say	1004
	12:27	of man, behold, *they of* the **h** of Israel say,	1004
	13: 5	neither made up the hedge for the **h** of	1004
	13: 9	be written in the writing of the **h** of Israel,	1004
	14: 4	Every man of the **h** of Israel that setteth up	1004
	14: 5	That *I* may take the **h** of Israel in their own	1004
	14: 6	Therefore say unto the **h** of Israel,	1004
	14: 7	For every one of the **h** of Israel, or of	1004
	14:11	That the **h** of Israel may go no more astray	1004
	17: 2	speak a parable unto the **h** of Israel;	1004
	17:12	Say now to the rebellious **h**, Know ye not	1004
	18: 6	up his eyes to the idols of the **h** of Israel,	1004
	18:15	up his eyes to the idols of the **h** of Israel,	1004
	18:25	Hear now, O **h** of Israel; Is not my way	1004
	18:29	Yet saith the **h** of Israel, The way of	1004
	18:29	O **h** of Israel, are not my ways equal?	1004
	18:30	Therefore I will judge you, O **h** of Israel,	1004
	18:31	for why will ye die, O **h** of Israel?	1004
	20: 5	lifted up mine hand unto the seed of the **h**	1004
	20:13	the **h** of Israel rebelled against me in	1004
	20:27	speak unto the **h** of Israel, and say unto	1004
	20:30	Wherefore say unto the **h** of Israel,	1004
	20:31	shall I be inquired of by you, O **h** of Israel?	1004
	20:39	As for you, O **h** of Israel, thus saith	1004
	20:40	Lord GOD, there shall all the **h** of Israel,	1004
	20:44	O ye **h** of Israel, saith the Lord GOD.	1004
	22:18	the **h** of Israel is to me become dross:	1004
	23:39	thus have they done in the midst of mine **h**.	1004
	24: 3	utter a parable unto the rebellious **h**, and	1004
	24:21	Speak unto the **h** of Israel, Thus saith	1004
	25: 3	against the **h** of Judah, when they went into	1004
	25: 8	the **h** of Judah *is* like unto all the heathen;	1004
	25:12	Because that Edom hath dealt against the **h**	1004
	27:14	They of the **h** of Togarmah traded in thy	1004
	28:24	more a pricking brier unto the **h** of Israel,	1004
	28:25	When I shall have gathered the **h** of Israel	1004
	29: 6	they have been a staff of reed to the **h** of	1004
	29:16	it shall be no more the confidence of the **h**	1004
	29:21	In that day will I cause the horn of the **h** of	1004
	33: 7	I have set thee a watchman unto the **h** of	1004
	33:10	thou son of man, speak unto the **h** of Israel;	1004
	33:11	for why will ye die, O **h** of Israel?	1004
	33:20	O ye **h** of Israel, I will judge you every one	1004
	34:30	*that* they, *even* the **h** of Israel, *are* my	1004
	35:15	rejoice at the inheritance of the **h** of Israel,	1004
	36:10	upon you, all the **h** of Israel, *even* all of it:	1004
	36:17	when the **h** of Israel dwelt in their own	1004
	36:21	which the **h** of Israel had profaned among	1004
	36:22	Therefore say unto the **h** of Israel,	1004
	36:22	O **h** of Israel, but for mine holy name's	1004
	36:32	for your own ways, O **h** of Israel.	1004
	36:37	I will yet *for* this be inquired of by the **h** of	1004
	37:11	these bones *are* the whole **h** of Israel:	1004
	37:16	and *for* all the **h** of Israel his companions:	1004
	38: 6	the **h** of Togarmah *of* the north quarters,	1004
	39:12	seven months shall the **h** of Israel be	1004
	39:22	So the **h** of Israel shall know that I *am*	1004
	39:23	the heathen shall know that the **h** of Israel	1004
	39:25	have mercy upon the whole **h** of Israel, and	1004
	39:29	for I have poured out my spirit upon the **h**	1004
	40: 4	declare all that thou seest to the **h** of Israel.	1004
	40: 5	behold a wall on the outside of the **h** round	1004
	40:45	the keepers of the charge of the **h**.	1004
	40:47	and the altar *that was* before the **h**.	1004
	40:48	he brought me to the porch of the **h**, and	1004
	41: 5	After he measured the wall of the **h**,	1004
	41: 5	round about the **h** on every side.	1004
	41: 6	of the **h** for the side chambers round about,	1004

Eze	41: 6	but they had not hold in the wall of the **h**.	1004
	41: 7	for the winding about of the **h** *went* still	1004
	41: 7	house *went* still upward round about the **h**:	1004
	41: 7	the breadth of the **h** *was still* upward,	1004
	41: 8	I saw also the height of the **h** round about:	1004
	41:10	cubits round about the **h** on every side.	1004
	41:13	So he measured the **h**, an hundred cubits	1004
	41:14	Also the breadth of the face of the **h**, and	1004
	41:17	even unto the inner **h**, and without, and	1004
	41:19	*it was* made through all the **h** round about.	1004
	41:26	*upon* the side chambers of the **h**, and thick	1004
	42:15	had made an end of measuring the inner **h**,	1004
	43: 4	the glory of the LORD came into the **h** by	1004
	43: 5	the glory of the LORD filled the **h**.	1004
	43: 6	I heard *him* speaking unto me out of the **h**;	1004
	43: 7	shall the **h** of Israel no more defile,	1004
	43:10	of man, shew the **h** to the house of Israel,	1004
	43:10	of man, shew the house to the **h** of Israel,	1004
	43:11	shew them the form of the **h**, and	1004
	43:12	This *is* the law of the **h**; Upon the top of	1004
	43:12	most holy. Behold, this *is* the law of the **h**.	1004
	43:21	shall burn it in the appointed place of the **h**,	1004
	44: 4	me the way of the north gate before the **h**:	1004
	44: 4	the glory of the LORD filled the **h** of	1004
	44: 5	all the ordinances of the **h** of the LORD,	1004
	44: 5	mark well the entering in of the **h**,	1004
	44: 6	*even* to the **h** of Israel, Thus saith the Lord	1004
	44: 6	O ye **h** of Israel, let it suffice you of all	1004
	44: 7	in my sanctuary, to pollute it, *even* my **h**,	1004
	44:11	*having* charge at the gates of the **h**, and	1004
	44:11	gates of the house, and ministering to the **h**:	1004
	44:12	caused the **h** of Israel to fall into iniquity;	1004
	44:14	make them keepers of the charge of the **h**,	1004
	44:22	they shall take maidens of the seed of the **h**	1004
	44:30	he may cause the blessing to rest in thine **h**.	1004
	45: 5	the ministers of the **h**, have for themselves,	1004
	45: 6	*portion:* it shall be for the whole **h** of Israel.	1004
	45: 8	*the rest of* the land shall they give to the **h**	1004
	45:17	in the sabbaths in all solemnities of the **h** of	1004
	45:17	to make reconciliation for the **h** of Israel.	1004
	45:19	put *it* upon the posts of the **h**, and upon	1004
	45:20	*that is* simple: so shall ye reconcile the **h**.	1004
	46:24	where the ministers of the **h** shall boil	1004
	47: 1	he brought me again unto the door of the **h**;	1004
	47: 1	from under the threshold of the **h** eastward:	1004
	47: 1	for the forefront of the **h** *stood toward*	1004
	47: 1	from under from the right side of the **h**,	1004
	48:21	the sanctuary of the **h** *shall be* in the midst	1004
Da	1: 2	with part of the vessels of the **h** of God:	1004
	1: 2	*into* the land of Shinar *to* the **h** of his god;	1004
	1: 2	he brought the vessels *into* the treasure **h** of	1004
	2:17	Daniel went to his **h**, and made the thing	1005
	4: 4	I Nebuchadnezzar was at rest in mine **h**,	1005
	4:30	that I have built for the **h** of the kingdom	1005
	5: 3	of the **h** of God which *was* at Jerusalem;	1005
	5:10	and his lords, came into the banquet **h**:	1005
	5:23	they have brought the vessels of his **h**	1005
	6:10	the writing *was* signed, he went into his **h**;	1005
Hos	1: 4	the blood of Jezreel upon the **h** of Jehu,	1004
	1: 4	will cause to cease the kingdom of the **h** of	1004
	1: 6	for I will no more have mercy upon the **h**	1004
	1: 7	I will have mercy upon the **h** of Judah, and	1004
	5: 1	and hearken, ye **h** of Israel; and give ye ear,	1004
	5: 1	of Israel; and give ye ear, O **h** of the king;	1004
	5:12	a moth, and to the **h** of Judah as rottenness.	1004
	5:14	and as a young lion to the **h** of Judah:	1004
	6:10	I have seen a horrible thing in the **h** of	1004
	8: 1	*He shall come* as an eagle against the **h** of	1004
	9: 4	shall not come *into* the **h** of the LORD.	1004
	9: 8	all his ways, *and* hatred in the **h** of his God.	1004
	9:15	doings I will drive them out of mine **h**,	1004
	11:12	with lies, and the **h** of Israel with deceit:	1004
Joel	1: 9	the drink offering is cut off from the **h** of	1004
	1:13	the drink offering is withholden from the **h**	1004
	1:14	all the inhabitants of the land *into* the **h** of	1004
	1:16	and gladness from the **h** of our God?	1004
	3:18	a fountain shall come forth of the **h** of	1004
Am	1: 4	I will send a fire into the **h** of Hazael,	1004
	1: 5	him that holdeth the sceptre from the **h** of	1004
	2: 8	of the condemned *in* the **h** of their god.	1004
	3:13	Hear ye, and testify in the **h** of Jacob,	1004
	3:15	I will smite the winter **h** with the summer	1004
	3:15	smite the winter house with the summer **h**;	1004
	5: 1	*even* a lamentation, O **h** of Israel.	1004
	5: 3	hundred shall leave ten, to the **h** of Israel.	1004
	5: 4	For thus saith the LORD unto the **h** of	1004
	5: 6	lest he break out like fire *in* the **h** of Joseph,	1004
	5:19	or went *into* the **h**, and leaned his hand on	1004
	5:25	in the wilderness forty years, O **h** of Israel?	1004
	6: 1	the nations, to whom the **h** of Israel came!	1004
	6: 9	if there remain ten men in one **h**, that they	1004
	6:10	to bring out the bones out of the **h**, and	1004
	6:10	say unto *him* that *is* by the sides of the **h**,	1004
	6:11	he will smite the great **h** *with* breaches, and	1004
	6:11	*with* breaches, and the little **h** *with* clefts.	1004
	6:14	O **h** of Israel, saith the LORD the God of	1004
	7: 9	I will rise against the **h** of Jeroboam with	1004
	7:10	against thee in the midst of the **h** of Israel:	1004
	7:16	drop not *thy word* against the **h** of Isaac.	1004
	9: 8	saving that I will not utterly destroy the **h**	1004
	9: 9	I will sift the **h** of Israel among all nations,	1004
Ob	1:17	the **h** of Jacob shall possess their	1004
	1:18	the **h** of Jacob shall be a fire, and the house	1004
	1:18	the **h** of Joseph a flame, and the house of	1004
	1:18	the **h** of Esau for stubble, and they shall	1004
	1:18	there shall not be *any* remaining of the **h** of	1004
Mic	1: 5	*is* all this, and for the sins of the **h** of Israel.	1004
	2: 2	so they oppress a man and his **h**, even a	1004
	2: 7	O *thou that art* named the **h** of Jacob, is	1004
	3: 1	of Jacob, and ye princes of the **h** of Israel;	1004
	3: 9	ye heads of the **h** of Jacob, and princes of	1004
	3: 9	princes of the **h** of Israel, that abhor	1004
	3:12	the mountain of the **h** as the high places of	1004
	4: 1	*that* the mountain of the **h** of the LORD	1004
	4: 2	and to the **h** of the God of Jacob;	1004
	6: 4	and redeemed thee out of the **h** of servants;	1004
	6:10	of wickedness *in* the **h** of the wicked,	1004
	6:16	all the works of the **h** of Ahab, and ye walk	1004
	7: 6	a man's enemies *are* the men of his own **h**.	1004
Na	1:14	out of the **h** of thy gods will I cut off	1004
Hab	2: 9	that coveteth an evil covetousness to his **h**,	1004
	2:10	Thou hast consulted shame to thy **h** by	1004
	3:13	thou woundedst the head out of the **h** of	1004
Zep	2: 7	the coast shall be for the remnant of the **h**	1004
Hag	1: 2	the time that the LORD'S **h** should be	1004
	1: 4	in your cieled houses, and this **h** *lie* waste?	1004
	1: 8	and bring wood, and build the **h**;	1004
	1: 9	Because of mine **h** that *is* waste, and ye run	1004
	1: 9	and ye run every man unto his own **h**.	1004
	1:14	did work in the **h** of the LORD of hosts,	1004
	2: 3	Who *is* left among you that saw this **h** in	1004
	2: 7	I will fill this **h** *with* glory, saith	1004
	2: 9	The glory of this latter **h** shall be greater	1004
Zec	1:16	my **h** shall be built in it, saith the LORD	1004
	3: 7	thou shalt also judge my **h**, and shalt also	1004
	4: 9	have laid the foundation of this **h**;	1004
	5: 4	it shall enter into the **h** of the thief, and	1004
	5: 4	into the **h** of him that sweareth falsely by	1004
	5: 4	it shall remain in the midst of his **h**, and	1004
	5:11	To build it a **h** in the land of Shinar:	1004
	6:10	go *into* the **h** of Josiah the son of	1004
	7: 2	When they had sent *unto* the **h** of God	1004
	7: 3	*were* in the **h** of the LORD of hosts,	1004
	8: 9	of the **h** of the LORD of hosts was laid,	1004
	8:13	O **h** of Judah, and house of Israel;	1004
	8:13	O house of Judah, and **h** of Israel;	1004
	8:15	well unto Jerusalem and to the **h** of Judah:	1004
	8:19	shall be to the **h** of Judah joy and gladness,	1004
	9: 8	I will encamp about mine **h** because of	1004
	10: 3	hosts hath visited his flock the **h** of Judah,	1004
	10: 6	I will strengthen the **h** of Judah, and I will	1004
	10: 6	I will save the **h** of Joseph, and I will bring	1004
	11:13	cast them to the potter *in* the **h** of	1004
	12: 4	I will open mine eyes upon the **h** of Judah,	1004
	12: 7	that the glory of the **h** of David and	1004
	12: 8	the **h** of David *shall be* as God, as the angel	1004
	12:10	I will pour upon the **h** of David, and	1004
	12:12	the family of the **h** of David apart, and	1004
	12:12	the family of the **h** of Nathan apart,	1004
	12:13	The family of the **h** of Levi apart, and	1004
	13: 1	shall be a fountain opened to the **h** of David	1004
	13: 6	*Those with* which I was wounded *in* the **h**	1004
	14:20	the pots in the LORD'S **h** shall be like	1004
	14:21	Canaanite in the **h** of the LORD of hosts.	1004
Mal	3:10	that there may be meat in mine **h**, and	1004
Mt	2:11	And when they were come into the **h**,	*3614*
	5:15	and it giveth light unto all that are in the **h**.	*3614*
	7:24	a wise man, which built his **h** upon a rock:	*3614*

Mt 7:25 and the winds blew, and beat upon that **h**; *3614*
7:26 which built his **h** upon the sand: *3614*
7:27 and the winds blew, and beat upon that **h**; *3614*
8:14 And when Jesus was come into Peter's **h**, *3614*
9: 6 Arise, take up thy bed, and go unto thine **h**. *3624*
9: 7 And he arose, and departed to his **h**. *3624*
9:10 as Jesus sat at meat in the **h**, behold, *3614*
9:23 And when Jesus came into the ruler's **h**, *3614*
9:28 And when he was come into the **h**, *3614*
10: 6 But go rather to the lost sheep of the **h** of *3624*
10:12 And when ye come into a **h** salute it. *3614*
10:13 And if the **h** be worthy, let your peace *3614*
10:14 when ye depart out of that **h** or city, *3614*
10:25 If they have called the **master of the h** *3617*
12: 4 How he entered into the **h** of God, and *3624*
12:25 or **h** divided against itself shall not stand: *3614*
12:29 how can one enter into a strong *man's* **h**, *3614*
12:29 strong *man?* and then he will spoil his **h**. *3614*
12:44 I will return into my **h** from whence I came *3624*
13: 1 The same day went Jesus out of the **h**, and *3614*
13:36 the multitude away, and went into the **h**: *3614*
13:57 save in his own country, and in his own **h**. *3614*
15:24 but unto the lost sheep of the **h** of Israel. *3624*
17:25 And when he was come into the **h**, *3614*
20:11 murmured against the **goodman of the h**, *3617*
21:13 My **h** shall be called the house of prayer; *3624*
21:13 My house shall be called the **h** of prayer; *3624*
23:38 Behold, your **h** is left unto you desolate. *3624*
24:17 come down to take any *thing* out of his **h**: *3614*
24:43 that if the **goodman of the h** had known in *3617*
24:43 would not have suffered his **h** to be broken *3614*
26: 6 in Bethany, in the **h** of Simon the leper, *3614*
26:18 I will keep the passover at thy **h** with my NIG
Mk 1:29 they entered into the **h** of Simon and *3614*
2: 1 and it was noised that he was in the **h**. *3624*
2:11 up thy bed, and go thy way into thine **h**. *3624*
2:15 that as *Jesus* sat at meat in his **h**, *3614*
2:26 How he went into the **h** of God in the days *3624*
3:19 also betrayed him. And they went into a **h**. *3624*
3:25 And if a **h** be divided against itself, *3614*
3:25 divided against itself, that **h** cannot stand. *3614*
3:27 No *man* can enter into a strong *man's* **h**, *3614*
3:27 the strong *man;* and then he will spoil his **h**. *3614*
5:35 of the synagogue's *h certain* which said, NIG
5:38 And he cometh to the **h** of the ruler of *3624*
6: 4 and among his own kin, and in his own **h**. *3614*
6:10 In what place soever ye enter into a **h**, *3614*
7:17 And when he was entered into *the* **h** from *3624*
7:24 and entered into a **h**, and would have no *3614*
7:30 And when she was come to her **h**, *3624*
8:26 And he sent him away to his **h**, saying, *3624*
9:28 And when he was come into *the* **h**, *3624*
9:33 and being in the **h** he asked them, *3614*
10:10 And in the **h** his disciples asked him again *3614*
10:29 There is no *man* that hath left **h**, or *3614*
11:17 My **h** shall be called of all nations *3624*
11:17 be called of all nations the **h** of prayer? *3624*
13:15 is on the housetop not go down into the **h**, *3614*
13:15 enter *therein,* to take any *thing* out of his **h**: *3614*
13:34 who left his **h**, and gave authority to his *3614*
13:35 for ye know not when the master of the **h** *3614*
14: 3 And being in Bethany in the **h** of Simon *3614*
14:14 say ye to the **goodman of the h**, The *3617*
Lk 1:23 he departed to his own **h**. *3624*
1:27 whose name was Joseph, of the **h** of David; *3624*
1:33 And he shall reign over the **h** of Jacob for *3624*
1:40 And entered into the **h** of Zacharias, and *3624*
1:56 three months, and returned to her own **h**. *3624*
1:69 for us in the **h** of his servant David; *3624*
2: 4 (because he was of the **h** and lineage of *3624*
4:38 the synagogue, and entered into Simon's **h**. *3614*
5:24 and take up thy couch, and go into thine **h**. *3624*
5:25 and departed to his own **h**, glorifying God. *3624*
5:29 Levi made him a great feast in his own **h**: *3614*
6: 4 How he went into the **h** of God, and *3624*
6:48 He is like a man which built a **h**, and *3614*
6:48 the stream beat vehemently upon that **h**, *3614*
6:49 a foundation built a **h** upon the earth; *3614*
6:49 it fell; and the ruin of that **h** was great. *3614*
7: 6 And when he was now not far from the **h**, *3614*
7:10 And they that were sent, returning to the **h**, *3624*
7:36 And he went into the Pharisee's **h**, *3614*
7:37 that *Jesus* sat at meat in the Pharisee's **h**, *3614*
7:44 I entered into thine **h**, thou gavest me no *3614*
8:27 neither abode in *any* **h**, but in the tombs. *3614*
8:39 Return to thine own **h**, and shew how great *3624*
8:41 him that *he* would come into his **h**: *3624*
8:49 ruler of the synagogue's *h*, saying to him, NIG
8:51 And when he came into the **h**, he suffered *3614*
9: 4 And whatsoever **h** ye enter into, *3614*
9:61 them farewell, which are *at home* in my **h**. *3624*
10: 5 And into whatsoever **h** ye enter, first say, *3614*
10: 5 house ye enter, first say, Peace *be* to this **h**. *3624*
10: 7 And in the same **h** remain, eating and *3614*
10: 7 worthy of his hire. Go not from **h** to house. *3614*
10: 7 worthy of his hire. Go not from house to **h**. *3614*
10:38 named Martha received him into her **h**. *3624*
11:17 and a **h** *divided* against a house falleth. *3624*
11:17 and a house *divided* against a **h** falleth. *3624*
11:24 I will return unto my **h** whence I came out. *3624*
12:39 that if the **goodman of the h** had known *3617*
12:39 not have suffered his **h** to be broken *3624*
12:52 there shall be five in one **h** divided, *3624*
13:25 When once the **master of the h** is risen up, *3617*
13:35 Behold, your **h** is left unto you desolate: *3624*
14: 1 as he went into the **h** of one of the chief *3624*
14:21 **master of the h** being angry said to his *3617*
14:23 *them* to come in, that my **h** may be filled. *3624*
15: 8 and sweep the **h**, and seek diligently till *3614*
15:25 and as he came and drew nigh to the **h**, *3614*
16:27 thou wouldest send him to my father's **h**: *3624*
17:31 be upon the housetop, and his stuff in the **h**, *3614*
18:14 this man went down to his **h** justified *rather* *3624*
18:29 There is no *man* that hath left **h**, or parents, *3614*
19: 5 for to day I must abide at thy **h**. *3624*
19: 9 This day is salvation come to this **h**, *3624*
19:46 It is written, My **h** is the house of prayer: *3624*
19:46 It is written, My house is the **h** of prayer: *3624*
22:10 follow him into the **h** where he entereth in. *3614*
22:11 ye shall say unto the goodman of the **h**, *3614*
22:54 and brought him into the high priest's **h**. *3624*
Jn 2:16 make not my Father's **h** a house of *3624*
2:16 make not my Father's house a **h** of *3624*
2:17 The zeal of thine **h** hath eaten me up. *3624*
4:53 and himself believed, and his whole **h**. *3614*
7:53 And every man went unto his own **h**. *3624*
8:35 And the servant abideth not in the **h** for *3614*
11:20 and met him: but Mary sat *still* in the **h**. *3624*
11:31 then which were with her in the **h**, *3614*
12: 3 the **h** was filled with the odour of *3614*
14: 2 In my Father's **h** are many mansions: if *it* *3614*
Ac 2: 2 it filled all the **h** where they were sitting. *3624*
2:36 Therefore let all the **h** of Israel know *3624*
2:46 and breaking bread **from h to house**, *2596+3624*
2:46 and breaking bread **from house to h**, *2596+3624*
5:42 and **in every h**, they ceased not to *2596+3624*
7:10 him governor over Egypt and all his **h**. *3624*
7:20 nourished up in his father's **h** three months: *3624*
7:42 O *ye* **h** of Israel, have ye offered to me *3624*
7:47 But Solomon built him a **h**. *3624*
7:49 what **h** will ye build me? saith the Lord: or *3624*
8: 3 of the church, entering into **every h**, *2596+3624*
9:11 inquire in the **h** of Judas for *one* called *3614*
9:17 went his way, and entered into the **h**; *3614*
10: 2 and one that feared God with all his **h**, *3624*
10: 6 Simon a tanner, whose **h** is by the sea side: *3614*
10: 9 Peter went up upon the **h** to pray about *1430*
10:17 Cornelius had made inquiry for Simon's **h**, *3614*
10:22 by a holy angel to send for thee into his **h**, *3624*
10:30 and at the ninth hour I prayed in my **h**, and *3624*
10:32 he is lodged in the **h** of *one* Simon a tanner *3614*
11:11 men already come unto the **h** where I was, *3614*
11:12 and we entered into the man's **h**: *3624*
11:13 us how he had seen an angel in his **h**, *3624*
11:14 whereby thou and all thy **h** shall be saved. *3624*
12:12 came to the **h** of Mary the mother of John, *3614*
16:15 come into my **h**, and abide *there.* And she *3624*
16:31 and thou shalt be saved, and thy **h**. *3624*
16:32 of the Lord, and to all that were in his **h**. *3614*
16:34 And when he had brought them into his **h**, *3624*
16:34 rejoiced, believing in God with **all** his **h**. *3832*
16:40 the prison, and entered into *the h of* Lydia: NIG
17: 5 and assaulted the **h** of Jason, and sought to *3614*
18: 7 and entered into a certain *man's* **h**, *3614*
18: 7 whose **h** joined hard to the synagogue. *3614*
18: 8 believed on the Lord with all his **h**; *3624*
19:16 so that *they* fled out of that **h** naked and *3624*
20:20 you publickly, and **from h to house**, *2596+3624*

Ac 20:20 you publickly, and **from house to h**, 2596+3624
21: 8 we entered into the **h** of Philip 3624
28:30 dwelt two whole years in his own **hired h**, 3410
Ro 16: 5 Likewise *greet* the church that is in their **h**. 3624
1Co 1:11 by them which are of the *h* of Chloe, NIG
16:15 brethren, (ye know the **h** of Stephanas, 3614
16:19 the Lord, with the church that is in their **h**. 3624
2Co 5: 1 For we know that if our earthly **h** of *this* 3614
5: 1 a **h** not made with hand, eternal in 3614
5: 2 upon with our **h** which is from heaven: 3613
Col 4:15 Nymphas, and the church which is in his **h**. 3624
1Ti 3: 4 One that ruleth well his own **h**, having *his* 3624
3: 5 if a man know not how to rule his own **h**, 3624
3:15 oughtest to behave thyself in the **h** of God, 3624
5: 8 and specially for those of his own **h**, 3609
5:13 wandering about **from h to house**; 3588+3614
5:13 wandering about **from house to h**; 3588+3614
5:14 *women* marry, bear children, **guide the h**, 3616
2Ti 1:16 The Lord give mercy unto the **h** of 3624
2:20 But in a great **h** there are not only vessels 3614
Phm 1: 2 and to the church in thy **h**: 3624
Heb 3: 2 as also Moses *was faithful* in all his **h**. 3624
3: 3 inasmuch as he who hath builded **the h**s 846
3: 3 the house hath more honour than the **h**. 3624
3: 4 For every **h** is builded by some *man;* but 3624
3: 5 And Moses verily *was* faithful in all his **h**, 3624
3: 6 But Christ as a Son over his own **h**; 3624
3: 6 whose **h** are we, if we hold fast 3624
8: 8 make a new covenant with the **h** of Israel 3624
8: 8 the house of Israel and with the **h** of Juda: 3624
8:10 make with the **h** of Israel after those days, 3624
10:21 And *having* a high priest over the **h** of God; 3624
11: 7 prepared an ark to the saving of his **h**; 3624
1Pe 2: 5 as lively stones, are built *up* a spiritual **h**, 3624
4:17 that judgment must begin at the **h** of God: 3624
2Jn 1:10 this doctrine, receive him not into *your* **h**, 3614

HOUSE OF APHRAH (1) [HOUSE]

Mic 1:10 in the **h** roll thyself *in* the dust. 1036

HOUSEHOLD (61) [HOUSE]

Ge 18:19 command his children and his **h** after him, 1004
31:37 what hast thou found of all thy **h** stuff? 1004
35: 2 Jacob said unto his **h**, and to all that *were* 1004
45:11 lest thou, and thy **h**, and all that thou hast, 1004
47:12 and all his father's **h**, *with* bread, 1004
Ex 1: 1 every man and his **h** came with Jacob. 1004
12: 4 if the **h** be too little for the lamb, let him 1004
Lev 16:17 for his **h**, and for all the congregation of 1004
Dt 6:22 upon Pharaoh, and upon all his **h**, 1004
14:26 and thou shalt rejoice, thou and thine **h**, 1004
15:20 the LORD shall choose, thou and thy **h**. 1004
Jos 2:18 and thy brethren, and all thy father's **h**, 1004
6:25 and her father's **h**, and all that she had; 1004
7:14 the **h** which the LORD shall take shall 1004
7:18 he brought his **h** man by man; and Achan, 1004
Jdg 6:27 because he feared his father's **h**, and 1004
18:25 thou lose thy life, with the lives of thy **h**. 1004
1Sa 25:17 against our master, and against all his **h**: 1004
27: 3 he and his men, every man with his **h**, 1004
2Sa 2: 3 did David bring up, every man with his **h**: 1004
6:11 LORD blessed Obed-edom, and all his **h**. 1004
6:20 David returned to bless his **h**. And Michal 1004
15:16 the king went forth, and all his **h** after him. 1004
16: 2 The asses *be* for the king's **h** to ride on; 1004
17:23 put his **h** in order, and hanged himself, and 1004
19:18 over a ferry boat to carry over the king's **h**, 1004
19:41 his **h**, and all David's men with him, 1004
1Ki 4: 6 Ahishar *was* over the **h**: and Adoniram 1004
4: 7 provided victuals for the king and his **h**: 1004
5: 9 my desire, in giving food for my **h**. 1004
5:11 measures of wheat *for* food to his **h**, 1004
11:20 Genubath was *in* Pharaoh's **h** among 1004
2Ki 7: 9 come, that we may go and tell the king's **h**. 1004
8: 1 go thou and thine **h**, and 1004
8: 2 she went with her **h**, and sojourned in 1004
18:18 which *was* over the **h**, and Shebna 1004
18:37 which *was* over the **h**, and Shebna 1004
19: 2 which *was* over the **h**, and Shebna 1004
1Ch 24: 6 one principal **h** being taken for Eleazar, and 1004
Ne 13: 8 I cast forth all the **h** stuff of Tobiah out of 1004
Job 1: 3 five hundred she asses, and a very great **h**; 5657
Pr 27:27 for the food of thy **h**, and *for* 1004
31:15 giveth meat to her **h**, and a portion to her 1004
31:21 She is not afraid of the snow for her **h**: 1004
31:21 for all her **h** *are* clothed with scarlet. 1004
31:27 She looketh well to the ways of her **h**, and 1004
Isa 36:22 that *was* over the **h**, and Shebna the scribe, 1004
37: 2 who *was* over the **h**, and Shebna the scribe, 1004
Mt 10:25 much more *shall they call* them **of** his **h**? 3615
10:36 a man's foes *shall be* they **of** his own **h**. 3615
24:45 whom his lord hath made ruler over his **h**, 2322
Lk 12:42 whom *his* lord shall make ruler over his **h**, 2322
Ac 10: 7 he called two of his **h servants**, and 3610
16:15 and her **h**, she besought *us,* saying, 3624
Ro 16:10 Salute them which are of Aristobulus' *h*. NIG
16:11 Greet them that be of the *h* of Narcissus, NIG
1Co 1:16 And I baptized also the **h** of Stephanas: 3624
Gal 6:10 unto them who are of the **h** of faith. 3609
Eph 2:19 with the saints, and **of** the **h** of God; 3609
Php 4:22 chiefly they that are of Cesar's **h**. 3614
2Ti 4:19 and Aquila, and the **h** of Onesiphorus. 3624

HOUSEHOLDER (4) [HOUSE]

Mt 13:27 So the servants of the **h** came and said unto 3617
13:52 of heaven is like unto a man *that is* a **h**, 3617
20: 1 of heaven is like unto a man *that is* a **h**, 3617
21:33 There was a certain **h**, which planted a 444+3617

HOUSEHOLDS (7) [HOUSE]

Ge 42:33 take *food for* the famine of your **h**, and 1004
45:18 take your father and your **h**, and come unto 1004
47:24 for them of your **h**, and for food for your 1004
Nu 18:31 ye shall eat it in every place, ye and your **h**: 1004
Dt 11: 6 their **h**, and their tents, and all 1004
12: 7 ye and your **h**, where*in* the LORD thy 1004
Jos 7:14 the LORD shall take shall come by **h**; 1004

HOUSES (136) [HOUSE]

Ge 42:19 go ye, carry corn *for* the famine of your **h**: 1004
Ex 1:21 midwives feared God, that he made them **h**. 1004
6:14 These *be* the heads of their fathers' **h**: 1004
8: 9 to destroy the frogs from thee and thy **h**, 1004
8:11 from thy **h**, and from thy servants, and 1004
8:13 the frogs died out of the **h**, out of 1004
8:21 and upon thy people, and into thy **h**: 1004
8:21 the **h** of the Egyptians shall be full of 1004
8:24 *into* his servants' **h**, and into all the land of 1004
9:20 his servants and his cattle flee into the **h**: 1004
10: 6 they shall fill thy **h**, and the houses of all 1004
10: 6 the **h** of all thy servants, and the houses of 1004
10: 6 thy servants, and the **h** of all the Egyptians; 1004
12: 7 and on the upper door post of the **h**, 1004
12:13 you for a token upon the **h** where you *are:* 1004
12:15 day ye shall put away leaven out of your **h**: 1004
12:19 shall there be no leaven found in your **h**: 1004
12:23 to come in unto your **h** to smite *you.* 1004
12:27 who passed over the **h** of the children of 1004
12:27 smote the Egyptians, and delivered our **h**. 1004
Lev 25:31 the **h** of the villages which have no wall 1004
25:32 *and* the **h** of the cities of their possession, 1004
25:33 for the **h** of the cities of the Levites *are* 1004
Nu 4:22 throughout the **h** of their fathers, by their 1004
16:32 their **h**, and all the men that *appertained* 1004
17: 6 according to their fathers' **h**, *even* twelve 1004
32:18 We will not return unto our **h**, until 1004
Dt 6:11 **h** full *of* all good *things,* which thou filledst 1004
8:12 and hast built goodly **h**, and dwelt *therein;* 1004
19: 1 and dwellest in their cities, and in their **h**; 1004
Jos 9:12 **h** on the day we came forth to go unto you; 1004
Jdg 18:14 Do ye know that there is in these **h** an 1004
18:22 the men that *were* in the **h** near to Micah's 1004
1Ki 9:10 when Solomon had built the two **h**, 1004
13:32 against all the **h** of the high places which 1004
20: 6 thine house, and the **h** of thy servants; 1004
2Ki 17:29 put *them* in the **h** of the high places which 1004
17:32 which sacrificed for them in the **h** of 1004
23: 7 he brake down the **h** of the sodomites, 1004
23:19 all the **h** also of the high places that *were* in 1004
25: 9 all the **h** of Jerusalem, and every great 1004
1Ch 15: 1 *David* made him **h** in the city of David, 1004
28:11 of the **h** thereof, and of the treasuries 1004
29: 4 to overlay the walls of the **h** *withal:* 1004
2Ch 25: 5 according to the **h** of *their* fathers, 1004
34:11 to floor the **h** which the kings of Judah had 1004
35: 4 prepare *yourselves* by the **h** of your fathers, 1004
Ne 4:14 your daughters, your wives, and your **h**. 1004
5: 3 vineyards, and **h**, that we might buy corn, 1004

Ne 5:11 their oliveyards, and their **h**, 1004
7: 4 few therein, and the **h** *were* not builded, 1004
9:25 a fat land, and possessed **h** full *of* all goods, 1004
10:34 after the **h** of our fathers, at times appointed 1004
Job 1: 4 his sons went and feasted *in their* **h**, 1004
3:15 that had gold, who filled their **h** *with* silver: 1004
4:19 How much less *in* them that dwell in **h** of 1004
15:28 *and* in **h** which no man inhabiteth, 1004
21: 9 Their **h** *are* safe from fear, neither *is* the rod 1004
22:18 Yet he filled their **h** *with* good *things:* but 1004
24:16 In the dark *they* dig *through* **h**, *which* they 1004
Ps 49:11 Their inward *thought is, that* their **h** *shall* 1004
83:12 Let us take to ourselves the **h** of God in 4999
Pr 1:13 we shall fill our **h** *with* spoil: 1004
30:26 yet make they their **h** in the rocks; 1004
Ecc 2: 4 I builded me **h**; I planted me vineyards: 1004
Isa 3:14 the spoil of the poor *is* in your **h**. 1004
5: 9 Of a truth many **h** shall be desolate, 1004
6:11 the **h** without man, and the land be utterly 1004
8:14 for a rock of offence to both the **h** of Israel, 1004
13:16 their **h** shall be spoiled, and their wives 1004
13:21 their **h** shall be full *of* doleful creatures; 1004
13:22 of the islands shall cry in their **desolate h**, 490
15: 3 on the **tops of** their **h**, and in their streets, 1406
22:10 ye have numbered the **h** of Jerusalem, and 1004
22:10 the **h** have ye broken down to fortify 1004
32:13 yea, upon all the **h** of joy *in* the joyous city: 1004
42:22 in holes, and they are hid in prison **h**: 1004
65:21 they shall build **h**, and inhabit *them;* and 1004
Jer 5: 7 themselves by troops *in* the harlots' **h**. 1004
5:27 *is* full *of* birds, so *are* their **h** full *of* deceit: 1004
6:12 their **h** shall be turned unto others, 1004
17:22 Neither carry forth a burden out of your **h** 1004
18:22 Let a cry be heard from their **h**, when thou 1004
19:13 the **h** of Jerusalem, and the houses of 1004
19:13 and the **h** of the kings of Judah, 1004
19:13 of all the **h** upon whose roofs they have 1004
29: 5 Build ye **h**, and dwell *in them;* and 1004
29:28 build ye **h**, and dwell *in them;* and 1004
32:15 **H** and fields and vineyards shall be 1004
32:29 set fire on this city, and burn it with the **h**, 1004
33: 4 concerning the **h** of this city, 1004
33: 4 concerning the **h** of the kings of Judah, 1004
35: 9 Nor to build **h** for us to dwell in: 1004
39: 8 the **h** of the people, with fire, and brake 1004
43:12 I will kindle a fire in the **h** of the gods of 1004
43:13 the **h** of the gods of the Egyptians shall he 1004
52:13 all the **h** of Jerusalem, and all the houses of 1004
52:13 all the **h** of the great *men,* burnt he with 1004
La 5: 2 is turned to strangers, our **h** to aliens. 1004
Eze 7:24 the heathen, and they shall possess their **h**: 1004
11: 3 Which say, *It is* not near; *let us* build **h**: 1004
16:41 they shall burn thine **h** with fire, and 1004
23:47 and burn up their **h** with fire. 1004
26:12 down thy walls, and destroy thy pleasant **h**: 1004
28:26 shall build **h**, and plant vineyards; 1004
33:30 thee by the walls and in the doors of the **h**, 1004
45: 4 it shall be a place for their **h**, and a holy 1004
Da 2: 5 and your **h** shall be made a dunghill. 1005
3:29 and their **h** shall be made a dunghill: 1005
Hos 11:11 I will place them in their **h**, saith 1004
Joel 2: 9 the wall, they shall climb up upon the **h**; 1004
Am 3:15 the **h** of ivory shall perish, and the great 1004
3:15 the great **h** shall have an end, saith 1004
5:11 ye have built **h** of hewn stone, but ye shall 1004
Mic 1:14 the **h** of Achzib *shall be* a lie to the kings of 1004
2: 2 by violence; and **h**, and take *them* away: 1004
2: 9 have ye cast out from their pleasant **h**; 1004
Zep 1: 9 which fill their masters' **h** *with* violence 1004
1:13 become a booty, and their **h** a desolation: 1004
1:13 they shall also build **h**, but not inhabit 1004
2: 7 in the **h** of Ashkelon shall they lie down in 1004
Hag 1: 4 to dwell in your cieled **h**, and this house *lie* 1004
Zec 14: 2 and the **h** rifled, and the women ravished; 1004
Mt 11: 8 they that wear soft *clothing* are in kings' **h**. *3624*
19:29 And every one that hath forsaken **h**, or *3614*
23:14 for ye devour widows' **h**, and for a pretence *3614*
Mk 8: 3 if I send them away fasting to their own **h**, *3624*
10:30 **h**, and brethren, and sisters, and mothers, *3614*
12:40 Which devour widows' **h**, and for a *3614*
Lk 16: 4 they may receive me into their **h**. *3624*
20:47 Which devour widows' **h**, and for a shew *3614*
Ac 4:34 as were possessors of lands or **h** sold them, *3614*
1Co 11:22 have ye not **h** to eat and to drink *in?* or *3614*
1Ti 3:12 ruling *their* children and their own **h** well. *3624*
2Ti 3: 6 For of this sort are they which creep into **h**, *3614*
Tit 1:11 must be stopped, who subvert whole **h**, *3624*

HOUSETOP (7) [HOUSE, TOP]
Ps 102: 7 and am as a sparrow alone upon the **h**. 1406
Pr 21: 9 *It is* better to dwell in a corner of the **h**, 1406
25:24 *It is* better to dwell in a corner of the **h**, 1406
Mt 24:17 Let him which is on the **h** not come down *1430*
Mk 13:15 And let him that is on the **h** not go down *1430*
Lk 5:19 they went upon the **h**, and let him down *1430*
17:31 he which shall be upon the **h**, and his stuff *1430*

HOUSETOPS (8) [HOUSE, TOP]
2Ki 19:26 *as* the grass on the **h**, and *as* corn blasted 1406
Ps 129: 6 Let them be as the grass upon the **h**, 1406
Isa 22: 1 that thou art wholly gone up to the **h**? 1406
37:27 *as* the grass on the **h**, and *as* corn blasted 1406
Jer 48:38 generally upon all the **h** of Moab, 1406
Zep 1: 5 that worship the host of heaven upon the **h**; 1406
Mt 10:27 hear in the ear, *that* preach ye upon the **h**. *1430*
Lk 12: 3 in closets shall be proclaimed upon the **h**. *1430*

HOW (543) [HOWBEIT, HOWSOEVER] See Index

HOWBEIT (64) [BE, HOW, IT] See Index

H

HOWL (29) [HOWLED, HOWLING, HOWLINGS]
Isa 13: 6 **H** ye; for the day of the LORD *is* at hand; 3213
14:31 **H**, O gate; cry, O city; thou, 3213
15: 2 Moab shall **h** over Nebo, and over Medeba: 3213
15: 3 in their streets, every one shall **h**, weeping 3213
16: 7 Therefore shall Moab **h** for Moab, 3213
16: 7 Moab howl for Moab, every one shall **h**: 3213
23: 1 **H**, ye ships of Tarshish; for it is laid waste, 3213
23: 6 to Tarshish; **h**, ye inhabitants of the isle. 3213
23:14 **H**, ye ships of Tarshish: for your strength is 3213
52: 5 they that rule over them **make** *them* **to h**, 3213
65:14 of heart, and shall **h** for vexation of spirit. 3213
Jer 4: 8 this gird you with sackcloth, lament and **h**: 3213
25:34 **H**, ye shepherds, and cry; and 3213
47: 2 and all the inhabitants of the land shall **h**. 3213
48:20 **h** and cry; tell ye *it* in Arnon, that Moab is 3213
48:31 Therefore will I **h** for Moab, and I will cry 3213
48:39 They shall **h**, *saying,* How is it broken 3213
49: 3 **H**, O Heshbon, for Ai is spoiled: cry, 3213
51: 8 **h** for her; take balm for her pain, if so 3213
Eze 21:12 Cry and **h**, son of man: for it shall be upon 3213
30: 2 the Lord GOD; **H** ye, Woe worth the day! 3213
Joel 1: 5 **h**, all ye drinkers of wine, because of 3213
1:11 **h**, O ye vinedressers, for the wheat and 3213
1:13 **h**, ye ministers of the altar: come, lie all 3213
Mic 1: 8 Therefore I will wail and **h**, I will go stript 3213
Zep 1:11 **H**, ye inhabitants of Maktesh, for all 3213
Zec 11: 2 **H**, fir tree; for the cedar is fallen; because 3213
11: 2 **h**, O ye oaks of Bashan; for the forest of 3213
Jas 5: 1 **h** for your miseries that shall come upon *3649*

HOWLED (1) [HOWL]
Hos 7:14 their heart, when they **h** upon their beds: 3213

HOWLING (6) [HOWL]
Dt 32:10 desert land, and in the waste **h** wilderness; 3214
Isa 15: 8 the **h** thereof unto Eglaim, and the howling 3215
15: 8 and the **h** thereof *unto* Beer-elim. 3215
Jer 25:36 and a **h** of the principal of the flock, 3215
Zep 1:10 a **h** from the second, and a great crashing 3215
Zec 11: 3 *There is* a voice of the **h** of the shepherds; 3215

HOWLINGS (1) [HOWL]
Am 8: 3 the songs of the temple shall be **h** in that 3213

HOWSOEVER (4) [EVER, HOW, SO]
Jdg 19:20 with thee; **h** *let* all thy wants *lie* upon me; 7535
2Sa 18:22 **h**, let me, I pray thee, also run after Cushi. 4100
18:23 **h**, *said he,* let me run. And he said unto 4100
Zep 3: 7 not be cut off, **h** I punished them: 834+3605

HUB See NAVES

HUGE (1)
2Ch 16: 8 and the Lubims a **h** host, 7230+3807.1

HUGE FISH See WHALE; WHALE'S; WHALES

HUKKOK (1)
Jos 19:34 goeth out from thence to **H**, and reacheth to 2712

HUKOK (1)
1Ch 6:75 **H** with her suburbs, and Rehob with her 2712

HUL (2)
Ge 10:23 Uz, and **H**, and Gether, and Mash. 2343
1Ch 1:17 and Uz, and **H**, and Gether, and Meshech. 2343

HULDAH (2)
2Ki 22:14 and Asahiah, went unto **H** the prophetess, 2468
2Ch 34:22 *they* that the king *had appointed*, went to **H** 2468

HUMBLE (25) [HUMBLED, HUMBLEDST, HUMBLENESS, HUMBLETH, HUMBLY]
Ex 10: 3 How long wilt thou refuse to **h** thyself 6031
Dt 8: 2 to **h** thee, *and* to prove thee, to know what 6031
8:16 that he might **h** thee, and that he might 6031
Jdg 19:24 **h** ye them, and do with them what seemeth 6031
2Ch 7:14 shall **h** themselves, and pray, and seek my 3665
34:27 and thou didst **h** thyself before God, 3665
Job 22:29 and he shall save the **h person**. 5869+7807
Ps 9:12 he forgetteth not the cry of the **h**. 6035
10:12 O God, lift up thine hand: forget not the **h**. 6035
10:17 LORD, thou hast heard the desire of the **h**: 6035
34: 2 the **h** shall hear *thereof*, and be glad. 6035
69:32 The **h** shall see *this, and* be glad: and 6035
Pr 6: 3 go, **h** thyself, and make sure thy friend. 7511
16:19 Better *it is to be* of an **h** spirit with 8217
29:23 but honour shall uphold the **h** in spirit. 8217
Isa 57:15 him also *that is* of a contrite and **h** spirit, 8217
57:15 to revive the spirit of the **h**, and to revive 8217
Jer 13:18 and to the queen, **H** yourselves, sit down: 8213
Mt 18: 4 therefore shall **h** himself as this little child, *5013*
23:12 and he that shall **h** himself shall be exalted. *5013*
2Co 12:21 my God will **h** *me* among you, and *that* I *5013*
Jas 4: 6 the proud, but giveth grace unto the **h**. *5011*
4:10 **H** yourselves in the sight of the Lord, and *5013*
1Pe 5: 5 the proud, and giveth grace to the **h**. *5011*
5: 6 **H** yourselves therefore under the mighty *5013*

HUMBLED (28) [HUMBLE]
Lev 26:41 if then their uncircumcised hearts be **h**, and 3665
Dt 8: 3 he **h** thee, and suffered thee to hunger, and 6031
21:14 of her, because thou hast **h** her. 6031
22:24 because he hath **h** his neighbour's wife: 6031
22:29 because he hath **h** her, he may not put her 6031
2Ki 22:19 and thou hast **h** thyself before the LORD, 3665
2Ch 12: 6 princes of Israel and the king **h** themselves; 3665
12: 7 when the LORD saw that they **h** 3665
12: 7 saying, They have **h** themselves; 3665
12:12 when he **h** himself, the wrath of 3665
30:11 Manasseh and of Zebulun **h** themselves, 3665
32:26 Notwithstanding Hezekiah **h** himself for 3665
33:12 **h** himself greatly before the God of his 3665
33:19 and graven images, before he was **h**: 3665
33:23 **h** not himself before the LORD, 3665
33:23 as Manasseh his father had **h** himself; 3665
36:12 **h** not himself before Jeremiah the prophet 3665
Ps 35:13 I **h** my soul with fasting; and my prayer 6031
Isa 2:11 The lofty looks of man shall be **h**, and 8213
5:15 the mighty man shall be **h**, and the eyes of 8213
5:15 and the eyes of the lofty shall be **h**: 8213
10:33 *be* hewn down, and the haughty shall be **h**. 8213
Jer 44:10 They are not **h** *even* unto this day, 1792
La 3:20 *them* still in remembrance, and is **h** in me. 7743
Eze 22:10 in thee have they **h** her that was set apart 6031
22:11 another in thee hath **h** his sister, his father's 6031
Da 5:22 O Belshazzar, hast not **h** thine heart, 8214
Php 2: 8 he **h** himself, and became obedient unto *5013*

HUMBLEDST (1) [HUMBLE]
2Ch 34:27 **h** thyself before me, and didst rend thy 3665

HUMBLENESS (1) [HUMBLE]
Col 3:12 kindness, **h of mind**, meekness, *5012*

HUMBLETH (7) [HUMBLE]
1Ki 21:29 Seest thou how Ahab **h** himself before me? 3665
21:29 because he **h** himself before me, I will not 3665
Ps 10:10 He croucheth, *and* **h** himself, that the poor 7817
113: 6 Who **h** *himself* to behold *the things that are* 8213
Isa 2: 9 boweth down, and the great man **h** himself; 8213
Lk 14:11 and he that **h** himself shall be exalted. *5013*
18:14 and he that **h** himself shall be exalted. *5013*

HUMBLY (2) [HUMBLE]
2Sa 16: 4 I **h beseech** thee *that* I may find grace in 7812
Mic 6: 8 to love mercy, and to walk **h** with thy God? 6800

HUMILIATION (1) [HUMILITY]
Ac 8:33 In his **h** his judgment was taken away: and *5014*

HUMILITY (7) [HUMILIATION]
Pr 15:33 of wisdom; and before honour *is* **h**. 6038
18:12 of man is haughty, and before honour *is* **h**. 6038
22: 4 By **h** *and* the fear of the LORD *are* riches, 6038
Ac 20:19 Serving the Lord with all **h of mind**, and *5012*
Col 2:18 beguile you of your reward in a voluntary **h** *5012*
2:23 and **h**, and neglecting of the body, not in *5012*
1Pe 5: 5 one to another, and be clothed with **h**: *5012*

HUMTAH (1)
Jos 15:54 **H**, and Kirjath-arba, which *is* Hebron, and 2547

HUNDRED (590) [HUNDREDFOLD, HUNDREDS, HUNDREDTH] See Index

HUNDREDFOLD (7) [HUNDRED]
Ge 26:12 received in the same year an **h**: 3967+8180
2Sa 24: 3 an **h**, and *that* the eyes of my lord 3967+6471
Mt 13: 8 some an **h**, some sixty*fold*, some *1540*
13:23 some an **h**, some sixty, some thirty. *1540*
19:29 shall receive an **h**, and shall inherit *1542*
Mk 10:30 But he shall receive an **h** now in this time, *1542*
Lk 8: 8 and sprang up, and bare fruit an **h**. *1542*

HUNDREDS (28) [HUNDRED] See Index

HUNDREDTH (3) [HUNDRED] See Index

HUNGER (24) [HUNGER-BITTEN, HUNGERED, HUNGRED, HUNGRY]
Ex 16: 3 to kill this whole assembly with **h**. 7458
Dt 8: 3 **suffered** thee **to h**, and fed thee with 7456
28:48 in **h**, and in thirst, and in nakedness, and 7458
32:24 *They shall be* burnt with **h**, and 7458
Ne 9:15 gavest them bread from heaven for their **h**, 7458
Ps 34:10 The young lions do lack, and **suffer h**: but 7456
Pr 19:15 deep sleep; and an idle soul shall **suffer h**. 7456
Isa 49:10 They shall not **h** nor thirst; neither shall 7456
Jer 38: 9 he is like to die for **h** in the place where he 7458
42:14 sound of the trumpet, nor have **h** of bread; 7456
La 2:19 that faint for **h** in the top of every street. 7458
4: 9 are better than *they that be* slain with **h**: 7458
Eze 34:29 they shall be no more consumed with **h** in 7458
Mt 5: 6 Blessed *are* they which do **h** and thirst after *3983*
Lk 6:21 Blessed *are ye* that **h** now: for ye shall be *3983*
6:25 for ye shall **h**. Woe unto you that laugh *3983*
15:17 and to spare, and I perish with **h**? *3042*
Jn 6:35 he that cometh to me shall never **h**; and *3983*
Ro 12:20 Therefore if thine enemy **h**, feed him; if he *3983*
1Co 4:11 Even unto this present hour we both **h**, and *3983*
11:34 And if any *man* **h**, let him eat at home; *3983*
2Co 11:27 in **h** and thirst, in fastings often, in cold and *3042*
Rev 6: 8 and with **h**, and with death, and with *3042*
7:16 They shall **h** no more, neither thirst any *3983*

HUNGER-BITTEN (1) [BITE, HUNGER]
Job 18:12 His strength shall be **h**, and 7457

HUNGERED (2) [HUNGER]
Mt 21:18 morning as he returned into the city, he **h**. *3983*
Lk 4: 2 and when they were ended, he afterward **h**. *3983*

HUNGRED (9) [HUNGER]
Mt 4: 2 and forty nights, he was afterward a **h**. *3983*
12: 1 and his disciples were a **h**, and began to *3983*
12: 3 when he was a **h**, and they that were with *3983*
25:35 For I was a **h**, and ye gave me meat: I was *3983*
25:37 when saw we thee a **h**, and fed *thee?* or *3983*
25:42 For I was a **h**, and ye gave me no meat: *3983*
25:44 when saw we thee a **h**, or athirst, or *3983*
Mk 2:25 and was a **h**, he, and they *that were* with *3983*
Lk 6: 3 when himself was a **h**, and they which were *3983*

HUNGRY (30) [HUNGER]
1Sa 2: 5 for bread; and *they that were* **h** ceased: 7457
2Sa 17:29 The people *is* **h**, and weary, and thirsty, 7457

2Ki 7:12 They know that we *be* **h**; therefore are they 7457
Job 5: 5 Whose harvest the **h** eateth up, and taketh it 7457
22: 7 and thou hast withholden bread from the **h**. 7457
24:10 and they take away the sheaf *from* the **h**; 7457
Ps 50:12 If I were **h**, I would not tell thee: for 7456
107: 5 **H** and thirsty, their soul fainted in them. 7457
107: 9 and filleth the **h** soul *with* goodness. 7457
107:36 there he maketh the **h** to dwell, that they 7457
146: 7 which giveth food to the **h**. The LORD 7457
Pr 6:30 if he steal to satisfy his soul when he is **h**; 7456
25:21 If thine enemy *be* **h**, give him bread to eat; 7457
27: 7 but *to* the **h** soul every bitter *thing is* sweet. 7457
Isa 8:21 shall pass through it, hardly bestead and **h**: 7457
8:21 come to pass, that when they shall be **h**, 7457
9:20 he shall snatch on the right hand, and be **h**; 7457
29: 8 It shall even be as when a **h** *man* dreameth, 7457
32: 6 to make empty the soul of the **h**, and 7457
44:12 yea, he is **h**, and his strength faileth: 7457
58: 7 *Is it* not to deal thy bread to the **h**, and 7457
58:10 *if* thou draw out thy soul to the **h**, and 7457
65:13 my servants shall eat, but ye shall be **h**: 7456
Eze 18: 7 hath given his bread to the **h**, and 7457
18:16 *but* hath given his bread to the **h**, and 7457
Mk 11:12 they were come from Bethany, he was **h**: *3983*
Lk 1:53 He hath filled the **h** with good *things;* and *3983*
Ac 10:10 And he became very **h**, and would have *4361*
1Co 11:21 and one is **h**, and another is drunken. *3983*
Php 4:12 I am instructed both to be full and to be **h**, *3983*

HUNT (12) [HUNTED, HUNTER, HUNTERS, HUNTEST, HUNTETH, HUNTING]
Ge 27: 5 And Esau went to the field to **h** for venison, 6679
1Sa 26:20 as when *one* doth **h** a partridge in 7291
Job 38:39 Wilt thou **h** the prey for the lion? or fill 6679
Ps 140:11 evil shall **h** the violent man to overthrow 6679
Pr 6:26 the adulteress will **h for** the precious life. 6679
Jer 16:16 and they shall **h** them from every mountain, 6679
La 4:18 They **h** our steps, that *we* cannot go in our 6679
Eze 13:18 upon the head of every stature to **h** souls! 6679
13:18 Will ye **h** the souls of my people, and 6679
13:20 where*with* ye there **h** the souls to make 6679
13:20 *even* the souls that ye **h** to make *them* fly. 6679
Mic 7: 2 they **h** every man his brother *with* a net. 6679

HUNTED (1) [HUNT]
Eze 13:21 they shall be no more in your hand to be **h**; 4686

HUNTER (4) [HUNT]
Ge 10: 9 He was a mighty **h** before the LORD: 6718
10: 9 *Even* as Nimrod the mighty **h** before 6718
25:27 Esau was a cunning **h**, a man of 376+6718
Pr 6: 5 thyself as a roe from the hand *of the h*, NIH

HUNTERS (1) [HUNT]
Jer 16:16 after will I send for many **h**, and they shall 6719

HUNTEST (2) [HUNT]
1Sa 24:11 against thee; yet thou **h** my soul to take it. 6658
Job 10:16 Thou **h** me as a fierce lion: and again thou 6679

HUNTETH (1) [HUNT]
Lev 17:13 which **h** and catcheth *any* beast or fowl that 6679

HUNTING (2) [HUNT]
Ge 27:30 that Esau his brother came in from his **h**. 6718
Pr 12:27 *man* roasteth not that which he **took in h**: 6718

HUPHAM (1) [HUPHAMITES]
Nu 26:39 of **H**, the family of the Huphamites. 2349

HUPHAMITES (1) [HUPHAM]
Nu 26:39 of Hupham, the family of the **H**. 2350

HUPPAH (1)
1Ch 24:13 The thirteenth to **H**, the fourteenth to 2647

HUPPIM (3)
Ge 46:21 Ehi, and Rosh, Muppim, and **H**, and Ard. 2650
1Ch 7:12 Shuppim also, and **H**, the children of Ir, 2650
7:15 And Machir took to wife *the sister* of **H** and 2650

HUR (16)
Ex 17:10 Aaron, and **H** went up *to* the top of the hill. 2354
17:12 Aaron and **H** stayed up his hands, the one 2354
24:14 behold, Aaron and **H** *are* with you: if any 2354
31: 2 of Uri, the son of **H**, of the tribe of Judah: 2354
35:30 of Uri, the son of **H**, of the tribe of Judah; 2354
38:22 of Uri, the son of **H**, of the tribe of Judah, 2354
Nu 31: 8 and Rekem, and Zur, and **H**, and Reba, 2354
Jos 13:21 Evi, and Rekem, and Zur, and **H**, and Reba, 2354
1Ki 4: 8 The son of **H**, in mount Ephraim: 2354
1Ch 2:19 took unto him Ephrath, which bare him **H**. 2354
2:20 And **H** begat Uri, and Uri begat Bezaleel. 2354
2:50 These were the sons of Caleb the son of **H**, 2354
4: 1 Hezron, and Carmi, and **H**, and Shobal. 2354
4: 4 These *are* the sons of **H**, the firstborn of 2354
2Ch 1: 5 the son of Uri, the son of **H**, had made, 2354
Ne 3: 9 unto them repaired Rephaiah the son of **H**, 2354

HURAI (1)
1Ch 11:32 **H** of the brooks of Gaash, Abiel 2360

HURAM (12)
1Ch 8: 5 And Gera, and Shephuphan, and **H**. 2361
2Ch 2: 3 Solomon sent to **H** the king of Tyre, 2361
2:11 **H** the king of Tyre answered in writing, 2361
2:12 **H** said moreover, Blessed *be* the LORD 2361
2:13 with understanding, of **H** my father's, 2361
4:11 **H** made the pots, and the shovels, and 2361
4:11 **H** finished the work that he was to make 2361
4:16 did **H** his father make to king Solomon for 2361
8: 2 That the cities which **H** had restored to 2361
8:18 **H** sent him by the hands of his servants 2361
9:10 the servants also of **H**, and the servants of 2361
9:21 went *to* Tarshish with the servants of **H**: 2361

HURI (1)
1Ch 5:14 *are* the children of Abihail the son of **H**, 2359

HURL (1) [HURLETH, HURLING]
Nu 35:20 or **h** at him by laying of wait, that he die; 7993

HURLETH (1) [HURL]
Job 27:21 and **as a storm h** him out of his place. 8175

HURLING (1) [HURL]
1Ch 12: 2 the right hand and the left in *h* stones and NIH

HURRIED See STRAIGHTWAY

HURT (63) [HURTFUL, HURTING]
Ge 4:23 to my wounding, and a young man to my **h**. 2250
26:29 That thou wilt do us no **h**, as we have not 7451
31: 7 but God suffered him not to **h** me. 7489
31:29 It is in the power of my hand to do you **h**: 7451
Ex 21:22 **h** a woman with child, so that her fruit 5062
21:35 if one man's ox **h** another's, that he die; 5062
22:10 it die, or be **h**, or driven away, no man 7665
22:14 it be **h**, or die, the owner thereof *being* not 7665
Nu 16:15 from them, neither have I **h** one of them. 7489
Jos 24:20 he will turn and **do** you **h**, and 7489
1Sa 20:21 for *there is* peace to thee, and no **h**; *as* 1697
24: 9 Behold, David seeketh thy **h**? 7451
25: 7 which were with us, we **h** them not, 3637
25:15 we were not **h**, neither missed we any 3637
2Sa 18:32 all that rise against thee to do *thee* **h**, be as 7451
2Ki 14:10 for why shouldest thou meddle to *thy* **h**, 7451
2Ch 25:19 why shouldest thou meddle to *thine* **h**, 7451
Ezr 4:22 why should damage grow to the **h** of 5142
Est 9: 2 to lay hand on such as sought their **h**: 7451
Job 35: 8 Thy wickedness *may* **h** a man as thou *art;* NIH
Ps 15: 4 *He that* sweareth to *his own* **h**, and 7489
35: 4 and brought to confusion that devise my **h**. 7451
35:26 to confusion together that rejoice at mine **h**: 7451
38:12 they that seek my **h** speak mischievous 7451
41: 7 against me do they devise my **h**. 7451
70: 2 and put to confusion, that desire my **h**. 7451
71:13 and dishonour that seek my **h**. 7451
71:24 are brought unto shame, that seek my **h**. 7451
105:18 Whose feet they **h** with fetters: he was laid 6031
Ecc 5:13 kept for the owners thereof to their **h**. 7451
8: 9 one man ruleth over another to his own **h**. 7451
10: 9 Whoso removeth stones shall be **h** 6087
Isa 11: 9 They shall not **h** nor destroy in all my holy 7489
27: 3 lest *any* **h** it, I will keep it night and day. 6485
65:25 They shall not **h** nor destroy in all my holy 7489
Jer 6:14 They have healed also the **h** of *the daughter* 7667
7: 6 neither walk after other gods to your **h**: 7451
8:11 For they have healed the **h** of the daughter 7667
8:21 For the **h** of the daughter of my people am I 7667

Jer 8:21 hurt of the daughter of my people am I **h**; 7665
10:19 Woe is me for my **h**! my wound *is* 7667
24: 9 all the kingdoms of the earth for *their* **h**, 7451
25: 6 of your hands; and I will do you no **h**. 7489
25: 7 the works of your hands to your own **h**. 7451
38: 4 not the welfare of this people, but the **h**. 7451
Da 3:25 in the midst of the fire, and they have no **h**; 2257
6:22 the lions' mouths, that they have not **h** me: 2255
6:22 also before thee, O king, have I done no **h**. 2248
6:23 no manner of **h** was found upon him, 2257
Mk 16:18 if they drink any deadly *thing,* it shall not **h** *984*
Lk 4:35 he came out of him, and **h** him not. *984*
10:19 and nothing shall by any means **h** you. *91*
Ac 18:10 and no *man* shall set on thee to **h** thee: *2559*
27:10 I perceive that *this* voyage will be with **h** *5196*
Rev 2:11 He that overcometh shall not be **h** of *91*
6: 6 and *see* thou **h** not the oil and the wine. *91*
7: 2 to whom it was given to **h** the earth and *91*
7: 3 Saying, **H** not the earth, neither the sea, *91*
9: 4 that they should not **h** the grass of the earth, *91*
9:10 and their power *was* to **h** men five months. *91*
9:19 and had heads, and with them they do **h**. *91*
11: 5 And if any *man* will **h** them, fire proceedeth *91*
11: 5 and if any *man* will **h** them, he must in this *91*

H

HURTFUL (3) [HURT]

Ezr 4:15 **h** unto kings and provinces, and that they 5142
Ps 144:10 David his servant from the **h** sword. 7451
1Ti 6: 9 a snare, and *into* many foolish and **h** lusts, *983*

HURTING (1) [HURT]

1Sa 25:34 which hath kept me back from **h** thee, 7489

HUSBAND (120) [HUSBAND'S, HUSBANDMAN, HUSBANDMEN, HUSBANDRY, HUSBANDS]

Ge 3: 6 did eat, and gave also unto her **h** with her; 376
3:16 thy desire *shall be* to thy **h**, and he shall rule 376
16: 3 and gave her to her **h** Abram to be his wife. 376
29:32 now therefore my **h** will love me. 376
29:34 Now *this* time will my **h** be joined unto me, 376
30:15 *it* a small matter that thou hast taken my **h**? 376
30:18 because I have given my maiden to my **h**: 376
30:20 now will my **h** dwell with me, because 376
Ex 4:25 and said, Surely a bloody **h** *art* thou to me. 2860
4:26 A bloody **h** *thou art,* because of 2860
21:22 according as the woman's **h** will lay upon 1167
Lev 19:20 betrothed to a **h**, and not at all redeemed, nor 376
21: 3 that is nigh unto him, which hath had no **h**; 376
21: 7 they take a woman put away from her **h**: 376
Nu 5:13 it be hid from the eyes of her **h**, and be kept 376
5:19 *to* uncleanness *with another* instead of thy **h**, 376
5:20 hast gone aside *to another* instead of thy **h**, 376
5:20 *some* man hath lain with thee beside thine **h**: 376
5:27 and have done trespass against her **h**, 376
5:29 wife goeth aside *to another* instead of her **h**, 376
30: 6 And if she had at all a **h**, when she vowed, or 376
30: 7 her **h** heard *it,* and held his peace at her in 376
30: 8 if her **h** disallow her on the day that he heard 376
30:11 And her **h** heard *it,* and held his peace at her, 376
30:12 if her **h** hath utterly made them void on 376
30:12 her **h** hath made them void; and the LORD 376
30:13 her **h** may establish it, or her husband may 376
30:13 may establish it, or her **h** may make it void. 376
30:14 if her **h** altogether hold his peace at her from 376
Dt 21:13 and be her **h**, and she shall be thy wife. 1166
22:22 found lying with a woman married to a **h**, 1167
22:23 damsel *that is* a virgin be betrothed unto a **h**, 376
24: 3 *if* the latter **h** hate her, and write her a bill of 376
24: 3 or if the latter **h** die, which took her *to be* his 376
24: 4 Her former **h**, which sent her away, 1167
25:11 **h** out of the hand of him that smiteth him, 376
28:56 her eye shall be evil towards the **h** of her 376
Jdg 13: 6 the woman came and told her **h**, saying, 376
13: 9 but Manoah her **h** *was* not with her. 376
13:10 ran, and shewed her **h**, and said unto him, 376
14:15 they said unto Samson's wife, Entice thy **h**, 376
19: 3 her **h** arose, and went after her, to speak 376
20: 4 the **h** of the woman that was slain, answered 376
Ru 1: 3 Elimelech Naomi's **h** died; and she was left, 376
1: 5 woman was left of her two sons and her **h**. 376
1: 9 find rest, each *of you in* the house of her **h**. 376
1:12 go *your way;* for I am too old to have a **h**. 376
1:12 *if* I should have a **h** also to night, and 376
2:11 thy mother in law since the death of thine **h**: 376
1Sa 1: 8 said Elkanah her **h** to her, Hannah, why 376
1:22 for she said unto her **h**, *I will not go up* until 376
1:23 Elkanah her **h** said unto her, Do what 376
2:19 when she came up with her **h** to offer 376
4:19 that her father in law and her **h** were dead, 376
4:21 and because of her father in law and her **h**. 376
25:19 come after you. But she told not her **h** Nabal. 376
2Sa 3:15 Ish-bosheth sent, and took her from *her* **h**, 376
3:16 her **h** went with her along weeping behind 376
11:26 of Uriah heard that Uriah her **h** was dead, 376
11:26 husband was dead, she mourned for her **h**. 1167
14: 5 indeed a widow woman, and mine **h** is dead. 376
14: 7 shall not leave to my **h** *neither* name nor 376
2Ki 4: 1 saying, Thy servant my **h** is dead; 376
4: 9 she said unto her **h**, Behold now, I perceive 376
4:14 Verily she hath no child, and her **h** is old. 376
4:22 she called unto her **h**, and said, Send me, 376
4:26 *is it* well with thy **h**? *is it* well with 376
Pr 12: 4 A virtuous woman *is* a crown to her **h**: but 1167
31:11 The heart of her **h** doth *safely* trust in her, 1167
31:23 Her **h** is known in the gates, when he sitteth 1167
31:28 her blessed; her **h** *also,* and he praiseth her. 1167
Isa 54: 5 For thy Maker *is* thine **h**; the LORD of 1166
Jer 3:20 a wife treacherously departeth from her **h**, 7453
6:11 for even the **h** with the wife shall be taken, 376
31:32 although I was a **h** unto them, saith 1166
Eze 16:32 *which* taketh strangers instead of her **h**. 376
16:45 that lotheth her **h** and her children; 376
44:25 for brother, or for sister that hath had no **h**, 376
Hos 2: 2 for she *is* not my wife, neither *am* I her **h**: 376
2: 7 she say, I will go and return to my first **h**; 376
Joel 1: 8 with sackcloth for the **h** of her youth. 1167
Mt 1:16 And Jacob begat Joseph the **h** of Mary, *435*
1:19 Then Joseph her **h**, being a just *man,* and *435*
Mk 10:12 And if a woman shall put away her **h**, and *435*
Lk 2:36 had lived with a **h** seven years from her *435*
16:18 is put away from *her* **h** committeth adultery. *435*
Jn 4:16 unto her, Go, call thy **h**, and come hither. *435*
4:17 The woman answered and said, I have no **h**. *435*
4:17 unto her, Thou hast well said, I have no **h**: *435*
4:18 and he whom thou now hast is not thy **h**: *435*
Ac 5: 9 the feet of them which have buried thy **h** *are* *435*
5:10 and, carrying *her* forth, buried *her* by her **h**. *435*
Ro 7: 2 For the woman which hath a **h** is bound by *5220*
7: 2 hath a husband is bound by the law to *her* **h** *435*
7: 2 but if the **h** be dead, she is loosed from *435*
7: 2 be dead, she is loosed from the law of the **h**. *435*
7: 3 So then if, while *her* **h** liveth, she be married *435*
7: 3 but if *her* **h** be dead, she is free from *that* *435*
1Co 7: 2 and let every woman have her own **h**. *435*
7: 3 Let the **h** render unto the wife due *435*
7: 3 and likewise also the wife unto the **h**. *435*
7: 4 hath not power of her own body, but the **h**: *435*
7: 4 likewise also the **h** hath not power of his *435*
7:10 the Lord, Let not the wife depart from *her* **h**: *435*
7:11 remain unmarried, or be reconciled to *her* **h**: *435*
7:11 and let not the **h** put away *his* wife. *435*
7:13 And the woman which hath a **h** that *435*
7:14 For the unbelieving **h** is sanctified by *435*
7:14 the unbelieving wife is sanctified by the **h**: *435*
7:16 O wife, whether thou shalt save *thy* **h**? *435*
7:34 of the world, how she may please *her* **h**. *435*
7:39 wife is bound by the law as long as her **h** *435*
7:39 but if her **h** be dead, she is at liberty to be *435*
2Co 11: 2 for I have espoused you to one **h**, that *I* may *435*
Gal 4:27 many moe children than she which hath a **h**. *435*
Eph 5:23 For the **h** is the head of the wife, even as *435*
5:33 and the wife *see* that she reverence *her* **h**. *435*
1Ti 3: 2 the **h** of one wife, vigilant, sober, of good *435*
Tit 1: 6 If any be blameless, the **h** of one wife, *435*
Rev 21: 2 prepared as a bride adorned for her **h**. *435*

HUSBAND'S (6) [HUSBAND]

Nu 30:10 if she vowed *in* her **h** house, or bound her 376
Dt 25: 5 her **h brother** shall go in unto her, and 2993
25: 5 **perform the duty of a h brother** unto her. 2992
25: 7 My **h brother** refuseth to raise up unto his 2993
25: 7 not **perform the duty of** my **h brother**. 2992
Ru 2: 1 Naomi had a kinsman of her **h**, a mighty 376

HUSBANDMAN (7) [HUSBAND, MAN]

Ge 9:20 Noah began *to be* a **h**, and 127+376+1886.1
Jer 51:23 and with thee will I break in pieces the **h** and 406
Am 5:16 they shall call the **h** to mourning, and 406

Zec 13: 5 I *am* no prophet, I *am* a **h**; 120+376+5647
Jn 15: 1 I am the true vine, and my Father is the **h**. *1092*
2Ti 2: 6 The **h** that laboureth must be first partaker *1092*
Jas 5: 7 the **h** waiteth for the precious fruit of *1092*

HUSBANDMEN (21) [HUSBAND, MAN]
2Ki 25:12 poor of the land to be vinedressers and **h**. 3009
2Ch 26:10 **h** *also,* and vinedressers in the mountains, 406
Jer 31:24 **h**, and they *that* go forth with flocks. 406
52:16 poor of the land for vinedressers and for **h**. 3009
Joel 1:11 Be ye ashamed, O ye **h**; howl, O ye 406
Mt 21:33 and let it out to **h**, and went into a far *1092*
21:34 he sent his servants to the **h**, that *they* *1092*
21:35 And the **h** took his servants, and beat one, *1092*
21:38 But when the **h** saw the son, they said *1092*
21:40 what will he do unto those **h**? *1092*
21:41 and will let out *his* vineyard unto other **h**, *1092*
Mk 12: 1 and let it out to **h**, and went into a far *1092*
12: 2 And at the season he sent to the **h** a servant, *1092*
12: 2 that he might receive from the **h** of the fruit *1092*
12: 7 But those **h** said amongst themselves, This *1092*
12: 9 he will come and destroy the **h**, and *1092*
Lk 20: 9 and let it forth to **h**, and went into a far *1092*
20:10 And at the season he sent a servant to the **h**, *1092*
20:10 but the **h** beat him, and sent *him* away *1092*
20:14 But when the **h** saw him, they reasoned *1092*
20:16 He shall come and destroy these **h**, and *1092*

HUSBANDRY (2) [HUSBAND]
2Ch 26:10 and in Carmel: for he loved **h**. 127
1Co 3: 9 ye are God's **h**, *ye are* God's building. *1091*

HUSBANDS (19) [HUSBAND]
Ru 1:11 sons in my womb, that they may be your **h**? 376
1:13 would ye stay for them from having **h**? nay, 376
Est 1:17 that *they* shall despise their **h** in their eyes, 1167
1:20 all the wives shall give to their **h** honour, 1167
Jer 29: 6 give your daughters to **h**, that they may bear 376
Eze 16:45 which lothed their **h** and their children: 376
Jn 4:18 For thou hast had five **h**; and he whom thou *435*
1Co 14:35 learn any *thing,* let them ask their **h** at home: *435*
Eph 5:22 Wives, submit yourselves unto your own **h**, *435*
5:24 *let* the wives *be* to their own **h** in every *435*
5:25 **H**, love your wives, even as Christ also *435*
Col 3:18 Wives, submit yourselves unto your own **h**, *435*
3:19 **H**, love *your* wives, and be not bitter against *435*
1Ti 3:12 Let the deacons be the **h** of one wife, *435*
Tit 2: 4 to **love** their **h**, to love their children, *1510+5362*
2: 5 at home, good, obedient to their own **h**, *435*
1Pe 3: 1 ye wives, *be* in subjection to your own **h**; *435*
3: 5 being in subjection unto their own **h**: *435*
3: 7 Likewise, ye **h**, dwell with *them* according *435*

HUSHAH (1)
1Ch 4: 4 father of Gedor, and Ezer the father of **H**. 2364

HUSHAI (14)
2Sa 15:32 **H** the Archite *came* to meet him with his 2365
15:37 So **H** David's friend came *into* the city, and 2365
16:16 when **H** the Archite, David's friend, 2365
16:16 that **H** said unto Absalom, God save 2365
16:17 Absalom said to **H**, *Is* this thy kindness to 2365
16:18 **H** said unto Absalom, Nay; but whom 2365
17: 5 Call now **H** the Archite also, and let us hear 2365
17: 6 when **H** was come to Absalom, 2365
17: 7 **H** said unto Absalom, The counsel that 2365
17: 8 For, (said **H**,) thou knowest thy father and 2365
17:14 The counsel of **H** the Archite *is* better than 2365
17:15 said **H** unto Zadok and to Abiathar 2365
1Ki 4:16 Baanah the son of **H** *was* in Asher and 2365
1Ch 27:33 **H** the Archite *was* the king's companion: 2365

HUSHAM (4)
Ge 36:34 **H** of the land of Temani reigned in his 2367
36:35 **H** died, and Hadad the son of Bedad, 2367
1Ch 1:45 **H** of the land of the Temanites reigned in 2367
1:46 when **H** was dead, Hadad the son of Bedad, 2367

HUSHATHITE (5)
2Sa 21:18 Sibbechai the **H** slew Saph, which *was* of 2843
23:27 Abiezer the Anethothite, Mebunnai the **H**, 2843
1Ch 11:29 Sibbecai the **H**, Ilai the Ahohite, 2843
20: 4 at which time Sibbechai the **H** slew Sippai, 2843
27:11 for the eighth month *was* Sibbecai the **H**, 2843

HUSHIM (4)
Ge 46:23 And the sons of Dan; **H**. 2366
1Ch 7:12 the children of Ir, *and* **H**, the sons of Aher. 2366
8: 8 them away; **H** and Baara *were* his wives. 2366
8:11 And of **H** he begat Abitub, and Elpaal. 2366

HUSK (2) [HUSKS]
Nu 6: 4 vine tree, from the kernels even to the **h**. 2085
2Ki 4:42 and full ears of corn in the **h** thereof. 6861

HUSKS (1) [HUSK]
Lk 15:16 his belly with the **h** that the swine did eat: *2769*

HUZ (1)
Ge 22:21 **H** his firstborn, and Buz his brother, and 5780

HUZZAB (1)
Na 2: 7 **H** shall be led away captive, she shall be 5324

HYMENEUS (2)
1Ti 1:20 Of whom is **H** and Alexander; whom I *5211*
2Ti 2:17 *doth* a canker: of whom is **H** and Philetus; *5211*

HYMN (2) [HYMNS]
Mt 26:30 And when they had **sung a h**, they went out *5214*
Mk 14:26 And when they had **sung a h**, they went out *5214*

HYMNS (2) [HYMN]
Eph 5:19 in psalms and **h** and spiritual songs, *5215*
Col 3:16 another in psalms and **h** and spiritual songs, *5215*

HYPOCRISIES (1) [HYPOCRISY]
1Pe 2: 1 and **h**, and envies, and all evil speakings, *5272*

HYPOCRISY (6) [HYPOCRISIES, HYPOCRITE, HYPOCRITE'S, HYPOCRITES, HYPOCRITICAL]
Isa 32: 6 to practise **h**, and to utter error against 2612
Mt 23:28 but within ye are full of **h** and iniquity. *5272*
Mk 12:15 But he, knowing their **h**, said unto them, *5272*
Lk 12: 1 of the leaven of the Pharisees, which is **h**. *5272*
1Ti 4: 2 Speaking lies in **h**, having their conscience *5272*
Jas 3:17 without partiality, and **without h**. *505*

HYPOCRITE (10) [HYPOCRISY]
Job 13:16 for a **h** shall not come before him. 2611
17: 8 innocent shall stir up himself against the **h**. 2611
20: 5 and the joy of the **h** *but* for a moment? 2611
27: 8 For what *is* the hope of the **h**, though he 2611
34:30 That the **h** reign not, lest the people be 120+2611
Pr 11: 9 A **h** with *his* mouth destroyeth his 2611
Isa 9:17 for every one *is* a **h** and an evildoer, and 2611
Mt 7: 5 *Thou* **h**, first cast out the beam out of thine *5273*
Lk 6:42 *Thou* **h**, cast out first the beam out of thine *5273*
13:15 then answered him, and said, *Thou* **h**, *5273*

HYPOCRITE'S (1) [HYPOCRISY]
Job 8:13 forget God; and the **h** hope shall perish: 2611

HYPOCRITES (20) [HYPOCRISY]
Job 15:34 For the congregation of **h** *shall be* desolate, 2611
36:13 the **h** in heart heap up wrath: they cry not 2611
Isa 33:14 are afraid; fearfulness hath surprised the **h**. 2611
Mt 6: 2 as the **h** do in the synagogues and in *5273*
6: 5 thou shalt not be as the **h** *are:* for they love *5273*
6:16 be not as the **h**, of a sad countenance: *5273*
15: 7 *Ye* **h**, well did Esaias prophesy of you, *5273*
16: 3 O *ye* **h**, ye can discern the face of the sky; *5273*
22:18 and said, Why tempt ye me, *ye* **h**? *5273*
23:13 But woe unto you, scribes and Pharisees, **h**! *5273*
23:14 Woe unto you, scribes and Pharisees, **h**! *5273*
23:15 Woe unto you, scribes and Pharisees, **h**! *5273*
23:23 Woe unto you, scribes and Pharisees, **h**! *5273*
23:25 Woe unto you, scribes and Pharisees, **h**! *5273*
23:27 Woe unto you, scribes and Pharisees, **h**! *5273*
23:29 Woe unto you, scribes and Pharisees, **h**! *5273*
24:51 and appoint *him* his portion with the **h**: *5273*
Mk 7: 6 Well hath Esaias prophesied of you **h**, as it *5273*
Lk 11:44 Woe unto you, scribes and Pharisees, **h**! *5273*
12:56 *Ye* **h**, ye can discern the face of the sky and *5273*

HYPOCRITICAL (2) [HYPOCRISY]
Ps 35:16 With **h** mockers in feasts, *they* gnashed 2611
Isa 10: 6 I will send him against a **h** nation, and 2611

HYSSOP (12)
Ex 12:22 ye shall take a bunch of **h**, and dip *it* in 231
Lev 14: 4 clean, and cedar wood, and scarlet, and **h**: 231
14: 6 the **h**, and shall dip them and the living bird 231
14:49 and cedar wood, and scarlet, and **h**: 231
14:51 the **h**, and the scarlet, and the living bird, 231
14:52 and with the **h**, and with the scarlet: 231
Nu 19: 6 **h**, and scarlet, and cast *it* into the midst of 231
19:18 a clean person shall take **h**, and dip *it* in 231
1Ki 4:33 unto the **h** that springeth out of the wall: 231
Ps 51: 7 Purge me with **h**, and I shall be clean: 231
Jn 19:29 and put *it* upon **h**, and put *it* to his mouth. *5301*
Heb 9:19 and **h**, and sprinkled both the book, and *5301*

I

I (8851) [ME, MINE, MY, MYSELF] See Index

IBEX See PYGARG

IBHAR (3)
2Sa 5:15 **I** also, and Elishua, and Nepheg, and 2984
1Ch 3: 6 **I** also, and Elishama, and Eliphelet, 2984
14: 5 And **I**, and Elishua, and Elpalet, 2984

IBLEAM (3)
Jos 17:11 **I** and her towns, and the inhabitants of Dor 2991
Jdg 1:27 nor the inhabitants of **I** and her towns, 2991
2Ki 9:27 *so* at the going up to Gur, which *is* by **I**. 2991

IBNEIAH (1)
1Ch 9: 8 **I** the son of Jeroham, and Elah the son of 2997

IBNIJAH (1)
1Ch 9: 8 the son of Reuel, the son of **I**; 2998

IBRI (1)
1Ch 24:27 Beno, and Shoham, and Zaccur, and **I**. 5681

IBSAM See JIBSAM

IBZAN (2)
Jdg 12: 8 And after him **I** of Beth-lehem judged Israel. 78
12:10 Then died **I**, and was buried at Beth-lehem. 78

ICE (3)
Job 6:16 Which are blackish by reason of the **i**, *and* 7140
38:29 Out of whose womb came the **i**? and 7140
Ps 147:17 He casteth forth his **i** like morsels: who can 7140

ICHABOD (1) [ICHABOD'S]
1Sa 4:21 she named the child **I**, saying, The glory is 350

ICHABOD'S (1) [ICHABOD]
1Sa 14: 3 Ahiah, the son of Ahitub, **I** brother, the son 350

ICONIUM (6)
Ac 13:51 of their feet against them, and came unto **I**. *2430*
14: 1 And it came to pass in **I**, that they went *2430*
14:19 thither *certain* Jews from Antioch and **I**, *2430*
14:21 *again* to Lystra, and *to* **I**, and Antioch, *2430*
16: 2 of by the brethren that were at Lystra and **I**. *2430*
2Ti 3:11 came unto me at Antioch, at **I**, at Lystra; *2430*

IDALAH (1)
Jos 19:15 and Shimron, and **I**, and Beth-lehem: 3030

IDBASH (1)
1Ch 4: 3 father of Etam; Jezreel, and Ishma, and **I**: 3031

IDDO (14)
1Ki 4:14 Ahinadab the son of **I** *had* Mahanaim: 5714
1Ch 6:21 Joah his son, **I** his son, Zerah his son, 5714
27:21 Manasseh in Gilead, **I** the son of Zechariah: 3035
2Ch 9:29 in the visions of **I** the seer against 3260
12:15 and of **I** the seer concerning genealogies? 5714
13:22 *are* written in the story of the prophet **I**. 5714
Ezr 5: 1 the prophet, and Zechariah the son of **I**, 5714
6:14 the prophet and Zechariah the son of **I**. 5714
8:17 I sent them with commandment unto **I** 112
8:17 and I told them what they should say unto **I**, 112
Ne 12: 4 **I**, Ginnetho, Abijah, 5714
12:16 Of **I**, Zechariah; of Ginnethon, Meshullam; 5714
Zec 1: 1 the son of **I** the prophet, saying, 5714
1: 7 the son of **I** the prophet, saying, 5714

IDEA See WIST

IDLE (11) [IDLENESS]
Ex 5: 8 for they *be* **i**; therefore they cry, saying, 7503
5:17 he said, Ye *are* **i**, *ye are* idle: therefore 7503
5:17 he said, Ye *are* idle, *ye are* **i**: therefore 7503
Pr 19:15 and an **i** soul shall suffer hunger. 7423
Mt 12:36 That every **i** word that men shall speak, *692*
20: 3 and saw others standing **i** in the marketplace, *692*
20: 6 and found others standing **i**, and saith unto *692*
20: 6 unto them, Why stand ye here all the day **i**? *692*
Lk 24:11 And their words seemed to them as **i tales**, *3026*
1Ti 5:13 And withal they learn *to be* **i**, *692*
5:13 and not only **i**, but tattlers also and *692*

IDLENESS (3) [IDLE]
Pr 31:27 her household, and eateth not the bread of **i**. 6104
Ecc 10:18 through **i** of the hands the house droppeth 8220
Eze 16:49 abundance of **i** was in her and in her 8252

IDOL (15) [IDOL'S, IDOLATER, IDOLATERS, IDOLATRIES, IDOLATROUS, IDOLATRY, IDOLS]
1Ki 15:13 because she had made an **i** in a grove; 4656
15:13 Asa destroyed her **i**, and burnt *it* by 4656
2Ch 15:16 because she had made an **i** in a grove: 4656
15:16 and Asa cut down her **i**, and stamped *it*, and 4656
33: 7 the **i** which he had made, in the house of 5566
33:15 the **i** out of the house of the LORD, and 5566
Isa 48: 5 Mine **i** hath done them, and my graven 6090
66: 3 he that burneth incense, *as if* he blessed an **i**. 205
Jer 22:28 *Is* this man Coniah a despised broken **i**? 6089
Zec 11:17 Woe to the **i** shepherd that leaveth the flock! 457
Ac 7:41 and offered sacrifice unto the **i**, and *1497*
1Co 8: 4 we know that an **i** *is* nothing in the world, *1497*
8: 7 for some with conscience of the **i** unto this *1497*
8: 7 eat *it* as a **thing offered unto an i**; *1494*
10:19 that the **i** is any *thing*, or that which is *1497*

IDOL'S (1) [IDOL]
1Co 8:10 hast knowledge sit at meat in the **i temple**, *1493*

IDOLATER (2) [IDOL]
1Co 5:11 or an **i**, or a railer, or a drunkard, or *1496*
Eph 5: 5 *person*, nor covetous man who is an **i**, *1496*

IDOLATERS (5) [IDOL]
1Co 5:10 with the covetous, or extortioners, or with **i**; *1496*
6: 9 nor **i**, nor adulterers, nor effeminate, *1496*
10: 7 Neither be ye **i**, as *were* some of them; as it *1496*
Rev 21: 8 and whoremongers, and sorcerers, and **i**, *1496*
22:15 and **i**, and whosoever loveth and maketh a *1496*

IDOLATRIES (1) [IDOL]
1Pe 4: 3 revellings, banquetings, and abominable **i**: *1495*

IDOLATROUS (1) [IDOL]
2Ki 23: 5 he put down the **i priests**, whom the kings 3649

IDOLATRY (5) [IDOL]
1Sa 15:23 and stubbornness *is as* iniquity and **i**. 8655
Ac 17:16 he saw the city **wholly given to i**. *1510+2712*
1Co 10:14 Wherefore, my dearly beloved, flee from **i**. *1495*
Gal 5:20 **I**, witchcraft, hatred, variance, emulations, *1495*
Col 3: 5 and covetousness, which is **i**: *1495*

IDOLS (101) [IDOL]
Lev 19: 4 Turn ye not unto **i**, nor make to yourselves 457
26: 1 Ye shall make you no **i** nor graven image, 457
26:30 your carcases upon the carcases of your **i**, 1544
Dt 29:17 and their **i**, wood and stone, silver and gold, 1544
1Sa 31: 9 to publish *it in* the house of their **i**, and 6091
1Ki 15:12 removed all the **i** that his fathers had made. 1544
21:26 he did very abominably in following **i**, 1544
2Ki 17:12 For they served **i**, whereof the LORD had 1544
21:11 and hath made Judah also to sin with his **i**: 1544
21:21 and served the **i** that his father served, 1544
23:24 the **i**, and all the abominations that were 1544
1Ch 10: 9 to carry tidings unto their **i**, and to 6091

1Ch 16:26 For all the gods of the people *are* i: but 457
2Ch 15: 8 put away the **abominable** i out of all 8251
24:18 of their fathers, and served groves and i: 6091
34: 7 cut down all the i throughout all the land of 2553
Ps 96: 5 For all the gods of the nations *are* i: but 457
97: 7 graven images, that boast themselves of i: 457
106:36 they served their i: which were a snare unto 6091
106:38 whom they sacrificed unto the i of Canaan: 6091
115: 4 Their i *are* silver and gold, the work of 6091
135:15 The i of the heathen *are* silver and gold, 6091
Isa 2: 8 Their land also is full *of* i; they worship 457
2:18 And the i he shall utterly abolish. 457
2:20 In that day a man shall cast his i of silver, 457
2:20 cast his idols of silver, and his i of gold, 457
10:10 my hand hath found the kingdoms of the i, 457
10:11 as I have done unto Samaria and her i, so 457
10:11 and her idols, so do to Jerusalem and her i? 6091
19: 1 the i of Egypt shall be moved at his 457
19: 3 they shall seek to the i, and to the charmers, 457
31: 7 day every man shall cast away his i of silver, 457
31: 7 his i of gold, which your own hands have 457
45:16 to confusion together *that are* makers of i. 6736
46: 1 their i were upon the beasts, and upon 6091
57: 5 Inflaming yourselves with i under every 410
Jer 50: 2 her i are confounded, her images are 6091
50:38 and they are mad upon *their* i. 367
Eze 6: 4 cast down your slain *men* before your i. 1544
6: 5 of the children of Israel before their i; 1544
6: 6 your i may be broken and cease, and 1544
6: 9 their eyes, which go a whoring after their i: 1544
6:13 when their slain *men* shall be among their i 1544
6:13 they did offer sweet savour to all their i. 1544
8:10 and all the i of the house of Israel, 1544
14: 3 these men have set up their i in their heart, 1544
14: 4 of Israel that setteth up his i in his heart, 1544
14: 4 cometh according to the multitude of his i; 1544
14: 5 are all estranged from me through their i. 1544
14: 6 Repent, and turn *yourselves* from your i; 1544
14: 7 setteth up his i in his heart, and putteth 1544
16:36 with all the i of thy abominations, and 1544
18: 6 neither hath lift up his eyes to the i of 1544
18:12 the pledge, and hath lift up his eyes to the i, 1544
18:15 neither hath lift up his eyes to the i of 1544
20: 7 defile not yourselves with the i of Egypt: 1544
20: 8 neither did they forsake the i of Egypt: 1544
20:16 for their heart went after their i. 1544
20:18 nor defile yourselves with their i: 1544
20:24 and their eyes were after their fathers' i. 1544
20:31 ye pollute yourselves with all your i, 1544
20:39 serve ye every one his i, and hereafter *also,* 1544
20:39 no more with your gifts, and with your i. 1544
22: 3 maketh i against herself to defile *herself.* 1544
22: 4 hast defiled *thyself* in thine i which thou 1544
23: 7 with all their i she defiled herself. 1544
23:30 *and* because thou art polluted with their i. 1544
23:37 with their i have they committed adultery, 1544
23:39 when they had slain their children to their i, 1544
23:49 and ye shall bear the sins of your i: 1544
30:13 I will also destroy the i, and I will cause 1544
33:25 lift up your eyes toward your i, and 1544
36:18 for their i *wherewith* they had polluted it: 1544
36:25 and from all your i, will I cleanse you. 1544
37:23 defile themselves any more with their i, 1544
44:10 went astray away from me after their i; 1544
44:12 they ministered unto them before their i, 1544
Hos 4:17 Ephraim *is* joined to i: let him alone. 6091
8: 4 and their gold have they made them i, 6091
13: 2 *and* i according to their own understanding, 6091
14: 8 *say,* What have I to do any more with i? 6091
Mic 1: 7 and all the i thereof will I lay desolate: 6091
Hab 2:18 of his work trusteth therein, to make dumb i? 457
Zec 10: 2 For the i have spoken vanity, and 8655
13: 2 *that* I will cut off the names of the i out of 6091
Ac 15:20 that *they* abstain from pollutions of i, and *1497*
15:29 That *ye* abstain from **meats offered to** i, *1494*
21:25 keep themselves from **things offered to** i, *1494*
Ro 2:22 thou that abhorrest i, dost thou commit *1497*
1Co 8: 1 Now as touching **things offered unto** i, *1494*
8: 4 **things** that are **offered in sacrifice unto** i, *1494*
8:10 to eat those **things** which are **offered to** i; *1494*
10:19 that which is **offered in sacrifice to** i is *1494*
10:28 This is **offered in sacrifice unto** i, *1494*
12: 2 carried away unto *these* dumb i, *even* as ye *1497*
2Co 6:16 agreement hath the temple of God with i? *1497*
1Th 1: 9 how ye turned to God from i to serve *1497*
1Jn 5:21 Little children, keep yourselves from i. *1497*
Rev 2:14 to eat **things sacrificed unto** i, and *1494*
2:20 and to eat **things sacrificed unto** i. *1494*
9:20 should not worship devils, and i of gold, *1497*

IDUMEA (5)
Isa 34: 5 it shall come down upon I, and upon 123
34: 6 and a great slaughter in the land of I. 123
Eze 35:15 O mount Seir, and all I, *even* all of it: 123
36: 5 the residue of the heathen, and against all I, 123
Mk 3: 8 and from I, and *from* beyond Jordan; *2401*

IEZER See JEEZER

IEZERITE See JEEZERITES

IF (1595) See Index

IGAL (2)
Nu 13: 7 Of the tribe of Issachar, I the son of Joseph. 3008
2Sa 23:36 I the son of Nathan of Zobah, Bani 3008

IGDALIAH (1)
Jer 35: 4 sons of Hanan, the son of I, a man of God, 3012

IGEAL (1)
1Ch 3:22 I, and Bariah, and Neariah, and Shaphat, 3008

IGNOMINY (1)
Pr 18: 3 cometh also contempt, and with i reproach. 7036

IGNORANCE (18) [IGNORANT, IGNORANTLY]
Lev 4: 2 If a soul shall sin through i against any of 7684
4:13 whole congregation of Israel **sin through** i, 7686
4:22 done somewhat through i against any of 7684
4:27 one of the common people sin through i, 7684
5:15 a soul commit a trespass, and sin through i, 7684
5:18 for him concerning his i wherein he erred 7684
Nu 15:24 if *ought* be committed by i without 7684
15:25 and it shall be forgiven them; for it *is* i: 7684
15:25 sin offering before the LORD, for their i: 7684
15:26 seeing all the people were in i. 7684
15:27 if any soul sin through i, then he shall bring 7684
15:28 when he sinneth by i before the LORD, 7684
15:29 him that **sinneth through** i, 6213+7684+871.1
Ac 3:17 I wot that through i ye did *it,* as *did* also your *52*
17:30 And the times of *this* i God winked at; but *52*
Eph 4:18 the life of God through the i that is in them, *52*
1Pe 1:14 according to the former lusts in your i: *52*
2:15 with well doing *ye* may put to silence the i *56*

IGNORANT (17) [IGNORANCE]
Ps 73:22 So foolish *was* I, and i: I was *as* a 3045+3808
Isa 56:10 they are all i, they *are* all dumb dogs, 3045+3808
63:16 though Abraham be i of us, and 3045+3808
Ac 4:13 that they were unlearned and i men, *2399*
Ro 1:13 Now I would not have you i, brethren, *50*
10: 3 For they being i of God's righteousness, and *50*
11:25 brethren, that ye should be i of this mystery, *50*
1Co 10: 1 I would not that ye should be i, *50*
12: 1 *gifts,* brethren, I would not have you i. *50*
14:38 But if any *man* be i, let him be ignorant. *50*
14:38 But if any *man* be ignorant, let him be i. *50*
2Co 1: 8 **have** you i of our trouble which came to us in *50*
2:11 of us: for we are not i of his devices. *50*
1Th 4:13 But I would not have you to be i, brethren, *50*
Heb 5: 2 Who can have compassion on the i, and *50*
2Pe 3: 5 For this they willingly are i of, that by *2990*
3: 8 be not i of this one *thing,* that one day *is* *2990*

IGNORANTLY (4) [IGNORANCE]
Nu 15:28 an atonement for the soul that **sinneth** i, 7683
Dt 19: 4 Whoso killeth his neighbour i, 1097+1847+871.1
Ac 17:23 Whom therefore ye i worship, him declare I *50*
1Ti 1:13 obtained mercy, because I did *it* i in unbelief. *50*

IIM (2)
Nu 33:45 they departed from I, and pitched in 5864
Jos 15:29 Baalah, and I, and Azem, 5864

IJE-ABARIM (2) [ABARIM]
Nu 21:11 journeyed from Oboth, and pitched at I, 5863
33:44 and pitched in I, in the border of Moab. 5863

I

IJON (3)
1Ki 15:20 smote **I**, and Dan, and Abel-beth-maachah, 5859
2Ki 15:29 took **I**, and Abel-beth-maachah, and 5859
2Ch 16: 4 and they smote **I**, and Dan, and Abel-maim, 5859

IKKESH (3)
2Sa 23:26 the Paltite, Ira the son of **I** the Tekoite, 6142
1Ch 11:28 Ira the son of **I** the Tekoite, Abi-ezer 6142
27: 9 month *was* Ira the son of **I** the Tekoite: 6142

ILAI (1)
1Ch 11:29 Sibbecai the Hushathite, **I** the Ahohite, 5866

ILL (15)
Ge 41: 3 out of the river, **i** favoured and leanfleshed; 7451
41: 4 the **i** favoured and leanfleshed kine did eat 7451
41:19 poor and very **i** favoured and leanfleshed, 7451
41:20 the **i favoured** kine did eat up the first 7451
41:21 they *were still* **i** favoured, as at 7451
41:27 **i favoured** kine that came up after them *are* 7451
43: 6 Wherefore **dealt** ye *so* **i** with me, 7489
Dt 15:21 *it be* lame, or blind, *or have* any **i** blemish, 7451
Job 20:26 it shall **go i** with him that is left in his 3415
Ps 106:32 so that it went **i** with Moses for their sakes: 3415
Isa 3:11 *it shall be* **i** *with him:* for the reward of his 7451
Jer 40: 4 if it seem **i** unto thee to come with me *into* 7489
Joel 2:20 his **i savour** shall come up, because he hath 6709
Mic 3: 4 as they have **behaved** themselves **i** in their 7489
Ro 13:10 Love worketh no **i** to *his* neighbour: *2556*

ILLUMINATED (1)
Heb 10:32 in which, after ye were **i**, ye endured a great *5461*

ILLYRICUM (1)
Ro 15:19 from Jerusalem, and round about unto **I**, *2437*

IMAGE (100) [IMAGE'S, IMAGERY, IMAGES]
Ge 1:26 God said, Let us make man in our **i**, 6754
1:27 So God created man in his own **i**, in 6754
1:27 own image, in the **i** of God created he him; 6754
5: 3 begat *a son* in his own likeness, after his **i**; 6754
9: 6 be shed: for in the **i** of God made he man. 6754
Ex 20: 4 shalt not make unto thee *any* **graven i**, 6459
Lev 26: 1 Ye shall make you no idols nor **graven i**, 6459
26: 1 neither rear you up a **standing i**, 4676
26: 1 neither shall ye set up *any* **i** of stone in your 4906
Dt 4:16 and make you a **graven i**, 6459
4:23 make you a **graven i**, *or* the likeness of any 6459
4:25 corrupt *yourselves,* and make a **graven i**, 6459
5: 8 Thou shalt not make thee *any* **graven i**, *or* 6459
9:12 they have made them a **molten i**. 4541
16:22 Neither shalt thou set thee up *any* **i**; 4676
27:15 man that maketh *any* graven or **molten i**, 4541
Jdg 17: 3 to make a **graven i** and a molten image: 6459
17: 3 to make a graven image and a **molten i**: 4541
17: 4 who made thereof a **graven i** and a molten 6459
17: 4 thereof a graven image and a **molten i**: 4541
18:14 and a **graven i**, and a molten image? 6459
18:14 and a graven image, and a **molten i**? 4541
18:17 *and* took the **graven i**, and the ephod, and 6459
18:17 and the teraphim, and the **molten i**: 4541
18:18 fetched the **carved i**, the ephod, and 6459
18:18 and the teraphim, and the **molten i**. 4541
18:20 the **graven i**, and went in the midst of 6459
18:30 the children of Dan set up the **graven i**: 6459
18:31 they set them up Micah's **graven i**, 6459
1Sa 19:13 And Michal took an **i**, and laid *it* in the bed, 8655
19:16 come in, behold *there was* an **i** in the bed, 8655
2Ki 3: 2 for he put away the **i** of Baal that his father 4676
10:27 they brake down the **i** of Baal, and 4676
21: 7 he set a **graven i** of the grove that he had 6459
2Ch 3:10 house he made two cherubims of **i** work, 6816
33: 7 he set a **carved i**, the idol which he had 6459
Job 4:16 an **i** *was* before mine eyes, *there was* 8544
Ps 73:20 *thou* awakest, thou shalt despise their **i**. 6754
106:19 calf in Horeb, and worshipped the **molten i**. 4541
Isa 40:19 The workman melteth a **graven i**, and 6459
40:20 a cunning workman to prepare a **graven i**, 6459
44: 9 They that make a **graven i** *are* all of them 6459
44:10 molten a **graven i** *that* is profitable for 6459
44:15 and worshippeth *it;* he maketh it a **graven i**, 6459
44:17 thereof he maketh a god, *even* his **graven i**: 6459
45:20 that set up the wood of their **graven i**, 6459
48: 5 my **graven i**, and my molten image, 6459
48: 5 my graven image, and my **molten i**, 5262
Jer 10:14 founder is confounded by the **graven i**: 6459
10:14 for his **molten i** *is* falsehood, and *there is* 5262
51:17 founder is confounded by the **graven i**: 6459
51:17 for his **molten i** *is* falsehood, and *there is* 5262
Eze 8: 3 where *was* the seat of the **i** of jealousy, 5566
8: 5 northward at the gate of the altar this **i** of 5566
Da 2:31 Thou, O king, sawest, and behold a great **i**. 6755
2:31 This great **i**, whose brightness *was* 6755
2:34 which smote the **i** upon his feet *that were* of 6755
2:35 the stone that smote the **i** became a great 6755
3: 1 Nebuchadnezzar the king made an **i** of 6755
3: 2 to come to the dedication of the **i** which 6755
3: 3 **i** that Nebuchadnezzar the king had set up; 6755
3: 3 they stood before the **i** that 6755
3: 5 worship the golden **i** that Nebuchadnezzar 6755
3: 7 worshipped the golden **i** that 6755
3:10 shall fall down and worship the golden **i**: 6755
3:12 nor worship the golden **i** which thou hast 6755
3:14 nor worship the golden **i** which I have set 6755
3:15 and worship the **i** which I have made; 6755
3:18 nor worship the golden **i** which thou hast 6755
Hos 3: 4 and without an **i**, and without an ephod, and 4676
Na 1:14 house of thy gods will I cut off the **graven i** 6459
1:14 I cut off the graven image and the **molten i**: 4541
Hab 2:18 What profiteth the **graven i** that the maker 6459
2:18 the **molten i**, and a teacher of lies, that 4541
Mt 22:20 Whose *is* this **i** and superscription? *1504*
Mk 12:16 Whose *is* this **i** and superscription? *1504*
Lk 20:24 Whose **i** and superscription hath it? *1504*
Ac 19:35 and of the *i* which fell down from Jupiter? NIG
Ro 1:23 God into an **i** made like to corruptible man, *1504*
8:29 *to be* conformed to the **i** of his Son, *1504*
11: 4 who have not bowed the knee to *the i of* NIG
1Co 11: 7 forasmuch as he is the **i** and glory of God: *1504*
15:49 And as we have borne the **i** of the earthy, *1504*
15:49 we shall also bear the **i** of the heavenly. *1504*
2Co 3:18 are changed *into* the same **i** from glory to *1504*
4: 4 who is the **i** of God, should shine unto *1504*
Col 1:15 Who is the **i** of the invisible God, *1504*
3:10 after the **i** of him that created him: *1504*
Heb 1: 3 and the **express i** of his person, and *5481*
10: 1 to come, *and* not the very **i** of the things, *1504*
Rev 13:14 that *they* should make an **i** to the beast, *1504*
13:15 And he had power to give life unto the **i** of *1504*
13:15 that the **i** of the beast should both speak, *1504*
13:15 worship the **i** of the beast should be killed. *1504*
14: 9 If any *man* worship the beast and his **i**, and *1504*
14:11 who worship the beast and his **i**, and *1504*
15: 2 the beast, and over his **i**, and over his mark, *1504*
16: 2 and *upon* them which worshipped his **i**. *1504*
19:20 the beast, and them that worshipped his **i**. *1504*
20: 4 had not worshipped the beast, neither his **i**, *1504*

IMAGE'S (1) [IMAGE]
Da 2:32 This **i** head *was* of fine gold, his breast and 6755

IMAGERY (1) [IMAGE]
Eze 8:12 every man in the chambers of his **i**? 4906

IMAGES (71) [IMAGE]
Ge 31:19 Rachel had stolen the **i** that *were* her 8655
31:34 Now Rachel had taken the **i**, and put them 8655
31:35 And he searched, but found not the **i**. 8655
Ex 23:24 and quite break down their **i**. 4676
34:13 break their **i**, and cut down their groves: 4676
Lev 26:30 cut down your **i**, and cast your carcases 2553
Nu 33:52 destroy all their molten **i**, and quite pluck 6754
Dt 7: 5 break down their **i**, and cut down their 4676
7: 5 and burn their **graven i** with fire. 6456
7:25 The **graven i** of their gods shall ye burn 6456
12: 3 you shall hew down the **graven i** of their 6456
1Sa 6: 5 Wherefore ye shall make **i** of your 6754
6: 5 and **i** of your mice that mar the land; 6754
6:11 the mice of gold and the **i** of their emerods. 6754
2Sa 5:21 there they left their **i**, and David and 6091
1Ki 14: 9 and made thee other gods, and **molten i**, 4541
14:23 **i**, and groves, on every high hill, and 4676
2Ki 10:26 they brought forth the **i** out of the house of 4676
11:18 and his **i** brake they in pieces throughly, 6754
17:10 they set them up **i** and groves in every high 4676
17:16 made them **molten i**, *even* two calves, and 4541
17:41 served their **graven i**, both their children, 6456
18: 4 brake the **i**, and cut down the groves, and 4676

2Ki 23:14 he brake in pieces the **i**, and cut down 4676
23:24 the **i**, and the idols, and all 8655
2Ch 14: 3 brake down the **i**, and cut down the groves: 4676
14: 5 the cities of Judah the high places and the **i**: 2553
23:17 brake his altars and his **i** in pieces, and slew 6754
28: 2 and made also **molten i** for Baalim. 4541
31: 1 brake the **i** *in pieces,* and cut down 4676
33:19 set up groves and **graven i**, before he was 6456
33:22 for Amon sacrificed unto all the **carved i** 6456
34: 3 and the **carved i**, and the molten images. 6456
34: 3 and the carved images, and the **molten i**. 4541
34: 4 the **i**, that *were* on high above them, he cut 2553
34: 4 and the **carved i**, and the molten images, 6456
34: 4 the **molten i**, he brake *in pieces,* and 4541
34: 7 had beaten the **graven i** into powder, and 6456
Ps 78:58 moved him to jealousy with their **graven i**. 6456
97: 7 Confounded be all they that serve **graven i**, 6459
Isa 10:10 whose **graven i** did excel *them of* 6456
17: 8 have made, either the groves, or the **i**. 2553
21: 9 all the **graven i** of her gods he hath broken 6456
27: 9 the groves and **i** shall not stand up. 2553
30:22 also the covering of thy **graven i** of silver, 6456
30:22 and the ornament of thy **molten i** of gold: 4541
41:29 their **molten i** *are* wind and confusion. 5262
42: 8 to another, neither my praise to **graven i**. 6456
42:17 that trust in **graven i**, that say to the molten 6459
42:17 that say to the **molten i**, Ye *are* our gods. 4541
Jer 8:19 provoked me to anger with their **graven i**, 6456
43:13 He shall break also the **i** of Beth-shemesh, 4676
50: 2 are confounded, her **i** are broken in pieces. 1544
50:38 for it *is* the land of **graven i**, and they are 6456
51:47 that I will do judgment upon the **graven i** 6456
51:52 that I will do judgment upon her **graven i**: 6456
Eze 6: 4 be desolate, and your **i** shall be broken: 2553
6: 6 your **i** may be cut down, and your works 2553
7:20 they made the **i** of their abominations *and* 6754
16:17 madest to thyself **i** of men, and 6754
21:21 he consulted with **i**, he looked in the liver. 8655
23:14 the **i** of the Chaldeans pourtrayed with 6754
30:13 and I will cause *their* **i** to cease out of Noph; 457
Hos 10: 1 of his land they have made goodly **i**. 4676
10: 2 down their altars, he shall spoil their **i**. 4676
11: 2 and burned incense to **graven i**. 6456
13: 2 have made them **molten i** of their silver, 4541
Am 5:26 of your Moloch and Chiun your **i**, 6754
Mic 1: 7 all the **graven i** thereof shall be beaten to 6456
5:13 Thy **graven i** also will I cut off, and 6456
5:13 and thy **standing i** out of the midst of thee; 4676

IMAGINATION (14) [IMAGINE]
Ge 6: 5 *that* every **i** of the thoughts of his heart *was* 3336
8:21 for the **i** of man's heart *is* evil from his 3336
Dt 29:19 though I walk in the **i** of mine heart, 8307
31:21 for I know their **i** which they go about, 3336
1Ch 29:18 keep this for ever in the **i** of the thoughts of 3336
Jer 3:17 neither shall they walk any more after the **i** 8307
7:24 the counsels *and* in the **i** of their evil heart, 8307
9:14 have walked after the **i** of their own heart, 8307
11: 8 walked every one in the **i** of their evil heart: 8307
13:10 which walk in the **i** of their heart, and 8307
16:12 ye walk every one after the **i** of his evil 8307
18:12 we will every one do the **i** of his evil heart. 8307
23:17 that walketh after the **i** of his own heart, 8307
Lk 1:51 he hath scattered the proud in the **i** of their *1271*

IMAGINATIONS (6) [IMAGINE]
1Ch 28: 9 and understandeth all the **i** of the thoughts: 3336
Pr 6:18 A heart that deviseth wicked **i**, feet that be 4284
La 3:60 their vengeance *and* all their **i** against me. 4284
3:61 O LORD, *and* all their **i** against me; 4284
Ro 1:21 but became vain in their **i**, and their foolish *1261*
2Co 10: 5 Casting down **i**, and every high thing that *3053*

IMAGINE (12) [IMAGINATION, IMAGINATIONS, IMAGINED, IMAGINETH]
Job 6:26 Do ye **i** to reprove words, and the speeches 2803
21:27 the devices *which* ye **wrongfully i** against 2554
Ps 2: 1 and the people **i** a vain *thing?* 1897
38:12 and **i** deceits all the day long. 1897
62: 3 How long will ye **i mischief** against a man? 2050
140: 2 Which **i** mischiefs in *their* heart; 2803
Pr 12:20 Deceit *is* in the heart of them that **i** evil: but 2790
Hos 7:15 yet do they **i** mischief against me. 2803
Na 1: 9 What do ye **i** against the LORD? he *will* 2803
Zec 7:10 let none of you **i** evil against his brother in 2803
8:17 let none of you **i** evil in your hearts against 2803
Ac 4:25 heathen rage, and the people **i** vain *things?* *3191*

IMAGINED (3) [IMAGINE]
Ge 11: 6 from them, which they have **i** to do. 2161
Ps 10: 2 be taken in the devices that they have **i**. 2803
21:11 they **i** a mischievous device, *which* they 2803

IMAGINETH (1) [IMAGINE]
Na 1:11 that **i** evil against the LORD, a wicked 2803

IMLA (2) [IMLAH]
2Ch 18: 7 the same *is* Micaiah the son of **I**. 3229
18: 8 said, Fetch quickly Micaiah the son of **I**. 3229

IMLAH (2) [IMLA]
1Ki 22: 8 *There is* yet one man, Micaiah the son of **I**, 3229
22: 9 said, Hasten *hither* Micaiah the son of **I**. 3229

IMMANUEL (2) [EMMANUEL]
Isa 7:14 and bear a Son, and shall call his name **I**. 6005
8: 8 wings shall fill the breadth of thy land, O **I**. 6005

IMMEDIATELY (55)
Mt 4:22 And they **i** left the ship and their father, and *2112*
8: 3 thou clean. And **i** his leprosy was cleansed. *2112*
14:31 And **i** Jesus stretched forth *his* hand, and *2112*
20:34 and **i** their eyes received sight, and *2112*
24:29 **I** after the tribulation of those days shall *2112*
26:74 I know not the man. And **i** *the* cock crew. *2112*
Mk 1:12 And **i** the Spirit driveth him into *2112*
1:28 And **i** his fame spread abroad throughout *2112*
1:31 and **i** the fever left her, and she ministered *2112*
1:42 **i** the leprosy departed from him, and he was *2112*
2: 8 And **i**, when Jesus perceived in his spirit *2112*
2:12 And **i** he arose, took up the bed, and *2112*
4: 5 and **i** it sprang up, because *it* had no depth *2112*
4:15 Satan cometh **i**, and taketh away the word *2112*
4:16 heard the word, **i** receive it with gladness; *2112*
4:17 for the word's sake, **i** they are offended. *2112*
4:29 **i** he putteth in the sickle, because *2112*
5: 2 **i** there met him out of the tombs a man with *2112*
5:30 And Jesus **i** knowing in himself that virtue *2112*
6:27 And **i** the king sent an executioner, and *2112*
6:50 And **i** he talked with them, and saith unto *2112*
10:52 And **i** he received his sight, and *2112*
14:43 And **i**, while he yet spake, cometh Judas, *2112*
Lk 1:64 And his mouth was opened **i**, and *3916*
4:39 and **i** she arose and ministered unto them. *3916*
5:13 And **i** the leprosy departed from him. *2112*
5:25 And **i** he rose up before them, and took up *3916*
6:49 stream did beat vehemently, and **i** it fell; *2112*
8:44 and **i** her issue of blood stanched. *3916*
8:47 touched him, and how she was healed **i**. *3916*
12:36 and knocketh, they may open unto him **i**. *2112*
13:13 and **i** she was made straight, and *3916*
18:43 And **i** he received his sight, and *3916*
19:11 that the kingdom of God should **i** appear. *3916*
19:40 hold their peace, the stones would **i** cry out. NIG
22:60 And **i**, while he yet spake, the cock crew. *3916*
Jn 5: 9 And **i** the man was made whole, and *2112*
6:21 **i** the ship was at the land whither they *2112*
13:30 He then having received the sop went **i** out: *2112*
18:27 then denied again: and **i** *the* cock crew. *2112*
21: 3 They went forth, and entered into a ship **i**; *2112*
Ac 3: 7 and **i** his feet and ankle bones received *3916*
9:18 And **i** there fell from his eyes as it had been *2112*
9:34 arise, and make thy bed. And he arose **i**. *2112*
10:33 **I** therefore I sent to thee; and thou hast well *1824*
11:11 **i** there were three men **already** come unto *1824*
12:23 And **i** *the* angel of the Lord smote him, *3916*
13:11 And **i** there fell on him a mist and *3916*
16:10 **i** we endeavoured to go into Macedonia, *2112*
16:26 and **i** all the doors were opened, and *3916*
17:10 And the brethren **i** sent away Paul and Silas *2112*
17:14 **i** the brethren sent away Paul to go as *it* *2112*
21:32 Who **i** took soldiers and centurions, and *1824*
Gal 1:16 **i** I conferred not with flesh and blood: *2112*
Rev 4: 2 And **i** I was in the spirit: and behold, *2112*

IMMER (10)
1Ch 9:12 the son of Meshillemith, the son of **I**; 564
24:14 The fifteenth to Bilgah, the sixteenth to **I**, 564
Ezr 2:37 The children of **I**, a thousand fifty and two. 564

Ezr 2:59 Tel-harsa, Cherub, Addan, *and* **I**: 564
10:20 And of the sons of **I**; Hanani, and Zebadiah. 564
Ne 3:29 After them repaired Zadok the son of **I** over 564
7:40 The children of **I**, a thousand fifty and two. 564
7:61 Tel-haresha, Cherub, Addon, and **I**: 564
11:13 the son of Meshillemoth, the son of **I**, 564
Jer 20: 1 Now Pashur the son of **I** the priest, who *was* 564

IMMORAL See WHOREMONGER; WHOREMONGERS

IMMORALITY See LASCIVIOUSNESS

IMMORTAL (1) [IMMORTALITY]
1Ti 1:17 **i**, invisible, the only wise God, *be* honour *862*

IMMORTALITY (5) [IMMORTAL]
Ro 2: 7 well doing seek for glory and honour and **i**, *861*
1Co 15:53 and this mortal *must* put on **i**. *110*
15:54 and this mortal shall have put on **i**, then *110*
1Ti 6:16 Who only hath **i**, dwelling in the light which *110*
2Ti 1:10 brought life and **i** to light through the gospel: *861*

IMMUTABILITY (1) [IMMUTABLE]
Heb 6:17 unto the heirs of promise the **i** of his counsel, *276*

IMMUTABLE (1) [IMMUTABILITY]
Heb 6:18 That by two **i** things, in which *it was* *276*

IMNA (1)
1Ch 7:35 Zophah, and **I**, and Shelesh, and Amal. 3234

IMNAH (2)
1Ch 7:30 **I**, and Isuah, and Ishuai, and Beriah, and 3232
2Ch 31:14 Kore the son of **I** the Levite, the porter 3232

IMNITE See JIMNITES

IMPART (2) [IMPARTED]
Lk 3:11 two coats, let him **i** to him that hath none; *3330*
Ro 1:11 that I may **i** unto you some spiritual gift, *3330*

IMPARTED (2) [IMPART]
Job 39:17 neither hath he **i** to her understanding. 2505
1Th 2: 8 we were willing to have **i** unto you, not *3330*

IMPEDIMENT (1)
Mk 7:32 *that was* deaf, and had an **i in** his **speech**; *3424*

IMPENITENT (1)
Ro 2: 5 **i** heart treasurest up unto thyself wrath *279*

IMPERIOUS (1)
Eze 16:30 *things,* the work of an **i** whorish woman; 7986

IMPERISHABLE See INCORRUPTIBLE; INCORRUPTION

IMPLACABLE (1)
Ro 1:31 without natural affection, **i**, unmerciful: *786*

IMPLEAD (1)
Ac 19:38 there are deputies: let them **i** one another. *1458*

IMPORTUNITY (1)
Lk 11: 8 yet because of his **i** he will rise and give him *335*

IMPOSE (1) [IMPOSED]
Ezr 7:24 it *shall* not *be* lawful to **i** toll, tribute, or 7412

IMPOSED (1) [IMPOSE]
Heb 9:10 **i** *on them* until the time of reformation. *1945*

IMPOSING See STOUT

IMPOSSIBLE (5) [UNPOSSIBLE]
Mk 10:27 With men *it is* **i**, but not with God: *102*
Lk 17: 1 It is **i** but that offences will come: *418*
Heb 6: 4 For *it is* **i** for those who were once *102*
6:18 in which *it was* **i** for God to lie, *102*
11: 6 But without faith *it is* **i** to please *him:* for he *102*

IMPOTENT (4)
Jn 5: 3 In these lay a great multitude of **i** *folk,* of *770*
5: 7 The **i** *man* answered him, Sir, I have no man, *770*
Ac 4: 9 of the good deed done to the **i** man, *772*
14: 8 there sat a certain man at Lystra, **i** in *his* feet, *102*

IMPOVERISH (1) [POVERTY]
Jer 5:17 they shall **i** thy fenced cities, wherein thou 7567

IMPOVERISHED (3) [POVERTY]
Jdg 6: 6 Israel was greatly **i** because of 1809
Isa 40:20 **so i** that he hath no oblation chooseth a tree 5533
Mal 1: 4 We are **i**, but we will return and build 7567

IMPRISONED (1) [PRISON]
Ac 22:19 they know that I **i** and beat in every *5439*

IMPRISONMENT (2) [PRISON]
Ezr 7:26 or to confiscation of goods, or to **i**. 613
Heb 11:36 scourgings, yea, moreover of bonds and **i**: *5438*

IMPRISONMENTS (1) [PRISON]
2Co 6: 5 In stripes, in **i**, in tumults, in labours, *5438*

IMPROPERLY See UNCOMELY

IMPUDENT (3)
Pr 7:13 and with an **i** face said unto him, 5810
Eze 2: 4 For *they are* **i** children and 6440+7186
3: 7 for all the house of Israel *are* **i** 2389+4696

IMPUTE (3) [IMPUTED, IMPUTETH, IMPUTING]
1Sa 22:15 let not the king **i** *any* thing unto his servant, 7760
2Sa 19:19 Let not my lord **i** iniquity unto me, 2803
Ro 4: 8 *is* the man to whom the Lord will not **i** sin. *3049*

IMPUTED (8) [IMPUTE]
Lev 7:18 neither shall it be **i** unto him that offereth it: 2803
17: 4 blood shall be **i** unto that man; he hath shed 2803
Ro 4:11 that righteousness might be **i** unto them *3049*
4:22 therefore it was **i** to him for righteousness. *3049*
4:23 for his sake alone, that it was **i** to him; *3049*
4:24 But for us also, to whom it shall be **i**, if we *3049*
5:13 but sin is not **i** when there is no law. *1677*
Jas 2:23 and it was **i** unto him for righteousness: *3049*

IMPUTETH (2) [IMPUTE]
Ps 32: 2 man unto whom the LORD **i** not iniquity, 2803
Ro 4: 6 unto whom God **i** righteousness without *3049*

IMPUTING (2) [IMPUTE]
Hab 1:11 and offend, *i* this his power unto his god. NIH
2Co 5:19 not **i** their trespasses unto them; *3049*

IMRAH (1)
1Ch 7:36 and Harnepher, and Shual, and Beri, and **I**, 3236

IMRI (2)
1Ch 9: 4 son of Omri, the son of **I**, the son of Bani, 566
Ne 3: 2 next to them builded Zaccur the son of **I**. 566

IN (12674) [HEREIN, INASMUCH, INSOMUCH, INTO, THEREIN, WHEREIN, WHEREINSOEVER, WITHIN] See Index

INASMUCH (9) [AS, IN, MUCH] See Index

INCENSE (129) [FRANKINCENSE]
Ex 25: 6 spices for anointing oil, and for sweet **i**, 7004
30: 1 thou shalt make an altar to burn **i** upon: 7004
30: 7 Aaron shall burn thereon sweet **i** every 7004
30: 7 dresseth the lamps, he shall **burn i** upon it. 6999
30: 8 the lamps at even, he shall **burn i** upon it, 6999
30: 8 a perpetual **i** before the LORD throughout 7004
30: 9 Ye shall offer no strange **i** thereon, nor 7004
30:27 and his vessels, and the altar of **i**, 7004
31: 8 with all his furniture, and the altar of **i**, 7004
31:11 sweet **i** for the holy *place:* according to all 7004
35: 8 spices for anointing oil, and for the sweet **i**, 7004
35:15 the **i** altar and his staves, and the anointing 7004
35:15 the sweet **i**, and the hanging for the door at 7004
35:28 for the anointing oil, and for the sweet **i**. 7004
37:25 he made the **i** altar *of* shittim wood: 7004
37:29 and the pure **i** of sweet spices, 7004
39:38 the sweet **i**, and the hanging for 7004
40: 5 thou shalt set the altar of gold for the **i** 7004
40:27 he burnt sweet **i** thereon; as the LORD 7004
Lev 4: 7 of the altar of sweet **i** before the LORD, 7004
10: 1 put **i** thereon, and offered strange fire 7004
16:12 his hands full of sweet **i** beaten small, and 7004
16:13 he shall put the **i** upon the fire before 7004
16:13 that the cloud of the **i** may cover the mercy 7004
Nu 4:16 and the sweet **i**, and the daily meat offering, 7004
7:14 One spoon of ten *shekels* of gold, full *of* **i**: 7004
7:20 One spoon of gold of ten *shekels,* full *of* **i**: 7004
7:26 One golden spoon of ten *shekels,* full *of* **i**: 7004

Nu 7:32 One golden spoon *of* ten *shekels,* full *of* **i**: 7004
7:38 One golden spoon of ten *shekels,* full *of* **i**: 7004
7:44 One golden spoon of ten *shekels,* full *of* **i**: 7004
7:50 One golden spoon of ten *shekels,* full *of* **i**: 7004
7:56 One golden spoon of ten *shekels,* full *of* **i**: 7004
7:62 One golden spoon of ten *shekels,* full *of* **i**: 7004
7:68 One golden spoon of ten *shekels,* full *of* **i**: 7004
7:74 One golden spoon of ten *shekels,* full *of* **i**: 7004
7:80 One golden spoon of ten *shekels,* full *of* **i**: 7004
7:86 full *of* **i**, *weighing* ten *shekels* apiece, 7004
16: 7 put **i** in them before the LORD to morrow: 7004
16:17 put **i** in them, and bring ye before 7004
16:18 laid **i** thereon, and stood *in* the door of 7004
16:35 two hundred and fifty men that offered **i**. 7004
16:40 come near to offer **i** before the LORD; 7004
16:46 put on **i**, and go quickly unto 7004
16:47 he put on **i**, and made an atonement for 7004
Dt 33:10 they shall put **i** before thee, and 6988
1Sa 2:28 to offer upon mine altar, to burn **i**, to wear 7004
1Ki 3: 3 he sacrificed and **burnt i** in high places. 6999
9:25 he **burnt i** upon the altar that *was* before 6999
11: 8 which **burnt i** and sacrificed unto their 6999
12:33 and he offered upon the altar, and **burnt i**. 6999
13: 1 and Jeroboam stood by the altar to **burn i**. 6999
13: 2 of the high places that **burn i** upon thee, 6999
22:43 *for* the people offered and **burnt i** 4480
2Ki 12: 3 and **burnt i** in the high places. 6999
14: 4 did sacrifice and **burnt i** on the high places. 6999
15: 4 and **burnt i** still on the high places. 6999
15:35 and **burnt i** still in the high places. 6999
16: 4 he sacrificed and **burnt i** in the high places, 6999
17:11 there they **burnt i** in all the high places, 6999
18: 4 days the children of Israel did **burn i** to it: 6999
22:17 and have **burnt i** unto other gods, 6999
23: 5 **burn i** in the high places in the cities of 6999
23: 5 them also that **burnt i** unto Baal, to the sun, 6999
23: 8 high places where the priests had **burnt i**, 6999
1Ch 6:49 on the altar of **i**, *and were appointed* for all 7004
23:13 sons for ever, to **burn i** before the LORD, 6999
28:18 for the altar of **i** refined gold by weight; 7004
2Ch 2: 4 *and* to burn before him sweet **i**, and *for* 7004
13:11 every evening burnt sacrifices and sweet **i**: 7004
25:14 before them, and **burned i** unto them. 6999
26:16 LORD to **burn i** upon the altar of incense. 6999
26:16 LORD to burn incense upon the altar of **i**. 7004
26:18 to **burn i** unto the LORD, but to 6999
26:18 of Aaron, that are consecrated to **burn i**: 6999
26:19 and *had* a censer in his hand to **burn i**: 6999
26:19 of the LORD, from beside the **i** altar. 7004
28: 3 Moreover he **burnt i** in the valley of 6999
28: 4 and **burnt i** in the high places, 6999
28:25 made high places to **burn i** unto other gods, 6999
29: 7 have not **burnt i** nor offered burnt 6999+7004
29:11 *you* should minister unto him, and **burn i**. 6999
30:14 all the **altars for i** took they away, and 6999
32:12 before one altar, and **burn i** upon it? 6999
34:25 and have **burned i** unto other gods, 6999
Ps 66:15 sacrifices of fatlings, with the **i** of rams; 7004
141: 2 Let my prayer be set forth before thee *as* **i**; 7004
Isa 1:13 **i** *is* an abomination unto me; the new 7004
43:23 with an offering, nor wearied thee with **i**. 3828
60: 6 they shall bring gold and **i**; and they shall 3828
65: 3 and **burneth i** upon altars of brick; 6999
65: 7 which have **burnt i** upon the mountains, 6999
66: 3 he that burneth **i**, *as if* he blessed an idol. 3828
Jer 1:16 have **burnt i** unto other gods, and 6999
6:20 To what purpose cometh there to me **i** from 3828
7: 9 **burn i** unto Baal, and walk after other gods 6999
11:12 cry unto the gods unto whom they **offer i**: 6999
11:13 *even* altars to **burn i** unto Baal. 6999
11:17 me to anger in **offering i** unto Baal. 6999
17:26 and **i**, and bringing *sacrifices of* praise, 3828
18:15 they have **burnt i** to vanity, and they have 6999
19: 4 and have **burnt i** in it unto other gods, 6999
19:13 have **burnt i** unto all the host of heaven, 6999
32:29 upon whose roofs they have **offered i** unto 6999
41: 5 with offerings and **i** in their hand, 3828
44: 3 in that *they* went to **burn i**, *and* to serve 6999
44: 5 to **burn** no **i** unto other gods. 6999
44: 8 **burning i** unto other gods in the land of 6999
44:15 their wives had **burnt i** unto other gods, 6999
44:17 to **burn i** unto the queen of heaven, and 6999
44:18 since we left off to **burn i** to the queen of 6999
44:19 when we **burnt i** to the queen of heaven, 6999
44:21 The **i** that ye burnt in the cities of Judah, 7002
44:23 Because you have **burnt i**, and because 6999
44:25 to **burn i** to the queen of heaven, and 6999
48:35 and him that **burneth i** to his gods. 6999
Eze 8:11 in his hand; and a thick cloud of **i** went up. 7004
16:18 hast set mine oil and mine **i** before them. 7004
23:41 whereupon thou hast set mine **i** and 7004
Hos 2:13 where*in* she **burnt i** to them, and 6999
4:13 **burn i** upon the hills, under oaks and 6999
11: 2 and **burned i** to graven images. 6999
Hab 1:16 unto their net, and **burn i** unto their drag; 6999
Mal 1:11 in every place **i** *shall be* offered unto my 6999
Lk 1: 9 his lot was to **burn i** when he went into *2370*
1:10 were praying without at the time of **i**. *2368*
1:11 standing on the right side of the altar of **i**. *2368*
Rev 8: 3 and there was given unto him much **i**, *2368*
8: 4 And the smoke of the **i**, *which came* with *2368*

INCENSED (2)

Isa 41:11 all they that were **i** against thee shall be 2734
45:24 all that are **i** against him shall be ashamed. 2734

INCLINE (16) [INCLINED, INCLINETH]

Jos 24:23 **i** your heart unto the LORD God of Israel. 5186
1Ki 8:58 That *he* may **i** our hearts unto him, to walk 5186
Ps 17: 6 **i** thine ear unto me, *and* hear my speech. 5186
45:10 O daughter, and consider, and **i** thine ear; 5186
49: 4 I will **i** mine ear to a parable: I will open 5186
71: 2 to escape: **i** thine ear unto me, and save me. 5186
78: 1 **i** your ears to the words of my mouth. 5186
88: 2 come before thee: **i** thine ear unto my cry; 5186
102: 2 *when* I am in trouble; **i** thine ear unto me: 5186
119:36 **I** my heart unto thy testimonies, and not to 5186
141: 4 **I** not my heart to *any* evil thing, to practise 5186
Pr 2: 2 So that *thou* **i** thine ear unto wisdom, *and* 7181
4:20 to my words; **i** thine ear unto my sayings. 5186
Isa 37:17 **I** thine ear, O LORD, and hear; open thine 5186
55: 3 **I** your ear, and come unto me: hear, and 5186
Da 9:18 O my God, **i** thine ear, and hear; open thine 5186

INCLINED (13) [INCLINE]

Jdg 9: 3 their hearts **i** to follow Abimelech; for they 5186
Ps 40: 1 and he **i** unto me, and heard my cry. 5186
116: 2 Because he hath **i** his ear unto me, therefore 5186
119:112 I have **i** mine heart to perform thy statutes 5186
Pr 5:13 nor **i** mine ear to them that instructed me! 5186
Jer 7:24 nor **i** their ear, but walked in the counsels 5186
7:26 nor **i** their ear, but hardened their neck: 5186
11: 8 nor **i** their ear, but walked every one in 5186
17:23 neither **i** their ear, but made their neck stiff, 5186
25: 4 have not hearkened, nor **i** your ear to hear. 5186
34:14 hearkened not unto me, neither **i** their ear. 5186
35:15 ye have not **i** your ear, nor hearkened unto 5186
44: 5 nor **i** their ear to turn from their 5186

INCLINETH (1) [INCLINE]

Pr 2:18 For her house **i** unto death, and her paths 7743

INCLOSE (1) [INCLOSED, INCLOSINGS]

SS 8: 9 a door, we will **i** her with boards of cedar. 6696

INCLOSED (8) [INCLOSE]

Ex 39: 6 they wrought onyx stones **i** *in* ouches *of* 5437
39:13 *they were* **i** *in* ouches *of* gold in their 5437
Jdg 20:43 *Thus* they **i** the Benjamites **round about**, 3803
Ps 17:10 They are **i** *in* their own fat: *with* their 5462
22:16 the assembly of the wicked have **i** me: 5362
SS 4:12 A garden **i** *is* my sister, *my* spouse; a spring 5274
La 3: 9 He hath **i** my ways with hewn stone, 1443
Lk 5: 6 this done, they **i** a great multitude of fishes: *4788*

INCLOSINGS (2) [INCLOSE]

Ex 28:20 a jasper: they shall be set in gold in their **i**. 4396
39:13 *were* inclosed *in* ouches *of* gold in their **i**. 4396

INCONTINENCY (1) [INCONTINENT]

1Co 7: 5 that Satan tempt you not for your **i**. *192*

INCONTINENT (1) [INCONTINENCY]

2Ti 3: 3 trucebreakers, false accusers, **i**, fierce, *193*

INCORRUPTIBLE (4) [INCORRUPTION]

1Co 9:25 *it* to obtain a corruptible crown; but we an **i**. *862*
15:52 and the dead shall be raised **i**, and we shall *862*
1Pe 1: 4 To an inheritance **i**, and undefiled, and *862*

1Pe 1:23 but *of* i, by the word of God, which liveth *862*

INCORRUPTION (4) [INCORRUPTIBLE]

1Co 15:42 It is sown in corruption; it is raised in i: *861*
15:50 of God; neither doth corruption inherit i. *861*
15:53 For this corruptible must put on i, and *861*
15:54 So when this corruptible shall have put on i, *861*

INCREASE (88) [INCREASED, INCREASEST, INCREASETH, INCREASING]

Ge 47:24 it shall come to pass in the i, that you shall 8393
Lev 19:25 that *it* may yield unto you the i thereof: 8393
25: 7 in thy land, shall all the i thereof be meat. 8393
25:12 ye shall eat the i thereof out of the field. 8393
25:16 of years thou shalt i the price thereof, 7235
25:20 we shall not sow, nor gather in our i: 8393
25:36 Take thou no usury of him, or i: but 8636
25:37 upon usury, nor lend him thy victuals for i. 4768
26: 4 the land shall yield her i, and the trees of 2981
26:20 for your land shall not yield her i, neither 2981
Nu 18:30 it shall be counted unto the Levites as the i 8393
18:30 and as the i of the winepress. 8393
32:14 up in your fathers' stead, an i of sinful men, 8635
Dt 6: 3 well with thee, and that ye may i mightily, 7235
7:13 the i of thy kine, and the flocks of thy 7698
7:22 lest the beasts of the field i upon thee. 7235
14:22 Thou shalt truly tithe all the i of thy seed, 8393
14:28 forth all the tithe of thine i the same year, 8393
16:15 thy God shall bless thee in all thy i, 8393
26:12 tithing all the tithes of thine i the third year, 8393
28: 4 the i of thy kine, and the flocks of thy 7698
28:18 the i of thy kine, and the flocks of thy 7698
28:51 *or* the i of thy kine, or flocks of thy sheep, 7698
32:13 that he might eat the i of the fields; 8570
32:22 shall consume the earth with her i, and 2981
Jdg 6: 4 destroyed the i of the earth, till thou come 2981
9:29 to Abimelech, I thine army, and come out. 7235
1Sa 2:33 all the i of thine house shall die in 4768
1Ch 27:23 the LORD had said *he* would i Israel like 7235
27:27 over the i of the vineyards for the wine 7945
2Ch 31: 5 oil, and honey, and of all the i of the field; 8393
32:28 Storehouses also for the i of corn, and 8393
Ezr 10:10 to i the trespass of Israel. 3254+5921
Ne 9:37 it **yieldeth** much i unto the kings whom 8393
Job 8: 7 yet thy latter end should greatly i. 7685
20:28 The i of his house shall depart, *and* 2981
31:12 and would root out all mine i. 8393
Ps 44:12 and dost not i *thy wealth* by their price. 7235
62:10 if riches i, set not *your* heart *upon them.* 5107
67: 6 *Then* shall the earth yield her i; *and* God, 2981
71:21 Thou shalt i my greatness, and comfort me 7235
73:12 who prosper in the world; they i *in* riches. 7685
78:46 He gave also their i unto the caterpillar, and 2981
85:12 *is* good; and our land shall yield her i. 2981
107:37 plant vineyards, which may yield fruits of i. 8393
115:14 The LORD shall i you **more and more**, 3254
Pr 1: 5 A wise *man* will hear, and will i learning; 3254
3: 9 and with the firstfruits of all thine i: 8393
9: 9 teach a just *man*, and he will i in learning. 3254
13:11 but he that gathereth by labour shall i. 7235
14: 4 but much i *is* by the strength of the ox. 8393
18:20 *and with* the i of his lips shall he be filled. 8393
22:16 He that oppresseth the poor to i his *riches*, 7235
28:28 but when they perish, the righteous i. 7235
Ecc 5:10 nor he that loveth abundance *with* i: 8393
5:11 When goods i, they are increased that eat 7235
6:11 Seeing there be many things that i vanity, 7235
Isa 9: 7 Of the i of *his* government and peace *there* 4766
29:19 The meek also shall i *their* joy in 3254
30:23 bread of the i of the earth, and it shall be fat 8393
57: 9 didst i thy perfumes, and didst send thy 7235
Jer 2: 3 unto the LORD, *and* the firstfruits of his i: 8393
23: 3 their folds; and they shall be fruitful and i. 7235
Eze 5:16 I *will* i the famine upon you, and will break 3254
18: 8 forth upon usury, neither hath taken any i, 8636
18:13 given forth upon usury, and hath taken i: 8636
18:17 *that* hath not received usury nor i, 8636
22:12 thou hast taken usury and i, and thou hast 8636
34:27 the earth shall yield her i, and they shall be 2981
36:11 and beast; and they shall i and bring fruit: 7235
36:29 and will i it, and lay no famine upon you. 7235
36:30 the fruit of the tree, and the i of the field, 8570
36:37 I will i them *with* men like a flock. 7235
48:18 the i thereof shall be for food unto them 8393
Da 11:39 he shall acknowledge *and* i *with* glory: 7235
Hos 4:10 shall commit whoredom, and shall not i: 6555
Zec 8:12 the ground shall give her i, and the heavens 2981
10: 8 and they shall i as they have increased. 7235
Lk 17: 5 the apostles said unto the Lord, I our faith. *4369*
Jn 3:30 He must i, but I *must* decrease. *837*
1Co 3: 6 Apollos watered; but God **gave the** i. *837*
3: 7 he that watereth; but God that **giveth** the i. *837*
2Co 9:10 and i the fruits of your righteousness;) *837*
Eph 4:16 maketh i of the body unto the edifying of *838*
Col 2:19 knit together, increaseth *with* the i of God. *838*
1Th 3:12 And the Lord **make** you **to** i and abound in *4121*
4:10 brethren, that *ye* i more *and more;* *4052*
2Ti 2:16 for they will i unto more ungodliness. *4298*

INCREASED (49) [INCREASE]

Ge 7:17 the waters i, and bare up the ark, and it was 7235
7:18 and were i greatly upon the earth; 7235
30:30 I *came,* and it is *now* i unto a multitude; 6555
30:43 the man i exceedingly, and had much cattle, 6555
Ex 1: 7 i **abundantly**, and multiplied, and 8317
23:30 until thou be i, and inherit the land. 6509
1Sa 14:19 in the host of the Philistines went on and i: 7227
2Sa 15:12 for the people i continually with Absalom. 7227
1Ki 22:35 the battle i that day: and the king was 5927
1Ch 4:38 and the house of their fathers i greatly. 6555
5:23 they i from Bashan unto Baal-hermon and 7235
2Ch 18:34 the battle i that day: howbeit the king of 5927
Ezr 9: 6 for our iniquities are i over *our* head, and 7235
Job 1:10 his hands, and his substance is i in the land. 6555
Ps 3: 1 LORD, how are they i that trouble me! 7231
4: 7 *in* the time *that* their corn and their wine i. 7231
49:16 made rich, when the glory of his house is i; 7235
105:24 he i his people greatly; and made them 6509
Pr 9:11 and the years of thy life shall be i. 3254
Ecc 2: 9 i **more** than all that were before me in 3254
5:11 goods increase, they are i that eat them: 7231
Isa 9: 3 hast multiplied the nation, *and* not i the joy: 1431
26:15 Thou hast i the nation, O LORD, thou hast 3254
26:15 O LORD, thou hast i the nation: 3254
51: 2 him alone, and blessed him, and i him. 7235
Jer 3:16 when ye be multiplied and i in the land, 6509
5: 6 are many, *and* their backslidings are i. 6105
15: 8 Their widows are i to me above the sand of 6105
29: 6 that ye may be i there, and not diminished. 7235
30:14 of thine iniquity; *because* thy sins were i. 6105
30:15 *because* thy sins were i, I have done these 6105
La 2: 5 hath i in the daughter of Judah mourning 7235
Eze 16: 7 thou hast i and waxen great, and thou art 7235
16:26 hast i thy whoredoms, to provoke me to 7235
23:14 *that* she i her whoredoms: for when she saw 3254
28: 5 *and* by thy traffick hast thou i thy riches, 7235
41: 7 i *from* the lowest *chamber* to the highest by 5927
Da 12: 4 run to and fro, and knowledge shall be i. 7235
Hos 4: 7 As they were i, so they sinned against me: 7230
10: 1 multitude of his fruit he hath i the altars; 7235
Am 4: 9 and your fig trees and your olive trees i, 7235
Zec 10: 8 and they shall increase as they have i. 7235
Mk 4: 8 and did yield fruit that sprang up and i; *837*
Lk 2:52 And Jesus i in wisdom and stature, and *4298*
Ac 6: 7 And the word of God i; and the number of *837*
9:22 But Saul i the more **in strength**, and *1743*
16: 5 in the faith, and i in number daily. *4052*
2Co 10:15 but having hope, when your faith is i, *837*
Rev 3:17 and i **with goods**, and have need of *4147*

INCREASEST (1) [INCREASE]

Job 10:17 and i thine indignation upon me; 7235

INCREASETH (15) [INCREASE]

Job 10:16 For it i. Thou huntest me as a fierce lion: 1342
12:23 He i the nations, and destroyeth them: 7679
Ps 74:23 those that rise up against thee i continually. 5927
Pr 11:24 There is that scattereth, and yet i; and 3254
16:21 and the sweetness of the lips i learning. 3254
23:28 a prey, and i the transgressors among men. 3254
24: 5 yea, a man of knowledge i strength. 553
28: 8 by usury and unjust gain i his substance, 7235
29:16 the wicked are multiplied, transgression i: 7235
Ecc 1:18 and he that i knowledge increaseth sorrow. 3254
1:18 and he that increaseth knowledge i sorrow. 3254
Isa 40:29 to *them that have* no might he i strength. 7235
Hos 12: 1 he daily i lies and desolation; and they do 7235
Hab 2: 6 say, Woe to him that i *that which is* not his! 7235

Col 2:19 and knit together, **i** *with* the increase of God. *837*

INCREASING (1) [INCREASE]
Col 1:10 good work, and **i** in the knowledge of God; *837*

INCREDIBLE (1)
Ac 26: 8 Why should it be thought *a thing* **i** with you, *571*

INCURABLE (6)
2Ch 21:18 him in his bowels with an **i** disease. 369+4832
Job 34: 6 my wound *is* **i** without transgression. 605
Jer 15:18 Why is my pain perpetual, and my wound **i**, 605
30:12 Thy bruise *is* **i**, *and* thy wound *is* grievous. 605
30:15 thy sorrow *is* **i** for the multitude of thine 605
Mic 1: 9 For her wound *is* **i**; for it is come unto Judah; 605

INDEBTED (1) [DEBT]
Lk 11: 4 for we also forgive every one *that is* **i** to us. *3784*

INDECENT See UNSEEMLY

INDECISIVE See TENDERHEARTED

INDEED (70) See Index

INDESCRIBABLE See UNSPEAKABLE

INDIA (2)
Est 1: 1 from **I** even unto Ethiopia, *over* an hundred 1912
8: 9 rulers of the provinces which *are* from **I** 1912

INDIGNATION (41)
Dt 29:28 in great **i**, and cast them into another land, 7110
2Ki 3:27 there was great **i** against Israel: and 7110
Ne 4: 1 **took** great **i**, and mocked the Jews. 3707
Est 5: 9 for him, he was full *of* **i** against Mordecai. 2534
Job 10:17 against me, and increasest thine **i** upon me; 3708
Ps 69:24 Pour out thine **i** upon them, and let thy 2195
78:49 wrath, and **i**, and trouble, *by* sending evil 2195
102:10 Because of thine **i** and thy wrath: for thou 2195
Isa 10: 5 and the staff in their hand *is* mine **i**. 2195
10:25 the **i** shall cease, and mine anger in their 2195
13: 5 *even* the LORD, and the weapons of his **i**, 2195
26:20 for a little moment, until the **i** be overpast. 2195
30:27 his lips are full *of* **i**, and his tongue as a 2195
30:30 with the **i** of *his* anger, and *with* the flame 2197
34: 2 For the **i** of the LORD *is* upon all nations, 7110
66:14 his servants, and *his* **i** towards his enemies. 2194
Jer 10:10 the nations shall not be able to abide his **i**. 2195
15:17 of thy hand: for thou hast filled me *with* **i**. 2195
50:25 and hath brought forth the weapons of his **i**: 2195
La 2: 6 hath despised in the **i** of his anger the king 2195
Eze 21:31 I will pour out mine **i** upon thee, I will blow 2195
22:24 nor rained upon in the day of **i**. 2195
22:31 Therefore have I poured out mine **i** upon 2195
Da 8:19 know what shall be in the last end of the **i**: 2195
11:30 and have **i** against the holy covenant: 2194
11:36 and shall prosper till the **i** be accomplished: 2195
Mic 7: 9 I will bear the **i** of the LORD, because 2197
Na 1: 6 Who can stand before his **i**? and who can 2195
Hab 3:12 Thou didst march through the land in **i**, 2195
Zep 3: 8 to pour upon them mine **i**, *even* all my 2195
Zec 1:12 *against* which thou hast had **i** these 2194
Mal 1: 4 *against* whom the LORD hath **i** for ever. 2194
Mt 20:24 were **moved with i** against the two brethren. *23*
26: 8 But when his disciples saw *it*, they **had i**, *23*
Mk 14: 4 And there were some that **had i** within *23*
Lk 13:14 the ruler of the synagogue answered with **i**, *23*
Ac 5:17 of the Sadducees,) and were filled with **i**, *2205*
Ro 2: 8 but obey unrighteousness, **i** and wrath, *2372*
2Co 7:11 yea, *what* **i**, yea, *what* fear, yea, *24*
Heb 10:27 fearful looking for of judgment and fiery **i**, *2205*
Rev 14:10 out without mixture into the cup of his **i**; *3709*

INDITING (1)
Ps 45: 1 My heart is **i** a good matter: I speak of 7370

INDUSTRIOUS (1)
1Ki 11:28 seeing the young man that he was **i**, 4399+6213

INEXCUSABLE (1)
Ro 2: 1 Therefore thou art **i**, O man, whosoever thou *379*

INEXPRESSIBLE See UNSPEAKABLE

INFALLIBLE (1)
Ac 1: 3 alive after his passion by many **i proofs**, *5039*

INFAMOUS (1) [INFAMY]
Eze 22: 5 *which art* **i** *and* much vexed. 2931+8034+1886.1

INFAMY (2) [INFAMOUS]
Pr 25:10 thee to shame, and thine **i** turn not away. 1681
Eze 36: 3 lips of talkers, and *are* an **i** of the people: 1681

INFANT (2) [INFANTS]
1Sa 15: 3 **i** and suckling, ox and sheep, camel and 5768
Isa 65:20 There shall be no more thence an **i** of days, 5764

INFANTS (3) [INFANT]
Job 3:16 I had not been; as **i** *which* never saw light. 5768
Hos 13:16 their **i** shall be dashed in pieces, and 5768
Lk 18:15 And they brought unto him also **i**, that he *1025*

INFERIOR (4)
Job 12: 3 as well as you; I *am* not **i** to you: 5307
13: 2 *same* do I know also. I *am* not **i** unto you. 5307
Da 2:39 after thee shall arise another kingdom **i** to 772
2Co 12:13 For what is it wherein ye were **i** to other *2274*

INFIDEL (2)
2Co 6:15 or what part hath he that believeth with an **i**? *571*
1Ti 5: 8 hath denied the faith, and is worse than an **i**. *571*

INFINITE (3)
Job 22: 5 and thine iniquities **i**? 369+7093
Ps 147: 5 of great power: his understanding *is* **i**. 369+4557
Na 3: 9 Egypt *were* her strength, and *it was* **i**; 369+7097

INFIRMITIES (12) [INFIRMITY]
Mt 8:17 saying Himself took our **i**, and bare our *769*
Lk 5:15 to hear, and to be healed by him of their **i**. *769*
7:21 in that *same* hour he cured many of *their* **i** *3554*
8: 2 which had been healed of evil spirits and **i**, *769*
Ro 8:26 Likewise the Spirit also helpeth our **i**: for we *769*
15: 1 that are strong ought to bear the **i** of *771*
2Co 11:30 glory of the *things* which concern mine **i**. *769*
12: 5 yet of myself I will not glory, but in mine **i**. *769*
12: 9 therefore will I rather glory in my **i**, *769*
12:10 Therefore I take pleasure in **i**, in reproaches, *769*
1Ti 5:23 for thy stomach's sake and thine often **i**. *769*
Heb 4:15 cannot be touched with the feeling of our **i**; *769*

INFIRMITY (10) [INFIRMITIES]
Lev 12: 2 the separation for her **i** shall she be unclean. 1738
Ps 77:10 I said, This *is* my **i**: *but I will remember* 2470
Pr 18:14 The spirit of a man will sustain his **i**; but 4245
Lk 13:11 there was a woman which had a spirit of **i** *769*
13:12 unto her, Woman, thou art loosed from thy **i**. *769*
Jn 5: 5 which had an **i** thirty *and* eight years. *769*
Ro 6:19 of men because of the **i** of your flesh: *769*
Gal 4:13 Ye know how through **i** of the flesh I *769*
Heb 5: 2 for that he himself also is compassed with **i**. *769*
7:28 law maketh men high priests which have **i**; *769*

INFLAME (1) [INFLAMING, INFLAMMATION]
Isa 5:11 that continue until night, *till* wine **i** them! 1814

INFLAMING (1) [INFLAME]
Isa 57: 5 **I** yourselves with idols under every green 2552

INFLAMMATION (2) [INFLAME]
Lev 13:28 him clean: for it *is* an **i** of the burning. 6867
Dt 28:22 with an **i**, and with an extreme burning, and 1816

INFLICTED (1)
2Co 2: 6 *is* this punishment, which *was* **i** of many. NIG

INFLUENCES (1)
Job 38:31 Canst thou bind the **sweet i** of Pleiades, or 4575

INFOLDING (1)
Eze 1: 4 a fire **i** itself, and a brightness *was* about it, 3947

INFORM (1) [INFORMED]
Dt 17:10 to do according to all that they **i** thee: 3384

INFORMED (6) [INFORM]
Da 9:22 he **i** *me*, and talked with me, and said, 995
Ac 21:21 And they are **i** of thee, that thou teachest all *2727*
21:24 whereof they were **i** concerning thee, *2727*
24: 1 who **i** the governor against Paul. *1718*
25: 2 the chief of the Jews **i** him against Paul, *1718*
25:15 the elders of the Jews **i** *me*, desiring *to have* *1718*

INGATHERING (2) [GATHER]
Ex 23:16 the feast of **i**, *which is* in the end of the year, 614
34:22 and the feast of **i** *at* the year's end. 614

INHABIT (10) [HABITABLE, HABITATION, HABITATIONS, INHABITANT, INHABITANTS, INHABITED, INHABITERS, INHABITEST, INHABITETH, INHABITING]
Nu 35:34 therefore the land which ye shall **i**, 3427
Pr 10:30 but the wicked shall not **i** the earth. 7931
Isa 42:11 *their voice,* the villages *that* Kedar doth **i**: 3427
65:21 **i** *them;* and they shall plant vineyards, and 3427
65:22 They shall not build, and another **i**; 3427
Jer 17: 6 shall **i** the parched places in the wilderness, 7931
48:18 Thou daughter that dost **i** Dibon, 3427
Eze 33:24 they that **i** those wastes of the land of Israel 3427
Am 9:14 **i** *them;* and they shall plant vineyards, and 3427
Zep 1:13 not **i** *them;* and they shall plant vineyards, 3427

INHABITANT (33) [INHABIT]
Job 28: 4 The flood breaketh out from the **i**; *even* 1481
Isa 5: 9 be desolate, *even* great and fair, without **i**. 3427
6:11 Until the cities be wasted without **i**, and 3427
9: 9 *even* Ephraim and the **i** of Samaria, that say 3427
12: 6 Cry out and shout, thou **i** of Zion: for great 3427
20: 6 the **i** of this isle shall say in that day, 3427
24:17 the snare, *are* upon thee, O **i** of the earth. 3427
33:24 the **i** shall not say, I am sick: the people that 7934
Jer 2:15 land waste: his cities are burnt without **i**. 3427
4: 7 thy cities shall be laid waste, without an **i**. 3427
9:11 the cities of Judah desolate, without an **i**. 3427
10:17 wares out of the land, O **i** of the fortress. 3427
21:13 O **i** of the valley, *and* rock of the plain, 3427
22:23 O **i** of Lebanon, that makest thy nest in 3427
26: 9 and this city shall be desolate without an **i**? 3427
33:10 and without **i**, and without beast, 3427
34:22 the cities of Judah a desolation without an **i**. 3427
44:22 and a curse, without an **i**, as *at* this day. 3427
46:19 shall be waste and desolate without an **i**. 3427
48:19 O **i** of Aroer, stand by the way and espy; 3427
48:43 upon thee, O **i** of Moab, saith the LORD. 3427
51:29 land of Babylon a desolation without an **i**. 3427
51:35 *be* upon Babylon, shall the **i** of Zion say; 3427
51:37 and a hissing, without an **i**. 3427
Am 1: 5 cut off the **i** from the plain of Aven, and 3427
1: 8 I will cut off the **i** from Ashdod, and 3427
Mic 1:11 Pass ye away, thou **i** of Saphir, having *thy* 3427
1:11 the **i** of Zaanan came not forth *in* 3427
1:12 For the **i** of Maroth waited carefully for 3427
1:13 O thou **i** of Lachish, bind the chariot to 3427
1:15 I bring an heir unto thee, O **i** of Mareshah: 3427
Zep 2: 5 even destroy thee, that there shall be no **i**. 3427
3: 6 so that there is no man, that there is none **i**. 3427

INHABITANTS (201) [INHABIT]
Ge 19:25 all the **i** of the cities, and that which grew 3427
34:30 make me to stink among the **i** of the land, 3427
50:11 when the **i** of the land, the Canaanites, saw 3427
Ex 15:14 sorrow shall take hold on the **i** of Palestina. 3427
15:15 all the **i** of Canaan shall melt away. 3427
23:31 for I will deliver the **i** of the land into your 3427
34:12 lest thou make a covenant with the **i** of 3427
34:15 Lest thou make a covenant with the **i** of 3427
Lev 18:25 and the land *itself* vomiteth out her **i**. 3427
25:10 *all* the land unto all the **i** thereof: 3427
Nu 13:32 *is* a land that eateth up the **i** thereof; 3427
14:14 they will tell *it* to the **i** of this land: *for* they 3427
32:17 fenced cities because of the **i** of the land. 3427
33:52 ye shall drive out all the **i** of the land from 3427
33:53 ye shall dispossess *the i of* the land, and NIH
33:55 if ye will not drive out the **i** of the land 3427
Dt 13:13 have withdrawn the **i** of their city, saying, 3427
13:15 Thou shalt surely smite the **i** of that city 3427
Jos 2: 9 that all the **i** of the land faint because of 3427
2:24 for even all the **i** of the country do faint 3427
7: 9 and all the **i** of the land shall hear *of it,* and 3427
8:24 an end of slaying all the **i** of Ai in the field, 3427
8:26 until *he* had utterly destroyed all the **i** of Ai. 3427
9: 3 when the **i** of Gibeon heard what Joshua 3427
9:11 and all the **i** of our country spake to us, 3427
9:24 to destroy all the **i** of the land from before 3427
10: 1 how the **i** of Gibeon had made peace with 3427
11:19 of Israel, save the Hivites the **i** of Gibeon: 3427
13: 6 All the **i** of the hill country from Lebanon 3427
15:15 he went up thence to the **i** of Debir: and 3427
15:63 As for the Jebusites the **i** of Jerusalem, 3427
17: 7 on the right hand unto the **i** of En-tappuah. 3427
17:11 the **i** of Dor and her towns, and 3427
17:11 the **i** of Endor and her towns, and 3427
17:11 the **i** of Taanach and her towns, and 3427
17:11 and the **i** of Megiddo and her towns, 3427
17:12 could not drive out *the i of* those cities; NIH
Jdg 1:11 from thence he went against the **i** of Debir: 3427
1:19 he drave out *the i of* the mountain; but NIH
1:19 could not drive out the **i** of the valley, 3427
1:27 Neither did Manasseh drive out *the i of* NIH
1:27 her towns, nor the **i** of Dor and her towns, 3427
1:27 nor the **i** of Ibleam and her towns, 3427
1:27 nor the **i** of Megiddo and her towns: 3427
1:30 Neither did Zebulun drive out the **i** of 3427
1:30 inhabitants of Kitron, nor the **i** of Nahalol; 3427
1:31 Neither did Asher drive out the **i** of Accho, 3427
1:31 nor the **i** of Zidon, nor of Ahlab, nor of 3427
1:32 among the Canaanites, the **i** of the land: 3427
1:33 Neither did Naphtali drive out the **i** of 3427
1:33 of Beth-shemesh, nor the **i** of Beth-anath; 3427
1:33 among the Canaanites, the **i** of the land: 3427
1:33 nevertheless the **i** of Beth-shemesh and 3427
2: 2 ye shall make no league with the **i** of this 3427
5: 7 *The i of* the villages ceased, they ceased in NIH
5:11 *even* the righteous acts *towards the i* of his NIH
5:23 the LORD, curse ye bitterly the **i** thereof; 3427
10:18 he shall be head over all the **i** of Gilead. 3427
11: 8 and be our head over all the **i** of Gilead. 3427
11:21 land of the Amorites, the **i** of that country. 3427
20:15 that drew sword, beside the **i** of Gibeah, 3427
21: 9 *there were* none of the **i** of Jabesh-gilead 3427
21:10 smite the **i** of Jabesh-gilead with the edge 3427
21:12 they found among the **i** of Jabesh-gilead 3427
Ru 4: 4 Buy *it* before the **i**, and before the elders of 3427
1Sa 6:21 they sent messengers to the **i** of 3427
23: 5 So David saved the **i** of Keilah. 3427
27: 8 for those *nations were* of old the **i** of 3427
31:11 when the **i** of Jabesh-gilead heard of that 3427
2Sa 5: 6 unto the Jebusites, the **i** of the land: 3427
1Ki 17: 1 *who was* of the **i** of Gilead, said unto Ahab, 8453
21:11 and the nobles who *were* the **i** in his city, 3427
2Ki 19:26 Therefore their **i** *were* of small power, 3427
22:16 evil upon this place, and upon the **i** thereof, 3427
22:19 against the **i** thereof, that *they* should 3427
23: 2 and all the **i** of Jerusalem with him, 3427
1Ch 8: 6 these *are* the heads of the fathers of the **i** of 3427
8:13 who *were* heads of the fathers of the **i** of 3427
8:13 of Aijalon, who drove away the **i** of Gath: 3427
9: 2 Now the first **i** that *dwelt* in their 3427
11: 4 where the Jebusites *were,* the **i** of the land. 3427
11: 5 the **i** of Jebus said to David, Thou shalt not 3427
22:18 for he hath given the **i** of the land into mine 3427
2Ch 15: 5 great vexations *were* upon all the **i** of 3427
20: 7 who didst drive out the **i** of this land before 3427
20:15 ye **i** of Jerusalem, and thou king 3427
20:18 the **i** of Jerusalem fell before the LORD, 3427
20:20 Hear me, O Judah, and ye **i** of Jerusalem; 3427
20:23 Moab stood up against the **i** of mount Seir, 3427
20:23 when they had made an end of the **i** of Seir, 3427
21:11 caused the **i** of Jerusalem to commit 3427
21:13 and the **i** of Jerusalem to go a whoring, 3427
22: 1 the **i** of Jerusalem made Ahaziah his 3427
32:22 the **i** of Jerusalem from the hand of 3427
32:26 *both* he and the **i** of Jerusalem, so that 3427
32:33 the **i** of Jerusalem did him honour at his 3427
33: 9 made Judah and the **i** of Jerusalem to err, 3427
34:24 evil upon this place, and upon the **i** thereof, 3427
34:27 against the **i** thereof, and humbledst thyself 3427
34:28 upon this place, and upon the **i** of the same. 3427
34:30 the **i** of Jerusalem, and the priests, and 3427
34:32 Benjamin to stand *to it.* And the **i** of 3427
35:18 that were present, and the **i** of Jerusalem. 3427
Ezr 4: 6 *him* an accusation against the **i** of Judah 3427
Ne 3:13 gate repaired Hanun, and the **i** of Zanoah; 3427
7: 3 and appoint watches of the **i** of Jerusalem, 3427
9:24 thou subduedst before them the **i** of 3427
Job 26: 5 from under the waters, and the **i** thereof. 7931
Ps 33: 8 let all the **i** of the world stand in awe of 3427
33:14 he looketh upon all the **i** of the earth. 3427
49: 1 all ye people; give ear, all ye **i** of the world: 3427
75: 3 and all the **i** thereof *are* dissolved: 3427
83: 7 Amalek; the Philistines with the **i** of Tyre; 3427
Isa 5: 3 O **i** of Jerusalem, and men of Judah, judge, 3427

Isa 8:14 a gin and for a snare to the i of Jerusalem. 3427
10:13 I have put down the i like a valiant *man:* 3427
10:31 the i of Gebim gather themselves to flee. 3427
18: 3 All ye i of the world, and dwellers on 3427
21:14 The i of the land of Tema brought water to 3427
22:21 he shall be a father to the i of Jerusalem, 3427
23: 2 Be still, ye i of the isle; thou whom 3427
23: 6 ye over to Tarshish; howl, ye i of the isle. 3427
24: 1 and scattereth abroad the i thereof. 3427
24: 5 The earth also is defiled under the i thereof; 3427
24: 6 therefore the i of the earth are burned, and 3427
26: 9 the i of the world will learn righteousness. 3427
26:18 neither have the i of the world fallen. 3427
26:21 punish the i of the earth for their iniquity: 3427
37:27 Therefore their i *were* of small power, 3427
38:11 I shall behold man no more with the i of 3427
40:22 and the i thereof *are* as grasshoppers; 3427
42:10 that is therein; the isles, and the i thereof. 3427
42:11 let the i of the rock sing, let them shout 3427
49:19 even now be too narrow by reason of the i, 3427
Jer 1:14 shall break forth upon all the i of the land. 3427
4: 4 ye men of Judah and i of Jerusalem: 3427
6:12 for I will stretch out my hand upon the i of 3427
8: 1 the bones of the i of Jerusalem, out of their 3427
10:18 I will sling out the i of the land at this once, 3427
11: 2 the men of Judah, and to the i of Jerusalem; 3427
11: 9 of Judah, and among the i of Jerusalem. 3427
11:12 the cities of Judah and i of Jerusalem go, 3427
13:13 Behold, I *will* fill all the i of this land, 3427
13:13 and the prophets, and all the i of Jerusalem, 3427
17:20 and all Judah, and all the i of Jerusalem, 3427
17:25 the men of Judah, and the i of Jerusalem: 3427
18:11 to the i of Jerusalem, saying, Thus saith 3427
19: 3 O kings of Judah, and i of Jerusalem; 3427
19:12 to the i thereof, and *even* make this city as 3427
21: 6 I will smite the i of this city, both man and 3427
23:14 as Sodom, and the i thereof as Gomorrah. 3427
25: 2 and to all the i of Jerusalem, saying, 3427
25: 9 against the i thereof, and against all these 3427
25:29 for I *will* call for a sword upon all the i of 3427
25:30 *the grapes,* against all the i of the earth. 3427
26:15 and upon this city, and upon the i thereof: 3427
32:32 the men of Judah, and the i of Jerusalem. 3427
35:13 the men of Judah and the i of Jerusalem, 3427
35:17 upon all the i of Jerusalem all the evil that I 3427
36:31 upon the i of Jerusalem, and upon the men 3427
42:18 my fury hath been poured forth upon the i 3427
46: 8 I will destroy the city and the i thereof. 3427
47: 2 and all the i of the land shall howl. 3427
49: 8 turn back, dwell deep, O i of Dedan; 3427
49:20 that he hath purposed against the i of 3427
49:30 get you far off, dwell deep, O ye i of Hazor, 3427
50:21 *even* against it, and against the i of Pekod: 3427
50:34 to the land, and disquiet the i of Babylon. 3427
50:35 upon the i of Babylon, and upon her 3427
51:12 done that which he spake against the i of 3427
51:24 to all the i of Chaldea all their evil that they 3427
51:35 my blood upon the i of Chaldea, 3427
La 4:12 kings of the earth, and all the i of the world, 3427
Eze 11:15 *are* they unto whom the i of Jerusalem have 3427
12:19 of the i of Jerusalem, *and* of the land of 3427
15: 6 for fuel, so will I give the i of Jerusalem. 3427
26:17 which wast strong in the sea, she and her i, 3427
27: 8 The i of Zidon and Arvad were thy 3427
27:35 All the i of the isles shall be astonished at 3427
29: 6 all the i of Egypt shall know that I *am* 3427
Da 4:35 all the i of the earth *are* reputed as nothing: 1753
4:35 of heaven, and *among* the i of the earth: 1753
9: 7 to the i of Jerusalem, and unto all Israel, 3427
Hos 4: 1 hath a controversy with the i of the land, 3427
10: 5 The i of Samaria shall fear because of 7934
Joel 1: 2 old men, and give ear, all ye i of the land. 3427
1:14 all the i of the land *into* the house of 3427
2: 1 let all the i of the land tremble: for the day 3427
Mic 6:12 the i thereof have spoken lies, and 3427
6:16 a desolation, and the i thereof a hissing: 3427
Zep 1: 4 and upon all the i of Jerusalem; 3427
1:11 Howl, ye i of Maktesh, for all the merchant 3427
2: 5 Woe unto the i of the sea coast, the nation 3427
Zec 8:20 shall come people, and the i of many cities: 3427
8:21 the i of one *city* shall go to another, saying, 3427
11: 6 For I will no more pity the i of the land, 3427
12: 5 The i of Jerusalem *shall be* my strength in 3427
12: 7 the glory of the i of Jerusalem do not 3427
12: 8 In that day shall the LORD defend the i of 3427
12:10 upon the i of Jerusalem, the spirit of grace 3427
13: 1 to the i of Jerusalem for sin and 3427

INHABITED (32) [INHABIT]

Ge 36:20 the sons of Seir the Horite, who i the land; 3427
Ex 16:35 forty years, until they came to a land i; 3427
Lev 16:22 him all their iniquities unto a land **not** i: 1509
Jdg 1:17 they slew the Canaanites that i Zephath, 3427
1:21 not drive out the Jebusites that i Jerusalem; 3427
1Ch 5: 9 eastward he i unto the entering in of 3427
Isa 13:20 It shall never be i, neither shall it be dwelt 3427
44:26 that saith to Jerusalem, Thou shalt be i; and 3427
45:18 created it not in vain, he formed it to be i: 3427
54: 3 and **make** the desolate cities **to be** i. 3427
Jer 6: 8 lest I make thee desolate, a land not i. 3427
17: 6 in the wilderness, *in* a salt land and not i. 3427
22: 6 thee a wilderness *and* cities *which* are not i. 3427
46:26 afterwards it shall be i, as *in* the days of 7931
50:13 of the wrath of the LORD it shall not be i, 3427
50:39 it shall be no more i for ever; neither shall 3427
Eze 12:20 the cities that are i shall be laid waste, and 3427
26:17 *that wast* i of seafaring men, the renowned 3427
26:19 a desolate city, like the cities that are not i; 3427
26:20 that go down to the pit, that thou be not i; 3427
29:11 through it, neither shall it be i forty years. 3427
34:13 and in all the i **places** of the country. 4186
36:10 the cities shall be i, and the wastes shall be 3427
36:35 ruined cities *are become* fenced, *and* are i. 3427
38:12 upon the desolate places *that are now* i, 3427
Zec 2: 4 Jerusalem shall be i *as* towns without walls 3427
7: 7 when Jerusalem was i and in prosperity, 3427
7: 7 when *men* i the south and the plain? 3427
9: 5 from Gaza, and Ashkelon shall not be i. 3427
12: 6 Jerusalem shall be i again in her own place, 3427
14:10 it shall be lifted up, and i in her place, from 3427
14:11 but Jerusalem shall be safely i. 3427

INHABITERS (3) [INHABIT]

Rev 8:13 to the i of the earth by reason of the other *2730*
12:12 Woe to the i of the earth and of the sea! *2730*
17: 2 the i of the earth have been made drunk *2730*

INHABITEST (1) [INHABIT]

Ps 22: 3 *art* holy, O thou that i the praises of Israel. 3427

INHABITETH (2) [INHABIT]

Job 15:28 *and* in houses which no man i, which are 3427
Isa 57:15 saith the high and lofty One that i eternity, 7931

INHABITING (1) [INHABIT]

Ps 74:14 *to be* meat to the people i **the wilderness**. 6728

INHERIT (62) [INHERITANCE, INHERITANCES, INHERITED, INHERITETH, INHERITOR]

Ge 15: 7 the Chaldees, to give thee this land to i it. 3423
15: 8 whereby shall I know that I shall i it? 3423
28: 4 that thou mayest i the land wherein thou art 3423
Ex 23:30 until thou be increased, and i the land. 5157
32:13 unto your seed, and they shall i *it* for ever. 5157
Lev 20:24 Ye shall i their land, and I will give it unto 3423
25:46 after you, to i *them for* a possession; 3423
Nu 18:24 I have given to the Levites to i: 5159
26:55 of the tribes of their fathers they shall i. 5157
32:19 For we will not i with them on *yonder* side 5157
33:54 to the tribes of your fathers ye shall i. 5157
34:13 This *is* the land which ye shall i by lot, 5157
Dt 1:38 for he shall **cause** Israel **to** i it. 5157
2:31 to possess, that *thou* mayest i his land. 3423
3:28 he shall **cause** them **to** i the land which 5157
12:10 the LORD your God **giveth** you **to** i, 5157
16:20 i the land which the LORD thy God 3423
19: 3 which the LORD thy God **giveth** thee **to** i, 5157
19:14 which thou shalt i in the land that 5157
21:16 when he **maketh** his sons **to** i *that* which he 5157
31: 7 and thou shalt **cause** them **to** i it. 5157
Jos 17:14 given me *but* one lot and one portion to i, 5159
Jdg 11: 2 Thou shalt not i in our father's house; 5157
1Sa 2: 8 and to **make** them i the throne of glory: 5157
2Ch 20:11 which thou hast **given** us **to** i. 3423
Ps 25:13 dwell at ease; and his seed shall i the earth. 3423
37: 9 upon the LORD, they shall i the earth. 3423
37:11 the meek shall i the earth; and shall delight 3423
37:22 For such as be blessed of him shall i 3423

I

Ps 37:29 The righteous shall i the land, and 3423
37:34 and he shall exalt thee to i the land: 3423
69:36 The seed also of his servants shall i it: and 5157
82: 8 judge the earth: for thou shalt i all nations. 5157
Pr 3:35 The wise shall i glory: but shame shall be 5157
8:21 That *I* may **cause** those that love me **to i** 5157
11:29 He that troubleth his own house shall i 5157
14:18 The simple i folly: but the prudent are 5157
Isa 49: 8 to **cause to i** the desolate heritages; 5157
54: 3 thy seed shall i the Gentiles, and make 3423
57:13 the land, and shall i my holy mountain; 3423
60:21 they shall i the land for ever, the branch of 3423
65: 9 mine elect shall i it, and my servants shall 3423
Jer 8:10 their fields to them that *shall* i *them:* for 3423
12:14 which I have **caused** my people Israel **to i**; 5157
49: 1 why *then* doth their king i Gad, and 3423
Eze 47:13 whereby ye shall i the land according to 5157
47:14 ye shall i it, one as well as another: 5157
Zec 2:12 the LORD shall i Judah his portion in 5157
Mt 5: 5 *are* the meek: for they shall i the earth. *2816*
19:29 an hundredfold, and shall i everlasting life. *2816*
25:34 i the kingdom prepared for you from *2816*
Mk 10:17 what shall I do that I may i eternal life? *2816*
Lk 10:25 Master, what shall I do to i eternal life? *2816*
18:18 what shall I do to i eternal life? *2816*
1Co 6: 9 Know ye not that the unrighteous shall not i *2816*
6:10 shall i the kingdom of God. *2816*
15:50 and blood cannot i the kingdom of God; *2816*
15:50 neither doth corruption i incorruption. *2816*
Gal 5:21 that they which do such *things* shall not i *2816*
Heb 6:12 through faith and patience i the promises. *2816*
1Pe 3: 9 thereunto called, that ye should i a blessing. *2816*
Rev 21: 7 He that overcometh shall i all *things;* and *2816*

INHERITANCE (239) [INHERIT]

Ge 31:14 or i for us in our father's house? 5159
48: 6 after the name of their brethren in their i. 5159
Ex 15:17 plant them in the mountain of thine i, *in* 5159
34: 9 and our sin, and **take** us **for** thine i. 5157
Lev 25:46 ye shall **take** them **as** an i for your children 5157
Nu 16:14 honey, or given us i of fields and vineyards: 5159
18:20 Thou shalt **have** no i in their land, 5157
18:20 and thine i among the children of Israel. 5159
18:21 of Levi all the tenth in Israel for an i, 5159
18:23 the children of Israel they **have** no i. 5157+5159
18:24 of Israel they shall **have** no i. 5157+5159
18:26 I have given you from them for your i, 5159
26:53 Unto these the land shall be divided for an i 5159
26:54 To many thou shalt give the more i, and 5159
26:54 to few thou shalt give the less i: 5159
26:54 *to* every one shall his i be given according 5159
26:62 there was no i given them among 5159
27: 7 of an i among their father's brethren; 5159
27: 7 thou shalt cause the i of their father to pass 5159
27: 8 ye shall cause his i to pass unto his 5159
27: 9 then ye shall give his i unto his brethren. 5159
27:10 ye shall give his i unto his father's brethren. 5159
27:11 ye shall give his i unto his kinsman that is 5159
32:18 of Israel have inherited every man his i. 5159
32:19 our i is fallen to us on *this* side Jordan 5159
32:32 that the possession of our i on *this* side 5159
33:54 **divide** the land by lot for **an i among** your 5157
33:54 *and* to the moe ye shall give the more i, and 5159
33:54 and to the fewer ye shall give the less i: 5159
33:54 every man's *i* shall be in the place where his NIH
34: 2 *is* the land that shall fall unto you for an i, 5159
34:14 have received *their i*; and half the tribe of NIH
34:14 the tribe of Manasseh have received their i: 5159
34:15 the half tribe have received their i on *this* 5159
34:18 of every tribe, to **divide** the land **by** i. 5157
34:29 **divide** the i **unto** the children of Israel in 5157
35: 2 that they give unto the Levites of the i of 5159
35: 8 according to his i which he inheriteth. 5159
36: 2 land for an i by lot to the children of Israel: 5159
36: 2 i of Zelophehad our brother unto his 5159
36: 3 shall their i be taken from the inheritance of 5159
36: 3 shall their inheritance be taken from the i of 5159
36: 3 shall be put to the i of the tribe whereinto 5159
36: 3 shall it be taken from the lot of our i. 5159
36: 4 shall their i be put unto the inheritance of 5159
36: 4 shall their inheritance be put unto the i of 5159
36: 4 shall their i be taken away from 5159
36: 4 away from the i of the tribe of our fathers. 5159
36: 7 So shall not the i of the children of Israel 5159
36: 7 himself to the i of the tribe of his fathers. 5159
36: 8 that possesseth an i in any tribe of 5159
36: 8 may enjoy every man the i of his fathers. 5159
36: 9 Neither shall the i remove from *one* tribe to 5159
36: 9 of Israel shall keep himself to his own i. 5159
36:12 their i remained in the tribe of the family of 5159
Dt 4:20 to be unto him a people of i, as *ye are* this 5159
4:21 the LORD thy God giveth thee *for* an i: 5159
4:38 to give thee their land *for* an i, as *it is* this 5159
9:26 destroy not thy people and thine i, 5159
9:29 Yet they *are* thy people and thine i, 5159
10: 9 Wherefore Levi hath no part nor i with his 5159
10: 9 the LORD *is* his i, according as 5159
12: 9 are not as yet come to the rest and to the i, 5159
12:12 forasmuch as he hath no part nor i with 5159
14:27 for he hath no part nor i with thee. 5159
14:29 (because he hath no part nor i with thee,) 5159
15: 4 thy God giveth thee *for* an i to possess it: 5159
18: 1 of Levi, shall have no part nor i with Israel: 5159
18: 1 of the LORD made by fire, and his i. 5159
18: 2 Therefore shall they have no i among their 5159
18: 2 the LORD *is* their i, as he hath said unto 5159
19:10 the LORD thy God giveth thee *for* an i, 5159
19:14 which they of old time have set in thine i, 5159
20:16 the LORD thy God doth give thee *for* an i, 5159
21:23 the LORD thy God giveth thee *for* an i. 5159
24: 4 the LORD thy God giveth thee *for* an i. 5159
25:19 thy God giveth thee *for* an i to possess it, 5159
26: 1 the LORD thy God giveth thee *for* an i, 5159
29: 8 gave it for an i unto the Reubenites, and 5159
32: 8 most High **divided** to the nations their i, 5157
32: 9 *is* his people; Jacob *is* the lot of his i. 5159
33: 4 *even* the i of the congregation of Jacob. 4181
Jos 1: 6 people shalt thou **divide for an** i the land, 5157
11:23 Joshua gave it for an i unto Israel according 5159
13: 6 thou it *by lot* unto the Israelites for an i, 5159
13: 7 divide this land for an i unto the nine tribes, 5159
13: 8 and the Gadites have received their i, 5159
13:14 Only unto the tribe of Levi he gave none i; 5159
13:14 God of Israel made by fire *are* their i, 5159
13:15 of Reuben *i* according to their families. NIH
13:23 the border *thereof.* This *was* the i of 5159
13:24 Moses gave *i* unto the tribe of Gad, NIH
13:28 This *is* the i of the children of Gad after 5159
13:29 Moses gave *i* unto the half tribe of NIH
13:32 did **distribute for** i in the plains of Moab, 5157
13:33 unto the tribe of Levi Moses gave not *any* i: 5159
13:33 the LORD God of Israel *was* their i, as he 5159
14: 1 of Israel, **distributed for** i to them. 5157
14: 2 By lot *was* their i, as the LORD 5159
14: 3 For Moses had given the i of two tribes and 5159
14: 3 unto the Levites he gave none i among 5159
14: 9 thy feet have trodden shall be thine i, 5159
14:13 the son of Jephunneh Hebron for an i. 5159
14:14 became the i of Caleb the son of Jephunneh 5159
15:20 This *is* the i of the tribe of the children of 5159
16: 4 Manasseh and Ephraim, **took** their i. 5157
16: 5 their i on the east side was Ataroth-addar, 5159
16: 8 This *is* the i of the tribe of the children of 5159
16: 9 among the i of the children of Manasseh, 5159
17: 4 Moses to give us an i among our brethren. 5159
17: 4 an i among the brethren of their father. 5159
17: 6 the daughters of Manasseh had an i 5159
18: 2 which had not *yet* received their i. 5159
18: 4 and describe it according to the i of them; 5159
18: 7 for the priesthood of the LORD *is* their i: 5159
18: 7 have received their i beyond Jordan on 5159
18:20 This *was* the i of the children of Benjamin, 5159
18:28 This *is* the i of the children of Benjamin 5159
19: 1 their i was within the inheritance of 5159
19: 1 their inheritance was within the i of 5159
19: 2 they had in their i Beer-sheba, or Sheba, 5159
19: 8 This *is* the i of the tribe of the children of 5159
19: 9 Judah *was* the i of the children of Simeon: 5159
19: 9 the children of Simeon had their i within 5157
19: 9 had their inheritance within the i of them. 5159
19:10 and the border of their i was unto Sarid: 5159
19:16 This *is* the i of the children of Zebulun 5159
19:23 This *is* the i of the tribe of the children of 5159
19:31 This *is* the i of the tribe of the children of 5159
19:39 This *is* the i of the tribe of the children of 5159
19:41 the coast of their i was Zorah, and Eshtaol, 5159
19:48 This *is* the i of the tribe of the children of 5159
19:49 of **dividing** the land **for** i by their coasts, 5157

Jos 19:49 the children of Israel gave an **i** to Joshua 5159
19:51 **divided for an i** by lot in Shiloh before 5157
21: 3 Israel gave unto the Levites out of their **i**, 5159
23: 4 to be an **i** for your tribes, from Jordan, 5159
24:28 let the people depart, every man unto his **i**. 5159
24:30 they buried him in the border of his **i** in 5159
24:32 it became the **i** of the children of Joseph. 5159
Jdg 2: 6 every man unto his **i** to possess the land. 5159
2: 9 they buried him in the border of his **i** in 5159
18: 1 **i** to dwell *in;* for unto that day *all their* 5159
18: 1 **i** had not fallen unto them among the tribes 5159
20: 6 sent her throughout all the country of the **i** 5159
21:17 *There must be* an **i** for them that be escaped 3425
21:23 they went and returned unto their **i**, and 5159
21:24 went out from thence every man to his **i**. 5159
Ru 4: 5 to raise up the name of the dead upon his **i**. 5159
4: 6 redeem *it* for myself, lest I mar mine own **i**: 5159
4:10 to raise up the name of the dead upon his **i**, 5159
1Sa 10: 1 hath anointed thee to be captain over his **i**? 5159
26:19 day from abiding in the **i** of the LORD, 5159
2Sa 14:16 and my son together out of the **i** of God. 5159
20: 1 neither have we **i** in the son of Jesse: 5159
20:19 why wilt thou swallow up the **i** of 5159
21: 3 that ye may bless the **i** of the LORD? 5159
1Ki 8:36 thou hast given to thy people for an **i**. 5159
8:51 For they *be* thy people, and thine **i**, 5159
8:53 to be thine **i**, as thou spakest by the hand of 5159
12:16 neither *have we* **i** in the son of Jesse: 5159
21: 3 that I should give the **i** of my fathers unto 5159
21: 4 I will not give thee the **i** of my fathers. 5159
2Ki 21:14 I will forsake the remnant of mine **i**, and 5159
1Ch 16:18 I give the land of Canaan, the lot of your **i**; 5159
28: 8 **leave** *it* **for an i** for your children after you 5157
2Ch 6:27 thou hast given unto thy people for an **i**. 5159
10:16 *we have* none **i** in the son of Jesse: 5159
Ezr 9:12 **leave** *it* for **an i** to your children for ever. 3423
Ne 11:20 in all the cities of Judah, every one in his **i**. 5159
Job 31: 2 and *what* **i** of the Almighty from on high? 5159
42:15 their father gave them **i** among their 5159
Ps 2: 8 I shall give *thee* the heathen *for* thine **i**, and 5159
16: 5 The LORD *is* the portion of mine **i** and 2506
28: 9 Save thy people, and bless thine **i**: 5159
33:12 people *whom* he hath chosen for his own **i**. 5159
37:18 of the upright: and their **i** shall be for ever. 5159
47: 4 He shall choose our **i** for us, the excellency 5159
68: 9 whereby thou didst confirm thine **i**, when it 5159
74: 2 the rod of thine **i**, *which* thou hast 5159
78:55 divided them an **i** by line, and made 5159
78:62 unto the sword; and was wroth with his **i**. 5159
78:71 to feed Jacob his people, and Israel his **i**. 5159
79: 1 O God, the heathen are come into thine **i**; 5159
94:14 off his people, neither will he forsake his **i**. 5159
105:11 I give the land of Canaan, the lot of your **i**: 5159
106: 5 of thy nation, that *I* may glory with thine **i**. 5159
106:40 insomuch that he abhorred his own **i**. 5159
Pr 13:22 A good *man* **leaveth an i** to *his* children's 5157
17: 2 shall have part of the **i** among the brethren. 5159
19:14 House and riches *are* the **i** of fathers: and 5159
20:21 An **i** *may be* gotten hastily at the beginning; 5159
Ecc 7:11 Wisdom *is* good with an **i**: and *by it there is* 5159
Isa 19:25 the work of my hands, and Israel mine **i**. 5159
47: 6 I have polluted mine **i**, and given them into 5159
63:17 for thy servants' sake, the tribes of thine **i**. 5159
Jer 3:18 that I have **given for an i** unto your fathers. 5157
10:16 of all *things;* and Israel *is* the rod of his **i**: 5159
12:14 that touch the **i** which I have caused my 5159
16:18 they have filled mine **i** with the carcases of 5159
32: 8 for the right of **i** *is* thine, and 3425
51:19 of all *things:* and *Israel is* the rod of his **i**: 5159
La 5: 2 Our **i** is turned to strangers, our houses to 5159
Eze 22:16 thou shalt **take** thine **i** in thyself in the sight 2490
33:24 but we *are* many; the land is given us for **i**. 4181
35:15 As thou didst rejoice at the **i** of the house of 5159
36:12 thou shalt be their **i**, and thou shalt no more 5159
44:28 it shall be unto them for an **i**: I *am* their 5159
44:28 I *am* their **i**: and ye shall give them no 5159
45: 1 when ye shall divide *by lot* the land for **i**, 5159
46:16 of his sons, the **i** thereof shall be his sons'; 5159
46:16 his sons'; it *shall be* their possession by **i**. 5159
46:17 if he give a gift of his **i** to one of his 5159
46:17 but his **i** shall be his sons' for them. 5159
46:18 the prince shall not take of the people's **i**, 5159
46:18 he shall **give** his sons **i** out of his own 5157
47:14 and this land shall fall unto you for **i**. 5159
47:22 *that* ye shall divide it *by lot* for an **i** unto 5159
47:22 they shall **have i** with you among 5159+5307
47:23 there shall ye give *him* his **i**, saith the Lord 5159
48:29 divide *by lot* unto the tribes of Israel for **i**, 5159
Mt 21:38 let us kill him, and let us seize on his **i**. *2817*
Mk 12: 7 let us kill him, and the **i** shall be ours. *2817*
Lk 12:13 to my brother, that *he* divide the **i** with me. *2817*
20:14 come, let us kill him, that the **i** may be ours. *2817*
Ac 7: 5 And he gave him none **i** in it, no, not so *2817*
20:32 to give you an **i** among all them which are *2817*
26:18 **i** among them which are sanctified by faith *2819*
Gal 3:18 For if the **i** *be* of the law, *it is* no more of *2817*
Eph 1:11 In whom also we have **obtained an i**, *2820*
1:14 Which is the earnest of our **i**, until *2817*
1:18 what the riches of the glory of his **i** in *2817*
5: 5 hath *any* **i** in the kingdom of Christ and *2817*
Col 1:12 to be partakers of the **i** of the saints in light: *2819*
3:24 Lord ye shall receive the reward of the **i**: *2817*
Heb 1: 4 as he hath by **i obtained** a more excellent *2816*
9:15 might receive the promise of eternal **i**. *2817*
11: 8 place which he should after receive for an **i**, *2817*
1Pe 1: 4 To an **i** incorruptible, and undefiled, and *2817*

INHERITANCES (1) [INHERIT]

Jos 19:51 These *are* the **i**, which Eleazar the priest, 5159

INHERITED (6) [INHERIT]

Nu 32:18 until the children of Israel have **i** every man 5157
Jos 14: 1 children of Israel **i** in the land of Canaan, 5157
Ps 105:44 and they **i** the labour of the people; 3423
Jer 16:19 Surely our fathers have **i** lies, vanity, and 5157
Eze 33:24 Abraham was one, and he **i** the land: 3423
Heb 12:17 when he would have **i** the blessing, he was *2816*

INHERITETH (1) [INHERIT]

Nu 35: 8 according to his inheritance which he **i**. 5157

INHERITOR (1) [INHERIT]

Isa 65: 9 and out of Judah an **i** of my mountains: 3423

INIQUITIES (56) [INIQUITY]

Lev 16:21 confess over him all the **i** of the children of 5771
16:22 the goat shall bear upon him all their **i** unto 5771
26:39 also in the **i** of their fathers shall they pine 5771
Nu 14:34 shall ye bear your **i**, *even* forty years, and 5771
Ezr 9: 6 for our **i** are increased over *our* head, and 5771
9: 7 for our **i** have we, our kings, *and* 5771
9:13 hast punished us less than our **i** *deserve,* 5771
Ne 9: 2 their sins, and the **i** of their fathers. 5771
Job 13:23 How many *are* mine **i** and sins? make me to 5771
13:26 makest me to possess the **i** of my youth. 5771
22: 5 thy wickedness great? and thine **i** infinite? 5771
Ps 38: 4 For mine **i** are gone *over* mine head: as a 5771
40:12 mine **i** have taken hold upon me, so that I 5771
51: 9 face from my sins, and blot out all mine **i**. 5771
64: 6 They search out **i**; they accomplish a 5766
65: 3 I prevail against me: *as for* our 1697+5771
79: 8 O remember not against us former **i**: let thy 5771
90: 8 Thou hast set our **i** before thee, our secret 5771
103: 3 Who forgiveth all thine **i**; who healeth all 5771
103:10 nor rewarded us according to our **i**. 5771
107:17 because of their **i**, are afflicted. 5771
130: 3 If thou, LORD, shouldest mark **i**, O Lord, 5771
130: 8 And he shall redeem Israel from all his **i**. 5771
Pr 5:22 His own **i** shall take the wicked himself, 5771
Isa 43:24 thy sins, thou hast wearied me with thine **i**. 5771
50: 1 for your **i** have you sold yourselves, and 5771
53: 5 our transgressions, *he was* bruised for our **i**: 5771
53:11 justify many; for he shall bear their **i**. 5771
59: 2 your **i** have separated between you 5771
59:12 with us; and *as for* our **i**, we know them; 5771
64: 6 our **i**, like the wind, have taken us away. 5771
64: 7 and hast consumed us, because of our **i**. 5771
65: 7 Your **i**, and the iniquities of your fathers 5771
65: 7 and the **i** of your fathers together, 5771
Jer 5:25 Your **i** have turned away these *things,* and 5771
11:10 They are turned back to the **i** of their 5771
14: 7 O LORD, though our **i** testify against us, 5771
33: 8 I will pardon all their **i**, whereby they have 5771
La 4:13 sins of her prophets, *and* the **i** of her priests, 5771
5: 7 *and are* not; *and* we have borne their **i**. 5771
Eze 24:23 ye shall pine away for your **i**, and 5771
28:18 thy sanctuaries by the multitude of thine **i**, 5771
32:27 but their **i** shall be upon their bones, 5771

Eze	36:31	yourselves in your own sight for your i	5771
	36:33	I shall have cleansed you from all your i,	5771
	43:10	that they may be ashamed of their i:	5771
Da	4:27	and thine i by shewing mercy to the poor;	5758
	9:13	that *we* might turn from our i, and	5771
	9:16	for the i of our fathers, Jerusalem and	5771
Am	3: 2	I will punish you for all your i.	5771
Mic	7:19	he will subdue our i; and thou wilt cast all	5771
Ac	3:26	turning away every one of you from *his* i.	*4189*
Ro	4: 7	*Saying,* Blessed *are they* whose i are	*458*
Heb	8:12	and their i will I remember no more.	*458*
	10:17	their sins and i will I remember no more.	*458*
Rev	18: 5	unto heaven, and God hath remembered her i.	*92*

INIQUITY (278) [INIQUITIES]

Ge	15:16	for the i of the Amorites *is* not yet full.	5771
	19:15	lest thou be consumed in the i of the city.	5771
	44:16	God hath found out the i of thy servants:	5771
Ex	20: 5	visiting the i of the fathers upon	5771
	28:38	that Aaron may bear the i of the holy	5771
	28:43	in the holy *place;* that they bear not i,	5771
	34: 7	forgiving i and transgression and sin, and	5771
	34: 7	the i of the fathers upon the children,	5771
	34: 9	pardon our i and our sin, and take us for	5771
Lev	5: 1	if he do not utter *it,* then he shall bear his i.	5771
	5:17	*it* not, yet is he guilty, and shall bear his i.	5771
	7:18	and the soul that eateth of it shall bear his i.	5771
	10:17	*God* hath given it you to bear the i of	5771
	17:16	nor bathe his flesh; then he shall bear his i.	5771
	18:25	therefore I do visit the i thereof upon it, and	5771
	19: 8	*every one* that eateth it shall bear his i,	5771
	20:17	his sister's nakedness; he shall bear his i.	5771
	20:19	his near kin: they shall bear their i.	5771
	22:16	Or suffer them to bear the i of trespass,	5771
	26:39	pine away in their i in your enemies' lands;	5771
	26:40	If they shall confess their i, and the iniquity	5771
	26:40	their iniquity, and the i of their fathers,	5771
	26:41	then accept of the **punishment of** their i:	5771
	26:43	shall accept of the **punishment of** their i:	5771
Nu	5:15	of memorial, bringing i to remembrance.	5771
	5:31	shall the man be guiltless from i, and this	5771
	5:31	and this woman shall bear her i.	5771
	14:18	forgiving i and transgression, and by no	5771
	14:18	i of the fathers upon the children unto	5771
	14:19	the i of this people according unto	5771
	15:31	utterly be cut off; his i *shall be* upon him.	5771
	18: 1	thy father's house with thee shall bear the i	5771
	18: 1	thy sons with thee shall bear the i of your	5771
	18:23	and they shall bear their i:	5771
	23:21	He hath not beheld i in Jacob, neither hath	205
	30:15	he hath heard *them;* then he shall bear her i.	5771
Dt	5: 9	visiting the i of the fathers upon	5771
	19:15	shall not rise up against a man for any i,	5771
	32: 4	a God of truth and without i, just and	5766
Jos	22:17	*Is* the i of Peor *too* little for us, from which	5771
	22:20	and that man perished not alone in his i.	5771
1Sa	3:13	house for ever for the i which he knoweth;	5771
	3:14	that the i of Eli's house shall not be purged	5771
	15:23	and stubbornness *is as* i and idolatry.	205
	20: 1	what *is* mine i? and what *is* my sin before	5771
	20: 8	if there be in me i, slay me thyself;	5771
	25:24	*upon* me *let this* i *be:* and let thine	5771
2Sa	7:14	If he **commit** i, I will chasten him with	5753
	14: 9	the i *be* on me, and on my father's house:	5771
	14:32	and if there be *any* i in me, let him kill me.	5771
	19:19	the king, Let not my lord impute i unto me,	5771
	22:24	and have kept myself from mine i.	5771
	24:10	O LORD, take away the i of thy servant;	5771
1Ch	21: 8	I beseech thee, do away the i of thy servant;	5771
2Ch	19: 7	do *it:* for *there is* no i with the LORD our	5766
Ne	4: 5	cover not their i, and let not their sin be	5771
Job	4: 8	they that plow i, and sow wickedness,	205
	5:16	poor hath hope, and i stoppeth her mouth.	5766
	6:29	Return, I pray you, let it not be i; yea,	5766
	6:30	Is there i in my tongue? cannot my taste	5766
	7:21	my transgression, and take away mine i?	5771
	10: 6	That thou inquirest after mine i, and	5771
	10:14	and thou wilt not acquit me from mine i.	5771
	11: 6	that God exacteth of thee *less* than thine i	5771
	11:14	If i *be* in thine hand, put it far away, and	205
	14:17	up in a bag, and thou sewest up mine i.	5771
	15: 5	For thy mouth uttereth thine i, and	5771
	15:16	filthy *is* man, which drinketh i like water?	5766
	20:27	The heaven shall reveal his i; and the earth	5771
	21:19	God layeth up his i for his children:	205
	22:23	thou shalt be built *up,* thou shalt put away i	5766
	31: 3	a strange punishment to the workers of i?	205
	31:11	yea, it *is* an i *to be punished by* the judges.	5771
	31:28	This also *were* an i *to be punished by*	5771
	31:33	as Adam, by hiding mine i in my bosom:	5771
	33: 9	I *am* innocent; neither *is there* i in me.	5771
	34: 8	goeth in company with the workers of i,	205
	34:10	the Almighty, *that he should commit* i.	5766
	34:22	where the workers of i may hide themselves.	205
	34:32	thou me: if I have done i, I will do no more.	5766
	36:10	and commandeth that they return from i.	205
	36:21	Take heed, regard not i: for this hast thou	205
	36:23	or who can say, Thou hast wrought i?	5766
Ps	5: 5	in thy sight: thou hatest all workers of i.	205
	6: 8	Depart from me, all ye workers of i; for	205
	7: 3	I have done this; if there be i in my hands;	5766
	7:14	he travaileth with i, and hath conceived	205
	14: 4	Have all the workers of i no knowledge?	205
	18:23	before him, and I kept myself from mine i.	5771
	25:11	thy name's sake, O LORD, pardon mine i;	5771
	28: 3	with the wicked, and with the workers of i,	205
	31:10	my strength faileth because of mine i, and	5771
	32: 2	man unto whom the LORD imputeth not i,	5771
	32: 5	my sin unto thee, and mine i have I not hid.	5771
	32: 5	and thou forgavest the i of my sin.	5771
	36: 2	own eyes, until his i be found to be hateful.	5771
	36: 3	The words of his mouth *are* i and deceit:	205
	36:12	There are the workers of i fallen: they are	205
	37: 1	be thou envious against the workers of i.	5766
	38:18	For I will declare mine i; I will be sorry for	5771
	39:11	thou with rebukes dost correct man for i,	5771
	41: 6	his heart gathereth i to itself; *when* he goeth	205
	49: 5	*when* the i of my heels shall compass me	5771
	51: 2	Wash me throughly from mine i, and	5771
	51: 5	Behold, I was shapen in i; and in sin did my	5771
	53: 1	are they, and have done abominable i:	5766
	53: 4	Have the workers of i no knowledge?	205
	55: 3	for they cast i upon me, and in wrath they	205
	56: 7	*Shall* they escape by i? in *thine* anger cast	205
	59: 2	Deliver me from the workers of i, and	205
	64: 2	from the insurrection of the workers of i:	205
	66:18	If I regard i in my heart, the Lord will not	205
	69:27	Add i unto their iniquity: and let them not	5771
	69:27	Add iniquity unto their i: and let them not	5771
	78:38	forgave *their* i, and destroyed *them* not:	5771
	85: 2	Thou hast forgiven the i of thy people,	5771
	89:32	with the rod, and their i with stripes.	5771
	92: 7	and when all the workers of i do flourish;	205
	92: 9	all the workers of i shall be scattered.	205
	94: 4	*and* all the workers of i boast themselves?	205
	94:16	stand up for me against the workers of i?	205
	94:20	Shall the throne of i have fellowship *with*	1942
	94:23	he shall bring upon them their own i, and	205
	106: 6	we have **committed** i, we have done	5753
	106:43	and were brought low for their i.	5771
	107:42	and rejoice: and all i shall stop her mouth.	5766
	109:14	Let the i of his fathers be remembered with	5771
	119: 3	They also do no i: they walk in his ways.	5766
	119:133	and let not any i have dominion over me.	205
	125: 3	the righteous put forth their hands unto i.	5766
	125: 5	shall lead them forth with the workers of i:	205
	141: 4	practise wicked works with men that work i:	205
	141: 9	laid for me, and the grins of the workers of i.	205
Pr	10:29	but destruction *shall be* to the workers of i.	205
	16: 6	By mercy and truth i is purged: and by	5771
	19:28	and the mouth of the wicked devoureth i.	205
	21:15	but destruction *shall be* to the workers of i.	205
	22: 8	He that soweth i shall reap vanity: and	5766
Ecc	3:16	the place of righteousness, *that* i *was* there.	7562
Isa	1: 4	Ah sinful nation, a people laden with i,	5771
	1:13	away with; *it is* i, even the solemn meeting.	205
	5:18	Woe unto them that draw i with cords of	5771
	6: 7	thine i is taken away, and thy sin purged.	5771
	13:11	for *their* evil, and the wicked for their i;	5771
	14:21	Prepare slaughter for his children for the i	5771
	22:14	Surely this i shall not be purged from you	5771
	26:21	the inhabitants of the earth for their i:	5771
	27: 9	therefore shall the i of Jacob be purged;	5771
	29:20	and all that watch for i are cut off:	205
	30:13	Therefore this i shall be to you as a breach	5771
	31: 2	and against the help of them that work i.	205
	32: 6	his heart will work i, to practise hypocrisy,	205
	33:24	that dwell therein *shall be* forgiven *their* i.	5771

Isa 40: 2 is accomplished, that her **i** is pardoned: 5771
53: 6 the LORD hath laid on him the **i** of us all. 5771
57:17 For the **i** of his covetousness was I wroth, 5771
59: 3 defiled with blood, and your fingers with **i**; 5771
59: 4 *they* conceive mischief, and bring forth **i**. 205
59: 6 their works *are* works of **i**, and the act of 205
59: 7 their thoughts *are* thoughts of **i**; wasting and 205
64: 9 O LORD, neither remember **i** for ever: 5771
Jer 2: 5 What **i** have your fathers found in me, 5766
2:22 much sope, *yet* thine **i** *is* marked before me, 5771
3:13 Only acknowledge thine **i**, that thou hast 5771
9: 5 *and* weary themselves to **commit i**. 5753
13:22 For the greatness of thine **i** are thy skirts 5771
14:10 he will now remember their **i**, and 5771
14:20 our wickedness, *and* the **i** of our fathers: 5771
16:10 or what *is* our **i**? or what *is* our sin that we 5771
16:17 neither is their **i** hid from mine eyes. 5771
16:18 first I will recompense their **i** and their sin 5771
18:23 against me to slay *me:* forgive not their **i**, 5771
25:12 for their **i**, and the land of the Chaldeans, 5771
30:14 of a cruel one, for the multitude of thine **i**; 5771
30:15 *is* incurable for the multitude of thine **i**: 5771
31:30 every one shall die for his own **i**: every man 5771
31:34 for I will forgive their **i**, and I will 5771
32:18 recompensest the **i** of the fathers into 5771
33: 8 I will cleanse them from all their **i**, 5771
36: 3 that I may forgive their **i** and their sin. 5771
36:31 and his seed and his servants for their **i**; 5771
50:20 the **i** of Israel shall be sought for, and 5771
51: 6 be not cut off in her **i**; for this *is* the time of 5771
La 2:14 they have not discovered thine **i**, to turn 5771
4: 6 For the **punishment of** the **i** of the daughter 5771
4:22 The **punishment of** thine **i** is 5771
4:22 he will visit thine **i**, O daughter of Edom; 5771
Eze 3:18 the same wicked *man* shall die in his **i**; 5771
3:19 from his wicked way, he shall die in his **i**; 5771
3:20 commit **i**, and I lay a stumblingblock before 5766
4: 4 lay the **i** of the house of Israel upon it: 5771
4: 4 thou shalt lie upon it thou shalt bear their **i**. 5771
4: 5 I have laid upon thee the years of their **i**, 5771
4: 5 shalt thou bear the **i** of the house of Israel. 5771
4: 6 thou shalt bear the **i** of the house of Judah 5771
4:17 with another, and consume away for their **i**. 5771
7:13 neither shall any strengthen himself in the **i** 5771
7:16 all of them mourning, every one for his **i**. 5771
7:19 because it is the stumblingblock of their **i**. 5771
9: 9 The **i** of the house of Israel and Judah *is* 5771
14: 3 put the stumblingblock of their **i** before 5771
14: 4 putteth the stumblingblock of his **i** before 5771
14: 7 putteth the stumblingblock of his **i** before 5771
14:10 they shall bear the **punishment of** their **i**: 5771
16:49 this was the **i** of thy sister Sodom, pride, 5771
18: 8 *that* hath withdrawn his hand from **i**, 5766
18:17 he shall not die for the **i** of his father, 5771
18:18 his people, lo, even he shall die in his **i**. 5771
18:19 doth not the son bear the **i** of the father? 5771
18:20 The son shall not bear the **i** of the father, 5771
18:20 neither shall the father bear the **i** of the son: 5771
18:24 committeth **i**, *and* doeth according to all 5766
18:26 and committeth **i**, and dieth in them; 5766
18:26 for his **i** that he hath done shall he die. 5766
18:30 so **i** shall not be your ruin. 5771
21:23 he will call to remembrance the **i**, that *they* 5771
21:24 Because ye have made your **i** to be 5771
21:25 day is come, when **i** *shall have* an end, 5771
21:29 day is come, when *their* **i** *shall have* an end. 5771
28:15 thou wast created, till **i** was found in thee. 5766
28:18 of thine iniquities, by the **i** of thy traffick; 5766
29:16 which bringeth *their* **i** to remembrance, 5771
33: 6 from among them, he is taken *away* in his **i**; 5771
33: 8 his way, that wicked *man* shall die in his **i**; 5771
33: 9 not turn from his way, he shall die in his **i**; 5771
33:13 to his own righteousness, and commit **i**, 5766
33:13 for his **i** that he hath committed, he shall 5766
33:15 in the statutes of life, without committing **i**; 5766
33:18 and committeth **i**, he shall even die thereby. 5766
35: 5 in the time *that their* **i** *had* an end: 5771
39:23 of Israel went into captivity for their **i**: 5771
44:10 after their idols; they shall even bear their **i**. 5771
44:12 and caused the house of Israel to fall into **i**; 5771
44:12 the Lord GOD, and they shall bear their **i**. 5771
Da 9: 5 have **committed i**, and have done 5753
9:24 to make reconciliation for **i**, and to bring in 5771
Hos 4: 8 and they set their heart on their **i**. 5771
5: 5 shall Israel and Ephraim fall in their **i**; 5771
6: 8 Gilead *is* a city of them that work **i**, *and* 205
7: 1 the **i** of Ephraim was discovered, and 5771
8:13 now will he remember their **i**, and 5771
9: 7 for the multitude of thine **i**, and the great 5771
9: 9 *therefore* he will remember their **i**, he will 5771
10: 9 the battle in Gibeah against the children of **i** 5932
10:13 have plowed wickedness, ye have reaped **i**; 5766
12: 8 *in* all my labours they shall find none **i** in 5771
12:11 *Is there* **i** *in* Gilead? surely they are vanity: 205
13:12 The **i** of Ephraim *is* bound up; his sin *is* hid. 5771
14: 1 thy God; for thou hast fallen by thine **i**. 5771
14: 2 Take away all **i**, and receive *us* graciously: 5771
Mic 2: 1 Woe to them that devise **i**, and work evil 205
3:10 up Zion with blood, and Jerusalem with **i**. 5766
7:18 that pardoneth **i**, and passeth by 5771
Hab 1: 3 Why dost thou shew me **i**, and cause *me* to 205
1:13 than to behold evil, and canst not look on **i**: 5999
2:12 town with blood, and stablisheth a city by **i**! 5766
Zep 3: 5 *is* in the midst thereof; he will not do **i**: 5766
3:13 The remnant of Israel shall not do **i**, 5766
Zec 3: 4 I have caused thine **i** to pass from thee, and 5771
3: 9 I will remove the **i** of that land in one day. 5771
Mal 2: 6 his mouth, and **i** was not found in his lips: 5766
2: 6 and equity, and did turn many away from **i**. 5771
Mt 7:23 knew you: depart from me, ye that work **i**. *458*
13:41 all things that offend, and them which do **i**; *458*
23:28 but within ye are full of hypocrisy and **i**. *458*
24:12 And because **i** shall abound, the love of *458*
Lk 13:27 you are; depart from me, all *ye* workers of **i**. *93*
Ac 1:18 *man* purchased a field with the reward of **i**; *93*
8:23 in the gall of bitterness, and *in* the bond of **i**. *93*
Ro 6:19 to uncleanness and to **i** unto iniquity; *458*
6:19 to uncleanness and to iniquity unto **i**; *458*
1Co 13: 6 Rejoiceth not in **i**, but rejoiceth in the truth; *93*
2Th 2: 7 For the mystery of **i** doth already work: *458*
2Ti 2:19 that nameth the name of Christ depart from **i**. *93*
Tit 2:14 that he might redeem us from all **i**, and *458*
Heb 1: 9 Thou hast loved righteousness, and hated **i**; *458*
Jas 3: 6 And the tongue *is* a fire, a world of **i**: so is *93*
2Pe 2:16 But was rebuked for his **i**: the dumb ass *3892*

INJURED (1) [INJURIOUS]
Gal 4:12 be as I *am;* for I *am* as ye *are:* ye have not **i** *91*

INJURIOUS (1) [INJURED]
1Ti 1:13 a blasphemer, and a persecutor, and **i**: *5197*

INJUSTICE (1)
Job 16:17 Not for *any* **i** in mine hands: also my prayer 2555

INK (4) [INKHORN]
Jer 36:18 and I wrote *them* with **i** in the book. 1773
2Co 3: 3 written not with **i**, but with the Spirit of *3188*
2Jn 1:12 I would not *write* with paper and **i**: *3188*
3Jn 1:13 but I will not with **i** and pen write unto *3188*

INKHORN (3) [HORN, INK]
Eze 9: 2 *with* linen, with a writer's **i** by his side: 7083
9: 3 which *had* the writer's **i** by his side; 7083
9:11 which *had* the **i** by his side, reported 7083

INN (5)
Ge 42:27 his sack to give his ass provender in the **i**, 4411
43:21 it came to pass, when we came to the **i**, 4411
Ex 4:24 it came to pass by the way in the **i**, that 4411
Lk 2: 7 there was no room for them in the **i**. *2646*
10:34 and brought him to an **i**, and took care of *3829*

INNER (37) [INNERMOST]
1Ki 6:27 he set the cherubims within the **i** house: 6442
6:36 he built the **i** court *with* three rows of 6442
7:12 both for the **i** court of the house of 6442
7:50 *of* gold, *both* for the doors of the **i** house, 6442
20:30 the city, into an **i chamber**. 2315+2315+871.1
22:25 an **i chamber** to hide thyself. 2315+2315+871.1
2Ki 9: 2 carry him *to* an **i chamber**: 2315+2315+871.1
1Ch 28:11 of the **i** parlours thereof, and of the place of 6442
2Ch 4:22 the **i** doors thereof for the most holy *place,* 6442
18:24 an **i chamber** to hide thyself. 2315+2315+871.1
29:16 the priests went into the **i part** *of* the house 6441
Est 4:11 shall come unto the king into the **i** court, 6442
5: 1 and stood in the **i** court of the king's house, 6442
Eze 8: 3 to the door of the **i** gate that looketh toward 6442
8:16 he brought me into the **i** court of 6442

Eze 10: 3 went in; and the cloud filled the i court. 6442
40:15 of the porch of the i gate *were* fifty cubits. 6442
40:19 unto the forefront of the i court without, 6442
40:23 the gate of the i court *was* over against 6442
40:27 *there was* a gate in the i court toward 6442
40:28 he brought me to the i court by the south 6442
40:32 he brought me into the i court toward 6442
40:44 without the i gate *were* the chambers of 6442
40:44 the chambers of the singers in the i court, 6442
41:15 with the i temple, and the porches of 6442
41:17 even unto the i house, and without, and 6442
42: 3 twenty *cubits* which *were* for the i court, 6442
42:15 had made an end of measuring the i house, 6442
43: 5 me up, and brought me into the i court; 6442
44:17 *that* when they enter in at the gates of the i 6442
44:17 whiles they minister in the gates of the i 6442
44:21 drink wine, when they enter into the i court. 6442
44:27 unto the i court, to minister in 6442
45:19 and upon the posts of the gate of the i court. 6442
46: 1 The gate of the i court that looketh *toward* 6442
Ac 16:24 thrust them into the i prison, and made their *2082*
Eph 3:16 with might by his Spirit in the i man; *2080*

INNERMOST (2) [INNER]
Pr 18: 8 they go down *into* the **i parts** of the belly. 2315
26:22 they go down *into* the **i parts** of the belly. 2315

INNOCENCY (5) [INNOCENT, INNOCENTS]
Ge 20: 5 and i of my hands have I done this. 5356
Ps 26: 6 I will wash mine hands in i: so will I 5356
73:13 heart *in* vain, and washed my hands in i. 5356
Da 6:22 forasmuch as before him i was found in 2136
Hos 8: 5 how long *will it be* ere they attain to i? 5356

INNOCENT (38) [INNOCENCY]
Ex 23: 7 and the i and righteous slay thou not: 5355
Dt 19:10 That i blood be not shed in thy land, 5355
19:13 thou shalt put away *the guilt of* i blood 5355
21: 8 lay not i blood unto thy people of Israel's 5355
21: 9 So shalt thou put away the *guilt of* i blood 5355
27:25 Cursed *be* he that taketh reward to slay an i 5355
1Sa 19: 5 then wilt thou sin against i blood, 5355
1Ki 2:31 that thou mayest take away the i blood, 2600
2Ki 21:16 Moreover Manasseh shed i blood very 5355
24: 4 also *for* the i blood that he shed: for he 5355
24: 4 for he filled Jerusalem *with* i blood; 5355
Job 4: 7 I pray thee, who *ever* perished, being i? 5355
9:23 he will laugh at the trial of the i. 5355
9:28 I know that thou wilt not **hold** me i. 5352
17: 8 the i shall stir up himself against 5355
22:19 and are glad: and the i laugh them to scorn. 5355
22:30 He shall deliver the island of the i: and it is 5355
27:17 put *it* on, and the i shall divide the silver. 5355
33: 9 I am clean without transgression, I *am* i; 2643
Ps 10: 8 in the secret places doth he murder the i: 5355
15: 5 to usury, nor taketh reward against the i. 5355
19:13 and I shall be i from *the* great transgression. 5352
94:21 of the righteous, and condemn the i blood. 5355
106:38 shed i blood, *even* the blood of their sons 5355
Pr 1:11 let us lurk privily for the i without cause: 5355
6:17 a lying tongue, and hands that shed i blood, 5355
6:29 whosoever toucheth her shall not be i. 5352
28:20 that maketh haste to be rich shall not be i. 5352
Isa 59: 7 and they make haste to shed i blood: 5355
Jer 2:35 Yet thou sayest, Because I am i, surely his 5352
7: 6 and shed not i blood in this place, 5355
22: 3 neither shed i blood in this place. 5355
22:17 for to shed i blood, and for oppression, and 5355
26:15 ye shall surely bring i blood upon 5355
Joel 3:19 they have shed i blood in their land. 5355
Jnh 1:14 this man's life, and lay not upon us i blood: 5355
Mt 27: 4 I have sinned in that I have betrayed *the* i *121*
27:24 I am i of the blood of this just *person:* see ye *121*

INNOCENTS (2) [INNOCENCY]
Jer 2:34 is found the blood of the souls of the poor i: 5355
19: 4 have filled this place *with* the blood of i; 5355

INNUMERABLE (7)
Job 21:33 after him, as *there are* i before him. 369+4557
Ps 40:12 For i evils have compassed me 369+4557+5704
104:25 wherein *are* things creeping i, 369+4557
Jer 46:23 more than the grasshoppers, and *are* i. 369+4557
Lk 12: 1 gathered together an **i multitude** of people, *3461*
Heb 11:12 and as the sand which is by the sea shore i. *382*
12:22 and to an **i company** of angels, *3461*

INORDINATE (2)
Eze 23:11 she was more corrupt in her **i love** than she, 5691
Col 3: 5 fornication, uncleanness, **i affection,** *3806*

INQUIRE (52) [INQUIRED, INQUIREST, INQUIRY]
Ge 24:57 We will call the damsel, and i at her mouth. 7592
25:22 I thus? And she went to i of the LORD. 1875
Ex 18:15 Because the people come unto me to i of 1875
Dt 12:30 that thou i not after their gods, saying, 1875
13:14 shalt thou i, and make search, and 1875
17: 9 the judge that shall be in those days, and i; 1875
Jdg 4:20 when any man doth come and i of thee, and 7592
1Sa 9: 9 when a man went to i of God, thus he 1875
17:56 king said, I thou whose son the stripling *is.* 7592
22:15 Did I then begin to i of God for him? be it 7592
28: 7 that I may go to her, and i of her. 1875
1Ki 22: 5 I, I pray thee, at the word of the LORD to 1875
22: 7 LORD besides, that we might i of him? 1875
22: 8 by whom *we* may i of the LORD: 1875
2Ki 1: 2 i of Baal-zebub the god of Ekron whether I 1875
1: 3 *that* ye go to i of Baal-zebub the god of 1875
1: 6 *that* thou sendest to i of Baal-zebub the god 1875
1:16 to i of Baal-zebub the god of Ekron, 1875
1:16 *there is* no God in Israel to i of his word? 1875
3:11 that we may i of the LORD by him? 1875
8: 8 and i of the LORD by him, saying, 1875
16:15 and the brasen altar shall be for me to i *by.* 1239
22:13 i of the LORD for me, and for the people, 1875
22:18 to the king of Judah which sent you to i of 1875
1Ch 10:13 of *one that had* a familiar spirit, to i *of it;* 1875
18:10 to i of his welfare, and to congratulate him, 7592
21:30 David could not go before it to i of God: 1875
2Ch 18: 4 I, I pray thee, at the word of the LORD to 1875
18: 6 LORD besides, that we might i of him? 1875
18: 7 by whom *we* may i of the LORD: 1875
32:31 who sent unto him to i of the wonder that 1875
34:21 i of the LORD for me, and for them that 1875
34:26 who sent you to i of the LORD, so 1875
Ezr 7:14 to i concerning Judah and Jerusalem, 1240
Job 8: 8 For i, I pray thee, of the former age, and 7592
Ps 27: 4 of the LORD, and to i in his temple. 1239
Ecc 7:10 for thou dost not i wisely concerning this. 7592
Isa 21:12 if ye will i, inquire ye: return, come. 1158
21:12 if ye will inquire, i ye: return, come. 1158
Jer 21: 2 I, I pray thee, of the LORD for us; for 1875
37: 7 of Judah, that sent you unto me to **i of** me; 1875
Eze 14: 7 cometh to a prophet to i of him concerning 1875
20: 1 elders of Israel came to **i of** the LORD, 1875
20: 3 the Lord GOD; Are ye come to **i of** me? 1875
Mt 10:11 or town ye shall enter, i who in it is worthy; *1833*
Lk 22:23 And they began to i among themselves, *4802*
Jn 16:19 Do ye i among yourselves of that I said, *2212*
Ac 9:11 i in the house of Judas for *one* called Saul, *2212*
19:39 But if ye i any *thing* concerning other *1934*
23:15 as though ye would i something more *1231*
23:20 as though they would i somewhat of him *4441*
2Co 8:23 Whether *any do* i of Titus, *he is* my partner NIG

INQUIRED (34) [INQUIRE]
Dt 17: 4 thou hast heard *of it,* and i diligently, and 1875
Jdg 6:29 when they i and asked, they said, 1875
8:14 man of the men of Succoth, and i of him: 7592
20:27 the children of Israel i of the LORD, 7592
1Sa 10:22 Therefore they i of the LORD further, 7592
22:10 he i of the LORD for him, and gave him 7592
22:13 and a sword, and hast i of God for him, 7592
23: 2 Therefore David i of the LORD, saying, 7592
23: 4 David i of the LORD yet again. And 7592
28: 6 when Saul i of the LORD, the LORD 7592
30: 8 David i at the LORD, saying, Shall I 7592
2Sa 2: 1 that David i of the LORD, saying, 7592
5:19 David i of the LORD, saying, Shall I go 7592
5:23 when David i of the LORD, he said, 7592
11: 3 David sent and i after the woman. And *one* 1875
16:23 *was* as if a man had i at the oracle of God: 7592
21: 1 and David **i of** the LORD. 1245+6440
1Ch 10:14 i not of the LORD: therefore he slew him, 1875
13: 3 to us: for we i not *at* it in the days of Saul. 1875
14:10 David i of God, saying, Shall I go up 7592
14:14 Therefore David i again of God; and God 7592
Ps 78:34 and they returned and **i early after** God. 7836

Eze 14: 3 should I be **i of at all** by them? 1875+1875
20: 3 the Lord GOD, I will not be **i of** by you. 1875
20:31 shall I be **i of** by you, O house of Israel? 1875
20:31 the Lord GOD, I will not be **i of** by you. 1875
36:37 I will yet *for* this be **i of** by the house of 1875
Da 1:20 *and* understanding, that the king **i** of them, 1245
Zep 1: 6 have not sought the LORD, nor **i for** him. 1875
Mt 2: 7 **i** of them **diligently** what time the star *198*
2:16 which he had **diligently i** of the wise men. *198*
Jn 4:52 Then **i** he of them the hour when he began *4441*
2Co 8:23 our brethren *be* **i** *of, they are* the messengers NIG
1Pe 1:10 Of which salvation the prophets have **i** and *1567*

INQUIREST (1) [INQUIRE]
Job 10: 6 That thou **i** after mine iniquity, and 1245

INQUIRY (2) [INQUIRE]
Pr 20:25 *which is* holy, and after vows to **make i**. 1239
Ac 10:17 Cornelius had **made i** for Simon's house, *1331*

INQUISITION (3)
Dt 19:18 the judges shall **make** diligent **i**: and 1875
Est 2:23 when **i was made** of the matter, it was 1245
Ps 9:12 When he **maketh i** for blood, he 1875

INSATIABLE See UNSATIABLE

INSCRIBED See GRAVED; GRAVEN

INSCRIPTION (1)
Ac 17:23 your devotions, I found an altar with this **i**, *1924*

INSIDE (1)
1Ki 6:15 *and* he covered *them* on the **i** with wood, 1004

INSOMUCH (20) [IN, MUCH, SO] See Index

INSPECTION GATE See MIPHKAD

INSPIRATION (2)
Job 32: 8 the **i** of the Almighty giveth them 5397
2Ti 3:16 All scripture *is* **given by i of God**, and *2315*

INSTANT (8) [INSTANTLY]
Isa 29: 5 yea, it shall be at an **i** suddenly. 6621
30:13 whose breaking cometh suddenly at an **i**. 6621
Jer 18: 7 *At what* **i** I shall speak concerning a nation 7281
18: 9 *at what* **i** I shall speak concerning a nation, 7281
Lk 2:38 And she coming in that **i** gave thanks *5610*
23:23 And they were **i** with loud voices, *1945*
Ro 12:12 in tribulation; **continuing i** in prayer; *4342*
2Ti 4: 2 be **i** in season, out of season; reprove, *2186*

INSTANTLY (2) [INSTANT]
Lk 7: 4 came to Jesus, they besought him **i**, saying, *4709*
Ac 26: 7 **i serving** *God* day and night, hope to *1616+1722*

INSTEAD (39) See Index

INSTRUCT (9) [INSTRUCTED, INSTRUCTING, INSTRUCTION, INSTRUCTOR, INSTRUCTORS]
Dt 4:36 thee to hear his voice, that he might **i** thee: 3256
Ne 9:20 Thou gavest also thy good spirit to **i** them, 7919
Job 40: 2 the Almighty **i** *him?* he that reproveth God, 3250
Ps 16: 7 my reins also **i** me *in* the night seasons. 3256
32: 8 I will **i** thee and teach thee in the way 7919
SS 8: 2 into my mother's house, *who* would **i** me: 3925
Isa 28:26 For his God doth **i** him to discretion, *and* 3256
Da 11:33 understand among the people shall **i** many: 995
1Co 2:16 the mind of the Lord, that he may **i** him? *4822*

INSTRUCTED (19) [INSTRUCT]
Dt 32:10 he led him about, he **i** him, he kept him as 995
2Ki 12: 2 his days where*in* Jehoiada the priest **i** him. 3384
1Ch 15:22 he **i** about the song, because he *was* skilful. 3256
25: 7 with their brethren *that were* **i** in the songs 3925
2Ch 3: 3 was **i** for the building of the house of God. 3245
Job 4: 3 thou hast **i** many, and thou hast 3256
Ps 2:10 O ye kings: be **i**, ye judges of the earth. 3256
Pr 5:13 nor inclined mine ear to them that **i** me! 3925
21:11 when the wise is **i**, he receiveth knowledge. 7919
Isa 8:11 **i** me that *I* should not walk in the way of 3256
40:14 *who* **i** him, and taught him in the path of 995
Jer 6: 8 Be thou **i**, O Jerusalem, lest my soul depart 3256
31:19 after that I was **i**, I smote upon *my* thigh: 3045
Mt 13:52 Therefore every scribe *which is* **i** unto *3100*
14: 8 And she, being **before i** of her mother, said, *4264*
Lk 1: 4 of *those* things, wherein thou hast been **i**. *2727*
Ac 18:25 This *man* was **i in** the way of the Lord; and *2727*
Ro 2:18 are more excellent, being **i** out of the law; *2727*
Php 4:12 and in all *things* I am **i** both to be full and *3453*

INSTRUCTING (1) [INSTRUCT]
2Ti 2:25 In meekness **i** those that oppose *3811*

INSTRUCTION (33) [INSTRUCT]
Job 33:16 openeth the ears of men, and sealeth their **i**. 4561
Ps 50:17 Seeing thou hatest **i**, and castest my words 4148
Pr 1: 2 To know wisdom and **i**; to perceive 4148
1: 3 To receive the **i** of wisdom, justice, and 4148
1: 7 *but* fools despise wisdom and **i**. 4148
1: 8 hear the **i** of thy father, and forsake not 4148
4: 1 the **i** of a father, and attend to know 4148
4:13 Take fast hold of **i**; let *her* not go: keep her; 4148
5:12 How have I hated **i**, and my heart despised 4148
5:23 He shall die without **i**; and in the greatness 4148
6:23 and reproofs of **i** *are* the way of life: 4148
8:10 Receive my **i**, and not silver; and 4148
8:33 Hear **i**, and be wise, and refuse *it* not. 4148
9: 9 Give *i* to a wise *man*, and he will be yet NIH
10:17 He *is in* the way of life that keepeth **i**: but 4148
12: 1 Whoso loveth **i** loveth knowledge: but 4148
13: 1 A wise son *heareth his* father's **i**: but 4148
13:18 and shame *shall be to* him that refuseth **i**: 4148
15: 5 A fool despiseth his father's **i**: but he that 4148
15:32 He that refuseth **i** despiseth his own soul: 4148
15:33 The fear of the LORD *is* the **i** of wisdom; 4148
16:22 him that hath it: but the **i** of fools *is* folly. 4148
19:20 Hear counsel, and receive **i**, that thou 4148
19:27 to hear the **i** *that causeth* to err from 4148
23:12 Apply thine heart unto **i**, and thine ears to 4148
23:23 *also* wisdom, and **i**, and understanding. 4148
24:32 *it* well: I looked upon *it, and* received **i**. 4148
Jer 17:23 that *they* might not hear, nor receive **i**. 4148
32:33 yet they have not hearkened to receive **i**. 4148
35:13 Will ye not receive **i** to hearken to my 4148
Eze 5:15 an **i** and an astonishment unto the nations 4148
Zep 3: 7 thou wilt fear me, thou wilt receive **i**; 4148
2Ti 3:16 for correction, for **i** in righteousness: *3809*

INSTRUCTOR (2) [INSTRUCT]
Ge 4:22 an **i** of every artificer in brass and iron: 3913
Ro 2:20 An **i** of the foolish, a teacher of babes, *3810*

INSTRUCTORS (1) [INSTRUCT]
1Co 4:15 For though you have ten thousand **i** in *3807*

INSTRUMENT (8) [INSTRUMENTS]
Nu 35:16 if he smite him with an **i** of iron, so that he 3627
Ps 33: 2 with the psaltery *and* an **i of ten strings**. 6218
92: 3 Upon an **i of ten strings**, and upon 6218
144: 9 an **i of ten strings** will I sing *praises* unto 6218
Isa 28:27 *i*, neither is a cart wheel turned about upon NIH
41:15 I will make thee a new sharp **threshing i** 4173
54:16 and that bringeth forth an **i** for his work; 3627
Eze 33:32 a pleasant voice, and can **play** well **on an i**: 5059

INSTRUMENTS (51) [INSTRUMENT]
Ge 49: 5 **i** of cruelty *are in* their habitations. 3627
Ex 25: 9 the pattern of all the **i** thereof, even so 3627
Nu 3: 8 they shall keep all the **i** of the tabernacle of 3627
4:12 they shall take all the **i** of ministry, 3627
4:26 all the **i** of their service, and all that is made 3627
4:32 with all their **i**, and with all their service: 3627
4:32 by name ye shall reckon the **i** of the charge 3627
7: 1 sanctified it, and all the **i** thereof, both 3627
31: 6 with the holy **i**, and the trumpets to blow in 3627
1Sa 8:12 to make his **i** of war, and instruments of his 3627
8:12 his instruments of war, and **i** of his chariots. 3627
18: 6 with joy, and with **i of musick**. 7991
2Sa 6: 5 on all *manner of i made of* fir wood, NIH
24:22 **threshing i** and *other* instruments of 4173
24:22 and *other* **i** of the oxen for wood. 3627
1Ki 19:21 and boiled their flesh with the **i** of the oxen, 3627
1Ch 9:29 all the **i** of the sanctuary, and the fine flour, 3627
12:33 expert in war, with all **i** of war, 3627
12:37 with all *manner of* **i** of war for the battle, 3627
15:16 brethren *to be* the singers with **i** of musick, 3627
16:42 make a sound, and with musical **i** of God. 3627
21:23 the **threshing i** for wood, and the wheat for 4173
23: 5 the LORD with the **i** which I made, 3627
28:14 *of* gold, for all **i** of all manner of service; 3627

1Ch 28:14 *silver also* for all **i** of silver by weight, 3627
28:14 by weight, for all **i** of every kind of service: 3627
2Ch 4:16 and the fleshhooks, and all their **i**, 3627
5: 1 the silver, and the gold, and all the **i**, put he 3627
5:13 the trumpets and cymbals and **i** of musick, 3627
7: 6 the Levites also with **i** of musick of 3627
23:13 also the singers with **i** of musick, and 3627
29:26 the Levites stood with the **i** of David, and 3627
29:27 with the **i** ordained by David king of Israel. 3627
30:21 *singing* with loud **i** unto the LORD. 3627
34:12 all that could skill of **i** of musick. 3627
Ne 12:36 with the musical **i** of David the man of 3627
Ps 7:13 He hath also prepared for him the **i** of 3627
68:25 the **players on i** *followed* after; 5059
87: 7 As well the singers as the **players on i** *shall* 2490
150: 4 praise him with **stringed i** and organs. 4482
Ecc 2: 8 *as* **musical i**, and that **of all sorts**. 7705+7705
Isa 32: 7 The **i** also of the churl *are* evil: he deviseth 3627
38:20 we will **sing** my songs *to* **the stringed i** all 5059
Eze 40:42 whereupon also they laid the **i** wherewith 3627
Da 6:18 neither were **i of musick** brought before 1761
Am 1: 3 they have threshed Gilead with threshing *i* NIH
6: 5 *and* invent to themselves **i** of musick, 3627
Hab 3:19 To the chief singer on my **stringed i**. 5058
Zec 11:15 Take unto thee yet the **i** of a foolish 3627
Ro 6:13 Neither yield ye your members *as* **i** of *3696*
6:13 your members *as* **i** of righteousness unto *3696*

INSURRECTION (5)
Ezr 4:19 city of old time *hath* **made i** against kings, 5376
Ps 64: 2 from the **i** of the workers of iniquity: 7285
Mk 15: 7 **made i with** *him,* who had committed *4955*
15: 7 *him,* who had committed murder in the **i**. *4714*
Ac 18:12 the Jews **made i** with one accord **against** *2721*

INTEGRITY (16)
Ge 20: 5 in the **i** of my heart and innocency of my 8537
20: 6 I know that thou didst this in the **i** of thy 8537
1Ki 9: 4 in **i** of heart, and in uprightness, 8537
Job 2: 3 still he holdeth fast his **i**, although thou 8538
2: 9 wife unto him, Dost thou still retain thine **i**? 8538
27: 5 till I die I will not remove my **i** from me. 8538
31: 6 even balance, that God may know mine **i**. 8538
Ps 7: 8 and according to mine **i** *that is* in me. 8537
25:21 Let **i** and uprightness preserve me; for I 8537
26: 1 O LORD; for I have walked in mine **i**: 8537
26:11 *as for* me, I will walk in mine **i**: redeem me, 8537
41:12 thou upholdest me in mine **i**, and settest me 8537
78:72 So he fed them according to the **i** of his 8537
Pr 11: 3 The **i** of the upright shall guide them: but 8538
19: 1 Better *is* the poor that walketh in his **i**, 8537
20: 7 The just *man* walketh in his **i**: his children 8537

INTELLIGENCE (1)
Da 11:30 have **i** with them that forsake the holy 995

INTEND (4) [INTENDED, INTENDEST, INTENDING, INTENT, INTENTS]
Jos 22:33 and did not **i** to go up against them in battle, 559
2Ch 28:13 LORD *already,* ye **i** to add *more* to our sins 559
Ac 5:28 and **i** to bring this man's blood upon us. *1014*
5:35 take heed to yourselves what ye **i** to do as *3195*

INTENDED (1) [INTEND]
Ps 21:11 For they **i** evil against thee: they imagined a 5186

INTENDEST (1) [INTEND]
Ex 2:14 **i** thou to kill me, as thou killedst 559

INTENDING (3) [INTEND]
Lk 14:28 For which of you, **i** to build a tower, *2309*
Ac 12: 4 **i** after Easter to bring him forth to *1014*
20:13 sailed unto Assos, there **i to** take in Paul: *3195*

INTENT (11) [INTEND]
2Sa 17:14 **to the i** that the LORD might bring evil 3807.1
2Ki 10:19 Jehu did *it* in subtilty, **to the i that** 4616+3807.1
2Ch 16: 1 **to the i that** *he* might let none go out or 3807.1
Eze 40: 4 for **to the i that** *I* might shew *them* 4616+3807.1
Da 4:17 to the **i** that the living may know that 1701
Jn 11:15 I was not there, **to the i** ye may believe; *2443*
13:28 Now no *man* at the table knew for what **i** he NIG
Ac 9:21 came hither for that *i,* that he might bring NIG
10:29 therefore for what **i** ye have sent for me? *3056*
1Co 10: 6 **to the i** we should not lust after evil *1519+3588*
Eph 3:10 **To the i that** now unto the principalities *2443*

INTENTS (2) [INTEND]
Jer 30:24 until he have performed the **i** of his heart: 4209
Heb 4:12 discerner of the thoughts and **i** of the heart. *1771*

INTERCEDE; INTERCEDED See INTREAT; INTREATED; INTREATIES; INTREATY

INTERCESSION (9) [INTERCESSIONS, INTERCESSOR]
Isa 53:12 of many, and **made i** for the transgressors. 6293
Jer 7:16 nor prayer for them, neither **make i** to me: 6293
27:18 let them now **make i** to the LORD of 6293
36:25 Gemariah had **made i** to the king that *he* 6293
Ro 8:26 the Spirit itself **maketh i** for us with *5241*
8:27 he **maketh i** for the saints according to *1793*
8:34 hand of God, who also **maketh i** for us. *1793*
11: 2 how he **maketh i** to God against Israel, *1793*
Heb 7:25 seeing he ever liveth to **make i** for them. *1793*

INTERCESSIONS (1) [INTERCESSION]
1Ti 2: 1 prayers, **i**, *and* giving of thanks, *1783*

INTERCESSOR (1) [INTERCESSION]
Isa 59:16 no man, and wondered that *there was* no **i**: 6293

INTERCOURSE See CARNALLY

INTERMARRY See AFFINITY

INTERMEDDLE (1) [INTERMEDDLETH]
Pr 14:10 and a stranger doth not **i** with his joy. 6148

INTERMEDDLETH (1) [INTERMEDDLE]
Pr 18: 1 seeketh *and* **i** with all wisdom. 1566

INTERMISSION (1)
La 3:49 and ceaseth not, without any **i**, 2014

INTERPRET (8) [INTERPRETATION, INTERPRETATIONS, INTERPRETED, INTERPRETER, INTERPRETING]
Ge 41: 8 *there was* none that could **i** them unto 6622
41:12 each man according to his dream he did **i**. 6622
41:15 a dream, and *there is* none that can **i** it: 6622
41:15 *that* thou canst understand a dream to **i** it. 6622
1Co 12:30 do all speak with tongues? do all **i**? *1329*
14: 5 except he **i**, that the church may receive *1329*
14:13 in an *unknown* tongue pray that he may **i**. *1329*
14:27 *by* three, and *that* by course; and let one **i**. *1329*

INTERPRETATION (46) [INTERPRET]
Ge 40: 5 each man according to the **i** of his dream, 6623
40:12 Joseph said unto him, This *is* the **i** of it: 6623
40:16 When the chief baker saw that the **i** was 6622
40:18 and said, This *is* the **i** thereof: 6623
41:11 we dreamed each man according to the **i** of 6623
Jdg 7:15 the **i** thereof, that he worshipped, and 7667
Pr 1: 6 To understand a proverb, and the **i**; 4426
Ecc 8: 1 and who knoweth the **i** of a thing? 6592
Da 2: 4 servants the dream, and we will shew the **i**. 6591
2: 5 with the **i** thereof, ye shall be cut in pieces, 6591
2: 6 if ye shew the dream, and the **i** thereof, 6591
2: 6 shew me the dream, and the **i** thereof. 6591
2: 7 the dream, and we will shew the **i** of it. 6591
2: 9 I shall know that ye can shew me the **i** 6591
2:16 and that *he* would shew the king the **i**. 6591
2:24 and I will shew unto the king the **i**. 6591
2:25 that will make known unto the king the **i**. 6591
2:26 dream which I have seen, and the **i** thereof? 6591
2:30 for *their* sakes that shall make known the **i** 6591
2:36 we will tell the **i** thereof before the king. 6591
2:45 the dream *is* certain, and the **i** thereof sure. 6591
4: 6 that they might make known unto me the **i** 6591
4: 7 they *did* not make known unto me the **i** 6591
4: 9 dream that I have seen, and the **i** thereof. 6591
4:18 O Belteshazzar, declare the **i** thereof, 6591
4:18 are not able to make known unto me the **i**: 6591
4:19 not the dream, or the **i** thereof, trouble thee. 6591
4:19 and the **i** thereof to thine enemies. 6591
4:24 This *is* the **i**, O king, and this *is* the decree 6591
5: 7 shew me the **i** thereof, shall be clothed with 6591
5: 8 nor make known to the king the **i** thereof. 6591
5:12 let Daniel be called, and he will shew the **i**. 6591
5:15 make known unto me the **i** thereof: 6591
5:15 but they could not shew the **i** of the thing: 6591
5:16 make known to me the **i** thereof, thou shalt 6591

Da 5:17 the king, and make known to him the **i**. 6591
5:26 This *is* the **i** of the thing: MENE; God hath 6591
7:16 and made me know the **i** of the things. 6591
Jn 1:42 be called Cephas, which is **by i**, A stone. *2059*
9: 7 in the pool of Siloam, (which is **by i**, Sent.) *2059*
Ac 9:36 which by **i** is called Dorcas: *1329*
13: 8 the sorcerer (for so is his name **by i**) *3177*
1Co 12:10 of tongues; to another the **i** of tongues: *2058*
14:26 hath a tongue, hath a revelation, hath an **i**. *2058*
Heb 7: 2 first being **by i** King of righteousness, and *2059*
2Pe 1:20 prophecy of the scripture is of *any* private **i**. *1955*

INTERPRETATIONS (2) [INTERPRET]
Ge 40: 8 said unto them, *Do* not **i** *belong* to God? 6623
Da 5:16 that thou canst **make i**, and dissolve 6590+6591

INTERPRETED (11) [INTERPRET]
Ge 40:22 the chief baker: as Joseph had **i** to them. 6622
41:12 and we told him, and he **i** to us our dreams; 6622
41:13 it came to pass, as he **i** to us, so it was; me 6622
Ezr 4: 7 Syrian tongue, and **i** in the Syrian tongue. 8638
Mt 1:23 which being **i** is, God with us. *3177*
Mk 5:41 which is, being **i**, Damsel (I say unto thee) *3177*
15:22 which is, being **i**, The place of a skull. *3177*
15:34 which is, being **i**, My God, my God, why *3177*
Jn 1:38 Rabbi, (which is to say, being **i**, Master,) *2059*
1:41 the Messias, which is, being **i**, the Christ. *3177*
Ac 4:36 (which is, being **i**, The son of consolation,) *3177*

INTERPRETER (4) [INTERPRET]
Ge 40: 8 dreamed a dream, and *there is* no **i** of it. 6622
42:23 *them;* for he spake unto them by an **i**. 3887
Job 33:23 with him, an **i**, one among a thousand, 3887
1Co 14:28 But if there be no **i**, let him keep silence in *1328*

INTERPRETING (1) [INTERPRET]
Da 5:12 **i** of dreams, and shewing of hard sentences, 6590

INTO (2015) [IN, TO, THEREINTO, WHEREINTO] See Index

INTREAT (15) [ENTREAT, INTREATED, INTREATIES, INTREATY]
Ge 23: 8 and **i** for me to Ephron the son of Zohar, 6293
Ex 8: 8 and Aaron, and said, I the LORD, 6279
8: 9 when shall I **i** for thee, and for thy servants, 6279
8:28 you shall not go very far away: **i** for me. 6279
8:29 I will **i** the LORD that the swarms *of flies* 6279
9:28 I the LORD (for *it is* enough) that there be 6279
10:17 only *this* once, and **i** the LORD your God, 6279
Ru 1:16 I me not to leave thee, *or* to return from 6293
1Sa 2:25 against the LORD, who shall **i** for him? 6419
1Ki 13: 6 I now the face of the LORD thy God, and 2470
Ps 45:12 among the people shall **i** thy **favour**. 2470+6440
Pr 19: 6 Many will **i** the favour of the prince: and 2470
1Co 4:13 Being defamed, we **i**: we are made as *3870*
Php 4: 3 And I **i** thee also, true yokefellow, *2065*
1Ti 5: 1 Rebuke not an elder, but **i** *him* as a father; *3870*

INTREATED (18) [INTREAT]
Ge 25:21 Isaac **i** the LORD for his wife, because 6279
25:21 the LORD was **i** of him, and Rebekah his 6279
Ex 8:30 went out from Pharaoh, and **i** the LORD. 6279
10:18 went out from Pharaoh, and **i** the LORD. 6279
Jdg 13: 8 Manoah **i** the LORD, and said, O my 6279
2Sa 21:14 And after that God was **i** for the land. 6279
24:25 So the LORD was **i** for the land, and 6279
1Ch 5:20 to God in the battle, and he was **i** of them; 6279
2Ch 33:13 he was **i** of him, and heard his supplication, 6279
33:19 *how God* was **i** of him, and all his sin, and 6279
Ezr 8:23 our God for this: and he was **i** of us. 6279
Job 19:16 gave *me* no answer; I **i** him with my mouth. 2603
19:17 though I **i** for the children's *sake* of mine 2589
Ps 119:58 I **i** thy favour with *my* whole heart: 2470
Isa 19:22 he shall be **i** of them, and shall heal them. 6279
Lk 15:28 therefore came his father out and **i** him. *3870*
Heb 12:19 which *voice* they that heard **i** that the word *3868*
Jas 3:17 then peaceable, gentle, *and* **easy to be i**, *2138*

INTREATIES (1) [INTREAT]
Pr 18:23 The poor **useth i**; but the rich answereth 8469

INTREATY (1) [INTREAT]
2Co 8: 4 Praying us with much **i** that we would *3874*

INTRUDING (1)
Col 2:18 **i into** *those things* which he hath not seen, *1687*

INVADE (2) [INVADED, INVASION]
2Ch 20:10 whom thou wouldest not let Israel **i**, 935+871.1
Hab 3:16 the people, he will **i** them **with his troops**. 1464

INVADED (5) [INVADE]
1Sa 23:27 come; for the Philistines have **i** the land. 6584
27: 8 **i** the Geshurites, and the Gezrites, and 6584
30: 1 that the Amalekites had **i** the south, and 6584
2Ki 13:20 the bands of the Moabites **i** the land 935+871.1
2Ch 28:18 The Philistines also had **i** the cities of 6584

INVALID See IMPOTENT

INVASION (1) [INVADE]
1Sa 30:14 We **made an i** *upon* the south of 6584

INVENT (1) [INVENTED, INVENTIONS, INVENTORS]
Am 6: 5 *and* **i** to themselves instruments of musick, 2803

INVENTED (1) [INVENT]
2Ch 26:15 **i** by cunning *men,* to be on the towers and 4284

INVENTIONS (5) [INVENT]
Ps 99: 8 though thou tookest vengeance of their **i**. 5949
106:29 they provoked *him* to anger with their **i**: 4611
106:39 and went a whoring with their own **i**. 4611
Pr 8:12 and find out knowledge of **witty i**. 4209
Ecc 7:29 but they have sought out many **i**. 2810

INVENTORS (1) [INVENT]
Ro 1:30 **i** of evil *things,* disobedient to parents, *2182*

INVESTIGATION See INQUISITION

INVISIBLE (5)
Ro 1:20 For the **i** *things* of him from the creation of *517*
Col 1:15 Who is the image of the **i** God, the firstborn *517*
1:16 in heaven, and that are in earth, visible and **i**, *517*
1Ti 1:17 immortal, **i**, the only wise God, *be* honour *517*
Heb 11:27 for he endured, as seeing *him who is* **i**. *517*

INVITED (3)
1Sa 9:24 for thee since *I* said, I have **i** the people. 7121
2Sa 13:23 and Absalom **i** all the king's sons. 7121
Est 5:12 to morrow *am* I **i** unto her also with 7121

INWARD (25) [INWARDLY, INWARDS]
Ex 28:26 which *is* in the side of the ephod **i**. 1004+1886.5
39:19 *was* on the side of the ephod **i**. 1004+1886.5
Lev 13:55 it *is* fret **i**, *whether* it *be* bare within or 871.1
2Sa 5: 9 built round about from Millo and **i**. 1004+1886.5
1Ki 7:25 and all their hinder parts *were* **i**. 1004+1886.5
2Ch 3:13 stood on their feet, and their faces *were* **i**. 1004
4: 4 and all their hinder parts *were* **i**. 1004+1886.5
Job 19:19 All my **i** friends abhorred me: and 5475
38:36 Who hath put wisdom in the **i parts**? or 2910
Ps 5: 9 their **i** *part is* very wickedness; their throat 7130
49:11 Their **i** *thought is, that* their houses *shall* 7130
51: 6 Behold, thou desirest truth in the **i parts**: 2910
64: 6 both the **i** *thought* of every one *of them,* 7130
Pr 20:27 searching all the **i parts** of the belly. 2315
20:30 so *do* stripes the **i parts** of the belly. 2315
Isa 16:11 for Moab, and mine **i parts** for Kir-haresh. 7130
Jer 31:33 I will put my law in their **i parts**, and 7130
Eze 40: 9 the porch of the gate *was* **i**. 1004+4480+1886.1
40:16 windows *were* round about **i**: 6441+3807.1
41: 3 went he **i**, and measured the post of 6441+3807.1
42: 4 a walk of ten cubits breadth **i**, 413+6442+1886.1
Lk 11:39 but your **i part** is full of ravening and *2081*
Ro 7:22 For I delight in the law of God after the **i** *2080*
2Co 4:16 yet the **i** *man* is renewed day by day. *2081*
7:15 And his **i affection** is more abundant *4698*

INWARDLY (3) [INWARD]
Ps 62: 4 with their mouth, but they curse **i**. 7130+871.1
Mt 7:15 but **i** they are ravening wolves. *2081*
Ro 2:29 But he *is* a Jew, which is one **i**; *1722+2927+3588*

INWARDS (20) [INWARD]
Ex 29:13 thou shalt take all the fat that covereth the **i**, 7130
29:17 wash the **i** of him, and his legs, and 7130
29:22 the fat that covereth the **i**, and the caul 7130
Lev 1: 9 his **i** and his legs shall he wash in water: 7130
1:13 he shall wash the **i** and the legs with water: 7130
3: 3 the fat that covereth the **i**, and all the fat 7130
3: 3 and all the fat that *is* upon the **i**, 7130

Lev 3: 9 the fat that covereth the i, and all the fat 7130
3: 9 and all the fat that *is* upon the i, 7130
3:14 the fat that covereth the i, and all the fat 7130
3:14 and all the fat that *is* upon the i, 7130
4: 8 the fat that covereth the i, and all the fat 7130
4: 8 and all the fat that *is* upon the i, 7130
4:11 and with his legs, and his i, and his dung, 7130
7: 3 the rump, and the fat that covereth the i, 7130
8:16 he took all the fat that *was* upon the i, and 7130
8:21 he washed the i and the legs in water; and 7130
8:25 all the fat that *was* upon the i, and the caul 7130
9:14 he did wash the i and the legs, and 7130
9:19 that which covereth *the* i, and the kidneys, NIH

IPHDEIAH See IPHEDEIAH

IPHEDEIAH (1)
1Ch 8:25 And I, and Penuel, the sons of Shashak; 3301

IPHTAH See JIPHTAH

IPHTAH EL See JIPHTHAH-EL

IR (1)
1Ch 7:12 and Huppim, the children of I, *and* Hushim, 5893

IRA (6)
2Sa 20:26 I also the Jairite was a chief ruler about 5896
23:26 the Paltite, I the son of Ikkesh the Tekoite, 5896
23:38 I an Ithrite, Gareb an Ithrite, 5896
1Ch 11:28 I the son of Ikkesh the Tekoite, 5896
11:40 I the Ithrite, Gareb the Ithrite, 5896
27: 9 The sixth *captain* for the sixth month *was* I 5896

IRAD (2)
Ge 4:18 unto Enoch was born I: and Irad begat 5897
4:18 I begat Mehujael: and Mehujael begat 5897

IRAM (2)
Ge 36:43 Duke Magdiel, duke I: these *be* the dukes 5902
1Ch 1:54 Duke Magdiel, duke I. These *are* the dukes 5902

IRI (1)
1Ch 7: 7 Uzzi, and Uzziel, and Jerimoth, and I, five; 5901

IRIJAH (2)
Jer 37:13 whose name *was* I, the son of Shelemiah, 3376
37:14 so I took Jeremiah, and brought him to 3376

IRNAHASH (1)
1Ch 4:12 and Paseah, and Tehinnah the father of I. 5904

IRON (101) [IRONS]
Ge 4:22 instructor of every artificer in brass and i: 1270
Lev 26:19 I will make your heaven as i, and your 1270
Nu 31:22 the brass, the i, the tin, and the lead, 1270
35:16 if he smite him with an instrument of i, 1270
Dt 3:11 behold, his bedstead *was* a bedstead of i; *is* 1270
4:20 brought you forth out of the i furnace, 1270
8: 9 a land whose stones *are* i, and out of whose 1270
27: 5 thou shalt not lift up *any* i *tool* upon them. 1270
28:23 and the earth that *is* under thee *shall be* i. 1270
28:48 and he shall put a yoke of i upon thy neck, 1270
33:25 Thy shoes *shall be* i and brass; and as thy 1270
Jos 6:19 and gold, and vessels of brass and i, 1270
6:24 the gold, and the vessels of brass and of i, 1270
8:31 over which no *man* hath lift up *any* i: 1270
17:16 in the land of the valley have chariots of i, 1270
17:18 though they have i chariots, *and* 1270
19:38 I, and Migdal-el, Horem, and Beth-anath, 3375
22: 8 and with i, and with very much raiment: 1270
Jdg 1:19 the valley, because they had chariots of i. 1270
4: 3 for he had nine hundred chariots of i; and 1270
4:13 *even* nine hundred chariots of i, and all 1270
1Sa 17: 7 head *weighed* six hundred shekels *of* i: 1270
2Sa 12:31 under harrows of i, and under axes of iron, 1270
12:31 under axes of i, and made them pass 1270
23: 7 *that* shall touch them must be fenced *with* i 1270
1Ki 6: 7 nor axe *nor* any tool of i heard in the house, 1270
8:51 of Egypt, from the midst of the furnace of i: 1270
22:11 the son of Chenaanah made him horns of i: 1270
2Ki 6: 6 and cast *it* in thither; and the i did swim. 1270
1Ch 20: 3 and with harrows of i, and with axes. 1270
22: 3 David prepared i in abundance for the nails 1270
22:14 of brass and i without weight; for it is in 1270
22:16 the gold, the silver, and the brass, and the i, 1270
29: 2 the i for *things of* iron, and wood for *things* 1270
29: 2 the iron for *things of* i, and wood for *things* 1270
29: 7 and one hundred thousand talents *of* i. 1270
2Ch 2: 7 in i, and in purple, and crimson, and blue, 1270
2:14 in brass, in i, in stone, and in timber, 1270
18:10 son of Chenaanah had made him horns of i, 1270
24:12 also such as wrought i and brass to mend 1270
Job 19:24 That they were graven with an i pen and 1270
20:24 He shall flee from the i weapon, *and* 1270
28: 2 I is taken out of the earth, and brass *is* 1270
40:18 pieces of brass; his bones *are* like bars of i. 1270
41:27 He esteemeth i as straw, *and* brass as rotten 1270
Ps 2: 9 Thou shalt break them with a rod of i; 1270
105:18 feet they hurt with fetters: he was laid *in* i: 1270
107:10 of death, *being* bound in affliction and i; 1270
107:16 of brass, and cut the bars of i in sunder. 1270
149: 8 and their nobles with fetters of i; 1270
Pr 27:17 I sharpeneth iron; so a man sharpeneth 1270
27:17 Iron sharpeneth i; so a man sharpeneth 1270
Ecc 10:10 If the i be blunt, and he do not whet 1270
Isa 10:34 cut down the thickets of the forest with i, 1270
45: 2 of brass, and cut in sunder the bars of i: 1270
48: 4 thy neck *is* an i sinew, and thy brow brass: 1270
60:17 for i I will bring silver, and for wood brass, 1270
60:17 and for wood brass, and for stones i: 1270
Jer 1:18 an i pillar, and brasen walls against 1270
6:28 *they are* brass and i; they *are* all corrupters. 1270
11: 4 from the i furnace, saying, Obey my voice, 1270
15:12 Shall i break the northern iron and 1270
15:12 Shall iron break the northern i and 1270
17: 1 The sin of Judah *is* written with a pen of i, 1270
28:13 but thou shalt make for them yokes of i. 1270
28:14 I have put a yoke of i upon the neck of all 1270
Eze 4: 3 Moreover take thou unto thee an i pan, and 1270
4: 3 set it *for* a wall of i between thee and 1270
22:18 all they *are* brass, and tin, and i, and lead, 1270
22:20 and brass, and i, and lead, and tin, 1270
27:12 with silver, i, tin, and lead, they traded in 1270
27:19 bright i, cassia, and calamus, were in thy 1270
Da 2:33 His legs of i, his feet part of iron and 6523
2:33 of iron, his feet part of i and part of clay. 6523
2:34 smote the image upon his feet *that were* of i 6523
2:35 was the i, the clay, the brass, the silver, 6523
2:40 the fourth kingdom shall be strong as i: 6523
2:40 forasmuch as i breaketh in pieces and 6523
2:40 all *things:* and as i that breaketh all these, 6523
2:41 and toes, part of potter's clay, and part of i, 6523
2:41 there shall be in it of the strength of the i, 6523
2:41 forasmuch as thou sawest the i mixed with 6523
2:42 *as* the toes of the feet *were* part of i, and 6523
2:43 whereas thou sawest i mixt with miry clay, 6523
2:43 to another, even as i is not mixed with clay. 6523
2:45 *that* it brake in pieces the i, the brass, 6523
4:15 even with a band of i and brass, in 6523
4:23 even with a band of i and brass, in 6523
5: 4 of brass, of i, of wood, and of stone. 6523
5:23 gold, of brass, i, wood, and stone, which 6523
7: 7 strong exceedingly; and it had great i teeth: 6523
7:19 whose teeth *were of* i, and his nails *of* 6523
Am 1: 3 Gilead with threshing *instruments* of i: 1270
Mic 4:13 for I will make thine horn i, and I will make 1270
Ac 12:10 they came unto the i gate that leadeth unto *4603*
1Ti 4: 2 their conscience **seared with a hot i**; *2743*
Rev 2:27 And he shall rule them with a rod **of i**; *4603*
9: 9 as *it were* breastplates **of i**; *4603*
12: 5 who was to rule all nations with a rod **of i**: *4603*
18:12 and of brass, and i, and marble, *4604*
19:15 and he shall rule them with a rod **of i**: and *4603*

IRONS (1) [IRON]
Job 41: 7 Canst thou fill his skin with **barbed** i? or 7905

IRPEEL (1)
Jos 18:27 And Rekem, and I, and Taralah, 3416

IR-SHEMESH (1)
Jos 19:41 inheritance was Zorah, and Eshtaol, and I, 5905

IRU (1)
1Ch 4:15 the son of Jephunneh; I, Elah, and Naam: 5900

IS (6993) [BE] See Index

ISAAC (128) [ISAAC'S]
Ge 17:19 a son indeed; and thou shalt call his name I: 3327

Ge 17:21 my covenant will I establish with I, 3327
21: 3 born unto him, whom Sarah bare to him, I. 3327
21: 4 Abraham circumcised his son I being eight 3327
21: 5 when his son I was born unto him. 3327
21: 8 great feast the *same* day that I was weaned. 3327
21:10 shall not be heir with my son, *even* with I. 3327
21:12 her voice; for in I shall thy seed be called. 3327
22: 2 he said, Take now thy son, thine only *son* I, 3327
22: 3 I his son, and clave the wood for the burnt 3327
22: 6 burnt offering, and laid *it* upon I his son; 3327
22: 7 I spake unto Abraham his father, and said, 3327
22: 9 bound I his son, and laid him on the altar 3327
24: 4 my kindred, and take a wife unto my son I. 3327
24:14 *that* thou hast appointed for thy servant I; 3327
24:62 I came from the way of the well Lahai-roi; 3327
24:63 I went out to meditate in the field at 3327
24:64 when she saw I, she lighted off the camel. 3327
24:66 the servant told I all things that he had 3327
24:67 I brought her into his mother Sarah's tent, 3327
24:67 I was comforted after his mother's *death*. 3327
25: 5 And Abraham gave all that he had unto I. 3327
25: 6 sent them away from I his son, while he yet 3327
25: 9 his sons I and Ishmael buried him in 3327
25:11 of Abraham, that God blessed his son I; 3327
25:11 and I dwelt by the well Lahai-roi. 3327
25:19 these *are* the generations of I, 3327
25:19 of Isaac, Abraham's son: Abraham begat I: 3327
25:20 I was forty years old when he took 3327
25:21 I intreated the LORD for his wife, 3327
25:26 I *was* threescore years old when she bare 3327
25:28 I loved Esau, because he did eat of *his* 3327
26: 1 I went unto Abimelech king of 3327
26: 6 And I dwelt in Gerar: 3327
26: 8 I *was* sporting with Rebekah his wife. 3327
26: 9 Abimelech called I, and said, Behold, of a 3327
26: 9 I said unto him, Because I said, Lest I die 3327
26:12 I sowed in that land, and received in 3327
26:16 Abimelech said unto I, Go from us; 3327
26:17 I departed thence, and pitched his tent in 3327
26:18 I digged again the wells of water, 3327
26:27 I said unto them, Wherefore come ye to 3327
26:31 I sent them away, and they departed from 3327
26:35 Which were a grief of mind unto I and 3327
27: 1 that when I was old, and his eyes were dim, 3327
27: 5 Rebekah heard when I spake to Esau his 3327
27:20 I said unto his son, How *is it that* thou hast 3327
27:21 I said unto Jacob, Come near, I pray thee, 3327
27:22 Jacob went near unto I his father; and 3327
27:26 his father I said unto him, Come near now, 3327
27:30 as soon as I had made an end of blessing 3327
27:30 gone out from the presence of I his father, 3327
27:32 I his father said unto him, Who *art* thou? 3327
27:33 I trembled very exceedingly, and said, 3327
27:37 I answered and said unto Esau, Behold, 3327
27:39 I his father answered and said unto him, 3327
27:46 Rebekah said to I, I am weary of my life 3327
28: 1 I called Jacob, and blessed him, and 3327
28: 5 I sent away Jacob: and he went to 3327
28: 6 When Esau saw that I had blessed Jacob, 3327
28: 8 of Canaan pleased not I his father; 3327
28:13 of Abraham thy father, and the God of I: 3327
31:18 for to go to I his father in the land of 3327
31:42 and the fear of I, had been with me, 3327
31:53 And Jacob sware by the fear of his father I. 3327
32: 9 father Abraham, and God of my father I, 3327
35:12 the land which I gave Abraham and I, 3327
35:27 Jacob came unto I his father unto Mamre, 3327
35:27 where Abraham and I sojourned. 3327
35:28 the days of I were an hundred 3327
35:29 I gave up the ghost, and died, and 3327
46: 1 sacrifices unto the God of his father I. 3327
48:15 whom my fathers Abraham and I did walk, 3327
48:16 and the name of my fathers Abraham and I; 3327
49:31 there they buried I and Rebekah his wife; 3327
50:24 he sware to Abraham, to I, and to Jacob. 3327
Ex 2:24 with Abraham, with I, and with Jacob. 3327
3: 6 the God of I, and the God of Jacob. 3327
3:15 the God of I, and the God of Jacob, 3327
3:16 of I, and of Jacob, appeared unto me, 3327
4: 5 the God of I, and the God of Jacob, 3327
6: 3 unto I, and unto Jacob, by *the name of* God 3327
6: 8 to give it to Abraham, to I, and to Jacob; 3327
32:13 I, and Israel, thy servants, 3327
33: 1 to I, and to Jacob, saying, Unto thy seed 3327
Lev 26:42 also my covenant with I, and also my 3327
Nu 32:11 unto Abraham, unto I, and unto Jacob; 3327
Dt 1: 8 Abraham, I, and Jacob, to give unto them 3327
6:10 to Abraham, to I, and to Jacob, to give thee 3327
9: 5 unto thy fathers, Abraham, I, and Jacob. 3327
9:27 thy servants, Abraham, I, and Jacob; 3327
29:13 thy fathers, to Abraham, to I, and to Jacob. 3327
30:20 to Abraham, to I, and to Jacob, to give 3327
34: 4 unto I, and unto Jacob, saying, I will give it 3327
Jos 24: 3 and multiplied his seed, and gave him I. 3327
24: 4 I gave unto I Jacob and Esau: and I gave 3327
1Ki 18:36 LORD God of Abraham, I, and of Israel, 3327
2Ki 13:23 I, and Jacob, and would not destroy them, 3327
1Ch 1:28 The sons of Abraham; I, and Ishmael. 3327
1:34 Abraham begat I. The sons of Isaac; Esau 3327
1:34 begat Isaac. The sons of I; Esau and Israel. 3327
16:16 made with Abraham, and of his oath unto I; 3327
29:18 of Abraham, I, and of Israel, our fathers, 3327
2Ch 30: 6 I, and Israel, and he will return to 3327
Ps 105: 9 made with Abraham, and his oath unto I; 3446
Jer 33:26 over the seed of Abraham, I, and Jacob: 3446
Am 7: 9 the high places of I shall be desolate, and 3446
7:16 drop not *thy word* against the house of I. 3446
Mt 1: 2 Abraham begat I; and Isaac begat Jacob; *2464*
1: 2 and I begat Jacob; and Jacob begat Judas *2464*
8:11 and I, and Jacob, in the kingdom of heaven. *2464*
22:32 and the God of I, and the God of Jacob? *2464*
Mk 12:26 and the God of I, and the God of Jacob? *2464*
Lk 3:34 *the son* of Jacob, which was *the son* of I, *2464*
13:28 and I, and Jacob, and all the prophets, *2464*
20:37 and the God of I, and the God of Jacob. *2464*
Ac 3:13 God of Abraham, and of I, and of Jacob, *2464*
7: 8 and so *Abraham* begat I, and *2464*
7: 8 and I *begat* Jacob; and Jacob *begat* *2464*
7:32 and the God of I, and the God of Jacob. *2464*
Ro 9: 7 but, In I shall thy seed be called. *2464*
9:10 had conceived by one, *even* by our father I; *2464*
Gal 4:28 Now we, brethren, as I was, are *2464*
Heb 11: 9 *country*, dwelling in tabernacles with I *2464*
11:17 when he was tried, offered up I: *2464*
11:18 was said, That in I shall thy seed be called: *2464*
11:20 By faith I blessed Jacob and Esau *2464*
Jas 2:21 when he had offered I his son upon *2464*

ISAAC'S (4) [ISAAC]

Ge 26:19 I servants digged in the valley, and 3327
26:20 the herdmen of Gerar did strive with I 3327
26:25 and there I servants digged a well. 3327
26:32 that I servants came, and told him 3327

ISACHAR (1) [ISSACHAR]

Rev 7: 7 Of the tribe of I *were* sealed twelve *2466*

ISAIAH (31) [ESAI, ESAIAS]

2Ki 19: 5 So the servants of king Hezekiah came to I. 3470
19: 6 I said unto them, Thus shall ye say to your 3470
19:20 I the son of Amoz sent to Hezekiah, saying, 3470
20: 1 the prophet I the son of Amoz came to him, 3470
20: 4 afore I was gone out *into* the middle court, 3470
20: 7 I said, Take a lump of figs. And they took 3470
20: 8 Hezekiah said unto I, What *shall be* 3470
20: 9 I said, This sign shalt thou have of 3470
20:11 I the prophet cried unto the LORD: and 3470
20:14 came I the prophet unto king Hezekiah, 3470
20:16 I said unto Hezekiah, Hear the word of 3470
20:19 said Hezekiah unto I, Good *is* the word of 3470
2Ch 26:22 first and last, did I the prophet, the son of 3470
32:20 the prophet I the son of Amoz, prayed and 3470
32:32 they *are* written in the vision of I 3470
Isa 1: 1 The vision of I the son of Amoz, which he 3470
2: 1 The word that I the son of Amoz saw 3470
7: 3 said the LORD unto I, Go forth now to 3470
13: 1 which I the son of Amoz did see. 3470
20: 2 At the same time spake the LORD by I 3470
20: 3 Like as my servant I hath walked naked 3470
37: 2 unto I the prophet the son of Amoz. 3470
37: 5 So the servants of king Hezekiah came to I. 3470
37: 6 I said unto them, Thus shall ye say unto 3470
37:21 I the son of Amoz sent unto Hezekiah, 3470
38: 1 I the prophet the son of Amoz came unto 3470
38: 4 came the word of the LORD to I, saying, 3470
38:21 For I had said, Let them take a lump of 3470
39: 3 came I the prophet unto king Hezekiah, 3470
39: 5 said I to Hezekiah, Hear the word of 3470

Isa 39: 8 said Hezekiah to I, Good *is* the word of 3470

ISCAH (1)
Ge 11:29 the father of Milcah, and the father of I. 3252

ISCARIOT (11)
Mt 10: 4 Simon the Canaanite, and Judas I, who also *2469*
26:14 Then one of the twelve, called Judas I, *2469*
Mk 3:19 And Judas I, which also betrayed him. *2469*
14:10 And Judas I, one of the twelve, went unto *2469*
Lk 6:16 and Judas I, which also was the traitor. *2469*
22: 3 Then entered Satan into Judas surnamed I, *2469*
Jn 6:71 He spake of Judas I *the son* of Simon: *2469*
12: 4 Then saith one of his disciples, Judas I, *2469*
13: 2 having now put into the heart of Judas I, *2469*
13:26 he gave *it* to Judas I, *the son* of Simon. *2469*
14:22 Judas saith unto him, not I, Lord, how is it *2469*

ISHBAH (1)
1Ch 4:17 and I the father of Eshtemoa. 3431

ISHBAK (2)
Ge 25: 2 and Medan, and Midian, and I, and Shuah. 3435
1Ch 1:32 and Medan, and Midian, and I, and Shuah. 3435

ISHBI-BENOB (1)
2Sa 21:16 I, which *was* of the sons of the giant, 3430

ISH-BOSHETH (12) [ESHBAAL]
2Sa 2: 8 took I the son of Saul, and brought him over 378
2:10 I Saul's son *was* forty years old when he 378
2:12 of Ner, and the servants of I the son of Saul, 378
2:15 which *pertained* to I the son of Saul, and 378
3: 7 *I* said to Abner, Wherefore hast thou gone NIH
3: 8 was Abner very wroth for the words of I, 378
3:14 David sent messengers to I Saul's son, 378
3:15 I sent, and took her from *her* husband, 378
4: 5 about the heat of the day to the house of I, 378
4: 8 they brought the head of I unto David *to* 378
4: 8 Behold the head of I the son of Saul thine 378
4:12 they took the head of I, and buried *it* in 378

ISHHOD See ISHOD

ISHI (6)
1Ch 2:31 the sons of Appaim; I. And the sons of Ishi; 3469
2:31 the sons of I; Sheshan. And the children of 3469
4:20 the sons of I *were,* Zoheth, and Ben-zoheth. 3469
4:42 and Rephaiah, and Uzziel, the sons of I. 3469
5:24 I, and Eliel, and Azriel, and Jeremiah, and 3469
Hos 2:16 saith the LORD, *that* thou shalt call *me* I; 376

ISHIAH (1)
1Ch 7: 3 Michael, and Obadiah, and Joel, I, five: 3449

ISHIJAH (1)
Ezr 10:31 Eliezer, I, Malchiah, Shemaiah, Shimeon, 3449

ISHMA (1)
1Ch 4: 3 father of Etam; Jezreel, and I, and Idbash: 3457

ISHMAEL (47) [ISHMAEL'S, ISHMAELITE, ISHMAELITES, ISHMEELITE, ISHMEELITES]
Ge 16:11 shalt bear a son, and shalt call his name I; 3458
16:15 called his son's name, which Hagar bare, I. 3458
16:16 six years old, when Hagar bare I to Abram. 3458
17:18 unto God, O that I might live before thee! 3458
17:20 as for I, I have heard thee: Behold, I have 3458
17:23 Abraham took I his son, and all that were 3458
17:25 I his son *was* thirteen years old, when he 3458
17:26 was Abraham circumcised, and I his son. 3458
25: 9 and I buried him in the cave of Machpelah, 3458
25:12 Now these *are* the generations of I, 3458
25:13 these *are* the names of the sons of I, 3458
25:13 the firstborn of I, Nebajoth; and Kedar, and 3458
25:16 These *are* the sons of I, and these *are* their 3458
25:17 these *are* the years of the life of I, 3458
28: 9 went Esau unto I, and took unto the wives 3458
28: 9 Mahalath the daughter of I Abraham's son, 3458
2Ki 25:23 even I the son of Nethaniah, and 3458
25:25 *that* I the son of Nethaniah, the son of 3458
1Ch 1:28 The sons of Abraham; Isaac, and I. 3458
1:29 The firstborn of I, Nebajoth; then Kedar, 3458
1:31 and Kedemah. These *are* the sons of I. 3458
8:38 I, and Sheariah, and Obadiah, and Hanan. 3458
9:44 I, and Sheariah, and Obadiah, and Hanan: 3458
2Ch 19:11 Zebadiah the son of I, the ruler of the house 3458
23: 1 I the son of Jehohanan, and Azariah the son 3458
Ezr 10:22 Elioenai, Maaseiah, I, Nethaneel, Jozabad, 3458
Jer 40: 8 even I the son of Nethaniah, and Johanan 3458
40:14 sent I the son of Nethaniah to slay thee? 3458
40:15 I will slay I the son of Nethaniah, and 3458
40:16 do this thing: for thou speakest falsely of I. 3458
41: 1 *that* I the son of Nethaniah the son of 3458
41: 2 arose I the son of Nethaniah, and the ten 3458
41: 3 I also slew all the Jews that were with him, 3458
41: 6 I the son of Nethaniah went forth from 3458
41: 7 that I the son of Nethaniah slew them, *and* 3458
41: 8 were found among them that said unto I, 3458
41: 9 Now the pit wherein I had cast all the dead 3458
41: 9 I the son of Nethaniah filled it *with them* 3458
41:10 I carried away captive all the residue of 3458
41:10 I the son of Nethaniah carried them away 3458
41:11 heard of all the evil that I the son of 3458
41:12 went to fight with I the son of Nethaniah, 3458
41:13 *that* when all the people which *were* with I 3458
41:14 So all the people that I had carried away 3458
41:15 I the son of Nethaniah escaped from 3458
41:16 had recovered from I the son of Nethaniah, 3458
41:18 I the son of Nethaniah had slain Gedaliah 3458

ISHMAEL'S (1) [ISHMAEL]
Ge 36: 3 Bashemath I daughter, sister of Nebajoth. 3458

ISHMAELITE (1) [ISHMAEL]
1Ch 27:30 Over the camels also *was* Obil the I: and 3459

ISHMAELITES (2) [ISHMAEL]
Jdg 8:24 had golden earrings, because they *were* I.) 3459
Ps 83: 6 The tabernacles of Edom, and the I; 3459

ISHMAIAH (1)
1Ch 27:19 Of Zebulun, I the son of Obadiah: 3460

ISHMEELITE (1) [ISHMAEL]
1Ch 2:17 and the father of Amasa *was* Jether the I. 3459

ISHMEELITES (4) [ISHMAEL]
Ge 37:25 a company of I came from Gilead with 3459
37:27 let us sell him to the I, and let not our hand 3459
37:28 sold Joseph to the I for twenty *pieces* of 3459
39: 1 bought him of the hand of the I, 3459

ISHMERAI (1)
1Ch 8:18 I also, and Jezliah, and Jobab, the sons of 3461

ISHOD (1)
1Ch 7:18 his sister Hammoleketh bare I, and Abiezer, 379

ISHPAH See ISPAH

ISHPAN (1)
1Ch 8:22 And I, and Heber, and Eliel, 3473

ISH-TOB (2)
2Sa 10: 6 and of I twelve thousand men. 382
10: 8 of Zoba, and of Rehob, and I, and Maacah, 382

ISHUAH (1)
Ge 46:17 I, and Ishui, and Beriah, and Serah their 3438

ISHUAI (1)
1Ch 7:30 and I, and Beriah, and Serah their sister. 3438

ISHUI (2) [JESUI]
Ge 46:17 and I, and Beriah, and Serah their sister: 3440
1Sa 14:49 Saul were Jonathan, and I, and Melchishua: 3440

ISHVAH See ISHUAH

ISHVI See ISHUAI; ISHUI; JESUI

ISHVITE See JESUITES

ISLAND (9) [ISLANDS, ISLE, ISLES]
Job 22:30 He shall deliver the i of the innocent: and 336
Isa 34:14 shall also meet with the **wild beasts of the i,** 338
Ac 27:16 And running under a certain i *which is* *3519*
27:26 Howbeit we must be cast upon a certain i. *3520*
28: 1 then they knew that the i was called Melita. *3520*
28: 7 were possessions of the chief *man* of the i, *3520*
28: 9 which had diseases in the i, came, and *3520*
Rev 6:14 and i were moved out of their places. *3520*

Rev 16:20 And every i fled *away,* and the mountains *3520*

ISLANDER See BARBARIANS

ISLANDERS See BARBAROUS

ISLANDS (7) [ISLAND]

Isa 11:11 and from Hamath, and from the i of the sea. 339
13:22 the **wild beasts of the i** shall cry in their 338
41: 1 Keep silence before me, O i; and let 339
42:12 the LORD, and declare his praise in the i. 339
42:15 I will make the rivers i, and I will dry up 339
59:18 to the i he will repay recompence. 339
Jer 50:39 the **wild beasts of the i** shall dwell *there,* 338

ISLE (6) [ISLAND]

Isa 20: 6 the inhabitant of this i shall say in that day, 339
23: 2 Be still, ye inhabitants of the i; thou whom 339
23: 6 to Tarshish; howl, ye inhabitants of the i. 339
Ac 13: 6 And when they had gone through the i unto *3520*
28:11 which had wintered in the i, *whose* sign *3520*
Rev 1: 9 was in the i that is called Patmos, for *3520*

ISLES (27) [ISLAND]

Ge 10: 5 By these were the i of the Gentiles divided in 339
Est 10: 1 upon the land, and *upon* the i of the sea. 339
Ps 72:10 of Tarshish and *of* the i shall bring presents: 339
97: 1 let the multitude of i be glad *thereof.* 339
Isa 24:15 the LORD God of Israel in the i of the sea. 339
40:15 he taketh up the i as a very little thing. 339
41: 5 The i saw *it,* and feared; the ends of the earth 339
42: 4 in the earth: and the i shall wait for his law. 339
42:10 is therein; the i, and the inhabitants thereof. 339
49: 1 Listen, O i, unto me; and hearken, ye people, 339
51: 5 the i shall wait upon me, and on mine arm 339
60: 9 Surely the i shall wait for me, and the ships 339
66:19 *to* Tubal, and Javan, *to* the i afar off, 339
Jer 2:10 For pass over the i of Chittim, and see; and 339
25:22 the kings of the i which *are* beyond the sea, 339
31:10 and declare *it* in the i afar off, and say, 339
Eze 26:15 Shall not the i shake at the sound of thy fall, 339
26:18 Now shall the i tremble *in* the day of thy fall; 339
26:18 the i that *are* in the sea shall be troubled at 339
27: 3 *art* a merchant of the people for many i, 339
27: 6 *of* ivory, *brought* out of the i of Chittim. 339
27: 7 purple from the i of Elishah was that which 339
27:15 many i *were* the merchandise of thine hand: 339
27:35 All the inhabitants of the i shall be 339
39: 6 among them that dwell carelessly in the i: 339
Da 11:18 After this shall he turn his face unto the i, 339
Zep 2:11 from his place, *even* all the i of the heathen. 339

ISMACHIAH (1)

2Ch 31:13 and Eliel, and I, and Mahath, and Benaiah, 3253

ISMAIAH (1)

1Ch 12: 4 I the Gibeonite, a mighty *man* among 3460

ISMAKIAH See ISMACHIAH

ISPAH (1)

1Ch 8:16 Michael, and I, and Joha, the sons of 3472

ISRAEL (2565) [EL-ELOHE-ISRAEL, ISRAEL'S, ISRAELITE, ISRAELITES, ISRAELITISH, JACOB]

Ge 32:28 name shall be called no more Jacob, but I: 3478
32:32 Therefore the children of I eat not *of* 3478
34: 7 he had wrought folly in I in lying with 3478
35:10 any more Jacob, but I shall be thy name: 3478
35:10 shall be thy name: and he called his name I. 3478
35:21 I journeyed, and spread his tent beyond 3478
35:22 when I dwelt in that land, that Reuben went 3478
35:22 I heard *it.* Now the sons of Jacob were 3478
36:31 reigned *any* king over the children of I. 3478
37: 3 Now I loved Joseph more than all his 3478
37:13 I said unto Joseph, Do not thy brethren feed 3478
42: 5 the sons of I came to buy *corn* among those 3478
43: 6 I said, Wherefore dealt ye *so* ill with me, 3478
43: 8 Judah said unto I his father, Send the lad 3478
43:11 their father I said unto them, If *it must be* 3478
45:21 the children of I did so: and Joseph gave 3478
45:28 I said, *It is* enough; Joseph my son *is* yet 3478
46: 1 I took his journey with all that he had, and 3478
46: 2 God spake unto I in the visions of 3478
46: 5 the sons of I carried Jacob their father, and 3478
46: 8 these *are* the names of the children of I, 3478
46:29 and went up to meet I his father, to Goshen, 3478
46:30 I said unto Joseph, Now let me die, since I 3478
47:27 I dwelt in the land of Egypt, in the country 3478
47:29 And the time drew nigh that I must die: and 3478
47:31 And I bowed himself upon the bed's head. 3478
48: 2 I strengthened himself, and sat upon 3478
48: 8 I beheld Joseph's sons, and said, Who *are* 3478
48:10 Now the eyes of I were dim for age, *so* 3478
48:11 I said unto Joseph, I had not thought to see 3478
48:14 I stretched out his right hand, and laid *it* 3478
48:20 saying, In thee shall I bless, saying, 3478
48:21 I said unto Joseph, Behold, I die: but 3478
49: 2 of Jacob; and hearken unto I your father. 3478
49: 7 divide them in Jacob, and scatter them in I. 3478
49:16 judge his people, as one of the tribes of I. 3478
49:24 thence *is* the shepherd, the stone of I:) 3478
49:28 All these *are* the twelve tribes of I: and 3478
50: 2 his father: and the physicians embalmed I. 3478
50:25 Joseph took an oath of the children of I, 3478
Ex 1: 1 these *are* the names of the children of I, 3478
1: 7 the children of I were fruitful, and 3478
1: 9 the people of the children of I *are* moe and 3478
1:12 were grieved because of the children of I. 3478
1:13 the Egyptians made the children of I to 3478
2:23 the children of I sighed by reason of 3478
2:25 And God looked upon the children of I, and 3478
3: 9 the cry of the children of I is come unto 3478
3:10 my people the children of I out of Egypt. 3478
3:11 that I should bring forth the children of I 3478
3:13 *when* I come unto the children of I, and 3478
3:14 Thus shalt thou say unto the children of I, 3478
3:15 Thus shalt thou say unto the children of I, 3478
3:16 gather the elders of I together, and say unto 3478
3:18 thou shalt come, thou and the elders of I, 3478
4:22 the LORD, I *is* my son, *even* my firstborn: 3478
4:29 together all the elders of the children of I: 3478
4:31 the LORD had visited the children of I, 3478
5: 1 Thus saith the LORD God of I, 3478
5: 2 that I should obey his voice to let I go? 3478
5: 2 not the LORD, neither will I let I go. 3478
5:14 the officers of the children of I, 3478
5:15 the officers of the children of I came and 3478
5:19 the officers of the children of I did see *that* 3478
6: 5 also heard the groaning of the children of I, 3478
6: 6 Wherefore say unto the children of I, I *am* 3478
6: 9 Moses spake so unto the children of I: but 3478
6:11 that he let the children of I go out of his 3478
6:12 the children of I have not hearkened unto 3478
6:13 gave them a charge unto the children of I, 3478
6:13 to bring the children of I out of the land of 3478
6:14 The sons of Reuben the firstborn of I; 3478
6:26 Bring out the children of I from the land of 3478
6:27 to bring out the children of I from Egypt: 3478
7: 2 that he send the children of I out of his 3478
7: 4 *and* my people the children of I, 3478
7: 5 bring out the children of I from among 3478
9: 4 LORD shall sever between the cattle of I 3478
9: 4 nothing die of all *that is* the children's of I. 3478
9: 6 of the cattle of the children of I died not 3478
9:26 where the children of I *were,* was there no 3478
9:35 neither would he let the children of I go; 3478
10:20 so that he would not let the children of I go. 3478
10:23 all the children of I had light in their 3478
11: 7 against any of the children of I shall not a 3478
11: 7 a difference between the Egyptians and I. 3478
11:10 that he would not let the children of I go 3478
12: 3 Speak ye unto all the congregation of I, 3478
12: 6 whole assembly of the congregation of I 3478
12:15 that soul shall be cut off from I. 3478
12:19 shall be cut off from the congregation of I, 3478
12:21 Moses called for all the elders of I, and 3478
12:27 the houses of the children of I in Egypt, 3478
12:28 the children of I went away, and did as 3478
12:31 my people, both you and the children of I; 3478
12:35 the children of I did according to the word 3478
12:37 the children of I journeyed from Rameses 3478
12:40 Now the sojourning of the children of I, 3478
12:42 of all the children of I in their generations. 3478
12:47 All the congregation of I shall keep it. 3478
12:50 Thus did all the children of I; as 3478
12:51 *that* the LORD did bring the children of I 3478
13: 2 openeth the womb among the children of I, 3478
13:18 the children of I went up harnessed out of 3478
13:19 for he had straitly sworn the children of I, 3478

Ge 14: 2 Speak unto the children of I, that they turn 3478
14: 3 For Pharaoh will say of the children of I, 3478
14: 5 that we have let I go from serving us? 3478
14: 8 and he pursued after the children of I: 3478
14: 8 the children of I went out with a high hand. 3478
14:10 the children of I lift up their eyes, and 3478
14:10 the children of I cried out unto the LORD. 3478
14:15 speak unto the children of I, that they go 3478
14:16 the children of I shall go on dry *ground* 3478
14:19 which went before the camp of I, removed 3478
14:20 camp of the Egyptians and the camp of I; 3478
14:22 the children of I went into the midst of 3478
14:25 Let us flee from the face of I; 3478
14:29 the children of I walked upon dry *land* in 3478
14:30 Thus the LORD saved I that day out of 3478
14:30 I saw the Egyptians dead upon the sea 3478
14:31 I saw *that* great work which the LORD 3478
15: 1 the children of I this song unto the LORD, 3478
15:19 the children of I went on dry *land* in 3478
15:22 So Moses brought I from the Red sea, and 3478
16: 1 all the congregation of the children of I 3478
16: 2 the whole congregation of the children of I 3478
16: 3 the children of I said unto them, Would to 3478
16: 6 and Aaron said unto all the children of I, 3478
16: 9 all the congregation of the children of I, 3478
16:10 the whole congregation of the children of I, 3478
16:12 heard the murmurings of the children of I: 3478
16:15 when the children of I saw *it,* they said one 3478
16:17 the children of I did so, and gathered, 3478
16:31 the house of I called the name thereof 3478
16:35 the children of I did eat manna forty years, 3478
17: 1 all the congregation of the children of I 3478
17: 5 and take with thee of the elders of I; 3478
17: 6 Moses did so in the sight of the elders of I. 3478
17: 7 because of the chiding of the children of I, 3478
17: 8 and fought with I in Rephidim. 3478
17:11 Moses held up his hand, that I prevailed: 3478
18: 1 for I his people, *and* that the LORD had 3478
18: 1 that the LORD had brought I out of 3478
18: 9 goodness which the LORD had done to I, 3478
18:12 Aaron came, and all the elders of I, to eat 3478
18:25 Moses chose able men out of all I, and 3478
19: 1 when the children of I were gone forth out 3478
19: 2 and there I camped before the mount. 3478
19: 3 house of Jacob, and tell the children of I; 3478
19: 6 thou shalt speak unto the children of I. 3478
20:22 Thus thou shalt say unto the children of I, 3478
24: 1 and Abihu, and seventy of the elders of I; 3478
24: 4 according to the twelve tribes of I. 3478
24: 5 And he sent young men of the children of I, 3478
24: 9 and Abihu, and seventy of the elders of I: 3478
24:10 they saw the God of I: and *there was* under 3478
24:11 upon the nobles of the children of I he laid 3478
24:17 the mount in the eyes of the children of I. 3478
25: 2 Speak unto the children of I, that they bring 3478
25:22 in commandment unto the children of I. 3478
27:20 thou shalt command the children of I, 3478
27:21 on the behalf of the children of I. 3478
28: 1 with him, from among the children of I, 3478
28: 9 on them the names of the children of I: 3478
28:11 stones with the names of the children of I: 3478
28:12 stones of memorial unto the children of I: 3478
28:21 shall be with the names of the children of I, 3478
28:29 I in the breastplate of judgment upon his 3478
28:30 I upon his heart before the LORD 3478
28:38 of I shall hallow in all their holy gifts; 3478
29:28 by a statute for ever from the children of I: 3478
29:28 of I of the sacrifice of their peace offerings, 3478
29:43 And there I will meet with the children of I, 3478
29:45 I will dwell amongst the children of I, and 3478
30:12 sum of the children of I after their number, 3478
30:16 the atonement money of the children of I, 3478
30:16 unto the children of I before the LORD, 3478
30:31 thou shalt speak unto the children of I, 3478
31:13 Speak thou also unto the children of I, 3478
31:16 Wherefore the children of I shall keep 3478
31:17 between me and the children of I for ever: 3478
32: 4 they said, These *be* thy gods, O I, 3478
32: 8 and said, These *be* thy gods, O I, 3478
32:13 Isaac, and I, thy servants, 3478
32:20 and made the children of I drink *of it.* 3478
32:27 unto them, Thus saith the LORD God of I, 3478
33: 5 Say unto the children of I, Ye *are* a 3478
33: 6 the children of I stript themselves of their 3478
34:23 before the Lord GOD, the God of I. 3478
34:27 have made a covenant with thee and with I. 3478
34:30 and all the children of I saw Moses, 3478
34:32 afterward all the children of I came nigh: 3478
34:34 spake unto the children of I *that* which he 3478
34:35 the children of I saw the face of Moses, 3478
35: 1 congregation of the children of I together, 3478
35: 4 all the congregation of the children of I, 3478
35:20 all the congregation of the children of I 3478
35:29 The children of I brought a willing offering 3478
35:30 Moses said unto the children of I, See, 3478
36: 3 which the children of I had brought for 3478
39: 6 with the names of the children of I. 3478
39: 7 stones for a memorial to the children of I; 3478
39:14 according to the names of the children of I, 3478
39:32 the children of I did according to all that 3478
39:42 so the children of I made all the work. 3478
40:36 the children of I went onward in all their 3478
40:38 it by night, in the sight of all the house of I, 3478
Lev 1: 2 Speak unto the children of I, and say unto 3478
4: 2 Speak unto the children of I, saying, If a 3478
4:13 if the whole congregation of I sin through 3478
7:23 Speak unto the children of I, saying, 3478
7:29 Speak unto the children of I, saying, 3478
7:34 I from off the sacrifices of their peace 3478
7:34 for ever from among the children of I. 3478
7:36 to be given them of the children of I, 3478
7:38 I to offer their oblations unto the LORD, 3478
9: 1 and his sons, and the elders of I; 3478
9: 3 unto the children of I thou shalt speak, 3478
10: 6 let your brethren, the whole house of I, 3478
10:11 that *ye* may teach the children of I all 3478
10:14 of peace offerings of the children of I. 3478
11: 2 Speak unto the children of I, saying, 3478
12: 2 Speak unto the children of I, saying, If a 3478
15: 2 Speak unto the children of I, and say unto 3478
15:31 Thus shall ye separate the children of I 3478
16: 5 of I two kids of the goats for a sin offering, 3478
16:16 of the uncleanness of the children of I, 3478
16:17 and for all the congregation of I. 3478
16:19 it from the uncleanness of the children of I. 3478
16:21 him all the iniquities of the children of I, 3478
16:34 to make an atonement for the children of I 3478
17: 2 unto all the children of I, and say unto 3478
17: 3 What man soever *there be* of the house of I, 3478
17: 5 To the end that the children of I may bring 3478
17: 8 Whatsoever man *there be* of the house of I, 3478
17:10 whatsoever man *there be* of the house of I, 3478
17:12 Therefore I said unto the children of I, No 3478
17:13 man *there be* of the children of I, 3478
17:14 therefore I said unto the children of I, 3478
18: 2 Speak unto the children of I, and say unto 3478
19: 2 all the congregation of the children of I, 3478
20: 2 Again, thou shalt say to the children of I, 3478
20: 2 Whosoever *he be* of the children of I, 376+3478
20: 2 or of the strangers that sojourn in I, 3478
21:24 to his sons, and unto all the children of I. 3478
22: 2 from the holy *things* of the children of I, 3478
22: 3 the children of I hallow unto the LORD, 3478
22:15 profane the holy *things* of the children of I, 3478
22:18 unto all the children of I, and say unto 3478
22:18 Whatsoever *he be* of the house of I, or 376+3478
22:18 the house of Israel, or of the strangers in I, 3478
22:32 I will be hallowed among the children of I: 3478
23: 2 Speak unto the children of I, and say unto 3478
23:10 Speak unto the children of I, and say unto 3478
23:24 Speak unto the children of I, saying, In 3478
23:34 Speak unto the children of I, saying, The 3478
23:43 I made the children of I to dwell in booths, 3478
23:44 Moses declared unto the children of I 3478
24: 2 Command the children of I, that they bring 3478
24: 8 *being taken* from the children of I *by* an 3478
24:10 went out among the children of I: 3478
24:10 and a man of I strove together in the camp; 3481
24:15 thou shalt speak unto the children of I, 3478
24:23 Moses spake to the children of I, that they 3478
24:23 the children of I did as the LORD 3478
25: 2 Speak unto the children of I, and say unto 3478
25:33 their possession among the children of I. 3478
25:46 over your brethren the children of I, 3478
25:55 For unto me the children of I *are* servants; 3478
26:46 the children of I in mount Sinai by the hand 3478
27: 2 Speak unto the children of I, and say unto 3478
27:34 Moses for the children of I in mount Sinai. 3478

Nu	1: 2	of all the congregation of the children of I,	3478
	1: 3	all that *are able to* go forth *to* war in I:	3478
	1:16	of their fathers, heads of thousands in I.	3478
	1:44	and Aaron numbered, and the princes of I,	3478
	1:45	that were numbered of the children of I,	3478
	1:45	all that *were able to* go forth *to* war in I;	3478
	1:49	the sum of them among the children of I:	3478
	1:52	the children of I shall pitch their tents,	3478
	1:53	upon the congregation of the children of I:	3478
	1:54	the children of I did according to all that	3478
	2: 2	Every man of the children of I shall pitch	3478
	2:32	children of I by the house of their fathers:	3478
	2:33	not numbered among the children of I;	3478
	2:34	the children of I did according to all that	3478
	3: 8	the charge of the children of I, to do	3478
	3: 9	given unto him out of the children of I.	3478
	3:12	I instead of all the firstborn that openeth	3478
	3:12	openeth the matrix among the children of I:	3478
	3:13	I hallowed unto me all the firstborn in I,	3478
	3:38	for the charge of the children of I;	3478
	3:40	males of the children of I from a month old	3478
	3:41	of all the firstborn among the children of I;	3478
	3:41	among the cattle of the children of I.	3478
	3:42	all the firstborn among the children of I.	3478
	3:45	of all the firstborn among the children of I,	3478
	3:46	thirteen of the firstborn of the children of I,	3478
	3:50	Of the firstborn of the children of I took he	3478
	4:46	and Aaron and the chief of I numbered,	3478
	5: 2	Command the children of I, that they put	3478
	5: 4	the children of I did so, and put them out	3478
	5: 4	spake unto Moses, so did the children of I.	3478
	5: 6	Speak unto the children of I, When a man	3478
	5: 9	of all the holy *things* of the children of I,	3478
	5:12	Speak unto the children of I, and say unto	3478
	6: 2	Speak unto the children of I, and say unto	3478
	6:23	On this wise ye shall bless the children of I,	3478
	6:27	shall put my name upon the children of I;	3478
	7: 2	That the princes of I, heads of the house of	3478
	7:84	when it was anointed, by the princes of I:	3478
	8: 6	the Levites from among the children of I,	3478
	8: 9	assembly of the children of I together:	3478
	8:10	the children of I shall put their hands upon	3478
	8:11	LORD *for* an offering of the children of I,	3478
	8:14	the Levites from among the children of I:	3478
	8:16	unto me from among the children of I;	3478
	8:16	*of* the firstborn of all the children of I,	3478
	8:17	For all the firstborn of the children of I *are*	3478
	8:18	for all the firstborn of the children of I.	3478
	8:19	to his sons from among the children of I,	3478
	8:19	to do the service of the children of I in	3478
	8:19	to make an atonement for the children of I:	3478
	8:19	there be no plague among the children of I,	3478
	8:19	when the children of I come nigh unto	3478
	8:20	all the congregation of the children of I,	3478
	8:20	so did the children of I unto them.	3478
	9: 2	Let the children of I also keep the passover	3478
	9: 4	Moses spake unto the children of I,	3478
	9: 5	so did the children of I.	3478
	9: 7	appointed season among the children of I?	3478
	9:10	Speak unto the children of I, saying, If any	3478
	9:17	then after that the children of I journeyed:	3478
	9:17	there the children of I pitched their tents.	3478
	9:18	of the LORD the children of I journeyed,	3478
	9:19	the children of I kept the charge of	3478
	9:22	the children of I abode in their tents, and	3478
	10: 4	*which are* heads of the thousands of I,	3478
	10:12	the children of I took their journeys out of	3478
	10:28	the children of I according to their armies,	3478
	10:29	the LORD hath spoken good concerning I.	3478
	10:36	O LORD, *unto* the many thousands of I.	3478
	11: 4	the children of I also wept again, and said,	3478
	11:16	unto me seventy men of the elders of I,	3478
	11:30	him into the camp, he and the elders of I.	3478
	13: 2	which I give unto the children of I:	3478
	13: 3	those men *were* heads of the children of I.	3478
	13:24	the children of I cut down from thence.	3478
	13:26	to all the congregation of the children of I,	3478
	13:32	they had searched unto the children of I,	3478
	14: 2	all the children of I murmured against	3478
	14: 5	of the congregation of the children of I.	3478
	14: 7	unto all the company of the children of I,	3478
	14:10	congregation before all the children of I.	3478
	14:27	heard the murmurings of the children of I,	3478
	14:39	told these sayings unto all the children of I:	3478
	15: 2	Speak unto the children of I, and say unto	3478
	15:18	Speak unto the children of I, and say unto	3478
	15:25	for all the congregation of the children of I,	3478
	15:26	all the congregation of the children of I,	3478
	15:29	him that is born amongst the children of I,	3478
	15:32	while the children of I were in	3478
	15:38	Speak unto the children of I, and bid them	3478
	16: 2	with certain of the children of I,	3478
	16: 9	that the God of I hath separated you from	3478
	16: 9	separated you from the congregation of I,	3478
	16:25	Abiram; and the elders of I followed him.	3478
	16:34	all I that *were* round about them fled at	3478
	16:38	they shall be a sign unto the children of I.	3478
	16:40	*To be* a memorial unto the children of I,	3478
	16:41	the children of I murmured against Moses	3478
	17: 2	Speak unto the children of I, and take of	3478
	17: 5	me the murmurings of the children of I,	3478
	17: 6	Moses spake unto the children of I, and	3478
	17: 9	the LORD unto all the children of I:	3478
	17:12	the children of I spake unto Moses, saying,	3478
	18: 5	no wrath any more upon the children of I.	3478
	18: 6	the Levites from among the children of I:	3478
	18: 8	all the hallowed *things* of the children of I;	3478
	18:11	all the wave offerings of the children of I:	3478
	18:14	Every thing devoted in I shall be thine.	3478
	18:19	the children of I offer unto the LORD,	3478
	18:20	thine inheritance among the children of I.	3478
	18:21	of Levi all the tenth in I for an inheritance,	3478
	18:22	Neither must the children of I henceforth	3478
	18:23	that among the children of I they have no	3478
	18:24	the tithes of the children of I, which they	3478
	18:24	Among the children of I they shall have no	3478
	18:26	When ye take of the children of I the tithes	3478
	18:28	which ye receive of the children of I;	3478
	18:32	pollute the holy *things* of the children of I,	3478
	19: 2	saying, Speak unto the children of I,	3478
	19: 9	the children of I for a water of separation:	3478
	19:10	it shall be unto the children of I, and	3478
	19:13	and that soul shall be cut off from I:	3478
	20: 1	came the children of I, *even* the whole	3478
	20:12	sanctify me in the eyes of the children of I,	3478
	20:13	the children of I strove with the LORD,	3478
	20:14	Thus saith thy brother I, Thou knowest all	3478
	20:19	the children of I said unto him, We will go	3478
	20:21	Thus Edom refused to give I passage	3478
	20:21	wherefore I turned away from him.	3478
	20:22	the children of I, *even* the whole	3478
	20:24	which I have given unto the children of I,	3478
	20:29	Aaron thirty days, *even* all the house of I.	3478
	21: 1	heard *tell* that I came *by* the way of	3478
	21: 1	he fought against I, and took *some* of them	3478
	21: 2	I vowed a vow unto the LORD, and said,	3478
	21: 3	the LORD hearkened to the voice of I,	3478
	21: 6	bit the people; and much people of I died.	3478
	21:10	the children of I set forward, and pitched in	3478
	21:17	I sang this song, Spring up, O well; sing ye	3478
	21:21	I sent messengers unto Sihon king of	3478
	21:23	Sihon would not suffer I to pass through	3478
	21:23	and went out against I into the wilderness:	3478
	21:23	and he came *to* Jahaz, and fought against I.	3478
	21:24	I smote him with the edge of the sword,	3478
	21:25	I took all these cities: and Israel dwelt in all	3478
	21:25	I dwelt in all the cities of the Amorites,	3478
	21:31	Thus I dwelt in the land of the Amorites.	3478
	22: 1	the children of I set forward, and pitched in	3478
	22: 2	Balak the son of Zippor saw all that I had	3478
	22: 3	was distressed because of the children of I.	3478
	23: 7	curse me Jacob, and come, defy I.	3478
	23:10	and the number *of* the fourth part of I?	3478
	23:21	neither hath he seen perverseness in I:	3478
	23:23	neither *is there* any divination against I:	3478
	23:23	*this* time it shall be said of Jacob and of I,	3478
	24: 1	saw that it pleased the LORD to bless I,	3478
	24: 2	he saw I abiding *in his tents* according to	3478
	24: 5	thy tents, O Jacob, *and* thy tabernacles, O I!	3478
	24:17	a Sceptre shall rise out of I, and shall smite	3478
	24:18	for his enemies; and I shall do valiantly.	3478
	25: 1	I abode in Shittim, and the people begun to	3478
	25: 3	I joined himself unto Baal-peor: and	3478
	25: 3	anger of the LORD was kindled against I.	3478
	25: 4	of the LORD may be turned away from I.	3478
	25: 5	Moses said unto the judges of I, Slay ye	3478
	25: 6	one of the children of I came and	3478
	25: 6	of all the congregation of the children of I,	3478

Nu 25: 8 he went after the man of I into the tent, 3478
25: 8 the man of I, and the woman through her 3478
25: 8 plague was stayed from the children of I. 3478
25:11 my wrath away from the children of I, 3478
25:11 that I consumed not the children of I in my 3478
25:13 made an atonement for the children of I. 3478
26: 2 of all the congregation of the children of I, 3478
26: 2 all that *are able to* go *to* war in I. 3478
26: 4 commanded Moses and the children of I, 3478
26: 5 Reuben, the eldest son of I: the children of 3478
26:51 *were* the numbered of the children of I, 3478
26:62 not numbered among the children of I, 3478
26:62 given them among the children of I. 3478
26:63 who numbered the children of I in 3478
26:64 when they numbered the children of I in 3478
27: 8 thou shalt speak unto the children of I, 3478
27:11 it shall be unto the children of I a statute of 3478
27:12 which I have given unto the children of I. 3478
27:20 that all the congregation of the children of I 3478
27:21 *both* he, and all the children of I with him, 3478
28: 2 Command the children of I, and say unto 3478
29:40 Moses told the children of I according to 3478
30: 1 of the tribes concerning the children of I, 3478
31: 2 Avenge the children of I of the Midianites: 3478
31: 4 throughout all the tribes of I, shall ye send 3478
31: 5 were delivered out of the thousands of I, 3478
31: 9 the children of I took *all* the women of 3478
31:12 unto the congregation of the children of I, 3478
31:16 Behold, these caused the children of I, 3478
31:54 *for* a memorial for the children of I before 3478
32: 4 LORD smote before the congregation of I, 3478
32: 7 I from going over into the land which 3478
32: 9 discouraged the heart of the children of I, 3478
32:13 the LORD'S anger was kindled against I, 3478
32:14 the fierce anger of the LORD toward I. 3478
32:17 go ready armed before the children of I, 3478
32:18 until the children of I have inherited every 3478
32:22 guiltless before the LORD, and before I; 3478
32:28 fathers of the tribes of the children of I: 3478
33: 1 These *are* the journeys of the children of I, 3478
33: 3 I went out with a high hand in the sight of 3478
33: 5 the children of I removed from Rameses, 3478
33:38 in the fortieth year after the children of I 3478
33:40 heard of the coming of the children of I. 3478
33:51 Speak unto the children of I, and say unto 3478
34: 2 Command the children of I, and say unto 3478
34:13 Moses commanded the children of I, 3478
34:29 unto the children of I in the land of Canaan. 3478
35: 2 Command the children of I, that they give 3478
35: 8 *be* of the possession of the children of I: 3478
35:10 Speak unto the children of I, and say unto 3478
35:15 *both* for the children of I, and for 3478
35:34 the LORD dwell among the children of I. 3478
36: 1 the chief fathers of the children of I: 3478
36: 2 an inheritance by lot to the children of I: 3478
36: 3 sons of the *other* tribes of the children of I, 3478
36: 4 when the jubile of the children of I shall be, 3478
36: 5 Moses commanded the children of I 3478
36: 7 the children of I remove from tribe to tribe: 3478
36: 7 for every one of the children of I shall keep 3478
36: 8 inheritance in any tribe of the children of I, 3478
36: 8 that the children of I may enjoy every man 3478
36: 9 every one of the tribes of the children of I 3478
36:13 I in the plains of Moab by Jordan *near* 3478
Dt 1: 1 all I on *this* side Jordan in the wilderness, 3478
1: 3 *that* Moses spake unto the children of I, 3478
1:38 for he shall cause I to inherit it. 3478
2:12 as I did unto the land of his possession, 3478
3:18 before your brethren the children of I, 3478
4: 1 Now therefore hearken, O I, unto 3478
4:44 which Moses set before the children of I: 3478
4:45 which Moses spake unto the children of I, 3478
4:46 whom Moses and the children of I smote, 3478
5: 1 Moses called all I, and said unto them, 3478
5: 1 Hear, O I, the statutes and judgments which 3478
6: 3 O I, and observe to do *it;* that it may be 3478
6: 4 Hear, O I: The LORD our God *is* one 3478
9: 1 Hear, O I: Thou art to pass over Jordan *this* 3478
10: 6 the children of I took their journey from 3478
10:12 now, I, what doth the LORD thy God 3478
11: 6 in their possession, in the midst of all I: 3478
13:11 all I shall hear, and fear, and shall do no 3478
17: 4 *that* such abomination is wrought in I: 3478
17:12 and thou shalt put away the evil from I. 3478
17:20 he, and his children, in the midst of I. 3478
18: 1 shall have no part nor inheritance with I: 3478
18: 6 come from any of thy gates out of all I, 3478
19:13 put away *the guilt of* innocent blood from I, 3478
20: 3 shall say unto them, Hear, O I, 3478
21: 8 Be merciful, O LORD, unto thy people I, 3478
21:21 among you; and all I shall hear, and fear. 3478
22:19 brought up an evil name upon a virgin of I: 3478
22:21 because she hath wrought folly in I, to play 3478
22:22 so shalt thou put away evil from I. 3478
23:17 shall be no whore of the daughters of I, 3478
23:17 of Israel, nor a sodomite of the sons of I. 3478
24: 7 any of his brethren of the children of I, 3478
25: 6 is dead, that his name be not put out of I. 3478
25: 7 to raise up unto his brother a name in I, 3478
25:10 his name shall be called in I, The house of 3478
26:15 bless thy people I, and the land which thou 3478
27: 1 Moses with the elders of I commanded 3478
27: 9 and the priests the Levites spake unto all I, 3478
27: 9 saying, Take heed, and hearken, O I; 3478
27:14 say unto all the men of I *with* a loud voice, 3478
29: 1 with the children of I in the land of Moab, 3478
29: 2 Moses called unto all I, and said unto them, 3478
29:10 and your officers, *with* all the men of I, 3478
29:21 him unto evil out of all the tribes of I, 3478
31: 1 and spake these words unto all I. 3478
31: 7 said unto him in the sight of all I, Be strong 3478
31: 9 of the LORD, and unto all the elders of I. 3478
31:11 When all I is come to appear before 3478
31:11 thou shalt read this law before all I in their 3478
31:19 song for you, and teach it the children of I: 3478
31:19 a witness for me against the children of I. 3478
31:22 same day, and taught it the children of I. 3478
31:23 for thou shalt bring the children of I into 3478
31:30 congregation of I the words of this song, 3478
32: 8 to the number of the children of I. 3478
32:45 an end of speaking all these words to all I: 3478
32:49 which I give unto the children of I for a 3478
32:51 of I at the waters of Meribah-Kadesh, 3478
32:51 me not in the midst of the children of I. 3478
32:52 unto the land which I give the children of I. 3478
33: 1 blessed the children of I before his death. 3478
33: 5 *and* the tribes of I were gathered together. 3478
33:10 teach Jacob thy judgments, and I thy law: 3478
33:21 of the LORD, and his judgments with I. 3478
33:28 I then shall dwell *in* safety alone: 3478
33:29 Happy *art* thou, O I: who *is* like unto thee, 3478
34: 8 the children of I wept for Moses in 3478
34: 9 the children of I hearkened unto him, and 3478
34:10 there arose not a prophet since in I like 3478
34:12 which Moses shewed in the sight of all I. 3478
Jos 1: 2 I do give to them, *even* to the children of I. 3478
2: 2 the children of I to search out the country. 3478
3: 1 he and all the children of I, and 3478
3: 7 I begin to magnify thee in the sight of all I, 3478
3: 9 Joshua said unto the children of I, 3478
3:12 take ye twelve men out of the tribes of I, 3478
4: 4 whom he had prepared of the children of I, 3478
4: 5 number of the tribes of the children of I: 3478
4: 7 a memorial unto the children of I for ever. 3478
4: 8 the children of I did so as Joshua 3478
4: 8 number of the tribes of the children of I, 3478
4:12 passed over armed before the children of I, 3478
4:14 magnified Joshua in the sight of all I; 3478
4:21 And he spake unto the children of I, saying, 3478
4:22 I came over this Jordan on dry *land.* 3478
5: 1 of Jordan from before the children of I, 3478
5: 1 any more, because of the children of I. 3478
5: 2 circumcise again the children of I 3478
5: 3 circumcised the children of I at the hill of 3478
5: 6 For the children of I walked forty years in 3478
5:10 the children of I encamped in Gilgal, and 3478
5:12 neither had the children of I manna any 3478
6: 1 straitly shut up because of the children of I: 3478
6:18 make the camp of I a curse, and trouble it. 3478
6:23 and left them without the camp of I. 3478
6:25 she dwelleth in I *even* unto this day; 3478
7: 1 the children of I committed a trespass in 3478
7: 1 was kindled against the children of I. 3478
7: 6 he and the elders of I, and put dust upon 3478
7: 8 when I turneth *their* backs before their 3478
7:11 I hath sinned, and they have also 3478
7:12 Therefore the children of I could not stand 3478
7:13 for thus saith the LORD God of I, 3478

Jos 7:13 an accursed thing in the midst of thee, O I: 3478
7:15 and because he hath wrought folly in I. 3478
7:16 the morning, and brought I by their tribes; 3478
7:19 glory to the LORD God of I, and 3478
7:20 I have sinned against the LORD God of I, 3478
7:23 unto all the children of I, and laid them out 3478
7:24 Joshua, and all I with him, took Achan 3478
7:25 all I stoned him *with* stones, and 3478
8:10 and went up, he and the elders of I, 3478
8:14 the men of the city went out against I to 3478
8:15 all I *made as if they* were beaten before 3478
8:17 in Ai or Beth-el, that went not out after I: 3478
8:17 they left the city open, and pursued after I. 3478
8:21 all I saw that the ambush had taken 3478
8:22 so they were in the midst of I, some on this 3478
8:24 when I had made an end of slaying all 3478
8:27 the spoil of that city I took for a prey unto 3478
8:30 unto the LORD God of I in mount Ebal, 3478
8:31 the LORD commanded the children of I, 3478
8:32 wrote in the presence of the children of I. 3478
8:33 all I, and their elders, and officers, and 3478
8:33 that they should bless the people of I. 3478
8:35 read not before all the congregation of I, 3478
9: 2 to fight with Joshua and with I, *with* one 3478
9: 6 said unto him, and to the men of I, We be 3478
9: 7 the men of I said unto the Hivites, 3478
9:17 the children of I journeyed, and came unto 3478
9:18 the children of I smote them not, because 3478
9:18 sworn unto them by the LORD God of I. 3478
9:19 sworn unto them by the LORD God of I: 3478
9:26 them out of the hand of the children of I, 3478
10: 1 of Gibeon had made peace with I, 3478
10: 4 with Joshua and with the children of I. 3478
10:10 And the LORD discomfited them before I, 3478
10:11 as they fled from before I, *and* were in 3478
10:11 the children of I slew with the sword. 3478
10:12 up the Amorites before the children of I, 3478
10:12 he said in the sight of I, Sun, stand thou 3478
10:14 of a man: for the LORD fought for I. 3478
10:15 Joshua returned, and all I with him, 3478
10:20 the children of I had made an end of 3478
10:21 his tongue against any of the children of I. 3478
10:24 that Joshua called for all the men of I, and 3478
10:29 all I with him, *unto* Libnah, and 3478
10:30 the king thereof, into the hand of I; 3478
10:31 all I with him, unto Lachish, and 3478
10:32 delivered Lachish into the hand of I, 3478
10:34 passed unto Eglon, and all I with him; 3478
10:36 and all I with him, unto Hebron; 3478
10:38 and all I with him, to Debir; 3478
10:40 as the LORD God of I commanded. 3478
10:42 the LORD God of I fought for Israel. 3478
10:42 the LORD God of Israel fought for I. 3478
10:43 Joshua returned, and all I with him, 3478
11: 5 at the waters of Merom, to fight against I. 3478
11: 6 will I deliver them up all slain before I: 3478
11: 8 LORD delivered them into the hand of I, 3478
11:13 I burned none of them, save Hazor only; 3478
11:14 the children of I took for a prey unto 3478
11:16 the mountain of I, and the valley of 3478
11:19 city that made peace with the children of I, 3478
11:20 that *they* should come against I *in* battle, 3478
11:21 of Judah, and from all the mountains of I: 3478
11:22 left in the land of the children of I: 3478
11:23 Joshua gave it for an inheritance unto I 3478
12: 1 which the children of I smote, and 3478
12: 6 of the LORD and the children of I smite: 3478
12: 7 the children of I smote on *this* side Jordan 3478
12: 7 which Joshua gave unto the tribes of I *for* a 3478
13: 6 I drive out from before the children of I: 3478
13:13 (Nevertheless the children of I expelled not 3478
13:14 the sacrifices of the LORD God of I made 3478
13:22 did the children of I slay with the sword 3478
13:33 the LORD God of I *was* their inheritance, 3478
14: 1 of I inherited in the land of Canaan, 3478
14: 1 the fathers of the tribes of the children of I, 3478
14: 5 so the children of I did, and they divided 3478
14:10 while *the children of* I wandered in 3478
14:14 he wholly followed the LORD God of I. 3478
17:13 when the children of I were waxen strong, 3478
18: 1 the whole congregation of the children of I 3478
18: 2 there remained among the children of I 3478
18: 3 Joshua said unto the children of I, How 3478
18:10 children of I according to their divisions. 3478
19:49 the children of I gave an inheritance to 3478
19:51 the fathers of the tribes of the children of I, 3478
20: 2 Speak to the children of I, saying, 3478
20: 9 the cities appointed for all the children of I, 3478
21: 1 the fathers of the tribes of the children of I; 3478
21: 3 the children of I gave unto the Levites out 3478
21: 8 the children of I gave by lot unto 3478
21:41 possession of the children of I *were* forty 3478
21:43 the LORD gave unto I all the land which 3478
21:45 the LORD had spoken unto the house of I; 3478
22: 9 departed from the children of I out of 3478
22:11 the children of I heard say, Behold, 3478
22:11 at the passage of the children of I. 3478
22:12 when the children of I heard *of it,* 3478
22:12 of I gathered themselves together *at* Shiloh, 3478
22:13 the children of I sent unto the children of 3478
22:14 a prince throughout all the tribes of I; 3478
22:14 of their fathers among the thousands of I. 3478
22:16 ye have committed against the God of I, 3478
22:18 be wroth with the whole congregation of I. 3478
22:20 and wrath fell on all the congregation of I? 3478
22:21 said unto the heads of the thousands of I, 3478
22:22 of gods, he knoweth, and I he shall know; 3478
22:24 have you to do with the LORD God of I? 3478
22:30 heads of the thousands of I which *were* 3478
22:31 now ye have delivered the children of I out 3478
22:32 to the children of I, and brought them word 3478
22:33 the thing pleased the children of I; and 3478
22:33 the children of I blessed God, and did not 3478
23: 1 unto I from all their enemies round about, 3478
23: 2 Joshua called for all I, *and* for their elders, 3478
24: 1 Joshua gathered all the tribes of I to 3478
24: 1 called for the elders of I, and for their 3478
24: 2 Thus saith the LORD God of I, 3478
24: 9 arose and warred against I, and sent and 3478
24:23 your heart unto the LORD God of I. 3478
24:31 I served the LORD all the days of Joshua, 3478
24:31 of the LORD, that he had done for I. 3478
24:32 which the children of I brought up out of 3478
Jdg 1: 1 that the children of I asked the LORD, 3478
1:28 it came to pass, when I was strong, 3478
2: 4 spake these words unto all the children of I, 3478
2: 6 the children of I went every man unto his 3478
2: 7 works of the LORD, that he did for I. 3478
2:10 nor yet the works which he had done for I. 3478
2:11 the children of I did evil in the sight of 3478
2:14 the anger of the LORD was hot against I, 3478
2:20 the anger of the LORD was hot against I; 3478
2:22 That through them I may prove I, 3478
3: 1 which the LORD left, to prove I by them, 3478
3: 1 *even* as many *of I* as had not known all NIH
3: 2 of the children of I might know, 3478
3: 4 they were to prove I by them, to know 3478
3: 5 the children of I dwelt among 3478
3: 7 the children of I did evil in the sight of 3478
3: 8 the anger of the LORD was hot against I, 3478
3: 8 the children of I served 3478
3: 9 when the children of I cried unto 3478
3: 9 raised up a deliverer to the children of I, 3478
3:10 and he judged I, and went out to war: 3478
3:12 the children of I did evil again in the sight 3478
3:12 Eglon the king of Moab against I, 3478
3:13 went and smote I, and possessed the city of 3478
3:14 So the children of I served Eglon the king 3478
3:15 when the children of I cried unto 3478
3:15 by him the children of I sent a present unto 3478
3:27 the children of I went down with him from 3478
3:30 was subdued that day under the hand of I. 3478
3:31 with an ox goad: and he also delivered I. 3478
4: 1 the children of I again did evil in the sight 3478
4: 3 the children of I cried unto the LORD: 3478
4: 3 he mightily oppressed the children of I. 3478
4: 4 wife of Lapidoth, she judged I at that time. 3478
4: 5 the children of I came up to her for 3478
4: 6 Hath not the LORD God of I commanded, 3478
4:23 the king of Canaan before the children of I. 3478
4:24 the hand of the children of I prospered, 3478
5: 2 Praise ye the LORD for the avenging of I, 3478
5: 3 I will sing *praise* to the LORD God of I. 3478
5: 5 Sinai from before the LORD God of I. 3478
5: 7 they ceased in I, until that I Deborah arose, 3478
5: 7 I Deborah arose, that I arose a mother in I. 3478
5: 8 or spear seen among forty thousand in I? 3478
5: 9 My heart *is* toward the governors of I, 3478

Jdg 5:11 *towards the inhabitants* of his villages in I: 3478
6: 1 the children of I did evil in the sight of 3478
6: 2 And the hand of Midian prevailed against I: 3478
6: 2 of the Midianites the children of I made 3478
6: 3 *so* it was, when I had sown, that 3478
6: 4 left no sustenance for I, neither sheep, 3478
6: 6 I was greatly impoverished because of 3478
6: 6 the children of I cried unto the LORD. 3478
6: 7 when the children of I cried unto 3478
6: 8 sent a prophet unto the children of I, 3478
6: 8 unto them, Thus saith the LORD God of I, 3478
6:14 thou shalt save I from the hand of 3478
6:15 O my Lord, wherewith shall I save I? 3478
6:36 If thou wilt save I by mine hand, as thou 3478
6:37 shall I know that thou wilt save I by mine 3478
7: 2 lest I vaunt themselves against me, saying, 3478
7: 8 he sent all *the rest of* I every man unto his 3478
7:14 of Gideon the son of Joash, a man of I: 3478
7:15 returned into the host of I, and said, Arise; 3478
7:23 the men of I gathered themselves together 3478
8:22 the men of I said unto Gideon, Rule thou 3478
8:27 all I went thither a whoring after it: 3478
8:28 Midian subdued before the children of I, 3478
8:33 that the children of I turned again, and 3478
8:34 the children of I remembered not 3478
8:35 the goodness which he had shewed unto I. 3478
9:22 Abimelech had reigned three years over I, 3478
9:55 when the men of I saw that Abimelech was 3478
10: 1 after Abimelech there arose to defend I 3478
10: 2 he judged I twenty and three years, and 3478
10: 3 and judged I twenty and two years. 3478
10: 6 the children of I did evil again in the sight 3478
10: 7 the anger of the LORD was hot against I, 3478
10: 8 they vexed and oppressed the children of I: 3478
10: 8 all the children of I that *were* on the *other* 3478
10: 9 of Ephraim; so that I was sore distressed. 3478
10:10 the children of I cried unto the LORD, 3478
10:11 And the LORD said unto the children of I, 3478
10:15 And the children of I said unto the LORD, 3478
10:16 his soul was grieved for the misery of I. 3478
10:17 the children of I assembled themselves 3478
11: 4 the children of Ammon made war against I. 3478
11: 5 the children of Ammon made war against I, 3478
11:13 Because I took away my land, when they 3478
11:15 I took not away the land of Moab, 3478
11:16 when I came up from Egypt, and 3478
11:17 I sent messengers unto the king of Edom, 3478
11:17 would not consent: and I abode in Kadesh. 3478
11:19 I sent messengers unto Sihon king of 3478
11:19 I said unto him, Let us pass, we pray thee, 3478
11:20 Sihon trusted not I to pass through his 3478
11:20 and pitched in Jahaz, and fought against I. 3478
11:21 the LORD God of I delivered Sihon and 3478
11:21 and all his people into the hand of I, 3478
11:21 so I possessed all the land of the Amorites, 3478
11:23 So now the LORD God of I hath 3478
11:23 the Amorites from before his people I, 3478
11:25 did he ever strive against I, or did he ever 3478
11:26 While I dwelt in Heshbon and her towns, 3478
11:27 be judge *this* day between the children of I 3478
11:33 were subdued before the children of I. 3478
11:39 she knew no man. And it was a custom in I, 3478
11:40 *That* the daughters of I went yearly to 3478
12: 7 Jephthah judged I six years. Then died 3478
12: 8 after him Ibzan of Beth-lehem judged I. 3478
12: 9 for his sons. And he judged I seven years. 3478
12:11 after him Elon, a Zebulonite, judged I; and 3478
12:11 judged Israel; and he judged I ten years. 3478
12:13 the son of Hillel, a Pirathonite, judged I. 3478
12:14 ten ass colts: and he judged I eight years. 3478
13: 1 the children of I did evil again in the sight 3478
13: 5 he shall begin to deliver I out of the hand 3478
14: 4 time the Philistines had dominion over I. 3478
15:20 he judged I in the days of the Philistines 3478
16:31 his father. And he judged I twenty years. 3478
17: 6 In those days *there was* no king in I, *but* 3478
18: 1 In those days *there was* no king in I: and 3478
18: 1 not fallen unto them among the tribes of I. 3478
18:19 be a priest unto a tribe and a family in I? 3478
18:29 of Dan their father, who was born unto I: 3478
19: 1 in those days, when *there was* no king in I, 3478
19:12 of a stranger, that *is* not of the children of I; 3478
19:29 and sent her into all the coasts of I. 3478
19:30 I came up out of the land of Egypt unto this 3478
20: 1 all the children of I went out, and 3478
20: 2 of all the people, *even* of all the tribes of I, 3478
20: 3 the children of I were gone up *to* Mizpeh.) 3478
20: 3 said the children of I, Tell *us,* how was this 3478
20: 6 all the country of the inheritance of I: 3478
20: 6 have committed lewdness and folly in I. 3478
20: 7 Behold, ye *are* all children of I; give here 3478
20:10 of an hundred throughout all the tribes of I, 3478
20:10 to all the folly that they have wrought in I. 3478
20:11 So all the men of I were gathered against 3478
20:12 the tribes of I sent men through all the tribe 3478
20:13 them to death, and put away evil from I. 3478
20:13 the voice of their brethren the children of I: 3478
20:14 to go out to battle against the children of I. 3478
20:17 the men of I, beside Benjamin, 3478
20:18 the children of I arose, and went up *to* 3478
20:19 the children of I rose up in the morning, 3478
20:20 the men of I went out to battle against 3478
20:20 the men of I put *themselves* in array to 3478
20:22 the people the men of I encouraged 3478
20:23 (And the children of I went up and 3478
20:24 the children of I came near against 3478
20:25 children of I again eighteen thousand men; 3478
20:26 all the children of I, and all the people, 3478
20:27 the children of I inquired of the LORD, 3478
20:29 And I set liers in wait round about Gibeah. 3478
20:30 the children of I went up against 3478
20:31 to Gibeah in the field, about thirty men of I. 3478
20:32 the children of I said, Let us flee, and 3478
20:33 all the men of I rose up out of their place, 3478
20:33 the liers in wait of I came forth out of their 3478
20:34 ten thousand chosen men out of all I, 3478
20:35 the LORD smote Benjamin before I: and 3478
20:35 the children of I destroyed of 3478
20:36 for the men of I gave place to 3478
20:38 an appointed sign between the men of I 3478
20:39 when the men of I retired in the battle, 3478
20:39 kill of the men of I about thirty persons: 3478
20:41 when the men of I turned *again,* the men of 3478
20:42 men of I unto the way of the wilderness; 3478
20:48 the men of I turned again upon the children 3478
21: 1 Now the men of I had sworn in Mizpeh, 3478
21: 3 said, O LORD God of I, why is this come 3478
21: 3 God of Israel, why is this come to pass in I, 3478
21: 3 should be to day one tribe lacking in I? 3478
21: 5 the children of I said, Who *is there* among 3478
21: 5 Who *is there* among all the tribes of I that 3478
21: 6 the children of I repented them for 3478
21: 6 There is one tribe cut off from I *this* day. 3478
21: 8 What one *is there* of the tribes of I that 3478
21:15 had made a breach in the tribes of I. 3478
21:17 that a tribe be not destroyed out of I. 3478
21:18 for the children of I have sworn, saying, 3478
21:24 the children of I departed thence at that 3478
21:25 In those days *there was* no king in I: 3478

Ru 2:12 be given thee of the LORD God of I, 3478
4: 7 in former time in I concerning redeeming 3478
4: 7 and this *was* a testimony in I. 3478
4:11 which two did build the house of I: 3478
4:14 that his name may be famous in I. 3478

1Sa 1:17 the God of I grant *thee* thy petition that 3478
2:22 and heard all that his sons did unto all I; 3478
2:28 did I choose him out of all the tribes of I to 3478
2:28 offerings made by fire of the children of I? 3478
2:29 chiefest of all the offerings of I my people? 3478
2:30 Wherefore the LORD God of I saith, 3478
2:32 in all *the wealth* which *God* shall give I: 3478
3:11 to Samuel, Behold, I will do a thing in I, 3478
3:20 all I from Dan even to Beer-sheba knew 3478
4: 1 the word of Samuel came to all I. 3478
4: 1 Now I went out against the Philistines to 3478
4: 2 put *themselves* in array against I: 3478
4: 2 I was smitten before the Philistines: 3478
4: 3 come into the camp, the elders of I said, 3478
4: 5 all I shouted *with* a great shout, so that 3478
4:10 I was smitten, and they fled every man into 3478
4:10 for there fell of I thirty thousand footmen. 3478
4:17 I is fled before the Philistines, and 3478
4:18 heavy. And he had judged I forty years. 3478
4:21 The glory is departed from I: 3478
4:22 she said, The glory is departed from I: 3478
5: 7 The ark of the God of I shall not abide with 3478
5: 8 shall we do with the ark of the God of I? 3478
5: 8 Let the ark of the God of I be carried about 3478

1Sa 5: 8 they carried the ark of the God of I about 3478
5:10 brought about the ark of the God of I to us, 3478
5:11 Send away the ark of the God of I, and 3478
6: 3 If ye send away the ark of the God of I, 3478
6: 5 and ye shall give glory unto the God of I: 3478
7: 2 all the house of I lamented after 3478
7: 3 Samuel spake unto all the house of I, 3478
7: 4 the children of I did put away Baalim and 3478
7: 5 Gather all I to Mizpeh, and I will pray for 3478
7: 6 Samuel judged the children of I in Mizpeh. 3478
7: 7 of I were gathered together to Mizpeh, 3478
7: 7 lords of the Philistines went up against I. 3478
7: 7 when the children of I heard *it,* they were 3478
7: 8 the children of I said to Samuel, Cease not 3478
7: 9 Samuel cried unto the LORD for I; and 3478
7:10 the Philistines drew near to battle against I: 3478
7:10 and they were smitten before I. 3478
7:11 the men of I went out of Mizpeh, and 3478
7:13 and they came no more into the coast of I: 3478
7:14 had taken from I were restored to Israel, 3478
7:14 had taken from Israel were restored to I, 3478
7:14 the coasts thereof did I deliver out of 3478
7:14 there was peace between I and 3478
7:15 Samuel judged I all the days of his life. 3478
7:16 and judged I in all those places. 3478
7:17 there he judged I; and there he built an altar 3478
8: 1 that he made his sons judges over I. 3478
8: 4 all the elders of I gathered themselves 3478
8:22 Samuel said unto the men of I, Go ye every 3478
9: 2 *there was* not among the children of I a 3478
9: 9 (Beforetime in I, when a man went to 3478
9:16 anoint him to be captain over my people I, 3478
9:20 on whom *is* all the desire of I? *Is it* not on 3478
9:21 of the smallest of the tribes of I? 3478
10:18 said unto the children of I, Thus saith 3478
10:18 Thus saith the LORD God of I, I brought 3478
10:18 I brought up I out of Egypt, and 3478
10:20 when Samuel had caused all the tribes of I 3478
11: 2 and lay it *for* a reproach upon all I. 3478
11: 3 send messengers unto all the coasts of I: 3478
11: 7 sent *them* throughout all the coasts of I by 3478
11: 8 the children of I were three hundred 3478
11:13 the LORD hath wrought salvation in I. 3478
11:15 and all the men of I rejoiced greatly. 3478
12: 1 Samuel said unto all I, Behold, I have 3478
13: 1 and when he had reigned two years over I, 3478
13: 2 Saul chose him three thousand *men* of I; 3478
13: 4 all I heard say *that* Saul had smitten a 3478
13: 4 *that* I also was had in abomination with 3478
13: 5 themselves together to fight with I, 3478
13: 6 When the men of I saw that they were in a 3478
13:13 established thy kingdom upon I for ever. 3478
13:19 no smith found throughout all the land of I: 3478
14:12 hath delivered them into the hand of I. 3478
14:18 God was at that time with the children of I. 3478
14:22 Likewise all the men of I which had hid 3478
14:23 So the LORD saved I that day: and 3478
14:24 the men of I were distressed that day: 3478
14:37 wilt thou deliver them into the hand of I? 3478
14:39 For, *as* the LORD liveth, which saveth I, 3478
14:40 said he unto all I, Be ye on one side, and 3478
14:41 Saul said unto the LORD God of I, 3478
14:45 who hath wrought this great salvation in I? 3478
14:47 So Saul took the kingdom over I, and 3478
14:48 delivered I out of the hands of them that 3478
15: 1 thee to be king over his people, over I: 3478
15: 2 I remember *that* which Amalek did to I, 3478
15: 6 ye shewed kindness to all the children of I, 3478
15:17 thou not *made* the head of the tribes of I, 3478
15:17 and the LORD anointed thee king over I? 3478
15:26 hath rejected thee from being king over I. 3478
15:28 The LORD hath rent the kingdom of I 3478
15:29 also the Strength of I will not lie nor 3478
15:30 and before I, and turn again with me, 3478
15:35 repented that he had made Saul king over I. 3478
16: 1 I have rejected him from reigning over I? 3478
17: 2 and the men of I were gathered together, 3478
17: 3 I stood on a mountain on the other side: 3478
17: 8 he stood and cried unto the armies of I, 3478
17:10 I defy the armies of I this day; 3478
17:11 all I heard those words of the Philistine, 3478
17:19 Now Saul, and they, and all the men of I, 3478
17:21 For I and the Philistines had put *the battle* 3478
17:24 all the men of I, when they saw the man, 3478
17:25 the men of I said, Have ye seen this man 3478
17:25 surely to defy I is he come up: and it shall 3478
17:25 and make his father's house free in I. 3478
17:26 and taketh away the reproach from I? 3478
17:45 the God of the armies of I, whom thou hast 3478
17:46 the earth may know that there is a God in I. 3478
17:52 the men of I and of Judah arose, and 3478
17:53 the children of I returned from chasing 3478
18: 6 that the women came out of all cities of I, 3478
18:16 all I and Judah loved David, because 3478
18:18 what *is* my life, *or* my father's family in I, 3478
19: 5 LORD wrought a great salvation for all I: 3478
20:12 said unto David, O LORD God of I, 3478
23:10 said David, O LORD God of I, 3478
23:11 O LORD God of I, I beseech thee, tell thy 3478
23:17 thou shalt be king over I, and I shall be 3478
24: 2 three thousand chosen men out of all I, 3478
24:14 After whom is the king of I come out? 3478
24:20 *that* the kingdom of I shall be established in 3478
25:30 and shall have appointed thee ruler over I; 3478
25:32 Blessed *be* the LORD God of I, 3478
25:34 very deed, *as* the LORD God of I liveth, 3478
26: 2 having three thousand chosen men of I with 3478
26:15 who *is* like to thee in I? wherefore then 3478
26:20 for the king of I is come out to seek a flea, 3478
27: 1 to seek me any more in any coast of I: 3478
27:12 He hath made his people I utterly to abhor 3478
28: 1 armies together for warfare, to fight with I. 3478
28: 3 all I had lamented him, and buried him in 3478
28: 4 Saul gathered all I together, and 3478
28:19 Moreover the LORD will also deliver I 3478
28:19 the LORD also shall deliver the host of I 3478
29: 3 this David, the servant of Saul the king of I, 3478
30:25 and an ordinance for I unto this day. 3478
31: 1 Now the Philistines fought against I: and 3478
31: 1 the men of I fled from before 3478
31: 7 when the men of I that *were* on the *other* 3478
31: 7 saw that the men of I fled, and that Saul 3478
2Sa 1: 3 Out of the camp of I am I escaped. 3478
1:12 of the LORD, and for the house of I; 3478
1:19 The beauty of I *is* slain upon thy high 3478
1:24 Ye daughters of I, weep over Saul, 3478
2: 9 and over Benjamin, and over all I. 3478
2:10 years old when he *began* to reign over I, 3478
2:17 Abner was beaten, and the men of I, before 3478
2:28 stood still, and pursued after I no more, 3478
3:10 and to set up the throne of David over I and 3478
3:12 *be* with thee, to bring about all I unto thee. 3478
3:17 had communication with the elders of I, 3478
3:18 people I out of the hand of the Philistines, 3478
3:19 David in Hebron all that seemed good to I, 3478
3:21 and will gather all I unto my lord the king, 3478
3:37 all I understood that day that it was not of 3478
3:38 and a great *man* fallen this day in I? 3478
5: 1 came all the tribes of I to David unto 3478
5: 2 wast he that leddest out and broughtest in I: 3478
5: 2 Thou shalt feed my people I, and thou shalt 3478
5: 2 and thou shalt be a captain over I. 3478
5: 3 So all the elders of I came to the king to 3478
5: 3 and they anointed David king over I. 3478
5: 5 and three years over all I and Judah. 3478
5:12 LORD had established him king over I, 3478
5:17 that they had anointed David king over I, 3478
6: 1 gathered together all the chosen *men* of I, 3478
6: 5 all the house of I played before the LORD 3478
6:15 all the house of I brought up the ark of 3478
6:19 *even* among the whole multitude of I, 3478
6:20 said, How glorious was the king of I to day, 3478
6:21 ruler over the people of the LORD, over I: 3478
7: 6 I brought up the children of I out of Egypt, 3478
7: 7 I spake I a word with any of the tribes of 3478
7: 7 spake I a word with any of the tribes of I, 3478
7: 7 whom I commanded to feed my people I, 3478
7: 8 to be ruler over my people, over I: 3478
7:10 I will appoint a place for my people I, 3478
7:11 commanded judges *to be* over my people I, 3478
7:23 *even* like I, whom God went to redeem for 3478
7:24 people I to be a people unto thee for ever; 3478
7:26 The LORD of hosts *is* the God over I: 3478
7:27 For thou, O LORD of hosts, God of I, 3478
8:15 David reigned over all I; and David 3478
10: 9 he chose of all the choice *men* of I, and 3478
10:15 saw that they were smitten before I, 3478
10:17 he gathered all I together, and passed over 3478

2Sa 10:18 the Syrians fled before I; and David slew 3478
10:19 saw that they were smitten before I, 3478
10:19 they made peace with I, and served them. 3478
11: 1 and his servants with him, and all I; 3478
11:11 The ark, and I, and Judah, abide in tents; 3478
12: 7 Thus saith the LORD God of I, I anointed 3478
12: 7 I anointed thee king over I, and I delivered 3478
12: 8 and gave thee the house of I and of Judah; 3478
12:12 I will do this thing before all I, and 3478
13:12 for no such thing ought to be done in I: 3478
13:13 thou shalt be as one of the fools in I. 3478
14:25 in all I there was none to be so 3478
15: 2 Thy servant *is* of one of the tribes of I. 3478
15: 6 on this manner did Absalom to all I that 3478
15: 6 so Absalom stole the hearts of the men of I. 3478
15:10 sent spies throughout all the tribes of I, 3478
15:13 The hearts of the men of I are after 3478
16: 3 To day shall the house of I restore me 3478
16:15 and all the people the men of I, 3478
16:18 this people, and all the men of I, choose, 3478
16:21 all I shall hear that thou art abhorred of thy 3478
16:22 his father's concubines in the sight of all I. 3478
17: 4 Absalom well, and all the elders of I. 3478
17:10 for all I knoweth that thy father *is* a mighty 3478
17:11 Therefore I counsel *that* all I be generally 3478
17:13 shall all I bring ropes to that city, and 3478
17:14 Absalom and all the men of I said, 3478
17:15 counsel Absalom and the elders of I; 3478
17:24 he and all the men of I with him. 3478
17:26 So I and Absalom pitched *in* the land of 3478
18: 6 the people went out *into* the field against I: 3478
18: 7 Where the people of I were slain before 3478
18:16 the people returned from pursuing after I: 3478
18:17 and all I fled every one to his tent. 3478
19: 8 for I had fled every man to his tent. 3478
19: 9 were at strife throughout all the tribes of I, 3478
19:11 seeing the speech of all I is come to 3478
19:22 there any man be put to death *this* day in I? 3478
19:22 not I know that I *am this* day king over I? 3478
19:40 the king, and also half the people of I. 3478
19:41 all the men of I came to the king, and 3478
19:42 all the men of Judah answered the men of I, 3478
19:43 the men of I answered the men of Judah, 3478
19:43 were fiercer than the words of the men of I. 3478
20: 1 son of Jesse: every man to his tents, O I. 3478
20: 2 So every man of I went up from after 3478
20:14 he went through all the tribes of I unto 3478
20:19 *of them that are* peaceable *and* faithful in I: 3478
20:19 seekest to destroy a city and a mother in I: 3478
20:23 Now Joab *was* over all the host of I: and 3478
21: 2 the Gibeonites *were* not of the children of I, 3478
21: 2 and the children of I had sworn unto them: 3478
21: 2 to slay them in his zeal to the children of I 3478
21: 4 neither for us *shalt thou* kill any man in I. 3478
21: 5 from remaining in any of the coasts of I, 3478
21:15 the Philistines had yet war again with I; 3478
21:17 to battle, that thou quench not the light of I. 3478
21:21 when he defied I, Jonathan the son of 3478
23: 1 of Jacob, and the sweet psalmist of I, said, 3478
23: 3 The God of I said, the Rock of Israel spake 3478
23: 3 of Israel said, the Rock of I spake to me, 3478
23: 9 to battle, and the men of I were gone away: 3478
24: 1 anger of the LORD was kindled against I, 3478
24: 1 them to say, Go, number I and Judah. 3478
24: 2 Go now through all the tribes of I, 3478
24: 4 of the king, to number the people *of* I. 3478
24: 9 there were in I eight hundred thousand 3478
24:15 So the LORD sent a pestilence upon I 3478
24:25 the land, and the plague was stayed from I. 3478
1Ki 1: 3 a fair damsel throughout all the coasts of I, 3478
1:20 lord O king, the eyes of all I *are* upon thee, 3478
1:30 I sware unto thee by the LORD God of I, 3478
1:34 the prophet anoint him there king over I: 3478
1:35 I have appointed him to be ruler over I and 3478
1:48 the king, Blessed *be* the LORD God of I, 3478
2: 4 fail thee (said he) a man on the throne of I. 3478
2: 5 he did to the two captains of the hosts of I, 3478
2:11 the days that David reigned over I *were* 3478
2:15 *that* all I set their faces on me, that *I* should 3478
2:32 captain of the host of I, and Amasa the son 3478
3:28 all I heard of the judgment which the king 3478
4: 1 So king Solomon was king over all I. 3478
4: 7 Solomon had twelve officers over all I, 3478
4:20 Judah and I *were* many, as the sand which 3478
4:25 Judah and I dwelt safely, every man under 3478
5:13 king Solomon raised a levy out of all I; 3478
6: 1 eightieth year after the children of I were 3478
6: 1 the fourth year of Solomon's reign over I, 3478
6:13 I will dwell among the children of I, and 3478
6:13 of Israel, and will not forsake my people I. 3478
8: 1 Solomon assembled the elders of I, 3478
8: 1 the chief of the fathers of the children of I, 3478
8: 2 all the men of I assembled themselves unto 3478
8: 3 all the elders of I came, and the priests took 3478
8: 5 and all the congregation of I, 3478
8: 9 made *a covenant* with the children of I, 3478
8:14 and blessed all the congregation of I: 3478
8:14 (and all the congregation of I stood;) 3478
8:15 he said, Blessed *be* the LORD God of I, 3478
8:16 I brought forth my people I out of Egypt, 3478
8:16 I chose no city out of all the tribes of I to 3478
8:16 but I chose David to be over my people I. 3478
8:17 for the name of the LORD God of I. 3478
8:20 sit on the throne of I, as the LORD 3478
8:20 for the name of the LORD God of I. 3478
8:22 in the presence of all the congregation of I, 3478
8:23 he said, LORD God of I, *there is* no God 3478
8:25 Therefore now, LORD God of I, 3478
8:25 a man in my sight to sit on the throne of I; 3478
8:26 now, O God of I, let thy word, I pray thee, 3478
8:30 of thy people I, when they shall pray 3478
8:33 When thy people I be smitten down before 3478
8:34 forgive the sin of thy people I, and 3478
8:36 the sin of thy servants, and of thy people I, 3478
8:38 be *made* by any man, *or* by all thy people I, 3478
8:41 that *is* not of thy people I, but cometh out 3478
8:43 thy name, to fear thee, as *do* thy people I; 3478
8:52 unto the supplication of thy people I, 3478
8:55 blessed all the congregation of I *with* a 3478
8:56 that hath given rest unto his people I, 3478
8:59 the cause of his people I at all times, as 3478
8:62 the king, and all I with him, 3478
8:63 all the children of I dedicated the house of 3478
8:65 and all I with him, a great congregation, 3478
8:66 for David his servant, and for I his people. 3478
9: 5 the throne of thy kingdom upon I for ever, 3478
9: 5 not fail thee a man upon the throne of I. 3478
9: 7 will I cut off I out of the land which I have 3478
9: 7 I shall be a proverb and a byword among 3478
9:20 which *were* not of the children of I, 3478
9:21 whom the children of I also were not able 3478
9:22 of the children of I did Solomon make no 3478
10: 9 in thee, to set thee on the throne of I: 3478
10: 9 because the LORD loved I for ever, 3478
11: 2 the LORD said unto the children of I, 3478
11: 9 was turned from the LORD God of I, 3478
11:16 six months did Joab remain there with all I, 3478
11:25 he was an adversary to I all the days of 3478
11:25 mischief that Hadad *did:* and he abhorred I, 3478
11:31 saith the LORD, the God of I, Behold, 3478
11:32 I have chosen out of all the tribes of I:) 3478
11:37 thy soul desireth, and shalt be king over I. 3478
11:38 I built for David, and will give I unto thee. 3478
11:42 in Jerusalem over all I *was* forty years. 3478
12: 1 for all I were come *to* Shechem to make 3478
12: 3 and all the congregation of I came, 3478
12:16 So when all I saw that the king hearkened 3478
12:16 to your tents, O I: now see to thine own 3478
12:16 David. So I departed unto their tents. 3478
12:17 *as for* the children of I which dwelt in 3478
12:18 all I stoned him with stones, that he died. 3478
12:19 So I rebelled against the house of David 3478
12:20 when all I heard that Jeroboam was come 3478
12:20 and made him king over all I: 3478
12:21 to fight against the house of I, 3478
12:24 against your brethren the children of I: 3478
12:28 behold thy gods, O I, which brought thee 3478
12:33 and ordained a feast unto the children of I: 3478
14: 7 Thus saith the LORD God of I, 3478
14: 7 and made thee prince over my people I, 3478
14:10 *and him that is* shut up and left in I, and 3478
14:13 all I shall mourn for him, and bury him: 3478
14:13 LORD God of I in the house of Jeroboam. 3478
14:14 LORD shall raise him up a king over I, 3478
14:15 For the LORD shall smite I, as a reed is 3478
14:15 he shall root up I out of this good land, 3478
14:16 he shall give I up because of the sins of 3478
14:16 who did sin, and who made I to sin. 3478

1Ki	14:18	all I mourned for him, according to	3478
	14:19	the book of the chronicles of the kings of I.	3478
	14:21	LORD did choose out of all the tribes of I,	3478
	14:24	LORD cast out before the children of I.	3478
	15: 9	in the twentieth year of Jeroboam king of I	3478
	15:16	and Baasha king of I all their days.	3478
	15:17	Baasha king of I went up against Judah,	3478
	15:19	*and* break thy league with Baasha king of I,	3478
	15:20	hosts which he had against the cities of I,	3478
	15:25	I in the second year of Asa king of Judah,	3478
	15:25	of Judah, and reigned over I two years.	3478
	15:26	and in his sin wherewith he made I to sin.	3478
	15:27	for Nadab and all I laid siege to Gibbethon.	3478
	15:30	which he sinned, and which he made I sin,	3478
	15:30	he provoked the LORD God of I to anger.	3478
	15:31	the book of the chronicles of the kings of I?	3478
	15:32	and Baasha king of I all their days.	3478
	15:33	son of Ahijah to reign over all I in Tirzah,	3478
	15:34	and in his sin wherewith he made I to sin.	3478
	16: 2	and made thee prince over my people I;	3478
	16: 2	hast made my people I to sin, to provoke	3478
	16: 5	the book of the chronicles of the kings of I?	3478
	16: 8	the son of Baasha to reign over I in Tirzah,	3478
	16:13	and *by* which they made I to sin,	3478
	16:13	in provoking the LORD God of I to anger	3478
	16:14	the book of the chronicles of the kings of I?	3478
	16:16	wherefore all I made Omri, the captain of	3478
	16:16	the host, king over I that day in the camp.	3478
	16:17	all I with him, and they besieged Tirzah.	3478
	16:19	and in his sin which he did, to make I sin.	3478
	16:20	the book of the chronicles of the kings of I?	3478
	16:21	were the people of I divided into two parts:	3478
	16:23	king of Judah *began* Omri to reign over I,	3478
	16:26	and in his sin wherewith he made I to sin,	3478
	16:26	to provoke the LORD God of I to anger	3478
	16:27	the book of the chronicles of the kings of I?	3478
	16:29	Ahab the son of Omri to reign over I:	3478
	16:29	Ahab the son of Omri reigned over I in	3478
	16:33	I to anger than all the kings of Israel that	3478
	16:33	than all the kings of I that were before him.	3478
	17: 1	unto Ahab, *As* the LORD God of I liveth,	3478
	17:14	For thus saith the LORD God of I,	3478
	18:17	said unto him, *Art* thou he that troubleth I?	3478
	18:18	he answered, I have not troubled I; but	3478
	18:19	*and* gather to me all I unto mount Carmel,	3478
	18:20	So Ahab sent unto all the children of I, and	3478
	18:31	LORD came, saying, I shall be thy name:	3478
	18:36	LORD God of Abraham, Isaac, and of I,	3478
	18:36	it be known *this* day that thou *art* God in I,	3478
	19:10	for the children of I have forsaken thy	3478
	19:14	the children of I have forsaken thy	3478
	19:16	Nimshi shalt thou anoint to be king over I:	3478
	19:18	Yet I have left *me* seven thousand in I,	3478
	20: 2	he sent messengers to Ahab king of I into	3478
	20: 4	the king of I answered and said, My lord,	3478
	20: 7	the king of I called all the elders of	3478
	20:11	the king of I answered and said, Tell *him,*	3478
	20:13	there came a prophet unto Ahab king of I,	3478
	20:15	*even* all the children of I, *being* seven	3478
	20:20	the Syrians fled; and I pursued them: and	3478
	20:21	the king of I went out, and smote the horses	3478
	20:22	the prophet came to the king of I, and	3478
	20:26	and went up to Aphek, to fight against I.	3478
	20:27	the children of I were numbered, and	3478
	20:27	the children of I pitched before them like	3478
	20:28	spake unto the king of I, and said,	3478
	20:29	the children of I slew *of* the Syrians an	3478
	20:31	kings of the house of I *are* merciful kings:	3478
	20:31	upon our heads, and go out to the king of I:	3478
	20:32	and came to the king of I, and said,	3478
	20:40	the king of I said unto him, So *shall* thy	3478
	20:41	the king of I discerned him that he *was* of	3478
	20:43	the king of I went to his house heavy and	3478
	21: 7	Dost thou now govern the kingdom of I?	3478
	21:18	Arise, go down to meet Ahab king of I,	3478
	21:21	and *him that is* shut up and left in I,	3478
	21:22	provoked *me* to anger, and made I to sin.	3478
	21:26	LORD cast out before the children of I).	3478
	22: 1	years without war between Syria and I.	3478
	22: 2	king of Judah came down to the king of I.	3478
	22: 3	the king of I said unto his servants, Know	3478
	22: 4	Jehoshaphat said to the king of I, I *am* as	3478
	22: 5	Jehoshaphat said unto the king of I,	3478
	22: 6	the king of I gathered the prophets	3478
	22: 8	the king of I said unto Jehoshaphat,	3478
	22: 9	the king of I called an officer, and said,	3478
	22:10	the king of I and Jehoshaphat the king of	3478
	22:17	he said, I saw all I scattered upon the hills,	3478
	22:18	the king of I said unto Jehoshaphat, Did I	3478
	22:26	the king of I said, Take Micaiah, and	3478
	22:29	So the king of I and Jehoshaphat the king	3478
	22:30	the king of I said unto Jehoshaphat, I will	3478
	22:30	the king of I disguised himself, and	3478
	22:31	nor great, save only with the king of I.	3478
	22:32	that they said, Surely it *is* the king of I.	3478
	22:33	perceived that it *was* not the king of I,	3478
	22:34	smote the king of I between the joints of	3478
	22:39	the book of the chronicles of the kings of I?	3478
	22:41	Judah in the fourth year of Ahab king of I.	3478
	22:44	Jehoshaphat made peace with the king of I.	3478
	22:51	I in Samaria the seventeenth year of	3478
	22:51	of Judah, and reigned two years over I.	3478
	22:52	the son of Nebat, who made I to sin:	3478
	22:53	provoked to anger the LORD God of I,	3478
2Ki	1: 1	Moab rebelled against I after the death of	3478
	1: 3	*Is it* not because *there is* not a God in I,	3478
	1: 6	*Is it* not because *there is* not a God in I,	3478
	1:16	*there is* no God in I to inquire of his word?	3478
	1:18	the book of the chronicles of the kings of I?	3478
	2:12	the chariot of I, and the horsemen thereof.	3478
	3: 1	I in Samaria the eighteenth year of	3478
	3: 3	the son of Nebat, which made I to sin;	3478
	3: 4	rendered unto the king of I an hundred	3478
	3: 5	king of Moab rebelled against the king of I.	3478
	3: 6	Samaria the same time, and numbered all I.	3478
	3: 9	So the king of I went, and the king of	3478
	3:10	the king of I said, Alas, that the LORD	3478
	3:12	So the king of I and Jehoshaphat and	3478
	3:13	Elisha said unto the king of I, What have I	3478
	3:13	the king of I said unto him, Nay: for	3478
	3:24	when they came to the camp of I,	3478
	3:27	there was great indignation against I: and	3478
	5: 2	captive out of the land of I a little maid;	3478
	5: 4	thus said the maid that *is* of the land of I.	3478
	5: 5	and I will send a letter unto the king of I.	3478
	5: 6	he brought the letter to the king of I,	3478
	5: 7	when the king of I had read the letter,	3478
	5: 8	heard that the king of I had rent his clothes,	3478
	5: 8	he shall know that there is a prophet in I.	3478
	5:12	better than all the waters of I?	3478
	5:15	*there is* no God in all the earth, but in I:	3478
	6: 8	the king of Syria warred against I, and	3478
	6: 9	And the man of God sent unto the king of I,	3478
	6:10	the king of I sent to the place which	3478
	6:11	shew me which of us *is* for the king of I?	3478
	6:12	Elisha, the prophet that *is* in I, telleth	3478
	6:12	telleth the king of I the words that thou	3478
	6:21	the king of I said unto Elisha, when he saw	3478
	6:23	of Syria came no more into the land of I.	3478
	6:26	as the king of I was passing by upon	3478
	7: 6	the king of I hath hired against us the kings	3478
	7:13	they *are* as all the multitude of I that are	3478
	8:12	evil that thou wilt do unto the children of I:	3478
	8:16	year of Joram the son of Ahab king of I,	3478
	8:18	he walked in the way of the kings of I,	3478
	8:25	I did Ahaziah the son of Jehoram king of	3478
	8:26	the daughter of Omri king of I.	3478
	9: 3	I have anointed thee king over I.	3478
	9: 6	unto him, Thus saith the LORD God of I,	3478
	9: 6	over the people of the LORD, *even* over I.	3478
	9: 8	and *him that is* shut up and left in I:	3478
	9:12	I have anointed thee king over I.	3478
	9:14	he and all I, because of Hazael king of	3478
	9:21	Joram king of I and Ahaziah king of Judah	3478
	10:21	Jehu sent through all I: and all	3478
	10:28	Thus Jehu destroyed Baal out of I.	3478
	10:29	who made I to sin, Jehu departed not from	3478
	10:30	*generation* shall sit on the throne of I.	3478
	10:31	of the LORD God of I with all his heart:	3478
	10:31	the sins of Jeroboam, which made I to sin.	3478
	10:32	In those days the LORD began to cut I	3478
	10:32	Hazael smote them in all the coasts of I;	3478
	10:34	the book of the chronicles of the kings of I?	3478
	10:36	the time that Jehu reigned over I in Samaria	3478
	13: 1	of Jehu *began* to reign over I in Samaria,	3478
	13: 2	the son of Nebat, which made I to sin;	3478
	13: 3	anger of the LORD was kindled against I,	3478
	13: 4	for he saw the oppression of I, because	3478

2Ki 13: 5 (And the LORD gave I a saviour, so 3478
13: 5 the children of I dwelt in their tents, 3478
13: 6 who made I sin, *but* walked therein: 3478
13: 8 the book of the chronicles of the kings of I? 3478
13:10 son of Jehoahaz to reign over I in Samaria, 3478
13:11 the son of Nebat, who made I sin: 3478
13:12 the book of the chronicles of the kings of I? 3478
13:13 was buried in Samaria with the kings of I. 3478
13:14 Joash the king of I came down unto him, 3478
13:14 the chariot of I, and the horsemen thereof. 3478
13:16 he said to the king of I, Put thine hand upon 3478
13:18 took *them*. And he said unto the king of I, 3478
13:22 Hazael king of Syria oppressed I all 3478
13:25 beat him, and recovered the cities of I. 3478
14: 1 I reigned Amaziah the son of Joash king of 3478
14: 8 son of Jehu, king of I, saying, Come, 3478
14: 9 Jehoash the king of I sent to Amaziah king 3478
14:11 Therefore Jehoash king of I went up; and 3478
14:12 Judah was put to the worse before I; and 3478
14:13 Jehoash king of I took Amaziah king of 3478
14:15 the book of the chronicles of the kings of I? 3478
14:16 was buried in Samaria with the kings of I; 3478
14:17 son of Jehoahaz king of I fifteen years. 3478
14:23 Joash king of I *began* to reign in Samaria, 3478
14:24 the son of Nebat, who made I to sin. 3478
14:25 He restored the coast of I from the entering 3478
14:25 to the word of the LORD God of I, 3478
14:26 For the LORD saw the affliction of I, 3478
14:26 shut up, nor any left, nor any helper for I. 3478
14:27 blot out the name of I from under heaven: 3478
14:28 *which belonged* to Judah, for I, 3478
14:28 the book of the chronicles of the kings of I? 3478
14:29 with his fathers, *even* with the kings of I; 3478
15: 1 seventh year of Jeroboam king of I *began* 3478
15: 8 reign over I in Samaria six months. 3478
15: 9 the son of Nebat, who made I to sin. 3478
15:11 the book of the chronicles of the kings of I. 3478
15:12 Thy sons shall sit on the throne of I unto 3478
15:15 the book of the chronicles of the kings of I. 3478
15:17 Menahem the son of Gadi to reign over I, 3478
15:18 the son of Nebat, who made I to sin. 3478
15:20 Menahem exacted the money of I, *even* of 3478
15:21 the book of the chronicles of the kings of I? 3478
15:23 Menahem *began* to reign over I in Samaria, 3478
15:24 the son of Nebat, who made I to sin. 3478
15:26 the book of the chronicles of the kings of I. 3478
15:27 Remaliah *began* to reign over I in Samaria, 3478
15:28 the son of Nebat, who made I to sin. 3478
15:29 In the days of Pekah king of I came 3478
15:31 the book of the chronicles of the kings of I. 3478
15:32 I *began* Jotham the son of Uzziah king of 3478
16: 3 he walked in the way of the kings of I, yea, 3478
16: 3 cast out from before the children of I. 3478
16: 5 Pekah son of Remaliah king of I came up 3478
16: 7 out of the hand of the king of I, which rise 3478
17: 1 Elah to reign in Samaria over I nine years. 3478
17: 2 not as the kings of I that were before him. 3478
17: 6 carried I away into Assyria, and 3478
17: 7 that the children of I had sinned against 3478
17: 8 cast out from before the children of I, 3478
17: 8 and of the kings of I, which they had made. 3478
17: 9 the children of I did secretly *those* things 3478
17:13 Yet the LORD testified against I, and 3478
17:18 the LORD was very angry with I, 3478
17:19 walked in the statutes of I which they 3478
17:20 the LORD rejected all the seed of I, and 3478
17:21 For he rent I from the house of David; and 3478
17:21 Jeroboam drave I from following 3478
17:22 For the children of I walked in all the sins 3478
17:23 Until the LORD removed I out of his 3478
17:23 So was I carried away out of their own land 3478
17:24 of Samaria instead of the children of I: 3478
17:34 the children of Jacob, whom he named I; 3478
18: 1 third year of Hoshea son of Elah king of I, 3478
18: 4 for unto those days the children of I did 3478
18: 5 He trusted in the LORD God of I; so 3478
18: 9 year of Hoshea son of Elah king of I, 3478
18:10 that *is* the ninth year of Hoshea king of I, 3478
18:11 the king of Assyria did carry away I unto 3478
19:15 said, O LORD God of I, which dwellest 3478
19:20 Thus saith the LORD God of I, 3478
19:22 on high? *even* against the Holy One of I. 3478
21: 2 LORD cast out before the children of I. 3478
21: 3 and made a grove, as did Ahab king of I; 3478
21: 7 which I have chosen out of all tribes of I, 3478
21: 8 Neither will I make the feet of I move any 3478
21: 9 LORD destroyed before the children of I. 3478
21:12 Therefore thus saith the LORD God of I, 3478
22:15 unto them, Thus saith the LORD God of I, 3478
22:18 to him, Thus saith the LORD God of I, 3478
23:13 which Solomon the king of I had builded 3478
23:15 who made I to sin, had made, both that 3478
23:19 which the kings of I had made to provoke 3478
23:22 from the days of the judges that judged I, 3478
23:22 nor *in* all the days of the kings of I, nor of 3478
23:27 as I have removed I, and will cast off this 3478
24:13 of I had made in the temple of the LORD, 3478
1Ch 1:34 begat Isaac. The sons of Isaac; Esau and I. 3478
1:43 *any* king reigned over the children of I; 3478
2: 1 These *are* the sons of I; Reuben, Simeon, 3478
2: 7 Achar, the troubler of I, who transgressed 3478
4:10 Jabez called on the God of I, saying, 3478
5: 1 Now the sons of Reuben the firstborn of I, 3478
5: 1 given unto the sons of Joseph the son of I: 3478
5: 3 *I say,* of Reuben the firstborn of I *were,* 3478
5:17 and in the days of Jeroboam king of I. 3478
5:26 the God of I stirred up the spirit of Pul king 3478
6:38 son of Kohath, the son of Levi, the son of I. 3478
6:49 most holy, and to make an atonement for I, 3478
6:64 the children of I gave to the Levites *these* 3478
7:29 dwelt the children of Joseph the son of I. 3478
9: 1 So all I were reckoned by genealogies; and 3478
9: 1 *were* written in the book of the kings of I 3478
10: 1 Now the Philistines fought against I; and 3478
10: 1 the men of I fled from before 3478
10: 7 when all the men of I that *were* in 3478
11: 1 all I gathered themselves to David unto 3478
11: 2 *wast* he that leddest out and broughtest in I: 3478
11: 2 Thou shalt feed my people I, and thou shalt 3478
11: 2 and thou shalt be ruler over my people I. 3478
11: 3 Therefore came all the elders of I to 3478
11: 3 they anointed David king over I, 3478
11: 4 David and all I went *to* Jerusalem, which *is* 3478
11:10 *and* with all I, to make him king, 3478
11:10 to the word of the LORD concerning I. 3478
12:32 of the times, to know what I ought to do; 3478
12:38 to Hebron, to make David king over all I: 3478
12:38 all the rest also of I *were of* one heart to 3478
12:40 sheep abundantly: for *there was* joy in I. 3478
13: 2 David said unto all the congregation of I, 3478
13: 2 that are left in all the land of I, and 3478
13: 5 So David gathered all I together, 3478
13: 6 David went up, and all I, to Baalah, *that is,* 3478
13: 8 all I played before God with all *their* might, 3478
14: 2 the LORD had confirmed him king over I, 3478
14: 2 *was* lift up on high, because of his people I. 3478
14: 8 that David was anointed king over all I, 3478
15: 3 David gathered all I together to Jerusalem, 3478
15:12 I unto *the place that* I have prepared for it. 3478
15:14 to bring up the ark of the LORD God of I. 3478
15:25 the elders of I, and the captains over 3478
15:28 Thus all I brought up the ark of 3478
16: 3 he dealt to every one of I, both man and 3478
16: 4 to thank and praise the LORD God of I: 3478
16:13 O ye seed of I his servant, ye children of 3478
16:17 a law, *and* to I *for* an everlasting covenant, 3478
16:36 Blessed *be* the LORD God of I for ever 3478
16:40 of the LORD, which he commanded I; 3478
17: 5 the day that I brought up I unto this day; 3478
17: 6 Wheresoever I have walked with all I, 3478
17: 6 spake I a word to any of the judges of I, 3478
17: 7 *thou* shouldest be ruler over my people I: 3478
17: 9 Also I will ordain a place for my people I, 3478
17:10 commanded judges *to be* over my people I. 3478
17:21 one nation in the earth *is* like thy people I, 3478
17:22 For thy people I didst thou make thine own 3478
17:24 The LORD of hosts *is* the God of I, 3478
17:24 hosts *is* the God of Israel, *even* a God to I: 3478
18:14 So David reigned over all I, and executed 3478
19:10 he chose out of all the choice of I, and 3478
19:16 that they were put to the worse before I, 3478
19:17 he gathered all I, and passed over Jordan, 3478
19:18 the Syrians fled before I; and David slew of 3478
19:19 that they were put to the worse before I, 3478
20: 7 when he defied I, Jonathan the son of 3478
21: 1 Satan stood *up* against I, and 3478
21: 1 and provoked David to number I. 3478
21: 2 number I from Beer-sheba even to Dan; 3478

1Ch 21: 3	why will he be a cause of trespass to I?	3478
21: 4	went throughout all I, and came *to*	3478
21: 5	all *they of* I were a thousand thousand and	3478
21: 7	with this thing; therefore he smote I.	3478
21:12	destroying throughout all the coasts of I.	3478
21:14	So the LORD sent pestilence upon I: and	3478
21:14	and there fell of I seventy thousand men.	3478
21:16	the elders *of I, who were* clothed in	NIH
22: 1	this *is* the altar of the burnt offering for I.	3478
22: 2	the strangers that *were* in the land of I;	3478
22: 6	to build a house for the LORD God of I.	3478
22: 9	give peace and quietness unto I in his days.	3478
22:10	the throne of his kingdom over I for ever.	3478
22:12	and give thee charge concerning I,	3478
22:13	LORD charged Moses with concerning I:	3478
22:17	David also commanded all the princes of I	3478
23: 1	he made Solomon his son king over I.	3478
23: 2	he gathered together all the princes of I,	3478
23:25	The LORD God of I hath given rest unto	3478
24:19	as the LORD God of I had commanded	3478
26:29	sons *were* for the outward business over I,	3478
26:30	*were* officers among them of I on *this* side	3478
27: 1	Now the children of I after their number,	3478
27:16	Furthermore over the tribes of I: the ruler	3478
27:22	These *were* the princes of the tribes of I.	3478
27:23	the LORD had said *he* would increase I	3478
27:24	because there fell wrath for it against I;	3478
28: 1	David assembled all the princes of I,	3478
28: 4	Howbeit the LORD God of I chose me	3478
28: 4	of my father to be king over I for ever:	3478
28: 4	he liked me to make *me* king over all I:	3478
28: 5	of the kingdom of the LORD over I.	3478
28: 8	in the sight of all I the congregation of	3478
29: 6	of the fathers and princes of the tribes of I,	3478
29:10	LORD God of I our father, for ever and	3478
29:18	of Abraham, Isaac, and of I, our fathers,	3478
29:21	and sacrifices in abundance for all I:	3478
29:23	and prospered; and all I obeyed him.	3478
29:25	Solomon exceedingly in the sight of all I,	3478
29:25	had not been on any king before him in I.	3478
29:26	David the son of Jesse reigned over all I.	3478
29:27	the time that he reigned over I *was* forty	3478
29:30	over I, and over all the kingdoms of	3478
2Ch 1: 2	Solomon spake unto all I, to the captains of	3478
1: 2	to the judges, and to every governor in all I,	3478
1:13	of the congregation, and reigned over I.	3478
2: 4	our God. This *is an ordinance* for ever to I.	3478
2:12	Blessed *be* the LORD God of I, that made	3478
2:17	all the strangers that *were* in the land of I,	3478
5: 2	Solomon assembled the elders of I, and	3478
5: 2	the chief of the fathers of the children of I,	3478
5: 3	Wherefore all the men of I assembled	3478
5: 4	all the elders of I came; and the Levites	3478
5: 6	all the congregation of I that were	3478
5:10	made *a covenant* with the children of I,	3478
6: 3	and blessed the whole congregation of I:	3478
6: 3	and all the congregation of I stood.	3478
6: 4	he said, Blessed *be* the LORD God of I,	3478
6: 5	I to build a house *in,* that my name might	3478
6: 5	I any man to be a ruler over my people I:	3478
6: 6	have chosen David to be over my people I.	3478
6: 7	for the name of the LORD God of I.	3478
6:10	am set on the throne of I, as the LORD	3478
6:10	for the name of the LORD God of I.	3478
6:11	that he made with the children of I.	3478
6:12	in the presence of all the congregation of I,	3478
6:13	his knees before all the congregation of I,	3478
6:14	said, O LORD God of I, *there is* no God	3478
6:16	Now therefore, O LORD God of I,	3478
6:16	man in my sight to sit upon the throne of I;	3478
6:17	Now then, O LORD God of I, let thy	3478
6:21	of thy servant, and of thy people I,	3478
6:24	if thy people I be put to the worse before	3478
6:25	forgive the sin of thy people I, and	3478
6:27	the sin of thy servants, and of thy people I,	3478
6:29	or of all thy people I, when every one shall	3478
6:32	which *is* not of thy people I, but is come	3478
6:33	as *doth* thy people I, and may know that	3478
7: 3	when all the children of I saw how the fire	3478
7: 6	trumpets before them, and all I stood.	3478
7: 8	all I with him, a very great congregation,	3478
7:10	and to Solomon, and to I his people.	3478
7:18	shall not fail thee a man *to be* ruler in I.	3478
8: 2	and caused the children of I to dwell there.	3478

8: 7	and the Jebusites, which *were* not of I,	3478
8: 8	whom the children of I consumed not,	3478
8: 9	of the children of I did Solomon make no	3478
8:11	not dwell in the house of David king of I,	3478
9: 8	because thy God loved I, to establish them	3478
9:30	Solomon reigned in Jerusalem over all I	3478
10: 1	for *to* Shechem were all I come to make	3478
10: 3	So Jeroboam and all I came and spake to	3478
10:16	when all I saw that the king would not	3478
10:16	every man to your tents, O I: *and* now,	3478
10:16	own house. So all I went to their tents.	3478
10:17	*as for* the children of I that dwelt in	3478
10:18	the children of I stoned him with stones,	3478
10:19	I rebelled against the house of David unto	3478
11: 1	to fight against I, that *he* might bring	3478
11: 3	and to all I in Judah and Benjamin, saying,	3478
11:13	the Levites that *were* in all I resorted to him	3478
11:16	after them out of all the tribes of I such as	3478
11:16	the LORD God of I came *to* Jerusalem,	3478
12: 1	the law of the LORD, and all I with him.	3478
12: 6	Whereupon the princes of I and the king	3478
12:13	had chosen out of all the tribes of I,	3478
13: 4	said, Hear me, *thou* Jeroboam, and all I;	3478
13: 5	I gave the kingdom over Israel to David for	3478
13: 5	gave the kingdom over I to David for ever,	3478
13:12	O children of I, fight ye not against	3478
13:15	and all I before Abijah and Judah.	3478
13:16	the children of I fled before Judah: and	3478
13:17	there fell down slain of I five hundred	3478
13:18	Thus the children of I were brought under	3478
15: 3	Now for a long season I *hath been* without	3478
15: 4	trouble did turn unto the LORD God of I,	3478
15: 9	for they fell to him out of I in abundance,	3478
15:13	LORD God of I should be put to death,	3478
15:17	high places were not taken away out of I:	3478
16: 1	Baasha king of I came up against Judah,	3478
16: 3	go, break thy league with Baasha king of I,	3478
16: 4	of his armies against the cities of I;	3478
16:11	in the book of the kings of Judah and I.	3478
17: 1	and strengthened himself against I.	3478
17: 4	and not after the doings of I.	3478
18: 3	Ahab king of I said unto Jehoshaphat king	3478
18: 4	Jehoshaphat said unto the king of I,	3478
18: 5	Therefore the king of I gathered together *of*	3478
18: 7	the king of I said unto Jehoshaphat,	3478
18: 8	the king of I called for one *of his* officers,	3478
18: 9	the king of I and Jehoshaphat king of Judah	3478
18:16	I did see all I scattered upon the mountains,	3478
18:17	the king of I said to Jehoshaphat, Did I not	3478
18:19	Who shall entice Ahab king of I, that he	3478
18:25	the king of I said, Take ye Micaiah, and	3478
18:28	So the king of I and Jehoshaphat the king	3478
18:29	the king of I said unto Jehoshaphat, I will	3478
18:29	So the king of I disguised himself; and	3478
18:30	or great, save only with the king of I.	3478
18:31	that they said, It *is* the king of I.	3478
18:32	perceived that it was not the king of I,	3478
18:33	smote the king of I between the joints of	3478
18:34	howbeit the king of I stayed *himself* up in	3478
19: 8	and of the chief of the fathers of I,	3478
20: 7	inhabitants of this land before thy people I,	3478
20:10	whom thou wouldest not let I invade,	3478
20:19	stood up to praise the LORD God of I	3478
20:29	LORD fought against the enemies of I.	3478
20:34	is mentioned in the book of the kings of I.	3478
20:35	Judah join himself with Ahaziah king of I,	3478
21: 2	*were* the sons of Jehoshaphat king of I.	3478
21: 4	and *divers* also of the princes of I.	3478
21: 6	he walked in the way of the kings of I,	3478
21:13	hast walked in the way of the kings of I,	3478
22: 5	I to war against Hazael king of Syria at	3478
23: 2	the chief of the fathers of I, and they came	3478
24: 5	gather of all I money to repair the house of	3478
24: 6	of the congregation of I, for the tabernacle	3478
24: 9	of God laid upon I in the wilderness.	3478
24:16	because he had done good in I,	3478
25: 6	out of I for an hundred talents of silver.	3478
25: 7	O king, let not the army of I go with thee;	3478
25: 7	for the LORD *is* not with I, *to wit, with* all	3478
25: 9	talents which I have given to the army of I?	3478
25:17	the son of Jehu, king of I, saying, Come,	3478
25:18	Joash king of I sent to Amaziah king of	3478
25:21	So Joash the king of I went up; and	3478
25:22	Judah was put to the worse before I, and	3478

I

2Ch 25:23 Joash the king of I took Amaziah king of 3478
25:25 son of Jehoahaz king of I fifteen years. 3478
25:26 in the book of the kings of Judah and I? 3478
27: 7 *are* written in the book of the kings of I 3478
28: 2 For he walked in the ways of the kings of I, 3478
28: 3 had cast out before the children of I. 3478
28: 5 delivered into the hand of the king of I, 3478
28: 8 the children of I carried away captive of 3478
28:13 is great, and *there is* fierce wrath against I. 3478
28:19 Judah low because of Ahaz king of I; 3478
28:23 But they were the ruin of him, and of all I. 3478
28:26 in the book of the kings of Judah and I. 3478
28:27 not into the sepulchres of the kings of I: 3478
29: 7 in the holy *place* unto the God of I. 3478
29:10 a covenant with the LORD God of I, 3478
29:24 the altar, to make an atonement for all I: 3478
29:24 the sin offering *should be made* for all I. 3478
29:27 instruments ordained by David king of I. 3478
30: 1 Hezekiah sent to all I and Judah, and 3478
30: 1 the passover unto the LORD God of I. 3478
30: 5 to make proclamation throughout all I, 3478
30: 5 unto the LORD God of I at Jerusalem: 3478
30: 6 and his princes throughout all I and Judah, 3478
30: 6 of the king, saying, Ye children of I, 3478
30: 6 I, and he will return to the remnant of you, 3478
30:21 the children of I that were present at 3478
30:25 all the congregation that came out of I, and 3478
30:25 the strangers that came out of the land of I, 3478
30:26 of I *there was* not the like in Jerusalem. 3478
31: 1 all I that were present went out to the cities 3478
31: 1 *all.* Then all the children of I returned, 3478
31: 5 the children of I brought in abundance 3478
31: 6 *concerning* the children of I and Judah, 3478
31: 8 they blessed the LORD, and his people I. 3478
32:17 also letters to rail on the LORD God of I, 3478
32:32 *and* in the book of the kings of Judah and I. 3478
33: 2 had cast out before the children of I. 3478
33: 7 I have chosen before all the tribes of I, 3478
33: 8 will I any more remove the foot of I 3478
33: 9 had destroyed before the children of I. 3478
33:16 Judah to serve the LORD God of I. 3478
33:18 to him in the name of the LORD God of I, 3478
33:18 *are written* in the book of the kings of I. 3478
34: 7 all the idols throughout all the land of I, 3478
34: 9 of all the remnant of I, and of all Judah and 3478
34:21 and for them that are left in I and in Judah, 3478
34:23 Thus saith the LORD God of I, 3478
34:26 Thus saith the LORD God of I *concerning* 3478
34:33 countries that *pertained* to the children of I, 3478
34:33 and made all that were present in I to serve, 3478
35: 3 said unto the Levites that taught all I, 3478
35: 3 the son of David king of I did build; 3478
35: 3 the LORD your God, and his people I, 3478
35: 4 according to the writing of David king of I, 3478
35:17 the children of I that were present kept 3478
35:18 kept in I from the days of Samuel 3478
35:18 neither did all the kings of I keep such a 3478
35:18 all Judah and I that were present, and 3478
35:25 *this* day, and made them an ordinance in I: 3478
35:27 *are* written in the book of the kings of I 3478
36: 8 *are* written in the book of the kings of I 3478
36:13 from turning unto the LORD God of I. 3478
Ezr 1: 3 build the house of the LORD God of I, 3478
2: 2 The number of the men of the people of I: 3478
2:59 and their seed, whether they *were* of I: 3478
2:70 dwelt in their cities, and all I in their cities. 3478
3: 1 and the children of I *were* in the cities, 3478
3: 2 and builded the altar of the God of I, 3478
3:10 after the ordinance of David king of I. 3478
3:11 for his mercy *endureth* for ever towards I. 3478
4: 1 the temple unto the LORD God of I; 3478
4: 3 and the rest of the chief of the fathers of I, 3478
4: 3 will build unto the LORD God of I, 3478
5: 1 and Jerusalem in the name of the God of I, 3479
5:11 which a great king of I builded and set up. 3479
6:14 to the commandment of the God of I, 3479
6:16 the children of I, the priests, and 3479
6:17 for a sin offering for all I, twelve he goats, 3479
6:17 according to the number of the tribes of I. 3479
6:21 the children of I, which were come again 3478
6:21 to seek the LORD God of I, did eat, 3478
6:22 the work of the house of God, the God of I. 3478
7: 6 which the LORD God of I had given: 3478
7: 7 there went up *some* of the children of I, 3478
7:10 to do *it,* and to teach in I statutes and 3478
7:11 of the LORD, and of his statutes to I. 3478
7:13 that all they of the people of I, and *of* his 3479
7:15 have freely offered unto the God of I, 3479
7:28 I gathered together out of I chief *men* to go 3478
8:18 sons of Mahli, the son of Levi, the son of I; 3478
8:25 his lords, and all I *there* present, had 3478
8:29 the Levites, and chief of the fathers of I, 3478
8:35 offered burnt offerings unto the God of I, 3478
8:35 twelve bullocks for all I, ninety and 3478
9: 1 The people of I, and the priests, and 3478
9: 4 that trembled at the words of the God of I, 3478
9:15 O LORD God of I, thou *art* righteous: 3478
10: 1 there assembled unto him out of I a very 3478
10: 2 yet now there is hope in I concerning this 3478
10: 5 the chief priests, the Levites, and all I, 3478
10:10 strange wives, to increase the trespass of I. 3478
10:25 Moreover of I: of the sons of Parosh; 3478
Ne 1: 6 for the children of I thy servants, and 3478
1: 6 confess the sins of the children of I, 3478
2:10 man to seek the welfare of the children of I. 3478
7: 7 *I say,* of the men of the people of I *was* 3478
7:61 nor their seed, whether they *were* of I. 3478
7:73 of the people, and the Nethinims, and all I, 3478
7:73 the children of I *were* in their cities. 3478
8: 1 which the LORD had commanded to I. 3478
8:14 that the children of I should dwell in booths 3478
8:17 that day had not the children of I done so. 3478
9: 1 fourth day of this month the children of I 3478
9: 2 the seed of I separated themselves from all 3478
10:33 sin offerings to make an atonement for I, 3478
10:39 For the children of I and the children of 3478
11: 3 *to wit,* I, the priests, and the Levites, and 3478
11:20 the residue of I, of the priests, *and* 3478
12:47 all I in the days of Zerubbabel, and in 3478
13: 2 Because they met not the children of I with 3478
13: 3 that they separated from I all the mixed 3478
13:18 yet ye bring more wrath upon I by 3478
13:26 Did not Solomon king of I sin by these 3478
13:26 his God, and God made him king over all I: 3478
Ps 14: 7 O that the salvation of I *were come* out of 3478
14: 7 Jacob shall rejoice, *and* I shall be glad. 3478
22: 3 O thou that inhabitest the praises of I. 3478
22:23 and fear him, all ye the seed of I. 3478
25:22 Redeem I, O God, out of all his troubles. 3478
41:13 Blessed *be* the LORD God of I from 3478
50: 7 O I, and I will testify against thee: 3478
53: 6 O that the salvation of I *were come* out of 3478
53: 6 Jacob shall rejoice, *and* I shall be glad. 3478
59: 5 O LORD God *of* hosts, the God of I, 3478
68: 8 at the presence of God, the God of I. 3478
68:26 *even* the Lord, from the fountain of I. 3478
68:34 his excellency *is* over I, and his strength *is* 3478
68:35 the God of I *is* he that giveth strength and 3478
69: 6 be confounded for my sake, O God of I. 3478
71:22 I sing with the harp, O thou Holy One of I. 3478
72:18 Blessed *be* the LORD God, the God of I, 3478
73: 1 Truly God *is* good to I, *even* to such as are 3478
76: 1 Judah *is* God known: his name *is* great in I. 3478
78: 5 appointed a law in I, which he commanded 3478
78:21 and anger also came up against I; 3478
78:31 and smote down the chosen *men* of I. 3478
78:41 and limited the Holy One of I. 3478
78:55 made the tribes of I to dwell in their tents. 3478
78:59 *this,* he was wroth, and greatly abhorred I: 3478
78:71 feed Jacob his people, and I his inheritance. 3478
80: 1 Give ear, O Shepherd of I, thou that leadest 3478
81: 4 For this *was* a statute for I, *and* a law of 3478
81: 8 O I, if thou wilt hearken unto me; 3478
81:11 to my voice; and I would none of me. 3478
81:13 unto me, *and* I had walked in my ways! 3478
83: 4 that the name of I may be no more in 3478
89:18 and the Holy One of I *is* our king. 3478
98: 3 and his truth toward the house of I: 3478
103: 7 unto Moses, his acts unto the children of I. 3478
105:10 a law, *and* to I *for* an everlasting covenant: 3478
105:23 I also came *into* Egypt; and 3478
106:48 Blessed *be* the LORD God of I from 3478
114: 1 When I went out of Egypt, the house of 3478
114: 2 was his sanctuary, *and* I his dominion. 3478
115: 9 O I, trust thou in the LORD: he *is* their 3478
115:12 will bless *us;* he will bless the house of I; 3478
118: 2 Let I now say, that his mercy *endureth* for 3478
121: 4 he that keepeth I shall neither slumber nor 3478

Ps 122: 4 of the LORD, *unto* the testimony of I, 3478
124: 1 who was on our side, now may I say; 3478
125: 5 of iniquity: *but* peace *shall be* upon I. 3478
128: 6 thy children's children, *and* peace upon I. 3478
129: 1 me from my youth, may I now say: 3478
130: 7 Let I hope in the LORD: for with 3478
130: 8 he shall redeem I from all his iniquities. 3478
131: 3 Let I hope in the LORD from henceforth 3478
135: 4 unto himself, *and* I for his peculiar treasure. 3478
135:12 an heritage, an heritage unto I his people. 3478
135:19 Bless the LORD, O house of I: bless 3478
136:11 brought out I from among them: for his 3478
136:14 made I to pass through the midst of it: 3478
136:22 *Even* an heritage unto I his servant: for his 3478
147: 2 he gathereth together the outcasts of I. 3478
147:19 his statutes and his judgments unto I. 3478
148:14 *even* of the children of I, a people near unto 3478
149: 2 Let I rejoice in him that made him: let 3478
Pr 1: 1 of Solomon the son of David, king of I. 3478
Ecc 1:12 I the Preacher was king over I in Jerusalem. 3478
SS 3: 7 valiant *men are* about it, of the valiant of I. 3478
Isa 1: 3 *but* I doth not know, my people doth not 3478
1: 4 they have provoked the Holy One of I unto 3478
1:24 LORD of hosts, the mighty One of I, Ah, 3478
4: 2 and comely for them that are escaped of I. 3478
5: 7 of the LORD of hosts *is* the house of I, 3478
5:19 let the counsel of the Holy One of I draw 3478
5:24 despised the word of the Holy One of I. 3478
7: 1 and Pekah the son of Remaliah, king of I, 3478
8:14 a rock of offence to both the houses of I, 3478
8:18 for wonders in I from the LORD of hosts, 3478
9: 8 word into Jacob, and it hath lighted upon I. 3478
9:12 they shall devour I with open mouth. 3478
9:14 Therefore the LORD will cut off from I 3478
10:17 the light of I shall be for a fire, and 3478
10:20 *that* the remnant of I, and such as are 3478
10:20 the LORD, the Holy One of I, in truth. 3478
10:22 For though thy people I be as the sand of 3478
11:12 shall assemble the outcasts of I, and 3478
11:16 like as it was to I in the day that he came 3478
12: 6 for great *is* the Holy One of I in the midst 3478
14: 1 will yet choose I, and set them in their own 3478
14: 2 the house of I shall possess them in 3478
17: 3 shall be as the glory of the children of I, 3478
17: 6 saith the LORD God of I. 3478
17: 7 shall have respect to the Holy One of I. 3478
17: 9 which they left because of the children of I: 3478
19:24 In that day shall I be the third with Egypt 3478
19:25 work of my hands, and I mine inheritance. 3478
21:10 the God of I, have I declared unto you. 3478
21:17 for the LORD God of I hath spoken *it.* 3478
24:15 *even* the name of the LORD God of I in 3478
27: 6 I shall blossom and bud, and fill the face of 3478
27:12 be gathered one by one, O ye children of I. 3478
29:19 men shall rejoice in the Holy One of I. 3478
29:23 One of Jacob, and shall fear the God of I. 3478
30:11 cause the Holy One of I to cease from 3478
30:12 Wherefore thus saith the Holy One of I, 3478
30:15 saith the Lord GOD, the Holy One of I; 3478
30:29 of the LORD, to the mighty One of I. 3478
31: 1 they look not unto the Holy One of I, 3478
31: 6 the children of I have deeply revolted. 3478
37:16 O LORD of hosts, God of I, that dwellest 3478
37:21 Thus saith the LORD God of I, 3478
37:23 on high? *even* against the Holy One of I. 3478
40:27 sayest thou, O Jacob, and speakest, O I, 3478
41: 8 thou, I, *art* my servant, Jacob whom I have 3478
41:14 thou worm Jacob, *and* ye men of I; 3478
41:14 and thy redeemer, the Holy One of I. 3478
41:16 *and* shalt glory in the Holy One of I. 3478
41:17 *I* the God of I will not forsake them. 3478
41:20 and the Holy One of I hath created it. 3478
42:24 gave Jacob for a spoil, and I to the robbers? 3478
43: 1 and he that formed thee, O I, Fear not: 3478
43: 3 thy God, the Holy One of I, thy Saviour: 3478
43:14 your redeemer, the Holy One of I; 3478
43:15 your Holy One, the creator of I, your King. 3478
43:22 but thou hast been weary of me, O I. 3478
43:28 Jacob to the curse, and I to reproaches. 3478
44: 1 my servant; and I, whom I have chosen: 3478
44: 5 and surname *himself* by the name of I. 3478
44: 6 Thus saith the LORD the King of I, and 3478
44:21 Remember these, O Jacob and I; for thou 3478
44:21 O I, thou shalt not be forgotten of me. 3478
44:23 redeemed Jacob, and glorified himself in I. 3478
45: 3 call *thee* by thy name, *am* the God of I. 3478
45: 4 Jacob my servant's sake, and I mine elect, 3478
45:11 the Holy One of I, and his maker, 3478
45:15 that hidest thyself, O God of I, the saviour. 3478
45:17 *But* I shall be saved in the LORD *with* an 3478
45:25 In the LORD shall all the seed of I be 3478
46: 3 and all the remnant of the house of I, 3478
46:13 I will place salvation in Zion for I my 3478
47: 4 of hosts *is* his name, the Holy One of I. 3478
48: 1 which are called by the name of I, and 3478
48: 1 make mention of the God of I, *but* not in 3478
48: 2 and stay themselves upon the God of I; 3478
48:12 unto me, O Jacob, and I my called; 3478
48:17 thy redeemer, the Holy One of I; 3478
49: 3 said unto me, Thou *art* my servant, O I, 3478
49: 5 again to him, Though I be not gathered, 3478
49: 6 of Jacob, and to restore the preserved of I: 3478
49: 7 the redeemer of I, *and* his Holy One, 3478
49: 7 *and* the Holy One of I, and he shall choose 3478
52:12 and the God of I *will be* your rereward. 3478
54: 5 and thy redeemer the Holy One of I; 3478
55: 5 thy God, and for the Holy One of I; 3478
56: 8 which gathereth the outcasts of I saith, 3478
60: 9 to the Holy One of I, because he hath 3478
60:14 the LORD, The Zion of the Holy One of I. 3478
63: 7 the great goodness towards the house of I, 3478
63:16 ignorant of us, and I acknowledge us not: 3478
66:20 as the children of I bring an offering in a 3478
Jer 2: 3 I *was* holiness unto the LORD, *and* 3478
2: 4 and all the families of the house of I: 3478
2:14 *Is* I a servant? *is* he a homeborn *slave?* why 3478
2:26 he is found, so is the house of I ashamed; 3478
2:31 Have I been a wilderness unto I? a land of 3478
3: 6 Hast thou seen *that* which backsliding I 3478
3: 8 I committed adultery I had put her away, 3478
3:11 The backsliding I hath justified herself 3478
3:12 say, Return, thou backsliding I, saith 3478
3:18 of Judah shall walk with the house of I, 3478
3:20 with me, O house of I, saith the LORD. 3478
3:21 *and* supplications of the children of I: 3478
3:23 in the LORD our God *is* the salvation of I. 3478
4: 1 O I, saith the LORD, return unto me: 3478
5:11 For the house of I and the house of Judah 3478
5:15 from far, O house of I, saith the LORD: 3478
6: 9 They shall throughly glean the remnant of I 3478
7: 3 the God of I, Amend your ways and 3478
7:12 did to it for the wickedness of my people I. 3478
7:21 saith the LORD of hosts, the God of I; 3478
9:15 saith the LORD of hosts, the God of I; 3478
9:26 all the house of I *are* uncircumcised in 3478
10: 1 LORD speaketh unto you, O house of I: 3478
10:16 and I *is* the rod of his inheritance: 3478
11: 3 unto them, Thus saith the LORD God of I; 3478
11:10 the house of I and the house of Judah have 3478
11:17 for the evil of the house of I and of 3478
12:14 which I have caused my people I to inherit; 3478
13:11 to cleave unto me the whole house of I 3478
13:12 Thus saith the LORD God of I, 3478
14: 8 O the hope of I, the saviour thereof in time 3478
16: 9 saith the LORD of hosts, the God of I; 3478
16:14 that brought up the children of I out of 3478
16:15 that brought up the children of I from 3478
17:13 O LORD, the hope of I, all that forsake 3478
18: 6 O house of I, cannot I do with you as this 3478
18: 6 so *are* ye in mine hand, O house of I. 3478
18:13 who hath heard such *things:* the virgin of I 3478
19: 3 saith the LORD of hosts, the God of I; 3478
19:15 saith the LORD of hosts, the God of I; 3478
21: 4 Thus saith the LORD God of I; Behold, 3478
23: 2 Therefore thus saith the LORD God of I 3478
23: 6 shall be saved, and I shall dwell safely: 3478
23: 7 which brought up the children of I out of 3478
23: 8 which led the seed of the house of I out of 3478
23:13 in Baal, and caused my people I to err. 3478
24: 5 Thus saith the LORD, the God of I; 3478
25:15 For thus saith the LORD God of I unto 3478
25:27 saith the LORD of hosts, the God of I; 3478
27: 4 saith the LORD of hosts, the God of I; 3478
27:21 saith the LORD of hosts, the God of I, 3478
28: 2 the LORD of hosts, the God of I, saying, 3478
28:14 saith the LORD of hosts, the God of I; 3478
29: 4 saith the LORD of hosts, the God of I; 3478
29: 8 saith the LORD of hosts, the God of I; 3478

Jer	29:21	the God of I, of Ahab the son of Kolaiah,	3478
	29:23	Because they have committed villany in I,	3478
	29:25	the LORD of hosts, the God of I, saying,	3478
	30: 2	Thus speaketh the LORD God of I,	3478
	30: 3	bring again the captivity of my people I	3478
	30: 4	words that the LORD spake concerning I	3478
	30:10	saith the LORD; neither be dismayed, O I:	3478
	31: 1	will I be the God of all the families of I,	3478
	31: 2	*even* I when *I* went to cause him to rest.	3478
	31: 4	and thou shalt be built, O virgin of I:	3478
	31: 7	save thy people, the remnant of I.	3478
	31: 9	for I am a father to I, and Ephraim *is* my	3478
	31:10	He that scattered I will gather him, and	3478
	31:21	turn again, O virgin of I, turn again to these	3478
	31:23	saith the LORD of hosts, the God of I;	3478
	31:27	that I will sow the house of I and the house	3478
	31:31	make a new covenant with the house of I,	3478
	31:33	that I will make with the house of I;	3478
	31:36	the seed of I also shall cease from being a	3478
	31:37	I will also cast off all the seed of I for all	3478
	32:14	saith the LORD of hosts, the God of I;	3478
	32:15	saith the LORD of hosts, the God of I;	3478
	32:20	this day, and in I, and amongst *other* men;	3478
	32:21	hast brought forth thy people I out of	3478
	32:30	For the children of I and the children of	3478
	32:30	for the children of I have only provoked me	3478
	32:32	Because of all the evil of the children of I	3478
	32:36	the God of I, concerning this city,	3478
	33: 4	For thus saith the LORD, the God of I,	3478
	33: 7	of Judah and the captivity of I to return,	3478
	33:14	which I have promised unto the house of I	3478
	33:17	to sit upon the throne of the house of I;	3478
	34: 2	Thus saith the LORD, the God of I; Go	3478
	34:13	Thus saith the LORD, the God of I;	3478
	35:13	saith the LORD of hosts, the God of I;	3478
	35:17	the LORD God of hosts, the God of I;	3478
	35:18	saith the LORD of hosts, the God of I;	3478
	35:19	saith the LORD of hosts, the God of I;	3478
	36: 2	that I have spoken unto thee against I,	3478
	37: 7	Thus saith the LORD, the God of I;	3478
	38:17	the LORD, the God of hosts, the God of I;	3478
	39:16	saith the LORD of hosts, the God of I;	3478
	41: 9	king had made for fear of Baasha king of I:	3478
	42: 9	Thus saith the LORD, the God of I,	3478
	42:15	saith the LORD of hosts, the God of I;	3478
	42:18	saith the LORD of hosts, the God of I;	3478
	43:10	saith the LORD of hosts, the God of I;	3478
	44: 2	saith the LORD of hosts, the God of I;	3478
	44: 7	the LORD, the God of hosts, the God of I;	3478
	44:11	saith the LORD of hosts, the God of I;	3478
	44:25	the LORD of hosts, the God of I, saying;	3478
	45: 2	the God of I, unto thee, O Baruch;	3478
	46:25	The LORD of hosts, the God of I, saith;	3478
	46:27	servant Jacob, and be not dismayed, O I:	3478
	48: 1	saith the LORD of hosts, the God of I;	3478
	48:13	as the house of I was ashamed of Beth-el	3478
	48:27	For was not I a derision unto thee? was he	3478
	49: 1	thus saith the LORD; Hath I no sons?	3478
	49: 2	shall I be heir unto them that were his	3478
	50: 4	the children of I shall come, they and	3478
	50:17	I *is* a scattered sheep; the lions have driven	3478
	50:18	saith the LORD of hosts, the God of I;	3478
	50:19	I will bring I again to his habitation, and	3478
	50:20	the iniquity of I shall be sought for, and	3478
	50:29	the LORD, against the Holy One of I.	3478
	50:33	The children of I and the children of Judah	3478
	51: 5	For I *hath* not *been* forsaken, nor Judah of	3478
	51: 5	filled *with* sin against the Holy One of I.	3478
	51:19	all *things:* and *I is* the rod of his inheritance:	NIH
	51:33	saith the LORD of hosts, the God of I;	3478
	51:49	As Babylon *hath caused* the slain of I to	3478
La	2: 1	from heaven *unto* the earth the beauty of I,	3478
	2: 3	cut off in *his* fierce anger all the horn of I:	3478
	2: 5	he hath swallowed up I, he hath swallowed	3478
Eze	2: 3	Son of man, I send thee to the children of I,	3478
	3: 1	this roll, and go speak unto the house of I.	3478
	3: 4	go, get thee unto the house of I, and	3478
	3: 5	of a hard language, *but* to the house of I;	3478
	3: 7	the house of I will not hearken unto thee;	3478
	3: 7	for all the house of I *are* impudent	3478
	3:17	made thee a watchman unto the house of I:	3478
	4: 3	This *shall be* a sign to the house of I.	3478
	4: 4	lay the iniquity of the house of I upon it:	3478
	4: 5	thou bear the iniquity of the house of I.	3478
	4:13	Even thus shall the children of I eat their	3478
	5: 4	a fire come forth into all the house of I.	3478
	6: 2	set thy face towards the mountains of I, and	3478
	6: 3	say, Ye mountains of I, hear the word of	3478
	6: 5	of the children of I before their idols;	3478
	6:11	all the evil abominations of the house of I:	3478
	7: 2	saith the Lord GOD unto the land of I;	3478
	8: 4	the glory of the God of I *was* there,	3478
	8: 6	that the house of I committeth here,	3478
	8:10	and all the idols of the house of I,	3478
	8:11	men of the ancients of the house of I,	3478
	8:12	ancients of the house of I do in the dark,	3478
	9: 3	the glory of the God of I was gone up from	3478
	9: 8	*wilt* thou destroy all the residue of I in thy	3478
	9: 9	The iniquity of the house of I and Judah *is*	3478
	10:19	the glory of the God of I *was* over them	3478
	10:20	under the God of I by the river of Chebar;	3478
	11: 5	Thus have ye said, O house of I:	3478
	11:10	I will judge you in the border of I; and	3478
	11:11	*but* I will judge you in the border of I:	3478
	11:13	thou make a full end of the remnant of I?	3478
	11:15	thy kindred, and all the house of I wholly,	3478
	11:17	and I will give you the land of I.	3478
	11:22	the glory of the God of I *was* over them	3478
	12: 6	have set thee *for* a sign unto the house of I.	3478
	12: 9	Son of man, hath not the house of I,	3478
	12:10	and all the house of I that *are* among them.	3478
	12:19	of Jerusalem, *and* of the land of I;	3478
	12:22	*is* that proverb *that* ye have in the land of I,	3478
	12:23	they shall no more use it as a proverb in I;	3478
	12:24	flattering divination within the house of I.	3478
	12:27	of man, behold, *they of* the house of I say,	3478
	13: 2	prophesy against the prophets of I that	3478
	13: 4	O I, thy prophets are like the foxes in	3478
	13: 5	I to stand in the battle in the day of	3478
	13: 9	be written in the writing of the house of I,	3478
	13: 9	neither shall they enter into the land of I;	3478
	13:16	*To wit,* the prophets of I which prophesy	3478
	14: 1	came certain of the elders of I unto me,	3478
	14: 4	Every man of the house of I that setteth up	3478
	14: 5	That *I* may take the house of I in their own	3478
	14: 6	Therefore say unto the house of I,	3478
	14: 7	For every one of the house of I, or of	3478
	14: 7	or of the stranger that sojourneth in I,	3478
	14: 9	destroy him from the midst of my people I.	3478
	14:11	That the house of I may go no more astray	3478
	17: 2	speak a parable unto the house of I;	3478
	17:23	In the mountain of the height of I will I	3478
	18: 2	use this proverb concerning the land of I,	3478
	18: 3	*occasion* any more to use this proverb in I.	3478
	18: 6	up his eyes to the idols of the house of I,	3478
	18:15	up his eyes to the idols of the house of I,	3478
	18:25	Hear now, O house of I; Is not my way	3478
	18:29	Yet saith the house of I, The way of	3478
	18:29	O house of I, are not my ways equal?	3478
	18:30	Therefore I will judge you, O house of I,	3478
	18:31	for why will ye die, O house of I?	3478
	19: 1	thou up a lamentation for the princes of I,	3478
	19: 9	no more be heard upon the mountains of I.	3478
	20: 1	*that* certain of the elders of I came to	3478
	20: 3	speak unto the elders of I, and say unto	3478
	20: 5	In the day when I chose I, and lifted up	3478
	20:13	the house of I rebelled against me in	3478
	20:27	speak unto the house of I, and say unto	3478
	20:30	Wherefore say unto the house of I,	3478
	20:31	shall I be inquired of by you, O house of I?	3478
	20:38	and they shall not enter into the land of I:	3478
	20:39	As for you, O house of I, thus saith	3478
	20:40	in the mountain of the height of I, saith	3478
	20:40	Lord GOD, there shall all the house of I,	3478
	20:42	when I shall bring you into the land of I,	3478
	20:44	O ye house of I, saith the Lord GOD.	3478
	21: 2	and prophesy against the land of I,	3478
	21: 3	say to the land of I, Thus saith the LORD;	3478
	21:12	it *shall be* upon all the princes of I:	3478
	21:25	thou, profane wicked prince of I,	3478
	22: 6	Behold, the princes of I, every one were in	3478
	22:18	the house of I is to me become dross:	3478
	24:21	Speak unto the house of I, Thus saith	3478
	25: 3	against the land of I, when it was desolate;	3478
	25: 6	with all thy despite against the land of I;	3478
	25:14	upon Edom by the hand of my people I:	3478
	27:17	Judah, and the land of I, they *were* thy	3478
	28:24	more a pricking brier unto the house of I,	3478

Ref	Text	Strong's
Eze 28:25	When I shall have gathered the house of I	3478
29: 6	have been a staff of reed to the house of I.	3478
29:16	no more the confidence of the house of I,	3478
29:21	the horn of the house of I to bud forth,	3478
33:24	inhabit those wastes of the land of I speak,	3478
33:28	the mountains of I shall be desolate,	3478
34: 2	prophesy against the shepherds of I,	3478
34: 2	Woe be to the shepherds of I that do feed	3478
34:13	feed them upon the mountains of I by	3478
34:14	upon the high mountains of I shall their	3478
34:14	shall they feed upon the mountains of I.	3478
34:30	that they, even the house of I, are my	3478
35: 5	hast shed the blood of the children of I by	3478
35:12	hast spoken against the mountains of I,	3478
36: 6	therefore concerning the land of I,	3478
36: 8	ye, O mountains of I, ye shall shoot forth	3478
36: 8	and yield your fruit to my people of I;	3478
36:10	upon you, all the house of I, even all of it:	3478
36:12	men to walk upon you, even my people I;	3478
36:17	when the house of I dwelt in their own	3478
36:21	which the house of I had profaned among	3478
36:22	Therefore say unto the house of I,	3478
36:22	O house of I, but for mine holy name's	3478
36:32	for your own ways, O house of I.	3478
36:37	yet for this be inquired of by the house of I,	3478
37:11	these bones are the whole house of I:	3478
37:12	and bring you into the land of I.	3478
37:16	and for the children of I his companions:	3478
37:16	and for all the house of I his companions:	3478
37:19	the tribes of I his fellows, and will put them	3478
37:21	I will take the children of I from among	3478
37:22	nation in the land upon the mountains of I;	3478
37:28	shall know that I the Lord do sanctify I,	3478
38: 8	against the mountains of I, which have	3478
38:14	In that day when my people of I dwelleth	3478
38:16	thou shalt come up against my people of I,	3478
38:19	shall be a great shaking in the land of I;	3478
39: 2	will bring thee upon the mountains of I:	3478
39: 4	Thou shalt fall upon the mountains of I,	3478
39: 7	name known in the midst of my people I;	3478
39: 7	that I am the Lord, the Holy One in I.	3478
39: 9	they that dwell in the cities of I shall go	3478
39:11	give unto Gog a place there of graves in I,	3478
39:12	seven months shall the house of I be	3478
39:17	a great sacrifice upon the mountains of I,	3478
39:22	So the house of I shall know that I am	3478
39:23	the heathen shall know that the house of I	3478
39:25	have mercy upon the whole house of I, and	3478
39:29	poured out my spirit upon the house of I,	3478
40: 2	of God brought he me into the land of I,	3478
40: 4	declare all that thou seest to the house of I.	3478
43: 2	the glory of the God of I came from	3478
43: 7	in the midst of the children of I for ever,	3478
43: 7	shall the house of I no more defile,	3478
44: 6	even to the house of I, Thus saith the Lord	3478
44: 6	O ye house of I, let it suffice you of all	3478
44: 9	any stranger that is among the children of I.	3478
44:10	away far from me, when I went astray,	3478
44:12	caused the house of I to fall into iniquity;	3478
44:15	the children of I went astray from me,	3478
44:22	take maidens of the seed of the house of I,	3478
44:28	ye shall give them no possession in I: I am	3478
44:29	and every dedicate thing in I shall be theirs.	3478
45: 6	portion: it shall be for the whole house of I.	3478
45: 8	In the land shall be his possession in I: and	3478
45: 8	to the house of I according to their tribes.	3478
45: 9	Let it suffice you, O princes of I:	3478
45:15	of two hundred, out of the fat pastures of I;	3478
45:16	shall give this oblation for the prince in I.	3478
45:17	in all solemnities of the house of I:	3478
45:17	to make reconciliation for the house of I:	3478
47:13	the land according to the twelve tribes of I:	3478

Ref	Text	Strong's
47:18	and from the land of I by Jordan,	3478
47:21	land unto you according to the tribes of I.	3478
47:22	in the country among the children of I;	3478
47:22	inheritance with you among the tribes of I.	3478
48:11	astray when the children of I went astray,	3478
48:19	city shall serve it out of all the tribes of I.	3478
48:29	by lot unto the tribes of I for inheritance,	3478
48:31	shall be after the names of the tribes of I:	3478
Da 1: 3	he should bring certain of the children of I,	3478
9: 7	unto all I, that are near, and that are far off,	3478
9:11	Yea, all I have transgressed thy law,	3478
9:20	my sin and the sin of my people I,	3478
Hos 1: 1	of Jeroboam the son of Joash, king of I.	3478
1: 4	to cease the kingdom of the house of I.	3478
1: 5	that I will break the bow of I in the valley	3478
1: 6	no more have mercy upon the house of I;	3478
3: 5	Afterward shall the children of I return, and	3478
4: 1	the word of the Lord, ye children of I:	3478
4:15	Though thou, I, play the harlot, yet let not	3478
4:16	For I slideth back as a backsliding heifer:	3478
5: 1	hearken, ye house of I; and give ye ear,	3478
5: 3	I know Ephraim, and I is not hid from me:	3478
5: 3	committest whoredom, and I is defiled.	3478
5: 5	the pride of I doth testify to his face:	3478
5: 5	therefore shall I and Ephraim fall in their	3478
5: 9	among the tribes of I have I made known	3478
6:10	have seen a horrible thing in the house of I:	3478
6:10	is the whoredom of Ephraim, I is defiled.	3478
7: 1	When I would have healed I, then	3478
7:10	the pride of I testifieth to his face: and	3478
8: 2	I shall cry unto me, My God, we know	3478
8: 3	I hath cast off the thing that is good:	3478
8: 6	For from I was it also: the workman made	3478
8: 8	I is swallowed up: now shall they be	3478
8:14	For I hath forgotten his Maker, and	3478
9: 1	Rejoice not, O I, for joy, as other people:	3478
9: 7	I shall know it: the prophet is a fool,	3478
9:10	I found I like grapes in the wilderness:	3478
10: 1	I is an empty vine, he bringeth forth fruit	3478
10: 6	and I shall be ashamed of his own counsel.	3478
10: 8	of Aven, the sin of I, shall be destroyed:	3478
10: 9	O I, thou hast sinned from the days of	3478
10:15	in a morning shall the king of I utterly be	3478
11: 1	When I was a child, then I loved him, and	3478
11: 8	how shall I deliver thee, I? how shall I	3478
11:12	with lies, and the house of I with deceit:	3478
12:12	I served for a wife, and for a wife he kept	3478
12:13	by a prophet the Lord brought I out of	3478
13: 1	spake trembling, he exalted himself in I;	3478
13: 9	O I, thou hast destroyed thyself; but in me	3478
14: 1	O I, return unto the Lord thy God;	3478
14: 5	I will be as the dew unto I: he shall grow as	3478
Joel 2:27	ye shall know that I am in the midst of I,	3478
3: 2	there for my people and for my heritage I,	3478
3:16	and the strength of the children of I.	3478
Am 1: 1	which he saw concerning I in the days of	3478
1: 1	of Jeroboam the son of Joash king of I,	3478
2: 6	For three transgressions of I, and for four,	3478
2:11	Is it not even thus, O ye children of I?	3478
3: 1	hath spoken against you, O children of I,	3478
3:12	shall the children of I be taken out that	3478
3:14	I upon him I will also visit the altars of	3478
4: 5	for this liketh you, O ye children of I,	3478
4:12	Therefore thus will I do unto thee, O I: and	3478
4:12	unto thee, prepare to meet thy God, O I.	3478
5: 1	even a lamentation, O house of I.	3478
5: 2	The virgin of I is fallen; she shall no more	3478
5: 3	hundred shall leave ten, to the house of I.	3478
5: 4	thus saith the Lord unto the house of I,	3478
5:25	in the wilderness forty years, O house of I?	3478
6: 1	the nations, to whom the house of I came!	3478
6:14	O house of I, saith the Lord the God of	3478
7: 8	set a plumbline in the midst of my people I:	3478
7: 9	and the sanctuaries of I shall be laid waste;	3478
7:10	priest of Beth-el sent to Jeroboam king of I,	3478
7:10	against thee in the midst of the house of I:	3478
7:11	I shall surely be led away captive out of	3478
7:15	unto me, Go, prophesy unto my people I.	3478
7:16	Prophesy not against I, and drop not thy	3478
7:17	I shall surely go into captivity forth of his	3478

Am	8: 2	The end is come upon my people *of* I;	3478
	9: 7	of the Ethiopians unto me, O children of I?	3478
	9: 7	Have not I brought up I out of the land of	3478
	9: 9	I will sift the house of I among all nations,	3478
	9:14	bring again the captivity of my people of I,	3478
Ob	1:20	the captivity of this host of the children of I	3478
Mic	1: 5	*is* all this, and for the sins of the house of I.	3478
	1:13	for the transgressions of I were found in	3478
	1:14	of Achzib *shall be* a lie to the kings of I.	3478
	1:15	he shall come unto Adullam the glory of I.	3478
	2:12	I will surely gather the remnant of I;	3478
	3: 1	of Jacob, and ye princes of the house of I;	3478
	3: 8	Jacob his transgression, and to I his sin.	3478
	3: 9	princes of the house of I, that abhor	3478
	5: 1	they shall smite the judge of I with a rod	3478
	5: 2	come forth unto me *that is* to be ruler in I;	3478
	5: 3	brethren shall return unto the children of I.	3478
	6: 2	with his people, and he will plead with I.	3478
Na	2: 2	excellency of Jacob, as the excellency of I:	3478
Zep	2: 9	saith the LORD of hosts, the God of I,	3478
	3:13	The remnant of I shall not do iniquity,	3478
	3:14	shout, O I; be glad and rejoice with all	3478
	3:15	the king of I, *even* the LORD, *is* in	3478
Zec	1:19	have scattered Judah, I, and Jerusalem.	3478
	8:13	O house of Judah, and house of I;	3478
	9: 1	the eyes of man, as of all the tribes of I,	3478
	11:14	break the brotherhood between Judah and I.	3478
	12: 1	burden of the word of the LORD for I,	3478
Mal	1: 1	The burden of the word of the LORD to I	3478
	1: 5	will be magnified from the border of I.	3478
	2:11	an abomination is committed in I and	3478
	2:16	*For* the LORD, the God of I, saith that he	3478
	4: 4	I commanded unto him in Horeb for all I,	3478
Mt	2: 6	a Governor, that shall rule my people I.	*2474*
	2:20	and his mother, and go into the land of I:	*2474*
	2:21	and his mother, and came into the land of I.	*2474*
	8:10	I have not found so great faith, no not in I.	*2474*
	9:33	saying, It was never so seen in I.	*2474*
	10: 6	go rather to the lost sheep of the house of I.	*2474*
	10:23	Ye shall not have gone over the cities of I,	*2474*
	15:24	but unto the lost sheep of the house of I.	*2474*
	15:31	to see: and they glorified the God of I.	*2474*
	19:28	judging the twelve tribes of I.	*2474*
	27: 9	whom they of the children of I did value;	*2474*
	27:42	If he be the King of I, let him now come	*2474*
Mk	12:29	first of all the commandments *is,* Hear, O I;	*2474*
	15:32	Let Christ the King of I descend now from	*2474*
Lk	1:16	And many of the children of I shall he turn	*2474*
	1:54	He hath holpen his servant I,	*2474*
	1:68	Blessed *be* the Lord God of I; for he hath	*2474*
	1:80	deserts till the day of his shewing unto I.	*2474*
	2:25	devout, waiting for the consolation of I:	*2474*
	2:32	the Gentiles, and the glory of thy people I.	*2474*
	2:34	for the fall and rising again of many in I;	*2474*
	4:25	many widows were in I in the days of	*2474*
	4:27	And many lepers were in I in the time of	*2474*
	7: 9	I have not found so great faith, no, not in I.	*2474*
	22:30	sit on thrones judging the twelve tribes of I.	*2474*
	24:21	had been he which should have redeemed I:	*2474*
Jn	1:31	but that he should be made manifest to I,	*2474*
	1:49	art the Son of God; thou art the King of I.	*2474*
	3:10	Art thou a master of I, and knowest not	*2474*
	12:13	Blessed *is* the King of I that cometh in	*2474*
Ac	1: 6	at this time restore again the kingdom to I?	*2474*
	2:22	Ye men of I, hear these words; Jesus of	*2475*
	2:36	Therefore let all the house of I know	*2474*
	3:12	Ye men of I, why marvel ye at this?	*2475*
	4: 8	Ye rulers of the people, and elders of I,	*2474*
	4:10	unto you all, and to all the people of I,	*2474*
	4:27	with the Gentiles, and the people of I,	*2474*
	5:21	and all the senate of the children of I, and	*2474*
	5:31	for to give repentance to I, and	*2474*
	5:35	And said unto them, Ye men of I, take heed	*2475*
	7:23	heart to visit his brethren the children of I.	*2474*
	7:37	which said unto the children of I,	*2474*
	7:42	O *ye* house of I, have ye offered to me slain	*2474*
	9:15	and kings, and the children of I:	*2474*
	10:36	word which *God* sent unto the children of I,	*2474*
	13:16	Men of I, and *ye* that fear God,	*2475*
	13:17	The God of this people of I chose our	*2474*
	13:23	to *his* promise raised unto I a Saviour,	*2474*
	13:24	baptism of repentance to all the people of I.	*2474*
	21:28	Crying out, Men of I, help: This is the man,	*2475*
	28:20	that for the hope of I I am bound with this	*2474*
Ro	9: 6	For they *are* not all I, which are of Israel:	*2474*
	9: 6	For they *are* not all Israel, which are of I:	*2474*
	9:27	Esaias also crieth concerning I, Though	*2474*
	9:27	Though the number of the children of I be	*2474*
	9:31	But I, which followed *after* the law of	*2474*
	10: 1	heart's desire and prayer to God for I is,	*2474*
	10:19	But I say, Did not I know? First Moses	*2474*
	10:21	But to I he saith, All day long have I	*2474*
	11: 2	he maketh intercession to God against I,	*2474*
	11: 7	I hath not obtained that which he seeketh	*2474*
	11:25	that blindness in part is happened to I,	*2474*
	11:26	And so all I shall be saved: as it is written,	*2474*
1Co	10:18	Behold I after the flesh: are not they which	*2474*
2Co	3: 7	that the children of I could not stedfastly	*2474*
	3:13	that the children of I could not stedfastly	*2474*
Gal	6:16	and mercy, and upon the I of God.	*2474*
Eph	2:12	being aliens from the commonwealth of I,	*2474*
Php	3: 5	of the stock of I, of the tribe of Benjamin,	*2474*
Heb	8: 8	make a new covenant with the house of I	*2474*
	8:10	make with the house of I after those days,	*2474*
	11:22	of the departing of the children of I;	*2474*
Rev	2:14	a stumblingblock before the children of I,	*2474*
	7: 4	of all the tribes of the children of I.	*2474*
	21:12	of the twelve tribes of the children of I:	*2474*

ISRAEL'S (10) [ISRAEL]

Ge	48:13	Ephraim in his right hand toward I left	3478
	48:13	Manasseh in his left hand towards I right	3478
Ex	18: 8	and to the Egyptians for I sake,	3478
Nu	1:20	I eldest son, *by* their generations, after their	3478
	31:30	of the children of I half, thou shalt take one	3478
	31:42	of the children of I half, which Moses	3478
	31:47	Even of the children of I half, Moses took	3478
Dt	21: 8	lay not innocent blood unto thy people of I	3478
2Sa	5:12	exalted his kingdom for his people I sake.	3478
2Ki	3:11	one of the king of I servants answered and	3478

ISRAELITE (4) [ISRAEL]

Nu	25:14	Now the name of the I that was slain,	376+3478
2Sa	17:25	a man's son, whose name *was* Ithra an I,	3481
Jn	1:47	and saith of him, Behold an I indeed,	*2475*
Ro	11: 1	For I also am an I, of the seed of Abraham,	*2475*

ISRAELITES (18) [ISRAEL]

Ex	9: 7	there was not one of the cattle of the I dead.	3478
Lev	23:42	all that are I born shall dwell in booths:	3478
Jos	3:17	all the I passed over on dry *ground,* until all	3478
	8:24	that all the I returned *unto* Ai, and smote it	3478
	13: 6	only divide thou it *by lot* unto the I for an	3478
	13:13	the Maachathites dwell among the I until	3478
Jdg	20:21	destroyed *down* to the ground of the I that	3478
1Sa	2:14	So they did in Shiloh unto all the I that	3478
	13:20	all the I went down *to* the Philistines,	3478
	14:21	even they also *turned* to be with the I that	3478
	25: 1	all the I were gathered together, and	3478
	29: 1	the I pitched by a fountain which *is* in	3478
2Sa	4: 1	were feeble, and all the I were troubled.	3478
2Ki	3:24	the I rose up and smote the Moabites, so	3478
	7:13	the multitude of the I that are consumed:)	3478
1Ch	9: 2	their possessions in their cities *were,* the I,	3478
Ro	9: 4	Who are I; to whom pertaineth	*2475*
2Co	11:22	Are they I? so *am* I. Are they the seed of	*2475*

ISRAELITISH (3) [ISRAEL]

Lev	24:10	the son of an I woman, whose father *was*	3482
	24:10	*this* son of the I *woman* and a man of Israel	3482
	24:11	the I woman's son blasphemed the name *of*	3482

ISSACHAR (43) [ISACHAR]

Ge	30:18	to my husband: and she called his name I.	3485
	35:23	and Levi, and Judah, and I, and Zebulun:	3485
	46:13	the sons of I; Tola, and Phuvah, and Job,	3485
	49:14	I *is* a strong ass couching down between	3485
Ex	1: 3	I, Zebulun, and Benjamin,	3485
Nu	1: 8	Of I; Nethaneel the son of Zuar.	3485
	1:28	Of the children of I, *by* their generations,	3485
	1:29	*even* of the tribe of I, *were* fifty and	3485
	2: 5	pitch next unto him *shall be* the tribe of I:	3485
	2: 5	of Zuar *shall be* captain of the children of I.	3485
	7:18	the son of Zuar, prince of I, did offer:	3485
	10:15	of I *was* Nethaneel the son of Zuar.	3485
	13: 7	Of the tribe of I, Igal the son of Joseph.	3485
	26:23	*Of* the sons of I after their families:	3485
	26:25	These *are* the families of I according to	3485

Nu 34:26 the prince of the tribe of the children of I, 3485
Dt 27:12 Judah, and I, and Joseph, and Benjamin: 3485
33:18 in thy going out; and, I, in thy tents. 3485
Jos 17:10 in Asher on the north, and in I on the east. 3485
17:11 Manasseh had in I and in Asher Beth-shean 3485
19:17 *And* the fourth lot came out to I, for 3485
19:17 for the children of I according to their 3485
19:23 the children of I according to their families, 3485
21: 6 by lot out of the families of the tribe of I, 3485
21:28 out of the tribe of I, Kishon with her 3485
Jdg 5:15 the princes of I *were* with Deborah; 3485
5:15 *were* with Deborah; even I, *and* also Barak: 3485
10: 1 son of Puah, the son of Dodo, a man of I; 3485
1Ki 4:17 Jehoshaphat the son of Paruah, in I: 3485
15:27 of the house of I, conspired against him; 3485
1Ch 2: 1 Simeon, Levi, and Judah, I, and Zebulun, 3485
6:62 their families out of the tribe of I, 3485
6:72 out of the tribe of I; Kedesh with her 3485
7: 1 Now the sons of I *were,* Tola, and Puah, 3485
7: 5 their brethren among all the families of I 3485
12:32 of the children of I, *which were men* that 3485
12:40 *even* unto I and Zebulun and Naphtali, 3485
26: 5 Ammiel the sixth, I the seventh, 3485
27:18 of David: of I, Omri the son of Michael: 3485
2Ch 30:18 of Ephraim, and Manasseh, I, and Zebulun, 3485
Eze 48:25 the east side unto the west side, I a *portion.* 3485
48:26 by the border of I, from the east side unto 3485
48:33 one gate of Simeon, one gate of I, one gate 3485

ISSHIAH (3)
1Ch 24:21 of the sons of Rehabiah, the first *was* I. 3449
24:25 The brother of Michah *was* I: of the sons of 3449
24:25 *was* Isshiah: of the sons of I; Zechariah. 3449

ISSUE (40) [ISSUED, ISSUES]
Ge 48: 6 thy i, which thou begettest after them, 4138
Lev 12: 7 she shall be cleansed from the i of her 4726
15: 2 When any man hath a **running** i out of his 2100
15: 2 of his flesh, *because of* his i he *is* unclean. 2101
15: 3 this shall be his uncleanness in his i: 2101
15: 3 *whether* his flesh run with his i, or his flesh 2101
15: 3 or his flesh be stopped from his i, it *is* his 2101
15: 4 whereon he lieth that hath the i, is unclean: 2100
15: 6 he sat that hath the i shall wash his clothes, 2100
15: 7 of him that hath the i shall wash his clothes, 2100
15: 8 if he that hath the i spit upon him that is 2100
15: 9 rideth upon that hath the i shall be unclean. 2100
15:11 whomsoever he toucheth that hath the i, 2100
15:12 that he toucheth which hath the i, shall be 2100
15:13 when he that hath an i is cleansed of his 2100
15:13 he that hath an issue is cleansed of his i; 2101
15:15 for him before the LORD for his i. 2101
15:19 if a woman have an i, *and* her issue in her 2100
15:19 an issue, *and* her i in her flesh be blood, 2101
15:25 if a woman **have an** i of her blood 2100+2101
15:25 all the days of the i of her uncleanness shall 2101
15:26 i shall be unto her as the bed of her 2101
15:28 if she be cleansed of her i, then she shall 2101
15:30 the LORD for the i of her uncleanness. 2101
15:32 This *is* the law of him that hath an i, and 2100
15:33 of him that hath an i, of the man, and of 2101
22: 4 of Aaron *is* a leper, or hath a **running** i; 2100
Nu 5: 2 every one that hath an i, and whosoever is 2100
2Sa 3:29 from the house of Joab one that **hath an** i, 2100
2Ki 20:18 of thy sons that shall i from thee, 3318
Isa 22:24 the offspring and the i, all vessels of small 6849
39: 7 of thy sons that shall i from thee, 3318
Eze 23:20 and whose i *is like* the issue of horses. 2231
23:20 and whose issue *is like* the i of horses. 2231
47: 8 These waters i **out** toward the east country, 3318
Mt 9:20 which was **diseased with an i of blood** *131*
22:25 and, having no i, left his wife unto his *4690*
Mk 5:25 which had an i of blood twelve years, *4511*
Lk 8:43 And a woman having an i of blood twelve *4511*
8:44 and immediately her i of blood stanched. *4511*

ISSUED (7) [ISSUE]
Jos 8:22 And the other i **out** of the city against them; 3318
Job 38: 8 brake forth, *as if* it had i **out** of the womb? 3318
Eze 47: 1 waters i **out** from under the threshold of 3318
47:12 their waters they i **out** of the sanctuary: 3318
Da 7:10 A fiery stream i and came forth from before 5047
Rev 9:17 and out of their mouths i fire and smoke *1607*
9:18 the brimstone, which i **out** of their mouths. *1607*

ISSUES (2) [ISSUE]
Ps 68:20 unto GOD the Lord *belong* the i from 8444
Pr 4:23 all diligence; for out of it *are* the i of life. 8444

ISUAH (1)
1Ch 7:30 I, and Ishuai, and Beriah, and Serah their 3440

IT (6132) [HOWBEIT, ITSELF] See Index

ITALIAN (1) [ITALY]
Ac 10: 1 a centurion of the band called the I *band,* *2483*

ITALY (5) [ITALIAN]
Ac 18: 2 born in Pontus, lately come from I, with his *2482*
27: 1 it was determined that we should sail into I, *2482*
27: 6 found a ship of Alexandria sailing into I; *2482*
Heb 13:24 and all the saints. They of I salute you. *2482*
13: S Written to the Hebrews from I by Timothy. *2482*

ITCH (1) [ITCHING]
Dt 28:27 and with the scab, and with the i, 2775

ITCHING (1) [ITCH]
2Ti 4: 3 heap to themselves teachers, having i ears; *2833*

ITHAI (1)
1Ch 11:31 I the son of Ribai of Gibeah, that pertained 863

ITHAMAR (21)
Ex 6:23 bare him Nadab, and Abihu, Eleazar, and I. 385
28: 1 Nadab and Abihu, Eleazar and I, 385
38:21 by the hand of I, son to Aaron the priest. 385
Lev 10: 6 unto Eleazar and unto I his sons, 385
10:12 and unto I his sons that were left, 385
10:16 I the sons of Aaron which were left *alive,* 385
Nu 3: 2 the firstborn, and Abihu, Eleazar, and I. 385
3: 4 I ministered in the priest's office in the sight 385
4:28 their charge *shall be* under the hand of I 385
4:33 under the hand of I the son of Aaron 385
7: 8 under the hand of I the son of Aaron 385
26:60 was born Nadab, and Abihu, Eleazar, and I. 385
1Ch 6: 3 of Aaron; Nadab, and Abihu, Eleazar, and I. 385
24: 1 of Aaron; Nadab, and Abihu, Eleazar, and I. 385
24: 2 Eleazar and I executed the priest's office. 385
24: 3 of Eleazar, and Ahimelech of the sons of I, 385
24: 4 of the sons of Eleazar than of the sons of I; 385
24: 4 eight among the sons of I according to 385
24: 5 of the sons of Eleazar, and of the sons of I. 385
24: 6 being taken for Eleazar, and *one* taken for I. 385
Ezr 8: 2 of the sons of I; Daniel: of the sons of 385

ITHIEL (3)
Ne 11: 7 of Maaseiah, the son of I, the son of Jesaiah. 384
Pr 30: 1 the man spake unto I, even unto Ithiel and 384
30: 1 man spake unto Ithiel, even unto I and Ucal. 384

ITHLAH See JETHLAH

ITHMAH (1)
1Ch 11:46 the sons of Elnaam, and I the Moabite, 3495

ITHNAN (1)
Jos 15:23 And Kedesh, and Hazor, and I, 3497

ITHRA (1)
2Sa 17:25 man's son, whose name *was* I an Israelite, 3501

ITHRAN (3)
Ge 36:26 Hemdan, and Eshban, and I, and Cheran. 3506
1Ch 1:41 Amram, and Eshban, and I, and Cheran. 3506
7:37 Shamma, and Shilshah, and I, and Beera. 3506

ITHREAM (2)
2Sa 3: 5 the sixth, I, by Eglah David's wife. 3507
1Ch 3: 3 of Abital: the sixth, I by Eglah his wife. 3507

ITHRITE (4)
2Sa 23:38 Ira an I, Gareb an Ithrite, 3505
23:38 Ira an Ithrite, Gareb an I, 3505
1Ch 11:40 Ira the I, Gareb the Ithrite, 3505
11:40 Ira the Ithrite, Gareb the I, 3505

ITHRITES (1)
1Ch 2:53 the I, and the Puhites, and the Shumathites, 3505

ITSELF (50) [IT, SELF] See Index

ITTAH-KAZIN (1)
Jos 19:13 to I, and goeth out *to* Remmon-methoar *to* 6278

ITTAI (8)
2Sa 15:19 said the king to I the Gittite, Wherefore 863
15:21 I answered the king, and said, *As* 863
15:22 David said to I, Go and pass over. And Ittai 863
15:22 I the Gittite passed over, and all his men, 863
18: 2 a third part under the hand of I the Gittite. 863
18: 5 king commanded Joab and Abishai and I, 863
18:12 the king charged thee and Abishai and I, 863
23:29 I the son of Ribai out of Gibeah of 863

ITUREA (1)
Lk 3: 1 and his brother Philip tetrarch of I and *2484*

IVAH (3)
2Ki 18:34 *are* the gods of Sepharvaim, Hena, and I? 5755
19:13 of the city of Sepharvaim, *of* Hena, and I? 5755
Isa 37:13 of the city of Sepharvaim, Hena, and I? 5755

IVORY (13)
1Ki 10:18 Moreover the king made a great throne of i, 8127
10:22 and silver, i, and apes, and peacocks. 8143
22:39 the i house which he made, and all 8127
2Ch 9:17 Moreover the king made a great throne of i, 8127
9:21 and silver, i, and apes, and peacocks. 8143
Ps 45: 8 and aloes, *and* cassia, out of the i palaces, 8127
SS 5:14 his belly *is as* bright i overlaid *with* 8127
7: 4 Thy neck *is* as a tower of i; thine eyes *like* 8127
Eze 27: 6 the Ashurites have made thy benches *of* i, 8127
27:15 they brought thee *for* a present horns of i 8127
Am 3:15 the houses of i shall perish, and the great 8127
6: 4 That lie upon beds of i, and 8127
Rev 18:12 and all *manner* vessels of i, and all *manner* *1661*

IVVAH See IVAH

IYE ABARIM See IJE-ABARIM

IZEHAR (1) [IZEHARITES]
Nu 3:19 Amram, and I, Hebron, and Uzziel. 3324

IZEHARITES (1) [IZEHAR]
Nu 3:27 the family of the I, and the family of 3325

IZHAR (8) [IZHARITES]
Ex 6:18 Amram, and I, and Hebron, and Uzziel: 3324
6:21 the sons of I; Korah, and Nepheg, and 3324
Nu 16: 1 Now Korah, the son of I, the son of 3324
1Ch 6: 2 Amram, and I, and Hebron, and Uzziel. 3324
6:18 and I, and Hebron, and Uzziel. 3324
6:38 The son of I, the son of Kohath, the son of 3324
23:12 Amram, I, Hebron, and Uzziel, four. 3324
23:18 *Of* the sons of I; Shelomith the chief. 3324

IZHARITES (3) [IZHAR]
1Ch 24:22 Of the I; Shelomoth: of the sons of 3325
26:23 *and* the I, the Hebronites, *and* 3325
26:29 Of the I, Chenaniah and his sons *were* for 3325

IZLIAH See JEZLIAH

IZRAHIAH (2)
1Ch 7: 3 the sons of Uzzi; I: and the sons of 3156
7: 3 the sons of I; Michael, and Obadiah, and 3156

IZRAHITE (1)
1Ch 27: 8 for the fifth month *was* Shamhuth the I: 3155

IZRI (1)
1Ch 25:11 The fourth to I, *he,* his sons, and 3339

IZZIAH See JEZIAH

J

JAAKAN (1) [BENE-JAAKAN]
Dt 10: 6 Beeroth of the children of J *to* Mosera: 3292

JAAKOBAH (1)
1Ch 4:36 J, and Jeshohaiah, and Asaiah, and Adiel, 3291

JAALA (1) [JAALAH]
Ne 7:58 The children of J, the children of Darkon, 3279

JAALAH (1) [JAALA]
Ezr 2:56 The children of J, the children of Darkon, 3279

JAALAM (4)
Ge 36: 5 Aholibamah bare Jeush, and J, and Korah: 3281
36:14 she bare to Esau Jeush, and J, and Korah. 3281
36:18 duke Jeush, duke J, duke Korah: 3281
1Ch 1:35 Reuel, and Jeush, and J, and Korah. 3281

JAANAI (1)
1Ch 5:12 the next, and J, and Shaphat in Bashan. 3285

JAARE-OREGIM (1)
2Sa 21:19 where Elhanan the son of J, 3296

JAARESHIAH See JARESIAH

JAASAU (1)
Ezr 10:37 Mattaniah, Mattenai, and J, 3299

JAASIEL (1)
1Ch 27:21 of Benjamin, J the son of Abner: 3300

JAASU See JAASAU

JAAZANIAH (4)
2Ki 25:23 J the son of a Maachathite, they and 2970
Jer 35: 3 I took J the son of Jeremiah, the son of 2970
Eze 8:11 in the midst of them stood J the son of 2970
11: 1 among whom I saw J the son of Azur, and 2970

JAAZER (2)
Nu 21:32 Moses sent to spy out J, and they took 3270
32:35 And Atroth, Shophan, and J, and Jogbehah, 3270

JAAZIAH (2)
1Ch 24:26 *were* Mahli and Mushi: the sons of J; Beno. 3269
24:27 The sons of Merari by J; Beno, and 3269

JAAZIEL (1)
1Ch 15:18 J, and Shemiramoth, and Jehiel, and Unni, 3268

JABAL (1)
Ge 4:20 Adah bare J: he was the father of such as 2989

JABBOK (7)
Ge 32:22 his eleven sons, and passed over the ford J. 2999
Nu 21:24 possessed his land from Arnon unto J, 2999
Dt 2:37 *nor unto* any place of the river J, nor *unto* 2999
3:16 and the border, even unto the river J, 2999
Jos 12: 2 and *from* half Gilead, even unto the river J, 2999
Jdg 11:13 from Arnon even unto J, and unto Jordan: 2999
11:22 from Arnon even unto J, and from 2999

JABESH (12) [JABESH-GILEAD]
1Sa 11: 1 all the men of J said unto Nahash, Make a 3003
11: 3 the elders of J said unto him, Give us seven 3003
11: 5 they told him the tidings of the men of J. 3003
11: 9 and shewed *it* to the men of J; 3003
11:10 Therefore the men of J said, To morrow we 3003
31:12 and came to J, and burnt them there. 3003
31:13 buried *them* under a tree at J, and 3003
2Ki 15:10 Shallum the son of J conspired against him, 3003
15:13 Shallum the son of J *began* to reign in 3003
15:14 smote Shallum the son of J in Samaria, and 3003
1Ch 10:12 brought them to J, and buried their bones 3003
10:12 buried their bones under the oak in J, and 3003

JABESH-GILEAD (12) [GILEAD, JABESH]
Jdg 21: 8 there came none to the camp from J to 3003
21: 9 *there were* none of the inhabitants of J 3003
21:10 smite the inhabitants of J with the edge of 3003
21:12 they found among the inhabitants of J four 3003
21:14 they had saved alive of the women of J: 3003
1Sa 11: 1 came up, and encamped against J: 3003
11: 9 Thus shall ye say unto the men of J, 3003
31:11 when the inhabitants of J heard of that 3003
2Sa 2: 4 *That* the men of J *were they* that buried 3003
2: 5 David sent messengers unto the men of J, 3003
21:12 of Jonathan his son from the men of J, 3003

J

1Ch 10:11 when all J heard all that the Philistines had 3003

JABEZ (4)
1Ch 2:55 the families of the scribes which dwelt at J; 3258
4: 9 J was more honourable than his brethren: 3258
4: 9 his mother called his name J, saying, 3258
4:10 J called on the God of Israel, saying, 3258

JABIN (7) [JABIN'S]
Jos 11: 1 when J king of Hazor had heard *those* 2985
Jdg 4: 2 the LORD sold them into the hand of J 2985
4:17 for *there was* peace between J the king of 2985
4:23 So God subdued on that day J the king of 2985
4:24 prevailed against J the king of Canaan, 2985
4:24 until they had destroyed J king of Canaan. 2985
Ps 83: 9 as *to* Sisera, as *to* J, at the brook of Kison: 2985

JABIN'S (1) [JABIN]
Jdg 4: 7 the captain of J army, with his chariots and 2985

JABNEEL (2)
Jos 15:11 *to* mount Baalah, and went out *unto* J; 2995
19:33 and Adami, Nekeb, and J, unto Lakum; 2995

JABNEH (1)
2Ch 26: 6 the wall of J, and the wall of Ashdod, and 2996

JACAN See JACHAN

JACHAN (1)
1Ch 5:13 and Jorai, and J, and Zia, and Heber, seven. 3275

JACHIN (8) [JACHINITES]
Ge 46:10 J, and Zohar, and Shaul the son of a 3199
Ex 6:15 J, and Zohar, and Shaul the son of a 3199
Nu 26:12 of J, the family of the Jachinites: 3199
1Ki 7:21 right pillar, and called the name thereof J: 3199
1Ch 9:10 of the priests; Jedaiah, and Jehoiarib, and J, 3199
24:17 The one and twentieth to J, the two and 3199
2Ch 3:17 called the name of *that on* the right hand J, 3199
Ne 11:10 Of the priests: Jedaiah the son of Joiarib, J, 3199

JACHINITES (1) [JACHIN]
Nu 26:12 the Jaminites: of Jachin, the family of the J: 3200

JACINTH (2)
Rev 9:17 breastplates of fire, and of j, and brimstone: *5191*
21:20 the eleventh, a j; the twelfth, an amethyst. *5192*

JACKAL; JACKALS See DRAGON; DRAGONS; FOXES; MONSTERS

JACOB (358) [ISRAEL, JACOB'S]
Ge 25:26 on Esau's heel; and his name was called J: 3290
25:27 and J *was* a plain man, dwelling in tents. 3290
25:28 did eat of *his* venison: but Rebekah loved J. 3290
25:29 J sod pottage: and Esau came from 3290
25:30 Esau said to J, Feed me, I pray thee, 3290
25:31 And J said, Sell me *this* day thy birthright. 3290
25:33 J said, Swear to me *this* day; and he sware 3290
25:33 to him: and he sold his birthright unto J. 3290
25:34 J gave Esau bread and pottage of lentiles; 3290
27: 6 Rebekah spake unto J her son, saying, 3290
27:11 J said to Rebekah his mother, Behold, 3290
27:15 and put them upon J her younger son: 3290
27:17 had prepared, into the hand of her son J. 3290
27:19 J said unto his father, I *am* Esau thy 3290
27:21 Isaac said unto J, Come near, I pray thee, 3290
27:22 J went near unto Isaac his father; and 3290
27:30 as Isaac had made an end of blessing J, 3290
27:30 J was yet scarce gone out from 3290
27:36 he said, Is not he rightly named J? for he 3290
27:41 Esau hated J because of the blessing 3290
27:41 are at hand; then will I slay my brother J. 3290
27:42 she sent and called J her younger son, and 3290
27:46 if J take a wife of the daughters of Heth, 3290
28: 1 Isaac called J, and blessed him, and 3290
28: 5 Isaac sent away J: and he went to 3290
28: 6 When Esau saw that Isaac had blessed J, 3290
28: 7 that J obeyed his father and his mother, 3290
28:10 J went out from Beer-sheba, and 3290
28:16 J awaked out of his sleep, and he said, 3290
28:18 J rose up early in the morning, and took 3290
28:20 J vowed a vow, saying, If God will be with 3290
29: 1 J went on his journey, and came into 3290
29: 4 J said unto them, My brethren, whence *be* 3290
29:10 when J saw Rachel the daughter of Laban 3290
29:10 that J went near, and rolled the stone from 3290
29:11 J kissed Rachel, and lifted up his voice, 3290
29:12 J told Rachel that he *was* her father's 3290
29:13 when Laban heard the tidings of J his 3290
29:15 Laban said unto J, Because thou *art* my 3290
29:18 J loved Rachel; and said, I will serve thee 3290
29:20 J served seven years for Rachel; and 3290
29:21 J said unto Laban, Give *me* my wife, 3290
29:28 J did so, and fulfilled her week: and 3290
30: 1 when Rachel saw that she bare J no 3290
30: 1 said unto J, Give me children, or else I die. 3290
30: 4 handmaid to wife: and J went in unto her. 3290
30: 5 And Bilhah conceived, and bare J a son. 3290
30: 7 conceived again, and bare J a second son. 3290
30: 9 Zilpah her maid, and gave her J to wife. 3290
30:10 And Zilpah Leah's maid bare J a son. 3290
30:12 Zilpah Leah's maid bare J a second son. 3290
30:16 J came out of the field in the evening, and 3290
30:17 and she conceived, and bare J the fifth son. 3290
30:19 conceived again, and bare J the sixth son. 3290
30:25 that J said unto Laban, Send me away, 3290
30:31 J said, Thou shalt not give me any thing: 3290
30:36 three days' journey betwixt himself and J: 3290
30:36 and J fed the rest of Laban's flocks. 3290
30:37 J took him rods of green poplar, and of 3290
30:40 J did separate the lambs, and set the faces 3290
30:41 that J laid the rods before the eyes of 3290
31: 1 J hath taken away all that *was* our father's; 3290
31: 2 J beheld the countenance of Laban, and 3290
31: 3 the LORD said unto J, Return unto 3290
31: 4 J sent and called Rachel and Leah to 3290
31:11 God spake unto me in a dream, *saying,* J: 3290
31:17 J rose up, and set his sons and his wives 3290
31:20 J stale away unawares to Laban the Syrian, 3290
31:22 it was told Laban on the third day that J 3290
31:24 Take heed that thou speak not to J either 3290
31:25 Laban overtook J. Now Jacob had pitched 3290
31:25 Now J had pitched his tent in the mount: 3290
31:26 Laban said to J, What hast thou done, 3290
31:29 Take thou heed that thou speak not to J 3290
31:31 J answered and said to Laban, Because I 3290
31:32 For J knew not that Rachel had stolen 3290
31:36 J was wroth, and chode with Laban: and 3290
31:36 J answered and said to Laban, What *is* my 3290
31:43 Laban answered and said unto J, *These* 3290
31:45 J took a stone, and set it up *for* a pillar. 3290
31:46 J said unto his brethren, Gather stones; 3290
31:47 it Jegar-sahadutha: but J called it Galeed. 3290
31:51 Laban said to J, Behold this heap, 3290
31:53 And J sware by the fear of his father Isaac. 3290
31:54 J offered sacrifice upon the mount, and 3290
32: 1 J went on his way, and the angels of God 3290
32: 2 when J saw them, he said, This *is* God's 3290
32: 3 J sent messengers before him to Esau his 3290
32: 4 Thy servant J saith thus, I have sojourned 3290
32: 6 the messengers returned to J, saying, 3290
32: 7 J was greatly afraid and distressed: and 3290
32: 9 J said, O God of my father Abraham, and 3290
32:20 Behold, thy servant J *is* behind us. 3290
32:24 J was left alone; and there wrestled a man 3290
32:27 What *is* thy name? And he said, J. 3290
32:28 Thy name shall be called no more J, but 3290
32:29 J asked *him,* and said, Tell *me,* I pray thee, 3290
32:30 J called the name of the place Peniel: for I 3290
33: 1 J lifted up his eyes, and looked, and 3290
33:10 J said, Nay, I pray thee, if now I have 3290
33:17 J journeyed to Succoth, and built him a 3290
33:18 J came to Shalem, a city of Shechem, 3290
34: 1 daughter of Leah, which she bare unto J, 3290
34: 3 his soul clave unto Dinah the daughter of J, 3290
34: 5 J heard that he had defiled Dinah his 3290
34: 5 and J held his peace until they were come. 3290
34: 6 went out unto J to commune with him. 3290
34: 7 the sons of J came out of the field when 3290
34:13 the sons of J answered Shechem and 3290
34:25 that two of the sons of J, Simeon and Levi, 3290
34:27 The sons of J came upon the slain, and 3290
34:30 J said to Simeon and Levi, Ye have 3290
35: 1 God said unto J, Arise, go up to Beth-el, 3290
35: 2 J said unto his household, and to all that 3290
35: 4 they gave unto J all the strange gods which 3290
35: 4 J hid them under the oak which *was* by 3290
35: 5 and they did not pursue after the sons of J. 3290

Ge 35: 6 So J came to Luz, which *is* in the land of 3290
35: 9 God appeared unto J again, when he came 3290
35:10 God said unto him, Thy name *is* J: 3290
35:10 thy name shall not be called any more J, 3290
35:14 J set up a pillar in the place where he 3290
35:15 J called the name of the place where God 3290
35:20 J set a pillar upon her grave: that *is* 3290
35:22 Israel heard *it.* Now the sons of J were 3290
35:26 these *are* the sons of J, which were born to 3290
35:27 J came unto Isaac his father unto Mamre, 3290
35:29 and his sons Esau and J buried him. 3290
36: 6 the country from the face of his brother J. 3290
37: 1 J dwelt in the land wherein his father was a 3290
37: 2 These *are* the generations of J. Joseph, 3290
37:34 J rent his clothes, and put sackcloth upon 3290
42: 1 Now when J saw that there was corn in 3290
42: 1 J said unto his sons, Why do ye look one 3290
42: 4 J sent not with his brethren; 3290
42:29 they came unto J their father unto the land 3290
42:36 J their father said unto them, Me have ye 3290
45:25 came *into* the land of Canaan unto J their 3290
45:27 the spirit of J their father revived: 3290
46: 2 the visions of the night, and said, J, Jacob. 3290
46: 2 the visions of the night, and said, Jacob, J. 3290
46: 5 J rose up from Beer-sheba: and the sons of 3290
46: 5 the sons of Israel carried J their father, and 3290
46: 6 into Egypt, J, and all his seed with him: 3290
46: 8 which came into Egypt, J and his sons: 3290
46:15 which she bare unto J in Padan-aram, 3290
46:18 these she bare unto J, *even* sixteen souls. 3290
46:22 the sons of Rachel, which were born to J: 3290
46:25 his daughter, and she bare these unto J: 3290
46:26 All the souls that came with J into Egypt, 3290
46:27 all the souls of the house of J, which came 3290
47: 7 Joseph brought in J his father, and set him 3290
47: 7 him before Pharaoh: and J blessed Pharaoh. 3290
47: 8 Pharaoh said unto J, How old *art* thou? 3290
47: 9 J said unto Pharaoh, The days of the years 3290
47:10 J blessed Pharaoh, and went out from 3290
47:28 J lived in the land of Egypt seventeen 3290
47:28 so the whole age of J was an hundred forty 3290
48: 2 *one* told J, and said, Behold, thy son Joseph 3290
48: 3 J said unto Joseph, God Almighty appeared 3290
49: 1 J called unto his sons, and said, 3290
49: 2 yourselves together, and hear, ye sons of J; 3290
49: 7 I will divide them in J, and scatter them in 3290
49:24 strong by the hands of the mighty *God* of J; 3290
49:33 when J had made an end of commanding 3290
50:24 he sware to Abraham, to Isaac, and to J. 3290
Ex 1: 1 every man and his household came with J. 3290
1: 5 all the souls that came *out of* the loins of J 3290
2:24 with Abraham, with Isaac, and with J. 3290
3: 6 the God of Isaac, and the God of J. 3290
3:15 the God of Isaac, and the God of J, 3290
3:16 of Isaac, and of J, appeared unto me, 3290
4: 5 the God of Isaac, and the God of J, 3290
6: 3 unto Isaac, and unto J, by *the name of* God 3290
6: 8 to give it to Abraham, to Isaac, and to J; 3290
19: 3 Thus shalt thou say to the house of J, and 3290
33: 1 to Isaac, and to J, saying, Unto thy seed 3290
Lev 26:42 will I remember my covenant with J, and 3290
Nu 23: 7 curse me J, and come, defy Israel. 3290
23:10 Who can count the dust of J, and 3290
23:21 He hath not beheld iniquity in J, 3290
23:23 Surely *there is* no enchantment against J, 3290
23:23 according to *this* time it shall be said of J 3290
24: 5 O J, *and* thy tabernacles, O Israel! 3290
24:17 there shall come a Star out of J, and 3290
24:19 Out of J shall come *he* that shall have 3290
32:11 unto Abraham, unto Isaac, and unto J; 3290
Dt 1: 8 Abraham, Isaac, and J, to give unto them 3290
6:10 to Abraham, to Isaac, and to J, to give thee 3290
9: 5 unto thy fathers, Abraham, Isaac, and J. 3290
9:27 thy servants, Abraham, Isaac, and J; 3290
29:13 thy fathers, to Abraham, to Isaac, and to J. 3290
30:20 to Abraham, to Isaac, and to J, to give 3290
32: 9 *is* his people; J *is* the lot of his inheritance. 3290
33: 4 the inheritance of the congregation of J. 3290
33:10 They shall teach J thy judgments, and 3290
33:28 the fountain of J *shall be* upon a land of 3290
34: 4 unto Isaac, and unto J, saying, I will give it 3290
Jos 24: 4 I gave unto Isaac J and Esau: and I gave 3290
24: 4 J and his children went down *into* Egypt. 3290
24:32 in a parcel of ground which J bought of 3290
1Sa 12: 8 When J was come *into* Egypt, and 3290
2Sa 23: 1 the anointed of the God of J, and the sweet 3290
1Ki 18:31 to the number of the tribes of the sons of J, 3290
2Ki 13:23 Isaac, and J, and would not destroy them, 3290
17:34 the LORD commanded the children of J, 3290
1Ch 16:13 ye children of J, his chosen *ones.* 3290
16:17 hath confirmed the same to J for a law, 3290
Ps 14: 7 J shall rejoice, *and* Israel shall be glad. 3290
20: 1 the name of the God of J defend thee; 3290
22:23 all ye the seed of J, glorify him; and 3290
24: 6 them that seek him, that seek thy face, O J. 3290
44: 4 O God: command deliverances for J. 3290
46: 7 hosts *is* with us; the God of J *is* our refuge. 3290
46:11 hosts *is* with us; the God of J *is* our refuge. 3290
47: 4 for us, the excellency of J whom he loved. 3290
53: 6 J shall rejoice, *and* Israel shall be glad. 3290
59:13 let them know that God ruleth in J unto 3290
75: 9 for ever; I will sing *praises* to the God of J. 3290
76: 6 At thy rebuke, O God of J, both the chariot 3290
77:15 thy people, the sons of J and Joseph. 3290
78: 5 For he established a testimony in J, and 3290
78:21 so a fire was kindled against J, and 3290
78:71 young he brought him to feed J his people, 3290
79: 7 For they have devoured J, and laid waste 3290
81: 1 make a joyful noise unto the God of J. 3290
81: 4 statute for Israel, *and* a law of the God of J. 3290
84: 8 my prayer: give ear, O God of J. Selah. 3290
85: 1 thou hast brought back the captivity of J. 3290
87: 2 of Zion more than all the dwellings of J. 3290
94: 7 neither shall the God of J regard *it.* 3290
99: 4 executest judgment and righteousness in J. 3290
105: 6 his servant, ye children of J, his chosen. 3290
105:10 confirmed the same unto J for a law, *and* 3290
105:23 and J sojourned in the land of Ham. 3290
114: 1 the house of J from a people of strange 3290
114: 7 of the Lord, at the presence of the God of J; 3290
132: 2 *and* vowed unto the mighty *God* of J; 3290
132: 5 a habitation for the mighty *God* of J. 3290
135: 4 For the LORD hath chosen J unto 3290
146: 5 Happy *is he* that *hath* the God of J for his 3290
147:19 He sheweth his word unto J, his statutes 3290
Isa 2: 3 the LORD, to the house of the God of J; 3290
2: 5 O house of J, come ye, and let us walk in 3290
2: 6 hast forsaken thy people the house of J, 3290
8:17 that hideth his face from the house of J, 3290
9: 8 The Lord sent a word into J, and it hath 3290
10:20 and such as are escaped of the house of J, 3290
10:21 *even* the remnant of J, unto the mighty 3290
14: 1 For the LORD will have mercy on J, and 3290
14: 1 and they shall cleave to the house of J. 3290
17: 4 *that* the glory of J shall be made thin, and 3290
27: 6 He shall cause them that come of J to take 3290
27: 9 shall the iniquity of J be purged; 3290
29:22 concerning the house of J, 3290
29:22 of Jacob, J shall not now be ashamed, 3290
29:23 sanctify the Holy One of J, and shall fear 3290
40:27 sayest thou, O J, and speakest, O Israel, 3290
41: 8 *art* my servant, J whom I have chosen, 3290
41:14 thou worm J, *and* ye men of Israel; 3290
41:21 your strong *reasons,* saith the King of J. 3290
42:24 Who gave J for a spoil, and Israel to 3290
43: 1 O J, and he that formed thee, O Israel, 3290
43:22 thou hast not called upon me, O J; but 3290
43:28 have given J to the curse, and Israel to 3290
44: 1 Yet now hear, O J my servant; and Israel, 3290
44: 2 Fear not, O J, my servant; and 3290
44: 5 another shall call *himself* by the name of J; 3290
44:21 Remember these, O J and Israel; for thou 3290
44:23 for the LORD hath redeemed J, and 3290
45: 4 For J my servant's sake, and Israel mine 3290
45:19 I said not unto the seed of J, Seek ye me in 3290
46: 3 O house of J, and all the remnant of 3290
48: 1 Hear ye this, O house of J, which are called 3290
48:12 unto me, O J, and Israel my called; 3290
48:20 The LORD hath redeemed his servant J. 3290
49: 5 to bring J again to him, Though Israel be 3290
49: 6 be my servant to raise up the tribes of J, 3290
49:26 and thy redeemer, the mighty One of J. 3290
58: 1 and the house of J their sins. 3290
58:14 feed thee with the heritage of J thy father: 3290
59:20 unto them that turn from transgression in J, 3290
60:16 and thy redeemer, the mighty One of J. 3290
65: 9 I will bring forth a seed out of J, and out of 3290
Jer 2: 4 O house of J, and all the families of 3290

Jer 5:20 Declare this in the house of J, and 3290
10:16 The portion of J *is* not like them: for he *is* 3290
10:25 for they have eaten up J, and 3290
30:10 thou not, O my servant J, saith the LORD; 3290
30:10 J shall return, and shall be in rest, and 3290
31: 7 Sing with gladness for J, and shout among 3290
31:11 For the LORD hath redeemed J, and 3290
33:26 will I cast away the seed of J, and 3290
33:26 over the seed of Abraham, Isaac, and J: 3290
46:27 O my servant J, and be not dismayed, 3290
46:27 J shall return, and be in rest and at ease, 3290
46:28 Fear thou not, O J my servant, saith 3290
51:19 The portion of J *is* not like them; for he *is* 3290
La 1:17 the LORD hath commanded concerning J, 3290
2: 2 hath swallowed up all the habitations of J, 3290
2: 3 he burned against J like a flaming fire, 3290
Eze 20: 5 mine hand unto the seed of the house of J, 3290
28:25 their land that I have given to my servant J. 3290
37:25 land that I have given unto J my servant, 3290
39:25 Now will I bring again the captivity of J, 3290
Hos 10:11 shall plow, *and* J shall break his clods. 3290
12: 2 and *will* punish J according to his ways; 3290
12:12 J fled *into* the country of Syria, and 3290
Am 3:13 Hear ye, and testify in the house of J, 3290
6: 8 I abhor the excellency of J, and hate his 3290
7: 2 *by* whom shall J arise? for he *is* small. 3290
7: 5 *by* whom shall J arise? for he *is* small. 3290
8: 7 LORD hath sworn by the excellency of J, 3290
9: 8 I will not utterly destroy the house of J, 3290
Ob 1:10 For *thy* violence against thy brother J 3290
1:17 the house of J shall possess their 3290
1:18 the house of J shall be a fire, and the house 3290
Mic 1: 5 For the transgression of J *is* all this, and 3290
1: 5 What *is* the transgression of J? *is it* not 3290
2: 7 O *thou that art* named the house of J, is 3290
2:12 I will surely assemble, O J, all of thee; 3290
3: 1 O heads of J, and ye princes of the house of 3290
3: 8 to declare unto J his transgression, and 3290
3: 9 ye heads of the house of J, and princes of 3290
4: 2 and to the house of the God of J; 3290
5: 7 the remnant of J shall be in the midst of 3290
5: 8 the remnant of J shall be among 3290
7:20 Thou wilt perform the truth to J, *and* 3290
Na 2: 2 hath turned *away* the excellency of J, 3290
Mal 1: 2 saith the LORD: yet I loved J, 3290
2:12 out of the tabernacles of J, and him that 3290
3: 6 therefore ye sons of J are not consumed. 3290
Mt 1: 2 and Isaac begat J; and Jacob begat Judas *2384*
1: 2 and J begat Judas and his brethren; *2384*
1:15 begat Matthan; and Matthan begat J; *2384*
1:16 And J begat Joseph the husband of Mary, *2384*
8:11 and Isaac, and J, in the kingdom of heaven. *2384*
22:32 and the God of Isaac, and the God of J? *2384*
Mk 12:26 and the God of Isaac, and the God of J? *2384*
Lk 1:33 And he shall reign over the house of J for *2384*
3:34 Which was *the son* of J, which was *the son* *2384*
13:28 and Isaac, and J, and all the prophets, in *2384*
20:37 and the God of Isaac, and the God of J. *2384*
Jn 4: 5 near to the parcel of ground that J gave to *2384*
4:12 Art thou greater than our father J, *2384*
Ac 3:13 God of Abraham, and of Isaac, and of J, *2384*
7: 8 and Isaac *begat* J; and Jacob *begat* *2384*
7: 8 and J *begat* the twelve patriarchs. *2384*
7:12 But when J heard that there was corn in *2384*
7:14 and called his father J to *him,* and all his *2384*
7:15 So J went down into Egypt, and died, he, *2384*
7:32 and the God of Isaac, and the God of J. *2384*
7:46 to find a tabernacle for the God of J. *2384*
Ro 9:13 As it is written, J have I loved, *2384*
11:26 and shall turn away ungodliness from J: *2384*
Heb 11: 9 dwelling in tabernacles with Isaac and J, *2384*
11:20 By faith Isaac blessed J and Esau *2384*
11:21 By faith J, when he was a dying, *2384*

JACOB'S (19) [JACOB]
Ge 27:22 The voice *is* J voice, but the hands *are* 3290
28: 5 brother of Rebekah, J and Esau's mother. 3290
30: 2 J anger was kindled against Rachel: and 3290
30:42 feebler were Laban's, and the stronger J. 3290
31:33 Laban went into J tent, and into Leah's 3290
32:18 thou shalt say, *They be* thy servant J; it *is* a 3290
32:25 the hollow of J thigh was out of joint, as he 3290
32:32 he touched the hollow of J thigh in 3290
34: 7 folly in Israel in lying with J daughter; 3290
34:19 because he had delight in J daughter: 3290
35:23 J firstborn, and Simeon, and Levi, and 3290
45:26 *J* heart fainted, for he believed them not. NIH
46: 8 Jacob and his sons: Reuben, J firstborn. 3290
46:19 The sons of Rachel J wife; Joseph, and 3290
46:26 out of his loins, besides J sons' wives, 3290
Jer 30: 7 it *is* even the time of J trouble; but he shall 3290
30:18 I *will* bring again the captivity of J tents, 3290
Mal 1: 2 *was* not Esau J brother? saith 3290+3807.1
Jn 4: 6 Now J well was there. Jesus therefore, *2384*

JADA (2)
1Ch 2:28 the sons of Onam were, Shammai, and J. 3047
2:32 the sons of J the brother of Shammai; 3047

JADAU (1)
Ezr 10:43 Zabad, Zebina, J, and Joel, Benaiah. 3035

JADDAI See JADAU

JADDUA (3)
Ne 10:21 Meshezabeel, Zadok, J, 3037
12:11 begat Jonathan, and Jonathan begat J. 3037
12:22 Joiada, and Johanan, and J, *were* recorded 3037

JADON (1)
Ne 3: 7 J the Meronothite, the men of Gibeon, and 3036

JAEL (6)
Jdg 4:17 the tent of J the wife of Heber the Kenite: 3278
4:18 J went out to meet Sisera, and said unto 3278
4:21 J Heber's wife took a nail of the tent, and 3278
4:22 J came out to meet him, and said unto him, 3278
5: 6 in the days of J, the highways were 3278
5:24 Blessed above women shall J the wife of 3278

JAGUR (1)
Jos 15:21 southward were Kabzeel, and Eder, and J, 3017

JAH (1) [LORD*]
Ps 68: 4 that rideth upon the heavens by his name J, 3050

JAHATH (8)
1Ch 4: 2 Reaiah the son of Shobal begat J; and 3189
4: 2 and J begat Ahumai, and Lahad. 3189
6:20 Libni his son, J his son, Zimmah his son, 3189
6:43 The son of J, the son of Gershom, the son 3189
23:10 the sons of Shimei *were,* J, Zina, and 3189
23:11 J was the chief, and Zizah the second: but 3189
24:22 Shelomoth: of the sons of Shelomoth; J. 3189
2Ch 34:12 the overseers of them *were* J and Obadiah, 3189

JAHAZ (5)
Nu 21:23 and he came *to* J, and fought against Israel. 3096
Dt 2:32 he and all his people, to fight *at* J. 3096
Jdg 11:20 and pitched in J, and fought against Israel. 3096
Isa 15: 4 their voice shall be heard *even* unto J: 3096
Jer 48:34 *and even* unto J, have they uttered their 3096

JAHAZAH (3)
Jos 13:18 And J, and Kedemoth, and Mephaath, 3096
21:36 with her suburbs, and J with her suburbs, 3096
Jer 48:21 and upon J, and upon Mephaath, 3096

JAHAZIAH (1)
Ezr 10:15 J the son of Tikvah were employed about 3167

JAHAZIEL (6)
1Ch 12: 4 J, and Johanan, and Josabad 3166
16: 6 J the priests with trumpets continually 3166
23:19 J the third, and Jekameam the fourth. 3166
24:23 J the third, Jekameam the fourth. 3166
2Ch 20:14 upon J the son of Zechariah, the son of 3166
Ezr 8: 5 the son of J, and with him three hundred 3166

JAHDAI (1)
1Ch 2:47 the sons of J; Regem, and Jotham, and 3056

JAHDIEL (1)
1Ch 5:24 Azriel, and Jeremiah, and Hodaviah, and J, 3164

JAHDO (1)
1Ch 5:14 of Jeshishai, the son of J, the son of Buz; 3163

JAHLEEL (2) [JAHLEELITES]
Ge 46:14 sons of Zebulun; Sered, and Elon, and J. 3177

Nu 26:26 of J, the family of the Jahleelites. 3177

JAHLEELITES (1) [JAHLEEL]
Nu 26:26 the Elonites: of Jahleel, the family of the J. 3178

JAHMAI (1)
1Ch 7: 2 and Jeriel, and J, and Jibsam, and Shemuel, 3181

JAHZAH (1)
1Ch 6:78 with her suburbs, and J with her suburbs, 3096

JAHZEEL (2) [JAHZEELITES, JAHZIEL]
Ge 46:24 J, and Guni, and Jezer, and Shillem. 3183
Nu 26:48 of J, the family of the Jahzeelites: of Guni, 3183

JAHZEELITES (1) [JAHZEEL]
Nu 26:48 of Jahzeel, the family of the J: of Guni, 3184

JAHZEIAH See JAHAZIAH

JAHZERAH (1)
1Ch 9:12 the son of J, the son of Meshullam, the son 3170

JAHZIEL (1) [JAHZEEL]
1Ch 7:13 J, and Guni, and Jezer, and Shallum, 3185

JAILOR (1)
Ac 16:23 charging the j to keep them safely: *1200*

JAIR (10) [BASHAN-HAVOTH-JAIR]
Nu 32:41 J the son of Manasseh went and took 2971
Dt 3:14 J the son of Manasseh took all the country 2971
Jos 13:30 and all the towns of J, which *are* in Bashan, 2971
Jdg 10: 3 after him arose J, a Gileadite, and 2971
10: 5 And J died, and was buried in Camon. 2971
1Ki 4:13 to him *pertained* the towns of J the son of 2971
1Ch 2:22 Segub begat J, who had three and 2971
2:23 Aram, with the towns of J, from them, 2971
20: 5 Elhanan the son of J slew Lahmi 3265
Est 2: 5 the son of J, the son of Shimei, the son of 2971

JAIRITE (1)
2Sa 20:26 Ira also the J was a chief ruler about David. 2972

JAIRUS (2)
Mk 5:22 of the rulers of the synagogue, J by name; *2383*
Lk 8:41 there came a man named J, and he was a *2383*

JAKAN (1)
1Ch 1:42 The sons of Ezer; Bilhan, and Zavan, *and* J. 3292

JAKEH (1)
Pr 30: 1 The words of Agur the son of J, *even* 3348

JAKIM (2)
1Ch 8:19 And J, and Zichri, and Zabdi, 3356
24:12 The eleventh to Eliashib, the twelfth to J, 3356

JAKIN See JACHIN

JAKINITE See JACHINITES

JALAM See JAALAM

JALON (1)
1Ch 4:17 *were,* Jether, and Mered, and Epher, and J: 3210

JAMBRES (1)
2Ti 3: 8 Now as Jannes and J withstood Moses, so *2387*

JAMES (42)
Mt 4:21 J the *son* of Zebedee, and John his brother, *2385*
10: 2 J, the *son* of Zebedee, and John his brother; *2385*
10: 3 J the *son* of Alpheus, and Lebbeus, *2385*
13:55 called Mary? and his brethren, J, and Joses, *2385*
17: 1 J, and John his brother, and bringeth them *2385*
27:56 and Mary the mother of J and Joses, and *2385*
Mk 1:19 he saw J the *son* of Zebedee, and John his *2385*
1:29 of Simon and Andrew, with J and John. *2385*
3:17 And J the *son* of Zebedee, and John *2385*
3:17 *son* of Zebedee, and John the brother of J; *2385*
3:18 and J the *son* of Alpheus, and Thaddeus, *2385*
5:37 and J, and John the brother of James. *2385*
5:37 and James, and John the brother of J. *2385*
6: 3 the brother of J, and Joses, and of Juda, and *2385*
9: 2 and J, and John, and leadeth them up into a *2385*
10:35 And J and John, the sons of Zebedee, *2385*
10:41 *it,* they began to be much displeased with J *2385*
13: 3 Peter and J and John and Andrew asked *2385*
14:33 he taketh with him Peter and J and John, *2385*
15:40 and Mary the mother of J the less and *2385*
16: 1 and Mary the *mother* of J, and Salome, *2385*
Lk 5:10 And so *was* also J, and John, *the* sons of *2385*
6:14 J and John, Philip and Bartholomew, *2385*
6:15 J the *son* of Alpheus, and Simon called *2385*
6:16 *And* Judas *the brother* of J, and *2385*
8:51 and J, and John, and the father and *2385*
9:28 he took Peter and John and J, and went up *2385*
9:54 And when his disciples J and John saw *2385*
24:10 and Mary *the mother* of J, and other *2385*
Ac 1:13 and J, and John, and Andrew, Philip, and *2385*
1:13 J *the son* of Alpheus, and Simon Zelotes, *2385*
1:13 Simon Zelotes, and Judas *the brother* of J. *2385*
12: 2 And he killed J the brother of John with *2385*
12:17 *Go* shew these *things* unto J, and to *2385*
15:13 J answered, saying, Men *and* brethren, *2385*
21:18 *day* following Paul went in with us unto J; *2385*
1Co 15: 7 After that, he was seen of J; then of all *2385*
Gal 1:19 saw I none, save J the Lord's brother. *2385*
2: 9 And when J, Cephas, and John, *2385*
2:12 For before that certain came from J, he did *2385*
Jas 1: 1 J, a servant of God and of the Lord Jesus *2385*
Jude 1: 1 servant of Jesus Christ, and brother of J, *2385*

JAMIN (6) [JAMINITES]
Ge 46:10 J, and Ohad, and Jachin, and Zohar, and 3226
Ex 6:15 J, and Ohad, and Jachin, and Zohar, and 3226
Nu 26:12 of J, the family of the Jaminites: of Jachin, 3226
1Ch 2:27 of Jerahmeel were, Maaz, and J, and Eker. 3226
4:24 and J, Jarib, Zerah, *and* Shaul: 3226
Ne 8: 7 Bani, and Sherebiah, J, Akkub, Shabbethai, 3226

JAMINITES (1) [JAMIN]
Nu 26:12 of Jamin, the family of the J: of Jachin, 3228

JAMLECH (1)
1Ch 4:34 and J, and Joshah the son of Amaziah, 3230

JANAI See JAANAI

JANGLING (1)
1Ti 1: 6 swerved have turned aside unto vain j; *3150*

JANIM See JANUM

JANNA (1)
Lk 3:24 which was *the son* of J, which was *the son* *2388*

JANNAI See JANNA

JANNES (1)
2Ti 3: 8 Now as J and Jambres withstood Moses, so *2389*

JANOAH (1)
2Ki 15:29 J, and Kedesh, and Hazor, and Gilead, and 3239

JANOHAH (2)
Jos 16: 6 and passed by it on the east *to* J; 3239
16: 7 it went down from J *to* Ataroth, and 3239

JANUM (1)
Jos 15:53 And J, and Beth-tappuah, and Aphekah, 3241

JAPHETH (11)
Ge 5:32 and Noah begat Shem, Ham, and J. 3315
6:10 Noah begat three sons, Shem, Ham, and J. 3315
7:13 Shem, and Ham, and J, the sons of Noah, 3315
9:18 of the ark, were Shem, and Ham, and J: 3315
9:23 Shem and J took a garment, and laid *it* 3315
9:27 God shall enlarge J, and he shall dwell in 3315
10: 1 of the sons of Noah, Shem, Ham, and J: 3315
10: 2 The sons of J; Gomer, and Magog, and 3315
10:21 the brother of J the elder, even to him were 3315
1Ch 1: 4 Noah, Shem, Ham, and J. 3315
1: 5 The sons of J; Gomer, and Magog, and 3315

JAPHIA (5)
Jos 10: 3 unto J king of Lachish, and unto Debir king 3309
19:12 goeth out to Daberath, and goeth up *to* J, 3309
2Sa 5:15 Ibhar also, and Elishua, and Nepheg, and J, 3309
1Ch 3: 7 And Nogah, and Nepheg, and J, 3309
14: 6 And Nogah, and Nepheg, and J, 3309

JAPHLET (3)
1Ch 7:32 Heber begat J, and Shomer, and Hotham, 3310

1Ch 7:33 the sons of J; Pasach, and Bimhal, and 3310
7:33 and Ashvath. These *are* the children of J. 3310

JAPHLETI (1)
Jos 16: 3 goeth down westward to the coast of J, 3311

JAPHLETITES See JAPHLETI

JAPHO (1)
Jos 19:46 and Rakkon, with the border before J. 3305

JAR; JARS See BARREL; BARRELS; CRUSE; WATERPOT; WATERPOTS

JARAH (2)
1Ch 9:42 Ahaz begat J; and Jarah begat Alemeth, 3294
9:42 J begat Alemeth, and Azmaveth, and 3294

JAREB (2)
Hos 5:13 to the Assyrian, and sent to king J: 3377
10: 6 carried unto Assyria *for* a present to king J: 3377

JARED (6)
Ge 5:15 lived sixty and five years, and begat J: 3382
5:16 Mahalaleel lived after he begat J eight 3382
5:18 J lived an hundred sixty and two years, 3382
5:19 J lived after he begat Enoch eight hundred 3382
5:20 all the days of J were nine hundred sixty 3382
Lk 3:37 *the son* of Enoch, which was *the son* of J, *2391*

JARESIAH (1)
1Ch 8:27 J, and Eliah, and Zichri, the sons of 3298

JARHA (2)
1Ch 2:34 a servant, an Egyptian, whose name *was* J. 3398
2:35 Sheshan gave his daughter to J his servant 3398

JARIB (3)
1Ch 4:24 and Jamin, J, Zerah, *and* Shaul: 3402
Ezr 8:16 and for J, and for Elnathan, and for Nathan, 3402
10:18 and Eliezer, and J, and Gedaliah. 3402

JARMUTH (7)
Jos 10: 3 unto Piram king of J, and unto Japhia king 3412
10: 5 the king of Hebron, the king of J, the king 3412
10:23 the king of Hebron, the king of J, the king 3412
12:11 The king of J, one; the king of Lachish, 3412
15:35 J, and Adullam, Socoh, and Azekah, 3412
21:29 J with her suburbs, En-gannim with her 3412
Ne 11:29 And at En-rimmon, and at Zareah, and at J, 3412

JAROAH (1)
1Ch 5:14 the son of J, the son of Gilead, the son of 3386

JASHAR See JASHER

JASHEN (1)
2Sa 23:32 the Shaalbonite, *of* the sons of J, Jonathan, 3464

JASHER (2)
Jos 10:13 *Is* not this written in the book of J? So 3477
2Sa 1:18 behold, *it is* written in the book of J.) 3477

JASHOBEAM (3)
1Ch 11:11 J, a Hachmonite, the chief of the captains: 3434
12: 6 and Jesiah, and Azareel, and Joezer, and J, 3434
27: 2 the first month *was* J the son of Zabdiel: 3434

JASHUB (3) [JASHUBITES]
Nu 26:24 Of J, the family of the Jashubites: 3437
1Ch 7: 1 *were,* Tola, and Puah, J, and Shimron, four. 3437
Ezr 10:29 and Adaiah, J, and Sheal, and Ramoth. 3437

JASHUBI-LEHEM (1)
1Ch 4:22 who had the dominion in Moab, and J. 3433

JASHUBITES (1) [JASHUB]
Nu 26:24 Of Jashub, the family of the J: of Shimron, 3432

JASIEL (1)
1Ch 11:47 Eliel, and Obed, and J the Mesobaite. 3300

JASON (5)
Ac 17: 5 and assaulted the house of J, and sought to *2394*
17: 6 they drew J and certain brethren unto *2394*
17: 7 Whom J hath received: and these all do *2394*
17: 9 And when they had taken security of J, and *2394*
Ro 16:21 and Lucius, and J, and Sosipater, *2394*

JASPER (7)
Ex 28:20 fourth row a beryl, and an onyx, and a j: 3471
39:13 the fourth row, a beryl, an onyx, and a j: 3471
Eze 28:13 the beryl, the onyx, and the j, the sapphire, 3471
Rev 4: 3 And he that sat was to look upon like a j *2393*
21:11 *even* like a j stone, clear as crystal; *2393*
21:18 And the building of the wall of it was *of* j: *2393*
21:19 The first foundation *was* j; the second, *2393*

JATHNIEL (1)
1Ch 26: 2 the second, Zebadiah the third, J the fourth, 3496

JATTIR (4)
Jos 15:48 the mountains, Shamir, and J, and Socoh, 3492
21:14 J with her suburbs, and Eshtemoa with her 3492
1Sa 30:27 and to *them* which *were* in J, 3492
1Ch 6:57 and J, and Eshtemoa, with their suburbs, 3492

JAVAN (7)
Ge 10: 2 and J, and Tubal, and Meshech, and Tiras. 3120
10: 4 the sons of J; Elishah, and Tarshish, 3120
1Ch 1: 5 and J, and Tubal, and Meshech, and Tiras. 3120
1: 7 the sons of J; Elishah, and Tarshish, 3120
Isa 66:19 Lud, that draw the bow, *to* Tubal, and J, 3120
Eze 27:13 J, Tubal, and Meshech, they *were* thy 3120
27:19 Dan also and J going to and fro occupied in 3120

JAVELIN (7)
Nu 25: 7 the congregation, and took a j in his hand; 7420
1Sa 18:10 and *there was* a j in Saul's hand. 2595
18:11 Saul cast the j; for he said, I will smite 2595
19: 9 as he sat in his house with his j in his hand: 2595
19:10 to smite David even to the wall with the j; 2595
19:10 and he smote the j into the wall: 2595
20:33 Saul cast a j at him to smite him: 2595

JAVELINS See DARTS

JAW (4) [JAWBONE, JAWS]
Jdg 15:16 with the j of an ass have I slain a thousand 3895
15:19 God clave a hollow place that *was* in the j, 3895
Job 41: 2 or bore his j through with a thorn? 3895
Pr 30:14 *are as* swords, and their **j teeth** *as* knives, 4973

JAWBONE (3) [BONE, JAW]
Jdg 15:15 he found a new j of an ass, and put forth his 3895
15:16 Samson said, With the j of an ass, 3895
15:17 that he cast away the j out of his hand, and 3895

JAWS (6) [JAW]
Job 29:17 I brake the j of the wicked, and pluckt 4973
Ps 22:15 my tongue cleaveth *to* my j; and thou hast 4455
Isa 30:28 *there shall be* a bridle in the j of the people, 3895
Eze 29: 4 I will put hooks in thy j, and I will cause 3895
38: 4 put hooks into thy j, and I will bring thee 3895
Hos 11: 4 as they that take off the yoke on their j, 3895

JAZER (11)
Nu 32: 1 when they saw the land of J, and the land 3270
32: 3 J, and Nimrah, and Heshbon, and Elealeh, 3270
Jos 13:25 their coast was J, and all the cities of 3270
21:39 with her suburbs, J with her suburbs; 3270
2Sa 24: 5 the midst of the river of Gad, and toward J: 3270
1Ch 6:81 with her suburbs, and J with her suburbs. 3270
26:31 them mighty *men* of valour at J of Gilead. 3270
Isa 16: 8 they are come *even* unto J, they wandered 3270
16: 9 with the weeping of J the vine of Sibmah: 3270
Jer 48:32 I will weep for thee with the weeping of J: 3270
48:32 the sea, they reach *even* to the sea of J: 3270

JAZIZ (1)
1Ch 27:31 over the flocks *was* J the Hagerite. 3151

JEALOUS (19) [JEALOUSY]
Ex 20: 5 for I the LORD thy God *am* a j God, 7067
34:14 for the LORD, whose name *is* J, *is* a 7067
34:14 whose name *is* Jealous, *is* a j God: 7067
Nu 5:14 and he be j of his wife, and she be defiled: 7065
5:14 he be j of his wife, and she be not defiled: 7065
5:30 he be j over his wife, and shall set 7065
Dt 4:24 thy God *is* a consuming fire, *even* a j God. 7067
5: 9 for I the LORD thy God *am* a j God, 7067
6:15 (For the LORD thy God *is* a j God among 7067
Jos 24:19 for he *is* a holy God; he *is* a j God; he will 7072

1Ki 19:10 I have been **very j** for the LORD 7065+7065
19:14 I have been **very j** for the LORD 7065+7065
Eze 39:25 of Israel, and will be j for my holy name; 7065
Joel 2:18 will the LORD be j for his land, and 7065
Na 1: 2 God *is* j, and the LORD revengeth; 7072
Zec 1:14 I am j for Jerusalem and for Zion *with* a 7065
8: 2 I was j for Zion *with* great jealousy, and 7065
8: 2 and I was j for her *with* great fury. 7065
2Co 11: 2 For I am j over you with godly jealousy: *2206*

JEALOUSIES (1) [JEALOUSY]
Nu 5:29 This *is* the law of j, when a wife goeth 7068

JEALOUSY (34) [JEALOUS, JEALOUSIES]
Nu 5:14 the spirit of j come upon him, and he be 7068
5:14 or if the spirit of j come upon him, and 7068
5:15 for it *is* an offering of j, an offering of 7068
5:18 in her hands, which *is* the j offering: 7068
5:25 the priest shall take the j offering out of 7068
5:30 Or when the spirit of j cometh upon him, 7068
25:11 consumed not the children of Israel in my j. 7068
Dt 29:20 and his j shall smoke against that man, 7068
32:16 They **provoked** him **to j** with strange *gods,* 7065
32:21 They have **moved** me **to j** with *that which* 7065
32:21 I will **move** them **to j** with *those which are* 7065
1Ki 14:22 they **provoked** him **to j** with their sins 7065
Ps 78:58 **moved** him **to j** with their graven images. 7065
79: 5 for ever? shall thy j burn like fire? 7068
Pr 6:34 For j *is* the rage of a man: therefore he will 7068
SS 8: 6 *is* strong as death; j *is* cruel as the grave: 7068
Isa 42:13 *man,* he shall stir up j like a man of war: 7068
Eze 8: 3 where *was* the seat of the image of j, 7068
8: 3 image of jealousy, which **provoketh to j**. 7069
8: 5 gate of the altar this image of j in the entry. 7068
16:38 and I will give thee blood in fury and j. 7068
16:42 my j shall depart from thee, and I will be 7068
23:25 I will set my j against thee, and they shall 7068
36: 5 Surely in the fire of my j have I spoken 7068
36: 6 I have spoken in my j and in my fury, 7068
38:19 For in my j *and* in the fire of my wrath 7068
Zep 1:18 land shall be devoured by the fire of his j: 7068
3: 8 shall be devoured with the fire of my j. 7068
Zec 1:14 for Jerusalem and for Zion *with* a great j. 7068
8: 2 I was jealous for Zion *with* great j, and 7068
Ro 10:19 I will **provoke** you **to j** by *them that are* no *3863*
11:11 unto the Gentiles, for to **provoke** them **to j**. *3863*
1Co 10:22 Do we **provoke** the Lord **to j**? are we *3863*
2Co 11: 2 For I am jealous over you with godly j: *2205*

JEARIM (1) [KIRJATH-JEARIM]
Jos 15:10 passed along unto the side of mount J, 3297

JEATERAI (1)
1Ch 6:21 Iddo his son, Zerah his son, J his son. 2979

JEATHERAI See JEATERAI

JEBERECHIAH (1)
Isa 8: 2 the priest, and Zechariah the son of J. 3000

JEBEREKIAH See JEBERECHIAH

JEBUS (4) [JEBUSI, JEBUSITE, JEBUSITES, JERUSALEM]
Jdg 19:10 and departed, and came over against J, 2982
19:11 *And* when they *were* by J, the day was far 2982
1Ch 11: 4 and all Israel went *to* Jerusalem, which *is* J; 2982
11: 5 the inhabitants of J said to David, 2982

JEBUSI (2) [JEBUS]
Jos 18:16 to the side of J on the south, and 2983
18:28 Zelah, Eleph, and J, which *is* Jerusalem, 2983

JEBUSITE (14) [JEBUS]
Ge 10:16 the J, and the Amorite, and the Girgashite, 2983
Ex 33: 2 and the Perizzite, the Hivite, and the J: 2983
34:11 and the Perizzite, and the Hivite, and the J. 2983
Jos 9: 1 the Perizzite, the Hivite, and the J, 2983
11: 3 the J in the mountains, and *to* the Hivite 2983
15: 8 son of Hinnom unto the south side of the J; 2983
2Sa 24:16 by the threshingplace of Araunah the J. 2983
24:18 in the threshingfloor of Araunah the J. 2983
1Ch 1:14 The J also, and the Amorite, and 2983
21:15 stood by the threshingfloor of Ornan the J. 2983
21:18 in the threshingfloor of Ornan the J. 2983
21:28 him in the threshingfloor of Ornan the J, 2983
2Ch 3: 1 in the threshingfloor of Ornan the J. 2983

Zec 9: 7 as a governor in Judah, and Ekron as a J. 2983

JEBUSITES (25) [JEBUS]
Ge 15:21 and the Girgashites, and the J. 2983
Ex 3: 8 the Perizzites, and the Hivites, and the J. 2983
3:17 the Perizzites, and the Hivites, and the J, 2983
13: 5 the Amorites, and the Hivites, and the J, 2983
23:23 and the Canaanites, the Hivites, and the J: 2983
Nu 13:29 the Hittites, and the J, and the Amorites, 2983
Dt 7: 1 the Perizzites, and the Hivites, and the J, 2983
20:17 and the Perizzites, the Hivites, and the J; 2983
Jos 3:10 and the Amorites, and the J. 2983
12: 8 the Perizzites, the Hivites, and the J: 2983
15:63 As for the J the inhabitants of Jerusalem, 2983
15:63 the J dwell with the children of Judah at 2983
24:11 and the Girgashites, the Hivites, and the J; 2983
Jdg 1:21 not drive out the J that inhabited Jerusalem; 2983
1:21 the J dwell with the children of Benjamin 2983
3: 5 and Perizzites, and Hivites, and J: 2983
19:11 let us turn in into this city of the J, and 2983
2Sa 5: 6 and his men went *to* Jerusalem unto the J, 2983
5: 8 smiteth the J, and the lame and the blind, 2983
1Ki 9:20 Hittites, Perizzites, Hivites, and J, 2983
1Ch 11: 4 where the J *were,* the inhabitants of 2983
11: 6 Whosoever smiteth the J first shall be chief 2983
2Ch 8: 7 the Perizzites, and the Hivites, and the J, 2983
Ezr 9: 1 the Hittites, the Perizzites, the J, 2983
Ne 9: 8 and the J, and the Girgashites, 2983

JECAMIAH (1)
1Ch 3:18 Pedaiah, and Shenazar, J, Hoshama, and 3359

JECHOLIAH (1) [JECOLIAH]
2Ki 15: 2 And his mother's name *was* J of Jerusalem. 3203

JECHONIAS (2) [JECONIAH]
Mt 1:11 And Josias begat J and his brethren, *2423*
1:12 were brought to Babylon, J begat Salathiel; *2423*

JECOLIAH (1) [JECHOLIAH]
2Ch 26: 3 His mother's name also *was* J of 3203

JECONIAH (7) [JECHONIAS]
1Ch 3:16 of Jehoiakim: J his son, Zedekiah his son. 3204
3:17 And the sons of J; Assir, Salathiel his son, 3204
Est 2: 6 been carried away with J king of Judah, 3204
Jer 24: 1 J the son of Jehoiakim king of Judah, 3204
27:20 when he carried away captive J the son of 3204
28: 4 I *will* bring again to this place J the son of 3204
29: 2 (After that J the king, and the queen, and 3204

JEDAIAH (13)
1Ch 4:37 the son of Allon, the son of J, the son of 3042
9:10 of the priests; J, and Jehoiarib, and Jachin, 3048
24: 7 lot came forth to Jehoiarib, the second to J, 3048
Ezr 2:36 the children of J, of the house of Jeshua, 3048
Ne 3:10 next unto them repaired J the son of 3042
7:39 the children of J, of the house of Jeshua, 3048
11:10 Of the priests: J the son of Joiarib, Jachin, 3048
12: 6 Shemaiah, and Joiarib, J, 3048
12: 7 Sallu, Amok, Hilkiah, J. These *were* 3048
12:19 And of Joiarib, Mattenai; of J, Uzzi; 3048
12:21 Of Hilkiah, Hashabiah; of J, Nethaneel. 3048
Zec 6:10 *even* of Heldai, of Tobijah, and of J, 3048
6:14 and to J, and to Hen the son of Zephaniah, 3048

JEDIAEL (6)
1Ch 7: 6 Bela, and Becher, and J, three. 3043
7:10 The sons also of J; Bilhan: and the sons of 3043
7:11 All these the sons of J, by the heads of *their* 3043
11:45 J the son of Shimri, and Joha his brother, 3043
12:20 J, and Michael, and Jozabad, and Elihu, 3043
26: 2 J the second, Zebadiah the third, 3043

JEDIDAH (1)
2Ki 22: 1 his mother's name *was* J, the daughter of 3040

JEDIDIAH (1) [SOLOMON]
2Sa 12:25 he called his name J, because of 3041

JEDUTHUN (17)
1Ch 9:16 the son of J, and Berechiah the son of Asa, 3038
16:38 Obed-edom also the son of J and Hosah to 3038
16:41 with them Heman and J, and the rest that 3038
16:42 with them Heman and J *with* trumpets and 3038

1Ch 16:42 of God. And the sons of J *were* porters. 3038
25: 1 of Heman, and of J, who should prophesy 3038
25: 3 Of J: the sons of Jeduthun; Gedaliah, and 3038
25: 3 the sons of J; Gedaliah, and Zeri, and 3038
25: 3 six, under the hands of their father J, 3038
25: 6 to the king's order *to* Asaph, J, and Heman. 3038
2Ch 5:12 of Heman, of J, with their sons and 3038
29:14 and of the sons of J; Shemaiah, and Uzziel. 3038
35:15 Asaph, and Heman, and J the king's seer; 3038
Ne 11:17 of Shammua, the son of Galal, the son of J. 3038
Ps 39: T *even* to J, A Psalm of David. 3038
62: T the chief Musician, to J, A Psalm of David. 3038
77: T the chief Musician, to J, A Psalm of Asaph. 3038

JEEZER (1) [JEEZERITES]
Nu 26:30 *of* J, the family of the Jeezerites: of Helek, 372

JEEZERITES (1) [JEEZER]
Nu 26:30 *of* Jeezer, the family of the J: of Helek, 373

JEGAR-SAHADUTHA (1)
Ge 31:47 Laban called it J: but Jacob called it 3026

JEHALELEEL (1)
1Ch 4:16 the sons of J; Ziph, and Ziphah, Tiria, and 3094

JEHALELEL (1)
2Ch 29:12 the son of Abdi, and Azariah the son of J: 3094

JEHALLELEL See JEHALELEEL; JEHALELEL

JEHDEIAH (2)
1Ch 24:20 Shubael: of the sons of Shubael; J. 3165
27:30 and over the asses *was* J the Meronothite: 3165

JEHEZEKEL (1)
1Ch 24:16 nineteenth to Pethahiah, the twentieth to J, 3168

JEHEZKEL See JEHEZEKEL

JEHIAH (1)
1Ch 15:24 and J *were* doorkeepers for the ark. 3174

JEHIEL (16)
1Ch 9:35 J, whose wife's name *was* Maachah: 3273
11:44 and J the sons of Hothan the Aroerite, 3273
15:18 J, and Unni, Eliab, and Benaiah, and 3171
15:20 J, and Unni, and Eliab, and Maaseiah, and 3171
16: 5 J, and Mattithiah, and Eliab, and Benaiah, 3171
23: 8 the chief *was* J, and Zetham, and Joel, 3171
27:32 J the son of Hachmoni *was* with the king's 3171
29: 8 by the hand of J the Gershonite. 3171
2Ch 21: 2 J, and Zechariah, and Azariah, and 3171
29:14 of the sons of Heman; J, and Shimei: and 3171
31:13 J, and Azaziah, and Nahath, and Asahel, 3171
35: 8 Hilkiah and Zechariah and J, rulers of 3171
Ezr 8: 9 Obadiah the son of J, and with him two 3171
10: 2 Shechaniah the son of J, *one* of the sons of 3171
10:21 Elijah, and Shemaiah, and J, and Uzziah. 3171
10:26 and J, and Abdi, and Jeremoth, and Eliah. 3171

JEHIELI (2)
1Ch 26:21 *even* of Laadan the Gershonite, *were* J. 3172
26:22 The sons of J; Zetham, and Joel his 3172

JEHIZKIAH (1)
2Ch 28:12 J the son of Shallum, and Amasa the son of 3169

JEHOADAH (2)
1Ch 8:36 Ahaz begat J; and Jehoadah begat Alemeth, 3085
8:36 J begat Alemeth, and Azmaveth, and 3085

JEHOADDAH See JEHOADAH

JEHOADDAN (2)
2Ki 14: 2 And his mother's name *was* J of Jerusalem. 3086
2Ch 25: 1 And his mother's name *was* J of Jerusalem. 3086

JEHOAHAZ (23)
2Ki 10:35 And J his son reigned in his stead. 3059
13: 1 J the son of Jehu *began* to reign over Israel 3059
13: 4 J besought the LORD, and the LORD 3059
13: 7 Neither did he leave *of* the people to J but 3059
13: 8 Now the rest of the acts of J, and all that he 3059
13: 9 J slept with his fathers; and they buried 3059
13:10 the son of J to reign over Israel in Samaria, 3059
13:22 of Syria oppressed Israel all the days of J. 3059
13:25 Jehoash the son of J took again out of 3059
13:25 which he had taken out of the hand of J his 3059
14: 1 In the second year of Joash son of J king of 3099
14: 8 the son of J son of Jehu, king of Israel, 3059
14:17 son of J king of Israel fifteen years. 3059
23:30 the people of the land took J the son of 3059
23:31 J *was* twenty and three years old when he 3059
23:34 took J *away*: and he came *to* Egypt, and 3059
2Ch 21:17 left him, save J, the youngest of his sons. 3059
25:17 sent to Joash, the son of J, the son of Jehu, 3059
25:23 the son of Joash, the son of J, 3059
25:25 Joash son of J king of Israel fifteen years. 3059
36: 1 the people of the land took J the son of 3059
36: 2 J *was* twenty and three years old when he 3099
36: 4 Necho took J his brother, and carried him 3099

JEHOASH (17)
2Ki 11:21 Seven years old *was* J when he *began* to 3060
12: 1 In the seventh year of Jehu J *began* to 3060
12: 2 J did *that* which *was* right in the sight of 3060
12: 4 J said to the priests, All the money of 3060
12: 6 twentieth year of king J the priests had not 3060
12: 7 king J called for Jehoiada the priest, and 3060
12:18 J king of Judah took all the hallowed *things* 3060
13:10 J the son of Jehoahaz to reign over Israel in 3060
13:25 J the son of Jehoahaz took again out of 3060
14: 8 Amaziah sent messengers to J, the son of 3060
14: 9 J the king of Israel sent to Amaziah king of 3060
14:11 Therefore J king of Israel went up; and he 3060
14:13 J king of Israel took Amaziah king of 3060
14:13 the son of J the son of Ahaziah, 3060
14:15 Now the rest of the acts of J which he did, 3060
14:16 J slept with his fathers, and was buried in 3060
14:17 J son of Jehoahaz king of Israel fifteen 3060

JEHOHANAN (6)
1Ch 26: 3 Elam the fifth, J the sixth, Elioenai 3076
2Ch 17:15 next to him *was* J the captain, and with him 3076
23: 1 Ishmael the son of J, and Azariah the son 3076
Ezr 10:28 of Bebai; J, Hananiah, Zabbai, *and* Athlai. 3076
Ne 12:13 Of Ezra, Meshullam; of Amariah, J; 3076
12:42 and J, and Malchijah, and Elam, and Ezer. 3076

JEHOIACHIN (10) [CONIAH, JEHOIACHIN'S]
2Ki 24: 6 and J his son reigned in his stead. 3078
24: 8 J *was* eighteen years old when he *began* to 3078
24:12 J the king of Judah went out to the king of 3078
24:15 he carried away J to Babylon, and 3078
25:27 thirtieth year of the captivity of J king of 3078
25:27 did lift up the head of J king of Judah out 3078
2Ch 36: 8 Judah: and J his son reigned in his stead. 3078
36: 9 J *was* eight years old when he *began* to 3078
Jer 52:31 thirtieth year of the captivity of J king of 3078
52:31 reign lifted up the head of J king of Judah, 3078

JEHOIACHIN'S (1) [JEHOIACHIN]
Eze 1: 2 which *was* the fifth year of king J captivity, 3112

JEHOIADA (52)
2Sa 8:18 Benaiah the son of J *was over* both 3077
20:23 Benaiah the son of J *was* over 3077
23:20 Benaiah the son of J, the son of a valiant 3077
23:22 These *things* did Benaiah the son of J, and 3077
1Ki 1: 8 Benaiah the son of J, and Nathan 3077
1:26 Benaiah the son of J, and thy servant 3077
1:32 the prophet, and Benaiah the son of J. 3077
1:36 Benaiah the son of J answered the king, 3077
1:38 Benaiah the son of J, and the Cherethites, 3077
1:44 Benaiah the son of J, and the Cherethites, 3077
2:25 sent by the hand of Benaiah the son of J; 3077
2:29 Solomon sent Benaiah the son of J, saying, 3077
2:34 So Benaiah the son of J went up, and 3077
2:35 the king put Benaiah the son of J in his 3077
2:46 the king commanded Benaiah the son of J; 3077
4: 4 Benaiah the son of J *was* over the host: 3077
2Ki 11: 4 the seventh year J sent and fet the rulers 3077
11: 9 to all *things* that J the priest commanded: 3077
11: 9 out on the sabbath, and came to J the priest. 3077
11:15 J the priest commanded the captains of 3077
11:17 J made a covenant between the LORD 3077
12: 2 days where*in* J the priest instructed him. 3077
12: 7 king Jehoash called for J the priest, and 3077
12: 9 J the priest took a chest, and bored a hole 3077
1Ch 11:22 Benaiah the son of J, the son of a valiant 3077

J

1Ch 11:24 These *things* did Benaiah the son of J, and 3077
12:27 J *was* the leader of the Aaronites, and 3077
18:17 Benaiah the son of J *was* over 3077
27: 5 the third month *was* Benaiah the son of J, 3077
27:34 after Ahithophel *was* J the son of Benaiah, 3077
2Ch 22:11 of king Jehoram, the wife of J the priest, 3077
23: 1 in the seventh year J strengthened himself, 3077
23: 8 all Judah did according to all *things* that J 3077
23: 8 for J the priest dismissed not the courses. 3077
23: 9 Moreover J the priest delivered to 3077
23:11 J and his sons anointed him, and said, 3077
23:14 J the priest brought out the captains of 3077
23:16 J made a covenant between him, and 3077
23:18 Also J appointed the offices of the house of 3077
24: 2 of the LORD all the days of J the priest. 3077
24: 3 J took for him two wives; and he begat 3077
24: 6 the king called for J the chief, and 3077
24:12 J gave it to such as did the work of 3077
24:14 the rest of the money before the king and J, 3077
24:14 of the LORD continually all the days of J. 3077
24:15 J waxed old, and was full *of* days when he 3077
24:17 Now after the death of J came the princes 3077
24:20 upon Zechariah the son of J the priest, 3077
24:22 which J his father had done to him, 3077
24:25 him for the blood of the sons of J the priest, 3077
Ne 3: 6 Moreover the old gate repaired J the son of 3111
Jer 29:26 made thee priest in the stead of J the priest, 3077

JEHOIAKIM (37) [ELIAKIM]

2Ki 23:34 turned his name *to* J, and took Jehoahaz 3079
23:35 J gave the silver and the gold to Pharaoh; 3079
23:36 J *was* twenty and five year old when he 3079
24: 1 and J became his servant three years: 3079
24: 5 Now the rest of the acts of J, and all that he 3079
24: 6 So J slept with his fathers: and 3079
24:19 according to all that J had done. 3079
1Ch 3:15 the second J, the third Zedekiah, the fourth 3079
3:16 the sons of J: Jeconiah his son, 3079
2Ch 36: 4 and Jerusalem, and turned his name *to* J. 3079
36: 5 J *was* twenty and five years old when he 3079
36: 8 Now the rest of the acts of J, and 3079
Jer 1: 3 It came also in the days of J the son of 3079
22:18 J the son of Josiah king of Judah; 3079
22:24 though Coniah the son of J king of Judah 3079
24: 1 captive Jeconiah the son of J king of Judah, 3079
25: 1 year of J the son of Josiah king of Judah, 3079
26: 1 In the beginning of the reign of J the son of 3079
26:21 when J the king, with all his mighty *men,* 3079
26:22 J the king sent men *into* Egypt, *namely,* 3079
26:23 of Egypt, and brought him unto J the king; 3079
27: 1 In the beginning of the reign of J the son of 3079
27:20 J king of Judah from Jerusalem to Babylon, 3079
28: 4 place Jeconiah the son of J king of Judah, 3079
35: 1 days of J the son of Josiah king of Judah, 3079
36: 1 it came to pass in the fourth year of J 3079
36: 9 it came to pass in the fifth year of J the son 3079
36:28 which J the king of Judah hath burnt. 3079
36:29 thou shalt say to J king of Judah, 3079
36:30 Therefore thus saith the LORD of J king 3079
36:32 which J king of Judah had burnt in the fire: 3079
37: 1 reigned instead of Coniah the son of J, 3079
45: 1 in the fourth year of J the son of Josiah 3079
46: 2 year of J the son of Josiah king of Judah. 3079
52: 2 according to all that J had done. 3079
Da 1: 1 In the third year of the reign of J king of 3079
1: 2 the Lord gave J king of Judah into his 3079

JEHOIARIB (2)

1Ch 9:10 of the priests; Jedaiah, and J, and Jachin, 3080
24: 7 Now the first lot came forth to J, 3080

JEHONADAB (3)

2Ki 10:15 he lighted on J the son of Rechab *coming* 3082
10:15 J answered, It is. If it be, give *me* thine 3082
10:23 Jehu went, and J the son of Rechab, 3082

JEHONATHAN (3)

1Ch 27:25 and in the castles, *was* J the son of Uzziah: 3083
2Ch 17: 8 J, and Adonijah, and Tobijah, and 3083
Ne 12:18 Of Bilgah, Shammua; of Shemaiah, J; 3083

JEHORAM (23)

1Ki 22:50 and J his son reigned in his stead. 3088
2Ki 1:17 J reigned in his stead in the second year of 3088
1:17 of J the son of Jehoshaphat king of Judah; 3088
3: 1 Now J the son of Ahab *began* to reign over 3088
3: 6 king J went out of Samaria the same time, 3088
8:16 J the son of Jehoshaphat king of Judah 3088
8:25 the son of J king of Judah *begin* to reign. 3088
8:29 Ahaziah the son of J king of Judah went 3088
9:24 smote J between his arms, and the arrow 3088
12:18 J, and Ahaziah, his fathers, kings of Judah, 3088
2Ch 17: 8 and with them Elishama and J, priests. 3088
21: 1 And J his son reigned in his stead. 3088
21: 3 the kingdom gave he to J; because he *was* 3088
21: 4 Now when J was risen up to the kingdom 3088
21: 5 J *was* thirty and two years old when he 3088
21: 9 J went forth with his princes, and all *his* 3088
21:16 Moreover the LORD stirred up against J 3088
22: 1 So Ahaziah the son of J king of Judah 3088
22: 5 went with J the son of Ahab king of Israel 3088
22: 6 Azariah the son of J king of Judah went 3088
22: 6 down to see J the son of Ahab at Jezreel, 3088
22: 7 he went out with J against Jehu the son of 3088
22:11 So Jehoshabeath, the daughter of king J, 3088

JEHOSHABEATH (2)

2Ch 22:11 J, the daughter of the king, took Joash 3090
22:11 So J, the daughter of king Jehoram, 3090

JEHOSHAPHAT (85) [JOSAPHAT]

2Sa 8:16 and J the son of Ahilud *was* recorder; 3092
20:24 and J the son of Ahilud *was* recorder: 3092
1Ki 4: 3 scribes; J the son of Ahilud, the recorder. 3092
4:17 J the son of Paruah, in Issachar: 3092
15:24 and J his son reigned in his stead. 3092
22: 2 that J the king of Judah came down to 3092
22: 4 he said unto J, Wilt thou go with me to 3092
22: 4 J said to the king of Israel, I *am* as thou *art,* 3092
22: 5 J said unto the king of Israel, Inquire, 3092
22: 7 J said, *Is there* not here a prophet of 3092
22: 8 the king of Israel said unto J, *There is* yet 3092
22: 8 And J said, Let not the king say so. 3092
22:10 J the king of Judah sat each on his throne, 3092
22:18 the king of Israel said unto J, Did I not tell 3092
22:29 J the king of Judah went up *to* 3092
22:30 the king of Israel said unto J, I will 3092
22:32 when the captains of the chariots saw J, 3092
22:32 aside to fight against him: and J cried out. 3092
22:41 J the son of Asa *began* to reign over Judah 3092
22:42 J *was* thirty and five years old when he 3092
22:44 And J made peace with the king of Israel. 3092
22:45 Now the rest of the acts of J, and his might 3092
22:48 J made ships of Tharshish to go to Ophir 3092
22:49 said Ahaziah the son of Ahab unto J, 3092
22:49 thy servants in the ships. But J would not. 3092
22:50 J slept with his fathers, and was buried 3092
22:51 the seventeenth year of J king of Judah, 3092
2Ki 1:17 year of Jehoram the son of J king of Judah; 3092
3: 1 the eighteenth year of J king of Judah, 3092
3: 7 he went and sent to J the king of Judah, 3092
3:11 J said, *Is there* not here a prophet of 3092
3:12 J said, The word of the LORD is with 3092
3:12 So the king of Israel and J and the king of 3092
3:14 were it not that I regard the presence of J 3092
8:16 king of Israel, J *being* then king of Judah, 3092
8:16 Jehoram the son of J king of Judah *began* 3092
9: 2 look out there Jehu the son of J the son of 3092
9:14 So Jehu the son of J the son of Nimshi 3092
12:18 of Judah took all the hallowed *things* that J, 3092
1Ch 3:10 Abia his son, Asa his son, J his son, 3092
15:24 J, and Nethaneel, and Amasai, and 3146
18:15 the host; and J the son of Ahilud, recorder. 3092
2Ch 17: 1 J his son reigned in his stead, and 3092
17: 3 the LORD was with J, because he walked 3092
17: 5 all Judah brought to J presents; and he had 3092
17:10 so that they made no war against J. 3092
17:11 Also *some* of the Philistines brought J 3092
17:12 J waxed great exceedingly; and he built in 3092
18: 1 Now J had riches and honour in 3092
18: 3 Ahab king of Israel said unto J king of 3092
18: 4 J said unto the king of Israel, Inquire, 3092
18: 6 J said, *Is there* not here a prophet of 3092
18: 7 the king of Israel said unto J, *There is* yet 3092
18: 7 of Imla. And J said, Let not the king say so. 3092
18: 9 J king of Judah sat either of them on his 3092
18:17 the king of Israel said to J, Did I not tell 3092
18:28 J the king of Judah went up to 3092

2Ch 18:29 the king of Israel said unto J, I will 3092
18:31 when the captains of the chariots saw J, 3092
18:31 J cried out, and the LORD helped him; 3092
19: 1 J the king of Judah returned to his house in 3092
19: 2 said to king J, Shouldest thou help 3092
19: 4 J dwelt at Jerusalem: and he went out again 3092
19: 8 Moreover in Jerusalem did J set of 3092
20: 1 the Ammonites, came against J to battle. 3092
20: 2 there came *some* that told J, saying, 3092
20: 3 J feared, and set himself to seek 3092
20: 5 J stood in the congregation of Judah and 3092
20:15 inhabitants of Jerusalem, and thou king J, 3092
20:18 J bowed his head *with his* face to 3092
20:20 J stood and said, Hear me, O Judah, and 3092
20:25 when J and his people came to take away 3092
20:27 Jerusalem, and J in the forefront of them, 3092
20:30 So the realm of J was quiet: for his God 3092
20:31 J reigned over Judah: *he was* thirty and 3092
20:34 Now the rest of the acts of J, first and last, 3092
20:35 after this did J king of Judah join himself 3092
20:37 of Mareshah prophesied against J, 3092
21: 1 Now J slept with his fathers, and 3092
21: 2 he had brethren the sons of J, Azariah, and 3092
21: 2 all these *were* the sons of J king of Israel. 3092
21:12 hast not walked in the ways of J thy father, 3092
22: 9 Because, said they, he *is* the son of J, 3092
Joel 3: 2 will bring them down into the valley of J, 3092
3:12 and come up to the valley of J: 3092

JEHOSHEBA (1)
2Ki 11: 2 J, the daughter of king Joram, sister of 3089

JEHOSHUA (2) [JOSHUA]
Nu 13:16 And Moses called Oshea the son of Nun, J. 3091
1Ch 7:27 Non his son, J his son. 3091

JEHOVAH (4) [GOD*, JEHOVAH-JIREH, JEHOVAH-NISSI, JEHOVAH-SHALOM, LORD*]
Ex 6: 3 *by* my name J was I not known to them. 3068
Ps 83:18 know that thou, whose name alone *is* J, 3068
Isa 12: 2 for the LORD J *is* my strength and 3068
26: 4 for in the LORD J *is* everlasting strength: 3068

JEHOVAH-JIREH (1) [JEHOVAH]
Ge 22:14 Abraham called the name of that place J: 3070

JEHOVAH-NISSI (1) [JEHOVAH]
Ex 17:15 built an altar, and called the name of it J: 3071

JEHOVAH-SHALOM (1) [JEHOVAH]
Jdg 6:24 altar there unto the LORD, and called it J: 3073

JEHOZABAD (4)
2Ki 12:21 J the son of Shomer, his servants, 3075
1Ch 26: 4 J the second, Joah the third, and Sacar 3075
2Ch 17:18 next him *was* J, and with him an hundred 3075
24:26 and J the son of Shimrith a Moabitess. 3075

JEHOZADAK (2)
1Ch 6:14 Azariah begat Seraiah, and Seraiah begat J, 3087
6:15 J went *into captivity,* when the LORD 3087

JEHU (59)
1Ki 16: 1 the word of the LORD came to J the son 3058
16: 7 also by the hand of the prophet J the son of 3058
16:12 which he spake against Baasha by J 3058
19:16 J the son of Nimshi shalt thou anoint to be 3058
19:17 escapeth the sword of Hazael shall J slay: 3058
19:17 him that escapeth from the sword of J shall 3058
2Ki 9: 2 look out there J the son of Jehoshaphat 3058
9: 5 J said, Unto which of all us? And he said, 3058
9:11 J came forth to the servants of his lord: 3058
9:13 and blew with trumpets, saying, J is king. 3058
9:14 So J the son of Jehoshaphat the son of 3058
9:15 J said, If it be your minds, *then* let none go 3058
9:16 So J rode *in a chariot,* and went to Jezreel; 3058
9:17 he spied the company of J as he came, and 3058
9:18 J said, What hast thou to do with peace? 3058
9:19 J answered, What hast thou to do with 3058
9:20 the driving *is* like the driving of J the son 3058
9:21 they went out against J, and met him in 3058
9:22 when Joram saw J, that he said, *Is it* peace, 3058
9:22 Joram saw Jehu, that he said, *Is it* peace, J? 3058
9:24 J drew a bow with his full strength, and 3058
9:25 said J to Bidkar his captain, Take up, *and* NIH
9:27 J followed after him, and said, Smite him 3058
9:30 when J was come to Jezreel, Jezebel heard 3058
9:31 as J entered in at the gate, she said, *Had* 3058
10: 1 J wrote letters, and sent *to* Samaria, 3058
10: 5 the bringers up *of the children,* sent to J, 3058
10:11 So J slew all that remained of the house of 3058
10:13 J met with the brethren of Ahaziah king of 3058
10:18 J gathered all the people together, and 3058
10:18 Baal a little; *but* J shall serve him much. 3058
10:19 J did *it* in subtility, to the intent that *he* 3058
10:20 J said, Proclaim a solemn assembly for 3058
10:21 J sent through all Israel: and all 3058
10:23 J went, and Jehonadab the son of Rechab, 3058
10:24 J appointed fourscore men without, and 3058
10:25 that J said to the guard and to the captains, 3058
10:28 Thus J destroyed Baal out of Israel. 3058
10:29 to sin, J departed not from after them, 3058
10:30 the LORD said unto J, Because thou hast 3058
10:31 J took no heed to walk in the law of 3058
10:34 Now the rest of the acts of J, and all that he 3058
10:35 J slept with his fathers: and they buried 3058
10:36 the time that J reigned over Israel in 3058
12: 1 In the seventh year of J Jehoash *began* to 3058
13: 1 of J *began* to reign over Israel in Samaria, 3058
14: 8 the son of Jehoahaz son of J, king of Israel, 3058
15:12 word of the LORD which he spake unto J, 3058
1Ch 2:38 And Obed begat J, and Jehu begat Azariah, 3058
2:38 And Obed begat Jehu, and J begat Azariah, 3058
4:35 Joel, and J the son of Josibiah, the son of 3058
12: 3 and Berachah, and J the Antothite, 3058
2Ch 19: 2 J the son of Hanani the seer went out to 3058
20:34 behold they *are* written in the book of J 3058
22: 7 he went out with Jehoram against J the son 3058
22: 8 that when J was executing judgment upon 3058
22: 9 *was* hid in Samaria,) and brought him to J: 3058
25:17 the son of J, king of Israel, saying, Come, 3058
Hos 1: 4 the blood of Jezreel upon the house of J, 3058

JEHUBBAH (1)
1Ch 7:34 of Shamer; Ahi, and Rohgah, J, and Aram. 3160

JEHUCAL (1)
Jer 37: 3 Zedekiah the king sent J the son of 3081

JEHUD (1)
Jos 19:45 And J, and Bene-berak, and Gath-rimmon, 3055

JEHUDI (4)
Jer 36:14 Therefore all the princes sent J the son of 3065
36:21 So the king sent J to fet the roll: and 3065
36:21 J read it in the ears of the king, and in 3065
36:23 *that* when J had read three or four leaves, 3065

JEHUDIJAH (1)
1Ch 4:18 his wife J bare Jered the father of Gedor, 3057

JEHUSH (1)
1Ch 8:39 J the second, and Eliphelet the third. 3266

JEIEL (11)
1Ch 5: 7 *were* the chief, J, and Zechariah, 3273
15:18 and Obed-edom, and J, the porters. 3273
15:21 and Obed-edom, and J, and Azaziah, 3273
16: 5 J, and Shemiramoth, and Jehiel, and 3273
16: 5 J with psalteries and with harps; but 3273
2Ch 20:14 the son of Benaiah, the son of J, the son of 3273
26:11 of their account by the hand of J the scribe 3273
29:13 of the sons of Elizaphan; Shimri, and J: 3273
35: 9 and Hashabiah and J and Jozabad, 3273
Ezr 8:13 J, and Shemaiah, and with them threescore 3273
10:43 J, Mattithiah, Zabad, Zebina, Jadau, and 3273

JEKABZEEL (1)
Ne 11:25 and at J, and *in* the villages thereof, 3343

JEKAMEAM (2)
1Ch 23:19 Jahaziel the third, and J the fourth. 3360
24:23 the second, Jahaziel the third, J the fourth. 3360

JEKAMIAH (2)
1Ch 2:41 Shallum begat J, and Jekamiah begat 3359
2:41 begat Jekamiah, and J begat Elishama. 3359

JEKUTHIEL (1)
1Ch 4:18 father of Socho, and J the father of Zanoah. 3354

JEMIMA (1)
Job 42:14 he called the name of the first, J; and 3224

JEMUEL (2)
Ge 46:10 J, and Jamin, and Ohad, and Jachin, and 3223
Ex 6:15 J, and Jamin, and Ohad, and Jachin, and 3223

JEOPARDED (1) [JEOPARDY]
Jdg 5:18 Naphtali *were* a people *that* j their lives 2778

JEOPARDY (6) [JEOPARDED]
2Sa 23:17 of the men that went in *j of* their lives? NIH
1Ch 11:19 of these men that **have put** their lives **in** j? 871.1
11:19 for with *the j of* their lives they brought it. NIH
12:19 He will fall to his master Saul to *the j of* our NIH
Lk 8:23 they were filled *with water,* and were **in** j. *2793*
1Co 15:30 And why **stand** we **in** j every hour? *2793*

JEPHTHAE (1) [JEPHTHAH]
Heb 11:32 and *of* Barak, and *of* Samson, and *of* J; *2422*

JEPHTHAH (29) [JEPHTHAE]
Jdg 11: 1 Now J the Gileadite was a mighty *man* of 3316
11: 1 *was* the son of a harlot: and Gilead begat J. 3316
11: 2 and they thrust out J, and said unto him, 3316
11: 3 J fled from his brethren, and dwelt in 3316
11: 3 there were gathered vain men to J, and 3316
11: 5 the elders of Gilead went to fetch J out of 3316
11: 6 they said unto J, Come, and be our captain, 3316
11: 7 J said unto the elders of Gilead, Did not ye 3316
11: 8 the elders of Gilead said unto J, 3316
11: 9 J said unto the elders of Gilead, If ye bring 3316
11:10 the elders of Gilead said unto J, 3316
11:11 J went with the elders of Gilead, and 3316
11:11 J uttered all his words before the LORD 3316
11:12 J sent messengers unto the king of 3316
11:13 answered unto the messengers of J, 3316
11:14 J sent messengers again unto the king of 3316
11:15 said unto him, Thus saith J, Israel took not 3316
11:28 not unto the words of J which he sent him. 3316
11:29 the spirit of the LORD came upon J, and 3316
11:30 J vowed a vow unto the LORD, and said, 3316
11:32 So J passed over unto the children of 3316
11:34 J came *to* Mizpeh unto his house, and 3316
11:40 of J the Gileadite four days in a year. 3316
12: 1 and went northward, and said unto J, 3316
12: 2 J said unto them, I and my people were at 3316
12: 4 J gathered together all the men of Gilead, 3316
12: 7 J judged Israel six years. Then died 3316
12: 7 died J the Gileadite, and was buried in *one* 3316
1Sa 12:11 J, and Samuel, and delivered you out of 3316

JEPHUNNEH (16)
Nu 13: 6 Of the tribe of Judah, Caleb the son of J. 3312
14: 6 the son of Nun, and Caleb the son of J, 3312
14:30 save Caleb the son of J, and Joshua the son 3312
14:38 the son of Nun, and Caleb the son of J, 3312
26:65 save Caleb the son of J, and Joshua the son 3312
32:12 Save Caleb the son of J the Kenezite, and 3312
34:19 Of the tribe of Judah, Caleb the son of J. 3312
Dt 1:36 Save Caleb the son of J, he shall see it, and 3312
Jos 14: 6 Caleb the son of J the Kenezite said unto 3312
14:13 gave unto Caleb the son of J Hebron for an 3312
14:14 the inheritance of Caleb the son of J 3312
15:13 unto Caleb the son of J he gave a part 3312
21:12 gave they to Caleb the son of J for his 3312
1Ch 4:15 the sons of Caleb the son of J; Iru, Elah, 3312
6:56 they gave to Caleb the son of J. 3312
7:38 the sons of Jether; J, and Pispah, and Ara. 3312

JERAH (2)
Ge 10:26 and Sheleph, and Hazarmaveth, and J, 3392
1Ch 1:20 and Sheleph, and Hazarmaveth, and J, 3392

JERAHMEEL (8) [JERAHMEELITES]
1Ch 2: 9 born unto him; J, and Ram, and Chelubai. 3396
2:25 the sons of J the firstborn of Hezron were, 3396
2:26 J had also another wife, whose name *was* 3396
2:27 the sons of Ram the firstborn of J were, 3396
2:33 Peleth, and Zaza. These were the sons of J. 3396
2:42 Now the sons of Caleb the brother of J 3396
24:29 Concerning Kish: the son of Kish *was* J. 3396
Jer 36:26 the king commanded J the son of 3396

JERAHMEELITES (2) [JERAHMEEL]
1Sa 27:10 against the south of the J, and against 3397
30:29 to *them* which *were* in the cities of the J, 3397

JERED (2)
1Ch 1: 2 Kenan, Mahalaleel, J, 3382
4:18 his wife Jehudijah bare J the father of 3382

JEREMAI (1)
Ezr 10:33 Zabad, Eliphelet, J, Manasseh, *and* Shimei. 3413

JEREMIAH (146) [JEREMIAH'S, JEREMIAS, JEREMIE]
2Ki 23:31 *was* Hamutal, the daughter of J of Libnah. 3414
24:18 *was* Hamutal, the daughter of J of Libnah. 3414
1Ch 5:24 Azriel, and J, and Hodaviah, and Jahdiel, 3414
12: 4 J, and Jahaziel, and Johanan, and 3414
12:10 Mishmannah the fourth, J the fifth, 3414
12:13 J the tenth, Machbanai the eleventh. 3414
2Ch 35:25 J lamented for Josiah: and all the singing 3414
36:12 humbled not himself before J the prophet 3414
36:21 the word of the LORD by the mouth of J, 3414
36:22 by the mouth of J might be accomplished, 3414
Ezr 1: 1 by the mouth of J might be fulfilled, 3414
Ne 10: 2 Seraiah, Azariah, J, 3414
12: 1 of Shealtiel, and Jeshua: Seraiah, J, Ezra, 3414
12:12 of Seraiah, Meraiah; of J, Hananiah; 3414
12:34 Judah, and Benjamin, and Shemaiah, and J, 3414
Jer 1: 1 The words of J the son of Hilkiah, of 3414
1:11 came unto me, saying, J, what seest thou? 3414
7: 1 The word that came to J from the LORD, 3414
11: 1 The word that came to J from the LORD, 3414
14: 1 The word of the LORD that came to J 3414
18: 1 The word which came to J from 3414
18:18 Come, and let us devise devices against J; 3414
19:14 came J from Tophet, whither the LORD 3414
20: 1 heard *that* J prophesied these things. 3414
20: 2 Pashur smote J the prophet, and put him in 3414
20: 3 that Pashur brought forth J out of 3414
20: 3 said J unto him, The LORD hath not 3414
21: 1 The word which came unto J from 3414
21: 3 said J unto them, Thus shall ye say to 3414
24: 3 the LORD unto me, What seest thou, J? 3414
25: 1 The word that came to J concerning all 3414
25: 2 The which J the prophet spake unto all 3414
25:13 which J hath prophesied against all 3414
26: 7 all the people heard J speaking these words 3414
26: 8 when J had made an end of speaking all 3414
26: 9 all the people were gathered against J in 3414
26:12 spake J unto all the princes and to all 3414
26:20 this land according to all the words of J: 3414
26:24 of Ahikam the son of Shaphan was with J, 3414
27: 1 came this word unto J from the LORD, 3414
28: 5 the prophet J said unto the prophet 3414
28: 6 Even the prophet J said, Amen: 3414
28:11 full years. And the prophet J went his way. 3414
28:12 the word of the LORD came unto J 3414
28:12 the yoke from off the neck of the prophet J, 3414
28:15 said the prophet J unto Hananiah 3414
29: 1 Now these *are* the words of the letter that J 3414
29:27 why hast thou not reproved J of Anathoth, 3414
29:29 read this letter in the ears of J the prophet. 3414
29:30 came the word of the LORD unto J, 3414
30: 1 The word that came to J from the LORD, 3414
32: 1 The word that came to J from the LORD 3414
32: 2 J the prophet was shut up in the court of 3414
32: 6 J said, The word of the LORD came unto 3414
32:26 came the word of the LORD unto J, 3414
33: 1 the LORD came unto J the second time, 3414
33:19 the word of the LORD came unto J, 3414
33:23 the word of the LORD came to J, 3414
34: 1 The word which came unto J from 3414
34: 6 J the prophet spake all these words unto 3414
34: 8 *This is* the word that came unto J from 3414
34:12 of the LORD came to J from the LORD, 3414
35: 1 The word which came unto J from 3414
35: 3 I took Jaazaniah the son of J, the son of 3414
35:12 came the word of the LORD unto J, 3414
35:18 J said unto the house of the Rechabites, 3414
36: 1 *that* this word came unto J from 3414
36: 4 J called Baruch the son of Neriah: and 3414
36: 4 Baruch wrote from the mouth of J all 3414
36: 5 J commanded Baruch, saying, I *am* shut 3414
36: 8 to all that J the prophet commanded him, 3414
36:10 read Baruch in the book the words of J *in* 3414

Jer 36:19 unto Baruch, Go, hide thee, thou and J; 3414
36:26 to take Baruch the scribe and J the prophet: 3414
36:27 the word of the LORD came to J, 3414
36:27 which Baruch wrote at the mouth of J, 3414
36:32 took J another roll, and gave it to Baruch 3414
36:32 who wrote therein from the mouth of J all 3414
37: 2 which he spake by the prophet J. 3414
37: 3 son of Maaseiah the priest to the prophet J, 3414
37: 4 Now J came in and went out among 3414
37: 6 the word of the LORD unto the prophet J, 3414
37:12 J went forth out of Jerusalem to go *into* 3414
37:13 he took J the prophet, saying, Thou fallest 3414
37:14 said J, *It is* false; I fall not away to 3414
37:14 so Irijah took J, and brought him to 3414
37:15 Wherefore the princes were wroth with J, 3414
37:16 When J was entered into the dungeon, 3414
37:16 and J had remained there many days; 3414
37:17 J said, There is: for, said he, thou shalt be 3414
37:18 Moreover J said unto king Zedekiah, 3414
37:21 commit J into the court of the prison, 3414
37:21 Thus J remained in the court of the prison. 3414
38: 1 heard the words that J had spoken unto all 3414
38: 6 took they J, and cast him into the dungeon 3414
38: 6 they let down J with cords. And in 3414
38: 6 no water, but mire: so J sunk in the mire. 3414
38: 7 heard that they had put J in the dungeon; 3414
38: 9 in all that they have done to J the prophet, 3414
38:10 take up J the prophet out of the dungeon, 3414
38:11 them down by cords into the dungeon to J. 3414
38:12 Ebed-melech the Ethiopian said unto J, 3414
38:12 armholes under the cords. And J did so. 3414
38:13 So they drew up J with cords, and took him 3414
38:13 and J remained in the court of the prison. 3414
38:14 took J the prophet unto him into the third 3414
38:14 the king said unto J, I *will* ask thee a thing; 3414
38:15 J said unto Zedekiah, If I declare *it* unto 3414
38:16 So Zedekiah the king sware secretly unto J, 3414
38:17 said J unto Zedekiah, Thus saith 3414
38:19 Zedekiah the king said unto J, I am afraid 3414
38:20 J said, They shall not deliver *thee.* Obey, 3414
38:24 said Zedekiah unto J, Let no man know of 3414
38:27 came all the princes unto J, and asked him: 3414
38:28 So J abode in the court of the prison until 3414
39:11 J to Nebuzar-adan the captain of the guard, 3414
39:14 took J out of the court of the prison, and 3414
39:15 Now the word of the LORD came unto J, 3414
40: 1 The word which came to J from 3414
40: 2 the captain of the guard took J, and 3414
40: 6 went J unto Gedaliah the son of Ahikam to 3414
42: 2 said unto J the prophet, Let, we beseech 3414
42: 4 J the prophet said unto them, I have heard 3414
42: 5 they said to J, The LORD be a true and 3414
42: 7 that the word of the LORD came unto J. 3414
43: 1 *that* when J had made an end of speaking 3414
43: 2 all the proud men, saying unto J, 3414
43: 6 J the prophet, and Baruch the son of 3414
43: 8 came the word of the LORD unto J in 3414
44: 1 The word that came to J concerning all 3414
44:15 of Egypt, in Pathros, answered J, saying, 3414
44:20 J said unto all the people, to the men, and 3414
44:24 Moreover J said unto all the people, and 3414
45: 1 The word that J the prophet spake unto 3414
45: 1 these words in a book at the mouth of J, 3414
46: 1 The word of the LORD which came to J 3414
46:13 The word that the LORD spake to J 3414
47: 1 The word of the LORD that came to J 3414
49:34 The word of the LORD that came to J 3414
50: 1 against the land of the Chaldeans by J 3414
51:59 The word which J the prophet commanded 3414
51:60 So J wrote in a book all the evil that should 3414
51:61 J said to Seraiah, When thou comest *to* 3414
51:64 shall be weary. Thus far *are* the words of J. 3414
52: 1 *was* Hamutal the daughter of J of Libnah. 3414
Da 9: 2 where*of* the word of the LORD came to J 3414

JEREMIAH'S (1) [JEREMIAH]

Jer 28:10 took the yoke from off the prophet J neck, 3414

JEREMIAS (1) [JEREMIAH]

Mt 16:14 Elias; and others, J, or one of the prophets. *2408*

JEREMIE (2) [JEREMIAH]

Mt 2:17 that which was spoken by J the prophet, *2408*
27: 9 that which was spoken by J the prophet, *2408*

JEREMOTH (5)

1Ch 8:14 And Ahio, Shashak, and J, 3406
23:23 of Mushi; Mahli, and Eder, and J, three. 3406
25:22 The fifteenth to J, *he,* his sons, and 3406
Ezr 10:26 and Jehiel, and Abdi, and J, and Eliah. 3406
10:27 Mattaniah, and J, and Zabad, and Aziza. 3406

JERIAH (2)

1Ch 23:19 J the first, Amariah the second, Jahaziel 3404
24:23 the sons *of Hebron; J the first,* Amariah 3404

JERIBAI (1)

1Ch 11:46 Eliel the Mahavite, and J, and Joshaviah, 3403

JERICHO (64)

Nu 22: 1 the plains of Moab on *this* side Jordan *by* J. 3405
26: 3 in the plains of Moab by Jordan *near* J, 3405
26:63 in the plains of Moab by Jordan *near* J. 3405
31:12 of Moab, which *are* by Jordan *near* J. 3405
33:48 in the plains of Moab by Jordan *near* J. 3405
33:50 in the plains of Moab by Jordan *near* J, 3405
34:15 on *this* side Jordan *near* J eastward, 3405
35: 1 in the plains of Moab by Jordan *near* J, 3405
36:13 in the plains of Moab by Jordan *near* J. 3405
Dt 32:49 in the land of Moab, that *is* over against J; 3405
34: 1 *to* the top of Pisgah, that *is* over against J. 3405
34: 3 the south, and the plain of the valley of J, 3405
Jos 2: 1 saying, Go view the land, even J. 3405
2: 2 it was told the king of J, saying, Behold, 3405
2: 3 the king of J sent unto Rahab, saying, 3405
3:16 and the people passed over right against J. 3405
4:13 the LORD unto battle, to the plains of J. 3405
4:19 encamped in Gilgal, in the east border of J. 3405
5:10 day of the month at even in the plains of J. 3405
5:13 And it came to pass, when Joshua was by J, 3405
6: 1 Now J was straitly shut up because of 3405
6: 2 I have given into thine hand J, and the king 3405
6:25 which Joshua sent to spy out J. 3405
6:26 that riseth up and buildeth this city J: 3405
7: 2 Joshua sent men from J *to* Ai, which *is* 3405
8: 2 her king as thou didst unto J and her king: 3405
9: 3 Gibeon heard what Joshua had done unto J 3405
10: 1 as he had done to J and her king, so he had 3405
10:28 of Makkedah as he did unto the king of J. 3405
10:30 king thereof as he did unto the king of J. 3405
12: 9 The king of J, one; the king of Ai, which *is* 3405
13:32 on the *other* side Jordan, *by* J, eastward. 3405
16: 1 children of Joseph fell from Jordan *by* J, 3405
16: 1 *by* Jericho, unto the water of J on the east, 3405
16: 1 *to* the wilderness that goeth up from J 3405
16: 7 and came to J, and went out *at* Jordan. 3405
18:12 the border went up to the side of J on 3405
18:21 according to their families were J, 3405
20: 8 And on the *other* side Jordan *by* J eastward, 3405
24:11 ye went over Jordan, and came unto J: and 3405
24:11 the men of J fought against you, 3405
2Sa 10: 5 Tarry at J until your beards be grown, and 3405
1Ki 16:34 In his days did Hiel the Bethelite build J: 3405
2Ki 2: 4 for the LORD hath sent me *to* J. 3405
2: 4 I will not leave thee. So they came *to* J. 3405
2: 5 the sons of the prophets that *were* at J came 3405
2:15 prophets which *were* to view at J saw him, 3405
2:18 came again to him, (for he tarried at J,) 3405
25: 5 and overtook him in the plains of J: 3405
1Ch 6:78 on the *other* side Jordan *by* J, on the east 3405
19: 5 Tarry at J until your beards be grown, and 3405
2Ch 28:15 brought them *to* J, the city of palm trees, 3405
Ezr 2:34 The children of J, three hundred forty and 3405
Ne 3: 2 next unto him builded the men of J. 3405
7:36 The children of J, three hundred forty and 3405
Jer 39: 5 and overtook Zedekiah in the plains of J: 3405
52: 8 and overtook Zedekiah in the plains of J; 3405
Mt 20:29 And as they departed from J, a great *2410*
Mk 10:46 And they came to J: and as he went out of *2410*
10:46 as he went out of J with his disciples and *2410*
Lk 10:30 man went down from Jerusalem to J, *2410*
18:35 to pass, *that* as he was come nigh unto J, *2410*
19: 1 And *Jesus* entered and passed through J. *2410*
Heb 11:30 By faith the walls of J fell down, after they *2410*

JERIEL (1)

1Ch 7: 2 J, and Jahmai, and Jibsam, and Shemuel, 3400

JERIJAH (1)
1Ch 26:31 Among the Hebronites *was* J the chief, 3404

JERIMOTH (8)
1Ch 7: 7 and Uzzi, and Uzziel, and J, and Iri, five; 3406
7: 8 J, and Abiah, and Anathoth, and Alameth. 3406
12: 5 J, and Bealiah, and Shemariah, and 3406
24:30 sons also of Mushi; Mahli, and Eder, and J. 3406
25: 4 Uzziel, Shebuel, and J, Hananiah, Hanani, 3406
27:19 of Naphtali, J the son of Azriel: 3406
2Ch 11:18 the daughter of J the son of David *to* wife, 3406
31:13 J, and Jozabad, and Eliel, and Ismachiah, 3406

JERIOTH (1)
1Ch 2:18 *children* of Azubah *his* wife, and of J: 3408

JEROBOAM (102) [JEROBOAM'S]
1Ki 11:26 J the son of Nebat, an Ephrathite of Zereda, 3379
11:28 the man J *was* a mighty *man* of valour: 3379
11:29 it came to pass at that time when J went out 3379
11:31 he said to J, Take thee ten pieces: for thus 3379
11:40 Solomon sought therefore to kill J. 3379
11:40 J arose, and fled *into* Egypt, unto Shishak 3379
12: 2 it came to pass, when J the son of Nebat, 3379
12: 2 of king Solomon, and J dwelt in Egypt;) 3379
12: 3 J and all the congregation of Israel came, 3379
12:12 So J and all the people came to Rehoboam 3379
12:15 the Shilonite unto J the son of Nebat. 3379
12:20 when all Israel heard that J was come 3379
12:25 J built Shechem in mount Ephraim, and 3379
12:26 J said in his heart, Now shall the kingdom 3379
12:32 J ordained a feast in the eighth month, 3379
13: 1 and J stood by the altar to burn incense. 3379
13: 4 when king J heard the saying of the man of 3379
13:33 After this thing J returned not from his evil 3379
13:34 this thing became sin unto the house of J, 3379
14: 1 At that time Abijah the son of J fell sick. 3379
14: 2 J said to his wife, Arise, I pray thee, and 3379
14: 2 that thou be not known to be the wife of J; 3379
14: 5 the wife of J cometh to ask a thing of thee 3379
14: 6 that he said, Come in, thou wife of J; 3379
14: 7 Go, tell J, Thus saith the LORD God of 3379
14:10 I will bring evil upon the house of J, and 3379
14:10 will cut off from J *him that* pisseth against 3379
14:10 take away the remnant of the house of J, 3379
14:11 Him that dieth of J in the city shall 3379
14:13 for he only of J shall come to the grave, 3379
14:13 the LORD God of Israel in the house of J. 3379
14:14 who shall cut off the house of J that day: 3379
14:16 shall give Israel up because of the sins of J, 3379
14:19 the rest of the acts of J, how he warred, 3379
14:20 the days which J reigned *were* two and 3379
14:30 between Rehoboam and J all *their* days. 3379
15: 1 Now in the eighteenth year of king J 3379
15: 6 and J all the days of his life. 3379
15: 7 And there was war between Abijam and J. 3379
15: 9 in the twentieth year of J king of Israel 3379
15:25 Nadab the son of J *began* to reign over 3379
15:29 he reigned, *that* he smote all the house of J; 3379
15:29 he left not to J any that breathed, until *he* 3379
15:30 Because of the sins of J which he sinned, 3379
15:34 walked in the way of J and in his sin 3379
16: 2 thou hast walked in the way of J, and 3379
16: 3 will make thy house like the house of J 3379
16: 7 of his hands, in being like the house of J; 3379
16:19 in walking in the way of J, and in his sin 3379
16:26 For he walked in all the way of J the son of 3379
16:31 to walk in the sins of J the son of Nebat, 3379
21:22 will make thine house like the house of J 3379
22:52 in the way of J the son of Nebat, who made 3379
2Ki 3: 3 Nevertheless he cleaved unto the sins of J 3379
9: 9 Ahab like the house of J the son of Nebat, 3379
10:29 Howbeit *from* the sins of J the son of 3379
10:31 *for* he departed not from the sins of J, 3379
13: 2 followed the sins of J the son of Nebat, 3379
13: 6 not from the sins of the house of J, 3379
13:11 he departed not from all the sins of J 3379
13:13 with his fathers; and J sat upon his throne: 3379
14:16 of Israel; and J his son reigned in his stead. 3379
14:23 J the son of Joash king of Israel *began* to 3379
14:24 he departed not from all the sins of J 3379
14:27 he saved them by the hand of J the son of 3379
14:28 Now the rest of the acts of J, and all that he 3379
14:29 J slept with his fathers, *even* with the kings 3379
15: 1 seventh year of J king of Israel *began* 3379
15: 8 J reign over Israel in Samaria six months. 3379
15: 9 he departed not from the sins of J the son 3379
15:18 days from the sins of J the son of Nebat, 3379
15:24 he departed not from the sins of J the son 3379
15:28 he departed not from the sins of J the son 3379
17:21 and they made J the son of Nebat king: 3379
17:21 J drave Israel from following the LORD, 3379
17:22 walked in all the sins of J which he did; 3379
23:15 the high place which J the son of Nebat, 3379
1Ch 5:17 and in the days of J king of Israel. 3379
2Ch 9:29 in the visions of Iddo the seer against J 3379
10: 2 when J the son of Nebat, who *was* in 3379
10: 2 heard *it,* that J returned out of Egypt. 3379
10: 3 So J and all Israel came and spake to 3379
10:12 So J and all the people came to Rehoboam 3379
10:15 Ahijah the Shilonite to J the son of Nebat. 3379
11: 4 and returned from going against J. 3379
11:14 for J and his sons had cast them off from 3379
12:15 wars between Rehoboam and J continually. 3379
13: 1 Now in the eighteenth year of king J *began* 3379
13: 2 And there was war between Abijah and J. 3379
13: 3 J also set the battle in array against him 3379
13: 4 and said, Hear me, *thou* J, and all Israel; 3379
13: 6 Yet J the son of Nebat, the servant of 3379
13: 8 golden calves, which J made you for gods. 3379
13:13 J caused an ambushment to come about 3379
13:15 that God smote J and all Israel before 3379
13:19 Abijah pursued after J, and took cities from 3379
13:20 Neither did J recover strength again in 3379
Hos 1: 1 in the days of J the son of Joash, king of 3379
Am 1: 1 in the days of J the son of Joash king of 3379
7: 9 I will rise against the house of J with 3379
7:10 Amaziah *the* priest of Beth-el sent to J king 3379
7:11 J shall die by the sword, and Israel shall 3379

JEROBOAM'S (2) [JEROBOAM]
1Ki 14: 4 J wife did so, and arose, and went *to* 3379
14:17 J wife arose, and departed, and came to 3379

JEROHAM (10)
1Sa 1: 1 the son of J, the son of Elihu, the son of 3395
1Ch 6:27 Eliab his son, J his son, Elkanah his son. 3395
6:34 the son of J, the son of Eliel, the son of 3395
8:27 and Eliah, and Zichri, the sons of J. 3395
9: 8 Ibneiah the son of J, and Elah the son of 3395
9:12 Adaiah the son of J, the son of Pashur, 3395
12: 7 and Zebadiah, the sons of J of Gedor. 3395
27:22 Of Dan, Azareel the son of J. These *were* 3395
2Ch 23: 1 Azariah the son of J, and Ishmael the son 3395
Ne 11:12 Adaiah the son of J, the son of Pelaliah, 3395

JERUBBAAL (14) [GIDEON, JERUBBESHETH]
Jdg 6:32 Therefore on that day he called him J, 3378
7: 1 J, who *is* Gideon, and all the people that 3378
8:29 J the son of Joash went and dwelt in his 3378
8:35 shewed they kindness to the house of J, 3378
9: 1 Abimelech the son of J went to Shechem 3378
9: 2 either that all the sons of J, *which are* 3378
9: 5 slew his brethren the sons of J, 3378
9: 5 yet Jotham the youngest son of J was left; 3378
9:16 if ye have dealt well with J and his house, 3378
9:19 have dealt truly and sincerely with J and 3378
9:24 and ten sons of J might come, 3378
9:28 *is* not *he* the son of J? and Zebul his 3378
9:57 came the curse of Jotham the son of J. 3378
1Sa 12:11 the LORD sent J, and Bedan, and 3378

JERUBBESHETH (1) [JERUBBAAL]
2Sa 11:21 Who smote Abimelech the son of J? 3380

JERUEL (1)
2Ch 20:16 of the brook, before the wilderness of J. 3385

JERUSALEM (811) [JEBUS, JERUSALEM'S, SALEM]
Jos 10: 1 when Adoni-zedek king of J had heard how 3389
10: 3 Wherefore Adoni-zedek king of J sent unto 3389
10: 5 the king of J, the king of Hebron, the king 3389
10:23 the king of J, the king of Hebron, the king 3389
12:10 The king of J, one; the king of Hebron, 3389
15: 8 the south side of the Jebusite; the same *is* J: 3389
15:63 As for the Jebusites the inhabitants of J, 3389
15:63 the children of Judah at J unto this day. 3389
18:28 Eleph, and Jebusi, which *is* J, Gibeath, *and* 3389
Jdg 1: 7 they brought him *to* J, and there he died. 3389

Jdg 1: 8 the children of Judah had fought against J, 3389
1:21 not drive out the Jebusites that inhabited J; 3389
1:21 the children of Benjamin in J unto this day. 3389
19:10 and came over against Jebus, which *is* J; 3389
1Sa 17:54 head of the Philistine, and brought it *to* J; 3389
2Sa 5: 5 in J he reigned thirty and three years over 3389
5: 6 and his men went *to* J unto the Jebusites, 3389
5:13 *him* mo concubines and wives out of J, 3389
5:14 of those that were born unto him in J; 3389
8: 7 of Hadadezer, and brought them *to* J. 3389
9:13 So Mephibosheth dwelt in J: for he did eat 3389
10:14 the children of Ammon, and came *to* J. 3389
11: 1 But David tarried *still* at J. 3389
11:12 So Uriah abode in J that day, and 3389
12:31 and all the people returned *unto* J. 3389
14:23 went to Geshur, and brought Absalom *to* J. 3389
14:28 So Absalom dwelt two full years in J, and 3389
15: 8 LORD shall bring me again indeed *to* J, 3389
15:11 Absalom went two hundred men out of J, 3389
15:14 all his servants that *were* with him at J, 3389
15:29 Abiathar carried the ark of God again *to* J: 3389
15:37 *into* the city, and Absalom came *into* J. 3389
16: 3 said unto the king, Behold, he abideth at J: 3389
16:15 came *to* J, and Ahithophel with him. 3389
17:20 and could not find *them,* they returned *to* J. 3389
19:19 the day that my lord the king went out of J, 3389
19:25 when he was come *to* J to meet the king, 3389
19:33 with me, and I will feed thee with me in J. 3389
19:34 that I should go up with the king *unto* J? 3389
20: 2 unto their king, from Jordan even to J. 3389
20: 3 David came to his house *at* J; and the king 3389
20: 7 all the mighty *men:* and they went out of J, 3389
20:22 And Joab returned *to* J unto the king. 3389
24: 8 they came *to* J at the end of nine months 3389
24:16 stretched out his hand *upon* J to destroy it, 3389
1Ki 2:11 and thirty and three years reigned he in J. 3389
2:36 Build thee a house in J, and dwell there, 3389
2:38 And Shimei dwelt in J many days. 3389
2:41 that Shimei had gone from J *to* Gath, 3389
3: 1 the LORD, and the wall of J round about. 3389
3:15 he came *to* J, and stood before the ark of 3389
8: 1 children of Israel, unto king Solomon *in* J, 3389
9:15 the wall of J, and Hazor, and Megiddo, and 3389
9:19 that which Solomon desired to build in J, 3389
10: 2 she came to J with a very great train, 3389
10:26 cities for chariots, and with the king at J. 3389
10:27 the king made silver *to be* in J as stones, 3389
11: 7 in the hill that *is* before J, and for Molech, 3389
11:29 at that time when Jeroboam went out of J, 3389
11:36 may have a light alway before me in J, 3389
11:42 the time that Solomon reigned in J over all 3389
12:18 to get *him* up to *his* chariot, to flee *to* J. 3389
12:21 when Rehoboam was come *to* J, he 3389
12:27 sacrifice in the house of the LORD at J, 3389
12:28 *It is* too much for you to go up *to* J: 3389
14:21 and he reigned seventeen years in J, 3389
14:25 Shishak king of Egypt came up against J: 3389
15: 2 Three years reigned he in J. And his 3389
15: 4 the LORD his God give him a lamp in J, 3389
15: 4 set up his son after him, and to establish J: 3389
15:10 forty and one years reigned he in J. And his 3389
22:42 and he reigned twenty and five years in J. 3389
2Ki 8:17 to reign; and he reigned eight years in J. 3389
8:26 to reign; and he reigned one year in J. 3389
9:28 his servants carried him *in a chariot* to J, 3389
12: 1 to reign; and forty years reigned he in J. 3389
12:17 and Hazael set his face to go up to J. 3389
12:18 king of Syria: and he went away from J. 3389
14: 2 and reigned twenty and nine years in J. 3389
14: 2 his mother's name *was* Jehoaddan of J. 3389
14:13 came *to* J, and brake down the wall of 3389
14:13 brake down the wall of J from the gate of 3389
14:19 they made a conspiracy against him in J: 3389
14:20 he was buried at J with his fathers in 3389
15: 2 and he reigned two and fifty years in J. 3389
15: 2 And his mother's name *was* Jecholiah of J. 3389
15:33 to reign, and he reigned sixteen years in J. 3389
16: 2 reigned sixteen years in J, and did not *that* 3389
16: 5 king of Israel came up *to* J to war: 3389
18: 2 and he reigned twenty and nine years in J. 3389
18:17 king Hezekiah with a great host *against* J. 3389
18:17 they went up and came *to* J. And when 3389
18:22 taken away, and hath said to Judah and J, 3389
18:22 Ye shall worship before this altar in J? 3389
18:35 that the LORD should deliver J out of 3389
19:10 J shall not be delivered into the hand of 3389
19:21 the daughter of J hath shaken her head at 3389
19:31 For out of J shall go forth a remnant, and 3389
21: 1 and reigned fifty and five years in J. 3389
21: 4 the LORD said, In J will I put my name. 3389
21: 7 to Solomon his son, In this house, and in J, 3389
21:12 I *am* bringing *such* evil upon J and Judah, 3389
21:13 I will stretch over J the line of Samaria, 3389
21:13 I will wipe J as *a man* wipeth a dish, 3389
21:16 till he had filled J from one end to another; 3389
21:19 to reign, and he reigned two years in J. 3389
22: 1 and he reigned thirty and one years in J. 3389
22:14 (now she dwelt in J in the college;) and 3389
23: 1 unto him all the elders of Judah and of J. 3389
23: 2 and all the inhabitants of J with him, 3389
23: 4 he burnt them without J in the fields of 3389
23: 5 of Judah, and in the places round about J; 3389
23: 6 without J, unto the brook Kidron, and 3389
23: 9 came not up to the altar of the LORD in J, 3389
23:13 the high places that *were* before J, 3389
23:20 men's bones upon them, and returned *to* J. 3389
23:23 passover was holden to the LORD in J. 3389
23:24 were spied in the land of Judah and in J, 3389
23:27 will cast off this city J which I have 3389
23:30 brought him *to* J, and buried him in his 3389
23:31 to reign; and he reigned three months in J. 3389
23:33 of Hamath, that *he* might not reign in J; 3389
23:36 to reign; and he reigned eleven years in J. 3389
24: 4 for he filled J *with* innocent blood; 3389
24: 8 to reign, and he reigned in J three months. 3389
24: 8 the daughter of Elnathan of J. 3389
24:10 king of Babylon came up *against* J, 3389
24:14 he carried away all J, and all the princes, 3389
24:15 *those* carried he *into* captivity from J to 3389
24:18 to reign, and he reigned eleven years in J. 3389
24:20 anger of the LORD it came to pass in J 3389
25: 1 his host, against J, and pitched against it; 3389
25: 8 a servant of the king of Babylon, *unto* J: 3389
25: 9 all the houses of J, and every great *man's* 3389
25:10 brake down the walls of J round about. 3389
1Ch 3: 4 and in J he reigned thirty and three years. 3389
3: 5 these were born unto him in J; Shimea, 3389
6:10 in the temple that Solomon built in J:) 3389
6:15 and J by the hand of Nebuchadnezzar. 3389
6:32 had built the house of the LORD in J: 3389
8:28 chief *men.* These dwelt in J. 3389
8:32 these also dwelt with their brethren in J, 3389
9: 3 in J dwelt of the children of Judah, and 3389
9:34 their generations; these dwelt at J. 3389
9:38 they also dwelt with their brethren at J, 3389
11: 4 David and all Israel went *to* J, which *is* 3389
14: 3 David took moe wives at J: and 3389
14: 4 names of *his* children which he had in J; 3389
15: 3 David gathered all Israel together to J, 3389
18: 7 of Hadarezer, and brought them *to* J. 3389
19:15 entered into the city. Then Joab came *to* J. 3389
20: 1 David tarried at J. And Joab smote Rabbah, 3389
20: 3 And David and all the people returned *to* J. 3389
21: 4 went throughout all Israel, and came to J. 3389
21:15 God sent an angel unto J to destroy it: and 3389
21:16 sword in his hand stretched out over J. 3389
23:25 that they may dwell in J for ever: 3389
28: 1 and with all the valiant men, unto J. 3389
29:27 and thirty and three *years* reigned he in J. 3389
2Ch 1: 4 for it: for he had pitched a tent for it at J. 3389
1:13 to the high place that *was* at Gibeon *to* J, 3389
1:14 in the chariot cities, and with the king at J. 3389
1:15 and gold at J *as plenteous* as stones, 3389
2: 7 *men* that *are* with me in Judah and in J, 3389
2:16 sea *to* Joppa; and thou shalt carry it up *to* J. 3389
3: 1 house of the LORD at J in mount Moriah, 3389
5: 2 the fathers of the children of Israel, unto J, 3389
6: 6 I have chosen J, that my name might be 3389
8: 6 all that Solomon desired to build in J, and 3389
9: 1 to prove Solomon with hard questions at J, 3389
9:25 in the chariot cities, and with the king at J. 3389
9:27 the king made silver in J as stones, and 3389
9:30 Solomon reigned in J over all Israel forty 3389
10:18 to get *him* up to *his* chariot, to flee *to* J. 3389
11: 1 when Rehoboam was come *to* J, he 3389
11: 5 Rehoboam dwelt in J, and built cities for 3389
11:14 their possession, and came to Judah and J: 3389
11:16 seek the LORD God of Israel came *to* J, 3389

2Ch 12: 2 Shishak king of Egypt came up against J, 3389
12: 4 which *pertained* to Judah, and came to J. 3389
12: 5 that were gathered together to J because 3389
12: 7 my wrath shall not be poured out upon J by 3389
12: 9 Shishak king of Egypt came up against J, 3389
12:13 king Rehoboam strengthened himself in J, 3389
12:13 and he reigned seventeen years in J, 3389
13: 2 He reigned three years in J. His mother's 3389
14:15 and camels in abundance, and returned *to* J. 3389
15:10 So they gathered themselves together *at* J 3389
17:13 of war, mighty *men* of valour, *were* in J. 3389
19: 1 Judah returned to his house in peace to J. 3389
19: 4 Jehoshaphat dwelt at J: and he went out 3389
19: 8 Moreover in J did Jehoshaphat set of 3389
19: 8 for controversies, when they returned *to* J. 3389
20: 5 stood in the congregation of Judah and J, 3389
20:15 ye inhabitants of J, and thou king 3389
20:17 of the LORD with you, O Judah and J: 3389
20:18 the inhabitants of J fell before the LORD, 3389
20:20 Hear me, O Judah, and ye inhabitants of J; 3389
20:27 every man of Judah and J, and 3389
20:27 forefront of them, to go again to J with joy; 3389
20:28 they came *to* J with psalteries and harps 3389
20:31 and he reigned twenty and five years in J. 3389
21: 5 to reign, and he reigned eight years in J. 3389
21:11 caused the inhabitants of J to commit 3389
21:13 and the inhabitants of J to go a whoring, 3389
21:20 he reigned in J eight years, and 3389
22: 1 the inhabitants of J made Ahaziah his 3389
22: 2 to reign, and he reigned one year in J. 3389
23: 2 of the fathers of Israel, and they came to J. 3389
24: 1 to reign, and he reigned forty years in J. 3389
24: 6 in out of Judah and out of J the collection, 3389
24: 9 made a proclamation through Judah and J, 3389
24:18 upon Judah and J for this their trespass. 3389
24:23 they came to Judah and J, and destroyed all 3389
25: 1 and he reigned twenty and nine years in J. 3389
25: 1 his mother's name *was* Jehoaddan of J. 3389
25:23 brought him *to* J, and brake down the wall 3389
25:23 brake down the wall of J from the gate of 3389
25:27 they made a conspiracy against him in J; 3389
26: 3 and he reigned fifty and two years in J. 3389
26: 3 His mother's name also *was* Jecoliah of J. 3389
26: 9 Moreover Uzziah built towers in J at 3389
26:15 he made in J engines, invented by cunning 3389
27: 1 to reign, and he reigned sixteen years in J. 3389
27: 8 to reign, and reigned sixteen years in J. 3389
28: 1 to reign, and he reigned sixteen years in J: 3389
28:10 J for bondmen and bondwomen unto you: 3389
28:24 he made him altars in every corner of J. 3389
28:27 and they buried him in the city, *even* in J: 3389
29: 1 and he reigned nine and twenty years in J. 3389
29: 8 of the LORD was upon Judah and J, 3389
30: 1 come to the house of the LORD at J, 3389
30: 2 his princes, and all the congregation in J, 3389
30: 3 people gathered themselves together to J. 3389
30: 5 unto the LORD God of Israel at J: 3389
30:11 humbled themselves, and came to J. 3389
30:13 there assembled *at* J much people to keep 3389
30:14 and took away the altars that *were* in J, 3389
30:21 the children of Israel that were present at J 3389
30:26 So there was great joy in J: for since 3389
30:26 king of Israel *there was* not the like in J. 3389
31: 4 dwelt in J to give the portion of the priests 3389
32: 2 and that he was purposed to fight against J, 3389
32: 9 king of Assyria send his servants to J, 3389
32: 9 and unto all Judah that *were* at J, saying, 3389
32:10 do ye trust, that ye abide in the siege in J? 3389
32:12 and commanded Judah and J, saying, 3389
32:18 unto the people of J that *were* on the wall, 3389
32:19 they spake against the God of J, as against 3389
32:22 the inhabitants of J from the hand of 3389
32:23 many brought gifts unto the LORD to J, 3389
32:25 wrath upon him, and upon Judah and J. 3389
32:26 *both* he and the inhabitants of J, so that 3389
32:33 the inhabitants of J did him honour at his 3389
33: 1 and he reigned fifty and five years in J: 3389
33: 4 had said, In J shall my name be for ever. 3389
33: 7 to Solomon his son, In this house, and in J, 3389
33: 9 made Judah and the inhabitants of J to err, 3389
33:13 brought him again *to* J into his kingdom. 3389
33:15 and in J, and cast *them* out of the city. 3389
33:21 *began* to reign, and reigned two years in J. 3389
34: 1 and he reigned in J one and thirty years. 3389
34: 3 to purge Judah and J from the high places, 3389
34: 5 upon their altars, and cleansed Judah and J. 3389
34: 7 all the land of Israel, he returned to J. 3389
34: 9 and Benjamin; and they returned *to* J. 3389
34:22 (now she dwelt in J in the college:) and 3389
34:29 together all the elders of Judah and J. 3389
34:30 the inhabitants of J, and the priests, and 3389
34:32 he caused all that were present in J and 3389
34:32 of J did according to the covenant of God, 3389
35: 1 kept a passover unto the LORD in J: 3389
35:18 that were present, and the inhabitants of J. 3389
35:24 they brought him *to* J, and he died, and 3389
35:24 And all Judah and J mourned for Josiah. 3389
36: 1 made him king in his father's stead in J. 3389
36: 2 to reign, and he reigned three months in J. 3389
36: 3 the king of Egypt put him down at J, and 3389
36: 4 Eliakim his brother king over Judah and J, 3389
36: 5 to reign, and he reigned eleven years in J: 3389
36: 9 he reigned three months and ten days in J: 3389
36:10 his brother king over Judah and J. 3389
36:11 to reign, and reigned eleven years in J. 3389
36:14 of the LORD which he had hallowed in J. 3389
36:19 brake down the wall of J, and burnt all 3389
36:23 hath charged me to build him a house in J, 3389
Ezr 1: 2 hath charged me to build him a house at J, 3389
1: 3 let him go up to J, which *is* in Judah, and 3389
1: 3 of Israel, (he *is* the God,) which *is* in J. 3389
1: 4 offering for the house of God that *is* in J. 3389
1: 5 the house of the LORD which *is* in J. 3389
1: 7 Nebuchadnezzar had brought forth out of J, 3389
1:11 that were brought up from Babylon unto J. 3389
2: 1 came again unto J and Judah, every one 3389
2:68 to the house of the LORD which *is* at J, 3389
3: 1 themselves together as one man to J. 3389
3: 8 of their coming unto the house of God at J, 3389
3: 8 that were come out of the captivity *unto* J; 3389
4: 6 against the inhabitants of Judah and J. 3389
4: 8 Shimshai the scribe wrote a letter against J 3390
4:12 came up from thee to us are come unto J, 3390
4:20 There have been mighty kings also over J, 3390
4:23 they went up in haste to J unto the Jews, 3390
4:24 work of the house of the God which *is* at J. 3390
5: 1 and J in the name of the God of Israel, 3390
5: 2 to build the house of God which *is* at J: 3390
5:14 took out of the temple that *was* in J, 3390
5:15 go, carry them into the temple that *is* in J, 3390
5:16 of the house of God which *is* in J: 3390
5:17 the king to build this house of God at J, 3390
6: 3 a decree *concerning* the house of God at J, 3390
6: 5 took forth out of the temple which *is* at J, 3390
6: 5 brought *again* unto the temple which *is* at J, 3390
6: 9 appointment of the priests which *are* at J, 3390
6:12 to destroy this house of God which *is* at J. 3390
6:18 for the service of God, which *is* at J; 3390
7: 7 and the porters, and the Nethinims, unto J, 3389
7: 8 he came *to* J in the fifth month, which *was* 3389
7: 9 first *day* of the fifth month came he to J, 3389
7:13 minded of their own freewill to go *up* to J, 3390
7:14 to inquire concerning Judah and J, 3390
7:15 the God of Israel, whose habitation *is* in J, 3390
7:16 for the house of their God which *is* in J: 3390
7:17 of the house of your God which *is* in J. 3390
7:19 *those* deliver thou before the God of J. 3390
7:27 the house of the LORD which *is* in J: 3389
8:29 and chief of the fathers of Israel, at J, 3389
8:30 to bring *them* to J unto the house of our 3389
8:31 twelfth *day* of the first month, to go *unto* J: 3389
8:32 we came *to* J, and abode there three days. 3389
9: 9 and to give us a wall in Judah and in J. 3389
10: 7 and J unto all the children of the captivity, 3389
10: 7 should gather themselves together *unto* J; 3389
10: 9 together *unto* J within three days. 3389
Ne 1: 2 were left of the captivity, and concerning J. 3389
1: 3 the wall of J also *is* broken down, and 3389
2:11 So I came to J, and was there three days. 3389
2:12 my God had put in my heart to do at J: 3389
2:13 to the dung port, and viewed the walls of J, 3389
2:17 how J *lieth* waste, and the gates thereof are 3389
2:17 come, and let us build *up* the wall of J, 3389
2:20 no portion, nor right, nor memorial, in J. 3389
3: 8 and they fortified J unto the broad wall. 3389
3: 9 son of Hur, the ruler of the half part of J. 3389
3:12 the ruler of the half part of J, he and 3389
4: 7 heard that the walls of J were made up, 3389

Ne	4: 8	together to come *and* to fight against J,	3389
	4:22	every one with his servant lodge within J,	3389
	6: 7	appointed prophets to preach of thee at J,	3389
	7: 2	the ruler of the palace, charge over J:	3389
	7: 3	Let not the gates of J be opened until	3389
	7: 3	and appoint watches of the inhabitants of J,	3389
	7: 6	came again to J and to Judah, every one	3389
	8:15	in J, saying, Go forth *unto* the mount, and	3389
	11: 1	the rulers of the people dwelt at J: the rest	3389
	11: 1	to bring one of ten to dwell in J the holy	3389
	11: 2	willingly offered themselves to dwell at J.	3389
	11: 3	*are* the chief of the province that dwelt in J:	3389
	11: 4	at J dwelt *certain* of the children of Judah,	3389
	11: 6	All the sons of Perez that dwelt at J *were*	3389
	11:22	The overseer also of the Levites at J *was*	3389
	12:27	at the dedication of the wall of J they	3389
	12:27	to bring them to J, to keep the dedication	3389
	12:28	both out of the plain country round about J,	3389
	12:29	had builded them villages round about J.	3389
	12:43	so that the joy of J was heard even afar off.	3389
	13: 6	in all this *time* was not I at J: for in the two	3389
	13: 7	I came to J, and understood of the evil that	3389
	13:15	which they brought *into* J on the sabbath	3389
	13:16	unto the children of Judah, and in J.	3389
	13:19	that when the gates of J began to be dark	3389
	13:20	sellers of all *kind of* ware lodged without J	3389
Est	2: 6	Who had been carried away from J with	3389
Ps	51:18	unto Zion: build thou the walls of J.	3389
	68:29	Because of thy temple at J shall kings bring	3389
	79: 1	they defiled; they have laid J on heaps.	3389
	79: 3	have they shed like water round about J;	3389
	102:21	of the LORD in Zion, and his praise in J;	3389
	116:19	LORD'S house, in the midst of thee, O J.	3389
	122: 2	Our feet shall stand within thy gates, O J.	3389
	122: 3	J *is* builded as a city that is compact	3389
	122: 6	Pray for the peace of J: they shall prosper	3389
	125: 2	*As* the mountains *are* round about J, so	3389
	128: 5	thou shalt see the good of J all the days of	3389
	135:21	LORD out of Zion, which dwelleth *at* J.	3389
	137: 5	If I forget thee, O J, let my right hand	3389
	137: 6	if I prefer not J above my chief joy.	3389
	137: 7	the children of Edom *in* the day of J;	3389
	147: 2	The LORD doth build up J: he gathereth	3389
	147:12	Praise the LORD, O J; praise thy God,	3389
Ecc	1: 1	of the Preacher, the son of David, king in J.	3389
	1:12	I the Preacher was king over Israel in J.	3389
	1:16	than all *they* that have been before me in J:	3389
	2: 7	small cattle above all that were in J before	3389
	2: 9	more than all that were before me in J:	3389
SS	1: 5	*am* black, but comely, O ye daughters of J,	3389
	2: 7	O ye daughters of J, by the roes, and by	3389
	3: 5	O ye daughters of J, by the roes, and by	3389
	3:10	paved *with* love, for the daughters of J.	3389
	5: 8	I charge you, O daughters of J, if ye find	3389
	5:16	and this *is* my friend, O daughters of J.	3389
	6: 4	O my love, as Tirzah, comely as J,	3389
	8: 4	I charge you, O daughters of J, that ye stir	3389
Isa	1: 1	and J in the days of Uzziah,	3389
	2: 1	son of Amoz saw concerning Judah and J.	3389
	2: 3	and the word of the LORD from J.	3389
	3: 1	doth take away from J and from Judah	3389
	3: 8	For J is ruined, and Judah is fallen: because	3389
	4: 3	he that remaineth in J, shall be called holy,	3389
	4: 3	one that is written among the living in J:	3389
	4: 4	shall have purged the blood of J from	3389
	5: 3	O inhabitants of J, and men of Judah,	3389
	7: 1	went up *towards* J to war against it, but	3389
	8:14	a gin and for a snare to the inhabitants of J.	3389
	10:10	whose graven images did excel *them of* J	3389
	10:11	and her idols, so do to J and her idols?	3389
	10:12	his whole work upon mount Zion and on J,	3389
	10:32	mount of the daughter of Zion, the hill of J.	3389
	22:10	And ye have numbered the houses of J, and	3389
	22:21	he shall be a father to the inhabitants of J,	3389
	24:23	and in J, and before his ancients gloriously.	3389
	27:13	worship the LORD in the holy mount at J.	3389
	28:14	that rule this people which *is* in J.	3389
	30:19	For the people shall dwell in Zion at J:	3389
	31: 5	so will the LORD of hosts defend J;	3389
	31: 9	whose fire *is* in Zion, and his furnace in J.	3389
	33:20	thine eyes shall see J a quiet habitation,	3389
	36: 2	to J unto king Hezekiah with a great army.	3389
	36: 7	said to Judah and to J, Ye shall worship	3389
	36:20	that the LORD should deliver J out of my	3389
	37:10	J shall not be given into the hand of	3389
	37:22	the daughter of J hath shaken her head at	3389
	37:32	For out of J shall go forth a remnant, and	3389
	40: 2	Speak ye comfortably to J, and cry unto	3389
	40: 9	O J, that bringest good tidings, lift up thy	3389
	41:27	I will give to J one that bringeth good	3389
	44:26	that saith to J, Thou shalt be inhabited; and	3389
	44:28	even saying to J, Thou shalt be built; and	3389
	51:17	Awake, awake, stand up, O J, which hast	3389
	52: 1	thy beautiful garments, O J, the holy city:	3389
	52: 2	from the dust; arise, *and* sit down, O J:	3389
	52: 9	sing together, ye waste places of J:	3389
	52: 9	comforted his people, he hath redeemed J.	3389
	62: 6	I have set watchmen upon thy walls, O J,	3389
	62: 7	and till he make J a praise in the earth.	3389
	64:10	Zion is a wilderness, J a desolation.	3389
	65:18	I create J a rejoicing, and her people a joy.	3389
	65:19	I will rejoice in J, and joy in my people:	3389
	66:10	Rejoice ye with J, and be glad with her,	3389
	66:13	and ye shall be comforted in J.	3389
	66:20	to my holy mountain J, saith the LORD,	3389
Jer	1: 3	unto the carrying away of J captive in	3389
	1:15	his throne *at* the entering of the gates of J,	3389
	2: 2	Go and cry in the ears of J, saying,	3389
	3:17	At that time they shall call J the throne of	3389
	3:17	unto it, to the name of the LORD, to J:	3389
	4: 3	the LORD to the men of Judah and J,	3389
	4: 4	ye men of Judah and inhabitants of J:	3389
	4: 5	Declare ye in Judah, and publish in J; and	3389
	4:10	hast greatly deceived this people and J,	3389
	4:11	time shall it be said to this people and to J,	3389
	4:14	O J, wash thine heart from wickedness, that	3389
	4:16	behold, publish against J, *that* watchers	3389
	5: 1	Run ye to and fro through the streets of J,	3389
	6: 1	yourselves to flee out of the midst of J,	3389
	6: 6	ye down trees, and cast a mount against J:	3389
	6: 8	Be thou instructed, O J, lest my soul depart	3389
	7:17	in the cities of Judah and in the streets of J?	3389
	7:29	*O J*, and cast *it* away, and take up a	NIH
	7:34	from the streets of J, the voice of mirth,	3389
	8: 1	the bones of the inhabitants of J, out of	3389
	8: 5	is this people of J slidden back *by* a	3389
	9:11	I will make J heaps, *and* a den of dragons;	3389
	11: 2	men of Judah, and to the inhabitants of J;	3389
	11: 6	in the streets of J, saying, Hear ye	3389
	11: 9	of Judah, and among the inhabitants of J.	3389
	11:12	the cities of Judah and inhabitants of J go,	3389
	11:13	*according to* the number of the streets of J	3389
	13: 9	the pride of Judah, and the great pride of J.	3389
	13:13	the prophets, and all the inhabitants of J,	3389
	13:27	Woe unto thee, O J! wilt thou not be made	3389
	14: 2	the ground; and the cry of J is gone up.	3389
	14:16	prophesy shall be cast out in the streets of J	3389
	15: 4	king of Judah, for *that* which he did in J.	3389
	15: 5	For who shall have pity upon thee, O J? or	3389
	17:19	which they go out, and in all the gates of J;	3389
	17:20	and all Judah, and all the inhabitants of J,	3389
	17:21	nor bring *it* in by the gates of J;	3389
	17:25	the men of Judah, and the inhabitants of J:	3389
	17:26	from the places about J, and from the land	3389
	17:27	even entering in at the gates of J on	3389
	17:27	it shall devour the palaces of J, and it shall	3389
	18:11	to the inhabitants of J, saying, Thus saith	3389
	19: 3	O kings of Judah, and inhabitants of J;	3389
	19: 7	the counsel of Judah and J in this place;	3389
	19:13	the houses of J, and the houses of the kings	3389
	22:19	drawn and cast forth beyond the gates of J.	3389
	23:14	I have seen also in the prophets of J a	3389
	23:15	for from the prophets of J is profaneness	3389
	24: 1	from J, and had brought them *to* Babylon.	3389
	24: 8	his princes, and the residue of J,	3389
	25: 2	and to all the inhabitants of J, saying,	3389
	25:18	*To wit*, J, and the cities of Judah, and	3389
	26:18	J shall become heaps, and the mountain of	3389
	27: 3	come *to* J unto Zedekiah king of Judah;	3389
	27:18	king of Judah, and at J, go not to Babylon.	3389
	27:20	king of Judah from J to Babylon,	3389
	27:20	and all the nobles of Judah and J;	3389
	27:21	*in* the house of the king of Judah and of J;	3389
	29: 1	J unto the residue of the elders which were	3389
	29: 1	carried away captive from J to Babylon;	3389
	29: 2	the princes of Judah and J, and	3389
	29: 2	and the smiths, were departed from J;)	3389
	29: 4	to be carried away from J unto Babylon;	3389

Jer	29:20	whom I have sent from J to Babylon:	3389
	29:25	in thy name unto all the people that *are* at J,	3389
	32: 2	the king of Babylon's army besieged J:	3389
	32:32	the men of Judah, and the inhabitants of J.	3389
	32:44	in the places about J, and in the cities of	3389
	33:10	in the streets of J, that are desolate, without	3389
	33:13	in the places about J, and in the cities of	3389
	33:16	Judah be saved, and J shall dwell safely:	3389
	34: 1	fought against J, and against all the cities	3389
	34: 6	words unto Zedekiah king of Judah in J,	3389
	34: 7	king of Babylon's army fought against J,	3389
	34: 8	with all the people which *were* at J,	3389
	34:19	the princes of J, the eunuchs, and	3389
	35:11	let us go *to* J for fear of the army of	3389
	35:11	the army of the Syrians: so we dwell at J.	3389
	35:13	the men of Judah and the inhabitants of J,	3389
	35:17	upon all the inhabitants of J all the evil that	3389
	36: 9	before the LORD *to* all the people in J,	3389
	36: 9	that came from the cities of Judah unto J.	3389
	36:31	upon the inhabitants of J, and upon the men	3389
	37: 5	when the Chaldeans that besieged J heard	3389
	37: 5	tidings of them, they departed from J.	3389
	37:11	up from J for fear of Pharaoh's army,	3389
	37:12	Jeremiah went forth out of J to go *into*	3389
	38:28	of the prison until the day that J was taken:	3389
	38:28	and he was *there* when J was taken.	3389
	39: 1	king of Babylon and all his army against J,	3389
	39: 8	with fire, and brake down the walls of J.	3389
	40: 1	all that were carried away captive of J	3389
	42:18	been poured forth upon the inhabitants of J;	3389
	44: 2	seen all the evil that I have brought upon J,	3389
	44: 6	in the cities of Judah and in the streets of J;	3389
	44: 9	in the land of Judah, and in the streets of J?	3389
	44:13	as I have punished J, by the sword, by	3389
	44:17	the cities of Judah, and in the streets of J:	3389
	44:21	in the streets of J, ye, and your fathers,	3389
	51:35	the inhabitants of Chaldea, shall J say.	3389
	51:50	afar off, and let J come into your mind.	3389
	52: 1	to reign, and he reigned eleven years in J.	3389
	52: 3	anger of the LORD it came to pass in J	3389
	52: 4	against J, and pitched against it, and	3389
	52:12	*which* served the king of Babylon, into J,	3389
	52:13	all the houses of J, and all the houses of	3389
	52:14	brake down all the walls of J round about.	3389
	52:29	away captive from J eight hundred thirty	3389
La	1: 7	J remembered in the days of her affliction	3389
	1: 8	J hath grievously sinned; therefore she is	3389
	1:17	J is as a menstruous *woman* among them.	3389
	2:10	the virgins of J hang down their heads to	3389
	2:13	*thing* shall I liken to thee, O daughter of J?	3389
	2:15	and wag their head at the daughter of J,	3389
	4:12	should have entered into the gates of J.	3389
Eze	4: 1	and pourtray upon it *the* city, *even* J:	3389
	4: 7	shalt set thy face toward the siege of J,	3389
	4:16	behold, I will break the staff of bread in J:	3389
	5: 5	Thus saith the Lord GOD; This *is* J:	3389
	8: 3	and brought me in the visions of God to J,	3389
	9: 4	the midst of the city through the midst of J,	3389
	9: 8	in thy pouring out of thy fury upon J?	3389
	11:15	*are* they unto whom the inhabitants of J	3389
	12:10	This burden *concerneth* the prince in J, and	3389
	12:19	of the inhabitants of J, *and* of the land of	3389
	13:16	of Israel which prophesy concerning J,	3389
	14:21	I send my four sore judgments upon J,	3389
	14:22	the evil that I have brought upon J,	3389
	15: 6	for fuel, so will I give the inhabitants of J.	3389
	16: 2	of man, cause J to know her abominations,	3389
	16: 3	And say, Thus saith the Lord GOD unto J;	3389
	17:12	the king of Babylon is come *to* J, and	3389
	21: 2	set thy face toward J, and drop *thy word*	3389
	21:20	and to Judah in J the defenced.	3389
	21:22	At his right hand was the divination for J,	3389
	22:19	I will gather you into the midst of J.	3389
	23: 4	Samaria *is* Aholah, and J Aholibah.	3389
	24: 2	the king of Babylon set himself against J	3389
	26: 2	because that Tyrus hath said against J, Aha,	3389
	33:21	*that* one that had escaped out of J came	3389
	36:38	as the flock of J in her solemn feasts;	3389
Da	1: 1	Nebuchadnezzar king of Babylon *unto* J,	3389
	5: 2	had taken out of the temple which *was* in J;	3390
	5: 3	temple of the house of God which *was* at J;	3390
	6:10	being open in his chamber toward J,	3390
	9: 2	seventy years in the desolations of J.	3389
	9: 7	to the inhabitants of J, and unto all Israel,	3389
	9:12	not been done as hath been done upon J.	3389
	9:16	thy fury be turned away from thy city J,	3389
	9:16	J and thy people *are become* a reproach to	3389
	9:25	to build J unto the Messiah the Prince *shall*	3389
Joel	2:32	mount Zion and in J shall be deliverance,	3389
	3: 1	bring again the captivity of Judah and J,	3389
	3: 6	the children of J have ye sold unto	3389
	3:16	roar out of Zion, and utter his voice from J;	3389
	3:17	shall J be holy, and there shall no strangers	3389
	3:20	and J from generation to generation.	3389
Am	1: 2	roar from Zion, and utter his voice from J;	3389
	2: 5	and it shall devour the palaces of J.	3389
Ob	1:11	cast lots upon J, even thou *wast* as one of	3389
	1:20	the captivity of J, which *is* in Sepharad,	3389
Mic	1: 1	which he saw concerning Samaria and J.	3389
	1: 5	the high places of Judah? *are they* not J?	3389
	1: 9	come unto the gate of my people, *even* to J.	3389
	1:12	down from the LORD unto the gate of J.	3389
	3:10	up Zion with blood, and J with iniquity.	3389
	3:12	J shall become heaps, and the mountain of	3389
	4: 2	and the word of the LORD from J.	3389
	4: 8	kingdom shall come to the daughter of J.	3389
Zep	1: 4	and upon all the inhabitants of J;	3389
	1:12	*that* I will search J with candles, and	3389
	3:14	rejoice with all the heart, O daughter of J.	3389
	3:16	In that day it shall be said to J, Fear thou	3389
Zec	1:12	how long wilt thou not have mercy on J	3389
	1:14	I am jealous for J and for Zion *with* a great	3389
	1:16	I am returned to J with mercies:	3389
	1:16	and a line shall be stretched forth upon J.	3389
	1:17	yet comfort Zion, and shall yet choose J.	3389
	1:19	which have scattered Judah, Israel, and J.	3389
	2: 2	he said unto me, To measure J, to see what	3389
	2: 4	J shall be inhabited *as* towns without walls	3389
	2:12	in the holy land, and shall choose J again.	3389
	3: 2	even the LORD that hath chosen J rebuke	3389
	7: 7	when J was inhabited and in prosperity,	3389
	8: 3	unto Zion, and will dwell in the midst of J:	3389
	8: 3	J shall be called a city of truth; and	3389
	8: 4	and old women dwell in the streets of J,	3389
	8: 8	and they shall dwell in the midst of J:	3389
	8:15	I thought in these days to do well unto J	3389
	8:22	come to seek the LORD of hosts in J,	3389
	9: 9	O daughter of Zion; shout, O daughter of J:	3389
	9:10	the horse from J, and the battle bow shall	3389
	12: 2	I *will* make J a cup of trembling unto all	3389
	12: 2	the siege both against Judah *and* against J.	3389
	12: 3	in that day will I make J a burdensome	3389
	12: 5	The inhabitants of J *shall be* my strength in	3389
	12: 6	J shall be inhabited again in her own place,	3389
	12: 6	inhabited again in her own place, *even* in J.	3389
	12: 7	the glory of the inhabitants of J do not	3389
	12: 8	the LORD defend the inhabitants of J;	3389
	12: 9	destroy all the nations that come against J.	3389
	12:10	upon the inhabitants of J, the spirit of grace	3389
	12:11	day shall there be a great mourning in J,	3389
	13: 1	to the inhabitants of J for sin and	3389
	14: 2	For I will gather all nations against J to	3389
	14: 4	which *is* before J on the east, and	3389
	14: 8	*that* living waters shall go out from J:	3389
	14:10	a plain from Geba to Rimmon south of J:	3389
	14:11	but J shall be safely inhabited.	3389
	14:12	all the people that have fought against J;	3389
	14:14	Judah also shall fight at J; and the wealth	3389
	14:16	J shall even go up from year to year to	3389
	14:17	of the earth unto J to worship the King,	3389
	14:21	every pot in J and in Judah shall be	3389
Mal	2:11	is committed in Israel and in J;	3389
	3: 4	and J be pleasant unto the LORD,	3389
Mt	2: 1	there came wise men from the east to J,	*2414*
	2: 3	*things,* he was troubled, and all J with him.	*2414*
	3: 5	Then went out to him J, and all Judea, and	*2414*
	4:25	and *from* J, and *from* Judea, and	*2414*
	5:35	neither by J; for it is the city of the great	*2414*
	15: 1	and Pharisees, which were of J, saying,	*2414*
	16:21	how that he must go unto J, and	*2414*
	20:17	And Jesus going up to J took the twelve	*2414*
	20:18	Behold, we go up to J; and the Son of man	*2414*
	21: 1	And when they drew nigh unto J, and	*2414*
	21:10	And when he was come into J, all the city	*2414*
	23:37	O J, Jerusalem, *thou* that killest	*2419*
	23:37	O Jerusalem, J, *thou* that killest	*2419*
Mk	1: 5	and they of J, and were all baptized of him	*2415*
	3: 8	And from J, and from Idumea, and	*2414*

Mk 3:22 And the scribes which came down from J *2414*
7: 1 certain of the scribes, which came from J. *2414*
10:32 And they were in the way going up to J; *2414*
10:33 *Saying,* Behold, we go up to J; and the Son *2414*
11: 1 And when they came nigh to J, *2419*
11:11 And Jesus entered into J, and into *2414*
11:15 And they come to J: and Jesus went into *2414*
11:27 And they come again to J: and as he was *2414*
15:41 *women* which came up with him unto J. *2414*
Lk 2:22 they brought him to J, to present *him* to *2414*
2:25 And behold, there was a man in J, *2419*
2:38 to all them that looked for redemption in J. *2419*
2:41 Now his parents went to J every year at *2419*
2:42 they went up to J after the custom of *2414*
2:43 the child Jesus tarried behind in J; *2419*
2:45 they turned back again to J, seeking him. *2419*
4: 9 And he brought him to J, and set him on a *2419*
5:17 of every town of Galilee, and Judea, and J: *2419*
6:17 multitude of people out of all Judea and J, *2419*
9:31 decease which he should accomplish at J. *2419*
9:51 he stedfastly set his face to go to J, *2419*
9:53 his face was *as though he* would go to J. *2419*
10:30 A certain man went down from J to *2419*
13: 4 were sinners above all men that dwelt in J? *2419*
13:22 teaching, and journeying towards J. *2419*
13:33 it cannot be that a prophet perish out of J. *2419*
13:34 O J, Jerusalem, which killest the prophets, *2419*
13:34 O Jerusalem, J, which killest the prophets, *2419*
17:11 And it came to pass, as he went to J, that he *2419*
18:31 we go up to J, and all *things* that are *2414*
19:11 because he was nigh to J, and *because* *2419*
19:28 he went before, ascending up to J. *2414*
21:20 And when ye shall see J compassed with *2419*
21:24 J shall be trodden down of the Gentiles, *2419*
23: 7 who himself also was at J at that time. *2414*
23:28 said, Daughters of J, weep not for me, but *2419*
24:13 which was from J *about* threescore *2419*
24:18 Art thou only a stranger in J, and hast not *2419*
24:33 and returned to J, and found the eleven *2419*
24:47 his name among all nations, beginning at J. *2419*
24:49 but tarry ye in the city of J, until ye be *2419*
24:52 and returned to J with great joy: *2419*
Jn 1:19 sent priests and Levites from J to ask him, *2414*
2:13 was at hand, and Jesus went up to J, *2414*
2:23 Now when he was in J at the passover, *2414*
4:20 that in J is the place where *men* ought to *2414*
4:21 nor *yet* at J, worship the Father. *2414*
4:45 having seen all *the things* that he did at J at *2414*
5: 1 a feast of the Jews; and Jesus went up to J. *2414*
5: 2 Now there is at J by the sheep *market* a *2414*
7:25 Then said some of them of J, Is not this he, *2415*
10:22 And it was at J *the feast of* the dedication, *2414*
11:18 Now Bethany was nigh unto J, *2414*
11:55 many went out of the country up to J *2414*
12:12 they heard that Jesus was coming to J, *2414*
Ac 1: 4 them that *they* should not depart from J, *2414*
1: 8 ye shall be witnesses unto me both in J, *2419*
1:12 Then returned they unto J from the mount *2419*
1:12 which is from J a sabbath day's journey. *2419*
1:19 it was known unto all the dwellers at J; *2419*
2: 5 And there were dwelling at J Jews, *2419*
2:14 Ye men of Judea, and all *ye* that dwell at J, *2419*
4: 6 the high priest, were gathered together at J. *2419*
4:16 them *is* manifest to all them that dwell in J; *2419*
5:16 *out* of the cities round about unto J, *2419*
5:28 ye have filled J with your doctrine, and *2419*
6: 7 the number of the disciples multiplied in J *2419*
8: 1 against the church which was at J; *2414*
8:14 Now when the apostles which were at J *2414*
8:25 returned to J, and preached the gospel in *2419*
8:26 the way that goeth down from J unto Gaza, *2419*
8:27 and had come to J for to worship, *2419*
9: 2 women, he might bring *them* bound unto J. *2419*
9:13 much evil he hath done to thy saints at J: *2419*
9:21 them which called on this name in J, *2419*
9:26 And when Saul was come to J, he assayed *2419*
9:28 with them coming in and going out at J. *2419*
10:39 did both in the land of the Jews, and in J; *2419*
11: 2 And when Peter was come up to J, *2414*
11:22 unto the ears of the church which was in J: *2414*
11:27 And in these days came prophets from J *2414*
12:25 And Barnabas and Saul returned from J, *2419*
13:13 John departing from them returned to J. *2414*
13:27 For they that dwell at J, and their rulers, *2419*
13:31 which came up with him from Galilee to J, *2419*
15: 2 should go up to J unto the apostles and *2419*
15: 4 And when they were come to J, they were *2419*
16: 4 of the apostles and elders which were at J. *2419*
18:21 all means keep *this* feast that cometh in J: *2414*
19:21 and Achaia, to go to J, saying, *2419*
20:16 for him, to be at J the day of Pentecost. *2414*
20:22 now behold, I go bound in the spirit unto J, *2419*
21: 4 the Spirit, that *he* should not go up to J. *2419*
21:11 So shall the Jews at J bind the man that *2419*
21:12 that place, besought him not to go up to J. *2419*
21:13 also to die at J for the name of the Lord *2419*
21:15 we took up our carriages, and went up to J. *2419*
21:17 And when we were come to J, the brethren *2414*
21:31 of the band, that all J was in an uproar. *2419*
22: 5 bound unto J, for to be punished. *2419*
22:17 to pass that, when I was come again to J, *2419*
22:18 Make haste, and get *thee* quickly out of J: *2419*
23:11 for as thou hast testified of me in J, so *2419*
24:11 twelve days since I went up to J for to *2419*
25: 1 three days he ascended from Cesarea to J. *2414*
25: 3 that he would send for him to J, *2419*
25: 7 the Jews which came down from J stood *2414*
25: 9 Wilt thou go up to J, and there be judged of *2414*
25:15 About whom, when I was at J, the chief *2414*
25:20 I asked *him* whether he would go to J, and *2419*
25:24 both at J, and *also* here, crying that he *2414*
26: 4 at the first among mine own nation at J, *2414*
26:10 Which *thing* I also did in J: and many of *2414*
26:20 and at J, and throughout all the coasts of *2414*
28:17 *yet* was I delivered prisoner from J into *2414*
Ro 15:19 so that from J, and round about unto *2419*
15:25 But now I go unto J to minister unto *2419*
15:26 for the poor saints which are at J. *2419*
15:31 that my service which I have for J may be *2419*
1Co 16: 3 will I send to bring your liberality unto J. *2419*
Gal 1:17 Neither went I up to J to them which were *2414*
1:18 Then after three years I went up to J to see *2414*
2: 1 after I went up again to J with Barnabas, *2414*
4:25 and answereth to J which now is, and is in *2419*
4:26 But J which is above is free, which is *2419*
Heb 12:22 the heavenly J, and to an innumerable *2419*
Rev 3:12 of the city of my God, *which is* new J, *2419*
21: 2 And I John saw the holy city, new J, *2419*
21:10 and shewed me *that* great city, the holy J, *2419*

JERUSALEM'S (3) [JERUSALEM]
1Ki 11:13 and for J sake, which I have chosen. 3389
11:32 my servant David's sake, and for J sake, 3389
Isa 62: 1 my peace, and for J sake I will not rest, 3389

JERUSHA (1) [JERUSHAH]
2Ki 15:33 his mother's name *was* J, the daughter of 3388

JERUSHAH (1) [JERUSHA]
2Ch 27: 1 His mother's name also *was* J, the daughter 3388

JESAIAH (2)
1Ch 3:21 the sons of Hananiah; Pelatiah, and J: 3470
Ne 11: 7 of Maaseiah, the son of Ithiel, the son of J. 3470

JESARELAH See JESHARELAH

JESHAIAH (5)
1Ch 25: 3 Gedaliah, and Zeri, and J, Hashabiah, and 3470
25:15 The eighth *to* J, *he,* his sons, and 3470
26:25 J his son, and Joram his son, and Zichri his 3470
Ezr 8: 7 J the son of Athaliah, and with him seventy 3470
8:19 with him J of the sons of Merari, 3470

JESHANAH (1)
2Ch 13:19 J with the towns thereof, and Ephrain with 3466

JESHARELAH (1)
1Ch 25:14 The seventh *to* J, *he,* his sons, and 3480

JESHEBEAB (1)
1Ch 24:13 thirteenth to Huppah, the fourteenth to J, 3428

JESHER (1)
1Ch 2:18 sons *are* these; J, and Shobab, and Ardon. 3475

JESHIMON (6)
Nu 21:20 the top of Pisgah, which looketh toward J. 3452
23:28 *unto* the top of Peor, that looketh toward J. 3452
1Sa 23:19 hill of Hachilah, which *is* on the south of J? 3452

1Sa 23:24 of Maon, in the plain on the south of J. 3452
26: 1 in the hill of Hachilah, *which is* before J? 3452
26: 3 of Hachilah, which *is* before J, by the way. 3452

JESHISHAI (1)
1Ch 5:14 the son of J, the son of Jahdo, the son of 3454

JESHOHAIAH (1)
1Ch 4:36 J, and Asaiah, and Adiel, and Jesimiel, and 3439

JESHUA (30) [JOSHUA]
1Ch 24:11 The ninth to J, the tenth to Shecaniah, 3442
2Ch 31:15 J, and Shemaiah, Amariah, and Shecaniah, 3442
Ezr 2: 2 J, Nehemiah, Seraiah, Reelaiah, Mordecai, 3442
2: 6 of the children of J *and* Joab, two thousand 3442
2:36 of the house of J, nine hundred seventy and 3442
2:40 the children of J and Kadmiel, of 3442
3: 2 stood up J the son of Jozadak, and 3442
3: 8 J the son of Jozadak, and the remnant of 3442
3: 9 stood J *with* his sons and his brethren, 3442
4: 3 J, and the rest of the chief of the fathers of 3442
5: 2 J the son of Jozadak, and began to build 3443
8:33 with them *was* Jozabad the son of J, and 3442
10:18 *namely,* of the sons of J the son of Jozadak, 3442
Ne 3:19 next to him repaired Ezer the son of J, 3442
7: 7 J, Nehemiah, Azariah, Raamiah, 3442
7:11 of the children of J and Joab, two thousand 3442
7:39 of the house of J, nine hundred seventy and 3442
7:43 the children of J, of Kadmiel, *and* of 3442
8: 7 Also J, and Bani, and Sherebiah, Jamin, 3442
8:17 for since the days of J the son of Nun unto 3442
9: 4 J, and Bani, Kadmiel, Shebaniah, Bunni, 3442
9: 5 J and Kadmiel, Bani, Hashabniah, 3442
10: 9 both J the son of Azaniah, Binnui of 3442
11:26 at J, and at Moladah, and at Beth-phelet, 3442
12: 1 with Zerubbabel the son of Shealtiel, and J: 3442
12: 7 and of their brethren in the days of J. 3442
12: 8 J, Binnui, Kadmiel, Sherebiah, Judah, *and* 3442
12:10 J begat Joiakim, Joiakim also begat 3442
12:24 Sherebiah, and J the son of Kadmiel, 3442
12:26 *were* in the days of Joiakim the son of J, 3442

JESHURUN (4)
Dt 32:15 J waxed fat, and kicked: thou art waxed fat, 3484
33: 5 he was king in J, when the heads of 3484
33:26 *There is* none like unto the God of J, 3484
Isa 44: 2 and *thou,* J, whom I have chosen. 3484

JESIAH (2)
1Ch 12: 6 J, and Azareel, and Joezer, and Jashobeam, 3449
23:20 Michah the first, and J the second. 3449

JESIMIEL (1)
1Ch 4:36 and Asaiah, and Adiel, and J, and Benaiah, 3450

JESSE (47)
Ru 4:17 he *is* the father of J, the father of David. 3448
4:22 And Obed begat J, and Jesse begat David. 3448
4:22 And Obed begat Jesse, and J begat David. 3448
1Sa 16: 1 go, I will send thee to J the Beth-lehemite: 3448
16: 3 call J to the sacrifice, and I will shew thee 3448
16: 5 he sanctified J and his sons, and 3448
16: 8 J called Abinadab, and made him pass 3448
16: 9 J made Shammah to pass by. And he said, 3448
16:10 J made seven of his sons to pass before 3448
16:10 Samuel said unto J, The LORD hath not 3448
16:11 Samuel said unto J, Are here all *thy* 3448
16:11 Samuel said unto J, Send and fetch him: 3448
16:18 I have seen a son of J the Beth-lehemite, 3448
16:19 Wherefore Saul sent messengers unto J, 3448
16:20 J took an ass *laden* with bread, and a bottle 3448
16:22 Saul sent to J, saying, Let David, I pray 3448
17:12 of Beth-lehem-judah, whose name *was* J; 3448
17:13 the three eldest sons of J went *and* 3448
17:17 J said unto David his son, Take now for thy 3448
17:20 took, and went, as J had commanded him; 3448
17:58 *I am* the son of thy servant J 3448
20:27 Wherefore cometh not the son of J to meat, 3448
20:30 chosen the son of J to thine own confusion, 3448
20:31 For as long as the son of J liveth upon 3448
22: 7 will the son of J give every one of you 3448
22: 8 son hath made *a league* with the son of J, 3448
22: 9 said, I saw the son of J coming to Nob, 3448
22:13 thou and the son of J, in that thou hast 3448
25:10 who *is* the son of J? there be many servants 3448
2Sa 20: 1 neither have we inheritance in the son of J: 3448
23: 1 David the son of J said, and the man *who* 3448
1Ki 12:16 neither *have we* inheritance in the son of J: 3448
1Ch 2:12 And Boaz begat Obed, and Obed begat J, 3448
2:13 J begat his firstborn Eliab, and 3448
10:14 the kingdom unto David the son of J. 3448
12:18 *we,* David, and on thy side, thou son of J: 3448
29:26 Thus David the son of J reigned over all 3448
2Ch 10:16 *we have* none inheritance in the son of J: 3448
11:18 Abihail the daughter of Eliab the son of J; 3448
Ps 72:20 The prayers of David the son of J are 3448
Isa 11: 1 shall come forth a rod out of the stem of J, 3448
11:10 in that day there shall be a root of J, 3448
Mt 1: 5 begat Obed of Ruth; and Obed begat J; *2421*
1: 6 And J begat David the king; and David *2421*
Lk 3:32 Which was *the son* of J, which was *the son* *2421*
Ac 13:22 and said, I have found David the *son* of J, *2421*
Ro 15:12 There shall be a root of J, and he that *shall* *2421*

JESTING (1)
Eph 5: 4 Neither filthiness, nor foolish talking, nor j, *2160*

JESUI (1) [ISHUI, JESUITES]
Nu 26:44 of J, the family of the Jesuites: of Beriah, 3440

JESUITES (1) [JESUI]
Nu 26:44 of Jesui, the family of the J: of Beriah, 3441

JESUS (973) [JESUS']
Mt 1: 1 The book of the generation of J Christ, *2424*
1:16 of whom was born J, who is called Christ. *2424*
1:18 Now the birth of J Christ was on this wise: *2424*
1:21 forth a son, and thou shalt call his name J: *2424*
1:25 her firstborn son: and *he* called his name J. *2424*
2: 1 Now when J was born in Bethlehem of *2424*
3:13 Then cometh J from Galilee to Jordan unto *2424*
3:15 And J answering said unto him, Suffer *it to* *2424*
3:16 And J, when he was baptized, went up *2424*
4: 1 Then was J led up of the Spirit into *2424*
4: 7 J said unto him, It is written again, *2424*
4:10 Then saith J unto him, Get thee hence, *2424*
4:12 Now when J had heard that John was cast *2424*
4:17 From that time J began to preach, and *2424*
4:18 And J, walking by the sea of Galilee, *2424*
4:23 And J went about all Galilee, teaching in *2424*
7:28 to pass, when J had ended these sayings, *2424*
8: 3 And J put forth *his* hand, and touched him, *2424*
8: 4 And J saith unto him, See thou tell no *man;* *2424*
8: 5 And when J was entered into Capernaum, *2424*
8: 7 And J saith unto him, I will come and *2424*
8:10 When J heard *it,* he marvelled, and said to *2424*
8:13 And J said unto the centurion, Go thy way; *2424*
8:14 And when J was come into Peter's house, *2424*
8:18 Now when J saw great multitudes about *2424*
8:20 And J saith unto him, The foxes have *2424*
8:22 But J said unto him, Follow me; and let *2424*
8:29 we to do with thee, J, *thou* Son of God? *2424*
8:34 the whole city came out to meet J: *2424*
9: 2 J seeing their faith said unto the sick of *2424*
9: 4 And J knowing their thoughts said, *2424*
9: 9 And as J passed forth from thence, he saw *2424*
9:10 as Js sat at meat in the house, behold, *846*
9:12 But when J heard *that,* he said unto them, *2424*
9:15 And J said unto them, Can the children of *2424*
9:19 And J arose, and followed him, and *so* *2424*
9:22 But J turned him about, and when he saw *2424*
9:23 And when J came into the ruler's house, *2424*
9:27 And when J departed thence, two blind *2424*
9:28 and J saith unto them, Believe ye that I am *2424*
9:30 and J straitly charged them, saying, *2424*
9:35 And J went about all the cities and villages, *2424*
10: 5 These twelve J sent forth, and *2424*
11: 1 when J had made an end of commanding *2424*
11: 4 J answered and said unto them, Go and *2424*
11: 7 J began to say unto the multitudes *2424*
11:25 At that time J answered and said, I thank *2424*
12: 1 At that time J went on the sabbath day *2424*
12:15 But when J knew *it,* he withdrew himself *2424*
12:25 And J knew their thoughts, and said unto *2424*
13: 1 The same day went J out of the house, and *2424*
13:34 All these *things* spake J unto the multitude *2424*
13:36 Then J sent the multitude away, and *2424*
13:51 J saith unto them, Have ye understood all *2424*
13:53 *that* when J had finished these parables, *2424*

Mt 13:57 But J said unto them, A prophet is not *2424*
14: 1 Herod the tetrarch heard of the fame of J, *2424*
14:12 and buried it, and went and told J. *2424*
14:13 When J heard *of it,* he departed thence by *2424*
14:14 And J went forth, and saw a great *2424*
14:16 But J said unto them, They need not depart; *2424*
14:22 And straightway J constrained his disciples *2424*
14:25 And in the fourth watch of the night J went *2424*
14:27 But straightway J spake unto them, saying, *2424*
14:29 the ship, he walked on the water, to go to J. *2424*
14:31 And immediately J stretched forth *his* *2424*
15: 1 Then came to J scribes and Pharisees, *2424*
15:16 And J said, Are ye also yet without *2424*
15:21 Then J went thence, and departed into *2424*
15:28 Then J answered and said unto her, *2424*
15:29 And J departed from thence, and came nigh *2424*
15:32 Then J called his disciples unto *him,* and *2424*
15:34 And J saith unto them, How many loaves *2424*
16: 6 Then J said unto them, Take heed and *2424*
16: 8 *Which* when J perceived, he said unto *2424*
16:13 When J came into the coasts of Cesarea *2424*
16:17 And J answered and said unto him, *2424*
16:20 should tell no *man* that he was J the Christ. *2424*
16:21 From that time forth began J to shew unto *2424*
16:24 Then said J unto his disciples, If any *man* *2424*
17: 1 And after six days J taketh Peter, James, *2424*
17: 4 answered Peter, and said unto J, Lord, *2424*
17: 7 And J came and touched them, and said, *2424*
17: 8 their eyes, they saw no *man,* save J only. *2424*
17: 9 from the mountain, J charged them, saying, *2424*
17:11 And J answered and said unto them, *2424*
17:17 Then J answered and said, O faithless and *2424*
17:18 And J rebuked the devil; and he departed *2424*
17:19 Then came the disciples to J apart, *2424*
17:20 And J said unto them, Because of your *2424*
17:22 they abode in Galilee, J said unto them, *2424*
17:25 J prevented him, saying, What thinkest *2424*
17:26 J saith unto him, Then are the children free. *2424*
18: 1 At the same time came the disciples unto J, *2424*
18: 2 And J called a little child unto *him,* and *2424*
18:22 J saith unto him, I say not unto thee, *2424*
19: 1 *that* when J had finished these sayings, *2424*
19:14 But J said, Suffer little children, and *2424*
19:18 J said, Thou shalt do no murder, Thou shalt *2424*
19:21 J said unto him, If thou wilt be perfect, go *2424*
19:23 Then said J unto his disciples, Verily I say *2424*
19:26 But J beheld *them,* and said unto them, *2424*
19:28 And J said unto them, Verily I say unto *2424*
20:17 And J going up to Jerusalem took *2424*
20:22 But J answered and said, Ye know not *2424*
20:25 But J called them unto *him,* and said, *2424*
20:30 when they heard that J passed by, cried out, *2424*
20:32 And J stood still, and called them, and said, *2424*
20:34 So J had compassion *on them,* and *2424*
21: 1 mount of Olives, then sent J two disciples, *2424*
21: 6 and did as J commanded them, *2424*
21:11 This is J the prophet of Nazareth of *2424*
21:12 And J went into the temple of God, and *2424*
21:16 And J saith unto them, Yea; have ye never *2424*
21:21 J answered and said unto them, Verily I say *2424*
21:24 And J answered and said unto them, I also *2424*
21:27 And they answered J, and said, We cannot *2424*
21:31 J saith unto them, Verily I say unto you, *2424*
21:42 J saith unto them, Did ye never read in *2424*
22: 1 And J answered and spake unto them again *2424*
22:18 But J perceived their wickedness, and said, *2424*
22:29 J answered and said unto them, Ye do err, *2424*
22:37 J said unto him, Thou shalt love the Lord *2424*
22:41 were gathered together, J asked them, *2424*
23: 1 Then spake J to the multitude, and to his *2424*
24: 1 And J went out, and departed from *2424*
24: 2 And J said unto them, See ye not all these *2424*
24: 4 And J answered and said unto them, *2424*
26: 1 when J had finished all these sayings, *2424*
26: 4 And consulted that they might take J by *2424*
26: 6 Now when J was in Bethany, in the house *2424*
26:10 When J understood *it,* he said unto them, *2424*
26:17 unleavened bread the disciples came to J, *2424*
26:19 And the disciples did as J had appointed *2424*
26:26 J took bread, and blessed *it,* and brake *it,* *2424*
26:31 Then saith J unto them, All ye shall be *2424*
26:34 J said unto him, Verily I say unto thee, *2424*
26:36 Then cometh J with them unto a place *2424*
26:49 And forthwith he came to J, and said, Hail, *2424*
26:50 And J said unto him, Friend, wherefore art *2424*
26:50 and laid hands on J, and took him. *2424*
26:51 one of them which were with J stretched *2424*
26:52 Then said J unto him, Put up again thy *2424*
26:55 In that *same* hour said J to the multitudes, *2424*
26:57 And they that had laid hold on J led *him* *2424*
26:59 the council, sought false witness against J, *2424*
26:63 But J held his peace. And the high priest *2424*
26:64 J saith unto him, Thou hast said: *2424*
26:69 saying, Thou also wast with J of Galilee. *2424*
26:71 This *fellow* was also with J of Nazareth. *2424*
26:75 And Peter remembered the word of J, *2424*
27: 1 elders of the people took counsel against J *2424*
27:11 And J stood before the governor: and *2424*
27:11 And J said unto him, Thou sayest. *2424*
27:17 Barabbas, or J which is called Christ? *2424*
27:20 they should ask Barabbas, and destroy J. *2424*
27:22 I do then with J which is called Christ? *2424*
27:26 and when he had scourged J, he delivered *2424*
27:27 Then the soldiers of the governor took J *2424*
27:37 THIS IS J THE KING OF THE JEWS. *2424*
27:46 And about the ninth hour J cried with a *2424*
27:50 J, when he had cried again with a loud *2424*
27:54 watching J, saw the earthquake, and *2424*
27:55 which followed J from Galilee, *2424*
27:58 went to Pilate, and begged the body of J. *2424*
28: 5 for I know that ye seek J, which was *2424*
28: 9 behold, J met them, saying, *All* hail. *2424*
28:10 Then said J unto them, Be not afraid: *2424*
28:16 into a mountain where J had appointed *2424*
28:18 And J came and spake unto them, saying, *2424*
Mk 1: 1 The beginning of the gospel of J Christ, *2424*
1: 9 *that* J came from Nazareth of Galilee, and *2424*
1:14 John was put in prison, J came into Galilee, *2424*
1:17 And J said unto them, Come ye after me, *2424*
1:24 we to do with thee, *thou* J of Nazareth? *2424*
1:25 And J rebuked him, saying, Hold thy *2424*
1:41 And J, moved with compassion, put forth *2424*
1:45 insomuch that *J* could no more openly enter NIG
2: 5 When J saw their faith, he said unto *2424*
2: 8 when J perceived in his spirit that they so *2424*
2:15 that as *J* sat at meat in his house, NIG
2:15 and sinners sat also together with J and *2424*
2:17 When J heard *it,* he saith unto them, They *2424*
2:19 And J said unto them, Can the children of *2424*
3: 7 But J withdrew himself with his disciples *2424*
5: 6 But when he saw J afar off, he ran and *2424*
5: 7 and said, What have I to do with thee, J, *2424*
5:13 And forthwith J gave them leave. And *2424*
5:15 And they come to J, and see him that was *2424*
5:19 Howbeit J suffered him not, but saith unto *2424*
5:20 how great *things* J had done for him: *2424*
5:21 And when J was passed over again by ship *2424*
5:24 And *J* went with him; and much people NIG
5:27 When she had heard of J, came in the press *2424*
5:30 And J immediately knowing in himself that *2424*
5:36 As soon as J heard the word *that was* *2424*
6: 4 But J said unto them, A prophet is not *2424*
6:30 gathered themselves together unto J, *2424*
6:34 And J, when he came out, saw much *2424*
7:27 But J said unto her, Let the children first be *2424*
8: 1 J called his disciples unto *him,* and *2424*
8:17 And when J knew *it,* he saith unto them, *2424*
8:27 And J went out, and his disciples, into *2424*
9: 2 And after six days J taketh with *him* Peter, *2424*
9: 4 with Moses: and they were talking with J. *2424*
9: 5 And Peter answered and said to J, Master, *2424*
9: 8 any more, save J only with themselves. *2424*
9:23 J said unto him, If thou canst believe, *2424*
9:25 When J saw that the people came running *2424*
9:27 But J took him by the hand, and lifted him *2424*
9:39 But J said, Forbid him not: for there is no *2424*
10: 5 And J answered and said unto them, *2424*
10:14 But when J saw *it,* he was much *2424*
10:18 And J said unto him, Why callest thou me *2424*
10:21 Then J beholding him loved him, and *2424*
10:23 And J looked round about, and saith unto *2424*
10:24 But J answereth again, and saith unto them, *2424*
10:27 And J looking upon them saith, With men *2424*
10:29 And J answered and said, Verily I say unto *2424*
10:32 up to Jerusalem; and J went before them: *2424*
10:38 But J said unto them, Ye know not what ye *2424*
10:39 And J said unto them, Ye shall indeed *2424*
10:42 But J called them to *him,* and saith unto *2424*

Mk	10:47	And when he heard that it was J of	*2424*
	10:47	and say, J, *thou* Son of David, have mercy	*2424*
	10:49	And J stood still, and commanded him to	*2424*
	10:50	away his garment, rose, and came to J.	*2424*
	10:51	And J answered and said unto him,	*2424*
	10:52	And J said unto him, Go thy way; thy faith	*2424*
	10:52	his sight, and followed J in the way.	*2424*
	11: 6	And they said unto them even as J had	*2424*
	11: 7	And they brought the colt to J, and	*2424*
	11:11	And J entered into Jerusalem, and into	*2424*
	11:14	And J answered and said unto it, No *man*	*2424*
	11:15	and J went into the temple, and began to	*2424*
	11:22	And J answering saith unto them,	*2424*
	11:29	And J answered and said unto them, I will	*2424*
	11:33	And they answered and said unto J,	*2424*
	11:33	And J answering saith unto them,	*2424*
	12:17	And J answering said unto them, Render to	*2424*
	12:24	And J answering said unto them, Do ye not	*2424*
	12:29	And J answered him, The first of all	*2424*
	12:34	And when J saw that he answered	*2424*
	12:35	And J answered and said, while he taught	*2424*
	12:41	And J sat over against the treasury, and	*2424*
	13: 2	And J answering said unto him, Seest thou	*2424*
	13: 5	And J answering them began to say,	*2424*
	14: 6	And J said, Let her alone; why trouble you	*2424*
	14:18	And as they sat and did eat, J said, Verily I	*2424*
	14:22	J took bread, and blessed, and brake *it,* and	*2424*
	14:27	And J saith unto them, All ye shall be	*2424*
	14:30	And J saith unto him, Verily I say unto	*2424*
	14:48	And J answered and said unto them, Are ye	*2424*
	14:53	And they led J away to the high priest: and	*2424*
	14:55	all the council sought for witness against J	*2424*
	14:60	and asked J, saying, Answerest thou	*2424*
	14:62	And J said, I am: and ye shall see the Son	*2424*
	14:67	*And* thou also wast with J of Nazareth.	*2424*
	14:72	And Peter called to mind the word that J	*2424*
	15: 1	and bound J, and carried *him* away, and	*2424*
	15: 5	But J yet answered nothing; so that Pilate	*2424*
	15:15	Barabbas unto them, and delivered J,	*2424*
	15:34	And at the ninth hour J cried with a loud	*2424*
	15:37	And J cried with a loud voice, and gave up	*2424*
	15:43	unto Pilate, and craved the body of J.	*2424*
	16: 6	Ye seek J of Nazareth, which was	*2424*
	16: 9	Now when *J* was risen early the first *day* of	NIG
Lk	1:31	bring forth a son, and shalt call his name J.	*2424*
	2:21	his name was called J, which was *so*	*2424*
	2:27	and when the parents brought in the child J,	*2424*
	2:43	the child J tarried behind in Jerusalem;	*2424*
	2:52	And J increased in wisdom and stature, and	*2424*
	3:21	*that* J also being baptized, and praying,	*2424*
	3:23	And J himself began *to be* about thirty	*2424*
	4: 1	And J being full of the Holy Ghost	*2424*
	4: 4	And J answered him, saying, It is written,	*2424*
	4: 8	And J answered and said unto him,	*2424*
	4:12	And J answering said unto him, It is said,	*2424*
	4:14	And J returned in the power of the Spirit	*2424*
	4:34	we to do with thee, *thou* J of Nazareth?	*2424*
	4:35	And J rebuked him, saying, Hold thy	*2424*
	5:10	And J said unto Simon, Fear not;	*2424*
	5:12	who seeing J fell on *his* face, and	*2424*
	5:19	with *his* couch into the midst before J.	*2424*
	5:22	But when J perceived their thoughts,	*2424*
	5:31	And J answering said unto them, They that	*2424*
	6: 3	And J answering them said, Have ye not	*2424*
	6: 9	Then said J unto them, I will ask you one	*2424*
	6:11	one with another what they might do to J.	*2424*
	7: 3	And when he heard of J, he sent unto him	*2424*
	7: 4	And when they came to J, they besought	*2424*
	7: 6	Then J went with them. And when he was	*2424*
	7: 9	When J heard these *things,* he marvelled at	*2424*
	7:19	*him* two of his disciples sent *them* to J,	*2424*
	7:22	Then J answering said unto them, Go *your*	*2424*
	7:37	when she knew that *J* sat at meat in	NIG
	7:40	And J answering said unto him, Simon,	*2424*
	8:28	When he saw J, he cried out, and fell down	*2424*
	8:28	with thee, J, *thou* Son of God most high?	*2424*
	8:30	And J asked him, saying, What is thy	*2424*
	8:35	and came to J, and found the man, out of	*2424*
	8:35	sitting at the feet of J, clothed, and in his	*2424*
	8:38	be with him: but J sent him away, saying,	*2424*
	8:39	city how great *things* J had done unto him.	*2424*
	8:40	it came to pass that, when J was returned,	*2424*
	8:45	And J said, Who touched me? When all	*2424*
	8:46	And J said, Somebody hath touched me:	*2424*
	8:50	But when J heard *it,* he answered him,	*2424*
	9:33	from him, Peter said unto J, Master,	*2424*
	9:36	the voice was past, J was found alone.	*2424*
	9:41	And J answering said, O faithless and	*2424*
	9:42	tare *him.* And J rebuked the unclean spirit,	*2424*
	9:43	every one at all *things* which J did,	*2424*
	9:47	And J, perceiving the thought of their	*2424*
	9:50	And J said unto him, Forbid *him* not: for he	*2424*
	9:58	And J said unto him, Foxes have holes, and	*2424*
	9:60	J said unto him, Let the dead bury their	*2424*
	9:62	And J said unto him, No *man* having put	*2424*
	10:21	In that hour J rejoiced in spirit, and said,	*2424*
	10:29	willing to justify himself, said unto J,	*2424*
	10:30	And J answering said, A certain man went	*2424*
	10:37	Then said J unto him, Go, and do thou	*2424*
	10:41	And J answered and said unto her, Martha,	*2424*
	13: 2	And J answering said unto them,	*2424*
	13:12	And when J saw her, he called *her* to *him,*	*2424*
	13:14	that J had healed on the sabbath day,	*2424*
	14: 3	And J answering spake unto the lawyers	*2424*
	17:13	and said, J, Master, have mercy on us.	*2424*
	17:17	And J answering said, Were there not ten	*2424*
	18:16	But J called them unto *him,* and said,	*2424*
	18:19	And J said unto him, Why callest thou me	*2424*
	18:22	Now when J heard these *things,* he said	*2424*
	18:24	And when J saw that he was very	*2424*
	18:37	told him, that J of Nazareth passeth by.	*2424*
	18:38	And he cried, saying, J, *thou* Son of David,	*2424*
	18:40	And J stood, and commanded him to be	*2424*
	18:42	And J said unto him, Receive thy sight:	*2424*
	19: 1	And *J* entered and passed through Jericho.	NIG
	19: 3	And he sought to see J who he was; and	*2424*
	19: 5	And when J came to the place, he looked	*2424*
	19: 9	And J said unto him, This day is salvation	*2424*
	19:35	And they brought him to J: and they cast	*2424*
	19:35	upon the colt, and they set J thereon.	*2424*
	20: 8	And J said unto them, Neither tell I you by	*2424*
	20:34	And J answering said unto them,	*2424*
	22:47	and drew near unto J to kiss him.	*2424*
	22:48	But J said unto him, Judas, betrayest thou	*2424*
	22:51	And J answered and said, Suffer ye thus	*2424*
	22:52	Then J said unto the chief priests, and	*2424*
	22:63	And the men that held J mocked him, and	*2424*
	23: 8	And when Herod saw J, he was exceeding	*2424*
	23:20	Pilate therefore, willing to release J, spake	*2424*
	23:25	had desired; but he delivered J to their will.	*2424*
	23:26	laid the cross, that *he* might bear *it* after J.	*2424*
	23:28	But J turning unto them, said, Daughters of	*2424*
	23:34	Then said J, Father, forgive them; for they	*2424*
	23:42	And he said unto J, Lord, remember me	*2424*
	23:43	And J said unto him, Verily I say unto thee,	*2424*
	23:46	And when J had cried with a loud voice,	*2424*
	23:52	went unto Pilate, and begged the body of J.	*2424*
	24: 3	and found not the body of the Lord J.	*2424*
	24:15	J himself drew near, and went with them.	*2424*
	24:19	Concerning J of Nazareth, which was a	*2424*
	24:36	J himself stood in the midst of them, and	*2424*
Jn	1:17	*but* grace and truth came by J Christ.	*2424*
	1:29	The next day John seeth J coming unto	*2424*
	1:36	And looking upon J as he walked, he saith,	*2424*
	1:37	heard him speak, and they followed J.	*2424*
	1:38	Then J turned,	*2424*
	1:42	And he brought him to J. And when Jesus	*2424*
	1:42	And when J beheld him, he said, Thou art	*2424*
	1:43	The day following J would go forth into	*2424*
	1:45	and the prophets, did write, J of Nazareth,	*2424*
	1:47	J saw Nathanael coming to him, and	*2424*
	1:48	J answered and said unto him, Before that	*2424*
	1:50	J answered and said unto him, Because I	*2424*
	2: 1	of Galilee; and the mother of J was there:	*2424*
	2: 2	And both J was called, and his disciples,	*2424*
	2: 3	the mother of J saith unto him, They have	*2424*
	2: 4	J saith unto her, Woman, what have I to do	*2424*
	2: 7	J saith unto them, Fill the waterpots with	*2424*
	2:11	This beginning of miracles did J in Cana of	*2424*
	2:13	was at hand, and J went up to Jerusalem,	*2424*
	2:19	J answered and said unto them,	*2424*
	2:22	and the word which J had said.	*2424*
	2:24	But J did not commit himself unto them,	*2424*
	3: 2	The same came to J by night, and said unto	*2424*
	3: 3	J answered and said unto him, Verily,	*2424*
	3: 5	J answered, Verily, verily, I say unto thee,	*2424*
	3:10	J answered and said unto him, Art thou a	*2424*
	3:22	After these *things* came J and his disciples	*2424*

Jn 4: 1 how the Pharisees had heard that J made 2424
4: 2 (Though J himself baptized not, but 2424
4: 6 J therefore, being wearied with *his* journey, 2424
4: 7 J saith unto her, Give me to drink. 2424
4:10 J answered and said unto her, If thou 2424
4:13 J answered and said unto her, 2424
4:16 J saith unto her, Go, call thy husband, and 2424
4:17 J said unto her, Thou hast well said, I have 2424
4:21 J saith unto her, Woman, believe me, 2424
4:26 J saith unto her, I that speak unto thee am 2424
4:34 J saith unto them, My meat is to do the will 2424
4:44 For J himself testified, that a prophet hath 2424
4:46 So J came again into Cana of Galilee, 2424
4:47 When he heard that J was come out of 2424
4:48 Then said J unto him, Except ye see signs 2424
4:50 J saith unto him, Go *thy way;* thy son 2424
4:50 And the man believed the word that J had 2424
4:53 in the which J said unto him, Thy son 2424
4:54 This *is* again the second miracle *that* J did, 2424
5: 1 of the Jews; and J went up to Jerusalem. 2424
5: 6 When J saw him lie, and knew that he had 2424
5: 8 J saith unto him, Rise, take up thy bed, and 2424
5:13 for J had conveyed himself away, 2424
5:14 Afterward J findeth him in the temple, and 2424
5:15 and told the Jews that it was J, 2424
5:16 And therefore did the Jews persecute J, and 2424
5:17 But J answered them, My Father worketh 2424
5:19 Then answered J and said unto them, 2424
6: 1 After these *things* J went over the sea of 2424
6: 3 And J went up into a mountain, and 2424
6: 5 When J then lift up *his* eyes, 2424
6:10 And J said, Make the men sit down. 2424
6:11 And J took the loaves; and when he had 2424
6:14 when they had seen the miracle that J did, 2424
6:15 When J therefore perceived that they 2424
6:17 was now dark, and J was not come to them. 2424
6:19 they see J walking on the sea, and drawing 2424
6:22 that J went not with his disciples into 2424
6:24 therefore saw that J was not there, 2424
6:24 and came to Capernaum, seeking for J. 2424
6:26 J answered them and said, Verily, verily, 2424
6:29 J answered and said unto them, This is 2424
6:32 Then J said unto them, Verily, verily, I say 2424
6:35 And J said unto them, I am the bread of 2424
6:42 And they said, Is not this J, the son of 2424
6:43 J therefore answered and said unto them, 2424
6:53 Then J said unto them, Verily, verily, I say 2424
6:61 When J knew in himself that his disciples 2424
6:64 For J knew from the beginning who they 2424
6:67 Then said J unto the twelve, Will ye also 2424
6:70 J answered them, Have not I chosen you 2424
7: 1 After these *things* J walked in Galilee: 2424
7: 6 Then J said unto them, My time is not yet 2424
7:14 Now about the midst of the feast J went up 2424
7:16 J answered them, and said, My doctrine is 2424
7:21 J answered and said unto them, I have done 2424
7:28 Then cried J in the temple as he taught, 2424
7:33 Then said J unto them, Yet a little while 2424
7:37 J stood and cried, saying, If any *man* thirst, 2424
7:39 because that J was not yet glorified.) 2424
7:50 (he that came to *J* by night, being one of NIG
8: 1 J went unto the mount of Olives. 2424
8: 6 But J stooped down, and with *his* finger 2424
8: 9 and J was left alone, and the woman 2424
8:10 When J had lift up *himself,* and saw none 2424
8:11 And J said unto her, Neither do I condemn 2424
8:12 Then spake J again unto them, saying, I am 2424
8:14 J answered and said unto them, Though I 2424
8:19 J answered, Ye neither know me, nor my 2424
8:20 These words spake J in the treasury, as he 2424
8:21 Then said J again unto them, I go my way, 2424
8:25 And J saith unto them, Even the same that I 2424
8:28 Then said J unto them, When ye have lift 2424
8:31 Then said J to those Jews which believed 2424
8:34 J answered them, Verily, verily, I say unto 2424
8:39 J saith unto them, If ye were Abraham's 2424
8:42 J said unto them, If God were your Father, 2424
8:49 J answered, I have not a devil; but I honour 2424
8:54 J answered, If I honour myself, my honour 2424
8:58 J said unto them, Verily, verily, I say unto 2424
8:59 but J hid himself, and went out of 2424
9: 1 And as *J* passed by, he saw a man *which* NIG
9: 3 J answered, Neither hath this *man* sinned, 2424
9:11 A man *that is* called J made clay, and 2424
9:14 And it was the sabbath day when J made 2424
9:35 J heard that they had cast him out; 2424
9:37 And J said unto him, Thou hast both seen 2424
9:39 And J said, For judgment I am come into 2424
9:41 J said unto them, If ye were blind, 2424
10: 6 This parable spake J unto them: but 2424
10: 7 Then said J unto them again, Verily, verily, 2424
10:23 And J walked in the temple in Solomon's 2424
10:25 J answered them, I told you, and ye believe 2424
10:32 J answered them, Many good works have I 2424
10:34 J answered them, Is it not written in your 2424
11: 4 When J heard *that,* he said, This sickness is 2424
11: 5 Now J loved Martha, and her sister, and 2424
11: 9 J answered, Are there not twelve hours in 2424
11:13 Howbeit J spake of his death: but 2424
11:14 Then said J unto them plainly, Lazarus is 2424
11:17 Then when J came, he found that he had 2424
11:20 as soon as she heard that J was coming, 2424
11:21 Then said Martha unto J, Lord, if thou 2424
11:23 J saith unto her, Thy brother shall rise 2424
11:25 J said unto her, I am the resurrection, and 2424
11:30 Now J was not yet come into the town, but 2424
11:32 Then when Mary was come where J was, 2424
11:33 When J therefore saw her weeping, and 2424
11:35 J wept. 2424
11:38 J therefore again groaning in himself 2424
11:39 J said, Take ye away the stone. Martha, 2424
11:40 J saith unto her, Said I not unto thee, that, 2424
11:41 And J lift up *his* eyes, and said, Father, 2424
11:44 J saith unto them, Loose him, and let *him* 2424
11:45 and had seen *the things* which J did, 2424
11:46 and told them what *things* J had done. 2424
11:51 he prophesied that J should die for *that* 2424
11:54 J therefore walked no more openly among 2424
11:56 Then sought they for J, and spake among 2424
12: 1 Then J six days before the passover came 2424
12: 3 and anointed the feet of J, and wiped his 2424
12: 7 Then said J, Let her alone: against the day 2424
12:11 of the Jews went away, and believed on J. 2424
12:12 when they heard that J was coming to 2424
12:14 And J, when he had found a young ass, 2424
12:16 but when J was glorified, then 2424
12:21 desired him, saying, Sir, we would see J. 2424
12:22 and again Andrew and Philip tell J. 2424
12:23 And J answered them, saying, The hour is 2424
12:30 J answered and said, This voice came not 2424
12:35 Then J said unto them, Yet a little while is 2424
12:36 These *things* spake J, and departed, and 2424
12:44 J cried and said, He that believeth on me, 2424
13: 1 when J knew that his hour was come that 2424
13: 3 J knowing that the Father had given all 2424
13: 7 J answered and said unto him, What I do 2424
13: 8 J answered him, If I wash thee not, 2424
13:10 J saith to him, He that is washed needeth 2424
13:21 When J had thus said, he was troubled in 2424
13:23 bosom one of his disciples, whom J loved. 2424
13:26 J answered, He it is, to whom I shall give a 2424
13:27 Then said J unto him, That thou doest, 2424
13:29 Judas had the bag, that J had said unto him, 2424
13:31 Therefore, when he was gone out, J said, 2424
13:36 J answered him, Whither I go, thou canst 2424
13:38 J answered him, Wilt thou lay down thy 2424
14: 6 J saith unto him, I am the way, the truth, 2424
14: 9 J saith unto him, Have I been so long time 2424
14:23 J answered and said unto him, If a man 2424
16:19 Now J knew that they were desirous to ask 2424
16:31 J answered them, Do ye now believe? 2424
17: 1 These *words* spake J, and lift up his eyes to 2424
17: 3 and J Christ, whom thou hast sent. 2424
18: 1 When J had spoken these *words,* he went 2424
18: 2 for J ofttimes resorted thither with his 2424
18: 4 J therefore, knowing all *things* that should 2424
18: 5 They answered him, J of Nazareth. 2424
18: 5 J saith unto them, I am *he.* And Judas also, 2424
18: 7 seek ye? And they said, J of Nazareth. 2424
18: 8 J answered, I have told you that I am *he:* if 2424
18:11 Then said J unto Peter, Put up thy sword 2424
18:12 the captain and officers of the Jews took J, 2424
18:15 And Simon Peter followed J, and *so* 2424
18:15 went in with J into the palace of the high 2424
18:19 high priest then asked J of his disciples, 2424
18:20 J answered him, I spake openly to 2424
18:22 one of the officers which stood by struck J 2424
18:23 J answered him, If I have spoken evil, 2424

Jn	18:28	Then led they **J** from Caiaphas unto	*2424*
	18:32	That the saying of **J** might be fulfilled,	*2424*
	18:33	and called **J**, and said unto him, Art thou	*2424*
	18:34	**J** answered him, Sayest thou this *thing* of	*2424*
	18:36	**J** answered, My kingdom is not of this	*2424*
	18:37	**J** answered, Thou sayest that I am a king.	*2424*
	19: 1	Then Pilate therefore took **J**, and	*2424*
	19: 5	Then came **J** forth, wearing the crown of	*2424*
	19: 9	and saith unto **J**, Whence art thou?	*2424*
	19: 9	art thou? But **J** gave him no answer.	*2424*
	19:11	**J** answered, Thou couldest have no power	*2424*
	19:13	he brought **J** forth, and sat down in	*2424*
	19:16	And they took **J**, and led *him* away.	*2424*
	19:18	on either side one, and **J** in the midst.	*2424*
	19:19	**J** OF NAZARETH THE KING OF THE	*2424*
	19:20	for the place where **J** was crucified was	*2424*
	19:23	the soldiers, when they had crucified **J**,	*2424*
	19:25	Now there stood by the cross of **J** his	*2424*
	19:26	When **J** therefore saw *his* mother, and	*2424*
	19:28	**J** knowing that all *things* were now	*2424*
	19:30	When **J** therefore had received the vinegar,	*2424*
	19:33	But when they came to **J**, and saw that he	*2424*
	19:38	being a disciple of **J**, but secretly for fear of	*2424*
	19:38	that he might take away the body of **J**:	*2424*
	19:38	He came therefore, and took the body of **J**.	*2424*
	19:39	which at the first came to **J** by night, and	*2424*
	19:40	Then took they the body of **J**, and wound it	*2424*
	19:42	There laid they **J** therefore because of	*2424*
	20: 2	whom **J** loved, and saith unto them,	*2424*
	20:12	at the feet, where the body of **J** had lain.	*2424*
	20:14	and saw **J** standing, and knew not that it	*2424*
	20:14	Jesus standing, and knew not that it was **J**.	*2424*
	20:15	**J** saith unto her, Woman, why weepest	*2424*
	20:16	**J** saith unto her, Mary. She turned herself,	*2424*
	20:17	**J** saith unto her, Touch me not; for I am not	*2424*
	20:19	came **J** and stood in the midst, and	*2424*
	20:21	Then said **J** to them again, Peace *be* unto	*2424*
	20:24	was not with them when **J** came.	*2424*
	20:26	*then* came **J**, the doors being shut,	*2424*
	20:29	**J** saith unto him, Thomas, because	*2424*
	20:30	And many other signs truly did **J** in	*2424*
	20:31	that ye might believe that **J** is the Christ,	*2424*
	21: 1	After these *things* **J** shewed himself again	*2424*
	21: 4	was now come, **J** stood on the shore:	*2424*
	21: 4	but the disciples knew not that it was **J**.	*2424*
	21: 5	Then **J** saith unto them, Children, have ye	*2424*
	21: 7	Therefore that disciple whom **J** loved saith	*2424*
	21:10	**J** saith unto them, Bring of the fish which	*2424*
	21:12	**J** saith unto them, Come *and* dine.	*2424*
	21:13	**J** then cometh, and taketh bread, and	*2424*
	21:14	This *is* now the third time *that* **J** shewed	*2424*
	21:15	**J** saith to Simon Peter, Simon, *son* of	*2424*
	21:17	love thee. **J** saith unto him, Feed my sheep.	*2424*
	21:20	seeth the disciple whom **J** loved following;	*2424*
	21:21	Peter seeing him saith to **J**, Lord, and	*2424*
	21:22	**J** saith unto him, If I will that he tarry till I	*2424*
	21:23	yet **J** said not unto him, He shall not die;	*2424*
	21:25	are also many other *things* which **J** did,	*2424*
Ac	1: 1	of all that **J** began both to do and teach,	*2424*
	1:11	this *same* **J**, which is taken up from you	*2424*
	1:14	and Mary the mother of **J**, and with his	*2424*
	1:16	which was guide to them that took **J**.	*2424*
	1:21	with us all the time that the Lord **J** went in	*2424*
	2:22	**J** of Nazareth, a man approved of God	*2424*
	2:32	This **J** hath God raised up, whereof we all	*2424*
	2:36	that God hath made that same **J**, whom ye	*2424*
	2:38	name of **J** Christ for the remission of sins,	*2424*
	3: 6	In the name of **J** Christ of Nazareth rise up	*2424*
	3:13	God of our fathers, hath glorified his Son **J**;	*2424*
	3:20	And he shall send **J** Christ, which before	*2424*
	3:26	you first God, having raised up his Son **J**,	*2424*
	4: 2	preached through **J** the resurrection from	*2424*
	4:10	that by the name of **J** Christ of Nazareth,	*2424*
	4:13	of them, that they had been with **J**.	*2424*
	4:18	to speak at all nor teach in the name of **J**.	*2424*
	4:27	For of a truth against thy holy child **J**,	*2424*
	4:30	be done by the name of thy holy child **J**.	*2424*
	4:33	witness of the resurrection of the Lord **J**:	*2424*
	5:30	The God of our fathers raised up **J**,	*2424*
	5:40	that *they* should not speak in the name of **J**,	*2424*
	5:42	ceased not to teach and preach **J** Christ.	*2424*
	6:14	that this **J** of Nazareth shall destroy this	*2424*
	7:45	with **J** into the possession of the Gentiles,	*2424*
	7:55	and **J** standing on the right hand of God,	*2424*
	7:59	calling upon *God*, and saying, Lord **J**,	*2424*
	8:12	and the name of **J** Christ, they were	*2424*
	8:16	were baptized in the name of the Lord **J**.)	*2424*
	8:35	same scripture, and preached unto him **J**.	*2424*
	8:37	I believe that **J** Christ is the Son of God.	*2424*
	9: 5	Lord said, I am **J** whom thou persecutest:	*2424*
	9:17	on him said, Brother Saul, the Lord, *even* **J**,	*2424*
	9:27	boldly at Damascus in the name of **J**.	*2424*
	9:29	he spake boldly in the name of the Lord **J**,	*2424*
	9:34	Aeneas, **J** Christ maketh thee whole:	*2424*
	10:36	of Israel, preaching peace by **J** Christ:	*2424*
	10:38	How God anointed **J** of Nazareth with	*2424*
	11:17	unto us, who believed on the Lord **J** Christ;	*2424*
	11:20	unto the Grecians, preaching the Lord **J**.	*2424*
	13:23	*his* promise raised unto Israel a Saviour, **J**:	*2424*
	13:33	in that he hath raised up **J** again;	*2424*
	15:11	of the Lord **J** Christ *we* shall be saved,	*2424*
	15:26	lives for the name of our Lord **J** Christ.	*2424*
	16:18	I command thee in the name of **J** Christ to	*2424*
	16:31	Believe on the Lord **J** Christ, and thou shalt	*2424*
	17: 3	and that this **J**, whom I preach unto you,	*2424*
	17: 7	saying that there is another king, *one* **J**.	*2424*
	17:18	because he preached unto them **J**, and	*2424*
	18: 5	and testified to the Jews *that* **J** *was* Christ.	*2424*
	18:28	shewing by the scriptures that **J** was Christ.	*2424*
	19: 4	should come after him, that is, on Christ **J**.	*2424*
	19: 5	were baptized in the name of the Lord **J**.	*2424*
	19:10	dwelt in Asia heard the word of the Lord **J**,	*2424*
	19:13	had evil spirits the name of the Lord **J**,	*2424*
	19:13	We adjure you by **J** whom Paul preacheth.	*2424*
	19:15	and said, **J** I know, and Paul I know;	*2424*
	19:17	and the name of the Lord **J** was magnified.	*2424*
	20:21	and faith toward our Lord **J** Christ.	*2424*
	20:24	which I have received of the Lord **J**,	*2424*
	20:35	and to remember the words of the Lord **J**,	*2424*
	21:13	die at Jerusalem for the name of the Lord **J**.	*2424*
	22: 8	And he said unto me, I am **J** of Nazareth,	*2424*
	25:19	and of one **J**, *which was* dead, whom Paul	*2424*
	26: 9	contrary to the name of **J** of Nazareth.	*2424*
	26:15	And he said, I am **J** whom thou persecutest.	*2424*
	28:23	persuading them concerning **J**, both out of	*2424*
	28:31	*things* which concern the Lord **J** Christ,	*2424*
Ro	1: 1	Paul, a servant of **J** Christ, called *to be* an	*2424*
	1: 3	Concerning his Son **J** Christ our Lord,	*2424*
	1: 6	Among whom are ye also *the* called of **J**	*2424*
	1: 7	God our Father, and the Lord **J** Christ.	*2424*
	1: 8	I thank my God through **J** Christ for you	*2424*
	2:16	of men by **J** Christ according to my gospel.	*2424*
	3:22	of God *which is* by faith of **J** Christ unto all	*2424*
	3:24	through the redemption that is in Christ **J**:	*2424*
	3:26	the justifier of him which believeth in **J**.	*2424*
	4:24	if we believe on him that raised up **J** our	*2424*
	5: 1	peace with God through our Lord **J** Christ:	*2424*
	5:11	we also joy in God through our Lord **J**	*2424*
	5:15	by grace, which is by one man, **J** Christ,	*2424*
	5:17	shall reign in life by one, **J** Christ.	*2424*
	5:21	unto eternal life by **J** Christ our Lord.	*2424*
	6: 3	many of us as were baptized into **J** Christ	*2424*
	6:11	alive unto God through **J** Christ our Lord.	*2424*
	6:23	the gift of God *is* eternal life through **J**	*2424*
	7:25	I thank God through **J** Christ our Lord. So	*2424*
	8: 1	*are* in Christ **J** who walk not after the flesh,	*2424*
	8: 2	For the law of the Spirit of life in Christ **J**	*2424*
	8:11	But if the Spirit of him that raised up **J**	*2424*
	8:39	love of God, which is in Christ **J** our Lord.	*2424*
	10: 9	shalt confess with thy mouth the Lord **J**,	*2424*
	13:14	But put ye on the Lord **J** Christ, and	*2424*
	14:14	I know, and am persuaded by the Lord **J**,	*2424*
	15: 5	one towards another according to Christ **J**:	*2424*
	15: 6	even the Father of our Lord **J** Christ.	*2424*
	15: 8	Now I say that **J** Christ was a minister of	*2424*
	15:16	That I should be the minister of **J** Christ to	*2424*
	15:17	whereof *I* may glory through **J** Christ *in*	*2424*
	15:30	for the Lord **J** Christ's sake, and for	*2424*
	16: 3	and Aquila my helpers in Christ **J**:	*2424*
	16:18	For *they that are* such serve not our Lord **J**	*2424*
	16:20	The grace of our Lord **J** Christ *be* with you.	*2424*
	16:24	The grace of our Lord **J** Christ *be* with you	*2424*
	16:25	and the preaching of **J** Christ, according to	*2424*
	16:27	*be* glory through **J** Christ for ever.	*2424*
1Co	1: 1	called *to be* an apostle of **J** Christ through	*2424*
	1: 2	to them that are sanctified in Christ **J**,	*2424*
	1: 2	call upon the name of **J** Christ our Lord,	*2424*
	1: 3	our Father, and *from* the Lord **J** Christ.	*2424*

J

1Co 1: 4 of God which is given you by J Christ; *2424*
1: 7 waiting for the coming of our Lord J *2424*
1: 8 blameless in the day of our Lord J Christ. *2424*
1: 9 the fellowship of his Son J Christ our Lord. *2424*
1:10 brethren, by the name of our Lord J Christ, *2424*
1:30 But of him are ye in Christ J, who of God *2424*
2: 2 save J Christ, and him crucified. *2424*
3:11 *man* lay than that is laid, which is J Christ. *2424*
4:15 for in Christ J I have begotten you through *2424*
5: 4 In the name of our Lord J Christ, when ye *2424*
5: 4 with the power of our Lord J Christ, *2424*
5: 5 may be saved in the day of the Lord J. *2424*
6:11 ye are justified in the name of the Lord J, *2424*
8: 6 and one Lord J Christ, by whom *are* all *2424*
9: 1 have I not seen J Christ our Lord? are not *2424*
11:23 That the Lord J the *same* night in which he *2424*
12: 3 by the Spirit of God calleth J accursed: *2424*
12: 3 and *that* no *man* can say that J is the Lord, *2424*
15:31 rejoicing which I have in Christ J our Lord, *2424*
15:57 us the victory through our Lord J Christ. *2424*
16:22 If any *man* love not the Lord J Christ, *2424*
16:23 The grace of *our* Lord J Christ *be* with you. *2424*
16:24 My love *be* with you all in Christ J. Amen. *2424*
2Co 1: 1 an apostle of J Christ by the will of God, *2424*
1: 2 our Father, and *from* the Lord J Christ. *2424*
1: 3 even the Father of our Lord J Christ, *2424*
1:14 as ye also *are* ours in the day of the Lord J. *2424*
1:19 For the Son of God, J Christ, who was *2424*
4: 5 preach not ourselves, but Christ J the Lord; *2424*
4: 6 of the glory of God in the face of J Christ. *2424*
4:10 about in the body the dying of the Lord J, *2424*
4:10 that the life also of J might be made *2424*
4:11 that the life also of J might be made *2424*
4:14 the Lord J shall raise up us also by Jesus, *2424*
4:14 the Lord Jesus shall raise up us also by J, *2424*
5:18 who hath reconciled us to himself by J *2424*
8: 9 For ye know the grace of our Lord J Christ, *2424*
11: 4 For if he that cometh preacheth another J, *2424*
11:31 The God and Father of our Lord J Christ, *2424*
13: 5 how that J Christ is in you, except ye be *2424*
13:14 The grace of the Lord J Christ, and the love *2424*
Gal 1: 1 but by J Christ, and God the Father, *2424*
1: 3 the Father, and *from* our Lord J Christ, *2424*
1:12 I taught *it,* but by the revelation of J Christ. *2424*
2: 4 out our liberty which we have in Christ J, *2424*
2:16 but by the faith of J Christ, even we have *2424*
2:16 even we have believed in J Christ, *2424*
3: 1 before whose eyes J Christ hath been *2424*
3:14 come on the Gentiles through J Christ; *2424*
3:22 that the promise by faith of J Christ might *2424*
3:26 all the children of God by faith in Christ J. *2424*
3:28 nor female: for ye are all one in Christ J. *2424*
4:14 me as an angel of God, *even* as Christ J. *2424*
5: 6 For in J Christ neither circumcision *2424*
6:14 save in the cross of our Lord J Christ, *2424*
6:15 For in Christ J neither circumcision *2424*
6:17 I bear in my body the marks of the Lord J. *2424*
6:18 the grace of our Lord J Christ *be* with your *2424*
Eph 1: 1 an apostle of J Christ by the will of God, *2424*
1: 1 at Ephesus, and to the faithful in Christ J: *2424*
1: 2 our Father, and *from* the Lord J Christ. *2424*
1: 3 *be* the God and Father of our Lord J Christ, *2424*
1: 5 adoption of children by J Christ to himself, *2424*
1:15 after I heard of your faith in the Lord J, and *2424*
1:17 That the God of our Lord J Christ, *2424*
2: 6 sit together in heavenly *places* in Christ J: *2424*
2: 7 in *his* kindness towards us through Christ J. *2424*
2:10 created in Christ J unto good works, *2424*
2:13 But now in Christ J ye who sometimes *2424*
2:20 J Christ himself being the chief corner *2424*
3: 1 the prisoner of J Christ for you Gentiles, *2424*
3: 9 in God, who created all *things* by J Christ: *2424*
3:11 which he purposed in Christ J our Lord: *2424*
3:14 knees unto the Father of our Lord J Christ, *2424*
3:21 Unto him *be* glory in the church by Christ J *2424*
4:21 been taught by him, as the truth is in J: *2424*
5:20 the Father in the name of our Lord J Christ; *2424*
6:23 from God the Father and the Lord J Christ. *2424*
6:24 Grace *be* with all them that love our Lord J *2424*
Php 1: 1 and Timotheus, the servants of J Christ, *2424*
1: 1 to all the saints in Christ J which are at *2424*
1: 2 our Father, and *from* the Lord J Christ. *2424*
1: 6 will perform *it* until the day of J Christ: *2424*
1: 8 long after you all in the bowels of J Christ. *2424*
1:11 which are by J Christ unto the glory and *2424*
1:19 and the supply of the Spirit of J Christ, *2424*
1:26 J Christ for me by my coming to you again. *2424*
2: 5 mind be in you, which *was* also in Christ J: *2424*
2:10 That at the name of J every knee should *2424*
2:11 And *that* every tongue should confess that J *2424*
2:19 But I trust in the Lord J to send Timotheus *2424*
2:21 not the *things which are* J Christ's. *2424*
3: 3 and rejoice in Christ J, and have no *2424*
3: 8 of the knowledge of Christ J my Lord: *2424*
3:12 which also I am apprehended of Christ J. *2424*
3:14 prize of the high calling of God in Christ J. *2424*
3:20 we look for the Saviour, the Lord J Christ: *2424*
4: 7 your hearts and minds through Christ J. *2424*
4:19 according to his riches in glory by Christ J. *2424*
4:21 Salute every saint in Christ J. The brethren *2424*
4:23 The grace of our Lord J Christ *be* with you *2424*
Col 1: 1 an apostle of J Christ by the will of God, *2424*
1: 2 from God our Father and the Lord J Christ. *2424*
1: 3 to God and the Father of our Lord J Christ, *2424*
1: 4 Since we heard of your faith in Christ J, *2424*
1:28 may present every man perfect in Christ J: *2424*
2: 6 therefore received Christ J the Lord, *2424*
3:17 or deed, *do* all in the name of the Lord J, *2424*
4:11 And J, which is called Justus, who are of *2424*
1Th 1: 1 in God the Father and *in* the Lord J Christ: *2424*
1: 1 God our Father, and the Lord J Christ. *2424*
1: 3 and patience of hope in our Lord J Christ, *2424*
1:10 whom he raised from the dead, *even* J, *2424*
2:14 of God which in Judea are in Christ J: *2424*
2:15 Who both killed the Lord J, and their own *2424*
2:19 of our Lord J Christ at his coming? *2424*
3:11 and our Father, and our Lord J Christ, *2424*
3:13 at the coming of our Lord J Christ with all *2424*
4: 1 brethren, and exhort *you* by the Lord J, *2424*
4: 2 commandments we gave you by the Lord J. *2424*
4:14 For if we believe that J died and rose again, *2424*
4:14 them also which sleep in J will God bring *2424*
5: 9 to obtain salvation by our Lord J Christ, *2424*
5:18 for this *is* the will of God in Christ J *2424*
5:23 unto the coming of our Lord J Christ. *2424*
5:28 The grace of our Lord J Christ *be* with you. *2424*
2Th 1: 1 in God our Father and the Lord J Christ: *2424*
1: 2 from God our Father and the Lord J Christ. *2424*
1: 7 when the Lord J shall be revealed from *2424*
1: 8 that obey not the gospel of our Lord J *2424*
1:12 That the name of our Lord J Christ may be *2424*
1:12 the grace of our God and the Lord J Christ. *2424*
2: 1 by the coming of our Lord J Christ, and *2424*
2:14 to the obtaining of the glory of our Lord J *2424*
2:16 Now our Lord J Christ himself, and God, *2424*
3: 6 brethren, in the name of our Lord J Christ, *2424*
3:12 and exhort by our Lord J Christ, *2424*
3:18 The grace of our Lord J Christ *be* with you *2424*
1Ti 1: 1 an apostle of J Christ by the commandment *2424*
1: 1 and Lord J Christ, *which is* our hope; *2424*
1: 2 from God our Father and J Christ our Lord. *2424*
1:12 And I thank Christ J our Lord, who hath *2424*
1:14 with faith and love which is in Christ J. *2424*
1:15 that Christ J came into the world to save *2424*
1:16 that in me first J Christ might shew forth *2424*
2: 5 between God and men, *the* man Christ J; *2424*
3:13 boldness in the faith which is in Christ J. *2424*
4: 6 thou shalt be a good minister of J Christ, *2424*
5:21 and the Lord J Christ, and the elect angels, *2424*
6: 3 *even* the *words* of our Lord J Christ, and *2424*
6:13 quickeneth all *things,* and *before* Christ J, *2424*
6:14 until the appearing of our Lord J Christ: *2424*
2Ti 1: 1 an apostle of J Christ by the will of God, *2424*
1: 1 to the promise of life which is in Christ J, *2424*
1: 2 from God the Father and Christ J our Lord. *2424*
1: 9 which was given us in Christ J before *2424*
1:10 by the appearing of our Saviour J Christ, *2424*
1:13 in faith and love which is in Christ J. *2424*
2: 1 be strong in the grace that is in Christ J. *2424*
2: 3 as a good soldier of J Christ. *2424*
2: 8 Remember that J Christ of the seed of *2424*
2:10 which is in Christ J with eternal glory. *2424*
3:12 all that will live godly in Christ J shall *2424*
3:15 salvation through faith which is in Christ J. *2424*
4: 1 before God, and the Lord J Christ, *2424*
4:22 The Lord J Christ *be* with thy spirit. Grace *2424*
Tit 1: 1 servant of God, and an apostle of J Christ, *2424*
1: 4 and the Lord J Christ our Saviour. *2424*

J

Tit 2:13 of the great God and our Saviour J Christ; *2424*
3: 6 Which he shed on us abundantly through J *2424*
Phm 1: 1 a prisoner of J Christ, and Timothy *our* *2424*
1: 3 from God our Father and the Lord J Christ. *2424*
1: 5 which thou hast toward the Lord J, and *2424*
1: 6 good *thing* which is in you in Christ J. *2424*
1: 9 and now also a prisoner of J Christ. *2424*
1:23 my fellowprisoner in Christ J; *2424*
1:25 The grace of our Lord J Christ *be* with your *2424*
Heb 2: 9 But we see J, who was made a little lower *2424*
3: 1 and High Priest of our profession, Christ J; *2424*
4: 8 For if J had given them rest, *then* would he *2424*
4:14 J the Son of God, let us hold fast *our* *2424*
6:20 the forerunner is for us entered, *even* J, *2424*
7:22 much was J made a surety of a better *2424*
10:10 of the body of J Christ once for all. *2424*
10:19 to enter into the holiest by the blood of J, *2424*
12: 2 Looking unto J the author and finisher of *2424*
12:24 And to J the mediator of the new covenant, *2424*
13: 8 J Christ the same yesterday, and to day, *2424*
13:12 Wherefore J also, that he might sanctify *2424*
13:20 brought again from the dead our Lord J, *2424*
13:21 well pleasing in his sight, through J Christ; *2424*
Jas 1: 1 a servant of God and of the Lord J Christ, *2424*
2: 1 have not the faith of our Lord J Christ, *2424*
1Pe 1: 1 Peter, an apostle of J Christ, to *2424*
1: 2 and sprinkling of the blood of J Christ: *2424*
1: 3 *be* the God and Father of our Lord J Christ, *2424*
1: 3 the resurrection of J Christ from the dead, *2424*
1: 7 and glory at the appearing of J Christ: *2424*
1:13 unto you at the revelation of J Christ; *2424*
2: 5 acceptable to God by J Christ. *2424*
3:21 by the resurrection of J Christ: *2424*
4:11 *things* may be glorified through J Christ, *2424*
5:10 called us into his eternal glory by Christ J, *2424*
5:14 Peace *be* with you all that are in Christ J. *2424*
2Pe 1: 1 a servant and an apostle of J Christ, *2424*
1: 1 of God and our Saviour J Christ: *2424*
1: 2 the knowledge of God, and of J our Lord. *2424*
1: 8 in the knowledge of our Lord J Christ. *2424*
1:11 kingdom of our Lord and Saviour J Christ. *2424*
1:14 even as our Lord J Christ hath shewed me. *2424*
1:16 the power and coming of our Lord J Christ, *2424*
2:20 of the Lord and Saviour J Christ, *2424*
3:18 of our Lord and Saviour J Christ. *2424*
1Jn 1: 3 with the Father, and with his Son J Christ. *2424*
1: 7 the blood of J Christ his Son cleanseth us *2424*
2: 1 with the Father, J Christ *the* righteous: *2424*
2:22 but he that denieth that J is the Christ? *2424*
3:23 believe on the name of his Son J Christ, *2424*
4: 2 Every spirit that confesseth that J Christ is *2424*
4: 3 And every spirit that confesseth not that J *2424*
4:15 Whosoever shall confess that J is the Son *2424*
5: 1 Whosoever believeth that J is the Christ is *2424*
5: 5 he that believeth that J is the Son of God? *2424*
5: 6 came by water and blood, *even* J Christ; *2424*
5:20 in him *that is* true, *even* in his Son J Christ. *2424*
2Jn 1: 3 God the Father, and from the Lord J Christ, *2424*
1: 7 who confess not that J Christ is come in *2424*
Jude 1: 1 the servant of J Christ, and brother of *2424*
1: 1 and preserved *in* J Christ, *and* called: *2424*
1: 4 the only Lord God, and our Lord J Christ. *2424*
1:17 before of the apostles of our Lord J Christ; *2424*
1:21 looking for the mercy of our Lord J Christ *2424*
Rev 1: 1 The Revelation of J Christ, which God *2424*
1: 2 and of the testimony of J Christ, and of all *2424*
1: 5 And from J Christ, *who is* the faithful *2424*
1: 9 in the kingdom and patience of J Christ, *2424*
1: 9 of God, and for the testimony of J Christ. *2424*
12:17 of God, and have the testimony of J Christ. *2424*
14:12 commandments of God, and the faith of J. *2424*
17: 6 and with the blood of the martyrs of J: *2424*
19:10 thy brethren that have the testimony of J: *2424*
19:10 for the testimony of J is the spirit of *2424*
20: 4 that were beheaded for the witness of J, *2424*
22:16 I J have sent mine angel to testify unto you *2424*
22:20 Amen. Even so, come, Lord J. *2424*
22:21 The grace of our Lord J Christ *be* with you *2424*

JESUS' (10) [JESUS]
Mt 15:30 many others, and cast them *down* at J feet; *2424*
27:57 who also himself was J disciple: *2424*
Lk 5: 8 When Simon Peter saw *it,* he fell down at J *2424*
8:41 and he fell down at J feet, and *2424*
10:39 which also sat at J feet, and heard his word. *2424*
Jn 12: 9 and they came not for J sake only, *2424*
13:23 Now there was leaning on J bosom one of *2424*
13:25 He then lying on J breast saith unto him, *2424*
2Co 4: 5 and ourselves your servants for J sake. *2424*
4:11 are alway delivered unto death for J sake, *2424*

JETHER (8)
Jdg 8:20 he said unto J his firstborn, Up, *and* 3500
1Ki 2: 5 unto Amasa the son of J, whom he slew, 3500
2:32 the host of Israel, and Amasa the son of J, 3500
1Ch 2:17 the father of Amasa *was* J the Ishmeelite. 3500
2:32 the brother of Shammai; J, and Jonathan: 3500
2:32 and Jonathan: and J died without children. 3500
4:17 the sons of Ezra *were,* J, and Mered, and 3500
7:38 the sons of J; Jephunneh, and Pispah, and 3500

JETHETH (2)
Ge 36:40 duke Timnah, duke Alvah, duke J, 3509
1Ch 1:51 duke Timnah, duke Aliah, duke J, 3509

JETHLAH (1)
Jos 19:42 And Shaalabbin, and Aijalon, and J, 3494

JETHRO (10)
Ex 3: 1 Now Moses kept the flock of J his father in 3503
4:18 and returned to J his father in law, 3500
4:18 And J said to Moses, Go in peace. 3503
18: 1 When J, the priest of Midian, Moses' father 3503
18: 2 J, Moses' father in law, took Zipporah, 3503
18: 5 J, Moses' father in law, came with his sons 3503
18: 6 I thy father in law J am come unto thee, 3503
18: 9 J rejoiced for all the goodness which 3503
18:10 J said, Blessed *be* the LORD, who hath 3503
18:12 J, Moses' father in law, took a burnt 3503

JETUR (3)
Ge 25:15 Hadar, and Tema, J, Naphish, and 3195
1Ch 1:31 J, Naphish, and Kedemah. These *are* 3195
5:19 with J, and Nephish, and Nodab. 3195

JEUEL (1)
1Ch 9: 6 J, and their brethren, six hundred and 3262

JEUSH (8)
Ge 36: 5 Aholibamah bare J, and Jaalam, and 3266
36:14 she bare to Esau J, and Jaalam, and Korah. 3266
36:18 duke J, duke Jaalam, duke Korah: 3266
1Ch 1:35 Reuel, and J, and Jaalam, and Korah. 3266
7:10 J, and Benjamin, and Ehud, and 3266
23:10 *were,* Jahath, Zina, and J, and Beriah. 3266
23:11 J and Beriah had not many sons; therefore 3266
2Ch 11:19 J, and Shamariah, and Zaham. 3266

JEUZ (1)
1Ch 8:10 J, and Shachia, and Mirma. These *were* his 3263

JEW (32) [JEWESS, JEWISH, JEWRY, JEWS, JEWS']
Est 2: 5 in Shushan the palace there was a certain J, 3064
3: 4 for he had told them that he *was* a J. 3064
5:13 long as I see Mordecai the J sitting at 3064
6:10 hast said, and do *even* so to Mordecai the J, 3064
8: 7 Esther the queen and to Mordecai the J, 3064
9:29 daughter of Abihail, and Mordecai the J, 3064
9:31 *appointed,* according as Mordecai the J 3064
10: 3 For Mordecai the J *was* next unto king 3064
Jer 34: 9 himself of them, *to wit,* of a J his brother. 3064
Zec 8:23 take hold of the skirt of him that is a J, 3064
Jn 4: 9 *is it that* thou, being a J, askest drink of me, *2453*
18:35 Pilate answered, Am I a J? Thine own *2453*
Ac 10:28 *thing* for a man *that is* a J to keep company, *2453*
13: 6 a false prophet, a J, whose name *was* *2453*
18: 2 And found a certain J named Aquila, born *2453*
18:24 And a certain J named Apollos, born at *2453*
19:14 a J, *and* chief of the priests, which did so. *2453*
19:34 But when *they* knew that he was a J, *2453*
21:39 I am a man *which am* a J of Tarsus, *2453*
22: 3 I am verily a man *which am* a J, born in *2453*
Ro 1:16 to the J first, and *also* to the Greek. *2453*
2: 9 of the J first, and *also* of the Gentile; *2453*
2:10 to the J first, and *also* to the Gentile: *2453*
2:17 thou art called a J, and restest in the law, *2453*
2:28 For he is not a J, which is one outwardly; *2453*
2:29 But he *is* a J, which is one inwardly; *2453*
3: 1 What advantage then hath the J? or *2453*

Ro 10:12 For there is no difference between the **J** 2453
1Co 9:20 And unto the Jews I became as a **J**, that I 2453
Gal 2:14 Peter before *them* all, If thou, being a **J**, 2453
3:28 There is neither **J** nor Greek, there is 2453
Col 3:11 Where there is neither Greek nor **J**, 2453

JEWEL (3) [JEWELS]
Pr 11:22 *As* a **j** of gold in a swine's snout, *so is* a fair 5141
20:15 but the lips of knowledge *are* a precious **j**. 3627
Eze 16:12 I put a **j** on thy forehead, and earrings in 5141

JEWELS (25) [JEWEL]
Ge 24:53 the servant brought forth **j** of silver, and 3627
24:53 **j** of gold, and raiment, and gave *them* to 3627
Ex 3:22 **j** of silver, and jewels of gold, and raiment: 3627
3:22 jewels of silver, and **j** of gold, and raiment: 3627
11: 2 **j** of silver, and jewels of gold. 3627
11: 2 jewels of silver, and **j** of gold. 3627
12:35 they borrowed of the Egyptians **j** of silver, 3627
12:35 jewels of silver, and **j** of gold, and raiment: 3627
35:22 and rings, and tablets, all **j** of gold: 3627
Nu 31:50 *of* **j** of gold, chains, and bracelets, rings, 3627
31:51 took the gold of them, *even* all wrought **j**. 3627
1Sa 6: 8 put the **j** of gold, which ye return him *for* a 3627
6:15 wherein the **j** of gold *were*, and put *them* on 3627
2Ch 20:25 precious **j**, which they stript off for 3627
32:27 for shields, and for all *manner of* pleasant **j**; 3627
Job 28:17 the exchange of it *shall not be for* **j** of fine 3627
SS 1:10 Thy cheeks are comely with rows *of* **j**, thy NIH
7: 1 the joints of thy thighs *are* like **j**, the work 2481
Isa 3:21 The rings, and nose **j**, 5141
61:10 and as a bride adorneth *herself* with her **j**. 3627
Eze 16:17 Thou hast also taken thy fair **j** of my gold 3627
16:39 shall take thy fair **j**, and leave thee naked 3627
23:26 out of thy clothes, and take away thy fair **j**. 3627
Hos 2:13 decked herself with her earrings and her **j**, 2484
Mal 3:17 of hosts, in that day when I make *up my* **j**; 5459

JEWESS (2) [JEW]
Ac 16: 1 *which was* a **J**, and believed; 2453
24:24 which was a **J**, he sent for Paul, and 2453

JEWISH (1) [JEW]
Tit 1:14 Not giving heed to **J** fables, and 2451

JEWRY (3) [JEW]
Da 5:13 whom the king my father brought out of **J**? 3061
Lk 23: 5 up the people, teaching throughout all **J**, 2449
Jn 7: 1 for he would not walk in **J**, because 2449

JEWS (243) [JEW]
2Ki 16: 6 Elath to Syria, and drave the **J** from Elath: 3064
25:25 the **J** and the Chaldees that were with him 3064
Ezr 4:12 that the **J** which came up from thee to us 3062
4:23 went up in haste to Jerusalem unto the **J**, 3062
5: 1 prophesied unto the **J** that *were* in Judah 3062
5: 5 of their God was upon the elders of the **J**, 3062
6: 7 let the governor of the **J** and the elders of 3062
6: 7 the elders of the **J** build this house of God 3062
6: 8 **J** for the building of this house of God: 3062
6:14 the elders of the **J** builded, and 3062
Ne 1: 2 I asked them concerning the **J** that had 3064
2:16 neither had I as yet told *it* to the **J**, nor to 3064
4: 1 took great indignation, and mocked the **J**. 3064
4: 2 and said, What do *these* feeble **J**? 3064
4:12 that when the **J** which dwelt by them came, 3064
5: 1 of their wives against their brethren the **J**. 3064
5: 8 ability have redeemed our brethren the **J**, 3064
5:17 an hundred and fifty of the **J** and rulers, 3064
6: 6 saith *it, that* thou and the **J** think to rebel: 3064
13:23 In those days also saw I **J** *that* had married 3064
Est 3: 6 **J** that *were* throughout the whole kingdom 3064
3:13 all **J**, both young and old, little children and 3064
4: 3 *there was* great mourning among the **J**, and 3064
4: 7 to pay to the king's treasuries for the **J**, 3064
4:13 *in* the king's house, more than all the **J**. 3064
4:14 deliverance arise to the **J** from another 3064
4:16 gather together all the **J** that are present in 3064
6:13 If Mordecai *be* of the seed of the **J**, 3064
8: 3 his device that he had devised against the **J**. 3064
8: 5 which he wrote to destroy the **J** which *are* 3064
8: 7 because he laid his hand upon the **J**. 3064
8: 8 Write ye also for the **J**, as it liketh you, 3064
8: 9 to all that Mordecai commanded unto the **J**, 3064
8: 9 to the **J** according to their writing, and 3064
8:11 Where*in* the king granted the **J** which *were* 3064
8:13 that the **J** should be ready against that day 3064
8:16 The **J** had light, and gladness, and joy, and 3064
8:17 the **J** had joy and gladness, a feast and 3064
8:17 many of the people of the land **became J**; 3054
8:17 for the fear of the **J** fell upon them. 3064
9: 1 in the day that the enemies of the **J** hoped 3064
9: 1 the **J** had rule over them that hated them;) 3064
9: 2 The **J** gathered themselves together in their 3064
9: 3 and officers of the king, helped the **J**; 3064
9: 5 Thus the **J** smote all their enemies *with* 3064
9: 6 in Shushan the palace the **J** slew and 3064
9:10 the enemy of the **J**, slew they; 3064
9:12 The **J** have slain and destroyed five 3064
9:13 let it be granted to the **J** which *are* in 3064
9:15 For the **J** that *were* in Shushan gathered 3064
9:16 the other **J** that *were* in the king's 3064
9:18 the **J** that *were* at Shushan assembled 3064
9:19 Therefore the **J** of the villages, that dwelt in 3064
9:20 sent letters unto all the **J** that *were* in all 3064
9:22 As the days wherein the **J** rested from their 3064
9:23 the **J** undertook to do as they had begun, 3064
9:24 the Agagite, the enemy of all the **J**, 3064
9:24 had devised against the **J** to destroy them, 3064
9:25 which he devised against the **J**, 3064
9:27 The **J** ordained, and took upon them, and 3064
9:28 of Purim should not fail from among the **J**, 3064
9:30 he sent the letters unto all the **J**, to 3064
10: 3 great among the **J**, and accepted of 3064
Jer 32:12 before all the **J** that sat in the court of 3064
38:19 I am afraid of the **J** that are fallen to 3064
40:11 Likewise when all the **J** that *were* in Moab, 3064
40:12 Even all the **J** returned out of all places 3064
40:15 that all the **J** which are gathered unto thee 3064
41: 3 Ishmael also slew all the **J** that were with 3064
44: 1 all the **J** which dwell in the land of Egypt, 3064
52:28 in the seventh year three thousand **J** and 3064
52:30 away captive *of* the **J** seven hundred forty 3064
Da 3: 8 Chaldeans came near, and accused the **J**. 3062
3:12 There are certain **J** whom thou hast set over 3062
Mt 2: 2 Where is he that is born King of the **J**? 2453
27:11 saying, Art thou the King of the **J**? 2453
27:29 mocked him, saying, Hail, King of the **J**! 2453
27:37 THIS IS JESUS THE KING OF THE **J**. 2453
28:15 reported among the **J** until this day. 2453
Mk 7: 3 For the Pharisees, and all the **J**, except they 2453
15: 2 asked him, Art thou the King of the **J**? 2453
15: 9 ye *that* I release unto you the King of the **J**? 2453
15:12 *unto him* whom ye call the King of the **J**? 2453
15:18 began to salute him, Hail, King of the **J**. 2453
15:26 was written over, THE KING OF THE **J**. 2453
Lk 7: 3 he sent unto him *the* elders of the **J**, 2453
23: 3 saying, Art thou the King of the **J**? 2453
23:37 And saying, If thou be the King of the **J**, 2453
23:38 Hebrew, THIS IS THE KING OF THE **J**. 2453
23:51 *he was* of Arimathea, a city of the **J**: 2453
Jn 1:19 when the **J** sent priests and Levites from 2453
2: 6 after the manner of the purifying of the **J**, 2453
2:18 Then answered the **J** and said unto him, 2453
2:20 Then said the **J**, Forty and six years was 2453
3: 1 named Nicodemus, a ruler of the **J**: 2453
3:25 John's disciples and the **J** about purifying. 2453
4: 9 For the **J** have no dealings with 2453
4:22 what we worship: for salvation is of the **J**. 2453
5: 1 After this there was a feast of the **J**; and 2453
5:10 The **J** therefore said unto him that was 2453
5:15 and told the **J** that it was Jesus, 2453
5:16 And therefore did the **J** persecute Jesus, 2453
5:18 Therefore the **J** sought the more to kill him, 2453
6: 4 the passover, a feast of the **J**, was nigh. 2453
6:41 The **J** then murmured at him, because 2453
6:52 The **J** therefore strove amongst themselves, 2453
7: 1 in Jewry, because the **J** sought to kill him. 2453
7:11 Then the **J** sought him at the feast, and 2453
7:13 *man* spake openly of him for fear of the **J**. 2453
7:15 And the **J** marvelled, saying, How knoweth 2453
7:35 Then said the **J** among themselves, 2453
8:22 Then said the **J**, Will he kill himself? 2453
8:31 Then said Jesus to those **J** which believed 2453
8:48 Then answered the **J**, and said unto him, 2453
8:52 Then said the **J** unto him, Now we know 2453
8:57 Then said the **J** unto him, Thou art not yet 2453
9:18 But the **J** did not believe concerning him, 2453
9:22 his parents, because they feared the **J**: 2453

Jn 9:22 for the J had agreed already, that if any 2453
10:19 again among the J for these sayings. 2453
10:24 Then came the J round about him, and 2453
10:31 Then the J took up stones again to stone 2453
10:33 The J answered him, saying, For a good 2453
11: 8 Master, the J of late sought to stone thee; 2453
11:19 And many of the J came to Martha and 2453
11:31 The J then which were with her in 2453
11:33 the J also weeping which came with her, 2453
11:36 Then said the J, Behold, how he loved him. 2453
11:45 Then many of the J which came to Mary, 2453
11:54 walked no more openly among the J; 2453
12: 9 Much people of the J therefore knew that 2453
12:11 by reason of him many of the J went away, 2453
13:33 and as I said unto the J, Whither I go, 2453
18:12 the captain and officers of the J took Jesus, 2453
18:14 was he, which gave counsel to the J, 2453
18:20 in the temple, whither the J always resort; 2453
18:31 The J therefore said unto him, It is not 2453
18:33 said unto him, Art thou the King of the J? 2453
18:36 that I should not be delivered to the J: 2453
18:38 he went out again unto the J, and saith unto 2453
18:39 *that* I release unto you the King of the J? 2453
19: 3 And said, Hail, King of the J: and 2453
19: 7 The J answered him, We have a law, and 2453
19:12 but the J cried out, saying, If thou let this 2453
19:14 and he saith unto the J, Behold your King. 2453
19:19 OF NAZARETH THE KING OF THE J. 2453
19:20 This title then read many of the J: for 2453
19:21 Then said the chief priests of the J to 2453
19:21 to Pilate, Write not, The King of the J; 2453
19:21 but that he said, I am King of the J. 2453
19:31 The J therefore, because it was 2453
19:38 of Jesus, but secretly for fear of the J, 2453
19:40 the spices, as the manner of the J is to bury. 2453
20:19 disciples were assembled for fear of the J, 2453
Ac 2: 5 And there were dwelling at Jerusalem J, 2453
2:10 and strangers of Rome, J and proselytes, 2453
9:22 confounded the J which dwelt at 2453
9:23 the J took counsel to kill him: 2453
10:22 good report among all the nation of the J, 2453
10:39 which he did both in the land of the J, 2453
11:19 the word to none but unto *the* J only. 2453
12: 3 And because he saw it pleased the J, 2453
12:11 all the expectation of the people of the J. 2453
13: 5 the word of God in the synagogues of the J: 2453
13:42 And when the J were gone out of 2453
13:43 many of the J and religious proselytes 2453
13:45 But when the J saw the multitudes, 2453
13:50 But the J stirred up the devout and 2453
14: 1 *both* together into the synagogue of the J, 2453
14: 1 that a great multitude both of the J and 2453
14: 2 But the unbelieving J stirred up 2453
14: 4 and part held with the J, and part with 2453
14: 5 and *also* of the J with their rulers, to use 2453
14:19 And there came thither *certain* J from 2453
16: 3 of the J which were in those quarters: 2453
16:20 saying, These men, being J, do exceedingly 2453
17: 1 where was a synagogue of the J: 2453
17: 5 But the J which believed not, moved with 2453
17:10 *thither* went into the synagogue of the J. 2453
17:13 But when the J of Thessalonica had 2453
17:17 disputed he in the synagogue with the J, 2453
18: 2 that Claudius had commanded all J to 2453
18: 4 and persuaded *the* J and *the* Greeks. 2453
18: 5 and testified to the J *that* Jesus *was* Christ. 2453
18:12 the J made insurrection with one accord 2453
18:14 Gallio said unto the J, If it were a matter of 2453
18:14 of wrong or wicked lewdness, O *ye* J, 2453
18:19 the synagogue, and reasoned with the J. 2453
18:28 For he mightily convinced the J, *and* 2453
19:10 word of the Lord Jesus, both J and Greeks. 2453
19:13 Then certain of the vagabond J, exorcists, 2453
19:17 And this was known to all the J and 2453
19:33 of the multitude, the J putting him forward. 2453
20: 3 and when the J laid wait for him, as he was 2453
20:19 befell me by the lying in wait of the J: 2453
20:21 Testifying both to the J, and *also* to 2453
21:11 So shall the J at Jerusalem bind the man 2453
21:20 how many thousands of J there are which 2453
21:21 that thou teachest all the J which are 2453
21:27 the J which were of Asia, when they saw 2453
22:12 having a good report of all the J which 2453
22:30 wherefore he was accused of the J, 2453
23:12 it was day, certain of the J banded together, 2453
23:20 The J have agreed to desire thee that thou 2453
23:27 This man was taken of the J, and 2453
23:30 And when it was told me how that the J 2453
24: 5 a mover of sedition among all the J 2453
24: 9 And the J also assented, saying that these 2453
24:18 Whereupon certain J from Asia found me 2453
24:27 and Felix, willing to shew the J a pleasure, 2453
25: 2 the chief of the J informed him against 2453
25: 7 the J which came down from Jerusalem 2453
25: 8 Neither against the law of the J, 2453
25: 9 But Festus, willing to do the J a pleasure, 2453
25:10 to the J have I done no wrong, as thou very 2453
25:15 the elders of the J informed *me,* desiring *to* 2453
25:24 the multitude of the J have dealt with me, 2453
26: 2 *the things* whereof I am accused of the J: 2453
26: 3 and questions which are among the J: 2453
26: 4 own nation at Jerusalem, know all the J; 2453
26: 7 king Agrippa, I am accused of the J. 2453
26:21 For these causes the J caught me in 2453
28:17 days Paul called the chief of the J together: 2453
28:19 But when the J spake against *it,* I was 2453
28:29 And when he had said these *words,* the J 2453
Ro 3: 9 for we have before proved both J and 2453
3:29 *Is he* the God of the J only? *is he* not also 2453
9:24 not of the J only, but also of the Gentiles? 2453
1Co 1:22 For the J require a sign, and the Greeks 2453
1:23 unto the J a stumblingblock, and unto 2453
1:24 both J and Greeks, Christ the power of 2453
9:20 And unto the J I became as a Jew, that I 2453
9:20 I became as a Jew, that I might gain *the* J; 2453
10:32 Give none offence, neither to the J, nor to 2453
12:13 whether *we be* J or Gentiles, whether *we be* 2453
2Co 11:24 Of the J five times received I forty *stripes* 2453
Gal 2:13 And the other J dissembled likewise with 2453
2:14 manner of Gentiles, and not **as do the J**, 2452
2:14 thou the Gentiles to **live as do the J**? 2450
2:15 We *who are* J by nature, and not sinners of 2453
1Th 2:14 even as they *have* of the J: 2453
Rev 2: 9 blasphemy of them which say they are J, 2453
3: 9 which say they are J, and are not, but 2453

JEWS' (14) [JEW]

2Ki 18:26 talk not with us **in the J language** in 3066
18:28 cried with a loud voice **in the J language**, 3066
2Ch 32:18 **in the J speech** unto the people of 3066
Ne 13:24 could not speak **in the J language**, but 3066
Est 3:10 of Hammedatha the Agagite, the J enemy. 3064
8: 1 Haman the J enemy unto Esther the queen. 3064
Isa 36:11 and speak not to us **in the J language**, 3066
36:13 cried with a loud voice **in the J language**, 3066
Jn 2:13 And the J passover was at hand, and 2453
7: 2 Now the J feast of tabernacles was at hand. 2453
11:55 And the J passover was nigh at hand: and 2453
19:42 of the J preparation *day;* for the sepulchre 2453
Gal 1:13 conversation in time past in the **J religion**, 2454
1:14 And profited in the **J religion** above many 2454

JEZANIAH (2)

Jer 40: 8 J the son of a Maachathite, they and 3153
42: 1 J the son of Hoshaiah, and all the people 3153

JEZEBEL (22) [JEZEBEL'S]

1Ki 16:31 that he took *to* wife J the daughter of 348
18: 4 when J cut off the prophets of the LORD, 348
18:13 Was it not told my lord what I did when J 348
19: 1 Ahab told J all that Elijah had done, and 348
19: 2 Then J sent a messenger unto Elijah, saying, 348
21: 5 J his wife came to him, and said unto him, 348
21: 7 J his wife said unto him, Dost thou now 348
21:11 did as J had sent unto them, *and* as *it was* 348
21:14 they sent to J, saying, Naboth is stoned, 348
21:15 when J heard that Naboth was stoned, and 348
21:15 and was dead, that J said to Ahab, Arise, 348
21:23 of J also spake the LORD, saying, 348
21:23 The dogs shall eat J by the wall of Jezreel. 348
21:25 of the LORD, whom J his wife stirred up. 348
2Ki 9: 7 the servants of the LORD, at the hand of J. 348
9:10 the dogs shall eat J in the portion of Jezreel, 348
9:22 so long as the whoredoms of thy mother J 348
9:30 J heard *of it;* and she painted her face, and 348
9:36 of Jezreel shall dogs eat the flesh of J: 348
9:37 the carcase of J shall be as dung upon 348
9:37 *so* that they shall not say, This *is* J. 348

Rev 2:20 because thou sufferest *that* woman J, *2403*

JEZEBEL'S (1) [JEZEBEL]
1Ki 18:19 groves four hundred, which eat *at* J table. 348

JEZER (3) [JEZERITES]
Ge 46:24 Jahzeel, and Guni, and J, and Shillem. 3337
Nu 26:49 Of J, the family of the Jezerites: 3337
1Ch 7:13 Jahziel, and Guni, and J, and Shallum, 3337

JEZERITES (1) [JEZER]
Nu 26:49 Of Jezer, the family of the J: of Shillem, 3340

JEZIAH (1)
Ezr 10:25 J, and Malchiah, and Miamin, and Eleazar, 3150

JEZIEL (1)
1Ch 12: 3 and J, and Pelet, the sons of Azmaveth; and 3149

JEZLIAH (1)
1Ch 8:18 Ishmerai also, and J, and Jobab, the sons of 3152

JEZOAR (1)
1Ch 4: 7 of Helah *were,* Zereth, and J, and Ethnan. 3328

JEZRAHIAH (1)
Ne 12:42 the singers sang loud, with J *their* overseer. 3156

JEZREEL (36) [JEZREELITE, JEZREELITESS]
Jos 15:56 And J, and Jokdeam, and Zanoah, 3157
17:16 and *they* who *are* of the valley of J. 3157
19:18 their border was toward J, and Chesulloth, 3157
Jdg 6:33 went over, and pitched in the valley of J. 3157
1Sa 25:43 David also took Ahinoam of J; and 3157
29: 1 pitched by a fountain which *is* in J. 3157
29:11 And the Philistines went up *to* J. 3157
2Sa 2: 9 over J, and over Ephraim, and 3157
4: 4 tidings came of Saul and Jonathan out of J, 3157
1Ki 4:12 which *is* by Zartanah beneath J, 3157
18:45 a great rain. And Ahab rode, and went to J. 3157
18:46 and ran before Ahab to the entrance of J. 3157
21: 1 Jezreelite had a vineyard, which *was* in J, 3157
21:23 The dogs shall eat Jezebel by the wall of J. 3157
2Ki 8:29 king Joram went back to be healed in J of 3157
8:29 down to see Joram the son of Ahab in J, 3157
9:10 dogs shall eat Jezebel in the portion of J, 3157
9:15 king Joram was returned to be healed in J 3157
9:15 escape out of the city to go to tell *it* in J. 3157
9:16 So Jehu rode *in a chariot,* and went to J; 3157
9:17 there stood a watchman on the tower in J, 3157
9:30 when Jehu was come to J, Jezebel heard *of* 3157
9:36 In the portion of J shall dogs eat the flesh 3157
9:37 the face of the field in the portion of J; 3157
10: 1 unto the rulers of J, to the elders, and 3157
10: 6 come to me to J by to morrow *this* time. 3157
10: 7 heads in baskets, and sent him *them* to J. 3157
10:11 all that remained of the house of Ahab in J, 3157
1Ch 4: 3 father of Etam; J, and Ishma, and Idbash: 3157
2Ch 22: 6 he returned to be healed in J because of 3157
22: 6 down to see Jehoram the son of Ahab at J, 3157
Hos 1: 4 the LORD said unto him, Call his name J; 3157
1: 4 I will avenge the blood of J upon the house 3157
1: 5 break the bow of Israel in the valley of J. 3157
1:11 of the land: for great *shall be* the day of J. 3157
2:22 the wine, and the oil; and they shall hear J. 3157

JEZREELITE (8) [JEZREEL]
1Ki 21: 1 *that* Naboth the J had a vineyard, 3158
21: 4 of the word which Naboth the J had spoken 3158
21: 6 Because I spake unto Naboth the J, and 3158
21: 7 will give thee the vineyard of Naboth the J. 3158
21:15 possession of the vineyard of Naboth the J, 3158
21:16 to go down to the vineyard of Naboth the J, 3158
2Ki 9:21 and met him in the portion of Naboth the J. 3158
9:25 in the portion of the field of Naboth the J: 3158

JEZREELITESS (5) [JEZREEL]
1Sa 27: 3 Ahinoam the J, and Abigail 3159
30: 5 Ahinoam the J, and Abigail the wife of 3159
2Sa 2: 2 Ahinoam the J, and Abigail Nabal's wife 3159
3: 2 firstborn was Amnon, of Ahinoam the J; 3159
1Ch 3: 1 the firstborn Amnon, of Ahinoam the J; 3159

JIBSAM (1)
1Ch 7: 2 and Jeriel, and Jahmai, and J, and Shemuel, 3005

JIDLAPH (1)
Ge 22:22 and Hazo, and Pildash, and J, and Bethuel. 3044

JIMNA (1) [JIMNAH, JIMNITES]
Nu 26:44 of J, the family of the Jimnites: of Jesui, 3232

JIMNAH (1) [JIMNA]
Ge 46:17 J, and Ishuah, and Ishui, and Beriah, and 3232

JIMNITES (1) [JIMNA]
Nu 26:44 of Jimna, the family of the J: of Jesui, 3232

JIPHTAH (1)
Jos 15:43 And J, and Ashnah, and Nezib, 3316

JIPHTHAH-EL (2)
Jos 19:14 the outgoings thereof are *in* the valley of J: 3317
19:27 to the valley of J toward the north side *of* 3317

JOAB (138) [JOAB'S]
1Sa 26: 6 the son of Zeruiah, brother to J, saying, 3097
2Sa 2:13 J the son of Zeruiah, and the servants of 3097
2:14 Abner said to J, Let the young men now 3097
2:14 play before us. And J said, Let them arise. 3097
2:18 Zeruiah there, J, and Abishai, and Asahel: 3097
2:22 should I hold up my face to J thy brother? 3097
2:24 J also and Abishai pursued after Abner: 3097
2:26 Abner called to J, and said, Shall the sword 3097
2:27 J said, *As* God liveth, unless thou hadst 3097
2:28 So J blew a trumpet, and all the people 3097
2:30 J returned from following Abner: and 3097
2:32 J and his men went all night, and they 3097
3:22 of David and J came from *pursuing* a troop, 3097
3:23 When J and all the host that *was* with him 3097
3:23 they told J, saying, Abner the son of Ner 3097
3:24 J came to the king, and said, What hast 3097
3:26 when J was come out from David, he sent 3097
3:27 J took him aside in the gate to speak with 3097
3:29 Let it rest on the head of J, and on all his 3097
3:29 let there not fail from the house of J one 3097
3:30 So J and Abishai his brother slew Abner, 3097
3:31 David said to J, and to all the people that 3097
8:16 And J the son of Zeruiah *was* over the host; 3097
10: 7 when David heard *of it,* he sent J, and all 3097
10: 9 When J saw that the front of the battle was 3097
10:13 J drew nigh, and the people that *were* with 3097
10:14 So J returned from the children of Ammon, 3097
11: 1 kings go forth *to battle,* that David sent J, 3097
11: 6 David sent to J, *saying,* Send me Uriah 3097
11: 6 the Hittite. And J sent Uriah to David. 3097
11: 7 David demanded *of him* how J did, and 3097
11:11 my lord J, and the servants of my lord, 3097
11:14 that David wrote a letter to J, and sent *it* by 3097
11:16 it came to pass, when J observed the city, 3097
11:17 of the city went out, and fought with J: 3097
11:18 J sent and told David all the things 3097
11:22 shewed David all that J had sent him for. 3097
11:25 Thus shalt thou say unto J, Let not this 3097
12:26 J fought against Rabbah of the children of 3097
12:27 J sent messengers to David, and said, 3097
14: 1 Now J the son of Zeruiah perceived that 3097
14: 2 J sent to Tekoah, and fetcht thence a wise 3097
14: 3 unto him. So J put the words in her mouth. 3097
14:19 *Is not* the hand of J with thee in all this? 3097
14:19 for thy servant J, he bade me, and he put all 3097
14:20 speech hath thy servant J done this thing: 3097
14:21 the king said unto J, Behold now, I have 3097
14:22 J fell to the ground on his face, and 3097
14:22 J said, To day thy servant knoweth that I 3097
14:23 So J arose and went to Geshur, and 3097
14:29 Therefore Absalom sent for J, to have sent 3097
14:31 J arose, and came to Absalom unto *his* 3097
14:32 Absalom answered J, Behold, I sent unto 3097
14:33 So J came to the king, and told him: and 3097
17:25 Amasa captain of the host instead of J: 3097
18: 2 third part of the people under the hand of J, 3097
18: 5 the king commanded J and Abishai and 3097
18:10 a certain man saw *it,* and told J, and said, 3097
18:11 J said unto the man that told him, 3097
18:12 the man said unto J, Though I should 3097
18:14 said J, I may not tarry thus with thee. 3097
18:16 J blew the trumpet, and the people returned 3097
18:16 after Israel: for J held back the people. 3097
18:20 J said unto him, Thou *shalt* not bear tidings 3097

2Sa 18:21 said J to Cushi, Go tell the king what thou 3097
18:21 And Cushi bowed himself unto J, and ran. 3097
18:22 Ahimaaz the son of Zadok yet again to J, 3097
18:22 J said, Wherefore wilt thou run, my son, 3097
18:29 When J sent the king's servant, and *me* thy 3097
19: 1 it was told J, Behold, the king weepeth 3097
19: 5 J came *into* the house to the king, and said, 3097
19:13 before me continually in the room of J. 3097
20: 9 J said to Amasa, *Art* thou in health, 3097
20: 9 J took Amasa by the beard with the right 3097
20:10 So J and Abishai his brother pursued after 3097
20:11 He that favoureth J, and he that *is* for 3097
20:11 and he that *is* for David, *let him go* after J. 3097
20:13 all the people went on after J, to pursue 3097
20:15 all the people that *were* with J battered 3097
20:16 say, I pray you, unto J, Come near hither, 3097
20:17 near unto her, the woman said, *Art* thou J? 3097
20:20 J answered and said, Far be it, far be it 3097
20:21 the woman said unto J, Behold, his head 3097
20:22 Sheba the son of Bichri, and cast *it* out to J. 3097
20:22 And J returned *to* Jerusalem unto the king. 3097
20:23 Now J *was* over all the host of Israel: and 3097
23:18 Abishai, the brother of J, the son of 3097
23:24 Asahel the brother of J *was* one of 3097
23:37 armourbearer to J the son of Zeruiah, 3097
24: 2 For the king said to J the captain of 3097
24: 3 J said unto the king, Now the LORD thy 3097
24: 4 the king's word prevailed against J, 3097
24: 4 J and the captains of the host went out from 3097
24: 9 J gave *up* the sum of the number of 3097
1Ki 1: 7 And he conferred with J the son of Zeruiah, 3097
1:19 the priest, and J the captain of the host: 3097
1:41 when J heard the sound of the trumpet, 3097
2: 5 Moreover thou knowest also what J the son 3097
2:22 the priest, and for J the son of Zeruiah. 3097
2:28 tidings came to J: for Joab had turned after 3097
2:28 for J had turned after Adonijah, though he 3097
2:28 J fled unto the tabernacle of the LORD, 3097
2:29 it was told king Solomon that J was fled 3097
2:30 Thus said J, and thus he answered me. 3097
2:31 which J shed, from me, and from the house 3097
2:33 therefore return upon the head of J, 3097
11:15 J the captain of the host was gone up to 3097
11:16 (For six months did J remain there with all 3097
11:21 that J the captain of the host was dead, 3097
1Ch 2:16 Abishai, and J, and Asahel, three. 3097
2:54 the house of J, and half of 3097
4:14 Seraiah begat J, the father of the valley of 3097
11: 6 So J the son of Zeruiah went first up, and 3097
11: 8 and J repaired the rest of the city. 3097
11:20 Abishai the brother of J, he was chief of 3097
11:26 of the armies *were,* Asahel the brother of J, 3097
11:39 the armourbearer of J the son of Zeruiah, 3097
18:15 And J the son of Zeruiah *was* over the host; 3097
19: 8 when David heard *of it,* he sent J, and all 3097
19:10 Now when J saw that the battle was set 3097
19:14 So J and the people that *were* with him 3097
19:15 into the city. Then J came *to* Jerusalem. 3097
20: 1 at the time that kings go out *to battle,* J led 3097
20: 1 And J smote Rabbah, and destroyed it. 3097
21: 2 David said to J and to the rulers of 3097
21: 3 J answered, The LORD make his people 3097
21: 4 the king's word prevailed against J. 3097
21: 4 Wherefore J departed, and went throughout 3097
21: 5 J gave the sum of the number of the people 3097
21: 6 for the king's word was abominable to J. 3097
26:28 and J the son of Zeruiah, had dedicated; 3097
27: 7 fourth month *was* Asahel the brother of J, 3097
27:24 J the son of Zeruiah began to number, but 3097
27:34 and the general of the king's army *was* J. 3097
Ezr 2: 6 of the children of Jeshua *and* J, 3097
8: 9 Of the sons of J; Obadiah the son of Jehiel, 3097
Ne 7:11 of the children of Jeshua and J, 3097
Ps 60: T when J returned, and smote of Edom in 3097

JOAB'S (8) [JOAB]
2Sa 14:30 J field is near mine, and he hath barley 3097
17:25 of Nahash, sister to Zeruiah J mother. 3097
18: 2 J brother, and a third part under the hand of 3097
18:15 ten young men that bare J armour 3097
20: 7 there went out after him J men, and 3097
20: 8 J garment that he had put on *was* girded 3097
20:10 no heed to the sword that *was* in J hand: 3097
20:11 one of J men stood by him, and said, 3097

J

JOAH (11)
2Ki 18:18 and J the son of Asaph the recorder. 3098
18:26 Shebna, and J, unto Rab-shakeh, Speak, 3098
18:37 and J the son of Asaph the recorder, 3098
1Ch 6:21 J his son, Iddo his son, Zerah his son, 3098
26: 4 J the third, and Sacar the fourth, and 3098
2Ch 29:12 J the son of Zimmah, and Eden the son of 3098
29:12 the son of Zimmah, and Eden the son of J: 3098
34: 8 and J the son of Joahaz the recorder, 3098
Isa 36: 3 the scribe, and J, Asaph's son, the recorder. 3098
36:11 and Shebna and J unto Rabshakeh, 3098
36:22 and J, the son of Asaph, the recorder, 3098

JOAHAZ (1)
2Ch 34: 8 the city, and Joah the son of J the recorder, 3099

JOANNA (3)
Lk 3:27 Which was *the son* of J, which was *the son* *2490*
8: 3 And J the wife of Chuza Herod's steward, *2489*
24:10 and J, and Mary *the mother* of James, and *2489*

JOASH (49)
Jdg 6:11 that *pertained* unto J the Abi-ezrite: 3101
6:29 Gideon the son of J hath done this thing. 3101
6:30 the men of the city said unto J, Bring out 3101
6:31 J said unto all that stood against him, Will 3101
7:14 else save the sword of Gideon the son of J, 3101
8:13 Gideon the son of J returned from battle 3101
8:29 Jerubbaal the son of J went and dwelt in his 3101
8:32 Gideon the son of J died in a good old age, 3101
8:32 was buried in the sepulchre of J his father, 3101
1Ki 22:26 of the city, and to J the king's son; 3101
2Ki 11: 2 took J the son of Ahaziah, and stale him 3101
12:19 the rest of the acts of J, and all that he did, 3101
12:20 slew J *in* the house of Millo, 3101
13: 1 twentieth year of J the son of Ahaziah king 3101
13: 9 and J his son reigned in his stead. 3101
13:10 seventh year of J king of Judah *began* 3101
13:12 the rest of the acts of J, and all that he did, 3101
13:13 J slept with his fathers; and Jeroboam sat 3101
13:13 J was buried in Samaria with the kings of 3101
13:14 J the king of Israel came down unto him, 3101
13:25 Three times did J beat him, and 3101
14: 1 In the second year of J son of Jehoahaz 3101
14: 1 Amaziah the son of J king of Judah. 3101
14: 3 he did according to all *things* as J his father 3101
14:17 Amaziah the son of J king of Judah lived 3101
14:23 J king of Judah Jeroboam the son of Joash 3101
14:23 J king of Israel *began* to reign in Samaria, 3101
14:27 them by the hand of Jeroboam the son of J. 3101
1Ch 3:11 Joram his son, Ahaziah his son, J his son, 3101
4:22 the men of Chozeba, and J, and Saraph, 3101
7: 8 J, and Eliezer, and Elioenai, and Omri, and 3135
12: 3 The chief *was* Ahiezer, then J, the sons of 3101
27:28 and over the cellars of oil *was* J: 3135
2Ch 18:25 of the city, and to J the king's son; 3101
22:11 took J the son of Ahaziah, and stole him 3101
24: 1 J *was* seven years old when he *began* to 3101
24: 2 J did *that* which *was* right in the sight of 3101
24: 4 *that* J was minded to repair the house of 3101
24:22 Thus J the king remembered not 3101
24:24 So they executed judgment against J. 3101
25:17 sent to J, the son of Jehoahaz, the son of 3101
25:18 J king of Israel sent to Amaziah king of 3101
25:21 So J the king of Israel went up; and 3101
25:23 J the king of Israel took Amaziah king of 3101
25:23 the son of J, the son of Jehoahaz, 3101
25:25 Amaziah the son of J king of Judah lived 3101
25:25 J son of Jehoahaz king of Israel fifteen 3101
Hos 1: 1 in the days of Jeroboam the son of J, 3101
Am 1: 1 in the days of Jeroboam the son of J king 3101

JOATHAM (2)
Mt 1: 9 And Ozias begat J; and Joatham begat *2488*
1: 9 and J begat Achaz; and Achaz begat *2488*

JOB (59) [JOB'S]
Ge 46:13 Tola, and Phuvah, and J, and Shimron. 3102
Job 1: 1 a man in the land of Uz, whose name *was* J; 347
1: 5 that J sent and sanctified them, and rose up 347
1: 5 for J said, It may be that my sons have 347
1: 5 God in their hearts. Thus did J continually. 347
1: 8 Hast thou considered my servant J, 347
1: 9 and said, Doth J fear God for nought? 347

Job 1:14 there came a messenger unto J, and said, 347
1:20 J arose, and rent his mantle, and shaved his 347
1:22 In all this J sinned not, nor charged God 347
2: 3 Hast thou considered my servant J, 347
2: 7 smote J with sore boils from the sole of his 347
2:10 In all this did not J sin with his lips. 347
3: 1 After this opened J his mouth, and 347
3: 2 And J spake, and said, 347
6: 1 But J answered and said, 347
9: 1 Then J answered and said, 347
12: 1 And J answered and said, 347
16: 1 Then J answered and said, 347
19: 1 Then J answered and said, 347
21: 1 But J answered and said, 347
23: 1 Then J answered and said, 347
26: 1 But J answered and said, 347
27: 1 Moreover J continued his parable, and said, 347
29: 1 Moreover J continued his parable, and said, 347
31:40 instead of barley. The words of J are ended. 347
32: 1 So these three men ceased to answer J, 347
32: 2 against J was his wrath kindled, because 347
32: 3 found no answer, and *yet* had condemned J. 347
32: 4 Now Elihu had waited till J had spoken, 347
32:12 *there was* none of you that convinced J, *or* 347
33: 1 Wherefore, J, I pray thee, hear my speeches, 347
33:31 Mark well, O J, hearken unto me: hold thy 347
34: 5 For J hath said, I am righteous: and 347
34: 7 What man *is* like J, *who* drinketh up 347
34:35 J hath spoken without knowledge, and 347
34:36 My desire *is that* J may be tried unto the end 347
35:16 Therefore doth J open his mouth in vain; 347
37:14 Hearken unto this, O J: stand still, and 347
38: 1 the LORD answered J out of 347
40: 1 Moreover the LORD answered J, and said, 347
40: 3 Then J answered the LORD, and said, 347
40: 6 answered the LORD unto J out of 347
42: 1 Then J answered the LORD, and said, 347
42: 7 the LORD had spoken these words unto J, 347
42: 7 *the thing that is* right, as my servant J *hath.* 347
42: 8 go to my servant J, and offer up for 347
42: 8 and my servant J shall pray for you: 347
42: 8 *the thing which is* right, like my servant J. 347
42: 9 the LORD also accepted J. 347
42:10 the LORD turned the captivity of J, 347
42:10 also the LORD gave J twice as much as he 347
42:12 So the LORD blessed the latter end of J 347
42:15 women found *so* fair as the daughters of J: 347
42:16 After this lived J an hundred and forty years, 347
42:17 So J died, *being* old and full of days. 347
Eze 14:14 Noah, Daniel, and J, were in it, they should 347
14:20 Daniel, and J, *were* in it, *as* I live, 347
Jas 5:11 Ye have heard of the patience of J, and *2492*

JOB'S (1) [JOB]
Job 2:11 Now when J three friends heard of all this 347

JOBAB (9)
Ge 10:29 Ophir, and Havilah, and J: all these *were* 3103
36:33 J the son of Zerah of Bozrah reigned in his 3103
36:34 J died, and Husham of the land of Temani 3103
Jos 11: 1 *things,* that he sent to J king of Madon, 3103
1Ch 1:23 Ophir, and Havilah, and J. All these *were* 3103
1:44 J the son of Zerah of Bozrah reigned in his 3103
1:45 when J was dead, Husham of the land of 3103
8: 9 J, and Zibia, and Mesha, and Malcham, 3103
8:18 Ishmerai also, and Jezliah, and J, the sons 3103

JOCHEBED (2)
Ex 6:20 Amram took him J his father's sister to 3115
Nu 26:59 the name of Amram's wife *was* J, 3115

JOED (1)
Ne 11: 7 the son of J, the son of Pedaiah, the son of 3133

JOEL (20)
1Sa 8: 2 Now the name of his firstborn was J; and 3100
1Ch 4:35 J, and Jehu the son of Josibiah, the son of 3100
5: 4 The sons of J; Shemaiah his son, Gog his 3100
5: 8 the son of Shema, the son of J, who dwelt 3100
5:12 J the chief, and Shapham the next, and 3100
6:33 Heman a singer, the son of J, the son of 3100
6:36 the son of J, the son of Azariah, 3100
7: 3 Michael, and Obadiah, and J, Ishiah, five: 3100
11:38 J the brother of Nathan, Mibhar the son of 3100
15: 7 J the chief, and his brethren an hundred and 3100
15:11 for Uriel, Asaiah, and J, Shemaiah, and 3100
15:17 the Levites appointed Heman the son of J; 3100
23: 8 chief *was* Jehiel, and Zetham, and J, three. 3100
26:22 Zetham, and J his brother, *which were* over 3100
27:20 tribe of Manasseh, J the son of Pedaiah: 3100
2Ch 29:12 son of Amasai, and J the son of Azariah, 3100
Ezr 10:43 Zabad, Zebina, Jadau, and J, Benaiah. 3100
Ne 11: 9 J the son of Zichri *was* their overseer: 3100
Joel 1: 1 The word of the LORD that came to J 3100
Ac 2:16 is that which was spoken by the prophet J; *2493*

JOELAH (1)
1Ch 12: 7 J, and Zebadiah, the sons of Jeroham of 3132

JOEZER (1)
1Ch 12: 6 Jesiah, and Azareel, and J, and Jashobeam, 3134

JOGBEHAH (2)
Nu 32:35 And Atroth, Shophan, and Jaazer, and J, 3011
Jdg 8:11 dwelt in tents on the east of Nobah and J, 3011

JOGLI (1)
Nu 34:22 of the children of Dan, Bukki the son of J. 3020

JOHA (2)
1Ch 8:16 Michael, and Ispah, and J, the sons of 3109
11:45 son of Shimri, and J his brother, the Tizite, 3109

JOHANAN (27)
2Ki 25:23 J the son of Careah, and Seraiah the son of 3110
1Ch 3:15 the sons of Josiah *were,* the firstborn J, 3110
3:24 and J, and Dalaiah, and Anani, seven. 3110
6: 9 begat Azariah, and Azariah begat J, 3110
6:10 J begat Azariah, (he *it is* that executed 3110
12: 4 and J, and Josabad the Gederathite, 3110
12:12 J the eighth, Elzabad the ninth, 3110
2Ch 28:12 Azariah the son of J, Berechiah the son of 3076
Ezr 8:12 J the son of Hakkatan, and with him an 3110
10: 6 went into the chamber of J the son of 3076
Ne 6:18 his son J had taken the daughter of 3076
12:22 Joiada, and J, and Jaddua, *were* recorded 3110
12:23 even until the days of J the son of Eliashib. 3110
Jer 40: 8 J and Jonathan the sons of Kareah, and 3110
40:13 Moreover J the son of Kareah, and all 3110
40:15 J the son of Kareah spake to Gedaliah in 3110
40:16 Gedaliah the son of Ahikam said unto J 3110
41:11 when J the son of Kareah, and all 3110
41:13 *were* with Ishmael saw J the son of Kareah, 3110
41:14 and went unto J the son of Kareah. 3110
41:15 Nethaniah escaped from J with eight men, 3110
41:16 took J the son of Kareah, and all 3110
42: 1 J the son of Kareah, and Jezaniah the son 3110
42: 8 called he J the son of Kareah, and all 3110
43: 2 J the son of Kareah, and all the proud men, 3110
43: 4 So J the son of Kareah, and all the captains 3110
43: 5 J the son of Kareah, and all the captains of 3110

JOHN (131) [JOHN'S]
Mt 3: 1 In those days came J the Baptist, *2491*
3: 4 And the same J had his raiment of camel's *2491*
3:13 Jesus from Galilee to Jordan unto J, *2491*
3:14 But J forbad him, saying, I have need to be *2491*
4:12 Now when Jesus had heard that J was cast *2491*
4:21 the *son* of Zebedee, and J his brother, *2491*
9:14 Then came to him the disciples of J, *2491*
10: 2 the *son* of Zebedee, and J his brother; *2491*
11: 2 Now when J had heard in the prison *2491*
11: 4 shew J again *those things* which ye do hear *2491*
11: 7 to say unto the multitudes concerning J, *2491*
11:11 hath not risen a greater than J the Baptist: *2491*
11:12 And from the days of J the Baptist until *2491*
11:13 the prophets and the law prophesied until J. *2491*
11:18 For J came neither eating nor drinking, and *2491*
14: 2 said unto his servants, This is J the Baptist; *2491*
14: 3 For Herod had laid hold on J, and *2491*
14: 4 For J said unto him, It is not lawful for thee *2491*
14: 8 Give me here J Baptist's head in a charger. *2491*
14:10 And he sent, and beheaded J in the prison. *2491*
16:14 Some *say that thou art* J the Baptist: *2491*
17: 1 and J his brother, and bringeth them up into *2491*
17:13 that he spake unto them of J the Baptist. *2491*
21:25 The baptism of J, whence was it? *2491*
21:26 fear the people; for all hold J as a prophet. *2491*
21:32 For J came unto you in the way of *2491*

J

Mk 1: 4 J did baptize in the wilderness, and 2491
1: 6 And J was clothed with camel's hair, and 2491
1: 9 of Galilee, and was baptized of J in Jordan. 2491
1:14 Now after that J was put in prison, Jesus 2491
1:19 the *son* of Zebedee, and J his brother, 2491
1:29 of Simon and Andrew, with James and J. 2491
2:18 And the disciples of J and of the Pharisees 2491
2:18 Why do the disciples of J and of 2491
3:17 *son* of Zebedee, and J the brother of James; 2491
5:37 and James, and J the brother of James. 2491
6:14 That J the Baptist was risen from the dead, 2491
6:16 *thereof,* he said, It is J, whom I beheaded: 2491
6:17 himself had sent forth and laid hold upon J, 2491
6:18 For J had said unto Herod, It is not lawful 2491
6:20 For Herod feared J, knowing that he *was* a 2491
6:24 And she said, The head of J the Baptist. 2491
6:25 by in a charger the head of J the Baptist. 2491
8:28 And they answered, J the Baptist: but 2491
9: 2 and J, and leadeth them up into a high 2491
9:38 And J answered him, saying, Master, 2491
10:35 And James and J, the sons of Zebedee, 2491
10:41 to be much displeased with James and J. 2491
11:30 The baptism of J, was *it* from heaven, or 2491
11:32 for all *men* counted J, that he was a prophet 2491
13: 3 Peter and James and J and Andrew asked 2491
14:33 he taketh with him Peter and James and J, 2491
Lk 1:13 thee a son, and thou shalt call his name J. 2491
1:60 and said, Not *so;* but he shall be called J. 2491
1:63 and wrote, saying, His name is J. 2491
3: 2 the word of God came unto J the son of 2491
3:15 and all *men* mused in their hearts of J, 2491
3:16 J answered, saying unto *them* all, I indeed 2491
3:20 this above all, that he shut up J in prison. 2491
5:10 And so *was* also James, and J, *the* sons of 2491
5:33 Why do the disciples of J fast often, and 2491
6:14 and J, Philip and Bartholomew, 2491
7:18 And the disciples of J shewed him of all 2491
7:19 And J calling unto *him* two of his disciples 2491
7:20 J Baptist hath sent us unto thee, saying, 2491
7:22 and tell J what *things* ye have seen and 2491
7:24 And when the messengers of J were 2491
7:24 to speak unto the people concerning J, 2491
7:28 is not a greater prophet than J the Baptist: 2491
7:29 being baptized *with* the baptism of J. 2491
7:33 For J the Baptist came neither eating bread 2491
8:51 and J, and the father and the mother of 2491
9: 7 of some, that J was risen from the dead; 2491
9: 9 And Herod said, J have I beheaded: but 2491
9:19 They answering said, J the Baptist; but 2491
9:28 he took Peter and J and James, and went up 2491
9:49 And J answered and said, Master, we saw 2491
9:54 disciples James and J saw *this,* they said, 2491
11: 1 us to pray, as J also taught his disciples. 2491
16:16 The law and the prophets *were* until J: 2491
20: 4 The baptism of J, was it from heaven, or 2491
20: 6 for they be persuaded that J was a prophet. 2491
22: 8 And he sent Peter and J, saying, Go and 2491
Jn 1: 6 a man sent from God, whose name *was* J. 2491
1:15 J bare witness of him, and cried, saying, 2491
1:19 And this is the record of J, when the Jews 2491
1:26 J answered them, saying, I baptize with 2491
1:28 beyond Jordan, where J was baptizing. 2491
1:29 The next day J seeth Jesus coming unto 2491
1:32 And J bare record, saying, I saw the Spirit 2491
1:35 Again the next day *after* J stood, and 2491
1:40 One of the two which heard J speak, and 2491
3:23 And J also was baptizing in Aenon near to 2491
3:24 For J was not yet cast into prison. 2491
3:26 And they came unto J, and said unto him, 2491
3:27 J answered and said, A man can receive 2491
4: 1 and baptized moe disciples than J, 2491
5:33 Ye sent unto J, and he bare witness unto 2491
5:36 But I have greater witness than *that of* J: 2491
10:40 into the place where J at first baptized; 2491
10:41 unto him, and said, J did no miracle: 2491
10:41 all *things* that J spake of this *man* were 2491
Ac 1: 5 For J truly baptized with water; but ye shall 2491
1:13 and J, and Andrew, Philip, and Thomas, 2491
1:22 Beginning from the baptism of J, unto *that* 2491
3: 1 J went up together into the temple at 2491
3: 3 and J about to go into the temple, 2491
3: 4 fastening his eyes upon him with J, said, 2491
3:11 *man* which was healed held Peter and J, 2491
4: 6 and J, and Alexander, and as many as were 2491
4:13 when they saw the boldness of Peter and J, 2491
4:19 But Peter and J answered and said unto 2491
8:14 of God, they sent unto them Peter and J: 2491
10:37 after the baptism which J preached; 2491
11:16 that he said, J indeed baptized with water; 2491
12: 2 And he killed James the brother of J with 2491
12:12 came to the house of Mary the mother of J, 2491
12:25 and took with *them* J, whose surname was 2491
13: 5 and they had also J to *their* minister. 2491
13:13 J departing from them returned to 2491
13:24 When J had first preached before his 2491
13:25 And as J fulfilled *his* course, he said, 2491
15:37 Barnabas determined to take with *them* J, 2491
18:25 of the Lord, knowing only the baptism of J. 2491
19: 4 J verily baptized *with* the baptism of 2491
Gal 2: 9 And when James, Cephas, and J, 2491
Rev 1: 1 signified *it* by his angel unto his servant J: 2491
1: 4 J to the seven churches which are in Asia: 2491
1: 9 I J, who also am your brother, and 2491
21: 2 And I J saw the holy city, new Jerusalem, 2491
22: 8 And I J saw these *things,* and heard *them.* 2491

JOHN'S (2) [JOHN]
Jn 3:25 a question between *some* of J disciples 2491
Ac 19: 3 And they said, Unto J baptism. 2491

JOIADA (4)
Ne 12:10 also begat Eliashib, and Eliashib begat J, 3111
12:11 J begat Jonathan, and Jonathan begat 3111
12:22 J, and Johanan, and Jaddua, *were* recorded 3111
13:28 *one* of the sons of J, the son of Eliashib 3111

JOIAKIM (4)
Ne 12:10 Jeshua begat J, Joiakim also begat Eliashib, 3113
12:10 J also begat Eliashib, and Eliashib begat 3113
12:12 in the days of J were priests, the chief of 3113
12:26 These *were* in the days of J the son of 3113

JOIARIB (5)
Ezr 8:16 chief *men;* also for J, and for Elnathan, 3114
Ne 11: 5 of Hazaiah, the son of Adaiah, the son of J, 3114
11:10 Of the priests: Jedaiah the son of J, Jachin, 3114
12: 6 Shemaiah, and J, Jedaiah, 3114
12:19 And of J, Mattenai; of Jedaiah, Uzzi; 3114

JOIN (14) [JOINED, JOINING, JOININGS, JOINT, JOINT-HEIRS, JOINTS]
Ex 1:10 they j also unto our enemies, and 3254
2Ch 20:35 after this did Jehoshaphat king of Judah j 2266
Ezr 9:14 **j in affinity** with the people of these 2859
Pr 11:21 *Though* hand *j* in hand, the wicked shall not NIH
16: 5 *though* hand *j* in hand, he shall not be NIH
Isa 5: 8 Woe unto them that j house to house, 5060
9:11 against him, and j his enemies **together**; 5526
56: 6 that j themselves to the LORD, to serve 3867
Jer 50: 5 let us j ourselves to the LORD *in* a 3867
Eze 37:17 j them one to another into one stick; and 7126
Da 11: 6 of years they shall j themselves **together**; 2266
Ac 5:13 And of the rest durst no *man* j himself to 2853
8:29 Go near, and j thyself **to** this chariot. 2853
9:26 he assayed to j himself to the disciples: 2853

JOINED (43) [JOIN]
Ge 14: 3 All these were j **together** in the vale of 2266
14: 8 they j battle with them in the vale of 6186
29:34 Now *this* time will my husband be j unto 3867
Ex 28: 7 *thereof* j at the two edges thereof; 2266
28: 7 edges thereof; and *so* it shall be j **together**. 2266
Nu 18: 2 that they may be j unto thee, and 3867
18: 4 they shall be j unto thee, and keep 3867
25: 3 Israel j himself **unto** Baal-peor: and 6775
25: 5 Slay ye every one his men that were j unto 6775
1Sa 4: 2 when they j battle, Israel was smitten 5203
1Ki 7:32 the axletrees of the wheels *were* j **to** 871.1
20:29 that in the seventh day the battle was j: 7126
2Ch 18: 1 in abundance, and j **affinity** with Ahab. 2859
20:36 he j himself with him to make ships to go 2266
20:37 Because thou hast j thyself with Ahaziah, 2266
Ezr 4:12 up the walls *thereof,* and j the foundations. 2338
Ne 4: 6 all the wall was **j together** unto the half 7194
Est 9:27 upon all such as j themselves unto them, 3867
Job 3: 6 let it not be j unto the days of the year, let it 2302
41:17 They are j one to another, they stick 1692
41:23 The flakes of his flesh are **j together**: 1692

Ps 83: 8 Assur also is j with them: they have holpen 3867
106:28 They j themselves also unto Baal-peor, and 6775
Ecc 9: 4 For to him that is j to all the living there is 2266
Isa 13:15 every one that is j *unto them* shall fall by 5595
14: 1 the strangers shall be j with them, and 3867
14:20 Thou shalt not be j **with** them in burial, 3161
56: 3 that hath j himself to the LORD, speak, 3867
Eze 1: 9 Their wings *were* j one to another; they 2266
1:11 two *wings* of every one *were* j one to 2266
46:22 *there were* courts j *of* forty *cubits* long 7000
Hos 4:17 Ephraim *is* j **to** idols: let him alone. 2266
Zec 2:11 many nations shall be j to the LORD in 3867
Mt 19: 6 What therefore God hath j **together**, let not *4801*
Mk 10: 9 What therefore God hath j **together**, let not *4801*
Lk 15:15 and j himself **to** a citizen of that country; *2853*
Ac 5:36 of men, about four hundred, j themselves: *4347*
18: 7 whose house j **hard to** the synagogue. *4927*
1Co 1:10 *that* ye be **perfectly** j **together** in the same *2675*
6:16 know ye not that he which is j **to** a harlot is *2853*
6:17 But he that is j unto the Lord is one spirit. *2853*
Eph 4:16 whom the whole body **fitly** j **together** *4883*
5:31 and shall be j unto his wife, and they two *4347*

JOINING (1) [JOIN]
2Ch 3:12 the other wing *was* five cubits *also*, j to 1695

JOININGS (1) [JOIN]
1Ch 22: 3 for the doors of the gates, and for the j; 4226

JOINT (4) [JOIN]
Ge 32:25 the hollow of Jacob's thigh was **out of** j, 3363
Ps 22:14 like water, and all my bones are **out of** j: 6504
Pr 25:19 *is like* a broken tooth, and a foot **out of** j. 4154
Eph 4:16 compacted by that which every j supplieth, *860*

JOINT-HEIRS (1) [HEIR, JOIN]
Ro 8:17 heirs of God, and j **with** Christ; if so be that *4789*

JOINTS (6) [JOIN]
1Ki 22:34 smote the king of Israel between the j of 1694
2Ch 18:33 smote the king of Israel between the j of 1694
SS 7: 1 the j of thy thighs *are* like jewels, the work 2542
Da 5: 6 so that the j of his loins were loosed, and 7001
Col 2:19 from which all the body by j and *860*
Heb 4:12 and of the j and marrow, and *is* a discerner *719*

JOKDEAM (1)
Jos 15:56 And Jezreel, and J, and Zanoah, 3347

JOKIM (1)
1Ch 4:22 J, and the men of Chozeba, and Joash, and 3137

JOKMEAM (1)
1Ch 6:68 J with her suburbs, and Beth-horon with 3361

JOKNEAM (4)
Jos 12:22 one; the king of J of Carmel, one; 3362
19:11 and reached to the river that *is* before J; 3362
21:34 J with her suburbs, and Kartah with her 3362
1Ki 4:12 *even* unto *the place that is* beyond J: 3361

JOKSHAN (4)
Ge 25: 2 J, and Medan, and Midian, and Ishbak, and 3370
25: 3 J begat Sheba, and Dedan. And the sons of 3370
1Ch 1:32 J, and Medan, and Midian, and Ishbak, and 3370
1:32 And the sons of J; Sheba, and Dedan. 3370

JOKTAN (6)
Ge 10:25 and his brother's name *was* J. 3355
10:26 J begat Almodad, and Sheleph, and 3355
10:29 and Jobab: all these *were* the sons of J. 3355
1Ch 1:19 was divided: and his brother's name *was* J. 3355
1:20 J begat Almodad, and Sheleph, and 3355
1:23 and Jobab. All these *were* the sons of J. 3355

JOKTHEEL (2)
Jos 15:38 And Dilean, and Mizpeh, and J, 3371
2Ki 14: 7 and called the name of it J unto this day. 3371

JONA (1)
Jn 1:42 he said, Thou art Simon the son of J: *2495*

JONADAB (12)
2Sa 13: 3 Amnon had a friend, whose name *was* J, 3122
13: 3 and J *was* a very subtil man. 3122
13: 5 J said unto him, Lay *thee* down on thy bed, 3082
13:32 J, the son of Shimeah David's brother, 3122
13:35 J said unto the king, Behold, the king's 3122
Jer 35: 6 for J the son of Rechab our father 3122
35: 8 Thus have we obeyed the voice of J the son 3082
35:10 done according to all that J our father 3122
35:14 The words of J the son of Rechab, that he 3082
35:16 Because the sons of J the son of Rechab 3082
35:18 obeyed the commandment of J your father, 3082
35:19 J the son of Rechab shall not want a man to 3122

JONAH (19) [JONAS]
2Ki 14:25 he spake by the hand of his servant J, 3124
Jnh 1: 1 Now the word of the LORD came unto J 3124
1: 3 J rose up to flee unto Tarshish from 3124
1: 5 J was gone down into the sides of the ship; 3124
1: 7 So they cast lots, and the lot fell upon J. 3124
1:15 So they took up J, and cast him forth into 3124
1:17 had prepared a great fish to swallow up J. 3124
1:17 J was in the belly of the fish three days 3124
2: 1 J prayed unto the LORD his God out of 3124
2:10 and it vomited out J upon the dry *land*. 3124
3: 1 the word of the LORD came unto J 3124
3: 3 So J arose, and went unto Nineveh, 3124
3: 4 J began to enter into the city a day's 3124
4: 1 it displeased J exceedingly, and he was 3124
4: 5 So J went out of the city, and sat on 3124
4: 6 a gourd, and made *it* to come up over J, 3124
4: 6 So J was exceeding glad of the gourd. 3124
4: 8 the sun beat upon the head of J, that he 3124
4: 9 God said to J, Doest thou well to be angry 3124

JONAM See JONAN

JONAN (1)
Lk 3:30 *the son* of Joseph, which was *the son* of J, *2494*

JONAS (12) [JONAH]
Mt 12:39 be given to it, but the sign of the prophet J: *2495*
12:40 For as J was three days and three nights in *2495*
12:41 because they repented at the preaching of J; *2495*
12:41 and behold, a greater than J *is* here. *2495*
16: 4 given unto it, but the sign of the prophet J. *2495*
Lk 11:29 be given it, but the sign of J the prophet. *2495*
11:30 For as J was a sign unto the Ninevites, so *2495*
11:32 for they repented at the preaching of J; and *2495*
11:32 and behold, a greater than J *is* here. *2495*
Jn 21:15 Jesus saith to Simon Peter, Simon, *son* of J, *2495*
21:16 Simon, *son* of J, lovest thou me? *2495*
21:17 third time, Simon, *son* of J, lovest thou me? *2495*

JONATHAN (118) [JONATHAN'S]
Jdg 18:30 J, the son of Gershom, the son of 3083
1Sa 13: 2 a thousand were with J in Gibeah of 3129
13: 3 J smote the garrison of the Philistines that 3129
13:16 J his son, and the people that were present 3129
13:22 of the people that *were* with Saul and J: 3129
13:22 and with J his son was there found. 3129
14: 1 that J the son of Saul said unto the young 3129
14: 3 And the people knew not that J was gone. 3129
14: 4 *by* which J sought to go over unto 3129
14: 6 J said to the young man that bare his 3083
14: 8 said J, Behold, we will pass over unto *these* 3083
14:12 the men of the garrison answered J and 3129
14:12 J said unto his armourbearer, Come up 3129
14:13 J climbed up upon his hands and upon his 3129
14:13 they fell before J; and his armourbearer 3129
14:14 which J and his armourbearer made, was 3129
14:17 behold J and his armourbearer *were* not 3129
14:21 the Israelites that *were* with Saul and J. 3129
14:27 J heard not when his father charged 3129
14:29 said J, My father hath troubled the land: 3129
14:39 though it be in J my son, he shall surely 3129
14:40 I and J my son will be on the other side. 3129
14:41 a perfect *lot*. And Saul and J were taken: 3129
14:42 Cast *lots* between me and J my son. 3129
14:42 and Jonathan my son. And J was taken. 3129
14:43 Saul said to J, Tell me what thou hast done. 3129
14:43 J told him, and said, I did but taste a little 3129
14:44 and more also: for thou shalt surely die, J. 3129
14:45 the people said unto Saul, Shall J die, 3129
14:45 So the people rescued J, that he died not. 3129
14:49 Now the sons of Saul were J, and Ishui, 3129
18: 1 that the soul of J was knit with the soul of 3083
18: 1 of David, and J loved him as his own soul. 3083
18: 3 J and David made a covenant, because 3083

J

1Sa 18: 4 J stript himself of the robe that *was* upon 3083
19: 1 Saul spake to J his son, and to all his 3129
19: 2 J Saul's son delighted much in David: and 3083
19: 2 J told David, saying, Saul my father 3083
19: 4 J spake good of David unto Saul his father, 3083
19: 6 Saul hearkened unto the voice of J: and 3083
19: 7 J called David, and Jonathan shewed him 3083
19: 7 and J shewed him all those things. 3083
19: 7 J brought David to Saul, and he was in his 3083
20: 1 came and said before J, What have I done? 3083
20: 3 he saith, Let not J know this, lest he be 3083
20: 4 said J unto David, Whatsoever thy soul 3083
20: 5 David said unto J, Behold, to morrow *is* 3083
20: 9 J said, Far be it from thee: for if I knew 3083
20:10 Then said David to J, Who shall tell me? or 3083
20:11 J said unto David, Come, and let us go out 3083
20:12 J said unto David, O LORD God of Israel, 3083
20:13 The LORD do so and much more to J: *but* 3083
20:16 So J made *a covenant* with the house of 3083
20:17 J caused David to swear again, because 3083
20:18 J said to *David,* To morrow *is* the new 3083
20:25 J arose, and Abner sat by Saul's side, and 3083
20:27 Saul said unto J his son, Wherefore cometh 3083
20:28 J answered Saul, David earnestly asked 3083
20:30 Saul's anger was kindled against J, and 3083
20:32 J answered Saul his father, and said unto 3083
20:33 whereby J knew that it was determined of 3083
20:34 So J arose from the table in fierce anger, 3083
20:35 that J went out *into* the field at the time 3083
20:37 to the place of the arrow which J had shot, 3083
20:37 J cried after the lad, and said, *Is* not 3083
20:38 J cried after the lad, Make speed, haste, 3083
20:39 only J and David knew the matter. 3083
20:40 J gave his artillery unto his lad, and 3083
20:42 J said to David, Go in peace, forasmuch as 3083
20:42 and departed: and J went *into* the city. 3083
23:16 J Saul's son arose, and went to David *into* 3083
23:18 abode in the wood, and J went to his house. 3083
31: 2 the Philistines slew J, and Abinadab, and 3083
2Sa 1: 4 dead; and Saul and J his son are dead also. 3083
1: 5 thou that Saul and J his son be dead? 3083
1:12 for J his son, and for the people of 3083
1:17 lamentation over Saul and over J his son: 3083
1:22 the bow of J turned not back, and 3083
1:23 Saul and J *were* lovely and pleasant in their 3083
1:25 O J, *thou wast* slain in thine high places. 3083
1:26 I am distressed for thee, my brother J: 3083
4: 4 J, Saul's son, had a son *that was* lame of 3083
4: 4 tidings came of Saul and J out of Jezreel, 3083
9: 3 J hath yet a son, *which is* lame on *his* feet. 3083
9: 6 the son of J, the son of Saul, was come 3083
9: 7 for I will surely shew thee kindness for J 3083
15:27 thy son, and J the son of Abiathar. 3083
15:36 Zadok's *son,* and J Abiathar's *son;* and 3083
17:17 Now J and Ahimaaz stayed by En-rogel; 3083
17:20 they said, Where *is* Ahimaaz and J? 3083
21: 7 the son of J the son of Saul, because of 3083
21: 7 between David and J the son of Saul. 3083
21:12 the bones of J his son from the men of 3083
21:13 bones of Saul and the bones of J his son; 3083
21:14 J his son buried they in the country of 3083
21:21 J the son of Shimea the brother of David 3083
23:32 the Shaalbonite, *of* the sons of Jashen, J, 3083
1Ki 1:42 J the son of Abiathar the priest came: 3129
1:43 J answered and said to Adonijah, 3129
1Ch 2:32 Jada the brother of Shammai; Jether, and J: 3129
2:33 the sons of J; Peleth, and Zaza. These were 3129
8:33 Saul begat J, and Malchishua, and 3083
8:34 the son of J *was* Merib-baal; and 3083
9:39 Saul begat J, and Malchishua, and 3083
9:40 the son of J *was* Merib-baal: and 3083
10: 2 the Philistines slew J, and Abinadab, and 3129
11:34 J the son of Shage the Hararite, 3129
20: 7 J the son of Shimea David's brother slew 3083
27:32 Also J David's uncle *was* a counseller, 3083
Ezr 8: 6 Ebed the son of J, and with him fifty males. 3129
10:15 Only J the son of Asahel and Jahaziah 3129
Ne 12:11 Joiada begat J, and Jonathan begat Jaddua. 3129
12:11 Joiada begat Jonathan, and J begat Jaddua. 3129
12:14 Of Melicu, J; of Shebaniah, Joseph; 3129
12:35 *namely,* Zechariah the son of J, the son of 3129
Jer 37:15 put him *in* prison *in* the house of J 3083
37:20 not to return *to* the house of J the scribe, 3083
40: 8 Johanan and J the sons of Kareah, and 3129

JONATHAN'S (3) [JONATHAN]
1Sa 20:38 J lad gathered up the arrows, and came to 3083
2Sa 9: 1 that I may shew him kindness for J sake? 3083
Jer 38:26 that *he* would not cause me to return *to* J 3083

JONATH-ELEM-RECHOKIM (1)
Ps 56: T To the chief Musician upon J, Michtam of 3128

JOPPA (13)
2Ch 2:16 we will bring it to thee *in* flotes by sea *to* J; 3305
Ezr 3: 7 cedar trees from Lebanon to the sea of J, 3305
Jnh 1: 3 of the LORD, and went down *to* J; 3305
Ac 9:36 Now there was at J a certain disciple *2445*
9:38 And forasmuch as Lydda was nigh to J, *2445*
9:42 And it was known throughout all J; and *2445*
9:43 that he tarried many days in J with one *2445*
10: 5 And now send men to J, and call for *one* *2445*
10: 8 *these things* unto them, he sent them to J. *2445*
10:23 certain brethren from J accompanied him. *2445*
10:32 Send therefore to J, and call hither Simon, *2445*
11: 5 I was in the city of J praying: and in a *2445*
11:13 Send men to J, and call for Simon, *2445*

JORAH (1)
Ezr 2:18 The children of J, an hundred and twelve. 3139

JORAI (1)
1Ch 5:13 J, and Jachan, and Zia, and Heber, seven. 3140

JORAM (29)
2Sa 8:10 Toi sent J his son unto king David, 3141
8:10 *J* brought with him vessels of silver, and NIH
2Ki 8:16 in the fifth year of J the son of Ahab king 3141
8:21 So J went over to Zair, and all the chariots 3141
8:23 the rest of the acts of J, and all that he did, 3141
8:24 J slept with his fathers, and was buried 3141
8:25 In the twelfth year of J the son of Ahab 3141
8:28 he went with J the son of Ahab to the war 3141
8:28 and the Syrians wounded J. 3141
8:29 king J went back to be healed in Jezreel of 3141
8:29 down to see J the son of Ahab in Jezreel, 3141
9:14 the son of Nimshi conspired against J. 3141
9:14 (Now J had kept Ramoth-gilead, he and 3141
9:15 king J was returned to be healed in Jezreel 3088
9:16 and went to Jezreel; for J lay there. 3141
9:16 king of Judah was come down to see J. 3141
9:17 J said, Take a horseman, and send to meet 3088
9:21 J said, Make ready. And his chariot was 3088
9:21 J king of Israel and Ahaziah king of Judah 3088
9:22 when J saw Jehu, that he said, *Is it* peace, 3088
9:23 J turned his hands, and fled, and said to 3088
9:29 in the eleventh year of J the son of Ahab 3141
11: 2 Jehosheba, the daughter of king J, sister of 3141
1Ch 3:11 J his son, Ahaziah his son, Joash his son, 3141
26:25 J his son, and Zichri his son, and 3141
2Ch 22: 5 at Ramoth-gilead: and the Syrians smote J. 3141
22: 7 of Ahaziah was of God by coming to J: 3141
Mt 1: 8 and Josaphat begat J; and Joram begat *2496*
1: 8 Josaphat begat Joram; and J begat Ozias; *2496*

JORDAN (197)
Ge 13:10 up his eyes, and beheld all the plain of J, 3383
13:11 Lot chose him all the plain of J; and 3383
32:10 for with my staff I passed over this J; 3383
50:10 which *is* beyond J, and there they mourned 3383
50:11 called Abel-mizraim, which *is* beyond J. 3383
Nu 13:29 dwell by the sea, and by the coast of J. 3383
22: 1 pitched in the plains of Moab on *this* side J 3383
26: 3 in the plains of Moab by J *near* Jericho, 3383
26:63 in the plains of Moab by J *near* Jericho. 3383
31:12 of Moab, which *are* by J *near* Jericho. 3383
32: 5 for a possession, *and* bring us not over J. 3383
32:19 will not inherit with them on *yonder* side J, 3383
32:19 our inheritance is fallen to us on *this* side J 3383
32:21 will go all of you armed over J before 3383
32:29 of Reuben will pass with you over J, 3383
32:32 our inheritance on *this* side J *may be* ours. 3383
33:48 pitched in the plains of Moab by J *near* 3383
33:49 they pitched by J, from Beth-jesimoth *even* 3383
33:50 in the plains of Moab by J *near* Jericho, 3383
33:51 When ye are passed over J into the land of 3383
34:12 the border shall go down to J, and 3383
34:15 on *this* side J *near* Jericho eastward, 3383
35: 1 in the plains of Moab by J *near* Jericho, 3383

Nu 35:10 When ye be come over J into the land of 3383
35:14 Ye shall give three cities on *this* side J, and 3383
36:13 in the plains of Moab by J *near* Jericho. 3383
Dt 1: 1 all Israel on *this* side J in the wilderness, 3383
1: 5 On *this* side J, in the land of Moab, 3383
2:29 until I shall pass over J into the land which 3383
3: 8 Amorites the land that *was* on *this* side J, 3383
3:17 J, and the coast *thereof,* from Chinnereth 3383
3:20 your God hath given them beyond J: 3383
3:25 and see the good land that *is* beyond J, 3383
3:27 thine eyes: for thou shalt not go over this J. 3383
4:21 sware that I should not go over J, and that *I* 3383
4:22 I *must* die in this land, I *must* not go over J: 3383
4:26 land whereunto you go over J to possess it; 3383
4:41 Moses severed three cities on *this* side J 3383
4:46 On *this* side J, in the valley over against 3383
4:47 which *were* on *this* side J *toward* 3383
4:49 all the plain on *this* side J eastward, even 3383
9: 1 Thou art to pass over J *this* day, to go in to 3383
11:30 *Are* they not on the *other* side J, by the way 3383
11:31 For ye shall pass over J to go in to possess 3383
12:10 *when* ye go over J and dwell in the land 3383
27: 2 J unto the land which the LORD thy God 3383
27: 4 it shall be when ye be gone over J, 3383
27:12 bless the people, when ye are come over J; 3383
30:18 whither thou passest over J to go to possess 3383
31: 2 said unto me, Thou shalt not go over this J. 3383
31:13 the land whither ye go over J to possess it. 3383
32:47 the land, whither ye go over J to possess it. 3383
Jos 1: 2 go over this J, thou, and all this people, 3383
1:11 within three days ye shall pass over this J, 3383
1:14 land which Moses gave you on *this* side J; 3383
1:15 you on *this* side J *toward* the sunrising. 3383
2: 7 the men pursued after them the way to J 3383
2:10 that *were* on the *other* side J, Sihon and Og, 3383
3: 1 came to J, he and all the children of Israel, 3383
3: 8 ye are come to the brink of the water of J, 3383
3: 8 the water of Jordan, ye shall stand still in J. 3383
3:11 all the earth passeth over before you into J. 3383
3:13 of all the earth, shall rest in the waters of J, 3383
3:13 *that* the waters of J shall be cut off *from* 3383
3:14 to pass over J, and the priests bearing 3383
3:15 as they that bare the ark were come unto J, 3383
3:15 (for J overfloweth all his banks all the time 3383
3:17 stood firm on dry *ground* in the midst of J, 3383
3:17 all the people were passed clean over J. 3383
4: 1 all the people were clean passed over J, 3383
4: 3 Take you hence out of the midst of J, 3383
4: 5 the LORD your God into the midst of J, 3383
4: 7 That the waters of J were cut off before 3383
4: 7 when it passed over J, the waters of Jordan 3383
4: 7 over Jordan, the waters of J were cut off: 3383
4: 8 took up twelve stones out of the midst of J, 3383
4: 9 set up twelve stones in the midst of J, 3383
4:10 which bare the ark stood in the midst of J, 3383
4:16 the Testimony, that they come up out of J. 3383
4:17 the priests, saying, Come ye up out of J. 3383
4:18 were come up out of the midst of J, 3383
4:18 the waters of J returned unto their place, 3383
4:19 the people came up out of J on the tenth 3383
4:20 twelve stones, which they took out of J, 3383
4:22 Israel came over this J on dry *land.* 3383
4:23 dried up the waters of J from before you, 3383
5: 1 which *were* on the side of J westward, 3383
5: 1 of J from before the children of Israel, 3383
7: 7 hast thou at all brought this people over J, 3383
7: 7 been content, and dwelt on the *other* side J! 3383
9: 1 all the kings which *were* on *this* side J, 3383
9:10 that *were* beyond J, to Sihon king of 3383
12: 1 possessed their land on the *other* side J 3383
12: 7 the children of Israel smote on *this* side J 3383
13: 8 Moses gave them, beyond J eastward, 3383
13:23 the border of the children of Reuben was J, 3383
13:27 of Sihon king of Heshbon, J and *his* border, 3383
13:27 of Cinnereth on the *other* side J eastward. 3383
13:32 on the *other* side J, *by* Jericho, eastward. 3383
14: 3 and a half tribe on the *other* side J: 3383
15: 5 *was* the salt sea, *even* unto the end of J. 3383
15: 5 the bay of the sea at the uttermost part of J: 3383
16: 1 the lot of the children of Joseph fell from J 3383
16: 7 and came to Jericho, and went out *at* J. 3383
17: 5 which *were* on the *other* side J; 3383
18: 7 have received their inheritance beyond J on 3383
18:12 their border on the north side was from J; 3383
18:19 bay of the salt sea at the south end of J: 3383
18:20 J was the border of it on the east side. 3383
19:22 and the outgoings of their border were *at* J: 3383
19:33 and the outgoings thereof were *at* J: 3383
19:34 and to Judah upon J *toward* the sunrising. 3383
20: 8 on the *other* side J *by* Jericho eastward, 3383
22: 4 of the LORD gave you on the *other* side J. 3383
22: 7 their brethren on *this* side J westward. 3383
22:10 when they came unto the borders of J, 3383
22:10 tribe of Manasseh built there an altar by J, 3383
22:11 in the borders of J, at the passage of 3383
22:25 For the LORD hath made J a border 3383
23: 4 to be an inheritance for your tribes, from J, 3383
24: 8 which dwelt on the *other* side J; 3383
24:11 ye went over J, and came unto Jericho: 3383
Jdg 3:28 took the fords of J toward Moab, and 3383
5:17 Gilead abode beyond J: and why did Dan 3383
7:24 them the waters unto Beth-barah and J. 3383
7:24 and took the waters unto Beth-barah and J. 3383
7:25 and Zeeb to Gideon on the *other* side J. 3383
8: 4 Gideon came to J, *and* passed over, he, 3383
10: 8 the *other* side J in the land of the Amorites, 3383
10: 9 passed over J to fight also against Judah, 3383
11:13 from Arnon even unto Jabbok, and unto J: 3383
11:22 and from the wilderness even unto J. 3383
12: 5 the Gileadites took the passages of J before 3383
12: 6 and slew him at the passages of J: 3383
1Sa 13: 7 *some of the* Hebrews went over J *to* 3383
31: 7 *they* that *were* on the *other* side J, saw that 3383
2Sa 2:29 passed over J, and went *through* all 3383
10:17 and passed over J, and came to Helam. 3383
17:22 that *were* with him, and they passed over J: 3383
17:22 not one *of them* that was not gone over J. 3383
17:24 Absalom passed over J, he and all the men 3383
19:15 So the king returned, and came to J. 3383
19:15 meet the king, to conduct the king over J. 3383
19:17 and they went over J before the king. 3383
19:18 before the king, as he was come over J; 3383
19:31 went over J with the king, to conduct him 3383
19:31 with the king, to conduct him *over* J. 3383
19:36 Thy servant will go a little *way* over J with 3383
19:39 all the people went over J. And when 3383
19:41 and all David's men with him, over J? 3383
20: 2 unto their king, from J even to Jerusalem. 3383
24: 5 they passed over J, and pitched in Aroer, 3383
1Ki 2: 8 he came down to meet me *at* J, and I sware 3383
7:46 In the plain of J did the king cast them, 3383
17: 3 by the brook Cherith, that *is* before J. 3383
17: 5 dwelt by the brook Cherith, that *is* before J. 3383
2Ki 2: 6 here; for the LORD hath sent me to J. 3383
2: 7 to view afar off: and they two stood by J. 3383
2:13 and went back, and stood by the bank of J; 3383
5:10 Go and wash in J seven times, and 3383
5:14 and dipped *himself* seven times in J, 3383
6: 2 unto J, and take thence every man a beam, 3383
6: 4 when they came to J, they cut down wood. 3383
7:15 they went after them unto J: and lo, all 3383
10:33 From J eastward, all the land of Gilead, 3383
1Ch 6:78 on the *other* side J *by* Jericho, on the east 3383
6:78 Jordan *by* Jericho, on the east *side* of J, 3383
12:15 These *are* they that went over J in the first 3383
12:37 on the *other* side of J, of the Reubenites, 3383
19:17 passed over J, and came upon them, and 3383
26:30 J westward in all the business of 3383
2Ch 4:17 In the plain of J did the king cast them, 3383
Job 40:23 he trusteth that he can draw up J into his 3383
Ps 42: 6 will I remember thee from the land of J, 3383
114: 3 The sea saw *it,* and fled: J was driven back. 3383
114: 5 thou J, *that* thou wast driven back? 3383
Isa 9: 1 the sea, beyond J, in Galilee of the nations. 3383
Jer 12: 5 then how wilt thou do in the swelling of J? 3383
49:19 of J against the habitation of the strong: 3383
50:44 of J unto the habitation of the strong: 3383
Eze 47:18 and from the land of Israel *by* J, 3383
Zec 11: 3 of young lions; for the pride of J is spoiled. 3383
Mt 3: 5 all Judea, and all the region round about J, *2446*
3: 6 And were baptized of him in J, *2446*
3:13 Then cometh Jesus from Galilee to J unto *2446*
4:15 *by* the way of the sea, beyond J, Galilee of *2446*
4:25 and *from* Judea, and *from* beyond J. *2446*
19: 1 came into the coasts of Judea beyond J; *2446*
Mk 1: 5 were all baptized of him in the river *of* J, *2446*
1: 9 of Galilee, and was baptized of John in J. *2446*
3: 8 and from Idumea, and *from* beyond J; *2446*

Mk 10: 1 the coasts of Judea by the farther side of J: *2446*
Lk 3: 3 And he came into all the country about J, *2446*
4: 1 full of the Holy Ghost returned from J, *2446*
Jn 1:28 *things* were done in Bethabara beyond J, *2446*
3:26 Rabbi, *he* that was with thee beyond J, *2446*
10:40 And went away again beyond J into *2446*

JORIM (1)
Lk 3:29 *the son* of Eliezer, which was *the son* of J, *2497*

JORKEAM See JORKOAM

JORKOAM (1)
1Ch 2:44 Shema begat Raham, the father of J: and 3421

JOSABAD (1)
1Ch 12: 4 and Johanan, and J the Gederathite, 3107

JOSAPHAT (2) [JEHOSHAPHAT]
Mt 1: 8 And Asa begat J; and Josaphat begat *2498*
1: 8 and J begat Joram; and Joram begat Ozias; *2498*

JOSE (1)
Lk 3:29 Which was *the son* of J, which was *the son* *2499*

JOSEDECH (6)
Hag 1: 1 to Joshua the son of J the high priest, 3087
1:12 Joshua the son of J the high priest, with all 3087
1:14 the spirit of Joshua the son of J the high 3087
2: 2 to Joshua the son of J the high priest and 3087
2: 4 be strong, O Joshua, son of J, the high 3087
Zec 6:11 head of Joshua the son of J the high priest; 3087

JOSEPH (228) [JOSEPH'S, JOSES]
Ge 30:24 she called his name J; and said, 3130
30:25 it came to pass, when Rachel had born J, 3130
33: 2 and Rachel and J hindermost. 3130
33: 7 after came J near and Rachel, and 3130
35:24 The sons of Rachel; J, and Benjamin: 3130
37: 2 J, *being* seventeen years old, was feeding 3130
37: 2 J brought unto his father their evil report. 3130
37: 3 Now Israel loved J more than all his 3130
37: 5 J dreamed a dream, and he told *it* his 3130
37:13 Israel said unto J, Do not thy brethren feed 3130
37:17 J went after his brethren, and found them in 3130
37:23 when J was come unto his brethren, 3130
37:23 that they stript J out of his coat, 3130
37:28 they drew and lift up J out of the pit, and 3130
37:28 sold J to the Ishmeelites for twenty *pieces* 3130
37:28 of silver: and they brought J into Egypt. 3130
37:29 behold, J *was* not in the pit; and he rent his 3130
37:33 J is without doubt rent in pieces. 3130
39: 1 J was brought down to Egypt; and 3130
39: 2 the LORD was with J, and he was a 3130
39: 4 J found grace in his sight, and he served 3130
39: 6 J was *a* goodly *person,* and well favoured. 3130
39: 7 that his master's wife cast her eyes upon J; 3130
39:10 came to pass, as she spake to J day by day, 3130
39:11 that *J* went into the house to do his NIH
39:21 the LORD was with J, and shewed him 3130
40: 3 the prison, the place where J *was* bound. 3130
40: 4 the captain of the guard charged J with 3130
40: 6 J came in unto them in the morning, and 3130
40: 8 J said unto them, *Do* not interpretations 3130
40: 9 the chief butler told his dream to J, and 3130
40:12 J said unto him, This *is* the interpretation of 3130
40:16 he said unto J, I also *was* in my dream, and 3130
40:18 J answered and said, This *is* 3130
40:22 chief baker: as J had interpreted to them. 3130
40:23 Yet did not the chief butler remember J, 3130
41:14 Pharaoh sent and called J, and they brought 3130
41:15 Pharaoh said unto J, I have dreamed a 3130
41:16 J answered Pharaoh, saying, *It is* not in me: 3130
41:17 Pharaoh said unto J, In my dream, behold, 3130
41:25 J said unto Pharaoh, The dream of Pharaoh 3130
41:39 Pharaoh said unto J, Forasmuch as God 3130
41:41 Pharaoh said unto J, See, I have set thee 3130
41:44 Pharaoh said unto J, I *am* Pharaoh, and 3130
41:45 And J went out over *all* the land of Egypt. 3130
41:46 J *was* thirty years old when he stood before 3130
41:46 J went out from the presence of Pharaoh, 3130
41:49 J gathered corn as the sand of the sea, 3130
41:50 unto J were born two sons before the years 3130
41:51 J called the name of the firstborn 3130
41:54 began to come, according as J had said: 3130
41:55 said unto all the Egyptians, Go unto J; 3130
41:56 J opened all the storehouses, and sold unto 3130
41:57 all countries came into Egypt to J for to 3130
42: 6 J *was* the governor over the land, *and* he *it* 3130
42: 7 J saw his brethren, and he knew them, but 3130
42: 8 J knew his brethren, but they knew not 3130
42: 9 J remembered the dreams which he 3130
42:14 J said unto them, That *is it* that I spake unto 3130
42:18 J said unto them the third day, This do, 3130
42:23 they knew not that J understood *them;* for 3130
42:25 J commanded to fill their sacks *with* corn, 3130
42:36 J *is* not, and Simeon *is* not, and ye will take 3130
43:15 went down *to* Egypt, and stood before J. 3130
43:16 when J saw Benjamin with them, he said to 3130
43:17 the man did as J bade; and the man brought 3130
43:25 they made ready the present against J came 3130
43:26 when J came home, they brought him 3130
43:30 J made haste; for his bowels did yern upon 3130
44: 2 he did according to the word that J had 3130
44: 4 not *yet* far off, J said unto his steward, Up, 3130
44:15 J said unto them, What deed *is* this that ye 3130
45: 1 J could not refrain himself before all them 3130
45: 1 while J made himself known unto his 3130
45: 3 J said unto his brethren, I *am* Joseph; doth 3130
45: 3 Joseph said unto his brethren, I *am* J; doth 3130
45: 4 J said unto his brethren, Come near to me, 3130
45: 4 he said, I *am* J your brother, whom ye sold 3130
45: 9 and say unto him, Thus saith thy son J, 3130
45:17 Pharaoh said unto J, Say unto thy brethren, 3130
45:21 J gave them wagons, according to 3130
45:26 J *is* yet alive, and he *is* governor over all 3130
45:27 they told him all the words of J, which he 3130
45:27 when he saw the wagons which J had sent 3130
45:28 *It is* enough; J my son *is* yet alive: 3130
46: 4 and J shall put his hand upon thine eyes. 3130
46:19 of Rachel Jacob's wife; J, and Benjamin. 3130
46:20 unto J in the land of Egypt were born 3130
46:27 the sons of J, which were born him in 3130
46:28 he sent Judah before him unto J, to direct 3130
46:29 J made ready his chariot, and went up to 3130
46:30 Israel said unto J, Now let me die, since I 3130
46:31 J said unto his brethren, and unto his 3130
47: 1 J came and told Pharaoh, and said, 3130
47: 5 Pharaoh spake unto J, saying, Thy father 3130
47: 7 J brought in Jacob his father, and set him 3130
47:11 J placed his father and his brethren, and 3130
47:12 J nourished his father, and his brethren, 3130
47:14 J gathered up all the money that was found 3130
47:14 J brought the money into Pharaoh's house. 3130
47:15 all the Egyptians came unto J, and said, 3130
47:16 J said, Give your cattle; and I will give you 3130
47:17 they brought their cattle unto J: and 3130
47:17 J gave them bread *in exchange* for horses, 3130
47:20 J bought all the land of Egypt for Pharaoh; 3130
47:23 J said unto the people, Behold, I have 3130
47:26 J made it a law over the land of Egypt unto 3130
47:29 he called his son J, and said unto him, 3130
48: 1 that *one* told J, Behold, thy father *is* sick: 3130
48: 2 said, Behold, thy son J cometh unto thee: 3130
48: 3 Jacob said unto J, God Almighty appeared 3130
48: 9 J said unto his father, They *are* my sons, 3130
48:11 Israel said unto J, I had not thought to see 3130
48:12 J brought them out from between his 3130
48:13 J took them both, Ephraim in his right hand 3130
48:15 he blessed J, and said, God, before whom 3130
48:17 when J saw that his father laid his right 3130
48:18 J said unto his father, Not so, my father: 3130
48:21 Israel said unto J, Behold, I die: but 3130
49:22 J *is* a fruitful bough, *even* a fruitful bough 3130
49:26 they shall be on the head of J, and on 3130
50: 1 J fell upon his father's face, and wept upon 3130
50: 2 J commanded his servants the physicians to 3130
50: 4 J spake unto the house of Pharaoh, saying, 3130
50: 7 J went up to bury his father: and with him 3130
50: 8 all the house of J, and his brethren, and 3130
50:14 J returned into Egypt, he, and his brethren, 3130
50:15 J will peradventure hate us, and 3130
50:16 they sent a messenger unto J, saying, 3130
50:17 So shall ye say unto J, Forgive, I pray thee 3130
50:17 And J wept when they spake unto him. 3130
50:19 J said unto them, Fear not: for *am* I in 3130
50:22 J dwelt in Egypt, he, and his father's 3130
50:22 and J lived an hundred and ten years. 3130
50:23 J saw Ephraim's children of the third 3130

Ge 50:24 J said unto his brethren, I die: and God will 3130
50:25 And J took an oath of the children of Israel, 3130
50:26 So J died, *being* an hundred and ten years 3130
Ex 1: 5 seventy souls: for J was in Egypt *already.* 3130
1: 6 J died, and all his brethren, and all that 3130
1: 8 a new king over Egypt, which knew not J. 3130
13:19 Moses took the bones of J with him: for he 3130
Nu 1:10 Of the children of J: of Ephraim; 3130
1:32 Of the children of J, *namely,* of 3130
13: 7 Of the tribe of Issachar, Igal the son of J. 3130
13:11 Of the tribe of J, *namely,* of the tribe of 3130
26:28 The sons of J after their families *were* 3130
26:37 These *are* the sons of J after their families. 3130
27: 1 of the families of Manasseh the son of J: 3130
32:33 half the tribe of Manasseh the son of J, 3130
34:23 The prince of the children of J, for the tribe 3130
36: 1 of the families of the sons of J, came near, 3130
36: 5 The tribe of the sons of J hath said well. 3130
36:12 of the sons of Manasseh the son of J, 3130
Dt 27:12 Judah, and Issachar, and J, and Benjamin: 3130
33:13 of J he said, Blessed of the Lord *be* his 3130
33:16 let *the blessing* come upon the head of J, 3130
Jos 14: 4 For the children of J were two tribes, 3130
16: 1 the lot of the children of J fell from Jordan 3130
16: 4 So the children of J, Manasseh and 3130
17: 1 for he *was* the firstborn of J; *to wit,* for 3130
17: 2 of Manasseh the son of J by their families. 3130
17:14 the children of J spake unto Joshua, saying, 3130
17:16 the children of J said, The hill is not 3130
17:17 Joshua spake unto the house of J, *even* to 3130
18: 5 the house of J shall abide in their coasts on 3130
18:11 the children of Judah and the children of J. 3130
24:32 the bones of J, which the children of Israel 3130
24:32 became the inheritance of the children of J. 3130
Jdg 1:22 the house of J, they also went up *against* 3130
1:23 the house of J sent to descry Beth-el. 3130
1:35 yet the hand of the house of J prevailed, so 3130
2Sa 19:20 of J to go down to meet my lord the king. 3130
1Ki 11:28 ruler over all the charge of the house of J. 3130
1Ch 2: 2 Dan, J, and Benjamin, Naphtali, Gad, and 3130
5: 1 his birthright was given unto the sons of J 3130
7:29 In these dwelt the children of J the son of 3130
25: 2 and J, and Nethaniah, and Asarelah, 3130
25: 9 Now the first lot came forth for Asaph to J: 3130
Ezr 10:42 Shallum, Amariah, *and* J. 3130
Ne 12:14 Of Melicu, Jonathan; of Shebaniah, J; 3130
Ps 77:15 thy people, the sons of Jacob and J. 3130
78:67 Moreover he refused the tabernacle of J, 3130
80: 1 of Israel, thou that leadest J like a flock; 3130
81: 5 This he ordained in J *for* a testimony, 3084
105:17 *even* J, *who* was sold for a servant: 3130
Eze 37:16 take another stick, and write upon it, For J, 3130
37:19 Behold, I *will* take the stick of J, which *is* 3130
47:13 tribes of Israel: J *shall have two* portions. 3130
48:32 one gate of J, one gate of Benjamin, 3130
Am 5: 6 lest he break out like fire *in* the house of J, 3130
5:15 will be gracious unto the remnant of J. 3130
6: 6 they are not grieved for the affliction of J. 3130
Ob 1:18 the house of J a flame, and the house of 3130
Zec 10: 6 I will save the house of J, and I will bring 3130
Mt 1:16 And Jacob begat J the husband of Mary, *2501*
1:18 as his mother Mary was espoused to J, *2501*
1:19 Then J her husband, being a just *man,* and *2501*
1:20 saying, J, *thou* son of David, fear not to *2501*
1:24 Then J being raised from sleep did as *2501*
2:13 *the* angel of the Lord appeareth to J in a *2501*
2:19 Lord appeareth in a dream to J in Egypt, *2501*
27:57 came a rich man of Arimathea, named J, *2501*
27:59 And when J had taken the body, *2501*
Mk 15:43 J of Arimathea, an honourable counseller, *2501*
15:45 *it* of the centurion, he gave the body to J. *2501*
Lk 1:27 espoused to a man whose name was J, *2501*
2: 4 And J also went up from Galilee, out of *2501*
2:16 and J, and the babe lying in a manger. *2501*
2:33 And J and his mother marvelled at those *2501*
2:43 and J and his mother knew not *of it.* *2501*
3:23 the son of J, which was *the son* of Heli, *2501*
3:24 *the son* of Janna, which was *the son* of J, *2501*
3:26 which was *the son* of J, which was *the son* *2501*
3:30 *the son* of Juda, which was *the son* of J, *2501*
23:50 And behold, *there was* a man named J, *2501*
Jn 1:45 did write, Jesus of Nazareth, the son of J. *2501*
4: 5 of ground that Jacob gave to his son J. *2501*
6:42 the son of J, whose father and mother we *2501*
19:38 And after this J of Arimathea, being a *2501*
Ac 1:23 And they appointed two, J called Barsabas, *2501*
7: 9 moved with envy, sold J into Egypt: *2501*
7:13 And at the second time J was made known *2501*
7:14 Then sent J, and called his father Jacob to *2501*
7:18 Till another king arose, which knew not J. *2501*
Heb 11:21 he was a dying, blessed both the sons of J; *2501*
11:22 By faith J, when he died, made mention of *2501*
Rev 7: 8 Of the tribe of J *were* sealed twelve *2501*

JOSEPH'S (22) [JOSEPH]
Ge 37:31 they took J coat, and killed a kid of 3130
39: 5 blessed the Egyptian's house for J sake; 3130
39: 6 he left all that he had in J hand; and 3130
39:20 J master took him, and put him into 3130
39:22 the keeper of the prison committed to J 3130
41:42 put it upon J hand, and arrayed him in 3130
41:45 Pharaoh called J name Zaphnath-paaneah; 3130
42: 3 J ten brethren went down to buy corn in 3130
42: 4 Benjamin, J brother, Jacob sent not with 3130
42: 6 J brethren came, and bowed down 3130
43:17 and the man brought the men into J house. 3130
43:18 because they were brought into J house; 3130
43:19 they came near to the steward of J house, 3130
43:24 the man brought the men into J house, and 3130
44:14 and his brethren came to J house; 3130
45:16 saying, J brethren are come: 3130
48: 8 Israel beheld J sons, and said, Who *are* 3130
50:15 when J brethren saw that their father was 3130
50:23 Manasseh were brought up upon J knees. 3130
1Ch 5: 2 the chief ruler; but the birthright *was* J:) 3130
Lk 4:22 his mouth. And they said, Is not this J son? *2501*
Ac 7:13 J kindred was made known unto Pharaoh. *2501*

JOSES (6) [BARNABAS, JOSEPH]
Mt 13:55 and his brethren, James, and J, *2500*
27:56 and Mary the mother of James and J, and *2500*
Mk 6: 3 of James, and J, and of Juda, and Simon? *2500*
15:40 Mary the mother of James the less and of J, *2500*
15:47 Mary *the mother* of J beheld where he was *2500*
Ac 4:36 And J, who by the apostles was surnamed *2500*

JOSHAH (1)
1Ch 4:34 and Jamlech, and J the son of Amaziah, 3144

JOSHAPHAT (1)
1Ch 11:43 the son of Maachah, and J the Mithnite, 3146

JOSHAVIAH (1)
1Ch 11:46 Eliel the Mahavite, and Jeribai, and J, 3145

JOSHBEKASHAH (2)
1Ch 25: 4 J, Mallothi, Hothir, *and* Mahazioth: 3436
25:24 The seventeenth to J, *he,* his sons, and 3436

JOSHIBIAH See JOSIBIAH

JOSHUA (216) [HOSHEA, JEHOSHUA, JESHUA, OSHEA]
Ex 17: 9 Moses said unto J, Choose us out men, 3091
17:10 So J did as Moses had said to him, and 3091
17:13 J discomfited Amalek and his people with 3091
17:14 in a book, and rehearse *it* in the ears of J: 3091
24:13 Moses rose up, and his minister J: and 3091
32:17 when J heard the noise of the people as 3091
33:11 his servant J, the son of Nun, a young man, 3091
Nu 11:28 J the son of Nun, the servant of Moses, 3091
14: 6 J the son of Nun, and Caleb the son of 3091
14:30 the son of Jephunneh, and J the son of Nun. 3091
14:38 J the son of Nun, and Caleb the son of 3091
26:65 the son of Jephunneh, and J the son of Nun. 3091
27:18 Take thee J the son of Nun, a man in whom 3091
27:22 he took J, and set him before Eleazar 3091
32:12 the Kenezite, and J the son of Nun: 3091
32:28 J the son of Nun, and the chief fathers of 3091
34:17 Eleazar the priest, and J the son of Nun. 3091
Dt 1:38 *But* J the son of Nun, which standeth 3091
3:21 I commanded J at that time, saying, 3091
3:28 charge J, and encourage him, and 3091
31: 3 *and* J, he shall go over before thee, as 3091
31: 7 Moses called unto J, and said unto him in 3091
31:14 call J, and present yourselves in 3091
31:14 Moses and J went, and 3091
31:23 And he gave J the son of Nun a charge, and 3091
34: 9 J the son of Nun was full *of* the spirit of 3091
Jos 1: 1 that the Lord spake unto J the son of 3091

Jos 1:10 J commanded the officers of the people, 3091
1:12 half the tribe of Manasseh, spake J, saying, 3091
1:16 they answered J, saying, All that thou 3091
2: 1 J the son of Nun sent out of Shittim two 3091
2:23 came to J the son of Nun, and told him all 3091
2:24 they said unto J, Truly the LORD hath 3091
3: 1 J rose early in the morning; and 3091
3: 5 J said unto the people, Sanctify yourselves: 3091
3: 6 J spake unto the priests, saying, Take up 3091
3: 7 the LORD said unto J, This day will I 3091
3: 9 J said unto the children of Israel, 3091
3:10 J said, Hereby ye shall know that the living 3091
4: 1 that the LORD spake unto J, saying, 3091
4: 4 J called the twelve men, whom he had 3091
4: 5 J said unto them, Pass over before the ark 3091
4: 8 children of Israel did so as J commanded, 3091
4: 8 of Jordan, as the LORD spake unto J, 3091
4: 9 J set up twelve stones in the midst of 3091
4:10 commanded J to speak unto the people, 3091
4:10 according to all that Moses commanded J: 3091
4:14 On that day the LORD magnified J in 3091
4:15 And the LORD spake unto J, saying, 3091
4:17 J therefore commanded the priests, saying, 3091
4:20 took out of Jordan, did J pitch in Gilgal. 3091
5: 2 At that time the LORD said unto J, 3091
5: 3 J made him sharp knives, and 3091
5: 4 this *is* the cause why J did circumcise: 3091
5: 7 up in their stead, them J circumcised: 3091
5: 9 the LORD said unto J, *This* day have I 3091
5:13 it came to pass, when J was by Jericho, 3091
5:13 J went unto him, and said unto him, 3091
5:14 J fell on his face to the earth, and 3091
5:15 captain of the LORD'S host said unto J, 3091
5:15 thou standest *is* holy. And J did so. 3091
6: 2 the LORD said unto J, See, I have given 3091
6: 6 And J the son of Nun called the priests, and 3091
6: 8 when J had spoken unto the people, 3091
6:10 J had commanded the people, saying, 3091
6:12 J rose early in the morning, and the priests 3091
6:16 the trumpets, J said unto the people, Shout; 3091
6:22 J had said unto the two men that had spied 3091
6:25 J saved Rahab the harlot alive, and her 3091
6:25 which J sent to spy out Jericho. 3091
6:26 J adjured *them* at that time, saying, 3091
6:27 So the LORD was with J; and his fame 3091
7: 2 J sent men from Jericho *to* Ai, which *is* 3091
7: 3 they returned to J, and said unto him, 3091
7: 6 J rent his clothes, and fell to the earth upon 3091
7: 7 J said, Alas, O Lord GOD, wherefore hast 3091
7:10 the LORD said unto J, Get thee up; 3091
7:16 So J rose up early in the morning, and 3091
7:19 J said unto Achan, My son, give, I pray 3091
7:20 Achan answered J, and said, Indeed I have 3091
7:22 So J sent messengers, and they ran unto 3091
7:23 brought them unto J, and unto all 3091
7:24 J, and all Israel with him, took Achan 3091
7:25 J said, Why hast thou troubled us? 3091
8: 1 the LORD said unto J, Fear not, 3091
8: 3 So J arose, and all the people of war, to go 3091
8: 3 J chose out thirty thousand mighty *men* of 3091
8: 9 J therefore sent them forth: and they went 3091
8: 9 but J lodged that night among the people. 3091
8:10 J rose up early in the morning, and 3091
8:13 J went that night into the midst of 3091
8:15 J and all Israel *made as if they* were beaten 3091
8:16 they pursued after J, and were drawn away 3091
8:18 the LORD said unto J, Stretch out 3091
8:18 J stretched out the spear that *he had* in his 3091
8:21 when J and all Israel saw that the ambush 3091
8:23 of Ai they took alive, and brought him to J. 3091
8:26 For J drew not his hand back, wherewith he 3091
8:27 of the LORD which he commanded J. 3091
8:28 J burnt Ai, and made it a heap for ever, 3091
8:29 J commanded that they should take his 3091
8:30 J built an altar unto the LORD God of 3091
8:35 which J read not before all 3091
9: 2 to fight with J and with Israel, *with* one 3091
9: 3 Gibeon heard what J had done unto Jericho 3091
9: 6 And they went to J unto the camp *at* Gilgal, 3091
9: 8 they said unto J, We *are* thy servants. 3091
9: 8 J said unto them, Who *are* ye? and 3091
9:15 J made peace with them, and made a 3091
9:22 J called for them, and he spake unto them, 3091
9:24 they answered J, and said, Because it was 3091
9:27 J made them that day hewers of wood and 3091
10: 1 of Jerusalem had heard how J had taken Ai, 3091
10: 4 for it hath made peace with J and with 3091
10: 6 the men of Gibeon sent unto J to the camp 3091
10: 7 So J ascended from Gilgal, he, and all 3091
10: 8 the LORD said unto J, Fear them not: 3091
10: 9 J therefore came unto them suddenly, *and* 3091
10:12 spake J to the LORD in the day when 3091
10:15 J returned, and all Israel with him, unto 3091
10:17 it was told J, saying, The five kings are 3091
10:18 J said, Roll great stones upon the mouth of 3091
10:20 when J and the children of Israel had made 3091
10:21 all the people returned to the camp to J *at* 3091
10:22 said J, Open the mouth of the cave, and 3091
10:24 when they brought out those kings unto J, 3091
10:24 that J called for all the men of Israel, and 3091
10:25 J said unto them, Fear not, nor be 3091
10:26 afterward J smote them, and slew them, 3091
10:27 *that* J commanded, and they took them 3091
10:28 that day J took Makkedah, and smote it 3091
10:29 J passed from Makkedah, and all Israel 3091
10:31 J passed from Libnah, and all Israel with 3091
10:33 J smote him and his people, until *he* had 3091
10:34 from Lachish J passed unto Eglon, and 3091
10:36 J went up from Eglon, and all Israel with 3091
10:38 J returned, and all Israel with him, 3091
10:40 So J smote all the country of the hills, and 3091
10:41 J smote them from Kadesh-barnea even 3091
10:42 and their land did J take *at* one time, 3091
10:43 J returned, and all Israel with him, unto 3091
11: 6 the LORD said unto J, Be not afraid 3091
11: 7 So J came, and all the people of war with 3091
11: 9 J did unto them as the LORD bade him: 3091
11:10 J at that time turned back, and took Hazor, 3091
11:12 did J take, and smote them with the edge of 3091
11:13 of them, save Hazor only; *that* did J burn. 3091
11:15 so did Moses command J, and so 3091
11:15 did Moses command Joshua, and so did J; 3091
11:16 So J took all that land, the hills, and all 3091
11:18 J made war a long time with all those 3091
11:21 at that time came J, and cut off 3091
11:21 J destroyed them utterly with their cities. 3091
11:23 So J took the whole land, according to all 3091
11:23 J gave it for an inheritance unto Israel 3091
12: 7 these *are* the kings of the country which J 3091
12: 7 which J gave unto the tribes of Israel *for* a 3091
13: 1 Now J was old *and* stricken in years; and 3091
14: 1 J the son of Nun, and the heads of 3091
14: 6 the children of Judah came unto J in 3091
14:13 J blessed him, and gave unto Caleb the son 3091
15:13 to the commandment of the LORD to J, 3091
17: 4 before J the son of Nun, and before 3091
17:14 the children of Joseph spake unto J, saying, 3091
17:15 J answered them, If thou *be* a great people, 3091
17:17 J spake unto the house of Joseph, *even* to 3091
18: 3 J said unto the children of Israel, How long 3091
18: 8 J charged them that went to describe 3091
18: 9 and came *again* to J to the host *at* Shiloh. 3091
18:10 J cast lots for them in Shiloh before 3091
18:10 there J divided the land unto the children of 3091
19:49 to J the son of Nun among them: 3091
19:51 J the son of Nun, and the heads of 3091
20: 1 The LORD also spake unto J, saying, 3091
21: 1 unto J the son of Nun, and unto the heads 3091
22: 1 J called the Reubenites, and the Gadites, 3091
22: 6 So J blessed them, and sent them away: 3091
22: 7 unto the *other* half thereof gave J among 3091
22: 7 when J sent them away also unto their 3091
23: 1 that J waxed old *and* stricken in age. 3091
23: 2 J called for all Israel, *and* for their elders, 3091
24: 1 J gathered all the tribes of Israel to 3091
24: 2 J said unto all the people, Thus saith 3091
24:19 J said unto the people, Ye cannot serve 3091
24:21 the people said unto J, Nay; but we will 3091
24:22 J said unto the people, Ye *are* witnesses 3091
24:24 the people said unto J, The LORD our 3091
24:25 So J made a covenant with the people that 3091
24:26 J wrote these words in the book of the law 3091
24:27 J said unto all the people, Behold, this 3091
24:28 So J let the people depart, every man unto 3091
24:29 that J the son of Nun, the servant of 3091
24:31 Israel served the LORD all the days of J, 3091
24:31 all the days of the elders that overlived J, 3091
Jdg 1: 1 Now after the death of J it came to pass, 3091

Jdg 2: 6 when J had let the people go, the children 3091
2: 7 people served the LORD all the days of J, 3091
2: 7 all the days of the elders that outlived J, 3091
2: 8 J the son of Nun, the servant of 3091
2:21 of the nations which J left when he died: 3091
2:23 delivered he them into the hand of J. 3091
1Sa 6:14 the cart came into the field of J, 3091
6:18 *remaineth* unto this day in the field of J, 3091
1Ki 16:34 which he spake by J the son of Nun. 3091
2Ki 23: 8 in of the gate of J the governor of the city, 3091
Hag 1: 1 and to J the son of Josedech the high priest, 3091
1:12 J the son of Josedech the high priest, 3091
1:14 the spirit of J the son of Josedech the high 3091
2: 2 to J the son of Josedech the high priest and 3091
2: 4 be strong, O J, son of Josedech, the high 3091
Zec 3: 1 he shewed me J the high priest standing 3091
3: 3 Now J was clothed with filthy garments, 3091
3: 6 the angel of the LORD protested unto J, 3091
3: 8 O J the high priest, thou, and thy fellows 3091
3: 9 behold the stone that I have laid before J; 3091
6:11 set *them* upon the head of J the son of 3091

JOSIAH (53) [JOSIAS]

1Ki 13: 2 born unto the house of David, J by name; 2977
2Ki 21:24 the people of the land made J his son king 2977
21:26 of Uzza: and J his son reigned in his stead. 2977
22: 1 J *was* eight years old when he *began* to 2977
22: 3 to pass in the eighteenth year of king J, 2977
23:16 as J turned himself, he spied the sepulchres 2977
23:19 J took away, and did to them according to 2977
23:23 in the eighteenth year of king J, 2977
23:24 of Judah and in Jerusalem, did J put away, 2977
23:28 Now the rest of the acts of J, and all that he 2977
23:29 king J went against him; and he slew him 2977
23:30 of the land took Jehoahaz the son of J, 2977
23:34 Pharaoh-nechoh made Eliakim the son of J 2977
23:34 of Josiah king in the room of J his father, 2977
1Ch 3:14 Amon his son, J his son. 2977
3:15 the sons of J *were,* the firstborn Johanan, 2977
2Ch 33:25 the people of the land made J his son king 2977
34: 1 J *was* eight years old when he *began* to 2977
34:33 J took away all the abominations out of all 2977
35: 1 Moreover J kept a passover unto 2977
35: 7 J gave to the people, *of* the flock, lambs 2977
35:16 according to the commandment of king J. 2977
35:18 of Israel keep such a passover as J kept, 2977
35:19 In the eighteenth year of the reign of J was 2977
35:20 all this, when J had prepared the temple, 2977
35:20 by Euphrates: and J went out against him. 2977
35:22 Nevertheless J would not turn his face from 2977
35:23 the archers shot at king J; and the king said 2977
35:24 all Judah and Jerusalem mourned for J. 2977
35:25 Jeremiah lamented for J: and all the singing 2977
35:25 the singing *women* spake of J in their 2977
35:26 Now the rest of the acts of J, and 2977
36: 1 of the land took Jehoahaz the son of J, 2977
Jer 1: 2 days of J the son of Amon king of Judah, 2977
1: 3 of Jehoiakim the son of J king of Judah, 2977
1: 3 of Zedekiah the son of J king of Judah, 2977
3: 6 said also unto me in the days of J the king, 2977
22:11 Shallum the son of J king of Judah, 2977
22:11 which reigned instead of J his father, 2977
22:18 Jehoiakim the son of J king of Judah; 2977
25: 1 of Jehoiakim the son of J king of Judah, 2977
25: 3 From the thirteenth year of J the son of 2977
26: 1 J king of Judah came this word from 2977
27: 1 J king of Judah came this word unto 2977
35: 1 of Jehoiakim the son of J king of Judah, 2977
36: 1 of Jehoiakim the son of J king of Judah, 2977
36: 2 from the days of J, even unto this day. 2977
36: 9 of Jehoiakim the son of J king of Judah, 2977
37: 1 king Zedekiah the son of J reigned instead 2977
45: 1 in the fourth year of Jehoiakim the son of J 2977
46: 2 of Jehoiakim the son of J king of Judah. 2977
Zep 1: 1 in the days of J the son of Amon, king of 2977
Zec 6:10 go *into* the house of J the son of 2977

JOSIAS (2) [JOSIAH]

Mt 1:10 Manasses begat Amon; and Amon begat J; *2502*
1:11 And J begat Jechonias and his brethren, *2502*

JOSIBIAH (1)

1Ch 4:35 Joel, and Jehu the son of J, the son of 3143

JOSIPHIAH (1)

Ezr 8:10 the son of J, and with him an hundred and 3131

JOT (1)

Mt 5:18 one j or one tittle shall in no wise pass from *2503*

JOTBAH (1)

2Ki 21:19 the daughter of Haruz of J. 3192

JOTBATH (1) [JOTBATHAH]

Dt 10: 7 from Gudgodah to J, a land of rivers of 3193

JOTBATHAH (2) [JOTBATH]

Nu 33:33 went from Hor-hagidgad, and pitched in J. 3193
33:34 they removed from J, and encamped at 3193

JOTHAM (24)

Jdg 9: 5 notwithstanding yet J the youngest son of 3147
9: 7 when they told *it* to J, he went and stood in 3147
9:21 J ran away, and fled, and went to Beer, 3147
9:57 upon them came the curse of J the son of 3147
2Ki 15: 5 J the king's son *was* over the house, 3147
15: 7 of David: and J his son reigned in his stead. 3147
15:30 in the twentieth year of J the son of Uzziah. 3147
15:32 J the son of Uzziah king of Judah to reign. 3147
15:36 Now the rest of the acts of J, and all that he 3147
15:38 J slept with his fathers, and was buried 3147
16: 1 the son of J king of Judah *began* to reign. 3147
1Ch 2:47 J, and Geshan, and Pelet, and Ephah, and 3147
3:12 his son, Azariah his son, J his son, 3147
5:17 genealogies in the days of J king of Judah, 3147
2Ch 26:21 J his son *was* over the king's house, 3147
26:23 a leper: and J his son reigned in his stead. 3147
27: 1 J *was* twenty and five years old when he 3147
27: 6 So J became mighty, because he prepared 3147
27: 7 Now the rest of the acts of J, and all his 3147
27: 9 J slept with his fathers, and they buried him 3147
Isa 1: 1 J, Ahaz, *and* Hezekiah, kings of Judah. 3147
7: 1 to pass in the days of Ahaz the son of J, 3147
Hos 1: 1 J, Ahaz, *and* Hezekiah, kings of Judah, and 3147
Mic 1: 1 to Micah the Morasthite in the days of J, 3147

JOURNEY (60) [JOURNEYED, JOURNEYING, JOURNEYINGS, JOURNEYS]

Ge 24:21 to wit whether the LORD had made his j 1870
29: 1 Jacob **went on** his j, and came into 5375+7272
30:36 he set three days' j betwixt himself and 1870
31:23 and pursued after him seven days' j; 1870
33:12 Let us **take** our j, and let us go, and I will 5265
46: 1 Israel **took** his j with all that he had, and 5265
Ex 3:18 three days' j into the wilderness, 1870
5: 3 three days' j into the desert, and 1870
8:27 We will go three days' j into 1870
13:20 they **took** their j from Succoth, and 5265
16: 1 they **took** their j from Elim, and all 5265
Nu 9:10 or *be* in a j afar off, yet he shall keep 1870
9:13 is not in a j, and forbeareth to keep 1870
10: 6 that lie on the south side shall **take** their j: 5265
10:13 they first **took** their j according to 5265
10:33 the mount of the LORD three days' j: 1870
10:33 went before them *in* the three days' j, 1870
11:31 as it were a day's j on this side, and as it 1870
11:31 as it were a day's j on the other side, 1870
33: 8 went three days' j in the wilderness of 1870
33:12 they **took** their j out of the wilderness of 5265
Dt 1: 2 (*There are* eleven days' *j* from Horeb *by* NIH
1: 7 **take** your j, and go *to* the mount of 5265
1:40 **take** your j into the wilderness *by* the way 5265
2: 1 **took** our j into the wilderness *by* the way of 5265
2:24 **take** your j, and pass over the river Arnon: 5265
10: 6 the children of Israel **took** their j from 5265
10:11 Arise, take thy j before the people, 4550
Jos 9:11 Take victuals with you for the j, and go to 1870
9:13 become old by reason of the very long j. 1870
Jdg 4: 9 notwithstanding the j that thou takest shall 1870
1Sa 15:18 the LORD sent thee on a j, and said, Go 1870
2Sa 11:10 unto Uriah, Camest thou not from *thy* j? 1870
1Ki 18:27 or he is in a j, *or* peradventure he sleepeth, 1870
19: 4 he himself went a day's j into 1870
19: 7 *and* eat; because the j *is* too great for thee. 1870
2Ki 3: 9 they fetcht a compass of seven days' j: and 1870
2Ch 1:13 Solomon came *from his* j to the high place NIH
Ne 2: 6 by him,) For how long shall thy j be? 4109
Pr 7:19 *is* not at home, he is gone a long j: 1870

Jnh 3: 3 an exceeding great city of three days' j. 4109
3: 4 Jonah began to enter into the city a day's j, 4109
Mt 10:10 Nor scrip for *your* j, neither two coats, *3598*
25:15 several ability; and straightway **took** his j. *589*
Mk 6: 8 that they should take nothing for *their* j, *3598*
13:34 *the Son of man is* as a man **taking a far** j, *590*
Lk 2:44 have been in the company, went a day's j; *3598*
9: 3 Take nothing for *your* j, neither staves, *3598*
11: 6 For a friend of mine in *his* j is come to me, *3598*
15:13 and **took** his j into a far country, and *589*
Jn 4: 6 Jesus therefore, being wearied with *his* j, *3597*
Ac 1:12 Jerusalem a **sabbath day's** j. *2192+3598+4521*
10: 9 as they **went on** their j, and drew nigh unto *3596*
22: 6 as I **made** my j, and was come nigh unto *4198*
Ro 1:10 **have a prosperous** j by the will of God to *2137*
15:24 Whensoever I **take** my j into Spain, I will *4198*
15:24 for I trust to see you **in** my j, and to be *1279*
1Co 16: 6 that ye may **bring** me **on** my j *4311*
Tit 3:13 **Bring** Zenas the lawyer and Apollos **on** their j *4311*
3Jn 1: 6 whom if thou **bring forward on** their j *4311*

JOURNEYED (33) [JOURNEY]

Ge 11: 2 And it came to pass, as they j from the east, 5265
12: 9 Abram j, going on still toward the south. 5265
13:11 him all the plain of Jordan; and Lot j east: 5265
20: 1 Abraham j from thence toward the south 5265
33:17 Jacob j to Succoth, and built him a house, 5265
35: 5 they j: and the terror of God was upon 5265
35:16 they j from Beth-el; and there was but 5265
35:21 Israel j, and spread his tent beyond 5265
Ex 12:37 the children of Israel j from Rameses to 5265
17: 1 of Israel j from the wilderness of Sin, 5265
40:37 they j not till the day that it was taken up. 5265
Nu 9:17 then after that the children of Israel j: 5265
9:18 of the LORD the children of Israel j, 5265
9:19 kept the charge of the LORD, and j not. 5265
9:20 to the commandment of the LORD they j. 5265
9:21 was taken up in the morning, then they j: 5265
9:21 by night that the cloud was taken up, they j. 5265
9:22 of Israel abode in their tents, and j not: 5265
9:22 but when it was taken up, they j. 5265
9:23 at the commandment of the LORD they j: 5265
11:35 *And* the people j from Kibroth-hattaavah 5265
12:15 the people j not till Miriam was brought in 5265
20:22 j from Kadesh, and came *unto* mount Hor. 5265
21: 4 they j from mount Hor *by* the way of 5265
21:11 they j from Oboth, and pitched at 5265
33:22 they j from Rissah, and pitched in 5265
Dt 10: 7 From thence they j *unto* Gudgodah; and 5265
Jos 9:17 the children of Israel j, and came unto their 5265
Jdg 17: 8 to the house of Micah, as he j. 1870+6213
Lk 10:33 as he j, came where he was: *3593*
Ac 9: 3 And as *he* j, he came near Damascus: and *4198*
9: 7 And the men which j **with** him stood *4922*
26:13 round about me and them which j with me. *4198*

JOURNEYING (3) [JOURNEY]

Nu 10: 2 of the assembly, and for the j of the camps. 4550
10:29 We *are* j unto the place of which 5265
Lk 13:22 teaching, and j towards Jerusalem. *4160+4197*

JOURNEYINGS (2) [JOURNEY]

Nu 10:28 Thus *were* the j of the children of Israel 4550
2Co 11:26 *In* j often, *in* perils of waters, *in* perils of *3597*

JOURNEYS (9) [JOURNEY]

Ge 13: 3 he went on his j from the south even to 4550
Ex 17: 1 after their j, according to 4550
40:36 children of Israel went onward in all their j: 4550
40:38 the house of Israel, throughout all their j. 4550
Nu 10: 6 they shall blow an alarm for their j. 4550
10:12 the children of Israel took their j out of 4550
33: 1 These *are* the j of the children of Israel, 4550
33: 2 j by the commandment of the LORD: 4550
33: 2 these *are* their j according to their goings 4550

JOY (165) [JOYED, JOYFUL, JOYFULLY, JOYFULNESS, JOYING, JOYOUS]

1Sa 18: 6 with j, and with instruments of musick. 8057
1Ki 1:40 rejoiced *with* great j, so that the earth rent 8057
1Ch 12:40 sheep abundantly: for *there was* j in Israel. 8057
15:16 sounding, by lifting up the voice with j. 8057
15:25 out of the house of Obed-edom with j. 8057
29: 9 David the king also rejoiced *with* great j. 8057
29:17 and now have I seen with j thy people, 8057
2Ch 20:27 of them, to go again to Jerusalem with j, 8057
30:26 So there was great j in Jerusalem: for since 8057
Ezr 3:12 a loud voice; and many shouted aloud for j: 8057
3:13 j from the noise of the weeping of 8057
6:16 the dedication of this house of God with j, 2305
6:22 of unleavened bread seven days with j: 8057
Ne 8:10 for the j of the LORD *is* your strength. 2304
12:43 God had made them rejoice *with* great j: 8057
12:43 that the j of Jerusalem was heard even afar 8057
Est 8:16 had light, and gladness, and j, and honour. 8342
8:17 the Jews had j and gladness, a feast and 8057
9:22 was turned unto them from sorrow to j, 8057
9:22 should make them days of feasting and j, 8057
Job 8:19 this *is* the j of his way, and out of the earth 4885
20: 5 the j of the hypocrite *but* for a moment? 8057
29:13 I **caused** the widow's heart **to sing for** j. 7442
33:26 he shall see his face with j: for he will 8643
38: 7 and all the sons of God **shouted for** j? 7321
41:22 and sorrow is **turned into** j before him. 1750
Ps 5:11 let them ever **shout for** j, because 7442
16:11 in thy presence *is* fulness of j; at thy right 8057
21: 1 The king shall j in thy strength, O LORD; 8055
27: 6 will I offer in his tabernacle sacrifices of j; 8643
30: 5 for a night, but j *cometh* in the morning. 7440
32:11 **shout for** j, all *ye that are* upright in heart. 7442
35:27 Let them **shout for** j, and be glad, 7442
42: 4 with the voice of j and praise, *with* a 7440
43: 4 the altar of God, unto God my exceeding j: 1524
48: 2 the j of the whole earth, *is* mount Zion, 4885
51: 8 Make me to hear j and gladness; *that* 8342
51:12 Restore unto me the j of thy salvation; and 8342
65:13 with corn; they **shout for** j, they also sing. 7321
67: 4 O let the nations be glad and **sing for** j: 7442
105:43 he brought forth his people with j, *and* 8342
126: 5 They that sow in tears shall reap in j. 7440
132: 9 and let thy saints **shout for** j. 7442
132:16 her saints shall **shout aloud for** j. 7442+7444
137: 6 if I prefer not Jerusalem above my chief j. 8057
Pr 12:20 but to the counsellers of peace *is* j. 8057
14:10 a stranger doth not intermeddle with his j. 8057
15:21 Folly *is* j to *him that is* destitute of wisdom: 8057
15:23 A man hath j by the answer of his mouth: 8057
17:21 and the father of a fool **hath** no j. 8055
21:15 *It is* j to the just to do judgment: but 8057
23:24 he that begetteth a wise *child* shall **have** j 8055
Ecc 2:10 I withheld not my heart from any j; 8057
2:26 in his sight wisdom, and knowledge, and j: 8057
5:20 God answereth *him* in the j of his heart. 8057
9: 7 Go *thy way,* eat thy bread with j, and 8057
Isa 9: 3 the nation, *and* not increased the j: 8057
9: 3 they j before thee according to the joy in 8055
9: 3 they joy before thee according to the j in 8057
9:17 Therefore the Lord shall have no j in their 8055
12: 3 Therefore with j shall ye draw water out of 8342
16:10 taken away, and j out of the plentiful field; 1524
22:13 behold j and gladness, slaying oxen, and 8342
24: 8 rejoice endeth, the j of the harp ceaseth. 4885
24:11 all j is darkened, the mirth of the land is 8057
29:19 The meek also shall increase *their* j in 8057
32:13 upon all the houses of j *in* the joyous city: 4885
32:14 a j of wild asses, a pasture of flocks; 4885
35: 2 rejoice even *with* j and singing: 1525
35:10 and everlasting j upon their heads: 8057
35:10 they shall obtain j and gladness, and sorrow 8342
51: 3 j and gladness shall be found therein, 8342
51:11 and everlasting j *shall be* upon their head: 8057
51:11 they shall obtain gladness and j; *and* sorrow 8057
52: 9 Break forth **into** j, **sing** together, ye waste 7442
55:12 For ye shall go out with j, and be led forth 8057
60:15 eternal excellency, a j of many generations. 4885
61: 3 beauty for ashes, the oil of j for mourning, 8342
61: 7 the double: everlasting j shall be unto them. 8057
65:14 my servants shall sing for j of heart, but 2898
65:18 Jerusalem a rejoicing, and her people a j. 4885
65:19 rejoice in Jerusalem, and j in my people: 7797
66: 5 he *shall* appear to your j, and they shall be 8057
66:10 rejoice for j with her, all ye that mourn for 4885
Jer 15:16 thy word was unto me the j and rejoicing of 8342
31:13 for I will turn their mourning into j, and 8342
33: 9 it shall be to me a name of j, a praise and 8342
33:11 The voice of j, and the voice of gladness, 8342
48:27 thou spakest of him, thou **skippedst for** j. 5110
48:33 j and gladness is taken from the plentiful 8057

Jer 49:25 the city of praise not left, the city of my j! 4885
La 2:15 of beauty, The j of the whole earth? 4885
5:15 The j of our heart is ceased; our dance is 4885
Eze 24:25 the j of their glory, the desire of their eyes, 4885
36: 5 their possession with the j of all *their* heart, 8057
Hos 9: 1 Rejoice not, O Israel, for j, as *other* people: 1524
Joel 1:12 j is withered away from the sons of men. 8342
1:16 *yea,* j and gladness from the house of our 8057
Hab 3:18 I will j in the God of my salvation. 1523
Zep 3:17 will save, he will rejoice over thee with j; 8057
3:17 in his love, he will j over thee with singing. 1523
Zec 8:19 shall be to the house of Judah j and 8342
Mt 2:10 they rejoiced *with* exceeding great j. 5479
13:20 the word, and anon with j receiveth it; *5479*
13:44 and for j thereof goeth and selleth all that *5479*
25:21 *things:* enter thou into the j of thy lord. *5479*
25:23 *things:* enter thou into the j of thy lord. *5479*
28: 8 from the sepulchre with fear and great j; *5479*
Lk 1:14 And thou shalt have j and gladness; and *5479*
1:44 mine ears, the babe leaped in my womb for j. *20*
2:10 I bring you good tidings of great j, *5479*
6:23 ye in that day, and leap *for j*: for behold, NIG
8:13 when they hear, receive the word with j; *5479*
10:17 And the seventy returned *again* with j, *5479*
15: 7 that likewise j shall be in heaven over one *5479*
15:10 there is j in the presence of the angels of *5479*
24:41 And while they yet believed not for j, and *5479*
24:52 and returned to Jerusalem with great j: *5479*
Jn 3:29 this my j therefore is fulfilled. *5479*
15:11 that my j might remain in you, and *5479*
15:11 remain in you, and *that* your j might be full. *5479*
16:20 but your sorrow shall be turned into j. *5479*
16:21 for j that a man is born into the world. *5479*
16:22 and your j no *man* taketh from you. *5479*
16:24 ye shall receive, that your j may be full. *5479*
17:13 that they might have my j fulfilled in *5479*
Ac 2:28 thou shalt make me full of j with thy *2167*
8: 8 And there was great j in that city. *5479*
13:52 And the disciples were filled with j, and *5479*
15: 3 they caused great j unto all the brethren. *5479*
20:24 so that *I* might finish my course with j, and *5479*
Ro 5:11 we also j in God through our Lord Jesus *2744*
14:17 and peace, and j in the Holy Ghost. *5479*
15:13 Now the God of hope fill you with all j and *5479*
15:32 That I may come unto you with j by *5479*
2Co 1:24 over your faith, but are helpers of your j: *5479*
2: 3 in you all, that my j is *the joy* of you all. *5479*
2: 3 in you all, that my joy is *the j* of you all. NIG
7:13 exceedingly the more joyed we for the j of *5479*
8: 2 trial of affliction the abundance of their j *5479*
Gal 5:22 j, peace, longsuffering, gentleness, *5479*
Php 1: 4 of mine for you all making request with j, *5479*
1:25 you all for your furtherance and j of faith; *5479*
2: 2 Fulfil ye my j, that ye be likeminded, *5479*
2:17 of your faith, I j, and rejoice with you all. *5463*
2:18 *For* the same *cause* also do ye j, and *5463*
4: 1 my j and crown, so stand fast in the Lord, *5479*
1Th 1: 6 much affliction, with j of the Holy Ghost: *5479*
2:19 *is* our hope, or j, or crown of rejoicing? *5479*
2:20 For ye are our glory and j. *5479*
3: 9 for all the j wherewith we joy for your *5479*
3: 9 for all the joy wherewith we j for your *5463*
2Ti 1: 4 of thy tears, that I may be filled with j; *5479*
Phm 1: 7 For we have great j and consolation in thy *5479*
1:20 brother, let me have j of thee in the Lord: *3685*
Heb 12: 2 who for the j that was set before him *5479*
13:17 that they may do it with j, and not with *5479*
Jas 1: 2 count *it* all j when ye fall into divers *5479*
4: 9 to mourning, and *your* j to heaviness. *5479*
1Pe 1: 8 ye rejoice with j unspeakable and full of *5479*
4:13 ye may be glad also with **exceeding** j. *21*
1Jn 1: 4 write we unto you, that your j may be full. *5479*
2Jn 1:12 speak face to face, that our j may be full. *5479*
3Jn 1: 4 I have no greater j than to hear that my *5479*
Jude 1:24 the presence of his glory with **exceeding** j, *20*

JOYED (1) [JOY]
2Co 7:13 exceedingly the more j we for the joy of *5463*

JOYFUL (25) [JOY]
1Ki 8:66 went unto their tents j and glad of heart for 8056
Ezr 6:22 for the LORD had **made** them j, and 8055
Est 5: 9 went Haman forth that day j and with a 8056
Job 3: 7 be solitary, let no j **voice** come therein. 7445
Ps 5:11 let them also that love thy name be j in 5970
35: 9 my soul shall be j in the LORD: it shall 1523
63: 5 and my mouth shall praise *thee with* j lips: 7445
66: 1 **Make a j noise** unto God, all ye lands: 7321
81: 1 **make a j noise** unto the God of Jacob. 7321
89:15 *is* the people that know the j **sound**: 8643
95: 1 let us **make a j noise** to the rock of our 7321
95: 2 *and* **make a j noise** unto him with psalms. 7321
96:12 Let the field be j, and all that *is* therein: 5937
98: 4 **Make a j noise** unto the LORD, all 7321
98: 6 sound of cornet **make a j noise** before 7321
98: 8 clap *their* hands: let the hills be j together 7442
100: 1 **Make a j noise** unto the LORD, all ye 7321
113: 9 to keep house, *to be* a j mother of children. 8056
149: 2 let the children of Zion be j in their King. 1523
149: 5 Let the saints be j in glory: let them sing 5937
Ecc 7:14 In the day of prosperity be j, but in the day 2896
Isa 49:13 be j, O earth; and break forth *into* singing, 1523
56: 7 and **make** them j in my house of prayer: 8055
61:10 the LORD, my soul shall be j in my God; 1523
2Co 7: 4 I am exceeding j in all our tribulation. *5479*

JOYFULLY (3) [JOY]
Ecc 9: 9 Live j with the wife whom thou lovest all 7200
Lk 19: 6 and came down, and received him j. *5463*
Heb 10:34 took j the spoiling of your goods, *3326+5479*

JOYFULNESS (2) [JOY]
Dt 28:47 servedst not the LORD thy God with j, 8057
Col 1:11 unto all patience and longsuffering with j; *5479*

JOYING (1) [JOY]
Col 2: 5 j and beholding your order, and *5463*

JOYOUS (4) [JOY]
Isa 22: 2 *art* full *of* stirs, a tumultuous city, a j city: 5947
23: 7 *Is* this your j *city,* whose antiquity *is* of 5947
32:13 yea, upon all the houses of joy *in* the j city: 5947
Heb 12:11 chastening for the present seemeth to be j, *5479*

JOZABAD (9)
1Ch 12:20 J, and Jediael, and Michael, and Jozabad, 3107
12:20 and Michael, and J, and Elihu, and Zilthai, 3107
2Ch 31:13 J, and Eliel, and Ismachiah, and Mahath, 3107
35: 9 and Hashabiah and Jeiel and J, 3107
Ezr 8:33 with them *was* J the son of Jeshua, and 3107
10:22 Ishmael, Nethaneel, J, and Elasah. 3107
10:23 J, and Shimei, and Kelaiah, (the same *is* 3107
Ne 8: 7 Azariah, J, Hanan, Pelaiah, and the Levites, 3107
11:16 Shabbethai and J, of the chief of 3107

JOZACHAR (1)
2Ki 12:21 For J the son of Shimeath, and 3108

JOZADAK (5)
Ezr 3: 2 stood up Jeshua the son of J, and 3136
3: 8 Jeshua the son of J, and the remnant of 3136
5: 2 Jeshua the son of J, and began to build 3136
10:18 *namely,* of the sons of Jeshua the son of J, 3136
Ne 12:26 the son of J, and in the days of Nehemiah 3136

JUBAL (1)
Ge 4:21 his brother's name *was* J: he was the father 3106

JUBILE (22)
Lev 25: 9 shalt thou cause the trumpet of the j to 8643
25:10 it shall be a j unto you; and ye shall return 3104
25:11 A j shall that fiftieth year be unto you: 3104
25:12 For it *is* the j; it shall be holy unto you: 3104
25:13 In the year of this j ye shall return every 3104
25:15 to the number of years after the j 3104
25:28 him that hath bought it until the year of j: 3104
25:28 in the j it shall go out, and he shall return 3104
25:30 his generations: it shall not go out in the j. 3104
25:31 be redeemed, and they shall go out in the j. 3104
25:33 his possession, shall go out in the *year of* j: 3104
25:40 *and* shall serve thee unto the year of j: 3104
25:50 that he was sold to him unto the year of j: 3104
25:52 but few years unto the year of j, 3104
25:54 then he shall go out in the year of j, 3104
27:17 If he sanctify his field from the year of j, 3104
27:18 if he sanctify his field after the j, then 3104
27:18 *even* unto the year of the j, and it shall be 3104
27:21 the field, when it goeth out in the j, shall be 3104
27:23 thy estimation, *even* unto the year of the j: 3104

Lev 27:24 In the year of the j the field shall return 3104
Nu 36: 4 when the j of the children of Israel shall be, 3104

JUBILEE See JUBILE

JUCAL (1)
Jer 38: 1 J the son of Shelemiah, and Pashur the son 3116

JUDA (11) [JUDAH]
Mt 2: 6 And thou Bethlehem, *in* the land of J, art *2448*
2: 6 art not the least among the princes of J: *2448*
Mk 6: 3 of James, and Joses, and of J, and Simon? *2455*
Lk 1:39 the hill country with haste, into a city of J; *2448*
3:26 *the son* of Joseph, which was *the son* of J, *2455*
3:30 which was *the son* of J, which was *the son* *2455*
3:33 *the son* of Phares, which was *the son* of J, *2455*
Heb 7:14 *it is* evident that our Lord sprang out of J; *2455*
8: 8 the house of Israel and with the house of J: *2455*
Rev 5: 5 behold, the Lion of the tribe of J, the root *2455*
7: 5 Of the tribe of J *were* sealed twelve *2455*

JUDAH (811) [BAALE OF JUDAH, BETH-LEHEM-JUDAH, JUDA, JUDAH'S, JUDAS, JUDEA]
Ge 29:35 therefore she called his name J; and 3063
35:23 and Levi, and J, and Issachar, and Zebulun: 3063
37:26 J said unto his brethren, What profit *is it* if 3063
38: 1 that J went down from his brethren, and 3063
38: 2 J saw there a daughter of a certain 3063
38: 6 J took a wife for Er his firstborn, 3063
38: 8 J said unto Onan, Go in unto thy brother's 3063
38:11 said J to Tamar his daughter in law, 3063
38:12 J was comforted, and went up unto his 3063
38:15 When J saw her, he thought her to be a 3063
38:20 J sent the kid by the hand of his friend 3063
38:22 he returned to J, and said, I cannot find her; 3063
38:23 J said, Let her take *it* to her, lest we be 3063
38:24 months after, that it was told J, saying, 3063
38:24 J said, Bring her forth, and let her be burnt. 3063
38:26 J acknowledged *them,* and said, She hath 3063
43: 3 J spake unto him, saying, The man did 3063
43: 8 J said unto Israel his father, Send the lad 3063
44:14 J and his brethren came to Joseph's house; 3063
44:16 J said, What shall we say unto my lord? 3063
44:18 J came near unto him, and said, O my lord, 3063
46:12 the sons of J; Er, and Onan, and Shelah, 3063
46:28 he sent J before him unto Joseph, to direct 3063
49: 8 J, thou *art he* whom thy brethren shall 3063
49: 9 J *is* a lion's whelp: from the prey, my son, 3063
49:10 The sceptre shall not depart from J, nor a 3063
Ex 1: 2 Reuben, Simeon, Levi, and J, 3063
31: 2 son of Uri, the son of Hur, of the tribe of J: 3063
35:30 son of Uri, the son of Hur, of the tribe of J; 3063
38:22 son of Uri, the son of Hur, of the tribe of J, 3063
Nu 1: 7 Of J; Nahshon the son of Amminadab. 3063
1:26 Of the children of J, *by* their generations, 3063
1:27 *even* of the tribe of J, *were* threescore and 3063
2: 3 camp of J pitch throughout their armies: 3063
2: 3 *shall be* captain of the children of J. 3063
2: 9 All that were numbered in the camp of J 3063
7:12 the son of Amminadab, of the tribe of J: 3063
10:14 the children of J according to their armies: 3063
13: 6 Of the tribe of J, Caleb the son of 3063
26:19 The sons of J *were* Er and Onan: and Er 3063
26:20 the sons of J after their families were, 3063
26:22 These *are* the families of J according to 3063
34:19 Of the tribe of J, Caleb the son of 3063
Dt 27:12 J, and Issachar, and Joseph, and Benjamin: 3063
33: 7 this *is the blessing* of J: and he said, Hear, 3063
33: 7 the voice of J, and bring him unto his 3063
34: 2 Manasseh, and all the land of J, unto 3063
Jos 7: 1 of Zabdi, the son of Zerah, of the tribe of J, 3063
7:16 by their tribes; and the tribe of J was taken: 3063
7:17 he brought the family of J; and he took 3063
7:18 son of Zerah, of the tribe of J, was taken. 3063
11:21 from all the mountains of J, and from all 3063
14: 6 the children of J came unto Joshua in 3063
15: 1 was the lot of the tribe of the children of J 3063
15:12 J round about according to their families. 3063
15:13 he gave a part among the children of J, 3063
15:20 children of J according to their families. 3063
15:21 J toward the coast of Edom southward 3063
15:63 the children of J could not drive them out: 3063
15:63 the Jebusites dwell with the children of J at 3063
18: 5 J shall abide in their coast on the south, and 3063
18:11 lot came forth between the children of J 3063
18:14 *is* Kirjath-jearim, a city of the children of J: 3063
19: 1 within the inheritance of the children of J. 3063
19: 9 Out of the portion of the children of J *was* 3063
19: 9 for the part of the children of J was too 3063
19:34 and to J upon Jordan *toward* the sunrising. 3063
20: 7 which *is* Hebron, in the mountain of J. 3063
21: 4 had by lot out of the tribe of J, and out of 3063
21: 9 gave out of the tribe of the children of J, 3063
21:11 *city is* Hebron, in the hill *country* of J, 3063
Jdg 1: 2 the LORD said, J shall go up: behold, 3063
1: 3 J said unto Simeon his brother, Come up 3063
1: 4 J went up; and the LORD delivered 3063
1: 8 Now the children of J had fought against 3063
1: 9 afterward the children of J went down to 3063
1:10 J went against the Canaanites that dwelt in 3063
1:16 children of J *into* the wilderness of Judah, 3063
1:16 children of Judah *into* the wilderness of J, 3063
1:17 J went with Simeon his brother, and 3063
1:18 Also J took Gaza with the coast thereof, 3063
1:19 the LORD was with J; and he drave out 3063
10: 9 passed over Jordan to fight also against J, 3063
15: 9 pitched in J, and spread themselves in Lehi. 3063
15:10 the men of J said, Why are ye come up 3063
15:11 three thousand men of J went to the top of 3063
17: 7 out of Beth-lehem-judah of the family of J, 3063
18:12 and pitched in Kirjath-jearim, in J: 3063
20:18 And the LORD said, J *shall go up* first. 3063
Ru 1: 7 on the way to return unto the land of J. 3063
4:12 house of Pharez, whom Tamar bare unto J, 3063
1Sa 11: 8 and the men of J thirty thousand. 3063
15: 4 and ten thousand men of J. 3063
17: 1 which *belongeth* to J, and pitched between 3063
17:52 the men of Israel and of J arose, and 3063
18:16 all Israel and J loved David, because 3063
22: 5 depart, and get thee *into* the land of J. 3063
23: 3 unto him, Behold, we *be* afraid here in J: 3063
23:23 him out throughout all the thousands of J. 3063
27: 6 pertaineth unto the kings of J unto this day. 3063
27:10 Against the south of J, and against 3063
30:14 upon *the coast* which *belongeth* to J, and 3063
30:16 of the Philistines, and out of the land of J. 3063
30:26 he sent of the spoil unto the elders of J, 3063
2Sa 1:18 (Also he bade *them* teach the children of J 3063
2: 1 Shall I go up into any of the cities of J? 3063
2: 4 the men of J came, and there they anointed 3063
2: 4 anointed David king over the house of J. 3063
2: 7 also the house of J have anointed me king 3063
2:10 But the house of J followed David. 3063
2:11 over the house of J was seven years 3063
3: 8 which against J do shew kindness *this* day 3063
3:10 the throne of David over Israel and over J, 3063
5: 5 In Hebron he reigned over J seven years 3063
5: 5 and three years over all Israel and J. 3063
11:11 The ark, and Israel, and J, abide in tents; 3063
12: 8 and gave thee the house of Israel and of J; 3063
19:11 Speak unto the elders of J, saying, 3063
19:14 he bowed the heart of all the men of J, 3063
19:15 J came to Gilgal, to go to meet the king, 3063
19:16 came down with the men of J to meet king 3063
19:40 all the people of J conducted the king, and 3063
19:41 Why have our brethren the men of J stolen 3063
19:42 all the men of J answered the men of Israel, 3063
19:43 the men of Israel answered the men of J, 3063
19:43 the words of the men of J were fiercer than 3063
20: 2 the men of J clave unto their king, 3063
20: 4 Assemble me the men of J *within* three 3063
20: 5 So Amasa went to assemble *the men of* J: 3063
21: 2 in his zeal to the children of Israel and J.) 3063
24: 1 them to say, Go, number Israel and J. 3063
24: 7 they went out to the south of J, *even to* 3063
24: 9 the men of J *were* five hundred thousand 3063
1Ki 1: 9 and all the men of J the king's servants: 3063
1:35 him to be ruler over Israel and over J. 3063
2:32 the son of Jether, captain of the host of J. 3063
4:20 J and Israel *were* many, as the sand which 3063
4:25 J and Israel dwelt safely, every man under 3063
12:17 of Israel which dwelt in the cities of J, 3063
12:20 the house of David, but the tribe of J only. 3063
12:21 he assembled all the house of J, with 3063
12:23 king of J, and unto all the house of Judah 3063
12:23 unto all the house of J and Benjamin, and 3063
12:27 *even* unto Rehoboam king of J, and 3063
12:27 and go again to Rehoboam king of J. 3063

1Ki 12:32	like unto the feast that *is* in J, and	3063
13: 1	there came a man of God out of J by	3063
13:12	the man of God went, which came from J.	3063
13:14	thou the man of God that camest from J?	3063
13:21	unto the man of God that came from J,	3063
14:21	the son of Solomon reigned in J.	3063
14:22	J did evil in the sight of the LORD, and	3063
14:29	book of the chronicles of the kings of J?	3063
15: 1	the son of Nebat reigned Abijam over J.	3063
15: 7	book of the chronicles of the kings of J?	3063
15: 9	Jeroboam king of Israel reigned Asa over J.	3063
15:17	Baasha king of Israel went up against J,	3063
15:17	*any* to go out or come in to Asa king of J.	3063
15:22	Asa made a proclamation throughout all J;	3063
15:23	book of the chronicles of the kings of J?	3063
15:25	Israel in the second year of Asa king of J,	3063
15:28	Even in the third year of Asa king of J did	3063
15:33	In the third year of Asa king of J *began*	3063
16: 8	sixth year of Asa king of J *began* Elah	3063
16:10	and seventh year of Asa king of J,	3063
16:15	seventh year of Asa king of J did Zimri	3063
16:23	first year of Asa king of J *began* Omri to	3063
16:29	eighth year of Asa king of J *began* Ahab	3063
19: 3	which *belongeth* to J, and left his servant	3063
22: 2	that Jehoshaphat the king of J came down	3063
22:10	Jehoshaphat the king of J sat each on his	3063
22:29	Jehoshaphat the king of J went up *to*	3063
22:41	J in the fourth year of Ahab king of Israel.	3063
22:45	book of the chronicles of the kings of J?	3063
22:51	seventeenth year of Jehoshaphat king of J,	3063
2Ki 1:17	Jehoram the son of Jehoshaphat king of J;	3063
3: 1	eighteenth year of Jehoshaphat king of J,	3063
3: 7	and sent to Jehoshaphat the king of J,	3063
3: 9	and the king of J, and the king of Edom:	3063
3:14	the presence of Jehoshaphat the king of J,	3063
8:16	of Israel, Jehoshaphat *being* then king of J,	3063
8:16	Jehoram the son of Jehoshaphat king of J	3063
8:19	Yet the LORD would not destroy J for	3063
8:20	Edom revolted from under the hand of J,	3063
8:22	Edom revolted from under the hand of J	3063
8:23	book of the chronicles of the kings of J?	3063
8:25	the son of Jehoram king of J *begin* to reign.	3063
8:29	Ahaziah the son of Jehoram king of J went	3063
9:16	Ahaziah king of J was come down to see	3063
9:21	of Israel and Ahaziah king of J went out,	3063
9:27	when Ahaziah the king of J saw *this,* he	3063
9:29	son of Ahab *began* Ahaziah to reign over J.	3063
10:13	met with the brethren of Ahaziah king of J,	3063
12:18	Jehoash king of J took all the hallowed	3063
12:18	and Ahaziah, his fathers, kings of J,	3063
12:19	book of the chronicles of the kings of J?	3063
13: 1	J Jehoahaz the son of Jehu *began* to reign	3063
13:10	seventh year of Joash king of J *began*	3063
13:12	he fought against Amaziah king of J,	3063
14: 1	Amaziah the son of Joash king of J.	3063
14: 9	king of Israel sent to Amaziah king of J,	3063
14:10	shouldest fall, *even* thou, and J with thee?	3063
14:11	Amaziah king of J looked one another *in*	3063
14:11	at Beth-shemesh, which *belongeth* to J.	3063
14:12	J was put to the worse before Israel; and	3063
14:13	king of Israel took Amaziah king of J,	3063
14:15	and how he fought with Amaziah king of J,	3063
14:17	Amaziah the son of Joash king of J lived	3063
14:18	book of the chronicles of the kings of J?	3063
14:21	all the people of J took Azariah, which *was*	3063
14:22	He built Elath, and restored it to J,	3063
14:23	J Jeroboam the son of Joash king of Israel	3063
14:28	Hamath, *which belonged* to J, for Israel,	3063
15: 1	Azariah son of Amaziah king of J to reign.	3063
15: 6	book of the chronicles of the kings of J?	3063
15: 8	eighth year of Azariah king of J did	3063
15:13	and thirtieth year of Uzziah king of J;	3063
15:17	thirtieth year of Azariah king of J *began*	3063
15:23	In the fiftieth year of Azariah king of J	3063
15:27	fiftieth year of Azariah king of J Pekah	3063
15:32	the son of Uzziah king of J to reign.	3063
15:36	book of the chronicles of the kings of J?	3063
15:37	to send against J Rezin the king of Syria,	3063
16: 1	the son of Jotham king of J *began* to reign.	3063
16:19	book of the chronicles of the kings of J?	3063
17: 1	In the twelfth year of Ahaz king of J *began*	3063
17:13	against J, by all the prophets, *and by* all	3063
17:18	there was none left but the tribe of J only.	3063
17:19	Also J kept not the commandments of	3063
18: 1	*that* Hezekiah the son of Ahaz king of J	3063
18: 5	was none like him among all the kings of J,	3063
18:13	come up against all the fenced cities of J,	3063
18:14	Hezekiah king of J sent to the king of	3063
18:14	king of J three hundred talents of silver	3063
18:16	*from* the pillars which Hezekiah king of J	3063
18:22	and hath said to J and Jerusalem,	3063
19:10	Thus shall ye speak to Hezekiah king of J,	3063
19:30	remnant that is escaped of the house of J	3063
20:20	book of the chronicles of the kings of J?	3063
21:11	Because Manasseh king of J hath done	3063
21:11	and hath made J also to sin with his idols:	3063
21:12	bringing *such* evil upon Jerusalem and J,	3063
21:16	beside his sin where*with* he made J to sin,	3063
21:17	book of the chronicles of the kings of J?	3063
21:25	book of the chronicles of the kings of J?	3063
22:13	for me, and for the people, and for all J,	3063
22:16	of the book which the king of J hath read:	3063
22:18	to the king of J which sent you to inquire	3063
23: 1	they gathered unto him all the elders of J	3063
23: 2	all the men of J and all the inhabitants of	3063
23: 5	whom the kings of J had ordained to burn	3063
23: 5	incense in the high places in the cities of J,	3063
23: 8	brought all the priests out of the cities of J,	3063
23:11	he took away the horses that the kings of J	3063
23:12	which the kings of J had made, and	3063
23:17	which came from J, and proclaimed these	3063
23:22	of the kings of Israel, nor of the kings of J;	3063
23:24	that were spied in the land of J	3063
23:26	where*with* his anger was kindled against J,	3063
23:27	I will remove J also out of my sight,	3063
23:28	book of the chronicles of the kings of J?	3063
24: 2	and sent them against J to destroy it,	3063
24: 3	of the LORD came *this* upon J,	3063
24: 5	book of the chronicles of the kings of J?	3063
24:12	Jehoiachin the king of J went out to	3063
24:20	LORD it came to pass in Jerusalem and J,	3063
25:21	So J was carried away out of their land.	3063
25:22	the people that remained in the land of J,	3063
25:27	of the captivity of Jehoiachin king of J,	3063
25:27	did lift up the head of Jehoiachin king of J	3063
1Ch 2: 1	Reuben, Simeon, Levi, and J, Issachar, and	3063
2: 3	The sons of J; Er, and Onan, and Shelah:	3063
2: 3	Er, the firstborn of J, was evil in the sight	3063
2: 4	and Zerah. All the sons of J *were* five.	3063
2:10	begat Nahshon, prince of the children of J;	3063
4: 1	The sons of J; Pharez, Hezron, and Carmi,	3063
4:21	The sons of Shelah the son of J *were,* Er	3063
4:27	family multiply, like to the children of J.	3063
4:41	came in the days of Hezekiah king of J,	3063
5: 2	For J prevailed above his brethren, and of	3063
5:17	in the days of Jotham king of J,	3063
6:15	*captivity,* when the LORD carried away J	3063
6:55	they gave them Hebron in the land of J,	3063
6:57	the sons of Aaron they gave the cities of J,	NIH
6:65	by lot out of the tribe of the children of J,	3063
9: 1	in the book of the kings of Israel and J,	3063
9: 3	in Jerusalem dwelt of the children of J,	3063
9: 4	of the children of Pharez the son of J.	3063
12:16	of Benjamin and J to the hold unto David.	3063
12:24	The children of J that bare shield and	3063
13: 6	*is,* to Kirjath-jearim, which *belonged* to J,	3063
21: 5	J *was* four hundred threescore and	3063
27:18	Of J, Elihu, *one* of the brethren of David:	3063
28: 4	for he hath chosen J to be the ruler; and	3063
28: 4	of the house of J, the house of my father;	3063
2Ch 2: 7	with the cunning *men* that *are* with me in J	3063
9:11	none such seen before in the land of J.	3063
10:17	of Israel that dwelt in the cities of J,	3063
11: 1	he gathered *of* the house of J and	3063
11: 3	king of J, and to all Israel in Judah and	3063
11: 3	and to all Israel in J and Benjamin, saying,	3063
11: 5	and built cities for defence in J.	3063
11:10	which *are* in J and in Benjamin,	3063
11:12	having J and Benjamin on his side.	3063
11:14	and came to J and Jerusalem:	3063
11:17	So they strengthened the kingdom of J, and	3063
11:23	children throughout all the countries of J	3063
12: 4	took the fenced cities which *pertained* to J,	3063
12: 5	*to* the princes of J, that were gathered	3063
12:12	and also in J things went well.	3063
13: 1	Jeroboam *began* Abijah to reign over J.	3063
13:13	so they were before J, and the ambushment	3063
13:14	when J looked back, behold, the battle *was*	3063

2Ch 13:15 the men of J gave a shout: and as the men 3063
13:15 as the men of J shouted, it came to pass, 3063
13:15 and all Israel before Abijah and J. 3063
13:16 the children of Israel fled before J: and 3063
13:18 the children of J prevailed, because 3063
14: 4 commanded J to seek the LORD God of 3063
14: 5 Also he took away out of all the cities of J 3063
14: 6 he built fenced cities in J: for the land had 3063
14: 7 Therefore he said unto J, Let us build these 3063
14: 8 spears, out of J three hundred thousand; 3063
14:12 the Ethiopians before Asa, and before J; 3063
15: 2 Hear ye me, Asa, and all J and Benjamin; 3063
15: 8 the abominable idols out of all the land of J 3063
15: 9 he gathered all J and Benjamin, and 3063
15:15 all J rejoiced at the oath: for they had 3063
16: 1 Baasha king of Israel came up against J, 3063
16: 1 let none go out or come in to Asa king of J. 3063
16: 6 Asa the king took all J; and they carried 3063
16: 7 time Hanani the seer came to Asa king of J, 3063
16:11 *are* written in the book of the kings of J 3063
17: 2 placed forces in all the fenced cities of J, 3063
17: 2 set garrisons in the land of J, and in 3063
17: 5 all J brought to Jehoshaphat presents; and 3063
17: 6 away the high places and groves out of J. 3063
17: 7 and to Michaiah, to teach in the cities of J. 3063
17: 9 they taught in J, and *had* the book of 3063
17: 9 went about throughout all the cities of J, 3063
17:10 of the lands that *were* round about J, 3063
17:12 he built in J castles, and cities of store. 3063
17:13 he had much business in the cities of J: 3063
17:14 Of J, the captains of thousands; Adnah 3063
17:19 put in the fenced cities throughout all J. 3063
18: 3 of Israel said unto Jehoshaphat king of J, 3063
18: 9 Jehoshaphat king of J sat either of them on 3063
18:28 Jehoshaphat the king of J went up to 3063
19: 1 Jehoshaphat the king of J returned to his 3063
19: 5 land throughout all the fenced cities of J, 3063
19:11 the ruler of the house of J, for all the king's 3063
20: 3 and proclaimed a fast throughout all J. 3063
20: 4 J gathered themselves together, to ask *help* 3063
20: 4 even out of all the cities of J they came to 3063
20: 5 Jehoshaphat stood in the congregation of J 3063
20:13 all J stood before the LORD, with their 3063
20:15 all J, and ye inhabitants of Jerusalem, and 3063
20:17 the LORD with you, O J and Jerusalem: 3063
20:18 all J and the inhabitants of Jerusalem fell 3063
20:20 O J, and ye inhabitants of Jerusalem; 3063
20:22 mount Seir, which were come against J; 3063
20:24 when J came toward the watch tower in 3063
20:27 every man of J and Jerusalem, and 3063
20:31 Jehoshaphat reigned over J: *he was* thirty 3063
20:35 after this did Jehoshaphat king of J join 3063
21: 3 of precious things, with fenced cities in J: 3063
21: 8 revolted from under the dominion of J, 3063
21:10 from under the hand of J unto this day. 3063
21:11 he made high places in the mountains of J, 3063
21:11 and compelled J *thereto.* 3063
21:12 thy father, nor in the ways of Asa king of J, 3063
21:13 hast made J and the inhabitants of 3063
21:17 they came up into J, and brake into it, and 3063
22: 1 So Ahaziah the son of Jehoram king of J 3063
22: 6 Azariah the son of Jehoram king of J went 3063
22: 8 found the princes of J, and the sons of 3063
22:10 all the seed royal of the house of J. 3063
23: 2 they went about in J, and gathered 3063
23: 2 the Levites out of all the cities of J, 3063
23: 8 all J did according to all *things* that 3063
24: 5 Go out unto the cities of J, and gather of all 3063
24: 6 required of the Levites to bring in out of J 3063
24: 9 they made a proclamation through J and 3063
24:17 the death of Jehoiada came the princes of J, 3063
24:18 wrath came upon J and Jerusalem for this 3063
24:23 they came to J and Jerusalem, and 3063
25: 5 Moreover Amaziah gathered J together, 3063
25: 5 throughout all J and Benjamin: 3063
25:10 their anger was greatly kindled against J, 3063
25:12 did the children of J carry away captive, 3063
25:13 fell upon the cities of J, from Samaria even 3063
25:17 Amaziah king of J took advice, and sent to 3063
25:18 king of Israel sent to Amaziah king of J, 3063
25:19 shouldest fall, *even* thou, and J with thee? 3063
25:21 *both* he and Amaziah king of J, 3063
25:21 at Beth-shemesh, which *belongeth* to J. 3063
25:22 J was put to the worse before Israel, and 3063
25:23 the king of Israel took Amaziah king of J, 3063
25:25 Amaziah the son of Joash king of J lived 3063
25:26 not written in the book of the kings of J 3063
25:28 buried him with his fathers in the city of J. 3063
26: 1 all the people of J took Uzziah, who *was* 3063
26: 2 He built Eloth, and restored it to J, 3063
27: 4 he built cities in the mountains of J, 3063
27: 7 in the book of the kings of Israel and J. 3063
28: 6 For Pekah the son of Remaliah slew in J an 3063
28: 9 God of your fathers was wroth with J, 3063
28:10 ye purpose to keep under the children of J 3063
28:17 the Edomites had come and smitten J, 3063
28:18 of the south of J, and had taken 3063
28:19 For the LORD brought J low because 3063
28:19 for he made J naked, and transgressed sore 3063
28:25 in every several city of J he made high 3063
28:26 *are* written in the book of the kings of J 3063
29: 8 the wrath of the LORD was upon J 3063
29:21 and for the sanctuary, and for J. 3063
30: 1 Hezekiah sent to all Israel and J, and 3063
30: 6 and his princes throughout all Israel and J, 3063
30:12 Also in J the hand of God was to give them 3063
30:24 For Hezekiah king of J did give to 3063
30:25 all the congregation of J, with the priests 3063
30:25 land of Israel, and that dwelt in J, rejoiced. 3063
31: 1 that were present went out to the cities of J, 3063
31: 1 and the altars out of all J and Benjamin, 3063
31: 6 *concerning* the children of Israel and J, 3063
31: 6 and Judah, that dwelt in the cities of J, 3063
31:20 thus did Hezekiah throughout all J, and 3063
32: 1 entered into J, and encamped against 3063
32: 8 upon the words of Hezekiah king of J. 3063
32: 9 unto Hezekiah king of J, and unto all Judah 3063
32: 9 unto all J that *were* at Jerusalem, saying, 3063
32:12 and commanded J and Jerusalem, saying, 3063
32:23 and presents to Hezekiah king of J: 3063
32:25 wrath upon him, and upon J and Jerusalem. 3063
32:32 *and* in the book of the kings of J and Israel. 3063
32:33 all J and the inhabitants of Jerusalem did 3063
33: 9 So Manasseh made J and the inhabitants of 3063
33:14 captains of war in all the fenced cities of J. 3063
33:16 commanded J to serve the LORD God of 3063
34: 3 in the twelfth year he began to purge J and 3063
34: 5 their altars, and cleansed J and Jerusalem. 3063
34: 9 of Israel, and of all J and Benjamin; 3063
34:11 to floor the houses which the kings of J had 3063
34:21 and for them that are left in Israel and in J, 3063
34:24 which they have read before the king of J: 3063
34:26 as for the king of J, who sent you to inquire 3063
34:29 and gathered together all the elders of J and 3063
34:30 all the men of J, and the inhabitants of 3063
35:18 all J and Israel that were present, and 3063
35:21 have I to do with thee, thou king of J? 3063
35:24 all J and Jerusalem mourned for Josiah. 3063
35:27 in the book of the kings of Israel and J. 3063
36: 4 Egypt made Eliakim his brother king over J 3063
36: 8 in the book of the kings of Israel and J: 3063
36:10 made Zedekiah his brother king over J and 3063
36:23 him a house in Jerusalem, which *is* in J. 3063
Ezr 1: 2 him a house at Jerusalem, which *is* in J. 3063
1: 3 which *is* in J, and build the house of 3063
1: 5 rose up the chief of the fathers of J and 3063
1: 8 them unto Sheshbazzar, the prince of J. 3063
2: 1 came again unto Jerusalem and J, 3063
3: 9 Kadmiel and his sons, the sons of J, 3063
4: 1 Now *when* the adversaries of J and 3063
4: 4 land weakened the hands of the people of J, 3063
4: 6 an accusation against the inhabitants of J 3063
5: 1 prophesied unto the Jews that *were* in J and 3061
7:14 to inquire concerning J and Jerusalem, 3061
9: 9 and to give us a wall in J and in Jerusalem. 3063
10: 7 they made proclamation throughout J and 3063
10: 9 all the men of J and Benjamin gathered 3063
10:23 same *is* Kelita,) Pethahiah, J, and Eliezer. 3063
Ne 1: 2 came, he and *certain* men of J; 3063
2: 5 that thou wouldest send me unto J, unto 3063
2: 7 they may convey me over till I come into J; 3063
4:10 J said, The strength of the bearers of 3063
4:16 the rulers *were* behind all the house of J. 3063
5:14 to be their governor in the land of J, 3063
6: 7 at Jerusalem, saying, *There is* a king in J: 3063
6:17 Moreover in those days the nobles of J sent 3063
6:18 For *there were* many in J sworn unto him, 3063
7: 6 came again to Jerusalem and to J, 3063

Ne 11: 3 in the cities of J dwelt every one in his 3063
11: 4 dwelt *certain* of the children of J, 3063
11: 4 Of the children of J; Athaiah the son of 3063
11: 9 J the son of Senuah *was* second over 3063
11:20 *and* the Levites, *were* in all the cities of J, 3063
11:24 of the children of Zerah the son of J, 3063
11:25 *some* of the children of J dwelt at 3063
11:36 of the Levites *were* divisions *in* J, *and* 3063
12: 8 Kadmiel, Sherebiah, J, *and* Mattaniah, 3063
12:31 I brought up the princes of J upon the wall, 3063
12:32 went Hoshaiah, and half of the princes of J, 3063
12:34 J, and Benjamin, and Shemaiah, and 3063
12:36 Gilalai, Maai, Nethaneel, and J, Hanani, 3063
12:44 for J rejoiced for the priests and for 3063
13:12 brought all J the tithe of the corn and 3063
13:15 In those days saw I in J *some* treading wine 3063
13:16 sold on the sabbath unto the children of J, 3063
13:17 I contended with the nobles of J, and 3063
Est 2: 6 been carried away with Jeconiah king of J, 3063
Ps 48:11 let the daughters of J be glad, because 3063
60: 7 strength of mine head; J *is* my lawgiver; 3063
63: T when he was in the wilderness of J. 3063
68:27 the princes of J *and* their council, 3063
69:35 save Zion, and will build the cities of J: 3063
76: 1 In J *is* God known: his name *is* great in 3063
78:68 chose the tribe of J, the mount Zion which 3063
97: 8 the daughters of J rejoiced, because of thy 3063
108: 8 strength of mine head; J *is* my lawgiver; 3063
114: 2 J was his sanctuary, *and* Israel his 3063
Pr 25: 1 which the men of Hezekiah king of J 3063
Isa 1: 1 which he saw concerning J and 3063
1: 1 Jotham, Ahaz, *and* Hezekiah, kings of J. 3063
2: 1 Isaiah the son of Amoz saw concerning J 3063
3: 1 and from J the stay and the staff, 3063
3: 8 For Jerusalem is ruined, and J is fallen: 3063
5: 3 and men of J, judge, I pray you, betwixt me 3063
5: 7 and the men of J his pleasant plant: 3063
7: 1 the son of Uzziah king of J, *that* Rezin 3063
7: 6 Let us go up against J, and vex it, and let us 3063
7:17 from the day that Ephraim departed from J; 3063
8: 8 he shall pass through J; he shall overflow 3063
9:21 *and* they together *shall be* against J. For all 3063
11:12 gather together the dispersed of J from 3063
11:13 and the adversaries of J shall be cut off: 3063
11:13 Ephraim shall not envy J, and Judah shall 3063
11:13 envy Judah, and J shall not vex Ephraim. 3063
19:17 the land of J shall be a terror unto Egypt, 3063
22: 8 he discovered the covering of J, and 3063
22:21 of Jerusalem, and to the house of J. 3063
26: 1 day shall this song be sung in the land of J; 3063
36: 1 came up against all the defenced cities of J, 3063
36: 7 said to J and to Jerusalem, Ye shall 3063
37:10 Thus shall ye speak to Hezekiah king of J, 3063
37:31 remnant that is escaped of the house of J 3063
38: 9 king of J, when he had been sick, and 3063
40: 9 say unto the cities of J, Behold your God. 3063
44:26 to the cities of J, Ye shall be built, and 3063
48: 1 and are come forth out of the waters of J, 3063
65: 9 and out of J an inheritor of my mountains: 3063
Jer 1: 2 days of Josiah the son of Amon king of J, 3063
1: 3 of Jehoiakim the son of Josiah king of J, 3063
1: 3 of Zedekiah the son of Josiah king of J, 3063
1:15 round about, and against all the cities of J. 3063
1:18 against the kings of J, against the princes 3063
2:28 the number of thy cities are thy gods, O J. 3063
3: 7 And her treacherous sister J saw *it*. 3063
3: 8 yet her treacherous sister J feared not, but 3063
3:10 yet for all this her treacherous sister J hath 3063
3:11 justified herself more than treacherous J. 3063
3:18 In those days the house of J shall walk with 3063
4: 3 For thus saith the LORD to the men of J 3063
4: 4 ye men of J and inhabitants of Jerusalem: 3063
4: 5 Declare ye in J, and publish in Jerusalem; 3063
4:16 give out their voice against the cities of J. 3063
5:11 the house of J have dealt very 3063
5:20 house of Jacob, and publish it in J, saying, 3063
7: 2 Hear the word of the LORD, all *ye of* J, 3063
7:17 thou not what they do in the cities of J 3063
7:30 For the children of J have done evil in my 3063
7:34 will I cause to cease from the cities of J, 3063
8: 1 shall bring out the bones of the kings of J, 3063
9:11 I will make the cities of J desolate, 3063
9:26 J, and Edom, and the children of Ammon, 3063
10:22 to make the cities of J desolate, *and* a den 3063
11: 2 speak unto the men of J, and to 3063
11: 6 Proclaim all these words in the cities of J, 3063
11: 9 A conspiracy is found among the men of J, 3063
11:10 the house of J have broken my covenant 3063
11:12 shall the cities of J and inhabitants of 3063
11:13 number of thy cities were thy gods, O J; 3063
11:17 of the house of Israel and of the house of J, 3063
12:14 pluck out the house of J from among them. 3063
13: 9 After this manner will I mar the pride of J, 3063
13:11 house of Israel and the whole house of J, 3063
13:19 none shall open *them:* J shall be carried 3063
14: 2 J mourneth, and the gates thereof languish; 3063
14:19 Hast thou utterly rejected J? hath thy soul 3063
15: 4 of Manasseh the son of Hezekiah king of J, 3063
17: 1 The sin of J *is* written with a pen of iron, 3063
17:19 whereby the kings of J come in, and by 3063
17:20 ye kings of J, and all Judah, and all 3063
17:20 all J, and all the inhabitants of Jerusalem, 3063
17:25 the men of J, and the inhabitants of 3063
17:26 they shall come from the cities of J, and 3063
18:11 speak to the men of J, and to 3063
19: 3 O kings of J, and inhabitants of Jerusalem; 3063
19: 4 nor the kings of J, and have filled this place 3063
19: 7 I will make void the counsel of J and 3063
19:13 and the houses of the kings of J, 3063
20: 4 I will give all J into the hand of the king of 3063
20: 5 all the treasures of the kings of J will I give 3063
21: 7 I will deliver Zedekiah king of J, and his 3063
21:11 touching the house of the king of J, 3063
22: 1 Go down *to* the house of the king of J, and 3063
22: 2 Hear the word of the LORD, O king of J, 3063
22: 6 the LORD unto the king's house of J; 3063
22:11 Shallum the son of Josiah king of J, 3063
22:18 Jehoiakim the son of Josiah king of J; 3063
22:24 of J were the signet upon my right hand, 3063
22:30 throne of David, and ruling any more in J. 3063
23: 6 In his days J shall be saved, and Israel shall 3063
24: 1 Jeconiah the son of Jehoiakim king of J, 3063
24: 1 the princes of J, with the carpenters and 3063
24: 5 them that are carried away captive of J, 3063
24: 8 So will I give Zedekiah the king of J, and 3063
25: 1 J in the fourth year of Jehoiakim the son of 3063
25: 1 of Jehoiakim the son of Josiah king of J, 3063
25: 2 the prophet spake unto all the people of J, 3063
25: 3 year of Josiah the son of Amon king of J, 3063
25:18 the cities of J, and the kings thereof, *and* 3063
26: 1 king of J came this word from the LORD, 3063
26: 2 and speak unto all the cities of J, 3063
26:10 When the princes of J heard these things, 3063
26:18 in the days of Hezekiah king of J, 3063
26:18 spake to all the people of J, saying, 3063
26:19 Did Hezekiah king of J and all Judah put 3063
26:19 of Judah and all J put him at all to death? 3063
27: 1 J came this word unto Jeremiah from 3063
27: 3 come *to* Jerusalem unto Zedekiah king of J; 3063
27:12 I spake also to Zedekiah king of J 3063
27:18 *in* the house of the king of J, and 3063
27:20 king of J from Jerusalem to Babylon, 3063
27:20 and all the nobles of J and Jerusalem; 3063
27:21 *in* the house of the king of J and 3063
28: 1 of the reign of Zedekiah king of J, 3063
28: 4 Jeconiah the son of Jehoiakim king of J, 3063
28: 4 with all the captives of J, that went into 3063
29: 2 the princes of J and Jerusalem, and 3063
29: 3 whom Zedekiah king of J sent unto 3063
29:22 all the captivity of J which *are* in Babylon, 3063
30: 3 the captivity of my people Israel and J, 3063
30: 4 spake concerning Israel and concerning J. 3063
31:23 they shall use this speech in the land of J 3063
31:24 there shall dwell in J itself, and *in* all 3063
31:27 and the house of J *with* the seed of man, 3063
31:31 the house of Israel, and with the house of J: 3063
32: 1 in the tenth year of Zedekiah king of J, 3063
32: 3 For Zedekiah king of J had shut him up, 3063
32: 4 Zedekiah king of J shall not escape out of 3063
32:30 the children of J have only done evil before 3063
32:32 children of Israel and of the children of J, 3063
32:32 the men of J, and the inhabitants of 3063
32:35 do this abomination, to cause J to sin. 3063
32:44 in the cities of J, and in the cities of 3063
33: 4 concerning the houses of the kings of J, 3063
33: 7 I will cause the captivity of J and 3063
33:10 *even* in the cities of J, and in the streets of 3063
33:13 about Jerusalem, and in the cities of J, 3063

Jer 33:14 the house of Israel and to the house of J. 3063
33:16 In those days shall J be saved, and 3063
34: 2 Go and speak to Zedekiah king of J, and 3063
34: 4 word of the Lord, O Zedekiah king of J; 3063
34: 6 unto Zedekiah king of J in Jerusalem, 3063
34: 7 against all the cities of J that were left, 3063
34: 7 defenced cities remained of the cities of J. 3063
34:19 The princes of J, and the princes of 3063
34:21 Zedekiah king of J and his princes will I 3063
34:22 I will make the cities of J a desolation 3063
35: 1 of Jehoiakim the son of Josiah king of J, 3063
35:13 Go and tell the men of J and the inhabitants 3063
35:17 I will bring upon J and upon all 3063
36: 1 of Jehoiakim the son of Josiah king of J, 3063
36: 2 against J, and against all the nations, 3063
36: 3 It may be that the house of J will hear all 3063
36: 6 also thou shalt read them in the ears of all J 3063
36: 9 of Jehoiakim the son of Josiah king of J, 3063
36: 9 came from the cities of J unto Jerusalem. 3063
36:28 which Jehoiakim the king of J hath burnt. 3063
36:29 thou shalt say to Jehoiakim king of J, 3063
36:30 saith the Lord of Jehoiakim king of J; 3063
36:31 of Jerusalem, and upon the men of J, 3063
36:32 Jehoiakim king of J had burnt in the fire: 3063
37: 1 king of Babylon made king in the land of J. 3063
37: 7 Thus shall ye say to the king of J, that sent 3063
39: 1 In the ninth year of Zedekiah king of J, 3063
39: 4 *that* when Zedekiah the king of J saw them, 3063
39: 6 king of Babylon slew all the nobles of J. 3063
39:10 in the land of J, and gave them vineyards 3063
40: 1 carried away captive of Jerusalem and J, 3063
40: 5 hath made governor over the cities of J, 3063
40:11 the king of Babylon had left a remnant of J, 3063
40:12 came *to* the land of J, to Gedaliah, unto 3063
40:15 be scattered, and the remnant in J perish? 3063
42:15 the word of the Lord, ye remnant of J; 3063
42:19 said concerning you, O ye remnant of J; 3063
43: 4 of the Lord, to dwell in the land of J. 3063
43: 5 of the forces, took all the remnant of J, 3063
43: 5 had been driven, to dwell in the land of J: 3063
43: 9 in Tahpanhes, in the sight of the men of J; 3064
44: 2 and upon all the cities of J; 3063
44: 6 was kindled in the cities of J and in 3063
44: 7 and woman, child and suckling, out of J, 3063
44: 9 the wickedness of the kings of J, and 3063
44: 9 they have committed in the land of J, 3063
44:11 against you for evil, and to cut off all J. 3063
44:12 I will take the remnant of J, that have set 3063
44:14 So that none of the remnant of J, which are 3063
44:14 that *they* should return *into* the land of J, 3063
44:17 in the cities of J, and in the streets of 3063
44:21 The incense that ye burnt in the cities of J, 3063
44:24 all J that *are* in the land of Egypt: 3063
44:26 all J that dwell in the land of Egypt; 3063
44:26 of any man of J in all the land of Egypt, 3063
44:27 all the men of J that *are* in the land of 3063
44:28 out of the land of Egypt *into* the land of J, 3063
44:28 all the remnant of J, that are gone into 3063
44:30 as I gave Zedekiah king of J into the hand 3063
45: 1 of Jehoiakim the son of Josiah king of J, 3063
46: 2 of Jehoiakim the son of Josiah king of J. 3063
49:34 of the reign of Zedekiah king of J, 3063
50: 4 they and the children of J together, going 3063
50:20 the sins of J, and they shall not be found: 3063
50:33 the children of J *were* oppressed together: 3063
51: 5 nor J of his God, of the Lord of hosts; 3063
51:59 when he went with Zedekiah the king of J 3063
52: 3 Lord it came to pass in Jerusalem and J, 3063
52:10 he slew also all the princes of J in Riblah. 3063
52:27 Thus J was carried away captive out of his 3063
52:31 of the captivity of Jehoiachin king of J, 3063
52:31 lifted up the head of Jehoiachin king of J, 3063
La 1: 3 J is gone into captivity because 3063
1:15 the daughter of J, *as in* a winepress. 3063
2: 2 wrath the strong holds of the daughter of J; 3063
2: 5 hath increased in the daughter of J 3063
5:11 in Zion, *and* the maids in the cities of J. 3063
Eze 4: 6 the iniquity of the house of J forty days: 3063
8: 1 and the elders of J sat before me, 3063
8:17 Is it a light thing to the house of J that *they* 3063
9: 9 the house of Israel and J *is* exceeding great, 3063
21:20 to J in Jerusalem the defenced. 3063
25: 3 against the house of J, when they went into 3063
25: 8 the house of J *is* like unto all the heathen; 3063
25:12 against the house of J by taking vengeance, 3063
27:17 J, and the land of Israel, they *were* thy 3063
37:16 For J, and for the children of Israel his 3063
37:19 *even* with the stick of J, and make them 3063
48: 7 east side unto the west side, a *portion for* J. 3063
48: 8 by the border of J, from the east side unto 3063
48:22 between the border of J and the border of 3063
48:31 of Reuben, one gate of J, one gate of Levi. 3063
Da 1: 1 J came Nebuchadnezzar king of Babylon 3063
1: 2 the Lord gave Jehoiakim king of J into his 3063
1: 6 Now among these were of the children of J, 3063
2:25 I have found a man of the captives of J, 3061
5:13 *art* of the children of the captivity of J, 3061
6:13 *is* of the children of the captivity of J, 3061
9: 7 to the men of J, and to the inhabitants of 3063
Hos 1: 1 kings of J, and in the days of Jeroboam 3063
1: 7 I will have mercy upon the house of J, and 3063
1:11 shall the children of J and the children of 3063
4:15 Israel, play the harlot, *yet* let not J offend; 3063
5: 5 in their iniquity; J also shall fall with them. 3063
5:10 The princes of J were like them that 3063
5:12 a moth, and to the house of J as rottenness. 3063
5:13 J *saw* his wound, then went Ephraim to 3063
5:14 and as a young lion to the house of J: 3063
6: 4 O J, what shall I do unto thee? for your 3063
6:11 Also, O J, he hath set a harvest for thee, 3063
8:14 and J hath multiplied fenced cities: 3063
10:11 J shall plow, *and* Jacob shall break his 3063
11:12 J yet ruleth with God, and is faithful with 3063
12: 2 The Lord hath also a controversy with J, 3063
Joel 3: 1 when I shall bring again the captivity of J 3063
3: 6 The children also of J and the children of 3063
3: 8 daughters into the hand of the children of J, 3063
3:18 all the rivers of J shall flow *with* waters, 3063
3:19 for the violence against the children of J, 3063
3:20 J shall dwell for ever, and Jerusalem from 3063
Am 1: 1 Israel in the days of Uzziah king of J, 3063
2: 4 For three transgressions of J, and for four, 3063
2: 5 I will send a fire upon J, and it shall devour 3063
7:12 go, flee thee away into the land of J, and 3063
Ob 1:12 children of J in the day of their destruction; 3063
Mic 1: 1 Ahaz, *and* Hezekiah, kings of J, which he 3063
1: 5 what *are* the high places of J? *are they* not 3063
1: 9 wound *is* incurable; for it is come unto J; 3063
5: 2 *thou* be little among the thousands of J, 3063
Na 1:15 O J, keep thy solemn feasts, perform thy 3063
Zep 1: 1 days of Josiah the son of Amon, king of J. 3063
1: 4 I will also stretch out mine hand upon J, 3063
2: 7 shall be for the remnant of the house of J; 3063
Hag 1: 1 governor of J, and to Joshua the son of 3063
1:14 governor of J, and the spirit of Joshua 3063
2: 2 governor of J, and to Joshua the son of 3063
2:21 Speak to Zerubbabel, governor of J, saying, 3063
Zec 1:12 mercy on Jerusalem and on the cities of J, 3063
1:19 These *are* the horns which have scattered J, 3063
1:21 These *are* the horns which have scattered J, 3063
1:21 which lift up *their* horn over the land of J 3063
2:12 the Lord shall inherit J his portion in 3063
8:13 O house of J, and house of Israel; 3063
8:15 well unto Jerusalem and to the house of J: 3063
8:19 shall be to the house of J joy and gladness, 3063
9: 7 he shall be as a governor in J, and Ekron as 3063
9:13 When I have bent J for me, filled the bow 3063
10: 3 hosts hath visited his flock the house of J, 3063
10: 6 I will strengthen the house of J, and I will 3063
11:14 I might break the brotherhood between J 3063
12: 2 they shall be in the siege both against J 3063
12: 4 I will open mine eyes upon the house of J, 3063
12: 5 the governors of J shall say in their heart, 3063
12: 6 In that day will I make the governors of J 3063
12: 7 The Lord also shall save the tents of J 3063
12: 7 do not magnify *themselves* against J. 3063
14: 5 earthquake in the days of Uzziah king of J: 3063
14:14 J also shall fight at Jerusalem; and 3063
14:21 in J shall be holiness unto the Lord of 3063
Mal 2:11 J hath dealt treacherously, and 3063
2:11 for J hath profaned the holiness of 3063
3: 4 shall the offering of J and Jerusalem be 3063

JUDAH'S (4) [JUDAH]

Ge 38: 7 Er, J firstborn, was wicked in the sight of 3063
38:12 in process of time the daughter of Shuah J 3063
Jer 32: 2 which *was in* the king of J house. 3063
38:22 all the women that are left in the king of J 3063

JUDAS (33) [JUDAH]
Mt 1: 2 and Jacob begat J and his brethren; *2455*
1: 3 And J begat Phares and Zara of Thamar; *2455*
10: 4 Simon the Canaanite, and J Iscariot, *2455*
13:55 James, and Joses, and Simon, and J? *2455*
26:14 Then one of the twelve, called J Iscariot, *2455*
26:25 Then J, which betrayed him, answered and *2455*
26:47 lo, J, one of the twelve, came, and with him *2455*
27: 3 Then J, which had betrayed him, when he *2455*
Mk 3:19 And J Iscariot, which also betrayed him. *2455*
14:10 And J Iscariot, one of the twelve, *2455*
14:43 cometh J, one of the twelve, and with him a *2455*
Lk 6:16 *And* J *the brother* of James, and *2455*
6:16 and J Iscariot, which also was the traitor. *2455*
22: 3 Then entered Satan into J surnamed *2455*
22:47 and he that was called J, one of the twelve, *2455*
22:48 But Jesus said unto him, J, betrayest thou *2455*
Jn 6:71 He spake of J Iscariot *the son* of Simon: *2455*
12: 4 Then saith one of his disciples, J Iscariot, *2455*
13: 2 the devil having now put into the heart of J *2455*
13:26 he gave *it* to J Iscariot, *the son* of Simon. *2455*
13:29 *of them* thought, because J had the bag, *2455*
14:22 J saith unto him, not Iscariot, Lord, how is *2455*
18: 2 And J also, which betrayed him, knew *2455*
18: 3 J then, having received a band *of men*, and *2455*
18: 5 I am *he*. And J also, which betrayed him, *2455*
Ac 1:13 Simon Zelotes, and J *the brother* of James. *2455*
1:16 mouth of David spake before concerning J, *2455*
1:25 from which J by transgression fell, *2455*
5:37 After this *man* rose up J of Galilee in *2455*
9:11 inquire in the house of J for *one* called *2455*
15:22 *namely*, J surnamed Barsabas, and Silas, *2455*
15:27 We have sent therefore J and Silas, *2455*
15:32 And J and Silas, being prophets also *2455*

JUDE (1)
Jude 1: 1 J, the servant of Jesus Christ, and *2455*

JUDEA (44) [JUDAH]
Ezr 5: 8 that we went into the province of J, 3061
Mt 2: 1 of J in the days of Herod the king, *2449*
2: 5 And they said unto him, In Bethlehem of J: *2449*
2:22 reign in J in the room of his father Herod, *2449*
3: 1 preaching in the wilderness of J, *2449*
3: 5 and all J, and all the region round about *2449*
4:25 and *from* J, and *from* beyond Jordan. *2449*
19: 1 came into the coasts of J beyond Jordan; *2449*
24:16 Then let them which be in J flee into *2449*
Mk 1: 5 there went out unto him all the land of J, *2449*
3: 7 from Galilee followed him, and from J, *2449*
10: 1 cometh into the coasts of J by the farther *2449*
13:14 let them that be in J flee to the mountains: *2449*
Lk 1: 5 was in the days of Herod, the king of J, *2449*
1:65 abroad throughout all the hill country of J. *2449*
2: 4 of Nazareth, into J, unto the city of David, *2449*
3: 1 Pontius Pilate being governor of J, and *2449*
5:17 town of Galilee, and J, and Jerusalem: *2449*
6:17 a great multitude of people out of all J and *2449*
7:17 rumour of him went forth throughout all J, *2449*
21:21 Then let them which are in J flee to *2449*
Jn 3:22 and his disciples into the land of J; *2453*
4: 3 He left J, and departed again into Galilee. *2449*
4:47 he heard that Jesus was come out of J *2449*
4:54 when he was come out of J into Galilee. *2449*
7: 3 said unto him, Depart hence, and go into J, *2449*
11: 7 he to *his* disciples, Let us go into J again. *2449*
Ac 1: 8 and in all J, and in Samaria, and unto *2449*
2: 9 and in J, and Cappadocia, in Pontus, and *2449*
2:14 Ye men of J, and all *ye* that dwell at *2453*
8: 1 abroad throughout the regions of J *2449*
9:31 Then had the churches rest throughout all J *2449*
10:37 which was published throughout all J, and *2449*
11: 1 brethren that were in J heard that *2449*
11:29 relief unto the brethren which dwelt in J: *2449*
12:19 And he went down from J to Cesarea, and *2449*
15: 1 And certain *men* which came down from J *2449*
21:10 there came down from J a certain prophet, *2449*
26:20 and throughout all the coasts of J, and *then* *2449*
28:21 We neither received letters out of J *2449*
Ro 15:31 from them that do not believe in J; *2449*
2Co 1:16 of you to be brought on *my* way toward J. *2449*
Gal 1:22 the churches of J which were in Christ: *2449*
1Th 2:14 of God which in J are in Christ Jesus: *2449*

JUDEAN See JEHUDIJAH; JUDAH

JUDGE (191) [JUDGED, JUDGES, JUDGEST, JUDGETH, JUDGING, JUDGMENT, JUDGMENTS]
Ge 15:14 that nation, whom they shall serve, will I j: 1777
16: 5 the LORD j between me and thee. 8199
18:25 Shall not the J of all the earth do right? 8199
19: 9 to sojourn, and he will **needs be a j**: 8199+8199
31:37 that they may j betwixt us both. 3198
31:53 the God of their father, j betwixt us. 8199
49:16 Dan shall j his people, as one of the tribes 1777
Ex 2:14 Who made thee a prince and a j over us? 8199
5:21 The LORD look upon you, and j; 8199
18:13 the morrow, that Moses sat to j the people: 8199
18:16 I j between one and another, and I do make 8199
18:22 let them j the people at all seasons: and 8199
18:22 but every small matter they shall j: 8199
Lev 19:15 in righteousness shalt thou j thy neighbour. 8199
Nu 35:24 the congregation shall j between the slayer 8199
Dt 1:16 j righteously between every man and his 8199
16:18 they shall j the people *with* just judgment. 8199
17: 9 unto the j that shall be in those days, 8199
17:12 or unto the j, even that man shall die: 8199
25: 1 unto judgment, that *the judges* may j them; 8199
25: 2 that the j shall cause him to lie down, and 8199
32:36 For the LORD shall j his people, and 1777
Jdg 2:18 the LORD was with the j, and 8199
2:18 hand of their enemies all the days of the j: 8199
2:19 when the j was dead, *that* they returned, 8199
11:27 the LORD the J be judge *this* day between 8199
11:27 the LORD the Judge be j *this* day between 8199
1Sa 2:10 the LORD shall j the ends of the earth; 1777
2:25 sin against another, the j shall judge him: 430
2:25 sin against another, the judge shall j him: 6419
3:13 For I have told him that I will j his house 8199
8: 5 now make us a king to j us like all 8199
8: 6 when they said, Give us a king to j us. 8199
8:20 that our king may j us, and go out before 8199
24:12 The LORD j between me and thee, and 8199
24:15 The LORD therefore be j, and 1781
24:15 j between me and thee, and see, and 8199
2Sa 15: 4 Oh that I were made j in the land, 8199
1Ki 3: 9 thy servant an understanding heart to j thy 8199
3: 9 for who is able to j this thy *so* great a 8199
7: 7 a porch for the throne where he might j, 8199
8:32 do, and j thy servants, condemning 8199
1Ch 16:33 because he cometh to j the earth. 8199
2Ch 1:10 for who can j this thy people, *that is so* 8199
1:11 for thyself, that thou mayest j my people, 8199
6:23 do, and j thy servants, by requiting 8199
19: 6 for ye j not for man, but for the LORD, 8199
20:12 O our God, wilt thou not j them? for we 8199
Ezr 7:25 which may j all the people that *are* beyond 1778
Job 9:15 *but* I would make supplication to my j. 8199
22:13 can he j through the dark *cloud*? 8199
23: 7 so should I be delivered for ever from my j. 8199
31:28 *were* an iniquity *to be punished by* the j: 6416
Ps 7: 8 The LORD shall j the people: judge me, 1777
7: 8 j me, O LORD, according to my 8199
9: 8 he shall j the world in righteousness, 8199
10:18 To j the fatherless and the oppressed, 8199
26: 1 J me, O LORD; for I have walked in mine 8199
35:24 J me, O LORD my God, according to thy 8199
43: 1 J me, O God, and plead my cause against 8199
50: 4 and to the earth, that *he* may j his people. 1777
50: 6 for God *is* j himself. Selah. 8199
54: 1 by thy name, and j me by thy strength. 1777
58: 1 do ye j uprightly, O ye sons of men? 8199
67: 4 for thou shalt j the people righteously, and 8199
68: 5 of the fatherless, and a j of the widows, 1781
72: 2 He shall j thy people with righteousness, 1777
72: 4 He shall j the poor of the people, he shall 8199
75: 2 receive the congregation I will j uprightly. 8199
75: 7 God *is* the j: he putteth down one, and 8199
82: 2 How long will ye j unjustly, and accept 8199
82: 8 Arise, O God, j the earth: for thou shalt 8199
94: 2 Lift up thyself, thou j of the earth: render a 8199
96:10 be moved: he shall j the people righteously. 1777
96:13 for he cometh, for he cometh to j the earth: 8199
96:13 he shall j the world with righteousness, and 8199
98: 9 the LORD; for he cometh to j the earth: 8199
98: 9 with righteousness shall he j the world, and 8199
110: 6 He shall j among the heathen, he shall fill 1777
135:14 For the LORD will j his people, and 1777

J

Pr	31: 9	j righteously, and plead the cause of	8199
Ecc	3:17	God shall j the righteous and the wicked:	8199
Isa	1:17	j the fatherless, plead for the widow.	8199
	1:23	they j not the fatherless, neither doth	8199
	2: 4	he shall j among the nations, and	8199
	3: 2	the j, and the prophet, and the prudent, and	8199
	3:13	*up* to plead, and standeth to j the people.	1777
	5: 3	j, I pray you, betwixt me and my vineyard.	8199
	11: 3	he shall not j after the sight of his eyes,	8199
	11: 4	with righteousness shall he j the poor, and	8199
	33:22	For the LORD *is* our j, the LORD *is* our	8199
	51: 5	and mine arms shall j the people;	8199
Jer	5:28	they j not the cause, the cause of	1777
	5:28	and the right of the needy do they not j.	8199
La	3:59	thou hast seen my wrong: j thou my cause.	8199
Eze	7: 3	will j thee according to thy ways, and	8199
	7: 8	I will j thee according to thy ways, and	8199
	7:27	and according to their deserts will I j them;	8199
	11:10	I will j you in the border of Israel; and	8199
	11:11	*but* I will j you in the border of Israel:	8199
	16:38	I will j thee, as *women* that break wedlock	8199
	18:30	Therefore I will j you, O house of Israel,	8199
	20: 4	Wilt thou j them, son of man, wilt thou	8199
	20: 4	wilt thou j *them?* cause them to know	8199
	21:30	I will j thee in the place where thou wast	8199
	22: 2	Now, thou son of man, wilt thou j, wilt	8199
	22: 2	wilt thou judge, wilt thou j the bloody city?	8199
	23:24	they shall j thee according to their	8199
	23:36	of man, wilt thou j Aholah and Aholibah?	8199
	23:45	they shall j them after the manner of	8199
	24:14	shall they j thee, saith the Lord GOD.	8199
	33:20	I will j you every one after his ways.	8199
	34:17	Behold, I j between cattle and cattle,	8199
	34:20	will j between the fat cattle and	8199
	34:22	and I will j between cattle and cattle.	8199
	44:24	they shall j it according to my judgments:	8199
Joel	3:12	for there will I sit to j all the heathen round	8199
Am	2: 3	I will cut off the j from the midst thereof,	8199
Ob	1:21	saviours shall come up on mount Zion to j	8199
Mic	3:11	The heads thereof j for reward, and	8199
	4: 3	he shall j among many people, and	8199
	5: 1	they shall smite the j of Israel with a rod	8199
	7: 3	prince asketh, and the j *asketh* for a reward;	8199
Zec	3: 7	thou shalt also j my house, and shalt also	1777
Mt	5:25	any time the adversary deliver thee to the j,	*2923*
	5:25	and the j deliver thee to the officer, and	*2923*
	7: 1	J not, that ye be not judged.	*2919*
	7: 2	For with what judgment ye j, ye shall be	*2919*
Lk	6:37	J not, and ye shall not be judged:	*2919*
	12:14	who made me a j or a divider over you?	*1348*
	12:57	why even of yourselves j ye not what *is*	*2919*
	12:58	lest he hale thee to the j, and the judge	*2923*
	12:58	and the j deliver thee to the officer, and	*2923*
	18: 2	Saying, There was in a city a j,	*2923*
	18: 6	the Lord said, Hear what the unjust j saith.	*2923*
	19:22	Out of thine own mouth will I j thee,	*2919*
Jn	5:30	as I hear, I j: and my judgment is just;	*2919*
	7:24	J not according to the appearance, but	*2919*
	7:24	the appearance, but j righteous judgment.	*2919*
	7:51	Doth our law j any man, before it hear him,	*2919*
	8:15	Ye j after the flesh; I judge no *man.*	*2919*
	8:15	Ye judge after the flesh; I j no *man.*	*2919*
	8:16	And yet if I j, my judgment is true: for I am	*2919*
	8:26	I have many *things* to say and to j of you:	*2919*
	12:47	hear my words, and believe not, I j him not:	*2919*
	12:47	for I came not to j the world, but to save	*2919*
	12:48	the same shall j him in the last day.	*2919*
	18:31	ye him, and j him according to your law.	*2919*
Ac	4:19	hearken unto you more than unto God, j ye.	*2919*
	7: 7	to whom they shall be in bondage will I j,	*2919*
	7:27	Who made thee a ruler and a j over us?	*1348*
	7:35	saying, Who made thee a ruler and a j?	*1348*
	10:42	was ordained of God *to be* the J of quick	*2923*
	13:46	j yourselves unworthy of everlasting life,	*2919*
	17:31	in the which he will j the world in	*2919*
	18:15	look ye *to it;* for I will be no j of such	*2923*
	23: 3	for sittest thou to j me after the law, and	*2919*
	24:10	been of many years a j unto this nation,	*2923*
Ro	2:16	In the day when God shall j the secrets of	*2919*
	2:27	j thee, who by the letter and	*2919*
	3: 6	for then how shall God j the world?	*2919*
	14: 3	let not him which eateth not j him that	*2919*
	14:10	But why dost thou j thy brother? or why	*2919*
	14:13	us not therefore j one another any more:	*2919*
	14:13	but j this rather, that no *man* put a	*2919*
1Co	4: 3	man's judgment: yea, I j not mine own self.	*350*
	4: 5	Therefore j nothing before the time,	*2919*
	5:12	For what have I to do to j them also that are	*2919*
	5:12	do not ye j them that are within?	*2919*
	6: 2	Do ye not know that the saints shall j	*2919*
	6: 2	are ye unworthy to j the smallest matters?	*2922*
	6: 3	Know ye not that we shall j angels?	*2919*
	6: 4	**set** them **to** j who are least esteemed in	*2523*
	6: 5	not one that shall be able to j between his	*1252*
	10:15	I speak as to wise *men;* j ye what I say.	*2919*
	11:13	J in yourselves: is it comely that a woman	*2919*
	11:31	For if we would j ourselves, we should not	*1252*
	14:29	speak two or three, and let the other j.	*1252*
2Co	5:14	because we thus j, that if one died for all,	*2919*
Col	2:16	Let no *man* therefore j you in meat,	*2919*
2Ti	4: 1	who shall j the quick and the dead at his	*2919*
	4: 8	which the Lord, the righteous j, shall give	*2923*
Heb	10:30	And again, The Lord shall j his people.	*2919*
	12:23	and to God the J of all, and to the spirits of	*2923*
	13: 4	whoremongers and adulterers God will j.	*2919*
Jas	4:11	but if thou j the law, thou art not a doer of	*2919*
	4:11	thou art not a doer of the law, but a j.	*2923*
	5: 9	the j standeth before the door.	*2923*
1Pe	4: 5	account to him that is ready to j the quick	*2919*
Rev	6:10	dost thou not j and avenge our blood on	*2919*
	19:11	and in righteousness he doth j and	*2919*

JUDGED (63) [JUDGE]

Ge	30: 6	God hath j me, and hath also heard my	1777
Ex	18:26	they j the people at all seasons: the hard	8199
	18:26	but every small matter they j themselves.	8199
Jdg	3:10	and he j Israel, and went out to war:	8199
	4: 4	wife of Lapidoth, she j Israel at that time.	8199
	10: 2	he j Israel twenty and three years, and died,	8199
	10: 3	and j Israel twenty and two years.	8199
	12: 7	Jephthah j Israel six years. Then died	8199
	12: 8	And after him Ibzan of Beth-lehem j Israel.	8199
	12: 9	for his sons. And he j Israel seven years.	8199
	12:11	after him Elon, a Zebulonite, j Israel; and	8199
	12:11	judged Israel; and he j Israel ten years.	8199
	12:13	the son of Hillel, a Pirathonite, j Israel.	8199
	12:14	ten ass colts: and he j Israel eight years.	8199
	15:20	he j Israel in the days of the Philistines	8199
	16:31	his father. And he j Israel twenty years.	8199
1Sa	4:18	and heavy. And he had j Israel forty years.	8199
	7: 6	Samuel j the children of Israel in Mizpeh.	8199
	7:15	And Samuel j Israel all the days of his life.	8199
	7:16	and Mizpeh, and j Israel in all those places.	8199
	7:17	there he j Israel; and there he built an altar	8199
1Ki	3:28	heard of the judgment which the king had j;	8199
2Ki	23:22	from the days of the judges that j Israel,	8199
Ps	9:19	let the heathen be j in thy sight.	8199
	37:33	in his hand, nor condemn him when he is j.	8199
	109: 7	When he shall be j, let him be condemned:	8199
Jer	22:16	He j the cause of the poor and needy; then	1777
Eze	16:38	that break wedlock and shed blood are j;	4941
	16:52	Thou also, which hast j thy sisters,	6419
	28:23	the wounded shall be j in the midst of her	5307
	35:11	known amongst them, when I have j thee.	8199
	36:19	and according to their doings I j them.	8199
Da	9:12	against us, and against our judges that j us,	8199
Mt	7: 1	Judge not, that ye be not j.	*2919*
	7: 2	with what judgment ye judge, ye shall be j:	*2919*
Lk	6:37	Judge not, and ye shall not be j:	*2919*
	7:43	And he said unto him, Thou hast rightly j.	*2919*
Jn	16:11	because the prince of this world is j.	*2919*
Ac	16:15	If ye have j me to be faithful to the Lord,	*2919*
	24: 6	and would have j according to our law.	*2919*
	25: 9	and there be j of these *things* before me?	*2919*
	25:10	judgment seat, where I ought to be j:	*2919*
	25:20	and there be j of these *matters.*	*2919*
	26: 6	am j for the hope of the promise made of	*2919*
Ro	2:12	as many as have sinned in the law shall be j	*2919*
	3: 4	and mightest overcome when thou art j.	*2919*
	3: 7	his glory; why yet am I also j as a sinner?	*2919*
1Co	2:15	all *things,* yet he himself is j of no *man.*	*350*
	4: 3	a very small *thing* that I should be j of you,	*350*
	5: 3	but present in spirit, have j already,	*2919*
	6: 2	and if the world shall be j by you, are ye	*2919*
	10:29	for why is my liberty j of another *man's*	*2919*
	11:31	would judge ourselves, we should not be j.	*2919*
	11:32	But when we are j, we are chastened of	*2919*
	14:24	he is convinced of all, he is j of all:	*350*

Heb 11:11 she j him faithful who had promised. 2233
Jas 2:12 as they that shall be j by the law of liberty. 2919
1Pe 4: 6 that they might be j according to men in 2919
Rev 11:18 that *they* should be j, and that *thou* 2919
16: 5 and shalt be, because thou hast j thus. 2919
19: 2 for he hath j the great whore, which did 2919
20:12 the dead were j out of those *things* which 2919
20:13 they were j every man according to their 2919

JUDGES (52) [JUDGE]

Ex 21: 6 his master shall bring him unto the j; he shall 430
21:22 and he shall pay as the j determine. 6414
22: 8 of the house shall be brought unto the j, 430
22: 9 cause of both parties shall come before the j; 430
22: 9 *and* whom the j shall condemn, he shall pay 430
Nu 25: 5 Moses said unto the j of Israel, Slay ye 8199
Dt 1:16 I charged your j at that time, saying, 8199
16:18 J and officers shalt thou make thee in all 8199
19:17 before the priests and the j, which shall be 8199
19:18 the j shall make diligent inquisition: and 8199
21: 2 thy elders and thy j shall come forth, and 8199
25: 1 unto judgment, that *the j* may judge them; NIH
32:31 even our enemies themselves *being* j. 6414
Jos 8:33 and their elders, and officers, and their j, 8199
23: 2 for their j, and for their officers, and 8199
24: 1 and for their j, and for their officers; 8199
Jdg 2:16 Nevertheless the LORD raised up j, 8199
2:17 yet they would not hearken unto their j, 8199
2:18 when the LORD raised them up j, then 8199
Ru 1: 1 Now it came to pass in the days when the j 8199
1Sa 8: 1 was old, that he made his sons j over Israel. 8199
8: 2 Abiah: *they were* j in Beer-sheba. 8199
2Sa 7:11 *as* since the time that I commanded j *to be* 8199
2Ki 23:22 from the days of the j that judged Israel, 8199
1Ch 17: 6 spake I a word to any of the j of Israel, 8199
17:10 since the time that I commanded j *to be* 8199
23: 4 and six thousand *were* officers and j: 8199
26:29 business over Israel, for officers and j. 8199
2Ch 1: 2 to the j, and to every governor in all Israel, 8199
19: 5 he set j in the land throughout all 8199
19: 6 said to the j, Take heed what ye do: for ye 8199
Ezr 7:25 that *is* in thine hand, set magistrates and j, 1782
10:14 the elders of every city, and the j thereof, 8199
Job 9:24 he covereth the faces of the j thereof; if not, 8199
12:17 away spoiled, and maketh the j fools. 8199
31:11 yea, it *is* an iniquity *to be punished by* the j. 6414
Ps 2:10 O ye kings: be instructed, ye j of the earth. 8199
141: 6 When their j are overthrown in stony 8199
148:11 all people; princes, and all j of the earth: 8199
Pr 8:16 and nobles, *even* all the j of the earth. 8199
Isa 1:26 I will restore thy j as at the first, and 8199
40:23 he maketh the j of the earth as vanity. 8199
Da 3: 2 and the captains, the j, the treasurers, 148
3: 3 the governors and captains, the j, 148
9:12 against us, and against our j that judged us, 8199
Hos 7: 7 hot as an oven, and have devoured their j; 8199
13:10 thy j *of* whom thou saidst, Give me a king 8199
Zep 3: 3 *are* roaring lions; her j *are* evening wolves; 8199
Mt 12:27 *them* out? therefore they shall be your j. *2923*
Lk 11:19 *them* out? therefore shall they be your j. *2923*
Ac 13:20 And after that he gave *unto them* j about *2923*
Jas 2: 4 and are become j of evil thoughts? *2923*

JUDGEST (8) [JUDGE]

Ps 51: 4 thou speakest, *and* be clear when thou j. 8199
Jer 11:20 that j righteously, that triest the reins and 8199
Ro 2: 1 O man, whosoever thou art that j: *2919*
2: 1 for wherein thou j another, *2919*
2: 1 for thou that j doest the same *things*. *2919*
2: 3 that j them which do such *things*, and *2919*
14: 4 Who art thou that j another *man's* servant? *2919*
Jas 4:12 and to destroy: who art thou that j another? *2919*

JUDGETH (17) [JUDGE]

Job 21:22 seeing he j those that are high. 8199
36:31 For by them j he the people; he giveth meat 1777
Ps 7:11 God j the righteous, and God is angry *with* 8199
58:11 verily he is a God that j in the earth. 8199
82: 1 of the mighty; he j among the gods. 8199
Pr 29:14 The king that faithfully j the poor, 8199
Jn 5:22 For the Father j no *man*, but *2919*
8:50 own glory: there is *one* that seeketh and j. *2919*
12:48 not my words, hath *one* that j him: *2919*
1Co 2:15 But he that is spiritual j all *things*, yet he *350*
4: 4 hereby justified: but he that j me is the Lord. *350*
5:13 But them that are without God j. *2919*
Jas 4:11 and j his brother, speaketh evil of the law, *2919*
4:11 speaketh evil of the law, and j the law: *2919*
1Pe 1:17 who without respect of persons j according *2919*
2:23 committed *himself* to him that j *2919*
Rev 18: 8 for strong *is* the Lord God who j her. *2919*

JUDGING (6) [JUDGE]

2Ki 15: 5 over the house, j the people of the land. 8199
2Ch 26:21 the king's house, j the people of the land. 8199
Ps 9: 4 my cause; thou satest in the throne j right. 8199
Isa 16: 5 j, and seeking judgment, and 8199
Mt 19:28 twelve thrones, j the twelve tribes of Israel. *2919*
Lk 22:30 sit on thrones j the twelve tribes of Israel. *2919*

JUDGMENT (294) [JUDGE]

Ge 18:19 the way of the LORD, to do justice and j; 4941
Ex 12:12 all the gods of Egypt I will execute j: 8201
21:31 according to this j shall it be done unto 4941
23: 2 in a cause to decline after many to wrest *j*: NIH
23: 6 Thou shalt not wrest the j of thy poor in his 4941
28:15 thou shalt make the breastplate of j *with* 4941
28:29 Israel in the breastplate of j upon his heart, 4941
28:30 thou shalt put in the breastplate of j 4941
28:30 Aaron shall bear the j of the children of 4941
Lev 19:15 Ye shall do no unrighteousness in j: 4941
19:35 Ye shall do no unrighteousness in j, 4941
Nu 27:11 be unto the children of Israel a statute of j, 4941
27:21 who shall ask *counsel* for him after the j of 4941
35:12 until he stand before the congregation in j. 4941
35:29 So these *things* shall be for a statute of j 4941
Dt 1:17 Ye shall not respect persons in j; *but* 4941
1:17 afraid of the face of man; for the j *is* God's: 4941
10:18 He doth execute the j of the fatherless and 4941
16:18 and they shall judge the people *with* just j. 4941
16:19 Thou shalt not wrest j; thou shalt not 4941
17: 8 If there arise a matter too hard for thee in j, 4941
17: 9 and they shall shew thee the sentence of j: 4941
17:11 according to the j which they shall tell thee, 4941
24:17 Thou shalt not pervert the j of the stranger, 4941
25: 1 they come unto j, that *the judges* may judge 4941
27:19 Cursed *be* he that perverteth the j of 4941
32: 4 for all his ways *are* j: a God of truth and 4941
32:41 and mine hand take hold on j; 4941
Jos 20: 6 until he stand before the congregation for j, 4941
Jdg 4: 5 the children of Israel came up to her for j. 4941
5:10 ye that sit in j, and walk by the way. 4055
1Sa 8: 3 after lucre, and took bribes, and perverted j. 4941
2Sa 8:15 David executed j and justice unto all his 4941
15: 2 had a controversy came to the king for j, 4941
15: 6 to all Israel that came to the king for j: 4941
1Ki 3:11 for thyself understanding to discern j; 4941
3:28 all Israel heard of the j which the king had 4941
3:28 that the wisdom of God *was* in him, to do j. 4941
7: 7 where he might judge, *even* the porch of j: 4941
10: 9 made he thee king, to do j and justice. 4941
20:40 So *shall* thy j *be*; thyself hast decided *it*. 4941
2Ki 25: 6 to Riblah; and they gave j upon him. 4941
1Ch 18:14 executed j and justice among all his people. 4941
2Ch 9: 8 he thee king over them, to do j and justice. 4941
19: 6 the LORD, who *is* with you in the j. 1697+4941
19: 8 for the j of the LORD, and 4941
20: 9 *as* the sword, j, or pestilence, or famine, 8196
22: 8 that when Jehu was **executing** j upon 8199
24:24 So they executed j against Joash. 8201
Ezr 7:26 let j be executed speedily upon him, 1780
Est 1:13 manner towards all that knew law and j: 1779
Job 8: 3 Doth God pervert j? or doth the Almighty 4941
9:19 if of j, who shall set me a time *to plead?* 4941
9:32 *and* we should come together in j. 4941
14: 3 a one, and bringest me into j with thee? 4941
19: 7 am not heard: I cry aloud, but *there is* no j. 4941
19:29 of the sword, that ye may know *there is* a j. 1779
22: 4 fear of thee? will he enter with thee into j? 4941
27: 2 *As* God liveth, *who* hath taken away my j; 4941
29:14 my j *was* as a robe and a diadem. 4941
32: 9 neither do the aged understand j. 4941
34: 4 Let us choose to us j: let us know among 4941
34: 5 and God hath taken away my j. 4941
34:12 neither will the Almighty pervert j. 4941
34:23 *right;* that *he* should enter into j with God. 4941
35:14 thou shalt not see him, *yet* j *is* before him; 1779
36:17 thou hast fulfilled the j of the wicked: 1779

Job	36:17	the wicked: j and justice take hold on *thee.*	1779
	37:23	in power, and *in* j, and *in* plenty of justice:	4941
	40: 8	Wilt thou also disannul my j? wilt thou	4941
Ps	1: 5	the ungodly shall not stand in the j,	4941
	7: 6	awake for me *to* the j *that* thou hast	4941
	9: 7	for ever: he hath prepared his throne for j.	4941
	9: 8	he shall **minister** j to the people in	1777
	9:16	The LORD is known *by* the j *which* he	4941
	25: 9	The meek will he guide in j: and the meek	4941
	33: 5	He loveth righteousness and j: the earth is	4941
	35:23	Stir up thyself, and awake to my j,	4941
	37: 6	as the light, and thy j as the noonday.	4941
	37:28	For the LORD loveth j, and forsaketh not	4941
	37:30	and his tongue talketh of j.	4941
	72: 2	with righteousness, and thy poor with j.	4941
	76: 8	Thou didst cause j to be heard from	1779
	76: 9	When God arose to j, to save all the meek	4941
	89:14	and j *are* the habitation of thy throne:	4941
	94:15	j shall return unto righteousness: and all	4941
	97: 2	and j *are* the habitation of his throne.	4941
	99: 4	The king's strength also loveth j; thou dost	4941
	99: 4	thou executest j and righteousness in Jacob.	4941
	101: 1	I will sing of mercy and j: unto thee,	4941
	103: 6	and j for all that are oppressed.	4941
	106: 3	Blessed *are* they that keep j, *and* he that	4941
	106:30	stood up Phinehas, and **executed** j: and	6419
	111: 7	The works of his hands *are* verity and j;	4941
	119:66	Teach me good j and knowledge: for I have	2940
	119:84	when wilt thou execute j on them that	4941
	119:121	I have done j and justice: leave me not to	4941
	119:149	O LORD, quicken me according to thy j.	4941
	122: 5	For there are set thrones of j, the thrones of	4941
	143: 2	enter not into j with thy servant: for in thy	4941
	146: 7	Which executeth j for the oppressed:	4941
	149: 9	To execute upon them the j written:	4941
Pr	1: 3	of wisdom, justice, and j, and equity;	4941
	2: 8	*He* keepeth the paths of j, and	4941
	2: 9	understand righteousness, and j, and equity;	4941
	8:20	in the midst of the paths of j:	4941
	13:23	but there is *that is* destroyed for want of j.	4941
	16:10	the king: his mouth transgresseth not in j.	4941
	17:23	out of the bosom to pervert the ways of j.	4941
	18: 5	the wicked, to overthrow the righteous in j.	4941
	19:28	An ungodly witness scorneth j: and	4941
	20: 8	A king that sitteth in the throne of j	1779
	21: 3	j *is* more acceptable to the LORD than	4941
	21: 7	destroy them; because they refuse to do j.	4941
	21:15	*It is* joy to the just to do j: but	4941
	24:23	*is* not good to have respect of persons in j.	4941
	28: 5	Evil men understand not j: but they that	4941
	29: 4	The king by j stablisheth the land: but	4941
	29:26	*every* man's j *cometh* from the LORD.	4941
	31: 5	and pervert the j of any of the afflicted.	1779
Ecc	3:16	I saw under the sun the place of j,	4941
	5: 8	violent perverting of j and justice in a	4941
	8: 5	*man's* heart discerneth *both* time and j.	4941
	8: 6	to every purpose there is time and j,	4941
	11: 9	all these *things* God will bring thee into j.	4941
	12:14	For God shall bring every work into j,	4941
Isa	1:17	seek j, relieve the oppressed, judge	4941
	1:21	*it was* full of j; righteousness lodged in it;	4941
	1:27	Zion shall be redeemed with j, and	4941
	3:14	The LORD will enter into j with	4941
	4: 4	from the midst thereof by the spirit of j,	4941
	5: 7	he looked for j, but behold oppression;	4941
	5:16	the LORD of hosts shall be exalted in j,	4941
	9: 7	to stablish it with j and with justice from	4941
	10: 2	To turn aside the needy from j, and to take	1779
	16: 3	Take counsel, execute j; make thy shadow	6415
	16: 5	and seeking j, and hasting righteousness.	4941
	28: 6	for a spirit of j to him that sitteth in	4941
	28: 6	a spirit of judgment to him that sitteth in j,	4941
	28: 7	they err in vision, they stumble *in* j.	6417
	28:17	J also will I lay to the line, and	4941
	30:18	for the LORD *is* a God of j: blessed *are* all	4941
	32: 1	in righteousness, and princes shall rule in j.	4941
	32:16	j shall dwell in the wilderness, and	4941
	33: 5	he hath filled Zion *with* j and	4941
	34: 5	and upon the people of my curse, to j.	4941
	40:14	taught him in the path of j, and taught him	4941
	40:27	and my j is passed over from my God?	4941
	41: 1	them speak: let us come near together to j.	4941
	42: 1	he shall bring forth j to the Gentiles.	4941
	42: 3	not quench: he shall bring forth j unto truth.	4941
	42: 4	till he have set j in the earth:	4941
	49: 4	*yet* surely my j *is* with the LORD, and	4941
	51: 4	I will make my j to rest for a light of	4941
	53: 8	He was taken from prison and from j: and	4941
	54:17	every tongue *that* shall rise against thee in j	4941
	56: 1	saith the LORD, Keep ye j, and do justice:	4941
	59: 8	know not; and *there is* no j in their goings:	4941
	59: 9	Therefore is j far from us, neither doth	4941
	59:11	we look for j, but *there is* none;	4941
	59:14	j is turned away backward, and	4941
	59:15	and it displeased him that *there was* no j.	4941
	61: 8	For I the LORD love j, I hate robbery for	4941
Jer	4: 2	in truth, in j, and in righteousness;	4941
	5: 1	find a man, if there be *any* that executeth j,	4941
	5: 4	way of the LORD, *nor* the j of their God.	4941
	5: 5	way of the LORD, *and* the j of their God:	4941
	7: 5	if you throughly execute j between a man	4941
	8: 7	my people know not the j of the LORD.	4941
	9:24	j, and righteousness, in the earth:	4941
	10:24	O LORD, correct me, but with j; not in	4941
	21:12	Execute j in the morning, and deliver *him*	4941
	22: 3	Execute ye j and righteousness, and	4941
	22:15	do j and justice, *and* then *it was* well with	4941
	23: 5	and shall execute j and justice in the earth.	4941
	33:15	he shall execute j and righteousness in	4941
	39: 5	land of Hamath, where he gave j upon him.	4941
	48:21	j is come upon the plain country;	4941
	48:47	saith the LORD. Thus far *is* the j of Moab.	4941
	49:12	they whose j *was* not to drink of the cup	4941
	51: 9	for her j reacheth unto heaven, and is lifted	4941
	51:47	that I will **do** j upon the graven images of	6485
	51:52	that I will **do** j upon her graven images:	6485
	52: 9	land of Hamath; where he gave j upon him.	4941
Eze	18: 8	hath executed true j between man and man,	4941
	23:10	for they had executed j upon her.	8196
	23:24	I will set j before them, and they shall	4941
	34:16	and the strong; I will feed them with j.	4941
	39:21	all the heathen shall see my j that I have	4941
	44:24	in controversy they shall stand in j; *and*	4941
	45: 9	and spoil, and execute j and justice,	4941
Da	4:37	all whose works *are* truth, and his ways j:	1780
	7:10	the j was set, and the books were opened.	1780
	7:22	j *was* given to the saints of the most High;	1780
	7:26	the j shall sit, and they shall take away his	1780
Hos	2:19	in j, and in lovingkindness, and in mercies.	4941
	5: 1	for j *is* toward you, because ye have been a	4941
	5:11	Ephraim *is* oppressed *and* broken in j,	4941
	10: 4	thus j springeth up as hemlock in	4941
	12: 6	keep mercy and j, and wait on thy God	4941
Am	5: 7	*Ye* who turn j to wormwood, and leave off	4941
	5:15	love the good, and establish j in the gate:	4941
	5:24	let j run down as waters, and	4941
	6:12	for ye have turned j into gall, and the fruit	4941
Mic	3: 1	house of Israel; *is it* not for you to know j?	4941
	3: 8	*of* j, and *of* might, to declare unto Jacob his	4941
	3: 9	that abhor j, and pervert all equity.	4941
	7: 9	he plead my cause, and execute j for me:	4941
Hab	1: 4	law is slacked, and j doth never go forth:	4941
	1: 4	therefore wrong j proceedeth.	4941
	1: 7	their j and their dignity shall proceed of	4941
	1:12	O LORD, thou hast ordained them for j;	4941
Zep	2: 3	of the earth, which have wrought his j;	4941
	3: 5	every morning doth he bring his j to light,	4941
Zec	7: 9	Execute true j, and shew mercy and	4941
	8:16	**execute the** j of truth and peace in	4941+8199
Mal	2:17	in them; or, Where *is* the God of j?	4941
	3: 5	I will come near to you to j; and I will be a	4941
Mt	5:21	shall kill shall be in danger of the j:	*2920*
	5:22	without a cause shall be in danger of the j:	*2920*
	7: 2	For with what j ye judge, ye shall be	*2917*
	10:15	of Sodom and Gomorrha in the day of j,	*2920*
	11:22	tolerable for Tyre and Sidon at the day of j,	*2920*
	11:24	for the land of Sodom in the day of j,	*2920*
	12:18	and he shall shew j to the Gentiles.	*2920*
	12:20	not quench, till he send forth j unto victory.	*2920*
	12:36	shall give account thereof in the day of j.	*2920*
	12:41	*The* men of Nineveh shall rise in j with this	*2920*
	12:42	*The* queen of the south shall rise up in the j	*2920*
	23:23	*matters* of the law, j, mercy, and faith:	*2920*
	27:19	When he was set down on the j **seat**,	*968*
Mk	6:11	for Sodom and Gomorrha in the day of j,	*2920*
Lk	10:14	more tolerable for Tyre and Sidon at the j,	*2920*
	11:31	*The* queen of the south shall rise up in the j	*2920*
	11:32	*The* men of Nineveh shall rise up in the j	*2920*

Lk	11:42	and pass over j and the love of God:	*2920*
Jn	5:22	but hath committed all j unto the Son:	*2920*
	5:27	And hath given him authority to execute j	*2920*
	5:30	and my j is just; because I seek not mine	*2920*
	7:24	to the appearance, but judge righteous j.	*2920*
	8:16	And yet if I judge, my j is true: for I am not	*2920*
	9:39	Jesus said, For j I am come into this world,	*2917*
	12:31	Now is the j of this world: now shall	*2920*
	16: 8	world of sin, and of righteousness, and of j:	*2920*
	16:11	Of j, because the prince of this world is	*2920*
	18:28	they Jesus from Caiaphas unto the **hall of j**:	*4232*
	18:28	they themselves went not into the **j hall**,	*4232*
	18:33	Then Pilate entered into the **j hall** again,	*4232*
	19: 9	And went again into the **j hall**, and	*4232*
	19:13	sat down in the **j seat** in a place *that is* called	*968*
Ac	8:33	In his humiliation his j was taken away:	*2920*
	18:12	against Paul, and brought him to the **j seat**,	*968*
	18:16	And he drave them from the **j seat**.	*968*
	18:17	and beat *him* before the **j seat**.	*968*
	23:35	him to be kept in Herod's **j hall**.	*4232*
	24:25	and j to come, Felix trembled,	*2917*
	25: 6	and the next day sitting in the **j seat**,	*968*
	25:10	Then said Paul, I stand at Cesar's **j seat**,	*968*
	25:15	*me,* desiring *to have* j against him.	*1349*
	25:17	on the morrow I sat on the **j seat**, and	*968*
Ro	1:32	Who knowing the j of God, that they which	*1345*
	2: 2	But we are sure that the j of God is	*2917*
	2: 3	that thou shalt escape the j of God?	*2917*
	2: 5	and revelation of the **righteous** j of God;	*1341*
	5:16	for the j *was* by one to condemnation, but	*2917*
	5:18	Therefore as by the offence of one *j came*	NIG
	14:10	for we shall all stand before the **j seat** of	*968*
1Co	1:10	in the same mind and in the same j.	*1106*
	4: 3	I should be judged of you, or of man's j:	*2250*
	7:25	yet I give *my* j, as one that hath obtained	*1106*
	7:40	she is happier if she so abide, after my j:	*1106*
2Co	5:10	For we must all appear before the **j seat** of	*968*
Gal	5:10	but he that troubleth you shall bear *his* j,	*2917*
Php	1: 9	yet more and more in knowledge and *in* all j;	*144*
2Th	1: 5	*Which is* a manifest token of the righteous j	*2920*
1Ti	5:24	sins are open beforehand, going before to j;	*2920*
Heb	6: 2	of resurrection of the dead, and of eternal j.	*2917*
	9:27	unto men once to die, but after this the j:	*2920*
	10:27	But a certain fearful looking for of j and	*2920*
Jas	2: 6	and draw you before the **j seats**?	*2922*
	2:13	For he shall have j without mercy, that hath	*2920*
	2:13	no mercy; and mercy rejoiceth against j.	*2920*
1Pe	4:17	For the time *is come* that j must begin at	*2917*
2Pe	2: 3	whose j now of a long time lingereth not,	*2917*
	2: 4	chains of darkness, *to be* reserved unto j;	*2920*
	2: 9	to reserve the unjust unto the day of j *to be*	*2920*
	3: 7	reserved unto fire against the day of j and	*2920*
1Jn	4:17	that we may have boldness in the day of j:	*2920*
Jude	1: 6	under darkness unto the j of the great day.	*2920*
	1:15	To execute j upon all, and to convince all	*2920*
Rev	14: 7	glory to him; for the hour of his j is come:	*2920*
	17: 1	I will shew unto thee the j of the great	*2917*
	18:10	mighty city! for in one hour is thy j come.	*2920*
	20: 4	sat upon them, and j was given unto them:	*2917*

JUDGMENTS (127) [JUDGE]

Ex	6: 6	with a stretched out arm, and with great j:	8201
	7: 4	out of the land of Egypt by great j.	8201
	21: 1	Now these *are* the j which thou shalt set	4941
	24: 3	all the words of the LORD, and all the j:	4941
Lev	18: 4	Ye shall do my j, and keep mine	4941
	18: 5	therefore keep my statutes, and my j:	4941
	18:26	therefore keep my statutes and my j,	4941
	19:37	all my statutes, and all my j, and do them:	4941
	20:22	all my statutes, and all my j, and do them:	4941
	25:18	my statutes, and keep my j, and do them;	4941
	26:15	or if your soul abhor my j, so that *ye* will	4941
	26:43	even because they despised my j, and	4941
	26:46	These *are* the statutes and j and laws,	4941
Nu	33: 4	their gods also the LORD executed j.	8201
	35:24	the revenger of blood according to these j:	4941
	36:13	These *are* the commandments and the j,	4941
Dt	4: 1	O Israel, unto the statutes and unto the j,	4941
	4: 5	Behold, I have taught you statutes and j,	4941
	4: 8	that hath statutes and j *so* righteous as all	4941
	4:14	me at that time to teach you statutes and j,	4941
	4:45	the testimonies, and the statutes, and the j,	4941
	5: 1	and j which I speak in your ears *this* day,	4941
	5:31	the statutes, and the j, which thou shalt	4941
	6: 1	the commandments, the statutes, and the j,	4941
	6:20	the testimonies, and the statutes, and the j,	4941
	7:11	and the statutes, and the j,	4941
	7:12	if ye hearken to these j, and keep, and	4941
	8:11	his j, and his statutes, which I command	4941
	11: 1	and his j, and his commandments alway.	4941
	11:32	and j which I set before you *this* day.	4941
	12: 1	These *are* the statutes and j, which ye shall	4941
	26:16	commanded thee to do these statutes and j:	4941
	26:17	and his j, and to hearken unto his voice:	4941
	30:16	and his statutes and his j,	4941
	33:10	They shall teach Jacob thy j, and Israel thy	4941
	33:21	justice of the LORD, and his j with Israel.	4941
2Sa	22:23	For all his j *were* before me: and *as for* his	4941
1Ki	2: 3	and his j, and his testimonies,	4941
	6:12	execute my j, and keep all my	4941
	8:58	and his statutes, and his j,	4941
	9: 4	*and* wilt keep my statutes and my j:	4941
	11:33	*to keep* my statutes and my j, as *did* David	4941
1Ch	16:12	his wonders, and the j of his mouth;	4941
	16:14	LORD our God; his j *are* in all the earth.	4941
	22:13	j which the LORD charged Moses with	4941
	28: 7	to do my commandments and my j,	4941
2Ch	7:17	and shalt observe my statutes and my j;	4941
	19:10	and commandment, statutes and j,	4941
Ezr	7:10	to do *it,* and to teach in Israel statutes and j.	4941
Ne	1: 7	nor the statutes, nor the j,	4941
	9:13	gavest them right j, and true laws,	4941
	9:29	sinned against thy j, (which if a man do,	4941
	10:29	LORD our Lord, and his j and his statutes;	4941
Ps	10: 5	thy j *are* far above out of his sight:	4941
	18:22	For all his j *were* before me, and I did not	4941
	19: 9	the j of the LORD *are* true *and*	4941
	36: 6	the great mountains; thy j *are* a great deep:	4941
	48:11	of Judah be glad, because of thy j.	4941
	72: 1	Give the king thy j, O God, and	4941
	89:30	forsake my law, and walk not in my j;	4941
	97: 8	because of thy j, O LORD.	4941
	105: 5	his wonders, and the j of his mouth;	4941
	105: 7	LORD our God: his j *are* in all the earth.	4941
	119: 7	when I shall have learned thy righteous j.	4941
	119:13	With my lips have I declared all the j of thy	4941
	119:20	longing *that it hath* unto thy j at all times.	4941
	119:30	way of truth: thy j have I laid *before me.*	4941
	119:39	reproach which I fear: for thy j *are* good.	4941
	119:43	out of my mouth; for I have hoped in thy j.	4941
	119:52	I remembered thy j of old, O LORD; and	4941
	119:62	thanks unto thee because of thy righteous j.	4941
	119:75	that thy j *are* right, and *that* thou *in*	4941
	119:102	I have not departed from thy j: for thou hast	4941
	119:106	perform *it,* that *I* will keep thy righteous j.	4941
	119:108	my mouth, O LORD, and teach me thy j.	4941
	119:120	for fear of thee; and I am afraid of thy j.	4941
	119:137	*art* thou, O LORD, and upright *are* thy j.	4941
	119:156	O LORD: quicken me according to thy j.	4941
	119:160	every one of thy righteous j *endureth* for	4941
	119:164	do I praise thee because of thy righteous j.	4941
	119:175	it shall praise thee; and let thy j help me.	4941
	147:19	his statutes and his j unto Israel.	4941
	147:20	*as for his* j, they have not known them.	4941
Pr	19:29	J are prepared for scorners, and stripes for	8201
Isa	26: 8	Yea, *in* the way of thy j, O LORD,	4941
	26: 9	for when thy j *are* in the earth,	4941
Jer	1:16	I will utter my j against them touching all	4941
	12: 1	yet let me talk with thee of *thy* j.	4941
Eze	5: 6	she hath changed my j into wickedness	4941
	5: 6	for they have refused my j, and my statutes,	4941
	5: 7	in my statutes, neither have kept my j,	4941
	5: 7	neither have done according to the j of	4941
	5: 8	will execute j in the midst of thee in	4941
	5:10	I will execute j in thee, and the whole	8201
	5:15	when I shall execute j in thee in anger and	8201
	11: 9	of strangers, and will execute j among you.	8201
	11:12	neither executed my j, but have done after	4941
	14:21	much more when I send my four sore j	8201
	16:41	execute j upon thee in the sight of many	8201
	18: 9	and hath kept my j, to deal truly;	4941
	18:17	hath executed my j, hath walked in my	4941
	20:11	shewed them my j, which *if* a man do, he	4941
	20:13	they despised my j, which *if* a man do, he	4941
	20:16	Because they despised my j, and walked	4941
	20:18	neither observe their j, nor defile	4941
	20:19	in my statutes, and keep my j, and do them;	4941
	20:21	neither kept my j to do them, which *if* a	4941

J

Eze 20:24 Because they had not executed my **j**, but 4941
20:25 and **j** whereby they should not live; 4941
23:24 they shall judge thee according to their **j**. 4941
25:11 I will execute **j** upon Moab; and they shall 8201
28:22 when I shall have executed **j** in her, and 8201
28:26 when I have executed **j** upon all those that 8201
30:14 set fire in Zoan, and will execute **j** in No. 8201
30:19 Thus will I execute **j** in Egypt: and 8201
36:27 and ye shall keep my **j**, and do *them.* 4941
37:24 they shall also walk in my **j**, and 4941
44:24 *and* they shall judge it according to my **j**: 4941
Da 9: 5 departing from thy precepts and from thy **j**: 4941
Hos 6: 5 and thy **j** *are as* the light *that* goeth forth. 4941
Zep 3:15 The LORD hath taken away thy **j**, he hath 4941
Mal 4: 4 Horeb for all Israel, *with* the statutes and **j**. 4941
Ro 11:33 how unsearchable *are* his **j**, and his ways *2917*
1Co 6: 4 ye have **j** *of things* pertaining to *this* life, *2922*
Rev 15: 4 before thee; for thy **j** are made manifest. *1345*
16: 7 God Almighty, true and righteous *are* thy **j**. *2920*
19: 2 For true and righteous *are* his **j**: for he hath *2920*

JUDITH (1)
Ge 26:34 to wife **J** the daughter of Beeri the Hittite, 3067

JUG See CRUSE

JUICE (1)
SS 8: 2 of spiced wine, of the **j** of my pomegranate. 6071

JULIA (1)
Ro 16:15 and **J**, Nereus, and his sister, and Olympas, *2456*

JULIUS (2)
Ac 27: 1 certain other prisoners unto *one* named **J**, *2457*
27: 3 And **J** courteously entreated Paul, and *2457*

JUMPING (1)
Na 3: 2 of the pransing horses, and of the **j** chariots. 7540

JUNIA (1)
Ro 16: 7 Salute Andronicus and **J**, my kinsmen, and *2458*

JUNIAS See JUNIA

JUNIPER (4)
1Ki 19: 4 and came and sat down under a **j tree**: 7574
19: 5 as he lay and slept under a **j tree**, 7574
Job 30: 4 by the bushes, and **j** roots *for* their meat. 7574
Ps 120: 4 Sharp arrows of the mighty, with coals of **j**. 7574

JUPITER (3)
Ac 14:12 And they called Barnabas, **J**; and Paul, *2203*
14:13 Then the priest of **J**, which was before their *2203*
19:35 and of the *image* which **fell down from J**? *1356*

JURISDICTION (1)
Lk 23: 7 he knew that he belonged unto Herod's **j**, *1849*

JUSHABHESED (1)
1Ch 3:20 Ohel, and Berechiah, and Hasadiah, **J**, five. 3142

JUST (94) [JUSTICE, JUSTIFICATION, JUSTIFIED, JUSTIFIER, JUSTIFIETH, JUSTIFY, JUSTIFYING, JUSTLY, UNJUST]
Ge 6: 9 Noah was a **j** man *and* perfect in his 6662
Lev 19:36 **J** balances, just weights, a just ephah, and 6664
19:36 **j** weights, a just ephah, and a just hin, 6664
19:36 just weights, a **j** ephah, and a just hin, 6664
19:36 just weights, a just ephah, and a **j** hin, 6664
Dt 16:18 they shall judge the people *with* **j** 6664
16:20 That which is **altogether j** shalt thou 6664+6664
25:15 *But* thou shalt have a perfect and **j** weight, 6664
25:15 a perfect and **j** measure shalt thou have: 6664
32: 4 and without iniquity, **j** and right *is* he. 6662
2Sa 23: 3 He that ruleth over men *must be* **j**, ruling *in* 6662
Ne 9:33 Howbeit thou *art* **j** in all that is brought 6662
Job 4:17 Shall mortal man be more **j** than God? 6663
9: 2 a truth: but how should man be **j** with God? 6663
12: 4 the **j** upright *man is* laughed to scorn. 6662
27:17 He may prepare *it,* but the **j** shall put *it* on, 6662
33:12 Behold, *in* this thou art not **j**: I will answer 6663
34:17 and wilt thou condemn him that is most **j**? 6662
Ps 7: 9 wicked come to an end; but establish the **j**: 6662
37:12 The wicked plotteth against the **j**, and 6662
Pr 3:33 but he blesseth the habitation of the **j**. 6662
4:18 the path of the **j** *is* as the shining light, 6662
9: 9 teach a **j** *man,* and he will increase in 6662
10: 6 Blessings *are* upon the head of the **j**: but 6662
10: 7 The memory of the **j** *is* blessed: but 6662
10:20 The tongue of the **j** *is as* choice silver: 6662
10:31 The mouth of the **j** bringeth forth wisdom: 6662
11: 1 to the LORD: but a **j** weight *is* his delight. 8003
11: 9 through knowledge shall the **j** be delivered. 6662
12:13 *his* lips: but the **j** shall come out of trouble. 6662
12:21 There shall no evil happen to the **j**: but 6662
13:22 the wealth of the sinner *is* laid up for the **j**. 6662
16:11 A **j** weight and balance *are* the LORD'S: 4941
17:15 the wicked, and he that condemneth the **j**, 6662
17:26 Also to punish the **j** *is* not good, *nor* to 6662
18:17 *He that is* first in his own cause *seemeth* **j**; 6662
20: 7 The **j** *man* walketh in his integrity: 6662
21:15 *It is* joy to the **j** to do judgment: but 6662
24:16 For a **j** *man* falleth seven *times,* and 6662
29:10 hate the upright: but the **j** seek his soul. 3477
29:27 An unjust man is an abomination to the **j**: 6662
Ecc 7:15 there is a **j** *man* that perisheth in his 6662
7:20 For *there is* not a **j** man upon earth, 6662
8:14 that there be **j** *men,* unto whom it 6662
Isa 26: 7 The way of the **j** *is* uprightness: thou, 6662
26: 7 most upright, dost weigh the path of the **j**. 6662
29:21 and turn aside the **j** for a thing of nought. 6662
45:21 a **j** God and a saviour; *there is* none beside 6662
La 4:13 that *have* shed the blood of the **j** in 6662
Eze 18: 5 if a man be **j**, and do that which is lawful 6662
18: 9 he *is* **j**, he shall surely live, saith the Lord 6662
45:10 Ye shall have **j** balances, and a just ephah, 6664
45:10 just balances, and a **j** ephah, and a just bath. 6664
45:10 just balances, and a just ephah, and a **j** bath. 6664
Hos 14: 9 *are* right, and the **j** shall walk in them: 6662
Am 5:12 they afflict the **j**, they take a bribe, and 6662
Hab 2: 4 in him: but the **j** shall live by his faith. 6662
Zep 3: 5 The **j** LORD *is* in the midst thereof; 6662
Zec 9: 9 he *is* **j**, and having salvation; lowly, and 6662
Mt 1:19 being a **j** *man,* and not willing to make her *1342*
5:45 and sendeth rain on the **j** and *on* the unjust. *1342*
13:49 and sever the wicked from among the **j**, *1342*
27:19 Have thou nothing to do with that **j** *man:* *1342*
27:24 I am innocent of the blood of this **j** *person:* *1342*
Mk 6:20 knowing that he *was* a **j** man and a holy, *1342*
Lk 1:17 and the disobedient to the wisdom of the **j**; *1342*
2:25 and the same man *was* **j** and devout, *1342*
14:14 be recompensed at the resurrection of the **j**. *1342*
15: 7 nine **j** *persons* which need no repentance. *1342*
20:20 which *should* feign themselves **j** *men,* that *1342*
23:50 *and he was* a good man, and a **j**: *1342*
Jn 5:30 and my judgment is **j**; because I seek not *1342*
Ac 3:14 But ye denied the Holy One and the **J**, and *1342*
7:52 shewed before of the coming of the **J One**; *1342*
10:22 a **j** man, and one that feareth God, and *1342*
22:14 and see *that* **J One**, and shouldest hear *1342*
24:15 of the dead, both of the **j** and unjust. *1342*
Ro 1:17 as it is written, The **j** shall live by faith. *1342*
2:13 (For not the hearers of the law *are* **j** before *1342*
3: 8 good may come? whose damnation is **j**. *1738*
3:26 that he might be **j**, and the justifier of him *1342*
7:12 the commandment holy, and **j**, and good. *1342*
Gal 3:11 *it is* evident: for, The **j** shall live by faith. *1342*
Php 4: 8 whatsoever *things are* **j**, whatsoever *things* *1342*
Col 4: 1 give unto *your* servants that which is **j** and *1342*
Tit 1: 8 of good *men,* sober, **j**, holy, temperate; *1342*
Heb 2: 2 disobedience received a **j recompence** of *1738*
10:38 Now the **j** shall live by faith: but if *any man* *1342*
12:23 and to the spirits of **j** *men* made perfect, *1342*
Jas 5: 6 Ye have condemned *and* killed the **j**; *and* *1342*
1Pe 3:18 the **j** for the unjust, that he might bring us *1342*
2Pe 2: 7 And delivered **j** Lot, vexed with the filthy *1342*
1Jn 1: 9 he is faithful and **j** to forgive us *our* sins, *1342*
Rev 15: 3 **j** and true *are* thy ways, thou King of saints. *1342*

JUSTICE (28) [JUST]
Ge 18:19 way of the LORD, to do **j** and judgment; 6666
Dt 33:21 he executed the **j** of the LORD, and 6666
2Sa 8:15 and **j** unto all his people. 6666
15: 4 might come unto me, and I would do him **j**. 6663
1Ki 10: 9 made he thee king, to do judgment and **j**. 6666
1Ch 18:14 and **j** among all his people. 6666
2Ch 9: 8 thee king over them, to do judgment and **j**. 6666
Job 8: 3 or doth the Almighty pervert **j**? 6664
36:17 judgment and **j** take hold on *thee.* 4941
37:23 and *in* judgment, and *in* plenty of **j**: 6666
Ps 82: 3 fatherless: **do j** to the afflicted and needy. 6663

Ps 89:14 **J** and judgment *are* the habitation of thy 6664
119:121 I have done judgment and **j**: leave me not 6664
Pr 1: 3 of wisdom, **j**, and judgment, and equity; 6664
8:15 By me kings reign, and princes decree **j**. 6664
21: 3 To do **j** and judgment *is* more acceptable to 6666
Ecc 5: 8 perverting of judgment and **j** in a province, 6664
Isa 9: 7 and with **j** from henceforth even for ever. 6666
56: 1 the LORD, Keep ye judgment, and do **j**: 6666
58: 2 they ask of me the ordinances of **j**; 6664
59: 4 None calleth for **j**, nor any pleadeth for 6664
59: 9 far from us, neither doth **j** overtake us: 6666
59:14 away backward, and **j** standeth afar off: 6666
Jer 22:15 do judgment and **j**, *and* then *it was* well 6666
23: 5 shall execute judgment and **j** in the earth. 6666
31:23 O habitation of **j**, *and* mountain of holiness. 6664
50: 7 the habitation of **j**, even the LORD, 6664
Eze 45: 9 and spoil, and execute judgment and **j**, 6666

JUSTIFICATION (3) [JUST]
Ro 4:25 and was raised *again* for our **j**. *1347*
5:16 but the free gift *is* of many offences unto **j**. *1345*
5:18 *free gift came* upon all men unto **j** of life. *1347*

JUSTIFIED (43) [JUST]
Job 11: 2 and should a man full of talk be **j**? 6663
13:18 ordered *my* cause; I know that I shall be **j**. 6663
25: 4 How then can man be **j** with God? or 6663
32: 2 because he **j** himself rather than God. 6663
Ps 51: 4 that thou mightest be **j** when thou speakest, 6663
143: 2 for in thy sight shall no *man* living be **j**. 6663
Isa 43: 9 forth their witnesses, that they may be **j**: 6663
43:26 declare thou, that thou mayest be **j**. 6663
45:25 the LORD shall all the seed of Israel be **j**, 6663
Jer 3:11 The backsliding Israel hath **j** herself more 6663
Eze 16:51 hast **j** thy sisters in all thine abominations 6663
16:52 thy shame, in that thou hast **j** thy sisters. 6663
Mt 11:19 sinners. But wisdom is **j** of her children. *1344*
12:37 For by thy words thou shalt be **j**, and by thy *1344*
Lk 7:29 that heard *him*, and the publicans, **j** God, *1344*
7:35 But wisdom is **j** of all her children. *1344*
18:14 this man went down to his house **j** *rather* *1344*
Ac 13:39 And by him all that believe are **j** from all *1344*
13:39 ye could not be **j** by the law of Moses. *1344*
Ro 2:13 but the doers of the law shall be **j**. *1344*
3: 4 That thou mightest be **j** in thy sayings, and *1344*
3:20 the law there shall no flesh be **j** in his sight: *1344*
3:24 Being **j** freely by his grace through *1344*
3:28 Therefore we conclude that a man is **j** by *1344*
4: 2 For if Abraham were **j** by works, he hath *1344*
5: 1 Therefore being **j** by faith, we have peace *1344*
5: 9 Much more then, being now **j** by his blood, *1344*
8:30 and whom he called, them he also **j**: and *1344*
8:30 and whom he **j**, them he also glorified. *1344*
1Co 4: 4 nothing by myself; yet am I not hereby **j**: *1344*
6:11 but ye are **j** in the name of the Lord Jesus, *1344*
Gal 2:16 Knowing that a man is not **j** by the works *1344*
2:16 that we might be **j** by the faith of Christ, *1344*
2:16 by the works of the law shall no flesh be **j**. *1344*
2:17 But if, while we seek to be **j** by Christ, *1344*
3:11 But that no *man* is **j** by the law in the sight *1344*
3:24 *us* unto Christ, that we might be **j** by faith. *1344*
5: 4 whosoever of you are **j** by the law; *1344*
1Ti 3:16 **j** in the Spirit, seen of angels, *1344*
Tit 3: 7 That being **j** by his grace, we should be *1344*
Jas 2:21 Was not Abraham our father **j** by works, *1344*
2:24 Ye see then how that by works a man is **j**, *1344*
2:25 Likewise also was not Rahab the harlot **j** by *1344*

JUSTIFIER (1) [JUST]
Ro 3:26 and the **j** of him which believeth in Jesus. *1344*

JUSTIFIETH (4) [JUST]
Pr 17:15 He that **j** the wicked, and he that 6663
Isa 50: 8 *He is* near that **j** me; who will contend with 6663
Ro 4: 5 but believeth on him that **j** the ungodly, *1344*
8:33 the charge of God's elect? *It is* God that **j**: *1344*

JUSTIFY (11) [JUST]
Ex 23: 7 slay thou not: for I will not **j** the wicked. 6663
Dt 25: 1 they shall **j** the righteous, and condemn 6663
Job 9:20 If I **j** myself, mine own mouth shall 6663
27: 5 God forbid that I should **j** you: till I die I 6663
33:32 answer me: speak, for I desire to **j** thee. 6663
Isa 5:23 Which **j** the wicked for reward, and 6663
53:11 shall my righteous servant **j** many; 6663
Lk 10:29 But he, willing to **j** himself, said unto Jesus, *1344*
16:15 Ye are they which **j** yourselves before men; *1344*
Ro 3:30 which shall **j** the circumcision by faith, and *1344*
Gal 3: 8 foreseeing that God would **j** the heathen *1344*

JUSTIFYING (2) [JUST]
1Ki 8:32 **j** the righteous, to give him according to his 6663
2Ch 6:23 by **j** the righteous, by giving him according 6663

JUSTLE (1)
Na 2: 4 they shall **j** one **against** another in 8264

JUSTLY (3) [JUST]
Mic 6: 8 to do **j**, and to love mercy, and to walk 4941
Lk 23:41 And we indeed **j**; for we receive the due *1346*
1Th 2:10 and God *also*, how holily and **j** and *1346*

JUSTUS (3)
Ac 1:23 who was surnamed **J**, and Matthias. *2459*
18: 7 named **J**, one that worshipped God, *2459*
Col 4:11 And Jesus, which is called **J**, who are of *2459*

JUTTAH (2)
Jos 15:55 Maon, Carmel, and Ziph, and **J**, 3194
21:16 **J** with her suburbs, *and* Beth-shemesh with 3194

K

KAB (1)
2Ki 6:25 the fourth part of a **k** of dove's dung for 6894

KABZEEL (3)
Jos 15:21 the coast of Edom southward were **K**, 6909
2Sa 23:20 the son of a valiant man, of **K**, who had 6909
1Ch 11:22 the son of a valiant man of **K**, who had 6909

KADESH (17) [KADESH-BARNEA, MERIBAH-KADESH]
Ge 14: 7 which *is* **K**, and smote all the country of 6946
16:14 behold, *it is* between **K** and Bered. 6946
20: 1 dwelled between **K** and Shur, and 6946
Nu 13:26 unto the wilderness of Paran, to **K**; 6946
20: 1 the people abode in **K**; and Miriam died 6946
20:14 Moses sent messengers from **K** unto 6946
20:16 behold, we *are* in **K**, a city in the uttermost 6946
20:22 journeyed from **K**, and came *unto* mount 6946
27:14 that *is* the water of Meribah in **K** *in* 6946
33:36 in the wilderness of Zin, which *is* **K**. 6946
33:37 they removed from **K**, and pitched in 6946
Dt 1:46 So ye abode in **K** many days, 6946
Jdg 11:16 unto the Red sea, and came to **K**; 6946
11:17 would not consent: and Israel abode in **K**. 6946
Ps 29: 8 the LORD shaketh the wilderness of **K**. 6946
Eze 47:19 Tamar *even* to the waters of strife *in* **K**, 6946
48:28 from Tamar *unto* the waters of strife *in* **K**, 6946

KADESH-BARNEA (10) [KADESH]
Nu 32: 8 when I sent them from **K** to see the land. 6947
34: 4 forth thereof shall be from the south to **K**, 6947
Dt 1: 2 Horeb *by* the way of mount Seir unto **K**.) 6947
1:19 God commanded us; and we came to **K**. 6947
2:14 the space in which we came from **K**, 6947
9:23 when the LORD sent you from **K**, 6947
Jos 10:41 Joshua smote them from **K** even unto Gaza, 6947
14: 6 man of God concerning me and thee in **K**. 6947
14: 7 sent me from **K** to espy out the land; 6947
15: 3 ascended up on the south side unto **K**, and 6947

KADMIEL (8)
Ezr 2:40 the children of Jeshua and **K**, of 6934
3: 9 his sons and his brethren, **K** and his sons, 6934
Ne 7:43 of **K**, *and* of the children of Hodevah, 6934
9: 4 Jeshua, and Bani, **K**, Shebaniah, Bunni, 6934
9: 5 Jeshua and **K**, Bani, Hashabniah, 6934
10: 9 Binnui of the sons of Henadad, **K**; 6934
12: 8 Jeshua, Binnui, **K**, Sherebiah, Judah, *and* 6934
12:24 Sherebiah, and Jeshua the son of **K**, 6934

KADMONITES (1)
Ge 15:19 The Kenites, and the Kenizzites, and the **K**, 6935

KALLAI (1)
Ne 12:20 Of Sallai, **K**; of Amok, Eber; 7040

KAMON See CAMON

KANAH (3)
Jos 16: 8 from Tappuah westward *unto* the river **K**; 7071
17: 9 the coast descended *unto* the river **K**, 7071
19:28 and Rehob, and Hammon, and **K**, 7071

KAREAH (13)
Jer 40: 8 Johanan and Jonathan the sons of **K**, and 7143
40:13 Moreover Johanan the son of **K**, and all 7143
40:15 Johanan the son of **K** spake to Gedaliah in 7143
40:16 of Ahikam said unto Johanan the son of **K**, 7143
41:11 when Johanan the son of **K**, and all 7143
41:13 with Ishmael saw Johanan the son of **K**, 7143
41:14 and went unto Johanan the son of **K**. 7143
41:16 took Johanan the son of **K**, and all 7143
42: 1 Johanan the son of **K**, and Jezaniah the son 7143
42: 8 called he Johanan the son of **K**, and all 7143
43: 2 Johanan the son of **K**, and all the proud 7143
43: 4 So Johanan the son of **K**, and all 7143
43: 5 Johanan the son of **K**, and all the captains 7143

KARKA See KARKAA

KARKAA (1)
Jos 15: 3 up to Adar, and fetched a compass to **K**: 7173

KARKOR (1)
Jdg 8:10 Now Zebah and Zalmunna *were* in **K**, and 7174

KARNAIM See ASHTEROTH KARNAIM

KARTAH (1)
Jos 21:34 with her suburbs, and **K** with her suburbs, 7177

KARTAN (1)
Jos 21:32 with her suburbs, and **K** with her suburbs; 7178

KATTATH (1)
Jos 19:15 **K**, and Nahallal, and Shimron, and Idalah, 7005

KEBAR See CHEBAR

KEDAR (12)
Ge 25:13 Nebajoth; and **K**, and Adbeel, and Mibsam, 6938
1Ch 1:29 then **K**, and Adbeel, and Mibsam, 6938
Ps 120: 5 *in* Mesech, *that* I dwell in the tents of **K**! 6938
SS 1: 5 as the tents of **K**, as the curtains of 6938
Isa 21:16 a hireling, and all the glory of **K** shall fail: 6938
21:17 the mighty *men* of the children of **K**, 6938
42:11 *their voice,* the villages *that* **K** doth inhabit: 6938
60: 7 All the flocks of **K** shall be gathered 6938
Jer 2:10 send *unto* **K**, and consider diligently, and 6938
49:28 Concerning **K**, and concerning 6938
49:28 go up to **K**, and spoil the men of the east. 6938
Eze 27:21 Arabia, and all the princes of **K**, 6938

KEDEMAH (2)
Ge 25:15 Hadar, and Tema, Jetur, Naphish, and **K**: 6929
1Ch 1:31 Jetur, Naphish, and **K**. These *are* the sons 6929

KEDEMOTH (4)
Dt 2:26 **K** unto Sihon king of Heshbon *with* words 6932
Jos 13:18 And Jahazah, and **K**, and Mephaath, 6932
21:37 **K** with her suburbs, and Mephaath with her 6932
1Ch 6:79 **K** also with her suburbs, and Mephaath 6932

KEDESH (11) [KEDESH-NAPHTALI]
Jos 12:22 The king of **K**, one; the king of Jokneam of 6943
15:23 And **K**, and Hazor, and Ithnan, 6943
19:37 And **K**, and Edrei, and En-hazor, 6943
20: 7 they appointed **K** in Galilee in mount 6943
21:32 of Naphtali, **K** in Galilee with her suburbs, 6943
Jdg 4: 9 Deborah arose, and went with Barak to **K**. 6943
4:10 Barak called Zebulun and Naphtali to **K**; 6943
4:11 unto the plain of Zaanaim, which *is* by **K**. 6943
2Ki 15:29 and **K**, and Hazor, and Gilead, and Galilee, 6943
1Ch 6:72 **K** with her suburbs, Daberath with her 6943
6:76 **K** in Galilee with her suburbs, and 6943

KEDESH-NAPHTALI (1) [KEDESH, NAPHTALI]
Jdg 4: 6 Barak the son of Abinoam out of **K**, 5321+6943

KEDORLAOMER See CHEDORLAOMER

KEEP (362) [DOORKEEPER, DOORKEEPERS, KEEPER, KEEPERS, KEEPEST, KEEPETH, KEEPING, KEPT]
Ge 2:15 the garden of Eden to dress it and to **k** it. 8104
3:24 every way, to **k** the way of the tree of life. 8104
6:19 into the ark, to **k** *them* **alive** with thee; 2421
6:20 *sort* shall come unto thee, to **k** *them* **alive**. 2421
7: 3 to **k** seed **alive** upon the face of all 2421
17: 9 Thou shalt **k** my covenant therefore, thou, 8104
17:10 which ye shall **k**, between me and you and 8104
18:19 they shall **k** the way of the LORD, to do 8104
28:15 will **k** thee in all *places* whither thou goest, 8104
28:20 will **k** me in this way that I go, and 8104
30:31 for me, I will again feed *and* **k** thy flock: 8104
33: 9 my brother; **k** that thou hast unto thyself. 1961
41:35 and let them **k** food in the cities. 8104
Ex 6: 5 whom the Egyptians **k in bondage**; 5647
12: 6 ye shall **k** it *up* until the fourteenth 1961+4931
12:14 you shall **k** it a feast to the LORD 2287
12:14 you shall **k** it **a feast** by an ordinance for 2287
12:25 hath promised, that ye shall **k** this service. 8104
12:47 All the congregation of Israel shall **k** it. 6213
12:48 will **k** the passover to the LORD, let all 6213
12:48 and then let him come near and **k** it; 6213
13: 5 that thou shalt **k** this service in this month. 5647
13:10 **k** this ordinance in his season from year to 8104
15:26 his commandments, and **k** all his statutes, 8104
16:28 How long refuse ye to **k** my 8104
19: 5 **k** my covenant, then ye shall be a peculiar 8104
20: 6 that love me, and **k** my commandments. 8104
20: 8 Remember the sabbath day, to **k** it **holy**. 6942
22: 7 unto his neighbour money or stuff to **k**, 8104
22:10 or an ox, or a sheep, or any beast, to **k**; 8104
23: 7 **K** thee **far** from a false matter; and 7368
23:14 Three times thou shalt **k** a **feast** unto me in 2287
23:15 Thou shalt **k** the feast of unleavened bread: 8104
23:20 to **k** thee in the way, and to bring thee into 8104
31:13 Verily my sabbaths ye shall **k**: 8104
31:14 Ye shall **k** the sabbath therefore; for it *is* 8104
31:16 Wherefore the children of Israel shall **k** 8104
34:18 The feast of unleavened bread shalt thou **k**: 8104
Lev 6: 2 in **that which was delivered** him **to k**, 6487
6: 4 which was **delivered** him **to k**, 854+6485+6487
8:35 **k** the charge of the LORD, that ye die not: 8104
18: 4 and **k** mine ordinances, to walk therein: 8104
18: 5 Ye shall therefore **k** my statutes, and my 8104
18:26 Ye shall therefore **k** my statutes and my 8104
18:30 Therefore ye shall **k** mine ordinance, 8104
19: 3 and his father, and **k** my sabbaths: 8104
19:19 Ye shall **k** my statutes. Thou shalt not let 8104
19:30 Ye shall **k** my sabbaths, and reverence my 8104
20: 8 ye shall **k** my statutes, and do them: I *am* 8104
20:22 Ye shall therefore **k** all my statutes, and all 8104
22: 9 They shall therefore **k** mine ordinance, 8104
22:31 Therefore shall ye **k** my commandments, 8104
23:39 ye shall **k** a feast unto the LORD seven 2287
23:41 ye shall **k** it **a feast** unto the LORD 2282+2287
25: 2 shall the land **k a sabbath** unto 7673+7676
25:18 and **k** my judgments, and do them; 8104
26: 2 Ye shall **k** my sabbaths, and reverence my 8104
26: 3 and **k** my commandments, and do them; 8104
Nu 1:53 the Levites shall **k** the charge of 8104
3: 7 they shall **k** his charge, and the charge of 8104
3: 8 they shall **k** all the instruments of 8104
3:32 *have* the oversight of them that **k** 8104
6:24 The LORD bless thee, and **k** thee: 8104
8:26 to **k** the charge, and shall do no service. 8104
9: 2 Let the children of Israel also **k** 6213
9: 3 ye shall **k** it in his appointed season: 6213
9: 3 to all the ceremonies thereof, shall ye **k** it. 6213
9: 4 of Israel, that they should **k** the passover. 6213
9: 6 that they could not **k** the passover on that 6213
9:10 yet he shall **k** the passover unto 6213
9:11 of the second month at even they shall **k** it, 6213
9:12 ordinances of the passover they shall **k** it. 6213
9:13 a journey, and forbeareth to **k** the passover, 6213
9:14 and will **k** the passover unto the LORD; 6213
18: 3 they shall **k** thy charge, and the charge of 8104
18: 4 **k** the charge of the tabernacle of 8104
18: 5 ye shall **k** the charge of the sanctuary, and 8104

Nu 18: 7 thy sons with thee shall **k** your priest's 8104
29:12 ye shall **k a feast** unto the LORD 2282+2287
31:18 by lying with him, **k alive** for yourselves. 2421
31:30 which **k** the charge of the tabernacle of 8104
36: 7 **k** himself to the inheritance of the tribe of 1692
36: 9 shall **k** himself to his own inheritance. 1692
Dt 4: 2 that *ye* may **k** the commandments of 8104
4: 6 **K** therefore and do *them;* for this *is* your 8104
4: 9 heed to thyself, and **k** thy soul diligently, 8104
4:40 Thou shalt **k** therefore his statutes, and his 8104
5: 1 ye may learn them, and **k**, and do them. 8104
5:10 that love me and **k** my commandments. 8104
5:12 **K** the sabbath day to sanctify it, as 8104
5:15 the LORD thy God commanded thee to **k** 6213
5:29 and **k** all my commandments always, 8104
6: 2 to **k** all his statutes and his commandments, 8104
6:17 You shall **diligently k** 8104+8104
7: 8 he would **k** the oath which he had sworn 8104
7: 9 **k** his commandments to a thousand 8104
7:11 Thou shalt therefore **k** the commandments, 8104
7:12 to these judgments, and **k**, and do them, 8104
7:12 that the LORD thy God shall **k** unto thee 8104
8: 2 whether thou wouldest **k** his 8104
8: 6 Therefore thou shalt **k** the commandments 8104
10:13 To **k** the commandments of the LORD, 8104
11: 1 **k** his charge, and his statutes, and 8104
11: 8 Therefore shall ye **k** all the commandments 8104
11:22 For if ye shall **diligently k** all these 8104+8104
13: 4 **k** his commandments, and obey his voice, 8104
13:18 to **k** all his commandments which I 8104
16: 1 **k** the passover unto the LORD thy God: 6213
16:10 thou shalt **k** the feast of weeks unto 6213
16:15 Seven days shalt thou **k a solemn feast** 2287
17:19 to **k** all the words of this law and 8104
19: 9 If thou shalt **k** all these commandments to 8104
23: 9 then **k** thee from every wicked thing. 8104
23:23 which is gone out of thy lips thou shalt **k** 8104
26:16 thou shalt therefore **k** and do them with all 8104
26:17 to **k** his statutes, and his commandments, 8104
26:18 that *thou* shouldest **k** all his 8104
27: 1 **K** all the commandments which I command 8104
28: 9 if thou shalt **k** the commandments of 8104
28:45 to **k** his commandments and his statutes 8104
29: 9 **K** therefore the words of this covenant, 8104
30:10 to **k** his commandments and his statutes 8104
30:16 to **k** his commandments and his statutes 8104
Jos 6:18 in any wise **k** *yourselves* from the accursed 8104
10:18 of the cave, and set men by it for to **k** them: 8104
22: 5 to **k** his commandments, and to cleave unto 8104
23: 6 Be ye therefore very courageous to **k** and 8104
Jdg 2:22 whether they will **k** the way of the LORD 8104
2:22 as their fathers did **k** *it,* or not. 8104
3:19 who said, **K silence**. And all that stood by 2013
Ru 2:21 Thou shalt **k fast** by my young men, 1692
1Sa 2: 9 He will **k** the feet of his saints, and 8104
7: 1 sanctified Eleazar his son to **k** the ark of 8104
2Sa 8: 2 to death, and *with* one full line to **k alive**. 2421
15:16 *which were* concubines, to **k** the house. 8104
16:21 which he hath left to **k** the house; 8104
18:18 no son to **k** my name **in remembrance**: 2142
20: 3 whom he had left to **k** the house, and 8104
1Ki 2: 3 **k** the charge of the LORD thy God, 8104
2: 3 to **k** his statutes, *and* his commandments, 8104
3:14 to **k** my statutes and my commandments, 8104
6:12 **k** all my commandments to walk in them; 8104
8:25 **k** with thy servant David my father that 8104
8:58 to **k** his commandments, and his statutes, 8104
8:61 and to **k** his commandments, as at this day. 8104
9: 4 *and* wilt **k** my statutes and my judgments: 8104
9: 6 will not **k** my commandments *and* 8104
11:33 *to* **k** my statutes and my judgments, as *did* NIH
11:38 to **k** my statutes and my commandments, 8104
20:39 a man unto me, and said, **K** this man: 8104
2Ki 11: 6 so shall ye **k** the watch of the house, that it 8104
11: 7 even they shall **k** the watch of the house of 8104
17:13 and **k** my commandments *and* my statutes, 8104
23: 3 to **k** his commandments and his testimonies 8104
23:21 **K** the passover unto the LORD your God, 6213
1Ch 4:10 that thou wouldest **k** *me* from evil, that it 6213
12:33 of war, fifty thousand, which could **k rank**: 5737
12:38 All these men of war, that could **k** rank, 5737
22:12 that *thou* mayest **k** the law of the LORD 8104
23:32 that they should **k** the charge of 8104
28: 8 **k** and seek for all the commandments of 8104
29:18 **k** this for ever in the imagination of 8104
29:19 to **k** thy commandments, thy testimonies, 8104
2Ch 6:16 **k** with thy servant David my father *that* 8104
13:11 for we **k** the charge of the LORD our 8104
22: 9 had no power to **k still** the kingdom. 6113
23: 6 all the people shall **k** the watch of 8104
28:10 now ye purpose to **k under** the children of 3533
30: 1 to **k** the passover unto the LORD God of 6213
30: 2 to **k** the passover in the second month. 6213
30: 3 For they could not **k** it at that time, because 6213
30: 5 that *they* should come to **k** the passover 6213
30:13 **k** the feast of unleavened bread in 6213
30:23 the whole assembly took counsel to **k** other 6213
34:31 to **k** his commandments, and 8104
35:16 to **k** the passover, and to offer burnt 6213
35:18 neither did all the kings of Israel **k** such a 6213
Ezr 8:29 **k** *them,* until ye weigh *them* before 8104
Ne 1: 9 and **k** my commandments, and do them; 8104
12:27 to **k** the dedication with gladness, both with 6213
13:22 *that* they should come *and* **k** the gates, 8104
Est 3: 8 all people; neither **k** they the king's laws: 6213
9:21 that they should **k** the fourteenth day of 6213
9:27 that they would **k** these two days according 6213
Job 14:13 that thou wouldest **k** me **secret**, until thy 5641
20:13 it not; but **k** it **still** within his mouth: 4513
Ps 12: 7 Thou shalt **k** them, O LORD, thou shalt 8104
17: 8 **K** me as the apple of the eye, hide me 8104
19:13 **K back** thy servant also from 2820
22:29 and none can **k alive** his own soul. 2421
25:10 truth unto such as **k** his covenant and 5341
25:20 O **k** my soul, and deliver me: let me not be 8104
31:20 thou shalt **k** them **secretly** in a pavilion 6845
33:19 from death, and to **k** them **alive** in famine. 2421
34:13 **K** thy tongue from evil, and thy lips from 5341
35:22 **k** not **silence**: O Lord, be not far from me. 2790
37:34 **k** his way, and he shall exalt thee to inherit 8104
39: 1 I will **k** my mouth with a bridle, while 8104
41: 2 LORD will preserve him, and **k** him **alive**; 2421
50: 3 God shall come, and shall not **k silence**: 2790
78: 7 works of God, but **k** his commandments: 5341
83: 1 **K** not thou **silence**, O God: hold not thy 1824
89:28 My mercy will I **k** for him for evermore, 8104
89:31 my statutes, and **k** not my commandments; 8104
91:11 charge over thee, to **k** thee in all thy ways. 8104
103: 9 neither will he **k** *his anger* for ever. 5201
103:18 To such as **k** his covenant, and to those that 8104
105:45 might observe his statutes, and **k** his laws. 5341
106: 3 Blessed *are* they that **k** judgment, *and* 8104
113: 9 He **maketh** the barren *woman* **to k** house, 3427
119: 2 Blessed *are* they that **k** his testimonies, *and* 5341
119: 4 Thou hast commanded *us* to **k** thy precepts 8104
119: 5 O that my ways were directed to **k** thy 8104
119: 8 I will **k** thy statutes: O forsake me not 8104
119:17 thy servant, *that* I may live, and **k** thy word. 8104
119:33 of thy statutes; and I shall **k** it *unto* the end. 5341
119:34 me understanding, and I shall **k** thy law; 5341
119:44 So shall I **k** thy law continually for ever 8104
119:57 I have said that *I* would **k** thy words. 8104
119:60 and delayed not to **k** thy commandments. 8104
119:63 fear thee, and of them that **k** thy precepts. 8104
119:69 I will **k** thy precepts with *my* whole heart. 5341
119:88 so shall I **k** the testimony of thy mouth. 8104
119:100 than the ancients, because I **k** thy precepts. 5341
119:101 every evil way, that I might **k** thy word. 8104
119:106 I will perform *it,* that *I* will **k** thy righteous 8104
119:115 for I will **k** the commandments of my God. 5341
119:129 therefore doth my soul **k** them. 5341
119:134 oppression of man: so will I **k** thy precepts. 8104
119:136 mine eyes, because they **k** not thy law. 8104
119:145 hear me, O LORD: I will **k** thy statutes. 5341
119:146 save me, and I shall **k** thy testimonies. 8104
127: 1 except the LORD **k** the city, 8104
132:12 If thy children will **k** my covenant and 8104
140: 4 **K** me, O LORD, from the hands of 8104
141: 3 before my mouth; **k** the door of my lips. 5341
141: 9 **K** me from the snare *which* they have laid 8104
Pr 2:11 preserve thee, understanding shall **k** thee: 5341
2:20 good *men,* and **k** the paths of the righteous. 8104
3: 1 but let thine heart **k** my commandments: 5341
3:21 thine eyes: **k** sound wisdom and discretion: 5341
3:26 and shall **k** thy foot from being taken. 8104
4: 4 my words: **k** my commandments, and live. 8104
4: 6 love her, and she shall **k** thee. 5341
4:13 let *her* not go: **k** her; for she *is* thy life. 5341

Pr 4:21 **k** them in the midst of thine heart. 8104
4:23 **K** thy heart with all diligence; for out of it 5341
5: 2 and *that* thy lips may **k** knowledge. 5341
6:20 **k** thy father's commandment, and 5341
6:22 when thou sleepest, it shall **k** thee; and 8104
6:24 To **k** thee from the evil woman, from 8104
7: 1 **k** my words, and lay up my commandments 8104
7: 2 **K** my commandments, and live; and 8104
7: 5 That *they* may **k** thee from the strange 8104
8:32 for blessed *are they that* **k** my ways. 8104
22: 5 he that doth **k** his soul shall be far from 8104
22:18 For *it is* a pleasant *thing* if thou **k** them 8104
28: 4 but such as **k** the law contend with them. 8104
Ecc 3: 6 a time to **k**, and a time to cast away; 8104
3: 7 a time to **k silence**, and a time to speak; 2814
5: 1 **K** thy foot when thou goest to the house of 8104
8: 2 I *counsel thee* to **k** the king's 8104
12:13 Fear God, and **k** his commandments: 8104
SS 8:12 those that **k** the fruit thereof two hundred. 5201
Isa 26: 3 Thou wilt **k** *him in* perfect peace, *whose* 5341
27: 3 I the LORD do **k** it; I will water it every 5341
27: 3 lest *any* hurt it, I will **k** it night and day. 5341
41: 1 **K silence** before me, O islands; and let 2790
42: 6 will **k** thee, and give thee for a covenant of 5341
43: 6 Give *up;* and to the south, **K** not **back**: 3607
56: 1 the LORD, **K** ye judgment, and do justice: 8104
56: 4 unto the eunuchs that **k** my sabbaths, 8104
62: 6 mention of the LORD, **k** not silence, 3807.1
65: 6 I will not **k** silence, but will recompense, NIH
Jer 3: 5 will he **k** *it* to the end? Behold, thou hast 8104
3:12 the LORD, *and* I will not **k** *anger* for ever. 5201
31:10 and **k** him as a shepherd *doth* his flock. 8104
42: 4 unto you; I will **k** nothing **back** from you. 4513
La 2:10 of Zion sit upon the ground, *and* **k silence**: 1826
Eze 11:20 and **k** mine ordinances, and do them: 8104
18:21 **k** all my statutes, and do that which is 8104
20:19 and **k** my judgments, and do them; 8104
36:27 and ye shall **k** my judgments, and do *them.* 8104
43:11 that they may **k** the whole form thereof, 8104
44:16 unto me, and they shall **k** my charge. 8104
44:24 they shall **k** my laws and my statutes in all 8104
Da 9: 4 and to them that **k** his commandments; 8104
Hos 12: 6 **k** mercy and judgment, and wait on thy 8104
Am 5:13 Therefore the prudent shall **k silence** in that 1826
Mic 7: 5 **k** the doors of thy mouth from her that lieth 8104
Na 1:15 O Judah, **k** thy solemn feasts, perform thy 2287
2: 1 **k** the munition, watch the way, make *thy* 5341
Hab 2:20 let all the earth **k silence** before him. 2013
Zec 3: 7 if thou wilt **k** my charge, then thou shalt 8104
3: 7 shalt also **k** my courts, and I will give thee 8104
13: 5 for man taught me *to* **k** cattle from my NIH
14:16 of hosts, and to **k** the feast of tabernacles. 2287
14:18 come not up to **k** the feast of tabernacles. 2287
14:19 come not up to **k** the feast of tabernacles. 2287
Mal 2: 7 For the priest's lips should **k** knowledge, 8104
Mt 19:17 wilt enter into life, **k** the commandments. *5083*
26:18 I will **k** the passover at thy house with my *4160*
Mk 7: 9 of God, that ye may **k** your own tradition. *5083*
Lk 4:10 give his angels charge over thee, to **k** thee: *1314*
8:15 **k** *it,* and bring forth fruit with patience. *2722*
11:28 *are* they that hear the word of God, and **k** it. *5442*
19:43 thee round, and **k** thee **in** on every side, *4912*
Jn 8:51 I say unto you, If a man **k** my saying, *5083*
8:52 and thou sayest, If a man **k** my saying, *5083*
8:55 unto you: but I know him, and **k** his saying. *5083*
12:25 he that hateth his life in this world shall **k** it *5442*
14:15 If ye love me, **k** my commandments. *5083*
14:23 If a man love me, he will **k** my words: *5083*
15:10 If ye **k** my commandments, ye shall abide *5083*
15:20 kept my saying, they will **k** yours also. *5083*
17:11 **k** through thine own name those whom *5083*
17:15 that thou shouldest **k** them from the evil. *5083*
Ac 5: 3 and to **k back** *part* of the price of the land? *3557*
10:28 *thing* for a man *that is* a Jew to **k company**, *2853*
12: 4 to four quaternions of soldiers to **k** him; *5442*
15: 5 to command *them* to **k** the law of Moses. *5083*
15:24 *Ye must* be circumcised, and **k** the law: *5083*
15:29 from which if ye **k** yourselves, ye shall do *1301*
16: 4 they delivered them the decrees for to **k**, *5442*
16:23 charging the jailor to **k** them safely: *5083*
18:21 I must by all means **k** *this* feast that cometh *4160*
21:25 **k** themselves **from** things offered to idols, *5442*
24:23 And he commanded a centurion to **k** Paul, *5083*
Ro 2:25 verily profiteth, if thou **k** the law: *4238*
2:26 Therefore if the uncircumcision **k** *5442*
1Co 5: 8 Therefore let us **k the feast**, not with old *1858*
5:11 I have written unto you not to **k company**, *4874*
7:37 decreed in his heart that *he* will **k** his *5083*
9:27 But I **k under** my body, and bring *it* into *5299*
11: 2 me in all *things,* and **k** the ordinances, *2722*
14:28 let him **k silence** in the church; *4601*
14:34 Let your women **k silence** in the churches: *4601*
15: 2 if ye **k in memory** what I preached unto *2722*
2Co 11: 9 burdensome to you, and *so* will I **k** *myself.* *5083*
Gal 6:13 themselves who are circumcised **k** the law; *5442*
Eph 4: 3 Endeavouring to **k** the unity of the Spirit in *5083*
Php 4: 7 shall **k** your hearts and minds through *5432*
2Th 3: 3 shall stablish you, and **k** *you* from evil. *5442*
1Ti 5:22 partaker of other *men's* sins: **k** thyself pure. *5083*
6:14 That thou **k** *this* commandment without *5083*
6:20 **k** that which is committed to *thy* trust, *5442*
2Ti 1:12 I am persuaded that he is able to **k** that *5442*
1:14 **k** by the Holy Ghost which dwelleth in us. *5442*
Jas 1:27 *and* to **k** himself unspotted from the world. *5083*
2:10 For whosoever shall **k** the whole law, and *5083*
1Jn 2: 3 we know him, if we **k** his commandments. *5083*
3:22 because we **k** his commandments, and *5083*
5: 2 we love God, and **k** his commandments. *5083*
5: 3 love of God, that we **k** his commandments: *5083*
5:21 Little children, **k** yourselves from idols. *5442*
Jude 1:21 **K** yourselves in the love of God, *5083*
1:24 Now unto him that is able to **k** you **from** *5442*
Rev 1: 3 **k** those *things* which are written therein: *5083*
3:10 I also will **k** thee from the hour of *5083*
12:17 which **k** the commandments of God, and *5083*
14:12 here *are* they that **k** the commandments of *5083*
22: 9 of them which **k** the sayings of this book: *5083*

KEEPER (21) [KEEP]

Ge 4: 2 Abel was a **k** of sheep, but Cain was a tiller 7462
4: 9 he said, I know not: *Am* I my brother's **k**? 8104
39:21 gave him favour in the sight of the **k** of 8269
39:22 the **k** of the prison committed to Joseph's 8269
39:23 The **k** of the prison looked not to any thing 8269
1Sa 17:20 left the sheep with a **k**, and took, and went, 8104
17:22 David left his carriage in the hand of the **k** 8104
28: 2 Therefore will I make thee **k** of mine head 8104
2Ki 22:14 the son of Harhas, **k** of the wardrobe; 8104
2Ch 34:22 the son of Hasrah, **k** of the wardrobe; 8104
Ne 2: 8 a letter unto Asaph the **k** of the king's 8104
3:29 son of Shechaniah, the **k** of the east gate. 8104
Est 2: 3 the king's chamberlain, **k** of the women; 8104
2: 8 to the custody of Hegai, **k** of the women. 8104
2:15 the **k** of the women, appointed. 8104
Job 27:18 as a moth, and as a booth *that* the **k** maketh. 5341
Ps 121: 5 The LORD *is* thy **k**: the LORD *is* thy 8104
SS 1: 6 they made me the **k** of the vineyards; *but* 5201
Jer 35: 4 the son of Shallum, the **k** of the door: 8104
Ac 16:27 And the **k of the prison** awaking out of his *1200*
16:36 And the **k of the prison** told this saying to *1200*

KEEPERS (21) [KEEP]

2Ki 11: 5 even be **k** of the watch of the king's house; 8104
22: 4 which the **k** of the door have gathered of 8104
23: 4 the **k** of the door, to bring forth out of 8104
25:18 second priest, and the three **k** of the door: 8104
1Ch 9:19 the service, **k** of the gates of the tabernacle: 8104
9:19 the host of the LORD, *were* **k** of the entry. 8104
Est 6: 2 the king's chamberlains, the **k** of the door, 8104
Ecc 12: 3 In the day when the **k** of the house shall 8104
SS 5: 7 the **k** of the walls took away my vail from 8104
8:11 he let out the vineyard unto **k**; 5201
Jer 4:17 As **k** of a field, are they against her round 8104
52:24 second priest, and the three **k** of the door: 8104
Eze 40:45 the priests, the **k** of the charge of the house. 8104
40:46 the priests, the **k** of the charge of the altar: 8104
44: 8 ye have set **k** of my charge in my sanctuary 8104
44:14 I will make them **k** of the charge of 8104
Mt 28: 4 And for fear of him the **k** did shake, and *5083*
Ac 5:23 the **k** standing without before the doors: *5441*
12: 6 and *the* **k** before the door kept the prison. *5441*
12:19 he examined the **k**, and commanded that *5441*
Tit 2: 5 *To be* discreet, chaste, **k at home**, good, *3626*

KEEPEST (4) [KEEP]

1Ki 8:23 who **k** covenant and mercy with thy 8104
2Ch 6:14 which **k** covenant, and *shewest* mercy unto 8104
Ne 9:32 terrible God, who **k** covenant and mercy, 8104

Ac 21:24 thyself also walkest orderly, and **k** the law. *5442*

KEEPETH (46) [KEEP]
Ex 21:18 with *his* fist, and he die not, but **k** *his* bed: 5307
Dt 7: 9 which **k** covenant and mercy with them that 8104
1Sa 16:11 the youngest, and behold, he **k** the sheep. 7462
Ne 1: 5 that **k** covenant and mercy for them that 8104
Job 33:18 He **k back** his soul from the pit, and his life 2820
Ps 34:20 He **k** all his bones: not one of them is 8104
121: 3 be moved: he that **k** thee will not slumber. 8104
121: 4 he that **k** Israel shall neither slumber nor 8104
146: 6 all that therein is: which **k** truth for ever: 8104
Pr 2: 8 *He* **k** the paths of judgment, and 5341
10:17 He *is in* the way of life that **k** instruction: 8104
13: 3 He that **k** his mouth keepeth his life: *but* 5341
13: 3 He that keepeth his mouth **k** his life: *but* 8104
13: 6 Righteousness **k** *him that is* upright in 5341
16:17 he that **k** his way preserveth his soul. 5341
19: 8 he that **k** understanding shall find good. 8104
19:16 He that **k** the commandment keepeth his 8104
19:16 He that keepeth the commandment **k** his 8104
21:23 Whoso **k** his mouth and his tongue keepeth 8104
21:23 and his tongue **k** his soul from troubles. 8104
24:12 the heart consider *it?* and he that **k** thy soul, 5341
27:18 Whoso **k** the fig tree shall eat the fruit 5341
28: 7 Whoso **k** the law *is* a wise son: but he that 5341
29: 3 he that **k company with** harlots spendeth 7462
29:11 but a wise *man* **k** it in *till* afterwards. 7623
29:18 but he that **k** the law, happy *is* he. 8104
Ecc 8: 5 Whoso **k** the commandment shall feel no 8104
Isa 26: 2 that the righteous nation which **k** the truth 8104
56: 2 that **k** the sabbath from polluting it, and 8104
56: 2 and **k** his hand from doing any evil. 8104
56: 6 every one that **k** the sabbath from polluting 8104
Jer 48:10 cursed *be* he that **k back** his sword from 4513
La 3:28 He sitteth alone and **k silence**, because 1826
Hab 2: 5 *he is* a proud man, neither **k at home**, 5115
Lk 11:21 When a strong *man* armed **k** his palace, his *5442*
Jn 7:19 you the law, and *yet* none of you **k** the law? *4160*
9:16 of God, because he **k** not the sabbath day. *5083*
14:21 and **k** them, he it is that loveth me: *5083*
14:24 He that loveth me not **k** not my sayings: *5083*
1Jn 2: 4 and **k** not his commandments, is a liar, and *5083*
2: 5 But whoso **k** his word, in him verily is *5083*
3:24 And he that **k** his commandments dwelleth *5083*
5:18 but he that is begotten of God **k** himself, *5083*
Rev 2:26 and **k** my works unto the end, *5083*
16:15 and **k** his garments, lest he walk naked, and *5083*
22: 7 blessed *is* he that **k** the sayings of *5083*

KEEPING (12) [KEEP]
Ex 34: 7 **K** mercy for thousands, forgiving iniquity 5341
Nu 3:28 six hundred, **k** the charge of the sanctuary. 8104
3:38 **k** the charge of the sanctuary for the charge 8104
Dt 8:11 in not **k** his commandments, and 8104
1Sa 25:16 all the while we were with them **k** 7462
Ne 12:25 *were* porters **k** the ward at the thresholds of 8104
Ps 19:11 *and* in **k** of them *there is* great reward. 8104
Eze 17:14 *but* that by **k** of his covenant it might stand. 8104
Da 9: 4 **k** the covenant and mercy to them that love 8104
Lk 2: 8 **k watch** over their flock by night. *5438+5442*
1Co 7:19 but the **k** of the commandments of God. *5084*
1Pe 4:19 **commit the k** of their souls *to him* in well *3908*

KEHELATHAH (2)
Nu 33:22 journeyed from Rissah, and pitched in **K**. 6954
33:23 they went from **K**, and pitched in mount 6954

KEILAH (18)
Jos 15:44 **K**, and Achzib, and Mareshah; nine cities 7084
1Sa 23: 1 the Philistines fight against **K**, and they rob 7084
23: 2 Go, and smite the Philistines, and save **K**. 7084
23: 3 if we come *to* **K** against the armies of 7084
23: 4 and said, Arise, go down *to* **K**; 7084
23: 5 So David and his men went *to* **K**, and 7084
23: 5 So David saved the inhabitants of **K**. 7084
23: 6 the son of Ahimelech fled to David *to* **K**, 7084
23: 7 it was told Saul that David was come *to* **K**. 7084
23: 8 to go down *to* **K**, to besiege David and his 7084
23:10 heard that Saul seeketh to come to **K**, 7084
23:11 Will the men of **K** deliver me up into his 7084
23:12 Will the men of **K** deliver me and my men 7084
23:13 arose and departed out of **K**, and 7084
23:13 told Saul that David was escaped from **K**; 7084
1Ch 4:19 the father of **K** the Garmite, and 7084
Ne 3:17 the ruler of the half part of **K**, in his part. 7084
3:18 of Henadad, the ruler of the half part of **K**. 7084

KELAIAH (1)
Ezr 10:23 Jozabad, and Shimei, and **K**, (the same *is* 7041

KELAL See CHELAL

KELITA (3)
Ezr 10:23 and Shimei, and Kelaiah, (the same *is* **K**,) 7042
Ne 8: 7 **K**, Azariah, Jozabad, Hanan, Pelaiah, and 7042
10:10 Shebaniah, Hodijah, **K**, Pelaiah, Hanan, 7042

KELUB See CHELUB

KELUHI See CHELLUH

KEMUEL (3)
Ge 22:21 Buz his brother, and **K** the father of Aram, 7055
Nu 34:24 children of Ephraim, **K** the son of Shiphtan. 7055
1Ch 27:17 Of the Levites, Hashabiah the son of **K**: 7055

KENAANAH See CHENAANAH

KENAN (1)
1Ch 1: 2 **K**, Mahalaleel, Jered, 7018

KENANI See CHENANI

KENANIAH See CHENANIAH

KENATH (2)
Nu 32:42 Nobah went and took **K**, and the villages 7079
1Ch 2:23 from them, with **K**, and the towns thereof, 7079

KENAZ (11)
Ge 36:11 Omar, Zepho, and Gatam, and **K**. 7073
36:15 duke Omar, duke Zepho, duke **K**, 7073
36:42 Duke **K**, duke Teman, duke Mibzar, 7073
Jos 15:17 Othniel the son of **K**, the brother of Caleb, 7073
Jdg 1:13 Othniel the son of **K**, Caleb's younger 7073
3: 9 delivered them, *even* Othniel the son of **K**, 7073
3:11 forty years. And Othniel the son of **K** died. 7073
1Ch 1:36 and Gatam, **K**, and Timna, and Amalek. 7073
1:53 Duke **K**, duke Teman, duke Mibzar, 7073
4:13 the sons of **K**; Othniel, and Seraiah: and 7073
4:15 and Naam: and the sons of Elah, even **K**. 7073

KENEZITE (3)
Nu 32:12 Save Caleb the son of Jephunneh the **K**, 7074
Jos 14: 6 Caleb the son of Jephunneh the **K** said unto 7074
14:14 the son of Jephunneh the **K** unto this day, 7074

KENITE (6) [KENITES]
Nu 24:22 Nevertheless the **K** shall be wasted, 7014
Jdg 1:16 the children of the **K**, Moses' father in law, 7017
4:11 Now Heber the **K**, *which was* of 7017
4:17 to the tent of Jael the wife of Heber the **K**: 7017
4:17 of Hazor and the house of Heber the **K**. 7017
5:24 shall Jael the wife of Heber the **K** be, 7017

KENITES (8) [KENITE]
Ge 15:19 The **K**, and the Kenizzites, and 7017
Nu 24:21 he looked on the **K**, and took up his 7017
Jdg 4:11 had severed himself from the **K**, and 7014
1Sa 15: 6 Saul said unto the **K**, Go, depart, get you 7017
15: 6 So the **K** departed from among 7017
27:10 and against the south of the **K**. 7017
30:29 to *them* which *were* in the cities of the **K**, 7017
1Ch 2:55 These *are* the **K** that came of Hemath, 7017

KENIZZITES (1)
Ge 15:19 and the **K**, and the Kadmonites, 7074

KEPHAR AMMONI See CHEPHAR-HAAMMONAI

KEPHIRAH See CHEPHIRAH

KEPT (175) [KEEP]
Ge 26: 5 **k** my charge, my commandments, 8104
29: 9 with her father's sheep: for she **k** them. 7462
39: 9 neither hath he **k back** any thing from me 2820
42:16 your brother, and ye shall be **k in prison**, 631
Ex 3: 1 Now Moses **k** the flock of Jethro his father 7462
16:23 lay up for you to be **k** until the morning. 4931
16:32 Fill an omer of it to be **k** for your 4931

Ex	16:33	the LORD, to be **k** for your generations.	4931
	16:34	laid it up before the Testimony, to be **k**.	4931
	21:29	he hath not **k** him in, but that he hath killed	8104
	21:36	time past, and his owner hath not **k** him in;	8104
Nu	5:13	be **k close**, and she be defiled, and *there be*	5641
	9: 5	they **k** the passover on the fourteenth day	6213
	9: 7	wherefore are we **k back**, that *we* may not	1639
	9:19	the children of Israel **k** the charge of	8104
	9:23	they **k** the charge of the LORD, at	8104
	17:10	to be **k** for a token against the rebels;	4931
	19: 9	it shall be **k** for the congregation of	4931
	24:11	the LORD hath **k** thee **back** from honour.	4513
	31:47	which **k** the charge of the tabernacle of	8104
Dt	32:10	he **k** him as the apple of his eye.	5341
	33: 9	observed thy word, and **k** thy covenant.	5341
Jos	5:10	**k** the passover on the fourteenth day of	6213
	14:10	the LORD hath **k** me **alive**, as he said,	2421
	22: 2	Ye have **k** all that Moses the servant of	8104
	22: 3	have **k** the charge of the commandment of	8104
Ru	2:23	So she **k fast** by the maidens of Boaz to	1692
1Sa	9:24	for unto *this* time *hath it* been **k** for thee	8104
	13:13	thou hast not **k** the commandment of	8104
	13:14	thou hast not **k** *that* which the LORD	8104
	17:34	Thy servant **k** his father's sheep, and	7462
	21: 4	if the young men have **k** themselves at least	8104
	21: 5	Of a truth women *have been* **k** from us	6113
	25:21	Surely in vain have I **k** all that this *fellow*	8104
	25:33	which hast **k** me this day from coming to	3607
	25:34	which hath **k** me **back** from hurting thee,	4513
	25:39	of Nabal, and hath **k** his servant from evil:	2820
	26:15	then hast thou not **k** thy lord the king?	8104
	26:16	to die, because ye have not **k** your master,	8104
2Sa	13:34	the young man that **k** the **watch** lift up his	6822
	22:22	For I have **k** the ways of the LORD, and	8104
	22:24	and have **k** myself from mine iniquity.	8104
	22:44	thou hast **k** me to be head of the heathen:	8104
1Ki	2:43	hast thou not **k** the oath of the LORD,	8104
	3: 6	thou hast **k** for him this great kindness, that	8104
	8:24	Who hast **k** with thy servant David my	8104
	11:10	he **k** not *that* which the LORD	8104
	11:11	thou hast not **k** my covenant and	8104
	11:34	because he **k** my commandments and	8104
	13:21	hast not **k** the commandment which	8104
	14: 8	who **k** my commandments, and	8104
	14:27	which **k** the door of the king's house.	8104
2Ki	9:14	(Now Joram had **k** Ramoth-gilead, he and	8104
	12: 9	the priests that **k** the door put therein all	8104
	17:19	Also Judah **k** not the commandments of	8104
	18: 6	following him, but **k** his commandments,	8104
1Ch	10:13	which he **k** not, and also for asking *counsel*	8104
	12: 1	while he yet **k** himself **close** because	6113
	12:29	for hitherto the greatest part of them had **k**	8104
2Ch	6:15	Thou which hast **k** with thy servant David	8104
	7: 8	Also at the same time Solomon **k** the feast	6213
	7: 9	for they **k** the dedication of the altar seven	6213
	12:10	that **k** the entrance of the king's house.	8104
	30:21	**k** the feast of unleavened bread seven days	6213
	30:23	and they **k** *other* seven days *with* gladness.	6213
	34: 9	which the Levites that **k** the doors had	8104
	34:21	our fathers have not **k** the word of	8104
	35: 1	Moreover Josiah **k** a passover unto	6213
	35:17	the children of Israel that were present **k**	6213
	35:18	**k** in Israel from the days of Samuel	6213
	35:18	of Israel keep such a passover as Josiah **k**,	6213
	35:19	of the reign of Josiah was this passover **k**.	6213
	36:21	as long as *she* lay desolate she **k sabbath**,	7673
Ezr	3: 4	They **k** also the feast of tabernacles, as it is	6213
	6:16	**k** the dedication of this house of God with	5648
	6:19	the children of the captivity **k** the passover	6213
	6:22	**k** the feast of unleavened bread seven days	6213
Ne	1: 7	have not **k** the commandments, nor	8104
	8:18	they **k** the feast seven days; and on	6213
	9:34	our priests, nor our fathers, **k** thy law,	6213
	11:19	Talmon, and their brethren that **k** the gates,	8104
	12:45	and the porters **k** the ward of their God,	8104
Est	2:14	which **k** the concubines:	8104
	2:21	and Teresh, of those which **k** the door,	8104
	9:28	and **k** throughout every generation,	6213
Job	23:11	his way have I **k**, and not declined.	8104
	28:21	and **k close** from the fowls of the air.	5641
	29:21	and waited, and **k silence** at my counsel.	1826
	31:34	that I **k silence**, *and* went not out *of*	1826
Ps	17: 4	by the word of thy lips I have **k** *me from*	8104
	18:21	For I have **k** the ways of the LORD, and	8104
	18:23	and I **k** myself from mine iniquity.	8104
	30: 3	thou hast **k** me **alive**, that I should not go	2421
	32: 3	When I **k silence**, my bones waxed old	2790
	42: 4	and praise, *with* a multitude that **k holyday**.	2287
	50:21	*things* hast thou done, and I **k silence**;	2790
	78:10	They **k** not the covenant of God, and	8104
	78:56	most high God, and **k** not his testimonies:	8104
	99: 7	they **k** his testimonies, and the ordinance	8104
	119:22	and contempt; for I have **k** thy testimonies.	5341
	119:55	in the night, and have **k** thy law.	8104
	119:56	This I had, because I **k** thy precepts.	5341
	119:67	I went astray: but now have I **k** thy word.	8104
	119:158	was grieved; because they **k** not thy word.	8104
	119:167	My soul hath **k** thy testimonies; and *I* love	8104
	119:168	I have **k** thy precepts and thy testimonies:	8104
Ecc	2:10	whatsoever mine eyes desired I **k** not from	680
	5:13	*namely,* riches **k** for the owners thereof to	8104
SS	1: 6	*but* mine own vineyard have I not **k**.	5201
Isa	30:29	as *in* the night when a **holy** solemnity is **k**;	6942
Jer	16:11	have forsaken me, and have not **k** my law;	8104
	35:18	**k** all his precepts, and done according unto	8104
Eze	5: 7	my statutes, neither have **k** my judgments,	6213
	18: 9	and hath **k** my judgments, to deal truly;	8104
	18:19	*and* hath **k** all my statutes, and hath done	8104
	20:21	neither **k** my judgments to do them,	8104
	44: 8	ye have not **k** the charge of mine holy	8104
	44:15	that **k** the charge of my sanctuary when	8104
	48:11	which have **k** my charge, which went not	8104
Da	5:19	whom he would he **k alive**; and whom he	2418
	7:28	in me: but I **k** the matter in my heart.	5202
Hos	12:12	for a wife, and for a wife he **k** *sheep*.	8104
Am	1:11	and he **k** his wrath for ever:	8104
	2: 4	have not **k** his commandments, and	8104
Mic	6:16	For the statutes of Omri are **k**, and all	8104
Mal	2: 9	according as ye have not **k** my ways, but	8104
	3: 7	have not **k** *them.* Return unto me, and I will	8104
	3:14	what profit *is it* that we have **k** his	8104
Mt	8:33	And they that **k** *them* fled, and went their	*1006*
	13:35	I will utter *things which have been* **k secret**	*2928*
	14: 6	But when Herod's birthday was **k**,	*71*
	19:20	All these *things* have I **k** from my youth up:	*5442*
Mk	4:22	neither was *any thing* **k secret**, but that it	*614*
	9:10	And they **k** *that* saying with themselves,	*2902*
Lk	2:19	But Mary **k** all these things, and	*4933*
	2:51	his mother **k** all these sayings in her heart.	*1301*
	8:29	and he was **k** bound with chains and	*5442*
	9:36	And they **k** *it* **close**, and told no *man* in	*4601*
	18:21	All these have I **k** from my youth up.	*5442*
	19:20	which I have **k** laid up in a napkin:	*2192*
Jn	2:10	*but* thou hast **k** the good wine until now.	*5083*
	12: 7	against the day of my burying hath she **k**	*5083*
	15:10	even as I have **k** my Father's	*5083*
	15:20	if they have **k** my saying, they will keep	*5083*
	17: 6	gavest them me; and they have **k** thy word.	*5083*
	17:12	them in the world, I **k** them in thy name:	*5083*
	17:12	*those* that thou gavest me I have **k**, and	*5442*
	18:16	and spake unto her that **k the door**, and	*2377*
	18:17	Then saith the damsel that **k the door** unto	*2377*
Ac	5: 2	And **k back** *part* of the price, his wife also	*3557*
	7:53	the disposition of angels, and have not **k** *it*.	*5442*
	9:33	which had **k** his bed eight years, and	*1909+2621*
	12: 5	Peter therefore was **k** in prison: but	*5083*
	12: 6	*the* keepers before the door **k** the prison.	*5083*
	15:12	Then all the multitude **k silence**, and	*4601*
	20:20	*And* how I **k back** nothing that was	*5288*
	22: 2	tongue to them, they **k** the more silence:	*3930*
	22:20	and **k** the raiment of them that slew him.	*5442*
	23:35	And he commanded him to be **k** in Herod's	*5442*
	25: 4	that Paul should be **k** at Cesarea, and	*5083*
	25:21	I commanded him to be **k** till I might send	*5083*
	27:43	to save Paul, **k** them **from** *their* purpose;	*2967*
	28:16	dwell by himself with a soldier that **k** him.	*5442*
Ro	16:25	which was **k secret** since the world began,	*4601*
2Co	11: 9	in all *things* I have **k** myself from being	*5083*
	11:32	**k** the city of the Damascenes *with a*	*5432*
Gal	3:23	faith came, we were **k** under the law,	*5432*
2Ti	4: 7	have finished *my* course, I have **k** the faith:	*5083*
Heb	11:28	Through faith he **k** the passover, and	*4160*
Jas	5: 4	which is of you **k back by fraud**, crieth:	*650*
1Pe	1: 5	Who are **k** by the power of God through	*5432*
2Pe	3: 7	are now, by the same word are **k in store**,	*2343*
Jude	1: 6	And the angels which **k** not their first	*5083*
Rev	3: 8	and hast **k** my word, and hast not denied	*5083*
	3:10	Because thou hast **k** the word of my	*5083*

KERAN See CHERAN

KERCHIEFS (2) [HANDKERCHIEFS]
Eze 13:18 make **k** upon the head of every stature to 4555
13:21 Your **k** also will I tear, and deliver my 4555

KEREN-HAPPUCH (1)
Job 42:14 Kezia; and the name of the third, **K**. 7163

KERETHITES See CHERETHIMS; CHERETHITES

KERIOTH (4)
Jos 15:25 Hazor, Hadattah, and **K**, *and* Hezron, 7152
Jer 48:24 upon **K**, and upon Bozrah, and upon all 7152
48:41 **K** is taken, and the strong holds are 7152
Am 2: 2 and it shall devour the palaces of **K**: 7152

KERITH See CHERITH

KERNELS (1)
Nu 6: 4 the vine tree, from the **k** even to the husk. 2785

KEROS (2)
Ezr 2:44 The children of **K**, the children of Siaha, 7026
Ne 7:47 The children of **K**, the children of Sia, 7026

KESALON See CHESALON

KESED See CHESED

KESIL See CHESIL

KESULLOTH See CHESULLOTH

KETTLE (1)
1Sa 2:14 *it* into the pan, or **k**, or caldron, or pot; 1731

KETURAH (4)
Ge 25: 1 Abraham took a wife, and her name *was* **K**. 6989
25: 4 Eldaah. All these *were* the children of **K**. 6989
1Ch 1:32 Now the sons of **K**, Abraham's concubine: 6989
1:33 and Eldaah. All these *are* the sons of **K**. 6989

KEY (6) [KEYS]
Jdg 3:25 therefore they took a **k**, and opened *them:* 4668
Isa 22:22 the **k** of the house of David will I lay upon 4668
Lk 11:52 for ye have taken away the **k** of knowledge: *2807*
Rev 3: 7 he *that is* true, he that hath the **k** of David, *2807*
9: 1 to him was given the **k** of the bottomless *2807*
20: 1 having the **k** of the bottomless *pit* and *2807*

KEYS (2) [KEY]
Mt 16:19 And I will give unto thee the **k** of *2807*
Rev 1:18 and have the **k** of hell and of death. *2807*

KEZIA (1)
Job 42:14 the name of the second, **K**; and the name of 7103

KEZIAH See KEZIA

KEZIB See CHEZIB

KEZIZ (1)
Jos 18:21 and Beth-hoglah, and the valley of **K**, 7104

KIBROTH-HATTAAVAH (5)
Nu 11:34 he called the name of that place **K**: because 6914
11:35 *And* the people journeyed from **K** *unto* 6914
33:16 from the desert of Sinai, and pitched at **K**. 6914
33:17 they departed from **K**, and encamped at 6914
Dt 9:22 at Taberah, and at Massah, and at **K**, 6914

KIBZAIM (1)
Jos 21:22 **K** with her suburbs, and Beth-horon with 6911

KICK (3) [KICKED]
1Sa 2:29 Wherefore **k** ye at my sacrifice and at mine 1163
Ac 9: 5 *it is* hard for thee to **k** against the pricks. *2979*
26:14 *it is* hard for thee to **k** against the pricks. *2979*

KICKED (1) [KICK]
Dt 32:15 Jeshurun waxed fat, and **k**: thou art waxed 1163

KID (43) [KIDS]
Ge 37:31 killed a **k** of the goats, and dipped the coat 8163
38:17 I will send *thee* a **k** from the flock. 1423+5795
38:20 Judah sent the **k** by the hand of his 1423+5795
38:23 I sent this **k**, and thou hast not found her. 1423
Ex 23:19 Thou shalt not seethe a **k** in his mother's 1423
34:26 Thou shalt not seethe a **k** in his mother's 1423
Lev 4:23 a **k** of the goats, a male without blemish; 8163
4:28 a **k** of the goats, a female without blemish, 8166
5: 6 a lamb or a **k** of the goats, for a sin 8166
9: 3 Take ye a **k** of the goats for a sin offering; 8163
23:19 ye shall sacrifice one **k** of the goats for a 8163
Nu 7:16 One **k** of the goats for a sin offering: 8163
7:22 One **k** of the goats for a sin offering: 8163
7:28 One **k** of the goats for a sin offering: 8163
7:34 One **k** of the goats for a sin offering: 8163
7:40 One **k** of the goats for a sin offering: 8163
7:46 One **k** of the goats for a sin offering: 8163
7:52 One **k** of the goats for a sin offering: 8163
7:58 One **k** of the goats for a sin offering: 8163
7:64 One **k** of the goats for a sin offering: 8163
7:70 One **k** of the goats for a sin offering: 8163
7:76 One **k** of the goats for a sin offering: 8163
7:82 One **k** of the goats for a sin offering: 8163
15:11 or for one ram, or for a lamb, or a **k**. 5795
15:24 and one **k** of the goats for a sin offering. 8163
28:15 one **k** of the goats for a sin offering unto 8163
28:30 *And* one **k** of the goats, to make an 8163
29: 5 one **k** of the goats for a sin offering, 8163
29:11 One **k** of the goats *for* a sin offering; beside 8163
29:16 one **k** of the goats *for* a sin offering; beside 8163
29:19 one **k** of the goats *for* a sin offering; beside 8163
29:25 one **k** of the goats *for* a sin offering; beside 8163
Dt 14:21 Thou shalt not seethe a **k** in his mother's 1423
Jdg 6:19 made ready a **k**, and 1423+5795
13:15 until we shall have made ready a **k** 1423+5795
13:19 So Manoah took a **k** with a meat 1423+5795
14: 6 he rent him as *he* would have rent a **k**, and 1423
15: 1 Samson visited his wife with a **k**; 1423+5795
1Sa 16:20 a **k**, and sent *them* by David his son 1423+5795
Isa 11: 6 and the leopard shall lie down with the **k**; 1423
Eze 43:22 on the second day thou shalt offer a **k** of 8163
45:23 and a **k** of the goats daily *for* a sin offering. 8163
Lk 15:29 and yet thou never gavest me a **k**, that I *2056*

KIDNEYS (18)
Ex 29:13 the two **k**, and the fat that *is* upon them, 3629
29:22 the two **k**, and the fat that *is* upon them, 3629
Lev 3: 4 the two **k**, and the fat that *is* on them, 3629
3: 4 the liver, with the **k**, it shall he take away. 3629
3:10 the two **k**, and the fat that *is* upon them, 3629
3:10 the liver, with the **k**, it shall he take away. 3629
3:15 the two **k**, and the fat that *is* upon them, 3629
3:15 the liver, with the **k**, it shall he take away. 3629
4: 9 the two **k**, and the fat that *is* upon them, 3629
4: 9 the liver, with the **k**, it shall he take away, 3629
7: 4 the two **k**, and the fat that *is* on them, 3629
7: 4 the liver, with the **k**, it shall he take away: 3629
8:16 the two **k**, and their fat, and Moses burned 3629
8:25 the two **k**, and their fat, and the right 3629
9:10 the **k**, and the caul above the liver of the sin 3629
9:19 that which covereth *the inwards,* and the **k**, 3629
Dt 32:14 and goats, with the fat of **k** of wheat; 3629
Isa 34: 6 and goats, with the fat of the **k** of rams: 3629

KIDON See CHIDON

KIDRON (11)
2Sa 15:23 king also *himself* passed over the brook **K**, 6939
1Ki 2:37 goest out, and passest over the brook **K**, 6939
15:13 her idol, and burnt *it* by the brook **K**. 6939
2Ki 23: 4 them without Jerusalem in the fields of **K**, 6939
23: 6 unto the brook **K**, and burnt it at the brook 6939
23: 6 burnt it at the brook **K**, and stampt *it* small 6939
23:12 and cast the dust of them into the brook **K**. 6939
2Ch 15:16 and stamped *it,* and burnt *it* at the brook **K**. 6939
29:16 *it,* to carry *it* out abroad into the brook **K**. 6939
30:14 they away, and cast *them* into the brook **K**. 6939
Jer 31:40 and all the fields unto the brook of **K**, 6939

KIDS (8) [KID]
Ge 27: 9 fetch me from thence two good **k** of 1423
27:16 she put the skins of the **k** of the goats upon 1423
Lev 16: 5 Israel two **k** of the goats for a sin offering, 8163
Nu 7:87 the **k** of the goats for sin offering twelve. 8163
1Sa 10: 3 one carrying three **k**, and another carrying 1423
1Ki 20:27 before them like two little flocks of **k**; 5795
2Ch 35: 7 the people, *of* the flock, lambs and **k**, 1121+5795
SS 1: 8 and feed thy **k** beside the shepherds' tents. 1429

KILEAB See CHILEAB

KILION See CHILION

KILL (126) [KILLED, KILLEDST, KILLEST, KILLETH, KILLING]

Ge 4:15 lest any finding him should **k** him. 5221
12:12 they will **k** me, but they will save thee 2026
26: 7 *said he,* the men of the place should **k** me 2026
27:42 doth comfort himself, *purposing* to **k** thee. 2026
37:21 of their hands; and said, Let us not **k** him. 5221
Ex 1:16 if it *be* a son, then ye shall **k** him: 4191
2:14 intendest thou to **k** me, as thou killedst 2026
4:24 the LORD met him, and sought to **k** him. 4191
12: 6 of Israel shall **k** it in the evening. 7819
12:21 to your families, and **k** the passover. 7819
16: 3 to **k** this whole assembly with hunger. 4191
17: 3 to **k** us and our children and our cattle with 4191
20:13 Thou shalt not **k**. 7523
22: 1 steal an ox, or a sheep, and **k** it, or sell it; 2873
22:24 wax hot, and I will **k** you with the sword; 2026
29:11 thou shalt **k** the bullock before the LORD, 7819
29:20 shalt thou **k** the ram, and take of his blood, 7819
Lev 1: 5 he shall **k** the bullock before the LORD: 7819
1:11 he shall **k** it on the side of the altar 7819
3: 2 **k** it *at* the door of the tabernacle of 7819
3: 8 **k** it before the tabernacle of 7819
3:13 **k** it before the tabernacle of 7819
4: 4 and **k** the bullock before the LORD. 7819
4:24 **k** it in the place where they kill the burnt 7819
4:24 kill it in the place where they **k** the burnt 7819
4:33 the place where they **k** the burnt offering. 7819
7: 2 In the place where they **k** the burnt offering 7819
7: 2 offering shall they **k** the trespass offering: 7819
14:13 the place where he shall **k** the sin offering 7819
14:19 and afterward he shall **k** the burnt offering: 7819
14:25 he shall **k** the lamb of the trespass offering, 7819
14:50 he shall **k** the one of the birds in an earthen 7819
16:11 shall **k** the bullock of the sin offering which 7819
16:15 shall he **k** the goat of the sin offering, 7819
20: 4 of his seed unto Molech, and **k** him not: 4191
20:16 thou shalt **k** the woman and the beast: 2026
22:28 ye shall not **k** it and her young both in one 7819
Nu 11:15 **k** me, I pray thee, **out of hand**, 2026+2026
14:15 Now *if* thou shalt **k** *all* this people as one 4191
16:13 and honey, to **k** us in the wilderness, 4191
22:29 in mine hand, for now would I **k** thee. 2026
31:17 **k** every male among the little ones, 2026
31:17 **k** every woman that hath known man by 2026
35:27 and the revenger of blood **k** the slayer; 7523
Dt 4:42 which should **k** his neighbour unawares, 7523
5:17 Thou shalt not **k**. 7523
12:15 Notwithstanding thou mayest **k** and 2076
12:21 thou shalt **k** of thy herd and of thy flock, 2076
13: 9 thou shalt **surely** **k** him; thine hand 2026+2026
32:39 I **k**, and I make alive; I wound, and I heal: 4191
Jdg 13:23 If the LORD were pleased to **k** us, 4191
15:13 **surely** we will not **k** thee. And they 4191+4191
16: 2 when it is day, we shall **k** him. 2026
20:31 *and* **k**, as at other times, in the highways, 2491
20:39 **k** of the men of Israel about thirty persons: 2491
1Sa 16: 2 if Saul hear *it,* he will **k** me. And 2026
17: 9 and *to* **k** me, then will we be your servants: 5221
17: 9 **k** him, then shall ye be our servants, and 5221
19: 1 all his servants, that they should **k** David. 4191
19: 2 Saul my father seeketh to **k** thee: 4191
19:17 unto me, Let me go; why should I **k** thee? 4191
24:10 *some* bade *me* **k** thee: but *mine eye* spared 2026
30:15 me by God, that thou wilt neither **k** me, 4191
2Sa 13:28 Smite Amnon; then **k** him, fear not: 4191
14: 7 that smote his brother, that we may **k** him, 4191
14:32 if there be *any* iniquity in me, let him **k** me. 4191
21: 4 neither for us *shalt thou* **k** any man in 4191
1Ki 11:40 Solomon sought therefore to **k** Jeroboam. 4191
12:27 they shall **k** me, and go again to Rehoboam 2026
2Ki 5: 7 and said, *Am* I God, to **k** and to make alive, 4191
7: 4 shall live; and if they **k** us, we shall but die. 4191
11:15 him that followeth her **k** with the sword. 4191
2Ch 35: 6 So **k** the passover, and sanctify yourselves, 7819
Est 3:13 to **k**, and to cause to perish, all Jews, 2026
Ps 59: T and they watcht the house to **k** him. 4191
Ecc 3: 3 A time to **k**, and a time to heal; a time to 2026
Isa 14:30 I will **k** thy root with famine, and he shall 4191
29: 1 add ye year to year; let them **k** sacrifices. 5362
Eze 34: 3 you with the wool, ye **k** them that are fed: 2076
Mt 5:21 said by them of old time, Thou shalt not **k**; 5407
5:21 whosoever shall **k** shall be in danger of 5407
10:28 And fear not them which **k** the body, but 615
10:28 kill the body, but are not able to **k** the soul: 615
17:23 And they shall **k** him, and the third day he 615
21:38 let us **k** him, and let us seize on his 615
23:34 and *some* of them ye shall **k** and crucify; and 615
24: 9 you up to be afflicted, and shall **k** you: 615
26: 4 might take Jesus by subtilty, and **k** *him.* 615
Mk 3: 4 to save life, or to **k**? But they held their 615
9:31 into the hands of men, and they shall **k** him; 615
10:19 commit adultery, Do not **k**, Do not steal, 5407
10:34 and shall spit upon him, and shall **k** him: 615
12: 7 let us **k** him, and the inheritance shall be 615
Lk 12: 4 Be not afraid of them that **k** the body, and 615
13:31 and depart hence: for Herod will **k** thee. 615
15:23 and **k** *it;* and let us eat, and be merry: 2380
18:20 commit adultery, Do not **k**, Do not steal, 5407
20:14 come, let us **k** him, that the inheritance may 615
22: 2 and scribes sought how they might **k** him; 337
Jn 5:18 Therefore the Jews sought the more to **k** 615
7: 1 in Jewry, because the Jews sought to **k** him. 615
7:19 keepeth the law? Why go ye about to **k** me? 615
7:20 hast a devil: who goeth about to **k** thee? 615
7:25 Is not this he, whom they seek to **k**? 615
8:22 Then said the Jews, Will he **k** himself? 615
8:37 but ye seek to **k** me, because my word hath 615
8:40 But now ye seek to **k** me, a man that hath 615
10:10 but for to steal, and to **k**, and to destroy: 2380
Ac 7:28 Wilt thou **k** me, as thou didst the Egyptian 337
9:23 the Jews took counsel to **k** him: 337
9:24 watched the gates day and night to **k** him. 337
10:13 came a voice to him, Rise, Peter; **k**, and eat. 2380
21:31 And as *they* went about to **k** him, 615
23:15 or ever he come near, are ready to **k** him. 337
25: 3 laying wait in the way to **k** him. 337
26:21 me in the temple, and went about to **k** *me.* 1315
27:42 And the soldiers' counsel was to **k** 615
Ro 13: 9 Thou shalt not **k**, Thou shalt not steal, 5407
Jas 2:11 not commit adultery, said also, Do not **k**. 5407
2:11 if thou commit no adultery, yet *if* thou **k**, 5407
4: 2 ye **k**, and desire *to have,* and cannot obtain: 5407
Rev 2:23 And I will **k** her children with death; and 615
6: 4 and that they should **k** one another: 4969
6: 8 to **k** with sword, and with hunger, and 615
9: 5 it was given that they should not **k** them, 615
11: 7 and shall overcome them, and **k** them. 615

KILLED (67) [KILL]

Ge 37:31 **k** a kid of the goats, and dipped the coat in 7819
Ex 21:29 but that he hath **k** a man or a woman; 4191
Lev 4:15 the bullock shall be **k** before the LORD. 7819
6:25 In the place where the burnt offering is **k** 7819
6:25 the sin offering be **k** before the LORD: 7819
8:19 he **k** *it;* and Moses sprinkled the blood 7819
14: 5 **k** in an earthen vessel over running water: 7819
14: 6 the bird *that was* **k** over the running water: 7819
Nu 16:41 Ye have **k** the people of the LORD. 4191
31:19 whosoever hath **k** *any* person, and 2026
1Sa 24:11 **k** thee not, know thou and see that *there is* 2026
25:11 my flesh that I have **k** for my shearers, and 2873
28:24 and **k** it, and took flour, and kneaded *it,* and 2076
2Sa 12: 9 thou hast **k** Uriah the Hittite with 5221
21:17 and smote the Philistine, and **k** him. 4191
1Ki 16: 7 house of Jeroboam; and because he **k** him. 5221
16:10 Zimri went in and smote him, and **k** him, 4191
21:19 Hast thou **k**, and also taken possession? 7523
2Ki 15:25 he **k** him, and reigned in his room. 4191
1Ch 19:18 **k** Shophach the captain of the host. 4191
2Ch 18: 2 Ahab **k** sheep and oxen for him in 2076
25: 3 that he slew his servants that had **k** the king 5221
29:22 So they **k** the bullocks, and the priests 7819
29:22 likewise, when they had **k** the rams, they 7819
29:22 they **k** also the lambs, and they sprinkled 7819
29:24 the priests **k** them, and they made 7819
30:15 they **k** the passover on the fourteenth *day* 7819
35: 1 they **k** the passover on the fourteenth *day* 7819
35:11 they **k** the passover, and the priests 7819
Ezr 6:20 **k** the passover for all the children of 7819
Ps 44:22 Yea, for thy sake are we **k** all the day long; 2026
Pr 9: 2 She hath **k** her beasts; she hath mingled her 2873
La 2:21 of thine anger; thou hast **k**, *and* not pitied. 2873
Mt 16:21 and be **k**, and be raised *again* the third day. 615
21:35 beat one, and **k** another, and stoned another. 615
22: 4 my oxen and *my* fatlings *are* **k**, and 2380
23:31 that ye are the children of them which **k** 5407

K

Mk 6:19 quarrel against him, and would have **k** him; *615*
8:31 and be **k**, and after three days rise again. *615*
9:31 and after that he is **k**, he shall rise the third *615*
12: 5 and him they **k**, and many others; *615*
12: 8 and **k** *him,* and cast *him* out of the vineyard. *615*
14:12 when they **k** the passover, his disciples said *2380*
Lk 11:47 of the prophets, and your fathers **k** them. *615*
11:48 for they indeed **k** them, and ye build their *615*
12: 5 which after *he* hath **k** hath power to cast into *615*
15:27 and thy father hath **k** the fatted calf, *2380*
15:30 thou hast **k** for him the fatted calf. *2380*
20:15 and **k** *him.* What therefore shall the lord of *615*
22: 7 when the passover must be **k**. *2380*
Ac 3:15 And **k** the Prince of life, whom God hath *615*
12: 2 And he **k** James the brother of John with *337*
16:27 out his sword, and would have **k** himself, *337*
23:12 neither eat nor drink till they had **k** Paul. *615*
23:21 neither eat nor drink till they have **k** him: *337*
23:27 of the Jews, and should have been **k** of them: *337*
Ro 8:36 For thy sake we are **k** all the day long; *2289*
11: 3 they have **k** thy prophets, and digged down *615*
2Co 6: 9 behold, we live; as chastened, and not **k**; *2289*
1Th 2:15 Who both **k** the Lord Jesus, and their own *615*
Jas 5: 6 Ye have condemned *and* **k** the just; *and* *5407*
Rev 6:11 that should be **k** as they *were,* should be *615*
9:18 By these three was the third *part* of men **k**, *615*
9:20 And the rest of the men which were not **k** by *615*
11: 5 will hurt them, he must in this manner be **k**. *615*
13:10 he that killeth with the sword must be **k** with *615*
13:15 worship the image of the beast should be **k**. *615*

KILLEDST (2) [KILL]
Ex 2:14 thou to kill me, as thou **k** the Egyptian? 2026
1Sa 24:18 me into thine hand, thou **k** me not. 2026

KILLEST (2) [KILL]
Mt 23:37 *thou* that **k** the prophets, and stonest them *615*
Lk 13:34 which **k** the prophets, and stonest them that *615*

KILLETH (23) [KILL]
Lev 17: 3 that **k** an ox, or lamb, or goat, in the camp, 7819
17: 3 in the camp, or that **k** *it* out of the camp, 7819
24:17 he that **k** any man shall surely be put 5221+5315
24:18 he that **k** a beast shall make it good; 5221+5315
24:21 he that **k** a beast, he shall restore it: and 5221
24:21 he that **k** a man, he shall be put to death. 5221
Nu 35:11 which **k** *any* person at unawares. 5221
35:15 that every one that **k** *any* person unawares 5221
35:30 Whoso **k** *any* person, the murderer shall be 5221
Dt 19: 4 Whoso **k** his neighbour ignorantly, whom 5221
Jos 20: 3 That the slayer that **k** *any* person unawares 5221
20: 9 that whosoever **k** *any* person at unawares 5221
1Sa 2: 6 The LORD **k**, and maketh alive: 4191
17:25 it shall be, *that* the man who **k** him, 5221
17:26 What shall be done to the man that **k** this 5221
17:27 So shall it be done to the man that **k** him. 5221
Job 5: 2 For wrath **k** the foolish man, and 2026
24:14 The murderer rising with the light **k** 6991
Pr 21:25 The desire of the slothful **k** him; for his 4191
Isa 66: 3 He that **k** an ox *is as if* he slew a man; 7819
Jn 16: 2 that whosoever **k** you will think that he *615*
2Co 3: 6 for the letter **k**, but the spirit giveth life. *615*
Rev 13:10 he that **k** with the sword must be killed with *615*

KILLING (5) [KILL]
Jdg 9:24 which aided him in the **k** of his brethren. 2026
2Ch 30:17 the Levites had the charge of the **k** of 7821
Isa 22:13 **k** sheep, eating flesh, and drinking wine: 7819
Hos 4: 2 **k**, and stealing, and committing adultery, 7523
Mk 12: 5 and many others; beating some, and **k** some. *615*

KILMAD See CHILMAD

KIMHAM See CHIMHAM

KIN (8) [KINDRED, KINDREDS, KINSFOLK, KINSFOLKS, KINSMAN, KINSMAN'S, KINSMEN, KINSWOMAN, KINSWOMEN]
Lev 18: 6 approach to any that is near of **k** to him, 1320
20:19 for he uncovereth his **near k**: they shall 7607
21: 2 for his **k**, that is near unto him, *that is,* for 7607
25:25 *if any of* his **k** come to redeem it, then 7138
25:49 *any* that is nigh of **k** unto him of his family 1320
Ru 2:20 The man *is* **near of k** unto us, one of our 7138
2Sa 19:42 Because the king *is* **near of k** to us: 7138

Mk 6: 4 and among his own **k**, and in his own *4773*

KINAH (1)
Jos 15:22 And **K**, and Dimonah, and Adadah, 7016

KIND (45) [KINDLY, KINDNESS, KINDS, LOVINGKINDNESS, LOVINGKINDNESSES]
Ge 1:11 *and* the fruit tree yielding fruit after his **k**, 4327
1:12 *and* herb yielding seed after his **k**, and 4327
1:12 whose seed *was* in itself, after his **k**: 4327
1:21 after their **k**, and every winged fowl after 4327
1:21 and every winged fowl after his **k**: 4327
1:24 bring forth the living creature after his **k**, 4327
1:24 and beast of the earth after his **k**: 4327
1:25 God made the beast of the earth after his **k**, 4327
1:25 cattle after their **k**, and every thing that 4327
1:25 that creepeth upon the earth after his **k**: 4327
6:20 Of fowls after their **k**, and of cattle after 4327
6:20 after their kind, and of cattle after their **k**, 4327
6:20 every creeping thing of the earth after his **k**, 4327
7:14 every beast after his **k**, and all the cattle 4327
7:14 all the cattle after their **k**, and 4327
7:14 that creepeth upon the earth after his **k**, 4327
7:14 every fowl after his **k**, every bird of every 4327
Lev 11:14 And the vulture, and the kite after his **k**; 4327
11:15 Every raven after his **k**; 4327
11:16 and the cuckow, and the hawk after his **k**, 4327
11:19 the heron after her **k**, and the lapwing, and 4327
11:22 the locust after his **k**, and the bald locust 4327
11:22 the bald locust after his **k**, and the beetle 4327
11:22 the beetle after his **k**, and the grasshopper 4327
11:22 his kind, and the grasshopper after his **k**. 4327
11:29 and the mouse, and the tortoise after his **k**, 4327
19:19 not let thy cattle gender with a **diverse k**: 3610
Dt 14:13 and the kite, and the vulture after his **k**, 4327
14:14 And every raven after his **k**, 4327
14:15 and the cuckow, and the hawk after his **k**, 4327
14:18 the heron after her **k**, and the lapwing, and 4327
1Ch 28:14 of **every k of service**: 5656+5656+2050.1
2Ch 10: 7 If thou be **k** to this people, and please them, 2896
Ne 13:20 sellers of all *k of* ware lodged without NIH
Ecc 2: 5 and I planted trees in them of all *k of* fruits: NIH
Eze 27:12 by reason of the multitude of all *k of* riches; NIH
Mt 13:47 cast into the sea, and gathered of every **k**: *1085*
17:21 Howbeit this **k** goeth not out but by prayer *1085*
Mk 9:29 This **k** can come forth by nothing, but by *1085*
Lk 6:35 for he is **k** unto the unthankful and *to* *5543*
1Co 13: 4 Charity suffereth long, *and* is **k**; *5541*
15:39 but *there is* one *k of* flesh of men, NIG
Eph 4:32 And be ye **k** one to another, tenderhearted, *5543*
Jas 1:18 that we should be a **k** of firstfruits of his *5100*
3: 7 For every **k** of beasts, and of birds, and *5449*

KINDLE (19) [KINDLED, KINDLETH]
Ex 35: 3 Ye shall **k** no fire throughout your 1197
Pr 26:21 to fire; so *is* a contentious man to **k** strife. 2787
Isa 9:18 shall **k** in the thickets of the forest, and 3341
10:16 under his glory he shall **k** a burning like 3344
30:33 like a stream of brimstone, doth **k** it. 1197
43: 2 neither shall the flame **k** upon thee. 1197
50:11 Behold, all ye that **k** a fire, that compass 6919
Jer 7:18 the fathers **k** the fire, and the women knead 1197
17:27 will I **k** a fire in the gates thereof, and 3341
21:14 I will **k** a fire in the forest thereof, and 3341
33:18 to **k** meat offerings, and to do sacrifice 6999
43:12 I will **k** a fire in the houses of the gods of 3341
49:27 I will **k** a fire in the wall of Damascus, and 3341
50:32 I will **k** a fire in his cities, and it shall 3341
Eze 20:47 I *will* **k** a fire in thee, and it shall devour 3341
24:10 Heap on wood, **k** the fire, consume 1814
Am 1:14 I will **k** a fire in the wall of Rabbah, and 3341
Ob 1:18 and they shall **k** in them, and devour them; 1814
Mal 1:10 neither do ye **k** *fire on* mine altar for nought. 215

KINDLED (66) [KINDLE]
Ge 30: 2 Jacob's anger was **k** against Rachel: and 2734
39:19 did thy servant to me; that his wrath was **k**. 2734
Ex 4:14 the anger of the LORD was **k** against 2734
22: 6 be consumed *therewith;* he that **k** the fire 1197
Lev 10: 6 the burning which the LORD hath **k**. 8313
Nu 11: 1 the LORD heard *it;* and his anger was **k**; 2734
11:10 the anger of the LORD was **k** greatly; 2734
11:33 the wrath of the LORD was **k** against 2734
12: 9 the anger of the LORD was **k** against 2734

Nu 22:22 God's anger was **k** because he went: and 2734
22:27 Balaam's anger was **k**, and he smote the ass 2734
24:10 Balak's anger was **k** against Balaam, and 2734
25: 3 the anger of the LORD was **k** against 2734
32:10 the LORD'S anger was **k** the same time, 2734
32:13 the LORD'S anger was **k** against Israel, 2734
Dt 6:15 lest the anger of the LORD thy God be **k** 2734
7: 4 will the anger of the LORD be **k** against 2734
11:17 *then* the LORD'S wrath be **k** against you, 2734
29:27 the anger of the LORD was **k** against this 2734
31:17 my anger shall be **k** against them in that 2734
32:22 For a fire is **k** in my anger, and shall burn 6919
Jos 7: 1 the anger of the LORD was **k** against 2734
23:16 shall the anger of the LORD be **k** against 2734
Jdg 9:30 of Gaal the son of Ebed, his anger was **k**. 2734
14:19 his anger was **k**, and he went up *to* his 2734
1Sa 11: 6 those tidings, and his anger was **k** greatly. 2734
17:28 Eliab's anger was **k** against David, and 2734
20:30 Saul's anger was **k** against Jonathan, and 2734
2Sa 6: 7 the anger of the LORD was **k** against 2734
12: 5 David's anger was greatly **k** against 2734
22: 9 of his mouth devoured: coals were **k** by it. 1197
22:13 brightness before him were coals of fire **k**. 1197
24: 1 again the anger of the LORD was **k** 2734
2Ki 13: 3 the anger of the LORD was **k** against 2734
22:13 wrath of the LORD that is **k** against us, 3341
22:17 my wrath shall be **k** against this place, 3341
23:26 where*with* his anger was **k** against Judah, 2734
1Ch 13:10 the anger of the LORD was **k** against 2734
2Ch 25:10 their anger was greatly **k** against Judah, 2734
25:15 Wherefore the anger of the LORD was **k** 2734
Job 19:11 He hath also **k** his wrath against me, and 2734
32: 2 was **k** the wrath of Elihu the son of 2734
32: 2 against Job was his wrath **k**, because 2734
32: 3 against his three friends was his wrath **k**, 2734
32: 5 of *these* three men, then his wrath was **k**. 2734
42: 7 My wrath is **k** against thee, and against thy 2734
Ps 2:12 the way, when his wrath is **k** but a little: 1197
18: 8 of his mouth devoured: coals were **k** by it. 1197
78:21 so a fire was **k** against Jacob, and 5400
106:18 a fire was **k** in their company; the flame 1197
106:40 Therefore was the wrath of the LORD **k** 2734
124: 3 when their wrath was **k** against us: 2734
Isa 5:25 Therefore is the anger of the LORD **k** 2734
50:11 your fire, and in the sparks *that* ye have **k**. 1197
Jer 11:16 with the noise of a great tumult he hath **k** 3341
15:14 for a fire is **k** in mine anger, *which* shall 6919
17: 4 for ye have **k** a fire in mine anger, 6919
44: 6 was **k** in the cities of Judah and in 1197
La 4:11 hath **k** a fire in Zion, and it hath devoured 3341
Eze 20:48 all flesh shall see that I the LORD have **k** 1197
Hos 8: 5 cast *thee* off; mine anger is **k** against them: 2734
11: 8 within me, my repentings are **k** together. 3648
Zec 10: 3 Mine anger was **k** against the shepherds, 2734
Lk 12:49 the earth; and what will I, if it be already **k**? *381*
22:55 And when they had **k** a fire in the midst of *681*
Ac 28: 2 for they **k** a fire, and received us every one, *381*

KINDLETH (3) [KINDLE]
Job 41:21 His breath **k** coals, and a flame goeth out of 3857
Isa 44:15 yea, he **k** *it*, and baketh bread; yea, 5400
Jas 3: 5 Behold, how great a matter a little fire **k**. *381*

KINDLY (10) [KIND]
Ge 24:49 now if ye will deal **k** and truly with my 2617
34: 3 and spake **k** unto the damsel. 3820+5921
47:29 my thigh, and deal **k** and truly with me; 2617
50:21 he comforted them, and spake **k** unto them. 3820
Jos 2:14 that we will deal **k** and truly with thee. 2617
Ru 1: 8 the LORD deal **k** with you, as ye have 2617
1Sa 20: 8 Therefore thou shalt deal **k** with thy 2617
2Ki 25:28 he spake **k** to him, and set his throne above 2896
Jer 52:32 spake **k** unto him, and set his throne above 2896
Ro 12:10 *Be* **k affectioned** one to another with *5387*

KINDNESS (48) [KIND]
Ge 20:13 This *is* thy **k** which thou shalt shew unto 2617
21:23 according to the **k** that I have done unto 2617
24:12 and shew **k** unto my master Abraham. 2617
24:14 that thou hast shewed **k** unto my master. 2617
40:14 shew **k**, I pray thee, unto me, and 2617
Jos 2:12 by the LORD, since I have shewed you **k**, 2617
2:12 that ye will also shew **k** unto my father's 2617
Jdg 8:35 Neither shewed they **k** to the house of 2617
Ru 2:20 who hath not left off his **k** to the living and 2617
3:10 *for* thou hast shewed more **k** in the latter 2617
1Sa 15: 6 for ye shewed **k** to all the children of Israel, 2617
20:14 yet I live shew me the **k** of the LORD, 2617
20:15 *also* thou shalt not cut off thy **k** from my 2617
2Sa 2: 5 that ye have shewed this **k** unto your lord, 2617
2: 6 now the LORD shew **k** and truth unto 2617
2: 6 I also will requite you this **k**, because 2896
3: 8 which against Judah do shew **k** *this* day 2617
9: 1 that I may shew him **k** for Jonathan's sake? 2617
9: 3 that I may shew the **k** of God unto him? 2617
9: 7 for I will surely shew thee **k** for Jonathan 2617
10: 2 I will shew **k** unto Hanun the son of 2617
10: 2 of Nahash, as his father shewed **k** unto me. 2617
16:17 said to Hushai, *Is* this thy **k** to thy friend? 2617
1Ki 2: 7 shew **k** unto the sons of Barzillai 2617
3: 6 thou hast kept for him this great **k**, that 2617
1Ch 19: 2 I will shew **k** unto Hanun the son of 2617
19: 2 because his father shewed **k** to me. 2617
2Ch 24:22 Thus Joash the king remembered not the **k** 2617
Ne 9:17 and of great **k**, and forsookest them not. 2617
Est 2: 9 pleased him, and she obtained **k** of him; 2617
Ps 31:21 for he hath shewed me his marvellous **k** in 2617
117: 2 For his **merciful k** is great toward us: and 2617
119:76 thy **merciful k** be for my comfort, 2617
141: 5 Let the righteous smite me; *it shall be* a **k**: 2617
Pr 19:22 The desire of a man *is* his **k**: and a poor 2617
31:26 and in her tongue *is* the law of **k**. 2617
Isa 54: 8 with everlasting **k** will I have mercy on 2617
54:10 my **k** shall not depart from thee, 2617
Jer 2: 2 I remember thee, the **k** of thy youth, 2617
Joel 2:13 of great **k**, and repenteth him of the evil. 2617
Jnh 4: 2 of great **k**, and repentest thee of the evil. 2617
Ac 28: 2 the barbarous people shewed us no little **k**: *5363*
2Co 6: 6 by knowledge, by longsuffering, by **k**, *5544*
Eph 2: 7 in *his* **k** towards us through Christ Jesus. *5544*
Col 3:12 holy and beloved, bowels of mercies, **k**, *5544*
Tit 3: 4 But after that the **k** and love of God our *5544*
2Pe 1: 7 And to godliness **brotherly k**; and *5360*
1: 7 and to **brotherly k** charity. *5360*

KINDRED (28) [KIN]
Ge 12: 1 from thy **k**, and from thy father's house, 4138
24: 4 to my **k**, and take a wife unto my son Isaac. 4138
24: 7 from the land of my **k**, and which spake 4138
24:38 and to my **k**, and take a wife unto my son. 4940
24:40 thou shalt take a wife for my son of my **k**, 4940
24:41 *this* my oath, when thou comest to my **k**; 4940
31: 3 unto the land of thy fathers, and to thy **k**; 4138
31:13 this land, and return unto the land of thy **k**. 4138
32: 9 and to thy **k**, and I will deal well with thee: 4138
43: 7 of our **k**, saying, *Is* your father yet alive? 4138
Nu 10:30 will depart to mine own land, and to my **k**. 4138
Jos 6:23 they brought out all her **k**, and left them 4940
Ru 2: 3 unto Boaz, who *was* of the **k** of Elimelech. 4940
3: 2 now *is* not Boaz of our **k**, with whose 4130
1Ch 12:29 of Benjamin, the **k** of Saul, three thousand: 251
Est 2:10 had not shewed her people nor her **k**: 4138
2:20 Esther had not *yet* shewed her **k** nor her 4138
8: 6 can I endure to see the destruction of my **k**? 4138
Job 32: 2 of Barachel the Buzite, of the **k** of Ram: 4940
Eze 11:15 the men of thy **k**, and all the house of Israel 1353
Lk 1:61 There is none of thy **k** that is called by this *4772*
Ac 4: 6 as many as were of the **k** of the high priest, *1085*
7: 3 and from thy **k**, and come into the land *4772*
7:13 Joseph's **k** was made known unto Pharaoh. *1085*
7:14 called his father Jacob to *him*, and all his **k**, *4772*
7:19 The same dealt subtilly with our **k**, and *1085*
Rev 5: 9 us to God by thy blood out of every **k**, *5443*
14: 6 and **k**, and tongue, and people, *5443*

KINDREDS (8) [KIN]
1Ch 16:28 Give unto the LORD, ye **k** of the people, 4940
Ps 22:27 all the **k** of the nations shall worship before 4940
96: 7 unto the LORD, O ye **k** of the people, 4940
Ac 3:25 And in thy seed shall all the **k** of the earth *3965*
Rev 1: 7 and all **k** of the earth shall wail because *5443*
7: 9 all nations, and **k**, and people, and tongues, *5443*
11: 9 *they* of the people and **k** and tongues and *5443*
13: 7 and power was given him over all **k**, and *5443*

KINDS (10) [KIND]
Ge 8:19 after their **k**, went forth out of the ark. 4940
2Ch 16:14 **divers k** *of spices* prepared by 2177

Jer 15: 3 I will appoint over them four **k**, saith 4940
Eze 47:10 their fish shall be according to their **k**, 4327
Da 3: 5 psaltery, dulcimer, and all **k** of musick, 2178
3: 7 sackbut, psaltery, and all **k** of musick, 2178
3:10 psaltery, and dulcimer, and all **k** of musick, 2178
3:15 psaltery, and dulcimer, and all **k** of musick, 2178
1Co 12:10 of spirits; to another *divers* **k** of tongues; *1085*
14:10 so many **k** of voices in the world, and *1085*

KINE (24)

Ge 32:15 forty **k**, and ten bulls, twenty she asses, and 6510
41: 2 up out of the river seven well favoured **k** 6510
41: 3 seven other **k** came up after them out of 6510
41: 3 stood by the *other* **k** upon the brink of 6510
41: 4 leanfleshed **k** did eat up the seven well 6510
41: 4 eat up the seven well favoured and fat **k**. 6510
41:18 there came up out of the river seven **k**, 6510
41:19 seven other **k** came up after them, poor and 6510
41:20 the ill favoured **k** did eat up the first seven 6510
41:20 kine did eat up the first seven fat **k**: 6510
41:26 The seven good **k** *are* seven years; and 6510
41:27 ill favoured **k** that came up after them *are* 6510
Dt 7:13 the increase of thy **k**, and the flocks of thy 504
28: 4 the increase of thy **k**, and the flocks of thy 504
28:18 the increase of thy **k**, and the flocks of thy 504
28:51 *or* the increase of thy **k**, or flocks of thy 504
32:14 Butter of **k**, and milk of sheep, with fat of 1241
1Sa 6: 7 make a new cart, and take two milch **k**, 6510
6: 7 tie the **k** to the cart, and bring their calves 6510
6:10 took two milch **k**, and tied them to the cart, 6510
6:12 the **k** took the straight way to the way of 6510
6:14 offered the **k** a burnt offering unto 6510
2Sa 17:29 butter, and sheep, and cheese of **k**, 1241
Am 4: 1 Hear this word, ye **k** of Bashan, that *are* in 6510

KING (2256) [KING'S, KINGDOM, KINGDOMS, KINGLY, KINGS, KINGS']

Ge 14: 1 it came to pass in the days of Amraphel **k** 4428
14: 1 Arioch **k** of Ellasar, Chedorlaomer king of 4428
14: 1 Chedorlaomer **k** of Elam, and Tidal king of 4428
14: 1 king of Elam, and Tidal **k** of nations; 4428
14: 2 *That these* made war with Bera **k** of 4428
14: 2 with Birsha **k** of Gomorrah, Shinab king of 4428
14: 2 Shinab **k** of Admah, and Shemeber king of 4428
14: 2 Shemeber **k** of Zeboiim, and the king of 4428
14: 2 and the **k** of Bela, which *is* Zoar. 4428
14: 8 there went out the **k** of Sodom, and 4428
14: 8 the **k** of Gomorrah, and the king of Admah, 4428
14: 8 the **k** of Admah, and the king of Zeboiim, 4428
14: 8 the **k** of Zeboiim, and the king of Bela 4428
14: 8 and the **k** of Bela (the same *is* Zoar); 4428
14: 9 With Chedorlaomer the **k** of Elam, and 4428
14: 9 *with* Tidal **k** of nations, and Amraphel king 4428
14: 9 Amraphel **k** of Shinar, and Arioch king of 4428
14: 9 king of Shinar, and Arioch **k** of Ellasar; 4428
14:17 the **k** of Sodom went out to meet him after 4428
14:18 Melchizedek **k** of Salem brought forth 4428
14:21 the **k** of Sodom said unto Abram, Give me 4428
14:22 Abram said to the **k** of Sodom, I have lift 4428
20: 2 Abimelech **k** of Gerar sent, and took Sarah. 4428
26: 1 Isaac went unto Abimelech **k** of 4428
26: 8 that Abimelech **k** of the Philistims looked 4428
36:31 before there reigned *any* **k** over the children 4428
40: 1 *that* the butler of the **k** of Egypt and *his* 4428
40: 1 *his* baker had offended their lord the **k** of 4428
40: 5 the butler and the baker of the **k** of Egypt, 4428
41:46 when he stood before Pharaoh **k** of Egypt. 4428
Ex 1: 8 Now there arose up a new **k** over Egypt, 4428
1:15 the **k** of Egypt spake to the Hebrew 4428
1:17 did not as the **k** of Egypt commanded them, 4428
1:18 the **k** of Egypt called for the midwives, 4428
2:23 in process of time, that the **k** of Egypt died: 4428
3:18 unto the **k** of Egypt, and you shall say unto 4428
3:19 I am sure that the **k** of Egypt will not let 4428
5: 4 the **k** of Egypt said unto them, Wherefore 4428
6:11 Go in, speak unto Pharaoh **k** of Egypt, 4428
6:13 of Israel, and unto Pharaoh **k** of Egypt, 4428
6:27 *These are* they which spake to Pharaoh **k** of 4428
6:29 speak thou unto Pharaoh **k** of Egypt all that 4428
14: 5 it was told the **k** of Egypt that the people 4428
14: 8 hardened the heart of Pharaoh **k** of Egypt, 4428
Nu 20:14 from Kadesh unto the **k** of Edom, 4428
21: 1 *when* **k** Arad the Canaanite, which dwelt *in* 4428
21:21 Israel sent messengers unto Sihon **k** of 4428
21:26 For Heshbon *was* the city of Sihon the **k** of 4428
21:26 who had fought against the former **k** of 4428
21:29 his daughters into captivity unto Sihon **k** of 4428
21:33 Og the **k** of Bashan went out against them, 4428
21:34 as thou didst unto Sihon **k** of the Amorites, 4428
22: 4 Balak the son of Zippor *was* **k** of 4428
22:10 **k** of Moab, hath sent unto me, *saying,* 4428
23: 7 Balak the **k** of Moab hath brought me from 4428
23:21 and the shout of a **k** *is* among them. 4428
24: 7 his **k** shall be higher than Agag, and 4428
32:33 the kingdom of Sihon **k** of the Amorites, 4428
32:33 the kingdom of Og **k** of Bashan, the land, 4428
33:40 **k** Arad the Canaanite, which dwelt in 4428
Dt 1: 4 After he had slain Sihon the **k** of 4428
1: 4 dwelt in Heshbon, and Og the **k** of Bashan, 4428
2:24 the Amorite, **k** of Heshbon, and his land: 4428
2:26 Sihon **k** of Heshbon *with* words of peace, 4428
2:30 Sihon **k** of Heshbon would not let us pass 4428
3: 1 Og the **k** of Bashan came out against us, 4428
3: 2 as thou didst unto Sihon **k** of the Amorites, 4428
3: 3 the **k** of Bashan, and all his people: 4428
3: 6 as we did unto Sihon **k** of Heshbon, 4428
3:11 For only Og **k** of Bashan remained of 4428
4:46 in the land of Sihon **k** of the Amorites, 4428
4:47 the land of Og **k** of Bashan, two kings of 4428
7: 8 from the hand of Pharaoh **k** of Egypt. 4428
11: 3 of Egypt unto Pharaoh the **k** of Egypt, 4428
17:14 shalt say, I will set a **k** over me, 4428
17:15 Thou shalt in any wise set *him* **k** over thee, 4428
17:15 thy brethren shalt thou set **k** over thee: 4428
28:36 and thy **k** which thou shalt set over thee, 4428
29: 7 Sihon the **k** of Heshbon, and Og the king of 4428
29: 7 king of Heshbon, and Og the **k** of Bashan, 4428
33: 5 he was **k** in Jeshurun, when the heads of 4428
Jos 2: 2 it was told the **k** of Jericho, saying, Behold, 4428
2: 3 the **k** of Jericho sent unto Rahab, saying, 4428
6: 2 the **k** thereof, *and* the mighty *men* of 4428
8: 1 I have given into thy hand the **k** of Ai, and 4428
8: 2 her **k** as thou didst unto Jericho and 4428
8: 2 king as thou didst unto Jericho and her **k**: 4428
8:14 when the **k** of Ai saw *it,* that they hasted 4428
8:23 the **k** of Ai they took alive, and 4428
8:29 the **k** of Ai he hanged on a tree until 4428
9:10 to Sihon **k** of Heshbon, and to Og king of 4428
9:10 to Og **k** of Bashan, which *was* at Ashtaroth. 4428
10: 1 when Adoni-zedek **k** of Jerusalem had 4428
10: 1 as he had done to Jericho and her **k**, so 4428
10: 1 her king, so he had done to Ai and her **k**; 4428
10: 3 Wherefore Adoni-zedek **k** of Jerusalem 4428
10: 3 of Jerusalem sent unto Hoham **k** of Hebron, 4428
10: 3 unto Piram **k** of Jarmuth, and unto Japhia 4428
10: 3 unto Japhia **k** of Lachish, and unto Debir 4428
10: 3 and unto Debir **k** of Eglon, saying, 4428
10: 5 the **k** of Jerusalem, the king of Hebron, 4428
10: 5 the **k** of Hebron, the king of Jarmuth, 4428
10: 5 the king of Hebron, the **k** of Jarmuth, 4428
10: 5 the **k** of Lachish, the king of Eglon, 4428
10: 5 the king of Lachish, the **k** of Eglon, 4428
10:23 the **k** of Jerusalem, the king of Hebron, 4428
10:23 the **k** of Hebron, the king of Jarmuth, 4428
10:23 the king of Hebron, the **k** of Jarmuth, 4428
10:23 the **k** of Lachish, *and* the king of Eglon. 4428
10:23 the king of Lachish, *and* the **k** of Eglon. 4428
10:28 the **k** thereof he utterly destroyed, them, 4428
10:28 he did to the **k** of Makkedah as he did unto 4428
10:28 Makkedah as he did unto the **k** of Jericho. 4428
10:30 the **k** thereof, into the hand of Israel; 4428
10:30 did unto the **k** thereof as he did unto 4428
10:30 king thereof as he did unto the **k** of Jericho. 4428
10:33 Horam **k** of Gezer came up to help 4428
10:37 the **k** thereof, and all the cities thereof, 4428
10:39 and the **k** thereof, and all the cities thereof; 4428
10:39 so he did to Debir, and to the **k** thereof; 4428
10:39 as he had done also to Libnah, and to her **k**. 4428
11: 1 when Jabin **k** of Hazor had heard *those* 4428
11: 1 *things,* that he sent to Jobab **k** of Madon, 4428
11: 1 to the **k** of Shimron, and to the king of 4428
11: 1 king of Shimron, and to the **k** of Achshaph, 4428
11:10 and smote the **k** thereof with the sword: 4428
12: 2 Sihon **k** of the Amorites, who dwelt in 4428
12: 4 the coast of Og **k** of Bashan, *which was* of 4428
12: 5 the border of Sihon **k** of Heshbon. 4428
12: 9 The **k** of Jericho, one; the king of Ai, 4428
12: 9 the **k** of Ai, which *is* beside Beth-el, one; 4428

Jos 12:10 The **k** of Jerusalem, one; the king of 4428
12:10 of Jerusalem, one; the **k** of Hebron, one; 4428
12:11 The **k** of Jarmuth, one; the king of Lachish, 4428
12:11 king of Jarmuth, one; the **k** of Lachish, one; 4428
12:12 The **k** of Eglon, one; the king of Gezer, 4428
12:12 king of Eglon, one; the **k** of Gezer, one; 4428
12:13 The **k** of Debir, one; the king of Geder, 4428
12:13 king of Debir, one; the **k** of Geder, one; 4428
12:14 The **k** of Hormah, one; the king of Arad, 4428
12:14 king of Hormah, one; the **k** of Arad, one; 4428
12:15 The **k** of Libnah, one; the king of Adullam, 4428
12:15 king of Libnah, one; the **k** of Adullam, one; 4428
12:16 The **k** of Makkedah, one; the king of 4428
12:16 of Makkedah, one; the **k** of Beth-el, one; 4428
12:17 The **k** of Tappuah, one; the king of Hepher, 4428
12:17 of Tappuah, one; the **k** of Hepher, one; 4428
12:18 The **k** of Aphek, one; the king of Lasharon, 4428
12:18 king of Aphek, one; the **k** of Lasharon, one; 4428
12:19 The **k** of Madon, one; the king of Hazor, 4428
12:19 king of Madon, one; the **k** of Hazor, one; 4428
12:20 The **k** of Shimron-meron, one; the king of 4428
12:20 one; the **k** of Achshaph, one; 4428
12:21 The **k** of Taanach, one; the king of 4428
12:21 of Taanach, one; the **k** of Megiddo, one; 4428
12:22 The **k** of Kedesh, one; the king of Jokneam 4428
12:22 one; the **k** of Jokneam of Carmel, one; 4428
12:23 The **k** of Dor in the coast of Dor, one; 4428
12:23 one; the **k** of the nations of Gilgal, one; 4428
12:24 The **k** of Tirzah, one: all the kings thirty 4428
13:10 all the cities of Sihon **k** of the Amorites, 4428
13:21 all the kingdom of Sihon **k** of the Amorites, 4428
13:27 the rest of the kingdom of Sihon **k** of 4428
13:30 all the kingdom of Og **k** of Bashan, and 4428
24: 9 **k** of Moab, arose and warred against Israel, 4428
Jdg 3: 8 of Chushan-rishathaim **k** of Mesopotamia: 4428
3:10 LORD delivered Chushan-rishathaim **k** 4428
3:12 the LORD strengthened Eglon the **k** of 4428
3:14 So the children of Israel served Eglon the **k** 4428
3:15 sent a present unto Eglon the **k** of Moab. 4428
3:17 he brought the present unto Eglon **k** of 4428
3:19 said, I have a secret errand unto thee, O **k**: 4428
4: 2 them into the hand of Jabin **k** of Canaan, 4428
4:17 for *there was* peace between Jabin the **k** of 4428
4:23 So God subdued on that day Jabin the **k** of 4428
4:24 prevailed against Jabin the **k** of Canaan, 4428
4:24 until they had destroyed Jabin **k** of Canaan. 4428
8:18 *each* one resembled the children of a **k**. 4428
9: 6 of Millo, and went, and made Abimelech **k**, 4428
9: 8 The trees went forth on a time to anoint a **k** 4428
9:15 If in truth ye anoint me **k** over you, *then* 4428
9:16 in that ye have **made** Abimelech **k**, and 4427
9:18 **made** Abimelech, the son of his maidservant, **k** 4427
11:12 Jephthah sent messengers unto the **k** of 4428
11:13 the **k** of the children of Ammon answered 4428
11:14 Jephthah sent messengers again unto the **k** 4428
11:17 Israel sent messengers unto the **k** of Edom, 4428
11:17 the **k** of Edom would not hearken *thereto*. 4428
11:17 like manner they sent unto the **k** of Moab: 4428
11:19 Israel sent messengers unto Sihon **k** of 4428
11:19 king of the Amorites, the **k** of Heshbon; 4428
11:25 than Balak the son of Zippor, **k** of Moab? 4428
11:28 Howbeit the **k** of the children of Ammon 4428
17: 6 In those days *there was* no **k** in Israel, *but* 4428
18: 1 In those days *there was* no **k** in Israel: and 4428
19: 1 those days, when *there was* no **k** in Israel, 4428
21:25 In those days *there was* no **k** in Israel: 4428
1Sa 2:10 he shall give strength unto his **k**, and 4428
8: 5 now make us a **k** to judge us like all 4428
8: 6 when they said, Give us a **k** to judge us. 4428
8: 9 shew them the manner of the **k** that shall 4428
8:10 unto the people that asked of him a **k**. 4428
8:11 This will be the manner of the **k** that shall 4428
8:18 of your **k** which ye shall have chosen you; 4428
8:19 Nay, but we will have a **k** over us; 4428
8:20 that our **k** may judge us, and go out before 4428
8:22 unto their voice, and **make** them a **k**. 4427+4428
10:19 said unto him, *Nay,* but set a **k** over us. 4428
10:24 people shouted, and said, God save the **k**. 4428
11:15 there they **made** Saul **k** before the LORD 4427
12: 1 and have **made a k** over you. 4427+4428
12: 2 now behold, the **k** walketh before you: and 4428
12: 9 into the hand of the **k** of Moab, and 4428
12:12 when ye saw that Nahash the **k** of 4428
12:12 unto me, Nay; but a **k** shall reign over us: 4428
12:12 when the LORD your God *was* your **k**. 4428
12:13 behold the **k** whom ye have chosen, 4428
12:13 behold, the LORD hath set a **k** over you. 4428
12:14 also the **k** that reigneth over you continue 4428
12:17 the sight of the LORD, in asking you a **k**. 4428
12:19 unto all our sins *this* evil, to ask us a **k**. 4428
12:25 ye shall be consumed, both ye and your **k**. 4428
15: 1 The LORD sent me to anoint thee to be **k** 4428
15: 8 he took Agag the **k** of the Amalekites alive, 4428
15:11 me that I have **set up** Saul **to be k**: 4427+4428
15:17 the LORD anointed thee **k** over Israel? 4428
15:20 have brought Agag the **k** of Amalek, and 4428
15:23 he hath also rejected thee from *being* **k**. 4428
15:26 the LORD hath rejected thee from being **k** 4428
15:32 Bring you hither to me Agag the **k** of 4428
15:35 that he had **made** Saul **k** over Israel. 4427
16: 1 for I have provided me a **k** among his sons. 4428
17:25 the **k** will enrich him *with* great riches, and 4428
17:55 *As* thy soul liveth, O **k**, I cannot tell. 4428
17:56 the **k** said, Inquire thou whose son 4428
18: 6 singing and dancing, to meet **k** Saul, 4428
18:18 that I should be son in law to the **k**? 4428
18:22 the **k** hath delight in thee, and all his 4428
18:25 The **k** desireth not *any* dowry, but an 4428
18:27 and they gave them in full tale to the **k**, 4428
19: 4 Let not the **k** sin against his servant, 4428
20: 5 I should not fail to sit with the **k** at meat: 4428
20:24 was come, the **k** sat him down to eat meat. 4428
20:25 the **k** sat upon his seat, as at other times, 4428
21: 2 The **k** hath commanded me a business, and 4428
21:10 of Saul, and went to Achish the **k** of Gath. 4428
21:11 *Is* not this David the **k** of the land? 4428
21:12 was sore afraid of Achish the **k** of Gath. 4428
22: 3 he said unto the **k** of Moab, Let my father 4428
22: 4 And he brought them before the **k** of Moab: 4428
22:11 the **k** sent to call Ahimelech the priest, 4428
22:11 in Nob: and they came all of them to the **k**. 4428
22:14 Ahimelech answered the **k**, and said, 4428
22:15 let not the **k** impute *any* thing unto his 4428
22:16 the **k** said, Thou shalt surely die, 4428
22:17 the **k** said unto the footmen that stood 4428
22:17 the servants of the **k** would not put forth 4428
22:18 the **k** said to Doeg, Turn thou, and fall upon 4428
23:17 thou shalt be **k** over Israel, and I shall be 4427
23:20 Now therefore, **O k**, come down according 4428
24: 8 and cried after Saul, saying, My lord the **k**. 4428
24:14 After whom is the **k** of Israel come out? 4428
24:20 well that thou shalt **surely be k**, 4427+4427
25:36 a feast in his house, like the feast of a **k**; 4428
26:14 and said, Who *art* thou *that* criest to the **k**? 4428
26:15 then hast thou not kept thy lord the **k**? 4428
26:15 of the people in to destroy the **k** thy lord. 4428
26:17 David said, *It is* my voice, my lord, O **k**. 4428
26:19 let my lord the **k** hear the words of his 4428
26:20 for the **k** of Israel is come out to seek a 4428
27: 2 unto Achish, the son of Maoch, **k** of Gath. 4428
28:13 the **k** said unto her, Be not afraid: for what 4428
29: 3 the servant of Saul the **k** of Israel, 4428
29: 8 fight against the enemies of my lord the **k**? 4428
2Sa 2: 4 there they anointed David **k** over the house 4428
2: 7 also the house of Judah have anointed me **k** 4428
2: 9 he **made** him **k** over Gilead, and over 4427
2:11 the time that David was **k** in Hebron over 4428
3: 3 the daughter of Talmai **k** of Geshur; 4428
3:17 Ye sought for David in times past to be **k** 4428
3:21 will gather all Israel unto my lord the **k**, 4428
3:23 Abner the son of Ner came to the **k**, and 4428
3:24 Joab came to the **k**, and said, What hast 4428
3:31 And **k** David *himself* followed the bier. 4428
3:32 the **k** lift up his voice, and wept at the grave 4428
3:33 the **k** lamented over Abner, and said, Died 4428
3:36 as whatsoever the **k** did, pleased all 4428
3:37 not of the **k** to slay Abner the son of Ner. 4428
3:38 the **k** said unto his servants, Know ye not 4428
3:39 And I *am this* day weak, though anointed **k**; 4428
4: 8 said to the **k**, Behold the head of 4428
4: 8 the LORD hath avenged my lord the **k** 4428
5: 2 Also in time past, when Saul was **k** over us, 4428
5: 3 So all the elders of Israel came to the **k** to 4428
5: 3 **k** David made a league with them in 4428
5: 3 and they anointed David **k** over Israel. 4428
5: 6 the **k** and his men went *to* Jerusalem unto 4428
5:11 Hiram **k** of Tyre sent messengers to David, 4428

2Sa 5:12	LORD had established him **k** over Israel,	4428
5:17	that they had anointed David **k** over Israel,	4428
6:12	it was told **k** David, saying, The LORD	4428
6:16	saw **k** David leaping and dancing before	4428
6:20	How glorious was the **k** of Israel to day,	4428
7: 1	when the **k** sat in his house, and	4428
7: 2	That the **k** said unto Nathan the prophet,	4428
7: 3	Nathan said to the **k**, Go, do all that *is* in	4428
7:18	went **k** David in, and sat before	4428
8: 3	the son of Rehob, **k** of Zobah,	4428
8: 5	came to succour Hadadezer **k** of Zobah,	4428
8: 8	**k** David took exceeding much brass.	4428
8: 9	When Toi **k** of Hamath heard that David	4428
8:10	Toi sent Joram his son unto **k** David,	4428
8:11	Which also **k** David did dedicate unto	4428
8:12	of Hadadezer, son of Rehob, **k** of Zobah.	4428
9: 2	the **k** said unto him, *Art* thou Ziba?	4428
9: 3	the **k** said, *Is there* not yet any of the house	4428
9: 3	Ziba said unto the **k**, Jonathan hath yet a	4428
9: 4	the **k** said unto him, Where *is* he? And Ziba	4428
9: 4	Ziba said unto the **k**, Behold, he *is in*	4428
9: 5	**k** David sent, and fet him out of the house	4428
9: 9	the **k** called to Ziba, Saul's servant, and	4428
9:11	said Ziba unto the **k**, According to all that	4428
9:11	According to all that my lord the **k** hath	4428
9:11	*said the* **k**, he shall eat at my table,	NIH
10: 1	that the **k** of the children of Ammon died,	4428
10: 5	the **k** said, Tarry at Jericho until your	4428
10: 6	of **k** Maacah a thousand men, and	4428
11: 8	followed him a mess *of meat* from the **k**.	4428
11:19	of telling the matters of the war unto the **k**,	4428
12: 7	I anointed thee **k** over Israel, and	4428
13: 6	when the **k** was come to see him, Amnon	4428
13: 6	Amnon said unto the **k**, I pray thee,	4428
13:13	I pray thee, speak unto the **k**;	4428
13:21	when **k** David heard of all these things, he	4428
13:24	Absalom came to the **k**, and said,	4428
13:24	let the **k**, I beseech thee, and his servants go	4428
13:25	the **k** said to Absalom, Nay, my son, let us	4428
13:26	the **k** said unto him, Why should he go with	4428
13:31	the **k** arose, and tare his garments, and	4428
13:33	let not my lord the **k** take the thing to his	4428
13:35	Jonadab said unto the **k**, Behold, the king's	4428
13:36	the **k** also and all his servants wept very	4428
13:37	the son of Ammihud, **k** of Geshur.	4428
13:39	*the soul of* **k** David longed to go forth unto	4428
14: 3	come to the **k**, and speak on this manner	4428
14: 4	when the woman of Tekoah spake to the **k**,	4428
14: 4	and did obeisance, and said, Help, O **k**.	4428
14: 5	the **k** said unto her, What aileth thee?	4428
14: 8	the **k** said unto the woman, Go to thine	4428
14: 9	the woman of Tekoah said unto the **k**,	4428
14: 9	My lord, O **k**, the iniquity *be* on me, and	4428
14: 9	and the **k** and his throne *be* guiltless.	4428
14:10	the **k** said, Whosoever saith *ought* unto	4428
14:11	let the **k** remember the LORD thy God,	4428
14:12	speak *one* word unto my lord the **k**.	4428
14:13	for the **k** doth speak this thing as one which	4428
14:13	in that the **k** doth not fetch *home* again his	4428
14:15	to speak of this thing unto my lord the **k**,	4428
14:15	handmaid said, I will now speak unto the **k**;	4428
14:15	it may be that the **k** will perform	4428
14:16	For the **k** will hear, to deliver his handmaid	4428
14:17	The word of my lord the **k** shall now be	4428
14:17	so *is* my lord the **k** to discern good and bad:	4428
14:18	the **k** answered and said unto the woman,	4428
14:18	woman said, Let my lord the **k** now speak.	4428
14:19	the **k** said, *Is not* the hand of Joab with thee	4428
14:19	and said, *As* thy soul liveth, my lord the **k**,	4428
14:19	to the left from ought that my lord the **k**	4428
14:21	the **k** said unto Joab, Behold now, I have	4428
14:22	and bowed himself, and thanked the **k**:	4428
14:22	my lord, O **k**, in that the king hath fulfilled	4428
14:22	in that the **k** hath fulfilled the request of his	4428
14:24	the **k** said, Let him turn to his own house,	4428
14:29	sent for Joab, to have sent him to the **k**;	4428
14:32	that I may send thee to the **k**, to say,	4428
14:33	So Joab came to the **k**, and told him: and	4428
14:33	he came to the **k**, and bowed himself on his	4428
14:33	on his face to the ground before the **k**:	4428
14:33	before the king: and the **k** kissed Absalom.	4428
15: 2	a controversy came to the **k** for judgment,	4428
15: 3	*there is* no man *deputed* of the **k** to hear	4428
15: 6	all Israel that came to the **k** for judgment:	4428
15: 7	that Absalom said unto the **k**, I pray thee,	4428
15: 9	the **k** said unto him, Go in peace. So he	4428
15:15	the king's servants said unto the **k**, Behold,	4428
15:15	*do* whatsoever my lord the **k** shall appoint.	4428
15:16	the **k** went forth, and all his household after	4428
15:16	the **k** left ten women, *which were*	4428
15:17	the **k** went forth, and all the people after	4428
15:18	him from Gath, passed on before the **k**.	4428
15:19	said the **k** to Ittai the Gittite, Wherefore	4428
15:19	return to thy place, and abide with the **k**:	4428
15:21	Ittai answered the **k**, and said, *As*	4428
15:21	LORD liveth, and *as* my lord the **k** liveth,	4428
15:21	surely in what place my lord the **k** shall be,	4428
15:23	the **k** also *himself* passed over the brook	4428
15:25	the **k** said unto Zadok, Carry back the ark	4428
15:27	The **k** said also unto Zadok the priest, *Art*	4428
15:34	unto Absalom, I will be thy servant, O **k**;	4428
16: 2	the **k** said unto Ziba, What meanest thou by	4428
16: 3	the **k** said, And where *is* thy master's son?	4428
16: 3	Ziba said unto the **k**, Behold, he abideth at	4428
16: 4	said the **k** to Ziba, Behold, thine *are* all that	4428
16: 4	I may find grace in thy sight, my lord, O **k**.	4428
16: 5	when **k** David came to Bahurim, behold,	4428
16: 6	at David, and at all the servants of **k** David:	4428
16: 9	said Abishai the son of Zeruiah unto the **k**,	4428
16: 9	should this dead dog curse my lord the **k**?	4428
16:10	And the **k** said, What have I to do with you,	4428
16:14	the **k**, and all the people that *were* with	4428
16:16	God save the **k**, God save the king.	4428
16:16	God save the king, God save the **k**.	4428
17: 2	him shall flee; and I will smite the **k** only:	4428
17:16	lest the **k** be swallowed up, and all	4428
17:17	told them; and they went and told **k** David.	4428
17:21	went and told **k** David, and said unto	4428
18: 2	the **k** said unto the people, I will surely go	4428
18: 4	the **k** said unto them, What seemeth you	4428
18: 4	the **k** stood by the gate side, and all	4428
18: 5	the **k** commanded Joab and Abishai and	4428
18: 5	all the people heard when the **k** gave all	4428
18:12	for in our hearing the **k** charged thee and	4428
18:13	for there is no matter hid from the **k**, and	4428
18:19	Let me now run, and bear the **k** tidings,	4428
18:21	to Cushi, Go tell the **k** what thou hast seen.	4428
18:25	the watchman cried, and told the **k**. And	4428
18:25	the **k** said, If he *be* alone, *there is* tidings in	4428
18:26	And the **k** said, He also bringeth tidings.	4428
18:27	the **k** said, He *is* a good man, and	4428
18:28	and said unto the **k**, All is well.	4428
18:28	to the earth upon his face before the **k**,	4428
18:28	that lift up their hand against my lord the **k**.	4428
18:29	the **k** said, *Is* the young man Absalom safe?	4428
18:30	the **k** said *unto him,* Turn aside, *and*	4428
18:31	and Cushi said, Tidings, my lord the **k**:	4428
18:32	the **k** said unto Cushi, *Is* the young man	4428
18:32	The enemies of my lord the **k**, and all that	4428
18:33	the **k** was much moved, and went up to	4428
19: 1	the **k** weepeth and mourneth for Absalom.	4428
19: 2	for the people heard say that day *how* the **k**	4428
19: 4	the **k** covered his face, and the king cried	4428
19: 4	the **k** cried *with* a loud voice, O my son	4428
19: 5	Joab came *into* the house to the **k**, and said,	4428
19: 8	the **k** rose, and sat in the gate. And they	4428
19: 8	Behold, the **k** doth sit in the gate.	4428
19: 8	all the people came before the **k**: for Israel	4428
19: 9	The **k** saved us out of the hand of our	4428
19:10	why speak ye not a word of bringing the **k**	4428
19:11	**k** David sent to Zadok and to Abiathar	4428
19:11	Why are ye the last to bring the **k** back to	4428
19:11	the speech of all Israel is come to the **k**,	4428
19:12	then are ye the last to bring back the **k**?	4428
19:14	so that they sent *this word* unto the **k**,	4428
19:15	So the **k** returned, and came to Jordan.	4428
19:15	Judah came to Gilgal, to go to meet the **k**,	4428
19:15	the king, to conduct the **k** over Jordan.	4428
19:16	with the men of Judah to meet **k** David.	4428
19:17	and they went over Jordan before the **k**.	4428
19:18	the son of Gera fell down before the **k**,	4428
19:19	said unto the **k**, Let not my lord impute	4428
19:19	that my lord the **k** went out of Jerusalem,	4428
19:19	that the **k** should take *it* to his heart.	4428
19:20	Joseph to go down to meet my lord the **k**.	4428
19:22	for do not I know that I *am this* day **k** over	4428
19:23	Therefore the **k** said unto Shimei,	4428
19:23	shalt not die. And the **k** sware unto him.	4428

2Sa 19:24	the son of Saul came down to meet the **k**,	4428
19:24	from the day the **k** departed until the day he	4428
19:25	he was come *to* Jerusalem to meet the **k**,	4428
19:25	that the **k** said unto him, Wherefore wentest	4428
19:26	he answered, My lord, O **k**, my servant	4428
19:26	that I may ride thereon, and go to the **k**;	4428
19:27	slandered thy servant unto my lord the **k**;	4428
19:27	but my lord the **k** *is* as an angel of God:	4428
19:28	but dead men before my lord the **k**:	4428
19:28	have I yet to cry any more unto the **k**?	4428
19:29	the **k** said unto him, Why speakest thou any	4428
19:30	Mephibosheth said unto the **k**, Yea, let him	4428
19:30	forasmuch as my lord the **k** is come *again*	4428
19:31	went over Jordan with the **k**, to conduct	4428
19:32	he had provided the **k** of sustenance while	4428
19:33	the **k** said unto Barzillai, Come thou over	4428
19:34	Barzillai said unto the **k**, How long have I	4428
19:34	that I should go up with the **k** *unto*	4428
19:35	servant be yet a burden unto my lord the **k**?	4428
19:36	will go a little *way* over Jordan with the **k**:	4428
19:36	why should the **k** recompense *it* me *with*	4428
19:37	let him go over with my lord the **k**; and	4428
19:38	the **k** answered, Chimham shall go over	4428
19:39	when the **k** was come over, the king kissed	4428
19:39	the **k** kissed Barzillai, and blessed him;	4428
19:40	the **k** went on to Gilgal, and Chimham went	4428
19:40	all the people of Judah conducted the **k**,	4428
19:41	all the men of Israel came to the **k**, and	4428
19:41	Israel came to the king, and said unto the **k**,	4428
19:41	have brought the **k**, and his household, and	4428
19:42	of Israel, Because the **k** *is* near of kin to us:	4428
19:43	We have ten parts in the **k**, and we have	4428
19:43	not be first had in bringing back our **k**?	4428
20: 2	the men of Judah clave unto their **k**,	4428
20: 3	the **k** took the ten women *his* concubines,	4428
20: 4	said the **k** to Amasa, Assemble me the men	4428
20:21	hath lift up his hand against the **k**,	4428
20:22	And Joab returned *to* Jerusalem unto the **k**.	4428
21: 2	the **k** called the Gibeonites, and said unto	4428
21: 5	they answered the **k**, The man that	4428
21: 6	And the **k** said, I will give *them.*	4428
21: 7	the **k** spared Mephibosheth, the son of	4428
21: 8	the **k** took the two sons of Rizpah	4428
21:14	they performed all that the **k** commanded.	4428
22:51	*He is* the tower of salvation for his **k**: and	4428
24: 2	For the **k** said to Joab the captain of	4428
24: 3	Joab said unto the **k**, Now the LORD thy	4428
24: 3	*that* the eyes of my lord the **k** may see *it:*	4428
24: 3	why doth my lord the **k** delight in this	4428
24: 4	host went out from the presence of the **k**,	4428
24: 9	sum of the number of the people unto the **k**:	4428
24:20	saw the **k** and his servants coming on	4428
24:20	bowed himself before the **k** *on* his face	4428
24:21	Wherefore is my lord the **k** come to his	4428
24:22	Let my lord the **k** take and offer up what	4428
24:23	did Araunah, *as* a **k**, give unto the king.	4428
24:23	did Araunah, *as* a king, give unto the **k**.	4428
24:23	Araunah said unto the **k**, The LORD thy	4428
24:24	the **k** said unto Araunah, Nay; but I will	4428
1Ki 1: 1	Now **k** David was old *and* stricken in years;	4428
1: 2	Let there be sought for my lord the **k** a	4428
1: 2	let her stand before the **k**, and let her	4428
1: 2	thy bosom, that my lord the **k** may get heat.	4428
1: 3	a Shunammite, and brought her to the **k**.	4428
1: 4	and cherished the **k**, and ministered to him:	4428
1: 4	ministered to him: but the **k** knew her not.	4428
1: 5	exalted himself, saying, I will be **k**:	4427
1:13	Go and get thee in unto **k** David, and	4428
1:13	say unto him, Didst not thou, my lord O **k**,	4428
1:14	while thou yet talkest there with the **k**,	4428
1:15	Bath-sheba went in unto the **k** into	4428
1:15	the **k** was very old; and Abishag	4428
1:15	the Shunammite ministered unto the **k**.	4428
1:16	and did obeisance unto the **k**.	4428
1:16	And the **k** said, What wouldest thou?	4428
1:18	now, my lord the **k**, thou knowest *it* not:	4428
1:19	hath called all the sons of the **k**, and	4428
1:20	thou, my lord O **k**, the eyes of all Israel *are*	4428
1:20	sit on the throne of my lord the **k** after him.	4428
1:21	when my lord the **k** shall sleep with his	4428
1:22	lo, while she yet talked with the **k**,	4428
1:23	they told the **k**, saying, Behold Nathan	4428
1:23	when he was come in before the **k**, he	4428
1:23	he bowed himself before the **k** with his face	4428
1:24	Nathan said, My lord O **k**, hast thou said,	4428
1:25	before him, and say, God save **k** Adonijah.	4428
1:27	Is this thing done by my lord the **k**, and	4428
1:27	sit on the throne of my lord the **k** after him?	4428
1:28	**k** David answered and said, Call me	4428
1:28	the king's presence, and stood before the **k**.	4428
1:29	the **k** sware, and said, *As* the LORD	4428
1:31	did reverence to the **k**, and said, Let my	4428
1:31	and said, Let my lord **k** David live for ever.	4428
1:32	**k** David said, Call me Zadok the priest,	4428
1:32	of Jehoiada. And they came before the **k**.	4428
1:33	The **k** also said unto them, Take with you	4428
1:34	Nathan the prophet anoint him there **k** over	4428
1:34	the trumpet, and say, God save **k** Solomon.	4428
1:35	my throne; for he shall be **k** in my stead:	4427
1:36	the son of Jehoiada answered the **k**,	4428
1:36	the LORD God of my lord the **k** say so	4428
1:37	the LORD hath been with my lord the **k**,	4428
1:37	greater than the throne of my lord **k** David.	4428
1:38	caused Solomon to ride upon **k** David's	4428
1:39	all the people said, God save **k** Solomon.	4428
1:43	Verily our lord **k** David hath made	4428
1:43	our lord king David hath **made** Solomon **k**.	4427
1:44	the **k** hath sent with him Zadok the priest,	4428
1:45	Nathan the prophet have anointed him **k** in	4428
1:47	servants came to bless our lord **k** David,	4428
1:47	And the **k** bowed himself upon the bed.	4428
1:48	also thus said the **k**, Blessed *be* the LORD	4428
1:51	Behold, Adonijah feareth **k** Solomon:	4428
1:51	Let **k** Solomon swear unto me to day that	4428
1:53	So **k** Solomon sent, and they brought him	4428
1:53	he came and bowed himself to **k** Solomon:	4428
2:17	Speak, I pray thee, unto Solomon the **k**,	4428
2:18	Well; I will speak for thee unto the **k**.	4428
2:19	Bath-sheba therefore went unto **k** Solomon,	4428
2:19	the **k** rose up to meet her, and	4428
2:20	the **k** said unto her, Ask on, my mother:	4428
2:22	**k** Solomon answered and said unto his	4428
2:23	**k** Solomon sware by the LORD, saying,	4428
2:25	**k** Solomon sent by the hand of Benaiah	4428
2:26	unto Abiathar the priest said the **k**, Get thee	4428
2:29	it was told **k** Solomon that Joab was fled	4428
2:30	unto him, Thus saith the **k**, Come forth.	4428
2:30	Benaiah brought the **k** word again, saying,	4428
2:31	the **k** said unto him, Do as he hath said,	4428
2:35	the **k** put Benaiah the son of Jehoiada in his	4428
2:35	Zadok the priest did the **k** put in the room	4428
2:36	the **k** sent and called for Shimei, and	4428
2:38	Shimei said unto the **k**, The saying *is* good:	4428
2:38	as my lord the **k** hath said, so will thy	4428
2:39	unto Achish son of Maachah **k** of Gath.	4428
2:42	the **k** sent and called for Shimei, and	4428
2:44	The **k** said moreover to Shimei,	4428
2:45	**k** Solomon *shall be* blessed, and the throne	4428
2:46	So the **k** commanded Benaiah the son of	4428
3: 1	Solomon made affinity with Pharaoh **k** of	4428
3: 4	the **k** went to Gibeon to sacrifice there;	4428
3: 7	thou hast **made** thy servant **k** instead of	4427
3:16	unto the **k**, and stood before him.	4428
3:22	*is* my son. Thus they spake before the **k**.	4428
3:23	said the **k**, The one saith, This *is* my son	4428
3:24	the **k** said, Bring me a sword. And they	4428
3:24	And they brought a sword before the **k**.	4428
3:25	the **k** said, Divide the living child in two,	4428
3:26	whose the living child *was* unto the **k**,	4428
3:27	the **k** answered and said, Give her	4428
3:28	all Israel heard of the judgment which the **k**	4428
3:28	the king had judged; and they feared the **k**:	4228
4: 1	So **k** Solomon was king over all Israel.	4428
4: 1	So king Solomon was **k** over all Israel.	4428
4: 7	which provided victuals for the **k** and his	4428
4:19	*in* the country of Sihon **k** of the Amorites,	4428
4:19	of the Amorites, and of Og **k** of Bashan;	4428
4:27	those officers provided victual for **k**	4428
4:27	for all that came unto **k** Solomon's table,	4428
5: 1	Hiram **k** of Tyre sent his servants unto	4428
5: 1	anointed him **k** in the room of his father:	4428
5:13	**k** Solomon raised a levy out of all Israel;	4428
5:17	the **k** commanded, and they brought great	4428
6: 2	the house which **k** Solomon built for	4428
7:13	**k** Solomon sent and fet Hiram out of Tyre.	4428
7:14	he came to **k** Solomon, and wrought all his	4428
7:40	**k** Solomon *for* the house of the LORD:	4428
7:45	which Hiram made to **k** Solomon *for*	4428

1Ki 7:46 In the plain of Jordan did the **k** cast them, 4428
7:51 So was ended all the work that **k** Solomon 4428
8: 1 of Israel, unto **k** Solomon *in* Jerusalem, 4428
8: 2 **k** Solomon at the feast in the month 4428
8: 5 **k** Solomon, and all the congregation of 4428
8:14 the **k** turned his face about, and blessed all 4428
8:62 the **k**, and all Israel with him, 4428
8:63 So the **k** and all the children of Israel 4428
8:64 The same day did the **k** hallow the middle 4428
8:66 they blessed the **k**, and went unto their tents 4428
9:11 (*Now* Hiram the **k** of Tyre had furnished 4428
9:11 **k** Solomon gave Hiram twenty cities in 4428
9:14 Hiram sent to the **k** sixscore talents of gold. 4428
9:15 this *is* the reason of the levy which **k** 4428
9:16 *For* Pharaoh **k** of Egypt had gone up, and 4428
9:26 **k** Solomon made a navy *of ships* in 4428
9:28 and brought *it* to **k** Solomon. 4428
10: 3 there was not *any* thing hid from the **k**, 4428
10: 6 she said to the **k**, It was a true report that I 4428
10: 9 therefore made he thee **k**, to do judgment 4428
10:10 she gave the **k** an hundred and 4428
10:10 the queen of Sheba gave to **k** Solomon. 4428
10:12 the **k** made *of* the almug trees pillars for 4428
10:13 **k** Solomon gave unto the queen of Sheba 4428
10:16 **k** Solomon made two hundred targets *of* 4428
10:17 the **k** put them *in* the house of the forest of 4428
10:18 Moreover the **k** made a great throne of 4428
10:21 all **k** Solomon's drinking vessels *were of* 4428
10:22 For the **k** had at sea a navy of Tharshish 4428
10:23 So **k** Solomon exceeded all the kings of 4428
10:26 for chariots, and with the **k** at Jerusalem. 4428
10:27 the **k** made silver *to be* in Jerusalem as 4428
11: 1 **k** Solomon loved many strange women, 4428
11:18 came *to* Egypt, unto Pharaoh **k** of Egypt; 4428
11:23 which fled from his lord Hadadezer **k** of 4428
11:26 even he lift up *his* hand against the **k**. 4428
11:27 cause that he lift up *his* hand against the **k**: 4428
11:37 thy soul desireth, and shalt be **k** over Israel. 4428
11:40 unto Shishak **k** of Egypt, and was in Egypt 4428
12: 1 were come *to* Shechem to **make** him **k**. 4427
12: 2 was fled from the presence of **k** Solomon, 4428
12: 6 **k** Rehoboam consulted with the old men, 4428
12:12 as the **k** had appointed, saying, Come to me 4428
12:13 the **k** answered the people roughly, and 4428
12:15 Wherefore the **k** hearkened not unto 4428
12:16 So when all Israel saw that the **k** hearkened 4428
12:16 the people answered the **k**, saying, 4428
12:18 **k** Rehoboam sent Adoram, who *was* over 4428
12:18 Therefore **k** Rehoboam made speed to get 4428
12:20 and **made** him **k** over all Israel: 4427
12:23 **k** of Judah, and unto all the house of Judah 4428
12:27 *even* unto Rehoboam **k** of Judah, and 4428
12:27 and go again to Rehoboam **k** of Judah. 4428
12:28 Whereupon the **k** took counsel, and 4428
13: 4 when **k** Jeroboam heard the saying of 4428
13: 6 the **k** answered and said unto the man of 4428
13: 7 the **k** said unto the man of God, 4428
13: 8 the man of God said unto the **k**, If thou wilt 4428
13:11 the words which he had spoken unto the **k**, 4428
14: 2 which told me that I should be **k** over this 4428
14:14 LORD shall raise him up a **k** over Israel, 4428
14:25 it came to pass in the fifth year of **k** 4428
14:25 *that* Shishak **k** of Egypt came up against 4428
14:27 **k** Rehoboam made in their stead brasen 4428
14:28 when the **k** went *into* the house of 4428
15: 1 Now in the eighteenth year of **k** Jeroboam 4428
15: 9 in the twentieth year of Jeroboam **k** of 4428
15:16 and Baasha **k** of Israel all their days. 4428
15:17 Baasha **k** of Israel went up against Judah, 4428
15:17 *any* to go out or come in to Asa **k** of Judah. 4428
15:18 **k** Asa sent them to Ben-hadad, the son of 4428
15:18 of Tabrimon, the son of Hezion, **k** of Syria, 4428
15:19 break thy league with Baasha **k** of Israel, 4428
15:20 So Ben-hadad hearkened unto **k** Asa, and 4428
15:22 **k** Asa made a proclamation throughout all 4428
15:22 **k** Asa built with them Geba of Benjamin, 4428
15:25 Israel in the second year of Asa **k** of Judah, 4428
15:28 Even in the third year of Asa **k** of Judah did 4428
15:32 and Baasha **k** of Israel all their days. 4428
15:33 In the third year of Asa **k** of Judah *began* 4428
16: 8 sixth year of Asa **k** of Judah *began* Elah 4428
16:10 and seventh year of Asa **k** of Judah, 4428
16:15 seventh year of Asa **k** of Judah did Zimri 4428
16:16 hath conspired, and hath also slain the **k**: 4428
16:16 Israel **made** Omri, the captain of the host, **k** 4427
16:21 Tibni the son of Ginath, to **make** him **k**; 4427
16:23 first year of Asa **k** of Judah *began* Omri to 4428
16:29 eighth year of Asa **k** of Judah *began* Ahab 4428
16:31 the daughter of Ethbaal **k** of the Zidonians, 4428
19:15 anoint Hazael to be **k** over Syria: 4428
19:16 shalt thou anoint to be **k** over Israel: 4428
20: 1 Ben-hadad the **k** of Syria gathered all his 4428
20: 2 he sent messengers to Ahab **k** of Israel into 4428
20: 4 the **k** of Israel answered and said, My lord, 4428
20: 4 of Israel answered and said, My lord, O **k**, 4428
20: 7 the **k** of Israel called all the elders of 4428
20: 9 of Ben-hadad, Tell my lord the **k**, 4428
20:11 the **k** of Israel answered and said, Tell *him*, 4428
20:13 there came a prophet unto Ahab **k** of Israel, 4428
20:20 Ben-hadad the **k** of Syria escaped on a 4428
20:21 the **k** of Israel went out, and smote 4428
20:22 the prophet came to the **k** of Israel, and 4428
20:22 for at the return of the year the **k** of Syria 4428
20:23 the servants of the **k** of Syria said unto him, 4428
20:28 spake unto the **k** of Israel, and said, 4428
20:31 our heads, and go out to the **k** of Israel: 4428
20:32 and came to the **k** of Israel, and said, 4428
20:38 waited for the **k** by the way, and 4428
20:39 as the **k** passed by, he cried unto the king: 4428
20:39 as the king passed by, he cried unto the **k**: 4428
20:40 the **k** of Israel said unto him, So *shall* thy 4428
20:41 the **k** of Israel discerned him that he *was* of 4428
20:43 the **k** of Israel went to his house heavy and 4428
21: 1 hard by the palace of Ahab **k** of Samaria. 4428
21:10 Thou didst blaspheme God and the **k**. 4428
21:13 Naboth did blaspheme God and the **k**. 4428
21:18 Arise, go down to meet Ahab **k** of Israel, 4428
22: 2 that Jehoshaphat the **k** of Judah came down 4428
22: 2 king of Judah came down to the **k** of Israel. 4428
22: 3 the **k** of Israel said unto his servants, Know 4428
22: 3 take it not out of the hand of the **k** of Syria? 4428
22: 4 Jehoshaphat said to the **k** of Israel, I *am* as 4428
22: 5 Jehoshaphat said unto the **k** of Israel, 4428
22: 6 the **k** of Israel gathered the prophets 4428
22: 6 Lord shall deliver *it* into the hand of the **k**. 4428
22: 8 the **k** of Israel said unto Jehoshaphat, 4428
22: 8 And Jehoshaphat said, Let not the **k** say so. 4428
22: 9 the **k** of Israel called an officer, and said, 4428
22:10 the **k** of Israel and Jehoshaphat the king of 4428
22:10 Jehoshaphat the **k** of Judah sat each on his 4428
22:13 *declare* good unto the **k** *with* one mouth: 4428
22:15 So he came to the **k**. And the king said unto 4428
22:15 the **k** said unto him, Micaiah, shall we go 4428
22:15 shall deliver *it* into the hand of the **k**. 4428
22:16 the **k** said unto him, How many times shall 4428
22:18 the **k** of Israel said unto Jehoshaphat, Did I 4428
22:26 the **k** of Israel said, Take Micaiah, and 4428
22:27 say, Thus saith the **k**, Put this *fellow in* 4428
22:29 So the **k** of Israel and Jehoshaphat the king 4428
22:29 Jehoshaphat the **k** of Judah went up *to* 4428
22:30 the **k** of Israel said unto Jehoshaphat, I will 4428
22:30 the **k** of Israel disguised himself, and 4428
22:31 the **k** of Syria commanded his thirty and 4428
22:31 nor great, save only with the **k** of Israel. 4428
22:32 that they said, Surely it *is* the **k** of Israel. 4428
22:33 perceived that it *was* not the **k** of Israel, 4428
22:34 smote the **k** of Israel between the joints of 4428
22:35 the **k** was stayed up in *his* chariot against 4428
22:37 So the **k** died, and was brought *to* Samaria; 4428
22:37 and they buried the **k** in Samaria. 4428
22:41 in the fourth year of Ahab **k** of Israel. 4428
22:44 Jehoshaphat made peace with the **k** of 4428
22:47 *There was* then no **k** in Edom: a deputy *was* 4428
22:47 then no king in Edom: a deputy *was* **k**. 4428
22:51 year of Jehoshaphat **k** of Judah, 4428
2Ki 1: 3 go up to meet the messengers of the **k** of 4428
1: 6 turn again unto the **k** that sent you, and 4428
1: 9 the **k** sent unto him a captain of fifty with NIH
1: 9 man of God, the **k** hath said, Come down. 4428
1:11 O man of God, thus hath the **k** said, 4428
1:15 and went down with him unto the **k**. 4428
1:17 Jehoram the son of Jehoshaphat **k** of Judah; 4428
3: 1 eighteenth year of Jehoshaphat **k** of Judah, 4428
3: 4 Mesha **k** of Moab was a sheepmaster, and 4428
3: 4 rendered unto the **k** of Israel an hundred 4428
3: 5 that the **k** of Moab rebelled against the king 4428
3: 5 that the king of Moab rebelled against the **k** 4428
3: 6 **k** Jehoram went out of Samaria the same 4428

2Ki 3: 7	and sent to Jehoshaphat the **k** of Judah,	4428
3: 7	The **k** of Moab hath rebelled against me:	4428
3: 9	So the **k** of Israel went, and the king of	4428
3: 9	and the **k** of Judah, and the king of Edom:	4428
3: 9	and the king of Judah, and the **k** of Edom:	4428
3:10	the **k** of Israel said, Alas, that the LORD	4428
3:11	one of the **k** of Israel's servants answered	4428
3:12	So the **k** of Israel and Jehoshaphat and	4428
3:12	and the **k** of Edom went down to him.	4428
3:13	Elisha said unto the **k** of Israel, What have	4428
3:13	the **k** of Israel said unto him, Nay: for	4428
3:14	the presence of Jehoshaphat the **k** of Judah,	4428
3:26	when the **k** of Moab saw that the battle was	4428
3:26	to break through *even* unto the **k** of Edom:	4428
4:13	wouldest thou be spoken for to the **k**, or	4428
5: 1	captain of the host of the **k** of Syria,	4428
5: 5	the **k** of Syria said, Go to, go, and I will	4428
5: 5	and I will send a letter unto the **k** of Israel.	4428
5: 6	he brought the letter to the **k** of Israel,	4428
5: 7	when the **k** of Israel had read the letter,	4428
5: 8	that the **k** of Israel had rent his clothes,	4428
5: 8	that he sent to the **k**, saying, Wherefore	4428
6: 8	the **k** of Syria warred against Israel, and	4428
6: 9	the man of God sent unto the **k** of Israel,	4428
6:10	the **k** of Israel sent to the place which	4428
6:11	Therefore the heart of the **k** of Syria was	4428
6:11	shew me which of us *is* for the **k** of Israel?	4428
6:12	of his servants said, None, my lord, O **k**:	4428
6:12	telleth the **k** of Israel the words that thou	4428
6:21	the **k** of Israel said unto Elisha, when he	4428
6:24	that Ben-hadad **k** of Syria gathered all his	4428
6:26	as the **k** of Israel was passing by upon	4428
6:26	unto him, saying, Help, my lord, O **k**.	4428
6:28	the **k** said unto her, What aileth thee?	4428
6:30	when the **k** heard the words of the woman,	4428
6:32	and *the* **k** sent a man from before him:	NIH
7: 2	a lord on whose hand the **k** leaned	4428
7: 6	the **k** of Israel hath hired against us	4428
7:12	the **k** arose in the night, and said unto his	4428
7:14	the **k** sent after the host of the Syrians,	4428
7:15	the messengers returned, and told the **k**.	4428
7:17	the **k** appointed the lord on whose hand he	4428
7:17	who spake when the **k** came down to him.	4428
7:18	as the man of God had spoken to the **k**,	4428
8: 3	she went forth to cry unto the **k** for her	4428
8: 4	the **k** talked with Gehazi the servant of	4428
8: 5	*as* he was telling the **k** how he had restored	4428
8: 5	cried to the **k** for her house and for her	4428
8: 5	Gehazi said, My lord, O **k**, this *is*	4428
8: 6	when the **k** asked the woman, she told him.	4428
8: 6	So the **k** appointed unto her a certain	4428
8: 7	Ben-hadad the **k** of Syria was sick; and	4428
8: 8	the **k** said unto Hazael, Take a present in	4428
8: 9	Thy son Ben-hadad **k** of Syria hath sent me	4428
8:13	shewed me *that* thou *shalt be* **k** over Syria.	4428
8:16	in the fifth year of Joram the son of Ahab **k**	4428
8:16	Jehoshaphat *being* then **k** of Judah,	4428
8:16	Jehoram the son of Jehoshaphat **k** of Judah	4428
8:20	and **made a k** over themselves.	4427+4428
8:25	**k** of Israel did Ahaziah the son of Jehoram	4428
8:25	son of Jehoram **k** of Judah *begin* to reign.	4428
8:26	the daughter of Omri **k** of Israel.	4428
8:28	Hazael **k** of Syria in Ramoth-gilead;	4428
8:29	**k** Joram went back to be healed in Jezreel	4428
8:29	when he fought against Hazael **k** of Syria.	4428
8:29	Ahaziah the son of Jehoram **k** of Judah	4428
9: 3	I have anointed thee **k** over Israel.	4428
9: 6	I have anointed thee **k** over the people of	4428
9:12	I have anointed thee **k** over Israel.	4428
9:13	and blew with trumpets, saying, Jehu is **k**.	4427
9:14	and all Israel, because of Hazael **k** of Syria.	4428
9:15	**k** Joram was returned to be healed in	4428
9:15	when he fought with Hazael **k** of Syria.)	4428
9:16	Ahaziah **k** of Judah was come down to see	4428
9:18	and said, Thus saith the **k**, *Is it* peace?	4428
9:19	and said, Thus saith the **k**, *Is it* peace?	4428
9:21	Joram **k** of Israel and Ahaziah king of	4428
9:21	of Israel and Ahaziah **k** of Judah went out,	4428
9:27	when Ahaziah the **k** of Judah saw *this,* he	4428
10: 5	thou shalt bid us; we will not **make** any **k**:	4427
10:13	Jehu met with the brethren of Ahaziah **k** of	4428
10:13	we go down to salute the children of the **k**	4428
11: 2	Jehosheba, the daughter of **k** Joram,	4428
11: 7	of the house of the LORD about the **k**.	4428
11: 8	ye shall compass the **k** round about,	4428
11: 8	be ye with the **k** as he goeth out and as he	4428
11:10	did the priest give **k** David's spears	4428
11:11	his weapons in his hand, round about the **k**,	4428
11:12	they **made** him **k**, and anointed him; and	4427
11:12	clapt their hands, and said, God save the **k**.	4428
11:14	behold, the **k** stood by a pillar, as	4428
11:14	and the princes and the trumpeters by the **k**,	4428
11:17	the LORD and the **k** and the people,	4428
11:17	between the **k** also and the people.	4428
11:19	they brought down the **k** from the house of	4428
12: 6	twentieth year of **k** Jehoash the priests had	4428
12: 7	**k** Jehoash called for Jehoiada the priest,	4428
12:17	Hazael **k** of Syria went up, and	4428
12:18	Jehoash **k** of Judah took all the hallowed	4428
12:18	and sent *it* to Hazael **k** of Syria:	4428
13: 1	**k** of Judah Jehoahaz the son of Jehu *began*	4428
13: 3	he delivered them into the hand of Hazael **k**	4428
13: 4	because the **k** of Syria oppressed them.	4428
13: 7	for the **k** of Syria had destroyed them, and	4428
13:10	seventh year of Joash **k** of Judah *began*	4428
13:12	he fought against Amaziah **k** of Judah,	4428
13:14	Joash the **k** of Israel came down unto him,	4428
13:16	he said to the **k** of Israel, Put thine hand	4428
13:18	he took *them.* And he said unto the **k** of	4428
13:22	Hazael **k** of Syria oppressed Israel all	4428
13:24	So Hazael **k** of Syria died; and	4428
14: 1	**k** of Israel reigned Amaziah the son of	4428
14: 1	Amaziah the son of Joash **k** of Judah.	4428
14: 5	servants which had slain the **k** his father.	4428
14: 8	son of Jehu, **k** of Israel, saying, Come,	4428
14: 9	Jehoash the **k** of Israel sent to Amaziah	4428
14: 9	king of Israel sent to Amaziah **k** of Judah,	4428
14:11	Therefore Jehoash **k** of Israel went up; and	4428
14:11	Amaziah **k** of Judah looked one another *in*	4428
14:13	Jehoash **k** of Israel took Amaziah king of	4428
14:13	Jehoash king of Israel took Amaziah **k** of	4428
14:15	how he fought with Amaziah **k** of Judah,	4428
14:17	Amaziah the son of Joash **k** of Judah lived	4428
14:17	son of Jehoahaz **k** of Israel fifteen years.	4428
14:21	**made** him **k** instead of his father Amaziah.	4427
14:22	after that the **k** slept with his fathers.	4428
14:23	**k** of Judah Jeroboam the son of Joash king	4428
14:23	Joash **k** of Israel *began* to reign in Samaria,	4428
15: 1	seventh year of Jeroboam **k** of Israel *began*	4428
15: 1	son of Amaziah **k** of Judah to reign.	4428
15: 5	the LORD smote the **k**, so that he was a	4428
15: 8	eighth year of Azariah **k** of Judah did	4428
15:13	thirtieth year of Uzziah **k** of Judah;	4428
15:17	thirtieth year of Azariah **k** of Judah *began*	4428
15:19	*And* Pul the **k** of Assyria came against	4428
15:20	*of* silver, to give to the **k** of Assyria.	4428
15:20	So the **k** of Assyria turned back, and	4428
15:23	In the fiftieth year of Azariah **k** of Judah	4428
15:27	fiftieth year of Azariah **k** of Judah Pekah	4428
15:29	In the days of Pekah **k** of Israel came	4428
15:29	of Israel came Tiglath-pileser **k** of Assyria,	4428
15:32	**k** of Israel *began* Jotham the son of Uzziah	4428
15:32	the son of Uzziah **k** of Judah to reign.	4428
15:37	to send against Judah Rezin the **k** of Syria,	4428
16: 1	son of Jotham **k** of Judah *began* to reign.	4428
16: 5	Rezin **k** of Syria and Pekah son of	4428
16: 5	Pekah son of Remaliah **k** of Israel came up	4428
16: 6	At that time Rezin **k** of Syria recovered	4428
16: 7	messengers to Tiglath-pileser **k** of Assyria,	4428
16: 7	save me out of the hand of the **k** of Syria,	4428
16: 7	out of the hand of the **k** of Israel, which rise	4428
16: 8	and sent *it for* a present to the **k** of Assyria.	4428
16: 9	the **k** of Assyria hearkened unto him:	4428
16: 9	for the **k** of Assyria went up against	4428
16:10	**k** Ahaz went *to* Damascus to meet	4428
16:10	to meet Tiglath-pileser **k** of Assyria,	4428
16:10	**k** Ahaz sent to Urijah the priest the fashion	4428
16:11	to all that **k** Ahaz had sent from Damascus:	4428
16:11	Urijah the priest made *it* against **k** Ahaz	4428
16:12	when the **k** was come from Damascus,	4428
16:12	come from Damascus, the **k** saw the altar:	4428
16:12	the **k** approached to the altar, and	4428
16:15	**k** Ahaz commanded Urijah the priest,	4428
16:16	according to all that **k** Ahaz commanded.	4428
16:17	**k** Ahaz cut off the borders of the bases,	4428
16:18	house of the LORD for the **k** of Assyria.	4428
17: 1	In the twelfth year of Ahaz **k** of Judah	4428
17: 3	Against him came up Shalmaneser **k** of	4428

2Ki 17: 4	the **k** of Assyria found conspiracy in	4428
17: 4	for he had sent messengers to So **k** of	4428
17: 4	brought no present to the **k** of Assyria,	4428
17: 4	therefore the **k** of Assyria shut him up, and	4428
17: 5	the **k** of Assyria came up throughout all	4428
17: 6	the **k** of Assyria took Samaria, and	4428
17: 7	from under the hand of Pharaoh **k** of Egypt,	4428
17:21	they **made** Jeroboam the son of Nebat **k**:	4427
17:24	the **k** of Assyria brought *men* from	4428
17:26	Wherefore they spake to the **k** of Assyria,	4428
17:27	the **k** of Assyria commanded, saying,	4428
18: 1	year of Hoshea son of Elah **k** of Israel,	4428
18: 1	*that* Hezekiah the son of Ahaz **k** of Judah	4428
18: 7	he rebelled against the **k** of Assyria, and	4428
18: 9	it came to pass in the fourth year of **k**	4428
18: 9	year of Hoshea son of Elah **k** of Israel,	4428
18: 9	*that* Shalmaneser **k** of Assyria came up	4428
18:10	that *is* the ninth year of Hoshea **k** of Israel,	4428
18:11	the **k** of Assyria did carry away Israel unto	4428
18:13	Now in the fourteenth year of **k** Hezekiah	4428
18:13	**k** of Assyria come up against all the fenced	4428
18:14	Hezekiah **k** of Judah sent to the king of	4428
18:14	Hezekiah king of Judah sent to the **k** of	4428
18:14	the **k** of Assyria appointed unto Hezekiah	4428
18:14	**k** of Judah three hundred talents of silver	4428
18:16	*from* the pillars which Hezekiah **k** of Judah	4428
18:16	and gave it to the **k** of Assyria.	4428
18:17	the **k** of Assyria sent Tartan and Rabsaris	4428
18:17	Rab-shakeh from Lachish to **k** Hezekiah	4428
18:18	when they had called to the **k**, there came	4428
18:19	Thus saith the great **k**, the king of Assyria,	4428
18:19	Thus saith the great king, the **k** of Assyria,	4428
18:21	*is* Pharaoh **k** of Egypt unto all that trust on	4428
18:23	give pledges to my lord the **k** of Assyria,	4428
18:28	spake, saying, Hear the word of the great **k**,	4428
18:28	the word of the great king, the **k** of Assyria:	4428
18:29	Thus saith the **k**, Let not Hezekiah deceive	4428
18:30	delivered into the hand of the **k** of Assyria.	4428
18:31	for thus saith the **k** of Assyria, Make *an*	4428
18:33	land out of the hand of the **k** of Assyria?	4428
19: 1	when **k** Hezekiah heard *it,* that he rent his	4428
19: 4	whom the **k** of Assyria his master hath sent	4428
19: 5	So the servants of **k** Hezekiah came to	4428
19: 6	*with* which the servants of the **k** of Assyria	4428
19: 8	found the **k** of Assyria warring against	4428
19: 9	when he heard say of Tirhakah **k** of	4428
19:10	Thus shall ye speak to Hezekiah **k** of	4428
19:10	delivered into the hand of the **k** of Assyria.	4428
19:13	Where *is* the **k** of Hamath, and the king of	4428
19:13	the **k** of Arpad, and the king of the city of	4428
19:13	the **k** of the city of Sepharvaim, *of* Hena,	4428
19:20	Sennacherib **k** of Assyria I have heard.	4428
19:32	the LORD concerning the **k** of Assyria,	4428
19:36	So Sennacherib **k** of Assyria departed, and	4428
20: 6	this city out of the hand of the **k** of Assyria;	4428
20:12	**k** of Babylon, sent letters and a present	4428
20:14	came Isaiah the prophet unto **k** Hezekiah,	4428
20:18	they shall be eunuchs in the palace of the **k**	4428
21: 3	and made a grove, as did Ahab **k** of Israel;	4428
21:11	Because Manasseh **k** of Judah hath done	4428
21:23	and slew the **k** in his own house.	4428
21:24	them that had conspired against **k** Amon;	4428
21:24	the land **made** Josiah his son **k** in his stead.	4427
22: 3	it came to pass in the eighteenth year of **k**	4428
22: 3	*that* the **k** sent Shaphan the son of Azaliah,	4428
22: 9	Shaphan the scribe came to the **k**, and	4428
22: 9	and brought the **k** word again, and said,	4428
22:10	Shaphan the scribe shewed the **k**, saying,	4428
22:10	a book. And Shaphan read it before the **k**.	4428
22:11	when the **k** had heard the words of the book	4428
22:12	the **k** commanded Hilkiah the priest, and	4428
22:16	*even* all the words of the book which the **k**	4428
22:18	to the **k** of Judah which sent you to inquire	4428
22:20	And they brought the **k** word again.	4428
23: 1	the **k** sent, and they gathered unto him all	4428
23: 2	the **k** went up *into* the house of	4428
23: 3	the **k** stood by a pillar, and made a	4428
23: 4	the **k** commanded Hilkiah the high priest,	4428
23:12	did the **k** beat down, and brake *them* down	4428
23:13	which Solomon the **k** of Israel had builded	4428
23:13	of the children of Ammon, did the **k** defile.	4428
23:21	the **k** commanded all the people, saying,	4428
23:23	in the eighteenth year of **k** Josiah,	4428
23:25	like unto him was there no **k** before him,	4428
23:29	In his days Pharaoh-nechoh **k** of Egypt	4428
23:29	the **k** of Assyria to the river Euphrates:	4428
23:29	**k** Josiah went against him; and he slew him	4428
23:30	and **made** him **k** in his father's stead.	4427
23:34	**made** Eliakim the son of Josiah **k** in	4427
24: 1	In his days Nebuchadnezzar **k** of Babylon	4428
24: 7	the **k** of Egypt came not again any more out	4428
24: 7	for the **k** of Babylon had taken from	4428
24: 7	all that pertained to the **k** of Egypt.	4428
24:10	**k** of Babylon came up *against* Jerusalem,	4428
24:11	Nebuchadnezzar **k** of Babylon came	4428
24:12	Jehoiachin the **k** of Judah went out to	4428
24:12	king of Judah went out to the **k** of Babylon,	4428
24:12	the **k** of Babylon took him in the eighth	4428
24:13	**k** of Israel had made in the temple of	4428
24:16	even them the **k** of Babylon brought	4428
24:17	the **k** of Babylon made Mattaniah his	4428
24:17	**made** Mattaniah his father's brother **k** in	4427
24:20	that Zedekiah rebelled against the **k** of	4428
25: 1	*that* Nebuchadnezzar **k** of Babylon came,	4428
25: 2	unto the eleventh year of **k** Zedekiah.	4428
25: 4	and *the* **k** went the way toward the plain.	NIH
25: 5	army of the Chaldees pursued after the **k**,	4428
25: 6	So they took the **k**, and brought him up to	4428
25: 6	brought him up to the **k** of Babylon to	4428
25: 8	which *is* the nineteenth year of **k**	4428
25: 8	year of king Nebuchadnezzar **k** of Babylon,	4428
25: 8	a servant of the **k** of Babylon,	4428
25:11	the fugitives that fell away to the **k** of	4428
25:20	brought them to the **k** of Babylon to	4428
25:21	the **k** of Babylon smote them, and	4428
25:22	whom Nebuchadnezzar **k** of Babylon had	4428
25:23	heard that the **k** of Babylon had made	4428
25:24	in the land, and serve the **k** of Babylon;	4428
25:27	of the captivity of Jehoiachin **k** of Judah,	4428
25:27	*that* Evil-merodach **k** of Babylon,	4428
25:27	did lift up the head of Jehoiachin **k** of	4428
25:30	a continual allowance given him of the **k**,	4428
1Ch 1:43	*any* **k** reigned over the children of Israel;	4428
3: 2	the daughter of Talmai **k** of Geshur:	4428
4:23	there they dwelt with the **k** for his work.	4428
4:41	came in the days of Hezekiah **k** of Judah,	4428
5: 6	whom Tilgath-pilneser **k** of Assyria carried	4428
5:17	in the days of Jotham **k** of Judah,	4428
5:17	and in the days of Jeroboam **k** of Israel.	4428
5:26	stirred up the spirit of Pul **k** of Assyria,	4428
5:26	the spirit of Tilgath-pilneser **k** of Assyria,	4428
11: 2	in time past, even when Saul was **k**,	4428
11: 3	all the elders of Israel to the **k** to Hebron;	4428
11: 3	they anointed David **k** over Israel,	4428
11:10	*and* with all Israel, to **make** him **k**,	4427
12:31	by name, to come and **make** David **k**.	4427
12:38	to Hebron, to **make** David **k** over all Israel:	4427
12:38	Israel *were of* one heart to **make** David **k**.	4427
14: 1	Now Hiram **k** of Tyre sent messengers to	4428
14: 2	LORD had confirmed him **k** over Israel,	4428
14: 8	that David was anointed **k** over all Israel,	4428
15:29	out at a window saw **k** David dancing	4428
17:16	David the **k** came and sat before	4428
18: 3	David smote Hadarezer **k** of Zobah unto	4428
18: 5	came to help Hadarezer **k** of Zobah,	4428
18: 9	Now when Tou **k** of Hamath heard how	4428
18: 9	all the host of Hadarezer **k** of Zobah;	4428
18:10	He sent Hadoram his son to **k** David,	4428
18:11	Them also **k** David dedicated unto	4428
18:17	the sons of David *were* chief about the **k**.	4428
19: 1	that Nahash the **k** of the children of	4428
19: 5	the **k** said, Tarry at Jericho until your	4428
19: 7	and the **k** of Maachah and his people;	4428
20: 2	David took the crown of their **k** from off	4428
21: 3	so many moe as they *be: but,* my lord the **k**,	4428
21:23	let my lord the **k** do *that* which *is* good in	4428
21:24	**k** David said to Ornan, Nay; but I will	4428
23: 1	he **made** Solomon his son **k** over Israel.	4427
24: 6	wrote them before the **k**, and the princes,	4428
24:31	of Aaron in the presence of David the **k**,	4428
25: 2	prophesied according to the order of the **k**.	4428
26:26	of the dedicate *things,* which David the **k**,	4428
26:30	of the LORD, and in the service of the **k**.	4428
26:32	whom **k** David made rulers over	4428
26:32	pertaining to God, and affairs of the **k**.	4428
27: 1	their officers that served the **k** in any matter	4428
27:24	in the account of the chronicles of **k** David.	4428
27:31	of the substance which *was* **k** David's.	4428

1Ch 28: 1 that ministered to the **k** by course, 4428
28: 1 all the substance and possession of the **k**, 4428
28: 2 David the **k** stood up upon his feet, and 4428
28: 4 of my father to be **k** over Israel for ever: 4428
28: 4 he liked me to **make** *me* **k** over all Israel: 4427
29: 1 Furthermore David the **k** said unto all 4428
29: 9 David the **k** also rejoiced *with* great joy. 4428
29:20 and worshipped the LORD, and the **k**. 4428
29:22 they **made** Solomon the son of David **k** 4427
29:23 LORD as **k** instead of David his father, 4428
29:24 and all the sons likewise of **k** David, 4428
29:24 submitted themselves unto Solomon the **k**. 4428
29:25 had not been on any **k** before him in Israel. 4428
29:29 Now the acts of David the **k**, first and last, 4428
2Ch 1: 9 for thou hast **made** me **k** over a people like 4427
1:11 my people, over whom I have **made** thee **k**: 4427
1:14 chariot cities, and with the **k** at Jerusalem. 4428
1:15 the **k** made silver and gold at Jerusalem *as* 4428
2: 3 Solomon sent to Huram the **k** of Tyre, 4428
2:11 Huram the **k** of Tyre answered in writing, 4428
2:11 his people, he hath made thee **k** over them. 4428
2:12 who hath given to David the **k** a wise son, 4428
4:11 make for **k** Solomon for the house of God; 4428
4:16 did Huram his father make to **k** Solomon 4428
4:17 In the plain of Jordan did the **k** cast them, 4428
5: 3 **k** in the feast which *was in* the seventh 4428
5: 6 Also **k** Solomon, and all the congregation 4428
6: 3 the **k** turned his face, and blessed the whole 4428
7: 4 the **k** and all the people offered sacrifices 4428
7: 5 **k** Solomon offered a sacrifice of twenty 4428
7: 5 so the **k** and all the people dedicated 4428
7: 6 which David the **k** had made to praise 4428
8:10 these *were* the chief of **k** Solomon's 4428
8:11 not dwell in the house of David **k** of Israel, 4428
8:15 the commandment of the **k** unto the priests 4428
8:18 of gold, and brought *them* to **k** Solomon. 4428
9: 5 she said to the **k**, *It was* a true report which 4428
9: 8 his throne, to be **k** for the LORD thy God: 4428
9: 8 therefore made he thee **k** over them, to do 4428
9: 9 she gave the **k** an hundred and 4428
9: 9 as the queen of Sheba gave **k** Solomon. 4428
9:11 the **k** made *of* the algum trees terraces to 4428
9:12 **k** Solomon gave to the queen of Sheba all 4428
9:12 *that* which she had brought unto the **k**. 4428
9:15 **k** Solomon made two hundred targets *of* 4428
9:16 the **k** put them in the house of the forest of 4428
9:17 Moreover the **k** made a great throne of 4428
9:20 all the drinking vessels of **k** Solomon *were* 4428
9:22 **k** Solomon passed all the kings of the earth 4428
9:25 chariot cities, and with the **k** at Jerusalem. 4428
9:27 the **k** made silver in Jerusalem as stones, 4428
10: 1 were all Israel come to **make** him **k**. 4427
10: 2 fled from the presence of Solomon the **k**, 4428
10: 6 **k** Rehoboam took counsel with the old men 4428
10:12 as the **k** bade, saying, Come again to me on 4428
10:13 the **k** answered them roughly; and king 4428
10:13 **k** Rehoboam forsook the counsel of the old 4428
10:15 So the **k** hearkened not unto the people: 4428
10:16 when all Israel saw that the **k** would not 4428
10:16 the people answered the **k**, saying, 4428
10:18 **k** Rehoboam sent Hadoram that *was* over 4428
10:18 **k** Rehoboam made speed to get *him* up to 4428
11: 3 **k** of Judah, and to all Israel in Judah and 4428
11:22 his brethren: for *he thought* to **make** him **k**. 4427
12: 2 *that* in the fifth year of **k** Rehoboam 4428
12: 2 **k** of Egypt came up against Jerusalem, 4428
12: 6 of Israel and the **k** humbled themselves; 4428
12: 9 So Shishak **k** of Egypt came up against 4428
12:10 Instead of which **k** Rehoboam made shields 4428
12:11 when the **k** entered *into* the house of 4428
12:13 So **k** Rehoboam strengthened himself in 4428
13: 1 Now in the eighteenth year of **k** Jeroboam 4428
15:16 Maachah the mother of Asa the **k**, 4428
16: 1 thirtieth year of the reign of Asa Baasha **k** 4428
16: 1 none go out or come in to Asa **k** of Judah. 4428
16: 2 and sent to Ben-hadad **k** of Syria, 4428
16: 3 break thy league with Baasha **k** of Israel, 4428
16: 4 Ben-hadad hearkened unto **k** Asa, and 4428
16: 6 Asa the **k** took all Judah; and they carried 4428
16: 7 at that time Hanani the seer came to Asa **k** 4428
16: 7 Because thou hast relied on the **k** of Syria, 4428
16: 7 is the host of the **k** of Syria escaped out of 4428
17:19 These waited on the **k**, besides *those* whom 4428
17:19 besides *those* whom the **k** put in the fenced 4428
18: 3 Ahab **k** of Israel said unto Jehoshaphat king 4428
18: 3 Ahab king of Israel said unto Jehoshaphat **k** 4428
18: 4 Jehoshaphat said unto the **k** of Israel, 4428
18: 5 Therefore the **k** of Israel gathered together 4428
18: 7 the **k** of Israel said unto Jehoshaphat, 4428
18: 7 And Jehoshaphat said, Let not the **k** say so. 4428
18: 8 the **k** of Israel called for one *of his* officers, 4428
18: 9 the **k** of Israel and Jehoshaphat king of 4428
18: 9 Jehoshaphat **k** of Judah sat either of them 4428
18:11 shall deliver *it* into the hand of the **k**. 4428
18:12 *declare* good to the **k** with one assent; 4428
18:14 when he was come to the **k**, the king said 4428
18:14 to the king, the **k** said unto him, Micaiah, 4428
18:15 the **k** said to him, How many times shall I 4428
18:17 the **k** of Israel said to Jehoshaphat, Did I 4428
18:19 Who shall entice Ahab **k** of Israel, that he 4428
18:25 the **k** of Israel said, Take ye Micaiah, and 4428
18:26 say, Thus saith the **k**, Put this *fellow in* 4428
18:28 So the **k** of Israel and Jehoshaphat the king 4428
18:28 Jehoshaphat the **k** of Judah went up to 4428
18:29 the **k** of Israel said unto Jehoshaphat, I will 4428
18:29 So the **k** of Israel disguised himself; and 4428
18:30 Now the **k** of Syria had commanded 4428
18:30 or great, save only with the **k** of Israel. 4428
18:31 that they said, It *is* the **k** of Israel. 4428
18:32 perceived that it was not the **k** of Israel, 4428
18:33 smote the **k** of Israel between the joints of 4428
18:34 howbeit the **k** of Israel stayed *himself* up in 4428
19: 1 Jehoshaphat the **k** of Judah returned to his 4428
19: 2 said to **k** Jehoshaphat, Shouldest thou help 4428
20:15 of Jerusalem, and thou **k** Jehoshaphat, 4428
20:35 after this did Jehoshaphat **k** of Judah join 4428
20:35 join himself with Ahaziah **k** of Israel, 4428
21: 2 all these *were* the sons of Jehoshaphat **k** of 4428
21: 8 of Judah, and **made** themselves **a k**. 4427+4428
21:12 nor in the ways of Asa **k** of Judah, 4428
22: 1 **made** Ahaziah his youngest son **k** in his 4427
22: 1 So Ahaziah the son of Jehoram **k** of Judah 4428
22: 5 went with Jehoram the son of Ahab **k** of 4428
22: 5 against Hazael **k** of Syria at Ramoth-gilead: 4428
22: 6 when he fought with Hazael **k** of Syria. 4428
22: 6 Azariah the son of Jehoram **k** of Judah 4428
22:11 Jehoshabeath, the daughter of the **k**, took 4428
22:11 the daughter of **k** Jehoram, 4428
23: 3 a covenant with the **k** in the house of God. 4428
23: 7 the Levites shall compass the **k** round 4428
23: 7 be you with the **k** when he cometh in, and 4428
23: 9 and shields, that *had been* **k** David's, 4428
23:10 and the temple, by the **k** round about. 4428
23:11 *gave him* the Testimony, and **made** him **k**. 4427
23:11 anointed him, and said, God save the **k**. 4428
23:12 of the people running and praising the **k**, 4428
23:13 the **k** stood at his pillar at the entering in, 4428
23:13 and the princes and the trumpets by the **k**: 4428
23:16 between all the people, and between the **k**, 4428
23:20 brought down the **k** from the house of 4428
23:20 set the **k** upon the throne of the kingdom. 4428
24: 6 the **k** called for Jehoiada the chief, and 4428
24:12 the **k** and Jehoiada gave it to such as did 4428
24:14 brought the rest of the money before the **k** 4428
24:17 of Judah, and made obeisance to the **k**. 4428
24:17 the king. Then the **k** hearkened unto them. 4428
24:21 **k** in the court of the house of the LORD. 4428
24:22 Thus Joash the **k** remembered not 4428
24:23 sent all the spoil of them unto the **k** of 4428
25: 3 his servants that had killed the **k** his father. 4428
25: 7 came a man of God to him, saying, O **k**, 4428
25:16 he talked with him, that *the* **k** said unto him, NIH
25:17 Amaziah **k** of Judah took advice, and 4428
25:17 the son of Jehu, **k** of Israel, saying, Come, 4428
25:18 Joash **k** of Israel sent to Amaziah king of 4428
25:18 Joash king of Israel sent to Amaziah **k** of 4428
25:21 So Joash the **k** of Israel went up; and 4428
25:21 *both* he and Amaziah **k** of Judah, 4428
25:23 Joash the **k** of Israel took Amaziah king of 4428
25:23 Joash the king of Israel took Amaziah **k** of 4428
25:25 Amaziah the son of Joash **k** of Judah lived 4428
25:25 son of Jehoahaz **k** of Israel fifteen years. 4428
26: 1 **made** him **k** in the room of his father 4427
26: 2 after that the **k** slept with his fathers. 4428
26:13 to help the **k** against the enemy. 4428
26:18 they withstood Uzziah the **k**, and said unto 4428
26:21 Uzziah the **k** was a leper unto the day of his 4428
27: 5 He fought also with the **k** of 4428

2Ch 28: 5 him into the hand of the **k** of Syria; 4428
28: 5 he was also delivered into the hand of the **k** 4428
28: 7 and Elkanah *that was* next to the **k**. 4428
28:16 At that time did **k** Ahaz send unto the kings 4428
28:19 Judah low because of Ahaz **k** of Israel; 4428
28:20 Tilgath-pilneser **k** of Assyria came unto 4428
28:21 *out* of the house of the **k**, and of 4428
28:21 and gave *it* unto the **k** of Assyria: 4428
28:22 against the LORD: this *is that* **k** Ahaz. 4428
29:15 according to the commandment of the **k**, 4428
29:18 they went in to Hezekiah the **k**, and said, 4428
29:19 which **k** Ahaz in his reign did cast away in 4428
29:20 Hezekiah the **k** rose early, and gathered 4428
29:23 he goats for the sin offering before the **k** 4428
29:24 for the **k** commanded *that* the burnt 4428
29:27 with the instruments ordained by David **k** 4428
29:29 the **k** and all that were present with him 4428
29:30 Moreover Hezekiah the **k** and the princes 4428
30: 2 For the **k** had taken counsel, and 4428
30: 4 the thing pleased the **k** and all 4428
30: 6 the posts went with the letters from the **k** 4428
30: 6 according to the commandment of the **k**, 4428
30:12 one heart to do the commandment of the **k** 4428
30:24 For Hezekiah **k** of Judah did give to 4428
30:26 **k** of Israel *there was* not the like in 4428
31:13 at the commandment of Hezekiah the **k**, 4428
32: 1 the establishment *thereof,* Sennacherib **k** of 4428
32: 7 be not afraid nor dismayed for the **k** of 4428
32: 8 upon the words of Hezekiah **k** of Judah. 4428
32: 9 After this did Sennacherib **k** of Assyria 4428
32: 9 unto Hezekiah **k** of Judah, and unto all 4428
32:10 Thus saith Sennacherib **k** of Assyria, 4428
32:11 us out of the hand of the **k** of Assyria? 4428
32:20 for this *cause* Hezekiah the **k**, and 4428
32:21 captains in the camp of the **k** of Assyria. 4428
32:22 the hand of Sennacherib the **k** of Assyria, 4428
32:23 and presents to Hezekiah **k** of Judah: 4428
33:11 the captains of the host of the **k** of Assyria, 4428
33:25 them that had conspired against **k** Amon; 4428
33:25 the land **made** Josiah his son **k** in his stead. 4427
34:16 Shaphan carried the book to the **k**, and 4428
34:16 brought the **k** word back again, saying, 4428
34:18 Shaphan the scribe told the **k**, saying, 4428
34:18 a book. And Shaphan read it before the **k**. 4428
34:19 when the **k** had heard the words of the law, 4428
34:20 the **k** commanded Hilkiah, and Ahikam 4428
34:22 *they* that the **k** *had appointed,* went to 4428
34:24 which they have read before the **k** of Judah: 4428
34:26 as for the **k** of Judah, who sent you to 4428
34:28 So they brought the **k** word again. 4428
34:29 the **k** sent and gathered together all 4428
34:30 the **k** went up *into* the house of 4428
34:31 the **k** stood in his place, and made a 4428
35: 3 the son of David **k** of Israel did build; 4428
35: 4 according to the writing of David **k** of 4428
35:16 according to the commandment of **k** Josiah. 4428
35:20 Necho **k** of Egypt came up to fight against 4428
35:21 have I to do with thee, thou **k** of Judah? 4428
35:23 the archers shot at **k** Josiah; and the king 4428
35:23 the **k** said to his servants, Have me away; 4428
36: 1 **made** him **k** in his father's stead in 4427
36: 3 the **k** of Egypt put him down at Jerusalem, 4428
36: 4 the **k** of Egypt made Eliakim his brother 4428
36: 4 **made** Eliakim his brother **k** over Judah 4427
36: 6 Against him came up Nebuchadnezzar **k** of 4428
36:10 **k** Nebuchadnezzar sent, and brought him to 4428
36:10 **made** Zedekiah his brother **k** over Judah 4427
36:13 he also rebelled against **k** Nebuchadnezzar, 4428
36:17 Therefore he brought upon them the **k** of 4428
36:18 the treasures of the **k**, and of his princes; 4428
36:22 Now in the first year of Cyrus **k** of Persia, 4428
36:22 the LORD stirred up the spirit of Cyrus **k** 4428
36:23 Thus saith Cyrus **k** of Persia, All 4428
Ezr 1: 1 Now in the first year of Cyrus **k** of Persia, 4428
1: 1 the LORD stirred up the spirit of Cyrus **k** 4428
1: 2 Thus saith Cyrus **k** of Persia, The LORD 4428
1: 7 Also Cyrus the **k** brought forth the vessels 4428
1: 8 Even those did Cyrus **k** of Persia bring 4428
2: 1 whom Nebuchadnezzar the **k** of Babylon 4428
3: 7 the grant that they had of Cyrus **k** of Persia. 4428
3:10 after the ordinance of David **k** of Israel. 4428
4: 2 since the days of Esar-haddon **k** of Assur, 4428
4: 3 as **k** Cyrus the king of Persia hath 4428
4: 3 as king Cyrus the **k** of Persia hath 4428
4: 5 all the days of Cyrus **k** of Persia, 4428
4: 5 even until the reign of Darius **k** of Persia. 4428
4: 7 unto Artaxerxes **k** of Persia; 4428
4: 8 Jerusalem to Artaxerxes the **k** in this sort: 4430
4:11 sent unto him, *even* unto Artaxerxes the **k**: 4430
4:12 Be it known unto the **k**, that the Jews which 4430
4:13 Be it known now unto the **k**, that, if this 4430
4:14 therefore have we sent and certified the **k**; 4430
4:16 We certify the **k** that, if this city be builded 4430
4:17 *Then* sent the **k** an answer unto Rehum 4430
4:23 Now when the copy of **k** Artaxerxes' letter 4430
4:24 year of the reign of Darius **k** of Persia. 4430
5: 6 *this* side the river, sent unto Darius the **k**: 4430
5: 7 written thus: Unto Darius the **k**, all peace. 4430
5: 8 Be it known unto the **k**, that we went into 4430
5:11 which a great **k** of Israel builded and set up. 4430
5:12 hand of Nebuchadnezzar the **k** of Babylon, 4430
5:13 in the first year of Cyrus the **k** of Babylon 4430
5:13 **k** Cyrus made a decree to build this house 4430
5:14 those did Cyrus the **k** take out of the temple 4430
5:17 Now therefore, if *it seem* good to the **k**, 4430
5:17 that a decree *was* made of Cyrus the **k** to 4430
5:17 let the **k** send his pleasure to us concerning 4430
6: 1 Darius the **k** made a decree, and search was 4430
6: 3 In the first year of Cyrus the **k** *the same* 4430
6: 3 **k** made a decree *concerning* the house of 4430
6:10 pray for the life of the **k**, and of his sons. 4430
6:13 according to that which Darius the **k** had 4430
6:14 and Darius, and Artaxerxes **k** of Persia. 4430
6:15 the sixth year of the reign of Darius the **k**. 4430
6:22 turned the heart of the **k** of Assyria unto 4428
7: 1 in the reign of Artaxerxes **k** of Persia, 4428
7: 6 the **k** granted him all his request, 4428
7: 7 in the seventh year of Artaxerxes the **k**. 4428
7: 8 which *was in* the seventh year of the **k**. 4428
7:11 Now this *is* the copy of the letter that the **k** 4428
7:12 Artaxerxes, **k** of kings, unto Ezra the priest, 4430
7:14 Forasmuch as *thou art* sent of the **k**, and 4430
7:15 which the **k** and his counsellers have freely 4430
7:21 I, *even* I Artaxerxes the **k**, do make a 4430
7:23 there be wrath against the realm of the **k** 4430
7:26 the law of the **k**, let judgment be executed 4430
7:28 hath extended mercy unto me before the **k**, 4428
8: 1 in the reign of Artaxerxes the **k**. 4428
8:22 For I was ashamed to require of the **k** a 4428
8:22 because we had spoken unto the **k**, saying, 4428
8:25 which the **k**, and his counsellers, and 4428
Ne 2: 1 *in* the twentieth year of Artaxerxes the **k**, 4428
2: 1 I took up the wine, and gave *it* unto the **k**. 4428
2: 2 Wherefore the **k** said unto me, Why *is* thy 4428
2: 3 said unto the **k**, Let the king live for ever: 4428
2: 3 said unto the king, Let the **k** live for ever: 4428
2: 4 the **k** said unto me, For what dost thou 4428
2: 5 I said unto the **k**, If it please the king, and 4428
2: 5 If it please the **k**, and if thy servant have 4428
2: 6 the **k** said unto me, (the queen also sitting 4428
2: 6 So it pleased the **k** to send me; and I set 4428
2: 7 Moreover I said unto the **k**, If it please 4428
2: 7 I said unto the king, If it please the **k**, 4428
2: 8 the **k** granted me, according to the good 4428
2: 9 Now the **k** had sent captains of the army 4428
2:19 that ye do? will ye rebel against the **k**? 4428
5:14 and thirtieth year of Artaxerxes the **k**, 4428
6: 6 that thou mayest be their **k**, according to 4428
6: 7 at Jerusalem, saying, *There is* a **k** in Judah: 4428
6: 7 now shall it be reported to the **k** according 4428
7: 6 whom Nebuchadnezzar the **k** of Babylon 4428
9:22 the land of the **k** of Heshbon, and the land 4428
9:22 and the land of Og **k** of Bashan. 4428
13: 6 thirtieth year of Artaxerxes **k** of Babylon 4428
13: 6 king of Babylon came I unto the **k**, 4428
13: 6 after certain days obtained I *leave* of the **k**: 4428
13:26 Did not Solomon **k** of Israel sin by these 4428
13:26 many nations was there no **k** like him, 4428
13:26 and God made him **k** over all Israel: 4428
Est 1: 2 when the **k** Ahasuerus sat on the throne of 4428
1: 5 the **k** made a feast unto all the people that 4428
1: 7 according to the state of the **k**. 4428
1: 8 the **k** had appointed to all the officers of his 4428
1: 9 house which *belonged* to **k** Ahasuerus. 4428
1:10 when the heart of the **k** was merry with 4428
1:10 served in the presence of Ahasuerus the **k**, 4428
1:11 To bring Vashti the queen before the **k** with 4428
1:12 therefore was the **k** very wroth, and 4428

Est 1:13 the **k** said to the wise *men,* which knew 4428
1:15 of the **k** Ahasuerus by the chamberlains? 4428
1:16 Memucan answered before the **k** and 4428
1:16 queen hath not done wrong to the **k** only, 4428
1:16 *are* in all the provinces of the **k** Ahasuerus. 4428
1:17 The **k** Ahasuerus commanded Vashti 4428
1:19 If it please the **k**, let there go a royal 4428
1:19 That Vashti come no *more* before **k** 4428
1:19 let the **k** give her royal estate unto another 4428
1:21 the saying pleased the **k** and the princes; 4428
1:21 the **k** did according to the word of 4428
2: 1 when the wrath of **k** Ahasuerus was 4428
2: 2 there be fair young virgins sought for the **k**: 4428
2: 3 let the **k** appoint officers in all 4428
2: 4 let the maiden which pleaseth the **k** be 4428
2: 4 And the thing pleased the **k**; and he did so. 4428
2: 6 carried away with Jeconiah **k** of Judah, 4428
2: 6 whom Nebuchadnezzar the **k** of Babylon 4428
2:12 turn was come to go in to **k** Ahasuerus, 4428
2:13 thus came *every* maiden unto the **k**; 4428
2:14 she came in unto the **k** no more, except 4428
2:14 except the **k** delighted in her, and *that* she 4428
2:15 was come to go in unto the **k**, she required 4428
2:16 So Esther was taken unto **k** Ahasuerus into 4428
2:17 the **k** loved Esther above all the women, 4428
2:18 the **k** made a great feast unto all his princes 4428
2:18 gave gifts, according to the state of the **k**. 4428
2:21 and sought to lay hand on the **k** Ahasuerus. 4428
2:22 Esther certified the **k** *thereof* in Mordecai's 4428
2:23 in the book of the chronicles before the **k**. 4428
3: 1 After these things did **k** Ahasuerus promote 4428
3: 2 for the **k** had so commanded concerning 4428
3: 7 in the twelfth year of **k** Ahasuerus, 4428
3: 8 Haman said unto **k** Ahasuerus, There is a 4428
3: 9 If it please the **k**, let it be written that they 4428
3:10 the **k** took his ring from his hand, and 4428
3:11 the **k** said unto Haman, The silver *is* given 4428
3:12 in the name of **k** Ahasuerus was it written, 4428
3:15 the **k** and Haman sat down to drink; but 4428
4: 8 charge her that *she* should go in unto the **k**, 4428
4:11 shall come unto the **k** into the inner court, 4428
4:11 except such to whom the **k** shall hold out 4428
4:11 I have not been called to come in unto the **k** 4428
4:16 so will I go in unto the **k**, which *is* not 4428
5: 1 the **k** sat upon his royal throne in the royal 4428
5: 2 when the **k** saw Esther the queen standing 4428
5: 2 the **k** held out to Esther the golden sceptre 4428
5: 3 said the **k** unto her, What wilt thou, queen 4428
5: 4 If *it seem* good unto the **k**, let the king and 4428
5: 4 let the **k** and Haman come *this* day unto 4428
5: 5 the **k** said, Cause Haman to make haste, 4428
5: 5 So the **k** and Haman came to the banquet 4428
5: 6 the **k** said unto Esther at the banquet of 4428
5: 8 If I have found favour in the sight of the **k**, 4428
5: 8 if it please the **k** to grant my petition, and 4428
5: 8 let the **k** and Haman come to the banquet 4428
5: 8 and I will do to morrow as the **k** hath said. 4428
5:11 all *the things* where*in* the **k** had promoted 4428
5:11 above the princes and servants of the **k**. 4428
5:12 **k** unto the banquet that she had prepared 4428
5:12 *am* I invited unto her also with the **k**. 4428
5:14 to morrow speak thou unto the **k** that 4428
5:14 go thou in merrily with the **k** unto 4428
6: 1 On that night could not the **k** sleep, and 4428
6: 1 and they were read before the **k**. 4428
6: 2 who sought to lay hand on the **k** Ahasuerus. 4428
6: 3 the **k** said, What honour and dignity hath 4428
6: 4 the **k** said, Who *is* in the court? 4428
6: 4 to speak unto the **k** to hang Mordecai on 4428
6: 5 the court. And the **k** said, Let him come in. 4428
6: 6 the **k** said unto him, What shall be done 4428
6: 6 the man whom the **k** delighteth to honour? 4428
6: 6 To whom would the **k** delight to do honour 4428
6: 7 Haman answered the **k**, *For* the man whom 4428
6: 7 *For* the man whom the **k** delighteth to 4428
6: 8 be brought which the **k** *useth* to wear, 4428
6: 8 the horse that the **k** rideth upon, and 4428
6: 9 *withal* whom the **k** delighteth to honour, 4428
6: 9 shall it be done to the man whom the **k** 4428
6:10 the **k** said to Haman, Make haste, *and* 4428
6:11 the man whom the **k** delighteth to honour. 4428
7: 1 So the **k** and Haman came to banquet with 4428
7: 2 the **k** said again unto Esther on the second 4428
7: 3 in thy sight, O **k**, and if it please the king, 4428
7: 3 in thy sight, O king, and if it please the **k**, 4428
7: 5 the **k** Ahasuerus answered and said unto 4428
7: 6 Haman was afraid before the **k** and 4428
7: 7 the **k** arising from the banquet of wine in 4428
7: 7 was evil determined against him by the **k**. 4428
7: 8 the **k** returned out of the palace garden into 4428
7: 8 bed whereon Esther *was.* Then said the **k**, 4428
7: 9 said before the **k**, Behold also, 4428
7: 9 who had spoken good for the **k**, standeth in 4428
7: 9 Then the **k** said, Hang him thereon. 4428
8: 1 On that day did the **k** Ahasuerus give 4428
8: 1 Mordecai came before the **k**; for Esther had 4428
8: 2 the **k** took off his ring, which he had taken 4428
8: 3 Esther spake yet again before the **k**, and 4428
8: 4 the **k** held out the golden sceptre toward 4428
8: 4 So Esther arose, and stood before the **k**, 4428
8: 5 If it please the **k**, and if I have found favour 4428
8: 5 the thing seem right before the **k**, and I *be* 4428
8: 7 the **k** Ahasuerus said unto Esther the queen 4428
8:10 he wrote in the **k** Ahasuerus' name, and 4428
8:11 Where*in* the **k** granted the Jews which *were* 4428
8:12 Upon one day in all the provinces of **k** 4428
8:15 presence of the **k** in royal apparel *of* blue 4428
9: 2 all the provinces of the **k** Ahasuerus, 4428
9: 3 and the deputies, and officers of the **k**, 4428
9:11 the palace was brought before the **k**. 4428
9:12 the **k** said unto Esther the queen, The Jews 4428
9:13 said Esther, If it please the **k**, let it be 4428
9:14 the **k** commanded it so to be done: and 4428
9:20 in all the provinces of the **k** Ahasuerus, 4428
9:25 when *Esther* came before the **k**, 4428
10: 1 the **k** Ahasuerus laid a tribute upon 4428
10: 2 where*unto* the **k** advanced him, 4428
10: 3 For Mordecai the Jew *was* next unto **k** 4428
Job 15:24 against him, as a **k** ready to the battle. 4428
18:14 and it shall bring him to the **k** of terrors. 4428
29:25 and sat chief, and dwelt as a **k** in the army, 4428
34:18 *Is it fit* to say to a **k**, *Thou art* wicked? *and* 4428
41:34 He beholdeth all high *things:* he *is* a **k** over 4428
Ps 2: 6 Yet have I set my **k** upon my holy hill of 4428
5: 2 the voice of my cry, my **K**, and my God: 4428
10:16 The LORD *is* **K** for ever and ever: 4428
18:50 Great deliverance giveth he to his **k**; and 4428
20: 9 LORD: let the **k** hear us when we call. 4428
21: 1 The **k** shall joy in thy strength, O LORD; 4428
21: 7 For the **k** trusteth in the LORD, and 4428
24: 7 and the **K** of glory shall come in. 4428
24: 8 Who *is* this **K** of glory? the LORD strong 4428
24: 9 and the **K** of glory shall come in. 4428
24:10 Who is this **K** of glory? The LORD of 4428
24:10 The LORD of hosts, he *is* the **K** of glory. 4428
29:10 yea, the LORD sitteth **K** for ever. 4428
33:16 There is no **k** saved by the multitude of a 4428
44: 4 Thou *art* my **K**, O God: 4428
45: 1 things which I have made touching *the* **k**: 4428
45:11 So shall the **k** greatly desire thy beauty: 4428
45:14 She shall be brought unto the **k** in raiment 4428
47: 2 *is* terrible; *he is* a great **K** over all the earth. 4428
47: 6 sing *praises:* sing *praises* unto our **K**, 4428
47: 7 For God *is* the **K** of all the earth: sing ye 4428
48: 2 sides of the north, the city of the great **K**. 4428
63:11 the **k** shall rejoice in God; every one that 4428
68:24 goings of my God, my **K**, in the sanctuary. 4428
72: 1 Give the **k** thy judgments, O God, and 4428
74:12 For God *is* my **K** of old, working salvation 4428
84: 3 O LORD of hosts, my **K**, and my God. 4428
89:18 and the Holy One of Israel *is* our **k**. 4428
95: 3 a great God, and a great **K** above all gods. 4428
98: 6 a joyful noise before the LORD, the **K**. 4428
105:20 The **k** sent and loosed him; *even* the ruler 4428
135:11 Sihon **k** of the Amorites, and Og king of 4428
135:11 Og **k** of Bashan, and all the kingdoms of 4428
136:19 Sihon **k** of the Amorites: for his mercy 4428
136:20 Og the **k** of Bashan: for his mercy *endureth* 4428
145: 1 I will extol thee, my God, O **k**; and I will 4428
149: 2 let the children of Zion be joyful in their **K**. 4428
Pr 1: 1 of Solomon the son of David, **k** of Israel. 4428
16:10 A divine sentence *is* in the lips of the **k**: 4428
16:14 The wrath of a **k** *is as* messengers of death: 4428
20: 2 The fear of a **k** *is* as the roaring of a lion: 4428
20: 8 A **k** that sitteth in the throne of judgment 4428
20:26 A wise **k** scattereth the wicked, and 4428
20:28 Mercy and truth preserve the **k**: and 4428
22:11 *for* the grace of his lips the **k** *shall be* his 4428

Pr	24:21	My son, fear thou the LORD and the **k**:	4428
	25: 1	which the men of Hezekiah **k** of Judah	4428
	25: 5	Take away the wicked *from* before the **k**,	4428
	25: 6	not forth thyself in the presence of the **k**,	4428
	29: 4	The **k** by judgment stablisheth the land: but	4428
	29:14	The **k** that faithfully judgeth the poor,	4428
	30:27	The locusts have no **k**, yet go they forth all	4428
	30:31	and a **k**, against whom *there is* no rising up.	4428
	31: 1	The words of **k** Lemuel, the prophecy that	4428
Ecc	1: 1	the son of David, **k** in Jerusalem.	4428
	1:12	I the Preacher was **k** over Israel in	4428
	2:12	*can* the man *do* that cometh after the **k**?	4428
	4:13	and a wise child than an old and foolish **k**,	4428
	5: 9	for all: the **k** *himself* is served by the field.	4428
	8: 4	Where the word of a **k** *is, there is* power:	4428
	9:14	there came a great **k** against it, and	4428
	10:16	when thy **k** *is* a child, and thy princes eat in	4428
	10:17	when thy **k** *is* the son of nobles, and	4428
	10:20	Curse not the **k**, no not in thy thought; and	4428
SS	1: 4	the **k** hath brought me *into* his chambers:	4428
	1:12	While the **k** *sitteth* at his table,	4428
	3: 9	**K** Solomon made himself a chariot of	4428
	3:11	behold **k** Solomon with the crown	4428
	7: 5	like purple; the **k** *is* held in the galleries.	4428
Isa	6: 1	In the year that **k** Uzziah died I saw also	4428
	6: 5	for mine eyes have seen the **K**, the LORD	4428
	7: 1	the son of Uzziah **k** of Judah, *that* Rezin	4428
	7: 1	*that* Rezin the **k** of Syria, and Pekah the son	4428
	7: 1	and Pekah the son of Remaliah, **k** of Israel,	4428
	7: 6	**set a k** in the midst of it, *even*	4427+4428
	7:17	departed from Judah; *even* the **k** of Assyria.	4428
	7:20	by the **k** of Assyria, the head, and the hair	4428
	8: 4	shall be taken away before the **k** of Assyria.	4428
	8: 7	*even* the **k** of Assyria, and all his glory:	4428
	8:21	curse their **k** and their God, and	4428
	10:12	fruit of the stout heart of the **k** of Assyria,	4428
	14: 4	up this proverb against the **k** of Babylon,	4428
	14:28	In the year that **k** Ahaz died was this	4428
	19: 4	a fierce **k** shall rule over them, saith	4428
	20: 1	(when Sargon the **k** of Assyria sent him,)	4428
	20: 4	So shall the **k** of Assyria lead away	4428
	20: 6	help to be delivered from the **k** of Assyria:	4428
	23:15	according to the days of one **k**:	4428
	30:33	yea, for the **k** it is prepared; he hath made *it*	4428
	32: 1	a **k** shall reign in righteousness, and princes	4428
	33:17	Thine eyes shall see the **k** in his beauty:	4428
	33:22	*is* our lawgiver, the LORD *is* our **k**;	4428
	36: 1	pass in the fourteenth year of **k** Hezekiah,	4428
	36: 1	*that* Sennacherib **k** of Assyria came up	4428
	36: 2	the **k** of Assyria sent Rabshakeh from	4428
	36: 2	unto **k** Hezekiah with a great army.	4428
	36: 4	Thus saith the great **k**, the king of Assyria,	4428
	36: 4	Thus saith the great king, the **k** of Assyria,	4428
	36: 6	*is* Pharaoh **k** of Egypt to all that trust in	4428
	36: 8	to my master the **k** of Assyria, and I will	4428
	36:13	said, Hear ye the words of the great **k**,	4428
	36:13	words of the great king, the **k** of Assyria.	4428
	36:14	Thus saith the **k**, Let not Hezekiah deceive	4428
	36:15	delivered into the hand of the **k** of Assyria.	4428
	36:16	for thus saith the **k** of Assyria, Make *an*	4428
	36:18	land out of the hand of the **k** of Assyria?	4428
	37: 1	when **k** Hezekiah heard *it*, that he rent his	4428
	37: 4	whom the **k** of Assyria his master hath sent	4428
	37: 5	So the servants of **k** Hezekiah came to	4428
	37: 6	where*with* the servants of the **k** of Assyria	4428
	37: 8	found the **k** of Assyria warring against	4428
	37: 9	he heard say concerning Tirhakah **k** of	4428
	37:10	Thus shall ye speak to Hezekiah **k** of	4428
	37:10	be given into the hand of the **k** of Assyria.	4428
	37:13	Where *is* the **k** of Hamath, and the king of	4428
	37:13	the **k** of Arphad, and the king of the city of	4428
	37:13	the **k** of the city of Sepharvaim, Hena, and	4428
	37:21	to me against Sennacherib **k** of Assyria:	4428
	37:33	the LORD concerning the **k** of Assyria,	4428
	37:37	So Sennacherib **k** of Assyria departed, and	4428
	38: 6	this city out of the hand of the **k** of Assyria:	4428
	38: 9	**k** of Judah, when he had been sick, and	4428
	39: 1	**k** of Babylon, sent letters and a present to	4428
	39: 3	came Isaiah the prophet unto **k** Hezekiah,	4428
	39: 7	they shall be eunuchs in the palace of the **k**	4428
	41:21	bring forth your strong *reasons*, saith the **K**	4428
	43:15	Holy One, the creator of Israel, your **K**.	4428
	44: 6	Thus saith the LORD the **K** of Israel, and	4428
	57: 9	thou wentest to the **k** with ointment, and	4428
Jer	1: 2	days of Josiah the son of Amon **k** of Judah,	4428
	1: 3	of Jehoiakim the son of Josiah **k** of Judah,	4428
	1: 3	of Zedekiah the son of Josiah **k** of Judah,	4428
	3: 6	also unto me in the days of Josiah the **k**,	4428
	4: 9	*that* the heart of the **k** shall perish, and	4428
	8:19	*is* not her **k** in her? Why have they	4428
	10: 7	Who would not fear thee, O **K** of nations?	4428
	10:10	he *is* the living God, and an everlasting **k**:	4428
	13:18	Say unto the **k** and to the queen,	4428
	15: 4	of Manasseh the son of Hezekiah **k** of	4428
	20: 4	I will give all Judah into the hand of the **k**	4428
	21: 1	when **k** Zedekiah sent unto him Pashur	4428
	21: 2	for Nebuchadrezzar **k** of Babylon maketh	4428
	21: 4	wherewith ye fight against the **k** of	4428
	21: 7	I will deliver Zedekiah **k** of Judah, and his	4428
	21: 7	into the hand of Nebuchadrezzar **k** of	4428
	21:10	it shall be given into the hand of the **k** of	4428
	21:11	touching the house of the **k** of Judah,	4428
	22: 1	Go down *to* the house of the **k** of Judah,	4428
	22: 2	the word of the LORD, O **k** of Judah,	4428
	22:11	Shallum the son of Josiah **k** of Judah,	4428
	22:18	Jehoiakim the son of Josiah **k** of Judah;	4428
	22:24	though Coniah the son of Jehoiakim **k** of	4428
	22:25	even into the hand of Nebuchadrezzar **k** of	4428
	23: 5	a **K** shall reign and prosper, and	4428
	24: 1	after that Nebuchadrezzar **k** of Babylon had	4428
	24: 1	Jeconiah the son of Jehoiakim **k** of Judah,	4428
	24: 8	So will I give Zedekiah the **k** of Judah, and	4428
	25: 1	of Jehoiakim the son of Josiah **k** of Judah,	4428
	25: 1	that *was* the first year of Nebuchadrezzar **k**	4428
	25: 3	year of Josiah the son of Amon **k** of Judah,	4428
	25: 9	Nebuchadrezzar the **k** of Babylon,	4428
	25:11	these nations shall serve the **k** of Babylon	4428
	25:12	*that* I will punish the **k** of Babylon, and that	4428
	25:19	Pharaoh **k** of Egypt, and his servants, and	4428
	25:26	the **k** of Sheshach shall drink after them.	4428
	26: 1	**k** of Judah came this word from	4428
	26:18	in the days of Hezekiah **k** of Judah,	4428
	26:19	Did Hezekiah **k** of Judah and all Judah put	4428
	26:21	when Jehoiakim the **k**, with all his mighty	4428
	26:21	his words, the **k** sought to put him to death:	4428
	26:22	Jehoiakim the **k** sent men *into* Egypt,	4428
	26:23	and brought him unto Jehoiakim the **k**;	4428
	27: 1	**k** of Judah came this word unto Jeremiah	4428
	27: 3	send them to the **k** of Edom, and to the king	4428
	27: 3	to the **k** of Moab, and to the king of	4428
	27: 3	to the **k** of the Ammonites, and to the king	4428
	27: 3	to the **k** of Tyrus, and to the king of Zidon,	4428
	27: 3	to the king of Tyrus, and to the **k** of Zidon,	4428
	27: 3	*to* Jerusalem unto Zedekiah **k** of Judah;	4428
	27: 6	hand of Nebuchadnezzar the **k** of Babylon,	4428
	27: 8	same Nebuchadnezzar the **k** of Babylon,	4428
	27: 8	neck under the yoke of the **k** of Babylon,	4428
	27: 9	saying, Ye shall not serve the **k** of Babylon:	4428
	27:11	neck under the yoke of the **k** of Babylon,	4428
	27:12	I spake also to Zedekiah **k** of Judah	4428
	27:12	Bring your necks under the yoke of the **k** of	4428
	27:13	nation that will not serve the **k** of Babylon?	4428
	27:14	saying, Ye shall not serve the **k** of Babylon:	4428
	27:17	serve the **k** of Babylon, and live:	4428
	27:18	*in* the house of the **k** of Judah, and	4428
	27:20	Which Nebuchadnezzar **k** of Babylon took	4428
	27:20	**k** of Judah from Jerusalem to Babylon,	4428
	27:21	*in* the house of the **k** of Judah and	4428
	28: 1	in the beginning of the reign of Zedekiah **k**	4428
	28: 2	I have broken the yoke of the **k** of Babylon.	4428
	28: 3	that Nebuchadnezzar **k** of Babylon took	4428
	28: 4	Jeconiah the son of Jehoiakim **k** of Judah,	4428
	28: 4	for I will break the yoke of the **k** of	4428
	28:11	will I break the yoke of Nebuchadnezzar **k**	4428
	28:14	that *they* may serve Nebuchadnezzar **k** of	4428
	29: 2	(After that Jeconiah the **k**, and the queen,	4428
	29: 3	whom Zedekiah **k** of Judah sent unto	4428
	29: 3	Babylon to Nebuchadnezzar **k** of Babylon,	4428
	29:16	*Know* that thus saith the LORD of the **k**	4428
	29:21	the hand of Nebuchadrezzar **k** of Babylon;	4428
	29:22	whom the **k** of Babylon roasted in the fire;	4428
	30: 9	David their **k**, whom I will raise up unto	4428
	32: 1	in the tenth year of Zedekiah **k** of Judah,	4428
	32: 2	the **k** of Babylon's army besieged	4428
	32: 2	which *was in* the **k** of Judah's house.	4428
	32: 3	For Zedekiah **k** of Judah had shut him up,	4428
	32: 3	I *will* give this city into the hand of the **k** of	4428
	32: 4	Zedekiah **k** of Judah shall not escape out of	4428

Jer 32: 4 delivered into the hand of the **k** of Babylon, 4428
32:28 into the hand of Nebuchadrezzar **k** of 4428
32:36 It shall be delivered into the hand of the **k** 4428
34: 1 when Nebuchadnezzar **k** of Babylon, and 4428
34: 2 Go and speak to Zedekiah **k** of Judah, and 4428
34: 2 I *will* give this city into the hand of the **k** of 4428
34: 3 thine eyes shall behold the eyes of the **k** of 4428
34: 4 of the LORD, O Zedekiah **k** of Judah; 4428
34: 6 unto Zedekiah **k** of Judah in Jerusalem, 4428
34: 7 When the **k** of Babylon's army fought 4428
34: 8 after that the **k** Zedekiah had made a 4428
34:21 Zedekiah **k** of Judah and his princes will I 4428
34:21 into the hand of the **k** of Babylon's army, 4428
35: 1 of Jehoiakim the son of Josiah **k** of Judah, 4428
35:11 when Nebuchadrezzar **k** of Babylon came 4428
36: 1 of Jehoiakim the son of Josiah **k** of Judah, 4428
36: 9 of Jehoiakim the son of Josiah **k** of Judah, 4428
36:16 We will surely tell the **k** of all these words. 4428
36:20 And they went in to the **k** into the court, but 4428
36:20 and told all the words in the ears of the **k**. 4428
36:21 So the **k** sent Jehudi to fet the roll: and 4428
36:21 Jehudi read it in the ears of the **k**, and in 4428
36:21 of all the princes which stood beside the **k**. 4428
36:22 Now the **k** sat *in* the winterhouse in 4428
36:24 nor rent their garments, *neither* the **k**, 4428
36:25 Gemariah had made intercession to the **k** 4428
36:26 the **k** commanded Jerahmeel the son of 4428
36:27 after that the **k** had burnt the roll, and 4428
36:28 which Jehoiakim the **k** of Judah hath burnt. 4428
36:29 And thou shalt say to Jehoiakim **k** of Judah, 4428
36:29 The **k** of Babylon shall certainly come 4428
36:30 saith the LORD of Jehoiakim **k** of Judah; 4428
36:32 Jehoiakim **k** of Judah had burnt in the fire: 4428
37: 1 **k** Zedekiah the son of Josiah reigned 4428
37: 1 whom Nebuchadrezzar **k** of Babylon made 4428
37: 1 of Babylon **made k** in the land of Judah. 4427
37: 3 Zedekiah the **k** sent Jehucal the son of 4428
37: 7 Thus shall ye say to the **k** of Judah, 4428
37:17 Zedekiah the **k** sent, and took him *out:* 4428
37:17 and the **k** asked him secretly in his house, 4428
37:17 delivered into the hand of the **k** of Babylon. 4428
37:18 Moreover Jeremiah said unto **k** Zedekiah, 4428
37:19 The **k** of Babylon shall not come against 4428
37:20 hear now, I pray thee, O my lord the **k**: 4428
37:21 Zedekiah the **k** commanded that they 4428
38: 3 into the hand of the **k** of Babylon's army, 4428
38: 4 Therefore the princes said unto the **k**, 4428
38: 5 Zedekiah the **k** said, Behold, he *is* in your 4428
38: 5 for the **k** *is* not *he that* can do *any* thing 4428
38: 7 the **k** then sitting in the gate of Benjamin; 4428
38: 8 king's house, and spake to the **k**, saying, 4428
38: 9 My lord the **k**, these men have done evil in 4428
38:10 the **k** commanded Ebed-melech 4428
38:11 went *into* the house of the **k** under 4428
38:14 Zedekiah the **k** sent, and took Jeremiah 4428
38:14 the **k** said unto Jeremiah, I *will* ask thee a 4428
38:16 So Zedekiah the **k** sware secretly unto 4428
38:17 If thou wilt assuredly go forth unto the **k** of 4428
38:18 if thou wilt not go forth to the **k** of 4428
38:19 Zedekiah the **k** said unto Jeremiah, I am 4428
38:22 all the women that are left in the **k** of 4428
38:22 brought forth to the **k** of Babylon's princes, 4428
38:23 shalt be taken by the hand of the **k** of 4428
38:25 unto us now what thou hast said unto the **k**, 4428
38:25 to death; also what the **k** said unto thee: 4428
38:26 I presented my supplication before the **k**, 4428
38:27 all these words that the **k** had commanded. 4428
39: 1 In the ninth year of Zedekiah **k** of Judah, 4428
39: 1 came Nebuchadrezzar **k** of Babylon and 4428
39: 3 all the princes of the **k** of Babylon came in, 4428
39: 3 with all the residue of the princes of the **k** 4428
39: 4 *that* when Zedekiah the **k** of Judah saw 4428
39: 5 they brought him up to Nebuchadnezzar **k** 4428
39: 6 the **k** of Babylon slew the sons of Zedekiah 4428
39: 6 also the **k** of Babylon slew all the nobles of 4428
39:11 Now Nebuchadrezzar **k** of Babylon gave 4428
39:13 and all the **k** of Babylon's princes; 4428
40: 5 whom the **k** of Babylon hath made 4428
40: 7 heard that the **k** of Babylon had made 4428
40: 9 in the land and serve the **k** of Babylon, 4428
40:11 heard that the **k** of Babylon had left a 4428
40:14 Dost thou certainly know that Baalis the **k** 4428
41: 1 of the seed royal, and the princes of the **k**, 4428
41: 2 whom the **k** of Babylon had made governor 4428
41: 9 *was* it which Asa the **k** had made for fear of 4428
41: 9 had made for fear of Baasha **k** of Israel: 4428
41:18 whom the **k** of Babylon made governor in 4428
42:11 Be not afraid of the **k** of Babylon, of whom 4428
43:10 and take Nebuchadrezzar the **k** of Babylon, 4428
44:30 I *will* give Pharaoh-hophra **k** of Egypt into 4428
44:30 as I gave Zedekiah **k** of Judah into the hand 4428
44:30 the hand of Nebuchadrezzar **k** of Babylon, 4428
45: 1 of Jehoiakim the son of Josiah **k** of Judah, 4428
46: 2 against the army of Pharaoh-necho **k** of 4428
46: 2 which Nebuchadrezzar **k** of Babylon smote 4428
46: 2 of Jehoiakim the son of Josiah **k** of Judah. 4428
46:13 how Nebuchadrezzar **k** of Babylon should 4428
46:17 Pharaoh **k** of Egypt *is but* a noise; 4428
46:18 *As* I live, saith the **K**, whose name *is* 4428
46:26 into the hand of Nebuchadrezzar **k** of 4428
48:15 saith the **K**, whose name *is* the LORD of 4428
49: 1 why *then* doth their **k** inherit Gad, and 4428
49: 3 for their **k** shall go into captivity, *and* 4428
49:28 which Nebuchadrezzar **k** of Babylon shall 4428
49:30 for Nebuchadrezzar **k** of Babylon hath 4428
49:34 of the reign of Zedekiah **k** of Judah, 4428
49:38 will destroy from thence the **k** and 4428
50:17 first the **k** of Assyria hath devoured him; 4428
50:17 last this Nebuchadrezzar **k** of Babylon hath 4428
50:18 I *will* punish the **k** of Babylon and his land, 4428
50:18 as I have punished the **k** of Assyria. 4428
50:43 The **k** of Babylon hath heard the report of 4428
51:31 to shew the **k** of Babylon that his city is 4428
51:34 Nebuchadrezzar the **k** of Babylon hath 4428
51:57 perpetual sleep, and not wake, saith the **K**, 4428
51:59 when he went with Zedekiah the **k** of Judah 4428
52: 3 that Zedekiah rebelled against the **k** of 4428
52: 4 *that* Nebuchadrezzar **k** of Babylon came, he 4428
52: 5 unto the eleventh year of **k** Zedekiah. 4428
52: 8 army of the Chaldeans pursued after the **k**, 4428
52: 9 they took the **k**, and carried him up unto 4428
52: 9 carried him up unto the **k** of Babylon to 4428
52:10 the **k** of Babylon slew the sons of Zedekiah 4428
52:11 the **k** of Babylon bound him in chains, and 4428
52:12 year of Nebuchadrezzar **k** of Babylon, 4428
52:12 *which* served the **k** of Babylon, 4428
52:15 that fell to the **k** of Babylon, and the rest of 4428
52:20 which **k** Solomon had made in the house of 4428
52:26 brought them to the **k** of Babylon to Riblah. 4428
52:27 the **k** of Babylon smote them, and put them 4428
52:31 of the captivity of Jehoiachin **k** of Judah, 4428
52:31 *that* Evil-merodach **k** of Babylon in the *first* 4428
52:31 lifted up the head of Jehoiachin **k** of Judah, 4428
52:34 diet given him of the **k** of Babylon, 4428
La 2: 6 in the indignation of his anger the **k** 4428
2: 9 her **k** and her princes *are* among 4428
Eze 1: 2 which *was* the fifth year of **k** Jehoiachin's 4428
7:27 The **k** shall mourn, and the prince shall be 4428
17:12 the **k** of Babylon is come *to* Jerusalem, and 4428
17:12 hath taken the **k** thereof, and the princes 4428
17:16 surely in the place *where* the **k** *dwelleth* 4428
17:16 *where* the king *dwelleth* that **made** him **k**, 4427
19: 9 and brought him to the **k** of Babylon: 4428
21:19 that the sword of the **k** of Babylon may 4428
21:21 For the **k** of Babylon stood at the parting of 4428
24: 2 the **k** of Babylon set himself against 4428
26: 7 I *will* bring upon Tyrus Nebuchadrezzar **k** 4428
26: 7 a **k** of kings, from the north, with horses, 4428
28:12 take up a lamentation upon the **k** of Tyrus, 4428
29: 2 set thy face against Pharaoh **k** of Egypt, 4428
29: 3 I *am* against thee, Pharaoh **k** of Egypt, 4428
29:18 Nebuchadrezzar **k** of Babylon caused his 4428
29:19 Egypt unto Nebuchadrezzar **k** of Babylon; 4428
30:10 the hand of Nebuchadrezzar **k** of Babylon. 4428
30:21 I have broken the arm of Pharaoh **k** of 4428
30:22 I *am* against Pharaoh **k** of Egypt, and 4428
30:24 I will strengthen the arms of the **k** of 4428
30:25 I will strengthen the arms of the **k** of 4428
30:25 sword into the hand of the **k** of Babylon, 4428
31: 2 speak unto Pharaoh **k** of Egypt, and to his 4428
32: 2 take up a lamentation for Pharaoh **k** of 4428
32:11 The sword of the **k** of Babylon shall come 4428
37:22 and one **k** shall be king to them all: 4428
37:22 and one king shall be **k** to them all: 4428
37:24 David my servant *shall be* **k** over them; 4428
Da 1: 1 In the third year of the reign of Jehoiakim **k** 4428
1: 1 **k** of Babylon *unto* Jerusalem, 4428
1: 2 the Lord gave Jehoiakim **k** of Judah into 4428

Da 1: 3 the **k** spake unto Ashpenaz the master of 4428
1: 5 the **k** appointed them a daily provision of 4428
1: 5 end thereof they might stand before the **k**. 4428
1:10 I fear my lord the **k**, who hath appointed 4428
1:10 ye make *me* endanger my head to the **k**. 4428
1:18 Now at the end of the days that the **k** had 4428
1:19 the **k** communed with them; and 4428
1:19 Azariah: therefore stood they before the **k**. 4428
1:20 understanding, that the **k** inquired of them, 4428
1:21 *even* unto the first year of **k** Cyrus. 4428
2: 2 the **k** commanded to call the magicians, 4428
2: 2 for to shew the **k** his dreams. 4428
2: 2 So they came and stood before the **k**. 4428
2: 3 the **k** said unto them, I have dreamed a 4428
2: 4 spake the Chaldeans to the **k** in Syriack, 4428
2: 4 to the king in Syriack, O **k**, live for ever: 4430
2: 5 The **k** answered and said to the Chaldeans, 4430
2: 7 Let the **k** tell his servants the dream, and 4430
2: 8 The **k** answered and said, I know of 4430
2:10 The Chaldeans answered before the **k**, and 4430
2:10 therefore *there is* no **k**, lord, nor ruler, 4430
2:11 *it is* a rare thing that the **k** requireth, and 4430
2:11 is none other that can shew it before the **k**, 4430
2:12 For this cause the **k** was angry and 4430
2:15 Why *is* the decree *so* hasty from the **k**? 4430
2:16 desired of the **k** that he would give him 4430
2:16 that *he* would shew the **k** the interpretation. 4430
2:24 whom the **k** had ordained to destroy 4430
2:24 bring me in before the **k**, and I will shew 4430
2:24 I will shew unto the **k** the interpretation. 4430
2:25 Arioch brought in Daniel before the **k** in 4430
2:25 that will make known unto the **k** 4430
2:26 The **k** answered and said to Daniel, 4430
2:27 Daniel answered in the presence of the **k**, 4430
2:27 The secret which the **k** hath demanded 4430
2:27 the soothsayers, shew unto the **k**; 4430
2:28 maketh known to the **k** Nebuchadnezzar 4430
2:29 *As for* thee, O **k**, thy thoughts came *into* 4430
2:30 make known the interpretation to the **k**, 4430
2:31 Thou, O **k**, sawest, and behold a great 4430
2:36 tell the interpretation thereof before the **k**. 4430
2:37 Thou, O **k**, *art* a king of kings: for the God 4430
2:37 Thou, O king, *art* a **k** of kings: for the God 4430
2:45 the great God hath made known to the **k** 4430
2:46 the **k** Nebuchadnezzar fell upon his face, 4430
2:47 The **k** answered unto Daniel, and said, Of a 4430
2:48 the **k** made Daniel a great man, and 4430
2:49 Daniel requested of the **k**, and he set 4430
2:49 but Daniel *sat* in the gate of the **k**. 4430
3: 1 Nebuchadnezzar the **k** made an image of 4430
3: 2 Nebuchadnezzar the **k** sent to gather 4430
3: 2 which Nebuchadnezzar the **k** had set up. 4430
3: 3 that Nebuchadnezzar the **k** had set up; 4430
3: 5 that Nebuchadnezzar the **k** hath set up: 4430
3: 7 that Nebuchadnezzar the **k** had set up. 4430
3: 9 and said to the **k** Nebuchadnezzar, 4430
3: 9 king Nebuchadnezzar, O **k**, live for ever. 4430
3:10 Thou, O **k**, hast made a decree, that every 4430
3:12 these men, O **k**, have not regarded thee: 4430
3:13 Then they brought these men before the **k**. 4430
3:16 and Abed-nego, answered and said to the **k**, 4430
3:17 he will deliver *us* out of thine hand, O **k**. 4430
3:18 if not, be it known unto thee, O **k**, that we 4430
3:24 Nebuchadnezzar the **k** was astonied, and 4430
3:24 They answered and said unto the **k**, True, O 4430
3:24 and said unto the king, True, O **k**. 4430
3:30 the **k** promoted Shadrach, Meshach, and 4430
4: 1 Nebuchadnezzar the **k**, unto all people, 4430
4:18 This dream I **k** Nebuchadnezzar have seen. 4430
4:19 The **k** spake, and said, Belteshazzar, let not 4430
4:22 It *is* thou, O **k**, that art grown and 4430
4:23 whereas the **k** saw a watcher and a holy one 4430
4:24 O **k**, and this *is* the decree of the most 4430
4:24 which is come upon my lord the **k**: 4430
4:27 Wherefore, O **k**, let my counsel be 4430
4:28 All this came upon the **k** Nebuchadnezzar. 4430
4:30 The **k** spake, and said, *Is* not this great 4430
4:31 *saying,* O **k** Nebuchadnezzar, to thee it is 4430
4:37 and extol and honour the **K** of heaven, 4430
5: 1 Belshazzar the **k** made a great feast to a 4430
5: 2 that the **k**, and his princes, his wives, and 4430
5: 3 the **k**, and his princes, his wives, and 4430
5: 5 the **k** saw the part of the hand that wrote. 4430
5: 7 The **k** cried aloud to bring in 4430
5: 7 *And* the **k** spake, and said to the wise *men* 4430
5: 8 nor make known to the **k** the interpretation 4430
5: 9 *was* **k** Belshazzar greatly troubled, and 4430
5:10 by reason of the words of the **k** and 4430
5:10 *and* the queen spake and said, O **k**, live for 4430
5:11 whom the **k** Nebuchadnezzar thy father, 4430
5:11 the **k**, *I say,* thy father, made master of 4430
5:12 whom the **k** named Belteshazzar: 4430
5:13 was Daniel brought in before the **k**. 4430
5:13 *And* the **k** spake and said unto Daniel, 4430
5:13 whom the **k** my father brought out of 4430
5:17 Daniel answered and said before the **k**, 4430
5:17 yet I will read the writing unto the **k**, and 4430
5:18 O thou **k**, the most high God gave 4430
5:30 In that night *was* Belshazzar the **k** of 4430
6: 2 and the **k** should have no damage. 4430
6: 3 the **k** thought to set him over the whole 4430
6: 6 princes assembled *together* to the **k**, 4430
6: 6 said thus unto him, **K** Darius, live for ever. 4430
6: 7 or man for thirty days, save of thee, O **k**, 4430
6: 8 Now, O **k**, establish the decree, and 4430
6: 9 Wherefore **k** Darius signed the writing and 4430
6:12 spake before the **k** concerning the king's 4430
6:12 man within thirty days, save of thee, O **k**, 4430
6:12 The **k** answered and said, The thing *is* true, 4430
6:13 answered they and said before the **k**, 4430
6:13 regardeth not thee, O **k**, nor the decree that 4430
6:14 the **k**, when he heard *these* words, was sore 4430
6:15 these men assembled unto the **k**, and 4430
6:15 said unto the **k**, Know, O king, that the law 4430
6:15 said unto the king, Know, O **k**, that the law 4430
6:15 which the **k** establisheth may be changed. 4430
6:16 the **k** commanded, and they brought 4430
6:16 *Now* the **k** spake and said unto Daniel, 4430
6:17 the **k** sealed it with his own signet, and 4430
6:18 the **k** went to his palace, and passed 4430
6:19 the **k** arose very early in the morning, and 4430
6:20 *and* the **k** spake and said to Daniel, 4430
6:21 said Daniel unto the **k**, O king, live for 4430
6:21 Daniel unto the king, O **k**, live for ever. 4430
6:22 also before thee, O **k**, have I done no hurt. 4430
6:23 Then was the **k** exceeding glad for him, and 4430
6:24 the **k** commanded, and they brought those 4430
6:25 **k** Darius wrote unto all people, nations, 4430
7: 1 In the first year of Belshazzar **k** of Babylon 4430
8: 1 In the third year of the reign of **k** 4428
8:21 the rough goat *is* the **k** of Grecia: and 4428
8:21 horn that *is* between his eyes *is* the first **k**. 4428
8:23 a **k** of fierce countenance, and 4428
9: 1 which was **made k** over the realm of 4427
10: 1 In the third year of Cyrus **k** of Persia a 4428
11: 3 a mighty **k** shall stand up, that shall rule 4428
11: 5 the **k** of the south shall be strong, and 4428
11: 6 to the **k** of the north to make an agreement: 4428
11: 7 shall enter into the fortress of the **k** of 4428
11: 8 he shall continue *more* years than the **k** of 4428
11: 9 So the **k** of the south shall come into *his* 4428
11:11 the **k** of the south shall be moved with 4428
11:11 with him, *even* with the **k** of the north: 4428
11:13 For the **k** of the north shall return, and 4428
11:14 many stand up against the **k** of the south: 4428
11:15 So the **k** of the north shall come, and 4428
11:25 his courage against the **k** of the south with 4428
11:25 the **k** of the south shall be stirred up to 4428
11:36 the **k** shall do according to his will; and 4428
11:40 at the time of the end shall the **k** of 4428
11:40 the **k** of the north shall come against him 4428
Hos 1: 1 of Jeroboam the son of Joash, **k** of Israel. 4428
3: 4 of Israel shall abide many days without a **k**, 4428
3: 5 the LORD their God, and David their **k**; 4428
5: 1 of Israel; and give ye ear, O house of the **k**; 4428
5:13 to the Assyrian, and sent to **k** Jareb: 4428
7: 3 They make the **k** glad with their 4428
7: 5 *In* the day of our **k** the princes have made 4428
8:10 a little for the burden of the **k** of princes. 4428
10: 3 We have no **k**, because we feared not 4428
10: 3 the LORD; what then should a **k** do to us? 4428
10: 6 unto Assyria *for* a present to **k** Jareb: 4428
10: 7 her **k** is cut off as the foam upon the water. 4428
10:15 in a morning shall the **k** of Israel utterly be 4428
11: 5 the Assyrian shall be his **k**, because 4428
13:10 I will be thy **k**: where *is any other* that may 4428
13:10 thou saidst, Give me a **k** and princes? 4428
13:11 I gave thee a **k** in mine anger, and took *him* 4428

Am	1: 1	Israel in the days of Uzziah **k** of Judah,	4428
	1: 1	in the days of Jeroboam the son of Joash **k**	4428
	1:15	their **k** shall go into captivity, he and	4428
	2: 1	he burnt the bones of the **k** of Edom into	4428
	7:10	of Beth-el sent to Jeroboam **k** of Israel,	4428
Jnh	3: 6	For word came unto the **k** of Nineveh, and	4428
	3: 7	through Nineveh by the decree of the **k**	4428
Mic	2:13	their **k** shall pass before them, and	4428
	4: 9	*is there* no **k** in thee? is thy counseller	4428
	6: 5	remember now what Balak **k** of Moab	4428
Na	3:18	Thy shepherds slumber, O **k** of Assyria:	4428
Zep	1: 1	days of Josiah the son of Amon, **k** of Judah.	4428
	3:15	the **k** of Israel, *even* the LORD, *is* in	4428
Hag	1: 1	In the second year of Darius the **k**, in	4428
	1:15	in the second year of Darius the **k**.	4428
Zec	7: 1	it came to pass in the fourth year of **k**	4428
	9: 5	the **k** shall perish from Gaza, and	4428
	9: 9	behold, thy **K** cometh unto thee: he *is* just,	4428
	11: 6	and into the hand of his **k**:	4428
	14: 5	in the days of Uzziah **k** of Judah:	4428
	14: 9	the LORD shall be **k** over all the earth:	4428
	14:16	go up from year to year to worship the **K**,	4428
	14:17	the earth unto Jerusalem to worship the **K**,	4428
Mal	1:14	the Lord a corrupt *thing:* for I *am* a great **K**,	4428
Mt	1: 6	And Jesse begat David the **k**; and David	*935*
	1: 6	David the **k** begat Solomon of *her that had*	*935*
	2: 1	of Judea in the days of Herod the **k**,	*935*
	2: 2	Where is he that is born **K** of the Jews?	*935*
	2: 3	When Herod the **k** had heard *these things,* he	*935*
	2: 9	When they had heard the **k**, they departed;	*935*
	5:35	by Jerusalem; for it is the city of the great **K**.	*935*
	14: 9	And the **k** was sorry: nevertheless for	*935*
	18:23	kingdom of heaven likened unto a certain **k**,	*935*
	21: 5	thy **K** cometh unto thee, meek, and	*935*
	22: 2	kingdom of heaven is like unto a certain **k**,	*935*
	22: 7	But when the **k** heard *thereof,* he was wroth:	*935*
	22:11	And when the **k** came in to see the guests,	*935*
	22:13	Then said the **k** to the servants, Bind him	*935*
	25:34	Then shall the **K** say unto them on his right	*935*
	25:40	And the **K** shall answer and say unto them,	*935*
	27:11	saying, Art thou the **K** of the Jews?	*935*
	27:29	mocked him, saying, Hail, **K** of the Jews!	*935*
	27:37	THIS IS JESUS THE **K** OF THE JEWS.	*935*
	27:42	If he be the **K** of Israel, let him now come	*935*
Mk	6:14	And **k** Herod heard *of him;* (for his name	*935*
	6:22	them that sat with *him,* the **k** said unto	*935*
	6:25	came in straightway with haste unto the **k**,	*935*
	6:26	And the **k** was exceeding sorry; *yet* for his	*935*
	6:27	And immediately the **k** sent an executioner,	*935*
	15: 2	asked him, Art thou the **K** of the Jews?	*935*
	15: 9	Will ye *that* I release unto you the **K** of	*935*
	15:12	*that* I shall do *unto him* whom ye call the **K**	*935*
	15:18	began to salute him, Hail, **K** of the Jews.	*935*
	15:26	was written over, THE **K** OF THE JEWS.	*935*
	15:32	Let Christ the **K** of Israel descend now from	*935*
Lk	1: 5	was in the days of Herod, the **k** of Judea,	*935*
	14:31	Or what **k**, going to make war against	*935*
	14:31	going to make war against another **k**,	*935*
	19:38	Blessed *be* the **K** that cometh in the name of	*935*
	23: 2	saying that he himself is Christ a **K**.	*935*
	23: 3	saying, Art thou the **K** of the Jews?	*935*
	23:37	And saying, If thou be the **K** of the Jews,	*935*
	23:38	Hebrew, THIS IS THE **K** OF THE JEWS.	*935*
Jn	1:49	art the Son of God; thou art the **K** of Israel.	*935*
	6:15	and take him by force, to make him a **k**,	*935*
	12:13	Blessed *is* the **K** of Israel that cometh in	*935*
	12:15	behold, thy **K** cometh, sitting on an ass's	*935*
	18:33	said unto him, Art thou the **K** of the Jews?	*935*
	18:37	therefore said unto him, Art thou a **k** then?	*935*
	18:37	Jesus answered, Thou sayest that I am a **k**.	*935*
	18:39	*that* I release unto you the **K** of the Jews?	*935*
	19: 3	And said, Hail, **K** of the Jews: and	*935*
	19:12	whosoever maketh himself a **k** speaketh	*935*
	19:14	and he saith unto the Jews, Behold your **K**.	*935*
	19:15	saith unto them, Shall I crucify your **K**?	*935*
	19:15	priests answered, We have no **k** but Cesar.	*935*
	19:19	JESUS OF NAZARETH THE **K** OF THE	*935*
	19:21	Jews to Pilate, Write not, The **K** of the Jews;	*935*
	19:21	but that he said, I am **K** of the Jews.	*935*
Ac	7:10	wisdom in the sight of Pharaoh **k** of Egypt;	*935*
	7:18	Till another **k** arose, which knew not Joseph.	*935*
	12: 1	Now about that time Herod the **k** stretched	*935*
	13:21	And afterward they desired a **k**: and God	*935*
	13:22	he raised up unto them David to be their **k**;	*935*
	17: 7	saying that there is another **k**, *one* Jesus.	*935*
	25:13	And after certain days **k** Agrippa and	*935*
	25:14	Festus declared Paul's cause unto the **k**,	*935*
	25:24	**K** Agrippa, and all men which are here	*935*
	25:26	and specially before thee, O **k** Agrippa, that,	*935*
	26: 2	**k** Agrippa, because I shall answer for myself	*935*
	26: 7	For which hope's sake, **k** Agrippa, I am	*935*
	26:13	At midday, O **k**, I saw in the way a light	*935*
	26:19	Whereupon, O **k** Agrippa, I was not	*935*
	26:26	For the **k** knoweth of these *things,* before	*935*
	26:27	**K** Agrippa, believest thou the prophets?	*935*
	26:30	thus spoken, the **k** rose up, and the governor,	*935*
2Co	11:32	**k** kept the city of the Damascenes *with a*	*935*
1Ti	1:17	Now unto the **K** eternal, immortal, invisible,	*935*
	6:15	the **K** of kings, and Lord of lords;	*935*
Heb	7: 1	For this Melchisedec, **k** of Salem, priest of	*935*
	7: 2	first being by interpretation **K** of	*935*
	7: 2	and after that also **K** of Salem, which is,	*935*
	7: 2	also King of Salem, which is, **K** of peace;	*935*
	11:27	not fearing the wrath of the **k**:	*935*
1Pe	2:13	whether *it be* to the **k**, as supreme;	*935*
	2:17	the brotherhood. Fear God. Honour the **k**.	*935*
Rev	9:11	And they had a **k** over them, *which is*	*935*
	15: 3	just and true *are* thy ways, thou **K** of saints.	*935*
	17:14	for he is Lord of lords, and **K** of kings: and	*935*
	19:16	**K** OF KINGS, AND LORD OF LORDS.	*935*

KING'S (284) [KING]

Ge	14:17	at the valley of Shaveh, which *is* the **k** dale.	4428
	39:20	a place where the **k** prisoners *were* bound:	4428
Nu	20:17	we will go *by* the **k** *high* way, we will not	4428
	21:22	*but* we will go along by the **k** *high* way,	4428
1Sa	18:22	now therefore be the **k** son in law.	4428+871.1
	18:23	a light *thing* to be a **k** son in law,	4428+871.1
	18:25	to be avenged of the **k** enemies.	4428
	18:26	it pleased David well to be the **k** son	4428+871.1
	18:27	that he might be the **k** son in law.	4428+871.1
	20:29	Therefore he cometh not unto the **k** table.	4428
	21: 8	because the **k** business required haste.	4428
	22:14	which *is* the **k** son in law, and goeth at thy	4428
	23:20	our part *shall be* to deliver him into the **k**	4428
	26:16	now see where the **k** spear *is,* and the cruse	4428
	26:22	and said, Behold, the **k** spear;	4428
2Sa	9:11	shall eat at my table, as one of the **k** sons.	4428
	9:13	for he did eat continually at the **k** table; and	4428
	11: 2	and walked upon the roof of the **k** house:	4428
	11: 8	Uriah departed out of the **k** house, and	4428
	11: 9	Uriah slept *at* the door of the **k** house with	4428
	11:20	if so be that the **k** wrath arise, and he say	4428
	11:24	*some* of the **k** servants be dead, and	4428
	12:30	he took their **k** crown from off his head,	4428
	13: 4	Why *art* thou, *being* the **k** son, lean from	4428
	13:18	for with such robes were the **k** daughters	4428
	13:23	and Absalom invited all the **k** sons.	4428
	13:27	let Amnon and all the **k** sons go with him.	4428
	13:29	all the **k** sons arose, and every man gat him	4428
	13:30	Absalom hath slain all the **k** sons, and	4428
	13:32	have slain all the young men the **k** sons;	4428
	13:33	to think *that* all the **k** sons are dead:	4428
	13:35	unto the king, Behold, the **k** sons come:	4428
	13:36	the **k** sons came, and lift up their voice and	4428
	14: 1	that the **k** heart *was* toward Absalom.	4428
	14:24	to his own house, and saw not the **k** face.	4428
	14:26	*at* two hundred shekels after the **k** weight.	4428
	14:28	years in Jerusalem, and saw not the **k** face.	4428
	14:32	now therefore let me see the **k** face; and	4428
	15:15	the **k** servants said unto the king, Behold,	4428
	15:35	soever thou shalt hear out of the **k** house,	4428
	16: 2	The asses *be* for the **k** household to ride on;	4428
	18:12	I not put forth mine hand against the **k** son:	4428
	18:18	for himself a pillar, which *is* in the **k** dale:	4428
	18:20	bear no tidings, because the **k** son is dead.	4428
	18:29	When Joab sent the **k** servant, and *me* thy	4428
	19:18	a ferry boat to carry over the **k** household,	4428
	19:42	have we eaten at all of the **k** *cost?* or	4428
	24: 4	Notwithstanding the **k** word prevailed	4428
1Ki	1: 9	called all his brethren the **k** sons, and all	4428
	1: 9	and all the men of Judah the **k** servants:	4428
	1:25	hath called all the **k** sons, and the captains	4428
	1:28	she came into the **k** presence, and	4428
	1:44	they have caused him to ride upon the **k**	4428
	1:47	moreover the **k** servants came to bless our	4428
	2:19	and caused a seat to be set for the **k** mother;	4428
	4: 5	*was* principal officer, *and* the **k** friend:	4428

1Ki 9: 1 the **k** house, and all Solomon's desire 4428
9:10 the house of the LORD, and the **k** house, 4428
10:12 for the **k** house, harps also and 4428
10:28 the **k** merchants received the linen yarn at a 4428
11:14 the Edomite: he *was* of the **k** seed in Edom. 4428
13: 6 the **k** hand was restored him again, and 4428
14:26 and the treasures of the **k** house; 4428
14:27 which kept the door of the **k** house. 4428
15:18 the treasures of the **k** house, and 4428
16:18 that he went into the palace of the **k** house, 4428
16:18 burnt the **k** house over him with fire, and 4428
22:12 for the LORD shall deliver *it* into the **k** 4428
22:26 governor of the city, and to Joash the **k** son; 4428
2Ki 7: 9 that we may go and tell the **k** household. 4428
7:11 and they told *it to* the **k** house within. 4428
9:34 and bury her: for she *is* a **k** daughter. 4428
10: 6 Now the **k** sons, *being* seventy persons, 4428
10: 7 that they took the **k** sons, and slew seventy 4428
10: 8 They have brought the heads of the **k** sons. 4428
11: 2 stale him from among the **k** sons which 4428
11: 4 of the LORD, and shewed them the **k** son. 4428
11: 5 be keepers of the watch of the **k** house; 4428
11:12 he brought forth the **k** son, and put 4428
11:16 the which the horses came *into* the **k** house: 4428
11:19 way of the gate of the guard *to* the **k** house. 4428
11:20 Athaliah with the sword *beside* the **k** house. 4428
12:10 that the **k** scribe and the high priest came 4428
12:18 *in* the **k** house, and sent *it* to Hazael king of 4428
13:16 and Elisha put his hands upon the **k** hands. 4428
14:14 in the treasures of the **k** house, and 4428
15: 5 Jotham the **k** son *was* over the house, 4428
15:25 in the palace of the **k** house, with Argob 4428
16: 8 in the treasures of the **k** house, and sent *it* 4428
16:15 the **k** burnt sacrifice, and his meat offering, 4428
16:18 built in the house, and the **k** entry without, 4428
18:15 and in the treasures of the **k** house. 4428
18:36 for the **k** commandment was, saying, 4428
22:12 and Asahiah a servant of the **k**, saying, 4428
24:13 the treasures of the **k** house, and cut in 4428
24:15 and the **k** mother, and the king's wives, and 4428
24:15 the **k** wives, and his officers, and 4428
25: 4 two walls, which *is* by the **k** garden: 4428
25: 9 the **k** house, and all the houses of 4428
25:19 five men of them that were in the **k** 4428
1Ch 9:18 Who hitherto *waited* in the **k** gate eastward: 4428
21: 4 Nevertheless the **k** word prevailed against 4428
21: 6 for the **k** word was abominable to Joab. 4428
25: 5 All these *were* the sons of Heman the **k** 4428
25: 6 according to the **k** order *to* Asaph, 4428
27:25 over the **k** treasures *was* Azmaveth the son 4428
27:32 Jehiel the son of Hachmoni *was* with the **k** 4428
27:33 Ahithophel *was* the **k** counseller: 4428+3807.1
27:33 Hushai the Archite *was* the **k** companion: 4428
27:34 and the general of the **k** army *was* Joab. 4428
29: 6 with the rulers over the **k** work, 4428
2Ch 1:16 the **k** merchants received the linen yarn at a 4428
7:11 the house of the LORD, and the **k** house: 4428
9:11 to the **k** palace, and harps and psalteries for 4428
9:21 For the **k** ships went *to* Tarshish with 4428
12: 9 and the treasures of the **k** house; 4428
12:10 that kept the entrance of the **k** house. 4428
16: 2 house of the LORD and of the **k** house, 4428
18: 5 for God will deliver *it* into the **k** hand. 4428
18:25 governor of the city, and to Joash the **k** son; 4428
19:11 of the house of Judah, for all the **k** matters: 4428
21:17 substance that was found in the **k** house, 4428
22:11 stole him from among the **k** sons that were 4428
23: 3 unto them, Behold, the **k** son shall reign, 4428
23: 5 And a third *part shall be* at the **k** house; and 4428
23:11 they brought out the **k** son, and put upon 4428
23:15 entering of the horse gate *by* the **k** house, 4428
23:20 they came through the high gate *into* the **k** 4428
24: 8 at the **k** commandment they made a chest, 4428
24:11 unto the **k** office by the hand of the Levites, 4428
24:11 the **k** scribe and the high priest's officer 4428
25:16 unto him, Art thou made of the **k** counsel? 4428
25:24 the treasures of the **k** house, the hostages 4428
26:11 hand of Hananiah, *one* of the **k** captains. 4428
26:21 Jotham his son *was* over the **k** house, 4428
28: 7 slew Maaseiah the **k** son, and Azrikam 4428
29:25 of Gad the **k** seer, and Nathan the prophet: 4428
31: 3 *He appointed* also the **k** portion of his 4428
34:20 and Asaiah a servant of the **k**, saying, 4428
35: 7 these *were* of the **k** substance. 4428
35:10 according to the **k** commandment. 4428
35:15 and Heman, and Jeduthun the **k** seer; 4428
Ezr 4:14 we have maintenance from *the* **k** palace, NIH
4:14 *it was* not meet for us to see the **k** 4428
5:17 let there be search made in the **k** treasure 4430
6: 4 let the expences be given out of the **k** 4430
6: 8 that of the **k** goods, *even* of the tribute 4430
7:20 bestow *it* out of the **k** treasure house. 4430
7:27 which hath put *such a thing* as this in the **k** 4428
7:28 and before all the **k** mighty princes. 4428
8:36 they delivered the **k** commissions unto 4428
8:36 king's commissions unto the **k** lieutenants, 4428
Ne 1:11 of this man. For I was the **k** cupbearer. 4428
2: 8 Asaph the keeper of the **k** forest, 4428+3807.1
2: 9 the river, and gave them the **k** letters. 4428
2:14 the gate of the fountain, and to the **k** pool: 4428
2:18 as also the **k** words that he had spoken unto 4428
3:15 the wall of the pool of Siloah by the **k** 4428
3:25 the tower which lieth out from the **k** high 4428
5: 4 We have borrowed money for the **k** tribute, 4428
11:23 For *it was* the **k** commandment concerning 4428
11:24 *was* at the **k** hand in all matters concerning 4428
Est 1: 5 in the court of the garden of the **k** palace; 4428
1:12 the queen Vashti refused to come at the **k** 4428
1:13 *was* the **k** manner towards all that knew 4428
1:14 which saw the **k** face, *and* which sat 4428
1:18 Media say this day unto all the **k** princes, 4428
1:20 when the **k** decree which he shall make 4428
1:22 For he sent letters into all the **k** provinces, 4428
2: 2 said the **k** servants that ministered unto 4428
2: 3 unto the custody of Hege the **k** 4428
2: 8 when the **k** commandment and his decree 4428
2: 8 that Esther was brought *also* unto the **k** 4428
2: 9 meet to be given her, out of the **k** house: 4428
2:13 the house of the women unto the **k** house. 4428
2:14 the **k** chamberlain, which kept 4428
2:15 but what Hegai the **k** chamberlain, 4428
2:19 then Mordecai sat in the **k** gate. 4428
2:21 while Mordecai sat in the **k** gate, 4428
2:21 two of the **k** chamberlains, Bigthan and 4428
3: 2 all the **k** servants, that *were* in the king's 4428
3: 2 that *were* in the **k** gate, bowed, and 4428
3: 3 the **k** servants, which *were* in the king's 4428
3: 3 which *were* in the **k** gate, said unto 4428
3: 3 Why transgressest thou the **k** 4428
3: 8 all people; neither keep they the **k** laws: 4428
3: 8 it *is* not for the **k** profit to suffer them. 4428
3: 9 to bring *it* into the **k** treasuries. 4428
3:12 were the **k** scribes called on the thirteenth 4428
3:12 had commanded unto the **k** lieutenants, 4428
3:12 was it written, and sealed with the **k** ring. 4428
3:13 the letters were sent by posts into all the **k** 4428
3:15 being hastened by the **k** commandment, 4428
4: 2 came even before the **k** gate: for none 4428
4: 2 for none might enter into the **k** gate clothed 4428
4: 3 whithersoever the **k** commandment and 4428
4: 5 for Hatach, *one* of the **k** chamberlains, 4428
4: 6 of the city, which *was* before the **k** gate. 4428
4: 7 to pay to the **k** treasuries for the Jews, 4428
4:11 All the **k** servants, and the people of 4428
4:11 and the people of the **k** provinces, do know, 4428
4:13 that *thou* shalt escape *in* the **k** house, 4428
5: 1 and stood in the inner court of the **k** house, 4428
5: 1 the king's house, over against the **k** house: 4428
5: 9 when Haman saw Mordecai in the **k** gate, 4428
5:13 I see Mordecai the Jew sitting at the **k** gate. 4428
6: 2 and Teresh, two of the **k** chamberlains, 4428
6: 3 said the **k** servants that ministered unto 4428
6: 4 come into the outward court of the **k** house, 4428
6: 5 the **k** servants said unto him, Behold, 4428
6: 9 hand of one of the **k** most noble princes, 4428
6:10 Mordecai the Jew, that sitteth at the **k** gate: 4428
6:12 Mordecai came again to the **k** gate. 4428
6:14 came the **k** chamberlains, and hasted to 4428
7: 4 enemy could not countervail the **k** damage. 4428
7: 8 As the word went out of the **k** mouth, 4428
7:10 Then was the **k** wrath pacified. 4428
8: 5 the Jews which *are* in all the **k** provinces: 4428
8: 8 in the **k** name, and seal *it* with the king's 4428
8: 8 the king's name, and seal *it* with the **k** ring: 4428
8: 8 for the writing which *is* written in the **k** 4428
8: 8 sealed with the **k** ring, may no man reverse. 4428
8: 9 were the **k** scribes called at that time in 4428
8:10 sealed *it* with the **k** ring, and sent letters by 4428

KINGDOM (342) [KING]

K

Ps	145:11	They shall speak of the glory of thy **k**, and	4438
	145:12	and the glorious majesty of his **k**.	4438
	145:13	Thy **k** *is* an everlasting kingdom, and	4438
	145:13	Thy kingdom *is* an everlasting **k**, and	4438
Ecc	4:14	whereas also *he that is* born in his **k**	4438
Isa	9: 7	upon his **k**, to order it, and to stablish it	4467
	17: 3	the **k** from Damascus, and the remnant of	4467
	19: 2	city against city, *and* **k** against kingdom.	4467
	19: 2	city against city, *and* kingdom against **k**.	4467
	34:12	They shall call the nobles thereof *to* the **k**,	4410
	60:12	and **k** that will not serve thee shall perish;	4467
Jer	18: 7	concerning a nation and concerning a **k**,	4467
	18: 9	and concerning a **k**, to build and to plant *it;*	4467
	27: 8	**k** which will not serve the same	4467
La	2: 2	he hath polluted the **k** and the princes	4467
Eze	16:13	and thou didst prosper into a **k**.	4410
	17:14	That the **k** might be base, that *it* might not	4467
	29:14	and they shall be there a base **k**.	4467
Da	2:37	for the God of heaven hath given thee a **k**,	4437
	2:39	after thee shall arise another **k** inferior to	4437
	2:39	another third **k** of brass, which shall bear	4437
	2:40	the fourth **k** shall be strong as iron:	4437
	2:41	and part of iron, the **k** shall be divided;	4437
	2:42	*so* the **k** shall be partly strong, and	4437
	2:44	kings shall the God of heaven set up a **k**,	4437
	2:44	the **k** shall not be left to other people, *but*	4437
	4: 3	his **k** *is* an everlasting kingdom, and	4437
	4: 3	his kingdom *is* an everlasting **k**, and	4437
	4:17	that the most High ruleth in the **k** of men,	4437
	4:18	forasmuch as all the wise *men* of my **k** are	4437
	4:25	that the most High ruleth in the **k** of men,	4437
	4:26	thy **k** *shall be* sure unto thee, after that thou	4437
	4:29	walked in the palace of the **k** of Babylon.	4437
	4:30	that I have built for the house of the **k** by	4437
	4:31	it is spoken; The **k** is departed from thee.	4437
	4:32	that the most High ruleth in the **k** of men,	4437
	4:34	and his **k** *is* from generation to generation:	4437
	4:36	for the glory of my **k**, mine honour and	4437
	4:36	I was established in my **k**, and	4437
	5: 7	and shall be the third ruler in the **k**.	4437
	5:11	There is a man in thy **k**, in whom *is*	4437
	5:16	and shalt be the third ruler in the **k**.	4437
	5:18	God gave Nebuchadnezzar thy father a **k**,	4437
	5:21	the most high God ruled in the **k** of men,	4437
	5:26	God hath numbered thy **k**, and finished it.	4437
	5:28	Thy **k** is divided, and given to the Medes	4437
	5:29	that *he* should be the third ruler in the **k**.	4437
	5:31	Darius the Median took the **k**, *being* about	4437
	6: 1	It pleased Darius to set over the **k** an	4437
	6: 1	which should be over the whole **k**;	4437
	6: 4	occasion against Daniel concerning the **k**;	4437
	6: 7	All the presidents of the **k**, the governors,	4437
	6:26	That in every dominion of my **k** *men*	4437
	6:26	his **k** *that* which shall not be destroyed, and	4437
	7:14	glory, and a **k**, that all people, nations,	4437
	7:14	and his **k** *that* which shall not be destroyed.	4437
	7:18	the saints of the most High shall take the **k**,	4437
	7:18	possess the **k** for ever, even for ever and	4437
	7:22	time came that the saints possessed the **k**.	4437
	7:23	The fourth beast shall be the fourth **k** upon	4437
	7:24	the ten horns out of this **k** *are* ten kings *that*	4437
	7:27	the **k** and dominion, and the greatness of	4437
	7:27	the greatness of the **k** under the whole	4437
	7:27	whose **k** *is* an everlasting kingdom, and	4437
	7:27	whose kingdom *is* an everlasting **k**, and	4437
	8:23	in the latter time of their **k**, when	4438
	10:13	the prince of the **k** of Persia withstood me	4438
	11: 4	his **k** shall be broken, and shall be divided	4438
	11: 4	for his **k** shall be pluckt up, even for others	4438
	11: 9	the king of the south shall come into *his* **k**,	4438
	11:17	to enter with the strength of his whole **k**,	4438
	11:20	estate a raiser of taxes *in* the glory of the **k**:	4438
	11:21	they shall not give the honour of the **k**:	4438
	11:21	in peaceably, and obtain the **k** by flatteries.	4438
Hos	1: 4	will cause to cease the **k** of the house of	4468
Am	9: 8	of the Lord GOD *are* upon the sinful **k**,	4467
Ob	1:21	of Esau; and the **k** shall be the LORD'S.	4410
Mic	4: 8	the **k** shall come to the daughter of	4467
Mt	3: 2	Repent ye: for the **k** of heaven is at hand.	*932*
	4:17	Repent: for the **k** of heaven is at hand.	*932*
	4:23	and preaching the gospel of the **k**,	*932*
	5: 3	poor in spirit: for theirs is the **k** of heaven.	*932*
	5:10	for theirs is the **k** of heaven.	*932*
	5:19	he shall be called the least in the **k** of	*932*
	5:19	same shall be called great in the **k** of heaven.	*932*
	5:20	ye shall in no case enter into the **k** of heaven.	*932*
	6:10	Thy **k** come. Thy will be done in earth, as *it*	*932*
	6:13	For thine is the **k**, and the power, and	*932*
	6:33	But seek ye first the **k** of God, and	*932*
	7:21	Lord, Lord, shall enter into the **k** of heaven;	*932*
	8:11	and Isaac, and Jacob, in the **k** of heaven.	*932*
	8:12	But the children of the **k** shall be cast out	*932*
	9:35	and preaching the gospel of the **k**, and	*932*
	10: 7	preach, saying, The **k** of heaven is at hand.	*932*
	11:11	notwithstanding he that is least in the **k** of	*932*
	11:12	until now the **k** of heaven suffereth violence,	*932*
	12:25	Every **k** divided against itself is brought to	*932*
	12:26	against himself; how shall then his **k** stand?	*932*
	12:28	of God, then the **k** of God is come unto you.	*932*
	13:11	to know the mysteries of the **k** of heaven,	*932*
	13:19	When any one heareth the word of the **k**, and	*932*
	13:24	The **k** of heaven is likened unto a man which	*932*
	13:31	The **k** of heaven is like unto a grain of	*932*
	13:33	The **k** of heaven is like unto leaven, which a	*932*
	13:38	the good seed are the children of the **k**; but	*932*
	13:41	they shall gather out of his **k** all things that	*932*
	13:43	shine forth as the sun in the **k** of their Father.	*932*
	13:44	the **k** of heaven is like unto treasure hid in a	*932*
	13:45	the **k** of heaven is like unto a merchant man,	*932*
	13:47	Again, the **k** of heaven is like unto a net,	*932*
	13:52	**k** of heaven is like unto a man *that is* a	*932*
	16:19	And I will give unto thee the keys of the **k** of	*932*
	16:28	till they see the Son of man coming in his **k**.	*932*
	18: 1	Who is the greatest in the **k** of heaven?	*932*
	18: 3	ye shall not enter into the **k** of heaven.	*932*
	18: 4	the same is greatest in the **k** of heaven.	*932*
	18:23	Therefore is the **k** of heaven likened unto a	*932*
	19:12	eunuchs for the **k** of heaven's sake.	*932*
	19:14	unto me: for of such is the **k** of heaven.	*932*
	19:23	That a rich *man* shall hardly enter into the **k**	*932*
	19:24	than for a rich *man* to enter into the **k** of	*932*
	20: 1	For the **k** of heaven is like unto a man *that is*	*932*
	20:21	right hand, and the other on the left, in thy **k**.	*932*
	21:31	the harlots go into the **k** of God before you.	*932*
	21:43	The **k** of God shall be taken from you, and	*932*
	22: 2	The **k** of heaven is like unto a certain king,	*932*
	23:13	for ye shut up the **k** of heaven against men:	*932*
	24: 7	rise against nation, and **k** against kingdom:	*932*
	24: 7	rise against nation, and kingdom against **k**:	*932*
	24:14	And this gospel of the **k** shall be preached in	*932*
	25: 1	Then shall the **k** of heaven be likened unto	*932*
	25:14	For *the k of heaven is* as a man travelling	NIG
	25:34	inherit the **k** prepared for you from	*932*
	26:29	I drink it new with you in my Father's **k**.	*932*
Mk	1:14	preaching the gospel of the **k** of God,	*932*
	1:15	time is fulfilled, and the **k** of God is at hand:	*932*
	3:24	And if a **k** be divided against itself,	*932*
	3:24	be divided against itself, that **k** cannot stand.	*932*
	4:11	given to know the mystery of the **k** of God:	*932*
	4:26	And he said, So is the **k** of God, as if a man	*932*
	4:30	Whereunto shall we liken the **k** of God?	*932*
	6:23	I will give *it* thee, unto the half of my **k**.	*932*
	9: 1	till they have seen the **k** of God come with	*932*
	9:47	it is better for thee to enter into the **k** of God	*932*
	10:14	forbid them not: for of such is the **k** of God.	*932*
	10:15	Whosoever shall not receive the **k** of God as	*932*
	10:23	they that have riches enter into the **k** of God!	*932*
	10:24	that trust in riches to enter into the **k** of God!	*932*
	10:25	than for a rich *man* to enter into the **k** of	*932*
	11:10	Blessed *be* the **k** of our father David,	*932*
	12:34	Thou art not far from the **k** of God.	*932*
	13: 8	rise against nation, and **k** against kingdom:	*932*
	13: 8	rise against nation, and kingdom against **k**:	*932*
	14:25	until that day that I drink it new in the **k** of	*932*
	15:43	which also waited for the **k** of God, came,	*932*
Lk	1:33	for ever; and of his **k** there shall be no end.	*932*
	4:43	I must preach the **k** of God to other cities	*932*
	6:20	*be ye* poor: for yours is the **k** of God.	*932*
	7:28	he that is least in the **k** of God is greater than	*932*
	8: 1	shewing the glad tidings of the **k** of God:	*932*
	8:10	given to know the mysteries of the **k** of God:	*932*
	9: 2	And he sent them to preach the **k** of God,	*932*
	9:11	and spake unto them of the **k** of God, and	*932*
	9:27	not taste of death, till they see the **k** of God.	*932*
	9:60	but go thou and preach the **k** of God.	*932*
	9:62	and looking back, is fit for the **k** of God.	*932*
	10: 9	The **k** of God is come nigh unto you.	*932*
	10:11	that the **k** of God is come nigh unto you.	*932*

Lk	11: 2	Thy **k** come. Thy will be done, as in heaven,	*932*
	11:17	Every **k** divided against itself is brought to	*932*
	11:18	against himself, how shall his **k** stand?	*932*
	11:20	no doubt the **k** of God is come upon you.	*932*
	12:31	But rather seek ye the **k** of God;	*932*
	12:32	Father's good pleasure to give you the **k**.	*932*
	13:18	said he, Unto what is the **k** of God like?	*932*
	13:20	Whereunto shall I liken the **k** of God?	*932*
	13:28	in the **k** of God, and you yourselves thrust	*932*
	13:29	the south, and shall sit down in the **k** of God.	*932*
	14:15	Blessed *is he* that shall eat bread in the **k** of	*932*
	16:16	since that time the **k** of God is preached, and	*932*
	17:20	when the **k** of God should come,	*932*
	17:20	The **k** of God cometh not with observation:	*932*
	17:21	for behold, the **k** of God is within you.	*932*
	18:16	forbid them not: for of such is the **k** of God.	*932*
	18:17	Whosoever shall not receive the **k** of God as	*932*
	18:24	they that have riches enter into the **k** of God!	*932*
	18:25	than for a rich *man* to enter into the **k** of	*932*
	18:29	or wife, or children, for the **k** of God's sake,	*932*
	19:11	they thought that the **k** of God should	*932*
	19:12	into a far country to receive for himself a **k**,	*932*
	19:15	having received the **k**, then he commanded	*932*
	21:10	rise against nation, and **k** against kingdom:	*932*
	21:10	rise against nation, and kingdom against **k**:	*932*
	21:31	know ye that the **k** of God is nigh at hand.	*932*
	22:16	until it be fulfilled in the **k** of God.	*932*
	22:18	of the vine, until the **k** of God shall come.	*932*
	22:29	And I appoint unto you a **k**, as my Father	*932*
	22:30	ye may eat and drink at my table in my **k**,	*932*
	23:42	remember me when thou comest into thy **k**.	*932*
	23:51	who also himself waited for the **k** of God.	*932*
Jn	3: 3	be born again, he cannot see the **k** of God.	*932*
	3: 5	the Spirit, he cannot enter into the **k** of God.	*932*
	18:36	Jesus answered, My **k** is not of this world:	*932*
	18:36	not of this world: if my **k** were of this world,	*932*
	18:36	to the Jews: but now is my **k** not from hence.	*932*
Ac	1: 3	speaking of the *things* pertaining to the **k** of	*932*
	1: 6	wilt thou at this time restore again the **k** to	*932*
	8:12	the *things* concerning the **k** of God,	*932*
	14:22	much tribulation enter into the **k** of God.	*932*
	19: 8	persuading the *things* concerning the **k** of	*932*
	20:25	among whom I have gone preaching the **k** of	*932*
	28:23	he expounded and testified the **k** of God,	*932*
	28:31	Preaching the **k** of God, and teaching those	*932*
Ro	14:17	For the **k** of God is not meat and drink; but	*932*
1Co	4:20	For the **k** of God *is* not in word, but	*932*
	6: 9	unrighteous shall not inherit the **k** of God?	*932*
	6:10	nor extortioners, shall inherit the **k** of God.	*932*
	15:24	when he shall have delivered up the **k** to	*932*
	15:50	and blood cannot inherit the **k** of God;	*932*
Gal	5:21	do such *things* shall not inherit the **k** of God.	*932*
Eph	5: 5	hath *any* inheritance in the **k** of Christ and	*932*
Col	1:13	hath translated *us* into the **k** of his dear Son:	*932*
	4:11	These only *are my* fellowworkers unto the **k**	*932*
1Th	2:12	who hath called you unto his **k** and glory.	*932*
2Th	1: 5	that ye may be counted worthy of the **k** of	*932*
2Ti	4: 1	and the dead at his appearing and his **k**;	*932*
	4:18	and will preserve *me* unto his heavenly **k**:	*932*
Heb	1: 8	of righteousness *is* the sceptre of thy **k**.	*932*
	12:28	Wherefore we receiving a **k** which cannot be	*932*
Jas	2: 5	heirs of the **k** which he hath promised to	*932*
2Pe	1:11	abundantly into the everlasting **k** of our Lord	*932*
Rev	1: 9	and in the **k** and patience of Jesus Christ,	*932*
	12:10	and the **k** of our God, and the power of his	*932*
	16:10	and his **k** was full of darkness; and	*932*
	17:12	ten kings, which have received no **k** as yet;	*932*
	17:17	and to agree, and give their **k** unto the beast,	*932*

KINGDOMS (57) [KING]

Dt	3:21	shall the LORD do unto all the **k** whither	4467
	28:25	shalt be removed into all the **k** of the earth.	4467
Jos	11:10	beforetime *was* the head of all those **k**.	4467
1Sa	10:18	out of the hand of all **k**, *and* of them that	4467
1Ki	4:21	Solomon reigned over all **k** from the river	4467
2Ki	19:15	*even* thou alone, of all the **k** of the earth;	4467
	19:19	that all the **k** of the earth may know that	4467
1Ch	29:30	and over all the **k** of the countries.	4467
2Ch	12: 8	and the service of the **k** of the countries.	4467
	17:10	the fear of the LORD fell upon all the **k** of	4467
	20: 6	rulest *not* thou over all the **k** of	4467
	20:29	the fear of God was on all the **k** of *those*	4467
	36:23	All the **k** of the earth hath the LORD God	4467
Ezr	1: 2	heaven hath given me all the **k** of the earth;	4467
Ne	9:22	Moreover thou gavest them **k** and nations,	4467
Ps	46: 6	The heathen raged, the **k** were moved:	4467
	68:32	Sing unto God, ye **k** of the earth; O sing	4467
	79: 6	upon the **k** that have not called upon thy	4467
	102:22	and the **k**, to serve the LORD.	4467
	135:11	king of Bashan, and all the **k** of Canaan:	4467
Isa	10:10	As my hand hath found the **k** of the idols,	4467
	13: 4	a tumultuous noise of the **k** of nations	4467
	13:19	Babylon, the glory of **k**, the beauty of	4467
	14:16	made the earth to tremble, that did shake **k**;	4467
	23:11	out his hand over the sea, he shook the **k**:	4467
	23:17	shall commit fornication with all the **k** of	4467
	37:16	*even* thou alone, of all the **k** of the earth:	4467
	37:20	that all the **k** of the earth may know that	4467
	47: 5	thou shalt no more be called, The lady of **k**.	4467
Jer	1:10	set thee over the nations and over the **k**,	4467
	1:15	I will call all the families of the **k** of	4467
	10: 7	in all their **k**, *there is* none like unto thee.	4438
	15: 4	I will cause them to be removed into all **k**	4467
	24: 9	into all the **k** of the earth for *their* hurt,	4467
	25:26	one with another, and all the **k** of the world,	4467
	28: 8	against great **k**, of war, and of evil, and	4467
	29:18	will deliver them to be removed to all the **k**	4467
	34: 1	all the **k** of the earth of his dominion,	4467
	34:17	to be removed into all the **k** of the earth.	4467
	49:28	and concerning the **k** of Hazor,	4467
	51:20	the nations, and with thee will I destroy **k**:	4467
	51:27	call together against her the **k** of Ararat,	4467
Eze	29:15	It shall be the basest of the **k**; neither shall	4467
	37:22	neither shall they be divided into two **k** any	4467
Da	2:44	break in pieces and consume all these **k**,	4437
	7:23	which shall be diverse from all **k**, and	4437
	8:22	four **k** shall stand up out of the nation, but	4438
Am	6: 2	*be they* better than these **k**? or their border	4467
Na	3: 5	nations thy nakedness, and the **k** thy shame.	4467
Zep	3: 8	that I may assemble the **k**, to pour upon	4467
Hag	2:22	I will overthrow the throne of **k**, and I will	4467
	2:22	I will destroy the strength of the **k** of	4467
Mt	4: 8	and sheweth him all the **k** of the world, and	*932*
Lk	4: 5	shewed unto him all the **k** of the world in a	*932*
Heb	11:33	Who through faith subdued **k**,	*932*
Rev	11:15	The **k** of *this* world are become	*932*
	11:15	of *this* world are become *the* **k** of our Lord,	NIG

KINGLY (1) [KING]

Da	5:20	he was deposed from his **k** throne, and	4437

KINGS (329) [KING]

Ge	14: 5	the **k** that *were* with him, and smote	4428
	14: 9	Arioch king of Ellasar; four **k** with five.	4428
	14:10	the **k** of Sodom and Gomorrah fled, and	4428
	14:17	of the **k** that *were* with him, at the valley of	4428
	17: 6	of thee, and **k** shall come out of thee.	4428
	17:16	of nations; **k** of people shall be of her.	4428
	35:11	of thee, and **k** shall come out of thy loins;	4428
	36:31	these *are* the **k** that reigned in the land of	4428
Nu	31: 8	they slew the **k** of Midian, beside *the rest*	4428
	31: 8	and Hur, and Reba, five **k** of Midian:	4428
Dt	3: 8	**k** of the Amorites the land that *was* on *this*	4428
	3:21	your God hath done unto these two **k**:	4428
	4:47	Og king of Bashan, two **k** of the Amorites,	4428
	7:24	he shall deliver their **k** into thine hand, and	4428
	31: 4	**k** of the Amorites, and unto the land of	4428
Jos	2:10	what you did unto the two **k** of	4428
	5: 1	to pass, when all the **k** of the Amorites,	4428
	5: 1	all the **k** of the Canaanites, which *were* by	4428
	9: 1	when all the **k** which *were* on *this* side	4428
	9:10	all that he did to the two **k** of the Amorites,	4428
	10: 5	Therefore the five **k** of the Amorites,	4428
	10: 6	for all the **k** of the Amorites that dwell in	4428
	10:16	these five **k** fled, and hid themselves in a	4428
	10:17	The five **k** are found hid in a cave at	4428
	10:22	bring out those five **k** unto me out of	4428
	10:23	brought forth those five **k** unto him out of	4428
	10:24	when they brought out those **k** unto Joshua,	4428
	10:24	put your feet upon the necks of these **k**.	4428
	10:40	the vale, and of the springs, and all their **k**:	4428
	10:42	all these **k** and their land did Joshua take *at*	4428
	11: 2	to the **k** that *were* on the north of	4428
	11: 5	when all these **k** were met together,	4428
	11:12	all the cities of those **k**, and all the kings of	4428
	11:12	all the **k** of them, did Joshua take, and	4428
	11:17	and all their **k** he took, and smote them, and	4428
	11:18	made war a long time with all those **k**.	4428

Jos 12: 1 Now these *are* the **k** of the land, which 4428
12: 7 these *are* the **k** of the country which Joshua 4428
12:24 king of Tirzah, one: all the **k** thirty and one. 4428
24:12 before you, *even* the two **k** of the Amorites; 4428
Jdg 1: 7 Threescore and ten **k**, having their thumbs 4428
5: 3 Hear, O ye **k**; give ear, O ye princes; I, 4428
5:19 The **k** came *and* fought, then fought 4428
5:19 fought the **k** of Canaan in Taanach by 4428
8: 5 after Zebah and Zalmunna, **k** of Midian. 4428
8:12 took the two **k** of Midian, Zebah and 4428
8:26 purple raiment that *was* on the **k** of Midian, 4428
1Sa 14:47 against the **k** of Zobah, and against 4428
27: 6 wherefore Ziklag pertaineth unto the **k** of 4428
2Sa 10:19 when all the **k** *that were* servants to 4428
11: 1 at the time when **k** go forth *to battle,* that 4428
1Ki 3:13 that there shall not be any among the **k** like 4428
4:24 over all the **k** on *this* side the river: 4428
4:34 from all **k** of the earth, which had heard of 4428
10:15 *of* all the **k** of Arabia, and *of* the governors 4428
10:23 So king Solomon exceeded all the **k** of 4428
10:29 so for all the **k** of the Hittites, and for 4428
10:29 kings of the Hittites, and for the **k** of Syria, 4428
14:19 the book of the chronicles of the **k** of Israel. 4428
14:29 book of the chronicles of the **k** of Judah? 4428
15: 7 book of the chronicles of the **k** of Judah? 4428
15:23 book of the chronicles of the **k** of Judah? 4428
15:31 book of the chronicles of the **k** of Israel? 4428
16: 5 book of the chronicles of the **k** of Israel? 4428
16:14 book of the chronicles of the **k** of Israel? 4428
16:20 book of the chronicles of the **k** of Israel? 4428
16:27 book of the chronicles of the **k** of Israel? 4428
16:33 all the **k** of Israel that were before him. 4428
20: 1 *there were* thirty and two **k** with him, and 4428
20:12 *was* drinking, he and the **k** in the pavilions, 4428
20:16 he and the **k**, the thirty and two kings that 4428
20:16 the thirty and two **k** that helped him. 4428
20:24 do this thing, Take the **k** away, every man 4428
20:31 we have heard that the **k** of the house of 4428
20:31 kings of the house of Israel *are* merciful **k**: 4428
22:39 book of the chronicles of the **k** of Israel? 4428
22:45 book of the chronicles of the **k** of Judah? 4428
2Ki 1:18 book of the chronicles of the **k** of Israel? 4428
3:10 that the LORD hath called these three **k** 4428
3:13 for the LORD hath called these three **k** 4428
3:21 when all the Moabites heard that the **k** were 4428
3:23 the **k** are surely slain, and they have smitten 4428
7: 6 the king of Israel hath hired against us the **k** 4428
7: 6 the **k** of the Egyptians, to come upon us. 4428
8:18 he walked in the way of the **k** of Israel, 4428
8:23 book of the chronicles of the **k** of Judah? 4428
10: 4 said, Behold, two **k** stood not before him: 4428
10:34 book of the chronicles of the **k** of Israel? 4428
11:19 And he sat on the throne of the **k**. 4428
12:18 and Ahaziah, his fathers, **k** of Judah, 4428
12:19 book of the chronicles of the **k** of Judah? 4428
13: 8 book of the chronicles of the **k** of Israel? 4428
13:12 book of the chronicles of the **k** of Israel? 4428
13:13 Joash was buried in Samaria with the **k** of 4428
14:15 book of the chronicles of the **k** of Israel? 4428
14:16 was buried in Samaria with the **k** of Israel; 4428
14:18 book of the chronicles of the **k** of Judah? 4428
14:28 book of the chronicles of the **k** of Israel? 4428
14:29 with his fathers, *even* with the **k** of Israel; 4428
15: 6 book of the chronicles of the **k** of Judah? 4428
15:11 the book of the chronicles of the **k** of Israel. 4428
15:15 the book of the chronicles of the **k** of Israel. 4428
15:21 book of the chronicles of the **k** of Israel? 4428
15:26 the book of the chronicles of the **k** of Israel. 4428
15:31 the book of the chronicles of the **k** of Israel. 4428
15:36 book of the chronicles of the **k** of Judah? 4428
16: 3 he walked in the way of the **k** of Israel, yea, 4428
16:19 book of the chronicles of the **k** of Judah? 4428
17: 2 not as the **k** of Israel that were before him. 4428
17: 8 of the **k** of Israel, which they had made. 4428
18: 5 none like him among all the **k** of Judah, 4428
19:11 thou hast heard what the **k** of Assyria have 4428
19:17 the **k** of Assyria have destroyed the nations 4428
20:20 book of the chronicles of the **k** of Judah? 4428
21:17 book of the chronicles of the **k** of Judah? 4428
21:25 book of the chronicles of the **k** of Judah? 4428
23: 5 whom the **k** of Judah had ordained to burn 4428
23:11 he took away the horses that the **k** of Judah 4428
23:12 which the **k** of Judah had made, and 4428
23:19 which the **k** of Israel had made to provoke 4428
23:22 nor *in* all the days of the **k** of Israel, nor of 4428
23:22 of the kings of Israel, nor of the **k** of Judah; 4428
23:28 book of the chronicles of the **k** of Judah? 4428
24: 5 book of the chronicles of the **k** of Judah? 4428
25:28 set his throne above the throne of the **k** that 4428
1Ch 1:43 Now these *are* the **k** that reigned in the land 4428
9: 1 they *were* written in the book of the **k** of 4428
16:21 yea, he reproved **k** for their sakes, 4428
19: 9 the **k** that were come *were* by themselves in 4428
20: 1 at the time that **k** go out *to battle,* Joab led 4428
2Ch 1:12 such as none of the **k** have had that *have* 4428
1:17 brought they out *horses* for all the **k** of 4428
1:17 and *for* the **k** of Syria, by their means. 4428
9:14 all the **k** of Arabia and governors of 4428
9:22 king Solomon passed all the **k** of the earth 4428
9:23 all the **k** of the earth sought the presence of 4428
9:26 he reigned over all the **k** from the river 4428
16:11 they *are* written in the book of the **k** of 4428
20:34 who is mentioned in the book of the **k** of 4428
21: 6 he walked in the way of the **k** of Israel, 4428
21:13 hast walked in the way of the **k** of Israel, 4428
21:20 of David, but not in the sepulchres of the **k**. 4428
24:16 him in the city of David among the **k**, 4428
24:25 buried him not in the sepulchres of the **k**. 4428
24:27 *are* written in the story of the book of the **k**. 4428
25:26 *are* they not written in the book of the **k** of 4428
26:23 field of the burial which *belonged* to the **k**; 4428
27: 7 lo they *are* written in the book of the **k** of 4428
28: 2 For he walked in the ways of the **k** of 4428
28:16 At that time did king Ahaz send unto the **k** 4428
28:23 Because the gods of the **k** of Syria help 4428
28:26 they *are* written in the book of the **k** of 4428
28:27 not into the sepulchres of the **k** of Israel: 4428
30: 6 that are escaped out of the hand of the **k** of 4428
32: 4 Why should the **k** of Assyria come, and 4428
32:32 *and* in the book of the **k** of Judah and 4428
33:18 they *are written* in the book of the **k** of 4428
34:11 to floor the houses which the **k** of Judah 4428
35:18 neither did all the **k** of Israel keep such a 4428
35:27 they *are* written in the book of the **k** of 4428
36: 8 they *are* written in the book of the **k** of 4428
Ezr 4:13 thou shalt endamage the revenue of the **k**. 4430
4:15 hurtful unto **k** and provinces, and that they 4430
4:19 old time *hath* made insurrection against **k**, 4430
4:20 There have been mighty **k** also over 4430
4:22 should damage grow to the hurt of the **k**? 4430
6:12 caused his name to dwell there destroy all **k** 4430
7:12 Artaxerxes, king of **k**, unto Ezra the priest, 4430
9: 7 iniquities have we, our **k**, *and* our priests, 4428
9: 7 been delivered into the hand of the **k** of 4428
9: 9 unto us in the sight of the **k** of Persia, 4428
Ne 9:24 with their **k**, and the people of the land, 4428
9:32 on our **k**, on our princes, and on our priests, 4428
9:32 since the time of the **k** of Assyria unto this 4428
9:34 Neither have our **k**, our princes, our priests, 4428
9:37 it yieldeth much increase unto the **k** whom 4428
Est 10: 2 book of the chronicles of the **k** of Media 4428
Job 3:14 With **k** and counsellers of the earth, 4428
12:18 He looseth the bond of **k**, and girdeth their 4428
36: 7 with **k** *are they* on the throne; yea, he doth 4428
Ps 2: 2 The **k** of the earth set themselves, and 4428
2:10 Be wise now therefore, O ye **k**: 4428
48: 4 For lo, the **k** were assembled, they passed 4428
68:12 **K** of armies did flee apace: and she that 4428
68:14 When the Almighty scattered **k** in it, it was 4428
68:29 Because of thy temple at Jerusalem shall **k** 4428
72:10 The **k** of Tarshish and *of* the isles shall 4428
72:10 the **k** of Sheba and Seba shall offer gifts. 4428
72:11 Yea, all **k** shall fall down before him: 4428
76:12 *he is* terrible to the **k** of the earth. 4428
89:27 *my* firstborn, higher than the **k** of the earth. 4428
102:15 and all the **k** of the earth thy glory. 4428
105:14 yea, he reproved **k** for their sakes; 4428
105:30 in abundance, in the chambers of their **k**. 4428
110: 5 strike through **k** in the day of his wrath. 4428
119:46 will speak of thy testimonies also before **k**, 4428
135:10 smote great nations, and slew mighty **k**; 4428
136:17 To him which smote great **k**: for his mercy 4428
136:18 slew famous **k**: for his mercy *endureth* for 4428
138: 4 All the **k** of the earth shall praise thee, 4428
144:10 *It is he* that giveth salvation unto **k**: 4428
148:11 **K** of the earth, and all people; princes, and 4428
149: 8 To bind their **k** with chains, and 4428
Pr 8:15 By me **k** reign, and princes decree justice. 4428

Pr 16:12 *It is* an abomination to **k** to commit 4428
16:13 Righteous lips *are* the delight of **k**; and 4428
22:29 he shall stand before **k**; he shall not stand 4428
25: 2 the honour of **k** *is* to search out a matter. 4428
25: 3 and the heart of **k** *is* unsearchable. 4428
31: 3 nor thy ways to *that which* destroyeth **k**. 4428
31: 4 *It is* not for **k**, O Lemuel, *it is* not for kings 4428
31: 4 O Lemuel, *it is* not for **k** to drink wine; 4428
Ecc 2: 8 the peculiar treasure of **k** and of 4428
Isa 1: 1 Jotham, Ahaz, *and* Hezekiah, **k** of Judah. 4428
7:16 abhorrest shall be forsaken of both her **k**. 4428
10: 8 he saith, *Are* not my princes altogether **k**? 4428
14: 9 it hath raised up from their thrones all the **k** 4428
14:18 All the **k** of the nations, *even* all of them, 4428
19:11 the son of the wise, the son of ancient **k**? 4428
24:21 and the **k** of the earth upon the earth. 4428
37:11 thou hast heard what the **k** of Assyria have 4428
37:18 the **k** of Assyria have laid waste all 4428
41: 2 before him, and made *him* rule over **k**? 4428
45: 1 I will loose the loins of **k**, to open before 4428
49: 7 to a servant of rulers, **K** shall see and arise, 4428
49:23 **k** shall be thy nursing fathers, and 4428
52:15 the **k** shall shut their mouths at him: 4428
60: 3 and **k** to the brightness of thy rising. 4428
60:10 and their **k** shall minister unto thee: 4428
60:11 and *that* their **k** *may be* brought. 4428
60:16 the Gentiles, and shalt suck the breast of **k**: 4428
62: 2 see thy righteousness, and all **k** thy glory: 4428
Jer 1:18 against the **k** of Judah, against the princes 4428
2:26 they, their **k**, their princes, and their priests, 4428
8: 1 they shall bring out the bones of the **k** of 4428
13:13 even the **k** that sit upon David's throne, and 4428
17:19 whereby the **k** of Judah come in, and by 4428
17:20 ye **k** of Judah, and all Judah, and all 4428
17:25 shall there enter into the gates of this city **k** 4428
19: 3 O **k** of Judah, and inhabitants of Jerusalem; 4428
19: 4 nor the **k** of Judah, and have filled this 4428
19:13 and the houses of the **k** of Judah, 4428
20: 5 all the treasures of the **k** of Judah will I 4428
22: 4 house **k** sitting upon the throne of David, 4428
25:14 great **k** shall serve themselves of them also: 4428
25:18 and the **k** thereof, *and* the princes thereof, 4428
25:20 all the **k** of the land of Uz, and all the kings 4428
25:20 all the **k** of the land of the Philistines, and 4428
25:22 all the **k** of Tyrus, and all the kings of 4428
25:22 all the **k** of Zidon, and the kings of the isles 4428
25:22 the **k** of the isles which *are* beyond the sea, 4428
25:24 all the **k** of Arabia, and all the kings of 4428
25:24 all the **k** of the mingled people that dwell in 4428
25:25 all the **k** of Zimri, and all the kings of 4428
25:25 all the **k** of Elam, and all the kings of 4428
25:25 kings of Elam, and all the **k** of the Medes, 4428
25:26 all the **k** of the north, far and near, one with 4428
27: 7 and great **k** shall serve themselves of him. 4428
32:32 they, their **k**, their princes, their priests, and 4428
33: 4 concerning the houses of the **k** of Judah, 4428
34: 5 the former **k** which were before thee, so 4428
44: 9 the wickedness of the **k** of Judah, and 4428
44:17 we, and our fathers, our **k**, and our princes, 4428
44:21 your **k**, and your princes, and the people of 4428
46:25 and Egypt, with their gods, and their **k**; 4428
50:41 many **k** shall be raised up from the coasts 4428
51:11 raised up the spirit of the **k** of the Medes: 4428
51:28 Prepare against her the nations with the **k** 4428
52:32 set his throne above the throne of the **k** that 4428
La 4:12 The **k** of the earth, and all the inhabitants of 4428
Eze 26: 7 a king of **k**, from the north, with horses, 4428
27:33 thou didst enrich the **k** of the earth with 4428
27:35 their **k** shall be sore afraid, they shall be 4428
28:17 I will lay thee before **k**, that *they* may 4428
32:10 and their **k** shall be horribly afraid for thee, 4428
32:29 There *is* Edom, her **k**, and all her princes, 4428
43: 7 *neither* they, nor their **k**, by their 4428
43: 7 nor by the carcases of their **k** *in* their high 4428
43: 9 the carcases of their **k**, far from me, and 4428
Da 2:21 he removeth **k**, and setteth up kings: 4430
2:21 he removeth kings, and setteth up **k**: 4430
2:37 Thou, O king, *art* a king of **k**: for the God 4430
2:44 in the days of these **k** shall the God of 4430
2:47 a Lord of **k**, and a revealer of secrets, 4430
7:17 great beasts, which *are* four, *are* four **k**, 4430
7:24 the ten horns out of this kingdom *are* ten **k** 4430
7:24 from the first, and he shall subdue three **k**. 4430
8:20 sawest having two horns *are* the **k** of Media 4428
9: 6 which spake in thy name to our **k**, 4428
9: 8 to our **k**, to our princes, and to our fathers, 4428
10:13 and I remained there with the **k** of Persia. 4428
11: 2 there *shall* stand up yet three **k** in Persia; 4428
Hos 1: 1 **k** of Judah, and in the days of Jeroboam 4428
7: 7 devoured their judges; all their **k** are fallen: 4428
8: 4 They have **set up k**, but not by me: 4427
Mic 1: 1 Ahaz, *and* Hezekiah, **k** of Judah, which he 4428
1:14 the houses of Achzib *shall be* a lie to the **k** 4428
Hab 1:10 they shall scoff at the **k**, and the princes 4428
Mt 10:18 brought before governors and **k** for my sake, *935*
17:25 of whom do the **k** of the earth take custom or *935*
Mk 13: 9 be brought before rulers and **k** for my sake, *935*
Lk 10:24 **k** have desired to see *those things* which ye *935*
21:12 being brought before **k** and rulers for my *935*
22:25 The **k** of the Gentiles exercise lordship over *935*
Ac 4:26 The **k** of the earth stood up, and the rulers *935*
9:15 and **k**, and the children of Israel: *935*
1Co 4: 8 ye are rich, ye have **reigned as k** without us: *936*
1Ti 2: 2 For **k**, and *for* all that are in authority; *935*
6:15 the King of **k**, and Lord of lords; *936*
Heb 7: 1 returning from the slaughter of the **k**, *935*
Rev 1: 5 the dead, and the prince of the **k** of the earth. *935*
1: 6 And hath made us **k** and priests unto God *935*
5:10 And hast made us unto our God **k** and *935*
6:15 And the **k** of the earth, and the great men, *935*
10:11 and nations, and tongues, and **k**. *935*
16:12 that the way of the **k** of the east might be *935*
16:14 which go forth unto the **k** of the earth and *935*
17: 2 With whom the **k** of the earth have *935*
17:10 And there are seven **k**: five are fallen, and *935*
17:12 the ten horns which thou sawest are ten **k**, *935*
17:12 receive power as **k** one hour with the beast. *935*
17:14 for he is Lord of lords, and King of **k**: and *935*
17:18 which reigneth over the **k** of the earth. *935*
18: 3 the **k** of the earth have committed *935*
18: 9 And the **k** of the earth, who have committed *935*
19:16 KING OF **K**, AND LORD OF LORDS. *935*
19:18 That ye may eat the flesh of **k**, and the flesh *935*
19:19 and the **k** of the earth, and their armies, *935*
21:24 the **k** of the earth do bring their glory and *935*

KINGS' (5) [KING]

Ps 45: 9 **K** daughters *were* among thy honourable 4428
Pr 30:28 hold with her hands, and *is* in **k** palaces. 4428
Da 11:27 both these **k** hearts *shall be* to do mischief, 4428
Mt 11: 8 they that wear soft *clothing* are in **k** houses. *935*
Lk 7:25 and live delicately, are in **k courts**. *933*

KINNERETH See CHINNERETH; CINNERETH

KINNEROTH See CINNEROTH

KINSFOLK (2) [FOLK, KIN]

Job 19:14 My **k** have failed, and my familiar friends 7138
Lk 2:44 and they sought him among *their* **k** and *4773*

KINSFOLKS (3) [FOLK, KIN]

1Ki 16:11 a wall, neither *of* his **k**, nor *of* his friends. 1350
2Ki 10:11 all his great *men*, and his **k**, and his priests, 3045
Lk 21:16 and brethren, and **k**, and friends; *4773*

KINSMAN (16) [KIN, MAN]

Nu 5: 8 if the man have no **k** to recompense 1350
27:11 ye shall give his inheritance unto his **k** that 7607
Ru 2: 1 Naomi had a **k** of her husband's, a mighty 4129
3: 9 over thine handmaid; for thou *art* a **near k**. 1350
3:12 now it is true that I *am thy* **near k**: 1350
3:12 howbeit there is a **k** nearer than I. 1350
3:13 he will **perform** unto thee **the part of a k**, 1350
3:13 if he will not **do the part of a k** to thee, 1350
3:13 will I **do the part of a k** to thee, *as* 1350
4: 1 the **k** of whom Boaz spake came by; 1350
4: 3 he said unto the **k**, Naomi, that is come 1350
4: 6 the **k** said, I cannot redeem *it* for myself, 1350
4: 8 Therefore the **k** said unto Boaz, Buy *it* for 1350
4:14 hath not left thee *this* day without a **k**, 1350
Jn 18:26 being *his* **k** whose ear Peter cut off, saith, *4773*
Ro 16:11 Salute Herodion my **k**. Greet them that be *4773*

KINSMAN'S (1) [KIN, MAN]

Ru 3:13 of a kinsman, well; let him **do the k part**: 1350

KINSMEN (7) [KIN, MAN]

Ru 2:20 *is* near of kin unto us, one of our **next k**. 1350

Ps 38:11 from my sore; and my **k** stand afar off. 7138
Lk 14:12 thy friends, nor thy brethren, neither thy **k**, *4773*
Ac 10:24 and had called together his **k** and near *4773*
Ro 9: 3 my brethren, my **k** according to the flesh: *4773*
16: 7 and Junia, my **k**, and my fellowprisoners, *4773*
16:21 and Lucius, and Jason, and Sosipater, my **k**, *4773*

KINSWOMAN (3) [KIN, WOMAN]
Lev 18:12 father's sister: she *is* thy father's **near k**. 7607
18:13 for she *is* thy mother's **near k**. 7607
Pr 7: 4 *art* my sister; and call understanding *thy* **k**: 4129

KINSWOMEN (1) [KIN, WOMAN]
Lev 18:17 her nakedness; *for* they *are* her **near k**: 7608

KIOS See CHIOS

KIR (5) [KIR-HARASETH, KIR-HARESETH, KIR-HARESH, KIR-HERES]
2Ki 16: 9 carried *the people of* it captive to **K**, and 7024
Isa 15: 1 in the night **K** of Moab is laid waste, 7024
22: 6 *and* horsemen, and **K** uncovered the shield. 7024
Am 1: 5 of Syria shall go into captivity unto **K**, 7024
9: 7 from Caphtor, and the Syrians from **K**? 7024

KIR-HARASETH (1) [KIR]
2Ki 3:25 only in **K** left *they* the stones thereof; 7025

KIR-HARESETH (1) [KIR]
Isa 16: 7 for the foundations of **K** shall ye mourn; 7025

KIR-HARESH (1) [KIR]
Isa 16:11 for Moab, and mine inward parts for **K**. 7025

KIR-HERES (2) [KIR]
Jer 48:31 *mine heart* shall mourn for the men of **K**. 7025
48:36 shall sound like pipes for the men of **K**: 7025

KIRIATH See KIRJATH

KIRIATH ARBA See KIRJATH-ARBA

KIRIATH ARIM See KIRJATH-ARIM

KIRIATH BAAL See KIRJATH-BAAL

KIRIATH HUZOTH See KIRJATH-HUZOTH

KIRIATH JEARIM See KIRJATH-JEARIM

KIRIATH SANNAH See KIRJATH-SANNAH

KIRIATH SEPHER See KIRJATH-SEPHER

KIRIATHAIM (3) [SHAVEH KIRIATHAIM]
Jer 48: 1 **K** is confounded *and* taken: Misgab is 7156
48:23 upon **K**, and upon Beth-gamul, and 7156
Eze 25: 9 Beth-jeshimoth, Baal-meon, and **K**, 7156

KIRJATH (1)
Jos 18:28 Jebusi, which *is* Jerusalem, Gibeath, *and* **K**; 7157

KIRJATHAIM (3)
Nu 32:37 Reuben built Heshbon, and Elealeh, and **K**, 7156
Jos 13:19 **K**, and Sibmah, and Zareth-shahar in 7156
1Ch 6:76 with her suburbs, and **K** with her suburbs. 7156

KIRJATH-ARBA (6) [ARBA]
Ge 23: 2 Sarah died in **K**; the same *is* Hebron in 7153
Jos 14:15 the name of Hebron before *was* **K**; 7153
15:54 Humtah, and **K**, which *is* Hebron, and Zior; 7153
20: 7 **K**, which *is* Hebron, in the mountain of 7153
Jdg 1:10 (now the name of Hebron before *was* **K**:) 7153
Ne 11:25 *some* of the children of Judah dwelt at **K**, 7153

KIRJATH-ARIM (1) [KIRJATH-JEARIM]
Ezr 2:25 The children of **K**, Chephirah, and Beeroth, 7157

KIRJATH-BAAL (2) [BAAL]
Jos 15:60 **K**, which *is* Kirjath-jearim, and Rabbah; 7154
18:14 the goings out thereof were at **K**, which *is* 7154

KIRJATH-HUZOTH (1)
Nu 22:39 went with Balak, and they came *unto* **K**. 7155

KIRJATH-JEARIM (18) [JEARIMKIRJATH-ARIM]
Jos 9:17 and Chephirah, and Beeroth, and **K**. 7157
15: 9 border was drawn *to* Baalah, which *is* **K**: 7157
15:60 Kirjath-baal, which *is* **K**, and Rabbah; 7157
18:14 which *is* **K**, a city of the children of Judah: 7157
18:15 the south quarter *was* from the end of **K**, 7157
Jdg 18:12 they went up, and pitched in **K**, in Judah: 7157
18:12 unto this day: behold, *it is* behind **K**. 7157
1Sa 6:21 sent messengers to the inhabitants of **K**, 7157
7: 1 the men of **K** came, and fetched up the ark 7157
7: 2 it came to pass, while the ark abode in **K**, 7157
1Ch 2:50 of Ephratah; Shobal the father of **K**, 7157
2:52 Shobal the father of **K** had sons; Haroeh, 7157
2:53 the families of **K**; the Ithrites, and 7157
13: 5 of Hemath, to bring the ark of God from **K**. 7157
13: 6 and all Israel, to Baalah, *that is,* to **K**, 7157
2Ch 1: 4 **K** to *the place which* David had prepared 7157
Ne 7:29 The men of **K**, Chephirah, and Beeroth, 7157
Jer 26:20 Urijah the son of Shemaiah of **K**, 7157

KIRJATH-SANNAH (1) [DEBIR]
Jos 15:49 And Dannah, and **K**, which *is* Debir, 7158

KIRJATH-SEPHER (4) [DEBIR]
Jos 15:15 and the name of Debir before *was* **K**. 7158
15:16 Caleb said, He that smiteth **K**, and taketh it, 7158
Jdg 1:11 and the name of Debir before *was* **K**. 7158
1:12 Caleb said, He that smiteth **K**, and taketh it, 7158

KISH (21)
1Sa 9: 1 whose name *was* **K**, the son of Abiel, 7027
9: 3 the asses of **K** Saul's father were lost. 7027
9: 3 **K** said to Saul his son, Take now one of 7027
10:11 What *is* this *that* is come unto the son of **K**? 7027
10:21 and Saul the son of **K** was taken: 7027
14:51 **K** *was* the father of Saul; and Ner the father 7027
2Sa 21:14 in Zelah, in the sepulchre of **K** his father: 7027
1Ch 8:30 and Zur, and **K**, and Baal, and Nadab, 7027
8:33 Ner begat **K**, and Kish begat Saul, and 7027
8:33 **K** begat Saul, and Saul begat Jonathan, and 7027
9:36 Zur, and **K**, and Baal, and Ner, and Nadab, 7027
9:39 Ner begat **K**; and Kish begat Saul; and 7027
9:39 **K** begat Saul; and Saul begat Jonathan, and 7027
12: 1 himself close because of Saul the son of **K**: 7027
23:21 Mushi. The sons of Mahli; Eleazar, and **K**. 7027
23:22 and their brethren the sons of **K** took them. 7027
24:29 Concerning **K**: the son of Kish *was* 7027
24:29 the son of **K** *was* Jerahmeel. 7027
26:28 Saul the son of **K**, and Abner the son of 7027
2Ch 29:12 **K** the son of Abdi, and Azariah the son of 7027
Est 2: 5 son of Shimei, the son of **K**, a Benjamite; 7027

KISHI (1)
1Ch 6:44 Ethan the son of **K**, the son of Abdi, 7029

KISHION (1)
Jos 19:20 And Rabbith, and **K**, and Abez, 7191

KISHON (6) [KISON]
Jos 21:28 **K** with her suburbs, Dabareh with her 7191
Jdg 4: 7 I will draw unto thee to the river **K** Sisera, 7028
4:13 of the Gentiles unto the river of **K**. 7028
5:21 The river of **K** swept them away, 7028
5:21 them away, *that* ancient river, the river **K**. 7028
1Ki 18:40 Elijah brought them down to the brook **K**, 7028

KISLEV See CHISLEU

KISLON See CHISLON

KISLOTH TABOR See CHISLOTH-TABOR

KISON (1) [KISHON]
Ps 83: 9 as *to* Sisera, as *to* Jabin, at the brook of **K**: 7028

KISS (20) [KISSED, KISSES]
Ge 27:26 Come near now, and **k** me, my son. 5401
31:28 hast not suffered me to **k** my sons and my 5401
2Sa 20: 9 by the beard with the right hand to **k** him. 5401
1Ki 19:20 **k** my father and my mother, and *then* I will 5401
Ps 2:12 **K** the Son, lest he be angry, and ye perish 5401
Pr 24:26 *Every man* shall **k** *his* lips that giveth a 5401
SS 1: 2 Let him **k** me with the kisses of his mouth: 5401
8: 1 I should find thee without, I would **k** thee; 5401
Hos 13: 2 Let the men that sacrifice **k** the calves. 5401
Mt 26:48 saying, Whomsoever I shall **k**, that *same* is *5368*
Mk 14:44 saying, Whomsoever I shall **k**, *that* same is *5368*
Lk 7:45 Thou gavest me no **k**: but this *woman* since *5370*
7:45 time I came in hath not ceased to **k** my feet. *2705*
22:47 and drew near unto Jesus to **k** him. *5368*

Lk 22:48 betrayest thou the Son of man with a **k**? *5370*
Ro 16:16 Salute one another with a holy **k**. The *5370*
1Co 16:20 Greet ye one another with a holy **k**. *5370*
2Co 13:12 Greet one another with a holy **k**. *5370*
1Th 5:26 Greet all the brethren with a holy **k**. *5370*
1Pe 5:14 Greet ye one another with a **k** of charity. *5370*

KISSED (26) [KISS]
Ge 27:27 he came near, and **k** him: and he smelled 5401
29:11 Jacob **k** Rachel, and lifted up his voice, 5401
29:13 and **k** him, and brought him to his house. 5401
31:55 **k** his sons and his daughters, and 5401
33: 4 and fell on his neck, and **k** him: 5401
45:15 Moreover he **k** all his brethren, and 5401
48:10 and he **k** them, and embraced them. 5401
50: 1 and wept upon him, and **k** him. 5401
Ex 4:27 met him in the mount of God, and **k** him. 5401
18: 7 father in law, and did obeisance, and **k** him; 5401
Ru 1: 9 she **k** them; and they lift up their voice, 5401
1:14 Orpah **k** her mother in law; but Ruth clave 5401
1Sa 10: 1 **k** him, and said, *Is it* not because 5401
20:41 they **k** one another, and wept one with 5401
2Sa 14:33 before the king: and the king **k** Absalom. 5401
15: 5 forth his hand, and took him, and **k** him. 5401
19:39 the king **k** Barzillai, and blessed him; 5401
1Ki 19:18 and every mouth which hath not **k** him. 5401
Job 31:27 or my mouth hath **k** my hand: 5401
Ps 85:10 righteousness and peace have **k** *each other.* 5401
Pr 7:13 **k** him, and with an impudent face said unto 5401
Mt 26:49 to Jesus, and said, Hail, master; and **k** him. *2705*
Mk 14:45 and saith, Master, master; and **k** him. *2705*
Lk 7:38 and **k** his feet, and anointed *them* with *2705*
15:20 and ran, and fell on his neck, and **k** him. *2705*
Ac 20:37 and fell on Paul's neck, and **k** him, *2705*

K

KISSES (2) [KISS]
Pr 27: 6 but the **k** of an enemy *are* deceitful. 5390
SS 1: 2 Let him kiss me with the **k** of his mouth: 5390

KITE (2)
Lev 11:14 And the vulture, and the **k** after his kind; 344
Dt 14:13 and the **k**, and the vulture after his kind, 344

KITHLISH (1)
Jos 15:40 And Cabbon, and Lahmam, and **K**, 3798

KITLISH See KITHLISH

KITRON (1)
Jdg 1:30 did Zebulun drive out the inhabitants of **K**, 7003

KITTIM (2)
Ge 10: 4 Elishah, and Tarshish, **K**, and Dodanim. 3794
1Ch 1: 7 Elishah, and Tarshish, **K**, and Dodanim. 3794

KNEAD (2) [KNEADED, KNEADINGTROUGHS]
Ge 18: 6 **k** *it,* and make cakes upon the hearth. 3888
Jer 7:18 the fire, and the women **k** *their* dough, 3888

KNEADED (3) [KNEAD]
1Sa 28:24 **k** *it,* and did bake unleavened bread 3888
2Sa 13: 8 **k** *it,* and made cakes in his sight, and 3888
Hos 7: 4 *who* ceaseth from raising after *he* hath **k** 3888

KNEADINGTROUGHS (2) [KNEAD, TROUGH]
Ex 8: 3 and into thine ovens, and into thy **k**: 4863
12:34 their **k** being bound up in their clothes upon 4863

KNEE (6) [KNEES]
Ge 41:43 he had; and they cried before him, **Bow the k**: 86
Isa 45:23 not return, That unto me every **k** shall bow, 1290
Mt 27:29 and they **bowed the k** before him, and *1120*
Ro 11: 4 who have not bowed the **k** to *the image of* *1119*
14:11 every **k** shall bow to me, and every tongue *1119*
Php 2:10 That at the name of Jesus every **k** should *1119*

KNEEL (2) [KNEELED, KNEELING]
Ge 24:11 he **made** *his* camels **to k down** without 1288
Ps 95: 6 let us **k** before the LORD our Maker. 1288

KNEELED (8) [KNEEL]
2Ch 6:13 **k** *down* upon his knees before all 1288
Da 6:10 he **k** upon his knees three times a day, and 1289
Mk 10:17 and **k** to him, and asked him, Good Master, *1120*
Lk 22:41 a stone's cast, and **k down**, *1119+3588+5087*
Ac 7:60 And he **k down**, *1119+3588+5087*
9:40 and **k down**, and prayed; *1119+3588+5087*
20:36 **k down**, and prayed with them *1119+3588+5087*
21: 5 **k down** on the shore, and *1119+3588+5087*

KNEELING (3) [KNEEL]
1Ki 8:54 from **k** on his knees with his hands spread 3766
Mt 17:14 a *certain* man, **k down** to him, and saying, *1120*
Mk 1:40 and **k down** to him, and saying unto him, If *1120*

KNEES (30) [KNEE]
Ge 30: 3 she shall bear upon my **k**, that I may also 1290
48:12 brought them out from between his **k**, 1290
50:23 were brought up upon Joseph's **k**. 1290
Dt 28:35 The LORD shall smite thee in the **k**, and 1290
Jdg 7: 5 one that boweth down upon his **k** to drink. 1290
7: 6 bowed down upon their **k** to drink water. 1290
16:19 she made him sleep upon her **k**; and 1290
1Ki 8:54 from kneeling on his **k** with his hands 1290
18:42 the earth, and put his face between his **k**, 1290
19:18 all the **k** which have not bowed unto Baal, 1290
2Ki 1:13 came and fell on his **k** before Elijah, and 1290
4:20 he sat on her **k** till noon, and *then* died. 1290
2Ch 6:13 kneeled *down* upon his **k** before all 1290
Ezr 9: 5 I fell upon my **k**, and spread out my hands 1290
Job 3:12 Why did the **k** prevent me? or why 1290
4: 4 and thou hast strengthened the feeble **k**. 1290
Ps 109:24 My **k** are weak through fasting; and 1290
Isa 35: 3 the weak hands, and confirm the feeble **k**. 1290
66:12 upon *her* sides, and be dandled upon *her* **k**. 1290
Eze 7:17 be feeble, and all **k** shall be weak *as* water. 1290
21: 7 shall faint, and all **k** shall be weak *as* water: 1290
47: 4 the waters; the waters *were to* the **k**. 1290
Da 5: 6 and his **k** smote one against another. 755
6:10 he kneeled upon his **k** three times a day, 1291
10:10 which set me upon my **k** and *upon* 1290
Na 2:10 the **k** smite together, and much pain *is* in all 1290
Mk 15:19 and bowing *their* **k** worshipped him. *1119*
Lk 5: 8 Peter saw *it,* he fell down at Jesus' **k**, *1119*
Eph 3:14 For this cause I bow my **k** unto the Father *1119*
Heb 12:12 hands which hang down, and the feeble **k**; *1119*

KNEW (169) [KNOW]
Ge 3: 7 and they **k** that they *were* naked; 3045
4: 1 Adam **k** Eve his wife; and she conceived, 3045
4:17 Cain **k** his wife; and she conceived, and 3045
4:25 Adam **k** his wife again; and she bare a son, 3045
8:11 Noah **k** that the waters were abated from 3045
9:24 **k** what his younger son had done unto him. 3045
28:16 the LORD is in this place; and I **k** *it* not. 3045
31:32 For Jacob **k** not that Rachel had stolen 3045
37:33 he **k** it, and said, *It is* my son's coat; an evil 5234
38: 9 And Onan **k** that the seed should not be his; 3045
38:16 (for he **k** not that she *was* his daughter in 3045
38:26 my son. And he **k** her again no more. 3045
39: 6 he **k** not ought he had, save the bread 3045
42: 7 he **k** them, but made himself strange unto 5234
42: 8 Joseph **k** his brethren, but they knew not 5234
42: 8 knew his brethren, but they **k** not him. 5234
42:23 they **k** not that Joseph understood *them;* for 3045
Ex 1: 8 a new king over Egypt, which **k** not Joseph. 3045
Nu 22:34 for I **k** not that thou stoodest in the way 3045
24:16 and **k** the knowledge of the most High, 3045
Dt 8:16 which thy fathers **k** not, that he might 3045
9:24 the LORD from the day that I **k** you. 3045
29:26 gods whom they **k** not, and *whom* he had 3045
32:17 *to* gods whom they **k** not, *to* new *gods that* 3045
33: 9 his brethren, nor **k** his own children: 3045
34:10 whom the LORD **k** face to face, 3045
Jdg 2:10 after them, which **k** not the LORD, 3045
3: 2 at the least such as before **k** nothing 3045
11:39 she **k** no man. And it was a custom in 3045
13:16 For Manoah **k** not that he *was* an angel of 3045
13:21 Manoah **k** that he *was* an angel of 3045
14: 4 his mother **k** not that it *was* of the LORD, 3045
18: 3 they **k** the voice of the young man 5234
19:25 they **k** her, and abused her all the night 3045
20:34 but they **k** not that evil *was* near them. 3045
1Sa 1:19 Elkanah **k** Hannah his wife; and 3045
2:12 *were* sons of Belial; they **k** not the LORD. 3045
3:20 all Israel from Dan even to Beer-sheba **k** 3045
10:11 when all that **k** him beforetime saw that 3045
14: 3 the people **k** not that Jonathan was gone. 3045
18:28 and **k** that the LORD *was* with David, 3045
20: 9 for if I **k certainly** that evil were 3045+3045

1Sa 20:33 whereby Jonathan **k** that it was determined 3045
20:39 the lad **k** not any thing: only Jonathan and 3045
20:39 only Jonathan and David **k** the matter. 3045
22:15 for thy servant **k** nothing of all this, less or 3045
22:17 because they **k** when he fled, and did not 3045
22:22 David said unto Abiathar, I **k** *it* that day, 3045
23: 9 David **k** that Saul secretly practised 3045
26:12 and no man saw *it,* nor **k** *it,* neither awaked: 3045
26:17 Saul **k** David's voice, and said, *Is* this thy 5234
2Sa 3:26 from the well of Sirah: but David **k** *it* not. 3045
11:16 a place where he **k** that valiant men *were.* 3045
11:20 **k** ye not that they would shoot from 3045
15:11 their simplicity, and they **k** not any thing. 3045
18:29 saw a great tumult, but I **k** not what *it was.* 3045
22:44 a people *which* I **k** not shall serve me. 3045
1Ki 1: 4 ministered to him: but the king **k** her not. 3045
18: 7 he **k** him, and fell on his face, and said, *Art* 5234
2Ki 4:39 into the pot of pottage: for they **k** *them* not. 3045
2Ch 33:13 Manasseh **k** that the LORD he *was* God. 3045
Ne 2:16 the rulers **k** not whither I went, or what I 3045
Est 1:13 the king said to the wise *men,* which **k** 3045
1:13 *was* the king's manner towards all that **k** 3045
Job 2:12 **k** him not, they lifted up their voice, and 5234
23: 3 O that I **k** where I might find him! *that* I 3045
29:16 and the cause *which* I **k** not I searched out. 3045
42: 3 *things* too wonderful for me, which I **k** not. 3045
Ps 35:11 they laid to my charge *things* that I **k** not. 3045
35:15 together against me, and I **k** *it* not; 3045
Pr 24:12 If thou sayest, Behold, we **k** it not; doth not 3045
Isa 42:16 I will bring the blind by a way *that* they **k** 3045
42:25 set him on fire round about, yet he **k** not; 3045
48: 4 Because I **k** that thou *art* obstinate, and 1847
48: 7 lest thou shouldest say, Behold, I **k** them. 3045
48: 8 for I **k** *that* thou wouldest deal very 3045
55: 5 nations *that* **k** not thee shall run unto thee 3045
Jer 1: 5 Before I formed thee in the belly I **k** thee; 3045
2: 8 they that handle the law **k** me not: 3045
11:19 I **k** not that they had devised devices 3045
32: 8 I **k** that this *was* the word of the LORD. 3045
41: 4 *he* had slain Gedaliah, and no man **k** *it,* 3045
44: 3 whom they **k** not, *neither* they, you, 3045
44:15 all the men which **k** that their wives had 3045
Eze 10:20 and I **k** that they *were the* cherubims. 3045
19: 7 he **k** their desolate palaces, and he laid 3045
Da 5:21 till he **k** that the most high God ruled in 3046
6:10 Now when Daniel **k** that the writing *was* 3046
11:38 a god whom his fathers **k** not shall he 3045
Hos 8: 4 they have made princes, and I **k** *it* not: 3045
11: 3 but they **k** not that I healed them. 3045
Jnh 1:10 For the men **k** that he fled from 3045
4: 2 for I **k** that thou *art* a gracious God, and 3045
Zec 7:14 among all the nations whom they **k** not: 3045
11:11 the poor of the flock that waited upon me **k** 3045
Mt 1:25 And **k** her not till she had brought forth her *1097*
7:23 will I profess unto them, I never **k** you: *1097*
12:15 But when Jesus **k** *it,* he withdrew himself *1097*
12:25 And Jesus **k** their thoughts, and said unto *1492*
17:12 and they **k** him not, but have done unto him *1921*
24:39 And **k** not until the flood came, and *1097*
25:24 Lord, I **k** thee that thou art a hard man, *1097*
27:18 For he **k** that for envy they had delivered *1492*
Mk 1:34 not the devils to speak, because they **k** him. *1492*
6:33 and many **k** him, and ran afoot thither out *1921*
6:38 And when they **k**, they say, Five, and *1097*
6:54 out of the ship, straightway they **k** him, *1921*
8:17 And when Jesus **k** *it,* he saith unto them, *1097*
12:12 for they **k** that he had spoken the parable *1097*
15:10 For he **k** that the chief priests had delivered *1097*
15:45 And when he **k** *it* of the centurion, he gave *1097*
Lk 2:43 and Joseph and his mother **k** not *of it.* *1097*
4:41 not to speak: for they **k** that he was Christ. *1492*
6: 8 But he **k** their thoughts, and said to the man *1492*
7:37 when she **k** that *Jesus* sat at meat in *1921*
9:11 the people, when they **k** *it,* followed him: *1097*
12:47 which **k** his lord's will, and prepared not *1097*
12:48 But he that **k** not, and did commit *things* *1097*
18:34 neither **k** they the *things* which were *1097*
23: 7 And as soon as he **k** that he belonged unto *1921*
24:31 their eyes were opened, and they **k** him; *1921*
Jn 1:10 was made by him, and the world **k** him not. *1097*
1:31 And I **k** him not: but that he should be *1492*
1:33 And I **k** him not: but he that sent me to *1492*
2: 9 *was* made wine, and **k** not whence it was: *1492*
2: 9 (but the servants which drew the water **k**;) *1492*
2:24 himself unto them, because he **k** all *men,* *1097*
2:25 testify of man: for he **k** what was in man. *1097*
4: 1 the Lord **k** how the Pharisees had heard *1097*
4:53 So the father **k** that *it was* at the same hour, *1097*
5: 6 **k** that he had been now a long time *in that* *1097*
6: 6 for he himself **k** what he would do. *1492*
6:61 When Jesus **k** in himself that his disciples *1492*
6:64 For Jesus **k** from the beginning who they *1492*
11:42 And I **k** that thou hearest me always: but *1492*
11:57 that, if any *man* **k** where he were, *1097*
12: 9 of the Jews therefore **k** that he was there: *1097*
13: 1 when Jesus **k** that his hour was come that *1492*
13:11 For he **k** who should betray him; therefore *1492*
13:28 Now no *man* at the table **k** for what intent *1097*
16:19 Now Jesus **k** that they were desirous to ask *1097*
18: 2 which betrayed him, **k** the place: *1492*
20: 9 For as yet they **k** not the scripture, that he *1492*
20:14 Jesus standing, and **k** not that it was Jesus. *1492*
21: 4 but the disciples **k** not that it was Jesus. *1492*
Ac 3:10 And they **k** that it was he which sat for *1921*
7:18 Till another king arose, which **k** not Joseph. *1492*
9:30 Which when the brethren **k**, they brought *1921*
12:14 And when she **k** Peter's voice, she opened *1921*
13:27 and their rulers, because they **k** him **not**, *50*
16: 3 for they **k** all that his father was a Greek. *1492*
19:32 the more part **k** not wherefore they were *1492*
19:34 But when *they* **k** that he was a Jew, all with *1921*
22:29 after he **k** that he was a Roman, and *1921*
26: 5 Which **k** me from the beginning, if they *4267*
27:39 And when it was day, they **k** not the land: *1921*
28: 1 they **k** that the island was called Melita. *1921*
Ro 1:21 Because that, when they **k** God, *1097*
1Co 1:21 of God the world by wisdom **k** not God, *1097*
2: 8 Which none of the princes of this world **k**: *1097*
2Co 5:21 made him *to be* sin for us, who **k** no sin; *1097*
12: 2 I **k** a man in Christ above fourteen years *1492*
12: 3 And I **k** such a man, (whether in the body, *1492*
Gal 4: 8 Howbeit then, when ye **k** not God, ye did *1492*
Col 1: 6 heard of *it,* and **k** the grace of God in truth: *1921*
2: 1 For I would that ye **k** what great conflict I *1492*
1Jn 3: 1 world knoweth us not, because it **k** him not. *1097*
Jude 1: 5 though ye once **k** this, how that the Lord, *1492*
Rev 19:12 that no *man* **k**, but he himself. *1492*

KNEWEST (10) [KNOW]

Dt 8: 3 and fed thee with manna, which thou **k** not, 3045
Ru 2:11 art come unto a people which thou **k** not 3045
Ne 9:10 for thou **k** that they dealt proudly against 3045
Ps 142: 3 within me, then thou **k** my path. 3045
Isa 48: 8 yea, thou **k** not; yea, from that time *that* 3045
Da 5:22 humbled thine heart, though thou **k** all this; 3046
Mt 25:26 thou **k** that I reap where I sowed not, and *1492*
Lk 19:22 Thou **k** that I was an austere man, taking up *1492*
19:44 thou **k** not the time of thy visitation. *1097*
Jn 4:10 If thou **k** the gift of God, and who it is that *1492*

KNIFE (6) [KNIVES]

Ge 22: 6 he took the fire in his hand, and a **k**; and 3979
22:10 his hand, and took the **k** to slay his son. 3979
Jdg 19:29 he took a **k**, and laid hold on his concubine, 3979
Pr 23: 2 put a **k** to thy throat, if thou *be* a man given 7915
Eze 5: 1 thou, son of man, take thee a sharp **k**, 2719
5: 2 a third *part, and* smite about it with a **k**: 2719

KNIT (6)

Jdg 20:11 against the city, **k together** as one man. 2270
1Sa 18: 1 that the soul of Jonathan was **k** with 7194
1Ch 12:17 mine heart shall be **k** unto you: 3162+3807.1
Ac 10:11 as *it had been* a great sheet **k** at the four *1210*
Col 2: 2 being **k together** in love, and unto all *4822*
2:19 and **k together**, increaseth *with* *4822*

KNITTED See WOOF

KNIVES (5) [KNIFE]

Jos 5: 2 Make thee sharp **k**, and circumcise again 2719
5: 3 Joshua made him sharp **k**, and 2719
1Ki 18:28 cut themselves after their manner with **k** 2719
Ezr 1: 9 chargers of silver, nine and twenty **k**, 4252
Pr 30:14 *are as* swords, and their jaw teeth *as* **k**, 3979

KNOCK (4) [KNOCKED, KNOCKETH, KNOCKING]

Mt 7: 7 **k**, and it shall be opened unto you: *2925*
Lk 11: 9 **k**, and it shall be opened unto you. *2925*
13:25 and to **k** at the door, saying, Lord, Lord, *2925*

Rev 3:20 Behold, I stand at the door, and **k**: if any *2925*

KNOCKED (1) [KNOCK]
Ac 12:13 And as Peter **k** at the door of the gate, *2925*

KNOCKETH (4) [KNOCK]
SS 5: 2 *it is* the voice of my beloved that **k** *saying,* 1849
Mt 7: 8 and to him that **k** it shall be opened. *2925*
Lk 11:10 and to him that **k** it shall be opened. *2925*
12:36 that when *he* cometh and **k**, they may open *2925*

KNOCKING (1) [KNOCK]
Ac 12:16 But Peter continued **k**: and when they had *2925*

KNOP (10) [KNOPS]
Ex 25:33 *with* a **k** and a flower in one branch; 3730
25:33 in the other branch, *with* a **k** and a flower: 3730
25:35 *there shall be* a **k** under two branches of 3730
25:35 a **k** under two branches of the same, and 3730
25:35 and a **k** under two branches of the same, 3730
37:19 of almonds in one branch, a **k** and a flower; 3730
37:19 in another branch, a **k** and a flower: 3730
37:21 a **k** under two branches of the same, and 3730
37:21 a **k** under two branches of the same, and 3730
37:21 and a **k** under two branches of the same, 3730

KNOPS (9) [KNOP]
Ex 25:31 his bowls, his **k**, and his flowers, 3730
25:34 *with* their **k** and their flowers. 3730
25:36 Their **k** and their branches shall be of 3730
37:17 his bowls, his **k**, and his flowers, 3730
37:20 made like almonds, his **k**, and his flowers: 3730
37:22 Their **k** and their branches were of 3730
1Ki 6:18 of the house within *was* carved with **k** 6497
7:24 the brim of it round about *there were* **k** 6497
7:24 the **k** *were* cast *in* two rows, when it was 6497

KNOW (763) [FOREKNEW, FOREKNOW, FOREKNOWLEDGE, KNEWEST, KNOWEST, KNOWETH, KNOWING, KNOWLEDGE, KNOWN, UNKNOWN]
Ge 3: 5 For God doth **k** that in the day ye eat 3045
3:22 is become as one of us, to **k** good and evil: 3045
4: 9 he said, I **k** not: *Am* I my brother's keeper? 3045
12:11 I **k** that thou *art* a fair woman to look upon: 3045
15: 8 whereby shall I **k** that I shall inherit it? 3045
15:13 **K of a surety** that thy seed shall be a 3045+3045
18:19 For I **k** him, that he will command his 3045
18:21 which is come unto me; and if not, I will **k**. 3045
19: 5 them out unto us, that we may **k** them. 3045
20: 6 I **k** that thou didst this in the integrity of thy 3045
20: 7 **k** thou that thou shalt surely die, thou, and 3045
22:12 for now I **k** that thou fearest God, 3045
24:14 thereby shall I **k** that thou hast shewed 3045
27: 2 I am old, I **k** not the day of my death: 3045
29: 5 unto them, **K** ye Laban the son of Nahor? 3045
29: 5 son of Nahor? And they said, We **k** *him.* 3045
31: 6 ye **k** that with all my power I have served 3045
37:32 **k** now whether it *be* thy son's coat or no. 5234
42:33 Hereby shall I **k** that ye *are* true *men;* leave 3045
42:34 shall I **k** that ye *are* no spies, but *that* ye *are* 3045
43: 7 could we **certainly k** that he would 3045+3045
44:27 Ye **k** that my wife bare me two *sons:* 3045
48:19 his father refused, and said, I **k** *it,* my son, 3045
48:19 I **k** *it:* he also shall become a people, and 3045
Ex 3: 7 of their taskmasters; for I **k** their sorrows; 3045
4:14 I **k** that he can speak well. And also, 3045
5: 2 I **k** not the LORD, neither will I let Israel 3045
6: 7 ye shall **k** that I *am* the LORD your God, 3045
7: 5 the Egyptians shall **k** that I *am* the LORD, 3045
7:17 In this thou shalt **k** that I *am* the LORD: 3045
8:10 that thou mayest **k** that *there is* none like 3045
8:22 to the end thou mayest **k** that I *am* 3045
9:14 that thou mayest **k** that *there is* none like 3045
9:29 that thou mayest **k** how that the earth *is* 3045
9:30 I **k** that ye will not yet fear the LORD 3045
10: 2 that ye may **k** how that I *am* the LORD. 3045
10:26 we **k** not with what we must serve 3045
11: 7 that ye may **k** how that the LORD doth 3045
14: 4 that the Egyptians may **k** that I *am* 3045
14:18 the Egyptians shall **k** that I *am* the LORD, 3045
16: 6 ye shall **k** that the LORD hath brought 3045
16:12 ye shall **k** that I *am* the LORD your God. 3045
18:11 Now I **k** that the LORD *is* greater than all 3045
18:16 I do **make** *them* **k** the statutes of God, and 3045
23: 9 for ye **k** the heart of a stranger, seeing ye 3045
29:46 they shall **k** that I *am* the LORD their 3045
31:13 that *ye* may **k** that I *am* the LORD that 3045
33: 5 that I may **k** what to do unto thee. 3045
33:12 thou hast not let me **k** whom thou wilt send 3045
33:12 I **k** thee by name, and thou hast also found 3045
33:13 shew me now thy way, that I may **k** thee, 3045
33:17 grace in my sight, and I **k** thee by name. 3045
36: 1 understanding to **k** how to work all *manner* 3045
Lev 23:43 That your generations may **k** that I made 3045
Nu 14:31 they shall **k** the land which ye have 3045
14:34 and ye shall **k** my breach of promise. 3045
16:28 Hereby ye shall **k** that the LORD hath 3045
22:19 that I may **k** what the LORD will say unto 3045
Dt 3:19 (*for* I **k** that ye have much cattle,) 3045
4:35 that thou mightest **k** that the LORD he *is* 3045
4:39 **K** therefore *this* day, and consider *it* in 3045
7: 9 **K** therefore that the LORD thy God, he *is* 3045
8: 2 to prove thee, to **k** what *was* in thine heart, 3045
8: 3 thou knewest not, neither did thy fathers **k**; 3045
8: 3 that he might **make** thee **k** that man doth 3045
11: 2 **k** you *this* day: for *I speak* not with your 3045
13: 3 to **k** whether you love the LORD your 3045
18:21 How shall we **k** the word which 3045
22: 2 or *if* thou **k** him not, then thou shalt bring it 3045
29: 6 that ye might **k** that I *am* the LORD your 3045
29:16 (For ye **k** how we have dwelt in the land of 3045
31:21 for I **k** their imagination which they go 3045
31:27 For I **k** thy rebellion, and thy stiff neck: 3045
31:29 For I **k** that after my death ye will utterly 3045
Jos 2: 9 I **k** that the LORD hath given you 3045
3: 4 that ye may **k** the way by which ye must 3045
3: 7 that they may **k** that, as I was with Moses, 3045
3:10 Hereby ye shall **k** that the living God *is* 3045
4:22 ye shall let your children **k**, saying, 3045
4:24 That all the people of the earth might **k** 3045
22:22 of gods, he knoweth, and Israel he shall **k**; 3045
23:13 **K for a certainty** that the LORD 3045+3045
23:14 ye **k** in all your hearts and in all your souls, 3045
Jdg 3: 2 of the children of Israel might **k**, 3045
3: 4 to **k** whether they would hearken unto 3045
6:37 shall I **k** that thou wilt save Israel by mine 3045
17:13 Now **k** I that the LORD will do me good, 3045
18: 5 that we may **k** whether our way which we 3045
18:14 Do ye **k** that there is in these houses an 3045
19:22 came into thine house, that we may **k** him. 3045
Ru 3:11 for all the city of my people doth **k** that 3045
3:14 she rose up before one could **k** another. 5234
3:18 until thou **k** how the matter will fall: 3045
4: 4 not redeem *it, then* tell me, that I may **k**: 3045
1Sa 3: 7 Now Samuel did not yet **k** the LORD, 3045
6: 9 we shall **k** that *it is* not his hand *that* smote 3045
14:38 **k** and see wherein this sin hath been *this* 3045
17:28 I **k** thy pride, and the naughtiness of thine 3045
17:46 that all the earth may **k** that there is a God 3045
17:47 all this assembly shall **k** that the LORD 3045
20: 3 he saith, Let not Jonathan **k** this, lest he be 3045
20:30 **k** that thou hast chosen the son of Jesse to 3045
21: 2 Let no man **k** any thing of the business 3045
22: 3 with you, till I **k** what God will do for me. 3045
23:22 **k** and see his place where his haunt is, *and* 3045
24:11 **k** thou and see that *there is* neither evil nor 3045
24:20 I **k well** that thou shalt surely be king, 3045
25:11 unto men, whom I **k** not whence they *be?* 3045
25:17 Now therefore **k** and consider what thou 3045
28: 1 said unto David, **K** thou **assuredly**, 3045+3045
28: 2 Surely thou shalt **k** what thy servant can do. 3045
29: 9 to David, I **k** that thou *art* good in my sight, 3045
2Sa 3:25 to **k** thy going out and thy coming in, and 3045
3:25 thy coming in, and to **k** all that thou doest. 3045
3:38 **K** ye not that there is a prince and a great 3045
7:21 great things, to **make** thy servant **k** *them.* 3045
14:20 of God, to **k** all *things* that *are* in the earth. 3045
19:20 For thy servant doth **k** that I have sinned: 3045
19:22 for do not I **k** that I *am this* day king over 3045
24: 2 that I may **k** the number of the people. 3045
1Ki 2:37 thou shalt **k for certain** that thou 3045+3045
2:42 unto thee, saying, **K for a certain**, 3045+3045
3: 7 I **k** not *how* to go out or come in. 3045
8:38 which shall **k** every man the plague of his 3045
8:43 that all people of the earth may **k** thy name, 3045
8:43 that *they* may **k** that this house, which I 3045
8:60 That all the people of the earth may **k** that 3045
17:24 Now *by* this I **k** that thou *art* a man of God, 3045

1Ki	18:12	the LORD shall carry thee whither I **k** not;	3045
	18:37	that this people may **k** that thou *art*	3045
	20:13	and thou shalt **k** that I *am* the LORD.	3045
	20:28	and ye shall **k** that I *am* the LORD.	3045
	22: 3	**K** ye that Ramoth in Gilead *is* ours, and	3045
2Ki	2: 3	he said, Yea, I **k** *it;* hold you your peace.	3045
	2: 5	Yea, I **k** *it;* hold you your peace.	3045
	5: 8	he shall **k** that there is a prophet in Israel.	3045
	5:15	now I **k** that *there is* no God in all the earth,	3045
	7:12	They **k** that we *be* hungry; therefore	3045
	8:12	Because I **k** the evil that thou wilt do unto	3045
	9:11	Ye **k** the man, and his communication.	3045
	10:10	**K** now that there shall fall unto the earth	3045
	17:26	**k** not the manner of the God of the land:	3045
	17:26	they **k** not the manner of the God of	3045
	19:19	that all the kingdoms of the earth may **k**	3045
	19:27	I **k** thy abode, and thy going out, and	3045
1Ch	12:32	of the times, to **k** what Israel ought to do;	3045
	21: 2	the number of them to me, that I may **k** *it.*	3045
	28: 9	**k** thou the God of thy father, and serve him	3045
	29:17	I **k** also, my God, that thou triest the heart,	3045
2Ch	2: 8	for I **k** that thy servants can skill to cut	3045
	6:29	when every one shall **k** his own sore and	3045
	6:33	that all people of the earth may **k** thy name,	3045
	6:33	may **k** that this house which I have built is	3045
	12: 8	that they may **k** my service, and the service	3045
	13: 5	Ought you not to **k** that the LORD God of	3045
	20:12	cometh against us; neither **k** we what to do:	3045
	25:16	I **k** that God hath determined to destroy	3045
	32:13	**K** ye not what I and my fathers have done	3045
	32:31	that *he* might **k** all *that was* in his heart.	3045
Ezr	4:15	**k** that this city *is* a rebellious city, and	3046
	7:25	the river, all such as **k** the laws of thy God;	3046
	7:25	and teach ye them that **k** *them* not.	3046
Ne	4:11	They shall not **k**, neither see,	3045
Est	2:11	to **k** how Esther did, and what should	3045
	4: 5	to **k** what it *was,* and why it *was.*	3045
	4:11	do **k**, that whosoever, *whether* man or	3045
Job	5:24	thou shalt **k** that thy tabernacle *shall be in*	3045
	5:25	Thou shalt **k** also that thy seed *shall be*	3045
	5:27	so it *is;* hear it, and **k** thou *it* for thy good.	3045
	7:10	neither shall his place **k** him any more.	5234
	8: 9	**k** nothing, because our days upon earth *are*	3045
	9: 2	I **k** *it is* so of a truth: but how should man	3045
	9: 5	removeth the mountains, and they **k** not:	3045
	9:21	I *were* perfect, *yet* would I not **k** my soul:	3045
	9:28	I **k** that thou wilt not hold me innocent.	3045
	10:13	hid in thine heart: I **k** that this *is* with thee.	3045
	11: 6	**K** therefore that God exacteth of thee *less*	3045
	11: 8	deeper than hell; what canst thou **k**?	3045
	13: 2	What ye **k**, *the same* do I know also. I *am*	1847
	13: 2	What ye know, *the same* do I **k** also. I *am*	3045
	13:18	*my* cause; I **k** that I shall be justified.	3045
	13:23	**make** me **to k** my transgression and	3045
	15: 9	What knowest thou, that we **k** not?	3045
	19: 6	**K** now that God hath overthrown me, and	3045
	19:25	For I **k** *that* my Redeemer liveth, and	3045
	19:29	that ye may **k** *there is* a judgment.	3045
	21:19	he rewardeth him, and he shall **k** *it.*	3045
	21:27	I **k** your thoughts, and the devices *which* ye	3045
	21:29	by the way? and do ye not **k** their tokens,	5234
	22:13	thou sayest, How doth God **k**? can he	3045
	23: 5	I would **k** the words *which* he would	3045
	24: 1	do they that **k** him not see his days?	3045
	24:13	they **k** not the ways thereof, nor abide in	5234
	24:16	in the daytime: they **k** not the light.	3045
	24:17	if *one* **k** *them, they are in* the terrors of	5234
	30:23	For I **k** *that* thou wilt bring me *to* death, and	3045
	31: 6	that God may **k** mine integrity.	3045
	32:22	For I **k** not to give flattering titles; *in so*	3045
	34: 4	let us **k** among ourselves what *is* good.	3045
	36:26	Behold, God *is* great, and we **k** *him* not,	3045
	37: 7	of every man; that all men may **k** his work.	3045
	37:15	Dost thou **k** when God disposed them, and	3045
	37:16	Dost thou **k** the balancings of the clouds,	3045
	38:12	*and* **caused** the dayspring **to k** his place;	3045
	38:20	that thou shouldest **k** the paths to the house	995
	42: 2	I **k** that thou canst do every *thing,* and	3045
Ps	4: 3	**k** that the LORD hath set apart *him that is*	3045
	9:10	they that **k** thy name will put their trust in	3045
	9:20	*that* the nations may **k** themselves *to be but*	3045
	20: 6	Now **k** I that the LORD saveth his	3045
	36:10	thy lovingkindness unto them that **k** thee;	3045
	39: 4	**make** me **to k** mine end, and the measure	3045
	39: 4	what it *is; that* I may **k** how frail I *am.*	3045
	41:11	By this I **k** that thou favourest me, because	3045
	46:10	Be still, and **k** that I *am* God: I will be	3045
	50:11	I **k** all the fowls of the mountains: and	3045
	51: 6	in the hidden *part* thou shalt **make me to k**	3045
	56: 9	turn back: this I **k**; for God *is* for me.	3045
	59:13	let them **k** that God ruleth in Jacob unto	3045
	71:15	all the day; for I **k** not the numbers *thereof.*	3045
	73:11	they say, How doth God **k**? and is there	3045
	73:16	When I thought to **k** this, it *was* too painful	3045
	78: 6	That the generation to come might **k** *them,*	3045
	82: 5	They **k** not, neither will they understand;	3045
	83:18	That *men* may **k** that thou, whose name	3045
	87: 4	of Rahab and Babylon to them that **k** me:	3045
	89:15	Blessed *is* the people that **k** the joyful	3045
	94:10	teacheth man knowledge, *shall not he k?*	NIH
	100: 3	**K** ye that the LORD he *is* God: *it is* he	3045
	101: 4	from me: I will not **k** a wicked *person.*	3045
	103:16	and the place thereof shall **k** it no more.	5234
	109:27	That they may **k** that this *is* thy hand;	3045
	119:75	I **k**, O LORD, that thy judgments *are*	3045
	119:125	that I may **k** thy testimonies.	3045
	135: 5	For I **k** that the LORD *is* great, and	3045
	139:23	Search me, O God, and **k** my heart: try me,	3045
	139:23	know my heart: try me, and **k** my thoughts:	3045
	140:12	I **k** that the LORD will maintain the cause	3045
	142: 4	but *there was* no man that would **k** me:	5234
	143: 8	**cause** me **to k** the way wherein I should	3045
Pr	1: 2	To **k** wisdom and instruction; to perceive	3045
	4: 1	of a father, and attend to **k** understanding.	3045
	4:19	they **k** not at what they stumble.	3045
	5: 6	are moveable, *that* thou canst not **k** *them.*	3045
	10:32	The lips of the righteous **k** what is	3045
	22:21	That *I* might **make** thee **k** the certainty of	3045
	24:12	doth *not* he **k** *it?* and shall *not* he render to	3045
	25: 8	lest *thou* **k** *not* what to do in the end thereof,	NIH
	27:23	Be thou **diligent to k** the state of thy	3045+3045
	29: 7	*but* the wicked regardeth not to **k** *it.*	1847
	30:18	wonderful for me, yea, four which I **k** not:	3045
Ecc	1:17	I gave my heart to **k** wisdom, and to know	3045
	1:17	know wisdom, and to **k** madness and folly:	3045
	3:12	I **k** that *there is* no good in them, but for *a*	3045
	3:14	I **k** that, whatsoever God doeth, it shall be	3045
	7:25	I applied mine heart to **k**, and to search, and	3045
	7:25	*of things,* and to **k** the wickedness of folly,	3045
	8:12	yet surely I **k** that it shall be well with them	3045
	8:16	When I applied mine heart to **k** wisdom,	3045
	8:17	though a wise *man* think to **k** *it,* yet shall	3045
	9: 5	For the living **k** that they shall die: but	3045
	9: 5	the dead **k** not any thing, neither have they	3045
	11: 9	**k** thou, that for all these *things* God will	3045
SS	1: 8	If thou **k** not, O thou fairest among women,	3045
Isa	1: 3	*but* Israel doth not **k**, my people doth not	3045
	5:19	draw nigh and come, that we may **k** *it.*	3045
	7:15	that he may **k** to refuse the evil, and	3045
	7:16	For before the child shall **k** to refuse	3045
	9: 9	all the people shall **k**, *even* Ephraim and	3045
	19:12	let them **k** what the LORD of hosts hath	3045
	19:21	the Egyptians shall **k** the LORD in that	3045
	37:20	that all the kingdoms of the earth may **k**	3045
	37:28	I **k** thy abode, and thy going out, and thy	3045
	41:20	**k**, and consider, and understand together,	3045
	41:22	consider *them,* and **k** the latter end of them;	3045
	41:23	that we may **k** that ye *are* gods:	3045
	41:26	from the beginning, that we may **k**?	3045
	43:10	that ye may **k** and believe me, and	3045
	43:19	now it shall spring forth; shall ye not **k** it?	3045
	44: 8	yea, *there is* no God; I **k** not *any.*	3045
	44: 9	they see not, nor **k**; that they may be	3045
	45: 3	that thou mayest **k** that I, the LORD,	3045
	45: 6	That they may **k** from the rising of the sun,	3045
	47: 8	neither shall I **k** the loss of children:	3045
	47:11	thou shalt not **k** from whence it riseth:	3045
	47:11	upon thee suddenly, *which* thou shalt not **k**.	3045
	48: 6	hidden *things,* and thou didst not **k** them.	3045
	49:23	and thou shalt **k** that I *am* the LORD:	3045
	49:26	all flesh shall **k** that I the LORD *am* thy	3045
	50: 4	that *I* should **k** how to speak a word in	3045
	50: 7	a flint, and I **k** that I shall not be ashamed.	3045
	51: 7	Hearken unto me, ye that **k** righteousness,	3045
	52: 6	Therefore my people shall **k** my name:	3045
	52: 6	*they shall* **k** in that day that I *am* he that	NIH
	58: 2	seek me daily, and delight to **k** my ways,	1847
	59: 8	The way of peace they **k** not; and *there is*	3045

Isa 59: 8 whosoever goeth therein shall not **k** peace. 3045
59:12 and *as for* our iniquities, we **k** them; 3045
60:16 thou shalt **k** that I the LORD *am* thy 3045
66:18 For I *k* their works and their thoughts: NIH
Jer 2:19 **k** therefore and see that *it is* an evil *thing* 3045
2:23 way in the valley, **k** what thou hast done: 3045
5: 1 and **k**, and seek in the broad places thereof, 3045
5: 4 for they **k** not the way of the LORD, 3045
6:18 Therefore hear, ye nations, and **k**, 3045
6:27 that thou mayest **k** and try their way. 3045
7: 9 and walk after other gods whom ye **k** not; 3045
8: 7 my people **k** not the judgment of 3045
9: 3 and they **k** not me, saith the LORD. 3045
9: 6 through deceit they refuse to **k** me, saith 3045
10:23 I **k** that the way of man *is* not in himself: 3045
10:25 Pour out thy fury upon the heathen that **k** 3045
11:18 I **k** *it:* then thou shewedst me their doings. 3045
13:12 Do we not **certainly k** that every 3045+3045
14:18 the priest go about into a land that they **k** 3045
15:15 **k** that for thy sake I have suffered rebuke. 3045
16:13 out of this land into a land that ye **k** not, 3045
16:21 I *will* this once **cause** them **to k**, 3045
16:21 I will **cause** them **to k** mine hand and my 3045
16:21 they shall **k** that my name *is* The LORD. 3045
17: 9 and desperately wicked: who can **k** it? 3045
22:16 *it was* well *with him: was* not this to **k** me? 1847
22:28 and are cast into a land which they **k** not? 3045
24: 7 I will give them a heart to **k** me, that I *am* 3045
26:15 **k** ye **for certain**, that if ye put me to 3045+3045
29:11 For I **k** the thoughts that I think towards 3045
29:16 *K* that thus saith the LORD of the king NIH
29:23 even I **k**, and *am* a witness, saith 3045
31:34 man his brother, saying, **K** the LORD: 3045
31:34 for they shall all **k** me, from the least of 3045
36:19 Jeremiah; and let no man **k** where ye *be.* 3045
38:24 Let no man **k** of these words, and thou shalt 3045
40:14 Dost thou **certainly k** that Baalis 3045+3045
40:15 no man shall **k** *it:* wherefore should he slay 3045
42:19 **k certainly** that I have admonished 3045+3045
42:22 **k certainly** that ye shall die by 3045+3045
44:28 shall **k** whose words shall stand, mine, or 3045
44:29 that ye may **k** that my words shall surely 3045
48:17 all ye that **k** his name, say, How is 3045
48:30 I **k** his wrath, saith the LORD; but *it shall* 3045
Eze 2: 5 yet shall **k** that there hath been a prophet 3045
5:13 they shall **k** that I the LORD have spoken 3045
6: 7 and ye shall **k** that I *am* the LORD. 3045
6:10 they shall **k** that I *am* the LORD, *and* 3045
6:13 shall ye **k** that I *am* the LORD, when their 3045
6:14 and they shall **k** that I *am* the LORD. 3045
7: 4 and ye shall **k** that I *am* the LORD. 3045
7: 9 ye shall **k** that I *am* the LORD that 3045
7:27 and they shall **k** that I *am* the LORD. 3045
11: 5 for I **k** the things that come into your mind, 3045
11:10 and ye shall **k** that I *am* the LORD. 3045
11:12 ye shall **k** that I *am* the LORD: for ye 3045
12:15 they shall **k** that I *am* the LORD, when I 3045
12:16 and they shall **k** that I *am* the LORD. 3045
12:20 and ye shall **k** that I *am* the LORD. 3045
13: 9 and ye shall **k** that I *am* the Lord GOD. 3045
13:14 and ye shall **k** that I *am* the LORD. 3045
13:21 and ye shall **k** that I *am* the LORD. 3045
13:23 and ye shall **k** that I *am* the LORD. 3045
14: 8 and ye shall **k** that I *am* the LORD. 3045
14:23 ye shall **k** that I have not done without 3045
15: 7 ye shall **k** that I *am* the LORD, when I set 3045
16: 2 **cause** Jerusalem **to k** her abominations, 3045
16:62 and thou shalt **k** that I *am* the LORD: 3045
17:12 **K** ye not what these *things mean?* tell *them,* 3045
17:21 ye shall **k** that I the LORD have spoken 3045
17:24 all the trees of the field shall **k** that I 3045
20: 4 wilt thou judge *them?* **cause** them **to k** 3045
20:12 that *they* might **k** that I *am* the LORD that 3045
20:20 that *ye* may **k** that I *am* the LORD your 3045
20:26 to the end that they might **k** that I *am* 3045
20:38 and ye shall **k** that I *am* the LORD. 3045
20:42 ye shall **k** that I *am* the LORD, when I 3045
20:44 ye shall **k** that I *am* the LORD, when I 3045
21: 5 That all flesh may **k** that I the LORD have 3045
22:16 and thou shalt **k** that I *am* the LORD. 3045
22:22 ye shall **k** that I the LORD have poured 3045
23:49 and ye shall **k** that I *am* the Lord GOD. 3045
24:24 ye shall **k** that I *am* the Lord GOD. 3045
24:27 and they shall **k** that I *am* the LORD. 3045
25: 5 and ye shall **k** that I *am* the LORD. 3045
25: 7 and thou shalt **k** that I *am* the LORD. 3045
25:11 and they shall **k** that I *am* the LORD. 3045
25:14 they shall **k** my vengeance, saith the Lord 3045
25:17 they shall **k** that I *am* the LORD, when I 3045
26: 6 and they shall **k** that I *am* the LORD. 3045
28:19 All they that **k** thee among the people shall 3045
28:22 they shall **k** that I *am* the LORD, when I 3045
28:23 and they shall **k** that I *am* the LORD. 3045
28:24 and they shall **k** that I *am* the Lord GOD. 3045
28:26 they shall **k** that I *am* the LORD their 3045
29: 6 all the inhabitants of Egypt shall **k** that I *am* 3045
29: 9 and they shall **k** that I *am* the LORD: 3045
29:16 but they shall **k** that I *am* the Lord GOD. 3045
29:21 and they shall **k** that I *am* the LORD. 3045
30: 8 they shall **k** that I *am* the LORD, when I 3045
30:19 and they shall **k** that I *am* the LORD. 3045
30:25 they shall **k** that I *am* the LORD, when I 3045
30:26 and they shall **k** that I *am* the LORD. 3045
32:15 shall they **k** that I *am* the LORD. 3045
33:29 shall they **k** that I *am* the LORD, when I 3045
33:33 shall they **k** that a prophet hath been among 3045
34:27 and shall **k** that I *am* the LORD, 3045
34:30 Thus shall they **k** that I the LORD their 3045
35: 4 and thou shalt **k** that I *am* the LORD. 3045
35: 9 and ye shall **k** that I *am* the LORD. 3045
35:12 thou shalt **k** that I *am* the LORD, *and* 3045
35:15 of it: and they shall **k** that I *am* the LORD. 3045
36:11 and ye shall **k** that I *am* the LORD. 3045
36:23 the heathen shall **k** that I *am* the LORD, 3045
36:36 **k** that I the LORD build the ruined *places,* 3045
36:38 and they shall **k** that I *am* the LORD. 3045
37: 6 and ye shall **k** that I *am* the LORD. 3045
37:13 ye shall **k** that I *am* the LORD, when I 3045
37:14 shall ye **k** that I the LORD have spoken *it,* 3045
37:28 the heathen shall **k** that I the LORD do 3045
38:14 Israel dwelleth safely, shalt thou not **k** *it?* 3045
38:16 my land, that the heathen may **k** me, 3045
38:23 and they shall **k** that I *am* the LORD. 3045
39: 6 and they shall **k** that I *am* the LORD. 3045
39: 7 the heathen shall **k** that I *am* the LORD, 3045
39:22 So the house of Israel shall **k** that I *am* 3045
39:23 the heathen shall **k** that the house of Israel 3045
39:28 shall they **k** that I *am* the LORD their 3045
Da 2: 3 and my spirit was troubled to **k** the dream. 3045
2: 8 I **k** of certainty that ye would gain the time, 3046
2: 9 I shall **k** that ye can shew me 3046
2:21 knowledge to them that **k** understanding: 3046
2:30 *that* thou mightest **k** the thoughts of thy 3046
4: 9 I **k** that the spirit of the holy gods *is* in thee, 3046
4:17 to the intent that the living may **k** that 3046
4:25 till thou **k** that the most High ruleth in 3046
4:32 until thou **k** that the most High ruleth in 3046
5:23 stone, which see not, nor hear, nor **k**: 3046
6:15 said unto the king, **K**, O king, that the law 3046
7:16 **made** me **k** the interpretation of the things. 3046
7:19 I would **k the truth** of the fourth beast, 3321
8:19 I *will* **make** thee **k** what shall be in the last 3045
9:25 **K** therefore and understand, *that* from 3045
11:32 the people that do **k** their God shall be 3045
Hos 2: 8 For she did not **k** that I gave her corn, and 3045
2:20 and thou shalt **k** the LORD. 3045
5: 3 I **k** Ephraim, and Israel is not hid from me: 3045
6: 3 shall we **k**, *if* we follow on to know 3045
6: 3 we know, *if* we follow on to **k** the LORD: 3045
8: 2 shall cry unto me, My God, we **k** thee. 3045
9: 7 Israel shall **k** *it:* the prophet *is* a fool, 3045
13: 4 of Egypt, and thou shalt **k** no god but me: 3045
13: 5 I did **k** thee in the wilderness, in the land of 3045
14: 9 these *things?* prudent, and he shall **k** them? 3045
Joel 2:27 ye shall **k** that I *am* in the midst of Israel, 3045
3:17 So shall ye **k** that I *am* the LORD your 3045
Am 3:10 For they **k** not to do right, saith 3045
5:12 For I **k** your manifold transgressions and 3045
Jnh 1: 7 that we may **k** for whose cause this evil *is* 3045
1:12 for I **k** that for my sake this great tempest *is* 3045
Mic 3: 1 of Israel; *is it* not for you to **k** judgment? 3045
4:12 they **k** not the thoughts of the LORD, 3045
6: 5 that *ye* may **k** the righteousness of 3045
Zec 2: 9 ye shall **k** that the LORD of hosts hath 3045
2:11 thou shalt **k** that the LORD of hosts hath 3045
4: 9 thou shalt **k** that the LORD of hosts hath 3045
6:15 ye shall **k** that the LORD of hosts hath 3045
Mal 2: 4 ye shall **k** that I have sent this 3045

Mt 6: 3 let not thy left hand **k** what thy right hand *1097*
7:11 **k how** to give good gifts unto your *1492*
7:16 Ye shall **k** them by their fruits. Do *men* *1921*
7:20 Wherefore by their fruits ye shall **k** them. *1921*
9: 6 But that ye may **k** that the Son of man hath *1492*
9:30 charged them, saying, See *that* no *man* **k** *it.* *1097*
13:11 Because it is given unto you to **k** *1097*
20:22 and said, Ye **k** not what ye ask. *1492*
20:25 Ye **k** that the princes of the Gentiles *1492*
22:16 we **k** that thou art true, and teachest *1492*
24:32 forth leaves, ye **k** that summer *is* nigh: *1097*
24:33 when ye shall see all these *things,* **k** that it *1097*
24:42 for ye **k** not what hour your Lord doth *1492*
24:43 But **k** this, that if the goodman of the house *1097*
25:12 and said, Verily I say unto you, I **k** you not. *1492*
25:13 for ye **k** neither the day nor the hour *1492*
26: 2 Ye **k** that after two days is *the feast of* *1492*
26:70 *them* all, saying, I **k** not what thou sayest. *1492*
26:72 he denied with an oath, I do not **k** the man. *1492*
26:74 and to swear, *saying,* I **k** not the man. *1492*
28: 5 for I **k** that ye seek Jesus, which was *1492*
Mk 1:24 I **k** thee who thou art, the Holy One of God. *1492*
2:10 But that ye may **k** that the Son of man hath *1492*
4:11 Unto you it is given to **k** the mystery of *1097*
4:13 he said unto them, **K** ye not this parable? *1492*
4:13 and how *then* will ye **k** all parables? *1097*
5:43 them straitly that no *man* should **k** it; *1097*
7:24 and would have no *man* **k** *it:* but he could *1097*
9:30 and he would not that any *man* should **k** *it.* *1097*
10:38 Jesus said unto them, Ye **k** not what ye ask: *1492*
10:42 Ye **k** that they which are accounted to rule *1492*
12:14 we **k** that thou art true, and carest for no *1492*
12:24 because ye **k** not the scriptures, *1492*
13:28 forth leaves, ye **k** that summer is near: *1097*
13:29 to pass, **k** that it is nigh, *even* at the doors. *1097*
13:33 and pray: for ye **k** not when the time is. *1492*
13:35 for ye **k** not when the master of the house *1492*
14:68 But he denied, saying, I **k** not, neither *1492*
14:71 *saying,* I **k** not this man of whom ye speak. *1492*
Lk 1: 4 That thou mightest **k** the certainty of *those* *1921*
1:18 said unto the angel, Whereby shall I **k** this? *1097*
1:34 How shall this be, seeing I **k** not a man? *1097*
4:34 I **k** thee who thou art, the Holy One of God. *1492*
5:24 But that ye may **k** that the Son of man hath *1492*
8:10 Unto you it is given to **k** the mysteries of *1097*
9:55 Ye **k** not what manner of spirit ye are of. *1492*
11:13 **k how** to give good gifts unto your *1492*
12:39 And this **k**, that if the goodman of *1097*
13:25 say unto you, I **k** you not whence you are: *1492*
13:27 I tell you, I **k** you not whence you are; *1492*
19:15 that he might **k** how much every *man* had *1097*
20:21 we **k** that thou sayest and teachest rightly, *1492*
21:20 then **k** that the desolation thereof is nigh. *1097*
21:30 **k** of your own selves that summer is now *1097*
21:31 **k** ye that the kingdom of God is nigh at *1097*
22:57 denied him, saying, Woman, I **k** him not. *1492*
22:60 Peter said, Man, I **k** not what thou sayest. *1492*
23:34 forgive them; for they **k** not what they do. *1492*
24:16 were holden that *they* should not **k** him. *1921*
Jn 1:26 standeth one among you, whom ye **k** not; *1492*
3: 2 we **k** that thou art a teacher come from *1492*
3:11 We speak that we do **k**, and testify that we *1492*
4:22 Ye worship ye **k** not what: we know what *1492*
4:22 we **k** what we worship: for salvation is of *1492*
4:25 I **k** that Messias cometh, which is called *1492*
4:32 I have meat to eat that ye **k** not of. *1492*
4:42 and **k** that this is indeed the Christ, *1492*
5:32 I **k** that the witness which he witnesseth of *1492*
5:42 But I **k** you, that ye have not the love of *1097*
6:42 of Joseph, whose father and mother we **k**? *1492*
7:17 he shall **k** of the doctrine, whether it be of *1097*
7:26 Do the rulers **k** indeed that this is the very *1097*
7:27 Howbeit we **k** this *man* whence he is: but *1492*
7:28 Ye both **k** me, and ye know whence I am: *1492*
7:28 Ye both know me, and ye **k** whence I am: *1492*
7:28 but he that sent me is true, whom ye **k** not. *1492*
7:29 But I **k** him: for I am from him, and he hath *1492*
7:51 before it hear him, and **k** what he doeth? *1097*
8:14 for I **k** whence I came, and whither I go; *1492*
8:19 Ye neither **k** me, nor my Father: *1492*
8:28 then shall ye **k** that I am *he,* and *that* I do *1097*
8:32 And ye shall **k** the truth, and the truth shall *1097*
8:37 I **k** that ye are Abraham's seed; but ye seek *1492*
8:52 unto him, Now we **k** that thou hast a devil. *1097*
8:55 Yet ye have not known him; but I **k** him: *1492*
8:55 and if I should say, I **k** him not, I shall be a *1492*
8:55 unto you: but I **k** him, and keep his saying. *1492*
9:12 unto him, Where is he? He said, I **k** not. *1492*
9:20 We **k** that this is our son, and that he was *1492*
9:21 But by what means he now seeth, we **k** not; *1492*
9:21 or who hath opened his eyes, we **k** not: *1492*
9:24 the praise: we **k** that this man is a sinner. *1492*
9:25 said, Whether he be a sinner *or no,* I **k** not: *1492*
9:25 one *thing* I **k**, that, whereas I was blind, *1492*
9:29 We **k** that God spake unto Moses: *as for* *1492*
9:29 *as for* this *fellow,* we **k** not from whence he *1492*
9:30 Why herein is a marvellous *thing,* that ye **k** *1492*
9:31 Now we **k** that God heareth not sinners: but *1492*
10: 4 the sheep follow him: for they **k** his voice. *1492*
10: 5 for they **k** not the voice of strangers. *1492*
10:14 and **k** my *sheep,* and am known of mine. *1097*
10:15 Father knoweth me, *even* so **k** I the Father: *1097*
10:27 and I **k** them, and they follow me: *1097*
10:38 that ye may **k**, and believe, that the Father *1097*
11:22 But I **k**, that even now, whatsoever thou *1492*
11:24 I **k** that he shall rise again in *1492*
11:49 said unto them, Ye **k** nothing at all, *1492*
12:50 And I **k** that his commandment is life *1492*
13: 7 not now; but thou shalt **k** hereafter. *1097*
13:12 unto them, **K** ye what I have done to you? *1097*
13:17 If ye **k** these *things,* happy are ye if ye do *1492*
13:18 I **k** whom I have chosen: but that *1492*
13:35 By this shall all *men* **k** that ye are my *1097*
14: 4 And whither I go ye **k**, and the way ye *1492*
14: 4 whither I go ye know, and the way ye **k**. *1492*
14: 5 Lord, we **k** not whither thou goest; *1492*
14: 5 thou goest; and how can we **k** the way? *1492*
14: 7 and from henceforth ye **k** him, and *1097*
14:17 but ye **k** him; for he dwelleth with you, and *1097*
14:20 At that day ye shall **k** that I *am* in my *1097*
14:31 But that the world may **k** that I love *1097*
15:18 ye **k** that it hated me before *it hated* you. *1097*
15:21 because they **k** not him that sent me. *1492*
17: 3 that they might **k** thee the only true God, *1097*
17:23 that the world may **k** that thou hast sent me, *1097*
18:21 said unto them: behold, they **k** what I said. *1492*
19: 4 that ye may **k** that I find no fault in him. *1097*
20: 2 and we **k** not where they have laid him. *1492*
20:13 and I **k** not where they have laid him. *1492*
21:24 and we **k** that his testimony is true. *1492*
Ac 1: 7 It is not for you to **k** *the* times or *1097*
2:22 in the midst of you, as ye yourselves also **k**: *1492*
2:36 Therefore let all the house of Israel **k** *1097*
3:16 made this *man* strong, whom ye see and **k**: *1492*
10:28 Ye **k** how that it is an unlawful *thing* for a *1987*
10:37 *That* word, *I say,* you **k**, which was *1492*
12:11 he said, Now I **k** of a surety, that the Lord *1492*
15: 7 ye **k** how that a good while ago God made *1987*
17:19 saying, May we **k** what this new doctrine, *1097*
17:20 we would **k** therefore what these *things* *1097*
19:15 and said, Jesus I **k**, and Paul I know; *1097*
19:15 and said, Jesus I know, and Paul I **k**; *1987*
19:25 ye **k** that by this craft we have our wealth. *1987*
20:18 were come to him, he said unto them, Ye **k**, *1987*
20:25 And now behold, I **k** that ye all, *1492*
20:29 For I **k** this, that after my departing shall *1492*
20:34 Yea, ye yourselves **k**, that these hands have *1097*
21:24 all may **k** that *those things,* whereof they *1097*
21:34 when he could not **k** the certainty for *1097*
22:14 that *thou* shouldest **k** his will, and see *that* *1097*
22:19 they **k** that I imprisoned and beat in every *1987*
22:24 that he might **k** wherefore they cried so *1921*
24:10 Forasmuch as I **k** that thou hast been of *1987*
24:22 I will **k the uttermost** of your matter. *1231*
26: 3 *I k* thee to be expert in all customs and NIG
26: 4 own nation at Jerusalem, **k** all the Jews; *2467*
26:27 thou the prophets? I **k** that thou believest. *1492*
28:22 **k** that every where it is spoken *1110+1510*
Ro 3:19 Now we **k** that what *things* soever the law *1492*
6: 3 **K** ye **not**, that so many of us as were baptized *50*
6:16 **K** ye not, that to whom ye yield yourselves *1492*
7: 1 **K** ye **not**, brethren, (for I speak to them that *50*
7: 1 (for I speak to them that **k** the law,) *1097*
7:14 For we **k** that the law is spiritual: but I am *1492*
7:18 For I **k** that in me (that is, in my flesh,) *1492*
8:22 For we **k** that the whole creation groaneth *1492*
8:26 for we **k** not what we should pray for as we *1492*
8:28 And we **k** that all *things* work together for *1492*

Ro 10:19 But I say, Did not Israel **k**? First Moses 1097
14:14 I **k**, and am persuaded by the Lord Jesus, 1492
1Co 1:16 I **k** not whether I baptized any other. 1492
2: 2 For I determined not to **k** any *thing* among 1492
2:12 that we might **k** the *things* that are freely 1492
2:14 neither can he **k** *them,* because they are 1097
3:16 **K** ye not that ye are the temple of God, and 1492
4: 4 For I **k** nothing by myself; yet am I not 4894
4:19 to you shortly, if the Lord will, and will **k**, 1097
5: 6 **K** ye not that a little leaven leaveneth 1492
6: 2 Do ye not **k** that the saints shall judge 1492
6: 3 **K** ye not that we shall judge angels? 1492
6: 9 **K** ye not that the unrighteous shall not 1492
6:15 **K** ye not that your bodies are the members 1492
6:16 **k** ye not that he which is joined to a harlot 1492
6:19 **k** ye not that your body is the temple of 1492
8: 1 we **k** that we all have knowledge. 1492
8: 2 he knoweth nothing yet as he ought to **k**. 1097
8: 4 we **k** that an idol *is* nothing in the world, 1492
9:13 Do ye not **k** that they which minister about 1492
9:24 **K** ye not that they which run in a race run 1492
11: 3 But I would have you **k**, that the head of 1492
12: 2 Ye **k** that ye were Gentiles, carried away 1492
13: 9 For we **k** in part, and we prophesy in part. 1097
13:12 now I **k** in part; but then shall I know even 1097
13:12 but then shall I **k** even as also I am known. 1921
14:11 Therefore if I **k** not the meaning of 1492
15:58 forasmuch as you **k** that your labour is not 1492
16:15 brethren, (ye **k** the house of Stephanas, 1492
2Co 2: 4 that ye might **k** the love which I have more 1097
2: 9 did I write, that I might **k** the proof of you, 1097
5: 1 For we **k** that if our earthly house of *this* 1492
5:16 Wherefore henceforth **k** we no *man* after 1492
5:16 yet now henceforth **k** we *him* no more. 1097
8: 9 For ye **k** the grace of our Lord Jesus Christ, 1097
9: 2 For I **k** the forwardness of your mind, 1492
13: 5 **K** ye not your own selves, how that Jesus 1921
13: 6 But I trust that ye shall **k** that we are not 1097
Gal 3: 7 **K** ye therefore that they which are of faith, 1097
4:13 Ye **k** how through infirmity of the flesh I 1492
Eph 1:18 that ye may **k** what is the hope of his 1492
3:19 And to **k** the love of Christ, which passeth 1097
5: 5 For this ye **k**, that no whoremonger, 1097
6:21 But that ye also may **k** my affairs, *and* 1492
6:22 that ye might **k** our affairs, and *that* he 1097
Php 1:19 For I **k** that this shall turn to my salvation 1492
1:25 I **k** that I shall abide and continue with you 1492
2:19 be of good comfort, when I **k** your state. 1097
2:22 But ye **k** the proof of him, that, as a son 1097
3:10 That *I* may **k** him, and the power of his 1097
4:12 I **k** both *how* to be abased, and I know *how* 1492
4:12 *how* to be abased, and I **k** *how* to abound: 1492
4:15 Now ye Philippians **k** also, that in 1492
Col 4: 6 that *you* may **k** how ye ought to answer 1492
4: 8 that he might **k** your estate, and 1097
1Th 1: 5 as ye **k** what manner of *men* we were 1492
2: 1 brethren, **k** our entrance in unto you, 1492
2: 2 shamefully entreated, as ye **k**, at Philippi, 1492
2: 5 as ye **k**, nor a cloke of covetousness; 1492
2:11 As you **k** how we exhorted and comforted 1492
3: 3 for yourselves **k** that we are appointed 1492
3: 4 even as it came to pass, and ye **k**. 1492
3: 5 no longer forbear, I sent to **k** your faith, 1097
4: 2 For ye **k** what commandments we gave you 1492
4: 4 That every one of you should **k** how to 1492
4: 5 even as the Gentiles which **k** not God: 1492
5: 2 For yourselves **k** perfectly that the day of 1492
5:12 to **k** them which labour among you, and 1492
2Th 1: 8 taking vengeance on them that **k** not God, 1492
2: 6 And now ye **k** what withholdeth that he 1492
3: 7 For yourselves **k** how *ye* ought to follow 1492
1Ti 1: 8 But we **k** that the law *is* good, if a man use 1492
3: 5 (For if a man **k** not how to rule his own 1492
3:15 that thou mayest **k** how *thou* oughtest to 1492
4: 3 of them which believe and **k** the truth. 1921
2Ti 1:12 for I **k** whom I have believed, and I am 1492
3: 1 This **k** also, that in the last days perilous 1097
Tit 1:16 They profess that *they* **k** God; but in works 1492
Heb 8:11 every man his brother, saying, **K** the Lord: 1097
8:11 for all shall **k** me, from the least to 1492
10:30 For we **k** him that hath said, 1492
12:17 For ye **k** how that afterward, when he 2467
13:23 **K** ye that *our* brother Timothy is set at 1097
Jas 2:20 But wilt thou **k**, O vain man, that faith 1097
4: 4 **k** ye not that the friendship of the world is 1492
4:14 Whereas ye **k** not what *shall be* on 1987
5:20 Let him **k**, that he which converteth 1097
1Pe 1:18 Forasmuch as ye **k** that ye were not 1492
2Pe 1:12 of these *things,* though ye **k** *them,* 1492
3:17 beloved, seeing ye **k** *these things* **before,** 4267
1Jn 2: 3 And hereby we do **k** that we know him, 1097
2: 3 And hereby we do know that we **k** him, 1097
2: 4 I **k** him, and keepeth not his 1097
2: 5 hereby **k** we that we are in him. 1097
2:18 whereby we **k** that it is the last time. 1097
2:20 from the Holy One, and ye **k** all *things.* 1492
2:21 written unto you because ye **k** not the truth, 1492
2:21 but because ye **k** it, and that no lie is of 1492
2:29 If ye **k** that he is righteous, ye know that 1492
2:29 ye **k** that every one which doeth 1097
3: 2 but we **k** that, when he shall appear, 1492
3: 5 And ye **k** that he was manifested to take 1492
3:14 We **k** that we have passed from death unto 1492
3:15 ye **k** that no murderer hath eternal life 1492
3:19 And hereby we **k** that we are of the truth, 1097
3:24 And hereby we **k** that he abideth in us, 1097
4: 2 Hereby **k** ye the Spirit of God: Every spirit 1097
4: 6 Hereby **k** we the spirit of truth, and 1097
4:13 Hereby **k** we that we dwell in him, and 1097
5: 2 By this we **k** that we love the children of 1097
5:13 that ye may **k** that ye have eternal life, and 1492
5:15 And if we **k** that he hear us, whatsoever we 1492
5:15 we **k** that we have the petitions that we 1492
5:18 We **k** that whosoever is born of God 1492
5:19 *And* we **k** that we are of God, and 1492
5:20 And we **k** that the Son of God is come, and 1492
5:20 that we may **k** him *that is* true, and we are 1097
3Jn 1:12 and ye **k** that our record is true. 1492
Jude 1:10 speak evil of those *things* which they **k** not: 1492
1:10 but what they **k** naturally, as brute beasts, 1987
Rev 2: 2 I **k** thy works, and thy labour, and 1492
2: 9 I **k** thy works, 1492
2: 9 *I k* the blasphemy of them which say they NIG
2:13 I **k** thy works, and where thou dwellest, 1492
2:19 I **k** thy works, and charity, and service, 1492
2:23 all the churches shall **k** that I am he which 1097
3: 1 I **k** thy works, that thou hast a name that 1492
3: 3 thou shalt not **k** what hour I will come upon 1097
3: 8 I **k** thy works: behold, I have set before 1492
3: 9 thy feet, and to **k** that I have loved thee. 1097
3:15 I **k** thy works, that thou art neither cold nor 1492

KNOWEST (89) [KNOW]

Ge 30:26 for thou **k** my service which I have done 3045
30:29 Thou **k** how I have served thee, and how 3045
47: 6 if thou **k** *any* man of activity amongst them, 3045
Ex 10: 7 **k** thou not yet that Egypt is destroyed? 3045
32:22 thou **k** the people, that they *are set* on 3045
Nu 10:31 forasmuch as thou **k** how we are to encamp 3045
11:16 whom thou **k** to be the elders of the people, 3045
20:14 Thou **k** all the travail that hath befallen us: 3045
Dt 7:15 diseases of Egypt, which thou **k**, upon thee; 3045
9: 2 whom thou **k**, and *of whom* thou hast heard 3045
20:20 Only the trees which thou **k** that they *be* not 3045
28:33 shall a nation which thou **k** not eat up; 3045
Jos 14: 6 Thou **k** the thing that the LORD said unto 3045
Jdg 15:11 **K** thou not that the Philistines *are* rulers 3045
1Sa 28: 9 Behold, thou **k** what Saul hath done, 3045
2Sa 1: 5 How **k** thou that Saul and Jonathan his son 3045
2:26 **k** thou not that it will be bitterness in 3045
3:25 Thou **k** Abner the son of Ner, that he came 3045
7:20 for thou, Lord GOD, **k** thy servant. 3045
17: 8 thou **k** thy father and his men, that they *be* 3045
1Ki 1:18 and now, my lord the king, thou **k** *it* not: 3045
2: 5 Moreover thou **k** also what Joab the son of 3045
2: 9 and **k** what thou oughtest to do unto him; 3045
2:15 Thou **k** that the kingdom was mine, and 3045
2:44 Thou **k** all the wickedness which thine 3045
5: 3 Thou **k** how that David my father could not 3045
5: 6 for thou **k** that *there is* not among us any 3045
8:39 according to his ways, whose heart thou **k**; 3045
8:39 **k** the hearts of all the children of men;) 3045
2Ki 2: 3 **K** thou that the LORD will take away thy 3045
2: 5 **K** thou that the LORD will take away thy 3045
4: 1 thou **k** that thy servant did fear the LORD: 3045
1Ch 17:18 of thy servant? for thou **k** thy servant. 3045
2Ch 6:30 unto all his ways, whose heart thou **k**; 3045
6:30 (for thou only **k** the hearts of the children 3045

Job	10: 7	Thou k that I am not wicked; and	1847+5921
	15: 9	What k thou, that we know not?	3045
	20: 4	K thou *not* this of old, since man was	3045
	34:33	and not I: therefore speak what thou k.	3045
	38: 5	hath laid the measures thereof, if thou k?	3045
	38:18	breadth of the earth? declare if thou k it all.	3045
	38:21	K thou *it,* because thou wast then born? or	3045
	38:33	K thou the ordinances of heaven? canst	3045
	39: 1	K thou the time when the wild goats of	3045
	39: 2	or k thou the time when they bring forth?	3045
Ps	40: 9	not refrained my lips, O LORD, thou k.	3045
	69: 5	O God, thou k my foolishness; and my sins	3045
	139: 2	Thou k my downsitting and mine uprising,	3045
	139: 4	*but* lo, O LORD, thou k it altogether.	3045
Pr	27: 1	for thou k not what a day may bring forth.	3045
Ecc	11: 2	for thou k not what evil shall be upon	3045
	11: 5	As thou k not what *is* the way of the spirit,	3045
	11: 5	thou k not the works of God who maketh	3045
	11: 6	for thou k not whether shall prosper,	3045
Isa	55: 5	thou shalt call a nation *that* thou k not, and	3045
Jer	5:15	a nation whose language thou k not,	3045
	12: 3	thou, O LORD, k me: thou hast seen me,	3045
	15:14	thine enemies into a land *which* thou k not:	3045
	15:15	O LORD, thou k: remember me, and	3045
	17: 4	thine enemies in the land which thou k not:	3045
	17:16	have I desired the woeful day; thou k:	3045
	18:23	thou k all their counsel against me to slay	3045
	33: 3	and mighty *things,* which thou k not.	3045
Eze	37: 3	And I answered, O Lord GOD, thou k.	3045
Da	10:20	K thou wherefore I come unto thee?	3045
Zec	4: 5	K thou not what these *be?* And I said, No,	3045
	4:13	K thou not what these *be?* And I said, No,	3045
Mt	15:12	K thou that the Pharisees were offended,	*1492*
Mk	10:19	Thou k the commandments, Do not commit	*1492*
Lk	18:20	Thou k the commandments, Do not commit	*1492*
	22:34	that thou shalt thrice deny that *thou* k me.	*1492*
Jn	1:48	saith unto him, Whence k thou me?	*1097*
	3:10	a master of Israel, and k not these *things?*	*1097*
	13: 7	said unto him, What I do thou k not now;	*1492*
	16:30	Now are we sure that thou k all *things,* and	*1492*
	19:10	k thou not that I have power to crucify	*1492*
	21:15	Yea, Lord; thou k that I love thee.	*1492*
	21:16	Yea, Lord; thou k that I love thee.	*1492*
	21:17	thou k all *things;* thou knowest that I love	*1492*
	21:17	thou knowest all *things;* thou k that I love	*1097*
Ac	1:24	which k the **hearts** of all *men,* shew	*2589*
	25:10	have I done no wrong, as thou very well k.	*1921*
Ro	2:18	And k *his* will, and approvest the *things*	*1097*
1Co	7:16	For what k thou, O wife, whether thou shalt	*1492*
	7:16	or how k thou, O man, whether thou shalt	*1492*
2Ti	1:15	This thou k, that all they which are in Asia	*1492*
	1:18	*unto me* at Ephesus, thou k very well.	*1097*
Rev	3:17	and k not that thou art wretched, and	*1492*
	7:14	And I said unto him, Sir, thou k. And he	*1492*

KNOWETH (104) [KNOW]

Ge	33:13	My lord k that the children *are* tender, and	3045
Lev	5: 3	when he k *of it,* then he shall be guilty.	3045
	5: 4	when he k *of it,* then he shall be guilty in	3045
Dt	2: 7	he k thy walking *through* this great	3045
	34: 6	but no man k of his sepulchre unto this day.	3045
Jos	22:22	of gods, he k, and Israel he shall know;	3045
1Sa	3:13	house for ever for the iniquity which he k;	3045
	20: 3	Thy father **certainly** k that I have	3045+3045
	23:17	unto thee; and that also Saul my father k.	3045
2Sa	14:22	To day thy servant k that I have found	3045
	17:10	for all Israel k that thy father *is* a mighty	3045
1Ki	1:11	doth reign, and David our lord k *it* not?	3045
Est	4:14	who k whether thou art come to	3045
Job	11:11	For he k vain men: he seeth wickedness	3045
	12: 3	to you: yea, who k not such *things* as these?	854
	12: 9	Who k not in all these that the hand of	3045
	14:21	His sons come to honour, and he k *it* not;	3045
	15:23	*saying,* Where *is it?* he k that the day of	3045
	18:21	and this *is* the place *of him that* k not God.	3045
	23:10	he k the way that I take: *when* he hath tried	3045
	28: 7	*There is* a path which no fowl k, and	3045
	28:13	Man k not the price thereof; neither is it	3045
	28:23	the way thereof, and he k the place thereof.	3045
	34:25	Therefore he k their works, and	5234
	35:15	his anger; yet he k *it* not in great extremity:	3045
Ps	1: 6	For the LORD k the way of the righteous:	3045
	37:18	The LORD k the days of the upright: and	3045
	39: 6	up *riches,* and k not who shall gather them.	3045
	44:21	this out? for he k the secrets of the heart.	3045
	74: 9	neither *is there* among us any that k how	3045
	90:11	Who k the power of thine anger?	3045
	92: 6	A brutish man k not; neither doth a fool	3045
	94:11	The LORD k the thoughts of man,	3045
	103:14	For he k our frame; he remembereth that	3045
	104:19	for seasons: the sun k his going down.	3045
	138: 6	unto the lowly: but the proud he k afar off.	3045
	139:14	thy works; and *that* my soul k right well.	3045
Pr	7:23	to the snare, and k not that it *is* for his life.	3045
	9:13	*is* clamorous: *she is* simple, and k nothing.	3045
	9:18	he k not that the dead *are* there; *and*	3045
	14:10	The heart k his own bitterness; and	3045
	24:22	and who k the ruin of them both?	3045
Ecc	2:19	who k whether he shall be a wise *man* or	3045
	3:21	Who k the spirit of man that goeth upward,	3045
	6: 8	the poor, that k to walk before the living?	3045
	6:12	For who k what *is* good for man in *this* life,	3045
	7:22	For oftentimes also thine own heart k that	3045
	8: 1	and who k the interpretation of a thing?	3045
	8: 7	For he k not that which shall be: for who	3045
	9: 1	no man k either love or hatred *by* all *that is*	3045
	9:12	For man also k not his time: as the fishes	3045
	10:15	because he k not how to go to the city.	3045
Isa	1: 3	The ox k his owner, and the ass his	3045
	29:15	and they say, Who seeth us? and who k us?	3045
Jer	8: 7	the stork in the heaven k her appointed	3045
	9:24	in this, that *he* understandeth and k me,	3045
Da	2:22	secret *things:* he k what *is* in the darkness,	3046
Hos	7: 9	have devoured his strength, and he k *it* not:	3045
	7: 9	are here and there upon him, yet he k not.	3045
Joel	2:14	Who k *if* he will return and repent, and	3045
Na	1: 7	of trouble; and he k them that trust in him.	3045
Zep	3: 5	he faileth not; but the unjust k no shame.	3045
Mt	6: 8	for your Father k what *things* ye have need	*1492*
	6:32	for your heavenly Father k that ye have	*1492*
	11:27	and no *man* k the Son, but the Father;	*1921*
	11:27	neither k any *man* the Father, save the Son,	*1921*
	24:36	But of that day and hour k no *man,* no,	*1492*
Mk	4:27	should spring and grow up, he k not how.	*1492*
	13:32	But of that day and *that* hour k no *man,* no,	*1492*
Lk	10:22	and no *man* k who the Son is, but	*1097*
	12:30	your Father k that ye have need of these	*1492*
	16:15	before men; but God k your hearts:	*1097*
Jn	7:15	saying, How k this *man* letters,	*1492*
	7:27	Christ cometh, no *man* k whence he is.	*1097*
	7:49	But this people who k not the law are	*1097*
	10:15	As the Father k me, *even* so know I	*1097*
	12:35	for he that walketh in darkness k not	*1492*
	14:17	because it seeth him not, neither k him:	*1097*
	15:15	for the servant k not what his lord doeth:	*1492*
	19:35	and he k that he saith true, that ye might	*1492*
Ac	15: 8	And God, which k the **hearts**, bare them	*2589*
	19:35	what man is there that k not how that	*1097*
	26:26	For the king k of these *things,* before whom	*1987*
Ro	8:27	And he that searcheth the hearts k what *is*	*1492*
1Co	2:11	For what man k the *things* of a man,	*1492*
	2:11	even so the *things* of God k no *man,* but	*1492*
	3:20	The Lord k the thoughts of the wise,	*1097*
	8: 2	And if any *man* think that *he* k any *thing,*	*1492*
	8: 2	he k nothing yet as he ought to know.	*1097*
2Co	11:11	because I love you not? God k.	*1492*
	11:31	is blessed for evermore, k that I lie not.	*1492*
	12: 2	God k;) such a one caught up to the third	*1492*
	12: 3	or out of the body, I cannot tell: God k;)	*1492*
2Ti	2:19	this seal, The Lord k them that are his.	*1097*
Jas	4:17	Therefore to him that k to do good, and	*1492*
2Pe	2: 9	The Lord k *how* to deliver the godly out of	*1492*
1Jn	2:11	and k not whither he goeth, because	*1492*
	3: 1	therefore the world k us not, because	*1097*
	3:20	is greater than our heart, and k all *things.*	*1097*
	4: 6	he that k God heareth us; *he* that is not of	*1097*
	4: 7	one that loveth is born of God, and k God.	*1097*
	4: 8	He that loveth not, k not God; for God is	*1097*
Rev	2:17	which no *man* k saving he that receiveth *it.*	*1097*
	12:12	because he k that he hath *but* a short time.	*1492*

KNOWING (51) [KNOW]

Ge	3: 5	and ye shall be as gods, k good and evil.	3045
1Ki	2:32	my father David not k *thereof, to wit,*	3045
Mt	9: 4	And Jesus k their thoughts said,	*1492*
	22:29	unto them, Ye do err, not k the scriptures,	*1492*
Mk	5:30	And Jesus immediately k in himself that	*1921*
	5:33	k what was done in her, came and	*1492*

Mk 6:20 **k** that he *was* a just man and a holy, and *1492*
12:15 But he, **k** their hypocrisy, said unto them, *1492*
Lk 8:53 laughed him to scorn, **k** that she was dead. *1492*
9:33 and one for Elias: not **k** what he said. *1492*
11:17 But he, **k** their thoughts, said unto them, *1492*
Jn 13: 3 Jesus **k** that the Father had given all *things* *1492*
18: 4 **k** all *things* that should come upon him, *1492*
19:28 Jesus **k** that all *things* were now *1492*
21:12 Who art thou? **k** that it was the Lord. *1492*
Ac 2:30 **k** that God had sworn with an oath to him, *1492*
5: 7 his wife, not **k** what was done, came in. *1492*
18:25 of the Lord, **k** only the baptism of John. *1987*
20:22 not **k** the *things* that shall befall me there: *1492*
Ro 1:32 Who **k** the judgment of God, that they *1921*
2: 4 **not k** that the goodness of God leadeth thee to *50*
5: 3 **k** that tribulation worketh patience; *1492*
6: 6 **K** this, that our old man is crucified with *1097*
6: 9 **k** that Christ being raised from the dead *1492*
13:11 And that, **k** the time, that now *it is* high *1492*
2Co 1: 7 And our hope of you *is* stedfast, **k**, that as *1492*
4:14 **K** that he which raised up the Lord Jesus *1492*
5: 6 **k** that, whilst we are at home in the body, *1492*
5:11 **K** therefore the terror of the Lord, *1492*
Gal 2:16 **K** that a man is not justified by the works *1492*
Eph 6: 8 **K** that whatsoever good *thing* any man *1492*
6: 9 **k** that your Master also is in heaven; *1492*
Php 1:17 **k** that I am set for the defence of *1492*
Col 3:24 **K** that of the Lord ye shall receive *1492*
4: 1 **k** that ye also have a Master in heaven. *1492*
1Th 1: 4 **K**, brethren beloved, your election of God. *1492*
1Ti 1: 9 **K** this, that the law is not made for a *1492*
6: 4 **k** nothing, but doting about questions and *1987*
2Ti 2:23 **k** that they do gender strifes. *1492*
3:14 **k** of whom thou hast learned *them;* *1492*
Tit 3:11 **K** that *he that is* such is subverted, and *1492*
Phm 1:21 **k** that thou wilt also do more than I say. *1492*
Heb 10:34 **k** in yourselves that *ye* have in heaven a *1097*
11: 8 and he went out, not **k** whither he went. *1987*
Jas 1: 3 **K** *this,* that the trying of your faith worketh *1097*
3: 1 **k** that we shall receive the greater *1492*
1Pe 3: 9 **k** that ye are thereunto called, that ye *1492*
5: 9 **k** that the same afflictions are *1492*
2Pe 1:14 **K** that shortly *I* must put off *this* my *1492*
1:20 **K** this first, that no prophecy of *1097*
3: 3 **K** this first, that there shall come in the last *1097*

KNOWLEDGE (172) [KNOW]

Ge 2: 9 and the tree of **k** of good and evil. 1847
2:17 of the tree of the **k** of good and evil, 1847
Ex 31: 3 in **k**, and in all *manner of* workmanship, 1847
35:31 in **k**, and in all *manner of* workmanship; 1847
Lev 4:23 wherein he hath sinned, **come to** his **k**, 3045
4:28 **come to** his **k**, then he shall bring his 3045
Nu 15:24 **without** the **k** of the congregation, 4480+5869
24:16 of God, and knew the **k** of the most High, 1847
Dt 1:39 which *in that* day **had** no **k** between good 3045
Ru 2:10 that *thou* shouldest **take k** of me, seeing I 5234
2:19 blessed be he that did **take k** of thee. 5234
1Sa 2: 3 for the LORD *is* a God of **k**, and by him 1844
23:23 **take k** of all the lurking places where he 3045
1Ki 9:27 shipmen that had **k** of the sea, with 3045
2Ch 1:10 Give me now wisdom and **k**, that I may go 4093
1:11 hast asked wisdom and **k** for thyself, 4093
1:12 Wisdom and **k** *is* granted unto thee; and 4093
8:18 and servants that had **k** of the sea; 3045
30:22 **taught** the good **k** of the LORD: 7919+7922
Ne 10:28 every one **having k**, *and* 3045
Job 15: 2 Should a wise *man* utter vain **k**, and fill his 1847
21:14 for we desire not the **k** of thy ways. 1847
21:22 Shall *any* teach God **k**? seeing he judgeth 1847
33: 3 my heart: and my lips shall utter **k** clearly. 1847
34: 2 and give ear unto me, ye that **have k**. 3045
34:35 Job hath spoken without **k**, and his words 1847
35:16 in vain; he multiplieth words without **k**. 1847
36: 3 I will fetch my **k** from afar, and will ascribe 1843
36: 4 *be* false: *he that is* perfect in **k** *is* with thee. 1844
36:12 by the sword, and they shall die without **k**. 1847
37:16 works of *him which is* perfect in **k**? 1843
38: 2 that darkeneth counsel by words without **k**? 1847
42: 3 Who *is* he that hideth counsel without **k**? 1847
Ps 14: 4 Have all the workers of iniquity no **k**? 3045
19: 2 and night unto night sheweth **k**. 1847
53: 4 Have the workers of iniquity no **k**? who eat 3045
73:11 and is there **k** in the most High? 1844
94:10 he that teacheth man **k**, *shall not he know?* 1847
119:66 Teach me good judgment and **k**: for I have 1847
139: 6 *Such* **k** *is* too wonderful for me; it is high, 1847
144: 3 what *is* man, that thou **takest k** of him? 3045
Pr 1: 4 to the young man **k** and discretion. 1847
1: 7 fear of the LORD *is* the beginning of **k**: 1847
1:22 delight in their scorning, and fools hate **k**? 1847
1:29 For that they hated **k**, and did not choose 1847
2: 3 if thou criest after **k**, *and* liftest up thy voice 998
2: 5 fear of the LORD, and find the **k** of God. 1847
2: 6 out of his mouth *cometh* **k** and 1847
2:10 thine heart, and **k** is pleasant unto thy soul; 1847
3:20 By his **k** the depths are broken up, and 1847
5: 2 and *that* thy lips may keep **k**. 1847
8: 9 and right to them that find **k**. 1847
8:10 not silver; and **k** rather than choice gold. 1847
8:12 and find out **k** of witty inventions. 1847
9:10 and the **k** of the holy *is* understanding. 1847
10:14 Wise *men* lay up **k**: but the mouth of 1847
11: 9 but through **k** shall the just be delivered. 1847
12: 1 Whoso loveth instruction loveth **k**: but 1847
12:23 A prudent man concealeth **k**: but the heart 1847
13:16 Every prudent *man* dealeth with **k**: but 1847
14: 6 but **k** *is* easy unto him that understandeth. 1847
14: 7 thou perceivest not *in him* the lips of **k**. 1847
14:18 but the prudent are crowned *with* **k**. 1847
15: 2 The tongue of the wise useth **k** aright: but 1847
15: 7 The lips of the wise disperse **k**: but 1847
15:14 of him that hath understanding seeketh **k**: 1847
17:27 He that **hath k** spareth his words: 1847+3045
18:15 The heart of the prudent getteth **k**; and 1847
18:15 and the ear of the wise seeketh **k**. 1847
19: 2 Also, *that* the soul *be* without **k**, *it is* not 1847
19:25 *and* he will understand **k**. 1847
19:27 *that causeth* to err from the words of **k**. 1847
20:15 but the lips of **k** *are* a precious jewel. 1847
21:11 when the wise is instructed, he receiveth **k**. 1847
22:12 The eyes of the LORD preserve **k**, and 1847
22:17 the wise, and apply thine heart unto my **k**. 1847
22:20 to thee excellent things in counsels and **k**, 1847
23:12 and thine ears to the words of **k**. 1847
24: 4 by **k** shall the chambers be filled *with* all 1847
24: 5 yea, a man of **k** increaseth strength. 1847
24:14 So shall the **k** of wisdom be unto thy soul: 3045
28: 2 *and* by **k** the state *thereof* shall be prolonged. 3045
30: 3 nor **have** the **k** of the holy. 1847+3045
Ecc 1:16 had great experience of wisdom and **k**. 1847
1:18 and he that increaseth **k** increaseth sorrow. 1847
2:21 *is* in wisdom, and in **k**, and in equity; 1847
2:26 *is* good in his sight wisdom, and **k**, and joy: 1847
7:12 the excellency of **k** *is, that* wisdom giveth 1847
9:10 nor device, nor **k**, nor wisdom, in the grave, 1847
12: 9 was wise, he still taught the people **k**; 1847
Isa 5:13 into captivity, because *they have* no **k**: 1847
8: 4 For before the child shall have **k** to cry, 3045
11: 2 the spirit of **k** and of the fear of 1847
11: 9 for the earth shall be full *of* the **k** of 1844
28: 9 Whom shall he teach **k**? and whom shall he 1844
32: 4 heart also of the rash shall understand **k**, 1847
33: 6 and **k** shall be the stability of thy times, 1847
40:14 taught him **k**, and shewed to him the way 1847
44:19 neither *is there* **k** nor understanding to say, 1847
44:25 *men* backward, and maketh their **k** foolish; 1847
45:20 they have no **k** that set up the wood of their 3045
47:10 Thy wisdom and thy **k**, it hath perverted 1847
53:11 by his **k** shall my righteous servant justify 1847
58: 3 we afflicted our soul, and thou **takest** no **k**? 3045
Jer 3:15 which shall feed you with **k** and 1844
4:22 to do evil, but to do good they have no **k**. 3045
10:14 Every man is brutish in *his* **k**: 1847
11:18 the LORD hath **given** me **k** *of it,* and 3045
51:17 Every man is brutish by *his* **k**; 1847
Da 1: 4 cunning in **k**, and understanding science, 1847
1:17 God gave them **k** and skill in all learning 4093
2:21 and **k** to them that know understanding: 4486
5:12 **k**, and understanding, interpreting of 4486
12: 4 run to and fro, and **k** shall be increased. 1847
Hos 4: 1 nor mercy, nor **k** of God in the land. 1847
4: 6 My people are destroyed for lack of **k**, 1847
4: 6 because thou hast rejected **k**, I will also 1847
6: 6 and the **k** of God more than burnt offerings. 1847
Hab 2:14 For the earth shall be filled with the **k** of 3045
Mal 2: 7 For the priest's lips should keep **k**, and 1847
Mt 14:35 And when the men of that place **had k** of *1921*

K

Lk 1:77 To give **k** of salvation unto his people by *1108*
11:52 for ye have taken away the key of **k**: *1108*
Ac 4:13 and they **took k** of them, that they had been *1921*
17:13 But when the Jews of Thessalonica had **k** *1097*
24: 8 **k** of all these *things,* whereof we accuse *1921*
24:22 *things,* having more perfect **k** of *that* way, *1492*
Ro 1:28 as they did not like to retain God in *their* **k**, *1922*
2:20 which hast the form of **k** and of the truth in *1108*
3:20 in his sight: for by the law *is* the **k** of sin. *1922*
10: 2 have a zeal of God, but not according to **k**. *1922*
11:33 riches both of the wisdom and **k** of God! *1108*
15:14 also are full of goodness, filled with all **k**, *1108*
1Co 1: 5 by him, in all utterance, and *in* all **k**; *1108*
8: 1 unto idols, we know that we all have **k**. *1108*
8: 1 **K** puffeth up, but charity edifieth. *1108*
8: 7 Howbeit *there is* not in every *man that* **k**: *1108*
8:10 For if any *man* see thee which hast **k** sit at *1108*
8:11 And through thy **k** shall the weak brother *1108*
12: 8 to another the word of **k** by the same Spirit; *1108*
13: 2 and understand all mysteries, and all **k**; *1108*
13: 8 whether *there be* **k**, it shall vanish away. *1108*
14: 6 or by **k**, or by prophesying, or by doctrine? *1108*
15:34 for some have **not** the **k** of God: I speak *this* *56*
2Co 2:14 maketh manifest the savour of his **k** by us *1108*
4: 6 to give the light of the **k** of the glory of *1108*
6: 6 By pureness, by **k**, by longsuffering, *1108*
8: 7 and **k**, and *in* all diligence, and *in* your love *1108*
10: 5 that exalteth itself against the **k** of God, *1108*
11: 6 though *I be* rude in speech, yet not in **k**; *1108*
Eph 1:17 of wisdom and revelation in the **k** of him: *1922*
3: 4 ye may understand my **k** in the mystery of *4907*
3:19 know the love of Christ, which passeth **k**, *1108*
4:13 and of the **k** of the Son of God, unto a *1922*
Php 1: 9 and more in **k** and *in* all judgment; *1922*
3: 8 loss for the excellency of the **k** of Christ *1108*
Col 1: 9 to desire that ye might be filled *with* the **k** *1922*
1:10 good work, and increasing in the **k** of God; *1922*
2: 3 are hid all the treasures of wisdom and **k**. *1108*
3:10 **k** after the image of him that created him: *1922*
1Ti 2: 4 and to come unto the **k** of the truth. *1922*
2Ti 3: 7 and never able to come to the **k** of the truth. *1922*
Heb 10:26 that *we* have received the **k** of the truth, *1922*
Jas 3:13 wise *man* and endued with **k** amongst you? *1990*
1Pe 3: 7 dwell with *them* according to **k**, *1108*
2Pe 1: 2 peace be multiplied unto you through the **k** *1922*
1: 3 through the **k** of him that hath called us to *1922*
1: 5 add to your faith virtue; and to virtue **k**; *1108*
1: 6 And to **k** temperance; and to temperance *1108*
1: 8 unfruitful in the **k** of our Lord Jesus Christ. *1922*
2:20 of the world through the **k** of the Lord *1922*
3:18 and *in* the **k** of our Lord and Saviour Jesus *1108*

KNOWN (222) [KNOW]

Ge 19: 8 I have two daughters which have not **k** 3045
24:16 a virgin, neither had any man **k** her: 3045
41:21 it could not be **k** that they had eaten them; 3045
41:31 the plenty shall not be **k** in the land by 3045
45: 1 while Joseph **made** himself **k** unto his 3045
Ex 2:14 and said, Surely *this* thing is **k**. 3045
6: 3 *by* my name JEHOVAH was I not **k** to 3045
21:36 Or *if* it be **k** that the ox *hath* used to push in 3045
33:16 For wherein shall it be **k** here that I and 3045
Lev 4:14 is **k**, then the congregation shall offer a 3045
5: 1 or **k** *of it;* if he do not utter *it,* then 3045
Nu 12: 6 *I* the LORD will **make** myself **k** unto him 3045
31:17 kill every woman that hath **k** man by lying 3045
31:18 that have not **k** a man by lying with him, 3045
31:35 of women that had not **k** man by lying with 3045
Dt 1:13 **k** among your tribes, and I will make them 3045
1:15 and **k**, and made them heads over you, 3045
11: 2 not with your children which have not **k**, 3045
11:28 to go after other gods, which ye have not **k**. 3045
13: 2 which thou hast not **k**, and let us serve 3045
13: 6 which thou hast not **k**, thou, nor thy fathers; 3045
13:13 and serve other gods, which ye have not **k**; 3045
21: 1 *and* it be not **k** who hath slain him: 3045
28:36 which neither thou nor thy fathers have **k**; 3045
28:64 which neither thou nor thy fathers have **k**, 3045
31:13 which have not **k** *any thing,* may hear, and 3045
Jos 24:31 which had **k** all the works of the LORD, 3045
Jdg 3: 1 *even* as many *of Israel* as had not **k** all 3045
16: 9 toucheth the fire. So his strength was not **k**. 3045
21:12 that had **k** no man by lying with *any* male: 3045
Ru 3: 3 *but* **make** not thyself **k** unto the man, 3045
3:14 Let it not be **k** that a woman came *into* 3045
1Sa 6: 3 it shall be **k** to you why his hand is not 3045
28:15 that *thou* mayest **make k** unto me what I 3045
2Sa 17:19 corn thereon; and the thing was not **k**. 3045
1Ki 14: 2 that thou be not **k** to be the wife of 3045
18:36 let it be **k** *this* day that thou *art* God in 3045
1Ch 16: 8 **make k** his deeds among the people. 3045
17:19 in **making k** all *these* great things. 3045
Ezr 4:12 Be it **k** unto the king, that the Jews which 3046
4:13 Be it **k** now unto the king, that, if this city 3046
5: 8 Be it **k** unto the king, that we went into 3046
Ne 4:15 when our enemies heard that it was **k** unto 3045
9:14 **madest k** unto them thy holy sabbath, and 3045
Est 2:22 the thing was **k** to Mordecai, who told *it* 3045
Ps 9:16 The LORD is **k** *by* the judgment *which* he 3045
18:43 a people *whom* I have not **k** shall serve me. 3045
31: 7 thou hast **k** my soul in adversities; 3045
48: 3 God is **k** in her palaces for a refuge. 3045
67: 2 That thy way may be **k** upon earth, 3045
69:19 Thou hast **k** my reproach, and my shame, 3045
76: 1 In Judah *is* God **k**: his name *is* great in 3045
77:19 great waters, and thy footsteps are not **k**. 3045
78: 3 Which we have heard and **k**, and 3045
78: 5 that *they* should **make** them **k** to their 3045
79: 6 upon the heathen that have not **k** thee, 3045
79:10 let him be **k** among the heathen in our sight 3045
88:12 Shall thy wonders be **k** in the dark? and 3045
89: 1 with my mouth will I **make k** thy 3045
91:14 him on high, because he hath **k** my name. 3045
95:10 *their* heart, and they have not **k** my ways: 3045
98: 2 The LORD hath **made k** his salvation: 3045
103: 7 He **made k** his ways unto Moses, his acts 3045
105: 1 **make k** his deeds among the people. 3045
106: 8 *he* might **make** his mighty power **to be k**. 3045
119:79 and those that have **k** thy testimonies. 3045
119:152 I have **k** of old that thou hast founded them 3045
139: 1 thou hast searched me, and **k** *me.* 3045
145:12 To **make k** to the sons of men his mighty 3045
147:20 *as for his* judgments, they have not **k** them. 3045
Pr 1:23 I will **make k** my words unto you. 3045
10: 9 but he that perverteth his ways shall be **k**. 3045
12:16 A fool's wrath is presently **k**: but a prudent 3045
14:33 *which is* in the midst of fools is **made k**. 3045
20:11 Even a child is **k** by his doings, whether his 5234
22:19 I have **made k** to thee *this* day, even *to* 3045
31:23 Her husband is **k** in the gates, when he 3045
Ecc 5: 3 a fool's voice *is k* by multitude of words. NIH
6: 5 nor **k** *any thing:* this hath more rest than 3045
6:10 is named already, and *it is* **k** that it *is* man: 3045
Isa 12: 5 excellent things: this *is* **k** in all the earth. 3045
19:21 the LORD shall be **k** to Egypt, and 3045
38:19 the father to the children shall **make k** thy 3045
40:21 Have ye not **k**? have ye not heard? hath it 3045
40:28 Hast thou not **k**? hast thou not heard, 3045
42:16 will lead them in paths *that* they have not **k**: 3045
44:18 They have not **k** nor understood: for he 3045
45: 4 surnamed thee, though thou hast not **k** me. 3045
45: 5 I girded thee though thou hast not **k** me: 3045
61: 9 their seed shall be **k** among the Gentiles, 3045
64: 2 to **make** thy name **k** to thine adversaries, 3045
66:14 the hand of the LORD shall be **k** towards 3045
Jer 4:22 my people *is* foolish, they have not **k** me; 3045
5: 5 for they have **k** the way of the LORD, *and* 3045
9:16 whom neither they nor their fathers have **k**: 3045
19: 4 whom neither they nor their fathers have **k**, 3045
28: 9 *then* shall the prophet be **k**, that the LORD 3045
La 4: 8 than a coal; they are not **k** in the streets: 5234
Eze 20: 5 **made** myself **k** unto them in the land of 3045
20: 9 in whose sight I **made** myself **k** unto them, 3045
32: 9 into the countries which thou hast not **k**. 3045
35:11 I will **make** myself **k** amongst them, 3045
36:32 *this,* saith the Lord GOD, be it **k** unto you: 3045
38:23 I will be **k** in the eyes of many nations, and 3045
39: 7 So will I **make** my holy name **k** in 3045
Da 2: 5 if ye will not **make k** unto me the dream, 3046
2: 9 if ye will not **make k** unto me the dream, 3046
2:15 Then Arioch **made** the thing **k** to Daniel. 3046
2:17 **made** the thing **k** to Hananiah, Mishael, 3046
2:23 hast **made k** unto me now what we desired 3046
2:23 for thou hast *now* **made k** unto us 3046
2:25 that will **make k** unto the king 3046
2:26 Art thou able to **make k** unto me the dream 3046
2:28 **maketh k** to the king Nebuchadnezzar 3046
2:29 he that revealeth secrets **maketh k** to thee 3046

Da 2:30 for *their* sakes that shall **make k** 3046
2:45 the great God hath **made k** to the king what 3046
3:18 if not, be it **k** unto thee, O king, that we 3046
4: 6 that they might **make k** unto me 3046
4: 7 they *did* not **make k** unto me 3046
4:18 able to **make k** unto me the interpretation: 3046
4:26 after that thou shalt have **k** that the heavens 3046
5: 8 nor **make k** to the king the interpretation 3046
5:15 **make k** unto me the interpretation thereof: 3046
5:16 **make k** to me the interpretation thereof, 3046
5:17 and **make k** to him the interpretation. 3046
Hos 5: 4 of them, and they have not **k** the LORD. 3045
5: 9 among the tribes of Israel have I **made k** 3045
Am 3: 2 You only have I **k** of all the families of 3045
Na 3:17 and their place is not **k** where they *are.* 3045
Hab 3: 2 the years, in the midst of the years **make k**; 3045
Zec 14: 7 it shall be one day which shall be **k** to 3045
Mt 10:26 not be revealed; and hid, that shall not be **k**. *1097*
12: 7 But if ye had **k** what *this* meaneth, I will *1097*
12:16 them that they should not make him **k**: *5318*
12:33 fruit corrupt: for the tree is **k** by *his* fruit. *1097*
24:43 that if the goodman of the house had **k** in *1492*
Mk 3:12 them that they should not make him **k**. *5318*
Lk 2:15 which the Lord hath **made k** unto us. *1107*
2:17 **made k abroad** the saying which was told *1232*
6:44 For every tree is **k** by his own fruit. For of *1097*
7:39 would have **k** who and what manner of *1097*
8:17 that shall not be **k** and come abroad. *1097*
12: 2 be revealed; neither hid, that shall not be **k**. *1097*
12:39 that if the goodman of the house had **k** *1492*
19:42 Saying, If thou hadst **k**, even thou, at least *1097*
24:18 hast not **k** the *things* which are come to *1097*
24:35 how he was **k** of them in breaking of bread. *1097*
Jn 7: 4 he himself seeketh to be **k openly**. *1722+3954*
8:19 if ye had **k** me, ye should have known my *1492*
8:19 ye should have **k** my Father also. *1492*
8:55 Yet ye have not **k** him; but I know him: and *1097*
10:14 and know my *sheep,* and am **k** of mine. *1097*
14: 7 If ye had **k** me, ye should have known my *1097*
14: 7 ye should have **k** my Father also: *1097*
14: 9 and *yet* hast thou not **k** me, Philip? *1097*
15:15 of my Father I have **made k** unto you. *1107*
16: 3 because they have not **k** the Father, nor me. *1097*
17: 7 Now they have **k** that all *things* whatsoever *1097*
17: 8 have **k** surely that I came out from thee, *1097*
17:25 righteous Father, the world hath not **k** thee: *1097*
17:25 but I have **k** thee, and these have known *1097*
17:25 and these have **k** that thou hast sent me. *1097*
18:15 that disciple was **k** unto the high priest, and *1110*
18:16 which was **k** unto the high priest, and *1110*
Ac 1:19 And it was **k** unto all the dwellers at *1110*
2:14 be this **k** unto you, and hearken to my *1110*
2:28 Thou hast **made k** to me the ways of life; *1107*
4:10 Be it **k** unto you all, and to all the people of *1110*
7:13 And at the second time Joseph was **made k** *319*
7:13 Joseph's kindred was made **k** unto Pharaoh. *5318*
9:24 But their laying await was **k** of Saul. *1097*
9:42 And it was **k** throughout all Joppa; and *1110*
13:38 Be it **k** unto you therefore, men *and* *1110*
15:18 **K** unto God are all his works from *1110*
19:17 And this was **k** to all the Jews and *1110*
22:30 he would have **k** the certainty wherefore he *1097*
23:28 And when I would have **k** the cause *1097*
28:28 Be it **k** therefore unto you, that *1110*
Ro 1:19 Because that which may be **k** of God is *1110*
3:17 And the way of peace have they not **k**: *1097*
7: 7 Nay, I had not **k** sin, but by the law: for I *1097*
7: 7 for I had not **k** lust, except the law had said, *1492*
9:22 shew *his* wrath, and to **make** his power **k**, *1107*
9:23 And that he might **make k** the riches of his *1107*
11:34 For who hath **k** the mind of the Lord? or *1097*
16:26 **made k** to all nations for the obedience of *1107*
1Co 2: 8 for had they **k** *it,* they would not have *1097*
2:16 For who hath **k** the mind of the Lord, *1097*
8: 3 if any *man* love God, the same is **k** of him. *1097*
13:12 but then shall I know even as also I am **k**. *1921*
14: 7 how shall it be **k** what is piped or harped? *1097*
14: 9 how shall it be **k** what is spoken? *1097*
2Co 3: 2 written in our hearts, **k** and read of all men: *1097*
5:16 though we have **k** Christ after the flesh, *1097*
6: 9 As unknown, and *yet* **well k**; as dying, and *1921*
Gal 4: 9 after that ye have **k** God, or rather are *1097*
4: 9 or rather are **k** of God, how turn ye again to *1097*
Eph 1: 9 Having **made k** unto us the mystery of his *1107*
3: 3 How that by revelation he **made k** unto me *1107*
3: 5 Which in other ages was not **made k** unto *1107*
3:10 powers in heavenly *places* might be **k** by *1107*
6:19 to **make k** the mystery of the gospel, *1107*
6:21 in the Lord, shall **make k** to you all *things:* *1107*
Php 4: 5 Let your moderation be **k** unto all men. *1097*
4: 6 let your requests be **made k** unto God. *1107*
Col 1:27 To whom God would **make k** what *is* *1107*
4: 9 They shall **make k** unto you all *things* *1107*
2Ti 3:10 But thou hast **fully k** my doctrine, manner *3877*
3:15 And that from a child thou hast **k** the holy *1492*
4:17 that by me the preaching might be **fully k**, *4135*
Heb 3:10 *their* heart; and they have not **k** my ways. *1097*
2Pe 1:16 when we **made k** unto you the power and *1107*
2:21 it had been better for them not to have **k** *1921*
2:21 after they have **k** *it,* to turn from the holy *1921*
1Jn 2:13 ye have **k** him that is from the beginning. *1097*
2:13 because ye have **k** the Father. *1097*
2:14 ye have **k** him that is from the beginning. *1097*
3: 6 sinneth hath not seen him, neither **k** him. *1097*
4:16 And we have **k** and believed the love that *1097*
2Jn 1: 1 but also all they that have **k** the truth; *1097*
Rev 2:24 and which have not **k** the depths of Satan, *1097*

KOA (1)

Eze 23:23 all the Chaldeans, Pekod, and Shoa, and **K**, 6970

KOHATH (32) [KOHATHITES]

Ge 46:11 the sons of Levi; Gershon, **K**, and Merari. 6955
Ex 6:16 Gershon, and **K**, and Merari: 6955
6:18 the sons of **K**; Amram, and Izhar, and 6955
6:18 the years of the life of **K** *were* an hundred 6955
Nu 3:17 their names; Gershon, and **K**, and Merari. 6955
3:19 the sons of **K** by their families; Amram, 6955
3:27 of **K** *was* the family of the Amramites, and 6955
3:29 The families of the sons of **K** shall pitch on 6955
4: 2 Take the sum of the sons of **K** from among 6955
4: 4 This *shall be* the service of the sons of **K** in 6955
4:15 the sons of **K** shall come to bear *it:* but 6955
4:15 of **K** in the tabernacle of the congregation. 6955
7: 9 unto the sons of **K** he gave none: because 6955
16: 1 the son of **K**, the son of Levi, and Dathan 6955
26:57 of **K**, the family of the Kohathites: 6955
26:58 of the Korahites. And **K** begat Amram. 6955
Jos 21: 5 the rest of the children of **K** had by lot out 6955
21:20 the families of the children of **K**, 6955
21:20 which remained of the children of **K**, 6955
21:26 families of the children of **K** that remained. 6955
1Ch 6: 1 The sons of Levi; Gershon, **K**, and Merari. 6955
6: 2 the sons of **K**; Amram, Izhar, and Hebron, 6955
6:16 The sons of Levi; Gershom, **K**, and Merari. 6955
6:18 And the sons of **K** *were,* Amram, and Izhar, 6955
6:22 The sons of **K**; Amminadab his son, 6955
6:38 the son of **K**, the son of Levi, the son of 6955
6:61 unto the sons of **K**, which were left of 6955
6:66 *the residue* of the families of the sons of **K** 6955
6:70 the family of the remnant of the sons of **K**. 6955
15: 5 Of the sons of **K**; Uriel the chief, and 6955
23: 6 of Levi, *namely,* Gershon, **K**, and Merari. 6955
23:12 The sons of **K**; Amram, Izhar, Hebron, and 6955

KOHATHITES (15) [KOHATH]

Nu 3:27 these *are* the families of the **K**. 6956
3:30 the **K** *shall be* Elizaphan the son of Uzziel. 6956
4:18 families of the **K** from among the Levites: 6956
4:34 the sons of the **K** after their families, 6956
4:37 were numbered of the families of the **K**, 6956
10:21 the **K** set forward, bearing the sanctuary: 6956
26:57 of Kohath, the family of the **K**: of Merari, 6956
Jos 21: 4 the lot came out for the families of the **K**: 6956
21:10 of Aaron, *being* of the families of the **K**, 6956
1Ch 6:33 Of the sons of the **K**: Heman a singer, 6956
6:54 the sons of Aaron, of the families of the **K**: 6956
9:32 of the sons of the **K**, *were* over 6956
2Ch 20:19 of the children of the **K**, and of the children 6956
29:12 the son of Azariah, of the sons of the **K**: 6956
34:12 and Meshullam, of the sons of the **K**, 6956

KOLAIAH (2)

Ne 11: 7 of Joed, the son of Pedaiah, the son of **K**, 6964
Jer 29:21 of Ahab the son of **K**, and of Zedekiah, 6964

KORAH (37) [KORAHITE, KORAHITES, KORHITES]

Ge 36: 5 bare Jeush, and Jaalam, and **K**: 7141

Ge 36:14 she bare to Esau Jeush, and Jaalam, and **K**. 7141
36:16 Duke **K**, duke Gatam, *and* duke Amalek: 7141
36:18 duke Jeush, duke Jaalam, duke **K**: 7141
Ex 6:21 sons of Izhar; **K**, and Nepheg, and Zichri. 7141
6:24 the sons of **K**; Assir, and Elkanah, and 7141
Nu 16: 1 Now **K**, the son of Izhar, the son of 7141
16: 5 he spake unto **K** and unto all his company, 7141
16: 6 Take you censers, **K**, and all his company; 7141
16: 8 Moses said unto **K**, Hear, I pray you, 7141
16:16 Moses said unto **K**, Be thou and all thy 7141
16:19 **K** gathered all the congregation against 7141
16:24 Get you up from about the tabernacle of **K**, 7141
16:27 So they gat up from the tabernacle of **K**, 7141
16:32 all the men that *appertained* unto **K**, and 7141
16:40 that he be not as **K**, and as his company: 7141
16:49 them that died about the matter of **K**. 7141
26: 9 and against Aaron in the company of **K**, 7141
26:10 swallowed them up together with **K**, 7141
26:11 Notwithstanding the children of **K** died not. 7141
27: 3 against the LORD in the company of **K**; 7141
1Ch 1:35 Reuel, and Jeush, and Jaalam, and **K**. 7141
2:43 **K**, and Tappuah, and Rekem, and Shema. 7141
6:22 his son, **K** his son, Assir his son, 7141
6:37 of Assir, the son of Ebiasaph, the son of **K**, 7141
9:19 of Ebiasaph, the son of **K**, and his brethren, 7141
Ps 42: T chief Musician, Maschil, for the sons of **K**. 7141
44: T To the chief Musician for the sons of **K**, 7141
45: T for the sons of **K**, Maschil, A Song of 7141
46: T To the chief Musician for the sons of **K**, 7141
47: T chief Musician, A Psalm for the sons of **K**. 7141
48: T A Song *and* Psalm for the sons of **K**. 7141
49: T chief Musician, A Psalm for the sons of **K**. 7141
84: T upon Gittith, A Psalm for the sons of **K**. 7141
85: T chief Musician, A Psalm for the sons of **K**. 7141
87: T A Psalm *or* Song for the sons of **K**. 7141
88: T A Song *or* Psalm for the sons of **K**. To 7141

KORAHITE (1) [KORAH]
1Ch 9:31 who *was* the firstborn of Shallum the **K**, 7145

KORAHITES (2) [KORAH]
Nu 26:58 family of the Mushites, the family of the **K**. 7145
1Ch 9:19 of the house of his father, the **K**, 7145

KORAZIN See CHORAZIN

KORE (4)
1Ch 9:19 Shallum the son of **K**, the son of Ebiasaph, 6981
26: 1 Korhites *was* Meshelemiah the son of **K**, 6981
26:19 of the porters among the sons of **K**, 7145
2Ch 31:14 **K** the son of Imnah the Levite, the porter 6981

KORHITES (4) [KORAH]
Ex 6:24 Abiasaph: these *are* the families of the **K**. 7145
1Ch 12: 6 Azareel, and Joezer, and Jashobeam, the **K**, 7145
26: 1 Of the **K** *was* Meshelemiah the son of 7145
2Ch 20:19 and of the children of the **K**, 7145

KOUM See CUMI

KOZ (4)
Ezr 2:61 the children of Habaiah, the children of **K**, 6976
Ne 3: 4 Meremoth the son of Urijah, the son of **K**. 6976
3:21 son of Urijah the son of **K** another piece, 6976
7:63 the children of Habaiah, the children of **K**, 6976

KUSHAIAH (1)
1Ch 15:17 Merari their brethren, Ethan the son of **K**; 6984

L

LAADAH (1)
1Ch 4:21 **L** the father of Mareshah, and the families 3935

LAADAN (7)
1Ch 7:26 **L** his son, Ammihud his son, Elishama his 3936
23: 7 Of the Gershonites *were*, **L**, and Shimei. 3936
23: 8 The sons of **L**; the chief *was* Jehiel, and 3936
23: 9 These *were* the chief of the fathers of **L**. 3936
26:21 *As concerning* the sons of **L**; the sons of 3936
26:21 the sons of the Gershonite **L**, chief fathers, 3936
26:21 *even* of **L** the Gershonite, *were* Jehieli. 3936

LABAN (51) [LABAN'S]
Ge 24:29 had a brother, and his name *was* **L**: 3837
24:29 and **L** ran out unto the man, unto the well. 3837
24:50 **L** and Bethuel answered and said, 3837
25:20 of Padan-aram, the sister to **L** the Syrian. 3837
27:43 arise, flee thou to **L** my brother to Haran; 3837
28: 2 of the daughters of **L** thy mother's brother. 3837
28: 5 he went to Padan-aram unto **L**, son of 3837
29: 5 unto them, Know ye **L** the son of Nahor? 3837
29:10 when Jacob saw Rachel the daughter of **L** 3837
29:10 the sheep of **L** his mother's brother, 3837
29:10 watered the flock of **L** his mother's brother. 3837
29:13 when **L** heard the tidings of Jacob his 3837
29:13 to his house. And he told **L** all these things. 3837
29:14 And **L** said to him, Surely thou *art* my bone 3837
29:15 **L** said unto Jacob, Because thou *art* my 3837
29:16 **L** had two daughters: the name of the elder 3837
29:19 **L** said, *It is* better that I give her to thee, 3837
29:21 Jacob said unto **L**, Give *me* my wife, 3837
29:22 **L** gathered together all the men of 3837
29:24 **L** gave unto his daughter Leah Zilpah his 3837
29:25 he said to **L**, What *is* this thou hast done 3837
29:26 **L** said, It must not be so done in our 3837
29:29 **L** gave to Rachel his daughter Bilhah his 3837
30:25 that Jacob said unto **L**, Send me away, 3837
30:27 **L** said unto him, I pray thee, if I have found 3837
30:34 **L** said, Behold, I would it might be 3837
30:40 and all the brown in the flock of **L**; 3837
31: 2 Jacob beheld the countenance of **L**, and 3837
31:12 for I have seen all that **L** doeth unto thee. 3837
31:19 **L** went to shear his sheep: and Rachel had 3837
31:20 Jacob stale away unawares to **L** the Syrian, 3837
31:22 it was told **L** on the third day that Jacob 3837
31:24 God came to **L** the Syrian in a dream by 3837
31:25 **L** overtook Jacob. Now Jacob had pitched 3837
31:25 **L** with his brethren pitched in the mount of 3837
31:26 **L** said to Jacob, What hast thou done, 3837
31:31 Jacob answered and said to **L**, Because I 3837
31:33 **L** went into Jacob's tent, and into Leah's 3837
31:34 **L** searched all the tent, but found *them* not. 3837
31:36 Jacob was wroth, and chode with **L**: and 3837
31:36 Jacob answered and said to **L**, What *is* my 3837
31:43 **L** answered and said unto Jacob, *These* 3837
31:47 **L** called it Jegar-sahadutha: but 3837
31:48 **L** said, This heap *is* a witness between me 3837
31:51 **L** said to Jacob, Behold this heap, 3837
31:55 early in the morning **L** rose up, and 3837
31:55 **L** departed, and returned unto his place. 3837
32: 4 I have sojourned with **L**, and stayed *there* 3837
46:18 whom **L** gave to Leah his daughter, and 3837
46:25 which **L** gave unto Rachel his daughter, 3837
Dt 1: 1 and **L**, and Hazeroth, and Dizahab. 3837

LABAN'S (4) [LABAN]
Ge 30:36 and Jacob fed the rest of **L** flocks. 3837
30:40 and put them not unto **L** cattle. 3837
30:42 so the feebler were **L**, and the stronger 3837
31: 1 he heard the words of **L** sons, saying, 3837

LABOR See TRAVAIL; TRAVAILED; TRAVAILEST; TRAVAILETH

LABORERS See HIRELING

LABOUR (89) [FELLOWLABOURER, FELLOWLABOURERS, LABOURED, LABOURER, LABOURERS, LABOURETH, LABOURING, LABOURS]
Ge 31:42 seen mine affliction and the **l** of my hands, 3018
35:16 and Rachel travailed, and she had hard **l**. 3205
35:17 it came to pass, when she was in hard **l**, 3205
Ex 5: 9 laid upon the men, that they may **l** therein; 6213
20: 9 Six days shalt thou **l**, and do all thy work: 5647
Dt 5:13 Six days thou shalt **l**, and do all thy work: 5647
26: 7 and our **l**, and our oppression: 5999
Jos 7: 3 *and* **make** not all the people **to l** thither; 3021
24:13 given you a land for which ye did not **l**, 3021
Ne 4:22 they may be a guard to us, and **l** on the day. 4399
5:13 from his **l**, that performeth not this promise, 3018
Job 9:29 *If* I be wicked, why then **l I** in vain? 3021
39:11 *is* great? or wilt thou leave thy **l** to him? 3018
39:16 *were* not hers: her **l** *is* in vain without fear; 3018

Ps 78:46 the caterpillar, and their l unto the locust. 3018
90:10 yet *is* their strength l and sorrow; 5999
104:23 unto his work and to his l until the evening. 5656
105:44 and they inherited the l of the people; 5999
107:12 he brought down their heart with l; 5999
109:11 he hath; and let the strangers spoil his l. 3018
127: 1 build the house, they l in vain that build it: 5998
128: 2 For thou shalt eat the l of thine hands: 3018
144:14 *That* our oxen *may be* **strong to l**; 5445
Pr 10:16 The l of the righteous *tendeth* to life: 6468
13:11 but he that gathereth by l shall increase. 3027
14:23 In all l there is profit: but the talk of the lips 6089
21:25 killeth him; for his hands refuse to l. 6213
23: 4 L not to be rich: cease from thine own 3021
Ecc 1: 3 What profit hath a man of all his l which he 5999
1: 8 All things *are* **full of l**; man cannot utter *it:* 3023
2:10 any joy; for my heart rejoiced in all my l: 5999
2:10 and this was my portion of all my l. 5999
2:11 and on the l that I had laboured to do: 5999
2:18 I hated all my l which I *had* taken under 5999
2:19 yet shall he have rule over all my l where*in* 5999
2:20 of all the l which I took under the sun. 5999
2:21 For there is a man whose l *is* in wisdom, 5999
2:22 For what hath man of all his l, and of 5999
2:24 he should make his soul enjoy good in his l. 5999
3:13 and drink, and enjoy the good of all his l, 5999
4: 8 yet *is there* no end of all his l; neither is his 5999
4: 8 neither *saith he,* For whom do I l, and 6001
4: 9 because they have a good reward for their l. 5999
5:15 shall take nothing of his l, which he may 5999
5:18 to enjoy the good of all his l that he taketh 5999
5:19 to take his portion, and to rejoice in his l; 5999
6: 7 All the l of man *is* for his mouth, and 5999
8:15 for that shall abide with him of his l 5999
8:17 because though a man l to seek *it* out, 5998
9: 9 in thy l which thou takest under the sun. 5999
10:15 The l of the foolish wearieth every one of 5999
Isa 22: 4 l not to comfort me, because of the spoiling 213
45:14 The l of Egypt, and merchandise of 3018
55: 2 your l for *that which* satisfieth not? hearken 3018
65:23 They shall not l in vain, nor bring forth for 3021
Jer 3:24 For shame hath devoured the l of our 3018
20:18 came I forth out of the womb to see l 5999
51:58 the people shall l in vain, and the folk in 3021
La 5: 5 under persecution: we l, *and* have no rest. 3021
Eze 23:29 shall take *away* all thy l, and shall leave 3018
29:20 I have given him the land of Egypt *for* his l 6468
Mic 4:10 Be in pain, and **l to bring forth**, 1518
Hab 2:13 hosts that the people shall l in the very fire, 3021
3:17 the l of the olive shall fail, and the fields 4639
Hag 1:11 upon cattle, and upon all the l of the hands. 3018
Mt 11:28 all *ye* that l and are heavy laden, and I will *2872*
Jn 4:38 you to reap *that* whereon ye **bestowed** no l: *2872*
6:27 L not for the meat which perisheth, but *2038*
Ro 16: 6 Greet Mary, who **bestowed** much l on us. *2872*
16:12 and Tryphosa, who l in the Lord. *2872*
1Co 3: 8 his own reward according to his own l. *2873*
4:12 And l, working with our own hands: *2872*
15:58 forasmuch as you know that your l is not in *2873*
2Co 5: 9 Wherefore we l, that, whether present or *5389*
Gal 4:11 lest I have **bestowed** upon you l in vain. *2872*
Eph 4:28 but rather let him l, working with *his* hands *2872*
Php 1:22 if *I* live in the flesh, this *is* the fruit of my l: *2041*
2:25 and **companion in l**, and fellowsoldier, but *4904*
Col 1:29 Whereunto I also l, striving according to *2872*
1Th 1: 3 and l of love, and patience of hope in our *2873*
2: 9 ye remember, brethren, our l and travail: *2873*
3: 5 have tempted you, and our l be in vain. *2873*
5:12 to know them which l among you, and *2872*
2Th 3: 8 but wrought with l and travail night and *2873*
1Ti 4:10 For therefore we both l and *2872*
5:17 especially they who l in the word and *2872*
Heb 4:11 Let us l therefore to enter into that rest, *4704*
6:10 to forget your work and l of love, *2873*
Rev 2: 2 and thy l, and thy patience, and how thou *2873*

LABOURED (19) [LABOUR]

Ne 4:21 So we l in the work: and half of them held 6213
Job 20:18 **That which** he l **for** shall he restore, and 3022
Ecc 2:11 and on the labour that I had l to do: 5998
2:19 rule over all my labour where*in* I have l, 5998
2:21 yet to a man that hath not l therein shall he 5998
2:22 his heart, wherein he *hath* l under the sun? 6001
5:16 what profit hath he that hath l for the wind? 5998
Isa 47:12 wherein thou hast l from thy youth; 3021
47:15 they be unto thee *with* whom thou hast l, 3021
49: 4 I said, I have l in vain, I have spent my 3021
62: 8 drink thy wine, for the which thou hast l: 3021
Da 6:14 he l till the going down of the sun to deliver 7712
Jnh 4:10 for the which thou hast not l, neither 5998
Jn 4:38 other *men* l, and ye are entered into their *2872*
Ro 16:12 beloved Persis, which l much in the Lord. *2872*
1Co 15:10 but I l more abundantly than they all: *2872*
Php 2:16 that I have not run in vain, neither l in vain. *2872*
4: 3 help those *women* which **l with** me in *4866*
Rev 2: 3 and for my name's sake hast l, and hast not *2872*

LABOURER (2) [LABOUR]

Lk 10: 7 for the l is worthy of his hire. Go not from *2040*
1Ti 5:18 And, The l *is* worthy of his reward. *2040*

LABOURERS (9) [LABOUR]

Mt 9:37 harvest truly is plenteous, but the l *are* few; *2040*
9:38 that he will send forth l into his harvest. *2040*
20: 1 in the morning to hire l into his vineyard. *2040*
20: 2 And when he had agreed with the l for a *2040*
20: 8 Call the l, and give them *their* hire, *2040*
Lk 10: 2 The harvest truly *is* great, but the l *are* few: *2040*
10: 2 that he would send forth l into his harvest. *2040*
1Co 3: 9 For we are l **together with** God: ye are *4904*
Jas 5: 4 the hire of the l which have reaped *down* *2040*

LABOURETH (5) [LABOUR]

Pr 16:26 He that l laboureth for himself; for his 6001
16:26 He that laboureth l for himself; for his 5998
Ecc 3: 9 *hath* he that worketh in *that* where*in* he l? 6001
1Co 16:16 and to every one that helpeth with *us,* and l. *2872*
2Ti 2: 6 The husbandman that l must be first *2872*

LABOURING (4) [LABOUR]

Ecc 5:12 The sleep of a l *man is* sweet, whether he 5647
Ac 20:35 how that so l *ye* ought to support the weak, *2872*
Col 4:12 always l **fervently** for you in prayers, *75*
1Th 2: 9 for l night and day, because *we* would not *2038*

LABOURS (13) [LABOUR]

Ex 23:16 the feast of harvest, the firstfruits of thy l, 4639
23:16 when thou hast gathered in thy l out of 4639
Dt 28:33 The fruit of thy land, and all thy l, shall a 3018
Pr 5:10 and thy l *be* in the house of a stranger; 6089
Isa 58: 3 fast you find pleasure, and exact all your l. 6092
Jer 20: 5 all the l thereof, and all the precious things 3018
Hos 12: 8 *in* all my l they shall find none iniquity in 3018
Hag 2:17 and with hail *in* all the l of your hands; 4639
Jn 4:38 and ye are entered into their l. *2873*
2Co 6: 5 in tumults, in l, in watchings, in fastings; *2873*
10:15 *our* measure, *that is,* of other *men's* l; *2873*
11:23 in l more abundant, in stripes above *2873*
Rev 14:13 the Spirit, that they may rest from their l; *2873*

LACE (4)

Ex 28:28 unto the rings of the ephod with a l of blue, 6616
28:37 thou shalt put it on a blue l, that it may be 6616
39:21 unto the rings of the ephod with a l of blue, 6616
39:31 they tied unto it a l of blue, to fasten *it* on 6616

LACHISH (24)

Jos 10: 3 unto Japhia king of **L**, and unto Debir king 3923
10: 5 the king of **L**, the king of Eglon, 3923
10:23 the king of **L**, *and* the king of Eglon. 3923
10:31 unto **L**, and encamped against it, and 3923
10:32 the LORD delivered **L** into the hand of 3923
10:33 Horam king of Gezer came up to help **L**; 3923
10:34 from **L** Joshua passed unto Eglon, and 3923
10:35 according to all that he had done to **L**. 3923
12:11 king of Jarmuth, one; the king of **L**, one; 3923
15:39 **L**, and Bozkath, and Eglon, 3923
2Ki 14:19 he fled to **L**; but they sent after him to 3923
14:19 they sent after him to **L**, and slew him 3923
18:14 of Judah sent to the king of Assyria to **L**, 3923
18:17 Rab-shakeh from **L** to king Hezekiah with 3923
19: 8 he had heard that he was departed from **L**. 3923
2Ch 11: 9 And Adoraim, and **L**, and Azekah, 3923
25:27 against him in Jerusalem; and he fled to **L**: 3923
25:27 they sent to **L** after him, and slew him 3923
32: 9 (but he *himself laid siege* against **L**, and 3923
Ne 11:30 *at* **L**, and the fields thereof, *at* Azekah, and 3923
Isa 36: 2 the king of Assyria sent Rabshakeh from **L** 3923
37: 8 he had heard that he was departed from **L**. 3923

Jer 34: 7 were left, against **L**, and against Azekah: 3923
Mic 1:13 O thou inhabitant of **L**, bind the chariot to 3923

LACK (15) [LACKED, LACKEST, LACKETH, LACKING]
Ge 18:28 Peradventure there shall **l** five of the fifty 2637
18:28 wilt thou destroy all the city for *l of* five? NIH
Ex 16:18 and he that gathered little **had** no **l**; 2637
Dt 8: 9 thou shalt not **l** any *thing* in it; 2637
Job 4:11 The old lion perisheth for **l** of prey, and 1097
38:41 cry unto God, they wander for **l** of meat. 1097
Ps 34:10 The young lions do **l**, and suffer hunger: 7326
Pr 28:27 He that giveth unto the poor *shall* not **l**: but 4270
Ecc 9: 8 and let thy head **l** no ointment. 2637
Hos 4: 6 My people are destroyed for **l** of 1097
Mt 19:20 have I kept from my youth up: what **l** I yet? *5302*
2Co 8:15 and he that *had gathered* little **had** no **l**. *1641*
Php 2:30 to supply your **l** of service toward me. 5303
1Th 4:12 and *that* ye may have **l** of nothing. 5532
Jas 1: 5 If any of you **l** wisdom, let him ask of God, *3007*

LACKED (11) [LACK]
Dt 2: 7 *hath been* with thee; thou hast **l** nothing. 2637
2Sa 2:30 there **l** of David's servants nineteen men 6485
17:22 by the morning light there **l** not one *of them* 5737
1Ki 4:27 every man *in* his month: they **l** nothing. 5737
11:22 But what *hast* thou **l** with me, that behold, 2638
Ne 9:21 in the wilderness, *so that* they **l** nothing; 2637
Lk 8: 6 withered away, because *it* **l** moisture. *2192+3361*
22:35 and shoes, **l** ye any *thing?* And they said, *5302*
Ac 4:34 Neither was there any among them that **l**: *1729*
1Co 12:24 more abundant honour to that *part* which **l**: *5302*
Php 4:10 ye were also careful, but ye **l** **opportunity**. *170*

LACKEST (2) [LACK]
Mk 10:21 and said unto him, One *thing* thou **l**: *5302*
Lk 18:22 Yet **l** thou one *thing*: sell all that thou hast, *3007*

LACKETH (5) [LACK]
Nu 31:49 our charge, and there **l** not one man of us. 6485
2Sa 3:29 or that falleth on the sword, or that **l** bread. 2638
Pr 6:32 adultery with a woman **l** understanding: 2638
12: 9 than he that honoureth himself, and **l** bread. 2638
2Pe 1: 9 But he that **l** these *things* is blind, *3361+3918*

LACKING (8) [LACK]
Lev 2:13 **suffer** the salt of the covenant of thy God **to be l** 7673
22:23 hath any thing superfluous or **l in** his **parts**, 7038
Jdg 21: 3 that there should be to day one tribe **l** in 6485
1Sa 30:19 there was nothing **l** to them, neither small 5737
Jer 23: 4 nor be dismayed, neither shall they be **l**, 6485
1Co 16:17 for that which was **l** on your part they have *5303*
2Co 11: 9 **l** to me the brethren which came from *5303*
1Th 3:10 might perfect that which is **l** in your faith? *5303*

LAD (33) [LAD'S, LADS]
Ge 21:12 be grievous in thy sight because of the **l**, 5288
21:17 God heard the voice of the **l**; and the angel 5288
21:17 for God hath heard the voice of the **l** where 5288
21:18 lift up the **l**, and hold him in thine hand; 5288
21:19 the bottle *with* water, and gave the **l** drink. 5288
21:20 God was with the **l**; and he grew, and 5288
22: 5 I and the **l** will go yonder and worship, and 5288
22:12 he said, Lay not thine hand upon the **l**, 5288
37: 2 the **l** *was* with the sons of Bilhah, and 5288
43: 8 Send the **l** with me, and we will arise and 5288
44:22 unto my lord, The **l** cannot leave his father: 5288
44:30 servant my father, and the **l** *be* not with us; 5288
44:31 when he seeth that the **l** *is* not *with us,* that 5288
44:32 For thy servant became surety for the **l** unto 5288
44:33 let thy servant abide instead of the **l** a 5288
44:33 and let the **l** go up with his brethren. 5288
44:34 up to my father, and the **l** *be* not with me? 5288
Jdg 16:26 Samson said unto the **l** that held him by 5288
1Sa 20:21 behold, I will send a **l**, *saying,* Go, find out 5288
20:21 If I expressly say unto the **l**, Behold, 5288
20:35 with David, and a little **l** with him. 5288
20:36 he said unto his **l**, Run, find out now 5288
20:36 *And* as the **l** ran, he shot an arrow beyond 5288
20:37 when the **l** was come to the place of 5288
20:37 Jonathan cried after the **l**, and said, *Is* not 5288
20:38 Jonathan cried after the **l**, Make speed, 5288
20:38 Jonathan's **l** gathered up the arrows, and 5288
20:39 But the **l** knew not any thing: only Jonathan 5288
20:40 Jonathan gave his artillery unto his **l**, and 5288
20:41 *And* as soon as the **l** was gone, David arose 5288
2Sa 17:18 Nevertheless a **l** saw them, and 5288
2Ki 4:19 And he said to a **l**, Carry him to his mother. 5288
Jn 6: 9 There is a **l** here, which hath five barley *3808*

LAD'S (1) [LAD]
Ge 44:30 seeing that his life *is* bound up in *the l* life; NIH

LADAN See LAADAN

LADDER (1)
Ge 28:12 behold a **l** set up on the earth, and the top of 5551

LADE (3) [LADED, LADEN, LADETH, LADING, UNLADE]
Ge 45:17 **l** your beasts, and go, get you unto the land 2943
1Ki 12:11 now whereas my father did **l** you with a 6006
Lk 11:46 for ye **l** men *with* burdens grievous to be *5412*

LADED (4) [LADE]
Ge 42:26 they **l** their asses with the corn, and 5375
44:13 **l** every man his ass, and returned to 6006
Ne 4:17 they that bare burdens, *with* those that **l**, 6006
Ac 28:10 they **l** *us* **with** such *things* as were *2007*

LADEN (6) [LADE]
Ge 45:23 ten asses **l** with the good things of Egypt, 5375
45:23 ten she asses **l** with corn and bread and 5375
1Sa 16:20 Jesse took an ass *l* with bread, and a bottle NIH
Isa 1: 4 Ah sinful nation, a people **l** with iniquity, 3515
Mt 11:28 all *ye* that labour and are **heavy l**, and I will *5412*
2Ti 3: 6 and lead captive silly women **l** with sins, *4987*

LADETH (1) [LADE]
Hab 2: 6 and to him that **l** himself **with** thick clay! 3513

LADIES (2) [LADY]
Jdg 5:29 Her wise **l** answered *her,* yea, she returned 8282
Est 1:18 Likewise shall the **l** of Persia and 8282

LADING (2) [LADE]
Ne 13:15 and bringing in sheaves, and **l** asses; 5921+6006
Ac 27:10 not only of the **l** and ship, but also of our *5414*

LADS (1) [LAD]
Ge 48:16 redeemed me from all evil, bless the **l**; 5288

LADY (4) [LADIES]
Isa 47: 5 shalt no more be called, The **l** of kingdoms. 1404
47: 7 thou saidst, I shall be a **l** for ever: *so* 1404
2Jn 1: 1 The elder unto the elect **l** and her children, *2959*
1: 5 And now I beseech thee, **l**, not as though I *2959*

LAEL (1)
Nu 3:24 Gershonites *shall be* Eliasaph the son of **L**. 3815

LAHAD (1)
1Ch 4: 2 and Jahath begat Ahumai, and **L**. 3855

LAHAI-ROI (2) [BEER-LAHAI-ROI]
Ge 24:62 And Isaac came from the way of the **well L**; 883
25:11 his son Isaac; and Isaac dwelt by the **well L**. 883

LAHMAM (1)
Jos 15:40 And Cabbon, and **L**, and Kithlish, 3903

LAHMAS See LAHMAM

LAHMI (1)
1Ch 20: 5 Elhanan the son of Jair slew **L** the brother 3902

LAID (279) [LAY]
Ge 9:23 **l** *it* upon both their shoulders, and 7760
15:10 and **l** each piece one against another: 5414
19:16 the men **l hold** upon his hand, and upon 2388
22: 6 burnt offering, and **l** *it* upon Isaac his son; 7760
22: 9 **l** the wood **in order**, and bound Isaac his 6186
22: 9 and **l** him on the altar upon the wood. 7760
30:41 that Jacob **l** the rods before the eyes of 7760
38:19 **l by** her vail from her, and put on 5493
39:16 she **l up** his garment by her, until his lord 3240
41:48 of Egypt, and **l up** the food in the cities: 5414
41:48 round about every city, **l** he **up** in the same. 5414
48:14 **l** *it* upon Ephraim's head, who *was* 7896
48:17 when Joseph saw that his father **l** his right 7896
Ex 2: 3 she **l** *it* in the flags by the river's brink. 7760
5: 9 Let there **more** work be **l** upon the men, 3513
16:24 they **l** it **up** till the morning, as Moses bade: 4340

Ex	16:34	so Aaron l it **up** before the Testimony,	3240
	19: 7	l before their faces all these words which	7760
	21:30	If there be l on him a sum of money, then	7896
	21:30	ransom of his life whatsoever is l upon him.	7896
	24:11	of the children of Israel he l not his hand:	7971
Lev	8:14	his sons l their hands upon the head of	5564
	8:18	his sons l their hands upon the head of	5564
	8:22	his sons l their hands upon the head of	5564
Nu	16:18	l incense thereon, and stood *in* the door of	7760
	17: 7	Moses l **up** the rods before the LORD in	4340
	21:30	we have l *them* **waste** even unto Nophah,	8074
	27:23	he l his hands upon him, and gave him a	5564
Dt	26: 6	afflicted us, and l upon us hard bondage:	5414
	29:22	the sicknesses which the LORD hath l	2470
	32:34	*Is* not this l **up in store** with me, *and*	3647
	34: 9	for Moses had l his hands upon him:	5564
Jos	2: 6	which she had l **in order** upon the roof.	6186
	2: 8	before they were l **down**, she came up unto	7901
	4: 8	where they lodged, and l them **down** there.	3240
	7:23	and l them **out** before the LORD.	3332
	10:27	l great stones in the cave's mouth,	7760
Jdg	9:24	their blood be l upon Abimelech their	7760
	9:34	they l **wait** against Shechem *in* four	693
	9:43	l **wait** in the field, and looked, and behold,	693
	9:48	l *it* on his shoulder, and said unto	7760
	16: 2	l **wait** for him all night in the gate of	693
	19:29	l **hold** on his concubine, and divided her,	2388
Ru	3: 7	and uncovered his feet, and l her **down**.	7901
	3:15	six *measures* of barley, and l *it* on her:	7896
	4:16	l it in her bosom, and became nurse unto it.	7896
1Sa	3: 2	when Eli *was* l **down** in his place, and	7901
	3: 3	God *was*, and Samuel was l **down** *to sleep;*	7901
	6:11	they l the ark of the LORD upon the cart,	7760
	10:25	*it* in a book, and l *it* **up** before the LORD.	3240
	15: 2	how he l *wait* for him in the way, when he	7760
	15: 5	a city of Amalek, and l **wait** in the valley.	7378
	15:27	he l **hold** upon the skirt of his mantle, and	2388
	19:13	l *it* in the bed, and put a pillow of goats'	7760
	21:12	David l **up** these words in his heart, and	7760
	25:18	hundred cakes *of figs*, and l *them* on asses.	7760
2Sa	13: 8	Amnon's house; and he was l **down**.	7901
	13:19	l her hand on her head, and went on crying.	7760
	18:17	and l a very great heap of stones upon him:	5324
1Ki	3:20	l it in her bosom, and laid her dead child in	7901
	3:20	and l her dead child in my bosom.	7901
	6:37	**foundation** of the house of the LORD **l**,	3245
	8:31	an oath be l upon him to cause him to	5375
	13:29	and l it upon the ass, and brought it back:	3240
	13:30	he l his carcase in his own grave; and	3240
	15:27	and all Israel l **siege** to Gibbethon.	6696
	16:34	he l the **foundation** thereof in Abiram his	3245
	17:19	he abode, and l him upon his own bed.	7901
	18:33	in pieces, and l *him* on the wood, and said,	7760
	19: 6	he did eat and drink, and l him **down** again.	7901
	21: 4	he l him **down** upon his bed, and	7901
2Ki	4:21	l him on the bed of the man of God, and	7901
	4:31	and l the staff upon the face of the child;	7760
	4:32	the child was dead, *and* l upon his bed.	7901
	5:23	and l *them* upon two of his servants;	5414
	9:25	the LORD l this burden upon him;	5375
	11:16	they l hands on her; and she went *by*	7760
	12:11	they l it **out** to the carpenters and builders,	3318
	12:12	for all that was l **out** for the house to repair	3318
	20: 7	they took and l *it* on the boil, and	7760
	20:17	*that* which thy fathers have l **up in store**	686
2Ch	6:22	an oath be l upon him to make him swear,	5375
	7:22	l **hold** on other gods, and worshipped them,	2388
	16:14	l him in the bed which was filled *with*	7901
	23:15	So they l hands on her; and when she was	7760
	24: 9	of God l **upon** Israel in the wilderness.	5921
	24:27	and the greatness of the burdens *l* upon him,	NIH
	29:23	and l their hands upon them:	5564
	31: 6	the LORD their God, and l *them* by heaps.	5414
	32: 9	(but he *himself l siege* against Lachish, and	NIH
Ezr	3: 6	**foundation** of the temple of the LORD was	
		not *yet* **l**.	3245
	3:10	when the builders l the **foundation** of	3245
	3:11	**foundation** of the house of the LORD was **l**.	3245
	3:12	when the **foundation** of this house was l	3245
	5: 8	timber *is* l in the walls, and this work goeth	7761
	5:16	l the foundation of the house of God which	3052
	6: 1	where the treasures were l **up** in Babylon.	5182
	6: 3	*let* the foundations thereof *be* **strongly** l;	5446
Ne	3: 3	who *also* l the **beams** thereof, and set up	7136
	3: 6	they l the **beams** thereof, and set up	7136
	13: 5	where aforetime they l the meat offerings,	5414
Est	8: 7	because he l his hand upon the Jews.	7971
	9:10	but on the spoil l they not their hand.	7971
	9:15	but on the prey they l not their hand.	7971
	9:16	but they l not their hands on the prey,	7971
	10: 1	the king Ahasuerus l a tribute upon	7760
Job	6: 2	my calamity l in the balances together!	5375
	18:10	The snare *is* l for him in the ground, and	2934
	29: 9	and l *their* hand on their mouth.	7760
	31: 9	or *if* I have l **wait** at my neighbour's door;	693
	38: 4	Where wast thou when I l the **foundations**	3245
	38: 5	Who hath l the measures thereof, if thou	7760
	38: 6	or who l the corner stone thereof;	3384
Ps	3: 5	I l me **down** and slept; I awaked; for	7901
	21: 5	honour and majesty hast thou l upon him.	7737
	31: 4	of the net that they have l **privily** for me:	2934
	31:19	which thou hast l **up** for them that fear	6845
	35:11	they l **to** my **charge** *things* that I knew not.	7592
	49:14	Like sheep they are l in the grave;	8371
	62: 9	to be l in the balance, they *are* altogether	5927
	79: 1	they have l Jerusalem on heaps.	7760
	79: 7	and l **waste** his dwelling place.	8074
	88: 6	Thou hast l me in the lowest pit,	7896
	89:19	I have l help upon *one that is* mighty;	7737
	102:25	Of old hast thou l the **foundation** of	3245
	104: 5	*Who* l the foundations of the earth, *that* it	3245
	105:18	feet they hurt with fetters: he was l *in* iron:	935
	119:30	of truth: thy judgments have I l *before me.*	7737
	119:110	The wicked have l a snare for me: yet I	5414
	139: 5	and before, and l thine hand upon me.	7896
	141: 9	Keep me from the snare *which* they have l	3369
	142: 3	I walked have they **privily** l a snare for me.	2934
Pr	13:22	the wealth of the sinner *is* l **up** for the just.	6845
SS	7:13	and old, *which* I have l **up** for thee,	6845
Isa	6: 7	he l *it* upon my mouth, and said, Lo,	5060
	10:28	at Michmash he hath l **up** his carriages:	6485
	14: 8	of Lebanon, *saying*, Since thou art l **down**,	7901
	15: 1	Because in the night Ar of Moab is l **waste**,	7703
	15: 1	because in the night Kir of Moab is l **waste**,	7703
	15: 7	have gotten, and **that** which they have l **up**,	6486
	23: 1	for it is l **waste**, so that *there is* no house,	7703
	23:14	of Tarshish: for your strength is l **waste**.	7703
	23:18	it shall not be treasured nor l **up**; for her	2630
	37:18	the kings of Assyria have l **waste** all	2717
	39: 6	*that* which thy fathers have l **up in store**	686
	42:25	and it burned him, yet he l *it* not to heart.	7760
	44:28	*to* the temple, Thy **foundation** shall be l.	3245
	47: 6	upon the ancient hast thou very **heavily** l	3513
	48:13	Mine hand also hath l the **foundation** of	3245
	51:13	and l the **foundations** of the earth;	3245
	51:23	thou hast l thy body as the ground, and	7760
	53: 6	the LORD hath l on him the iniquity of us	6293
	57:11	not remembered me, nor l *it* to thy heart?	7760
	64:11	and all our pleasant things are l **waste**.	2723
Jer	4: 7	*and* thy cities shall be l **waste**, without an	5327
	27:17	live: wherefore should this city be l **waste**?	2723
	36:20	they l **up** the roll in the chamber of	6485
	50:24	I have l **a snare** for thee, and thou art also	3369
La	4:19	they l **wait** for us in the wilderness.	693
Eze	4: 5	For I have l upon thee the years of their	5414
	6: 6	dwelling places the cities shall be l **waste**,	2717
	6: 6	that your altars may be l **waste** and	2717
	11: 7	Your slain whom ye have l in the midst of	7760
	12:20	the cities that are inhabited shall be l **waste**,	2717
	19: 7	desolate palaces, and he l **waste** their cities;	2717
	26: 2	I shall be replenished, *now* she is l **waste**:	2717
	29:12	her cities among the cities *that are* l **waste**	2717
	32:19	and be thou l with the uncircumcised.	7901
	32:27	they have l their swords under their heads,	5414
	32:29	which with their might are l by *them that*	5414
	32:32	he shall be l in the midst of	7901
	33:29	when I have l the land most desolate	5414
	35:12	saying, They are l **desolate**, they are given	8074
	39:21	and my hand that I have l upon them.	7760
	40:42	whereupon also they l the instruments	3240
Da	6:17	and l upon the mouth of the den;	7761
Hos	11: 4	yoke on their jaws, and I l meat unto them.	5186
Joel	1: 7	He hath l my vine waste, and barked my fig	7760
	1:17	the garners are l **desolate**, the barns are	8074
Am	2: 8	upon clothes l **to pledge** by every altar,	2254
	7: 9	the sanctuaries of Israel shall be l **waste**;	2717
Ob	1: 7	*they that eat* thy bread have l a wound	7760
	1:13	nor have l *hands* on their substance in	7971

Jnh 3: 6 he l his robe from him, and covered *him* 5674
Mic 5: 1 he hath l siege against us: they shall smite 7760
Na 3: 7 flee from thee, and say, Nineveh is l **waste**: 7703
Hab 2:19 it *is* l **over** *with* gold and silver, and *there is* 8610
Hag 2:15 from before a stone was l upon a stone in 7760
2:18 **foundation** of the LORD'S temple was l, 3245
Zec 3: 9 For behold the stone that I have l before 5414
4: 9 have l the **foundation** of this house; 3245
7:14 for they l the pleasant land desolate. 7760
8: 9 **foundation** of the house of the LORD of hosts was l, 3245
Mal 1: 3 l his mountains and his heritage waste for 7760
Mt 3:10 And now also the axe is l unto the root of *2749*
8:14 he saw his wife's mother l, and sick of a *906*
14: 3 For Herod had l **hold on** John, and *2902*
18:28 and he l **hands on** him, and took *him* by *2902*
19:15 And he l *his* hands **on** them, and *2007*
26:50 and l hands on Jesus, and took him. *1911*
26:55 in the temple, and ye l no **hold** on me. *2902*
26:57 And they that had l **hold** on Jesus led *him* *2902*
27:60 And l it in his own new tomb, which he had *5087*
Mk 6: 5 save that he l *his* hands **upon** a few sick *2007*
6:17 had sent forth and l **hold upon** John, *2902*
6:29 and took up his corpse, and l it in a tomb. *5087*
6:56 they l the sick in the streets, and *5087*
7:30 gone out, and *her* daughter l upon the bed. *906*
14:46 And they l their hands on him, and *1911*
14:51 and the young men l **hold on** him: *2902*
15:46 l him in a sepulchre which was hewn out of *2698*
15:47 *the mother* of Joses beheld where he was l. *5087*
16: 6 not here: behold the place where they l him. *5087*
Lk 1:66 And all they that heard *them* l *them* **up** in *5087*
2: 7 in swaddling clothes, and l him in a manger; *347*
3: 9 And now also the axe is l unto the root of *2749*
4:40 and he l *his* hands **on** every one of them, *2007*
6:48 and l the foundation on a rock: *5087*
12:19 thou hast much goods l **up** for many years; *2749*
13:13 And he l *his* hands **on** her: and *2007*
14:29 after he hath l the foundation, and is not *5087*
16:20 which was l at his gate, full of sores, *906*
19:20 which I have kept l **up** in a napkin: *606*
19:22 taking up that I l not **down**, and *5087*
23:26 they l **hold upon** one Simon, a Cyrenian, *1949*
23:26 of the country, and **on** him they l the cross, *2007*
23:53 l it in a sepulchre *that was* hewn in stone, *5087*
23:53 in stone, wherein never man before was l. *2749*
23:55 the sepulchre, and how his body was l. *5087*
24:12 he beheld the linen clothes l by themselves, *2749*
Jn 7:30 but no *man* l hands on him, because *1911*
7:44 have taken him; but no *man* l hands on him. *1911*
8:20 and no *man* l **hands on** him; for his hour *4084*
11:34 And said, Where have ye l him? They say *5087*
11:41 stone *from the place* where the dead was l. *2749*
13: 4 from supper, and l **aside** *his* garments; *5087*
19:41 wherein was never man yet l. *5087*
19:42 There l they Jesus therefore because of *5087*
20: 2 and we know not where they have l him. *5087*
20:13 and I know not where they have l him. *5087*
20:15 him *hence,* tell me where thou hast l him, *5087*
21: 9 coals there, and fish l **thereon**, and bread. *1945*
Ac 3: 2 whom they l daily at the gate of the temple *5087*
4: 3 And they l hands **on** them, and put *them* in *1911*
4:35 And l *them down* at the apostles' feet: and *5087*
4:37 the money, and l *it* at the apostles' feet. *5087*
5: 2 a certain part, and l *it* at the apostles' feet. *5087*
5:15 the streets, and l *them* on beds and couches, *5087*
5:18 And l their hands on the apostles, and *1911*
6: 6 had prayed, they l *their* hands **on** them. *2007*
7:16 l in the sepulchre that Abraham bought for *5087*
7:58 the witnesses l **down** their clothes at a young *659*
8:17 Then l they *their* hands **on** them, and *2007*
9:37 they l *her* in an upper chamber. *5087*
13: 3 and prayed, and l *their* hands **on** them, *2007*
13:29 from the tree, and l *him* in a sepulchre. *5087*
13:36 and was l unto his fathers, and *4369*
16:23 And when they had l many stripes upon *2007*
19: 6 And when Paul had l *his* hands **upon** them, *2007*
20: 3 and when the Jews l **wait for** him, *1096+1917*
21:27 up all the people, and l hands on him, *1911*
23:29 to have nothing l **to** his **charge** worthy of *1462*
23:30 me how that the Jews l **wait** for the man, *1917*
25: 7 and l many and grievous complaints against *5342*
25:16 concerning the **crime** l *against him.* *1462*
25:27 not withal to signify the crimes *l* against NIG
28: 3 and l *them* on the fire, there came a viper *2007*
28: 8 and l *his* hands **on** him, and healed him. *2007*
Ro 16: 4 Who have for my life l **down** their own *5294*
1Co 3:10 I have l the foundation, and *5087*
3:11 foundation can no *man* lay than that is l, *2749*
9:16 for necessity is l **upon** me; yea, woe is unto *1945*
Col 1: 5 For the hope which is l **up** for you in heaven, *606*
2Ti 4: 8 Henceforth there is l **up** for me a crown of *606*
4:16 *God* that it may not be l **to** their **charge**. *3049*
Heb 1:10 in the beginning hast l **the foundation** of *2311*
1Jn 3:16 *of God,* because he l **down** his life for us: *5087*
Rev 1:17 And he l his right hand upon me, *2007*
20: 2 And he l **hold on** the dragon, *that* old *2902*

LAIDST (1) [LAY]
Ps 66:11 into the net; thou l affliction upon our loins. 7760

LAIN (3) [LIE]
Nu 5:19 If no man have l with thee, and if thou hast 7901
5:20 *some* man hath l with thee beside thine 7903
Jn 20:12 at the feet, where the body of Jesus had l. *2749*

LAISH (7)
Jdg 18: 7 came to **L**, and saw the people that *were* 3919
18:14 men that went to spy out the country of **L**, 3919
18:27 the priest which he had, and came unto **L**, 3919
18:29 howbeit the name of the city *was* **L** at 3919
1Sa 25:44 David's wife, to Phalti the son of **L**, 3919
2Sa 3:15 *even* from Phaltiel the son of **L**. 3919
Isa 10:30 cause *it* to be heard unto **L**, O poor 3919

LAKE (10)
Lk 5: 1 of God, he stood by the l of Gennesaret, *3041*
5: 2 And saw two ships standing by the l: but *3041*
8:22 Let us go over unto the other side of the l. *3041*
8:23 there came down a storm of wind on the l; *3041*
8:33 ran violently down a steep place into the l, *3041*
Rev 19:20 *These* both were cast alive into a l of fire *3041*
20:10 deceived them was cast into the l of fire *3041*
20:14 and hell were cast into the l of fire. *3041*
20:15 in the book of life was cast into the l of fire. *3041*
21: 8 shall have their part in the l which burneth *3041*

LAKKUM See LAKUM

LAKUM (1)
Jos 19:33 and Adami, Nekeb, and Jabneel, unto **L**; 3946

LAMA (2)
Mt 27:46 saying, ELI, ELI, **L** SABACHTHANI? *2982*
Mk 15:34 saying, ELOI, ELOI, **L** SABACHTHANI? *2982*

LAMB (105) [LAMB'S, LAMBS]
Ge 22: 7 but where *is* the l for a burnt offering? 7716
22: 8 God will provide himself a l for a burnt 7716
Ex 12: 3 they shall take to them every man a l, 7716
12: 3 to the house of *their* fathers, a l for a house: 7716
12: 4 if the household be too little for the l, 7716
12: 4 his eating shall make your count for the l. 7716
12: 5 Your l shall be without blemish, a male of 7716
12:21 and take you a l according to your families, 6629
13:13 of an ass thou shalt redeem with a l; 7716
29:39 The one l thou shalt offer in the morning; 3532
29:39 and the other l thou shalt offer at even: 3532
29:40 with the one l a tenth deal of flour mingled 3532
29:41 the other l thou shalt offer at even, *and* 3532
34:20 of an ass thou shalt redeem with a l: 7716
Lev 3: 7 If he offer a l for his offering, then shall he 3775
4:32 if he bring a l for a sin offering, he shall 3532
4:35 as the fat of the l is taken away from 3775
5: 6 a l or a kid of the goats, for a sin offering; 3776
5: 7 if he be not able to bring a l, then he shall 7716
9: 3 a calf and a l, both of the first year, 3532
12: 6 she shall bring a l of the first year for a 3532
12: 8 if she be not able to bring a l, then she shall 7716
14:10 one **ewe** l of the first year without blemish, 3535
14:12 the priest shall take one **he** l, and offer him 3532
14:13 he shall slay the l in the place where he 3532
14:21 he shall take one l *for* a trespass offering to 3532
14:24 the priest shall take the l of the trespass 3532
14:25 he shall kill the l of the trespass offering, 3532
17: 3 or l, or goat, in the camp, or that killeth *it* 3775
22:23 or a l that hath any thing superfluous or 7716
23:12 **he** l without blemish of the first year for a 3532
Nu 6:12 shall bring a l of the first year for a trespass 3532

L

Nu 6:14 one **he l** of the first year without blemish 3532
6:14 one **ewe l** of the first year without blemish 3535
7:15 one ram, one l of the first year, 3532
7:21 one ram, one l of the first year, 3532
7:27 one ram, one l of the first year, 3532
7:33 one ram, one l of the first year, 3532
7:39 one ram, one l of the first year, 3532
7:45 one ram, one l of the first year, 3532
7:51 one ram, one l of the first year, 3532
7:57 one ram, one l of the first year, 3532
7:63 one ram, one l of the first year, 3532
7:69 one ram, one l of the first year, 3532
7:75 one ram, one l of the first year, 3532
7:81 one ram, one l of the first year, 3532
15: 5 the burnt offering or sacrifice, for one l. 3532
15:11 or for one ram, or for a l, or a kid. 3532+7716
28: 4 The one l shalt thou offer in the morning, 3532
28: 4 and the other l shalt thou offer at even; 3532
28: 7 *be* the fourth *part* of a hin for the one l: 3532
28: 8 the other l shalt thou offer at even: as 3532
28:13 with oil *for* a meat offering unto one l; 3532
28:14 a ram, and a fourth *part* of a hin unto a l: 3532
28:21 tenth deal shalt thou offer for every l, 3532
28:29 A several tenth deal unto one l, throughout 3532
29: 4 one tenth deal for one l, throughout 3532
29:10 A several tenth deal for one l, throughout 3532
29:15 a several tenth deal to each l of the fourteen 3532
1Sa 7: 9 Samuel took a sucking l, and offered it *for* 2924
17:34 and a bear, and took a l out of the flock: 7716
2Sa 12: 3 save one little **ewe l**, which he had bought 3535
12: 4 took the poor man's l, and dressed it for 3535
12: 6 he shall restore the l fourfold, because he 3535
Isa 11: 6 The wolf also shall dwell with the l, and 3532
16: 1 Send ye the l *to* the ruler of the land from 3733
53: 7 he is brought as a l to the slaughter, and 7716
65:25 The wolf and the l shall feed together, and 2924
66: 3 he that sacrificeth a l, *as if* he cut off a 7716
Jer 11:19 I *was* like a l *or* an ox *that* is brought to 3532
Eze 45:15 one l out of the flock, out of two hundred, 7716
46:13 *of* a l of the first year without blemish: 3532
46:15 Thus shall they prepare the l, and the meat 3532
Hos 4:16 now the LORD will feed them as a l in a 3532
Jn 1:29 and saith, Behold the L of God, which taketh *286*
1:36 as he walked, he saith, Behold the L of God. *286*
Ac 8:32 and like a l dumb before his shearer, so *286*
1Pe 1:19 as of a l without blemish and without spot: *286*
Rev 5: 6 stood a L as *it had been* slain, having seven *721*
5: 8 *and* twenty elders fell down before the L, *721*
5:12 Worthy is the L that was slain to receive *721*
5:13 the throne, and unto the L for ever and ever. *721*
6: 1 And I saw when the L opened one of *721*
6:16 on the throne, and from the wrath of the L: *721*
7: 9 stood before the throne, and before the L, *721*
7:10 sitteth upon the throne, and unto the L. *721*
7:14 and made them white in the blood of the L. *721*
7:17 For the L which is in the midst of the throne *721*
12:11 they overcame him by the blood of the L, *721*
13: 8 the L slain from the foundation of the world. *721*
13:11 and he had two horns like a l, and he spake *721*
14: 1 and lo, a L stood on the mount Sion, and *721*
14: 4 These are they which follow the L *721*
14: 4 *being* the firstfruits unto God and to the L. *721*
14:10 the holy angels, and in the presence of the L: *721*
15: 3 and the song of the L, saying, Great and *721*
17:14 These shall make war with the L, and *721*
17:14 the Lamb, and the L shall overcome them: *721*
19: 7 for the marriage of the L is come, and *721*
19: 9 are called unto the marriage supper of the L. *721*
21:14 the names of the twelve apostles of the L. *721*
21:22 God Almighty and the L are the temple of it. *721*
21:23 did lighten it, and the L *is* the light thereof. *721*
22: 1 out of the throne of God and of the L. *721*
22: 3 the throne of God and of the L shall be in it; *721*

LAMB'S (2) [LAMB]

Rev 21: 9 I will shew thee the bride, the L wife. *721*
21:27 they which are written in the L book of life. *721*

LAMBS (81) [LAMB]

Ge 21:28 Abraham set seven **ewe l** of the flock by 3535
21:29 What *mean* these seven **ewe l** which thou 3535
21:30 For *these* seven **ewe l** shalt thou take of my 3535
30:40 Jacob did separate the l, and set the faces of 3775
Ex 29:38 two l of the first year day by day 3532
Lev 14:10 on the eighth day he shall take two **he l** 3532
23:18 ye shall offer with the bread seven l 3532
23:19 two l of the first year for a sacrifice of 3532
23:20 offering before the LORD, with the two l: 3532
Nu 7:17 five he goats, five l of the first year: 3532
7:23 five he goats, five l of the first year: 3532
7:29 five he goats, five l of the first year: 3532
7:35 five he goats, five l of the first year: 3532
7:41 five he goats, five l of the first year: 3532
7:47 five he goats, five l of the first year: 3532
7:53 five he goats, five l of the first year: 3532
7:59 five he goats, five l of the first year: 3532
7:65 five he goats, five l of the first year: 3532
7:71 five he goats, five l of the first year: 3532
7:77 five he goats, five l of the first year: 3532
7:83 five he goats, five l of the first year: 3532
7:87 rams twelve, the l of the first year twelve, 3532
7:88 he goats sixty, the l of the first year sixty. 3532
28: 3 two l of the first year without spot day by 3532
28: 9 on the sabbath day two l of the first year 3532
28:11 seven l of the first year without spot; 3532
28:19 and one ram, and seven l of the first year: 3532
28:21 for every lamb, throughout the seven l; 3532
28:27 one ram, seven l of the first year; 3532
28:29 deal unto one lamb, throughout the seven l; 3532
29: 2 seven l of the first year without blemish: 3532
29: 4 deal for one lamb, throughout the seven l: 3532
29: 8 one ram, *and* seven l of the first year; 3532
29:10 deal for one lamb, throughout the seven l: 3532
29:13 two rams, *and* fourteen l of the first year; 3532
29:15 tenth deal to each lamb of the fourteen l: 3532
29:17 fourteen l of the first year without spot: 3532
29:18 for the rams, and for the l, *shall be* 3532
29:20 fourteen l of the first year without blemish; 3532
29:21 for the rams, and for the l, *shall be* 3532
29:23 fourteen l of the first year without blemish: 3532
29:24 for the rams, and for the l, *shall be* 3532
29:26 *and* fourteen l of the first year without spot: 3532
29:27 for the rams, and for the l, *shall be* 3532
29:29 fourteen l of the first year without blemish: 3532
29:30 for the rams, and for the l, *shall be* 3532
29:32 fourteen l of the first year without blemish: 3532
29:33 for the rams, and for the l, *shall be* 3532
29:36 seven l of the first year without blemish: 3532
29:37 for the ram, and for the l, *shall be* according 3532
Dt 32:14 with fat of l, and rams of the breed of 3733
1Sa 15: 9 the l, and all *that was* good, and would not 3733
2Ki 3: 4 the king of Israel an hundred thousand l, 3733
1Ch 29:21 a thousand rams, *and* a thousand l, 3532
2Ch 29:21 and seven l, and seven he goats, 3532
29:22 they killed also the l, and they sprinkled 3532
29:32 an hundred rams, *and* two hundred l: 3532
35: 7 gave to the people, *of* the flock, l and kids, 3532
Ezr 6: 9 both young bullocks, and rams, and l, 563
6:17 two hundred rams, four hundred l; 563
7:17 rams, l, with their meat offerings and 563
8:35 ninety and six rams, seventy and seven l, 3532
Ps 37:20 of the LORD *shall be* as the fat of l: 3733
114: 4 like rams, *and* the little hills like l. 1121+6629
114: 6 like rams; *and* ye little hills, like l? 1121+6629
Pr 27:26 The l *are* for thy clothing, and the goats *are* 3532
Isa 1:11 blood of bullocks, or of l, or of he goats. 3532
5:17 Then shall the l feed after their manner, and 3532
34: 6 *and* with the blood of l and goats, 3733
40:11 he shall gather the l with his arm, and 2922
Jer 51:40 I will bring them down like l to 3733
Eze 27:21 they occupied with thee in l, and rams, and 3733
39:18 of rams, of l, and of goats, of bullocks, 3733
46: 4 sabbath day *shall be* six l without blemish, 3532
46: 5 the meat offering for the l as he shall be 3532
46: 6 without blemish, and six l, and a ram: 3532
46: 7 for the l according as his hand shall attain 3532
46:11 to the l as he is able to give, and a hin of oil 3532
Am 6: 4 eat the l out of the flock, and the calves out 3733
Lk 10: 3 behold, I send you forth as l among wolves. *704*
Jn 21:15 I love thee. He saith unto him, Feed my l. *721*

LAME (27)

Lev 21:18 or a l, or he that hath a flat nose, or 6455
Dt 15:21 *as if it be* l, or blind, *or have* any ill 6455
2Sa 4: 4 had a son *that was* l of *his* feet, *and* 5223
4: 4 haste to flee, that he fell, and **became l**. 6452
5: 6 Except thou take away the blind and the l, 6455
5: 8 the Jebusites, and the l and the blind, 6455

2Sa	5: 8	and the l shall not come into the house.	6455
	9: 3	hath yet a son, *which is* l on *his* feet.	5223
	9:13	the king's table; and *was* l on both his feet.	6455
	19:26	go to the king; because thy servant *is* l.	6455
Job	29:15	eyes to the blind, and feet *was* I to the l.	6455
Pr	26: 7	The legs of the l are not equal: so *is* a	6455
Isa	33:23	of a great spoil divided; the l take the prey.	6455
	35: 6	shall the l *man* leap as a hart, and	6455
Jer	31: 8	*and* with them the blind and the l,	6455
Mal	1: 8	if ye offer the l and sick, *is it* not evil?	6455
	1:13	*that which was* torn, and the l, and the sick;	6455
Mt	11: 5	and the l walk, the lepers are cleansed, and	*5560*
	15:30	having with them *those that were* l, blind,	*5560*
	15:31	the l to walk, and the blind to see:	*5560*
	21:14	and *the* l came to him in the temple;	*5560*
Lk	7:22	how that the blind see, the l walk, the lepers	*5560*
	14:13	call the poor, the maimed, the l, the blind:	*5560*
Ac	3: 2	And a certain man l from his mother's	*5560*
	3:11	And as the l *man* which was healed held	*5560*
	8: 7	with palsies, and *that were* l, were healed.	*5560*
Heb	12:13	lest *that which is* l be turned out of the way;	*5560*

LAMECH (12)

Ge	4:18	begat Methusael: and Methusael begat **L**.	3929
	4:19	**L** took unto him two wives: the name of	3929
	4:23	**L** said unto his wives, Adah and Zillah,	3929
	4:23	ye wives of **L**, hearken unto my speech:	3929
	4:24	truly **L** seventy and sevenfold.	3929
	5:25	and seven years, and begat **L**:	3929
	5:26	Methuselah lived after he begat **L** seven	3929
	5:28	**L** lived an hundred eighty and two years,	3929
	5:30	**L** lived after he begat Noah five hundred	3929
	5:31	all the days of **L** were seven hundred	3929
1Ch	1: 3	Henoch, Methuselah, **L**,	3929
Lk	3:36	*the son* of Noe, which was *the son* of **L**,	*2984*

LAMENT (21) [LAMENTABLE, LAMENTATION, LAMENTATIONS, LAMENTED]

Jdg	11:40	*That* the daughters of Israel went yearly to l	8567
Isa	3:26	her gates shall l and mourn; and she *being*	578
	19: 8	all they that cast angle into the brooks shall l,	56
	32:12	They *shall* l for the teats, for the pleasant	5594
Jer	4: 8	this gird you with sackcloth, l and howl:	5594
	16: 5	neither go to l nor bemoan them:	5594
	16: 6	neither shall *men* l for them, nor cut	5594
	22:18	They shall not l for him, *saying,* Ah my	5594
	22:18	they shall not l for him, *saying,* Ah lord! or,	5594
	34: 5	and they will l thee, *saying,* Ah lord!	5594
	49: 3	l, and run to and fro by the hedges;	5594
La	2: 8	he **made** the rampart and the wall **to** l;	56
Eze	27:32	l over thee, *saying,* What *city is* like Tyrus,	6969
	32:16	the lamentation wherewith they shall l her:	6969
	32:16	the daughters of the nations shall l her:	6969
	32:16	they shall l for her, *even* for Egypt, and	6969
Joel	1: 8	**L** like a virgin girded with sackcloth for	421
	1:13	Gird yourselves, and l, ye priests: howl,	5594
Mic	2: 4	l with a doleful lamentation, *and* say,	5091
Jn	16:20	That ye shall weep and l, but the world	*2354*
Rev	18: 9	with her, shall bewail her, and l for her,	*2875*

LAMENTABLE (1) [LAMENT]

Da	6:20	the den, he cried with a l voice unto Daniel:	6088

LAMENTATION (25) [LAMENT]

Ge	50:10	they mourned with a great and very sore l:	4553
2Sa	1:17	David lamented with this l over Saul and	7015
Ps	78:64	by the sword; and their widows **made** no l.	1058
Jer	6:26	*as* for an only *son,* most bitter l:	4553
	7:29	cast *it* away, and take up a l on high places;	7015
	9:10	and for the habitations of the wilderness a l,	7015
	9:20	and every one her neighbour l.	7015
	31:15	was heard in Ramah, l, *and* bitter weeping;	5092
	48:38	*There shall be* l generally upon all	4553
La	2: 5	in the daughter of Judah mourning and l.	592
Eze	19: 1	Moreover take thou up a l for the princes of	7015
	19:14	This *is* a l, and shall be for a lamentation.	7015
	19:14	This *is* a lamentation, and shall be for a l.	7015
	26:17	they shall take up a l for thee, and say to	7015
	27: 2	thou son of man, take up a l for Tyrus;	7015
	27:32	in their wailing they shall take up a l for	7015
	28:12	take up a l upon the king of Tyrus, and	7015
	32: 2	take up a l for Pharaoh king of Egypt, and	7015
	32:16	This *is* the l wherewith they shall lament	7015
Am	5: 1	up against you, *even* a l, O house of Israel.	7015
	5:16	and such as are skilful of l to wailing.	5092
	8:10	into mourning, and all your songs into l;	7015
Mic	2: 4	lament with a **doleful** l, *and* say, We be	5093
Mt	2:18	l, and weeping, and great mourning,	*2355*
Ac	8: 2	*to his burial,* and made great l over him.	*2870*

LAMENTATIONS (3) [LAMENT]

2Ch	35:25	singing *women* spake of Josiah in their l	7015
	35:25	and behold, they *are* written in the l.	7015
Eze	2:10	*there was* written therein l, and mourning,	7015

LAMENTED (11) [LAMENT]

1Sa	6:19	the people l, because the LORD had smitten	56
	7: 2	all the house of Israel l after the LORD.	5091
	25: 1	l him, and buried him in his house at	5594
	28: 3	all Israel had l him, and buried him in	5594
2Sa	1:17	David l with this lamentation over Saul	6969
	3:33	the king l over Abner, and said, Died Abner	6969
2Ch	35:25	Jeremiah l for Josiah: and all the singing	6969
Jer	16: 4	they shall not be l; neither shall they be	5594
	25:33	they shall not be l, neither gathered,	5594
Mt	11:17	have mourned unto you, and ye have not l.	*2875*
Lk	23:27	of women, which also bewailed and l him.	*2354*

LAMENTS See LAMENTATIONS

LAMP (13) [LAMPS]

Ge	15:17	a burning l that passed between those	3940
Ex	27:20	for the light, to cause the l to burn always.	5216
1Sa	3: 3	ere the l of God went out in the temple of	5216
2Sa	22:29	For thou *art* my l, O LORD: and	5216
1Ki	15: 4	LORD his God give him a l in Jerusalem,	5216
Job	12: 5	He that is ready to slip with *his* feet *is as* a l	3940
Ps	119:105	Thy word *is* a l unto my feet, and a light	5216
	132:17	I have ordained a l for mine anointed.	5216
Pr	6:23	For the commandment *is* a l; and the law *is*	5216
	13: 9	but the l of the wicked shall be put out.	5216
	20:20	his l shall be put out in obscure darkness.	5216
Isa	62: 1	and the salvation thereof as a l *that* burneth.	3940
Rev	8:10	burning as *it were* a l, and it fell upon	*2985*

LAMPS (37) [LAMP]

Ex	25:37	thou shalt make the seven l thereof: and	5216
	25:37	they shall light the l thereof, that they may	5216
	30: 7	when he dresseth the l, he shall burn	5216
	30: 8	when Aaron lighteth the l at even, he shall	5216
	35:14	his furniture, and his l, with the oil for	5216
	37:23	he made his seven l, and his snuffers, and	5216
	39:37	The pure candlestick, *with* the l thereof,	5216
	39:37	*even with* the l to be set in order, and all	5216
	40: 4	in the candlestick, and light the l thereof.	5216
	40:25	he lighted the l before the LORD; as	5216
Lev	24: 2	the light, to cause the l to burn continually.	5216
	24: 4	He shall order the l upon the pure	5216
Nu	4: 9	and his l, and his tongs, and his snuffdishes,	5216
	8: 2	and say unto him, When thou lightest the l,	5216
	8: 2	the seven l shall give light over against	5216
	8: 3	he lighted the l thereof over against	5216
Jdg	7:16	empty pitchers, and l within the pitchers.	3940
	7:20	held the l in their left hands, and	3940
1Ki	7:49	and the l, and the tongs *of* gold,	5216
1Ch	28:15	*for* their l of gold, by weight for every	5216
	28:15	for every candlestick, and *for* the l thereof:	5216
	28:15	the candlestick, and *also for* the l thereof,	5216
2Ch	4:20	Moreover the candlesticks with their l,	5216
	4:21	the flowers, and the l, and the tongs,	5216
	13:11	the candlestick of gold with the l thereof,	5216
	29: 7	put out the l, and have not burnt incense	5216
Job	41:19	Out of his mouth go **burning** l, *and*	3940
Eze	1:13	coals of fire, *and* like the appearance of l:	3940
Da	10: 6	his eyes as l of fire, and his arms and	3940
Zec	4: 2	his seven l thereon, and seven pipes to	5216
	4: 2	and seven pipes to the seven l,	5216
Mt	25: 1	which took their l, and went forth to meet	*2985*
	25: 3	They that *were* foolish took their l, and	*2985*
	25: 4	wise took oil in their vessels with their l.	*2985*
	25: 7	all those virgins arose, and trimmed their l.	*2985*
	25: 8	Give us of your oil; for our l are gone out.	*2985*
Rev	4: 5	*there were* seven l of fire burning before	*2985*

LAMPSTAND; LAMPSTANDS See CANDLESTICK; CANDLESTICKS

LANCE (1) [LANCETS]

Jer	50:42	They shall hold the bow and the l: they *are*	3591

LANCETS (1) [LANCE]

1Ki 18:28 after their manner with knives and l, 7420

LAND (1717) [LANDED, LANDING, LANDMARK, LANDMARKS, LANDS]

Ge 1: 9 unto one place, and let the dry *l* appear: NIH
1:10 God called the dry *l* Earth; and NIH
2:11 that *is it* which compasseth the whole l of 776
2:12 the gold of that l *is* good: there *is* bdellium 776
2:13 the same *is it* that compasseth the whole l of 776
4:16 dwelt in the l of Nod, on the east of Eden. 776
7:22 of life, of all that *was* in the dry *l*, died. NIH
10:10 and Accad, and Calneh, in the l of Shinar. 776
10:11 Out of that l went forth Asshur, and 776
11: 2 that they found a plain in the l of Shinar; 776
11:28 Haran died before his father Terah in the l of 776
11:31 of the Chaldees, to go into the l of Canaan; 776
12: 1 father's house, unto a l that I will shew thee: 776
12: 5 they went forth to go into the l of Canaan; 776
12: 5 and into the l of Canaan they came. 776
12: 6 Abram passed through the l unto the place of 776
12: 6 And the Canaanite *was* then in the l. 776
12: 7 and said, Unto thy seed will I give this l: 776
12:10 there was a famine in the l: and Abram went 776
12:10 for the famine *was* grievous in the l. 776
13: 6 the l was not able to bear them, that they 776
13: 7 and the Perizzite dwelled then in the l. 776
13: 9 *Is* not the whole l before thee? 776
13:10 like the l of Egypt, as thou comest unto Zoar. 776
13:12 Abram dwelled in the l of Canaan, and 776
13:15 For all the l which thou seest, to thee will I 776
13:17 walk through the l in the length of it and 776
15: 7 the Chaldees, to give thee this l to inherit it. 776
15:13 shall be a stranger in a l *that is* not theirs, 776
15:18 saying, Unto thy seed have I given this l, 776
16: 3 after Abram had dwelt ten years in the l of 776
17: 8 after thee, the l wherein thou art a stranger, 776
17: 8 all the l of Canaan, for an everlasting 776
19:28 and toward all the l of the plain, and beheld, 776
20:15 Abimelech said, Behold, my l *is* before thee: 776
21:21 his mother took him a wife out of the l of 776
21:23 and to the l wherein thou hast sojourned. 776
21:32 and they returned into the l of the Philistines. 776
21:34 Abraham sojourned in the Philistines' l 776
22: 2 and get thee into the l of Moriah; 776
23: 2 the same *is* Hebron in the l of Canaan: 776
23: 7 and bowed himself to the people of the l, 776
23:12 down himself before the people of the l. 776
23:13 Ephron in the audience of the people of the l, 776
23:15 the l *is worth* four hundred shekels of silver; 776
23:19 the same *is* Hebron in the l of Canaan. 776
24: 5 will not be willing to follow me unto this l: 776
24: 5 must I needs bring thy son again unto the l 776
24: 7 from the l of my kindred, and which spake 776
24: 7 saying, Unto thy seed will I give this l; 776
24:37 of the Canaanites, in whose l I dwell: 776
26: 1 there was a famine in the l, besides the first 776
26: 2 dwell in the l which I shall tell thee of: 776
26: 3 Sojourn in this l, and I will be with thee, and 776
26:12 Isaac sowed in that l, and received in 776
26:22 room for us, and we shall be fruitful in the l. 776
27:46 as these *which are* of the daughters of the l, 776
28: 4 that thou mayest inherit the l wherein thou 776
28:13 the l whereon thou liest, to thee will I give it, 776
28:15 and will bring thee again into this l; 127
29: 1 and came into the l of the people of the east. 776
31: 3 Return unto the l of thy fathers, and to thy 776
31:13 get thee out from this l, and return unto 776
31:13 and return unto the l of thy kindred. 776
31:18 for to go to Isaac his father in the l of 776
32: 3 him to Esau his brother unto the l of Seir, 776
33:18 city of Shechem, which *is* in the l of Canaan, 776
34: 1 went out to see the daughters of the l. 776
34:10 the l shall be before you; dwell and trade you 776
34:21 therefore let them dwell in the l, and 776
34:21 for the l, behold, *it is* large enough for them; 776
34:30 me to stink among the inhabitants of the l, 776
35: 6 which *is* in the l of Canaan, that *is,* Beth-el, 776
35:12 the l which I gave Abraham and Isaac, 776
35:12 and to thy seed after thee will I give the l. 776
35:22 when Israel dwelt in that l, that Reuben went 776
36: 5 which were born unto him in the l of 776
36: 6 which he had got in the l of Canaan; 776
36: 7 the l wherein they were strangers could not 776
36:16 dukes *that came* of Eliphaz in the l of Edom; 776
36:17 dukes *that came* of Reuel in the l of Edom; 776
36:20 sons of Seir the Horite, who inhabited the l; 776
36:21 the children of Seir in the l of Edom. 776
36:30 of Hori, among their dukes in the l of Seir. 776
36:31 these *are* the kings that reigned in the l of 776
36:34 Husham of the l of Temani reigned in his 776
36:43 according to their habitations in the l of their 776
37: 1 Jacob dwelt in the l wherein his father was a 776
37: 1 his father was a stranger, in the l of Canaan. 776
40:15 For indeed I was stolen away out of the l of 776
41:19 such as I never saw in all the l of Egypt for 776
41:29 of great plenty throughout all the l of Egypt: 776
41:30 all the plenty shall be forgotten in the l of 776
41:30 and the famine shall consume the l; 776
41:31 the plenty shall not be known in the l by 776
41:33 and wise, and set him over the l of Egypt. 776
41:34 and let him appoint officers over the l, 776
41:34 take up the fifth *part* of the l of Egypt in 776
41:36 *that* food shall be for store to the l against 776
41:36 of famine, which shall be in the l of Egypt; 776
41:36 that the l perish not through the famine. 776
41:41 See, I have set thee over all the l of Egypt. 776
41:43 he made him *ruler* over all the l of Egypt. 776
41:44 lift up his hand or foot in all the l of Egypt. 776
41:45 And Joseph went out over *all* the l of Egypt. 776
41:46 and went throughout all the l of Egypt. 776
41:48 which were in the l of Egypt, and laid up 776
41:52 me to be fruitful in the l of my affliction. 776
41:53 that was in the l of Egypt, were ended. 776
41:54 but in all the l of Egypt there was bread. 776
41:55 when all the l of Egypt was famished, 776
41:56 and the famine waxed sore in the l of Egypt. 776
42: 5 for the famine was in the l of Canaan. 776
42: 6 And Joseph *was* the governor over the l, *and* 776
42: 6 he *it was* that sold to all the people of the l: 776
42: 7 they said, From the l of Canaan to buy food. 776
42: 9 to see the nakedness of the l you are come. 776
42:12 to see the nakedness of the l you are come. 776
42:13 the sons of one man in the l of Canaan; 776
42:29 they came unto Jacob their father unto the l 776
42:30 The man, *who is* the lord of the l, 776
42:32 *is this* day with our father in the l of Canaan. 776
42:34 your brother, and ye shall traffick in the l. 776
43: 1 And the famine *was* sore in the l. 776
43:11 take of the best fruits in the l in your vessels, 776
44: 8 we brought again unto thee out of the l of 776
45: 6 these two years *hath* the famine *been* in the l: 776
45: 8 and a ruler throughout all the l of Egypt. 776
45:10 And thou shalt dwell in the l of Goshen, and 776
45:17 and go, get you unto the l of Canaan; 776
45:18 I will give you the good of the l of Egypt, 776
45:18 of Egypt, and ye shall eat the fat of the l. 776
45:19 take you wagons out of the l of Egypt for 776
45:20 for the good of all the l of Egypt *is* yours. 776
45:25 came *into* the l of Canaan unto Jacob their 776
45:26 and he *is* governor over all the l of Egypt. 776
46: 6 which they had gotten in the l of Canaan, 776
46:12 Er and Onan died in the l of Canaan. And 776
46:20 unto Joseph in the l of Egypt were born 776
46:28 and they came into the l of Goshen. 776
46:31 which *were* in the l of Canaan, are come 776
46:34 that ye may dwell in the l of Goshen; 776
47: 1 they have, are come out of the l of Canaan; 776
47: 1 and behold, they *are* in the l of Goshen. 776
47: 4 For to sojourn in the l are we come; 776
47: 4 for the famine *is* sore in the l of Canaan: 776
47: 4 let thy servants dwell in the l of Goshen. 776
47: 6 The l of Egypt *is* before thee; in the best of 776
47: 6 in the best of the l make thy father and 776
47: 6 to dwell; in the l of Goshen let them dwell: 776
47:11 and gave them a possession in the l of Egypt, 776
47:11 in the best of the l, in the land of Rameses, 776
47:11 in the best of the land, in the l of Rameses, 776
47:13 *there was* no bread in all the l; for the famine 776
47:13 so that the l of Egypt and *all* the land of 776
47:13 *all* the l of Canaan fainted by reason of 776
47:14 the money that was found in the l of Egypt, 776
47:14 in the l of Canaan, for the corn which they 776
47:15 when money failed in the l of Egypt, and 776
47:15 in the l of Canaan, all the Egyptians came 776
47:19 we die before thine eyes, both we and our l? 127
47:19 buy us and our l for bread, and we and 127

Ge	47:19	we and our l will be servants unto Pharaoh:	127
	47:19	and not die, that the l be not desolate.	127
	47:20	Joseph bought all the l of Egypt for Pharaoh;	127
	47:20	over them: so the l became Pharaoh's.	776
	47:22	Only the l of the priests bought he not;	127
	47:23	bought you *this* day and your l for Pharaoh:	127
	47:23	*here is* seed for you, and ye shall sow the l.	127
	47:26	Joseph made it a law over the l of Egypt	127
	47:26	the fifth *part;* except the l of the priests only,	127
	47:27	Israel dwelt in the l of Egypt, in the country	776
	47:28	Jacob lived in the l of Egypt seventeen	776
	48: 3	appeared unto me at Luz in the l of Canaan,	776
	48: 4	will give this l to thy seed after thee *for* an	776
	48: 5	which were born unto thee in the l of Egypt	776
	48: 7	Rachel died by me in the l of Canaan in	776
	48:21	bring you again unto the l of your fathers.	776
	49:15	rest *was* good, and the l that *it was* pleasant;	776
	49:30	which *is* before Mamre, in the l of Canaan,	776
	50: 5	I have digged for me in the l of Canaan,	776
	50: 7	and all the elders of the l of Egypt,	776
	50: 8	and their herds, they left in the l of Goshen.	776
	50:11	when the inhabitants of the l, the Canaanites,	776
	50:13	For his sons carried him into the l of Canaan,	776
	50:24	bring you out of this l unto the land which he	776
	50:24	bring you out of this land unto the l which he	776
Ex	1: 7	and the l was filled with them.	776
	1:10	against us, and *so* get them up out of the l.	776
	2:15	of Pharaoh, and dwelt in the l of Midian:	776
	2:22	he said, I have been a stranger in a strange l.	776
	3: 8	to bring them up out of that l unto a good	776
	3: 8	bring them up out of that land unto a good l	776
	3: 8	unto a l flowing with milk and honey;	776
	3:17	of Egypt unto the l of the Canaanites,	776
	3:17	unto a l flowing with milk and honey.	776
	4: 9	pour *it upon* the dry *l*: and the water which	NIH
	4: 9	the river shall become blood upon the dry *l*.	NIH
	4:20	an ass, and he returned to the l of Egypt:	776
	5: 5	the people of the l now *are* many, and	776
	5:12	l of Egypt to gather stubble instead of straw.	776
	6: 1	a strong hand shall he drive them out of his l.	776
	6: 4	to give them the l of Canaan, the land of	776
	6: 4	the l of their pilgrimage, wherein they were	776
	6: 8	I will bring you in unto the l, *concerning*	776
	6:11	he let the children of Israel go out of his l.	776
	6:13	to bring the children of Israel out of the l of	776
	6:26	Bring out the children of Israel from the l of	776
	6:28	LORD spake unto Moses in the l of Egypt,	776
	7: 2	he send the children of Israel out of his l.	776
	7: 3	my signs and my wonders in the l of Egypt.	776
	7: 4	out of the l of Egypt by great judgments.	776
	7:19	*that* there may be blood throughout all the l	776
	7:21	there was blood throughout all the l of	776
	8: 5	cause frogs to come up upon the l of Egypt.	776
	8: 6	frogs came up, and covered the l of Egypt.	776
	8: 7	and brought up frogs upon the l of Egypt.	776
	8:14	them together upon heaps: and the l stank.	776
	8:16	out thy rod, and smite the dust of the l,	776
	8:16	that it may become lice throughout all the l	776
	8:17	all the dust of the l became lice throughout	776
	8:17	became lice throughout all the l of Egypt.	776
	8:22	And I will sever in that day the l of Goshen,	776
	8:24	servants' houses, and into all the l of Egypt:	776
	8:24	the l was corrupted by reason of the swarm	776
	8:25	said, Go ye, sacrifice to your God in the l.	776
	9: 5	the LORD shall do this thing in the l.	776
	9: 9	it shall become small dust in all the l of	776
	9: 9	upon beast, throughout all the l of Egypt.	776
	9:22	that there may be hail in all the l of Egypt,	776
	9:22	herb of the field, throughout the l of Egypt.	776
	9:23	the LORD rained hail upon the l of Egypt.	776
	9:24	such as there was none like it in all the l of	776
	9:25	the hail smote throughout all the l of Egypt	776
	9:26	Only in the l of Goshen, where the children	776
	10:12	Stretch out thine hand over the l of Egypt for	776
	10:12	that they may come up upon the l of Egypt,	776
	10:12	eat every herb of the l, *even* all that the hail	776
	10:13	Moses stretched forth his rod over the l of	776
	10:13	the LORD brought an east wind upon the l	776
	10:14	the locusts went up over all the l of Egypt,	776
	10:15	the whole earth, so that the l was darkened;	776
	10:15	they did eat every herb of the l, and all	776
	10:15	herbs of the field, through all the l of Egypt.	776
	10:21	that there may be darkness over the l of	776
	10:22	there was a thick darkness in all the l of	776
	11: 3	man Moses *was* very great in the l of Egypt,	776
	11: 5	all the firstborn in the l of Egypt shall die,	776
	11: 6	there shall be a great cry throughout all the l	776
	11: 9	that my wonders may be multiplied in the l	776
	11:10	not let the children of Israel go out of his l.	776
	12: 1	unto Moses and Aaron in the l of Egypt,	776
	12:12	For I will pass through the l of Egypt this	776
	12:12	will smite all the firstborn in the l of Egypt,	776
	12:13	to destroy *you,* when I smite the l of Egypt.	776
	12:17	I brought your armies out of the l of Egypt:	776
	12:19	whether he be a stranger, or born in the l.	776
	12:25	when ye be come to the l which the LORD	776
	12:29	smote all the firstborn in the l of Egypt,	776
	12:33	that they might send them out of the l in	776
	12:41	of the LORD went out from the l of Egypt.	776
	12:42	for bringing them out from the l of Egypt:	776
	12:48	and he shall be as one that is born in the l:	776
	12:51	Israel out of the l of Egypt by their armies.	776
	13: 5	shall bring thee into the l of the Canaanites,	776
	13: 5	give thee, a l flowing with milk and honey,	776
	13:11	shall bring thee into the l of the Canaanites,	776
	13:15	that the LORD slew all the firstborn in the l	776
	13:17	*through* the way of the l of the Philistines,	776
	13:18	went up harnessed out of the l of Egypt.	776
	14: 3	They *are* entangled in the l, the wilderness	776
	14:21	made the sea dry *l*, and the waters were	NIH
	14:29	the children of Israel walked upon dry *l* in	NIH
	15:19	the children of Israel went on dry *l* in	NIH
	16: 1	after their departing out of the l of Egypt.	776
	16: 3	by the hand of the LORD in the l of Egypt,	776
	16: 6	hath brought you out from the l of Egypt:	776
	16:32	when I brought you forth from the l of	776
	16:35	forty years, until they came to a l inhabited;	776
	16:35	until they came unto the borders of the l of	776
	18: 3	he said, I have been an alien in a strange l:	776
	18:27	and he went his way into his own l.	776
	19: 1	Israel were gone forth out of the l of Egypt,	776
	20: 2	which have brought thee out of the l of	776
	20:12	that thy days may be long upon the l which	127
	22:21	for ye were strangers in the l of Egypt.	776
	23: 9	seeing ye were strangers in the l of Egypt.	776
	23:10	six years thou shalt sow thy l, and	776
	23:19	The first of the firstfruits of thy l thou shalt	127
	23:26	cast their young, nor be barren, in thy l:	776
	23:29	lest the l become desolate, and the beast of	776
	23:30	until thou be increased, and inherit the l.	776
	23:31	for I will deliver the inhabitants of the l into	776
	23:33	They shall not dwell in thy l, lest they make	776
	29:46	that brought them forth out of the l of Egypt,	776
	32: 1	the man that brought us up out of the l of	776
	32: 4	which brought thee up out of the l of Egypt.	776
	32: 7	which thou broughtest out of the l of Egypt,	776
	32: 8	which have brought thee up out of the l of	776
	32:11	which thou hast brought forth out of the l of	776
	32:13	all this l that I have spoken of will I give	776
	32:23	the man that brought us up out of the l of	776
	33: 1	thou hast brought up out of the l of Egypt,	776
	33: 1	unto the l which I sware unto Abraham,	776
	33: 3	Unto a l flowing with milk and honey: for I	776
	34:12	the inhabitants of the l whither thou goest,	776
	34:15	a covenant with the inhabitants of the l,	776
	34:24	neither shall any man desire thy l, when thou	776
	34:26	The first of the firstfruits of thy l thou shalt	127
Lev	11:45	that bringeth you up out of the l of Egypt,	776
	14:34	When ye be come into the l of Canaan,	776
	14:34	I put the plague of leprosy in a house of the l	776
	16:22	him all their iniquities unto a l not inhabited:	776
	18: 3	After the doings of the l of Egypt,	776
	18: 3	after the doings of the l of Canaan, whither I	776
	18:25	the l is defiled: therefore I do visit	776
	18:25	and the l *itself* vomiteth out her inhabitants.	776
	18:27	abominations have the men of the l done,	776
	18:27	which *were* before you, and the l is defiled;)	776
	18:28	That the l spue not you out also, when ye	776
	19: 9	when ye reap the harvest of your l, thou shalt	776
	19:23	when ye shall come into the l, and shall have	776
	19:29	lest the l fall to whoredom, and the land	776
	19:29	and the l become full of wickedness.	776
	19:33	And if a stranger sojourn with thee in your l,	776
	19:34	for ye were strangers in the l of Egypt:	776
	19:36	which brought you out of the l of Egypt.	776
	20: 2	the people of the l shall stone him with	776
	20: 4	if the people of the l do any ways hide their	776
	20:22	that the l, whither I bring you to dwell	776

Lev 20:24 Ye shall inherit their l, and I will give it unto 127
20:24 a l that floweth with milk and honey: 776
22:24 you make *any* offering *thereof* in your l. 776
22:33 That brought you out of the l of Egypt, to be 776
23:10 When ye be come into the l which I give 776
23:22 when ye reap the harvest of your l, thou shalt 776
23:39 when ye have gathered in the fruit of the l, 776
23:43 when I brought them out of the l of Egypt: 776
24:16 well the stranger, as he **that is born in** the l, 249
25: 2 When ye come into the l which I give you, 776
25: 2 shall the l keep a sabbath unto the LORD. 776
25: 4 year shall be a sabbath of rest unto the l, 776
25: 5 *for* it is a year of rest unto the l. 776
25: 6 the sabbath of the l shall be meat for you; 776
25: 7 thy cattle, and for the beast that *are* in thy l, 776
25: 9 the trumpet sound throughout all your l. 776
25:10 proclaim liberty throughout *all* the l unto all 776
25:18 do them; and ye shall dwell in the l in safety. 776
25:19 the l shall yield her fruit, and ye shall eat 776
25:23 The l shall not be sold for ever: for the land 776
25:23 for the l *is* mine; for ye *were* strangers and 776
25:24 in all the l of your possession ye shall grant a 776
25:24 ye shall grant a redemption for the l. 776
25:38 which brought you forth out of the l of 776
25:38 to give you the l of Canaan, *and* to be your 776
25:42 which I brought forth out of the l of Egypt: 776
25:45 that *are* with you, which they begat in your l: 776
25:55 whom I brought forth out of the l of Egypt: 776
26: 1 shall ye set up *any* image of stone in your l, 776
26: 4 the l shall yield her increase, and the trees of 776
26: 5 bread to the full, and dwell in your l safely. 776
26: 6 I will give peace in the l, and ye shall lie 776
26: 6 I will rid evil beasts out of the l, neither shall 776
26: 6 neither shall the sword go through your l. 776
26:13 which brought you forth out of the l of 776
26:20 for your l shall not yield her increase, neither 776
26:20 neither shall the trees of the l yield their 776
26:32 I will bring the l into desolation: and 776
26:33 your l shall be desolate, and your cities 776
26:34 shall the l enjoy her sabbaths, as long as it 776
26:34 lieth desolate, and ye *be* in your enemies' l; 776
26:34 *even* then shall the l rest, and enjoy her 776
26:38 and the l of your enemies shall eat you up. 776
26:41 have brought them into the l of their 776
26:42 will I remember; and I will remember the l. 776
26:43 The l also shall be left of them, and 776
26:44 when they be in the l of their enemies, 776
26:45 whom I brought forth out of the l of Egypt in 776
27:24 *even* to him to whom the possession of the l 776
27:30 all the tithe of the l, *whether* of the seed of 776
27:30 *whether* of the seed of the l, *or* of the fruit of 776
Nu 1: 1 after they were come out of the l of Egypt, 776
3:13 l of Egypt I hallowed unto me all 776
8:17 that I smote every firstborn in the l of Egypt, 776
9: 1 after they were come out of the l of Egypt, 776
9:14 and for him that was born in the l. 776
10: 9 if ye go *to* war in your l against the enemy 776
10:30 I will depart to mine own l, and to my 776
11:12 unto the l which thou swarest unto their 127
13: 2 that they may search the l of Canaan, 776
13:16 the men which Moses sent to spy out the l. 776
13:17 Moses sent them to spy out the l of Canaan, 776
13:18 see the l, what it *is;* and the people that 776
13:19 what the l *is* that they dwell in, whether it *be* 776
13:20 what the l *is,* whether it *be* fat or lean, 776
13:20 good courage, and bring of the fruit of the l. 776
13:21 searched the l from the wilderness of Zin 776
13:25 they returned from searching of the l after 776
13:26 and shewed them the fruit of the l. 776
13:27 We came unto the l whither thou sentest us, 776
13:28 the people *be* strong that dwell in the l, 776
13:29 The Amalekites dwell in the l of the south: 776
13:32 they brought up an evil report of the l which 776
13:32 saying, The l, through which we have gone 776
13:32 *is* a l that eateth up the inhabitants thereof; 776
14: 2 Would God that we had died in the l of 776
14: 3 *hath* the LORD brought us unto this l, 776
14: 6 *which were* of them that searched the l, 776
14: 7 saying, The l, which we passed through to 776
14: 7 through to search it, *is* an exceeding good **l.** 776
14: 8 he will bring us into this l, and give it us; 776
14: 8 it us; a l which floweth with milk and honey. 776
14: 9 neither fear ye the people of the l; 776
14:14 they will tell *it* to the inhabitants of this l: 776
14:16 people into the l which he sware unto them, 776
14:23 Surely they shall not see the l which I sware 776
14:24 him will I bring into the l whereinto he went; 776
14:30 Doubtless ye shall not come into the l, 776
14:31 they shall know the l which ye have 776
14:34 of the days *in* which ye searched the l, 776
14:36 the men, which Moses sent to search the l, 776
14:36 by bringing up a slander upon the l, 776
14:37 that did bring up the evil report upon the l, 776
14:38 *were* of the men that went to search the l, 776
15: 2 When ye be come into the l of your 776
15:18 When ye come into the l whither I bring you, 776
15:19 *that* when ye eat of the bread of the l, 776
15:30 *whether he be* **born in the** l, or a stranger, 249
15:41 which brought you out of the l of Egypt, 776
16:13 us up out of a l that floweth with milk 776
16:14 Moreover thou hast not brought us into a l 776
18:13 *And* whatsoever is first ripe in the l, 776
18:20 Thou shalt have no inheritance in their l, 776
20:12 ye shall not bring this congregation into the l 776
20:23 by the coast of the l of Edom, saying, 776
20:24 for he shall not enter into the l which I have 776
21: 4 of the Red sea, to compass the l of Edom: 776
21:22 Let me pass through thy l: we will not turn 776
21:24 and possessed his l from Arnon unto Jabbok, 776
21:26 taken all his l out of his hand, *even* unto 776
21:31 Thus Israel dwelt in the l of the Amorites. 776
21:34 into thy hand, and all his people, and his l; 776
21:35 none left him alive: and they possessed his l. 776
22: 5 which *is* by the river *of* the l of the children 776
22: 6 and *that* I may drive them out of the l: 776
22:13 the princes of Balak, Get you into your l: 776
26: 4 which went forth out of the l of Egypt. 776
26:19 and Er and Onan died in the l of Canaan. 776
26:53 Unto these the l shall be divided for an 776
26:55 Notwithstanding the l shall be divided by lot: 776
27:12 see the l which I have given unto 776
32: 1 when they saw the l of Jazer, and the land of 776
32: 1 the l of Gilead, that behold, the place *was* a 776
32: 4 *is* a l for cattle, and thy servants have cattle: 776
32: 5 let this l be given unto thy servants for a 776
32: 7 the l which the LORD hath given them? 776
32: 8 I sent them from Kadesh-barnea to see the l. 776
32: 9 up unto the valley of Eshcol, and saw the l, 776
32: 9 that *they* should not go into the l which 776
32:11 shall see the l which I sware unto Abraham, 127
32:17 because of the inhabitants of the l. 776
32:22 the l be subdued before the LORD: then 776
32:22 this l shall be your possession before 776
32:29 and the l shall be subdued before you; 776
32:29 ye shall give them the l of Gilead for a 776
32:30 possessions among you in the l of Canaan. 776
32:32 before the LORD *into* the l of Canaan, 776
32:33 the l, with the cities thereof in the coasts, 776
33: 1 which went forth out of the l of Egypt with 776
33:37 in mount Hor, in the edge of the l of Edom. 776
33:38 of Israel were come out of the l of Egypt, 776
33:40 which dwelt in the south in the l of Canaan, 776
33:51 When ye are passed over Jordan into the l of 776
33:52 ye shall drive out all the inhabitants of the l 776
33:53 ye shall dispossess *the inhabitants of* the l, 776
33:53 for I have given you the l to possess it. 776
33:54 ye shall divide the l by lot for an inheritance 776
33:55 out the inhabitants of the l from before you; 776
33:55 and shall vex you in the l wherein ye dwell. 776
34: 2 When ye come into the l of Canaan; 776
34: 2 (this *is* the l that shall fall unto you for an 776
34: 2 *even* the l of Canaan with the coasts 776
34:12 this shall be your l with the coasts thereof 776
34:13 This *is* the l which ye shall inherit by lot, 776
34:17 of the men which shall divide the l unto you: 776
34:18 of every tribe, to divide the l by inheritance. 776
34:29 unto the children of Israel in the l of Canaan. 776
35:10 When ye be come over Jordan into the l of 776
35:14 three cities shall ye give in the l of Canaan, 776
35:28 shall return into the l of his possession. 776
35:32 that he should come again to dwell in the l, 776
35:33 So ye shall not pollute the l wherein ye *are:* 776
35:33 wherein ye *are:* for blood it defileth the l: 776
35:33 the l cannot be cleansed of the blood that is 776
35:34 therefore the l which ye shall inhabit, 776
36: 2 l for an inheritance by lot to the children of 776
Dt 1: 5 On *this* side Jordan, in the l of Moab, 776
1: 7 *to* the l of the Canaanites, and *unto* Lebanon, 776

Dt 1: 8 Behold, I have set the l before you: go in and 776
1: 8 possess the l which the LORD sware unto 776
1:21 the LORD thy God hath set the l before 776
1:22 they shall search us out the l, and bring us 776
1:25 they took of the fruit of the l in their hands, 776
1:25 *It is* a good l which the LORD our God 776
1:27 he hath brought us forth out of the l of 776
1:35 men of this evil generation see that good l, 776
1:36 to him will I give the l that he hath trodden 776
2: 5 for I will not give you of their l, no, not so 776
2: 9 for I will not give thee of their l *for* a 776
2:12 as Israel did unto the l of his possession, 776
2:19 for I will not give thee of the l of 776
2:20 (That also was accounted a l of giants: 776
2:24 the Amorite, king of Heshbon, and his l: 776
2:27 Let me pass through thy l: I will go along by 776
2:29 until I shall pass over Jordan into the l which 776
2:31 begun to give Sihon and his l before thee: 776
2:31 to possess, that *thou* mayest inherit his l. 776
2:37 Only unto the l of the children of Ammon 776
3: 2 and all his people, and his l, into thy hand; 776
3: 8 Amorites the l that *was* on *this* side Jordan, 776
3:12 And this l, *which* we possessed at that time, 776
3:13 all Bashan, which was called the l of giants. 776
3:18 The LORD your God hath given you this l 776
3:20 *until* they also possess the l which 776
3:25 and see the good l that *is* beyond Jordan, 776
3:28 he shall cause them to inherit the l which 776
4: 1 possess the l which the LORD God of your 776
4: 5 so in the l whither ye go to possess it. 776
4:14 that ye might do them in the l whither ye go 776
4:21 and that *I* should not go in unto *that* good l, 776
4:22 I *must* die in this l, I *must* not go over 776
4:22 but ye *shall* go over, and possess that good l. 776
4:25 and ye shall have remained long in the l, and 776
4:26 ye shall soon utterly perish from off the l 776
4:38 to give thee their l *for* an inheritance, as *it is* 776
4:46 in the l of Sihon king of the Amorites, 776
4:47 they possessed his l, and the land of Og king 776
4:47 the l of Og king of Bashan, two kings of 776
5: 6 which brought thee out of the l of Egypt, 776
5:15 remember that thou wast a servant in the l of 776
5:16 in the l which the LORD thy God giveth 127
5:31 that they may do *them* in the l which I give 776
5:33 *that* ye may prolong *your* days in the l which 776
6: 1 that ye might do *them* in the l whither ye go 776
6: 3 *in* the l that floweth with milk and honey. 776
6:10 into the l which he sware unto thy fathers, 776
6:12 which brought thee forth out of the l of 776
6:18 possess the good l which the LORD sware 776
6:23 to give us the l which he sware unto our 776
7: 1 into the l whither thou goest to possess it, 776
7:13 and the fruit of thy l, thy corn, and thy wine, 127
7:13 in the l which he sware unto thy fathers to 127
8: 1 possess the l which the LORD sware unto 776
8: 7 LORD thy God bringeth thee into a good l, 776
8: 7 a l of brooks of water, of fountains and 776
8: 8 A l of wheat, and barley, and vines, and 776
8: 8 pomegranates; a l of oil olive, and honey; 776
8: 9 A l wherein thou shalt eat bread without 776
8: 9 a l whose stones *are* iron, and out of whose 776
8:10 God for the good l which he hath given thee. 776
8:14 which brought thee forth out of the l of 776
9: 4 LORD hath brought me in to possess this l: 776
9: 5 of thine heart, dost thou go to possess their l: 776
9: 6 good l to possess it for thy righteousness; 776
9: 7 that thou didst depart out of the l of Egypt, 776
9:23 and possess the l which I have given you; 776
9:28 Lest the l whence thou broughtest us out say, 776
9:28 them into the l which he promised them, 776
10: 7 Gudgodah to Jotbath, a l of rivers of waters. 776
10:11 that they may go in and possess the l, 776
10:19 for ye were strangers in the l of Egypt. 776
11: 3 Pharaoh the king of Egypt, and unto all his l; 776
11: 8 may be strong, and go in and possess the l, 776
11: 9 that ye may prolong *your* days in the l, 127
11: 9 a l that floweth with milk and honey. 776
11:10 For the l, whither thou goest in to possess it, 776
11:10 *is* not as the l of Egypt, from whence ye 776
11:11 the l, whither ye go to possess it, *is* a land of 776
11:11 *is* a l of hills and valleys, *and* drinketh water 776
11:12 A l which the LORD thy God careth for: 776
11:14 That I will give *you* the rain of your l in his 776
11:17 be no rain, and *that* the l yield not her fruit; 127
11:17 *lest* ye perish quickly from off the good l 776
11:21 in the l which the LORD sware unto your 127
11:25 the dread of you upon all the l that ye shall 776
11:29 in unto the l whither thou goest to possess it, 776
11:30 sun goeth down, in the l of the Canaanites, 776
11:31 l which the LORD your God giveth you, 776
12: 1 which ye shall observe to do in the l, 776
12:10 dwell in the l which the LORD your God 776
12:29 thou succeedest them, and dwellest in their l; 776
13: 5 which brought you out of the l of Egypt, and 776
13:10 which brought thee out of the l of Egypt, 776
15: 4 l which the LORD thy God giveth thee *for* 776
15: 7 thy l which the LORD thy God giveth thee, 776
15:11 For the poor shall never cease out of the l: 776
15:11 to thy poor, and to thy needy, in thy l. 776
15:15 that thou wast a bondman in the l of Egypt, 776
16: 3 for thou camest forth out of the l of Egypt in 776
16: 3 out of the l of Egypt all the days of thy life. 776
16:20 inherit the l which the LORD thy God 776
17:14 When thou art come unto the l which 776
18: 9 When thou art come into the l which 776
19: 1 whose l the LORD thy God giveth thee, 776
19: 2 three cities for thee in the midst of thy l, 776
19: 3 thee a way, and divide the coasts of thy l, 776
19: 8 give thee all the l which he promised to give 776
19:10 That innocent blood be not shed in thy l, 776
19:14 which thou shalt inherit in the l that 776
20: 1 which brought thee up out of the l of Egypt. 776
21: 1 If *one* be found slain in the l which 127
21:23 that thy l be not defiled, which the LORD 127
23: 7 because thou wast a stranger in his l. 776
23:20 to in the l whither thou goest to possess it. 776
24: 4 thou shalt not cause the l to sin, which 776
24:14 of thy strangers that *are* in thy l within thy 776
24:22 that thou wast a bondman in the l of Egypt: 776
25:15 that thy days may be lengthened in the l 127
25:19 in the l which the LORD thy God giveth 776
26: 1 when thou art come in unto the l which 776
26: 2 which thou shalt bring of thy l that 776
26: 9 hath given us this l, *even* a land that floweth 776
26: 9 *even* a l that floweth with milk and honey. 776
26:10 behold, I have brought the firstfruits of the l, 127
26:15 and the l which thou hast given us, 127
26:15 a l that floweth with milk and honey. 776
27: 2 the l which the LORD thy God giveth thee, 776
27: 3 that thou mayest go in unto the l which 776
27: 3 a l that floweth with milk and honey; 776
28: 8 he shall bless thee in the l which the LORD 776
28:11 in the l which the LORD sware unto thy 127
28:12 the heaven to give the rain unto thy l in his 776
28:18 the fruit of thy l, the increase of thy kine, 127
28:21 until he have consumed thee from off the l, 127
28:24 The LORD shall make the rain of thy l 776
28:33 The fruit of thy l, and all thy labours, shall a 127
28:42 and fruit of thy l shall the locust consume. 127
28:51 and the fruit of thy l, until thou be destroyed: 127
28:52 wherein thou trustedst, throughout all thy l: 776
28:52 thee in all thy gates throughout all thy l, 776
28:63 ye shall be plucked from off the l whither 127
29: 1 with the children of Israel in the l of Moab, 776
29: 2 your eyes in the l of Egypt unto Pharaoh, 776
29: 2 and unto all his servants, and unto all his l; 776
29: 8 we took their l, and gave it for an inheritance 776
29:16 (For ye know how we have dwelt in the l of 776
29:22 and the stranger that shall come from a far l, 776
29:22 when they see the plagues of that l, and 776
29:23 *And that* the whole l thereof *is* brimstone, 776
29:24 hath the LORD done thus unto this l? 776
29:25 he brought them forth out of the l of Egypt: 776
29:27 of the LORD was kindled against this l, 776
29:28 the LORD rooted them out of their l in 127
29:28 and cast them into another l, as *it is* this day. 776
30: 5 the LORD thy God will bring thee into the l 776
30: 9 thy cattle, and in the fruit of thy l, for good: 127
30:16 the LORD thy God shall bless thee in the l 776
30:18 ye shall not prolong *your* days upon the l, 127
30:20 that thou mayest dwell in the l which 127
31: 4 and unto the l of them, whom he destroyed. 776
31: 7 for thou must go with this people unto the l 776
31:13 as long as ye live in the l whither ye go over 127
31:16 after the gods of the strangers of the l, 776
31:20 *For* when I shall have brought them into the l 127
31:21 before I have brought them into the l which I 776
31:23 of Israel into the l which I sware unto them: 776

L

Dt 32:10 He found him in a desert l, and in the waste 776
32:43 will be merciful *unto* his l, *and to* his people. 127
32:47 this thing ye shall prolong *your* days in the l, 127
32:49 *unto* mount Nebo, which *is* in the l of Moab, 776
32:49 behold the l of Canaan, which I give unto 776
32:52 Yet thou shalt see the l before *thee;* but 776
32:52 thou shalt not go thither unto the l which I 776
33:13 he said, Blessed of the LORD *be* his l, 776
33:28 the fountain of Jacob *shall be* upon a l of 776
34: 1 the LORD shewed him all the l of Gilead, 776
34: 2 the l of Ephraim, and Manasseh, and all 776
34: 2 Manasseh, and all the l of Judah, unto 776
34: 4 This *is* the l which I sware unto Abraham, 776
34: 5 of the LORD died there in the l of Moab, 776
34: 6 he buried him in a valley in the l of Moab, 776
34:11 which the LORD sent him to do in the l of 776
34:11 and to all his servants, and to all his l, 776
Jos 1: 2 unto the l which I do give to them, 776
1: 4 all the l of the Hittites, and unto the great sea 776
1: 6 shalt thou divide for an inheritance the l, 776
1:11 over this Jordan, to go in to possess the l, 776
1:13 given you rest, and hath given you this l. 776
1:14 shall remain in the l which Moses gave you 776
1:15 they also have possessed the l which 776
1:15 ye shall return unto the l of your possession, 776
2: 1 saying, Go view the l, even Jericho. 776
2: 9 I know that the LORD hath given you the l, 776
2: 9 that all the inhabitants of the l faint because 776
2:14 when the LORD hath given us the l, 776
2:18 Behold, *when* we come into the l, thou shalt 776
2:24 hath delivered into our hands all the l; 776
4:18 *l,* that the waters of Jordan returned unto NIH
4:22 Israel came over this Jordan on dry *l.* NIH
5: 6 sware that *he* would not shew them the l, 776
5: 6 a l that floweth with milk and honey. 776
5:11 they did eat of the old corn of the l on 776
5:12 after they had eaten of the old corn of the l; 776
5:12 they did eat of the fruit of the l of Canaan 776
7: 9 all the inhabitants of the l shall hear *of it,* 776
8: 1 of Ai, and his people, and his city, and his l: 776
9:24 his servant Moses to give you all the l, 776
9:24 to destroy all the inhabitants of the l from 776
10:42 and their l did Joshua take *at* one time, 776
11: 3 *to* the Hivite under Hermon in the l of 776
11:16 So Joshua took all that l, the hills, and all 776
11:16 all the south *country,* and all the l of Goshen, 776
11:22 There was none of the Anakims left in the l 776
11:23 So Joshua took the whole l, according to all 776
11:23 by their tribes. And the l rested from war. 776
12: 1 Now these *are* the kings of the l, which 776
12: 1 possessed their l on the *other* side Jordan 776
13: 1 there remaineth *yet* very much l to be 776
13: 2 This is the l that *yet* remaineth: all 776
13: 4 all the l of the Canaanites, and Mearah that 776
13: 5 the l of the Giblites, and all Lebanon, 776
13: 7 divide this l for an inheritance unto the nine 776
13:25 and half the l of the children of Ammon, 776
14: 1 of Israel inherited in the l of Canaan, 776
14: 4 they gave no part unto the Levites in the l, 776
14: 5 children of Israel did, and they divided the l. 776
14: 7 me from Kadesh-barnea to espy out the l; 776
14: 9 Surely the l whereon thy feet have trodden 776
14:15 the Anakims. And the l had rest from war. 776
15:19 a blessing; for thou hast given me a south l; 776
17: 5 beside the l of Gilead and Bashan, 776
17: 6 the rest of Manasseh's sons had the l of 776
17: 8 *Now* Manasseh had the l of Tappuah: but 776
17:12 but the Canaanites would dwell in that l. 776
17:15 cut down for thyself there in the l of 776
17:16 all the Canaanites that dwell in the l of 776
18: 1 And the l was subdued before them. 776
18: 3 long *are* you slack to go to possess the l, 776
18: 4 go through the l, and describe it according to 776
18: 6 therefore describe the l *into* seven parts, 776
18: 8 charged them that went to describe the l, 776
18: 8 Go and walk through the l, and describe it, 776
18: 9 And the men went and passed through the l, 776
18:10 there Joshua divided the l unto the children 776
19:49 When they had made an end of dividing the l 776
21: 2 they spake unto them at Shiloh in the l of 776
21:43 the LORD gave unto Israel all the l which 776
22: 4 your tents, *and* unto the l of your possession, 776
22: 9 which *is* in the l of Canaan, to go unto 776
22: 9 to the l of their possession, whereof they 776
22:10 that *are* in the l of Canaan, the children of 776
22:11 built an altar over against the l of Canaan, 776
22:13 half tribe of Manasseh, into the l of Gilead, 776
22:15 unto the l of Gilead, and they spake with 776
22:19 if the l of your possession *be* unclean, *then* 776
22:19 pass ye over unto the l of the possession of 776
22:32 out of the l of Gilead, unto the land of 776
22:32 unto the l of Canaan, to the children of 776
22:33 to destroy the l wherein the children of 776
23: 5 ye shall possess their l, as the LORD your 776
23:13 until ye perish from off this good l which 127
23:15 l which the LORD your God hath given 127
23:16 ye shall perish quickly from off the good l 776
24: 3 led him throughout all the l of Canaan, and 776
24: 8 And I brought you into the l of the Amorites, 776
24: 8 into your hand, that ye might possess their l; 776
24:13 I have given you a l for which ye did not 776
24:15 gods of the Amorites, in whose l ye dwell: 776
24:17 us up and our fathers out of the l of Egypt, 776
24:18 even the Amorites which dwelt in the l: 776
Jdg 1: 2 behold, I have delivered the l into his hand. 776
1:15 for thou hast given me a south l; give me 776
1:26 the man went *into* the l of the Hittites, and 776
1:27 but the Canaanites would dwell in that l. 776
1:32 the Canaanites, the inhabitants of the l: 776
1:33 the Canaanites, the inhabitants of the l: 776
2: 1 have brought you unto the l which I sware 776
2: 2 make no league with the inhabitants of this l; 776
2: 6 man unto his inheritance to possess the l. 776
2:12 which brought them out of the l of Egypt, 776
3:11 the l had rest forty years. And Othniel 776
3:30 of Israel. And the l had rest fourscore years. 776
5:31 in his might. And the l had rest forty years. 776
6: 5 and they entered into the l to destroy it. 776
6: 9 out from before you, and gave you their l; 776
6:10 gods of the Amorites, in whose l ye dwell: 776
9:37 come people down by the middle of the l, 776
10: 4 unto this day, which *are* in the l of Gilead. 776
10: 8 *other* side Jordan in the l of the Amorites, 776
11: 3 from his brethren, and dwelt in the l of Tob: 776
11: 5 went to fetch Jephthah out of the l of Tob: 776
11:12 thou art come against me to fight in my l? 776
11:13 Because Israel took away my l, when they 776
11:15 Israel took not away the l of Moab, 776
11:15 nor the l of the children of Ammon: 776
11:17 Let me, I pray thee, pass through thy l: 776
11:18 compassed the l of Edom, and the land of 776
11:18 the l of Moab, and came by the east side of 776
11:18 came by the east side of the l of Moab, and 776
11:19 we pray thee, through thy l into my place. 776
11:21 so Israel possessed all the l of the Amorites, 776
12:15 was buried in Pirathon in the l of Ephraim, 776
18: 2 to spy out the l, and to search it; 776
18: 2 and they said unto them, Go, search the l: 776
18: 7 *there was* no magistrate in the l, that might 776
18: 9 for we have seen the l, and behold, it *is* very 776
18: 9 slothful to go, *and* to enter to possess the l. 776
18:10 come unto a people secure, and to a large l: 776
18:17 the five men that went to spy out the l went 776
18:30 of Dan until the day of the captivity of the l. 776
19:30 came up out of the l of Egypt unto this day: 776
20: 1 with the l of Gilead, unto the LORD *in* 776
21:12 camp *to* Shiloh, which *is* in the l of Canaan. 776
21:21 of Shiloh, and go *to* the l of Benjamin. 776
Ru 1: 1 judges ruled, that there was a famine in the l. 776
1: 7 they went on the way to return unto the l of 776
2:11 the l of thy nativity, and art come unto a 776
4: 3 selleth a parcel of l, which *was* our brother 7704
1Sa 6: 5 and images of your mice that mar the l; 776
6: 5 and from off your gods, and from off your l. 776
9: 4 passed through the l of Shalisha, but 776
9: 4 then they passed through the l of Shalim, and 776
9: 4 he passed through the l of the Benjamites, 776
9: 5 *And* when they were come to the l of Zuph, 776
9:16 send thee a man out of the l of Benjamin, 776
12: 6 that brought your fathers up out of the l of 776
13: 3 Saul blew the trumpet throughout all the l, 776
13: 7 Hebrews went over Jordan *to* the l of Gad 776
13:17 that leadeth to Ophrah, unto the l of Shual: 776
13:19 no smith found throughout all the l of Israel: 776
14:14 within as it were a half acre of l, 7704
14:25 all *they of* the l came to a wood; and 776
14:29 said Jonathan, My father hath troubled the l: 776
21:11 unto him, *Is* not this David the king of the l? 776

1Sa 22: 5 depart, and get thee *into* the l of Judah. 776
23:23 it shall come to pass, if he be in the l, that I 776
23:27 come; for the Philistines have invaded the l. 776
27: 1 speedily escape into the l of the Philistines; 776
27: 8 the inhabitants of the l as thou goest to Shur, 776
27: 8 thou goest to Shur, even unto the l of Egypt. 776
27: 9 David smote the l, and left neither man nor 776
28: 3 familiar spirits, and the wizards, out of the l. 776
28: 9 familiar spirits, and the wizards, out of the l: 776
29:11 to return into the l of the Philistines. 776
30:16 they had taken out of the l of the Philistines, 776
30:16 of the Philistines, and out of the l of Judah. 776
31: 9 sent into the l of the Philistines round about, 776
2Sa 3:12 David on his behalf, saying, Whose *is* the l? 776
5: 6 unto the Jebusites, the inhabitants of the l: 776
7:23 do for you great things and terrible, for thy l, 776
9: 7 will restore thee all the l of Saul thy father; 7704
9:10 shall till the l for him, and thou shalt bring in 127
10: 2 David's servants came *into* the l of 776
15: 4 Oh that I were made judge in the l, 776
17:26 and Absalom pitched *in* the l of Gilead. 776
19: 9 and now he is fled out of the l for Absalom. 776
19:29 I have said, Thou and Ziba divide the l. 7704
21:14 And after that God was intreated for the l. 776
24: 6 to Gilead, and to the l of Tahtim-hodshi; 776
24: 8 So when they had gone through all the l, 776
24:13 years of famine come unto thee in thy l? 776
24:13 that there be three days' pestilence in thy l? 776
24:25 So the LORD was intreated for the l, and 776
1Ki 4:10 *pertained* Sochoh, and all the l of Hepher: 776
4:19 *he was* the only officer which *was* in the l. 776
4:21 from the river *unto* the l of the Philistines, 776
6: 1 of Israel were come out of the l of Egypt, 776
8: 9 when they came out of the l of Egypt. 776
8:21 when he brought them out of the l of Egypt. 776
8:34 bring them again unto the l which thou 127
8:36 give rain upon thy l, which thou hast given 776
8:37 If there be in the l famine, if there be 776
8:37 if their enemy besiege them in the l of their 776
8:40 in the l which thou gavest unto our fathers. 127
8:46 that they carry them away captives unto the l 776
8:47 *Yet* if they shall bethink themselves in the l 776
8:47 make supplication unto thee in the l of them 776
8:48 with all their soul, in the l of their enemies, 776
8:48 and pray unto thee toward their l, 776
9: 7 will I cut off Israel out of the l which I have 127
9: 8 Why hath the LORD done thus unto this l, 776
9: 9 who brought forth their fathers out of the l of 776
9:11 gave Hiram twenty cities in the l of Galilee. 776
9:13 he called them the l of Cabul unto this day. 776
9:18 and Tadmor in the wilderness, in the l, 776
9:19 in Lebanon, and in all the l of his dominion. 776
9:21 children that were left after them in the l, 776
9:26 on the shore of the Red sea, in the l of Edom. 776
10: 6 report that I heard in mine own l of thy acts 776
11:18 and appointed him victuals, and gave him l. 776
12:28 which brought thee up out of the l of Egypt. 776
14:15 and he shall root up Israel out of this good l, 127
14:24 there were also sodomites in the l: *and* 776
15:12 And he took away the sodomites out of the l, 776
15:20 and all Cinneroth, with all the l of Naphtali. 776
17: 7 because there had been no rain in the l. 776
18: 5 Go into the l, unto all fountains of water, and 776
18: 6 So they divided the l between them to pass 776
20: 7 king of Israel called all the elders of the l, 776
22:46 days of his father Asa, he took out of the l. 776
2Ki 2:21 be from thence any more death or barren *l*. NIH
3:19 and mar every good **piece of** l with stones. 2513
3:25 *on* every good **piece of** l cast every man his 2513
3:27 from him, and returned to *their own* l. 776
4:38 *there was* a dearth in the l; and the sons of 776
5: 2 had brought away captive out of the l of 776
5: 4 thus said the maid that *is* of the l of Israel. 776
6:23 of Syria came no more into the l of Israel. 776
8: 1 and it shall also come upon the l seven years. 776
8: 2 sojourned in the l of the Philistines seven 776
8: 3 that the woman returned out of the l of 776
8: 3 unto the king for her house and for her l. 7704
8: 5 cried to the king for her house and for her l. 7704
8: 6 of the field since the day that she left the l, 776
10:33 all the l of Gilead, the Gadites, and 776
11: 3 six years. And Athaliah *did* reign over the l. 776
11:14 all the people of the l rejoiced, and 776
11:18 all the people of the l went *into* the house of 776
11:19 and the guard, and all the people of the l; 776
11:20 all the people of the l rejoiced, and the city 776
13:20 the bands of the Moabites invaded the l *at* 776
15: 5 over the house, judging the people of the l. 776
15:19 Pul the king of Assyria came against the l: 776
15:20 turned back, and stayed not there in the l. 776
15:29 all the l of Naphtali, and carried them 776
16:15 the burnt offering of all the people of the l, 776
17: 5 king of Assyria came up throughout all the l, 776
17: 7 which had brought them up out of the l of 776
17:23 So was Israel carried away out of their own l 127
17:26 know not the manner of the God of the l: 776
17:26 know not the manner of the God of the l. 776
17:27 teach them the manner of the God of the l. 776
17:36 who brought you up out of the l of Egypt 776
18:25 to me, Go up against this l, and destroy it. 776
18:32 and take you away to a l like your own land, 776
18:32 and take you away to a land like your own l, 776
18:32 a l of corn and wine, a land of bread and 776
18:32 of corn and wine, a l of bread and vineyards, 776
18:32 and vineyards, a l of oil olive and of honey, 776
18:33 his l out of the hand of the king of Assyria? 776
19: 7 hear a rumour, and shall return to his own l; 776
19: 7 cause him to fall by the sword in his own l. 776
19:37 they escaped *into* the l of Armenia. 776
21: 8 more out of the l which I gave their fathers; 127
21:24 the people of the l slew all them that had 776
21:24 the people of the l made Josiah his son king 776
23:24 all the abominations that were spied in the l 776
23:30 the people of the l took Jehoahaz the son of 776
23:33 him in bands at Riblah in the l of Hamath, 776
23:33 put the l to a tribute of an hundred talents of 776
23:35 he taxed the l to give the money according to 776
23:35 the silver and the gold of the people of the l, 776
24: 7 Egypt came not again any more out of his l: 776
24:14 save the poorest sort of the people of the l. 776
24:15 and his officers, and the mighty of the l, 776
25: 3 there was no bread for the people of the l. 776
25:12 left of the poor of the l to be vinedressers 776
25:19 which mustered the people of the l, and 776
25:19 threescore men of the people of the l that 776
25:21 and slew them at Riblah in the l of Hamath. 776
25:21 So Judah was carried away out of their l. 127
25:22 *as for* the people that remained in the l of 776
25:24 dwell in the l, and serve the king of Babylon; 776
1Ch 1:43 Now these *are* the kings that reigned in the l 776
1:45 Husham of the l of the Temanites reigned in 776
2:22 had three and twenty cities in the l of Gilead. 776
4:40 and the l *was* wide, and quiet, and peaceable; 776
5: 9 their cattle were multiplied in the l of Gilead. 776
5:10 tents throughout all the east *l* of Gilead. NIH
5:11 in the l of Bashan unto Salchah: 776
5:23 of the half tribe of Manasseh dwelt in the l: 776
5:25 whoring after the gods of the people of the l, 776
6:55 they gave them Hebron in the l of Judah, 776
7:21 men of Gath that were born in *that* l slew, 776
10: 9 sent into the l of the Philistines round about, 776
11: 4 the Jebusites *were*, the inhabitants of the l. 776
13: 2 that are left in all the l of Israel, and 776
16:18 Unto thee will I give the l of Canaan, 776
19: 2 So the servants of David came into the l of 776
19: 3 and to overthrow, and to spy out the l? 776
21:12 in the l, and the angel of the LORD 776
22: 2 the strangers that *were* in the l of Israel; 776
22:18 for he hath given the inhabitants of the l into 776
22:18 and the l is subdued before the LORD, and 776
28: 8 that ye may possess *this* good l, and leave *it* 776
2Ch 2:17 all the strangers that *were* in the l of Israel, 776
6: 5 l of Egypt I chose no city among all 776
6:25 bring them again unto the l which thou 127
6:27 send rain upon thy l, which thou hast given 776
6:28 If there be dearth in the l, if there be 776
6:28 enemies besiege them in the cities of their l; 776
6:31 long as they live in the l which thou gavest 127
6:36 they carry them away captives unto a l far 776
6:37 *Yet* if they bethink themselves in the l 776
6:37 and pray unto thee in the l of their captivity, 776
6:38 with all their soul in the l of their captivity, 776
6:38 pray toward their l, which thou gavest unto 776
7:13 or if I command the locusts to devour the l, 776
7:14 will forgive their sin, and will heal their l. 776
7:20 will I pluck them up by the roots out of my l 127
7:21 Why hath the LORD done thus unto this l, 776
7:22 which brought them forth out of the l of 776

2Ch 8: 6 and throughout all the l of his dominion. 776
8: 8 who were left after them in the l, 776
8:17 and to Eloth, at the sea side in the l of Edom. 776
9: 5 which I heard in mine own l of thine acts, 776
9:11 there were none such seen before in the l of 776
9:12 went away to her own l, she and 776
9:26 the river even unto the l of the Philistines, 776
14: 1 In his days the l was quiet ten years. 776
14: 6 for the l had rest, and he had no war in those 776
14: 7 gates, and bars, *while* the l *is* yet before us; 776
15: 8 put away the abominable idols out of all the l 776
17: 2 set garrisons in the l of Judah, and in 776
19: 3 thou hast taken away the groves out of the l, 776
19: 5 he set judges in the l throughout all 776
20: 7 who didst drive out the inhabitants of this l 776
20:10 when they came out of the l of Egypt, but 776
22:12 six years: and Athaliah reigned over the l. 776
23:13 all the people of the l rejoiced, and 776
23:20 all the people of the l, and brought down 776
23:21 all the people of the l rejoiced: and the city 776
26:21 the king's house, judging the people of the l. 776
30: 9 so that *they shall* come again into this l: 776
30:25 the strangers that came out of the l of Israel, 776
32: 4 the brook that ran through the midst of the l, 776
32:21 he returned with shame of face to his own l. 776
32:31 inquire of the wonder that was *done* in the l, 776
33: 8 l which I have appointed for your fathers; 127
33:25 the people of the l slew all them that had 776
33:25 the people of the l made Josiah his son king 776
34: 7 cut down all the idols throughout all the l of 776
34: 8 when he had purged the l, and the house, 776
36: 1 the people of the l took Jehoahaz the son of 776
36: 3 condemned the l in an hundred talents of 776
36:21 until the l had enjoyed her sabbaths: 776
Ezr 4: 4 the people of the l weakened the hands of 776
6:21 from the filthiness of the heathen of the l, 776
9:11 saying, The l, *unto* which ye go to possess it, 776
9:11 *is* an unclean l with the filthiness of 776
9:12 eat the good of the l, and leave *it* for an 776
10: 2 taken strange wives of the people of the l: 776
10:11 separate yourselves from the people of the l, 776
Ne 4: 4 and give them for a prey in the l of captivity: 776
5:14 to be their governor in the l of Judah, 776
5:16 work of this wall, neither bought we *any* l: 7704
9: 8 madest a covenant with him to give the l of 776
9:10 all his servants, and on all the people of his l: 776
9:11 through the midst of the sea on the dry *l*; NIH
9:15 the l which thou hadst sworn to give them. 776
9:22 so they possessed the l of Sihon, and 776
9:22 the l of the king of Heshbon, and the land of 776
9:22 of Heshbon, and the l of Og king of Bashan. 776
9:23 broughtest them into the l, *concerning* which 776
9:24 So the children went in and possessed the l, 776
9:24 before them the inhabitants of the l, 776
9:24 with their kings, and the people of the l, 776
9:25 a fat l, and possessed houses full *of* all 127
9:35 and fat l which thou gavest before them, 776
9:36 *for* the l that thou gavest unto our fathers to 776
10:30 give our daughters unto the people of the l, 776
10:31 *if* the people of the l bring ware or 776
Est 8:17 many of the people of the l became Jews; 776
10: 1 the king Ahasuerus laid a tribute upon the l, 776
Job 1: 1 There was a man in the l of Uz, whose name 776
1:10 and his substance is increased in the l. 776
10:21 *even* to the l of darkness and the shadow of 776
10:22 A l of darkness, as darkness itself; *and of* 776
28:13 neither is it found in the l of the living. 776
31:38 If my l cry against me, or that the furrows 127
37:13 for correction, or for his l, or for mercy. 776
39: 6 and the barren *l* his dwellings. NIH
42:15 in all the l were no women found *so* fair as 776
Ps 10:16 ever: the heathen are perished out of his l. 776
27:13 of the LORD in the l of the living. 776
35:20 matters against *them that are* quiet in the l. 776
37: 3 *so* shalt thou dwell in the l, and verily thou 776
37:29 The righteous shall inherit the l, and 776
37:34 and he shall exalt thee to inherit the l: 776
42: 6 will I remember thee from the l of Jordan, 776
44: 3 For they got not the l in possession by their 776
52: 5 and root thee out of the l of the living. 776
63: 1 in a dry and thirsty l, where no water is; 776
66: 6 He turned the sea into dry *l*: they went NIH
68: 6 but the rebellious dwell *in* a dry *l*. NIH
74: 8 burnt up all the synagogues of God in the l. 776
78:12 in the l of Egypt, *in* the field of Zoan. 776
80: 9 cause it to take deep root, and it filled the l. 776
81: 5 when he went out through the l of Egypt: 776
81:10 which brought thee out of the l of Egypt: 776
85: 1 thou hast been favourable unto thy l: 776
85: 9 that fear him; that glory may dwell in our l. 776
85:12 *is* good; and our l shall yield her increase. 776
88:12 thy righteousness in the l of forgetfulness? 776
95: 5 he made it: and his hands formed the dry *l*. NIH
101: 6 Mine eyes *shall be* upon the faithful of the l, 776
101: 8 I will early destroy all the wicked of the l; 776
105:11 Unto thee will I give the l of Canaan, 776
105:16 Moreover, he called *for* a famine upon the l: 776
105:23 and Jacob sojourned in the l of Ham. 776
105:27 among them, and wonders in the l of Ham. 776
105:30 Their l brought forth frogs in abundance, 776
105:32 them hail *for* rain, *and* flaming fire in their l. 776
105:35 did eat up all the herbs in their l, and 776
105:36 He smote also all the firstborn in their l, 776
106:22 Wondrous works in the l of Ham, *and* 776
106:24 Yea, they despised the pleasant l, 776
106:38 and the l was polluted with blood. 776
107:34 A fruitful l into barrenness, for 776
116: 9 I will walk before the LORD in the l of 776
135:12 gave their l *for* an heritage, an heritage unto 776
136:21 gave their l for an heritage: for his mercy 776
137: 4 we sing the LORD'S song in a strange l? 127
142: 5 *and* my portion in the l of the living. 776
143: 6 my soul *thirsteth* after thee, as a thirsty l. 776
143:10 *is* good; lead me into the l of uprightness. 776
Pr 2:21 For the upright shall dwell *in* the l, and 776
12:11 He that tilleth his l shall be satisfied *with* 127
28: 2 For the transgression of a l many *are* 776
28:19 He that tilleth his l shall have plenty *of* 127
29: 4 The king by judgment stablisheth the l: but 776
31:23 when he sitteth among the elders of the l. 776
Ecc 10:16 Woe to thee, O l, when thy king *is* a child, 776
10:17 Blessed *art* thou, O l, when thy king *is* 776
SS 2:12 and the voice of the turtle is heard in our l; 776
Isa 1: 7 your l, strangers devour it in your presence, 127
1:19 and obedient, ye shall eat the good of the l: 776
2: 7 Their l also is full *of* silver and gold, 776
2: 7 their l is also full *of* horses, neither *is there* 776
2: 8 Their l also is full *of* idols; they worship 776
5:30 if *one* look unto the l, behold darkness *and* 776
6:11 without man, and the l be utterly desolate, 127
6:12 *be* a great forsaking in the midst of the l. 776
7:16 the l that thou abhorrest shall be forsaken of 127
7:18 and for the bee that *is* in the l of Assyria. 776
7:22 honey shall every *one* eat that is left in the l. 776
7:24 all the l shall become briers and thorns. 776
8: 8 out of his wings shall fill the breadth of thy l, 776
9: 1 when at the first he lightly afflicted the l of 776
9: 1 the land of Zebulun and the l of Naphtali, 776
9: 2 they that dwell in the l of the shadow of 776
9:19 of the LORD of hosts is the l darkened, 776
10:23 even determined, *in* the midst of all *the l*. NIH
11:16 the day that he came up out of the l of Egypt. 776
13: 5 of his indignation, to destroy the whole l. 776
13: 9 and fierce anger, to lay the l desolate: 776
13:14 and flee every one into his own l. 776
14: 1 choose Israel, and set them in their own l: 127
14: 2 the house of Israel shall possess them in the l 127
14:20 because thou hast destroyed thy l, *and* 776
14:21 *that* they do not rise, nor possess the l, 776
14:25 That *I* will break the Assyrian in my l, and 776
15: 9 of Moab, and upon the remnant of the l. 127
16: 1 Send ye the lamb *to* the ruler of the l from 776
16: 4 the oppressors are consumed out of the l. 776
18: 1 Woe to the l shadowing with wings, which *is* 776
18: 2 whose l the rivers have spoiled. 776
18: 7 under foot, whose l the rivers have spoiled, 776
19:17 the l of Judah shall be a terror unto Egypt, 127
19:18 In that day shall five cities in the l of Egypt 776
19:19 to the LORD in the midst of the l of Egypt, 776
19:20 unto the LORD of hosts in the l of Egypt: 776
19:24 *even* a blessing in the midst of the l: 776
21: 1 it cometh from the desert, from a terrible l. 776
21:14 The inhabitants of the l of Tema brought 776
23: 1 from the l of Chittim it is revealed to them. 776
23:10 Pass through thy l as a river, O daughter of 776
23:13 Behold the l of the Chaldeans; this people 776
24: 3 The l shall be utterly emptied, and 776
24:11 all joy is darkened, the mirth of the l is gone. 776

L

Isa 24:13 When thus it shall be in the midst of the l 776
26: 1 In that day shall this song be sung in the l of 776
26:10 in the l of uprightness will he deal unjustly, 776
27:13 were ready to perish in the l of Assyria, 776
27:13 the outcasts in the l of Egypt, and 776
30: 6 into the l of trouble and anguish, 776
32: 2 as the shadow of a great rock in a weary l. 776
32:13 Upon the l of my people shall come up 127
33:17 they shall behold the l that is very far off. 776
34: 6 and a great slaughter in the l of Idumea. 776
34: 7 their l shall be soaked with blood, and 776
34: 9 and the l thereof shall become burning pitch. 776
35: 7 a pool, and the **thirsty** l springs of water: 6774
36:10 the LORD against this l to destroy it? 776
36:10 unto me, Go up against this l, and destroy it. 776
36:17 and take you away to a l like your own land, 776
36:17 and take you away to a land like your own l, 776
36:17 a l of corn and wine, a land of bread and 776
36:17 of corn and wine, a l of bread and vineyards. 776
36:18 his l out of the hand of the king of Assyria? 776
36:20 that have delivered their l out of my hand, 776
37: 7 shall hear a rumour, and return to his own l; 776
37: 7 cause him to fall by the sword in his own l. 776
37:38 and they escaped *into* the l of Armenia: 776
38:11 *even* the LORD, in the l of the living: 776
41:18 pool of water, and the dry l springs of water. 776
49:12 from the west; and these from the l of Sinim. 776
49:19 desolate places, and the l of thy destruction, 776
53: 8 for he was cut off out of the l of the living: 776
57:13 putteth his trust in me shall possess the l, 776
60:18 Violence shall no more be heard in thy l, 776
60:21 they shall inherit the l for ever, the branch of 776
61: 7 in their l they shall possess the double: 776
62: 4 neither shall thy l any more be termed 776
62: 4 shalt be called Hephzi-bah, and thy l Beulah: 776
62: 4 delighteth in thee, and thy l shall be married. 776
Jer 1: 1 of the priests that *were* in Anathoth in the l 776
1:14 break forth upon all the inhabitants of the l. 776
1:18 and brasen walls against the whole l, 776
1:18 and against the people of the l. 776
2: 2 in the wilderness, in a l *that was* not sown. 776
2: 6 that brought us up out of the l of Egypt, 776
2: 6 through a l of deserts and of pits, through a 776
2: 6 through a l of drought, and of the shadow of 776
2: 6 through a l that no man passed through, and 776
2: 7 ye defiled my l, and made mine heritage an 776
2:15 *and* yelled, and they made his l waste: 776
2:31 a l of darkness? wherefore say my people, 776
3: 1 shall not that l be greatly polluted? but 776
3: 2 thou hast polluted the l with thy whoredoms 776
3: 9 that she defiled the l, and 776
3:16 when ye be multiplied and increased in the l, 776
3:18 they shall come together out of the l of 776
3:18 l that I have given for an inheritance unto 776
3:19 the children, and give thee a pleasant l, 776
4: 5 and say, Blow ye the trumpet in the l: 776
4: 7 he is gone forth from his place to make thy l 776
4:20 is cried; for the whole l is spoiled: 776
4:27 LORD said, The whole l shall be desolate; 776
5:19 served strange gods in your l, so shall ye 776
5:19 shall ye serve strangers in a l *that is* not 776
5:30 and horrible thing is committed in the l; 776
6: 8 lest I make thee desolate, a l not inhabited. 776
6:12 out my hand upon the inhabitants of the l, 776
7: 7 in the l that I gave to your fathers, for ever 776
7:22 day that I brought them out of the l of Egypt, 776
7:25 forth out of the l of Egypt unto this day, 776
7:34 voice of the bride: for the l shall be desolate. 776
8:16 the whole l trembled at the sound of 776
8:16 and have devoured the l, and all that is in it; 776
9:12 for what the l perisheth *and* is burnt up like a 776
9:19 because we have forsaken the l, because 776
10:17 Gather up thy wares out of the l, 776
10:18 I will sling out the inhabitants of the l at this 776
11: 4 I brought them forth out of the l of Egypt, 776
11: 5 to give them a l flowing with milk and 776
11: 7 that I brought them up out of the l of Egypt, 776
11:19 let us cut him off from the l of the living, 776
12: 4 How long shall the l mourn, and the herbs of 776
12: 5 *if* in the l of peace, *wherein* thou trustedst, 776
12:11 the whole l is made desolate, because 776
12:12 end of the l even to the *other* end of the land: 776
12:12 end of the land even to the *other* end of the l: 776
12:14 I will pluck them out of their l, and pluck out 127
12:15 man to his heritage, and every man to his l. 776
13:13 Behold, I *will* fill all the inhabitants of this l, 776
14: 8 why shouldest thou be as a stranger in the l, 776
14:15 Sword and famine shall not be in this l; 776
14:18 the priest go about into a l that they know 776
15: 7 will fan them with a fan in the gates of the l; 776
15:14 enemies into a l *which* thou knowest not: 776
16: 3 their fathers that begat them in this l; 776
16: 6 the great and the small shall die in this l: 776
16:13 Therefore will I cast you out of this l into a 776
16:13 you out of this land into a l that ye know not, 776
16:14 the children of Israel out of the l of Egypt; 776
16:15 the children of Israel from the l of the north, 776
16:15 I will bring them again into their l that I gave 127
16:18 because they have defiled my l, they have 776
17: 4 enemies in the l which thou knowest not: 776
17: 6 the wilderness, *in* a salt l and not inhabited. 776
17:26 from the l of Benjamin, and from the plain, 776
18:16 To make their l desolate, *and* a perpetual 776
22:12 led him captive, and shall see this l no more. 776
22:27 to the l whereunto they desire to return, 776
22:28 and are cast into a l which they know not? 776
23: 7 the children of Israel out of the l of Egypt; 776
23: 8 and they shall dwell in their own l. 127
23:10 For the l is full *of* adulterers; for because 776
23:10 for because of swearing the l mourneth; 776
23:15 is profaneness gone forth into all the l. 776
24: 5 whom I have sent out of this place *into* the l 776
24: 6 and I will bring them again to this l: 776
24: 8 that remain in this l, and them that dwell in 776
24: 8 and them that dwell in the l of Egypt: 776
24:10 till they be consumed from off the l that I 127
25: 5 dwell in the l that the LORD hath given 127
25: 9 will bring them against this l, and against 776
25:11 this whole l shall be a desolation, *and* 776
25:12 the l of the Chaldeans, and will make it 776
25:13 I will bring upon that l all my words which I 776
25:20 all the kings of the l of Uz, and all the kings 776
25:20 all the kings of the l of the Philistines, and 776
25:38 for their l is desolate because of 776
26:17 rose up certain of the elders of the l, and 776
26:20 against this l according to all the words of 776
27: 7 son's son, until the very time of his l come: 776
27:10 lie unto you, to remove you far from your l; 127
27:11 those will I let remain still in their own l, 127
30: 3 I will cause them to return to the l that I gave 776
30:10 and thy seed from the l of their captivity; 776
31:16 they shall come again from the l of 776
31:23 As yet they shall use this speech in the l of 776
31:32 the hand, to bring them out of the l of Egypt; 776
32:15 vineyards shall be possessed again in this l. 776
32:20 hast set signs and wonders in the l of Egypt, 776
32:21 people Israel out of the l of Egypt with signs, 776
32:22 hast given them this l, which thou didst 776
32:22 give them, a l flowing with milk and honey; 776
32:41 I will plant them in this l assuredly with my 776
32:43 fields shall be bought in this l, whereof ye 776
32:44 and take witnesses in the l of Benjamin, 776
33:11 to return the captivity of the l as at the first, 776
33:13 in the l of Benjamin, and in the places about 776
33:15 execute judgment and righteousness in the l. 776
34:13 I brought them forth out of the l of Egypt, 776
34:19 and the priests, and all the people of the l, 776
35: 7 that ye may live many days in the l where ye 127
35:11 king of Babylon came up into the l, 776
35:15 ye shall dwell in the l which I have given to 127
36:29 shall certainly come and destroy this l, 776
37: 1 king of Babylon made king in the l of Judah. 776
37: 2 nor his servants, nor the people of the l, 776
37: 7 shall return *to* Egypt into their own l. 776
37:12 of Jerusalem to go *into* the l of Benjamin, 776
37:19 not come against you, nor against this l? 776
39: 5 of Babylon to Riblah in the l of Hamath, 776
39:10 in the l of Judah, and gave them vineyards 776
40: 4 behold, all the l *is* before thee: whither it 776
40: 6 him among the people that were left in the l. 776
40: 7 the son of Ahikam governor in the l, 776
40: 7 and children, and of the poor of the l, 776
40: 9 dwell in the l and serve the king of Babylon, 776
40:12 came *to* the l of Judah, to Gedaliah, unto 776
41: 2 of Babylon had made governor over the l. 776
41:18 the king of Babylon made governor in the l. 776
42:10 If ye will still abide in this l, then will I build 776
42:12 and cause you to return to your own l. 127

Jer	42:13	if ye say, We will not dwell in this l, neither	776
	42:14	we will go *into* the l of Egypt, where we	776
	42:16	shall overtake you there in the l of Egypt,	776
	43: 4	of the LORD, to dwell in the l of Judah.	776
	43: 5	had been driven, to dwell in the l of Judah:	776
	43: 7	So they came *into* the l of Egypt: for they	776
	43:11	he shall smite the l of Egypt, *and*	776
	43:12	he shall array himself with the l of Egypt,	776
	43:13	of Beth-shemesh, that *is* in the l of Egypt;	776
	44: 1	all the Jews which dwell in the l of Egypt,	776
	44: 8	burning incense unto other gods in the l of	776
	44: 9	which they have committed in the l of Judah,	776
	44:12	that have set their faces to go *into* the l of	776
	44:12	all be consumed, *and* fall in the l of Egypt;	776
	44:13	For I will punish them that dwell in the l of	776
	44:14	which are gone into the l of Egypt to sojourn	776
	44:14	that *they* should return *into* the l of Judah,	776
	44:15	even all the people that dwelt in the l of	776
	44:21	and your princes, and the people of the l,	776
	44:22	therefore is your l a desolation, and an	776
	44:24	all Judah that *are* in the l of Egypt:	776
	44:26	all Judah that dwell in the l of Egypt;	776
	44:26	of any man of Judah in all the l of Egypt,	776
	44:27	all the men of Judah that *are* in the l of Egypt	776
	44:28	out of the l of Egypt *into* the land of Judah,	776
	44:28	out of the land of Egypt *into* the l of Judah,	776
	44:28	that are gone into the l of Egypt to sojourn	776
	45: 4	planted I *will* pluck up, even this whole l.	776
	46:12	*of* thy shame, and thy cry hath filled the l:	776
	46:13	should come and smite the l of Egypt.	776
	46:16	to the l of our nativity, from the oppressing	776
	46:27	and thy seed from the l of their captivity;	776
	47: 2	shall overflow the l, and all that is therein;	776
	47: 2	and all the inhabitants of the l shall howl.	776
	48:24	upon all the cities of the l of Moab, far or	776
	48:33	the plentiful field, and from the l of Moab;	776
	50: 1	against the l of the Chaldeans by Jeremiah	776
	50: 3	which shall make her l desolate, and	776
	50: 8	go forth out of the l of the Chaldeans, and	776
	50:12	*shall be* a wilderness, a **dry** l, and a desert.	6723
	50:16	and they shall flee every one to his own l.	776
	50:18	I *will* punish the king of Babylon and his l,	776
	50:21	Go up against the l of Merethaim,	776
	50:22	A sound of battle *is* in the l, and of great	776
	50:25	GOD of hosts in the l of the Chaldeans.	776
	50:28	that flee and escape out of the l of Babylon,	776
	50:34	that he may give rest to the l, and	776
	50:38	for it *is* the l of graven images, and they are	776
	50:45	that he hath purposed against the l of	776
	51: 2	that shall fan her, and shall empty her l:	776
	51: 4	Thus the slain shall fall in the l of	776
	51: 5	though their l was filled *with* sin against	776
	51:27	Set ye up a standard in the l, blow	776
	51:28	rulers thereof, and all the l of his dominion.	776
	51:29	the l shall tremble and sorrow: for every	776
	51:29	to make the l of Babylon a desolation	776
	51:43	are a desolation, a dry l, and a wilderness,	776
	51:43	a wilderness, a l wherein no man dwelleth,	776
	51:46	for the rumour that shall be heard in the l;	776
	51:46	and violence in the l, ruler against ruler.	776
	51:47	her whole l shall be confounded, and all her	776
	51:52	through all her l the wounded shall groan.	776
	51:54	great destruction from the l of	776
	52: 6	there was no bread for the people of the l.	776
	52: 9	of Babylon to Riblah in the l of Hamath;	776
	52:16	*certain* of the poor of the l for vinedressers	776
	52:25	the host, who mustered the people of the l;	776
	52:25	threescore men of the people of the l,	776
	52:27	put them to death in Riblah in the l of	776
	52:27	was carried away captive out of his own l.	127
La	4:21	of Edom, that dwellest in the l of Uz;	776
Eze	1: 3	in the l of the Chaldeans by the river Chebar;	776
	6:14	upon them, and make the l desolate, yea,	776
	7: 2	thus saith the Lord GOD unto the l of	127
	7: 2	end is come upon the four corners of the l.	776
	7: 7	come unto thee, O thou that dwellest in the l:	776
	7:23	for the l is full *of* bloody crimes, and the city	776
	7:27	the hands of the people of the l shall be	776
	8:17	for they have filled the l *with* violence, and	776
	9: 9	the l is full *of* blood, and the city full *of*	776
	11:15	unto us is this l given in possession.	776
	11:17	and I will give you the l of Israel.	127
	12:13	I will bring him to Babylon *to* the l of	776
	12:19	say unto the people of the l, Thus saith	776
	12:19	of Jerusalem, *and* of the l of Israel;	127
	12:19	that her l may be desolate from all that is	776
	12:20	be laid waste, and the l shall be desolate;	776
	12:22	what *is* that proverb *that* ye have in the l of	127
	13: 9	neither shall they enter into the l of Israel;	127
	14:13	when the l sinneth against me by trespassing	776
	14:15	I cause noisome beasts to pass through the l,	776
	14:16	shall be delivered, but the l shall be desolate.	776
	14:17	Or *if* I bring a sword upon that l, and say,	776
	14:17	that land, and say, Sword, go through the l;	776
	14:19	Or *if* I send a pestilence into that l, and	776
	15: 8	I will make the l desolate, because they have	776
	16: 3	and thy nativity *is* of the l of Canaan;	776
	16:29	fornication in the l of Canaan unto Chaldea;	776
	17: 4	and carried it into a l of traffick;	776
	17: 5	He took also of the seed of the l, and	776
	17:13	he hath also taken the mighty of the l:	776
	18: 2	that ye use this proverb concerning the l of	127
	19: 4	they brought him with chains unto the l of	776
	19: 7	the l was desolate, and the fulness thereof,	776
	20: 5	made myself known unto them in the l of	776
	20: 6	to bring them forth of the l of Egypt into a	776
	20: 6	of Egypt into a l that I had espied for them,	776
	20: 8	against them in the midst of the l of Egypt.	776
	20: 9	in bringing them forth out of the l of Egypt.	776
	20:10	caused them to go forth out of the l of Egypt,	776
	20:15	that *I* would not bring them into the l which I	776
	20:28	*For* when I had brought them into the l,	776
	20:36	fathers in the wilderness of the l of Egypt,	776
	20:38	and they shall not enter into the l of Israel:	127
	20:40	of Israel, all of them in the l, serve me:	776
	20:42	when I shall bring you into the l of Israel,	127
	21: 2	and prophesy against the l of Israel,	127
	21: 3	say to the l of Israel, Thus saith the LORD;	127
	21:19	both twain shall come forth out of one l: and	776
	21:30	thou wast created, in the l of thy nativity.	776
	21:32	thy blood shall be in the midst of the l;	776
	22:24	unto her, Thou *art* the l that is not cleansed,	776
	22:29	The people of the l have used oppression,	776
	22:30	stand in the gap before me for the l, that *I*	776
	23:15	of Chaldea, the l of their nativity:	776
	23:19	wherein she had played the harlot in the l of	776
	23:27	thy whoredom *brought* from the l of Egypt:	776
	23:48	will I cause lewdness to cease out of the l,	776
	25: 3	against the l of Israel, when it was desolate;	127
	25: 6	with all thy despite against the l of Israel;	127
	26:20	and I shall set glory in the l of the living;	776
	27:17	Judah, and the l of Israel, they *were* thy	776
	27:29	from their ships, they shall stand upon the l;	776
	28:25	shall they dwell in their l that I have given to	127
	29: 9	the l of Egypt shall be desolate and waste;	776
	29:10	I will make the l of Egypt utterly waste *and*	776
	29:12	I will make the l of Egypt desolate in	776
	29:14	will cause them to return *into* the l of	776
	29:14	land of Pathros, into the l of their habitation;	776
	29:19	I *will* give the l of Egypt unto	776
	29:20	I have given him the l of Egypt *for* his	776
	30: 5	Chub, and the men of the l that is in league,	776
	30:11	the nations, *shall be* brought to destroy the l:	776
	30:11	against Egypt, and fill the l *with* the slain.	776
	30:12	and sell the l into the hand of the wicked:	776
	30:12	I will make the l waste, and all that is	776
	30:13	there shall be no more a prince of the l of	776
	30:13	and I will put a fear in the l of Egypt.	776
	30:25	he shall stretch it out upon the l of Egypt.	776
	31:12	boughs are broken by all the rivers of the l;	776
	32: 4	will I leave thee upon the l, I will cast thee	776
	32: 6	I will also water with thy blood the l wherein	776
	32: 8	set darkness upon thy l, saith the Lord	776
	32:15	When I shall make the l of Egypt desolate,	776
	32:23	which caused terror in the l of the living.	776
	32:24	which caused their terror in the l of	776
	32:25	though their terror was caused in the l of	776
	32:26	though they caused their terror in the l of	776
	32:27	the terror of the mighty in the l of the living.	776
	32:32	For I have caused my terror in the l of	776
	33: 2	unto them, When I bring the sword upon a l,	776
	33: 2	if the people of the l take a man of their	776
	33: 3	*If* when he seeth the sword come upon the l,	776
	33:24	they that inhabit those wastes of the l of	127
	33:24	Abraham was one, and he inherited the l:	776
	33:24	*are* many; the l is given us for inheritance.	776
	33:25	and shed blood: and shall ye possess the l?	776
	33:26	neighbour's wife: and shall ye possess the l?	776

Eze 33:28 For I will lay the l most desolate, and 776
33:29 when I have laid the l most desolate because 776
34:13 will bring them to their own l, and feed them 127
34:25 cause the evil beasts to cease out of the l: 776
34:27 they shall be safe in their l, and shall know 127
34:28 neither shall the beast of the l devour them; 776
34:29 be no more consumed with hunger in the l, 776
36: 5 which have appointed my l into their 776
36: 6 Prophesy therefore concerning the l of Israel, 127
36:13 Thou *l* devourest up men, and hast bereaved NIH
36:17 the house of Israel dwelt in their own l, 127
36:18 for the blood that they had shed upon the l, 776
36:20 the LORD, and are gone forth out of his l. 776
36:24 and will bring you into your own l. 127
36:28 ye shall dwell in the l that I gave to your 776
36:34 the desolate l shall be tilled, whereas it lay 776
36:35 This l that was desolate is become like 776
37:12 and bring you into the l of Israel. 127
37:14 and I shall place you in your own l: 127
37:21 every side, and bring them into their own l: 127
37:22 I will make them one nation in the l upon 776
37:25 they shall dwell in the l that I have given 776
38: 2 set thy face against Gog, the l of Magog, 776
38: 8 in the latter years thou shalt come into the l 776
38: 9 thou shalt be like a cloud to cover the l, thou, 776
38:11 I will go up to the l of unwalled villages; 776
38:12 and goods, that dwell in the midst of the l. 776
38:16 my people of Israel, as a cloud to cover the l; 776
38:16 and I will bring thee against my l, 776
38:18 when Gog shall come against the l of Israel, 127
38:19 shall be a great shaking in the l of Israel; 127
39:12 burying of them, that *they* may cleanse the l. 776
39:13 all the people of the l shall bury *them;* and 776
39:14 passing through the l to bury with 776
39:15 the passengers *that* pass through the l, 776
39:16 *be* Hamonah. Thus shall they cleanse the l. 776
39:26 when they dwelt safely in their l, and 127
39:28 I have gathered them unto their own l, and 127
40: 2 of God brought he me into the l of Israel, 776
45: 1 when ye shall divide *by lot* the l for 776
45: 1 unto the LORD, a holy *portion* of the l: 776
45: 4 The holy *portion* of the l shall be for 776
45: 8 In the l shall be his possession in Israel: and 776
45: 8 *the rest of* the l shall they give to the house 776
45:16 All the people of the l shall give this oblation 776
45:22 for all the people of the l a bullock *for* a sin 776
46: 3 Likewise the people of the l shall worship *at* 776
46: 9 when the people of the l shall come before 776
47:13 whereby ye shall inherit the l according to 776
47:14 and this l shall fall unto you for inheritance. 776
47:15 this *shall be* the border of the l toward 776
47:18 and from the l of Israel *by* Jordan, 776
47:21 So shall ye divide this l unto you according 776
48:12 *this* oblation of the l that is offered shall be 776
48:14 nor alienate the firstfruits of the l: 776
48:29 This *is* the l which ye shall divide *by lot* unto 776
Da 1: 2 which he carried *into* the l of Shinar *to* 776
8: 9 toward the east, and toward the pleasant *l.* NIH
9: 6 and our fathers, and to all the people of the l. 776
9:15 that hast brought thy people forth out of the l 776
11: 9 *his* kingdom, and shall return into his own l. 127
11:16 he shall stand in the glorious l, which by his 776
11:19 turn his face towards the fort of his own l: 776
11:28 shall he return *into* his l with great riches; 776
11:28 he shall do *exploits,* and return to his own l. 776
11:39 over many, and shall divide the l for gain. 127
11:41 He shall enter also into the glorious l, and 776
11:42 and the l of Egypt shall not escape. 776
Hos 1: 2 for the l hath committed great whoredom, 776
1:11 and they shall come up out of the l: 776
2: 3 set her like a dry l, and slay her with thirst. 776
2:15 as *in* the day when she came up out of the l 776
4: 1 a controversy with the inhabitants of the l, 776
4: 1 nor mercy, nor knowledge of God in the l. 776
4: 3 Therefore shall the l mourn, and every one 776
7:16 this *shall be* their derision in the l of Egypt. 776
9: 3 They shall not dwell in the LORD'S l; but 776
10: 1 according to the goodness of his l they have 776
11: 5 He shall not return into the l of Egypt, but 776
11:11 and as a dove out of the l of Assyria: 776
12: 9 I *that am* the LORD thy God from the l of 776
13: 4 Yet I *am* the LORD thy God from the l of 776
13: 5 in the wilderness, in the l of great drought. 776
Joel 1: 2 and give ear, all ye inhabitants of the l. 776
1: 6 For a nation is come up upon my l, strong, 776
1:10 The field is wasted, the l mourneth; for 127
1:14 all the inhabitants of the l *into* the house of 776
2: 1 let all the inhabitants of the l tremble: for 776
2: 3 the l *is* as the garden of Eden before them, 776
2:18 will the LORD be jealous for his l, and 776
2:20 will drive him into a l barren and desolate, 776
2:21 Fear not, O l; be glad and rejoice: for 127
3: 2 among the nations, and parted my l. 776
3:19 they have shed innocent blood in their l. 776
Am 2:10 Also I brought you up from the l of Egypt, 776
2:10 to possess the l of the Amorite. 776
3: 1 which I brought up from the l of Egypt, 776
3: 9 and in the palaces in the l of Egypt, and say, 776
3:11 *there shall be* even round about the l; 776
5: 2 she is forsaken upon her l; *there is* none to 127
7: 2 had made an end of eating the grass of the l, 776
7:10 the l is not able to bear all his words. 776
7:11 surely be led away captive out of their own l. 127
7:12 go, flee thee away into the l of Judah, and 776
7:17 the sword, and thy l shall be divided by line; 127
7:17 by line; and thou shalt die in a polluted l: 127
7:17 shall surely go into captivity forth of his l. 127
8: 4 even to make the poor of the l to fail, 776
8: 8 Shall not the l tremble for this, and 776
8:11 that I will send a famine in the l, 776
9: 5 Lord GOD of hosts *is* he that toucheth the l, 776
9: 7 Have not I brought up Israel out of the l of 776
9:15 I will plant them upon their l, and they shall 127
9:15 they shall no more be pulled up out of their l 127
Jnh 1: 9 which hath made the sea and the dry *l.* NIH
1:13 the men rowed hard to bring *it* to the l; 3004
2:10 and it vomited out Jonah upon the dry *l.* NIH
Mic 5: 5 when the Assyrian shall come into our l: 776
5: 6 they shall waste the l of Assyria with 776
5: 6 and the l of Nimrod in the entrances thereof: 776
5: 6 when he cometh into our l, and when he 776
5:11 I will cut off the cities of thy l, and 776
6: 4 For I brought thee up out of the l of Egypt, 776
7:13 Notwithstanding the l shall be desolate 776
7:15 l of Egypt will I shew unto him marvellous 776
Na 3:13 the gates of thy l shall be set wide open unto 776
Hab 1: 6 *shall* march through the breadth of the l, 776
2: 8 and *for* the violence of the l, *of* the city, and 776
2:17 and *for* the violence of the l, *of* the city, and 776
3: 7 the curtains of the l of Midian did tremble. 776
3:12 Thou didst march through the l in 776
Zep 1: 2 will utterly consume all *things* from off the l, 127
1: 3 I will cut off man from off the l, saith 127
1:18 the whole l shall be devoured by the fire of 776
1:18 riddance of all them that dwell in the l. 776
2: 5 O Canaan, the l of the Philistines, I will even 776
3:19 fame in every l where they have been put to 776
Hag 1:11 I called *for* a drought upon the l, and 776
2: 4 be strong, all ye people of the l, saith 776
2: 6 and the earth, and the sea, and the dry *l;* NIH
Zec 1:21 which lift up *their* horn over the l of Judah to 776
2: 6 *come forth,* and flee from the l of the north, 776
2:12 shall inherit Judah his portion in the holy l, 127
3: 9 I will remove the iniquity of that l in one 776
5:11 To build it a house in the l of Shinar: 776
7: 5 Speak unto all the people of the l, and to 776
7:14 thus the l was desolate after them, that no 776
7:14 for they laid the pleasant l desolate. 776
9: 1 the word of the LORD in the l of Hadrach, 776
9:16 of a crown, lifted up as an ensign upon his l. 127
10:10 I will bring them again also out of the l of 776
10:10 and I will bring them into the l of Gilead and 776
11: 6 I will no more pity the inhabitants of the l, 776
11: 6 they shall smite the l, and out of their hand I 776
11:16 For lo, I *will* raise up a shepherd in the l, 776
12:12 the l shall mourn, every family apart; 776
13: 2 cut off the names of the idols out of the l, 776
13: 2 and the unclean spirit to pass out of the l. 776
13: 8 to pass, *that* in all the l, saith the LORD, 776
14:10 All the l shall be turned as a plain from Geba 776
Mal 3:12 for ye shall be a delightsome l, saith 776
Mt 2: 6 And thou Bethlehem, *in* the l of Juda, art *1093*
2:20 and his mother, and go into the l of Israel: *1093*
2:21 his mother, and came into the l of Israel. *1093*
4:15 The l of Zabulon, and the land of *1093*
4:15 land of Zabulon, and the l of Nephthalim, *1093*
9:26 the fame hereof went abroad into all that l. *1093*
10:15 It shall be more tolerable for the l of Sodom *1093*

Mt 11:24 that it shall be more tolerable for the l of *1093*
14:34 they came into the l of Gennesaret. *1093*
23:15 compass sea and l to make one proselyte, *3584*
27:45 darkness over all the l unto the ninth hour. *1093*
Mk 1: 5 And there went out unto him all the l of *5561*
4: 1 the whole multitude was by the sea on the l. *1093*
6:47 the midst of the sea, and he alone on the l. *1093*
6:53 they came into the l of Genesaret, and *1093*
15:33 there was darkness over the whole l until *1093*
Lk 4:25 when great famine was throughout all the l; *1093*
5: 3 that *he* would thrust out a little from the l. *1093*
5:11 And when they had brought *their* ships to l, *1093*
8:27 And when he went forth to l, there met him *1093*
14:35 It is neither fit for the l, nor yet for *1093*
15:14 there arose a mighty famine in that l; *5561*
21:23 for there shall be great distress in the l, and *1093*
Jn 3:22 and his disciples into the l of Judea; *1093*
6:21 immediately the ship was at the l whither *1093*
21: 8 (for they were not far from l, but as it were *1093*
21: 9 As soon then as they were come to l, *1093*
21:11 and drew the net to l full of great fishes, *1093*
Ac 4:37 Having l, sold *it,* and brought the money, and *68*
5: 3 and to keep back *part* of the price of the l? *5564*
5: 8 Tell me whether ye sold the l for so much? *5564*
7: 3 and come into the l which I shall shew thee. *1093*
7: 4 Then came he out of the l of the Chaldeans, *1093*
7: 4 he removed him into this l, wherein ye now *1093*
7: 6 That his seed should sojourn in a strange l; *1093*
7:11 Now there came a dearth over all the l of *1093*
7:29 and was a stranger in the l of Madian, *1093*
7:36 and signs in the l of Egypt, *1093*
7:40 which brought us out of the l of Egypt, *1093*
10:39 which he did both in the l of the Jews, *5561*
13:17 *they* dwelt as strangers in the l of Egypt, *1093*
13:19 destroyed seven nations in the l of Canaan, *1093*
13:19 of Canaan, he divided their l to them by lot. *1093*
27:39 And when it was day, they knew not the l: *1093*
27:43 *themselves* first into *the sea,* and get to l: *1093*
27:44 came to pass, that *they* escaped all safe to l. *1093*
Heb 8: 9 the hand to lead them out of the l of Egypt; *1093*
11: 9 By faith he sojourned in the l of promise, *1093*
11:29 *l*: which the Egyptians assaying to do were NIG
Jude 1: 5 having saved the people out of the l of *1093*

LANDED (2) [LAND]
Ac 18:22 And when he had l at Cesarea, and gone up, *2718*
21: 3 and sailed into Syria, and l at Tyre: *2609*

LANDING (1) [LAND]
Ac 28:12 And l at Syracuse, we tarried *there* three *2609*

LANDMARK (4) [LAND, MARK]
Dt 19:14 Thou shalt not remove thy neighbour's l, 1366
27:17 *be* he that removeth his neighbour's l. 1366
Pr 22:28 Remove not the ancient l, which thy fathers 1366
23:10 Remove not the old l; and enter not into 1366

LANDMARKS (1) [LAND, MARK]
Job 24: 2 *Some* remove the l; they violently take 1367

LANDOWNER See GOODMAN

LANDS (46) [LAND]
Ge 10: 5 the isles of the Gentiles divided in their l; 776
10:31 their tongues, in their l, after their nations. 776
41:54 the dearth was in all l; but in all the land of 776
41:57 because that the famine was *so* sore in all l. 776
47:18 sight of my lord, but our bodies, and our l: 127
47:22 gave them: wherefore they sold not their l. 127
Lev 26:36 into their hearts in the l of their enemies; 776
26:39 away in their iniquity in your enemies' l; 776
Jdg 11:13 therefore restore those *l* again peaceably. NIH
2Ki 19:11 what the kings of Assyria have done to all l, 776
19:17 have destroyed the nations and their l, 776
1Ch 14:17 the fame of David went out into all l; and 776
2Ch 9:28 horses out of Egypt, and out of all l. 776
13: 9 after the manner of the nations of *other* l? 776
17:10 of the l that *were* round about Judah, 776
32:13 have done unto all the people of *other* l? 776
32:13 were the gods of the nations of *those* l any 776
32:13 able to deliver their l out of mine hand? 776
32:17 As the gods of the nations of *other* l have not 776
Ezr 9: 1 themselves from the people of the l, 776
9: 2 themselves with the people of *those* l: 776
9: 7 delivered into the hand of the kings of the l, 776
9:11 land with the filthiness of the people of the l, 776
Ne 5: 3 We *have* mortgaged our l, vineyards, and 7704
5: 4 *and that upon* our l and vineyards. 7704
5: 5 *to redeem them;* for other men have our l 7704
5:11 I pray you, to them, even *this* day, their l, 7704
9:30 them into the hand of the people of the l. 776
10:28 from the people of the l unto the law of God, 776
Ps 49:11 they call *their* l after their own names. 127
66: 1 Make a joyful noise unto God, all ye l: 776
100: 1 a joyful noise unto the LORD, all ye l. 776
105:44 gave them the l of the heathen: and 776
106:27 the nations, and to scatter them in the l. 776
107: 3 gathered them out of the l, from the east, 776
Isa 36:20 Who *are they* amongst all the gods of these l, 776
37:11 have done to all l by destroying them utterly; 776
Jer 16:15 from all the l whither he had driven them: 776
27: 6 now have I given all these l into the hand of 776
Eze 20: 6 and honey, which *is* the glory of all l: 776
20:15 and honey, which *is* the glory of all l; 776
39:27 gathered them out of their enemies' l, and 776
Mt 19:29 or father, or mother, or wife, or children, or l, *68*
Mk 10:29 or father, or mother, or wife, or children, or l, *68*
10:30 and sisters, and mothers, and children, and l, *68*
Ac 4:34 for as many as were possessors of l or *5564*

LANES (1)
Lk 14:21 out quickly into the streets and l of the city, *4505*

LANGUAGE (27) [LANGUAGES]
Ge 11: 1 the whole earth was *of* one l, and *of* one 8193
11: 6 the people *is* one, and they have all one l; 8193
11: 7 let us go down, and there confound their l, 8193
11: 9 the LORD did there confound the l of all 8193
2Ki 18:26 I pray thee, to thy servants **in the Syrian** l; 762
18:26 talk not with us **in the Jews'** l in the ears of 3066
18:28 and cried with a loud voice **in the Jews'** l, 3066
Ne 13:24 could not speak **in the Jews'** l, but 3066
13:24 but according to the l of each people. 3956
Est 1:22 to every people after their l, that every man 3956
1:22 according to the l of every people. 3956
3:12 and *to* every people after their l; 3956
8: 9 *unto* every people after their l, and to 3956
8: 9 to their writing, and according to their l. 3956
Ps 19: 3 *There is* no speech nor l, *where* their voice 1697
81: 5 *where* I heard a l *that* I understood not. 8193
114: 1 house of Jacob from a people of **strange** l; 3937
Isa 19:18 in the land of Egypt speak the l of Canaan, 8193
36:11 pray thee, unto thy servants **in the Syrian** l; 762
36:11 and speak not unto us **in the Jews'** l, 3066
36:13 cried with a loud voice **in the Jews'** l, and 3066
Jer 5:15 a nation whose l thou knowest not, 3956
Eze 3: 5 a people of a strange speech and of a hard l, 3956
3: 6 people of a strange speech and of a hard l, 3956
Da 3:29 a decree, That every people, nation, and l, 3961
Zep 3: 9 For then will I turn to the people a pure l, 8193
Ac 2: 6 every man heard them speak in his own l. *1258*

LANGUAGES (7) [LANGUAGE]
Da 3: 4 it is commanded, O people, nations, and l, 3961
3: 7 the l, fell down *and* worshipped the golden 3961
4: 1 unto all people, nations, and l, that dwell in 3961
5:19 nations, and l, trembled and feared before 3961
6:25 and l, that dwell in all the earth; 3961
7:14 a kingdom, that all people, nations, and l, 3961
Zec 8:23 shall take hold out of all l of the nations, 3956

LANGUISH (5) [LANGUISHED, LANGUISHETH, LANGUISHING]
Isa 16: 8 For the fields of Heshbon l, *and* the vine of 535
19: 8 they that spread nets upon the waters shall l. 535
24: 4 the haughty people of the earth do l. 535
Jer 14: 2 Judah mourneth, and the gates thereof l; 535
Hos 4: 3 every one that dwelleth therein shall l, 535

LANGUISHED (1) [LANGUISH]
La 2: 8 and the wall to lament; they l together. 535

LANGUISHETH (8) [LANGUISH]
Isa 24: 4 fadeth away, the world l *and* fadeth away, 535
24: 7 The new wine mourneth, the vine l, all 535
33: 9 The earth mourneth *and* l: Lebanon is 535
Jer 15: 9 She that hath borne seven l: she hath given 535
Joel 1:10 is wasted, the new wine is dried up, the oil l. 535
1:12 The vine is dried up, and the fig tree l; 535

Na 1: 4 Bashan l, and Carmel, and the flower of 535
1: 4 and Carmel, and the flower of Lebanon l. 535

LANGUISHING (1) [LANGUISH]
Ps 41: 3 will strengthen him upon the bed of l: 1741

LANTERNS (1)
Jn 18: 3 cometh thither with l and torches and 5322

LAODICEA (6) [LAODICEANS]
Col 2: 1 and *for* them at L, and *for* as many as have 2993
4:13 and them that are in L, and them in 2993
4:15 Salute the brethren which are in L, and 2993
4:16 that ye likewise read the *epistle* from L. 2993
1Ti 6: S The first to Timothy was written from L, 2993
Rev 1:11 and unto Philadelphia, and unto L. 2993

LAODICEANS (2) [LAODICEA]
Col 4:16 that it be read also in the church of the L; 2994
Rev 3:14 And unto the angel of the church of the L 2994

LAP (3) [LAPPED, LAPPETH]
2Ki 4:39 gathered thereof wild gourds his l full, and 899
Ne 5:13 Also I shook my l, and said, So God shake 2684
Pr 16:33 The lot is cast into the l; but the whole 2436

LAPIDOTH (1)
Jdg 4: 4 Deborah, a prophetess, the wife of L, 3941

LAPPED (2) [LAP]
Jdg 7: 6 the number of them that l, putting their 3952
7: 7 By the three hundred men that l will I save 3952

LAPPETH (2) [LAP]
Jdg 7: 5 Every one that l of the water with his 3952
7: 5 as a dog l, him shalt thou set by himself; 3952

LAPPIDOTH See LAPIDOTH

LAPWING (2)
Lev 11:19 heron after her kind, and the l, and the bat. 1744
Dt 14:18 heron after her kind, and the l, and the bat. 1744

LARGE (21) [LARGENESS]
Ge 34:21 behold, *it is* l **enough** for them; 3027+7342
Ex 3: 8 up out of that land unto a good land and a l, 7342
Jdg 18:10 unto a people secure, and to a l land: 3027+7342
2Sa 22:20 He brought me forth also into a l **place**: he 4800
Ne 4:19 The work *is* great and l, and we *are* 7342
7: 4 Now the city *was* l and great: but 3027+7342
9:35 in the l and fat land which thou gavest 7342
Ps 18:19 He brought me forth also into a l **place**; 4800
31: 8 thou hast set my feet in a l **room**. 4800
118: 5 answered me, *and set me* in a l **place**. 4800
Isa 22:18 toss thee like a ball into a l country: 3027+7342
30:23 in that day shall thy cattle feed *in* l 7337
30:33 it is prepared; he hath made *it* deep *and* l: 7337
Jer 22:14 will build me a wide house and l chambers, 7304
Eze 23:32 shalt drink *of* thy sister's cup deep and l: 7342
Hos 4:16 will feed them as a lamb in a l **place**. 4800
Mt 28:12 they gave l money unto the soldiers, 2425
Mk 14:15 And he will shew you a l upper room 3173
Lk 22:12 And he shall shew you a l upper room 3173
Gal 6:11 Ye see **how** l a letter I have written unto 4080
Rev 21:16 and the length is as l as the breadth: 5118

LARGENESS (1) [LARGE]
1Ki 4:29 exceeding much, and l of heart, 7341

LASCIVIOUSNESS (6)
Mk 7:22 deceit, l, an evil eye, blasphemy, pride, 766
2Co 12:21 and l which they have committed. 766
Gal 5:19 *these;* Adultery, fornication, uncleanness, l, 766
Eph 4:19 feeling have given themselves over unto l, 766
1Pe 4: 3 when we walked in l, lusts, excess of wine, 766
Jude 1: 4 *men,* turning the grace of our God into l, 766

LASEA (1)
Ac 27: 8 nigh whereunto was the city *of* L. 2996

LASH; LASHES See SCOURGES; SCOURGETH; SCOURGING; SCOURGINGS; STRIPE; STRIPES

LASHA (1)
Ge 10:19 and Admah, and Zeboim, even unto L. 3962

LASHARON (1)
Jos 12:18 The king of Aphek, one; the king of L, one; 8289

LAST (85) [LASTED, LASTING]
Ge 49: 1 you *that* which shall befall you in the l days. 319
49:19 but he shall overcome at the l. 6119
Nu 23:10 of the righteous, and let my l **end** be like his! 319
2Sa 19:11 Why are ye the l to bring the king back to his 314
19:12 then are ye the l to bring back the king? 314
23: 1 Now these *be* the l words of David. 314
1Ch 23:27 For by the l words of David, the Levites 314
29:29 acts of David the king, first and l, behold, 314
2Ch 9:29 the rest of the acts of Solomon, first and l, 314
12:15 Now the acts of Rehoboam, first and l, *are* 314
16:11 behold, the acts of Asa, first and l, lo, 314
20:34 the rest of the acts of Jehoshaphat, first and l, 314
25:26 of the acts of Amaziah, first and l, behold, 314
26:22 first and l, did Isaiah the prophet, the son of 314
28:26 and of all his ways, first and l, behold, 314
35:27 his deeds, first and l, behold, they *are* written 314
Ezr 8:13 of the l sons of Adonikam, whose names *are* 314
Ne 8:18 day by day, from the first day unto the l day, 314
Pr 5:11 And thou mourn at the l, when thy flesh and 319
23:32 At the l it biteth like a serpent, and 319
Isa 2: 2 it shall come to pass in the l days, *that* 319
41: 4 I the LORD, the first, and with the l; I *am* 314
44: 6 I *am* the first, and I *am* the l; and besides me 314
48:12 I *am* he; I *am* the first, I also *am* the l. 314
Jer 12: 4 because they said, He shall not see our l **end**. 319
50:17 l this Nebuchadrezzar king of Babylon hath 314
La 1: 9 she remembereth not her l **end**; therefore 319
Da 4: 8 at the l Daniel came in before me, 318
8: 3 and the higher came up l. 314+871.1+1886.1
8:19 what shall be in the l **end** of the indignation: 319
Am 9: 1 and I will slay the l of them with the sword: 319
Mic 4: 1 in the l days it shall come to pass, *that* 319
Mt 12:45 the l *state* of that man is worse than 2078
19:30 But many *that are* first shall be l; and 2078
19:30 *are* first shall be last; and *the* l *shall be* first. 2078
20: 8 beginning from the l unto the first. 2078
20:12 These l have wrought *but* one hour, and 2078
20:14 I will give unto this l, even as unto thee. 2078
20:16 So the l shall be first, and the first last: 2078
20:16 So the last shall be first, and the first l: 2078
21:37 But l *of all* he sent unto them his son, 5306
22:27 And l of all the woman died also. 5306
26:60 **At the** l came two false witnesses, 5306
27:64 so the l error shall be worse than the first. 2078
Mk 9:35 *the same* shall be l of all, and servant of all. 2078
10:31 But many *that are* first shall be l; and 2078
10:31 *that are* first shall be last; and the l first. 2078
12: 6 he sent him also l unto them, saying, 2078
12:22 left no seed: l of all the woman died also. 2078
Lk 11:26 the l *state* of that man is worse than 2078
12:59 till thou hast paid the very l mite. 2078
13:30 there are l which shall be first, and there are 2078
13:30 be first, and there are first which shall be l. 2078
20:32 L of all the woman died also. 5306
Jn 6:39 but should raise it up *again* at the l day. 2078
6:40 and I will raise him up *at* the l day. 2078
6:44 and I will raise him up *at* the l day. 2078
6:54 and I will raise him up *at* the l day. 2078
7:37 In the l day, *that* great *day* of the feast, 2078
8: 9 beginning at the eldest, *even* unto the l: 2078
11:24 rise again in the resurrection at the l day. 2078
12:48 the same shall judge him in the l day. 2078
Ac 2:17 And it shall come to pass in the l days, 2078
1Co 4: 9 that God hath set forth us the apostles l, 2078
15: 8 And l of all he was seen of me also, as of 2078
15:26 The l enemy *that* shall be destroyed *is* 2078
15:45 the l Adam *was made* a quickening spirit. 2078
15:52 in the twinkling of an eye, at the l trump: 2078
Php 4:10 that now **at** the l your care of me hath 4218
2Ti 3: 1 that in the l days perilous times shall come. 2078
Heb 1: 2 Hath in these l days spoken unto us by *his* 2078
Jas 5: 3 ye have heaped treasure together for the l 2078
1Pe 1: 5 salvation ready to be revealed in the l time. 2078
1:20 but was manifest in *these* l times for you, 2078
2Pe 3: 3 that there shall come in the l days scoffers, 2078
1Jn 2:18 Little children, it is the l time: and as ye 2078
2:18 whereby we know that it is the l time. 2078
Jude 1:18 you there should be mockers in the l time, 2078
Rev 1:11 I am Alpha and Omega, the first and the l: 2078

L

Rev 1:17 unto me, Fear not; I am the first and the l: *2078*
2: 8 These *things* saith the first and the l, *2078*
2:19 and the l *to be* more than the first. *2078*
15: 1 seven angels having the seven l plagues; *2078*
21: 9 the seven vials full of the seven l plagues, *2078*
22:13 and the end, the first and the l. *2078*

LASTED (1) [LAST]
Jdg 14:17 him the seven days, while their feast l: 1961

LASTING (1) [LAST]
Dt 33:15 and for the precious things of the l hills, 5769

LATCHET (4) [SHOELATCHET]
Isa 5:27 nor the l of their shoes be broken: 8288
Mk 1: 7 the l of whose shoes I am not worthy to *2438*
Lk 3:16 the l of whose shoes I am not worthy to *2438*
Jn 1:27 whose shoe's l I am not worthy to unloose. *2438*

LATE (3) [LATELY, LATTER]
Ps 127: 2 to sit up l, to eat the bread of sorrows: 309
Mic 2: 8 Even of l my people is risen up as an enemy: 865
Jn 11: 8 Master, the Jews **of l** sought to stone thee; *3568*

LATELY (1) [LATE]
Ac 18: 2 born in Pontus, l come from Italy, with his *4373*

LATIN (2)
Lk 23:38 and L, and Hebrew, THIS IS THE KING *4513*
Jn 19:20 was written in Hebrew, *and* Greek, *and* L. *4515*

LATRINE See DRAUGHT

LATTER (42) [LATE]
Ex 4: 8 that they will believe the voice of the l sign. 314
Nu 24:14 people shall do to thy people in the l days. 319
24:20 but his l **end** *shall be* that he perish for ever. 319
Dt 4:30 *even* in the l days, if thou turn to the LORD 319
8:16 prove thee, to do thee good at thy l **end**; 319
11:14 the first rain and the l **rain**, that thou 4456
24: 3 *if* the l husband hate her, and write her a bill 314
24: 3 or if the l husband die, which took her *to be* 314
31:29 and evil will befall you in the l days; because 319
32:29 *that* they would consider their l **end**! 319
Ru 3:10 kindness in the l **end** than at the beginning, 314
2Sa 2:26 not that it will be bitterness in the l **end**? 314
Job 8: 7 yet thy l **end** should greatly increase. 319
19:25 *that* he shall stand *at* the l *day* upon 314
29:23 opened their mouth wide *as* for the l **rain**. 4456
42:12 So the LORD blessed the l **end** of Job more 319
Pr 16:15 and his favour *is* as a cloud of the l **rain**. 4456
19:20 that thou mayest be wise in thy l **end**. 319
Isa 41:22 consider *them,* and know the l **end** of them; 319
47: 7 neither didst remember the l **end** of it. 319
Jer 3: 3 and there hath been no l **rain**; 4456
5:24 both the former and the l, in his season: 4456
23:20 in the l days ye shall consider it perfectly. 319
30:24 of his heart: in the l days ye shall consider it. 319
48:47 again the captivity of Moab in the l days, 319
49:39 it shall come to pass in the l days, *that* I will 319
Eze 38: 8 in the l years thou shalt come into the land 319
38:16 it shall be in the l days, and I will bring thee 319
Da 2:28 Nebuchadnezzar what shall be in the l days. 320
8:23 in the l **time** of their kingdom, when 319
10:14 what shall befall thy people in the l days: 319
11:29 but it shall not be as the former, or as the l. 314
Hos 3: 5 the LORD and his goodness in the l days. 319
6: 3 as the l *and* former rain *unto* the earth. 4456
Joel 2:23 and the l **rain** in the first *month.* 4456
Am 7: 1 of the shooting up of the l **growth**; 3954
7: 1 *it was* the l **growth** after the king's 3954
Hag 2: 9 The glory of this l house shall be greater 314
Zec 10: 1 of the LORD rain in the time of the l **rain**; 4456
1Ti 4: 1 that in the l times some shall depart from 5306
Jas 5: 7 for it, until he receive the early and l rain. 3797
2Pe 2:20 the l *end* is worse with them than 2078

LATTICE (3)
Jdg 5:28 and cried through the l, Why is his chariot *so* 822
2Ki 1: 2 Ahaziah fell down through a l in his upper 7639
SS 2: 9 shewing himself through the l. 2762

LAUD (1)
Ro 15:11 all ye Gentiles; and l him, all ye people. *1867*

LAUGH (18) [LAUGHED, LAUGHETH, LAUGHING, LAUGHTER]
Ge 18:13 Wherefore did Sarah l, saying, 6711
18:15 And he said, Nay; but thou didst l. 6711
21: 6 God hath made me to l, *so that* all that hear 6712
21: 6 to laugh, *so that* all that hear will l with me. 6711
Job 5:22 At destruction and famine thou shalt l: 7832
9:23 he will l at the trial of the innocent. 3932
22:19 are glad: and the innocent l them **to scorn**. 3932
Ps 2: 4 He that sitteth in the heavens shall l: 7832
22: 7 All they that see me l me **to scorn**: 3932
37:13 The Lord shall l at him: for he seeth that his 7832
52: 6 also shall see, and fear, and shall l at him: 7832
59: 8 thou, O LORD, shalt l at them; thou shalt 7832
80: 6 and our enemies l among themselves. 3932
Pr 1:26 I also will l at your calamity; I will mock 7832
29: 9 whether he rage or l, *there is* no rest. 7832
Ecc 3: 4 A time to weep, and a time to l; a time to 7832
Lk 6:21 *are ye* that weep now: for ye shall l. *1070*
6:25 Woe unto you that l now: for ye shall *1070*

LAUGHED (13) [LAUGH]
Ge 17:17 upon his face, and l, and said in his heart, 6711
18:12 Therefore Sarah l within herself, saying, 6711
18:15 Sarah denied, saying, I l not; for she was 6711
2Ki 19:21 hath despised thee, *and* l thee **to scorn**; 3932
2Ch 30:10 but they l them **to scorn**, and mocked them. 7832
Ne 2:19 heard *it,* they l us **to scorn**, and 3932
Job 12: 4 the just upright *man is* l **to scorn**. 7814
29:24 *If* I l on them, they believed *it* not; and 7832
Isa 37:22 hath despised thee, *and* l thee **to scorn**; 3932
Eze 23:32 thou shalt be l **to scorn** and had in derision; 6712
Mt 9:24 but sleepeth. And they l him **to scorn**. *2606*
Mk 5:40 And they l him **to scorn**. But when he had *2606*
Lk 8:53 And they l him **to scorn**, knowing that she *2606*

LAUGHETH (1) [LAUGH]
Job 41:29 as stubble: he l at the shaking of a spear. 7832

LAUGHING (1) [LAUGH]
Job 8:21 Till he fill thy mouth *with* l, and thy lips 7814

LAUGHTER (7) [LAUGH]
Ps 126: 2 was our mouth filled *with* l, and our tongue 7814
Pr 14:13 Even in l the heart is sorrowful; and the end 7814
Ecc 2: 2 I said of l, *It is* mad: and of mirth, 7814
7: 3 Sorrow *is* better than l: for by the sadness 7814
7: 6 of thorns under a pot, so *is* the l of the fool: 7814
10:19 A feast is made for l, and wine maketh 7814
Jas 4: 9 let your l be turned to mourning, and *1071*

LAUNCH (1) [LAUNCHED]
Lk 5: 4 **L out** into the deep, and let down your nets *1877*

LAUNCHED (4) [LAUNCH]
Lk 8:22 the other side of the lake. And they l **forth**. *321*
Ac 21: 1 after we were gotten from them, and had l, *321*
27: 2 we l, meaning to sail by the coasts of Asia; *321*
27: 4 And when we had l from thence, we sailed *321*

LAUNDERER'S SOAP See SOPE

LAVER (15) [LAVERS]
Ex 30:18 Thou shalt also make a l *of* brass, and 3595
30:28 with all his vessels, and the l and his foot. 3595
31: 9 with all his furniture, and the l and his foot, 3595
35:16 and all his vessels, the l and his foot, 3595
38: 8 he made the l *of* brass, and the foot of it *of* 3595
39:39 and all his vessels, the l and his foot, 3595
40: 7 thou shalt set the l between the tent of 3595
40:11 And thou shalt anoint the l and his foot, and 3595
40:30 he set the l between the tent of 3595
Lev 8:11 and all his vessels, both the l and his foot, 3595
1Ki 7:30 under the l *were* undersetters molten, at 3595
7:38 one l contained forty baths: *and* every laver 3595
7:38 *and* every l was four cubits: *and* upon every 3595
7:38 *and* upon every one of the ten bases one l. 3595
2Ki 16:17 the bases, and removed the l from off them; 3595

LAVERS (5) [LAVER]
1Ki 7:38 made he ten l of brass: one laver contained 3595
7:40 And Hiram made the l, and the shovels, and 3595
7:43 And the ten bases, and ten l on the bases; 3595
2Ch 4: 6 He made also ten l, and put five on the right 3595
4:14 also bases and l made he upon the bases; 3595

LAVISH (1)
Isa 46: 6 They l gold out of the bag, and weigh silver 2107

LAW (523) [LAWFUL, LAWFULLY, LAWGIVER, LAWLESS, LAWS, LAWYER, LAWYERS, UNLAWFUL]
Ge 11:31 Sarai his **daughter in l**, his son Abram's 3618
19:12 **son in l**, and thy sons, and thy daughters, 2860
19:14 Lot went out, and spake unto his **sons in l**, 2860
19:14 as one that mocked unto his **sons in l**. 2860
38:11 said Judah to Tamar his **daughter in l**, 3618
38:13 Behold thy **father in l** goeth up to Timnath 2524
38:16 knew not that she *was* his **daughter in l**:) 3618
38:24 Tamar thy **daughter in l** hath played 3618
38:25 she sent to her **father in l**, saying, By 2524
47:26 Joseph made it a l over the land of Egypt 2706
Ex 3: 1 kept the flock of Jethro his **father in l**, 2859
4:18 and returned to Jethro his **father in l**, 2859
12:49 One l shall be to him that is homeborn, and 8451
13: 9 that the LORD's l may be in thy mouth: 8451
16: 4 whether they will walk in my l, or no. 8451
18: 1 the priest of Midian, Moses' **father in l**, 2859
18: 2 Jethro, Moses' **father in l**, took Zipporah, 2859
18: 5 Jethro, Moses' **father in l**, came with his 2859
18: 6 I thy **father in l** Jethro am come unto thee, 2859
18: 7 Moses went out to meet his **father in l**, 2859
18: 8 Moses told his **father in l** all that 2859
18:12 Jethro, Moses' **father in l**, took a burnt 2859
18:12 to eat bread with Moses' **father in l** before 2859
18:14 when Moses' **father in l** saw all that he did 2859
18:15 Moses said unto his **father in l**, 2859
18:17 Moses' **father in l** said unto him, The thing 2859
18:24 hearkened to the voice of his **father in l**, 2859
18:27 Moses let his **father in l** depart; and 2859
24:12 a l, and commandments which I have 8451
Lev 6: 9 This *is* the l of the burnt offering: 8451
6:14 this *is* the l of the meat offering: the sons of 8451
6:25 This *is* the l of the sin offering: 8451
7: 1 Likewise this *is* the l of the trespass 8451
7: 7 *there is* one l for them: the priest that 8451
7:11 this *is* the l of the sacrifice of peace 8451
7:37 This *is* the l of the burnt offering, of 8451
11:46 This *is* the l of the beasts, and of the fowl, 8451
12: 7 This *is* the l for her that hath born a male or 8451
13:59 This *is* the l of the plague of leprosy in a 8451
14: 2 This shall be the l of the leper in the day of 8451
14:32 This *is* the l *of him* in whom *is* the plague 8451
14:54 This *is* the l for all *manner of* plague of 8451
14:57 and when *it is* clean: this *is* the l of leprosy. 8451
15:32 This *is* the l of him that hath an issue, and 8451
18:15 the nakedness of thy **daughter in l**: 3618
20:12 if a man lie with his **daughter in l**, both of 3618
24:22 Ye shall have one manner of l, as well for 4941
Nu 5:29 This *is* the l of jealousies, when a wife 8451
5:30 the priest shall execute upon her all this l. 8451
6:13 this *is* the l of the Nazarite, when the days 8451
6:21 This *is* the l of the Nazarite who hath 8451
6:21 so he must do after the l of his separation. 8451
10:29 Raguel the Midianite, Moses' **father in l**, 2859
15:16 One l and one manner shall be for you, and 8451
15:29 You shall have one l for him that sinneth 8451
19: 2 This *is* the ordinance of the l which 8451
19:14 This *is* the l, when a man dieth in a tent: 8451
31:21 This *is* the ordinance of the l which 8451
Dt 1: 5 began Moses to declare this l, saying, 8451
4: 8 and judgments *so* righteous as all this l, 8451
4:44 this *is* the l which Moses set before 8451
17:11 According to the sentence of the l which 8451
17:18 that he shall write him a copy of this l in a 8451
17:19 to keep all the words of this l and 8451
27: 3 write upon them all the words of this l, 8451
27: 8 stones all the words of this l very plainly. 8451
27:23 *be* he that lieth with his **mother in l**. 2859
27:26 not *all* the words of this l to do them. 8451
28:58 words of this l that are written in this book, 8451
28:61 which *is* not written in the book of this l, 8451
29:21 that are written in this book of the l: 8451
29:29 that *we* may do all the words of this l. 8451
30:10 which are written in this book of the l, 8451
31: 9 Moses wrote this l, and delivered it unto 8451
31:11 thou shalt read this l before all Israel in 8451
31:12 and observe to do all the words of this l: 8451
31:24 end of writing the words of this l in a book, 8451
31:26 Take this book of the l, and put it in 8451
32:46 to observe to do, all the words of this l. 8451
33: 2 from his right hand *went* a fiery l for them. 1881
33: 4 Moses commanded us a l, *even* 8451
33:10 teach Jacob thy judgments, and Israel thy l: 8451
Jos 1: 7 mayest observe to do according to all the l, 8451
1: 8 This book of the l shall not depart out of 8451
8:31 as it is written in the book of the l of 8451
8:32 upon the stones a copy of the l of Moses, 8451
8:34 afterward he read all the words of the l, 8451
8:34 to all that is written in the book of the l. 8451
22: 5 heed to do the commandment and the l, 8451
23: 6 to do all that is written in the book of the l 8451
24:26 these words in the book of the l of God, 8451
Jdg 1:16 children of the Kenite, Moses' **father in l**, 2859
4:11 children of Hobab the **father in l** of Moses, 2859
15: 6 the **son in l** of the Timnite, because he had 2860
19: 4 his **father in l**, the damsel's father, 2859
19: 5 the damsel's father said unto his **son in l**, 2860
19: 7 rose up to depart, his **father in l** urged him: 2859
19: 9 and his servant, his **father in l**, 2859
Ru 1: 6 she arose with her **daughters in l**, that she 3618
1: 7 and her two **daughters in l** with her; 3618
1: 8 Naomi said unto her two **daughters in l**, 3618
1:14 Orpah kissed her **mother in l**; but 2545
1:15 thy **sister in l** is gone back unto her people, 2994
1:15 her gods: return thou after thy **sister in l**. 2994
1:22 the Moabitess, her **daughter in l**, with her, 3618
2:11 all that thou hast done unto thy **mother in l** 2545
2:18 her **mother in l** saw what she had gleaned: 2545
2:19 her **mother in l** said unto her, Where hast 2545
2:19 she shewed her **mother in l** with whom she 2545
2:20 Naomi said unto her **daughter in l**, 3618
2:22 Naomi said unto Ruth her **daughter in l**, 3618
2:23 and dwelt with her **mother in l**. 2545
3: 1 Naomi her **mother in l** said unto her, 2545
3: 6 did according to all that her **mother in l** 2545
3:16 when she came to her **mother in l**, she said, 2545
3:17 to me, Go not empty unto thy **mother in l**. 2545
4:15 for thy **daughter in l**, which loveth thee, 3618
1Sa 4:19 his **daughter in l**, Phinehas' wife, was with 3618
4:19 that her **father in l** and her husband were 2524
4:21 because of her **father in l** and her husband. 2524
18:18 that I should be **son in l** to the king? 2860
18:21 Thou shalt *this* day be my **son in l** in 2859
18:22 now therefore be the king's **son in l**. 2859
18:23 to you a light *thing* to be a king's **son in l**, 2859
18:26 David well to be the king's **son in l**: 2859
18:27 that he might be the king's **son in l**. 2859
22:14 which *is* the king's **son in l**, and goeth at 2860
1Ki 2: 3 as *it is* written in the l of Moses, 8451
2Ki 8:27 for he *was* the **son in l** of the house of 2860
10:31 Jehu took no heed to walk in the l of 8451
14: 6 is written in the book of the l of Moses, 8451
17:13 according to all the l which I commanded 8451
17:34 or after the l and commandment which 8451
17:37 and the l, and the commandment, 8451
21: 8 according to all the l that my servant Moses 8451
22: 8 I have found the book of the l in the house 8451
22:11 had heard the words of the book of the l, 8451
23:24 that he might perform the words of the l 8451
23:25 his might, according to all the l of Moses; 8451
1Ch 2: 4 Tamar his **daughter in l** bare him Pharez 3618
16:17 hath confirmed the same to Jacob for a l, 2706
16:40 *to do* according to all that is written in the l 8451
22:12 that *thou* mayest keep the l of the LORD 8451
2Ch 6:16 take heed to their way to walk in my l, 8451
12: 1 he forsook the l of the LORD, and 8451
14: 4 and to do the l and the commandment. 8451
15: 3 and without a teaching priest, and without l. 8451
17: 9 *had* the book of the l of the LORD with 8451
19:10 and blood, between l and commandment, 8451
23:18 as it is written in the l of Moses, 8451
25: 4 *did* as it is written in the l in the book of 8451
30:16 according to the l of Moses the man of 8451
31: 3 as it is written in the l of the LORD. 8451
31: 4 that they might be encouraged in the l of 8451
31:21 in the l, and in the commandments, to seek 8451
33: 8 according to the whole l and the statutes 8451
34:14 Hilkiah the priest found a book of the l of 8451
34:15 I have found the book of the l in the house 8451
34:19 when the king had heard the words of the l, 8451
35:26 according to that which was written in the l 8451
Ezr 3: 2 as it is written in the l of Moses the man of 8451
7: 6 he *was* a ready scribe in the l of Moses, 8451

Ezr 7:10 his heart to seek the l of the LORD, 8451
7:12 a scribe of the l of the God of heaven, 1882
7:14 according to the l of thy God which *is* in 1882
7:21 the scribe of the l of the God of heaven, 1882
7:26 whosoever will not do the l of thy God, 1882
7:26 the l of the king, let judgment be executed 1882
10: 3 and let it be done according to the l. 8451
Ne 6:18 he *was* the **son in** l of Shechaniah the son 2860
8: 1 scribe to bring the book of the l of Moses, 8451
8: 2 Ezra the priest brought the l before 8451
8: 3 *were attentive* unto the book of the l. 8451
8: 7 caused the people to understand the l: 8451
8: 8 So they read in the book in the l of God 8451
8: 9 when they heard the words of the l. 8451
8:13 even to understand the words of the l. 8451
8:14 they found written in the l which 8451
8:18 he read in the book of the l of God. 8451
9: 3 read in the book of the l of the LORD 8451
9:26 cast thy l behind their backs, and slew thy 8451
9:29 *thou* mightest bring them again unto thy l: 8451
9:34 our priests, nor our fathers, kept thy l, 8451
10:28 the people of the lands unto the l of God, 8451
10:29 and into an oath, to walk in God's l, 8451
10:34 LORD our God, as it is written in the l: 8451
10:36 as it is written in the l, and the firstlings of 8451
12:44 the cities the portions of the l for the priests 8451
13: 3 it came to pass, when they had heard the l, 8451
13:28 *was* **son in** l to Sanballat the Horonite: 2860
Est 1: 8 the drinking *was* according to the l; 1881
1:13 the king's manner towards all that knew l 1881
1:15 *we* do unto the queen Vashti according to l, 1881
4:11 *there is* one l of his to put *him* to death, 1881
4:16 the king, which *is* not according to the l: 1881
Job 22:22 the l from his mouth, and lay up his words 8451
Ps 1: 2 his delight *is* in the l of the LORD; and 8451
1: 2 and in his l doth he meditate day and night. 8451
19: 7 The l of the LORD *is* perfect, 8451
37:31 The l of his God *is* in his heart; none of his 8451
40: 8 O my God: yea, thy l *is* within my heart. 8451
78: 1 Give ear, O my people, to my l: 8451
78: 5 appointed a l in Israel, which he 8451
78:10 of God, and refused to walk in his l; 8451
81: 4 for Israel, *and* a l of the God of Jacob. 4941
89:30 If his children forsake my l, and walk not in 8451
94:12 O LORD, and teachest him out of thy l; 8451
94:20 *with* thee, which frameth mischief by a l? 2706
105:10 confirmed the same unto Jacob for a l, *and* 2706
119: 1 the way, who walk in the l of the LORD. 8451
119:18 I may behold wondrous *things* out of thy l. 8451
119:29 way of lying: and grant me thy l graciously. 8451
119:34 me understanding, and I shall keep thy l; 8451
119:44 So shall I keep thy l continually for ever 8451
119:51 *yet* have I not declined from thy l. 8451
119:53 because of the wicked that forsake thy l. 8451
119:55 in the night, and have kept thy l. 8451
119:61 robbed me: *but* I have not forgotten thy l. 8451
119:70 is as fat as grease; *but* I delight *in* thy l. 8451
119:72 The l of thy mouth *is* better unto me than 8451
119:77 that I may live: for thy l *is* my delight. 8451
119:85 pits for me, which *are* not after thy l. 8451
119:92 Unless thy l *had been* my delights, I should 8451
119:97 O how love I thy l! it *is* my meditation all 8451
119:109 in my hand: yet do I not forget thy l. 8451
119:113 I hate *vain* thoughts: but thy l do I love. 8451
119:126 to work: *for* they have made void thy l. 8451
119:136 mine eyes, because they keep not thy l. 8451
119:142 and thy l *is* the truth. 8451
119:150 after mischief: they are far from thy l. 8451
119:153 and deliver me: for I do not forget thy l. 8451
119:163 I hate and abhor lying: *but* thy l do I love. 8451
119:165 Great peace have they which love thy l: and 8451
119:174 O LORD; and thy l *is* my delight. 8451
Pr 1: 8 and forsake not the l of thy mother: 8451
3: 1 My son, forget not my l; but let thine heart 8451
4: 2 you good doctrine, forsake you not my l. 8451
6:20 and forsake not the l of thy mother: 8451
6:23 the l *is* light; and reproofs of instruction *are* 8451
7: 2 and live; and my l as the apple of thine eye. 8451
13:14 The l of the wise *is* a fountain of life, 8451
28: 4 They that forsake the l praise the wicked: 8451
28: 4 but such as keep the l contend with them. 8451
28: 7 Whoso keepeth the l *is* a wise son: but 8451
28: 9 that turneth away his ear from hearing the l, 8451
29:18 but he that keepeth the l, happy *is* he. 8451
31: 5 forget the l, and pervert the judgment of 2710
31:26 and in her tongue *is* the l of kindness. 8451
Isa 1:10 give ear unto the l of our God, ye people of 8451
2: 3 for out of Zion shall go forth the l, and 8451
5:24 they have cast away the l of the LORD of 8451
8:16 seal the l among my disciples. 8451
8:20 To the l and to the testimony: if they speak 8451
30: 9 children *that* will not hear the l of 8451
42: 4 the earth: and the isles shall wait for his l. 8451
42:21 he will magnify the l, and make *it* 8451
42:24 neither were they obedient unto his l. 8451
51: 4 for a l shall proceed from me, and I will 8451
51: 7 the people in whose heart *is* my l; 8451
Jer 2: 8 they that handle the l knew me not: 8451
6:19 unto my words, nor *to* my l, but rejected it. 8451
8: 8 and the l of the LORD *is* with us? 8451
9:13 Because they have forsaken my l which I 8451
16:11 have forsaken me, and have not kept my l; 8451
18:18 for the l shall not perish from the priest, 8451
26: 4 to walk in my l, which I have set before 8451
31:33 I will put my l in their inward parts, and 8451
32:11 that which was sealed *according to* the l 4687
32:23 not thy voice, neither walked in thy l; 8451
44:10 nor walked in my l, nor in my statutes, 8451
44:23 nor walked in his l, nor in his statutes, 8451
La 2: 9 the l *is no more;* her prophets also find no 8451
Eze 7:26 the l shall perish from the priest, and 8451
22:11 hath lewdly defiled his **daughter in** l; 3618
22:26 Her priests have violated my l, and 8451
43:12 This *is* the l of the house; Upon the top of 8451
43:12 Behold, this *is* the l of the house. 8451
Da 6: 5 *it* against him concerning the l of his God. 1882
6: 8 according to the l of the Medes and 1882
6:12 according to the l of the Medes and 1882
6:15 that the l of the Medes and Persians *is,* That 1882
9:11 Yea, all Israel have transgressed thy l, 8451
9:11 the oath that *is* written in the l of Moses 8451
9:13 As *it is* written in the l of Moses, all this 8451
Hos 4: 6 seeing thou hast forgotten the l of thy God, 8451
8: 1 my covenant, and trespassed against my l. 8451
8:12 written to him the great things of my l, 8451
Am 2: 4 they have despised the l of the LORD, 8451
Mic 4: 2 for the l shall go forth of Zion, and 8451
7: 6 the **daughter in** l against her mother in 3618
7: 6 the daughter in law against her **mother in** l; 2545
Hab 1: 4 Therefore the l is slacked, and 8451
Zep 3: 4 they have done violence to the l. 8451
Hag 2:11 Ask now the priests *concerning* the l, 8451
Zec 7:12 lest *they* should hear the l, and the words 8451
Mal 2: 6 The l of truth was in his mouth, and 8451
2: 7 and they should seek the l at his mouth: 8451
2: 8 ye have caused many to stumble at the l; 8451
2: 9 my ways, but have been partial in the l. 8451
4: 4 Remember ye the l of Moses my servant, 8451
Mt 5:17 Think not that I am come to destroy the l, *3551*
5:18 or one tittle shall in no wise pass from the l, *3551*
5:40 And if any man will **sue** thee **at the** l, and *2919*
7:12 so to them: for this is the l and the prophets. *3551*
10:35 the **daughter in** l against her mother in *3565*
10:35 the daughter in law against her **mother in** l. *3994*
11:13 and the l prophesied until John. *3551*
12: 5 Or have ye not read in the l, how that on *3551*
22:36 which *is* the great commandment in the l? *3551*
22:40 On these two commandments hang all the l *3551*
23:23 have omitted the weightier *matters* of the l, *3551*
Lk 2:22 to the l of Moses were accomplished, *3551*
2:23 (As it is written in the l of the Lord, Every *3551*
2:24 to that which is said in the l of the Lord, *3551*
2:27 to do for him after the custom of the l, *3551*
2:39 all *things* according to the l of the Lord, *3551*
5:17 **doctors of the** l sitting *by,* which were *3547*
10:26 He said unto him, What is written in the l? *3551*
12:53 the **mother in** l against her daughter in law, *3994*
12:53 mother in law against her **daughter in** l, *3565*
12:53 the **daughter in** l against her mother in *3565*
12:53 the daughter in law against her **mother in** l. *3994*
16:16 The l and the prophets *were* until John: *3551*
16:17 earth to pass, than one tittle of the l to fail. *3551*
24:44 which were written in the l of Moses, and *3551*
Jn 1:17 For the l was given by Moses, *but* grace *3551*
1:45 of whom Moses in the l, and the prophets, *3551*
7:19 Did not Moses give you the l, and *yet* none *3551*
7:19 the law, and *yet* none of you keepeth the l? *3551*
7:23 that the l of Moses should not be broken; *3551*

Jn 7:49 But this people who knoweth not the l are *3551*
7:51 Doth our l judge any man, before it hear *3551*
8: 5 Now Moses in the l commanded us, *3551*
8:17 It is also written in your l, that *3551*
10:34 Is it not written in your l, I said, Ye are *3551*
12:34 We have heard out of the l that Christ *3551*
15:25 might be fulfilled that is written in their l, *3551*
18:13 for he was **father in** l to Caiaphas, *3995*
18:31 ye him, and judge him according to your l. *3551*
19: 7 We have a l, and by our law he ought to *3551*
19: 7 and by our l he ought to die, because *3551*
Ac 5:34 a Pharisee, named Gamaliel, a **doctor of** l, *3547*
6:13 words against this holy place, and the l: *3551*
7:53 Who have received the l by the disposition *3551*
13:15 And after the reading of the l and *3551*
13:39 ye could not be justified by the l of Moses. *3551*
15: 5 to command *them* to keep the l of Moses. *3551*
15:24 *Ye must* be circumcised, and keep the l: *3551*
18:13 men to worship God contrary to the l. *3551*
18:15 question of words and names, and *of* your l, *3551*
19:38 have a matter against any *man,* the l is open, *60*
21:20 and they are all zealous of the l: *3551*
21:24 also walkest orderly, and keepest the l. *3551*
21:28 against the people, and the l, and this place: *3551*
22: 3 to the perfect manner of the l of the fathers, *3551*
22:12 a devout man according to the l, *3551*
23: 3 for sittest thou to judge me after the l, and *3551*
23: 3 me to be smitten **contrary to** the l? *3891*
23:29 to be accused of questions of their l, *3551*
24: 6 and would have judged according to our l. *3551*
24:14 all *things* which are written in the l *3551*
25: 8 Neither against the l of the Jews, *3551*
28:23 both out of the l of Moses, and *out of* *3551*
Ro 2:12 For as many as have sinned **without** l shall *460*
2:12 without law shall also perish **without** l: *460*
2:12 as many as have sinned in the l shall be *3551*
2:12 sinned in the law shall be judged by the l; *3551*
2:13 (For not the hearers of the l *are* just before *3551*
2:13 but the doers of the l shall be justified. *3551*
2:14 when *the* Gentiles, which have not the l, *3551*
2:14 do by nature the *things* contained in the l, *3551*
2:14 these, having not the l, are a law unto *3551*
2:14 having not the law, are a l unto themselves: *3551*
2:15 Which shew the work of the l written in *3551*
2:17 and restest in the l, and makest thy boast of *3551*
2:18 being instructed out of the l; *3551*
2:20 form of knowledge and of the truth in the l. *3551*
2:23 Thou that makest thy boast of the l, *3551*
2:23 through breaking the l dishonourest thou *3551*
2:25 verily profiteth, if thou keep the l: *3551*
2:25 but if thou be a breaker of the l, *3551*
2:26 keep the righteousness of the l, *3551*
2:27 if it fulfil the l, judge thee, who by the letter *3551*
2:27 and circumcision dost transgress the l? *3551*
3:19 Now we know that what *things* soever the l *3551*
3:19 it saith to them who are under the l: *3551*
3:20 Therefore by the deeds of the l there shall *3551*
3:20 for by the l *is* the knowledge of sin. *3551*
3:21 of God without the l is manifested, *3551*
3:21 being witnessed by the l and the prophets; *3551*
3:27 By what l? of works? Nay: but by the law *3551*
3:27 of works? Nay: but by the l of faith. *3551*
3:28 justified by faith without the deeds of the l. *3551*
3:31 Do we then make void the l through faith? *3551*
3:31 God forbid: yea, we establish the l. *3551*
4:13 through the l, but through the righteousness *3551*
4:14 For if they which are of the l *be* heirs, faith *3551*
4:15 Because the l worketh wrath: for where no *3551*
4:15 for where no l is, *there is* no transgression. *3551*
4:16 not to that only which is of the l, but to that *3551*
5:13 For until the l sin was in the world: but *3551*
5:13 but sin is not imputed when there is no l. *3551*
5:20 Moreover the l entered, that the offence *3551*
6:14 for ye are not under the l, but under grace. *3551*
6:15 because we are not under the l, but *3551*
7: 1 (for I speak to them that know the l,) *3551*
7: 1 how that the l hath dominion over a man, *3551*
7: 2 a husband is bound by the l to *her* husband *3551*
7: 2 she is loosed from the l of the husband. *3551*
7: 3 *her* husband be dead, she is free from *that* l; *3551*
7: 4 ye also are become dead to the l by *3551*
7: 5 the motions of sins, which were by the l, *3551*
7: 6 But now we are delivered from the l, *3551*
7: 7 *Is* the l sin? God forbid. Nay, I had not *3551*
7: 7 Nay, I had not known sin, but by the l: for I *3551*
7: 7 except the l had said, Thou shalt not covet. *3551*
7: 8 For without the l sin *was* dead. *3551*
7: 9 For I was alive without the l once: but *3551*
7:12 Wherefore the l *is* holy, and *3551*
7:14 For we know that the l is spiritual: but I am *3551*
7:16 I consent unto the l that *it is* good. *3551*
7:21 I find then a l, that, when I would do good, *3551*
7:22 For I delight in the l of God after *3551*
7:23 But I see another l in my members, *3551*
7:23 warring against the l of my mind, and *3551*
7:23 bringing me into captivity to the l of sin *3551*
7:25 with the mind I myself serve the l of God; *3551*
7:25 law of God; but with the flesh the l of sin. *3551*
8: 2 For the l of the Spirit of life in Christ Jesus *3551*
8: 2 Jesus hath made me free from the l of sin *3551*
8: 3 For what the l could not do, in that it was *3551*
8: 4 That the righteousness of the l might be *3551*
8: 7 for it is not subject to the l of God, *3551*
9: 4 and the **giving of the** l, and the service *of* *3548*
9:31 which followed *after* the l of righteousness, *3551*
9:31 hath not attained to the l of righteousness. *3551*
9:32 but as *it were* by the works of the l. *3551*
10: 4 For Christ *is* the end of the l for *3551*
10: 5 the righteousness which is of the l, *3551*
13: 8 he that loveth another hath fulfilled the l. *3551*
13:10 therefore love *is* the fulfilling of the l. *3551*
1Co 6: 1 **go to** l before the unjust, and not before *2919*
6: 6 But brother **goeth to** l with brother, and *2919*
6: 7 because ye **go to** l one with another. *2192+2917*
7:39 The wife is bound by the l as long as her *3551*
9: 8 as a man? or saith not the l the same also? *3551*
9: 9 For it is written in the l of Moses, *3551*
9:20 to them that are under the l, as under *3551*
9:20 them that are under the law, as under the l, *3551*
9:20 that I might gain them that are under the l; *3551*
9:21 To them *that are* **without** l, as without law, *459*
9:21 To them *that are* without law, as **without** l, *459*
9:21 (being not **without** l to God, but under *459*
9:21 law to God, but **under** the l to Christ,) *1772*
9:21 that I might gain them *that are* **without** l. *459*
14:21 In the l it is written, With *men* of other *3551*
14:34 to be under obedience, as also saith the l. *3551*
15:56 death *is* sin; and the strength of sin *is* the l. *3551*
Gal 2:16 a man is not justified by the works of the l, *3551*
2:16 of Christ, and not by the works of the l: *3551*
2:16 for by the works of the l shall no flesh be *3551*
2:19 For I through the l am dead to the law, *3551*
2:19 For I through the law am dead to the l, *3551*
2:21 for if righteousness *come* by the l, then *3551*
3: 2 ye the Spirit by the works of the l, *3551*
3: 5 *doeth he it* by the works of the l, or by *3551*
3:10 For as many as are of the works of the l are *3551*
3:10 are written in the book of the l to do them. *3551*
3:11 But that no *man* is justified by the l in *3551*
3:12 And the l is not of faith: but, The man that *3551*
3:13 hath redeemed us from the curse of the l, *3551*
3:17 the l, which was four hundred and *3551*
3:18 For if the inheritance *be* of the l, *it is* no *3551*
3:19 Wherefore then *serveth* the l? It was added *3551*
3:21 *Is* the l then against the promises of God? *3551*
3:21 for if there had been a l given which could *3551*
3:21 righteousness should have been by the l. *3551*
3:23 faith came, we were kept under the l, *3551*
3:24 Wherefore the l was our schoolmaster *to* *3551*
4: 4 made of a woman, made under the l, *3551*
4: 5 To redeem them that were under the l, *3551*
4:21 Tell me, ye that desire to be under the l, *3551*
4:21 to be under the law, do ye not hear the l? *3551*
5: 3 that he is a debtor to do the whole l. *3551*
5: 4 whosoever of you are justified by the l; *3551*
5:14 For all the l is fulfilled in one word, *even* in *3551*
5:18 be led of the Spirit, ye are not under the l. *3551*
5:23 against such there is no l. *3551*
6: 2 and so fulfil the l of Christ. *3551*
6:13 themselves who are circumcised keep the l; *3551*
Eph 2:15 *even* the l of commandments *contained* in *3551*
Php 3: 5 the Hebrews; as touching the l, a Pharisee; *3551*
3: 6 touching the righteousness which is in the l, *3551*
3: 9 which is of the l, but that which is through *3551*
1Ti 1: 7 Desiring to be **teachers of the** l; *3547*
1: 8 But we know that the l *is* good, if a man *3551*
1: 9 that the l is not made for a righteous *man,* *3551*
Tit 3: 9 and contentions, and strivings **about** the l; *3544*

Heb 7: 5 take tithes of the people according to the l, *3551*
7:11 (for under it the people **received** the l,) *3549*
7:12 is made of necessity a change also of the l. *3551*
7:16 not after the l of a carnal commandment, *3551*
7:19 For the l made nothing perfect, but *3551*
7:28 For the l maketh men high priests which *3551*
7:28 which was since the l, *maketh* the Son, *3551*
8: 4 are priests that offer gifts according to the l: *3551*
9:19 precept to all the people according to the l, *3551*
9:22 And almost all *things* are by the l purged *3551*
10: 1 For the l having a shadow of good *things* to *3551*
10: 8 pleasure *therein:* which are offered by the l; *3551*
10:28 He that despised Moses' l died without *3551*
Jas 1:25 But whoso looketh into the perfect l of *3551*
2: 8 If ye fulfil the royal l according to *3551*
2: 9 and are convinced of the l as transgressors. *3551*
2:10 For whosoever shall keep the whole l, and *3551*
2:11 thou art become a transgressor of the l. *3551*
2:12 as they that shall be judged by the l of *3551*
4:11 speaketh evil of the l, and judgeth the law: *3551*
4:11 speaketh evil of the law, and judgeth the l: *3551*
4:11 but if thou judge the l, thou art not a doer of *3551*
4:11 thou art not a doer of the l, but a judge. *3551*
1Jn 3: 4 sin **transgresseth** also the l: *458+4160*
3: 4 the law: for sin is the **transgression of** the l. *458*

LAWFUL (39) [LAW]
Ezr 7:24 it *shall* not *be* l to impose toll, tribute, or 7990
Isa 49:24 from the mighty, or the l captive delivered? 6662
Eze 18: 5 be just, and do **that which is** l and right, 4941
18:19 When the son hath done **that which is** l and 4941
18:21 do **that which is** l and right, he shall surely 4941
18:27 doeth **that which is** l and right, he shall 4941
33:14 his sin, and do **that which is** l and right; 4941
33:16 he hath done **that which is** l and right; 4941
33:19 do **that which is** l and right, he shall live 4941
Mt 12: 2 thy disciples do *that* which is not l to do *1832*
12: 4 which was not l for him to eat, *1832*
12:10 saying, Is it l to heal on the sabbath days? *1832*
12:12 Wherefore it is l to do well on the sabbath *1832*
14: 4 unto him, It is not l for thee to have her. *1832*
19: 3 Is it l for a man to put away his wife for *1832*
20:15 Is it not l for me to do what I will with *1832*
22:17 Is it l to give tribute unto Cesar, or not? *1832*
27: 6 It is not l for to put them into the treasury, *1832*
Mk 2:24 they on the sabbath day *that* which is not l? *1832*
2:26 which is not l to eat but for the priests, and *1832*
3: 4 Is it l to do good on the sabbath days, or *1832*
6:18 It is not l for thee to have thy brother's *1832*
10: 2 Is it l for a man to put away *his* wife? *1832*
12:14 Is it l to give tribute to Cesar, or not? *1832*
Lk 6: 2 Why do ye *that* which is not l to do on *1832*
6: 4 which it is not l to eat but for the priests *1832*
6: 9 I will ask you one *thing;* Is it l on *1832*
14: 3 saying, Is it l to heal on the sabbath day? *1832*
20:22 Is it l for us to give tribute unto Cesar, or *1832*
Jn 5:10 it is not l for thee to carry *thy* bed. *1832*
18:31 It is not l for us to put any *man* to death: *1832*
Ac 16:21 which are not l for us to receive, neither to *1832*
19:39 it shall be determined in a l assembly. *1772*
22:25 l for you to scourge a man *that is* a Roman, *1832*
1Co 6:12 All *things* are l unto me, but all *things* are *1832*
6:12 all *things* are l for me, but I will not be *1832*
10:23 All *things* are l for me, but all *things* are not *1832*
10:23 all *things* are l for me, but all *things* edify *1832*
2Co 12: 4 which *it is* not l for a man to utter. *1832*

LAWFULLY (2) [LAW]
1Ti 1: 8 know that the law *is* good, if a man use it l; *3545*
2Ti 2: 5 *yet* is he not crowned, except he strive l. *3545*

LAWGIVER (7) [GIVE, LAW]
Ge 49:10 nor a l from between his feet, until Shiloh 2710
Nu 21:18 by the direction of the l, with their staves. 2710
Dt 33:21 because there, *in* a portion of the l, *was he* 2710
Ps 60: 7 *is* the strength of mine head; Judah *is* my l; 2710
108: 8 *is* the strength of mine head; Judah *is* my l; 2710
Isa 33:22 the LORD *is* our l, the LORD *is* our 2710
Jas 4:12 There is one l, who is able to save and *3550*

LAWLESS (1) [LAW]
1Ti 1: 9 righteous *man,* but for the l and disobedient, *459*

LAWS (20) [LAW]
Ge 26: 5 my commandments, my statutes, and my l. 8451
Ex 16:28 ye to keep my commandments and my l? 8451
18:16 *them* know the statutes of God, and his l. 8451
18:20 And thou shalt teach them ordinances and l, 8451
Lev 26:46 These *are* the statutes and judgments and l, 8451
Ezr 7:25 the river, all such as know the l of thy God; 1882
Ne 9:13 true l, good statutes and commandments: 8451
9:14 them precepts, statutes, and l, 8451
Est 1:19 let it be written among the l of the Persians 1881
3: 8 their l *are* diverse from all people; 1881
3: 8 all people; neither keep they the king's l: 1881
Ps 105:45 might observe his statutes, and keep his l. 8451
Isa 24: 5 because they have transgressed the l, 8451
Eze 43:11 all the forms thereof, and all the l thereof: 8451
44: 5 house of the LORD, and all the l thereof; 8451
44:24 they shall keep my l and my statutes in all 8451
Da 7:25 most High, and think to change times and l: 1882
9:10 to walk in his l, which he set before us by 8451
Heb 8:10 I will put my l into their mind, and *3551*
10:16 I will put my l into their hearts, and in their *3551*

LAWYER (3) [LAW]
Mt 22:35 Then one of them, *which was* a l, *3544*
Lk 10:25 a certain l stood up, and tempted him, *3544*
Tit 3:13 Bring Zenas the l and Apollos on their *3544*

LAWYERS (5) [LAW]
Lk 7:30 l rejected the counsel of God against *3544*
11:45 Then answered one of the l, and said unto *3544*
11:46 And he said, Woe unto you also, *ye* l! *3544*
11:52 Woe unto you, l! for ye have taken away *3544*
14: 3 And Jesus answering spake unto the l and *3544*

LAY (241) [LAID, LAIDST, LAYEDST, LAYEST, LAYETH, LAYING, OVERLAY]
Ge 19: 4 But before they l **down**, the men of the city, 7901
19:33 the firstborn went in, and l with her father; 7901
19:33 he perceived not when she l **down**, 7901
19:34 Behold, I l yesternight with my father: 7901
19:35 the younger arose, and l with him; and 7901
19:35 he perceived not when she l **down**, 7901
22:12 he said, **L** not thine hand upon the lad, 7971
28:11 and l **down** in that place **to sleep**. 7901
30:16 And he l with her that night. 7901
34: 2 he took her, and l with her, and defiled her. 7901
35:22 and l with Bilhah his father's concubine: 7901
37:22 l no hand upon him, that he might rid him 7971
41:35 l **up** corn under the hand of Pharaoh, and 6651
Ex 5: 8 did make heretofore, you shall l upon them; 7760
7: 4 that I may l my hand upon Egypt, and 5414
16:13 in the morning the dew l round about 7902
16:14 when the dew that l was gone up, behold, 7902
16:14 upon the face of the wilderness *there l* a NIH
16:23 that which remaineth over l **up** for you to 3240
16:33 l it **up** before the LORD, to be kept for 3240
21:22 according as the woman's husband will l 7896
22:25 neither shalt thou l upon him usury. 7760
Lev 1: 7 and l the wood **in order** upon the fire: 6186
1: 8 l the parts, the head, and the fat, **in order** 6186
1:12 the priest shall l them **in order** on the wood 6186
2:15 put oil upon it, and l frankincense thereon: 7760
3: 2 he shall l his hand upon the head of his 5564
3: 8 he shall l his hand upon the head of his 5564
3:13 he shall l his hand upon the head of it, and 5564
4: 4 shall l his hand upon the bullock's head, 5564
4:15 the elders of the congregation shall l their 5564
4:24 he shall l his hand upon the head of 5564
4:29 he shall l his hand upon the head of the sin 5564
4:33 he shall l his hand upon the head of the sin 5564
6:12 l the burnt offering **in order** upon it; 6186
16:21 Aaron shall l both his hands upon the head 5564
24:14 let all that heard *him* l their hands upon his 5564
Nu 8:12 the Levites shall l their hands upon 5564
12:11 I beseech thee, l not the sin upon us, 7896
17: 4 thou shalt l them **up** in the tabernacle of 3240
19: 9 l *them* **up** without the camp in a clean 3240
24: 9 he l **down** as a lion, and as a great lion: 7901
27:18 *is* the spirit, and l thine hand upon him; 5564
Dt 7:15 but will l them upon all *them* that hate thee. 5414
11:18 Therefore shall ye l **up** these my words in 7760
11:25 *for* the LORD your God shall l the fear of 5414
14:28 and shalt l *it* **up** within thy gates: 3240
21: 8 l not innocent blood unto thy people of 5414

Dt 21:19 his father and his mother l **hold** on him, 8610
22:22 *both* the man that l with the woman, and 7901
22:25 then the man only that l with her shall die: 7901
22:28 l **hold on** her, and lie with her, and they be 8610
22:29 the man that l with her shall give unto 7901
Jos 6:26 he shall l the **foundation** thereof in his 3245
8: 2 l thee an ambush for the city behind it. 7760
15:46 all that *I* near Ashdod, with their villages: NIH
Jdg 4:22 Sisera l dead, and the nail *was* in his 5307
5:27 At her feet he bowed, he fell, he l **down**: 7901
6:20 and l *them* upon this rock, 3240
7:12 all the children of the east l **along** in 5307
7:13 and overturned it, that the tent l **along**. 5307
14:17 he told her, because she l **sore upon** him: 6693
16: 3 Samson l till midnight, and arose at 7901
18:19 l thine hand upon thy mouth, and go with 7760
Ru 3: 4 and uncover his feet, and l thee **down**; 7901
3: 8 and behold, a woman l *at* his feet. 7901
3:14 she l *at* his feet until the morning: and 7901
1Sa 2:22 how they l with the women that assembled 7901
3: 5 lie down again. And he went and l **down**. 7901
3: 9 So Samuel went and l **down** in his place. 7901
3:15 Samuel l until the morning, and opened 7901
6: 8 ark of the LORD, and l it upon the cart; 5414
11: 2 and l it *for* a reproach upon all Israel. 7760
19:24 l **down** naked all that day and all *that* night. 5307
26: 5 David beheld the place where Saul l, and 7901
26: 5 Saul l in the trench, and the people pitched 7901
26: 7 Saul l sleeping within the trench, and 7901
26: 7 Abner and the people l round about him. 7901
2Sa 2:21 l thee **hold on** one of the young men, and 270
4: 5 who l **on a bed** at noon. 4904+7901
4: 7 he l on his bed in his bedchamber, and 7901
11: 4 she came in unto him, and he l with her; 7901
12: 3 l in his bosom, and was unto him as a 7901
12:16 and went in, and l all night upon the earth. 7901
12:24 and went in unto her, and l with her: 7901
13: 5 **L** *thee* **down** on thy bed, and make thyself 7901
13: 6 So Amnon l **down**, and made himself sick: 7901
13:14 than she, forced her, and l with her. 7901
13:31 and tare his garments, and l on the earth; 7901
19:32 king of sustenance while he l at Mahanaim; 7871
1Ki 5:17 to l **the foundation** of the house. 3245
7: 3 that *l* on forty five pillars, fifteen *in* a row. NIH
13: 4 hand from the altar, saying, **L hold on** him. 8610
13:31 God *is* buried; l my bones beside his bones: 3240
18:23 l *it* on wood, and put no fire *under*: and 7760
18:23 and l *it* on wood, and put no fire *under*: 5414
19: 5 as he l and slept under a juniper tree, 7901
21:27 fasted, and l in sackcloth, and went softly. 7901
2Ki 4:11 he turned into the chamber, and l there. 7901
4:29 and l my staff upon the face of the child. 7760
4:34 l upon the child, and put his mouth upon 7901
9:16 and went to Jezreel; for Joram l there. 7901
10: 8 **L** ye them *in* two heaps *at* the entering in of 7760
19:25 that thou shouldest be to l **waste** fenced 7582
2Ch 31: 7 began to l the **foundation** of the heaps, 3245
36:21 *for* as long as *she* l **desolate** she kept 8074
Ezr 8:31 and of such as l **in wait** by the way. 693
Ne 13:21 if ye do *so* again, I will l hands on you. 7971
Est 2:21 and sought to l hand on the king Ahasuerus. 7971
3: 6 he thought scorn to l hands on Mordecai 7971
4: 3 wailing; *and* many l in sackcloth and ashes. 3331
6: 2 who sought to l hand on the king 7971
9: 2 to l hand on such as sought their hurt: 7971
Job 9:33 *that* might l his hand upon us both. 7896
17: 3 **L down** now, put me in a surety with thee; 7760
21: 5 and l *your* hand upon *your* mouth. 7760
22:22 and l **up** his words in thine heart. 7760
22:24 shalt thou l **up** gold as dust, and *the gold of* 7896
29:19 and the dew l **all night** upon my branch. 3885
34:23 For he will not l upon man more *than right*; 7760
40: 4 I will l my hand upon my mouth. 7760
41: 8 **L** thine hand upon him, remember 7760
Ps 4: 8 I will both l me **down** in peace, and sleep: 7901
7: 5 the earth, and l mine honour in the dust. 7931
38:12 They also that seek after my life l **snares** 5367
71:10 they that l **wait** for my soul take counsel 8104
84: 3 where she may l her young, *even* thine 7896
104:22 and l them **down** in their dens. 7257
Pr 1:11 Come with us, let us l **wait** for blood, 693
1:18 they l **wait** for their own blood; they lurk 693
3:18 She *is* a tree of life to them that l **hold** upon 2388
7: 1 and l **up** my commandments with thee. 6845

10:14 Wise *men* l **up** knowledge: but the mouth 6845
24:15 **L** not **wait**, O wicked *man*, against 693
30:32 thought evil, *l thine* hand upon thy mouth. NIH
Ecc 2: 3 to l **hold** on folly, till I might see what *was* 270
7: 2 all men; and the living will l *it* to his heart. 5414
Isa 5: 6 I will l it waste: it shall not be pruned, nor 7896
5: 8 *that* l field to field, till *there be* no place, 7126
5:29 l **hold** of the prey, and shall carry *it* away 270
11:14 they shall l their hand **upon** Edom and 4916
13: 9 and fierce anger, to l the land desolate: 7760
13:11 will l **low** the haughtiness of the terrible. 8213
22:22 the key of the house of David will I l upon 5414
25:12 l **low**, *and* bring to the ground, *even* to 8213
28:16 I l in Zion **for a foundation** a stone, 3245
28:17 Judgment also will I l to the line, and 7760
29: 3 will l **siege** against thee *with* a mount, and 6696
29:21 l **a snare** for him that reproveth in the gate, 6983
30:32 which the LORD shall l upon him, *it* shall 5117
34:15 l, and hatch, and gather under her shadow: 4422
35: 7 **where** each l, *shall be* grass with reeds and 7258
37:26 that thou shouldest be to l **waste** defenced 7582
38:21 l *it* **for a plaister** upon the boil, and 4799
47: 7 that thou didst not l these *things* to thy 7760
51:16 l the **foundations** of the earth, and say unto 3245
54:11 I will l thy stones with fair colours, and 7257
54:11 and l thy **foundations** with sapphires. 3245
Jer 5:26 people are found wicked *men*: they l **wait**, 7789
6:21 I will l stumblingblocks before this people, 5414
6:23 They shall l **hold on** bow and spear; 2388
Eze 3:20 I l a stumblingblock before him, he shall 5414
4: 1 l it before thee, and pourtray upon it 5414
4: 2 l siege against it, and build a fort against it, 5414
4: 3 and thou shalt l **siege** against it. 6696
4: 4 l the iniquity of the house of Israel upon it: 7760
4: 8 I will l bands upon thee, and thou shalt not 5414
6: 5 I will l the dead carcases of the children of 5414
19: 2 she l **down** among lions, she nourished her 7257
23: 8 for in her youth they l with her, and 7901
25:14 I will l my vengeance upon Edom by 5414
25:17 when I shall l my vengeance upon them. 5414
26:12 they shall l thy stones and thy timber and 7760
26:16 l **away** their robes, and put off their 5493
28:17 I will l thee before kings, that *they* may 5414
32: 5 I will l thy flesh upon the mountains, and 5414
33:28 For I will l the land most desolate, and 5414
35: 4 I will l thy cities waste, and thou shalt be 7760
36:29 will increase it, and l no famine upon you. 5414
36:34 whereas it l desolate in the sight of all that 1961
37: 6 I will l sinews upon you, and will bring up 5414
42:13 there shall they l the most holy *things*, 3240
42:14 there they shall l their garments wherein 3240
44:19 l them in the holy chambers, and they shall 3240
Am 2: 8 they l *themselves* **down** upon clothes laid 5186
Jnh 1: 5 of the ship; and he l, and was fast asleep. 7901
1:14 and l not upon us innocent blood: 5414
Mic 1: 7 and all the idols thereof will I l desolate: 7760
7:16 they shall l *their* hand upon *their* mouth, 7760
Zec 14:13 they shall l **hold** every one on the hand of 2388
Mal 2: 2 will not hear, and if ye will not l *it* to heart, 7760
2: 2 because ye do not l *it* to heart. 7760
Mt 6:19 **L** not **up** for yourselves treasures upon *2343*
6:20 But l **up** for yourselves treasures in heaven, *2343*
8:20 the Son of man hath not where to l *his* *2827*
9:18 but come and l thy hand upon her, and *2007*
12:11 will he not l **hold on** it, and lift *it* out? *2902*
21:46 But when they sought to l **hands on** him, *2902*
23: 4 and l *them* **on** men's shoulders; *2007*
28: 6 Come, see the place where the Lord l. *2749*
Mk 1:30 But Simon's wife's mother l sick of a fever, *2621*
2: 4 the bed wherein the sick of the palsy l. *2621*
3:21 heard *of it*, they went out to l **hold on** him: *2902*
5:23 *I pray thee*, come and l *thy* hands **on** her, *2007*
12:12 And they sought to l **hold on** him, but *2902*
15: 7 *which I* bound with them that had made NIG
16:18 they shall l hands on the sick, and *2007*
Lk 5:18 to bring him in, and to l *him* before him. *5087*
5:25 and took up *that* whereon he l, and *2621*
8:42 about twelve years of age, and she l a dying. NIG
9:58 the Son of man hath not where to l *his* *2827*
19:44 And shall l thee **even with the ground**, and *1474*
20:19 same hour sought to l hands **on** him; *1911*
21:12 they shall l their hands **on** you, and *1911*
Jn 5: 3 In these l a great multitude of impotent *2621*
10:15 and I l **down** my life for the sheep. *5087*

L

Jn 10:17 because I l **down** my life, that I might take 5087
10:18 taketh it from me, but I l it **down** of myself. 5087
10:18 I have power to l it **down**, and I have power 5087
11:38 It was a cave, and a stone l upon it. 1945
13:37 I will l **down** my life for thy sake. 5087
13:38 Wilt thou l **down** thy life for my sake? 5087
15:13 that a man l **down** his life for his friends. 5087
Ac 7:60 Lord, l not this sin **to** their **charge**. 2476
8:19 this power, that **on** whomsoever I l hands, 2007
15:28 to l **upon** you no greater burden than these 2007
27:20 no small tempest l **on** *us*, all hope that we 1945
28: 8 that the father of Publius l sick of a fever 2621
Ro 8:33 Who shall l any thing **to the charge** of 1458
9:33 I l in Sion a stumblingstone and rock of 5087
1Co 3:11 For other foundation can no *man* l than that 5087
16: 2 week let every one of you l by him in store, 5087
2Co 12:14 for the children ought not to l **up** for 2343
1Ti 5:22 L hands suddenly **on** no *man*, neither be 2007
6:12 good fight of faith, l **hold on** eternal life, 1949
6:19 that they may l **hold on** eternal life. 1949
Heb 6:18 who have fled for refuge to l **hold upon** 2902
12: 1 let us l **aside** every weight, and the sin which 659
Jas 1:21 Wherefore l **apart** all filthiness and 659
1Pe 2: 6 I l in Sion a chief corner stone, elect, 5087
1Jn 3:16 we ought to l **down** *our* lives for 5087

LAYEDST (1) [LAY]
Lk 19:21 thou takest up that thou l not **down**, and 5087

LAYEST (2) [LAY]
Nu 11:11 that *thou* l the burden of all this people 7760
1Sa 28: 9 wherefore then l thou **a snare** for my life, 5367

LAYETH (18) [LAY]
Job 21:19 God l **up** his iniquity for his children: 6845
24:12 crieth out: yet God l not folly *to them*. 7760
41:26 The sword of him that l at him cannot hold: 5381
Ps 33: 7 as a heap: he l **up** the depth in storehouses. 5414
104: 3 Who l the **beams** of his chambers in 7136
Pr 2: 7 He l **up** sound wisdom for the righteous: 6845
13:16 with knowledge: but a fool l **open** *his* folly. 6566
26:24 with his lips, and l **up** deceit within him; 7896
31:19 She l her hands to the spindle, and 7971
Isa 26: 5 the lofty city, he l it **low**; he layeth it low, 8213
26: 5 it low; he l it **low**, *even* to the ground; 8213
56: 2 and the son of man *that* l **hold** on it; 2388
57: 1 and no man l *it* to heart: 7760
Jer 9: 8 with his mouth, but in heart he l his wait. 7760
12:11 made desolate, because no man l *it* to heart. 7760
Zec 12: 1 l the **foundation** of the earth, and 3245
Lk 12:21 So *is* he that l **up treasure** for himself, and 2343
15: 5 And when he hath found *it*, he l *it* on his 2007

LAYING (13) [LAY]
Nu 35:20 or hurl at him by l **of wait**, that he die; 6660
35:22 cast upon him any thing without l **of wait**, 6660
Ps 64: 5 they commune of l snares **privily**; they say, 2934
Mk 7: 8 For l **aside** the commandment of God, 863
Lk 11:54 L **wait for** him, and seeking to catch 1748
Ac 8:18 And when Simon saw that through l **on** of 1936
9:24 But their l **await** was known of Saul. 1917
25: 3 l **wait** in the way to kill him. 1747+4160
1Ti 4:14 with the l **on** of the hands of the presbytery. 1936
6:19 L **up in store** for themselves a good 597
Heb 6: 1 not l again the foundation of repentance 2598
6: 2 and of l **on** of hands, and of resurrection of 1936
1Pe 2: 1 Wherefore l **aside** all malice, and all guile, 659

LAZARUS (15)
Lk 16:20 And there was a certain beggar named L, 2976
16:23 Abraham afar off, and L in his bosom. 2976
16:24 have mercy on me, and send L, 2976
16:25 and likewise L evil *things*: but now he is 2976
Jn 11: 1 *named* L, of Bethany, the town of Mary 2976
11: 2 with her hair, whose brother L was sick.) 2976
11: 5 Jesus loved Martha, and her sister, and L. 2976
11:11 he saith unto them, Our friend L sleepeth; 2976
11:14 said Jesus unto them plainly, L is dead. 2976
11:43 he cried with a loud voice, L, come forth. 2976
12: 1 where L was which had been dead, 2976
12: 2 L was one of them that sat at the table with 2976
12: 9 sake only, but that they might see L also, 2976
12:10 that they might put L also to death; 2976
12:17 that was with him when he called L out of 2976

LAZINESS See SLOTHFUL

LAZY See SLOTHFUL

LEAD (60) [LEADER, LEADERS, LEADEST, LEADETH, LED, LEDDEST, RINGLEADER]
Ge 33:14 I will l **on** softly, according as the cattle 5095
Ex 13:21 day in a pillar of a cloud, to l them the way; 5148
15:10 they sank as l in the mighty waters. 5777
32:34 l the people unto *the place* of which I have 5148
Nu 27:17 which may l them **out**, and which may 3318
31:22 the brass, the iron, the tin, and the l, 5777
Dt 4:27 whither the LORD shall l you. 5090
20: 9 make captains of the armies to l the people. 7218
28:37 all nations whither the LORD shall l thee. 5090
32:12 *So* the LORD alone did l him, and 5148
Jdg 5:12 arise, Barak, and l thy captivity **captive**, 7617
1Sa 30:22 that they may l *them* **away**, and depart. 5090
2Ch 30: 9 before them that l them **captive**, 7617
Ne 9:19 not from them by day, to l them in the way; 5148
Job 19:24 with an iron pen and l in the rock for ever! 5777
Ps 5: 8 L me, O LORD, in thy righteousness 5148
25: 5 L me in thy truth, and teach me: for thou 1869
27:11 l me in a plain path, because of mine 5148
31: 3 therefore for thy name's sake l me, and 5148
43: 3 let them l me; let them bring me unto thy 5148
60: 9 the strong city? who will l me into Edom? 5148
61: 2 l me to the rock *that* is higher than I. 5148
108:10 the strong city? who will l me into Edom? 5148
125: 5 the LORD shall l them **forth** with 1980
139:10 Even there shall thy hand l me, and 5148
139:24 way in me, and l me in the way everlasting. 5148
143:10 *is* good; l me into the land of uprightness. 5148
Pr 6:22 When thou goest, it shall l thee; when thou 5148
8:20 I l in the way of righteousness, in the midst 1980
SS 8: 2 I would l thee, *and* bring thee into my 5090
Isa 3:12 they which l thee cause *thee* to err, and 833
11: 6 and a little child shall l them. 5090
20: 4 So shall the king of Assyria l **away** 5090
40:11 *and* shall **gently** l those that are with young. 5095
42:16 I will l them in paths *that* they have not 1869
49:10 for he that hath mercy on them shall l them, 5090
57:18 I will l him also, and restore comforts unto 5148
63:14 so didst thou l thy people, to make thyself a 5090
Jer 6:29 are burnt, the l is consumed of the fire; 5777
31: 9 and with supplications will I l them: 2986
32: 5 he shall l Zedekiah *to* Babylon, and 1980
Eze 22:18 all they *are* brass, and tin, and iron, and l, 5777
22:20 and brass, and iron, and l, and tin, 5777
27:12 with silver, iron, tin, and l, they traded in 5777
Na 2: 7 her maids *shall* l *her* as *with* the voice of 5090
Zec 5: 7 behold, there *was* lift up a talent of l: and 5777
5: 8 he cast the weight of l upon the mouth 5777
Mt 6:13 And l us not into temptation, but deliver us 1533
15:14 And if the blind l the blind, both shall fall 3594
Mk 13:11 But when they shall l *you*, and deliver you up, 71
14:44 same is he; take him, and l *him* **away** safely. 520
Lk 6:39 unto them, Can the blind l the blind? 3594
11: 4 And l us not **into** temptation; but 1533
13:15 from the stall, and l *him* **away** to watering? 520
Ac 13:11 about seeking *some* to l him **by the hand**. 5497
1Co 9: 5 Have we not power to l **about** a sister, 4013
1Ti 2: 2 that we may l a quiet and peaceable life in 1236
2Ti 3: 6 and l **captive** silly women laden with sins, 162
Heb 8: 9 the hand to l them **out** of the land of Egypt; 1806
Rev 7:17 shall l them unto living fountains of waters: 3594

LEADER (3) [LEAD]
1Ch 12:27 Jehoiada *was* the l of the Aaronites, and 5057
13: 1 and hundreds, *and* with every l. 5057
Isa 55: 4 a l and commander to the people. 5057

LEADERS (3) [LEAD]
2Ch 32:21 the l and captains in the camp of the king of 5057
Isa 9:16 For the l of this people cause *them* to err; 833
Mt 15:14 they be blind l of the blind. And if the blind 3595

LEADERSHIP See BISHOPRICK

LEADEST (1) [LEAD]
Ps 80: 1 of Israel, thou that l Joseph like a flock; 5090

LEADETH (14) [LEAD]
1Sa 13:17 one company turned unto the way that l to NIH
Job 12:17 He l counsellers **away** spoiled, and 1980

Job 12:19 He l princes **away** spoiled, and 1980
Ps 23: 2 he l me beside the still waters. 5095
23: 3 he l me in the paths of righteousness for his 5148
Pr 16:29 and l him into the way *that is* not good. 1980
Isa 48:17 which l thee by the way *that* thou shouldest 1869
Mt 7:13 that l to destruction, and many there be *520*
7:14 which l unto life, and few there be that find *520*
Mk 9: 2 l them **up** into a high mountain apart by *399*
Jn 10: 3 his own sheep by name, and l them **out**. *1806*
Ac 12:10 they came unto the iron gate that l unto *5342*
Ro 2: 4 not knowing that the goodness of God l thee *71*
Rev 13:10 He that l into captivity *shall* go into *4863*

LEAF (11) [LEAVES]
Ge 8:11 lo, in her mouth *was* an olive l pluckt off: 5929
Lev 26:36 the sound of a shaken l shall chase them; 5929
Job 13:25 Wilt thou break a l driven to and fro? and 5929
Ps 1: 3 his l also shall not wither; and 5929
Isa 1:30 For ye shall be as an oak whose l fadeth, 5929
34: 4 as the l falleth off from the vine, and as a 5929
64: 6 we all do fade as a l; and our iniquities, 5929
Jer 8:13 nor figs on the fig tree, and the l shall fade; 5929
17: 8 when heat cometh, but her l shall be green; 5929
Eze 47:12 all trees for meat, whose l shall not fade, 5929
47:12 be for meat, and the l thereof for medicine. 5929

LEAGUE (19)
Jos 9: 6 now therefore make ye a l with us. 1285
9: 7 and how shall we make a l with you? 1285
9:11 therefore now make ye a l with us. 1285
9:15 and made a l with them, to let them live: 1285
9:16 days after they had made a l with them, 1285
Jdg 2: 2 ye shall make no l with the inhabitants of 1285
1Sa 22: 8 my son hath made *a l* with the son of Jesse, NIH
2Sa 3:12 saying *also,* Make thy l with me, and 1285
3:13 he said, Well; I will make a l with thee: 1285
3:21 that they may make a l with thee, and 1285
5: 3 king David made a l with them in Hebron 1285
1Ki 5:12 and they two made a l *together.* 1285
15:19 *There is* a l between me and thee, *and* 1285
15:19 *and* break thy l with Baasha king of Israel, 1285
2Ch 16: 3 *There is* a l between me and thee, as *there* 1285
16: 3 go, break thy l with Baasha king of Israel, 1285
Job 5:23 For thou shalt be **in** l with the stones of 1285
Eze 30: 5 Chub, and the men of the land that is **in** l, 1285
Da 11:23 after the l *made* with him he shall work 2266

LEAH (29) [LEAH'S]
Ge 29:16 the name of the elder *was* L, and the name 3812
29:17 L was tender eyed; but Rachel was 3812
29:23 that he took L his daughter, and 3812
29:24 Laban gave unto his daughter L Zilpah his 3812
29:25 that in the morning, behold, it *was* L: 3812
29:30 he loved also Rachel more than L, and 3812
29:31 when the LORD saw that L *was* hated, 3812
29:32 L conceived, and bare a son, and she called 3812
30: 9 When L saw that she had left bearing, she 3812
30:11 L said, A troop cometh: and she called his 3812
30:13 L said, Happy am I, for the daughters will 3812
30:14 and brought them unto his mother L. 3812
30:14 Rachel said to L, Give me, I pray thee, 3812
30:16 L went out to meet him, and said, 3812
30:17 God hearkened unto L, and she conceived, 3812
30:18 L said, God hath given *me* my hire, 3812
30:19 L conceived again, and bare Jacob the sixth 3812
30:20 L said, God hath endued me with a good 3812
31: 4 and L to the field unto his flock, 3812
31:14 Rachel and L answered and said unto him, 3812
33: 1 he divided the children unto L, and 3812
33: 2 L and her children after, and Rachel and 3812
33: 7 L also with her children came near, and 3812
34: 1 Dinah the daughter of L, which she bare 3812
35:23 The sons of L; Reuben, Jacob's firstborn, 3812
46:15 These *be* the sons of L, which she bare 3812
46:18 whom Laban gave to L his daughter, and 3812
49:31 and Rebekah his wife; and there I buried L. 3812
Ru 4:11 into thine house like Rachel and like L, 3812

LEAH'S (5) [LEAH]
Ge 30:10 And Zilpah L maid bare Jacob a son. 3812
30:12 Zilpah L maid bare Jacob a second son. 3812
31:33 into L tent, and into the two maidservants' 3812
31:33 went he out of L tent, and entered into 3812
35:26 the sons of Zilpah, L handmaid; Gad, and 3812

LEAN (11) [LEANED, LEANETH, LEANFLESHED, LEANING, LEANNESS]
Ge 41:20 the l and the ill favoured kine did eat up 7534
Nu 13:20 what the land *is,* whether it *be* fat or l, 7330
Jdg 16:26 the house standeth, that I may l upon them. 8172
2Sa 13: 4 *being* the king's son, l from day to day? 1800
2Ki 18:21 *even* upon Egypt, on which if a man l, it 5564
Job 8:15 He shall l upon his house, but it shall not 8172
Pr 3: 5 and l not unto thine own understanding. 8172
Isa 17: 4 and the fatness of his flesh shall **wax** l. 7329
36: 6 whereon if a man l, it will go into his hand, 5564
Eze 34:20 the fat cattle and between the l cattle. 7330
Mic 3:11 yet will they l upon the LORD, and say, *Is* 8172

LEANED (6) [LEAN]
2Sa 1: 6 behold, Saul l upon his spear; 8172
2Ki 7: 2 a lord on whose hand the king l answered 8172
7:17 hand he l to have the charge of the gate: 8172
Eze 29: 7 when they l upon thee, thou brakest, and 8172
Am 5:19 l his hand on the wall, and a serpent bit 5564
Jn 21:20 which also l on his breast at supper, and said, *377*

LEANETH (2) [LEAN]
2Sa 3:29 or that l on a staff, or that falleth on 2388
2Ki 5:18 he l on my hand, and I bow myself *in* 8172

LEANFLESHED (3) [FLESH, LEAN]
Ge 41: 3 out of the river, ill favoured and l; 1320+1851
41: 4 l kine did eat up the seven well 1320+1851
41:19 poor and very ill favoured and l, 1320+7534

LEANING (3) [LEAN]
SS 8: 5 from the wilderness, l upon her beloved? 7514
Jn 13:23 Now there was l on Jesus' bosom one of his *345*
Heb 11:21 and worshipped, *l* upon the top of his staff. NIG

LEANNESS (5) [LEAN]
Job 16: 8 my l rising up in me beareth witness to my 3585
Ps 106:15 them their request; but sent l into their soul. 7332
Isa 10:16 Lord of hosts, send among his fat ones l; 7332
24:16 I said, My l, my leanness, woe unto me! 7334
24:16 I said, My leanness, my l, woe unto me! 7334

LEANNOTH (1)
Ps 88: T To the chief Musician upon Mahalath L, 6031

LEAP (9) [LEAPED, LEAPING, LEAPT]
Ge 31:12 all the rams which l upon the cattle *are* 5927
Lev 11:21 above their feet, to l withal upon the earth; 5425
Dt 33:22 *is* a lion's whelp: he shall l from Bashan. 2187
Job 41:19 go burning lamps, *and* sparks of fire **l out**. 4422
Ps 68:16 Why l ye, ye high hills? *this is* the hill 7520
Isa 35: 6 shall the lame *man* l as a hart, and 1801
Joel 2: 5 on the tops of mountains shall they l, 7540
Zep 1: 9 I punish all those that l on the threshold, 1801
Lk 6:23 ye in that day, and l *for joy:* for behold, *4640*

LEAPED (6) [LEAP]
Ge 31:10 the rams which l upon the cattle *were* 5927
2Sa 22:30 a troop: by my God have I l **over** a wall. 1801
Ps 18:29 and by my God have I l **over** a wall. 1801
Lk 1:41 salutation of Mary, the babe l in her womb; *4640*
1:44 mine ears, the babe l in my womb for joy. *4640*
Ac 14:10 upright on thy feet. And he l and walked. *242*

LEAPING (4) [LEAP]
2Sa 6:16 saw king David l and dancing before 6339
SS 2: 8 behold, he cometh l upon the mountains, 1801
Ac 3: 8 And he l **up** stood, and walked, and *1814*
3: 8 the temple, walking, and l, and praising God. *242*

LEAPT (2) [LEAP]
1Ki 18:26 And they l upon the altar which was made. 6452
Ac 19:16 whom the evil spirit was **l on** them, *2177*

LEARN (32) [LEARNED, LEARNING, UNLEARNED]
Dt 4:10 that they may l to fear me all the days that 3925
5: 1 that ye may l them, and keep, and do them. 3925
14:23 that thou mayest l to fear the LORD thy 3925
17:19 that he may l to fear the LORD his God, 3925
18: 9 thou shalt not l to do after the abominations 3925
31:12 that they may l, and fear the LORD your 3925
31:13 and l to fear the LORD your God, 3925
Ps 119:71 been afflicted; that I might l thy statutes. 3925
119:73 that I may l thy commandments. 3925

L

Pr 22:25 Lest thou l his ways, and get a snare to thy 502
Isa 1:17 L to do well; seek judgment, relieve 3925
2: 4 neither shall they l war any more. 3925
26: 9 the inhabitants of the world will l 3925
26:10 the wicked, *yet* will he not l righteousness: 3925
29:24 and they that murmured shall l doctrine. 3925
Jer 10: 2 L not the way of the heathen, and be not 3925
12:16 if they will **diligently** l the ways of 3925+3925
Mic 4: 3 neither shall they l war any more. 3925
Mt 9:13 But go ye and l what *that* meaneth, I will *3129*
11:29 Take my yoke upon you, and l of me; for I *3129*
24:32 Now l a parable of the fig tree; When his *3129*
Mk 13:28 Now l a parable of the fig tree; When her *3129*
1Co 4: 6 that ye might l in us not to think *of men* *3129*
14:31 that all may l, and all may be comforted. *3129*
14:35 And if they will l any *thing,* let them ask *3129*
Gal 3: 2 This only would I l of you, Received ye *3129*
1Ti 1:20 that they may l not to blaspheme. *3811*
2:11 Let the woman l in silence with all *3129*
5: 4 let them l first to shew piety at home, and *3129*
5:13 And withal they l *to be* idle, *3129*
Tit 3:14 And let ours also l to maintain good works *3129*
Rev 14: 3 and no *man* could l *that* song but *3129*

LEARNED (22) [LEARN]

Ge 30:27 *tarry: for* I have l **by experience** that 5172
Ps 106:35 among the heathen, and l their works. 3925
119: 7 when I shall have l thy righteous 3925
Pr 30: 3 I neither l wisdom, nor have the knowledge 3925
Isa 29:11 which *men* deliver to one that is l, 3045+5612
29:12 book is delivered to *him* that is not l, 3045+5612
29:12 I pray thee: and he saith, I am not l. 3045+5612
50: 4 GOD hath given me the tongue of the l, 3928
50: 4 he wakeneth mine ear to hear as the l. 3928
Eze 19: 3 a young lion, and it l to catch the prey; 3925
19: 6 and l to catch the prey, *and* devoured men. 3925
Jn 6:45 that hath heard, and hath l of the Father, *3129*
7:15 knoweth this *man* letters, having never l? *3129*
Ac 7:22 And Moses was l in all the wisdom of *3811*
Ro 16:17 contrary to the doctrine which ye have l; *3129*
Eph 4:20 But ye have not so l Christ; *3129*
Php 4: 9 Those *things,* which ye have both l, and *3129*
4:11 for I have l, in whatsoever *state* I am, *3129*
Col 1: 7 As ye also l of Epaphras our dear *3129*
2Ti 3:14 thou in *the things* which thou hast l *3129*
3:14 knowing of whom thou hast l *them;* *3129*
Heb 5: 8 *yet* l he obedience by *the things* which he *3129*

LEARNING (9) [LEARN]

Pr 1: 5 A wise *man* will hear, and will increase l; 3948
9: 9 teach a just *man,* and he will increase in l. 3948
16:21 and the sweetness of the lips increaseth l. 3948
16:23 teacheth his mouth, and addeth l to his lips. 3948
Da 1: 4 whom *they* might teach the l and the tongue 5612
1:17 and skill in all l and wisdom: 5612
Ac 26:24 beside thyself; much l doth make thee mad. *1121*
Ro 15: 4 written aforetime were written for our l, *1319*
2Ti 3: 7 Ever l, and never able to come to *3129*

LEASING (2)

Ps 4: 2 *long* will ye love vanity, *and* seek after l? 3577
5: 6 Thou shalt destroy them that speak l: 3577

LEAST (39) [LESS]

Ge 24:55 abide with us *a few* days, **at the** l ten; 176
32:10 I am not worthy **of the** l of all the mercies, 4480
Nu 11:32 he that **gathered** l gathered ten homers: and 4591
Jdg 3: 2 **at the** l such as before knew nothing 7535
6:15 and I *am* the l in my father's house. 6810
1Sa 9:21 my family the l of all the families of 6810
21: 4 if the young men have kept themselves **at l** 389
2Ki 18:24 captain of the l of my master's servants, 6996
1Ch 12:14 one of the l *was* over an hundred, and 6996
Isa 36: 9 captain of the l of my master's servants, 6996
Jer 6:13 For from the l of them even unto 6996
8:10 l even unto the greatest is given to 6996
31:34 from the l of them unto the greatest of 6996
42: 1 all the people from the l even unto 6996
42: 8 all the people from the l even to 6996
44:12 from the l even unto the greatest, by 6996
49:20 Surely the l of the flock shall draw them 6810
50:45 Surely the l of the flock shall draw them 6810
Am 9: 9 yet shall not the l **grain** fall *upon* the earth. 6872
Jnh 3: 5 from the greatest of them even to the l of 6996
Mt 2: 6 art not the l among the princes of Juda: *1646*
5:19 shall break one of these l commandments, *1646*
5:19 he shall be called the l in the kingdom of *1646*
11:11 notwithstanding he that is l in the kingdom *3398*
13:32 Which indeed is the l of all seeds: but *3398*
25:40 *it* unto one of the l of these my brethren, *1646*
25:45 Inasmuch as ye did *it* not to one of the l of *1646*
Lk 7:28 he that is l in the kingdom of God is greater *3398*
9:48 for he that is l among you all, the same *3398*
12:26 then be not able *to do that thing which is* l, *1646*
16:10 He that is faithful in *that which is* l is *1646*
16:10 he that is unjust in the l is unjust also in *1646*
19:42 even thou, **at** l in this thy day, *1065+2532*
Ac 5:15 that **at the** l the shadow of Peter passing by *2579*
8:10 from the l to the greatest, saying, *3398*
1Co 6: 4 set them to judge who are l **esteemed** in *1848*
15: 9 For I am the l of the apostles, that am not *1646*
Eph 3: 8 *who am* less than the l of all saints, *1647*
Heb 8:11 shall know me, from the l to the greatest. *3398*

LEATHER (1) [LEATHERN]

2Ki 1: 8 girt *with* a girdle of l about his loins. 5785

LEATHERN (1) [LEATHER]

Mt 3: 4 camel's hair, and a l girdle about his loins; *1193*

LEAVE (115) [LEAVED, LEAVETH, LEAVING, LEFT, LEFTEST]

Ge 2:24 Therefore shall a man l his father and his 5800
28:15 for I will not l thee, until I have done *that* 5800
33:15 Let me now l with thee *some* of the folk 3322
42:33 Hereby shall I know that ye *are* true *men;* l 3240
44:22 unto my lord, The lad cannot l his father: 5800
44:22 for *if* he should l his father, *his father* 5800
Ex 16:19 Let no man l of it till the morning. 3498
23:11 what they l the beasts of the field shall eat. 3499
Lev 7:15 he shall not l *any* of it until the morning. 3240
16:23 into the holy *place,* and shall l them there: 3240
19:10 thou shalt l them for the poor and stranger: 5800
22:30 ye shall l none of it until the morrow: 3498
23:22 thou shalt l them unto the poor, and to 5800
Nu 9:12 They shall l none of it unto the morning, 7604
10:31 he said, L us not, I pray thee; forasmuch as 5800
22:13 for the LORD refuseth to **give** me l to go 5414
32:15 he will yet again l them in the wilderness; 3240
Dt 28:51 which *also* shall not l thee *either* corn, 7604
28:54 remnant of his children which he shall l: 3498
Jos 4: 3 l them in the lodging place, where you shall 3240
Jdg 9: 9 tree said unto them, Should I l my fatness, 2308
9:13 Should I l my wine, which cheereth God 2308
Ru 1:16 Intreat me not to l thee, *or* to return from 5800
2:16 l *them,* that she may glean *them,* and 5800
1Sa 9: 5 lest my father l *caring* for the asses, and 2308
14:36 and let us not l a man of them. 7604
20: 6 David earnestly asked *l* of me that *he* might NIH
20:28 David earnestly asked *l* of me *to go* to NIH
25:22 if I l of all that *pertain* to him by 7604
2Sa 14: 7 shall not l to my husband *neither* name nor 7760
1Ki 8:57 our fathers: let him not l us, nor forsake us: 5800
2Ki 2: 2 and *as* thy soul liveth, I will not l thee. 5800
2: 4 and *as* thy soul liveth, I will not l thee. 5800
2: 6 and *as* thy soul liveth, I will not l thee. 5800
4:30 and *as* thy soul liveth, I will not l thee. 5800
4:43 They shall eat, and shall l *thereof.* 3498
13: 7 Neither did he l *of* the people to Jehoahaz 7604
1Ch 28: 8 l *it* **for an inheritance** for your children 5157
Ezr 9: 8 to l us a remnant to escape, and to give us a 7604
9:12 l *it* for **an inheritance** to your children for 3423
Ne 5:10 and corn: I pray you, let us l **off** this usury. 5800
6: 3 whilst I l it, and come down to you? 7503
10:31 *that* we would l the seventh year, and 5203
13: 6 after certain days obtained I *l* of the king: NIH
Job 9:27 I will l **off** my heaviness, and 5800
10: 1 my life; I will l my complaint upon myself; 5800
39:11 *is* great? or wilt thou l thy labour to him? 5800
Ps 16:10 For thou wilt not l my soul in hell; 5800
17:14 l the rest of their *substance* to their babes. 3240
27: 9 l me not, neither forsake me, O God of my 5203
37:33 The LORD will not l him in his hand, 5800
49:10 person perish, and l their wealth to others. 5800
119:121 and justice: l me not to mine oppressors. 3240
141: 8 in thee is my trust; l not my soul **destitute**. 6168
Pr 2:13 Who l the paths of uprightness, to walk in 5800
17:14 therefore l **off** contention, before *it* be 5203
Ecc 2:18 I should l it unto the man that shall be after 3240

Ecc 2:21 laboured therein shall he l it *for* his portion. 5414
10: 4 ruler rise up against thee, l not thy place; 3240
Isa 10: 3 for help? and where will ye l your glory? 5800
65:15 ye shall l your name for a curse unto my 3240
Jer 9: 2 that I might l my people, and go from 5800
14: 9 and we are called by thy name; l us not. 3240
17:11 shall l them in the midst of his days, and 5800
18:14 Will *a man* l the snow of Lebanon *which* 5800
30:11 not l thee **altogether unpunished**. 5352+5352
44: 7 out of Judah, to l you none to remain; 3498
46:28 will I not l thee **wholly unpunished**. 5352+5352
48:28 l the cities, and dwell in the rock, and 5800
49: 9 would they not l *some* gleaning grapes? 7604
49:11 **L** thy fatherless children, I will preserve 5800
Eze 6: 8 Yet will I l **a remnant**, that ye may have 3498
12:16 I will l a few men of them from the sword, 3498
16:39 thy fair jewels, and l thee naked and bare. 3240
22:20 and I will l *you there,* and melt you. 3240
23:29 thy labour, and shall l thee naked and bare: 5800
29: 5 I will l thee *thrown* into the wilderness, 5203
32: 4 will I l thee upon the land, I will cast thee 5203
39: 2 l but **the sixth part** of thee, and will cause 8338
Da 4:15 Nevertheless l the stump of his roots in 7662
4:23 yet l the stump of the roots thereof in 7662
4:26 whereas they commanded to l the stump of 7662
Hos 12:14 therefore shall he l his blood upon him, and 5203
Joel 2:14 and repent, and l a blessing behind him; 7604
Am 5: 3 The city that went out *by* a thousand shall l 7604
5: 3 that which went forth *by* an hundred shall l 7604
5: 7 and l **off** righteousness in the earth, 3240
Ob 1: 5 to thee, would they not l *some* grapes? 7604
Zep 3:12 I will also l in the midst of thee an afflicted 7604
Mal 4: 1 that it shall l them neither root nor branch. 5800
Mt 5:24 **L** there thy gift before the altar, and go thy *863*
18:12 doth he not l the ninety and nine, and *863*
19: 5 For this cause shall a man l father and *2641*
23:23 to have done, and not to l the other **undone**. *863*
Mk 5:13 And forthwith Jesus **gave** them l. And *2010*
10: 7 For this cause shall a man l his father and *2641*
12:19 and l *his* wife *behind him,* and leave no *2641*
12:19 leave *his* wife *behind him,* and l no children, *863*
Lk 11:42 to have done, and not to l the other **undone**. *863*
15: 4 doth not l the ninety and nine in *2641*
19:44 they shall not l in thee one stone upon *863*
Jn 14:18 I will not l you comfortless: I will come to *863*
14:27 Peace I l with you, my peace I give unto *863*
16:28 again, I l the world, and go to the Father. *863*
16:32 every man to his own, and shall l me alone: *863*
19:38 and Pilate **gave** *him* l. He came therefore, *2010*
Ac 2:27 Because thou wilt not l my soul in hell, *1459*
6: 2 It is not reason that we should l the word of *2641*
18:18 and then **took** his l of the brethren, and *657*
21: 6 And when we had **taken** our l one of *782*
1Co 7:13 pleased to dwell with her, let her not l him. *863*
2Co 2:13 but **taking** my l **of** them, I went from *thence* *657*
Eph 5:31 For this cause shall a man l his father and *2641*
Heb 13: 5 for he hath said, I will never l thee, *447*
Rev 11: 2 But the court which is without the temple l *1544*

LEAVED (1) [LEAVE]
Isa 45: 1 to open before him the **two l gates**; 1817

LEAVEN (23) [LEAVENED, LEAVENETH, UNLEAVENED]
Ex 12:15 even the first day ye shall put away l out of 7603
12:19 Seven days shall there be no l found in your 7603
13: 7 neither shall there be l seen with thee in all 7603
34:25 not offer the blood of my sacrifice with l; 2557
Lev 2:11 unto the LORD, shall be made *with* l: 2557
2:11 for ye shall burn no l, nor any honey, *in* any 7603
6:17 It shall not be baken *with* l. I have given it 2557
10:12 by fire, and eat it **without** l beside the altar: 4682
23:17 be *of* fine flour; they shall be baken *with* l; 2557
Am 4: 5 And offer a sacrifice of thanksgiving with l, 2557
Mt 13:33 The kingdom of heaven is like unto l, *2219*
16: 6 and beware of the l of the Pharisees and *2219*
16:11 that *ye* should beware of the l of *2219*
16:12 he bade *them* not beware of the l of bread, *2219*
Mk 8:15 beware of the l of the Pharisees, and *of* *2219*
8:15 of the Pharisees, and *of* the l of Herod. *2219*
Lk 12: 1 *of all,* Beware ye of the l of the Pharisees, *2219*
13:21 It is like l, which a woman took and hid in *2219*
1Co 5: 6 Know ye not that a little l leaveneth *2219*
5: 7 Purge out therefore the old l, that ye may *2219*
5: 8 let us keep the feast, not with old l, *2219*
5: 8 neither with the l of malice and *2219*
Gal 5: 9 A little l leaveneth the whole lump. *2219*

LEAVENED (14) [LEAVEN]
Ex 12:15 for whosoever eateth l **bread** from the first 2557
12:19 for whosoever eateth **that which is** l, 2556
12:20 Ye shall eat nothing l; in all your 2556
12:34 the people took their dough before it was l, 2556
12:39 brought forth out of Egypt, for it was not l; 2556
13: 3 this *place:* there shall no l **bread** be eaten. 2557
13: 7 there shall no l **bread** be seen with thee, 2557
23:18 the blood of my sacrifice with l **bread**; 2557
Lev 7:13 he shall offer *for* his offering l bread with 2557
Dt 16: 3 Thou shalt eat no l **bread** with it; 2557
16: 4 there shall be no l **bread** seen with thee in 7603
Hos 7: 4 *he* hath kneaded the dough, until it be l. 2556
Mt 13:33 measures of meal, till the whole was l. *2220*
Lk 13:21 measures of meal, till the whole was l. *2220*

LEAVENETH (2) [LEAVEN]
1Co 5: 6 Know ye not that a little leaven l the whole *2220*
Gal 5: 9 A little leaven l the whole lump. *2220*

LEAVES (19) [LEAF]
Ge 3: 7 they sewed fig l together, and 5929
1Ki 6:34 the two l of the one door *were* folding, and 6763
6:34 the two l of the other door *were* folding. 7050
Isa 6:13 when they cast *their l*: *so* the holy seed *shall* NIH
Jer 36:23 *that* when Jehudi had read three or four l, 1817
Eze 17: 9 it shall wither *in* all the l of her spring, 2964
41:24 the doors had two l *apiece,* two turning 1817
41:24 doors had two leaves *apiece,* two turning l; 1817
41:24 two *l* for the one door, and two leaves for NIH
41:24 the one door, and two l for the other *door.* 1817
Da 4:12 The l thereof *were* fair, and the fruit thereof 6074
4:14 shake off his l, and scatter his fruit: 6074
4:21 Whose l *were* fair, and the fruit thereof 6074
Mt 21:19 but l only, and said unto it, *5444*
24:32 and putteth forth l, ye know that summer *is* *5444*
Mk 11:13 And seeing a fig tree afar off having l, *5444*
11:13 when he came to it, he found nothing but l; *5444*
13:28 and putteth forth l, ye know that summer is *5444*
Rev 22: 2 the l of the tree *were* for the healing of *5444*

LEAVETH (6) [LEAVE]
Job 39:14 Which l her eggs in the earth, and 5800
Pr 13:22 A good *man* l **an inheritance** to *his* 5157
28: 3 *is like* a sweeping rain which l no food. NIH
Zec 11:17 Woe to the idol shepherd that l the flock! 5800
Mt 4:11 Then the devil l him, and behold, *863*
Jn 10:12 the wolf coming, and l the sheep, and fleeth: *863*

LEAVING (5) [LEAVE]
Mt 4:13 And l Nazareth, he came and dwelt in *2641*
Lk 10:30 wounded *him,* and departed, l *him* half dead. *863*
Ro 1:27 also the men, l the natural use of the woman, *863*
Heb 6: 1 Therefore l the principles of the doctrine of *863*
1Pe 2:21 Christ also suffered for us, l us an example, *5277*

LEBANA (1) [LEBANAH]
Ne 7:48 The children of **L**, the children of Hagaba, 3838

LEBANAH (1) [LEBANA]
Ezr 2:45 The children of **L**, the children of Hagabah, 3838

LEBANON (71)
Dt 1: 7 *unto* **L**, unto the great river, the river 3844
3:25 that goodly mountain, and **L**. 3844
11:24 from the wilderness and **L**, from the river, 3844
Jos 1: 4 and this **L** even unto the great river, 3844
9: 1 the coasts of the great sea over against **L**, 3844
11:17 even unto Baal-gad in the valley of **L** under 3844
12: 7 from Baal-gad in the valley of **L** even unto 3844
13: 5 and all **L**, *toward* the sunrising, 3844
13: 6 hill country from **L** unto Misrephoth-maim, 3844
Jdg 3: 3 and the Hivites that dwelt in mount **L**, 3844
9:15 of the bramble, and devour the cedars of **L**. 3844
1Ki 4:33 from the cedar tree that *is* in **L** even unto 3844
5: 6 thou that they hew me cedar trees out of **L**; 3844
5: 9 My servants shall bring *them* down from **L** 3844
5:14 he sent them to **L**, ten thousand a month *by* 3844
5:14 a month they were in **L**, *and* two months at 3844
7: 2 He built also the house of the forest of **L**; 3844
9:19 in **L**, and in all the land of his dominion. 3844
10:17 put them *in* the house of the forest of **L**. 3844

L

1Ki 10:21 house of the forest of **L** *were of* pure gold: 3844
2Ki 14: 9 The thistle that *was* in **L** sent to the cedar 3844
14: 9 in Lebanon sent to the cedar that *was* in **L**, 3844
14: 9 there passed by a wild beast that *was* in **L**, 3844
19:23 *to* the sides of **L**, and will cut down the tall 3844
2Ch 2: 8 fir trees, and algum trees, out of **L**: 3844
2: 8 thy servants can skill to cut timber in **L**; 3844
2:16 we will cut wood out of **L**, as much as thou 3844
8: 6 in **L**, and throughout all the land of his 3844
9:16 put them in the house of the forest of **L**. 3844
9:20 house of the forest of **L** *were of* pure gold: 3844
25:18 The thistle that *was* in **L** sent to the cedar 3844
25:18 in Lebanon sent to the cedar that *was* in **L**, 3844
25:18 there passed by a wild beast that *was* in **L**, 3844
Ezr 3: 7 to bring cedar trees from **L** to the sea of 3844
Ps 29: 5 yea, the LORD breaketh the cedars of **L**. 3844
29: 6 a calf; **L** and Sirion like a young unicorn. 3844
72:16 the fruit thereof shall shake like **L**: 3844
92:12 palm tree: he shall grow like a cedar in **L**. 3844
104:16 the LORD are full *of sap;* the cedars of **L**, 3844
SS 3: 9 made himself a chariot of the wood of **L**. 3844
4: 8 Come with me from **L**, *my* spouse, with me 3844
4: 8 from Lebanon, *my* spouse, with me from **L**: 3844
4:11 smell of thy garments *is* like the smell of **L**. 3844
4:15 a well of living waters, and streams from **L**. 3844
5:15 his countenance *is* as **L**, excellent as 3844
7: 4 thy nose *is* as the tower of **L** which looketh 3844
Isa 2:13 upon all the cedars of **L**, that are high and 3844
10:34 with iron, and **L** shall fall by a mighty one. 3844
14: 8 fir trees rejoice at thee, *and* the cedars of **L**, 3844
29:17 **L** shall be turned into a fruitful field, and 3844
33: 9 **L** is ashamed *and* hewn down: Sharon is 3844
35: 2 the glory of **L** shall be given unto it, 3844
37:24 height of the mountains, *to* the sides of **L**; 3844
40:16 **L** *is* not sufficient to burn, nor the beasts 3844
60:13 The glory of **L** shall come unto thee, the fir 3844
Jer 18:14 Will *a man* leave the snow of **L** *which* 3844
22: 6 *art* Gilead unto me, *and* the head of **L**: 3844
22:20 Go up *to* **L**, and cry; and lift up thy voice in 3844
22:23 O inhabitant of **L**, that makest thy nest in 3844
Eze 17: 3 came unto **L**, and took the highest branch 3844
27: 5 they have taken cedars from **L** to make 3844
31: 3 the Assyrian *was* a cedar in **L** with fair 3844
31:15 I caused **L** to mourn for him, and all 3844
31:16 the choice and best of **L**, all that drink 3844
Hos 14: 5 as the lily, and cast forth his roots as **L**. 3844
14: 6 be as the olive tree, and his smell as **L**. 3844
14: 7 the sent thereof *shall be* as the wine of **L**. 3844
Na 1: 4 Carmel, and the flower of **L** languisheth. 3844
Hab 2:17 For the violence of **L** shall cover thee, and 3844
Zec 10:10 bring them into the land of Gilead and **L**; 3844
11: 1 Open thy doors, O **L**, that the fire may 3844

LEBAOTH (1)
Jos 15:32 **L**, and Shilhim, and Ain, and Rimmon: 3822

LEBBEUS (1)
Mt 10: 3 James the *son* of Alpheus, and **L**, *3002*

LEBONAH (1)
Jdg 21:19 Beth-el to Shechem, and on the south of **L**. 3829

LECAH (1)
1Ch 4:21 the son of Judah *were,* Er the father of **L**, 3922

LECTURE HALL See SCHOOL

LED (68) [LEAD]
Ge 24:27 the LORD **l** me to the house of my 5148
24:48 which had **l** me in the right way to take my 5148
Ex 3: 1 he **l** the flock to the backside of the desert, 5090
13:17 that God **l** them not *through* the way of 5148
13:18 God **l** the people **about**, *through* the way of 5437
15:13 Thou in thy mercy hast **l** **forth** the people 5148
Dt 8: 2 **l** thee these forty years in the wilderness, 1980
8:15 Who **l** thee through *that* great and terrible 1980
29: 5 I have **l** you forty years in the wilderness: 1980
32:10 he **l** him **about**, he instructed him, he kept 5437
Jos 24: 3 **l** him throughout all the land of Canaan, 1980
1Ki 8:48 which **l** them **away captive**, and pray unto 7617
2Ki 6:19 whom ye seek. But he **l** them to Samaria. 1980
1Ch 20: 1 *battle,* Joab **l** **forth** the power of the army, 5090
2Ch 25:11 **l** **forth** his people, and went *to* the valley of 5090
Ps 68:18 on high, thou hast **l** captivity **captive**: 7617
78:14 In the daytime also he **l** them with a cloud, 5148
78:53 he **l** them **on** safely, so that they feared not: 5148
106: 9 so he **l** them through the depths, as *through* 1980
107: 7 he **l** them **forth** by the right way, that *they* 1869
136:16 To him which **l** his people through 1980
Pr 4:11 way of wisdom; I have **l** thee in right paths. 1869
Isa 9:16 and *they that are* **l** of them *are* destroyed. 833
48:21 they thirsted not *when* he **l** them through 1980
55:12 go out with joy, and be **l** **forth** with peace: 2986
63:12 That **l** *them* by the right hand of Moses 1980
63:13 That **l** them through the deep, as a horse in 1980
Jer 2: 6 that **l** us through the wilderness, through a 1980
2:17 thy God, when he **l** thee by the way? 1980
22:12 the place whither they have **l** him **captive**, 1540
23: 8 which **l** the seed of the house of Israel out of 935
La 3: 2 He hath **l** me, and brought *me into* 5090
Eze 17:12 and **l** them with him to Babylon; 935
39:28 which **caused** them **to be l into captivity** 1540
47: 2 **l** me **about** the way without unto the utter 5437
Am 2:10 **l** you forty years through the wilderness, 1980
7:11 Israel shall **surely** be **l** **away captive** 1540+1540
Na 2: 7 Huzzab shall be **l** **away captive**, she shall 1540
Mt 4: 1 Then was Jesus **l** **up** of the Spirit into *321*
26:57 Jesus **l** *him* **away** to Caiaphas the high priest, *520*
27: 2 they **l** *him* **away**, and delivered him to *520*
27:31 on him, and **l** him **away** to crucify *him.* *520*
Mk 8:23 by the hand, and **l** him **out** of the town; *1806*
14:53 And they **l** Jesus **away** to the high priest: and *520*
15:16 And the soldiers **l** him **away** into the hall, *520*
15:20 on him, and **l** him **out** to crucify him. *1806*
Lk 4: 1 and was **l** by the Spirit into the wilderness, *71*
4:29 **l** him unto the brow of the hill whereon their *71*
21:24 and shall be **l** **away captive** into all nations: *163*
22:54 and **l** *him,* and brought him into the high *71*
22:66 and **l** him into their council, saying, *321*
23: 1 of them arose, and **l** him unto Pilate. *71*
23:26 And as they **l** him **away**, they laid hold upon *520*
23:32 malefactors, **l** with him to be put to death. *71*
24:50 And he **l** them **out** as far as to *1806*
Jn 18:13 And **l** him **away** to Annas first; for he was *520*
18:28 Then **l** they Jesus from Caiaphas unto the hall *71*
19:16 And they took Jesus, and **l** *him* **away**. *520*
Ac 8:32 was this, He was **l** as a sheep to the slaughter; *71*
9: 8 saw no *man:* but they **l** him **by the hand**, *5496*
21:37 And as Paul was to be **l** **into** *1521*
22:11 being **l** **by the hand** of them that were with *5496*
Ro 8:14 For as many as are **l** by the Spirit of God, *71*
1Co 12: 2 unto these dumb idols, *even* as ye were **l**. *71*
Gal 5:18 But if ye be **l** of the Spirit, ye are not under *71*
Eph 4: 8 he **l** captivity **captive**, and gave gifts unto *162*
2Ti 3: 6 laden with sins, **l** **away** with divers lusts, *71*
2Pe 3:17 being **l** **away with** the error of the wicked, *4879*

LEDDEST (5) [LEAD]
2Sa 5: 2 thou wast he that **l** **out** and broughtest in 3318
1Ch 11: 2 thou *wast* he that **l** **out** and broughtest in 3318
Ne 9:12 Moreover thou **l** them in the day by a 5148
Ps 77:20 Thou **l** thy people like a flock by the hand 5148
Ac 21:38 **l** **out** into the wilderness four thousand men *1806*

LEDGES (5)
1Ki 7:28 and the borders *were* between the **l**: 7948
7:29 on the borders that *were* between the **l** *were* 7948
7:29 upon the **l** *there was* a base above: and 7948
7:35 on the top of the base the **l** thereof and 3027
7:36 For on the plates of the **l** thereof, and on 3027

LEECH See HORSELEACH

LEEKS (1)
Nu 11: 5 and the **l**, and the onions, and the garlick: 2682

LEES (4)
Isa 25: 6 a feast of **wines on the l**, of fat things full 8105
25: 6 of marrow, of **wines on the l** well refined. 8105
Jer 48:11 he *hath* settled on his **l**, and hath not been 8105
Zep 1:12 punish the men that are settled on their **l**: 8105

LEESE (1)
1Ki 18: 5 and mules alive, that we **l** not all the beasts. 3772

LEFT (348) [LEAVE, LEFTHANDED]
Ge 11: 8 all the earth: and they **l** off to build the city. NIH
13: 9 if *thou wilt take* the **l** **hand**, then I will go 8040
13: 9 *to* the right hand, then I will **go to the l**. 8041
14:15 which *is* on the **l** **hand** of Damascus. 8040

Ge	17:22	he l **off** talking with him, and God went up	3615
	18:33	as soon as he had l communing with	3615
	24:27	who hath not l **destitute** my master of his	5800
	24:49	that I may turn to the right hand, or to the l.	8040
	29:35	she called his name Judah; and l bearing.	5975
	30: 9	When Leah saw that she had l bearing, she	5975
	32: 8	the *other* company which is l shall escape.	7604
	32:24	Jacob was l alone; and there wrestled a man	3498
	39: 6	he l all that he had in Joseph's hand; and	5800
	39:12	he l his garment in her hand, and fled, and	5800
	39:13	when she saw that he had l his garment in	5800
	39:15	that he l his garment with me, and fled, and	5800
	39:18	that he l his garment with me, and fled out.	5800
	41:49	of the sea, very much, until he l numbering;	2308
	42:38	for his brother is dead, and he is l alone:	7604
	44:12	began at the eldest, and l at the youngest:	3615
	44:20	he alone is l of his mother, and his father	3498
	47:18	there is not ought l in the sight of my lord,	7604
	48:13	in his right hand toward Israel's **l hand**,	8040
	48:13	Manasseh in his **l hand** towards Israel's	8040
	48:14	and his **l hand** upon Manasseh's head,	8040
	50: 8	their herds, they l in the land of Goshen.	5800
Ex	2:20	why *is it that* ye have l the man? call him,	5800
	9:21	not the word of the LORD l his servants	5800
	10:12	of the land, *even* all that the hail hath l.	7604
	10:15	all the fruit of the trees which the hail had l:	3498
	10:26	with us; there shall not a hoof be **l behind**;	7604
	14:22	them on their right hand, and on their l.	8040
	14:29	them on their right hand, and on their l.	8040
	16:20	some of them l of it until the morning, and	3498
	34:25	feast of the passover be l unto the morning.	3885
Lev	2:10	that which is l of the meat offering *shall be*	3498
	10:12	and unto Ithamar his sons that were l,	3498
	10:16	Ithamar the sons of Aaron which were l	3498
	14:15	and pour *it* into the palm of his own l hand:	8042
	14:16	right finger in the oil that *is* in his l hand,	8042
	14:26	of the oil into the palm of his own l hand:	8042
	14:27	his l hand seven times before the LORD:	8042
	26:36	*upon* them that are l *alive* of you I will send	7604
	26:39	they that are l of you shall pine away in	7604
	26:43	The land also shall be l of them, and	5800
Nu	20:17	will not turn *to* the right hand nor *to* the l,	8040
	21:35	his people, until there was none l him alive:	7604
	22:26	to turn *either to* the right hand or *to* the l.	8040
	26:65	there was not l a man of them, save Caleb	3498
Dt	2:27	neither turn *unto* the right hand nor to the l.	8040
	2:34	of every city, we l none to remain:	7604
	3: 3	we smote him until none was l to him	7604
	4:27	ye shall be l few in number among	7604
	5:32	not turn aside *to* the right hand or *to* the l.	8040
	7:20	until they that are l, and hide themselves	7604
	17:11	shew thee, *to* the right hand, nor *to* the l.	8040
	17:20	*to* the right hand, or *to* the l:	8040
	28:14	*to* the right hand, or *to* the l, to go after	8040
	28:55	because he hath nothing l him in the siege,	7604
	28:62	ye shall be l few in number, whereas ye	7604
	32:36	is gone, and *there is* none shut up, or l.	5800
Jos	1: 7	turn not from it *to* the right hand or *to* the l,	8040
	6:23	and l them without the camp of Israel.	3240
	8:17	there was not a man l in Ai or Beth-el,	7604
	8:17	they l the city open, and pursued after	5800
	10:33	until *he* had l him none remaining.	7604
	10:37	he l none remaining, according to all that	7604
	10:39	that *were* therein; he l none remaining:	7604
	10:40	he l none remaining, but utterly destroyed	7604
	11: 8	until *they* l them none remaining.	7604
	11:11	utterly destroying *them:* there was not any l	3498
	11:14	neither l they any to breathe.	7604
	11:15	he l nothing **undone** of all that the LORD	5493
	11:22	There was none of the Anakims l in	3498
	19:27	and goeth out to Cabul on the **l hand**,	8040
	22: 3	Ye have not l your brethren these many	5800
	23: 6	aside therefrom *to* the right hand or *to* the l;	8040
Jdg	2:21	of the nations which Joshua l when he died:	5800
	2:23	Therefore the LORD l those nations,	3240
	3: 1	these *are* the nations which the LORD l,	3240
	3:21	Ehud put forth his l hand, and took	8040
	4:16	of the sword; *and* there was not a man l.	7604
	6: 4	l no sustenance for Israel, neither sheep,	7604
	7:20	held the lamps in their l hands, and	8040
	8:10	about fifteen thousand *men,* all that were l	3498
	9: 5	the youngest son of Jerubbaal was l;	3498
	16:29	his right hand, and of the other with his l.	8040
Ru	1: 3	and she was l, and her two sons.	7604
	1: 5	the woman was l of her two sons and	7604
	1:18	to go with her, then she l speaking unto her.	2308
	2:11	*how* thou hast l thy father and thy mother,	5800
	2:14	and she did eat, and was sufficed, and l.	3498
	2:20	who hath not l **off** his kindness to the living	5800
	4:14	which hath not l thee *this* day **without** a	7673
1Sa	2:36	*that* every one that is l in thine house shall	3498
	5: 4	only *the stump of* Dagon was l to him.	7604
	6:12	not aside *to* the right hand or *to* the l;	8040
	9:24	*Samuel* said, Behold that which is l; set *it*	7604
	10: 2	lo, thy father hath l the care of the asses,	5203
	11:11	so that two of them were not l together.	7604
	17:20	and l the sheep with a keeper, and took, and	5203
	17:22	David l his carriage in the hand of	5203
	17:28	with whom hast thou l those few sheep in	5203
	25:34	surely there had not been l unto Nabal by	3498
	27: 9	l neither man nor woman **alive**, and	2421
	30: 9	where those that were **l behind** stayed.	3498
	30:13	my master l me, because three days agone I	5800
2Sa	2:19	hand nor to the l from following Abner.	8040
	2:21	Turn thee aside to thy right hand or to thy l,	8040
	5:21	there they l their images, and David and	5800
	9: 1	Is there yet *any* that is l of the house of	3498
	13:30	king's sons, and there is not one of them l.	3498
	14: 7	*so* they shall quench my coal which is l,	7604
	14:19	to the l from ought that my lord the king	8041
	15:16	the king l ten women, *which were*	5800
	16: 6	*men were* on his right hand and on his l.	8040
	16:21	which he hath l to keep the house;	3240
	17:12	men that *are* with him there shall not be l	3498
	20: 3	whom he had l to keep the house, and	3240
1Ki	7:21	he set up the l pillar, and called the name	8042
	7:39	and five on the l side of the house:	8040
	7:47	Solomon l all the vessels *unweighed,*	3240
	7:49	five on the l, before the oracle, with	8040
	9:20	*And* all the people that were l of	3498
	9:21	Their children that were l after them in	3498
	14:10	*and him that is* shut up and l in Israel, and	5800
	15:18	the gold that were l in the treasures of	3498
	15:21	when Baasha heard *thereof,* that he l **off**	2308
	15:29	he l not to Jeroboam any that breathed,	7604
	16:11	he l him not *one that* pisseth against a wall,	7604
	17:17	so sore, that there was no breath l in him.	3498
	19: 3	*belongeth* to Judah, and l his servant there.	3240
	19:10	I, *even* I only, am l; and they seek my life,	3498
	19:14	I, *even* I only, am l; and they seek my life,	3498
	19:18	Yet I have l *me* seven thousand in Israel,	7604
	19:20	he l the oxen, and ran after Elijah, and said,	5800
	20:30	and seven thousand of the men that were l.	3498
	21:21	and *him that is* shut up and l in Israel,	5800
	22:19	by him on his right hand and on his l.	8040
2Ki	3:25	only in Kir-haraseth l *they* the stones	7604
	4:44	l *thereof,* according to the word of	3498
	7: 7	l their tents, and their horses, and their	5800
	7:13	that remain, which are l in the city, (behold,	7604
	7:13	as all the multitude of Israel that are l in it:	7604
	8: 6	of the field since the day that she l the land,	5800
	9: 8	and *him that is* shut up and l in Israel:	5800
	10:11	his priests, until *he* l him none remaining.	7604
	10:14	and forty men; neither l he any of them.	7604
	10:21	so that there was not a man l that came not.	7604
	11:11	from the right corner of the temple to the l	8042
	14:26	shut up, nor any l, nor any helper for Israel.	5800
	17:16	they l all the commandments of the LORD	5800
	17:18	there was none l but the tribe of Judah only.	7604
	19: 4	lift up *thy* prayer for the remnant that are l.	4672
	20:17	nothing shall be l, saith the LORD.	3498
	22: 2	turned not aside *to* the right hand or *to* the l.	8040
	23: 8	which *were* on a man's **l hand** at the gate	8040
	25:11	Now the rest of the people that were l in	7604
	25:12	the captain of the guard l of the poor of	7604
	25:22	Nebuchadnezzar king of Babylon had l,	7604
1Ch	6:44	the sons of Merari *stood* on the **l hand**:	8040
	6:61	which were l of the family of *that* tribe,	3498
	12: 2	right hand and the l in *hurling* stones and	8041
	13: 2	that are l in all the land of Israel, and	7604
	14:12	when they had l their gods there, David	5800
	16:37	So he l there before the ark of the covenant	5800
2Ch	3:17	on the right hand, and the other on the l;	8040
	3:17	and the name of *that on* the l Boaz.	8042
	4: 6	and five on the l, to wash in them:	8040
	4: 7	five on the right hand, and five on the l.	8040
	4: 8	five on the right side, and five on the l.	8040
	8: 7	*As for* all the people that were l of	3498

2Ch	8: 8	who were l after them in the land,	3498
	11:14	For the Levites l their suburbs and	5800
	12: 5	have I also l you in the hand of Shishak.	5800
	16: 5	when Baasha heard *it,* that he **l off** building	2308
	18:18	standing on his right hand and *on* his l.	8040
	21:17	so that there was never a son l him,	7604
	23:10	from the right side of the temple to the l	8042
	24:18	they l the house of the LORD God of their	5800
	24:25	from him, (for they l him in great diseases,)	5800
	25:12	*other* ten thousand *l* alive did the children of	NIH
	28:14	So the armed men l the captives and	5800
	31:10	have had enough to eat, and have l plenty:	3498
	31:10	and that which is l *is* this great store.	3498
	32:31	God l him, to try him, that *he* might know	5800
	34: 2	neither *to* the right hand, nor *to* the l.	8040
	34:21	for them that are l in Israel and in Judah,	7604
Ne	1: 2	which were l of the captivity, and	7604
	1: 3	The remnant that are l of the captivity there	7604
	6: 1	and *that* there was no breach l therein;	3498
	8: 4	on his **l hand**, Pedaiah, and Mishael, and	8040
Job	20:21	*There shall* none of his meat *be* l; therefore	8300
	20:26	it shall go ill with him that is l in his	8300
	23: 9	*On* the **l hand**, where he doth work, but	8040
	32:15	no more: they **l off** speaking.	4480+6275
Ps	36: 3	he hath **l off** to be wise, *and* to do good.	2308
	106:11	their enemies: there was not one of them l.	3498
Pr	3:16	and in her **l hand** riches and honour.	8040
	4:27	Turn not *to* the right hand nor *to* the l:	8040
	29:15	a child l *to himself* bringeth his mother to	7971
Ecc	10: 2	at his right hand; but a fool's heart at his l.	8040
SS	2: 6	His **l hand** *is* under my head, and his right	8040
	8: 3	His **l hand** *should be* under my head, and	8040
Isa	1: 8	the daughter of Zion is l as a cottage in a	3498
	1: 9	Except the LORD of hosts had l unto us a	3498
	4: 3	*that* he that is l in Zion, and he that	7604
	7:22	honey shall every one eat that is l in	3498
	9:20	he shall eat on the **l hand**, and they shall	8040
	10:14	as *one* gathereth eggs *that are* l, have I	5800
	11:11	which shall be l from Assyria, and	7604
	11:16	his people, which shall be l from Assyria;	7604
	17: 6	Yet gleaning grapes shall be l in it, as	7604
	17: 9	which they l because of the children of	5800
	18: 6	They shall be l together unto the fowls of	5800
	24: 6	of the earth are burned, and few men l.	7604
	24:12	In the city is l desolation, and the gate is	7604
	27:10	habitation forsaken, and l like a wilderness:	5800
	30:17	till ye be l as a beacon upon the top of a	3498
	30:21	the right hand, and when ye **turn to the l**.	8041
	32:14	the multitude of the city shall be l; the forts	5800
	37: 4	lift up *thy* prayer for the remnant that is l.	4672
	39: 6	nothing shall be l, saith the LORD.	3498
	49:21	Behold, I was l alone; these, where *had*	7604
	54: 3	break forth *on* the right hand and *on* the l;	8040
Jer	12: 7	mine house, I have l mine heritage;	5203
	21: 7	such as are l in this city from the pestilence,	7604
	27:18	that the vessels which are l in the house of	3498
	31: 2	The people which were l of the sword	8300
	34: 7	against all the cities of Judah that were l,	3498
	38:22	all the women that are l in the king of	7604
	38:27	So they **l off speaking** with him; for	2790
	39:10	Nebuzar-adan the captain of the guard l of	7604
	40: 6	among the people that were l in the land.	7604
	40:11	heard that the king of Babylon had l a	5414
	42: 2	(for we are l *but* a few of many, as thine	7604
	43: 6	l with Gedaliah the son of Ahikam the son	3240
	44:18	since we **l off** to burn incense to the queen	2308
	49:25	How is the city of praise not l, the city of	5800
	50:26	destroy her utterly: let nothing of her be l.	7611
	52:16	Nebuzar-adan the captain of the guard l	7604
Eze	1:10	four had the face of an ox on the **l side**;	8040
	4: 4	Lie thou also upon thy l side, and lay	8042
	9: 8	I *was* l, that I fell upon my face, and cried,	7604
	14:22	therein shall be l a remnant that shall be	3498
	16:46	and her daughters that dwell at thy **l hand**:	8040
	21:16	other, *either* on the right hand, *or* **on the l**,	8041
	23: 8	Neither l she her whoredoms *brought* from	5800
	24:21	your daughters whom ye have l shall fall by	5800
	31:12	have cut him off, and have l him:	5203
	31:12	down from his shadow, and have l him.	5203
	36:36	the heathen that are l round about you shall	7604
	39: 3	I will smite thy bow out of thy l hand, and	8040
	39:28	and have l none of them any more there.	3498
	41: 9	*that* which *was* l *was* the place of the side	3240
	41:11	chambers *were* toward *the place* that *was* l,	3240
	41:11	the breadth of the place that was l *was* five	3240
	48:15	that are l in the breadth over against	3498
Da	2:44	the kingdom shall not be l to other people,	7662
	10: 8	Therefore I was l alone, and saw this great	7604
	10:17	in me, neither is there breath l in me.	7604
	12: 7	his right hand and his **l hand** unto heaven,	8040
Hos	4:10	they have **l off** to take heed to the LORD.	5800
	9:12	*that there shall* not *be* a man *l*: yea,	NIH
Joel	1: 4	That which the palmerworm hath l hath	3499
	1: 4	that which the locust hath l hath	3499
	1: 4	that which the cankerworm hath l hath	3499
Jnh	4:11	between their right hand and their **l hand**;	8040
Hag	2: 3	Who *is* l among you that saw this house in	7604
Zec	4: 3	and the other upon the l *side* thereof.	8040
	4:11	the candlestick and upon the l *side* thereof?	8040
	12: 6	round about, on the right hand and on the l:	8040
	13: 8	*and* die; but the third shall be l therein.	3498
	14:16	*that* every one that is l of all the nations	3498
Mt	4:20	And they straightway l *their* nets, and	*863*
	4:22	And they immediately l the ship and	*863*
	6: 3	let not thy **l hand** know what thy right hand	*710*
	8:15	he touched her hand, and the fever l her:	*863*
	15:37	they took up of the broken *meat* that was l	*4052*
	16: 4	And he l them, and departed.	*2641*
	20:21	and the other on the l, in thy kingdom.	*2176*
	20:23	and on my l, is not mine to give, but *it shall*	*2176*
	21:17	And he l them, and went out of the city into	*2641*
	22:22	and l him, and went their way.	*863*
	22:25	having no issue, l his wife unto his brother:	*863*
	23:38	Behold, your house is l unto you desolate.	*863*
	24: 2	There shall not be l here one stone upon	*863*
	24:40	the one shall be taken, and the other l.	*863*
	24:41	*the* one shall be taken, and *the* other l.	*863*
	25:33	on his right hand, but the goats on the l.	*2176*
	25:41	shall he say also unto them on the **l hand**,	*2176*
	26:44	And he l them, and went away again, and	*863*
	27:38	one on the right hand, and another on the l.	*2176*
Mk	1:20	they l their father Zebedee in the ship with	*863*
	1:31	and immediately the fever l her, and	*863*
	8: 8	they took up of the broken *meat* that was l	*4051*
	8:13	And he l them, and entering into the ship	*863*
	10:28	Lo, we have l all, and have followed thee.	*863*
	10:29	There is no *man* that hath l house, or	*863*
	10:37	and the other on thy **l hand**, in thy glory.	*2176*
	10:40	and on my **l hand** is not mine to give;	*2176*
	12:12	and they l him, and went their way.	*863*
	12:20	and the first took a wife, and dying l no seed.	*863*
	12:21	took her, and died, neither l he *any* seed:	*863*
	12:22	And the seven had her, and l no seed: last of	*863*
	13: 2	there shall not be l one stone upon another,	*863*
	13:34	who l his house, and gave authority to his	*863*
	14:52	And he l the linen cloth, and fled from	*2641*
	15:27	on *his* right hand, and the other on his l.	*2176*
Lk	4:39	over her, and rebuked the fever; and it l her:	*863*
	5: 4	Now when he had l speaking, he said unto	*3973*
	5:28	And he l all, rose up, and followed him.	*2641*
	10:40	dost thou not care that my sister hath l me	*2641*
	13:35	Behold, your house is l unto you desolate:	*863*
	17:34	one shall be taken, and the other shall be l.	*863*
	17:35	the one shall be taken, and the other l.	*863*
	17:36	the one shall be taken, and the other l.	*863*
	18:28	Then Peter said, Lo, we have l all,	*863*
	18:29	There is no *man* that hath l house, or parents,	*863*
	20:31	seven also: and they l no children, and died.	*2641*
	21: 6	in the which there shall not be l one stone	*863*
	23:33	one on the right hand, and the other on the l.	*710*
Jn	4: 3	He l Judea, and departed again into Galilee.	*863*
	4:28	The woman then l her waterpot, and	*863*
	4:52	Yesterday at the seventh hour the fever l	*863*
	8: 9	and Jesus was l alone, and the woman	*2641*
	8:29	the Father hath not l me alone; for I do	*863*
Ac	2:31	of Christ, that his soul was not l in hell,	*2641*
	14:17	Nevertheless he l not himself without	*863*
	18:19	And he came to Ephesus, and l them there:	*2641*
	21: 3	we l it on the left hand, and sailed into	*2641*
	21: 3	we left it on the **l hand**, and sailed into	*2176*
	21:32	and the soldiers, they l beating of Paul.	*3973*
	23:32	On the morrow they l the horsemen to go	*1439*
	24:27	to shew the Jews a pleasure, l Paul bound.	*2641*
	25:14	There is a certain man l in bonds by Felix:	*2641*
Ro	9:29	Except the Lord of sabaoth had l us a seed,	*1459*
	11: 3	and I am l alone, and they seek my life.	*5275*
2Co	6: 7	righteousness on the right hand and on the l,	*710*
1Th	3: 1	we thought it good to be l at Athens alone;	*2641*

2Ti 4:13 The cloke that I l at Troas with Carpus, *620*
4:20 but Trophimus have I l at Miletum sick. *620*
Tit 1: 5 For this cause l I thee in Crete, that thou *2641*
Heb 2: 8 he l nothing *that is* not put under him. *863*
4: 1 a promise being l *us* of entering into his *2641*
Jude 1: 6 their first estate, but l their own habitation, *620*
Rev 2: 4 because thou hast l thy first love. *863*
10: 2 upon the sea, and *his* l *foot* on the earth, *2176*

LEFTEST (1) [LEAVE]
Ne 9:28 l thou them in the hand of their enemies, 5800

LEFTHANDED (2) [HAND, LEFT]
Jdg 3:15 of Gera, a Benjamite, a man l: 334+3027+3225
20:16 seven hundred chosen men l; 334+3027+3225

LEG (1) [LEGS]
Isa 47: 2 make bare the l, uncover the thigh, 7640

LEGION (3) [LEGIONS]
Mk 5: 9 And he answered, saying, My name *is* L: *3003*
5:15 and had the l, sitting, and clothed, and *3003*
Lk 8:30 And he said, L: because many devils were *3003*

LEGIONS (1) [LEGION]
Mt 26:53 give me more than twelve l of angels? *3003*

LEGS (19) [LEG]
Ex 12: 9 his head with his l, and with the purtenance 3767
29:17 his l, and put *them* unto his pieces, and 3767
Lev 1: 9 and his l shall he wash in water: 3767
1:13 shall wash the inwards and the l with water: 3767
4:11 with his l, and his inwards, and his dung, 3767
8:21 he washed the inwards and the l in water; 3767
9:14 he did wash the inwards and the l, and 3767
11:21 which have l above their feet, to leap withal 3767
Dt 28:35 in the l, with a sore botch that cannot be 7785
1Sa 17: 6 *he had* greaves of brass upon his l, and 7272
Ps 147:10 he taketh not pleasure in the l of a man. 7785
Pr 26: 7 The l of the lame are not equal: so *is* a 7785
SS 5:15 His l *are as* pillars of marble, set upon 7785
Isa 3:20 the **ornaments of the** l, and the headbands, 6807
Da 2:33 His l of iron, his feet part of iron and 8243
Am 3:12 taketh out of the mouth of the lion two l, 3767
Jn 19:31 besought Pilate that their l might be broken, *4628*
19:32 and brake the l of the first, and of the other *4628*
19:33 he was dead already, they brake not his l: *4628*

LEHABIM (2)
Ge 10:13 and Anamim, and L, and Naphtuhim, 3853
1Ch 1:11 and Anamim, and L, and Naphtuhim, 3853

LEHABITES See LEHABIM

LEHI (3) [RAMATH-LEHI]
Jdg 15: 9 in Judah, and spread themselves in L. 3896
15:14 *And* when he came unto L, the Philistines 3896
15:19 which *is* in L unto this day. 3896

LEISURE (1)
Mk 6:31 and they **had** no l so much as to eat. *2119*

LEMUEL (2)
Pr 31: 1 The words of king L, the prophecy that his 3927
31: 4 *It is* not for kings, O L, *it is* not for kings to 3927

LEND (16) [LENDER, LENDETH, LENT]
Ex 22:25 If thou l money to *any of* my people *that is* 3867
Lev 25:37 nor l him thy victuals for increase. 5414
Dt 15: 6 thou shalt l unto many nations, but 5670
15: 8 **surely** l him sufficient for his need, 5670+5670
23:19 Thou shalt not l **upon usury** to thy brother; 5391
23:20 Unto a stranger thou mayest l **upon usury**; 5391
23:20 thy brother thou shalt not l **upon usury**: 5391
24:10 When thou dost l thy brother any 4859+5383
24:11 the man to whom thou dost l shall bring out 5383
28:12 thou shalt l unto many nations, and 3867
28:44 He shall l to thee, and thou shalt not lend to 3867
28:44 lend to thee, and thou shalt not l to him: 3867
Lk 6:34 And if ye l *to them* of whom ye hope to *1155*
6:34 for sinners also l to sinners, to receive as *1155*
6:35 and do good, and l, hoping for nothing *1155*
11: 5 and say unto him, Friend, l me three loaves; *5531*

LENDER (2) [LEND]
Pr 22: 7 and the borrower *is* servant to the l. 376+3867
Isa 24: 2 as *with* the l, so *with* the borrower; 3867

LENDETH (4) [LEND]
Dt 15: 2 Every creditor that l *ought* unto his 5383
Ps 37:26 *He is* ever merciful, and l; and his seed *is* 3867
112: 5 A good man sheweth favour, and l: he will 3867
Pr 19:17 He that hath pity upon the poor l unto 3867

LENGTH (77) [LENGTHEN, LENGTHENED, LENGTHENING, LONG, LONGER, LONGSUFFERING, LONGWINGED]
Ge 6:15 the l of the ark *shall be* three hundred cubits, 753
13:17 walk through the land in the l of it and in 753
Ex 25:10 two cubits and a half *shall be* the l thereof, 753
25:17 two cubits and a half *shall be* the l thereof, 753
25:23 two cubits *shall be* the l thereof, and a cubit 753
26: 2 The l of one curtain *shall be* eight and 753
26: 8 The l of one curtain *shall be* thirty cubits, 753
26:13 remaineth in the l of the curtains of the tent, 753
26:16 Ten cubits *shall be* the l of a board, and 753
27:11 likewise for the north side in l *there shall be* 753
27:18 The l of the court *shall be* an hundred cubits, 753
28:16 a span *shall be* the l thereof, and a span *shall* 753
30: 2 A cubit *shall be* the l thereof, and a cubit 753
36: 9 The l of one curtain *was* twenty and 753
36:15 The l of one curtain *was* thirty cubits, and 753
36:21 The l of a board *was* ten cubits, and 753
37: 1 two cubits and a half *was* the l of it, and 753
37: 6 two cubits and a half *was* the l thereof, and 753
37:10 two cubits *was* the l thereof, and a cubit 753
37:25 the l of it *was* a cubit, and the breadth of it a 753
38: 1 five cubits *was* the l thereof, and five cubits 753
38:18 twenty cubits *was* the l, and the height in 753
39: 9 a span *was* the l thereof, and a span 753
Dt 3:11 nine cubits *was* the l thereof, and four cubits 753
30:20 for he *is* thy life, and the l of thy days: 753
Jdg 3:16 a dagger which had two edges, of a cubit l; 753
1Ki 6: 2 the l thereof *was* threescore cubits, and 753
6: 3 twenty cubits *was* the l thereof, according to 753
6:20 oracle in the forepart *was* twenty cubits in l, 753
7: 2 the l thereof *was* an hundred cubits, and 753
7: 6 the l thereof *was* fifty cubits, and the breadth 753
7:27 four cubits *was* the l of one base, and 753
2Ch 3: 3 The l *by* cubits after the first measure *was* 753
3: 4 l *of it was* according to the breadth of 753
3: 8 the l whereof *was* according to the breadth 753
4: 1 twenty cubits the l thereof, and twenty cubits 753
Job 12:12 *is* wisdom; and *in* l of days understanding. 753
Ps 21: 4 *it* him, *even* l of days for ever and ever. 753
Pr 3: 2 For l of days, and long life, and peace, 753
3:16 L of days *is* in her right hand; and in her left 753
29:21 child shall have him become *his* son at the l. 319
Eze 31: 7 fair in his greatness, in the l of his branches: 753
40:11 *and* the l of the gate, thirteen cubits. 753
40:18 the l of the gates *was* the lower pavement. 753
40:20 he measured the l thereof, and the breadth 753
40:21 the l thereof *was* fifty cubits, and the breadth 753
40:25 the l *was* fifty cubits, and the breadth five 753
40:36 the l *was* fifty cubits, and the breadth five 753
40:49 The l of the porch *was* twenty cubits, and 753
41: 2 he measured the l thereof, forty cubits: and 753
41: 4 So he measured the l thereof, twenty cubits; 753
41:12 round about, and the l thereof ninety cubits. 753
41:15 he measured the l of the building over 753
41:22 cubits high, and the l thereof two cubits; 753
41:22 the l thereof, and the walls thereof, *were of* 753
42: 2 Before the l of an hundred cubits *was* 753
42: 7 the chambers, the l thereof *was* fifty cubits. 753
42: 8 For the l of the chambers that *were* in 753
45: 1 the l *shall be* the length *of* five and 753
45: 1 the length *shall be* the l *of* five and 753
45: 2 *l*, with five hundred *in breadth*, square NIH
45: 3 of this measure shalt thou measure the l of 753
45: 5 *the* five and twenty thousand of l, and *the* ten 753
45: 7 the l *shall be* over against one of 753
48: 8 *in* breadth, and *in* l as one of the *other* parts, 753
48: 9 *shall be of* five and twenty thousand *in* l, 753
48:10 the north five and twenty thousand *in* l, and NIH
48:10 the south five and twenty thousand *in* l: 753
48:13 *shall have* five and twenty thousand *in* l, 753
48:13 all the l *shall be* five and twenty thousand, 753
48:18 the residue in l over against the oblation of 753
Zec 2: 2 the breadth thereof, and what *is* the l thereof. 753
5: 2 the l thereof *is* twenty cubits, and the breadth 753
Ro 1:10 if by any means now **at** l I might have a *4218*

Eph 3:18 *is* the breadth, and l, and depth, and height; *3372*
Rev 21:16 and the l is as large as the breadth: *3372*
21:16 The l and the breadth and the height of it *3372*

LENGTHEN (2) [LENGTH]
1Ki 3:14 father David did walk, then I will l thy days. 748
Isa 54: 2 l thy cords, and strengthen thy stakes; 748

LENGTHENED (1) [LENGTH]
Dt 25:15 that thy days may be l in the land which 748

LENGTHENING (1) [LENGTH]
Da 4:27 the poor; if it may be a l of thy tranquillity. 754

LENT (7) [LEND]
Ex 12:36 that they l unto them *such things as they* 7592
Dt 23:19 usury of any thing that is l **upon usury**: 5391
1Sa 1:28 Therefore also I have l him to the LORD; 7592
1:28 as long as he liveth he *shall be* l to 7592
2:20 for the loan which is l to the LORD. 7592
Jer 15:10 I have neither l **on usury**, nor *men* have 5383
15:10 on usury, nor *men* have l to me **on usury**; 5383

LENTILES (4)
Ge 25:34 Jacob gave Esau bread and pottage of l; 5742
2Sa 17:28 and beans, and l, and parched *pulse*, 5742
23:11 where was a piece of ground full *of* l: 5742
Eze 4: 9 l, and millet, and fitches, and put them in 5742

LENTILS See LENTILES

LEOPARD (6) [LEOPARDS]
Isa 11: 6 and the l shall lie down with the kid; 5246
Jer 5: 6 spoil them, a l shall watch over their cities: 5246
13:23 change his skin, or the l his spots? 5246
Da 7: 6 After this I beheld, and lo another, like a l, 5245
Hos 13: 7 as a l by the way will I observe *them:* 5246
Rev 13: 2 the beast which I saw was like unto a l, *3917*

LEOPARDS (2) [LEOPARD]
SS 4: 8 the lions' dens, from the mountains of the l. 5246
Hab 1: 8 Their horses also are swifter than the l, and 5246

LEPER (17) [LEPROSY]
Lev 13:45 the l in whom the plague *is,* his clothes 6879
14: 2 This shall be the law of the l in the day of 6879
14: 3 *if* the plague of leprosy be healed in the l; 6879
22: 4 man soever of the seed of Aaron *is* a l, 6879
Nu 5: 2 that they put out of the camp every l, and 6879
2Sa 3:29 or that is a l, or that leaneth on a staff, or 6879
2Ki 5: 1 also a mighty *man* in valour, *but he was* a l. 6879
5:11 his hand over the place, and recover the l. 6879
5:27 he went out from his presence a l *as white* 6879
15: 5 so that he was a l unto the day of his death, 6879
2Ch 26:21 Uzziah the king was a l unto the day of his 6879
26:21 and dwelt *in* a several house, *being* a l; 6879
26:23 to the kings; for they said, He *is* a l: 6879
Mt 8: 2 there came a l and worshipped him, saying, *3015*
26: 6 in Bethany, in the house of Simon the l, *3015*
Mk 1:40 And there came a l to him, beseeching him, *3015*
14: 3 in Bethany in the house of Simon the l, *3015*

LEPERS (6) [LEPROSY]
2Ki 7: 8 when these l came to the uttermost part of 6879
Mt 10: 8 Heal the sick, cleanse the l, raise the dead, *3015*
11: 5 the l are cleansed, and the deaf hear, *3015*
Lk 4:27 And many l were in Israel in the time of *3015*
7:22 lame walk, the l are cleansed, the deaf hear, *3015*
17:12 there met him ten men *that were* l, *3015*

LEPROSY (39) [LEPER, LEPERS, LEPROUS]
Lev 13: 2 in the skin of his flesh like the plague of l; 6883
13: 3 than the skin of his flesh, it *is* a plague of l: 6883
13: 8 priest shall pronounce him unclean: it *is* a l. 6883
13: 9 When the plague of l is in a man, then 6883
13:11 It *is* an old l in the skin of his flesh, and 6883
13:12 if a l break out abroad in the skin, and 6883
13:12 the l cover all the skin of *him that hath* 6883
13:13 behold, *if* the l have covered all his flesh, 6883
13:15 *for* the raw flesh *is* unclean: it *is* a l. 6883
13:20 it *is* a plague of l broken out of the boil. 6883
13:25 the skin; it *is* a l broken out of the burning: 6883
13:25 him unclean: it *is* the plague of l. 6883
13:27 him unclean: it *is* the plague of l. 6883
13:30 a dry scall, *even* a l upon the head or beard. 6883
13:42 it *is* a l sprung up in his bald head, or his 6883
13:43 as the l appeareth in the skin of the flesh; 6883
13:47 The garment also that the plague of l is in, 6883
13:49 it *is* a plague of l, and shall be shewed unto 6883
13:51 the plague *is* a fretting l; it *is* unclean. 6883
13:52 for it *is* a fretting l; it shall be burnt in 6883
13:59 This *is* the law of the plague of l in a 6883
14: 3 *if* the plague of l be healed in the leper; 6883
14: 7 is to be cleansed from the l seven times, 6883
14:32 the law *of him* in whom *is* the plague of l, 6883
14:34 I put the plague of l in a house of the land 6883
14:44 in the house, it *is* a fretting l in the house: 6883
14:54 *is* the law for all *manner of* plague of l, 6883
14:55 And for the l of a garment, and of a house, 6883
14:57 and when *it is* clean: this *is* the law of l. 6883
Dt 24: 8 Take heed in the plague of l, that *thou* 6883
2Ki 5: 3 for he would recover him of his l. 6883
5: 6 that thou mayest recover him of his l. 6883
5: 7 send unto me to recover a man of his l? 6883
5:27 The l therefore of Naaman shall cleave unto 6883
2Ch 26:19 the l even rose up in his forehead before 6883
Mt 8: 3 And immediately his l was cleansed. *3014*
Mk 1:42 immediately the l departed from him, and *3014*
Lk 5:12 was in a certain city, behold a man full of l: *3014*
5:13 And immediately the l departed from him. *3014*

LEPROUS (6) [LEPROSY]
Ex 4: 6 took it out, behold, his hand *was* l as snow. 6879
Lev 13:44 He *is* a l man, he *is* unclean: the priest shall 6879
Nu 12:10 behold, Miriam *became* l, *white* as snow: 6879
12:10 looked upon Miriam, and behold, *she was* l. 6879
2Ki 7: 3 there were four l men *at* the entering in of 6879
2Ch 26:20 he *was* l in his forehead, and they thrust 6879

LESHEM (2) [DAN]
Jos 19:47 children of Dan went up to fight against L, 3959
19:47 and dwelt therein, and called L, Dan, 3959

LESS (27) [LEAST, LESSER]
Ex 16:17 did so, and gathered, some more, some l. 4591
30:15 the poor shall not **give** l than half a shekel, 4591
Nu 22:18 of the LORD my God, to do l or more. 6996
26:54 to few thou shalt **give** the l inheritance: 4591
33:54 to the fewer ye shall **give** the l inheritance: 4591
1Sa 22:15 servant knew nothing of all this, l or more. 6996
25:36 l or more, until the morning light. 6996
1Ki 8:27 **how much l** this house that I have 637+3588
2Ch 6:18 **how much l** this house which I have 637+3588
32:15 **how much l** shall your God 637+3588+3808
Ezr 9:13 seeing that thou our God hast punished us **l** 4295
Job 4:19 **How much l** *in* them that dwell in houses of 637
9:14 **How much l** shall I answer him, *and* 637+3588
11: 6 that God exacteth of thee *l* than thine NIH
25: 6 **How much l** man, *that is* a worm? and 637+3588
34:19 *How much l to him* that accepteth not NIH
Pr 17: 7 a fool: **much l** do lying lips a prince. 637+3588
19:10 **much l for** a servant to have rule over 637+3588
Isa 40:17 they are counted to him **l than** nothing, and 4480
Eze 15: 5 **how much l** shall it be meet yet for 637+3588
Mk 4:31 is **l than** all the seeds that be in the earth: *3398*
15:40 and Mary the mother of James the l and *3398*
1Co 12:23 which we think to be **l honourable**, *820*
2Co 12:15 abundantly I love you, the l I be loved. *2276*
Eph 3: 8 *who am* l than the least of all saints, NIG
Php 2:28 and *that* I may be the **l sorrowful**. *253*
Heb 7: 7 And without all contradiction the l is *1640*

LESSER (3) [LESS]
Ge 1:16 the day, and the l light to rule the night: 6996
Isa 7:25 of oxen, and for the treading of **l cattle**. 7716
Eze 43:14 from the l settle *even* to the greater settle 6996

LEST (240) See Index

LET (1511) [LETTEST, LETTETH, LETTING] See Index

LETTER (37) [LETTERS]
2Sa 11:14 that David wrote a l to Joab, and sent *it* by 5612
11:15 he wrote in the l, saying, Set ye Uriah in 5612
2Ki 5: 5 and I will send a l unto the king of Israel. 5612
5: 6 he brought the l to the king of Israel, 5612
5: 6 saying, Now when this l is come unto thee, 5612
5: 7 when the king of Israel had read the l, 5612
10: 2 Now as soon as this l cometh to you, 5612
10: 6 he wrote a l the second time to them, 5612
10: 7 it came to pass, when the l came to them, 5612

2Ki 19:14 Hezekiah received the l of the hand of 5612
Ezr 4: 7 the writing of the l *was* written in 5406
4: 8 Shimshai the scribe wrote a l against 104
4:11 This *is* the copy of the l that they sent unto 104
4:18 The l which ye sent unto us *hath been* 5407
4:23 Now when the copy of king Artaxerxes' l 5407
5: 5 they returned answer by l concerning this 5407
5: 6 The copy of the l that Tatnai, governor on 104
5: 7 They sent a l unto him, wherein *was* written 6600
7:11 Now this *is* the copy of the l that the king 5406
Ne 2: 8 a l unto Asaph the keeper of the king's 107
6: 5 the fifth time with an open l in his hand; 107
Est 9:26 Therefore for all the words of this l, and 107
9:29 to confirm this second l of Purim. 107
Isa 37:14 Hezekiah received the l from the hand of 5612
Jer 29: 1 Now these *are* the words of the l that 5612
29:29 Zephaniah the priest read this l in the ears 5612
Ac 23:25 And he wrote a l after this manner: *1992*
23:34 And when the governor had read *the l*, he NIG
Ro 2:27 who by the l and circumcision dost *1121*
2:29 of the heart, in the spirit, *and* not *in* the l; *1121*
7: 6 of spirit, and not *in* the oldness of the l. *1121*
2Co 3: 6 new testament; not of the l, but of the spirit: *1121*
3: 6 for the l killeth, but the spirit giveth life. *1121*
7: 8 For though I made you sorry with a l, I do *1992*
Gal 6:11 Ye see how large a l I have written unto *1121*
2Th 2: 2 by spirit, nor by word, nor by l as from us, *1992*
Heb 13:22 for I have **written a l** unto you in few *1989*

LETTERS (34) [LETTER]
1Ki 21: 8 So she wrote l in Ahab's name, and 5612
21: 8 sent the l unto the elders and to the nobles 5612
21: 9 she wrote in the l, saying, Proclaim a fast, 5612
21:11 as *it was* written in the l which she had sent 5612
2Ki 10: 1 Jehu wrote l, and sent *to* Samaria, unto 5612
20:12 sent l and a present unto Hezekiah: 5612
2Ch 30: 1 and wrote l also to Ephraim and Manasseh, 107
30: 6 So the posts went with the l from the king 107
32:17 He wrote also l to rail on the LORD God 5612
Ne 2: 7 let l be given me to the governors beyond 107
2: 9 beyond the river, and gave them the king's l. 107
6:17 the nobles of Judah sent many l unto Tobiah, 107
6:17 and *the l* of Tobiah came unto them. NIH
6:19 to him. *And* Tobiah sent l to put me in fear. 107
Est 1:22 For he sent l into all the king's provinces, 5612
3:13 the l were sent by posts into all the king's 5612
8: 5 let it be written to reverse the l devised by 5612
8:10 sent l by posts on horseback, *and* riders on 5612
9:20 sent l unto all the Jews that *were* in all 5612
9:25 he commanded by l *that* his wicked device, 5612
9:30 he sent the l unto all the Jews, to 5612
Isa 39: 1 sent l and a present to Hezekiah: 5612
Jer 29:25 Because thou hast sent l in thy name unto 5612
Lk 23:38 also was written over him in l of Greek, *1121*
Jn 7:15 saying, How knoweth this *man* l, *1121*
Ac 9: 2 And desired of him l to Damascus to *1992*
15:23 And they wrote *l* by them after this manner; NIG
22: 5 from whom also I received l unto *1992*
28:21 We neither received l out of Judea *1121*
1Co 16: 3 whomsoever you shall approve by *your* l, *1992*
2Co 3: 1 to you, or *l* of commendation from you? NIG
10: 9 may not seem as if *I* would terrify you by l. *1992*
10:10 For *his* l, say they, *are* weighty and *1992*
10:11 such as we are in word by l when we are *1992*

LETTEST (3) [LET]
Job 15:13 and l *such* words go out of thy mouth? NIH
41: 1 his tongue with a cord *which* thou l **down**? 8257
Lk 2:29 now l thou thy servant depart in peace, NIG

LETTETH (3) [LET]
2Ki 10:24 *he that l him go,* his life *shall be* for the life NIH
Pr 17:14 The beginning of strife *is as* when one **l out** 6362
2Th 2: 7 only he who now l *will let,* until he be *2722*

LETTING (1) [LET]
Ex 8:29 l the people **go** to sacrifice to the LORD. 7971

LETUSHIM (1)
Ge 25: 3 were Asshurim, and L, and Leummim. 3912

LETUSHITES See LETUSHIM

LEUMMIM (1)
Ge 25: 3 were Asshurim, and Letushim, and L. 3817

LEUMMITES See LEUMMIM

LEVI (72) [LEVITE, LEVITES, LEVITICAL]
Ge 29:34 therefore was his name called L. 3878
34:25 Simeon and L, Dinah's brethren, took each 3878
34:30 Jacob said to Simeon and L, Ye have 3878
35:23 L, and Judah, and Issachar, and Zebulun: 3878
46:11 the sons of L; Gershon, Kohath, and 3878
49: 5 Simeon and L *are* brethren; instruments of 3878
Ex 1: 2 Reuben, Simeon, L, and Judah, 3878
2: 1 there went a man of the house of L, and 3878
2: 1 of Levi, and took *to wife* a daughter of L. 3878
6:16 these *are* the names of the sons of L 3878
6:16 the years of the life of L *were* an hundred 3878
6:19 these *are* the families of L according to 3878
32:26 all the sons of L gathered themselves 3878
32:28 the children of L did according to the word 3878
Nu 1:49 Only thou shalt not number the tribe of L, 3878
3: 6 Bring the tribe of L near, and present them 3878
3:15 Number the children of L after the house of 3878
3:17 these were the sons of L by their names; 3878
4: 2 sons of Kohath from among the sons of L, 3878
16: 1 the son of L, and Dathan and Abiram, 3878
16: 7 *ye take* too much upon you, ye sons of L. 3878
16: 8 unto Korah, Hear, I pray you, ye sons of L: 3878
16:10 and all thy brethren the sons of L with thee: 3878
17: 3 write Aaron's name upon the rod of L: 3878
17: 8 the rod of Aaron for the house of L was 3878
18: 2 thy brethren also *of* the tribe of L, the tribe 3878
18:21 I have given the children of L all the tenth 3878
26:59 the daughter of L, whom *her mother* bare to 3878
26:59 whom *her mother* bare to L in Egypt: 3878
Dt 10: 8 time the LORD separated the tribe of L, 3878
10: 9 Wherefore L hath no part nor inheritance 3878
18: 1 priests the Levites, *and* all the tribe of L, 3878
21: 5 the priests the sons of L shall come near; 3878
27:12 and L, and Judah, and Issachar, and Joseph, 3878
31: 9 delivered it unto the priests the sons of L, 3878
33: 8 of L he said, *Let* thy Thummim and 3878
Jos 13:14 Only unto the tribe of L he gave none 3878
13:33 unto the tribe of L Moses gave not *any* 3878
21:10 *who were* of the children of L, had: 3878
1Ki 12:31 which were not of the sons of L. 3878
1Ch 2: 1 Reuben, Simeon, L, and Judah, Issachar, 3878
6: 1 The sons of L; Gershon, Kohath, and 3878
6:16 The sons of L; Gershom, Kohath, and 3878
6:38 of Kohath, the son of L, the son of Israel. 3878
6:43 the son of Gershom, the son of L. 3878
6:47 of Mushi, the son of Merari, the son of L. 3878
9:18 in the companies of the children of L. 3878
12:26 Of the children of L four thousand and 3878
21: 6 L and Benjamin counted he not among 3878
23: 6 them *into* courses among the sons of L, 3878
23:14 his sons were named of the tribe of L. 3878
23:24 These *were* the sons of L after the house of 3878
24:20 the rest of the sons of L *were these:* Of 3878
Ezr 8:15 and found there none of the sons of L. 3878
8:18 of Mahli, the son of L, the son of Israel; 3878
Ne 10:39 the children of L shall bring the offering of 3878
12:23 The sons of L, the chief of the fathers, 3878
Ps 135:20 Bless the LORD, O house of L: ye that 3878
Eze 40:46 *are* the sons of Zadok among the sons of L, 3878
48:31 one gate of Judah, one gate of L. 3878
Zec 12:13 The family of the house of L apart, 3878
Mal 2: 4 that my covenant might be with L, saith 3878
2: 8 ye have corrupted the covenant of L, 3878
3: 3 he shall purify the sons of L, and 3878
Mk 2:14 he saw L the *son* of Alpheus sitting at *3018*
Lk 3:24 which was *the son* of L, which was *the son* *3017*
3:29 *the son* of Matthat, which was *the son* of L, *3017*
5:27 and saw a publican, named L, sitting at *3018*
5:29 And L made him a great feast in his own *3018*
Heb 7: 5 And verily they that are of the sons of L *3017*
7: 9 And as *I* may so say, L also, who receiveth *3017*
Rev 7: 7 Of the tribe of L *were* sealed twelve *3017*

LEVIATHAN (5)
Job 41: 1 Canst thou draw out l with a hook? or 3882
Ps 74:14 Thou brakest the heads of l in pieces, *and* 3882
104:26 *there is* that l, *whom* thou hast made to play 3882
Isa 27: 1 strong sword shall punish l the piercing 3882
27: 1 even l *that* crooked serpent; 3882

LEVITE (28) [LEVI]
Ex 4:14 and he said, Is not Aaron the **L** thy brother? 3881
Dt 12:12 and the **L** that *is* within your gates; 3881
12:18 and the **L** that *is* within thy gates: 3881
12:19 the **L** as long as thou livest upon the earth. 3881
14:27 the **L** that *is* within thy gates; thou shalt not 3881
14:29 the **L**, (because he hath no part nor 3881
16:11 the **L** that *is* within thy gates, and 3881
16:14 the **L**, the stranger, and the fatherless, and 3881
18: 6 if a **L** come from any of thy gates out of all 3881
26:11 the **L**, and the stranger that *is* among you. 3881
26:12 hast given *it* unto the **L**, the stranger, 3881
26:13 also have given them unto the **L**, and 3881
Jdg 17: 7 who *was* a **L**, and he sojourned there. 3881
17: 9 I *am* a **L** of Beth-lehem-judah, and I go to 3881
17:10 and thy victuals. So the **L** went *in*. 3881
17:11 the **L** was content to dwell with the man; 3881
17:12 Micah consecrated the **L**; and the young 3881
17:13 do me good, seeing I have a **L** to *my* priest. 3881
18: 3 knew the voice of the young man the **L**: 3881
18:15 came to the house of the young man the **L**, 3881
19: 1 that there was a certain **L** sojourning on 3881
20: 4 the **L**, the husband of the woman that was 3881
2Ch 20:14 son of Mattaniah, a **L** of the sons of Asaph, 3881
31:12 over which Cononiah the **L** *was* ruler, and 3881
31:14 Kore the son of Imnah the **L**, the porter 3881
Ezr 10:15 and Shabbethai the **L** helped them. 3881
Lk 10:32 And likewise a **L**, when he was at *3019*
Ac 4:36 a **L**, *and* of the country of Cyprus, *3019*

LEVITES (265) [LEVI]
Ex 6:25 these *are* the heads of the fathers of the **L** 3881
38:21 *for* the service of the **L**, by the hand of 3881
Lev 25:32 Notwithstanding the cities of the **L**, *and* 3881
25:32 may the **L** redeem at any time. 3881
25:33 if a man purchase of the **L**, then the house 3881
25:33 for the houses of the cities of the **L** *are* their 3881
Nu 1:47 the **L** after the tribe of their fathers were 3881
1:50 thou shalt appoint the **L** over the tabernacle 3881
1:51 setteth forward, the **L** shall take it down: 3881
1:51 is to be pitched, the **L** shall set it up: 3881
1:53 the **L** shall pitch round about the tabernacle 3881
1:53 the **L** shall keep the charge of 3881
2:17 the camp of the **L** in the midst of the camp: 3881
2:33 the **L** were not numbered among 3881
3: 9 thou shalt give the **L** unto Aaron and to his 3881
3:12 I have taken the **L** from among the children 3881
3:12 of Israel: therefore the **L** shall be mine; 3881
3:20 These *are* the families of the **L** according to 3881
3:32 priest *shall be* chief over the chief of the **L**, 3881
3:39 All that were numbered of the **L**, 3881
3:41 thou shalt take the **L** for me (I *am* 3881
3:41 the cattle of the **L** instead of all 3881
3:45 Take the **L** instead of all the firstborn 3881
3:45 the cattle of the **L** instead of their cattle; 3881
3:45 of their cattle; and the **L** shall be mine: 3881
3:46 of Israel, which are more than the **L**; 3881
3:49 above them that were redeemed by the **L**: 3881
4:18 of the Kohathites from among the **L**: 3881
4:46 All those that were numbered of the **L**, 3881
7: 5 thou shalt give them unto the **L**, to every 3881
7: 6 and the oxen, and gave them unto the **L**. 3881
8: 6 Take the **L** from among the children of 3881
8: 9 thou shalt bring the **L** before the tabernacle 3881
8:10 thou shalt bring the **L** before the LORD: 3881
8:10 of Israel shall put their hands upon the **L**: 3881
8:11 Aaron shall offer the **L** before the LORD 3881
8:12 the **L** shall lay their hands upon the heads 3881
8:12 to make an atonement for the **L**. 3881
8:13 thou shalt set the **L** before Aaron, and 3881
8:14 Thus shalt thou separate the **L** from among 3881
8:14 children of Israel: and the **L** shall be mine. 3881
8:15 after that shall the **L** go in to do the service 3881
8:18 I have taken the **L** for all the firstborn of 3881
8:19 I have given the **L** *as* a gift to Aaron and 3881
8:20 did to the **L** according unto all that 3881
8:20 commanded Moses concerning the **L**, 3881
8:21 the **L** were purified, and they washed their 3881
8:22 after that went the **L** in to do their service 3881
8:22 had commanded Moses concerning the **L**, 3881
8:24 This *is it* that *belongeth* unto the **L**: 3881
8:26 Thus shalt thou do unto the **L** touching 3881
18: 6 I have taken your brethren the **L** from 3881
18:23 the **L** shall do the service of the tabernacle 3881
18:24 I have given to the **L** to inherit: 3881
18:26 Thus speak unto the **L**, and say unto them, 3881
18:30 it shall be counted unto the **L** as 3881
26:57 these *are* they that were numbered of the **L** 3881
26:58 These *are* the families of the **L**: the family 3881
31:30 *of* beasts, and give them unto the **L**, 3881
31:47 and of beast, and gave them unto the **L**, 3881
35: 2 that they give unto the **L** of the inheritance 3881
35: 2 ye shall give *also* unto the **L** suburbs for 3881
35: 4 of the cities, which ye shall give unto the **L**, 3881
35: 6 the **L** *there shall be* six cities for refuge, 3881
35: 7 *So* all the cities which ye shall give to the **L** 3881
35: 8 every one shall give of his cities unto the **L** 3881
Dt 17: 9 thou shalt come unto the priests the **L**, and 3881
17:18 out of *that which is* before the priests the **L**: 3881
18: 1 The priests the **L**, *and* all the tribe of Levi, 3881
18: 7 as all his brethren the **L** *do*, which stand 3881
24: 8 do according to all that the priests the **L** 3881
27: 9 and the priests the **L** spake unto all Israel, 3881
27:14 the **L** shall speak, and say unto all the men 3881
31:25 That Moses commanded the **L**, which bare 3881
Jos 3: 3 the priests the **L** bearing it, then ye shall 3881
8:33 and on that side before the priests the **L**, 3881
14: 3 unto the **L** he gave none inheritance among 3881
14: 4 they gave no part unto the **L** in the land, 3881
18: 7 the **L** have no part among you; for 3881
21: 1 came near the heads of the fathers of the **L** 3881
21: 3 the children of Israel gave unto the **L** out of 3881
21: 4 of Aaron the priest, *which were* of the **L**, 3881
21: 8 the children of Israel gave by lot unto the **L** 3881
21:20 the **L** which remained of the children of 3881
21:27 of Gershon, of the families of the **L**, 3881
21:34 the rest of the **L**, out of the tribe of 3881
21:40 were remaining of the families of the **L**, 3881
21:41 All the cities of the **L** within the possession 3881
1Sa 6:15 the **L** took down the ark of the LORD, 3881
2Sa 15:24 lo Zadok also, and all the **L** *were* with him, 3881
1Ki 8: 4 those did the priests and the **L** bring up. 3881
1Ch 6:19 these *are* the families of the **L** according to 3881
6:48 Their brethren also the **L** *were* appointed 3881
6:64 the children of Israel gave to the **L** *these* 3881
9: 2 the priests, **L**, and the Nethinims. 3881
9:14 of the **L**; Shemaiah the son of Hasshub, 3881
9:26 For these **L**, the four chief porters, *were* in 3881
9:31 Mattithiah, *one* of the **L**, who *was* 3881
9:33 *are* the singers, chief of the fathers of the **L**, 3881
9:34 These chief fathers of the **L** *were* chief 3881
13: 2 and **L** *which are* in their cities *and* suburbs, 3881
15: 2 ought to carry the ark of God but the **L**: 3881
15: 4 the children of Aaron, and the **L**: 3881
15:11 for the **L**, for Uriel, Asaiah, and Joel, 3881
15:12 Ye *are* the chief of the fathers of the **L**: 3881
15:14 the **L** sanctified themselves to bring up 3881
15:15 the children of the **L** bare the ark of God 3881
15:16 David spake to the chief of the **L** to appoint 3881
15:17 So the **L** appointed Heman the son of Joel; 3881
15:22 chief of the **L**, *was* for song: 3881
15:26 when God helped the **L** that bare the ark of 3881
15:27 all the **L** that bare the ark, and the singers, 3881
16: 4 he appointed *certain* of the **L** to minister 3881
23: 2 princes of Israel, with the priests and the **L**. 3881
23: 3 Now the **L** were numbered from the age of 3881
23:26 also unto the **L**; *they* shall no *more* carry 3881
23:27 the **L** *were* numbered from twenty 1121+3878
24: 6 *one* of the **L**, wrote them before the king, 3881
24: 6 the chief of the fathers of the priests and **L**: 3881
24:30 These *were* the sons of the **L** after 3881
24:31 the chief of the fathers of the priests and **L**, 3881
26:17 Eastward *were* six **L**, northward four a day, 3881
26:20 *of* the **L**, Ahijah *was* over the treasures of 3881
27:17 Of the **L**, Hashabiah the son of Kemuel: 3881
28:13 for the courses of the priests and the **L**, 3881
28:21 the courses of the priests and the **L**, 3881
2Ch 5: 4 of Israel came; and the **L** took up the ark. 3881
5: 5 these did the priests *and* the **L** bring up. 3881
5:12 Also the **L** *which were* the singers, all of 3881
7: 6 the **L** also with instruments of musick of 3881
8:14 the **L** to their charges, to praise and 3881
8:15 the priests and **L** concerning any matter, 3881
11:13 the **L** that *were* in all Israel resorted to him 3881
11:14 For the **L** left their suburbs and 3881
13: 9 the **L**, and have made you priests after 3881
13:10 and the **L** *wait* upon *their* business: 3881

2Ch 17: 8 with them *he sent* L, *even* Shemaiah, and 3881
17: 8 and Tobijah, and Tob-adonijah, L; 3881
19: 8 in Jerusalem did Jehoshaphat set of the L, 3881
19:11 also the L *shall be* officers before you. 3881
20:19 the L, of the children of the Kohathites, 3881
23: 2 gathered the L out of all the cities of Judah, 3881
23: 4 of the priests and of the L, *shall be* porters 3881
23: 6 the priests, and they that minister of the L; 3881
23: 7 the L shall compass the king round about, 3881
23: 8 So the L and all Judah did according to all 3881
23:18 LORD by the hand of the priests the L, 3881
24: 5 he gathered together the priests and the L, 3881
24: 5 the matter. Howbeit the L hastened *it* not. 3881
24: 6 Why hast thou not required of the L to 3881
24:11 unto the king's office by the hand of the L, 3881
29: 4 he brought in the priests and the L, and 3881
29: 5 said unto them, Hear me, ye L, 3881
29:12 the L arose, Mahath the son of Amasai, 3881
29:16 the L took *it,* to carry *it* out abroad into 3881
29:25 he set the L *in* the house of the LORD 3881
29:26 the L stood with the instruments of David, 3881
29:30 the princes commanded the L to *sing* praise 3881
29:34 wherefore their brethren the L did help 3881
29:34 for the L *were* more upright in heart to 3881
30:15 the priests and the L were ashamed, and 3881
30:16 *which they received* of the hand of the L. 3881
30:17 the L had the charge of the killing of 3881
30:21 the L and the priests praised the LORD 3881
30:22 Hezekiah spake comfortably unto all the L 3881
30:25 with the priests and the L, and all 3881
30:27 the priests the L arose and blessed 3881
31: 2 of the priests and the L after their courses, 3881
31: 2 the priests and L for burnt offerings and 3881
31: 4 to give the portion of the priests and the L, 3881
31: 9 the priests and the L concerning the heaps. 3881
31:17 the L from twenty years old and upward, 3881
31:19 reckoned by genealogies among the L. 3881
34: 9 which the L that kept the doors had 3881
34:12 of them *were* Jahath and Obadiah, the L, 3881
34:12 *other of* the L, all that could skill of 3881
34:13 of the L *there were* scribes, and officers, 3881
34:30 the L, and all the people, great and small: 3881
35: 3 said unto the L that taught all Israel, 3881
35: 5 *after* the division of the families of the L. 3881
35: 8 unto the people, to the priests, and to the L: 3881
35: 9 and Jeiel and Jozabad, chief of the L, 3881
35: 9 gave unto the L for passover *offerings* five 3881
35:10 in their place, and the L in their courses, 3881
35:11 from their hands, and the L flayed *them.* 3881
35:14 therefore the L prepared for themselves, 3881
35:15 for their brethren the L prepared for them. 3881
35:18 the L, and all Judah and Israel that were 3881
Ezr 1: 5 and Benjamin, and the priests, and the L, 3881
2:40 The L: the children of Jeshua and Kadmiel, 3881
2:70 the L, and *some* of the people, and 3881
3: 8 of their brethren the priests and the L, 3881
3: 8 appointed the L from twenty years old and 3881
3: 9 *with* their sons and their brethren the L. 3881
3:10 the L the sons of Asaph with cymbals, 3881
3:12 of the priests and L and chief of the fathers, 3881
6:16 the L, and the rest of the children of 3879
6:18 the L in their courses, for the service of 3879
6:20 the priests and the L were purified together, 3881
7: 7 the L, and the singers, and the porters, and 3881
7:13 and *of* his priests and L, in my realm, 3879
7:24 that *touching* any of the priests and L, 3879
8:20 had appointed for the service of the L, 3881
8:29 before the chief of the priests and the L, 3881
8:30 and the L the weight of the silver, 3881
8:33 and Noadiah the son of Binnui, L; 3881
9: 1 people of Israel, and the priests, and the L, 3881
10: 5 made the chief priests, the L, and all Israel, 3881
10:23 Also of the L; Jozabad, and Shimei, and 3881
Ne 3:17 After him repaired the L, Rehum the son of 3881
7: 1 and the singers and the L were appointed, 3881
7:43 The L: the children of Jeshua, of Kadmiel, 3881
7:73 the L, and the porters, and the singers, and 3881
8: 7 Jozabad, Hanan, Pelaiah, and the L, 3881
8: 9 the L that taught the people, said unto all 3881
8:11 So the L stilled all the people, saying, 3881
8:13 the priests, and the L, unto Ezra the scribe, 3881
9: 4 stood up upon the stairs of the L, Jeshua, 3881
9: 5 the L, Jeshua and Kadmiel, Bani, 3881
9:38 write *it;* and our princes, L, *and* priests, 3881
10: 9 the L: both Jeshua the son of Azaniah, 3881
10:28 the priests, the L, the porters, the singers, 3881
10:34 the L, and the people, for the wood 3881
10:37 the tithes of our ground unto the L, that 3881
10:37 that the same L *might* have the tithes in all 3881
10:38 priest the son of Aaron shall be with the L, 3881
10:38 be with the Levites, when the L take tithes: 3881
10:38 the L shall bring up the tithe of the tithes 3881
11: 3 the L, and the Nethinims, and the children 3881
11:15 Also of the L: Shemaiah the son of Hashub, 3881
11:16 and Jozabad, of the chief of the L, 3881
11:18 All the L in the holy city *were* two hundred 3881
11:20 residue of Israel, of the priests, *and* the L, 3881
11:22 The overseer also of the L at Jerusalem *was* 3881
11:36 of the L *were* divisions *in* Judah, *and* 3881
12: 1 the L that went up with Zerubbabel the son 3881
12: 8 Moreover the L: Jeshua, Binnui, Kadmiel, 3881
12:22 The L in the days of Eliashib, Joiada, and 3881
12:24 the chief of the L: Hashabiah, Sherebiah, 3881
12:27 they sought the L out of all their places, 3881
12:30 the priests and the L purified themselves, 3881
12:44 portions of the law for the priests and L: 3881
12:44 for the priests and for the L that waited. 3881
12:47 they sanctified *holy things* unto the L; and 3881
12:47 the L sanctified *them* unto the children of 3881
13: 5 was commanded *to be given* to the L, 3881
13:10 I perceived that the portions of the L had 3881
13:10 Levites had not been given *them:* for the L 3881
13:13 Zadok the scribe, and of the L, Pedaiah: 3881
13:22 I commanded the L that they should 3881
13:29 covenant of the priesthood, and of the L. 3881
13:30 the wards of the priests and the L, 3881
Isa 66:21 will also take of them for priests *and* for L, 3881
Jer 33:18 Neither shall the priests the L want a man 3881
33:21 and with the L the priests, my ministers. 3881
33:22 and the L that minister unto me. 3881
Eze 43:19 thou shalt give to the priests the L that *be* 3881
44:10 the L that are gone away far from me, 3881
44:15 the priests the L, the sons of Zadok, 3881
45: 5 shall also the L, the ministers of the house, 3881
48:11 of Israel went astray, as the L went astray. 3881
48:12 *a thing* most holy by the border of the L. 3881
48:13 the L *shall have* five and twenty thousand 3881
48:22 Moreover from the possession of the L, *and* 3881
Jn 1:19 and L from Jerusalem to ask him, *3019*

LEVITICAL (1) [LEVI]
Heb 7:11 perfection were by the L priesthood, *3020*

LEVY (6)
Nu 31:28 l a tribute unto the LORD of the men of 7311
1Ki 5:13 king Solomon raised a l out of all Israel; 4522
5:13 and the l was thirty thousand men. 4522
5:14 at home: and Adoniram *was* over the l. 4522
9:15 this *is* the reason of the l which king 4522
9:21 **upon** those did Solomon l a tribute of 5927

LEWD (3) [LEWDLY, LEWDNESS]
Eze 16:27 which are ashamed of thy l way. 2154
23:44 and unto Aholibah, the l women. 2154
Ac 17: 5 took unto *them* certain l fellows of *4190*

LEWDLY (1) [LEWD]
Eze 22:11 hath l defiled his daughter in law; 2154+871.1

LEWDNESS (17) [LEWD]
Jdg 20: 6 for they have committed l and folly in 2154
Jer 11:15 *seeing* she hath wrought l *with* many, and 4209
13:27 the l of thy whoredom, *and* 2154
Eze 16:43 thou shalt not commit *this* l above all thine 2154
16:58 Thou hast borne thy l and thine 2154
22: 9 in the midst of thee they commit l. 2154
23:21 Thus thou calledst to remembrance the l of 2154
23:27 Thus will I make thy l to cease from thee, 2154
23:29 both thy l and thy whoredoms. 2154
23:35 therefore bear thou also thy l and thy 2154
23:48 Thus will I cause l to cease out of the land, 2154
23:48 may be taught not to do after your l. 2154
23:49 they shall recompense your l upon you, 2154
24:13 In thy filthiness *is* l: because I have purged 2154
Hos 2:10 now will I discover her l in the sight of her 5040
6: 9 *in* the way by consent: for they commit l. 2154
Ac 18:14 If it were a matter of wrong or wicked l, *4467*

LIAR (13) [LIE]
Job 24:25 who will **make** me **a l**, and make my 3576
Pr 17: 4 *and* a l giveth ear to a naughty tongue. 8267
19:22 and a poor *man is* better than a l. 376+3577
30: 6 lest he reprove thee, and thou be **found a l**. 3576
Jer 15:18 wilt thou be altogether unto me as a l, *and* 391
Jn 8:44 of his own: for he is a l, and the father of it. *5583*
8:55 I know him not, I shall be a l like unto you: *5583*
Ro 3: 4 yea, let God be true, but every man a l; as it *5583*
1Jn 1:10 we make him a l, and his word is not in us. *5583*
2: 4 is a l, and the truth is not in him. *5583*
2:22 Who is a l but he that denieth that Jesus is *5583*
4:20 I love God, and hateth his brother, he is a l: *5583*
5:10 that believeth not God hath made him a l; *5583*

LIARS (8) [LIE]
Dt 33:29 thine enemies shall be **found** l unto thee; 3584
Ps 116:11 I said in my haste, All men *are* l. 3576
Isa 44:25 That frustrateth the tokens of the l, and 907
Jer 50:36 A sword *is* upon the l; and they shall dote: 907
1Ti 1:10 for menstealers, for l, for perjured *persons,* *5583*
Tit 1:12 said, The Cretians *are* alway l, evil beasts, *5583*
Rev 2: 2 and are not, and hast found them l: *5571*
21: 8 and sorcerers, and idolaters, and all l, *5571*

LIBERAL (6) [LIBERALITY, LIBERALLY, LIBERTINES]
Pr 11:25 The l soul shall be made fat: and he that 1293
Isa 32: 5 The vile person shall be no more called l, 5081
32: 8 the l deviseth liberal *things;* and by liberal 5081
32: 8 the liberal deviseth l *things;* and by liberal 5082
32: 8 and by l *things* shall he stand. 5082
2Co 9:13 and *for your* l distribution unto them, and *572*

LIBERALITY (2) [LIBERAL]
1Co 16: 3 them will I send to bring your l unto *5485*
2Co 8: 2 poverty abounded unto the riches of their l. *572*

LIBERALLY (2) [LIBERAL]
Dt 15:14 Thou shalt **furnish** him l out of thy 6059+6059
Jas 1: 5 that giveth to all *men* l, and upbraideth not; *574*

LIBERTINES (1) [LIBERAL]
Ac 6: 9 which is called *the synagogue* of the L, and *3032*

LIBERTY (27)
Lev 25:10 proclaim l throughout *all* the land unto all 1865
Ps 119:45 And I will walk at l: for I seek thy precepts. 7342
Isa 61: 1 to proclaim l to the captives, and 1865
Jer 34: 8 *were* at Jerusalem, to proclaim l unto them; 1865
34:15 in proclaiming l every man to his 1865
34:16 whom ye had set at l at their pleasure, 2670
34:17 in proclaiming l, every one to his brother, 1865
34:17 behold, I proclaim a l for you, saith 1865
Eze 46:17 then it shall be his to the year of l; 1865
Lk 4:18 to the blind, to set at l *them that are* bruised, *859*
Ac 24:23 and to let *him* have l, and that *he* should *425*
26:32 This man might have been **set at** l, *630*
27: 3 **gave** *him* l to go unto *his* friends to refresh *2010*
Ro 8:21 into the glorious l of the children of God. *1657*
1Co 7:39 she is at l to be married to whom she will; *1658*
8: 9 But take heed lest by any means this l of *1849*
10:29 for why is my l judged of another *man's* *1657*
2Co 3:17 where the Spirit of the Lord *is,* there *is* l. *1657*
Gal 2: 4 who came in privily to spy out our l which *1657*
5: 1 in the l wherewith Christ hath made us free, *1657*
5:13 For, brethren, ye have been called unto l; *1657*
5:13 only *use* not l for an occasion to the flesh, *1657*
Heb 13:23 Know ye that *our* brother Timothy is **set at** l; *630*
Jas 1:25 But whoso looketh into the perfect law of l, *1657*
2:12 as they that shall be judged by the law of l. *1657*
1Pe 2:16 not using *your* l for a cloke of *1657*
2Pe 2:19 While they promise them l, they themselves *1657*

LIBNAH (18)
Nu 33:20 from Rimmon-parez, and pitched in L. 3841
33:21 they removed from L, and pitched at 3841
Jos 10:29 *unto* L, and fought against Libnah: 3841
10:29 *unto* Libnah, and fought against L: 3841
10:31 Joshua passed from L, and all Israel with 3841
10:32 according to all that he had done to L. 3841
10:39 as he had done also to L, and to her king. 3841
12:15 The king of L, one; the king of Adullam, 3841
15:42 L, and Ether, and Ashan, 3841
21:13 for the slayer; and L with her suburbs, 3841
2Ki 8:22 this day. Then L revolted at the same time. 3841
19: 8 the king of Assyria warring against L: 3841
23:31 the daughter of Jeremiah of L. 3841
24:18 the daughter of Jeremiah of L. 3841
1Ch 6:57 L with her suburbs, and Jattir, and 3841
2Ch 21:10 The same time also did L revolt from under 3841
Isa 37: 8 the king of Assyria warring against L: 3841
Jer 52: 1 Hamutal the daughter of Jeremiah of L. 3841

LIBNI (5) [LIBNITES]
Ex 6:17 L, and Shimi, according to their families. 3845
Nu 3:18 Gershon by their families; L, and Shimei. 3845
1Ch 6:17 of the sons of Gershom; L, and Shimei. 3845
6:20 L his son, Jahath his son, Zimmah his son, 3845
6:29 Mahli, L his son, Shimei his son, Uzza his 3845

LIBNITES (2) [LIBNI]
Nu 3:21 Of Gershon *was* the family of the L, and 3846
26:58 the family of the L, the family of 3846

LIBYA (3) [LIBYANS]
Eze 30: 5 L, and Lydia, and all the mingled people, 6316
38: 5 Persia, Ethiopia, and L with them; all of 6316
Ac 2:10 and in the parts of L about Cyrene, and *3033*

LIBYANS (2) [LIBYA]
Jer 46: 9 the Ethiopians and the L, that handle 6316
Da 11:43 the L and the Ethiopians *shall be* at his 3864

LICE (6)
Ex 8:16 that it may become l throughout all the land 3654
8:17 and it became l in man, and in beast; 3654
8:17 all the dust of the land became l throughout 3654
8:18 so with their enchantments to bring forth l, 3654
8:18 so there were l upon man, and upon beast. 3654
Ps 105:31 divers sorts *of flies, and* l in all their coasts. 3654

LICENCE (2)
Ac 21:40 And when he had **given** *him* l, Paul stood *2010*
25:16 have l to answer for himself concerning *5117*

LICK (5) [LICKED, LICKETH]
Nu 22: 4 Now shall *this* company l **up** all *that are* 3897
1Ki 21:19 the blood of Naboth shall dogs l thy blood, 3952
Ps 72: 9 before him; and his enemies shall l the dust. 3897
Isa 49:23 the earth, and l **up** the dust of thy feet; 3897
Mic 7:17 They shall l the dust like a serpent, 3897

LICKED (4) [LICK]
1Ki 18:38 and l **up** the water that *was* in the trench. 3897
21:19 In the place where dogs l the blood of 3952
22:38 the dogs l **up** his blood; and they washed 3952
Lk 16:21 moreover the dogs came and l his sores. *621*

LICKETH (1) [LICK]
Nu 22: 4 as the ox l **up** the grass of the field. 3897

LID (1)
2Ki 12: 9 bored a hole in the l of it, and set it beside 1817

LIE (155) [LAIN, LIAR, LIARS, LIED, LIEN, LIERS, LIES, LIEST, LIETH, LYING]
Ge 19:32 father drink wine, and we will l with him, 7901
19:34 go thou in, *and* l with him, that we may 7901
30:15 Therefore he shall l with thee to night for 7901
39: 7 eyes upon Joseph; and she said, L with me. 7901
39:10 not unto her, to l by her, *or* to be with her. 7901
39:12 him by his garment, saying, L with me: 7901
39:14 he came in unto me to l with me, and 7901
47:30 I will l with my fathers, and thou shalt 7901
Ex 21:13 if a man l not **in wait**, but God deliver *him* 6658
22:16 l with her, he shall surely endow her to be 7901
23:11 seventh *year* thou shalt let it rest and **l still**; 5203
Lev 6: 2 **l** unto his neighbour in that which was 3584
15:18 The woman also with whom man shall l 7901
15:24 if any man l **with** her **at all**, 854+7901+7901
18:20 **l carnally** with thy 2233+5414+7903+3807.1
18:22 Thou shalt not l with mankind, as with 7901
18:23 Neither shalt thou l with any beast to 5414+7903
18:23 stand before a beast to **l down** thereto: 7250
19:11 deal falsely, neither l one to another. 8266
20:12 if a man l with his daughter in law, both of 7901
20:13 If a man also l with mankind, as he lieth 7901
20:15 if a man **l with** a beast, he shall 5414+7903
20:16 **l down** thereto, thou shalt kill the woman 7250

Lev 20:18 if a man shall l with a woman having her 7901
20:20 if a man shall l with his uncle's wife, 7901
26: 6 ye shall l **down**, and none shall make *you* 7901
Nu 5:13 a man l with her carnally, and it be hid 7901
10: 5 the camps that l on the east parts shall go 2583
10: 6 the camps that l on the south side shall take 2583
23:19 God *is* not a man, that he should l; 3576
23:24 he shall not l **down** until he eat *of* the prey, 7901
Dt 19:11 **l in wait** for him, and rise up against him, 693
22:23 a man find her in the city, and l with her; 7901
22:25 and the man force her, and l with her: 7901
22:28 on her, and l with her, and they be found; 7901
25: 2 that the judge shall **cause** him **to l down**, 5307
28:30 a wife, and another man shall l **with** her: 7901
29:20 are written in this book shall l upon him, 7257
Jos 8: 4 Behold, ye shall l **in wait against** the city, 693
8: 9 they went to l **in ambush**, and 3993
8:12 set them to l **in ambush** between Beth-el 693
Jdg 9:32 that *is* with thee, *and* l **in wait** in the field: 693
19:20 howsoever *let* all thy wants *l* upon me; NIH
21:20 Go and l **in wait** in the vineyards; 693
Ru 3: 4 thou shalt mark the place where he shall l, 7901
3: 7 he went to l **down** at the end of the heap *of* 7901
3:13 LORD liveth: l **down** until the morning. 7901
1Sa 3: 5 he said, I called not; l **down** again. And he 7901
3: 6 I called not, my son; l **down** again. 7901
3: 9 Eli said unto Samuel, Go, l **down**: 7901
15:29 also the Strength of Israel will not l nor 8266
22: 8 against me, to l **in wait**, as at this day? 693
22:13 rise against me, to l **in wait**, as at this day? 693
2Sa 11:11 to eat and to drink, and to l with my wife? 7901
11:13 at even he went out to l on his bed with 7901
12:11 he shall l with thy wives in the sight of this 7901
13:11 said unto her, Come l with me, my sister. 7901
1Ki 1: 2 her cherish him, and let her l in thy bosom, 7901
2Ki 4:16 man of God, do not l unto thine handmaid. 3576
Job 6:28 upon me; for *it is* evident unto you if I l. 3576
7: 4 When I l **down**, I say, When shall I arise, 7901
11:19 Also thou shalt l **down**, and none shall 7257
20:11 which shall l **down** with him in the dust. 7901
21:26 They shall l **down** alike in the dust, and 7901
27:19 The rich *man* shall l **down**, but he shall not 7901
34: 6 Should I l against my right? my wound *is* 3576
38:40 *and* abide in the covert to l **in wait**? 695
Ps 23: 2 He **maketh** me **to l down** in green 7257
57: 4 I l *even among* them that are set on fire, 7901
59: 3 For lo, they l **in wait** for my soul: the mighty 693
62: 9 *are* vanity, *and* men of high degree *are* a l: 3577
88: 5 the dead, like the slain that l in the grave, 7901
89:35 by my holiness that I will not l unto David. 3576
119:69 The proud have forged a l against me: *but* 8267
Pr 3:24 thou shalt l **down**, and thy sleep shall be 7901
12: 6 The words of the wicked *are* to l **in wait** *for* 693
14: 5 A faithful witness will not l: but a false 3576
Ecc 4:11 if two l **together**, then they have heat: 7901
SS 1:13 he shall l **all night** betwixt my breasts. 3885
Isa 11: 6 and the leopard shall l **down** with the kid; 7257
11: 7 their young ones shall l **down** together: 7257
13:21 wild beasts of the desert shall l there; and 7257
14:18 of the nations, *even* all of them, l in glory, 7901
14:30 and the needy shall l **down** in safety: 7257
17: 2 which shall l **down**, and none shall make 7257
27:10 there shall he l **down**, and consume 7257
33: 8 The highways l **waste**, the wayfaring man 8074
34:10 generation to generation it shall l **waste**; 2717
43:17 they shall l **down** together, they shall not 7901
44:20 nor say, *Is there* not a l in my right hand? 8267
50:11 of mine hand; ye shall l **down** in sorrow. 7901
51:20 they l at the head of all the streets, as a wild 7901
63: 8 they *are* my people, children *that* will not l: 8266
65:10 of Achor a **place** for the herds **to l down in**, 7258
Jer 3:25 We l **down** in our shame, and 7901
27:10 For they prophesy a l unto you, to remove 8267
27:14 of Babylon: for they prophesy a l unto you. 8267
27:15 yet they prophesy a l in my name; 8267
27:16 for they prophesy a l unto you. 8267
28:15 but thou makest this people to trust in a l. 8267
29:21 which prophesy a l unto you in my name; 8267
29:31 him not, and he caused you to trust in a l: 8267
33:12 shepherds **causing** *their* flocks **to l down**. 7257
La 2:21 and the old l on the ground in the streets: 7901
Eze 4: 4 L thou also upon thy left side, and lay 7901
4: 4 shalt l upon it thou shalt bear their iniquity. 7901
4: 6 l again on thy right side, and thou shalt bear 7901
4: 9 of the days that thou shalt l upon thy side, 7901
21:29 unto thee, whiles *they* divine a l unto thee, 3577
31:18 thou shalt l in the midst of 7901
32:21 they l uncircumcised, slain by the sword. 7901
32:27 they shall not l with the mighty *that are* 7901
32:28 shalt l with *them that are* slain with 7901
32:29 they shall l with the uncircumcised, and 7901
32:30 they l uncircumcised with *them that be* 7901
34:14 there shall they l in a good fold, and *in* a fat 7257
34:15 my flock, and I will **cause** them **to l down**, 7257
Hos 2:18 and will **make** them **to l down** safely. 7901
7: 6 heart like an oven, whiles they l **in wait**: 693
Joel 1:13 come, l **all night** in sackcloth, ye ministers 3885
Am 6: 4 That l upon beds of ivory, and 7901
Mic 1:14 the houses of Achzib *shall be* a l to the kings 391
2:11 walking *in* the spirit and falsehood do l, 3576
7: 2 they all l **in wait** for blood; they hunt every 693
Hab 2: 3 but at the end it shall speak, and not l: 3576
Zep 2: 7 Ashkelon shall they l **down** in the evening: 7257
2:14 And flocks shall l **down** in the midst of her, 7257
2:15 a **place** for beasts **to l down in**! 4769
3:13 for they shall feed and l **down**, and 7257
Hag 1: 4 your cieled houses, and this house *l* waste? NIH
Zec 10: 2 the diviners have seen a l, and have told 8267
Jn 5: 6 When Jesus saw him l, and knew that he *2621*
8:44 When he speaketh a l, he speaketh of his *5579*
20: 6 the sepulchre, and seeth the linen clothes l, *2749*
Ac 5: 3 why hath Satan filled thine heart to l to *5574*
23:21 for there l **in wait for** him of them moe *1748*
Ro 1:25 Who changed the truth of God into a l, and *5579*
3: 7 abounded through my l unto his glory; *5582*
9: 1 I say the truth in Christ, I l not, *5574*
2Co 11:31 blessed for evermore, knoweth that I l not. *5574*
Gal 1:20 write unto you, behold, before God, I l not. *5574*
Eph 4:14 whereby they l **in wait** to deceive; *3180*
Col 3: 9 L not one to another, seeing that ye have *5574*
2Th 2:11 that they should believe a l: *5579*
1Ti 2: 7 (I speak the truth in Christ, *and* l not;) *5574*
Tit 1: 2 of eternal life, which God, that **cannot** l, *893*
Heb 6:18 in which *it was* impossible for God to l, *5574*
Jas 3:14 glory not, and l *not* against the truth. *5574*
1Jn 1: 6 walk in darkness, we l, and do not the truth: *5574*
2:21 ye know it, and that no l is of the truth. *5579*
2:27 and is no l, and even as it hath taught you, *5579*
Rev 3: 9 say they are Jews, and are not, but do l; *5574*
11: 8 And their dead bodies *shall l* in the street of NIG
21:27 worketh abomination, or *maketh* a l: *5579*
22:15 and whosoever loveth and maketh a l. *5579*

LIED (4) [LIE]

1Ki 13:18 and drink water. *But* he l unto him. 3584
Ps 78:36 and they l unto him with their tongues. 3576
Isa 57:11 that thou hast l, and hast not remembered 3576
Ac 5: 4 thou hast not l unto men, but unto God. *5574*

LIEN (6) [LIE]

Ge 26:10 might lightly have l **with** thy wife, 854+7901
Jdg 21:11 and every woman that hath l by man. 4904
Job 3:13 For now should I have l *still* and 7901
Ps 68:13 Though ye have l among the pots, *yet shall* 7901
Jer 3: 2 and see where thou hast not been l with. 7693
Jn 11:17 he found that he had *l* in the grave four days NIG

LIERS (10) [LIE]

Jos 8:13 and their l **in wait** on the west of the city, 6119
8:14 he wist not that *there were* l **in ambush** 693
Jdg 9:25 the men of Shechem set l **in wait** for him in 693
16:12 *there were* l **in wait** abiding in the chamber. 693
20:29 And Israel set l **in wait** round about Gibeah. 693
20:33 the l **in wait** of Israel came forth out of their 693
20:36 they trusted unto the l **in wait** which they 693
20:37 the l **in wait** hasted, and rushed upon 693
20:37 and the l **in wait** drew *themselves* along, and 693
20:38 between the men of Israel and the l **in wait**, 693

LIES (51) [LIE]

Jdg 16:10 thou hast mocked me, and told me l: 3577
16:13 thou hast mocked me, and told me l: 3577
Job 11: 3 Should thy l make men hold their peace? and 907
13: 4 ye *are* forgers of l, ye *are* all physicians of 8267
Ps 40: 4 not the proud, nor such as turn aside to l. 3577
58: 3 astray as soon as they be born, speaking l. 3577
62: 4 they delight in l: they bless with their 3577
63:11 the mouth of them that speak l shall be 8267

Ps 101: 7 he that telleth l shall not tarry in my sight. 8267
Pr 6:19 A false witness *that* speaketh l, and he that 3577
14: 5 will not lie: but a false witness will utter l. 3577
14:25 but a deceitful *witness* speaketh l. 3577
19: 5 and *he that* speaketh l shall not escape. 3577
19: 9 and *he that* speaketh l shall perish. 3577
29:12 If a ruler hearken to l, all his servants 1697+8267
30: 8 Remove far from me vanity and l: 1697+3577
Isa 9:15 the prophet that teacheth l, he *is* the tail. 8267
16: 6 and his wrath: *but* his l *shall* not *be* so. 907
28:15 for we have made l our refuge, and 3577
28:17 the hail shall sweep away the refuge of l, 3577
59: 3 your lips have spoken l, your tongue hath 8267
59: 4 *they* trust in vanity, and speak l; 7723
Jer 9: 3 they bend their tongues *like* their bow *for* l: 8267
9: 5 they have taught their tongue to speak l, 8267
14:14 The prophets prophesy l in my name: 8267
16:19 Surely our fathers have inherited l, vanity, 8267
20: 6 to whom thou hast prophesied l. 8267
23:14 *they* commit adultery, and walk in l: 8267
23:25 that prophesy l in my name, saying, I have 8267
23:26 in the heart of the prophets that prophesy l? 8267
23:32 cause my people to err by their l, and 8267
48:30 *it shall* not *be* so; his l shall not so effect *it.* 907
Eze 13: 8 seen l, therefore behold, I *am* against you, 3577
13: 9 prophets that see vanity, and that divine l: 3577
13:19 your lying to my people that hear *your* l? 3577
13:22 Because *with* l *ye* have made the heart of 8267
22:28 divining l unto them, saying, Thus saith 3577
24:12 She hath wearied *herself with* l, and 8383
Da 11:27 and they shall speak l at one table; 3577
Hos 7: 3 and the princes with their l. 3585
7:13 yet they have spoken l against me. 3577
10:13 reaped iniquity; ye have eaten the fruit of l: 3585
11:12 Ephraim compasseth me about with l, and 3585
12: 1 he daily increaseth l and desolation; and 3577
Am 2: 4 and their l caused them to err, 3577
Mic 6:12 the inhabitants thereof have spoken l, and 8267
Na 3: 1 it *is* all full *of* l *and* robbery; the prey 3585
Hab 2:18 the molten image, and a teacher of l, 8267
Zep 3:13 of Israel shall not do iniquity, nor speak l; 3577
Zec 13: 3 for thou speakest l in the name of 8267
1Ti 4: 2 **Speaking** l in hypocrisy, having their *5573*

LIEST (5) [LIE]

Ge 28:13 the land whereon thou l, to thee will I give 7901
Dt 6: 7 when thou l **down**, and when thou risest up. 7901
11:19 when thou l **down**, and when thou risest up. 7901
Jos 7:10 wherefore l thou thus upon thy face? 5307
Pr 3:24 When thou l **down**, thou shalt not be afraid: 7901

LIETH (59) [LIE]

Ge 4: 7 if thou doest not well, sin l at the door. 7257
49:25 blessings of the deep that l under, 7257
Ex 22:19 Whosoever l with a beast shall surely be 7901
Lev 6: 3 and l concerning it, and sweareth falsely; 3584
14:47 he that l in the house shall wash his clothes; 7901
15: 4 whereon he l that hath the issue, is unclean: 7901
15:20 every *thing* that she l upon in her separation 7901
15:24 all the bed whereon he l shall be unclean. 7901
15:26 Every bed whereon she l all the days of her 7901
15:33 him that l **with** her which is unclean. 5973+7901
19:20 **l carnally with** a woman 854+2233+7901+7902
20:11 the man that l with his father's wife hath 7901
20:13 lie with mankind, as he l **with** a woman, 4904
26:34 as long as it l **desolate**, and ye *be* in your 8074
26:35 As long as it l **desolate** it shall rest; because 8074
26:43 while she l **desolate** without them: 8074
Nu 21:15 of Ar, and l upon the border of Moab. 8172
Dt 27:20 Cursed *be* he that l with his father's wife; 7901
27:21 Cursed *be* he that l with any *manner of* 7901
27:22 Cursed *be* he that l with his sister, 7901
27:23 Cursed *be* he that l with his mother in law. 7901
Jos 15: 8 *I* before the valley of Hinnom westward, NIH
17: 7 *to* Michmethah, that *I* before Shechem; NIH
18:13 near the hill that *I* on the south side of NIH
18:14 from the hill that *I* before Beth-horon NIH
18:16 *I* before the valley of the son of Hinnom, NIH
Jdg 1:16 of Judah, which *I* in the south of Arad; NIH
16: 5 see wherein his great strength *I*, and by what NIH
16: 6 wherein thy great strength *I*, and NIH
16:15 not told me wherein thy great strength *I*. NIH
18:28 and it was in the valley that *I* by Beth-rehob. NIH
Ru 3: 4 it shall be, when he l **down**, that thou shalt 7901
2Sa 2:24 that *I* before Giah *by* the way of NIH
24: 5 *on* the right side of the city that *I* in NIH
Ne 2: 3 *I* waste, and the gates thereof are consumed NIH
2:17 how Jerusalem *I* waste, and the gates NIH
3:25 the tower which l **out** from the king's high 3318
3:26 toward the east, and the tower that l **out**. 3318
3:27 over against the great tower that l **out**, 3318
Job 14:12 So man l **down**, and riseth not: till 7901
40:21 He l under the shady trees, in the covert of 7901
Ps 10: 9 He l **in wait** secretly as a lion in his den: 693
10: 9 he l **in wait** to catch the poor: he doth catch 693
41: 8 and *now* that he l he shall rise up no more. 7901
88: 7 Thy wrath l **hard** upon me, and thou hast 5564
Pr 7:12 in the streets, and l **in wait** at every corner.) 693
23:28 She also l **in wait** as *for* a prey, and 693
23:34 thou shalt be as he that l **down** in the midst 7901
23:34 or as he that l upon the top of a mast. 7901
Eze 9: 2 which l toward the north, and every man a 6437
29: 3 the great dragon that l in the midst of his 7257
Mic 7: 5 keep the doors of thy mouth from her that l 7901
Mt 8: 6 Lord, my servant l at home sick of the palsy, *906*
Mk 5:23 daughter **l at the point of death**: *2079+2192*
Ac 14: 6 and *unto* the **region that l round about**: *4066*
27:12 and l toward the south west and north west. *991*
Ro 12:18 If *it be* possible, **as much as l in** you, *1537*
1Jn 5:19 and the whole world l in wickedness. *2749*
Rev 21:16 And the city l foursquare, and the length is *2749*

LIEUTENANTS (4)

Ezr 8:36 the king's commissions unto the king's l, 323
Est 3:12 Haman had commanded unto the king's l, 323
8: 9 to the l, and the deputies and rulers of 323
9: 3 the l, and the deputies, and officers of 323

LIFE (450) [LIVE]

Ge 1:20 abundantly the moving creature that hath l, 2416
1:30 wherein *there is* l, *I have given* every 2416+5315
2: 7 breathed into his nostrils the breath of l; 2416
2: 9 the tree of l also in the midst of the garden, 2416
3:14 and dust shalt thou eat all the days of thy l: 2416
3:17 shalt thou eat *of* it all the days of thy l; 2416
3:22 take also of the tree of l, and eat, and 2416
3:24 every way, to keep the way of the tree of l. 2416
6:17 destroy all flesh, wherein *is* the breath of l, 2416
7:11 In the six hundredth year of Noah's l, in 2416
7:15 two of all flesh, wherein *is* the breath of l. 2416
7:22 All in whose nostrils *was* the breath of l, 2416
9: 4 flesh with the l thereof, *which is* the blood 5315
9: 5 man's brother will I require the l of man. 5315
18:10 return unto thee according to the time of l; 2416
18:14 according to the time of l, and Sarah shall 2416
19:17 forth abroad, that he said, Escape for thy l; 5315
19:19 thou hast shewed unto me in saving my l; 5315
23: 1 *these were* the years of the l of Sarah. 2416
25: 7 of the years of Abraham's l which he lived, 2416
25:17 these *are* the years of the l of Ishmael, 2416
27:46 I am weary of my l because of 2416
27:46 of the land, what good shall my l do me? 2416
32:30 God face to face, and my l is preserved. 5315
42:15 By the l of Pharaoh ye shall not go forth 2416
42:16 else by the l of Pharaoh surely ye *are* spies. 2416
44:30 seeing that his l *is* bound up in *the lad's* 5315
44:30 that his life *is* bound up in *the lad's* l; 5315
45: 5 God did send me before you to **preserve** l. 4241
47: 9 evil have the days of the years of my l 2416
47: 9 l of my fathers in the days of their 2416
48:15 the God which fed me **all** my **l long** 4480+5750
Ex 4:19 for all the men are dead which sought thy l. 5315
6:16 the years of the l of Levi *were* an hundred 2416
6:18 the years of the l of Kohath *were* an 2416
6:20 the years of the l of Amram *were* an 2416
21:23 then thou shalt give l for life, 5315
21:23 then thou shalt give life for l, 5315
21:30 he shall give *for* the ransom of his l 5315
Lev 17:11 For the l of the flesh *is* in the blood: and 5315
17:14 For *it is* the l of all flesh; the blood of it *is* 5315
17:14 all flesh; the blood of it *is* for the l thereof: 5315
17:14 for the l of all flesh *is* the blood thereof: 5315
18:18 besides the other in her l *time.* 2416
Nu 35:31 take no satisfaction for the l of a murderer, 5315
Dt 4: 9 depart from thy heart all the days of thy l: 2416
6: 2 and thy son's son, all the days of thy l; 2416
12:23 for the blood *is* the l; and thou mayest not 5315
12:23 and thou mayest not eat the l with the flesh. 5315

Dt 16: 3 of the land of Egypt all the days of thy l. 2416
17:19 he shall read therein all the days of his l: 2416
19:21 *but* l *shall go* for life, eye for eye, tooth for 5315
19:21 *but* life *shall go* for l, eye for eye, tooth for 5315
20:19 down (for the tree of the field *is* man's *l*) NIH
24: 6 to pledge: for he taketh *a man's* l to pledge. 5315
28:66 thy l shall hang in doubt before thee; and 2416
28:66 and shalt have none assurance of thy l: 2416
30:15 I have set before thee *this* day l and good, 2416
30:19 *that* I have set before you l and death, 2416
30:19 therefore choose l, that *both* thou and 2416
30:20 for he *is* thy l, and the length of thy days: 2416
32:47 a vain thing for you; because it *is* your l: 2416
Jos 1: 5 *to* stand before thee all the days of thy l: 2416
2:14 the men answered her, Our l for yours, if ye 5315
4:14 as they feared Moses, all the days of his l. 2416
Jdg 9:17 adventured his l far, and delivered you out 5315
12: 3 I put my l in my hands, and passed over 5315
16:30 were moe than *they* which he slew in his l. 2416
18:25 thou lose thy l, with the lives of thy 5315
Ru 4:15 And he shall be unto thee a restorer of *thy* l, 5315
1Sa 1:11 him unto the LORD all the days of his l, 2416
7:15 Samuel judged Israel all the days of his l. 2416
18:18 what *is* my l, *or* my father's family in 2416
19: 5 For he did put his l in his hand, and 5315
19:11 saying, If thou save not thy l to night, 5315
20: 1 sin before thy father, that he seeketh my l? 5315
22:23 for he that seeketh my l seeketh thy life: but 5315
22:23 for he that seeketh my life seeketh thy l: but 5315
23:15 saw that Saul was come out to seek his l: 5315
25:29 in the bundle of l with the LORD thy God; 2416
26:24 as thy l was much set by this day in mine 5315
26:24 let my l be much set by in the eyes of 5315
28: 9 wherefore then layest thou a snare for my l, 5315
28:21 I have put my l in my hand, and 5315
2Sa 1: 9 upon me, because my l *is* yet whole in me. 5315
4: 8 of Saul thine enemy, which sought thy l; 5315
14: 7 for the l of his brother whom he slew; 5315
15:21 whether in death or l, even there *also* will 2416
16:11 came forth of my bowels, seeketh my l: 5315
18:13 wrought falsehood against mine own l: 5315
19: 5 which *this* day have saved thy l, and 5315
1Ki 1:12 that thou mayest save thine own l, and 5315
1:12 own life, and the l of thy son Solomon. 5315
2:23 not spoken this word against his own l. 5315
3:11 and hast not asked for thyself long l; 3117
3:11 nor hast asked the l of thine enemies; 5315
4:21 and served Solomon all the days of his l. 2416
11:34 I will make him prince all the days of his l 2416
15: 5 he commanded him all the days of his l, 2416
15: 6 and Jeroboam all the days of his l. 2416
19: 2 if I make not thy l as the life of one of them 5315
19: 2 if I make not thy life as the l of one of them 5315
19: 3 went for his l, and came *to* Beer-sheba, 5315
19: 4 now, O LORD, take away my l; 5315
19:10 am left; and they seek my l, to take it away. 5315
19:14 am left; and they seek my l, to take it away. 5315
20:31 of Israel: peradventure he will save thy l. 5315
20:39 shall thy l be for his life, or else thou shalt 5315
20:39 shall thy life be for his l, or else thou shalt 5315
20:42 therefore thy l shall go for his life, and 5315
20:42 therefore thy life shall go for his l, and 5315
2Ki 1:13 let my l, and the life of these fifty thy 5315
1:13 my life, and the l of these fifty thy servants, 5315
1:14 let my l now be precious in thy sight. 5315
4:16 this season, according to the time of l, 2416
4:17 said unto her, according to the time of l. 2416
7: 7 *even* the camp as it *was,* and fled for their l. 5315
8: 1 whose son he had **restored to l**, saying, 2421
8: 5 king how he had **restored** a dead *body* **to l**, 2421
8: 5 whose son he had **restored to l**, 2421
8: 5 this *is* her son, whom Elisha **restored to l**. 2421
10:24 *he that letteth him go,* his l *shall be* for 5315
10:24 *him go,* his life *shall be* for the l of him. 5315
25:29 continually before him all the days of his l. 2416
25:30 rate for every day, all the days of his l. 2416
2Ch 1:11 or honour, nor the l of thine enemies, 5315
1:11 thine enemies, neither yet hast asked long l; 3117
Ezr 6:10 pray for the l of the king, and of his sons. 2417
Ne 6:11 *am,* would go into the temple to **save** his l? 2421
Est 7: 3 let my l be given me at my petition, and 5315
7: 7 Haman stood *up* to make request for his l to 5315
8:11 to stand for their l, to destroy, to slay, and 5315
Job 2: 4 all that a man hath will he give for his l. 5315
2: 6 Behold, he *is* in thine hand; but save his l. 5315
3:20 is in misery, and l unto the bitter in soul; 2416
6:11 *is* mine end, that I should prolong my l? 5315
7: 7 O remember that my l *is* wind: mine eye 2416
7:15 *and* death rather than my l. 6106
9:21 I not know my soul: I would despise my l. 2416
10: 1 My soul is weary of my l; I will leave my 2416
10:12 Thou hast granted me l and favour, and 2416
13:14 in my teeth, and put my l in mine hand? 5315
24:22 he riseth up, and no *man* is sure of l. 2416
31:39 caused the owners thereof to lose their l: 5315
33: 4 the breath of the Almighty hath **given** me l. 2421
33:18 and his l from perishing by the sword. 2416
33:20 So that his l abhorreth bread, and his soul 2416
33:22 unto the grave, and his l to the destroyers. 2416
33:28 into the pit, and his l shall see the light. 2416
36: 6 He **preserveth** not the l of the wicked: but 2421
36:14 in youth, and their l *is* among the unclean. 2416
Ps 7: 5 let him tread down my l upon the earth, and 2416
16:11 Thou wilt shew me the path of l: in thy 2416
17:14 *which have* their portion in *this* l, and 2416
21: 4 He asked l of thee, *and* thou gavest *it* him, 2416
23: 6 mercy shall follow me all the days of my l: 2416
26: 9 with sinners, nor my l with bloody men: 2416
27: 1 the LORD *is* the strength of my l; 2416
27: 4 house of the LORD all the days of my l, 2416
30: 5 *but* a moment; in his favour *is* l: 2416
31:10 For my l is spent with grief, and my years 2416
31:13 against me, they devised to take away my l. 5315
34:12 What man *is he that* desireth l, *and* 2416
36: 9 For with thee *is* the fountain of l: in thy 2416
38:12 They also that seek after my l lay snares *for* 5315
42: 8 *and my* prayer unto the God of my l. 2416
61: 6 wilt **prolong** the king's l: 3117+3117+5921
63: 3 Because thy lovingkindness *is* better than l, 2416
64: 1 preserve my l from fear of the enemy. 2416
66: 9 Which holdeth our soul in l, and 2416
78:50 but gave their l over to the pestilence; 2416
88: 3 and my l draweth nigh unto the grave. 2416
91:16 *With* long l will I satisfy him, and 3117
103: 4 Who redeemeth thy l from destruction; 2416
128: 5 the good of Jerusalem all the days of thy l. 2416
133: 3 the blessing, *even* l for evermore. 2416
143: 3 he hath smitten my l down to the ground; 2416
Pr 1:19 *which* taketh away the l of the owners 5315
2:19 neither take they hold of the paths of l. 2416
3: 2 For length of days, and long l, and peace, 2416
3:18 She *is* a tree of l to them that lay hold upon 2416
3:22 So shall they be l unto thy soul, and 2416
4:10 and the years of thy l shall be many. 2416
4:13 let *her* not go: keep her; for she *is* thy l. 2416
4:22 For they *are* l unto those that find them, and 2416
4:23 all diligence; for out of it *are* the issues of l. 2416
5: 6 Lest thou shouldest ponder the path of l, 2416
6:23 and reproofs of instruction *are* the way of l: 2416
6:26 the adulteress will hunt for the precious l. 5315
7:23 and knoweth not that it *is* for his l. 5315
8:35 For whoso findeth me findeth l, and 2416
9:11 and the years of thy l shall be increased. 2416
10:11 The mouth of a righteous *man is* a well of l: 2416
10:16 The labour of the righteous *tendeth* to l: 2416
10:17 He *is in* the way of l that keepeth 2416
11:19 As righteousness *tendeth* to l: so he that 2416
11:30 The fruit of the righteous *is* a tree of l; and 2416
12:10 A righteous *man* regardeth the l of his 5315
12:28 In the way of righteousness *is* l; and *in* 2416
13: 3 He that keepeth his mouth keepeth his l: 5315
13: 8 The ransom of a man's l *are* his riches: but 5315
13:12 but *when* the desire cometh, *it is* a tree of l. 2416
13:14 The law of the wise *is* a fountain of l, 2416
14:27 The fear of the LORD *is* a fountain of l, 2416
14:30 A sound heart *is* the l of the flesh: but 2416
15: 4 A wholesome tongue *is* a tree of l: but 2416
15:24 The way of l *is* above to the wise, that *he* 2416
15:31 The ear that heareth the reproof of l abideth 2416
16:15 In the light of the king's countenance *is* l; 2416
16:22 Understanding *is* a wellspring of l unto him 2416
18:21 Death and l *are* in the power of the tongue: 2416
19:23 The fear of the LORD *tendeth* to l: and 2416
21:21 after righteousness and mercy findeth l, 2416
22: 4 the LORD *are* riches, and honour, and l. 2416
31:12 him good and not evil all the days of her l. 2416
Ecc 2: 3 do under the heaven all the days of their l. 2416
2:17 Therefore I hated l; because the work that 2416

Ecc	3:12	for *a man* to rejoice, and to do good in his l.	2416
	5:18	he taketh under the sun all the days of his l,	2416
	5:20	shall not much remember the days of his l;	2416
	6:12	knoweth what *is* good for man in *this* l,	2416
	6:12	all the days of his vain l which he spendeth	2416
	7:12	*that* wisdom **giveth** l to them that have it.	2421
	7:15	there is a wicked *man* that prolongeth *his l*	NIH
	8:15	with him of his labour the days of his l,	2416
	9: 9	lovest all the days of the l of thy vanity,	2416
	9: 9	for that *is* thy portion in *this* l, and in thy	2416
Isa	15: 4	cry out; his l shall be grievous unto him.	5315
	38:12	I have cut off like a weaver my l: he will	2416
	38:16	and in all these *things is* the l of my spirit:	2416
	38:20	days of our l in the house of the LORD.	2416
	43: 4	I give men for thee, and people for thy l.	5315
	57:10	thou hast found the l of thine hand;	2416
Jer	4:30	will despise thee, they will seek thy l.	5315
	8: 3	death shall be chosen rather than l by all	2416
	11:21	that seek thy l, saying, Prophesy not in	5315
	21: 7	and into the hand of those that seek their l:	5315
	21: 8	I set before you the way of l, and the way	2416
	21: 9	and his l shall be unto him for a prey.	5315
	22:25	thee into the hand of them that seek thy l,	5315
	34:20	and into the hand of them that seek their l:	5315
	34:21	into the hand of them that seek their l, and	5315
	38: 2	for he shall have his l for a prey, and	5315
	38:16	into the hand of these men that seek thy l.	5315
	39:18	but thy l shall be for a prey unto thee:	5315
	44:30	and into the hand of them that seek his l;	5315
	44:30	his enemy, and that sought his l.	5315
	45: 5	thy l will I give unto thee for a prey in all	5315
	49:37	and before them that seek their l:	5315
	52:33	eat bread before him all the days of his l.	2416
	52:34	the day of his death, all the days of his l.	2416
La	2:19	lift up thy hands toward him for the l of thy	5315
	3:53	They have cut off my l in the dungeon, and	2416
	3:58	of my soul; thou hast redeemed my l.	2416
Eze	3:18	wicked from his wicked way, to **save** his l;	2421
	7:13	strengthen himself in the iniquity of his l.	2416
	13:22	from his wicked way, by **promising** him l:	2421
	32:10	every man for his own l, in the day of thy	5315
	33:15	walk in the statutes of l,	2416
Da	12: 2	some to everlasting l, and some to shame	2416
Jnh	1:14	let us not perish for this man's l, and	5315
	2: 6	yet hast thou brought up my l from	2416
	4: 3	take, I beseech thee, my l from me;	5315
Mal	2: 5	My covenant was with him of l and peace;	2416
Mt	2:20	are dead which sought the young child's l.	*5590*
	6:25	Take no thought for your l, what ye shall	*5590*
	6:25	ye shall put on. Is not the l more than meat,	*5590*
	7:14	which leadeth unto l, and few there be that	*2222*
	10:39	He that findeth his l shall lose it: and	*5590*
	10:39	he that loseth his l for my sake shall find it.	*5590*
	16:25	For whosoever will save his l shall lose it:	*5590*
	16:25	whosoever will lose his l for my sake shall	*5590*
	18: 8	it is better for thee to enter into l halt or	*2222*
	18: 9	it is better for thee to enter into l with one	*2222*
	19:16	*thing* shall I do, that I may have eternal l?	*2222*
	19:17	but if thou wilt enter into l, keep	*2222*
	19:29	and shall inherit everlasting l.	*2222*
	20:28	and to give his l a ransom for many.	*5590*
	25:46	but the righteous into l eternal.	*2222*
Mk	3: 4	to save l, or to kill? But they held their	*5590*
	8:35	For whosoever will save his l shall lose it;	*5590*
	8:35	but whosoever shall lose his l for my sake	*5590*
	9:43	it is better for thee to enter into l maimed,	*2222*
	9:45	it is better for thee to enter halt into l,	*2222*
	10:17	what shall I do that I may inherit eternal l?	*2222*
	10:30	and in the world to come eternal l.	*2222*
	10:45	and to give his l a ransom for many.	*5590*
Lk	1:75	before him, all the days of our l.	*2222*
	6: 9	or to do evil? to save l, or to destroy *it?*	*5590*
	8:14	with cares and riches and pleasures of *this* l,	*979*
	9:24	For whosoever will save his l shall lose it:	*5590*
	9:24	but whosoever will lose his l for my sake,	*5590*
	10:25	Master, what shall I do to inherit eternal l?	*2222*
	12:15	for a man's l consisteth not in	*2222*
	12:22	Take no thought for your l, what ye shall	*5590*
	12:23	The l is more than meat, and the body *is*	*5590*
	14:26	and sisters, yea, and his own l also,	*5590*
	17:33	Whosoever shall seek to save his l shall	*5590*
	17:33	whosoever shall lose *his l* shall preserve it.	NIG
	18:18	what shall I do to inherit eternal l?	*2222*
	18:30	and in the world to come l everlasting.	*2222*
	21:34	and cares **of** *this* l, and *so* that day come	*982*
Jn	1: 4	In him was l; and the life was the light of	*2222*
	1: 4	him was life; and the l was the light of men.	*2222*
	3:15	in him should not perish, but have eternal l.	*2222*
	3:16	should not perish, but have everlasting l.	*2222*
	3:36	that believeth on the Son hath everlasting l:	*2222*
	3:36	he that believeth not the Son shall not see l;	*2222*
	4:14	of water springing up into everlasting l.	*2222*
	4:36	and gathereth fruit unto l eternal:	*2222*
	5:24	hath everlasting l, and shall not come into	*2222*
	5:24	but is passed from death unto l.	*2222*
	5:26	For as the Father hath l in himself; so	*2222*
	5:26	hath he given to the Son to have l in	*2222*
	5:29	have done good, unto the resurrection of l;	*2222*
	5:39	for in them ye think ye have eternal l:	*2222*
	5:40	will not come to me, that ye might have l.	*2222*
	6:27	*that* meat which endureth unto everlasting l,	*2222*
	6:33	from heaven, and giveth l unto the world.	*2222*
	6:35	Jesus said unto them, I am the bread of l:	*2222*
	6:40	believeth on him, may have everlasting l:	*2222*
	6:47	He that believeth on me hath everlasting l.	*2222*
	6:48	I am *that* bread of l.	*2222*
	6:51	which I will give for the l of the world.	*2222*
	6:53	and drink his blood, ye have no l in you.	*2222*
	6:54	and drinketh my blood, hath eternal l;	*2222*
	6:63	unto you, *they* are spirit, and *they* are l.	*2222*
	6:68	we go? thou hast the words of eternal l.	*2222*
	8:12	in darkness, but shall have the light of l.	*2222*
	10:10	I am come that they might have l, and	*2222*
	10:11	the good shepherd giveth his l for	*5590*
	10:15	and I lay down my l for the sheep.	*5590*
	10:17	because I lay down my l, that I might take	*5590*
	10:28	And I give unto them eternal l; and	*2222*
	11:25	unto her, I am the resurrection, and the l:	*2222*
	12:25	He that loveth his l shall lose it; and he that	*5590*
	12:25	he that hateth his l in this world shall keep	*5590*
	12:25	life in this world shall keep it unto l eternal.	*2222*
	12:50	And I know that his commandment is l	*2222*
	13:37	I will lay down my l for thy sake.	*5590*
	13:38	Wilt thou lay down thy l for my sake?	*5590*
	14: 6	unto him, I am the way, the truth, and the l:	*2222*
	15:13	that a man lay down his l for his friends.	*5590*
	17: 2	that he should give eternal l to as many as	*2222*
	17: 3	And this is l eternal, that they might know	*2222*
	20:31	that believing ye might have l through his	*2222*
Ac	2:28	Thou hast made known to me the ways of l;	*2222*
	3:15	And killed the Prince of l, whom God hath	*2222*
	5:20	temple to the people all the words of this l.	*2222*
	8:33	for his l is taken from the earth.	*2222*
	11:18	to the Gentiles granted repentance unto l.	*2222*
	13:46	judge yourselves unworthy of everlasting l,	*2222*
	13:48	as many as were ordained to eternal l	*2222*
	17:25	needed any *thing,* seeing he giveth to all l,	*2222*
	20:10	Trouble not yourselves; for his l is in him.	*5590*
	20:24	neither count I my l dear unto myself, so	*5590*
	26: 4	My **manner of** l from *my* youth, which was	*981*
	27:22	for there shall be no loss of *any man's* l	*5590*
Ro	2: 7	and honour and immortality, eternal l:	*2222*
	5:10	we shall be saved by his l.	*2222*
	5:17	of the gift of righteousness shall reign in l	*2222*
	5:18	*came* upon all men unto justification of l.	*2222*
	5:21	unto eternal l by Jesus Christ our Lord.	*2222*
	6: 4	so we also should walk in newness of l.	*2222*
	6:22	unto holiness, and the end everlasting l.	*2222*
	6:23	the gift of God *is* eternal l through Jesus	*2222*
	7:10	which was *ordained* to l,	*2222*
	8: 2	For the law of the Spirit of l in Christ Jesus	*2222*
	8: 6	but to be spiritually minded *is* l and peace.	*2222*
	8:10	but the Spirit *is* l because of righteousness.	*2222*
	8:38	nor l, nor angels, nor principalities,	*2222*
	11: 3	and I am left alone, and they seek my l.	*5590*
	11:15	receiving *of them be,* but l from the dead?	*2222*
	16: 4	Who have for my l laid down their own	*5590*
1Co	3:22	or l, or death, or *things* present, or *things* to	*2222*
	6: 3	much more *things* **that pertain to** *this* l?	*982*
	6: 4	judgments *of things* **pertaining to** *this* l,	*982*
	14: 7	*And* even *things* **without** l giving sound,	*895*
	15:19	If in this l only we have hope in Christ,	*2222*
2Co	1: 8	insomuch that we despaired even of l:	*2198*
	2:16	and to the other the savour of l unto life.	*2222*
	2:16	and to the other the savour of life unto l.	*2222*
	3: 6	for the letter killeth, but the spirit **giveth** l.	*2227*
	4:10	that the l also of Jesus might be made	*2222*
	4:11	that the l also of Jesus might be made	*2222*

2Co 4:12 So then death worketh in us, but l in you. 2222
5: 4 that mortality might be swallowed up of l. 2222
Gal 2:20 the I which I now live in the flesh I live by NIG
3:21 a law given which could have given l, 2227
6: 8 Spirit shall of the Spirit reap l everlasting. 2222
Eph 4:18 being alienated from the l of God through 2222
Php 1:20 in my body, whether it be by l, or by death. 2222
2:16 Holding forth the word of l; that I may 2222
2:30 not regarding his l, to supply your lack of 5590
4: 3 whose names are in the book of l. 2222
Col 3: 3 and your l is hid with Christ in God. 2222
3: 4 who is our l, shall appear, then shall ye also 2222
1Ti 1:16 hereafter believe on him to l everlasting. 2222
2: 2 and peaceable l in all godliness and honesty. 979
4: 8 things, having promise of the l that now is, 2222
6:12 the good fight of faith, lay hold on eternal l, 2222
6:19 that they may lay hold on eternal l. 2222
2Ti 1: 1 according to the promise of l which is in 2222
1:10 and hath brought l and immortality to light 2222
2: 4 entangleth himself with the affairs of this l; 979
3:10 manner of l, purpose, faith, longsuffering, 72
Tit 1: 2 In hope of eternal l, which God, that cannot 2222
3: 7 heirs according to the hope of eternal l. 2222
Heb 7: 3 neither beginning of days, nor end of l; 2222
7:16 but after the power of an endless l. 2222
11:35 received their dead raised to l again: 386+1537
Jas 1:12 he is tried, he shall receive the crown of l, 2222
4:14 for what is your l? It is even a vapour, 2222
1Pe 3: 7 and as being heirs together of the grace of l; 2222
3:10 For he that will love l, and see good days, 2222
4: 3 For the time past of our l may suffice us to 979
2Pe 1: 3 given unto us all things that pertain unto l 2222
1Jn 1: 1 our hands have handled, of the Word of l; 2222
1: 2 (For the l was manifested, and we have 2222
1: 2 and shew unto you that eternal l, 2222
2:16 and the lust of the eyes, and the pride of l, 979
2:25 that he hath promised us, even eternal l. 2222
3:14 that we have passed from death unto l, 2222
3:15 ye know that no murderer hath eternal l 2222
3:16 of God, because he laid down his l for us: 5590
5:11 that God hath given to us eternal l, and 2222
5:11 to us eternal life, and this l is in his Son. 2222
5:12 He that hath the Son hath l; and he that hath 2222
5:12 he that hath not the Son of God hath not l. 2222
5:13 that ye may know that ye have eternal l, 2222
5:16 he shall give him l for them that sin not 2222
5:20 This is the true God, and eternal l. 2222
Jude 1:21 of our Lord Jesus Christ unto eternal l. 2222
Rev 2: 7 will I give to eat of the tree of l, 2222
2:10 and I will give thee a crown of l. 2222
3: 5 not blot out his name out of the book of l, 2222
8: 9 which were in the sea, and had l, died; 5590
11:11 a half the spirit of l from God entered into 2222
13: 8 names are not written in the book of l 2222
13:15 And he had power to give l unto the image 4151
17: 8 book of l from the foundation of the world, 2222
20:12 book was opened, which is the book of l: 2222
20:15 the book of l was cast into the lake of fire. 2222
21: 6 of the fountain of the water of l freely. 2222
21:27 which are written in the Lamb's book of l. 2222
22: 1 he shewed me a pure river of water of l, 2222
22: 2 side of the river, was there the tree of l, 2222
22:14 that they may have right to the tree of l, and 2222
22:17 let him take the water of l freely. 2222
22:19 shall take away his part out of the book of l, 2222

LIFELESS See DUMB

LIFETIME (3) [LIVE, TIME]

2Sa 18:18 Now Absalom in his l had taken and 2416
Lk 16:25 remember that thou in thy l receivedst thy 2222
Heb 2:15 of death were all their l subject to bondage. 2198

LIFT (193) [LIFTED, LIFTER, LIFTEST, LIFTETH, LIFTING]

Ge 7:17 up the ark, and it was l up above the earth. 7311
13:14 L up now thine eyes, and look from 5375
14:22 I have l up mine hand unto the LORD, 7311
18: 2 he l up his eyes and looked, and lo, 5375
21:16 sat over against him, and l up her voice, 5375
21:18 l up the lad, and hold him in thine hand; 5375
22: 4 on the third day Abraham l up his eyes, 5375
24:63 he l up his eyes, and saw, and behold, 5375
24:64 Rebekah l up her eyes, and when she saw 5375
27:38 And Esau l up his voice, and wept. 5375
31:12 he said, L up now thine eyes, and see, 5375
33: 5 he l up his eyes, and saw the women and 5375
37:25 they l up their eyes and looked, and behold, 5375
37:28 they drew and l up Joseph out of the pit, 5927
39:18 came to pass, as I l up my voice and cried, 7311
40:13 Yet within three days shall Pharaoh l up 5375
40:19 Yet within three days shall Pharaoh l up 5375
41:44 without thee shall no man l up his hand or 7311
43:29 he l up his eyes, and saw his brother 5375
Ex 7:20 he l up the rod, and smote the waters that 7311
14:10 the children of Israel l up their eyes, and 5375
14:16 l thou up thy rod, and stretch out thine 7311
20:25 for if thou l up thy tool upon it, thou hast 5130
Lev 9:22 Aaron l up his hand towards the people, 5375
Nu 6:26 The LORD l up his countenance upon 5375
16: 3 l you up yourselves above the congregation 5375
20:11 Moses l up his hand, and with his rod he 7311
23:24 great lion, and l up himself as a young lion: 5375
24: 2 Balaam l up his eyes, and he saw Israel 5375
Dt 3:27 l up thine eyes westward, and northward, 5375
4:19 lest thou l up thine eyes unto heaven, and 5375
22: 4 surely help him to l them up again. 6965+6965
27: 5 thou shalt not l up any iron tool upon them. 5130
32:40 For I l up my hand to heaven, and say, 5375
Jos 4:18 the soles of the priests' feet were l up unto 5423
5:13 that he l up his eyes and looked, and 5375
8:31 over which no man hath l up any iron: 5130
Jdg 2: 4 that the people l up their voice, and wept. 5375
9: 7 l up his voice, and cried, and said unto 5375
19:17 when he had l up his eyes, he saw a 5375
21: 2 and l up their voices, and wept sore; 5375
Ru 1: 9 and they l up their voice, and wept. 5375
1:14 they l up their voice, and wept again: and 5375
1Sa 11: 4 all the people l up their voices, and wept. 5375
24:16 And Saul l up his voice, and wept. 5375
30: 4 the people that were with him l up their 5375
2Sa 3:32 the king l up his voice, and wept at 5375
13:34 the young man that kept the watch l up his 5375
13:36 sons came, and l up their voice and wept: 5375
18:24 l up his eyes, and looked, and behold a man 5375
18:28 which hath delivered up the men that l up 5375
20:21 hath l up his hand against the king, 5375
23: 8 he l up his spear against eight hundred, NIH
23:18 he l up his spear against three hundred, 5782
1Ki 11:26 even he l up his hand against the king. 7311
11:27 this was the cause that he l up his hand 7311
2Ki 9:32 he l up his face to the window, and said, 5375
19: 4 wherefore l up thy prayer for the remnant 5375
19:22 thy voice, and l up thine eyes on high? 5375
25:27 did l up the head of Jehoiachin king of 5375
1Ch 11:11 he l up his spear against three hundred 5782
14: 2 for his kingdom was l up on high, because 5375
21:16 David l up his eyes, and saw the angel of 5375
25: 5 seer in the words of God, to l up the horn. 7311
2Ch 5:13 when they l up their voice with 7311
17: 6 his heart was l up in the ways of 1361
Ezr 9: 6 and blush to l up my face to thee, 7311
Job 2:12 when they l up their eyes afar off, and 5375
10:15 I be righteous, yet will I not l up my head. 5375
11:15 then shalt thou l up thy face without spot; 5375
22:26 and shalt l up thy face unto God. 5375
31:21 If I have l up my hand against 5130
31:29 or l up myself when evil found him: 5782
38:34 Canst thou l up thy voice to the clouds, 7311
Ps 4: 6 l thou up the light of thy countenance upon 5375
7: 6 l up thyself because of the rage of mine 5375
10:12 Arise, O LORD; O God, l up thine hand: 5375
24: 4 who hath not l up his soul unto vanity, 5375
24: 7 L up your heads, O ye gates; and be ye lift 5375
24: 7 be ye l up, ye everlasting doors; and 5375
24: 9 L up your heads, O ye gates; even lift them 5375
24: 9 even l them up, ye everlasting doors; and 5375
25: 1 Unto thee, O LORD, do I l up my soul. 5375
28: 2 when I l up my hands toward thy holy 5375
28: 9 feed them also, and l them up for ever. 5375
41: 9 of my bread, hath l up his heel against me. 1431
63: 4 I live: I will l up my hands in thy name. 5375
74: 3 L up thy feet unto the perpetual 7311
75: 4 and to the wicked, L not up the horn: 7311
75: 5 L not up your horn on high: speak not with 7311
83: 2 and they that hate thee have l up the head. 5375
86: 4 for unto thee, O Lord, do I l up my soul. 5375
93: 3 up their voice; the floods l up their waves. 5375
94: 2 L up thyself, thou judge of the earth: 5375

Ps 110: 7 in the way: therefore shall he **l up** the head. 7311
119:48 My hands also will I **l up** unto thy 5375
121: 1 I will **l up** mine eyes unto the hills, 5375
123: 1 Unto thee I **l up** mine eyes, O thou that 5375
134: 2 **L up** your hands *in* the sanctuary, and 5375
143: 8 I should walk; for I **l up** my soul unto thee. 5375
Ecc 4:10 For if they fall, the one will **l up** his fellow: 6965
Isa 2: 4 nation shall not **l up** sword against nation, 5375
5:26 he will **l up** an ensign to the nations from 5375
10:15 should shake *itself against* them that **l** it **up**, 7311
10:15 as if the staff should **l up** *itself, as if it were* 7311
10:24 shall **l up** his staff against thee, after 5375
10:26 shall he **l** it **up** after the manner of Egypt. 5375
10:30 **L up** thy voice, O daughter of Gallim: 6670
13: 2 **L** ye **up** a banner upon the high mountain, 5375
24:14 They shall **l up** their voice, they shall sing, 5375
33:10 will I be exalted; now will I **l up** myself. 5375
37: 4 wherefore **l up** *thy* prayer for the remnant 5375
40: 9 good tidings, **l up** thy voice with strength; 7311
40: 9 **l** *it* **up**, be not afraid; say unto the cities of 7311
40:26 **L up** your eyes on high, and behold who 5375
42: 2 He shall not cry, nor **l up**, nor cause his 5375
42:11 the cities thereof **l up** *their voice,* 5375
49:18 **L up** thine eyes round about, and behold: 5375
49:22 I will **l up** mine hand to the Gentiles, and 5375
51: 6 **L up** your eyes to the heavens, and 5375
52: 8 Thy watchmen shall **l up** the voice; 5375
58: 1 **l up** thy voice like a trumpet, and shew my 7311
59:19 LORD shall **l up a standard** against him. 5127
60: 4 **L up** thine eyes round about, and see: 5375
62:10 the stones; **l up** a standard for the people. 7311
Jer 3: 2 **L up** thine eyes unto the high places, and 5375
7:16 neither **l up** cry nor prayer for them, 5375
11:14 neither **l up** a cry or prayer for them: 5375
13:20 **L up** your eyes, and behold them that come 5375
22:20 **l up** thy voice in Bashan, and cry from 5414
51:14 and they shall **l up** a shout against thee. 6030
La 2:19 **l up** thy hands toward him for the life of 5375
3:41 Let us **l up** our heart with *our* hands unto 5375
Eze 1:19 when the living creatures were **l up** from 5375
1:19 lift up from the earth, the wheels were **l up**. 5375
8: 3 and the spirit **l** me **up** between the earth and 5375
8: 5 **l up** thine eyes now the way towards 5375
8: 5 So I **l up** mine eyes the way toward 5375
10:16 when the cherubims **l up** their wings to 5375
10:17 *these* **l up** themselves *also:* for the spirit of 7426
10:19 the cherubims **l up** their wings, and 5375
11: 1 Moreover the spirit **l** me **up**, and 5375
11:22 did the cherubims **l up** their wings, and 5375
17:14 that *it* might not **l** itself **up**, *but* that by 5375
18: 6 neither hath **l up** his eyes to the idols of 5375
18:12 and hath **l up** his eyes to the idols, 5375
18:15 neither hath **l up** his eyes to the idols of 5375
21:22 to **l up** the voice with shouting, 7311
23:27 that thou shalt not **l up** thine eyes unto 5375
26: 8 and **l up** the buckler against thee. 6965
33:25 **l up** your eyes toward your idols, and 5375
44:12 have I **l up** mine hand against them, 5375
Da 4:34 **l up** mine eyes unto heaven, 5191
10: 5 I **l up** mine eyes, and looked, and behold, 5375
Mic 4: 3 nation shall not **l up** a sword against nation, 5375
5: 9 Thine hand shall be **l up** upon thine 7311
Hab 3:10 his voice, *and* **l up** his hands on high. 5375
Zec 1:18 I **l up** mine eyes, and saw, and behold four 5375
1:21 so that no man did **l up** his head: 5375
1:21 which **l up** *their* horn over the land of 5375
2: 1 I **l up** mine eyes again, and looked, and 5375
5: 1 **l up** mine eyes, and looked, and behold, 5375
5: 5 **L up** now thine eyes, and see what *is* this 5375
5: 7 behold, there *was* **l up** a talent of lead: and 5375
5: 9 I **l up** mine eyes, and looked, and behold, 5375
5: 9 they **l up** the ephah between the earth and 5375
6: 1 **l up** mine eyes, and looked, and behold, 5375
Mt 12:11 will he not lay hold on it, and **l** *it* **out**? *1453*
17: 8 And when they had **l up** their eyes, *1869*
Mk 1:31 and took her by the hand, and **l** her **up**; *1453*
Lk 11:27 woman of the company **l up** her voice, *1869*
13:11 and could in no wise **l up** *herself.* *352*
16:23 And in hell he **l up** his eyes, being in *1869*
18:13 would not **l up** so much as *his* eyes unto *1869*
21:28 to pass, *then* look up, and **l up** your heads; *1869*
24:50 and he **l up** his hands, and blessed them. *1869*
Jn 4:35 **L up** your eyes, and look on the fields; *1869*
6: 5 When Jesus then **l up** *his* eyes, *1869*
8: 7 he **l up** *himself,* and said unto them, He that *352*
8:10 When Jesus had **l up** *himself,* and saw none *352*
8:28 When ye have **l up** the Son of man, then *5312*
11:41 And Jesus **l up** *his* eyes, and said, Father, *142*
12:34 sayest thou, The Son of man must be **l up**? *5312*
13:18 He that eateth bread with me hath **l up** his *1869*
17: 1 and **l up** his eyes to heaven, and said, *1869*
Ac 2:14 **l up** his voice, and said unto them, Ye men *1869*
3: 7 took him by the right hand, and **l** *him* **up**: *1453*
4:24 And when they heard *that,* they **l up** their *142*
9:41 and **l** her **up**, and when he had called *450*
14:11 they **l up** their voices, saying in the speech *1869*
22:22 and *then* **l up** their voices, and said, *1869*
Heb 12:12 Wherefore **l up** the hands which hang down, *461*
Jas 4:10 the sight of the Lord, and he shall **l** you **up**. *5312*

LIFTED (69) [LIFT]

Ge 13:10 Lot **l up** his eyes, and beheld all the plain 5375
22:13 Abraham **l up** his eyes, and looked, and 5375
29:11 kissed Rachel, and **l up** his voice, and wept. 5375
31:10 that I **l up** mine eyes, and saw in a dream, 5375
33: 1 Jacob **l up** his eyes, and looked, and 5375
39:15 when he heard that I **l up** my voice and 7311
40:20 he **l up** the head of the chief butler and of 5375
Nu 14: 1 all the congregation **l up** their voice, and 5375
Dt 8:14 thine heart be **l up**, and thou forget 7311
17:20 That his heart be not **l up** above his 7311
Jdg 8:28 so that they **l up** their heads no more. 5375
1Sa 6:13 they **l up** their eyes, and saw the ark, and 5375
2Sa 22:49 thou also hast **l** me **up on high** above them 7311
2Ki 14:10 and thine heart hath **l** thee **up**: 5375
2Ch 26:16 his heart was **l up** to *his* destruction: 1361
32:25 *done* unto him; for his heart was **l up**: 1361
Job 2:12 him not, they **l up** their voice, and wept; 5375
Ps 27: 6 now shall mine head be **l up** above mine 7311
30: 1 for thou hast **l** me **up**, and hast not made 1802
74: 5 *A man* was famous according as he had **l** up 935
93: 3 The floods have **l up**, O LORD, the floods 5375
93: 3 O LORD, the floods have **l up** their voice; 5375
102:10 for thou hast **l** me **up**, and cast me down. 5375
106:26 Therefore he **l up** his hand against them, 5375
Pr 30:13 are their eyes! and their eyelids are **l up**. 5375
Isa 2:12 and lofty, and upon every one that is **l up**; 5375
2:13 that are high and **l up**, and upon all the oaks 5375
2:14 upon all the hills that are **l up**, 5375
6: 1 high and **l up**, and his train filled 5375
26:11 LORD, *when* thy hand is **l up**, they will 7311
37:23 *thy* voice, and **l up** thine eyes on high? 5375
Jer 51: 9 unto heaven, and is **l up** *even* to the skies. 5375
52:31 **l up** the head of Jehoiachin king of Judah, 5375
Eze 1:20 the wheels were **l up** over against them: 5375
1:21 when those were **l up** from the earth, 5375
1:21 the wheels were **l up** over against them: 5375
3:14 So the spirit **l** me **up**, and took me away, 5375
10:15 the cherubims were **l up**. This *is* the living 7426
10:17 when they were **l up**, *these* lift up 7311
20: 5 **l up** mine hand unto the seed of the house 5375
20: 5 when I **l up** mine hand unto them, saying, 5375
20: 6 In the day *that* I **l up** mine hand unto them, 5375
20:15 Yet also I **l up** my hand unto them in 5375
20:23 I **l up** mine hand unto them also in 5375
20:28 *for* the which I **l up** mine hand to give it to 5375
20:42 into the country *for* the which I **l up** mine 5375
28: 2 Because thine heart *is* **l up**, and thou hast 1361
28: 5 thine heart is **l up** because of thy riches: 1361
28:17 Thine heart was **l up** because of thy beauty, 1361
31:10 Because thou hast **l up** thyself in height, 1361
31:10 and his heart is **l up** in his height; 7311
36: 7 I have **l up** mine hand, Surely the heathen 5375
47:14 *concerning* the which I **l up** mine hand to 5375
Da 5:20 when his heart was **l up**, and his mind 7313
5:23 hast **l up** thyself against the Lord of 7313
7: 4 it was **l up** from the earth, and made stand 5191
8: 3 I **l up** mine eyes, and saw, and behold, 5375
11:12 away the multitude, his heart shall be **l up**; 7311
Hab 2: 4 his soul *which* is **l up** is not upright in him: 6075
Zec 9:16 a crown, **l up as an ensign** upon his land. 5264
14:10 it shall be **l up**, and inhabited in her place, 7213
Mk 9:27 Jesus took him by the hand, and **l** him **up**; *1453*
Lk 6:20 And he **l up** his eyes on his disciples, and *1869*
17:13 And they **l up** *their* voices, and said, Jesus, *142*
Jn 3:14 And as Moses **l up** the serpent in *5312*
3:14 *even* so must the Son of man be **l up**: *5312*
12:32 And I, if I be **l up** from the earth, will draw *5312*

1Ti 3: 6 lest being **l up with pride** he fall into *5187*
Rev 10: 5 and upon the earth **l up** his hand to heaven, *142*

LIFTER (1) [LIFT]
Ps 3: 3 my glory, and the **l up** of mine head. 7311

LIFTEST (4) [LIFT]
Job 30:22 Thou **l** me **up** to the wind; thou causest me 5375
Ps 9:13 thou that **l** me **up** from the gates of death: 7311
18:48 thou **l** me **up** above those that rise up 7311
Pr 2: 3 *and* **l up** thy voice for understanding; 5414

LIFTETH (10) [LIFT]
1Sa 2: 7 and maketh rich: he bringeth low, and **l up**. 7311
2: 8 *and* **l up** the beggar from the dunghill, 7311
2Ch 25:19 and thine heart **l** thee **up** to boast: 5375
Job 39:18 What time she **l up** herself on high, 4754
Ps 107:25 stormy wind, which **l up** the waves thereof. 7311
113: 7 *and* **l** the needy out of the dunghill; 7311
147: 6 The LORD **l up** the meek: he casteth 5749
Isa 18: 3 when *he* **l up** an ensign *on* the mountains; 5375
Jer 51: 3 against *him that* **l** himself **up** in his 5927
Na 3: 3 The horseman **l up** both the bright sword 5927

LIFTING (9) [LIFT]
1Ch 11:20 for **l up** his spear against three hundred, 5782
15:16 sounding, by **l up** the voice with joy. 7311
Ne 8: 6 Amen, Amen, with **l up** their hands: 4607
Job 22:29 then thou shalt say, *There is* **l up**; 1466
Ps 141: 2 the **l up** of my hands *as* the evening 4864
Pr 30:32 If thou hast done foolishly in **l up** thyself, 5375
Isa 9:18 they shall mount up *like* the **l up** of smoke. 1348
33: 3 at the **l up** of thyself the nations were 7427
1Ti 2: 8 **l up** holy hands, without wrath and *1869*

LIGHT (272) [ENLIGHTEN, ENLIGHTENED, ENLIGHTENING, LIGHTED, LIGHTEN, LIGHTENED, LIGHTENETH, LIGHTER, LIGHTEST, LIGHTETH, LIGHTING, LIGHTLY, LIGHTNESS, LIGHTS]
Ge 1: 3 God said, Let there be **l**: and there was light. 216
1: 3 God said, Let there be light: and there was **l**. 216
1: 4 God saw the **l**, that *it was* good: and 216
1: 4 and God divided the **l** from the darkness. 216
1: 5 God called the **l** Day, and the darkness he 216
1:15 of the heaven to **give l** upon the earth: 215
1:16 the greater **l** to rule the day, and the lesser 3974
1:16 the day, and the lesser **l** to rule the night: 3974
1:17 of the heaven to **give l** upon the earth, 215
1:18 and to divide the **l** from the darkness: 216
44: 3 As soon as the morning was **l**, the men were 215
Ex 10:23 all the children of Israel had **l** in their 216
13:21 by night in a pillar of fire, to **give** them **l**; 215
14:20 *to them,* but it **gave l** by night *to these:* so 215
25: 6 Oil for the **l**, spices for anointing oil, and 3974
25:37 they shall **l** the lamps thereof, that they may 5927
25:37 that they may **give l** over against it. 215
27:20 bring thee pure oil olive beaten for the **l**, 3974
35: 8 oil for the **l**, and spices for anointing oil, 3974
35:14 The candlestick also for the **l**, and his 3974
35:14 and his lamps, with the oil for the **l**, 3974
35:28 oil for the **l**, and for the anointing oil, and 3974
39:37 and all the vessels thereof, and the oil for **l**, 3974
40: 4 in the candlestick, and **l** the lamps thereof. 5927
Lev 24: 2 unto thee pure oil olive beaten for the **l**, 3974
Nu 4: 9 cover the candlestick of the **l**, and his 3974
4:16 Aaron the priest *pertaineth* the oil for the **l**, 3974
8: 2 the seven lamps shall **give l** over against 215
21: 5 and our soul loatheth *this* **l** bread. 7052
Dt 27:16 Cursed *be* he that **setteth l** by his father or 7034
Jdg 9: 4 Abimelech hired vain and **l** persons, 6348
19:26 man's house where her lord *was,* till it was **l**. 216
Ru 2: 3 her hap was to **l on** a part of the field 7136
1Sa 14:36 spoil them until the morning **l**, and let us not 216
18:23 Seemeth it to you a **l** *thing* to be a king's 7043
25:22 morning **l** *any that* pisseth against the wall. 216
25:34 morning **l** *any that* pisseth against the wall. 216
25:36 less or more, until the morning **l**. 216
29:10 up early in the morning, and **have l**, depart. 215
2Sa 2:18 and Asahel *was as* **l** of foot as a wild roe. 7031
17:12 we *will l* upon him as the dew falleth on NIH
17:22 by the morning **l** there lacked not one *of* 216
21:17 that thou quench not the **l** of Israel. 5216
23: 4 *he shall be* as the **l** of the morning, *when* 216
1Ki 7: 4 and **l** *was* against light *in* three ranks. 4237
7: 4 and light *was* against **l** *in* three ranks. 4237
7: 5 and **l** *was* against light *in* three ranks. 4237
7: 5 and light *was* against **l** *in* three ranks. 4237
11:36 that David my servant may have a **l** alway 5216
16:31 as if it had been a **l thing** for him to walk in 7043
2Ki 3:18 *but* a **l thing** in the sight of the LORD: 7043
7: 9 if we tarry till the morning **l**, *some* mischief 216
8:19 he promised him to give to him alway a **l**, 5216
20:10 It is a **l thing** for the shadow to go down 7043
2Ch 21: 7 as he promised to give a **l** to him and to his 5216
Ne 9:12 to **give** them **l** in the way wherein they 215
9:19 to **shew** them **l**, and the way wherein they 215
Est 8:16 The Jews had **l**, and gladness, and joy, and 219
Job 3: 4 it from above, neither let the **l** shine upon it. 5105
3: 9 let it look for **l**, but *have* none; neither let it 216
3:16 I had not been; as infants *which* never saw **l**. 216
3:20 Wherefore is **l** given to him that is in misery, 216
3:23 *Why is l given* to a man whose way is hid, NIH
10:22 any order, and *where* the **l** is as darkness. 3313
12:22 and bringeth out to **l** the shadow of death. 216
12:25 They grope *in* the dark without **l**, and 216
17:12 into day: the **l** *is* short, because of darkness. 216
18: 5 the **l** of the wicked shall be put out, and 216
18: 6 The **l** shall be dark in his tabernacle, and 216
18:18 He shall be driven from **l** into darkness, and 216
22:28 and the **l** shall shine upon thy ways. 216
24:13 They are of those that rebel against the **l**; 216
24:14 The murderer rising with the **l** killeth 216
24:16 in the daytime: they know not the **l**. 216
25: 3 and upon whom doth not his **l** arise? 216
28:11 the thing that is hid bringeth he forth *to* **l**. 216
29: 3 *when* by his **l** I walked *through* darkness; 216
29:24 the **l** of my countenance they cast not down. 216
30:26 evil came *unto me:* and when I waited for **l**, 216
33:28 going into the pit, and his life shall see the **l**. 216
33:30 to be enlightened with the **l** of the living. 216
36:30 he spreadeth his **l** upon it, and covereth 216
36:32 With clouds he covereth the **l**; and 216
37:15 and caused the **l** of his cloud to shine? 216
37:21 now *men* see not the bright **l** which *is* in 216
38:15 from the wicked their **l** is withholden, and 216
38:19 Where *is* the way *where* **l** dwelleth? and 216
38:24 By what way is the **l** parted, *which* scattereth 216
41:18 *By* his neesings a **l** doth shine, and his eyes 216
Ps 4: 6 lift thou up the **l** of thy countenance upon us. 216
18:28 For thou wilt **l** my candle: the LORD my 215
27: 1 The LORD *is* my **l** and my salvation; 216
36: 9 fountain of life: in thy **l** shall we see light. 216
36: 9 fountain of life: in thy light shall we see **l**. 216
37: 6 shall bring forth thy righteousness as the **l**, 216
38:10 as for the **l** of mine eyes, it also is gone from 216
43: 3 O send out thy **l** and thy truth: let them lead 216
44: 3 the **l** of thy countenance, because thou hadst 216
49:19 of his fathers; they shall never see **l**. 216
56:13 that *I* may walk before God in the **l** of 216
74:16 thou hast prepared the **l** and the sun. 3974
78:14 a cloud, and all the night with a **l** of fire. 216
89:15 O LORD, in the **l** of thy countenance. 216
90: 8 our secret *sins* in the **l** of thy countenance. 3974
97:11 **L** is sown for the righteous, and gladness for 216
104: 2 Who coverest *thyself with* **l** as *with* a 216
105:39 for a covering; and fire to **give l** in the night. 215
112: 4 Unto the upright there ariseth **l** in 216
118:27 God *is* the LORD, which hath **shewed** us **l**: 215
119:105 *is* a lamp unto my feet, and a **l** unto my path. 216
119:130 The entrance of thy words **giveth l**; it giveth 215
139:11 cover me; even the night *shall be* **l** about me. 216
139:12 the darkness and the **l** *are* both alike *to thee.* 219
148: 3 sun and moon: praise him, all ye stars of **l**. 216
Pr 4:18 the path of the just *is* as the shining **l**, 216
6:23 the law *is* **l**; and reproofs of instruction *are* 216
13: 9 The **l** of the righteous rejoiceth: but the lamp 216
15:30 The **l** of the eyes rejoiceth the heart: *and* 3974
16:15 In the **l** of the king's countenance *is* life; and 216
Ecc 2:13 excelleth folly, as far as **l** excelleth darkness. 216
11: 7 Truly the **l** *is* sweet, and a pleasant *thing it is* 216
12: 2 the sun, or the **l**, or the moon, or the stars, 216
Isa 2: 5 and let us walk in the **l** of the LORD. 216
5:20 that put darkness for **l**, and light for 216
5:20 put darkness for light, and **l** for darkness; 216
5:30 and the **l** is darkened in the heavens thereof. 216
8:20 *it is* because *there is* no **l** in them. 7837
9: 2 that walked in darkness have seen a great **l**: 216
9: 2 of death, upon them hath the **l** shined. 216

L

Isa 10:17 the l of Israel shall be for a fire, and his Holy 216
13:10 constellations thereof shall not give their l: 216
13:10 and the moon shall not cause her l to shine. 216
30:26 Moreover the l of the moon shall be as 216
30:26 light of the moon shall be as the l of the sun, 216
30:26 the l of the sun shall be sevenfold, as 216
30:26 shall be sevenfold, as the l of seven days, 216
42: 6 of the people, for a l of the Gentiles; 216
42:16 I will make darkness l before them, and 216
45: 7 I form the l, and create darkness: I make 216
49: 6 It is a l thing that thou shouldest be my 7043
49: 6 I will also give thee for a l to the Gentiles, 216
50:10 that walketh *in* darkness, and hath no l? 5051
50:11 walk in the l of your fire, and in the sparks 217
51: 4 I will make my judgment to rest for a l of 216
58: 8 shall thy l break forth as the morning, and 216
58:10 shall thy l rise in obscurity, and thy darkness 216
59: 9 we wait for l, but behold obscurity; 216
60: 1 for thy l is come, and the glory of 216
60: 3 the Gentiles shall come to thy l, and kings to 216
60:19 The sun shall be no more thy l by day; 216
60:19 neither for brightness shall the moon **give l** 215
60:19 LORD shall be unto thee an everlasting l, 216
60:20 for the LORD shall be thine everlasting l, 216
Jer 4:23 and void; and the heavens, and they *had* no l. 216
13:16 and, while ye look for l, he turn it into 216
25:10 of the millstones, and the l of the candle. 216
31:35 which giveth the sun for a l by day, *and* 216
31:35 of the moon and of the stars for a l by night, 216
La 3: 2 and brought *me into* darkness, but not *into* l. 216
Eze 8:17 Is it a l **thing** to the house of Judah that 7043
22: 7 In thee have they **set** l by father and 7043
32: 7 and the moon shall not **give** her l. 215+216
Da 2:22 the darkness, and the l dwelleth with him. 5094
5:11 in the days of thy father l and 5094
5:14 *that* l and understanding and 5094
Hos 6: 5 thy judgments *are as* the l *that* goeth forth. 216
Am 5:18 the day of the LORD *is* darkness, and not l. 216
5:20 day of the LORD *be* darkness, and not l? 216
Mic 2: 1 when the morning is l, they practise it, 216
7: 8 in darkness, the LORD *shall be* a l unto me. 216
7: 9 he will bring me forth to the l, *and* I shall 216
Hab 3: 4 *his* brightness was as the l; he had horns 216
3:11 at the l of thine arrows they went, *and* at 216
Zep 3: 4 Her prophets *are* l *and* treacherous persons: 6348
3: 5 morning doth he bring his judgment to l, 216
Zec 14: 6 *that* the l shall not be clear, *nor* dark: 216
14: 7 to pass, *that* at evening time it shall be l. 216
Mt 4:16 people which sat in darkness saw great l; *5457*
4:16 and shadow of death l is sprung up. *5457*
5:14 Ye are the l of the world. A city that is set *5457*
5:15 Neither do men l a candle, and put it under *2545*
5:15 and it **giveth** l unto all that are in the house. *2989*
5:16 Let your l so shine before men, that they *5457*
6:22 The l of the body is the eye: if therefore *3088*
6:22 be single, thy whole body shall be **full of** l. *5460*
6:23 If therefore the l that is in thee be darkness, *5457*
10:27 I tell you in darkness, *that* speak ye in l: *5457*
11:30 For my yoke *is* easy, and my burden is l. *1645*
17: 2 the sun, and his raiment was white as the l. *5457*
22: 5 But they **made** l **of** *it,* and went their ways, *272*
24:29 and the moon shall not give her l, and *5338*
Mk 13:24 and the moon shall not give her l, *5338*
Lk 1:79 To **give** l to them that sit in darkness and *2014*
2:32 A l to lighten the Gentiles, and the glory of *5457*
8:16 that they which enter in may see the l. *5457*
11:33 that they which come in may see the l. *5338*
11:34 The l of the body is the eye: *3088*
11:34 is single, thy whole body also is **full of** l; *5460*
11:35 that the l which is in thee be not darkness. *5457*
11:36 If thy whole body therefore *be* **full of** l, *5460*
11:36 no part dark, the whole shall be **full of** l, *5460*
11:36 bright shining of a candle doth **give** thee l. *5461*
12: 3 spoken in darkness shall be heard in the l; *5457*
15: 8 doth not l a candle, and sweep the house, and *681*
16: 8 their generation wiser than the children of l. *5457*
Jn 1: 4 him was life; and the life was the l of men. *5457*
1: 5 And the l shineth in darkness; and *5457*
1: 7 for a witness, to bear witness of the L, *5457*
1: 8 He was not *that* L, but *was sent* to bear *5457*
1: 8 but *was sent* to bear witness of *that* L. *5457*
1: 9 *That* was the true L, which lighteth every *5457*
3:19 that l is come into the world, and men *5457*
3:19 and men loved darkness rather than l, *5457*
3:20 For every one that doeth evil hateth the l, *5457*
3:20 neither cometh to the l, lest his deeds *5457*
3:21 But he that doeth truth cometh to the l, *5457*
5:35 He was a burning and a shining l: and *3088*
5:35 were willing for a season to rejoice in his l. *5457*
8:12 unto them, saying, I am the l of the world: *5457*
8:12 in darkness, but shall have the l of life. *5457*
9: 5 I am in the world, I am the l of the world. *5457*
11: 9 because he seeth the l of this world. *5457*
11:10 he stumbleth, because there is no l in him. *5457*
12:35 Yet a little while is the l with you. *5457*
12:35 Walk while ye have the l, lest darkness *5457*
12:36 While ye have l, believe in the light, that ye *5457*
12:36 While ye have light, believe in the l, that ye *5457*
12:36 in the light, that ye may be the children of l. *5457*
12:46 I am come a l into the world, *5457*
Ac 9: 3 suddenly there shined round about him a l *5457*
12: 7 upon *him,* and a l shined in the prison: *5457*
13:47 *saying,* I have set thee to be a l of *5457*
16:29 Then he called for a l, and sprang in, and *5457*
22: 6 suddenly there shone from heaven a great l *5457*
22: 9 they that were with me saw indeed the l, *5457*
22:11 when I could not see for the glory of that l, *5457*
26:13 O king, I saw in the way a l from heaven, *5457*
26:18 *and* to turn *them* from darkness to l, and *5457*
26:23 and should shew l unto the people, and *5457*
Ro 2:19 the blind, a l of them which are in darkness, *5457*
13:12 and let us put on the armour of l. *5457*
1Co 4: 5 who both will **bring to** l the hidden *things* *5461*
2Co 4: 4 lest the l of the glorious gospel of Christ, *5462*
4: 6 who commanded the l to shine out of *5457*
4: 6 to give the l of the knowledge of the glory *5462*
4:17 For our l affliction, which is but for a *1645*
6:14 and what communion hath l with darkness? *5457*
11:14 himself is transformed into an angel of l. *5457*
Eph 5: 8 but now *are ye* l in the Lord: *5457*
5: 8 *ye* light in the Lord: walk as children of l: *5457*
5:13 are reproved are made manifest by the l: *5457*
5:13 for whatsoever doth make manifest is l. *5457*
5:14 from the dead, and Christ shall **give** thee l. *2017*
Col 1:12 of the inheritance of the saints in l: *5457*
1Th 5: 5 Ye are all the children of l, and the children *5457*
1Ti 6:16 dwelling in the l which no *man* can *5457*
2Ti 1:10 hath **brought** life and immortality **to l** *5461*
1Pe 2: 9 you out of darkness into his marvellous l: *5457*
2Pe 1:19 as unto a l that shineth in a dark place, *3088*
1Jn 1: 5 that God is l, and in him is no darkness at *5457*
1: 7 But if we walk in the l, as he is in the light, *5457*
1: 7 But if we walk in the light, as he is in the l, *5457*
2: 8 darkness is past, and the true l now shineth. *5457*
2: 9 He that saith *he* is in the l, and hateth his *5457*
2:10 He that loveth his brother abideth in the l, *5457*
Rev 7:16 neither shall the sun l on them, nor any *4098*
18:23 And the l of a candle shall shine no more at *5457*
21:11 her l *was* like unto a stone most precious, *5458*
21:23 did lighten it, and the Lamb *is* the l thereof. *3088*
21:24 which are saved shall walk in the l of it: *5457*
22: 5 they need no candle, neither l of the sun; *5457*
22: 5 of the sun; for the Lord God **giveth** them l: *5461*

LIGHTED (13) [LIGHT]

Ge 24:64 when she saw Isaac, she l off the camel. 5307
28:11 he l upon a *certain* place, and tarried there 6293
Ex 40:25 he l the lamps before the LORD; as 5927
Nu 8: 3 he l the lamps thereof over against 5927
Jos 15:18 she l **off** *her* ass; and 4480+5921+6795
Jdg 1:14 she l from off *her* ass; and Caleb said unto 6795
4:15 so that Sisera l **down** off *his* chariot, and 3381
1Sa 25:23 l off the ass, and fell before David on her 3381
2Ki 5:21 he l **down** from the chariot to meet him, 5307
10:15 he l **on** Jehonadab the son of Rechab 4672
Isa 9: 8 a word into Jacob, and it hath l upon Israel. 5307
Lk 8:16 No *man,* when he hath l a candle, covereth it *681*
11:33 No *man,* when he hath l a candle, putteth *it* *681*

LIGHTEN (7) [LIGHT]

1Sa 6: 5 peradventure he will l his hand from off 7043
2Sa 22:29 and the LORD will l my darkness. 5050
Ezr 9: 8 that our God may l our eyes, and give us a 215
Ps 13: 3 l mine eyes, lest I sleep the *sleep of* death; 215
Jnh 1: 5 *were* in the ship into the sea, to l *it* of them. 7043
Lk 2:32 A light to l the Gentiles, and the glory of thy *602*
Rev 21:23 for the glory of God did l it, and the Lamb *5461*

LIGHTENED (5) [LIGHT]
Ps 34: 5 They looked unto him, and were l: and 5102
77:18 the lightnings l the world: the earth trembled 215
Ac 27:18 the next *day* they l **the ship**; *1546+4160*
27:38 they l the ship, and cast out the wheat into *2893*
Rev 18: 1 and the earth was l with his glory. *5461*

LIGHTENETH (2) [LIGHT]
Pr 29:13 meet together: the LORD l both their eyes. 215
Lk 17:24 that l out of the one *part* under heaven, *797*

LIGHTER (5) [LIGHT]
1Ki 12: 4 **make** thou the grievous service of thy father, and his heavy yoke which he put upon us, l, 7043
12: 9 **Make** the yoke which thy father did put upon us l? 7043
12:10 our yoke heavy, but **make** thou *it* l unto us; 7043
2Ch 10:10 but **make** thou *it* **somewhat** l for us; 7043
Ps 62: 9 they *are* altogether *l* than vanity. NIH

LIGHTEST (1) [LIGHT]
Nu 8: 2 and say unto him, When thou l the lamps, 5927

LIGHTETH (3) [LIGHT]
Ex 30: 8 when Aaron l the lamps at even, he shall 5927
Dt 19: 5 and l **upon** his neighbour, that he die; 4672
Jn 1: 9 which l every man *that* cometh into *5461*

LIGHTING (2) [LIGHT]
Isa 30:30 shall shew the l **down** of his arm, with 5183
Mt 3:16 descending like a dove, and l upon him: *2064*

LIGHTLY (7) [LIGHT]
Ge 26:10 one of the people might l have lien 4592+3509.1
Dt 32:15 and l **esteemed** the Rock of his salvation. 5034
1Sa 2:30 they that despise me shall be l **esteemed**. 7043
18:23 that I *am* a poor man, and l **esteemed**? 7034
Isa 9: 1 when at the first he l **afflicted** the land of 7043
Jer 4:24 lo, they trembled, and all the hills **moved** l. 7043
Mk 9:39 in my name, that can l speak evil of me. *5036*

LIGHTNESS (3) [LIGHT]
Jer 3: 9 it came to pass through the l of her 6963
23:32 people to err by their lies, and by their l; 6350
2Co 1:17 therefore was thus minded, did I use l? *1644*

LIGHTNING (13) [LIGHTNINGS]
2Sa 22:15 scattered them; l, and discomfited them. 1300
Job 28:26 the rain, and a way for the l of the thunder: 2385
37: 3 and his l unto the ends of the earth. 216
38:25 of waters, or a way for the l of thunder; 2385
Ps 144: 6 **Cast forth** l, and scatter them: 1299+1300
Eze 1:13 was bright, and out of the fire went forth l. 1300
1:14 returned as the appearance of a **flash of** l. 965
Da 10: 6 his face as the appearance of l, and his eyes 1300
Zec 9:14 and his arrow shall go forth as the l: 1300
Mt 24:27 For as the l cometh out of the east, and *796*
28: 3 His countenance was like l, and his raiment *796*
Lk 10:18 I beheld Satan as l fall from heaven. *796*
17:24 For as the l, that lighteneth out of the one *796*

LIGHTNINGS (14) [LIGHTNING]
Ex 19:16 that there were thunders and l, and a thick 1300
20:18 the l, and the noise of the trumpet, and 3940
Job 38:35 Canst thou send l, that they may go, and 1300
Ps 18:14 and he shot out l, and discomfited them. 1300
77:18 the l lightened the world: the earth trembled 1300
97: 4 His l enlightened the world: the earth saw, 1300
135: 7 he maketh l for the rain; he bringeth 1300
Jer 10:13 he maketh l with rain, and bringeth forth 1300
51:16 he maketh l with rain, and bringeth forth 1300
Na 2: 4 seem like torches, they shall run like the l. 1300
Rev 4: 5 And out of the throne proceeded l and *796*
8: 5 and thunderings, and l, and an earthquake. *796*
11:19 and there were l, and voices, and *796*
16:18 And there were voices, and thunders, and l; *796*

LIGHTS (10) [LIGHT]
Ge 1:14 Let there be l in the firmament of 3974
1:15 let them be for l in the firmament of 3974
1:16 God made two great l; the greater light to 3974
1Ki 6: 4 the house he made windows of narrow l. 8261
Ps 136: 7 To him that made great l: for his mercy 216
Eze 32: 8 All the bright l of heaven will I make dark 216
Lk 12:35 loins be girded about, and *your* l burning; *3088*
Ac 20: 8 And there were many l in the upper *2985*
Php 2:15 among whom ye shine as l in the world; *5458*
Jas 1:17 and cometh down from the Father of l, *5457*

LIGN (1)
Nu 24: 6 as the **trees of l aloes** *which* the LORD 174

LIGURE (2)
Ex 28:19 the third row a l, an agate, and an amethyst. 3958
39:12 third row, a l, an agate, and an amethyst. 3958

LIKE (669) [ALIKE, LIKED, LIKEMINDED, LIKEN, LIKENED, LIKENESS, LIKETH, LIKEWISE, LIKING] See Index

LIKED (1) [LIKE]
1Ch 28: 4 among the sons of my father he l me to 7521

LIKEMINDED (3) [LIKE, MIND]
Ro 15: 5 consolation grant you to be l *846+3588+5426*
Php 2: 2 Fulfil ye my joy, that ye be l, *846+3588+5426*
2:20 For I have no *man* l, who will naturally *2473*

LIKEN (9) [LIKE]
Isa 40:18 To whom then will ye l God? or 1819
40:25 To whom then will ye l me, or shall I be 1819
46: 5 To whom will ye l me, and make *me* equal, 1819
La 2:13 what *thing* shall I l to thee, O daughter of 1819
Mt 7:24 doeth them, I will l him unto a wise man, *3666*
11:16 But whereunto shall I l this generation? It is *3666*
Mk 4:30 Whereunto shall we l the kingdom of God? *3666*
Lk 7:31 then shall I l the men of this generation? *3666*
13:20 Whereunto shall I l the kingdom of God? *3666*

LIKENED (6) [LIKE]
Ps 89: 6 *who* among the sons of the mighty can be l 1819
Jer 6: 2 I have l the daughter of Zion *to* a comely 1819
Mt 7:26 them not, shall be l unto a foolish man, *3666*
13:24 The kingdom of heaven is l unto a man *3666*
18:23 Therefore is the kingdom of heaven l unto a *3666*
25: 1 Then shall the kingdom of heaven be l unto *3666*

LIKENESS (34) [LIKE]
Ge 1:26 Let us make man in our image, after our l: 1823
5: 1 created man, in the l of God made he him; 1823
5: 3 thirty years, and begat *a son* in his own l, 1823
Ex 20: 4 any l *of any thing* that *is* in heaven above, 8544
Dt 4:16 of any figure, the l of male or female, 8403
4:17 The l of any beast that *is* on the earth, 8403
4:17 the l of any winged fowl that flieth in 8403
4:18 The l of any *thing* that creepeth on 8403
4:18 the l of any fish that *is* in the waters 8403
4:23 the l of any *thing,* which the LORD thy 8544
4:25 *or* the l of any *thing,* and shall do evil in 8544
5: 8 any l *of any thing* that *is* in heaven above, 8544
Ps 17:15 shall be satisfied, when *I* awake, *with* thy l. 8544
Isa 40:18 or what l will ye compare unto him? 1823
Eze 1: 5 Also out of the midst thereof *came* the l of 1823
1: 5 their appearance; they had the l of a man. 1823
1:10 As for the l of their faces, they four had 1823
1:13 As for the l of the living creatures, 1823
1:16 they four had one l: and their appearance 1823
1:22 the l of the firmament upon the heads of 1823
1:26 *was* over their heads *was* the l of a throne, 1823
1:26 upon the l of the throne *was* the likeness as 1823
1:26 upon the likeness of the throne *was* the l as 1823
1:28 This *was* the appearance of the l of 1823
8: 2 and lo, a l as the appearance of fire: 1823
10: 1 as the appearance of the l of a throne. 1823
10:10 *for* their appearances, they four had one l, 1823
10:21 the l of the hands of a man *was* under their 1823
10:22 the l of their faces *was* the same faces 1823
Ac 14:11 The gods are come down to us in the l of *3666*
Ro 6: 5 if we have been planted together **in** the l *3667*
6: 5 we shall be also *in the l* of *his* resurrection: NIG
8: 3 God sending his own Son in the l of sinful *3667*
Php 2: 7 of a servant, and was made in the l of men: *3667*

LIKETH (3) [LIKE]
Dt 23:16 where it l him **best**: 2896+871.1+1886.1
Est 8: 8 as it l you, in the king's name, 2896+5869+871.1
Am 4: 5 for this l you, O ye children of Israel, 157

LIKEWISE (107) [LIKE] See Index

LIKHI (1)
1Ch 7:19 Ahian, and Shechem, and L, and Aniam. 3949

LIKING (2) [LIKE]
Job 39: 4 Their young ones are **in good l**, they grow 2492
Da 1:10 for why should he see your faces **worse l** 2196

LILIES (10) [LILY]
1Ki 7:26 like the brim of a cup, *with* flowers of l: 7799
2Ch 4: 5 of the brim of a cup, *with* flowers of l; 7799
SS 2:16 and I *am* his: he feedeth among the l. 7799
4: 5 roes *that are* twins, which feed among the l. 7799
5:13 his lips *like* l, dropping sweet smelling 7799
6: 2 to feed in the gardens, and to gather l. 7799
6: 3 beloved *is* mine: he feedeth among the l. 7799
7: 2 *is like* a heap of wheat set about with l. 7799
Mt 6:28 Consider the l of the field, how they grow; *2918*
Lk 12:27 Consider the l how they grow: they toil not, *2918*

LILY (5) [LILIES]
1Ki 7:19 of the pillars *were* of l work in the porch, 7799
7:22 upon the top of the pillars *was* l work: so 7799
SS 2: 1 the rose of Sharon, *and* the l of the valleys. 7799
2: 2 As the l among thorns, so *is* my love 7799
Hos 14: 5 he shall grow as the l, and cast forth his 7799

LIME (2)
Isa 33:12 the people shall be *as* the burnings of l: 7875
Am 2: 1 burnt the bones of the king of Edom into l: 7875

LIMIT (1) [LIMITED, LIMITETH]
Eze 43:12 Upon the top of the mountain the whole l 1366

LIMITED (1) [LIMIT]
Ps 78:41 tempted God, and l the Holy One of Israel. 8428

LIMITETH (1) [LIMIT]
Heb 4: 7 Again he l a certain day, saying in David, *3724*

LINE (31) [LINEAGE, LINES, PLUMBLINE]
Jos 2:18 thou shalt bind this l of scarlet thread in 8615
2:21 and she bound the scarlet l in the window. 8615
2Sa 8: 2 smote Moab, and measured them with a l, 2256
8: 2 to death, and *with* one full l to keep alive. 2256
1Ki 7:15 a l of twelve cubits did compass either of 2339
7:23 a l of thirty cubits did compass it round 6957
2Ki 21:13 I will stretch over Jerusalem the l of 6957
2Ch 4: 2 a l of thirty cubits did compass it round 6957
Job 38: 5 or who hath stretched the l upon it? 6957
Ps 19: 4 Their l is gone out through all the earth, 6957
78:55 divided them an inheritance by l, and 2256
Isa 28:10 l upon line, line upon line; here a little, *and* 6957
28:10 line upon l, line upon line; here a little, *and* 6957
28:10 line upon line, l upon line; here a little, *and* 6957
28:10 line upon line, line upon l; here a little, *and* 6957
28:13 l upon line, line upon line; here a little, *and* 6957
28:13 line upon l, line upon line; here a little, *and* 6957
28:13 line upon line, l upon line; here a little, *and* 6957
28:13 line upon line, line upon l; here a little, *and* 6957
28:17 Judgment also will I lay to the l, and 6957
34:11 he shall stretch out upon it the l of 6957
34:17 and his hand hath divided it unto them by l: 6957
44:13 he marketh it out with a l; he fitteth it with 8279
Jer 31:39 the measuring l shall yet go forth over 6957
La 2: 8 he hath stretched out a l, he hath not 6957
Eze 40: 3 with a l of flax in his hand, and a measuring 6616
47: 3 when the man that had the l in his hand 6957
Am 7:17 and thy land shall be divided by l; 2256
Zec 1:16 a l shall be stretched forth upon Jerusalem. 6957
2: 1 a man with a measuring l in his hand. 2256
2Co 10:16 not to boast in another *man's* l of *things* *2583*

LINEAGE (1) [LINE]
Lk 2: 4 he was of the house and l of David:) *3965*

LINEN (104)
Ge 41:42 arrayed him in vestures of **fine** l, and put a 8336
Ex 25: 4 and scarlet, and **fine** l, and goats' *hair,* 8336
26: 1 *with* ten curtains *of* **fine** twined l, 8336
26:31 scarlet, and **fine** twined l *of* cunning work: 8336
26:36 and purple, and scarlet, and **fine** twined l, 8336
27: 9 **fine** twined l of an hundred cubits long for 8336
27:16 and purple, and scarlet, and **fine** twined l, 8336
27:18 the height five cubits *of* **fine** twined l, and 8336
28: 5 and blue, and purple, and scarlet, and **fine** l. 8336
28: 6 and *of* purple, *of* scarlet, and **fine** twined l, 8336
28: 8 and purple, and scarlet, and **fine** twined l. 8336
28:15 and *of* scarlet, and *of* **fine** twined l, 8336
28:39 thou shalt embroider the coat of **fine** l, and 8336
28:39 thou shalt make the mitre *of* **fine** l, and 8336
28:42 thou shalt make them l breeches to cover 906
35: 6 and scarlet, and **fine** l, and goats' *hair,* 8336
35:23 **fine** l, and goats' *hair,* and red skins of 8336
35:25 and of purple, *and* of scarlet, and of **fine** l. 8336
35:35 in scarlet, and in **fine** l, and of the weaver, 8336
36: 8 made ten curtains *of* **fine** twined l, 8336
36:35 and purple, and scarlet, and **fine** twined l: 8336
36:37 purple, and scarlet, and **fine** twined l, 8336
38: 9 hangings of the court *were of* **fine** twined l, 8336
38:16 the court round about *were of* **fine** twined l. 8336
38:18 and purple, and scarlet, and **fine** twined l: 8336
38:23 and in purple, and in scarlet, and **fine** l. 8336
39: 2 and purple, and scarlet, and **fine** twined l. 8336
39: 3 and in the scarlet, and in the **fine** l, 8336
39: 5 and purple, and scarlet, and **fine** twined l; 8336
39: 8 and purple, and scarlet, and **fine** twined l. 8336
39:24 and purple, and scarlet, *and* twined *l.* NIH
39:27 they made coats *of* **fine** l *of* woven work 8336
39:28 a mitre *of* **fine** l, and goodly bonnets *of* fine 8336
39:28 goodly bonnets *of* **fine** l, and linen breeches 8336
39:28 and l breeches *of* fine twined linen, 906
39:28 and linen breeches *of* **fine** twined l, 8336
39:29 a girdle *of* **fine** twined l, and blue, and 8336
Lev 6:10 And the priest shall put on his l garment, and 906
6:10 *his* l breeches shall he put upon his flesh, 906
13:47 *it be* a woollen garment, or a l garment; 6593
13:48 *be* in the warp, or woof; of l, or of woollen; 6593
13:52 in woollen or in l, or any thing of skin, 6593
13:59 of leprosy in a garment of woollen or l, 6593
16: 4 He shall put on the holy l coat, and he shall 906
16: 4 he shall have the l breeches upon his flesh, 906
16: 4 shall be girded with a l girdle, and with 906
16: 4 and with the l mitre shall he be attired: 906
16:23 shall put off the l garments, which he put on 906
16:32 shall put on the l clothes, *even* the holy 906
19:19 a garment **mingled of l and woollen** 3610+8162
Dt 22:11 of divers sorts, *as* of woollen and l together. 6593
1Sa 2:18 *being* a child, girded *with* a l ephod. 906
22:18 and five persons that did wear a l ephod. 906
2Sa 6:14 and David *was* girded *with* a l ephod. 906
1Ki 10:28 horses brought out of Egypt, and l **yarn**: 4723
10:28 the king's merchants received the l **yarn** at 4723
1Ch 4:21 of the house of them that wrought **fine** l, 948
15:27 And David *was* clothed with a robe of **fine** l, 948
15:27 David also *had* upon him an ephod of l. 906
2Ch 1:16 horses brought out of Egypt, and l **yarn**: 4723
1:16 the king's merchants received the l **yarn** at 4723
2:14 in blue, and in **fine** l, and in crimson; 948
3:14 and **fine** l, and wrought cherubims thereon. 948
5:12 and their brethren, *being* arrayed in **white** l, 948
Est 1: 6 blue *hangings,* fastened with cords of **fine** l 948
8:15 and *with* a garment of **fine** l and purple: 948
Pr 7:16 *with* carved *works, with* **fine** l of Egypt. 330
31:24 She maketh **fine** l, and selleth *it;* and 5466
Isa 3:23 and the **fine** l, and the hoods, and the vails. 5466
Jer 13: 1 Go and get thee a l girdle, and put it upon 6593
Eze 9: 2 one man among them *was* clothed *with* l, 906
9: 3 he called to the man clothed *with* l, 906
9:11 behold, the man clothed with l, which *had* 906
10: 2 he spake unto the man clothed with l, and 906
10: 6 he had commanded the man clothed with l, 906
10: 7 into the hands of *him that was* clothed with l: 906
16:10 and I girded thee about with **fine** l, 8336
16:13 thy raiment *was of* **fine** l, and silk, and 8336
27: 7 **Fine** l with broidered work from Egypt was 8336
27:16 and **fine** l, and coral, and agate. 948
44:17 they shall be clothed with l garments; 6593
44:18 They shall have l bonnets upon their heads, 6593
44:18 and shall have l breeches upon their loins; 6593
Da 10: 5 and behold, a certain man clothed *in* l, 906
12: 6 *one* said to the man clothed in l, which *was* 906
12: 7 I heard the man clothed in l, which *was* upon 906
Mt 27:59 the body, he wrapped it in a clean l **cloth**, *4616*
Mk 14:51 having a l **cloth** cast about *his* naked *body;* *4616*
14:52 And he left the l **cloth**, and fled from them *4616*
15:46 And he bought **fine** l, and took him down, *4616*
15:46 and wrapped *him* in the l, and laid him in a *4616*
Lk 16:19 which was clothed in purple and **fine** l, and *1040*
23:53 and wrapped it in l, and laid it in a *4616*
24:12 he beheld the l **clothes** laid by themselves, *3608*
Jn 19:40 and wound it in l **clothes** with the spices, *3608*
20: 5 and looking in, saw the l **clothes** lying; *3608*

Jn 20: 6 the sepulchre, and seeth the l **clothes** lie, *3608*
20: 7 not lying with the l **clothes**, but *3608*
Rev 15: 6 clothed in pure and white l, and *3043*
18:12 and **fine** l, and purple, and silk, and scarlet, *1040*
18:16 that was clothed in **fine** l, and purple, and *1039*
19: 8 granted that she should be arrayed in **fine** l, *1039*
19: 8 for the **fine** l is the righteousness of saints. *1039*
19:14 clothed in **fine** l, white and clean. *1039*

LINES (2) [LINE]
2Sa 8: 2 even *with* two l measured he to put to 2256
Ps 16: 6 The l are fallen unto me in pleasant *places;* 2256

LINGERED (2) [LINGERETH]
Ge 19:16 while he l, the men laid hold upon his hand, 4102
43:10 For except we had l, surely now we had 4102

LINGERETH (1) [LINGERED]
2Pe 2: 3 whose judgment now of a long time l not, *691*

LINTEL (4) [LINTELS]
Ex 12:22 strike the l and the two side posts with 4947
12:23 and when he seeth the blood upon the l, and 4947
1Ki 6:31 the l *and* side posts *were* a fifth *part of* 352
Am 9: 1 he said, Smite the **l of the door**, that 3730

LINTELS (1) [LINTEL]
Zep 2:14 the bittern shall lodge in the **upper** l of it; 3730

LINUS (1)
2Ti 4:21 and L, and Claudia, and all the brethren. *3044*

LION (98) [LION'S, LIONESS, LIONESSES, LIONLIKE, LIONS, LIONS']
Ge 49: 9 he couched as a l, and as an old lion; 738
49: 9 he couched as a lion, and as an **old** l; 3833
Nu 23:24 the people shall rise up as a **great** l, and 3833
23:24 a great lion, and lift up himself as a **young** l: 738
24: 9 he lay down as a l, and as a great lion: 738
24: 9 he lay down as a lion, and as a **great** l: 3833
Dt 33:20 he dwelleth as a l, and teareth the arm with 3833
Jdg 14: 5 behold, a young l roared against him. 738
14: 8 he turned aside to see the carcase of the l: 738
14: 8 of bees and honey in the carcase of the l. 738
14: 9 taken the honey out of the carcase of the l. 738
14:18 what *is* stronger than a l? And he said unto 738
1Sa 17:34 there came a l and a bear, and took a lamb 738
17:36 Thy servant slew both the l and the bear: and 738
17:37 that delivered me out of the paw of the l, 738
2Sa 17:10 whose heart *is* as the heart of a l, shall utterly 738
23:20 slew a l in the midst of a pit in time of snow: 738
1Ki 13:24 a l met him by the way, and slew him: 738
13:24 stood by it, the l also stood by the carcase. 738
13:25 in the way, and the l standing by the carcase: 738
13:26 the LORD hath delivered him unto the l, 738
13:28 and the ass and the l standing by the carcase: 738
13:28 the l had not eaten the carcase, nor torn 738
20:36 thou art departed from me, a l shall slay thee. 738
20:36 from him, a l found him, and slew him. 738
1Ch 11:22 and slew a l in a pit in a snowy day. 738
Job 4:10 The roaring of the l, and the voice of 738
4:10 the voice of the **fierce** l, and the teeth of 7826
4:11 The **old** l perisheth for lack of prey, and 3918
10:16 Thou huntest me as a **fierce** l: and 7826
28: 8 not trodden it, nor the **fierce** l passed by it. 7826
38:39 Wilt thou hunt the prey for the l? or fill 3833
Ps 7: 2 Lest he tear my soul like a l, rending *it* in 738
10: 9 He lieth in wait secretly as a l in his den: 738
17:12 Like as a l *that* is greedy of his prey, and 738
17:12 as it were a **young** l lurking in secret 3715
22:13 their mouths, *as* a ravening and a roaring l. 738
91:13 Thou shalt tread upon the l and adder: 7826
91:13 the **young** l and the dragon shalt thou 3715
Pr 19:12 The king's wrath *is* as the roaring of a l; but 3715
20: 2 The fear of a king *is* as the roaring of a l: 3715
22:13 The slothful *man* saith, *There is* a l without, 738
26:13 slothful *man* saith, *There is* a l in the way; 7826
26:13 *is* a lion in the way; a l *is* in the streets. 738
28: 1 but the righteous are bold as a l. 3715
28:15 *As* a roaring l, and a ranging bear; *so is* a 738
30:30 A l *which is* strongest among beasts, and 3918
Ecc 9: 4 for a living dog *is* better than a dead l. 738
Isa 5:29 Their roaring *shall be* like a l, they shall 3833
11: 6 the calf and the **young** l and the fatling 3715
11: 7 and the l shall eat straw like the ox. 738
21: 8 he cried, A l: My lord, I stand continually 738
30: 6 from whence *come* the young and **old** l, 3918
31: 4 Like as the l and the young lion roaring on 738
31: 4 and the **young** l roaring on his prey, 3715
35: 9 No l shall be there, nor *any* ravenous beast 738
38:13 *that,* as a l, so will he break all my bones: 738
65:25 and the l shall eat straw like the bullock: 738
Jer 2:30 devoured your prophets, like a destroying l. 738
4: 7 The l is come up from his thicket, and 738
5: 6 Wherefore a l out of the forest shall slay 738
12: 8 Mine heritage is unto me as a l in the forest; 738
25:38 He hath forsaken his covert, as the l: 3715
49:19 he shall come up like a l from the swelling 738
50:44 he shall come up like a l from the swelling 738
La 3:10 bear lying in wait, *and as* a l in secret places. 738
Eze 1:10 a man, and the face of a l, on the right side: 738
10:14 the third the face of a l, and the fourth 738
19: 3 it became a **young** l, and it learned to catch 3715
19: 5 of her whelps, *and* made him a **young** l. 3715
19: 6 he became a **young** l, and learned to catch 3715
22:25 like a roaring l ravening the prey; 738
32: 2 Thou art like a **young** l of the nations, and 3715
41:19 the face of a **young** l toward the palm tree 3715
Da 7: 4 The first *was* like a l, and had eagle's wings: 744
Hos 5:14 For I *will be* unto Ephraim as a l, and as a 7826
5:14 and as a **young** l to the house of Judah: 3715
11:10 he shall roar like a l: when he shall roar, then 738
13: 7 Therefore I will be unto them as a l: as a 7826
13: 8 and there will I devour them like a l: 3833
Joel 1: 6 whose teeth *are* the teeth of a l, and he hath 738
1: 6 and he hath the cheek-teeth of a **great** l. 3833
Am 3: 4 Will a l roar in the forest, when he hath no 738
3: 4 will a **young** l cry out of his den, if he have 3715
3: 8 The l hath roared, who will not fear? 738
3:12 taketh out of the mouth of the l two legs, 738
5:19 As if a man did flee from a l, and a bear met 738
Mic 5: 8 people as a l among the beasts of the forest, 738
5: 8 as a **young** l among the flocks of sheep: 3715
Na 2:11 where the l, *even* the old lion, walked, *and* 738
2:11 *even* the **old** l, walked, *and* the lion's 3833
2:12 The l did tear in pieces enough for his 738
2Ti 4:17 I was delivered out of the mouth of the l. *3023*
1Pe 5: 8 the devil, as a roaring l, walketh about, *3023*
Rev 4: 7 And the first beast *was* like a l, and *3023*
5: 5 behold, the L of the tribe of Juda, the root *3023*
10: 3 cried with a loud voice, as *when* a l roareth: *3023*
13: 2 a bear, and his mouth as the mouth of a l: *3023*

LION'S (6) [LION]
Ge 49: 9 Judah *is* a l whelp: from the prey, my son, 738
Dt 33:22 of Dan he said, Dan *is* a l whelp: he shall 738
Job 4:11 and the **stout** l whelps are scattered abroad. 3833
28: 8 The l whelps have not trodden it, nor 7830
Ps 22:21 Save me from the l mouth: for thou hast 738
Na 2:11 *and* the l whelp, and none made *them* afraid? 738

LIONESS (1) [LION]
Eze 19: 2 A l: she lay down among lions, 3833

LIONESSES (1) [LION]
Na 2:12 strangled for his l, and filled his holes *with* 3833

LIONLIKE (2) [LION]
2Sa 23:20 done many acts, he slew two l **men** of Moab: 739
1Ch 11:22 done many acts; he slew two l **men** of Moab: 739

LIONS (43) [LION]
2Sa 1:23 than eagles, they were stronger than l. 738
1Ki 7:29 borders that *were* between the ledges *were* l, 738
7:29 beneath the l and oxen *were certain* additions 738
7:36 he graved cherubims, l, and palm trees, 738
10:19 of the seat, and two l stood beside the stays. 738
10:20 And twelve l stood there on the one side and 738
2Ki 17:25 therefore the LORD sent l among them, 738
17:26 therefore he hath sent l among them, 738
1Ch 12: 8 whose faces *were like* the faces of l, and 738
2Ch 9:18 sitting place, and two l standing by the stays: 738
9:19 And twelve l stood there on the one side and 738
Job 4:10 and the teeth of the **young** l, are broken. 3715
38:39 the lion? or fill the appetite of the **young** l, 3715
Ps 34:10 The **young** l do lack, and suffer hunger: 3715
35:17 their destructions, my darling from the l. 3715
57: 4 My soul *is* among l: *and* I lie *even among* 3833
58: 6 break out the great teeth of the **young** l, 3715

Ps 104:21 The **young** l roar after *their* prey, and seek 3715
Isa 5:29 *be* like a lion, they shall roar like **young** l: 3715
15: 9 l upon him that escapeth of Moab, and 738
Jer 2:15 The **young** l roared upon him, *and* yelled, 3715
50:17 scattered sheep; the l have driven *him* away: 738
51:38 They shall roar together like l: they shall 3715
Eze 19: 2 she lay down among l, she nourished her 738
19: 2 she nourished her whelps among **young** l. 3715
19: 6 he went up and down among the l, 738
38:13 with all the **young** l thereof, shall say unto 3715
Da 6: 7 O king, he shall be cast into the den of l. 744
6:12 O king, shall be cast into the den of l? 744
6:16 and cast *him* into the den of l. 744
6:19 and went in haste unto the den of l. 744
6:20 able to deliver thee from the l? 744
6:24 they cast *them* into the den of l, them, 744
6:24 the l had the mastery of them, and brake all 744
6:27 delivered Daniel from the power of the l. 744
Na 2:11 Where *is* the dwelling of the l, and 738
2:11 the feeding place of the **young** l, where 3715
2:13 and the sword shall devour thy **young** l: 3715
Zep 3: 3 Her princes within her *are* roaring l; 738
Zec 11: 3 a voice of the roaring of **young** l; for 3715
Heb 11:33 obtained promises, stopped the mouths of l, *3023*
Rev 9: 8 and their teeth were as *the teeth* of l. *3023*
9:17 heads of the horses *were* as the heads of l; *3023*

LIONS' (3) [LION]
SS 4: 8 top of Shenir and Hermon, from the l dens, 738
Jer 51:38 like lions: they shall yell as l whelps, 738
Da 6:22 hath shut the l mouths, that they have not 744

LIP (3) [LIPS]
Lev 13:45 he shall put a covering upon *his* **upper** l, 8222
Ps 22: 7 they shoot out the l, they shake the head, 8193
Pr 12:19 The l of truth shall be established for ever: 8193

LIPS (119) [LIP]
Ex 6:12 hear me, who *am* of uncircumcised l? 8193
6:30 I *am* of uncircumcised l, and how shall 8193
Lev 5: 4 pronouncing with *his* l to do evil, or to do 8193
Nu 30: 6 she vowed, or uttered ought out of her l, 8193
30: 8 that which she uttered with her l, 8193
30:12 whatsoever proceeded out of her l 8193
Dt 23:23 That which is gone out of thy l thou shalt 8193
1Sa 1:13 only her l moved, but her voice was not 8193
2Ki 19:28 my bridle in thy l, and I will turn thee back 8193
Job 2:10 In all this did not Job sin with his l. 8193
8:21 *with* laughing, and thy l *with* rejoicing. 8193
11: 5 would speak, and open his l against thee; 8193
13: 6 and hearken to the pleadings of my l. 8193
15: 6 not I; yea, thine own l testify against thee. 8193
16: 5 the moving of my l should asswage *your* 8193
23:12 gone back from the commandment of his l; 8193
27: 4 My l shall not speak wickedness, nor my 8193
32:20 be refreshed: I will open my l and answer. 8193
33: 3 and my l shall utter knowledge clearly. 8193
Ps 12: 2 *with* flattering l *and* with a double heart do 8193
12: 3 The LORD shall cut off all flattering l, 8193
12: 4 tongue will we prevail; our l *are* our own: 8193
16: 4 not offer, nor take up their names into my l. 8193
17: 1 my prayer, *that goeth* not out of feigned l. 8193
17: 4 by the word of thy l I have kept *me from* 8193
21: 2 and hast not withholden the request of his l. 8193
31:18 Let the lying l be put to silence; 8193
34:13 from evil, and thy l from speaking guile. 8193
40: 9 lo, I have not refrained my l, O LORD, 8193
45: 2 grace is poured into thy l: therefore 8193
51:15 O Lord, open thou my l; and my mouth 8193
59: 7 swords *are* in their l: for who, *say they,* 8193
59:12 the words of their l let them even be taken 8193
63: 3 *is* better than life, my l shall praise thee. 8193
63: 5 my mouth shall praise *thee with* joyful l: 8193
66:14 Which my l have uttered, and my mouth 8193
71:23 My l shall greatly rejoice when I sing unto 8193
89:34 nor alter the thing that is gone out of my l. 8193
106:33 so that he spake unadvisedly with his l. 8193
119:13 With my l have I declared all the judgments 8193
119:171 My l shall utter praise, when thou hast 8193
120: 2 from lying l, *and* from a deceitful tongue. 8193
140: 3 a serpent; adder's poison *is* under their l. 8193
140: 9 let the mischief of their own l cover them. 8193
141: 3 before my mouth; keep the door of my l. 8193
Pr 4:24 and perverse l put far from thee. 8193
5: 2 and *that* thy l may keep knowledge. 8193
5: 3 For the l of a strange *woman* drop *as* a 8193
7:21 with the flattering of her l she forced him. 8193
8: 6 the opening of my l *shall be* right things. 8193
8: 7 and wickedness *is* an abomination to my l. 8193
10:13 In the l of him that hath understanding 8193
10:18 He that hideth hatred *with* lying l, and 8193
10:19 not sin: but he that refraineth his l *is* wise. 8193
10:21 The l of the righteous feed many: but 8193
10:32 The l of the righteous know what is 8193
12:13 is snared by the transgression of *his* l: 8193
12:22 Lying l *are* abomination to the LORD: but 8193
13: 3 he that openeth wide his l shall have 8193
14: 3 but the l of the wise shall preserve them. 8193
14: 7 when thou perceivest not *in him* the l of 8193
14:23 but the talk of the l *tendeth* only to penury. 8193
15: 7 The l of the wise disperse knowledge: but 8193
16:10 A divine sentence *is* in the l of the king: 8193
16:13 Righteous l *are* the delight of kings; and 8193
16:21 the sweetness of the l increaseth learning. 8193
16:23 his mouth, and addeth learning to his l. 8193
16:27 and in his l *there is* as a burning fire. 8193
16:30 moving his l he bringeth evil to pass. 8193
17: 4 A wicked doer giveth heed to false l; *and* 8193
17: 7 not a fool: much less do lying l a prince. 8193
17:28 he that shutteth his l *is esteemed a man* of 8193
18: 6 A fool's l enter into contention, and 8193
18: 7 and his l *are* the snare of his soul. 8193
18:20 *with* the increase of his l shall he be filled. 8193
19: 1 than *he that is* perverse in his l, and *is* a 8193
20:15 but the l of knowledge *are* a precious jewel. 8193
20:19 not with him that flattereth *with* his l. 8193
22:11 *for* the grace of his l the king *shall be* his 8193
22:18 they shall withal be fitted in thy l. 8193
23:16 shall rejoice, when thy l speak right things. 8193
24: 2 and their l talk of mischief. 8193
24:26 *Every man* shall kiss *his* l that giveth a right 8193
24:28 without cause; and deceive not with thy l. 8193
26:23 Burning l and a wicked heart *are like* a 8193
26:24 He that hateth dissembleth with his l, and 8193
27: 2 own mouth; a stranger, and not thine own l. 8193
Ecc 10:12 but the l of a fool will swallow up himself. 8193
SS 4: 3 Thy l *are* like a thread of scarlet, and 8193
4:11 Thy l, O *my* spouse, drop *as* 8193
5:13 his l *like* lilies, dropping sweet smelling 8193
7: 9 causing the l of *those that are* asleep to 8193
Isa 6: 5 because I *am* a man of unclean l, and 8193
6: 5 dwell in the midst of a people of unclean l: 8193
6: 7 and said, Lo, this hath touched thy l; 8193
11: 4 with the breath of his l shall he slay 8193
28:11 For with stammering l and another tongue 8193
29:13 with their l do honour me, but 8193
30:27 his l are full *of* indignation, and his tongue 8193
37:29 my bridle in thy l, and I will turn thee back 8193
57:19 I create the fruit of the l; Peace, peace to 8193
59: 3 your l have spoken lies, your tongue hath 8193
Jer 17:16 that which came out of my l was right 8193
La 3:62 The l of those that rose up against me, and 8193
Eze 24:17 cover not *thy* l, and eat not the bread of 8222
24:22 ye shall not cover *your* l, nor eat the bread 8222
36: 3 ye are taken up in the l of talkers, and 8193
Da 10:16 similitude of the sons of men touched my l: 8193
Hos 14: 2 so will we render the calves of our l. 8193
Mic 3: 7 yea, they shall all cover their l; for *there is* 8222
Hab 3:16 belly trembled; my l quivered at the voice: 8193
Mal 2: 6 and iniquity was not found in his l: 8193
2: 7 For the priest's l should keep knowledge, 8193
Mt 15: 8 their mouth, and honoureth me with *their* l; *5491*
Mk 7: 6 This people honoureth me with *their* l, but *5491*
Ro 3:13 the poison of asps *is* under their l: *5491*
1Co 14:21 and other l will I speak unto this people; *5491*
Heb 13:15 the fruit of *our* l giving thanks to his name. *5491*
1Pe 3:10 and his l that *they* speak no guile: *5491*

LIQUOR (2) [LIQUORS]
Nu 6: 3 neither shall he drink any l of grapes, 4952
SS 7: 2 *is like* a round goblet, *which* wanteth not l: 4197

LIQUORS (1) [LIQUOR]
Ex 22:29 *offer the first of* thy ripe fruits, and *of* thy l: 1831

LISTED (2) [LISTETH]
Mt 17:12 but have done unto him whatsoever they l. *2309*
Mk 9:13 they have done unto him whatsoever they l, *2309*

LISTEN (1)
Isa 49: 1 **L**, O isles, unto me; and hearken, 8085

LISTETH (2) [LISTED]
Jn 3: 8 The wind bloweth where it l, and *2309*
Jas 3: 4 whithersoever the governor l. *1014+2116*

LITTERS (1)
Isa 66:20 in l, and upon mules, and upon swift beasts, 6632

LITTLE (242)
Ge 18: 4 Let a l water, I pray you, be fetched, and 4592
19:20 city *is* near to flee unto, and it *is* a **l one**: 4705
19:20 Oh, let me escape thither, (*is* it not a **l one**?) 4705
24:17 I pray thee, drink a l water of thy pitcher. 4592
24:43 I pray thee, a l water of thy pitcher to drink; 4592
30:30 For *it was* l which thou hadst before I 4592
34:29 all their **l ones**, and their wives took they 2945
35:16 a **l way** to come to Ephrath: 776+3530+1886.1
43: 2 said unto them, Go again, buy us a l food. 4592
43: 8 both we, and thou, *and* also our **l ones**. 2945
43:11 a l balm, and a little honey, spices, and 4592
43:11 a l honey, spices, and myrrh, nuts, and 4592
44:20 old man, and a child of *his* old age, a **l one**; 6996
44:25 father said, Go again, *and* buy us a l food. 4592
45:19 out of the land of Egypt for your **l ones**, 2945
46: 5 and their **l ones**, and their wives, 2945
47:24 and for food for your **l ones**. 2945
48: 7 but a l way to come unto Ephrath: 3530
50: 8 only their **l ones**, and their flocks, and 2945
50:21 I will nourish you and your **l ones**. And he 2945
Ex 10:10 as I will let you go, and your **l ones**: 2945
10:24 be stayed: let your **l ones** also go with you. 2945
12: 4 if the household be too l for the lamb, 4591
16:18 and he that **gathered** l had no lack; 4591
23:30 By l and little I will drive them out from 4592
23:30 l I will drive them out from before thee, 4592
Lev 11:17 the **l owl**, and the cormorant, and the great 3563
Nu 14:31 your **l ones**, which ye said should be a prey, 2945
16:27 and their sons, and their **l children**. 2945
31: 9 their **l ones**, and took the spoil of all their 2945
31:17 therefore kill every male among the **l ones**, 2945
32:16 here for our cattle, and cities for our **l ones**: 2945
32:17 our **l ones** shall dwell in the fenced cities 2945
32:24 Build ye cities for your **l ones**, and folds for 2945
32:26 Our **l ones**, our wives, our flocks, and 2945
Dt 1:39 Moreover your **l ones**, which ye said 2945
2:34 the women, and the **l ones**, of every city, 2945
3:19 and your **l ones**, and your cattle, 2945
7:22 nations before thee **by l and little**: 4592+4592
7:22 nations before thee **by little and l**: 4592+4592
14:16 The **l owl**, and the great owl, and the swan, 3563
20:14 the **l ones**, and the cattle, and all that is in 2945
28:38 out *into* the field, and shalt gather *but* l in; 4592
29:11 Your **l ones**, your wives, and thy stranger 2945
Jos 1:14 Your wives, your **l ones**, and your cattle, 2945
8:35 the **l ones**, and the strangers that were 2945
19:47 the children of Dan went out *too l* for them: NIH
22:17 *Is* the iniquity of Peor *too* l for us, from 4592
Jdg 4:19 Give me, I pray thee, a l water to drink; 4592
18:21 put the **l ones** and the cattle and 2945
Ru 2: 7 until now, that she tarried a l in the house. 4592
1Sa 2:19 Moreover his mother made him a l coat, 6996
14:29 because I tasted a l of this honey. 4592
14:43 taste a l honey with the end of the rod that 4592
15:17 When thou *wast* l in thine own sight, 6996
20:35 appointed with David, and a l lad with him. 6996
2Sa 12: 3 save one l ewe lamb, which he had bought 6996
12: 8 if *that had been* too l, I would moreover 4592
15:22 and all the **l ones** that *were* with him. 2945
16: 1 when David was a l past the top *of the hill*, 4592
19:36 Thy servant will go a l *way* over Jordan 4592
1Ki 3: 7 I *am but* a l child: I know not *how* to go out 6996
8:64 *was* too l to receive the burnt offerings, 6996
11:17 to go *into* Egypt; Hadad *being yet* a l child. 6996
12:10 My l *finger* shall be thicker than my 6995
17:10 Fetch me, I pray thee, a l water in a vessel, 4592
17:12 of meal in a barrel, and a l oil in a cruse: 4592
17:13 make me thereof a l cake first, and bring *it* 6996
18:44 there ariseth a l cloud out of the sea, 6996
20:27 before them like two **l flocks** of kids; 2835
2Ki 2:23 there came forth l children out of the city, 6996
4:10 Let us make a l chamber, I pray thee, on 6996
5: 2 captive out of the land of Israel a l maid; 6996
5:14 came again like unto the flesh of a l child, 6996
5:19 in peace. So he departed from him a l way. 3530
10:18 and said unto them, Ahab served Baal a l; 4592
2Ch 10:10 My l *finger* shall be thicker than my 6995
20:13 with their **l ones**, their wives, and 2945
31:18 to the genealogy of all their **l ones**, 2945
Ezr 8:21 for our **l ones**, and for all our substance. 2945
9: 8 now for a l space grace hath been *shewed* 4592
9: 8 and give us a l reviving in our bondage. 4592
Ne 9:32 let not all the trouble seem l before thee, 4591
Est 3:13 both young and old, **l children** and women, 2945
8:11 *both* **l ones** and women, and *to take* 2945
Job 4:12 to me, and mine ear received a l thereof. 8102
10:20 let me alone, that I may take comfort a l, 4592
21:11 They send forth their **l ones** like a flock, 5759
24:24 They are exalted for a **l while**, but are gone 4592
26:14 how l a portion is heard of him? but 8102
36: 2 Suffer me a l, and I will shew thee that *I* 2191
Ps 2:12 the way, when his wrath is kindled but a l: 4592
8: 5 For thou hast made him a l lower than 4592
37:10 For yet a **l while**, and the wicked *shall* not 4592
37:16 A l that a righteous *man* hath *is* better than 4592
65:12 and the **l hills** rejoice on every side. 1389
68:27 There *is* l Benjamin *with* their ruler, 6810
72: 3 the people, and the **l hills**, by righteousness. 1389
114: 4 like rams, *and* the **l hills** like lambs. 1389
114: 6 like rams; *and* ye **l hills**, like lambs? 1389
137: 9 and dasheth thy **l ones** against the stones. 5768
Pr 6:10 *Yet* a l sleep, a little slumber, a little 4592
6:10 *Yet* a little sleep, a l slumber, a little 4592
6:10 a l folding of the hands to sleep: 4592
10:20 the heart of the wicked *is* **l worth**. 4592+3509.1
15:16 Better *is* l with the fear of the LORD than 4592
16: 8 Better *is* a l with righteousness than great 4592
24:33 *Yet* a l sleep, a little slumber, a little 4592
24:33 *Yet* a little sleep, a l slumber, a little 4592
24:33 a l folding of the hands to sleep: 4592
30:24 There be four *things which are* l upon 6996
Ecc 5:12 *man is* sweet, whether he eat l or much: 4592
9:14 *There was* a l city, and few men within it; 6996
10: 1 *doth* a l folly *him that is* in reputation for 4592
SS 2:15 Take us the foxes, the l foxes, that spoil 6996
3: 4 *It was* but a l that I passed from them, but I 4592
8: 8 We have a l sister, and she hath no breasts: 6996
Isa 10:25 For yet a **very l while**, and 4213+4592
11: 6 and a l child shall lead them. 6996
26:20 hide thyself as it were for a l moment, 4592
28:10 line upon line; here a l, *and* there a little: 2191
28:10 line upon line; here a little, *and* there a l: 2191
28:13 line upon line; here a l, *and* there a little; 2191
28:13 line upon line; here a little, *and* there a l; 2191
29:17 *Is* it not yet a **very l while**, 4213+4592
40:15 he taketh up the isles as a **very l thing**. 1851
54: 8 In a l wrath I hid my face from thee for a 8241
60:22 A **l one** shall become a thousand, and 6996
63:18 thy holiness have possessed *it* but a **l while**: 4705
Jer 14: 3 their nobles have sent their **l ones** to 6810
48: 4 her **l ones** have caused a cry to be heard. 6810
51:33 yet a **l while**, and the time of her harvest 4592
Eze 9: 6 both maids, and **l children**, and women: 2945
11:16 yet will I be to them as a l sanctuary in 4592
16:47 as *if that were* a **very l** *thing*, thou 4592+6985
31: 4 sent out her **l rivers** unto all the trees of 8585
40: 7 *every* **l chamber** *was* one reed long, and 8372
40: 7 between the **l chambers** *were* five cubits; 8372
40:10 the **l chambers** of the gate eastward *were* 8372
40:12 The space also before the **l chambers** *was* 8372
40:12 the **l chambers** *were* six cubits on this side, 8372
40:13 the gate from the roof of *one* **l chamber** to 8372
40:16 *were* narrow windows to the **l chambers**, 8372
40:21 the **l chambers** thereof *were* three on this 8372
40:29 the **l chambers** thereof, and the posts 8372
40:33 the **l chambers** thereof, and the posts 8372
40:36 The **l chambers** thereof, the posts thereof, 8372
Da 7: 8 there came up among them another l horn, 2192
8: 9 out of one of them came forth a l horn, 4704
11:34 shall fall, they shall be holpen *with* a l help: 4592
Hos 1: 4 for yet a l *while*, and I will avenge 4592
8:10 they shall sorrow a l for the burden of 4592
Am 6:11 *with* breaches, and the l house *with* clefts. 6996
Mic 5: 2 *though thou* be l among the thousands of 6810
Hag 1: 6 Ye have sown much, and bring in l; *ye* eat, 4592
1: 9 *Ye* looked for much, and lo, *it came* to l; 4592
2: 6 it *is* a **l while**, and I *will* shake the heavens, 4592

Zec 1:15 for I was *but* a l displeased, and they helped 4592
13: 7 and I will turn mine hand upon the **l ones**. 6819
Mt 6:30 not much more *clothe* you, O ye **of l faith**? 3640
8:26 Why are ye fearful, O ye **of l faith**? 3640
10:42 **l ones** a cup of cold *water* only in the name 3398
14:31 and said unto him, O thou **of l faith**, 3640
15:34 And they said, Seven, and a few **l fishes**. 2485
16: 8 he said unto them, O ye **of l faith**, 3640
18: 2 And Jesus called a **l child** unto *him,* and 3813
18: 3 ye be converted, and become as **l children**, 3813
18: 4 shall humble himself as this **l child**, 3813
18: 5 And whoso shall receive one such **l child** in 3813
18: 6 But whoso shall offend one of these **l ones** 3398
18:10 heed that ye despise not one of these **l ones**; 3398
18:14 that one of these **l ones** should perish. 3398
19:13 were there brought unto him **l children**, 3813
19:14 Suffer **l children**, and forbid them not, 3813
26:39 And he went a l further, and fell on his 3398
Mk 1:19 And when he had gone a l further thence, 3641
4:36 And there were also with him other **l ships**. 4142
5:23 My **l daughter** lieth at the point of death: 2365
9:42 one of *these* **l ones** that believe in me, 3398
10:14 Suffer the **l children** to come unto me, and 3813
10:15 receive the kingdom of God as a **l child**, 3813
14:35 And he went forward a l, and fell on 3398
14:70 And a l after, they that stood by said again 3398
Lk 5: 3 prayed him that *he* would thrust out a l 3641
7:47 but to whom l is forgiven, *the same* loveth 3641
7:47 whom little is forgiven, *the same* loveth l. 3641
12:28 more *will he clothe* you, O ye **of l faith**? 3640
12:32 Fear not, l flock; for it is your Father's 3398
17: 2 that he should offend one of these **l ones**. 3398
18:16 Suffer **l children** to come unto me, and 3813
18:17 as a **l child** shall in no wise enter therein. 3813
19: 3 for the press, because he was l of stature. 3398
19:17 because thou hast been faithful in a **very l**, 1646
22:58 And after a **l while** another saw him, and 1024
Jn 6: 7 that every one of them may take a l. 1024
7:33 Yet a l while am I with you, and *then* I go 3398
12:35 Yet a l while is the light with you. 3398
13:33 **L children**, yet a little while I am with you. 5040
13:33 Little children, yet a **l while** I am with you. 3398
14:19 Yet a l while, and the world seeth me no 3398
16:16 A **l while**, and ye shall not see me: and 3398
16:16 and again, a **l while**, and ye shall see me, 3398
16:17 unto us, A **l while**, and ye shall not see me: 3398
16:17 and again, a **l while**, and ye shall see me: 3398
16:18 What is this that he saith, A **l while**? 3398
16:19 I said, A **l while**, and ye shall not see me: 3398
16:19 and again, a **l while**, and ye shall see me? 3398
21: 8 And the other disciples came in a **l ship**; 4142
Ac 5:34 to put the apostles forth a **l space**; 1024
20:12 man alive, and were not a l comforted. 3357
27:28 and when they had gone a l further, 1024
28: 2 And the barbarous people shewed us no l 5177
1Co 5: 6 Know ye not that a l leaven leaveneth 3398
2Co 8:15 and he that *had gathered* l had no lack. 3641
11: 1 Would *to God* you could bear with me a l 3398
11:16 fool receive me, that I may boast myself a l. 3398
Gal 4:19 My **l children**, of whom I travail in birth 5040
5: 9 A l leaven leaveneth the whole lump. 3398
1Ti 4: 8 For bodily exercise profiteth l: 3641
5:23 but use a l wine for thy stomach's sake and 3641
Heb 2: 7 Thou madest him a l lower than the angels; 1024
2: 9 who was made a l lower than the angels, 1024
10:37 For yet a **l while**, 3398+3745+3745
Jas 3: 5 Even so the tongue is a l member, and 3398
3: 5 Behold, how great a matter a l fire kindleth. 3641
4:14 that appeareth for a l *time,* and then 3641
1Jn 2: 1 My **l children**, these *things* write I unto 5040
2:12 **l children**, because *your* sins are forgiven 5040
2:13 **l children**, because ye have known 3813
2:18 **L children**, it is the last time: and as ye 3813
2:28 And now, **l children**, abide in him; that, 5040
3: 7 **L children**, let no *man* deceive you: he that 5040
3:18 My **l children**, let us not love in word, 5040
4: 4 **l children**, and have overcome them: 5040
5:21 **L children**, keep yourselves from idols. 5040
Rev 3: 8 for thou hast a l strength, and hast kept my 3398
6:11 that they should rest yet for a l season, 3398
10: 2 And he had in his hand a **l book** open: and 974
10: 8 take the **l book** which is open in the hand of 974
10: 9 and said unto him, Give me the **l book**. 974
10:10 And I took the **l book** out of the angel's 974
20: 3 and after that he must be loosed a l season. 3398

LIVE (247) [ALIVE, LIFE, LIFETIME, LIVED, LIVELY, LIVES, LIVEST, LIVETH, LIVING, OUTLIVED, OVERLIVED]

Ge 3:22 of the tree of life, and eat, and l for ever: 2421
12:13 and my soul shall l because of thee. 2421
17:18 O that Ishmael might l before thee! 2421
19:20 (*is* it not a little one?) and my soul shall l. 2421
20: 7 and he shall pray for thee, and thou shalt l: 2421
27:40 by thy sword shalt thou l, and shalt serve 2421
31:32 thou findest thy gods, let him not l: 2421
42: 2 us from thence; that we may l, and not die. 2421
42:18 said unto them the third day, This do, and l; 2421
43: 8 that we may l, and not die, both we, and 2421
45: 3 I *am* Joseph; doth my father yet l? 2416
47:19 give *us* seed, that we may l, and not die, 2421
Ex 1:16 but if it *be* a daughter, then she shall l. 2421
19:13 whether *it be* beast or man, it shall not l: 2421
21:35 they shall sell the l ox, and divide 2416
22:18 Thou shalt not **suffer** a witch **to l**. 2421
33:20 for there shall no man see me, and l. 2421
Lev 16:20 and the altar, he shall bring the l goat: 2416
16:21 both his hands upon the head of the l goat, 2416
18: 5 which if a man do, he shall l in them: I *am* 2421
25:35 or a sojourner; that he may l with thee. 2416
25:36 thy God; that thy brother may l with thee. 2416
Nu 4:19 do unto them, that they may l, and not die, 2421
14:21 *as* truly *as* I l, all the earth shall be filled 2416
14:28 Say unto them, *As truly as* I l, saith 2416
21: 8 is bitten, when he looketh upon it, shall l. 2421
24:23 Alas, who shall l when God doeth this! 2421
Dt 4: 1 for to do *them,* that ye may l, and go in and 2421
4:10 all the days that they shall l upon the earth, 2416
4:33 midst of the fire, as thou hast heard, and l? 2421
4:42 fleeing unto one of these cities he might l: 2421
5:33 that ye may l, and *that it may be* well with 2421
8: 1 that ye may l, and multiply, and go in and 2421
8: 3 know that man doth not l by bread only, 2421
8: 3 out of the mouth of the LORD doth man l. 2421
12: 1 all the days that ye l upon the earth. 2416
16:20 that thou mayest l, and inherit the land 2421
19: 4 which shall flee thither, that he may l: 2421
19: 5 he shall flee unto one of those cities, and l: 2421
30: 6 and with all thy soul, that thou mayest l. 2416
30:16 that thou mayest l and multiply: 2421
30:19 that *both* thou and thy seed may l: 2421
31:13 as long as ye l in the land whither ye go 2416
32:40 up my hand to heaven, and say, I l for ever. 2416
33: 6 Let Reuben l, and not die; and let *not* his 2421
Jos 6:17 only Rahab the harlot shall l, she and 2421
9:15 and made a league with them, to let them l: 2421
9:20 we will even let them l, lest wrath be upon 2421
9:21 the princes said unto them, Let them l; but 2421
1Sa 20:14 thou shalt not only while yet I l shew me 2416
2Sa 1:10 I was sure that he could not l after *that* he 2421
12:22 will be gracious to me, that the child may l? 2416
19:34 said unto the king, How long have I to l, 2416
1Ki 1:31 and said, Let my lord king David l for ever. 2421
8:40 l in the land which thou gavest unto our 2416
20:32 Ben-hadad saith, I pray thee, let me l. 2421
2Ki 4: 7 and l thou and thy children of the rest. 2421
7: 4 if they save us alive, we shall l; and if they 2421
10:19 whosoever shall be wanting, he shall not l. 2421
18:32 and of honey, that ye may l, and not die: 2421
20: 1 house in order; for thou shalt die, and not l. 2421
2Ch 6:31 long as they l in the land which thou gavest 2416
Ne 2: 3 said unto the king, Let the king l for ever: 2421
5: 2 up corn *for them,* that we may eat, and l. 2421
9:29 (which if a man do, he shall l in them;) 2421
Est 4:11 hold out the golden sceptre, that he may l: 2421
Job 7:16 I loathe *it;* I would not l alway: let me 2421
14:14 shall he l *again?* all the days of my 2421
21: 7 Wherefore do the wicked l, become old, 2421
27: 6 heart shall not reproach *me* so long as I l. 3117
Ps 22:26 that seek him: your heart shall l for ever. 2421
49: 9 That he should still l for ever, *and* not see 2421
55:23 deceitful men shall not **l out half** their 2673
63: 4 Thus will I bless thee while I l: I will lift up 2416
69:32 and your heart shall l that seek God. 2421
72:15 he shall l, and to him shall be given of 2421
104:33 I will sing unto the LORD as long as I l: 2416
116: 2 therefore will I call upon *him* as long as I l. 3117
118:17 but l, and declare the works of the LORD. 2421

Ps	119:17	*that* I may l, and keep thy word.	2421
	119:77	tender mercies come *unto* me, that I may l:	2421
	119:116	me according unto thy word, that I may l:	2421
	119:144	give me understanding, and I shall l.	2421
	119:175	Let my soul l, and it shall praise thee; and	2421
	146: 2	While I l will I praise the LORD: I will	2416
Pr	4: 4	my words: keep my commandments, and l.	2421
	7: 2	Keep my commandments, and l; and	2421
	9: 6	Forsake the foolish, and l; and go in	2421
	15:27	own house; but he that hateth gifts shall l.	2421
Ecc	6: 3	an hundred *children,* and l many years,	2421
	6: 6	though he l a thousand years twice *told,* yet	2421
	9: 3	madness *is* in their heart while they l, and	2416
	9: 9	L joyfully with the wife whom thou lovest	2416
	11: 8	if a man l many years, *and* rejoice in them	2421
Isa	6: 6	unto me, having a l **coal** in his hand,	7531
	26:14	*They are* dead, they shall not l; *they are*	2421
	26:19	Thy dead *men* shall l, *together with* my	2421
	38: 1	house in order: for thou shalt die, and not l.	2421
	38:16	by these *things men* l, and in all these	2421
	38:16	so wilt thou recover me, and **make** me **to** l.	2421
	49:18	*As* I l, saith the LORD, thou shalt surely	2416
	55: 3	hear, and your soul shall l; and I will make	2421
Jer	21: 9	he shall l, and his life shall be unto him for	2421
	22:24	*As* I l, saith the LORD, though Coniah	2416
	27:12	and serve him and his people, and l.	2421
	27:17	serve the king of Babylon, and l:	2421
	35: 7	that ye may l many days in the land where	2421
	38: 2	he that goeth forth to the Chaldeans shall l;	2421
	38: 2	he shall have his life for a prey, and shall l.	2421
	38:17	thy soul shall l, and this city shall not be	2421
	38:17	with fire; and thou shalt l, and thine house:	2421
	38:20	shall be well unto thee, and thy soul shall l.	2421
	46:18	*As* I l, saith the King, whose name *is*	2416
La	4:20	Under his shadow we shall l among	2421
Eze	3:21	shall **surely** l, because he is warned;	2421+2421
	5:11	Wherefore, *as* I l, saith the Lord GOD;	2416
	13:19	and to save the souls alive that should not l,	2421
	14:16	men *were* in it, *as* I l, saith the Lord GOD,	2416
	14:18	men *were* in it, *as* I l, saith the Lord GOD,	2416
	14:20	Daniel, and Job, *were* in it, *as* I l,	2416
	16: 6	unto thee *when thou wast* in thy blood, L;	2421
	16: 6	unto thee *when thou wast* in thy blood, L.	2421
	16:48	*As* I l, saith the Lord GOD, Sodom thy	2416
	17:16	*As* I l, saith the Lord GOD, surely in	2416
	17:19	*As* I l, surely mine oath that he hath	2416
	18: 3	*As* I l, saith the Lord GOD, ye shall not	2416
	18: 9	he *is* just, he shall **surely** l, saith	2421+2421
	18:13	shall he then l? he shall not live: he hath	2421
	18:13	he shall not l: he hath done all these	2421
	18:17	of his father, he shall **surely** l.	2421+2421
	18:19	hath done them, he shall **surely** l.	2421+2421
	18:21	is lawful and right, he shall **surely** l,	2421+2421
	18:22	righteousness that he hath done he shall l.	2421
	18:23	that he should return from his ways, and l?	2421
	18:24	that the wicked *man* doeth, shall he l?	2421
	18:28	he shall **surely** l, he shall not die.	2421+2421
	18:32	wherefore turn *yourselves,* and l ye.	2421
	20: 3	*As* I l, saith the Lord GOD, I will not be	2416
	20:11	which *if* a man do, he shall even l in them.	2421
	20:13	which *if* a man do, he shall even l in them;	2421
	20:21	which *if* a man do, he shall even l in them;	2421
	20:25	and judgments whereby they should not l;	2421
	20:31	*As* I l, saith the Lord GOD, I will not be	2416
	20:33	*As* I l, saith the Lord GOD, surely with a	2416
	33:10	pine away in them, how should we then l?	2421
	33:11	Say unto them, *As* I l, saith the Lord	2416
	33:11	but that the wicked turn from his way and l:	2421
	33:12	neither shall the righteous be able to l for	2421
	33:13	the righteous, *that* he shall **surely** l;	2421+2421
	33:15	he shall **surely** l, he shall not die.	2421+2421
	33:16	is lawful and right; he shall **surely** l.	2421+2421
	33:19	is lawful and right, he shall l thereby.	2421
	33:27	*As* I l, surely *they* that *are* in the wastes	2416
	34: 8	*As* I l, saith the Lord GOD, surely because	2416
	35: 6	Therefore, *as* I l, saith the Lord GOD, I	2416
	35:11	Therefore, *as* I l, saith the Lord GOD,	2416
	37: 3	unto me, Son of man, can these bones l?	2421
	37: 5	breath to enter into you, and ye shall l:	2421
	37: 6	and put breath in you, and ye shall l;	2421
	37: 9	breathe upon these slain, that they may l.	2421
	37:14	ye shall l, and I shall place you in your own	2421
	47: 9	whithersoever the rivers shall come, shall l:	2421
	47: 9	every *thing* shall l whither the river cometh.	2416
Da	2: 4	to the king in Syriack, O king, l for ever:	2418
	3: 9	king Nebuchadnezzar, O king, l for ever.	2418
	5:10	queen spake and said, O king, l for ever:	2418
	6: 6	said thus unto him, King Darius, l for ever.	2418
	6:21	Daniel unto the king, O king, l for ever.	2418
Hos	6: 2	will raise us up, and we shall l in his sight.	2421
Am	5: 4	house of Israel, Seek ye me, and ye shall l:	2421
	5: 6	Seek the LORD, and ye shall l; lest he	2421
	5:14	Seek good, and not evil, that ye may l: and	2421
Jnh	4: 3	for *it is* better for me to die than to l.	2416
	4: 8	and said, *It is* better for me to die than to l.	2416
Hab	2: 4	in him: but the just shall l by his faith.	2421
Zep	2: 9	Therefore *as* I l, saith the LORD of hosts,	2416
Zec	1: 5	and the prophets, do they l for ever?	2421
	10: 9	they shall l with their children, and	2421
	13: 3	him shall say unto him, Thou shalt not l;	2421
Mt	4: 4	Man shall not l by bread alone, but	*2198*
	9:18	and lay thy hand upon her, and she shall l.	*2198*
Mk	5:23	that she may be healed; and she shall l.	*2198*
Lk	4: 4	That man shall not l by bread alone, but	*2198*
	7:25	and l delicately, are in kings' courts.	*5225*
	10:28	answered right: this do, and thou shalt l.	*2198*
	20:38	but of the living: for all l unto him.	*2198*
Jn	5:25	the Son of God: and they that hear shall l.	*2198*
	6:51	*man* eat of this bread, he shall l for ever:	*2198*
	6:57	Father hath sent me, and I l by the Father:	*2198*
	6:57	so he that eateth me, even he shall l by me.	*2198*
	6:58	he that eateth *of* this bread shall l for ever.	*2198*
	11:25	in me, though he were dead, *yet* shall he l:	*2198*
	14:19	ye see me: because I l, ye shall live also.	*2198*
	14:19	ye see me: because I live, ye shall l also.	*2198*
Ac	7:19	young children, to the end *they* might not l.	*2225*
	17:28	For in him we l, and move, and have our	*2198*
	22:22	the earth: for it is not fit that he should l.	*2198*
	25:24	crying that he ought not to l any longer.	*2198*
	28: 4	the sea, yet Vengeance suffereth not to l.	*2198*
Ro	1:17	as it is written, The just shall l by faith.	*2198*
	6: 2	that are dead to sin, l any longer therein?	*2198*
	6: 8	we believe that we shall also **l with** him:	*4800*
	8:12	not to the flesh, to l after the flesh.	*2198*
	8:13	For if ye l after the flesh, ye shall die: but	*2198*
	8:13	do mortify the deeds of the body, ye shall l.	*2198*
	10: 5	which doeth those *things* shall l by them.	*2198*
	12:18	as lieth in you, **l peaceably** with all men.	*1514*
	14: 8	For whether we l, we live unto the Lord;	*2198*
	14: 8	For whether we live, we l unto the Lord;	*2198*
	14: 8	whether we l therefore, or die, we are	*2198*
	14:11	For it is written, *As* I l, saith the Lord,	*2198*
1Co	9:13	holy *things* l of *the things of* the temple?	*2068*
	9:14	preach the gospel should l of the gospel.	*2198*
2Co	4:11	For we which l are alway delivered unto	*2198*
	5:15	that they which l should not henceforth live	*2198*
	5:15	that they which live should not henceforth l	*2198*
	6: 9	as dying, and behold, we l; as chastened,	*2198*
	7: 3	you are in our hearts to die and **l with** *you.*	*4800*
	13: 4	we shall l with him by the power of God	*2198*
	13:11	good comfort, be of one mind, **l in peace**;	*1514*
Gal	2:14	thou the Gentiles to l **as do the Jews**?	*2450*
	2:19	am dead to the law, that I might l unto God.	*2198*
	2:20	nevertheless I l; yet not I, but Christ liveth	*2198*
	2:20	*the life* which I now l in the flesh I live by	*2198*
	2:20	*the life* which I now live in the flesh I l by	*2198*
	3:11	*it is* evident: for, The just shall l by faith.	*2198*
	3:12	The man that doeth them shall l in them.	*2198*
	5:25	If we l in the Spirit, let us also walk in	*2198*
Eph	6: 3	and thou mayest **l long** on the earth.	*1510+3118*
Php	1:21	For to me to l *is* Christ, and to die *is* gain.	*2198*
	1:22	But if I l in the flesh, this *is* the fruit of my	*2198*
1Th	3: 8	For now we l, if ye stand fast in the Lord.	*2198*
	5:10	or sleep, we should l together with him.	*2198*
2Ti	2:11	be dead with *him,* we shall also **l with** *him:*	*4800*
	3:12	all that will l godly in Christ Jesus shall	*2198*
Tit	2:12	and worldly lusts we should l soberly,	*2198*
Heb	10:38	Now the just shall l by faith: but if *any man*	*2198*
	12: 9	subjection unto the Father of spirits, and l?	*2198*
	13:18	in all *things* willing to l honestly.	*390*
Jas	4:15	Lord will, we shall l, and do this, or that.	*2198*
1Pe	2:24	dead to sins, should l unto righteousness:	*2198*
	4: 2	That *he* no longer should l the rest of *his*	*980*
	4: 6	but l according to God in the spirit.	*2198*
2Pe	2: 6	unto **those that** after should **l ungodly**;	*764*
	2:18	clean escaped from them who l in error.	*390*
1Jn	4: 9	into the world, that we might l through him.	*2198*
Rev	13:14	which had the wound by a sword, and did l.	*2198*

LIVED (58) [LIVE]

Ge	5: 3	Adam l an hundred and thirty years, and	2421
	5: 5	all the days that Adam l were nine hundred	2421
	5: 6	Seth l an hundred and five years, and	2421
	5: 7	Seth l after he begat Enos eight hundred	2421
	5: 9	And Enos l ninety years, and begat Cainan:	2421
	5:10	Enos l after he begat Cainan eight hundred	2421
	5:12	Cainan l seventy years, and	2421
	5:13	Cainan l after he begat Mahalaleel eight	2421
	5:15	Mahalaleel l sixty and five years, and	2421
	5:16	Mahalaleel l after he begat Jared eight	2421
	5:18	And Jared l an hundred sixty and two years,	2421
	5:19	Jared l after he begat Enoch eight hundred	2421
	5:21	Enoch l sixty and five years, and	2421
	5:25	Methuselah l an hundred eighty and seven	2421
	5:26	Methuselah l after he begat Lamech seven	2421
	5:28	Lamech l an hundred eighty and two years,	2421
	5:30	Lamech l after he begat Noah five hundred	2421
	9:28	Noah l after the flood three hundred and	2421
	11:11	Shem l after he begat Arphaxad five	2421
	11:12	Arphaxad l five and thirty years, and	2421
	11:13	Arphaxad l after he begat Salah four	2421
	11:14	And Salah l thirty years, and begat Eber:	2421
	11:15	Salah l after he begat Eber four hundred	2421
	11:16	Eber l four and thirty years, and	2421
	11:17	Eber l after he begat Peleg four hundred	2421
	11:18	And Peleg l thirty years, and begat Reu:	2421
	11:19	And Peleg l after he begat Reu two hundred	2421
	11:20	Reu l two and thirty years, and begat Serug:	2421
	11:21	Reu l after he begat Serug two hundred	2421
	11:22	And Serug l thirty years, and begat Nahor:	2421
	11:23	Serug l after he begat Nahor two hundred	2421
	11:24	Nahor l nine and twenty years, and	2421
	11:25	Nahor l after he begat Terah an hundred	2421
	11:26	Terah l seventy years, and begat Abram,	2421
	25: 6	while he yet l, eastward, unto the east	2416
	25: 7	of the years of Abraham's life which he l,	2421
	47:28	Jacob l in the land of Egypt seventeen	2421
	50:22	and Joseph l an hundred and ten years.	2421
Nu	14:38	the men that went to search the land, l *still.*	2421
	21: 9	when he beheld the serpent of brass, he l.	2421
Dt	5:26	of the midst of the fire, as we *have,* and l?	2421
2Sa	19: 6	that if Absalom had l, and all we had died	2416
1Ki	12: 6	Solomon his father while he *yet* l,	1961+2416
2Ki	14:17	Amaziah the son of Joash king of Judah l	2421
2Ch	10: 6	before Solomon his father while he *yet* l,	2416
	25:25	Amaziah the son of Joash king of Judah l	2421
Job	42:16	After this l Job an hundred and forty years,	2421
Ps	49:18	Though whiles he l he blessed his soul: and	2416
Eze	37:10	they l, and stood up upon their feet,	2421
Lk	2:36	had l with a husband seven years from her	*2198*
Ac	23: 1	I have l in all good conscience before God	*4176*
	26: 5	straitest sect of our religion I l a Pharisee.	*2198*
Col	3: 7	also walked sometime, when ye l in them.	*2198*
Jas	5: 5	Ye have **l in pleasure** on the earth, and	*5171*
Rev	18: 7	and l **deliciously**, so much torment and	*4763*
	18: 9	and l **deliciously** with her,	*4763*
	20: 4	and they l and reigned with Christ a	*2198*
	20: 5	But the rest of the dead l not **again** until	*326*

LIVELY (5) [LIVE]

Ex	1:19	for they *are* l, and are delivered ere	2422
Ps	38:19	mine enemies *are* l, *and* they are strong:	2416
Ac	7:38	who received *the* l oracles to give unto us:	*2198*
1Pe	1: 3	l hope by the resurrection of Jesus Christ	*2198*
	2: 5	Ye also, as l stones, are built *up* a spiritual	*2198*

LIVER (14)

Ex	29:13	the caul *that is* above the l, and the two	3516
	29:22	the caul *above* the l, and the two kidneys,	3516
Lev	3: 4	the caul above the l, with the kidneys,	3516
	3:10	the caul above the l, with the kidneys,	3516
	3:15	the caul above the l, with the kidneys,	3516
	4: 9	the caul above the l, with the kidneys,	3516
	7: 4	the caul *that is* above the l, with	3516
	8:16	the caul *above* the l, and the two kidneys,	3516
	8:25	the caul *above* the l, and the two kidneys,	3516
	9:10	and the caul above the l of the sin offering,	3516
	9:19	and the kidneys, and the caul *above* the l:	3516
Pr	7:23	Till a dart strike through his l; as a bird	3516
La	2:11	are troubled, my l is poured upon the earth,	3516
Eze	21:21	consulted with images, he looked in the l.	3516

LIVES (28) [LIFE]

Ge	9: 5	surely your blood of your l will I require;	5315
	45: 7	and to **save** your l by a great deliverance.	2421
	47:25	they said, Thou hast **saved** our l: let us find	2421
Ex	1:14	they made their l bitter with hard bondage,	2416
Jos	2:13	that they have, and deliver our l from death.	5315
	9:24	we were sore afraid of our l because of you,	5315
Jdg	5:18	l unto the death in the high places of	5315
	18:25	lose thy life, with the l of thy household.	5315
2Sa	1:23	*were* lovely and pleasant in their l,	2416
	19: 5	the l of thy sons and of thy daughters, and	5315
	19: 5	the l of thy wives, and the lives of thy	5315
	19: 5	of thy wives, and the l of thy concubines;	5315
	23:17	of the men that went in *jeopardy of* their l?	5315
1Ch	11:19	these men that have put their l in jeopardy?	5315
	11:19	for with *the jeopardy of* their l they brought	5315
Est	9:16	stood for their l, and had rest from their	5315
Pr	1:18	own blood; they lurk privily for their own l.	5315
Jer	19: 7	and by the hands of them that seek their l:	5315
	19: 9	they that seek their l, shall straiten them.	5315
	46:26	them into the hand of those that seek their l,	5315
	48: 6	save your l, and be like the heath in	5315
La	5: 9	We gat our bread with *the peril of* our l	5315
Da	7:12	yet their l were prolonged for a season and	2417
Lk	9:56	Son of man is not come to destroy men's l,	*5590*
Ac	15:26	Men that have hazarded their l for the name	*5590*
	27:10	of the lading and ship, but also of our l.	*5590*
1Jn	3:16	we ought to lay down *our* l for the brethren.	*5590*
Rev	12:11	and they loved not their l unto the death.	*5590*

LIVEST (4) [LIVE]

Dt	12:19	the Levite as long as thou ls upon the earth.	3117
2Sa	11:11	*as* thou l, and *as* thy soul liveth, I will not	2416
Gal	2:14	l after the manner of Gentiles, and not as do	*2198*
Rev	3: 1	that thou hast a name that thou l, and	*2198*

LIVETH (96) [LIVE]

Ge	9: 3	Every moving thing that l shall be meat for	2416
Dt	5:24	day that God doth talk with man, and he l.	2421
Jdg	8:19	*as* the LORD l, if ye had saved them alive,	2416
Ru	3:13	part of a kinsman to thee, *as* the LORD l:	2416
1Sa	1:26	she said, O my lord, *as* thy soul l, my lord,	2416
	1:28	as long as he l he *shall be* lent to	1961
	14:39	For, *as* the LORD l, which saveth Israel,	2416
	14:45	*as* the LORD l, there shall not one hair of	2416
	17:55	*As* thy soul l, O king, I cannot tell.	2416
	19: 6	Saul sware, *As* the LORD l, he shall not	2416
	20: 3	truly *as* the LORD l, and *as* thy soul	2416
	20: 3	*as* thy soul l, *there is* but a step between me	2416
	20:21	peace to thee, and no hurt; *as* the LORD l.	2416
	20:31	For as long as the son of Jesse l upon	2416
	25: 6	thus shall ye say to him that l *in prosperity,*	2416
	25:26	*as* the LORD l, and *as* thy soul liveth,	2416
	25:26	*as* the LORD liveth, and *as* thy soul l,	2416
	25:34	in very deed, *as* the LORD God of Israel l,	2416
	26:10	David said furthermore, *As* the LORD l,	2416
	26:16	*As* the LORD l, ye *are* worthy to die,	2416
	28:10	by the LORD, saying, *As* the LORD l,	2416
	29: 6	said unto him, Surely, *as* the LORD l,	2416
2Sa	2:27	Joab said, *As* God l, unless thou hadst	2416
	4: 9	and said unto them, *As* the LORD l,	2416
	11:11	*as* thou livest, and *as* thy soul l, I will not	2416
	12: 5	he said to Nathan, *As* the LORD l,	2416
	14:11	he said, *As* the LORD l, there shall not	2416
	14:19	woman answered and said, *As* thy soul l,	2416
	15:21	*As* the LORD l, and *as* my lord the king	2416
	15:21	LORD liveth, and *as* my lord the king l,	2416
	22:47	The LORD l; and blessed *be* my rock; and	2416
1Ki	1:29	the king sware, and said, *As* the LORD l,	2416
	2:24	Now therefore, *as* the LORD l, which hath	2416
	3:23	This *is* my son that l, and thy son *is*	2416
	17: 1	unto Ahab, *As* the LORD God of Israel l,	2416
	17:12	she said, *As* the LORD thy God l, I have	2416
	17:23	his mother: and Elijah said, See, thy son l.	2416
	18:10	*As* the LORD thy God l, there is no nation	2416
	18:15	Elijah said, *As* the LORD of hosts l,	2416
	22:14	Micaiah said, *As* the LORD l, what	2416
2Ki	2: 2	And Elisha said *unto him, As* the LORD l,	2416
	2: 2	and *as* thy soul l, I will not leave thee.	2416
	2: 4	*As* the LORD l, and *as* thy soul liveth,	2416
	2: 4	and *as* thy soul l, I will not leave thee.	2416
	2: 6	*As* the LORD l, and *as* thy soul liveth,	2416
	2: 6	and *as* thy soul l, I will not leave thee.	2416
	3:14	Elisha said, *As* the LORD of hosts l,	2416

L

2Ki 4:30 *As* the LORD l, and *as* thy soul liveth, 2416
4:30 and *as* thy soul l, I will not leave thee. 2416
5:16 he said, *As* the LORD l, before whom I 2416
5:20 but, *as* the LORD l, I will run after him, 2416
2Ch 18:13 Micaiah said, As the LORD l, even what 2416
Job 19:25 For I know *that* my Redeemer l, and *that* he 2416
27: 2 *As* God l, *who* hath taken away my 2416
Ps 18:46 The LORD l; and blessed *be* my rock; and 2416
89:48 What man *is he that* l, and shall not see 2421
Jer 4: 2 The LORD l, in truth, in judgment, and 2416
5: 2 though they say, The LORD l; surely they 2416
12:16 to swear by my name, The LORD l; 2416
16:14 that it shall no more be said, The LORD l, 2416
16:15 But, The LORD l, that brought up 2416
23: 7 that they shall no more say, The LORD l, 2416
23: 8 But, The LORD l, which brought up and 2416
38:16 saying, *As* the LORD l, that made us this 2416
44:26 land of Egypt, saying, The Lord GOD l. 2416
Eze 47: 9 *that* every thing that l, which moveth, 2416
Da 4:34 I praised and honoured him that l for ever, 2417
12: 7 sware by him that l for ever that *it shall be* 2416
Hos 4:15 up *to* Beth-aven, nor swear, The LORD l. 2416
Am 8:14 sin of Samaria, and say, Thy god, O Dan, l; 2416
8:14 liveth; and, The manner of Beer-sheba l; 2416
Jn 4:50 Jesus saith unto him, Go *thy way;* thy son l. 2198
4:51 met him, and told *him,* saying, Thy son l. 2198
4:53 in the which Jesus said unto him, Thy son l: 2198
11:26 And whosoever l and believeth in me shall 2198
Ro 6:10 but in that he l, he liveth unto God. 2198
6:10 but in that he liveth, he l unto God. 2198
7: 1 hath dominion over a man, as long as he l? 2198
7: 2 by the law to *her* husband so long as he l; 2198
7: 3 So then if, while *her* husband l, she be 2198
14: 7 For none of us l to himself, and no *man* 2198
1Co 7:39 bound by the law as long as her husband l; 2198
2Co 13: 4 yet he l by the power of God. 2198
Gal 2:20 I live; yet not I, but Christ l in me: 2198
1Ti 5: 6 But she that l **in pleasure** is dead while she 4684
5: 6 that liveth in pleasure is dead while she l. 2198
Heb 7: 8 *them,* of whom it is witnessed that he l. 2198
7:25 seeing he ever l to make intercession for 2198
9:17 is of no strength at all whilst the testator l. 2198
1Pe 1:23 word of God, which l and abideth for ever. 2198
Rev 1:18 I am he that l, and was dead; and behold, 2198
4: 9 sat on the throne, who l for ever and ever, 2198
4:10 and worship him that l for ever and ever, 2198
5:14 and worshipped him that l for ever and 2198
10: 6 And sware by him that l for ever and ever, 2198
15: 7 the wrath of God, who l for ever and ever. 2198

LIVING (147) [LIVE]
Ge 1:21 and every l creature that moveth, 2416
1:24 Let the earth bring forth the l creature after 2416
1:28 over every l **thing** that moveth upon 2416
2: 7 the breath of life; and man became a l soul. 2416
2:19 whatsoever Adam called every l creature, 2416
3:20 because she was the mother of all l. 2416
6:19 of every l *thing* of all flesh, two of every 2416
7: 4 every l **substance** that I have made will I 3351
7:23 every l **substance** was destroyed which 3351
8: 1 every l **thing**, and all the cattle that *was* 2416
8:17 Bring forth with thee every l **thing** that *is* 2416
8:21 will I again smite any more every *thing* l, 2416
9:10 with every l creature that *is* with you, of 2416
9:12 and every l creature that *is* with you, 2416
9:15 and you and every l creature of all flesh; 2416
9:16 every l creature of all flesh that *is* upon 2416
Lev 11:10 and of any l thing which *is* in the waters, 2416
11:46 of every l creature that moveth in 2416
14: 6 As for the l bird, he shall take it, and 2416
14: 6 the l bird in the blood of the bird *that was* 2416
14: 7 shall let the l bird loose into the open field. 2416
14:51 the l bird, and dip them in the blood of 2416
14:52 with the l bird, and with the cedar wood, 2416
14:53 he shall let go the l bird out of the city into 2416
20:25 by any *manner of l thing* that creepeth *on* NIH
Nu 16:48 he stood between the dead and the l; and 2416
Dt 5:26 that hath heard the voice of the l God 2416
Jos 3:10 Hereby ye shall know that the l God *is* 2416
Ru 2:20 who hath not left off his kindness to the l 2416
1Sa 17:26 that he should defy the armies of the l God? 2416
17:36 seeing he hath defied the armies of the l 2416
2Sa 20: 3 unto the day of their death, l in widowhood. 2424
1Ki 3:22 but the l *is* my son, and the dead *is* thy son. 2416
3:22 but the dead *is* thy son, and the l *is* my son. 2416
3:23 but thy son *is* the dead, and my son *is* the l. 2416
3:25 Divide the l child in two, and give half to 2416
3:26 spake the woman whose the l child *was* 2416
3:26 give her the l child, and in no wise slay it. 2416
3:27 Give her the l child, and in no wise slay it: 2416
2Ki 19: 4 his master hath sent to reproach the l God; 2416
19:16 which hath sent him to reproach the l God. 2416
Job 12:10 In whose hand *is* the soul of every l *thing,* 2416
28:13 neither is it found in the land of the l. 2416
28:21 Seeing it is hid from the eyes of all l, and 2416
30:23 and *to* the house appointed for all l. 2416
33:30 to be enlightened with the light of the l. 2416
Ps 27:13 goodness of the LORD in the land of the l. 2416
42: 2 My soul thirsteth for God, for the l God: 2416
52: 5 and root thee out of the land of the l. 2416
56:13 *I* may walk before God in the light of the l? 2416
58: 9 with a whirlwind, both l, and in *his* wrath. 2416
69:28 Let them be blotted out of the book of the l, 2416
84: 2 and my flesh crieth out for the l God. 2416
116: 9 walk before the LORD in the land of the l. 2416
142: 5 *and* my portion in the land of the l. 2416
143: 2 for in thy sight shall no *man* l be justified. 2416
145:16 and satisfiest the desire of every **l thing**. 2416
Ecc 4: 2 dead more than the l which are yet alive. 2416
4:15 I considered all the l which walk under 2416
6: 8 the poor, that knoweth to walk before the l? 2416
7: 2 of all men; and the l will lay *it* to his heart. 2416
9: 4 For to him that is joined to all the l there is 2416
9: 4 for a l dog *is* better than a dead lion. 2416
9: 5 For the l know that they shall die: but 2416
SS 4:15 a well of l waters, and streams from 2416
Isa 4: 3 *even* every one that is written among the l 2416
8:19 seek unto their God? for the l to the dead? 2416
37: 4 his master hath sent to reproach the l God, 2416
37:17 which hath sent to reproach the l God. 2416
38:11 *even* the LORD, in the land of the l: 2416
38:19 The l, the living, he shall praise thee, as I 2416
38:19 The living, the l, he shall praise thee, as I 2416
53: 8 for he was cut off out of the land of the l: 2416
Jer 2:13 they have forsaken me the fountain of l 2416
10:10 he *is* the l God, and an everlasting king: 2416
11:19 and let us cut him off from the land of the l, 2416
17:13 the LORD, the fountain of l waters. 2416
23:36 for ye have perverted the words of the l 2416
La 3:39 Wherefore doth a l man complain, a man 2416
Eze 1: 5 *came* the likeness of four l **creatures**. 2416
1:13 As for the likeness of the l **creatures**, 2416
1:13 went up and down among the l **creatures**; 2416
1:14 the l **creatures** ran and returned as 2416
1:15 Now as I beheld the l **creatures**, behold 2416
1:15 wheel upon the earth by the l **creatures**, 2416
1:19 when the l **creatures** went, the wheels went 2416
1:19 when the l **creatures** were lift up from 2416
1:20 for the spirit of the l **creature** *was* in 2416
1:21 for the spirit of the l **creature** *was* in 2416
1:22 l **creature** *was* as the colour of the terrible 2416
3:13 of the l **creatures** that touched one another, 2416
10:15 This *is* the l **creature** that I saw by the river 2416
10:17 for the spirit of the l **creature** *was* in them. 2416
10:20 This *is* the l **creature** that I saw under 2416
26:20 and I shall set glory in the land of the l; 2416
32:23 which caused terror in the land of the l. 2416
32:24 caused their terror in the land of the l; 2416
32:25 their terror was caused in the land of the l, 2416
32:26 they caused their terror in the land of the l. 2416
32:27 the terror of the mighty in the land of the l. 2416
32:32 I have caused my terror in the land of the l: 2416
Da 2:30 for *any* wisdom that I have more than any l, 2417
4:17 to the intent that the l may know that 2417
6:20 O Daniel, servant of the l God, is thy God, 2417
6:26 for he *is* the l God, and stedfast for ever, 2417
Hos 1:10 unto them, *Ye are* the sons of the l God. 2416
Zec 14: 8 *that* l waters shall go out from Jerusalem; 2416
Mt 16:16 Thou art the Christ, the Son of the l God. 2198
22:32 God is not the God of the dead, but of the l. 2198
26:63 said unto him, I adjure thee by the l God, 2198
Mk 12:27 the God of the dead, but the God of the l: 2198
12:44 did cast in all that she had, *even* all her l. 979
Lk 8:43 which had spent all *her* l upon physicians, 979
15:12 to *me.* And he divided unto them *his* l. 979
15:13 there wasted his substance with riotous l. 2198
15:30 which hath devoured thy l with harlots, 979
20:38 For he is not a God of the dead, but of the l: 2198

Lk 21: 4 she of her penury hath cast in all the l that *979*
24: 5 Why seek ye the l among the dead? *2198*
Jn 4:10 and he would have given thee l water. *2198*
4:11 from whence then hast thou *that* l water? *2198*
6:51 I am the l bread which came down from *2198*
6:57 As the l Father hath sent me, and I live by *2198*
6:69 thou art *that* Christ, the Son of the l God. *2198*
7:38 out of his belly shall flow rivers of l water. *2198*
Ac 14:15 turn from these vanities unto the l God, *2198*
Ro 9:26 they be called the children of the l God. *2198*
12: 1 that *ye* present your bodies a l sacrifice, *2198*
14: 9 he might be Lord both of the dead and l. *2198*
1Co 15:45 The first man Adam was made a l soul; *2198*
2Co 3: 3 with ink, but with the Spirit of the l God; *2198*
6:16 for ye are the temple of the l God; as God *2198*
Col 2:20 why, as though l in the world, are ye *2198*
1Th 1: 9 ye turned to God from idols to serve the l *2198*
1Ti 3:15 which is the church of the l God, the pillar *2198*
4:10 because we trust in the l God, *2198*
6:17 trust in uncertain riches, but in the l God, *2198*
Tit 3: 3 l in malice and envy, hateful, *and* *1236*
Heb 3:12 of unbelief, in departing from the l God. *2198*
9:14 from dead works to serve the l God? *2198*
10:20 *By* a new and l way, which he hath *2198*
10:31 *thing* to fall into the hands of the l God. *2198*
12:22 and unto the city of the l God, the heavenly *2198*
1Pe 2: 4 To whom coming, *as unto* a l stone, *2198*
Rev 7: 2 from the east, having the seal of the l God: *2198*
7:17 shall lead them unto l fountains of waters: *2198*
16: 3 dead *man:* and every l soul died in the sea. *2198*

LIZARD (1)
Lev 11:30 and the l, and the snail, and the mole. 3911

LO (159) See Index

LOAD See LADE; LADED; LADING

LOADEN (1) [LOADETH]
Isa 46: 1 your carriages *were* **heavy l**; *they are* a 6006

LOADETH (1) [LOADEN]
Ps 68:19 *who* daily l us *with benefits, even* the God 6006

LOAF (3) [LOAVES]
Ex 29:23 one l of bread, and one cake of oiled bread, 3603
1Ch 16: 3 to every one a l of bread, and a good piece 3603
Mk 8:14 they in the ship with them more than one l. *740*

LO-AMMI (1) [AMMI]
Hos 1: 9 said *God,* Call his name L: for ye *are* not 3818

LOAN (1)
1Sa 2:20 for the l which is lent to the LORD. 7596

LOATHE (1) [LOATHETH, LOATHSOME, LOTHE]
Job 7:16 I l *it;* I would not live alway: let me alone; 3988

LOATHETH (2) [LOATHE]
Nu 21: 5 *any* water; and our soul l *this* light bread. 6973
Pr 27: 7 The full soul l a honeycomb; but *to* 947

LOATHSOME (4) [LOATHE]
Nu 11:20 out at your nostrils, and it be l unto you: 2214
Job 7: 5 of dust; my skin is broken, and **become l**. 3988
Ps 38: 7 For my loins are filled *with* a l *disease:* and 7033
Pr 13: 5 but a wicked *man* is l, and cometh to shame. 887

LOAVES (32) [LOAF]
Lev 23:17 habitations two wave l of two tenth deals: 3899
Jdg 8: 5 l of bread unto the people that follow me; 3603
1Sa 10: 3 another carrying three l of bread, and 3603
10: 4 salute thee, and give thee two *l* of bread; NIH
17:17 ephah of this parched *corn,* and these ten l, 3899
21: 3 give *me* five *l of* bread in mine hand, or NIH
25:18 took two hundred l, and two bottles of 3899
2Sa 16: 1 upon them two hundred *l of* bread, and NIH
1Ki 14: 3 And take with thee ten l, and cracknels, and 3899
2Ki 4:42 twenty l of barley, and full ears of corn in 3899
Mt 14:17 We have here but five l, and two fishes. *740*
14:19 and took the five l, and the two fishes, and *740*
14:19 and gave the l to *his* disciples, and *740*
15:34 Jesus saith unto them, How many l have ye? *740*
15:36 And he took the seven l and the fishes, and *740*
16: 9 neither remember the five l of the five *740*
16:10 Neither the seven l of the four thousand, and *740*
Mk 6:38 He saith unto them, How many l have ye? go *740*
6:41 And when he had taken the five l and *740*
6:41 and brake the l, and gave *them* to his *740*
6:44 And they that did eat *of* the l were about five *740*
6:52 For they considered not *the miracle* of the l: *740*
8: 5 And he asked them, How many l have ye? *740*
8: 6 and he took the seven l, and gave thanks, and *740*
8:19 When I brake the five l among five *740*
Lk 9:13 We have no more but five l and two fishes; *740*
9:16 Then he took the five l and the two fishes, *740*
11: 5 and say unto him, Friend, lend me three l; *740*
Jn 6: 9 which hath five barley l, and two small *740*
6:11 And Jesus took the l; and when he had given *740*
6:13 with the fragments of the five barley l, *740*
6:26 but because ye did eat of the l, and *740*

LOCK (2) [LOCKED, LOCKS]
SS 5: 5 smelling myrrh, upon the handles of the l. 4514
Eze 8: 3 of a hand, and took me by a l of mine head; 6734

LOCKED (2) [LOCK]
Jdg 3:23 doors of the parlour upon him, and l *them.* 5274
3:24 the doors of the parlour *were* l, they said, 5274

LOCKS (15) [LOCK]
Nu 6: 5 shall let the l of the hair of his head grow. 6545
Jdg 16:13 If thou weavest the seven l of my head with 4253
16:19 she caused *him* to shave off the seven l of 4253
Ne 3: 3 the l thereof, and the bars thereof. 4514
3: 6 and the l thereof, and the bars thereof. 4514
3:13 the l thereof, and the bars thereof, and 4514
3:14 the l thereof, and the bars thereof. 4514
3:15 the l thereof, and the bars thereof, and 4514
SS 4: 1 *art* fair; thou *hast* doves' eyes within thy l: 6777
4: 3 like a piece of a pomegranate within thy l. 6777
5: 2 *and* my l *with* the drops of the night. 6977
5:11 his l *are* bushy, *and* black as a raven. 6977
6: 7 a pomegranate *are* thy temples within thy l. 6777
Isa 47: 2 uncover thy l, make bare the leg, 6777
Eze 44:20 their heads, nor suffer *their* l to grow long; 6545

LOCUST (11) [LOCUSTS]
Ex 10:19 there remained not one l in all the coasts of 697
Lev 11:22 the l after his kind, and the bald locust after 697
11:22 the **bald l** after his kind, and the beetle after 5556
Dt 28:38 *but* little in; for the l shall consume it. 697
28:42 and fruit of thy land shall the l consume. 6767
1Ki 8:37 blasting, mildew, l, *or* if there be caterpillar; 697
Ps 78:46 the caterpillar, and their labour unto the l. 697
109:23 I am tossed up and down as the l. 697
Joel 1: 4 the palmerworm hath left hath the l eaten; 697
1: 4 that which the l hath left hath 697
2:25 I will restore to you the years that the l hath 697

LOCUSTS (17) [LOCUST]
Ex 10: 4 to morrow will I bring the l into thy coast: 697
10:12 thine hand over the land of Egypt for the l, 697
10:13 it was morning, the east wind brought the l. 697
10:14 And the l went up over all the land of Egypt, 697
10:14 before them there were no such l as they, 697
10:19 which took away the l, and cast them into 697
2Ch 6:28 be blasting, or mildew, l, or caterpillars; 697
7:13 or if I command the l to devour the land, or 2284
Ps 105:34 the l came, and caterpillars, and that without 697
Pr 30:27 The l have no king, yet go they forth all of 697
Isa 33: 4 and fro of l shall he run upon them. 1357
Na 3:15 the cankerworm, make thyself many as the l. 697
3:17 Thy crowned *are* as the l, and thy captains as 697
Mt 3: 4 his loins; and his meat was l and wild honey. *200*
Mk 1: 6 his loins; and he did eat l and wild honey; *200*
Rev 9: 3 And there came out of the smoke l upon *200*
9: 7 And the shapes of the l *were* like unto horses *200*

LOD (4)
1Ch 8:12 and Shamed, who built Ono, and L, 3850
Ezr 2:33 The children of L, Hadid, and Ono, 3850
Ne 7:37 The children of L, Hadid, and Ono, 3850
11:35 L, and Ono, the valley of craftsmen. 3850

LO-DEBAR (3)
2Sa 9: 4 house of Machir, the son of Ammiel, in L. 3810
9: 5 of Machir, the son of Ammiel, from L. 3810
17:27 Machir the son of Ammiel of L, and 3810

LODGE (27) [LODGED, LODGEST, LODGETH, LODGING, LODGINGS]
Ge 24:23 room *in* thy father's house for us to **l in**? 3885
24:25 and provender enough, and room to **l in**. 3885
Nu 22: 8 L here *this* night, and I will bring you word 3885
Jos 4: 3 lodging place, where you shall l *this* night. 3885
Jdg 19: 9 behold, the day groweth to an end, l here, 3885
19:11 in into this city of the Jebusites, and l in it. 3885
19:13 near to one of *these* places to **l all night**, 3885
19:15 aside thither, to go in *and* to l in Gibeah: 3885
19:20 wants *lie* upon me; only l not in the street. 3885
20: 4 to Benjamin, I and my concubine, to l. 3885
Ru 1:16 I will go; and where thou lodgest, I will l: 3885
2Sa 17: 8 man of war, and will not l with the people. 3885
17:16 L not *this* night in the plains of 3885
Ne 4:22 Let every one with his servant l within 3885
13:21 said unto them, Why l ye about the wall? 3885
Job 24: 7 They **cause** the naked **to** l without clothing, 3885
31:32 The stranger did not l in the street: *but* 3885
SS 7:11 forth *into* the field; let us l in the villages. 3885
Isa 1: 8 as a l in a garden of cucumbers, as a 4412
21:13 In the forest in Arabia shall ye l, O ye 3885
65: 4 l in the monuments, which eat swine's 3885
Jer 4:14 How long shall thy vain thoughts l within 3885
Zep 2:14 the bittern shall l in the upper lintels of it; 3885
Mt 13:32 the air come and l in the branches thereof. *2681*
Mk 4:32 that the fowls of the air may l under *2681*
Lk 9:12 round about, and l, and get victuals: *2647*
Ac 21:16 an old disciple, with whom we should l. *3579*

LODGED (21) [LODGE]
Ge 32:13 he l there that *same* night; and took of that 3885
32:21 and himself l that night in the company. 3885
Jos 2: 1 a harlot's house, named Rahab, and l there. 7901
3: 1 and l there before they passed over. 3885
4: 8 with them unto the **place where** they l, 4411
6:11 they came *into* the camp, and l in the camp. 3885
8: 9 but Joshua l that night among the people. 3885
Jdg 18: 2 to the house of Micah, they l there. 3885
19: 4 so they did eat and drink, and l there. 3885
19: 7 in law urged him: therefore he l there again. 3885
1Ki 19: 9 he came thither unto a cave, and l there; 3885
1Ch 9:27 they l round about the house of God, 3885
Ne 13:20 sellers of all *kind of* ware l without 3885
Isa 1:21 righteousness l in it; but now murderers. 3885
Mt 21:17 out of the city into Bethany; and he l there. *835*
Lk 13:19 the fowls of the air l in the branches of it. *2681*
Ac 10:18 which was surnamed Peter, were l there. *3579*
10:23 l *them*. And on the morrow Peter went *3579*
10:32 he is l in the house of *one* Simon a tanner *3579*
28: 7 and l *us* three days courteously. *3579*
1Ti 5:10 up children, if she have **l strangers**, *3580*

LODGEST (1) [LODGE]
Ru 1:16 I will go; and where thou l, I will lodge: 3885

LODGETH (1) [LODGE]
Ac 10: 6 He l with one Simon a tanner, whose house *3579*

LODGING (6) [LODGE]
Jos 4: 3 leave them in the **l place**, where you shall 4411
Jdg 19:15 no man that took them into *his* house to l. 3885
Isa 10:29 they have **taken up** their l at Geba; Ramah 4411
Jer 9: 2 O that I had in the wilderness a **l place** of 4411
Ac 28:23 a day, there came many to him into *his* l; *3578*
Phm 1:22 But withal prepare me also a l: for I trust *3578*

LODGINGS (1) [LODGE]
2Ki 19:23 and I will enter *into* the l of his borders, *and* 4411

LOFT (2)
1Ki 17:19 and carried him up into a l, where he abode, 5944
Ac 20: 9 and fell down from the **third** l, and *5152*

LOFTILY (1) [LOFTY]
Ps 73: 8 *concerning* oppression: they speak l. 4480+4791

LOFTINESS (2) [LOFTY]
Isa 2:17 the l of man shall be bowed down, and 1365
Jer 48:29 his l, and his arrogancy, and his pride, and 1363

LOFTY (8) [LOFTILY, LOFTINESS]
Ps 131: 1 my heart is not haughty, nor mine eyes l: 7311
Pr 30:13 *is* a generation, O how l are their eyes! 7311
Isa 2:11 The l looks of man shall be humbled, and 1365
2:12 *shall be* upon every one *that is* proud and l, 7311
5:15 and the eyes of the l shall be humbled: 1364
26: 5 the l city, he layeth it low; he layeth it low, 7682
57: 7 Upon a l and high mountain hast thou set 1364
57:15 the high and l One that inhabiteth eternity, 5375

LOG (5)
Lev 14:10 mingled with oil, and one l of oil. 3849
14:12 the l of oil, and wave them *for* a wave 3849
14:15 the priest shall take *some* of the l of oil, 3849
14:21 with oil for a meat offering, and a l of oil; 3849
14:24 the l of oil, and the priest shall wave them 3849

LOINS (63)
Ge 35:11 of thee, and kings shall come out of thy l; 2504
37:34 put sackcloth upon his l, and mourned for 4975
46:26 which came out of his l, besides Jacob's 3409
Ex 1: 5 all the souls that came *out of* the l of Jacob 3409
12:11 *with* your l girded, your shoes on your feet, 4975
28:42 from the l even unto the thighs they shall 4975
Dt 33:11 smite through the l of them that rise against 4975
2Sa 20: 8 fastened upon his l in the sheath thereof; 4975
1Ki 2: 5 of war upon his girdle that *was* about his l, 4975
8:19 thy son that shall come forth out of thy l, 2504
12:10 *finger* shall be thicker than my father's l. 4975
18:46 he girded up his l, and ran before Ahab to 4975
20:31 put sackcloth on our l, and ropes upon our 4975
20:32 So they girded sackcloth on their l, and 4975
2Ki 1: 8 girt *with* a girdle of leather about his l. 4975
4:29 Gird up thy l, and take my staff in thine 4975
9: 1 Gird up thy l, and take this box of oil in 4975
2Ch 6: 9 thy son which shall come forth out of thy l, 2504
10:10 *finger* shall be thicker than my father's l. 4975
Job 12:18 of kings, and girdeth their l with a girdle. 4975
31:20 If his l have not blessed me, and *if* he were 2504
38: 3 Gird up now thy l like a man; for I will 2504
40: 7 Gird up thy l now like a man: I will 2504
40:16 his strength *is* in his l, and his force *is* in 4975
Ps 38: 7 For my l are filled *with* a loathsome 3689
66:11 the net; thou laidst affliction upon our l. 4975
69:23 and make their l continually to shake. 4975
Pr 31:17 She girdeth her l with strength, and 4975
Isa 5:27 neither shall the girdle of their l be loosed, 2504
11: 5 righteousness shall be the girdle of his l, 4975
20: 2 Go and loose the sackcloth from off thy l, 4975
21: 3 Therefore are my l filled *with* pain: 4975
32:11 ye bare, and gird *sackcloth* upon *your* l. 2504
45: 1 I will loose the l of kings, to open before 4975
Jer 1:17 Thou therefore gird up thy l, and arise, and 4975
13: 1 put it upon thy l, and put it not in water. 4975
13: 2 the word of the LORD, and put *it* on my l. 4975
13: 4 which *is* upon thy l, and arise, go to 4975
13:11 For as the girdle cleaveth to the l of a man, 4975
30: 6 do I see every man *with* his hands on his l, 2504
48:37 *shall be* cuttings, and upon the l sackcloth. 4975
Eze 1:27 from the appearance of his l even upward, 4975
1:27 from the appearance of his l even 4975
8: 2 from the appearance of his l even 4975
8: 2 from his l even upward, as the appearance 4975
21: 6 thou son of man, with the breaking of *thy* l; 4975
23:15 Girded with girdles upon their l, 4975
29: 7 and madest all their l to be at a stand. 4975
44:18 and shall have linen breeches upon their l; 4975
47: 4 me through; the waters *were* to the l. 4975
Da 5: 6 so that the joints of his l were loosed, and 2783
10: 5 whose l *were* girded with fine gold of 4975
Am 8:10 I will bring up sackcloth upon all l, and 4975
Na 2: 1 watch the way, make *thy* l strong, 4975
2:10 much pain *is* in all l, and the faces of them 4975
Mt 3: 4 and a leathern girdle about his l; *3751*
Mk 1: 6 and with a girdle of a skin about his l; *3751*
Lk 12:35 Let your l be girded about, and *your* lights *3751*
Ac 2:30 that of the fruit of his l, according to *3751*
Eph 6:14 having your l girt about with truth, and *3751*
Heb 7: 5 though they come out of the l of Abraham: *3751*
7:10 For he was yet in the l of his father, *3751*
1Pe 1:13 Wherefore gird up the l of your mind, *3751*

LOIS (1)
2Ti 1: 5 which dwelt first in thy grandmother **L**, and *3090*

LONG (211) [LENGTH, LONGED, LONGEDST, LONGETH, LONGING]
Ge 26: 8 to pass, when he had been there a l time, 748

L

Ge 48:15 the God which fed me **all** my **life l** 4480+5750
Ex 10: 3 LORD God of the Hebrews, **How l** 4970+5704
10: 7 servants said unto him, **How l** 4970+5704
16:28 said unto Moses, **How l** 575+5704+1886.5
19:13 when the trumpet **soundeth l**, they shall 4900
19:19 when the voice of the trumpet **sounded l**, 1980
20:12 that thy days may be l upon the land which 748
27: 1 five cubits **l**, and five cubits broad; 753
27: 9 linen of an hundred cubits l for one side: 753
27:11 *shall be* hangings of an hundred *cubits* **l**, 753
Lev 18:19 **as l as** she is put apart for her uncleanness. 871.1
26:34 **as l as** it lieth desolate, and ye *be* in 3117+3605
26:35 **As l as** it lieth desolate it shall rest; 3117+3605
Nu 9:18 **as l as** the cloud abode upon 3117+3605
9:19 when the cloud **tarried l** upon the tabernacle 748
14:11 said unto Moses, **How l** 575+5704+1886.5
14:11 **how l** will it be ere they 575+5704+1886.5
14:27 **How l** *shall I bear* with this evil 4970+5704
20:15 and we have dwelt in Egypt a l time; 7227
Dt 1: 6 Ye have dwelt **l enough** in this mount: 7227
2: 3 have compassed this mountain **l enough**: 7227
4:25 ye shall have **remained l** in the land, and 3462
12:19 the Levite **as l as** thou livest upon the earth. 3605
14:24 if the way be too l for thee, so that thou art 7235
19: 6 because the way is **l**, and slay him; 7235
20:19 When thou shalt besiege a city a l time, 7227
28:32 and fail *with longing* for them all the day **l**: NIH
28:59 of **l continuance**, and sore sicknesses, and 539
28:59 and sore sicknesses, and of **l continuance**. 539
31:13 **as l as** ye live in 834+3117+3605+1886.1
33:12 *the* LORD shall cover him all the day **l**, NIH
Jos 6: 5 *that* when *they* **make a l blast** with 4900
9:13 become old by reason of the very l journey. 7230
11:18 Joshua made war a l time with all those 7227
18: 3 the children of Israel, **How l** 575+5704+1886.5
23: 1 it came to pass a l time after that 7227
24: 7 and ye dwelt in the wilderness a l season. 7227
Jdg 5:28 Why is his chariot *so* **l** in coming? 954
1Sa 1:14 Eli said unto her, **How l** wilt thou be 4970+5704
1:28 **as l as** he liveth he *shall* 834+3117+3605+1886.1
7: 2 abode in Kirjath-jearim, that the time was **l**: 7235
16: 1 the LORD said unto Samuel, **How l** 4970+5704
20:31 For **as l as** the son of Jesse 3117+3605+1886.1
25:15 **as l as** we were conversant with 3117+3605
29: 8 **so l as** I have been with thee unto 3117+4480
2Sa 2:26 be bitterness in the latter end? **how l** 4970+5704
3: 1 Now there was l war between the house of 752
14: 2 be as a woman *that had* a l time mourned 7227
19:34 unto the king, **How l** 3117+4100+8141+3509.1
1Ki 3:11 and hast not asked for thyself l life; 7227
6:17 *is*, the temple before it, was forty cubits *l*. NIH
18:21 **How l** halt ye between two opinions? 4970+5704
2Ki 9:22 **so l as** the whoredoms of thy mother 5704
19:25 Hast thou not heard **l ago** 4480+7350+3807.1
2Ch 1:11 thine enemies, neither yet hast asked l life; 7227
3:11 wings of the cherubims *were* twenty cubits **l**: 753
6:13 of five cubits **l**, and five cubits broad, 753
6:31 **so l as** they live in the land 3117+3605+1886.1
15: 3 Now for a l season Israel *hath been* without 7227
26: 5 **as l as** he sought the LORD, God 3117+871.1
30: 5 for they had not done *it* of a l *time in such* 7230
36:21 *for* **as l as** *she* lay desolate she kept 3117+3605
Ne 2: 6 **For how l** shall thy journey be? 4970+5704
Est 5:13 **so l as** I see Mordecai the Jew 3605+871.1
Job 3:21 Which **l for** death, but it *cometh* not; and 2442
6: 8 God would grant *me* the **thing** that I **l for**! 8615
7:19 **How l** wilt thou not depart from 4100+3509.1
8: 2 **How l** wilt thou speak these *things?* 575+5704
8: 2 *how l shall* the words of thy mouth *be like* a NIH
18: 2 **How l** *will it be ere* you make 575+5704+1886.5
19: 2 **How l** will ye vex my soul, 575+5704+1886.5
27: 6 heart shall not reproach *me* **so l as** I live. 4480
Ps 4: 2 **how l** *will ye turn* my glory into 4100+5704
4: 2 *how l* will ye love vanity, *and* seek after NIH
6: 3 but thou, O LORD, **how l?** 4970+5704
13: 1 **How l** wilt thou forget me, 575+5704+1886.5
13: 1 for ever? **how l** wilt thou hide 575+5704+1886.5
13: 2 **How l** shall I take counsel in 575+5704+1886.5
13: 2 **how l** shall mine enemy be 575+5704+1886.5
32: 3 waxed old through my roaring all the day **l**. NIH
35:17 Lord, **how l** wilt thou look on? 4100+3509.1
35:28 *and* of thy praise all the day **l**. NIH
38: 6 down greatly; I go mourning all the day **l**. NIH
38:12 and imagine deceits all the day **l**. NIH
44: 8 In God we boast all the day **l**, and praise thy NIH
44:22 Yea, for thy sake are we killed all the day **l**; NIH
62: 3 **How l** will ye imagine 575+5704+1886.5
71:24 shall talk of thy righteousness all the day **l**: NIH
72: 5 They shall fear thee **as l as** the sun and 5973
72: 7 of peace **so l as** the moon **endureth**. 1097+5704
72:17 his name shall be continued **as l as** 6440+3807.1
73:14 For all the day l have I been plagued, and NIH
74: 9 among us any that knoweth **how l**. 4100+5704
74:10 O God, **how l** shall the adversary 4970+5704
79: 5 **How l**, LORD? wilt thou be angry, 4100+5704
80: 4 O LORD God *of* hosts, **how l** wilt 4970+5704
82: 2 **How l** will ye judge unjustly, and 4970+5704
89:46 **How l**, LORD? wilt thou hide 4100+5704
90:13 Return, O LORD, **how l?** and let it 4970+5704
91:16 *With* l life will I satisfy him, and shew him 753
94: 3 LORD, **how l** shall the wicked, 4970+5704
94: 3 **how l** shall the wicked triumph? 4970+5704
94: 4 *How l* shall they utter *and* speak hard NIH
95:10 Forty years l was I grieved with *this* NIH
104:33 I will sing unto the LORD **as l as** I live: 871.1
116: 2 therefore will I call upon *him* **as l as** I live. 871.1
120: 6 My soul hath l dwelt with him that hateth 7227
129: 3 upon my back: they **made l** their furrows. 748
143: 3 in darkness, as those that have been l dead. 5769
Pr 1:22 **How l**, ye simple ones, will ye love 4970+5704
3: 2 For length of days, and l life, and peace, 8141
6: 9 **How l** wilt thou sleep, O sluggard? 4970+5704
7:19 *is* not at home, he is gone a l journey: 4480+7350
21:26 He coveteth greedily all the day **l**: but NIH
23:17 *thou* in the fear of the LORD all the day **l**. NIH
23:30 They that **tarry l** at the wine; they that go to 309
25:15 By l forbearing is a prince persuaded, and 753
Ecc 12: 5 because man goeth to his l home, and 5769
Isa 6:11 said I, Lord, **how l?** And he 4970+5704
22:11 unto him that fashioned it **l ago**. 4480+7350
37:26 Hast thou not heard **l ago**, 4480+7350+3807.1
42:14 I have **l time** holden my peace; I have been 5769
65:22 mine elect shall **l enjoy** the work of their 1086
Jer 4:14 that thou mayest be saved. **How l** 4970+5704
4:21 **How l** shall I see the standard, *and* 4970+5704
12: 4 **How l** shall the land mourn, and 4970+5704
23:26 **How l** shall *this* be in the heart of 4970+5704
29:28 us *in* Babylon, saying, This *captivity is* **l**: 752
31:22 **How l** wilt thou go about, O thou 4970+5704
47: 5 the remnant of their valley: **how l** 4970+5704
47: 6 sword of the LORD, **how l** 575+5704+1886.5
La 2:20 eat their fruit, *and* children of a **span l?** 2949
5:20 forget us for ever, *and* forsake us **so l** time? 753
Eze 31: 5 his branches became **l** because of 748
40: 5 a measuring reed of six cubits *l* by the cubit NIH
40: 7 And *every* little chamber *was* one reed **l**, and 753
40:29 *it was* fifty cubits **l**, and five and 753
40:30 round about *were* five and twenty cubits **l**, 753
40:33 *it was* fifty cubits **l**, and five and 753
40:42 of a cubit and a half **l**, and a cubit and a half 753
40:47 an hundred cubits **l**, and an hundred cubits 753
41:13 he measured the house, an hundred cubits **l**; 753
41:13 with the walls thereof, an hundred cubits **l**; 753
42:11 the north, as l as they, *and* as broad as they: 753
42:20 five hundred *reeds* **l**, and five hundred broad, 753
43:16 the altar *shall be* twelve *cubits* **l**, twelve 753
43:17 the settle *shall be* fourteen *cubits* **l** and 753
44:20 nor **suffer** *their* locks **to grow l**; 7971
45: 6 and five and twenty thousand **l**, 753
46:22 *there were* courts joined *of* forty *cubits* **l** 753
Da 8:13 that certain *saint* which spake, **How l** 4970+5704
10: 1 *was* true, but the time appointed *was* **l**: 1419
12: 6 upon the waters of the river, **How l** 4970+5704
Hos 8: 5 anger is kindled against them: **how l** 4970+5704
13:13 for he should not stay **l** in *the place of* 6256
Hab 1: 2 O LORD, **how l** shall I cry, 575+5704+1886.5
2: 6 *that which is* not his! **how l?** 4970+5704
Zec 1:12 O LORD of hosts, **how l** wilt thou 4970+5704
Mt 9:15 **as l as** the bridegroom is with them? *1909+3745*
11:21 Sidon they would have repented **l ago** in *3819*
17:17 **how l** shall I be with you? *2193+4219*
17:17 **how l** shall I suffer you? bring him *2193+4219*
23:14 and for a pretence make **l** prayer: *3117*
25:19 After a l time the lord of those servants *4183*
Mk 2:19 **as l as** they have the bridegroom *3745+5550*
9:19 **how l** shall I be with you? *2193+4219*
9:19 **how l** shall I suffer you? bring him *2193+4219*
9:21 How l is it **ago** since this came unto him? *5550*

L

Mk 12:38 which love to go in **l clothing**, and *4749*
12:40 and for a pretence make l prayers: *3117*
16: 5 the right side, clothed in a l white **garment**; *4749*
Lk 1:21 marvelled that he **tarried** *so* l in the temple. *5549*
8:27 which had devils l time, and ware no *2425*
9:41 **how** l shall I be with you, and *2193+4219*
18: 7 unto him, though he **bear** l with them? *3114*
20: 9 and went into a far country for a l time. *2425*
20:46 which desire to walk in l **robes**, and *4749*
20:47 and for a shew make l prayers: *3117*
23: 8 for he was desirous to see him of a l *season*, *2425*
Jn 5: 6 knew that he had been now a l time *in that* *4183*
9: 5 **As l as** I am in the world, I am the light of *3752*
10:24 **How** l dost thou make us to doubt? *2193+4219*
14: 9 Have I been **so** l time with you, and *5118*
Ac 8:11 that of l time *he* had bewitched them with *2425*
14: 3 L time therefore abode they speaking *2425*
14:28 And there they abode l time with *3641+3756*
20: 9 and as Paul was l preaching, he sunk *1909+4183*
20:11 and eaten, and talked a l **while**, *1909+2425*
27:14 But not l after there arose against it a *4183*
27:21 But after l abstinence Paul stood *forth* in *4183*
Ro 1:11 For I l to see you, that I may impart unto *1971*
7: 1 over a man, **as** l **as** he liveth? *1909+3745+5550*
7: 2 by the law to *her* husband so l as he liveth; NIG
8:36 For thy sake we are killed all the day l; NIG
10:21 **All** day l have I stretched forth my hands *3650*
1Co 7:39 law **as** l **as** her husband liveth; *1909+3745+5550*
11:14 that, if a man **have l hair**, it is a shame unto *2863*
11:15 But if a woman **have l hair**, it is a glory to *2863*
13: 4 Charity **suffereth** l, *and* is kind; *3114*
2Co 9:14 which l **after** you for the exceeding grace *1971*
Gal 4: 1 the heir, **as** l **as** he is a child, *1909+3745+5550*
Eph 6: 3 and thou mayest **live** l on the earth. *1510+3118*
Php 1: 8 how *greatly* I l **after** you all in the bowels *1971*
1Ti 3:15 But if I **tarry** l, that thou mayest know how *1019*
Heb 4: 7 saying in David, To day, after **so** l a time; *5118*
Jas 5: 7 and **hath** l **patience** for it, until he receive *3114*
1Pe 3: 6 as l as ye do well, and are not afraid *with* NIG
2Pe 1:13 **as** l **as** I am in this tabernacle, *1909+3745*
2: 3 whose judgment now **of a** l **time** lingereth *1597*
Rev 6:10 saying, **How** l, O Lord, holy and *2193+4219*

LONGED (8) [LONG]

2Sa 13:39 *the soul of* king David l to go forth unto 3615
23:15 David l, and said, Oh that one would give 183
1Ch 11:17 David l, and said, Oh that one would give 183
Ps 119:40 Behold, I have l after thy precepts: 8373
119:131 and panted: for I l for thy commandments. 2968
119:174 I have l for thy salvation, O LORD; and 8373
Php 2:26 For he l **after** you all, and *was* full of *1971*
4: 1 my brethren dearly beloved and l **for**, *1973*

LONGEDST (1) [LONG]

Ge 31:30 thou **sore** l after thy father's house, 3700+3700

LONGER (17) [LENGTH]

Ex 2: 3 when she could not l hide him, she took for 5750
9:28 and I will let you go, and ye shall stay no l. 3254
Jdg 2:14 that they could not **any** l stand before their 5750
2Sa 20: 5 he **tarried** l than the set time which he had 309
2Ki 6:33 what should I wait for the LORD **any** l? 5750
Job 11: 9 The measure thereof *is* l than the earth, and 752
Jer 44:22 So that the LORD could no l bear, 5750
Lk 16: 2 for thou mayest be no l steward. *2089*
Ac 18:20 When they desired *him* to tarry l *1909+4183*
25:24 crying that he ought not to live **any** l. *3371*
Ro 6: 2 that are dead to sin, live **any** l therein? *2089*
Gal 3:25 is come, we are **no** l under a schoolmaster. *3765*
1Th 3: 1 Wherefore when we could **no** l forbear, *3371*
3: 5 For this cause, when I could **no** l forbear, *3371*
1Ti 5:23 Drink **no** l water, but use a little wine for *3371*
1Pe 4: 2 That *he* **no** l should live the rest of *his* time *3371*
Rev 10: 6 are therein, that there should be time no l: *2089*

LONGETH (4) [LONG]

Ge 34: 8 The soul of my son Shechem l for your 2836
Dt 12:20 will eat flesh, because thy soul l to eat flesh; 183
Ps 63: 1 my flesh l for thee, in a dry and 3642
84: 2 My soul l, yea, even fainteth for the courts 3700

LONGING (3) [LONG]

Dt 28:32 and fail *with* l for them all the day long: NIH
Ps 107: 9 For he satisfieth the l soul, and filleth 8264

119:20 My soul breaketh for the l *that it hath* unto 8375

LONGSUFFERING (17) [LENGTH, SUFFER]

Ex 34: 6 l, and abundant in goodness and truth, 639+750
Nu 14:18 The LORD *is* l, and of great mercy, 639+750
Ps 86:15 l, and plenteous in mercy and truth. 639+750
Jer 15:15 take me not away in thy l: 639+750
Ro 2: 4 of his goodness and forbearance and l; *3115*
9:22 endured with much l *the* vessels of wrath *3115*
2Co 6: 6 by knowledge, by l, by kindness, *3115*
Gal 5:22 joy, peace, l, gentleness, goodness, faith, *3115*
Eph 4: 2 With all lowliness and meekness, with l, *3115*
Col 1:11 unto all patience and l with joyfulness; *3115*
3:12 kindness, humbleness of mind, meekness, l; *3115*
1Ti 1:16 me first Jesus Christ might shew forth all l, *3115*
2Ti 3:10 of life, purpose, faith, l, charity, patience, *3115*
4: 2 rebuke, exhort with all l and doctrine. *3115*
1Pe 3:20 when once the l of God waited in the days *3115*
2Pe 3: 9 but is l to us-ward, not willing that any *3114*
3:15 And account *that* the l of our Lord *is* *3115*

LONGWINGED (1) [LENGTH, WING]

Eze 17: 3 l, full *of* feathers, which had divers 83+750

LOOK (155) [LOOKED, LOOKEST, LOOKETH, LOOKING, LOOKING-GLASSES, LOOKS]

Ge 9:16 I will l upon it, that I may remember 7200
12:11 know that thou *art* a fair woman to l **upon**: 4758
13:14 l from the place where thou *art* northward, 7200
15: 5 L now towards heaven, and tell the stars, 5027
19:17 l not behind thee, neither stay thou in all 5027
24:16 the damsel *was* very fair to l **upon**, a virgin, 4758
26: 7 because she *was* fair to l **upon**. 4758
40: 7 Wherefore l ye *so* sadly to day? 6440
41:33 let Pharaoh **l out** a man discreet and wise, 7200
42: 1 his sons, Why do ye l one upon another? 7200
Ex 3: 6 his face; for he was afraid to l upon God. 5027
5:21 The LORD l upon you, and judge; 7200
10:10 little ones: l *to it;* for evil *is* before you. 7200
25:20 and their faces *shall l* one to another; NIH
25:40 l that thou make *them* after their pattern, 7200
39:43 Moses did l upon all the work, and behold, 7200
Lev 13: 3 the priest shall l on the plague in the skin of 7200
13: 3 the priest shall l on him, and 7200
13: 5 the priest shall l on him the seventh day: 7200
13: 6 the priest shall l on him again the seventh 7200
13:21 if the priest l on it, and behold, *there be* no 7200
13:25 the priest shall l upon it: and behold, *if* 7200
13:26 if the priest l on it, and behold, *there be* no 7200
13:27 the priest shall l upon him the seventh day: 7200
13:31 And if the priest l on the plague of the scall, 7200
13:32 in the seventh day the priest shall l on 7200
13:34 in the seventh day the priest shall l on 7200
13:36 the priest shall l on him: and behold, *if* 7200
13:39 the priest shall l: and behold, *if* the bright 7200
13:43 the priest shall l upon it: and behold, *if* 7200
13:50 the priest shall l upon the plague, and 7200
13:51 he shall l on the plague on the seventh day: 7200
13:53 if the priest shall l, and behold, the plague 7200
13:55 the priest shall l on the plague, after *that* it 7200
13:56 if the priest l, and behold, the plague *be* 7200
14: 3 the priest shall l, and behold, *if* the plague 7200
14:37 he shall l on the plague, and behold, *if* 7200
14:39 come again the seventh day, and shall l: 7200
14:44 the priest shall come and l, and behold, 7200
14:48 shall come in, and l *upon it,* and behold, 7200
Nu 15:39 that ye may l upon it, and remember all 7200
Dt 9:27 l not unto the stubbornness of this people, 6437
26:15 L **down** from thy holy habitation, 8259
28:32 thine eyes shall l, and fail *with longing* for 7200
Jdg 7:17 said unto them, L on me, and do likewise: 7200
1Sa 1:11 if thou wilt **indeed** l on the affliction 7200+7200
16: 7 L not on his countenance, or on the height 5027
16:12 a beautiful countenance, and goodly to **l to**. 7210
17:18 l how thy brethren fare, and take their 6485
2Sa 9: 8 that thou shouldest l upon such a dead dog 6437
11: 2 the woman *was* very beautiful to **l upon**. 4758
16:12 It may be that the LORD will l on mine 7200
1Ki 18:43 to his servant, Go up now, l toward the sea. 5027
2Ki 3:14 I would not l toward thee, nor see thee. 5027
6:32 l, when the messenger cometh, shut 7200
9: 2 **l out** there Jehu the son of Jehoshaphat 7200
10: 3 L even out the best and meetest of your 7200
10:23 l that there be here with you none of 7200

2Ki	14: 8	Come, let us l one another *in* the face.	7200
1Ch	12:17	the God of our fathers l *thereon,* and	7200
2Ch	24:22	The LORD l upon *it,* and require *it.*	7200
Est	1:11	princes her beauty: for she *was* fair to **l on**.	4758
Job	3: 9	let it l for light, but *have* none; neither let it	6960
	6:28	Now therefore be content, l upon me; for *it*	6437
	20:21	therefore shall no *man* l **for** his goods.	2342
	35: 5	L unto the heavens, and see; and behold	5027
	40:12	L on every one *that is* proud, *and* bring him	7200
Ps	5: 3	I direct *my prayer* unto thee, and will **l up**.	6822
	22:17	tell all my bones: they l *and* stare upon me.	5027
	25:18	L upon mine affliction and my pain; and	7200
	35:17	Lord, how long wilt thou l on? rescue my	7200
	40:12	that I am not able to l *up;* they are moe than	7200
	80:14	**l down** from heaven, and behold, and	5027
	84: 9	and **l upon** the face of thine anointed.	5027
	85:11	righteousness shall **l down** from heaven.	8259
	101: 5	him that hath a high l and a proud heart will	5869
	119:132	L thou upon me, and be merciful unto me,	6437
	123: 2	as the eyes of servants *l* unto the hand of	NIH
Pr	4:25	Let thine eyes l right on, and let thine	5027
	4:25	and let thine eyelids **l straight** before thee.	3474
	6:17	A proud l, a lying tongue, and hands that	5869
	21: 4	A high l, and a proud heart, *and*	5869
	23:31	L not thou upon the wine when it is red,	7200
	27:23	state of thy flocks, *and* l well to thy herds.	7896
Ecc	12: 3	those that l out of the windows be	7200
SS	1: 6	L not upon me, because I *am* black,	7200
	4: 8	l from the top of Amana, from the top of	7789
	6:13	return, return, that we may l upon thee.	2372
Isa	5:30	if *one* l unto the land, behold darkness *and*	5027
	8:17	the house of Jacob, and I will l for him.	6960
	8:21	their king and their God, and l upward.	6437
	8:22	they shall l unto the earth; and	5027
	14:16	They that see thee shall **narrowly** l upon	7688
	17: 7	At that day shall a man l to his Maker, and	8159
	17: 8	he shall not l to the altars, the work of his	8159
	22: 4	Therefore said I, **L away** from me; I will	8159
	22: 8	thou didst l in that day to the armour of	5027
	31: 1	they l not unto the Holy One of Israel,	8159
	33:20	L upon Zion, the city of our solemnities:	2372
	42:18	ye deaf; and l, ye blind, that *ye* may see.	5027
	45:22	L unto me, and be ye saved, all the ends of	6437
	51: 1	l unto the rock *whence* ye are hewn, and	5027
	51: 2	L unto Abraham your father, and	5027
	51: 6	the heavens, and l upon the earth beneath:	5027
	56:11	they all l to their own way, every one for	6437
	59:11	we l for judgment, but *there is* none;	6960
	63:15	**L down** from heaven, and behold from	5027
	66: 2	to this *man* will I l, *even* to *him that is* poor	5027
	66:24	l upon the carcases of the men that have	7200
Jer	13:16	and, while ye l for light, he turn it into	6960
	39:12	**l well** to him, and do him no harm;	5869+7760
	40: 4	come; and I will **l well** unto thee:	5869+7760
	46: 5	and are fled apace, and l not **back**:	6437
	47: 3	the fathers shall not **l back** to *their* children	6437
La	3:50	Till the LORD **l down**, and behold from	8259
Eze	23:15	upon their heads, all of them princes to **l to**,	4758
	29:16	upon when they shall l after them:	6437
	43:17	and his stairs *shall* **l toward** the east.	6437
Da	7:20	whose l *was* more stout than his fellows.	2376
Hos	3: 1	who l to other gods, and love flagons of	6437
Jnh	2: 4	yet I will l again toward thy holy temple.	5027
Mic	4:11	her be defiled, and let our eye l upon Zion.	2372
	7: 7	Therefore I will l unto the LORD; I will	6822
Na	2: 8	stand, *shall they cry;* but none shall **l back**.	6437
	3: 7	*that* all they that l upon thee shall flee from	7200
Hab	1:13	to behold evil, and canst not l on iniquity:	5027
	2:15	that thou mayest l on their nakedness!	5027
Zec	12:10	they shall l upon me whom they have	5027
Mt	11: 3	that should come, or do we l **for** another?	*4328*
Mk	8:25	again upon his eyes, and made him **l up**:	*308*
Lk	7:19	he that should come? or l we **for** another?	*4328*
	7:20	he that should come? or l we **for** another?	*4328*
	9:38	I beseech thee, **l upon** my son:	*1914*
	21:28	to pass, *then* **l up**, and lift up your heads;	*352*
Jn	4:35	Lift up your eyes, and **l on** the fields;	*2300*
	7:52	Search, and l: for out of Galilee ariseth no	*2396*
	19:37	They shall l on *him* whom they pierced.	*3700*
Ac	3: 4	his eyes upon him with John, said, L on us.	*991*
	3:12	or why l ye *so* **earnestly** on us, as though by	*816*
	6: 3	l ye **out** among you seven men of honest	*1980*
	18:15	l ye *to it;* for I will be no judge of such	*3700*
1Co	16:11	unto me: for I l **for** him with the brethren.	*1551*
2Co	3:13	**stedfastly** l to the end of that which is	*816*
	4:18	While we l not **at** the *things* which are	*4648*
	10: 7	Do ye **l on** *things* after the outward	*991*
Php	2: 4	L not every man on his own *things,* but	*4648*
	3:20	from whence also we l **for** the Saviour,	*553*
Heb	9:28	unto them that l **for** him shall he appear	*553*
1Pe	1:12	which *things the* angels desire to l into.	*3879*
2Pe	3:13	**l for** new heavens and a new earth,	*4328*
	3:14	seeing that ye l **for** such *things,* be diligent	*4328*
2Jn	1: 8	L to yourselves, that we lose not *those things*	*991*
Rev	4: 3	And he that sat was to l upon like a jasper	*3706*
	5: 3	able to open the book, neither to l thereon.	*991*
	5: 4	and to read the book, neither to l thereon.	*991*

LOOKED (143) [LOOK]

Ge	6:12	God l upon the earth, and behold, it was	7200
	8:13	l, and behold, the face of the ground was	7200
	16:13	Have I also here l after him that seeth me?	7200
	18: 2	he lift up his eyes and l, and lo, three men	7200
	18:16	rose up from thence, and l toward Sodom:	8259
	19:26	his wife l back from behind him, and	5027
	19:28	And he l toward Sodom and Gomorrah, and	8259
	22:13	l, and behold behind *him* a ram caught in a	7200
	26: 8	that Abimelech king of the Philistims **l out**	8259
	29: 2	And he l, and behold a well in the field, and	7200
	29:32	Surely the LORD hath l upon my	7200
	33: 1	l, and behold, Esau came, and with him	7200
	37:25	and they lift up their eyes and l, and behold,	7200
	39:23	The keeper of the prison l not to any thing	7200
	40: 6	l upon them, and behold, they *were* sad.	7200
Ex	2:11	unto his brethren, and l on their burdens:	7200
	2:12	he l this way and that way, and when he	6437
	2:25	God **l upon** the children of Israel, and	7200
	3: 2	he l, and behold, the bush burned with fire,	7200
	4:31	that he had **l upon** their affliction, then	7200
	14:24	that in the morning watch the LORD l	8259
	16:10	that they l toward the wilderness, and	6437
	33: 8	man *at* his tent door, and l after Moses,	5027
Nu	12:10	Aaron l upon Miriam, and behold, *she was*	6437
	16:42	that they l toward the tabernacle of	6437
	17: 9	and they l, and took every man his rod.	7200
	24:20	when he l on Amalek, he took up his	7200
	24:21	he l on the Kenites, and took up his parable,	7200
Dt	9:16	I l, and behold, ye had sinned against	7200
	26: 7	l on our affliction, and our labour, and	7200
Jos	5:13	that he lift up his eyes and l, and behold,	7200
	8:20	when the men of Ai l behind them, they	6437
Jdg	5:28	The mother of Sisera **l out** at a window,	8259
	6:14	the LORD l upon him, and said, Go in this	6437
	9:43	and laid wait in the field, and l, and behold,	7200
	13:19	and Manoah and his wife **l on**.	7200
	13:20	Manoah and his wife **l on** *it,* and fell on	7200
	20:40	the Benjamites l behind them, and behold,	6437
1Sa	6:19	they had l into the ark of the LORD,	7200
	9:16	for I have l upon my people, because	7200
	14:16	watchmen of Saul in Gibeah of Benjamin l;	7200
	16: 6	were come, that he l on Eliab, and said,	7200
	17:42	when the Philistine **l about**, and saw David,	5027
	24: 8	when Saul l behind him, David stooped	5027
2Sa	1: 7	when he l behind him, he saw me, and	6437
	2:20	Abner l behind him, and said, *Art* thou	6437
	6:16	Michal Saul's daughter l through a	8259
	13:34	watch lift up his eyes, and l, and behold,	7200
	18:24	and l, and behold a man running alone.	7200
	22:42	They l, but *there was* none to save;	8159
	24:20	Araunah l, and saw the king and his	8259
1Ki	18:43	he went up, and l, and said, *There is*	5027
	19: 6	he l, and behold, *there was* a cake baken on	5027
2Ki	2:24	l on them, and cursed them in the name of	7200
	6:30	upon the wall, and the people l, and behold,	7200
	9:30	and tired her head, and **l out** at a window.	8259
	9:32	there **l out** to him two *or* three eunuchs.	8259
	11:14	when she l, behold, the king stood by a	7200
	14:11	Amaziah king of Judah l one another *in*	7200
1Ch	21:21	Ornan l and saw David, and went out of	5027
2Ch	13:14	when Judah **l back**, behold, the battle *was*	6437
	20:24	they l unto the multitude, and behold,	6437
	23:13	she l, and behold, the king stood at his	7200
	26:20	and all the priests, l upon him, and behold,	6437
Ne	4:14	I l, and rose up, and said unto the nobles,	7200
Est	2:15	in the sight of all them that l upon her.	7200
Job	6:19	The troops of Tema l, the companies of	5027
	30:26	When I l for good, then evil came *unto me:*	6960
Ps	14: 2	The LORD **l down** from heaven upon	8259

Ps 34: 5 They **l** unto him, and were lightened: and 5027
53: 2 God **l down** from heaven upon the children 8259
69:20 I **l** *for some* to take pity, but *there was* 6960
102:19 For he hath **l down** from the height of his 8259
109:25 *when* they **l** upon me they shaked their 7200
142: 4 I **l** *on my* right hand, and beheld, but 5027
Pr 7: 6 For at the window of my house I **l** through 8259
24:32 *it* well: I **l** upon *it, and* received instruction. 7200
Ecc 2:11 I **l** on all the works that my hands had 6437
SS 1: 6 I *am* black, because the sun hath **l** upon me: 7805
Isa 5: 2 he **l** that *it* should bring forth grapes, and 6960
5: 4 when I **l** that *it* should bring forth grapes, 6960
5: 7 he **l** for judgment, but behold oppression; 6960
22:11 ye have not **l** unto the Maker thereof, 5027
63: 5 I **l**, and *there was* none to help; and 5027
64: 3 When thou didst terrible things *which* we **l** 6960
Jer 8:15 *We* **l** for peace, but no good *came; and* for a 6960
14:19 *we* **l** for peace, and *there is* no good; and 6960
La 2:16 certainly this *is* the day that we **l for**; we 6960
Eze 1: 4 I **l**, and behold, a whirlwind came out of 7200
2: 9 when I **l**, behold, a hand *was* sent unto me; 7200
8: 7 and when I **l**, behold a hole in the wall. 7200
10: 1 I **l**, and behold, in the firmament that *was* 7200
10: 9 when I **l**, behold the four wheels by 7200
10:11 *to* the place whither the head **l** they 6437
16: 8 I passed by thee, and **l** upon thee, behold, 7200
21:21 he consulted with images, he **l** in the liver. 7200
40:20 the gate of the outward court that **l** toward 6440
44: 4 I **l**, and behold, the glory of the LORD 7200
46:19 of the priests, which **l toward** the north: 6437
Da 1:13 let our countenances be **l** upon before thee, 7200
10: 5 I lift up mine eyes, and **l**, and behold, 7200
12: 5 I Daniel **l**, and behold, there stood other 7200
Ob 1:12 thou shouldest not have **l** on the day of thy 7200
1:13 thou shouldest not have **l** on their affliction 7200
Hag 1: 9 *Ye* **l** for much, and lo, *it came* to little; and 6437
Zec 2: 1 I lift up mine eyes again, and **l**, and behold, 7200
4: 2 I said, I have **l**, and behold, a candlestick all 7200
5: 1 mine eyes, and **l**, and behold, a flying roll. 7200
5: 9 lift I up mine eyes, and **l**, and behold, 7200
6: 1 and lift up mine eyes, and **l**, and behold, 7200
Mk 3: 5 And when he had **l round about** on them *4017*
3:34 And he **l** round about on them which sat *4017*
5:32 And he **l round about** to see her that had *4017*
6:41 he **l up** to heaven, and blessed, and brake *308*
8:24 And he **l up**, and said, I see men as trees, *308*
8:33 he had turned about and **l on** his disciples, *1492*
9: 8 when they had **l round about**, *4017*
10:23 And Jesus **l round about**, and saith unto *4017*
11:11 when he had **l round about** upon all *things, 4017*
14:67 warming himself, she **l upon** him, and said, *1689*
16: 4 And when they **l**, they saw that the stone was *308*
Lk 1:25 **l on** *me,* to take away my reproach among *1896*
2:38 spake of him to all them that **l for** *4327*
10:32 came and **l** *on him,* and passed by on *1492*
19: 5 he **l up**, and saw him, and said unto him, *308*
21: 1 And he **l up**, and saw the rich *men* casting *308*
22:56 and **earnestly** **l** upon him, and said, *816*
22:61 And the Lord turned, and **l upon** Peter. *1689*
Jn 13:22 Then the disciples **l** one on another, *991*
20:11 she **stooped down, and l** into *3879*
Ac 1:10 And while they **l stedfastly** toward heaven *816*
7:55 **l up stedfastly** into heaven, and saw *816*
10: 4 And when he **l** on him, he was afraid, and *816*
22:13 And the same hour I **l up** upon him. *308*
28: 6 Howbeit they **l** when he should have *4328*
28: 6 but after they had **l** a great while, and *4328*
Heb 11:10 For he **l for** a city which hath foundations, *1551*
1Jn 1: 1 which we have **l upon**, and our hands have *2300*
Rev 4: 1 After this I **l**, and behold, a door *was* *1492*
6: 8 And I **l**, and behold a pale horse: and *1492*
14: 1 And I **l**, and lo, a Lamb stood on the mount *1492*
14:14 And I **l**, and behold a white cloud, and *1492*
15: 5 And after that I **l**, and behold, the temple of *1492*

LOOKEST (2) [LOOK]

Job 13:27 and **l narrowly** unto all my paths; 8104
Hab 1:13 wherefore **l** thou upon them that deal 5027

LOOKETH (33) [LOOK]

Lev 13:12 to his foot, wheresoever the priest **l**; 4758+5869
Nu 21: 8 that is bitten, when he **l** upon it, shall live. 7200
21:20 the top of Pisgah, which **l** toward Jeshimon. 8259
23:28 the top of Peor, that **l** toward Jeshimon. 8259
Jos 15: 2 the salt sea, from the bay that **l** southward: 6437
1Sa 13:18 **l** to the valley of Zeboim toward 8259
16: 7 for man **l** on the outward appearance, but 7200
16: 7 but the LORD **l** on the heart. 7200
Job 7: 2 as a hireling **l** for the reward of his work: 6960
28:24 For he **l** to the ends of the earth, *and* 5027
33:27 He **l** upon men, and *if any* say, I have 7789
Ps 33:13 The LORD **l** from heaven; he beholdeth 5027
33:14 From the place of his habitation he **l** upon 7688
104:32 He **l** on the earth, and it trembleth: 5027
Pr 14:15 but the prudent *man* **l well** to his going. 995
31:27 She **l well** to the ways of her household, 6822
SS 2: 9 behind our wall, he **l** forth at the windows, 7688
6:10 Who *is* she that **l forth** as the morning, 8259
7: 4 thy nose *is* as the tower of Lebanon which **l** 6822
Isa 28: 4 which *when* he that **l** upon it seeth, while it 7200
Eze 8: 3 to the door of the inner gate that **l** toward 6437
11: 1 of the LORD'S house, which **l** eastward: 6437
40: 6 came he unto the gate which **l** toward 6440
40:22 *were* after the measure of the gate that **l** 6440
43: 1 *even* the gate that **l** toward the east: 6437
44: 1 outward sanctuary which **l** *toward* the east; 6437
46: 1 The gate of the inner court that **l** *toward* 6437
46:12 open him the gate that **l** *toward* the east, 6437
47: 2 the utter gate *by* the way that **l** east*ward;* 6437
Mt 5:28 That whosoever **l on** a woman to lust after *991*
24:50 shall come in a day when he **l** not for *him,* *4328*
Lk 12:46 will come in a day when he **l** not **for** *him,* *4328*
Jas 1:25 But whoso **l** into the perfect law of liberty, *3879*

LOOKING (30) [LOOK]

Jos 15: 7 *so* northward, **l** toward Gilgal, that *is* before 6437
1Ki 7:25 three **l** toward the north, and three looking 6437
7:25 three **l** toward the west, and three looking 6437
7:25 three **l** toward the south, and three looking 6437
7:25 the south, and three **l** toward the east: 6437
1Ch 15:29 that Michal the daughter of Saul **l** out at a 8259
2Ch 4: 4 three **l** toward the north, and three looking 6437
4: 4 three **l** toward the west, and three looking 6437
4: 4 three **l** toward the south, and three looking 6437
4: 4 the south, and three **l** toward the east: 6437
Job 37:18 *which is* strong, *and* as a molten **l glass**? 7209
Isa 38:14 mine eyes fail *with l* upward: O LORD, NIH
Mt 14:19 and **l up** to heaven, he blessed, and brake, *308*
Mk 7:34 And **l up** to heaven, he sighed, and *308*
10:27 And Jesus **l upon** them saith, With men *it* *1689*
15:40 There were also women **l on** afar off: *2334*
Lk 6:10 And **l round about** upon them all, he said *4017*
9:16 and the two fishes, and **l up** to heaven, *308*
9:62 and **l** back, is fit for the kingdom of God. *991*
21:26 *for* **l after** those *things* which are coming *4329*
Jn 1:36 And **l upon** Jesus as he walked, he saith, *1689*
20: 5 And he **stooping down, and l** in, saw *3879*
Ac 6:15 that sat in the council, **l stedfastly** on him, *816*
23:21 are they ready, **l for** a promise from thee. *4327*
Tit 2:13 **L for** *that* blessed hope, and the glorious *4327*
Heb 10:27 But a certain fearful **l for** of judgment and *1561*
12: 2 **L** unto Jesus the author and finisher of *our* *872*
12:15 **L diligently** lest any *man* fail of the grace *1983*
2Pe 3:12 **L for** and hasting *unto* the coming of *4328*
Jude 1:21 **l for** the mercy of our Lord Jesus Christ *4327*

LOOKING-GLASSES (1) [GLASS, LOOK]

Ex 38: 8 *of* brass, of the **l** of *the women* assembling, 4759

LOOKS (5) [LOOK]

Ps 18:27 afflicted people; but wilt bring down high **l**. 5869
Isa 2:11 The lofty **l** of man shall be humbled, and 5869
10:12 king of Assyria, and the glory of his high **l**. 5869
Eze 2: 6 of their words, nor be dismayed at their **l**, 6440
3: 9 them not, neither be dismayed at their **l**, 6440

LOOPS (13)

Ex 26: 4 thou shalt make **l** of blue upon the edge of 3924
26: 5 Fifty **l** shalt thou make in the one curtain, 3924
26: 5 fifty **l** shalt thou make in the edge of 3924
26: 5 that the **l** may take hold one of another. 3924
26:10 thou shalt make fifty **l** on the edge of 3924
26:10 fifty **l** in the edge of the curtain which 3924
26:11 put the taches into the **l**, and couple the tent 3924
36:11 he made **l** of blue on the edge of one 3924
36:12 Fifty **l** made he in one curtain, and 3924
36:12 fifty **l** made he in the edge of the curtain 3924
36:12 the **l** held one *curtain* to another. 3924

Ex 36:17 he made fifty l upon the uttermost edge of 3924
36:17 fifty l made he upon the edge of the curtain 3924

LOOSE (29) [LOOSED, LOOSETH, LOOSING, UNLOOSE]
Ge 49:21 Naphtali *is* a hind **let** l: he giveth goodly 7971
Lev 14: 7 shall **let** the living bird l into the open field. 7971
Dt 25: 9 l his shoe from off his foot, and spit in his 2502
Jos 5:15 unto Joshua, L thy shoe from off thy foot; 5394
Job 6: 9 *that* he would let l his hand, and cut me off! 5425
30:11 they have also let l the bridle before me. 7971
38:31 of Pleiades, or l the bands of Orion? 6605
Ps 102:20 to l those that are appointed to death; 6605
Isa 20: 2 Go and l the sackcloth from off thy loins, 6605
45: 1 I will l the loins of kings, to open before 6605
52: 2 l thyself **from** the bands of thy neck, 6605
58: 6 to l the bands of wickedness, to undo 6605
Jer 40: 4 I l thee *this* day from the chains which *were* 6605
Da 3:25 He answered and said, Lo, I see four men l, 8271
Mt 16:19 whatsoever thou shalt l on earth shall be *3089*
18:18 whatsoever ye shall l on earth shall be *3089*
21: 2 with her: l *them,* and bring *them* unto me. *3089*
Mk 11: 2 never man sat; l him, and bring *him.* *3089*
11: 4 place where two ways met; and they l him. *3089*
Lk 13:15 doth not each one of you on the sabbath l *3089*
19:30 never man sat: l him, and bring *him hither.* *3089*
19:31 Why do ye l *him?* thus shall ye say unto *3089*
19:33 thereof said unto them, Why l ye the colt? *3089*
Jn 11:44 saith unto them, L him, and let *him* go. *3089*
Ac 13:25 shoes of *his* feet I am not worthy to l. *3089*
24:26 given him of Paul, that he might l him: *3089*
Rev 5: 2 to open the book, and to l the seals thereof? *3089*
5: 5 the book, and to l the seven seals thereof. *3089*
9:14 L the four angels which are bound in *3089*

LOOSED (32) [LOOSE]
Ex 28:28 that the breastplate be not l from the ephod. 2118
39:21 that the breastplate might not be l from 2118
Dt 25:10 The house of him that hath his shoe l. 2502
Jdg 15:14 and his bands l from off his hands. 4549
Job 30:11 Because he hath l my cord, and 6605
39: 5 or who hath l the bands of the wild ass? 6605
Ps 105:20 The king sent and l him; *even* the ruler of 5425
116:16 son of thy handmaid: thou hast l my bonds. 6605
Ecc 12: 6 Or ever the silver cord be l, or the golden 7576
Isa 5:27 neither shall the girdle of their loins be l, 6605
33:23 Thy tacklings are l; they could not well 5203
51:14 captive exile hasteneth that *he* may be l, 6605
Da 5: 6 so that the joints of his loins were l, and 8271
Mt 16:19 shalt loose on earth shall be l in heaven. *3089*
18:18 ye shall loose on earth shall be l in heaven. *3089*
18:27 and l him, and forgave him the debt. *630*
Mk 7:35 and the string of his tongue was l, and *3089*
Lk 1:64 and his tongue *l,* and he spake, and NIG
13:12 Woman, thou art l from thy infirmity. *630*
13:16 be l from this bond on the sabbath day? *3089*
Ac 2:24 hath raised up, having l the pains of death: *3089*
13:13 when Paul and his company l from Paphos, *321*
16:26 were opened, and every one's bands were l. *447*
22:30 he l him from *his* bands, and *3089*
27:21 and not have l from Crete, and to have *321*
27:40 and l the rudder bands, and hoised up *447*
Ro 7: 2 she is l from the law of the husband. *2673*
1Co 7:27 seek not to be l. Art thou loosed from a *3080*
7:27 Art thou l from a wife? seek not a wife. *3089*
Rev 9:15 And the four angels were l, which were *3089*
20: 3 and after that he must be l a little season. *3089*
20: 7 Satan shall be l out of his prison, *3089*

LOOSETH (2) [LOOSE]
Job 12:18 He l the bond of kings, and girdeth their 6605
Ps 146: 7 to the hungry. The Lord l the prisoners: 5425

LOOSING (4) [LOOSE]
Mk 11: 5 said unto them, What do ye, l the colt? *3089*
Lk 19:33 And as they were l the colt, the owners *3089*
Ac 16:11 Therefore l from Troas, we came with a *321*
27:13 l *thence,* they sailed close by Crete. *142*

LOP (1)
Isa 10:33 of hosts, shall l the bough with terror: 5586

LORD (1367) [LORD'S, LORDLY, LORDS, LORDSHIP; see also LORD*]
Ge 15: 2 Abram said, L God, what wilt thou give 136
15: 8 he said, L God, whereby shall I know that 136
18: 3 said, My L, if now I have found favour in 136
18:12 shall I have pleasure, my l being old also? 113
18:27 I have taken upon me to speak unto the L, 136
18:30 he said *unto him,* Oh let not the L be angry, 136
18:31 I have taken upon me to speak unto the L: 136
18:32 Oh let not the L be angry, and I will speak 136
19:18 And Lot said unto them, Oh, not so, my L: 113
20: 4 he said, L, wilt thou slay also a righteous 136
23: 6 Hear us, my l: thou *art* a mighty prince 113
23:11 Nay, my l, hear me: the field give I thee, and 113
23:15 My l, hearken unto me: the land *is worth* 113
24:18 she said, Drink, my l: and she hasted, and 113
27:29 be l over thy brethren, and let thy mother's 1376
27:37 I have made him thy l, and all his brethren 1376
31:35 Let it not displease my l that I cannot rise up 113
32: 4 saying, Thus shall ye speak unto my l Esau; 113
32: 5 I have sent to tell my l, that I may find grace 113
32:18 it *is* a present sent unto my l Esau: 113
33: 8 *These are* to find grace in the sight of my l. 113
33:13 My l knoweth that the children *are* tender, 113
33:14 Let my l, I pray thee, pass over before his 113
33:14 to endure, until I come unto my l unto Seir. 113
33:15 let me find grace in the sight of my l. 113
39:16 up his garment by her, until his l came home. 113
40: 1 *his* baker had offended their l the king of 113
42:10 my l, but to buy food are thy servants come. 113
42:30 The man, *who is* the l of the land, 113
42:33 the man, the l of the country, said unto us, 113
44: 5 *Is* not this *it* in which my l drinketh, and 113
44: 7 unto him, Wherefore saith my l these words? 113
44:16 Judah said, What shall we say unto my l? 113
44:18 and said, O my l, let thy servant, I pray thee, 113
44:19 My l asked his servants, saying, Have ye a 113
44:20 we said unto my l, We have a father, an old 113
44:22 we said unto my l, The lad cannot leave his 113
44:24 my father, we told him the words of my l. 113
44:33 abide instead of the lad a bondman to my l; 113
45: 8 l of all his house, and a ruler throughout all 113
45: 9 God hath made me l of all Egypt: 113
47:18 said unto him, We will not hide *it* from my l, 113
47:18 is spent; my l also had our herds of cattle; 113
47:18 there is not ought left in the sight of my l, 113
47:25 let us find grace in the sight of my l, and 113
Ex 4:10 O my L, I *am* not eloquent, neither 136
4:13 he said, O my L, send, I pray thee, by 136
5:22 said, L, wherefore hast thou *so* evil entreated 136
15:17 *in* the Sanctuary, O L, *which* thy hands have 136
23:17 thy males shall appear before the L God. 113
32:22 Let not the anger of my l wax hot: 113
34: 9 O L, let my Lord, I pray thee, go amongst 136
34: 9 O Lord, let my L, I pray thee, go amongst 136
34:23 men children appear before the L God, 113
Nu 11:28 answered and said, My l Moses, forbid them. 113
12:11 Alas, my l, I beseech thee, lay not the sin 113
14:17 beseech thee, let the power of my L be great, 136
32:25 Thy servants will do as my l commandeth. 113
32:27 before the Lord to battle, as my l saith. 113
36: 2 The Lord commanded my l to give 113
36: 2 my l was commanded by the Lord to give 113
Dt 3:24 O L God, thou hast begun to shew thy 136
9:26 unto the Lord, and said, O L God, 136
10:17 L of lords, a great God, a mighty, and 113
Jos 3:11 *even* the L of all the earth passeth over 113
3:13 the L of all the earth, shall rest in the waters 113
5:14 unto him, What saith my l unto his servant? 113
7: 7 Joshua said, Alas, O L God, 136
7: 8 O L, what shall I say, when Israel turneth 136
Jdg 3:25 their l *was* fallen down dead on the earth. 113
4:18 said unto him, Turn in, my l, turn in to me; 113
6:13 O my l, if the Lord be with us, why then 113
6:15 he said unto him, O my L, wherewith shall I 136
6:22 the Lord, Gideon said, Alas, O L God! 136
13: 8 intreated the Lord, and said, O my L, 136
16:28 said, O L God, remember me, I pray thee, 136
19:26 house where her l *was,* till it was light. 113
19:27 her l rose up in the morning, and opened 113
Ru 2:13 Let me find favour in thy sight, my l; 113
1Sa 1:15 Hannah answered and said, No, my l, I *am* a 113
1:26 she said, O my l, *as* thy soul liveth, my lord, 113
1:26 she said, O my lord, *as* thy soul liveth, my l, 113
16:16 Let our l now command thy servants *which* 113
22:12 And he answered, Here I *am,* my l. 113
24: 8 and cried after Saul, saying, My l the king. 113

1Sa	24:10	I will not put forth mine hand against my l;	113
	25:24	And fell at his feet, and said, Upon me, my l,	113
	25:25	Let not my l, I pray thee, regard this man of	113
	25:25	handmaid saw not the young men of my l,	113
	25:26	Now therefore, my l, *as* the LORD liveth,	113
	25:26	and they that seek evil to my l, be as Nabal.	113
	25:27	thine handmaid hath brought unto my l,	113
	25:27	given unto the young men that follow my l.	113
	25:28	for the LORD will certainly make my l a	113
	25:28	my l fighteth the battles of the LORD,	113
	25:29	the soul of my l shall be bound in the bundle	113
	25:30	when the LORD shall have done to my l	113
	25:31	unto thee, nor offence of heart unto my l,	113
	25:31	or that my l hath avenged himself:	113
	25:31	the LORD shall have dealt well with my l,	113
	25:41	to wash the feet of the servants of my l.	113
	26:15	then hast thou not kept thy l the king?	113
	26:15	one of the people in to destroy the king thy l.	113
	26:17	And David said, *It is* my voice, my l, O king.	113
	26:18	Wherefore doth my l thus pursue after his	113
	26:19	let my l the king hear the words of his	113
	29: 8	fight against the enemies of my l the king?	113
2Sa	1:10	and have brought them hither unto my l.	113
	2: 5	ye have shewed this kindness unto your l,	113
	3:21	and will gather all Israel unto my l the king,	113
	4: 8	the LORD hath avenged my l the king this	113
	7:18	and he said, Who *am* I, O L GOD?	136
	7:19	yet a small thing in thy sight, O L GOD;	136
	7:19	And *is* this the manner of man, O L GOD?	136
	7:20	for thou, L GOD, knowest thy servant.	136
	7:28	And now, O L GOD, thou *art* that God, and	136
	7:29	for thou, O L GOD, hast spoken *it*: and	136
	9:11	According to all that my l the king hath	113
	10: 3	children of Ammon said unto Hanun their l,	113
	11: 9	king's house with all the servants of his l,	113
	11:11	my l Joab, and the servants of my lord,	113
	11:11	my lord Joab, and the servants of my l,	113
	11:13	to lie on his bed with the servants of his l,	113
	13:32	Let not my l suppose *that* they have slain all	113
	13:33	let not my l the king take the thing to his	113
	14: 9	My l, O king, the iniquity *be* on me, and	113
	14:12	speak *one* word unto my l the king.	113
	14:15	to speak of this thing unto my l the king,	113
	14:17	The word of my l the king shall now be	113
	14:17	so *is* my l the king to discern good and bad:	113
	14:18	woman said, Let my l the king now speak.	113
	14:19	and said, *As* thy soul liveth, my l the king,	113
	14:19	to the left from ought that my l the king hath	113
	14:20	my l *is* wise, according to the wisdom of an	113
	14:22	my l, O king, in that the king hath fulfilled	113
	15:15	thy servants *are ready to do* whatsoever my l	113
	15:21	LORD liveth, and *as* my l the king liveth,	113
	15:21	surely in what place my l the king shall be,	113
	16: 4	I may find grace in thy sight, my l, O king.	113
	16: 9	Why should this dead dog curse my l	113
	18:28	that lift up their hand against my l the king.	113
	18:31	and Cushi said, Tidings, my l the king:	113
	18:32	The enemies of my l the king, and all that	113
	19:19	Let not my l impute iniquity unto me,	113
	19:19	day that my l the king went out of Jerusalem,	113
	19:20	of Joseph to go down to meet my l the king.	113
	19:26	he answered, My l, O king, my servant	113
	19:27	he hath slandered thy servant unto my l	113
	19:27	but my l the king *is* as an angel of God:	113
	19:28	but dead men before my l the king:	113
	19:30	forasmuch as my l the king is come *again* in	113
	19:35	should thy servant be yet a burden unto my l	113
	19:37	let him go over with my l the king; and do to	113
	24: 3	*that* the eyes of my l the king may see *it*: but	113
	24: 3	why doth my l the king delight in this thing?	113
	24:21	Wherefore is my l the king come to his	113
	24:22	Let my l the king take and offer up what	113
1Ki	1: 2	Let there be sought for my l the king a	113
	1: 2	thy bosom, that my l the king may get heat.	113
	1:11	doth reign, and David our l knoweth *it* not?	113
	1:13	say unto him, Didst not thou, my l O king,	113
	1:17	she said unto him, My l, thou swarest by	113
	1:18	and now, my l the king, thou knowest *it* not:	113
	1:20	thou, my l O king, the eyes of all Israel *are*	113
	1:20	sit on the throne of my l the king after him.	113
	1:21	when my l the king shall sleep with his	113
	1:24	Nathan said, My l O king, hast thou said,	113
	1:27	Is this thing done by my l the king, and	113
	1:27	who should sit on the throne of my l the king	113
	1:31	and said, Let my l king David live for ever.	113
	1:33	Take with you the servants of your l, and	113
	1:36	the LORD God of my l the king say so *too*.	113
	1:37	As the LORD hath been with my l the king,	113
	1:37	greater than the throne of my l king David.	113
	1:43	Verily our l king David hath made Solomon	113
	1:47	servants came to bless our l king David,	113
	2:26	thou barest the ark of the L GOD before	136
	2:38	as my l the king hath said, so will thy servant	113
	3:10	the speech pleased the L, that Solomon had	136
	3:17	O my l, I and this woman dwell in one	113
	3:26	she said, O my l, give her the living child,	113
	8:53	our fathers out of Egypt, O L GOD.	136
	11:23	which fled from his l Hadadezer king of	113
	12:27	heart of this people turn again unto their l,	113
	18: 7	his face, and said, *Art* thou that my l Elijah?	113
	18: 8	I *am*: go, tell thy l, Behold, Elijah *is here*.	113
	18:10	whither my l hath not sent to seek thee:	113
	18:11	Go, tell thy l, Behold, Elijah *is here*.	113
	18:13	Was it not told my l what I did when Jezebel	113
	18:14	Go, tell thy l, Behold, Elijah *is here*: and	113
	20: 4	the king of Israel answered and said, My l,	113
	20: 9	of Ben-hadad, Tell my l the king,	113
	22: 6	for the L shall deliver *it* into the hand of	136
2Ki	2:19	of *this* city *is* pleasant, as my l seeth:	113
	4:16	she said, Nay, my l, thou man of God, do not	113
	4:28	she said, Did I desire a son of my l? did I not	113
	5: 3	Would God my l *were* with the prophet that	113
	5: 4	told his l, saying, Thus and thus said	113
	6:12	one of his servants said, None, my l, O king:	113
	6:26	unto him, saying, Help, my l, O king.	113
	7: 2	a l on whose hand the king leaned	7991
	7: 6	For the L had made the host of the Syrians	136
	7:17	the king appointed the l on whose hand he	7991
	7:19	*that* l answered the man of God, and said,	7991
	8: 5	Gehazi said, My l, O king, this *is*	113
	8:12	Hazael said, Why weepeth my l? And he	113
	9:11	Then Jehu came forth to the servants of his l:	113
	18:23	give pledges to my l the king of Assyria, and	113
	19:23	thy messengers thou hast reproached the L,	136
1Ch	21: 3	so many moe as they *be*: *but*, my l the king,	113
	21: 3	doth my l require this *thing*? why will he be	113
	21:23	let my l the king do *that* which *is* good in his	113
2Ch	2:14	with the cunning *men* of my l David thy	113
	2:15	and the wine, which my l hath spoken of,	113
	13: 6	is risen up, and hath rebelled against his l.	113
Ezr	10: 3	according to the counsel of my l, and	113
Ne	1:11	O L, I beseech thee, let now thine ear be	136
	3: 5	put not their necks to the work of their L.	113
	4:14	remember the L, *which is* great and terrible,	136
	8:10	for *this* day *is* holy unto our L: neither be ye	113
	10:29	all the commandments of the LORD our L,	113
Job	28:28	Behold, the fear of the L, that *is* wisdom;	136
Ps	8: 1	O LORD our L, how excellent *is* thy name	113
	8: 9	O LORD our L, how excellent *is* thy name	113
	12: 4	our lips *are* our own: who *is* l over us?	113
	16: 2	hast said unto the LORD, Thou *art* my L:	136
	22:30	it shall be accounted to the L for a	136
	35:17	L, how long wilt thou look on? rescue my	136
	35:22	keep not silence: O L, be not far from me.	136
	35:23	*even* unto my cause, my God and my L.	136
	37:13	The L shall laugh at him: for he seeth that	136
	38: 9	L, all my desire *is* before thee; and	136
	38:15	do I hope: thou wilt hear, O L my God.	136
	38:22	Make haste to help me, O L my salvation.	136
	39: 7	now, L, what wait I for? my hope *is* in thee.	136
	40:17	and needy; *yet* the L thinketh upon me:	136
	44:23	Awake, why sleepest thou, O L? arise,	136
	45:11	for he *is* thy L; and worship thou him.	113
	51:15	O L, open thou my lips; and my mouth shall	136
	54: 4	the L *is* with them that uphold my soul.	136
	55: 9	Destroy, O L, *and* divide their tongues: for I	136
	57: 9	I will praise thee, O L, among the people:	136
	59:11	and bring them down, O L our shield.	136
	62:12	Also unto thee, O L, *belongeth* mercy:	136
	66:18	iniquity in my heart, the L will not hear *me*:	136
	68:11	The L gave the word: great *was*	136
	68:17	the L *is* among them, *as in* Sinai, in the holy	136
	68:19	Blessed *be* the L, *who* daily loadeth us *with*	136
	68:20	unto GOD the L *belong* the issues from	136
	68:22	The L said, I will bring again from Bashan,	136
	68:26	*even* the L, from the fountain of Israel.	136
	68:32	the earth; O sing *praises unto* the L; Selah.	136
	69: 6	O L GOD of hosts, be ashamed for my	136

Ps	71: 5	For thou *art* my hope, O L GOD: *thou art*	136
	71:16	I will go in the strength of the L GOD:	136
	73:20	*so,* O L, when *thou* awakest, thou shalt	136
	73:28	I have put my trust in the L GOD, that *I*	136
	77: 2	In the day of my trouble I sought the L:	136
	77: 7	Will the L cast off for ever? and will he be	136
	78:65	the L awaked as one out of sleep, *and* like a	136
	79:12	wherewith they have reproached thee, O L.	136
	86: 3	Be merciful unto me, O L: for I cry unto	136
	86: 4	for unto thee, O L, do I lift up my soul.	136
	86: 5	For thou, L, *art* good, and ready to forgive;	136
	86: 8	the gods *there is* none like unto thee, O L;	136
	86: 9	shall come and worship before thee, O L;	136
	86:12	I will praise thee, O L my God, with all my	136
	86:15	But thou, O L, *art* a God full of compassion,	136
	89:49	L, where *are* thy former lovingkindnesses,	136
	89:50	Remember, L, the reproach of thy servants;	136
	90: 1	L, thou hast been our dwelling place in all	136
	97: 5	at the presence of the L of the whole earth.	113
	105:21	He made him l of his house, and ruler of all	113
	109:21	do thou for me, O GOD the L, for thy	136
	110: 1	The LORD said unto my L, Sit thou at my	113
	110: 5	The L at thy right hand shall strike through	136
	114: 7	Tremble, thou earth, at the presence of the L,	113
	130: 2	L, hear my voice: let thine ears be attentive	136
	130: 3	mark iniquities, O L, who shall stand?	136
	130: 6	My soul *waiteth* for the L more than they	136
	135: 5	*is* great, and *that* our L *is* above all gods.	113
	136: 3	O give thanks to the L of lords: for his	113
	140: 7	O GOD the L, the strength of my salvation,	136
	141: 8	But mine eyes *are* unto thee, O GOD the L:	136
	147: 5	Great *is* our L, and of great power:	113
Isa	1:24	Therefore saith the L, the LORD of hosts,	113
	3: 1	For behold, the L, the LORD of hosts,	113
	3:15	of the poor? saith the L GOD of hosts.	136
	3:17	Therefore the L will smite with a scab	136
	3:18	In that day the L will take away the bravery	136
	4: 4	When the L shall have washed away the filth	136
	6: 1	died I saw also the L sitting upon a throne,	136
	6: 8	Also I heard the voice of the L, saying,	136
	6:11	Then said I, L, how long? And he answered,	136
	7: 7	Thus saith the L GOD, It shall not stand,	136
	7:14	Therefore the L himself shall give you a	136
	7:20	In the same day shall the L shave with a	136
	8: 7	the L bringeth up upon them the waters of	136
	9: 8	The L sent a word into Jacob, and it hath	136
	9:17	Therefore the L shall have no joy in their	136
	10:12	*that* when the L hath performed his whole	136
	10:16	Therefore shall the L, the Lord of hosts,	113
	10:16	Therefore shall the Lord, the L of hosts,	136
	10:23	For the L GOD of hosts shall make a	136
	10:24	Therefore thus saith the L GOD of hosts,	136
	10:33	Behold, the L, the LORD of hosts, shall lop	113
	11:11	*that* the L shall set his hand again the second	136
	19: 4	will I give over into the hand of a cruel l;	113
	19: 4	over them, saith the L, the LORD of hosts.	113
	21: 6	For thus hath the L said unto me, Go, set a	136
	21: 8	My l, I stand continually upon	136
	21:16	For thus hath the L said unto me, Within a	136
	22: 5	of perplexity by the L GOD of hosts in	136
	22:12	in that day did the L GOD of hosts call to	136
	22:14	you till ye die, saith the L GOD of hosts.	136
	22:15	Thus saith the L GOD of hosts, Go,	136
	25: 8	the L GOD will wipe away tears from off	136
	28:16	Therefore thus saith the L GOD, Behold,	136
	28:22	for I have heard from the L GOD of hosts a	136
	29:13	Wherefore the L said, Forasmuch as this	136
	30:15	For thus saith the L GOD, the Holy One of	136
	30:20	*though* the L give you the bread of adversity,	136
	37:24	By thy servants hast thou reproached the L,	136
	38:16	O L, by these *things men* live, and in all	136
	40:10	the L GOD will come with strong *hand,*	136
	48:16	now the L GOD, and his Spirit, hath sent	136
	49:14	forsaken me, and my L hath forgotten me.	136
	49:22	Thus saith the L GOD, Behold, I will lift	136
	50: 4	The L GOD hath given me the tongue of	136
	50: 5	The L GOD hath opened mine ear, and	136
	50: 7	For the L GOD will help me; therefore	136
	50: 9	Behold, the L GOD will help me; who *is* he	136
	51:22	Thus saith thy L the LORD, and thy God	113
	52: 4	For thus saith the L GOD, My people went	136
	56: 8	The L GOD which gathereth the outcasts of	136
	61: 1	The Spirit of the L GOD *is* upon me;	136
	61:11	so the L GOD will cause righteousness and	136

	65:13	Therefore thus saith the L GOD, Behold,	136
	65:15	for the L GOD shall slay thee, and call his	136
Jer	1: 6	said I, Ah, L GOD, behold, I cannot speak:	136
	2:19	*is* not in thee, saith the L GOD of hosts.	136
	2:22	*is* marked before me, saith the L GOD.	136
	4:10	(Then said I, Ah, L GOD! surely thou hast	136
	7:20	Therefore thus saith the L GOD; Behold,	136
	14:13	said I, Ah L GOD! behold, the prophets say	136
	22:18	they shall not lament for him, *saying,* Ah l!	113
	32:17	Ah L GOD! behold, thou hast made	136
	32:25	thou hast said unto me, O L GOD,	136
	34: 5	and they will lament thee, *saying,* Ah l!	113
	37:20	hear now, I pray thee, O my l the king:	113
	38: 9	My l the king, these men have done evil in	113
	44:26	land of Egypt, saying, The L GOD liveth.	136
	46:10	For this *is* the day of the L GOD of hosts,	136
	46:10	for the L GOD of hosts hath a sacrifice in	136
	49: 5	a fear upon thee, saith the L GOD of hosts,	136
	50:25	for this *is* the work of the L GOD of hosts	136
	50:31	*thou* most proud, saith the L GOD of hosts:	136
La	1:14	the L hath delivered me into *their* hands,	136
	1:15	The L hath trodden under foot all my mighty	136
	1:15	the L hath trodden the virgin, the daughter of	136
	2: 1	How hath the L covered the daughter of	136
	2: 2	The L hath swallowed up all the habitations	136
	2: 5	The L was as an enemy: he hath swallowed	136
	2: 7	The L hath cast off his altar, he hath	136
	2:18	Their heart cried unto the L, O wall of	136
	2:19	heart like water before the face of the L:	136
	2:20	prophet be slain in the sanctuary of the L?	136
	3:31	For the L will not cast off for ever:	136
	3:36	a man in his cause, the L approveth not.	136
	3:37	to pass, *when* the L commandeth *it* not?	136
	3:58	O L, thou hast pleaded the causes of my	136
Eze	2: 4	shalt say unto them, Thus saith the L GOD.	136
	3:11	and tell them, Thus saith the L GOD;	136
	3:27	shalt say unto them, Thus saith the L GOD;	136
	4:14	said I, Ah L GOD, behold, my soul *hath*	136
	5: 5	Thus saith the L GOD; This *is* Jerusalem:	136
	5: 7	Therefore thus saith the L GOD;	136
	5: 8	Therefore thus saith the L GOD; Behold, I,	136
	5:11	Wherefore, *as* I live, saith the L GOD;	136
	6: 3	of Israel, hear the word of the L GOD;	136
	6: 3	Thus saith the L GOD to the mountains,	136
	6:11	Thus saith the L GOD; Smite with thine	136
	7: 2	thus saith the L GOD unto the land of	136
	7: 5	Thus saith the L GOD; An evil, an only	136
	8: 1	that the hand of the L GOD fell there upon	136
	9: 8	my face, and cried, and said, Ah L GOD,	136
	11: 7	Therefore thus saith the L GOD; Your slain	136
	11: 8	bring a sword upon you, saith the L GOD.	136
	11:13	*with* a loud voice, and said, Ah L GOD,	136
	11:16	Therefore say, Thus saith the L GOD;	136
	11:17	Therefore say, Thus saith the L GOD;	136
	11:21	upon their own heads, saith the L GOD.	136
	12:10	Say thou unto them, Thus saith the L GOD;	136
	12:19	Thus saith the L GOD, of the inhabitants of	136
	12:23	Tell them therefore, Thus saith the L GOD;	136
	12:25	and will perform it, saith the L GOD.	136
	12:28	say unto them, Thus saith the L GOD;	136
	12:28	spoken shall be done, saith the L GOD.	136
	13: 3	Thus saith the L GOD; Woe unto	136
	13: 8	Therefore thus saith the L GOD;	136
	13: 8	behold, I *am* against you, saith the L GOD.	136
	13: 9	and ye shall know that I *am* the L GOD.	136
	13:13	Therefore thus saith the L GOD; I will	136
	13:16	and *there is* no peace, saith the L GOD.	136
	13:18	say, Thus saith the L GOD; Woe to	136
	13:20	Wherefore thus saith the L GOD; Behold,	136
	14: 4	and say unto them, Thus saith the L GOD;	136
	14: 6	the house of Israel, Thus saith the L GOD;	136
	14:11	and I may be their God, saith the L GOD.	136
	14:14	by their righteousness, saith the L GOD.	136
	14:16	men *were* in it, *as* I live, saith the L GOD,	136
	14:18	men *were* in it, *as* I live, saith the L GOD,	136
	14:20	Job, *were* in it, *as* I live, saith the L GOD,	136
	14:21	For thus saith the L GOD; How much more	136
	14:23	all that I have done in it, saith the L GOD.	136
	15: 6	Therefore thus saith the L GOD; As	136
	15: 8	committed a trespass, saith the L GOD.	136
	16: 3	Thus saith the L GOD unto Jerusalem;	136
	16: 8	saith the L GOD, and thou becamest mine.	136
	16:14	I had put upon thee, saith the L GOD.	136
	16:19	and *thus* it was, saith the L GOD.	136

Eze 16:23 (woe, woe unto thee! saith the L GOD;) 136
16:30 How weak is thine heart, saith the L GOD, 136
16:36 Thus saith the L GOD; Because thy 136
16:43 thy way upon *thine* head, saith the L GOD: 136
16:48 *As* I live, saith the L GOD, Sodom thy 136
16:59 For thus saith the L GOD; I will even deal 136
16:63 all that thou hast done, saith the L GOD. 136
17: 3 say, Thus saith the L GOD; A great eagle 136
17: 9 Say thou, Thus saith the L GOD; Shall it 136
17:16 *As* I live, saith the L GOD, surely in 136
17:19 Therefore thus saith the L GOD; *As* I live, 136
17:22 Thus saith the L GOD; I will also take of 136
18: 3 *As* I live, saith the L GOD, ye shall not 136
18: 9 he shall surely live, saith the L GOD. 136
18:23 saith the L GOD: *and* not that he should 136
18:25 Yet ye say, The way of the L is not equal. 136
18:29 of Israel, The way of the L is not equal. 136
18:30 according to his ways, saith the L GOD. 136
18:32 death of him that dieth, saith the L GOD: 136
20: 3 and say unto them, Thus saith the L GOD; 136
20: 3 *As* I live, saith the L GOD, I will not be 136
20: 5 And say unto them, Thus saith the L GOD; 136
20:27 and say unto them, Thus saith the L GOD; 136
20:30 the house of Israel, Thus saith the L GOD; 136
20:31 *As* I live, saith the L GOD, I will not be 136
20:33 *As* I live, saith the L GOD, surely with a 136
20:36 so will I plead with you, saith the L GOD. 136
20:39 O house of Israel, thus saith the L GOD; 136
20:40 saith the L GOD, there shall all the house 136
20:44 O ye house of Israel, saith the L GOD. 136
20:47 Thus saith the L GOD; Behold, I *will* 136
20:49 said I, Ah L GOD, they say of me, Doth he 136
21: 7 shall be brought to pass, saith the L GOD. 136
21:13 it shall be no *more,* saith the L GOD. 136
21:24 Therefore thus saith the L GOD; 136
21:26 Thus saith the L GOD; Remove 136
21:28 Thus saith the L GOD concerning 136
22: 3 say thou, Thus saith the L GOD, The city 136
22:12 and hast forgotten me, saith the L GOD. 136
22:19 Therefore thus saith the L GOD; 136
22:28 unto them, saying, Thus saith the L GOD, 136
22:31 upon their heads, saith the L GOD. 136
23:22 O Aholibah, thus saith the L GOD; 136
23:28 For thus saith the L GOD; Behold, I *will* 136
23:32 Thus saith the L GOD; Thou shalt drink *of* 136
23:34 for I have spoken *it,* saith the L GOD. 136
23:35 Therefore thus saith the L GOD; 136
23:46 For thus saith the L GOD; *I will* bring up a 136
23:49 and ye shall know that I *am* the L GOD. 136
24: 3 and say unto them, Thus saith the L GOD; 136
24: 6 Wherefore thus saith the L GOD; Woe to 136
24: 9 Therefore thus saith the L GOD; Woe to 136
24:14 shall they judge thee, saith the L GOD. 136
24:21 the house of Israel, Thus saith the L GOD; 136
24:24 ye shall know that I *am* the L GOD. 136
25: 3 Hear the word of the L GOD; 136
25: 3 Thus saith the L GOD; Because thou 136
25: 6 For thus saith the L GOD; Because thou 136
25: 8 Thus saith the L GOD; Because that Moab 136
25:12 Thus saith the L GOD; Because that Edom 136
25:13 Therefore thus saith the L GOD; I will also 136
25:14 know my vengeance, saith the L GOD. 136
25:15 Thus saith the L GOD; Because 136
25:16 Therefore thus saith the L GOD; Behold, 136
26: 3 Therefore thus saith the L GOD; Behold, 136
26: 5 for I have spoken *it,* saith the L GOD: and 136
26: 7 For thus saith the L GOD; Behold, I *will* 136
26:14 for I the LORD have spoken *it,* saith the L 136
26:15 Thus saith the L GOD to Tyrus; Shall not 136
26:19 For thus saith the L GOD; When I shall 136
26:21 never be found again, saith the L GOD. 136
27: 3 for many isles, Thus saith the L GOD; 136
28: 2 the prince of Tyrus, Thus saith the L GOD; 136
28: 6 Therefore thus saith the L GOD; 136
28:10 for I have spoken *it,* saith the L GOD. 136
28:12 and say unto him, Thus saith the L GOD; 136
28:22 say, Thus saith the L GOD; Behold, I *am* 136
28:24 and they shall know that I *am* the L GOD. 136
28:25 Thus saith the L GOD; When I shall have 136
29: 3 Speak, and say, Thus saith the L GOD; 136
29: 8 Therefore thus saith the L GOD; Behold, 136
29:13 Yet thus saith the L GOD; At the end of 136
29:16 but they shall know that I *am* the L GOD. 136
29:19 Therefore thus saith the L GOD; Behold, 136
29:20 they wrought for me, saith the L GOD. 136
30: 2 prophesy and say, Thus saith the L GOD; 136
30: 6 fall in it by the sword, saith the L GOD. 136
30:10 Thus saith the L GOD; I will also make 136
30:13 Thus saith the L GOD; I will also destroy 136
30:22 Therefore thus saith the L GOD; Behold, 136
31:10 Therefore thus saith the L GOD; 136
31:15 Thus saith the L GOD; In the day when he 136
31:18 and all his multitude, saith the L GOD. 136
32: 3 Thus saith the L GOD; I will therefore 136
32: 8 darkness upon thy land, saith the L GOD. 136
32:11 For thus saith the L GOD; The sword of 136
32:14 their rivers to run like oil, saith the L GOD. 136
32:16 and for all her multitude, saith the L GOD. 136
32:31 army slain by the sword, saith the L GOD. 136
32:32 and all his multitude, saith the L GOD. 136
33:11 Say unto them, *As* I live, saith the L GOD, 136
33:17 people say, The way of the L is not equal: 136
33:20 Yet ye say, The way of the L is not equal. 136
33:25 say unto them, Thus saith the L GOD; 136
33:27 thus unto them, Thus saith the L GOD; 136
34: 2 Thus saith the L GOD unto the shepherds; 136
34: 8 saith the L GOD, surely because my flock 136
34:10 Thus saith the L GOD; Behold, I *am* 136
34:11 For thus saith the L GOD; Behold, I, 136
34:15 cause them to lie down, saith the L GOD. 136
34:17 *for* you, O my flock, thus saith the L GOD; 136
34:20 Therefore thus saith the L GOD unto them; 136
34:30 of Israel, *are* my people, saith the L GOD. 136
34:31 *and* I *am* your God, saith the L GOD. 136
35: 3 say unto it, Thus saith the L GOD; Behold, 136
35: 6 Therefore, *as* I live, saith the L GOD, I will 136
35:11 Therefore, *as* I live, saith the L GOD, I will 136
35:14 Thus saith the L GOD; When the whole 136
36: 2 Thus saith the L GOD; Because the enemy 136
36: 3 and say, Thus saith the L GOD; 136
36: 4 of Israel, hear the word of the L GOD; 136
36: 4 Thus saith the L GOD to the mountains, 136
36: 5 Therefore thus saith the L GOD; Surely in 136
36: 6 and to the valleys, Thus saith the L GOD; 136
36: 7 Therefore thus saith the L GOD; I have 136
36:13 Thus saith the L GOD; Because they say 136
36:14 thy nations any more, saith the L GOD. 136
36:15 nations to fall any more, saith the L GOD. 136
36:22 the house of Israel, Thus saith the L GOD; 136
36:23 that I *am* the LORD, saith the L GOD, 136
36:32 Not for your sakes do I *this,* saith the L 136
36:33 Thus saith the L GOD; In the day that I 136
36:37 Thus saith the L GOD; I will yet *for* this be 136
37: 3 And I answered, O L GOD, thou knowest. 136
37: 5 Thus saith the L GOD unto these bones; 136
37: 9 and say to the wind, Thus saith the L GOD; 136
37:12 and say unto them, Thus saith the L GOD; 136
37:19 Say unto them, Thus saith the L GOD; 136
37:21 And say unto them, Thus saith the L GOD; 136
38: 3 say, Thus saith the L GOD; Behold, I *am* 136
38:10 Thus saith the L GOD; It shall also come to 136
38:14 and say unto Gog, Thus saith the L GOD; 136
38:17 Thus saith the L GOD; *Art* thou he of 136
38:18 saith the L GOD, *that* my fury shall come 136
38:21 all my mountains, saith the L GOD: 136
39: 1 and say, Thus saith the L GOD; 136
39: 5 for I have spoken *it,* saith the L GOD. 136
39: 8 it is come, and it is done, saith the L GOD; 136
39:10 those that robbed them, saith the L GOD. 136
39:13 that I shall be glorified, saith the L GOD. 136
39:17 thou son of man, thus saith the L GOD; 136
39:20 and *with* all men of war, saith the L GOD. 136
39:25 Therefore thus saith the L GOD; Now will 136
39:29 upon the house of Israel, saith the L GOD. 136
43:18 Son of man, thus saith the L GOD; 136
43:19 to minister unto me, saith the L GOD, 136
43:27 and I will accept you, saith the L GOD. 136
44: 6 the house of Israel, Thus saith the L GOD; 136
44: 9 Thus saith the L GOD; No stranger, 136
44:12 saith the L GOD, and they shall bear their 136
44:15 me the fat and the blood, saith the L GOD: 136
44:27 offer his sin offering, saith the L GOD. 136
45: 9 Thus saith the L GOD; Let it suffice you, 136
45: 9 from my people, saith the L GOD. 136
45:15 reconciliation for them, saith the L GOD. 136
45:18 Thus saith the L GOD; In the first *month,* 136
46: 1 Thus saith the L GOD; The gate of 136
46:16 Thus saith the L GOD; If the prince give a 136

Eze	47:13	Thus saith the **L** GOD; This *shall be*	136
	47:23	give *him* his inheritance, saith the **L** GOD.	136
	48:29	these *are* their portions, saith the **L** GOD.	136
Da	1: 2	the **L** gave Jehoiakim king of Judah into his	136
	1:10	I fear my **l** the king, who hath appointed	113
	2:10	therefore *there is* no king, **l**, nor ruler,	7229
	2:47	a **L** of kings, and a revealer of secrets,	4756
	4:19	Belteshazzar answered and said, My **l**,	4756
	4:24	which is come upon my **l** the king:	4756
	5:23	hast lifted up thyself against the **L** of	4756
	9: 3	I set my face unto the **L** God, to seek *by*	136
	9: 4	and said, O **L**, the great and dreadful God,	136
	9: 7	O **L**, righteousness *belongeth* unto thee, but	136
	9: 8	O **L**, to us *belongeth* confusion of face,	136
	9: 9	To the **L** our God *belong* mercies and	136
	9:15	now, O **L** our God, that hast brought thy	136
	9:16	O **L**, according to all thy righteousness,	136
	9:19	O **L**, hear; O Lord, forgive; O Lord, hearken	136
	9:19	O Lord, hear; O **L**, forgive; O Lord, hearken	136
	9:19	hear; O Lord, forgive; O **L**, hearken and do;	136
	10:16	said unto him that stood before me, O my **l**,	113
	10:17	For how can the servant of this my **l** talk	113
	10:17	servant of this my lord talk with this my **l**?	113
	10:19	I was strengthened, and said, Let my **l** speak;	113
	12: 8	said I, O my **l**, what *shall be* the end of these	113
Hos	12:14	and his reproach shall his **L** return unto him.	113
Am	1: 8	Philistines shall perish, saith the **L** GOD.	136
	3: 7	Surely the **L** GOD will do nothing, but he	136
	3: 8	the **L** GOD hath spoken, who can but	136
	3:11	Therefore thus saith the **L** GOD;	136
	3:13	saith the **L** GOD, the God of hosts,	136
	4: 2	The **L** GOD hath sworn by his holiness,	136
	4: 5	O ye children of Israel, saith the **L** GOD.	136
	5: 3	For thus saith the **L** GOD; The city that	136
	5:16	the God of hosts, the **L**, saith thus;	136
	6: 8	The **L** GOD hath sworn by himself, saith	136
	7: 1	Thus hath the **L** GOD shewed unto me; and	136
	7: 2	I said, O **L** GOD, forgive, I beseech thee:	136
	7: 4	Thus hath the **L** GOD shewed unto me: and	136
	7: 4	the **L** GOD called to contend by fire, and	136
	7: 5	said I, O **L** GOD, cease, I beseech thee:	136
	7: 6	This also shall not be, saith the **L** GOD.	136
	7: 7	the **L** stood upon a wall made by a	136
	7: 8	said the **L**, Behold, I *will* set a plumbline in	136
	8: 1	Thus hath the **L** GOD shewed unto me: and	136
	8: 3	be howlings in that day, saith the **L** GOD:	136
	8: 9	come to pass in that day, saith the **L** GOD,	136
	8:11	Behold, the days come, saith the **L** GOD,	136
	9: 1	I saw the **L** standing upon the altar: and	136
	9: 5	the **L** GOD of hosts *is* he that toucheth	136
	9: 8	the eyes of the **L** GOD *are* upon the sinful	136
Ob	1: 1	Thus saith the **L** GOD concerning Edom;	136
Mic	1: 2	and let the **L** GOD be witness against you,	136
	1: 2	against you, the **L** from his holy temple.	136
	4:13	their substance unto the **L** of the whole	113
Hab	3:19	The **L** GOD *is* my strength, and he will	136
Zep	1: 7	Hold thy peace at the presence of the **L**	136
Zec	1: 9	said I, O my **l**, what *are* these? And the angel	113
	4: 4	with me, saying, What *are* these, my **l**?	113
	4: 5	not what these *be?* And I said, No, my **l**.	113
	4:13	not what these *be?* And I said, No, my **l**.	113
	4:14	that stand by the **L** of the whole earth.	113
	6: 4	that talked with me, What *are* these, my **l**?	113
	6: 5	*which* go forth from standing before the **L** of	113
	9: 4	the **L** will cast her out, and he will smite her	136
	9:14	and the **L** GOD shall blow the trumpet, and	136
Mal	1:14	sacrificeth unto the **L** a corrupt *thing:* for I	136
Mt	1:20	*the* angel of the **L** appeared unto him in a	*2962*
	1:22	which was spoken of the **L** by the prophet,	*2962*
	1:24	did as the angel of the **L** had bidden him,	*2962*
	2:13	*the* angel of the **L** appeareth to Joseph in a	*2962*
	2:15	which was spoken of the **L** by the prophet,	*2962*
	2:19	an angel of the **L** appeareth in a dream to	*2962*
	3: 3	Prepare ye the way of the **L**, make his paths	*2962*
	4: 7	Thou shalt not tempt the **L** thy God.	*2962*
	4:10	Thou shalt worship the **L** thy God, and	*2962*
	5:33	but shalt perform unto the **L** thine oaths:	*2962*
	7:21	Not every one that saith unto me, **L**, Lord,	*2962*
	7:21	Not every one that saith unto me, Lord, **L**,	*2962*
	7:22	Many will say to me in that day, **L**, Lord,	*2962*
	7:22	Many will say to me in that day, Lord, **L**,	*2962*
	8: 2	worshipped him, saying, **L**, if thou wilt,	*2962*
	8: 6	And saying, **L**, my servant lieth at home	*2962*
	8: 8	The centurion answered and said, **L**, I am	*2962*
	8:21	**L**, suffer me first to go and bury my father.	*2962*
	8:25	to *him,* and awoke him, saying, **L**, save us:	*2962*
	9:28	to do this? They said unto him, Yea, **L**.	*2962*
	9:38	Pray ye therefore the **L** of the harvest,	*2962*
	10:24	*his* master, nor the servant above his **l**.	*2962*
	10:25	he be as his master, and the servant as his **l**.	*2962*
	11:25	**L** of heaven and earth, because thou hast	*2962*
	12: 8	For the Son of man is **L** even of the sabbath	*2962*
	13:51	these *things?* They say unto him, Yea, **L**.	*2962*
	14:28	And Peter answered him and said, **L**, if it	*2962*
	14:30	to sink, he cried, saying, **L**, save me.	*2962*
	15:22	mercy on me, O **L**, *thou* Son of David;	*2962*
	15:25	and worshipped him, saying, **L**, help me.	*2962*
	15:27	And she said, Truth, **L**: yet the dogs eat of	*2962*
	16:22	rebuke him, saying, Be it far from thee, **L**:	*2962*
	17: 4	answered Peter, and said unto Jesus, **L**,	*2962*
	17:15	**L**, have mercy on my son: for he is	*2962*
	18:21	Then came Peter to him, and said, **L**,	*2962*
	18:25	his **l** commanded him to be sold, and	*2962*
	18:26	fell down, and worshipped him, saying, **L**,	*2962*
	18:27	Then the **l** of that servant was moved with	*2962*
	18:31	came and told unto their **l** all that was done.	*2962*
	18:32	Then his **l**, after that he had called him,	*2962*
	18:34	And his **l** was wroth, and delivered him to	*2962*
	20: 8	the **l** of the vineyard saith unto his steward,	*2962*
	20:30	cried out, saying, Have mercy on us, O **L**,	*2962*
	20:31	saying, Have mercy on us, O **L**, *thou* Son	*2962*
	20:33	They say unto him, **L**, that our eyes may be	*2962*
	21: 3	ye shall say, The **L** hath need of them;	*2962*
	21: 9	*is* he that cometh in the name of the **L**;	*2962*
	21:40	When the **l** therefore of the vineyard	*2962*
	22:37	Thou shalt love the **L** thy God with all thy	*2962*
	22:43	How then doth David in spirit call him **L**,	*2962*
	22:44	The **L** said unto my Lord, Sit thou on my	*2962*
	22:44	The LORD said unto my **L**, Sit thou on my	*2962*
	22:45	If David then call him **L**, how is he his son?	*2962*
	23:39	is he that cometh in the name of the **L**.	*2962*
	24:42	for ye know not what hour your **L** doth	*2962*
	24:45	whom his **l** hath made ruler over his	*2962*
	24:46	whom his **l** when he cometh shall find so	*2962*
	24:48	say in his heart, My **l** delayeth his coming;	*2962*
	24:50	The **l** of that servant shall come in a day	*2962*
	25:11	other virgins, saying, **L**, Lord, open to us.	*2962*
	25:11	other virgins, saying, Lord, **L**, open to us.	*2962*
	25:19	After a long time the **l** of those servants	*2962*
	25:20	and brought other five talents, saying, **L**,	*2962*
	25:21	His **l** said unto him, Well *done, thou* good	*2962*
	25:21	*things:* enter thou into the joy of thy **l**.	*2962*
	25:22	had received two talents came and said, **L**,	*2962*
	25:23	His **l** said unto him, Well *done,* good and	*2962*
	25:23	*things:* enter thou into the joy of thy **l**.	*2962*
	25:24	received the one talent came and said, **L**,	*2962*
	25:26	His **l** answered and said unto him,	*2962*
	25:37	saying, **L**, when saw we thee a hungred,	*2962*
	25:44	saying, **L**, when saw we thee a hungred, or	*2962*
	26:22	one of them to say unto him, **L**, is it I?	*2962*
	27:10	the potter's field, as the **L** appointed me.	*2962*
	28: 2	for *the* angel of the **L** descended from	*2962*
	28: 6	Come, see the place where the **L** lay.	*2962*
Mk	1: 3	Prepare ye the way of the **L**, make his paths	*2962*
	2:28	Therefore the Son of man is **L** also of	*2962*
	5:19	tell them how great *things* the **L** hath done	*2962*
	7:28	she answered and said unto him, Yes, **L**:	*2962*
	9:24	cried out, and said with tears, **L**, I believe;	*2962*
	10:51	unto him, **L**, that I might receive my sight.	*4462*
	11: 3	say ye that the **L** hath need of him; and	*2962*
	11: 9	*is* he that cometh in the name of the **L**:	*2962*
	11:10	that cometh in the name of the **L**:	*2962*
	12: 9	therefore the **l** of the vineyard do?	*2962*
	12:29	O Israel; The **L** our God is one Lord:	*2962*
	12:29	O Israel; The Lord our God is one **L**:	*2962*
	12:30	And thou shalt love the **L** thy God with all	*2962*
	12:36	The **L** said to my Lord, Sit thou on my	*2962*
	12:36	The LORD said to my **L**, Sit thou on my	*2962*
	12:37	David therefore himself calleth him **L**; and	*2962*
	13:20	And except that the **L** had shortened *those*	*2962*
	16:19	So then after the **L** had spoken unto them,	*2962*
	16:20	the **L** working with *them,* and	*2962*
Lk	1: 6	and ordinances of the **L** blameless.	*2962*
	1: 9	when he went into the temple of the **L**.	*2962*
	1:11	**L** standing on the right side of the altar of	*2962*
	1:15	For he shall be great in the sight of the **L**,	*2962*
	1:16	of Israel shall he turn to the **L** their God.	*2962*
	1:17	to make ready a people prepared for the **L**.	*2962*

Lk 1:25 Thus hath the **L** dealt with me in the days *2962*
1:28 *that art* highly favoured, the **L** *is* with thee: *2962*
1:32 the **L** God shall give unto him the throne of *2962*
1:38 Mary said, Behold the handmaid of the **L**; *2962*
1:43 that the mother of my **L** should come to *2962*
1:45 *things* which were told her from the **L**. *2962*
1:46 Mary said, My soul doth magnify the **L**, *2962*
1:58 her cousins heard how the **L** had shewed *2962*
1:66 And the hand of the **L** was with him. *2962*
1:68 Blessed *be* the **L** God of Israel; for he hath *2962*
1:76 for thou shalt go before the face of the **L** to *2962*
2: 9 *the* angel of the **L** came upon them, and *2962*
2: 9 the glory of the **L** shone round about them: *2962*
2:11 of David a Saviour, which is Christ the **L**. *2962*
2:15 which the **L** hath made known unto us. *2962*
2:22 him to Jerusalem, to present *him* to the **L**; *2962*
2:23 (As it is written in the law of the **L**, Every *2962*
2:23 the womb shall be called holy to the **L**;) *2962*
2:24 to that which is said in the law of the **L**, *2962*
2:29 **L**, now lettest thou thy servant depart in *1203*
2:38 instant gave thanks *likewise* unto the **L**, *2962*
2:39 all *things* according to the law of the **L**, *2962*
3: 4 Prepare ye the way of the **L**, make his paths *2962*
4: 8 Thou shalt worship the **L** thy God, and *2962*
4:12 is said, Thou shalt not tempt the **L** thy God. *2962*
4:18 The Spirit of the **L** *is* upon me, *2962*
4:19 To preach the acceptable year of the **L**. *2962*
5: 8 from me; for I am a sinful man, O **L**. *2962*
5:12 and besought him, saying, **L**, if thou wilt, *2962*
5:17 the power of the **L** was *present* to heal *2962*
6: 5 That the Son of man is **L** also of *2962*
6:46 **L**, Lord, and do not *the things* which I say? *2962*
6:46 Lord, **L**, and do not *the things* which I say? *2962*
7: 6 saying unto him, **L**, trouble not thyself: *2962*
7:13 And when the **L** saw her, he had *2962*
7:31 And the **L** said, Whereunto then shall I *2962*
9:54 and John saw *this,* they said, **L**, *2962*
9:57 a certain *man* said unto him, **L**, I will *2962*
9:59 But he said, **L**, suffer me first to go and *2962*
9:61 And another also said, **L**, I will follow thee; *2962*
10: 1 After these *things* the **L** appointed other *2962*
10: 2 pray ye therefore the **L** of the harvest, *2962*
10:17 seventy returned *again* with joy, saying, **L**, *2962*
10:21 O Father, **L** of heaven and earth, *2962*
10:27 Thou shalt love the **L** thy God with all thy *2962*
10:40 and came to *him,* and said, **L**, *2962*
11: 1 **L**, teach us to pray, as John also taught his *2962*
11:39 And the **L** said unto him, Now do ye *2962*
12:36 like unto men that wait for their **l**, *2962*
12:37 whom the **l** when he cometh shall find *2962*
12:41 Then Peter said unto him, **L**, speakest thou *2962*
12:42 And the **L** said, Who then is *that* faithful *2962*
12:42 whom *his* **l** shall make ruler over his *2962*
12:43 whom his **l** when he cometh shall find so *2962*
12:45 say in his heart, My **l** delayeth his coming; *2962*
12:46 The **l** of that servant will come in a day *2962*
13: 8 **L**, let it alone this year also, till I shall dig *2962*
13:15 The **L** then answered him, and said, *2962*
13:23 Then said one unto him, **L**, are there few *2962*
13:25 at the door, saying, **L**, Lord, open unto us; *2962*
13:25 at the door, saying, Lord, **L**, open unto us; *2962*
13:35 *is* he that cometh in the name of the **L**. *2962*
14:21 shewed his **l** these *things.* Then the master *2962*
14:22 And the servant said, **L**, it is done as thou *2962*
14:23 And the **l** said unto the servant, Go out into *2962*
16: 3 for my **l** taketh away from me *2962*
16: 5 the first, How much owest thou unto my **l**? *2962*
16: 8 And the **l** commended the unjust steward, *2962*
17: 5 And the apostles said unto the **L**, *2962*
17: 6 And the **L** said, If ye had faith as a grain of *2962*
17:37 and said unto him, Where, **L**? *2962*
18: 6 And the **L** said, Hear what the unjust judge *2962*
18:41 And he said, **L**, that I may receive my *2962*
19: 8 And Zaccheus stood, and said unto the **L**; *2962*
19: 8 Behold, **L**, the half of my goods I give to *2962*
19:16 Then came the first, saying, **L**, thy pound *2962*
19:18 And the second came, saying, **L**, thy pound *2962*
19:20 saying, **L**, behold, *here is* thy pound, *2962*
19:25 they said unto him, **L**, he hath ten pounds.) *2962*
19:31 unto him, Because the **L** hath need of him. *2962*
19:34 And they said, The **L** hath need of him. *2962*
19:38 the King that cometh in the name of the **L**: *2962*
20:13 Then said the **l** of the vineyard, What shall *2962*
20:15 shall the **l** of the vineyard do unto them? *2962*
20:37 when he calleth the **L** the God of Abraham, *2962*
20:42 The **L** said to my Lord, Sit thou on my *2962*
20:42 The LORD said to my **L**, Sit thou on my *2962*
20:44 David therefore calleth him **L**, how is he *2962*
22:31 And the **L** said, Simon, Simon, behold, *2962*
22:33 And he said unto him, **L**, I am ready to go *2962*
22:38 And they said, **L**, behold, here *are* two *2962*
22:49 they said unto him, **L**, shall we smite with *2962*
22:61 And the **L** turned, and looked upon Peter. *2962*
22:61 And Peter remembered the word of the **L**, *2962*
23:42 And he said unto Jesus, **L**, remember me *2962*
24: 3 and found not the body of the **L** Jesus. *2962*
24:34 The **L** is risen indeed, and hath appeared to *2962*
Jn 1:23 Make straight the way of the **L**, as said *2962*
4: 1 the **L** knew how the Pharisees had heard *2962*
6:23 after that the **L** had given thanks:) *2962*
6:34 Then said they unto him, **L**, evermore give *2962*
6:68 answered him, **L**, to whom shall we go? *2962*
8:11 She said, No *man,* **L**. And Jesus said unto *2962*
9:36 He answered and said, Who is he, **L**, that I *2962*
9:38 And he said, **L**, I believe. And he *2962*
11: 2 (It was *that* Mary which anointed the **L** *2962*
11: 3 saying, **L**, behold, he whom thou lovest is *2962*
11:12 **L**, if he sleep, he shall do well. *2962*
11:21 **L**, if thou hadst been here, my brother had *2962*
11:27 She saith unto him, Yea, **L**: I believe that *2962*
11:32 saying unto him, **L**, if thou hadst been here, *2962*
11:34 They say unto him, **L**, come and see. *2962*
11:39 saith unto him, **L**, by this time he stinketh: *2962*
12:13 of Israel that cometh in the name of the **L**. *2962*
12:38 which he spake, **L**, who hath believed our *2962*
12:38 to whom hath the arm of the **L** been *2962*
13: 6 and *Peter* saith unto him, **L**, dost thou wash *2962*
13: 9 **L**, not my feet only, but also *my* hands and *2962*
13:13 Ye call me Master and **L**: and ye say well; *2962*
13:14 If I then, *your* **L** and Master, have washed *2962*
13:16 The servant is not greater than his **l**; *2962*
13:25 Jesus' breast saith unto him, **L**, who is it? *2962*
13:36 Peter said unto him, **L**, whither goest thou? *2962*
13:37 Peter said unto him, **L**, why cannot I follow *2962*
14: 5 Thomas saith unto him, **L**, we know not *2962*
14: 8 **L**, shew us the Father, and it sufficeth us. *2962*
14:22 Judas saith unto him, not Iscariot, **L**, how is *2962*
15:15 for the servant knoweth not what his **l** *2962*
15:20 The servant is not greater than his **l**. *2962*
20: 2 They have taken away the **L** out of *2962*
20:13 Because they have taken away my **L**, and *2962*
20:18 told the disciples that she had seen the **L**, *2962*
20:20 the disciples glad, when they saw the **L**. *2962*
20:25 said unto him, We have seen the **L**. *2962*
20:28 and said unto him, My **L** and my God. *2962*
21: 7 Jesus loved saith unto Peter, It is the **L**. *2962*
21: 7 when Simon Peter heard that it was the **L**, *2962*
21:12 Who art thou? knowing that it was the **L**. *2962*
21:15 He saith unto him, Yea, **L**; thou knowest *2962*
21:16 He saith unto him, Yea, **L**; thou knowest *2962*
21:17 And he said unto him, **L**, thou knowest all *2962*
21:20 and said, **L**, which is he that betrayeth *2962*
21:21 to Jesus, **L**, and what *shall* this *man do?* *2962*
Ac 1: 6 they asked of him, saying, **L**, *2962*
1:21 with us all the time that the **L** Jesus went in *2962*
1:24 And they prayed, and said, Thou, **L**, *2962*
2:20 *that* great and notable day of the **L** come: *2962*
2:21 call on the name of the **L** shall be saved. *2962*
2:25 I foresaw the **L** always before my face, *2962*
2:34 he saith himself, The **L** said unto my Lord, *2962*
2:34 saith himself, The LORD said unto my **L**, *2962*
2:36 ye have crucified, both **L** and Christ. *2962*
2:39 *even* as many as the **L** our God shall call. *2962*
2:47 And the **L** added to the church daily such *2962*
3:19 shall come from the presence of the **L**; *2962*
3:22 A prophet shall the **L** your God raise up *2962*
4:24 and said, **L**, thou *art* God, which hast made *1203*
4:26 rulers were gathered together against the **L**, *2962*
4:29 And now, **L**, behold their threatenings: and *2962*
4:33 witness of the resurrection of the **L** Jesus: *2962*
5: 9 together to tempt the Spirit of the **L**? *2962*
5:14 believers were the more added to the **L**, *2962*
5:19 But *the* angel of the **L** by night opened *2962*
7:30 angel of the **L** in a flame of fire in a bush. *2962*
7:31 behold *it,* the voice of the **L** came unto him, *2962*
7:33 Then said the **L** to him, Put off *thy* shoes *2962*
7:37 A prophet shall the **L** your God raise up *2962*
7:49 saith the **L**: or what *is* the place of my rest? *2962*

Ac 7:59 calling upon *God,* and saying, L Jesus, *2962*
7:60 and cried with a loud voice, L, *2962*
8:16 were baptized in the name of the L Jesus.) *2962*
8:24 and said, Pray ye to the L for me, *2962*
8:25 and preached the word of the L, *2962*
8:26 And *the* angel of the L spake unto Philip, *2962*
8:39 the Spirit of the L caught away Philip, *2962*
9: 1 and slaughter against the disciples of the L, *2962*
9: 5 And he said, Who art thou, L? And *2962*
9: 5 And the L said, I am Jesus whom thou *2962*
9: 6 And he trembling and astonished said, L, *2962*
9: 6 And the L *said* unto him, Arise, and go into *2962*
9:10 and to him said the L in a vision, Ananias. *2962*
9:10 And he said, Behold, I *am here,* L. *2962*
9:11 And the L *said* unto him, Arise, and go into *2962*
9:13 Then Ananias answered, L, I have heard by *2962*
9:15 But the L said unto him, Go *thy way:* for he *2962*
9:17 him said, Brother Saul, the L, *even* Jesus, *2962*
9:27 declared unto them how he had seen the L *2962*
9:29 And he spake boldly in the name of the L *2962*
9:31 and walking in the fear of the L, and in *2962*
9:35 and Saron saw him, and turned to the L. *2962*
9:42 all Joppa; and many believed in the L. *2962*
10: 4 he was afraid, and said, What is it, L? *2962*
10:14 But Peter said, Not so, L; for I have never *2962*
10:36 peace by Jesus Christ: (he is L of all:) *2962*
10:48 them to be baptized in the name of the L. *2962*
11: 8 But I said, Not so, L: for nothing common *2962*
11:16 Then remembered I the word of the L, *2962*
11:17 who believed on the L Jesus Christ; *2962*
11:20 unto the Grecians, preaching the L Jesus. *2962*
11:21 And the hand of the L was with them: and *2962*
11:21 number believed, and turned unto the L. *2962*
11:23 of heart *they* would cleave unto the L. *2962*
11:24 and much people was added unto the L. *2962*
12: 7 *the* angel of the L came upon *him,* and *2962*
12:11 that the L hath sent his angel, and *2962*
12:17 declared unto them how the L had brought *2962*
12:23 And immediately *the* angel of the L smote *2962*
13: 2 As they ministered to the L, and fasted, *2962*
13:10 cease to pervert the right ways of the L? *2962*
13:11 the hand of the L *is* upon thee, and *2962*
13:12 being astonished at the doctrine of the L. *2962*
13:47 For so hath the L commanded us, *saying,* I *2962*
13:48 were glad, and glorified the word of the L: *2962*
13:49 And the word of the L was published *2962*
14: 3 abode they speaking boldly in the L, *2962*
14:23 they commended them to the L, on whom *2962*
15:11 of the L Jesus Christ *we* shall be saved, *2962*
15:17 the residue of men might seek after the L, *2962*
15:17 saith the L, who doeth all these *things.* *2962*
15:26 lives for the name of our L Jesus Christ. *2962*
15:35 teaching and preaching the word of the L, *2962*
15:36 where we have preached the word of the L, *2962*
16:10 assuredly gathering that the L had called us *2962*
16:14 heard *us:* whose heart the L opened, *2962*
16:15 If ye have judged me to be faithful to the L, *2962*
16:31 Believe on the L Jesus Christ, and *2962*
16:32 And they spake unto him the word of the L, *2962*
17:24 seeing that he is L of heaven and earth, *2962*
17:27 That *they* should seek the L, if haply they *2962*
18: 8 believed on the L with all his house; *2962*
18: 9 Then spake the L to Paul in the night by a *2962*
18:25 *man* was instructed in the way of the L; *2962*
18:25 and taught diligently the *things* of the L, *2962*
19: 5 were baptized in the name of the L Jesus. *2962*
19:10 in Asia heard the word of the L Jesus, *2962*
19:13 had evil spirits the name of the L Jesus, *2962*
19:17 and the name of the L Jesus was magnified. *2962*
20:19 Serving the L with all humility of mind, *2962*
20:21 and faith toward our L Jesus Christ. *2962*
20:24 which I have received of the L Jesus, *2962*
20:35 and to remember the words of the L Jesus, *2962*
21:13 at Jerusalem for the name of the L Jesus. *2962*
21:14 saying, The will of the L be done. *2962*
21:20 when they heard *it,* they glorified the L, *2962*
22: 8 And I answered, Who art thou, L? And he *2962*
22:10 And I said, What shall I do, L? And *2962*
22:10 And the L said unto me, Arise, and go into *2962*
22:16 away thy sins, calling on the name of the L. *2962*
22:19 And I said, L, they know that I imprisoned *2962*
23:11 And the night following the L stood by *2962*
25:26 I have no certain *thing* to write unto *my* l. *2962*
26:15 And I said, Who art thou, L? And he said, *2962*
28:31 teaching those *things* which concern the L *2962*

Ro 1: 3 Concerning his Son Jesus Christ our L, *2962*
1: 7 God our Father, and the L Jesus Christ. *2962*
4: 8 Blessed *is* the man to whom the L will not *2962*
4:24 that raised up Jesus our L from the dead; *2962*
5: 1 we have peace with God through our L *2962*
5:11 we also joy in God through our L Jesus *2962*
5:21 unto eternal life by Jesus Christ our L. *2962*
6:11 alive unto God through Jesus Christ our L. *2962*
6:23 *is* eternal life through Jesus Christ our L. *2962*
7:25 I thank God through Jesus Christ our L. So *2962*
8:39 love of God, which is in Christ Jesus our L. *2962*
9:28 a short work will the L make upon *2962*
9:29 Except the L of sabaoth had left us a seed, *2962*
10: 9 shalt confess with thy mouth the L Jesus, *2962*
10:12 for the same L over all *is* rich unto all that *2962*
10:13 call upon the name of the L shall be saved. *2962*
10:16 For Esaias saith, L, who hath believed our *2962*
11: 3 L, they have killed thy prophets, and *2962*
11:34 For who hath known the mind of the L? or *2962*
12:11 in business; fervent in spirit; serving the L; *2962*
12:19 *is* mine; I will repay, saith the L. *2962*
13:14 But put ye on the L Jesus Christ, and *2962*
14: 6 regardeth the day, regardeth *it* unto the L; *2962*
14: 6 to the L he doth not regard *it.* He that *2962*
14: 6 eateth to the L, for he giveth God thanks; *2962*
14: 6 to the L he eateth not, and giveth God *2962*
14: 8 For whether we live, we live unto the L; *2962*
14: 8 and whether we die, we die unto the L: *2962*
14: 9 that he might be L both of the dead and *2961*
14:11 For it is written, *As* I live, saith the L, *2962*
14:14 I know, and am persuaded by the L Jesus, *2962*
15: 6 even the Father of our L Jesus Christ. *2962*
15:11 And again, Praise the L, all ye Gentiles; *2962*
15:30 for the L Jesus Christ's sake, and for *2962*
16: 2 That ye receive her in the L, as becometh *2962*
16: 8 Greet Amplias my beloved in the L. *2962*
16:11 *household* of Narcissus, which are in the L. *2962*
16:12 and Tryphosa, who labour in the L. *2962*
16:12 which laboured much in the L. *2962*
16:13 Salute Rufus chosen in the L, and *2962*
16:18 For *they that are* such serve not our L Jesus *2962*
16:20 The grace of our L Jesus Christ *be* with *2962*
16:22 who wrote *this* epistle, salute you in the L. *2962*
16:24 The grace of our L Jesus Christ *be* with you *2962*

1Co 1: 2 call upon the name of Jesus Christ our L, *2962*
1: 3 our Father, and *from* the L Jesus Christ. *2962*
1: 7 waiting for the coming of our L Jesus *2962*
1: 8 blameless in the day of our L Jesus Christ. *2962*
1: 9 fellowship of his Son Jesus Christ our L. *2962*
1:10 by the name of our L Jesus Christ, *2962*
1:31 He that glorieth, let him glory in the L. *2962*
2: 8 would not have crucified the L of glory. *2962*
2:16 For who hath known the mind of the L, *2962*
3: 5 even as the L gave to every man? *2962*
3:20 The L knoweth the thoughts of the wise, *2962*
4: 4 but he that judgeth me is the L. *2962*
4: 5 nothing before the time, until the L come, *2962*
4:17 is my beloved son, and faithful in the L, *2962*
4:19 to you shortly, if the L will, and will know, *2962*
5: 4 In the name of our L Jesus Christ, when ye *2962*
5: 4 with the power of our L Jesus Christ, *2962*
5: 5 may be saved in the day of the L Jesus. *2962*
6:11 ye are justified in the name of the L Jesus, *2962*
6:13 body *is* not for fornication, but for the L; *2962*
6:13 but for the Lord; and the L for the body. *2962*
6:14 And God hath both raised up the L, and *2962*
6:17 But he that is joined unto the L is one *2962*
7:10 married I command, *yet* not I, but the L, *2962*
7:12 But to the rest speak I, not the L: If any *2962*
7:17 as the L hath called every one, so let him *2962*
7:22 For he that is called in the L, *being* a *2962*
7:25 virgins I have no commandment of the L: *2962*
7:25 as one that hath obtained mercy of the L to *2962*
7:32 careth for the *things* that belong to the L, *2962*
7:32 to the Lord, how he may please the L: *2962*
7:34 *woman* careth for the *things* of the L, *2962*
7:35 that you may attend upon the L without *2962*
7:39 be married to whom she will; only in the L. *2962*
8: 6 and one L Jesus Christ, by whom *are* all *2962*
9: 1 have I not seen Jesus Christ our L? are not *2962*
9: 1 our Lord? are not you my work in the L? *2962*
9: 2 the seal of mine apostleship are ye in the L. *2962*
9: 5 and *as* the brethren of the L, and Cephas? *2962*

1Co 9:14 hath the **L** ordained that they which preach 2962
10:21 Ye cannot drink the cup of the **L**, and 2962
10:22 Do we provoke the **L** to jealousy? are we 2962
11:11 the woman without the man, in the **L**. 2962
11:23 For I have received of the **L** *that* which also 2962
11:23 That the **L** Jesus the *same* night in which he 2962
11:27 and drink *this* cup of the **L** unworthily, 2962
11:27 be guilty of the body and blood of the **L**. 2962
11:32 we are judged, we are chastened of the **L**, 2962
12: 3 and *that* no *man* can say that Jesus is the **L**, 2962
12: 5 of administrations, but the same **L**. 2962
14:21 all that will they not hear me, saith the **L**. 2962
14:37 unto you are the commandments of the **L**. 2962
15:31 which I have in Christ Jesus our **L**, 2962
15:47 the second man *is* the **L** from heaven. 2962
15:57 which giveth us the victory through our **L** 2962
15:58 always abounding in the work of the **L**, 2962
15:58 that your labour is not in vain in the **L**. 2962
16: 7 to tarry a while with you, if the **L** permit. 2962
16:10 for he worketh the work of the **L**, as I also 2962
16:19 and Priscilla salute you much in the **L**, 2962
16:22 If any *man* love not the **L** Jesus Christ, 2962
16:23 The grace of *our* **L** Jesus Christ *be* with 2962
2Co 1: 2 our Father, and *from* the **L** Jesus Christ. 2962
1: 3 even the Father of our **L** Jesus Christ, 2962
1:14 even as ye also *are* ours in the day of the **L** 2962
2:12 and a door was opened unto me of the **L**, 2962
3:16 Nevertheless when *it* shall turn to the **L**, 2962
3:17 Now the **L** is *that* Spirit: and where 2962
3:17 where the Spirit of the **L** *is*, there *is* liberty. 2962
3:18 beholding as in a glass the glory of the **L**, 2962
3:18 to glory, even as by the Spirit of the **L**. 2962
4: 5 not ourselves, but Christ Jesus the **L**; 2962
4:10 about in the body the dying of the **L** Jesus, 2962
4:14 Knowing that he which raised up the **L** 2962
5: 6 in the body, we are absent from the **L**: 2962
5: 8 the body, and to be present with the **L**. 2962
5:11 Knowing therefore the terror of the **L**, 2962
6:17 saith the **L**, and touch not the unclean 2962
6:18 and daughters, saith the **L** Almighty. 2962
8: 5 but first gave their own selves to the **L**, and 2962
8: 9 For ye know the grace of our **L** Jesus 2962
8:19 by us to the glory of the same **L**, 2962
8:21 honest *things*, not only in the sight of the **L**, 2962
10: 8 which the **L** hath given us for edification, 2962
10:17 But he that glorieth, let him glory in the **L**. 2962
10:18 is approved, but whom the **L** commendeth. 2962
11:17 I speak *it* not after the **L**, but as *it were* 2962
11:31 The God and Father of our **L** Jesus Christ, 2962
12: 1 come to visions and revelations of the **L**. 2962
12: 8 For this *thing* I besought the **L** thrice, that it 2962
13:10 according to the power which the **L** hath 2962
13:14 The grace of the **L** Jesus Christ, and 2962
Gal 1: 3 the Father, and *from* our **L** Jesus Christ, 2962
4: 1 from a servant, though he be **l** of all; 2962
5:10 I have confidence in you through the **L**, 2962
6:14 save in the cross of our **L** Jesus Christ, 2962
6:17 for I bear in my body the marks of the **L** 2962
6:18 the grace of our **L** Jesus Christ *be* with your 2962
Eph 1: 2 our Father, and *from* the **L** Jesus Christ. 2962
1: 3 the God and Father of our **L** Jesus Christ, 2962
1:15 after I heard of your faith in the **L** Jesus, 2962
1:17 That the God of our **L** Jesus Christ, 2962
2:21 groweth unto a holy temple in the **L**: 2962
3:11 which he purposed in Christ Jesus our **L**: 2962
3:14 knees unto the Father of our **L** Jesus Christ, 2962
4: 1 I therefore, the prisoner of the **L**, 2962
4: 5 One **L**, one faith, one baptism, 2962
4:17 This I say therefore, and testify in the **L**, 2962
5: 8 but now *are ye* light in the **L**: 2962
5:10 Proving what is acceptable unto the **L**. 2962
5:17 but understanding what the will of the **L** *is*. 2962
5:19 and making melody in your heart to the **L**; 2962
5:20 the Father in the name of our **L** Jesus 2962
5:22 unto your own husbands, as unto the **L**. 2962
5:29 and cherisheth it, even as the **L** the church: 2962
6: 1 Children, obey your parents in the **L**: 2962
6: 4 up in the nurture and admonition of the **L**. 2962
6: 7 doing service, as to the **L**, and not to men: 2962
6: 8 the same shall he receive of the **L**, 2962
6:10 be strong in the **L**, and in the power of his 2962
6:21 and faithful minister in the **L**, 2962
6:23 from God the Father and the **L** Jesus Christ. 2962
6:24 Grace *be* with all them that love our **L** 2962
Php 1: 2 our Father, and *from* the **L** Jesus Christ. 2962
1:14 And many of the brethren in the **L**, 2962
2:11 should confess that Jesus Christ *is* **L**, 2962
2:19 But I trust in the **L** Jesus to send Timotheus 2962
2:24 But I trust in the **L** that I also myself shall 2962
2:29 therefore in the **L** with all gladness; 2962
3: 1 Finally, my brethren, rejoice in the **L**. 2962
3: 8 of the knowledge of Christ Jesus my **L**: 2962
3:20 we look for the Saviour, the **L** Jesus Christ: 2962
4: 1 my joy and crown, so stand fast in the **L**, 2962
4: 2 that *they* be of the same mind in the **L**. 2962
4: 4 Rejoice in the **L** alway: *and* again I say, 2962
4: 5 be known unto all men. The **L** *is* at hand. 2962
4:10 But I rejoiced in the **L** greatly, that now at 2962
4:23 The grace of our **L** Jesus Christ *be* with you 2962
Col 1: 2 God our Father and the **L** Jesus Christ. 2962
1: 3 and the Father of our **L** Jesus Christ, 2962
1:10 That ye might walk worthy of the **L** unto 2962
2: 6 therefore received Christ Jesus the **L**, 2962
3:16 singing with grace in your hearts to the **L**. 2962
3:17 or deed, *do* all in the name of the **L** Jesus, 2962
3:18 your own husbands, as it is fit in the **L**. 2962
3:20 *things*: for this is well pleasing unto the **L**. 2962
3:23 *it* heartily, as to the **L**, and not unto men; 2962
3:24 Knowing that of the **L** ye shall receive 2962
3:24 of the inheritance: for ye serve the **L** Christ. 2962
4: 7 faithful minister and fellowservant in the **L**: 2962
4:17 ministry which thou hast received in the **L**, 2962
1Th 1: 1 in God the Father and *in* the **L** Jesus Christ: 2962
1: 1 God our Father, and the **L** Jesus Christ. 2962
1: 3 and patience of hope in our **L** Jesus Christ, 2962
1: 6 ye became followers of us, and of the **L**, 2962
1: 8 from you sounded out the word of the **L** 2962
2:15 Who both killed the **L** Jesus, and their own 2962
2:19 *Are* not even ye in the presence of our **L** 2962
3: 8 For now we live, if ye stand fast in the **L**. 2962
3:11 and our Father, and our **L** Jesus Christ, 2962
3:12 And the **L** make you to increase and 2962
3:13 at the coming of our **L** Jesus Christ with all 2962
4: 1 brethren, and exhort *you* by the **L** Jesus, 2962
4: 2 we gave you by the **L** Jesus. 2962
4: 6 that the **L** *is* the avenger of all such, 2962
4:15 this we say unto you by the word of the **L**, 2962
4:15 remain unto the coming of the **L** shall not 2962
4:16 For the **L** himself shall descend from 2962
4:17 them in the clouds, to meet the **L** in the air: 2962
4:17 the air: and so shall we ever be with the **L**. 2962
5: 2 know perfectly that the day of the **L** 2962
5: 9 to obtain salvation by our **L** Jesus Christ, 2962
5:12 and are over you in the **L**, and 2962
5:23 unto the coming of our **L** Jesus Christ. 2962
5:27 I charge you by the **L** that *this* epistle be 2962
5:28 The grace of our **L** Jesus Christ *be* with 2962
2Th 1: 1 in God our Father and the **L** Jesus Christ: 2962
1: 2 God our Father and the **L** Jesus Christ. 2962
1: 7 when the **L** Jesus shall be revealed from 2962
1: 8 that obey not the gospel of our **L** Jesus 2962
1: 9 destruction from the presence of the **L**, 2962
1:12 That the name of our **L** Jesus Christ may be 2962
1:12 grace of our God and the **L** Jesus Christ. 2962
2: 1 by the coming of our **L** Jesus Christ, and 2962
2: 8 whom the **L** shall consume with the spirit 2962
2:13 brethren beloved of the **L**, because God 2962
2:14 to the obtaining of the glory of our **L** Jesus 2962
2:16 Now our **L** Jesus Christ himself, and God, 2962
3: 1 that the word of the **L** may have *free* 2962
3: 3 But the **L** is faithful, who shall stablish 2962
3: 4 And we have confidence in the **L** touching 2962
3: 5 And the **L** direct your hearts into the love 2962
3: 6 brethren, in the name of our **L** Jesus Christ, 2962
3:12 and exhort by our **L** Jesus Christ, 2962
3:16 Now the **L** of peace himself give you peace 2962
3:16 always by all means. The **L** *be* with you all. 2962
3:18 The grace of our **L** Jesus Christ *be* with you 2962
1Ti 1: 1 and **L** Jesus Christ, *which is* our hope; 2962
1: 2 God our Father and Jesus Christ our **L**. 2962
1:12 And I thank Christ Jesus our **L**, who hath 2962
1:14 And the grace of our **L** was exceeding 2962
5:21 and the **L** Jesus Christ, and the elect angels, 2962
6: 3 *even* the *words* of our **L** Jesus Christ, and 2962
6:14 until the appearing of our **L** Jesus Christ: 2962
6:15 the King of kings, and **L** of lords; 2962
2Ti 1: 2 God the Father and Christ Jesus our **L**. 2962
1: 8 ashamed of the testimony of our **L**, 2962

2Ti 1:16 The **L** give mercy unto the house of *2962*
1:18 The **L** grant unto him that *he* may find *2962*
1:18 that *he* may find mercy of the **L** in that day: *2962*
2: 7 the **L** give thee understanding in all *things*. *2962*
2:14 charging *them* before the **L** that *they* strive *2962*
2:19 this seal, The **L** knoweth them that are his. *2962*
2:22 with them that call on the **L** out of a pure *2962*
2:24 And the servant of the **L** must not strive; *2962*
3:11 but out of *them* all the **L** delivered me. *2962*
4: 1 before God, and the **L** Jesus Christ, *2962*
4: 8 which the **L**, the righteous judge, shall give *2962*
4:14 the **L** reward him according to his works: *2962*
4:17 Notwithstanding the **L** stood with me, and *2962*
4:18 And the **L** shall deliver me from every evil *2962*
4:22 The **L** Jesus Christ *be* with thy spirit. Grace *2962*
Tit 1: 4 and the **L** Jesus Christ our Saviour. *2962*
Phm 1: 3 God our Father and the **L** Jesus Christ. *2962*
1: 5 which thou hast toward the **L** Jesus, and *2962*
1:16 unto thee, both in the flesh, and in the **L**? *2962*
1:20 brother, let me have joy of thee in the **L**: *2962*
1:20 in the Lord: refresh my bowels in the **L**. *2962*
1:25 The grace of our **L** Jesus Christ *be* with *2962*
Heb 1:10 And, Thou, **L**, in the beginning hast laid *2962*
2: 3 at the first began to be spoken by the **L**, *2962*
7:14 For *it is* evident that our **L** sprang out of *2962*
7:21 unto him, The **L** sware and will not repent, *2962*
8: 2 which the **L** pitched, and not man. *2962*
8: 8 Behold, the days come, saith the **L**, *2962*
8: 9 and I regarded them not, saith the **L**. *2962*
8:10 house of Israel after those days, saith the **L**; *2962*
8:11 every man his brother, saying, Know the **L**: *2962*
10:16 saith the **L**, I will put my laws into their *2962*
10:30 unto me, I will recompense, saith the **L**. *2962*
10:30 And again, The **L** shall judge his people. *2962*
12: 5 despise not thou the chastening of the **L**, *2962*
12: 6 For whom the **L** loveth he chasteneth, and *2962*
12:14 without which no *man* shall see the **L**: *2962*
13: 6 The **L** *is* my helper, and I will not fear what *2962*
13:20 that brought again from the dead our **L** *2962*
Jas 1: 1 a servant of God and of the **L** Jesus Christ, *2962*
1: 7 that he shall receive any *thing* of the **L**. *2962*
1:12 which the **L** hath promised to them that *2962*
2: 1 have not the faith of our **L** Jesus Christ, *2962*
2: 1 *the* **L** of glory, with respect of persons. NIG
4:10 Humble yourselves in the sight of the **L**, *2962*
4:15 If the **L** will, we shall live, and do this, or *2962*
5: 4 entered into the ears of the **L** of sabaoth. *2962*
5: 7 brethren, unto the coming of the **L**. *2962*
5: 8 for the coming of the **L** draweth nigh. *2962*
5:10 who have spoken in the name of the **L**, *2962*
5:11 of Job, and have seen the end of the **L**; *2962*
5:11 that the **L** is very pitiful, and of tender *2962*
5:14 anointing him with oil in the name of the **L**: *2962*
5:15 save the sick, and the **L** shall raise him up; *2962*
1Pe 1: 3 the God and Father of our **L** Jesus Christ, *2962*
1:25 But the word of the **L** endureth for ever. *2962*
2: 3 so be ye have tasted that the **L** *is* gracious. *2962*
3: 6 as Sara obeyed Abraham, calling him **l**: *2962*
3:12 For the eyes of the **L** *are* over the righteous, *2962*
3:12 the face of the **L** *is* against them that do *2962*
3:15 But sanctify the **L** God in your hearts: and *2962*
2Pe 1: 2 the knowledge of God, and of Jesus our **L**. *2962*
1: 8 in the knowledge of our **L** Jesus Christ. *2962*
1:11 into the everlasting kingdom of our **L** *2962*
1:14 even as our **L** Jesus Christ hath shewed me. *2962*
1:16 and coming of our **L** Jesus Christ, *2962*
2: 1 even denying the **L** that bought them, and *1203*
2: 9 The **L** knoweth *how* to deliver the godly *2962*
2:11 accusation against them before the **L**. *2962*
2:20 the world through the knowledge of the **L** *2962*
3: 2 commandment of us the apostles of the **L** *2962*
3: 8 one day *is* with the **L** as a thousand years, *2962*
3: 9 The **L** is not slack concerning *his* promise, *2962*
3:10 But the day of the **L** will come as a thief in *2962*
3:15 And account *that* the longsuffering of our **L** *2962*
3:18 and *in* the knowledge of our **L** and *2962*
2Jn 1: 3 the Father, and from the **L** Jesus Christ, *2962*
Jude 1: 4 and denying the only **L** God, and our Lord *1203*
1: 4 the only Lord God, and our **L** Jesus Christ. *2962*
1: 5 though ye once knew this, how that the **L**, *2962*
1: 9 but said, The **L** rebuke thee. *2962*
1:14 the **L** cometh with ten thousands of his *2962*
1:17 before of the apostles of our **L** Jesus Christ; *2962*
1:21 looking for the mercy of our **L** Jesus Christ *2962*
Rev 1: 8 saith the **L**, which is, and which was, and *2962*
4: 8 saying, Holy, holy, holy, **L** God Almighty, *2962*
4:11 O **L**, to receive glory and honour and *2962*
6:10 saying, How long, O **L**, holy and true, *1203*
11: 8 and Egypt, where also our **L** was crucified. *2962*
11:15 world are become *the kingdoms* of our **L**, *2962*
11:17 O **L** God Almighty, which art, and wast, *2962*
14:13 Blessed *are* the dead which die in the **L** *2962*
15: 3 *are* thy works, **L** God Almighty; *2962*
15: 4 not fear thee, O **L**, and glorify thy name? *2962*
16: 5 O **L**, which art, and wast, and shalt be, *2962*
16: 7 **L** God Almighty, true and righteous *are* thy *2962*
17:14 for he is **L** of lords, and King of kings: and *2962*
18: 8 for strong *is* the **L** God who judgeth her. *2962*
19: 1 honour, and power, unto the **L** our God: *2962*
19: 6 for the **L** God Omnipotent reigneth. *2962*
19:16 KING OF KINGS, AND **L** OF LORDS. *2962*
21:22 for the **L** God Almighty and the Lamb are *2962*
22: 5 of the sun; for the **L** God giveth them light: *2962*
22: 6 the **L** God of the holy prophets sent his *2962*
22:20 Amen. Even so, come, **L** Jesus. *2962*
22:21 The grace of our **L** Jesus Christ *be* with you *2962*

LORD* (6469) [GOD*, JAH, JEHOVAH, LORD'S*; this is the proper name of God, *Yahweh* or *Jehovah*]

Ge 2: 4 in the day that **the L** God made the earth 3068
2: 5 for **the L** God had not caused it to rain 3068
2: 7 **the L** God formed man *of* the dust of 3068
2: 8 **the L** God planted a garden eastward in 3068
2: 9 out of the ground made **the L** God to grow 3068
2:15 **the L** God took the man, and put him into 3068
2:16 **the L** God commanded the man, saying, 3068
2:18 **the L** God said, *It is* not good that the man 3068
2:19 out of the ground **the L** God formed every 3068
2:21 **the L** God caused a deep sleep to fall upon 3068
2:22 which **the L** God had taken from man, 3068
3: 1 of the field which **the L** God had made. 3068
3: 8 they heard the voice of **the L** God walking 3068
3: 8 **the L** God amongst the trees of the garden. 3068
3: 9 **the L** God called unto Adam, and said unto 3068
3:13 **the L** God said unto the woman, What *is* 3068
3:14 **the L** God said unto the serpent, 3068
3:21 to his wife did **the L** God make coats of 3068
3:22 **the L** God said, Behold, the man is become 3068
3:23 Therefore **the L** God sent him forth from 3068
4: 1 and said, I have gotten a man from **the L**. 3068
4: 3 fruit of the ground an offering unto **the L**. 3068
4: 4 **the L** had respect unto Abel and to his 3068
4: 6 **the L** said unto Cain, Why art thou wroth? 3068
4: 9 **the L** said unto Cain, Where *is* Abel thy 3068
4:13 Cain said unto **the L**, My punishment *is* 3068
4:15 **the L** said unto him, Therefore whosoever 3068
4:15 **the L** set a mark upon Cain, lest any 3068
4:16 Cain went out from the presence of **the L**, 3068
4:26 began *men* to call upon the name of **the L**. 3068
5:29 of the ground which **the L** hath cursed. 3068
6: 3 **the L** said, My spirit shall not always strive 3068
6: 6 it repented **the L** that he had made man on 3068
6: 7 **the L** said, I will destroy man whom I have 3068
6: 8 But Noah found grace in the eyes of **the L**. 3068
7: 1 **the L** said unto Noah, Come thou and 3068
7: 5 Noah did according unto all that **the L** 3068
7:16 commanded him: and **the L** shut him in. 3068
8:20 Noah builded an altar unto **the L**; and 3068
8:21 **the L** smelled a sweet savour; and 3068
8:21 **the L** said in his heart, I will not again 3068
9:26 he said, Blessed *be* **the L** God of Shem; 3068
10: 9 He was a mighty hunter before **the L**: 3068
10: 9 as Nimrod the mighty hunter before **the L**. 3068
11: 5 **the L** came down to see the city and 3068
11: 6 **the L** said, Behold, the people *is* one, and 3068
11: 8 So **the L** scattered them abroad from 3068
11: 9 **the L** did there confound the language of 3068
11: 9 from thence did **the L** scatter them abroad 3068
12: 1 Now **the L** had said unto Abram, Get thee 3068
12: 4 as **the L** had spoken unto him; 3068
12: 7 **the L** appeared unto Abram, and said, 3068
12: 7 there builded he an altar unto **the L**, 3068
12: 8 there he builded an altar unto **the L**, and 3068
12: 8 and called upon the name of **the L**. 3068
12:17 **the L** plagued Pharaoh and his house with 3068
13: 4 there Abram called on the name of **the L**. 3068
13:10 before **the L** destroyed Sodom and 3068
13:10 and Gomorrah, *even* as the garden of **the L**, 3068

Ge	13:13	and sinners before **the L** exceedingly.	3068
	13:14	**the L** said unto Abram, after that Lot was	3068
	13:18	and built there an altar unto **the L**.	3068
	14:22	I have lift up mine hand unto **the L**,	3068
	15: 1	After these things the word of **the L** came	3068
	15: 4	the word of **the L** *came* unto him, saying,	3068
	15: 6	he believed in **the L**; and he counted it to	3068
	15: 7	I *am* **the L** that brought thee out of Ur of	3068
	15:18	In the same day **the L** made a covenant	3068
	16: 2	**the L** hath restrained me from bearing:	3068
	16: 5	her eyes: **the L** judge between me and thee.	3068
	16: 7	the angel of **the L** found her by a fountain	3068
	16: 9	the angel of **the L** said unto her, Return to	3068
	16:10	the angel of **the L** said unto her, I will	3068
	16:11	the angel of **the L** said unto her, Behold,	3068
	16:11	because **the L** hath heard thy affliction.	3068
	16:13	she called the name of **the L** that spake	3068
	17: 1	**the L** appeared to Abram, and said unto	3068
	18: 1	**the L** appeared unto him in the plains of	3068
	18:13	**the L** said unto Abraham, Wherefore did	3068
	18:14	Is any thing too hard for **the L**? At the time	3068
	18:17	**the L** said, Shall I hide from Abraham *that*	3068
	18:19	they shall keep the way of **the L**, to do	3068
	18:19	that **the L** may bring upon Abraham that	3068
	18:20	**the L** said, Because the cry of Sodom and	3068
	18:22	but Abraham stood yet before **the L**.	3068
	18:26	**the L** said, If I find in Sodom fifty	3068
	18:33	**the L** went his way, as soon as he had left	3068
	19:13	is waxen great before the face of **the L**;	3068
	19:13	and **the L** hath sent us to destroy it.	3068
	19:14	this place; for **the L** will destroy this city.	3068
	19:16	**the L** being merciful unto him:	3068
	19:24	**the L** rained upon Sodom and	3068
	19:24	and fire from **the L** out of heaven;	3068
	19:27	to the place where he stood before **the L**:	3068
	20:18	For **the L** had fast closed up all the wombs	3068
	21: 1	**the L** visited Sarah as he had said, and	3068
	21: 1	and **the L** did unto Sarah as he had spoken.	3068
	21:33	called there on the name of **the L**,	3068
	22:11	the angel of **the L** called unto him out of	3068
	22:14	In the mount of **the L** it shall be seen.	3068
	22:15	the angel of **the L** called unto Abraham out	3068
	22:16	saith **the L**, for because thou hast done this	3068
	24: 1	**the L** had blessed Abraham in all things.	3068
	24: 3	I will make thee swear by **the L**, the God of	3068
	24: 7	**The L** God of heaven, which took me from	3068
	24:12	O **L** God of my master Abraham, I pray	3068
	24:21	to wit whether **the L** had made his journey	3068
	24:26	down his head, and worshipped **the L**.	3068
	24:27	Blessed *be* **the L** God of my master	3068
	24:27	**the L** led me to the house of my master's	3068
	24:31	he said, Come in, thou blessed of **the L**;	3068
	24:35	**the L** hath blessed my master greatly; and	3068
	24:40	said unto me, **The L**, before whom I walk,	3068
	24:42	and said, O **L** God of my master Abraham,	3068
	24:44	*let* the same *be* the woman whom **the L**	3068
	24:48	worshipped **the L**, and blessed the LORD	3068
	24:48	blessed **the L** God of my master Abraham,	3068
	24:50	and said, The thing proceedeth from **the L**:	3068
	24:51	master's son's wife, as **the L** hath spoken.	3068
	24:52	he worshipped **the L**, *bowing himself* to	3068
	24:56	seeing **the L** hath prospered my way;	3068
	25:21	Isaac intreated **the L** for his wife, because	3068
	25:21	**the L** was intreated of him, and	3068
	25:22	I thus? And she went to inquire of **the L**.	3068
	25:23	**the L** said unto her, Two nations *are* in thy	3068
	26: 2	**the L** appeared unto him, and said, Go not	3068
	26:12	an hundredfold: and **the L** blessed him.	3068
	26:22	For now **the L** hath made room for us, and	3068
	26:24	**the L** appeared unto him the same night,	3068
	26:25	called upon the name of **the L**, and	3068
	26:28	We saw certainly that **the L** was with thee:	3068
	26:29	in peace: thou *art* now the blessed of **the L**.	3068
	27: 7	bless thee before **the L** before my death.	3068
	27:20	Because **the L** thy God brought *it* to me.	3068
	27:27	smell of a field which **the L** hath blessed:	3068
	28:13	behold, **the L** stood above it, and said, I *am*	3068
	28:13	I *am* **the L** God of Abraham thy father, and	3068
	28:16	and he said, Surely **the L** is in this place;	3068
	28:21	in peace; then shall **the L** be my God:	3068
	29:31	when **the L** saw that Leah *was* hated,	3068
	29:32	Surely **the L** hath looked upon my	3068
	29:33	Because **the L** hath heard that I *was* hated,	3068
	29:35	she said, Now will I praise **the L**: therefore	3068
	30:24	said, **The L** shall add to me another son.	3068
	30:27	that **the L** hath blessed me for thy sake.	3068
	30:30	**the L** hath blessed thee since my coming:	3068
	31: 3	**the L** said unto Jacob, Return unto the land	3068
	31:49	he said, **The L** watch between me and thee,	3068
	32: 9	father Isaac, **the L** which saidst unto me,	3068
	38: 7	was wicked in the sight of **the L**;	3068
	38: 7	sight of the LORD; and **the L** slew him.	3068
	38:10	*the thing* which he did displeased **the L**:	3068
	39: 2	**the L** was with Joseph, and he was a	3068
	39: 3	his master saw that **the L** *was* with him,	3068
	39: 3	*that* **the L** made all that he did to prosper in	3068
	39: 5	that **the L** blessed the Egyptian's house for	3068
	39: 5	the blessing of **the L** was upon all that he	3068
	39:21	**the L** was with Joseph, and shewed him	3068
	39:23	because **the L** *was* with him, and	3068
	39:23	*that* which he did, **the L** made *it* to prosper.	3068
	49:18	I have waited for thy salvation, O **L**.	3068
Ex	3: 2	the angel of **the L** appeared unto him in a	3068
	3: 4	when **the L** saw that he turned aside to see,	3068
	3: 7	**the L** said, I have surely seen the affliction	3068
	3:15	**The L** God of your fathers, the God of	3068
	3:16	say unto them, **The L** God of your fathers,	3068
	3:18	**The L** God of the Hebrews hath met with	3068
	3:18	that we may sacrifice to **the L** our God.	3068
	4: 1	**The L** hath not appeared unto thee.	3068
	4: 2	**the L** said unto him, What *is* that in thine	3068
	4: 4	**the L** said unto Moses, Put forth thine	3068
	4: 5	That they may believe that **the L** God of	3068
	4: 6	**the L** said furthermore unto him, Put now	3068
	4:10	Moses said unto **the L**, O my Lord, I *am*	3068
	4:11	**the L** said unto him, Who hath made man's	3068
	4:11	the seeing, or the blind? have not I **the L**?	3068
	4:14	the anger of **the L** was kindled against	3068
	4:19	**the L** said unto Moses in Midian, Go,	3068
	4:21	**the L** said unto Moses, When thou goest to	3068
	4:22	Thus saith **the L**, Israel *is* my son, *even* my	3068
	4:24	that **the L** met him, and sought to kill him.	3068
	4:27	**the L** said to Aaron, Go into the wilderness	3068
	4:28	Moses told Aaron all the words of **the L**	3068
	4:30	Aaron spake all the words which **the L** had	3068
	4:31	when they heard that **the L** had visited	3068
	5: 1	Thus saith **the L** God of Israel,	3068
	5: 2	Pharaoh said, Who *is* **the L**, that I should	3068
	5: 2	I know not **the L**, neither will I let Israel	3068
	5: 3	and sacrifice unto **the L** our God;	3068
	5:17	ye say, Let us go *and* do sacrifice to **the L**.	3068
	5:21	**The L** look upon you, and judge;	3068
	5:22	Moses returned unto **the L**, and said, Lord,	3068
	6: 1	**the L** said unto Moses, Now shalt thou see	3068
	6: 2	unto Moses, and said unto him, I *am* **the L**:	3068
	6: 6	I *am* **the L**, and I will bring you out from	3068
	6: 7	ye shall know that I *am* **the L** your God,	3068
	6: 8	will give it you *for* an heritage: I *am* **the L**.	3068
	6:10	And **the L** spake unto Moses, saying,	3068
	6:12	Moses spake before **the L**, saying, Behold,	3068
	6:13	**the L** spake unto Moses and unto Aaron,	3068
	6:26	that Aaron and Moses, to whom **the L** said,	3068
	6:28	it came to pass on the day *when* **the L**	3068
	6:29	That **the L** spake unto Moses, saying, I *am*	3068
	6:29	spake unto Moses, saying, I *am* **the L**:	3068
	6:30	Moses said before **the L**, Behold, I *am* of	3068
	7: 1	**the L** said unto Moses, See, I have made	3068
	7: 5	the Egyptians shall know that I *am* **the L**,	3068
	7: 6	and Aaron did as **the L** commanded them,	3068
	7: 8	**the L** spake unto Moses and unto Aaron,	3068
	7:10	and they did so as **the L** had commanded:	3068
	7:13	hearkened not unto them; as **the L** had said.	3068
	7:14	**the L** said unto Moses, Pharaoh's heart *is*	3068
	7:16	**The L** God of the Hebrews hath sent me	3068
	7:17	Thus saith **the L**, In this thou shalt know	3068
	7:17	In this thou shalt know that I *am* **the L**:	3068
	7:19	**the L** spake unto Moses, Say unto Aaron,	3068
	7:20	and Aaron did so, as **the L** commanded;	3068
	7:22	he hearken unto them; as **the L** had said.	3068
	7:25	after *that* **the L** had smitten the river.	3068
	8: 1	**the L** spake unto Moses, Go unto Pharaoh,	3068
	8: 1	and say unto him, Thus saith **the L**,	3068
	8: 5	**the L** spake unto Moses, Say unto Aaron,	3068
	8: 8	and Aaron, and said, Intreat **the L**,	3068
	8: 8	that they may do sacrifice unto **the L**.	3068
	8:10	that *there is* none like unto **the L** our God.	3068
	8:12	Moses cried unto **the L** because of	3068
	8:13	**the L** did according to the word of Moses;	3068

Ex 8:15	hearkened not unto them; as **the L** had said.	3068
8:16	**the L** said unto Moses, Say unto Aaron,	3068
8:19	hearkened not unto them; as **the L** had said.	3068
8:20	**the L** said unto Moses, Rise up early in	3068
8:20	say unto him, Thus saith **the L**, Let my	3068
8:22	that I *am* **the L** in the midst of the earth.	3068
8:24	**the L** did so; and there came a grievous	3068
8:26	of the Egyptians to **the L** our God:	3068
8:27	sacrifice to **the L** our God, as he shall	3068
8:28	that ye may sacrifice to **the L** your God in	3068
8:29	I will intreat **the L** that the swarms *of flies*	3068
8:29	letting the people go to sacrifice to **the L**.	3068
8:30	out from Pharaoh, and intreated **the L**.	3068
8:31	**the L** did according to the word of Moses;	3068
9: 1	**the L** said unto Moses, Go in unto Pharaoh,	3068
9: 1	Thus saith **the L** God of the Hebrews,	3068
9: 3	the hand of **the L** is upon thy cattle which	3068
9: 4	**the L** shall sever between the cattle of	3068
9: 5	**the L** appointed a set time, saying,	3068
9: 5	To morrow **the L** shall do this thing in	3068
9: 6	**the L** did that thing on the morrow, and	3068
9: 8	**the L** said unto Moses and unto Aaron,	3068
9:12	**the L** hardened the heart of Pharaoh, and	3068
9:12	as **the L** had spoken unto Moses.	3068
9:13	**the L** said unto Moses, Rise up early in	3068
9:13	Thus saith **the L** God of the Hebrews,	3068
9:20	He that feared the word of **the L** amongst	3068
9:21	he that regarded not the word of **the L** left	3068
9:22	**the L** said unto Moses, Stretch forth thine	3068
9:23	**the L** sent thunder and hail, and the fire ran	3068
9:23	**the L** rained hail upon the land of Egypt.	3068
9:27	**the L** *is* righteous, and I and my people *are*	3068
9:28	Intreat **the L** (for *it is* enough) that there be	3068
9:29	I will spread abroad my hands unto **the L**;	3068
9:30	I know that ye will not yet fear **the L** God.	3068
9:33	spread abroad his hands unto **the L**:	3068
9:35	of Israel go; as **the L** had spoken by Moses.	3068
10: 1	**the L** said unto Moses, Go in unto Pharaoh:	3068
10: 2	that ye may know how that I *am* **the L**.	3068
10: 3	Thus saith **the L** God of the Hebrews,	3068
10: 7	that they may serve **the L** their God:	3068
10: 8	said unto them, Go, serve **the L** your God:	3068
10: 9	we go; for we *must hold* a feast unto **the L**.	3068
10:10	Let **the L** be so with you, as I will let you	3068
10:11	go now ye *that are* men, and serve **the L**;	3068
10:12	**the L** said unto Moses, Stretch out thine	3068
10:13	**the L** brought an east wind upon the land	3068
10:16	I have sinned against **the L** your God, and	3068
10:17	only *this* once, and intreat **the L** your God,	3068
10:18	out from Pharaoh, and intreated **the L**.	3068
10:19	**the L** turned a mighty strong west wind,	3068
10:20	**the L** hardened Pharaoh's heart, so that he	3068
10:21	**the L** said unto Moses, Stretch out thine	3068
10:24	unto Moses, and said, Go ye, serve **the L**;	3068
10:25	that we may sacrifice unto **the L** our God.	3068
10:26	for thereof must we take to serve **the L** our	3068
10:26	know not with what we must serve **the L**,	3068
10:27	**the L** hardened Pharaoh's heart, and	3068
11: 1	(And **the L** said unto Moses, Yet will I	3068
11: 3	**the L** gave the people favour in the sight of	3068
11: 4	Moses said, Thus saith **the L**,	3068
11: 7	that ye may know how that **the L** doth put	3068
11: 9	**the L** said unto Moses, Pharaoh shall not	3068
11:10	**the L** hardened Pharaoh's heart, so that he	3068
12: 1	**the L** spake unto Moses and Aaron in	3068
12:12	Egypt I will execute judgment: I *am* **the L**.	3068
12:14	you shall keep it a feast to **the L** throughout	3068
12:23	For **the L** will pass through to smite	3068
12:23	**the L** will pass over the door, and will not	3068
12:25	when ye be come to the land which **the L**	3068
12:28	did as **the L** had commanded Moses and	3068
12:29	that at midnight **the L** smote all	3068
12:31	and go, serve **the L**, as ye have said.	3068
12:36	**the L** gave the people favour in the sight of	3068
12:41	*that* all the hosts of **the L** went out from	3068
12:42	**the L** for bringing them out from the land	3068
12:42	this *is* that night of **the L** to be observed of	3068
12:43	**the L** said unto Moses and Aaron, This *is*	3068
12:48	will keep the passover to **the L**, let all his	3068
12:50	as **the L** commanded Moses and Aaron, so	3068
12:51	*that* **the L** did bring the children of Israel	3068
13: 1	And **the L** spake unto Moses, saying,	3068
13: 3	for by strength of hand **the L** brought you	3068
13: 5	it shall be when **the L** shall bring thee into	3068
13: 6	in the seventh day *shall be* a feast to **the L**.	3068
13: 8	of that *which* **the L** did unto me when I	3068
13: 9	for with a strong hand hath **the L** brought	3068
13:11	it shall be when **the L** shall bring thee into	3068
13:12	That thou shalt set apart unto **the L** all that	3068
13:14	By strength of hand **the L** brought us out	3068
13:15	that **the L** slew all the firstborn in the land	3068
13:15	I sacrifice to **the L** all that openeth	3068
13:16	for by strength of hand **the L** brought us	3068
13:21	**the L** went before them by day in a pillar	3068
14: 1	And **the L** spake unto Moses, saying,	3068
14: 4	the Egyptians may know that I *am* **the L**.	3068
14: 8	**the L** hardened the heart of Pharaoh king	3068
14:10	the children of Israel cried out unto **the L**.	3068
14:13	stand still, and see the salvation of **the L**,	3068
14:14	**The L** shall fight for you, and ye shall hold	3068
14:15	**the L** said unto Moses, Wherefore criest	3068
14:18	the Egyptians shall know that I *am* **the L**,	3068
14:21	**the L** caused the sea to go *back* by a strong	3068
14:24	that in the morning watch **the L** looked	3068
14:25	for **the L** fighteth for them against	3068
14:26	**the L** said unto Moses, Stretch out thine	3068
14:27	**the L** overthrew the Egyptians in the midst	3068
14:30	Thus **the L** saved Israel that day out of	3068
14:31	Israel saw *that* great work which **the L** did	3068
14:31	the people feared **the L**, and believed	3068
14:31	and believed **the L**, and his servant Moses.	3068
15: 1	the children of Israel this song unto **the L**,	3068
15: 1	spake, saying, I will sing unto **the L**, for he	3068
15: 2	**The L** *is* my strength and song, and he is	3050
15: 3	**The L** *is* a man of war: the LORD *is* his	3068
15: 3	LORD *is* a man of war: **the L** *is* his name.	3068
15: 6	Thy right hand, **O L**, is become glorious in	3068
15: 6	thy right hand, **O L**, hath dashed in pieces	3068
15:11	*is* like unto thee, **O L**, among the gods?	3068
15:16	pass over, **O L**, till the people pass over,	3068
15:17	*in* the place, **O L**, *which* thou hast made for	3068
15:18	**The L** shall reign for ever and ever.	3068
15:19	**the L** brought again the waters of the sea	3068
15:21	Miriam answered them, Sing ye to **the L**,	3068
15:25	he cried unto **the L**; and the LORD	3068
15:25	**the L** shewed him a tree, *which* when he	3068
15:26	hearken to the voice of **the L** thy God,	3068
15:26	for I *am* **the L** that healeth thee.	3068
16: 3	by the hand of **the L** in the land of Egypt,	3068
16: 4	said **the L** unto Moses, Behold, I will rain	3068
16: 6	ye shall know that **the L** hath brought you	3068
16: 7	then ye shall see the glory of **the L**;	3068
16: 7	he heareth your murmurings against **the L**:	3068
16: 8	*This shall be,* when **the L** shall give you in	3068
16: 8	for that **the L** heareth your murmurings	3068
16: 8	*are* not against us, but against **the L**.	3068
16: 9	children of Israel, Come near before **the L**:	3068
16:10	the glory of **the L** appeared in the cloud.	3068
16:11	And **the L** spake unto Moses, saying,	3068
16:12	ye shall know that I *am* **the L** your God.	3068
16:15	This *is* the bread which **the L** hath given	3068
16:16	This *is* the thing which **the L** hath	3068
16:23	This *is that* which **the L** hath said,	3068
16:23	*is* the rest of the holy sabbath unto **the L**:	3068
16:25	to day; for to day *is* a sabbath unto **the L**:	3068
16:28	**the L** said unto Moses, How long refuse ye	3068
16:29	for that **the L** hath given you the sabbath,	3068
16:32	This *is* the thing which **the L** commandeth,	3068
16:33	lay it up before **the L**, to be kept for your	3068
16:34	As **the L** commanded Moses, so Aaron laid	3068
17: 1	according to the commandment of **the L**,	3068
17: 2	with me? wherefore do ye tempt **the L**?	3068
17: 4	Moses cried unto **the L**, saying, What shall	3068
17: 5	**the L** said unto Moses, Go on before	3068
17: 7	because they tempted **the L**, saying, Is	3068
17: 7	Is **the L** amongst us, or not?	3068
17:14	**the L** said unto Moses, Write this *for* a	3068
17:16	Because **the L** hath sworn *that* the LORD	3050
17:16	Because the LORD hath sworn *that* **the L**	3068
18: 1	that **the L** had brought Israel out of Egypt;	3068
18: 8	Moses told his father in law all that **the L**	3068
18: 8	by the way, and *how* **the L** delivered them.	3068
18: 9	goodness which **the L** had done to Israel,	3068
18:10	Jethro said, Blessed *be* **the L**, who hath	3068
18:11	Now I know that **the L** *is* greater than all	3068
19: 3	**the L** called unto him out of the mountain,	3068
19: 7	these words which **the L** commanded him.	3068
19: 8	said, All that **the L** hath spoken we will do.	3068

Ex 19: 8 the words of the people unto **the L**. 3068
19: 9 **the L** said unto Moses, Lo, I come unto 3068
19: 9 told the words of the people unto **the L**. 3068
19:10 **the L** said unto Moses, Go unto the people, 3068
19:11 for the third day **the L** will come down in 3068
19:18 **the L** descended upon it in fire: 3068
19:20 **the L** came down upon mount Sinai, on 3068
19:20 **the L** called Moses *up* to the top of 3068
19:21 **the L** said unto Moses, Go down, 3068
19:21 lest they break through unto **the L** to gaze, 3068
19:22 which come near to **the L**, 3068
19:22 lest **the L** break forth upon them. 3068
19:23 Moses said unto **the L**, The people cannot 3068
19:24 **the L** said unto him, Away, get thee down, 3068
19:24 break through to come up unto **the L**, 3068
20: 2 I *am* **the L** thy God, which have brought 3068
20: 5 for I **the L** thy God *am* a jealous God, 3068
20: 7 Thou shalt not take the name of **the L** thy 3068
20: 7 for **the L** will not hold him guiltless that 3068
20:10 the seventh day *is* the sabbath of **the L** thy 3068
20:11 For *in* six days **the L** made heaven and 3068
20:11 wherefore **the L** blessed the sabbath day, 3068
20:12 the land which **the L** thy God giveth thee. 3068
20:22 **the L** said unto Moses, Thus thou shalt say 3068
22:11 *Then* shall an oath of **the L** be between 3068
22:20 save unto **the L** only, he shall be utterly 3068
23:19 shalt bring *into* the house of **the L** thy God. 3068
23:25 ye shall serve **the L** your God, and he shall 3068
24: 1 Come up unto **the L**, thou, and Aaron, 3068
24: 2 Moses alone shall come near **the L**: but 3068
24: 3 and told the people all the words of **the L**, 3068
24: 3 All the words which **the L** hath said will 3068
24: 4 Moses wrote all the words of **the L**, and 3068
24: 5 peace offerings *of* oxen unto **the L**. 3068
24: 7 All that **the L** hath said will we do, and 3068
24: 8 which **the L** hath made with you 3068
24:12 **the L** said unto Moses, Come up to me into 3068
24:16 the glory of **the L** abode upon mount Sinai, 3068
24:17 the sight of the glory of **the L** *was* like 3068
25: 1 And **the L** spake unto Moses, saying, 3068
27:21 it from evening to morning before **the L**: 3068
28:12 Aaron shall bear their names before **the L** 3068
28:29 for a memorial before **the L** continually. 3068
28:30 when he goeth in before **the L**: 3068
28:30 upon his heart before **the L** continually. 3068
28:35 goeth in unto the holy *place* before **the L**, 3068
28:36 of a signet, HOLINESS TO **THE L**. 3068
28:38 that they may be accepted before **the L**. 3068
29:11 thou shalt kill the bullock before **the L**, 3068
29:18 it *is* a burnt offering unto **the L**: it *is* a 3068
29:18 an offering made by fire unto **the L**. 3068
29:23 the unleavened bread that *is* before **the L**: 3068
29:24 them *for* a wave offering before **the L**. 3068
29:25 for a sweet savour before **the L**: 3068
29:25 it *is* an offering made by fire unto **the L**. 3068
29:26 wave it *for* a wave offering before **the L**: 3068
29:28 *even* their heave offering unto **the L**. 3068
29:41 an offering made by fire unto **the L**. 3068
29:42 of the congregation before **the L**: 3068
29:46 they shall know that I *am* **the L** their God, 3068
29:46 dwell amongst them: I *am* **the L** their God. 3068
30: 8 a perpetual incense before **the L** 3068
30:10 it *is* most holy unto **the L**. 3068
30:11 And **the L** spake unto Moses, saying, 3068
30:12 man a ransom for his soul unto **the L**, 3068
30:13 a half shekel *shall be* the offering of **the L**. 3068
30:14 above, shall give an offering unto **the L**. 3068
30:15 when *they* give an offering unto **the L**, 3068
30:16 unto the children of Israel before **the L**, 3068
30:17 And **the L** spake unto Moses, saying, 3068
30:20 to burn offering made by fire unto **the L**: 3068
30:22 Moreover **the L** spake unto Moses, saying, 3068
30:34 **the L** said unto Moses, Take unto thee 3068
30:37 it shall be unto thee holy for **the L**. 3068
31: 1 And **the L** spake unto Moses, saying, 3068
31:12 And **the L** spake unto Moses, saying, 3068
31:13 that *ye* may know that I *am* **the L** that doth 3068
31:15 *is* the sabbath of rest, holy to **the L**: 3068
31:17 for *in* six days **the L** made heaven and 3068
32: 5 and said, To morrow *is* a feast to **the L**. 3068
32: 7 **the L** said unto Moses, Go, get thee down; 3068
32: 9 **the L** said unto Moses, I have seen this 3068
32:11 Moses besought **the L** his God, and said, 3068
32:11 besought the LORD his God, and said, L, 3068
32:14 **the L** repented of the evil which he thought 3068
32:27 unto them, Thus saith **the L** God of Israel, 3068
32:29 Consecrate yourselves to day to **the L**, 3068
32:30 now I will go up unto **the L**; peradventure I 3068
32:31 Moses returned unto **the L**, and said, Oh, 3068
32:33 **the L** said unto Moses, Whosoever hath 3068
32:35 **the L** plagued the people, because they 3068
33: 1 **the L** said unto Moses, Depart, *and* go up 3068
33: 5 For **the L** had said unto Moses, Say unto 3068
33: 7 *that* every one which sought **the L** went out 3068
33: 9 the tabernacle, and *the L* talked with Moses. NIH
33:11 **the L** spake unto Moses face to face, as a 3068
33:12 Moses said unto **the L**, See, thou sayest 3068
33:17 **the L** said unto Moses, I will do this thing 3068
33:19 I will proclaim the name of **the L** before 3068
33:21 **the L** said, Behold, *there is* a place by me, 3068
34: 1 **the L** said unto Moses, Hew thee two 3068
34: 4 as **the L** had commanded him, and took in 3068
34: 5 **the L** descended in the cloud, and 3068
34: 5 and proclaimed the name of **the L**. 3068
34: 6 **the L** passed by before him, and 3068
34: 6 proclaimed, **The L**, The LORD God, 3068
34: 6 **The L** God, merciful and gracious, 3068
34:10 which thou *art* shall see the work of **the L**: 3068
34:14 for **the L**, whose name *is* Jealous, *is* a 3068
34:24 before **the L** thy God thrice in the year. 3068
34:26 bring *unto* the house of **the L** thy God. 3068
34:27 **the L** said unto Moses, Write thou these 3068
34:28 he was there with **the L** forty days and 3068
34:32 **the L** had spoken with him in mount Sinai. 3068
34:34 when Moses went in before **the L** to speak 3068
35: 1 These *are* the words which **the L** hath 3068
35: 2 you a holy *day,* a sabbath of rest to **the L**: 3068
35: 4 This *is* the thing which **the L** commanded, 3068
35: 5 from amongst you an offering unto **the L**: 3068
35: 5 let him bring it, an offering of **the L**; 3068
35:10 and make all that **the L** hath commanded; 3068
35:22 *offered* an offering of gold unto **the L**. 3068
35:29 brought a willing offering unto **the L**, 3068
35:29 which **the L** had commanded to be made 3068
35:30 **the L** hath called by name Bezaleel the son 3068
36: 1 in whom **the L** put wisdom and 3068
36: 1 according to all that **the L** had commanded. 3068
36: 2 in whose heart **the L** had put wisdom, 3068
36: 5 which **the L** commanded to make. 3068
38:22 made all that **the L** commanded Moses. 3068
39: 1 for Aaron; as **the L** commanded Moses. 3068
39: 5 twined linen; as **the L** commanded Moses. 3068
39: 7 of Israel; as **the L** commanded Moses. 3068
39:21 the ephod; as **the L** commanded Moses. 3068
39:26 to minister *in;* as **the L** commanded Moses. 3068
39:29 as **the L** commanded Moses. 3068
39:30 of a signet, HOLINESS TO **THE L**. 3068
39:31 the mitre; as **the L** commanded Moses. 3068
39:32 to all that **the L** commanded Moses, 3068
39:42 According to all that **the L** commanded 3068
39:43 they had done it as **the L** had commanded, 3068
40: 1 And **the L** spake unto Moses, saying, 3068
40:16 according to all that **the L** commanded 3068
40:19 above upon it; as **the L** commanded Moses. 3068
40:21 as **the L** commanded Moses. 3068
40:23 set the bread in order upon it before **the L**; 3068
40:23 as **the L** had commanded Moses. 3068
40:25 he lighted the lamps before **the L**; as 3068
40:25 the LORD; as **the L** commanded Moses. 3068
40:27 as **the L** commanded Moses. 3068
40:29 meat offering; as **the L** commanded Moses. 3068
40:32 they washed; as **the L** commanded Moses. 3068
40:34 and the glory of **the L** filled the tabernacle. 3068
40:35 the glory of **the L** filled the tabernacle. 3068
40:38 For the cloud of **the L** *was* upon 3068
Lev 1: 1 **the L** called unto Moses, and spake unto 3068
1: 2 man of you bring an offering unto **the L**, 3068
1: 3 of the congregation before **the L**. 3068
1: 5 he shall kill the bullock before **the L**: and 3068
1: 9 made by fire, of a sweet savour unto **the L**. 3068
1:11 side of the altar northward before **the L**: 3068
1:13 made by fire, of a sweet savour unto **the L**. 3068
1:14 for his offering to **the L** *be* of fowls, 3068
1:17 made by fire, of a sweet savour unto **the L**. 3068
2: 1 any will offer a meat offering unto **the L**, 3068
2: 2 made by fire, of a sweet savour unto **the L**: 3068
2: 3 holy of the offerings of **the L** made by fire. 3068
2: 8 that is made of these *things* unto **the L**: 3068

Lev 2: 9 made by fire, of a sweet savour unto **the L**. 3068
2:10 holy of the offerings of **the L** made by fire. 3068
2:11 which ye shall bring unto **the L**, 3068
2:11 *in* any offering of **the L** made by fire. 3068
2:12 ye shall offer them unto **the L**: 3068
2:14 a meat offering of *thy* firstfruits unto **the L**, 3068
2:16 *it is* an offering made by fire unto **the L**. 3068
3: 1 shall offer it without blemish before **the L**. 3068
3: 3 an offering made by fire unto **the L**; 3068
3: 5 made by fire, of a sweet savour unto **the L**. 3068
3: 6 peace offering unto **the L** *be* of the flock, 3068
3: 7 then shall he offer it before **the L**. 3068
3: 9 an offering made by fire unto **the L**; 3068
3:11 of the offering made by fire unto **the L**. 3068
3:12 a goat, then he shall offer it before **the L**. 3068
3:14 *even* an offering made by fire unto the **L**; 3068
4: 1 And **the L** spake unto Moses, saying, 3068
4: 2 **the L** (*concerning things* which ought not 3068
4: 3 blemish unto **the L** for a sin offering. 3068
4: 4 of the congregation before **the L**; 3068
4: 4 and kill the bullock before **the L**. 3068
4: 6 of the blood seven times before **the L**, 3068
4: 7 of the altar of sweet incense before **the L**, 3068
4:13 **the L** *concerning things* which should not 3068
4:15 upon the head of the bullock before **the L**: 3068
4:15 and the bullock shall be killed before **the L**. 3068
4:17 sprinkle *it* seven times before **the L**, 3068
4:18 the horns of the altar which *is* before **the L**, 3068
4:22 **the L** his God *concerning things* which 3068
4:24 they kill the burnt offering before **the L**: 3068
4:27 **the L** *concerning things* which ought not to 3068
4:31 the altar for a sweet savour unto **the L**; 3068
4:35 to the offerings made by fire unto **the L**; 3068
5: 6 unto **the L** for his sin which he hath sinned, 3068
5: 7 or two young pigeons, unto **the L**; 3068
5:12 to the offerings made by fire unto **the L**: 3068
5:14 And **the L** spake unto Moses, saying, 3068
5:15 in the holy *things* of **the L**; 3068
5:15 he shall bring for his trespass unto **the L** a 3068
5:17 to be done by the commandments of **the L**; 3068
5:19 he hath certainly trespassed against **the L**. 3068
6: 1 And **the L** spake unto Moses, saying, 3068
6: 2 commit a trespass against **the L**, and 3068
6: 6 shall bring his trespass offering unto **the L**, 3068
6: 7 make an atonement for him before **the L**: 3068
6: 8 And **the L** spake unto Moses, saying, 3068
6:14 sons of Aaron shall offer it before **the L**, 3068
6:15 *even* the memorial of it, unto **the L**. 3068
6:18 the offerings of **the L** made by fire: 3068
6:19 And **the L** spake unto Moses, saying, 3068
6:20 which they shall offer unto **the L** in the day 3068
6:21 thou offer *for* a sweet savour unto **the L**. 3068
6:22 *it is* a statute for ever unto **the L**; it shall be 3068
6:24 And **the L** spake unto Moses, saying, 3068
6:25 shall the sin offering be killed before **the L**: 3068
7: 5 *for* an offering made by fire unto **the L**: 3068
7:11 which he shall offer unto **the L**. 3068
7:14 oblation *for* a heave offering unto **the L**, 3068
7:20 that *pertain* unto **the L**, having his 3068
7:21 which *pertain* unto **the L**, even that soul 3068
7:22 And **the L** spake unto Moses, saying, 3068
7:25 offer an offering made by fire unto **the L**, 3068
7:28 And **the L** spake unto Moses, saying, 3068
7:29 **the L** shall bring his oblation unto 3068
7:29 **the L** of the sacrifice of his peace offerings. 3068
7:30 bring the offerings of **the L** made by fire, 3068
7:30 be waved *for* a wave offering before **the L**. 3068
7:35 out of the offerings of **the L** made by fire, 3068
7:35 to minister unto **the L** in the priest's office; 3068
7:36 Which **the L** commanded to be given them 3068
7:38 Which **the L** commanded Moses in mount 3068
7:38 of Israel to offer their oblations unto **the L**, 3068
8: 1 And **the L** spake unto Moses, saying, 3068
8: 4 Moses did as **the L** commanded him; and 3068
8: 5 This *is* the thing which **the L** commanded 3068
8: 9 holy crown; as **the L** commanded Moses. 3068
8:13 upon them; as **the L** commanded Moses. 3068
8:17 the camp; as **the L** commanded Moses. 3068
8:21 *and* an offering made by fire unto **the L**; 3068
8:21 the LORD; as **the L** commanded Moses. 3068
8:26 that *was* before **the L**, he took one 3068
8:27 them *for* a wave offering before **the L**. 3068
8:28 it *is* an offering made by fire unto **the L**. 3068
8:29 waved it *for* a wave offering before **the L**: 3068
8:29 Moses' part; as **the L** commanded Moses. 3068
8:34 this day, *so* **the L** hath commanded to do, 3068
8:35 keep the charge of **the L**, that ye die not: 3068
8:36 his sons did all things which **the L** 3068
9: 2 and offer *them* before **the L**. 3068
9: 4 peace offerings, to sacrifice before **the L**; 3068
9: 4 for to day **the L** will appear unto you. 3068
9: 5 drew near and stood before **the L**. 3068
9: 6 This *is* the thing which **the L** commanded 3068
9: 6 the glory of **the L** shall appear unto you. 3068
9: 7 atonement for them; as **the L** commanded. 3068
9:10 the altar; as **the L** commanded Moses. 3068
9:21 waved *for* a wave offering before **the L**; 3068
9:23 the glory of **the L** appeared unto all 3068
9:24 there came a fire out from before **the L**, 3068
10: 1 offered strange fire before **the L**, 3068
10: 2 there went out fire from **the L**, and 3068
10: 2 devoured them, and they died before **the L**. 3068
10: 3 This *is it* that **the L** spake, saying, 3068
10: 6 bewail the burning which **the L** hath 3068
10: 7 for the anointing oil of **the L** *is* upon you. 3068
10: 8 And **the L** spake unto Aaron, saying, 3068
10:11 **the L** hath spoken unto them by the hand of 3068
10:12 of the offerings of **the L** made by fire, 3068
10:13 of the sacrifices of **the L** made by fire: 3068
10:15 to wave *it for* a wave offering before **the L**; 3068
10:15 statute for ever; as **the L** hath commanded. 3068
10:17 to make atonement for them before **the L**? 3068
10:19 and their burnt offering before **the L**; 3068
10:19 it have been accepted in the sight of the **L**? 3068
11: 1 **the L** spake unto Moses and to Aaron, 3068
11:44 For I *am* **the L** your God: ye shall therefore 3068
11:45 For I *am* **the L** that bringeth you up out of 3068
12: 1 And **the L** spake unto Moses, saying, 3068
12: 7 Who shall offer it before **the L**, and 3068
13: 1 **the L** spake unto Moses and Aaron, saying, 3068
14: 1 And **the L** spake unto Moses, saying, 3068
14:11 those *things*, before **the L**, *at* the door of 3068
14:12 them *for* a wave offering before **the L**: 3068
14:16 with his finger seven times before **the L**: 3068
14:18 make an atonement for him before **the L**. 3068
14:23 of the congregation, before **the L**. 3068
14:24 them *for* a wave offering before **the L**: 3068
14:27 *is* in his left hand seven times before **the L**: 3068
14:29 to make an atonement for him before **the L**. 3068
14:31 for him that is to be cleansed before **the L**. 3068
14:33 **the L** spake unto Moses and unto Aaron, 3068
15: 1 **the L** spake unto Moses and to Aaron, 3068
15:14 come before **the L** unto the door of 3068
15:15 for him before **the L** for his issue. 3068
15:30 **the L** for the issue of her uncleanness. 3068
16: 1 **the L** spake unto Moses after the death of 3068
16: 1 when they offered before **the L**, and died; 3068
16: 2 **the L** said unto Moses, Speak unto Aaron 3068
16: 7 present them before **the L** *at* the door of 3068
16: 8 one lot for **the L**, and the other lot for 3068
16:10 shall be presented alive before **the L**, 3068
16:12 coals of fire from off the altar before **the L**, 3068
16:13 put the incense upon the fire before **the L**, 3068
16:18 go out unto the altar that *is* before **the L**, 3068
16:30 be clean from all your sins before **the L**. 3068
16:34 And he did as **the L** commanded Moses. 3068
17: 1 And **the L** spake unto Moses, saying, 3068
17: 2 This *is* the thing which **the L** hath 3068
17: 4 to offer an offering unto **the L** before 3068
17: 4 the LORD before the tabernacle of **the L**; 3068
17: 5 even that they may bring them unto **the L**, 3068
17: 5 offer them *for* peace offerings unto **the L**. 3068
17: 6 **the L** *at* the door of the tabernacle of 3068
17: 6 burn the fat for a sweet savour unto **the L**. 3068
17: 9 of the congregation, to offer it unto **the L**; 3068
18: 1 And **the L** spake unto Moses, saying, 3068
18: 2 and say unto them, I *am* **the L** your God. 3068
18: 4 to walk therein: I *am* **the L** your God. 3068
18: 5 a man do, he shall live in them: I *am* **the L**. 3068
18: 6 to uncover *their* nakedness: I *am* **the L**. 3068
18:21 profane the name of thy God: I *am* **the L**. 3068
18:30 yourselves therein: I *am* **the L** your God. 3068
19: 1 And **the L** spake unto Moses, saying, 3068
19: 2 be holy: for I **the L** your God *am* holy. 3068
19: 3 keep my sabbaths: I *am* **the L** your God. 3068
19: 4 molten gods: I *am* **the L** your God. 3068
19: 5 a sacrifice of peace offerings unto **the L**, 3068
19: 8 hath profaned the hallowed *thing* of **the L**: 3068

Lev	19:10	and stranger: I *am* **the L** your God.	3068
	19:12	profane the name of thy God: I *am* **the L**.	3068
	19:14	but shalt fear thy God: I *am* **the L**.	3068
	19:16	the blood of thy neighbour: I *am* **the L**.	3068
	19:18	love thy neighbour as thyself: I *am* **the L**.	3068
	19:21	shall bring his trespass offering unto **the L**,	3068
	19:22	**the L** for his sin which he hath done:	3068
	19:24	shall be holy to praise **the L** *withal.*	3068
	19:25	the increase thereof: I *am* **the L** your God.	3068
	19:28	nor print any marks upon you: I *am* **the L**.	3068
	19:30	and reverence my sanctuary: I *am* **the L**.	3068
	19:31	be defiled by them: I *am* **the L** your God.	3068
	19:32	the old man, and fear thy God: I *am* **the L**.	3068
	19:34	in the land of Egypt: I *am* **the L** your God.	3068
	19:36	I *am* **the L** your God, which brought you	3068
	19:37	all my judgments, and do them: I *am* **the L**.	3068
	20: 1	And **the L** spake unto Moses, saying,	3068
	20: 7	and be ye holy: for I *am* **the L** your God.	3068
	20: 8	do them: I *am* **the L** which sanctify you.	3068
	20:24	I *am* **the L** your God, which have separated	3068
	20:26	for I **the L** *am* holy, and have severed you	3068
	21: 1	**the L** said unto Moses, Speak unto	3068
	21: 6	for the offerings of **the L** made by fire, *and*	3068
	21: 8	for I **the L**, which sanctify you, *am* holy.	3068
	21:12	oil of his God *is* upon him: I *am* **the L**.	3068
	21:15	his people: for I **the L** do sanctify him.	3068
	21:16	And **the L** spake unto Moses, saying,	3068
	21:21	to offer the offerings of **the L** made by fire:	3068
	21:23	for I **the L** do sanctify them.	3068
	22: 1	And **the L** spake unto Moses, saying,	3068
	22: 2	which they hallow unto me: I *am* **the L**.	3068
	22: 3	the children of Israel hallow unto **the L**,	3068
	22: 3	be cut off from my presence: I *am* **the L**.	3068
	22: 8	eat to defile *himself* therewith: I *am* **the L**.	3068
	22: 9	if they profane it: I **the L** do sanctify them.	3068
	22:15	of Israel, which they offer unto **the L**;	3068
	22:16	when they eat their holy *things:* for I **the L**	3068
	22:17	And **the L** spake unto Moses, saying,	3068
	22:18	which they will offer unto **the L** for a burnt	3068
	22:21	unto **the L** to accomplish *his* vow,	3068
	22:22	ye shall not offer these unto **the L**,	3068
	22:22	by fire of them upon the altar unto **the L**.	3068
	22:24	Ye shall not offer unto **the L** that which is	3068
	22:26	And **the L** spake unto Moses, saying,	3068
	22:27	for an offering made by fire unto **the L**.	3068
	22:29	offer a sacrifice of thanksgiving unto **the L**,	3068
	22:30	none of it until the morrow: I *am* **the L**.	3068
	22:31	and do them: I *am* **the L**.	3068
	22:32	of Israel: I *am* **the L** which hallow you,	3068
	22:33	land of Egypt, to be your God: I *am* **the L**.	3068
	23: 1	And **the L** spake unto Moses, saying,	3068
	23: 2	unto them, *Concerning* the feasts of **the L**,	3068
	23: 3	the sabbath of **the L** in all your dwellings.	3068
	23: 4	These *are* the feasts of **the L**, *even* holy	3068
	23: 6	*is* the feast of unleavened bread unto **the L**:	3068
	23: 8	made by fire unto **the L** seven days:	3068
	23: 9	And **the L** spake unto Moses, saying,	3068
	23:11	he shall wave the sheaf before **the L**, to be	3068
	23:12	first year for a burnt offering unto **the L**.	3068
	23:13	an offering made by fire unto **the L** *for* a	3068
	23:16	shall offer a new meat offering unto **the L**.	3068
	23:17	*they are* the firstfruits unto **the L**.	3068
	23:18	shall be *for* a burnt offering unto **the L**,	3068
	23:18	made by fire, of sweet savour unto **the L**.	3068
	23:20	firstfruits *for* a wave offering before **the L**,	3068
	23:20	they shall be holy to **the L** for the priest.	3068
	23:22	and to the stranger: I *am* **the L** your God.	3068
	23:23	And **the L** spake unto Moses, saying,	3068
	23:25	offer an offering made by fire unto **the L**.	3068
	23:26	And **the L** spake unto Moses, saying,	3068
	23:27	offer an offering made by fire unto **the L**.	3068
	23:28	to make an atonement for you before **the L**	3068
	23:33	And **the L** spake unto Moses, saying,	3068
	23:34	of tabernacles *for* seven days unto **the L**.	3068
	23:36	offer an offering made by fire unto **the L**:	3068
	23:36	offer an offering made by fire unto **the L**:	3068
	23:37	These *are* the feasts of **the L**, which ye	3068
	23:37	offer an offering made by fire unto **the L**,	3068
	23:38	Beside the sabbaths of **the L**, and	3068
	23:38	which ye give unto **the L**.	3068
	23:39	ye shall keep a feast unto **the L** seven days:	3068
	23:40	ye shall rejoice before **the L** your God	3068
	23:41	ye shall keep it a feast unto **the L** seven	3068
	23:43	of the land of Egypt: I *am* **the L** your God.	3068
	23:44	the children of Israel the feasts of **the L**.	3068
	24: 1	And **the L** spake unto Moses, saying,	3068
	24: 3	unto the morning before **the L** continually:	3068
	24: 4	pure candlestick before **the L** continually.	3068
	24: 6	on a row, upon the pure table before **the L**.	3068
	24: 7	*even* an offering made by fire unto **the L**.	3068
	24: 8	set it in order before **the L** continually,	3068
	24: 9	him of the offerings of **the L** made by fire,	3068
	24:11	son blasphemed the name *of the L,*	NIH
	24:12	that the mind of **the L** might be shewed	3068
	24:13	And **the L** spake unto Moses, saying,	3068
	24:16	he that blasphemeth the name of **the L**,	3068
	24:16	when he blasphemeth the name *of the L,*	NIH
	24:22	own country: for I *am* **the L** your God.	3068
	24:23	the children of Israel did as **the L**	3068
	25: 1	**the L** spake unto Moses in mount Sinai,	3068
	25: 2	shall the land keep a sabbath unto **the L**.	3068
	25: 4	of rest unto the land, a sabbath for **the L**:	3068
	25:17	fear thy God: for I *am* **the L** your God.	3068
	25:38	I *am* **the L** your God, which brought you	3068
	25:55	of the land of Egypt: I *am* **the L** your God.	3068
	26: 1	bow down unto it: for I *am* **the L** your God.	3068
	26: 2	and reverence my sanctuary: I *am* **the L**.	3068
	26:13	I *am* **the L** your God, which brought you	3068
	26:44	with them: for I *am* **the L** their God.	3068
	26:45	that *I* might be their God: I *am* **the L**.	3068
	26:46	which **the L** made between him and	3068
	27: 1	And **the L** spake unto Moses, saying,	3068
	27: 2	the persons *shall be* for **the L** by thy	3068
	27: 9	whereof *men* bring an offering unto **the L**,	3068
	27: 9	all that *any man* giveth of such unto **the L**	3068
	27:11	they do not offer a sacrifice unto **the L**,	3068
	27:14	sanctify his house *to be* holy unto **the L**,	3068
	27:16	if a man shall sanctify unto **the L** *some part*	3068
	27:21	shall be holy unto **the L**, as a field devoted;	3068
	27:22	if *a man* sanctify unto **the L** a field which	3068
	27:23	in that day, *as* a holy *thing* unto **the L**.	3068
	27:28	that a man shall devote unto **the L** of all	3068
	27:28	devoted thing *is* most holy unto **the L**.	3068
	27:30	*is* the LORD'S: *it is* holy unto **the L**.	3068
	27:32	the rod, the tenth shall be holy unto **the L**.	3068
	27:34	which **the L** commanded Moses for	3068
Nu	1: 1	**the L** spake unto Moses in the wilderness	3068
	1:19	As **the L** commanded Moses, so	3068
	1:48	For **the L** had spoken unto Moses, saying,	3068
	1:54	to all that **the L** commanded Moses,	3068
	2: 1	**the L** spake unto Moses and unto Aaron,	3068
	2:33	of Israel; as **the L** commanded Moses.	3068
	2:34	to all that **the L** commanded Moses:	3068
	3: 1	Moses in the day that **the L** spake with	3068
	3: 4	Nadab and Abihu died before **the L**,	3068
	3: 4	they offered strange fire before **the L**,	3068
	3: 5	And **the L** spake unto Moses, saying,	3068
	3:11	And **the L** spake unto Moses, saying,	3068
	3:13	and beast: mine they shall be: I *am* **the L**.	3068
	3:14	**the L** spake unto Moses in the wilderness	3068
	3:16	them according to the word of **the L**,	3068
	3:39	numbered at the commandment of **the L**,	3068
	3:40	**the L** said unto Moses, Number all	3068
	3:41	shalt take the Levites for me (I *am* **the L**)	3068
	3:42	as **the L** commanded him,	3068
	3:44	And **the L** spake unto Moses, saying,	3068
	3:45	and the Levites shall be mine: I *am* **the L**.	3068
	3:51	to his sons, according to the word of **the L**,	3068
	3:51	the LORD, as **the L** commanded Moses.	3068
	4: 1	**the L** spake unto Moses and unto Aaron,	3068
	4:17	**the L** spake unto Moses and unto Aaron,	3068
	4:21	And **the L** spake unto Moses, saying,	3068
	4:37	of **the L** by the hand of Moses.	3068
	4:41	according to the commandment of **the L**.	3068
	4:45	to the word of **the L** by the hand of Moses.	3068
	4:49	According to the commandment of **the L**	3068
	4:49	of him, as **the L** commanded Moses.	3068
	5: 1	And **the L** spake unto Moses, saying,	3068
	5: 4	as **the L** spake unto Moses, so did	3068
	5: 5	And **the L** spake unto Moses, saying,	3068
	5: 6	to do a trespass against **the L**, and	3068
	5: 8	*let* the trespass *be* recompensed unto **the L**,	3068
	5:11	And **the L** spake unto Moses, saying,	3068
	5:16	bring her near, and set her before **the L**:	3068
	5:18	the priest shall set the woman before **the L**,	3068
	5:21	**The L** make thee a curse and an oath	3068
	5:21	when **the L** doth make thy thigh to rot, and	3068
	5:25	shall wave the offering before **the L**, and	3068

Nu 5:30 shall set the woman before **the L**, and 3068
6: 1 And **the L** spake unto Moses, saying, 3068
6: 2 to separate *themselves* unto **the L**: 3068
6: 5 the which he separateth *himself* unto **the L**, 3068
6: 6 unto **the L** he shall come at no dead body. 3068
6: 8 of his separation he *is* holy unto **the L**. 3068
6:12 he shall consecrate unto **the L** the days of 3068
6:14 he shall offer his offering unto **the L**, 3068
6:16 the priest shall bring *them* before **the L**, 3068
6:17 a sacrifice of peace offerings unto **the L**, 3068
6:20 them *for* a wave offering before **the L**: 3068
6:21 *of* his offering unto **the L** for his 3068
6:22 And **the L** spake unto Moses, saying, 3068
6:24 **The L** bless thee, and keep thee: 3068
6:25 **The L** make his face shine upon thee, and 3068
6:26 **The L** lift up his countenance upon thee, 3068
7: 3 they brought their offering before **the L**, 3068
7: 4 And **the L** spake unto Moses, saying, 3068
7:11 **the L** said unto Moses, They shall offer 3068
8: 1 And **the L** spake unto Moses, saying, 3068
8: 3 as **the L** commanded Moses. 3068
8: 4 according unto the pattern which **the L** had 3068
8: 5 And **the L** spake unto Moses, saying, 3068
8:10 thou shalt bring the Levites before **the L**: 3068
8:11 Aaron shall offer the Levites before **the L** 3068
8:11 that they may execute the service of **the L**. 3068
8:12 the other *for* a burnt offering, unto **the L**, 3068
8:13 and offer them *for* an offering unto **the L**. 3068
8:20 **the L** commanded Moses concerning 3068
8:21 offered them *as* an offering before **the L**; 3068
8:22 as **the L** had commanded Moses 3068
8:23 And **the L** spake unto Moses, saying, 3068
9: 1 **the L** spake unto Moses in the wilderness 3068
9: 5 according to all that **the L** commanded 3068
9: 7 that *we* may not offer an offering of **the L** 3068
9: 8 I will hear what **the L** will command 3068
9: 9 And **the L** spake unto Moses, saying, 3068
9:10 yet he shall keep the passover unto **the L**. 3068
9:13 he brought not the offering of **the L** in his 3068
9:14 and will keep the passover unto **the L**; 3068
9:18 At the commandment of **the L** the children 3068
9:18 at the commandment of **the L** they pitched: 3068
9:19 children of Israel kept the charge of **the L**, 3068
9:20 according to the commandment of **the L** 3068
9:20 according to the commandment of **the L** 3068
9:23 At the commandment of **the L** they rested 3068
9:23 at the commandment of **the L** they 3068
9:23 they kept the charge of **the L**, at 3068
9:23 at the commandment of **the L** by the hand 3068
10: 1 And **the L** spake unto Moses, saying, 3068
10: 9 ye shall be remembered before **the L** your 3068
10:10 before your God: I *am* **the L** your God. 3068
10:13 of **the L** by the hand of Moses. 3068
10:29 unto the place of which **the L** said, 3068
10:29 for **the L** hath spoken good concerning 3068
10:32 *that* what goodness **the L** shall do unto us, 3068
10:33 they departed from the mount of **the L** 3068
10:33 the ark of the covenant of **the L** went 3068
10:34 the cloud of **the L** *was* upon them by day, 3068
10:35 **L**, and let thine enemies be scattered; 3068
10:36 when it rested, he said, Return, O **L**, 3068
11: 1 the people complained, it displeased **the L**: 3068
11: 1 **the L** heard *it;* and his anger was kindled; 3068
11: 1 the fire of **the L** burnt among them, and 3068
11: 2 when Moses prayed unto **the L**, the fire 3068
11: 3 the fire of **the L** burnt among them. 3068
11:10 the anger of **the L** was kindled greatly; 3068
11:11 Moses said unto **the L**, Wherefore hast 3068
11:16 **the L** said unto Moses, Gather unto me 3068
11:18 for you have wept in the ears of **the L**, 3068
11:18 therefore **the L** will give you flesh, and 3068
11:20 that ye have despised **the L** which *is* 3068
11:23 **the L** said unto Moses, Is the LORD'S 3068
11:24 told the people the words of **the L**, and 3068
11:25 **the L** came down in a cloud, and 3068
11:29 that **the L** would put his spirit upon them! 3068
11:31 there went forth a wind from **the L**, and 3068
11:33 the wrath of **the L** was kindled against 3068
11:33 **the L** smote the people *with* a very great 3068
12: 2 Hath **the L** indeed spoken only by Moses? 3068
12: 2 not spoken also by us? And **the L** heard *it.* 3068
12: 4 **the L** spake suddenly unto Moses, and 3068
12: 5 **the L** came down in the pillar of the cloud, 3068
12: 6 *I* **the L** will make myself known unto him 3068
12: 8 and the similitude of **the L** shall he behold: 3068
12: 9 the anger of **the L** was kindled against 3068
12:13 Moses cried unto **the L**, saying, Heal her 3068
12:14 **the L** said unto Moses, If her father had 3068
13: 1 And **the L** spake unto Moses, saying, 3068
13: 3 Moses by the commandment of **the L** sent 3068
14: 3 wherefore *hath* **the L** brought us unto this 3068
14: 8 If **the L** delight in us, then he will bring us 3068
14: 9 Only rebel not ye against **the L**, 3068
14: 9 departed from them, and **the L** *is* with us: 3068
14:10 the glory of **the L** appeared in 3068
14:11 **the L** said unto Moses, How long will this 3068
14:13 Moses said unto **the L**, Then the Egyptians 3068
14:14 *for* they have heard that thou **L** *art* among 3068
14:14 that thou **L** *art* seen face to face, and 3068
14:16 Because **the L** was not able to bring this 3068
14:18 **The L** *is* longsuffering, and of great mercy, 3068
14:20 **the L** said, I have pardoned according to 3068
14:21 earth shall be filled *with* the glory of **the L**. 3068
14:26 **the L** spake unto Moses and unto Aaron, 3068
14:28 unto them, *As truly as* I live, saith **the L**, 3068
14:35 I **the L** have said, I will surely do it unto all 3068
14:37 the land, died by the plague before **the L**. 3068
14:40 will go up unto the place which **the L** hath 3068
14:41 ye transgress the commandment of **the L**? 3068
14:42 Go not up, for **the L** *is* not among you; 3068
14:43 because ye are turned away from **the L**, 3068
14:43 therefore **the L** will not be with you. 3068
14:44 the ark of the covenant of **the L**, 3068
15: 1 And **the L** spake unto Moses, saying, 3068
15: 3 will make an offering by fire unto **the L**, 3068
15: 3 to make a sweet savour unto **the L**, of 3068
15: 4 **the L** bring a meat offering of a tenth deal 3068
15: 7 hin *of* wine, *for* a sweet savour unto **the L**. 3068
15: 8 a vow, or peace offerings unto **the L**: 3068
15:10 made by fire, of a sweet savour unto **the L**. 3068
15:13 made by fire, of a sweet savour unto **the L**. 3068
15:14 made by fire, of a sweet savour unto **the L**; 3068
15:15 so shall the stranger be before **the L**. 3068
15:17 And **the L** spake unto Moses, saying, 3068
15:19 shall offer up a heave offering unto **the L**. 3068
15:21 **the L** a heave offering in your generations. 3068
15:22 which **the L** hath spoken unto Moses, 3068
15:23 *Even* all that **the L** hath commanded you 3068
15:23 from the day that **the L** commanded 3068
15:24 for a sweet savour unto **the L**, with his 3068
15:25 a sacrifice made by fire unto **the L**, and 3068
15:25 their sin offering before **the L**, for their 3068
15:28 when he sinneth by ignorance before **the L**, 3068
15:30 or a stranger, the same reproacheth **the L**; 3068
15:31 he hath despised the word of **the L**, 3068
15:35 **the L** said unto Moses, The man shall be 3068
15:36 and he died; as **the L** commanded Moses. 3068
15:37 And **the L** spake unto Moses, saying, 3068
15:39 remember all the commandments of **the L**, 3068
15:41 I *am* **the L** your God, which brought you 3068
15:41 to be your God: I *am* **the L** your God. 3068
16: 3 one of them, and **the L** *is* among them: 3068
16: 3 above the congregation of **the L**? 3068
16: 5 Even to morrow **the L** will shew who *are* 3068
16: 7 put incense in them before **the L** to 3068
16: 7 it shall be *that* the man whom **the L** doth 3068
16: 9 to do the service of the tabernacle of **the L**, 3068
16:11 *are* gathered together against **the L**: 3068
16:15 was very wroth, and said unto **the L**, 3068
16:16 Be thou and all thy company before **the L**, 3068
16:17 bring ye before **the L** every man his censer, 3068
16:19 the glory of **the L** appeared unto all 3068
16:20 **the L** spake unto Moses and unto Aaron, 3068
16:23 And **the L** spake unto Moses, saying, 3068
16:28 Hereby ye shall know that **the L** hath sent 3068
16:29 of all men; *then* **the L** hath not sent me. 3068
16:30 if **the L** make a new thing, and the earth 3068
16:30 that these men have provoked **the L**. 3068
16:35 there came out a fire from **the L**, and 3068
16:36 And **the L** spake unto Moses, saying, 3068
16:38 for they offered them before **the L**, 3068
16:40 come near to offer incense before **the L**; 3068
16:40 as **the L** said to him by the hand of Moses. 3068
16:41 Ye have killed the people of **the L**. 3068
16:42 covered it, and the glory of **the L** appeared. 3068
16:44 And **the L** spake unto Moses, saying, 3068
16:46 for there is wrath gone out from **the L**; 3068
17: 1 And **the L** spake unto Moses, saying, 3068

Nu 17: 7 Moses laid up the rods before **the L** in 3068
17: 9 before **the L** unto all the children of Israel: 3068
17:10 **the L** said unto Moses, Bring Aaron's rod 3068
17:11 Moses did *so:* as **the L** commanded him, 3068
17:13 near unto the tabernacle of **the L** shall die: 3068
18: 1 **the L** said unto Aaron, Thou and thy sons 3068
18: 6 to you *they are* given *as* a gift for **the L**, 3068
18: 8 **the L** spake unto Aaron, Behold, I also 3068
18:12 of them which they shall offer unto **the L**, 3068
18:13 which they shall bring unto **the L**, shall be 3068
18:15 which they bring unto **the L**, *whether it be* 3068
18:17 by fire, for a sweet savour unto **the L**. 3068
18:19 the children of Israel offer unto **the L**, 3068
18:19 it *is* a covenant of salt for ever before **the L** 3068
18:20 **the L** spake unto Aaron, Thou shalt have 3068
18:24 they offer *as* a heave offering unto **the L**, 3068
18:25 And **the L** spake unto Moses, saying, 3068
18:26 offer up a heave offering of it for **the L**, 3068
18:28 heave offering unto **the L** of all your tithes, 3068
18:29 shall offer every heave offering of **the L**, 3068
19: 1 **the L** spake unto Moses and unto Aaron, 3068
19: 2 of the law which **the L** hath commanded, 3068
19:13 defileth the tabernacle of **the L**; 3068
19:20 he hath defiled the sanctuary of **the L**: 3068
20: 3 died when our brethren died before **the L**! 3068
20: 4 congregation of **the L** into this wilderness, 3068
20: 6 and the glory of **the L** appeared unto them. 3068
20: 7 And **the L** spake unto Moses, saying, 3068
20: 9 Moses took the rod from before **the L**, 3068
20:12 **the L** spake unto Moses and Aaron, 3068
20:13 the children of Israel strove with **the L**, 3068
20:16 when we cried unto **the L**, he heard our 3068
20:23 **the L** spake unto Moses and Aaron in 3068
20:27 Moses did as **the L** commanded: and 3068
21: 2 Israel vowed a vow unto **the L**, and said, 3068
21: 3 **the L** hearkened to the voice of Israel, and 3068
21: 6 **the L** sent fiery serpents among the people, 3068
21: 7 for we have spoken against **the L**, and 3068
21: 7 pray unto **the L**, that he take away 3068
21: 8 **the L** said unto Moses, Make thee a fiery 3068
21:14 it is said in the book of the wars of **the L**, 3068
21:16 that *is* the well whereof **the L** spake unto 3068
21:34 **the L** said unto Moses, Fear him not: for I 3068
22: 8 word again, as **the L** shall speak unto me: 3068
22:13 for **the L** refuseth to give me leave to go 3068
22:18 I cannot go beyond the word of **the L** my 3068
22:19 that I may know what **the L** will say unto 3068
22:22 the angel of **the L** stood in the way for an 3068
22:23 the ass saw the angel of **the L** standing in 3068
22:24 the angel of **the L** stood in a path of 3068
22:25 when the ass saw the angel of **the L**, she 3068
22:26 the angel of **the L** went further, and 3068
22:27 when the ass saw the angel of **the L**, she 3068
22:28 **the L** opened the mouth of the ass, and 3068
22:31 Then **the L** opened the eyes of Balaam, and 3068
22:31 he saw the angel of **the L** standing in 3068
22:32 the angel of **the L** said unto him, 3068
22:34 Balaam said unto the angel of **the L**, I have 3068
22:35 the angel of **the L** said unto Balaam, 3068
23: 3 peradventure **the L** will come to meet me: 3068
23: 5 **the L** put a word in Balaam's mouth, and 3068
23: 8 shall I defy, *whom* **the L** hath not defied? 3068
23:12 that which **the L** hath put in my mouth? 3068
23:15 burnt offering, while I meet *the L* yonder. NIH
23:16 **the L** met Balaam, and put a word in his 3068
23:17 said unto him, What hath **the L** spoken? 3068
23:21 **the L** his God *is* with him, and the shout of 3068
23:26 saying, All that **the L** speaketh, that I must 3068
24: 1 when Balaam saw that it pleased **the L** to 3068
24: 6 as the trees of lign aloes *which* **the L** hath 3068
24:11 lo, **the L** hath kept thee back from honour. 3068
24:13 go beyond the commandment of **the L**, 3068
24:13 *but* what **the L** saith, that will I speak? 3068
25: 3 the anger of **the L** was kindled against 3068
25: 4 **the L** said unto Moses, Take all the heads 3068
25: 4 hang them up before **the L** against the sun, 3068
25: 4 that the fierce anger of **the L** may be turned 3068
25:10 And **the L** spake unto Moses, saying, 3068
25:16 And **the L** spake unto Moses, saying, 3068
26: 1 that **the L** spake unto Moses and 3068
26: 4 as **the L** commanded Moses and 3068
26: 9 of Korah, when they strove against **the L**: 3068
26:52 And **the L** spake unto Moses, saying, 3068
26:61 they offered strange fire before **the L**. 3068
26:65 For **the L** had said of them, They shall 3068
27: 3 against **the L** in the company of Korah; 3068
27: 5 Moses brought their cause before **the L**. 3068
27: 6 And **the L** spake unto Moses, saying, 3068
27:11 of judgment, as **the L** commanded Moses. 3068
27:12 **the L** said unto Moses, Get thee up into 3068
27:15 And Moses spake unto **the L**, saying, 3068
27:16 Let **the L**, the God of the spirits of all flesh, 3068
27:17 that the congregation of **the L** be not as 3068
27:18 **the L** said unto Moses, Take thee Joshua 3068
27:21 after the judgment of Urim before **the L**: 3068
27:22 Moses did as **the L** commanded him: and 3068
27:23 as **the L** commanded by the hand of Moses. 3068
28: 1 And **the L** spake unto Moses, saying, 3068
28: 3 by fire which ye shall offer unto **the L**; 3068
28: 6 a sacrifice made by fire unto **the L**. 3068
28: 7 be poured unto **the L** *for* a drink offering. 3068
28: 8 made by fire, *of* a sweet savour unto **the L**. 3068
28:11 ye shall offer a burnt offering unto **the L**; 3068
28:13 a sacrifice made by fire unto **the L**. 3068
28:15 a sin offering unto **the L** shall be offered, 3068
28:16 of the first month *is* the passover of **the L**. 3068
28:19 by fire *for* a burnt offering unto **the L**; 3068
28:24 made by fire, *of* a sweet savour unto **the L**: 3068
28:26 ye bring a new meat offering unto **the L**, 3068
28:27 offering for a sweet savour unto **the L**; 3068
29: 2 offering for a sweet savour unto **the L**; 3068
29: 6 a sacrifice made by fire unto **the L**. 3068
29: 8 ye shall offer a burnt offering unto **the L** 3068
29:12 ye shall keep a feast unto **the L** seven days: 3068
29:13 made by fire, *of* a sweet savour unto **the L**; 3068
29:36 made by fire, *of* a sweet savour unto **the L**: 3068
29:39 These *things* ye shall do unto **the L** in your 3068
29:40 to all that **the L** commanded Moses. 3068
30: 1 This *is* the thing which **the L** hath 3068
30: 2 If a man vow a vow unto **the L**, or 3068
30: 3 If a woman also vow a vow unto **the L**, and 3068
30: 5 **the L** shall forgive her, because her father 3068
30: 8 of none effect: and **the L** shall forgive her. 3068
30:12 them void; and **the L** shall forgive her. 3068
30:16 which **the L** commanded Moses, between a 3068
31: 1 And **the L** spake unto Moses, saying, 3068
31: 3 and avenge **the L** of Midian. 3068
31: 7 as **the L** commanded Moses; 3068
31:16 to commit trespass against **the L** in 3068
31:16 a plague among the congregation of **the L**. 3068
31:21 *is* the ordinance of the law which **the L** 3068
31:25 And **the L** spake unto Moses, saying, 3068
31:28 levy a tribute unto **the L** of the men of war 3068
31:29 the priest, *for* a heave offering of **the L**. 3068
31:30 keep the charge of the tabernacle of **the L**. 3068
31:31 Eleazar the priest did as **the L** commanded 3068
31:41 the priest, as **the L** commanded Moses. 3068
31:47 kept the charge of the tabernacle of **the L**; 3068
31:47 the LORD; as **the L** commanded Moses. 3068
31:50 therefore brought an oblation for **the L**, 3068
31:50 an atonement for our souls before **the L**. 3068
31:52 the offering that they offered up to **the L**, 3068
31:54 for the children of Israel before **the L**. 3068
32: 4 *Even* the country which **the L** smote before 3068
32: 7 into the land which **the L** hath given them? 3068
32: 9 into the land which **the L** had given them. 3068
32:12 for they have wholly followed **the L**. 3068
32:13 that had done evil in the sight of **the L**, 3068
32:14 to augment yet the fierce anger of **the L** 3068
32:20 if ye will go armed before **the L** to war, 3068
32:21 all of you armed over Jordan before **the L**, 3068
32:22 And the land be subdued before **the L**: then 3068
32:22 be guiltless before **the L**, and before Israel; 3068
32:22 land shall be your possession before **the L**. 3068
32:23 behold, ye have sinned against **the L**: 3068
32:27 before **the L** to battle, as my lord saith. 3068
32:29 before **the L**, and the land shall be subdued 3068
32:31 As **the L** hath said unto thy servants, so 3068
32:32 We will pass over armed before **the L** *into* 3068
33: 2 journeys by the commandment of **the L**: 3068
33: 4 which **the L** had smitten among them: 3068
33: 4 upon their gods also **the L** executed 3068
33:38 mount Hor at the commandment of **the L**, 3068
33:50 **the L** spake unto Moses in the plains of 3068
34: 1 And **the L** spake unto Moses, saying, 3068
34:13 which **the L** commanded to give unto 3068
34:16 And **the L** spake unto Moses, saying, 3068
34:29 These *are they* whom **the L** commanded to 3068

Nu 35: 1 **the L** spake unto Moses in the plains of 3068
35: 9 And **the L** spake unto Moses, saying, 3068
35:34 for I **the L** dwell among the children of 3068
36: 2 **The L** commanded my lord to give the land 3068
36: 2 my lord was commanded by **the L** to give 3068
36: 5 of Israel according to the word of **the L**, 3068
36: 6 This *is* the thing which **the L** doth 3068
36:10 Even as **the L** commanded Moses, so 3068
36:13 which **the L** commanded by the hand of 3068
Dt 1: 3 according unto all that **the L** had given him 3068
1: 6 **The L** our God spake unto us in Horeb, 3068
1: 8 possess the land which **the L** sware unto 3068
1:10 **The L** your God hath multiplied you, and 3068
1:11 (**The L** God of your fathers make you a 3068
1:19 as **the L** our God commanded us; 3068
1:20 which **the L** our God doth give unto us. 3068
1:21 **the L** thy God hath set the land before thee: 3068
1:21 possess *it,* as **the L** God of thy fathers hath 3068
1:25 *It is* a good land which **the L** our God doth 3068
1:26 rebelled against the commandment of **the L** 3068
1:27 and said, Because **the L** hated us, 3068
1:30 **The L** your God which goeth before you, 3068
1:31 where thou hast seen how that **the L** thy 3068
1:32 Yet in this thing ye did not believe **the L** 3068
1:34 **the L** heard the voice of your words, and 3068
1:36 because he hath wholly followed **the L**. 3068
1:37 Also **the L** was angry with me for your 3068
1:41 unto me, We have sinned against **the L**, 3068
1:41 according to all that **the L** our God 3068
1:42 **the L** said unto me, Say unto them, Go not 3068
1:43 against the commandment of **the L**, 3068
1:45 And ye returned and wept before **the L**; but 3068
1:45 **the L** would not hearken to your voice, 3068
2: 1 of the Red sea, as **the L** spake unto me: 3068
2: 2 And **the L** spake unto me, saying, 3068
2: 7 For **the L** thy God hath blessed thee in all 3068
2: 7 these forty years **the L** thy God *hath been* 3068
2: 9 **the L** said unto me, Distress not 3068
2:12 which **the L** gave unto them.) 3068
2:14 among the host, as **the L** sware unto them. 3068
2:15 For indeed the hand of **the L** was against 3068
2:17 That **the L** spake unto me, saying, 3068
2:21 **the L** destroyed them before them; and 3068
2:29 the land which **the L** our God giveth us. 3068
2:30 for **the L** thy God hardened his spirit, and 3068
2:31 **the L** said unto me, Behold, I have begun 3068
2:33 **the L** our God delivered him before us; 3068
2:36 for us: **the L** our God delivered all unto us: 3068
2:37 nor *unto* whatsoever **the L** our God forbad 3068
3: 2 **the L** said unto me, Fear him not: for I will 3068
3: 3 So **the L** our God delivered into our hands 3068
3:18 **The L** your God hath given you this land to 3068
3:20 Until **the L** have given rest unto your 3068
3:20 *until* they also possess the land which **the L** 3068
3:21 Thine eyes have seen all that **the L** your 3068
3:21 shall **the L** do unto all the kingdoms 3068
3:22 for **the L** your God he shall fight for you. 3068
3:23 And I besought **the L** at that time, saying, 3068
3:26 **the L** was wroth with me for your sakes, 3068
3:26 **the L** said unto me, Let it suffice thee; 3068
4: 1 possess the land which **the L** God of your 3068
4: 2 of **the L** your God which I command you. 3068
4: 3 Your eyes have seen what **the L** did 3068
4: 3 **the L** thy God hath destroyed them from 3068
4: 4 ye that did cleave unto **the L** your God *are* 3068
4: 5 even as **the L** my God commanded me, 3068
4: 7 as **the L** our God *is* in all *things that* we 3068
4:10 stoodest before **the L** thy God in Horeb 3068
4:10 when **the L** said unto me, Gather me 3068
4:12 **the L** spake unto you out of the midst of 3068
4:14 **the L** commanded me at that time to teach 3068
4:15 **the L** spake unto you in Horeb out of 3068
4:19 which **the L** thy God hath divided unto all 3068
4:20 **the L** hath taken you, and brought you 3068
4:21 Furthermore **the L** was angry with me for 3068
4:21 which **the L** thy God giveth thee *for* an 3068
4:23 lest ye forget the covenant of **the L** your 3068
4:23 the likeness of any *thing,* which **the L** thy 3068
4:24 For **the L** thy God *is* a consuming fire, 3068
4:25 shall do evil in the sight of **the L** thy God, 3068
4:27 **the L** shall scatter you among the nations, 3068
4:27 the heathen, whither **the L** shall lead you. 3068
4:29 if from thence thou shalt seek **the L** thy 3068
4:30 if thou turn to **the L** thy God, and shalt be 3068

4:31 (For **the L** thy God *is* a merciful God;) 3068
4:34 according to all that **the L** your God did for 3068
4:35 that thou mightest know that **the L** he *is* 3068
4:39 that **the L** he *is* God in heaven above, and 3068
4:40 which **the L** thy God giveth thee, for ever. 3068
5: 2 **The L** our God made a covenant with us in 3068
5: 3 **The L** made not this covenant with our 3068
5: 4 **The L** talked with you face to face in 3068
5: 5 (I stood between **the L** and you at that 3068
5: 5 at that time, to shew you the word of **the L**: 3068
5: 6 I *am* **the L** thy God, which brought thee out 3068
5: 9 for I **the L** thy God *am* a jealous God, 3068
5:11 Thou shalt not take the name of **the L** thy 3068
5:11 for **the L** will not hold *him* guiltless that 3068
5:12 as **the L** thy God hath commanded thee. 3068
5:14 the seventh day *is* the sabbath of **the L** thy 3068
5:15 *that* **the L** thy God brought thee out thence 3068
5:15 **the L** thy God commanded thee to keep 3068
5:16 as **the L** thy God hath commanded thee; 3068
5:16 in the land which **the L** thy God giveth 3068
5:22 These words **the L** spake unto all your 3068
5:24 **the L** our God hath shewed us his glory 3068
5:25 if we hear the voice of **the L** our God any 3068
5:27 and hear all that **the L** our God shall say: 3068
5:27 speak thou unto us all that **the L** our God 3068
5:28 **the L** heard the voice of your words, 3068
5:28 **the L** said unto me, I have heard the voice 3068
5:32 as **the L** your God hath commanded you: 3068
5:33 You shall walk in all the ways which **the L** 3068
6: 1 which **the L** your God commanded to teach 3068
6: 2 That thou mightest fear **the L** thy God, 3068
6: 3 as **the L** God of thy fathers hath promised 3068
6: 4 O Israel: **The L** our God *is* one LORD: 3068
6: 4 O Israel: The LORD our God *is* one **L**: 3068
6: 5 thou shalt love **the L** thy God with all thine 3068
6:10 when **the L** thy God shall have brought 3068
6:12 *Then* beware lest thou forget **the L**, 3068
6:13 Thou shalt fear **the L** thy God, and 3068
6:15 (For **the L** thy God *is* a jealous God among 3068
6:15 lest the anger of **the L** thy God be kindled 3068
6:16 Ye shall not tempt **the L** your God, as ye 3068
6:17 the commandments of **the L** your God, 3068
6:18 *is* right and good in the sight of **the L**: 3068
6:18 possess the good land which **the L** sware 3068
6:19 from before thee, as **the L** hath spoken. 3068
6:20 which **the L** our God hath commanded 3068
6:21 **the L** brought us out of Egypt with a 3068
6:22 **the L** shewed signs and wonders, great 3068
6:24 **the L** commanded us to do all these 3068
6:24 to fear **the L** our God, for our good always, 3068
6:25 commandments before **the L** our God, 3068
7: 1 When **the L** thy God shall bring thee into 3068
7: 2 when **the L** thy God shall deliver them 3068
7: 4 will the anger of **the L** be kindled against 3068
7: 6 For thou *art* a holy people unto **the L** thy 3068
7: 6 **the L** thy God hath chosen thee to be a 3068
7: 7 **The L** did not set his love upon you, 3068
7: 8 because **the L** loved you, and because 3068
7: 8 hath **the L** brought you out with a mighty 3068
7: 9 Know therefore that **the L** thy God, he *is* 3068
7:12 that **the L** thy God shall keep unto thee 3068
7:15 **the L** will take away from thee all sickness, 3068
7:16 which **the L** thy God shall deliver thee; 3068
7:18 shalt well remember what **the L** thy God 3068
7:19 where*by* **the L** thy God brought thee out: 3068
7:19 shall **the L** thy God do unto all the people 3068
7:20 Moreover **the L** thy God will send 3068
7:21 for **the L** thy God *is* among you, a mighty 3068
7:22 **the L** thy God will put out those nations 3068
7:23 **the L** thy God shall deliver them unto thee, 3068
7:25 for it *is* an abomination to **the L** thy God. 3068
8: 1 possess the land which **the L** sware unto 3068
8: 2 **the L** thy God led thee these forty years in 3068
8: 3 out of the mouth of **the L** doth man live. 3068
8: 5 his son, *so* **the L** thy God chasteneth thee. 3068
8: 6 keep the commandments of **the L** thy God, 3068
8: 7 For **the L** thy God bringeth thee into a 3068
8:10 thou shalt bless **the L** thy God for the good 3068
8:11 Beware that thou forget not **the L** thy God, 3068
8:14 be lifted up, and thou forget **the L** thy God, 3068
8:18 thou shalt remember **the L** thy God: for *it* 3068
8:19 if thou do at all forget **the L** thy God, and 3068
8:20 As the nations which **the L** destroyeth 3068
8:20 obedient unto the voice of **the L** your God. 3068

Dt	9: 3	that **the L** thy God *is* he which goeth over	3068
	9: 3	them quickly, as **the L** hath said unto thee.	3068
	9: 4	after that **the L** thy God hath cast them out	3068
	9: 4	For my righteousness **the L** hath brought	3068
	9: 4	for the wickedness of these nations **the L**	3068
	9: 5	for the wickedness of these nations **the L**	3068
	9: 5	that he may perform the word which **the L**	3068
	9: 6	that **the L** thy God giveth thee not this	3068
	9: 7	how thou provokedst **the L** thy God to	3068
	9: 7	ye have been rebellious against **the L**.	3068
	9: 8	Also in Horeb ye provoked **the L** to wrath,	3068
	9: 8	that **the L** was angry with you to have	3068
	9: 9	*even* the tables of the covenant which **the L**	3068
	9:10	**the L** delivered unto me two tables of stone	3068
	9:10	which **the L** spake with you in the mount	3068
	9:11	*that* **the L** gave me the two tables of stone,	3068
	9:12	**the L** said unto me, Arise, get thee down	3068
	9:13	Furthermore **the L** spake unto me, saying,	3068
	9:16	ye had sinned against **the L** your God, *and*	3068
	9:16	the way which **the L** had commanded you.	3068
	9:18	And I fell down before **the L**, as at the first,	3068
	9:18	in doing wickedly in the sight of **the L**,	3068
	9:19	where*with* **the L** was wroth against you to	3068
	9:19	**the L** hearkened unto me at that time also.	3068
	9:20	**the L** was very angry with Aaron to have	3068
	9:22	ye provoked **the L** to wrath.	3068
	9:23	Likewise when **the L** sent you from	3068
	9:23	the commandment of **the L** your God,	3068
	9:24	You have been rebellious against **the L**	3068
	9:25	Thus I fell down before **the L** forty days	3068
	9:25	**the L** had said he would destroy you.	3068
	9:26	I prayed therefore unto **the L**, and said,	3068
	9:28	Because **the L** was not able to bring them	3068
	10: 1	At that time **the L** said unto me, Hew thee	3068
	10: 4	which **the L** spake unto you in the mount	3068
	10: 4	and **the L** gave them unto me.	3068
	10: 5	and there they be, as **the L** commanded me.	3068
	10: 8	At that time **the L** separated the tribe of	3068
	10: 8	to bear the ark of the covenant of **the L**,	3068
	10: 8	to stand before **the L** to minister unto him,	3068
	10: 9	**the L** *is* his inheritance, according as	3068
	10: 9	according as **the L** thy God promised him.	3068
	10:10	the **L** hearkened unto me at that time also,	3068
	10:10	*and* **the L** would not destroy thee.	3068
	10:11	**the L** said unto me, Arise, take thy journey	3068
	10:12	what doth **the L** thy God require of thee,	3068
	10:12	to fear **the L** thy God, to walk in all his	3068
	10:12	to serve **the L** thy God with all thy heart	3068
	10:13	To keep the commandments of **the L**, and	3068
	10:15	Only **the L** had a delight in thy fathers to	3068
	10:17	For **the L** your God *is* God of gods, and	3068
	10:20	Thou shalt fear **the L** thy God; him shalt	3068
	10:22	now **the L** thy God hath made thee as	3068
	11: 1	Therefore thou shalt love **the L** thy God,	3068
	11: 2	seen the chastisement of **the L** your God,	3068
	11: 4	*how* **the L** hath destroyed them unto this	3068
	11: 7	all the great acts of **the L** which he did.	3068
	11: 9	which **the L** sware unto your fathers to	3068
	11:12	A land which **the L** thy God careth for:	3068
	11:12	the eyes of **the L** thy God *are* always upon	3068
	11:13	to love **the L** your God, and to serve him	3068
	11:17	off the good land which **the L** giveth you.	3068
	11:21	in the land which **the L** sware unto your	3068
	11:22	to do them, to love **the L** your God, to walk	3068
	11:23	will **the L** drive out all these nations from	3068
	11:25	*for* **the L** your God shall lay the fear of you	3068
	11:27	if ye obey the commandments of **the L**	3068
	11:28	the commandments of **the L** your God,	3068
	11:29	when **the L** thy God hath brought thee in	3068
	11:31	the land which **the L** your God giveth you,	3068
	12: 1	which **the L** God of thy fathers giveth thee	3068
	12: 4	Ye shall not do so unto **the L** your God.	3068
	12: 5	unto the place which **the L** your God shall	3068
	12: 7	there ye shall eat before **the L** your God,	3068
	12: 7	where*in* **the L** thy God hath blessed thee.	3068
	12: 9	which **the L** your God giveth you.	3068
	12:10	dwell in the land which **the L** your God	3068
	12:11	there shall be a place which **the L** your	3068
	12:11	choice vows which ye vow unto **the L**:	3068
	12:12	ye shall rejoice before **the L** your God,	3068
	12:14	in the place which **the L** shall choose in	3068
	12:15	according to the blessing of **the L** thy God	3068
	12:18	thou must eat them before **the L** thy God in	3068
	12:18	place which **the L** thy God shall choose,	3068
	12:18	thou shalt rejoice before **the L** thy God in	3068
	12:20	When **the L** thy God shall enlarge thy	3068
	12:21	If the place which **the L** thy God hath	3068
	12:21	of thy flock, which **the L** hath given thee,	3068
	12:25	do *that which is* right in the sight of **the L**.	3068
	12:26	go unto the place which **the L** shall choose:	3068
	12:27	the blood, upon the altar of **the L** thy God:	3068
	12:27	poured out upon the altar of **the L** thy God,	3068
	12:28	and right in the sight of **the L** thy God.	3068
	12:29	When **the L** thy God shall cut off	3068
	12:31	Thou shalt not do so unto **the L** thy God:	3068
	12:31	for every abomination to **the L**, which he	3068
	13: 3	for **the L** your God proveth you, to know	3068
	13: 3	to know whether you love **the L** your God	3068
	13: 4	Ye shall walk after **the L** your God, and	3068
	13: 5	to turn *you* away from **the L** your God,	3068
	13: 5	to thrust thee out of the way which **the L**	3068
	13:10	to thrust thee away from **the L** thy God,	3068
	13:12	which **the L** thy God hath given thee to	3068
	13:16	spoil thereof every whit, for **the L** thy God:	3068
	13:17	that **the L** may turn from the fierceness of	3068
	13:18	shalt hearken to the voice of **the L** thy God,	3068
	13:18	*which is* right in the eyes of **the L** thy God.	3068
	14: 1	Ye *are* the children of **the L** your God:	3068
	14: 2	For thou *art* a holy people unto **the L** thy	3068
	14: 2	**the L** hath chosen thee to be a peculiar	3068
	14:21	for thou *art* a holy people unto **the L** thy	3068
	14:23	thou shalt eat before **the L** thy God, in	3068
	14:23	that thou mayest learn to fear **the L** thy	3068
	14:24	which **the L** thy God shall choose to set his	3068
	14:24	when **the L** thy God hath blessed thee:	3068
	14:25	shalt go unto the place which **the L** thy	3068
	14:26	thou shalt eat there before **the L** thy God,	3068
	14:29	that **the L** thy God may bless thee in all	3068
	15: 4	for **the L** shall greatly bless thee in the land	3068
	15: 4	**the L** thy God giveth thee *for* an	3068
	15: 5	hearken unto the voice of **the L** thy God,	3068
	15: 6	For **the L** thy God blesseth thee, as he	3068
	15: 7	thy land which **the L** thy God giveth thee,	3068
	15: 9	he cry unto **the L** against thee, and it be sin	3068
	15:10	that for this thing **the L** thy God shall bless	3068
	15:14	*of that* where*with* **the L** thy God hath	3068
	15:15	and **the L** thy God redeemed thee:	3068
	15:18	**the L** thy God shall bless thee in all that	3068
	15:19	of thy flock thou shalt sanctify unto **the L**	3068
	15:20	Thou shalt eat it before **the L** thy God year	3068
	15:20	year in the place which **the L** shall choose,	3068
	15:21	thou shalt not sacrifice it unto **the L** thy	3068
	16: 1	and keep the passover unto **the L** thy God:	3068
	16: 1	for in the month of Abib **the L** thy God	3068
	16: 2	sacrifice the passover unto **the L** thy God,	3068
	16: 2	in the place which **the L** shall choose to	3068
	16: 5	thy gates, which **the L** thy God giveth thee:	3068
	16: 6	at the place which **the L** thy God shall	3068
	16: 7	eat *it* in the place which **the L** thy God	3068
	16: 8	*be* a solemn assembly to **the L** thy God:	3068
	16:10	**the L** thy God *with* a tribute of a freewill	3068
	16:10	which thou shalt give *unto the L thy God,*	NIH
	16:10	as **the L** thy God hath blessed thee:	3068
	16:11	thou shalt rejoice before **the L** thy God,	3068
	16:11	in the place which **the L** thy God hath	3068
	16:15	**the L** thy God in the place which	3068
	16:15	God in the place which **the L** shall choose:	3068
	16:15	**the L** thy God shall bless thee in all thy	3068
	16:16	**the L** thy God in the place which he shall	3068
	16:16	they shall not appear before **the L** empty:	3068
	16:17	according to the blessing of **the L** thy God	3068
	16:18	which **the L** thy God giveth thee,	3068
	16:20	inherit the land which **the L** thy God giveth	3068
	16:21	trees near unto the altar of **the L** thy God,	3068
	16:22	up *any* image; which **the L** thy God hateth.	3068
	17: 1	Thou shalt not sacrifice unto **the L** thy God	3068
	17: 1	for that *is* an abomination unto **the L** thy	3068
	17: 2	within any of thy gates which **the L** thy	3068
	17: 2	wickedness in the sight of **the L** thy God,	3068
	17: 8	get thee up into the place which **the L** thy	3068
	17:10	which *they* of that place which **the L** shall	3068
	17:12	to minister there before **the L** thy God,	3068
	17:14	the land which **the L** thy God giveth thee,	3068
	17:15	whom **the L** thy God shall choose:	3068
	17:16	forasmuch as **the L** hath said unto you,	3068
	17:19	that he may learn to fear **the L** his God,	3068
	18: 1	they shall eat the offerings of **the L** made	3068
	18: 2	**the L** *is* their inheritance, as he hath said	3068

Dt 18: 5 For **the L** thy God hath chosen him out of 3068
18: 5 to stand to minister in the name of **the L,** 3068
18: 6 unto the place which **the L** shall choose; 3068
18: 7 he shall minister in the name of **the L** his 3068
18: 7 Levites *do,* which stand there before **the L.** 3068
18: 9 the land which **the L** thy God giveth thee, 3068
18:12 these *things are* an abomination unto **the L:** 3068
18:12 of these abominations **the L** thy God doth 3068
18:13 Thou shalt be perfect with **the L** thy God. 3068
18:14 **the L** thy God hath not suffered thee so 3068
18:15 **The L** thy God will raise up unto thee a 3068
18:16 **the L** thy God in Horeb in the day of 3068
18:16 Let me not hear again the voice of **the L** 3068
18:17 **the L** said unto me, They have well *spoken* 3068
18:21 How shall we know the word which **the L** 3068
18:22 a prophet speaketh in the name of **the L,** 3068
18:22 that *is* the thing which **the L** hath not 3068
19: 1 When **the L** thy God hath cut off 3068
19: 1 whose land **the L** thy God giveth thee, 3068
19: 2 which **the L** thy God giveth thee to possess 3068
19: 3 which **the L** thy God giveth thee to inherit, 3068
19: 8 if **the L** thy God enlarge thy coast, as he 3068
19: 9 to love **the L** thy God, and to walk ever in 3068
19:10 which **the L** thy God giveth thee *for* an 3068
19:14 that **the L** thy God giveth thee to possess it. 3068
19:17 the controversy *is,* shall stand before **the L,** 3068
20: 1 for **the L** thy God *is* with thee, 3068
20: 4 For **the L** your God *is* he that goeth with 3068
20:13 when **the L** thy God hath delivered it into 3068
20:14 which **the L** thy God hath given thee. 3068
20:16 which **the L** thy God doth give thee *for* an 3068
20:17 as **the L** thy God hath commanded thee: 3068
20:18 so should ye sin against **the L** your God. 3068
21: 1 **the L** thy God giveth thee to possess it, 3068
21: 5 for them **the L** thy God hath chosen to 3068
21: 5 unto him, and to bless in the name of **the L;** 3068
21: 8 Be merciful, **O L,** unto thy people Israel, 3068
21: 9 do *that which is* right in the sight of **the L.** 3068
21:10 **the L** thy God hath delivered them into 3068
21:23 which **the L** thy God giveth thee *for* an 3068
22: 5 so *are* abomination unto **the L** thy God. 3068
23: 1 not enter into the congregation of **the L.** 3068
23: 2 not enter into the congregation of **the L;** 3068
23: 2 he not enter into the congregation of **the L.** 3068
23: 3 not enter into the congregation of **the L;** 3068
23: 3 into the congregation of **the L** for ever: 3068
23: 5 Nevertheless **the L** thy God would not 3068
23: 5 **the L** thy God turned the curse into a 3068
23: 5 because **the L** thy God loved thee. 3068
23: 8 of **the L** *in* their third generation. 3068
23:14 For **the L** thy God walketh in the midst of 3068
23:18 *into* the house of **the L** thy God for any 3068
23:18 these *are* abomination unto **the L** thy God. 3068
23:20 that **the L** thy God may bless thee in all 3068
23:21 When thou shalt vow a vow unto **the L** thy 3068
23:21 for **the L** thy God will surely require it of 3068
23:23 according as thou hast vowed unto **the L** 3068
24: 4 for that *is* abomination before **the L:** 3068
24: 4 which **the L** thy God giveth thee *for* an 3068
24: 9 Remember what **the L** thy God did unto 3068
24:13 unto thee before **the L** thy God. 3068
24:15 lest he cry against thee unto **the L,** and it be 3068
24:18 and **the L** thy God redeemed thee thence: 3068
24:19 that **the L** thy God may bless thee in all 3068
25:15 the land which **the L** thy God giveth thee. 3068
25:16 *are* an abomination unto **the L** thy God. 3068
25:19 when **the L** thy God hath given thee rest 3068
25:19 in the land which **the L** thy God giveth thee 3068
26: 1 **the L** thy God giveth thee *for* an 3068
26: 2 thou shalt bring of thy land that **the L** 3068
26: 2 shalt go unto the place which **the L** thy 3068
26: 3 I profess *this* day unto **the L** thy God, 3068
26: 3 **the L** sware unto our fathers for to give us. 3068
26: 4 set it down before the altar of **the L** thy 3068
26: 5 shalt speak and say before **the L** thy God, 3068
26: 7 when we cried unto **the L** God of our 3068
26: 7 **the L** heard our voice, and looked on our 3068
26: 8 **the L** brought us forth out of Egypt with a 3068
26:10 the land, which thou, **O L,** hast given me. 3068
26:10 thou shalt set it before **the L** thy God, and 3068
26:10 and worship before **the L** thy God: 3068
26:11 which **the L** thy God hath given unto thee, 3068
26:13 thou shalt say before **the L** thy God, I have 3068
26:14 I have hearkened to the voice of **the L** my 3068
26:16 This day **the L** thy God hath commanded 3068
26:17 Thou hast avouched **the L** *this* day to be 3068
26:18 **the L** hath avouched thee *this* day to be his 3068
26:19 be a holy people unto **the L** thy God, 3068
27: 2 the land which **the L** thy God giveth thee, 3068
27: 3 the land which **the L** thy God giveth thee, 3068
27: 3 as **the L** God of thy fathers hath promised 3068
27: 5 there shalt thou build an altar unto **the L** 3068
27: 6 Thou shalt build the altar of **the L** thy God 3068
27: 6 burnt offerings thereon unto **the L** thy God: 3068
27: 7 eat there, and rejoice before **the L** thy God. 3068
27: 9 art become the people of **the L** thy God. 3068
27:10 therefore obey the voice of **the L** thy God, 3068
27:15 molten image, an abomination unto **the L,** 3068
28: 1 diligently unto the voice of **the L** thy God, 3068
28: 1 that **the L** thy God will set thee on high 3068
28: 2 hearken unto the voice of **the L** thy God. 3068
28: 7 **The L** shall cause thine enemies that rise 3068
28: 8 **The L** shall command the blessing upon 3068
28: 8 he shall bless thee in the land which **the L** 3068
28: 9 **The L** shall establish thee a holy people 3068
28: 9 keep the commandments of **the L** thy God, 3068
28:10 that thou art called by the name of **the L;** 3068
28:11 **the L** shall make thee plenteous in goods, 3068
28:11 in the land which **the L** sware unto thy 3068
28:12 **The L** shall open unto thee his good 3068
28:13 **the L** shall make thee the head, and not 3068
28:13 unto the commandments of **the L** thy God, 3068
28:15 hearken unto the voice of **the L** thy God, 3068
28:20 **The L** shall send upon thee cursing, 3068
28:21 **The L** shall make the pestilence cleave 3068
28:22 **The L** shall smite thee with a consumption, 3068
28:24 **The L** shall make the rain of thy land 3068
28:25 **The L** shall cause thee *to be* smitten before 3068
28:27 **The L** will smite thee with the botch of 3068
28:28 **The L** shall smite thee with madness, and 3068
28:35 **The L** shall smite thee in the knees, and 3068
28:36 **The L** shall bring thee, and thy king which 3068
28:37 among all nations whither **the L** shall lead 3068
28:45 not unto the voice of **the L** thy God, 3068
28:47 Because thou servedst not **the L** thy God 3068
28:48 which **the L** shall send against thee, 3068
28:49 **The L** shall bring a nation against thee 3068
28:52 which **the L** thy God hath given thee. 3068
28:53 which **the L** thy God hath given thee, in 3068
28:58 and fearful name, **THE L THY GOD;** 3068
28:59 **the L** will make thy plagues wonderful, 3068
28:61 them will **the L** bring upon thee, until thou 3068
28:62 thou wouldest not obey the voice of **the L** 3068
28:63 *that* as **the L** rejoiced over you to do you 3068
28:63 **the L** will rejoice over you to destroy you, 3068
28:64 **the L** shall scatter thee among all people, 3068
28:65 **the L** shall give thee there a trembling 3068
28:68 **the L** shall bring thee *into* Egypt again with 3068
29: 1 which **the L** commanded Moses to make 3068
29: 2 Ye have seen all that **the L** did before your 3068
29: 4 Yet **the L** hath not given you a heart to 3068
29: 6 that ye might know that I *am* **the L** your 3068
29:10 Ye stand *this* day all of you before **the L** 3068
29:12 enter into covenant with **the L** thy God, 3068
29:12 which **the L** thy God maketh with thee *this* 3068
29:15 here with us *this* day before **the L** our God, 3068
29:18 turneth away *this* day from **the L** our God, 3068
29:20 **The L** will not spare him, but then 3068
29:20 then the anger of **the L** and his jealousy 3068
29:20 **the L** shall blot out his name from under 3068
29:21 **the L** shall separate him unto evil out of all 3068
29:22 the sicknesses which **the L** hath laid upon 3068
29:23 which **the L** overthrew in his anger, and 3068
29:24 Wherefore hath **the L** done thus unto this 3068
29:25 the covenant of **the L** God of their fathers, 3068
29:27 the anger of **the L** was kindled against this 3068
29:28 **the L** rooted them out of their land in 3068
29:29 The secret *things belong* unto **the L** our 3068
30: 1 whither **the L** thy God hath driven thee, 3068
30: 2 shalt return unto **the L** thy God, and 3068
30: 3 then **the L** thy God will turn thy captivity, 3068
30: 3 whither **the L** thy God hath scattered thee. 3068
30: 4 from thence will **the L** thy God gather thee, 3068
30: 5 **the L** thy God will bring thee into the land 3068
30: 6 **the L** thy God will circumcise thine heart, 3068
30: 6 to love **the L** thy God with all thine heart, 3068
30: 7 **the L** thy God will put all these curses 3068
30: 8 shalt return and obey the voice of **the L,** 3068

Dt 30: 9 **the L** thy God will make thee plenteous in 3068
30: 9 for **the L** will again rejoice over thee for 3068
31: 2 also **the L** hath said unto me, Thou shalt 3068
31: 3 **The L** thy God, he will go over before thee, 3068
31: 3 go over before thee, as **the L** hath said. 3068
31: 4 **the L** shall do unto them as he did to Sihon 3068
31: 5 **the L** shall give them up before your face, 3068
31: 6 for **the L** thy God, he *it is* that doth go with 3068
31: 7 **the L** hath sworn unto their fathers to give 3068
31: 8 **the L**, he *it is* that doth go before thee; 3068
31: 9 bare the ark of the covenant of **the L**, 3068
31:11 **the L** thy God in the place which he shall 3068
31:12 fear **the L** your God, and observe to do all 3068
31:13 may hear, and learn to fear **the L** your God, 3068
31:14 **the L** said unto Moses, Behold, thy days 3068
31:15 **the L** appeared in the tabernacle in a pillar 3068
31:16 **the L** said unto Moses, Behold, thou shalt 3068
31:25 bare the ark of the covenant of **the L**, 3068
31:26 the ark of the covenant of **the L** your God, 3068
31:27 ye have been rebellious against **the L**; 3068
32: 6 Do ye thus requite **the L**, O foolish people 3068
32:12 *So* **the L** alone did lead him, and *there was* 3068
32:19 when **the L** saw *it*, he abhorred *them*, 3068
32:27 is high, and **the L** hath not done all this. 3068
32:30 sold them, and **the L** had shut them up? 3068
32:36 For **the L** shall judge his people, and 3068
32:48 **the L** spake unto Moses that selfsame day, 3068
33: 2 **The L** came from Sinai, and rose up from 3068
33: 7 he said, Hear, **L**, the voice of Judah, and 3068
33:11 Bless, **L**, his substance, and accept 3068
33:12 The beloved of **the L** shall dwell in safety 3068
33:12 *and* **the L** shall cover him all the day long, NIH
33:13 he said, Blessed of **the L** *be* his land, 3068
33:21 he executed the justice of **the L**, and 3068
33:23 and full *with* the blessing of **the L**: 3068
33:29 *is* like unto thee, O people saved by **the L**, 3068
34: 1 **the L** shewed him all the land of Gilead, 3068
34: 4 **the L** said unto him, This *is* the land which 3068
34: 5 So Moses the servant of **the L** died there in 3068
34: 5 of Moab, according to the word of **the L**. 3068
34: 9 and did as **the L** commanded Moses. 3068
34:10 whom **the L** knew face to face, 3068
34:11 which **the L** sent him to do in the land of 3068
Jos 1: 1 Moses the servant of **the L** it came to pass, 3068
1:13 **The L** your God hath given you rest, and 3068
1:15 Until **the L** have given your brethren rest, 3068
1:15 land which **the L** your God giveth them: 3068
1:17 only **the L** thy God be with thee, as he was 3068
2: 9 I know that **the L** hath given you the land, 3068
2:10 For we have heard how **the L** dried up 3068
2:11 for **the L** your God, he *is* God in heaven 3068
2:12 I pray you, swear unto me by **the L**, 3068
2:14 shall be, when **the L** hath given us the land, 3068
2:24 Truly **the L** hath delivered into our hands 3068
3: 3 the ark of the covenant of **the L** your God, 3068
3: 5 for to morrow **the L** will do wonders 3068
3: 7 **the L** said unto Joshua, This day will I 3068
3: 9 and hear the words of **the L** your God. 3068
3:13 feet of the priests that bear the ark of **the L**, 3068
3:17 **the L** stood firm on dry *ground* in the midst 3068
4: 1 that **the L** spake unto Joshua, saying, 3068
4: 5 Pass over before the ark of **the L** your God 3068
4: 7 off before the ark of the covenant of **the L**; 3068
4: 8 of Jordan, as **the L** spake unto Joshua, 3068
4:10 until every thing was finished that **the L** 3068
4:11 that the ark of **the L** passed over, and 3068
4:13 war passed over before **the L** unto battle, 3068
4:14 On that day **the L** magnified Joshua in 3068
4:15 And **the L** spake unto Joshua, saying, 3068
4:18 **the L** were come up out of the midst of 3068
4:23 For **the L** your God dried up the waters of 3068
4:23 as **the L** your God did to the Red sea, 3068

5: 1 heard that **the L** had dried up the waters of 3068
5: 2 At that time **the L** said unto Joshua, 3068
5: 6 because they obeyed not the voice of **the L**: 3068
5: 6 unto whom **the L** sware that *he* would not 3068
5: 6 which **the L** sware unto their fathers that he 3068
5: 9 **the L** said unto Joshua, This day have I 3068
5:14 *as* captain of the host of **the L** am I now 3068
6: 2 **the L** said unto Joshua, See, I have given 3068
6: 6 of rams' horns before the ark of **the L**. 3068
6: 7 is armed pass on before the ark of **the L**. 3068
6: 8 of rams' horns passed on before **the L**, 3068
6: 8 the ark of the covenant of **the L** followed 3068
6:11 So the ark of **the L** compassed the city, 3068
6:12 and the priests took up the ark of **the L**. 3068
6:13 before the ark of **the L** went on continually, 3068
6:13 the rereward came after the ark of **the L**, 3068
6:16 Shout; for **the L** hath given you the city. 3068
6:17 *even* it, and all that *are* therein, to **the L**: 3068
6:19 and iron, *are* consecrated unto **the L**: 3068
6:19 they shall come *into* the treasury of **the L**. 3068
6:24 put *into* the treasury of the house of **the L**. 3068
6:26 saying, Cursed *be* the man before **the L**, 3068
6:27 So **the L** was with Joshua; and his fame 3068
7: 1 the anger of **the L** was kindled against 3068
7: 6 before the ark of **the L** until the eventide, 3068
7:10 **the L** said unto Joshua, Get thee up; 3068
7:13 for thus saith **the L** God of Israel, *There is* 3068
7:14 *that* the tribe which **the L** taketh shall come 3068
7:14 the family which **the L** shall take shall 3068
7:14 the household which **the L** shall take shall 3068
7:15 he hath transgressed the covenant of **the L**, 3068
7:19 glory to **the L** God of Israel, and 3068
7:20 Indeed I have sinned against **the L** God of 3068
7:23 of Israel, and laid them out before **the L**. 3068
7:25 **the L** shall trouble thee this day. And all 3068
7:26 So **the L** turned from the fierceness of his 3068
8: 1 **the L** said unto Joshua, Fear not, neither be 3068
8: 7 for **the L** your God will deliver it into your 3068
8: 8 according to the commandment of **the L** 3068
8:18 **the L** said unto Joshua, Stretch out 3068
8:33 bare the ark of the covenant of **the L**, 3068
8:33 as Moses the servant of **the L** had 3068
9: 9 because of the name of **the L** thy God: 3068
9:14 asked not *counsel* at the mouth of **the L**. 3068
9:18 sworn unto them by **the L** God of Israel. 3068
9:19 We have sworn unto them by **the L** God of 3068
9:24 how that **the L** thy God commanded his 3068
9:27 for the altar of **the L**, *even* unto this day, 3068
10: 8 **the L** said unto Joshua, Fear them not: for I 3068
10:10 **the L** discomfited them before Israel, and 3068
10:11 that **the L** cast down great stones from 3068
10:12 spake Joshua to **the L** in the day when 3068
10:12 **the L** delivered up the Amorites before 3068
10:14 that **the L** hearkened unto the voice of a 3068
10:14 voice of a man: for **the L** fought for Israel. 3068
10:19 for **the L** your God hath delivered them 3068
10:25 for thus shall **the L** do to all your enemies 3068
10:30 **the L** delivered it also, and the king 3068
10:32 **the L** delivered Lachish into the hand of 3068
10:40 as **the L** God of Israel commanded. 3068
10:42 **the L** God of Israel fought for Israel. 3068
11: 6 **the L** said unto Joshua, Be not afraid 3068
11: 8 **the L** delivered them into the hand of 3068
11: 9 Joshua did unto them as **the L** bade him: 3068
11:12 as Moses the servant of **the L** commanded. 3068
11:15 As **the L** commanded Moses his servant, so 3068
11:15 he left nothing undone of all that **the L** 3068
11:20 For it was of **the L** to harden their hearts, 3068
13: 1 **the L** said unto him, Thou art old *and* 3068
13: 8 *even* as Moses the servant of **the L** gave 3068
13:14 the sacrifices of **the L** God of Israel made 3068
13:33 **the L** God of Israel *was* their inheritance, 3068
14: 2 as **the L** commanded by the hand of Moses, 3068
14: 5 As **the L** commanded Moses, so 3068

L

Jos 14: 6 Thou knowest the thing that **the L** said 3068
14: 7 **the L** sent me from Kadesh-barnea to espy 3068
14: 8 but I wholly followed **the L** my God. 3068
14: 9 thou hast wholly followed **the L** my God. 3068
14:10 **the L** hath kept me alive, as he said, 3068
14:10 *even* since **the L** spake this word unto 3068
14:12 whereof **the L** spake in that day; 3068
14:12 if so be **the L** *will be* with me, then I shall 3068
14:12 *be able to* drive them out, as **the L** said. 3068
14:14 that he wholly followed **the L** God of 3068
15:13 according to the commandment of **the L** to 3068
17: 4 **The L** commanded Moses to give us an 3068
17: 4 **the L** he gave them an inheritance among 3068
17:14 forasmuch as **the L** hath blessed me 3068
18: 3 which **the L** God of your fathers hath given 3068
18: 6 cast lots for you here before **the L** our God. 3068
18: 7 for the priesthood of **the L** *is* their 3068
18: 7 which Moses the servant of **the L** gave 3068
18: 8 cast lots for you before **the L** in Shiloh. 3068
18:10 cast lots for them in Shiloh before **the L**: 3068
19:50 According to the word of **the L** they gave 3068
19:51 inheritance by lot in Shiloh before **the L**, 3068
20: 1 **The L** also spake unto Joshua, saying, 3068
21: 2 **The L** commanded by the hand of Moses 3068
21: 3 at the commandment of **the L**, these cities 3068
21: 8 as **the L** commanded by the hand of Moses. 3068
21:43 **the L** gave unto Israel all the land which he 3068
21:44 **the L** gave them rest round about, 3068
21:44 **the L** delivered all their enemies into their 3068
21:45 **the L** had spoken unto the house of Israel; 3068
22: 2 the servant of **the L** commanded you, 3068
22: 3 of the commandment of **the L** your God. 3068
22: 4 now **the L** your God hath given rest unto 3068
22: 4 which Moses the servant of **the L** gave you 3068
22: 5 which Moses the servant of **the L** charged 3068
22: 5 to love **the L** your God, and to walk in all 3068
22: 9 according to the word of **the L** by the hand 3068
22:16 saith the whole congregation of **the L**, 3068
22:16 to turn away *this* day from following **the L**, 3068
22:16 that ye might rebel *this* day against **the L**? 3068
22:17 was a plague in the congregation of **the L**, 3068
22:18 turn away *this* day from following **the L**? 3068
22:18 *seeing* ye rebel to day against **the L**, 3068
22:19 unto the land of the possession of **the L**, 3068
22:19 rebel not against **the L**, nor rebel against 3068
22:19 an altar beside the altar of **the L** our God. 3068
22:22 **The L** God of gods, the LORD God of 3068
22:22 **the L** God of gods, he knoweth, and 3068
22:22 or if in transgression against **the L**, 3068
22:23 us an altar to turn from following **the L**; 3068
22:23 let **the L** himself require *it;* 3068
22:24 What have you to do with **the L** God of 3068
22:25 For **the L** hath made Jordan a border 3068
22:25 children of Gad; ye have no part in **the L**: 3068
22:25 our children cease from fearing **the L**: 3068
22:27 that *we* might do the service of **the L** 3068
22:27 in time to come, Ye have no part in **the L**. 3068
22:28 Behold the pattern of the altar of **the L**, 3068
22:29 forbid that we should rebel against **the L**, 3068
22:29 turn *this* day from following **the L**, to build 3068
22:29 besides the altar of **the L** our God that *is* 3068
22:31 *This* day we perceive that **the L** *is* among 3068
22:31 not committed this trespass against **the L**: 3068
22:31 children of Israel out of the hand of **the L**. 3068
22:34 *be* a witness between us that **the L** *is* God. 3068
23: 1 it came to pass a long time after that **the L** 3068
23: 3 ye have seen all that **the L** your God hath 3068
23: 3 for **the L** your God *is* he that hath fought 3068
23: 5 **the L** your God, he shall expel them from 3068
23: 5 as **the L** your God hath promised unto you. 3068
23: 8 cleave unto **the L** your God, as ye have 3068
23: 9 For **the L** hath driven out from before you 3068
23:10 for **the L** your God, he *it is* that fighteth for 3068
23:11 that ye love **the L** your God. 3068
23:13 Know for a certainty that **the L** your God 3068
23:13 land which **the L** your God hath given you. 3068
23:14 **the L** your God spake concerning you; 3068
23:15 which **the L** your God promised you; 3068
23:15 shall **the L** bring upon you all evil things, 3068
23:15 land which **the L** your God hath given you. 3068
23:16 the covenant of **the L** your God, 3068
23:16 shall the anger of **the L** be kindled against 3068
24: 2 the people, Thus saith **the L** God of Israel, 3068
24: 7 when they cried unto **the L**, he put 3068
24:14 Now therefore fear **the L**, and serve him in 3068
24:14 the flood, and in Egypt; and serve ye **the L**. 3068
24:15 if it seem evil unto you to serve **the L**, 3068
24:15 for me and my house, we will serve **the L**. 3068
24:16 God forbid that we should forsake **the L**, 3068
24:17 For **the L** our God, he *it is* that brought us 3068
24:18 **the L** drave out from before us all 3068
24:18 *therefore* will we also serve **the L**; for he *is* 3068
24:19 unto the people, Ye cannot serve **the L**: 3068
24:20 If ye forsake **the L**, and serve strange gods, 3068
24:21 unto Joshua, Nay; but we will serve **the L**. 3068
24:22 yourselves that ye have chosen you **the L**, 3068
24:23 incline your heart unto **the L** God of Israel. 3068
24:24 **The L** our God will we serve, and his voice 3068
24:26 an oak, that *was* by the sanctuary of **the L**. 3068
24:27 for it hath heard all the words of **the L** 3068
24:29 the servant of **the L**, died, *being* an 3068
24:31 Israel served **the L** all the days of Joshua, 3068
24:31 which had known all the works of **the L**, 3068
Jdg 1: 1 that the children of Israel asked **the L**, 3068
1: 2 **the L** said, Judah shall go up: behold, 3068
1: 4 **the L** delivered the Canaanites and 3068
1:19 **the L** was with Judah; and he drave out 3068
1:22 *against* Beth-el: and **the L** *was* with them. 3068
2: 1 an angel of **the L** came up from Gilgal to 3068
2: 4 when the angel of **the L** spake these words 3068
2: 5 and they sacrificed there unto **the L**. 3068
2: 7 the people served **the L** all the days of 3068
2: 7 who had seen all the great works of **the L**, 3068
2: 8 the servant of **the L**, died, *being* an 3068
2:10 after them, which knew not **the L**, 3068
2:11 of Israel did evil in the sight of **the L**, 3068
2:12 they forsook **the L** God of their fathers, 3068
2:12 unto them, and provoked **the L** to anger. 3068
2:13 they forsook **the L**, and served Baal and 3068
2:14 the anger of **the L** was hot against Israel, 3068
2:15 the hand of **the L** was against them for evil, 3068
2:15 as **the L** had said, and as the LORD had 3068
2:15 and as **the L** had sworn unto them: 3068
2:16 Nevertheless **the L** raised up judges, 3068
2:17 obeying the commandments of **the L**; 3068
2:18 when **the L** raised them up judges, then 3068
2:18 **the L** was with the judge, and 3068
2:18 for it repented **the L** because of their 3068
2:20 the anger of **the L** was hot against Israel; 3068
2:22 whether they will keep the way of **the L** to 3068
2:23 Therefore **the L** left those nations, without 3068
3: 1 Now these *are* the nations which **the L** left, 3068
3: 4 hearken unto the commandments of **the L**, 3068
3: 7 of Israel did evil in the sight of **the L**, 3068
3: 7 forgat **the L** their God, and served Baalim 3068
3: 8 Therefore the anger of **the L** was hot 3068
3: 9 the children of Israel cried unto **the L**, 3068
3: 9 **the L** raised up a deliverer to the children 3068
3:10 the spirit of **the L** came upon him, and 3068
3:10 **the L** delivered Chushan-rishathaim king 3068
3:12 of Israel did evil again in the sight of **the L**: 3068
3:12 **the L** strengthened Eglon the king of Moab 3068
3:12 they had done evil in the sight of **the L**. 3068
3:15 the children of Israel cried unto **the L**, 3068
3:15 **the L** raised them up a deliverer, Ehud 3068
3:28 for **the L** hath delivered your enemies 3068
4: 1 of Israel again did evil in the sight of **the L**, 3068
4: 2 **the L** sold them into the hand of Jabin king 3068
4: 3 the children of Israel cried unto **the L**: 3068
4: 6 Hath not **the L** God of Israel commanded, 3068
4: 9 for **the L** shall sell Sisera into the hand of a 3068
4:14 for this *is* the day in which **the L** hath 3068
4:14 is not **the L** gone out before thee? So Barak 3068
4:15 **the L** discomfited Sisera, and all *his* 3068
5: 2 Praise ye **the L** for the avenging of Israel, 3068
5: 3 ye princes; I, *even* I, will sing unto **the L**; 3068
5: 3 I will sing *praise* to **the L** God of Israel. 3068
5: 4 **L**, when thou wentest out of Seir, 3068
5: 5 The mountains melted from before **the L**, 3068
5: 5 *even* that Sinai from before **the L** God of 3068
5: 9 willingly among the people. Bless ye **the L**. 3068
5:11 they rehearse the righteous acts of **the L**, 3068
5:11 shall the people of **the L** go down to 3068
5:13 **the L** made me have dominion over 3068
5:23 Curse ye Meroz, said the angel of **the L**, 3068
5:23 because they came not to the help of **the L**, 3068
5:23 to the help of **the L** against the mighty. 3068
5:31 So let all thine enemies perish, O **L**: but 3068

Jdg	6: 1	of Israel did evil in the sight of **the L**:	3068
	6: 1	**the L** delivered them into the hand of	3068
	6: 6	and the children of Israel cried unto **the L**.	3068
	6: 7	when the children of Israel cried unto **the L**	3068
	6: 8	That **the L** sent a prophet unto the children	3068
	6: 8	unto them, Thus saith **the L** God of Israel,	3068
	6:10	I said unto you, I *am* **the L** your God;	3068
	6:11	there came an angel of **the L**, and sat under	3068
	6:12	the angel of **the L** appeared unto him, and	3068
	6:12	said unto him, **The L** *is* with thee,	3068
	6:13	if **the L** be with us, why then is all this	3068
	6:13	Did not **the L** bring us up from Egypt?	3068
	6:13	now **the L** hath forsaken us, and	3068
	6:14	**the L** looked upon him, and said, Go in this	3068
	6:16	**the L** said unto him, Surely I will be with	3068
	6:21	the angel of **the L** put forth the end of	3068
	6:21	the angel of **the L** departed out of his sight.	3068
	6:22	perceived that he *was* an angel of **the L**,	3068
	6:22	I have seen an angel of **the L** face to face.	3068
	6:23	**the L** said unto him, Peace *be* unto thee;	3068
	6:24	Then Gideon built an altar there unto **the L**,	3068
	6:25	that **the L** said unto him, Take thy father's	3068
	6:26	build an altar unto **the L** thy God upon	3068
	6:27	and did as **the L** had said unto him:	3068
	6:34	the spirit of **the L** came upon Gideon, and	3068
	7: 2	**the L** said unto Gideon, The people that *are*	3068
	7: 4	**the L** said unto Gideon, The people *are* yet	3068
	7: 5	**the L** said unto Gideon, Every one that	3068
	7: 7	**the L** said unto Gideon, By the three	3068
	7: 9	that **the L** said unto him, Arise, get thee	3068
	7:15	for **the L** hath delivered into your hand	3068
	7:18	say, *The sword* of **the L**, and of Gideon.	3068
	7:20	The sword of **the L**, and of Gideon.	3068
	7:22	**the L** set every man's sword against his	3068
	8: 7	Therefore when **the L** hath delivered Zebah	3068
	8:19	*as* **the L** liveth, if ye had saved them alive,	3068
	8:23	rule over you: **the L** shall rule over you.	3068
	8:34	the children of Israel remembered not **the L**	3068
	10: 6	of Israel did evil again in the sight of **the L**,	3068
	10: 6	and forsook **the L**, and served not him.	3068
	10: 7	the anger of **the L** was hot against Israel,	3068
	10:10	the children of Israel cried unto **the L**,	3068
	10:11	**the L** said unto the children of Israel, *Did*	3068
	10:15	the children of Israel said unto **the L**,	3068
	10:16	gods from among them, and served **the L**:	3068
	11: 9	**the L** deliver them before me, shall I be	3068
	11:10	**The L** be witness between us, if we do not	3068
	11:11	Jephthah uttered all his words before **the L**	3068
	11:21	**the L** God of Israel delivered Sihon and	3068
	11:23	So now **the L** God of Israel hath	3068
	11:24	So whomsoever **the L** our God shall drive	3068
	11:27	**the L** the Judge be judge *this* day between	3068
	11:29	the spirit of **the L** came upon Jephthah,	3068
	11:30	And Jephthah vowed a vow unto **the L**, and	3068
	11:32	and **the L** delivered them into his hands.	3068
	11:35	for I have opened my mouth unto **the L**,	3068
	11:36	*if* thou hast opened thy mouth unto **the L**,	3068
	11:36	forasmuch as **the L** hath taken vengeance	3068
	12: 3	and **the L** delivered them into my hand:	3068
	13: 1	of Israel did evil again in the sight of **the L**;	3068
	13: 1	**the L** delivered them into the hand of	3068
	13: 3	the angel of **the L** appeared unto	3068
	13: 8	Manoah intreated **the L**, and said, O my	3068
	13:13	the angel of **the L** said unto Manoah, Of all	3068
	13:15	Manoah said unto the angel of **the L**, I pray	3068
	13:16	the angel of **the L** said unto Manoah,	3068
	13:16	thou must offer it unto **the L**.	3068
	13:16	knew not that he *was* an angel of **the L**.	3068
	13:17	Manoah said unto the angel of **the L**,	3068
	13:18	the angel of **the L** said unto him, Why	3068
	13:19	and offered *it* upon a rock unto **the L**:	3068
	13:20	that the angel of **the L** ascended in	3068
	13:21	the angel of **the L** did no more appear to	3068
	13:21	knew that he *was* an angel of **the L**.	3068
	13:23	unto him, If **the L** were pleased to kill us,	3068
	13:24	and the child grew, and **the L** blessed him.	3068
	13:25	the spirit of **the L** began to move him at	3068
	14: 4	his mother knew not that it *was* of **the L**,	3068
	14: 6	the spirit of **the L** came mightily upon him,	3068
	14:19	the spirit of **the L** came upon him, and	3068
	15:14	the spirit of **the L** came mightily upon him,	3068
	15:18	sore athirst, and called on **the L**, and said,	3068
	16:20	he wist not that **the L** was departed from	3068
	16:28	Samson called unto **the L**, and said, O Lord	3068
	17: 2	Blessed *be thou* of **the L**, my son.	3068
	17: 3	silver unto **the L** from my hand for my son,	3068
	17:13	Now know I that **the L** will do me good,	3068
	18: 6	before **the L** *is* your way wherein ye go.	3068
	19:18	I am *now* going *to* the house of **the L**;	3068
	20: 1	the land of Gilead, unto **the L** *in* Mizpeh.	3068
	20:18	And **the L** said, Judah *shall go up* first.	3068
	20:23	went up and wept before **the L** until even,	3068
	20:23	and asked *counsel* of **the L**, saying,	3068
	20:23	And **the L** said, Go up against him.)	3068
	20:26	sat there before **the L**, and fasted that day	3068
	20:26	and peace offerings before **the L**.	3068
	20:27	the children of Israel inquired of **the L**,	3068
	20:28	**the L** said, Go up; for to morrow I will	3068
	20:35	**the L** smote Benjamin before Israel: and	3068
	21: 3	said, O **L** God of Israel, why is this come to	3068
	21: 5	not up with the congregation unto **the L**?	3068
	21: 5	*him* that came not up to **the L** *to* Mizpeh,	3068
	21: 7	seeing we have sworn by **the L** that *we* will	3068
	21: 8	Israel that came not up *to* Mizpeh to **the L**?	3068
	21:15	that **the L** had made a breach in the tribes	3068
	21:19	*there is* a feast of **the L** in Shiloh yearly *in*	3068
Ru	1: 6	**the L** had visited his people in giving them	3068
	1: 8	**the L** deal kindly with you, as ye have	3068
	1: 9	**The L** grant you that you may find rest,	3068
	1:13	the hand of **the L** is gone out against me.	3068
	1:17	**the L** do so to me, and more also, *if ought*	3068
	1:21	**the L** hath brought me *home* again empty:	3068
	1:21	seeing **the L** hath testified against me, and	3068
	2: 4	said unto the reapers, **The L** *be* with you.	3068
	2: 4	And they answered him, **The L** bless thee.	3068
	2:12	**The L** recompense thy work, and a full	3068
	2:12	a full reward be given thee of **the L** God of	3068
	2:20	her daughter in law, Blessed *be* he of **the L**,	3068
	3:10	he said, Blessed *be* thou of **the L**,	3068
	3:13	part of a kinsman to thee, *as* **the L** liveth:	3068
	4:11	**The L** make the woman that is come into	3068
	4:12	of the seed which **the L** shall give thee of	3068
	4:13	**the L** gave her conception, and she bare a	3068
	4:14	women said unto Naomi, Blessed *be* **the L**,	3068
1Sa	1: 3	to sacrifice unto **the L** of hosts in Shiloh.	3068
	1: 3	Hophni and Phinehas, the priests of **the L**,	3068
	1: 5	but **the L** had shut up her womb.	3068
	1: 6	because **the L** had shut up her womb.	3068
	1: 7	when she went up to the house of **the L**, so	3068
	1: 9	a seat by a post of the temple of **the L**.	3068
	1:10	and prayed unto **the L**, and wept sore.	3068
	1:11	she vowed a vow, and said, O **L** of hosts,	3068
	1:11	I will give him unto **the L** all the days of	3068
	1:12	as she continued praying before **the L**,	3068
	1:15	but have poured out my soul before **the L**.	3068
	1:19	worshipped before **the L**, and returned, and	3068
	1:19	his wife; and **the L** remembered her.	3068
	1:20	*saying,* Because I have asked him of **the L**.	3068
	1:21	went up to offer unto **the L** the yearly	3068
	1:22	that he may appear before **the L**, and	3068
	1:23	weaned him; only **the L** establish his word.	3068
	1:24	brought him *unto* the house of **the L** *in*	3068
	1:26	that stood by thee here, praying unto **the L**.	3068
	1:27	**the L** hath given me my petition which I	3068
	1:28	Therefore also I have lent him to **the L**;	3068
	1:28	long as he liveth he *shall be* lent to **the L**.	3068
	1:28	And he worshipped **the L** there.	3068
	2: 1	and said, My heart rejoiceth in **the L**,	3068
	2: 1	the LORD, mine horn is exalted in **the L**:	3068
	2: 2	*There is* none holy as **the L**: for *there is*	3068
	2: 3	for **the L** *is* a God of knowledge, and	3068
	2: 6	**The L** killeth, and maketh alive:	3068
	2: 7	**The L** maketh poor, and maketh rich:	3068
	2:10	The adversaries of **the L** shall be broken to	3068
	2:10	**the L** shall judge the ends of the earth; and	3068
	2:11	the child did minister unto **the L** before Eli	3068
	2:12	*were* sons of Belial; they knew not **the L**.	3068
	2:17	young men was very great before **the L**:	3068
	2:17	for men abhorred the offering of **the L**.	3068
	2:18	Samuel ministered before **the L**, *being* a	3068
	2:20	**The L** give thee seed of this woman for	3068
	2:20	woman for the loan which is lent to **the L**.	3068
	2:21	**the L** visited Hannah, so that she	3068
	2:21	And the child Samuel grew before **the L**.	3068
	2:25	if a man sin against **the L**, who shall intreat	3068
	2:25	because **the L** would slay them.	3068
	2:26	was in favour both with **the L**, and	3068
	2:27	and said unto him, Thus saith **the L**,	3068

1Sa 2:30 Wherefore **the L** God of Israel saith, I said 3068
2:30 now **the L** saith, Be it far from me; 3068
3: 1 the child Samuel ministered unto **the L** 3068
3: 1 the word of **the L** was precious in those 3068
3: 3 of God went out in the temple of **the L**, 3068
3: 4 That **the L** called Samuel: and 3068
3: 6 **the L** called yet again, Samuel. 3068
3: 7 Now Samuel did not yet know **the L**, 3068
3: 7 neither was the word of **the L** yet revealed 3068
3: 8 **the L** called Samuel again the third time. 3068
3: 8 Eli perceived that **the L** had called 3068
3: 9 if he call thee, that thou shalt say, Speak, **L**; 3068
3:10 **the L** came, and stood, and called as at 3068
3:11 **the L** said to Samuel, Behold, I will do a 3068
3:15 and opened the doors of the house of **the L**. 3068
3:17 What *is* the thing that *the L* hath said unto NIH
3:18 he said, It *is* **the L**: let him do what 3068
3:19 **the L** was with him, and did let none of his 3068
3:20 *was* established to be a prophet of **the L**. 3068
3:21 **the L** appeared again in Shiloh: for 3068
3:21 for **the L** revealed himself to Samuel in 3068
3:21 to Samuel in Shiloh by the word of **the L**. 3068
4: 3 Wherefore hath **the L** smitten us to day 3068
4: 3 us fetch the ark of the covenant of **the L** 3068
4: 4 the ark of the covenant of **the L** of hosts, 3068
4: 5 when the ark of the covenant of **the L** came 3068
4: 6 they understood that the ark of **the L** was 3068
5: 3 his face to the earth before the ark of **the L**. 3068
5: 4 face to the ground before the ark of **the L**; 3068
5: 6 the hand of **the L** was heavy upon them of 3068
5: 9 the hand of **the L** was against the city *with* 3068
6: 1 the ark of **the L** was in the country of 3068
6: 2 What shall we do to the ark of **the L**? 3068
6: 8 take the ark of **the L**, and lay it upon 3068
6:11 they laid the ark of **the L** upon the cart, 3068
6:14 the kine a burnt offering unto **the L**. 3068
6:15 the Levites took down the ark of **the L**, 3068
6:15 sacrifices the same day unto **the L**. 3068
6:17 returned *for* a trespass offering unto **the L**; 3068
6:18 whereon they set down the ark of **the L**: 3068
6:19 they had looked into the ark of **the L**, 3068
6:19 **the L** had smitten *many* of the people *with* 3068
6:20 Who is able to stand before this holy **L** 3068
6:21 have brought again the ark of **the L**; 3068
7: 1 fetched up the ark of **the L**, and brought it 3068
7: 1 Eleazar his son to keep the ark of **the L**. 3068
7: 2 all the house of Israel lamented after **the L**. 3068
7: 3 If ye do return unto **the L** with all your 3068
7: 3 prepare your hearts unto **the L**, and 3068
7: 4 and Ashtaroth, and served **the L** only. 3068
7: 5 and I will pray for you unto **the L**. 3068
7: 6 poured *it* out before **the L**, and fasted on 3068
7: 6 said there, We have sinned against **the L**. 3068
7: 8 Cease not to cry unto **the L** our God for us, 3068
7: 9 it *for* a burnt offering wholly unto **the L**: 3068
7: 9 Samuel cried unto **the L** for Israel; and 3068
7: 9 the LORD for Israel; and **the L** heard him. 3068
7:10 **the L** thundered with a great thunder on 3068
7:12 Hitherto hath **the L** helped us. 3068
7:13 the hand of **the L** was against 3068
7:17 and there he built an altar unto **the L**. 3068
8: 6 judge us. And Samuel prayed unto **the L**. 3068
8: 7 **the L** said unto Samuel, Hearken unto 3068
8:10 Samuel told all the words of **the L** unto 3068
8:18 and **the L** will not hear you in that day. 3068
8:21 and he rehearsed them in the ears of **the L**. 3068
8:22 **the L** said to Samuel, Hearken unto their 3068
9:15 Now **the L** had told Samuel in his ear a day 3068
9:17 Samuel saw Saul, **the L** said unto him, 3068
10: 1 **the L** hath anointed thee to be captain over 3068
10: 6 the spirit of **the L** will come upon thee, 3068
10:17 the people together unto **the L** *to* Mizpeh; 3068
10:18 Thus saith **the L** God of Israel, I brought 3068
10:19 present yourselves before **the L** by your 3068
10:22 Therefore they inquired of **the L** further, 3068
10:22 **the L** answered, Behold, he hath hid 3068
10:24 See ye him whom **the L** hath chosen, 3068
10:25 *it* in a book, and laid *it* up before **the L**. 3068
11: 7 the fear of **the L** fell on the people, and 3068
11:13 for to day **the L** hath wrought salvation in 3068
11:15 there they made Saul king before **the L** in 3068
11:15 sacrifices *of* peace offerings before **the L**; 3068
12: 3 here I *am*: witness against me before **the L**, 3068
12: 5 **The L** *is* witness against you, and 3068

12: 6 *It is* **the L** that advanced Moses and Aaron, 3068
12: 7 that I may reason with you before **the L** of 3068
12: 7 LORD of all the righteous acts of **the L**, 3068
12: 8 your fathers cried unto **the L**, then 3068
12: 8 then **the L** sent Moses and Aaron, 3068
12: 9 when they forgat **the L** their God, he sold 3068
12:10 they cried unto **the L**, and said, We have 3068
12:10 because we have forsaken **the L**, and 3068
12:11 **the L** sent Jerubbaal, and Bedan, and 3068
12:12 when **the L** your God *was* your king. 3068
12:13 and behold, **the L** hath set a king over you. 3068
12:14 If ye will fear **the L**, and serve him, and 3068
12:14 rebel against the commandment of **the L**, 3068
12:14 you continue following **the L** your God: 3068
12:15 if ye will not obey the voice of **the L**, but 3068
12:15 rebel against the commandment of **the L**, 3068
12:15 shall the hand of **the L** be against you, as *it* 3068
12:16 which **the L** will do before your eyes. 3068
12:17 I will call unto **the L**, and he shall send 3068
12:17 which ye have done in the sight of **the L**, 3068
12:18 So Samuel called unto **the L**; and 3068
12:18 and **the L** sent thunder and rain that day: 3068
12:18 all the people greatly feared **the L** and 3068
12:19 Pray for thy servants unto **the L** thy God, 3068
12:20 yet turn not aside from following **the L**, but 3068
12:20 but serve **the L** with all your heart; 3068
12:22 For **the L** will not forsake his people for his 3068
12:22 it hath pleased **the L** to make you his 3068
12:23 God forbid that I should sin against **the L** 3068
12:24 Only fear **the L**, and serve him in truth 3068
13:12 I have not made supplication unto **the L**: 3068
13:13 kept the commandment of **the L** thy God, 3068
13:13 for now would **the L** have established thy 3068
13:14 **the L** hath sought him a man after his own 3068
13:14 **the L** hath commanded him to be captain 3068
13:14 thou hast not kept *that* which **the L** 3068
14: 6 it may be that **the L** will work for us: 3068
14: 6 for *there is* no restraint to **the L** to save by 3068
14:10 for **the L** hath delivered them into our 3068
14:12 for **the L** hath delivered them into the hand 3068
14:23 So **the L** saved Israel that day: and 3068
14:33 Behold, the people sin against **the L**, 3068
14:34 sin not against **the L** in eating with 3068
14:35 Saul built an altar unto **the L**: the same was 3068
14:35 was the first altar that he built unto **the L**. 3068
14:39 For, *as* **the L** liveth, which saveth Israel, 3068
14:41 Therefore Saul said unto **the L** God of 3068
14:45 *as* **the L** liveth, there shall not one hair of 3068
15: 1 **The L** sent me to anoint thee to be king 3068
15: 1 thou unto the voice of the words of **the L**. 3068
15: 2 Thus saith **the L** of hosts, I remember *that* 3068
15:10 came the word of **the L** unto Samuel, 3068
15:11 and he cried unto **the L** all night. 3068
15:13 said unto him, Blessed *be* thou of **the L**: 3068
15:13 performed the commandment of **the L**. 3068
15:15 the oxen, to sacrifice unto **the L** thy God; 3068
15:16 I will tell thee what **the L** hath said to me 3068
15:17 and **the L** anointed thee king over Israel? 3068
15:18 **the L** sent thee on a journey, and said, Go 3068
15:19 didst thou not obey the voice of **the L**, 3068
15:19 and didst evil in the sight of **the L**? 3068
15:20 I have obeyed the voice of **the L**, and 3068
15:20 have gone the way which **the L** sent me, 3068
15:21 to sacrifice unto **the L** thy God in Gilgal. 3068
15:22 Hath **the L** *as great* delight in burnt 3068
15:22 sacrifices, as in obeying the voice of **the L**? 3068
15:23 thou hast rejected the word of **the L**, 3068
15:24 transgressed the commandment of **the L**, 3068
15:25 again with me, that I may worship **the L**. 3068
15:26 for thou hast rejected the word of **the L**, 3068
15:26 **the L** hath rejected thee from being king 3068
15:28 **The L** hath rent the kingdom of Israel from 3068
15:30 with me, that I may worship **the L** thy God. 3068
15:31 after Saul; and Saul worshipped **the L**. 3068
15:33 Samuel hewed Agag in pieces before **the L** 3068
15:35 **the L** repented that he had made Saul king 3068
16: 1 **the L** said unto Samuel, How long wilt 3068
16: 2 **the L** said, Take a heifer with thee, 3068
16: 2 say, I am come to sacrifice to **the L**. 3068
16: 4 Samuel did *that* which **the L** spake, and 3068
16: 5 I am come to sacrifice unto **the L**: 3068
16: 7 **the L** said unto Samuel, Look not on his 3068
16: 7 for *the L seeth* not as man seeth; for man NIH
16: 7 but **the L** looketh on the heart. 3068

1Sa 16: 8 he said, Neither hath **the L** chosen this. 3068
16: 9 he said, Neither hath **the L** chosen this. 3068
16:10 unto Jesse, **The L** hath not chosen these. 3068
16:12 **the L** said, Arise, anoint him: for this *is* he. 3068
16:13 the spirit of **the L** came upon David from 3068
16:14 the spirit of **the L** departed from Saul, and 3068
16:14 and an evil spirit from **the L** troubled him. 3068
16:18 a comely person, and **the L** *is* with him. 3068
17:37 **The L** that delivered me out of the paw of 3068
17:37 unto David, Go, and **the L** be with thee. 3068
17:45 I come to thee in the name of **the L** of 3068
17:46 This day will **the L** deliver thee into mine 3068
17:47 all this assembly shall know that **the L** 3068
18:12 because **the L** was with him, and 3068
18:14 in all his ways; and **the L** *was* with him. 3068
18:28 and knew that **the L** *was* with David, 3068
19: 5 **the L** wrought a great salvation for all 3068
19: 6 Saul sware, *As* **the L** liveth, he shall not be 3068
19: 9 the evil spirit from **the L** was upon Saul, 3068
20: 3 truly *as* **the L** liveth, and *as* thy soul liveth, 3068
20: 8 servant into a covenant of **the L** with thee: 3068
20:12 said unto David, O **L** God of Israel, 3068
20:13 **The L** do so and much more to Jonathan: 3068
20:13 **the L** be with thee, as he hath been with my 3068
20:14 yet I live shew me the kindness of **the L**, 3068
20:15 not when **the L** hath cut off the enemies of 3068
20:16 *saying,* Let **the L** even require *it* at 3068
20:21 peace to thee, and no hurt; *as* **the L** liveth. 3068
20:22 go *thy way:* for **the L** hath sent thee away. 3068
20:23 **the L** *be* between thee and me for ever. 3068
20:42 have sworn both of us in the name of **the L**, 3068
20:42 **The L** be between me and thee, and 3068
21: 6 that was taken from before **the L**, 3068
21: 7 *was* there that day, detained before **the L**; 3068
22:10 he inquired of **the L** for him, and gave him 3068
22:17 Turn, and slay the priests of **the L**; 3068
22:17 their hand to fall upon the priests of **the L**. 3068
23: 2 Therefore David inquired of **the L**, saying, 3068
23: 2 **the L** said unto David, Go, and smite 3068
23: 4 David inquired of **the L** yet again. And 3068
23: 4 **the L** answered him and said, Arise, 3068
23:10 said David, O **L** God of Israel, thy servant 3068
23:11 O **L** God of Israel, I beseech thee, tell thy 3068
23:11 And **the L** said, He will come down. 3068
23:12 And **the L** said, They will deliver *thee* up. 3068
23:18 they two made a covenant before **the L**: 3068
23:21 Saul said, Blessed *be* ye of **the L**; for ye 3068
24: 4 Behold the day of which **the L** said unto 3068
24: 6 **The L** forbid that I should do this thing 3068
24: 6 seeing he *is* the anointed of **the L**. 3068
24:10 day thine eyes have seen how that **the L** 3068
24:12 **The L** judge between me and thee, and 3068
24:12 and thee, and **the L** avenge me of thee: 3068
24:15 **The L** therefore be judge, and 3068
24:18 forasmuch as when **the L** had delivered me 3068
24:19 wherefore **the L** reward thee good for that 3068
24:21 Swear now therefore unto me by **the L**, 3068
25:26 *as* **the L** liveth, and *as* thy soul liveth, 3068
25:26 seeing **the L** hath withholden thee 3068
25:28 for **the L** will certainly make my lord a 3068
25:28 my lord fighteth the battles of **the L**, 3068
25:29 in the bundle of life with **the L** thy God; 3068
25:30 when **the L** shall have done to my lord 3068
25:31 when **the L** shall have dealt well with my 3068
25:32 to Abigail, Blessed *be* **the L** God of Israel, 3068
25:34 in very deed, *as* **the L** God of Israel liveth, 3068
25:38 ten days *after,* that **the L** smote Nabal, 3068
25:39 Nabal was dead, he said, Blessed *be* **the L**, 3068
25:39 for **the L** hath returned the wickedness of 3068
26:10 David said furthermore, *As* **the L** liveth, 3068
26:10 the LORD liveth, **the L** shall smite him; 3068
26:11 **The L** forbid that *I* should stretch forth 3068
26:12 a deep sleep from **the L** was fallen upon 3068
26:16 *As* **the L** liveth, ye *are* worthy to die, 3068
26:19 If **the L** have stirred thee up against me, 3068
26:19 of men, cursed *be* they before **the L**; 3068
26:19 from abiding in the inheritance of **the L**, 3068
26:20 fall to the earth before the face of **the L**: 3068
26:23 **The L** render to every man his 3068
26:23 for **the L** delivered thee into *my* hand to 3068
26:24 my life be much set by in the eyes of **the L**, 3068
28: 6 when Saul inquired of **the L**, the LORD 3068
28: 6 **the L** answered him not, neither by dreams, 3068
28:10 Saul sware to her by **the L**, saying, *As* 3068
28:10 her by the LORD, saying, *As* **the L** liveth, 3068
28:16 seeing **the L** is departed from thee, and 3068
28:17 **the L** hath done to him, as he spake by me: 3068
28:17 for **the L** hath rent the kingdom out of thine 3068
28:18 thou obeyedst not the voice of **the L**, 3068
28:18 hath **the L** done this thing unto thee this 3068
28:19 Moreover **the L** will also deliver Israel 3068
28:19 **the L** also shall deliver the host of Israel 3068
29: 6 said unto him, Surely, *as* **the L** liveth, 3068
30: 6 David encouraged himself in **the L** his 3068
30: 8 David inquired at **the L**, saying, Shall I 3068
30:23 with *that* which **the L** hath given us, 3068
30:26 you of the spoil of the enemies of **the L**; 3068
2Sa 1:12 for the people of **the L**, and for the house 3068
2: 1 that David inquired of **the L**, saying, 3068
2: 1 **the L** said unto him, Go up. And David 3068
2: 5 said unto them, Blessed *be* ye of **the L**, 3068
2: 6 now **the L** shew kindness and truth unto 3068
3: 9 as **the L** hath sworn to David, even so I do 3068
3:18 then do *it:* for **the L** hath spoken of David, 3068
3:28 my kingdom *are* guiltless before **the L** for 3068
3:39 **the L** shall reward the doer of evil 3068
4: 8 **the L** hath avenged my lord the king this 3068
4: 9 and said unto them, *As* **the L** liveth, 3068
5: 2 **the L** said to thee, Thou shalt feed my 3068
5: 3 a league with them in Hebron before **the L**: 3068
5:10 and **the L** God of hosts *was* with him. 3068
5:12 David perceived that **the L** had established 3068
5:19 David inquired of **the L**, saying, Shall I go 3068
5:19 **the L** said unto David, Go up: for I will 3068
5:20 **The L** hath broken forth upon mine 3068
5:23 And when David inquired of **the L**, he said, 3068
5:24 for then shall **the L** go out before thee, 3068
5:25 did so, as **the L** had commanded him; 3068
6: 2 whose name is called *by* the name of **the L** 3068
6: 5 all the house of Israel played before **the L** 3068
6: 7 the anger of **the L** was kindled against 3068
6: 8 **the L** had made a breach upon Uzzah: 3068
6: 9 David was afraid of **the L** that day, 3068
6: 9 How shall the ark of **the L** come to me? 3068
6:10 of **the L** unto him into the city of David: 3068
6:11 the ark of **the L** continued *in* the house of 3068
6:11 **the L** blessed Obed-edom, and all his 3068
6:12 **The L** hath blessed the house of 3068
6:13 that when they that bare the ark of **the L** 3068
6:14 David danced before **the L** with all *his* 3068
6:15 brought up the ark of **the L** with shouting, 3068
6:16 as the ark of **the L** came *into* the city of 3068
6:16 David leaping and dancing before **the L**; 3068
6:17 they brought in the ark of **the L**, and set it 3068
6:17 and peace offerings before **the L**. 3068
6:18 he blessed the people in the name of **the L** 3068
6:21 said unto Michal, *It was* before **the L**, 3068
6:21 appoint me ruler over the people of **the L**, 3068
6:21 therefore will I play before **the L**. 3068
7: 1 **the L** had given him rest round about from 3068
7: 3 that *is* in thine heart; for **the L** *is* with thee. 3068
7: 4 that the word of **the L** came unto Nathan, 3068
7: 5 tell my servant David, Thus saith **the L**, 3068
7: 8 Thus saith **the L** of hosts, I took thee from 3068
7:11 Also **the L** telleth thee that he will make 3068
7:18 sat before **the L**, and he said, Who *am* I, 3068
7:22 Wherefore thou art great, O **L** God: 3068
7:24 for ever; and thou, **L**, art become their God. 3068
7:25 now, O **L** God, the word that thou hast 3068
7:26 **The L** of hosts *is* the God over Israel: 3068
7:27 For thou, O **L** of hosts, God of Israel, 3068
8: 6 **the L** preserved David whithersoever he 3068
8:11 also king David did dedicate unto **the L**, 3068
8:14 **the L** preserved David whithersoever he 3068
10:12 and **the L** do that which seemeth him good. 3068
11:27 thing that David had done displeased **the L**. 3068
12: 1 **the L** sent Nathan unto David. And he 3068
12: 5 he said to Nathan, *As* **the L** liveth, the man 3068
12: 7 Thus saith **the L** God of Israel, I anointed 3068
12: 9 thou despised the commandment of **the L**, 3068
12:11 Thus saith **the L**, Behold, I will raise up 3068
12:13 unto Nathan, I have sinned against **the L**. 3068
12:13 **The L** also hath put away thy sin; 3068
12:14 to the enemies of **the L** to blaspheme, 3068
12:15 **the L** strake the child that Uriah's wife 3068
12:20 came *into* the house of **the L**, and 3068
12:24 his name Solomon: and **the L** loved him. 3068
12:25 called his name Jedidiah, because of **the L**. 3068

2Sa 14:11	let the king remember **the L** thy God,	3068
14:11	he said, *As* **the L** liveth, there shall not one	3068
14:17	therefore **the L** thy God will be with thee.	3068
15: 7	which I have vowed unto **the L**, in Hebron.	3068
15: 8	If **the L** shall bring me again indeed *to*	3068
15: 8	*to* Jerusalem, then I will serve **the L**.	3068
15:21	*As* **the L** liveth, and *as* my lord the king	3068
15:25	if I shall find favour in the eyes of **the L**,	3068
15:31	David said, O L, I pray thee, turn	3068
16: 8	**The L** hath returned upon thee all the blood	3068
16: 8	**the L** hath delivered the kingdom into	3068
16:10	because **the L** hath said unto him,	3068
16:11	let him curse; for **the L** hath bidden him.	3068
16:12	It may be that **the L** will look on mine	3068
16:12	that **the L** will requite me good for his	3068
16:18	whom **the L**, and this people, and all	3068
17:14	For **the L** had appointed to defeat the good	3068
17:14	to the intent that **the L** might bring evil	3068
18:19	how that **the L** hath avenged him of his	3068
18:28	and said, Blessed *be* **the L** thy God,	3068
18:31	for **the L** hath avenged thee *this* day of all	3068
19: 7	for I swear by **the L**, if thou go not forth,	3068
20:19	thou swallow up the inheritance of **the L**?	3068
21: 1	after year; and David inquired of **the L**.	3068
21: 1	**the L** answered, *It is* for Saul, and for *his*	3068
21: 3	that ye may bless the inheritance of **the L**?	3068
21: 6	we will hang them up unto **the L** in Gibeah	3068
21: 6	in Gibeah of Saul, whom **the L** did choose.	3068
21: 9	they hanged them in the hill before **the L**:	3068
22: 1	David spake unto **the L** the words of this	3068
22: 1	**the L** had delivered him out of the hand of	3068
22: 2	**The L** *is* my rock, and my fortress, and	3068
22: 4	I will call on **the L**, who is *worthy* to be	3068
22: 7	In my distress I called upon **the L**, and	3068
22:14	**The L** thundered from heaven, and	3068
22:16	at the rebuking of **the L**, at the blast of	3068
22:19	day of my calamity: but **the L** was my stay.	3068
22:21	**The L** rewarded me according to my	3068
22:22	For I have kept the ways of **the L**, and	3068
22:25	Therefore **the L** hath recompensed me	3068
22:29	For thou *art* my lamp, O L: and the LORD	3068
22:29	and **the L** will lighten my darkness.	3068
22:31	way *is* perfect; the word of **the L** *is* tried:	3068
22:32	For who *is* God, save **the L**? and who *is* a	3068
22:42	*even* unto **the L**, but he answered them not.	3068
22:47	**The L** liveth; and blessed *be* my rock; and	3068
22:50	O L, among the heathen, and I will sing	3068
23: 2	The Spirit of **the L** spake by me, and	3068
23:10	**the L** wrought a great victory that day;	3068
23:12	and **the L** wrought a great victory.	3068
23:16	drink thereof, but poured it out unto **the L**.	3068
23:17	he said, Be it far from me, O L, that I	3068
24: 1	again the anger of **the L** was kindled	3068
24: 3	Now **the L** thy God add unto the people,	3068
24:10	David said unto **the L**, I have sinned	3068
24:10	now, I beseech thee, O L, take away	3068
24:11	the word of **the L** came unto the prophet	3068
24:12	Go and say unto David, Thus saith **the L**,	3068
24:14	let us fall now into the hand of **the L**;	3068
24:15	So **the L** sent a pestilence upon Israel from	3068
24:16	**the L** repented him of the evil, and said to	3068
24:16	the angel of **the L** was by	3068
24:17	David spake unto **the L** when he saw	3068
24:18	rear an altar unto **the L** in	3068
24:19	of Gad, went up as **the L** commanded.	3068
24:21	of thee, to build an altar unto **the L**,	3068
24:23	unto the king, **The L** thy God accept thee.	3068
24:24	**the L** my God of that which doth cost me	3068
24:25	David built there an altar unto **the L**, and	3068
24:25	So **the L** was intreated for the land, and	3068
1Ki 1:17	thou swarest by **the L** thy God unto thine	3068
1:29	the king sware, and said, *As* **the L** liveth,	3068
1:30	Even as I sware unto thee by **the L** God of	3068
1:36	**the L** God of my lord the king say so *too*.	3068
1:37	As **the L** hath been with my lord the king,	3068
1:48	the king, Blessed *be* **the L** God of Israel,	3068
2: 3	keep the charge of **the L** thy God, to walk	3068
2: 4	That **the L** may continue his word which	3068
2: 8	and I sware to him by **the L**, saying,	3068
2:15	my brother's: for it was his from **the L**.	3068
2:23	king Solomon sware by **the L**, saying,	3068
2:24	Now therefore, *as* **the L** liveth, which hath	3068
2:27	out Abiathar from being priest unto **the L**;	3068
2:27	that *he* might fulfil the word of **the L**,	3068
2:28	Joab fled unto the tabernacle of **the L**, and	3068
2:29	Joab was fled unto the tabernacle of **the L**;	3068
2:30	Benaiah came to the tabernacle of **the L**,	3068
2:32	**the L** shall return his blood upon his own	3068
2:33	shall there be peace for ever from **the L**.	3068
2:42	Did I not make thee to swear by **the L**, and	3068
2:43	then hast thou not kept the oath of **the L**,	3068
2:44	**the L** shall return thy wickedness upon	3068
2:45	shall be established before **the L** for ever.	3068
3: 1	the house of **the L**, and the wall of	3068
3: 2	was no house built unto the name of **the L**,	3068
3: 3	Solomon loved **the L**, walking in	3068
3: 5	In Gibeon **the L** appeared to Solomon in a	3068
3: 7	now, O L my God, thou hast made thy	3068
3:15	before the ark of the covenant of **the L**,	3068
5: 3	**the L** his God for the wars which were	3068
5: 3	until **the L** put them under the soles of his	3068
5: 4	now **the L** my God hath given me rest on	3068
5: 5	a house unto the name of **the L** my God,	3068
5: 5	as **the L** spake unto David my father,	3068
5: 7	and said, Blessed *be* **the L** *this* day,	3068
5:12	**the L** gave Solomon wisdom, as he	3068
6: 1	that he *began* to build the house of **the L**.	3068
6: 2	house which king Solomon built for **the L**,	3068
6:11	the word of **the L** came to Solomon,	3068
6:19	set there the ark of the covenant of **the L**.	3068
6:37	the foundation of the house of **the L** laid,	3068
7:12	for the inner court of the house of **the L**,	3068
7:40	made king Solomon *for* the house of **the L**:	3068
7:45	to king Solomon *for* the house of **the L**,	3068
7:48	that *pertained unto* the house of **the L**:	3068
7:51	king Solomon made *for* the house of **the L**.	3068
7:51	among the treasures of the house of **the L**.	3068
8: 1	covenant of **the L** out of the city of David,	3068
8: 4	they brought up the ark of **the L**, and	3068
8: 6	ark of the covenant of **the L** unto his place,	3068
8: 9	when **the L** made *a covenant* with	3068
8:10	that the cloud filled the house of **the L**,	3068
8:11	for the glory of **the L** had filled the house	3068
8:11	the LORD had filled the house of **the L**.	3068
8:12	**The L** said that *he* would dwell in the thick	3068
8:15	he said, Blessed *be* **the L** God of Israel,	3068
8:17	house for the name of **the L** God of Israel.	3068
8:18	**the L** said unto David my father,	3068
8:20	**the L** hath performed his word that he	3068
8:20	as **the L** promised, and have built a house	3068
8:20	have built a house for the name of **the L**	3068
8:21	wherein *is* the covenant of **the L**, which he	3068
8:22	Solomon stood before the altar of **the L** in	3068
8:23	he said, L God of Israel, *there is* no God	3068
8:25	Therefore now, L God of Israel, keep with	3068
8:28	to his supplication, O L my God,	3068
8:44	shall pray unto **the L** toward the city which	3068
8:54	all this prayer and supplication unto **the L**,	3068
8:54	he arose from before the altar of **the L**,	3068
8:56	Blessed *be* **the L**, that hath given rest unto	3068
8:57	**The L** our God be with us, as he was with	3068
8:59	I have made supplication before **the L**,	3068
8:59	be nigh unto **the L** our God day and night,	3068
8:60	of the earth may know that **the L** *is* God,	3068
8:61	therefore be perfect with **the L** our God,	3068
8:62	with him, offered sacrifice before **the L**.	3068
8:63	which he offered unto **the L**, two and	3068
8:63	of Israel dedicated the house of **the L**.	3068
8:64	court that *was* before the house of **the L**:	3068
8:64	the brasen altar that *was* before **the L** *was*	3068
8:65	before **the L** our God, seven days and	3068
8:66	glad of heart for all the goodness that **the L**	3068
9: 1	finished the building of the house of **the L**,	3068
9: 2	That **the L** appeared to Solomon the second	3068
9: 3	**the L** said unto him, I have heard thy	3068
9: 8	Why hath **the L** done thus unto this land,	3068
9: 9	Because they forsook **the L** their God,	3068
9: 9	hath **the L** brought upon them all this evil.	3068
9:10	the house of **the L**, and the king's house,	3068
9:15	for to build the house of **the L**, and his own	3068
9:25	upon the altar which he built unto **the L**,	3068
9:25	upon the altar that *was* before **the L**.	3068
10: 1	of Solomon concerning the name of **the L**,	3068
10: 5	which he went up *unto* the house of **the L**;	3068
10: 9	Blessed be **the L** thy God, which delighted	3068
10: 9	because **the L** loved Israel for ever,	3068
10:12	almug trees pillars for the house of **the L**,	3068
11: 2	Of the nations *concerning* which **the L** said	3068

1Ki 11: 4 his heart was not perfect with **the L** his 3068
11: 6 Solomon did evil in the sight of **the L**, and 3068
11: 6 went not fully after **the L**, as *did* David his 3068
11: 9 **the L** was angry with Solomon, because 3068
11: 9 his heart was turned from **the L** God of 3068
11:10 he kept not *that* which **the L** commanded. 3068
11:11 Wherefore **the L** said unto Solomon, 3068
11:14 **the L** stirred up an adversary unto 3068
11:31 for thus saith **the L**, the God of Israel, 3068
12:15 for the cause was from **the L**, that *he* might 3068
12:15 which **the L** spake by Ahijah the Shilonite 3068
12:24 Thus saith **the L**, Ye shall not go up, 3068
12:24 therefore to the word of **the L**, 3068
12:24 to depart, according to the word of **the L**. 3068
12:27 sacrifice in the house of **the L** at Jerusalem, 3068
13: 1 of Judah by the word of **the L** unto Beth-el: 3068
13: 2 cried against the altar in the word of **the L**, 3068
13: 2 and said, O altar, altar, thus saith **the L**; 3068
13: 3 This *is* the sign which **the L** hath spoken; 3068
13: 5 of God had given by the word of **the L**. 3068
13: 6 Intreat now the face of **the L** thy God, and 3068
13: 6 the man of God besought **the L**, and 3068
13: 9 so was it charged me by the word of **the L**, 3068
13:17 For it was said to me by the word of **the L**, 3068
13:18 angel spake unto me by the word of **the L**, 3068
13:20 that the word of **the L** came unto 3068
13:21 came from Judah, saying, Thus saith **the L**, 3068
13:21 as thou hast disobeyed the mouth of **the L**, 3068
13:21 which **the L** thy God commanded thee, 3068
13:22 of the which *the L* did say to thee, Eat no NIH
13:26 was disobedient unto the word of **the L**: 3068
13:26 **the L** hath delivered him unto the lion, 3068
13:26 slain him, according to the word of **the L**, 3068
13:32 word of **the L** against the altar in Beth-el, 3068
14: 5 **the L** said unto Ahijah, Behold, the wife of 3068
14: 7 Thus saith **the L** God of Israel, 3068
14:11 of the air eat: for **the L** hath spoken *it*. 3068
14:13 **the L** God of Israel in the house of 3068
14:14 Moreover **the L** shall raise him up a king 3068
14:15 For **the L** shall smite Israel, as a reed is 3068
14:15 their groves, provoking **the L** to anger. 3068
14:18 for him, according to the word of **the L**, 3068
14:21 the city which **the L** did choose out of all 3068
14:22 Judah did evil in the sight of **the L**, and 3068
14:24 **the L** cast out before the children of Israel. 3068
14:26 away the treasures of the house of **the L**, 3068
14:28 when the king went *into* the house of **the L**, 3068
15: 3 his heart was not perfect with **the L** his 3068
15: 4 Nevertheless for David's sake did **the L** his 3068
15: 5 *that* which *was* right in the eyes of **the L**, 3068
15:11 *that* which *was* right in the eyes of **the L**, 3068
15:14 heart was perfect with **the L** all his days. 3068
15:15 *into* the house of **the L**, silver, and gold, 3068
15:18 left in the treasures of the house of **the L**, 3068
15:26 he did evil in the sight of **the L**, and 3068
15:29 according unto the saying of **the L**, 3068
15:30 he provoked **the L** God of Israel to anger. 3068
15:34 he did evil in the sight of **the L**, and 3068
16: 1 the word of **the L** came to Jehu the son of 3068
16: 7 came the word of **the L** against Baasha, 3068
16: 7 all the evil that he did in the sight of **the L**, 3068
16:12 of Baasha, according to the word of **the L**, 3068
16:13 in provoking **the L** God of Israel to anger 3068
16:19 sinned in doing evil in the sight of **the L**, 3068
16:25 But Omri wrought evil in the eyes of **the L**, 3068
16:26 to provoke **the L** God of Israel to anger 3068
16:30 of **the L** above all that *were* before him. 3068
16:33 Ahab did more to provoke **the L** God of 3068
16:34 according to the word of **the L**, which he 3068
17: 1 unto Ahab, *As* **the L** God of Israel liveth, 3068
17: 2 the word of **the L** came unto him, saying, 3068
17: 5 and did according unto the word of **the L**: 3068
17: 8 the word of **the L** came unto him, saying, 3068
17:12 she said, *As* **the L** thy God liveth, I have 3068
17:14 For thus saith **the L** God of Israel, 3068
17:14 until the day *that* **the L** sendeth rain upon 3068
17:16 according to the word of **the L**, which he 3068
17:20 he cried unto **the L**, and said, O LORD 3068
17:20 unto the LORD, and said, O **L** my God, 3068
17:21 cried unto **the L**, and said, O LORD my 3068
17:21 and said, O **L** my God, I pray thee, 3068
17:22 **the L** heard the voice of Elijah; and 3068
17:24 *that* the word of **the L** in thy mouth *is* truth. 3068
18: 1 that the word of **the L** came to Elijah in 3068
18: 3 (Now Obadiah feared **the L** greatly: 3068
18: 4 when Jezebel cut off the prophets of **the L**, 3068
18:10 *As* **the L** thy God liveth, there is no nation 3068
18:12 that the spirit of **the L** shall carry thee 3068
18:12 but *I* thy servant fear **the L** from my youth. 3068
18:13 when Jezebel slew the prophets of **the L**, 3068
18:15 Elijah said, *As* **the L** of hosts liveth, before 3068
18:18 have forsaken the commandments of **the L**, 3068
18:21 if **the L** *be* God, follow him: but if Baal, 3068
18:22 I, *even* I only, remain a prophet of **the L**; 3068
18:24 and I will call on the name of **the L**: 3068
18:30 he repaired the altar of **the L** that was 3068
18:31 unto whom the word of **the L** came, 3068
18:32 he built an altar in the name of **the L**: 3068
18:36 said, **L** God of Abraham, Isaac, and 3068
18:37 Hear me, O **L**, hear me, that this people 3068
18:37 people may know that thou *art* **the L** God, 3068
18:38 the fire of **the L** fell, and consumed 3068
18:39 they said, **The L**, he *is* the God; 3068
18:39 he *is* the God; **the L**, he *is* the God. 3068
18:46 the hand of **the L** was on Elijah; and 3068
19: 4 *It is* enough; now, O **L**, take away my life; 3068
19: 7 the angel of **the L** came again the second 3068
19: 9 the word of **the L** *came* to him, and he said 3068
19:10 I have been very jealous for **the L** God of 3068
19:11 and stand upon the mount before **the L**. 3068
19:11 **the L** passed by, and a great and 3068
19:11 and brake in pieces the rocks before **the L**; 3068
19:11 the LORD; *but* **the L** *was* not in the wind: 3068
19:11 *but* **the L** *was* not in the earthquake: 3068
19:12 a fire; *but* **the L** *was* not in the fire: 3068
19:14 I have been very jealous for **the L** God of 3068
19:15 **the L** said unto him, Go, return on thy way 3068
20:13 saying, Thus saith **the L**, Hast thou seen all 3068
20:13 and thou shalt know that I *am* **the L**. 3068
20:14 he said, Thus saith **the L**, *Even* by 3068
20:28 king of Israel, and said, Thus saith **the L**, 3068
20:28 **The L** *is* God of the hills, but he *is* not God 3068
20:28 and ye shall know that I *am* **the L**. 3068
20:35 unto his neighbour in the word of **the L**, 3068
20:36 thou hast not obeyed the voice of **the L**, 3068
20:42 he said unto him, Thus saith **the L**, 3068
21: 3 Naboth said to Ahab, **The L** forbid it me, 3068
21:17 the word of **the L** came to Elijah 3068
21:19 saying, Thus saith **the L**, Hast thou killed, 3068
21:19 speak unto him, saying, Thus saith **the L**, 3068
21:20 thyself to work evil in the sight of **the L**, 3068
21:23 of Jezebel also spake **the L**, saying, 3068
21:25 to work wickedness in the sight of **the L**, 3068
21:26 whom **the L** cast out before the children of 3068
21:28 the word of **the L** came to Elijah 3068
22: 5 I pray thee, at the word of **the L** to day. 3068
22: 7 *Is there* not here a prophet of **the L** besides, 3068
22: 8 by whom *we* may inquire of **the L**: 3068
22:11 he said, Thus saith **the L**, With these shalt 3068
22:12 for **the L** shall deliver *it* into the king's 3068
22:14 Micaiah said, *As* **the L** liveth, what 3068
22:14 what **the L** saith unto me, that will I speak. 3068
22:15 for **the L** shall deliver *it* into the hand of 3068
22:16 but *that which is* true in the name of **the L**? 3068
22:17 **the L** said, These have no master: let them 3068
22:19 Hear thou therefore the word of **the L**: 3068
22:19 I saw **the L** sitting on his throne, and all 3068
22:20 **the L** said, Who shall persuade Ahab, 3068
22:21 stood before **the L**, and said, I will 3068
22:22 **the L** said unto him, Wherewith? And he 3068
22:23 **the L** hath put a lying spirit in the mouth of 3068
22:23 **the L** hath spoken evil concerning thee. 3068
22:24 Which way went the spirit of **the L** from 3068
22:28 all in peace, **the L** hath not spoken by me. 3068
22:38 according unto the word of **the L** which he 3068
22:43 *that* which *was* right in the eyes of **the L**: 3068
22:52 he did evil in the sight of **the L**, and 3068
22:53 and provoked to anger **the L** God of Israel, 3068
2Ki 1: 3 the angel of **the L** said to Elijah 3068
1: 4 Now therefore thus saith **the L**, Thou shalt 3068
1: 6 Thus saith **the L**, *Is it* not because *there is* 3068
1:15 the angel of **the L** said unto Elijah, 3068
1:16 he said unto him, Thus saith **the L**, 3068
1:17 So he died according to the word of **the L** 3068
2: 1 when **the L** would take up Elijah *into* 3068
2: 2 for **the L** hath sent me to Beth-el. 3068
2: 2 Elisha said *unto him*, *As* **the L** liveth, and 3068
2: 3 Knowest thou that **the L** will take away thy 3068

2Ki 2: 4	for **the L** hath sent me *to* Jericho.	3068
2: 4	*As* **the L** liveth, and *as* thy soul liveth,	3068
2: 5	Knowest thou that **the L** will take away thy	3068
2: 6	here; for **the L** hath sent me to Jordan.	3068
2: 6	*As* **the L** liveth, and *as* thy soul liveth,	3068
2:14	and said, Where *is* **the L** God of Elijah?	3068
2:16	lest peradventure the spirit of **the L** hath	3068
2:21	the salt in there, and said, Thus saith **the L**,	3068
2:24	and cursed them in the name of **the L**.	3068
3: 2	he wrought evil in the sight of **the L**; but	3068
3:10	that **the L** hath called these three kings	3068
3:11	*Is there* not here a prophet of **the L**,	3068
3:11	that we may inquire of **the L** by him?	3068
3:12	The word of **the L** is with him.	3068
3:13	for **the L** hath called these three kings	3068
3:14	Elisha said, *As* **the L** of hosts liveth, before	3068
3:15	that the hand of **the L** came upon him.	3068
3:16	he said, Thus saith **the L**, Make this valley	3068
3:17	For thus saith **the L**, Ye shall not see wind,	3068
3:18	this is *but* a light thing in the sight of **the L**:	3068
4: 1	knowest that thy servant did fear **the L**:	3068
4:27	**the L** hath hid *it* from me, and hath not told	3068
4:30	*As* **the L** liveth, and *as* thy soul liveth,	3068
4:33	upon them twain, and prayed unto **the L**.	3068
4:43	for thus saith **the L**, They shall eat, and	3068
4:44	left *thereof,* according to the word of **the L**.	3068
5: 1	by him **the L** had given deliverance unto	3068
5:11	call on the name of **the L** his God, and	3068
5:16	he said, *As* **the L** liveth, before whom I	3068
5:17	sacrifice unto other gods, but unto **the L**.	3068
5:18	In this thing **the L** pardon thy servant,	3068
5:18	**the L** pardon thy servant in this thing.	3068
5:20	but, *as* **the L** liveth, I will run after him,	3068
6:17	said, **L**, I pray thee, open his eyes, that he	3068
6:17	**the L** opened the eyes of the young man;	3068
6:18	Elisha prayed unto **the L**, and said,	3068
6:20	come *into* Samaria, that Elisha said, **L**,	3068
6:20	**the L** opened their eyes, and they saw; and	3068
6:27	he said, *If* **the L** do not help thee, whence	3068
6:33	he said, Behold, this evil *is* of **the L**;	3068
6:33	what should I wait for **the L** any longer?	3068
7: 1	Elisha said, Hear ye the word of **the L**;	3068
7: 1	Thus saith **the L**, To morrow about *this*	3068
7: 2	*if* **the L** would make windows in heaven,	3068
7:16	a shekel, according to the word of **the L**.	3068
7:19	*if* **the L** should make windows in heaven,	3068
8: 1	for **the L** hath called for a famine; and	3068
8: 8	and inquire of **the L** by him, saying,	3068
8:10	howbeit **the L** hath shewed me that he shall	3068
8:13	**The L** hath shewed me *that* thou *shalt be*	3068
8:18	and he did evil in the sight of **the L**.	3068
8:19	Yet **the L** would not destroy Judah for	3068
8:27	did evil in the sight of **the L**, as *did*.	3068
9: 3	*it* on his head, and say, Thus saith **the L**,	3068
9: 6	unto him, Thus saith **the L** God of Israel,	3068
9: 6	thee king over the people of **the L**,	3068
9: 7	the blood of all the servants of **the L**, at	3068
9:12	spake he to me, saying, Thus saith **the L**,	3068
9:25	his father, **the L** laid this burden upon him;	3068
9:26	and the blood of his sons, saith **the L**;	3068
9:26	I will requite thee in this plat, saith **the L**.	3068
9:26	*of ground,* according to the word of **the L**.	3068
9:36	he said, This *is* the word of **the L**, which he	3068
10:10	unto the earth nothing of the word of **the L**,	3068
10:10	which **the L** spake concerning the house of	3068
10:10	for **the L** hath done *that* which he spake by	3068
10:16	Come with me, and see my zeal for **the L**.	3068
10:17	according to the saying of **the L**, which he	3068
10:23	with you none of the servants of **the L**,	3068
10:30	**the L** said unto Jehu, Because thou hast	3068
10:31	of **the L** God of Israel with all his heart:	3068
10:32	In those days **the L** began to cut Israel	3068
11: 3	he was with her hid *in* the house of **the L**	3068
11: 4	them to him *into* the house of **the L**,	3068
11: 4	took an oath of them in the house of **the L**,	3068
11: 7	watch of the house of **the L** about the king.	3068
11:10	that *were* in the temple of **the L**.	3068
11:13	to the people *into* the temple of **the L**.	3068
11:15	Let her not be slain *in* the house of **the L**.	3068
11:17	Jehoiada made a covenant between **the L**	3068
11:18	appointed officers over the house of **the L**.	3068
11:19	down the king from the house of **the L**,	3068
12: 2	**the L** all his days where*in* Jehoiada	3068
12: 4	that is brought *into* the house of **the L**,	3068
12: 4	heart to bring *into* the house of **the L**,	3068
12: 9	side as one cometh *into* the house of **the L**:	3068
12: 9	that was brought *into* the house of **the L**.	3068
12:10	that was found *in* the house of **the L**.	3068
12:11	had the oversight *of* the house of **the L**:	3068
12:11	that wrought upon the house of **the L**,	3068
12:12	to repair the breaches of the house of **the L**,	3068
12:13	*for* the house of **the L** bowls of silver,	3068
12:13	that was brought *into* the house of **the L**:	3068
12:14	repaired therewith the house of **the L**.	3068
12:16	was not brought *into* the house of **the L**:	3068
12:18	in the treasures of the house of **the L**,	3068
13: 2	*that* which *was* evil in the sight of **the L**,	3068
13: 3	the anger of **the L** was kindled against	3068
13: 4	Jehoahaz besought **the L**, and the LORD	3068
13: 4	and **the L** hearkened unto him:	3068
13: 5	(And **the L** gave Israel a saviour, so	3068
13:11	*that* which *was* evil in the sight of **the L**;	3068
13:23	**the L** was gracious unto them, and	3068
14: 3	*that* which *was* right in the sight of **the L**,	3068
14: 6	where*in* **the L** commanded, saying,	3068
14:14	that were found *in* the house of **the L**,	3068
14:24	*that* which *was* evil in the sight of **the L**:	3068
14:25	according to the word of **the L** God of	3068
14:26	For **the L** saw the affliction of Israel, *that it*	3068
14:27	**the L** said not that *he* would blot out	3068
15: 3	*that* which *was* right in the sight of **the L**,	3068
15: 5	**the L** smote the king, so that he was a leper	3068
15: 9	*that* which *was* evil in the sight of **the L**,	3068
15:12	This *was* the word of **the L** which he spake	3068
15:18	*that* which *was* evil in the sight of **the L**:	3068
15:24	*that* which *was* evil in the sight of **the L**:	3068
15:28	*that* which *was* evil in the sight of **the L**:	3068
15:34	*that* which *was* right in the sight of **the L**:	3068
15:35	built the higher gate of the house of **the L**.	3068
15:37	In those days **the L** began to send against	3068
16: 2	*was* right in the sight of **the L** his God,	3068
16: 3	whom **the L** cast out from before	3068
16: 8	gold that was found *in* the house of **the L**,	3068
16:14	which *was* before **the L**, from the forefront	3068
16:14	between the altar and the house of **the L**,	3068
16:18	turned he *from* the house of **the L** for	3068
17: 2	*that* which *was* evil in the sight of **the L**,	3068
17: 7	Israel had sinned against **the L** their God,	3068
17: 8	whom **the L** cast out from before	3068
17: 9	that *were* not right against **the L** their God,	3068
17:11	as *did* the heathen whom **the L** carried	3068
17:11	wrought wicked things to provoke **the L** to	3068
17:12	whereof **the L** had said unto them,	3068
17:13	Yet **the L** testified against Israel, and	3068
17:14	that did not believe in **the L** their God.	3068
17:15	*concerning* whom **the L** had charged them,	3068
17:16	they left all the commandments of **the L**	3068
17:17	themselves to do evil in the sight of **the L**,	3068
17:18	Therefore **the L** was very angry with Israel,	3068
17:19	not the commandments of **the L** their God,	3068
17:20	**the L** rejected all the seed of Israel, and	3068
17:21	drave Israel from following **the L**,	3068
17:23	Until **the L** removed Israel out of his sight,	3068
17:25	dwelling there, *that* they feared not **the L**:	3068
17:25	therefore **the L** sent lions among them,	3068
17:28	taught them how they should fear **the L**.	3068
17:32	So they feared **the L**, and made unto	3068
17:33	They feared **the L**, and served their own	3068
17:34	they fear not **the L**, neither do they after	3068
17:34	commandment which **the L** commanded	3068
17:35	With whom **the L** had made a covenant,	3068
17:36	**the L**, who brought you up out of the land	3068
17:39	**the L** your God ye shall fear; and he shall	3068
17:41	So these nations feared **the L**, and served	3068
18: 3	*that* which *was* right in the sight of **the L**,	3068
18: 5	He trusted in **the L** God of Israel; so	3068
18: 6	For he clave to **the L**, *and* departed not	3068
18: 6	which **the L** commanded Moses.	3068
18: 7	**the L** was with him; *and* he prospered	3068
18:12	Because they obeyed not the voice of **the L**	3068
18:12	all that Moses the servant of **the L**	3068
18:15	silver that was found *in* the house of **the L**,	3068
18:16	*gold from* the doors of the temple of **the L**,	3068
18:22	ye say unto me, We trust in **the L** our God:	3068
18:25	Am I now come up without **the L** against	3068
18:25	**The L** said to me, Go up against this land,	3068
18:30	let Hezekiah make you trust in **the L**,	3068
18:30	**The L** will surely deliver us, and this city	3068

2Ki	18:32	saying, **The L** will deliver us.	3068
	18:35	that **the L** should deliver Jerusalem out of	3068
	19: 1	and went *into* the house of **the L.**	3068
	19: 4	It may be **the L** thy God will hear all	3068
	19: 4	will reprove the words which **the L** thy	3068
	19: 6	ye say to your master, Thus saith **the L,**	3068
	19:14	Hezekiah went up *into* the house of **the L,**	3068
	19:14	of the LORD, and spread it before **the L.**	3068
	19:15	Hezekiah prayed before **the L,** and said,	3068
	19:15	said, O **L** God of Israel, which dwellest	3068
	19:16	**L,** bow down thine ear, and hear: open,	3068
	19:16	open, **L,** thine eyes, and see: and hear	3068
	19:17	Of a truth, **L,** the kings of Assyria have	3068
	19:19	O **L** our God, I beseech thee,	3068
	19:19	earth may know that thou *art* **the L** God,	3068
	19:20	Thus saith **the L** God of Israel,	3068
	19:21	This *is* the word that **the L** hath spoken	3068
	19:31	the zeal of **the L** *of hosts* shall do this.	3068
	19:32	Therefore thus saith **the L** concerning	3068
	19:33	shall not come into this city, saith **the L.**	3068
	19:35	that the angel of **the L** went out, and	3068
	20: 1	said unto him, Thus saith **the L,** Set thine	3068
	20: 2	to the wall, and prayed unto **the L,** saying,	3068
	20: 3	I beseech thee, O **L,** remember now how I	3068
	20: 4	that the word of **the L** came to him, saying,	3068
	20: 5	Thus saith **the L,** the God of David thy	3068
	20: 5	thou shalt go up *unto* the house of **the L.**	3068
	20: 8	What *shall be* the sign that **the L** will heal	3068
	20: 8	*that* I shall go up *into* the house of **the L**	3068
	20: 9	This sign shalt thou have of **the L,**	3068
	20: 9	that **the L** will do the thing that he hath	3068
	20:11	Isaiah the prophet cried unto **the L:** and	3068
	20:16	unto Hezekiah, Hear the word of **the L.**	3068
	20:17	nothing shall be left, saith **the L.**	3068
	20:19	Good *is* the word of **the L** which thou hast	3068
	21: 2	*that* which *was* evil in the sight of **the L,**	3068
	21: 2	whom **the L** cast out before the children of	3068
	21: 4	he built altars in the house of **the L,**	3068
	21: 4	of which **the L** said, In Jerusalem will I put	3068
	21: 5	in the two courts of the house of **the L.**	3068
	21: 6	much wickedness in the sight of **the L,**	3068
	21: 7	of which **the L** said to David, and	3068
	21: 9	**the L** destroyed before the children of	3068
	21:10	**the L** spake by his servants the prophets,	3068
	21:12	Therefore thus saith **the L** God of Israel,	3068
	21:16	*that* which *was* evil in the sight of **the L.**	3068
	21:20	*that* which *was* evil in the sight of **the L,**	3068
	21:22	he forsook **the L** God of his fathers, and	3068
	21:22	and walked not in the way of **the L.**	3068
	22: 2	*that* which *was* right in the sight of **the L,**	3068
	22: 3	the scribe, *to* the house of **the L,** saying,	3068
	22: 4	which is brought *into* the house of **the L,**	3068
	22: 5	have the oversight of the house of **the L:**	3068
	22: 5	of the work which *is* in the house of **the L,**	3068
	22: 8	the book of the law in the house of **the L.**	3068
	22: 9	have the oversight *of* the house of **the L.**	3068
	22:13	inquire of **the L** for me, and for the people,	3068
	22:13	for great *is* the wrath of **the L** that is	3068
	22:15	unto them, Thus saith **the L** God of Israel,	3068
	22:16	Thus saith **the L,** Behold, I will bring evil	3068
	22:18	Judah which sent you to inquire of **the L,**	3068
	22:18	say to him, Thus saith **the L** God of Israel,	3068
	22:19	thou hast humbled thyself before **the L,**	3068
	22:19	I also have heard *thee,* saith **the L.**	3068
	23: 2	the king went up *into* the house of **the L,**	3068
	23: 2	which was found in the house of **the L.**	3068
	23: 3	made a covenant before **the L,** to walk after	3068
	23: 3	to walk after **the L,** and to keep his	3068
	23: 4	to bring forth out of the temple of **the L** all	3068
	23: 6	out the grove from the house of **the L,**	3068
	23: 7	that *were* by the house of **the L,** where	3068
	23: 9	not up to the altar of **the L** in Jerusalem,	3068
	23:11	at the entering in of the house of **the L,**	3068
	23:12	in the two courts of the house of **the L,**	3068
	23:16	according to the word of **the L** which	3068
	23:19	Israel had made to provoke *the L* to anger,	NIH
	23:21	Keep the passover unto **the L** your God,	3068
	23:23	*wherein* this passover was holden to **the L**	3068
	23:24	the priest found *in* the house of **the L.**	3068
	23:25	that turned to **the L** with all his heart, and	3068
	23:26	Notwithstanding **the L** turned not from	3068
	23:27	**the L** said, I will remove Judah also out of	3068
	23:32	*that* which *was* evil in the sight of **the L,**	3068
	23:37	*that* which *was* evil in the sight of **the L,**	3068
	24: 2	**the L** sent against him bands of	3068
	24: 2	destroy it, according to the word of **the L,**	3068
	24: 3	Surely at the commandment of **the L** came	3068
	24: 4	which **the L** would not pardon.	3068
	24: 9	*that* which *was* evil in the sight of **the L,**	3068
	24:13	all the treasures of the house of **the L,**	3068
	24:13	of Israel had made in the temple of **the L,**	3068
	24:13	temple of the LORD, as **the L** had said.	3068
	24:19	*that* which *was* evil in the sight of **the L,**	3068
	24:20	For through the anger of **the L** it came to	3068
	25: 9	he burnt the house of **the L,** and the king's	3068
	25:13	of brass that *were in* the house of **the L,**	3068
	25:13	brasen sea that *was* in the house of **the L,**	3068
	25:16	Solomon had made for the house of **the L;**	3068
1Ch	2: 3	of Judah, was evil in the sight of **the L;**	3068
	6:15	Jehozadak went *into captivity,* when **the L**	3068
	6:31	the service of song *in* the house of **the L,**	3068
	6:32	until Solomon had built the house of **the L**	3068
	9:19	their fathers, *being* over the host of **the L,**	3068
	9:20	them in time past, *and* **the L** *was* with him.	3068
	9:23	oversight of the gates of the house of **the L,**	3068
	10:13	which he committed against **the L,**	3068
	10:13	*even* against the word of **the L,** which he	3068
	10:14	inquired not of **the L:** therefore he slew	3068
	11: 2	**the L** thy God said unto thee, Thou shalt	3068
	11: 3	with them in Hebron before **the L;**	3068
	11: 3	according to the word of **the L** by Samuel.	3068
	11: 9	greater: for **the L** of hosts *was* with him.	3068
	11:10	according to the word of **the L** concerning	3068
	11:14	**the L** saved *them by* a great deliverance.	3068
	11:18	not drink *of* it, but poured it out to **the L,**	3068
	12:23	to him, according to the word of **the L.**	3068
	13: 2	unto you, and *that it be* of **the L** our God,	3068
	13: 6	to bring up thence the ark of God **the L,**	3068
	13:10	the anger of **the L** was kindled against	3068
	13:11	**the L** had made a breach upon Uzza:	3068
	13:14	**the L** blessed the house of Obed-edom,	3068
	14: 2	David perceived that **the L** had confirmed	3068
	14:10	**the L** said unto him, Go up; for I will	3068
	14:17	**the L** brought the fear of him upon all	3068
	15: 2	for them hath **the L** chosen to carry the ark	3068
	15: 3	to bring up the ark of **the L** unto his place,	3068
	15:12	that you may bring up the ark of **the L** God	3068
	15:13	**the L** our God made a breach upon us,	3068
	15:14	to bring up the ark of **the L** God of Israel.	3068
	15:15	according to the word of **the L.**	3068
	15:25	**the L** out of the house of Obed-edom with	3068
	15:26	that bare the ark of the covenant of **the L,**	3068
	15:28	ark of the covenant of **the L** with shouting,	3068
	15:29	*as* the ark of the covenant of **the L** came to	3068
	16: 2	he blessed the people in the name of **the L.**	3068
	16: 4	Levites to minister before the ark of **the L,**	3068
	16: 4	and to thank and praise **the L** God of Israel:	3068
	16: 7	to thank **the L** into the hand of Asaph	3068
	16: 8	Give thanks unto **the L,** call upon his	3068
	16:10	let the heart of them rejoice that seek **the L.**	3068
	16:11	Seek **the L** and his strength, seek his face	3068
	16:14	He *is* **the L** our God; his judgments *are* in	3068
	16:23	Sing unto **the L,** all the earth; shew forth	3068
	16:25	For great *is* **the L,** and greatly to be	3068
	16:26	*are* idols: but **the L** made the heavens.	3068
	16:28	Give unto **the L,** ye kindreds of the people,	3068
	16:28	give unto **the L** glory and strength.	3068
	16:29	Give unto **the L** the glory due unto his	3068
	16:29	worship **the L** in the beauty of holiness.	3068
	16:31	say among the nations, **The L** reigneth.	3068
	16:33	the wood sing out at the presence of **the L,**	3068
	16:34	O give thanks unto **the L;** for *he is* good;	3068
	16:36	Blessed *be* **the L** God of Israel for ever and	3068
	16:36	the people said, Amen, and praised **the L.**	3068
	16:37	the ark of the covenant of **the L** Asaph	3068
	16:39	before the tabernacle of **the L** in the high	3068
	16:40	To offer burnt offerings unto **the L** upon	3068
	16:40	to all that is written in the law of **the L,**	3068
	16:41	to give thanks to **the L,** because his mercy	3068
	17: 1	the ark of the covenant of **the L** *remaineth*	3068
	17: 4	tell David my servant, Thus saith **the L,**	3068
	17: 7	Thus saith **the L** of hosts, I took thee from	3068
	17:10	Furthermore I tell thee that **the L** will build	3068
	17:16	David the king came and sat before **the L,**	3068
	17:16	*am* I, O **L** God, and what *is* mine house,	3068
	17:17	estate of a man of high degree, O **L** God.	3068
	17:19	O **L,** for thy servant's sake, and	3068
	17:20	O **L,** *there is* none like thee, neither *is there*	3068

1Ch 17:22 for ever; and thou, **L**, becamest their God. 3068
17:23 Therefore now, **L**, let the thing that thou 3068
17:24 saying, **The L** of hosts *is* the God of Israel, 3068
17:26 now, **L**, thou *art* God, and hast promised 3068
17:27 O **L**, and *it shall be* blessed for ever. 3068
18: 6 Thus **the L** preserved David whithersoever 3068
18:11 also king David dedicated unto **the L**, 3068
18:13 Thus **the L** preserved David whithersoever 3068
19:13 let **the L** do *that* which *is* good in his sight. 3068
21: 3 **The L** make his people an hundred times 3068
21: 9 **the L** spake unto Gad, David's seer, 3068
21:10 and tell David, saying, Thus saith **the L**, 3068
21:11 unto him, Thus saith **the L**, Choose thee 3068
21:12 or else three days the sword of **the L**, 3068
21:12 the angel of **the L** destroying throughout all 3068
21:13 let me fall now into the hand of **the L**; 3068
21:14 So **the L** sent pestilence upon Israel: and 3068
21:15 **the L** beheld, and he repented him of 3068
21:15 the angel of **the L** stood by 3068
21:16 saw the angel of **the L** stand between 3068
21:17 O **L** my God, be on me, and on my father's 3068
21:18 the angel of **the L** commanded Gad to say 3068
21:18 set up an altar unto **the L** in 3068
21:19 which he spake in the name of **the L**. 3068
21:22 that I may build an altar therein unto **the L**: 3068
21:24 I will not take *that* which *is* thine for **the L**, 3068
21:26 David built there an altar unto **the L**, and 3068
21:26 and peace offerings, and called upon **the L**; 3068
21:27 **the L** commanded the angel; and he put up 3068
21:28 At that time when David saw that **the L** 3068
21:29 For the tabernacle of **the L**, which Moses 3068
21:30 of the sword of the angel of **the L**. 3068
22: 1 This *is* the house of **the L** God, and this *is* 3068
22: 5 the house *that is* to be builded for **the L** 3068
22: 6 charged him to build a house for **the L** God 3068
22: 7 a house unto the name of **the L** my God: 3068
22: 8 the word of **the L** came to me, saying, 3068
22:11 Now, my son, **the L** be with thee; and 3068
22:11 and build the house of **the L** thy God, 3068
22:12 Only **the L** give thee wisdom and 3068
22:12 that *thou* mayest keep the law of **the L** thy 3068
22:13 judgments which **the L** charged Moses 3068
22:14 **the L** an hundred thousand talents *of* gold, 3068
22:16 and be doing, and **the L** be with thee. 3068
22:18 *Is* not **the L** your God with you? and 3068
22:18 the land is subdued before **the L**, and 3068
22:19 and your soul to seek **the L** your God; 3068
22:19 and build ye the sanctuary of **the L** God, 3068
22:19 to bring the ark of the covenant of **the L**, 3068
22:19 that is *to be* built to the name of **the L**. 3068
23: 4 set forward the work of the house of **the L**; 3068
23: 5 four thousand praised **the L** with 3068
23:13 sons for ever, to burn incense before **the L**, 3068
23:24 work for the service of the house of **the L**, 3068
23:25 **The L** God of Israel hath given rest unto 3068
23:28 Aaron for the service of the house of **the L**, 3068
23:30 every morning to thank and praise **the L**, 3068
23:31 to offer all burnt sacrifices unto **the L** in 3068
23:31 unto them, continually before **the L**: 3068
23:32 in the service of the house of **the L**. 3068
24:19 service to come into the house of **the L**, 3068
24:19 as **the L** God of Israel had commanded 3068
25: 3 a harp, to give thanks and to praise **the L**. 3068
25: 6 their father for song *in* the house of **the L**, 3068
25: 7 *that were* instructed in the songs of **the L**, 3068
26:12 to minister in the house of **the L**. 3068
26:22 over the treasures of the house of **the L**. 3068
26:27 dedicate to maintain the house of **the L**. 3068
26:30 westward in all the business of **the L**, 3068
27:23 **the L** had said *he* would increase Israel like 3068
28: 2 of rest for the ark of the covenant of **the L**, 3068
28: 4 Howbeit **the L** God of Israel chose me 3068
28: 5 (for **the L** hath given me many sons,) 3068
28: 5 throne of the kingdom of **the L** over Israel. 3068
28: 8 sight of all Israel the congregation of **the L**, 3068
28: 8 seek for all the commandments of **the L** 3068
28: 9 for **the L** searcheth all hearts, and 3068
28:10 for **the L** hath chosen thee to build a house 3068
28:12 of the courts of the house of **the L**, and 3068
28:13 work of the service of the house of **the L**, 3068
28:13 the vessels of service in the house of **the L**. 3068
28:18 covered the ark of the covenant of **the L**. 3068
28:19 All *this, said David,* **the L** made me 3068
28:20 for **the L** God, *even* my God, *will be* with 3068
28:20 work for the service of the house of **the L**. 3068
29: 1 palace *is* not for man, but for **the L** God. 3068
29: 5 consecrate his service *this* day unto **the L**? 3068
29: 8 *them* to the treasure of the house of **the L**, 3068
29: 9 heart they offered willingly to **the L**: 3068
29:10 Wherefore David blessed **the L** before all 3068
29:10 **L** God of Israel our father, for ever and 3068
29:11 Thine, O **L**, *is* the greatness, and the power, 3068
29:11 O **L**, and *thou* art exalted as head above all. 3068
29:16 O **L** our God, all this store that we have 3068
29:18 O **L** God of Abraham, Isaac, and of Israel, 3068
29:20 Now bless **the L** your God. 3068
29:20 all the congregation blessed **the L** God of 3068
29:20 and worshipped **the L**, and the king. 3068
29:21 they sacrificed sacrifices unto **the L**, and 3068
29:21 offered burnt offerings unto **the L**, on 3068
29:22 drink before **the L** on that day with great 3068
29:22 anointed *him* unto **the L** to be the chief 3068
29:23 Solomon sat on the throne of **the L** as king 3068
29:25 **the L** magnified Solomon exceedingly in 3068
2Ch 1: 1 **the L** his God *was* with him, and 3068
1: 3 which Moses the servant of **the L** had 3068
1: 5 he put before the tabernacle of **the L**: 3068
1: 6 up thither to the brasen altar before **the L**, 3068
1: 9 Now, O **L** God, let thy promise unto David 3068
2: 1 to build a house for the name of **the L**, 3068
2: 4 I build a house to the name of **the L** my 3068
2: 4 and on the solemn feasts of **the L** our God. 3068
2:11 Because **the L** hath loved his people, 3068
2:12 Blessed *be* **the L** God of Israel, that made 3068
2:12 that might build a house for **the L**, and 3068
3: 1 Solomon began to build the house of **the L** 3068
3: 1 where *the L* appeared unto David his father, NIH
4:16 for the house of **the L** *of* bright brass. 3068
5: 1 made for the house of **the L** was finished: 3068
5: 2 to bring up the ark of the covenant of **the L** 3068
5: 7 ark of the covenant of **the L** unto his place, 3068
5:10 when **the L** made *a covenant* with 3068
5:13 to be heard in praising and thanking **the L**; 3068
5:13 and praised **the L**, *saying,* For *he is* good; 3068
5:13 *with* a cloud, *even* the house of **the L**; 3068
5:14 for the glory of **the L** had filled the house 3068
6: 1 **The L** hath said that *he* would dwell in 3068
6: 4 he said, Blessed *be* **the L** God of Israel, 3068
6: 7 house for the name of **the L** God of Israel. 3068
6: 8 **the L** said to David my father, 3068
6:10 **The L** therefore hath performed his word 3068
6:10 as **the L** promised, and have built the house 3068
6:10 have built the house for the name of **the L** 3068
6:11 the ark, wherein *is* the covenant of **the L**, 3068
6:12 he stood before the altar of **the L** in 3068
6:14 said, O **L** God of Israel, *there is* no God 3068
6:16 Now therefore, O **L** God of Israel, 3068
6:17 Now then, O **L** God of Israel, let thy word 3068
6:19 to his supplication, O **L** my God, 3068
6:41 Now therefore arise, O **L** God, into thy 3068
6:41 let thy priests, O **L** God, be clothed *with* 3068
6:42 O **L** God, turn not away the face of thine 3068
7: 1 and the glory of **the L** filled the house. 3068
7: 2 could not enter into the house of **the L**, 3068
7: 2 the glory of **the L** had filled the LORD'S 3068
7: 3 and the glory of **the L** upon the house, 3068
7: 3 worshipped, and praised **the L**, *saying,* For 3068
7: 4 the people offered sacrifices before **the L**. 3068
7: 6 also with instruments of musick of **the L**, 3068
7: 6 David the king had made to praise **the L**, 3068
7: 7 court that *was* before the house of **the L**: 3068
7:10 merry in heart for the goodness that **the L** 3068
7:11 Thus Solomon finished the house of **the L**, 3068
7:11 heart to make in the house of **the L**, 3068
7:12 **the L** appeared to Solomon by night, and 3068
7:21 Why hath **the L** done thus unto this land, 3068
7:22 Because they forsook **the L** God of their 3068
8: 1 Solomon had built the house of **the L**, 3068
8:11 whereunto the ark of **the L** hath come. 3068
8:12 Solomon offered burnt offerings unto **the L** 3068
8:12 unto the LORD on the altar of **the L**, 3068
8:16 day of the foundation of the house of **the L**, 3068
8:16 *So* the house of **the L** was perfected. 3068
9: 4 which he went up *into* the house of **the L**; 3068
9: 8 Blessed be **the L** thy God, which delighted 3068
9: 8 on his throne, to be king for **the L** thy God: 3068
9:11 algum trees terraces to the house of **the L**, 3068
10:15 of God, that **the L** might perform his word, 3068

2Ch 11: 2 the word of **the L** came to Shemaiah 3068
11: 4 Thus saith **the L**, Ye shall not go up, 3068
11: 4 they obeyed the words of **the L**, and 3068
11:14 executing the priest's office unto **the L**: 3068
11:16 **the L** God of Israel came *to* Jerusalem, 3068
11:16 to sacrifice unto **the L** God of their fathers. 3068
12: 1 he forsook the law of **the L**, and all Israel 3068
12: 2 they had transgressed against **the L**, 3068
12: 5 and said unto them, Thus saith **the L**, 3068
12: 6 and they said, **The L** *is* righteous. 3068
12: 7 when **the L** saw that they humbled 3068
12: 7 the word of **the L** came to Shemaiah, 3068
12: 9 away the treasures of the house of **the L**, 3068
12:11 the king entered *into* the house of **the L**, 3068
12:12 the wrath of **the L** turned from him, 3068
12:13 the city which **the L** had chosen out of all 3068
12:14 he prepared not his heart to seek **the L**. 3068
13: 5 Ought you not to know that **the L** God of 3068
13: 8 of **the L** in the hand of the sons of David; 3068
13: 9 Have ye not cast out the priests of **the L**, 3068
13:10 **the L** *is* our God, and we have not forsaken 3068
13:10 the priests, which minister unto **the L**, 3068
13:11 they burn unto **the L** every morning 3068
13:11 for we keep the charge of **the L** our God; 3068
13:12 fight ye not against **the L** God of your 3068
13:14 they cried unto **the L**, and the priests 3068
13:18 they relied upon **the L** God of their fathers. 3068
13:20 and **the L** struck him, and he died. 3068
14: 2 and right in the eyes of **the L** his God: 3068
14: 4 commanded Judah to seek **the L** God of 3068
14: 6 because **the L** had given him rest. 3068
14: 7 because we have sought **the L** our God, 3068
14:11 Asa cried unto **the L** his God, and said, 3068
14:11 said, **L**, *it is* nothing with thee to help, 3068
14:11 help us, O **L** our God; for we rest on thee, 3068
14:11 O **L**, thou *art* our God; let not man prevail 3068
14:12 So **the L** smote the Ethiopians before Asa, 3068
14:13 for they were destroyed before **the L**, and 3068
14:14 for the fear of **the L** came upon them: 3068
15: 2 **The L** *is* with you, while ye be with him; 3068
15: 4 trouble did turn unto **the L** God of Israel, 3068
15: 8 renewed the altar of **the L**, that *was* before 3068
15: 8 that *was* before the porch of **the L**. 3068
15: 9 when they saw that **the L** his God *was* with 3068
15:11 they offered unto **the L** the same time, 3068
15:12 they entered into a covenant to seek **the L** 3068
15:13 That whosoever would not seek **the L** God 3068
15:14 they sware unto **the L** with a loud voice, 3068
15:15 and **the L** gave them rest round about. 3068
16: 2 out of the treasures of the house of **the L** 3068
16: 7 not relied on **the L** thy God, therefore is 3068
16: 8 yet, because thou didst rely on **the L**, 3068
16: 9 For the eyes of **the L** run to and 3068
16:12 yet in his disease he sought not *to* **the L**, 3068
17: 3 **the L** was with Jehoshaphat, because 3068
17: 4 sought to the *L* God of his father, and NIH
17: 5 Therefore **the L** stablished the kingdom in 3068
17: 6 his heart was lift up in the ways of **the L**: 3068
17: 9 *had* the book of the law of **the L** with them, 3068
17:10 the fear of **the L** fell upon all the kingdoms 3068
17:16 who willingly offered himself unto **the L**; 3068
18: 4 I pray thee, at the word of **the L** to day. 3068
18: 6 *Is there* not here a prophet of **the L** besides, 3068
18: 7 by whom *we* may inquire of **the L**: 3068
18:10 said, Thus saith **the L**, With these thou 3068
18:11 for **the L** shall deliver *it* into the hand of 3068
18:13 Micaiah said, *As* **the L** liveth, even what 3068
18:15 but the truth to me in the name of **the L**? 3068
18:16 **the L** said, These have no master; let them 3068
18:18 he said, Therefore hear the word of **the L**; 3068
18:18 I saw **the L** sitting upon his throne, and 3068
18:19 **the L** said, Who shall entice Ahab king of 3068
18:20 stood before **the L**, and said, I will entice 3068
18:20 And **the L** said unto him, Wherewith? 3068
18:21 *the L* said, Thou shalt entice *him*, and NIH
18:22 **the L** hath put a lying spirit in the mouth of 3068
18:22 and **the L** hath spoken evil against thee. 3068
18:23 Which way went the spirit of **the L** from 3068
18:27 in peace, *then* hath not **the L** spoken by me. 3068
18:31 cried out, and **the L** helped him; 3068
19: 2 the ungodly, and love them that hate **the L**? 3068
19: 2 *is* wrath upon thee from before **the L**. 3068
19: 4 brought them back unto **the L** God of their 3068
19: 6 for ye judge not for man, but for **the L**, 3068
19: 7 Wherefore now let the fear of **the L** be 3068
19: 7 do *it*: for *there is* no iniquity with **the L** our 3068
19: 8 for the judgment of **the L**, and 3068
19: 9 Thus shall ye do in the fear of **the L**, 3068
19:10 them that they trespass not against **the L**, 3068
19:11 priest *is* over you in all matters of **the L**; 3068
19:11 and **the L** shall be with the good. 3068
20: 3 set himself to seek **the L**, and proclaimed a 3068
20: 4 themselves together, to ask *help* of **the L**: 3068
20: 4 the cities of Judah they came to seek **the L**. 3068
20: 5 and Jerusalem, in the house of **the L**, 3068
20: 6 said, O **L** God of our fathers, *art* not thou 3068
20:13 all Judah stood before **the L**, with their 3068
20:14 came the spirit of **the L** in the midst of 3068
20:15 Thus saith **the L** unto you, 3068
20:17 and see the salvation of **the L** with you, 3068
20:17 against them: for **the L** *will be* with you. 3068
20:18 inhabitants of Jerusalem fell before **the L**, 3068
20:18 fell before the LORD, worshipping **the L**. 3068
20:19 stood up to praise **the L** God of Israel with 3068
20:20 Believe in **the L** your God, so shall you be 3068
20:21 he appointed singers unto **the L**, and 3068
20:21 before the army, and to say, Praise **the L**; 3068
20:22 **the L** set ambushments against the children 3068
20:26 of Berachah; for there they blessed **the L**: 3068
20:27 for **the L** had made them to rejoice over 3068
20:28 harps and trumpets unto the house of **the L**. 3068
20:29 when they had heard that **the L** fought 3068
20:32 *that* which *was* right in the sight of **the L**. 3068
20:37 with Ahaziah, **the L** hath broken thy works. 3068
21: 6 *that* which *was* evil in the eyes of **the L**. 3068
21: 7 Howbeit **the L** would not destroy the house 3068
21:10 he had forsaken **the L** God of his fathers. 3068
21:12 Thus saith **the L** God of David thy father, 3068
21:14 *with* a great plague will **the L** smite thy 3068
21:16 Moreover **the L** stirred up against Jehoram 3068
21:18 after all this **the L** smote him in his bowels 3068
22: 4 Wherefore he did evil in the sight of **the L**, 3068
22: 7 whom **the L** had anointed to cut off 3068
22: 9 who sought **the L** with all his heart. 3068
23: 3 as **the L** hath said of the sons of David. 3068
23: 5 *shall be* in the courts of the house of **the L**. 3068
23: 6 let none come *into* the house of **the L**, 3068
23: 6 the people shall keep the watch of **the L**. 3068
23:12 came to the people *into* the house of **the L**: 3068
23:14 Slay her not *in* the house of **the L**. 3068
23:18 **the L** by the hand of the priests the Levites, 3068
23:18 David had distributed in the house of **the L**, 3068
23:18 to offer the burnt offerings of **the L**, as it is 3068
23:19 porters at the gates of the house of **the L**, 3068
23:20 down the king from the house of **the L**: 3068
24: 2 of **the L** all the days of Jehoiada the priest. 3068
24: 4 was minded to repair the house of **the L**. 3068
24: 6 of Moses the servant of **the L**, 3068
24: 7 of **the L** did they bestow upon Baalim. 3068
24: 8 it without at the gate of the house of **the L**. 3068
24: 9 to bring in to **the L** the collection that 3068
24:12 work of the service of the house of **the L**, 3068
24:12 and carpenters to repair the house of **the L**, 3068
24:12 and brass to mend the house of **the L**. 3068
24:14 were made vessels for the house of **the L**, 3068
24:14 **the L** continually all the days of Jehoiada. 3068
24:18 they left the house of **the L** God of their 3068
24:19 to them, to bring them again unto **the L**; 3068
24:20 transgress ye the commandments of **the L**, 3068
24:20 because ye have forsaken **the L**, he hath 3068
24:21 the king in the court of the house of **the L**. 3068
24:22 he said, **The L** look upon *it*, and require *it*. 3068
24:24 **the L** delivered a very great host into their 3068
24:24 they had forsaken **the L** God of their 3068
25: 2 *that* which *was* right in the sight of **the L**, 3068
25: 4 where **the L** commanded, saying, 3068
25: 7 for **the L** *is* not with Israel, *to wit, with* all 3068
25: 9 **The L** is able to give thee much more than 3068
25:15 Wherefore the anger of **the L** was kindled 3068
25:27 **the L** they made a conspiracy against him 3068
26: 4 *that* which *was* right in the sight of **the L**, 3068
26: 5 as long as he sought **the L**, God made him 3068
26:16 for he transgressed against **the L** his God, 3068
26:16 went into the temple of **the L** to burn 3068
26:17 with him fourscore priests of **the L**, 3068
26:18 to burn incense unto **the L**, but to 3068
26:18 *shall it be* for thine honour from **the L** God. 3068
26:19 before the priests in the house of **the L**, 3068

2Ch 26:20	to go out, because **the L** had smitten him.	3068
26:21	for he was cut off from the house of **the L**:	3068
27: 2	*that* which *was* right in the sight of **the L**,	3068
27: 2	he entered not into the temple of **the L**.	3068
27: 3	built the high gate of the house of **the L**,	3068
27: 6	he prepared his ways before **the L** his God.	3068
28: 1	*that* which *was* right in the sight of **the L**,	3068
28: 3	**the L** had cast out before the children of	3068
28: 5	Wherefore **the L** his God delivered him	3068
28: 6	they had forsaken **the L** God of their	3068
28: 9	a prophet of **the L** was there, whose name	3068
28: 9	**the L** God of your fathers was wroth with	3068
28:10	with you, sins against **the L** your God?	3068
28:11	for the fierce wrath of **the L** *is* upon you.	3068
28:13	**the L** *already,* ye intend to add *more* to our	3068
28:19	For **the L** brought Judah low because	3068
28:19	and transgressed sore against **the L**.	3068
28:21	away a portion *out* of the house of **the L**,	3068
28:22	did he trespass yet more against **the L**:	3068
28:24	and shut up the doors of the house of **the L**,	3068
28:25	provoked to anger **the L** God of his fathers.	3068
29: 2	*that* which *was* right in the sight of **the L**,	3068
29: 3	opened the doors of the house of **the L**, and	3068
29: 5	sanctify the house of **the L** God of your	3068
29: 6	*was* evil in the eyes of **the L** our God,	3068
29: 6	their faces from the habitation of **the L**,	3068
29: 8	Wherefore the wrath of **the L** was upon	3068
29:10	make a covenant with **the L** God of Israel,	3068
29:11	for **the L** hath chosen you to stand before	3068
29:15	by the words of **the L**, to cleanse the house	3068
29:15	the LORD, to cleanse the house of **the L**.	3068
29:16	into the inner part *of* the house of **the L**,	3068
29:16	**the L** into the court of the house of	3068
29:16	into the court of the house of **the L**.	3068
29:17	the month came they to the porch of **the L**:	3068
29:17	they sanctified the house of **the L** in eight	3068
29:18	We have cleansed all the house of **the L**,	3068
29:19	behold, they *are* before the altar of **the L**.	3068
29:20	the city, and went up *to* the house of **the L**.	3068
29:21	Aaron to offer *them* on the altar of **the L**.	3068
29:25	he set the Levites *in* the house of **the L**	3068
29:25	*was* the commandment of **the L** by his	3068
29:27	the song of **the L** began *also* with	3068
29:30	praise unto **the L** with the words of David,	3068
29:31	ye have consecrated yourselves unto **the L**,	3068
29:31	and thank offerings into the house of **the L**.	3068
29:32	all these *were* for a burnt offering to **the L**.	3068
29:35	So the service of the house of **the L** was set	3068
30: 1	that *they* should come to the house of **the L**	3068
30: 1	to keep the passover unto **the L** God of	3068
30: 5	unto **the L** God of Israel at Jerusalem:	3068
30: 6	turn again unto **the L** God of Abraham,	3068
30: 7	which trespassed against **the L** God of their	3068
30: 8	*but* yield yourselves unto **the L**,	3068
30: 8	serve **the L** your God, that the fierceness of	3068
30: 9	For if ye turn again unto **the L**,	3068
30: 9	for **the L** your God *is* gracious and	3068
30:12	and of the princes, by the word of **the L**.	3068
30:15	the burnt offerings *into* the house of **the L**.	3068
30:17	*was* not clean, to sanctify *them* unto **the L**.	3068
30:18	**The** good **L** pardon every one	3068
30:19	heart to seek God, **the L** God of his fathers,	3068
30:20	**the L** hearkened to Hezekiah, and	3068
30:21	and the priests praised **the L** day by day,	3068
30:21	*singing* with loud instruments unto **the L**.	3068
30:22	that taught the good knowledge of **the L**:	3068
30:22	making confession to **the L** God of their	3068
31: 2	to praise in the gates of the tents of **the L**.	3068
31: 3	as it is written in the law of **the L**.	3068
31: 4	might be encouraged in the law of **the L**.	3068
31: 6	were consecrated unto **the L** their God,	3068
31: 8	they blessed **the L**, and his people Israel.	3068
31:10	bring the offerings *into* the house of **the L**,	3068
31:10	for **the L** hath blessed his people; and	3068
31:11	to prepare chambers in the house of **the L**;	3068
31:14	to distribute the oblations of **the L**, and	3068
31:16	one that entereth into the house of **the L**,	3068
31:20	and right and truth before **the L** his God.	3068
32: 8	but with us *is* **the L** our God to help us, and	3068
32:11	**The L** our God shall deliver us out of	3068
32:16	his servants spake yet *more* against **the L**	3068
32:17	He wrote also letters to rail on **the L** God	3068
32:21	**the L** sent an angel, which cut off all	3068
32:22	Thus **the L** saved Hezekiah and	3068
32:23	many brought gifts unto **the L** to	3068
32:24	sick to the death, and prayed unto **the L**:	3068
32:26	that the wrath of **the L** came not upon them	3068
33: 2	*that* which *was* evil in the sight of **the L**,	3068
33: 2	whom **the L** had cast out before	3068
33: 4	Also he built altars in the house of **the L**,	3068
33: 4	whereof **the L** had said, In Jerusalem shall	3068
33: 5	in the two courts of the house of **the L**.	3068
33: 6	he wrought much evil in the sight of **the L**,	3068
33: 9	whom **the L** had destroyed before	3068
33:10	**the L** spake to Manasseh, and to his	3068
33:11	Wherefore **the L** brought upon them	3068
33:12	he besought **the L** his God, and	3068
33:13	Manasseh knew that **the L** he *was* God.	3068
33:15	the idol out of the house of **the L**, and	3068
33:15	built in the mount of the house of **the L**,	3068
33:16	he repaired the altar of **the L**, and	3068
33:16	commanded Judah to serve **the L** God of	3068
33:17	high places, *yet* unto **the L** their God only.	3068
33:18	to him in the name of **the L** God of Israel,	3068
33:22	*that* which *was* evil in the sight of **the L**,	3068
33:23	humbled not himself before **the L**,	3068
34: 2	*that* which *was* right in the sight of **the L**,	3068
34: 8	to repair the house of **the L** his God.	3068
34:10	had the oversight of the house of **the L**,	3068
34:10	that wrought in the house of **the L**,	3068
34:14	that was brought *into* the house of **the L**,	3068
34:14	a book of the law of **the L** *given* by Moses.	3068
34:15	the book of the law in the house of **the L**.	3068
34:17	that was found in the house of **the L**,	3068
34:21	inquire of **the L** for me, and for them that	3068
34:21	for great *is* the wrath of **the L** that is	3068
34:21	our fathers have not kept the word of **the L**,	3068
34:23	Thus saith **the L** God of Israel,	3068
34:24	Thus saith **the L**, Behold, I will bring evil	3068
34:26	who sent you to inquire of **the L**, so	3068
34:26	Thus saith **the L** God of Israel *concerning*	3068
34:27	I have even heard *thee* also, saith **the L**.	3068
34:30	the king went up *into* the house of **the L**,	3068
34:30	that was found *in* the house of **the L**.	3068
34:31	made a covenant before **the L**, to walk after	3068
34:31	to walk after **the L**, and to keep his	3068
34:33	to serve, *even* to serve **the L** their God.	3068
34:33	they departed not from following **the L**,	3068
35: 1	kept a passover unto **the L** in Jerusalem:	3068
35: 2	them to the service of the house of **the L**,	3068
35: 3	all Israel, which were holy unto **the L**,	3068
35: 3	serve now **the L** your God, and his people	3068
35: 6	to the word of **the L** by the hand of Moses.	3068
35:12	to offer unto **the L**, as it is written in	3068
35:16	So all the service of **the L** was prepared	3068
35:16	burnt offerings upon the altar of **the L**,	3068
35:26	that which was written in the law of **the L**,	3068
36: 5	*was* evil in the sight of **the L** his God.	3068
36: 7	vessels of the house of **the L** to Babylon,	3068
36: 9	*that* which *was* evil in the sight of **the L**.	3068
36:10	the goodly vessels of the house of **the L**,	3068
36:12	*was* evil in the sight of **the L** his God,	3068
36:12	prophet *speaking* from the mouth of **the L**.	3068
36:13	hardened his heart from turning unto **the L**	3068
36:14	polluted the house of **the L** which he had	3068
36:15	**the L** God of their fathers sent to them by	3068
36:16	until the wrath of **the L** arose against his	3068
36:18	the treasures of the house of **the L**, and	3068
36:21	To fulfil the word of **the L** by the mouth of	3068
36:22	that the word of **the L** *spoken* by the mouth	3068
36:22	**the L** stirred up the spirit of Cyrus king of	3068
36:23	All the kingdoms of the earth hath **the L**	3068
36:23	**The L** his God *be* with him, and let him go	3068
Ezr 1: 1	that the word of **the L** by the mouth of	3068
1: 1	**the L** stirred up the spirit of Cyrus king of	3068
1: 2	**The L** God of heaven hath given me all	3068
1: 3	build the house of **the L** God of Israel,	3068
1: 5	to go up to build the house of **the L** which	3068
1: 7	forth the vessels of the house of **the L**,	3068
2:68	when they came to the house of **the L**	3068
3: 3	offered burnt offerings thereon unto **the L**,	3068
3: 5	of all the set feasts of **the L** that were	3068
3: 5	offered a freewill offering unto **the L**.	3068
3: 6	they to offer burnt offerings unto **the L**.	3068
3: 6	the foundation of the temple of **the L** was	3068
3: 8	set forward the work of the house of **the L**.	3068
3:10	laid the foundation of the temple of **the L**,	3068
3:10	to praise **the L**, after the ordinance of	3068

Ezr 3:11 in praising and giving thanks unto **the L**; 3068
3:11 when they praised **the L**, because 3068
3:11 the foundation of the house of **the L** was 3068
4: 1 the temple unto **the L** God of Israel; 3068
4: 3 we ourselves together will build unto **the L** 3068
6:21 to seek **the L** God of Israel, did eat, 3068
6:22 for **the L** had made them joyful, and 3068
7: 6 which **the L** God of Israel had given: 3068
7: 6 according to the hand of **the L** his God 3068
7:10 prepared his heart to seek the law of **the L**, 3068
7:11 the words of the commandments of **the L**, 3068
7:27 Blessed *be* **the L** God of our fathers, 3068
7:27 to beautify the house of **the L** which *is* in 3068
7:28 I was strengthened as the hand of **the L** my 3068
8:28 I said unto them, Ye *are* holy unto **the L**; 3068
8:28 the gold *are* a freewill offering unto **the L** 3068
8:29 *in* the chambers of the house of **the L**. 3068
8:35 all *this was* a burnt offering unto **the L**. 3068
9: 5 spread out my hands unto **the L** my God, 3068
9: 8 hath been *shewed* from **the L** our God, 3068
9:15 **O L** God of Israel, thou *art* righteous: 3068
10:11 make confession unto **the L** God of your 3068
Ne 1: 5 **O L** God of heaven, the great and terrible 3068
5:13 Amen, and praised **the L**. 3068
8: 1 which **the L** had commanded to Israel. 3068
8: 6 Ezra blessed **the L**, the great God. And all 3068
8: 6 worshipped **the L** *with their* faces to 3068
8: 9 *This* day *is* holy unto **the L** your God; 3068
8:10 for the joy of **the L** *is* your strength. 3068
8:14 they found written in the law which **the L** 3068
9: 3 read in the book of the law of **the L** their 3068
9: 3 and worshipped **the L** their God. 3068
9: 4 cried with a loud voice unto **the L** their 3068
9: 5 *and* bless **the L** your God for ever and ever: 3068
9: 6 Thou, *even* thou, *art* **L** alone; thou hast 3068
9: 7 Thou *art* **the L** the God, who didst choose 3068
10:29 do all the commandments of **the L** our 3068
10:34 to burn upon the altar of **the L** our God, 3068
10:35 year by year, unto the house of **the L**: 3068
Job 1: 6 came to present themselves before **the L**, 3068
1: 7 **the L** said unto Satan, Whence comest 3068
1: 7 Satan answered **the L**, and said, 3068
1: 8 **the L** said unto Satan, Hast thou considered 3068
1: 9 Satan answered **the L**, and said, Doth Job 3068
1:12 **the L** said unto Satan, Behold, all that he 3068
1:12 went forth from the presence of **the L**. 3068
1:21 **the L** gave, and the LORD hath taken 3068
1:21 **the L** hath taken *away;* blessed be the name 3068
1:21 taken *away;* blessed be the name of **the L**. 3068
2: 1 came to present themselves before **the L**, 3068
2: 1 them to present himself before **the L**. 3068
2: 2 **the L** said unto Satan, From whence 3068
2: 2 Satan answered **the L**, and said, 3068
2: 3 **the L** said unto Satan, Hast thou considered 3068
2: 4 Satan answered **the L**, and said, Skin for 3068
2: 6 **the L** said unto Satan, Behold, he *is* in 3068
2: 7 Satan forth from the presence of **the L**, 3068
12: 9 that the hand of **the L** hath wrought this? 3068
38: 1 **the L** answered Job out of the whirlwind, 3068
40: 1 Moreover **the L** answered Job, and said, 3068
40: 3 Then Job answered **the L**, and said, 3068
40: 6 answered **the L** unto Job out of 3068
42: 1 Then Job answered **the L**, and said, 3068
42: 7 that after **the L** had spoken these words 3068
42: 7 **the L** said to Eliphaz the Temanite, 3068
42: 9 did according as **the L** commanded them: 3068
42: 9 commanded them: **the L** also accepted Job. 3068
42:10 **the L** turned the captivity of Job, when he 3068
42:10 also **the L** gave Job twice as much as he 3068
42:11 comforted him over all the evil that **the L** 3068
42:12 So **the L** blessed the latter end of Job more 3068
Ps 1: 2 his delight *is* in the law of **the L**; and in his 3068
1: 6 For **the L** knoweth the way of 3068
2: 2 against **the L**, and against his anointed, 3068
2: 4 **the L** shall have them in derision. 3068
2: 7 **the L** hath said unto me, Thou *art* my Son; 3068
2:11 Serve **the L** with fear, and rejoice with 3068
3: 1 **L**, how are they increased that trouble me! 3068
3: 3 thou, **O L**, *art* a shield for me; my glory, 3068
3: 4 I cried unto **the L** *with* my voice, and 3068
3: 5 slept; I awaked; for **the L** sustained me. 3068
3: 7 Arise, **O L**; save me, O my God: for thou 3068
3: 8 Salvation *belongeth* unto **the L**: 3068
4: 3 know that **the L** hath set apart *him that is* 3068
4: 3 **the L** will hear when I call unto him. 3068
4: 5 and put your trust in **the L**. 3068
4: 6 **L**, lift thou up the light of thy countenance 3068
4: 8 for thou, **L**, only makest me dwell in safety. 3068
5: 1 Give ear to my words, **O L**, consider my 3068
5: 3 voice shalt thou hear *in* the morning, **O L**; 3068
5: 6 **the L** will abhor the bloody and 3068
5: 8 Lead me, **O L**, in thy righteousness because 3068
5:12 For thou, **L**, wilt bless the righteous; 3068
6: 1 **O L**, rebuke me not in thine anger, 3068
6: 2 Have mercy upon me, **O L**; for I *am* weak: 3068
6: 2 **O L**, heal me; for my bones are vexed. 3068
6: 3 also sore vexed: but thou, **O L**, how long? 3068
6: 4 Return, **O L**, deliver my soul: O save me 3068
6: 8 for **the L** hath heard the voice of my 3068
6: 9 **The L** hath heard my supplication; 3068
6: 9 **the L** will receive my prayer. 3068
7: T of David, which he sang unto **the L**, 3068
7: 1 **O L** my God, in thee do I put my trust: 3068
7: 3 **O L** my God, if I have done this; if there be 3068
7: 6 Arise, **O L**, in thine anger, lift up thyself 3068
7: 8 **The L** shall judge the people: judge me, 3068
7: 8 judge me, **O L**, according to my 3068
7:17 I will praise **the L** according to his 3068
7:17 will sing *praise* to the name of **the L** most 3068
8: 1 **O L** our Lord, how excellent *is* thy name in 3068
8: 9 **O L** our Lord, how excellent *is* thy name in 3068
9: 1 I will praise *thee,* **O L**, with my whole 3068
9: 7 **the L** shall endure for ever: he hath 3068
9: 9 **The L** also will be a refuge for 3068
9:10 for thou, **L**, hast not forsaken them that 3068
9:11 Sing *praises* to **the L**, which dwelleth in 3068
9:13 Have mercy upon me, **O L**; consider my 3068
9:16 **The L** is known *by* the judgment *which* he 3068
9:19 Arise, **O L**; let not man prevail: let 3068
9:20 Put them in fear, **O L**: *that* the nations may 3068
10: 1 Why standest thou afar off, **O L**? 3068
10: 3 the covetous, *whom* **the L** abhorreth. 3068
10:12 Arise, **O L**; O God, lift up thine hand: 3068
10:16 **The L** *is* King for ever and ever: 3068
10:17 **L**, thou hast heard the desire of the humble: 3068
11: 1 In **the L** put I my trust: how say ye to my 3068
11: 4 **The L** *is* in his holy temple, the LORD'S 3068
11: 5 **The L** trieth the righteous: but the wicked 3068
11: 7 For **the** righteous **L** loveth righteousness; 3068
12: 1 Help, **L**; for the godly *man* ceaseth; for 3068
12: 3 **The L** shall cut off all flattering lips, *and* 3068
12: 5 of the needy, now will I arise, saith **the L**; 3068
12: 6 The words of **the L** *are* pure words: 3068
12: 7 Thou shalt keep them, **O L**, thou shalt 3068
13: 1 How long wilt thou forget me, **O L**? 3068
13: 3 Consider *and* hear me, **O L** my God: 3068
13: 6 I will sing unto **the L**, because he hath 3068
14: 2 **The L** looked down from heaven upon 3068
14: 4 *as* they eat bread, *and* call not upon **the L**. 3068
14: 6 of the poor, because **the L** *is* his refuge. 3068
14: 7 when **the L** bringeth back the captivity of 3068
15: 1 **L**, who shall abide in thy tabernacle? 3068
15: 4 but he honoureth them that fear **the L**. 3068
16: 2 *O my soul,* thou hast said unto **the L**, 3068
16: 5 **The L** *is* the portion of mine inheritance 3068
16: 7 I will bless **the L**, who hath given me 3068
16: 8 I have set **the L** always before me: because 3068
17: 1 Hear the right, **O L**, attend unto my cry, 3068
17:13 Arise, **O L**, disappoint him, cast him down: 3068
17:14 *are* thy hand, **O L**, from men of the world, 3068
18: T *A Psalm* of David, the servant of **the L**, 3068
18: T who spake unto **the L** the words of this 3068
18: T **the L** delivered him from the hand of all 3068
18: 1 I will love thee, **O L**, my strength. 3068
18: 2 **The L** *is* my rock, and my fortress, and 3068
18: 3 I will call upon **the L**, who is *worthy* to be 3068
18: 6 In my distress I called upon **the L**, and 3068
18:13 **The L** also thundered in the heavens, and 3068
18:15 **O L**, at the blast of the breath of thy 3068
18:18 day of my calamity: but **the L** was my stay. 3068
18:20 **The L** rewarded me according to my 3068
18:21 For I have kept the ways of **the L**, and 3068
18:24 Therefore hath **the L** recompensed me 3068
18:28 **the L** my God will enlighten my darkness. 3068
18:30 the word of **the L** is tried: he *is* a buckler to 3068
18:31 For who *is* God save **the L**? or who *is* a 3068
18:41 *was* none to save *them: even* unto **the L**, 3068
18:46 **The L** liveth; and blessed *be* my rock; and 3068

Ps 18:49 **O L**, among the heathen, and sing *praises* 3068
19: 7 The law of **the L** *is* perfect, converting 3068
19: 7 the testimony of **the L** *is* sure, making wise 3068
19: 8 The statutes of **the L** *are* right, rejoicing 3068
19: 8 the commandment of **the L** *is* pure, 3068
19: 9 The fear of **the L** *is* clean, enduring for 3068
19: 9 the judgments of **the L** *are* true *and* 3068
19:14 **O L**, my strength, and my redeemer. 3068
20: 1 **The L** hear thee in the day of trouble; 3068
20: 5 *our* banners: **the L** fulfil all thy petitions. 3068
20: 6 Now know I that **the L** saveth his anointed; 3068
20: 7 we will remember the name of **the L** our 3068
20: 9 Save, **L**: let the king hear us when we call. 3068
21: 1 The king shall joy in thy strength, **O L**; and 3068
21: 7 For the king trusteth in **the L**, and 3068
21: 9 **the L** shall swallow them up in his wrath, 3068
21:13 Be thou exalted, **L**, in thine own strength: 3068
22: 8 He trusted on **the L** *that* he would deliver 3068
22:19 be not thou far *from me*, **O L**: O my 3068
22:23 Ye that fear **the L**, praise him; all ye 3068
22:26 they shall praise **the L** that seek him: 3068
22:27 world shall remember and turn unto **the L**: 3068
23: 1 **The L** *is* my shepherd; I shall not want. 3068
23: 6 I will dwell in the house of **the L** for ever. 3068
24: 3 Who shall ascend into the hill of **the L**? 3068
24: 5 He shall receive the blessing from **the L**, 3068
24: 8 **the L** strong and mighty, the LORD 3068
24: 8 and mighty, **the L** mighty *in* battle. 3068
24:10 **The L** of hosts, he *is* the King of glory. 3068
25: 1 Unto thee, **O L**, do I lift up my soul. 3068
25: 4 Shew me thy ways, **O L**; teach me thy 3068
25: 6 Remember, **O L**, thy tender mercies and 3068
25: 7 thou me for thy goodness' sake, **O L**. 3068
25: 8 Good and upright *is* **the L**: therefore 3068
25:10 All the paths of **the L** *are* mercy and 3068
25:11 For thy name's sake, **O L**, pardon mine 3068
25:12 What man *is* he that feareth **the L**? 3068
25:14 The secret of **the L** *is* with them that fear 3068
25:15 Mine eyes *are* ever towards **the L**; for he 3068
26: 1 Judge me, **O L**; for I have walked in mine 3068
26: 1 I have trusted also in **the L**; *therefore* 3068
26: 2 Examine me, **O L**, and prove me; try my 3068
26: 6 so will I compass thine altar, **O L**: 3068
26: 8 **L**, I have loved the habitation of thy house, 3068
26:12 in the congregations will I bless **the L**. 3068
27: 1 **The L** *is* my light and my salvation; whom 3068
27: 1 **the L** *is* the strength of my life; of whom 3068
27: 4 One *thing* have I desired of **the L**, that will 3068
27: 4 that I may dwell in the house of **the L** all 3068
27: 4 to behold the beauty of **the L**, and 3068
27: 6 yea, I will sing *praises* unto **the L**. 3068
27: 7 Hear, **O L**, *when* I cry *with* my voice: 3068
27: 8 said unto thee, Thy face, **L**, will I seek. 3068
27:10 forsake me, then **the L** will take me up. 3068
27:11 **O L**, and lead me in a plain path, because 3068
27:13 goodness of **the L** in the land of the living. 3068
27:14 Wait on **the L**: be of good courage, and 3068
27:14 strengthen thine heart: wait, I say, on **the L**. 3068
28: 1 Unto thee will I cry, **O L**, my rock; be not 3068
28: 5 they regard not the works of **the L**, 3068
28: 6 Blessed *be* **the L**, because he hath heard 3068
28: 7 **The L** *is* my strength and my shield; 3068
28: 8 **The L** *is* their strength, and he *is* the saving 3068
29: 1 Give unto **the L**, O ye mighty, give unto 3068
29: 1 give unto **the L** glory and strength. 3068
29: 2 Give unto **the L** the glory due unto his 3068
29: 2 worship **the L** in the beauty of holiness. 3068
29: 3 The voice of **the L** *is* upon the waters: 3068
29: 3 **the L** *is* upon many waters. 3068
29: 4 The voice of **the L** *is* powerful; the voice of 3068
29: 4 the voice of **the L** *is* full of majesty. 3068
29: 5 The voice of **the L** breaketh the cedars; 3068
29: 5 yea, **the L** breaketh the cedars of Lebanon. 3068
29: 7 The voice of **the L** divideth the flames of 3068
29: 8 The voice of **the L** shaketh the wilderness; 3068
29: 8 **the L** shaketh the wilderness of Kadesh. 3068
29: 9 The voice of **the L** maketh the hinds to 3068
29:10 **The L** sitteth upon the flood; yea, 3068
29:10 the flood; yea, **the L** sitteth King for ever. 3068
29:11 **The L** will give strength unto his people; 3068
29:11 **the L** will bless his people with peace. 3068
30: 1 I will extol thee, **O L**; for thou hast lifted 3068
30: 2 **O L** my God, I cried unto thee, and 3068
30: 3 **O L**, thou hast brought up my soul from 3068
30: 4 Sing unto **the L**, O ye saints of his, and 3068
30: 7 **L**, by thy favour thou hast made my 3068
30: 8 I cried to thee, **O L**; and unto the LORD I 3068
30: 8 and unto **the L** I made supplication. 3068
30:10 Hear, **O L**, and have mercy upon me: 3068
30:10 have mercy upon me: **L**, be thou my helper. 3068
30:12 **O L** my God, I will give thanks unto thee 3068
31: 1 In thee, **O L**, do I put my trust; let me never 3068
31: 5 thou hast redeemed me, **O L** God of truth. 3068
31: 6 regard lying vanities: but I trust in **the L**. 3068
31: 9 mercy upon me, **O L**, for I am in trouble: 3068
31:14 I trusted in thee, **O L**: I said, Thou *art* my 3068
31:17 Let me not be ashamed, **O L**; for I have 3068
31:21 Blessed *be* **the L**: for he hath shewed me 3068
31:23 O love **the L**, all ye his saints: *for* 3068
31:23 *for* **the L** preserveth the faithful, and 3068
31:24 your heart, all ye that hope in **the L**. 3068
32: 2 Blessed *is* the man unto whom **the L** 3068
32: 5 will confess my transgressions unto **the L**; 3068
32:10 he that trusteth in **the L**, mercy shall 3068
32:11 Be glad in **the L**, and rejoice, ye righteous: 3068
33: 1 Rejoice in **the L**, O ye righteous: *for* praise 3068
33: 2 Praise **the L** with harp: sing unto him with 3068
33: 4 For the word of **the L** *is* right; and all his 3068
33: 5 the earth is full *of* the goodness of **the L**. 3068
33: 6 By the word of **the L** were the heavens 3068
33: 8 Let all the earth fear **the L**: let all 3068
33:10 **The L** bringeth the counsel of the heathen 3068
33:11 The counsel of **the L** standeth for ever, 3068
33:12 Blessed *is* the nation whose God *is* **the L**; 3068
33:13 **The L** looketh from heaven; he beholdeth 3068
33:18 the eye of **the L** *is* upon them that fear him, 3068
33:20 Our soul waiteth for **the L**: he *is* our help 3068
33:22 Let thy mercy, **O L**, be upon us, 3068
34: 1 I will bless **the L** at all times: his praise 3068
34: 2 My soul shall make her boast in **the L**: 3068
34: 3 O magnify **the L** with me, and let us exalt 3068
34: 4 I sought **the L**, and he heard me, and 3068
34: 6 **the L** heard *him*, and saved him out of all 3068
34: 7 The angel of **the L** encampeth round about 3068
34: 8 O taste and see that **the L** *is* good: 3068
34: 9 O fear **the L**, ye his saints: for *there is* no 3068
34:10 they that seek **the L** shall not want any 3068
34:11 unto me: I will teach you the fear of **the L**. 3068
34:15 The eyes of **the L** *are* upon the righteous, 3068
34:16 The face of **the L** *is* against them that do 3068
34:17 **the L** heareth, and delivereth them out of 3068
34:18 **The L** *is* nigh unto them that are of a 3068
34:19 but **the L** delivereth him out of them all. 3068
34:22 **The L** redeemeth the soul of his servants: 3068
35: 1 Plead *my cause*, **O L**, with them that strive 3068
35: 5 and let the angel of **the L** chase *them*. 3068
35: 6 and let the angel of **the L** persecute them. 3068
35: 9 my soul shall be joyful in **the L**: it shall 3068
35:10 bones shall say, **L**, who *is* like unto thee, 3068
35:22 *This* thou hast seen, **O L**: keep not silence: 3068
35:24 Judge me, **O L** my God, according to thy 3068
35:27 say continually, Let **the L** be magnified, 3068
36: T *A Psalm* of David the servant of **the L**. 3068
36: 5 Thy mercy, **O L**, *is* in the heavens; *and* 3068
36: 6 **O L**, thou preservest man and beast. 3068
37: 3 Trust in **the L**, and do good; *so* shalt thou 3068
37: 4 Delight thyself also in **the L**; and he shall 3068
37: 5 Commit thy way unto **the L**; trust also in 3068
37: 7 Rest in **the L**, and wait patiently for him: 3068
37: 9 those that wait upon **the L**, they shall 3068
37:17 but **the L** upholdeth the righteous. 3068
37:18 **The L** knoweth the days of the upright: and 3068
37:20 the enemies of **the L** *shall be* as the fat of 3068
37:23 steps of a *good* man are ordered by **the L**: 3068
37:24 for **the L** upholdeth *him with* his hand. 3068
37:28 For **the L** loveth judgment, and 3068
37:33 **The L** will not leave him in his hand, 3068
37:34 Wait on **the L**, and keep his way, and 3068
37:39 the salvation of the righteous *is* of **the L**: 3068
37:40 **the L** shall help them, and deliver them: 3068
38: 1 **O L**, rebuke me not in thy wrath: 3068
38:15 For in thee, **O L**, do I hope: thou wilt hear, 3068
38:21 Forsake me not, **O L**: O my God, be not far 3068
39: 4 **L**, make me to know mine end, and 3068
39:12 my prayer, **O L**, and give ear unto my cry; 3068
40: 1 I waited patiently for **the L**; and he inclined 3068
40: 3 see *it*, and fear, and shall trust in **the L**. 3068
40: 4 Blessed *is that* man that maketh **the L** his 3068

Ps 40: 5	Many, O **L** my God, *are* thy wonderful	3068
40: 9	not refrained my lips, O **L**, thou knowest.	3068
40:11	not thou thy tender mercies from me, O **L**:	3068
40:13	Be pleased, O **L**, to deliver me: O LORD,	3068
40:13	to deliver me: O **L**, make haste to help me.	3068
40:16	say continually, **The L** be magnified.	3068
41: 1	**the L** will deliver him in time of trouble.	3068
41: 2	**The L** will preserve him, and keep him	3068
41: 3	**The L** will strengthen him upon the bed of	3068
41: 4	I said, **L**, be merciful unto me: heal my	3068
41:10	thou, O **L**, be merciful unto me, and	3068
41:13	Blessed *be* **the L** God of Israel from	3068
42: 8	*Yet* **the L** will command his	3068
46: 7	**The L** of hosts *is* with us; the God of Jacob	3068
46: 8	Come, behold the works of **the L**,	3068
46:11	**The L** of hosts *is* with us; the God of Jacob	3068
47: 2	For **the L** most High *is* terrible; *he is* a	3068
47: 5	a shout, **the L** with the sound of a trumpet.	3068
48: 1	Great *is* **the L**, and greatly to be praised in	3068
48: 8	have we seen in the city of **the L** of hosts,	3068
50: 1	*even* **the L**, hath spoken, and called	3068
54: 6	I will praise thy name, O **L**; for *it is* good.	3068
55:16	call upon God; and **the L** shall save me.	3068
55:22	Cast thy burden upon **the L**, and he shall	3068
56:10	*his* word: in **the L** will I praise *his* word.	3068
58: 6	out the great teeth of the young lions, O **L**.	3068
59: 3	*for* my transgression, nor *for* my sin, O **L**.	3068
59: 5	Thou therefore, O **L** God *of* hosts, the God	3068
59: 8	thou, O **L**, shalt laugh at them; thou shalt	3068
64:10	The righteous shall be glad in **the L**, and	3068
68:16	yea, **the L** will dwell *in it* for ever.	3068
68:18	that **the L** God might dwell *among them.*	3050
69:13	*is* unto thee, O **L**, *in* an acceptable time:	3068
69:16	Hear me, O **L**; for thy lovingkindness *is*	3068
69:31	*This* also shall please **the L** better than an	3068
69:33	For **the L** heareth the poor, and despiseth	3068
70: 1	to deliver me; make haste to help me, O **L**.	3068
70: 5	and my deliverer; O **L**, make no tarrying.	3068
71: 1	In thee, O **L**, do I put my trust: let me never	3068
72:18	Blessed *be* **the L** God, the God of Israel,	3068
74:18	O **L**, and *that* the foolish people have	3068
75: 8	For in the hand of **the L** *there is* a cup, and	3068
76:11	Vow, and pay unto **the L** your God: let all	3068
77:11	I will remember the works of **the L**:	3050
78: 4	the generation to come the praises of **the L**,	3068
78:21	Therefore **the L** heard *this,* and was wroth:	3068
79: 5	How long, **L**? wilt thou be angry, for ever?	3068
80: 4	O **L** God *of* hosts, how long wilt thou be	3068
80:19	Turn us again, O **L** God *of* hosts, cause thy	3068
81:10	I *am* **the L** thy God, which brought thee out	3068
81:15	The haters of **the L** should have submitted	3068
83:16	that they may seek thy name, O **L**.	3068
84: 1	amiable *are* thy tabernacles, O **L** of hosts!	3068
84: 2	yea, even fainteth for the courts of **the L**:	3068
84: 3	O **L** of hosts, my King, and my God.	3068
84: 8	O **L** God *of* hosts, hear my prayer: give ear,	3068
84:11	For **the L** God *is* a sun and shield:	3068
84:11	**the L** will give grace and glory: no good	3068
84:12	O **L** of hosts, blessed *is* the man that	3068
85: 1	**L**, thou hast been favourable unto thy land:	3068
85: 7	thy mercy, O **L**, and grant us thy salvation.	3068
85: 8	I will hear what God **the L** will speak:	3068
85:12	Yea, **the L** shall give *that which is* good;	3068
86: 1	Bow down thine ear, O **L**, hear me: for I	3068
86: 6	Give ear, O **L**, unto my prayer; and	3068
86:11	Teach me thy way, O **L**; I will walk in thy	3068
86:17	because thou, **L**, hast holpen me, and	3068
87: 2	**The L** loveth the gates of Zion more than	3068
87: 6	**The L** shall count, when he writeth *up*	3068
88: 1	O **L** God of my salvation, I have cried day	3068
88: 9	**L**, I have called daily upon thee, I have	3068
88:13	unto thee have I cried, O **L**; and in	3068
88:14	**L**, why castest thou off my soul?	3068
89: 1	I will sing of the mercies of **the L** for ever:	3068
89: 5	the heavens shall praise thy wonders, O **L**:	3068
89: 6	in the heaven can be compared unto **the L**?	3068
89: 6	of the mighty can be likened unto **the L**?	3068
89: 8	O **L** God of hosts, who *is* a strong LORD	3068
89: 8	of hosts, who *is* a strong **L** like unto thee?	3050
89:15	they shall walk, O **L**, in the light of thy	3068
89:18	For **the L** *is* our defence; and the Holy One	3068
89:46	How long, **L**? wilt thou hide thyself,	3068
89:51	thine enemies have reproached, O **L**;	3068
89:52	Blessed *be* **the L** for evermore. Amen, and	3068

90:13	Return, O **L**, how long? and let it repent	3068
90:17	let the beauty of **the L** our God be upon us:	3068
91: 2	I will say of **the L**, *He is* my refuge and	3068
91: 9	Because thou hast made **the L**, *which is* my	3068
92: 1	*It is a* good *thing* to give thanks unto **the L**,	3068
92: 4	For thou, **L**, hast made me glad through thy	3068
92: 5	O **L**, how great are thy works! *and*	3068
92: 8	But thou, **L**, *art most* high for evermore.	3068
92: 9	For lo, thine enemies, O **L**, for lo,	3068
92:13	Those that be planted in the house of **the L**	3068
92:15	To shew that **the L** *is* upright: *he is* my	3068
93: 1	**The L** reigneth, he is clothed with majesty;	3068
93: 1	**the L** is clothed with strength,	3068
93: 3	The floods have lifted up, O **L**, the floods	3068
93: 4	**The L** on high *is* mightier than the noise of	3068
93: 5	becometh thine house, O **L**, for ever.	3068
94: 1	O **L** God, to whom vengeance belongeth;	3068
94: 3	**L**, how long shall the wicked, how long	3068
94: 5	thy people, O **L**, and afflict thine heritage.	3068
94: 7	Yet they say, **The L** shall not see,	3050
94:11	**The L** knoweth the thoughts of man,	3068
94:12	O **L**, and teachest him out of thy law;	3050
94:14	For **the L** will not cast off his people,	3068
94:17	Unless **the L** *had been* my help, my soul	3068
94:18	foot slippeth; thy mercy, O **L**, held me up.	3068
94:22	**the L** is my defence; and my God *is*	3068
94:23	*yea,* **the L** our God shall cut them off.	3068
95: 1	O come, let us sing unto **the L**: let us make	3068
95: 3	For **the L** *is* a great God, and a great King	3068
95: 6	let us kneel before **the L** our Maker.	3068
96: 1	O sing unto **the L** a new song: sing unto	3068
96: 1	a new song: sing unto **the L**, all the earth.	3068
96: 2	Sing unto **the L**, bless his name; shew forth	3068
96: 4	For **the L** *is* great, and greatly to be	3068
96: 5	*are* idols: but **the L** made the heavens.	3068
96: 7	Give unto **the L**, O ye kindreds of	3068
96: 7	give unto **the L** glory and strength.	3068
96: 8	Give unto **the L** the glory due unto his	3068
96: 9	O worship **the L** in the beauty of holiness:	3068
96:10	Say among the heathen *that* **the L** reigneth:	3068
96:13	Before **the L**, for he cometh, for he cometh	3068
97: 1	**The L** reigneth; let the earth rejoice; let	3068
97: 5	melted like wax at the presence of **the L**,	3068
97: 8	because of thy judgments, O **L**.	3068
97: 9	For thou, **L**, *art* High above all the earth:	3068
97:10	Ye that love **the L**, hate evil: he preserveth	3068
97:12	Rejoice in **the L**, ye righteous; and	3068
98: 1	O sing unto **the L** a new song; for he hath	3068
98: 2	**The L** hath made known his salvation:	3068
98: 4	Make a joyful noise unto **the L**, all	3068
98: 5	Sing unto **the L** with the harp; with	3068
98: 6	of cornet make a joyful noise before **the L**,	3068
98: 9	Before **the L**; for he cometh to judge	3068
99: 1	**The L** reigneth; let the people tremble:	3068
99: 2	**The L** *is* great in Zion; and he *is* high	3068
99: 5	Exalt ye **the L** our God, and worship at his	3068
99: 6	they called upon **the L**, and he answered	3068
99: 8	Thou answeredst them, O **L** our God:	3068
99: 9	Exalt **the L** our God, and worship at his	3068
99: 9	at his holy hill; for **the L** our God *is* holy.	3068
100: 1	Make a joyful noise unto **the L**, all ye	3068
100: 2	Serve **the L** with gladness: come before his	3068
100: 3	Know ye that **the L** he *is* God: *it is* he *that*	3068
100: 5	For **the L** *is* good; his mercy *is* everlasting;	3068
101: 1	and judgment: unto thee, O **L**, will I sing.	3068
101: 8	off all wicked doers from the city of **the L**.	3068
102: T	and poureth out his complaint before **the L**.	3068
102: 1	O **L**, and let my cry come unto thee.	3068
102:12	thou, O **L**, shalt endure for ever; and	3068
102:15	So the heathen shall fear the name of **the L**,	3068
102:16	When **the L** shall build up Zion, he shall	3068
102:18	which *shall be* created shall praise **the L**.	3050
102:19	from heaven did **the L** behold the earth;	3068
102:21	To declare the name of **the L** in Zion, and	3068
102:22	and the kingdoms, to serve **the L**.	3068
103: 1	Bless **the L**, O my soul: and all that is	3068
103: 2	Bless **the L**, O my soul, and forget not all	3068
103: 6	**The L** executeth righteousness and	3068
103: 8	**The L** *is* merciful and gracious, slow to	3068
103:13	*so* **the L** pitieth them that fear him.	3068
103:17	the mercy of **the L** *is* from everlasting to	3068
103:19	**The L** hath prepared his throne in	3068
103:20	Bless **the L**, ye his angels, that excel in	3068
103:21	Bless ye **the L**, all ye his hosts;	3068

Ps 103:22	Bless **the L**, all his works in all places of	3068
103:22	of his dominion: bless **the L**, O my soul.	3068
104: 1	Bless **the L**, O my soul. O LORD my	3068
104: 1	O **L** my God, thou art very great; thou art	3068
104:16	The trees of **the L** are full *of sap;*	3068
104:24	O **L**, how manifold are thy works!	3068
104:31	The glory of **the L** shall endure for ever:	3068
104:31	for ever: **the L** shall rejoice in his works.	3068
104:33	I will sing unto **the L** as long as I live:	3068
104:34	him shall be sweet: I will be glad in **the L**.	3068
104:35	Bless thou **the L**, O my soul. Praise ye	3068
104:35	the LORD, O my soul. Praise ye **the L**.	3050
105: 1	O give thanks unto **the L**; call upon his	3068
105: 3	let the heart of them rejoice that seek **the L**.	3068
105: 4	Seek **the L**, and his strength: seek his face	3068
105: 7	He *is* **the L** our God: his judgments *are* in	3068
105:19	word came: the word of **the L** tried him.	3068
105:45	and keep his laws. Praise ye **the L**.	3050
106: 1	Praise ye **the L**. O give thanks unto	3050
106: 1	O give thanks unto **the L**; for *he is* good:	3068
106: 2	Who can utter the mighty acts of **the L**?	3068
106: 4	Remember me, O **L**, with the favour *that*	3068
106:16	in the camp, *and* Aaron the saint of **the L**.	3068
106:25	*and* hearkened not unto the voice of **the L**.	3068
106:34	*concerning* whom **the L** commanded them:	3068
106:40	Therefore was the wrath of **the L** kindled	3068
106:47	O **L** our God, and gather us from among	3068
106:48	Blessed *be* **the L** God of Israel from	3068
106:48	all the people say, Amen. Praise ye **the L**.	3050
107: 1	O give thanks unto **the L**, for *he is* good:	3068
107: 2	Let the redeemed of **the L** say *so,* whom he	3068
107: 6	they cried unto **the L** in their trouble, *and*	3068
107: 8	Oh that *men* would praise **the L** *for* his	3068
107:13	they cried unto **the L** in their trouble, *and*	3068
107:15	Oh that *men* would praise **the L** *for* his	3068
107:19	they cry unto **the L** in their trouble,	3068
107:21	Oh that *men* would praise **the L** *for* his	3068
107:24	These see the works of **the L**, and	3068
107:28	they cry unto **the L** in their trouble, and	3068
107:31	Oh that *men* would praise **the L** *for* his	3068
107:43	understand the lovingkindness of **the L**.	3068
108: 3	I will praise thee, O **L**, among the people:	3068
109:14	of his fathers be remembered with **the L**;	3068
109:15	Let them be before **the L** continually,	3068
109:20	the reward of mine adversaries from **the L**,	3068
109:26	Help me, O **L** my God: O save me	3068
109:27	this *is* thy hand; *that* thou, **L**, hast done it.	3068
109:30	I will greatly praise **the L** with my mouth;	3068
110: 1	**The L** said unto my Lord, Sit thou at my	3068
110: 2	**The L** shall send the rod of thy strength out	3068
110: 4	**The L** hath sworn, and will not repent,	3068
111: 1	Praise ye **the L**. I will praise the LORD	3050
111: 1	I will praise **the L** with *my* whole heart,	3068
111: 2	The works of **the L** *are* great, sought out of	3068
111: 4	**the L** *is* gracious and full of compassion.	3068
111:10	The fear of **the L** *is* the beginning of	3068
112: 1	Praise ye **the L**. Blessed *is* the man *that*	3050
112: 1	Blessed *is* the man *that* feareth **the L**,	3068
112: 7	his heart is fixed, trusting in **the L**.	3068
113: 1	Praise ye **the L**. Praise, O ye servants of	3050
113: 1	Praise, O ye servants of **the L**, praise	3068
113: 1	of the LORD, praise the name of **the L**.	3068
113: 2	Blessed be the name of **the L** from this	3068
113: 4	**The L** *is* high above all nations, *and*	3068
113: 5	Who *is* like unto **the L** our God, who	3068
113: 9	joyful mother of children. Praise ye **the L**.	3050
115: 1	O **L**, not unto us, but unto thy name give	3068
115: 9	O Israel, trust thou in **the L**: he *is* their help	3068
115:10	O house of Aaron, trust in **the L**: he *is* their	3068
115:11	Ye that fear **the L**, trust in the LORD:	3068
115:11	Ye that fear the LORD, trust in **the L**:	3068
115:12	**The L** hath been mindful of us: he will	3068
115:13	He will bless them that fear **the L**, *both*	3068
115:14	**The L** shall increase you more and more,	3068
115:15	You *are* blessed of **the L** which made	3068
115:17	The dead praise not **the L**, neither any that	3050
115:18	But we will bless **the L** from this time forth	3050
115:18	time forth and for evermore. Praise **the L**.	3050
116: 1	I love **the L**, because he hath heard my	3068
116: 4	called I upon the name of **the L**;	3068
116: 4	O **L**, I beseech thee, deliver my soul.	3068
116: 5	Gracious *is* **the L**, and righteous; yea,	3068
116: 6	**The L** preserveth the simple: I was brought	3068
116: 7	for **the L** hath dealt bountifully with thee.	3068
116: 9	I will walk before **the L** in the land of	3068
116:12	What shall I render unto **the L** *for* all his	3068
116:13	and call upon the name of **the L**.	3068
116:14	I will pay my vows unto **the L** now in	3068
116:15	Precious in the sight of **the L** *is* the death	3068
116:16	Oh **L**, truly I *am* thy servant; I *am* thy	3068
116:17	and will call upon the name of **the L**.	3068
116:18	I will pay my vows unto **the L** now in	3068
116:19	midst of thee, O Jerusalem. Praise ye **the L**.	3050
117: 1	O praise **the L**, all ye nations: praise him,	3068
117: 2	the truth of **the L** *endureth* for ever.	3068
117: 2	LORD *endureth* for ever. Praise ye **the L**.	3050
118: 1	O give thanks unto **the L**; for *he is* good:	3068
118: 4	Let them now that fear **the L** say, that his	3068
118: 5	I called upon **the L** in distress: the LORD	3050
118: 5	**the L** answered me, *and set me* in a large	3050
118: 6	**The L** *is* on my side; I will not fear:	3068
118: 7	**The L** taketh my part with them that help	3068
118: 8	*It is* better to trust in **the L** than to put	3068
118: 9	*It is* better to trust in **the L** than to put	3068
118:10	in the name of **the L** will I destroy them.	3068
118:11	in the name of **the L** I will destroy them.	3068
118:12	for in the name of **the L** I will destroy	3068
118:13	me that *I* might fall: but **the L** helped me.	3068
118:14	**The L** *is* my strength and song, and	3050
118:15	the right hand of **the L** doeth valiantly.	3068
118:16	The right hand of **the L** is exalted: the right	3068
118:16	the right hand of **the L** doeth valiantly.	3068
118:17	but live, and declare the works of **the L**.	3050
118:18	**The L** hath chastened me sore: but he hath	3050
118:19	I will go into them, *and* I will praise **the L**:	3050
118:20	This gate of **the L**, into which the righteous	3068
118:24	This *is* the day *which* **the L** hath made;	3068
118:25	Save now, I beseech thee, O **L**: O LORD,	3068
118:25	O **L**, I beseech thee, send now prosperity.	3068
118:26	*be* he that cometh in the name of **the L**:	3068
118:26	have blessed you out of the house of **the L**.	3068
118:27	God *is* **the L**, which hath shewed us light:	3068
118:29	O give thanks unto **the L**; for *he is* good:	3068
119: 1	in the way, who walk in the law of **the L**.	3068
119:12	Blessed *art* thou, O **L**: teach me thy	3068
119:31	thy testimonies: O **L**, put me not to shame.	3068
119:33	Teach me, O **L**, the way of thy statutes; and	3068
119:41	O **L**, *even* thy salvation, according to thy	3068
119:52	I remembered thy judgments of old, O **L**;	3068
119:55	O **L**, in the night, and have kept thy law.	3068
119:57	*Thou art* my portion, O **L**: I have said that *I*	3068
119:64	The earth, O **L**, is full *of* thy mercy:	3068
119:65	thy servant, O **L**, according unto thy word.	3068
119:75	I know, O **L**, that thy judgments *are* right,	3068
119:89	For ever, O **L**, thy word *is* settled in	3068
119:107	quicken me, O **L**, according unto thy word.	3068
119:108	O **L**, and teach me thy judgments.	3068
119:126	*It is* time for *thee,* **L**, to work: *for* they have	3068
119:137	O **L**, and upright *are* thy judgments.	3068
119:145	I cried with *my* whole heart; hear me, O **L**:	3068
119:149	O **L**, quicken me according to thy	3068
119:151	Thou *art* near, O **L**; and all thy	3068
119:156	Great *are* thy tender mercies, O **L**:	3068
119:159	quicken me, O **L**, according to thy	3068
119:166	**L**, I have hoped for thy salvation, and	3068
119:169	Let my cry come near before thee, O **L**:	3068
119:174	I have longed for thy salvation, O **L**; and	3068
120: 1	In my distress I cried unto **the L**, and	3068
120: 2	O **L**, from lying lips, *and* from a deceitful	3068
121: 2	My help *cometh* from **the L**, which made	3068
121: 5	**The L** *is* thy keeper: the LORD *is* thy	3068
121: 5	**the L** *is* thy shade upon thy right hand.	3068
121: 7	**The L** shall preserve thee from all evil:	3068
121: 8	**The L** shall preserve thy going out and	3068
122: 1	unto me, Let us go *into* the house of **the L**.	3068
122: 4	the tribes go up, the tribes of **the L**,	3050
122: 4	to give thanks unto the name of **the L**.	3068
122: 9	Because of the house of **the L** our God I	3068
123: 2	so our eyes *wait* upon **the L** our God,	3068
123: 3	mercy upon us, O **L**, have mercy upon us:	3068
124: 1	If *it had* not *been* **the L** who was on our	3068
124: 2	If *it had* not *been* **the L** who was on our	3068
124: 6	Blessed *be* **the L**, who hath not given us *as*	3068
124: 8	Our help *is* in the name of **the L**, who made	3068
125: 1	They that trust in **the L** *shall be* as mount	3068
125: 2	**the L** *is* round about his people from	3068
125: 4	Do good, O **L**, unto *those that be* good, and	3068
125: 5	**the L** shall lead them forth with	3068

Ps 126: 1	When **the L** turned again the captivity of	3068
126: 2	**The L** hath done great things for them.	3068
126: 3	**The L** hath done great things for us;	3068
126: 4	Turn again our captivity, O **L**, as	3068
127: 1	Except **the L** build the house, they labour	3068
127: 1	except **the L** keep the city, the watchman	3068
127: 3	Lo, children *are* an heritage of **the L**: *and*	3068
128: 1	Blessed *is* every one that feareth **the L**;	3068
128: 4	shall the man be blessed that feareth **the L**.	3068
128: 5	**The L** shall bless thee out of Zion: and	3068
129: 4	**The L** *is* righteous: he hath cut asunder	3068
129: 8	by say, The blessing of **the L** *be* upon you:	3068
129: 8	we bless you in the name of **the L**.	3068
130: 1	of the depths have I cried unto thee, O **L**.	3068
130: 3	If thou, **L**, shouldest mark iniquities,	3050
130: 5	I wait for **the L**, my soul doth wait, and	3068
130: 7	Let Israel hope in **the L**: for with	3068
130: 7	for with **the L** *there is* mercy, and with him	3068
131: 1	**L**, my heart is not haughty, nor mine eyes	3068
131: 3	Let Israel hope in **the L** from henceforth	3068
132: 1	**L**, remember David, *and* all his afflictions:	3068
132: 2	How he sware unto **the L**, *and* vowed unto	3068
132: 5	Until I find out a place for **the L**,	3068
132: 8	Arise, O **L**, into thy rest; thou, and the ark	3068
132:11	**The L** hath sworn *in* truth unto David;	3068
132:13	For **the L** hath chosen Zion; he hath	3068
133: 3	for there **the L** commanded the blessing,	3068
134: 1	Behold, bless ye **the L**, all ye servants of	3068
134: 1	ye the LORD, all ye servants of **the L**,	3068
134: 1	which by night stand in the house of **the L**.	3068
134: 2	hands *in* the sanctuary, and bless **the L**.	3068
134: 3	**The L** that made heaven and earth bless	3068
135: 1	Praise ye **the L**. Praise ye the name of	3050
135: 1	Praise ye the name of **the L**; praise *him,* O	3068
135: 1	praise *him,* O ye servants of **the L**.	3068
135: 2	Ye that stand in the house of **the L**, in	3068
135: 3	Praise **the L**; for the LORD *is* good:	3050
135: 3	Praise the LORD; for **the L** *is* good:	3068
135: 4	For **the L** hath chosen Jacob unto himself,	3050
135: 5	For I know that **the L** *is* great, and *that* our	3068
135: 6	Whatsoever **the L** pleased, *that* did he in	3068
135:13	Thy name, O **L**, *endureth* for ever; *and*	3068
135:13	*and* thy memorial, O **L**, throughout all	3068
135:14	For **the L** will judge his people, and he will	3068
135:19	Bless **the L**, O house of Israel: bless	3068
135:19	of Israel: bless **the L**, O house of Aaron:	3068
135:20	Bless **the L**, O house of Levi: ye that fear	3068
135:20	ye that fear **the L**, bless the LORD.	3068
135:20	ye that fear the LORD, bless **the L**.	3068
135:21	Blessed *be* **the L** out of Zion,	3068
135:21	dwelleth *at* Jerusalem. Praise ye **the L**.	3050
136: 1	O give thanks unto **the L**; for *he is* good:	3068
137: 7	Remember, O **L**, the children of Edom *in*	3068
138: 4	O **L**, when they hear the words of thy	3068
138: 5	Yea, they shall sing in the ways of **the L**:	3068
138: 5	the LORD: for great *is* the glory of **the L**.	3068
138: 6	Though **the L** *be* high, yet hath he respect	3068
138: 8	**The L** will perfect that which concerneth	3068
138: 8	thy mercy, O **L**, *endureth* for ever:	3068
139: 1	O **L**, thou hast searched me, and	3068
139: 4	*but* lo, O **L**, thou knowest it altogether.	3068
139:21	Do not I hate them, O **L**, that hate thee?	3068
140: 1	Deliver me, O **L**, from the evil man:	3068
140: 4	Keep me, O **L**, from the hands of	3068
140: 6	I said unto **the L**, Thou *art* my God:	3068
140: 6	hear the voice of my supplications, O **L**.	3068
140: 8	Grant not, O **L**, the desires of the wicked:	3068
140:12	I know that **the L** will maintain the cause	3068
141: 1	**L**, I cry unto thee: make haste unto me;	3068
141: 3	Set a watch, O **L**, before my mouth;	3068
142: 1	I cried unto **the L** *with* my voice; *with* my	3068
142: 1	*with* my voice unto **the L** did I make my	3068
142: 5	I cried unto thee, O **L**: I said, Thou *art* my	3068
143: 1	Hear my prayer, O **L**, give ear to my	3068
143: 7	Hear me speedily, O **L**: my spirit faileth:	3068
143: 9	Deliver me, O **L**, from mine enemies: I flee	3068
143:11	Quicken me, O **L**, for thy name's sake:	3068
144: 1	Blessed *be* **the L** my strength,	3068
144: 3	**L**, what *is* man, that thou takest knowledge	3068
144: 5	Bow thy heavens, O **L**, and come down:	3068
144:15	happy *is that* people, whose God *is* **the L**.	3068
145: 3	Great *is* **the L**, and greatly to be praised;	3068
145: 8	**The L** *is* gracious, and full of compassion;	3068
145: 9	**The L** *is* good to all: and his tender mercies	3068
145:10	All thy works shall praise thee, O **L**; and	3068
145:14	**The L** upholdeth all that fall, and raiseth up	3068
145:17	**The L** *is* righteous in all his ways, and	3068
145:18	**The L** *is* nigh unto all them that call upon	3068
145:20	**The L** preserveth all them that love him:	3068
145:21	My mouth shall speak the praise of **the L**:	3068
146: 1	Praise ye **the L**. Praise the LORD, O my	3050
146: 1	ye the LORD. Praise **the L**, O my soul.	3068
146: 2	While I live will I praise **the L**: I will sing	3068
146: 5	his help, whose hope *is* in **the L** his God:	3068
146: 7	to the hungry. **The L** looseth the prisoners:	3068
146: 8	**The L** openeth *the eyes of* the blind:	3068
146: 8	**the L** raiseth them that are bowed down:	3068
146: 8	bowed down: **the L** loveth the righteous:	3068
146: 9	**The L** preserveth the strangers; he relieveth	3068
146:10	**The L** shall reign for ever, *even* thy God,	3068
146:10	unto all generations. Praise ye **the L**.	3050
147: 1	Praise ye **the L**: for *it is* good to sing	3050
147: 2	**The L** doth build up Jerusalem:	3068
147: 6	**The L** lifteth up the meek: he casteth	3068
147: 7	Sing unto **the L** with thanksgiving;	3068
147:11	**The L** taketh pleasure in them that fear	3068
147:12	Praise **the L**, O Jerusalem; praise thy God,	3068
147:20	they have not known them. Praise ye **the L**.	3050
148: 1	Praise ye **the L**. Praise ye the LORD from	3050
148: 1	Praise ye **the L** from the heavens:	3068
148: 5	Let them praise the name of **the L**: for he	3068
148: 7	Praise **the L** from the earth, ye dragons,	3068
148:13	Let them praise the name of **the L**: for his	3068
148:14	a people near unto him. Praise ye **the L**.	3050
149: 1	Praise ye **the L**. Sing unto the LORD a	3050
149: 1	Sing unto **the L** a new song, *and* his praise	3068
149: 4	For **the L** taketh pleasure in his people:	3068
149: 9	honour have all his saints. Praise ye **the L**.	3050
150: 1	Praise ye **the L**. Praise God in his	3050
150: 6	every *thing that hath* breath praise **the L**.	3050
150: 6	breath praise the LORD. Praise ye **the L**.	3050
Pr 1: 7	The fear of **the L** *is* the beginning of	3068
1:29	and did not choose the fear of **the L**:	3068
2: 5	shalt thou understand the fear of **the L**,	3068
2: 6	For **the L** giveth wisdom: out of his mouth	3068
3: 5	Trust in **the L** with all thine heart; and	3068
3: 7	own eyes: fear **the L**, and depart from evil.	3068
3: 9	Honour **the L** with thy substance, and	3068
3:11	despise not the chastening of **the L**;	3068
3:12	For whom **the L** loveth he correcteth;	3068
3:19	**The L** by wisdom hath founded the earth;	3068
3:26	For **the L** shall be thy confidence, and	3068
3:32	For the froward *is* abomination to **the L**:	3068
3:33	The curse of **the L** *is* in the house of	3068
5:21	ways of man *are* before the eyes of **the L**,	3068
6:16	These six *things* doth **the L** hate: yea,	3068
8:13	The fear of **the L** *is* to hate evil: pride, and	3068
8:22	**The L** possessed me *in* the beginning of his	3068
8:35	and shall obtain favour of **the L**.	3068
9:10	The fear of **the L** *is* the beginning of	3068
10: 3	**The L** will not suffer the soul of	3068
10:22	The blessing of **the L**, it maketh rich, and	3068
10:27	The fear of **the L** prolongeth days: but	3068
10:29	The way of **the L** *is* strength to the upright:	3068
11: 1	A false balance *is* abomination to **the L**:	3068
11:20	froward heart *are* abomination unto **the L**:	3068
12: 2	A good *man* obtaineth favour of **the L**: but	3068
12:22	Lying lips *are* abomination to **the L**: but	3068
14: 2	walketh in his uprightness feareth **the L**:	3068
14:26	In the fear of **the L** *is* strong confidence:	3068
14:27	The fear of **the L** *is* a fountain of life,	3068
15: 3	The eyes of **the L** *are* in every place,	3068
15: 8	of the wicked *is* an abomination to **the L**:	3068
15: 9	the wicked *is* an abomination unto **the L**:	3068
15:11	Hell and destruction *are* before **the L**:	3068
15:16	Better *is* little with the fear of **the L** than	3068
15:25	**The L** will destroy the house of the proud:	3068
15:26	of the wicked *are* an abomination to **the L**:	3068
15:29	**The L** *is* far from the wicked: but	3068
15:33	The fear of **the L** *is* the instruction of	3068
16: 1	the answer of the tongue, *is* from **the L**.	3068
16: 2	own eyes; but **the L** weigheth the spirits.	3068
16: 3	Commit thy works unto **the L**, and	3068
16: 4	**The L** hath made all *things* for himself:	3068
16: 5	proud in heart *is* an abomination to **the L**:	3068
16: 6	by the fear of **the L** *men* depart from evil.	3068
16: 7	When a man's ways please **the L**,	3068
16: 9	his way: but **the L** directeth his steps.	3068

Pr	16:20	and whoso trusteth in **the L**, happy *is* he.	3068
	16:33	but the whole disposing thereof *is* of **the L**.	3068
	17: 3	furnace for gold: but **the L** trieth the hearts.	3068
	17:15	even they both *are* abomination to **the L**.	3068
	18:10	The name of **the L** *is* a strong tower:	3068
	18:22	good *thing,* and obtaineth favour of **the L**.	3068
	19: 3	and his heart fretteth against **the L**.	3068
	19:14	and a prudent wife *is* from **the L**.	3068
	19:17	hath pity upon the poor lendeth unto **the L**;	3068
	19:21	nevertheless the counsel of **the L**, that shall	3068
	19:23	The fear of **the L** *tendeth* to life: and	3068
	20:10	of them *are* alike abomination to **the L**.	3068
	20:12	**the L** hath made even both of them.	3068
	20:22	*but* wait on **the L**, and he shall save thee.	3068
	20:23	weights *are* an abomination unto **the L**;	3068
	20:24	Man's goings *are* of **the L**; how can a man	3068
	20:27	The spirit of man *is* the candle of **the L**,	3068
	21: 1	The king's heart *is* in the hand of **the L**,	3068
	21: 2	own eyes: but **the L** pondereth the hearts.	3068
	21: 3	judgment *is* more acceptable to **the L** than	3068
	21:30	understanding nor counsel against **the L**.	3068
	21:31	the day of battle: but safety *is* of **the L**.	3068
	22: 2	**the L** *is* the Maker of them all.	3068
	22: 4	*and* the fear of **the L** *are* riches,	3068
	22:12	The eyes of **the L** preserve knowledge, and	3068
	22:14	he that is abhorred of **the L** shall fall	3068
	22:19	That thy trust may be in **the L**, I have made	3068
	22:23	For **the L** will plead their cause, and	3068
	23:17	*be thou* in the fear of **the L** all the day long.	3068
	24:18	Lest **the L** see *it,* and it displease him, and	3068
	24:21	My son, fear thou **the L** and the king: *and*	3068
	25:22	upon his head, and **the L** shall reward thee.	3068
	28: 5	they that seek **the L** understand all *things.*	3068
	28:25	he that putteth his trust in **the L** shall be	3068
	29:13	**the L** lighteneth both their eyes.	3068
	29:25	whoso putteth his trust in **the L** shall be	3068
	29:26	*every* man's judgment *cometh* from **the L**.	3068
	30: 9	and deny *thee,* and say, Who *is* **the L**?	3068
	31:30	*but* a woman that feareth **the L**, she shall	3068
Isa	1: 2	for **the L** hath spoken, I have nourished and	3068
	1: 4	they have forsaken **the L**, they have	3068
	1: 9	Except **the L** of hosts had left unto us a	3068
	1:10	Hear the word of **the L**, ye rulers of	3068
	1:11	saith **the L**: I am full *of* the burnt offerings	3068
	1:18	and let us reason together, saith **the L**:	3068
	1:20	for the mouth of **the L** hath spoken *it.*	3068
	1:24	Therefore saith the Lord, **the L** of hosts,	3068
	1:28	they that forsake **the L** shall be consumed.	3068
	2: 3	and let us go up to the mountain of **the L**,	3068
	2: 3	and the word of **the L** from Jerusalem.	3068
	2: 5	and let us walk in the light of **the L**.	3068
	2:10	for fear of **the L**, and for the glory of his	3068
	2:11	and **the L** alone shall be exalted in that day.	3068
	2:12	For the day of **the L** of hosts *shall be* upon	3068
	2:17	and **the L** alone shall be exalted in that day.	3068
	2:19	for fear of **the L**, and for the glory of his	3068
	2:21	for fear of **the L**, and for the glory of his	3068
	3: 1	For behold, the Lord, **the L** of hosts,	3068
	3: 8	and their doings *are* against **the L**,	3068
	3:13	**The L** standeth *up* to plead, and standeth to	3068
	3:14	**The L** will enter into judgment with	3068
	3:16	Moreover **the L** saith, Because	3068
	3:17	and **the L** will discover their secret parts.	3068
	4: 2	In that day shall the branch of **the L** be	3068
	4: 5	**the L** will create upon every dwelling place	3068
	5: 7	For the vineyard of **the L** of hosts *is*	3068
	5: 9	In mine ears *said* **the L** of hosts, Of a truth	3068
	5:12	they regard not the work of **the L**,	3068
	5:16	**the L** of hosts shall be exalted in judgment,	3068
	5:24	they have cast away the law of **the L** of	3068
	5:25	Therefore is the anger of **the L** kindled	3068
	6: 3	said, Holy, holy, holy, *is* **the L** of hosts:	3068
	6: 5	eyes have seen the King, **the L** of hosts.	3068
	6:12	**the L** have removed men far away, and	3068
	7: 3	said **the L** unto Isaiah, Go forth now to	3068
	7:10	Moreover **the L** spake again unto Ahaz,	3068
	7:11	Ask thee a sign of **the L** thy God; ask it	3068
	7:12	I will not ask, neither will I tempt **the L**.	3068
	7:17	**The L** shall bring upon thee, and upon thy	3068
	7:18	*that* **the L** shall hiss for the fly that *is* in	3068
	8: 1	Moreover **the L** said unto me, Take thee a	3068
	8: 3	said **the L** to me, Call his name	3068
	8: 5	**The L** spake also unto me again, saying,	3068
	8:11	For **the L** spake thus to me with a strong	3068
	8:13	Sanctify **the L** of hosts himself; and *let* him	3068
	8:17	I will wait upon **the L**, that hideth his face	3068
	8:18	the children whom **the L** hath given me *are*	3068
	8:18	for wonders in Israel from **the L** of hosts,	3068
	9: 7	The zeal of **the L** of hosts will perform	3068
	9:11	Therefore **the L** shall set up the adversaries	3068
	9:13	neither do they seek **the L** of hosts.	3068
	9:14	Therefore **the L** will cut off from Israel	3068
	9:19	Through the wrath of **the L** of hosts is	3068
	10:20	shall stay upon **the L**, the Holy One of	3068
	10:26	**the L** of hosts shall stir up a scourge for	3068
	10:33	Behold, the Lord, **the L** of hosts, shall lop	3068
	11: 2	the Spirit of **the L** shall rest upon him,	3068
	11: 2	of knowledge and of the fear of **the L**;	3068
	11: 3	of quick understanding in the fear of **the L**:	3068
	11: 9	shall be full *of* the knowledge of **the L**,	3068
	11:15	**the L** shall utterly destroy the tongue of	3068
	12: 1	day thou shalt say, O **L**, I will praise thee:	3068
	12: 2	for **the L** JEHOVAH *is* my strength and	3050
	12: 4	ye say, Praise **the L**, call upon his name,	3068
	12: 5	Sing unto **the L**; for he hath done excellent	3068
	13: 4	**the L** of hosts mustereth the host of	3068
	13: 5	*even* **the L**, and the weapons of his	3068
	13: 6	Howl ye; for the day of **the L** *is* at hand;	3068
	13: 9	Behold, the day of **the L** cometh,	3068
	13:13	in the wrath of **the L** of hosts, and in	3068
	14: 1	For **the L** will have mercy on Jacob, and	3068
	14: 2	them in the land of **the L** for servants	3068
	14: 3	it shall come to pass in the day that **the L**	3068
	14: 5	**The L** hath broken the staff of the wicked,	3068
	14:22	saith **the L** of hosts, and cut off from	3068
	14:22	remnant, and son, and nephew, saith **the L**.	3068
	14:23	besom of destruction, saith **the L** of hosts.	3068
	14:24	**The L** of hosts hath sworn, saying,	3068
	14:27	For **the L** of hosts hath purposed, and	3068
	14:32	That **the L** hath founded Zion, and the poor	3068
	16:13	This *is* the word that **the L** hath spoken	3068
	16:14	now **the L** hath spoken, saying,	3068
	17: 3	the children of Israel, saith **the L** of hosts.	3068
	17: 6	branches thereof, saith **the L** God of Israel.	3068
	18: 4	For so **the L** said unto me, I will take my	3068
	18: 7	unto **the L** of hosts *of* a people scattered	3068
	18: 7	to the place of the name of **the L** of hosts,	3068
	19: 1	**the L** rideth upon a swift cloud, and	3068
	19: 4	over them, saith the Lord, **the L** of hosts.	3068
	19:12	let them know what **the L** of hosts hath	3068
	19:14	**The L** hath mingled a perverse spirit in	3068
	19:16	of the shaking of the hand of **the L** of	3068
	19:17	because of the counsel of **the L** of hosts,	3068
	19:18	of Canaan, and swear to **the L** of hosts:	3068
	19:19	In that day shall there be an altar to **the L**	3068
	19:19	and a pillar at the border thereof to **the L**.	3068
	19:20	for a witness unto **the L** of hosts in the land	3068
	19:20	for they shall cry unto **the L** because of	3068
	19:21	**the L** shall be known to Egypt, and	3068
	19:21	the Egyptians shall know **the L** in that day,	3068
	19:21	they shall vow a vow unto **the L**, and	3068
	19:22	**the L** shall smite Egypt: *he* shall smite and	3068
	19:22	heal *it:* and they shall return *even* to **the L**,	3068
	19:25	Whom **the L** of hosts shall bless, saying,	3068
	20: 2	At the same time spake **the L** by Isaiah	3068
	20: 3	**the L** said, Like as my servant Isaiah hath	3068
	21:10	that which I have heard of **the L** of hosts,	3068
	21:17	for **the L** God of Israel hath spoken *it.*	3068
	22:14	it was revealed in mine ears *by* **the L** of	3068
	22:17	**the L** will carry thee away with a mighty	3068
	22:25	In that day, saith **the L** of hosts, shall	3068
	22:25	it shall be cut off: for **the L** hath spoken *it.*	3068
	23: 9	**The L** of hosts hath purposed it, to stain	3068
	23:11	**the L** hath given a commandment against	3068
	23:17	*that* **the L** will visit Tyre, and she shall turn	3068
	23:18	and her hire shall be holiness to **the L**:	3068
	23:18	shall be for them that dwell before **the L**,	3068
	24: 1	**the L** maketh the earth empty, and	3068
	24: 3	for **the L** hath spoken this word.	3068
	24:14	they shall sing, for the majesty of **the L**,	3068
	24:15	Wherefore glorify ye **the L** in the fires,	3068
	24:15	*even* the name of **the L** God of Israel in	3068
	24:21	*that* **the L** shall punish the host of the high	3068
	24:23	when **the L** of hosts shall reign in mount	3068
	25: 1	O **L**, thou *art* my God; I will exalt thee,	3068
	25: 6	in this mountain shall **the L** of hosts make	3068
	25: 8	off all the earth: for **the L** hath spoken *it.*	3068
	25: 9	this *is* **the L**; we have waited for him,	3068

Isa 25:10 For in this mountain shall the hand of **the L** 3068
26: 4 Trust ye in **the L** for ever: for in 3068
26: 4 for in **the L** JEHOVAH *is* everlasting 3050
26: 8 O **L**, have we waited for thee; 3068
26:10 and will not behold the majesty of **the L**. 3068
26:11 **L**, *when* thy hand is lifted up, they will not 3068
26:12 **L**, thou wilt ordain peace for us: for thou 3068
26:13 O **L** our God, *other* lords besides thee have 3068
26:15 O **L**, thou hast increased the nation: 3068
26:16 **L**, in trouble have they visited thee, 3068
26:17 so have we been in thy sight, O **L**. 3068
26:21 **the L** cometh out of his place to punish 3068
27: 1 In that day **the L** with his sore and great 3068
27: 3 I **the L** do keep it; I will water it every 3068
27:12 *that* **the L** shall beat off from the channel of 3068
27:13 shall worship **the L** in the holy mount at 3068
28: 2 **the L** hath a mighty and strong one, 3068
28: 5 In that day shall **the L** of hosts be for a 3068
28:13 the word of **the L** was unto them precept 3068
28:14 Wherefore hear the word of **the L**, 3068
28:21 For **the L** shall rise up as *in* mount 3068
28:29 This also cometh forth from **the L** of hosts, 3068
29: 6 Thou shalt be visited of **the L** of hosts with 3068
29:10 For **the L** hath poured out upon you 3068
29:15 seek deep to hide *their* counsel from **the L**, 3068
29:19 meek also shall increase *their* joy in **the L**, 3068
29:22 Therefore thus saith **the L**, who redeemed 3068
30: 1 saith **the L**, that take counsel, but not of 3068
30: 9 children *that* will not hear the law of **the L**: 3068
30:18 therefore will **the L** wait, that *he* may be 3068
30:18 for **the L** *is* a God of judgment: blessed *are* 3068
30:26 in the day that **the L** bindeth up the breach 3068
30:27 the name of **the L** cometh from far, 3068
30:29 a pipe to come into the mountain of **the L**, 3068
30:30 **the L** shall cause his glorious voice to be 3068
30:31 For through the voice of **the L** shall 3068
30:32 which **the L** shall lay upon him, *it* shall be 3068
30:33 the breath of **the L**, like a stream of 3068
31: 1 the Holy One of Israel, neither seek **the L**. 3068
31: 3 When **the L** shall stretch out his hand, 3068
31: 4 For thus hath **the L** spoken unto me, 3068
31: 4 shall **the L** of hosts come down to fight for 3068
31: 5 so will **the L** of hosts defend Jerusalem; 3068
31: 9 saith **the L**, whose fire *is* in Zion, and his 3068
32: 6 and to utter error against **the L**, 3068
33: 2 O **L**, be gracious unto us; we have waited 3068
33: 5 **The L** *is* exalted; for he dwelleth on high: 3068
33: 6 the fear of **the L** *is* his treasure. 3068
33:10 Now will I rise, saith **the L**; now will I be 3068
33:21 there **the** glorious **L** *will be* unto us a place 3068
33:22 For **the L** *is* our judge, the LORD *is* our 3068
33:22 **the L** *is* our lawgiver, the LORD *is* our 3068
33:22 LORD *is* our lawgiver, **the L** *is* our king; 3068
34: 2 For the indignation of **the L** *is* upon all 3068
34: 6 The sword of **the L** is filled *with* blood, 3068
34: 6 for **the L** hath a sacrifice in Bozrah, and 3068
34:16 Seek ye out of the book of **the L**, and read: 3068
35: 2 they shall see the glory of **the L**, *and* 3068
35:10 the ransomed of **the L** shall return, and 3068
36: 7 thou say to me, We trust in **the L** our God: 3068
36:10 am I now come up without **the L** against 3068
36:10 **the L** said unto me, Go up against this land, 3068
36:15 let Hezekiah make you trust in **the L**, 3068
36:15 **The L** will surely deliver us: 3068
36:18 saying, **The L** will deliver us. 3068
36:20 that **the L** should deliver Jerusalem out of 3068
37: 1 and went *into* the house of **the L**. 3068
37: 4 It may be **the L** thy God will hear 3068
37: 4 will reprove the words which **the L** thy 3068
37: 6 ye say unto your master, Thus saith **the L**, 3068
37:14 Hezekiah went up *unto* the house of **the L**, 3068
37:14 of the LORD, and spread it before **the L**. 3068
37:15 And Hezekiah prayed unto **the L**, saying, 3068
37:16 O **L** of hosts, God of Israel, that dwellest 3068
37:17 Incline thine ear, O **L**, and hear; open thine 3068
37:17 and hear; open thine eyes, O **L**, and see: 3068
37:18 Of a truth, **L**, the kings of Assyria have laid 3068
37:20 Now therefore, O **L** our God, save us from 3068
37:20 of the earth may know that thou *art* **the L**, 3068
37:21 Thus saith **the L** God of Israel, 3068
37:22 This *is* the word which **the L** hath spoken 3068
37:32 the zeal of **the L** of hosts shall do this. 3068
37:33 Therefore thus saith **the L** concerning 3068
37:34 shall not come into this city, saith **the L**. 3068
37:36 the angel of **the L** went forth, and smote in 3068
38: 1 said unto him, Thus saith **the L**, Set thine 3068
38: 2 toward the wall, and prayed unto **the L**, 3068
38: 3 Remember now, O **L**, I beseech thee, 3068
38: 4 came the word of **the L** to Isaiah, saying, 3068
38: 5 Go and say to Hezekiah, Thus saith **the L**, 3068
38: 7 this *shall be* a sign unto thee from **the L**, 3068
38: 7 that **the L** will do this thing that he hath 3068
38:11 I said, I shall not see **the L**, *even* 3050
38:11 *even* **the L**, in the land of the living: 3050
38:14 O **L**, I am oppressed; undertake for me. 3068
38:20 **The L** *was ready* to save me: therefore 3068
38:20 the days of our life in the house of **the L**. 3068
38:22 that I shall go up *to* the house of **the L**? 3068
39: 5 Hear the word of **the L** of hosts: 3068
39: 6 nothing shall be left, saith **the L**. 3068
39: 8 Good *is* the word of **the L** which thou hast 3068
40: 3 Prepare ye the way of **the L**, 3068
40: 5 the glory of **the L** shall be revealed, and 3068
40: 5 for the mouth of **the L** hath spoken *it*. 3068
40: 7 because the spirit of **the L** bloweth upon it: 3068
40:13 Who hath directed the spirit of **the L**, or 3068
40:27 My way is hid from **the L**, and 3068
40:28 not heard, *that* the everlasting God, **the L**, 3068
40:31 they that wait upon **the L** shall renew *their* 3068
41: 4 I **the L**, the first, and with the last; I *am* he. 3068
41:13 For I **the L** thy God will hold thy right 3068
41:14 help thee, saith **the L**, and thy redeemer, 3068
41:16 thou shalt rejoice in **the L**, *and* shalt glory 3068
41:17 faileth for thirst, I **the L** will hear them, 3068
41:20 that the hand of **the L** hath done this, and 3068
41:21 Produce your cause, saith **the L**; bring forth 3068
42: 5 Thus saith God **the L**, he that created 3068
42: 6 I **the L** have called thee in righteousness, 3068
42: 8 I *am* **the L**: that *is* my name: and my glory 3068
42:10 Sing unto **the L** a new song, *and* his praise 3068
42:12 Let them give glory unto **the L**, and 3068
42:13 **The L** shall go forth as a mighty *man*, he 3068
42:21 **The L** is well pleased for his righteousness' 3068
42:24 did not **the L**, he against whom we have 3068
43: 1 now thus saith **the L** that created thee, 3068
43: 3 For I *am* **the L** thy God, the Holy One of 3068
43:10 saith **the L**, and my servant whom I have 3068
43:11 I, *even* I, *am* **the L**; and beside me *there is* 3068
43:12 my witnesses, saith **the L**, that I *am* God. 3068
43:14 Thus saith **the L**, your redeemer, the Holy 3068
43:15 I *am* **the L**, your Holy One, the creator of 3068
43:16 Thus saith **the L**, which maketh a way in 3068
44: 2 Thus saith **the L** that made thee, and 3068
44: 5 shall subscribe *with* his hand unto **the L**, 3068
44: 6 Thus saith **the L** the King of Israel, and 3068
44: 6 of Israel, and his redeemer **the L** of hosts; 3068
44:23 for **the L** hath done *it:* shout, ye lower parts 3068
44:23 for **the L** hath redeemed Jacob, and 3068
44:24 Thus saith **the L**, thy redeemer, and he that 3068
44:24 I *am* **the L** that maketh all *things;* that 3068
45: 1 Thus saith **the L** to his anointed, to Cyrus, 3068
45: 3 **the L**, which call *thee* by thy name, *am* 3068
45: 5 I *am* **the L**, and *there is* none else, *there is* 3068
45: 6 I *am* **the L**, and *there is* none else. 3068
45: 7 and create evil: I **the L** do all these *things.* 3068
45: 8 spring up together; I **the L** have created it. 3068
45:11 Thus saith **the L**, the Holy One of Israel, 3068
45:13 for price nor reward, saith **the L** of hosts. 3068
45:14 Thus saith **the L**, The labour of Egypt, and 3068
45:17 *But* Israel shall be saved in **the L** *with* an 3068
45:18 For thus saith **the L** that created 3068
45:18 I *am* **the L**; and *there is* none else. 3068
45:19 I **the L** speak righteousness, I declare 3068
45:21 *have* not I **the L**? and *there is* no God else 3068
45:24 in **the L** have I righteousness and strength: 3068
45:25 In **the L** shall all the seed of Israel be 3068
47: 4 our redeemer, **the L** of hosts *is* his name, 3068
48: 1 which swear by the name of **the L**, and 3068
48: 2 God of Israel; **The L** of hosts *is* his name. 3068
48:14 these *things?* **The L** hath loved him: 3068
48:17 Thus saith **the L**, thy redeemer, the Holy 3068
48:17 I *am* **the L** thy God which teacheth thee to 3068
48:20 **The L** hath redeemed his servant Jacob. 3068
48:22 *is* no peace, saith **the L**, unto the wicked. 3068
49: 1 **The L** hath called me from the womb; 3068
49: 4 *yet* surely my judgment *is* with **the L**, and 3068
49: 5 saith **the L** that formed me from the womb 3068
49: 5 yet shall I be glorious in the eyes of **the L**, 3068

Isa	49: 7	Thus saith **the L**, the redeemer of Israel,	3068
	49: 7	because of **the L** that *is* faithful, *and*	3068
	49: 8	Thus saith **the L**, In an acceptable time	3068
	49:13	for **the L** hath comforted his people, and	3068
	49:14	**The L** hath forsaken me, and my Lord hath	3068
	49:18	*As* I live, saith **the L**, thou shalt surely	3068
	49:23	and thou shalt know that I *am* **the L**:	3068
	49:25	thus saith **the L**, Even the captives of	3068
	49:26	all flesh shall know that I **the L** *am* thy	3068
	50: 1	Thus saith **the L**, Where *is* the bill of your	3068
	50:10	Who *is* among you that feareth **the L**,	3068
	50:10	let him trust in the name of **the L**, and	3068
	51: 1	after righteousness, ye that seek **the L**:	3068
	51: 3	For **the L** shall comfort Zion: he will	3068
	51: 3	and her desert like the garden of **the L**;	3068
	51: 9	awake, put on strength, O arm of **the L**;	3068
	51:11	Therefore the redeemed of **the L** shall	3068
	51:13	forgettest **the L** thy Maker, that hath	3068
	51:15	I *am* **the L** thy God, that divided the sea,	3068
	51:15	waves roared: **The L** of hosts *is* his name.	3068
	51:17	which hast drunk at the hand of **the L**	3068
	51:20	*they are* full *of* the fury of **the L**, the rebuke	3068
	51:22	Thus saith thy Lord **the L**, and thy God *that*	3068
	52: 3	For thus saith **the L**, Ye have sold	3068
	52: 5	what have I here, saith **the L**,	3068
	52: 5	over them make *them* to howl, saith **the L**;	3068
	52: 8	to eye, when **the L** shall bring again Zion.	3068
	52: 9	for **the L** hath comforted his people,	3068
	52:10	**The L** hath made bare his holy arm in	3068
	52:11	be ye clean, that bear the vessels of **the L**.	3068
	52:12	for **the L** will go before you; and the God	3068
	53: 1	and to whom is the arm of **the L** revealed?	3068
	53: 6	**the L** hath laid on him the iniquity of us all.	3068
	53:10	Yet it pleased **the L** to bruise him; he hath	3068
	53:10	the pleasure of **the L** shall prosper in his	3068
	54: 1	children of the married wife, saith **the L**.	3068
	54: 5	**the L** of hosts *is* his name; and	3068
	54: 6	For **the L** hath called thee as a woman	3068
	54: 8	mercy on thee, saith **the L** thy redeemer.	3068
	54:10	saith **the L** that hath mercy on thee.	3068
	54:13	all thy children *shall be* taught of **the L**;	3068
	54:17	This *is* the heritage of the servants of **the L**,	3068
	54:17	their righteousness *is* of me, saith **the L**.	3068
	55: 5	run unto thee because of **the L** thy God,	3068
	55: 6	Seek ye **the L** while he may be found,	3068
	55: 7	let him return unto **the L**, and he will have	3068
	55: 8	*are* your ways my ways, saith **the L**.	3068
	55:13	it shall be to **the L** for a name, for an	3068
	56: 1	Thus saith **the L**, Keep ye judgment, and	3068
	56: 3	that hath joined himself to **the L**, speak,	3068
	56: 3	**The L** hath utterly separated me from his	3068
	56: 4	For thus saith **the L** unto the eunuchs that	3068
	56: 6	that join themselves to **the L**, to serve him,	3068
	56: 6	serve him, and to love the name of **the L**,	3068
	57:19	far off, and to *him that is* near, saith **the L**;	3068
	58: 5	this a fast, and an acceptable day to **the L**?	3068
	58: 8	the glory of **the L** shall be thy rereward.	3068
	58: 9	shalt thou call, and **the L** shall answer;	3068
	58:11	**the L** shall guide thee continually, and	3068
	58:13	a delight, the holy of **the L**, honourable;	3068
	58:14	shalt thou delight thyself in **the L**; and	3068
	58:14	for the mouth of **the L** hath spoken *it*.	3068
	59:13	In transgressing and lying against **the L**,	3068
	59:15	**the L** saw *it*, and it displeased him that	3068
	59:19	So shall they fear the name of **the L** from	3068
	59:19	the spirit of **the L** shall lift up a standard	3068
	59:20	from transgression in Jacob, saith **the L**.	3068
	59:21	this *is* my covenant with them, saith **the L**;	3068
	59:21	saith **the L**, from henceforth and for ever.	3068
	60: 1	and the glory of **the L** is risen upon thee.	3068
	60: 2	**the L** shall arise upon thee, and his glory	3068
	60: 6	they shall shew forth the praises of **the L**.	3068
	60: 9	unto the name of **the L** thy God, and to	3068
	60:14	they shall call thee, The city of **the L**,	3068
	60:16	thou shalt know that I **the L** *am* thy Saviour	3068
	60:19	**the L** shall be unto thee an everlasting	3068
	60:20	for **the L** shall be thine everlasting light,	3068
	60:22	I **the L** will hasten it in his time.	3068
	61: 1	**the L** hath anointed me to preach good	3068
	61: 2	To proclaim the acceptable year of **the L**,	3068
	61: 3	the planting of **the L**, that *he* might be	3068
	61: 6	ye shall be named the Priests of **the L**:	3068
	61: 8	For I **the L** love judgment, I hate robbery	3068
	61: 9	that they *are* the seed *which* **the L** hath	3068
	61:10	I will greatly rejoice in **the L**, my soul shall	3068
	62: 2	which the mouth of **the L** shall name.	3068
	62: 3	be a crown of glory in the hand of **the L**,	3068
	62: 4	for **the L** delighteth in thee, and thy land	3068
	62: 6	ye that make mention of **the L**, keep not	3068
	62: 8	**The L** hath sworn by his right hand, and	3068
	62: 9	gathered it shall eat it, and praise **the L**;	3068
	62:11	**the L** hath proclaimed unto the end of	3068
	62:12	The holy people, The redeemed of **the L**:	3068
	63: 7	will mention the lovingkindnesses of **the L**,	3068
	63: 7	of the LORD, *and* the praises of **the L**,	3068
	63: 7	according to all that **the L** hath bestowed	3068
	63:14	the Spirit of **the L** caused him to rest:	3068
	63:16	thou, O **L**, *art* our father, our redeemer;	3068
	63:17	O **L**, why hast thou made us to err from thy	3068
	64: 8	now, O **L**, thou *art* our father; we *are*	3068
	64: 9	Be not wroth very sore, O **L**,	3068
	64:12	thou refrain thyself for these *things,* O **L**?	3068
	65: 7	of your fathers together, saith **the L**,	3068
	65: 8	Thus saith **the L**, As the new wine is found	3068
	65:11	ye *are* they that forsake **the L**, that forget	3068
	65:23	they *are* the seed of the blessed of **the L**,	3068
	65:25	in all my holy mountain, saith **the L**.	3068
	66: 1	Thus saith **the L**, The heaven *is* my throne,	3068
	66: 2	and all those *things* have been, saith **the L**:	3068
	66: 5	Hear the word of **the L**, ye that tremble at	3068
	66: 5	name's sake, said, Let **the L** be glorified:	3068
	66: 6	a voice of **the L** that rendereth recompence	3068
	66: 9	saith **the L**: shall I cause to bring forth, and	3068
	66:12	For thus saith **the L**, Behold, I will extend	3068
	66:14	the hand of **the L** shall be known towards	3068
	66:15	**the L** will come with fire, and with his	3068
	66:16	by his sword will **the L** plead with all flesh:	3068
	66:16	and the slain of **the L** shall be many.	3068
	66:17	shall be consumed together, saith **the L**.	3068
	66:20	unto **the L** out of all nations upon horses,	3068
	66:20	my holy mountain Jerusalem, saith **the L**,	3068
	66:20	in a clean vessel *into* the house of **the L**.	3068
	66:21	for priests *and* for Levites, saith **the L**.	3068
	66:22	saith **the L**, so shall your seed and	3068
	66:23	come to worship before me, saith **the L**.	3068
Jer	1: 2	To whom the word of **the L** came in	3068
	1: 4	the word of **the L** came unto me, saying,	3068
	1: 7	**the L** said unto me, Say not, I *am* a child:	3068
	1: 8	I *am* with thee to deliver thee, saith **the L**.	3068
	1: 9	**the L** put forth his hand, and touched my	3068
	1: 9	**the L** said unto me, Behold, I have put my	3068
	1:11	the word of **the L** came unto me, saying,	3068
	1:12	said **the L** unto me, Thou hast well seen:	3068
	1:13	the word of **the L** came unto me the second	3068
	1:14	**the L** said unto me, Out of the north an evil	3068
	1:15	of the kingdoms of the north, saith **the L**;	3068
	1:19	I *am* with thee, saith **the L**, to deliver thee.	3068
	2: 1	Moreover the word of **the L** came to me,	3068
	2: 2	ears of Jerusalem, saying, Thus saith **the L**;	3068
	2: 3	Israel *was* holiness unto **the L**, *and*	3068
	2: 3	evil shall come upon them, saith **the L**.	3068
	2: 4	Hear ye the word of **the L**, O house of	3068
	2: 5	Thus saith **the L**, What iniquity have your	3068
	2: 6	Where *is* **the L** that brought us up out of	3068
	2: 8	The priests said not, Where *is* **the L**? and	3068
	2: 9	saith **the L**, and with your children's	3068
	2:12	be ye very desolate, saith **the L**.	3068
	2:17	in that thou hast forsaken **the L** thy God,	3068
	2:19	that thou hast forsaken **the L** thy God, and	3068
	2:29	have transgressed against me, saith **the L**.	3068
	2:31	O generation, see ye the word of **the L**.	3068
	2:37	for **the L** hath rejected thy confidences, and	3068
	3: 1	yet return again to me, saith **the L**.	3068
	3: 6	**The L** said also unto me in the days of	3068
	3:10	her whole heart, but feignedly, saith **the L**.	3068
	3:11	**the L** said unto me, The backsliding Israel	3068
	3:12	Return, thou backsliding Israel, saith **the L**;	3068
	3:12	saith **the L**, *and* I will not keep *anger* for	3068
	3:13	that thou hast transgressed against **the L**	3068
	3:13	ye have not obeyed my voice, saith **the L**.	3068
	3:14	Turn, O backsliding children, saith **the L**;	3068
	3:16	in the land, in those days, saith **the L**,	3068
	3:16	no more, The ark of the covenant of **the L**:	3068
	3:17	shall call Jerusalem the throne of **the L**;	3068
	3:17	unto it, to the name of **the L**, to Jerusalem:	3068
	3:20	with me, O house of Israel, saith **the L**.	3068
	3:21	*and* they have forgotten **the L** their God.	3068
	3:22	come unto thee; for thou *art* **the L** our God.	3068

Jer 3:23 truly in **the L** our God *is* the salvation of 3068
3:25 for we have sinned against **the L** our God, 3068
3:25 have not obeyed the voice of **the L** our 3068
4: 1 O Israel, saith **the L**, return unto me: 3068
4: 2 **The L** liveth, in truth, in judgment, and 3068
4: 3 For thus saith **the L** to the men of Judah 3068
4: 4 Circumcise yourselves to **the L**, and 3068
4: 8 for the fierce anger of **the L** is not turned 3068
4: 9 shall come to pass at that day, saith **the L**, 3068
4:17 been rebellious against me, saith **the L**. 3068
4:26 were broken down at the presence of **the L**, 3068
4:27 For thus hath **the L** said, The whole land 3068
5: 2 though they say, **The L** liveth; surely they 3068
5: 3 O **L**, *are* not thine eyes upon the truth? 3068
5: 4 for they know not the way of **the L**, *nor* 3068
5: 5 for they have known the way of **the L**, *and* 3068
5: 9 I not visit for these *things?* saith **the L**: 3068
5:11 very treacherously against me, saith **the L**. 3068
5:12 They have belied **the L**, and said, *It is* not 3068
5:14 Wherefore thus saith **the L** God of hosts, 3068
5:15 you from far, O house of Israel, saith **the L**: 3068
5:18 Nevertheless in those days, saith **the L**, 3068
5:19 Wherefore doth **the L** our God all these 3068
5:22 saith **the L**: will ye not tremble at my 3068
5:24 Let us now fear **the L** our God, that giveth 3068
5:29 I not visit for these *things?* saith **the L**: 3068
6: 6 For thus hath **the L** of hosts said, Hew ye 3068
6: 9 Thus saith **the L** of hosts, They shall 3068
6:10 the word of **the L** is unto them a reproach; 3068
6:11 Therefore I am full *of* the fury of **the L**; 3068
6:12 the inhabitants of the land, saith **the L**. 3068
6:15 them they shall be cast down, saith **the L**. 3068
6:16 Thus saith **the L**, Stand ye in the ways, and 3068
6:21 Therefore thus saith **the L**, Behold, I will 3068
6:22 Thus saith **the L**, Behold, a people cometh 3068
6:30 because **the L** hath rejected them. 3068
7: 1 word that came to Jeremiah from **the L**, 3068
7: 2 say, Hear the word of **the L**, all *ye of* 3068
7: 2 enter in at these gates to worship **the L**. 3068
7: 3 Thus saith **the L** of hosts, the God of Israel, 3068
7: 4 saying, The temple of **the L**, The temple of 3068
7: 4 The temple of **the L**, The temple of 3068
7: 4 the LORD, The temple of **the L**, *are* these. 3068
7:11 Behold, even I have seen *it,* saith **the L**. 3068
7:13 saith **the L**, and I spake unto you, rising up 3068
7:19 saith **the L**: *do they* not *provoke* 3068
7:21 Thus saith **the L** of hosts, the God of Israel; 3068
7:28 obeyeth not the voice of **the L** their God, 3068
7:29 for **the L** hath rejected and forsaken 3068
7:30 have done evil in my sight, saith **the L**: 3068
7:32 the days come, saith **the L**, 3068
8: 1 At that time, saith **the L**, they shall bring 3068
8: 3 I have driven them, saith **the L** of hosts. 3068
8: 4 thou shalt say unto them, Thus saith **the L**; 3068
8: 7 my people know not the judgment of **the L**. 3068
8: 8 *are* wise, and the law of **the L** *is* with us? 3068
8: 9 lo, they have rejected the word of **the L**; 3068
8:12 they shall be cast down, saith **the L**. 3068
8:13 I will surely consume them, saith **the L**: 3068
8:14 for **the L** our God hath put us to silence, 3068
8:14 because we have sinned against **the L**. 3068
8:17 and they shall bite you, saith **the L**. 3068
8:19 *Is* not **the L** in Zion? *is* not her king in her? 3068
9: 3 to evil, and they know not me, saith **the L**. 3068
9: 6 deceit they refuse to know me, saith **the L**. 3068
9: 7 Therefore thus saith **the L** of hosts, Behold, 3068
9: 9 not visit them for these *things?* saith **the L**: 3068
9:12 *who is he* to whom the mouth of **the L** hath 3068
9:13 **the L** saith, Because they have forsaken my 3068
9:15 Therefore thus saith **the L** of hosts, the God 3068
9:17 Thus saith **the L** of hosts, Consider ye, and 3068
9:20 Yet hear the word of **the L**, O ye women, 3068
9:22 Speak, Thus saith **the L**, Even the carcases 3068
9:23 Thus saith **the L**, Let not the wise *man* 3068
9:24 that I *am* **the L** which exercise 3068
9:24 for in these *things* I delight, saith **the L**. 3068
9:25 Behold, the days come, saith **the L**, that I 3068
10: 1 Hear ye the word which **the L** speaketh 3068
10: 2 Thus saith **the L**, Learn not the way of 3068
10: 6 as *there is* none like unto thee, O **L**; 3068
10:10 **the L** *is* the true God, he *is* the living God, 3068
10:16 his inheritance: **The L** of hosts *is* his name. 3068
10:18 For thus saith **the L**, Behold, I will sling 3068
10:21 become brutish, and have not sought **the L**: 3068
10:23 O **L**, I know that the way of man *is* not in 3068
10:24 O **L**, correct me, but with judgment; not in 3068
11: 1 word that came to Jeremiah from **the L**, 3068
11: 3 unto them, Thus saith **the L** God of Israel; 3068
11: 5 Then answered I, and said, So be it, O **L**. 3068
11: 6 **the L** said unto me, Proclaim all these 3068
11: 9 **the L** said unto me, A conspiracy is found 3068
11:11 Therefore thus saith **the L**, Behold, I *will* 3068
11:16 **The L** called thy name, A green olive tree, 3068
11:17 For **the L** of hosts, that planted thee, 3068
11:18 **the L** hath given me knowledge *of it,* and 3068
11:20 But, O **L** of hosts, that judgest righteously, 3068
11:21 Therefore thus saith **the L** of the men of 3068
11:21 Prophesy not in the name of **the L**, 3068
11:22 Therefore thus saith **the L** of hosts, Behold, 3068
12: 1 Righteous *art* thou, O **L**, when I plead with 3068
12: 3 thou, O **L**, knowest me: thou hast seen me, 3068
12:12 for the sword of **the L** *shall* devour from 3068
12:13 because of the fierce anger of **the L**. 3068
12:14 Thus saith **the L** against all mine evil 3068
12:16 to swear by my name, **The L** liveth; 3068
12:17 and destroy that nation, saith **the L**. 3068
13: 1 Thus saith **the L** unto me, Go and get thee 3068
13: 2 according to the word of **the L**, and put *it* 3068
13: 3 the word of **the L** came unto me the second 3068
13: 5 it by Euphrates, as **the L** commanded me. 3068
13: 6 that **the L** said unto me, Arise, go to 3068
13: 8 the word of **the L** came unto me, saying, 3068
13: 9 Thus saith **the L**, After this manner will I 3068
13:11 and the whole house of Judah, saith **the L**; 3068
13:12 Thus saith **the L** God of Israel, Every bottle 3068
13:13 say unto them, Thus saith **the L**, Behold, 3068
13:14 and the sons together, saith **the L**: 3068
13:15 be not proud: for **the L** hath spoken. 3068
13:16 Give glory to **the L** your God, before he 3068
13:25 of thy measures from me, saith **the L**; 3068
14: 1 The word of **the L** that came to Jeremiah 3068
14: 7 O **L**, though our iniquities testify against 3068
14: 9 yet thou, O **L**, *art* in the midst of us, and 3068
14:10 Thus saith **the L** unto this people, Thus 3068
14:10 therefore **the L** doth not accept them; 3068
14:11 said **the L** unto me, Pray not for this people 3068
14:14 **the L** said unto me, The prophets prophesy 3068
14:15 Therefore thus saith **the L** concerning 3068
14:20 O **L**, our wickedness, *and* the iniquity of 3068
14:22 *art* not thou he, O **L** our God? therefore 3068
15: 1 said **the L** unto me, Though Moses and 3068
15: 2 thou shalt tell them, Thus saith **the L**; 3068
15: 3 appoint over them four kinds, saith **the L**: 3068
15: 6 Thou hast forsaken me, saith **the L**, 3068
15: 9 the sword before their enemies, saith **the L**. 3068
15:11 **The L** said, Verily it shall be well with thy 3068
15:15 O **L**, thou knowest: remember me, and 3068
15:16 I am called by thy name, O **L** God of hosts. 3068
15:19 Therefore thus saith **the L**, If thou return, 3068
15:20 to save thee and to deliver thee, saith **the L**. 3068
16: 1 The word of **the L** came also unto me, 3068
16: 3 For thus saith **the L** concerning the sons 3068
16: 5 For thus saith **the L**, Enter not *into* 3068
16: 5 saith **the L**, *even* lovingkindness and 3068
16: 9 For thus saith **the L** of hosts, the God of 3068
16:10 Wherefore hath **the L** pronounced all this 3068
16:10 we have committed against **the L** our God? 3068
16:11 saith **the L**, and have walked after other 3068
16:14 the days come, saith **the L**, 3068
16:14 that it shall no more be said, **The L** liveth, 3068
16:15 But, **The L** liveth, that brought up 3068
16:16 saith **the L**, and they shall fish them; 3068
16:19 O **L**, my strength, and my fortress, and 3068
16:21 they shall know that my name *is* **The L**. 3068
17: 5 Thus saith **the L**; Cursed *be* the man that 3068
17: 5 and whose heart departeth from **the L**. 3068
17: 7 Blessed *is* the man that trusteth in **the L**, 3068
17: 7 in the LORD, and whose hope **the L** is. 3068
17:10 I **the L** search the heart, *I* try the reins, 3068
17:13 O **L**, the hope of Israel, all that forsake thee 3068
17:13 because they have forsaken **the L**, 3068
17:14 Heal me, O **L**, and I shall be healed; 3068
17:15 say unto me, Where *is* the word of **the L**? 3068
17:19 Thus said **the L** unto me; Go and stand in 3068
17:20 Hear ye the word of **the L**, ye kings of 3068
17:21 Thus saith **the L**; Take heed to yourselves, 3068
17:24 ye diligently hearken unto me, saith **the L**, 3068
17:26 *of* praise, *unto* the house of **the L**. 3068

Jer 18: 1	word which came to Jeremiah from **the L**,	3068
18: 5	the word of **the L** came to me, saying,	3068
18: 6	saith **the L**. Behold, as the clay *is* in	3068
18:11	of Jerusalem, saying, Thus saith **the L**;	3068
18:13	Therefore thus saith **the L**; Ask ye now	3068
18:19	O **L**, and hearken to the voice of them that	3068
18:23	Yet, **L**, thou knowest all their counsel	3068
19: 1	Thus saith **the L**, Go and get a potter's	3068
19: 3	say, Hear ye the word of **the L**, O kings of	3068
19: 3	Thus saith **the L** of hosts, the God of Israel;	3068
19: 6	the days come, saith **the L**,	3068
19:11	say unto them, Thus saith **the L** of hosts;	3068
19:12	saith **the L**, and to the inhabitants thereof,	3068
19:14	whither **the L** had sent him to prophesy;	3068
19:15	Thus saith **the L** of hosts, the God of Israel;	3068
20: 1	also chief governor in the house of **the L**,	3068
20: 2	which *was* by the house of **the L**.	3068
20: 3	**The L** hath not called thy name Pashur, but	3068
20: 4	For thus saith **the L**, Behold, I will make	3068
20: 7	O **L**, thou hast deceived me, and I was	3068
20: 8	the word of **the L** was made a reproach	3068
20:11	**the L** *is* with me as a mighty terrible one:	3068
20:12	But, O **L** of hosts, that triest the righteous,	3068
20:13	Sing unto **the L**, praise ye the LORD:	3068
20:13	Sing unto the LORD, praise ye **the L**:	3068
20:16	let that man be as the cities which **the L**	3068
21: 1	which came unto Jeremiah from **the L**,	3068
21: 2	Inquire, I pray thee, of **the L** for us; for	3068
21: 2	be that **the L** will deal with us according to	3068
21: 4	Thus saith **the L** God of Israel; Behold,	3068
21: 7	afterward, saith **the L**, I will deliver	3068
21: 8	this people thou shalt say, Thus saith **the L**;	3068
21:10	city for evil, and not for good, saith **the L**:	3068
21:11	of Judah, *say,* Hear ye the word of **the L**.	3068
21:12	O house of David, thus saith **the L**;	3068
21:13	*and* rock of the plain, saith **the L**;	3068
21:14	to the fruit of your doings, saith **the L**:	3068
22: 1	Thus saith **the L**; Go down *to* the house of	3068
22: 2	say, Hear the word of **the L**, O king of	3068
22: 3	Thus saith **the L**; Execute ye judgment and	3068
22: 5	these words, I swear by myself, saith **the L**,	3068
22: 6	For thus saith **the L** unto the king's house	3068
22: 8	Wherefore hath **the L** done thus unto this	3068
22: 9	forsaken the covenant of **the L** their God,	3068
22:11	For thus saith **the L** touching Shallum	3068
22:16	*him: was* not this to know me? saith **the L**.	3068
22:18	Therefore thus saith **the L** concerning	3068
22:24	*As* I live, saith **the L**, though Coniah	3068
22:29	earth, earth, hear the word of **the L**.	3068
22:30	Thus saith **the L**, Write ye this man	3068
23: 1	scatter the sheep of my pasture! saith **the L**.	3068
23: 2	Therefore thus saith **the L** God of Israel	3068
23: 2	you the evil of your doings, saith **the L**.	3068
23: 4	neither shall they be lacking, saith **the L**.	3068
23: 5	Behold, the days come, saith **the L**, that I	3068
23: 6	**THE L** OUR RIGHTEOUSNESS.	3068
23: 7	the days come, saith **the L**,	3068
23: 7	that they shall no more say, **The L** liveth,	3068
23: 8	But, **The L** liveth, which brought up and	3068
23: 9	because of **the L**, and because of the words	3068
23:11	have I found their wickedness, saith **the L**.	3068
23:12	the year of their visitation, saith **the L**.	3068
23:15	Therefore thus saith **the L** of hosts	3068
23:16	Thus saith **the L** of hosts, Hearken not unto	3068
23:16	*and* not out of the mouth of **the L**.	3068
23:17	**The L** hath said, Ye shall have peace;	3068
23:18	For who hath stood in the counsel of **the L**,	3068
23:19	a whirlwind of **the L** is gone forth *in* fury,	3068
23:20	The anger of **the L** shall not return, until he	3068
23:23	saith **the L**, and not a God afar off?	3068
23:24	saith **the L**. Do not I fill heaven and earth?	3068
23:24	Do not I fill heaven and earth? saith **the L**.	3068
23:28	What *is* the chaff to the wheat? saith **the L**.	3068
23:29	saith **the L**; and like a hammer *that*	3068
23:30	I *am* against the prophets, saith **the L**,	3068
23:31	saith **the L**, that use their tongues, and say,	3068
23:32	saith **the L**, and do tell them, and cause my	3068
23:32	not profit this people at all, saith **the L**.	3068
23:33	saying, What *is* the burden of **the L**?	3068
23:33	I will even forsake you, saith **the L**.	3068
23:34	that shall say, The burden of **the L**,	3068
23:35	to his brother, What hath **the L** answered?	3068
23:35	and, What hath **the L** spoken?	3068
23:36	the burden of **the L** shall ye mention no	3068
23:36	the living God, of **the L** of hosts our God.	3068
23:37	What hath **the L** answered thee?	3068
23:37	and, What hath **the L** spoken?	3068
23:38	sith ye say, The burden of **the L**; therefore	3068
23:38	of the LORD; therefore thus saith **the L**;	3068
23:38	The burden of **the L**, and I have sent unto	3068
23:38	Ye shall not say, The burden of **the L**;	3068
24: 1	**The L** shewed me, and behold, two baskets	3068
24: 1	of figs *were* set before the temple of **the L**,	3068
24: 3	said **the L** unto me, What seest thou,	3068
24: 4	Again the word of **the L** came unto me,	3068
24: 5	Thus saith **the L**, the God of Israel;	3068
24: 7	them a heart to know me, that I *am* **the L**:	3068
24: 8	surely thus saith **the L**, So will I give	3068
25: 3	the word of **the L** hath come unto me, and	3068
25: 4	**the L** hath sent unto you all his servants	3068
25: 5	dwell in the land that **the L** hath given unto	3068
25: 7	have not hearkened unto me, saith **the L**;	3068
25: 8	Therefore thus saith **the L** of hosts;	3068
25: 9	saith **the L**, and Nebuchadrezzar the king	3068
25:12	that nation, saith **the L**, for their iniquity,	3068
25:15	For thus saith **the L** God of Israel unto me;	3068
25:17	to drink, unto whom **the L** had sent me:	3068
25:27	Thus saith **the L** of hosts, the God of Israel;	3068
25:28	say unto them, Thus saith **the L** of hosts;	3068
25:29	of the earth, saith **the L** of hosts.	3068
25:30	**The L** shall roar from on high, and utter his	3068
25:31	for **the L** hath a controversy with	3068
25:31	*that are* wicked to the sword, saith **the L**.	3068
25:32	Thus saith **the L** of hosts, Behold, evil *shall*	3068
25:33	the slain of **the L** shall be at that day from	3068
25:36	*shall be heard:* for **the L** *hath* spoiled their	3068
25:37	because of the fierce anger of **the L**.	3068
26: 1	king of Judah came this word from **the L**,	3068
26: 2	Thus saith **the L**; Stand in the court of	3068
26: 4	thou shalt say unto them, Thus saith **the L**;	3068
26: 7	speaking these words in the house of **the L**.	3068
26: 8	**the L** had commanded *him* to speak unto	3068
26: 9	hast thou prophesied in the name of **the L**,	3068
26: 9	against Jeremiah in the house of **the L**.	3068
26:10	the king's house *unto* the house of **the L**,	3068
26:12	**The L** sent me to prophesy against this	3068
26:13	and obey the voice of **the L** your God;	3068
26:13	**the L** will repent him of the evil that he	3068
26:15	for of a truth **the L** hath sent me unto you	3068
26:16	spoken to us in the name of **the L** our God.	3068
26:18	of Judah, saying, Thus saith **the L** of hosts;	3068
26:19	did he not fear **the L**, and besought	3068
26:19	besought **the L**, and the LORD repented	3068
26:19	**the L** repented him of the evil which he	3068
26:20	a man that prophesied in the name of **the L**,	3068
27: 1	came this word unto Jeremiah from **the L**,	3068
27: 2	Thus saith **the L** to me; Make thee bonds	3068
27: 4	Thus saith **the L** of hosts, the God of Israel;	3068
27: 8	saith **the L**, with the sword, and with	3068
27:11	remain still in their own land, saith **the L**;	3068
27:13	as **the L** hath spoken against the nation that	3068
27:15	For I have not sent them, saith **the L**,	3068
27:16	to all this people, saying, Thus saith **the L**;	3068
27:18	and if the word of **the L** be with them,	3068
27:18	let them now make intercession to **the L** of	3068
27:18	vessels which are left in the house of **the L**,	3068
27:19	For thus saith **the L** of hosts concerning	3068
27:21	Yea, thus saith **the L** of hosts, the God of	3068
27:21	vessels that remain *in* the house of **the L**,	3068
27:22	until the day that I visit them, saith **the L**;	3068
28: 1	spake unto me in the house of **the L**,	3068
28: 2	Thus speaketh **the L** of hosts, the God of	3068
28: 4	that went into Babylon, saith **the L**:	3068
28: 5	the people that stood in the house of **the L**,	3068
28: 6	**the L** do so: the LORD perform thy words	3068
28: 6	**the L** perform thy words which thou hast	3068
28: 9	be known, that **the L** hath truly sent him.	3068
28:11	of all the people, saying, Thus saith **the L**;	3068
28:12	the word of **the L** came unto Jeremiah	3068
28:13	and tell Hananiah, saying, Thus saith **the L**;	3068
28:14	For thus saith **the L** of hosts, the God of	3068
28:15	**The L** hath not sent thee; but thou makest	3068
28:16	Therefore thus saith **the L**; Behold, I will	3068
28:16	thou hast taught rebellion against **the L**.	3068
29: 4	Thus saith **the L** of hosts, the God of Israel,	3068
29: 7	away captives, and pray unto **the L** for it:	3068
29: 8	For thus saith **the L** of hosts, the God of	3068
29: 9	my name: I have not sent them, saith **the L**.	3068

Jer 29:10 For thus saith **the L**, That after seventy 3068
29:11 saith **the L**, thoughts of peace, and not of 3068
29:14 And I will be found of you, saith **the L**: and 3068
29:14 whither I have driven you, saith **the L**; 3068
29:15 **The L** hath raised us up prophets in 3068
29:16 *Know* that thus saith **the L** of the king that 3068
29:17 Thus saith **the L** of hosts; Behold, I will 3068
29:19 not hearkened to my words, saith **the L**, 3068
29:19 but ye would not hear, saith **the L**. 3068
29:20 Hear ye therefore the word of **the L**, all *ye* 3068
29:21 Thus saith **the L** of hosts, the God of Israel, 3068
29:22 **The L** make thee like Zedekiah and 3068
29:23 even I know, and *am* a witness, saith **the L**. 3068
29:25 Thus speaketh **the L** of hosts, the God of 3068
29:26 **The L** hath made thee priest in the stead of 3068
29:26 *ye* should be officers in the house of **the L**, 3068
29:30 came the word of **the L** unto Jeremiah, 3068
29:31 Thus saith **the L** concerning Shemaiah 3068
29:32 Therefore thus saith **the L**; Behold, I will 3068
29:32 that I will do for my people, saith **the L**; 3068
29:32 he hath taught rebellion against **the L**. 3068
30: 1 word that came to Jeremiah from **the L**, 3068
30: 2 Thus speaketh **the L** God of Israel, saying, 3068
30: 3 For lo, the days come, saith **the L**, that I 3068
30: 3 of my people Israel and Judah, saith **the L**: 3068
30: 4 these *are* the words that **the L** spake 3068
30: 5 For thus saith **the L**; We have heard a voice 3068
30: 8 to pass in that day, saith **the L** of hosts, 3068
30: 9 they shall serve **the L** their God, and David 3068
30:10 thou not, O my servant Jacob, saith **the L**; 3068
30:11 I *am* with thee, saith **the L**, to save thee: 3068
30:12 For thus saith **the L**, Thy bruise *is* 3068
30:17 I will heal thee of thy wounds, saith **the L**; 3068
30:18 Thus saith **the L**: Behold, I *will* bring again 3068
30:21 his heart to approach unto me? saith **the L**. 3068
30:23 the whirlwind of **the L** goeth forth *with* 3068
30:24 The fierce anger of **the L** shall not return, 3068
31: 1 At the same time, saith **the L**, will I be 3068
31: 2 Thus saith **the L**, The people which were 3068
31: 3 **The L** hath appeared of old unto me, 3068
31: 6 let us go up *to* Zion unto **the L** our God. 3068
31: 7 For thus saith **the L**; Sing with gladness for 3068
31: 7 publish ye, praise ye, and say, O **L**, save 3068
31:10 Hear the word of **the L**, O ye nations, and 3068
31:11 For **the L** hath redeemed Jacob, and 3068
31:12 flow *together* to the goodness of **the L**, 3068
31:14 be satisfied with my goodness, saith **the L**. 3068
31:15 Thus saith **the L**; A voice was heard in 3068
31:16 Thus saith **the L**, Refrain thy voice from 3068
31:16 for thy work shall be rewarded, saith **the L**; 3068
31:17 there is hope in thine end, saith **the L**, 3068
31:18 shall be turned; for thou *art* **the L** my God. 3068
31:20 surely have mercy upon him, saith **the L**. 3068
31:22 for **the L** hath created a new *thing* in 3068
31:23 Thus saith **the L** of hosts, the God of Israel; 3068
31:23 **The L** bless thee, O habitation of justice, 3068
31:27 Behold, the days come, saith **the L**, that I 3068
31:28 to build, and to plant, saith **the L**. 3068
31:31 Behold, the days come, saith **the L**, that I 3068
31:32 I was a husband unto them, saith **the L**: 3068
31:33 After those days, saith **the L**, I will put my 3068
31:34 every man his brother, saying, Know **the L**: 3068
31:34 them unto the greatest of them, saith **the L**: 3068
31:35 Thus saith **the L**, which giveth the sun for a 3068
31:35 thereof roar; **The L** of hosts *is* his name: 3068
31:36 saith **the L**, *then* the seed of Israel also 3068
31:37 Thus saith **the L**; If heaven above can be 3068
31:37 for all that they have done, saith **the L**. 3068
31:38 Behold, the days come, saith **the L**, that 3068
31:38 that the city shall be built to **the L** from 3068
31:40 towards the east, *shall be* holy unto **the L**; 3068
32: 1 The word that came to Jeremiah from **the L** 3068
32: 3 and say, Thus saith **the L**, Behold, 3068
32: 5 shall he be until I visit him, saith **the L**: 3068
32: 6 The word of **the L** came unto me, saying, 3068
32: 8 the prison according to the word of **the L**, 3068
32: 8 I knew that this *was* the word of **the L**. 3068
32:14 Thus saith **the L** of hosts, the God of Israel; 3068
32:15 For thus saith **the L** of hosts, the God of 3068
32:16 son of Neriah, I prayed unto **the L**, saying, 3068
32:18 Mighty God, **the L** of hosts, *is* his name, 3068
32:26 came the word of **the L** unto Jeremiah, 3068
32:27 Behold, I *am* **the L**, the God of all flesh: is 3068
32:28 Therefore thus saith **the L**; Behold, I *will* 3068
32:30 with the work of their hands, saith **the L**. 3068
32:36 now therefore thus saith **the L**, the God of 3068
32:42 For thus saith **the L**; Like as I have brought 3068
32:44 cause their captivity to return, saith **the L**. 3068
33: 1 Moreover the word of **the L** came unto 3068
33: 2 Thus saith **the L** the maker thereof, 3068
33: 2 **the L** that formed it, to establish it; 3068
33: 2 formed it, to establish it; **the L** *is* his name; 3068
33: 4 For thus saith **the L**, the God of Israel, 3068
33:10 Thus saith **the L**; Again there shall be 3068
33:11 them that shall say, Praise **the L** of hosts: 3068
33:11 for **the L** *is* good; for his mercy *endureth* 3068
33:11 sacrifice of praise *into* the house of **the L**. 3068
33:11 of the land as at the first, saith **the L**. 3068
33:12 Thus saith **the L** of hosts, Again in this 3068
33:13 hands of him that telleth *them,* saith **the L**. 3068
33:14 Behold, the days come, saith **the L**, that I 3068
33:16 shall be called, **The L** our righteousness. 3068
33:17 For thus saith **the L**; David shall never 3068
33:19 And the word of **the L** came unto Jeremiah, 3068
33:20 Thus saith **the L**; If you can break my 3068
33:23 Moreover the word of **the L** came to 3068
33:24 The two families which **the L** hath chosen, 3068
33:25 Thus saith **the L**; If my covenant *be* not 3068
34: 1 which came unto Jeremiah from **the L**, 3068
34: 2 Thus saith **the L**, the God of Israel; Go and 3068
34: 2 of Judah, and tell him, Thus saith **the L**; 3068
34: 4 Yet hear the word of **the L**, O Zedekiah 3068
34: 4 Thus saith **the L** of thee, Thou shalt not die 3068
34: 5 I have pronounced the word, saith **the L**. 3068
34: 8 word that came unto Jeremiah from **the L**, 3068
34:12 Therefore the word of **the L** came to 3068
34:12 the LORD came to Jeremiah from **the L**, 3068
34:13 Thus saith **the L**, the God of Israel; I made 3068
34:17 Therefore thus saith **the L**; Ye have not 3068
34:17 saith **the L**, to the sword, to the pestilence, 3068
34:22 saith **the L**, and cause them to return to this 3068
35: 1 **the L** in the days of Jehoiakim the son of 3068
35: 2 and bring them *into* the house of **the L**, 3068
35: 4 I brought them *into* the house of **the L**, 3068
35:12 came the word of **the L** unto Jeremiah, 3068
35:13 Thus saith **the L** of hosts, the God of Israel; 3068
35:13 to hearken to my words? saith **the L**. 3068
35:17 Therefore thus saith **the L** God of hosts, 3068
35:18 Thus saith **the L** of hosts, the God of Israel; 3068
35:19 Therefore thus saith **the L** of hosts, the God 3068
36: 1 this word came unto Jeremiah from **the L**, 3068
36: 4 mouth of Jeremiah all the words of **the L**, 3068
36: 5 I cannot go *into* the house of **the L**: 3068
36: 6 the words of **the L** in the ears of the people 3068
36: 7 will present their supplication before **the L**, 3068
36: 7 the fury that **the L** hath pronounced against 3068
36: 8 reading in the book the words of **the L** *in* 3068
36: 9 *that* they proclaimed a fast before **the L** *to* 3068
36:10 words of Jeremiah *in* the house of **the L**, 3068
36:11 out of the book all the words of **the L**, 3068
36:26 Jeremiah the prophet: but **the L** hid them. 3068
36:27 the word of **the L** came to Jeremiah, 3068
36:29 Jehoiakim king of Judah, Thus saith **the L**; 3068
36:30 Therefore thus saith **the L** of Jehoiakim 3068
37: 2 did hearken unto the words of **the L**, 3068
37: 3 Pray now unto **the L** our God for us. 3068
37: 6 came the word of **the L** unto the prophet 3068
37: 7 Thus saith **the L**, the God of Israel; 3068
37: 9 Thus saith **the L**; Deceive not yourselves, 3068
37:17 and said, Is there *any* word from **the L**? 3068
38: 2 Thus saith **the L**, He that remaineth in this 3068
38: 3 Thus saith **the L**, This city shall surely be 3068
38:14 the third entry that *is* in the house of **the L**: 3068
38:16 saying, *As* **the L** liveth, that made us this 3068
38:17 Thus saith **the L**, the God of hosts, the God 3068
38:20 I beseech thee, the voice of **the L**, which I 3068
38:21 this *is* the word that **the L** hath shewed me: 3068
39:15 Now the word of **the L** came unto 3068
39:16 saying, Thus saith **the L** of hosts, the God 3068
39:17 I will deliver thee in that day, saith **the L**: 3068
39:18 thou hast put thy trust in me, saith **the L**. 3068
40: 1 word which came to Jeremiah from **the L**, 3068
40: 2 **The L** thy God hath pronounced this evil 3068
40: 3 Now **the L** hath brought *it,* and 3068
40: 3 because ye have sinned against **the L**, and 3068
41: 5 to bring *them to* the house of **the L**. 3068
42: 2 pray for us unto **the L** thy God, *even* for all 3068
42: 3 That **the L** thy God may shew us the way 3068

Jer 42: 4 I *will* pray unto **the L** your God according 3068
42: 4 *that* whatsoever thing **the L** shall answer 3068
42: 5 **The L** be a true and faithful witness 3068
42: 5 which **the L** thy God shall send thee to us. 3068
42: 6 we will obey the voice of **the L** our God, 3068
42: 6 when we obey the voice of **the L** our God. 3068
42: 7 that the word of **the L** came unto Jeremiah. 3068
42: 9 Thus saith **the L**, the God of Israel, 3068
42:11 *are* afraid; be not afraid of him, saith **the L**: 3068
42:13 neither obey the voice of **the L** your God, 3068
42:15 now therefore hear the word of **the L**, 3068
42:15 Thus saith **the L** of hosts, the God of Israel; 3068
42:18 For thus saith **the L** of hosts, the God of 3068
42:19 **The L** hath said concerning you, O ye 3068
42:20 when ye sent me unto **the L** your God, 3068
42:20 Pray for us unto **the L** our God; 3068
42:20 according unto all that **the L** our God shall 3068
42:21 ye have not obeyed the voice of **the L** your 3068
43: 1 the people all the words of **the L** their God, 3068
43: 1 *for* which **the L** their God had sent him to 3068
43: 2 **the L** our God hath not sent thee to say, 3068
43: 4 the people, obeyed not the voice of **the L**, 3068
43: 7 for they obeyed not the voice of **the L**: 3068
43: 8 came the word of **the L** unto Jeremiah in 3068
43:10 Thus saith **the L** of hosts, the God of Israel; 3068
44: 2 Thus saith **the L** of hosts, the God of Israel; 3068
44: 7 Therefore now thus saith **the L**, the God of 3068
44:11 Therefore thus saith **the L** of hosts, the God 3068
44:16 hast spoken unto us in the name of **the L**, 3068
44:21 did not **the L** remember them, and came it 3068
44:22 So that **the L** could no longer bear, because 3068
44:23 because ye have sinned against **the L**, and 3068
44:23 have not obeyed the voice of **the L**, 3068
44:24 to all the women, Hear the word of **the L**, 3068
44:25 Thus saith **the L** of hosts, the God of Israel, 3068
44:26 Therefore hear ye the word of **the L**, 3068
44:26 have sworn by my great name, saith **the L**, 3068
44:29 this *shall be* a sign unto you, saith **the L**, 3068
44:30 Thus saith **the L**; Behold, I *will* give 3068
45: 2 Thus saith **the L**, the God of Israel, 3068
45: 3 for **the L** hath added grief to my sorrow; 3068
45: 4 shalt thou say unto him, **The L** saith thus; 3068
45: 5 I *will* bring evil upon all flesh, saith **the L**: 3068
46: 1 The word of **the L** which came to Jeremiah 3068
46: 5 *for* fear *was* round about, saith **the L**. 3068
46:13 The word that **the L** spake to Jeremiah 3068
46:15 stood not, because **the L** did drive them. 3068
46:18 the King, whose name *is* **the L** of hosts, 3068
46:23 saith **the L**, though it cannot be searched; 3068
46:25 **The L** of hosts, the God of Israel, saith; 3068
46:26 as *in* the days of old, saith **the L**. 3068
46:28 thou not, O Jacob my servant, saith **the L**: 3068
47: 1 The word of **the L** that came to Jeremiah 3068
47: 2 Thus saith **the L**; Behold, waters rise up 3068
47: 4 for **the L** *will* spoil the Philistines, 3068
47: 6 O thou sword of **the L**, how long *will it be* 3068
47: 7 seeing **the L** hath given it a charge against 3068
48: 1 Against Moab thus saith **the L** of hosts, 3068
48: 8 shall be destroyed, as **the L** hath spoken. 3068
48:10 Cursed *be* he that doeth the work of **the L** 3068
48:12 the days come, saith **the L**, 3068
48:15 the King, whose name *is* **the L** of hosts. 3068
48:25 cut off, and his arm is broken, saith **the L**. 3068
48:26 for he magnified *himself* against **the L**: 3068
48:30 I know his wrath, saith **the L**; but *it shall* 3068
48:35 saith **the L**, him that offereth *in* the high 3068
48:38 a vessel wherein *is* no pleasure, saith **the L**. 3068
48:40 For thus saith **the L**; Behold, he shall fly as 3068
48:42 he hath magnified *himself* against **the L**. 3068
48:43 O inhabitant of Moab, saith **the L**. 3068
48:44 the year of their visitation, saith **the L**. 3068
48:47 of Moab in the latter days, saith **the L**. 3068
49: 1 the Ammonites, thus saith **the L**; 3068
49: 2 the days come, saith **the L**, 3068
49: 2 unto them that were his heirs, saith **the L**. 3068
49: 6 of the children of Ammon, saith **the L**. 3068
49: 7 thus saith **the L** of hosts; 3068
49:12 For thus saith **the L**; Behold, they whose 3068
49:13 For I have sworn by myself, saith **the L**, 3068
49:14 I have heard a rumour from **the L**, and 3068
49:16 bring thee down from thence, saith **the L**. 3068
49:18 saith **the L**, no man shall abide there, 3068
49:20 Therefore hear the counsel of **the L**, that he 3068
49:26 be cut off in that day, saith **the L** of hosts. 3068
49:28 of Babylon shall smite, thus saith **the L**; 3068
49:30 O ye inhabitants of Hazor, saith **the L**; 3068
49:31 that dwelleth without care, saith **the L**, 3068
49:32 calamity from all sides thereof, saith **the L**. 3068
49:34 The word of **the L** that came to Jeremiah 3068
49:35 Thus saith **the L** of hosts; Behold, I *will* 3068
49:37 *even* my fierce anger, saith **the L**; 3068
49:38 thence the king and the princes, saith **the L**. 3068
49:39 again the captivity of Elam, saith **the L**. 3068
50: 1 The word that **the L** spake against Babylon 3068
50: 4 In those days, and in that time, saith **the L**, 3068
50: 4 they shall go, and seek **the L** their God. 3068
50: 5 let us join ourselves to **the L** *in* a perpetual 3068
50: 7 because they have sinned against **the L**, 3068
50: 7 the habitation of justice, even **the L**, 3068
50:10 that spoil her shall be satisfied, saith **the L**. 3068
50:13 Because of the wrath of **the L** it shall not 3068
50:14 for she hath sinned against **the L**. 3068
50:15 for it *is* the vengeance of **the L**: 3068
50:18 Therefore thus saith **the L** of hosts, the God 3068
50:20 In those days, and in that time, saith **the L**, 3068
50:21 saith **the L**, and do according to all that I 3068
50:24 because thou hast striven against **the L**. 3068
50:25 **The L** hath opened his armoury, and 3068
50:28 to declare in Zion the vengeance of **the L** 3068
50:29 for she hath been proud against **the L**, 3068
50:30 war shall be cut off in that day, saith **the L**. 3068
50:33 Thus saith **the L** of hosts; The children of 3068
50:34 *is* strong; **the L** of hosts *is* his name: 3068
50:35 saith **the L**, and upon the inhabitants of 3068
50:40 the neighbour *cities* thereof, saith **the L**; 3068
50:45 Therefore hear ye the counsel of **the L**, 3068
51: 1 Thus saith **the L**; Behold, I *will* raise up 3068
51: 5 nor Judah of his God, of **the L** of hosts; 3068
51:10 **The L** hath brought forth our 3068
51:10 let us declare in Zion the work of **the L** our 3068
51:11 **the L** hath raised up the spirit of the kings 3068
51:11 because it *is* the vengeance of **the L**, 3068
51:12 for **the L** hath both devised and done that 3068
51:14 **The L** of hosts hath sworn by himself, 3068
51:19 his inheritance: **the L** of hosts *is* his name. 3068
51:24 done in Zion in your sight, saith **the L**. 3068
51:25 O destroying mountain, saith **the L**, 3068
51:26 thou shalt be desolate for ever, saith **the L**. 3068
51:29 for every purpose of **the L** shall be 3068
51:33 For thus saith **the L** of hosts, the God of 3068
51:36 Therefore thus saith **the L**; Behold, I *will* 3068
51:39 perpetual sleep, and not wake, saith **the L**. 3068
51:45 man his soul from the fierce anger of **the L**. 3068
51:48 come unto her from the north, saith **the L**. 3068
51:50 remember **the L** afar off, and let Jerusalem 3068
51:52 the days come, saith **the L**, 3068
51:53 shall spoilers come unto her, saith **the L**. 3068
51:55 Because **the L** *hath* spoiled Babylon, and 3068
51:56 for **the L** God of recompences shall surely 3068
51:57 the King, whose name *is* **the L** of hosts. 3068
51:58 Thus saith **the L** of hosts; The broad walls 3068
51:62 shalt thou say, O **L**, thou hast spoken 3068
52: 2 *that* which *was* evil in the eyes of **the L** 3068
52: 3 For through the anger of **the L** it came to 3068
52:13 burnt the house of **the L**, and the king's 3068
52:17 of brass that *were* in the house of **the L**, 3068
52:17 brasen sea that *was* in the house of **the L**, 3068
52:20 Solomon had made in the house of **the L**: 3068
La 1: 5 for **the L** hath afflicted her for 3068
1: 9 O **L**, behold my affliction: for the enemy 3068
1:11 see, O **L**, and consider; for I am become 3068
1:12 wherewith **the L** hath afflicted *me* in 3068
1:17 **the L** hath commanded concerning Jacob, 3068
1:18 **The L** *is* righteous; for I have rebelled 3068
1:20 Behold, O **L**; for I *am* in distress: my 3068
2: 6 **the L** hath caused the solemn feasts and 3068
2: 7 have made a noise in the house of **the L**, 3068
2: 8 **The L** hath purposed to destroy the wall of 3068
2: 9 her prophets also find no vision from **the L**. 3068
2:17 **The L** hath done *that* which he had 3068
2:20 O **L**, and consider to whom thou hast done 3068
3:18 and my hope is perished from **the L**: 3068
3:24 **The L** *is* my portion, saith my soul; 3068
3:25 **The L** *is* good unto them that wait for him, 3068
3:26 and quietly wait for the salvation of **the L**. 3068
3:40 and try our ways, and turn again to **the L**. 3068
3:50 Till **the L** look down, and behold from 3068
3:55 I called upon thy name, O **L**, out of the low 3068

La 3:59 O L, thou hast seen my wrong: judge thou 3068
3:61 O L, *and* all their imaginations against me; 3068
3:64 Render unto them a recompence, O L, 3068
3:66 in anger from under the heavens of **the L**. 3068
4:11 **The L** hath accomplished his fury; he hath 3068
4:16 The anger of **the L** hath divided them; 3068
4:20 the anointed of **the L**, was taken in their 3068
5: 1 Remember, O L, what is come upon us: 3068
5:19 Thou, O L, remainest for ever; thy throne 3068
5:21 us unto thee, O L, and we shall be turned; 3068
Eze 1: 3 The word of **the L** came expressly unto 3068
1: 3 and the hand of **the L** was there upon him. 3068
1:28 of the likeness of the glory of **the L**. 3068
3:12 *saying,* Blessed *be* the glory of **the L** from 3068
3:14 but the hand of **the L** was strong upon me. 3068
3:16 that the word of **the L** came unto me, 3068
3:22 the hand of **the L** was there upon me; and 3068
3:23 behold, the glory of **the L** stood there, 3068
4:13 **the L** said, Even thus shall the children of 3068
5:13 they shall know that I **the L** have spoken *it* 3068
5:15 in furious rebukes. I **the L** have spoken *it.* 3068
5:17 sword upon thee. I **the L** have spoken *it.* 3068
6: 1 the word of **the L** came unto me, saying, 3068
6: 7 of you, and ye shall know that I *am* **the L**. 3068
6:10 they shall know that I *am* **the L**, *and that* I 3068
6:13 shall ye know that I *am* **the L**, when their 3068
6:14 and they shall know that I *am* **the L**. 3068
7: 1 Moreover the word of **the L** came unto me, 3068
7: 4 of thee: and ye shall know that I *am* **the L**. 3068
7: 9 ye shall know that I *am* **the L** that smiteth. 3068
7:19 them in the day of the wrath of **the L**: 3068
7:27 and they shall know that I *am* **the L**. 3068
8:12 for they say, **The L** seeth us not; 3068
8:12 seeth us not; **the L** hath forsaken the earth. 3068
8:16 behold, *at* the door of the temple of **the L**, 3068
8:16 their backs toward the temple of **the L**, 3068
9: 4 **the L** said unto him, Go through the midst 3068
9: 9 **The L** hath forsaken the earth, and 3068
9: 9 forsaken the earth, and **the L** seeth not. 3068
10: 4 the glory of **the L** went up from the cherub, 3068
10:18 the glory of **the L** departed from off 3068
11: 5 the Spirit of **the L** fell upon me, and 3068
11: 5 and said unto me, Speak; Thus saith **the L**; 3068
11:10 and ye shall know that I *am* **the L**. 3068
11:12 ye shall know that I *am* **the L**: for ye have 3068
11:14 Again the word of **the L** came unto me, 3068
11:15 Jerusalem have said, Get ye far from **the L**: 3068
11:23 the glory of **the L** went up from the midst 3068
11:25 all the things that **the L** had shewed me. 3068
12: 1 The word of **the L** also came unto me, 3068
12: 8 in the morning came the word of **the L** 3068
12:15 they shall know that I *am* **the L**, when I 3068
12:16 and they shall know that I *am* **the L**. 3068
12:17 Moreover the word of **the L** came to me, 3068
12:20 and ye shall know that I *am* **the L**. 3068
12:21 the word of **the L** came unto me, saying, 3068
12:25 For I *am* **the L**: I will speak, and the word 3068
12:26 Again the word of **the L** came to me, 3068
13: 1 the word of **the L** came unto me, saying, 3068
13: 2 own hearts, Hear ye the word of **the L**; 3068
13: 5 to stand in the battle in the day of **the L**. 3068
13: 6 and lying divination, saying, **The L** saith: 3068
13: 6 **the L** hath not sent them: and they have 3068
13: 7 **The L** saith *it;* albeit I have not spoken? 3068
13:14 and ye shall know that I *am* **the L**. 3068
13:21 and ye shall know that I *am* **the L**. 3068
13:23 and ye shall know that I *am* **the L**. 3068
14: 2 the word of **the L** came unto me, saying, 3068
14: 4 I **the L** will answer him that cometh 3068
14: 7 I **the L** will answer him by myself: 3068
14: 8 and ye shall know that I *am* **the L**. 3068
14: 9 I **the L** have deceived that prophet, and 3068
14:12 The word of **the L** came again to me, 3068
15: 1 the word of **the L** came unto me, saying, 3068
15: 7 ye shall know that I *am* **the L**, when I set 3068
16: 1 Again the word of **the L** came unto me, 3068
16:35 O harlot, hear the word of **the L**: 3068
16:58 and thine abominations, saith **the L**. 3068
16:62 and thou shalt know that I *am* **the L**: 3068
17: 1 the word of **the L** came unto me, saying, 3068
17:11 Moreover the word of **the L** came unto me, 3068
17:21 ye shall know that I **the L** have spoken *it.* 3068
17:24 I **the L** have brought down the high tree, 3068
17:24 I **the L** have spoken and have done *it.* 3068
18: 1 the word of **the L** came unto me again, 3068
20: 1 elders of Israel came to inquire of **the L**, 3068
20: 2 came the word of **the L** unto me, saying, 3068
20: 5 unto them, saying, I *am* **the L** your God; 3068
20: 7 the idols of Egypt: I *am* **the L** your God. 3068
20:12 that *they* might know that I *am* **the L** that 3068
20:19 I *am* **the L** your God; walk in my statutes, 3068
20:20 that *ye* may know that I *am* **the L** your 3068
20:26 end that they might know that I *am* **the L**. 3068
20:38 and ye shall know that I *am* **the L**. 3068
20:42 ye shall know that I *am* **the L**, when I shall 3068
20:44 ye shall know that I *am* **the L**, when I have 3068
20:45 Moreover the word of **the L** came unto me, 3068
20:47 forest of the south, Hear the word of **the L**; 3068
20:48 all flesh shall see that I **the L** have kindled 3068
21: 1 the word of **the L** came unto me, saying, 3068
21: 3 say to the land of Israel, Thus saith **the L**; 3068
21: 5 That all flesh may know that I **the L** have 3068
21: 8 Again the word of **the L** came unto me, 3068
21: 9 prophesy, and say, Thus saith **the L**; 3068
21:17 cause my fury to rest: I **the L** have said *it.* 3068
21:18 The word of **the L** came unto me again, 3068
21:32 for I **the L** have spoken *it.* 3068
22: 1 Moreover the word of **the L** came unto me, 3068
22:14 I **the L** have spoken *it,* and will do *it.* 3068
22:16 and thou shalt know that I *am* **the L**. 3068
22:17 the word of **the L** came unto me, saying, 3068
22:22 ye shall know that I **the L** have poured out 3068
22:23 the word of **the L** came unto me, saying, 3068
22:28 Lord GOD, when **the L** hath not spoken. 3068
23: 1 The word of **the L** came again unto me, 3068
23:36 **The L** said moreover unto me; Son of man, 3068
24: 1 the word of **the L** came unto me, saying, 3068
24:14 I **the L** have spoken *it:* it shall come to 3068
24:15 Also the word of **the L** came unto me, 3068
24:20 The word of **the L** came unto me, saying, 3068
24:27 and they shall know that I *am* **the L**. 3068
25: 1 The word of **the L** came again unto me, 3068
25: 5 and ye shall know that I *am* **the L**. 3068
25: 7 and thou shalt know that I *am* **the L**. 3068
25:11 and they shall know that I *am* **the L**. 3068
25:17 they shall know that I *am* **the L**, when I 3068
26: 1 *that* the word of **the L** came unto me, 3068
26: 6 and they shall know that I *am* **the L**. 3068
26:14 for I **the L** have spoken *it,* saith the Lord 3068
27: 1 The word of **the L** came again unto me, 3068
28: 1 The word of **the L** came again unto me, 3068
28:11 Moreover the word of **the L** came unto me, 3068
28:20 Again the word of **the L** came unto me, 3068
28:22 they shall know that I *am* **the L**, when I 3068
28:23 and they shall know that I *am* **the L**. 3068
28:26 they shall know that I *am* **the L** their God. 3068
29: 1 the word of **the L** came unto me, saying, 3068
29: 6 of Egypt shall know that I *am* **the L**, 3068
29: 9 waste; and they shall know that I *am* **the L**: 3068
29:17 the word of **the L** came unto me, saying, 3068
29:21 and they shall know that I *am* **the L**. 3068
30: 1 The word of **the L** came again unto me, 3068
30: 3 even the day of **the L** *is* near, a cloudy day; 3068
30: 6 Thus saith **the L**; They also that uphold 3068
30: 8 they shall know that I *am* **the L**, when I 3068
30:12 hand of strangers: I **the L** have spoken *it.* 3068
30:19 and they shall know that I *am* **the L**. 3068
30:20 *that* the word of **the L** came unto me, 3068
30:25 they shall know that I *am* **the L**, when I 3068
30:26 and they shall know that I *am* **the L**. 3068
31: 1 *that* the word of **the L** came unto me, 3068
32: 1 *that* the word of **the L** came unto me, 3068
32:15 shall they know that I *am* **the L**. 3068
32:17 *that* the word of **the L** came unto me, 3068
33: 1 Again the word of **the L** came unto me, 3068
33:22 Now the hand of **the L** was upon me in 3068
33:23 the word of **the L** came unto me, saying, 3068
33:29 shall they know that I *am* **the L**, when I 3068
33:30 *is* the word that cometh forth from **the L**. 3068
34: 1 the word of **the L** came unto me, saying, 3068
34: 7 ye shepherds, hear the word of **the L**; 3068
34: 9 O ye shepherds, hear the word of **the L**; 3068
34:24 I **the L** will be their God, and my servant 3068
34:24 among them; I **the L** have spoken *it.* 3068
34:27 their land, and shall know that I *am* **the L**, 3068
34:30 Thus shall they know that I **the L** their God 3068
35: 1 Moreover the word of **the L** came unto me, 3068
35: 4 and thou shalt know that I *am* **the L**. 3068

Eze 35: 9 and ye shall know that I *am* **the L**. 3068
35:10 will possess it; whereas **the L** was there: 3068
35:12 thou shalt know that I *am* **the L**, *and that* I 3068
35:15 of it: and they shall know that I *am* **the L**. 3068
36: 1 mountains of Israel, hear the word of **the L**: 3068
36:11 and ye shall know that I *am* **the L**. 3068
36:16 Moreover the word of **the L** came unto me, 3068
36:20 These *are* the people of **the L**, and are gone 3068
36:23 the heathen shall know that I *am* **the L**, 3068
36:36 know that I **the L** build the ruined *places,* 3068
36:36 I **the L** have spoken *it,* and I will do *it.* 3068
36:38 and they shall know that I *am* **the L**. 3068
37: 1 The hand of **the L** was upon me, and 3068
37: 1 carried me out in the spirit of **the L**, and 3068
37: 4 O ye dry bones, hear the word of **the L**. 3068
37: 6 and ye shall know that I *am* **the L**. 3068
37:13 ye shall know that I *am* **the L**, when I have 3068
37:14 shall ye know that I **the L** have spoken *it,* 3068
37:14 spoken *it,* and performed *it,* saith **the L**. 3068
37:15 The word of **the L** came again unto me, 3068
37:28 the heathen shall know that I **the L** do 3068
38: 1 the word of **the L** came unto me, saying, 3068
38:23 and they shall know that I *am* **the L**. 3068
39: 6 and they shall know that I *am* **the L**. 3068
39: 7 the heathen shall know that I *am* **the L**, 3068
39:22 that I *am* **the L** their God from that day 3068
39:28 shall they know that I *am* **the L** their God, 3068
40: 1 in the selfsame day the hand of **the L** was 3068
40:46 which come near to **the L** to minister unto 3068
41:22 This *is* the table that *is* before **the L**. 3068
42:13 where the priests that approach unto **the L** 3068
43: 4 the glory of **the L** came into the house by 3068
43: 5 behold, the glory of **the L** filled the house. 3068
43:24 And thou shalt offer them before **the L**, and 3068
43:24 them up *for* a burnt offering unto **the L**. 3068
44: 2 said **the L** unto me; This gate shall be shut, 3068
44: 2 because **the L**, the God of Israel, 3068
44: 3 he shall sit in it to eat bread before **the L**; 3068
44: 4 the glory of **the L** filled the house of 3068
44: 4 of the LORD filled the house of **the L**: 3068
44: 5 **the L** said unto me, Son of man, mark well, 3068
44: 5 all the ordinances of the house of **the L**, 3068
45: 1 ye shall offer an oblation unto **the L**, a holy 3068
45: 4 shall come near to minister unto **the L**: 3068
45:23 he shall prepare a burnt offering to **the L**, 3068
46: 3 of this gate before **the L** in the sabbaths 3068
46: 4 **the L** in the sabbath day *shall be* six lambs 3068
46: 9 come before **the L** in the solemn feasts, 3068
46:12 or peace offerings voluntarily unto **the L**, 3068
46:13 **the L** *of* a lamb of the first year without 3068
46:14 *by* a perpetual ordinance unto **the L**. 3068
48: 9 The oblation that ye shall offer unto **the L** 3068
48:10 the sanctuary of **the L** shall be in the midst 3068
48:14 of the land: for *it is* holy unto **the L**. 3068
48:35 city from *that* day *shall be,* **The L** *is* there. 3068
Da 9: 2 where*of* the word of **the L** came to 3068
9: 4 I prayed unto **the L** my God, and made my 3068
9:10 Neither have we obeyed the voice of **the L** 3068
9:13 yet made we not our prayer before **the L** 3068
9:14 Therefore hath **the L** watched upon 3068
9:14 for **the L** our God *is* righteous in all his 3068
9:20 presenting my supplication before **the L** 3068
Hos 1: 1 The word of **the L** that came unto Hosea, 3068
1: 2 The beginning of the word of **the L** by 3068
1: 2 **the L** said to Hosea, Go, take unto thee a 3068
1: 2 great whoredom, *departing* from **the L**. 3068
1: 4 **the L** said unto him, Call his name Jezreel; 3068
1: 7 will save them by **the L** their God, and 3068
2:13 after her lovers, and forgat me, saith **the L**. 3068
2:16 it shall be at that day, saith **the L**, *that* thou 3068
2:20 in faithfulness: and thou shalt know **the L**. 3068
2:21 I will hear, saith **the L**, I will hear 3068
3: 1 said **the L** unto me, Go yet, love a woman 3068
3: 1 according to the love of **the L** toward 3068
3: 5 seek **the L** their God, and David their king; 3068
3: 5 shall fear **the L** and his goodness in 3068
4: 1 Hear the word of **the L**, ye children of 3068
4: 1 for **the L** hath a controversy with 3068
4:10 they have left off to take heed to **the L**. 3068
4:15 up *to* Beth-aven, nor swear, **The L** liveth. 3068
4:16 now **the L** will feed them as a lamb in a 3068
5: 4 of them, and they have not known **the L**. 3068
5: 6 and with their herds to seek **the L**; 3068
5: 7 have dealt treacherously against **the L**: 3068
6: 1 Come and let us return unto **the L**: for he 3068
6: 3 we know, *if* we follow on to know **the L**: 3068
7:10 they do not return to **the L** their God, 3068
8: 1 as an eagle against the house of **the L**, 3068
8:13 and eat *it; but* **the L** accepteth them not; 3068
9: 4 shall not offer wine *offerings* to **the L**, 3068
9: 4 soul shall not come *into* the house of **the L**. 3068
9: 5 and in the day of the feast of **the L**? 3068
9:14 Give them, **O L**: what wilt thou give? 3068
10: 3 have no king, because we feared not **the L**; 3068
10:12 for *it is* time to seek **the L**, till he come and 3068
11:10 They shall walk after **the L**: he shall roar 3068
11:11 will place them in their houses, saith **the L**. 3068
12: 2 **The L** hath also a controversy with Judah, 3068
12: 5 Even **the L** God of hosts; the LORD *is* his 3068
12: 5 God of hosts; **the L** *is* his memorial. 3068
12: 9 I *that am* **the L** thy God from the land of 3068
12:13 by a prophet **the L** brought Israel out of 3068
13: 4 Yet I *am* **the L** thy God from the land of 3068
13:15 the wind of **the L** *shall* come up from 3068
14: 1 O Israel, return unto **the L** thy God; 3068
14: 2 Take with you words, and turn to **the L**: 3068
14: 9 for the ways of **the L** *are* right, and the just 3068
Joel 1: 1 The word of **the L** that came to Joel the son 3068
1: 9 offering is cut off from the house of **the L**; 3068
1:14 the land *into* the house of **the L** your God, 3068
1:14 the LORD your God, and cry unto **the L**, 3068
1:15 for the day of **the L** *is* at hand, and as a 3068
1:19 **O L**, to thee will I cry: for the fire hath 3068
2: 1 for the day of **the L** cometh, for *it is* nigh at 3068
2:11 **the L** shall utter his voice before his army: 3068
2:11 for the day of **the L** *is* great and 3068
2:12 Therefore also now, saith **the L**, turn ye 3068
2:13 and turn unto **the L** your God: 3068
2:14 and a drink offering unto **the L** your God? 3068
2:17 Let the priests, the ministers of **the L**, 3068
2:17 **O L**, and give not thine heritage to 3068
2:18 will **the L** be jealous for his land, and 3068
2:19 **the L** will answer and say unto his people, 3068
2:21 and rejoice: for **the L** will do great things. 3068
2:23 of Zion, and rejoice in **the L** your God: 3068
2:26 and praise the name of **the L** your God, 3068
2:27 *that* I *am* **the L** your God, and none else: 3068
2:31 and the terrible day of **the L** come. 3068
2:32 on the name of **the L** shall be delivered: 3068
2:32 as **the L** hath said, and in the remnant 3068
2:32 and in the remnant whom **the L** *shall* call. 3068
3: 8 a people far off: for **the L** hath spoken *it.* 3068
3:11 cause thy mighty ones to come down, **O L**. 3068
3:14 for the day of **the L** *is* near in the valley of 3068
3:16 **The L** also shall roar out of Zion, and 3068
3:16 **the L** *will be* the hope of his people, and 3068
3:17 So shall ye know that I *am* **the L** your God 3068
3:18 shall come forth of the house of **the L**, 3068
3:21 not cleansed: for **the L** dwelleth in Zion. 3068
Am 1: 2 **The L** will roar from Zion, and utter his 3068
1: 3 Thus saith **the L**; For three transgressions 3068
1: 5 shall go into captivity unto Kir, saith **the L**. 3068
1: 6 Thus saith **the L**; For three transgressions 3068
1: 9 Thus saith **the L**; For three transgressions 3068
1:11 Thus saith **the L**; For three transgressions 3068
1:13 Thus saith **the L**; For three transgressions 3068
1:15 he and his princes together, saith **the L**. 3068
2: 1 Thus saith **the L**; For three transgressions 3068
2: 3 the princes thereof with him, saith **the L**. 3068
2: 4 Thus saith **the L**; For three transgressions 3068
2: 4 they have despised the law of **the L**, 3068
2: 6 Thus saith **the L**; For three transgressions 3068
2:11 O ye children of Israel? saith **the L**. 3068
2:16 flee away naked in that day, saith **the L**. 3068
3: 1 Hear this word that **the L** hath spoken 3068
3: 6 evil in a city, and **the L** hath not done *it?* 3068
3:10 saith **the L**, who store up violence and 3068
3:12 Thus saith **the L**; As the shepherd taketh 3068
3:15 great houses shall have an end, saith **the L**. 3068
4: 3 shall cast *them* into the palace, saith **the L**. 3068
4: 6 have ye not returned unto me, saith **the L**. 3068
4: 8 have ye not returned unto me, saith **the L**. 3068
4: 9 have ye not returned unto me, saith **the L**. 3068
4:10 have ye not returned unto me, saith **the L**. 3068
4:11 have ye not returned unto me, saith **the L**. 3068
4:13 **The L**, The God of hosts, *is* his name. 3068
5: 4 For thus saith **the L** unto the house of 3068
5: 6 Seek **the L**, and ye shall live; lest he break 3068

Am	5: 8	the face of the earth: **The L** *is* his name:	3068
	5:14	so **the L**, the God of hosts, shall be with	3068
	5:15	it may be that **the L** God of hosts will be	3068
	5:16	Therefore **the L**, the God of hosts,	3068
	5:17	for I will pass through thee, saith **the L**.	3068
	5:18	Woe unto *you* that desire the day of **the L**!	3068
	5:18	the day of **the L** *is* darkness, and not light.	3068
	5:20	*Shall* not the day of **the L** *be* darkness, and	3068
	5:27	saith **the L**, whose name *is* The God of	3068
	6: 8	saith **the L** the God of hosts, I abhor	3068
	6:10	not make mention of the name of **the L**.	3068
	6:11	**the L** commandeth, and he will smite	3068
	6:14	of Israel, saith **the L** the God of hosts;	3068
	7: 3	**The L** repented for this: It shall not be,	3068
	7: 3	for this: It shall not be, saith **the L**.	3068
	7: 6	**The L** repented for this: This also shall not	3068
	7: 8	**the L** said unto me, Amos, what seest	3068
	7:15	**the L** took me as I followed the flock, and	3068
	7:15	**the L** said unto me, Go, prophesy unto my	3068
	7:16	Now therefore hear thou the word of **the L**:	3068
	7:17	Therefore thus saith **the L**; Thy wife shall	3068
	8: 2	said **the L** unto me, The end is come upon	3068
	8: 7	**The L** hath sworn by the excellency of	3068
	8:11	but of hearing the words of **the L**:	3068
	8:12	run to and fro to seek the word of **the L**,	3068
	9: 6	the face of the earth: **The L** *is* his name.	3068
	9: 7	saith **the L**. Have not I brought up Israel	3068
	9: 8	destroy the house of Jacob, saith **the L**.	3068
	9:12	by my name, saith **the L** that doeth this.	3068
	9:13	Behold, the days come, saith **the L**, that	3068
	9:15	I have given them, saith **the L** thy God.	3068
Ob	1: 1	We have heard a rumour from **the L**, and	3068
	1: 4	thence will I bring thee down, saith **the L**.	3068
	1: 8	Shall I not in that day, saith **the L**,	3068
	1:15	For the day of **the L** *is* near upon all	3068
	1:18	house of Esau; for **the L** hath spoken *it*.	3068
Jnh	1: 1	Now the word of **the L** came unto Jonah	3068
	1: 3	unto Tarshish from the presence of **the L**,	3068
	1: 3	unto Tarshish from the presence of **the L**.	3068
	1: 4	But **the L** sent out a great wind into the sea,	3068
	1: 9	I fear **the L**, the God of heaven, which hath	3068
	1:10	that he fled from the presence of **the L**,	3068
	1:14	Wherefore they cried unto **the L**, and said,	3068
	1:14	We beseech thee, **O L**, we beseech thee,	3068
	1:14	for thou, **O L**, hast done as it pleased thee.	3068
	1:16	the men feared **the L** exceedingly, and	3068
	1:16	offered a sacrifice unto **the L**, and	3068
	1:17	Now **the L** had prepared a great fish to	3068
	2: 1	Jonah prayed unto **the L** his God out of	3068
	2: 2	by reason of mine affliction unto **the L**,	3068
	2: 6	up my life from corruption, **O L** my God.	3068
	2: 7	soul fainted within me I remembered **the L**:	3068
	2: 9	that I have vowed. Salvation *is* of **the L**.	3068
	2:10	**the L** spake unto the fish, and it vomited	3068
	3: 1	the word of **the L** came unto Jonah	3068
	3: 3	according to the word of **the L**.	3068
	4: 2	he prayed unto **the L**, and said, I pray thee,	3068
	4: 2	said, I pray thee, **O L**, *was* not this my	3068
	4: 3	Therefore now, **O L**, take, I beseech thee,	3068
	4: 4	said **the L**, Doest thou well to be angry?	3068
	4: 6	**the L** God prepared a gourd, and made *it* to	3068
	4:10	said **the L**, Thou hast had pity on	3068
Mic	1: 1	The word of **the L** that came to Micah	3068
	1: 3	**the L** cometh forth out of his place, and	3068
	1:12	evil came down from **the L** unto the gate of	3068
	2: 3	Therefore thus saith **the L**; Behold,	3068
	2: 5	a cord by lot in the congregation of **the L**.	3068
	2: 7	of Jacob, is the spirit of **the L** straitened?	3068
	2:13	and **the L** on the head of them.	3068
	3: 4	shall they cry unto **the L**, but he will not	3068
	3: 5	Thus saith **the L** concerning the prophets	3068
	3: 8	I am full *of* power by the spirit of **the L**,	3068
	3:11	yet will they lean upon **the L**, and say, *Is*	3068
	3:11	and say, *Is* not **the L** among us?	3068
	4: 1	*that* the mountain of the house of **the L**	3068
	4: 2	let us go up to the mountain of **the L**, and	3068
	4: 2	and the word of **the L** from Jerusalem.	3068
	4: 4	for the mouth of **the L** of hosts hath	3068
	4: 5	we will walk in the name of **the L** our God	3068
	4: 6	In that day, saith **the L**, will I assemble her	3068
	4: 7	**the L** shall reign over them in mount Zion	3068
	4:10	there **the L** shall redeem thee from	3068
	4:12	they know not the thoughts of **the L**,	3068
	4:13	I will consecrate their gain unto **the L**, and	3068

	5: 4	and feed in the strength of **the L**,	3068
	5: 4	in the majesty of the name of **the L** his	3068
	5: 7	midst of many people as a dew from **the L**,	3068
	5:10	shall come to pass in that day, saith **the L**,	3068
	6: 1	Hear ye now what **the L** saith; Arise,	3068
	6: 2	for **the L** hath a controversy with his	3068
	6: 5	*ye* may know the righteousness of **the L**.	3068
	6: 6	Wherewith shall I come before **the L**, *and*	3068
	6: 7	Will **the L** be pleased with thousands of	3068
	6: 8	what doth **the L** require of thee, but to do	3068
	7: 7	Therefore I will look unto **the L**; I will wait	3068
	7: 8	in darkness, **the L** *shall be* a light unto me.	3068
	7: 9	I will bear the indignation of **the L**,	3068
	7:10	said unto me, Where is **the L** thy God?	3068
	7:17	they shall be afraid of **the L** our God, and	3068
Na	1: 2	God *is* jealous, and **the L** revengeth;	3068
	1: 2	**the L** revengeth, and *is* furious;	3068
	1: 2	**the L** will take vengeance on his	3068
	1: 3	**The L** *is* slow to anger, and great in power,	3068
	1: 3	will not at all acquit *the wicked*: **the L** *hath*	3068
	1: 7	**The L** *is* good, a strong hold in the day of	3068
	1: 9	What do ye imagine against **the L**? he *will*	3068
	1:11	that imagineth evil against **the L**, a wicked	3068
	1:12	Thus saith **the L**; Though *they be* quiet,	3068
	1:14	**the L** hath given a commandment	3068
	2: 2	For **the L** hath turned *away* the excellency	3068
	2:13	saith **the L** of hosts, and I will burn her	3068
	3: 5	I *am* against thee, saith **the L** of hosts;	3068
Hab	1: 2	**O L**, how long shall I cry, and thou wilt not	3068
	1:12	**O L** my God, mine Holy One?	3068
	1:12	**O L**, thou hast ordained them for judgment;	3068
	2: 2	**the L** answered me, and said, Write	3068
	2:13	*is it* not of **the L** of hosts that the people	3068
	2:14	with the knowledge of the glory of **the L**,	3068
	2:20	**the L** *is* in his holy temple: let all the earth	3068
	3: 2	**O L**, I have heard thy speech, *and*	3068
	3: 2	**O L**, revive thy work in the midst of	3068
	3: 8	Was **the L** displeased against the rivers?	3068
	3:18	Yet I will rejoice in **the L**, I will joy in	3068
Zep	1: 1	The word of **the L** which came unto	3068
	1: 2	all *things* from off the land, saith **the L**.	3068
	1: 3	cut off man from off the land, saith **the L**.	3068
	1: 5	them that worship *and* that swear by **the L**,	3068
	1: 6	them that are turned back from **the L**; and	3068
	1: 6	*those* that have not sought **the L**, nor	3068
	1: 7	for the day of **the L** *is* at hand: for	3068
	1: 7	for **the L** hath prepared a sacrifice, he hath	3068
	1:10	shall come to pass in that day, saith **the L**,	3068
	1:12	say in their heart, **The L** will not do good,	3068
	1:14	The great day of **the L** *is* near, *it is* near,	3068
	1:14	*even* the voice of the day of **the L**:	3068
	1:17	because they have sinned against **the L**:	3068
	2: 2	before the fierce anger of **the L** come upon	3068
	2: 3	Seek ye **the L**, all ye meek of the earth,	3068
	2: 5	the word of **the L** *is* against you;	3068
	2: 7	for **the L** their God shall visit them, and	3068
	2: 9	saith **the L** of hosts, the God of Israel,	3068
	2:10	against the people of **the L** of hosts.	3068
	2:11	**The L** *will be* terrible unto them: for he	3068
	3: 2	not correction; she trusted not in **the L**;	3068
	3: 5	**The** just **L** *is* in the midst thereof; he will	3068
	3: 8	Therefore wait ye upon me, saith **the L**,	3068
	3: 9	they may all call upon the name of **the L**,	3068
	3:12	and they shall trust in the name of **the L**.	3068
	3:15	**The L** hath taken away thy judgments,	3068
	3:15	the king of Israel, *even* **the L**, *is* in	3068
	3:17	**The L** thy God in the midst of thee *is*	3068
	3:20	captivity before your eyes, saith **the L**.	3068
Hag	1: 1	came the word of **the L** by Haggai	3068
	1: 2	Thus speaketh **the L** of hosts, saying, This	3068
	1: 3	came the word of **the L** by Haggai	3068
	1: 5	Now therefore thus saith **the L** of hosts;	3068
	1: 7	Thus saith **the L** of hosts; Consider your	3068
	1: 8	in it, and I will be glorified, saith **the L**.	3068
	1: 9	saith **the L** of hosts. Because of mine house	3068
	1:12	obeyed the voice of **the L** their God, and	3068
	1:12	as **the L** their God had sent him, and	3068
	1:12	and the people did fear before **the L**.	3068
	1:13	saying, I *am* with you, saith **the L**.	3068
	1:14	**the L** stirred up the spirit of Zerubbabel	3068
	1:14	and did work in the house of **the L** of hosts,	3068
	2: 1	came the word of **the L** by the prophet	3068
	2: 4	now be strong, O Zerubbabel, saith **the L**;	3068
	2: 4	people of the land, saith **the L**, and work:	3068

Hag 2: 4 for I *am* with you, saith **the L** of hosts: 3068
2: 6 For thus saith **the L** of hosts; Yet once, it *is* 3068
2: 7 this house *with* glory, saith **the L** of hosts. 3068
2: 8 and the gold *is* mine, saith **the L** of hosts. 3068
2: 9 than of the former, saith **the L** of hosts: 3068
2: 9 place will I give peace, saith **the L** of hosts. 3068
2:10 came the word of **the L** by Haggai 3068
2:11 Thus saith **the L** of hosts; Ask now 3068
2:14 and so *is* this nation before me, saith **the L**; 3068
2:15 laid upon a stone in the temple of **the L**: 3068
2:17 yet ye *turned* not to me, saith **the L**. 3068
2:20 again the word of **the L** came unto Haggai 3068
2:23 In that day, saith **the L** of hosts, will I take 3068
2:23 saith **the L**, and will make thee as a signet: 3068
2:23 for I have chosen thee, saith **the L** of hosts. 3068
Zec 1: 1 came the word of **the L** unto Zechariah, 3068
1: 2 **The L** hath been sore displeased with your 3068
1: 3 thou unto them, Thus saith **the L** of hosts; 3068
1: 3 saith **the L** of hosts, and I will turn unto 3068
1: 3 I will turn unto you, saith **the L** of hosts. 3068
1: 4 saying, Thus saith **the L** of hosts; 3068
1: 4 not hear, nor hearken unto me, saith **the L**. 3068
1: 6 Like as **the L** of hosts thought to do unto 3068
1: 7 came the word of **the L** unto Zechariah, 3068
1:10 These *are they* whom **the L** hath sent to 3068
1:11 they answered the angel of **the L** that stood 3068
1:12 the angel of **the L** answered and said, 3068
1:12 Lord answered and said, O **L** of hosts, 3068
1:13 **the L** answered the angel that talked with 3068
1:14 Cry thou, saying, Thus saith **the L** of hosts; 3068
1:16 Therefore thus saith **the L**; I am returned to 3068
1:16 saith **the L** of hosts, and a line shall be 3068
1:17 Cry yet, saying, Thus saith **the L** of hosts; 3068
1:17 **the L** shall yet comfort Zion, and shall yet 3068
1:20 And **the L** shewed me four carpenters. 3068
2: 5 For I, saith **the L**, will be unto her a wall of 3068
2: 6 flee from the land of the north, saith **the L**: 3068
2: 6 the four winds of the heaven, saith **the L**. 3068
2: 8 For thus saith **the L** of hosts; After 3068
2: 9 ye shall know that **the L** of hosts hath sent 3068
2:10 will dwell in the midst of thee, saith **the L**. 3068
2:11 many nations shall be joined to **the L** in 3068
2:11 thou shalt know that **the L** of hosts hath 3068
2:12 **the L** shall inherit Judah his portion in 3068
2:13 Be silent, O all flesh, before **the L**: for he is 3068
3: 1 priest standing before the angel of **the L**, 3068
3: 2 **the L** said unto Satan, The Lord rebuke 3068
3: 2 unto Satan, **The L** rebuke thee, O Satan; 3068
3: 2 even **the L** that hath chosen Jerusalem 3068
3: 5 And the angel of **the L** stood *by*. 3068
3: 6 the angel of **the L** protested unto Joshua, 3068
3: 7 Thus saith **the L** of hosts; If thou wilt walk 3068
3: 9 saith **the L** of hosts, and I will remove 3068
3:10 In that day, saith **the L** of hosts, shall ye 3068
4: 6 This *is* the word of **the L** unto Zerubbabel, 3068
4: 6 but by my spirit, saith **the L** of hosts. 3068
4: 8 Moreover the word of **the L** came unto me, 3068
4: 9 thou shalt know that **the L** of hosts hath 3068
4:10 they *are* the eyes of **the L**, which run to and 3068
5: 4 saith **the L** of hosts, and it shall enter into 3068
6: 9 the word of **the L** came unto me, saying, 3068
6:12 Thus speaketh **the L** of hosts, saying, 3068
6:12 and he shall build the temple of **the L**: 3068
6:13 Even he shall build the temple of **the L**; 3068
6:14 for a memorial in the temple of **the L**. 3068
6:15 and build in the temple of **the L**, 3068
6:15 ye shall know that **the L** of hosts hath sent 3068
6:15 if ye will diligently obey the voice of **the L** 3068
7: 1 *that* the word of **the L** came unto Zechariah 3068
7: 2 and their men, to pray before **the L**, 3068
7: 3 which *were* in the house of **the L** of hosts, 3068
7: 4 came the word of **the L** of hosts unto me, 3068
7: 7 *Should* ye not *hear* the words which **the L** 3068
7: 8 the word of **the L** came unto Zechariah, 3068
7: 9 Thus speaketh **the L** of hosts, saying, 3068
7:12 the words which **the L** of hosts hath sent in 3068
7:12 came a great wrath from **the L** of hosts. 3068
7:13 and I would not hear, saith **the L** of hosts: 3068
8: 1 Again the word of **the L** of hosts came *to* 3068
8: 2 Thus saith **the L** of hosts; I was jealous for 3068
8: 3 Thus saith **the L**; I am returned unto Zion, 3068
8: 3 the mountain of **the L** of hosts the holy 3068
8: 4 Thus saith **the L** of hosts; There shall yet 3068
8: 6 Thus saith **the L** of hosts; If it be 3068
8: 6 in my eyes? saith **the L** of hosts. 3068
8: 7 Thus saith **the L** of hosts; Behold, I *will* 3068
8: 9 Thus saith **the L** of hosts; Let your hands 3068
8: 9 of the house of **the L** of hosts was laid, 3068
8:11 as *in* the former days, saith **the L** of hosts. 3068
8:14 For thus saith **the L** of hosts; As I thought 3068
8:14 saith **the L** of hosts, and I repented not: 3068
8:17 all these *are things* that I hate, saith **the L**. 3068
8:18 the word of **the L** of hosts came unto me, 3068
8:19 Thus saith **the L** of hosts; The fast of 3068
8:20 Thus saith **the L** of hosts; *It shall* yet *come* 3068
8:21 Let us go speedily to pray before **the L**, 3068
8:21 the Lord, and to seek **the L** of hosts: 3068
8:22 strong nations shall come to seek **the L** of 3068
8:22 in Jerusalem, and to pray before **the L**. 3068
8:23 Thus saith **the L** of hosts; In those days *it* 3068
9: 1 The burden of the word of **the L** in the land 3068
9: 1 the tribes of Israel, *shall be* toward **the L**. 3068
9:14 **the L** shall be seen over them, and 3068
9:15 **The L** of hosts shall defend them; and 3068
9:16 **the L** their God shall save them in that day 3068
10: 1 Ask ye of **the L** rain in the time of the latter 3068
10: 1 *so* **the L** *shall* make bright clouds, and 3068
10: 3 for **the L** of hosts hath visited his flock 3068
10: 5 because **the L** *is* with them, and the riders 3068
10: 6 for I *am* **the L** their God, and will hear 3068
10: 7 be glad; their heart shall rejoice in **the L**. 3068
10:12 I will strengthen them in **the L**; and 3068
10:12 walk up and down in his name, saith **the L**. 3068
11: 4 Thus saith **the L** my God; Feed the flock of 3068
11: 5 they that sell them say, Blessed *be* **the L**; 3068
11: 6 pity the inhabitants of the land, saith **the L**: 3068
11:11 me knew that it *was* the word of **the L**. 3068
11:13 **the L** said unto me, Cast it unto the potter: 3068
11:13 them to the potter *in* the house of **the L**. 3068
11:15 **the L** said unto me, Take unto thee yet 3068
12: 1 The burden of the word of **the L** for Israel, 3068
12: 1 saith **the L**, which stretcheth forth 3068
12: 4 In that day, saith **the L**, I will smite every 3068
12: 5 *be* my strength in **the L** of hosts their God. 3068
12: 7 **The L** also shall save the tents of Judah 3068
12: 8 In that day shall **the L** defend 3068
12: 8 as God, as the angel of **the L** before them. 3068
13: 2 to pass in that day, saith **the L** of hosts, 3068
13: 3 for thou speakest lies in the name of **the L**: 3068
13: 7 man *that is* my fellow, saith **the L** of hosts: 3068
13: 8 to pass, *that* in all the land, saith **the L**, 3068
13: 9 and they shall say, **The L** *is* my God. 3068
14: 1 the day of **the L** cometh, and thy spoil shall 3068
14: 3 shall **the L** go forth, and fight against those 3068
14: 5 **the L** my God shall come, *and* all the saints 3068
14: 7 be one day which shall be known to **the L**, 3068
14: 9 **the L** shall be king over all the earth: 3068
14: 9 in that day shall there be one **L**, and 3068
14:12 this shall be the plague where*with* **the L** 3068
14:13 *that* a great tumult from **the L** shall be 3068
14:16 **the L** of hosts, and to keep the feast of 3068
14:17 **the L** of hosts, even upon them shall be no 3068
14:18 where*with* **the L** will smite the heathen that 3068
14:20 of the horses, HOLINESS UNTO **THE L**; 3068
14:21 in Judah shall be holiness unto **the L** of 3068
14:21 Canaanite in the house of **the L** of hosts. 3068
Mal 1: 1 The burden of the word of **the L** to Israel 3068
1: 2 I have loved you, saith **the L**. Yet ye say, 3068
1: 2 saith **the L**: yet I loved Jacob, 3068
1: 4 thus saith **the L** of hosts, They shall build, 3068
1: 4 The people *against* whom **the L** hath 3068
1: 5 **The L** will be magnified from the border of 3068
1: 6 saith **the L** of hosts unto you, O priests, 3068
1: 7 ye say, The table of **the L** *is* contemptible. 3068
1: 8 or accept thy person? saith **the L** of hosts. 3068
1: 9 regard your persons? saith **the L** of hosts. 3068
1:10 no pleasure in you, saith **the L** of hosts, 3068
1:11 among the heathen, saith **the L** of hosts. 3068
1:12 that ye say, The table of **the L** *is* polluted; 3068
1:13 ye have snuffed at it, saith **the L** of hosts; 3068
1:13 I accept this of your hand? saith **the L**. 3068
1:14 saith **the L** of hosts, and my name *is* 3068
2: 2 glory unto my name, saith **the L** of hosts, 3068
2: 4 might be with Levi, saith **the L** of hosts. 3068
2: 7 for he *is* the messenger of **the L** of hosts. 3068
2: 8 the covenant of Levi, saith **the L** of hosts. 3068
2:11 the holiness of **the L** which he loved, 3068
2:12 **The L** will cut off the man that doth this, 3068

L

Mal 2:12 him that offereth an offering unto **the L** of 3068
2:13 covering the altar of **the L** *with* tears, *with* 3068
2:14 Because **the L** hath been witness between 3068
2:16 *For* **the L**, the God of Israel, saith that he 3068
2:16 with his garment, saith **the L** of hosts: 3068
2:17 Ye have wearied **the L** with your words. 3068
2:17 that doeth evil *is* good in the sight of **the L**, 3068
3: 1 **the L**, whom ye seek, shall suddenly come 3068
3: 1 behold, he *shall* come, saith **the L** of hosts. 3068
3: 3 that they may offer unto **the L** an offering 3068
3: 4 and Jerusalem be pleasant unto **the L**, 3068
3: 5 and fear not me, saith **the L** of hosts. 3068
3: 6 For I *am* **the L**, I change not; therefore 3068
3: 7 I will return unto you, saith **the L** of hosts. 3068
3:10 me now herewith, saith **the L** of hosts, 3068
3:11 the time in the field, saith **the L** of hosts. 3068
3:12 be a delightsome land, saith **the L** of hosts. 3068
3:13 have been stout against me, saith **the L**. 3068
3:14 walked mournfully before **the L** of hosts? 3068
3:16 they that feared **the L** spake often one to 3068
3:16 **the L** hearkened, and heard *it*, and a book 3068
3:16 before him for them that feared **the L**, 3068
3:17 they shall be mine, saith **the L** of hosts, 3068
4: 1 shall burn them up, saith **the L** of hosts, 3068
4: 3 day that I *shall* do *this*, saith **the L** of hosts. 3068
4: 5 of the great and dreadful day of **the L**: 3068

LORD IS MY BANNER See JEHOVAH-NISSI

LORD IS PEACE See JEHOVAH-SHALOM

LORD WILL PROVIDE See JEHOVAH-JIREH

LORD'S (26) [LORD]

Ge 40: 7 *were* with him in the ward of his l house, 113
44: 8 should we steal out of thy l house silver or 113
44: 9 and we also will be my l bondmen. 113+3807.1
44:16 behold, we *are* my l servants, both 113+3807.1
44:18 speak a word in my l ears, and let not thine 113
2Sa 20: 6 take thou thy l servants, and pursue after 113
1Ch 21: 3 *are* they not all my l servants? 113+3807.1
Isa 22:18 thy glory *shall be* the shame of thy l house. 113
Da 9:17 thy sanctuary that is desolate, for the L sake. 136
Mt 21:42 this is the L doing, and it is marvellous in *2962*
25:18 digged in the earth, and hid his l money. *2962*
Mk 12:11 This was the L doing, and it is marvellous *2962*
Lk 2:26 see death, before he had seen the L Christ. *2962*
12:47 which knew his l will, and prepared not *2962*
16: 5 So he called every one of his l debtors unto *2962*
Ro 14: 8 we live therefore, or die, we are the L. *2962*
1Co 7:22 the Lord, *being* a servant, is the L freeman: *2962*
10:21 ye cannot be partakers of the L table, and *2962*
10:26 For the earth *is* the L, and the fulness *2962*
10:28 *for* conscience *sake:* for the earth *is* the L, *2962*
11:20 one place, *this* is not to eat the L supper. *2960*
11:26 ye do shew the L death till he come. *2962*
11:29 to himself, not discerning the L body. *2962*
Gal 1:19 saw I none, save James the L brother. *2962*
1Pe 2:13 to every ordinance of man for the L sake: *2962*
Rev 1:10 I was in the spirit on the L day, and *2960*

LORD'S* (108) [LORD*]

Ex 9:29 know how that the earth *is* **the L**. 3068+3807.1
12:11 eat it in haste: it *is* **the L** passover. 3068+3807.1
12:27 It *is* the sacrifice of **the L** passover, 3068+3807.1
13: 9 that **the L** law may be in thy mouth: 3068
13:12 thou hast; the males *shall be* **the L**. 3068+3807.1
32:26 the camp, and said, Who *is* on **the L** side? 3068
35:21 they brought **the L** offering to the work of 3068
35:24 of silver and brass brought **the L** offering: 3068
Lev 3:16 a sweet savour: all the fat *is* **the L**. 3068+3807.1
16: 9 the goat upon which **the L** lot fell, 3068+3807.1
23: 5 month at even *is* **the L** passover. 3068+3807.1
27:26 which should be **the L** firstling, no 3068+3807.1
27:26 *it be* ox, or sheep: it *is* **the L**. 3068+3807.1
27:30 *or* of the fruit of the tree, *is* **the L**: 3068+3807.1
Nu 11:23 unto Moses, Is **the L** hand waxed short? 3068
11:29 would God that all **the L** people were 3068
18:28 ye shall give thereof **the L** heave offering 3068
31:37 **the L** tribute of the sheep was six hundred 3068
31:38 of which **the L** tribute *was* threescore and 3068
31:39 of which **the L** tribute *was* 3068+3807.1
31:40 of which **the L** tribute *was* thirty 3068+3807.1
31:41 *which was* **the L** heave offering, 3068
32:10 **the L** anger was kindled the same time, 3068
32:13 And **the L** anger was kindled against Israel, 3068
Dt 10:14 of heavens *is* **the L** thy God, 3068+3807.1
11:17 *then* **the L** wrath be kindled against you, 3068
15: 2 because it is called **the L** release. 3068+3807.1
32: 9 For **the L** portion *is* his people; Jacob *is* 3068
Jos 1:15 which Moses **the L** servant gave you on 3068
5:15 the captain of **the L** host said unto Joshua, 3068
22:19 wherein **the L** tabernacle dwelleth, and 3068
Jdg 11:31 shall surely be **the L**, and I will 3068+3807.1
1Sa 2: 8 the pillars of the earth *are* **the L**, 3068+3807.1
2:24 I hear: *ye* make **the L** people to transgress. 3068
14: 3 the son of Eli, **the L** priest in Shiloh, 3068
16: 6 said, Surely **the L** anointed *is* before him. 3068
17:47 for the battle *is* **the L**, and he will 3068+3807.1
18:17 thou valiant for me, and fight **the L** battles. 3068
22:21 David that Saul had slain **the L** priests. 3068
24: 6 do this thing unto my master, **the L** 3068+3807.1
24:10 against my lord; for he *is* **the L** anointed. 3068
26: 9 forth his hand against **the L** anointed, 3068
26:11 forth mine hand against **the L** anointed: 3068
26:16 have not kept your master, **the L** anointed. 3068
26:23 forth mine hand against **the L** anointed. 3068
2Sa 1:14 forth thine hand to destroy **the L** anointed? 3068
1:16 saying, I have slain **the L** anointed. 3068
19:21 for this, because he cursed **the L** anointed? 3068
21: 7 of **the L** oath that *was* between them, 3068
1Ki 18:13 how I hid an hundred men of **the L** 3068
2Ki 11:17 that *they* should be **the L** people; 3068+3807.1
13:17 The arrow of **the L** deliverance, 3068+3807.1
2Ch 7: 2 the glory of the LORD had filled **the L** 3068
23:16 that *they* should be **the L** people. 3068+3807.1
Ps 11: 4 his holy temple, **the L** throne *is* in heaven: 3068
22:28 For the kingdom *is* **the L**: and *he is* 3068+3807.1
24: 1 The earth *is* **the L**, and the fulness 3068+3807.1
113: 3 of the same **the L** name *is* to be praised. 3068
115:16 *even* the heavens, *are* **the L**: 3068+3807.1
116:19 In the courts of **the L** house, in the midst of 3068
118:23 This is **the L** doing; it is marvellous in our 3068
137: 4 How shall we sing **the L** song in a strange 3068
Pr 16:11 just weight and balance *are* **the L**: 3068+3807.1
Isa 2: 2 *that* the mountain of **the L** house shall be 3068
34: 8 For *it is* the day of **the L** vengeance, *and* 3068
40: 2 for she hath received of **the L** hand double 3068
42:19 that is perfect, and blind as **the L** servant? 3068
44: 5 One shall say, I *am* **the L**; and 3068+3807.1
59: 1 Behold, **the L** hand is not shortened, that *it* 3068
Jer 5:10 for they *are* not **the L**. 3068+3807.1
7: 2 Stand in the gate of **the L** house, and 3068
13:17 **the L** flock is carried away captive. 3068
19:14 he stood in the court of **the L** house; and 3068
25:17 took I the cup at **the L** hand, and made all 3068
26: 2 Stand in the court of **the L** house, and 3068
26: 2 which come to worship *in* the **L** house, 3068
26:10 the entry of the new gate of **the L** *house*. 3068
27:16 the vessels of **the L** house *shall* now 3068
28: 3 this place all the vessels of **the L** house, 3068
28: 6 to bring again the vessels of **the L** house, 3068
36: 6 people *in* **the L** house upon the fasting day: 3068
36: 8 the words of the LORD *in* **the L** house. 3068
36:10 *at* the entry of the new gate of **the L** house, 3068
51: 6 for this *is* the time of **the L** vengeance; 3068
51: 7 Babylon *hath been* a golden cup in **the L** 3068
51:51 come into the sanctuaries of **the L** house. 3068
La 2:22 that in the day of **the L** anger none escaped 3068
3:22 *It is of* **the L** mercies that we are not 3068
Eze 8:14 **the L** house which *was* towards the north; 3068
8:16 he brought me into the inner court of **the L** 3068
10: 4 the court was full of the brightness of **the L** 3068
10:19 *at* the door of the east gate of **the L** house; 3068
11: 1 brought me unto the east gate of **the L** 3068
Hos 9: 3 They shall not dwell in **the L** land; but 3068
Joel 1: 9 the priests, **the L** ministers, mourn. 3068
Ob 1:21 and the kingdom shall be **the L**. 3068+3807.1
Mic 6: 2 **the L** controversy, and ye strong 3068
6: 9 **The L** voice crieth unto the city, and 3068
Hab 2:16 the cup of **the L** right hand shall be turned 3068
Zep 1: 8 it shall come to pass in the day of **the L** 3068
1:18 to deliver them in the day of **the L** wrath; 3068
2: 2 before the day of **the L** anger come upon 3068
2: 3 it may be ye shall be hid in the day of **the L** 3068
Hag 1: 2 the time that **the L** house should be built. 3068
1:13 spake Haggai **the L** messenger in 3068
1:13 in **the L** message unto the people, 3068
2:18 the foundation of **the L** temple was laid, 3068

Zec 14:20 the pots in **the L** house shall be like 3068

LORDLY (1) [LORD]
Jdg 5:25 *him* milk; she brought forth butter in a l dish. 117

LORDS (42) [LORD]
Ge 19: 2 Behold now, my l, turn in, I pray you, 113
Nu 21:28 *and* the l of the high places of Arnon. 1167
Dt 10:17 Lord of l, a great God, a mighty, and 113
Jos 13: 3 five l of the Philistines; the Gazathites, and 5633
Jdg 3: 3 *Namely,* five l of the Philistines, and all 5633
16: 5 the l of the Philistines came up unto her, 5633
16: 8 the l of the Philistines brought up to her 5633
16:18 and called for the l of the Philistines, 5633
16:18 the l of the Philistines came up unto her, 5633
16:23 the l of the Philistines gathered them 5633
16:27 all the l of the Philistines *were* there; 5633
16:30 the house fell upon the l, and upon all 5633
1Sa 5: 8 gathered all the l of the Philistines unto 5633
5:11 gathered together all the l of the Philistines, 5633
6: 4 *according to* the number of the l of 5633
6: 4 one plague *was* on you all, and on your l. 5633
6:12 the l of the Philistines went after them unto 5633
6:16 when the five l of the Philistines had seen 5633
6:18 of the Philistines *belonging* to the five l, 5633
7: 7 the l of the Philistines went up against 5633
29: 2 the l of the Philistines passed on by 5633
29: 6 this day: nevertheless the l favour thee not. 5633
29: 7 that thou displease not the l of 5633
1Ch 12:19 for the l of the Philistines upon advisement 5633
Ezr 8:25 his l, and all Israel *there* present, had 8269
Ps 136: 3 O give thanks to the Lord of l: for his mercy 113
Isa 16: 8 the l of the heathen have broken down 1167
26:13 *other* l besides thee have had dominion over 113
Jer 2:31 wherefore say my people, We are l; we will 7300
Eze 23:23 captains and rulers, **great** l and renowned, 7991
Da 4:36 my counsellers and my l sought unto me; 7261
5: 1 made a great feast to a thousand of his l, 7261
5: 9 changed in him, and his l *were* astonied. 7261
5:10 by reason of the words of the king and his l, 7261
5:23 thou, and thy l, thy wives, and 7261
6:17 his own signet, and with the signet of his l; 7261
Mk 6:21 on his birthday made a supper to his l, *3175*
1Co 8: 5 (as there be gods many, and l many,) *2962*
1Ti 6:15 the King of kings, and Lord of l; *2961*
1Pe 5: 3 Neither as being l **over** *God's* heritage, but *2634*
Rev 17:14 for he is Lord of l, and King of kings: and *2962*
19:16 KING OF KINGS, AND LORD OF L. *2962*

LORDSHIP (2) [LORD]
Mk 10:42 rule over the Gentiles **exercise l over** them; *2634*
Lk 22:25 The kings of the Gentiles **exercise l over** *2961*

LO-RUHAMAH (2) [RUHAMAH]
Hos 1: 6 *God* said unto him, Call her name L: for I 3819
1: 8 Now when she had weaned L, 3819

LOSE (23) [LOSETH, LOSS, LOST]
Jdg 18:25 thou l thy life, with the lives of thy 622
Job 31:39 have **caused** the owners thereof **to l** their 5301
Pr 23: 8 shalt thou vomit up, and l thy sweet words. 7843
Ecc 3: 6 A time to get, and a time to l; a time to keep, 6
Mt 10:39 He that findeth his life shall l it: and he that *622*
10:42 unto you, he shall in no wise l his reward. *622*
16:25 For whosoever will save his life shall l it: *622*
16:25 whosoever will l his life for my sake shall *622*
16:26 gain the whole world, and l his own soul? *2210*
Mk 8:35 For whosoever will save his life shall l it; but *622*
8:35 but whosoever shall l his life for my sake *622*
8:36 gain the whole world, and l his own soul? *2210*
9:41 I say unto you, he shall not l his reward. *622*
Lk 9:24 For whosoever will save his life shall l it: but *622*
9:24 but whosoever will l his life for my sake, *622*
9:25 whole world, and l himself, or be cast away? *622*
15: 4 if he l one of them, doth not leave the ninety *622*
15: 8 if she l one piece, doth not light a candle, *622*
17:33 Whosoever shall seek to save his life shall l *622*
17:33 whosoever shall l *his life* shall preserve it. *622*
Jn 6:39 that of all which he hath given me I should l *622*
12:25 He that loveth his life shall l it; and he that *622*
2Jn 1: 8 that we l not *those things* which we have *622*

LOSETH (1) [LOSE]
Mt 10:39 and he that l his life for my sake shall find it. *622*

LOSS (10) [LOSE]
Ge 31:39 I **bare** the l of it; of my hand didst thou 2398
Ex 21:19 only he shall pay *for* the l **of** his **time**, and 7674
Isa 47: 8 neither shall I know the **l of children**: 7908
47: 9 one day, the **l of children**, and widowhood: 7908
Ac 27:21 and to have gained this harm and l. *2209*
27:22 for there shall be no l of *any man's* life *580*
1Co 3:15 *man's* work shall be burnt, he shall **suffer** l: *2210*
Php 3: 7 gain to me, those I counted l for Christ. *2209*
3: 8 l for the excellency of the knowledge of *2209*
3: 8 for whom I have **suffered** the l of all *2210*

LOST (33) [LOSE]
Ex 22: 9 for any manner of l *thing,* which *another* 9
Lev 6: 3 Or have found **that which was** l, and 9
6: 4 him to keep, or the l *thing* which he found, 9
Nu 6:12 the days that were before shall be l, because 5307
Dt 22: 3 with all l *thing* of thy brother's, which he hath 9
22: 3 which he hath l, and thou hast found, shalt thou 6
1Sa 9: 3 the asses of Kish Saul's father were l. 6
9:20 as for thine asses that were l three days ago, 6
1Ki 20:25 like the army that thou hast l, horse for 5307
Ps 119:176 I have gone astray like a l sheep; seek thy 6
Isa 49:20 after thou hast **l** the other, shall say again in 7923
49:21 seeing I have l my **children**, and 7921
Jer 50: 6 My people hath been l sheep: their shepherds 6
Eze 19: 5 *and* her hope was l, then she took another of 6
34: 4 neither have ye sought that which was l; 6
34:16 I will seek that which was l, and bring again 6
37:11 Our bones are dried, and our hope is l: 6
Mt 5:13 but if the salt have l his **savour**, *3471*
10: 6 But go rather to the l sheep of the house of *622*
15:24 but unto the l sheep of the house of Israel. *622*
18:11 Son of man is come to save that which was l. *622*
Mk 9:50 but if the salt have l his **saltness**, *358*
Lk 14:34 but if the salt have l his **savour**, *3471*
15: 4 and go after that which is l, until he find it? *622*
15: 6 for I have found my sheep which was l. *622*
15: 9 for I have found the piece which I had l. *622*
15:24 and is alive again; he was l, and is found. *622*
15:32 and is alive again; and was l, and is found. *622*
19:10 is come to seek and to save that which was l. *622*
Jn 6:12 the fragments that remain, that nothing be l. *622*
17:12 and none of them is l, but the son of *622*
18: 9 Of them which thou gavest me have I l none. *622*
2Co 4: 3 our gospel be hid, it is hid to them that are l: *622*

LOT (111) [LOT'S, LOTS]
Ge 11:27 and Haran; and Haran begat **L**. 3876
11:31 **L** the son of Haran his son's son, and Sarai 3876
12: 4 had spoken unto him; and **L** went with him: 3876
12: 5 **L** his brother's son, and all their substance 3876
13: 1 that he had, and **L** with him, into the south. 3876
13: 5 **L** also, which went with Abram, 3876
13: 8 Abram said unto **L**, Let there be no strife, 3876
13:10 **L** lifted up his eyes, and beheld all the plain 3876
13:11 **L** chose him all the plain of Jordan; and 3876
13:11 the plain of Jordan; and **L** journeyed east: 3876
13:12 **L** dwelled in the cities of the plain, and 3876
13:14 after that **L** was separated from him, Lift up 3876
14:12 they took **L**, Abram's brother's son, 3876
14:16 also brought again his brother **L**, and 3876
19: 1 at even; and **L** sat in the gate of Sodom: 3876
19: 1 **L** seeing *them* rose up to meet them; and 3876
19: 5 they called unto **L**, and said unto him, 3876
19: 6 **L** went out at the door unto them, and 3876
19: 9 *even* **L**, and came near to break the door. 3876
19:10 pulled **L** into the house to them, and shut to 3876
19:12 the men said unto **L**, Hast thou here any 3876
19:14 **L** went out, and spake unto his sons in law, 3876
19:15 the angels hastened **L**, saying, Arise, 3876
19:18 **L** said unto them, Oh, not so, my Lord: 3876
19:23 The sun was risen upon the earth when **L** 3876
19:29 sent **L** out of the midst of the overthrow, 3876
19:29 overthrew the cities in the which **L** dwelt. 3876
19:30 **L** went up out of Zoar, and dwelt in 3876
19:36 Thus were both the daughters of **L** with 3876
Lev 16: 8 one l for the LORD, and the other lot for 1486
16: 8 and the other l for the scapegoat. 1486
16: 9 the goat upon which the LORD'S l fell, 1486
16:10 on which the l fell to be the scapegoat, 1486
Nu 26:55 the land shall be divided by l: 1486
26:56 According to the l shall the possession 1486
33:54 ye shall divide the land by l for an 1486

Nu 33:54 shall be in the place where his l falleth; 1486
34:13 This *is* the land which ye shall inherit by l, 1486
36: 2 an inheritance by l to the children of Israel: 1486
36: 3 shall it be taken from the l of our 1486
Dt 2: 9 I have given Ar unto the children of L *for a* 3876
2:19 I have given it unto the children of L *for* a 3876
32: 9 his people; Jacob *is* the l of his inheritance. 2256
Jos 13: 6 only divide thou it *by l* unto the Israelites NIH
14: 2 By l *was* their inheritance, as the LORD 1486
15: 1 was the l of the tribe of the children of 1486
16: 1 the l of the children of Joseph fell from 1486
17: 1 There was also a l for the tribe of 1486
17: 2 There was also *a l* for the rest of NIH
17:14 *but* one l and one portion to inherit, 1486
17:17 thou shalt not have one l *only:* 1486
18:11 the l of the tribe of the children of 1486
18:11 the coast of their l came forth between 1486
19: 1 the second l came forth to Simeon, *even* for 1486
19:10 the third l came up for the children of 1486
19:17 *And* the fourth l came out to Issachar, 1486
19:24 the fifth l came out for the tribe of 1486
19:32 The sixth l came out to the children of 1486
19:40 *And* the seventh l came out for the tribe of 1486
19:51 divided for an inheritance by l in Shiloh 1486
21: 4 the l came out for the families of 1486
21: 4 had by l out of the tribe of Judah, and 1486
21: 5 the rest of the children of Kohath had by l 1486
21: 6 the children of Gershon *had* by l out of 1486
21: 8 the children of Israel gave by l unto 1486
21:10 of Levi, had: for theirs was the first l. 1486
21:20 even they had the cities of their l out of 1486
21:40 of the Levites, were *by* their l twelve cities. 1486
23: 4 I have divided unto you *by l* these nations NIH
Jdg 1: 3 his brother, Come up with me into my l, 1486
1: 3 and I likewise will go with thee into thy l. 1486
20: 9 do to Gibeah; *we will go up* by l against it; 1486
1Sa 14:41 Give a perfect *l*. And Saul and NIH
1Ch 6:54 of the Kohathites: for theirs was the l. 1486
6:61 the half *tribe* of Manasseh, by l, ten cities. 1486
6:63 Unto the sons of Merari *were given* by l, 1486
6:65 they gave by l out of the tribe of 1486
16:18 land of Canaan, the l of your inheritance; 2256
24: 5 Thus were they divided by l, one *sort* with 1486
24: 7 Now the first l came forth to Jehoiarib, 1486
25: 9 Now the first l came forth for Asaph to 1486
26:14 the l eastward fell to Shelemiah. Then *for* 1486
26:14 cast lots; and his l came out northward. 1486
26:16 and Hosah *the l came forth* westward, NIH
Est 3: 7 they cast Pur, that *is,* the l, before Haman 1486
9:24 had cast Pur, that *is,* the l, to consume 1486
Ps 16: 5 and of my cup: thou maintainest my l. 1486
83: 8 they have holpen the children of L. Selah. 3876
105:11 land of Canaan, the l of your inheritance: 2256
125: 3 shall not rest upon the l of the righteous; 1486
Pr 1:14 Cast in thy l among us; let us all have one 1486
16:33 The l is cast into the lap; but the whole 1486
18:18 The l causeth contentions to cease, and 1486
Isa 17:14 that spoil us, and the l of them that rob us. 1486
34:17 he hath cast the l for them, and his hand 1486
57: 6 stream *is* thy portion; they, they *are* thy l: 1486
Jer 13:25 This *is* thy l, the portion of thy measures 1486
Eze 24: 6 it out piece by piece; let no l fall upon it. 1486
45: 1 when ye shall divide *by l* the land for NIH
47:22 *that* ye shall divide it *by l* for an inheritance NIH
48:29 This *is* the land which ye shall divide *by l* NIH
Da 12:13 and stand in thy l at the end of the days. 1486
Jnh 1: 7 So they cast lots, and the l fell upon Jonah. 1486
Mic 2: 5 by l in the congregation of the LORD. 1486
Lk 1: 9 his l was to burn incense when he went into *2975*
17:28 Likewise also as it was in the days of L; *3091*
17:29 But the *same* day that L went out of Sodom *3091*
Ac 1:26 and the l fell upon Matthias; and he was *2819*
8:21 Thou hast neither part nor l in this matter: *2819*
13:19 he **divided** their land to them **by l**. *2624*
2Pe 2: 7 And delivered just L, vexed with the filthy *3091*

LOT'S (2) [LOT]
Ge 13: 7 Abram's cattle and the herdmen of L cattle: 3876
Lk 17:32 Remember L wife. *3091*

LOTAN (5) [LOTAN'S]
Ge 36:20 L, and Shobal, and Zibeon, and Anah, 3877
36:22 the children of L were Hori and Hemam; 3877
36:29 duke L, duke Shobal, duke Zibeon, 3877
1Ch 1:38 L, and Shobal, and Zibeon, and Anah, and 3877
1:39 the sons of L; Hori, and Homam: and 3877

LOTAN'S (2) [LOTAN]
Ge 36:22 and Hemam; and L sister *was* Timna. 3877
1Ch 1:39 Hori, and Homam: and Timna *was* L sister. 3877

LOTHE (4) [LOATHE, LOTHED, LOTHETH, LOTHING]
Ex 7:18 the Egyptians shall l to drink of the water 3811
Eze 6: 9 they shall l themselves for the evils which 6962
20:43 ye shall l yourselves in your own sight for 6962
36:31 shall l yourselves in your own sight for 6962

LOTHED (3) [LOTHE]
Jer 14:19 hath thy soul l Zion? why hast thou smitten 1602
Eze 16:45 which l their husbands and their children: 1602
Zec 11: 8 my soul l them, and their soul also abhorred 7114

LOTHETH (1) [LOTHE]
Eze 16:45 that l her husband and her children; 1602

LOTHING (1) [LOTHE]
Eze 16: 5 to the l of thy person, in the day that thou 1604

LOTS (24) [LOT]
Lev 16: 8 Aaron shall cast l upon the two goats; 1486
Jos 18: 6 that I may cast l for you here before 1486
18: 8 that I may here cast l for you before 1486
18:10 Joshua cast l for them in Shiloh before 1486
1Sa 14:42 Cast *l* between me and Jonathan my son. NIH
1Ch 24:31 These likewise cast l over against their 1486
25: 8 they cast l, ward against *ward,* as well 1486
26:13 they cast l, as well the small as the great, 1486
26:14 his son, a wise counseller, they cast l; 1486
Ne 10:34 we cast the l *among* the priests, the Levites, 1486
11: 1 the rest of the people also cast l, to bring 1486
Ps 22:18 among them, and cast l upon my vesture. 1486
Joel 3: 3 they have cast l for my people; and 1486
Ob 1:11 cast l upon Jerusalem, even thou *wast* as 1486
Jnh 1: 7 one to his fellow, Come, and let us cast l, 1486
1: 7 So they cast l, and the lot fell upon Jonah. 1486
Na 3:10 they cast l for her honourable *men,* and 1486
Mt 27:35 and parted his garments, casting l: *2819*
27:35 and upon my vesture did they cast l. *2819*
Mk 15:24 parted his garments, casting l upon them, *2819*
Lk 23:34 And they parted his raiment, and cast l. *2819*
Jn 19:24 Let us not rent it, but **cast** l for it, whose it *2975*
19:24 and for my vesture they did cast l. *2819*
Ac 1:26 And they gave forth their l; and the lot fell *2819*

LOUD (61) [ALOUD, LOUDER]
Ge 39:14 to lie with me, and I cried with a l voice: 1419
Ex 19:16 and the voice of the trumpet exceeding l; 2389
Dt 27:14 say unto all the men of Israel *with* a l voice, 7311
1Sa 28:12 saw Samuel, she cried with a l voice: 1419
2Sa 15:23 And all the country wept *with* a l voice, and 1419
19: 4 the king cried *with* a l voice, O my son 1419
1Ki 8:55 all the congregation of Israel *with* a l voice, 1419
18:28 they cried l, and 1419+6963+871.1
2Ki 18:28 cried with a l voice in the Jews' language, 1419
2Ch 15:14 they sware unto the LORD with a l voice, 1419
20:19 God of Israel with a l voice on high. 1419
30:21 *singing* with l instruments unto 5797
32:18 they cried with a l voice in the Jews' 1419
Ezr 3:12 laid before their eyes, wept with a l voice; 1419
3:13 for the people shouted *with* a l shout, and 1419
10:12 and said *with* a l voice, 1419
Ne 9: 4 cried with a l voice unto the LORD their 1419
12:42 the singers **sang l**, with Jezrahiah *their* 8085
Est 4: 1 the city, and cried *with* a l and a bitter cry; 1419
Ps 33: 3 a new song; play skilfully with a l **noise**. 8643
98: 4 **make a l noise**, and rejoice, and 6476
150: 5 Praise him upon the l cymbals: praise him 8088
Pr 7:11 (She *is* l and stubborn; her feet abide not in 1993
27:14 He that blesseth his friend with a l voice, 1419
Isa 36:13 cried with a l voice in the Jews' language, 1419
Eze 8:18 though they cry in mine ears *with* a l voice, 1419
9: 1 He cried also in mine ears *with* a l voice, 1419
11:13 cried *with* a l voice, and said, Ah Lord 1419
Mt 27:46 the ninth hour Jesus cried with a l voice, *3173*
27:50 when he had cried again with a l voice, *3173*
Mk 1:26 and cried with a l voice, he came out of *3173*
5: 7 And cried with a l voice, and said, *3173*
15:34 And at the ninth hour Jesus cried with a l *3173*
15:37 And Jesus cried with a l voice, and gave up *3173*

L

Lk 1:42 And she spake out with a l voice, *3173*
4:33 unclean devil, and cried out with a l voice, *3173*
8:28 down before him, and with a l voice said, *3173*
17:15 and with a l voice glorified God, *3173*
19:37 praise God with a l voice for all the mighty *3173*
23:23 And they were instant with l voices, *3173*
23:46 And when Jesus had cried with a l voice, *3173*
Jn 11:43 he cried with a l voice, Lazarus, *3173*
Ac 7:57 Then they cried out with a l voice, and *3173*
7:60 and cried with a l voice, Lord, *3173*
8: 7 For unclean spirits, crying with l voice, *3173*
14:10 Said with a l voice, Stand upright on thy *3173*
16:28 But Paul cried with a l voice, saying, *3173*
26:24 Festus said with a l voice, Paul, thou art *3173*
Rev 5: 2 a strong angel proclaiming with a l voice, *3173*
5:12 Saying with a l voice, Worthy is the Lamb *3173*
6:10 And they cried with a l voice, saying, *3173*
7: 2 he cried with a l voice to the four angels, *3173*
7:10 And cried with a l voice, saying, Salvation *3173*
8:13 saying with a l voice, Woe, woe, woe, *3173*
10: 3 And cried with a l voice, as *when* a lion *3173*
12:10 And I heard a l voice saying in heaven, *3173*
14: 7 Saying with a l voice, Fear God, and *3173*
14: 9 saying with a l voice, If any *man* worship *3173*
14:15 crying with a l voice to him that sat on *3173*
14:18 cried with a l cry to him that had the sharp *3173*
19:17 and he cried with a l voice, saying to all *3173*

LOUDER (2) [LOUD]
Ex 19:19 **waxed l and louder**, Moses spake, 2390+3966
19:19 **waxed louder and l**, Moses spake, 2390+3966

LOVE (310) [BELOVED, BELOVED'S, LOVE'S, LOVED, LOVEDST, LOVELY, LOVER, LOVERS, LOVES, LOVEST, LOVETH, LOVING, LOVINGKINDNESS, LOVINGKINDNESSES, WELLBELOVED, WELL-BELOVED]
Ge 27: 4 such as I l, and bring *it* to me, that I may eat; 157
29:20 *but* a few days, for the l he had to her. 160
29:32 now therefore my husband will l me. 157
Ex 20: 6 shewing mercy unto thousands of them that l 157
21: 5 I l my master, my wife, and my children; 157
Lev 19:18 but thou shalt l thy neighbour as thyself: 157
19:34 amongst you, and thou shalt l him as thyself; 157
Dt 5:10 shewing mercy unto thousands of them that l 157
6: 5 thou shalt l the LORD thy God with all 157
7: 7 The LORD did not **set** his l upon you, 2836
7: 9 and mercy with them that l him and 157
7:13 he will l thee, and bless thee, and 157
10:12 to l him, and to serve the LORD thy God 157
10:15 had a delight in thy fathers to l them, 157
10:19 L ye therefore the stranger: for ye were 157
11: 1 Therefore thou shalt l the LORD thy God, 157
11:13 to l the LORD your God, and to serve him 157
11:22 to do them, to l the LORD your God, 157
13: 3 to know whether you l the LORD your God 157
19: 9 to l the LORD thy God, and to walk ever in 157
30: 6 to l the LORD thy God with all thine heart, 157
30:16 In that I command thee *this* day to l 157
30:20 That thou mayest l the LORD thy God, *and* 157
Jos 22: 5 to l the LORD your God, and to walk in all 157
23:11 that ye l the LORD your God. 157
Jdg 5:31 *let* them that l him *be* as the sun when he 157
16:15 said unto him, How canst thou say, I l thee, 157
1Sa 18:22 delight in thee, and all his servants l thee: 157
2Sa 1:26 thy l to me was wonderful, passing the love 160
1:26 me was wonderful, passing the l of women. 160
13: 4 Amnon said unto him, I l Tamar, my brother 157
13:15 than the l wherewith he had loved her. 160
1Ki 11: 2 their gods: Solomon clave unto these in l. 157
2Ch 19: 2 and l them that hate the LORD? 157
Ne 1: 5 and mercy for them that l him and 157
Ps 4: 2 *how long* will ye l vanity, *and* seek after 157
5:11 let them also that l thy name be joyful in 157
18: 1 I will l thee, O LORD, my strength. 7355
31:23 O l the LORD, all ye his saints: *for* 157
40:16 let such as l thy salvation say continually, 157
69:36 and they that l his name shall dwell therein. 157
70: 4 let such as l thy salvation say continually, 157
91:14 Because he hath **set** his l upon me, 2836
97:10 Ye that l the LORD, hate evil: 157
109: 4 For my l they are my adversaries: but I *give* 160
109: 5 me evil for good, and hatred for my l. 160
116: 1 I l the LORD, because he hath heard my 157
119:97 O how I l thy law! it *is* my meditation all 157
119:113 I hate *vain* thoughts: but thy law do I l. 157
119:119 earth *like* dross: therefore I l thy testimonies. 157
119:127 Therefore I l thy commandments above 157
119:132 as thou usest to do unto those that l thy 157
119:159 Consider how I l thy precepts: quicken me, 157
119:163 I hate and abhor lying: *but* thy law do I l. 157
119:165 Great peace have they which l thy law: and 157
119:167 thy testimonies; and *I* l them exceedingly. 157
122: 6 of Jerusalem: they shall prosper that l thee. 157
145:20 The LORD preserveth all them that l him: 157
Pr 1:22 ye simple ones, will ye l simplicity? 157
4: 6 preserve thee: l her, and she shall keep thee. 157
5:19 and be thou ravisht always with her l. 160
7:18 let us take our fill of l until the morning: 1730
8:17 I l them that love me; and those that seek me 157
8:17 I love them that l me; and those that seek me 157
8:21 That *I* may cause those that l me to inherit 157
8:36 his own soul: all they that hate me l death. 157
9: 8 rebuke a wise *man*, and he will l thee. 157
10:12 stirreth up strifes: but l covereth all sins. 160
15:17 Better *is* a dinner of herbs where l is, than a 160
16:13 of kings; and *they* l him that speaketh right. 157
17: 9 He that covereth a transgression seeketh l; 160
18:21 and they that l it shall eat the fruit thereof. 157
20:13 L not sleep, lest thou come to poverty; 157
27: 5 Open rebuke *is* better than secret l. 160
Ecc 3: 8 A time to l, and a time to hate; a time of war, 157
9: 1 no man knoweth either l or hatred *by* all *that* 160
9: 6 Also their l, and their hatred, and their envy, 160
SS 1: 2 of his mouth: for thy l *is* better than wine. 1730
1: 3 poured forth, therefore do the virgins l thee. 157
1: 4 we will remember thy l more than wine: 1730
1: 4 thy love more than wine: the upright l thee. 157
1: 9 I have compared thee, O my l, to a 7474
1:15 Behold, thou *art* fair, my l; behold, thou *art* 7474
2: 2 so *is* my l among the daughters. 7474
2: 4 and his banner over me *was* l. 160
2: 5 comfort me with apples: for I *am* sick of l. 160
2: 7 ye stir not up, nor awake *my* l, till he please. 160
2:10 Rise up, my l, my fair one, and come away. 7474
2:13 Arise, my l, my fair one, and come away. 7474
3: 5 ye stir not up, nor awake *my* l, till he please. 160
3:10 the midst thereof being paved *with* l, 160
4: 1 Behold, thou *art* fair, my l; behold, thou *art* 7474
4: 7 Thou *art* all fair, my l; *there is* no spot in 7474
4:10 How fair is thy l, my sister, *my* spouse! 1730
4:10 how much better is thy l than wine! and 1730
5: 2 my sister, my l, my dove, my undefiled: 7474
5: 8 that ye tell him, that I *am* sick of l. 160
6: 4 Thou *art* beautiful, O my l, as Tirzah, 7474
7: 6 and how pleasant art thou, O l, for delights! 160
8: 4 stir not up, nor awake *my* l, until he please. 160
8: 6 for l *is* strong as death; jealousy *is* cruel as 160
8: 7 Many waters cannot quench l, neither can 160
8: 7 give all the substance of his house for l, 160
Isa 38:17 thou hast **in** l to my soul *delivered it* from 2836
56: 6 serve him, and to l the name of the LORD, 157
61: 8 For I the LORD l judgment, I hate robbery 157
63: 9 in his l and in his pity he redeemed them; 160
66:10 and be glad with her, all ye that l her: 157
Jer 2: 2 of thy youth, the l of thine espousals, 160
2:33 Why trimmest thou thy way to seek l? 160
5:31 their means; and my people l *to have it* so: 157
31: 3 I have loved thee *with* an everlasting l; 160
Eze 16: 8 behold, thy time *was* the time of l; 1730
23:11 more corrupt in her **inordinate** l than she, 5691
23:17 Babylonians came to her into the bed of l, 1730
33:31 for with their mouth they shew **much** l, *but* 5690
Da 1: 9 and **tender** l with the prince of the eunuchs. 7356
9: 4 the covenant and mercy to them that l him, 157
Hos 3: 1 Go yet, l a woman beloved of *her* friend, 157
3: 1 according to the l of the LORD toward 160
3: 1 look to other gods, and l flagons of wine. 157
4:18 her rulers *with* shame do l, Give ye. 157
9:15 out of mine house, I will l them no more: 160
11: 4 them with cords of a man, with bands of l: 160
14: 4 heal their backsliding, I will l them freely: 157
Am 5:15 l the good, and establish judgment in 157
Mic 3: 2 Who hate the good, and l the evil; who pluck 157
6: 8 to l mercy, and to walk humbly with thy 160
Zep 3:17 he will rest in his l, he will joy over thee 160
Zec 8:17 against his neighbour; and l no false oath: 157
8:19 therefore l the truth and peace. 157
Mt 5:43 Thou shalt l thy neighbour, and hate thine *25*

Mt	5:44	But I say unto you, **L** your enemies,	*25*
	5:46	For if ye **l** them which love you, what reward	*25*
	5:46	For if ye love them which **l** you, what reward	*25*
	6: 5	they **l** to pray standing in the synagogues	*5368*
	6:24	for either he will hate the one, and **l** the other;	*25*
	19:19	and, Thou shalt **l** thy neighbour as thyself.	*25*
	22:37	Thou shalt **l** the Lord thy God with all thy	*25*
	22:39	unto it, Thou shalt **l** thy neighbour as thyself.	*25*
	23: 6	And **l** the uppermost rooms at feasts, and	*5368*
	24:12	shall abound, the **l** of many shall wax cold.	*26*
Mk	12:30	And thou shalt **l** the Lord thy God with all thy	*25*
	12:31	Thou shalt **l** thy neighbour as thyself.	*25*
	12:33	And to **l** him with all the heart, and with all	*25*
	12:33	the strength, and to **l** *his* neighbour as himself,	*25*
	12:38	which **l** to go in long clothing, and	*2309*
	12:38	and *l* salutations in the marketplaces,	NIG
Lk	6:27	I say unto you which hear, **L** your enemies,	*25*
	6:32	For if ye **l** them which love you, what thank	*25*
	6:32	For if ye love them which **l** you, what thank	*25*
	6:32	for sinners also **l** those that love them.	*25*
	6:32	for sinners also love those that **l** them.	*25*
	6:35	But **l** ye your enemies, and do good, and lend,	*25*
	7:42	me therefore, which of them will **l** him most?	*25*
	10:27	Thou shalt **l** the Lord thy God with all thy	*25*
	11:42	and pass over judgment and the **l** of God:	*26*
	11:43	for ye **l** the uppermost seats in	*25*
	16:13	for either he will hate the one, and **l** the other;	*25*
	20:46	and **l** greetings in the markets, and	*5368*
Jn	5:42	that ye have not the **l** of God in you.	*26*
	8:42	If God were your Father, ye would **l** me:	*25*
	10:17	Therefore doth *my* Father **l** me, because I lay	*25*
	13:34	I give unto you, That ye **l** one another;	*25*
	13:34	as I have loved you, that ye also **l** one another.	*25*
	13:35	are my disciples, if ye have **l** one to another.	*26*
	14:15	If ye **l** me, keep my commandments.	*25*
	14:21	and I will **l** him, and will manifest myself to	*25*
	14:23	and said unto him, If a man **l** me,	*25*
	14:23	and my Father will **l** him, and we will come	*25*
	14:31	But that the world may know that I **l**	*25*
	15: 9	so have I loved you: continue ye in my **l**.	*26*
	15:10	my commandments, ye shall abide in my **l**;	*26*
	15:10	Father's commandments, and abide in his **l**.	*26*
	15:12	That ye **l** one another, as I have loved you.	*25*
	15:13	Greater **l** hath no *man* than this, that a man lay	*26*
	15:17	*things* I command you, that ye **l** one another.	*25*
	15:19	of the world, the world would **l** his own:	*5368*
	17:26	will declare *it:* that the **l** where*with* thou hast	*26*
	21:15	Yea, Lord; thou knowest that I **l** thee.	*5368*
	21:16	Yea, Lord; thou knowest that I **l** thee.	*5368*
	21:17	all *things;* thou knowest that I **l** thee.	*5368*
Ro	5: 5	the **l** of God is shed abroad in our hearts by	*26*
	5: 8	But God commendeth his **l** toward us, in that,	*26*
	8:28	work together for good to them that **l** God,	*25*
	8:35	Who shall separate us from the **l** of Christ?	*26*
	8:39	shall be able to separate us from the **l** of God,	*26*
	12: 9	*Let* **l** *be* without dissimulation. Abhor *that*	*26*
	12:10	one to another with **brotherly l**;	*5360*
	13: 8	Owe no *man* any *thing,* but to **l** one another:	*25*
	13: 9	namely, Thou shalt **l** thy neighbour as thyself.	*25*
	13:10	**L** worketh no ill to *his* neighbour: therefore	*26*
	13:10	therefore **l** *is* the fulfilling of the law.	*26*
	15:30	Jesus Christ's sake, and for the **l** of the Spirit,	*26*
1Co	2: 9	which God hath prepared for them that **l** him.	*25*
	4:21	a rod, or in **l**, and *in* the spirit of meekness?	*26*
	8: 3	But if any *man* **l** God, the same is known of	*25*
	16:22	If any *man* **l** not the Lord Jesus Christ,	*5368*
	16:24	My **l** *be* with you all in Christ Jesus. Amen.	*26*
2Co	2: 4	that ye might know the **l** which I have more	*26*
	2: 8	that *you* would confirm *your* **l** towards him.	*26*
	5:14	For the **l** of Christ constraineth us; because	*26*
	6: 6	by the Holy Ghost, by **l** unfeigned,	*26*
	8: 7	and *in* all diligence, and *in* your **l** to us,	*26*
	8: 8	of others, and to prove the sincerity of your **l**.	*26*
	8:24	the proof of your **l**, and of our boasting on	*26*
	11:11	because I **l** you not? God knoweth.	*25*
	12:15	though the more abundantly I **l** you, the less I	*25*
	13:11	and the God of **l** and peace shall be with you.	*26*
	13:14	and the **l** of God, and the communion of	*26*
Gal	5: 6	but faith which worketh by **l**.	*26*
	5:13	to the flesh, but by **l** serve one another.	*26*
	5:14	*even* in *this;* Thou shalt **l** thy neighbour as	*25*
	5:22	But the fruit of the Spirit is **l**, joy, peace,	*26*
Eph	1: 4	be holy and without blame before him in **l**:	*26*
	1:15	in the Lord Jesus, and **l** unto all the saints,	*26*
	2: 4	for his great **l** wherewith he loved us,	*26*
	3:17	that ye, being rooted and grounded in **l**,	*26*
	3:19	And to know the **l** of Christ, which passeth	*26*
	4: 2	forbearing one another in **l**;	*26*
	4:15	But speaking the truth in **l**, may grow *up* into	*26*
	4:16	of the body unto the edifying of itself in **l**.	*26*
	5: 2	And walk in **l**, as Christ also hath loved us,	*26*
	5:25	Husbands, **l** your wives, even as Christ also	*25*
	5:28	So ought men to **l** their wives as their own	*25*
	5:33	you in particular so **l** his wife even as himself;	*25*
	6:23	and **l** with faith, from God the Father and	*26*
	6:24	Grace *be* with all them that **l** our Lord Jesus	*25*
Php	1: 9	that your **l** may abound yet more and more in	*26*
	1:17	But the other of **l**, knowing that I am set for	*26*
	2: 1	any consolation in Christ, if any comfort of **l**,	*26*
	2: 2	having the same **l**, *being* of one accord, of one	*26*
Col	1: 4	and of the **l** which *ye have* to all the saints,	*26*
	1: 8	Who also declared unto us your **l** in the Spirit.	*26*
	2: 2	being knit together in **l**, and unto all riches of	*26*
	3:19	**l** *your* wives, and be not bitter against them.	*25*
1Th	1: 3	and labour of **l**, and patience of hope in our	*26*
	3:12	and abound in **l** one towards another,	*26*
	4: 9	But as touching **brotherly l** ye need not	*5360*
	4: 9	for ye yourselves are taught of God to **l** one	*25*
	5: 8	putting on the breastplate of faith and **l**;	*26*
	5:13	And to esteem them very highly in **l** for their	*26*
2Th	2:10	because they received not the **l** of the truth,	*26*
	3: 5	And the Lord direct your hearts into the **l** of	*26*
1Ti	1:14	with faith and **l** which is in Christ Jesus.	*26*
	6:10	For the **l of money** is the root of all evil:	*5365*
	6:11	godliness, faith, **l**, patience, meekness.	*26*
2Ti	1: 7	but of power, and of **l**, and of a sound mind.	*26*
	1:13	of me, in faith and **l** which is in Christ Jesus.	*26*
	4: 8	but unto all them also that **l** his appearing.	*25*
Tit	2: 4	**l** their **husbands**, to love their	*1510+5362*
	2: 4	to love their husbands, to **l** their **children**,	*5388*
	3: 4	**l** of God our Saviour **toward man**	*5363*
	3:15	Greet them that **l** us in the faith. Grace *be*	*5368*
Phm	1: 5	Hearing of thy **l** and faith, which thou hast	*26*
	1: 7	we have great joy and consolation in thy **l**,	*26*
Heb	6:10	to forget your work and labour of **l**,	*26*
	10:24	let us consider one another to provoke unto **l**	*26*
	13: 1	Let **brotherly l** continue.	*5360*
Jas	1:12	which the Lord hath promised to them that **l**	*25*
	2: 5	which he hath promised to them that **l** him?	*25*
	2: 8	Thou shalt **l** thy neighbour as thyself, ye do	*25*
1Pe	1: 8	Whom having not seen, ye **l**; in whom,	*25*
	1:22	the Spirit unto unfeigned **l of the brethren**,	*5360*
	1:22	*see that ye* **l** one another with a pure heart	*25*
	2:17	Honour all *men.* **L** the brotherhood. Fear God.	*25*
	3: 8	**l as brethren**, *be* pitiful, *be* courteous:	*5361*
	3:10	For he that will **l** life, and see good days,	*25*
1Jn	2: 5	in him verily is the **l** of God perfected:	*26*
	2:15	**L** not the world, neither the *things* that are in	*25*
	2:15	If any *man* **l** the world, the love of the Father	*25*
	2:15	the world, the **l** of the Father is not in him.	*26*
	3: 1	what manner of **l** the Father hath bestowed	*26*
	3:11	the beginning, that we should **l** one another.	*25*
	3:14	death unto life, because we **l** the brethren.	*25*
	3:16	Hereby perceive we the **l** *of God,* because	*26*
	3:17	from him, how dwelleth the **l** of God in him?	*26*
	3:18	let us not **l** in word, neither in tongue;	*25*
	3:23	and **l** one another, as he gave us	*25*
	4: 7	Beloved, let us **l** one another: for love is of	*25*
	4: 7	for **l** is of God; and every one that loveth is	*26*
	4: 8	that loveth not, knoweth not God; for God is **l**.	*26*
	4: 9	In this was manifested the **l** of God towards	*26*
	4:10	Herein is **l**, not that we loved God, but that he	*26*
	4:11	so loved us, we ought also to **l** one another.	*25*
	4:12	If we **l** one another, God dwelleth in us, and	*25*
	4:12	dwelleth in us, and his **l** is perfected in us.	*26*
	4:16	and believed the **l** that God hath to us.	*26*
	4:16	God is **l**; and he that dwelleth in love dwelleth	*26*
	4:16	and he that dwelleth in **l** dwelleth in God, and	*26*
	4:17	Herein is our **l** made perfect, that we may	*26*
	4:18	There is no fear in **l**; but perfect love casteth	*26*
	4:18	no fear in love; but perfect **l** casteth out fear:	*26*
	4:18	He that feareth is not made perfect in **l**.	*26*
	4:19	We **l** him, because he first loved us.	*25*
	4:20	I **l** God, and hateth his brother, he is a liar:	*25*
	4:20	how can he **l** God whom he hath not seen?	*25*
	4:21	That he who loveth God **l** his brother also.	*25*
	5: 2	By this we know that we **l** the children of	*25*
	5: 2	when we **l** God, and keep his commandments.	*25*

1Jn 5: 3 For this is the l of God, that we keep his *26*
2Jn 1: 1 and her children, whom I l in the truth; *25*
1: 3 the Son of the Father, in truth and l. *26*
1: 5 had from the beginning, that we l one another. *25*
1: 6 And this is l, that we walk after his *26*
3Jn 1: 1 the wellbeloved Gaius, whom I l in the truth. *25*
Jude 1: 2 unto you, and peace, and l, be multiplied. *26*
1:21 Keep yourselves in the l of God, looking for *26*
Rev 2: 4 against thee, because thou hast left thy first l. *26*
3:19 As many as I l, I rebuke and chasten: *5368*

LOVE'S (1) [LOVE]
Phm 1: 9 *Yet* for l sake I rather beseech *thee,* being *26*

LOVED (98) [LOVE]
Ge 24:67 and she became his wife; and he l her: 157
25:28 Isaac l Esau, because he did eat of *his* 157
25:28 did eat of *his* venison: but Rebekah l Jacob. 157
27:14 made savoury meat, such as his father l. 157
29:18 Jacob l Rachel; and said, I will serve thee 157
29:30 he l also Rachel more than Leah, and 157
34: 3 he l the damsel, and spake kindly unto 157
37: 3 Now Israel l Joseph more than all his 157
37: 4 when his brethren saw that their father l him 157
Dt 4:37 because he l thy fathers, therefore he chose 157
7: 8 because the LORD l you, and because 160
23: 5 because the LORD thy God l thee. 157
33: 3 Yea, he l the people; all his saints *are* in thy 2245
Jdg 16: 4 that he l a woman in the valley of Sorek, 157
1Sa 1: 5 he gave a worthy portion; for he l Hannah: 157
16:21 he l him greatly; and he became his 157
18: 1 and Jonathan l him as his own soul. 157
18: 3 because he l him as his own soul. 160
18:16 all Israel and Judah l David, because he went 157
18:20 Michal Saul's daughter l David: and 157
18:28 and *that* Michal Saul's daughter l him. 157
20:17 David to swear again, because he l him: 160
20:17 for he l him as he loved his own soul. 157
20:17 for he loved him as he l his own soul. 160
2Sa 12:24 his name Solomon: and the LORD l him. 157
13: 1 and Amnon the son of David l her. 157
13:15 greater than the love wherewith he had l her. 157
1Ki 3: 3 Solomon l the LORD, walking in 157
10: 9 because the LORD l Israel for ever, 160
11: 1 king Solomon l many strange women, 157
2Ch 2:11 Because the LORD hath l his people, 160
9: 8 because thy God l Israel, to establish them 160
11:21 Rehoboam l Maachah the daughter of 157
26:10 and in Carmel: for he l husbandry. 157
Est 2:17 the king l Esther above all the women, and 157
Job 19:19 and they whom I l are turned against me. 157
Ps 26: 8 I have l the habitation of thy house, and 157
47: 4 for us, the excellency of Jacob whom he l. 157
78:68 tribe of Judah, the mount Zion which he l. 157
109:17 As he l cursing, so let it come *unto* him: as 157
119:47 in thy commandments, which I have l. 157
119:48 up unto thy commandments, which I have l; 157
Isa 43: 4 thou hast been honourable, and I have l thee: 157
48:14 these *things?* The LORD hath l him: 157
Jer 2:25 for I have l strangers, and after them will I 157
8: 2 whom they have l, and whom they have 157
14:10 Thus have they l to wander, they have not 157
31: 3 I have l thee *with* an everlasting love; 157
Eze 16:37 all *them* that thou hast l, with all *them* that 157
Hos 9: 1 thou hast l a reward upon every cornfloor. 157
9:10 *their* abominations were according as they l. 157
11: 1 then I l him, and called my son out of Egypt. 157
Mal 1: 2 I have l you, saith the LORD. Yet ye say, 157
1: 2 Yet ye say, Wherein hast thou l us? *was* not 157
1: 2 saith the LORD: yet I l Jacob, 157
2:11 the holiness of the LORD which he l, 157
Mk 10:21 Then Jesus beholding him l him, and *25*
Lk 7:47 which are many, are forgiven; for she l much: *25*
Jn 3:16 For God so l the world, that he gave his only *25*
3:19 and men l darkness rather than light, because *25*
11: 5 Now Jesus l Martha, and her sister, and *25*
11:36 Then said the Jews, Behold, how he l him. *5368*
12:43 For they l the praise of men more than *25*
13: 1 having l his own which were in the world, *25*
13: 1 were in the world, he l them unto the end. *25*
13:23 bosom one of his disciples, whom Jesus l. *25*
13:34 as I have l you, that ye also love one another. *25*
14:21 and he that loveth me shall be l of my Father, *25*
14:28 If ye l me, ye would rejoice, because I said, *25*
15: 9 As the Father hath l me, so have I loved you: *25*
15: 9 As the Father hath loved me, so have I l you: *25*
15:12 That ye love one another, as I have l you. *25*
16:27 because ye have l me, and have believed *5368*
17:23 and hast l them, as thou hast loved me. *25*
17:23 and hast loved them, as thou hast l me. *25*
17:26 where*with* thou hast l me may be in them, *25*
19:26 and the disciple standing by, whom he l, *25*
20: 2 whom Jesus l, and saith unto them, *5368*
21: 7 Therefore that disciple whom Jesus l saith *25*
21:20 seeth the disciple whom Jesus l following; *25*
Ro 8:37 more than conquerors through him that l us. *25*
9:13 As it is written, Jacob have I l, *25*
2Co 12:15 the more abundantly I love you, the less I be l. *25*
Gal 2:20 of God, who l me, and gave himself for me. *25*
Eph 2: 4 in mercy, for his great love wherewith he l us, *25*
5: 2 as Christ also hath l us, and hath given *25*
5:25 even as Christ also l the church, and *25*
2Th 2:16 which hath l us, and hath given *us* everlasting *25*
2Ti 4:10 having l *this* present world, and is departed *25*
Heb 1: 9 Thou hast l righteousness, and hated iniquity; *25*
2Pe 2:15 of Bosor, who l the wages of unrighteousness; *25*
1Jn 4:10 not that we l God, but that he loved us, and *25*
4:10 but that he l us, and sent his Son *to be* *25*
4:11 Beloved, if God so l us, we ought also to love *25*
4:19 We love him, because he first l us. *25*
Rev 1: 5 Unto him that l us, and washed us from our *25*
3: 9 before thy feet, and to know that I have l thee. *25*
12:11 and they l not their lives unto the death. *25*

LOVEDST (2) [LOVE]
Isa 57: 8 thou l their bed where thou sawest *it.* 157
Jn 17:24 for thou l me before the foundation of *25*

LOVELY (4) [LOVE]
2Sa 1:23 Saul and Jonathan *were* l and pleasant in 157
SS 5:16 yea, he *is* altogether l. This *is* my beloved, 4261
Eze 33:32 thou *art* unto them as a **very** l song *of* one 5690
Php 4: 8 *things are* pure, whatsoever *things are* l, *4375*

LOVER (4) [LOVE]
1Ki 5: 1 his father: for Hiram was ever a l of David. 157
Ps 88:18 L and friend hast thou put far from me, *and* 157
Tit 1: 8 But a l **of hospitality**, a lover of good *men,* *5382*
1: 8 a l **of good** *men,* sober, just, holy, *5358*

LOVERS (23) [LOVE]
Ps 38:11 My l and my friends stand aloof from my 157
Jer 3: 1 thou hast played the harlot with many l; 7453
4:30 *thy* l will despise thee, they will seek thy 5689
22:20 from the passages: for all thy l are destroyed. 157
22:22 thy pastors, and thy l shall go into captivity: 157
30:14 All thy l have forgotten thee; they seek thee 157
La 1: 2 among all her l she hath none to comfort *her:* 157
1:19 I called for my l, *but* they deceived me: 157
Eze 16:33 thou givest thy gifts to all thy l, and 157
16:36 through thy whoredoms with thy l, 157
16:37 Behold therefore, I will gather all thy l, 157
23: 5 she doted on her l, on the Assyrians *her* 157
23: 9 I have delivered her into the hand of her l, 157
23:22 Behold, I will raise up thy l against thee, 157
Hos 2: 5 for she said, I will go after my l, that give *me* 157
2: 7 she shall follow after her l, but she shall not 157
2:10 I discover her lewdness in the sight of her l, 157
2:12 These *are* my rewards that my l have given 157
2:13 and she went after her l, and forgat me, 157
8: 9 ass alone by himself: Ephraim hath hired l. 158
2Ti 3: 2 For men shall be l **of** their **own selves,** *5367*
3: 4 **l of pleasures** more than lovers of God; *5369*
3: 4 lovers of pleasures more than **l of God;** *5377*

LOVES (3) [LOVE]
Ps 45: T the sons of Korah, Maschil, A Song of l. 3039
Pr 7:18 the morning: let us solace ourselves with l. 159
SS 7:12 bud forth: there will I give thee my l. 1730

LOVEST (12) [LOVE]
Ge 22: 2 whom thou l, and get thee into the land of 157
Jdg 14:16 said, Thou dost but hate me, and l me not: 157
2Sa 19: 6 In that thou l thine enemies, and hatest thy 157
Ps 45: 7 Thou l righteousness, and hatest wickedness: 157
52: 3 Thou l evil more than good; *and* lying rather 157
52: 4 Thou l all devouring words, O thou deceitful 157
Ecc 9: 9 Live joyfully with the wife whom thou l all 157
Jn 11: 3 Lord, behold, he whom thou l is sick. *5368*

Jn 21:15 *son* of Jonas, l thou me more than these? *25*
21:16 second time, Simon, *son* of Jonas, l thou me? *25*
21:17 third time, Simon, *son* of Jonas, l thou me? *5368*
21:17 he said unto him the third time, L thou me? *5368*

LOVETH (65) [LOVE]
Ge 27: 9 savoury meat for thy father, such as he l: 157
44:20 is left of his mother, and his father l him. 157
Dt 10:18 the fatherless and widow, and l the stranger, 157
15:16 because he l thee and thine house, because 157
Ru 4:15 for thy daughter in law, which l thee, 157
Ps 11: 5 and him that l violence his soul hateth. 157
11: 7 For the righteous LORD l righteousness; 157
33: 5 He l righteousness and judgment: the earth is 157
34:12 *and* l *many* days, that *he* may see good? 157
37:28 For the LORD l judgment, and 157
87: 2 The LORD l the gates of Zion more than all 157
99: 4 The king's strength also l judgment; 157
119:140 word *is* very pure: therefore thy servant l it. 157
146: 8 are bowed down: the LORD l the righteous: 157
Pr 3:12 For whom the LORD l he correcteth; 157
12: 1 Whoso l instruction loveth knowledge: but 157
12: 1 Whoso loveth instruction l knowledge: but 157
13:24 but he that l him chasteneth him betimes. 157
15: 9 he l him that followeth after righteousness. 157
15:12 A scorner l not one that reproveth him: 157
17:17 A friend l at all times, and a brother is born 157
17:19 He l transgression that loveth strife: *and* 157
17:19 He loveth transgression that l strife: *and* 157
19: 8 He that getteth wisdom l his own soul: 157
21:17 He that l pleasure *shall be* a poor man: 157
21:17 he that l wine and oil shall not be rich. 157
22:11 He that l pureness of heart, *for* the grace of 157
29: 3 Whoso l wisdom rejoiceth his father: but 157
Ecc 5:10 He that l silver shall not be satisfied *with* 157
5:10 nor he that l abundance *with* increase: 157
SS 1: 7 Tell me, O thou whom my soul l, where thou 157
3: 1 on my bed I sought *him* whom my soul l: 157
3: 2 broad ways, I will seek *him* whom my soul l: 157
3: 3 *whom I said,* Saw ye *him* whom my soul l? 157
3: 4 from them, but I found *him* whom my soul l: 157
Isa 1:23 every one l gifts, and followeth after 157
Hos 10:11 *and* l to tread out *the corn;* but I passed over 157
12: 7 of deceit *are* in his hand: he l to oppress. 157
Mt 10:37 He that l father or mother more than me is *5368*
10:37 and he that l son or daughter more than me *5368*
Lk 7: 5 For he l our nation, and he hath built us a *25*
7:47 but to whom little is forgiven, *the same* l little. *25*
Jn 3:35 The Father l the Son, and hath given all *things* *25*
5:20 For the Father l the Son, and sheweth him *5368*
12:25 He that l his life shall lose it; and he that *5368*
14:21 and keepeth them, he it is that l me: *25*
14:21 and he that l me shall be loved of my Father, *25*
14:24 He that l me not keepeth not my sayings: and *25*
16:27 For the Father himself l you, because *5368*
Ro 13: 8 for he that l another hath fulfilled the law. *25*
2Co 9: 7 or of necessity: for God l a cheerful giver. *25*
Eph 5:28 own bodies. He that l his wife loveth himself. *25*
5:28 own bodies. He that loveth his wife l himself. *25*
Heb 12: 6 For whom the Lord l he chasteneth, and *25*
1Jn 2:10 He that l his brother abideth in the light, and *25*
3:10 is not of God, neither he that l not his brother. *25*
3:14 He that l not *his* brother abideth in death. *25*
4: 7 and every one that l is born of God, and *25*
4: 8 He that l not, knoweth not God; for God is *25*
4:20 for he that l not his brother whom he hath *25*
4:21 That he who l God love his brother also. *25*
5: 1 every one that l him that begat loveth him also *25*
5: 1 every one that loveth him that begat l him also *25*
3Jn 1: 9 who l **to have** the **preeminence among** *5383*
Rev 22:15 idolaters, and whosoever l and maketh a lie. *5368*

LOVING (3) [LOVE]
Pr 5:19 *Let her be as* the l hind and pleasant roe; 158
22: 1 *and* l favour rather than silver and gold. 2896
Isa 56:10 sleeping, lying down, l to slumber. 157

LOVINGKINDNESS (26) [KIND, LOVE]
Ps 17: 7 Shew thy marvellous l, O thou that savest 2617
26: 3 For thy l *is* before mine eyes: and I have 2617
36: 7 How excellent *is* thy l, O God! therefore 2617
36:10 O continue thy l unto them that know thee; 2617
40:10 I have not concealed thy l and thy truth 2617
40:11 let thy l and thy truth continually preserve 2617
42: 8 *Yet* the LORD will command his l in 2617
48: 9 We have thought of thy l, O God, in 2617
51: 1 mercy upon me, O God, according to thy l: 2617
63: 3 Because thy l *is* better than life, my lips 2617
69:16 Hear me, O LORD; for thy l *is* good: 2617
88:11 Shall thy l be declared in the grave? *or* 2617
89:33 Nevertheless my l will I not utterly take 2617
92: 2 To shew forth thy l in the morning, and 2617
103: 4 who crowneth thee *with* l and 2617
107:43 they shall understand the l of the LORD. 2617
119:88 Quicken me after thy l; so shall I keep 2617
119:149 Hear my voice according unto thy l: 2617
119:159 quicken me, O LORD, according to thy l. 2617
138: 2 praise thy name for thy l and for thy truth: 2617
143: 8 Cause me to hear thy l in the morning; 2617
Jer 9:24 that I *am* the LORD which exercise l, 2617
16: 5 saith the LORD, *even* l and mercies. 2617
31: 3 therefore *with* l have I drawn thee. 2617
32:18 Thou shewest l unto thousands, and 2617
Hos 2:19 and in judgment, and in l, and in mercies. 2617

LOVINGKINDNESSES (4) [KIND, LOVE]
Ps 25: 6 O LORD, thy tender mercies and thy l; 2617
89:49 Lord, where *are* thy former l, *which* thou 2617
Isa 63: 7 I will mention the l of the LORD, *and* 2617
63: 7 and according to the multitude of his l. 2617

LOW (46) [LOWER, LOWEST, LOWLINESS, LOWLY]
Dt 28:43 thou shalt come down **very** l. 4295+4295
Jdg 11:35 thou hast **brought** me **very** l, 3766+3766
1Sa 2: 7 maketh rich: he **bringeth** l, and lifteth up. 8213
1Ch 27:28 the sycomore trees that *were* in the l **plains** 8219
2Ch 9:27 trees that *are* in the l **plains** in abundance. 8219
26:10 both in the l **country**, and in the plains: 8219
28:18 also had invaded the cities of the l **country**, 8219
28:19 For the LORD **brought** Judah l because 3665
Job 5:11 To set up on high those that be l; that those 8217
14:21 they are **brought** l, but he perceiveth *it* not 6819
24:24 a little while, but are gone and **brought** l, 4355
40:12 on every one *that is* proud, *and* **bring** him l; 3665
Ps 49: 2 Both ls and high, rich and poor, 120+1121
62: 9 Surely **men of** l **degree** *are* vanity, 120+1121
79: 8 prevent us: for we are **brought** very l. 1809
106:43 and were **brought** l for their iniquity. 4355
107:39 and **brought** l through oppression, 7817
116: 6 I was **brought** l, and he helped me. 1809
136:23 Who remembered us in our l **estate**: for his 8216
142: 6 unto my cry; for I am **brought** very l: 1809
Pr 29:23 A man's pride shall **bring** him l: but 8213
Ecc 10: 6 in great dignity, and the rich sit in l **place**. 8216
12: 4 when the sound of the grinding is l, and 8217
12: 4 the daughters of musick shall be **brought** l; 7817
Isa 2:12 that is lifted up; and he shall be **brought** l: 8213
2:17 the haughtiness of men shall be **made** l: 8213
13:11 will **lay** l the haughtiness of the terrible. 8213
25: 5 of the terrible ones shall be **brought** l. 6030
25:12 **lay** l, *and* bring to the ground, *even* to 8213
26: 5 the lofty city, he **layeth** it l; he layeth it 8213
26: 5 it low; he **layeth** it l, *even* to the ground; 8213
29: 4 thy speech shall be l out of the dust, and 7817
32:19 and the city shall be l in a low place. 8213
32:19 and the city shall be low in a l **place**. 8218
40: 4 every mountain and hill shall be **made** l: 8213
La 3:55 thy name, O LORD, out of the l dungeon. 8482
Eze 17: 6 and became a spreading vine of l stature, 8217
17:24 have exalted the l tree, have dried up 8217
21:26 exalt *him that is* l, and abase *him that is* 8217
26:20 shall set thee **in** the l **parts** of the earth, 8482
Lk 1:48 For he hath regarded the l **estate** of his *5014*
1:52 *their* seats, and exalted them of l **degree**. *5011*
3: 5 every mountain and hill shall be **brought** l; *5013*
Ro 12:16 *things,* but condescend to *men* **of** l **estate**. *5011*
Jas 1: 9 Let the brother of l **degree** rejoice in that he *5011*
1:10 But the rich, in that he is **made** l: because *5014*

LOWBORN See DEGREE; DEGREES

LOWER (18) [LOW]
Ge 6:16 *with* l, second, and third *stories* shalt thou 8482
Lev 13:20 it *be* in sight l than the skin, and the hair 8217
13:21 *if* it *be* not l than the skin, but *be* somewhat 8217
13:26 it *be* no l than the *other* skin, but *be* 8217
14:37 reddish, which in sight *are* l than the wall; 8217
Ne 4:13 Therefore set I in the l places behind 8482

Ps 8: 5 For thou hast **made** him a little l than 2637
63: 9 to destroy *it,* shall go into the l **parts** of 8482
Pr 25: 7 than that thou shouldest be **put** l in 8213
Isa 22: 9 ye gathered together the waters of the l 8481
44:23 hath done *it:* shout, ye l **parts** of the earth: 8482
Eze 40:18 the length of the gates *was* the l pavement. 8481
40:19 l gate unto the forefront of the inner court 8481
42: 5 than the l, and than the middlemost of 8481
43:14 *even* to the l settle *shall be* two cubits, 8481
Eph 4: 9 that he also descended first into the l parts *2737*
Heb 2: 7 Thou **madest** him a little l than the angels; *1642*
2: 9 who was **made** a little l than the angels, *1642*

LOWEST (11) [LOW]
Dt 32:22 shall burn unto the l hell, and 8482
1Ki 12:31 made priests of the l of the people, 7098
13:33 made again of the l of the people priests of 7098
2Ki 17:32 made unto themselves of the l of them 7098
Ps 86:13 thou hast delivered my soul from the l hell. 8482
88: 6 Thou hast laid me in the l pit, in darkness, 8482
139:15 curiously wrought in the l **parts** of 8482
Eze 41: 7 increased *from* the l *chamber* to the highest 8481
42: 6 *the building* was straitened more than the l 8481
Lk 14: 9 thou begin with shame to take the l room. *2078*
14:10 art bidden, go and sit down in the l room; *2078*

LOWETH (1) [LOWING]
Job 6: 5 he hath grass? or l the ox over his fodder? 1600

LOWING (2) [LOWETH]
1Sa 6:12 l as they went, and turned not aside *to* 1600
15:14 and the l of the oxen which I hear? 6963

LOWLINESS (2) [LOW]
Eph 4: 2 With all l and meekness, with *5012*
Php 2: 3 in **l of mind** *let* each esteem other better *5012*

LOWLY (6) [LOW]
Ps 138: 6 *be* high, yet hath he respect unto the l: 8217
Pr 3:34 the scorners: but he giveth grace unto the l. 6035
11: 2 cometh shame: but with the l *is* wisdom. 6800
16:19 *it is to be* of an humble spirit with the l, 6035
Zec 9: 9 l, and riding upon an ass, and upon a colt 6041
Mt 11:29 learn of me; for I am meek and l in heart: *5011*

LOWRING (1)
Mt 16: 3 for the sky is red and l. O *ye* hypocrites, *4768*

LUBIM (1) [LUBIMS]
Na 3: 9 *it was* infinite; Put and L were thy helpers. 3864

LUBIMS (2) [LUBIM]
2Ch 12: 3 the L, the Sukkiims, and the Ethiopians. 3864
16: 8 not the Ethiopians and the L a huge host, 3864

LUCAS (2)
2Co 13: S *a city* of Macedonia, by Titus and L. *3065*
Phm 1:24 Marcus, Aristarchus, Demas, L, *3065*

LUCIFER (1)
Isa 14:12 from heaven, O L, son of the morning! 1966

LUCIUS (2)
Ac 13: 1 and L of Cyrene, and Manaen, *3066*
Ro 16:21 and L, and Jason, and Sosipater, *3066*

LUCRE (5) [LUCRE'S]
1Sa 8: 3 turned aside after l, and took bribes, and 1215
1Ti 3: 3 to wine, no striker, not **greedy of filthy** l; *146*
3: 8 given to much wine, not **greedy of filthy** l; *146*
Tit 1: 7 to wine, no striker, not **given to filthy** l; *146*
1Pe 5: 2 not **for filthy** l, but of a ready mind; *147*

LUCRE'S (1) [LUCRE]
Tit 1:11 which *they* ought not, for filthy l sake. *2771*

LUD (4)
Ge 10:22 Asshur, and Arphaxad, and L, and Aram. 3865
1Ch 1:17 L, and Aram, and Uz, and Hul, and Gether, 3865
Isa 66:19 *to* Tarshish, Pul, and L, that draw the bow, 3865
Eze 27:10 They of Persia and of L and of Phut were 3865

LUDIM (2)
Ge 10:13 Mizraim begat L, and Anamim, and 3865
1Ch 1:11 Mizraim begat L, and Anamim, and 3865

LUDITES See LUDIM

LUHITH (2)
Isa 15: 5 for *by* the mounting up of L with weeping 3872
Jer 48: 5 For *in* the going up of L continual weeping 3872

LUKE (2)
Col 4:14 L, the beloved physician, and Demas, *3065*
2Ti 4:11 Only L is with me. Take Mark, and *3065*

LUKEWARM (1) [WARM]
Rev 3:16 So *then* because thou art l, and neither cold *5513*

LUMP (7)
2Ki 20: 7 Isaiah said, Take a l of figs. And they took 1690
Isa 38:21 Let them take a l of figs, and lay *it* for a 1690
Ro 9:21 of the same l to make one vessel unto *5445*
11:16 the l *is* also *holy:* and if the root *be* holy, so *5445*
1Co 5: 6 that a little leaven leaveneth the whole l? *5445*
5: 7 the old leaven, that ye may be a new l, *5445*
Gal 5: 9 A little leaven leaveneth the whole l. *5445*

LUNATICK (2)
Mt 4:24 and those which were l, and those that had *4583*
17:15 for he is l, and sore vexed: for ofttimes he *4583*

LURK (2) [LURKING]
Pr 1:11 let us l **privily** for the innocent without 6845
1:18 they l **privily** for their own lives. 6845

LURKING (3) [LURK]
1Sa 23:23 take knowledge of all the l **places** where he 4224
Ps 10: 8 He sitteth in the l **places** of the villages: 3993
17:12 as it were a young lion l in secret places. 3427

LUST (19) [LUSTED, LUSTETH, LUSTING, LUSTS, LUSTY]
Ex 15: 9 the spoil; my l shall be satisfied upon them; 5315
Ps 78:18 in their heart by asking meat for their l. 5315
78:30 They were not estranged from their l. 8378
81:12 So I gave them up unto their own heart's l: 8307
Pr 6:25 L **not after** her beauty in thine heart; 2530
Mt 5:28 **l after** her hath committed adultery with *1937*
Ro 1:27 burned in their l one towards another; *3715*
7: 7 for I had not known l, except the law had *1939*
1Co 10: 6 to the intent we should not **l after** evil *1938*
Gal 5:16 and ye shall not fulfil the l of the flesh. *1939*
1Th 4: 5 Not in the l of concupiscence, even as *3806*
Jas 1:14 when he is drawn away of his own l, and *1939*
1:15 Then when l hath conceived, it bringeth *1939*
4: 2 Ye l, and have not: ye kill, and desire *to* *1937*
2Pe 1: 4 the corruption that is in the world through l: *1939*
2:10 walk after the flesh in the l of uncleanness, *1939*
1Jn 2:16 the l of the flesh, and the lust of the eyes, *1939*
2:16 and the l of the eyes, and the pride of life, *1939*
2:17 the world passeth away, and the l thereof: *1939*

LUSTED (4) [LUST]
Nu 11:34 because there they buried the people that l. 183
Ps 106:14 **l exceedingly** in the wilderness, and 183+8378
1Co 10: 6 not lust after evil *things,* as they also l. *1937*
Rev 18:14 And the fruits that thy soul **l after** are *1939*

LUSTETH (6) [LUST]
Dt 12:15 in all thy gates, whatsoever thy soul **l after,** 185
12:20 mayest eat flesh, whatsoever thy soul **l after.** 185
12:21 eat in thy gates whatsoever thy soul **l after.** 185
14:26 *that* money for whatsoever thy soul **l after,** 183
Gal 5:17 For the flesh l against the Spirit, and *1937*
Jas 4: 5 the spirit that dwelleth in us l to envy? *1971*

LUSTING (1) [LUST]
Nu 11: 4 that *was* among them **fell a l:** 183+8378

LUSTS (24) [LUST]
Mk 4:19 and the l of other *things* entering in, *1939*
Jn 8:44 and the l of your father ye will do. *1939*
Ro 1:24 through the l of their own hearts, *1939*
6:12 that *ye* should obey it in the l thereof. *1939*
13:14 for the flesh, to *fulfil* the l *thereof.* *1939*
Gal 5:24 crucified the flesh with the affections and l. *1939*
Eph 2: 3 in times past in the l of our flesh, *1939*
4:22 is corrupt according to the deceitful l; *1939*
1Ti 6: 9 a snare, and *into* many foolish and hurtful l, *1939*
2Ti 2:22 Flee also youthful l: but *1939*
3: 6 laden with sins, led away with divers l, *1939*

2Ti 4: 3 after their own l shall they heap to 1939
Tit 2:12 and worldly l we should live soberly, 1939
3: 3 deceived, serving divers l and pleasures, 1939
Jas 4: 1 even of your l that war in your members? 2237
4: 3 that ye may consume it upon your l. 2237
1Pe 1:14 according to the former l in your ignorance: 1939
2:11 and pilgrims, abstain from fleshly l, 1939
4: 2 rest of his time in the flesh to the l of men, 1939
4: 3 l, excess of wine, revellings, banquetings, 1939
2Pe 2:18 they allure through the l of the flesh, 1939
3: 3 last days scoffers, walking after their own l, 1939
Jude 1:16 complainers, walking after their own l; 1939
1:18 who should walk after their own ungodly l. 1939

LUSTY (1) [LUST]
Jdg 3:29 thousand men, all l, and all men of valour; 8082

LUXURY See SUMPTUOUSLY

LUZ (8)
Ge 28:19 the name of that city was called L at 3870
35: 6 So Jacob came to L, which is in the land of 3870
48: 3 God Almighty appeared unto me at L in 3870
Jos 16: 2 goeth out from Beth-el to L, and 3870
18:13 the border went over from thence toward L, 3870
18:13 to the side of L, which is Beth-el, 3870
Jdg 1:23 (Now the name of the city before was L.) 3870
1:26 built a city, and called the name thereof L: 3870

LYCAONIA (2)
Ac 14: 6 cities of L, and unto the region that lieth 3071
14:11 up their voices, saying in the speech of L, 3072

LYCIA (1)
Ac 27: 5 Pamphylia, we came to Myra, a city of L. 3073

LYDDA (3)
Ac 9:32 down also to the saints which dwelt at L. 3069
9:35 And all that dwelt at L and Saron saw him, 3069
9:38 And forasmuch as L was nigh to Joppa, and 3069

LYDIA (3) [LYDIANS]
Eze 30: 5 L, and all the mingled people, and Chub, 3865
Ac 16:14 And a certain woman named L, a seller of 3070
16:40 the prison, and entered into the house of L: 3070

LYDIANS (1) [LYDIA]
Jer 46: 9 and the L, that handle and bend the bow. 3865

LYING (57) [LIE]
Ge 29: 2 lo, there were three flocks of sheep l by it; 7257
34: 7 he had wrought folly in Israel in l with 7901
Ex 23: 5 If thou see the ass of him that hateth thee l 7257
Nu 31:17 woman that hath known man by l with him. 4904
31:18 that have not known a man by l with him, 4904
31:35 that had not known man by l with him. 4904
Dt 21: 1 l in the field, and it be not known who hath 5307
22:22 If a man be found l with a woman married 7901
Jdg 9:35 people that were with him, from l in wait. 3993
16: 9 Now there were men l in wait, abiding with 693
21:12 that had known no man by l with any male: 4904
1Ki 22:22 I will be a l spirit in the mouth of all his 8267
22:23 the LORD hath put a l spirit in the mouth 8267
2Ch 18:21 be a l spirit in the mouth of all his prophets. 8267
18:22 the LORD hath put a l spirit in the mouth 8267
Ps 31: 6 I have hated them that regard l vanities: but 7723
31:18 Let the l lips be put to silence; which speak 8267
52: 3 and l rather than to speak righteousness. 8267
59:12 and for cursing and l which they speak. 3585
109: 2 they have spoken against me with a l 8267
119:29 Remove from me the way of l: and 8267
119:163 I hate and abhor l: but thy law do I love. 8267
120: 2 from l lips, and from a deceitful tongue. 8267
139: 3 Thou compassest my path and my l down, 7252
Pr 6:17 a l tongue, and hands that shed innocent 8267
10:18 He that hideth hatred with l lips, and he that 8267
12:19 for ever: but a l tongue is but for a moment. 8267
12:22 L lips are abomination to the LORD: but 8267
13: 5 A righteous man hateth l: but 1697+8267
17: 7 not a fool: much less do l lips a prince. 8267
21: 6 The getting of treasures by a l tongue is a 8267
26:28 A l tongue hateth those that are afflicted by 8267
Isa 30: 9 That this is a rebellious people, l children, 3586
32: 7 devices to destroy the poor with l words, 8267
56:10 sleeping, l down, loving to slumber. 7901
59:13 In transgressing and l against the LORD, 3584
Jer 7: 4 Trust ye not in l words, saying, The temple 8267
7: 8 Behold, ye trust in l words, that cannot 8267
29:23 have spoken l words in my name, which I 8267
La 3:10 He was unto me as a bear l in wait, and as a 693
Eze 13: 6 They have seen vanity and l divination, 3577
13: 7 have ye not spoken a l divination, 3577
13:19 by your l to my people that hear your lies? 3576
Da 2: 9 for ye have prepared l and corrupt words to 3538
Hos 4: 2 l, and killing, and stealing, and 3584
Jnh 2: 8 They that observe l vanities forsake their 7723
Mt 9: 2 to him a man sick of the palsy, l on a bed: 906
Mk 5:40 and entereth in where the damsel was l. 345
Lk 2:12 in swaddling clothes, l in a manger. 2749
2:16 and Joseph, and the babe l in a manger. 2749
Jn 13:25 He then l on Jesus' breast saith unto him, 1968
20: 5 and looking in, saw the linen clothes l; 2749
20: 7 not l with the linen clothes, but 2749
Ac 20:19 which befell me by the l in wait of 1917
23:16 Paul's sister's son heard of their l in wait, 1747
Eph 4:25 Wherefore putting away l, speak every man 5579
2Th 2: 9 with all power and signs and l wonders, 5579

LYRE See SACKBUT

LYSANIAS (1)
Lk 3: 1 and L the tetrarch of Abilene, 3078

LYSIAS (3)
Ac 23:26 Claudius L unto the most excellent 3079
24: 7 But the chief captain L came upon us, and 3079
24:22 When L the chief captain shall come down, 3079

LYSTRA (6)
Ac 14: 6 were ware of it, and fled unto L and Derbe, 3082
14: 8 And there sat a certain man at L, 3082
14:21 they returned again to L, and to Iconium, 3082
16: 1 Then came he to Derbe and L: and behold, 3082
16: 2 reported of by the brethren that were at L 3082
2Ti 3:11 came unto me at Antioch, at Iconium, at L; 3082

M

M

MAACAH (3) [MAACHAH]
2Sa 3: 3 Absalom the son of M the daughter of 4601
10: 6 of king M a thousand men, and of Ish-tob 4601
10: 8 of Zoba, and of Rehob, and Ish-tob, and M, 4601

MAACATHITE; MAACATHITES See MAACHATHI; MAACHATHITE; MAACHATHITES

MAACHAH (18) [MAACAH, MAACHATHI, MAACHATHITE, MAACHATHITES]
Ge 22:24 and Gaham, and Thahash, and M. 4601
1Ki 2:39 away unto Achish son of M king of Gath. 4601
15: 2 his mother's name was M, the daughter of 4601
15:10 his mother's name was M, the daughter of 4601
15:13 also M his mother, even her he removed 4601
1Ch 2:48 M, Caleb's concubine, bare Sheber, and 4601
3: 2 Absalom the son of M the daughter of 4601
7:15 and Shuppim, whose sister's name was M;) 4601
7:16 M the wife of Machir bare a son, and 4601
8:29 of Gibeon; whose wife's name was M: 4601
9:35 Jehiel, whose wife's name was M: 4601
11:43 Hanan the son of M, and Joshaphat 4601
19: 7 and the king of M and his people; 4601
27:16 the Simeonites, Shephatiah the son of M: 4601
2Ch 11:20 after her he took M the daughter of 4601
11:21 Rehoboam loved M the daughter of 4601
11:22 Rehoboam made Abijah the son of M 4601
15:16 also concerning M the mother of Asa 4601

MAACHATHI (1) [MAACHAH]
Dt 3:14 of Argob unto the coasts of Geshuri and M; 4602

MAACHATHITE (4) [MAACHAH]
2Sa 23:34 the son of Ahasbai, the son of the M, 4602
2Ki 25:23 Jaazaniah the son of a M, they and 4602

1Ch 4:19 Keilah the Garmite, and Eshtemoa the **M**. 4602
Jer 40: 8 Jezaniah the son of a **M**, they and 4602

MAACHATHITES (4) [MAACHAH]
Jos 12: 5 the border of the Geshurites and the **M**, 4602
13:11 the border of the Geshurites and **M**, and 4602
Jos 13:13 expelled not the Geshurites, nor the **M**: 4602
13:13 the **M** dwell among the Israelites until this 4601

MAADAI (1)
Ezr 10:34 Of the sons of Bani; **M**, Amram, and Uel, 4572

MAADIAH (1)
Ne 12: 5 Miamin, **M**, Bilgah, 4573

MAAI (1)
Ne 12:36 Shemaiah, and Azarael, Milalai, Gilalai, **M**, 4597

MAALEH-ACRABBIM (1)
Jos 15: 3 it went out to the south side to **M**, and 4610

MAARATH (1)
Jos 15:59 **M**, and Beth-anoth, and Eltekon; six cities 4638

MAASEIAH (25)
1Ch 15:18 **M**, and Mattithiah, and Elipheleh, and 4641
15:20 and Unni, and Eliab, and **M**, and Benaiah, 4641
2Ch 23: 1 **M** the son of Adaiah, and Elishaphat 4641
26:11 the hand of Jeiel the scribe and **M** the ruler, 4641
28: 7 slew **M** the king's son, and Azrikam 4641
34: 8 **M** the governor of the city, and Joah 4641
Ezr 10:18 **M**, and Eliezer, and Jarib, and Gedaliah. 4641
10:21 **M**, and Elijah, and Shemaiah, and Jehiel, 4641
10:22 Elioenai, **M**, Ishmael, Nethaneel, Jozabad, 4641
10:30 Adna, and Chelal, Benaiah, **M**, Mattaniah, 4641
Ne 3:23 After him repaired Azariah the son of **M** 4641
8: 4 Anaiah, and Urijah, and Hilkiah, and **M**, 4641
8: 7 **M**, Kelita, Azariah, Jozabad, Hanan, 4641
10:25 Rehum, Hashabnah, **M**, 4641
11: 5 **M** the son of Baruch, the son of Col-hozeh, 4641
11: 7 the son of **M**, the son of Ithiel, the son of 4641
12:41 Eliakim, **M**, Miniamin, Michaiah, Elioenai, 4641
12:42 **M**, and Shemaiah, and Eleazar, and Uzzi, 4641
Jer 21: 1 Zephaniah the son of **M** the priest, saying, 4641
29:21 of Kolaiah, and of Zedekiah, the son of **M**, 4641
29:25 to Zephaniah the son of **M** the priest, and 4641
32:12 the son of **M**, in the sight of Hanameel 4271
35: 4 which *was* above the chamber of **M** the son 4641
37: 3 Zephaniah the son of **M** the priest to 4641
51:59 Seraiah the son of Neriah, the son of **M**, 4271

MAASIAI (1)
1Ch 9:12 **M** the son of Adiel, the son of Jahzerah, 4640

MAATH (1)
Lk 3:26 Which was *the son* of **M**, which was *3092*

MAAZ (1)
1Ch 2:27 Jerahmeel were, **M**, and Jamin, and Eker. 4619

MAAZIAH (2)
1Ch 24:18 to Delaiah, the four and twentieth to **M**. 4590
Ne 10: 8 **M**, Bilgai, Shemaiah: these *were* 4590

MACBANNAI See MACHBANAI

MACBENAH See MACHBENAH

MACEDONIA (28) [MACEDONIAN]
Ac 16: 9 There stood a man of **M**, and prayed him, *3110*
16: 9 Come over into **M**, and help us. *3109*
16:10 immediately we endeavoured to go into **M**, *3109*
16:12 which is the chief city of *that* part of **M**, *3109*
18: 5 and Timotheus were come from **M**, *3109*
19:21 when he had passed through **M** and Achaia, *3109*
19:22 So he sent into **M** two of them that *3109*
19:29 caught Gaius and Aristarchus, men of **M**, *3110*
20: 1 and departed for to go into **M**. *3109*
20: 3 he purposed to return through **M**. *3109*
Ro 15:26 For it hath pleased *them of* **M** and *3109*
1Co 16: 5 unto you, when I shall pass through **M**: *3109*
16: 5 for I do pass through **M**. *3109*
2Co 1:16 And to pass by you into **M**, and to come *3109*
1:16 and to come again out of **M** unto you, and *3109*
2:13 leave of them, I went from *thence* into **M**. *3109*
7: 5 For, when we were come into **M**, our flesh *3109*
8: 1 of God bestowed on the churches of **M**; *3109*
9: 2 for which I boast of you to them of **M**, *3110*
9: 4 Lest haply if they of **M** come with me, and *3110*
11: 9 the brethren which came from **M** supplied: *3109*
13: S *a city* of **M**, by Titus and Lucas. *3109*
Php 4:15 of the gospel, when I departed from **M**, *3109*
1Th 1: 7 ye were ensamples to all that believe in **M** *3109*
1: 8 out the word of the Lord not only in **M** *3109*
4:10 towards all the brethren which are in all **M**: *3109*
1Ti 1: 3 abide *still* at Ephesus, when I went into **M**, *3109*
Tit 3: S of the Cretians, from Nicopolis of **M**. *3109*

MACEDONIAN (1) [MACEDONIA]
Ac 27: 2 a **M** of Thessalonica, being with us. *3110*

MACHBANAI (1)
1Ch 12:13 Jeremiah the tenth, **M** the eleventh. 4344

MACHBENAH (1)
1Ch 2:49 Sheva the father of **M**, and the father of 4343

MACHI (1)
Nu 13:15 Of the tribe of Gad, Geuel the son of **M**. 4352

MACHIR (22) [MACHIRITES]
Ge 50:23 **M** the son of Manasseh were brought up 4353
Nu 26:29 of **M**, the family of the Machirites: and 4353
26:29 **M** begat Gilead: of Gilead *come* the family 4353
27: 1 of Hepher, the son of Gilead, the son of **M**, 4353
32:39 the children of **M** the son of Manasseh 4353
32:40 Moses gave Gilead unto **M** the son of 4353
36: 1 the son of **M**, the son of Manasseh, of 4353
Dt 3:15 And I gave Gilead unto **M**. 4353
Jos 13:31 *were pertaining* unto the children of **M** 4353
13:31 *even* to the one half of the children of **M** by 4353
17: 1 *to wit*, for **M** the firstborn of Manasseh, 4353
17: 3 of Hepher, the son of Gilead, the son of **M**, 4353
Jdg 5:14 out of **M** came down governors, and out of 4353
2Sa 9: 4 Behold, he *is in* the house of **M**, the son of 4353
9: 5 fet him out of the house of **M**, the son of 4353
17:27 **M** the son of Ammiel of Lo-debar, and 4353
1Ch 2:21 to the daughter of **M** the father of Gilead, 4353
2:23 All these *belonged to* the sons of **M** 4353
7:14 his concubine the Aramitess bare **M** 4353
7:15 **M** took to wife *the sister* of Huppim and 4353
7:16 Maachah the wife of **M** bare a son, and 4353
7:17 the son of **M**, the son of Manasseh. 4353

MACHIRITES (1) [MACHIR]
Nu 26:29 of Machir, the family of the **M**: and 4354

MACHNADEBAI (1)
Ezr 10:40 **M**, Shashai, Sharai, 4367

MACHPELAH (6)
Ge 23: 9 That he may give me the cave of **M**, 4375
23:17 the field of Ephron, which *was* in **M**, 4375
23:19 in the cave of the field of **M** before Mamre: 4375
25: 9 and Ishmael buried him in the cave of **M**, 4375
49:30 In the cave that *is* in the field of **M**, 4375
50:13 buried him in the cave of the field of **M**, 4375

MACNADEBAI See MACHNADEBAI

MAD (22) [MADNESS]
Dt 28:34 So that thou shalt be **m** for the sight of 7696
1Sa 21:13 **feigned** himself **m** in their hands, and 1984
21:14 unto his servants, Lo, you see the man *is* **m**: 7696
21:15 *Have* I need of **m men**, that ye have 7696
21:15 *fellow* to **play the m man** in my presence? 7696
2Ki 9:11 wherefore came this **m** *fellow* to thee? 7696
Ps 102: 8 they that are **m** against me are sworn 1984
Pr 26:18 As a **m** *man* who casteth firebrands, 3856
Ecc 2: 2 I said of laughter, *It is* **m**: and of mirth, 1984
7: 7 Surely oppression **maketh** a wise *man* **m**; 1984
Isa 44:25 tokens of the liars, and **maketh** diviners **m**; 1984
Jer 25:16 be **m**, because of the sword that I will send 1984
29:26 for every man *that is* **m**, and 7696
50:38 and they are **m** upon *their* idols. 1984
51: 7 of her wine; therefore the nations are **m**. 1984
Hos 9: 7 the spiritual man *is* **m**, for the multitude of 7696
Jn 10:20 of them said, He hath a devil, and is **m**; *3105*
Ac 12:15 And they said unto her, Thou art **m**. *3105*
26:11 and being exceedingly **m against** them, *1693*
26:24 learning doth **make** thee **m**. *1519+3130+4062*

Ac 26:25 But he said, I am not **m**, most noble Festus; *3105*
1Co 14:23 will they not say that ye are **m**? *3105*

MADAI (2)
Ge 10: 2 **M**, and Javan, and Tubal, and Meshech, 4074
1Ch 1: 5 **M**, and Javan, and Tubal, and Meshech, 4074

MADE (1406) [MAKE] See Index

MADEST (10) [MAKE] See Index

MADIAN (1) [MIDIAN]
Ac 7:29 and was a stranger in the land of **M**, *3099*

MADMANNAH (2)
Jos 15:31 And Ziklag, and **M**, and Sansannah, 4089
1Ch 2:49 She bare also Shaaph the father of **M**, 4089

MADMEN (1)
Jer 48: 2 Also thou shalt be cut down, O **M**; 4086

MADMENAH (1)
Isa 10:31 **M** is removed; the inhabitants of Gebim 4088

MADNESS (9) [MAD]
Dt 28:28 The LORD shall smite thee with **m**, and 7697
Ecc 1:17 to know wisdom, and to know **m** and folly: 1947
2:12 myself to behold wisdom, and **m**, and folly: 1947
7:25 of folly, even of foolishness *and* **m**: 1947
9: 3 **m** *is* in their heart while they live, and 1947
10:13 and the end of his talk *is* mischievous **m**. 1948
Zec 12: 4 with astonishment, and his rider with **m**: 7697
Lk 6:11 And they were filled with **m**; and *454*
2Pe 2:16 man's voice forbad the **m** of the prophet. *3913*

MADON (2)
Jos 11: 1 *things*, that he sent to Jobab king of **M**, 4068
12:19 The king of **M**, one; the king of Hazor, one; 4068

MAGADAN See MAGDALA

MAGBISH (1)
Ezr 2:30 The children of **M**, an hundred fifty and 4019

MAGDALA (1) [MAGDALENE]
Mt 15:39 took ship, and came into the coasts of **M**. *3093*

MAGDALENE (12) [MAGDALA]
Mt 27:56 Among which was Mary **M**, and Mary *3094*
27:61 And there was Mary **M**, and the other *3094*
28: 1 came Mary **M** and the other Mary to see *3094*
Mk 15:40 among whom was Mary **M**, and Mary *3094*
15:47 And Mary **M** and Mary *the mother* of Joses *3094*
16: 1 Mary **M**, and Mary the *mother* of James, *3094*
16: 9 he appeared first to Mary **M**, out of whom *3094*
Lk 8: 2 evil spirits and infirmities, Mary called **M**, *3094*
24:10 It was Mary **M**, and Joanna, and Mary *3094*
Jn 19:25 Mary the *wife* of Cleophas, and Mary **M**. *3094*
20: 1 The first *day* of the week cometh Mary **M** *3094*
20:18 Mary **M** came and told the disciples that *3094*

MAGDIEL (2)
Ge 36:43 Duke **M**, duke Iram: these *be* the dukes of 4025
1Ch 1:54 Duke **M**, duke Iram. These *are* the dukes of 4025

MAGICIAN (1) [MAGICIANS]
Da 2:10 *that* asked such things at any **m**, or 2749

MAGICIANS (15) [MAGICIAN]
Ge 41: 8 he sent and called for all the **m** of Egypt, 2748
41:24 I told *this* unto the **m**; but *there was* none 2748
Ex 7:11 now the **m** of Egypt, they also did in like 2748
7:22 the **m** of Egypt did so with their 2748
8: 7 the **m** did so with their enchantments, and 2748
8:18 the **m** did so with their enchantments to 2748
8:19 the **m** said unto Pharaoh, This *is* the finger 2748
9:11 the **m** could not stand before Moses 2748
9:11 for the boil was upon the **m**, and upon all 2748
Da 1:20 found them ten times better than all the **m** 2748
2: 2 the king commanded to call the **m**, and 2748
2:27 the **m**, the soothsayers, shew unto the king; 2749
4: 7 came in the **m**, the astrologers, 2749
4: 9 master of the **m**, because I know that 2749
5:11 made master of the **m**, astrologers, 2749

MAGISTRATE (2) [MAGISTRATES]
Jdg 18: 7 *there was* no **m** in the land, 3423+6114
Lk 12:58 thou goest with thine adversary to the **m**, *758*

MAGISTRATES (8) [MAGISTRATE]
Ezr 7:25 that *is* in thine hand, set **m** and judges, 8200
Lk 12:11 and *unto* **m**, and powers, take ye no thought *746*
Ac 16:20 And brought them to the **m**, saying, *4755*
16:22 and the **m** rent off their clothes, and *4755*
16:35 the **m** sent the sergeants, saying, Let those *4755*
16:36 to Paul, The **m** have sent to let you go: *4755*
16:38 the sergeants told these words unto the **m**: *4755*
Tit 3: 1 to principalities and powers, to **obey m**, *3980*

MAGNIFICAL (1) [MAGNIFY]
1Ch 22: 5 for the LORD *must be* exceeding **m**, 1431

MAGNIFICENCE (1) [MAGNIFY]
Ac 19:27 and her **m** should be destroyed, whom all *3168*

MAGNIFIED (21) [MAGNIFY]
Ge 19:19 in thy sight, and thou hast **m** thy mercy, 1431
Jos 4:14 On that day the LORD **m** Joshua in 1431
2Sa 7:26 let thy name be **m** for ever, saying, 1431
1Ch 17:24 that thy name may be **m** for ever, saying, 1431
29:25 the LORD **m** Solomon exceedingly in 1431
2Ch 1: 1 God *was* with him, and **m** him exceedingly. 1431
32:23 that he was **m** in the sight of all nations 5375
Ps 35:27 say continually, Let the LORD be **m**, 1431
40:16 say continually, The LORD be **m**. 1431
70: 4 salvation say continually, Let God be **m**. 1431
138: 2 for thou hast **m** thy word above all thy 1431
Jer 48:26 for he **m** *himself* against the LORD: 1431
48:42 he hath **m** *himself* against the LORD. 1431
La 1: 9 for the enemy hath **m** *himself*. 1431
Da 8:11 he **m** *himself even* to the prince of the host, 1431
Zep 2: 8 and **m** *themselves* against their border. 1431
2:10 **m** *themselves* against the people of 1431
Mal 1: 5 The LORD will be **m** from the border of 1431
Ac 5:13 himself to them: but the people **m** them. *3170*
19:17 and the name of the Lord Jesus was **m**. *3170*
Php 1:20 *so* now also Christ shall be **m** in my body, *3170*

MAGNIFY (19) [MAGNIFICAL, MAGNIFICENCE, MAGNIFIED]
Jos 3: 7 This day will I begin to **m** thee in the sight 1431
Job 7:17 What *is* man, that thou shouldest **m** him? 1431
19: 5 If indeed ye will **m** *yourselves* against me, 1431
36:24 Remember that thou **m** his work, 7679
Ps 34: 3 O **m** the LORD with me, and let us exalt 1431
35:26 dishonour that **m** *themselves* against me. 1431
38:16 they **m** *themselves* against me. 1431
55:12 hated me *that* did **m** *himself* against me; 1431
69:30 a song; and will **m** him with thanksgiving. 1431
Isa 10:15 shall the saw **m** itself against him that 1431
42:21 he will **m** the law, and make *it* honourable. 1431
Eze 38:23 Thus will I **m** myself, and sanctify myself; 1431
Da 8:25 he shall **m** *himself* in his heart, and 1431
11:36 **m** himself above every god, and shall speak 1431
11:37 any god: for he shall **m** himself above all. 1431
Zec 12: 7 do not **m** *themselves* against Judah. 1431
Lk 1:46 And Mary said, My soul doth **m** the Lord, *3170*
Ac 10:46 them speak with tongues, and **m** God. *3170*
Ro 11:13 the apostle of the Gentiles, I **m** mine office: *1392*

MAGOG (5)
Ge 10: 2 **M**, and Madai, and Javan, and Tubal, and 4031
1Ch 1: 5 **M**, and Madai, and Javan, and Tubal, and 4031
Eze 38: 2 set thy face against Gog, the land of **M**, 4031
39: 6 I will send a fire on **M**, and among them 4031
Rev 20: 8 Gog and **M**, to gather them together to *3098*

MAGOR-MISSABIB (1)
Jer 20: 3 hath not called thy name Pashur, but **M**. 4036

MAGPIASH (1)
Ne 10:20 **M**, Meshullam, Hezir, 4047

MAHALAH (1)
1Ch 7:18 bare Ishod, and Abiezer, and **M**. 4244

MAHALALEEL (7)
Ge 5:12 Cainan lived seventy years, and begat **M**: 4111
5:13 Cainan lived after he begat **M** eight 4111
5:15 **M** lived sixty and five years, and 4111
5:16 **M** lived after he begat Jared eight hundred 4111
5:17 all the days of **M** were eight hundred ninety 4111
1Ch 1: 2 Kenan, **M**, Jered, 4111

Ne 11: 4 the son of Shephatiah, the son of **M**, 4111

MAHALALEL See MAHALALEEL; MALELEEL

MAHALATH (4)
Ge 28: 9 took unto the wives which he had **M** 4258
2Ch 11:18 Rehoboam took him **M** the daughter of 4258
Ps 53: T To the chief Musician upon **M**, Maschil, 4257
88: T To the chief Musician upon **M** Leannoth, 4257

MAHALI (1)
Ex 6:19 the sons of Merari; **M** and Mushi: these *are* 4249

MAHANAIM (13)
Ge 32: 2 and he called the name of that place **M**. 4266
Jos 13:26 and from **M** unto the border of Debir; 4266
13:30 their coast was from **M**, all Bashan, all 4266
21:38 for the slayer; and **M** with her suburbs, 4266
2Sa 2: 8 son of Saul, and brought him over *to* **M**; 4266
2:12 son of Saul, went out from **M** to Gibeon. 4266
2:29 *through* all Bithron, and they came *to* **M**. 4266
17:24 David came to **M**. And Absalom passed 4266
17:27 came to pass, when David was come to **M**, 4266
19:32 the king of sustenance while he lay at **M**; 4266
1Ki 2: 8 curse in the day when I went *to* **M**: 4266
4:14 Ahinadab the son of Iddo *had* **M**: 4266
1Ch 6:80 with her suburbs, and **M** with her suburbs, 4266

MAHANEH-DAN (1) [DAN]
Jdg 18:12 wherefore they called that place **M** unto 4265

MAHARAI (3)
2Sa 23:28 Zalmon the Ahohite, **M** the Netophathite, 4121
1Ch 11:30 **M** the Netophathite, Heled the son of 4121
27:13 the tenth month *was* **M** the Netophathite, 4121

MAHATH (3)
1Ch 6:35 the son of **M**, the son of Amasai, 4287
2Ch 29:12 **M** the son of Amasai, and Joel the son of 4287
31:13 Eliel, and Ismachiah, and **M**, and Benaiah, 4287

MAHAVITE (1)
1Ch 11:46 Eliel the **M**, and Jeribai, and Joshaviah, 4233

MAHAZIOTH (2)
1Ch 25: 4 Joshbekashah, Mallothi, Hothir, *and* **M**: 4238
25:30 The three and twentieth to **M**, *he,* his sons, 4238

MAHER-SHALAL-HASH-BAZ (2)
Isa 8: 1 write in it with a man's pen concerning **M**. 4122
8: 3 said the LORD to me, Call his name **M**. 4122

MAHLAH (4)
Nu 26:33 of the daughters of Zelophehad *were* **M**, 4244
27: 1 **M**, Noah, and Hoglah, and Milcah, and 4244
36:11 For **M**, Tirzah, and Hoglah, and Milcah, 4244
Jos 17: 3 **M**, and Noah, Hoglah, Milcah, and Tirzah. 4244

MAHLI (11) [MAHLITES]
Nu 3:20 of Merari by their families; **M**, and Mushi. 4249
1Ch 6:19 The sons of Merari; **M**, and Mushi. 4249
6:29 **M**, Libni his son, Shimei his son, Uzza his 4249
6:47 The son of **M**, the son of Mushi, the son of 4249
23:21 The sons of Merari; **M**, and Mushi. 4249
23:21 Mushi. The sons of **M**; Eleazar, and Kish. 4249
23:23 **M**, and Eder, and Jeremoth, three. 4249
24:26 The sons of Merari *were* **M** and Mushi: 4249
24:28 Of **M** *came* Eleazar, who had no sons. 4249
24:30 also of Mushi; **M**, and Eder, and Jerimoth. 4249
Ezr 8:18 of the sons of **M**, the son of Levi, the son of 4249

MAHLITES (2) [MAHLI]
Nu 3:33 Of Merari *was* the family of the **M**, and 4250
26:58 the family of the **M**, the family of 4250

MAHLON (3) [MAHLON'S]
Ru 1: 2 the name of his two sons **M** and Chilion, 4248
1: 5 **M** and Chilion died also both of them; and 4248
4:10 Ruth the Moabitess, the wife of **M**, 4248

MAHLON'S (1) [MAHLON]
Ru 4: 9 all that *was* Chilion's and **M**, of the hand of 4248

MAHOL (1)
1Ki 4:31 and Chalcol, and Darda, the sons of **M**: 4235

MAID (36) [BONDMAID, BONDMAIDS, HANDMAID, HANDMAIDEN, HANDMAIDENS, HANDMAIDS, MAID'S, MAIDEN, MAIDENS, MAIDS, MAIDSERVANT, MAIDSERVANT'S, MAIDSERVANTS, MAIDSERVANTS']
Ge 16: 2 I pray thee, go in unto my **m**; it may be that 8198
16: 3 Sarai Abram's wife took Hagar her **m** 8198
16: 5 I have given my **m** into thy bosom; and 8198
16: 6 unto Sarai, Behold, thy **m** *is* in thy hand; 8198
16: 8 he said, Hagar, Sarai's **m**, whence camest 8198
29:24 Leah Zilpah his **m** *for* a handmaid. 8198
29:29 daughter Bilhah his handmaid to be her **m**. 8198
30: 3 she said, Behold my **m** Bilhah, go in unto 519
30: 7 Bilhah Rachel's **m** conceived again, and 8198
30: 9 she took Zilpah her **m**, and gave her Jacob 8198
30:10 And Zilpah Leah's **m** bare Jacob a son. 8198
30:12 Zilpah Leah's **m** bare Jacob a second son. 8198
Ex 2: 5 among the flags, she sent her **m** to fetch it. 519
2: 8 the **m** went and called the child's mother. 5959
21:20 or his **m**, with a rod, and he die under his 519
21:26 or the eye of his **m**, that it perish; 519
22:16 if a man entice a **m** that is not betrothed, 1330
Lev 12: 5 if she bear a **m child**, then she shall be 5347
25: 6 and for thy **m**, and for thy hired servant, and 519
Dt 22:14 when I came to her, I found her not a **m**: 1331
22:17 *her,* saying, I found not thy daughter a **m**; 1331
2Ki 5: 2 captive out of the land of Israel a little **m**; 5291
5: 4 thus said the **m** that *is* of the land of Israel. 5291
Est 2: 7 and the **m** *was* fair and beautiful; 5291
Job 31: 1 why then should I think upon a **m**? 1330
Pr 30:19 of the sea; and the way of a man with a **m**. 5959
Isa 24: 2 as *with* the **m**, so *with* her mistress; 8198
Jer 2:32 Can a **m** forget her ornaments, *or* a bride 1330
51:22 I break in pieces the young man and the **m**; 1330
Am 2: 7 and his father will go in unto the *same* **m**, 5291
Mt 9:24 for the **m** is not dead, but sleepeth. *2877*
9:25 and took her by the hand, and the **m** arose. *2877*
26:71 another *m* saw him, and said unto them that NIG
Mk 14:69 And a **m** saw him again, and began to say *3814*
Lk 8:54 by the hand, and called, saying, **M**, arise. *3816*
22:56 But a certain **m** beheld him as he sat by *3814*

MAID'S (1) [MAID]
Est 2:12 Now when **every m** turn was 5291+5291+2050.1

MAIDEN (8) [MAID]
Ge 30:18 because I have given my **m** to my husband: 8198
Jdg 19:24 *here is* my daughter a **m**, and 1330
2Ch 36:17 had no compassion upon young man or **m**, 1330
Est 2: 4 let the **m** which pleaseth the king be queen 5291
2: 9 the **m** pleased him, and she obtained 5291
2:13 thus came *every* **m** unto the king; 5291
Ps 123: 2 as the eyes of a **m** unto the hand of her 8198
Lk 8:51 and the father and the mother of the **m**. *3816*

MAIDENS (19) [MAID]
Ex 2: 5 her **m** walked along by the river's side; and 5291
Ru 2: 8 from hence, but abide here fast by my **m**: 5291
2:22 my daughter, that thou go out with his **m**, 5291
2:23 So she kept fast by the **m** of Boaz to glean 5291
3: 2 of our kindred, with whose **m** thou wast? 5291
1Sa 9:11 they found **young m** going out to draw 5291
Est 2: 8 when many **m** were gathered together unto 5291
2: 9 seven **m**, *which were* meet to be given her, 5291
4:16 I also and my **m** will fast likewise; and so 5291
Job 19:15 and my **m**, count me for a stranger: 519
41: 5 a bird? or wilt thou bind him for thy **m**? 5291
Ps 78:63 and their **m** were not given to marriage. 1330
148:12 Both young men, and **m**; old men, and 1330
Pr 9: 3 She hath sent forth her **m**: she crieth upon 5291
27:27 and *for* the maintenance for thy **m**. 5291
31:15 to her household, and a portion to her **m**. 5291
Ecc 2: 7 I got *me* servants and **m**, and had servants 8198
Eze 44:22 they shall take **m** of the seed of the house 1330
Lk 12:45 shall begin to beat the menservants and **m**, *3814*

MAIDS (8) [MAID]
Ezr 2:65 Beside their servants and their **m**, of whom 519
Est 2: 9 her **m** unto the best *place* of the house of 5291
4: 4 So Esther's **m** and her chamberlains came 5291
La 5:11 in Zion, *and* the **m** in the cities of Judah. 1330
Eze 9: 6 both **m**, and little children, and women: 1330
Na 2: 7 her **m** *shall* lead *her* as *with* the voice of 519
Zec 9:17 young men cheerful, and new wine the **m**. 1330
Mk 14:66 there cometh one of the **m** of the high *3814*

MAIDSERVANT (16) [MAID, SERVE]
Ex 11: 5 *even* unto the firstborn of the **m** that *is* 8198
20:10 thy manservant, nor thy **m**, nor thy cattle, 519
20:17 nor his **m**, nor his ox, nor his ass, 519
21: 7 if a man sell his daughter to be a **m**, she shall 519
21:32 If the ox shall push a manservant or a **m**; 519
Dt 5:14 nor thy **m**, nor thine ox, nor thine ass, 519
5:14 and thy **m** may rest as well as thou. 519
5:21 or his **m**, his ox, or his ass, or any *thing* that 519
12:18 thy **m**, and the Levite that *is* within thy 519
15:17 And also unto thy **m** thou shalt do likewise. 519
16:11 thy **m**, and the Levite that *is* within thy 519
16:14 thy **m**, and the Levite, the stranger, and 519
Jdg 9:18 and have made Abimelech, the son of his **m**, 519
Job 31:13 the cause of my manservant or of my **m**, 519
Jer 34: 9 every man his **m**, *being* a Hebrew or 8198
34:10 and every one his **m**, go free, 8198

MAIDSERVANT'S (1) [MAID, SERVE]
Ex 21:27 out his manservant's tooth, or his **m** tooth; 519

MAIDSERVANTS (9) [MAID, SERVE]
Ge 12:16 and **m**, and she asses, and camels. 8198
20:17 healed Abimelech, and his wife, and his **m**; 519
24:35 menservants, and **m**, and camels, and asses. 8198
30:43 **m**, and menservants, and camels, and asses. 8198
Dt 12:12 your **m**, and the Levite that *is* within your 519
1Sa 8:16 and your **m**, and your goodliest young men, 8198
2Sa 6:22 of the **m** which thou hast spoken of, of them 519
2Ki 5:26 sheep, and oxen, and menservants, and **m**? 8198
Ne 7:67 Beside their manservants and their **m**, 519

MAIDSERVANTS' (1) [MAID, SERVE]
Ge 31:33 into Leah's tent, and into the two **m** tents; 519

MAIL (2)
1Sa 17: 5 and he *was* armed with a coat of **m**; 7193
17:38 also he armed him with a coat *of* **m**. NIH

MAIMED (7)
Lev 22:22 or **m**, or having a wen, or scurvy, or 2782
Mt 15:30 **m**, and many others, and cast them *down* at *2948*
15:31 the **m** *to be* whole, the lame to walk, and *2948*
18: 8 is better for thee to enter into life halt or **m**, *2948*
Mk 9:43 it is better for thee to enter into life **m**, *2948*
Lk 14:13 call the poor, the **m**, the lame, the blind: *376*
14:21 and the **m**, and the halt, and the blind. *376*

MAINSAIL (1)
Ac 27:40 and hoised up the **m** to the wind, and *736*

MAINTAIN (10) [MAINTAINED, MAINTAINEST, MAINTENANCE]
1Ki 8:45 and their supplication, and **m** their cause. 6213
8:49 thy dwelling place, and **m** their cause, 6213
8:59 that *he* **m** the cause of his servant, and 6213
1Ch 26:27 dedicate to **m** the house of the LORD. 2388
2Ch 6:35 and their supplication, and **m** their cause. 6213
6:39 **m** their cause, and forgive thy people 6213
Job 13:15 but I will **m** mine own ways before him. 3198
Ps 140:12 I know that the LORD will **m** the cause of 6213
Tit 3: 8 in God might be careful to **m** good works. *4291*
3:14 And let ours also learn to **m** good works for *4291*

MAINTAINED (1) [MAINTAIN]
Ps 9: 4 For thou hast **m** my right and my cause; 6213

MAINTAINEST (1) [MAINTAIN]
Ps 16: 5 and of my cup: thou **m** my lot. 8551

MAINTENANCE (2) [MAINTAIN]
Ezr 4:14 we **have m** from *the king's* palace, 4415+4416
Pr 27:27 and *for* the **m** for thy maidens. 2416

MAJESTY (29)
1Ch 29:11 and the glory, and the victory, and the **m**: 1935
29:25 bestowed upon him *such* royal **m** as had 1935
Est 1: 4 the honour of his excellent **m** many days, 1420
Job 37:22 out of the north: with God *is* terrible **m**. 1935
40:10 Deck thyself now with **m** and excellency; 1347
Ps 21: 5 honour and **m** hast thou laid upon him. 1926
29: 4 the voice of the LORD *is* **full of m**. 1926
45: 3 O *most* mighty, *with* thy glory and thy **m**. 1926
45: 4 *in* thy **m** ride prosperously because of truth 1926
93: 1 The LORD reigneth, he is clothed with **m**; 1348
96: 6 Honour and **m** *are* before him: strength and 1926
104: 1 thou art clothed with honour and **m**. 1926
145: 5 will speak of the glorious honour of thy **m**, 1935
145:12 and the glorious **m** of his kingdom. 1926
Isa 2:10 of the LORD, and for the glory of his **m**. 1347
2:19 of the LORD, and for the glory of his **m**, 1347
2:21 of the LORD, and for the glory of his **m**, 1347
24:14 they shall sing, for the **m** of the LORD, 1347
26:10 and will not behold the **m** of the LORD. 1348
Eze 7:20 the beauty of his ornament, he set it in **m**: 1347
Da 4:30 of my power, and for the honour of my **m**? 1923
4:36 and excellent **m** was added unto me. 7238
5:18 a kingdom, and **m**, and glory, and honour: 7238
5:19 for the **m** that he gave him, all people, 7238
Mic 5: 4 in the **m** of the name of the LORD his 1347
Heb 1: 3 sat down on the right hand of the **M** on *3172*
8: 1 hand of the throne of the **M** in the heavens; *3172*
2Pe 1:16 but were eyewitnesses of his **m**. *3168*
Jude 1:25 *be* glory and **m**, dominion and power, *3172*

MAKAZ (1)
1Ki 4: 9 in **M**, and in Shaalbim, and Beth-shemesh, 4739

MAKE (1055) [MADE, MADEST, MAKER, MAKERS, MAKEST, MAKETH, MAKING, TENTMAKERS] See Index

MAKER (20) [MAKE]
Job 4:17 shall a man be more pure than his **M**? 6213
32:22 *so doing* my **M** would soon take me away. 6213
35:10 none saith, Where *is* God my **M**, 6213
36: 3 and will ascribe righteousness to my **M**. 6466
Ps 95: 6 let us kneel before the LORD our **M**. 6213
Pr 14:31 that oppresseth the poor reproacheth his **M**: 6213
17: 5 mocketh the poor reproacheth his **M**: 6213
22: 2 the LORD *is* the **M** of them all. 6213
Isa 1:31 the **m** of it as a spark, and they shall both 6467
17: 7 At that day shall a man look to his **M**, and 6213
22:11 ye have not looked unto the **M** thereof, 6213
45: 9 Woe unto him that striveth with his **m**! 3335
45:11 the Holy One of Israel, and his **m**, 3335
51:13 forgettest the LORD thy **M**, that hath 6213
54: 5 For thy **M** *is* thine husband; the LORD of 6213
Jer 33: 2 Thus saith the LORD the **m** thereof, 6213
Hos 8:14 For Israel hath forgotten his **M**, and 6213
Hab 2:18 What profiteth the graven image that the **m** 3335
2:18 that the **m** of his work trusteth therein, 3335
Heb 11:10 whose builder and **m** *is* God. *1217*

MAKERS (1) [MAKE]
Isa 45:16 go to confusion together *that are* **m** of idols. 2796

MAKEST (26) [MAKE] See Index

MAKETH (126) [MAKE] See Index

MAKHELOTH (2)
Nu 33:25 removed from Haradah, and pitched in **M**. 4722
33:26 they removed from **M**, and encamped at 4722

MAKI See MACHI

MAKING (30) [MAKE] See Index

MAKIR See MACHIR

MAKIRITE See MACHIRITES

MAKKEDAH (9)
Jos 10:10 and smote them to Azekah, and unto **M**. 4719
10:16 and hid themselves in a cave at **M**. 4719
10:17 The five kings are found hid in a cave at **M**. 4719
10:21 to the camp to Joshua *at* **M** in peace: 4719
10:28 that day Joshua took **M**, and smote it with 4719
10:28 he did to the king of **M** as he did unto 4719
10:29 Joshua passed from **M**, and all Israel with 4719
12:16 The king of **M**, one; the king of Beth-el, 4719
15:41 Beth-dagon, and Naamah, and **M**; 4719

MAKTESH (1)
Zep 1:11 Howl, ye inhabitants of **M**, for all 4389

MALACHI (1)
Mal 1: 1 of the word of the LORD to Israel by **M**. 4401

MALCAM See MALCHAM

MALCHAM (2) [MOLOCH]
1Ch 8: 9 Jobab, and Zibia, and Mesha, and **M**, 4445

M

Zep 1: 5 swear by the LORD, and that swear by **M**; 4445

MALCHIAH (9)
1Ch 6:40 the son of Baaseiah, the son of **M**, 4441
Ezr 10:25 **M**, and Miamin, and Eleazar, and 4441
10:31 Eliezer, Ishijah, **M**, Shemaiah, Shimeon, 4441
Ne 3:14 the dung gate repaired **M** the son of 4441
3:31 After him repaired **M** the goldsmith's son 4441
8: 4 and **M**, and Hashum, and Hashbadana, 4441
11:12 the son of Pashur, the son of **M**, 4441
Jer 38: 1 son of Shelemiah, and Pashur the son of **M**, 4441
38: 6 cast him into the dungeon of **M** the son of 4441

MALCHIEL (3)
Ge 46:17 and the sons of Beriah; Heber, and **M**. 4439
Nu 26:45 of **M**, the family of the Malchielites. 4439
1Ch 7:31 Heber, and **M**, who *is* the father of 4439

MALCHIELITES (1)
Nu 26:45 of Malchiel, the family of the **M**. 4440

MALCHIJAH (6)
1Ch 9:12 the son of **M**, and Maasiai the son of Adiel, 4441
24: 9 The fifth to **M**, the sixth to Mijamin, 4441
Ezr 10:25 Miamin, and Eleazar, and **M**, and Benaiah. 4441
Ne 3:11 **M** the son of Harim, and Hashub the son of 4441
10: 3 Pashur, Amariah, **M**, 4441
12:42 Jehohanan, and **M**, and Elam, and Ezer. 4441

MALCHIRAM (1)
1Ch 3:18 **M** also, and Pedaiah, and Shenazar, 4443

MALCHISHUA (4)
1Sa 31: 2 and Abinadab, and **M**, Saul's sons. 4444
1Ch 8:33 and **M**, and Abinadab, and Eshbaal. 4444
9:39 and **M**, and Abinadab, and Eshbaal. 4444
10: 2 and Abinadab, and **M**, the sons of Saul. 4444

MALCHUS (1)
Jn 18:10 his right ear. The servant's name was **M**. *3124*

MALE (46) [MALES]
Ge 1:27 he him; **m** and female created he them. 2145
5: 2 **M** and female created he them; and 2145
6:19 alive with thee; they shall be **m** and female. 2145
7: 2 take to thee by sevens, the **m** and his female: 376
7: 2 *are* not clean by two, the **m** and his female. 376
7: 3 of the air by sevens, the **m** and the female; 2145
7: 9 Noah into the ark, the **m** and the female, 2145
7:16 went in, went in **m** and female of all flesh, 2145
17:23 every **m** among the men of Abraham's 2145
34:15 If ye will be as we *be*, that every **m** of you 2145
34:22 if every **m** among us be circumcised, 2145
34:24 every **m** was circumcised, all that went out 2145
Ex 12: 5 be without blemish, a **m** of the first year: 2145
34:19 thy cattle, *whether* ox or sheep, *that* is **m**. 2142
Lev 1: 3 the herd, let him offer a **m** without blemish: 2145
1:10 he shall bring it a **m** without blemish. 2145
3: 1 whether *it be* a **m** or female, he shall offer 2145
3: 6 **m** or female, he shall offer it without 2145
4:23 a kid of the goats, a **m** without blemish; 2145
7: 6 Every **m** among the priests shall eat 2145
12: 7 This *is* the law for her that hath born a **m** or 2145
22:19 *Ye shall offer* at your own will a **m** without 2145
27: 3 of the **m** from twenty years old even unto 2145
27: 5 thy estimation shall be of the **m** twenty 2145
27: 6 thy estimation shall be of the **m** five 2145
27: 7 if *it be* a **m**, then thy estimation shall be 2145
Nu 1: 2 of *their* names, every **m** by their polls; 2145
1:20 every **m** from twenty years old and upward, 2145
1:22 every **m** from twenty years old and upward, 2145
3:15 every **m** from a month old and 2145
5: 3 Both **m** and female shall ye put out, 2145
18:10 *place* shalt thou eat it; every **m** shall eat it: 2145
31:17 kill every **m** among the little ones, 2145
Dt 4:16 of any figure, the likeness of **m** or female, 2145
7:14 there shall not be **m**s or female barren 6135
20:13 thou shalt smite every **m** thereof with 2138
Jos 17: 2 these *were* the **m** children of Manasseh 2145
Jdg 21:11 Ye shall utterly destroy every **m**, and 2145
21:12 had known no man by lying with *any* **m**: 2145
1Ki 11:15 after he had smitten every **m** in Edom; 2145
11:16 until he had cut off every **m** in Edom:) 2145
Mal 1:14 which hath in his flock a **m**, and voweth, 2145
Mt 19: 4 made *them* at the beginning made them **m** *730*
Mk 10: 6 beginning of the creation God made them **m** *730*
Lk 2:23 Every **m** that openeth the womb shall be *730*
Gal 3:28 bond nor free, there is neither **m** nor female: *730*

MALE PROSTITUTES See EFFEMINATE

MALE SHRINE PROSTITUTES See SODOMITE; SODOMITES

MALEFACTOR (1) [MALEFACTORS]
Jn 18:30 and said unto him, If he were not a **m**, *2555*

MALEFACTORS (3) [MALEFACTOR]
Lk 23:32 And there were also two other, **m**, led with *2557*
23:33 and the **m**, one on the right hand, and *2557*
23:39 And one of the **m** which were hanged *2557*

MALELEEL (1)
Lk 3:37 *the son* of Jared, which was *the son* of **M**, *3121*

MALES (32) [MALE]
Ge 34:25 upon the city boldly, and slew all the **m**. 2145
Ex 12:48 let all his **m** be circumcised, and then 2145
13:12 thou hast; the **m** *shall be* the LORD'S. 2145
13:15 all that openeth the matrix, being **m**; 2145
23:17 Three times in the year all thy **m** shall 2138
Lev 6:18 All the **m** among the children of Aaron 2145
6:29 All the **m** among the priests shall eat 2145
Nu 3:22 according to the number of all the **m**, 2145
3:28 In the number of all the **m**, from a month 2145
3:34 according to the number of all the **m**, 2145
3:39 all the **m** from a month old and upward, 2145
3:40 Number all the firstborn of the **m** of 2145
3:43 all the firstborn **m** by the number of names, 2145
26:62 all **m** from a month old and upward: 2145
31: 7 and they slew all the **m**. 2145
Dt 15:19 All the firstling **m** that come of thy herd 2145
16:16 Three times in a year shall all thy **m** appear 2138
Jos 5: 4 *that were* **m**, *even* all the men of war, 2145
2Ch 31:16 Beside their genealogy of **m**, from three 2145
31:19 to give portions to all the **m** among 2145
Ezr 8: 3 by genealogy of the **m** an hundred 2145
8: 4 of Zerahiah, and with him two hundred **m**. 2145
8: 5 of Jahaziel, and with him three hundred **m**. 2145
8: 6 the son of Jonathan, and with him fifty **m**. 2145
8: 7 son of Athaliah, and with him seventy **m**. 2145
8: 8 son of Michael, and with him fourscore **m**. 2145
8: 9 and with him two hundred and eighteen **m**. 2145
8:10 and with him an hundred and threescore **m**. 2145
8:11 of Bebai, and with him twenty and eight **m**. 2145
8:12 and with him an hundred and ten **m**. 2145
8:13 and Shemaiah, and with them threescore **m**. 2145
8:14 and Zabbud, and with them seventy **m**. 2145

MALICE (6) [MALICIOUS, MALICIOUSNESS]
1Co 5: 8 neither with the leaven of **m** and *2549*
14:20 howbeit in **m** be ye children, *2549*
Eph 4:31 be put away from you, with all **m**: *2549*
Col 3: 8 wrath, **m**, blasphemy, filthy communication *2549*
Tit 3: 3 living in **m** and envy, hateful, *and* *2549*
1Pe 2: 1 Wherefore laying aside all **m**, and all guile, *2549*

MALICIOUS (1) [MALICE]
3Jn 1:10 he doeth, prating against us with **m** words: *4190*

MALICIOUSNESS (2) [MALICE]
Ro 1:29 fornication, wickedness, covetousness, **m**; *2549*
1Pe 2:16 and not using *your* liberty for a cloke of **m**, *2549*

MALIGNITY (1)
Ro 1:29 full of envy, murder, debate, deceit, **m**; *2550*

MALKI-SHUA See MELCHISHUA

MALKIEL See MALCHIEL

MALKIELITE See MALCHIELITES

MALKIJAH See MALCHIAH; MALCHIJAH; MELCHIAH

MALKIRAM See MALCHIRAM

MALLOTHI (2)
1Ch 25: 4 Joshbekashah, **M**, Hothir, *and* Mahazioth: 4413
25:26 The nineteenth to **M**, *he*, his sons, and 4413

MALLOWS (1)
Job 30: 4 Who cut up **m** by the bushes, and 4408

M

MALLUCH (6)
1Ch 6:44 son of Kishi, the son of Abdi, the son of **M**, 4409
Ezr 10:29 **M**, and Adaiah, Jashub, and Sheal, and 4409
10:32 Benjamin, **M**, *and* Shemariah. 4409
Ne 10: 4 Hattush, Shebaniah, **M**, 4409
10:27 **M**, Harim, Baanah. 4409
12: 2 Amariah, **M**, Hattush, 4409

MALTA See MELITA

MAMMON (4)
Mt 6:24 the other. Ye cannot serve God and **m**. *3126*
Lk 16: 9 Make to yourselves friends of the **m** of *3126*
16:11 have not been faithful in the unrighteous **m**, *3126*
16:13 the other. Ye cannot serve God and **m**. *3126*

MAMRE (10)
Ge 13:18 came and dwelt in the plain of **M**, which *is* 4471
14:13 for he dwelt in the plain of **M** the Amorite, 4471
14:24 which went with me, Aner, Eshcol, and **M**; 4471
18: 1 appeared unto him in the plains of **M**: 4471
23:17 which *was* before **M**, the field, and the cave 4471
23:19 cave of the field of Machpelah before **M**: 4471
25: 9 son of Zohar the Hittite, which *is* before **M**; 4471
35:27 Jacob came unto Isaac his father unto **M**, 4471
49:30 which *is* before **M**, in the land of Canaan, 4471
50:13 of Ephron the Hittite, before **M**. 4471

MAN (2616) [BONDMAN, BONDMEN, BOWMEN, CHAPMEN, COUNTRYMEN, CRAFTSMAN, CRAFTSMEN, DAYSMAN, FISHERMEN, FOOTMEN, FREEMAN, GOODMAN, HARVESTMAN, HERDMAN, HERDMEN, HORSEMAN, HORSEMEN, HUSBANDMAN, HUSBANDMEN, KINSMAN, KINSMAN'S, KINSMEN, MAN'S, MANKIND, MANSERVANT, MANSERVANT'S, MANSERVANTS, MANSLAYER, MANSLAYERS, MEN, MEN'S, MENPLEASERS, MENSERVANTS, MENSTEALERS, NOBLEMAN, PLOWMAN, PLOWMEN, SHIPMEN, SPEARMEN, SPOKESMAN, WATCHMAN, WATCHMAN'S, WATCHMEN, WORKWORKMAN, WORKMANSHIP, WORKMEN, WORKMEN'S]
Ge 1:26 And God said, Let us make **m** in our image, 120
1:27 So God created **m** in his own image, in 120
2: 5 and *there was* not a **m** to till the ground. 120
2: 7 the LORD God formed **m** *of* the dust of 120
2: 7 breath of life; and **m** became a living soul. 120
2: 8 and there he put the **m** whom he had formed. 120
2:15 the LORD God took the **m**, and put him 120
2:16 the LORD God commanded the **m**, saying, 120
2:18 *It is* not good that the **m** should be alone; 120
2:22 which the LORD God had taken from **m**, 120
2:22 he a woman, and brought her unto the **m**. 120
2:23 because she was taken out of **M**. 376
2:24 Therefore shall a **m** leave his father and his 376
2:25 the **m** and his wife, and were not ashamed. 120
3:12 the **m** said, The woman whom thou gavest *to* 120
3:22 Behold, the **m** is become as one of us, 120
3:24 So he drove out the **m**; and he placed at 120
4: 1 said, I have gotten a **m** from the LORD. 376
4:23 for I have slain a **m** to my wounding, and 376
4:23 my wounding, and a **young m** to my hurt. 3206
5: 1 In the day that God created **m**, in 120
6: 3 My spirit shall not always strive with **m**, 120
6: 5 GOD saw that the wickedness of **m** *was* 120
6: 6 it repented the LORD that he had made **m** 120
6: 7 I will destroy **m** whom I have created from 120
6: 7 both **m**, and beast, and the creeping thing, 120
6: 9 Noah was a just **m** *and* perfect in his 376
7:21 that creepeth upon the earth, and every **m**: 120
7:23 both **m**, and cattle, and the creeping things, 120
9: 5 beast will I require it, and at the hand of **m**; 120
9: 5 man's brother will I require the life of **m**. 120
9: 6 man's blood, by **m** shall his blood be shed: 120
9: 6 be shed: for in the image of God made he **m**. 120
13:16 that if a **m** can number the dust of the earth, 376
16:12 he will be a wild **m**; his hand *will be* against 120
16:12 his hand *will be* against **every m**, and 3605
17:10 Every **m** *child* among you shall be 2145
17:12 every **m** *child* in your generations, he that 2145
17:14 the uncircumcised **m** *child* whose flesh of 2145
18: 7 and good, and gave *it* unto a **young m**; 5288
19: 8 two daughters which have not known **m**; 376
19: 9 And they pressed sore upon the **m**, *even* Lot, 376
19:31 *there is* not a **m** in the earth to come in unto 376
20: 3 said to him, Behold, thou *art but* a dead **m**, NIH
20: 7 Now therefore restore the **m** *his* wife; for he 376
24:16 a virgin, neither had **any m** known her: 376
24:21 the **m** wondering at her held his peace, to wit 376
24:22 that the **m** took a golden earring of half a 376
24:26 the **m** bowed down his head, and 376
24:29 and Laban ran out unto the **m**, unto the well. 376
24:30 his sister, saying, Thus spake the **m** unto me; 376
24:30 that he came unto the **m**; and behold, 376
24:32 the **m** came into the house: and he ungirded 376
24:58 and said unto her, Wilt thou go with this **m**? 376
24:61 rode upon the camels, and followed the **m**: 376
24:65 What **m** *is* this that walketh in the field to 376
25: 8 an **old m**, and full *of years;* and 2205
25:27 Esau was a cunning hunter, a **m** of the field; 376
25:27 and Jacob *was* a plain **m**, dwelling in tents. 376
26:11 He that toucheth this **m** or his wife shall 376
26:13 the **m** waxed great, and went forward, 376
27:11 Esau my brother *is* a hairy **m**, and I *am* a 376
27:11 brother *is* a hairy man, and I *am* a smooth **m**: 376
29:19 than that I should give her to another **m**: 376
30:43 the **m** increased exceedingly, and had much 376
31:50 wives beside my daughters, no **m** *is* with us; 376
32:24 there wrestled a **m** with him until 376
34:19 the **young m** deferred not to do the thing, 5288
34:25 took **each m** his sword, and came upon 376
37:15 a *certain* **m** found him, and behold, *he was* 376
37:15 the **m** asked him, saying, What seekest thou? 376
37:17 the **m** said, They are departed hence; for I 376
38:25 sent to her father in law, saying, By the **m**, 376
39: 2 with Joseph, and he was a prosperous **m**; 376
40: 5 both of them, **each m** his dream in one night, 376
40: 5 **each m** according to the interpretation of his 376
41:11 we dreamed **each m** according to 376
41:12 *there was* there with us a **young m**, 5288
41:12 to **each m** according to his dream he did 376
41:33 let Pharaoh look out a **m** discreet and wise, 376
41:38 Can we find *such a one* as this *is*, a **m** in 376
41:44 without thee shall no **m** lift up his hand or 376
42:13 the sons of one **m** in the land of Canaan; 376
42:30 The **m**, *who is* the lord of the land, 376
42:33 the **m**, the lord of the country, said unto us, 376
43: 3 The **m** did solemnly protest unto us, saying, 376
43: 5 for the **m** said unto us, Ye shall not see my 376
43: 6 *as* to tell the **m** whether ye had yet a brother? 376
43: 7 The **m** asked us straitly of our state, and 376
43:11 carry down the **m** a present, a little balm, 376
43:13 your brother, and arise, go again unto the **m**: 376
43:14 God Almighty give you mercy before the **m**, 376
43:17 the **m** did as Joseph bade; and the man 376
43:17 the **m** brought the men into Joseph's house. 376
43:24 the **m** brought the men into Joseph's house, 376
43:27 father well, the **old m** of whom ye spake? 2205
44:11 they speedily took down **every m** his sack to 376
44:11 to the ground, and opened **every m** his sack. 376
44:13 laded **every m** his ass, and returned to 376
44:15 wot ye not that such a **m** as I can certainly 376
44:17 *but* the **m** in whose hand the cup is found, 376
44:20 an **old m**, and a child of *his* old age, a little 2205
45: 1 he cried, Cause every **m** to go out from me. 376
45: 1 there stood no **m** with him, while Joseph 376
45:22 To all of them he gave **each m** changes of 376
47: 6 if thou knowest *any* **m** of activity amongst 376
47:20 for the Egyptians sold **every m** his field, 376
49: 6 for in their anger they slew a **m**, and in their 376
Ex 1: 1 **every m** and his household came with Jacob. 376
2: 1 there went a **m** of the house of Levi, and 376
2:12 and when he saw that *there was* no **m**, 376
2:20 why *is* it *that* ye have left the **m**? call him, 376
2:21 And Moses was content to dwell with the **m**: 376
7:12 For they cast down **every m** his rod, and 376
8:17 and it became lice in **m**, and in beast; 120
8:18 so there were lice upon **m**, and upon beast. 120
9: 9 be a boil breaking forth *with* blains upon **m**, 120
9:10 a boil breaking forth *with* blains upon **m**, 120
9:19 *for upon* every **m** and beast which shall be 120
9:22 upon **m**, and upon beast, and upon every 120
9:25 all that *was* in the field, both **m** and beast; 120
10: 7 How long shall this *m* be a snare unto us? NIH
11: 2 let **every m** borrow of his neighbour, and 376
11: 3 Moreover the **m** Moses *was* very great in 376
11: 7 a dog move his tongue, against **m** or beast: 376
12: 3 they shall take to them **every m** a lamb, 376

Ex	12: 4	**every m** according to his eating shall make	376
	12:12	in the land of Egypt, both **m** and beast;	120
	12:16	save *that* which every **m** must eat, that only	5315
	13: 2	children of Israel, *both* of **m** and of beast:	120
	13:13	all the firstborn of **m** amongst thy children	120
	13:15	both the firstborn of **m**, and the firstborn of	120
	15: 3	The LORD *is* a **m** of war: the LORD *is*	376
	16:16	Gather of it **every m** according to his eating,	376
	16:16	an omer for **every m**, *according to*	1538
	16:16	take ye **every m** for *them* which *are* in his	376
	16:18	they gathered **every m** according to his	376
	16:19	Let no **m** leave of it till the morning.	376
	16:21	**every m** according to his eating:	376
	16:22	two omers for one *m*: and all the rulers of	NIH
	16:29	abide ye **every m** in his place, let no man go	376
	16:29	let no **m** go out of his place on the seventh	376
	19:13	whether *it be* beast or **m**, it shall not live:	376
	21: 7	if a **m** sell his daughter to be a maidservant,	376
	21:12	He that smiteth a **m**, so that he die, shall be	376
	21:13	if a **m**s lie not in wait, but God deliver *him*	834
	21:14	if a **m** come presumptuously upon his	376
	21:16	And he that stealeth a **m**, and selleth him, or	376
	21:20	if a **m** smite his servant, or his maid, with a	376
	21:26	if a **m** smite the eye of his servant, or the eye	376
	21:28	If an ox gore a **m** or a woman, that they die:	376
	21:29	but that he hath killed a **m** or a woman;	376
	21:33	if a **m** shall open a pit, or if a man shall dig a	376
	21:33	or if a **m** shall dig a pit, and not cover it, and	376
	22: 1	If a **m** shall steal an ox, or a sheep, and	376
	22: 5	If a **m** shall cause a field or vineyard to be	376
	22: 7	If a **m** shall deliver unto his neighbour	376
	22:10	If a **m** deliver unto his neighbour an ass, or	376
	22:10	or be hurt, or driven away, **no m** seeing *it:*	369
	22:14	if a **m** borrow *ought* of his neighbour, and	376
	22:16	if a **m** entice a maid that is not betrothed,	376
	23: 3	Neither shalt thou countenance a poor *m* in	NIH
	24:14	if any **m** have any matters to do, let him	1167
	25: 2	of every **m** that giveth it willingly with his	376
	30:12	shall they give **every m** a ransom for his	376
	32: 1	the **m** that brought us up out of the land of	376
	32:23	the **m** that brought us up out of the land of	376
	32:27	Put **every m** his sword by his side, *and* go in	376
	32:27	slay **every m** his brother, and every man his	376
	32:27	**every m** his companion, and every man his	376
	32:27	his companion, and **every m** his neighbour.	376
	32:29	even **every m** upon his son, and upon his	376
	33: 4	and no **m** did put on him his ornaments.	376
	33: 8	stood **every m** *at* his tent door, and	376
	33:10	and worshipped, **every m** *in* his tent door.	376
	33:11	face to face, as a **m** speaketh unto his friend.	376
	33:11	servant Joshua, the son of Nun, a **young m**,	5288
	33:20	for there shall no **m** see me, and live.	120
	34: 3	no **m** shall come up with thee, neither let any	376
	34: 3	neither let **any m** be seen throughout all	376
	34:24	neither shall **any m** desire thy land,	376
	35:22	every **m** that offered *offered* an offering of	376
	35:23	every **m**, with whom was found blue, and	376
	35:24	**every m**, with whom was found shittim	3605
	35:29	every **m** and woman, whose heart made	376
	36: 1	and Aholiab, and every wise hearted **m**,	376
	36: 2	and Aholiab, and every wise hearted **m**,	376
	36: 4	came **every m** from his work which	376+376
	36: 6	Let neither **m** nor woman make any more	376
	36: 8	every wise hearted *m* among them that	NIH
	38:26	A bekah for every **m**, *that is,* half a shekel,	1538
Lev	1: 2	If *any* **m** of you bring an offering unto	120
	5: 3	Or if he touch the uncleanness of **m**,	120
	5: 3	whatsoever uncleanness *it be* that a **m** shall	NIH
	5: 4	whatsoever *it be* that a **m** shall pronounce	120
	6: 3	in any of all *these* that a **m** doeth, sinning	120
	7:21	any unclean *thing, as* the uncleanness of **m**,	120
	12: 2	have conceived seed, and born a **m child**:	2145
	13: 2	When a **m** shall have in the skin of his flesh	120
	13: 9	When the plague of leprosy is in a **m**, then	120
	13:29	If a **m** or woman hath a plague upon	376
	13:38	If a **m** also or a woman have in the skin of	376
	13:40	And the **m** whose hair is fallen off his head,	376
	13:44	He *is* a leprous **m**, he *is* unclean: the priest	376
	14:11	shall present the **m** that is to be made clean,	376
	15: 2	When **any m** hath a running issue out	376+376
	15:18	The woman also with whom **m** shall lie *with*	376
	15:24	if **any m** lie with her at all, and her flowers	376
	15:33	of the **m**, and of the woman, and of him	2145
	16:17	there shall be no **m** in the tabernacle of	120
	16:21	shall send *him* away by the hand of a fit **m**	376
	17: 3	**What m soever** *there be* of the house	376+376
	17: 4	blood shall be imputed unto that **m**; he hath	376
	17: 4	that **m** shall be cut off from among his	376
	17: 8	**Whatsoever m** *there be* of the house of	376+376
	17: 9	even that **m** shall be cut off from among his	376
	17:10	**whatsoever m** *there be* of the house of	376+376
	17:13	**whatsoever m** *there be* of the children	376+376
	18: 5	which if a **m** do, he shall live in them: I *am*	120
	19: 3	Ye shall fear **every m** his mother, and	376
	19:32	honour the face of the **old m**, and fear thy	2205
	20: 3	I will set my face against that **m**, and will cut	376
	20: 4	land do any ways hide their eyes from the **m**,	376
	20: 5	I will set my face against that **m**, and	376
	20:10	the **m** that committeth adultery with *another*	376
	20:11	the **m** that lieth with his father's wife hath	376
	20:12	if a **m** lie with his daughter in law, both of	376
	20:13	If a **m** also lie with mankind, as he lieth with	376
	20:14	if a **m** take a wife and her mother, it *is*	376
	20:15	if a **m** lie with a beast, he shall surely be put	376
	20:17	if a **m** shall take his sister, his father's	376
	20:18	if a **m** shall lie with a woman having her	376
	20:20	if a **m** shall lie with his uncle's wife, he hath	376
	20:21	if a **m** shall take his brother's wife, it *is* an	376
	20:27	A **m** also or woman that hath a familiar	376
	21: 4	*being* a **chief m** among his people,	1167
	21:18	For whatsoever **m** *he be* that hath a blemish,	376
	21:18	a blind **m**, or a lame, or he that hath a flat	376
	21:19	Or a **m** that is brokenfooted,	376
	21:21	No **m** that hath a blemish, of the seed of	376
	22: 4	**What m soever** of the seed of Aaron *is*	376+376
	22: 4	the dead, or a **m** whose seed goeth from him;	376
	22: 5	or a **m** of whom he may take uncleanness,	120
	22:14	And if a **m** eat *of* the holy *thing* unwittingly,	376
	24:10	a **m** of Israel strove together in the camp;	376
	24:17	he that killeth any **m** shall surely be put to	120
	24:19	And if a **m** cause a blemish in his neighbour;	376
	24:20	as he hath caused a blemish in a **m**, so	120
	24:21	he that killeth a **m**, he shall be put to death.	120
	25:10	ye shall return **every m** unto his possession,	376
	25:10	and ye shall return **every m** unto his family.	376
	25:13	ye shall return **every m** unto his possession.	376
	25:26	if the **m** have none to redeem *it,* and	376
	25:27	restore the overplus unto the **m** to whom he	376
	25:29	if a **m** sell a dwelling house in a walled city,	376
	25:33	if a **m** purchase of the Levites, then	NIH
	27: 2	When a **m** shall make a singular vow,	376
	27: 9	all that *any m* giveth of such unto	NIH
	27:14	when a **m** shall sanctify his house *to be* holy	376
	27:16	if a **m** shall sanctify unto the LORD *some*	376
	27:20	or if he have sold the field to another **m**,	376
	27:22	if *a m* sanctify unto the LORD a field	NIH
	27:26	LORD'S firstling, no **m shall sanctify** it;	376
	27:28	that a **m** shall devote unto the LORD of all	376
	27:28	*both* of **m** and beast, and of the field of his	120
	27:31	if a **m** will at all redeem *ought* of his tithes,	376
Nu	1: 4	with you there shall be a **m** of every tribe;	376
	1:52	**every m** by his own camp, and every man	376
	1:52	**every m** by his own standard,	376
	2: 2	**Every m** of the children of Israel shall pitch	376
	2:17	**every m** in his place by their standards.	376
	3:13	all the firstborn in Israel, both **m** and beast:	120
	5: 6	When a **m** or woman shall commit any sin	376
	5: 8	if the **m** have no kinsman to recompense	376
	5:10	whatsoever **any m** giveth the priest, it shall	376
	5:13	a **m** lie with her **carnally**, and	376+2233+7902
	5:15	shall the **m** bring his wife unto the priest,	376
	5:19	If no **m** have lain with thee, and if thou hast	376
	5:20	*some* **m** hath lain with thee beside thine	376
	5:31	shall the **m** be guiltless from iniquity, and	376
	6: 2	When either **m** or woman shall separate	376
	6: 9	And if any **m** die very suddenly by him, and	NIH
	7: 5	to **every m** according to his service.	376
	8:17	of Israel *are* mine, *both* **m** and beast:	120
	9: 6	who were defiled by the dead body of a **m**,	120
	9: 7	We *are* defiled by the dead body of a **m**:	120
	9:10	If any **m** of you or of your posterity shall be	376
	9:13	the **m** that *is* clean, and is not in a journey,	376
	9:13	appointed season, that **m** shall bear his sin.	376
	11:10	**every m** in the door of his tent:	376
	11:27	there ran a **young m**, and told Moses, and	5288
	12: 3	(Now the **m** Moses *was* very meek, above all	376
	13: 2	every tribe of their fathers shall ye send a **m**,	376
	14:15	*if* thou shalt kill *all* this people as one **m**,	376

Nu	15:32	they found a **m** that gathered sticks upon	376
	15:35	The **m** shall be surely put to death:	376
	16: 7	it shall be *that* the **m** whom the LORD doth	376
	16:17	take **every m** his censer, and put incense in	376
	16:17	bring ye before the LORD **every m** his	376
	16:18	they took **every m** his censer, and put fire in	376
	16:22	shall one **m** sin, and wilt thou be wroth with	376
	17: 9	and they looked, and took **every m** his rod.	376
	18:15	nevertheless the firstborn of **m** shalt thou	120
	19: 9	a **m** *that is* clean shall gather up the ashes of	376
	19:11	of any **m** shall be unclean seven days.	120+5315
	19:13	the dead *body* of *any* **m** that is dead,	120+5315
	19:14	This *is* the law, when a **m** dieth in a tent:	120
	19:16	or a dead *body,* or a bone of a **m**, or a grave,	120
	19:20	the **m** that shall be unclean, and shall not	376
	21: 9	to pass, that if a serpent had bitten *any* **m**,	376
	23:19	God *is* not a **m**, that he should lie; neither	376
	23:19	neither the son of **m**, that he should repent:	120
	24: 3	and the **m** whose eyes are open hath said:	1397
	24:15	and the **m** whose eyes are open hath said:	1397
	25: 8	he went after the **m** of Israel into the tent,	376
	25: 8	the **m** of Israel, and the woman through her	376
	26:64	among these there was not a **m** of them	376
	26:65	there was not left a **m** of them, save Caleb	376
	27: 8	If a **m** die, and have no son, then ye shall	376
	27:16	of all flesh, set a **m** over the congregation,	376
	27:18	a **m** in whom *is* the spirit, and lay thine hand	376
	30: 2	If a **m** vow a vow unto the LORD, or	376
	30:16	between a **m** and his wife, between	376
	31:17	kill every woman that hath known **m** by	376
	31:18	that have not known a **m** by lying with him,	2145
	31:26	*both* of **m** and of beast, thou, and Eleazar	120
	31:35	of women that had not known **m** by lying	2145
	31:47	*both* of **m** and of beast, and gave them unto	120
	31:49	and there lacketh not **one m** of us.	376
	31:50	what **every m** hath gotten, *of* jewels of gold,	376
	31:53	of war had taken spoil, **every m** for himself.)	376
	32:18	have inherited **every m** his inheritance.	376
	32:27	**every m** armed for war, before the LORD	3605
	32:29	**every m** armed to battle, before	3605
	35:23	wherewith *a m* may die, seeing *him* not, and	NIH
	36: 8	enjoy **every m** the inheritance of his fathers.	376
Dt	1:16	and judge righteously between every **m** and	376
	1:17	you shall not be afraid of the face of **m**;	376
	1:31	as a **m** doth bear his son, in all the way that	376
	1:41	when ye had girded on **every m** his weapons	376
	3:11	the breadth of it, after the cubit of a **m**.	376
	3:20	shall ye return **every m** unto his possession,	376
	4:32	since the day that God created **m** upon	120
	5:24	seen this day that God doth talk with **m**,	120
	7:24	there shall no **m** *be able to* stand before thee,	376
	8: 3	that he might make thee know that **m** doth	120
	8: 3	out of the mouth of the LORD doth **m** live.	120
	8: 5	as a **m** chasteneth his son, *so* the LORD thy	376
	11:25	There shall no **m** *be able to* stand before	376
	12: 8	**every m** whatsoever *is* right in his own eyes.	376
	15: 7	If there be among you a **poor m** of one of thy	34
	15:12	a **Hebrew m**, or a Hebrew woman, be sold	5680
	16:17	**Every m** *shall give* as he is able, according	376
	17: 2	LORD thy God giveth thee, **m** or woman,	376
	17: 5	shalt thou bring forth that **m** or that woman,	376
	17: 5	*even that* **m** or *that* woman, and shalt stone	376
	17:12	And the **m** that will do presumptuously, and	376
	17:12	or unto the judge, even that **m** shall die:	376
	19: 5	As when *a m* goeth into the wood with his	NIH
	19:11	if **any m** hate his neighbour, and lie in wait	376
	19:15	One witness shall not rise up against a **m** for	376
	19:16	If a false witness rise up against **any m** to	376
	20: 5	What **m** *is there* that hath built a new house,	376
	20: 5	die in the battle, and another **m** dedicate it.	376
	20: 6	what **m** *is he* that hath planted a vineyard,	376
	20: 6	he die in the battle, and another **m** eat of it.	376
	20: 7	what **m** *is there* that hath betrothed a wife,	376
	20: 7	he die in the battle, and another **m** take her.	376
	20: 8	What **m** *is there that is* fearful and	376
	21: 3	*that* the city *which is* next unto the slain *m*,	NIH
	21: 6	*that are* next unto the slain *m*, shall wash	NIH
	21:15	If a **m** have two wives, one beloved, and	376
	21:18	If a **m** have a stubborn and rebellious son,	376
	21:22	if a **m** have committed a sin worthy of death,	376
	22: 5	not wear that which pertaineth unto a **m**,	1397
	22: 5	neither shall a **m** put on a woman's	1397
	22: 8	thine house, if any **m**s fall from thence.	5307
	22:13	If **any m** take a wife, and go in unto her, and	376
	22:16	I gave my daughter unto this **m** to wife, and	376
	22:18	the elders of that city shall take *that* **m** and	376
	22:22	If a **m** be found lying with a woman married	376
	22:22	*both* the **m** that lay with the woman, and	376
	22:23	and a **m** find her in the city, and lie with her;	376
	22:24	the **m**, because he hath humbled his	376
	22:25	if a **m** find a betrothed damsel in the field,	376
	22:25	and the **m** force her, and lie with her:	376
	22:25	then the **m** only that lay with her shall die:	376
	22:26	for as when a **m** riseth against his neighbour,	376
	22:28	If a **m** find a damsel *that is* a virgin, which is	376
	22:29	the **m** that lay with her shall give unto	376
	22:30	A **m** shall not take his father's wife,	376
	23:10	If there be among you **any m**, that is not	376
	24: 1	When a **m** hath taken a wife, and	376
	24: 5	When a **m** hath taken a new wife, he shall	376
	24: 6	No *m* shall take the nether or the upper	NIH
	24: 7	If a **m** be found stealing any of his brethren	376
	24:11	the **m** to whom thou dost lend shall bring out	376
	24:12	if the **m** *be* poor, thou shalt not sleep with	376
	24:16	**every m** shall be put to death for his own	376
	25: 2	if the wicked *m be* worthy to be beaten,	NIH
	25: 7	if the **m** like not to take his brother's wife,	376
	25: 9	So shall it be done unto *that* **m** that will not	376
	27:15	Cursed *be* the **m** that maketh *any* graven or	376
	28:26	of the earth, and **no m** shall fray *them* away.	369
	28:29	spoiled evermore, and **no m** shall save *thee.*	369
	28:30	a wife, and another **m** shall lie with her:	376
	28:54	*So that* the **m** *that is* tender among you, and	376
	28:68	and bondwomen, and **no m** shall buy *you.*	369
	29:18	Lest there should be among you **m**, or	376
	29:20	and his jealousy shall smoke against that **m**,	376
	32:25	shall destroy both the **young m** and	970
	32:25	the suckling *also* with the **m** of gray hairs.	376
	33: 1	wherewith Moses the **m** of God blessed	376
	34: 6	no **m** knoweth of his sepulchre unto this day.	376
Jos	1: 5	There shall not **any m** *be able to* stand	376
	2:11	there remain any more courage in **any m**,	376
	3:12	of the tribes of Israel, out of every tribe a **m**.	376
	4: 2	out of the people, out of every tribe a **m**,	376
	4: 4	the children of Israel, out of every tribe a **m**:	376
	4: 5	take ye up **every m** of you a stone upon his	376
	5:13	there stood a **m** over against him with his	376
	6: 5	the people shall ascend up **every m** straight	376
	6:20	**every m** straight before him, and they took	376
	6:21	both **m** and woman, young and old, and ox,	376
	6:26	saying, Cursed *be* the **m** before the LORD,	376
	7:14	LORD shall take shall come **m** by man.	1397
	7:14	LORD shall take shall come man by **m**.	NIH
	7:17	he brought the family of the Zarhites **m** by	1397
	7:17	the family of the Zarhites man by **m**;	NIH
	7:18	he brought his household **m** by man; and	1397
	7:18	he brought his household man by **m**; and	NIH
	8:17	there was not a **m** left in Ai or Beth-el,	376
	8:31	over which no *m* hath lift up *any* iron:	NIH
	10: 8	there shall not a **m** of them stand before	376
	10:14	LORD hearkened unto the voice of a **m**:	376
	11:14	every **m** they smote with the edge of	120
	14: 6	unto Moses the **m** of God concerning me	376
	14:15	which *Arba was* a great **m** among	120
	17: 1	because he was a **m** of war, therefore he had	376
	21:44	there stood not a **m** of all their enemies	376
	22:20	and that **m** perished not alone in his iniquity.	376
	23: 9	no **m** hath *been able to* stand before you unto	376
	23:10	One **m** of you shall chase a thousand: for	376
	24:28	people depart, **every m** unto his inheritance.	376
Jdg	1:24	the spies saw a **m** come forth out of the city,	376
	1:25	but they let go the **m** and all his family.	376
	1:26	And the **m** went *into* the land of the Hittites,	376
	2: 6	the children of Israel went **every m** unto his	376
	3:15	son of Gera, a Benjamite, a **m** lefthanded:	376
	3:17	king of Moab: and Eglon *was* a very fat **m**.	376
	3:28	and suffered not a **m** to pass over.	376
	3:29	all men of valour; and there escaped not a **m**.	376
	4:16	of the sword; *and* there was not a **m** left.	259
	4:20	when any **m** doth come and inquire of thee,	376
	4:20	inquire of thee, and say, Is there any **m** here?	376
	4:22	I will shew thee the **m** whom thou seekest.	376
	5:30	the prey; to every **m** a damsel *or* two;	1397
	6:12	*is* with thee, thou mighty *m* of valour.	NIH
	6:16	thou shalt smite the Midianites as one **m**.	376
	7: 7	let all the *other* people go **every m** unto his	376
	7: 8	he sent all *the rest of* Israel **every m** unto his	376
	7:13	*there was* a **m** that told a dream unto his	376

Jdg 7:14 of Gideon the son of Joash, a **m** of Israel: 376
7:21 they stood **every m** in his place round about 376
8:14 caught a **young m** of the men of Succoth, 5288
8:21 for as the **m** *is, so is* his strength. 376
8:24 that you would give me **every m** the earrings 376
8:25 did cast therein **every m** the earrings of his 376
9: 9 wherewith by me they honour God and **m**, 376
9:13 which cheereth God and **m**, and go to be 376
9:49 all the people likewise cut down **every m** his 376
9:54 he called hastily unto the **young m** his 5288
9:54 his **young m** thrust him through, and 5288
9:55 they departed **every m** unto his place. 376
10: 1 of Puah, the son of Dodo, a **m** of Issachar; 376
10:18 What **m** *is he* that will begin to fight against 376
11: 1 Now Jephthah the Gileadite was a mighty *m* NIH
11:39 she knew no **m**. And it was a custom in 376
13: 2 there was a certain **m** of Zorah, of the family 376
13: 6 A **m** of God came unto me, and 376
13: 8 let the **m** of God which thou didst send come 376
13:10 Behold, the **m** hath appeared unto me, 376
13:11 and came to the **m**, and said unto him, 376
13:11 *Art* thou the **m** that spakest unto the woman? 376
16: 7 then shall I be weak, and be as another **m**. 120
16:11 shall I be weak, and be as another **m**. 120
16:17 shall become weak, and be like any *other* **m**. 120
16:19 she called for a **m**, and she caused *him* to 376
17: 1 there was a **m** of mount Ephraim, whose 376
17: 5 the **m** Micah had a house of gods, and 376
17: 6 **every m** did *that* which *was* right in his own 376
17: 7 there was a **young m** out of 5288
17: 8 the **m** departed out of the city from 376
17:11 the Levite was content to dwell with the **m**; 376
17:11 the **young m** was unto him as one of his 5288
17:12 the **young m** became his priest, and was in 5288
18: 3 they knew the voice of the **young m** 5288
18: 7 and had no business with *any* **m**. 120
18:15 came to the house of the **young m** 5288
18:19 thee to be a priest unto the house of one **m**, 376
18:28 and they had no business with *any* **m**; 120
19: 6 for the damsel's father had said unto the **m**, 376
19: 7 when the **m** rose up to depart, his father in 376
19: 9 when the **m** rose up to depart, he, and 376
19:10 the **m** would not tarry *that* night, but he rose 376
19:15 for *there was* no **m** that took them into *his* 376
19:16 there came an old **m** from his work out of 376
19:17 he saw a wayfaring **m** in the street of 376
19:17 and the old **m** said, Whither goest thou? and 376
19:18 and there *is* no **m** that receiveth me to house. 376
19:19 for the **young m** *which is* with thy servants: 5288
19:20 the old **m** said, Peace *be* with thee; 376
19:22 the master of the house, the **old m**, saying, 2205
19:22 Bring forth the **m** that came into thine house, 376
19:23 the **m**, the master of the house, went out unto 376
19:23 seeing that this **m** is come into mine house, 376
19:24 but unto this **m** do not so vile a thing. 376
19:25 so the **m** took his concubine, and brought *her* 376
19:28 the **m** took her *up* upon an ass, and the man NIH
19:28 the **m** rose up, and gat him unto his place. 376
20: 1 was gathered together as one **m**, 376
20: 8 all the people arose as one **m**, saying, 376
20:11 against the city, knit together as one **m**. 376
21:11 and every woman that hath lien by **m**. 2145
21:12 that had known no **m** by lying with *any* 376
21:21 catch you **every m** his wife of the daughters 376
21:22 we reserved not to **each m** his wife in 376
21:24 **every m** to his tribe and to his family, and 376
21:24 they went out from thence **every m** to his 376
21:25 **every m** did *that* which *was* right in his own 376
Ru 1: 1 a *certain* **m** of Beth-lehem-judah went to 376
1: 2 the name of the **m** *was* Elimelech, and 376
2: 1 a mighty **m** of wealth, of the family of 376
2:20 The **m** *is* near of kin unto us, one of our next 376
3: 3 *but* make not thyself known unto the **m**, 376
3: 8 that the **m** was afraid, and turned himself: 376
3:16 she told her all that the **m** had done to her. 376
3:18 for the **m** will not be in rest, until he have 376
4: 7 a **m** plucked off his shoe, and gave *it* to his 376
1Sa 1: 1 Now there was a certain **m** of 376
1: 3 this **m** went up out of his city yearly to 376
1:11 but wilt give unto thine handmaid a **m** child, 376
1:21 the **m** Elkanah, and all his house, went up to 376
2: 9 for by strength shall no **m** prevail. 376
2:13 *was, that* when any **m** offered sacrifice, 376
2:15 and said to the **m** that sacrificed, 376
2:16 *if any* **m** said unto him, Let them not fail to 376
2:25 If **one m** sin against another, the judge shall 376
2:25 if a **m** sin against the LORD, who shall 376
2:27 there came a **m** of God unto Eli, and 376
2:31 that there shall not be an **old m** in thine 2205
2:32 there shall not be an **old m** in thine house 2205
2:33 the **m** of thine, *whom* I shall not cut off from 376
4:10 and they fled **every m** into his tent: 376
4:12 there ran a **m** of Benjamin out of the army, 376
4:13 when the **m** came into the city, and told *it*, 376
4:14 And the **m** came in hastily, and told Eli. 376
4:16 the **m** said unto Eli, I *am* he that came out of 376
4:18 for he was an old **m**, and heavy. And he had 376
8:22 men of Israel, Go ye **every m** unto his city. 376
9: 1 Now there was a **m** of Benjamin, whose 376
9: 1 a Benjamite, a mighty *m* of power. NIH
9: 2 *was* Saul, a choice *young m*, and a goodly: NIH
9: 6 *there is* in this city a **m** of God, and *he is* an 376
9: 6 a man of God, and *he is* an honourable **m**; 376
9: 7 *if* we go, what shall we bring the **m**? 376
9: 7 *there is* not a present to bring to the **m** of 376
9: 8 *that* will I give to the **m** of God, to tell us our 376
9: 9 when a **m** went to inquire of God, thus he 376
9:10 So they went unto the city where the **m** of 376
9:16 send thee a **m** out of the land of Benjamin, 376
9:17 Behold the **m** whom I spake to thee of: 376
10: 6 and shalt be turned into another **m**. 376
10:22 if the **m** should yet come thither. 376
10:25 all the people away, **every m** to his house. 376
10:27 of Belial said, How shall this *m* save us? NIH
11: 3 then, if *there be* **no m** to save us, we will 369
11:13 There shall not a **m** be put to death this day: 376
13: 2 the rest of the people he sent **every m** to his 376
13:14 the LORD hath sought him a **m** after his 376
13:20 to sharpen **every m** his share, and his 376
14: 1 said unto the **young m** that bare his armour, 5288
14: 6 Jonathan said to the **young m** that bare his 5288
14:24 Cursed *be* the **m** that eateth *any* food until 376
14:26 but **no m** put his hand to his mouth: 369
14:28 Cursed *be* the **m** that eateth *any* food *this* 376
14:34 Bring me hither **every m** his ox, and 376
14:34 **every m** his sheep, and slay *them* here, and 376
14:34 all the people brought **every m** his ox with 376
14:36 and let us not leave a **m** of them. 376
14:39 *there was* not *a m* among all the people *that* NIH
14:52 when Saul saw any strong **m**, or any valiant 376
14:52 or any valiant **m**, he took him unto him. 1121
15: 3 slay both **m** and woman, infant and suckling, 376
15:29 for he *is* not a **m**, that *he* should repent. 120
16: 7 for *the LORD seeth* not as **m** seeth; for man 120
16: 7 for **m** looketh on the outward appearance, 120
16:16 to seek out a **m**, *who is* a cunning player on 376
16:17 Provide me now a **m** that can play well, and 376
16:18 a mighty valiant *m*, and a man of war, and NIH
16:18 a mighty valiant *man*, and a **m** of war, and 376
17: 8 choose you a **m** for you, and let him come 376
17:10 give me a **m**, that we may fight together. 376
17:12 the **m** went among men *for* an old man in 376
17:12 the man went among men *for* an **old m** in 2204
17:24 when they saw the **m**, fled from him, and 376
17:25 Have ye seen this **m** that is come up? 376
17:25 it shall be, *that* the **m** who killeth him, 376
17:26 What shall be done to the **m** that killeth this 376
17:27 So shall it be done to the **m** that killeth him. 376
17:33 a youth, and he a **m** of war from his youth. 376
17:41 the **m** that bare the shield *went* before him. 376
17:58 to him, Whose son *art* thou, *thou* **young m**? 5288
18:23 seeing that I *am* a poor **m**, and 376
20:22 if I say thus unto the **young m**, Behold, 5958
21: 1 Why *art* thou alone, and no **m** with thee? 376
21: 2 Let no **m** know any thing of the business 376
21: 7 Now a *certain* **m** of the servants of Saul *was* 376
21:14 unto his servants, Lo, you see the **m** *is* mad: 376
21:15 *fellow* to **play the mad m** in my presence? 7696
24:19 For if a **m** find his enemy, will he let him go 376
25: 2 *there was* a **m** in Maon, whose possessions 376
25: 2 the **m** *was* very great, and he had three 376
25: 3 Now the name of the **m** *was* Nabal; and 376
25: 3 the **m** *was* churlish and evil *in* his doings; 376
25:10 that break away **every m** from his master. 376
25:13 his men, Gird you on **every m** his sword. 376
25:13 And they girded on **every m** his sword; and 376
25:17 son of Belial, that *a m* cannot speak to him. NIH
25:25 I pray thee, regard this **m** of Belial, 376

1Sa 25:29 Yet a **m** is risen to pursue thee, and to seek 120
26:12 **no m** saw *it,* nor knew *it,* neither awaked: 369
26:15 said to Abner, *Art* not thou a *valiant* **m**? 376
26:23 The LORD render to **every m** his 376
27: 3 he and his men, **every m** with his household, 376
27: 9 left neither **m** nor woman alive, and 376
27:11 David saved neither **m** nor woman alive, 376
28:14 she said, An old **m** cometh up; and he *is* 376
30: 6 **every m** for his sons and for his daughters: 376
30:13 he said, I *am* a **young m** of Egypt, 5288
30:17 there escaped not a **m** of them, save four 376
30:22 save *to* **every m** his wife and his children, 376
2Sa 1: 2 a **m** came out of the camp from Saul with his 376
1: 5 David said unto the **young m** that told him, 5288
1: 6 the **young m** that told him said, As I 5288
1:13 David said unto the **young m** that told him, 5288
2: 3 David bring up, **every m** with his household: 376
3:34 as *a m* falleth before wicked men, *so* NIH
3:38 and a great *m* fallen this day in Israel? NIH
7:19 And *is* this the manner of **m**, O Lord GOD? 120
12: 2 The rich *m* had exceeding many flocks and NIH
12: 3 the poor *m* had nothing, save one little ewe NIH
12: 4 there came a traveller unto the rich **m**, and 376
12: 4 to dress for the **wayfaring m** that was come 732
12: 4 dressed it for the **m** that was come to him. 376
12: 5 anger was greatly kindled against the **m**; 376
12: 5 the **m** that hath done this *thing* shall surely 376
12: 7 Nathan said to David, Thou *art* the **m**. 376
13: 3 and Jonadab *was* a very subtil **m**. 376
13: 9 And they went out every **m** from him. 376
13:29 and **every m** gat him up upon his mule, and 376
13:34 the **young m** that kept the watch lift up his 5288
14:16 of the hand of the **m** *that would* destroy me 376
14:21 bring the **young m** Absalom again. 5288
15: 2 *that when* any **m** that had a controversy 376
15: 3 *there is* **no m** *deputed* of the king to hear 369
15: 4 that every **m** which hath *any* suit or 376
15: 5 that when **any m** came nigh *to him* to do 376
15:30 that *was* with him covered **every m** his head, 376
16: 5 thence came out a **m** of the family of 376
16: 7 thou bloody **m**, and thou man of Belial: 376
16: 7 thou bloody man, and thou **m** of Belial: 376
16: 8 to thy mischief, because thou *art* a bloody **m**. 376
16:23 *was* as if a **m** had inquired at the oracle of 376
17: 3 the **m** whom thou seekest *is* as if all 376
17: 8 thy father *is* a **m** of war, and will not lodge 376
17:10 Israel knoweth that thy father *is* a mighty *m*, NIH
18: 5 *Deal* gently for my sake with the **young m**, 5288
18:10 a certain **m** saw *it,* and told Joab, and said, 376
18:11 Joab said unto the **m** that told him, 376
18:12 the **m** said unto Joab, Though I should 376
18:12 Beware *that* none *touch* the **young m** 5288
18:24 and looked, and behold a **m** running alone. 376
18:26 the watchman saw another **m** running: and 376
18:26 and said, Behold *another* **m** running alone. 376
18:27 He *is* a good **m**, and cometh with good 376
18:29 king said, *Is* the **young m** Absalom safe? 5288
18:32 unto Cushi, *Is* the **young m** Absalom safe? 5288
18:32 thee to do *thee* hurt, be as *that* **young m** *is.* 5288
19: 8 for Israel had fled **every m** to his tent. 376
19:14 men of Judah, *even* as *the heart of* one **m**; 376
19:22 shall there **any m** be put to death *this* day in 376
19:32 Now Barzillai was a very **aged m**, 2204
19:32 lay at Mahanaim; for he *was* a very great **m**. 376
20: 1 there happened to be there a **m** of Belial, 376
20: 1 son of Jesse: **every m** to his tents, O Israel. 376
20: 2 So every **m** of Israel went up from after 376
20:12 when the **m** saw that all the people stood 376
20:21 a **m** of mount Ephraim, Sheba the son of 376
20:22 retired from the city, **every m** to his tent. 376
21: 4 neither for us *shalt thou* kill **any m** in Israel. 376
21: 5 The **m** that consumed us, and that devised 376
21:20 where was a **m** of *great* stature, that had on 376
22:26 with the upright **m** thou wilt shew thyself 1368
22:49 thou hast delivered me from the violent **m**. 376
23: 1 and the **m** *who* was raised up on high, 1397
23: 7 the **m** *that* shall touch them must be fenced 376
23:20 the son of a valiant **m**, of Kabzeel, who had 376
23:21 he slew an Egyptian, a goodly **m**: and 376
24:14 and let me not fall into the hand of **m**. 120
1Ki 1: 6 he also *was* a very goodly *m*; and NIH
1:42 for thou *art* a valiant **m**, and bringest good 376
1:49 and rose up, and went **every m** his way. 376
1:52 If he will shew himself a worthy **m**, 1121
2: 2 thou strong therefore, and shew thyself a **m**; 376
2: 4 fail thee (said he) a **m** on the throne of Israel. 376
2: 9 for thou *art* a wise **m**, and knowest what 376
4: 7 **each m** *his* month in a year made provision. 259
4:25 **every m** under his vine and under his fig 376
4:27 king Solomon's table, **every m** *in* his month: 376
4:28 **every m** according to his charge. 376
7:14 his father *was* a **m** of Tyre, a worker in 376
8:25 There shall not fail thee a **m** in my sight to 376
8:31 If **any m** trespass against his neighbour, and 376
8:38 and supplication soever be *made* by any **m**, 120
8:38 which shall know **every m** the plague of his 376
8:39 and give to **every m** according to his ways, 376
8:46 (for *there is* no **m** that sinneth not,) 120
9: 5 There shall not fail thee a **m** upon the throne 376
10:25 they brought **every m** his present, vessels of 376
11:28 the **m** Jeroboam *was* a mighty *man* of 376
11:28 the man Jeroboam *was* a mighty *m* of NIH
11:28 Solomon seeing the **young m** that he was 5288
12:22 the word of God came unto Shemaiah the **m** 376
12:24 return **every m** to his house; for this thing is 376
13: 1 there came a **m** of God out of Judah by 376
13: 4 Jeroboam heard the saying of the **m** of God, 376
13: 5 according to the sign which the **m** of God 376
13: 6 king answered and said unto the **m** of God, 376
13: 6 And the **m** of God besought the LORD, and 376
13: 7 the king said unto the **m** of God, 376
13: 8 the **m** of God said unto the king, If thou wilt 376
13:11 told him all the works that the **m** of God had 376
13:12 For his sons had seen what way the **m** of 376
13:14 went after the **m** of God, and found him 376
13:14 *Art* thou the **m** of God that camest from 376
13:21 he cried unto the **m** of God that came from 376
13:26 It *is* the **m** of God, who was disobedient unto 376
13:29 the prophet took up the carcase of the **m** of 376
13:31 bury me in the sepulchre wherein the **m** of 376
14:10 as *a m* taketh away dung, till it be all gone. NIH
17:18 have I to do with thee, O thou **m** of God? 376
17:24 Now *by* this I know that thou *art* a **m** of 376
20: 7 and see how this *m* seeketh mischief: NIH
20:20 they slew every one his **m**: and the Syrians 376
20:24 **every m** out of his place, and put captains in 376
20:28 there came a **m** of God, and spake unto 376
20:35 a certain **m** of the sons of the prophets said 376
20:35 I pray thee. And the **m** refused to smite him. 376
20:37 he found another **m**, and said, Smite me, 376
20:37 the **m** smote him, so that in smiting he 376
20:39 a **m** turned aside, and brought a man unto 376
20:39 brought a **m** unto me, and said, Keep this 376
20:39 a man unto me, and said, Keep this **m**: 376
20:42 Because thou hast let go out of *thy* hand a **m** 376
22: 8 *There is* yet one **m**, Micaiah the son of 376
22:17 let them return **every m** to his house in 376
22:34 a *certain* **m** drew a bow at a venture, 376
22:36 **Every m** to his city, and every man to his 376
22:36 to his city, and **every m** to his own country. 376
2Ki 1: 6 There came a **m** up to meet us, and said unto 376
1: 7 What manner of **m** *was he* which came up to 376
1: 8 *He was* a hairy **m**, and girt *with* a girdle of 376
1: 9 Thou **m** of God, the king hath said, 376
1:10 If I *be* a **m** of God, then let fire come down 376
1:11 he answered and said unto him, O **m** of God, 376
1:12 and said unto them, If I *be* a **m** of God, 376
1:13 O **m** of God, I pray thee, let my life, and 376
3:25 *on* every good piece of land cast **every m** his 376
4: 7 she came and told the **m** of God. And he 376
4: 9 I perceive that this *is* a holy **m** of God, 376
4:16 And she said, Nay, my lord, thou **m** of God, 376
4:21 and laid him on the bed of the **m** of God, and 376
4:22 that I may run to the **m** of God, and 376
4:25 came unto the **m** of God to mount Carmel. 376
4:25 to pass, when the **m** of God saw her afar off, 376
4:27 when she came to the **m** of God to the hill, 376
4:27 the **m** of God said, Let her alone; for her 376
4:29 go *thy way:* if thou meet **any m**, salute him 376
4:40 they cried out, and said, O thou **m** of God, 376
4:42 And there came a **m** from Baal-shalisha, and 376
4:42 brought the **m** of God bread of the firstfruits, 376
5: 1 was a great **m** with his master, and 376
5: 1 he was also a mighty **m** in valour, *but* NIH
5: 7 that this *m* doth send unto me to recover a NIH
5: 7 send unto me to recover a **m** of his leprosy? 376
5: 8 when Elisha the **m** of God had heard that 376
5:14 according to the saying of the **m** of God: 376

2Ki	5:15	he returned to the **m** of God, he and all his	376
	5:20	the servant of Elisha the **m** of God, said,	376
	5:26	Went not mine heart *with thee,* when the **m**	376
	6: 2	take thence **every m** a beam, and let us make	376
	6: 6	the **m** of God said, Where fell it? And he	376
	6: 9	the **m** of God sent unto the king of Israel,	376
	6:10	to the place which the **m** of God told him	376
	6:15	when the servant of the **m** of God was risen	376
	6:17	LORD opened the eyes of the **young m**;	5288
	6:19	and I will bring you to the **m** whom ye seek.	376
	6:32	and *the king* sent a **m** from before him:	376
	7: 2	the king leaned answered the **m** of God,	376
	7: 5	camp of Syria, behold, *there was* no **m** there.	376
	7:10	behold, *there was* no **m** there, neither voice	376
	7:10	neither voice of **m**, but horses tied, and asses	120
	7:17	and he died, as the **m** of God had said,	376
	7:18	it came to pass as the **m** of God had spoken	376
	7:19	*that* lord answered the **m** of God, and said,	376
	8: 2	and did after the saying of the **m** of God:	376
	8: 4	with Gehazi the servant of the **m** of God,	376
	8: 7	saying, The **m** of God is come hither.	376
	8: 8	go, meet the **m** of God, and inquire of	376
	8:11	*he* was ashamed: and the **m** of God wept.	376
	9: 4	So the **young m**, *even* the young man	5288
	9: 4	young man, *even* the **young m** the prophet,	5288
	9:11	Ye know the **m**, and his communication.	376
	9:13	took **every m** his garment, and put *it* under	376
	10:21	so that there was not a **m** left that came not.	376
	11: 8	**every m** with his weapons in his hand:	376
	11: 9	they took **every m** his men that were to	376
	11:11	**every m** with his weapons in his hand,	376
	12: 4	*account,* the money that every **m** is set at,	5315
	12: 5	take *it* to them, **every m** of his acquaintance:	376
	13:19	And the **m** of God was wroth with him, and	376
	13:21	as they were burying a **m**, that behold,	376
	13:21	they cast the **m** into the sepulchre of Elisha:	376
	13:21	when the **m** was let down, and touched	376
	14: 6	**every m** shall be put to death for his own	376
	14:12	and they fled **every m** to their tents.	376
	15:20	of each **m** fifty shekels *of* silver, to give to	376
	18:21	*even* upon Egypt, on which if a **m** lean, it	376
	18:31	and *then* eat ye **every m** of his own vine, and	376
	21:13	I will wipe Jerusalem as *a m* wipeth a dish,	NIH
	22:15	God of Israel, Tell the **m** that sent you to me,	376
	23:10	that no **m** might make his son or his	376
	23:16	the LORD which the **m** of God proclaimed,	376
	23:17	*It is* the sepulchre of the **m** of God,	376
	23:18	Let him alone; let no **m** move his bones.	376
1Ch	11:22	the son of a valiant **m** of Kabzeel, who had	376
	11:23	a **m** of *great* stature, five cubits *high;* and	376
	12: 4	a mighty *m* among the thirty, and over	NIH
	12:28	a **young m** mighty of valour, and *of* his	5288
	16: 3	both **m** and woman, to every one a loaf of	376
	16:21	He suffered no **m** to do them wrong: yea,	376
	16:43	all the people departed **every m** to his house:	376
	17:17	to the estate of a **m** of high degree,	120
	20: 6	where was a **m** of *great* stature, whose	376
	21:13	but let me not fall into the hand of **m**.	120
	22: 9	*be* born to thee, who shall be a **m** of rest;	376
	23: 3	**m** by man, was thirty and eight thousand.	NIH
	23: 3	man by **m**, was thirty and eight thousand.	1397
	23:14	Now *concerning* Moses the **m** of God,	376
	27:32	*was* a counseller, a wise **m**, and a scribe:	376
	28: 3	because thou *hast been* a **m** of war, and	376
	28:21	willing skilful *m*, for any *manner of* service:	NIH
	29: 1	for the palace *is* not for **m**, but for	120
2Ch	2: 7	therefore a **m** cunning to work in gold,	376
	2:13	now I have sent a cunning **m**, endued with	376
	2:14	his father *was* a **m** of Tyre, skilful to work in	376
	6: 5	neither chose I **any m** to be a ruler over my	376
	6:16	There shall not fail thee a **m** in my sight to	376
	6:22	If a **m** sin against his neighbour, and an oath	376
	6:29	supplication soever shall be *made* of any **m**,	120
	6:30	render unto **every m** according unto all his	376
	6:36	(for *there is* no **m** which sinneth not,)	120
	7:18	There shall not fail thee a **m** *to be* ruler in	376
	8:14	for so had David the **m** of God commanded.	376
	9:24	they brought **every m** his present, vessels of	376
	10:16	**every m** to your tents, O Israel: *and* now,	376
	11: 2	LORD came to Shemaiah the **m** of God,	376
	11: 4	return **every m** to his house, for this thing is	376
	14:11	*art* our God; let not **m** prevail against thee.	582
	15:13	or great, whether **m** or woman.	376
	17:17	Eliada a mighty *m* of valour, and with him	NIH
	18: 7	*There is* yet one **m**, by whom *we* may	376
	18:16	*therefore* **every m** to his house in peace.	376
	18:33	a *certain* **m** drew a bow at a venture,	376
	18:33	therefore he said to *his* **chariot m**,	7395
	19: 6	for ye judge not for **m**, but for the LORD,	120
	20:27	every **m** of Judah and Jerusalem, and	376
	23: 7	**every m** with his weapons in his hand;	376
	23: 8	took **every m** his men that were to come in	376
	23:10	**every m** having his weapon in his hand,	376
	25: 4	but **every m** shall die for his own sin.	376
	25: 7	there came a **m** of God to him, saying,	376
	25: 9	Amaziah said to the **m** of God, But what	376
	25: 9	the **m** of God answered, The LORD is able	376
	25:22	and they fled **every m** to his tent.	376
	28: 7	Zichri, a mighty *m* of Ephraim, slew	NIH
	30:16	according to the law of Moses the **m** of God:	376
	31: 1	**every m** to his possession, into their own	376
	31: 2	**every m** according to his service, the priests	376
	32:19	*which were* the work of the hands of **m**.	120
	34:23	of Israel, Tell ye the **m** that sent you to me,	376
	36:17	had no compassion upon **young m** or	970
	36:17	maiden, **old m**, or him that stooped for age:	2205
Ezr	3: 1	themselves together as one **m** to Jerusalem.	376
	3: 2	as it is written in the law of Moses the **m** of	376
	8:18	us they brought us a **m** of understanding,	376
Ne	1:11	and grant him mercy in the sight of this **m**.	376
	2:10	**m** to seek the welfare of the children of	120
	2:12	neither told I *any* **m** what my God had put in	120
	5:13	So God shake out every **m** from his house,	376
	6:11	I said, Should such a **m** as I flee? and who *is*	376
	7: 2	for he *was* a faithful **m**, and feared God	376
	8: 1	**m** into the street that *was* before the water	376
	9:29	(which if a **m** do, he shall live in them;)	120
	12:24	to the commandment of David the **m** of God,	376
	12:36	with the musical instruments of David the **m**	376
Est	1:22	that every **m** should bear rule in his own	376
	4:11	that whosoever, *whether* **m** or woman,	376
	5:12	Esther the queen did let no *m* come in with	NIH
	6: 6	What shall be done unto the **m** whom	376
	6: 7	*For* the **m** whom the king delighteth to	376
	6: 9	that they may array the **m** *withal* whom	376
	6: 9	Thus shall it be done to the **m** whom	376
	6:11	Thus shall it be done unto the **m** whom	376
	8: 8	with the king's ring, may **no m** reverse.	369
	9: 2	no **m** could withstand them; for the fear of	376
	9: 4	for *this* **m** Mordecai waxed greater and	376
Job	1: 1	There was a **m** in the land of Uz,	376
	1: 1	that **m** was perfect and upright, and one that	376
	1: 3	that this **m** was the greatest of all the men of	376
	1: 8	a perfect and an upright **m**, one that feareth	376
	2: 3	a perfect and an upright **m**, one that feareth	376
	2: 4	yea, all that a **m** hath will he give for his life.	376
	3: 3	*it was* said, There is a **m child** conceived.	1397
	3:23	*Why is light given* to a **m** whose way is	1397
	4:17	Shall **mortal m** be more just than God?	582
	4:17	shall a **m** be more pure than his Maker?	1397
	5: 2	For wrath killeth the **foolish m**, and	191
	5: 7	Yet **m** is born unto trouble, as the sparks fly	120
	5:17	happy *is* the **m** whom God correcteth:	582
	7: 1	*Is there* not an appointed time to **m** upon	582
	7:17	What *is* **m**, that thou shouldest magnify him?	582
	8:20	God will not cast away a perfect *m*, neither	NIH
	9: 2	a truth: but how should **m** be just with God?	582
	9:32	For *he is* not a **m**, as I *am, that* I should	376
	10: 4	thou eyes of flesh? or seest thou as **m** seeth?	582
	10: 5	*Are* thy days as the days of **m**? *are* thy years	582
	11: 2	and should a **m** full of talk be justified?	376
	11: 3	shall **no m** make *thee* ashamed?	369
	11:12	For vain **m** would be wise, though man be	376
	11:12	though **m** be born *like* a wild ass's colt.	120
	12: 4	the just upright *m is* laughed to scorn.	NIH
	12:14	it cannot be built *again:* he shutteth up a **m**,	376
	12:25	maketh them to stagger like a drunken *m*.	NIH
	13: 9	or as *one* **m** mocketh another, do ye *so*	NIH
	14: 1	**M** *that is* born of a woman *is* of few days,	120
	14:10	**m** dieth, and wasteth away: yea, man giveth	1397
	14:10	yea, **m** giveth up the ghost, and where *is* he?	120
	14:12	So **m** lieth down, and riseth not: till	376
	14:14	If a **m** die, shall he live *again?* all the days	1397
	14:19	the earth; and thou destroyest the hope of **m**.	582
	15: 2	Should a wise *m* utter vain knowledge, and	NIH
	15: 7	*Art* thou the first **m** *that* was born? or	120
	15:14	What *is* **m**, that he should be clean? and	582
	15:16	How much more abominable and filthy *is* **m**,	376

Job 15:20 The wicked *m* travaileth with pain all his NIH
15:28 *and* in houses which no **m** inhabiteth, NIH
16:21 O that *one* might plead for a **m** with God, 1397
16:21 as a **m** *pleadeth* for his neighbour. 120+1121
17:10 for I cannot find *one* wise **m** among you. NIH
20: 4 this of old, since **m** was placed upon earth, 120
20:21 therefore shall no *m* look for his goods. NIH
20:29 This *is* the portion of a wicked **m** from God, 120
21: 4 *As for* me, *is* my complaint to **m**? and if *it* 120
21:33 every **m** shall draw after him, as *there are* 120
22: 2 Can a **m** be profitable unto God, as he that 1397
22: 8 *as for* the mighty **m**, he had the earth; and 376
22: 8 the earth; and the honourable *m* dwelt in it. NIH
24:22 he riseth up, and no *m* is sure of life. NIH
25: 4 How then can **m** be justified with God? or 582
25: 6 How much less **m**, *that is* a worm? and 582
25: 6 a worm? and the son of **m**, *which is* a worm? 120
27:13 This *is* the portion of a wicked **m** with God, 120
27:19 The rich *m* shall lie down, but he shall not NIH
28:13 **M** knoweth not the price thereof; neither is it 582
28:28 unto **m** he said, Behold, the fear of the Lord, 120
32: 8 *there is* a spirit in **m**: and the inspiration of 582
32:13 out wisdom: God thrusteth him down, not **m**. 376
32:21 neither let me give flattering titles unto **m**. 120
33:12 will answer thee, that God is greater than **m**. 582
33:14 yea twice, *yet m* perceiveth it not. NIH
33:17 That *he* may withdraw **m** *from his* purpose, 120
33:17 *from his* purpose, and hide pride from **m**. 1397
33:23 a thousand, to shew unto **m** his uprightness: 120
33:26 for he will render unto **m** his righteousness. 582
33:29 *things* worketh God oftentimes with **m**, 1397
34: 7 What **m** *is* like Job, *who* drinketh up 1397
34: 9 It profiteth a **m** nothing that he should 1397
34:11 For the work of a **m** shall he render unto 120
34:11 cause **every m** to find according to *his* ways. 376
34:14 If he set his heart upon *m*, *if* he gather unto NIH
34:15 and **m** shall turn again unto dust. 120
34:21 For his eyes *are* upon the ways of **m**, and 376
34:23 For he will not lay upon **m** more *than right;* 376
34:29 *done* against a nation, or against a **m** only: 120
34:34 tell me, and let a wise **m** hearken unto me. 1397
35: 8 Thy wickedness *may hurt* a **m** as thou *art;* 376
35: 8 thy righteousness *may profit* the son of **m**. 120
36:25 Every **m** may see it; man may behold *it* afar 120
36:25 man may see it; **m** may behold *it* afar off. 582
36:28 do drop *and* distil upon **m** abundantly. 120
37: 7 He sealeth up the hand of every **m**; that all 120
37:20 if a **m** speak, surely he shall be swallowed 376
38: 3 Gird up now thy loins like a **m**; for I will 1397
38:26 *where* no **m** *is; on* the wilderness, 376
38:26 *is; on* the wilderness, wherein *there is* no **m**; 120
40: 7 Gird up thy loins now like a **m**: I will 1397
42:11 **every m** also gave him a piece of money, 376
Ps 1: 1 Blessed *is* the **m** that walketh not in 376
5: 6 will abhor the bloody and deceitful **m**. 376
8: 4 What *is* **m**, that thou art mindful of him? and 582
8: 4 and the son of **m**, that thou visitest him? 120
9:19 Arise, O LORD; let not **m** prevail: let 582
10:15 the evil **m**: seek out his wickedness *till* thou NIH
10:18 that the **m** of the earth may no more oppress. 582
12: 1 Help, LORD; for the godly *m* ceaseth; NIH
18:25 with an upright **m** thou wilt shew thyself 1399
18:48 thou hast delivered me from the violent **m**. 376
19: 5 *and* rejoiceth as a strong *m* to run a race. NIH
22: 6 I *am* a worm, and no **m**; a reproach of men, 376
25:12 What **m** *is* he that feareth the LORD? 376
31:12 I am forgotten as a **dead m** out of mind: 4191
31:20 secret of thy presence from the pride of **m**: 376
32: 2 Blessed *is* the **m** unto whom the LORD 120
33:16 a mighty *m* is not delivered by much NIH
34: 6 This poor *m* cried, and the LORD heard NIH
34: 8 blessed *is* the **m** *that* trusteth in him. 1397
34:12 What **m** *is he that* desireth life, *and* 376
36: 6 O LORD, thou preservest **m** and beast. 120
37: 7 of the **m** who bringeth wicked devices to 376
37:16 A little that a righteous *m* hath *is* better than NIH
37:23 The steps of a *good* **m** are ordered by 1397
37:37 Mark the perfect *m*, and behold the upright: NIH
37:37 the upright: for the end of *that* **m** *is* peace. 376
38:13 I, as a deaf *m*, heard not; and *I was* as a NIH
38:13 *I was* as a dumb *m that* openeth not his NIH
38:14 Thus I was as a **m** that heareth not, and 376
39: 5 verily every **m** at his best state *is* altogether 120
39: 6 Surely **every m** walketh in a vain shew: 376
39:11 When thou with rebukes dost correct **m** for 376
39:11 like a moth: surely every **m** *is* vanity. Selah. 120
40: 4 Blessed *is that* **m** that maketh the LORD 1397
43: 1 deliver me from the deceitful and unjust **m**. 376
49:12 Nevertheless **m** *being* in honour abideth not: 120
49:20 **M** *that is* in honour, and understandeth not, 120
52: 1 O mighty *m*? the goodness of God *endureth* NIH
52: 7 *this is* the **m** *that* made not God his 1397
55:13 a **m** mine equal, my guide, and 582
56: 1 for **m** would swallow me up; he fighting 582
56:11 I will not be afraid what **m** can do unto me. 120
58:11 So that a **m** shall say, Verily *there is* a 120
60:11 help from trouble: for vain *is* the help of **m**. 120
62: 3 long will ye imagine mischief against a **m**? 376
62:12 for thou renderest to *every* **m** according to 376
65: 4 Blessed *is the m whom* thou choosest, and NIH
71: 4 of the hand of the unrighteous and cruel *m*. NIH
74: 5 *A m* was famous according as he had lifted NIH
74:22 remember how the foolish *m* reproacheth NIH
76:10 Surely the wrath of **m** shall praise thee: 120
78:25 **M** did eat angels' food: he sent them meat to 376
78:65 like a mighty *m* that shouteth by reason of NIH
80:17 Let thy hand be upon the **m** of thy right 376
80:17 upon the son of **m** *whom* thou madest strong 120
84: 5 Blessed *is* the **m** whose strength *is* in thee; 120
84:12 blessed *is* the **m** that trusteth in thee. 120
87: 4 Tyre, with Ethiopia; this *m* was born there. NIH
87: 5 be said, This and that **m** was born in her: 376
87: 6 *up* the people, *that* this *m* was born there. NIH
88: 4 the pit: I am as a **m** *that hath* no strength: 1397
89:48 What **m** *is he that* liveth, and shall not see 1397
90: T A Prayer of Moses the **m** of God. 376
90: 3 Thou turnest **m** to destruction; and sayest, 582
92: 6 A brutish **m** knoweth not; neither doth a fool 376
94:10 he that teacheth **m** knowledge, *shall not he* 120
94:11 The LORD knoweth the thoughts of **m**, 120
94:12 Blessed *is* the **m** whom thou chastenest, 1397
103:15 *As for* **m**, his days *are* as grass: as a flower 582
104:14 for the cattle, and herb for the service of **m**: 120
104:15 wine *that* maketh glad the heart of **m**, 582
104:23 **M** goeth forth unto his work and to his 120
105:14 He suffered no **m** to do them wrong: yea, 120
105:17 He sent a **m** before them, *even* Joseph, 376
107:27 stagger like a drunken *m*, and are at their NIH
108:12 help from trouble: for vain *is* the help of **m**. 120
109: 6 Set thou a wicked *m* over him: and let Satan NIH
109:16 persecuted the poor and needy **m**, that *he* 376
112: 1 Blessed *is* the **m** *that* feareth the LORD, 376
112: 5 A good **m** sheweth favour, and lendeth: 376
118: 6 I will not fear: what can **m** do unto me? 120
118: 8 in the LORD than to put confidence in **m**. 120
119: 9 Wherewithal shall a **young m** cleanse his 5288
119:134 Deliver me from the oppression of **m**: so 120
127: 4 As arrows *are* in the hand of a mighty *m*; so NIH
127: 5 Happy *is* the **m** that hath his quiver full of 1397
128: 4 that thus shall the **m** be blessed that feareth 1397
135: 8 the firstborn of Egypt, both of **m** and beast. 120
140: 1 Deliver me, O LORD, from the evil **m**: 120
140: 1 evil man: preserve me from the violent **m**; 376
140: 4 the wicked; preserve me from the violent **m**; 376
140:11 evil shall hunt the violent **m** to overthrow 376
142: 4 but *there was* **no m** that would know me: 369
142: 4 refuge failed me; **no m** cared for my soul. 369
143: 2 for in thy sight shall no *m* living be NIH
144: 3 LORD, what *is* **m**, that thou takest 120
144: 3 *or* the son of **m**, that thou makest account of 582
144: 4 **M** is like to vanity: his days *are* as a shadow 120
146: 3 *nor* in the son of **m**, in whom *there is* no 120
147:10 he taketh not pleasure in the legs of a **m**. 376
Pr 1: 4 to the **young m** knowledge and discretion. 5288
1: 5 A wise *m* will hear, and will increase NIH
1: 5 a *m* of understanding shall attain unto wise NIH
1:24 stretched out my hand, and no *m* regarded; NIH
2:12 To deliver thee from the way of the evil *m*, NIH
2:12 from the **m** that speaketh froward things; 376
3: 4 understanding in the sight of God and **m**. 120
3:13 Happy *is* the **m** *that* findeth wisdom, and 120
3:13 and the **m** *that* getteth understanding. 120
3:30 Strive not with a **m** without cause, if he have 120
5:21 For the ways of **m** *are* before the eyes of 376
6:11 that travelleth, and thy want as an armed **m**. 376
6:12 A naughty person, a wicked **m**, walketh *with* 376
6:26 For by means of a whorish woman *a m is* NIH
6:27 Can a **m** take fire in his bosom, and 376

M

Pr 6:34 For jealousy *is* the rage of a **m**: therefore 1397
7: 7 a **young m** void of understanding, 5288
8: 4 I call; and my voice *is* to the sons of **m**. 120
8:34 Blessed *is* the **m** that heareth me, watching 120
9: 7 he that rebuketh a wicked *m getteth* himself NIH
9: 8 rebuke a wise *m*, and he will love thee. NIH
9: 9 Give *instruction* to a wise *m*, and he will be NIH
9: 9 teach a just *m*, and he will increase in NIH
10:11 The mouth of a righteous *m is* a well of life: NIH
10:23 but a **m** of understanding hath wisdom. 376
11: 7 When a wicked **m** dieth, *his* expectation 120
11:12 but a **m** of understanding holdeth his peace. 376
11:17 The merciful **m** doeth good to his own soul: 376
12: 2 A good *m* obtaineth favour of the LORD: NIH
12: 2 but a **m** of wicked devices will he condemn. 376
12: 3 A **m** shall not be established by wickedness: 120
12: 8 A **m** shall be commended according to his 376
12:10 A righteous *m* regardeth the life of his NIH
12:14 A **m** shall be satisfied *with* good by the fruit 376
12:16 but a prudent *m* covereth shame. NIH
12:23 A prudent **m** concealeth knowledge: but 120
12:25 Heaviness in the heart of **m** maketh it stoop: 376
12:27 The slothful *m* roasteth not that which he NIH
12:27 but the substance of a diligent **m** *is* precious. 120
13: 2 A **m** shall eat good by the fruit of *his* mouth: 376
13: 5 A righteous *m* hateth lying: but a wicked NIH
13: 5 a wicked *m* is loathsome, and cometh to NIH
13:16 Every prudent *m* dealeth with knowledge: NIH
13:22 A good *m* leaveth an inheritance to *his* NIH
14: 7 Go from the presence of a foolish **m**, 376
14:12 is a way which seemeth right unto a **m**, 376
14:14 and a good **m** *shall be satisfied* from himself. 376
14:15 but the prudent *m* looketh well to his going. NIH
14:16 A wise *m* feareth, and departeth from evil: NIH
14:17 and a **m** of wicked devices is hated. 376
15:18 A wrathful **m** stirreth up strife: but *he that is* 376
15:19 The way of the slothful *m is* as a hedge of NIH
15:20 but a foolish **m** despiseth his mother. 120
15:21 but a **m** of understanding walketh uprightly. 376
15:23 A **m** hath joy by the answer of his mouth: 376
16: 1 The preparations of the heart in **m**, and 120
16: 2 All the ways of a **m** *are* clean in his own 376
16:14 of death: but a wise **m** will pacify it. 376
16:25 There is a way that seemeth right unto a **m**, 376
16:27 An ungodly **m** diggeth up evil: and in his 376
16:28 A froward **m** soweth strife: and a whisperer 376
16:29 A violent **m** enticeth his neighbour, and 376
17:10 A reproof entereth more into a wise *m* than NIH
17:11 An evil *m* seeketh only rebellion: therefore NIH
17:12 *Let* a bear robbed of her whelps meet a **m**, 376
17:18 A **m** void of understanding striketh hands, 120
17:23 A wicked *m* taketh a gift out of the bosom NIH
17:27 a **m** of understanding is of an excellent 376
17:28 he that shutteth his lips *is esteemed a m* of NIH
18: 1 Through desire a *m*, having separated NIH
18:12 Before destruction the heart of **m** is haughty, 376
18:14 The spirit of a **m** will sustain his infirmity; 376
18:24 A **m** that hath friends must shew himself 376
19: 3 The foolishness of **m** perverteth his way: and 120
19: 6 every *m is* a friend to him that giveth gifts. NIH
19:11 The discretion of a **m** deferreth his anger; 120
19:19 *A m* of great wrath *shall* suffer punishment: NIH
19:22 The desire of a **m** *is* his kindness: and a poor 120
19:22 and a poor *m is* better than a liar. NIH
19:24 A slothful *m* hideth his hand in *his* bosom, NIH
20: 3 *It is* an honour for a **m** to cease from strife: 376
20: 5 Counsel in the heart of **m** *is like* deep water; 376
20: 5 but a **m** of understanding will draw it out. 376
20: 6 but a faithful **m** who can find? 376
20: 7 The just *m* walketh in his integrity: NIH
20:17 Bread of deceit *is* sweet to a **m**; but 376
20:24 how can a **m** then understand his own way? 120
20:25 *It is* a snare to the **m** *who* devoureth *that* 120
20:27 The spirit of **m** *is* the candle of the LORD, 120
21: 2 Every way of a **m** *is* right in his own eyes: 376
21: 8 The way of **m** *is* froward and strange: but 376
21:12 The righteous *m* wisely considereth NIH
21:16 The **m** that wandereth out of the way of 120
21:17 He that loveth pleasure *shall be* a poor **m**: 376
21:20 of the wise; but a foolish **m** spendeth it up. 120
21:22 A wise *m* scaleth the city of the mighty, and NIH
21:28 but the **m** that heareth, speaketh constantly. 376
21:29 A wicked **m** hardeneth his face: but *as for* 376
22: 3 A prudent *m* foreseeth the evil, and NIH
22:13 The slothful *m* saith, *There is* a lion NIH
22:24 Make no friendship with an angry **m**; and 1167
22:24 and with a furious **m** thou shalt not go: 376
22:29 Seest thou a **m** diligent in his business? 376
23: 2 thy throat, if thou *be* a **m** given to appetite. 1167
23:21 and drowsiness shall clothe *a m* with rags. NIH
24: 5 A wise **m** *is* strong; yea, a man of 1397
24: 5 yea, a **m** of knowledge increaseth strength. 376
24:12 shall *not* he render to *every* **m** according to 120
24:15 O wicked *m*, against the dwelling of NIH
24:16 For a just *m* falleth seven *times,* and NIH
24:20 For there shall be no reward to the evil *m*; NIH
24:26 *Every m* shall kiss *his* lips that giveth a NIH
24:29 I will render to the **m** according to his work. 376
24:30 by the vineyard of the **m** void of 120
24:34 that travelleth; and thy want as an armed **m**. 376
25:18 A **m** that beareth false witness against his 376
25:19 Confidence in an unfaithful *m* in time of NIH
25:26 A righteous *m* falling down before NIH
26:12 Seest thou a **m** wise in his own conceit? 376
26:13 The slothful *m* saith, *There is* a lion in NIH
26:18 As a mad *m* who casteth firebrands, arrows, NIH
26:19 So *is* the **m** *that* deceiveth his neighbour, and 376
26:21 to fire; so *is* a contentious **m** to kindle strife. 376
27: 2 Let another *m* praise thee, and not thine NIH
27: 8 so *is* a **m** that wandereth from his place. 376
27:12 A prudent *m* foreseeth the evil, *and* NIH
27:17 a **m** sharpeneth the countenance of his 376
27:19 *answereth* to face, so the heart of **m** to man. 120
27:19 *answereth* to face, so the heart of man to **m**. 120
27:20 so the eyes of **m** are never satisfied. 120
27:21 the furnace for gold; so *is* a **m** to his praise. 376
28: 1 The wicked flee when **no m** pursueth: but 369
28: 2 by a **m** of understanding *and* knowledge 120
28: 3 A poor **m** that oppresseth the poor *is like* a 1397
28:11 The rich **m** *is* wise in his own conceit; but 376
28:12 but when the wicked rise, a **m** is hidden. 120
28:14 Happy *is* the **m** that feareth alway: but 120
28:17 A **m** that doeth violence to the blood of *any* 120
28:17 shall flee to the pit; let no **m** stay him. NIH
28:20 A faithful **m** shall abound with blessings: but 376
28:21 for for a piece of bread *that* **m** will 1397
28:23 He that rebuketh a **m**, afterwards shall find 120
29: 5 A **m** that flattereth his neighbour spreadeth 1397
29: 6 In the transgression of an evil **m** *there is* a 376
29: 9 If a wise **m** contendeth with a foolish man, 376
29: 9 If a wise man contendeth with a foolish **m**, 376
29:11 but a wise *m* keepeth it in *till* afterwards. NIH
29:13 The poor and the deceitful **m** meet together: 376
29:20 Seest thou a **m** that is hasty in his words? 376
29:22 An angry **m** stirreth up strife, and a furious 376
29:22 and a furious **m** aboundeth in transgression. 1167
29:25 The fear of **m** bringeth a snare: but 120
29:27 An unjust **m** is an abomination to the just: 376
30: 1 the **m** spake unto Ithiel, even unto Ithiel 1397
30: 2 Surely I *am* more brutish than *any* **m**, and 376
30: 2 and have not the understanding of a **m**. 120
30:19 of the sea; and the way of a **m** with a maid. 1397
Ecc 1: 3 What profit hath a **m** of all his labour which 120
1: 8 **m** cannot utter *it:* the eye is not satisfied with 376
1:13 to the sons of **m** to be exercised therewith. 120
2:12 for what *can* the **m** *do* that cometh after 120
2:16 And how dieth the wise *m*? as the fool. NIH
2:18 I should leave it unto the **m** that shall be 120
2:19 who knoweth whether he shall be a wise *m* NIH
2:21 For there is a **m** whose labour *is* in wisdom, 120
2:21 yet to a **m** that hath not laboured therein 120
2:22 For what hath **m** of all his labour, and of 120
2:24 *There is* nothing better for a **m**, *than* that he 120
2:26 For *God* giveth to a **m** that *is* good in his 120
3:11 that no **m** can find out the work that God 120
3:12 for *a m* to rejoice, and to do good in his life. NIH
3:13 And also that every **m** should eat and drink, 120
3:19 that a **m** hath no preeminence above a beast: 120
3:21 Who knoweth the spirit of **m** that 120+1121
3:22 than that a **m** should rejoice in his own 120
4: 4 that for this a **m** is envied of his neighbour. 376
5:12 The sleep of a labouring *m is* sweet, NIH
5:19 Every **m** also to whom God hath given 120
6: 2 A **m** to whom God hath given riches, wealth, 376
6: 3 If a **m** beget an hundred *children,* and 376
6: 7 All the labour of **m** *is* for his mouth, and 120
6:10 named already, and *it is* known that it *is* **m**: 120
6:11 that increase vanity, what *is* **m** the better? 120

M

Ecc	6:12	For who knoweth what *is* good for **m** in *this*	120
	6:12	for who can tell a **m** what shall be after him	120
	7: 5	than for a **m** to hear the song of fools.	376
	7: 7	Surely oppression maketh a wise *m* mad;	NIH
	7:14	to the end that **m** should find nothing after	120
	7:15	there is a just *m* that perisheth in his	NIH
	7:15	there is a wicked *m* that prolongeth *his life*	NIH
	7:20	For *there is* not a just **m** upon earth,	120
	7:28	one **m** among a thousand have I found; but	120
	7:29	have I found, that God hath made **m** upright;	120
	8: 1	Who *is* as the wise *m*? and who knoweth	NIH
	8: 6	therefore the misery of **m** *is* great upon him.	120
	8: 8	*There is* no **m** that hath power over the spirit	120
	8: 9	*there is* a time wherein one **m** ruleth over	120
	8:15	a **m** hath no better *thing* under the sun,	120
	8:17	that a **m** cannot find out the work that is	120
	8:17	because though a **m** labour to seek *it* out,	120
	8:17	though a wise *m* think to know *it,* yet shall	NIH
	9: 1	no **m** knoweth either love or hatred *by* all	120
	9:12	For **m** also knoweth not his time: as	120
	9:15	Now there was found in it a poor wise **m**,	376
	9:15	yet no **m** remembered that *same* poor man.	120
	9:15	yet no man remembered that *same* poor **m**.	376
	10:14	a **m** cannot tell what shall be; and what shall	120
	11: 8	if a **m** live many years, *and* rejoice in them	120
	11: 9	Rejoice, O **young m**, in thy youth; and	970
	12: 5	because **m** goeth to his long home, and	120
	12:13	for this *is* the whole *duty of* **m**.	120
SS	3: 8	**every m** *hath* his sword upon his thigh	376
	8: 7	if a **m** would give all the substance of his	376
Isa	2: 9	the mean **m** boweth down, and the great man	120
	2: 9	and the great **m** humbleth himself;	376
	2:11	The lofty looks of **m** shall be humbled, and	120
	2:17	And the loftiness of **m** shall be bowed down,	120
	2:20	In that day a **m** shall cast his idols of silver,	120
	2:22	Cease ye from **m**, whose breath *is* in his	120
	3: 2	The mighty *m*, and the man of war,	NIH
	3: 2	The mighty *man,* and the **m** of war,	376
	3: 3	the honourable *m*, and the counseller, and	NIH
	3: 6	When a **m** shall take hold of his brother *of*	376
	4: 1	day seven women shall take hold of one **m**,	376
	5:15	And the mean **m** shall be brought down, and	120
	5:15	the mighty **m** shall be humbled, and the eyes	376
	6: 5	because I *am* a **m** of unclean lips, and	376
	6:11	the houses without **m**, and the land be utterly	120
	7:21	*that* a **m** shall nourish a young cow, and	376
	9:19	fuel of the fire: no **m** shall spare his brother.	376
	9:20	they shall eat **every m** the flesh of his own	376
	10:13	put down the inhabitants like a valiant *m*:	NIH
	13:12	I will make a **m** more precious than fine	582
	13:12	even a **m** than the golden wedge of Ophir.	120
	13:14	and as a sheep that no *m* taketh up:	NIH
	13:14	they shall **every m** turn to his own people,	376
	14:16	*saying, Is* this the **m** that made the earth to	376
	17: 7	At that day shall a **m** look to his Maker, and	120
	19:14	as a drunken *m* staggereth in his vomit.	NIH
	24:10	house is shut up, that no *m may* come in.	NIH
	28:20	For the bed is shorter than that *a m* can	NIH
	29: 8	It shall even be as when a hungry *m*	NIH
	29: 8	or as when a thirsty *m* dreameth, and	NIH
	29:21	That make a **m** an offender for a word, and	120
	31: 7	For in that day **every m** shall cast away his	376
	31: 8	fall with the sword, not of a mighty **m**;	376
	31: 8	the sword, not of a mean **m**, shall devour	120
	32: 2	a **m** shall be as a hiding place from the wind,	376
	33: 8	lie waste, the **wayfaring m** ceaseth:	734+5674
	33: 8	hath despised the cities, he regardeth no **m**.	582
	35: 6	shall the lame *m* leap as a hart, and	NIH
	36: 6	whereon if a **m** lean, it will go into his hand,	376
	38:11	I shall behold **m** no more with	120
	41: 2	Who raised up the righteous *m* from	NIH
	41:28	For I beheld, and *there was* no **m**;	376
	42:13	The LORD shall go forth as a mighty *m*,	NIH
	42:13	he shall stir up jealousy like a **m** of war:	376
	44:13	maketh it after the figure of a **m**,	376
	44:13	of a man, according to the beauty of a **m**;	120
	44:15	shall it be for a **m** to burn: for he will take	120
	45:12	have made the earth, and created **m** upon it:	120
	46:11	the **m** that executeth my counsel from a far	376
	47: 3	and I will not meet *thee as* a **m**.	120
	49: 7	his Holy One, to him whom **m** despiseth,	5315
	50: 2	Wherefore, when I came, *was there* no **m**?	376
	51:12	that thou shouldest be afraid of a **m** *that* shall	582
	51:12	of the son of **m** *which* shall be made *as*	120
	52:14	his visage *was* so marred more than *any* **m**,	376
	53: 3	a **m** of sorrows, and acquainted with grief:	376
	55: 7	his way, and the unrighteous **m** his thoughts:	376
	56: 2	Blessed *is* the **m** *that* doeth this, and the son	582
	56: 2	and the son of **m** *that* layeth hold on it;	120
	57: 1	and no **m** layeth *it* to heart:	376
	58: 5	a day for a **m** to afflict his soul? *is it* to bow	120
	59:16	he saw that *there was* no **m**, and	376
	60:15	that **no m** went through *thee,* I will make	369
	62: 5	For *as* a **young m** marrieth a virgin, *so*	970
	65:20	nor an **old m** that hath not filled his days:	2205
	66: 2	to this *m* will I look, *even to him that is*	NIH
	66: 3	He that killeth an ox *is as if* he slew a **m**;	376
	66: 7	pain came, she was delivered of a **m child**.	2145
Jer	2: 6	through a land that no **m** passed through, and	376
	2: 6	man passed through, and where no **m** dwelt?	120
	3: 1	If a **m** put away his wife, and she go from	376
	4:25	lo, *there was* no **m**, and all the birds of	120
	4:29	*shall be* forsaken, and not a **m** dwell therein.	376
	5: 1	the broad places thereof, if ye can find a **m**,	376
	7: 5	throughly execute judgment between a **m**	376
	7:20	upon **m**, and upon beast, and upon the trees	120
	8: 6	no **m** repented him of his wickedness,	376
	9:12	Who *is* the wise **m**, that may understand	376
	9:23	Let not the wise *m* glory in his wisdom,	NIH
	9:23	neither let the mighty *m* glory in his might,	NIH
	9:23	let not the rich *m* glory in his riches:	NIH
	10:14	Every **m** is brutish in *his* knowledge:	120
	10:23	I know that the way of **m** *is* not in himself:	120
	10:23	*it is* not in **m** that walketh to direct his steps.	376
	11: 3	Cursed *be* the **m** that obeyeth not the words	376
	12:11	because no **m** layeth *it* to heart.	376
	12:15	**every m** to his heritage, and every man to	376
	12:15	man to his heritage, and **every m** to his land.	376
	13:11	For as the girdle cleaveth to the loins of a **m**,	376
	14: 8	as a **wayfaring m** *that* turneth aside to tarry	732
	14: 9	Why shouldest thou be as a **m** astonied, as a	376
	14: 9	as a mighty *m that* cannot save?	NIH
	15:10	that thou hast borne me a **m** of strife and	376
	15:10	and a **m** of contention to the whole earth!	376
	16:20	Shall a **m** make gods unto himself, and	120
	17: 5	Cursed *be* the **m** that trusteth in man, and	1397
	17: 5	Cursed *be* the man that trusteth in **m**, and	120
	17: 7	Blessed *is* the **m** that trusteth in	1397
	17:10	even to give **every m** according to his ways,	376
	18:14	Will *a m* leave the snow of Lebanon *which*	NIH
	20:15	Cursed *be* the **m** who brought tidings to my	376
	20:15	saying, A **m** child is born unto thee;	2145
	20:16	let that **m** be as the cities which the LORD	376
	21: 6	the inhabitants of this city, both **m** and beast:	120
	22: 8	and they shall say **every m** to his neighbour,	376
	22:28	*Is* this **m** Coniah a despised broken idol?	376
	22:30	saith the LORD, Write ye this **m** childless,	376
	22:30	a **m** *that* shall not prosper in his days:	1397
	22:30	for no **m** of his seed shall prosper,	376
	23: 9	I am like a drunken **m**, and like a man whom	376
	23: 9	like a **m** whom wine hath overcome,	1397
	23:27	which they tell **every m** to his neighbour,	376
	23:34	I will even punish that **m** and his house.	376
	26: 3	and turn **every m** from his evil way,	376
	26:11	the people, saying, This **m** *is* worthy to die;	376
	26:16	to the prophets; This **m** *is* not worthy to die:	376
	26:20	there was also a **m** that prophesied in	376
	27: 5	the **m** and the beast that *are* upon the ground,	120
	29:26	for every **m** *that is* mad, and maketh himself	376
	29:32	he shall not have a **m** to dwell among this	376
	30: 6	see whether a **m** doth travail with child?	2145
	30: 6	wherefore do I see every **m** *with* his hands	1397
	30:17	This *is* Zion, whom **no m** seeketh after.	369
	31:22	in the earth, A woman shall compass a **m**.	1397
	31:27	and the house of Judah *with* the seed of **m**,	120
	31:30	every **m** that eateth the sour grape, his teeth	120
	31:34	they shall teach no more **every m** his	376
	31:34	**every m** his brother, saying, Know	376
	32:43	ye say, *It is* desolate without **m** or beast;	120
	33:10	which ye say *shall be* desolate without **m**	120
	33:10	without **m**, and without inhabitant, and	120
	33:12	*which is* desolate without **m** and	120
	33:17	David shall never want a **m** to sit upon	376
	33:18	shall the priests the Levites want a **m**	376
	34: 9	That **every m** should let his manservant, and	376
	34: 9	**every m** his maidservant, *being* a Hebrew	376
	34:14	At the end of seven years let ye go **every m**	376
	34:15	in proclaiming liberty **every m** to his	376

Jer	34:16	caused **every m** his servant, and every man	376
	34:16	man his servant, and **every m** his handmaid,	376
	34:17	to his brother, and **every m** to his neighbour:	376
	35: 4	of Hanan, the son of Igdaliah, a **m** of God,	376
	35:15	Return ye now **every m** from his evil way,	376
	35:19	not want a **m** to stand before me for ever.	376
	36: 3	that they may return **every m** from his evil	376
	36:19	Jeremiah; and let no **m** know where ye *be.*	376
	36:29	shall cause to cease from thence **m** and	120
	37:10	*yet* should they rise up **every m** in his tent,	376
	38: 4	We beseech thee, let this **m** be put to death:	376
	38: 4	for this **m** seeketh not the welfare of this	376
	38:24	Let no **m** know of these words, and	376
	40:15	no **m** shall know *it:* wherefore should he slay	376
	41: 4	*he* had slain Gedaliah, and no **m** knew *it,*	376
	44: 2	*are* a desolation, and **no m** dwelleth therein,	369
	44: 7	to cut off from you **m** and woman, child and	376
	44:26	of any **m** of Judah in all the land of Egypt,	376
	46: 6	swift flee away, nor the mighty *m* escape;	NIH
	46:12	for the mighty *m* hath stumbled against	NIH
	49: 5	ye shall be driven out **every m** right forth;	376
	49:18	saith the LORD, no **m** shall abide there,	376
	49:18	neither shall a son of **m** dwell in it.	120
	49:19	who *is* a chosen *m, that* I may appoint over	NIH
	49:33	there shall no **m** abide there, nor *any* son of	376
	49:33	abide there, nor *any* son of **m** dwell in it.	120
	50: 3	they shall depart, both **m** and beast.	120
	50: 9	mighty expert *m;* none shall return in vain.	NIH
	50:40	*so* shall no **m** abide there, neither shall any	376
	50:40	neither shall any son of **m** dwell therein.	120
	50:42	in array, like a **m** to the battle, against thee,	376
	50:44	who *is* a chosen *m, that* I may appoint over	NIH
	51: 6	of Babylon, and deliver **every m** his soul:	376
	51:17	Every **m** is brutish by *his* knowledge;	120
	51:22	With thee also will I break in pieces **m** and	376
	51:22	with thee will I break in pieces the **young m**	970
	51:43	a wilderness, a land wherein no **m** dwelleth,	376
	51:43	neither doth *any* son of **m** pass thereby.	120
	51:45	deliver ye **every m** his soul from the fierce	376
	51:62	neither **m** nor beast, but that it shall be	120
La	3: 1	I *am* the **m** *that* hath seen affliction by	1397
	3:26	*It is* good *that a* **m** *should* both hope and	NIH
	3:27	*It is* good for a **m** that he bear the yoke in	1397
	3:35	To turn aside the right of a **m** before	1397
	3:36	To subvert a **m** in his cause, the Lord	120
	3:39	Wherefore doth a living **m** complain, a man	120
	3:39	a **m** for the punishment of his sins?	1397
	4: 4	ask bread, *and* **no m** breaketh *it* unto them.	369
Eze	1: 5	they had the likeness of a **m.**	120
	1: 8	*they had* the hands of a **m** under their wings	120
	1:10	they four had the face of a **m,** and the face of	120
	1:26	as the appearance of a **m** above upon it.	120
	2: 1	Son of **m,** stand upon thy feet, and I will	120
	2: 3	he said unto me, Son of **m,** I send thee to	120
	2: 6	thou, son of **m,** be not afraid of them,	120
	2: 8	thou, son of **m,** hear what I say unto thee;	120
	3: 1	said unto me, Son of **m,** eat that thou findest;	120
	3: 3	he said unto me, Son of **m,** cause thy belly to	120
	3: 4	he said unto me, Son of **m,** go, get thee unto	120
	3:10	Moreover he said unto me, Son of **m,** all my	120
	3:17	Son of **m,** I have made thee a watchman	120
	3:18	the same wicked *m* shall die in his iniquity;	NIH
	3:20	When a righteous *m* doth turn from his	NIH
	3:21	Nevertheless if thou warn the righteous *m,*	NIH
	3:25	thou, O son of **m,** behold, they shall put	120
	4: 1	Thou also, son of **m,** take thee a tile, and	120
	4:12	shalt bake it with dung that cometh out of **m,**	120
	4:16	he said unto me, Son of **m,** behold,	120
	5: 1	And thou, son of **m,** take thee a sharp knife,	120
	6: 2	Son of **m,** set thy face towards the mountains	120
	7: 2	Also, thou son of **m,** thus saith the Lord	120
	8: 5	said he unto me, Son of **m,** lift up thine eyes	120
	8: 6	unto me, Son of **m,** seest thou what they do?	120
	8: 8	he unto me, Son of **m,** dig now in the wall:	120
	8:11	with **every m** his censer in his hand;	376
	8:12	said he unto me, Son of **m,** hast thou seen	120
	8:12	**every m** in the chambers of his imagery?	376
	8:15	he unto me, Hast thou seen *this,* O son of **m?**	120
	8:17	unto me, Hast thou seen *this,* O son of **m?**	120
	9: 1	even **every m** *with* his destroying weapon in	376
	9: 2	and **every m** a slaughter weapon in his hand;	376
	9: 2	one **m** among them *was* clothed *with* linen,	376
	9: 3	he called to the **m** clothed *with* linen,	376
	9: 6	come not near any **m** upon whom *is*	376
	9:11	behold, the **m** clothed with linen, which *had*	376
	10: 2	And he spake unto the **m** clothed with linen,	376
	10: 3	right side of the house, when the **m** went in;	376
	10: 6	*that* when he had commanded the **m** clothed	376
	10:14	and the second face *was* the face of a **m,** and	120
	10:21	the likeness of the hands of a **m** *was* under	120
	11: 2	said he unto me, Son of **m,** these *are* the men	120
	11: 4	against them, prophesy, O son of **m.**	120
	11:15	Son of **m,** thy brethren, *even* thy brethren,	120
	12: 2	Son of **m,** thou dwellest in the midst of a	120
	12: 3	Therefore thou son of **m,** prepare thee stuff	120
	12: 9	Son of **m,** hath not the house of Israel,	120
	12:18	Son of **m,** eat thy bread with quaking, and	120
	12:22	Son of **m,** what *is* that proverb *that* ye have	120
	12:27	Son of **m,** behold, *they of* the house of Israel	120
	13: 2	Son of **m,** prophesy against the prophets of	120
	13:17	Likewise thou son of **m,** set thy face against	120
	14: 3	Son of **m,** these men have set up their idols	120
	14: 4	**Every m** of the house of Israel that	376+376
	14: 8	I will set my face against that **m,** and	376
	14:13	Son of **m,** when the land sinneth against me	120
	14:13	upon it, and will cut off **m** and beast from it:	120
	14:15	that **no m** may pass through because of	1097
	14:17	so that I cut off **m** and beast from it:	120
	14:19	it in blood, to cut off from it **m** and beast:	120
	14:21	to cut off from it **m** and beast?	120
	15: 2	Son of **m,** What is the vine tree more than	120
	16: 2	Son of **m,** cause Jerusalem to know her	120
	17: 2	Son of **m,** put forth a riddle, and speak a	120
	18: 5	if a **m** be just, and do that which is lawful	376
	18: 8	hath executed true judgment between **m** and	376
	18: 8	executed true judgment between man and **m,**	376
	18:24	the abominations that the wicked *m* doeth,	NIH
	18:26	When a righteous *m* turneth away from his	NIH
	18:27	when the wicked *m* turneth away from his	NIH
	20: 3	Son of **m,** speak unto the elders of Israel,	120
	20: 4	Wilt thou judge them, son of **m,** wilt thou	120
	20: 7	Cast ye away **every m** the abominations of	376
	20: 8	they did not **every m** cast away	376
	20:11	which *if* a **m** do, he shall even live in them.	120
	20:13	which *if* a **m** do, he shall even live in them;	120
	20:21	which *if* a **m** do, he shall even live in them;	120
	20:27	Therefore, son of **m,** speak unto the house of	120
	20:46	Son of **m,** set thy face toward the south, and	120
	21: 2	Son of **m,** set thy face toward Jerusalem, and	120
	21: 6	Sigh therefore, thou son of **m,** with	120
	21: 9	Son of **m,** prophesy, and say, Thus saith	120
	21:12	Cry and howl, son of **m:** for it shall be upon	120
	21:14	son of **m,** prophesy, and smite *thine* hands	120
	21:19	Also, thou son of **m,** appoint thee two ways,	120
	21:28	thou, son of **m,** prophesy and say, Thus saith	120
	22: 2	Now, thou son of **m,** wilt thou judge, wilt	120
	22:18	Son of **m,** the house of Israel is to me	120
	22:24	Son of **m,** say unto her, Thou *art* the land	120
	22:30	I sought for a **m** among them, that *should*	376
	23: 2	Son of **m,** there were two women,	120
	23:36	Son of **m,** wilt thou judge Aholah and	120
	24: 2	Son of **m,** write thee the name of the day,	120
	24:16	Son of **m,** behold, I take away from thee	120
	24:25	Also, thou son of **m,** *shall it* not *be* in the day	120
	25: 2	Son of **m,** set thy face against	120
	25:13	and will cut off **m** and beast from it;	120
	26: 2	Son of **m,** because that Tyrus hath said	120
	27: 2	Now, thou son of **m,** take up a lamentation	120
	28: 2	Son of **m,** say unto the prince of Tyrus,	120
	28: 2	yet thou *art* a **m,** and not God, though thou	120
	28: 9	thou *shalt be* a **m,** and no God, in the hand of	120
	28:12	Son of **m,** take up a lamentation upon	120
	28:21	Son of **m,** set thy face against Zidon, and	120
	29: 2	Son of **m,** set thy face against Pharaoh king	120
	29: 8	and cut off **m** and beast out of thee.	120
	29:11	No foot of **m** shall pass through it, nor foot	120
	29:18	Son of **m,** Nebuchadrezzar king of Babylon	120
	30: 2	Son of **m,** prophesy and say, Thus saith	120
	30:21	Son of **m,** I have broken the arm of Pharaoh	120
	30:24	*with* the groanings of a deadly wounded *m.*	NIH
	31: 2	Son of **m,** speak unto Pharaoh king of Egypt,	120
	32: 2	Son of **m,** take up a lamentation for Pharaoh	120
	32:10	**every m** for his own life, in the day of thy	376
	32:13	neither shall the foot of **m** trouble them any	120
	32:18	Son of **m,** wail for the multitude of Egypt,	120
	33: 2	Son of **m,** speak to the children of thy	120
	33: 2	if the people of the land take a **m** of their	376
	33: 7	So thou, O son of **m,** I have set thee a	120

Eze	33: 8	O wicked *m*, thou shalt surely die;	NIH
	33: 8	that wicked *m* shall die in his iniquity;	NIH
	33:10	Therefore, O thou son of **m**, speak unto	120
	33:12	Therefore, thou son of **m**, say unto	120
	33:24	Son of **m**, they that inhabit those wastes of	120
	33:30	Also, thou son of **m**, the children of thy	120
	34: 2	Son of **m**, prophesy against the shepherds of	120
	35: 2	Son of **m**, set thy face against mount Seir,	120
	36: 1	Also, thou son of **m**, prophesy unto	120
	36:11	I will multiply upon you **m** and beast; and	120
	36:17	Son of **m**, when the house of Israel dwelt in	120
	37: 3	unto me, Son of **m**, can these bones live?	120
	37: 9	prophesy, son of **m**, and say to the wind,	120
	37:11	he said unto me, Son of **m**, these bones *are*	120
	37:16	Moreover, thou son of **m**, take thee one	120
	38: 2	Son of **m**, set thy face against Gog, the land	120
	38:14	son of **m**, prophesy and say unto Gog,	120
	39: 1	Therefore thou son of **m**, prophesy against	120
	39:17	thou son of **m**, thus saith the Lord GOD;	120
	40: 3	me thither, and behold, *there was* a **m**,	376
	40: 4	the **m** said unto me, Son of man, behold with	376
	40: 4	Son of **m**, behold with thine eyes, and	120
	41:19	So that the face of a **m** *was* toward the palm	120
	43: 6	me out of the house; and *the* **m** stood by me.	376
	43: 7	he said unto me, Son of **m**, the place of my	120
	43:10	Thou son of **m**, shew the house to the house	120
	43:18	he said unto me, Son of **m**, thus saith	120
	44: 2	not be opened, and no **m** shall enter in by it;	376
	44: 5	Son of **m**, mark well, and behold with thine	120
	46:18	that my people be not scattered **every m**	376
	47: 3	when the **m** that had the line in his hand	376
	47: 6	he said unto me, Son of **m**, hast thou seen	120
	47:20	till *a m* come over against Hamath.	NIH
Da	2:10	There is not a **m** upon the earth that can	606
	2:25	I have found a **m** of the captives of Judah,	1400
	2:48	the king made Daniel a great **m**, and	NIH
	3:10	that every **m** that shall hear the sound of	606
	5:11	There is a **m** in thy kingdom, in whom *is*	1400
	6: 7	a petition of any God or **m** for thirty days,	606
	6:12	that every **m** that shall ask *a petition* of any	606
	6:12	*petition* of any God or **m** within thirty days,	606
	7: 4	made stand upon the feet as a **m**, and	606
	7: 8	in this horn *were* eyes like the eyes of **m**,	606
	7:13	*one* like the Son of **m** came with the clouds	606
	8:15	stood before me as the appearance of a **m**.	1397
	8:16	make this *m* to understand the vision.	NIH
	8:17	he said unto me, Understand, O son of **m**:	120
	9:21	*was* speaking in prayer, even the **m** Gabriel,	376
	10: 5	and behold, a certain **m** clothed *in* linen,	376
	10:11	said unto me, O Daniel, a **m** greatly beloved,	376
	10:18	touched me *one* like the appearance of a **m**,	120
	10:19	said, O **m** greatly beloved, fear not: peace *be*	376
	12: 6	*one* said to the **m** clothed in linen,	376
	12: 7	I heard the **m** clothed in linen, which *was*	376
Hos	3: 3	and thou shalt not be for *another* **m**:	376
	4: 4	Yet let no **m** strive, nor reprove another:	376
	6: 9	as troops *of robbers* wait for a **m**, *so*	376
	9: 7	the spiritual **m** *is* mad, for the multitude of	376
	9:12	*that there shall* not *be* a **m** *left*: yea,	120
	11: 4	I drew them with cords of a **m**, with bands of	120
	11: 9	for I *am* God, and not **m**; the Holy One in	376
Am	2: 7	a **m** and his father will go in unto the *same*	376
	4:13	and declareth unto **m** what *is* his thought,	120
	5:19	As if a **m** did flee from a lion, and a bear met	376
Jnh	1: 5	cried **every m** unto his god, and cast forth	376
	3: 7	his nobles, saying, Let neither **m** nor beast,	120
	3: 8	let **m** and beast be covered with sackcloth,	120
Mic	2: 2	so they oppress a **m** and his house, even a	1397
	2: 2	and his house, even a **m** and his heritage.	376
	2:11	If a **m** walking *in* the spirit and falsehood do	376
	4: 4	But they shall sit **every m** under his vine and	376
	5: 5	this *m* shall be *the* peace, when the Assyrian	NIH
	5: 7	upon the grass, that tarrieth not for **m**,	376
	6: 8	He hath shewed thee, O **m**, what *is* good;	120
	6: 9	and *the m of* wisdom shall see thy name:	NIH
	7: 2	The good *m* is perished out of the earth: and	NIH
	7: 2	they hunt **every m** his brother *with* a net.	376
	7: 3	the great *m*, he uttereth his mischievous	NIH
Na	3:18	the mountains, and no **m** gathereth *them*.	NIH
Hab	1:13	*the m that is* more righteous than he?	NIH
	2: 5	*he is* a proud **m**, neither keepeth at home,	1397
Zep	1: 3	I will consume **m** and beast; I will consume	120
	1: 3	I will cut off **m** from off the land, saith	120
	1:14	the mighty *m* shall cry there bitterly.	NIH
	3: 6	cities are destroyed, so that there is no **m**,	376
Hag	1: 9	and ye run **every m** unto his own house.	376
Zec	1: 8	and behold a **m** riding upon a red horse, and	376
	1:10	the **m** that stood among the myrtle trees	376
	1:21	so that no **m** did lift up his head:	376
	2: 1	a **m** with a measuring line in his hand.	376
	2: 4	Run, speak to this **young m**, saying,	5288
	3:10	shall ye call **every m** his neighbour, under	376
	4: 1	as a **m** that is wakened out of his sleep,	376
	6:12	Behold the **m** whose name *is* The BRANCH;	376
	7: 9	and compassions **every m** to his brother:	376
	7:14	that no **m** passed through nor returned:	NIH
	8: 4	**every m** with his staff in his hand for very	376
	8:10	before these days there was no hire for **m**,	120
	8:16	Speak ye **every m** the truth to his neighbour;	376
	9: 1	when the eyes of **m**, as of all the tribes of	120
	9:13	and made thee as the sword of a mighty *m*.	NIH
	10: 7	*they of* Ephraim shall be like a mighty *m*,	NIH
	12: 1	and formeth the spirit of **m** within him.	120
	13: 5	for **m** taught me *to keep cattle* from my	120
	13: 7	and against the **m** *that is* my fellow,	1397
Mal	2:10	why do we deal treacherously **every m**	376
	2:12	The LORD will cut off the **m** that doth this,	376
	3: 8	Will a **m** rob God? Yet ye *have* robbed me.	120
	3:17	as a **m** spareth his own son that serveth him.	376
Mt	1:19	being a just *m*, and not willing to make her	NIG
	4: 4	**M** shall not live by bread alone, but by every	*444*
	5:40	And if any **m** will sue thee at the law, and	NIG
	6:24	No *m* can serve two masters: for either he	NIG
	7: 9	Or what **m** is there of you, whom if his son	*444*
	7:24	doeth them, I will liken him unto a wise **m**,	*435*
	7:26	them not, shall be likened unto a foolish **m**,	*435*
	8: 4	See thou tell no *m*; but go thy way,	NIG
	8: 9	For I am a **m** under authority,	*444*
	8: 9	and I say to this *m*, Go, and he goeth; and	NIG
	8:20	the Son of **m** hath not where to lay *his* head.	*444*
	8:27	saying, **What manner of m** is this,	*4217*
	8:28	so that no *m* might pass by that way.	NIG
	9: 2	they brought to him a **m sick of the palsy**,	*3885*
	9: 3	within themselves, This *m* blasphemeth.	NIG
	9: 6	But that ye may know that the Son of **m** hath	*444*
	9: 9	he saw a **m**, named Matthew, sitting at	*444*
	9:16	No *m* putteth a piece of new cloth unto an	NIG
	9:30	saying, See *that* no **m** know *it*.	NIG
	9:32	they brought to him a dumb **m** possessed	*444*
	10:23	the cities of Israel, till the Son of **m** be come.	*444*
	10:35	For I am come to set a **m** at variance against	*444*
	10:41	he that receiveth a righteous *m* in the name	NIG
	10:41	*m* shall receive a righteous *man's* reward.	NIG
	11: 8	A **m** clothed in soft raiment? behold,	*444*
	11:19	The Son of **m** came eating and drinking, and	*444*
	11:19	Behold a **m** gluttonous, and a winebibber,	*444*
	11:27	and no *m* knoweth the Son, but the Father;	NIG
	11:27	neither knoweth any *m* the Father, save	NIG
	12: 8	For the Son of **m** is Lord even of the sabbath	*444*
	12:10	there was a **m** which had *his* hand withered.	*444*
	12:11	What **m** shall there be among you,	*444*
	12:12	How much then is a **m** better than a sheep?	*444*
	12:13	Then saith he to the **m**, Stretch forth thine	*444*
	12:19	neither shall any *m* hear his voice in	NIG
	12:29	except he first bind the strong *m*? and then	NIG
	12:32	speaketh a word against the Son of **m**,	*444*
	12:35	A good **m** out of the good treasure of	*444*
	12:35	an evil **m** out of the evil treasure bringeth	*444*
	12:40	so shall the Son of **m** be three days and	*444*
	12:43	When the unclean spirit is gone out of a **m**,	*444*
	12:45	the last *state* of that **m** is worse than the first.	*444*
	13:24	The kingdom of heaven is likened unto a **m**	*444*
	13:31	which a **m** took, and sowed in his field:	*444*
	13:37	that soweth the good seed is the Son of **m**;	*444*
	13:41	The Son of **m** shall send forth his angels,	*444*
	13:44	the which when a **m** hath found, he hideth,	*444*
	13:45	of heaven is like unto a merchant **m**,	*444*
	13:52	heaven is like unto a **m** *that is* a householder,	*444*
	13:54	Whence hath this *m* this wisdom, and	NIG
	13:56	Whence then hath this *m* all these *things*?	NIG
	15:11	which goeth into the mouth defileth a **m**;	*444*
	15:11	cometh out of the mouth, this defileth the **m**.	*444*
	15:18	forth from the heart; and they defile the **m**.	*444*
	15:20	These are *the things* which defile a **m**: but	*444*
	15:20	to eat with unwashen hands defileth not a **m**.	*444*
	16:13	Whom do men say that I the Son of **m** am?	*444*
	16:20	tell no *m* that he was Jesus the Christ.	NIG
	16:24	If any *m* will come after me, let him deny	NIG

Mt	16:26	For what is a **m** profited, if he shall gain	*444*
	16:26	what shall a **m** give in exchange for his soul?	*444*
	16:27	For the Son of **m** shall come in the glory of	*444*
	16:27	he shall reward **every m** according to his	*1538*
	16:28	till they see the Son of **m** coming in his	*444*
	17: 8	their eyes, they saw no *m*, save Jesus only.	NIG
	17: 9	Tell the vision to no *m*, until the Son of man	NIG
	17: 9	Tell the vision to no *man*, until the Son of **m**	*444*
	17:12	Likewise shall also the Son of **m** suffer of	*444*
	17:14	there came to him a *certain* **m**,	*444*
	17:22	The Son of **m** shall be betrayed into	*444*
	18: 7	woe to that **m** by whom the offence cometh.	*444*
	18:11	For the Son of **m** is come to save that which	*444*
	18:12	if a **m** have an hundred sheep, and one of	*444*
	18:17	let him be unto thee as a heathen *m* and	NIG
	19: 3	Is it lawful for a **m** to put away his wife for	*444*
	19: 5	For this cause shall a **m** leave father and	*444*
	19: 6	hath joined together, let not **m** put asunder.	*444*
	19:10	If the case of the **m** be so with *his* wife, it is	*444*
	19:20	The **young m** saith unto him, All these	*3495*
	19:22	But when the **young m** heard *that* saying,	*3495*
	19:23	That a rich *m* shall hardly enter into	NIG
	19:24	than for a rich *m* to enter into the kingdom	NIG
	19:28	when the Son of **m** shall sit in the throne of	*444*
	20: 1	For the kingdom of heaven is like unto a **m**	*444*
	20: 7	say unto him, Because no *m* hath hired us.	NIG
	20: 9	they received **every m** a penny.	*303*
	20:10	and they likewise received **every m** a penny.	*303*
	20:18	the Son of **m** shall be betrayed unto the chief	*444*
	20:28	Even as the Son of **m** came not to be	*444*
	21: 3	And if any *m* say ought unto you, ye shall	NIG
	21:28	A *certain* **m** had two sons; and he came to	*444*
	22:11	he saw there a **m** which had not on a	*444*
	22:16	neither carest thou for any *m*: for thou	NIG
	22:24	Saying, Master, Moses said, If a **m** die,	*5100*
	22:46	And no *m* was able to answer him a word,	NIG
	22:46	neither durst any *m* from that day forth ask	NIG
	23: 9	And call no *m* your father upon the earth:	NIG
	24: 4	Take heed that no *m* deceive you.	NIG
	24:23	Then if any *m* shall say unto you, Lo,	NIG
	24:27	so shall also the coming of the Son of **m** be.	*444*
	24:30	shall appear the sign of the Son of **m** in	*444*
	24:30	they shall see the Son of **m** coming in	*444*
	24:36	But of that day and hour knoweth no *m*, no,	NIG
	24:37	so shall also the coming of the Son of **m** be.	*444*
	24:39	so shall also the coming of the Son of **m** be.	*444*
	24:44	hour as you think not the Son of **m** cometh.	*444*
	25:13	nor the hour wherein the Son of **m** cometh.	*444*
	25:14	For *the kingdom of heaven is* as a **m**	*444*
	25:15	to **every m** according to his several ability;	*1538*
	25:24	Lord, I knew thee that thou art a hard **m**,	*444*
	25:31	When the Son of **m** shall come in his glory,	*444*
	26: 2	and the Son of **m** is betrayed to be crucified.	*444*
	26:18	Go into the city to **such a m**, and say unto	*1170*
	26:24	The Son of **m** goeth as it is written of him:	*444*
	26:24	woe unto that **m** by whom the Son of man is	*444*
	26:24	woe unto that man by whom the Son of **m** is	*444*
	26:24	it had been good for that **m** if he had not	*444*
	26:45	the Son of **m** is betrayed into the hands of	*444*
	26:64	Hereafter shall ye see the Son of **m** sitting on	*444*
	26:72	he denied with an oath, I do not know the **m**.	*444*
	26:74	and to swear, *saying,* I know not the **m**.	*444*
	27:19	Have thou nothing to do with that just *m*:	NIG
	27:32	they found a **m** of Cyrene, Simon by name:	*444*
	27:47	heard *that,* said, This *m* calleth for Elias.	NIG
	27:57	there came a rich **m** of Arimathea,	*444*
Mk	1:23	And there was in their synagogue a **m** with	*444*
	1:44	See thou say nothing to any *m*: but go thy	NIG
	2: 7	Why doth this *m* thus speak blasphemies?	NIG
	2:10	But that ye may know that the Son of **m** hath	*444*
	2:21	No *m* also seweth a piece of new cloth on	NIG
	2:22	And no *m* putteth new wine into old bottles:	NIG
	2:27	The sabbath was made for **m**, *and* not man	*444*
	2:27	made for man, *and* not **m** for the sabbath:	*444*
	2:28	Therefore the Son of **m** is Lord also of	*444*
	3: 1	there was a **m** there which had a withered	*444*
	3: 3	And he saith unto the **m** which had	*444*
	3: 5	he saith unto the **m**, Stretch forth thine hand.	*444*
	3:27	No *m* can enter into a strong *man's* house,	NIG
	3:27	except he will first bind the strong *m*; and	NIG
	4:23	If any *m* have ears to hear, let him hear.	NIG
	4:26	as if a **m** should cast seed into the ground,	*444*
	4:41	**What** *manner of* **m** is this, that even	*687+5101*
	5: 2	out of the tombs a **m** with an unclean spirit,	*444*
	5: 3	and no *m* could bind him, no, not with	NIG
	5: 4	in pieces: neither could any *m* tame him.	NIG
	5: 8	Come out of the **m**, *thou* unclean spirit.	*444*
	5:37	And he suffered no *m* to follow him,	NIG
	5:43	And he charged them straitly that no *m*	NIG
	6: 2	From whence hath this *m* these *things?* and	NIG
	6:20	knowing that he *was* a just **m** and a holy, and	*435*
	7:11	If a **m** shall say to *his* father or mother,	*444*
	7:15	There is nothing from without a **m**,	*444*
	7:15	out of him, those are they that defile the **m**.	*444*
	7:16	If any *m* have ears to hear, let him hear.	NIG
	7:18	*thing* from without entereth into the **m**,	*444*
	7:20	he said, That which cometh out of the **m**,	*444*
	7:20	cometh out of the man, that defileth the **m**.	*444*
	7:23	*things* come from within, and defile the **m**.	*444*
	7:24	and would have no *m* know *it:* but he could	NIG
	7:36	he charged them that they should tell no *m*:	NIG
	8: 4	From whence can a **m** satisfy these *men*	*5100*
	8:22	and they bring a **blind m** unto him, and	*5185*
	8:23	And he took the **blind m** by the hand, and	*5185*
	8:25	he was restored, and saw every *m* clearly.	NIG
	8:30	them that they should tell no *m* of him.	NIG
	8:31	that the Son of **m** must suffer many *things,*	*444*
	8:36	For what shall it profit a **m**, if he shall gain	*444*
	8:37	Or what shall a **m** give in exchange for his	*444*
	8:38	of him also shall the Son of **m** be ashamed,	*444*
	9: 8	they saw no *m* any more, save Jesus only	NIG
	9: 9	he charged them that they should tell no *m*	NIG
	9: 9	till the Son of **m** were risen from the dead.	*444*
	9:12	and how it is written of the Son of **m**,	*444*
	9:30	he would not that any *m* should know *it.*	NIG
	9:31	The Son of **m** is delivered into the hands of	*444*
	9:35	saith unto them, If any *m* desire to be first,	NIG
	9:39	for there is no *m* which shall do a miracle in	NIG
	10: 2	Is it lawful for a **m** to put away *his* wife?	*435*
	10: 7	For this cause shall a **m** leave his father and	*444*
	10: 9	hath joined together, let not **m** put asunder.	*444*
	10:25	than for a rich *m* to enter into the kingdom	NIG
	10:29	There is no *m* that hath left house, or	NIG
	10:33	the Son of **m** shall be delivered unto	*444*
	10:45	For even the Son of **m** came not to be	*444*
	10:49	And they call the **blind m**, saying unto	*5185*
	10:51	The **blind m** said unto him, Lord, that I	*5185*
	11: 2	shall find a colt tied, whereon never **m** sat;	*444*
	11: 3	And if any *m* say unto you, Why do ye this?	NIG
	11:14	No *m* eat fruit of thee hereafter for ever.	NIG
	11:16	And would not suffer that any *m* should	NIG
	12: 1	A *certain* **m** planted a vineyard, and set a	*444*
	12:14	carest for no *m*: for thou regardest not	NIG
	12:34	And no *m* after that durst ask him *any*	NIG
	13: 5	to say, Take heed lest any *m* deceive you:	NIG
	13:21	And then if any *m* shall say to you, Lo, here	NIG
	13:26	shall they see the Son of **m** coming in	*444*
	13:32	of that day and *that* hour knoweth no *m*, no,	NIG
	13:34	*For the Son of m is* as a man taking a far	NIG
	13:34	*For the Son of man is* as a **m** taking a far	*444*
	13:34	and to **every m** his work, and	*1538*
	14:13	there shall meet you a **m** bearing a pitcher of	*444*
	14:21	The Son of **m** indeed goeth, as it is written	*444*
	14:21	woe to that **m** by whom the Son of man is	*444*
	14:21	woe to that man by whom the Son of **m** is	*444*
	14:21	good were it for that **m** if he had never been	*444*
	14:41	the Son of **m** is betrayed into the hands of	*444*
	14:51	And there followed him a certain **young m**,	*3495*
	14:62	ye shall see the Son of **m** sitting on the right	*444*
	14:71	*saying,* I know not this **m** of whom ye speak.	*444*
	15:24	lots upon them, what every *m* should take.	NIG
	15:39	he said, Truly this **m** was the Son of God.	*444*
	16: 5	they saw a **young m** sitting on the right	*3495*
	16: 8	neither said they any *thing* to any *m*; for	NIG
Lk	1:18	for I am an **old m**, and my wife well	*4246*
	1:27	To a virgin espoused to a **m** whose name	*435*
	1:34	How shall this be, seeing I know not a **m**?	*435*
	2:25	And behold, there was a **m** in Jerusalem,	*444*
	2:25	and the same **m** *was* just and devout,	*444*
	2:52	and stature, and in favour with God and **m**.	*444*
	3:14	he said unto them, Do violence to **no m**,	*3367*
	4: 4	That **m** shall not live by bread alone, but	*444*
	4:33	And in the synagogue there was a **m**,	*444*
	5: 8	from me; for I am a sinful **m**, O Lord.	*435*
	5:12	in a certain city, behold a **m** full of leprosy:	*435*
	5:14	And he charged him to tell no *m*: but go,	NIG
	5:18	men brought in a bed a **m** which was taken	*444*
	5:20	he said unto him, **M**, thy sins are forgiven	*444*

M

Lk	5:24	But that ye may know that the Son of **m** hath	*444*
	5:36	No *m* putteth a piece of a new garment	NIG
	5:37	And no *m* putteth new wine into old bottles;	NIG
	5:39	No *m* also having drunk old *wine*	NIG
	6: 5	That the Son of **m** is Lord also of	*444*
	6: 6	there was a **m** whose right hand was	*444*
	6: 8	said to the **m** which had the withered hand,	*444*
	6:10	he said unto the **m**, Stretch forth thy hand.	*444*
	6:30	Give to **every m** that asketh of thee; and	*3956*
	6:45	A good **m** out of the good treasure of his	*444*
	6:45	an evil **m** out of the evil treasure of his heart	*444*
	6:48	He is like a **m** which built a house, and	*444*
	6:49	is like a **m** that without a foundation built a	*444*
	7: 8	For I also am a **m** set under authority,	*444*
	7:12	behold, there was a **dead m** carried out,	*2348*
	7:14	And he said, **Young m**, I say unto thee,	*3495*
	7:25	A **m** clothed in soft raiment? Behold,	*444*
	7:34	The Son of **m** is come eating and drinking;	*444*
	7:34	Behold a gluttonous **m**, and a winebibber,	*444*
	7:39	saying, This *m*, if he were a prophet,	NIG
	8:16	No *m*, when he hath lighted a candle,	NIG
	8:25	one to another, What *manner of m* is this?	NIG
	8:27	there met him out of the city a certain **m**,	*435*
	8:29	the unclean spirit to come out of the **m**.	*444*
	8:33	Then went the devils out of the **m**, and	*444*
	8:35	and came to Jesus, and found the **m**, out of	*444*
	8:38	Now the **m** out of whom the devils were	*435*
	8:41	there came a **m** named Jairus, and he was a	*435*
	8:51	he suffered no *m* to go in, save Peter,	NIG
	8:56	he charged them that they should tell no *m*	NIG
	9:21	commanded *them* to tell no *m* that *thing;*	NIG
	9:22	The Son of **m** must suffer many *things,* and	*444*
	9:23	If any *m* will come after me, let him deny	NIG
	9:25	For what is a **m** advantaged, if he gain	*444*
	9:26	of him shall the Son of **m** be ashamed,	*444*
	9:36	told no *m* in those days any of *those things*	NIG
	9:38	a **m** of the company cried out, saying,	*435*
	9:44	for the Son of **m** shall be delivered into	*444*
	9:56	For the Son of **m** is not come to destroy	*444*
	9:57	a certain *m* said unto him, Lord, I will	NIG
	9:58	the Son of **m** hath not where to lay *his* head.	*444*
	9:62	No *m* having put his hand to the plough,	NIG
	10: 4	nor shoes: and salute no *m* by the way.	NIG
	10:22	and no *m* knoweth who the Son is, but	NIG
	10:30	A certain **m** went down from Jerusalem to	*444*
	11:21	When a strong *m* armed keepeth his palace,	NIG
	11:24	When the unclean spirit is gone out of a **m**,	*444*
	11:26	the last *state* of that **m** is worse than the first.	*444*
	11:30	shall also the Son of **m** be to this generation.	*444*
	11:33	No *m*, when he hath lighted a candle,	NIG
	12: 8	him shall the Son of **m** also confess before	*444*
	12:10	shall speak a word against the Son of **m**,	*444*
	12:14	And he said unto him, **M**, who made me a	*444*
	12:16	The ground of a certain rich **m** brought forth	*444*
	12:40	for the Son of **m** cometh at an hour when ye	*444*
	13: 6	A certain *m* had a fig tree planted in his	NIG
	13:19	which a **m** took, and cast into his garden;	*444*
	14: 2	there was a certain **m** before him,	*444*
	14: 8	When thou art bidden of any *m* to a	NIG
	14: 8	lest a more honourable *m* than thou be	NIG
	14: 9	and say to thee, Give this *m* place;	NIG
	14:16	A certain **m** made a great supper, and	*444*
	14:26	If any *m* come to me, and hate not his	NIG
	14:30	This **m** began to build, and was not able to	*444*
	15: 2	This *m* receiveth sinners, and eateth with	NIG
	15: 4	What **m** of you, having an hundred sheep,	*444*
	15:11	And he said, A certain **m** had two sons:	*444*
	15:16	the swine did eat: and no *m* gave unto him.	NIG
	16: 1	There was a certain rich **m**, which had a	*444*
	16:16	is preached, and every *m* presseth into it.	NIG
	16:19	There was a certain rich **m**, which was	*444*
	16:22	the rich *m* also died, and was buried;	NIG
	17:22	desire to see one of the days of the Son of **m**,	*444*
	17:24	so shall also the Son of **m** be in his day.	*444*
	17:26	shall it be also in the days of the Son of **m**.	*444*
	17:30	be in the day when the Son of **m** is revealed.	*444*
	18: 2	which feared not God, neither regarded **m**:	*444*
	18: 4	Though I fear not God, nor regard **m**;	*444*
	18: 8	Nevertheless when the Son of **m** cometh,	*444*
	18:14	this *m* went down to his house justified	NIG
	18:25	than for a rich *m* to enter into the kingdom	NIG
	18:29	There is no *m* that hath left house, or	NIG
	18:31	the Son of **m** shall be accomplished.	*444*
	18:35	a certain **blind m** sat by the way side	*5185*
	19: 2	And behold, *there was* a **m** named Zaccheus,	*435*
	19: 7	That he was gone to be guest with a **m** *that is*	*435*
	19: 8	if I have taken any *thing* from any *m* by	NIG
	19:10	For the Son of **m** is come to seek and to save	*444*
	19:14	We will not have this *m* to reign over us.	NIG
	19:15	that he might know how much every *m* had	NIG
	19:21	I feared thee, because thou art an austere **m**:	*444*
	19:22	Thou knewest that I was an austere **m**,	*444*
	19:30	find a colt tied, whereon yet never **m** sat:	*444*
	19:31	And if any *m* ask you, Why do ye loose	NIG
	20: 9	A certain **m** planted a vineyard, and let it	*444*
	21:27	shall they see the Son of **m** coming in a	*444*
	21:36	to pass, and to stand before the Son of **m**.	*444*
	22:10	there shall a **m** meet you, bearing a pitcher	*444*
	22:22	And truly the Son of **m** goeth, as it was	*444*
	22:22	woe unto that **m** by whom he is betrayed.	*444*
	22:48	betrayest thou the Son of **m** with a kiss?	*444*
	22:56	and said, This *m* was also with him.	NIG
	22:58	also of them. And Peter said, **M**, I am not.	*444*
	22:60	And Peter said, **M**, I know not what thou	*444*
	22:69	Hereafter shall the Son of **m** sit on the right	*444*
	23: 4	and *to* the people, I find no fault in this **m**.	*444*
	23: 6	he asked whether the **m** were a Galilean.	*444*
	23:14	unto them, Ye have brought this **m** unto me,	*444*
	23:14	have found no fault in this **m** *touching those*	*444*
	23:18	Away with this *m*, and release unto us	NIG
	23:41	but this *m* hath done nothing amiss.	NIG
	23:47	saying, Certainly this was a righteous **m**.	*444*
	23:50	And behold, *there was* a **m** named Joseph,	*435*
	23:50	*and he was* a good **m**, and a just:	*435*
	23:52	This *m* went unto Pilate, and begged	NIG
	23:53	in stone, wherein never **m** before was laid.	*3762*
	24: 7	The Son of **m** must be delivered into	*444*
Jn	1: 6	There was a **m** sent from God, whose name	*444*
	1: 9	which lighteth every **m** *that* cometh into	*444*
	1:13	of the flesh, nor of the will of **m**, but of God.	*435*
	1:18	No *m* hath seen God at any time; the only	NIG
	1:30	After me cometh a **m** which is preferred	*435*
	1:51	and descending upon the Son of **m**.	*444*
	2:10	Every **m** at the beginning doth set forth good	*444*
	2:25	And needed not that any should testify of **m**:	*444*
	2:25	testify of man: for he knew what was in **m**.	*444*
	3: 1	There was a **m** of the Pharisees,	*444*
	3: 2	for no *m* can do these miracles that thou	NIG
	3: 3	I say unto thee, Except a **m** be born again,	*5100*
	3: 4	How can a **m** be born when he is old?	*444*
	3: 5	Except a **m** be born of water and *of*	*5100*
	3:13	And no *m* hath ascended up to heaven, but	NIG
	3:13	*even* the Son of **m** which is in heaven.	*444*
	3:14	*even* so must the Son of **m** be lifted up:	*444*
	3:27	and said, A **m** can receive nothing,	*444*
	3:32	and no *m* receiveth his testimony.	NIG
	4:27	yet no *m* said, What seekest thou? or,	NIG
	4:29	Come, see a **m**, which told me all *things* that	*444*
	4:33	Hath any *m* brought him *ought* to eat?	NIG
	4:50	And the **m** believed the word that Jesus had	*444*
	5: 5	And a certain **m** was there, which had an	*444*
	5: 7	The impotent *m* answered him, Sir, I have	NIG
	5: 7	Sir, I have no **m**, when the water is troubled,	*444*
	5: 9	And immediately the **m** was made whole,	*444*
	5:12	What **m** is that which said unto thee,	*444*
	5:15	The **m** departed, and told the Jews that it	*444*
	5:22	For the Father judgeth no *m*, but	NIG
	5:27	judgment also, because he is the Son of **m**.	*444*
	5:34	But I receive not testimony from **m**:	*444*
	6:27	which the Son of **m** shall give unto you:	*444*
	6:44	No *m* can come to me, except the Father	NIG
	6:45	Every *m* therefore that hath heard, and	NIG
	6:46	Not that any *m* hath seen the Father, save he	NIG
	6:50	from heaven, that a **m** may eat thereof,	*5100*
	6:51	if any *m* eat of this bread, he shall live for	NIG
	6:52	How can this *m* give us *his* flesh to eat?	NIG
	6:53	Except ye eat the flesh of the Son of **m**, and	*444*
	6:62	if ye shall see the Son of **m** ascend up where	*444*
	6:65	I unto you, that no *m* can come unto me,	NIG
	7: 4	For *there is* no *m that* doeth any *thing* in	NIG
	7:12	He is a good *m*: others said, Nay;	NIG
	7:13	Howbeit no *m* spake openly of him for fear	NIG
	7:15	saying, How knoweth this *m* letters,	NIG
	7:17	If any *m* will do his will, he shall know of	NIG
	7:22	and ye on the sabbath day circumcise a **m**.	*444*
	7:23	If a **m** on the sabbath day receive	*444*
	7:23	I have made a **m** every whit whole on	*444*
	7:27	Howbeit we know this *m* whence he is: but	NIG

Jn	7:27	Christ cometh, no *m* knoweth whence he is.	NIG
	7:30	but no *m* laid hands on him, because	NIG
	7:31	miracles than these which this *m* hath done?	NIG
	7:37	and cried, saying, If any *m* thirst,	NIG
	7:44	taken him; but no *m* laid hands on him.	NIG
	7:46	Never **m** spake like this man.	444
	7:46	Never man spake like this **m**.	444
	7:51	Doth our law judge any **m**, before it hear	444
	7:53	And **every m** went unto his own house.	1538
	8:10	thine accusers? hath no *m* condemned thee?	NIG
	8:11	She said, No *m*, Lord. And Jesus said unto	NIG
	8:15	Ye judge after the flesh; I judge no *m*.	NIG
	8:20	and no *m* laid hands on him; for his hour	NIG
	8:28	When ye have lift up the Son of **m**, then	444
	8:33	were never in bondage to any *m*: how	NIG
	8:40	a **m** that hath told you the truth, which I have	444
	8:51	I say unto you, If a **m** keep my saying,	5100
	8:52	and thou sayest, If a **m** keep my saying,	5100
	9: 1	he saw a **m** *which was* blind from *his* birth.	444
	9: 2	Master, who did sin, this *m*, or his parents,	NIG
	9: 3	Neither hath this *m* sinned, nor his parents:	NIG
	9: 4	the night cometh, when no *m* can work.	NIG
	9: 6	he anointed the eyes of the **blind m** with	5185
	9:11	A **m** *that is* called Jesus made clay, and	444
	9:16	This **m** is not of God, because he keepeth	444
	9:16	How can a **m** *that is* a sinner do such	444
	9:17	They say unto the **blind m** again,	5185
	9:22	that if any *m* did confess that he *was* Christ,	NIG
	9:24	Then again called they the **m** that was blind,	444
	9:24	the praise: we know that this **m** is a sinner.	444
	9:30	The **m** answered and said unto them,	444
	9:31	but if any *m* be a worshipper of God, and	NIG
	9:32	*m* opened the eyes of one that was born	NIG
	9:33	If this *m* were not of God, he could do	NIG
	10: 9	by me if any *m* enter in, he shall be saved,	NIG
	10:18	No *m* taketh it from me, but I lay it down of	NIG
	10:28	neither shall any *m* pluck them out of my	NIG
	10:29	no *m* is able to pluck *them* out of my	NIG
	10:33	and because that thou, being a **m**,	444
	10:41	all *things* that John spake of this *m* were	NIG
	11: 1	Now a certain *m* was sick, *named* Lazarus,	NIG
	11: 9	If any *m* walk in the day, he stumbleth not,	NIG
	11:10	But if a **m** walk in the night, he stumbleth,	5100
	11:37	Could not this *m*, which opened the eyes of	NIG
	11:37	have caused that even this *m* should not	NIG
	11:47	do we? for this **m** doeth many miracles.	444
	11:50	that one **m** should die for the people, and	444
	11:57	that, if any *m* knew where he were,	NIG
	12:23	that the Son of **m** should be glorified.	444
	12:26	If any *m* serve me, let him follow me; and	NIG
	12:26	if any *m* serve me, him will *my* Father	NIG
	12:34	sayest thou, The Son of **m** must be lift up?	444
	12:34	man must be lift up? who is this Son of **m**?	444
	12:47	And if any *m* hear my words, and	NIG
	13:28	Now no *m* at the table knew for what intent	NIG
	13:31	Now is the Son of **m** glorified, and God is	444
	14: 6	no *m* cometh unto the Father, but by me.	NIG
	14:23	and said unto him, If a **m** love me,	5100
	15: 6	If a **m** abide not in me, he is cast forth as a	5100
	15:13	Greater love hath no *m* than this, that a man	NIG
	15:13	that a **m** lay down his life for his friends.	5100
	15:24	them the works which none other *m* did,	NIG
	16:21	for joy that a **m** is born into the world.	444
	16:22	and your joy no *m* taketh from you.	NIG
	16:30	and needest not that any *m* should ask thee:	NIG
	16:32	every *m* to his own, and shall leave me	NIG
	18:14	that it was expedient that one **m** should die	444
	18:29	What accusation bring you against this **m**?	444
	18:31	It is not lawful for us to put any *m* to death:	NIG
	18:40	all again, saying, Not this *m*, but Barabbas.	NIG
	19: 5	And *Pilate* saith unto them, Behold the **m**.	444
	19:12	Jews cried out, saying, If thou let this *m* go,	NIG
	19:41	wherein was never **m** yet laid.	3762
	21:21	to Jesus, Lord, and what *shall* this *m do?*	NIG
Ac	1:18	Now this *m* purchased a field with	NIG
	1:20	be desolate, and let no **m** dwell therein:	3588
	2: 6	that every **m** heard them speak in his own	1520
	2: 8	And how hear we **every m** in our own	1538
	2:22	a **m** approved of God among you by	435
	2:45	parted them to all *men,* as every *m* had	NIG
	3: 2	And a certain **m** lame from his mother's	435
	3:11	And as the lame *m* which was healed held	NIG
	3:12	or holiness we had made this *m* to walk?	NIG
	3:16	faith in his name hath made this *m* strong,	NIG
	4: 9	of the good deed done to the impotent **m**,	444
	4:10	*even* by him doth this *m* stand here before	NIG
	4:14	And beholding the **m** which was healed	444
	4:17	that *they* speak henceforth to no **m** in this	444
	4:22	For the **m** was above forty years old,	444
	4:35	distribution was made unto **every m**	1538
	5: 1	But a certain **m** named Ananias,	435
	5:13	And of the rest durst no *m* join himself to	NIG
	5:23	we had opened, we found no *m* within.	NIG
	5:37	After this *m* rose up Judas of Galilee in	NIG
	6: 5	a **m** full of faith and of the Holy Ghost, and	435
	6:13	This **m** ceaseth not to speak blasphemous	444
	7:56	the Son of **m** standing on the right hand of	444
	8: 9	But there was a certain **m**, called Simon,	435
	8:10	saying, This *m* is the great power of God.	NIG
	8:27	and behold, a **m** of Ethiopia, an eunuch of	435
	8:31	can I, except some *m* should guide me?	NIG
	8:34	of himself, or of some other *m*?	NIG
	9: 7	hearing a voice, but seeing no *m*.	NIG
	9: 8	he saw no *m*: but they led him by the hand,	NIG
	9:12	And hath seen in a vision a **m** named	435
	9:13	Lord, I have heard by many of this **m**,	435
	9:33	And there he found a certain **m** named	444
	10: 1	There was a certain **m** in Cesarea called	435
	10: 2	A devout *m*, and one that feared God with	NIG
	10:22	a just **m**, and one that feareth God, and	435
	10:26	saying, Stand up; I myself also am a **m**.	444
	10:28	*thing* for a **m** *that is* a Jew to keep company,	435
	10:28	me that *I* should not call any **m** common	444
	10:30	a **m** stood before me in bright clothing,	435
	10:47	Can any *m* forbid water, that these should	NIG
	11:24	For he was a good **m**, and full of the Holy	435
	11:29	**every m** according to his ability,	1538
	12:22	*It is* the voice of a god, and not of a **m**.	444
	13: 7	*of the country,* Sergius Paulus, a prudent **m**;	435
	13:21	a **m** of the tribe of Benjamin, *by the space of*	435
	13:22	a **m** after mine own heart, which shall fulfil	435
	13:38	that through this *m* is preached unto you	NIG
	13:41	though a **m** declare it unto you.	5100
	14: 8	And there sat a certain **m** at Lystra,	435
	16: 9	There stood a **m** of Macedonia, and	435
	17:31	by *that* **m** whom he hath ordained;	435
	18:10	and no *m* shall set on thee to hurt thee:	NIG
	18:24	an eloquent **m**, *and* mighty in the scriptures,	435
	18:25	This *m* was instructed in the way of	NIG
	19:16	And the **m** in whom the evil spirit was leapt	444
	19:24	For a certain *m* named Demetrius,	NIG
	19:35	what **m** is there that knoweth not how that	444
	19:38	have a matter against any *m*, the law is	NIG
	20: 9	a certain **young m** named Eutychus,	3494
	20:12	And they brought the **young m** alive, and	3816
	21: 9	And the same *m* had four daughters,	NIG
	21:11	So shall the Jews at Jerusalem bind the **m**	435
	21:28	This is the **m**, that teacheth all *men* every	444
	21:39	I am a **m** *which am* a Jew of Tarsus,	444
	22: 3	I am verily a **m** *which am* a Jew, born in	435
	22:12	a devout **m** according to the law,	435
	22:25	for you to scourge a **m** *that is* a Roman,	444
	22:26	heed what thou doest: for this **m** is a Roman.	444
	23: 9	and strove, saying, We find no evil in this **m**:	444
	23:17	Bring this **young m** unto the chief captain:	3494
	23:18	prayed *me* to bring this **young m** unto thee,	3494
	23:22	chief captain then let the **young m** depart,	3494
	23:22	charged *him, See thou* tell no *m* that thou	NIG
	23:27	This **m** was taken of the Jews, and	435
	23:30	me how that the Jews laid wait for the **m**,	435
	24: 5	For we have found this **m** a pestilent *fellow,*	435
	24:12	with any *m*, neither raising up the people,	NIG
	25: 5	go down with *me,* and accuse this **m**,	435
	25:11	accuse me, no *m* may deliver me unto them.	NIG
	25:14	There is a certain **m** left in bonds by Felix:	435
	25:16	of the Romans to deliver any **m** to die,	444
	25:17	and commanded the **m** to be brought *forth.*	435
	25:22	unto Festus, I would also hear the **m** myself.	444
	25:24	ye see this *m*, about whom all the multitude	NIG
	26:31	This **m** doeth nothing worthy of death or	444
	26:32	This **m** might have been set at liberty,	444
	28: 4	No doubt this **m** is a murderer, whom,	444
	28: 7	possessions of the chief *m* of the island,	NIG
	28:31	with all confidence, no **m** forbidding him.	NIG
Ro	1:23	into an image made like to corruptible **m**,	444
	2: 1	Therefore thou art inexcusable, O **m**,	444
	2: 3	And thinkest thou this, O **m**, that judgest	444
	2: 6	Who will render to every *m* according to his	NIG

Ro 2: 9 upon every soul of **m** that doeth evil, *444*
2:10 and peace, to every *m* that worketh good, NIG
2:21 thou that preachest *a m* should not steal, NIG
2:22 Thou that sayest *a m* should not commit NIG
3: 4 yea, let God be true, but every **m** a liar; as it *444*
3: 5 who taketh vengeance? (I speak as a **m**) *444*
3:28 Therefore we conclude that a **m** is justified *444*
4: 6 also describeth the blessedness of the **m**, *444*
4: 8 Blessed *is* the **m** to whom the Lord will not *435*
5: 7 For scarcely for a righteous *m* will one die: NIG
5: 7 yet peradventure for a good *m* some would NIG
5:12 as by one **m** sin entered into the world, and *444*
5:15 by grace, which is by one **m**, Jesus Christ, *444*
6: 6 that our old **m** is crucified with *him,* that *444*
7: 1 how that the law hath dominion over a **m**, *444*
7: 3 husband liveth, she be married to another **m**, *435*
7: 3 though she be married to another **m**. *435*
7:22 delight in the law of God after the inward **m**: *444*
7:24 O wretched **m** that I am! who shall deliver *444*
8: 9 Now if any *m* have not the Spirit of Christ, NIG
8:24 for what a **m** seeth, why doth he yet hope *5100*
9:20 Nay but, O **m**, who art thou that repliest *444*
10: 5 That the **m** which doeth those *things* shall *444*
10:10 For with the heart *m* believeth unto NIG
12: 3 unto me, to every *m* that is among you, NIG
12: 3 according as God hath dealt to **every m** *1538*
12:17 Recompense to no *m* evil for evil. NIG
13: 8 Owe no *m* any *thing,* but to love one NIG
14: 5 **One m** esteemeth one day above another: *3739*
14: 5 **every m** be fully persuaded in his own *1538*
14: 7 liveth to himself, and no *m* dieth to himself. NIG
14:13 that no *m* put a stumblingblock or NIG
14:20 *it is* evil for *that* **m** who eateth with offence. *444*
1Co 2: 9 neither have entered into the heart of **m**, *444*
2:11 For what **m** knoweth the *things* of a man, *444*
2:11 For what man knoweth the *things* of a **m**, *444*
2:11 a man, save the spirit of **m** which is in him? *444*
2:11 so the *things* of God knoweth no *m*, but NIG
2:14 But the natural **m** receiveth not the *things* of *444*
2:15 all *things,* yet he himself is judged of no *m*. NIG
3: 5 even as the Lord gave to **every m**? *1538*
3: 8 **every m** shall receive his own reward *1538*
3:10 But let **every m** take heed how he buildeth *1538*
3:11 For other foundation can no *m* lay than that NIG
3:12 Now if any *m* build upon this foundation NIG
3:17 If any *m* defile the temple of God, him shall NIG
3:18 Let no *m* deceive himself. If any *man* NIG
3:18 If any *m* among you seemeth to be wise in NIG
3:21 Therefore let no *m* glory in men. For all NIG
4: 1 Let a **m** so account of us, as of the ministers *444*
4: 2 in stewards, that a **m** be found faithful. *5100*
4: 5 and then shall **every m** have praise of God. *1538*
5:11 if any *m that is* called a brother be a NIG
6: 5 that there is not a wise *m* amongst you? NIG
6:18 Every sin that a **m** doeth is without the body; *444*
7: 1 *It is* good for a **m** not to touch a woman. *444*
7: 2 let **every m** have his own wife, and *1538*
7: 7 But **every m** hath his proper gift of God, *1538*
7:16 or how knowest thou, O **m**, whether thou *435*
7:17 But as God hath distributed to **every m**, *1538*
7:18 Is any *m* called being circumcised? let him NIG
7:20 Let **every m** abide in the same calling *1538*
7:24 Brethren, let **every m**, wherein he is called, *1538*
7:26 *I say,* that *it is* good for a **m** so to be. *444*
7:36 But if any *m* think that *he* behaveth himself NIG
8: 2 And if any *m* think that *he* knoweth any NIG
8: 3 But if any *m* love God, the same is known NIG
8: 7 Howbeit *there is* not in every *m that* NIG
8:10 For if any *m* see thee which hast knowledge NIG
9: 8 Say I these *things* as a **m**? or saith not *444*
9:15 than that any *m* should make my glorying NIG
9:25 And every *m* that striveth for the mastery is NIG
10:13 taken you but such as is **common to m**: *442*
10:24 Let no *m* seek his own, but every man NIG
10:24 his own, but **every m** another's *wealth.* *1538*
10:28 But if any *m* say unto you, This is offered in NIG
11: 3 that the head of every **m** is Christ; *435*
11: 3 and the head of the woman *is* the **m**; and *435*
11: 4 Every **m** praying or prophesying, having *his* *435*
11: 7 For a **m** indeed ought not to cover *his* head, *435*
11: 7 of God: but the woman is the glory of the **m**. *435*
11: 8 For the **m** is not of the woman; but *435*
11: 8 not of the woman; but the woman of the **m**. *435*
11: 9 Neither was the **m** created for the woman; *435*
11: 9 for the woman; but the woman for the **m**. *435*
11:11 Nevertheless neither *is* the **m** without *435*
11:11 neither the woman without the **m**, in *435*
11:12 For as the woman *is* of the **m**, *even* so *is* *435*
11:12 *even* so *is* the **m** also by the woman; *435*
11:14 that, if a **m** have long hair, it is a shame unto *435*
11:16 But if any *m* seem to be contentious, NIG
11:28 But let a **m** examine himself, and so let him *444*
11:34 And if any *m* hunger, let him eat at home; NIG
12: 3 that no *m* speaking by the Spirit of God NIG
12: 3 and *that* no *m* can say that Jesus is the Lord, NIG
12: 7 Spirit is given to **every m** to profit withal. *1538*
12:11 dividing to **every m** severally as he will. *1538*
13:11 but when I became a **m**, I put away childish *435*
14: 2 for no *m* understandeth *him;* howbeit in NIG
14:27 If any *m* speak in an *unknown* tongue, *let it* NIG
14:37 If any *m* think himself to be a prophet, or NIG
14:38 But if any *m* be ignorant, let him be NIG
15:21 For since by **m** *came* death, by man *came* *444*
15:21 by **m** *came* also the resurrection of the dead. *444*
15:23 But **every m** in his own order: Christ *1538*
15:35 But some *m* will say, How are the dead NIG
15:45 The first **m** Adam was made a living soul; *444*
15:47 The first **m** *is* of the earth, earthy: the second *444*
15:47 the second **m** *is* the Lord from heaven. *444*
16:11 Let no *m* therefore despise him: but NIG
16:22 If any *m* love not the Lord Jesus Christ, NIG
2Co 2: 6 Sufficient to such *a m is* this punishment, NIG
4:16 but though our outward **m** perish, yet *444*
4:16 yet the inward *m* is renewed day by day. NIG
5:16 Wherefore henceforth know we no *m* after NIG
5:17 Therefore if any *m be* in Christ, *he is* a new NIG
7: 2 we have wronged no *m*, we have corrupted NIG
7: 2 no *m*, we have defrauded no *man.* NIG
7: 2 no *man,* we have defrauded no *m*. NIG
8:12 *it is* accepted according to that a **m** hath, *5100*
8:20 that no *m* should blame us in this NIG
9: 7 **Every m** according as he purposeth in *his* *1538*
10: 7 If any *m* trust to himself that *he* is Christ's, NIG
11: 9 I was chargeable to no *m*: for that which NIG
11:10 no *m* shall stop me of this boasting in NIG
11:16 I say again, Let no *m* think me a fool; NIG
11:20 ye suffer, **if a m** bring you into bondage, *1536*
11:20 **if a m** devour *you,* if a man take *of you,* if a *1536*
11:20 if a man devour *you,* **if a m** take *of you,* if a *1536*
11:20 if a man take *of you,* **if a m** exalt himself, *1536*
11:20 exalt himself, **if a m** smite you on the face. *1536*
12: 2 I knew a **m** in Christ above fourteen years *444*
12: 3 And I knew such a **m**, (whether in the body, *444*
12: 4 which *it is* not lawful for a **m** to utter. *444*
12: 6 lest any *m* should think of me above *that* NIG
Gal 1: 1 neither by **m**, but by Jesus Christ, and *444*
1: 9 If any *m* preach any other gospel unto you NIG
1:11 which was preached of me is not after **m**. *444*
1:12 For I neither received it of **m**, neither was I *444*
2:16 Knowing that a **m** is not justified by *444*
3:11 But that no *m* is justified by the law in NIG
3:12 The **m** that doeth them shall live in them. *444*
3:15 no *m* disannulleth, or added thereto. NIG
5: 3 For I testify again to every **m** that is *444*
6: 1 Brethren, if a **m** be overtaken in a fault, *444*
6: 3 For if a **m** think himself to be something, *5100*
6: 4 But let **every m** prove his own work, and *1538*
6: 5 For **every m** shall bear his own burden. *1538*
6: 7 for whatsoever a **m** soweth, that shall he also *444*
6:17 From henceforth let no *m* trouble me: for I NIG
Eph 2: 9 Not of works, lest any *m* should boast. NIG
2:15 for to make in himself of twain one new **m**, *444*
3:16 with might by his Spirit in the inner **m**; *444*
4:13 of the Son of God, unto a perfect **m**, *435*
4:22 the former conversation the old **m**, *444*
4:24 And that *ye* put on the new **m**, which after *444*
4:25 speak **every m** truth with his neighbour: *1538*
5: 5 nor unclean *person,* nor **covetous m** who is *4123*
5: 6 Let no *m* deceive you with vain words: for NIG
5:29 For no *m* ever yet hated his own flesh; but NIG
5:31 For this cause shall a **m** leave his father and *444*
6: 8 that whatsoever good *thing* **any m** doeth, *1538*
Php 2: 4 Look not **every m** on his own *things,* but *1538*
2: 4 but **every m** also on the *things* of others. *1538*
2: 8 And being found in fashion as a **m**, *444*
2:20 For I have no *m* likeminded, who will NIG
3: 4 If any other *m* thinketh that *he hath whereof* NIG
Col 1:28 warning every **m**, and teaching every man in *444*

Col 1:28 and teaching every **m** in all wisdom; *444*
1:28 that we may present every **m** perfect in *444*
2: 4 lest any ***m*** should beguile you with enticing NIG
2: 8 Beware lest any ***m*** spoil you through NIG
2:16 Let no ***m*** therefore judge you in meat, NIG
2:18 Let no ***m*** beguile you of your reward in a NIG
3: 9 seeing that ye have put off the old **m** with *444*
3:10 And have put on the new ***m***, which is NIG
3:13 if any ***m*** have a quarrel against any: NIG
4: 6 know how ye ought to answer every **m**. *1520*
1Th 3: 3 That no ***m*** should be moved by these NIG
4: 6 That no ***m*** go beyond and defraud his NIG
4: 8 that despiseth, despiseth not **m**, but God, *444*
5:15 that none render evil for evil unto any ***m***; NIG
2Th 2: 3 Let no ***m*** deceive you by any means: NIG
2: 3 and *that* **m** of sin be revealed, the son of *444*
3:14 And if any ***m*** obey not our word by *this* NIG
3:14 note that ***m***, and have no company with NIG
1Ti 1: 8 that the law *is* good, if a **m** use it lawfully; *5100*
1: 9 that the law is not made for a righteous ***m***, NIG
2: 5 between God and men, *the* **m** Christ Jesus; *444*
2:12 nor to usurp authority over the **m**, but to be *435*
3: 1 **If a m** desire the office of a bishop, *1536*
3: 5 (For if a **m** know not how to rule his own *5100*
4:12 Let no ***m*** despise thy youth; but be thou an NIG
5: 9 years old, having been the wife of one **m**, *435*
5:16 If any **m**[s] or woman that believeth have *4103*
5:22 Lay hands suddenly on no ***m***, neither be NIG
6: 3 If any ***m*** teach otherwise, and consent not to NIG
6:11 But thou, O **m** of God, flee these *things;* and *444*
6:16 dwelling in the light which no ***m*** can NIG
6:16 whom no **m** hath seen, nor can see: *444*
2Ti 2: 4 No ***m*** that warreth entangleth himself with NIG
2: 5 And if a **m** also strive for masteries, *yet* is *5100*
2:21 If a **m** therefore purge himself from these, *5100*
3:17 That the **m** of God may be perfect, *444*
4:16 At my first answer no ***m*** stood with me, but NIG
Tit 2:15 with all authority. Let no ***m*** despise thee. NIG
3: 2 To speak evil of no ***m***, to be no brawlers, NIG
3: 4 **love** of God our Saviour **toward m** *5363*
3:10 A **m** *that is* a heretick after the first and *444*
Heb 2: 6 saying, What is **m**, that thou art mindful of *444*
2: 6 or the son of **m**, that thou visitest him? *444*
2: 9 of God should taste death for every ***m***. NIG
3: 3 For this ***m*** was counted worthy of more NIG
3: 4 For every house is builded by some ***m***; but NIG
4:11 lest any ***m*** fall after the same example of NIG
5: 4 And no ***m*** taketh *this* honour unto himself, NIG
7: 4 Now consider how great this ***m*** *was,* unto NIG
7:13 of which no ***m*** gave attendance at the altar. NIG
7:24 But this ***m***, because he continueth ever, hath NIG
8: 2 which the Lord pitched, and not **m**. *444*
8: 3 wherefore *it is* of necessity that this ***m*** have NIG
8:11 And they shall not teach **every m** his *1538*
8:11 and **every m** his brother, saying, Know *1538*
10:12 But this ***m***, after he had offered one NIG
10:38 but if *any* ***m*** draw back, my soul shall have NIG
12:14 without which no ***m*** shall see the Lord: NIG
12:15 Looking diligently lest any ***m*** fail of NIG
13: 6 and I will not fear what **m** shall do unto me. *444*
Jas 1: 7 For let not that **m** think that he shall receive *444*
1: 8 A double minded **m** *is* unstable in all his *435*
1:11 also shall the rich ***m*** fade away in his ways. NIG
1:12 Blessed *is* the **m** that endureth temptation: *435*
1:13 Let no ***m*** say when he is tempted, I am NIG
1:13 with evil, neither tempteth he any ***m***: NIG
1:14 But **every m** is tempted, when he is drawn *1538*
1:19 let every **m** be swift to hear, slow to speak, *444*
1:20 For the wrath of **m** worketh not *435*
1:23 he is like unto a **m** beholding his natural face *435*
1:24 straightway forgetteth what manner of ***m*** he NIG
1:25 this ***m*** shall be blessed in his deed. NIG
1:26 If any ***m*** among you seem to be religious, NIG
2: 2 For if there come unto your assembly a **m** *435*
2: 2 there come in also a poor ***m*** in vile raiment; NIG
2:14 though a **m** say *he* hath faith, and have not *5100*
2:18 Yea, a **m** may say, Thou hast faith, and I *5100*
2:20 But wilt thou know, O vain **m**, that faith *444*
2:24 then how that by works a **m** is justified, *444*
3: 2 If any ***m*** offend not in word, the same *is* a NIG
3: 2 the same *is* a perfect **m**, *and* able also to *435*
3: 8 But the tongue can no **m** tame; *it is* an *444*
3:13 Who *is* a wise ***m*** and endued with NIG
5:16 prayer of a righteous ***m*** availeth much. NIG

5:17 Elias was a **m** subject to like passions as we *444*
1Pe 1:24 and all the glory of **m** as the flower of grass. *444*
2:13 Submit yourselves to every ordinance **of m** *442*
2:19 if a **m** for conscience toward God endure *5100*
3: 4 But *let it be* the hidden **m** of the heart, in *that* *444*
3:15 ***m*** that asketh you a reason of the hope that NIG
4:10 As **every m** hath received *the* gift, *even so* *1538*
4:11 If any ***m*** speak, *let him speak* as the oracles NIG
4:11 if any ***m*** minister, *let him do it* as of NIG
4:16 Yet if *any* ***m*** *suffer* as a Christian, let him NIG
2Pe 1:21 came not in old time by the will of **m**: *444*
2: 8 (For *that* righteous ***m*** dwelling among them, NIG
2:19 for of whom a **m** is overcome, of the same *5100*
1Jn 2: 1 And if any ***m*** sin, we have an advocate with NIG
2:15 If any ***m*** love the world, the love of NIG
2:27 and ye need not that any ***m*** teach you: NIG
3: 3 And every ***m*** that hath this hope in him NIG
3: 7 Little children, let no ***m*** deceive you: he that NIG
4:12 No ***m*** hath seen God at any time. If we love NIG
4:20 If a **m** say, I love God, and hateth his *5100*
5:16 If any ***m*** see his brother sin a sin *which is* NIG
Rev 1:13 candlesticks one like unto the Son of **m**, *444*
2:17 which no ***m*** knoweth saving he that NIG
3: 7 he that openeth, and no ***m*** shutteth; NIG
3: 7 and shutteth, and no ***m*** openeth; NIG
3: 8 thee an open door, and no ***m*** can shut it: NIG
3:11 which thou hast, that no ***m*** take thy crown. NIG
3:20 if any ***m*** hear my voice, and open the door, NIG
4: 7 and the third beast had a face as a **m**, and *444*
5: 3 And no ***m*** in heaven, nor in earth, NIG
5: 4 no ***m*** was found worthy to open and NIG
6:15 every free ***m***, hid themselves in the dens NIG
7: 9 which no ***m*** could number, of all nations, NIG
9: 5 torment of a scorpion, when he striketh a **m**. *444*
11: 5 And if any ***m*** will hurt them, fire proceedeth NIG
11: 5 and if any ***m*** will hurt them, he must in this NIG
12: 5 And she brought forth a **m** child, who was to *730*
12:13 the woman which brought forth the **m** *child.* *730*
13: 9 If any ***m*** have an ear, let him hear. NIG
13:17 And that no ***m*** might buy or sell, save he NIG
13:18 for it is the number of a **m**; and his number *444*
14: 3 and no ***m*** could learn *that* song but NIG
14: 9 If any ***m*** worship the beast and his image, NIG
14:14 the cloud one sat like unto the Son of **m**, *444*
15: 8 and no ***m*** was able to enter into the temple, NIG
16: 3 and it became as the blood of a dead ***m***: and NIG
18:11 for no ***m*** buyeth their merchandise any NIG
19:12 that no ***m*** knew, but he himself. NIG
20:13 they were judged **every m** according to *1538*
21:17 *according to* the measure of a **m**, that is, *444*
22:12 to give **every m** according as his work shall *1538*
22:18 For I testify unto every ***m*** that heareth NIG
22:18 If any ***m*** shall add unto these *things,* God NIG
22:19 And if any ***m*** shall take away from NIG

MAN'S (122) [MAN]

Ge 8:21 again curse the ground any more for **m** sake; 120
8:21 for the imagination of **m** heart *is* evil from 120
9: 5 at the hand of every **m** brother will I require 376
9: 6 Whoso sheddeth **m** blood, by man shall his 120
16:12 every man, and **every m** hand against him; 3605
20: 3 which thou hast taken; for she *is* a **m** wife. 1167
42:11 We *are* all one **m** sons; we *are* true *men,* thy 376
42:25 to restore every **m** money into his sack, and 376
42:35 every **m** bundle of money *was* in his sack: 376
43:21 every **m** money *was* in the mouth of his 376
44: 1 and put **every m** money in his sack's mouth. 376
44:26 for we may not see the **m** face, except our 376
Ex 4:11 said unto him, Who hath made **m** mouth? 120
12:44 every **m** servant that is bought for money, 376
21:35 if **one m** ox hurt another's, that he die; then 376
22: 5 his beast, and shall feed in **another m** field; 312
22: 7 to keep, and it be stolen out of the **m** house; 376
30:32 Upon **m** flesh shall it not be poured, 120
Lev 7: 8 the priest that offereth *any* **m** burnt offering, 376
15:16 if **any m** seed of copulation go out from 376
20:10 committeth adultery with *another* **m** wife, 376
Nu 5:10 **every m** hallowed *things* shall be his: 376
5:12 If any **m** wife go aside, and commit a 376
17: 2 write thou **every m** name upon his rod. 376
17: 5 *that* the **m** rod, whom I shall choose, shall 376
33:54 every **m**[s] *inheritance* shall be in 2050.2+3807.1
Dt 20:19 them down (for the tree of the field *is* **m** *life*) 120

Dt 24: 2 she may go and be another **m** *wife.* 376
24: 6 to pledge: for he taketh *a* **m** life to pledge. NIH
Jdg 7:16 he put a trumpet in every **m**s hand, 3963.1
7:22 the LORD set **every m** sword against his 376
19:26 fell down *at* the door of the **m** house where 376
Ru 2:19 The **m** name with whom I wrought to day *is* 376
1Sa 12: 4 neither hast thou taken ought of **any m** hand. 376
14:20 **every m** sword was against his fellow, *and* 376
17:32 to Saul, Let no **m** heart fail because of him; 120
2Sa 12: 4 took the poor **m** lamb, and dressed it for 376
17:18 came to a **m** house in Bahurim, which had a 376
17:25 which Amasa *was* a **m** son, whose name *was* 376
1Ki 18:44 a little cloud out of the sea, like a **m** hand. 376
2Ki 12: 4 all the money that cometh into **any m** heart 376
23: 8 which *were* on a **m** left hand at the gate of 376
25: 9 and every great *m* house burnt he with fire. NIH
Est 1: 8 according to **every m** pleasure. 376+376+2050.1
Job 10: 5 the days of man? *are* thy years as **m** days, 1397
32:21 Let me not, I pray you, accept *any* **m** person, 376
Ps 104:15 and bread *which* strengtheneth **m** heart. 582
Pr 10:15 The rich *m* wealth *is* his strong city: NIH
12:14 the recompence of a **m** hands shall be 120
13: 8 The ransom of a **m** life *are* his riches: but 376
16: 7 When a **m** ways please the LORD, 376
16: 9 A **m** heart deviseth his way: but the LORD 120
18: 4 The words of a **m** mouth *are as* deep waters, 376
18:11 The rich *m* wealth *is* his strong city, and NIH
18:16 A **m** gift maketh room for him, and 120
18:20 A **m** belly shall be satisfied with the fruit of 376
19:21 *There are* many devices in a **m** heart; 376
20:24 **M** goings *are* of the LORD; how can a 1397
27: 9 *doth* the sweetness of a **m**s friend by 1930.2
29:23 A **m** pride shall bring him low: but 120
29:26 *every* **m** judgment *cometh* from the LORD. 376
Ecc 2:14 The wise *m* eyes *are* in his head; but NIH
8: 1 a **m** wisdom maketh his face to shine, and 120
8: 5 and a wise *m* heart discerneth *both* time and NIH
9:16 nevertheless the poor *m* wisdom *is* NIH
10: 2 A wise *m* heart *is* at his right hand; but NIH
10:12 The words of a wise *m* mouth *are* gracious; NIH
Isa 8: 1 write in it with a **m** pen concerning 582
13: 7 hands be faint, and every **m** heart shall melt: 582
Jer 3: 1 she go from him, and become another **m,** 376
23:36 for **every m** word shall be his 376+3807.1
Eze 4:15 I have given thee cow's dung for **m** dung, 120
10: 8 the form of a **m** hand under their wings. 120
38:21 **every m** sword shall be against his brother. 376
39:15 when *any* seeth a **m** bone, then shall he set 120
40: 5 in the **m** hand a measuring reed of six cubits 376
Da 4:16 Let his heart be changed from **m,** and let a 606
5: 5 In the same hour came forth fingers of a **m** 606
7: 4 feet as a man, and a **m** heart was given to it. 606
8:16 I heard a **m** voice between *the banks of* Ulai, 120
Am 6:10 a **m**s uncle shall take him up, and he that 2050.2
Jnh 1:14 let us not perish for this **m** life, and lay not 376
Mic 7: 6 a **m** enemies *are* the men of his own house. 376
Mt 10:36 And a **m** foes *shall be* they of his own *444*
10:41 *man* shall receive a righteous **m** reward. NIG
12:29 Or else how can one enter into a strong *m* NIG
Mk 3:27 No *man* can enter into a strong **m** house, NIG
12:19 If a **m** brother die, and leave *his* wife *5100*
Lk 6:22 out your name as evil, for the Son of **m** sake. *444*
12:15 for a **m** life consisteth not in the abundance *846*
16:12 *m,* who shall give you that which is your NIG
16:21 the crumbs which fell from the rich *m* table: NIG
20:28 If any *m* brother die, having a wife, and NIG
Jn 18:17 Art not thou also *one* of this **m** disciples? *444*
Ac 5:28 and intend to bring this **m** blood upon us. *444*
7:58 laid down their clothes at a **young m** feet, *3494*
11:12 and we entered into the **m** house: *435*
13:23 Of this **m** seed hath God according to *his* NIG
17:29 silver, or stone, graven by art and **m** device. *444*
18: 7 and entered into a certain *m* house, NIG
20:33 I have coveted no *m* silver, or gold, or NIG
27:22 for there shall be no loss of *any* **m** life NIG
Ro 5:17 For if by one **m** offence death reigned by NIG
5:19 For as by one **m** disobedience many were *444*
14: 4 Who art thou that judgest another *m* NIG
15:20 lest I should build upon another *m* NIG
1Co 2: 4 *was* not with enticing words of **m** wisdom, *442*
2:13 not in the words which **m** wisdom teacheth, *442*
3:13 **Every m** work shall be made manifest: *1538*
3:13 the fire shall try **every m** work of what sort *1538*
3:14 If any *m* work abide which he hath built NIG
3:15 If any *m* work shall be burnt, he shall suffer NIG
4: 3 I should be judged of you, or of **m** judgment: *442*
10:29 for why is my liberty judged of another *m* NIG
2Co 4: 2 to every **m** conscience in the sight of God. *444*
10:16 not to boast in another *m* line of *things* NIG
Gal 2: 6 God accepteth no **m** person:) for they who *444*
3:15 Though *it be* but a **m** covenant, *yet if it be* *444*
2Th 3: 8 Neither did we eat any *m* bread for nought; NIG
Jas 1:26 his own heart, this *m* religion *is* vain. NIG
1Pe 1:17 judgeth according to **every m** work, *1538*
2Pe 2:16 the dumb ass speaking with **m** voice forbad *444*

MANAEN (1)

Ac 13: 1 called Niger, and Lucius of Cyrene, and **M,** *3127*

MANAHATH (3) [MANAHETHITES]

Ge 36:23 Alvan, and **M,** and Ebal, Shepho, and 4506
1Ch 1:40 Alian, and **M,** and Ebal, Shephi, and Onam. 4506
8: 6 of Geba, and they removed them to **M:** 4506

MANAHETHITES (2) [MANAHATH]

1Ch 2:52 had sons; Haroeh, *and* half of the **M.** 2679
2:54 of Joab, and half of the **M,** the Zorites. 2680

MANASSEH (143) [MANASSEH'S, MANASSES, MANASSITES]

Ge 41:51 Joseph called the name of the firstborn **M:** 4519
46:20 Joseph in the land of Egypt were born **M** 4519
48: 1 with him his two sons, **M** and Ephraim. 4519
48: 5 now thy two sons, Ephraim and **M,** 4519
48:13 **M** in his left hand towards Israel's right 4519
48:14 hands wittingly; for **M** *was* the firstborn. 4519
48:20 God make thee as Ephraim and as **M:** 4519
48:20 as Manasseh: and he set Ephraim before **M.** 4519
50:23 of **M** were brought up upon Joseph's knees. 4519
Nu 1:10 of **M;** Gamaliel the son of Pedahzur. 4519
1:34 Of the children of **M,** *by* their generations, 4519
1:35 *even* of the tribe of **M,** *were* thirty and 4519
2:20 by him *shall be* the tribe of **M:** and 4519
2:20 the captain of the children of **M** *shall be* 4519
7:54 of Pedahzur, prince of the children of **M:** 4519
10:23 of **M** *was* Gamaliel the son of Pedahzur. 4519
13:11 *namely,* of the tribe of **M,** Gaddi the son of 4519
26:28 sons of Joseph after their families *were* **M** 4519
26:29 *Of* the sons of **M:** of Machir, the family of 4519
26:34 These *are* the families of **M,** and those that 4519
27: 1 of Gilead, the son of Machir, the son of **M,** 4519
27: 1 of the families of **M** the son of Joseph: 4519
32:33 unto half the tribe of **M** the son of Joseph, 4519
32:39 the children of Machir the son of **M** went to 4519
32:40 gave Gilead unto Machir the son of **M;** 4519
32:41 Jair the son of **M** went and took the small 4519
34:14 half the tribe of **M** have received their 4519
34:23 for the tribe of the children of **M,** 4519
36: 1 the son of Machir, the son of **M,** of 4519
36:12 families of the sons of **M** the son of Joseph, 4519
Dt 3:13 of Og, gave I unto the half tribe of **M;** 4519
3:14 Jair the son of **M** took all the country of 4519
29: 8 to the Gadites, and to the half tribe of **M.** 4520
33:17 and they *are* the thousands of **M.** 4519
34: 2 **M,** and all the land of Judah, unto 4519
Jos 1:12 to half the tribe of **M,** spake Joshua, saying, 4519
4:12 the children of Gad, and half the tribe of **M,** 4519
12: 6 and the Gadites, and the half tribe of **M.** 4519
13: 7 unto the nine tribes, and the half tribe of **M,** 4519
13:29 gave *inheritance* unto the half tribe of **M:** 4519
13:29 tribe of the children of **M** by their families. 4519
13:31 unto the children of Machir the son of **M,** 4519
14: 4 of Joseph were two tribes, **M** and Ephraim: 4519
16: 4 **M** and Ephraim, took their inheritance. 4519
16: 9 among the inheritance of the children of **M,** 4519
17: 1 There was also a lot for the tribe of **M;** 4519
17: 1 *to wit,* for Machir the firstborn of **M,** 4519
17: 2 rest of the children of **M** by their families; 4519
17: 2 these *were* the male children of **M** the son 4519
17: 3 the son of **M,** had no sons, but daughters: 4519
17: 5 there fell ten portions to **M,** beside the land 4519
17: 6 Because the daughters of **M** had an 4519
17: 7 the coast of **M** was from Asher *to* 4519
17: 8 *Now* **M** had the land of Tappuah: but 4519
17: 8 Tappuah on the border of **M** *belonged* to 4519
17: 9 of Ephraim *are* among the cities of **M:** 4519
17: 9 the coast of **M** also *was* on the north side of 4519
17:11 **M** had in Issachar and in Asher Beth-shean 4519
17:12 Yet the children of **M** could not drive out 4519

M

Jos 17:17 *even* to Ephraim and to **M**, saying, Thou *art* 4519
18: 7 Gad, and Reuben, and half the tribe of **M**, 4519
20: 8 and Golan in Bashan out of the tribe of **M**. 4519
21: 5 and out of the half tribe of **M**, ten cities. 4519
21: 6 out of the half tribe of **M** in Bashan, 4519
21:25 out of the half tribe of **M**, Tanach with her 4519
21:27 out of the *other* half tribe of **M** *they gave* 4519
22: 1 and the Gadites, and the half tribe of **M**, 4519
22: 7 Now to the *one* half of the tribe of **M** 4519
22: 9 of Gad and the half tribe of **M** returned, 4519
22:10 the half tribe of **M** built there an altar by 4519
22:11 the half tribe of **M** have built an altar over 4519
22:13 children of Gad, and to the half tribe of **M**, 4519
22:15 children of Gad, and to the half tribe of **M**, 4519
22:21 of Gad and the half tribe of **M** answered, 4519
22:30 of Gad and the children of **M** spake, 4519
22:31 children of Gad, and to the children of **M**, 4519
Jdg 1:27 Neither did **M** drive out *the inhabitants of* 4519
6:15 my family *is* poor in **M**, and I *am* the least 4519
6:35 he sent messengers throughout all **M**; who 4519
7:23 out of all **M**, and pursued after 4519
11:29 he passed over Gilead and **M**, and 4519
18:30 the son of **M**, he and his sons were priests 4519
1Ki 4:13 *pertained* the towns of Jair the son of **M**, 4519
2Ki 20:21 and **M** his son reigned in his stead. 4519
21: 1 **M** *was* twelve years old when he *began* to 4519
21: 9 **M** seduced them to do more evil than did 4519
21:11 Because **M** king of Judah hath done these 4519
21:16 Moreover **M** shed innocent blood very 4519
21:17 Now the rest of the acts of **M**, and all that 4519
21:18 **M** slept with his fathers, and was buried in 4519
21:20 sight of the LORD, as his father **M** did. 4519
23:12 the altars which **M** had made in the two 4519
23:26 of all the provocations that **M** had 4519
24: 3 for the sins of **M**, according to all that he 4519
1Ch 3:13 Ahaz his son, Hezekiah his son, **M** his son, 4519
5:18 the Gadites, and half the tribe of **M**, 4519
5:23 the children of the half tribe of **M** dwelt in 4519
5:26 the half tribe of **M**, and brought them unto 4519
6:61 *namely, out of* the half *tribe* of **M**, by lot, 4519
6:62 out of the tribe of **M** in Bashan, 4519
6:70 out of the half tribe of **M**; Aner with her 4519
6:71 out of the family of the half tribe of **M**, 4519
7:14 The sons of **M**; Ashriel, whom she bare: 4519
7:17 of Gilead, the son of Machir, the son of **M**. 4519
7:29 by the borders of the children of **M**, 4519
9: 3 and of the children of Ephraim, and **M**; 4519
12:19 there fell *some* of **M** to David, when he 4519
12:20 there fell to him of **M**, Adnah, and Jozabad, 4519
12:20 captains of the thousands that *were* of **M**. 4519
12:31 of the half tribe of **M** eighteen thousand, 4519
12:37 and the Gadites, and of the half tribe of **M**, 4519
26:32 the Gadites, and the half tribe of **M**, 4520
27:20 of the half tribe of **M**, Joel the son of 4519
27:21 Of the half *tribe* of **M** in Gilead, Iddo 4519
2Ch 15: 9 strangers with them out of Ephraim and **M**, 4519
30: 1 and wrote letters also to Ephraim and **M**, 4519
30:10 of Ephraim and **M** even unto Zebulun: 4519
30:11 Nevertheless divers of Asher and **M** and 4519
30:18 of Ephraim, and **M**, Issachar, and Zebulun, 4519
31: 1 and Benjamin, in Ephraim also and **M**, 4519
32:33 And **M** his son reigned in his stead. 4519
33: 1 **M** *was* twelve years old when he *began* to 4519
33: 9 So **M** made Judah and the inhabitants of 4519
33:10 the LORD spake to **M**, and to his people: 4519
33:11 which took **M** among the thorns, and 4519
33:13 Then **M** knew that the LORD he *was* God. 4519
33:18 Now the rest of the acts of **M**, and 4519
33:20 So **M** slept with his fathers, and they buried 4519
33:22 sight of the LORD, as did **M** his father: 4519
33:22 images which **M** his father had made, 4519
33:23 as **M** his father had humbled himself; 4519
34: 6 *so did he* in the cities of **M**, and Ephraim, 4519
34: 9 the doors had gathered of the hand of **M** 4519
Ezr 10:30 Mattaniah, Bezaleel, and Binnui, and **M**. 4519
10:33 Zabad, Eliphelet, Jeremai, **M**, *and* Shimei. 4519
Ps 60: 7 Gilead *is* mine, and **M** *is* mine; 4519
80: 2 and Benjamin and **M** stir up thy strength, 4519
108: 8 Gilead *is* mine; **M** *is* mine; Ephraim also *is* 4519
Isa 9:21 **M**, Ephraim; and Ephraim, Manasseh: *and* 4519
9:21 Manasseh, Ephraim; and Ephraim, **M**: *and* 4519
Jer 15: 4 of **M** the son of Hezekiah king of Judah, 4519
Eze 48: 4 side unto the west side, a *portion for* **M**. 4519
48: 5 by the border of **M**, from the east side unto 4519

MANASSEH'S (4) [MANASSEH]
Ge 48:14 and his left hand upon **M** head, 4519
48:17 to remove it from Ephraim's head unto **M** 4519
Jos 17: 6 the rest of **M** sons had the land of Gilead. 4519
17:10 northward *it was* **M**, and the sea is 4519+3807.1

MANASSES (3) [MANASSEH]
Mt 1:10 And Ezekias begat **M**; and Manasses begat *3128*
1:10 and **M** begat Amon; and Amon begat *3128*
Rev 7: 6 Of the tribe of **M** *were* sealed twelve *3128*

MANASSITES (3) [MANASSEH]
Dt 4:43 and Golan in Bashan, of the **M**. 4520
Jdg 12: 4 among the Ephraimites, *and* among the **M**. 4519
2Ki 10:33 and the Reubenites, and the **M**, from Aroer, 4520

MANDRAKES (6)
Ge 30:14 found **m** in the field, and brought them unto 1736
30:14 Give me, I pray thee, of thy son's **m**. 1736
30:15 wouldest thou take away my son's **m** also? 1736
30:15 shall lie with thee to night for thy son's **m**. 1736
30:16 surely I have hired thee with my son's **m**. 1736
SS 7:13 The **m** give a smell, and at our gates *are* all 1736

MANEH (1)
Eze 45:12 fifteen shekels, shall be your **m**. 4488

MANGER (3)
Lk 2: 7 in swaddling clothes, and laid him in a **m**; *5336*
2:12 wrapped in swaddling clothes, lying in a **m**. *5336*
2:16 and Joseph, and the babe lying in a **m**. *5336*

MANIFEST (39) [MANIFESTATION, MANIFESTED, MANIFESTLY]
Ecc 3:18 that God might **m** them, and that *they* 1305
Lk 8:17 nothing is secret, that shall not be made **m**; *5318*
Jn 1:31 but that he should be **made m** to Israel, *5319*
3:21 that his deeds may be **made m**, that they *5319*
9: 3 that the works of God should be **made m** in *5319*
14:21 I will love him, and will **m** myself to him. *1718*
14:22 how is it that thou wilt **m** thyself unto us, *1718*
Ac 4:16 *is* **m** to all them that dwell in Jerusalem; *5318*
Ro 1:19 which may be known of God is **m** in them; *5318*
10:20 I was made **m** unto them that asked not *1717*
16:26 But now is **made m**, and by the scriptures *5319*
1Co 3:13 Every man's work shall be made **m**: for *5318*
4: 5 and will **make m** the counsels of the hearts: *5319*
11:19 *are* approved may be made **m** among you. *5318*
14:25 thus are the secrets of his heart made **m**; *5318*
15:27 all *things* are put under *him, it is* **m** that he *1212*
2Co 2:14 **maketh m** the savour of his knowledge by *5319*
4:10 that the life also of Jesus might be **made m** *5319*
4:11 that the life also of Jesus might be **made m** *5319*
5:11 but we are **made m** unto God; and I trust *5319*
5:11 I trust also are **made m** in your *5319*
11: 6 we *have been* throughly **made m** among *5319*
Gal 5:19 Now the works of the flesh are **m**, *5318*
Eph 5:13 But all *things* that are reproved are **made m** *5319*
5:13 for whatsoever doth **make m** is light. *5319*
Php 1:13 So that my bonds in Christ are **m** in all *5318*
Col 1:26 but now is **made m** to his saints: *5319*
4: 4 That I may **make** it **m**, as I ought to speak. *5319*
2Th 1: 5 *Which is* a **m token** of the righteous *1730*
1Ti 3:16 God was **m** in the flesh, justified in *5319*
5:25 the good works *of some* are **m beforehand**; *4271*
2Ti 1:10 But is now **made m** by the appearing of our *5319*
3: 9 for their folly shall be **m** unto all *men*, as *1552*
Heb 4:13 Neither is there any creature *that is* **not m** in *852*
9: 8 into the holiest *of all* was not yet **made m**, *5319*
1Pe 1:20 but was **m** in *these* last times for you, *5319*
1Jn 2:19 *they went out*, that they might be **made m** *5319*
3:10 In this the children of God are **m**, and *5318*
Rev 15: 4 before thee; for thy judgments are **made m**. *5319*

MANIFESTATION (3) [MANIFEST]
Ro 8:19 waiteth for the **m** of the sons of God. *602*
1Co 12: 7 But the **m** of the Spirit is given to every *5321*
2Co 4: 2 by **m** of the truth commending ourselves to *5321*

MANIFESTED (10) [MANIFEST]
Mk 4:22 there is nothing hid, which shall not be **m**; *5319*
Jn 2:11 in Cana of Galilee, and **m forth** his glory; *5319*
17: 6 I have **m** thy name unto the men which *5319*
Ro 3:21 righteousness of God without the law is **m**, *5319*

Tit 1: 3 But hath in due times **m** his word through *5319*
1Jn 1: 2 (For the life was **m**, and we have seen *it*, *5319*
1: 2 was with the Father, and was **m** unto us;) *5319*
1: 5 And ye know that he was **m** to take away *5319*
3: 8 For this purpose the Son of God was **m**, *5319*
4: 9 In this was **m** the love of God towards us, *5319*

MANIFESTLY (1) [MANIFEST]
2Co 3: 3 Forasmuch as ye are **m declared** to be *5319*

MANIFOLD (8)
Ne 9:19 Yet thou in thy **m** mercies forsookest them 7227
9:27 according to thy **m** mercies thou gavest 7227
Ps 104:24 O LORD, how **m** are thy works! 7231
Am 5:12 For I know your **m** transgressions and 7227
Lk 18:30 Who shall not receive **m more** in this *4179*
Eph 3:10 by the church the **m** wisdom of God, *4182*
1Pe 1: 6 ye are in heaviness through **m** temptations: *4164*
4:10 as good stewards of the **m** grace of God. *4164*

MANKIND (6) [MAN]
Lev 18:22 Thou shalt not lie with **m**, as with 2145
20:13 If a man also lie with **m**, as he lieth with a 2145
Job 12:10 living *thing*, and the breath of all **m**. 376+1320
1Co 6: 9 nor **abusers** of themselves **with m**, *733*
1Ti 1:10 for **them that defile** themselves **with m**, *733*
Jas 3: 7 the sea, is tamed, and hath been tamed **of m**: *442*

MANNA (19)
Ex 16:15 saw *it*, they said one to another, It *is* **m**: 4478
16:31 house of Israel called the name thereof **M**: 4478
16:33 put an omer full of **m** therein, and lay it up 4478
16:35 the children of Israel did eat **m** forty years, 4478
16:35 they did eat **m**, until they came unto 4478
Nu 11: 6 at all, beside *this* **m**, *before* our eyes. 4478
11: 7 the **m** *was* as coriander seed, and the colour 4478
11: 9 the camp in the night, the **m** fell upon it. 4478
Dt 8: 3 thee to hunger, and fed thee with **m**, 4478
8:16 Who fed thee in the wilderness with **m**, 4478
Jos 5:12 the **m** ceased on the morrow after they had 4478
5:12 neither had the children of Israel **m** any 4478
Ne 9:20 withheldest not thy **m** from their mouth, 4478
Ps 78:24 had rained down **m** upon them to eat, and 4478
Jn 6:31 Our fathers did eat **m** in the desert; as it is *3131*
6:49 Your fathers did eat **m** in the wilderness, *3131*
6:58 not as your fathers did eat **m**, and are dead: *3131*
Heb 9: 4 wherein *was* the golden pot that had **m**, and *3131*
Rev 2:17 will I give to eat of the hidden **m**, *3131*

MANNER (196) [MANNERS]
Ge 18:11 it ceased to be with Sarah after the **m** of 734
18:25 That be far from thee to do after this **m**, to 1697
19:31 come in unto us after the **m** of all the earth: 1870
25:23 two **m** of people shall be separated from thy NIH
32:19 On this **m** shall you speak unto Esau, 1697
39:19 After this **m** did thy servant to me; 1697
40:13 after the former **m** when thou wast his 4941
40:17 in the uppermost basket *there was* of all *m* NIH
45:23 to his father he sent after this **m**; ten asses NIH
Ex 1:14 in brick, and in **all m** of service in the field: 3605
7:11 they also did **in like m** with their 3651
12:16 no *m of* work shall be done in them, NIH
21: 9 he shall deal with her after the **m** of 4941
22: 9 For all **m** of trespass, *whether it be* for ox, 1697
22: 9 for **any m** of lost *thing*, which *another* 3605
23:11 **In like m** thou shalt deal with thy vineyard, 3651
31: 3 in knowledge, and in all *m of* workmanship, NIH
31: 5 of timber, to work in all *m of* workmanship. NIH
35:29 them willing to bring for all *m of* work, NIH
35:31 in knowledge, and in all *m of* workmanship; NIH
35:33 of wood, to make any *m of* cunning work. NIH
35:35 to work all *m of* work, of the engraver, and NIH
36: 1 understanding to know how to work all *m* NIH
Lev 5:10 *for* a burnt offering, according to the **m**: 4941
7:23 Ye shall eat no *m* fat, of ox, or of sheep, or NIH
7:26 Moreover ye shall eat no *m of* blood, NIH
7:27 Whatsoever soul *it be* that eateth any *m of* NIH
9:16 and offered it according to the **m**. 4941
11:27 among all *m of* beasts that go on *all* four, NIH
11:44 shall ye defile yourselves with any *m* NIH
14:54 This *is* the law for all *m of* plague of NIH
17:10 among you, that eateth any *m of* blood; NIH
17:14 Ye shall eat the blood of no *m of* flesh: NIH
19:23 shall have planted all *m of* trees for food, NIH
20:25 by any *m of living thing* that creepeth *on* NIH
23:31 Ye shall do no *m of* work: *it shall be* a NIH
24:22 Ye shall have **one m** of law, as well for 259
Nu 5:13 neither she be taken *with the m*; NIH
9:14 according to the **m** thereof, so shall he do: 4941
15:13 country shall do these *things* **after this m**, 3602
15:16 One law and one **m** shall be for you, and 4941
15:24 according to the **m**, and one kid of 4941
28:18 ye shall do no *m of* servile work *therein:* NIH
28:24 **After** this **m** ye shall offer daily, 3509.1
29: 6 according unto their **m**, for a sweet savour, 4941
29:18 *be* according to their number, after the **m**: 4941
29:21 *be* according to their number, after the **m**: 4941
29:24 *be* according to their number, after the **m**: 4941
29:27 *be* according to their number, after the **m**: 4941
29:30 *be* according to their number, after the **m**: 4941
29:33 *be* according to their number, after the **m**: 4941
29:37 *be* according to their number, after the **m**: 4941
31:30 of all *m of* beasts, and give them unto NIH
Dt 4:15 for ye saw no *m of* similitude on the day NIH
15: 2 this *is* the **m** of the release: Every creditor 1697
22: 3 **In like m** shalt thou do with his ass; and so 3651
27:21 Cursed *be* he that lieth with any *m of* beast. NIH
Jos 6:15 compassed the city after the same **m** seven 4941
Jdg 8:18 **What m** of men *were they* whom ye slew at 375
11:17 **in like m** they sent unto the king of Moab: 1571
18: 7 after the **m** of the Zidonians, quiet and 4941
Ru 4: 7 Now this *was the m* in former time in Israel NIH
1Sa 8: 9 shew them the **m** of the king that shall 4941
8:11 This will be the **m** of the king that shall 4941
10:25 Samuel told the people the **m** of 4941
17:27 the people answered him after this **m**, 1697
17:30 and spake after the same **m**: 1697
17:30 answered him again after the former **m**. 1697
18:24 told him, saying, On this **m** spake David. 1697
19:24 prophesied before Samuel **in like m**, and 1571
21: 5 and *the bread is in* a **m** common, yea, 1870
27:11 *will be* his **m** all the while he dwelleth in 4941
2Sa 6: 5 on all *m of instruments made of* fir wood, NIH
7:19 And *is* this the **m** of man, O Lord GOD? 8452
14: 3 to the king, and speak on this **m** unto him. 1697
15: 6 on this **m** did Absalom to all Israel that 1697
17: 6 Ahithophel hath spoken after this **m**: 1697
1Ki 7:28 the work of the bases *was on* this *m*: they NIH
7:37 After this *m* he made the ten bases: all of NIH
18:28 cut themselves after their **m** with knives 4941
22:20 one said on **this m**, and another said on that 3541
22:20 on this manner, and another said on **that m**. 3541
2Ki 1: 7 What **m** of man *was he* which came up to 4941
11:14 as the **m** *was*, and the princes and 4941
17:26 know not the **m** of the God of the land: 4941
17:26 they know not the **m** of the God of the land. 4941
17:27 let him teach them the **m** of the God of 4941
17:33 after the **m** of the nations whom they 4941
17:40 but they did after their former **m**. 4941
1Ch 6:48 *m of* service of the tabernacle of the house NIH
12:37 with all *m of* instruments of war for NIH
18:10 *with him* all *m of* vessels of gold and silver NIH
22:15 all *m of* cunning *men* for every *manner of* NIH
22:15 all *manner of* cunning *men* for every *m of* NIH
23:29 is fried, and for all *m of* measure and size; NIH
24:19 according to their **m**, under Aaron their 4941
28:14 of **all m of service**; 5656+5656+2050.1
28:21 *there shall be* with thee for all *m of* NIH
28:21 willing skilful *man*, for any *m of* service: NIH
29: 2 all *m of* precious stones, and marble stones NIH
29: 5 for all *m of* work *to be made* by the hands NIH
2Ch 2:14 also to grave any *m of* graving, and to find NIH
4:20 that they should burn after the **m** before 4941
13: 9 have made you priests **after the m of** 3509.1
18:19 one spake saying **after this m**, and 3602
18:19 and another saying **after that m**. 3602
30:16 they stood in their place after their **m**, 4941
32:15 nor persuade you on this *m*, neither yet NIH
32:27 for shields, and for all *m of* pleasant jewels; NIH
32:28 stalls for all *m of* beasts, and cotes for NIH
34:13 work in **any m of service:** 5656+5656+2050.1
Ezr 5: 4 said we unto them **after this m**, What are 3660
Ne 6: 4 and I answered them after the same **m**. 1697
6: 5 sent Sanballat his servant unto me in like **m** 1697
8:18 a solemn assembly, according unto the **m**. 4941
10:37 the fruit of all *m of* trees, of wine and of oil, NIH
13:15 grapes, and figs, and all *m of* burdens, NIH
13:16 all *m of* ware, and sold on the sabbath unto NIH

Est 1:13 *was* the king's **m** towards all that knew law 1697
2:12 according to the **m** of the women, (for so 1881
Ps 107:18 Their soul abhorreth all *m of* meat; and NIH
144:13 affording **all m of store**: 413+2177+2177+4480
SS 7:13 at our gates *are* all *m of* pleasant *fruits,* new NIH
Isa 5:17 shall the lambs feed after their **m**, and 1699
10:24 his staff against thee, after the **m** of Egypt. 1870
10:26 so shall he lift it up after the **m** of Egypt. 1870
51: 6 they that dwell therein shall die **in like m**: 3654
Jer 13: 9 **After this m** will I mar the pride of Judah, 3602
22:21 This *hath been* thy **m** from thy youth, 1870
30:18 the palace shall remain after the **m** thereof. 4941
Eze 20:30 Are ye polluted after the **m** of your fathers? 1870
23:15 *after* the **m** of the Babylonians of Chaldea, 1823
23:45 they shall judge them **after the m** of 4941
23:45 and **after the m** of *women* that shed blood; 4941
Da 6:23 no **m** of hurt was found upon him, because 3606
Am 4:10 you the pestilence after the **m** of Egypt: 1870
8:14 liveth; and, The **m** of Beer-sheba liveth; 1870
Mt 4:23 and healing all *m of* sickness and NIG
4:23 and all *m of* disease among the people. NIG
5:11 shall say **all m** of evil against you falsely, *3956*
6: 9 **After this m** therefore pray ye: Our Father *3779*
8:27 saying, **What m of man** is this, that even *4217*
10: 1 and to heal all *m of* sickness and all *manner* NIG
10: 1 all *manner of* sickness and all *m of* disease. NIG
12:31 All *m of* sin and blasphemy shall be NIG
Mk 4:41 What *m of* man is this, that even the wind NIG
13: 1 see **what m** of stones and what buildings *4217*
13:29 **So** ye **in like m**, when ye shall see *2532+3779*
Lk 1:29 cast in her mind **what m** of salutation this *4217*
1:66 saying, What *m of* child shall this be! NIG
6:23 for **in the like m** did their *846+2596+3588*
7:39 **what m of** woman *this is* that toucheth *4217*
8:25 one to another, What *m of man* is this? NIG
9:55 Ye know not **what m** of spirit ye are of. *3634*
11:42 for ye tithe mint and rue and all *m of* herbs, NIG
20:31 third took her; and **in like m** the seven also: *5615*
24:17 What *m of* communications *are* these that NIG
Jn 2: 6 **after the m** of the purifying of the Jews, *2596*
7:36 What *m of* saying is this that he said, NIG
19:40 the spices, as the **m** of the Jews is to bury. *1485*
Ac 1:11 come *in* like **m** as ye have seen him go into *5158*
10:12 Wherein were all *m of* fourfooted beasts of NIG
15: 1 *said,* Except ye be circumcised after the **m** *1485*
15:23 they wrote *letters* by them **after this m**; *3592*
17: 2 And Paul, as his **m** was, went in unto them, *1486*
Ac 20:18 **after what m** I have been with you at all *4459*
22: 3 taught according to the **perfect m** of the law *195*
23:25 And he wrote a letter after this **m**: *5179*
25:16 It is not the **m** of the Romans to deliver any *1485*
25:20 because I doubted of such *m of* questions, NIG
26: 4 My **m of life** from *my* youth, which was at *981*
Ro 6:19 I speak **after the m of men** because of *442*
7: 8 wrought in me all *m of* concupiscence. NIG
1Co 7: 7 his proper gift of God, one **after this m**, *3779*
11:25 **After the same m** also *he took* the cup, *5615*
15:32 If **after the m of** men I have fought with *2596*
2Co 7: 9 for ye were made sorry **after a** godly **m**, *2596*
Gal 2:14 livest **after the m of Gentiles**, and not as *1483*
3:15 Brethren, I speak **after the m** of men; *2596*
1Th 1: 5 as ye know **what m** of *men* we were among *3634*
1: 9 For they themselves shew of us **what m of** *3697*
1Ti 2: 9 **In like m** also, that women adorn *5615*
2Ti 3:10 **m of life**, purpose, faith, longsuffering, *72*
Heb 10:25 as the **m** of some *is;* but exhorting *one* *1485*
Jas 1:24 straightway forgetteth **what m of** *man* he *3697*
1Pe 1:11 **what m** of time the Spirit of Christ which *4169*
1:15 so be ye holy in all *m of* conversation; NIG
3: 5 For **after this m** in the old time the holy *3779*
2Pe 3:11 **what m** *of persons* ought ye to be in all *4217*
1Jn 3: 1 **what m** of love the Father hath bestowed *4217*
Jude 1: 7 in like **m** giving themselves over to *5158*
Rev 11: 5 will hurt them, he must **in this m** be killed. *3779*
18:12 and all *m* vessels of ivory, and all *manner* NIG
18:12 and all *m* vessels of most precious wood, NIG
21:19 garnished with all *m of* precious stones. NIG
22: 2 which bare twelve *m of* fruits, *and* NIG

MANNERS (6) [MANNER]
Lev 20:23 ye shall not walk in the **m** of the nation, 2708
2Ki 17:34 Unto this day they do after the former **m**: 4941
Eze 11:12 have done after the **m** of the heathen that 4941
Ac 13:18 years **suffered** he their **m** in the wilderness. *5159*
1Co 15:33 evil communications corrupt good **m**. *2239*
Heb 1: 1 in divers **m** spake in time past unto *4187*

MANOAH (18)
Jdg 13: 2 family of the Danites, whose name *was* **M**; 4495
13: 8 **M** intreated the LORD, and said, O my 4495
13: 9 God hearkened to the voice of **M**; and 4495
13: 9 but **M** her husband *was* not with her. 4495
13:11 **M** arose, and went after his wife, and 4495
13:12 **M** said, Now let thy words come to pass. 4495
13:13 the angel of the LORD said unto **M**, Of all 4495
13:15 **M** said unto the angel of the LORD, 4495
13:16 the angel of the LORD said unto **M**, 4495
13:16 For **M** knew not that he *was* an angel of 4495
13:17 **M** said unto the angel of the LORD, 4495
13:19 So **M** took a kid with a meat offering, and 4495
13:19 and **M** and his wife looked on. 4495
13:20 **M** and his wife looked on *it,* and fell on 4495
13:21 of the LORD did no more appear to **M** 4495
13:21 **M** knew that he *was* an angel of 4495
13:22 **M** said unto his wife, We shall surely die, 4495
16:31 Eshtaol in the buryingplace of **M** his father. 4495

MANSERVANT (12) [MAN, SERVE]
Ex 20:10 thou, nor thy son, nor thy daughter, thy **m**, 5650
20:17 nor his **m**, nor his maidservant, nor his ox, 5650
21:32 If the ox shall push a **m** or a maidservant; 5650
Dt 5:14 nor thy son, nor thy daughter, nor thy **m**, 5650
5:14 that thy **m** and thy maidservant may rest as 5650
5:21 or his **m**, or his maidservant, his ox, or 5650
12:18 thy **m**, and thy maidservant, and the Levite 5650
16:11 thy **m**, and thy maidservant, and the Levite 5650
16:14 thy **m**, and thy maidservant, and the Levite, 5650
Job 31:13 If I did despise the cause of my **m** or of my 5650
Jer 34: 9 That every man should let his **m**, and 5650
34:10 heard that every one should let his **m**, and 5650

MANSERVANT'S (1) [MAN, SERVE]
Ex 21:27 if he smite out his **m** tooth, or 5650

MANSERVANTS (1) [MAN, SERVE]
Ne 7:67 Beside their **m** and their maidservants, 5650

MANSIONS (1)
Jn 14: 2 In my Father's house are many **m**: if *it* *3438*

MANSLAYER (2) [MAN, SLAY]
Nu 35: 6 which ye shall appoint for the **m**, that he 7523
35:12 that the **m** die not, until he stand before 7523

MANSLAYERS (1) [MAN, SLAY]
1Ti 1: 9 of fathers and murderers of mothers, for **m**, *409*

MANTLE (13) [MANTLES]
Jdg 4:18 her into the tent, she covered him with a **m**. 8063
1Sa 15:27 he laid hold upon the skirt of his **m**, and 4598
28:14 cometh up; and he *is* covered with a **m**. 4598
1Ki 19:13 heard *it,* that he wrapped his face in his **m**, 155
19:19 passed by him, and cast his **m** upon him. 155
2Ki 2: 8 And Elijah took his **m**, and wrapt *it* together, 155
2:13 He took up also the **m** of Elijah that fell 155
2:14 he took the **m** of Elijah that fell from him, 155
Ezr 9: 3 I rent my garment and my **m**, and 4598
9: 5 having rent my garment and my **m**, I fell 4598
Job 1:20 rent his **m**, and shaved his head, and 4598
2:12 they rent every one his **m**, and 4598
Ps 109:29 *with* their own confusion, as *with* a **m**. 4598

MANTLES (1) [MANTLE]
Isa 3:22 the **m**, and the wimples, and the crisping 4595

MANURE PILE See DUNGHILL

MANY (556) See Index

MAOCH (1)
1Sa 27: 2 unto Achish, the son of **M**, king of Gath. 4582

MAON (7) [MAONITES]
Jos 15:55 **M**, Carmel, and Ziph, and Juttah, 4584
1Sa 23:24 and his men *were* in the wilderness of **M**, 4584
23:25 a rock, and abode in the wilderness of **M**. 4584
23:25 pursued after David *in* the wilderness of **M**. 4584
25: 2 *there was* a man in **M**, whose possessions 4584
1Ch 2:45 the son of Shammai *was* **M**: and Maon *was* 4584
2:45 and **M** *was* the father of Beth-zur. 4584

MAONITES (1) [MAON]
Jdg 10:12 the Amalekites, and the **M**, did oppress 4584

MAR (6) [MARRED]
Lev 19:27 neither shalt thou **m** the corners of thy 7843
Ru 4: 6 for myself, lest I **m** mine own inheritance: 7843
1Sa 6: 5 and images of your mice that **m** the land; 7843
2Ki 3:19 **m** every good piece of land with stones. 3510
Job 30:13 They **m** my path, they set forward my 5420
Jer 13: 9 After this manner will I **m** the pride of 7843

MARA (1)
Ru 1:20 unto them, Call me not Naomi, call me **M**: 4755

MARAH (5)
Ex 15:23 when they came to **M**, they could not drink 4785
15:23 they could not drink of the waters of **M**, 4785
15:23 the name of it was called **M**. 4785
Nu 33: 8 the wilderness of Etham, and pitched in **M**. 4785
33: 9 they removed from **M**, and came unto 4785

MARALAH (1)
Jos 19:11 **M**, and reached to Dabbasheth, and 4831

MARAN-ATHA (1)
1Co 16:22 Lord Jesus Christ, let him be anathema, **M**. *3134*

MARBLE (5)
1Ch 29: 2 and **m** stones in abundance. 7893
Est 1: 6 and purple to silver rings and pillars of **m**: 8336
1: 6 of red, and **blue**, and white, and black **m**. 8336
SS 5:15 His legs *are as* pillars of **m**, set upon 8336
Rev 18:12 and of brass, and iron, and **m**, *3139*

MARCH (5) [MARCHED, MARCHEDST]
Ps 68: 7 when thou didst **m** through the wilderness; 6805
Jer 46:22 for they shall **m** with an army, and 1980
Joel 2: 7 they shall **m** every one on his ways, and 1980
Hab 1: 6 which *shall* **m** through the breadth of 1980
3:12 Thou didst **m through** the land in 6805

MARCHED (1) [MARCH]
Ex 14:10 and behold, the Egyptians **m** after them; 5265

MARCHEDST (1) [MARCH]
Jdg 5: 4 when thou **m** out of the field of Edom, 6805

MARCUS (3) [MARK]
Col 4:10 and **M**, sister's son to Barnabas, *3138*
Phm 1:24 **M**, Aristarchus, Demas, Lucas, *3138*
1Pe 5:13 *you,* saluteth you; and *so doth* **M** my son. *3138*

MARDUK See MERODACH

MARESHAH (8)
Jos 15:44 Keilah, and Achzib, and **M**; nine cities with 4762
1Ch 2:42 and the sons of **M** the father of Hebron. 4762
4:21 Laadah the father of **M**, and the families of 4762
2Ch 11: 8 And Gath, and **M**, and Ziph, 4762
14: 9 three hundred chariots; and came unto **M**. 4762
14:10 in array in the valley of Zephathah at **M**. 4762
20:37 Eliezer the son of Dodavah of **M** 4762
Mic 1:15 bring an heir unto thee, O inhabitant of **M**: 4762

MARINERS (5)
Eze 27: 8 of Zidon and Arvad were thy **m**: 7751
27: 9 all the ships of the sea with their **m** were in 4419
27:27 thy **m**, and thy pilots, thy calkers, and 4419
27:29 the oar, the **m**, *and* all the pilots of the sea, 4419
Jnh 1: 5 the **m** were afraid, and cried every man 4419

MARISHES (1)
Eze 47:11 and the **m** thereof shall not be healed; 1360

MARITAL UNFAITHFULNESS See FORNICATION

MARK (37) [LANDMARK, LANDMARKS, MARCUS, MARKED, MARKEST, MARKETH, MARKS, WAYMARKS]
Ge 4:15 the LORD set a **m** upon Cain, lest any 226
Ru 3: 4 that thou shalt **m** the place where he shall 3045
1Sa 20:20 on the side *thereof,* as *though* I shot at a **m**. 4307
2Sa 13:28 **M** ye now when Amnon's heart is merry 7200
1Ki 20: 7 said, **M**, I pray you, and see how this *man* 3045
20:22 and **m**, and see what thou doest: 3045
Job 7:20 why hast thou set me as a **m** against thee, 4645
16:12 me to pieces, and set me up for his **m**. 4307
18: 2 of words? **m**, and afterwards we will speak. 995
21: 5 **M** me, and be astonished, and 413+6437
33:31 **M well**, O Job, hearken unto me: hold thy 7181
39: 1 *or* canst thou **m** when the hinds do calve? 8104
Ps 37:37 **M** the perfect *man,* and behold the upright: 8104
48:13 **M** ye well her bulwarks, consider her 7896
56: 6 they hide themselves, they **m** my steps, 8104
130: 3 LORD, shouldest **m** iniquities, O Lord, 8104
La 3:12 his bow, and set me as a **m** for the arrow. 4307
Eze 9: 4 **set a m** upon the foreheads of 8420+8427
9: 6 not near any man upon whom *is* the **m**; 8420
44: 5 **m well**, and behold with thine eyes, 3820+7760
44: 5 **m well** the entering in of the house, 3820+7760
Ac 12:12 the mother of John, whose surname was **M**; *3138*
12:25 with *them* John, whose surname was **M**. *3138*
15:37 with *them* John, whose surname was **M**. *3138*
15:39 and *so* Barnabas took **M**, and sailed unto *3138*
Ro 16:17 **m** them which cause divisions and offences *4648*
Php 3:14 I press toward the **m** for the prize of *4649*
3:17 and **m** them which walk so as ye have us *4648*
2Ti 4:11 Take **M**, and bring *him* with thee: for he is *3138*
Rev 13:16 to receive a **m** in their right hand, or in their *5480*
13:17 save he that had the **m**, or the name of *5480*
14: 9 and receive *his* **m** in his forehead, or in his *5480*
14:11 whosoever receiveth the **m** of his name. *5480*
15: 2 and over his image, and over his **m**, *5480*
16: 2 upon the men which had the **m** of the beast, *5480*
19:20 them that had received the **m** of the beast, *5480*
20: 4 neither had received *his* **m** upon their *5480*

MARKED (6) [MARK]
1Sa 1:12 before the LORD, that Eli **m** her mouth. 8104
Job 22:15 Hast thou **m** the old way which wicked 8104
24:16 *which* they had **m** for themselves in 2856
Jer 2:22 *yet* thine iniquity *is* **m** before me, 3799
23:18 who hath **m** his word, and heard *it?* 7181
Lk 14: 7 when he **m** how they chose out the chief *1907*

MARKEST (1) [MARK]
Job 10:14 thou **m** me, and thou wilt not acquit me 8104

MARKET (7) [MARKETPLACE, MARKET-PLACE, MARKETPLACES, MARKETS]
Eze 27:13 of men and vessels of brass in thy **m**. 4627
27:17 they traded in thy **m** wheat of Minnith, and 4627
27:19 cassia, and calamus, were in thy **m**. 4627
27:25 ships of Tarshish did sing of thee *in* thy **m**: 4627
Mk 7: 4 And *when they come* from the **m**, except they *58*
Jn 5: 2 Now there is at Jerusalem by the sheep *m* a NIG
Ac 17:17 in the **m** daily with them that met with *him.* *58*

MARKETH (3) [MARK]
Job 33:11 my feet in the stocks, he **m** all my paths. 8104
Isa 44:13 he **m** it **out** with a line; he fitteth it with 8388
44:13 he **m** it **out** with the compass, and 8388

MARKETPLACE, MARKET-PLACE (3) [MARKET, PLACE]
Mt 20: 3 and saw others standing idle in the **m**, *58*
Lk 7:32 They are like unto children sitting in the **m**, *58*
Ac 16:19 and drew *them* into the **m** unto the rulers, *58*

MARKETPLACES (1) [MARKET, PLACE]
Mk 12:38 long clothing, and *love* salutations in the **m**, *58*

MARKETS (4) [MARKET]
Mt 11:16 It is like unto children sitting in the **m**, and *58*
23: 7 And greetings in the **m**, and to be called of *58*
Lk 11:43 in the synagogues, and greetings in the **m**. *58*
20:46 and love greetings in the **m**, and the highest *58*

MARKS (2) [MARK]
Lev 19:28 for the dead, nor print any **m** upon you: 7085
Gal 6:17 for I bear in my body the **m** of the Lord *4742*

MAROTH (1)
Mic 1:12 For the inhabitant of **M** waited carefully for 4796

MARRED (5) [MAR]
Isa 52:14 his visage *was* so **m** more than *any* man, 4893
Jer 13: 7 behold, the girdle was **m**, it was profitable 7843
18: 4 the vessel that he made of clay was **m** in 7843
Na 2: 2 them out, and **m** their vine branches. 7843
Mk 2:22 the wine is spilled, and the bottles will be **m**: *622*

M

MARRIAGE (19) [MARRY]
Ex 21:10 her raiment, and her **duty of m**, shall he not 5772
Ps 78:63 and their maidens were not **given to m**. 1984
Mt 22: 2 a certain king, which made a **m** for his son, *1062*
22: 4 and all *things are* ready: come unto the **m**. *1062*
22: 9 and as many as ye shall find, bid to the **m**. *1062*
22:30 they neither marry, nor are **given in m**, *1547*
24:38 and drinking, marrying and **giving in m**, *1547*
25:10 *that were* ready went in with him to the **m**: *1062*
Mk 12:25 they neither marry, nor are **given in m**; *1061*
Lk 17:27 they married *wives,* they were **given in m**, *1547*
20:34 of this world marry, and are **given in m**: *1548*
20:35 the dead, neither marry, nor are **given in m**: *1548*
Jn 2: 1 And the third day there was a **m** in Cana of *1062*
2: 2 was called, and his disciples, to the **m**. *1062*
1Co 7:38 So then he that **giveth** *her* **in m** doeth well; *1547*
7:38 but he that **giveth** *her* not **in m** doeth better. *1547*
Heb 13: 4 **M** *is* honourable in all, and the bed *1062*
Rev 19: 7 for the **m** of the Lamb is come, and his wife *1062*
19: 9 are called unto the **m** supper of the Lamb. *1062*

MARRIAGES (3) [MARRY]
Ge 34: 9 **make** ye **m** with us, *and* give your 2859
Dt 7: 3 Neither shalt thou **make m** with them; 2859
Jos 23:12 shall **make m** with them, and go in unto 2859

MARRIED (30) [MARRY]
Ge 19:14 which **m** his daughters, and said, Up, get ye 3947
Ex 21: 3 if he *were* **m**, then his wife shall go 802+1167
Lev 22:12 If the priest's daughter also be *m* unto a NIH
Nu 12: 1 of the Ethiopian woman whom he had **m**: 3947
12: 1 for he had **m** an Ethiopian woman. 3947
36: 3 *if* they be **m** to any of the sons of 802+3807.1
36:11 **m** unto their father's brothers' 802+1961+3807.1
36:12 *And* they were **m** into 802+1961+3807.1
Dt 22:22 If a man be found lying with a woman **m** to 1166
24: 1 **m** her, and it come to pass that she find no 1166
1Ch 2:21 whom he **m** when he *was* threescore years 3947
2Ch 13:21 **m** fourteen wives, and 5375+3807.1
Ne 13:23 In those days also saw I Jews *that* had **m** 3427
Pr 30:23 For an odious *woman* when she is **m**; and 1166
Isa 54: 1 desolate than the children of the **m wife**, 1166
62: 4 delighteth in thee, and thy land shall be **m**. 1166
Jer 3:14 saith the LORD; for I am **m** unto you: 1166
Mal 2:11 and hath **m** the daughter of a strange god. 1166
Mt 22:25 when he had **m** *a wife,* deceased, and, *1060*
Mk 6:17 his brother Philip's wife: for he had **m** her. *1060*
10:12 and be **m** to another, she committeth *1060*
Lk 14:20 I have **m** a wife, and therefore I cannot *1060*
17:27 they **m** *wives,* they were given in marriage, *1060*
Ro 7: 3 husband liveth, she be **m** to another man, *1096*
7: 3 though she be **m** to another man. *1096*
7: 4 that ye should be **m** to another, *even* to him *1096*
1Co 7:10 And unto the **m** I command, *yet* not I, but *1060*
7:33 But he that is **m** careth for the *things that* *1060*
7:34 she that is **m** careth for the *things* of *1060*
7:39 she is at liberty to be **m** to whom she will; *1060*

MARRIETH (4) [MARRY]
Isa 62: 5 For *as* a young man **m** a virgin, *so* shall thy 1166
Mt 19: 9 whoso **m** her *which is* put away doth *1060*
Lk 16:18 and **m** another, committeth adultery: *1060*
16:18 whosoever **m** her that is put away from *her* *1060*

MARROW (5)
Job 21:24 and his bones are moistened with **m**. 4221
Ps 63: 5 My soul shall be satisfied as *with* **m** and 2459
Pr 3: 8 be health to thy navel, and **m** to thy bones. 8250
Isa 25: 6 of wines on the lees, of fat things **full of m**, 4229
Heb 4:12 and of the joints and **m**, and *is* a discerner *3452*

MARRY (22) [MARRIAGE, MARRIAGES, MARRIED, MARRIETH, MARRYING, UNMARRIED]
Ge 38: 8 and **m** her, and raise up seed to thy brother. 2992
Nu 36: 6 **m** to whom they think best; 802+1961+3807.1
36: 6 of their father shall they **m**. 802+1961+3807.1
Dt 25: 5 the wife of the dead shall not **m** without 1961
Isa 62: 5 marrieth a virgin, *so* shall thy sons **m** thee: 1166
Mt 5:32 whosoever shall **m** her that is divorced *1060*
19: 9 and shall **m** another, committeth adultery: *1060*
19:10 so with *his* wife, it is not good to **m**. *1060*
22:24 his brother shall **m** his wife, and raise up *1918*
22:30 For in the resurrection they neither **m**, *1060*
Mk 10:11 and **m** another, committeth adultery against *1060*
12:25 they neither **m**, nor are given in marriage; *1060*
Lk 20:34 The children of this world **m**, and are given *1060*
20:35 neither **m**, nor are given in marriage: *1060*
1Co 7: 9 But if they cannot contain, let them **m**: *1060*
7: 9 for it is better to **m** than to burn. *1060*
7:28 But and if thou **m**, thou hast not sinned; *1060*
7:28 and if a virgin **m**, she hath not sinned. *1060*
7:36 do what he will, he sinneth not: let them **m**. *1060*
1Ti 4: 3 Forbidding to **m**, *and commanding* to *1060*
5:11 *to* wax wanton against Christ, they will **m**; *1060*
5:14 I will therefore that the younger *women* **m**, *1060*

MARRYING (2) [MARRY]
Ne 13:27 to transgress against our God in **m** strange 3427
Mt 24:38 and drinking, **m** and giving in marriage, *1060*

MARS' HILL (1) [AREOPAGUS]
Ac 17:22 Then Paul stood in the midst of **M**, and *697*

MARSENA (1)
Est 1:14 Tarshish, Meres, **M**, *and* Memucan, 4826

MARSHES See MARISHES

MART (1)
Isa 23: 3 *is* her revenue; and she is a **m** of nations. 5505

MARTHA (13)
Lk 10:38 a certain woman named **M** received him *3136*
10:40 But **M** was cumbered about much serving, *3136*
10:41 and said unto her, **M**, Martha, *3136*
10:41 and said unto her, Martha, **M**, *3136*
Jn 11: 1 the town of Mary and her sister **M**. *3136*
11: 5 Now Jesus loved **M**, and her sister, and *3136*
11:19 And many of the Jews came to **M** and *3136*
11:20 Then **M**, as soon as she heard that Jesus *3136*
11:21 Then said **M** unto Jesus, Lord, if thou hadst *3136*
11:24 **M** saith unto him, I know that he shall rise *3136*
11:30 but was in *that* place where **M** met him. *3136*
11:39 **M**, the sister of him that was dead, saith *3136*
12: 2 they made him a supper; and **M** served: *3136*

MARTYR (2) [MARTYRS]
Ac 22:20 And when the blood of thy **m** Stephen was *3144*
Rev 2:13 days wherein Antipas *was* my faithful **m**, *3144*

MARTYRS (1) [MARTYR]
Rev 17: 6 and with the blood of the **m** of Jesus: *3144*

MARVEL (11) [MARVELLED, MARVELLOUS, MARVELLOUSLY, MARVELS]
Ecc 5: 8 justice in a province, **m** not at the matter: 8539
Mk 5:20 Jesus had done for him: and all *men* did **m**. *2296*
Jn 3: 7 **M** not that I said unto thee, Ye must be *2296*
5:20 greater works than these, that ye may **m**. *2296*
5:28 **M** not at this: for the hour is coming, in *2296*
7:21 I have done one work, and ye all **m**. *2296*
Ac 3:12 Ye men of Israel, why **m** ye at this? *2296*
2Co 11:14 And no **m**; for Satan himself is transformed *2298*
Gal 1: 6 I **m** that you are so soon removed from him *2296*
1Jn 3:13 **M** not, my brethren, if the world hate you. *2296*
Rev 17: 7 said unto me, Wherefore didst thou **m**? *2296*

MARVELLED (23) [MARVEL]
Ge 43:33 to his youth: and the men **m** one at another. 8539
Ps 48: 5 They saw *it, and* so they **m**; they were 8539
Mt 8:10 When Jesus heard *it,* he **m**, and said to *2296*
8:27 But the men **m**, saying, What manner of *2296*
9: 8 But when the multitudes saw *it,* they **m**, *2296*
9:33 and the multitudes **m**, saying, It was never *2296*
21:20 And when the disciples saw *it,* they **m**, *2296*
22:22 When they had heard *these words,* they **m**, *2296*
27:14 insomuch that the governor **m** greatly. *2296*
Mk 6: 6 And he **m** because of their unbelief. And he *2296*
12:17 *things* that are God's. And they **m** at him. *2296*
15: 5 yet answered nothing; so that Pilate **m**. *2296*
15:44 And Pilate **m** if he were already dead: and *2296*
Lk 1:21 and **m** that he tarried *so* long in the temple. *2296*
1:63 saying, His name is John. And they **m** all. *2296*
2:33 his mother **m** at those *things* which were *2296*
7: 9 When Jesus heard these *things,* he **m** at *2296*
11:38 And when the Pharisee saw *it,* he **m** that he *2296*
20:26 and they **m** at his answer, and held their *2296*
Jn 4:27 and **m** that he talked with *the* woman: *2296*
7:15 And the Jews **m**, saying, How knoweth this *2296*

Ac 2: 7 And they were all amazed and **m**, *2296*
4:13 were unlearned and ignorant men, they **m**; *2296*

MARVELLOUS (24) [MARVEL]
1Ch 16:12 Remember his **m works** that he hath done, 6381
16:24 his **m works** among all nations. 6381
Job 5: 9 unsearchable; **m** *things* without number: 6381
10:16 and again thou **shewest** thyself **m** upon me. 6381
Ps 9: 1 I will shew forth all thy **m works**. 6381
17: 7 **Shew** thy **m** lovingkindness, O thou that 6395
31:21 for he hath **shewed** me his **m** kindness in a 6381
78:12 **M things** did he in the sight of their 6382
98: 1 for he hath done **m** *things*: his right hand, 6381
105: 5 Remember his **m works** that he hath done; 6381
118:23 is the LORD'S doing; it is **m** in our eyes. 6381
139:14 **m** *are* thy works; and *that* my soul knoweth 6395
Isa 29:14 I will proceed to **do a m work** amongst this 6381
29:14 this people, *even* a **m work** and a wonder: 6381
Da 11:36 shall speak **m** *things* against the God of 6381
Mic 7:15 of Egypt will I shew unto him **m** *things*. 6381
Zec 8: 6 If it be **m** in the eyes of the remnant of this 6381
8: 6 these days, should it also be **m** in my eyes? 6381
Mt 21:42 is the Lord's doing, and it is **m** in our eyes? *2298*
Mk 12:11 the Lord's doing, and it is **m** in our eyes? *2298*
Jn 9:30 Why herein is a **m** *thing*, that ye know not *2298*
1Pe 2: 9 called you out of darkness into his **m** light: *2298*
Rev 15: 1 I saw another sign in heaven, great and **m**, *2298*
15: 3 saying, Great and **m** *are* thy works, *2298*

MARVELLOUSLY (3) [MARVEL]
2Ch 26:15 for he was **m** helped, till he was strong. 6381
Job 37: 5 God thundereth **m** with his voice; 6381
Hab 1: 5 the heathen, and regard, and wonder **m**: 8539

MARVELS (1) [MARVEL]
Ex 34:10 before all thy people I will do **m**, such as 6381

MARY (54)
Mt 1:16 And Jacob begat Joseph the husband of **M**, *3137*
1:18 When as his mother **M** was espoused to *3137*
1:20 fear not to take unto *thee* **M** thy wife: *3137*
2:11 they saw the young child with **M** his *3137*
13:55 is not his mother called **M**? and *3137*
27:56 Among which was **M** Magdalene, and *3137*
27:56 and **M** the mother of James and Joses, and *3137*
27:61 And there was **M** Magdalene, and the other *3137*
27:61 was Mary Magdalene, and the other **M**, *3137*
28: 1 came **M** Magdalene and the other Mary to *3137*
28: 1 and the other **M** to see the sepulchre. *3137*
Mk 6: 3 the son of **M**, the brother of James, and *3137*
15:40 among whom was **M** Magdalene, and *3137*
15:40 and **M** the mother of James the less and *3137*
15:47 And **M** Magdalene and Mary *the mother* of *3137*
15:47 **M** *the mother* of Joses beheld where he was *3137*
16: 1 **M** Magdalene, and Mary the *mother* of *3137*
16: 1 and **M** the *mother* of James, and Salome, *3137*
16: 9 he appeared first to **M** Magdalene, out of *3137*
Lk 1:27 of David; and the virgin's name *was* **M**. *3137*
1:30 And the angel said unto her, Fear not, **M**: *3137*
1:34 Then said **M** unto the angel, How shall this *3137*
1:38 And **M** said, Behold the handmaid of *3137*
1:39 And **M** arose in those days, and went into *3137*
1:41 when Elisabeth heard the salutation of **M**, *3137*
1:46 And **M** said, My soul doth magnify *3137*
1:56 And **M** abode with her about three months, *3137*
2: 5 To be taxed with **M** his espoused wife, *3137*
2:16 and found **M**, and Joseph, and the babe *3137*
2:19 But **M** kept all these things, and *3137*
2:34 and said unto **M** his mother, Behold, *3137*
8: 2 and infirmities, **M** called Magdalene, *3137*
10:39 And she had a sister called **M**, which also *3137*
10:42 and **M** hath chosen *that* good part, *3137*
24:10 It was **M** Magdalene, and Joanna, and *3137*
24:10 and **M** *the mother* of James, and other *3137*
Jn 11: 1 the town of **M** and her sister Martha. *3137*
11: 2 (It was *that* **M** which anointed the Lord *3137*
11:19 many of the Jews came to Martha and **M**, *3137*
11:20 and met him: but **M** sat *still* in the house. *3137*
11:28 and called **M** her sister secretly, saying, *3137*
11:31 and comforted her, when they saw **M**, *3137*
11:32 Then when **M** was come where Jesus was, *3137*
11:45 Then many of the Jews which came to **M**, *3137*
12: 3 Then took **M** a pound of ointment of *3137*
19:25 **M** the *wife* of Cleophas, and *3137*
19:25 the *wife* of Cleophas, and **M** Magdalene. *3137*
20: 1 The first *day* of the week cometh **M** *3137*
20:11 But **M** stood without at the sepulchre *3137*
20:16 Jesus saith unto her, **M**. She turned herself, *3137*
20:18 **M** Magdalene came and told the disciples *3137*
Ac 1:14 and **M** the mother of Jesus, and with his *3137*
12:12 came to the house of **M** the mother of John, *3137*
Ro 16: 6 Greet **M**, who bestowed much labour on us. *3137*

MASCHIL (13)
Ps 32: T *A Psalm* of David, **M**. 4905
42: T chief Musician, **M**, for the sons of Korah. 4905
44: T chief Musician for the sons of Korah, **M**. 4905
45: T for the sons of Korah, **M**, A Song of loves. 4905
52: T the chief Musician, **M**, *A Psalm* of David, 4905
53: T upon Mahalath, **M**, *A Psalm* of David. 4905
54: T **M**, *A Psalm* of David, when the Ziphims 4905
55: T on Neginoth, **M**, *A Psalm* of David. 4905
74: T **M** of Asaph. 4905
78: T **M** of Asaph. 4905
88: T **M** of Heman the Ezrahite. 4905
89: T **M** of Ethan the Ezrahite. 4905
142: T **M** of David; A Prayer when he was in 4905

MASH (1)
Ge 10:23 of Aram; Uz, and Hul, and Gether, and **M**. 4851

MASHAL (1)
1Ch 6:74 **M** with her suburbs, and Abdon with her 4913

MASONS (7)
2Sa 5:11 and carpenters, and **m**: 68+2796+7023
2Ki 12:12 to **m**, and hewers of stone, and to buy 1443
22: 6 **m**, and to buy timber and hewn stone to 1443
1Ch 14: 1 of cedars, with **m** and carpenters, 2796+7023
22: 2 he set **m** to hew wrought stones to build 2672
2Ch 24:12 hired **m** and carpenters to repair the house 2672
Ezr 3: 7 They gave money also unto the **m**, and 2672

MASREKAH (2)
Ge 36:36 and Samlah of **M** reigned in his stead. 4957
1Ch 1:47 Samlah of **M** reigned in his stead. 4957

MASSA (2)
Ge 25:14 And Mishma, and Dumah, and **M**, 4854
1Ch 1:30 and Dumah, **M**, Hadad, and Tema, 4854

MASSAH (4)
Ex 17: 7 he called the name of the place **M**, and 4532
Dt 6:16 LORD your God, as ye tempted *him* in **M**. 4532
9:22 and at **M**, and at Kibroth-hattaavah, 4532
33: 8 whom thou didst prove at **M**, *and* 4532

MAST (2) [MASTS]
Pr 23:34 or as he that lieth upon the top of a **m**. 2260
Isa 33:23 they could not well strengthen their **m**, 8650

MASTER (157) [MASTER'S, MASTERBUILDER, MASTERIES, MASTERS, MASTERS', MASTERY, SCHOOLMASTER, SHEEPMASTER, SHIPMASTER, TASKMASTERS]
Ge 24: 9 his hand under the thigh of Abraham his **m**, 113
24:10 took ten camels of the camels of his **m**, 113
24:10 for all the goods of his **m** *were* in his hand: 113
24:12 O LORD God of my **m** Abraham, I pray 113
24:12 and shew kindness unto my **m** Abraham. 113
24:14 that thou hast shewed kindness unto my **m**. 113
24:27 Blessed *be* the LORD God of my **m** 113
24:27 who hath not left destitute my **m** of his 113
24:35 And the LORD hath blessed my **m** greatly; 113
24:36 Sarah my master's wife bare a son to my **m** 113
24:37 my **m** made me swear, saying, Thou shalt 113
24:39 I said unto my **m**, Peradventure the woman 113
24:42 and said, O LORD God of my **m** Abraham, 113
24:48 blessed the LORD God of my **m** Abraham, 113
24:49 if ye will deal kindly and truly with my **m**, 113
24:54 and he said, Send me away unto my **m**. 113
24:56 send me away that I may go to my **m**. 113
24:65 the servant had said, It *is* my **m**: therefore 113
39: 2 he was in the house of his **m** the Egyptian. 113
39: 3 his **m** saw that the LORD *was* with him, 113
39: 8 my **m** wotteth not what *is* with me in 113
39:19 when his **m** heard the words of his wife, 113
39:20 Joseph's **m** took him, and put him into 113
Ex 21: 4 If his **m** have given him a wife, and she have 113
21: 5 I love my **m**, my wife, and my children; 113

M

Ex 21: 6 Then his **m** shall bring him unto the judges; 113
21: 6 his **m** shall bore his ear through with an aul; 113
21: 8 If she please not her **m**, who hath betrothed 113
21:32 he shall give unto their **m** thirty shekels *of* 113
22: 8 the **m** of the house shall be brought unto 1167
Dt 23:15 Thou shalt not deliver unto his **m** the servant 113
23:15 which is escaped from his **m** unto thee: 113
Jdg 19:11 the servant said unto his **m**, Come, I pray 113
19:12 his **m** said unto him, We will not turn aside 113
19:22 spake to the **m** of the house, the old 376+1167
19:23 the man, the **m** of the house, went out unto 1167
1Sa 20:38 gathered up the arrows, and came to his **m**. 113
24: 6 forbid that I should do this thing unto my **m**, 113
25:10 days that break away every man from his **m**. 113
25:14 out of the wilderness to salute our **m**; 113
25:17 for evil is determined against our **m**, and 113
26:16 to die, because ye have not kept your **m**, 113
29: 4 should he reconcile himself unto his **m**? 113
30:13 my **m** left me, because three days agone I 113
30:15 nor deliver me into the hands of my **m**, and 113
2Sa 2: 7 for your **m** Saul is dead, and also the house 113
1Ki 22:17 the LORD said, These have no **m**: let them 113
2Ki 2: 3 will take away thy **m** from thy head to day? 113
2: 5 will take away thy **m** from thy head to day? 113
2:16 let them go, we pray thee, and seek thy **m**: 113
5: 1 was a great man with his **m**, and honourable, 113
5:18 *that* when my **m** goeth *into* the house of 113
5:20 my **m** hath spared Naaman this Syrian, 113
5:22 My **m** hath sent me, saying, Behold, 113
5:25 he went in, and stood before his **m**. 113
6: 5 he cried, and said, Alas, **m**, for it *was* 113
6:15 unto him, Alas, my **m**, how shall we do? 113
6:22 they may eat and drink, and go to their **m**. 113
6:23 he sent them away, and they went to their **m**. 113
8:14 he departed from Elisha, and came to his **m**; 113
9: 7 thou shalt smite the house of Ahab thy **m**, 113
9:31 she said, *Had* Zimri peace, who slew his **m**? 113
10: 9 I conspired against my **m**, and slew him: 113
18:27 Hath my **m** sent me to thy master, and 113
18:27 Hath my master sent me to thy **m**, and 113
19: 4 whom the king of Assyria his **m** hath sent to 113
19: 6 Thus shall ye say to your **m**, Thus saith 113
1Ch 12:19 He will fall to his **m** Saul to *the jeopardy of* 113
15:27 Chenaniah the **m** of the song *with* 8269
2Ch 18:16 the LORD said, These have no **m**; let them 113
Job 3:19 *are* there; and the servant *is* free from his **m**. 113
Pr 27:18 he that waiteth on his **m** shall be honoured. 113
30:10 Accuse not a servant unto his **m**, lest he 113
Isa 24: 2 the priest; as *with* the servant, so *with* his **m**; 113
36: 8 to my **m** the king of Assyria, and I will give 113
36:12 Hath my **m** sent me to thy master and to thee 113
36:12 Hath my master sent me to thy **m** and to thee 113
37: 4 whom the king of Assyria his **m** hath sent to 113
37: 6 Thus shall ye say unto your **m**, Thus saith 113
Da 1: 3 the king spake unto Ashpenaz the **m** of his 7227
4: 9 **m** of the magicians, because I know that 7229
5:11 made **m** of the magicians, astrologers, 7229
Mal 1: 6 honoureth *his* father, and a servant his **m**: 113
1: 6 if I *be* a **m**, where *is* my fear? saith 113
2:12 the **m** and the scholar, out of 5782
Mt 8:19 certain scribe came, and said unto him, **M**, 1320
9:11 Why eateth your **M** with publicans and 1320
10:24 The disciple is not above *his* **m**, nor 1320
10:25 enough for the disciple that he be as his **m**, 1320
10:25 If they have called the **m of the house** 3617
12:38 and of the Pharisees answered, saying, **M**, 1320
17:24 and said, Doth not your **m** pay tribute? 1320
19:16 one came and said unto him, Good **M**, 1320
22:16 saying, **M**, we know that thou art true, and 1320
22:24 Saying, **M**, Moses said, If a man die, 1320
22:36 **M**, which *is* the great commandment in 1320
23: 8 for one is your **M**, *even* Christ; 2519
23:10 for one is your **M**, *even* Christ. 2519
26:18 and say unto him, The **M** saith, My time is 1320
26:25 betrayed him, answered and said, **M**, is it I? 4461
26:49 he came to Jesus, and said, Hail, **m**; 4461
Mk 4:38 and they awake him, and say unto him, **M**, 1320
5:35 why troublest thou the **M** any further? 1320
9: 5 And Peter answered and said to Jesus, **M**, 4461
9:17 one of the multitude answered and said, **M**, 1320
9:38 And John answered him, saying, **M**, 1320
10:17 kneeled to him, and asked him, Good **M**, 1320
10:20 And he answered and said unto him, **M**, 1320
10:35 of Zebedee, come unto him, saying, **M**, 1320
11:21 **M**, behold, the fig tree which thou cursedst 4461
12:14 they say unto him, **M**, we know that thou 1320
12:19 **M**, Moses wrote unto us, If a man's brother 1320
12:32 unto him, Well, **M**, thou hast said the truth: 1320
13: 1 **M**, see what manner of stones and 1320
13:35 for ye know not when the **m** of the house 2962
14:14 The **M** saith, Where is the guestchamber, 1320
14:45 straightway to him, and saith, **M**, master; 4461
14:45 straightway to him, and saith, Master, **m**; 4461
Lk 3:12 and said unto him, **M**, what shall we do? 1320
5: 5 **M**, we have toiled all the night, and 1988
6:40 The disciple is not above his **m**: but 1320
6:40 every one *that is* perfect shall be as his **m**. 1320
7:40 to say unto thee. And he saith, **M**, say *on*. 1320
8:24 awoke him, saying, **M**, master, we perish. 1988
8:24 awoke him, saying, Master, **m**, we perish. 1988
8:45 **M**, the multitude throng thee and 1988
8:49 Thy daughter is dead; trouble not the **M**. 1320
9:33 from him, Peter said unto Jesus, **M**, 1988
9:38 saying, **M**, I beseech thee, look upon my 1320
9:49 And John answered and said, **M**, we saw 1988
10:25 stood up, and tempted him, saying, **M**, 1320
11:45 one of the lawyers, and said unto him, **M**, 1320
12:13 **M**, speak to my brother, that *he* divide 1320
13:25 When once the **m of the house** is risen up, 3617
14:21 **m of the house** being angry said to his 3617
17:13 and said, Jesus, **M**, have mercy on us. 1988
18:18 a certain ruler asked him, saying, Good **M**, 1320
19:39 said unto him, **M**, rebuke thy disciples. 1320
20:21 And they asked him, saying, **M**, we know 1320
20:28 Saying, **M**, Moses wrote unto us, If any 1320
20:39 answering said, **M**, thou hast well said. 1320
21: 7 And they asked him, saying, **M**, 1320
22:11 The **M** saith unto thee, Where is 1320
Jn 1:38 (which is to say, being interpreted, **M**,) 1320
3:10 Art thou a **m** of Israel, and knowest not 1320
4:31 *his* disciples prayed him, saying, **M**, eat. 4461
8: 4 They say unto him, **M**, this woman was 1320
9: 2 saying, **M**, who did sin, this *man*, or 4461
11: 8 *His* disciples say unto him, **M**, the Jews of 4461
11:28 The **M** is come, and calleth for thee. 1320
13:13 Ye call me **M** and Lord: and ye say well; 1320
13:14 If I then, *your* Lord and **M**, have washed 1320
20:16 unto him, Rabboni; which is to say, **M**. 1320
Ac 27:11 Nevertheless the centurion believed the **m** 2942
Ro 14: 4 to his own **m** he standeth or falleth. Yea, 2962
Eph 6: 9 knowing that your **M** also is in heaven; 2962
Col 4: 1 knowing that ye also have a **M** in heaven. 2962

MASTER'S (24) [MASTER]

Ge 24:27 the LORD led me to the house of my **m** 113
24:36 Sarah my **m** wife bare a son to my master 113
24:44 LORD hath appointed out for my **m** son. 113
24:48 take my **m** brother's daughter unto his son. 113
24:51 and go, and let her be thy **m** son's wife, 113
39: 7 that his **m** wife cast her eyes upon Joseph; 113
39: 8 and said unto his **m** wife, Behold, 113
Ex 21: 4 the wife and her children shall be her **m**, and 113
1Sa 29:10 with thy **m** servants that are come with thee: 113
2Sa 9: 9 I have given unto thy **m** son all that 113
9:10 thou shalt bring in *the fruits,* that thy **m** son 113
9:10 Mephibosheth thy **m** son shall eat bread 113
12: 8 I gave thee thy **m** house, and thy master's 113
12: 8 thy **m** wives into thy bosom, and gave thee 113
16: 3 And the king said, And where *is* thy **m** son? 113
2Ki 6:32 *is* not the sound of his **m** feet behind him? 113
10: 2 seeing your **m** sons *are* with you, and 113
10: 3 out the best and meetest of your **m** sons, 113
10: 3 father's throne, and fight for your **m** house. 113
10: 6 take ye the heads of the men your **m** sons, 113
18:24 of one captain of the least of my **m** servants, 113
Isa 1: 3 knoweth his owner, and the ass his **m** crib: 1167
36: 9 of one captain of the least of my **m** servants, 113
2Ti 2:21 and meet for the **m** use, *and* prepared unto 1203

MASTERBUILDER (1) [BUILD, MASTER]

1Co 3:10 as a wise **m**, I have laid the foundation, and 753

MASTERIES (1) [MASTER]

2Ti 2: 5 And if a man also **strive for m**, *yet* is he not 118

MASTERS (20) [MASTER]

Ps 123: 2 of servants *look* unto the hand of their **m**, 113
Pr 25:13 send him: for he refresheth the soul of his **m**. 113

Ecc 12:11 as nails fastened *by* the **m** of assemblies, 1167
Jer 27: 4 command them to say unto their **m**, 113
27: 4 of Israel; Thus shall ye say unto your **m**; 113
Am 4: 1 which say to their **m**, Bring, and let us drink. 113
Mt 6:24 No *man* can serve two **m**: for either he will *2962*
23:10 Neither be ye called **m**: for one is your *2519*
Lk 16:13 No servant can serve two **m**: for either he *2962*
Ac 16:16 which brought her **m** much gain by *2962*
16:19 And when her **m** saw that the hope of their *2962*
Eph 6: 5 be obedient to *them that are your* **m** *2962*
6: 9 And, ye **m**, do the same *things* unto them, *2962*
Col 3:22 obey in all *things your* **m** according to *2962*
4: 1 **M**, give unto *your* servants that which is *2962*
1Ti 6: 1 count their own **m** worthy of all honour, *1203*
6: 2 And they that have believing **m**, let them *1203*
Tit 2: 9 servants to be obedient unto their own **m**, *1203*
Jas 3: 1 My brethren, be not many **m**, knowing that *1320*
1Pe 2:18 Servants, *be* subject to *your* **m** with all fear; *1203*

MASTERS' (2) [MASTER]
Zep 1: 9 which fill their **m** houses *with* violence and 113
Mt 15:27 of the crumbs which fall from their **m** table. *2962*

MASTERY (3) [MASTER]
Ex 32:18 *It is* not the voice of *them that* shout for **m**, 1369
Da 6:24 the lions had the **m** of them, and brake all 7981
1Co 9:25 And every *man* that **striveth for the m** is *75*

MASTS (1) [MAST]
Eze 27: 5 cedars from Lebanon to make **m** for thee. 8650

MATE (2)
Isa 34:15 also be gathered, every one *with* her **m**. 7468
34:16 of these shall fail, none shall want her **m**: 7468

MATERIAL See CARNAL

MATHUSALA (1) [METHUSELAH]
Lk 3:37 Which was *the son* of **M**, which was *3103*

MATRED (2)
Ge 36:39 the daughter of **M**, the daughter of 4308
1Ch 1:50 the daughter of **M**, the daughter of 4308

MATRI (1)
1Sa 10:21 the family of **M** was taken, and Saul 4309

MATRIX (5)
Ex 13:12 unto the LORD all that openeth the **m**, 7358
13:15 to the LORD all that openeth the **m**, 7358
34:19 All that openeth the **m** *is* mine; and 7358
Nu 3:12 openeth the **m** among the children of Israel: 7358
18:15 Every thing that openeth the **m** in all flesh, 7358

MATTAN (3)
2Ki 11:18 slew **M** the priest of Baal before the altars. 4977
2Ch 23:17 slew **M** the priest of Baal before the altars. 4977
Jer 38: 1 Shephatiah the son of **M**, and Gedaliah 4977

MATTANAH (2)
Nu 21:18 And from the wilderness *they went* to **M**: 4980
21:19 from **M** *to* Nahaliel: and from Nahaliel *to* 4980

MATTANIAH (16)
2Ki 24:17 the king of Babylon made **M** his father's 4983
1Ch 9:15 Heresh, and Galal, and **M** the son of Micah, 4983
25: 4 **M**, Uzziel, Shebuel, and Jerimoth, 4983
25:16 The ninth *to* **M**, *he*, his sons, and 4983
2Ch 20:14 of Benaiah, the son of Jeiel, the son of **M**, 4983
29:13 of the sons of Asaph; Zechariah, and **M**: 4983
Ezr 10:26 **M**, Zechariah, and Jehiel, and Abdi, and 4983
10:27 **M**, and Jeremoth, and Zabad, and Aziza. 4983
10:30 **M**, Bezaleel, and Binnui, and Manasseh. 4983
10:37 **M**, Mattenai, and Jaasau, 4983
Ne 11:17 **M** the son of Micha, the son of Zabdi, 4983
11:22 the son of **M**, the son of Micha. 4983
12: 8 Binnui, Kadmiel, Sherebiah, Judah, *and* **M**, 4983
12:25 **M**, and Bakbukiah, Obadiah, Meshullam, 4983
12:35 the son of **M**, the son of Michaiah, the son 4983
13:13 *was* Hanan the son of Zaccur, the son of **M**: 4983

MATTATHA (1)
Lk 3:31 *the son* of Menan, which was *the son* of **M**, *3160*

MATTATHAH (1)
Ezr 10:33 Mattenai, **M**, Zabad, Eliphelet, Jeremai, 4992

MATTATHIAS (2)
Lk 3:25 Which was *the son* of **M**, which was *3161*
3:26 which was *the son* of **M**, which was *the son* *3161*

MATTATTAH See MATTATHAH

MATTENAI (3)
Ezr 10:33 **M**, Mattathah, Zabad, Eliphelet, Jeremai, 4982
10:37 Mattaniah, **M**, and Jaasau, 4982
Ne 12:19 And of Joiarib, **M**; of Jedaiah, Uzzi; 4982

MATTER (80) [MATTERS]
Ge 24: 9 and sware to him concerning that **m**. 1697
30:15 *Is it* a **small m** that thou hast taken my 4592
Ex 18:16 When they have a **m**, they come unto me; 1697
18:22 *that* every great **m** they shall bring unto 1697
18:22 but every small **m** they shall judge: 1697
18:26 but every small **m** they judged themselves. 1697
23: 7 Keep thee far from a false **m**; and 1697
Nu 16:49 beside them that died about the **m** of 1697
25:18 wherewith they have beguiled you in the **m** 1697
25:18 in the **m** of Cozbi, the daughter of a prince 1697
31:16 against the LORD in the **m** of Peor, 1697
Dt 3:26 speak no more unto me of this **m**. 1697
17: 8 If there arise a **m** too hard for thee in 1697
19:15 three witnesses, shall the **m** be stablished. 1697
22:26 and slayeth him, even so *is* this **m**: 1697
Ru 3:18 until thou know how the **m** will fall: 1697
1Sa 10:16 of the **m** of the kingdom, whereof Samuel 1697
20:23 *as touching* the **m** which thou and I have 1697
20:39 only Jonathan and David knew the **m**. 1697
30:24 For who will hearken unto you in this **m**? 1697
2Sa 1: 4 David said unto him, How went the **m**? 1697
18:13 for there is no **m** hid from the king, and 1697
19:42 wherefore then be ye angry for this **m**? 1697
20:18 *counsel* at Abel: and so they ended *the m*. NIH
20:21 The **m** *is* not so: but a man of mount 1697
1Ki 8:59 Israel at all times, **as the m** shall **require**: 1697
15: 5 save only in the **m** of Urijah the Hittite. 1697
1Ch 26:32 for every **m** pertaining to God, and 1697
27: 1 their officers that served the king in any **m** 1697
2Ch 8:15 the priests and Levites concerning any **m**, 1697
24: 5 year to year, and *see that* ye haste the **m**. 1697
Ezr 5: 5 them to cease, till the **m** came to Darius: 2941
5: 5 answer by letter concerning this *m*. NIH
5:17 send his pleasure to us concerning this *m*. NIH
10: 4 Arise; for *this* **m** *belongeth* unto thee: 1697
10: 9 trembling because of *this* **m**, and for 1697
10:14 until the fierce wrath of our God for this **m** 1697
10:15 son of Tikvah were employed about this *m*: NIH
10:16 day of the tenth month to examine the **m**. 1697
Ne 6:13 *that* they might have *m* for an evil report, NIH
Est 2:23 when inquisition was made of the **m**, it was 1697
9:26 *that* which they had seen concerning this *m*, NIH
Job 19:28 seeing the root of the **m** is found in me; 1697
32:18 For I am full *of* **m**, the spirit within me 4405
Ps 45: 1 My heart is inditing a good **m**: I speak of 1697
64: 5 They encourage themselves *in* an evil **m**: 1697
Pr 11:13 that is of a faithful spirit concealeth the **m**. 1697
16:20 He that handleth a **m** wisely shall find 1697
17: 9 he that repeateth a **m** separateth very 1697
18:13 He that answereth a **m** before he heareth *it*, 1697
25: 2 the honour of kings *is* to search out a **m**. 1697
Ecc 5: 8 justice in a province, marvel not at the **m**: 2656
10:20 and that which hath wings shall tell the **m**. 1697
12:13 Let us hear the conclusion of the whole **m**: 1697
Jer 38:27 with him; for the **m** was not perceived. 1697
Eze 9:11 inkhorn by his side, reported the **m**, saying, 1697
16:20 *Is this* of thy whoredoms a **small m**, 4592
Da 1:14 So he consented to them in this **m**, and 1697
2:10 upon the earth that can shew the king's **m**: 4406
2:23 *now* made known unto us the king's **m**. 4406
3:16 we *are* not careful to answer thee in this **m**. 6600
4:17 *This* **m** *is* by the decree of the watchers, 6600
7:28 Hitherto *is* the end of the **m**. *As for* me 4406
7:28 in me: but I kept the **m** in my heart. 4406
9:23 therefore understand the **m**, and 1697
Mk 1:45 publish *it* much, and to blaze abroad the **m**, *3056*
10:10 disciples asked him again of the same *m*. NIG
Ac 8:21 Thou hast neither part nor lot in this **m**: *3056*
11: 4 But Peter *rehearsed the* **m** from NIG
15: 6 came together for to consider of this **m**. *3056*
17:32 We will hear thee again of this *m*. NIG
18:14 If it were a **m** of wrong or *5100*

M

Ac 19:38 have a **m** against any *man,* the law is open, *3056*
24:22 I will know the uttermost of your **m**. *2596+3588*
1Co 6: 1 any of you, having a **m** against another, *4229*
2Co 7:11 approved yourselves to be clear in *this* **m**. *4229*
9: 5 as *a* **m** *of* **bounty**, and not as *of* NIG
Gal 2: 6 they were, it **maketh** no **m** to me: *1308*
1Th 4: 6 and defraud his brother in *any* **m**: *4229*
Jas 3: 5 Behold, how great a **m** a little fire kindleth. *5208*

MATTERS (23) [MATTER]
Ex 24:14 if any man have any **m** to do, let him come 1697
Dt 17: 8 *being* **m** of controversy within thy gates: 1697
1Sa 16:18 and prudent in **m**, and a comely person, and 1697
2Sa 11:19 of telling the **m** of the war unto the king, 1697
15: 3 unto him, See, thy **m** *are* good and right; 1697
19:29 Why speakest thou any more of thy **m**? 1697
2Ch 19:11 priest *is* over you in all **m** of the LORD; 1697
19:11 of the house of Judah, for all the king's **m**: 1697
Ne 11:24 *was* at the king's hand in all **m** concerning 1697
Est 3: 4 to see whether Mordecai's **m** would stand: 1697
9:31 the **m** of the fastings and their cry. 1697
9:32 the decree of Esther confirmed these **m** of 1697
Job 33:13 for he giveth not account of any of his **m**. 1697
Ps 35:20 they devise deceitful **m** against *them that* 1697
131: 1 neither do I exercise myself in great *m*, or NIH
Da 1:20 *in* all **m** of wisdom *and* understanding, 1697
7: 1 wrote the dream, *and* told the sum of the **m**. 4406
Mt 23:23 have omitted the weightier *m* of the law, NIG
Ac 18:15 ye *to it;* for I will be no judge of such *m*. NIG
19:39 *m*, it shall be determined in a lawful NIG
25:20 and there be judged of these *m*. NIG
1Co 6: 2 are ye unworthy to judge the **smallest m**? *1646*
1Pe 4:15 or as a **busybody in other men's m**. *244*

MATTHAN (2)
Mt 1:15 and Eleazar begat **M**; and Matthan begat *3157*
1:15 Eleazar begat Matthan; and **M** begat Jacob; *3157*

MATTHAT (2)
Lk 3:24 Which was *the son* of **M**, which was *3158*
3:29 which was *the son* of **M**, which was *the son* *3158*

MATTHEW (5)
Mt 9: 9 he saw a man, named **M**, sitting at *3156*
10: 3 Thomas, and **M** the publican; *3156*
Mk 3:18 and **M**, and Thomas, and James the *son* of *3156*
Lk 6:15 **M** and Thomas, James the *son* of Alpheus, *3156*
Ac 1:13 Philip, and Thomas, Bartholomew, and **M**, *3156*

MATTHIAS (2)
Ac 1:23 who was surnamed Justus, and **M**. *3159*
1:26 and the lot fell upon **M**; and he was *3159*

MATTITHIAH (8)
1Ch 9:31 **M**, *one* of the Levites, who *was* 4993
15:18 **M**, and Elipheleh, and Mikneiah, and 4993
15:21 **M**, and Elipheleh, and Mikneiah, and 4993
16: 5 **M**, and Eliab, and Benaiah, and 4993
25: 3 Zeri, and Jeshaiah, Hashabiah, and **M**, six, 4993
25:21 The fourteenth *to* **M**, *he,* his sons, and 4993
Ezr 10:43 Jeiel, **M**, Zabad, Zebina, Jadau, and Joel, 4993
Ne 8: 4 beside him stood **M**, and Shema, and 4993

MATTOCK (2) [MATTOCKS]
1Sa 13:20 and his coulter, and his axe, and his **m**. 4281
Isa 7:25 *on* all hills that shall be digged with the **m**, 4576

MATTOCKS (2) [MATTOCK]
1Sa 13:21 Yet they had a file for the **m**, and for 4281
2Ch 34: 6 unto Naphtali, with their **m** round about. 2719

MAUL (1)
Pr 25:18 false witness against his neighbour *is* a **m**, 4650

MAULED See TARE

MAW (1)
Dt 18: 3 and the two cheeks, and the **m**. 6896

MAY (1027) [MAYEST] See Index

MAYEST (114) [MAY] See Index

MAZZAROTH (1)
Job 38:32 Canst thou bring forth **M** in his season? or 4216

ME (4096) [I] See Index

MEADOW (2) [MEADOWS]
Ge 41: 2 and fatfleshed; and they fed in a **m**. 260
41:18 well favoured; and they fed in a **m**: 260

MEADOWS (1) [MEADOW]
Jdg 20:33 their places, *even* out of the **m** of Gibeah. 4629

MEAH (2)
Ne 3: 1 even unto the tower of **M** they sanctified it, 3968
12:39 the tower of Hananeel, and the tower of **M**, 3968

MEAL (12) [MEALTIME]
Ge 18: 6 ready quickly three measures of fine **m**, 7058
Nu 5:15 the tenth *part* of an ephah of barley **m**; 7058
1Ki 4:22 of fine flour, and threescore measures of **m**, 7058
17:12 a handful of **m** in a barrel, and a little oil in 7058
17:14 The barrel of **m** shall not waste, 7058
17:16 *And* the barrel of **m** wasted not, neither did 7058
2Ki 4:41 he said, Then bring **m**. And he cast *it* into 7058
1Ch 12:40 and on mules, and on oxen, *and* meat, **m**, 7058
Isa 47: 2 Take the millstones, and grind **m**: 7058
Hos 8: 7 the bud shall yield no **m**: if so be it yield, 7058
Mt 13:33 and hid in three measures of **m**, *224*
Lk 13:21 woman took and hid in three measures of **m**, *224*

MEALTIME (1) [MEAL, TIME]
Ru 2:14 At **m** come thou hither, and 400+6256+1886.1

MEAN (22) [MEANEST, MEANETH, MEANING, MEANS, MEANT]
Ge 21:29 What *m* these seven ewe lambs which thou NIH
Ex 12:26 unto you, What **m** you by this service? 3807.1
Dt 6:20 What *m* the testimonies, and the statutes, NIH
Jos 4: 6 What **m** you by these stones? 3807.1
4:21 time to come, saying, What *m* these stones? NIH
1Ki 18:45 **in the m while,** 3541+3541+5704+5704+2050.1
Pr 22:29 he shall not stand before **m** *men.* 2823
Isa 2: 9 the **m** man boweth down, and the great man NIH
3:15 What **m** ye *that* ye beat my people to 3807.1
5:15 the **m** man shall be brought down, and NIH
31: 8 the sword, not of a **m** man, shall devour NIH
Eze 17:12 Know ye not what these *things* **m**? tell NIH
18: 2 What **m** ye, that ye use this proverb 3807.1
Mk 9:10 what the rising from the dead should **m**. *1510*
Lk 12: 1 **In the m time**, when there were *1722+3739*
Jn 4:31 In the **m while** *his* disciples prayed him, *3342*
Ac 10:17 *this* vision which he had seen should **m**, *1510*
17:20 would know therefore what these *things* **m**. *2309*
21:13 **What m** ye to weep and to break mine *5101*
21:39 *a city* in Cilicia, a citizen of no **m** city: *767*
Ro 2:15 and *their* thoughts the **m** while accusing or NIG
2Co 8:13 For *I* **m** not that other *men* be eased, and NIG

MEANEST (4) [MEAN]
Ge 33: 8 **m** thou by all this drove which I met? 3807.1
2Sa 16: 2 said unto Ziba, What **m** thou by these? 3807.1
Eze 37:18 Wilt thou not shew us what thou **m** by 3807.1
Jnh 1: 6 said unto him, What **m** thou, O sleeper? 3807.1

MEANETH (8) [MEAN]
Dt 29:24 what *m* the heat of this great anger? NIH
1Sa 4: 6 What *m* the noise of this great shout in NIH
4:14 he said, What *m* the noise of this tumult? NIH
15:14 What *m* then this bleating of the sheep in NIH
Isa 10: 7 Howbeit he **m** not so, neither doth his heart 1819
Mt 9:13 But go ye and learn what *that* **m**, I will *1510*
12: 7 But if ye had known what *this* **m**, I will *1510*
Ac 2:12 saying one to another, What **m** this? *1510+2309*

MEANING (3) [MEAN]
Da 8:15 and sought for the **m**, then behold, 998
Ac 27: 2 **m to** sail by the coasts of Asia; *3195*
1Co 14:11 Therefore if I know not the **m** of the voice, *1411*

MEANINGLESS See VANITIES; VANITY

MEANS (35) [MEAN]
Ex 34: 7 *that* will **by no m** clear *the guilty;* visiting 3808
Nu 14:18 **by no m** clearing *the guilty,* visiting 3808
Jdg 5:22 were the horsehoofs broken **by the m of** 4480
16: 5 and by what *m* we may prevail against him, NIH
2Sa 14:14 yet doth he devise **m**, that *his* banished be 4284
1Ki 10:29 did they bring *them* out by their **m**. 3027
20:39 if **by any m** he be **missing**, then 6485+6485
2Ch 1:17 and *for* the kings of Syria, by their **m**. 3027

Ezr 4:16 by this **m** thou shalt have no portion on *this* 6903
Ps 49: 7 None *of them* can **by any m redeem** 6299+6299
Pr 6:26 For **by m of** a whorish woman *a man is* 1157
Jer 5:31 and the priests bear rule by their **m**; 3027
Mal 1: 9 this hath been by your **m**: will he regard 3027
Mt 5:26 Thou shalt **by no m** come out thence, *3364*
Lk 5:18 and they sought *m* to bring him in, and NIG
8:36 **by what m** he that was possessed of *4459*
10:19 and nothing shall **by any m** hurt you. *3364*
Jn 9:21 But **by what m** he now seeth, we know *4459*
Ac 4: 9 impotent man, by what *m* he is made whole; NIG
18:21 I must **by all m** keep *this* feast that cometh *3843*
27:12 **if by any m** they might attain to Phenice, *1513*
Ro 1:10 **if by any m** now at length I might have a *1513*
11:14 **If by any m** I may provoke to emulation *1513*
1Co 8: 9 But take heed **lest by any m** this liberty of *3381*
9:22 to all *men,* that I might **by all m** save some. *3843*
9:27 **lest that by any m**, when I have preached *3381*
2Co 1:11 **by the m of** many persons thanks may be *1537*
11: 3 But I fear, **lest by any m**, as the serpent *3381*
Gal 2: 2 **lest by any m** I should run, or had run, *3381*
Php 3:11 **If by any m** I might attain unto *1513*
1Th 3: 5 **lest by some m** the tempter have tempted *3381*
2Th 2: 3 Let no *man* deceive you by any **m**: for *that* *5158*
3:16 himself give you peace always by all **m**. *5158*
Heb 9:15 of the new testament, that by **m** of death, NIG
Rev 13:14 **by the m of** *those* miracles which he had *1223*

MEANT (3) [MEAN]
Ge 50:20 *but* God **m** it unto good, to bring to pass, 2803
Lk 15:26 and asked what these *things* **m**. *1510*
18:36 the multitude pass by, he asked what it **m**. *1510*

MEARAH (1)
Jos 13: 4 **M** that *is* beside the Sidonians, unto Aphek, 4632

MEASURE (69) [MEASURED, MEASURES, MEASURING]
Ex 26: 2 every one of the curtains shall have one **m**. 4060
26: 8 the eleven curtains *shall be all* of one **m**. 4060
Lev 19:35 in meteyard, in weight, or in **m**. 4884
Nu 35: 5 ye shall **m** from without the city *on* the east 4058
Dt 21: 2 they shall **m** unto the cities which *are* round 4058
25:15 a perfect and just **m** shalt thou have: 374
Jos 3: 4 and it, about two thousand cubits by **m**: 4060
1Ki 6:25 both the cherubims *were* of one **m** and 4060
7:37 them had one casting, one **m**, *and* one size. 4060
2Ki 7: 1 To morrow about *this* time *shall* a **m** of fine 5429
7:16 So a **m** of fine flour was *sold* for a shekel, 5429
7:18 a shekel, and a **m** of fine flour for a shekel, 5429
1Ch 23:29 is fried, and for all *manner of* **m** and size; 4884
2Ch 3: 3 The length *by* cubits after the first **m** *was* 4060
Job 11: 9 The **m** thereof *is* longer than the earth, and 4055
28:25 and he weigheth the waters by **m**. 4060
Ps 39: 4 to know mine end, and the **m** of my days, 4060
80: 5 and givest them tears to drink *in great* **m**. 7991
Isa 5:14 and opened her mouth without **m**: 2706
27: 8 In **m**, when it shooteth forth, thou wilt 5432
40:12 comprehended the dust of the earth in a **m**, 7991
65: 7 will I **m** their former work into their 4058
Jer 30:11 I will correct thee in **m**, and will not leave 4941
46:28 a full end of thee, but correct thee in **m**; 4941
51:13 end is come, *and* the **m** of thy covetousness. 520
Eze 4:11 Thou shalt drink also water by **m**, the sixth 4884
4:16 they shall drink water by **m**, and 4884
40:10 on that side; they three *were* of one **m**: 4060
40:10 the posts had one **m** on this side and on that 4060
40:21 the arches thereof were after the **m** of 4060
40:22 *were* after the **m** of the gate that looketh 4060
41:17 wall round about within and without, *by* **m**. 4060
43:10 their iniquities: and let them **m** the pattern. 4058
45: 3 of this **m** shalt thou measure the length of 4060
45: 3 of this measure shalt thou **m** the length of 4058
45:11 The ephah and the bath shall be of one **m**, 8506
45:11 the **m** thereof shall be after the homer. 4971
46:22 these four corners *were* of one **m**. 4060
47:18 the east side ye shall **m** from Hauran, and 4058
Mic 6:10 and the scant **m** *that is* abominable? 374
Zec 2: 2 he said unto me, To **m** Jerusalem, to see 4058
Mt 7: 2 and with what **m** ye mete, it shall be *3358*
23:32 Fill ye up then the **m** of your fathers. *3358*
Mk 4:24 with what **m** ye mete, it shall be measured *3358*
6:51 were sore amazed in themselves beyond **m**, *4053*
7:37 And were **beyond m** astonished, saying, *5249*
10:26 And they were astonished **out of m**, *4057*
Lk 6:38 good **m**, pressed down, and *3358*
6:38 For with the same **m** that ye mete withal it *3358*
Jn 3:34 for God giveth not the Spirit by **m** *unto* *3358*
Ro 12: 3 God hath dealt to every man the **m** of faith. *3358*
2Co 1: 8 that we were pressed **out of m**, *2596+5236*
10:13 we will not boast of *things* **without** *our* **m**, *280*
10:13 according to the **m** of the rule which God *3358*
10:13 to us, a **m** to reach even unto you. *3358*
10:14 For we stretch not ourselves beyond *our* **m**, NIG
10:15 Not boasting of *things* **without** *our* **m**, *280*
11:23 in stripes **above m**, in prisons more *5234*
12: 7 And lest I should be **exalted above m** *5229*
12: 7 lest I should be **exalted above m**. *5229*
Gal 1:13 how that **beyond m** I persecuted *2596+5236*
Eph 4: 7 according to the **m** of the gift of Christ. *3358*
4:13 unto the **m** of the stature of the fulness of *3358*
4:16 according to the effectual working in the **m** *3358*
Rev 6: 6 A **m** of wheat for a penny, and *5518*
11: 1 and **m** the temple of God, and the altar, and *3354*
11: 2 without the temple leave out, and **m** it not; *3354*
21:15 with me had a golden reed to **m** the city, *3354*
21:17 *according to* the **m** of a man, that is, *3358*

MEASURED (46) [MEASURE]
Ru 3:15 he **m** six *measures* of barley, and laid *it* on 4058
2Sa 8: 2 he smote Moab, and **m** them with a line, 4058
8: 2 even *with* two lines **m** he to put to death, 4058
Isa 40:12 Who hath **m** the waters in the hollow of his 4058
Jer 31:37 If heaven above can be **m**, and 4058
33:22 neither the sand of the sea **m**: 3808+4058
Eze 40: 5 so he **m** the breadth of the building, 4058
40: 6 and **m** the threshold of the gate, 4058
40: 8 He **m** also the porch of the gate within, one 4058
40: 9 **m** he the porch of the gate, eight cubits; 4058
40:11 he **m** the breadth of the entry of the gate, 4058
40:13 He **m** then the gate from the roof of *one* 4058
40:19 he **m** the breadth from the forefront of 4058
40:20 he **m** the length thereof, and the breadth 4058
40:23 he **m** from gate to gate an hundred cubits. 4058
40:24 he **m** the posts thereof and the arches 4058
40:27 he **m** from gate to gate toward the south an 4058
40:28 he **m** the south gate according to these 4058
40:32 he **m** the gate according to these measures. 4058
40:35 and **m** *it* according to these measures; 4058
40:47 So he **m** the court, an hundred cubits long, 4058
40:48 **m** *each* post of the porch, five cubits on this 4058
41: 1 **m** the posts, six cubits broad on the one 4058
41: 2 he **m** the length thereof, forty cubits: and 4058
41: 3 **m** the post of the door, two cubits; 4058
41: 4 So he **m** the length thereof, twenty cubits; 4058
41: 5 After he **m** the wall of the house, six cubits; 4058
41:13 So he **m** the house, an hundred cubits long; 4058
41:15 he **m** the length of the building over against 4058
42:15 *is* toward the east, and **m** it round about. 4058
42:16 He **m** the east side with the measuring reed, 4058
42:17 He **m** the north side, five hundred reeds, 4058
42:18 He **m** the south side, five hundred reeds, 4058
42:19 **m** five hundred reeds with the measuring 4058
42:20 He **m** it by the four sides: it had a wall 4058
47: 3 forth east*ward,* he **m** a thousand cubits, 4058
47: 4 Again he **m** a thousand, and brought me 4058
47: 4 Again he **m** a thousand, and brought me 4058
47: 5 Afterward he **m** a thousand; *and it was* a 4058
Hos 1:10 the sea, which cannot be **m** nor numbered; 4058
Hab 3: 6 He stood, and **m** the earth: he beheld, and 4128
Mt 7: 2 measure ye mete, it shall be **m** to you **again**. *488*
Mk 4:24 what measure ye mete, it shall be **m** to you: *3354*
Lk 6:38 ye mete withal it shall be **m** to you **again**. *488*
Rev 21:16 and he **m** the city with the reed, *3354*
21:17 And he **m** the wall thereof, an hundred *and* *3354*

MEASURES (39) [MEASURE]
Ge 18: 6 Make ready quickly three **m** of fine meal, 5429
Dt 25:14 have in thine house **divers m**, 374+374+2050.1
Ru 3:15 he measured six *m* of barley, and laid *it* on NIH
3:17 she said, These six *m* of barley gave he me; NIH
1Sa 25:18 five **m** of parched *corn,* and an hundred 5429
1Ki 4:22 for one day was thirty **m** of fine flour, 3734
4:22 of fine flour, and threescore **m** of meal, 3734
5:11 Solomon gave Hiram twenty thousand **m** of 3734
5:11 to his household, and twenty **m** of pure oil: 3734
7: 9 according to the **m** of hewed stones, 4060
7:11 after the **m** of hewed stones, and cedars. 4060
18:32 as great as would contain **two m** of seed. 5429

M

2Ki 7: 1 **two m** of barley for a shekel, in the gate of 5429
7:16 **two m** of barley for a shekel, according to 5429
7:18 **Two m** of barley for a shekel, and 5429
2Ch 2:10 twenty thousand **m** of beaten wheat, and 3734
2:10 twenty thousand **m** of wheat, and 3734
27: 5 ten thousand **m** of wheat, and ten thousand 3734
Ezr 7:22 to an hundred **m** *of* wheat, and to an 3734
Job 38: 5 Who hath laid the **m** thereof, if thou 4461
Pr 20:10 Divers weights, *and* **divers m**, 374+374+2050.1
Jer 13:25 *is* thy lot, the portion of thy **m** from me, 4055
Eze 40:24 the arches thereof according to these **m**. 4060
40:28 the south gate according to these **m**; 4060
40:29 the arches thereof, according to these **m**: 4060
40:32 he measured the gate according to these **m**. 4060
40:33 arches thereof, *were* according to these **m**: 4060
40:35 and measured *it* according to these **m**; 4060
43:13 these *are* the **m** of the altar after the cubits: 4060
48:16 these *shall be* the **m** thereof; the north side 4060
48:30 four thousand and five hundred **m**. 4060
48:33 side four thousand and five hundred **m**: 4060
48:35 *It was* round about eighteen thousand *m*: NIH
Hag 2:16 when *one* came to a heap of twenty *m*, there NIH
Mt 13:33 a woman took, and hid in three **m** of meal, *4568*
Lk 13:21 a woman took and hid in three **m** of meal, *4568*
16: 6 And he said, An hundred **m** of oil. And he *943*
16: 7 And he said, An hundred **m** of wheat. *2884*
Rev 6: 6 a penny, and three **m** of barley for a penny; *5518*

MEASURING (11) [MEASURE]
Jer 31:39 the **m** line shall yet go forth over against it 4060
Eze 40: 3 a line of flax in his hand, and a **m** reed; 4060
40: 5 in the man's hand a **m** reed of six cubits 4060
42:15 Now when he had made an end of **m** 4060
42:16 He measured the east side with the **m** reed, 4060
42:16 with the **m** reed round about. 4060
42:17 with the **m** reed round about. 4060
42:18 five hundred reeds, with the **m** reed. 4060
42:19 measured five hundred reeds with the **m** 4060
Zec 2: 1 behold, a man with a **m** line in his hand. 4060
2Co 10:12 but they **m** themselves by themselves, and *3354*

MEAT (290) [BAKEMEATS, MEATS]
Ge 1:29 a tree yielding seed; to you it shall be for **m**. 402
1:30 *is* life, *I have given* every green herb for **m**: 402
9: 3 Every moving thing that liveth shall be **m** 402
24:33 there was set *m* before him to eat: but NIH
27: 4 make me **savoury m**, such as I love, and 4303
27: 7 make me **savoury m**, that I may eat, and 4303
27: 9 I will make them **savoury m** for thy father, 4303
27:14 his mother made **savoury m**, such as his 4303
27:17 And she gave the **savoury m** and the bread, 4303
27:31 he also had made **savoury m**, and 4303
45:23 and bread and **m** for his father by the way. 4202
Ex 29:41 shalt do thereto according to the **m offering** 4503
30: 9 nor burnt sacrifice, nor **m offering**; 4503
40:29 it the burnt offering and the **m offering**; 4503
Lev 2: 1 when any will offer a **m offering** unto 4503
2: 3 the remnant of the **m offering** *shall be* 4503
2: 4 if thou bring an oblation of a **m offering** 4503
2: 5 if thy oblation *be* a **m offering** *baken* in a 4503
2: 6 and pour oil thereon: it *is* a **m offering**. 4503
2: 7 if thy oblation *be* a **m offering** *baken* in 4503
2: 8 thou shalt bring the **m offering** that is made 4503
2: 9 the priest shall take from the **m offering** a 4503
2:10 that which is left of the **m offering** *shall be* 4503
2:11 No **m offering**, which ye shall bring unto 4503
2:13 every oblation of thy **m offering** shalt thou 4503
2:13 thy God to be lacking from thy **m offering**: 4503
2:14 if thou offer a **m offering** of *thy* firstfruits 4503
2:14 thou shalt offer for the **m offering** of thy 4503
2:15 lay frankincense thereon: it *is* a **m offering**. 4503
5:13 shall be the priest's, as a **m offering**. 4503
6:14 this *is* the law of the **m offering**: the sons 4503
6:15 of the flour of the **m offering**, and of the oil 4503
6:15 frankincense which *is* upon the **m offering**, 4503
6:20 of fine flour *for* a **m offering** perpetual, 4503
6:21 the baken pieces of the **m offering** shalt 4503
6:23 For every **m offering** for the priest shall be 4503
7: 9 all the **m offering** that is baken in the oven, 4503
7:10 every **m offering**, mingled with oil, and 4503
7:37 of the **m offering**, and of the sin offering, 4503
9: 4 and a **m offering** mingled with oil: 4503
9:17 he brought the **m offering**, and took a 4503
10:12 Take the **m offering** that remaineth of 4503
11:34 Of all **m** which may be eaten, *that* on which 400
14:10 tenth deals of fine flour *for* a **m offering**, 4503
14:20 and the **m offering** upon the altar: 4503
14:21 flour mingled with oil for a **m offering**, 4503
14:31 *for* a burnt offering, with the **m offering**: 4503
22:11 is born in his house: they shall eat of his **m**. 3899
22:13 *in* her youth, she shall eat of her father's **m**: 3899
23:13 the **m offering** thereof *shall be* two tenth 4503
23:16 ye shall offer a new **m offering** unto 4503
23:18 with their **m offering**, and their drink 4503
23:37 a **m offering**, a sacrifice, and 4503
25: 6 the sabbath of the land shall be **m** for you; 402
25: 7 thy land, shall all the increase thereof be **m**. 398
Nu 4:16 the daily **m offering**, and the anointing oil, 4503
6:15 their **m offering**, and their drink offerings. 4503
6:17 the priest shall offer also his **m offering**, 4503
7:13 flour mingled with oil for a **m offering**: 4503
7:19 flour mingled with oil for a **m offering**: 4503
7:25 flour mingled with oil for a **m offering**: 4503
7:31 flour mingled with oil for a **m offering**: 4503
7:37 flour mingled with oil for a **m offering**: 4503
7:43 flour mingled with oil for a **m offering**: 4503
7:49 flour mingled with oil for a **m offering**: 4503
7:55 flour mingled with oil for a **m offering**: 4503
7:61 flour mingled with oil for a **m offering**: 4503
7:67 flour mingled with oil for a **m offering**: 4503
7:73 flour mingled with oil for a **m offering**: 4503
7:79 flour mingled with oil for a **m offering**: 4503
7:87 the first year twelve, with their **m offering**: 4503
8: 8 take a young bullock with his **m offering**, 4503
15: 4 **m offering** of a tenth deal *of* flour mingled 4503
15: 6 thou shalt prepare *for* a **m offering** two 4503
15: 9 shall he bring with a bullock a **m offering** 4503
15:24 with his **m offering**, and his drink offering, 4503
18: 9 every **m offering** of theirs, and every sin 4503
28: 5 *part* of an ephah *of* flour for a **m offering**, 4503
28: 8 as the **m offering** of the morning, and 4503
28: 9 two tenth deals *of* flour *for* a **m offering**, 4503
28:12 three tenth deals *of* flour *for* a **m offering**, 4503
28:12 two tenth deals *of* flour *for* a **m offering**, 4503
28:13 with oil *for* a **m offering** unto one lamb; 4503
28:20 their **m offering** *shall be of* flour mingled 4503
28:24 the **m** of the sacrifice made by fire, 3899
28:26 when ye bring a new **m offering** unto 4503
28:28 their **m offering** *of* flour mingled with oil, 4503
28:31 his **m offering**, (they shall be unto you 4503
29: 3 their **m offering** *shall be of* flour mingled 4503
29: 6 his **m offering**, and the daily burnt 4503
29: 6 his **m offering**, and their drink offerings, 4503
29: 9 their **m offering** *shall be of* flour mingled 4503
29:11 the **m offering** of it, and their drink 4503
29:14 their **m offering** *shall be of* flour mingled 4503
29:16 his **m offering**, and his drink offering. 4503
29:18 their **m offering** and their drink offerings 4503
29:19 the **m offering** thereof, and their drink 4503
29:21 their **m offering** and their drink offerings 4503
29:22 and his **m offering**, and his drink offering. 4503
29:24 Their **m offering** and their drink offerings 4503
29:25 his **m offering**, and his drink offering. 4503
29:27 their **m offering** and their drink offerings 4503
29:28 and his **m offering**, and his drink offering. 4503
29:30 their **m offering** and their drink offerings 4503
29:31 his **m offering**, and his drink offering. 4503
29:33 their **m offering** and their drink offerings 4503
29:34 his **m offering**, and his drink offering. 4503
29:37 Their **m offering** and their drink offerings 4503
29:38 and his **m offering**, and his drink offering. 4503
29:39 for your **m offerings**, and for your drink 4503
Dt 2: 6 Ye shall buy **m** of them for money, that ye 400
2:28 Thou shalt sell me **m** for money, that I may 400
20:20 thou knowest that they *be* not trees for **m**, 3978
28:26 thy carcase shall be **m** unto all fowls of 3978
Jos 22:23 offer thereon burnt offering or **m offering**, 4503
22:29 for **m offerings**, or for sacrifices, 4503
Jdg 1: 7 cut off, gathered *their m* under my table: NIH
13:19 So Manoah took a kid with a **m offering**, 4503
13:23 and a **m offering** at our hands, 4503
14:14 Out of the eater came forth **m**, and out of 3978
1Sa 20: 5 I should not fail to sit with the king at **m**: 398
20:24 was come, the king sat him down to eat **m**. 3899
20:27 cometh not the son of Jesse to **m**, 3899
20:34 did eat no **m** the second day of the month: 3899
2Sa 3:35 cause David to eat **m** while it was yet day, 3899
11: 8 there followed him a mess *of m* from NIH

2Sa 12: 3 it did eat of his own **m**, and drank of his 6595
13: 5 give me **m**, and dress the meat in my sight, 3899
13: 5 give me meat, and dress the **m** in my sight, 1279
13: 7 brother Amnon's house, and dress him **m**. 1279
13:10 Bring the **m** *into* the chamber, that I may 1279
1Ki 8:64 **m offerings**, and the fat of the peace 4503
8:64 **m offerings**, and the fat of the peace 4503
10: 5 the **m** of his table, and the sitting of his 3978
19: 8 went in the strength of that **m** forty days and 396
2Ki 3:20 when the **m offering** was offered, 4503
16:13 burnt his burnt offering and his **m offering**, 4503
16:15 the evening **m offering**, and the king's 4503
16:15 king's burnt sacrifice, and his **m offering**, 4503
16:15 their **m offering**, and their drink offerings; 4503
1Ch 12:40 and on mules, and on oxen, *and* **m**, meal, 3978
21:23 for wood, and the wheat for the **m offering**; 4503
23:29 for the fine flour for **m offering**, and 4503
2Ch 7: 7 and the **m offerings**, and the fat. 4503
9: 4 the **m** of his table, and the sitting of his 3978
Ezr 3: 7 **m**, and drink, and oil, unto them of Zidon, 3978
7:17 with their **m offerings** and their drink 4504
Ne 10:33 *for* the continual **m offering**, and for 4503
13: 5 where aforetime they laid the **m offerings**, 4503
13: 9 with the **m offering** and the frankincense. 4503
Job 6: 7 refused to touch *are* as my sorrowful **m**. 3899
12:11 ear try words? and the mouth taste his **m**? 400
20:14 *Yet* his **m** in his bowels is turned, *it is* 3899
20:21 *There shall* none of his **m** *be* left; therefore 400
30: 4 by the bushes, and juniper roots *for* their **m**. 3899
33:20 life abhorreth bread, and his soul dainty **m**. 3978
34: 3 the ear trieth words, as the mouth tasteth **m**. 398
36:31 he the people; he giveth **m** in abundance. 400
38:41 cry unto God, they wander for lack of **m**. 400
Ps 42: 3 My tears have been my **m** day and night, 3899
44:11 hast given us like sheep appointed for **m**; 3978
59:15 Let them wander up and down for **m**, and 398
69:21 They gave me also gall for my **m**; and 1267
74:14 gavest him *to be* **m** to the people inhabiting 3978
78:18 they tempted God in their heart by asking **m** 400
78:25 eat angels' food: he sent them **m** to the full. 6720
78:30 But while their **m** *was* yet in their mouths, 400
79: 2 given *to be* **m** unto the fowls of the heaven, 3978
104:21 after *their* prey, and seek their **m** from God. 400
104:27 that *thou* mayest give *them* their **m** in due 400
107:18 Their soul abhorreth all *manner of* **m**; and 400
111: 5 He hath given **m** unto them that fear him: 2964
145:15 and thou givest them their **m** in due season. 400
Pr 6: 8 Provideth her **m** in the summer, *and* 3899
23: 3 of his dainties: for they *are* deceitful **m**. 3899
30:22 and a fool when he is filled *with* **m**; 3899
30:25 yet they prepare their **m** in the summer; 3899
31:15 giveth **m** to her household, and a portion to 2964
Isa 57: 6 thou hast offered a **m offering**. 4503
62: 8 Surely I will no more give thy corn *to be* **m** 3978
65:25 dust *shall be* the serpent's **m**. They shall 3899
Jer 7:33 the carcases of this people shall be **m** for 3978
16: 4 their carcases shall be **m** for the fowls of 3978
17:26 **m offerings**, and incense, and 4503
19: 7 their carcases will I give to be **m** for 3978
33:18 to kindle **m offerings**, and to do sacrifice 4503
34:20 their dead bodies shall be for **m** unto 3978
La 1:11 they have given their pleasant things for **m** 400
1:19 while they sought their **m**, to relieve their 400
4:10 they were their **m** in the destruction of 1262
Eze 4:10 thy **m** which thou shalt eat *shall be* by 3978
16:19 My **m** also which I gave thee, fine flour, 3899
29: 5 I have given thee for **m** to the beasts of 402
34: 5 they became **m** to all the beasts of the field, 402
34: 8 my flock became **m** to every beast of 402
34:10 that they may not be **m** for them. 402
42:13 the most holy *things,* and the **m offering**, 4503
44:29 They shall eat the **m offering**, and the sin 4503
45:15 for a **m offering**, and for a burnt offering, 4503
45:17 **m offerings**, and drink offerings, in 4503
45:17 the **m offering**, and the burnt offering, and 4503
45:24 he shall prepare a **m offering** *of* an ephah 4503
45:25 according to the **m offering**, and 4503
46: 5 the **m offering** *shall be* an ephah for a ram, 4503
46: 5 the **m offering** for the lambs as he shall be 4503
46: 7 he shall prepare a **m offering**, an ephah for 4503
46:11 in the solemnities the **m offering** shall be 4503
46:14 thou shalt prepare a **m offering** for it every 4503
46:14 a **m offering** continually *by* a perpetual 4503
46:15 the lamb, and the **m offering**, and the oil, 4503
46:20 where they shall bake the **m offering**; 4503
47:12 and on that side, shall grow all trees for **m**, 3978
47:12 the fruit thereof shall be for **m**, and the leaf 3978
Da 1: 5 them a daily provision of the king's **m**, 6598
1: 8 himself with the **portion of** the king's **m**, 6598
1:10 who hath appointed your **m** and your drink: 3978
1:13 that eat *of* the **portion of** the king's **m**: 6598
1:15 which did eat the **portion of** the king's **m**. 6598
1:16 Melzar took away the **portion of** their **m**, 6598
4:12 fruit thereof much, and in it *was* **m** for all: 4203
4:21 fruit thereof much, and in it *was* **m** for all; 4203
11:26 they that feed of the **portion of** his **m** shall 6598
Hos 11: 4 yoke on their jaws, and I laid **m** unto them. 398
Joel 1: 9 The **m offering** and the drink offering is 4503
1:13 for the **m offering** and the drink offering is 4503
1:16 Is not the **m** cut off before our eyes, *yea,* joy 400
2:14 *even* a **m offering** and a drink offering unto 4503
Am 5:22 me burnt offerings and your **m offerings**, 4503
Hab 1:16 their portion *is* fat, and their **m** plenteous. 3978
3:17 shall fail, and the fields shall yield no **m**; 400
Hag 2:12 or pottage, or wine, or oil, or any **m**, shall it 3978
Mal 1:12 the fruit thereof, *even* his **m**, *is* contemptible. 400
3:10 that there may be **m** in mine house, and 2964
Mt 3: 4 and his **m** was locusts and wild honey. *5160*
6:25 ye shall put on. Is not the life more than **m**, *5160*
9:10 as Jesus **sat at m** in the house, behold, *345*
10:10 for the workman is worthy of his **m**. *5160*
14: 9 and them which **sat with** him **at m**, *4873*
15:37 they took up of the broken *m* that was left NIG
24:45 to give them **m** in due season? *5160*
25:35 For I was a hungred, and ye gave me **m**: *5315*
25:42 For I was a hungred, and ye gave me no **m**: *5315*
26: 7 and poured *it* on his head, as he **sat at m**. *345*
Mk 2:15 that as *Jesus* **sat at m** in his house, *2621*
8: 8 they took up of the broken *m* that was left NIG
14: 3 house of Simon the leper, as he **sat at m**, *2621*
16:14 appeared unto the eleven as they **sat at m**, *345*
Lk 3:11 and he that hath **m**, let him do likewise. *1033*
7:36 the Pharisee's house, and **sat down to m**. *347*
7:37 when she knew that *Jesus* **sat at m** in *345*
7:49 And they that **sat at m with** *him* began to *4873*
8:55 and he commanded to give her **m**. *5315*
9:13 we should go and buy **m** for all this people. *1033*
11:37 and he went in, and **sat down to m**. *377*
12:23 The life is more than **m**, and the body *is* *5160*
12:37 and **make** them to **sit down to m**, and *347*
12:42 to give *them their* **portion of m** in due *4620*
14:10 presence of them that **sit at m with** thee. *4873*
14:15 And when one of them that **sat at m with** *4873*
17: 7 come from the field, Go and **sit down to m**? *377*
22:27 he that **sitteth at m**, or he that serveth? *345*
22:27 *is* not he that **sitteth at m**? but I am among *345*
24:30 as he **sat at m** with them, he took bread, *2625*
24:41 he said unto them, Have ye here any **m**? *1034*
Jn 4: 8 were gone away unto the city to buy **m**.) *5160*
4:32 I have **m** to eat that ye know not of. *1035*
4:34 My **m** is to do the will of him that sent me, *1033*
6:27 Labour not for the **m** which perisheth, but *1035*
6:27 for *that* **m** which endureth unto everlasting *1035*
6:55 For my flesh is **m** indeed, *1035*
21: 5 saith unto them, Children, have ye any **m**? *4371*
Ac 2:46 did eat *their* **m** with gladness and *5160*
9:19 And when he had received **m**, he was *5160*
16:34 he **set m before** *them,* and rejoiced, *3908+5132*
27:33 Paul besought *them* all to take **m**, saying, *5160*
27:34 Wherefore I pray you to take *some* **m**: *5160*
27:36 of good cheer, and they also took *some* **m**. *5160*
Ro 14:15 But if thy brother be grieved with *thy* **m**, *1033*
14:15 Destroy not him with thy **m**, for whom *1033*
14:17 For the kingdom of God is not **m** and drink; *1035*
14:20 For **m** destroy not the work of God. *1033*
1Co 3: 2 I have fed you with milk, and not with **m**: *1033*
8: 8 But **m** commendeth us not to God: *1033*
8:10 knowledge **sit at m** in the idol's temple, *2621*
8:13 if **m** make my brother to offend, *1033*
10: 3 And did all eat the same spiritual **m**; *1033*
Col 2:16 Let no *man* therefore judge you in **m**, *1035*
Heb 5:12 as have need of milk, and not of strong **m**. *5160*
5:14 But strong **m** belongeth to *them that are* of *5160*
12:16 who for one **morsel of m** sold his *1035*

MEAT MARKET See SHAMBLES

M

MEATS (8) [MEAT]
Pr 23: 6 evil eye, neither desire thou his **dainty m**: 4303
Mk 7:19 goeth out into the draught, purging all **m**? *1033*
Ac 15:29 That *ye* abstain from **m offered to idols**, *1494*
1Co 6:13 **M** for the belly, and the belly for meats: but *1033*
6:13 Meats for the belly, and the belly for **m**: but *1033*
1Ti 4: 3 *and commanding* to abstain from **m**, *1033*
Heb 9:10 *Which stood* only in **m** and drinks, and *1033*
13: 9 not with **m**, which have not profited them *1033*

MEBUNNAI (1)
2Sa 23:27 Abiezer the Anethothite, **M** the Hushathite, 4012

MECHERATHITE (1)
1Ch 11:36 Hepher the **M**, Ahijah the Pelonite, 4382

MECONAH See MEKONAH

MEDAD (2)
Nu 11:26 *was* Eldad, and the name of the other **M**: 4312
11:27 Eldad and **M** do prophesy in the camp. 4312

MEDAN (2) [MEDANITES]
Ge 25: 2 and **M**, and Midian, and Ishbak, and Shuah. 4091
1Ch 1:32 and **M**, and Midian, and Ishbak, and Shuah. 4091

MEDANITES (1) [MEDAN]
Ge 37:36 the **M** sold him into Egypt unto Potiphar, 4084

MEDDLE (6) [MEDDLED, MEDDLETH, MEDDLING]
Dt 2: 5 **M** not with them; for I will not give you of 1624
2:19 distress them not, nor **m** with them: 1624
2Ki 14:10 for why shouldest thou **m** to *thy* hurt, 1624
2Ch 25:19 why shouldest thou **m** to *thine* hurt, 1624
Pr 20:19 **m** not with him that flattereth *with* his lips. 6148
24:21 **m** not with them that are given to change: 6148

MEDDLED (1) [MEDDLE]
Pr 17:14 leave off contention, before *it* be **m with**. 1566

MEDDLER See BUSYBODY

MEDDLETH (1) [MEDDLE]
Pr 26:17 *and* **m** with strife *belonging* not to him, 5674

MEDDLING (2) [MEDDLE]
2Ch 35:21 forbear thee from **m** with God, who *is* with NIH
Pr 20: 3 cease from strife: but every fool will be **m**. 1566

MEDE (1) [MEDIA]
Da 11: 1 Also I in the first year of Darius the **M**, 4075

MEDEBA (5)
Nu 21:30 even unto Nophah, which *reacheth* unto **M**. 4311
Jos 13: 9 and all the plain of **M** unto Dibon; 4311
13:16 midst of the river, and all the plain by **M**; 4311
1Ch 19: 7 who came and pitched before **M**. 4311
Isa 15: 2 Moab shall howl over Nebo, and over **M**: 4311

MEDES (14) [MEDIA]
2Ki 17: 6 river of Gozan, and in the cities of the **M**. 4074
18:11 river of Gozan, and in the cities of the **M**: 4074
Ezr 6: 2 the palace that *is* in the province of the **M**, 4076
Est 1:19 among the laws of the Persians and the **M**, 4074
Isa 13:17 Behold, I will stir up the **M** against them, 4074
Jer 25:25 kings of Elam, and all the kings of the **M**, 4074
51:11 raised up the spirit of the kings of the **M**: 4074
51:28 her the nations with the kings of the **M**, 4074
Da 5:28 is divided, and given to the **M** and Persians. 4076
6: 8 according to the law of the **M** and Persians, 4076
6:12 according to the law of the **M** and Persians, 4076
6:15 that the law of the **M** and Persians *is*, That 4076
9: 1 the son of Ahasuerus, of the seed of the **M**, 4074
Ac 2: 9 and **M**, and Elamites, and the dwellers in *3370*

MEDIA (6) [MEDE, MEDES, MEDIAN]
Est 1: 3 the power of Persia and **M**, the nobles and 4074
1:14 the seven princes of Persia and **M**, 4074
1:18 **M** say this day unto all the king's princes, 4074
10: 2 book of the chronicles of the kings of **M** 4074
Isa 21: 2 besiege, O **M**; all the sighing thereof have I 4074
Da 8:20 sawest having two horns *are* the kings of **M** 4074

MEDIAN (1) [MEDIA]
Da 5:31 Darius the **M** took the kingdom, 4076

MEDIATOR (7)
Gal 3:19 *was* ordained by angels in the hand of a **m**. *3316*
3:20 Now a **m** is not *a mediator* of one, but God *3316*
3:20 Now a mediator is not *a* **m** of one, but God NIG
1Ti 2: 5 and one **m** between God and men, *3316*
Heb 8: 6 by how much also he is the **m** of a better *3316*
9:15 And for this cause he is the **m** of the new *3316*
12:24 And to Jesus the **m** of the new covenant, *3316*

MEDICINE (2) [MEDICINES]
Pr 17:22 A merry heart doeth good *like* a **m**: but 1456
Eze 47:12 be for meat, and the leaf thereof for **m**. 8644

MEDICINES (2) [MEDICINE]
Jer 30:13 be bound up: thou hast no healing **m**. 7499
46:11 in vain shalt thou use many **m**; *for* thou 7499

MEDITATE (14) [MEDITATION]
Ge 24:63 Isaac went out to **m** in the field at 7742
Jos 1: 8 thou shalt **m** therein day and night, that 1897
Ps 1: 2 and in his law doth he **m** day and night. 1897
63: 6 *and* **m** on thee in the *night* watches. 1897
77:12 I will **m** also of all thy work, and talk of thy 1897
119:15 I will **m** in thy precepts, and have respect 7878
119:23 *but* thy servant did **m** in thy statutes. 7878
119:48 I have loved; and I will **m** in thy statutes. 7878
119:78 a cause: *but* I will **m** in thy precepts. 7878
119:148 *night* watches, that *I* might **m** in thy word. 7878
143: 5 the days of old; I **m** on all thy works; 1897
Isa 33:18 Thine heart shall **m** terror. Where *is* 1897
Lk 21:14 not to **m before** *what ye* shall answer: *4304*
1Ti 4:15 **M upon** these *things;* give thyself wholly *3191*

MEDITATION (6) [MEDITATE]
Ps 5: 1 to my words, O LORD, consider my **m**. 1901
19:14 the **m** of my heart, be acceptable in thy 1902
49: 3 the **m** of my heart *shall be of* 1900
104:34 My **m** of him shall be sweet: I will be glad 7879
119:97 how love I thy law! it *is* my **m** all the day. 7881
119:99 my teachers: for thy testimonies *are* my **m**. 7881

MEEK (17) [MEEKNESS]
Nu 12: 3 (Now the man Moses *was* very **m**, 6035
Ps 22:26 The **m** shall eat and be satisfied: they shall 6035
25: 9 The **m** will he guide in judgment: and 6035
25: 9 and the **m** will he teach his way. 6035
37:11 the **m** shall inherit the earth; and 6035
76: 9 to judgment, to save all the **m** of the earth. 6035
147: 6 The LORD lifteth up the **m**: he casteth 6035
149: 4 he will beautify the **m** with salvation. 6035
Isa 11: 4 reprove with equity for the **m** of the earth: 6035
29:19 The **m** also shall increase *their* joy in 6035
61: 1 me to preach good tidings unto the **m**; 6035
Am 2: 7 the poor, and turn aside the way of the **m**: 6035
Zep 2: 3 Seek ye the LORD, all ye **m** of the earth, 6035
Mt 5: 5 Blessed *are* the **m**: for they shall inherit *4239*
11:29 learn of me; for I am **m** and lowly in heart: *4235*
21: 5 **m**, and sitting upon an ass, and a colt *4239*
1Pe 3: 4 *even the ornament* of a **m** and quiet spirit, *4239*

MEEKNESS (14) [MEEK]
Ps 45: 4 of truth and **m** *and* righteousness; 6037
Zep 2: 3 his judgment; seek righteousness, seek **m**: 6038
1Co 4:21 a rod, or in love, and *in* the spirit of **m**? *4236*
2Co 10: 1 Now I Paul myself beseech you by the **m** *4236*
Gal 5:23 **M**, temperance: against such there is no *4236*
6: 1 restore such a one in the spirit of **m**; *4236*
Eph 4: 2 With all lowliness and **m**, with *4236*
Col 3:12 humbleness of mind, **m**, longsuffering; *4236*
1Ti 6:11 godliness, faith, love, patience, **m**. *4236*
2Ti 2:25 In **m** instructing those that oppose *4236*
Tit 3: 2 *but* gentle, shewing all **m** unto all men. *4236*
Jas 1:21 and receive with **m** the engrafted word, *4240*
3:13 conversation his works with **m** of wisdom. *4240*
1Pe 3:15 a reason of the hope that is in you with **m** *4240*

MEET (132) [MEETEST, MEETETH, MEETING, MET]
Ge 2:18 I will make him a help **m for** him. 5048+3509.1
2:20 was not found a help **m for** him. 5048+3509.1
14:17 the king of Sodom went out to **m** him after 7125
18: 2 when he saw *them,* he ran to **m** them from 7125
19: 1 Lot seeing *them* rose up to **m** them; and 7125
24:17 the servant ran to **m** her, and said, Let me, 7125
24:65 *is* this that walketh in the field to **m** us? 7125

Ge 29:13 that he ran to **m** him, and embraced him, 7125
30:16 Leah went out to **m** him, and said, 7125
32: 6 also he cometh to **m** thee, and four hundred 7125
33: 4 And Esau ran to **m** him, and embraced him, 7125
46:29 went up to **m** Israel his father, to Goshen, 7125
Ex 4:14 behold, he cometh forth to **m** thee: 7125
4:27 Go into the wilderness to **m** Moses. 7125
8:26 Moses said, It is not **m** so to do; for we 3559
18: 7 Moses went out to **m** his father in law, and 7125
19:17 the people out of the camp to **m with** God; 7125
23: 4 If thou **m** thine enemy's ox or his ass going 6293
25:22 there I will **m** with thee, and I will 3259
29:42 where I will **m** you, to speak there unto 3259
29:43 there I will **m** with the children of Israel, 3259
30: 6 the Testimony, where I will **m** with thee. 3259
30:36 the congregation, where I will **m** with thee: 3259
Nu 17: 4 the Testimony, where I will **m** with you. 3259
22:36 he went out to **m** him unto a city of Moab, 7125
23: 3 peradventure the LORD will come to **m** 7125
23:15 while I **m** *the* LORD yonder. 7136
31:13 went forth to **m** them without the camp. 7125
Dt 3:18 of Israel, all *that are* **m for the war**. 1121+2428
Jos 2:16 to the mountain, lest the pursuers **m** you; 6293
9:11 go to **m** them, and say unto them, We *are* 7125
Jdg 4:18 Jael went out to **m** Sisera, and said unto 7125
4:22 Jael came out to **m** him, and said unto him, 7125
5:30 *m* for the necks of *them that take* the spoil? NIH
6:35 and they came up to **m** them. 7125
11:31 forth of the doors of my house to **m** me, 7125
11:34 his daughter came out to **m** him with 7125
19: 3 the damsel saw him, he rejoiced to **m** him. 7125
Ru 2:22 that they **m** thee not in *any* other field. 6293
1Sa 10: 3 there shall **m** thee three men going up to 4672
10: 5 that thou shalt **m** a company of prophets 6293
13:10 Saul went out to **m** him, that he might 7125
15:12 when Samuel rose early to **m** Saul in 7125
17:48 came and drew nigh to **m** David, that David 7125
17:48 ran *toward* the army to **m** the Philistine. 7125
18: 6 singing and dancing, to **m** king Saul, 7125
25:32 of Israel, which sent thee this day to **m** me: 7125
25:34 thou hadst hasted and come to **m** me, 7125
30:21 they went forth to **m** David, and to meet 7125
30:21 and to **m** the people that *were* with him: 7125
2Sa 6:20 Michal the daughter of Saul came out to **m** 7125
10: 5 he sent to **m** them, because the men were 7125
15:32 Hushai the Archite *came* to **m** him with his 7125
19:15 Judah came to Gilgal, to go to **m** the king, 7125
19:16 came down with the men of Judah to **m** 7125
19:20 Joseph to go down to **m** my lord the king. 7125
19:24 the son of Saul came down to **m** the king, 7125
19:25 when he was come *to* Jerusalem to **m** 7125
1Ki 2: 8 he came down to **m** me *at* Jordan, and 7125
2:19 the king rose up to **m** her, and 7125
18:16 So Obadiah went to **m** Ahab, and told him: 7125
18:16 and told him: and Ahab went to **m** Elijah. 7125
21:18 Arise, go down to **m** Ahab king of Israel, 7125
2Ki 1: 3 go up to **m** the messengers of the king of 7125
1: 6 There came a man up to **m** us, and 7125
1: 7 of man *was he* which came up to **m** you, 7125
2:15 they came to **m** him, and bowed themselves 7125
4:26 I pray thee, to **m** her, and say unto her, 7125
4:29 go *thy way:* if thou **m** any man, salute him 4672
4:31 Wherefore he went again to **m** him, and 7125
5:21 he lighted down from the chariot to **m** him, 7125
5:26 turned *again* from his chariot to **m** thee? 7125
8: 8 go, **m** the man of God, and inquire of 7125
8: 9 So Hazael went to **m** him, and took a 7125
9:17 send to **m** them, and let him say, *Is it* 7125
9:18 So there went one on horseback to **m** him, 7125
10:15 the son of Rechab *coming* to **m** him: 7125
16:10 king Ahaz went *to* Damascus to **m** 7125
1Ch 12:17 David went out to **m** them, and answered 6440
19: 5 he sent to **m** them: for the men were greatly 7125
2Ch 15: 2 he went out to **m** Asa, and said unto him, 6440
19: 2 son of Hanani the seer went out to **m** him, 6440
Ezr 4:14 *it was* not **m** for us to see the king's 749
Ne 6: 2 let us **m** together in *some one of* 3259
6:10 Let us **m together** in the house of God, 3259
Est 2: 9 *which were* **m** to be given her, 7200
Job 5:14 They **m** with darkness in the daytime, and 6298
34:31 Surely it is *m to be* said unto God, I have NIH
39:21 He goeth on to **m** the armed men. 7125
Pr 7:15 Therefore came I forth to **m** thee, 7125
11:24 *there is* that withholdeth more than is **m**, 3476
17:12 *Let* a bear robbed of her whelps **m** a man, 6298
22: 2 The rich and poor **m together**: the LORD 6298
29:13 and the deceitful man **m together**: 6298
Isa 7: 3 Go forth now to **m** Ahaz, thou, and 7125
14: 9 Hell from beneath is moved for thee to **m** 7125
34:14 The wild beasts of the desert shall also **m** 6298
47: 3 and I will not **m** *thee as* a man. 6293
Jer 26:14 with me as seemeth good and **m** unto you. 3477
27: 5 have given it unto whom it seemed **m** unto 3474
41: 6 went forth from Mizpah to **m** them, 7125
51:31 One post shall run to **m** another, and 7125
51:31 and one messenger to **m** another, 7125
Eze 15: 4 midst of it is burnt. Is it **m** for *any* work? 6743
15: 5 when it was whole, it was **m** for no work: 6213
15: 5 how much less shall it be **m** yet for *any* 6213
Hos 13: 8 I will **m** them as a bear *that is* bereaved of 6298
Am 4:12 unto thee, prepare to **m** thy God, O Israel. 7125
Zec 2: 3 and another angel went out to **m** him, 7125
Mt 3: 8 therefore fruits **m for** repentance: *514*
8:34 the whole city came out to **m** Jesus: *4877*
15:26 It is not **m** to take the children's bread, and *2570*
25: 1 and went forth to **m** the bridegroom. *529*
25: 6 the bridegroom cometh; go ye out to **m** him. *529*
Mk 7:27 for it is not **m** to take the children's bread, *2570*
14:13 there shall **m** you a man bearing a pitcher of *528*
Lk 14:31 **m** him that cometh against him with twenty *528*
15:32 It was **m** that *we* should make merry, and *1163*
22:10 there shall a man **m** you, bearing a pitcher *4876*
Jn 12:13 and went forth to **m** him, and cried, *5222*
Ac 26:20 turn to God, and do works **m for** repentance. *514*
28:15 they came to **m** us as far as Appii forum, and *529*
Ro 1:27 recompence of their error which was **m**. *1163*
1Co 15: 9 that am not **m** to be called an apostle, *2425*
16: 4 And if it be **m** that I go also, they shall go *514*
Php 1: 7 Even as it is **m** for me to think this of you *1342*
Col 1:12 which hath **made** us **m** to be partakers of *2427*
1Th 4:17 them in the clouds, to **m** the Lord in the air: *529*
2Th 1: 3 as it is **m**, because that your faith groweth *514*
2Ti 2:21 and **m for** the master's **use**, *and* *2173*
Heb 6: 7 bringeth forth herbs **m** for them by whom it *2111*
2Pe 1:13 Yea, I think it **m**, as long as I am in this *1342*

MEETEST (2) [MEET]
2Ki 10: 3 out the best and **m** of your master's sons, 3477
Isa 64: 5 Thou **m** him that rejoiceth and 6293

MEETETH (3) [MEET]
Ge 32:17 When Esau my brother **m** thee, and 6298
Nu 35:19 when he **m** him, he shall slay him. 6293
35:21 shall slay the murderer, when he **m** him. 6293

MEETING (2) [MEET]
1Sa 21: 1 Ahimelech was afraid at the **m** of David, 7125
Isa 1:13 *it is* iniquity, even the **solemn m**. 6116

MEGIDDO (11) [MEGIDDON]
Jos 12:21 king of Taanach, one; the king of **M**, one; 4023
17:11 and the inhabitants of **M** and her towns, 4023
Jdg 1:27 nor the inhabitants of **M** and her towns: 4023
5:19 of Canaan in Taanach by the waters of **M**; 4023
1Ki 4:12 *to him pertained* Taanach and **M**, and 4023
9:15 and Hazor, and **M**, and Gezer. 4023
2Ki 9:27 And he fled *to* **M**, and died there. 4023
23:29 he slew him at **M**, when he had seen him. 4023
23:30 carried him *in a chariot* dead from **M**, 4023
1Ch 7:29 **M** and her towns, Dor and her towns. 4023
2Ch 35:22 and came to fight in the valley of **M**. 4023

MEGIDDON (1) [MEGIDDO]
Zec 12:11 of Hadadrimmon in the valley of **M**. 4023

MEHETABEEL (1)
Ne 6:10 Shemaiah the son of Delaiah the son of **M**, 4105

MEHETABEL (2)
Ge 36:39 his wife's name *was* **M**, the daughter of 4105
1Ch 1:50 his wife's name *was* **M**, the daughter of 4105

MEHIDA (2)
Ezr 2:52 the children of **M**, the children of Harsha, 4240
Ne 7:54 the children of **M**, the children of Harsha, 4240

MEHIR (1)
1Ch 4:11 Chelub the brother of Shuah begat **M**, 4243

MEHOLATHITE (2)
1Sa 18:19 that she was given unto Adriel the **M** to 4259
2Sa 21: 8 up for Adriel the son of Barzillai the **M**: 4259

MEHUJAEL (2)
Ge 4:18 Irad begat **M**: and Mehujael begat 4232
4:18 **M** begat Methusael: and Methusael begat 4232

MEHUMAN (1)
Est 1:10 he commanded **M**, Biztha, Harbona, 4104

MEHUNIM (1) [MEHUNIMS, MEUNIM]
Ezr 2:50 The children of Asnah, the children of **M**, 4586

MEHUNIMS (1) [MEHUNIM]
2Ch 26: 7 Arabians that dwelt in Gur-baal, and the **M**. 4586

ME-JARKON (1)
Jos 19:46 **M**, and Rakkon, with the border before 4313

MEKERATHITE See MECHERATHITE

MEKONAH (1)
Ne 11:28 and at **M**, and in the villages thereof, 4368

MELATIAH (1)
Ne 3: 7 next unto them repaired **M** the Gibeonite, 4424

MELCHI (2)
Lk 3:24 *the son* of Levi, which was *the son* of **M**, *3197*
3:28 Which was *the son* of **M**, which was *3197*

MELCHIAH (1)
Jer 21: 1 sent unto him Pashur the son of **M**, 4441

MELCHISEDEC (9) [MELCHIZEDEK]
Heb 5: 6 *art* a priest for ever after the order of **M**. *3198*
5:10 of God a high priest after the order of **M**. *3198*
6:20 a high priest for ever after the order of **M**. *3198*
7: 1 For this **M**, king of Salem, priest of *3198*
7:10 in the loins of his father, when **M** met him. *3198*
7:11 priest should rise after the order of **M**, *3198*
7:15 for that after the similitude of **M** there *3198*
7:17 *art* a priest for ever after the order of **M**. *3198*
7:21 *art* a priest for ever after the order of **M**:) *3198*

MELCHISHUA (1)
1Sa 14:49 of Saul were Jonathan, and Ishui, and **M**: 4444

MELCHIZEDEK (2) [MELCHISEDEC]
Ge 14:18 **M** king of Salem brought forth bread and 4442
Ps 110: 4 *art* a priest for ever after the order of **M**. 4442

MELEA (1)
Lk 3:31 Which was *the son* of **M**, which was *3190*

MELECH (2)
1Ch 8:35 *were,* Pithon, and **M**, and Tarea, and Ahaz. 4429
9:41 and **M**, and Tahrea, *and Ahaz.* 4429

MELICU (1)
Ne 12:14 Of **M**, Jonathan; of Shebaniah, Joseph; 4409

MELITA (1)
Ac 28: 1 they knew that the island was called **M**. *3194*

MELKI See MELCHI

MELODY (4)
Isa 23:16 make sweet **m**, sing many songs, that thou 5059
51: 3 thanksgiving, and the voice of **m**. 2172
Am 5:23 for I will not hear the **m** of thy viols. 2172
Eph 5:19 and **making m** in your heart to the Lord; *5567*

MELONS (1)
Nu 11: 5 and the **m**, and the leeks, and the onions, and 20

MELT (17) [MELTED, MELTETH, MELTING, MOLTEN]
Ex 15:15 all the inhabitants of Canaan shall **m away**. 4127
Jos 2:11 had heard *these things,* our hearts did **m**, 4549
14: 8 with me **made** the heart of the people **m**: 4529
2Sa 17:10 the heart of a lion, shall **utterly m**: 4549+4549
Ps 58: 7 Let them **m away** as waters *which* run 3988
112:10 he shall gnash *with* his teeth, and **m away**: 4549
Isa 13: 7 be faint, and every man's heart shall **m**: 4549
19: 1 the heart of Egypt shall **m** in the midst of it. 4549
Jer 9: 7 Behold, I will **m** them, and try them; 6884
Eze 21: 7 every heart shall **m**, and all hands shall be 4549
22:20 to **m** *it;* so will I gather *you* in mine anger 5413
22:20 and I will leave *you there,* and **m** you. 5413
Am 9: 5 it shall **m**, and all that dwell therein shall 4127
9:13 drop sweet wine, and all the hills shall **m**. 4127
Na 1: 5 the hills **m**, and the earth is burnt at his 4127
2Pe 3:10 and the elements shall **m** with fervent heat, *3089*
3:12 and the elements shall **m** with fervent heat? *5080*

MELTED (13) [MELT]
Ex 16:21 and when the sun waxed hot, it **m**. 4549
Jos 5: 1 we were passed over, that their heart **m**, 4549
7: 5 wherefore the hearts of the people **m**, and 4549
Jdg 5: 5 The mountains **m** from before the LORD, 5140
1Sa 14:16 the multitude **m away**, and they went on 4127
Ps 22:14 like wax; it is **m** in the midst of my bowels. 4549
46: 6 he uttered his voice, the earth **m**. 4127
97: 5 The hills **m** like wax at the presence of 4549
107:26 their soul is **m** because of trouble. 4127
Isa 34: 3 the mountains shall be **m** with their blood. 4549
Eze 22:21 and ye shall be **m** in the midst thereof. 5413
22:22 As silver is **m** in the midst of the furnace, 2046
22:22 so shall ye be **m** in the midst thereof; 5413

MELTETH (7) [MELT]
Ps 58: 8 As a snail *which* **m**, let *every one of them* 8557
68: 2 as wax **m** before the fire, *so* let the wicked 4549
119:28 My soul **m** for heaviness: strengthen thou 1811
147:18 He sendeth out his word, and **m** them: 4529
Isa 40:19 The workman **m** a graven image, and 5258
Jer 6:29 of the fire; the founder **m** in vain: 6884
Na 2:10 the heart **m**, and the knees smite together, 4549

MELTING (1) [MELT]
Isa 64: 2 As *when* the **m** fire burneth, the fire 2003

MELZAR (2)
Da 1:11 said Daniel to **M**, whom the prince of 4453
1:16 Thus **M** took away the portion of their 4453

MEMBER (6) [MEMBERS]
Dt 23: 1 in the stones, or hath *his* **privy m** cut off, 8212
1Co 12:14 For the body is not one **m**, but many. *3196*
12:19 And if they were all one **m**, where *were* *3196*
12:26 And whether one **m** suffer, all the members *3196*
12:26 suffer with *it;* or one **m** be honoured, *3196*
Jas 3: 5 Even so the tongue is a little **m**, and *3196*

MEMBERS (32) [MEMBER]
Job 17: 7 of sorrow, and all my **m** *are* as a shadow. 3338
Ps 139:16 in thy book all *my* **m** were written, *which* in NIH
Mt 5:29 for it is profitable for thee that one of thy **m** *3196*
5:30 for it is profitable for thee that one of thy **m** *3196*
Ro 6:13 Neither yield ye your **m** *as* instruments of *3196*
6:13 your **m** *as* instruments of righteousness *3196*
6:19 for as ye have yielded your **m** servants to *3196*
6:19 now yield your **m** servants to righteousness *3196*
7: 5 did work in our **m** to bring forth fruit unto *3196*
7:23 But I see another law in my **m**, *3196*
7:23 to the law of sin which is in my **m**. *3196*
12: 4 For as we have many **m** in one body, and *3196*
12: 4 and all **m** have not the same office: *3196*
12: 5 in Christ, and every one **m** one of another. *3196*
1Co 6:15 Know ye not that your bodies are the **m** of *3196*
6:15 shall I then take the **m** of Christ, and *3196*
6:15 of Christ, and make *them* the **m** of a harlot? *3196*
12:12 and hath many **m**, and all the members of *3196*
12:12 and all the **m** of *that* one body, being many, *3196*
12:18 But now hath God set the **m** every one of *3196*
12:20 But now *are they* many **m**, yet *but* *3196*
12:22 Nay, much more those **m** of the body, *3196*
12:23 And those *m* of the body, which we think to NIG
12:25 *that* the **m** should have the same care one *3196*
12:26 all the **m** suffer with *it;* or one member be *3196*
12:26 be honoured, all the **m** rejoice with *it.* *3196*
12:27 are the body of Christ, and **m** in particular. *3196*
Eph 4:25 his neighbour: for we are **m** one of another. *3196*
5:30 For we are **m** of his body, of his flesh, and *3196*
Col 3: 5 therefore your **m** which are upon the earth; *3196*
Jas 3: 6 so is the tongue amongst our **m**, that it *3196*
4: 1 *even* of your lusts that war in your **m**? *3196*

MEMORIAL (32)
Ex 3:15 and this *is* my **m** unto all generations. 2143
12:14 this day shall be unto you for a **m**; and 2146

Ex 13: 9 for a **m** between thine eyes, that 2146
17:14 Write this *for* a **m** in a book, and rehearse *it* 2146
28:12 *for* stones of **m** unto the children of Israel: 2146
28:12 LORD upon his two shoulders for a **m**. 2146
28:29 for a **m** before the LORD continually. 2146
30:16 that it may be a **m** unto the children of 2146
39: 7 *that they should be* stones for a **m** to 2146
Lev 2: 2 the priest shall burn the **m** of it upon 234
2: 9 take from the meat offering a **m** thereof, 234
2:16 the priest shall burn the **m** of it, *part* of 234
5:12 *even* a **m** thereof, and burn *it* on the altar, 234
6:15 *even* the **m** of it, unto the LORD. 234
23:24 a **m** of blowing of trumpets, a holy 2146
24: 7 that it may be on the bread for a **m**, *even* an 234
Nu 5:15 *is* an offering of jealousy, an offering of **m**, 2146
5:18 and put the offering of **m** in her hands, 2146
5:26 *even* the **m** thereof, and burn *it* upon 234
10:10 that they may be to you for a **m** before your 2146
16:40 *To be* a **m** unto the children of Israel, that 2146
31:54 *for* a **m** for the children of Israel before 2146
Jos 4: 7 these stones shall be for a **m** unto 2146
Ne 2:20 no portion, nor right, nor **m**, in Jerusalem. 2146
Est 9:28 nor the **m** of them perish from their seed. 2143
Ps 9: 6 their **m** is perished *with* them. 2143
135:13 *and* thy **m**, O LORD, throughout all 2143
Hos 12: 5 LORD God of hosts; the LORD *is* his **m**. 2143
Zec 6:14 for a **m** in the temple of the LORD. 2146
Mt 26:13 *woman* hath done, be told for a **m** of her. *3422*
Mk 14: 9 hath done shall be spoken of for a **m** of her. *3422*
Ac 10: 4 thine alms are come up for a **m** before God. *3422*

MEMORY (6)
Ps 109:15 that he may cut off the **m** of them from 2143
145: 7 They shall abundantly utter the **m** of thy 2143
Pr 10: 7 The **m** of the just *is* blessed: but the name 2143
Ecc 9: 5 a reward; for the **m** of them is forgotten. 2143
Isa 26:14 and made all their **m** to perish. 2143
1Co 15: 2 if ye **keep in m** what I preached unto you, *2722*

MEMPHIS (1)
Hos 9: 6 shall gather them up, **M** shall bury them: 4644

MEMUCAN (3)
Est 1:14 Tarshish, Meres, Marsena, *and* **M**, 4462
1:16 **M** answered before the king and 4462
1:21 the king did according to the word of **M**: 4462

MEN (1652) [MAN]
Ge 4:26 began *m* to call upon the name of NIH
6: 1 when **m** began to multiply on the face of 120
6: 2 That the sons of God saw the daughters of **m** 120
6: 4 of God came in unto the daughters of **m**, 120
6: 4 the same *became* mighty **m** which *were* of NIH
6: 4 *men* which *were* of old, **m** of renown. 376
11: 5 the tower, which the children of **m** builded. 120
12:20 Pharaoh commanded *his* **m** concerning him: 376
13:13 the **m** of Sodom *were* wicked and 376
14:24 Save only that which the **young m** have 5288
14:24 the portion of the **m** which went with me, 376
17:23 every male among the **m** of Abraham's 376
17:27 all the **m** of his house, born in the house, 376
18: 2 and looked, and lo, three **m** stood by him: 376
18:16 the **m** rose up from thence, and 376
18:22 the **m** turned their faces from thence, and 376
19: 4 the **m** of the city, *even* the men of Sodom, 376
19: 4 the men of the city, *even* the **m** of Sodom, 376
19: 5 Where *are* the **m** which came in to thee this 376
19: 8 only unto these **m** do nothing; for therefore 376
19:10 the **m** put forth their hand, and pulled Lot 376
19:11 they smote the **m** that *were at* the door of 376
19:12 the **m** said unto Lot, Hast thou here any 376
19:16 the **m** laid hold upon his hand, and upon 376
20: 8 in their ears: and the **m** were sore afraid. 376
22: 3 took two of his **young m** with him, and 5288
22: 5 Abraham said unto his **young m**, 5288
22:19 So Abraham returned unto his **young m**, 5288
24:13 the daughters of the **m** of the city come out 376
24:54 he and the **m** that *were* with him, and 376
24:59 and Abraham's servant, and his **m**. 376
26: 7 the **m** of the place asked *him* of his wife; 376
26: 7 *said he,* the **m** of the place should kill me for 376
29:22 Laban gathered together all the **m** of 376
32: 6 to meet thee, and four hundred **m** with him. 376
32:28 hast thou power with God and with **m**, 376
33: 1 Esau came, and with him four hundred **m**. 376
33:13 if *m* should overdrive them one day, all NIH
34: 7 when they heard *it:* and the **m** were grieved, 376
34:20 communed with the **m** of their city, saying, 376
34:21 These **m** *are* peaceable with us; therefore 376
34:22 Only herein will the **m** consent unto us for to 376
38:21 he asked the **m** of that place, saying, 376
38:22 also the **m** of the place said, *that* there was 376
39:11 *there was* none of the **m** of the house there 376
39:14 That she called unto the **m** of her house, and 376
41: 8 of Egypt, and all the **wise m** thereof: 2450
42:11 we *are* true *m*, thy servants are no spies. NIH
42:19 If ye *be* true *m*, let one of your brethren be NIH
42:31 unto him, We *are* true *m*; we are no spies: NIH
42:33 Hereby shall I know that ye *are* true *m*; NIH
42:34 *that* ye *are* true *m*: *so* will I deliver you your NIH
43:15 the **m** took that present, and they took 376
43:16 Bring *these* **m** home, and slay, and 376
43:16 for *these* **m** shall dine with me at noon. 376
43:17 the **m** brought the **m** into Joseph's house. 376
43:18 the **m** were afraid, because they were 376
43:24 the man brought the **m** into Joseph's house, 376
43:33 and the **m** marvelled one at another. 376
44: 3 the **m** were sent away, they and their asses. 376
44: 4 unto his steward, Up, follow after the **m**; 376
46:32 the **m** *are* shepherds, for their trade hath 376
47: 2 *even* five **m**, and presented them unto 376
Ex 1:17 but saved the **m children** alive. 3206
1:18 have saved the **m children** alive? 3206
2:13 two **m** of the Hebrews strove together: 376
4:19 for all the **m** are dead which sought thy life. 376
5: 9 Let there more work be laid upon the **m**, 376
7:11 Pharaoh also called the **wise m** and 2450
10: 7 let the **m** go, that they may serve the LORD 376
10:11 go now ye *that are* **m**, and serve 1397
12:33 in haste; for they said, We *be* all dead *m*. NIH
12:37 six hundred thousand on foot *that were* **m**, 1397
15:15 the **mighty m** of Moab, trembling shall take 352
17: 9 Choose us out **m**, and go out, fight with 376
18:21 shalt provide out of all the people able **m**, 376
18:21 such as fear God, **m** of truth, 376
18:25 Moses chose able **m** out of all Israel, and 376
21:18 if **m** strive together, and one smite another 376
21:22 If **m** strive, and hurt a woman with child, so 376
22:31 ye shall be holy **m** unto me: neither shall ye 376
24: 5 he sent **young m** of the children of Israel, 5288
32:28 the people that day about three thousand **m**. 376
34:23 Thrice in the year shall all your **m children** 2138
35:22 they came, both **m** and women, as many as 376
36: 4 all the wise *m*, that wrought all the work of NIH
38:26 and five hundred and fifty *m*. NIH
Lev 7:25 of which *m* offer an offering made by fire NIH
18:27 (For all these abominations have the **m** of 376
27: 9 whereof *m* bring an offering unto NIH
27:29 None devoted, which shall be devoted of **m**, 120
Nu 1: 5 these *are* the names of the **m** that shall stand 376
1:17 Aaron took these **m** which are expressed by 376
1:44 and the princes of Israel, *being* twelve *m*: NIH
5: 6 woman shall commit any sin that **m** commit, 120
9: 6 there were *certain* **m**, who were defiled by 376
9: 7 those **m** said unto him, We *are* defiled by 376
11:16 Gather unto me seventy **m** of the elders of 376
11:24 gathered the seventy **m** of the elders of 376
11:26 there remained two *of the* **m** in the camp, 376
11:28 *one* of his **young m**, answered and said, 979
12: 3 above all the **m** which *were* upon the face of 120
13: 2 Send thou **m**, that they may search the land 376
13: 3 all those **m** *were* heads of the children of 376
13:16 These *are* the names of the **m** which Moses 376
13:21 of Zin unto Rehob, as *m* come to Hamath. NIH
13:31 the **m** that went up with him said, We be not 376
13:32 all the people that we saw in it *are* **m** of a 376
14:22 Because all *those* **m** which have seen my 376
14:36 the **m**, which Moses sent to search the land, 376
14:37 Even *those* **m** that did bring up the evil 376
14:38 *which were* of the **m** that went to search 376
16: 1 the son of Peleth, sons of Reuben, took *m*: NIH
16: 2 famous in the congregation, **m** of renown: 376
16:14 wilt thou put out the eyes of these **m**? 376
16:26 from the tents of these wicked **m**, and 376
16:29 If these *m* die the common death of all men, NIH
16:29 If these *men* die the common death of all **m**, 120
16:29 if they be visited after the visitation of all **m**; 120
16:30 ye shall understand that these **m** have 376

Nu	16:32	all the **m** that *appertained* unto Korah, and	120
	16:35	and fifty **m** that offered incense.	376
	18:15	*whether it be* of **m** or beasts, shall be thine:	120
	22: 9	and said, What **m** *are* these with thee?	376
	22:20	If the **m** come to call thee, rise up, *and*	376
	22:35	LORD said unto Balaam, Go with the **m**:	376
	25: 5	Slay ye every one his **m** that were joined	376
	26:10	the fire devoured two hundred and fifty **m**:	376
	31:11	and all the prey, *both* of **m** and of beasts.	120
	31:21	Eleazar the priest said unto the **m** of war	376
	31:28	levy a tribute unto the LORD of the **m** of	376
	31:32	*being* the rest of the prey which the **m** of	5971
	31:42	which Moses divided from the **m** that	376
	31:49	Thy servants have taken the sum of the **m** of	376
	31:53	(*For* the **m** of war had taken spoil,	376
	32:11	Surely none of the **m** that came up out of	376
	32:14	your fathers' stead, an increase of sinful **m**,	376
	34:17	These *are* the names of the **m** which shall	376
	34:19	the names of the **m** *are* these: Of the tribe of	376
Dt	1:13	Take ye wise **m**, and understanding, and	376
	1:15	wise **m**, and known, and made them heads	376
	1:22	We will send **m** before us, and they shall	376
	1:23	I took twelve **m** of you, one of a tribe:	376
	1:35	Surely there shall not one of these **m** of this	376
	2:14	until all the generation of the **m** of war were	376
	2:16	when all the **m** of war were consumed and	376
	2:34	utterly destroyed the **m**, and the women,	4962
	3: 6	utterly destroying the **m**, women, and	4962
	4: 3	for all the **m** that followed Baal-peor,	376
	13:13	*Certain* **m**, the children of Belial, are gone	376
	19:17	both the **m**, between whom the controversy	376
	21:21	all the **m** of his city shall stone him with	376
	22:21	the **m** of her city shall stone her with stones	376
	25: 1	If there be a controversy between **m**, and	376
	25:11	When **m** strive together one with another,	376
	27:14	say unto all the **m** of Israel *with* a loud	376
	29:10	and your officers, *with* all the **m** of Israel,	376
	29:25	*m* shall say, Because they have forsaken	NIH
	31:12	**m**, and women, and children, and	376
	32:26	of them to cease from among **m**:	582
	33: 6	and not die; and let *not* his **m** be few.	4962
Jos	1:14	all the mighty *m* of valour, and help them;	NIH
	2: 1	sent out of Shittim two **m** to spy secretly,	376
	2: 2	there came **m** in hither to night of	376
	2: 3	Bring forth the **m** that are come to thee,	376
	2: 4	the woman took the two **m**, and hid them,	376
	2: 4	There came **m** unto me, but I wist not	376
	2: 5	when it was dark, that the **m** went out:	376
	2: 5	whither the **m** went I wot not: pursue after	376
	2: 7	the **m** pursued after them the way to Jordan	376
	2: 9	she said unto the **m**, I know that the LORD	376
	2:14	And the **m** answered her, Our life for yours,	376
	2:17	the **m** said unto her, We *will be* blameless of	376
	2:23	So the two **m** returned, and descended from	376
	3:12	take ye twelve **m** out of the tribes of Israel,	376
	4: 2	Take you twelve **m** out of the people, out of	376
	4: 4	Joshua called the twelve **m**, whom he had	376
	5: 4	*that were* males, *even* all the **m** of war,	376
	5: 6	till all the people *that were* **m** of war,	376
	6: 2	king thereof, *and* the mighty *m* of valour.	NIH
	6: 3	all *ye* **m** of war, *and* go round about the city	376
	6: 9	the armed **m** went before the priests that	NIH
	6:13	the armed **m** went before them; but	NIH
	6:22	Joshua had said unto the two **m** that had	376
	6:23	the **young m** that were spies went in, and	5288
	7: 2	Joshua sent **m** from Jericho *to* Ai, which *is*	376
	7: 2	And the **m** went up and viewed Ai.	376
	7: 3	or three thousand **m** go up and smite Ai;	376
	7: 4	thither of the people about three thousand **m**:	376
	7: 4	and they fled before the **m** of Ai.	376
	7: 5	the **m** of Ai smote of them about thirty and	376
	7: 5	of Ai smote of them about thirty and six **m**:	376
	8: 3	Joshua chose out thirty thousand mighty *m*	NIH
	8:12	he took about five thousand **m**, and set them	376
	8:14	the **m** of the city went out against Israel to	376
	8:20	when the **m** of Ai looked behind them, they	376
	8:21	then they turned again, and slew the **m** of Ai.	376
	8:25	both of **m** and women, *were* twelve	376
	8:25	*were* twelve thousand, *even* all the **m** of Ai.	376
	9: 6	said unto him, and to the **m** of Israel, We be	376
	9: 7	the **m** of Israel said unto the Hivites,	376
	9:14	the **m** took of their victuals, and asked not	376
	10: 2	than Ai, and all the **m** thereof *were* mighty.	376
	10: 6	the **m** of Gibeon sent unto Joshua to	376
	10: 7	with him, and all the mighty *m* of valour.	NIH
	10:18	of the cave, and set **m** by it for to keep them:	376
	10:24	that Joshua called for all the **m** of Israel, and	376
	10:24	said unto the captains of the **m** of war which	376
	18: 4	Give out from among you three **m** for *each*	376
	18: 8	the **m** arose, and went away: and	376
	18: 9	the **m** went and passed through the land,	376
	24:11	the **m** of Jericho fought against you,	1167
Jdg	1: 4	they slew *of* them in Bezek ten thousand **m**.	376
	3:29	*of* Moab at that time about ten thousand **m**,	376
	3:29	thousand men, all lusty, and all **m** of valour;	376
	3:31	which slew *of* the Philistines six hundred **m**	376
	4: 6	take with thee ten thousand **m** of	376
	4:10	he went up with ten thousand **m** at his feet:	376
	4:14	mount Tabor, and ten thousand **m** after him.	376
	6:27	Then Gideon took ten **m** of his servants, and	376
	6:27	the **m** of the city, that *he* could not do *it* by	376
	6:28	when the **m** of the city arose early in	376
	6:30	the **m** of the city said unto Joash, Bring out	376
	7: 6	hand to their mouth, were three hundred **m**:	376
	7: 7	By the three hundred **m** that lapped will I	376
	7: 8	his tent, and retained *those* three hundred **m**:	376
	7:11	of the armed *m* that *were* in the host.	NIH
	7:16	he divided the three hundred **m** *into* three	376
	7:19	and the hundred **m** that *were* with him,	376
	7:23	the **m** of Israel gathered themselves together	376
	7:24	all the **m** of Ephraim gathered themselves	376
	8: 1	the **m** of Ephraim said unto him, Why hast	376
	8: 4	and the three hundred **m** that *were* with him,	376
	8: 5	he said unto the **m** of Succoth, Give, I pray	376
	8: 8	the **m** of Penuel answered him as the men of	376
	8: 8	the men of Penuel answered him as the **m** of	376
	8: 9	he spake also unto the **m** of Penuel, saying,	376
	8:10	about fifteen thousand *m*, all that were left	NIH
	8:10	and twenty thousand **m** that drew sword.	376
	8:14	caught a young man of the **m** of Succoth,	376
	8:14	*even* threescore and seventeen **m**.	376
	8:15	he came unto the **m** of Succoth, and said,	376
	8:15	that we should give bread unto thy **m** *that*	376
	8:16	and with them he taught the **m** of Succoth.	376
	8:17	tower of Penuel, and slew the **m** of the city.	376
	8:18	What manner of **m** *were they* whom ye slew	376
	8:22	the **m** of Israel said unto Gideon, Rule thou	376
	9: 2	in the ears of all the **m** of Shechem,	1167
	9: 3	of all the **m** of Shechem all these words:	1167
	9: 6	all the **m** of Shechem gathered together,	1167
	9: 7	Hearken unto me, you **m** of Shechem,	1167
	9:18	king over the **m** of Shechem, because he *is*	1167
	9:20	devour the **m** of Shechem, and the house of	1167
	9:20	let fire come out from the **m** of Shechem,	1167
	9:23	between Abimelech and the **m** of Shechem;	1167
	9:23	the **m** of Shechem dealt treacherously with	1167
	9:24	upon the **m** of Shechem, which aided him	1167
	9:25	the **m** of Shechem set liers in wait for him	1167
	9:26	the **m** of Shechem put their confidence in	1167
	9:28	serve the **m** of Hamor the father of	376
	9:36	shadow of the mountains as *if they were* **m**.	376
	9:39	Gaal went out before the **m** of Shechem,	1167
	9:46	when all the **m** of the tower of Shechem	1167
	9:47	that all the **m** of the tower of Shechem were	1167
	9:49	that all the **m** of the tower of Shechem died	376
	9:49	died also, about a thousand **m** and women.	376
	9:51	thither fled all the **m** and women, and	376
	9:54	and slay me, that *m* say not of me,	NIH
	9:55	when the **m** of Israel saw that Abimelech	376
	9:57	all the evil of the **m** of Shechem did God	376
	11: 3	and there were gathered vain **m** to Jephthah,	376
	12: 1	the **m** of Ephraim gathered themselves	376
	12: 4	Jephthah gathered together all the **m** of	376
	12: 4	and the **m** of Gilead smote Ephraim, because	376
	12: 5	that the **m** of Gilead said unto him, *Art* thou	376
	14:10	there a feast; for so used the **young m** to do.	970
	14:18	the **m** of the city said unto him on	376
	14:19	slew thirty **m** of them, and took their spoil,	376
	15:10	the **m** of Judah said, Why are ye come up	376
	15:11	three thousand **m** of Judah went to the top of	376
	15:15	took it, and slew a thousand **m** therewith.	376
	15:16	the jaw of an ass have I slain a thousand **m**.	376
	16: 9	Now *there were* **m** lying in wait,	NIH
	16:27	Now the house was full *of* **m** and women;	376
	16:27	*were* upon the roof about three thousand **m**	376
	18: 2	sent of their family five **m** from their coasts,	376
	18: 2	**m** of valour, from Zorah and	376+1121
	18: 7	the five **m** departed, and came to Laish,	376

Jdg 18:11 six hundred **m** appointed *with* weapons of 376
18:14 answered the five **m** that went to spy out 376
18:16 the six hundred **m** appointed *with* their 376
18:17 the five **m** that went to spy out the land went 376
18:17 **m** that were appointed *with* weapons of war. 376
18:22 the **m** that *were* in the houses near to 376
19:16 but the **m** of the place *were* Benjamites. 376
19:22 behold, the **m** of the city, certain sons of 376
19:25 the **m** would not hearken to him: so the man 376
20: 5 the **m** of Gibeah rose against me, and 1167
20:10 we will take ten **m** of an hundred throughout 376
20:11 So all the **m** of Israel were gathered against 376
20:12 the tribes of Israel sent **m** through all 376
20:13 Now therefore deliver *us* the **m**, the children 376
20:15 and six thousand **m** that drew sword, 376
20:15 were numbered seven hundred chosen **m**. 376
20:16 *were* seven hundred chosen **m** lefthanded; 376
20:17 the **m** of Israel, beside Benjamin, 376
20:17 were numbered four hundred thousand **m** 376
20:17 that drew sword: all these *were* **m** of war. 376
20:20 the **m** of Israel went out to battle against 376
20:20 the **m** of Israel put *themselves* in array to 376
20:21 that day twenty and two thousand **m**. 376
20:22 the people the **m** of Israel encouraged 376
20:25 of Israel again eighteen thousand **m**; 376
20:31 Gibeah in the field, about thirty **m** of Israel. 376
20:33 all the **m** of Israel rose up out of their place, 376
20:34 ten thousand chosen **m** out of all Israel, 376
20:35 and five thousand and an hundred **m**: 376
20:36 for the **m** of Israel gave place to 376
20:38 an appointed sign between the **m** of Israel 376
20:39 when the **m** of Israel retired in the battle, 376
20:39 kill of the **m** of Israel about thirty persons: 376
20:41 when the **m** of Israel turned *again,* the men 376
20:41 when the men of Israel turned *again,* the **m** 376
20:42 **m** of Israel unto the way of the wilderness; 376
20:44 there fell of Benjamin eighteen thousand **m**; 376
20:44 thousand men; all these *were* **m** of valour. 376
20:45 of them in the highways five thousand **m**; 376
20:45 and slew two thousand **m** of them. 376
20:46 and five thousand **m** that drew the sword; 376
20:46 drew the sword; all these *were* **m** of valour. 376
20:47 six hundred **m** turned and fled to 376
20:48 the **m** of Israel turned again upon 376
20:48 as well the **m** of *every* city, as the beast, 4974
21: 1 Now the **m** of Israel had sworn in Mizpeh, 376
21:10 thither twelve thousand **m** of the valiantest, 376
Ru 2: 9 have I not charged the **young m** that *they* 5288
2: 9 drink of *that* which the **young m** have 5288
2:15 Boaz commanded his **young m**, saying, 5288
2:21 Thou shalt keep fast by my **young m**, 5288
3:10 inasmuch as *thou* followedst not **young m**, 970
4: 2 he took ten **m** of the elders of the city, and 376
1Sa 2: 4 The bows of the mighty *m are* broken, and NIH
2:17 Wherefore the sin of the **young m** was very 5288
2:17 for **m** abhorred the offering of the LORD. 376
2:26 both with the LORD, and also with **m**. 376
4: 2 the army in the field about four thousand **m**. 376
4: 9 Be strong, and quit yourselves like **m**, O ye 376
4: 9 to you: quit yourselves like **m**, and fight. 376
5: 7 when the **m** of Ashdod saw that *it was* so, 376
5: 9 he smote the **m** of the city, both small and 376
5:12 the **m** that died not were smitten with 376
6:10 the **m** did so; and took two milch kine, and 376
6:15 the **m** of Beth-shemesh offered burnt 376
6:19 he smote the **m** of Beth-shemesh, because 376
6:19 fifty thousand and threescore and ten **m**: 376
6:20 the **m** of Beth-shemesh said, Who is able to 376
7: 1 the **m** of Kirjath-jearim came, and 376
7:11 And the **m** of Israel went out of Mizpeh, and 376
8:16 and your goodliest **young m**, and your asses, 970
8:22 Samuel said unto the **m** of Israel, Go ye 376
10: 2 thou shalt find two **m** by Rachel's sepulchre 376
10: 3 there shall meet thee three **m** going up to 376
10:26 there went with him a **band of m**, 2428
11: 1 all the **m** of Jabesh said unto Nahash, 376
11: 5 they told him the tidings of the **m** of Jabesh. 376
11: 8 and the **m** of Judah thirty thousand. 376
11: 9 Thus shall ye say unto the **m** of 376
11: 9 and shewed *it* to the **m** of Jabesh; 376
11:10 Therefore the **m** of Jabesh said, To morrow 376
11:12 bring the **m**, that we may put them to death. 376
11:15 and all the **m** of Israel rejoiced greatly. 376
13: 2 Saul chose him three thousand *m* of Israel; NIH
13: 6 When the **m** of Israel saw that they were in a 376
13:15 were present with him, about six hundred **m**. 376
14: 2 *were* with him *were* about six hundred **m**; 376
14: 8 we will pass over unto *these* **m**, and we will 376
14:12 the **m** of the garrison answered Jonathan 376
14:14 his armourbearer made, was about twenty **m**, 376
14:22 Likewise all the **m** of Israel which had hid 376
14:24 And the **m** of Israel were distressed that day: 376
15: 4 and ten thousand **m** of Judah. 376
17: 2 and the **m** of Israel were gathered together, 376
17:12 the man went among **m** *for* an old man in 376
17:19 Now Saul, and they, and all the **m** of Israel, 376
17:24 all the **m** of Israel, when they saw the man, 376
17:25 the **m** of Israel said, Have ye seen this man 376
17:26 And David spake to the **m** that stood by him, 376
17:28 brother heard when he spake unto the **m**; 376
17:52 the **m** of Israel and of Judah arose, and 376
18: 5 Saul set him over the **m** of war, and he was 376
18:27 he and his **m**, and slew of the Philistines two 376
18:27 and slew of the Philistines two hundred **m**; 376
21: 4 if the **young m** have kept themselves at 5288
21: 5 the vessels of the **young m** are holy, and 5288
21:15 *Have* I need of **mad m**, that ye have 7696
22: 2 there were with him about four hundred **m**. 376
22: 6 and the **m** that *were* with him, 376
22:19 both **m** and women, children and sucklings, 376
23: 3 David's **m** said unto him, Behold, we *be* 376
23: 5 So David and his **m** went *to* Keilah, and 376
23: 8 down *to* Keilah, to besiege David and his **m**. 376
23:11 Will the **m** of Keilah deliver me up into his 1167
23:12 Will the **m** of Keilah deliver me and my 1167
23:12 deliver me and my **m** into the hand of Saul? 376
23:13 David and his **m**, *which were* about six 376
23:24 and his **m** *were* in the wilderness of Maon, 376
23:25 his **m** went to seek *him.* And they told 376
23:26 and his **m** on that side of the mountain: 376
23:26 for Saul and his **m** compassed David and his 376
23:26 and his **m** round about to take them. 376
24: 2 Saul took three thousand chosen **m** out of all 376
24: 2 and his **m** upon the rocks of the wild goats. 376
24: 3 and his **m** remained in the sides of the cave. 376
24: 4 the **m** of David said unto him, Behold 376
24: 6 he said unto his **m**, The LORD forbid that I 376
24:22 David and his **m** gat them up unto the hold. 376
25: 5 David sent out ten **young m**, and 5288
25: 5 David said unto the **young m**, Get you up 5288
25: 8 Ask thy **young m**, and they will shew thee. 5288
25: 8 Wherefore let the **young m** find favour in 5288
25: 9 when David's **young m** came, they spake 5288
25:11 give *it* unto **m**, whom I know not whence 376
25:12 So David's **young m** turned their way, and 5288
25:13 David said unto his **m**, Gird you on every 376
25:13 went up after David about four hundred **m**; 376
25:14 one of the **young m** told Abigail, 5288
25:15 the **m** *were* very good unto us, and we were 376
25:20 David and his **m** came down against her; 376
25:25 I thine handmaid saw not the **young m** of 5288
25:27 let it even be given unto the **young m** that 5288
26: 2 having three thousand chosen **m** of Israel 376
26:19 if *they be* the children of **m**, cursed *be* they 120
26:22 let one of the **young m** come over and 5288
27: 2 he passed over with the six hundred **m** that 376
27: 3 he and his **m**, every man with his household, 376
27: 8 David and his **m** went up, and invaded 376
28: 1 go out with me to battle, thou and thy **m**. 376
28: 8 two **m** with him, and they came to 376
29: 2 his **m** passed on in the rereward with Achish. 376
29: 4 *should it* not *be* with the heads of these **m**? 376
29:11 his **m** rose up early to depart in the morning, 376
30: 1 his **m** were come *to* Ziklag on the third day, 376
30: 3 So David and his **m** came to the city, and 376
30: 9 and the six hundred **m** that *were* with him, 376
30:10 But David pursued, he and four hundred **m**: 376
30:17 save four hundred **young m**, 376+5288
30:21 David came to the two hundred **m**, 376
30:22 answered all the wicked **m** and *men* of 376
30:22 all the wicked men and *m* of Belial, NIH
30:31 David himself and his **m** were wont to haunt. 376
31: 1 the **m** of Israel fled from before 376
31: 6 and his armourbearer, and all his **m**, 376
31: 7 when the **m** of Israel that *were* on the *other* 376
31: 7 saw that the **m** of Israel fled, and that Saul 376
31:12 All the valiant **m** arose, and went all night, 376
2Sa 1:11 and likewise all the **m** that *were* with him: 376

2Sa	1:15	David called one of the **young m**, and said,	5288
	2: 3	his **m** that *were* with him did David bring	376
	2: 4	the **m** of Judah came, and there they	376
	2: 4	*That* the **m** of Jabesh-gilead *were they* that	376
	2: 5	David sent messengers unto the **m** of	376
	2:14	Let the **young m** now arise, and play before	5288
	2:17	Abner was beaten, and the **m** of Israel,	376
	2:21	lay thee hold on one of the **young m**, and	5288
	2:29	his **m** walked all that night through the plain,	376
	2:30	there lacked of David's servants nineteen **m**	376
	2:31	and of Abner's **m**, *so that* three hundred and	376
	2:31	*so that* three hundred and threescore **m** died.	376
	2:32	Joab and his **m** went all night, and they came	376
	3:20	to David *to* Hebron, and twenty **m** with him.	376
	3:20	and the **m** that *were* with him a feast.	376
	3:34	as *a man* falleth before wicked **m**, *so*	1121
	3:39	these **m** the sons of Zeruiah *be* too hard for	376
	4: 2	Saul's son had two **m** *that were* captains of	376
	4:11	when wicked **m** have slain a righteous	376
	4:12	David commanded *his* **young m**, and	5288
	5: 6	his **m** went *to* Jerusalem unto the Jebusites,	376
	5:21	and David and his **m** burnt them.	376
	6: 1	David gathered together all the chosen *m* of	NIH
	6:19	as well to the women as **m**, to every one a	376
	7: 9	like unto the name of the great *m* that *are* in	NIH
	7:14	I will chasten him with the rod of **m**, and	376
	7:14	and with the stripes of the children of **m**:	120
	8: 5	of the Syrians two and twenty thousand **m**.	376
	8:13	valley of salt, *being* eighteen thousand *m*.	NIH
	10: 5	because the **m** were greatly ashamed:	376
	10: 6	of king Maacah a thousand **m**, and of Ish-tob	376
	10: 6	and of Ish-tob twelve thousand **m**.	376
	10: 7	sent Joab, and all the host *of* the mighty *m*.	NIH
	10: 9	he chose of all the choice *m* of Israel, and	NIH
	10:12	let us **play the m** for our people, and	2388
	10:18	David slew *the m of* seven hundred chariots	NIH
	11:16	a place where he knew that valiant **m** *were*.	376
	11:17	the **m** of the city went out, and fought with	376
	11:23	Surely the **m** prevailed against us, and	376
	12: 1	said unto him, There were two **m** in one city;	376
	13: 9	Amnon said, Have out all **m** from me.	376
	13:32	have slain all the **young m** the king's sons;	5288
	15: 1	and horses, and fifty **m** to run before him.	376
	15: 6	Absalom stole the hearts of the **m** of Israel.	376
	15:11	with Absalom went two hundred **m** out of	376
	15:13	The hearts of the **m** of Israel are after	376
	15:18	six hundred **m** which came after him from	376
	15:22	all his **m**, and all the little ones that *were*	376
	16: 2	and summer fruit for the **young m** to eat;	5288
	16: 6	all the mighty *m were* on his right hand and	NIH
	16:13	as David and his **m** went by the way, Shimei	376
	16:15	and all the people the **m** of Israel,	376
	16:18	this people, and all the **m** of Israel, choose,	376
	17: 1	Let me now choose out twelve thousand **m**,	376
	17: 8	thou knowest thy father and his **m**, that they	376
	17: 8	that they *be* mighty *m*, and they *be* chafed	NIH
	17:10	and *they* which *be* with him *are* valiant **m**.	1121
	17:12	of all the **m** that *are* with him there shall not	376
	17:14	Absalom and all the **m** of Israel said,	376
	17:24	he and all the **m** of Israel with him.	376
	18: 7	slaughter that day *of* twenty thousand *m*.	NIH
	18:15	ten **young m** that bare Joab's armour	5288
	18:28	which hath delivered up the **m** that lift up	376
	19:14	he bowed the heart of all the **m** of Judah,	376
	19:16	came down with the **m** of Judah to meet king	376
	19:17	*there were* a thousand **m** of Benjamin with	376
	19:28	but dead **m** before my lord the king:	376
	19:35	can I hear any more the voice of singing *m*	NIH
	19:41	all the **m** of Israel came to the king, and	376
	19:41	Why have our brethren the **m** of Judah	376
	19:41	and all David's **m** with him, over Jordan?	376
	19:42	all the **m** of Judah answered the men of	376
	19:42	all the men of Judah answered the **m** of	376
	19:43	the **m** of Israel answered the men of Judah,	376
	19:43	the men of Israel answered the **m** of Judah,	376
	19:43	the words of the **m** of Judah were fiercer	376
	19:43	fiercer than the words of the **m** of Israel.	376
	20: 2	the **m** of Judah clave unto their king,	376
	20: 4	Assemble me the **m** of Judah *within* three	376
	20: 5	So Amasa went to assemble *the m of* Judah:	NIH
	20: 7	there went out after him Joab's **m**, and	376
	20: 7	all the mighty *m*: and they went out of	NIH
	20:11	one of Joab's **m** stood by him, and said,	5288
	21: 6	Let seven **m** of his sons be delivered unto us,	376
	21:12	the bones of Jonathan his son from the **m** of	1167
	21:17	the **m** of David sware unto him, saying,	376
	22: 5	the floods of **ungodly m** made me afraid;	1100
	23: 3	He that ruleth over **m** *must be* just, ruling *in*	120
	23: 8	These *be* the names of the mighty *m* whom	NIH
	23: 9	*one* of the three mighty *m* with David,	NIH
	23: 9	and the **m** of Israel were gone away:	376
	23:16	the three mighty *m* brake through the host	NIH
	23:17	*is not this* the blood of the **m** that went in	376
	23:17	These *things* did *these* three mighty *m*.	NIH
	23:20	many acts, he slew two **lionlike m** of Moab:	739
	23:22	and had the name among three mighty *m*.	NIH
	24: 9	thousand valiant **m** that drew the sword;	376
	24: 9	the **m** of Judah *were* five hundred thousand	376
	24: 9	of Judah *were* five hundred thousand **m**.	376
	24:15	Dan even to Beer-sheba seventy thousand **m**.	376
1Ki	1: 5	and horsemen, and fifty **m** to run before him.	376
	1: 8	and the mighty *m* which *belonged* to David,	NIH
	1: 9	and all the **m** of Judah the king's servants:	376
	1:10	and the mighty *m*, and Solomon his brother,	NIH
	2:32	who fell upon two **m** more righteous and	376
	4:31	For he was wiser than all **m**; than Ethan	120
	5:13	and the levy was thirty thousand **m**.	376
	8: 2	all the **m** of Israel assembled themselves	376
	8:39	knowest the hearts of all the children of **m**;)	120
	9:22	they *were* **m** of war, and his servants, and	376
	10: 8	Happy *are* thy **m**, happy *are* these thy	376
	11:18	and they took **m** with them out of Paran, and	376
	11:24	he gathered **m** unto him, and became captain	376
	12: 6	king Rehoboam consulted with the **old m**,	2205
	12: 8	he forsook the counsel of the **old m**,	2205
	12: 8	consulted with the **young m** that were	3206
	12:10	the **young m** that were grown up with him	3206
	12:14	to them after the counsel of the **young m**,	3206
	12:21	fourscore thousand chosen *m*, which were	NIH
	13:25	**m** passed by, and saw the carcase cast in	376
	18:13	how I hid an hundred **m** of the LORD's	376
	18:22	prophets *are* four hundred and fifty **m**.	376
	20:14	*Even* by the **young m** of the princes of	5288
	20:15	he numbered the **young m** of the princes of	5288
	20:17	the **young m** of the princes of the provinces	5288
	20:17	There are **m** come out of Samaria.	376
	20:19	So these **young m** of the princes of	5288
	20:30	and seven thousand of the **m** that were left.	376
	20:33	Now the **m** did diligently observe whether	376
	21:10	set two **m**, sons of Belial, before him, to bear	376
	21:11	the **m** of his city, *even* the elders and	376
	21:13	And there came in two **m**, children of Belial,	376
	21:13	the **m** of Belial witnessed against him,	376
	22: 6	about four hundred **m**, and said unto them,	376
2Ki	2: 7	And fifty **m** of the sons of the prophets went,	376
	2:16	there be with thy servants fifty strong **m**;	376
	2:17	They sent therefore fifty **m**; and they sought	376
	2:19	the **m** of the city said unto Elisha, Behold,	376
	3:26	he took with him seven hundred **m** that drew	376
	4:22	one of the **young m**, and one of the asses,	5288
	4:40	So they poured out for the **m** to eat. And it	376
	4:43	What, should I set this before an hundred **m**?	376
	5:22	two **young m** of the sons of the prophets:	5288
	5:24	and he let the **m** go, and they departed.	376
	6:20	open the eyes of these *m*, that they may see.	NIH
	7: 3	there were four leprous **m** *at* the entering in	376
	8:12	their young *m* wilt thou slay with the sword,	NIH
	10: 6	take ye the heads of the **m** your master's	376
	10: 6	*were* with the great *m* of the city,	NIH
	10:11	all his great *m*, and his kinsfolks, and	NIH
	10:14	of the shearing house, *even* two and forty **m**;	376
	10:24	Jehu appointed fourscore **m** without, and	376
	10:24	*If* any of the **m** whom I *have* brought into	376
	11: 9	they took every man his **m** that were to come	376
	12:15	Moreover they reckoned not with the **m**,	376
	13:21	they spied a band *of m*; and they cast	NIH
	15:20	*even* of all the mighty *m* of wealth, of each	NIH
	15:25	and with him fifty **m** of the Gileadites:	376
	17:24	the king of Assyria brought *m* from	NIH
	17:30	the **m** of Babylon made Succoth-benoth,	376
	17:30	the **m** of Cuth made Nergal, and the men of	376
	17:30	and the **m** of Hamath made Ashima,	376
	18:27	*hath he* not *sent me* to the **m** which sit on	376
	20:14	and said unto him, What said these **m**?	376
	23: 2	all the **m** of Judah and all the inhabitants of	376
	23:14	and filled their places *with* the bones of **m**.	120
	23:17	the **m** of the city told him, *It is* the sepulchre	376
	24:14	the princes, and all the mighty *m* of valour,	NIH

2Ki 24:16 all the **m** of might, *even* seven thousand, 376
25: 4 all the **m** of war *fled* by night *by* the way of 376
25:19 an officer that was set over the **m** of war, 376
25:19 five **m** of them that were in the king's 376
25:19 threescore **m** of the people of the land that 376
25:23 the captains of the armies, they and *their* **m**, 376
25:23 the son of a Maachathite, they and their **m**. 376
25:24 to them, and to their **m**, and said unto them, 376
25:25 and ten **m** with him, and smote Gedaliah, 376
1Ch 4:12 of Irnahash. These *are* the **m** of Rechah. 376
4:22 the **m** of Chozeba, and Joash, and Saraph, 376
4:42 five hundred **m**, went to mount Seir, 376
5:18 of valiant **m**, men *able to* bear buckler and 1121
5:18 **m** *able to* bear buckler and sword, and 376
5:21 and *of* **m** an hundred thousand. 120+5315
5:24 Hodaviah, and Jahdiel, mighty *m* of valour, NIH
5:24 famous **m**, *and* heads of the house of their 376
7: 2 *they were* valiant **m** of might in their NIH
7: 3 and Joel, Ishiah, five: all of them chief *m*. NIH
7: 4 thirty thousand *m*: for they had many wives NIH
7: 5 the families of Issachar *were* **m** of might, 1368
7: 7 house of *their* fathers, mighty *m* of valour; NIH
7: 9 mighty *m* of valour, *was* twenty thousand NIH
7:11 mighty *m* of valour, *were* seventeen NIH
7:21 whom the **m** of Gath that were born in *that* 376
7:40 choice *and* mighty **m** of valour, chief of NIH
7:40 *and* to battle *was* twenty and six thousand **m**. 376
8:28 chief *m*. These dwelt in Jerusalem. NIH
8:40 the sons of Ulam were mighty **m** of valour, 376
9: 9 All these **m** *were* chief of the fathers in 376
9:13 very able **m** *for* the work of the service of 1368
10: 1 the **m** of Israel fled from before 376
10: 7 when all the **m** of Israel that *were* in 376
10:12 all the valiant **m**, and took away the body of 376
11:10 These also *are* the chief of the mighty *m* NIH
11:11 this *is* the number of the mighty *m* whom NIH
11:19 these **m** that have put their lives in jeopardy? 376
11:22 many acts; he slew two **lionlike m** of Moab: 739
11:26 Also the valiant *m* of the armies *were*, NIH
12: 1 they *were* among the mighty *m*, helpers of NIH
12: 8 into the hold to the wilderness **m** of might, 1368
12: 8 *and* **m** of war *fit* for the battle, that could 376
12:21 for they *were* all mighty *m* of valour, NIH
12:25 mighty *m* of valour for the war, NIH
12:30 and eight hundred, mighty *m* of valour, NIH
12:32 *which were* **m** that had understanding of NIH
12:38 All these **m** of war, that could keep rank, 376
16:31 let *m* say among the nations, The LORD NIH
17: 8 the name of the great *m* that *are* in the earth. NIH
18: 5 of the Syrians two and twenty thousand **m**. 376
19: 5 and told David how the **m** were served. 376
19: 5 for the **m** were greatly ashamed. And 376
19: 8 sent Joab, and all the host *of* the mighty *m*. NIH
19:18 David slew of the Syrians seven thousand *m* NIH
21: 5 and an hundred thousand **m** that drew sword: 376
21: 5 and ten thousand **m** that drew sword. 376
21:14 and there fell of Israel seventy thousand **m**. 376
22:15 all *manner of* cunning *m* for every *manner* NIH
24: 4 there were moe chief **m** found of the sons 1397
24: 4 sixteen chief *m* of the house of *their* fathers, NIH
26: 6 for they *were* mighty *m* of valour. NIH
26: 7 whose brethren *were* strong **m**, Elihu, and 1121
26: 8 able **m** for strength for the service, 376
26: 9 had sons and brethren, strong **m**, 1121
26:12 *even* among the chief **m**, *having* wards one 1397
26:30 **m** of valour, a thousand and seven hundred, 1121
26:31 there were found among them mighty *m* of NIH
26:32 his brethren, **m** of valour, *were* two 1121
28: 1 *with* the mighty *m*, and with all the valiant NIH
28: 1 the mighty *men*, and with all the valiant **m**, 1368
29:24 the mighty *m*, and all the sons likewise of NIH
2Ch 2: 2 and ten thousand **m** to bear burdens, 376
2: 7 that can skill to grave with the cunning *m* NIH
2:14 with thy cunning *m*, and with the cunning NIH
2:14 with the cunning *m* of my lord David thy NIH
5: 3 Wherefore all the **m** of Israel assembled 376
6:18 will God in very deed dwell with **m** on 120
6:30 knowest the hearts of the children of **m**:) 120
8: 9 they *were* **m** of war, and chief of his 376
9: 7 Happy *are* thy **m**, and happy *are* these thy 376
10: 6 Rehoboam took counsel with the **old m** 2205
10: 8 he forsook the counsel which the **old m** 2205
10: 8 took counsel with the **young m** that were 3206
10:10 the **young m** that were brought up with him 3206
10:13 forsook the counsel of the **old m**, 2205
10:14 them after the advice of the **young m**, 3206
11: 1 fourscore thousand chosen *m*, which were NIH
13: 3 in array with an army of valiant *m* of war, NIH
13: 3 *even* four hundred thousand chosen **m**: 376
13: 3 him with eight hundred thousand chosen **m**, 376
13: 3 chosen men, *being* mighty *m* of valour. NIH
13: 7 there are gathered unto him vain **m**, 376
13:15 the **m** of Judah gave a shout: and as the men 376
13:15 as the **m** of Judah shouted, it came to pass, 376
13:17 of Israel five hundred thousand chosen **m**. 376
14: 8 And Asa had an army *of m* that bare targets NIH
14: 8 all these *were* mighty *m* of valour. NIH
17:13 the **m** of war, mighty *men* of valour, *were* in 376
17:13 the men of war, mighty *m* of valour, *were* in NIH
17:14 with him mighty *m* of valour three hundred NIH
17:16 with him two hundred thousand mighty *m* NIH
17:17 with him armed *m* with bow and shield two NIH
18: 5 together *of* prophets four hundred **m**, 376
22: 1 for the band *of m* that came with NIH
23: 8 took every man his **m** that were to come in 376
24:24 Syrians came with a small *company* of **m**, 376
25: 5 thousand choice *m*, *able to* go forth *to* war, NIH
25: 6 *m* of valour out of Israel for an hundred NIH
26:11 Moreover Uzziah had a host of fighting *m*, NIH
26:12 the mighty *m* of valour *were* two thousand NIH
26:15 invented by cunning *m*, to be on the towers NIH
26:17 priests of the LORD, *that were* valiant **m**: 1121
28: 6 in one day, *which were* all valiant **m**; 1121
28:14 So the armed *m* left the captives and NIH
28:15 the **m** which were expressed by name rose 376
31:19 the **m** that were expressed by name, 376
32: 3 his mighty *m* to stop the waters of NIH
32:21 which cut off all the mighty *m* of valour, NIH
34:12 the **m** did the work faithfully: and 376
34:30 all the **m** of Judah, and the inhabitants of 376
35:25 all the singing *m* and the singing *women* NIH
36:17 who slew their **young m** with the sword in 970
Ezr 1: 4 let the **m** of his place help him with silver, 376
2: 2 The number of the **m** of the people of Israel: 376
2:22 The **m** of Netophah, fifty and six. 376
2:23 The **m** of Anathoth, an hundred twenty and 376
2:27 The **m** of Michmas, an hundred twenty and 376
2:28 The **m** of Beth-el and Ai, two hundred 376
2:65 *were* among them two hundred singing *m* NIH
3:12 *who were* **ancient m** that had seen the first 2205
4:11 Thy servants the **m** *on this* side the river, and 606
4:21 commandment to cause these **m** to cease, 1400
5: 4 What are the names of the **m** that make this 1400
5:10 that we might write the names of the **m** that 1400
6: 8 forthwith expences be given unto these **m**, 1400
7:28 I gathered together out of Israel chief *m* to NIH
8:16 chief *m*; also for Joiarib, and for Elnathan, NIH
8:16 and for Elnathan, *m* of understanding. NIH
10: 1 out of Israel a very great congregation *of* **m** 376
10: 9 all the **m** of Judah and Benjamin gathered 376
10:17 they made an end with all the **m** that had 376
Ne 1: 2 came, he and *certain* **m** of Judah; 376
2:12 in the night, I and *some* few **m** with me; 376
3: 2 And next unto him builded the **m** of Jericho. 376
3: 7 the **m** of Gibeon, and of Mizpah, 376
3:22 him repaired the priests, the **m** of the plain. 376
4:23 nor the **m** of the guard which followed me, 376
5: 5 *to redeem them;* for **other m** have our lands 312
7: 7 *I say,* of the **m** of the people of Israel *was* 376
7:26 The **m** of Beth-lehem and Netophah, 376
7:27 The **m** of Anathoth, an hundred twenty and 376
7:28 The **m** of Beth-azmaveth, forty and two. 376
7:29 The **m** of Kirjath-jearim, Chephirah, and 376
7:30 The **m** of Ramah and Geba, six hundred 376
7:31 The **m** of Michmas, an hundred and twenty 376
7:32 The **m** of Beth-el and Ai, an hundred twenty 376
7:33 The **m** of the other Nebo, fifty and two. 376
7:67 and five singing *m* and singing *women*. NIH
8: 2 the law before the congregation both of **m** 376
8: 3 before the **m** and the women, and those that 376
11: 2 the people blessed all the **m**, that willingly 376
11: 6 four hundred threescore and eight valiant **m**. 376
11:14 mighty *m* of valour, an hundred twenty and NIH
11:14 *was* Zabdiel, the son of *one of* the great *m*. NIH
13:16 There dwelt **m of Tyre** also therein, which 6876
Est 1:13 the king said to the wise *m*, which knew NIH
6:13 said his wise *m* and Zeresh his wife unto NIH
9: 6 the Jews slew and destroyed five hundred **m**. 376

Est	9:12	destroyed five hundred **m** in Shushan	376
	9:15	and slew three hundred **m** at Shushan;	376
Job	1: 3	that this man was the greatest of all the **m**	1121
	1:19	it fell upon the **young m**, and they are	5288
	4:13	of the night, when deep sleep falleth on **m**.	376
	7:20	shall I do unto thee, O thou preserver of **m**?	120
	11: 3	Should thy lies make **m** hold their peace?	4962
	11:11	For he knoweth vain **m**: he seeth	4962
	15:10	*are* both the grayheaded and **very aged m**,	3453
	15:18	Which wise ***m*** have told from their fathers,	NIH
	17: 8	Upright ***m*** shall be astonied at this, and	NIH
	22:15	the old way which wicked **m** have trodden?	4962
	22:29	When ***m*** are cast down, then thou shalt say,	NIH
	24:12	**M** groan from out of the city, and the soul	4962
	27:23	***M*** shall clap their hands at him, and	NIH
	28: 4	are dried up, they are gone away from **m**.	582
	29: 8	The **young m** saw me, and hid themselves:	5288
	29:21	Unto me ***m*** gave ear, and waited, and	NIH
	30: 5	They were driven forth from among **m**,	NIH
	30: 8	of fools, yea, children of **base m**:	1097+8034
	31:31	If the **m** of my tabernacle said not, O that	4962
	32: 1	So these three **m** ceased to answer Job,	376
	32: 5	no answer in the mouth of *these* three **m**,	376
	32: 9	**Great m** are not *always* wise: neither do	7227
	33:15	the night, when deep sleep falleth upon **m**,	376
	33:16	he openeth the ears of **m**, and sealeth their	376
	33:27	He looketh upon **m**, and *if any* say, I have	376
	34: 2	O ye wise ***m***; and give ear unto me,	NIH
	34: 8	of iniquity, and walketh with wicked **m**.	376
	34:10	hearken unto me, ye **m** of understanding:	376
	34:24	He shall break in pieces mighty ***m*** without	NIH
	34:26	He striketh them as wicked ***m*** in the open	NIH
	34:34	Let **m** of understanding tell me, and let a	376
	34:36	because of *his* answers for wicked **m**.	376
	35:12	because of the pride of **evil m**.	7451
	36:24	that thou magnify his work, which **m** behold.	376
	37: 7	of every man; that all **m** may know his work.	376
	37:21	now ***m*** see not the bright light which *is* in	NIH
	37:24	**M** do therefore fear him: he respecteth not	376
	39:21	He goeth on to meet the **armed m**.	5402
Ps	4: 2	O ye sons of **m**, how long *will ye turn* my	376
	9:20	nations may know themselves *to be but* **m**.	582
	11: 4	his eyelids try, the children of **m**.	120
	12: 1	faithful fail from among the children of **m**.	120
	12: 8	when the vilest **m** are exalted.	120+1121
	14: 2	down from heaven upon the children of **m**,	120
	17: 4	Concerning the works of **m**, by the word of	120
	17:14	From **m** *which are* thy hand, O LORD,	4962
	17:14	thy hand, O LORD, from **m** of the world,	4962
	18: 4	the floods of **ungodly m** made me afraid.	1100
	21:10	their seed from among the children of **m**.	120
	22: 6	a reproach of **m**, and despised of the people.	120
	26: 9	with sinners, nor my life with bloody **m**:	376
	31:19	them that trust in thee before the sons of **m**!	120
	33:13	from heaven; he beholdeth all the sons of **m**.	120
	36: 7	the children of **m** put their trust under	120
	45: 2	Thou art fairer than the children of **m**:	120
	49:10	For he seeth *that* wise ***m*** die, likewise	NIH
	49:18	***m*** will praise thee, when thou doest well to	NIH
	53: 2	down from heaven upon the children of **m**,	120
	55:23	deceitful **m** shall not live out half their days;	376
	57: 4	*even* the sons of **m**, whose teeth *are* spears	120
	58: 1	do ye judge uprightly, O ye sons of **m**?	120
	59: 2	of iniquity, and save me from bloody **m**.	376
	62: 9	Surely **m of low degree** *are* vanity,	120+1121
	62: 9	*and* **m of high degree** *are* a lie:	376+1121
	64: 9	all **m** shall fear, and shall declare the work	120
	66: 5	*in his* doing toward the children of **m**.	120
	66:12	Thou hast caused **m** to ride over our heads;	582
	68:18	thou hast received gifts for **m**; yea, *for*	120
	72:17	***m*** shall be blessed in him: all nations shall	NIH
	73: 5	They *are* not in trouble *as other* **m**;	582
	73: 5	neither are they plagued like *other* **m**.	120
	76: 5	none of the **m** of might have found their	376
	78:31	and smote down the chosen ***m*** of Israel.	NIH
	78:60	the tent *which* he placed among **m**;	120
	78:63	The fire consumed their **young m**; and	970
	82: 7	ye shall die like **m**, and fall like one of	120
	83:18	That ***m*** may know that thou, whose name	NIH
	86:14	the assemblies of violent ***m*** have sought	NIH
	89:47	hast thou made all **m** in vain?	120+1121
	90: 3	and sayest, Return, ye children of **m**.	120
	105:12	When they were *but a few* **m** in number;	4962
	107: 8	Oh that ***m*** would praise the LORD *for* his	NIH
	107: 8	his wonderful works to the children of **m**!	120
	107:15	Oh that ***m*** would praise the LORD *for* his	NIH
	107:15	his wonderful works to the children of **m**!	120
	107:21	Oh that ***m*** would praise the LORD *for* his	NIH
	107:21	his wonderful works to the children of **m**!	120
	107:31	Oh that ***m*** would praise the LORD *for* his	NIH
	107:31	his wonderful works to the children of **m**!	120
	115:16	the earth hath he given to the children of **m**.	120
	116:11	I said in my haste, All **m** *are* liars.	120
	124: 2	was on our side, when **m** rose up against us:	120
	139:19	depart from me therefore, ye bloody **m**.	376
	141: 4	to practise wicked works with **m** that work	376
	145: 6	***m*** shall speak of the might of thy terrible	NIH
	145:12	To make known to the sons of **m** his mighty	120
	148:12	Both **young m**, and maidens; old men, and	970
	148:12	and maidens; **old m**, and children:	2205
Pr	2:20	thou mayest walk in the way of good ***m***,	NIH
	4:14	and go not in the way of evil ***m***.	NIH
	6:30	***M*** do not despise a thief, if he steal to	NIH
	7:26	yea, many strong ***m*** *have been* slain by her.	NIH
	8: 4	Unto you, O **m**, I call; and my voice *is* to	376
	8:31	and my delights *were* with the sons of **m**.	120
	10:14	Wise ***m*** lay up knowledge: but the mouth of	NIH
	11: 7	and the hope of unjust ***m*** perisheth.	NIH
	11:16	retaineth honour: and strong ***m*** retain riches.	NIH
	12:12	The wicked desireth the net of evil ***m***: but	NIH
	13:20	He that walketh with wise ***m*** shall be wise:	NIH
	15:11	then the hearts of the children of **m**?	120
	16: 6	by the fear of the LORD ***m*** depart from	NIH
	17: 6	Children's children *are* the crown of **old m**;	2205
	18:16	for him, and bringeth him before great ***m***.	NIH
	20: 6	Most **m** will proclaim every one his own	120
	20:29	The glory of **young m** *is* their strength: and	970
	20:29	and the beauty of **old m** *is* the gray head.	2205
	22:29	he shall not stand before mean ***m***.	NIH
	23:28	and increaseth the transgressors among **m**.	120
	24: 1	Be not thou envious against evil **m**,	376
	24: 9	and the scorner *is* an abomination to **m**.	120
	24:19	of evil ***m***, neither be thou envious at	NIH
	25: 1	which the **m** of Hezekiah king of Judah	376
	25: 6	and stand not in the place of great ***m***:	NIH
	25:27	*for* ***m*** to search their own glory *is not* glory.	NIH
	26:16	than seven ***m*** that can render a reason.	NIH
	28: 5	Evil **m** understand not judgment: but	376
	28: 7	he that is a companion of riotous ***m*** shameth	NIH
	28:12	When righteous ***m*** do rejoice, *there is* great	NIH
	28:28	When the wicked rise, **m** hide themselves:	120
	29: 8	Scornful **m** bring a city into a snare: but	376
	29: 8	into a snare: but wise ***m*** turn away wrath.	NIH
	30:14	off the earth, and the needy from *among* **m**.	120
Ecc	2: 3	see what *was* that good for the sons of **m**,	120
	2: 8	I gat me ***m*** singers and *women* singers, and	NIH
	2: 8	and the delights of the sons of **m**,	120
	3:10	which God hath given to the sons of **m** to be	120
	3:14	God doeth *it*, that ***m*** should fear before him.	NIH
	3:18	heart concerning the estate of the sons of **m**,	120
	3:19	For that which befalleth the sons of **m**	120
	6: 1	under the sun, and it *is* common among **m**:	120
	7: 2	for that *is* the end of all **m**; and the living	120
	7:19	than ten mighty ***m*** which are in the city.	NIH
	8:11	the heart of the sons of **m** is fully set in them	120
	8:14	that there be just ***m***, unto whom it	NIH
	8:14	there be wicked ***m***, to whom it happeneth	NIH
	9: 3	also the heart of the sons of **m** is full *of* evil,	120
	9:11	nor yet riches to **m**s of understanding,	1886.1
	9:11	nor yet favour to **m**s of skill;	1886.1
	9:12	so *are* the sons of **m** snared in an evil time,	120
	9:14	*There was* a little city, and few **m** within it;	376
	9:17	The words of wise ***m*** *are* heard in quiet,	NIH
	12: 3	and the strong **m** shall bow themselves, and	376
SS	3: 7	threescore valiant ***m*** *are* about it, of	NIH
	4: 4	thousand bucklers, all shields of mighty ***m***.	NIH
Isa	2:11	the haughtiness of **m** shall be bowed down,	376
	2:17	and the haughtiness of **m** shall be made low:	376
	3:25	Thy **m** shall fall by the sword, and	4962
	5: 3	**m** of Judah, judge, I pray you, betwixt me	376
	5: 7	and the **m** of Judah his pleasant plant:	376
	5:13	their honourable **m** *are* famished, and	4962
	5:22	and **m** of strength to mingle strong drink:	376
	6:12	And the LORD have removed **m** far away,	120
	7:13	*Is it* a small thing for you to weary **m**, but	376
	7:24	and with bows shall ***m*** come thither;	NIH
	9: 3	*and* as ***m*** rejoice when they divide the spoil.	NIH
	9:17	the Lord shall have no joy in their **young m**,	970

Isa 11:15 and make *m* go over dryshod. NIH
13:18 *Their* bows also shall dash the **young m** to 5288
19:12 where *are* thy wise *m*? and let them tell thee NIH
21: 9 behold, here cometh a chariot of **m**, *with* a 376
21:17 the mighty *m* of the children of Kedar, NIH
22: 2 thy slain *m are* not slain with the sword, nor NIH
22: 6 And Elam bare the quiver with chariots of **m** 120
23: 4 neither do I nourish up **young m**, *nor* bring 970
24: 6 of the earth are burned, and few **m** left. 582
26:19 Thy dead *m* shall live, *together with* my NIH
28:14 hear the word of the LORD, ye scornful **m**, 376
29:11 which *m* deliver to one that is learned, NIH
29:13 towards me is taught *by* the precept of **m**: 376
29:14 for the wisdom of their wise *m* shall perish, NIH
29:14 the understanding of their prudent *m* shall NIH
29:19 the poor among **m** shall rejoice in the Holy 120
31: 3 Now the Egyptians *are* **m**, and not God; and 120
31: 8 and his **young m** shall be discomfited. 970
35: 8 the **wayfaring m**, though fools, 1870+1980
36:12 *hath he* not *sent me* to the **m** that sit upon 376
38:16 by these *things m* live, and in all these NIH
39: 3 and said unto him, What said these **m**? 376
40:30 be weary, and the **young m** shall utterly fall: 970
41: 9 and called thee from the **chief m** thereof, and 678
41:14 thou worm Jacob, *and* ye **m** of Israel; 4962
43: 4 therefore will I give **m** for thee, and 120
44:11 the workmen, they *are* of **m**: let them all be 120
44:25 that turneth wise *m* backward, and NIH
45:14 of Ethiopia and of the Sabeans, **m** of stature, 376
45:24 *even* to him shall *m* come; and all that are NIH
46: 8 Remember this, and **shew yourselves m**: 377
51: 7 fear ye not the reproach of **m**, neither be ye 582
52:14 and his form more than the sons of **m**: 120
53: 3 He is despised and rejected of **m**; a man of 376
57: 1 merciful *m are* taken away, none 376
59:10 *we are* in desolate places as dead *m*. NIH
60:11 that *m* may bring unto thee the forces of NIH
61: 6 *m* shall call you the Ministers of our God: NIH
64: 4 For since the beginning of the world *m* have NIH
66:24 look upon the carcases of the **m** that have 376
Jer 4: 3 For thus saith the LORD to the **m** of Judah 376
4: 4 ye **m** of Judah and inhabitants of Jerusalem: 376
5: 5 I will get me unto the **great m**, and 1419
5:16 an open sepulchre, they *are* all mighty *m*. NIH
5:26 For among my people are found wicked *m*: NIH
5:26 setteth snares; they set a trap, they catch **m**. 376
6:11 and upon the assembly of **young m** together: 970
6:23 set in array as **m** for war against thee, 376
6:30 Reprobate silver shall *m* call them, because NIH
8: 9 The wise *m* are ashamed, they are dismayed NIH
9: 2 wilderness a lodging place of **wayfaring m**; 732
9: 2 an assembly of treacherous *m*. NIH
9:10 neither can *m* hear the voice of the cattle; NIH
9:21 *and* the **young m** from the streets. 970
9:22 Even the carcases of **m** shall fall as dung 120
10: 7 forasmuch as among all the wise *m* of NIH
10: 9 they *are* all the work of cunning *m*. NIH
11: 2 speak unto the **m** of Judah, and to 376
11: 9 A conspiracy is found among the **m** of 376
11:21 Therefore thus saith the LORD of the **m** of 376
11:22 the **young m** shall die by the sword; 970
11:23 for I will bring evil upon the **m** of Anathoth, 376
15: 8 mother of the **young m** a spoiler at noonday: 970
15:10 on usury, nor *m* have lent to me on usury; NIH
16: 6 neither shall *m* lament for them, nor cut NIH
16: 7 Neither shall *m* tear *themselves* for them in NIH
16: 7 neither shall *m* give them the cup of NIH
17:25 the **m** of Judah, and the inhabitants of 376
18:11 speak to the **m** of Judah, and to 376
18:21 *be* widows; and let their **m** be put to death; 376
18:21 *let* their **young m** *be* slain by the sword in 970
19:10 bottle in the sight of the **m** that go with thee. 376
26:21 with all his mighty *m*, and all the princes, NIH
26:22 Jehoiakim the king sent **m** *into* Egypt, 376
26:22 and *certain* **m** with him into Egypt. 376
31:13 in the dance, both **young m** and old together: 970
32:19 *are* open upon all the ways of the sons of **m**: 120
32:20 this day, and in Israel, and amongst *other* **m**; 120
32:32 the **m** of Judah, and the inhabitants of 376
32:44 *M* shall buy fields for money, and NIH
33: 5 *it is* to fill them with the dead bodies of **m**, 120
34:18 I will give the **m** that have transgressed my 376
35:13 Go and tell the **m** of Judah and 376
36:31 of Jerusalem, and upon the **m** of Judah, 376
37:10 there remained *but* wounded **m** among them, 376
38: 4 for thus he weakeneth the hands of the **m** of 376
38: 9 these **m** have done evil in all that they have 376
38:10 Take from hence thirty **m** with thee, and 376
38:11 So Ebed-melech took the **m** with him, and 376
38:16 into the hand of these **m** that seek thy life. 376
39: 4 all the **m** of war, then they fled, and 376
39:17 shalt not be given into the hand of the **m** 376
40: 7 *were* in the fields, *even* they and their **m**, 376
40: 7 and had committed unto him **m**, and women, 376
40: 8 the son of a Maachathite, they and their **m**. 376
40: 9 of Shaphan sware unto them and to their **m**, 376
41: 1 the princes of the king, even ten **m** with him, 376
41: 2 the ten **m** that were with him, and 376
41: 3 that were found there, *and* the **m** of war. 376
41: 5 and from Samaria, *even* fourscore **m**, 376
41: 7 of the pit, he, and the **m** that *were* with him. 376
41: 8 ten **m** were found among them that said unto 376
41: 9 had cast all the dead bodies of the **m**, 376
41:12 they took all the **m**, and went to fight with 376
41:15 escaped from Johanan with eight **m**, 376
41:16 *even* mighty **m** of war, and the women, and 376
42:17 So shall it be with all the **m** that set their 376
43: 2 all the proud **m**, saying unto Jeremiah, 376
43: 6 *Even* **m**, and women, and children, and 1397
43: 9 in Tahpanhes, in the sight of the **m** of Judah; 376
44:15 all the **m** which knew that their wives had 376
44:19 out drink offerings unto her, without our **m**? 376
44:20 to the **m**, and to the women, and to all 1397
44:27 all the **m** of Judah that *are* in the land of 376
46: 9 and let the mighty *m* come forth; NIH
46:15 Why are thy valiant *m* swept away? NIH
46:21 Also her **hired m** *are* in the midst of her 7916
47: 2 the **m** shall cry, and all the inhabitants of 120
48:14 We *are* mighty and strong **m** for the war? 376
48:15 his chosen **young m** are gone down to 970
48:31 *mine heart* shall mourn for the **m** of 376
48:36 mine heart shall sound like pipes for the **m** 376
49:15 among the heathen, *and* despised among **m**. 120
49:22 at that day shall the heart of the mighty *m* NIH
49:26 Therefore her **young m** shall fall in her 970
49:26 all the **m** of war shall be cut off in that day, 376
49:28 go up to Kedar, and spoil the **m** of the east. 1121
50:30 Therefore shall her **young m** fall in 970
50:30 all her **m** of war shall be cut off in that day, 376
50:35 and upon her princes, and upon her wise *m*. NIH
50:36 a sword *is* upon her mighty *m*; and NIH
51: 3 spare ye not her **young m**; destroy ye utterly 970
51:14 *saying,* Surely I will fill thee *with* **m**, as *with* 120
51:30 The mighty *m* of Babylon have forborn to NIH
51:32 with fire, and the **m** of war are affrighted. 376
51:56 upon Babylon, and her mighty *m* are taken, NIH
51:57 and her wise *m*, her captains, and her rulers, NIH
51:57 her mighty *m*: and they shall sleep a NIH
52: 7 all the **m** of war fled, and went forth out of 376
52:13 all the houses of the great *m*, burnt he with NIH
52:25 which had the charge of the **m** of war; 376
52:25 seven **m** of them that were near the king's 376
52:25 threescore **m** of the people of the land, 376
La 1:15 foot all my mighty *m* in the midst of me: NIH
1:15 assembly against me to crush my **young m**: 970
1:18 and my **young m** are gone into captivity. 970
2:15 *saying, Is* this the city that *m* call The NIH
2:21 and my **young m** are fallen by the sword; 970
3:33 afflict willingly nor grieve the children of **m**. 376
4:14 They have wandered *as* blind *m* in NIH
4:14 so that *m* could not touch their garments. NIH
5:13 They took the **young m** to grind, and 970
5:14 the gate, the **young m** from their musick. 970
Eze 6: 4 I will cast down your slain *m* before your NIH
6:13 when their slain *m* shall be among their NIH
8:11 there stood before them seventy **m** of 376
8:16 and the altar, *were* about five and twenty **m**, 376
9: 2 six **m** came from the way of the higher gate, 376
9: 4 set a mark upon the foreheads of the **m** that 376
9: 6 they began at the ancient **m** which *were* 376
11: 1 at the door of the gate five and twenty **m**; 376
11: 2 these *are* the **m** that devise mischief, and 376
11:15 the **m** of thy kindred, and all the house of 376
12:16 I will leave a few **m** of them from the sword, 376
14: 3 these **m** have set up their idols in their heart, 376
14:14 Though these three **m**, Noah, Daniel, and 376
14:16 *Though* these three **m** *were* in it, *as* I live, 376
14:18 Though these three **m** *were* in it, *as* I live, 376

Eze 15: 3 will *m* take a pin of it to hang any vessel NIH
16:17 madest to thyself images of **m**, and 2145
19: 3 it learned to catch the prey; it devoured **m**. 120
19: 6 learned to catch the prey, *and* devoured **m**. 120
21:14 it *is* the sword of the great *m that are* slain, NIH
21:31 deliver thee into the hand of brutish **m**, *and* 376
22: 9 In thee are **m** that carry tales to shed blood: 376
23: 6 and rulers, all of them desirable **young m**, 970
23: 7 *with* all them *that were* the chosen **m** of 1121
23:12 upon horses, all of them desirable **young m**. 970
23:14 for when she saw **m** pourtrayed upon 376
23:23 all of them desirable **young m**, captains and 970
23:40 that ye have sent for **m** to come from far, 376
23:42 with the **m** of the common sort *were* brought 376
23:45 *the* righteous **m**, they shall judge them after 376
24:17 not *thy* lips, and eat not the bread of **m**. 376
24:22 not cover *your* lips, nor eat the bread of **m**. 376
25: 4 I *will* deliver thee to the **m** of the east for a 1121
25:10 Unto the **m** of the east with the Ammonites, 1121
26:10 as **m** enter into a city wherein is made a NIH
26:17 *that wast* inhabited of seafaring **m**, NIH
27: 8 thy wise *m*, O Tyrus, *that* were in thee, NIH
27: 9 the wise *m* thereof were in thee thy calkers: NIH
27:10 of Phut were in thine army, thy **m** of war: 376
27:11 The **m** of Arvad with thine army *were* upon 1121
27:13 they traded the persons of **m** and vessels of 120
27:15 The **m** of Dedan *were* thy merchants; 1121
27:27 all thy **m** of war, that *are* in thee, and in all 376
30: 5 and the **m** of the land that is in league, 1121
30:17 The **young m** of Aven and of Phi-beseth 970
31:14 the earth, in the midst of the children of **m**, 120
34:31 *are* **m**, *and* I *am* your God, saith the Lord 120
35: 8 I will fill his mountains *with* his slain *m*: in NIH
36:10 I will multiply **m** upon you, all the house of 120
36:12 Yea, I will cause **m** to walk upon you, 120
36:12 no more henceforth **bereave** them **of m**. 7921
36:13 Thou *land* devourest up **m**, and 120
36:14 Therefore thou shalt devour **m** no more, 120
36:15 Neither will I cause **m** to hear in thee NIH
36:37 I will increase them *with* **m** like a flock. 120
36:38 the waste cities be filled *with* flocks of **m**: 120
38:20 all the **m** that *are* upon the face of the earth, 120
39:14 they shall sever out **m** of continual 376
39:20 with mighty *m*, and *with* all men of war, NIH
39:20 with mighty *men*, and *with* all **m** of war, 376
47:15 the way of Hethlon, as *m* go to Zedad; NIH
Da 2:12 commanded to destroy all the wise *m* of NIH
2:13 the decree went forth that the wise *m* should NIH
2:14 which was gone forth to slay the wise *m* of NIH
2:18 with the rest of the wise *m* of Babylon. NIH
2:24 ordained to destroy the wise *m* of Babylon: NIH
2:24 Destroy not the wise *m* of Babylon: NIH
2:27 cannot the wise *m*, the astrologians, NIH
2:38 wheresoever the children of **m** dwell, 606
2:43 shall mingle themselves with the seed of **m**: 606
2:48 chief of the governors over all the wise *m* of NIH
3:12 these **m**, O king, have not regarded thee: 1400
3:13 Then they brought these **m** before the king. 1400
3:20 **most mighty m** that *were* in 1400+1401+2429
3:21 these **m** were bound in their coats, 1400
3:22 the flame of the fire slew those **m** that took 1400
3:23 these three **m**, Shadrach, Meshach, and 1400
3:24 Did not we cast three **m** bound into 1400
3:25 and said, Lo, I see four **m** loose, 1400
3:27 being gathered together, saw these **m**, 1400
4: 6 in all the wise *m* of Babylon before me, NIH
4:17 the most High ruleth in the kingdom of **m**, 606
4:17 and setteth up over it the basest of **m**. 606
4:18 forasmuch as all the wise *m* of my kingdom NIH
4:25 That they *shall* drive thee from **m**, and 606
4:25 the most High ruleth in the kingdom of **m**, 606
4:32 they *shall* drive thee from **m**, and 606
4:32 the most High ruleth in the kingdom of **m**, 606
4:33 he *was* driven from **m**, and did eat grass as 606
5: 7 and said to the wise *m* of Babylon, NIH
5: 8 came in all the king's wise *m*: but NIH
5:15 now the wise *m*, the astrologers, have been NIH
5:21 he *was* driven from the sons of **m**; and 606
5:21 most high God ruled in the kingdom of **m**, 606
6: 5 said these **m**, We shall not find any 1400
6:11 these **m** assembled, and found Daniel 1400
6:15 these **m** assembled unto the king, and 1400
6:24 they brought those **m** which had accused 1400
6:26 That in every dominion of my kingdom *m* NIH
9: 7 to the **m** of Judah, and to the inhabitants of 376
10: 7 for the **m** that were with me saw not 376
10:16 *one* like the similitude of the sons of **m** 120
Hos 6: 7 they like **m** have transgressed the covenant: 120
10:13 thy way, in the multitude of thy mighty *m*. NIH
13: 2 Let the **m** that sacrifice kiss the calves. 120
Joel 1: 2 Hear this, ye **old m**, and give ear, all ye 2205
1:12 joy is withered away from the sons of **m**. 120
2: 7 They shall run like mighty *m*; they shall NIH
2: 7 *men;* they shall climb the wall like **m** of war; 376
2:28 your **old m** shall dream dreams, 2205
2:28 your **young m** shall see visions: 970
3: 9 wake up the mighty *m*, let all the men of NIH
3: 9 wake up the mighty *men*, let all the **m** of war 376
Am 2:11 and of your **young m** for Nazarites. 970
4:10 your **young m** have I slain with the sword, 970
6: 9 if there remain ten **m** in one house, that they 376
8:13 the fair virgins and **young m** faint for thirst. 970
Ob 1: 7 All the **m** of thy confederacy have brought 376
1: 7 the **m** that were at peace with thee have 376
1: 8 even destroy the wise *m* out of Edom, and NIH
1: 9 thy mighty *m*, O Teman, shall be dismayed, NIH
Jnh 1:10 were the **m** exceedingly afraid, and said unto 376
1:10 For the **m** knew that he fled from 376
1:13 Nevertheless the **m** rowed hard to bring *it* to 376
1:16 Then the **m** feared the LORD exceedingly, 376
Mic 2: 8 that pass by securely *as m* averse from war. NIH
2:12 great noise by reason of *the multitude of* **m**. 120
5: 5 him seven shepherds, and eight principal **m**. 120
5: 7 not for man, nor waiteth for the sons of **m**. 120
6:12 For the rich **m** thereof are full *of* violence, NIH
7: 2 *there is* none upright among **m**: they all lie in 120
7: 6 a man's enemies *are* the **m** of his own house. 376
Na 2: 3 The shield of his mighty *m is* made red, NIH
2: 3 *men is* made red, the valiant **m** *are* in scarlet: 376
3:10 and they cast lots for her honourable *m*, and NIH
3:10 and all her great *m* were bound in chains. NIH
Hab 1:14 makest **m** as the fishes of the sea, as 120
Zep 1:12 punish the **m** that are settled on their lees: 376
1:17 I will bring distress upon **m**, that they shall 120
1:17 that they shall walk like blind *m*, because NIH
2:11 *m* shall worship him, every one from his NIH
Hag 1:11 upon **m**, and upon cattle, and upon all 120
Zec 2: 4 towns without walls for the multitude of **m** 120
3: 8 for they *are* **m** wondered at: for behold, 376
7: 2 and Regemmelech, and their **m**, 376
7: 7 when *m* inhabited the south and the plain? NIH
8: 4 There shall yet **old m** and old women dwell 2205
8:10 for I set all **m** every one against his 120
8:23 **m** shall take hold out of all languages of 376
9:17 corn shall make the **young m** cheerful, and 970
10: 5 they shall be as mighty *m*, which tread NIH
11: 6 I *will* deliver the **m** every one into his 120
14:11 *m* shall dwell in it, and there shall be no NIH
Mt 2: 1 there came **wise m** from the east to *3097*
2: 7 when he had privily called the **wise m**, *3097*
2:16 he saw that he was mocked of the **wise m**, *3097*
2:16 he had diligently inquired of the **wise m**. *3097*
4:19 and I will make you fishers of **m**. *444*
5:11 when *m* shall revile you, and persecute *you*, NIG
5:13 cast out, and to be trodden under foot of **m**. *444*
5:15 Neither do **m** light a candle, and put it under NIG
5:16 Let your light so shine before **m**, that they *444*
5:19 least commandments, and shall teach **m** so, *444*
6: 1 heed that *ye* do not your alms before **m**, *444*
6: 2 in the streets, that they may have glory of **m**. *444*
6: 5 of the streets, that they may be seen of **m**. *444*
6:14 For if ye forgive **m** their trespasses, *444*
6:15 But if ye forgive not **m** their trespasses, *444*
6:16 that they may appear unto **m** to fast. *444*
6:18 That thou appear not unto **m** to fast, but *444*
7:12 ye would that **m** should do to you, *444*
7:16 Do *m* gather grapes of thorns, or figs of NIG
8:27 But the **m** marvelled, saying, What manner *444*
9: 8 which had given such power unto **m**. *444*
9:17 Neither do *m* put new wine into old bottles: NIG
9:27 two **blind m** followed him, crying, and *5185*
9:28 into the house, the **blind m** came to him: *5185*
10:17 But beware of **m**: for they will deliver you *444*
10:22 And ye shall be hated of all *m* for my NIG
10:32 therefore shall confess me before **m**, *444*
10:33 But whosoever shall deny me before **m**, *444*
12:31 and blasphemy shall be forgiven unto **m**: *444*
12:31 the *Holy* Ghost shall not be forgiven unto **m**. *444*

Mt 12:36 That every idle word that **m** shall speak, *444*
12:41 *The* **m** of Nineveh shall rise in judgment *435*
13:17 righteous **m** have desired to see *those things* NIG
13:25 But while **m** slept, his enemy came and *444*
14:21 that had eaten were about five thousand **m**, *435*
14:35 And when the **m** of that place had *435*
15: 9 for doctrines the commandments of **m**. *444*
15:38 And they that did eat were four thousand **m**, *435*
16:13 Whom do **m** say that I the Son of man am? *444*
16:23 *things* that be of God, but *those* that be of **m**. *444*
17:22 man shall be betrayed into the hands of **m**: *444*
19:11 unto them, All *m* cannot receive this saying, NIG
19:12 which were made eunuchs of **m**: *444*
19:26 said unto them, With **m** this is unpossible; *444*
20:30 two **blind m** sitting by the way side, *5185*
21:25 from heaven, or of **m**? And they reasoned *444*
21:26 But if we shall say, Of **m**; we fear *444*
21:41 He will miserably destroy those wicked *m*, NIG
22:16 *man:* for thou regardest not the person of **m**. *444*
23: 5 all their works they do for to be seen of **m**: *444*
23: 7 and to be called of **m**, Rabbi, Rabbi. *444*
23:13 ye shut up the kingdom of heaven against **m**: *444*
23:28 ye also outwardly appear righteous unto **m**, *444*
23:34 unto you prophets, and wise *m*, and scribes: NIG
26:33 Though all *m* shall be offended because NIG
28: 4 keepers did shake, and became as dead *m*. NIG
Mk 1:17 and I will make you to become fishers of **m**. *444*
1:37 they said unto him, All *m* seek for thee. NIG
3:28 All sins shall be forgiven unto the sons of **m**, *444*
5:20 had done for him: and all *m* did marvel. NIG
6:12 and preached that *m* should repent. NIG
6:44 *of* the loaves were about five thousand **m**. *435*
7: 7 for doctrines the commandments of **m**. *444*
7: 8 ye hold the tradition of **m**, *as* the washing of *444*
7:21 For from within, out of the heart of **m**, *444*
8: 4 From whence can a man satisfy these *m* NIG
8:24 and said, I see **m** as trees, walking. *444*
8:27 unto them, Whom do **m** say that I am? *444*
8:33 that be of God, but the *things* that be of **m**. *444*
9:31 Son of man is delivered into the hands of **m**, *444*
10:27 With **m** *it is* impossible, but not with God: *444*
11:30 of John, was *it* from heaven, or of **m**? *444*
11:32 But if we shall say, Of **m**; they feared *444*
11:32 for all *m* counted John, that he was a NIG
12:14 *man:* for thou regardest not the person of **m**, *444*
13:13 And ye shall be hated of all *m* for my NIG
14:51 and the **young m** laid hold on him: *3495*
Lk 1:25 on *me,* to take away my reproach among **m**. *444*
2:14 and on earth peace, good will towards **m**. *444*
3:15 and all *m* mused in their hearts of John, NIG
5:10 from henceforth thou shalt catch **m**. *444*
5:18 **m** brought in a bed a man which was taken *435*
6:22 when **m** shall hate you, and when they shall *444*
6:26 when all **m** shall speak well of you: *444*
6:31 And as ye would that **m** should do to you, *444*
6:38 running over, shall *m* give into your bosom. NIG
6:44 For of thorns *m* do not gather figs, nor of a NIG
7:20 When the **m** were come unto him, they said, *435*
7:31 then shall I liken the **m** of this generation? *444*
9:14 For they were about five thousand **m**. *435*
9:30 And behold, there talked with him two **m**, *435*
9:32 his glory, and the two **m** that stood with him. *435*
9:44 man shall be delivered into the hands of **m**. *444*
11:31 the judgment with the **m** of this generation, *435*
11:32 *The* **m** of Nineveh shall rise up in *435*
11:44 the **m** that walk over *them* are not aware *of* *444*
11:46 for ye lade **m** *with* burdens grievous to be *444*
12: 8 Whosoever shall confess me before **m**, *444*
12: 9 But he that denieth me before **m** shall be *444*
12:36 And ye yourselves like unto **m** that wait for *444*
12:48 and to whom *m* have committed much, NIG
13: 4 think ye that they were sinners above all **m** *444*
13:14 There are six days in which *m* ought to NIG
14:24 That none of those **m** which were bidden *435*
14:35 nor yet for the dunghill; *but m* cast it out. NIG
16:15 are they which justify yourselves before **m**; *444*
16:15 for that which is highly esteemed amongst **m** *444*
17:12 there met him ten **m** *that were* lepers, *435*
17:34 in that night there shall be two *m* in one NIG
17:36 Two *m* shall be in the field; the one shall be NIG
18: 1 *to this end,* that *m* ought always to pray, NIG
18:10 Two **m** went up into the temple to pray; *444*
18:11 that I am not as other **m** *are,* extortioners, *444*
18:27 The *things which are* unpossible with **m** are *444*
20: 4 of John, was it from heaven, or of **m**? *444*
20: 6 But *and* if we say, Of **m**; all the people will *444*
20:20 which *should* feign themselves just *m*, that NIG
21: 1 saw the rich *m* casting their gifts into NIG
21:17 And ye shall be hated of all *m* for my NIG
22:63 And the **m** that held Jesus mocked him, and *435*
23:11 And Herod with his **m of war** set him at *4753*
24: 4 two **m** stood by them in shining garments: *435*
24: 7 must be delivered into the hands of sinful **m**, *444*
Jn 1: 4 him was life; and the life was the light of **m**. *444*
1: 7 that all *m* through him might believe. NIG
2:10 and when *m* have well drunk, then NIG
2:24 himself unto them, because he knew all *m*, NIG
3:19 and **m** loved darkness rather than light, *444*
3:26 the same baptizeth, and all *m* come to him. NIG
4:20 that in Jerusalem is the place where *m* NIG
4:28 her way into the city, and saith to the **m**, *444*
4:38 other *m* laboured, and ye are entered into NIG
5:23 That all *m* should honour the Son, even as NIG
5:41 I receive not honour from **m**. *444*
6:10 And Jesus said, Make the **m** sit down. *444*
6:10 So the **m** sat down, *in* number about five *435*
6:14 Then *those* **m**, when they had seen *444*
8:17 your law, that the testimony of two **m** is true. *444*
11:48 him thus alone, all *m* will believe on him: NIG
12:32 up from the earth, will draw all *m* unto me. NIG
12:43 For they loved the praise of **m** more than *444*
13:35 By this shall all *m* know that ye are my NIG
15: 6 and *m* gather them, and cast *them* into NIG
17: 6 I have manifested thy name unto the **m** *444*
18: 3 having received a band *of m*, and NIG
Ac 1:10 two **m** stood by them in white apparel; *435*
1:11 Which also said, Ye **m** of Galilee, why stand *435*
1:16 **M** *and* brethren, this scripture must needs *435*
1:21 Wherefore of these **m** which have *435*
1:24 which knowest the hearts of all *m*, shew NIG
2: 5 devout **m**, out of every nation under heaven. *435*
2:13 *These m* are full of new wine. NIG
2:14 Ye **m** of Judea, and all *ye* that dwell at *435*
2:17 and your **young m** shall see visions, and *3495*
2:17 and your **old m** shall dream dreams: *4245*
2:22 Ye **m** of Israel, hear these words; Jesus of *435*
2:29 **M** *and* brethren, let *me* freely speak unto you *435*
2:37 **M** *and* brethren, what shall we do? *435*
2:45 parted them to all *m*, as every *man* had NIG
3:12 Ye **m** of Israel, why marvel ye at this? *435*
4: 4 the number of the **m** was about five *435*
4:12 other name under heaven given among **m**, *444*
4:13 that they were unlearned and ignorant **m**, *444*
4:16 Saying, What shall we do to these **m**? *444*
4:21 for all *m* glorified God for that which was NIG
5: 4 thou hast not lied unto **m**, but unto God. *444*
5: 6 And the **young m** arose, wound him up, *3501*
5:10 and the **young m** came in, and found her *3495*
5:14 the Lord, multitudes both of **m** and women.) *435*
5:25 the **m** whom ye put in prison are standing in *435*
5:29 said, We ought to obey God rather than **m**. *444*
5:35 And said unto them, Ye **m** of Israel, *435*
5:35 what ye intend to do as touching these **m**. *444*
5:36 to whom a number of **m**, about four *435*
5:38 Refrain from these **m**, and let them alone: *444*
5:38 for if this counsel or this work be of **m**, *444*
6: 3 look ye out among you seven **m** of honest *435*
6:11 Then they suborned **m**, which said, We have *435*
7: 2 he said, **M**, brethren, and fathers, hearken; *435*
8: 2 And devout **m** carried Stephen *to his burial,* *435*
8: 3 and haling **m** and women committed *them* *435*
8:12 they were baptized, both **m** and women. *435*
9: 2 of *this* way, whether they were **m** or women, *435*
9: 7 And the **m** which journeyed with him stood *435*
9:38 Peter was there, they sent unto him two **m**, *435*
10: 5 And now send **m** to Joppa, and call for *one* *435*
10:17 the **m** which were sent from Cornelius had *435*
10:19 said unto him, Behold, three **m** seek thee: *435*
10:21 Then Peter went down to the **m** which were *435*
11: 3 Thou wentest in to **m** uncircumcised, *435*
11:11 immediately there were three **m** already *435*
11:13 Send **m** to Joppa, and call for Simon, *435*
11:20 And some of them were **m** of Cyprus and *435*
13:15 saying, *Ye m and* brethren, if ye have *any* *435*
13:16 **M** of Israel, and *ye* that fear God, *435*
13:26 **M** *and* brethren, children of the stock of *435*
13:38 it known unto you therefore, **m** *and* brethren, *435*
13:50 and the chief *m* of the city, and NIG

Ac 14:11 are come down to us in the likeness of **m**. *444*
14:15 why do ye these *things?* We also are **m** of *444*
15: 1 And certain *m* which came down from NIG
15: 7 rose up, and said unto them, **M** *and* brethren, *435*
15:13 James answered, saying, **M** *and* brethren, *435*
15:17 That the residue of **m** might seek after *444*
15:22 to send chosen **m** of their own company to *435*
15:22 and Silas, chief *m* among the brethren: NIG
15:25 to send chosen **m** unto you with our beloved *435*
15:26 **M** that have hazarded their lives for *444*
16:17 These **m** are the servants of the most high *444*
16:20 saying, These **m**, being Jews, do exceedingly *444*
16:35 sent the sergeants, saying, Let those **m** go. *444*
17:12 which were Greeks, and of **m**, not a few. *435*
17:22 of Mars' hill, and said, *Ye* **m** of Athens, *435*
17:26 And hath made of one blood all nations of **m** *444*
17:30 now commandeth all **m** every where to *444*
17:31 *whereof* he hath given assurance unto all *m*, NIG
17:34 Howbeit certain **m** clave unto him, and *435*
18:13 This *fellow* persuadeth **m** to worship God *444*
19: 7 And all the **m** were about twelve. *435*
19:19 and burned *them* before all *m*: and NIG
19:29 and Aristarchus, **m** of Macedonia, NIG
19:35 the people, he said, *Ye* **m** of Ephesus, *435*
19:37 For ye have brought *hither* these **m**, *435*
20:26 that I *am* pure from the blood of all *m*. NIG
20:30 Also of your own selves shall **m** arise, *435*
21:23 We have four **m** which have a vow on them; *435*
21:26 Then Paul took the **m**, and the next day *435*
21:28 Crying out, **M** of Israel, help: This is *435*
21:28 that teacheth all *m* every where against NIG
21:38 four thousand **m** that were murderers? *435*
22: 1 **M**, brethren, and fathers, hear ye my defence *435*
22: 4 and delivering into prisons both **m** and *435*
22:15 For thou shalt be his witness unto all **m** of *444*
23: 1 beholding the council, said, **M** *and* brethren, *435*
23: 6 **M** *and* brethren, I am a Pharisee, the son of a *435*
23:21 lie in wait for him of them moe *than* forty **m**, *435*
24:16 void of offence toward God, and *toward* **m**. *444*
25:23 chief captains, and principal **m** of the city, *435*
25:24 and all **m** which are here present with us, *435*
28:17 he said unto them, **M** *and* brethren, *435*
Ro 1:18 all ungodliness and unrighteousness of **m**, *444*
1:27 And likewise also the **m**, leaving the natural *730*
1:27 **m** with men working that which is *730*
1:27 men with **m** working that which is *730*
2:16 of **m** by Jesus Christ according to my gospel. *444*
2:29 whose praise *is* not of **m**, but of God. *444*
5:12 and so death passed upon all **m**, for that all *444*
5:18 *judgment came* upon all **m** to condemnation; *444*
5:18 *came* upon all **m** unto justification of life. *444*
6:19 I speak **after the manner of m** because *442*
11: 4 I have reserved to myself seven thousand **m**, *435*
12:16 *things,* but condescend to *m* of low estate. NIG
12:17 Provide *things* honest in the sight of all **m**. *444*
12:18 as lieth in you, live peaceably with all **m**. *444*
14:18 *is* acceptable to God, and approved of **m**. *444*
16:19 is come abroad unto all *m*. I am glad NIG
1Co 1:25 the foolishness of God is wiser than **m**; *444*
1:25 and the weakness of God is stronger than **m**. *444*
1:26 how that not many wise *m* after the flesh, NIG
2: 5 faith should not stand in the wisdom of **m**, *444*
3: 3 divisions, are ye not carnal, and walk as **m**? *444*
3:21 Therefore let no *man* glory in **m**. For all *444*
4: 6 that ye might learn in us not to think *of m* NIG
4: 9 unto the world, and to angels, and to **m**. *444*
7: 7 For I would that all **m** were even as I myself. *444*
7:23 with a price; be not ye the servants of **m**. *444*
9:19 For though I be free from all *m*, yet have I NIG
9:22 I am made all *things* to all *m*, that I might NIG
10:15 I speak as to wise *m*; judge ye what I say. NIG
10:33 Even as I please all *m* in all *things,* not NIG
13: 1 Though I speak with the tongues of **m** and *444*
14: 2 in an *unknown* tongue speaketh not unto **m**, *444*
14: 3 But he that prophesieth speaketh unto **m** *to* *444*
14:20 be ye children, but in understanding be **m**. *5046*
14:21 With *m* of other tongues and other lips will NIG
15:19 in Christ, we are of all **m** most miserable. *444*
15:32 If after the manner of **m** I have fought with *444*
15:39 but *there is* one *kind of* flesh of **m**, *444*
16:13 fast in the faith, **quit** you **like m**, be strong. *407*
2Co 3: 2 in our hearts, known and read of all **m**: *444*
5:11 the terror of the Lord, we persuade **m**; *444*
8:13 For *I mean* not that other *m* be eased, and NIG
8:21 sight of the Lord, but also in the sight of **m**. *444*
9:13 distribution unto them, and unto all *m*; NIG
Gal 1: 1 Paul, an apostle, (not of **m**, neither by man, *444*
1:10 For do I now persuade **m**, or God? or do I *444*
1:10 or do I seek to please **m**? for if I yet pleased *444*
1:10 for if I yet pleased **m**, I should not be *444*
3:15 Brethren, I speak after the manner of **m**; *444*
6:10 let us do good unto all *m*, especially unto NIG
Eph 3: 5 was not made known unto the sons of **m**, *444*
3: 9 And to make all *m* see what *is* NIG
4: 8 led captivity captive, and gave gifts unto **m**. *444*
4:14 every wind of doctrine, by the sleight of **m**, *444*
5:28 So ought **m** to love their wives as their own *435*
6: 7 doing service, as to the Lord, and not to **m**: *444*
Php 2: 7 and was made in the likeness of **m**: *444*
4: 5 Let your moderation be known unto all **m**. *444*
Col 2: 8 and vain deceit, after the tradition of **m**, *444*
2:22 the commandments and doctrines of **m**? *444*
3:23 do *it* heartily, as to the Lord, and not unto **m**; *444*
1Th 1: 5 as ye know what manner of *m* we were NIG
2: 4 not as pleasing **m**, but God, which trieth our *444*
2: 6 Nor of **m** sought we glory, neither of you, *444*
2:13 ye received *it* not as the word of **m**, but as it *444*
2:15 please not God, and are contrary to all **m**: *444*
3:12 towards all *m*, even as we *do* towards you: NIG
5:14 support the weak, be patient toward all *m*. NIG
5:15 both among yourselves, and to all *m*. NIG
2Th 3: 2 delivered from unreasonable and wicked **m**: *444*
3: 2 and wicked men: for all *m* have not faith. NIG
1Ti 2: 1 *and* giving of thanks, be made for all **m**; *444*
2: 4 Who will have all **m** to be saved, and *444*
2: 5 and one mediator between God and **m**, *444*
2: 8 I will therefore that **m** pray every where, *435*
4:10 the living God, who is the Saviour of all **m**, *444*
5: 1 as a father; *and* the younger *m* as brethren; NIG
5:24 to judgment; and some *m* they follow after. NIG
6: 5 Perverse disputings of **m** of corrupt minds, *444*
6: 9 which drown **m** in destruction and perdition. *444*
2Ti 2: 2 the same commit thou to faithful **m**, *444*
2:24 but be gentle unto all *m*, apt to teach, NIG
3: 2 For **m** shall be lovers of their own selves, *444*
3: 8 **m** of corrupt minds, reprobate concerning *444*
3: 9 for their folly shall be manifest unto all *m*, NIG
3:13 But evil **m** and seducers shall wax worse and *444*
4:16 *man* stood with me, but all *m* forsook me: NIG
Tit 1: 8 a lover of good *m*, sober, just, holy, NIG
1:14 and commandments of **m**, that turn from *444*
2: 2 That the **aged m** be sober, grave, *4246*
2: 6 Young *m* likewise exhort to be sober NIG
2:11 bringeth salvation hath appeared to all **m**, *444*
3: 2 *but* gentle, shewing all meekness unto all **m**. *444*
3: 8 These *things* are good and profitable unto **m**. *444*
Heb 5: 1 For every high priest taken from among **m** is *444*
5: 1 ordained for **m** *in things* pertaining to God, *444*
6:16 For **m** verily swear by the greater: and *444*
7: 8 And here **m** that die receive tithes; but *444*
7:28 For the law maketh **m** high priests which *444*
9:17 For a testament *is* of force after *m* are dead: NIG
9:27 And as it is appointed unto **m** once to die, *444*
12:14 Follow peace with all *m*, and holiness, NIG
12:23 and to the spirits of just *m* made perfect, NIG
Jas 1: 5 that giveth to all *m* liberally, and NIG
2: 6 Do not rich *m* oppress you, and draw you NIG
3: 9 and therewith curse we **m**, which are made *444*
5: 1 ye rich *m*, weep and howl for your miseries NIG
1Pe 2: 4 disallowed indeed of **m**, but chosen of God, *444*
2:15 put to silence the ignorance of foolish **m**: *444*
2:17 Honour all *m*. Love the brotherhood. NIG
4: 2 rest of *his* time in the flesh to the lusts of **m**, *444*
4: 6 that they might be judged according to **m** in *444*
2Pe 1:21 holy **m** of God spake *as they were* moved by *444*
3: 7 day of judgment and perdition of ungodly **m**. *444*
3: 9 *his* promise, as some *m* count slackness; NIG
1Jn 2:13 **young m**, because you have overcome *3495*
2:14 **young m**, because ye are strong, and *3495*
5: 9 If we receive the witness of **m**, the witness *444*
3Jn 1:12 Demetrius hath good report of all *m*, and NIG
Jude 1: 4 For there are certain **m** crept in unawares, *444*
1: 4 ungodly *m*, turning the grace of our God NIG
Rev 6:15 and the **great m**, and the rich *men,* and *3175*
6:15 and the rich *m*, and the chief captains, and NIG
6:15 and the mighty *m*, and every bondman, and NIG
8:11 and many **m** died of the waters, because *444*
9: 4 only *those* **m** which have not the seal of God *444*

Rev 9: 6 And in those days shall **m** seek death, and *444*
9: 7 and their faces *were* as the faces of **m**. *444*
9:10 and their power *was* to hurt **m** five months. *444*
9:15 and a year, for to slay the third *part* of **m**. *444*
9:18 By these three was the third *part* of **m** killed, *444*
9:20 And the rest of the **m** which were not killed *444*
11:13 in the earthquake were slain of **m** *444+3686*
13:13 from heaven on the earth in the sight of **m**, *444*
14: 4 These were redeemed from among **m**, *444*
16: 2 grievous sore upon the **m** which had *444*
16: 8 *power* was given unto him to scorch **m** with *444*
16: 9 And **m** were scorched *with* great heat, and *444*
16:18 such as was not since **m** were upon the earth, *444*
16:21 And there fell upon **m** a great hail out of *444*
16:21 and **m** blasphemed God because of *444*
18:13 and chariots, and slaves, and souls of **m**. *444*
18:23 for thy merchants were the **great m** of *3175*
19:18 and the flesh of mighty *m*, and the flesh of NIG
19:18 and the flesh of all *m*, both free and bond, NIG
21: 3 the tabernacle of God *is* with **m**, and he will *444*

MEN OF TOB See ISH-TOB

MEN'S (24) [MAN]
Ge 24:32 his feet, and the **m** feet that *were* with him. 376
44: 1 saying, Fill the **m** sacks *with* food, as much 376
Dt 4:28 the work of **m** hands, wood and stone, 120
1Sa 24: 9 Wherefore hearest thou **m** words, saying, 120
1Ki 12:13 forsook the **old m** counsel that they gave 2205
13: 2 and **m** bones shall be burnt upon thee. 120
2Ki 19:18 but the work of **m** hands, wood and stone: 120
23:20 burnt **m** bones upon them, and returned *to* 120
Ps 115: 4 *are* silver and gold, the work of **m** hands. 120
135:15 *are* silver and gold, the work of **m** hands. 120
Isa 37:19 but the work of **m** hands, wood and stone: 120
Jer 48:41 the mighty *m* hearts in Moab at that day NIH
Hab 2: 8 because of **m** blood, and *for* the violence of 120
2:17 because of **m** blood, and *for* the violence of 120
Mt 23: 4 to be borne, and lay *them* on **m** shoulders; *444*
23:27 but are within full of dead *m* bones, and NIG
Lk 9:56 For the Son of man is not come to destroy **m** *444*
21:26 **M** hearts failing them for fear, and *444*
Ac 17:25 Neither is worshipped with **m** hands, *444*
2Co 10:15 *our* measure, *that is,* of other *m* labours; NIG
1Ti 5:22 no *man,* neither be partaker of other *m* sins: NIG
5:24 Some **m** sins are open beforehand, *444*
1Pe 4:15 or as a **busybody in other m matters**. *244*
Jude 1:16 *words,* having *m* persons in admiration NIG

MENAHEM (8)
2Ki 15:14 For **M** the son of Gadi went up from 4505
15:16 **M** smote Tiphsah, and all that *were* therein, 4505
15:17 **M** the son of Gadi to reign over Israel, 4505
15:19 and **M** gave Pul a thousand talents of silver, 4505
15:20 **M** exacted the money of Israel, *even* of all 4505
15:21 the rest of the acts of **M**, and all that he did, 4505
15:22 **M** slept with his fathers; and Pekahiah his 4505
15:23 of **M** *began* to reign over Israel in Samaria, 4505

MENAN (1)
Lk 3:31 *the son* of Melea, which was *the son* of **M**, *3104*

MEND (2) [MENDING]
2Ch 24:12 and brass to **m** the house of the LORD. 2388
34:10 of the LORD, to repair and **m** the house: 2388

MENDING (2) [MEND]
Mt 4:21 ship with Zebedee their father, **m** their nets; *2675*
Mk 1:19 who also *were* in the ship **m** *their* nets. *2675*

MENE (3)
Da 5:25 **M**, MENE, TEKEL, UPHARSIN. 4484
5:25 MENE, **M**, TEKEL, UPHARSIN. 4484
5:26 **M**; God hath numbered thy kingdom, and 4484

MENNA See MENAN

MENPLEASERS (2) [MAN, PLEASE]
Eph 6: 6 Not with eyeservice, as **m**; but as *441*
Col 3:22 not with eyeservice, as **m**; but in singleness *441*

MENSERVANTS (10) [MAN, SERVE]
Ge 12:16 **m**, and maidservants, and she asses, and 5650
20:14 **m**, and womenservants, and gave *them* 5650
24:35 **m**, and maidservants, and camels, and 5650
30:43 and **m**, and camels, and asses. 5650
32: 5 asses, flocks, and **m**, and womenservants: 5650
Ex 21: 7 she shall not go out as the **m** do. 5650
Dt 12:12 your **m**, and your maidservants, and 5650
1Sa 8:16 he will take your **m**, and your 5650
2Ki 5:26 sheep, and oxen, and **m**, and maidservants? 5650
Lk 12:45 and shall begin to beat the **m** and maidens, *3816*

MENSTEALERS (1) [MAN, STEAL]
1Ti 1:10 for **m**, for liars, for perjured *persons,* and *405*

MENSTRUOUS (3)
Isa 30:22 thou shalt cast them away as a **m cloth**; 1739
La 1:17 Jerusalem is as a **m** *woman* among them. 5079
Eze 18: 6 neither hath come near to a **m** woman, 5079

MENTION (23) [MENTIONED]
Ge 40:14 **make m** of me unto Pharaoh, and bring me 2142
Ex 23:13 **make** no **m** of the name of other gods, 2142
Jos 23: 7 neither **make m** of the name of their gods, 2142
1Sa 4:18 when he **made m** of the ark of God, 2142
Job 28:18 No **m** shall be **made** of coral, or of pearls: 2142
Ps 71:16 I will **make m** of thy righteousness, *even* of 2142
87: 4 I will **make m** of Rahab and Babylon to 2142
Isa 12: 4 **make m** that his name *is* exalted. 2142
19:17 every one that **maketh m** thereof shall be 2142
26:13 by thee only will we **make m** of thy name. 2142
48: 1 **make m** of the God of Israel, *but* not in 2142
49: 1 of my mother hath he **made m of** my name. 2142
62: 6 ye that **make m** of the LORD, keep not 2142
63: 7 I will **m** the lovingkindnesses of 2142
Jer 4:16 **Make** ye **m** to the nations; behold, 2142
20: 9 I said, I will not **make m** of him, nor speak 2142
23:36 the burden of the LORD shall ye **m** no 2142
Am 6:10 for *we may* not **make m** of the name of 2142
Ro 1: 9 that without ceasing I make **m** of you, *3417*
Eph 1:16 for you, making **m** of you in my prayers; *3417*
1Th 1: 2 you all, making **m** of you in our prayers; *3417*
Phm 1: 4 making **m** of thee always in my prayers, *3417*
Heb 11:22 **made m** of the departing of the children of *3421*

MENTIONED (7) [MENTION]
Jos 21: 9 these cities which are *here* **m** by name, 7121
1Ch 4:38 These **m** by *their* names *were* princes in their 935
2Ch 20:34 who is **m** in the book of the kings of Israel. 5927
Eze 16:56 For thy sister Sodom was not **m** by thy 8052
18:22 they shall not be **m** unto him: 2142
18:24 that he hath done shall not be **m**: 2142
33:16 he hath committed shall be **m** unto him: 2142

MEONENIM (1)
Jdg 9:37 company come along by the plain of **M**. 6049

MEONOTHAI (1)
1Ch 4:14 **M** begat Ophrah: and Seraiah begat Joab, 4587

MEPHAATH (4)
Jos 13:18 And Jahazah, and Kedemoth, and **M**, 4158
21:37 with her suburbs, and **M** with her suburbs; 4158
1Ch 6:79 with her suburbs, and **M** with her suburbs: 4158
Jer 48:21 and upon Jahazah, and upon **M**, 4158

MEPHIBOSHETH (15) [MERIB-BAAL]
2Sa 4: 4 and became lame. And his name *was* **M**. 4648
9: 6 Now when **M**, the son of Jonathan, the son 4648
9: 6 David said, **M**. And he answered, 4648
9:10 **M** thy master's son shall eat bread alway at 4648
9:11 As for **M**, *said the king,* he shall eat at my 4648
9:12 **M** had a young son, whose name *was* 4648
9:12 in the house of Ziba *were* servants unto **M**. 4648
9:13 So **M** dwelt in Jerusalem: for he did eat 4648
16: 1 Ziba the servant of **M** met him, with a 4648
16: 4 Behold, thine *are* all that *pertained* unto **M**. 4648
19:24 **M** the son of Saul came down to meet 4648
19:25 Wherefore wentest not thou with me, **M**? 4648
19:30 **M** said unto the king, Yea, let him take all, 4648
21: 7 the king spared **M**, the son of Jonathan 4648
21: 8 whom she bare unto Saul, Armoni and **M**; 4648

MERAB (3)
1Sa 14:49 *were these;* the name of the firstborn **M**, 4764
18:17 to David, Behold my elder daughter **M**, 4764
18:19 it came to pass at the time when **M** Saul's 4764

MERAIAH (1)
Ne 12:12 of Seraiah, **M**; of Jeremiah, Hananiah; 4811

M

MERAIOTH (7)

1Ch 6: 6 begat Zerahiah, and Zerahiah begat **M**, 4812
6: 7 **M** begat Amariah, and Amariah begat 4812
6:52 **M** his son, Amariah his son, Ahitub his 4812
9:11 the son of Zadok, the son of **M**, the son of 4812
Ezr 7: 3 the son of Azariah, the son of **M**, 4812
Ne 11:11 the son of Zadok, the son of **M**, the son of 4812
Ne 12:15 Of Harim, Adna; of **M**, Helkai; 4812

MERARI (39) [MERARITES]

Ge 46:11 the sons of Levi; Gershon, Kohath, and **M**. 4847
Ex 6:16 Gershon, and Kohath, and **M**: 4847
6:19 the sons of **M**; Mahali and Mushi: these *are* 4847
Nu 3:17 their names; Gershon, and Kohath, and **M**. 4847
3:20 the sons of **M** by their families; Mahli, and 4847
3:33 Of **M** *was* the family of the Mahlites, and 4847
3:33 the Mushites: these *are* the families of **M**. 4847
3:35 of **M** *was* Zuriel the son of Abihail: 4847
3:36 charge of the sons of **M** *shall be* the boards 4847
4:29 *As for* the sons of **M**, thou shalt number 4847
4:33 the service of the families of the sons of **M**, 4847
4:42 numbered of the families of the sons of **M**, 4847
4:45 numbered of the families of the sons of **M**, 4847
7: 8 and eight oxen he gave unto the sons of **M**, 4847
10:17 of Gershon and the sons of **M** set forward, 4847
26:57 of **M**, the family of the Merarites. 4847
Jos 21: 7 The children of **M** by their families *had* out 4847
21:34 unto the families of the children of **M**, 4847
21:40 So all the cities for the children of **M** by 4847
1Ch 6: 1 The sons of Levi; Gershon, Kohath, and **M**. 4847
6:16 sons of Levi; Gershom, Kohath, and **M**. 4847
6:19 The sons of **M**; Mahli, and Mushi. 4847
6:29 The sons of **M**; Mahli, Libni his son, 4847
6:44 their brethren the sons of **M** *stood* on 4847
6:47 of Mushi, the son of **M**, the son of Levi. 4847
6:63 Unto the sons of **M** *were given* by lot, 4847
6:77 Unto the rest of the children of **M** *were* 4847
9:14 the son of Hashabiah, of the sons of **M**; 4847
15: 6 Of the sons of **M**; Asaiah the chief, and 4847
15:17 of the sons of **M** their brethren, Ethan 4847
23: 6 of Levi, *namely,* Gershon, Kohath, and **M**. 4847
23:21 The sons of **M**; Mahli, and Mushi. 4847
24:26 The sons of **M** *were* Mahli and Mushi: 4847
24:27 The sons of **M** by Jaaziah; Beno, and 4847
26:10 Also Hosah, of the children of **M**, had sons; 4847
26:19 the sons of Kore, and among the sons of **M**. 4847
2Ch 29:12 of the sons of **M**, Kish the son of Abdi, and 4847
34:12 and Obadiah, the Levites, of the sons of **M**; 4847
Ezr 8:19 with him Jeshaiah of the sons of **M**, 4847

MERARITES (1) [MERARI]

Nu 26:57 of Merari, the family of the **M**. 4848

MERCHANDISE (22) [MERCHANT]

Dt 21:14 thou shalt not **make m** of her, because thou 6014
24: 7 and **maketh m** of him, or selleth him; 6014
Pr 3:14 For the **m** of it *is* better than 5504
3:14 of it *is* better than the **m** of silver, 5505
31:18 She perceiveth that her **m** *is* good: 5504
Isa 23:18 her **m** and her hire shall be holiness to 5504
23:18 for her **m** shall be for them that dwell 5504
45:14 **m** of Ethiopia and of the Sabeans, men of 5505
Eze 26:12 of thy riches, and make a prey of thy **m**: 7404
27: 9 mariners were in thee to occupy thy **m**. 4627
27:15 many isles *were* the **m** of thine hand: 5506
27:24 and made of cedar, among thy **m**. 4819
27:27 Thy riches, and thy fairs, thy **m**, 4627
27:27 the occupiers of thy **m**, and all thy men of 4627
27:33 the multitude of thy riches and of thy **m**. 4627
27:34 thy **m** and all thy company in the midst of 4627
28:16 By the multitude of thy **m** they have filled 7404
Mt 22: 5 one to his farm, another to his **m**: *1711*
Jn 2:16 make not my Father's house a house of **m**. *1712*
2Pe 2: 3 they with feigned words **make m** of you: *1710*
Rev 18:11 for no *man* buyeth their **m** any more: *1117*
18:12 The **m** of gold, and silver, and *1117*

MERCHANT (12) [MERCHANDISE, MERCHANT'S, MERCHANTMEN, MERCHANTS]

Ge 23:16 of silver, current *money* with the **m**. 5503
Pr 31:24 selleth *it;* and delivereth girdles unto the **m**. 3669
SS 3: 6 frankincense, with all powders of the **m**? 7402
Isa 23:11 **m** *city,* to destroy the strong holds thereof. 3667
Eze 27: 3 *which art* a **m** of the people for many isles, 7402
27:12 Tarshish *was* thy **m** by reason of 5503
27:16 Syria *was* thy **m** by reason of the multitude 5503
27:18 Damascus *was* thy **m** in the multitude of 5503
27:20 Dedan *was* thy **m** in precious clothes for 7402
Hos 12: 7 *He is* a **m**, the balances of deceit *are* in his 3667
Zep 1:11 for all the **m** people are cut down; 3667
Mt 13:45 the kingdom of heaven is like unto a **m** *1713*

MERCHANT'S (1) [MERCHANT]

Pr 31:14 She is like the **m** ships; she bringeth her 5503

MERCHANTMEN (2) [MERCHANT]

Ge 37:28 there passed by Midianites **m**; and 376+5503
1Ki 10:15 Besides *that he had* of the **m**, and *of* 376

MERCHANTS (28) [MERCHANT]

1Ki 10:15 *of* the traffick of the *spice* **m**, and *of* all 7402
10:28 the king's **m** received the linen yarn at a 5503
2Ch 1:16 the king's **m** received the linen yarn at a 5503
9:14 *that which* chapmen and **m** brought. 5503
Ne 3:31 *of* the **m**, over against the gate Miphkad, 7402
3:32 gate repaired the goldsmiths and the **m**. 7402
13:20 So the **m** and sellers of all *kind of* ware 7402
Job 41: 6 of him? shall they part him among the **m**? 3669
Isa 23: 2 thou whom the **m** of Zidon, that pass over 5503
23: 8 the crowning *city,* whose **m** *are* princes, 5503
47:15 hast laboured, *even* thy **m**, from thy youth: 5503
Eze 17: 4 a land of traffick; he set it in a city of **m**. 7402
27:13 Tubal, and Meshech, they *were* thy **m**: 7402
27:15 The men of Dedan *were* thy **m**; many isles 7402
27:17 and the land of Israel, they *were* thy **m**: 7402
27:21 rams, and goats: in these *were they* thy **m**. 5503
27:22 The **m** of Sheba and Raamah, they *were* thy 7402
27:22 of Sheba and Raamah, they *were* thy **m**: 7402
27:23 Eden, the **m** of Sheba, Asshur, *and* 7402
27:23 Asshur, *and* Chilmad, *were* thy **m**. 7402
27:24 These *were* thy **m** in all sorts of things, 7402
Eze 27:36 The **m** among the people shall hiss at thee; 5503
38:13 Sheba, and Dedan, and the **m** of Tarshish, 5503
Na 3:16 Thou hast multiplied thy **m** above the stars 7402
Rev 18: 3 the **m** of the earth are waxed rich through *1713*
18:11 And the **m** of the earth *shall* weep and *1713*
18:15 The **m** of these *things,* which were made *1713*
18:23 for thy **m** were the great men of the earth; *1713*

MERCIES (40) [MERCY]

Ge 32:10 I am not worthy of the least of all the **m**, 2617
2Sa 24:14 hand of the LORD; for his **m** *are* great: 7356
1Ch 21:13 of the LORD; for very great *are* his **m**: 7356
2Ch 6:42 remember the **m** of David thy servant. 2617
Ne 9:19 Yet thou in thy manifold **m** forsookest 7356
9:27 according to thy manifold **m** thou gavest 7356
9:28 didst thou deliver them according to thy **m**; 7356
Ps 25: 6 thy **tender m** and thy lovingkindnesses; 7356
40:11 Withhold not thou thy **tender m** from me, 7356
51: 1 of thy **tender m** blot out my transgressions. 7356
69:16 according to the multitude of thy **tender m**. 7356
77: 9 hath he in anger shut up his **tender m**? 7356
79: 8 let thy **tender m** speedily prevent us: 7356
89: 1 I will sing of the **m** of the LORD for ever: 2617
103: 4 thee *with* lovingkindness and **tender m**; 7356
106: 7 remembered not the multitude of thy **m**; 2617
106:45 according to the multitude of his **m**. 2617
119:41 Let thy **m** come also *unto* me, O LORD, 2617
119:77 Let thy **tender m** come *unto* me, that I may 7356
119:156 Great *are* thy **tender m**, O LORD: 7356
145: 9 and his **tender m** *are* over all his works. 7356
Pr 12:10 but the **tender m** of the wicked *are* cruel. 7356
Isa 54: 7 but with great **m** will I gather thee. 7356
55: 3 with you, *even* the sure **m** of David. 2617
63: 7 hath bestowed on them according to his **m**, 7356
63:15 of thy bowels and of thy **m** towards me? 7356
Jer 16: 5 the LORD, *even* lovingkindness and **m**. 7356
42:12 I will shew **m** unto you, that he may have 7356
La 3:22 *It is of* the LORD'S **m** that we are not 2617
3:32 according to the multitude of his **m**. 2617
Da 2:18 That *they* would desire **m** of the God of 7359
9: 9 To the Lord our God *belong* **m** and 7356
9:18 for our righteousnesses, but for thy great **m**. 7356
Hos 2:19 and in lovingkindness, and in **m**. 7356
Zec 1:16 I am returned to Jerusalem with **m**: 7356
Ac 13:34 I will give you the sure **m** of David. *3741*
Ro 12: 1 you therefore, brethren, by the **m** of God, *3628*
2Co 1: 3 the Father of **m**, and the God of all *3628*

Php 2: 1 of the Spirit, if any bowels and **m**, *3628*
Col 3:12 holy and beloved, bowels of **m**, kindness, *3628*

MERCIES' (1) [MERCY]
Ne 9:31 Nevertheless for thy great **m** sake thou 7356

MERCIFUL (40) [MERCY]
Ge 19:16 the LORD being **m** unto him: 2551
Ex 34: 6 **m** and gracious, longsuffering, 7349
Dt 4:31 (For the LORD thy God *is* a **m** God;) 7349
21: 8 Be **m**, O LORD, unto thy people Israel, 3722
32:43 will be **m** *unto* his land, *and to* his people. 3722
2Sa 22:26 With the **m** thou wilt shew thyself merciful, 2623
22:26 the merciful thou wilt **shew** thyself **m**, 2616
1Ki 20:31 the kings of the house of Israel *are* **m** kings: 2617
2Ch 30: 9 the LORD your God *is* gracious and **m**, 7349
Ne 9:17 gracious and **m**, slow to anger, and of great 7349
9:31 for thou *art* a gracious and **m** God. 7349
Ps 18:25 With the **m** thou wilt shew thyself merciful; 2623
18:25 the merciful thou wilt **shew** thyself **m**; 2616
26:11 redeem me, and be **m** unto me. 2603
37:26 *He is* ever **m**, and lendeth; and his seed *is* 2603
41: 4 I said, LORD, be **m** unto me: heal my 2603
41:10 O LORD, be **m** unto me, and raise me up, 2603
56: 1 Be **m** unto me, O God: for man would 2603
57: 1 Be **m** unto me, O God, be merciful unto 2603
57: 1 merciful unto me, O God, be **m** unto me: 2603
59: 5 be not **m** to any wicked transgressors. 2603
67: 1 God be **m** unto us, and bless us; *and* 2603
86: 3 Be **m** unto me, O Lord: for I cry unto thee 2603
103: 8 The LORD *is* **m** and gracious, slow to 7349
116: 5 and righteous; yea, our God *is* **m**. 7355
117: 2 For his **m kindness** is great toward us: and 2617
119:58 be **m** unto me according to thy word. 2603
119:76 thy **m kindness** be for my comfort, 2617
119:132 Look thou upon me, and be **m** unto me, 2603
Pr 11:17 The **m** man doeth good to his own soul: but 2617
Isa 57: 1 **m** men *are* taken away, none considering 2617
Jer 3:12 for I *am* **m**, saith the LORD, *and* I will not 2623
Joel 2:13 for he *is* gracious and **m**, slow to anger, and 7349
Jnh 4: 2 **m**, slow to anger, and of great kindness, 7349
Mt 5: 7 Blessed *are* the **m**: for they shall obtain *1655*
Lk 6:36 Be ye therefore **m**, as your Father also is *3629*
6:36 therefore merciful, as your Father also is **m**. *3629*
18:13 his breast, saying, God be **m** to me a sinner. *2433*
Heb 2:17 that he might be a **m** and faithful high *1655*
8:12 For I will be **m** to their unrighteousness, *2436*

MERCURIUS (1)
Ac 14:12 and Paul, **M**, because he was the chief *2060*

MERCY (277) [MERCIES, MERCIES', MERCIFUL, MERCY'S, UNMERCIFUL]
Ge 19:19 in thy sight, and thou hast magnified thy **m**, 2617
24:27 hath not left destitute my master of his **m** 2617
39:21 shewed him **m**, and gave him favour in 2617
43:14 God Almighty give you **m** before the man, 7356
Ex 15:13 Thou in thy **m** hast led forth the people 2617
20: 6 shewing **m** unto thousands of them that 2617
25:17 thou shalt make a **m seat** *of* pure gold: 3727
25:18 make them, in the two ends of the **m seat**. 3727
25:19 *even* of the **m seat** shall ye make 3727
25:20 covering the **m seat** with their wings, 3727
25:20 toward the **m seat** shall the faces of 3727
25:21 thou shalt put the **m seat** above upon 3727
25:22 commune with thee from above the **m seat**, 3727
26:34 thou shalt put the **m seat** upon the ark of 3727
30: 6 before the **m seat** that *is* over 3727
31: 7 the **m seat** that *is* thereupon, and all 3727
33:19 will **shew m** on whom I will shew mercy. 7355
33:19 will shew mercy on whom I will **shew m**. 7355
34: 7 Keeping **m** for thousands, 2617
35:12 *with* the **m seat**, and the vail of 3727
37: 6 he made the **m seat** *of* pure gold: 3727
37: 7 he them, on the two ends of the **m seat**; 3727
37: 8 out of the **m seat** made he the cherubims on 3727
37: 9 covered with their wings over the **m seat**, 3727
37: 9 *even* to the **m seatward** were the faces of 3727
39:35 and the staves thereof, and the **m seat**, 3727
40:20 and put the **m seat** above upon the ark: 3727
Lev 16: 2 *place* within the vail before the **m seat**, 3727
16: 2 I will appear in the cloud upon the **m seat**. 3727
16:13 the **m seat** that *is* upon the Testimony, 3727
16:14 sprinkle *it* with his finger upon the **m seat** 3727
16:14 before the **m seat** shall he sprinkle of 3727
16:15 sprinkle it upon the **m seat**, and before 3727
16:15 upon the mercy seat, and before the **m seat**: 3727
Nu 7:89 **m seat** that *was* upon the ark of Testimony, 3727
14:18 of great **m**, forgiving iniquity and 2617
14:19 according unto the greatness of thy **m**, 2617
Dt 5:10 shewing **m** unto thousands of them that 2617
7: 2 with them, nor **shew m** unto them: 2603
7: 9 and **m** with them that love him and 2617
7:12 and the **m** which he sware unto thy fathers: 2617
13:17 shew thee **m**, and have compassion upon 7356
Jdg 1:24 into the city, and we will shew thee **m**. 2617
2Sa 7:15 my **m** shall not depart away from him, as I 2617
15:20 back thy brethren: **m** and truth *be* with thee. 2617
22:51 sheweth **m** to his anointed, unto David, and 2617
1Ki 3: 6 unto thy servant David my father great **m**, 2617
8:23 **m** with thy servants that walk before thee 2617
1Ch 16:34 for *he is* good; for his **m** *endureth* for ever. 2617
16:41 because his **m** *endureth* for ever; 2617
17:13 I will not take my **m** away from him, as I 2617
28:11 and of the place of the **m seat**, 3727
2Ch 1: 8 Thou hast shewed great **m** unto David my 2617
5:13 For *he is* good; for his **m** *endureth* for ever: 2617
6:14 and *shewest* **m** unto thy servants, 2617
7: 3 For *he is* good; for his **m** *endureth* for ever. 2617
7: 6 because his **m** *endureth* for ever, 2617
20:21 the LORD; for his **m** *endureth* for ever. 2617
Ezr 3:11 for his **m** *endureth* for ever towards Israel. 2617
7:28 hath extended **m** unto me before the king, 2617
9: 9 hath extended **m** unto us in the sight of 2617
Ne 1: 5 and **m** for them that love him and 2617
1:11 and grant him **m** in the sight of this man. 7356
9:32 terrible God, who keepest covenant and **m**, 2617
13:22 me according to the greatness of thy **m**. 2617
Job 37:13 for correction, or for his land, or for **m**. 2617
Ps 4: 1 **have m** upon me, and hear my prayer. 2603
5: 7 *into* thy house in the multitude of thy **m**: 2617
6: 2 **Have m** upon me, O LORD; for I *am* 2603
9:13 **Have m** upon me, O LORD; consider my 2603
13: 5 I have trusted in thy **m**; my heart shall 2617
18:50 sheweth **m** to his anointed, to David, and 2617
21: 7 through the **m** of the most High he shall not 2617
23: 6 **m** shall follow me all the days of my life: 2617
25: 7 according to thy **m** remember thou me for 2617
25:10 All the paths of the LORD *are* **m** and 2617
25:16 Turn thee unto me, and **have m** upon me; 2603
27: 7 **have m** also upon me, and answer me. 2603
30:10 Hear, O LORD, and **have m** upon me: 2603
31: 7 I will be glad and rejoice in thy **m**: for thou 2617
31: 9 **Have m** upon me, O LORD, for I am in 2603
32:10 in the LORD, **m** shall compass him about. 2617
33:18 fear him, upon them that hope in his **m**; 2617
33:22 Let thy **m**, O LORD, be upon us, 2617
36: 5 Thy **m**, O LORD, *is* in the heavens; *and* 2617
37:21 but the righteous **sheweth m**, and giveth. 2603
51: 1 **Have m** upon me, O God, according to thy 2603
52: 8 I trust in the **m** of God for ever and ever. 2617
57: 3 God shall send forth his **m** and his truth. 2617
57:10 For thy **m** *is* great unto the heavens, and 2617
59:10 The God of my **m** shall prevent me: 2617
59:16 I will sing aloud of thy **m** in the morning: 2617
59:17 God *is* my defence, *and* the God of my **m**. 2617
61: 7 O prepare **m** and truth, *which* may preserve 2617
62:12 Also unto thee, O Lord, *belongeth* **m**: 2617
66:20 turned away my prayer, nor his **m** from me. 2617
69:13 O God, in the multitude of thy **m** hear me, 2617
77: 8 Is his **m** clean gone for ever? doth *his* 2617
85: 7 Shew us thy **m**, O LORD, and grant us thy 2617
85:10 **M** and truth are met together; righteousness 2617
86: 5 plenteous in **m** unto all them that call upon 2617
86:13 For great *is* thy **m** toward me: and thou hast 2617
86:15 plenteous in **m** and truth. 2617
86:16 O turn unto me, and **have m** upon me; 2603
89: 2 I have said, **M** shall be built up for ever: 2617
89:14 **m** and truth shall go before thy face. 2617
89:24 and my **m** *shall be* with him: 2617
89:28 My **m** will I keep for him for evermore, 2617
90:14 O satisfy us early *with* thy **m**; that we may 2617
94:18 thy **m**, O LORD, held me up. 2617
98: 3 He hath remembered his **m** and his truth 2617
100: 5 his **m** *is* everlasting; and his truth *endureth* 2617
101: 1 I will sing of **m** and judgment: unto thee, 2617
102:13 Thou shalt arise, *and* **have m** upon Zion: 7355
103: 8 slow to anger, and plenteous in **m**. 2617

Ps 103:11 *so* great is his **m** toward them that fear him. 2617
103:17 the **m** of the LORD *is* from everlasting to 2617
106: 1 for *he is* good: for his **m** *endureth* for ever. 2617
107: 1 for *he is* good: for his **m** *endureth* for ever. 2617
108: 4 For thy **m** *is* great above the heavens: and 2617
109:12 Let there be none to extend **m** unto him: 2617
109:16 that he remembered not to shew **m**, 2617
109:21 because thy **m** *is* good, deliver thou me. 2617
109:26 my God: O save me according to thy **m**: 2617
115: 1 for thy **m**, *and* for thy truth's sake. 2617
118: 1 *is* good: because his **m** *endureth* for ever. 2617
118: 2 now say, that his **m** *endureth* for ever. 2617
118: 3 now say, that his **m** *endureth* for ever. 2617
118: 4 LORD say, that his **m** *endureth* for ever. 2617
118:29 for *he is* good: for his **m** *endureth* for ever. 2617
119:64 The earth, O LORD, is full *of* thy **m**: 2617
119:124 with thy servant according unto thy **m**, 2617
123: 2 our God, until that he **have m** upon us. 2603
123: 3 **Have m** upon us, O LORD, have mercy 2603
123: 3 upon us, O LORD, **have m** upon us: 2603
130: 7 for with the LORD *there is* **m**, and 2617
136: 1 for *he is* good: for his **m** *endureth* for ever. 2617
136: 2 God of gods: for his **m** *endureth* for ever. 2617
136: 3 Lord of lords: for his **m** *endureth* for ever. 2617
136: 4 great wonders: for his **m** *endureth* for ever. 2617
136: 5 the heavens: for his **m** *endureth* for ever. 2617
136: 6 the waters: for his **m** *endureth* for ever. 2617
136: 7 great lights: for his **m** *endureth* for ever: 2617
136: 8 to rule by day: for his **m** *endureth* for ever: 2617
136: 9 rule by night: for his **m** *endureth* for ever. 2617
136:10 their firstborn: for his **m** *endureth* for ever: 2617
136:11 among them: for his **m** *endureth* for ever: 2617
136:12 out arm: for his **m** *endureth* for ever. 2617
136:13 sea into parts: for his **m** *endureth* for ever: 2617
136:14 the midst of it: for his **m** *endureth* for ever: 2617
136:15 in the Red sea: for his **m** *endureth* for ever. 2617
136:16 the wilderness: for his **m** *endureth* for ever. 2617
136:17 great kings: for his **m** *endureth* for ever: 2617
136:18 famous kings: for his **m** *endureth* for ever: 2617
136:19 the Amorites: for his **m** *endureth* for ever: 2617
136:20 of Bashan: for his **m** *endureth* for ever: 2617
136:21 for an heritage: for his **m** *endureth* for ever: 2617
136:22 his servant: for his **m** *endureth* for ever. 2617
136:23 our low estate: for his **m** *endureth* for ever: 2617
136:24 our enemies: for his **m** *endureth* for ever. 2617
136:25 to all flesh: for his **m** *endureth* for ever. 2617
136:26 God of heaven: for his **m** *endureth* for ever. 2617
138: 8 thy **m**, O LORD, *endureth* for ever: 2617
143:12 of thy **m** cut off mine enemies, and 2617
145: 8 slow to anger, and of great **m**. 2617
147:11 that fear him, in those that hope in his **m**. 2617
Pr 3: 3 Let not **m** and truth forsake thee: bind them 2617
14:21 he that **hath m** on the poor, happy *is* he. 2603
14:22 **m** and truth *shall be to* them that devise 2617
14:31 he that honoureth him **hath m** on the poor. 2603
16: 6 By **m** and truth iniquity is purged: and 2617
20:28 **M** and truth preserve the king: and 2617
20:28 the king: and his throne is upholden by **m**. 2617
21:21 after righteousness and **m** findeth life, 2617
28:13 and forsaketh *them* shall **have m**. 7355
Isa 9:17 neither shall **have m** on their fatherless and 7355
14: 1 For the LORD will **have m** on Jacob, and 7355
16: 5 in **m** shall the throne be established: and 2617
27:11 he that made them will not **have m** on 7355
30:18 be exalted, that *he* may **have m** upon you: 7355
47: 6 thou didst shew them no **m**; upon 7356
49:10 for he that **hath m** on them shall lead them, 7355
49:13 and will **have m** upon his afflicted. 7355
54: 8 with everlasting kindness will I **have m** on 7355
54:10 saith the LORD that **hath m** on thee. 7355
55: 7 the LORD, and he will **have m** upon him; 7355
60:10 but in my favour have I **had m** on thee. 7355
Jer 6:23 and spear; they *are* cruel, and **have** no **m**; 7355
13:14 nor spare, nor **have m**, but destroy them. 7355
21: 7 spare them, neither have pity, nor **have m**. 7355
30:18 and **have m** on his dwelling places; 7355
31:20 I will **surely have m** upon him, 7355+7355
33:11 *is* good; for his **m** *endureth* for ever: 2617
33:26 captivity to return, and **have m** on them. 7355
42:12 that he may **have m** upon you, and 7355
50:42 they *are* cruel, and will not **shew m**: 7355
Eze 39:25 and **have m** upon the whole house of Israel, 7355
Da 4:27 thine iniquities by **shewing m** to the poor; 2604
9: 4 the covenant and **m** to them that love him, 2617
Hos 1: 6 for I will no more **have m** upon the house 7355
1: 7 I will **have m** upon the house of Judah, and 7355
2: 4 I will not **have m** upon her children; 7355
2:23 I will **have m** upon her that had not 7355
2:23 mercy upon her that had not **obtained m**; 7355
4: 1 because *there is* no truth, nor **m**, 2617
6: 6 For I desired **m**, and not sacrifice; and 2617
10:12 to yourselves in righteousness, reap in **m**; 2617
12: 6 keep **m** and judgment, and wait on thy God 2617
14: 3 for in thee the fatherless **findeth m**. 7355
Jnh 2: 8 observe lying vanities forsake their own **m**. 2617
Mic 6: 8 to love **m**, and to walk humbly with thy 2617
7:18 anger for ever, because he delighteth in **m**. 2617
7:20 the truth to Jacob, *and* the **m** to Abraham, 2617
Hab 3: 2 years make known; in wrath remember **m**. 7355
Zec 1:12 how long wilt thou not **have m** on 7355
7: 9 shew **m** and compassions every man to his 2617
10: 6 to place them; for I **have m** upon them: 7355
Mt 5: 7 *are* the merciful: for they shall **obtain m**. *1653*
9:13 I will have **m**, and not sacrifice: *1656*
9:27 saying, *Thou* Son of David, **have m** on us. *1653*
12: 7 I will have **m**, and not sacrifice, *1656*
15:22 unto him, saying, **Have m** on me, O Lord, *1653*
17:15 Lord, **have m** on my son: for he is lunatick, *1653*
20:30 cried out, saying, **Have m** on us, O Lord, *1653*
20:31 saying, **Have m** on us, O Lord, *thou* Son of *1653*
23:23 *matters* of the law, judgment, **m**, and faith: *1656*
Mk 10:47 Jesus, *thou* Son of David, **have m** on me. *1653*
10:48 *Thou* Son of David, **have m** on me. *1653*
Lk 1:50 And his **m** *is* on them that fear him from *1656*
1:54 his servant Israel, in remembrance of *his* **m**, *1656*
1:58 the Lord had shewed great **m** upon her; *1656*
1:72 To perform the **m** *promised* to our fathers, *1656*
1:78 Through the **tender m** of our God; *1656+4698*
10:37 And he said, He that shewed **m** on him. *1656*
16:24 **have m** on me, and send Lazarus, *1653*
17:13 and said, Jesus, Master, **have m** on us. *1653*
18:38 Jesus, *thou* Son of David, **have m** on me. *1653*
18:39 *Thou* Son of David, **have m** on me. *1653*
Ro 9:15 I will **have m** on whom I will have mercy, *1653*
9:15 I will have mercy on whom I will **have m**, *1653*
9:16 that runneth, but of God that **sheweth m**. *1653*
9:18 Therefore **hath** he **m** on whom he will *have* *1653*
9:18 hath he mercy on whom he will *have* **m**, NIG
9:23 the riches of his glory on the vessels of **m**, *1656*
11:30 yet have now **obtained m** through their *1653*
11:31 that through your **m** they also may obtain *1656*
11:31 your mercy they also may **obtain m**. *1653*
11:32 in unbelief, that he might **have m** upon all. *1653*
12: 8 he that **sheweth m**, with cheerfulness. *1653*
15: 9 the Gentiles might glorify God for *his* **m**; *1656*
1Co 7:25 as one that hath **obtained m** of the Lord to *1653*
2Co 4: 1 as we have **received m**, we faint not; *1653*
Gal 6:16 to this rule, peace *be* on them, and **m**, *1656*
Eph 2: 4 But God, who is rich in **m**, for his great *1656*
Php 2:27 but God **had m** on him; and not on him *1653*
1Ti 1: 2 Grace, **m**, *and* peace, from God our Father *1656*
1:13 but I **obtained m**, because I did *it* *1653*
1:16 Howbeit for this cause I **obtained m**, *1653*
2Ti 1: 2 Grace, **m**, *and* peace, from God the Father *1656*
1:16 The Lord give **m** unto the house of *1656*
1:18 Lord grant unto him that *he* may find **m** *1656*
Tit 1: 4 Grace, **m**, *and* peace, from God the Father *1656*
3: 5 but according to his **m** he saved us, by *1656*
Heb 4:16 that we may obtain **m**, and find grace to *1656*
9: 5 cherubims of glory shadowing the **m seat**; *2435*
10:28 Moses' law died without **m** under two *3628*
Jas 2:13 For he shall have judgment **without m**, *448*
2:13 without mercy, that hath shewed no **m**; *1656*
2:13 and **m** rejoiceth against judgment. *1656*
3:17 full of **m** and good fruits, without partiality, *1656*
5:11 the Lord is very pitiful, and of **tender m**. *3629*
1Pe 1: 3 which according to his abundant **m** hath *1656*
2:10 which had not **obtained m**, but now have *1653*
2:10 obtained mercy, but now have **obtained m**. *1653*
2Jn 1: 3 Grace be with you, **m**, *and* peace, from God *1656*
Jude 1: 2 **M** unto you, and peace, and love, *1656*
1:21 looking for the **m** of our Lord Jesus Christ *1656*

MERCY'S (3) [MERCY]

Ps 6: 4 deliver my soul: O save me for thy **m** sake. 2617
31:16 upon thy servant: save me for thy **m** sake. 2617
44:26 for our help, and redeem us for thy **m** sake. 2617

MERED (2)
1Ch 4:17 *were,* Jether, and **M**, and Epher, and Jalon: 4778
4:18 the daughter of Pharaoh, which **M** took. 4778

MEREMOTH (6)
Ezr 8:33 the hand of **M** the son of Uriah the priest; 4822
10:36 Vaniah, **M**, Eliashib, 4822
Ne 3: 4 next unto them repaired **M** the son of 4822
3:21 After him repaired **M** the son of Urijah 4822
10: 5 Harim, **M**, Obadiah, 4822
12: 3 Shechaniah, Rehum, **M**, 4822

MERES (1)
Est 1:14 Tarshish, **M**, Marsena, *and* Memucan, 4825

MERETHAIM (1)
Jer 50:21 Go up against the land of **M**, *even* against 4850

MERIBAH (6) [MERIBAH-KADESH]
Ex 17: 7 **M**, because of the chiding of the children of 4809
Nu 20:13 This *is* the water of **M**; because 4809
20:24 rebelled against my word at the water of **M**. 4809
27:14 that *is* the water of **M** in Kadesh *in* 4809
Dt 33: 8 whom thou didst strive at the waters of **M**; 4809
Ps 81: 7 I proved thee at the waters of **M**. Selah. 4809

MERIBAH-KADESH (1) [MERIBAH, KADESH]
Dt 32:51 the children of Israel at the waters of **M**, 4809

MERIB-BAAL (4) [MEPHIBOSHETH]
1Ch 8:34 the son of Jonathan *was* **M**; and 4807
8:34 *was* Merib-baal; and **M** begat Micah. 4807
9:40 the son of Jonathan *was* **M**: and 4807
9:40 *was* Merib-baal: and **M** begat Micah. 4810

MERODACH (1)
Jer 50: 2 Bel is confounded, **M** is broken in pieces; 4781

MERODACH-BALADAN (1) [BERODACH-BALADAN]
Isa 39: 1 At that time **M**, the son of Baladan, king of 4757

MEROM (2)
Jos 11: 5 and pitched together at the waters of **M**, 4792
11: 7 against them by the waters of **M** suddenly; 4792

MERONOTHITE (2)
1Ch 27:30 and over the asses *was* Jehdeiah the **M**: 4824
Ne 3: 7 Jadon the **M**, the men of Gibeon, and of 4824

MEROZ (1)
Jdg 5:23 Curse ye **M**, said the angel of the LORD, 4789

MERRILY (1) [MERRY]
Est 5:14 go thou in **m** with the king unto 8056

MERRY (28) [MERRILY, MERRYHEARTED]
Ge 43:34 And they drunk, and were **m** with him. 7937
Jdg 9:27 trode *the grapes,* and made **m**, and 1974
16:25 when their hearts were **m**, that they said, 2896
19: 6 and tarry all night, and let thine heart be **m**. 3190
19: 9 lodge here, that thine heart may be **m**; 3190
19:22 *Now* as they were **making** their hearts **m**, 3190
Ru 3: 7 had eaten and drunk, and his heart was **m**, 3190
1Sa 25:36 Nabal's heart *was* **m** within him, for he *was* 2896
2Sa 13:28 Mark ye now when Amnon's heart is **m** 2896
1Ki 4:20 eating and drinking, and **making m**. 8056
21: 7 *and* eat bread, and let thine heart be **m**: 3190
2Ch 7:10 **m** in heart for the goodness that 2896
Est 1:10 when the heart of the king was **m** with 2896
Pr 15:13 A **m** heart maketh a cheerful countenance: 8056
15:15 *he that is* of a **m** heart *hath* a continual 2896
17:22 A **m** heart doeth good *like* a medicine: but 8056
Ecc 8:15 than to eat, and to drink, and to be **m**: 8055
9: 7 and drink thy wine with a **m** heart; 2896
10:19 for laughter, and wine **maketh m**: 2416+8055
Jer 30:19 and the voice of them that **make m**: 7832
31: 4 forth in the dances of them that **make m**. 7832
Lk 12:19 take thine ease, eat, drink, *and* be **m**. *2165*
15:23 and kill *it;* and let us eat, and be **m**: *2165*
15:24 and is found. And they began to be **m**. *2165*
15:29 that I might **make m** with my friends: *2165*
15:32 It was meet that *we* should **make m**, and *2165*
Jas 5:13 let him pray. Is any **m**? let him sing psalms. *2114*
Rev 11:10 and **make m**, and shall send gifts one to *2165*

MERRYHEARTED (1) [HEART, MERRY]
Isa 24: 7 vine languisheth, all the **m** do sigh. 3820+8056

MESECH (1)
Ps 120: 5 Woe is me, that I sojourn *in* **M**, *that* I dwell 4902

MESHA (4)
Ge 10:30 their dwelling was from **M**, as thou goest 4852
2Ki 3: 4 **M** king of Moab was a sheepmaster, and 4338
1Ch 2:42 brother of Jerahmeel *were,* **M** his firstborn, 4337
8: 9 and Zibia, and **M**, and Malcham, 4331

MESHACH (15)
Da 1: 7 to Mishael, of **M**; and to Azariah, 4335
2:49 and he set Shadrach, **M**, and Abed-nego, 4336
3:12 of Babylon, Shadrach, **M**, and Abed-nego; 4336
3:13 to bring Shadrach, **M**, and Abed-nego. 4336
3:14 *Is it* true, O Shadrach, **M**, and Abed-nego, 4336
3:16 **M**, and Abed-nego, answered and said to 4336
3:19 against Shadrach, **M**, and Abed-nego: 4336
3:20 **M**, and Abed-nego, *and* to cast *them* into 4336
3:22 that took up Shadrach, **M**, and Abed-nego. 4336
3:23 three men, Shadrach, **M**, and Abed-nego, 4336
3:26 and said, Shadrach, **M**, and Abed-nego, 4336
3:26 *hither.* Then Shadrach, **M**, and Abed-nego, 4336
3:28 **M**, and Abed-nego, who hath sent his 4336
3:29 **M**, and Abed-nego, shall be cut in pieces, 4336
3:30 **M**, and Abed-nego, in the province of 4336

MESHECH (8)
Ge 10: 2 and Javan, and Tubal, and **M**, and Tiras. 4902
1Ch 1: 5 and Javan, and Tubal, and **M**, and Tiras. 4902
1:17 and Uz, and Hul, and Gether, and **M**. 4902
Eze 27:13 Javan, Tubal, and **M**, they *were* thy 4902
32:26 There *is* **M**, Tubal, and all her multitude: 4902
38: 2 the chief prince of **M** and Tubal, and 4902
38: 3 O Gog, the chief prince of **M** and Tubal: 4902
39: 1 O Gog, the chief prince of **M** and Tubal: 4902

MESHELEMIAH (4)
1Ch 9:21 *And* Zechariah the son of **M** *was* porter of 4920
26: 1 Of the Korhites *was* **M** the son of Kore, 4920
26: 2 the sons of **M** *were,* Zechariah 4920
26: 9 **M** had sons and brethren, strong men, 4920

MESHEZABEEL (3)
Ne 3: 4 the son of Berechiah, the son of **M**. 4898
10:21 **M**, Zadok, Jaddua, 4898
11:24 Pethahiah the son of **M**, of the children of 4898

MESHEZABEL See MESHEZABEEL

MESHILLEMITH (1) [MESHILLEMOTH]
1Ch 9:12 the son of **M**, the son of Immer; 4921

MESHILLEMOTH (2) [MESHILLEMITH]
2Ch 28:12 Berechiah the son of **M**, and Jehizkiah 4919
Ne 11:13 of Ahasai, the son of **M**, the son of Immer, 4919

MESHOBAB (1)
1Ch 4:34 **M**, and Jamlech, and Joshah the son of 4877

MESHULLAM (25)
2Ki 22: 3 the son of **M**, the scribe, *to* the house of 4918
1Ch 3:19 **M**, and Hananiah, and Shelomith their 4918
5:13 **M**, and Sheba, and Jorai, and Jachan, and 4918
8:17 and **M**, and Hezeki, and Heber, 4918
9: 7 Sallu the son of **M**, the son of Hodaviah, 4918
9: 8 **M** the son of Shephathiah, the son of 4918
9:11 the son of **M**, the son of Zadok, the son of 4918
9:12 the son of Jahzerah, the son of **M**, the son 4918
2Ch 34:12 Zechariah and **M**, of the sons of 4918
Ezr 8:16 for Nathan, and for Zechariah, and for **M**, 4918
10:15 **M** and Shabbethai the Levite helped them. 4918
10:29 **M**, Malluch, and Adaiah, Jashub, and 4918
Ne 3: 4 next unto them repaired **M** the son of 4918
3: 6 son of Paseah, and **M** the son of Besodeiah; 4918
3:30 After him repaired **M** the son of Berechiah 4918
6:18 the daughter of **M** the son of Berechiah. 4918
8: 4 and Hashbadana, Zechariah, *and* **M**. 4918
10: 7 **M**, Abijah, Mijamin, 4918
10:20 Magpiash, **M**, Hezir, 4918
11: 7 Sallu the son of **M**, the son of Joed, the son 4918
11:11 the son of **M**, the son of Zadok, the son of 4918
12:13 Of Ezra, **M**; of Amariah, Jehohanan; 4918

Ne 12:16 Of Iddo, Zechariah; of Ginnethon, **M**; 4918
12:25 Bakbukiah, Obadiah, **M**, Talmon, Akkub, 4918
12:33 And Azariah, Ezra, and **M**, 4918

MESHULLEMETH (1)
2Ki 21:19 his mother's name *was* **M**, the daughter of 4922

MESOBAITE (1)
1Ch 11:47 Eliel, and Obed, and Jasiel the **M**. 4677

MESOPOTAMIA (7)
Ge 24:10 he arose, and went to **M**, unto the city of 763
Dt 23: 4 thee Balaam the son of Beor of Pethor of **M**, 763
Jdg 3: 8 the hand of Chushan-rishathaim king of **M**: 763
3:10 Chushan-rishathaim king of **M** into his hand; 758
1Ch 19: 6 hire them chariots and horsemen out of **M**, 763
Ac 2: 9 and the dwellers in **M**, and in Judea, and *3318*
7: 2 when he was in **M**, before he dwelt in *3318*

MESS (2) [MESSES]
Ge 43:34 Benjamin's **m** was five times so much as 4864
2Sa 11: 8 there followed him a **m** *of meat* from 4864

MESSAGE (7) [MESSENGER, MESSENGERS]
Jdg 3:20 Ehud said, I have a **m** from God unto thee. 1697
1Ki 20:12 when *Ben-hadad* heard this **m**, as he *was* 1697
Pr 26: 6 He that sendeth a **m** by the hand of a fool 1697
Hag 1:13 in the LORD'S **m** unto the people, 4400
Lk 19:14 hated him, and sent a **m** after him, saying, *4242*
1Jn 1: 5 then is the **m** which we have heard of him, *1860*
3:11 For this is the **m** that ye heard from *31*

MESSENGER (34) [MESSAGE]
Ge 50:16 they **sent a m** unto Joseph, saying, 6680
1Sa 4:17 the **m** answered and said, Israel is fled 1319
23:27 there came a **m** unto Saul, saying, 4397
2Sa 11:19 charged the **m**, saying, When thou hast 4397
11:22 So the **m** went, and came and 4397
11:23 the **m** said unto David, Surely the men 4397
11:25 David said unto the **m**, Thus shalt thou say 4397
15:13 there came a **m** to David, saying, 5046
1Ki 19: 2 Jezebel sent a **m** unto Elijah, saying, So let 4397
22:13 the **m** that was gone to call Micaiah spake 4397
2Ki 5:10 Elisha sent a **m** unto him, saying, Go and 4397
6:32 ere the **m** came to him, he said to 4397
6:32 look, when the **m** cometh, shut the door, 4397
6:33 behold, the **m** came down unto him: 4397
9:18 The **m** came to them, but he cometh not 4397
10: 8 there came a **m**, and told him, saying, 4397
2Ch 18:12 the **m** that went to call Micaiah spake to 4397
Job 1:14 there came a **m** unto Job, and said, 4397
33:23 If there be a **m** with him, an interpreter, 4397
Pr 13:17 A wicked **m** falleth into mischief: but 4397
17:11 a cruel **m** shall be sent against him. 4397
25:13 *so is* a faithful **m** to them that send him: 6735
Isa 42:19 or deaf, as my **m** *that* I sent? who *is* blind 4397
Jer 51:31 meet another, and one **m** to meet another, 5046
Eze 23:40 to come from far, unto whom a **m** *was* sent; 4397
Hag 1:13 spake Haggai the LORD'S **m** in 4397
Mal 2: 7 for he *is* the **m** of the LORD of hosts. 4397
3: 1 I *will* send my **m**, and he shall prepare 4397
3: 1 even the **m** of the covenant, whom ye 4397
Mt 11:10 Behold, I send my **m** before thy face, *32*
Mk 1: 2 Behold, I send my **m** before thy face, *32*
Lk 7:27 Behold, I send my **m** before thy face, *32*
2Co 12: 7 the **m** of Satan to buffet me, lest I should be *32*
Php 2:25 but your **m**, and he that ministered to my *652*

MESSENGERS (79) [MESSAGE]
Ge 32: 3 Jacob sent **m** before him to Esau his 4397
32: 6 the **m** returned to Jacob, saying, We came 4397
Nu 20:14 Moses sent **m** from Kadesh unto the king 4397
21:21 Israel sent **m** unto Sihon king of 4397
22: 5 He sent **m** therefore unto Balaam the son of 4397
24:12 Spake I not also to thy **m** which thou 4397
Dt 2:26 I sent **m** out of the wilderness of Kedemoth 4397
Jos 6:17 because she hid the **m** that we sent. 4397
6:25 because she hid the **m**, which Joshua sent 4397
7:22 So Joshua sent **m**, and they ran unto 4397
Jdg 6:35 he sent **m** throughout all Manasseh; who 4397
6:35 he sent **m** unto Asher, and unto Zebulun, 4397
7:24 Gideon sent **m** throughout all mount 4397
9:31 he sent **m** unto Abimelech privily, saying, 4397
11:12 Jephthah sent **m** unto the king of 4397
11:13 Ammon answered unto the **m** of Jephthah, 4397
11:14 Jephthah sent **m** again unto the king of 4397
11:17 Israel sent **m** unto the king of Edom, 4397
11:19 Israel sent **m** unto Sihon king of 4397
1Sa 6:21 they sent **m** to the inhabitants of 4397
11: 3 that we may send **m** unto all the coasts of 4397
11: 4 came the **m** *to* Gibeah of Saul, and told 4397
11: 7 all the coasts of Israel by the hands of **m**, 4397
11: 9 they said unto the **m** that came, Thus shall 4397
11: 9 the **m** came and shewed *it* to the men of 4397
16:19 Wherefore Saul sent **m** unto Jesse, and 4397
19:11 Saul also sent **m** unto David's house, 4397
19:14 when Saul sent **m** to take David, she said, 4397
19:15 Saul sent the **m** *again* to see David, saying, 4397
19:16 when the **m** were come in, behold *there* 4397
19:20 Saul sent **m** to take David: and when they 4397
19:20 the spirit of God was upon the **m** of Saul, 4397
19:21 he sent other **m**, and they prophesied 4397
19:21 Saul sent **m** again the third time, and 4397
25:14 David sent **m** out of the wilderness to 4397
25:42 she went after the **m** of David, and 4397
2Sa 2: 5 David sent **m** unto the men of 4397
3:12 Abner sent **m** to David on his behalf, 4397
3:14 David sent **m** to Ish-bosheth Saul's son, 4397
3:26 out from David, he sent **m** after Abner, 4397
5:11 Hiram king of Tyre sent **m** to David, and 4397
11: 4 David sent **m**, and took her; and she came 4397
12:27 Joab sent **m** to David, and said, I have 4397
1Ki 20: 2 he sent **m** to Ahab king of Israel into 4397
20: 5 the **m** came again, and said, Thus speaketh 4397
20: 9 Wherefore he said unto the **m** of 4397
20: 9 the **m** departed, and brought him word 4397
2Ki 1: 2 he sent **m**, and said unto them, Go, 4397
1: 3 go up to meet the **m** of the king of Samaria, 4397
1: 5 when the **m** turned back unto him, he said 4397
1:16 Forasmuch as thou hast sent **m** to inquire of 4397
7:15 And the **m** returned, and told the king. 4397
14: 8 Amaziah sent **m** to Jehoash, the son of 4397
16: 7 So Ahaz sent **m** to Tiglath-pileser king of 4397
17: 4 for he had sent **m** to So king of Egypt, and 4397
19: 9 he sent **m** again unto Hezekiah, saying, 4397
19:14 received the letter of the hand of the **m**, 4397
19:23 By thy **m** thou hast reproached the Lord, 4397
1Ch 14: 1 Now Hiram king of Tyre sent **m** to David, 4397
19: 2 David sent **m** to comfort him concerning 4397
19:16 they sent **m**, and drew forth the Syrians that 4397
2Ch 36:15 God of their fathers sent to them by his **m**, 4397
36:16 they mocked the **m** of God, and 4397
Ne 6: 3 I sent **m** unto them, saying, I *am* doing a 4397
Pr 16:14 The wrath of a king *is as* **m** of death: but 4397
Isa 14:32 shall *one* then answer the **m** of the nation? 4397
18: 2 *saying*, Go, ye swift **m**, to a nation 4397
37: 9 when he heard *it*, he sent **m** to Hezekiah, 4397
37:14 received the letter from the hand of the **m**, 4397
44:26 and performeth the counsel of his **m**; 4397
57: 9 didst send thy **m** far off, and didst debase 6735
Jer 27: 3 by the hand of the **m** which come *to* 4397
Eze 23:16 and sent **m** unto them into Chaldea. 4397
30: 9 In that day shall **m** go forth from me in 4397
Na 2:13 the voice of thy **m** shall no more be heard. 4397
Lk 7:24 And when the **m** of John were departed, *32*
9:52 And sent **m** before his face: and they went, *32*
2Co 8:23 our brethren *be inquired of, they are* the **m** *652*
Jas 2:25 when she had received the **m**, and had sent *32*

MESSES (1) [MESS]
Ge 43:34 *and sent* **m** unto them from before him: 4864

MESSIAH (2) [MESSIAS]
Da 9:25 to build Jerusalem unto the **M** the Prince 4899
9:26 and two weeks shall **M** be cut off, 4899

MESSIAS (2) [MESSIAH]
Jn 1:41 unto him, We have found the **M**, which is, *3323*
4:25 I know that **M** cometh, which is called *3323*

MET (45) [MEET]
Ge 32: 1 on his way, and the angels of God **m** him. 6293
33: 8 meanest thou by all this drove which I **m**? 6298
Ex 3:18 The LORD God of the Hebrews hath **m** 7136
4:24 that the LORD **m** him, and sought to kill 6298
4:27 **m** him in the mount of God, and 6298
5: 3 The God of the Hebrews hath **m** with us: 7122
5:20 they **m** Moses and Aaron, who stood in 6293
Nu 23: 4 God **m** Balaam: and he said unto him, I 7136

Nu 23:16 the LORD **m** Balaam, and put a word in 7136
Dt 23: 4 Because they **m** you not with bread and 6923
25:18 How he **m** thee by the way, and smote 7136
Jos 11: 5 when all these kings were **m together**, 3259
17:10 they **m together** in Asher on the north, and 6293
1Sa 10:10 behold, a company of prophets **m** him; 7125
25:20 came down against her; and she **m** them. 6298
2Sa 2:13 and **m** together by the pool of Gibeon: 6298
16: 1 Ziba the servant of Mephibosheth **m** him, 7125
18: 9 Absalom **m** the servants of David. 7122
1Ki 13:24 a lion **m** him by the way, and slew him: 4672
18: 7 was in the way, behold Elijah **m** him: 7125
2Ki 9:21 **m** him in the portion of Naboth 4672
10:13 Jehu **m** with the brethren of Ahaziah king 4672
Ne 13: 2 Because they **m** not the children of Israel 6923
Ps 85:10 Mercy and truth are **m together**; 6298
Pr 7:10 there **m** him a woman *with* the attire of a 7125
Jer 41: 6 it came to pass, as he **m** them, he said unto 6298
Am 5:19 man did flee from a lion, and a bear **m** him; 6293
Mt 8:28 there **m** him two possessed with devils, *5221*
28: 9 behold, Jesus **m** them, saying, *All* hail. *528*
Mk 5: 2 immediately there **m** him out of the tombs a *528*
11: 4 door without in a place where two ways **m**; *296*
Lk 8:27 there **m** him out of the city a certain man, *5221*
9:37 down from the hill, much people **m** him. *4876*
17:12 there **m** him ten men *that were* lepers, *528*
Jn 4:51 his servants **m** him, and told *him,* saying, *528*
11:20 that Jesus was coming, **went and m** him: *5221*
11:30 but was in *that* place where Martha **m** him. *5221*
12:18 For this cause the people also **m** him, *5221*
Ac 10:25 Cornelius **m** him, and fell down at *his* feet, *4876*
16:16 possessed with a spirit of divination **m** us, *528*
17:17 in the market daily with them that **m with** *3909*
20:14 And when he **m with** us at Assos, we took *4820*
27:41 And falling into a place **where two seas m**, *1337*
Heb 7: 1 who **m** Abraham returning from *4876*
7:10 of his father, when Melchisedec **m** him. *4876*

METALWORKER See COPPERSMITH

METE (6) [METED]
Ex 16:18 when they did **m** *it* with an omer, he that 4058
Ps 60: 6 and **m out** the valley of Succoth. 4058
108: 7 and **m out** the valley of Succoth. 4058
Mt 7: 2 and with what measure ye **m**, it shall be *3354*
Mk 4:24 with what measure ye **m**, it shall be *3354*
Lk 6:38 For with the same measure that ye **m** withal *3354*

METED (3) [METE]
Isa 18: 2 a nation **m out** and trodden down, 6978+6978
18: 7 a nation **m out** and trodden under 6978+6978
40:12 **m out** heaven with the span, and 8505

METEYARD (1)
Lev 19:35 in **m**, in weight, or in measure. 4060

METHEG-AMMAH (1) [AMMAH]
2Sa 8: 1 David took **M** out of the hand of 4964

METHUSAEL (2)
Ge 4:18 Mehujael begat **M**: and Methusael begat 4967
4:18 begat Methusael: and **M** begat Lamech. 4967

METHUSELAH (6) [MATHUSALA]
Ge 5:21 lived sixty and five years, and begat **M**: 4968
5:22 Enoch walked with God after he begat **M** 4968
5:25 **M** lived an hundred eighty and seven years, 4968
5:26 **M** lived after he begat Lamech seven 4968
5:27 all the days of **M** were nine hundred sixty 4968
1Ch 1: 3 Henoch, **M**, Lamech, 4968

METHUSHAEL See METHUSAEL

MEUNIM (1) [MEHUNIM]
Ne 7:52 The children of Besai, the children of **M**, 4586

MEUNITES See MEHUNIMS

MEZAHAB (2)
Ge 36:39 the daughter of Matred, the daughter of **M**. 4314
1Ch 1:50 the daughter of Matred, the daughter of **M**. 4314

MEZOBAITE See MESOBAITE

MIAMIN (2)
Ezr 10:25 **M**, and Eleazar, and Malchijah, and 4326
Ne 12: 5 **M**, Maadiah, Bilgah, 4326

MIBHAR (1)
1Ch 11:38 brother of Nathan, **M** the son of Haggeri, 4006

MIBSAM (3)
Ge 25:13 Nebajoth; and Kedar, and Adbeel, and **M**, 4017
1Ch 1:29 Nebajoth; then Kedar, and Adbeel, and **M**, 4017
4:25 his son, **M** his son, Mishma his son. 4017

MIBZAR (2)
Ge 36:42 Duke Kenaz, duke Teman, duke **M**, 4014
1Ch 1:53 Duke Kenaz, duke Teman, duke **M**, 4014

MICAH (27) [MICAH'S, MICHA]
Jdg 17: 1 of mount Ephraim, whose name *was* **M**. 4321
17: 4 and they were in the house of **M**. 4321
17: 5 the man **M** had a house of gods, and 4318
17: 8 came *to* mount Ephraim to the house of **M**, 4318
17: 9 **M** said unto him, Whence comest thou? 4318
17:10 **M** said unto him, Dwell with me, and 4318
17:12 **M** consecrated the Levite; and the young 4318
17:12 his priest, and was in the house of **M**. 4318
17:13 said **M**, Now know I that the LORD will 4318
18: 2 to the house of **M**, they lodged there. 4318
18: 3 When they *were* by the house of **M**, they 4318
18: 4 Thus and thus dealeth **M** with me, and 4318
18:13 and came unto the house of **M**. 4318
18:15 *even unto* the house of **M**, and saluted him. 4318
18:22 they were a good way from the house of **M**, 4318
18:23 and said unto **M**, What aileth thee, 4318
18:26 when **M** saw that they *were* too strong for 4318
18:27 they took *the things* which **M** had made, 4318
1Ch 5: 5 **M** his son, Reaia his son, Baal his son, 4318
8:34 *was* Merib-baal; and Merib-baal begat **M**. 4318
8:35 the sons of **M** *were,* Pithon, and Melech, 4318
9:15 and Galal, and Mattaniah the son of **M**, 4316
9:40 *was* Merib-baal: and Merib-baal begat **M**. 4318
9:41 the sons of **M** *were,* Pithon, and Melech, 4318
2Ch 34:20 Abdon the son of **M**, and Shaphan 4318
Jer 26:18 **M** the Morasthite prophesied in the days of 4318
Mic 1: 1 The word of the LORD that came to **M** 4318

MICAH'S (3) [MICAH]
Jdg 18:18 these went *into* **M** house, and fetched 4318
18:22 the men that *were* in the houses near to **M** 4318
18:31 they set them up **M** graven image, which he 4318

MICAIAH (18)
1Ki 22: 8 *There is* yet one man, **M** the son of Imlah, 4321
22: 9 and said, Hasten *hither* **M** the son of Imlah. 4321
22:13 the messenger that was gone to call **M** 4321
22:14 **M** said, *As* the LORD liveth, what 4321
22:15 the king said unto him, **M**, shall we go 4321
22:24 and smote **M** on the cheek, and said, 4321
22:25 **M** said, Behold, thou shalt see in that day, 4321
22:26 Take **M**, and carry him back unto Amon 4321
22:28 **M** said, If thou return at all in peace, 4321
2Ch 18: 7 the same *is* **M** the son of Imla. 4321
18: 8 and said, Fetch quickly **M** the son of Imla. 4321
18:12 the messenger that went to call **M** spake to 4321
18:13 **M** said, *As* the LORD liveth, even what 4321
18:14 to the king, the king said unto him, **M**, 4318
18:23 and smote **M** upon the cheek, and said, 4321
18:24 **M** said, Behold, thou shalt see on that day 4321
18:25 Take ye **M**, and carry him back to Amon 4321
18:27 **M** said, If thou certainly return in peace, 4321

MICE (4) [MOUSE]
1Sa 6: 4 Five golden emerods, and five golden **m**, 5909
6: 5 and images of your **m** that mar the land; 5909
6:11 the coffer with the **m** of gold and 5909
6:18 the golden **m**, *according to* the number of 5909

MICHA (4) [MICAH]
2Sa 9:12 had a young son, whose name *was* **M**. 4316
Ne 10:11 **M**, Rehob, Hashabiah, 4316
11:17 Mattaniah the son of **M**, the son of Zabdi, 4316
11:22 the son of Mattaniah, the son of **M**. 4316

MICHAEL (15)
Nu 13:13 Of the tribe of Asher, Sethur the son of **M**. 4317
1Ch 5:13 of the house of their fathers *were,* **M**, 4317
5:14 of Jaroah, the son of Gilead, the son of **M**, 4317
6:40 The son of **M**, the son of Baaseiah, the son 4317

1Ch 7: 3 **M**, and Obadiah, and Joel, Ishiah, five: 4317
8:16 **M**, and Ispah, and Joha, the sons of Beriah; 4317
12:20 and **M**, and Jozabad, and Elihu, and Zilthai, 4317
27:18 of David: of Issachar, Omri the son of **M**: 4317
2Ch 21: 2 and Azariah, and **M**, and Shephatiah: 4317
Ezr 8: 8 Zebadiah the son of **M**, and with him 4317
Da 10:13 lo, **M**, one of the chief princes, came to 4317
10:21 with me in these *things*, but **M** your prince. 4317
12: 1 at that time shall **M** stand up, the great 4317
Jude 1: 9 Yet **M** the archangel, when contending *3413*
Rev 12: 7 **M** and his angels fought against the dragon; *3413*

MICHAH (4)
1Ch 23:20 **M** the first, and Jesiah the second. 4318
24:24 *Of* the sons of Uzziel; **M**: of the sons of 4318
24:24 Michah: of the sons of **M**; Shamir. 4318
24:25 The brother of **M** *was* Isshiah: of the sons 4318

MICHAIAH (7)
2Ki 22:12 Achbor the son of **M**, and Shaphan 4320
2Ch 13: 2 His mother's name also *was* **M** 4322
17: 7 to Zechariah, and to Nethaneel, and to **M**, 4322
Ne 12:35 the son of **M**, the son of Zaccur, the son of 4320
12:41 Eliakim, Maaseiah, Miniamin, **M**, Elioenai, 4320
Jer 36:11 When **M** the son of Gemariah, the son of 4321
36:13 **M** declared unto them all the words that he 4321

MICHAL (18)
1Sa 14:49 and the name of the younger **M**: 4324
18:20 **M** Saul's daughter loved David: and 4324
18:27 And Saul gave him **M** his daughter to wife. 4324
18:28 and *that* **M** Saul's daughter loved him. 4324
19:11 **M** David's wife told him, saying, If thou 4324
19:12 So **M** let David down through a window: 4324
19:13 **M** took an image, and laid *it* in the bed, 4324
19:17 Saul said unto **M**, Why hast thou deceived 4324
19:17 **M** answered Saul, He said unto me, Let me 4324
25:44 Saul had given **M** his daughter, 4324
2Sa 3:13 except thou first bring **M** Saul's daughter, 4324
3:14 Saul's son, saying, Deliver *me* my wife **M**, 4324
6:16 **M** Saul's daughter looked through a 4324
6:20 **M** the daughter of Saul came out to meet 4324
6:21 David said unto **M**, *It was* before 4324
6:23 Therefore **M** the daughter of Saul had no 4324
21: 8 the five sons of **M** the daughter of Saul, 4324
1Ch 15:29 that **M** the daughter of Saul looking out at a 4324

MICHMAS (2) [MICHMASH]
Ezr 2:27 The men of **M**, an hundred twenty and two. 4363
Ne 7:31 The men of **M**, an hundred and twenty and 4363

MICHMASH (9) [MICHMAS]
1Sa 13: 2 *whereof* two thousand were with Saul in **M** 4363
13: 5 they came up, and pitched in **M**, 4363
13:11 gathered themselves together *at* **M**; 4363
13:16 but the Philistines encamped in **M**. 4363
13:23 Philistines went out to the passage of **M**. 4363
14: 5 one *was* situate northward over against **M**, 4363
14:31 they smote the Philistines that day from **M** 4363
Ne 11:31 also of Benjamin from Geba *dwelt at* **M**, 4363
Isa 10:28 at **M** he hath laid up his carriages: 4363

MICHMETHAH (2)
Jos 16: 6 the border went out toward the sea *to* **M** on 4366
17: 7 coast of Manasseh was from Asher *to* **M**, 4366

MICHRI (1)
1Ch 9: 8 the son of **M**, and Meshullam the son of 4381

MICHTAM (6)
Ps 16: T **M** of David. 4387
56: T **M** of David, when the Philistines took him 4387
57: T chief Musician, Al-taschith, **M** of David, 4387
58: T chief Musician, Al-taschith, **M** of David. 4387
59: T chief Musician, Al-taschith, **M** of David; 4387
60: T upon Shushan-eduth, **M** of David, to teach; 4387

MICMASH See MICHMAS; MICHMASH

MICMETHATH See MICHMETHAH

MICRI See MICHRI

MIDDAY (3) [DAY, MIDDLE]
1Ki 18:29 when **m** was past, and they prophesied until 6672
Ne 8: 3 from the morning until **m**, 3117+4276+1886.1
Ac 26:13 **At m**, O king, I saw in the way a *2250+3319*

MIDDIN (1)
Jos 15:61 Beth-arabah, **M**, and Secacah, 4081

MIDDLE (18) [MIDDAY, MIDDLEMOST, MIDNIGHT, MIDST]
Ex 26:28 the **m** bar in the midst of the boards shall 8484
36:33 he made the **m** bar to shoot through 8484
Jos 12: 2 *from* the **m** of the river, and *from* half 8432
Jdg 7:19 the camp *in* the beginning of the **m** watch; 8484
9:37 See there come people down by the **m** of 2872
16:29 Samson took hold of the two **m** pillars 8432
1Sa 25:29 them shall he sling out *as out* of the **m** of a 3709
2Sa 10: 4 cut off their garments in the **m**, *even* to 2677
1Ki 6: 6 the **m** *was* six cubits broad, and the third 8484
6: 8 The door for the **m** chamber *was* in 8484
6: 8 they went up with winding stairs into the **m** 8484
6: 8 and out of the **m** into the third. 8484
8:64 The same day did the king hallow the **m** of 8432
2Ki 20: 4 afore Isaiah was gone out *into* the **m** court, 8484
2Ch 7: 7 Moreover Solomon hallowed the **m** of 8432
Jer 39: 3 and sat in the **m** gate, *even* Nergal-sharezer, 8432
Eze 1:16 their work *was* as it were a wheel in the **m** 8432
Eph 2:14 hath broken down the **m wall** of partition *3320*

MIDDLEMOST (2) [MIDDLE]
Eze 42: 5 the lower, and than the **m** of the building. 8484
42: 6 than the lowest and the **m** from the ground. 8484

MIDIAN (39) [MADIAN, MIDIANITE, MIDIANITES, MIDIANITISH]
Ge 25: 2 and Medan, and **M**, and Ishbak, and Shuah. 4080
25: 4 the sons of **M**; Ephah, and Epher, and 4080
36:35 who smote **M** in the field of Moab, 4080
Ex 2:15 of Pharaoh, and dwelt in the land of **M**: 4080
2:16 Now the priest of **M** had seven daughters: 4080
3: 1 of Jethro his father in law, the priest of **M**: 4080
4:19 the LORD said unto Moses in **M**, Go, 4080
18: 1 When Jethro, the priest of **M**, Moses' father 4080
Nu 22: 4 Moab said unto the elders of **M**, Now shall 4080
22: 7 the elders of **M** departed with the rewards 4080
25:15 over a people, *and* of a chief house in **M**. 4080
25:18 the daughter of a prince of **M**, their sister, 4080
31: 3 and avenge the LORD of **M**. 4080
31: 8 they slew the kings of **M**, beside *the rest of* 4080
31: 8 and Hur, and Reba, five kings of **M**: 4080
31: 9 of Israel took *all* the women of **M** captives, 4080
Jos 13:21 whom Moses smote with the princes of **M**, 4080
Jdg 6: 1 them into the hand of **M** seven years. 4080
6: 2 the hand of **M** prevailed against Israel: *and* 4080
7: 8 the host of **M** was beneath him in 4080
7:13 of barley bread tumbled into the host of **M**, 4080
7:14 *for* into his hand hath God delivered **M**, 4080
7:15 delivered into your hand the host of **M**. 4080
7:25 pursued **M**, and brought the heads of Oreb 4080
8: 3 delivered into your hands the princes of **M**, 4080
8: 5 after Zebah and Zalmunna, kings of **M**. 4080
8:12 took the two kings of **M**, Zebah and 4080
8:22 thou hast delivered us from the hand of **M**. 4080
8:26 purple raiment that *was* on the kings of **M**, 4080
8:28 Thus was **M** subdued before the children of 4080
9:17 and delivered you out of the hand of **M**: 4080
1Ki 11:18 they arose out of **M**, and came *to* Paran: 4080
1Ch 1:32 and Medan, and **M**, and Ishbak, and Shuah. 4080
1:33 the sons of **M**; Ephah, and Epher, and 4080
1:46 which smote **M** in the field of Moab, 4080
Isa 9: 4 the rod of his oppressor, as *in* the day of **M**. 4080
10:26 to the slaughter of **M** at the rock Oreb: 4080
60: 6 the dromedaries of **M** and Ephah; 4080
Hab 3: 7 the curtains of the land of **M** did tremble. 4080

MIDIANITE (1) [MIDIAN]
Nu 10:29 the son of Raguel the **M**, Moses' father in 4084

MIDIANITES (23) [MIDIAN]
Ge 37:28 there passed by **M** merchantmen; and 4084
Nu 25:17 Vex the **M**, and smite them: 4084
31: 2 Avenge the children of Israel of the **M**: 4084
31: 3 let them go against the **M**, and avenge 4080
31: 7 they warred against the **M**, as the LORD 4080
Jdg 6: 2 of the **M** the children of Israel made them 4080
6: 3 that the **M** came up, and the Amalekites, 4080
6: 6 greatly impoverished because of the **M**; 4080
6: 7 cried unto the LORD because of the **M**, 4080

Jdg 6:11 by the winepress, to hide *it* from the **M**. 4080
6:13 and delivered us into the hands of the **M**. 4080
6:14 shalt save Israel from the hand of the **M**: 4080
6:16 and thou shalt smite the **M** as one man. 4080
6:33 all the **M** and the Amalekites and 4080
7: 1 that the host of the **M** were on the north 4080
7: 2 many for me to give the **M** into their hands, 4080
7: 7 and deliver the **M** into thine hand: 4080
7:12 the **M** and the Amalekites and all 4080
7:23 of all Manasseh, and pursued after the **M**. 4080
7:24 Come down against the **M**, and take before 4080
7:25 they took two princes of the **M**, Oreb and 4080
8: 1 when thou wentest to fight with the **M**? 4080
Ps 83: 9 Do unto them as *unto* the **M**; as *to* Sisera, 4080

MIDIANITISH (3) [MIDIAN]
Nu 25: 6 brought unto his brethren a **M** *woman* in 4084
25:14 *even* that was slain with the **M woman**, 4084
25:15 the name of the **M** woman that was slain 4084

MIDNIGHT (14) [MIDDLE, NIGHT]
Ex 11: 4 About **m** will I go out into 2676+3915+1886.1
12:29 that at **m** the LORD smote 2677+3915+1886.1
Jdg 16: 3 Samson lay till **m**, and 2677+3915+1886.1
16: 3 arose at **m**, and took 2677+3915+1886.1
Ru 3: 8 it came to pass at **m**, that 2677+3915+1886.1
1Ki 3:20 she rose at **m**, and took my 3915+8432+1886.1
Job 34:20 the people shall be troubled **at m**, 2676+3915
Ps 119:62 **At m** I will rise to give thanks unto 2676+3915
Mt 25: 6 And **at m** there was a cry made, *3319+3571*
Mk 13:35 or **at m**, or at the cockcrowing, or in *3317*
Lk 11: 5 and shall go unto him at **m**, and say unto *3317*
Ac 16:25 And at **m** Paul and Silas prayed, and *3317*
20: 7 and continued *his* speech until **m**. *3317*
27:27 about **m** the shipmen deemed *3319+3571+3588*

MIDST (364) [MIDDLE] See Index

MIDWIFE (3) [MIDWIVES]
Ge 35:17 that the **m** said unto her, Fear not; 3205
38:28 the **m** took and bound upon his hand a 3205
Ex 1:16 When ye **do the office of a m** to 3205

MIDWIVES (7) [MIDWIFE]
Ex 1:15 the king of Egypt spake to the Hebrew **m**, 3205
1:17 the **m** feared God, and did not as the king 3205
1:18 And the king of Egypt called for the **m**, and 3205
1:19 the **m** said unto Pharaoh, Because 3205
1:19 are delivered ere the **m** come in unto them. 3205
1:20 Therefore God dealt well with the **m**: and 3205
1:21 it came to pass, because the **m** feared God, 3205

MIGDAL-EL (1)
Jos 19:38 **M**, Horem, and Beth-anath, and 4027

MIGDAL-GAD (1)
Jos 15:37 Zenan, and Hadashah, and **M**, 4028

MIGDOL (4)
Ex 14: 2 between **M** and the sea, over against 4024
Nu 33: 7 and they pitched before **M**. 4024
Jer 44: 1 which dwell at **M**, and at Tahpanhes, and 4024
46:14 publish in **M**, and publish in Noph and 4024

MIGHT (475) [ALMIGHTY, MIGHTEST, MIGHTIER, MIGHTIES, MIGHTIEST, MIGHTILY, MIGHTY] See Index

MIGHTEST (19) [MIGHT] See Index

MIGHTIER (13) [MIGHT]
Ge 26:16 Go from us; for thou art much **m** than we. 6105
Ex 1: 9 children of Israel *are* moe and **m** than we: 6099
Nu 14:12 of thee a greater nation and **m** than they. 6099
Dt 4:38 and **m** than thou *art*, to bring thee in, 6099
7: 1 seven nations greater and **m** than thou; 6099
9: 1 possess nations greater and **m** than thyself, 6099
9:14 I will make of thee a nation **m** and 6099
11:23 greater nations and **m** than yourselves. 6099
Ps 93: 4 The LORD on high *is* **m** than the noise of 117
Ecc 6:10 neither may he contend with him that *is* **m** 8623
Mt 3:11 but he that cometh after me is **m than** I, *2478*
Mk 1: 7 There cometh one **m than** I after me, *2478*
Lk 3:16 but one **m than** I cometh, the latchet of *2478*

MIGHTIES (2) [MIGHT]
1Ch 11:12 the Ahohite, who *was one* of the three **m**. 1368
11:24 and had the name among the three **m**. 1368

MIGHTIEST (1) [MIGHT]
1Ch 11:19 not drink it. These *things* did *these* three **m**. 1368

MIGHTILY (11) [MIGHT]
Dt 6: 3 well with thee, and that ye may increase **m**, 3966
Jdg 4: 3 twenty years he **m** oppressed 2393+871.1
14: 6 the spirit of the LORD **came m** upon him, 6743
15:14 the spirit of the LORD **came m** upon him, 6743
Jer 25:30 he shall **m roar** upon his habitation; 7580+7580
Jnh 3: 8 with sackcloth, and cry **m** unto God: 2394+871.1
Na 2: 1 make *thy* loins strong, fortify *thy* power **m**. 3966
Ac 18:28 For he **m** convinced the Jews, *and* *2159*
19:20 So **m** grew the word of God and *2596+2904*
Col 1:29 to his working, which worketh in me **m**. *1411*
Rev 18: 2 And he cried **m** with a strong voice, saying, *2479*

MIGHTY (284) [MIGHT]
Ge 6: 4 the same *became* **m** *men* which *were* of 1368
10: 8 he began to be a **m** *one* in the earth. 1368
10: 9 He was a **m** hunter before the LORD: 1368
10: 9 *Even* as Nimrod the **m** hunter before 1368
18:18 shall surely become a great and **m** nation, 6099
23: 6 thou *art* a **m** prince among us: in the choice 430
49:24 strong by the hands of the **m** *God* of Jacob; 46
Ex 1: 7 and multiplied, and **waxed** exceeding **m**; 6105
1:20 the people multiplied, and **waxed** very **m**. 6105
3:19 will not let you go, no, not by a **m** hand. 2389
9:28 that there be no *more* **m** thunderings and 430
10:19 the LORD turned a **m** strong west wind, 3966
15:10 they sank as lead in the **m** waters. 117
15:15 the **m men** of Moab, trembling shall take 352
32:11 with great power, and with a **m** hand? 2389
Lev 19:15 the poor, nor honour the person of the **m**: 1419
Nu 22: 6 me this people; for they *are* too **m** for me: 6099
Dt 3:24 thy servant thy greatness, and thy **m** hand: 2389
4:34 by a **m** hand, and by a stretched out arm, 2389
4:37 brought thee out in his sight with his **m** 1419
5:15 brought thee out thence through a **m** hand 2389
6:21 brought us out of Egypt with a **m** hand: 2389
7: 8 hath the LORD brought you out with a **m** 2389
7:19 and the **m** hand, and the stretched out arm, 2389
7:21 God *is* among you, a **m** God and terrible. 1419
7:23 shall destroy them *with* a **m** destruction, 1419
9:26 brought forth out of Egypt with a **m** hand. 2389
9:29 which thou broughtest out by thy **m** power 1419
10:17 of lords, a great God, a **m**, and a terrible, 1368
11: 2 his **m** hand, and his stretched out arm, 2389
26: 5 there a nation, great, **m**, and populous: 6099
26: 8 us forth out of Egypt with a **m** hand, 2389
34:12 in all *that* **m** hand, and in all the great terror 2389
Jos 1:14 all the **m** *men* of valour, and help them; 1368
4:24 know the hand of the LORD, that it *is* **m**: 2389
6: 2 the king thereof, *and* the **m** *men* of valour. 1368
8: 3 Joshua chose out thirty thousand **m** *men* of 1368
10: 2 than Ai, and all the men thereof *were* **m**. 1368
10: 7 war with him, and all the **m** *men* of valour. 1368
Jdg 5:13 made me have dominion over the **m**. 1368
5:22 the pransings, the pransings of their **m** *ones*. 47
5:23 to the help of the LORD against the **m**. 1368
6:12 LORD *is* with thee, thou **m** *man* of valour. 1368
11: 1 Now Jephthah the Gileadite was a **m** *man* 1368
Ru 2: 1 a **m** man of wealth, of the family of 1368
1Sa 2: 4 The bows of the **m** *men are* broken, and 1368
4: 8 deliver us out of the hand of these **m** Gods? 117
9: 1 of Aphiah, a Benjamite, a **m** *man* of power. 1368
16:18 and a **m** valiant *man*, and a man of war, and 1368
2Sa 1:19 upon thy high places: how are the **m** fallen! 1368
1:21 for there the shield of the **m** is vilely cast 1368
1:22 the blood of the slain, from the fat of the **m**, 1368
1:25 How are the **m** fallen in the midst of 1368
1:27 How are the **m** fallen, and the weapons of 1368
10: 7 he sent Joab, and all the host *of* the **m** *men*. 1368
16: 6 all the **m** *men were* on his right hand and 1368
17: 8 that they *be* **m** *men*, and they *be* chafed in 1368
17:10 for all Israel knoweth that thy father *is* a **m** 1368
20: 7 all the **m** *men*: and they went out of 1368
23: 8 These *be* the names of the **m** *men* whom 1368
23: 9 *one* of the three **m** *men* with David, 1368
23:16 the three **m** *men* brake through the host of 1368
23:17 These *things* did *these* three **m** *men*. 1368
23:22 and had the name among three **m** *men*. 1368
1Ki 1: 8 and the **m** *men* which *belonged* to David, 1368

1Ki	1:10	and the **m** *men,* and Solomon his brother,	1368
	11:28	the man Jeroboam *was* a **m** *man* of valour:	1368
2Ki	5: 1	he was also a **m** *man* in valour, *but he was*	1368
	15:20	*even* of all the **m** *men* of wealth, of each	1368
	24:14	all the princes, and all the **m** *men* of valour,	1368
	24:15	and his officers, and the **m** of the land,	352
1Ch	1:10	he began to be **m** upon the earth.	1368
	5:24	Hodaviah, and Jahdiel, **m** *men* of valour,	1368
	7: 7	the house of *their* fathers, **m** *men* of valour;	1368
	7: 9	**m** *men* of valour, *was* twenty thousand and	1368
	7:11	**m** *men* of valour, *were* seventeen thousand	1368
	7:40	choice *and* **m** *men* of valour, chief of	1368
	8:40	the sons of Ulam were **m** men of valour,	1368
	11:10	These also *are* the chief of the **m** *men*	1368
	11:11	this *is* the number of the **m** *men* whom	1368
	12: 1	they *were* among the **m** *men,* helpers of	1368
	12: 4	a **m** *man* among the thirty, and over	1368
	12:21	*rovers:* for they *were* all **m** *men* of valour,	1368
	12:25	**m** *men* of valour for the war,	1368
	12:28	a young man **m** of valour, and *of* his	1368
	12:30	and eight hundred, **m** *men* of valour,	1368
	19: 8	he sent Joab, and all the host *of* the **m** *men.*	1368
	26: 6	their father: for they *were* **m** *men* of valour.	1368
	26:31	there were found among them **m** *men* of	1368
	27: 6	*who was* **m** among the thirty, and above	1368
	28: 1	*with* the **m** *men,* and with all the valiant	1368
	29:24	the **m** *men,* and all the sons likewise of	1368
2Ch	6:32	and thy **m** hand, and thy stretched out arm;	2389
	13: 3	chosen men, *being* **m** *men* of valour.	1368
	13:21	Abijah **waxed m**, and married fourteen	2388
	14: 8	all these *were* **m** *men* of valour.	1368
	17:13	the men of war, **m** *men* of valour, *were* in	1368
	17:14	with him **m** *men* of valour three hundred	1368
	17:16	with him two hundred thousand **m** *men* of	1368
	17:17	Eliada a **m** *man* of valour, and with him	1368
	25: 6	He hired also an hundred thousand **m** *men*	1368
	26:12	of the **m** *men* of valour *were* two thousand	1368
	26:13	five hundred, that made war with **m** power,	2428
	27: 6	So Jotham **became m**, because he prepared	2388
	28: 7	Zichri, a **m** *man* of Ephraim, slew	1368
	32: 3	his **m** *men* to stop the waters of	1368
	32:21	which cut off all the **m** *men* of valour, and	1368
Ezr	4:20	There have been **m** kings also over	8624
	7:28	and before all the king's **m** princes.	1368
Ne	3:16	was made, and unto the house of the **m**.	1368
	9:11	into the deeps, as a stone into the **m** waters.	5794
	9:32	the great, the **m**, and the terrible God,	1368
	11:14	**m** *men* of valour, an hundred twenty and	1368
Job	5:15	their mouth, and from the hand of the **m**.	2389
	6:23	or, Redeem me from the hand of the **m**?	6184
	9: 4	*He is* wise in heart, and **m** in strength:	533
	12:19	away spoiled, and overthroweth the **m**.	386
	12:21	and weakeneth the strength of the **m**.	650
	21: 7	become old, yea, are **m** *in* power?	1396
	22: 8	*as for* the **m** man, he had the earth; and	2220
	24:22	He draweth also the **m** with his power:	47
	34:20	and the **m** shall be taken away without hand.	47
	34:24	He shall break in pieces **m** *men* without	3524
	35: 9	they cry out by reason of the arm of the **m**.	7227
	36: 5	God *is* **m**, and despiseth not *any: he is*	3524
	36: 5	despiseth not *any: he is* **m** in strength *and*	3524
	41:25	When he raiseth up *himself,* the **m** are	352
Ps	24: 8	the LORD strong and **m**, the LORD	1368
	24: 8	and mighty, the LORD **m** *in* battle.	1368
	29: 1	Give unto the LORD, O ye **m**, give	410+1121
	33:16	a **m** *man* is not delivered by much strength.	1368
	45: 3	O *most* **m**, *with* thy glory and thy majesty.	1368
	50: 1	The **m** God, *even* the LORD, hath spoken,	410
	52: 1	O **m** *man?* the goodness of God *endureth*	1368
	59: 3	the **m** are gathered against me; not *for* my	5794
	68:33	doth send out his voice, *and that* a **m** voice.	5797
	69: 4	*being* mine enemies wrongfully, are **m**:	6105
	74:15	and the flood: thou driedst up **m** rivers.	386
	78:65	like a **m** *man* that shouteth by reason of	1368
	82: 1	God standeth in the congregation of the **m**;	410
	89: 6	*who* among the sons of the **m** can be likened	410
	89:13	Thou hast a **m** arm: strong is thy	1369+5973
	89:19	saidst, I have laid help upon *one that is* **m**;	1368
	89:50	my bosom *the reproach of* all the **m** people;	7227
	93: 4	*yea, than* the **m** waves of the sea.	117
	106: 2	Who can utter the **m acts** of the LORD?	1369
	106: 8	that *he* might make his **m power** to be	1369
	112: 2	His seed shall be **m** upon earth:	1368
	120: 4	Sharp arrows of the **m**, with coals of	1368
	127: 4	As arrows *are* in the hand of a **m** *man;* so	1368
	132: 2	*and* vowed unto the **m** *God* of Jacob;	46
	132: 5	a habitation for the **m** *God* of Jacob.	46
	135:10	smote great nations, and slew **m** kings;	6099
	145: 4	to another, and shall declare thy **m acts**.	1369
	145:12	make known to the sons of men his **m acts**,	1369
	150: 2	Praise him for his **m acts**: praise him	1369
Pr	16:32	*that is* slow to anger *is* better than the **m**;	1368
	18:18	to cease, and parteth between the **m**.	6099
	21:22	A wise *man* scaleth the city of the **m**, and	1368
	23:11	For their Redeemer *is* **m**; he shall plead	2389
Ecc	7:19	more than ten **m** *men* which are in the city.	7989
SS	4: 4	a thousand bucklers, all shields of **m** *men.*	1368
Isa	1:24	the LORD of hosts, the **m One** of Israel, Ah,	46
	3: 2	The **m** *man,* and the man of war, the judge,	1368
	3:25	fall by the sword, and thy **m** in the war.	1369
	5:15	the **m** man shall be humbled, and the eyes	NIH
	5:22	Woe unto *them that are* **m** to drink wine,	1368
	9: 6	Counseller, The **m** God, The everlasting	1368
	10:21	*even* the remnant of Jacob, unto the **m** God.	1368
	10:34	with iron, and Lebanon shall fall by a **m one**.	117
	11:15	with his **m** wind shall he shake his hand	5868
	13: 3	I have also called my **m ones** for mine	1368
	17:12	*that* make a rushing like the rushing of **m**	3524
	21:17	the **m** *men* of the children of Kedar,	1368
	22:17	the LORD will carry thee away with a **m**	1397
	28: 2	the LORD hath a **m** and strong one,	2389
	28: 2	as a flood of **m** waters overflowing,	3524
	30:29	of the LORD, to the **m One** of Israel.	6697
	31: 8	fall with the sword, not of a **m** man;	NIH
	42:13	The LORD shall go forth as a **m** *man,* he	1368
	43:16	way in the sea, and a path in the **m** waters;	5794
	49:24	Shall the prey be taken from the **m**, or	1368
	49:25	Even the captives of the **m** shall be taken	1368
	49:26	and thy redeemer, the **m One** of Jacob.	46
	60:16	and thy redeemer, the **m One** of Jacob.	46
	63: 1	I that speak in righteousness, **m** to save.	7227
Jer	5:15	it *is* a **m** nation, it *is* an ancient nation,	386
	5:16	as an open sepulchre, they *are* all **m** *men.*	1368
	9:23	neither let the **m** *man* glory in his might,	1368
	14: 9	man astonied, as a **m** *man that* cannot save?	1368
	20:11	the LORD *is* with me as a **m** terrible one:	1368
	26:21	with all his **m** *men,* and all the princes,	1368
	32:18	the Great, the **M** God, the LORD of hosts,	1368
	32:19	Great in counsel, and **m** in work: for thine	7227
	33: 3	and **m** *things,* which thou knowest not.	1219
	41:16	*even* **m** men of war, and the women, and	1397
	46: 5	their **m ones** are beaten down, and are fled	1368
	46: 6	the swift flee away, nor the **m** *man* escape;	1368
	46: 9	ye chariots; and let the **m** *men* come forth;	1368
	46:12	for the **m** *man* hath stumbled against	1368
	46:12	mighty *man* hath stumbled against the **m**,	1368
	48:14	We *are* **m** and strong men for the war?	1368
	48:41	the **m** *men's* hearts in Moab at that day	1368
	49:22	at that day shall the heart of the **m** *men* of	1368
	50: 9	their arrows *shall be* as of a **m** expert *man;*	1368
	50:36	a sword *is* upon her **m** *men;* and they shall	1368
	51:30	The **m** *men* of Babylon have forborn to	1368
	51:56	upon Babylon, and her **m** *men* are taken,	1368
	51:57	her **m** *men:* and they shall sleep a perpetual	1368
La	1:15	The Lord hath trodden under foot all my **m**	47
Eze	17:13	of him: he hath also taken the **m** of the land:	352
	17:17	Neither shall Pharaoh with *his* **m** army and	1419
	20:33	surely with a **m** hand, and with a stretched	2389
	20:34	with a **m** hand, and with a stretched out	2389
	31:11	delivered him into the hand of the **m one** of	410
	32:12	By the swords of the **m** will I cause thy	1368
	32:21	The strong among the **m** shall speak to him	1368
	32:27	they shall not lie with the **m** *that are* fallen	1368
	32:27	though *they were* the terror of the **m** in	1368
	38:15	a great company, and a **m** army:	7227
	39:18	Ye shall eat the flesh of the **m**, and	1368
	39:20	with **m** *men,* and *with* all men of war,	1368
Da	3:20	**most m men** that *were* in his	1400+1401+2429
	4: 3	how **m** *are* his wonders! his kingdom *is* an	8624
	8:24	his power shall be **m**, but not by his own	6105
	8:24	shall destroy the **m** and the holy people.	6099
	9:15	out of the land of Egypt with a **m** hand,	2389
	11: 3	a **m** king shall stand up, that shall rule *with*	1368
	11:25	up to battle with a very great and **m** army;	6099
Hos	10:13	in thy way, in the multitude of thy **m** *men.*	1368
Joel	2: 7	They shall run like **m** *men;* they shall climb	1368
	3: 9	wake up the **m** *men,* let all the men of war	1368
	3:11	thither cause thy **m ones** to come down,	1368

Am 2:14 neither shall the **m** deliver himself: 1368
2:16 he *that is* courageous among the **m** shall 1368
5:12 manifold transgressions and your **m** sins: 6099
5:24 as waters, and righteousness as a **m** stream. 386
Ob 1: 9 thy **m** *men,* O Teman, shall be dismayed, 1368
Jnh 1: 4 there was a **m** tempest in the sea, so that 1419
Na 2: 3 The shield of his **m** *men is* made red, 1368
Hab 1:12 and, O **m God**, thou hast established them 6697
Zep 1:14 the **m** *man* shall cry there bitterly. 1368
3:17 LORD thy God in the midst of thee *is* **m**; 1368
Zec 9:13 and made thee as the sword of a **m** *man.* 1368
10: 5 they shall be as **m** *men,* which tread down 1368
10: 7 And *they of* Ephraim shall be like a **m** *man,* 1368
11: 2 cedar is fallen; because the **m** are spoiled: 117
Mt 11:20 wherein most of his **m works** were done, *1411*
11:21 for if the **m works** which were done in you, *1411*
11:23 for if the **m works**, which have been done *1411*
13:54 this *man* this wisdom, and *these* **m works**? *1411*
13:58 And he did not many **m works** there, *1411*
14: 2 **m works** do shew forth themselves in him. *1411*
Mk 6: 2 that even such **m works** are wrought by his *1411*
6: 5 And he could there do no **m work**, *1411*
6:14 **m works** do shew forth themselves in him. *1411*
Lk 1:49 For he *that is* **m** hath done to me great *1415*
1:52 He hath put down the **m** from *their* seats, *1413*
9:43 And they were all amazed at the **m power** *3168*
10:13 for if the **m works** had been done in Tyre *1411*
15:14 there arose a **m** famine in that land; *2478*
19:37 for all the **m works** that they had seen; *1411*
24:19 which was a prophet **m** in deed and *1415*
Ac 2: 2 a sound from heaven as of a rushing **m** wind, *972*
7:22 and was **m** in words and in deeds. *1415*
18:24 an eloquent man, *and* **m** in the scriptures, *1415*
Ro 15:19 Through **m** signs and wonders, by *1411*
1Co 1:26 not many **m**, not many noble, *are called:* *1415*
1:27 world to confound the *things which are* **m**; *2478*
2Co 10: 4 **m** through God to the pulling down of *1415*
12:12 in signs, and wonders, and **m deeds**. *1411*
13: 3 to you-ward is not weak, but is **m** in you. *1414*
Gal 2: 8 *the same* was **m in** me towards *1754*
Eph 1:19 according to the working of his **m** power, *2904*
2Th 1: 7 be revealed from heaven with his **m** angels, *1411*
1Pe 5: 6 therefore under the **m** hand of God, *2900*
Rev 6:13 when she is shaken of a **m** wind. *3173*
6:15 and the **m** *men,* and every bondman, and *1415*
10: 1 And I saw another **m** angel come down *2478*
16:18 the earth, so **m** an earthquake, *and* so great. *5082*
18:10 alas, *that* great city Babylon, *that* **m** city! *2478*
18:21 And a **m** angel took up a stone like a great *2478*
19: 6 and as the voice of **m** thunderings, saying, *2478*
19:18 and the flesh of **m** *men,* and the flesh of *2478*

MIGRON (2)
1Sa 14: 2 under a pomegranate tree which *is* in **M**: 4051
Isa 10:28 He is come to Aiath, he is passed to **M**; 4051

MIJAMIN (2)
1Ch 24: 9 The fifth to Malchijah, the sixth to **M**, 4326
Ne 10: 7 Meshullam, Abijah, **M**, 4326

MIKLOTH (4)
1Ch 8:32 **M** begat Shimeah. And these also dwelt 4732
9:37 and Ahio, and Zechariah, and **M**. 4732
9:38 **M** begat Shimeam. And they also dwelt 4732
27: 4 and *of* his course *was* **M** also the ruler: 4732

MIKNEIAH (2)
1Ch 15:18 and **M**, and Obed-edom, and Jeiel, 4737
15:21 **M**, and Obed-edom, and Jeiel, and 4737

MILALAI (1)
Ne 12:36 Shemaiah, and Azarael, **M**, Gilalai, Maai, 4450

MILCAH (11)
Ge 11:29 **M**, the daughter of Haran, the father of 4435
11:29 the father of **M**, and the father of Iscah. 4435
22:20 it was told Abraham, saying, Behold, **M**, 4435
22:23 these eight **M** did bear to Nahor, 4435
24:15 son of **M**, the wife of Nahor, 4435
24:24 I *am* the daughter of Bethuel the son of **M**, 4435
24:47 Nahor's son, whom **M** bare unto him: 4435
Nu 26:33 and Noah, Hoglah, **M**, and Tirzah. 4435
27: 1 Noah, and Hoglah, and **M**, and Tirzah. 4435
36:11 Tirzah, and Hoglah, and **M**, and Noah, 4435
Jos 17: 3 Mahlah, and Noah, Hoglah, **M**, and Tirzah. 4435

MILCH (3) [MILK]
Ge 32:15 Thirty **m** camels with their colts, forty kine, 3243
1Sa 6: 7 make a new cart, and take two **m** kine, 5763
6:10 took two **m** kine, and tied them to the cart, 5763

MILCOM (3) [MOLOCH]
1Ki 11: 5 after **M** the abomination of the Ammonites. 4445
11:33 **M** the god of the children of Ammon, and 4445
2Ki 23:13 for **M** the abomination of the children of 4445

MILDEW (5)
Dt 28:22 the sword, and with blasting, and with **m**; 3420
1Ki 8:37 **m**, locust, *or* if there be caterpillar; 3420
2Ch 6:28 be blasting, or **m**, locusts, or caterpillars; 3420
Am 4: 9 I have smitten you with blasting and **m**: 3420
Hag 2:17 I smote you with blasting and with **m** and 3420

MILE (1)
Mt 5:41 whosoever shall compel thee to go a **m**, *3400*

MILES See FURLONGS

MILETUM (1) [MILETUS]
2Ti 4:20 but Trophimus have I left at **M** sick. *3399*

MILETUS (2) [MILETUM]
Ac 20:15 and the next *day* we came to **M**. *3399*
20:17 And from **M** he sent to Ephesus, and *3399*

MILK (48) [MILCH]
Ge 18: 8 **m**, and the calf which he had dressed, and 2461
49:12 red with wine, and *his* teeth white with **m**. 2461
Ex 3: 8 unto a land flowing with **m** and honey; 2461
3:17 unto a land flowing with **m** and honey. 2461
13: 5 a land flowing with **m** and honey, 2461
23:19 shalt not seethe a kid in his mother's **m**. 2461
33: 3 Unto a land flowing with **m** and honey: 2461
34:26 shalt not seethe a kid in his mother's **m**. 2461
Lev 20:24 a land that floweth with **m** and honey: 2461
Nu 13:27 and surely it floweth with **m** and honey; 2461
14: 8 a land which floweth with **m** and honey. 2461
16:13 us up out of a land that floweth with **m** 2461
16:14 brought us into a land that floweth with **m** 2461
Dt 6: 3 *in* the land that floweth with **m** and honey. 2461
11: 9 a land that floweth with **m** and honey. 2461
14:21 shalt not seethe a kid in his mother's **m**. 2461
26: 9 *even* a land that floweth with **m** and honey. 2461
26:15 a land that floweth with **m** and honey. 2461
27: 3 a land that floweth with **m** and honey; 2461
31:20 that floweth with **m** and honey; 2461
32:14 Butter of kine, and **m** of sheep, with fat of 2461
Jos 5: 6 a land that floweth with **m** and honey. 2461
Jdg 4:19 she opened a bottle of **m**, and gave him 2461
5:25 He asked water, *and* she gave *him* **m**; 2461
Job 10:10 Hast thou not poured me out as **m**, and 2461
21:24 His breasts are full *of* **m**, and his bones are 2461
Pr 27:27 *thou shalt have* goats' **m** enough for thy 2461
30:33 Surely the churning of **m** bringeth forth 2461
SS 4:11 honey and **m** *are* under thy tongue; and 2461
5: 1 I have drunk my wine with my **m**: 2461
5:12 of waters, washed with **m**, *and* fitly set. 2461
Isa 7:22 for the abundance of **m** *that they* shall give 2461
28: 9 them that are weaned from the **m**, *and* 2461
55: 1 buy wine and **m** without money and 2461
60:16 Thou shalt also suck the **m** of the Gentiles, 2461
66:11 that ye may **m out**, and be delighted with 4711
Jer 11: 5 to give them a land flowing with **m** and 2461
32:22 a land flowing with **m** and honey; 2461
La 4: 7 purer than snow, they were whiter than **m**, 2461
Eze 20: 6 flowing with **m** and honey, which *is* 2461
20:15 which I had given *them,* flowing with **m** 2461
25: 4 eat thy fruit, and they shall drink thy **m**. 2461
Joel 3:18 the hills shall flow *with* **m**, and all 2461
1Co 3: 2 I have fed you with **m**, and not with meat: *1051*
9: 7 and eateth not of the **m** of the flock? *1051*
Heb 5:12 and are become such as have need of **m**, *1051*
5:13 For every one that useth **m** *is* unskilful in *1051*
1Pe 2: 2 desire the sincere **m** of the word, *1051*

MILL (2) [MILLS, MILLSTONE, MILLSTONES]
Ex 11: 5 of the maidservant that *is* behind the **m**; 7347
Mt 24:41 Two *women shall be* grinding at the **m**; *3459*

MILLET (1)
Eze 4: 9 **m**, and fitches, and put them in one vessel, 1764

M

MILLIONS (1)
Ge 24:60 be thou *the mother* of thousands of **m**, and 7233

MILLO (10)
Jdg 9: 6 all the house of **M**, and went, and 4407
9:20 the men of Shechem, and the house of **M**; 4407
9:20 from the house of **M**, and 4407
2Sa 5: 9 David built round about from **M** and 4407
1Ki 9:15 **M**, and the wall of Jerusalem, and Hazor, 4407
9:24 had built for her: then did he build **M**. 4407
11:27 Solomon built **M**, *and* repaired the breaches 4407
2Ki 12:20 slew Joash *in* the house of **M**, 4407
1Ch 11: 8 round about, even from **M** round about: 4407
2Ch 32: 5 repaired **M** *in* the city of David, and 4407

MILLS (1) [MILL]
Nu 11: 8 gathered *it*, and ground *it* in **m**, or beat *it* in 7347

MILLSTONE (9) [MILL]
Dt 24: 6 take the nether or the **upper m** to pledge: 7393
Jdg 9:53 a certain woman cast a piece of a **m** upon 7393
2Sa 11:21 did not a woman cast a piece of a **m** upon 7393
Job 41:24 yea, as hard as a piece of the nether *m*. NIH
Mt 18: 6 it were better for him that a **m** were *3458+3684*
Mk 9:42 it is better for him that a **m** were *3037+3457*
Lk 17: 2 It were better for him that a **m** were *3458+3684*
Rev 18:21 angel took up a stone like a great **m**, *3458*
18:22 the sound of a **m** shall be heard no more at *3458*

MILLSTONES (2) [MILL]
Isa 47: 2 Take the **m**, and grind meal: uncover thy 7347
Jer 25:10 the sound of the **m**, and the light of 7347

MINAH See MANEH

MINCING (1)
Isa 3:16 walking and **m** *as* they go, and making a 2952

MINDED See below.

MIND (95) [FEEBLEMINDED, HIGHMINDED, HIGH-MINDED, LIKEMINDED, MINDED, MINDFUL, MINDING, MINDS, UNMINDFUL]
Ge 23: 8 If it be your **m** that I should bury my dead 5315
26:35 Which were a grief of **m** unto Isaac and 7307
Lev 24:12 that the **m** of the LORD might be shewed 6310
Nu 16:28 for *I have* not *done them* of mine own **m**. 3820
24:13 to do *either* good or bad of mine own **m**; 3820
Dt 18: 6 come with all the desire of his **m** unto 5315
28:65 and failing of eyes, and sorrow of **m**: 5315
30: 1 thou shalt call *them* to **m** among all 3824
1Sa 2:35 to *that* which *is* in my heart and in my **m**: 5315
9:20 lost three days ago, set not thy **m** on them; 3820
1Ch 22: 7 it was in my **m** to build a house unto 3824
28: 9 with a perfect heart and with a willing **m**: 5315
Ne 4: 6 for the people had a **m** to work. 3820
Job 23:13 he *is* in one **m**, and who can turn him? and NIH
34:33 *Should it be* **according to** thy **m**? 4480+5973
Ps 31:12 I am forgotten as a dead man out of **m**: 3820
Pr 21:27 *when* he bringeth it with a **wicked m**? 2154
29:11 A fool uttereth all his **m**: but a wise *man* 7307
Isa 26: 3 *whose* **m** *is* stayed *on thee:* because 3336
46: 8 bring *it* again to **m**, O ye transgressors. 3820
65:17 shall not be remembered, nor come into **m**. 3820
Jer 3:16 neither shall it come to **m**: neither shall 3820
15: 1 *yet* my **m** *could* not *be* toward this people: 5315
19: 5 nor spake *it*, neither came *it* into my **m**: 3820
32:35 them not, neither came it into my **m**, 3820
44:21 and came it *not* into his **m**? 3820
51:50 and let Jerusalem come into your **m**. 3824
La 3:21 This I recall to my **m**, therefore have I 3820
Eze 11: 5 I know the things that come into your **m**, 7307
20:32 that which cometh into your **m** shall not be 7307
23:17 and her **m** was alienated from them. 5315
23:18 my **m** was alienated from her, like as my 5315
23:18 like as my **m** was alienated from her sister. 5315
23:22 from whom thy **m** is alienated, and I will 5315
23:28 into the hand *of them* from whom thy **m** is 5315
38:10 the same time shall things come into thy **m**, 3824
Da 2:29 thy thoughts came *into thy* **m** upon thy bed, NIH
5:20 was lifted up, and his **m** hardened in pride, 7308
Hab 1:11 shall *his* **m** change, and he shall pass over, 7307
Mt 22:37 and with all thy soul, and with all thy **m**. *1271*
Mk 5:15 sitting, and clothed, and **in** his **right m**: *4993*
12:30 and with all thy **m**, and with all thy *1271*
14:72 And Peter **called to m** the word that Jesus *363*
Lk 1:29 **cast in** her **m** what manner of salutation *1260*
8:35 feet of Jesus, clothed, and **in** his **right m**: *4993*
10:27 with all thy strength, and with all thy **m**; *1271*
12:29 ye shall drink, neither be ye of **doubtful m**. *3349*
Ac 17:11 received the word with all **readiness of m**, *4288*
20:19 Serving the Lord with all **humility of m**, *5012*
Ro 1:28 God gave them over to a reprobate **m**, to do *3563*
7:23 warring against the law of my **m**, and *3563*
7:25 with the **m** I myself serve the law of God; *3563*
8: 5 For they that are after the flesh do **m** *5426*
8: 7 Because the carnal **m** *is* enmity against *5427*
8:27 hearts knoweth what *is* the **m** of the Spirit, *5427*
11:34 For who hath known the **m** of the Lord? or *3563*
12: 2 ye transformed by the renewing of your **m**, *3563*
12:16 *Be* of the same **m** one towards another. *5426*
12:16 **M** not high *things*, but condescend to *men* *5426*
14: 5 every man be fully persuaded in his own **m**. *3563*
15: 6 That ye may with **one m** *and* one mouth *3661*
15:15 as **putting** you **in m**, because of the grace *1878*
1Co 1:10 be perfectly joined together in the same **m** *3563*
2:16 For who hath known the **m** of the Lord, *3563*
2:16 instruct him? But we have the **m** of Christ. *3563*
2Co 7: 7 your mourning, your **fervent m** toward me; *2205*
8:12 For if there be first a **willing m**, *it is* *4288*
8:19 and *declaration of* your **ready m**: *4288*
9: 2 For I know the **forwardness of** your **m**, *4288*
13:11 good comfort, be of one **m**, live in peace; *5426*
Eph 2: 3 the desires of the flesh and of the **m**; *1271*
4:17 Gentiles walk, in the vanity of their **m**, *3563*
4:23 And be renewed in the spirit of your **m**; *3563*
Php 1:27 with one **m** striving together for the faith of *5590*
2: 2 same love, *being* of one accord, of one **m**. *5426*
2: 3 in **lowliness of m** *let* each esteem other *5012*
2: 5 Let this **m** be in you, which *was* also in *5426*
3:16 by the same rule, *let us* **m** the same *thing*. *5426*
3:19 *is* in their shame, who **m** earthly *things*.) *5426*
4: 2 that *they* be of the same **m** in the Lord. *5426*
Col 1:21 and enemies in *your* **m** by wicked works, *1271*
2:18 not seen, vainly puft up by his fleshly **m**, *3563*
3:12 kindness, **humbleness of m**, meekness, *5012*
2Th 2: 2 That ye be not soon shaken in **m**, or *3563*
2Ti 1: 7 of power, and of love, and of a **sound m**. *4995*
Tit 1:15 but even their **m** and conscience is defiled. *3563*
3: 1 **Put** them **in m** to be subject to *5279*
Phm 1:14 But without thy **m** would I do nothing; *1106*
Heb 8:10 I will put my laws into their **m**, and *1271*
1Pe 1:13 Wherefore gird up the loins of your **m**, *1271*
3: 8 Finally, *be ye* all of **one m**, *3675*
4: 1 arm yourselves likewise with the same **m**: *1771*
5: 2 not for filthy lucre, but **of a ready m**; *4290*
Rev 17: 9 *And* here *is* the **m** which hath wisdom. *3563*
17:13 These have one **m**, and shall give their *1106*

MINDED (15) [MIND]
Ru 1:18 When she saw that she *was* **stedfastly m** to 553
2Ch 24: 4 *that* Joash was **m** to repair the house 3820+5973
Ezr 7:13 *which are* **m of** their **own freewill** to go *up* 5069
Mt 1:19 was **m** to put her away privily. *1014*
Ac 27:39 into the which they were **m**, if it were *1011*
Ro 8: 6 For to be carnally **m** *is* death; *5427*
8: 6 but to be spiritually **m** *is* life and peace. *5427*
2Co 1:15 And in this confidence I was **m** to come *1014*
1:17 When I therefore was thus **m**, did I use *1011*
Gal 5:10 that you will be none otherwise **m**: *5426*
Php 3:15 as many as *be* perfect, be thus **m**: *5426*
3:15 and if in any *thing* ye be otherwise **m**, *5426*
Tit 2: 6 Young *men* likewise exhort to be **sober m**. *4993*
Jas 1: 8 A **double m** man *is* unstable in all his *1374*
4: 8 and purify *your* hearts, *ye* **double m**. *1374*

MINDFUL (10) [MIND]
1Ch 16:15 Be ye **m** always of his covenant; the word 2142
Ne 9:17 neither were **m** of thy wonders that thou 2142
Ps 8: 4 What *is* man, that thou art **m** of him? and 2142
111: 5 fear him: he will ever be **m** of his covenant. 2142
115:12 The LORD hath been **m** of us: he will 2142
Isa 17:10 hast not been **m** of the rock of thy strength, 2142
2Ti 1: 4 desiring to see thee, being **m** of thy tears, *3415*
Heb 2: 6 What is man, that thou art **m** of him? *3403*
11:15 if they had been **m** of that *country* from *3421*
2Pe 3: 2 That *ye* may be **m** of the words which were *3415*

MINDING (1) [MIND]
Ac 20:13 so had he appointed, **m** himself to go afoot. *3195*

M

MINDS (16) [MIND]
Jdg 19:30 of it, take advice, and speak *your* **m**. NIH
2Sa 17: 8 mighty *men*, and they *be* chafed in their **m**, 5315
2Ki 9:15 If it be your **m**, *then* let none go forth *nor* 5315
Eze 24:25 that whereupon they set their **m**, their sons 5315
36: 5 with despiteful **m**, to cast it out for a prey. 5315
Ac 14: 2 made their **m** evil affected against *5590*
28: 6 they changed *their* **m**, and said that he was a NIG
2Co 3:14 But their **m** were blinded: for until this day *3540*
4: 4 blinded the **m** of them which believe not, *3540*
11: 3 your **m** should be corrupted from *3540*
Php 4: 7 your hearts and **m** through Christ Jesus. *3540*
1Ti 6: 5 Perverse disputings of men of corrupt **m**, *3563*
2Ti 3: 8 men of corrupt **m**, reprobate concerning *3563*
Heb 10:16 and in their **m** will I write them; *1271*
12: 3 lest ye be wearied and faint in your **m**. *5590*
2Pe 3: 1 in both which I stir up your pure **m** by way *1271*

MINE (647) [I] See Index

MINGLE (2) [MINGLED]
Isa 5:22 and men of strength to **m** strong drink: 4537
Da 2:43 they shall **m** themselves with the seed of 6151

MINGLED (55) [MINGLE]
Ex 9:24 and fire **m** with the hail, very grievous, 3947
29:40 with the one lamb a tenth deal of flour **m** 1101
Lev 2: 4 *it shall be* unleavened cakes of fine flour **m** 1101
2: 5 be *of* fine flour unleavened, **m** with oil. 1101
7:10 every meat offering, **m** with oil, and dry, 1101
7:12 thanksgiving unleavened cakes **m** with oil, 1101
7:12 and cakes **m** with oil, of fine flour, fried. 1101
9: 4 and a meat offering **m** with oil: 1101
14:10 **m** with oil, and one log of oil. 1101
14:21 one tenth deal of fine flour **m** with oil for a 1101
19:19 thou shalt not sow thy field with **m** seed: 3610
19:19 a garment **m of linen and woollen** 3610+8162
23:13 *be* two tenth deals *of* fine flour **m** with oil, 1101
Nu 6:15 cakes *of* fine flour **m** with oil, and 1101
7:13 both of them *were* full *of* fine flour **m** with 1101
7:19 both of them full *of* fine flour **m** with oil 1101
7:25 both of them full *of* fine flour **m** with oil 1101
7:31 both of them full *of* fine flour **m** with oil 1101
7:37 both of them full *of* fine flour **m** with oil 1101
7:43 both of them full *of* fine flour **m** with oil 1101
7:49 both of them full *of* fine flour **m** with oil 1101
7:55 both of them full *of* fine flour **m** with oil 1101
7:61 both of them full *of* fine flour **m** with oil 1101
7:67 both of them full *of* fine flour **m** with oil 1101
7:73 both of them full *of* fine flour **m** with oil 1101
7:79 both of them full *of* fine flour **m** with oil 1101
8: 8 *even* fine flour **m** with oil, and 1101
15: 4 flour **m** with the fourth *part* of a hin of oil. 1101
15: 6 *of* flour **m** with the third *part* of a hin of oil. 1101
15: 9 tenth deals *of* flour **m** with half a hin of oil. 1101
28: 5 **m** with the fourth *part* of a hin of beaten 1101
28: 9 **m** with oil, and the drink offering thereof: 1101
28:12 meat offering, **m** with oil, for one bullock; 1101
28:12 a meat offering, **m** with oil, for one ram; 1101
28:13 a several tenth deal of flour **m** with oil *for* a 1101
28:20 their meat offering *shall be of* flour **m** with 1101
28:28 their meat offering *of* flour **m** with oil, 1101
29: 3 their meat offering *shall be of* flour **m** with 1101
29: 9 their meat offering *shall be of* flour **m** with 1101
29:14 their meat offering *shall be of* flour **m** with 1101
Ezr 9: 2 that the holy seed have **m** themselves with 6148
Ps 102: 9 like bread, and **m** my drink with weeping, 4537
106:35 were **m** among the heathen, and 6148
Pr 9: 2 hath killed her beasts; she hath **m** her wine; 4537
9: 5 and drink of the wine *which* I have **m**. 4537
Isa 19:14 The LORD hath **m** a perverse spirit in 4537
Jer 25:20 all the **m people**, and all the kings of 6153
25:24 all the kings of the **m people** that dwell in 6153
50:37 upon all the **m** people that *are* in the midst NIH
Eze 30: 5 all the **m people**, and Chub, and the men of 6153
Mt 27:34 They gave him vinegar to drink **m** with *3396*
Mk 15:23 gave him to drink wine **m with myrrh**: *4669*
Lk 13: 1 whose blood Pilate had **m** with their *3396*
Rev 8: 7 there followed hail and fire **m** with blood, *3396*
15: 2 And I saw as *it were* a sea of glass **m** with *3396*

MINIAMIN (3)
2Ch 31:15 **M**, and Jeshua, and Shemaiah, Amariah, 4509
Ne 12:17 Of Abijah, Zichri; of **M**, of Moadiah, Piltai; 4509
12:41 Eliakim, Maaseiah, **M**, Michaiah, Elioenai, 4509

MINISH (1) [MINISHED]
Ex 5:19 Ye shall not **m** *ought* from your bricks of 1639

MINISHED (1) [MINISH]
Ps 107:39 they are **m** and brought low through 4591

MINISTER (100) [MINISTERED, MINISTERETH, MINISTERING, MINISTERS, MINISTRATION, MINISTRY]
Ex 24:13 Moses rose up, and his **m** Joshua: and 8334
28: 1 he may **m** unto me **in the priest's office**, 3547
28: 3 he may **m** unto me **in the priest's office**. 3547
28: 4 he may **m** unto me **in the priest's office**. 3547
28:35 it shall be upon Aaron to **m**: and his sound 8334
28:41 they may **m** unto me **in the priest's office**. 3547
28:43 when they come near unto the altar to **m** in 8334
29: 1 to **m** unto me **in the priest's office**: 3547
29:30 of the congregation to **m** in the holy *place*. 8334
29:44 his sons, to **m** to me **in the priest's office**. 3547
30:20 or when they come near to the altar to **m**, 8334
30:30 *they* may **m** unto me **in the priest's office**. 3547
31:10 of his sons, to **m in the priest's office**, 3547
35:19 of his sons, to **m in the priest's office**. 3547
39:26 round about the hem of the robe to **m** *in;* as 8334
39:41 sons' garments, to **m in the priest's office**. 3547
40:13 he may **m** unto me **in the priest's office**. 3547
40:15 they may **m** unto me **in the priest's office**: 3547
Lev 7:35 **m** unto the LORD **in the priest's office**; 3547
16:32 **m in the priest's office** in his father's 3547
Nu 1:50 they shall **m** unto it, and shall encamp 8334
3: 3 he consecrated to **m in the priest's office**. 3547
3: 6 Aaron the priest, that they may **m** unto him. 8334
3:31 vessels of the sanctuary wherewith they **m**, 8334
4: 9 vessels thereof, wherewith they **m** unto it: 8334
4:12 wherewith they **m** in the sanctuary, and 8334
4:14 wherewith they **m** about it, *even* 8334
8:26 shall **m** with their brethren in the tabernacle 8334
16: 9 to stand before the congregation to **m** unto 8334
18: 2 may be joined unto thee, and **m** unto thee: 8334
18: 2 thy sons with thee *shall* **m** before NIH
Dt 10: 8 to stand before the LORD to **m** unto him, 8334
17:12 to **m** there before the LORD thy God, 8334
18: 5 to stand to **m** in the name of the LORD, 8334
18: 7 he shall **m** in the name of the LORD his 8334
21: 5 thy God hath chosen to **m** unto him, 8334
Jos 1: 1 Joshua the son of Nun, Moses' **m**, saying, 8334
1Sa 2:11 the child did **m** unto the LORD before Eli 8334
1Ki 8:11 So that the priests could not stand to **m** 8334
1Ch 15: 2 the ark of God, and to **m** unto him for ever. 8334
16: 4 he appointed *certain* of the Levites to **m** 8334
16:37 to **m** before the ark continually, 8334
23:13 to **m** unto him, and to bless in his name for 8334
26:12 to **m** in the house of the LORD. 8334
2Ch 5:14 So that the priests could not stand to **m** by 8334
8:14 to praise and **m** before the priests, 8334
13:10 the priests, which **m** unto the LORD, 8334
23: 6 the priests, and they that **m** of the Levites; 8334
24:14 *even* vessels to **m**, and to offer *withal,* and 8335
29:11 that *you* should **m** unto him, and 8334
31: 2 to **m**, and to give thanks, and to praise in 8334
Ne 10:36 unto the priests that **m** in the house of our 8334
10:39 the priests that **m**, and the porters, and 8334
Ps 9: 8 he shall **m judgment** to the people in 1777
Isa 60: 7 the rams of Nebajoth shall **m** unto thee: 8334
60:10 thy walls, and their kings shall **m** unto thee: 8334
Jer 33:22 and the Levites that **m** unto me. 8334
Eze 40:46 which come near to the LORD to **m** unto 8334
42:14 shall lay their garments wherein they **m**; 8334
43:19 to **m** unto me, saith the Lord GOD, 8334
44:11 they shall stand before them to **m** unto 8334
44:15 they shall come near to me to **m** unto me, 8334
44:16 to **m** unto me, and they shall keep my 8334
44:17 whiles they **m** in the gates of the inner 8334
44:27 unto the inner court, to **m** in the sanctuary, 8334
45: 4 which shall come near to **m** unto 8334
Mt 20:26 be great among you, let him be your **m**; *1249*
20:28 but to **m**, and to give his life a ransom for *1247*
25:44 sick, or in prison, and did not **m** unto thee? *1247*
Mk 10:43 will be great among you, shall be your **m**: *1249*
10:45 but to **m**, and to give his life a ransom for *1247*
Lk 4:20 and he gave *it* again to the **m**, and *5257*
Ac 13: 5 the Jews: and they had also John to *their* **m**. *5257*
24:23 forbid none of his acquaintance to **m** *5256*

Ac 26:16 thee for this *purpose,* to make thee a **m** *5257*
Ro 13: 4 For he is the **m** of God to thee for good. *1249*
13: 4 for he is the **m** of God, a revenger to *1249*
15: 8 Now I say that Jesus Christ was a **m** of *1249*
15:16 That I should be the **m** of Jesus Christ to *3011*
15:25 But now I go unto Jerusalem to **m** unto *1247*
15:27 is also to **m** unto them in carnal *things.* *3008*
1Co 9:13 Do ye not know that they which **m** about *2038*
2Co 9:10 to the sower both **m** bread for *your* food, *5524*
Gal 2:17 *is* therefore Christ the **m** of sin? *1249*
Eph 3: 7 Whereof I was made a **m**, according to *1249*
4:29 that it may **m** grace unto the hearers. *1325*
6:21 beloved brother and faithful **m** in the Lord, *1249*
Col 1: 7 who is for you a faithful **m** of Christ; *1249*
1:23 whereof I Paul am made a **m**; *1249*
1:25 Whereof I am made a **m**, according to *1249*
4: 7 and a faithful **m** and fellowservant in *1249*
1Th 3: 2 and **m** of God, and our fellowlabourer in *1249*
1Ti 1: 4 endless genealogies, which **m** questions, *3930*
4: 6 thou shalt be a good **m** of Jesus Christ, *1249*
Heb 1:14 sent forth to **m** for them who shall be heirs *1248*
6:10 ye have ministered to the saints, and do **m**. *1247*
8: 2 A **m** of the sanctuary, and of the true *3011*
1Pe 1:12 but unto us they did **m** the things, *1247*
4:10 *the* gift, *even so* **m** the same one to another, *1247*
4:11 if any *man* **m**, *let him do it* as of the ability *1247*

MINISTERED (37) [MINISTER]

Nu 3: 4 Ithamar **m in the priest's office** in the sight 3547
Dt 10: 6 Eleazar his son **m in the priest's office** in 3547
1Sa 2:18 Samuel **m** before the LORD, *being* a 8334
3: 1 the child Samuel **m** unto the LORD before 8334
2Sa 13:17 he called his servant that **m** unto him, and 8334
1Ki 1: 4 and cherished the king, and **m** to him: 8334
1:15 Abishag the Shunammite **m** unto the king. 8334
19:21 and went after Elijah, and **m** unto him. 8334
2Ki 25:14 all the vessels of brass wherewith they **m**, 8334
1Ch 6:32 they **m** before the dwelling place of 8334
28: 1 the captains of the companies that **m** to 8334
2Ch 22: 8 that **m** to Ahaziah, he slew them. 8334
Est 2: 2 said the king's servants that **m** unto him, 8334
6: 3 said the king's servants that **m** unto him, 8334
Jer 52:18 all the vessels of brass wherewith they **m**, 8334
Eze 44:12 Because they **m** unto them before their 8334
44:19 put off their garments wherein they **m**, 8334
Da 7:10 thousand thousands **m** unto him, and 8120
Mt 4:11 and behold, angels came and **m** unto him. *1247*
8:15 left her: and she arose, and **m** unto them. *1247*
20:28 Even as the Son of man came not to be **m** *1247*
Mk 1:13 the wild beasts; and the angels **m** unto him. *1247*
1:31 the fever left her, and she **m** unto them. *1247*
10:45 For even the Son of man came not to be **m** *1247*
15:41 in Galilee, followed him, and **m** unto him;) *1247*
Lk 4:39 immediately she arose and **m** unto them. *1247*
8: 3 which **m** unto him of their substance. *1247*
Ac 13: 2 As they **m** to the Lord, and fasted, the Holy *3008*
19:22 Macedonia two of them that **m** unto him, *1247*
20:34 that these hands have **m** unto my *5256*
2Co 3: 3 declared to be the epistle of Christ **m** by us, *1247*
Php 2:25 and he that **m** to my wants. *3011*
Col 2:19 and bands having **nourishment m**, *2023*
2Ti 1:18 in how many *things* he **m** *unto me* at *1247*
Phm 1:13 that in thy stead he might have **m** unto me *1247*
Heb 6:10 in that ye have **m** to the saints, and *1247*
2Pe 1:11 an entrance shall be **m** unto you abundantly *2023*

MINISTERETH (2) [MINISTER]

2Co 9:10 Now he that **m** seed to the sower both *2023*
Gal 3: 5 He therefore that **m** to you the Spirit, and *2023*

MINISTERING (9) [MINISTER]

1Ch 9:28 *certain* of them had the charge of the **m** 5656
Eze 44:11 the gates of the house, and **m** to the house: 8334
Mt 27:55 followed Jesus from Galilee, **m** unto him: *1247*
Ro 12: 7 Or ministry, *let us wait* on *our* **m**: or he that *1248*
15:16 **m** the gospel of God, that the offering up of *2418*
2Co 8: 4 *take upon us* the fellowship of the **m** to *1248*
9: 1 For as touching the **m** to the saints, it is *1248*
Heb 1:14 Are they not all **m** spirits, sent forth to *3010*
10:11 And every priest standeth daily **m** and *3008*

MINISTERS (26) [MINISTER]

1Ki 10: 5 the attendance of his **m**, and their apparel, 8334
2Ch 9: 4 the attendance of his **m**, and their apparel; 8334
Ezr 7:24 or **m** of this house of God, 6399
8:17 that *they* should bring unto us **m** for 8334
Ps 103:21 his hosts; ye **m** of his, that do his pleasure. 8334
104: 4 his angels spirits; his **m** a flaming fire: 8334
Isa 61: 6 *men* shall call you the **M** of our God: 8334
Jer 33:21 and with the Levites the priests, my **m**. 8334
Eze 44:11 Yet they shall be **m** in my sanctuary, 8334
45: 4 be for the priests the **m** of the sanctuary, 8334
45: 5 the **m** of the house, have for themselves, 8334
46:24 where the **m** of the house shall boil 8334
Joel 1: 9 the priests, the LORD'S **m**, mourn. 8334
1:13 howl, ye **m** of the altar: come, lie all night 8334
1:13 lie all night in sackcloth, ye **m** of my God; 8334
2:17 Let the priests, the **m** of the LORD, 8334
Lk 1: 2 were eyewitnesses, and **m** of the word; *5257*
Ro 13: 6 for they are God's **m**, *3011*
1Co 3: 5 *is* Apollos, but **m** by whom ye believed, *1249*
4: 1 as of the **m** of Christ, and stewards of *5257*
2Co 3: 6 Who also hath made us able **m** of the new *1249*
6: 4 approving ourselves as the **m** of God, *1249*
11:15 Therefore *it is* no great *thing* if his **m** also *1249*
11:15 be transformed as the **m** of righteousness; *1249*
11:23 Are they **m** of Christ? (I speak as a fool) *1249*
Heb 1: 7 his angels spirits, and his **m** a flame of fire. *3011*

MINISTRATION (7) [MINISTER]

Lk 1:23 as the days of his **m** were accomplished, *3009*
Ac 6: 1 their widows were neglected in the daily **m**. *1248*
2Co 3: 7 But if the **m** of death, written *and* *1248*
3: 8 How shall not the **m** of the spirit be rather *1248*
3: 9 For if the **m** of condemnation *be* glory, *1248*
3: 9 much more doth the **m** of righteousness *1248*
9:13 Whiles by the experiment of this **m** they *1248*

MINISTRY (22) [MINISTER]

Nu 4:12 they shall take all the instruments of **m**, 8335
4:47 one that came to do the service of the **m**, 5656
2Ch 7: 6 for ever, when David praised by their **m**; 3027
Hos 12:10 used similitudes by the **m** of the prophets. 3027
Ac 1:17 with us, and had obtained part of this **m**. *1248*
1:25 That *he* may take part of this **m** and *1248*
6: 4 to prayer, and to the **m** of the word. *1248*
12:25 when they had fulfilled *their* **m**, and *1248*
20:24 might finish my course with joy, and the **m**, *1248*
21:19 had wrought among the Gentiles by his **m**. *1248*
Ro 12: 7 Or **m**, *let us wait* on *our* ministering: or *1248*
1Co 16:15 *that* they have addicted themselves to the **m** *1248*
2Co 4: 1 Therefore seeing we have this **m**, as we *1248*
5:18 hath given to us the **m** of reconciliation; *1248*
6: 3 Giving no offence in any *thing,* that the **m** *1248*
Eph 4:12 of the saints for the work of the **m**, *1248*
Col 4:17 Take heed to the **m** which thou hast *1248*
1Ti 1:12 counted me faithful, putting *me* into the **m**; *1248*
2Ti 4: 5 of an evangelist, make full proof of thy **m**. *1248*
4:11 for he is profitable to me for the **m**. *1248*
Heb 8: 6 now hath he obtained a more excellent **m**, *3009*
9:21 the tabernacle, and all the vessels of the **m**. *3009*

MINNI (1)

Jer 51:27 kingdoms of Ararat, **M**, and Ashchenaz; 4508

MINNITH (2)

Jdg 11:33 even till thou come *to* **M**, *even* twenty 4511
Eze 27:17 they traded in thy market wheat of **M**, and 4511

MINSTREL (2) [MINSTRELS]

2Ki 3:15 now bring me a **m**. And it came to pass, 5059
3:15 it came to pass, when the **m** played, that 5059

MINSTRELS (1) [MINSTREL]

Mt 9:23 and saw the **m** and the people making a *834*

MINT (2)

Mt 23:23 for ye pay tithe of **m** and anise and *2238*
Lk 11:42 for ye tithe **m** and rue and all *manner of* *2238*

MIPHKAD (1)

Ne 3:31 over against the gate **M**, and to the going 4662

MIRACLE (10) [MIRACLES]

Ex 7: 9 speak unto you, saying, Shew a **m** for you: 4159
Mk 6:52 For they considered not *the* **m** of the loaves: NIG
9:39 for there is no *man* which shall do a **m** in *1411*
Lk 23: 8 he hoped to have seen some **m** done by *4592*
Jn 4:54 This *is* again the second **m** *that* Jesus did, *4592*

Jn 6:14 when they had seen the **m** that Jesus did, *4592*
10:41 resorted unto him, and said, John did no **m**: *4592*
12:18 for that they heard that he had done this **m**. *4592*
Ac 4:16 for that indeed a notable **m** hath been done *4592*
4:22 on whom this **m** of healing was shewed. *4592*

MIRACLES (27) [MIRACLE]
Nu 14:22 my **m**, which I did in Egypt and in 226
Dt 11: 3 his **m**, and his acts, which he did in the midst 226
29: 3 have seen, the signs, and those great **m**: 4159
Jdg 6:13 where *be* all his **m** which our fathers told us 6381
Jn 2:11 This beginning of **m** did Jesus in Cana of *4592*
2:23 when they saw the **m** which he did. *4592*
3: 2 for no *man* can do these **m** that thou doest, *4592*
6: 2 they saw his **m** which he did on them that *4592*
6:26 not because ye saw *the* **m**, but because *4592*
7:31 will he do moe **m** than these which this *4592*
9:16 How can a man *that is* a sinner do such **m**? *4592*
11:47 What do we? for this man doeth many **m**. *4592*
12:37 he had done so many **m** before them, *4592*
Ac 2:22 a man approved of God among you by **m** *1411*
6: 8 did great wonders and **m** among the people. *4592*
8: 6 hearing and seeing the **m** which he did. *4592*
8:13 beholding *the* **m** and signs *which were* *1411*
15:12 declaring what **m** and wonders God had *4592*
19:11 And God wrought special **m** by the hands *1411*
1Co 12:10 To another the working of **m**; to another *1411*
12:28 after that **m**, then gifts of healings, helps, *1411*
12:29 *are* all teachers? *are* all **workers of m**? *1411*
Gal 3: 5 you the Spirit, and worketh **m** among you, *1411*
Heb 2: 4 and with divers **m**, and gifts of the Holy *1411*
Rev 13:14 **m** which he had power to do in the sight of *4592*
16:14 they are the spirits of devils, working **m**, *4592*
19:20 with him the false prophet that wrought **m** *4592*

MIRE (15) [MIRY]
2Sa 22:43 I did stamp them as the **m** of the street, *and* 2916
Job 8:11 Can the rush grow up without **m**? can 1207
30:19 He hath cast me into the **m**, and I am 2563
41:30 spreadeth sharp pointed *things* upon the **m**. 2916
Ps 69: 2 I sink in deep **m**, where *there is* no 3121
69:14 Deliver me out of the **m**, and let me not 2916
Isa 10: 6 to tread them down like the **m** of 2563
57:20 whose waters cast up **m** and dirt. 7516
Jer 38: 6 in the dungeon *there was* no water, but **m**: 2916
38: 6 but mire: so Jeremiah sunk in the **m**. 2916
38:22 thy feet are sunk in the **m**, *and* they are 1206
Mic 7:10 now shall she be trodden down as the **m** of 2916
Zec 9: 3 and fine gold as the **m** of the streets. 2916
10: 5 *enemies* in the **m** of the streets in the battle: 2916
2Pe 2:22 that was washed to *her* wallowing in the **m**. *1004*

MIRIAM (15)
Ex 15:20 **M** the prophetess, the sister of Aaron, took 4813
15:21 **M** answered them, Sing ye to the LORD, 4813
Nu 12: 1 **M** and Aaron spake against Moses because 4813
12: 4 unto Moses, and unto Aaron, and unto **M**, 4813
12: 5 of the tabernacle, and called Aaron and **M**: 4813
12:10 behold, **M** *became* leprous, *white* as snow: 4813
12:10 Aaron looked upon **M**, and behold, *she was* 4813
12:15 **M** was shut out from the camp seven days: 4813
12:15 the people journeyed not till **M** was 4813
20: 1 and **M** died there, and was buried there. 4813
26:59 and Moses, and **M** their sister. 4813
Dt 24: 9 LORD thy God did unto **M** by the way, 4813
1Ch 4:17 she bare **M**, and Shammai, and Ishbah 4813
6: 3 of Amram; Aaron, and Moses, and **M**. 4813
Mic 6: 4 I sent before thee Moses, Aaron, and **M**. 4813

MIRMA (1)
1Ch 8:10 Jeuz, and Shachia, and **M**. These *were* his 4821

MIRROR See GLASSES; LOOKINGGLASSES

MIRTH (15)
Ge 31:27 that I might have sent thee away with **m**, 8057
Ne 8:12 to make great **m**, because they had 8057
Ps 137: 3 they that wasted us *required of us* **m**, 8057
Pr 14:13 and the end of that **m** *is* heaviness. 8057
Ecc 2: 1 I will prove thee with **m**, therefore 8057
2: 2 *It is* mad: and of **m**, What doeth it? 8057
7: 4 but the heart of fools *is* in the house of **m**. 8057
8:15 I commended **m**, because a man hath no 8057
Isa 24: 8 The **m** of tabrets ceaseth, the noise of them 4885
24:11 joy is darkened, the **m** of the land is gone. 4885

Jer 7:34 the voice of **m**, and the voice of gladness, 8342
16: 9 the voice of **m**, and the voice of gladness, 8342
25:10 I will take from them the voice of **m**, 8342
Eze 21:10 should we then **make m**? it contemneth 7797
Hos 2:11 I will also cause all her **m** to cease, 4885

MIRY (4) [MIRE]
Ps 40: 2 out of the **m** clay, and set my feet upon a 3121
Eze 47:11 the **m places** thereof and the marishes 1207
Da 2:41 as thou sawest the iron mixed with **m** clay. 2917
2:43 whereas thou sawest iron mixt with **m** clay, 2917

MISCARRYING (1)
Hos 9:14 give them a **m** womb and dry breasts. 7921

MISCHIEF (47) [MISCHIEFS, MISCHIEVOUS]
Ge 42: 4 for he said, Lest peradventure **m** befall him. 611
42:38 if **m** befall him by the way in the which ye 611
44:29 ye take this also from me, and **m** befall him, 611
Ex 21:22 fruit depart *from her,* and yet no **m** follow: 611
21:23 if *any* **m** follow, then thou shalt give life for 611
32:12 say, For **m** did he bring them out, to slay 7451
32:22 knowest the people, that they *are set* on **m**. 7451
1Sa 23: 9 David knew that Saul secretly practised **m** 7451
2Sa 16: 8 and, behold, thou *art taken* to thy **m**, 7451
1Ki 11:25 beside the **m** that Hadad *did:* and 7451
20: 7 pray you, and see how this *man* seeketh **m**: 7451
2Ki 7: 9 morning light, *some* **m** will come upon us: 5771
Ne 6: 2 plain of Ono. But they thought to do me **m**. 7451
Est 8: 3 besought him with tears to put away the **m** 7451
Job 15:35 They conceive **m**, and bring forth vanity, 5999
Ps 7:14 hath conceived **m**, and brought forth 5999
7:16 His **m** shall return upon his own head, and 5999
10: 7 fraud: under his tongue *is* **m** and vanity. 5999
10:14 Thou hast seen *it;* for thou beholdest **m** and 5999
26:10 In whose hands *is* **m**, and their right hand is 2154
28: 3 to their neighbours, but **m** *is* in their hearts. 7451
36: 4 He deviseth **m** upon his bed; he setteth 205
52: 1 Why boastest thou thyself in **m**, O mighty 7451
55:10 **m** also and sorrow *are* in the midst of it. 205
62: 3 How long will ye **imagine m** against a 2050
94:20 *with* thee, which frameth **m** by a law? 5999
119:150 They draw nigh that follow after **m**: 2154
140: 9 let the **m** of their own lips cover them. 5999
Pr 4:16 they sleep not, except they have **done m**; 7489
6:14 *is* in his heart, he deviseth **m** continually; 7451
6:18 feet that be swift in running to **m**, 7451
10:23 *It is* as sport to a fool to do **m**: but a man of 2154
11:27 he that seeketh **m**, it shall come *unto* him. 7451
12:21 but the wicked shall be filled *with* **m**. 7451
13:17 A wicked messenger falleth into **m**: but 7451
17:20 that hath a perverse tongue falleth into **m**. 7451
24: 2 and their lips talk of **m**. 5999
24:16 up *again:* but the wicked shall fall into **m**. 7451
28:14 he that hardeneth his heart shall fall into **m**. 7451
Isa 47:11 **m** shall fall upon thee; thou shalt not be 1943
59: 4 *they* conceive **m**, and bring forth iniquity. 5999
Eze 7:26 **M** shall come upon mischief, and 1943
7:26 Mischief shall come upon **m**, and 1943
11: 2 these *are* the men that devise **m**, and give 205
Da 11:27 both these kings' hearts *shall be* to **do m**, 4827
Hos 7:15 yet do they imagine **m** against me. 7451
Ac 13:10 And said, O full of all subtilty and all **m**, *4468*

MISCHIEFS (3) [MISCHIEF]
Dt 32:23 I will heap **m** upon them; I will spend mine 7451
Ps 52: 2 Thy tongue deviseth **m**; like a sharp rasor, 1942
140: 2 Which imagine **m** in *their* heart; 7451

MISCHIEVOUS (5) [MISCHIEF]
Ps 21:11 they imagined a **m device**, *which* they are 4209
38:12 and they that seek my hurt speak **m things**, 1942
Pr 24: 8 to do evil shall be called a **m** person. 4209
Ecc 10:13 and the end of his talk *is* **m** madness. 7451
Mic 7: 3 and the great *man,* he uttereth his **m** desire: 1942

MISERABLE (3) [MISERY]
Job 16: 2 I have heard many such *things:* **m** 5999
1Co 15:19 hope in Christ, we are of all men **most m**. *1652*
Rev 3:17 and **m**, and poor, and blind, and naked: *1652*

MISERABLY (1) [MISERY]
Mt 21:41 He will **m** destroy those wicked *men,* and *2560*

MISERIES (2) [MISERY]
La 1: 7 of her **m** all her pleasant things that she had 4788
Jas 5: 1 howl for your **m** that shall come upon *you.* *5004*

MISERY (7) [MISERABLE, MISERABLY, MISERIES]
Jdg 10:16 his soul was grieved for the **m** of Israel. 5999
Job 3:20 is light given to him that is **in m,** 6001
11:16 Because thou shalt forget *thy* **m,** *and* 5999
Pr 31: 7 his poverty, and remember his **m** no more. 5999
Ecc 8: 6 therefore the **m** of man *is* great upon him. 7451
La 3:19 Remembering mine affliction and my **m,** 4788
Ro 3:16 Destruction and **m** *are* in their ways: *5004*

MISFORTUNE See TRAVAIL; TRAVAILED; TRAVAILEST; TRAVAILETH

MISGAB (1)
Jer 48: 1 *and* taken: **M** is confounded and dismayed. 4869

MISHAEL (8)
Ex 6:22 of Uzziel; **M,** and Elzaphan, and Zithri. 4332
Lev 10: 4 Moses called **M** and Elzaphan, the sons of 4332
Ne 8: 4 **M,** and Malchiah, and Hashum, and 4332
Da 1: 6 Daniel, Hananiah, **M,** and Azariah: 4332
1: 7 to **M,** of Meshach; and to Azariah, 4332
1:11 set over Daniel, Hananiah, **M,** and Azariah, 4332
1:19 like Daniel, Hananiah, **M,** and Azariah: 4332
2:17 **M,** and Azariah, his companions: 4333

MISHAL (1)
Jos 21:30 **M** with her suburbs, Abdon with her 4861

MISHAM (1)
1Ch 8:12 Eber, and **M,** and Shamed, who built Ono, 4936

MISHEAL (1)
Jos 19:26 Alammelech, and Amad, and **M;** and 4861

MISHMA (4)
Ge 25:14 And **M,** and Dumah, and Massa, 4927
1Ch 1:30 **M,** and Dumah, Massa, Hadad, and Tema, 4927
4:25 his son, Mibsam his son, **M** his son. 4927
4:26 the sons of **M;** Hamuel his son, Zacchur his 4927

MISHMANNAH (1)
1Ch 12:10 **M** the fourth, Jeremiah the fifth, 4925

MISHRAITES (1)
1Ch 2:53 and the Shumathites, and the **M;** 4954

MISPAR See MIZPAR

MISPERETH (1)
Ne 7: 7 Bilshan, **M,** Bigvai, Nehum, Baanah. 4559

MISREPHOTH-MAIM (2)
Jos 11: 8 unto **M,** and unto the valley of Mizpeh 4956
13: 6 of the hill country from Lebanon unto **M,** 4956

MISS (2) [AMISS, MISSED, MISSING]
Jdg 20:16 sling stones at a hair *breadth,* and not **m.** 2398
1Sa 20: 6 If thy father **at all m** me, then say, 6485+6485

MISSED (3) [MISS]
1Sa 20:18 thou shalt be **m,** because thy seat will be 6485
25:15 we were not hurt, neither **m** we any thing, 6485
25:21 that nothing was **m** of all that *pertained* 6485

MISSING (2) [MISS]
1Sa 25: 7 neither was there ought **m** unto them, 6485
1Ki 20:39 if **by any means** he be **m,** then 6485+6485

MIST (3)
Ge 2: 6 there went up a **m** from the earth, and 108
Ac 13:11 And immediately there fell on him a **m** and *887*
2Pe 2:17 to whom the **m** of darkness is reserved for *2217*

MISTREAT; MISTREATED See VEX; VEXATION; VEXED

MISTRESS (9)
Ge 16: 4 her **m** was despised in her eyes. 1404
16: 8 I flee from the face of my **m** Sarai. 1404
16: 9 Return to thy **m,** and submit thyself under 1404
1Ki 17:17 of the woman, the **m** of the house, fell sick; 1172
2Ki 5: 3 she said unto her **m,** Would God my lord 1404
Ps 123: 2 eyes of a maiden unto the hand of her **m;** 1404
Pr 30:23 and a handmaid that is heir to her **m.** 1404
Isa 24: 2 his master; as *with* the maid, so *with* her **m;** 1404
Na 3: 4 the **m** of witchcrafts, that selleth nations 1172

MISUSED (1)
2Ch 36:16 despised his words, and **m** his prophets, 8591

MITE (1) [MITES]
Lk 12:59 till thou hast paid the very last **m.** *3016*

MITES (2) [MITE]
Mk 12:42 and she threw in two **m,** which make a *3016*
Lk 21: 2 poor widow casting in thither two **m.** *3016*

MITHCAH (2)
Nu 33:28 removed from Tarah, and pitched in **M.** 4989
33:29 they went from **M,** and pitched in 4989

MITHNITE (1)
1Ch 11:43 the son of Maachah, and Joshaphat the **M,** 4981

MITHREDATH (2)
Ezr 1: 8 bring forth by the hand of **M** the treasurer, 4990
4: 7 **M,** Tabeel, and the rest of their 4990

MITRE (13)
Ex 28: 4 and a broidered coat, a **m,** and a girdle: 4701
28:37 it on a blue lace, that it may be upon the **m;** 4701
28:37 upon the forefront of the **m** it shall be. 4701
28:39 thou shalt make the **m** *of* fine linen, and 4701
29: 6 thou shalt put the **m** upon his head, and 4701
29: 6 and put the holy crown upon the **m.** 4701
39:28 a **m** *of* fine linen, and goodly bonnets *of* 4701
39:31 of blue, to fasten *it* on high upon the **m;** 4701
Lev 8: 9 he put the **m** upon his head; also upon 4701
8: 9 also upon the **m,** *even* upon his forefront, 4701
16: 4 and with the linen **m** shall he be attired: 4701
Zec 3: 5 I said, Let them set a fair **m** upon his head. 6797
3: 5 So they set a fair **m** upon his head, and 6797

MITYLENE (1)
Ac 20:14 at Assos, we took him in, and came to **M.** *3412*

MIXED (6) [MIXTURE]
Ex 12:38 a **m** multitude went up also with them; and 6154
Ne 13: 3 separated from Israel all the **m multitude.** 6154
Da 2:41 forasmuch as thou sawest the iron **m** with 6151
2:43 to another, even as iron is not **m** with clay. 6151
Hos 7: 8 he hath **m** himself among the people; 1101
Heb 4: 2 not being **m** with faith in them that heard *4786*

MIXT (4) [MIXTURE]
Nu 11: 4 the **m multitude** that *was* among them fell a 628
Pr 23:30 at the wine; they that go to seek **m wine.** 4469
Isa 1:22 is become dross, thy wine **m** with water: 4107
Da 2:43 whereas thou sawest iron **m** with miry clay, 6151

MIXTURE (3) [MIXED, MIXT]
Ps 75: 8 it is full *of* **m;** and he poureth out of 4538
Jn 19:39 and brought a **m** of myrrh and aloes, *3395*
Rev 14:10 which is poured out **without m** into the cup *194*

MIZAR (1)
Ps 42: 6 and of the Hermonites, from the hill **M.** 4706

MIZPAH (23) [MIZPEH]
Ge 31:49 **M;** for he said, The LORD watch between 4709
1Ki 15:22 built with them Geba of Benjamin, and **M.** 4709
2Ki 25:23 there came to Gedaliah *to* **M,** even Ishmael 4709
25:25 and the Chaldees that were with him at **M.** 4709
2Ch 16: 6 and he built therewith Geba and **M.** 4709
Ne 3: 7 the men of Gibeon, and of **M,** 4709
3:15 son of Col-hozeh, the ruler of part of **M;** 4709
3:19 Ezer the son of Jeshua, the ruler of **M,** 4709
Jer 40: 6 unto Gedaliah the son of Ahikam to **M;** 4708
40: 8 they came to Gedaliah to **M,** even Ishmael 4708
40:10 I *will* dwell at **M** to serve the Chaldeans, 4709
40:12 unto **M,** and gathered wine and 4708
40:13 *were* in the fields, came to Gedaliah to **M,** 4708
40:15 of Kareah spake to Gedaliah in **M** secretly, 4709
41: 1 unto Gedaliah the son of Ahikam to **M;** 4709
41: 1 and there they did eat bread together in **M.** 4708
41: 3 *even* with Gedaliah at **M,** and 4709
41: 6 went forth from **M** to meet them, 4709
41:10 all the residue of the people that *were* in **M,** 4709
41:10 and all the people that remained in **M,** 4709
41:14 carried away captive from **M** cast about 4709

Jer 41:16 from **M**, after *that* he had slain Gedaliah 4709
Hos 5: 1 because ye have been a snare on **M**, and 4709

MIZPAR (1)
Ezr 2: 2 Bilshan, **M**, Bigvai, Rehum, Baanah. 4558

MIZPEH (23) [MIZPAH, RAMATH-MIZPEH]
Jos 11: 3 the Hivite under Hermon in the land of **M**. 4709
11: 8 and unto the valley of **M** eastward; 4708
15:38 And Dilean, and **M**, and Joktheel, 4708
18:26 And **M**, and Chephirah, and Mozah, 4708
Jdg 10:17 themselves together, and encamped in **M**. 4709
11:11 all his words before the LORD in **M**. 4709
11:29 passed over **M** of Gilead, and from Mizpeh 4708
11:29 from **M** of Gilead he passed over *unto* 4708
11:34 Jephthah came *to* **M** unto his house, and 4709
20: 1 the land of Gilead, unto the LORD *in* **M**. 4709
20: 3 the children of Israel were gone up *to* **M**.) 4709
21: 1 Now the men of Israel had sworn in **M**, 4709
21: 5 *him* that came not up to the LORD *to* **M**, 4709
21: 8 that came not up *to* **M** to the LORD? 4709
1Sa 7: 5 Gather all Israel to **M**, and I will pray for 4708
7: 6 they gathered together to **M**, and 4709
7: 6 Samuel judged the children of Israel in **M**. 4708
7: 7 of Israel were gathered together to **M**, 4708
7:11 the men of Israel went out of **M**, and 4709
7:12 set *it* between **M** and Shen, and called 4709
7:16 **M**, and judged Israel in all those places. 4709
10:17 the people together unto the LORD *to* **M**; 4709
22: 3 David went thence *to* **M** of Moab: and 4708

MIZRAIM (4)
Ge 10: 6 Cush, and **M**, and Phut, and Canaan. 4714
10:13 **M** begat Ludim, and Anamim, and 4714
1Ch 1: 8 of Ham; Cush, and **M**, Put, and Canaan. 4714
1:11 **M** begat Ludim, and Anamim, and 4714

MIZZAH (3)
Ge 36:13 Nahath, and Zerah, Shammah, and **M**: 4199
36:17 duke Zerah, duke Shammah, duke **M**: 4199
1Ch 1:37 of Reuel; Nahath, Zerah, Shammah, and **M**. 4199

MNASON (1)
Ac 21:16 and brought *with them* one **M** of Cyprus, *3416*

MO (1) [= MORE] See Index

MOAB (168) [MOABITE, MOABITES, MOABITESS, MOABITISH]
Ge 19:37 bare a son, and called his name **M**: 4124
36:35 who smote Midian in the field of **M**, 4124
Ex 15:15 the mighty men of **M**, trembling shall take 4124
Nu 21:11 in the wilderness which *is* before **M**, 4124
21:13 for Arnon *is* the border of **M**, 4124
21:13 of Moab, between **M** and the Amorites. 4124
21:15 of Ar, and lieth upon the border of **M**. 4124
21:20 that *is* in the country of **M**, *to* the top of 4124
21:26 had fought against the former king of **M**, 4124
21:28 it hath consumed Ar of **M**, *and* the lords of 4124
21:29 Woe to thee, **M**! thou art undone, O people 4124
22: 1 pitched in the plains of **M** on *this* side 4124
22: 3 **M** was sore afraid of the people, because 4124
22: 3 **M** was distressed because of the children of 4124
22: 4 **M** said unto the elders of Midian, 4124
22: 7 the elders of **M** and the elders of Midian 4124
22: 8 and the princes of **M** abode with Balaam. 4124
22:10 king of **M**, hath sent unto me, *saying*, 4124
22:14 the princes of **M** rose up, and they went 4124
22:21 his ass, and went with the princes of **M**. 4124
22:36 he went out to meet him unto a city of **M**, 4124
23: 6 burnt sacrifice, he, and all the princes of **M**. 4124
23: 7 Balak the king of **M** hath brought me from 4124
23:17 and the princes of **M** with him. 4124
24:17 shall smite the corners of **M**, and 4124
25: 1 whoredom with the daughters of **M**. 4124
26: 3 in the plains of **M** by Jordan *near* Jericho, 4124
26:63 in the plains of **M** by Jordan *near* Jericho. 4124
31:12 unto the camp at the plains of **M**, which *are* 4124
33:44 pitched in Ije-abarim, in the border of **M**. 4124
33:48 pitched in the plains of **M** by Jordan *near* 4124
33:49 *even* unto Abel-shittim in the plains of **M**. 4124
33:50 in the plains of **M** by Jordan *near* Jericho, 4124
35: 1 in the plains of **M** by Jordan *near* Jericho, 4124
36:13 in the plains of **M** by Jordan *near* Jericho. 4124
Dt 1: 5 On *this* side Jordan, in the land of **M**, 4124
2: 8 passed *by* the way of the wilderness of **M**. 4124
2:18 over *through* Ar, the coast of **M**, *this* day: 4124
29: 1 with the children of Israel in the land of **M**, 4124
32:49 mount Nebo, which *is* in the land of **M**, 4124
34: 1 Moses went up from the plains of **M** unto 4124
34: 5 of the LORD died there in the land of **M**, 4124
34: 6 he buried him in a valley in the land of **M**, 4124
34: 8 for Moses in the plains of **M** thirty days: 4124
Jos 13:32 distribute for inheritance in the plains of **M**, 4124
24: 9 king of **M**, arose and warred against Israel, 4124
Jdg 3:12 Eglon the king of **M** against Israel, 4124
3:14 served Eglon the king of **M** eighteen years. 4124
3:15 sent a present unto Eglon the king of **M**. 4124
3:17 brought the present unto Eglon king of **M**: 4124
3:28 took the fords of Jordan toward **M**, and 4124
3:29 they slew *of* **M** at that time about ten 4124
3:30 So **M** was subdued that day under the hand 4124
10: 6 the gods of **M**, and the gods of the children 4124
11:15 Israel took not away the land of **M**, 4124
11:17 like manner they sent unto the king of **M**: 4124
11:18 the land of **M**, and came by the east side of 4124
11:18 came by the east side of the land of **M**, and 4124
11:18 but came not within the border of **M**: 4124
11:18 of Moab: for Arnon *was* the border of **M**. 4124
11:25 than Balak the son of Zippor, king of **M**? 4124
Ru 1: 1 went to sojourn in the country of **M**, 4124
1: 2 they came *into* the country of **M**, and 4124
1: 4 they took them wives of the **women of M**; 4125
1: 6 she might return from the country of **M**: 4124
1: 6 for she had heard in the country of **M** how 4124
1:22 which returned out of the country of **M**: 4124
2: 6 back with Naomi out of the country of **M**: 4124
4: 3 that is come again out of the country of **M**, 4124
1Sa 12: 9 into the hand of the king of **M**, and 4124
14:47 against **M**, and against the children of 4124
22: 3 David went thence *to* Mizpeh of **M**: and 4124
22: 3 he said unto the king of **M**, Let my father 4124
22: 4 he brought them before the king of **M**: and 4124
2Sa 8: 2 he smote **M**, and measured them with a 4124
8:12 of **M**, and of the children of Ammon, and 4124
23:20 many acts, he slew two lionlike men of **M**: 4124
1Ki 11: 7 the abomination of **M**, in the hill that *is* 4124
2Ki 1: 1 **M** rebelled against Israel after the death of 4124
3: 4 Mesha king of **M** was a sheepmaster, and 4124
3: 5 that the king of **M** rebelled against the king 4124
3: 7 The king of **M** hath rebelled against me: 4124
3: 7 wilt thou go with me against **M** to battle? 4124
3:10 to deliver them into the hand of **M**. 4124
3:13 to deliver them into the hand of **M**. 4124
3:23 one another: now therefore, **M**, to the spoil. 4124
3:26 when the king of **M** saw that the battle was 4124
1Ch 1:46 which smote Midian in the field of **M**, 4124
4:22 who had the dominion in **M**, and 4124
8: 8 begat *children* in the country of **M**, 4124
11:22 many acts; he slew two lionlike men of **M**: 4124
18: 2 he smote **M**; and the Moabites became 4124
18:11 from **M**, and from the children of Ammon, 4124
2Ch 20: 1 *that* the children of **M**, and the children of 4124
20:10 children of Ammon and **M** and mount Seir, 4124
20:22 **M**, and mount Seir, which were come 4124
20:23 **M** stood up against the inhabitants of 4124
Ne 13:23 wives of Ashdod, of Ammon, *and* **of M**: 4125
Ps 60: 8 **M** *is* my washpot; over Edom will I cast 4124
83: 6 the Ishmaelites; of **M**, and the Hagarenes; 4124
108: 9 **M** *is* my washpot; over Edom will I cast 4124
Isa 11:14 shall lay their hand upon Edom and **M**; 4124
15: 1 The burden of **M**. Because in the night Ar 4124
15: 1 Because in the night Ar of **M** is laid waste, 4124
15: 1 because in the night Kir of **M** is laid waste, 4124
15: 2 **M** shall howl over Nebo, and over Medeba: 4124
15: 4 the armed soldiers of **M** shall cry out; 4124
15: 5 My heart shall cry out for **M**; his fugitives 4124
15: 8 cry is gone round about the borders of **M**; 4124
15: 9 lions upon him that escapeth of **M**, and 4124
16: 2 the daughters of **M** shall be *at* the fords of 4124
16: 4 Let mine outcasts dwell with thee, **M**; 4124
16: 6 We have heard of the pride of **M**; *he is* very 4124
16: 7 Therefore shall **M** howl for Moab, 4124
16: 7 Therefore shall Moab howl for **M**, 4124
16:11 my bowels shall sound like a harp for **M**, 4124
16:12 when it is seen that **M** is weary on the high 4124
16:13 hath spoken concerning **M** since that time. 4124
16:14 and the glory of **M** shall be contemned, 4124
25:10 **M** shall be trodden down under him, 4124

M

Jer 9:26 **M**, and all *that are* in the utmost corners, 4124
25:21 Edom, and **M**, and the children of Ammon, 4124
27: 3 to the king of **M**, and to the king of 4124
40:11 Likewise when all the Jews that *were* in **M**, 4124
48: 1 Against **M** thus saith the LORD of hosts, 4124
48: 2 *There shall be* no more praise of **M**: 4124
48: 4 **M** is destroyed; her little ones have caused 4124
48: 9 Give wings unto **M**, that it may flee and 4124
48:11 **M** hath been at ease from his youth, and 4124
48:13 **M** shall be ashamed of Chemosh, as 4124
48:15 **M** is spoiled, and gone up *out of* her cities, 4124
48:16 The calamity of **M** *is* near to come, and 4124
48:18 for the spoiler of **M** shall come upon thee, 4124
48:20 **M** is confounded; for it is broken down: 4124
48:20 cry; tell ye *it* in Arnon, that **M** is spoiled, 4124
48:24 upon all the cities of the land of **M**, far or 4124
48:25 The horn of **M** is cut off, and his arm is 4124
48:26 **M** also shall wallow in his vomit, and 4124
48:28 O ye that dwell in **M**, leave the cities, and 4124
48:29 We have heard the pride of **M**; *he is* 4124
48:31 Therefore will I howl for **M**, and I will cry 4124
48:31 howl for Moab, and I will cry out for all **M**; 4124
48:33 the plentiful field, and from the land of **M**; 4124
48:35 Moreover I will cause to cease in **M**, 4124
48:36 Therefore mine heart shall sound for **M** like 4124
48:38 generally upon all the housetops of **M**, 4124
48:38 for I have broken **M** like a vessel wherein 4124
48:39 how hath **M** turned the back with shame! 4124
48:39 so shall **M** be a derision and a dismaying to 4124
48:40 and shall spread his wings over **M**. 4124
48:41 the mighty *men's* hearts in **M** at that day 4124
48:42 **M** shall be destroyed from *being* a people, 4124
48:43 O inhabitant of **M**, saith the LORD. 4124
48:44 for I will bring upon it, *even* upon **M**, 4124
48:45 shall devour the corner of **M**, and 4124
48:46 Woe be unto thee, O **M**! the people of 4124
48:47 Yet will I bring again the captivity of **M** in 4124
48:47 the LORD. Thus far *is* the judgment of **M**. 4124
Eze 25: 8 Because that **M** and Seir do say, Behold, 4124
25: 9 I *will* open the side of **M** from the cities, 4124
25:11 I will execute judgments upon **M**; and 4124
Da 11:41 **M**, and the chief of the children of Ammon. 4124
Am 2: 1 For three transgressions of **M**, and for four, 4124
2: 2 I will send a fire upon **M**, and it shall 4124
2: 2 **M** shall die with tumult, with shouting, *and* 4124
Mic 6: 5 remember now what Balak king of **M** 4124
Zep 2: 8 I have heard the reproach of **M**, and 4124
2: 9 Surely **M** shall be as Sodom, and 4124

MOABITE (3) [MOAB]
Dt 23: 3 **M** shall not enter into the congregation of 4125
1Ch 11:46 the sons of Elnaam, and Ithmah the **M**, 4125
Ne 13: 1 the **M** should not come into 4125

MOABITES (19) [MOAB]
Ge 19:37 the same *is* the father of the **M** unto *this* 4124
Nu 22: 4 Balak the son of Zippor *was* king of the **M** 4124
Dt 2: 9 LORD said unto me, Distress not the **M**, 4124
2:11 the Anakims; but the **M** call them Emims. 4125
2:29 and the **M** which dwell in Ar, did unto me;) 4125
Jdg 3:28 your enemies the **M** into your hand. 4124
2Sa 8: 2 *so* the **M** became David's servants, and 4124
1Ki 11: 1 *women of the* **M**, Ammonites, Edomites, 4125
11:33 Chemosh the god of the **M**, and Milcom 4124
2Ki 3:18 he will deliver the **M** also into your hand. 4124
3:21 when all the **M** heard that the kings were 4124
3:22 the **M** saw the water on the other side *as* 4124
3:24 the Israelites rose up and smote the **M**, so 4124
3:24 they went forward smiting the **M**, even in 4124
13:20 the bands of the **M** invaded the land *at* 4124
23:13 for Chemosh the abomination of the **M**, 4124
24: 2 bands of the **M**, and bands of the children 4124
1Ch 18: 2 the **M** became David's servants, and 4124
Ezr 9: 1 the **M**, the Egyptians, and the Amorites. 4125

MOABITESS (6) [MOAB]
Ru 1:22 So Naomi returned, and Ruth the **M**, 4125
2: 2 Ruth the **M** said unto Naomi, Let me now 4125
2:21 And Ruth the **M** said, He said unto me also, 4125
4: 5 thou must buy *it* also of Ruth the **M**, 4125
4:10 Moreover Ruth the **M**, the wife of Mahlon, 4125
2Ch 24:26 and Jehozabad the son of Shimrith a **M**. 4125

MOABITISH (1) [MOAB]
Ru 2: 6 It *is* the **M** damsel that came back with 4125

MOADIAH (1)
Ne 12:17 Zichri; of Miniamin, of **M**, Piltai; 4153

MOCK (12) [MOCKED, MOCKER, MOCKERS, MOCKEST, MOCKETH, MOCKING, MOCKINGS]
Ge 39:14 he hath brought in a Hebrew unto us to **m** 6711
39:17 brought unto us, came in unto me to **m** me: 6711
Job 13: 9 *one* man mocketh another, do ye *so* **m** him? 2048
21: 3 and after that I have spoken, **m** on. 3932
Pr 1:26 I will **m** when your fear cometh; 3932
14: 9 Fools **make a m at** sin: but among 3887
Jer 38:19 deliver me into their hand, and they **m** me. 5953
La 1: 7 saw her, *and* did **m** at her sabbaths. 7832
Eze 22: 5 shall **m** thee, *which art* infamous *and* 7046
Mt 20:19 And shall deliver him to the Gentiles to **m**, *1702*
Mk 10:34 And they shall **m** him, and shall scourge *1702*
Lk 14:29 finish *it*, all that behold *it* begin to **m** him, *1702*

MOCKED (21) [MOCK]
Ge 19:14 he seemed as one that **m** unto his sons in 6711
Nu 22:29 said unto the ass, Because thou hast **m** me: 5953
Jdg 16:10 Behold, thou hast **m** me, and told me lies: 2048
16:13 Hitherto thou hast **m** me, and told me lies: 2048
16:15 thou hast **m** me these three times, and 2048
1Ki 18:27 that Elijah **m** them, and said, Cry aloud: 2048
2Ki 2:23 **m** him, and said unto him, Go up, thou bald 7046
2Ch 30:10 they laughed them to scorn, and **m** them. 3932
36:16 they **m** the messengers of God, and 3931
Ne 4: 1 took great indignation, and **m** the Jews. 3932
Job 12: 4 I am *as* **one m** of his neighbour, 7814
Mt 2:16 when he saw that he was **m** of the wise *1702*
27:29 and **m** him, saying, Hail, King of the Jews! *1702*
27:31 And after that they had **m** him, they took *1702*
Mk 15:20 And when they had **m** him, they took off *1702*
Lk 18:32 and shall be **m**, and spitefully entreated, *1702*
22:63 And the men that held Jesus **m** him, and *1702*
23:11 and **m** *him*, and arrayed him in a gorgeous *1702*
23:36 And the soldiers also **m** him, coming to *1702*
Ac 17:32 of the resurrection of the dead, some **m**: *5512*
Gal 6: 7 Be not deceived; God is not **m**: *3456*

MOCKER (1) [MOCK]
Pr 20: 1 Wine *is* a **m**, strong drink *is* raging: and 3887

MOCKERS (5) [MOCK]
Job 17: 2 *Are there* not **m** with me? and *doth not* 2049
Ps 35:16 With hypocritical **m** in feasts, *they* gnashed 3934
Isa 28:22 Now therefore be ye not **m**, lest your bands 3887
Jer 15:17 I sat not in the assembly of the **m**, 7832
Jude 1:18 How that they told you there should be **m** *1703*

MOCKEST (1) [MOCK]
Job 11: 3 when thou **m**, shall no man make *thee* 3932

MOCKETH (5) [MOCK]
Job 13: 9 or as *one* man **m** another, do ye *so* 2048
39:22 He **m** at fear, and is not affrighted; 7832
Pr 17: 5 Whoso **m** the poor reproacheth his Maker: 3932
30:17 The eye *that* **m** at *his* father, and 3932
Jer 20: 7 I am in derision daily, every one **m** me. 3932

MOCKING (5) [MOCK]
Ge 21: 9 which she had born unto Abraham, **m**. 6711
Eze 22: 4 unto the heathen, and a **m** to all countries. 7048
Mt 27:41 Likewise also the chief priests **m** *him*, with *1702*
Mk 15:31 Likewise also the chief priests **m** said *1702*
Ac 2:13 Others **m** said, *These men* are full of new *5512*

MOCKINGS (1) [MOCK]
Heb 11:36 And others had trial of *cruel* **m** and *1701*

MODEL See ENSAMPLE

MODERATELY (1) [MODERATION]
Joel 2:23 hath given you the former rain **m**, 6666+3807.1

MODERATION (1) [MODERATELY]
Php 4: 5 Let your **m** be known unto all men. *1933*

MODEST (1)
1Ti 2: 9 that women adorn themselves in **m** apparel, *2887*

MOE (28) [= MORE] See Index

MOIST (1) [MOISTENED, MOISTURE]
Nu 6: 3 liquor of grapes, nor eat **m** grapes, or dried. 3892

MOISTENED (1) [MOIST]
Job 21:24 *of* milk, and his bones are **m** with marrow. 8248

MOISTURE (2) [MOIST]
Ps 32: 4 my **m** is turned into the drought of summer. 3955
Lk 8: 6 it withered away, because *it* lacked **m**. *2429*

MOLADAH (4)
Jos 15:26 Amam, and Shema, and **M**, 4137
19: 2 inheritance Beer-sheba, or Sheba, and **M**, 4137
1Ch 4:28 at Beer-sheba, and **M**, and Hazar-shual, 4137
Ne 11:26 at Jeshua, and at **M**, and at Beth-phelet, 4137

MOLDY See MOULDY

MOLE (1) [MOLES]
Lev 11:30 and the lizard, and the snail, and the **m**. 8580

MOLECH (8)
Lev 18:21 *any* of thy seed pass through *the fire* to **M**, 4432
20: 2 that giveth *any* of his seed unto **M**; 4432
20: 3 because he hath given of his seed unto **M**, 4432
20: 4 when he giveth of his seed unto **M**, and 4432
20: 5 to commit whoredom with **M**, from among 4432
1Ki 11: 7 the hill that *is* before Jerusalem, and for **M**, 4432
2Ki 23:10 his daughter to pass through the fire to **M**. 4432
Jer 32:35 daughters to pass through *the fire* unto **M**; 4432

MOLES (1) [MOLE]
Isa 2:20 to worship, to the **m** and to the bats; 2661+6512

MOLID (1)
1Ch 2:29 and she bare him Ahban, and **M**. 4140

MOLLIFIED (1)
Isa 1: 6 neither bound up, neither **m** with ointment. 7401

MOLOCH (2) [MALCHAM, MILCOM]
Am 5:26 ye have borne the tabernacle of your **M** and 4429
Ac 7:43 ye took up the tabernacle of **M**, and the star *3434*

MOLTEN (39) [MELT]
Ex 32: 4 graving tool, after he had made it a **m** calf: 4541
32: 8 they have made them a **m** calf, and 4541
34:17 Thou shalt make thee no **m** gods. 4541
Lev 19: 4 unto idols, nor make to yourselves **m** gods: 4541
Nu 33:52 destroy all their **m** images, and quite pluck 4541
Dt 9:12 they have made them a **m image**. 4541
9:16 your God, *and* had made you a **m** calf: 4541
27:15 man that maketh *any* graven or **m image**, 4541
Jdg 17: 3 to make a graven image and a **m image**: 4541
17: 4 thereof a graven image and a **m image**: 4541
18:14 and a graven image, and a **m image**? 4541
18:17 and the teraphim, and the **m image**: 4541
18:18 and the teraphim, and the **m image**. 4541
1Ki 7:16 he made two chapiters *of* **m** brass, to set 3332
7:23 he made a **m** sea, ten cubits from the one 3332
7:30 under the laver *were* undersetters **m**, at 3332
7:33 their felloes, and their spokes, *were* all **m**. 3332
14: 9 and made thee other gods, and **m images**, 4541
2Ki 17:16 and made them **m images**, *even* two calves, 4541
2Ch 4: 2 Also he made a **m** sea of ten cubits from 3332
28: 2 and made also **m images** for Baalim. 4541
34: 3 and the carved images, and the **m images**. 4541
34: 4 the **m images**, he brake *in pieces,* and 4541
Ne 9:18 when they had made them a **m** calf, and 4541
Job 28: 2 of the earth, and brass *is* **m** *out of* the stone. 6694
37:18 *which is* strong, *and* as a **m** looking glass? 3332
Ps 106:19 in Horeb, and worshipped the **m image**. 4541
Isa 30:22 and the ornament of thy **m images** of gold: 4541
41:29 their **m images** *are* wind and confusion. 5262
42:17 that say to the **m images**, Ye *are* our gods. 4541
44:10 **m** a graven image *that* is profitable for 5258
48: 5 my graven image, and my **m image**, 5262
Jer 10:14 for his **m image** *is* falsehood, and *there is* 5262
51:17 for his **m image** *is* falsehood, and *there is* 5262
Eze 24:11 and *that* the filthiness of it may be **m** in it, 5413
Hos 13: 2 have made them **m images** of their silver, 4541
Mic 1: 4 the mountains shall be **m** under him, and 4549
Na 1:14 cut off the graven image and the **m image**: 4541
Hab 2:18 the **m image**, and a teacher of lies, that 4541

MOMENT (22)
Ex 33: 5 will come up into the midst of thee in a **m**, 7281
Nu 16:21 that I may consume them **in a m**. 7281+3509.1
16:45 that I may consume them as **in a m**. 7281
Job 7:18 him every morning, *and* try him every **m**? 7281
20: 5 and the joy of the hypocrite *but* for a **m**? 7281
21:13 in wealth, and in a **m** go down *to* the grave. 7281
34:20 *In* a **m** shall they die, and the people shall 7281
Ps 30: 5 For his anger *endureth but* a **m**; in his 7281
73:19 are they *brought* into desolation, as *in* a **m**! 7281
Pr 12:19 for ever: but a lying tongue *is* but for a **m**. 7280
Isa 26:20 hide thyself as it were for a little **m**, 7281
27: 3 do keep it; I will water it **every m**: 7281+3807.1
47: 9 these two *things* shall come to thee *in* a **m** 7281
54: 7 For a small **m** have I forsaken thee; but 7281
54: 8 little wrath I hid my face from thee for a **m**; 7281
Jer 4:20 my tents spoiled, *and* my curtains **in a m**. 7281
La 4: 6 that was overthrown as **in a m**, and 7281
Eze 26:16 shall tremble at every **m**, and be astonished 7281
32:10 they shall tremble at every **m**, every man 7281
Lk 4: 5 the kingdoms of the world in a **m** of time. *4743*
1Co 15:52 In a **m**, in the twinkling of an eye, at the last *823*
2Co 4:17 our light affliction, which is but **for a m**, *3910*

MONEY (140) [MONEYCHANGERS, MONEY-CHANGERS]
Ge 17:12 or bought with **m** of any stranger, which *is* 3701
17:13 he that is bought with thy **m**, must needs be 3701
17:23 and all that were bought with his **m**, 3701
17:27 and bought with **m** of the stranger, 3701
23: 9 for as much **m** as it is worth he shall give it 3701
23:13 I will give *thee* **m** for the field; take *it* of 3701
23:16 of silver, current *m* with the merchant. NIH
31:15 and hath quite devoured also our **m**. 3701
33:19 for an hundred **pieces of m**. 7192
42:25 to restore every man's **m** into his sack, and 3701
42:27 ass provender in the inn, he espied his **m**; 3701
42:28 he said unto his brethren, My **m** is restored; 3701
42:35 every man's bundle of **m** *was* in his sack: 3701
42:35 and their father saw the bundles of **m**, 3701
43:12 take double **m** in your hand; and the money 3701
43:12 the **m** that was brought again in the mouth 3701
43:15 they took double **m** in their hand, and 3701
43:18 Because of the **m** that was returned in our 3701
43:21 every man's **m** *was* in the mouth of his 3701
43:21 the mouth of his sack, our **m** in full weight: 3701
43:22 other **m** have we brought down in our 3701
43:22 we cannot tell who put our **m** in our sacks. 3701
43:23 I had your **m**. And he brought Simeon out 3701
44: 1 and put every man's **m** in his sack's mouth. 3701
44: 2 mouth of the youngest, and his corn **m**. 3701
44: 8 Behold, the **m**, which we found in our 3701
47:14 Joseph gathered up all the **m** that was 3701
47:14 Joseph brought the **m** into Pharaoh's house. 3701
47:15 when **m** failed in the land of Egypt, and 3701
47:15 we die in thy presence? for the **m** faileth. 3701
47:16 and I will give you for your cattle, if **m** fail. 3701
47:18 *it* from my lord, how that our **m** is spent; 3701
Ex 12:44 every man's servant that is bought for **m**, 3701
21:11 then shall she go out free without **m**. 3701
21:21 he shall not be punished: for he *is* his **m**. 3701
21:30 If there be laid on him a **sum of m**, then 3724
21:34 *and* give **m** unto the owner of them; 3701
21:35 shall sell the live ox, and divide the **m** of it; 3701
22: 7 If a man shall deliver unto his neighbour **m** 3701
22:17 he shall pay **m** according to the dowry of 3701
22:25 If thou lend **m** to *any of* my people *that is* 3701
30:16 thou shalt take the atonement **m** of 3701
Lev 22:11 if the priest buy *any* soul with his **m**, 3701
25:37 Thou shalt not give him thy **m** upon usury, 3701
25:51 out of the **m** that he was bought for. 3701
27:15 he shall add the fifth *part* of the **m** of thy 3701
27:18 the priest shall reckon unto him the **m** 3701
27:19 he shall add the fifth *part* of the **m** of thy 3701
Nu 3:48 thou shalt give the **m**, wherewith the odd 3701
3:49 Moses took the redemption **m** of them that 3701
3:50 of the children of Israel took he the **m**; 3701
3:51 Moses gave the **m** of them that were 3701
18:16 thine estimation, *for* the **m** of five shekels, 3701
Dt 2: 6 Ye shall buy meat of them for **m**, that ye 3701
2: 6 ye shall also buy water of them for **m**, 3701
2:28 Thou shalt sell me meat for **m**, that I may 3701

Dt 2:28 and give me water for **m**, that I may drink: 3701
14:25 shalt thou turn *it* into **m**, and bind up 3701
14:25 bind up the **m** in thine hand, and shalt go 3701
14:26 thou shalt bestow *that* **m** for whatsoever thy 3701
21:14 thou shalt not sell her at all for **m**, 3701
23:19 usury of **m**, usury of victuals, usury of any 3701
Jdg 5:19 waters of Megiddo; they took no gain of **m**. 3701
16:18 up unto her, and brought **m** in their hand. 3701
17: 4 Yet he restored the **m** unto his mother; and 3701
1Ki 21: 2 to thee, I will give thee the worth of it *in* **m**. 3701
21: 6 said unto him, Give me thy vineyard for **m**; 3701
21:15 which he refused to give thee for **m**: 3701
2Ki 5:26 *Is it* a time to receive **m**, and to receive 3701
12: 4 All the **m** of the dedicated *things* that is 3701
12: 4 *even* the **m** of every one that passeth 3701
12: 4 *the account,* the **m** that every man is set at, 3701
12: 4 all the **m** that cometh into any man's heart 3701
12: 7 receive no *more* **m** of your acquaintance, 3701
12: 8 the priests consented to receive no *more* **m** 3701
12: 9 **m** that was brought *into* the house of 3701
12:10 when they saw that *there was* much **m** in 3701
12:10 told the **m** that was found *in* the house of 3701
12:11 they gave the **m**, being told, into the hands 3701
12:13 of the **m** that was brought *into* the house of 3701
12:15 into whose hand they delivered the **m** to be 3701
12:16 The trespass **m** and sin money was not 3701
12:16 sin **m** was not brought *into* the house of 3701
15:20 Menahem exacted the **m** of Israel, *even* of 3701
22: 7 of the **m** that was delivered into their hand, 3701
22: 9 Thy servants have gathered the **m** that was 3701
23:35 he taxed the land to give the **m** according to 3701
2Ch 24: 5 gather of all Israel **m** to repair the house of 3701
24:11 when they saw that *there was* much **m**, 3701
24:11 day by day, and gathered **m** in abundance. 3701
24:14 brought the rest of the **m** before the king 3701
34: 9 they delivered the **m** that was brought *into* 3701
34:14 when they brought out the **m** that was 3701
34:17 they have gathered together the **m** that was 3701
Ezr 3: 7 They gave **m** also unto the masons, and 3701
7:17 That thou mayest buy speedily with this **m** 3702
Ne 5: 4 We have borrowed **m** for the king's tribute, 3701
5:10 *might* exact of them **m** and corn: 3701
5:11 also the hundredth *part* of the **m**, and *of* 3701
Est 4: 7 of the sum of the **m** that Haman had 3701
Job 31:39 If I have eaten the fruits thereof without **m**, 3701
42:11 every man also gave him a **piece of m**, and 7192
Ps 15: 5 *He that* putteth not out his **m** to usury, 3701
Pr 7:20 He hath taken a bag of **m** with him, 3701
Ecc 7:12 wisdom *is* a defence, *and* **m** *is* a defence: 3701
10:19 maketh merry: but **m** answereth all *things.* 3701
Isa 43:24 hast bought me no sweet cane with **m**, 3701
52: 3 and ye shall be redeemed without **m**. 3701
55: 1 ye to the waters, and he that hath no **m**; 3701
55: 1 buy wine and milk without **m** and without 3701
55: 2 Wherefore do ye spend **m** for *that which is* 3701
Jer 32: 9 *was* in Anathoth, and weighed him the **m**, 3701
32:10 weighed *him* the **m** in the balances. 3701
32:25 Buy thee the field for **m**, and 3701
32:44 *Men* shall buy fields for **m**, and 3701
La 5: 4 We have drunken our water for **m**; 3701
Mic 3:11 and the prophets thereof divine for **m**: 3701
Mt 17:24 they that received **tribute m** came to Peter, *1323*
17:27 his mouth, thou shalt find a **piece of m**: *4715*
22:19 Shew me the tribute **m**. And they brought *3546*
25:18 and digged in the earth, and hid his lord's **m**. *694*
25:27 to have put my **m** to the exchangers, *694*
28:12 they gave large **m** unto the soldiers, *694*
28:15 So they took the **m**, and did as they were *694*
Mk 6: 8 no scrip, no bread, no **m** in *their* purse: *5475*
12:41 beheld how the people cast **m** into *5475*
14:11 they were glad, and promised to give him **m**. *694*
Lk 9: 3 nor scrip, neither bread, neither **m**; *694*
19:15 unto him, to whom he had given the **m**, *694*
19:23 then gavest not thou my **m** into the bank, *694*
22: 5 were glad, and covenanted to give him **m**. *694*
Jn 2:14 and doves, and the **changers of m** sitting: *2773*
2:15 and poured out the changers' **m**, and *2772*
Ac 4:37 sold *it,* and brought the **m**, and laid *it* at *5536*
7:16 **m** of the sons of Emmor the *father* of *694*
8:18 Holy Ghost was given, he offered them **m**, *5536*
8:20 Thy **m** perish with thee, because thou hast *694*
8:20 the gift of God may be purchased with **m**. *5536*
24:26 He hoped also that **m** should have been *5536*
1Ti 6:10 For the **love of m** is the root of all evil: *5365*

MONEYCHANGERS, MONEY-CHANGERS (2) [MONEY]
Mt 21:12 and overthrew the tables of the **m**, and *2855*
Mk 11:15 and overthrew the tables of the **m**, and *2855*

MONEYLENDER See USURER

MONSTER See WHALE; WHALE'S; WHALES

MONSTERS (1)
La 4: 3 Even the **sea m** draw out the breast, 8577

MONTH (250) [MONTHLY, MONTHS]
Ge 7:11 in the second **m**, the seventeenth day of 2320
7:11 the seventeenth day of the **m**, 2320
8: 4 the ark rested in the seventh **m**, on 2320
8: 4 on the seventeenth day of the **m**, upon 2320
8: 5 decreased continually until the tenth **m**: 2320
8: 5 in the tenth **m**, on the first *day* of the month, NIH
8: 5 the tenth *month,* on the first *day* of the **m**, 2320
8:13 in the first **m**, the first *day* of the month, NIH
8:13 in the first *month,* the first *day* of the **m**, 2320
8:14 in the second **m**, on the seven and 2320
8:14 on the seven and twentieth day of the **m**, 2320
29:14 And he abode with him the space of a **m**. 2320
Ex 12: 2 This **m** *shall be* unto you the beginning of 2320
12: 2 it *shall be* the first **m** of the year to you. 2320
12: 3 In the tenth *day* of this **m** they shall take to 2320
12: 6 *up* until the fourteenth day of the same **m**: 2320
12:18 In the first *m*, on the fourteenth day of NIH
12:18 on the fourteenth day of the **m** at even, 2320
12:18 the one and twentieth day of the **m** at even. 2320
13: 4 *This* day came ye out in the **m** Abib. 2320
13: 5 that thou shalt keep this service in this **m**. 2320
16: 1 on the fifteenth day of the second **m** after 2320
19: 1 In the third **m**, when the children of Israel 2320
23:15 in the time appointed of the **m** Abib; 2320
34:18 in the time of the **m** Abib: 2320
34:18 for in the **m** Abib thou camest out from 2320
40: 2 On the first day of the first **m** shalt thou set 2320
40:17 it came to pass in the first **m** in the second 2320
40:17 on the first *day* of the **m**, *that* the tabernacle 2320
Lev 16:29 *that* in the seventh **m**, on the tenth *day* of 2320
16:29 on the tenth *day* of the **m**, ye shall afflict 2320
23: 5 In the fourteenth *day* of the first **m** at even 2320
23: 6 on the fifteenth day of the same **m** *is* 2320
23:24 saying, In the seventh **m**, in the first *day* of 2320
23:24 the seventh month, in the first *day* of the **m**, 2320
23:27 Also on the tenth *day* of this seventh **m** 2320
23:32 in the ninth *day* of the **m** at even, from even 2320
23:34 The fifteenth day of this seventh **m** *shall be* 2320
23:39 Also in the fifteenth day of the seventh **m**, 2320
23:41 ye shall celebrate it in the seventh **m**. 2320
25: 9 to sound on the tenth *day* of the seventh **m**, 2320
27: 6 if *it be* from a **m** old even unto five years 2320
Nu 1: 1 on the first *day* of the second **m**, 2320
1:18 together on the first *day* of the second **m**, 2320
3:15 every male from a **m** old and upward shalt 2320
3:22 of all the males, from a **m** old and upward, 2320
3:28 from a **m** old and upward, *were* eight 2320
3:34 from a **m** old and upward, *were* six 2320
3:39 all the males from a **m** old and upward, 2320
3:40 males of the children of Israel from a **m** old 2320
3:43 from a **m** old and upward, of those that 2320
9: 1 in the first **m** of the second year after they 2320
9: 3 In the fourteenth day of this **m**, at even, 2320
9: 5 first **m** at even in the wilderness of Sinai: 2320
9:11 The fourteenth day of the second **m** at even 2320
9:22 *whether it were* two days, or a **m**, or a year, 2320
10:11 pass on the twentieth *day* of the second **m**, 2320
11:20 *But* even a whole **m**, until it come out at 2320
11:21 them flesh, that they may eat a whole **m**. 2320
18:16 those that are *to be* redeemed from a **m** old 2320
20: 1 *into* the desert of Zin in the first **m**: 2320
26:62 all males from a **m** old and upward: 2320
28:14 **every m** throughout 2320+2320+871.1
28:16 in the fourteenth day of the first **m** *is* 2320
28:17 in the fifteenth day of this **m** *is* the feast: 2320
29: 1 in the seventh **m**, on the first *day* of 2320
29: 1 seventh month, on the first *day* of the **m**, 2320
29: 6 Beside the burnt offering of the **m**, and 2320
29: 7 *day* of this seventh **m** a holy convocation; 2320
29:12 on the fifteenth day of the seventh **m** ye 2320
33: 3 they departed from Rameses in the first **m**, 2320
33: 3 on the fifteenth day of the first **m**; 2320

M

Nu 33:38 of Egypt, in the first *day* of the fifth **m**. 2320
Dt 1: 3 in the eleventh **m**, on the first *day* of 2320
1: 3 eleventh month, on the first *day* of the **m**, 2320
16: 1 Observe the **m** of Abib, and keep 2320
16: 1 for in the **m** of Abib the LORD thy God 2320
21:13 her father and her mother a **full m**: 3117+3391
Jos 4:19 of Jordan on the tenth *day* of the first **m**, 2320
5:10 of the **m** at even in the plains of Jericho. 2320
1Sa 20:27 *which was* the second *day* of the **m**, 2320
20:34 did eat no meat the second day of the **m**: 2320
1Ki 4: 7 each man *his* **m** in a year made provision. 2320
4:27 king Solomon's table, every man *in* his **m**: 2320
5:14 to Lebanon, ten thousand a **m** *by* courses: 2320
5:14 a **m** they were in Lebanon, *and* two months 2320
6: 1 in the **m** Zif, which *is* the second month, 2320
6: 1 in the month Zif, which *is* the second **m**, 2320
6:37 the house of the LORD laid, in the **m** Zif: 3391
6:38 in the eleventh year, in the **m** Bul, which *is* 3391
6:38 in the month Bul, which *is* the eighth **m**, 2320
8: 2 Solomon at the feast in the **m** Ethanim, 3391
8: 2 month Ethanim, which *is* the seventh **m**. 2320
12:32 Jeroboam ordained a feast in the eighth **m**, 2320
12:32 on the fifteenth day of the **m**, like unto 2320
12:33 in Beth-el the fifteenth day of the eighth **m**, 2320
12:33 *even* in the **m** which he had devised of his 2320
2Ki 15:13 and he reigned a **full m** in Samaria. 3117+3391
25: 1 in the tenth **m**, in the tenth *day* of 2320
25: 1 the tenth month, in the tenth *day* of the **m**, 2320
25: 3 on the ninth *day* of the *fourth* **m** the famine 2320
25: 8 in the fifth **m**, on the seventh *day* of 2320
25: 8 fifth month, on the seventh *day* of the **m**, 2320
25:25 it came to pass in the seventh **m**, 2320
25:27 in the twelfth **m**, on the seven and 2320
25:27 on the seven and twentieth *day* of the **m**, 2320
1Ch 12:15 they that went over Jordan in the first **m**, 2320
27: 1 went out **m** by month throughout all 2320
27: 1 went out month by **m** throughout all 2320
27: 2 Over the first course for the first **m** *was* 2320
27: 3 all the captains of the host for the first **m**. 2320
27: 4 over the course of the second **m** *was* Dodai 2320
27: 5 The third captain of the host for the third **m** 2320
27: 7 The fourth *captain* for the fourth **m** *was* 2320
27: 8 The fifth captain for the fifth **m** *was* 2320
27: 9 The sixth *captain* for the sixth **m** *was* Ira 2320
27:10 The seventh *captain* for the seventh **m** *was* 2320
27:11 The eighth *captain* for the eighth **m** *was* 2320
27:12 The ninth *captain* for the ninth **m** *was* 2320
27:13 The tenth *captain* for the tenth **m** *was* 2320
27:14 The eleventh *captain* for the eleventh **m** 2320
27:15 The twelfth *captain* for the twelfth **m** *was* 2320
2Ch 3: 2 to build in the second *day* of the second **m**, 2320
5: 3 in the feast which *was in* the seventh **m**. 2320
7:10 twentieth day of the seventh **m** he sent 2320
15:10 together *at* Jerusalem in the third **m**, 2320
29: 3 in the first year of his reign, in the first **m**, 2320
29:17 on the first *day* of the first **m** to sanctify, 2320
29:17 on the eighth day of the **m** came they to 2320
29:17 in the sixteenth day of the first **m** they 2320
30: 2 to keep the passover in the second **m**. 2320
30:13 feast of unleavened bread in the second **m**, 2320
30:15 on the fourteenth *day* of the second **m**: 2320
31: 7 In the third **m** they began to lay 2320
31: 7 and finished *them* in the seventh **m**. 2320
35: 1 on the fourteenth *day* of the first **m**. 2320
Ezr 3: 1 when the seventh **m** was come, and 2320
3: 6 From the first day of the seventh **m** began 2320
3: 8 in the second **m**, began Zerubbabel the son 2320
6:15 finished on the third day of the **m** Adar, 3393
6:19 upon the fourteenth *day* of the first **m**. 2320
7: 8 he came *to* Jerusalem in the fifth **m**, 2320
7: 9 For upon the first *day* of the first **m** began 2320
7: 9 on the first *day* of the fifth **m** came he to 2320
8:31 of Ahava on the twelfth *day* of the first **m**, 2320
10: 9 It *was* the ninth **m**, on the twentieth *day* of 2320
10: 9 ninth month, on the twentieth *day* of the **m**; 2320
10:16 sat down in the first day of the tenth **m** to 2320
10:17 strange wives by the first day of the first **m**. 2320
Ne 1: 1 it came to pass in the **m** Chisleu, *in* 2320
2: 1 it came to pass in the **m** Nisan, *in* 2320
6:15 in the twenty and fifth *day* of *the* **m** Elul, NIH
7:73 when the seventh **m** came, the children of 2320
8: 2 upon the first day of the seventh **m**. 2320
8:14 in booths in the feast of the seventh **m**: 2320
9: 1 fourth day of this **m** the children of Israel 2320
Est 2:16 into his house royal in the tenth **m**, 2320
2:16 which *is* the **m** Tebeth, in the seventh year 2320
3: 7 In the first **m**, that *is*, the month Nisan, 2320
3: 7 In the first month, that *is*, the **m** Nisan, 2320
3: 7 from day to day, and from **m** to month, 2320
3: 7 from day to day, and from month to **m**, 2320
3: 7 *to* the twelfth **m**, that *is*, the month Adar. NIH
3: 7 *to* the twelfth *month*, that *is*, the **m** Adar. 2320
3:12 called on the thirteenth day of the first **m**, 2320
3:13 upon the thirteenth *day* of the twelfth **m**, 2320
3:13 which *is* the **m** Adar, and *to take* the spoil 2320
8: 9 scribes called at that time in the third **m**, 2320
8: 9 that *is*, the **m** Sivan, on the three and 2320
8:12 upon the thirteenth *day* of the twelfth **m**, 2320
8:12 of the twelfth month, which *is* the **m** Adar. 2320
9: 1 Now in the twelfth **m**, that *is*, the month 2320
9: 1 in the twelfth month, that *is*, the **m** Adar, 2320
9:15 on the fourteenth day also of the **m** Adar, 2320
9:17 On the thirteenth day of the **m** Adar; and 2320
9:19 made the fourteenth day of the **m** Adar *a* 2320
9:21 keep the fourteenth day of the **m** Adar, 2320
9:22 the **m** which was turned unto them from 2320
Jer 1: 3 away of Jerusalem captive in the fifth **m**. 2320
2:24 in her **m** they shall find her. 2320
28: 1 in the fourth year, *and* in the fifth **m**, 2320
28:17 died the same year in the seventh **m**. 2320
36: 9 in the ninth **m**, *that* they proclaimed a fast 2320
36:22 king sat *in* the winterhouse in the ninth **m**: 2320
39: 1 in the tenth **m**, came Nebuchadrezzar king 2320
39: 2 in the fourth **m**, the ninth *day* of the month, 2320
39: 2 in the fourth month, the ninth *day* of the **m**, 2320
41: 1 Now it came to pass in the seventh **m**, 2320
52: 4 in the tenth **m**, in the tenth *day* of 2320
52: 4 the tenth month, in the tenth *day* of the **m**, 2320
52: 6 in the fourth **m**, in the ninth *day* of 2320
52: 6 the fourth month, in the ninth *day* of the **m**, 2320
52:12 Now in the fifth **m**, in the tenth *day* of 2320
52:12 the fifth month, in the tenth *day* of the **m**, 2320
52:31 in the twelfth **m**, in the five and 2320
52:31 in the five and twentieth *day* of the **m**, 2320
Eze 1: 1 in the fourth **m**, in the fifth *day* of NIH
1: 1 the fourth *month*, in the fifth *day* of the **m**, 2320
1: 2 In the fifth *day* of the **m**, which *was* 2320
8: 1 in the sixth **m**, in the fifth *day* of the month, NIH
8: 1 in the sixth *month*, in the fifth *day* of the **m**, 2320
20: 1 in the fifth **m**, the tenth *day* of the month, NIH
20: 1 in the fifth *month*, the tenth *day* of the **m**, 2320
24: 1 Again in the ninth year, in the tenth **m**, 2320
24: 1 the tenth month, in the tenth *day* of the **m**, 2320
26: 1 the eleventh year, in the first *day* of the **m**, 2320
29: 1 in the tenth **m**, in the twelfth *day* of NIH
29: 1 tenth *month*, in the twelfth *day* of the **m**, 2320
29:17 in the first **m**, in the first *day* of the month, NIH
29:17 in the first *month*, in the first *day* of the **m**, 2320
30:20 in the first **m**, in the seventh *day* of NIH
30:20 the first *month*, in the seventh *day* of the **m**, 2320
31: 1 in the third **m**, in the first *day* of the month, NIH
31: 1 in the third *month*, in the first *day* of the **m**, 2320
32: 1 in the twelfth **m**, in the first *day* of 2320
32: 1 the twelfth month, in the first *day* of the **m**, 2320
32:17 twelfth year, in the fifteenth *day* of the **m**, 2320
33:21 in the tenth **m**, in the fifth *day* of the month, NIH
33:21 the tenth *month*, in the fifth *day* of the **m**, 2320
40: 1 of the year, in the tenth *day* of the **m**, 2320
45:18 In the first **m**, in the first *day* of the month, NIH
45:18 In the first *month*, in the first *day* of the **m**, 2320
45:20 thou shalt do the seventh *day* of the **m** for 2320
45:21 In the first **m**, in the fourteenth day of NIH
45:21 first *month*, in the fourteenth day of the **m**, 2320
45:25 In the seventh **m**, in the fifteenth day of NIH
45:25 *month*, in the fifteenth day of the **m**, 2320
Da 10: 4 in the four and twentieth day of the first **m**, 2320
Hos 5: 7 now shall a **m** devour them with their 2320
Joel 2:23 and the latter rain in the first **m**. NIH
Hag 1: 1 in the sixth **m**, in the first day of the month, 2320
1: 1 in the sixth month, in the first day of the **m**, 2320
1:15 the four and twentieth day of the sixth **m**, 2320
2: 1 In the seventh **m**, in the one and NIH
2: 1 in the one and twentieth *day* of the **m**, 2320
2:10 twentieth *day* of the ninth **m**, in the second NIH
2:18 twentieth day of the ninth **m**, *even* from NIH
2:20 in the four and twentieth *day* of the **m**, 2320
Zec 1: 1 In the eighth **m**, in the second year of 2320
1: 7 and twentieth day of the eleventh **m**, 2320

Zec 1: 7 which *is* the m Sebat, in the second year of 2320
7: 1 Zechariah in the fourth *day* of the ninth m, 2320
7: 3 Should I weep in the fifth m, 2320
7: 5 and seventh *m*, even those seventy years, NIH
8:19 The fast of the fourth *m*, and the fast of NIH
11: 8 Three shepherds also I cut off in one m; 3391
Lk 1:26 And in the sixth m the angel Gabriel was 3376
1:36 and this is the sixth m with her, who was 3376
Rev 9:15 and a day, and a m, and a year, for to slay 3376
22: 2 *of* fruits, *and* yielded her fruit every m: 3376

MONTHLY (1) [MONTH]

Isa 47:13 the m prognosticators, stand *up*, and 2320

MONTHS (59) [MONTH]

Ge 38:24 it came to pass about three m after, that it 2320
Ex 2: 2 he *was a* goodly *child*, she hid him three m. 3391
12: 2 *shall be* unto you the beginning of m: 2320
Nu 10:10 and in the beginnings of your m, 2320
28:11 in the beginnings of your m ye shall offer a 2320
28:14 every month throughout the m of the year. 2320
Jdg 11:37 let me alone two m, that I may go up and 2320
11:38 he sent her away *for* two m: and she went 2320
11:39 it came to pass at the end of two m, that she 2320
19: 2 was there four whole m. 2320
20:47 and abode in the rock Rimmon four m. 2320
1Sa 6: 1 in the country of the Philistines seven m. 2320
27: 7 the Philistines was a full year and four m. 2320
2Sa 2:11 house of Judah was seven years and six m. 2320
5: 5 reigned over Judah seven years and six m: 2320
6:11 house of Obed-edom the Gittite three m: 2320
24: 8 came *to* Jerusalem at the end of nine m 2320
24:13 wilt thou flee three m before thine enemies, 2320
1Ki 5:14 they were in Lebanon, *and* two m at home: 2320
11:16 (For six m did Joab remain there with all 2320
2Ki 15: 8 reign over Israel in Samaria six m. 2320
23:31 and he reigned three m in Jerusalem. 2320
24: 8 and he reigned in Jerusalem three m. 2320
1Ch 3: 4 and there he reigned seven years and six m: 2320
13:14 family of Obed-edom in his house three m. 2320
21:12 or three m to be destroyed before thy foes, 2320
27: 1 by month throughout all the m of the year, 2320
2Ch 36: 2 and he reigned three m in Jerusalem. 2320
36: 9 he reigned three m and ten days in 2320
Est 2:12 after that she had been twelve m, 2320
2:12 *to wit*, six m with oil of myrrh, and 2320
2:12 six m with sweet odours, and with *other* 2320
Job 3: 6 let it not come into the number of the m. 3391
7: 3 So am I made to possess m of vanity, and 3391
14: 5 the number of his m *are* with thee, 2320
21:21 when the number of his m is cut off in 2320
29: 2 O that I were as *in* m past, as *in* the days 3391
39: 2 Canst thou number the m *that* they fulfil? 3391
Eze 39:12 seven m shall the house of Israel be 2320
39:14 after the end of seven m shall they search. 2320
47:12 bring forth new fruit according to his m, 2320
Da 4:29 At the end of twelve m he walked in 3393
Am 4: 7 when *there were* yet three m to the harvest: 2320
Lk 1:24 and hid herself five m, saying, 3376
1:56 And Mary abode with her about three m, 3376
4:25 heaven was shut up three years and six m, 3376
Jn 4:35 There are yet **four m**, and *then* cometh 5072
Ac 7:20 nourished up in his father's house three m: 3376
18:11 And he continued *there* a year and six m, 3376
19: 8 and spake boldly for the space of three m, 3376
20: 3 And *there* abode three m: and when 3376
28:11 And after three m we departed in a ship of 3376
Gal 4:10 observe days, and m, and times, and years. 3376
Heb 11:23 was hid **three m** of his parents, because 5150
Jas 5:17 earth *by the space of* three years and six m. 3376
Rev 9: 5 but that they should be tormented five m: 3376
9:10 and their power *was* to hurt men five m. 3376
11: 2 shall they tread under foot forty *and* two m. 3376
13: 5 unto him to continue forty *and* two m. 3376

MONUMENTS (1)

Isa 65: 4 lodge in the m, which eat swine's flesh, 5341

MOON (51) [MOONS]

Ge 37: 9 the sun and the m and the eleven stars 3394
Dt 4:19 thou seest the sun, and the m, and the stars, 3394
17: 3 the sun, or m, or any of the host of heaven, 3394
33:14 for the precious things put forth by the m, 3391
Jos 10:12 and thou, M, in the valley of Ajalon. 3394
10:13 the sun stood still, and the m stayed, 3394
1Sa 20: 5 to morrow *is* the **new m**, and I should not 2320
20:18 said to *David*, To morrow *is* the **new m**: 2320
20:24 when the **new m** was come, the king sat 2320
2Ki 4:23 *it is* neither **new m**, nor sabbath. And she 2320
23: 5 to the m, and to the planets, and to all 3394
Job 25: 5 Behold *even* to the m, and it shineth not; 3394
31:26 it shined, or the m walking *in* brightness; 3394
Ps 8: 3 the work of thy fingers, the m and the stars, 3394
72: 5 fear thee as long as the sun and m endure, 3394
72: 7 of peace so long as the m endureth. 3394
81: 3 Blow up the trumpet in the **new m**, in 2320
89:37 It shall be established for ever as the m, 3394
104:19 He appointed the m for seasons: the sun 3394
121: 6 not smite thee by day, nor the m by night. 3394
136: 9 The m and stars to rule by night: for his 3394
148: 3 Praise ye him, sun and m: praise him, all ye 3394
Ecc 12: 2 the sun, or the light, or the m, or the stars, 3394
SS 6:10 fair as the m, clear as the sun, *and* 3842
Isa 3:18 and *their* **round tires like the m**, 7720
13:10 and the m shall not cause her light to shine. 3394
24:23 the m shall be confounded, and the sun 3842
30:26 Moreover the light of the m shall be as 3842
60:19 neither for brightness shall the m give light 3394
60:20 neither shall thy m withdraw itself: 3391
66:23 *that* from one **new m** to another, and 2320
Jer 8: 2 the m, and all the host of heaven, 3394
31:35 *and* the ordinances of the m and of the stars 3394
Eze 32: 7 a cloud, and the m shall not give her light. 3394
46: 1 in the day of the **new m** it shall be opened. 2320
46: 6 in the day of the **new m** *it shall be* a young 2320
Joel 2:10 the sun and the m shall be dark, and 3394
2:31 the m into blood, before the great and 3394
3:15 The sun and the m shall be darkened, and 3394
Am 8: 5 Saying, When will the **new m** be gone, 2320
Hab 3:11 *and* m stood still in *their* habitation: 3394
Mt 24:29 and the m shall not give her light, and 4582
Mk 13:24 and the m shall not give her light, 4582
Lk 21:25 in the sun, and in the m, and in the stars; 4582
Ac 2:20 and the m into blood, before *that* great and 4582
1Co 15:41 and another glory of the m, and 4582
Col 2:16 or of the **new m**, or of the sabbath days: 3561
Rev 6:12 of hair, and the m became as blood; 4582
8:12 and the third *part* of the m, and the third 4582
12: 1 and the m under her feet, and upon her 4582
21:23 of the sun, neither of the m, to shine in it: 4582

MOONS (11) [MOON]

1Ch 23:31 in the **new m**, and on the set feasts, 2320
2Ch 2: 4 on the **new m**, and on the solemn feasts of 2320
8:13 on the **new m**, and on the solemn feasts, 2320
31: 3 and for the **new m**, and for the set feasts, 2320
Ezr 3: 5 both of the **new m**, and of all the set feasts 2320
Ne 10:33 of the sabbaths, of the **new m**, for the set 2320
Isa 1:13 the **new m** and sabbaths, the calling of 2320
1:14 Your **new m** and your appointed feasts my 2320
Eze 45:17 in the **new m**, and in the sabbaths in all 2320
46: 3 LORD in the sabbaths and in the **new m**. 2320
Hos 2:11 her feast *days*, her **new m**, and 2320

MORASTHITE (2) [MORESHETH-GATH]

Jer 26:18 Micah the M prophesied in the days of 4183
Mic 1: 1 to Micah the M in the days of Jotham, 4183

MORDECAI (58) [MORDECAI'S]

Ezr 2: 2 M, Bilshan, Mizpar, Bigvai, Rehum, 4782
Ne 7: 7 M, Bilshan, Mispereth, Bigvai, Nehum, 4782
Est 2: 5 whose name *was* M, the son of Jair, the son 4782
2: 7 whom M, when her father and mother were 4782
2:10 for M had charged her that she should not 4782
2:11 M walked every day before the court of 4782
2:15 the daughter of Abihail the uncle of M, 4782
2:19 second time, then M sat in the king's gate. 4782
2:20 nor her people; as M had charged her: 4782
2:20 for Esther did the commandment of M, 4782
2:21 those days, while M sat in the king's gate, 4782
2:22 the thing was known to M, who told *it* unto 4782
3: 2 But M bowed not, nor did *him* reverence. 4782
3: 3 which *were* in the king's gate, said unto M, 4782
3: 5 when Haman saw that M bowed not, 4782
3: 6 he thought scorn to lay hands on M alone; 4782
3: 6 for they had shewed him the people of M: 4782
3: 6 of Ahasuerus, *even* the people of M. 4782
4: 1 When M perceived all that was done, 4782

M

Est 4: 1 **M** rent his clothes, and put on sackcloth 4782
4: 4 she sent raiment to clothe **M**, and to take 4782
4: 5 gave him a commandment to **M**, to know 4782
4: 6 So Hatach went forth to **M** unto the street 4782
4: 7 **M** told him of all that had happened unto 4782
4: 9 and told Esther the words of **M**. 4782
4:10 and gave him commandment unto **M**: 4782
4:12 And they told to **M** Esther's words. 4782
4:13 **M** commanded to answer Esther, Think not 4782
4:15 Esther bade *them* return **M** *this answer:* 4782
4:17 So **M** went his way, and did according to 4782
5: 9 when Haman saw **M** in the king's gate, 4782
5: 9 he was full *of* indignation against **M**. 4782
5:13 long as I see **M** the Jew sitting at the king's 4782
5:14 to morrow speak thou unto the king that **M** 4782
6: 2 that **M** had told of Bigthana and Teresh, 4782
6: 3 and dignity hath been done to **M** for this? 4782
6: 4 to speak unto the king to hang **M** on 4782
6:10 hast said, and do *even* so to **M** the Jew, 4782
6:11 arrayed **M**, and brought him on horseback 4782
6:12 **M** came again to the king's gate. 4782
6:13 unto him, If **M** *be* of the seed of the Jews, 4782
7: 9 cubits high, which Haman had made for **M**, 4782
7:10 on the gallows that he had prepared for **M**. 4782
8: 1 **M** came before the king; for Esther had 4782
8: 2 had taken from Haman, and gave it unto **M**. 4782
8: 2 Esther set **M** over the house of Haman. 4782
8: 7 unto Esther the queen and to **M** the Jew, 4782
8: 9 it was written according to all that **M** 4782
8:15 **M** went out from the presence of the king 4782
9: 3 because the fear of **M** fell upon them. 4782
9: 4 For **M** *was* great in the king's house, and 4782
9: 4 for *this* man **M** waxed greater and greater. 4782
9:20 **M** wrote these things, and sent letters unto 4782
9:23 and as **M** had written unto them; 4782
9:29 the daughter of Abihail, and **M** the Jew, 4782
9:31 times *appointed,* according as **M** the Jew 4782
10: 2 and the declaration of the greatness of **M**, 4782
10: 3 For **M** the Jew *was* next unto king 4782

MORDECAI'S (2) [MORDECAI]
Est 2:22 Esther certified the king *thereof* in **M** 4782
3: 4 to see whether **M** matters would stand: 4782

MORE (657) [= MO, = MOE, MOREOVER, MUCH] See Index

MOREH (3)
Ge 12: 6 the place of Sichem, unto the plain of **M**. 4176
Dt 11:30 over against Gilgal, beside the plains of **M**? 4176
Jdg 7: 1 side of them, by the hill of **M**, in the valley. 4176

MOREOVER (171) [MORE] See Index

MORESHETH-GATH (1) [GATH, MORASTHITE]
Mic 1:14 Therefore shalt thou give presents to **M**: 4182

MORIAH (2)
Ge 22: 2 thou lovest, and get thee into the land of **M**; 4179
2Ch 3: 1 of the LORD at Jerusalem in mount **M**, 4179

MORNING (227)
Ge 1: 5 the evening and the **m** were the first day. 1242
1: 8 the evening and the **m** were the second day. 1242
1:13 the evening and the **m** were the third day. 1242
1:19 the evening and the **m** were the fourth day. 1242
1:23 the evening and the **m** were the fifth day. 1242
1:31 the evening and the **m** were the sixth day. 1242
19:15 when the **m** arose, then the angels hastened 7837
19:27 Abraham gat up early in the **m** to the place 1242
20: 8 Therefore Abimelech rose early in the **m**, 1242
21:14 Abraham rose up early in the **m**, and 1242
22: 3 Abraham rose up early in the **m**, and 1242
24:54 they rose up in the **m**, and he said, Send me 1242
26:31 they rose up betimes in the **m**, and 1242
28:18 Jacob rose up early in the **m**, and took 1242
29:25 to pass, that in the **m**, behold, it *was* Leah: 1242
31:55 early in the **m** Laban rose up, and 1242
40: 6 Joseph came in unto them in the **m**, and 1242
41: 8 it came to pass in the **m** that his spirit was 1242
44: 3 As soon as the **m** was light, the men were 1242
49:27 in the **m** he shall devour the prey, and 1242
Ex 7:15 Get thee unto Pharaoh in the **m**; lo, 1242
8:20 Rise up early in the **m**, and stand before 1242
9:13 Rise up early in the **m**, and stand before 1242
10:13 *and* when it was **m**, the east wind brought 1242
12:10 ye shall let nothing of it remain until the **m**; 1242
12:10 that which remaineth of it until the **m** ye 1242
12:22 go out at the door of his house until the **m**. 1242
14:24 that in the **m** watch the LORD looked 1242
14:27 the sea returned to his strength when the **m** 1242
16: 7 in the **m**, then ye shall see the glory of 1242
16: 8 flesh to eat, and in the **m** bread to the full; 1242
16:12 and in the **m** ye shall be filled *with* bread; 1242
16:13 in the **m** the dew lay round about the host. 1242
16:19 Let no man leave of it till the **m**. 1242
16:20 some of them left of it until the **m**, and 1242
16:21 they gathered it **every m**, 1242+1242+871.1+871.1+1886.1+1886.1
16:23 over lay up for you to be kept until the **m**. 1242
16:24 they laid it up till the **m**, as Moses bade: 1242
18:13 the people stood by Moses from the **m** unto 1242
18:14 all the people stand by thee from **m** unto 1242
19:16 it came to pass on the third day in the **m**, 1242
23:18 the fat of my sacrifice remain until the **m**. 1242
24: 4 rose up early in the **m**, and builded an altar 1242
27:21 his sons shall order it from evening to **m** 1242
29:34 remain unto the **m**, then thou shalt burn 1242
29:39 The one lamb thou shalt offer in the **m**; and 1242
29:41 according to the meat offering of the **m**, 1242
30: 7 burn thereon sweet incense **every m**: 1242+1242+871.1+871.1+1886.1+1886.1
34: 2 be ready in the **m**, and come up in 1242
34: 2 come up in the **m** unto mount Sinai, and 1242
34: 4 Moses rose up early in the **m**, and went up 1242
34:25 the feast of the passover be left unto the **m**. 1242
36: 3 free offerings **every m**. 1242+1242+871.1+871.1+1886.1+1886.1
Lev 6: 9 burning upon the altar all night unto the **m**, 1242
6:12 burn wood on it **every m**, 1242+1242+871.1+871.1+1886.1+1886.1
6:20 half of it in the **m**, and half thereof at night. 1242
7:15 he shall not leave *any* of it until the **m**. 1242
9:17 beside the burnt sacrifice of the **m**. 1242
19:13 not abide with thee all night until the **m**. 1242
24: 3 unto the **m** before the LORD continually: 1242
Nu 9:12 They shall leave none of it unto the **m**, 1242
9:15 it were the appearance of fire, until the **m**. 1242
9:21 the cloud abode from even unto the **m**, 1242
9:21 *that* the cloud was taken up in the **m**, then 1242
14:40 they rose up early in the **m**, and gat them 1242
22:13 Balaam rose up in the **m**, and said unto 1242
22:21 Balaam rose up in the **m**, and saddled his 1242
28: 4 The one lamb shalt thou offer in the **m**, and 1242
28: 8 as the meat offering of the **m**, and as 1242
28:23 these beside the burnt offering in the **m**, 1242
Dt 16: 4 day at even, remain all night until the **m**. 1242
16: 7 thou shalt turn in the **m**, and go unto thy 1242
28:67 In the **m** thou shalt say, Would God it were 1242
28:67 even thou shalt say, Would God it were **m**! 1242
Jos 3: 1 Joshua rose early in the **m**; and 1242
6:12 Joshua rose early in the **m**, and the priests 1242
7:14 In the **m** therefore ye shall be brought 1242
7:16 So Joshua rose up early in the **m**, and 1242
8:10 Joshua rose up early in the **m**, and 1242
Jdg 6:28 the men of the city arose early in the **m**, 1242
6:31 let him be put to death whilst *it is yet* **m**: 1242
9:33 it shall be, *that* in the **m**, as soon as the sun 1242
16: 2 saying, In the **m**, when it is day, we shall 1242
19: 5 when they arose early in the **m**, that he rose 1242
19: 8 he arose early in the **m** on the fifth day to 1242
19:25 and abused her all the night until the **m**: 1242
19:27 her lord rose up in the **m**, and opened 1242
20:19 the children of Israel rose up in the **m**, and 1242
Ru 2: 7 hath continued even from the **m** until now, 1242
3:13 Tarry this night, and it shall be in the **m**, 1242
3:13 *as* the LORD liveth: lie down until the **m**. 1242
3:14 she lay *at* his feet until the **m**: and she rose 1242
1Sa 1:19 they rose up in the **m** early, and 1242
3:15 Samuel lay until the **m**, and opened 1242
5: 4 when they arose early on the morrow **m**, 1242
11:11 into the midst of the host in the **m** watch, 1242
14:36 spoil them until the **m** light, and let us not 1242
15:12 Samuel rose early to meet Saul in the **m**, 1242
17:16 the Philistine drew near **m** and evening, 7925
17:20 David rose up early in the **m**, and left 1242
19: 2 take heed to thyself until the **m**, and 1242
19:11 to watch him, and to slay him in the **m**: 1242
20:35 it came to pass in the **m**, that Jonathan went 1242
25:22 if I leave of all that *pertain* to him by the **m** 1242

M

1Sa 25:34 **m** light *any that* pisseth against the wall. 1242
25:36 him nothing, less or more, until the **m** light. 1242
25:37 it came to pass in the **m**, when the wine 1242
29:10 Wherefore now rise up early in the **m** with 1242
29:10 as soon as ye be up early in the **m**, and 1242
29:11 his men rose up early to depart in the **m**, 1242
2Sa 2:27 in the **m** the people had gone up every one 1242
11:14 it came to pass in the **m**, that David wrote a 1242
17:22 by the **m** light there lacked not one *of them* 1242
23: 4 *he shall be* as the light of the **m**, *when* 1242
23: 4 the sun riseth, *even* a **m** without clouds; 1242
24:11 For when David was up in the **m**, the word 1242
24:15 from the **m** even to the time appointed: 1242
1Ki 3:21 when I rose in the **m** to give my child suck, 1242
3:21 when I had considered it in the **m**, behold, 1242
17: 6 brought him bread and flesh in the **m**, 1242
18:26 called on the name of Baal from **m** even 1242
2Ki 3:20 it came to pass in the **m**, when the meat 1242
3:22 they rose up early in the **m**, and the sun 1242
7: 9 if we tarry till the **m** light, *some* mischief 1242
10: 8 *at* the entering in of the gate until the **m**. 1242
10: 9 it came to pass in the **m**, that he went out, 1242
16:15 Upon the great altar burn the **m** burnt 1242
19:35 and when they arose early in the **m**, behold, 1242
1Ch 9:27 the opening *thereof* **every m**
1242+1242+1886.1+1886.1+3807.1+3807.1
16:40 the altar of the burnt offering continually **m** 1242
23:30 **every m** to thank and praise the LORD,
1242+1242+871.1+871.1+1886.1+1886.1
2Ch 2: 4 *for* the burnt offerings **m** and evening, 1242
13:11 burn unto the LORD **every m**
1242+1242+871.1+871.1+1886.1+1886.1
20:20 they rose early in the **m**, and went forth 1242
31: 3 *to wit,* for the **m** and evening burnt 1242
Ezr 3: 3 *even* burnt offerings **m** and evening. 1242
Ne 4:21 the rising of the **m** till the stars appeared. 7837
8: 3 the water gate from the **m** until midday, 216
Job 1: 5 rose up early in the **m**, and offered burnt 1242
4:20 They are destroyed from **m** to evening: 1242
7:18 *that* thou shouldest visit him every **m**, *and* 1242
7:21 thou shalt **seek** me **in the m**, but I *shall* not 7836
11:17 shalt shine forth, thou shalt be as the **m**. 1242
24:17 For the **m** *is* to them even as the shadow of 1242
38: 7 When the **m** stars sang together, and all 1242
38:12 Hast thou commanded the **m** since thy 1242
41:18 and his eyes *are* like the eyelids of the **m**. 7837
Ps 5: 3 My voice shalt thou hear *in* the **m**, 1242
5: 3 *in* the **m** will I direct *my prayer* unto thee, 1242
30: 5 endure for a night, but joy *cometh* in the **m**. 1242
49:14 shall have dominion over them in the **m**; 1242
55:17 Evening, and **m**, and at noon, will I pray, 1242
59:16 I will sing aloud of thy mercy in the **m**: 1242
65: 8 thou makest the outgoings of the **m** and 1242
73:14 I been plagued, and chastened every **m**. 1242
88:13 and in the **m** shall my prayer prevent thee. 1242
90: 5 in the **m** *they are* like grass *which* groweth 1242
90: 6 In the **m** it flourisheth, and groweth up; 1242
92: 2 To shew forth thy lovingkindness in the **m**, 1242
110: 3 of holiness from the womb of the **m**: 4891
119:147 I prevented the **dawning of the m**, and 5399
130: 6 Lord more than they that watch for the **m**: 1242
130: 6 *I say, more than* they that watch for the **m**. 1242
139: 9 *If* I take the wings of the **m**, *and* dwell in 7837
143: 8 me to hear thy lovingkindness in the **m**; 1242
Pr 7:18 let us take our fill of love until the **m**: 1242
27:14 rising early in the **m**, it shall be counted a 1242
Ecc 10:16 king *is* a child, and thy princes eat in the **m**. 1242
11: 6 In the **m** sow thy seed, and in the evening 1242
SS 6:10 Who *is* she that looketh forth as the **m**, 7837
Isa 5:11 Woe unto them that rise up early in the **m**, 1242
14:12 from heaven, O Lucifer, son of the **m**! 7837
17:11 in the **m** shalt thou make thy seed to 1242
17:14 *and* before the **m** he *is* not. 1242
21:12 The **m** cometh, and also the night: 1242
28:19 for **m** by morning shall it pass over, by day 1242
28:19 for morning by **m** shall it pass over, by day 1242
33: 2 be thou their arm every **m**, our salvation 1242
37:36 and when they arose early in the **m**, behold, 1242
38:13 I reckoned till **m**, *that,* as a lion, so will he 1242
50: 4 he wakeneth **m** by morning, he wakeneth 1242
50: 4 he wakeneth morning by **m**, he wakeneth 1242
58: 8 shall thy light break forth as the **m**, and 7837
Jer 5: 8 They were *as* fed horses in the **m**: 7904
20:16 let him hear the cry in the **m**, and 1242
21:12 Execute judgment in the **m**, and 1242
La 3:23 *They are* new every **m**: great *is* thy 1242
Eze 7: 7 The **m** is come unto thee, O thou that 6843
7:10 the **m** is gone forth; the rod hath 6843
12: 8 in the **m** came the word of the LORD unto 1242
24:18 So I spake unto the people in the **m**: and 1242
24:18 and I did in the **m** as I was commanded. 1242
33:22 my mouth, until *he* came to me in the **m**; 1242
46:13 thou shalt prepare it **every m**.
1242+1242+871.1+871.1+1886.1+1886.1
46:14 a meat offering for it **every m**,
1242+1242+871.1+871.1+1886.1+1886.1
46:15 **every m** *for* a continual burnt offering.
1242+1242+871.1+871.1+1886.1+1886.1
Da 6:19 the king arose very early in the **m**, and 5053
8:26 and the **m** which was told *is* true: 1242
Hos 6: 3 his going forth *is* prepared as the **m**; and 7837
6: 4 for your goodness *is* as a **m** cloud, and 1242
7: 6 *in* the **m** it burneth as a flaming fire. 1242
10:15 in a **m** shall the king of Israel utterly be cut 7837
13: 3 Therefore they shall be as the **m** cloud, and 1242
Joel 2: 2 as the **m** spread upon the mountains: 7837
Am 4: 4 bring your sacrifices *every* **m**, *and* 1242
4:13 that maketh the **m** darkness, and 7837
5: 8 turneth the shadow of death into the **m**, and 1242
Jnh 4: 7 God prepared a worm when the **m** rose 7837
Mic 2: 1 when the **m** is light, they practise it, 1242
Zep 3: 5 **every m** doth he bring his judgment
1242+1242+871.1+871.1+1886.1+1886.1
Mt 16: 3 And **in the m**, *It will be* foul weather to *4404*
20: 1 which went out **early in the m** to hire *260+4404*
21:18 Now **in the m** as he returned into the city, *4405*
27: 1 When the **m** was come, all the chief priests *4405*
Mk 1:35 And **in the m**, rising up a great while *4404*
11:20 And **in the m**, as they passed by, they saw *4404*
13:35 or at the cockcrowing, or **in the m**: *4404*
15: 1 And straightway in the **m** the chief priests *4404*
16: 2 And very **early in the m** the first *day* of *4404*
Lk 21:38 And all the people **came early in the m** to *3719*
24: 1 **very early in the m**, they came unto *901+3722*
Jn 8: 2 And **early in the m** he came again into *3722*
21: 4 But when the **m** was now come, *4405*
Ac 5:21 into the temple **early in the m**, *3588+3722+5259*
28:23 *out of* the prophets, from **m** till evening. *4404*
Rev 2:28 And I will give him the **m** star. *4407*
22:16 of David, *and* the bright and **m** star. *3720*

MORROW (103)

Ge 19:34 it came to pass on the **m**, that the firstborn 4283
Ex 8:10 he said, **To m**. And he said, *Be it* according 4279
8:23 and thy people: **to m** shall this sign be. 4279
8:29 his servants, and from his people, **to m**: 4279
9: 5 **To m** the LORD shall do this thing in 4279
9: 6 the LORD did that thing on the **m**, and 4283
9:18 **to m** about *this* time I will cause it to rain a 4279
10: 4 **to m** will I bring the locusts into thy coast: 4279
16:23 **To m** *is* the rest of the holy sabbath unto 4279
17: 9 **to m** I will stand on the top of the hill with 4279
18:13 it came to pass on the **m**, that Moses sat to 4283
19:10 sanctify them to day and **to m**, and let them 4279
32: 5 and said, **To m** *is* a feast to the LORD. 4279
32: 6 they rose up early on the **m**, and 4283
32:30 it came to pass on the **m**, that Moses said 4283
Lev 7:16 on the **m** also the remainder of it shall be 4283
19: 6 the *same* day ye offer it, and on the **m**: 4283
22:30 ye shall leave none of it until the **m**: 1242
23:11 on the **m** after the sabbath the priest shall 4283
23:15 ye shall count unto you from the **m** after 4283
23:16 Even unto the **m** after the seventh sabbath 4283
Nu 11:18 Sanctify yourselves against **to m**, and 4279
14:25 **To m** turn you, and get you *into* 4279
16: 5 Even **to m** the LORD will shew who *are* 1242
16: 7 incense in them before the LORD **to m**: 4279
16:16 thou, and they, and Aaron, **to m**: 4279
16:41 on the **m** all the congregation of 4283
17: 8 that on the **m** Moses went into 4283
22:41 it came to pass on the **m**, that Balak took 1242
33: 3 on the **m** after the passover the children of 4283
Jos 3: 5 for **to m** the LORD will do wonders 4279
5:11 of the land on the **m after** the passover, 4283
5:12 the manna ceased on the **m after** they had 4283
7:13 and say, Sanctify yourselves against **to m**: 4279
11: 6 for **to m** about this time will I deliver them 4279
22:18 that **to m** he will be wroth with the whole 4279

M

Jdg 6:38 for he rose up early on the **m**, and thrust 4283
9:42 it came to pass on the **m**, that the people 4283
19: 9 **to m** get you early on your way, that thou 4279
20:28 for **to m** I will deliver them into thine hand. 4279
21: 4 it came to pass on the **m**, that the people 4283
1Sa 5: 3 when they of Ashdod arose early on the **m**, 4283
5: 4 when they arose early on the **m** morning, 4283
9:16 **To m** about *this* time I will send thee a man 4279
9:19 **to m** I will let thee go, and 1242+871.1+1886.1
11: 9 **To m**, by *that time* the sun be hot, ye shall 4279
11:10 **To m** we will come out unto you, and 4279
11:11 it was *so* on the **m**, that Saul put the people 4283
18:10 it came to pass on the **m**, that the evil spirit 4283
19:11 thy life to night, **to m** thou *shalt be* slain. 4279
20: 5 **to m** *is* the new moon, and I should not fail 4279
20:12 when I have sounded my father about **to m** 4279
20:18 Jonathan said to *David,* **To m** *is* the new 4279
20:27 it came to pass on the **m**, *which was* 4283
28:19 **to m** *shalt* thou and thy sons *be* with me: 4279
31: 8 it came to pass on the **m**, when 4283
2Sa 11:12 to day also, and **to m** I will let thee depart. 4279
11:12 abode in Jerusalem that day, and the **m**. 4283
1Ki 19: 2 life of one of them *by* **to m** about *this* time. 4279
20: 6 Yet I will send my servants unto thee **to m** 4279
2Ki 6:28 him to day, and we will eat my son **to m**. 4279
7: 1 **To m** about *this* time *shall* a measure of 4279
7:18 shall be **to m** about *this* time in the gate of 4279
8:15 it came to pass on the **m**, that he took a 4283
10: 6 come to me to Jezreel by **to m** *this* time. 4279
1Ch 10: 8 it came to pass on the **m**, when 4283
29:21 on the **m after** that day, *even* a thousand 4283
2Ch 20:16 **To m** go ye down against them: behold, 4279
20:17 nor be dismayed; **to m** go out against them: 4279
Est 2:14 on the **m** she returned into the second 1242
5: 8 and I will do **to m** as the king hath said. 4279
5:12 **to m** *am* I invited unto her also with 4279
5:14 **to m** speak thou unto the king that 1242
9:13 **to m** also according unto *this* day's decree, 4279
Pr 3:28 Go, and come again, and **to m** I will give; 4279
27: 1 Boast not thyself of **to m**; for thou 3117+4279
Isa 22:13 let us eat and drink; for **to m** we shall die. 4279
56:12 **to m** shall be as this day, *and* much more 4279
Jer 20: 3 it came to pass on the **m**, that Pashur 4283
Zep 3: 3 they gnaw not the bones till the **m**. 1242
Mt 6:30 to day is, and **to m** is cast into the oven, *839*
6:34 Take therefore no thought for the **m**: for *839*
6:34 for the **m** shall take thought for the *things* of *839*
Mk 11:12 And **on** the **m**, when they were come from *1887*
Lk 10:35 And on the **m** when he departed, he took out *839*
12:28 in the field, and **to m** is cast into the oven; *839*
13:32 and I do cures to day and **to m**, and the third *839*
13:33 to day, and **to m**, and the *day* following: *839*
Ac 4: 5 And it came to pass on the **m**, that their *839*
10: 9 **On** the **m**, as they went on their journey, *1887*
10:23 lodged *them.* And **on** the **m** Peter went *1887*
10:24 And the **m** *after* they entered into Cesarea. *1887*
20: 7 unto them, ready to depart **on** the **m**; *1887*
22:30 **On** the **m**, because he would have known *1887*
23:15 that he bring him down unto you **to m**, *839*
23:20 bring down Paul **to m** into the council, *839*
23:32 **On** the **m** they left the horsemen to go with *1887*
25:17 **on** the **m** I sat on the judgment seat, and *1836*
25:22 **To m**, said he, thou shalt hear him. *839*
25:23 And **on** the **m**, when Agrippa was come, *1887*
1Co 15:32 let us eat and drink; for **to m** we die. *839*
Jas 4:13 To day or **to m** we will go into such a city, *839*
4:14 ye know not what *shall be* **on** the **m**: *839*

MORSEL (10) [MORSELS]
Ge 18: 5 I will fetch a **m** of bread, and comfort ye 6595
Jdg 19: 5 Comfort thine heart *with* a **m** of bread, and 6595
Ru 2:14 of the bread, and dip thy **m** in the vinegar. 6595
1Sa 2:36 him for a piece of silver and a **m** of bread, 3603
28:22 and let me set a **m** of bread before thee; 6595
1Ki 17:11 I pray thee, a **m** of bread in thine hand. 6595
Job 31:17 Or have eaten my **m** myself alone, and 6595
Pr 17: 1 Better *is* a dry **m**, and quietness therewith, 6595
23: 8 The **m** *which* thou hast eaten shalt thou 6595
Heb 12:16 who for one **m of meat** sold his birthright. *1035*

MORSELS (1) [MORSEL]
Ps 147:17 He casteth forth his ice like **m**: who can 6595

MORTAL (6) [MORTALITY, MORTALLY]
Job 4:17 Shall **m man** be more just than God? shall a 582
Ro 6:12 Let not sin therefore reign in your **m** body, *2349*
8:11 **m** bodies by his Spirit that dwelleth in you. *2349*
1Co 15:53 and this **m** *must* put on immortality. *2349*
15:54 and this **m** shall have put on immortality, *2349*
2Co 4:11 might be made manifest in our **m** flesh. *2349*

MORTALITY (1) [MORTAL]
2Co 5: 4 that **m** might be swallowed up of life. *2349*

MORTALLY (1) [MORTAL]
Dt 19:11 smite him **m** that he die, and fleeth into one 5315

MORTAR (2) [MORTER]
Nu 11: 8 or beat *it* in a **m**, and baked *it* in pans, and 4085
Pr 27:22 Though thou shouldest bray a fool in a **m** 4388

MORTER (11) [MORTAR]
Ge 11: 3 brick for stone, and slime had they for **m**. 2563
Ex 1:14 in **m**, and in brick, and in all manner of 2563
Lev 14:42 he shall take other **m**, and shall plaister 6083
14:45 timber thereof, and all the **m** of the house; 6083
Isa 41:25 he shall come *upon* princes as *upon* **m**, and 2563
Eze 13:10 lo, others daubed it *with* untempered **m**: NIH
13:11 daub *it with* untempered **m**, that it shall fall: NIH
13:14 that ye have daubed *with* untempered **m**, NIH
13:15 that have daubed it *with* untempered **m**, NIH
22:28 them *with* untempered **m**, seeing vanity, NIH
Na 3:14 go into clay, and tread the **m**, make strong 2563

MORTGAGED (1)
Ne 5: 3 We *have* **m** our lands, vineyards, and 6148

MORTIFY (2)
Ro 8:13 if ye through the Spirit do **m** the deeds of *2289*
Col 3: 5 **M** therefore your members which are upon *3499*

MOSERA (1)
Dt 10: 6 Beeroth of the children of Jaakan *to* **M**: 4149

MOSEROTH (2)
Nu 33:30 from Hashmonah, and encamped at **M**. 4149
33:31 they departed from **M**, and pitched in 4149

MOSES (829) [MOSES']
Ex 2:10 she called his name **M**: and she said, 4872
2:11 to pass in those days, when **M** was grown, 4872
2:14 **M** feared, and said, Surely *this* thing is 4872
2:15 heard this thing, he sought to slay **M**. 4872
2:15 **M** fled from the face of Pharaoh, and 4872
2:17 **M** stood up and helped them, and 4872
2:21 **M** was content to dwell with the man: and 4872
2:21 and he gave **M** Zipporah his daughter. 4872
3: 1 Now **M** kept the flock of Jethro his father 4872
3: 3 **M** said, I will now turn aside, and see this 4872
3: 4 the midst of the bush, and said, **M**, Moses. 4872
3: 4 the midst of the bush, and said, Moses, **M**. 4872
3: 6 **M** hid his face; for he was afraid to look 4872
3:11 **M** said unto God, Who *am* I, that I should 4872
3:13 **M** said unto God, Behold, *when* I come 4872
3:14 God said unto **M**, I AM THAT I AM: and 4872
3:15 God said moreover unto **M**, Thus shalt thou 4872
4: 1 **M** answered and said, But behold, they will 4872
4: 3 a serpent; and **M** fled from before it. 4872
4: 4 the LORD said unto **M**, Put forth thine 4872
4:10 **M** said unto the LORD, O my Lord, I *am* 4872
4:14 of the LORD was kindled against **M**, 4872
4:18 **M** went and returned to Jethro his father in 4872
4:18 And Jethro said to **M**, Go in peace. 4872
4:19 the LORD said unto **M** in Midian, Go, 4872
4:20 **M** took his wife and his sons, and set them 4872
4:20 and **M** took the rod of God in his hand. 4872
4:21 the LORD said unto **M**, When thou goest 4872
4:27 Go into the wilderness to meet **M**. 4872
4:28 **M** told Aaron all the words of the LORD 4872
4:29 **M** and Aaron went and gathered together 4872
4:30 which the LORD had spoken unto **M**, 4872
5: 1 afterward **M** and Aaron went in, and 4872
5: 4 Wherefore do ye, **M** and Aaron, let 4872
5:20 they met **M** and Aaron, who stood in 4872
5:22 And **M** returned unto the LORD, and said, 4872
6: 1 the LORD said unto **M**, Now shalt thou 4872
6: 2 God spake unto **M**, and said unto him, I *am* 4872
6: 9 **M** spake so unto the children of Israel: but 4872

Ex 6: 9	they hearkened not unto **M** for anguish of	4872
6:10	And the LORD spake unto **M**, saying,	4872
6:12	**M** spake before the LORD, saying,	4872
6:13	the LORD spake unto **M** and unto Aaron,	4872
6:20	to wife; and she bare him Aaron and **M**:	4872
6:26	*These are* that Aaron and **M**, to whom	4872
6:27	from Egypt: *these are* that **M** and Aaron.	4872
6:28	LORD spake unto **M** in the land of Egypt,	4872
6:29	That the LORD spake unto **M**, saying,	4872
6:30	**M** said before the LORD, Behold, I *am* of	4872
7: 1	the LORD said unto **M**, See, I have made	4872
7: 6	**M** and Aaron did as the LORD	4872
7: 7	**M** *was* fourscore years old, and	4872
7: 8	the LORD spake unto **M** and unto Aaron,	4872
7:10	**M** and Aaron went in unto Pharaoh, and	4872
7:14	the LORD said unto **M**, Pharaoh's heart *is*	4872
7:19	the LORD spake unto **M**, Say unto Aaron,	4872
7:20	**M** and Aaron did so, as the LORD	4872
8: 1	the LORD spake unto **M**, Go unto	4872
8: 5	the LORD spake unto **M**, Say unto Aaron,	4872
8: 8	Pharaoh called for **M** and Aaron, and said,	4872
8: 9	**M** said unto Pharaoh, Glory over me: when	4872
8:12	**M** and Aaron went out from Pharaoh: and	4872
8:12	**M** cried unto the LORD because of	4872
8:13	LORD did according to the word of **M**;	4872
8:16	the LORD said unto **M**, Say unto Aaron,	4872
8:20	the LORD said unto **M**, Rise up early in	4872
8:25	Pharaoh called for **M** and for Aaron, and	4872
8:26	**M** said, It is not meet so to do; for we shall	4872
8:29	**M** said, Behold, I go out from thee, and	4872
8:30	**M** went out from Pharaoh, and intreated	4872
8:31	LORD did according to the word of **M**;	4872
9: 1	the LORD said unto **M**, Go in unto	4872
9: 8	the LORD said unto **M** and unto Aaron,	4872
9: 8	let **M** sprinkle it towards the heaven in	4872
9:10	**M** sprinkled it *up* toward heaven; and	4872
9:11	the magicians could not stand before **M**	4872
9:12	as the LORD had spoken unto **M**.	4872
9:13	the LORD said unto **M**, Rise up early in	4872
9:22	the LORD said unto **M**, Stretch forth thine	4872
9:23	**M** stretched forth his rod toward heaven:	4872
9:27	called for **M** and Aaron, and said unto	4872
9:29	**M** said unto him, As soon as I am gone out	4872
9:33	**M** went out of the city from Pharaoh,	4872
9:35	Israel go; as the LORD had spoken by **M**.	4872
10: 1	the LORD said unto **M**, Go in unto	4872
10: 3	**M** and Aaron came in unto Pharaoh, and	4872
10: 8	**M** and Aaron were brought again unto	4872
10: 9	**M** said, We will go with our young and	4872
10:12	the LORD said unto **M**, Stretch out thine	4872
10:13	**M** stretched forth his rod over the land of	4872
10:16	Pharaoh called for **M** and Aaron in haste;	4872
10:21	the LORD said unto **M**, Stretch out thine	4872
10:22	**M** stretched forth his hand toward heaven;	4872
10:24	Pharaoh called unto **M**, and said, Go ye,	4872
10:25	**M** said, Thou must give us also sacrifices	4872
10:29	**M** said, Thou hast spoken well, I will see	4872
11: 1	(And the LORD said unto **M**, Yet will I	4872
11: 3	Moreover the man **M** *was* very great in	4872
11: 4	**M** said, Thus saith the LORD,	4872
11: 9	the LORD said unto **M**, Pharaoh shall not	4872
11:10	**M** and Aaron did all these wonders before	4872
12: 1	the LORD spake unto **M** and Aaron in	4872
12:21	**M** called for all the elders of Israel, and	4872
12:28	did as the LORD had commanded **M** and	4872
12:31	he called for **M** and Aaron by night, and	4872
12:35	of Israel did according to the word of **M**;	4872
12:43	the LORD said unto **M** and Aaron, This *is*	4872
12:50	as the LORD commanded **M** and Aaron,	4872
13: 1	And the LORD spake unto **M**, saying,	4872
13: 3	**M** said unto the people, Remember this	4872
13:19	**M** took the bones of Joseph with him:	4872
14: 1	And the LORD spake unto **M**, saying,	4872
14:11	they said unto **M**, Because *there were* no	4872
14:13	**M** said unto the people, Fear ye not,	4872
14:15	the LORD said unto **M**, Wherefore criest	4872
14:21	**M** stretched out his hand over the sea; and	4872
14:26	the LORD said unto **M**, Stretch out thine	4872
14:27	**M** stretched forth his hand over the sea,	4872
14:31	believed the LORD, and his servant **M**.	4872
15: 1	sang **M** and the children of Israel this song	4872
15:22	So **M** brought Israel from the Red sea, and	4872
15:24	the people murmured against **M**, saying,	4872
16: 2	the children of Israel murmured against **M**	4872
16: 4	said the LORD unto **M**, Behold, I will	4872
16: 6	**M** and Aaron said unto all the children of	4872
16: 8	**M** said, *This shall be,* when the LORD	4872
16: 9	**M** spake unto Aaron, Say unto all	4872
16:11	And the LORD spake unto **M**, saying,	4872
16:15	for they wist not what it *was*. And **M** said	4872
16:19	**M** said, Let no man leave of it till	4872
16:20	they hearkened not unto **M**;	4872
16:20	and stank: and **M** was wroth with them.	4872
16:22	of the congregation came and told **M**.	4872
16:24	they laid it up till the morning, as **M** bade:	4872
16:25	**M** said, Eat that to day; for to day *is* a	4872
16:28	the LORD said unto **M**, How long refuse	4872
16:32	**M** said, This *is* the thing which the LORD	4872
16:33	**M** said unto Aaron, Take a pot, and put an	4872
16:34	As the LORD commanded **M**, so	4872
17: 2	Wherefore the people did chide with **M**,	4872
17: 2	**M** said unto them, Why chide you with	4872
17: 3	the people murmured against **M**, and said,	4872
17: 4	**M** cried unto the LORD, saying,	4872
17: 5	the LORD said unto **M**, Go on before	4872
17: 6	**M** did so in the sight of the elders of Israel.	4872
17: 9	**M** said unto Joshua, Choose us out men,	4872
17:10	So Joshua did as **M** had said to him, and	4872
17:10	**M**, Aaron, and Hur went up *to* the top of	4872
17:11	it came to pass, when **M** held up his hand,	4872
17:14	the LORD said unto **M**, Write this *for* a	4872
17:15	**M** built an altar, and called the name of it	4872
18: 1	heard of all that God had done for **M**, and	4872
18: 5	and his wife unto **M** into the wilderness,	4872
18: 6	he said unto **M**, I thy father in law Jethro	4872
18: 7	**M** went out to meet his father in law, and	4872
18: 8	**M** told his father in law all that the LORD	4872
18:13	the morrow, that **M** sat to judge the people:	4872
18:13	the people stood by **M** from the morning	4872
18:15	**M** said unto his father in law, Because	4872
18:24	So **M** hearkened to the voice of his father	4872
18:25	**M** chose able men out of all Israel, and	4872
18:26	the hard causes they brought unto **M**, but	4872
18:27	**M** let his father in law depart; and he went	4872
19: 3	**M** went up unto God, and the LORD	4872
19: 7	**M** came and called for the elders of	4872
19: 8	**M** returned the words of the people unto	4872
19: 9	the LORD said unto **M**, Lo, I come unto	4872
19: 9	**M** told the words of the people unto	4872
19:10	the LORD said unto **M**, Go unto	4872
19:14	**M** went down from the mount unto	4872
19:17	**M** brought forth the people out of the camp	4872
19:19	**M** spake, and God answered him by a	4872
19:20	the LORD called **M** *up* to the top of	4872
19:20	*up* to the top of the mount; and **M** went up.	4872
19:21	the LORD said unto **M**, Go down,	4872
19:23	**M** said unto the LORD, The people	4872
19:25	So **M** went down unto the people, and	4872
20:19	they said unto **M**, Speak thou with us, and	4872
20:20	**M** said unto the people, Fear not: for God	4872
20:21	**M** drew near unto the thick darkness	4872
20:22	the LORD said unto **M**, Thus thou shalt	4872
24: 1	he said unto **M**, Come up unto the LORD,	4872
24: 2	**M** alone shall come near the LORD: but	4872
24: 3	**M** came and told the people all the words	4872
24: 4	**M** wrote all the words of the LORD, and	4872
24: 6	**M** took half of the blood, and put *it* in	4872
24: 8	**M** took the blood, and sprinkled *it* on	4872
24: 9	went up **M**, and Aaron, Nadab, and Abihu,	4872
24:12	the LORD said unto **M**, Come up to me	4872
24:13	**M** rose up, and his minister Joshua: and	4872
24:13	and **M** went up into the mount of God.	4872
24:15	**M** went up into the mount, and a cloud	4872
24:16	the seventh day he called unto **M** out of	4872
24:18	**M** went into the midst of the cloud, and	4872
24:18	**M** was in the mount forty days and	4872
25: 1	And the LORD spake unto **M**, saying,	4872
30:11	And the LORD spake unto **M**, saying,	4872
30:17	And the LORD spake unto **M**, saying,	4872
30:22	Moreover the LORD spake unto **M**,	4872
30:34	the LORD said unto **M**, Take unto thee	4872
31: 1	And the LORD spake unto **M**, saying,	4872
31:12	And the LORD spake unto **M**, saying,	4872
31:18	he gave unto **M**, when he had made an end	4872
32: 1	when the people saw that **M** delayed to	4872
32: 1	for *as for* this **M**, the man that brought us	4872
32: 7	the LORD said unto **M**, Go, get thee	4872
32: 9	the LORD said unto **M**, I have seen this	4872

Ex	32:11	**M** besought the LORD his God, and said,	4872
	32:15	**M** turned, and went down from the mount,	4872
	32:17	he said unto **M**, *There is* a noise of war in	4872
	32:21	**M** said unto Aaron, What did this people	4872
	32:23	for *as for* this **M**, the man that brought us	4872
	32:25	when **M** saw that the people *were* naked;	4872
	32:26	**M** stood in the gate of the camp, and said,	4872
	32:28	of Levi did according to the word of **M**:	4872
	32:29	For **M** had said, Consecrate yourselves to	4872
	32:30	that **M** said unto the people, Ye have	4872
	32:31	And **M** returned unto the LORD, and said,	4872
	32:33	the LORD said unto **M**, Whosoever hath	4872
	33: 1	the LORD said unto **M**, Depart, *and* go up	4872
	33: 5	For the LORD had said unto **M**, Say unto	4872
	33: 7	**M** took the tabernacle, and pitched it	4872
	33: 8	when **M** went out unto the tabernacle,	4872
	33: 8	man *at* his tent door, and looked after **M**,	4872
	33: 9	to pass, as **M** entered into the tabernacle,	4872
	33: 9	and *the LORD* talked with **M**.	4872
	33:11	And the LORD spake unto **M** face to face,	4872
	33:12	**M** said unto the LORD, See, thou sayest	4872
	33:17	the LORD said unto **M**, I will do this	4872
	34: 1	the LORD said unto **M**, Hew thee two	4872
	34: 4	**M** rose up early in the morning, and	4872
	34: 8	**M** made haste, and bowed his head toward	4872
	34:27	the LORD said unto **M**, Write thou these	4872
	34:29	when **M** came down from mount Sinai with	4872
	34:29	that **M** wist not that the skin of his face	4872
	34:30	and all the children of Israel saw **M**,	4872
	34:31	**M** called unto them; and Aaron and all	4872
	34:31	returned unto him: and **M** talked with them.	4872
	34:33	*till* **M** had done speaking with them, he put	4872
	34:34	when **M** went in before the LORD to	4872
	34:35	the children of Israel saw the face of **M**,	4872
	34:35	**M** put the vail upon his face again, until he	4872
	35: 1	**M** gathered all the congregation of	4872
	35: 4	**M** spake unto all the congregation of	4872
	35:20	of Israel departed from the presence of **M**.	4872
	35:29	commanded to be made by the hand of **M**.	4872
	35:30	And **M** said unto the children of Israel, See,	4872
	36: 2	**M** called Bezaleel and Aholiab, and every	4872
	36: 3	they received of **M** all the offering,	4872
	36: 5	they spake unto **M**, saying, The people	4872
	36: 6	**M** gave commandment, and they caused it	4872
	38:21	according to the commandment of **M**,	4872
	38:22	made all that the LORD commanded **M**.	4872
	39: 1	for Aaron; as the LORD commanded **M**.	4872
	39: 5	as the LORD commanded **M**.	4872
	39: 7	of Israel; as the LORD commanded **M**.	4872
	39:21	the ephod; as the LORD commanded **M**.	4872
	39:26	minister *in;* as the LORD commanded **M**.	4872
	39:29	as the LORD commanded **M**.	4872
	39:31	the mitre; as the LORD commanded **M**.	4872
	39:32	to all that the LORD commanded **M**,	4872
	39:33	they brought the tabernacle unto **M**,	4872
	39:42	to all that the LORD commanded **M**,	4872
	39:43	**M** did look upon all the work, and behold,	4872
	39:43	so had they done it: and **M** blessed them.	4872
	40: 1	And the LORD spake unto **M**, saying,	4872
	40:16	Thus did **M**: according to all that	4872
	40:18	**M** reared up the tabernacle, and	4872
	40:19	upon it; as the LORD commanded **M**.	4872
	40:21	as the LORD commanded **M**.	4872
	40:23	as the LORD had commanded **M**.	4872
	40:25	the LORD; as the LORD commanded **M**.	4872
	40:27	as the LORD commanded **M**.	4872
	40:29	as the LORD commanded **M**.	4872
	40:31	**M** and Aaron and his sons washed their	4872
	40:32	as the LORD commanded **M**.	4872
	40:33	of the court gate. So **M** finished the work.	4872
	40:35	**M** was not able to enter into the tent of	4872
Lev	1: 1	the LORD called unto **M**, and spake unto	4872
	4: 1	And the LORD spake unto **M**, saying,	4872
	5:14	And the LORD spake unto **M**, saying,	4872
	6: 1	And the LORD spake unto **M**, saying,	4872
	6: 8	And the LORD spake unto **M**, saying,	4872
	6:19	And the LORD spake unto **M**, saying,	4872
	6:24	And the LORD spake unto **M**, saying,	4872
	7:22	And the LORD spake unto **M**, saying,	4872
	7:28	And the LORD spake unto **M**, saying,	4872
	7:38	Which the LORD commanded **M** in	4872
	8: 1	And the LORD spake unto **M**, saying,	4872
	8: 4	**M** did as the LORD commanded him;	4872
	8: 5	**M** said unto the congregation, This *is*	4872
	8: 6	**M** brought Aaron and his sons, and	4872
	8: 9	holy crown; as the LORD commanded **M**.	4872
	8:10	**M** took the anointing oil, and anointed	4872
	8:13	**M** brought Aaron's sons, and put coats	4872
	8:13	upon them; as the LORD commanded **M**.	4872
	8:15	he slew *it;* and **M** took the blood, and put *it*	4872
	8:16	their fat, and **M** burned *it* upon the altar.	4872
	8:17	the camp; as the LORD commanded **M**.	4872
	8:19	**M** sprinkled the blood upon the altar round	4872
	8:20	**M** burnt the head, and the pieces, and	4872
	8:21	and **M** burnt the whole ram upon the altar:	4872
	8:21	the LORD; as the LORD commanded **M**.	4872
	8:23	he slew *it;* and **M** took of the blood of it,	4872
	8:24	**M** put of the blood upon the tip of their	4872
	8:24	**M** sprinkled the blood upon the altar round	4872
	8:28	**M** took them from off their hands, and	4872
	8:29	**M** took the breast, and waved it *for* a wave	4872
	8:29	as the LORD commanded **M**.	4872
	8:30	**M** took of the anointing oil, and of	4872
	8:31	**M** said unto Aaron and to his sons, Boil	4872
	8:36	the LORD commanded by the hand of **M**.	4872
	9: 1	*that* **M** called Aaron and his sons, and	4872
	9: 5	they brought *that* which **M** commanded	4872
	9: 6	**M** said, This *is* the thing which the LORD	4872
	9: 7	**M** said unto Aaron, Go unto the altar, and	4872
	9:10	the altar; as the LORD commanded **M**.	4872
	9:21	before the LORD; as **M** commanded.	4872
	9:23	**M** and Aaron went into the tabernacle of	4872
	10: 3	**M** said unto Aaron, This *is it* that	4872
	10: 4	**M** called Mishael and Elzaphan, the sons of	4872
	10: 5	their coats out of the camp; as **M** had said.	4872
	10: 6	**M** said unto Aaron, and unto Eleazar and	4872
	10: 7	And they did according to the word of **M**.	4872
	10:11	hath spoken unto them by the hand of **M**.	4872
	10:12	**M** spake unto Aaron, and unto Eleazar and	4872
	10:16	**M** diligently sought the goat of the sin	4872
	10:19	Aaron said unto **M**, Behold, *this* day have	4872
	10:20	And when **M** heard *that,* he was content.	4872
	11: 1	the LORD spake unto **M** and to Aaron,	4872
	12: 1	And the LORD spake unto **M**, saying,	4872
	13: 1	the LORD spake unto **M** and Aaron,	4872
	14: 1	And the LORD spake unto **M**, saying,	4872
	14:33	the LORD spake unto **M** and unto Aaron,	4872
	15: 1	the LORD spake unto **M** and to Aaron,	4872
	16: 1	the LORD spake unto **M** after the death of	4872
	16: 2	the LORD said unto **M**, Speak unto Aaron	4872
	16:34	And he did as the LORD commanded **M**.	4872
	17: 1	And the LORD spake unto **M**, saying,	4872
	18: 1	And the LORD spake unto **M**, saying,	4872
	19: 1	And the LORD spake unto **M**, saying,	4872
	20: 1	And the LORD spake unto **M**, saying,	4872
	21: 1	the LORD said unto **M**, Speak unto	4872
	21:16	And the LORD spake unto **M**, saying,	4872
	21:24	**M** told *it* unto Aaron, and to his sons, and	4872
	22: 1	And the LORD spake unto **M**, saying,	4872
	22:17	And the LORD spake unto **M**, saying,	4872
	22:26	And the LORD spake unto **M**, saying,	4872
	23: 1	And the LORD spake unto **M**, saying,	4872
	23: 9	And the LORD spake unto **M**, saying,	4872
	23:23	And the LORD spake unto **M**, saying,	4872
	23:26	And the LORD spake unto **M**, saying,	4872
	23:33	And the LORD spake unto **M**, saying,	4872
	23:44	**M** declared unto the children of Israel	4872
	24: 1	And the LORD spake unto **M**, saying,	4872
	24:11	they brought him unto **M**: (and	4872
	24:13	And the LORD spake unto **M**, saying,	4872
	24:23	**M** spake to the children of Israel, that they	4872
	24:23	of Israel did as the LORD commanded **M**.	4872
	25: 1	the LORD spake unto **M** in mount Sinai,	4872
	26:46	of Israel in mount Sinai by the hand of **M**.	4872
	27: 1	And the LORD spake unto **M**, saying,	4872
	27:34	which the LORD commanded **M** for	4872
Nu	1: 1	the LORD spake unto **M** in the wilderness	4872
	1:17	**M** and Aaron took these men which are	4872
	1:19	As the LORD commanded **M**, so	4872
	1:44	which **M** and Aaron numbered, and	4872
	1:48	For the LORD had spoken unto **M**,	4872
	1:54	to all that the LORD commanded **M**,	4872
	2: 1	the LORD spake unto **M** and unto Aaron,	4872
	2:33	of Israel; as the LORD commanded **M**.	4872
	2:34	to all that the LORD commanded **M**:	4872
	3: 1	**M** in the day that the LORD spake with	4872
	3: 1	the LORD spake with **M** in mount Sinai.	4872
	3: 5	And the LORD spake unto **M**, saying,	4872

Nu 3:11 And the LORD spake unto **M**, saying, 4872
3:14 the LORD spake unto **M** in the wilderness 4872
3:16 **M** numbered them according to the word of 4872
3:38 *shall be* **M**, and Aaron and his sons, 4872
3:39 which **M** and Aaron numbered at 4872
3:40 the LORD said unto **M**, Number all 4872
3:42 **M** numbered, as the LORD commanded 4872
3:44 And the LORD spake unto **M**, saying, 4872
3:49 **M** took the redemption money of them that 4872
3:51 **M** gave the money of them that were 4872
3:51 the LORD, as the LORD commanded **M**. 4872
4: 1 the LORD spake unto **M** and unto Aaron, 4872
4:17 the LORD spake unto **M** and unto Aaron, 4872
4:21 And the LORD spake unto **M**, saying, 4872
4:34 **M** and Aaron and the chief of 4872
4:37 which **M** and Aaron did number according 4872
4:37 of the LORD by the hand of **M**. 4872
4:41 whom **M** and Aaron did number according 4872
4:45 whom **M** and Aaron numbered according 4872
4:45 the word of the LORD by the hand of **M**. 4872
4:46 whom **M** and Aaron and the chief of Israel 4872
4:49 they were numbered by the hand of **M**, 4872
4:49 of him, as the LORD commanded **M**. 4872
5: 1 And the LORD spake unto **M**, saying, 4872
5: 4 as the LORD spake unto **M**, so did 4872
5: 5 And the LORD spake unto **M**, saying, 4872
5:11 And the LORD spake unto **M**, saying, 4872
6: 1 And the LORD spake unto **M**, saying, 4872
6:22 And the LORD spake unto **M**, saying, 4872
7: 1 it came to pass on the day that **M** had fully 4872
7: 4 And the LORD spake unto **M**, saying, 4872
7: 6 **M** took the wagons and the oxen, and 4872
7:11 the LORD said unto **M**, They shall offer 4872
7:89 when **M** was gone into the tabernacle of 4872
8: 1 And the LORD spake unto **M**, saying, 4872
8: 3 as the LORD commanded **M**. 4872
8: 4 pattern which the LORD had shewed **M**, 4872
8: 5 And the LORD spake unto **M**, saying, 4872
8:20 **M**, and Aaron, and all the congregation of 4872
8:20 commanded **M** concerning the Levites, 4872
8:22 as the LORD had commanded **M** 4872
8:23 And the LORD spake unto **M**, saying, 4872
9: 1 the LORD spake unto **M** in the wilderness 4872
9: 4 **M** spake unto the children of Israel, 4872
9: 5 to all that the LORD commanded **M**, 4872
9: 6 they came before **M** and before Aaron on 4872
9: 8 **M** said unto them, Stand still, and I will 4872
9: 9 And the LORD spake unto **M**, saying, 4872
9:23 of the LORD by the hand of **M**. 4872
10: 1 And the LORD spake unto **M**, saying, 4872
10:13 of the LORD by the hand of **M**. 4872
10:29 **M** said unto Hobab, the son of Raguel 4872
10:35 that **M** said, Rise up, LORD, and let thine 4872
11: 2 the people cried unto **M**; and when Moses 4872
11: 2 when **M** prayed unto the LORD, the fire 4872
11:10 **M** heard the people weep throughout their 4872
11:10 kindled greatly; **M** also was displeased. 4872
11:11 **M** said unto the LORD, Wherefore hast 4872
11:16 the LORD said unto **M**, Gather unto me 4872
11:21 **M** said, The people, amongst whom I *am*, 4872
11:23 the LORD said unto **M**, Is the LORD'S 4872
11:24 **M** went out, and told the people the words 4872
11:27 told **M**, and said, Eldad and Medad do 4872
11:28 the servant of **M**, *one* of his young men, 4872
11:28 answered and said, My lord **M**, 4872
11:29 **M** said unto him, Enviest thou for my sake? 4872
11:30 **M** gat him into the camp, he and the elders 4872
12: 1 and Aaron spake against **M** because 4872
12: 2 the LORD indeed spoken only by **M**? 4872
12: 3 (Now the man **M** *was* very meek, above all 4872
12: 4 the LORD spake suddenly unto **M**, and 4872
12: 7 My servant **M** *is* not so, who *is* faithful in 4872
12: 8 not afraid to speak against my servant **M**? 4872
12:11 Aaron said unto **M**, Alas, my lord, 4872
12:13 **M** cried unto the LORD, saying, Heal her 4872
12:14 the LORD said unto **M**, If her father had 4872
13: 1 And the LORD spake unto **M**, saying, 4872
13: 3 **M** by the commandment of the LORD 4872
13:16 These *are* the names of the men which **M** 4872
13:16 **M** called Oshea the son of Nun, Jehoshua. 4872
13:17 **M** sent them to spy out the land of Canaan, 4872
13:26 they went and came to **M**, and to Aaron, 4872
13:30 Caleb stilled the people before **M**, and said, 4872
14: 2 the children of Israel murmured against **M** 4872
14: 5 **M** and Aaron fell on their faces before all 4872
14:11 the LORD said unto **M**, How long will 4872
14:13 **M** said unto the LORD, Then 4872
14:26 the LORD spake unto **M** and unto Aaron, 4872
14:36 the men, which **M** sent to search the land, 4872
14:39 **M** told these sayings unto all the children 4872
14:41 **M** said, Wherefore now do ye transgress 4872
14:44 and **M**, departed not out of the camp. 4872
15: 1 And the LORD spake unto **M**, saying, 4872
15:17 And the LORD spake unto **M**, saying, 4872
15:22 which the LORD hath spoken unto **M**, 4872
15:23 hath commanded you by the hand of **M**, 4872
15:23 the day that the LORD commanded *M*, NIH
15:33 him gathering sticks brought him unto **M** 4872
15:35 the LORD said unto **M**, The man shall be 4872
15:36 and he died; as the LORD commanded **M**. 4872
15:37 And the LORD spake unto **M**, saying, 4872
16: 2 they rose up before **M**, with certain of 4872
16: 3 gathered themselves together against **M** 4872
16: 4 And when **M** heard *it*, he fell upon his face: 4872
16: 8 **M** said unto Korah, Hear, I pray you, 4872
16:12 **M** sent to call Dathan and Abiram, the sons 4872
16:15 **M** was very wroth, and said unto 4872
16:16 **M** said unto Korah, Be thou and all thy 4872
16:18 the tabernacle of the congregation with **M** 4872
16:20 the LORD spake unto **M** and unto Aaron, 4872
16:23 And the LORD spake unto **M**, saying, 4872
16:25 **M** rose up and went unto Dathan and 4872
16:28 **M** said, Hereby ye shall know that 4872
16:36 And the LORD spake unto **M**, saying, 4872
16:40 the LORD said to him by the hand of **M**. 4872
16:41 the children of Israel murmured against **M** 4872
16:42 the congregation was gathered against **M** 4872
16:43 **M** and Aaron came before the tabernacle of 4872
16:44 And the LORD spake unto **M**, saying, 4872
16:46 **M** said unto Aaron, Take a censer, and 4872
16:47 Aaron took as **M** commanded, and ran into 4872
16:50 Aaron returned unto **M** unto the door of 4872
17: 1 And the LORD spake unto **M**, saying, 4872
17: 6 **M** spake unto the children of Israel, and 4872
17: 7 **M** laid up the rods before the LORD in 4872
17: 8 that on the morrow **M** went into 4872
17: 9 **M** brought out all the rods from before 4872
17:10 the LORD said unto **M**, Bring Aaron's 4872
17:11 **M** did *so*: as the LORD commanded him, 4872
17:12 the children of Israel spake unto **M**, saying, 4872
18:25 And the LORD spake unto **M**, saying, 4872
19: 1 the LORD spake unto **M** and unto Aaron, 4872
20: 2 gathered themselves together against **M** 4872
20: 3 the people chode with **M**, and spake, 4872
20: 6 **M** and Aaron went from the presence of 4872
20: 7 And the LORD spake unto **M**, saying, 4872
20: 9 **M** took the rod from before the LORD, 4872
20:10 **M** and Aaron gathered the congregation 4872
20:11 **M** lift up his hand, and with his rod he 4872
20:12 the LORD spake unto **M** and Aaron, 4872
20:14 **M** sent messengers from Kadesh unto 4872
20:23 the LORD spake unto **M** and Aaron in 4872
20:27 And **M** did as the LORD commanded: and 4872
20:28 And **M** stripped Aaron of his garments, and 4872
20:28 **M** and Eleazar came down from the mount. 4872
21: 5 people spake against God, and against **M**, 4872
21: 7 Therefore the people came to **M**, and said, 4872
21: 7 from us. And **M** prayed for the people. 4872
21: 8 the LORD said unto **M**, Make thee a fiery 4872
21: 9 **M** made a serpent of brass, and put it upon 4872
21:16 well whereof the LORD spake unto **M**, 4872
21:32 **M** sent to spy out Jaazer, and they took 4872
21:34 the LORD said unto **M**, Fear him not: 4872
25: 4 the LORD said unto **M**, Take all the heads 4872
25: 5 **M** said unto the judges of Israel, Slay ye 4872
25: 6 a Midianitish *woman* in the sight of **M**, 4872
25:10 And the LORD spake unto **M**, saying, 4872
25:16 And the LORD spake unto **M**, saying, 4872
26: 1 that the LORD spake unto **M** and 4872
26: 3 **M** and Eleazar the priest spake with them 4872
26: 4 as the LORD commanded **M** and 4872
26: 9 who strove against **M** and against Aaron in 4872
26:52 And the LORD spake unto **M**, saying, 4872
26:59 she bare unto Amram Aaron and **M**, and 4872
26:63 These *are* they that were numbered by **M** 4872
26:64 these there was not a man of them whom **M** 4872
27: 2 they stood before **M**, and before Eleazar 4872
27: 5 **M** brought their cause before the LORD. 4872

Nu	27: 6	And the LORD spake unto **M**, saying,	4872
	27:11	as the LORD commanded **M**.	4872
	27:12	the LORD said unto **M**, Get thee up into	4872
	27:15	And **M** spake unto the LORD, saying,	4872
	27:18	the LORD said unto **M**, Take thee Joshua	4872
	27:22	**M** did as the LORD commanded him:	4872
	27:23	the LORD commanded by the hand of **M**.	4872
	28: 1	And the LORD spake unto **M**, saying,	4872
	29:40	**M** told the children of Israel according to	4872
	29:40	to all that the LORD commanded **M**.	4872
	30: 1	**M** spake unto the heads of the tribes	4872
	30:16	which the LORD commanded **M**,	4872
	31: 1	And the LORD spake unto **M**, saying,	4872
	31: 3	**M** spake unto the people, saying,	4872
	31: 6	**M** sent them to the war, a thousand of	4872
	31: 7	as the LORD commanded **M**;	4872
	31:12	unto **M**, and Eleazar the priest, and unto	4872
	31:13	**M**, and Eleazar the priest, and all	4872
	31:14	**M** was wroth with the officers of the host,	4872
	31:15	**M** said unto them, Have ye saved all	4872
	31:21	the law which the LORD commanded **M**;	4872
	31:25	And the LORD spake unto **M**, saying,	4872
	31:31	**M** and Eleazar the priest did as the LORD	4872
	31:31	priest did as the LORD commanded **M**.	4872
	31:41	**M** gave the tribute, *which was*	4872
	31:41	the priest, as the LORD commanded **M**.	4872
	31:42	which **M** divided from the men that warred,	4872
	31:47	**M** took one portion of fifty, *both* of man	4872
	31:47	the LORD; as the LORD commanded **M**.	4872
	31:48	captains of hundreds, came near unto **M**:	4872
	31:49	they said unto **M**, Thy servants have taken	4872
	31:51	**M** and Eleazar the priest took the gold of	4872
	31:54	**M** and Eleazar the priest took the gold of	4872
	32: 2	of Reuben came and spake unto **M**,	4872
	32: 6	**M** said unto the children of Gad and to	4872
	32:20	**M** said unto them, If ye will do this thing,	4872
	32:25	and the children of Reuben spake unto **M**,	4872
	32:28	So concerning them **M** commanded Eleazar	4872
	32:29	**M** said unto them, If the children of Gad	4872
	32:33	**M** gave unto them, *even* to the children of	4872
	32:40	**M** gave Gilead unto Machir the son of	4872
	33: 1	with their armies under the hand of **M**	4872
	33: 2	**M** wrote their goings out according to their	4872
	33:50	the LORD spake unto **M** in the plains of	4872
	34: 1	And the LORD spake unto **M**, saying,	4872
	34:13	**M** commanded the children of Israel,	4872
	34:16	And the LORD spake unto **M**, saying,	4872
	35: 1	the LORD spake unto **M** in the plains of	4872
	35: 9	And the LORD spake unto **M**, saying,	4872
	36: 1	and spake before **M**, and before the princes,	4872
	36: 5	**M** commanded the children of Israel	4872
	36:10	Even as the LORD commanded **M**, so	4872
	36:13	**M** unto the children of Israel in the plains	4872
Dt	1: 1	These *be* the words which **M** spake unto all	4872
	1: 3	*that* **M** spake unto the children of Israel,	4872
	1: 5	began **M** to declare this law, saying,	4872
	4:41	**M** severed three cities on *this* side Jordan	4872
	4:44	this *is* the law which **M** set before	4872
	4:45	which **M** spake unto the children of Israel,	4872
	4:46	whom **M** and the children of Israel smote,	4872
	5: 1	**M** called all Israel, and said unto them,	4872
	27: 1	**M** with the elders of Israel commanded	4872
	27: 9	**M** and the priests the Levites spake unto all	4872
	27:11	**M** charged the people the same day, saying,	4872
	29: 1	which the LORD commanded **M** to make	4872
	29: 2	**M** called unto all Israel, and said unto	4872
	31: 1	**M** went and spake these words unto all	4872
	31: 7	**M** called unto Joshua, and said unto him in	4872
	31: 9	**M** wrote this law, and delivered it unto	4872
	31:10	**M** commanded them, saying, At the end of	4872
	31:14	the LORD said unto **M**, Behold, thy days	4872
	31:14	**M** and Joshua went, and	4872
	31:16	the LORD said unto **M**, Behold, thou shalt	4872
	31:22	**M** therefore wrote this song the same day,	4872
	31:24	when **M** had made an end of writing	4872
	31:25	That **M** commanded the Levites,	4872
	31:30	**M** spake in the ears of all the congregation	4872
	32:44	**M** came and spake all the words of this	4872
	32:45	**M** made an end of speaking all these words	4872
	32:48	the LORD spake unto **M** that selfsame	4872
	33: 1	wherewith **M** the man of God blessed	4872
	33: 4	**M** commanded us a law, *even*	4872
	34: 1	**M** went up from the plains of Moab unto	4872
	34: 5	So **M** the servant of the LORD died there	4872
	34: 7	**M** *was* an hundred and twenty years old	4872
	34: 8	the children of Israel wept for **M** in	4872
	34: 8	*and* mourning for **M** were ended.	4872
	34: 9	for **M** had laid his hands upon him:	4872
	34: 9	and did as the LORD commanded **M**.	4872
	34:10	not a prophet since in Israel like unto **M**,	4872
	34:12	in all the great terror which **M** shewed in	4872
Jos	1: 1	Now after the death of **M** the servant of	4872
	1: 2	**M** my servant is dead; now therefore arise,	4872
	1: 3	have I given unto you, as I said unto **M**.	4872
	1: 5	as I was with **M**, *so* I will be with thee:	4872
	1: 7	which **M** my servant commanded thee:	4872
	1:13	Remember the word which **M** the servant	4872
	1:14	shall remain in the land which **M** gave you	4872
	1:15	which **M** the LORD'S servant gave you	4872
	1:17	According as we hearkened unto **M** in all	4872
	1:17	thy God be with thee, as he was with **M**.	4872
	3: 7	as I was with **M**, *so* I will be with thee.	4872
	4:10	according to all that **M** commanded Joshua:	4872
	4:12	children of Israel, as **M** spake unto them:	4872
	4:14	they feared him, as they feared **M**, all	4872
	8:31	As **M** the servant of the LORD	4872
	8:31	as it is written in the book of the law of **M**,	4872
	8:32	upon the stones a copy of the law of **M**,	4872
	8:33	as **M** the servant of the LORD had	4872
	8:35	There was not a word of all that **M**	4872
	9:24	his servant **M** to give you all the land,	4872
	11:12	as **M** the servant of the LORD	4872
	11:15	As the LORD commanded **M** his servant,	4872
	11:15	so did **M** command Joshua, and so	4872
	11:15	of all that the LORD commanded **M**.	4872
	11:20	as the LORD commanded **M**.	4872
	11:23	to all that the LORD said unto **M**;	4872
	12: 6	Them did **M** the servant of the LORD and	4872
	12: 6	**M** the servant of the LORD gave it *for* a	4872
	13: 8	which **M** gave them, beyond Jordan	4872
	13: 8	*even* as **M** the servant of the LORD gave	4872
	13:12	for these did **M** smite, and cast them out.	4872
	13:15	**M** gave unto the tribe of the children of	4872
	13:21	whom **M** smote with the princes of Midian,	4872
	13:24	**M** gave *inheritance* unto the tribe of Gad,	4872
	13:29	**M** gave *inheritance* unto the half tribe of	4872
	13:32	These *are the countries* which **M** did	4872
	13:33	unto the tribe of Levi **M** gave not *any*	4872
	14: 2	the LORD commanded by the hand of **M**,	4872
	14: 3	For **M** had given the inheritance of two	4872
	14: 5	As the LORD commanded **M**, so	4872
	14: 6	said unto **M** the man of God concerning me	4872
	14: 7	Forty years old *was* I when **M** the servant	4872
	14: 9	**M** sware on that day, saying, Surely	4872
	14:10	since the LORD spake this word unto **M**,	4872
	14:11	*this* day as *I was* in the day that **M** sent me:	4872
	17: 4	The LORD commanded **M** to give us an	4872
	18: 7	which **M** the servant of the LORD gave	4872
	20: 2	I spake unto you by the hand of **M**:	4872
	21: 2	The LORD commanded by the hand of **M**	4872
	21: 8	the LORD commanded by the hand of **M**.	4872
	22: 2	Ye have kept all that **M** the servant of	4872
	22: 4	which **M** the servant of the LORD gave	4872
	22: 5	which **M** the servant of the LORD	4872
	22: 7	**M** had given *possession* in Bashan:	4872
	22: 9	the word of the LORD by the hand of **M**.	4872
	23: 6	that is written in the book of the law of **M**,	4872
	24: 5	I sent **M** also and Aaron, and I plagued	4872
Jdg	1:20	they gave Hebron unto Caleb, as **M** said:	4872
	3: 4	commanded their fathers by the hand of **M**.	4872
	4:11	children of Hobab the father in law of **M**,	4872
1Sa	12: 6	*It is* the LORD that advanced **M** and	4872
	12: 8	then the LORD sent **M** and Aaron,	4872
1Ki	2: 3	as *it is* written in the law of **M**,	4872
	8: 9	of stone, which **M** put there at Horeb,	4872
	8:53	as thou spakest by the hand of **M** thy	4872
	8:56	which he promised by the hand of **M** his	4872
2Ki	14: 6	is written in the book of the law of **M**,	4872
	18: 4	brake in pieces the brasen serpent that **M**	4872
	18: 6	which the LORD commanded **M**.	4872
	18:12	all that **M** the servant of the LORD	4872
	21: 8	according to all the law that my servant **M**	4872
	23:25	all his might, according to all the law of **M**;	4872
1Ch	6: 3	of Amram; Aaron, and **M**, and Miriam.	4872
	6:49	according to all that **M** the servant of God	4872
	15:15	as **M** commanded according to the word of	4872
	21:29	which **M** made in the wilderness, and	4872
	22:13	judgments which the LORD charged **M**	4872

1Ch 23:13 The sons of Amram; Aaron and **M**: and 4872
23:14 Now *concerning* **M** the man of God, 4872
23:15 The sons of **M** *were*, Gershom, and Eliezer. 4872
26:24 the son of **M**, *was* ruler of the treasures. 4872
2Ch 1: 3 which **M** the servant of the LORD had 4872
5:10 two tables which **M** put *therein* at Horeb, 4872
8:13 according to the commandment of **M**, 4872
23:18 as it is written in the law of **M**, 4872
24: 6 *according to the commandment* of **M** 4872
24: 9 **M** the servant of God laid upon Israel in 4872
25: 4 as it is written in the law in the book of **M**, 4872
30:16 according to the law of **M** the man of God: 4872
33: 8 and the ordinances by the hand of **M**. 4872
34:14 book of the law of the LORD *given* by **M**. 4872
35: 6 the word of the LORD by the hand of **M**. 4872
35:12 as it is written in the book of **M**. 4872
Ezr 3: 2 as it is written in the law of **M** the man of 4872
6:18 as it is written in the book of **M**. 4873
7: 6 he *was* a ready scribe in the law of **M**, 4872
Ne 1: 7 which thou commandedst thy servant **M**. 4872
1: 8 that thou commandedst thy servant **M**, 4872
8: 1 scribe to bring the book of the law of **M**, 4872
8:14 which the LORD had commanded by **M**, 4872
9:14 and laws, by the hand of **M** thy servant: 4872
10:29 which was given by **M** the servant of God, 4872
13: 1 On that day they read in the book of **M** in 4872
Ps 77:20 thy people like a flock by the hand of **M** 4872
90: T A Prayer of **M** the man of God. 4872
99: 6 **M** and Aaron among his priests, and 4872
103: 7 He made known his ways unto **M**, his acts 4872
105:26 He sent **M** his servant; *and* Aaron whom he 4872
106:16 They envied **M** also in the camp, *and* 4872
106:23 had not **M** his chosen stood before him in 4872
106:32 so that it went ill with **M** for their sakes: 4872
Isa 63:11 the days of old, **M**, *and* his people, 4872
63:12 That led *them* by the right hand of **M** *with* 4872
Jer 15: 1 Though **M** and Samuel stood before me, 4872
Da 9:11 the oath that *is* written in the law of **M** 4872
9:13 As *it is* written in the law of **M**, all this evil 4872
Mic 6: 4 I sent before thee **M**, Aaron, and Miriam. 4872
Mal 4: 4 Remember ye the law of **M** my servant, 4872
Mt 8: 4 offer the gift that **M** commanded for a *3475*
17: 3 there appeared unto them **M** and *3475*
17: 4 for thee, and one for **M**, and one for Elias. *3475*
19: 7 Why did **M** then command to give a *3475*
19: 8 **M** because of the hardness of your hearts *3475*
22:24 Saying, Master, **M** said, If a man die, *3475*
Mk 1:44 *those things* which **M** commanded, *3475*
7:10 For **M** said, Honour thy father and *3475*
9: 4 there appeared unto them Elias with **M**: *3475*
9: 5 for thee, and one for **M**, and one for Elias. *3475*
10: 3 unto them, What did **M** command you? *3475*
10: 4 **M** suffered to write a bill of divorcement, *3475*
12:19 Master, **M** wrote unto us, If a man's *3475*
12:26 have ye not read in the book of **M**, how in *3475*
Lk 2:22 to the law of **M** were accomplished, *3475*
5:14 thy cleansing, according as **M** commanded, *3475*
9:30 him two men, which were **M** and Elias: *3475*
9:33 for thee, and one for **M**, and one for Elias: *3475*
16:29 unto him, They have **M** and the prophets; *3475*
16:31 If they hear not **M** and the prophets, *3475*
20:28 Saying, Master, **M** wrote unto us, If any *3475*
20:37 are raised, even **M** shewed at the bush, *3475*
24:27 And beginning at **M** and all the prophets, *3475*
24:44 which were written in the law of **M**, and *3475*
Jn 1:17 For the law was given by **M**, *but* grace and *3475*
1:45 of whom **M** in the law, and the prophets, *3475*
3:14 And as **M** lifted up the serpent in *3475*
5:45 accuseth you, *even* **M**, in whom ye trust. *3475*
5:46 For had ye believed **M**, ye would have *3475*
6:32 **M** gave you not *that* bread from heaven; *3475*
7:19 Did not **M** give you the law, and *yet* none *3475*
7:22 **M** therefore gave unto you circumcision, *3475*
7:22 not because it is of **M**, but of the fathers; *3475*
7:23 that the law of **M** should not be broken; *3475*
8: 5 Now **M** in the law commanded us, *3475*
9:29 We know that God spake unto **M**: *as for* *3475*
Ac 3:22 For **M** truly said unto the fathers, A prophet *3475*
6:11 him speak blasphemous words against **M**, *3475*
6:14 shall change the customs which **M** *3475*
7:20 In which time **M** was born, and *3475*
7:22 And **M** was learned in all the wisdom of *3475*
7:29 Then fled **M** at this saying, and was a *3475*
7:31 When **M** saw *it*, he wondered at the sight: *3475*
7:32 and the God of Jacob. Then **M** trembled, *3475*
7:35 This **M** whom they refused, saying, *3475*
7:37 This is *that* **M**, which said unto the children *3475*
7:40 for *as for* this **M**, which brought us out of *3475*
7:44 as he had appointed, speaking unto **M**, *3475*
13:39 ye could not be justified by the law of **M**. *3475*
15: 1 ye be circumcised after the manner of **M**, *3475*
15: 5 to command *them* to keep the law of **M**. *3475*
15:21 For **M** of old time hath in every city them *3475*
21:21 are among the Gentiles to forsake **M**, *3475*
26:22 the prophets and **M** did say should come: *3475*
28:23 both out of the law of **M**, and *out of* *3475*
Ro 5:14 death reigned from Adam to **M**, *3475*
9:15 For he saith to **M**, I will have mercy on *3475*
10: 5 For **M** describeth the righteousness which *3475*
10:19 First **M** saith, I will provoke you to *3475*
1Co 9: 9 For it is written in the law of **M**, Thou shalt *3475*
10: 2 And were all baptized unto **M** in the cloud *3475*
2Co 3: 7 face of **M** for the glory of his countenance; *3475*
3:13 And not as **M**, *which* put a vail over his *3475*
3:15 But *even* unto this day, when **M** is read, *3475*
2Ti 3: 8 Now as Jannes and Jambres withstood **M**, *3475*
Heb 3: 2 as also **M** *was faithful* in all his house. *3475*
3: 3 was counted worthy of more glory than **M**, *3475*
3: 5 And **M** verily *was* faithful in all his house, *3475*
3:16 not all that came out of Egypt by **M**. *3475*
7:14 of which tribe **M** spake nothing concerning *3475*
8: 5 shadow of heavenly *things*, as **M** was *3475*
9:19 For when **M** had spoken every precept to *3475*
11:23 By faith **M**, when he was born, was hid *3475*
11:24 By faith **M**, when he was come to years, *3475*
12:21 *that* **M** said, I exceedingly fear and quake;) *3475*
Jude 1: 9 the devil he disputed about the body of **M**, *3475*
Rev 15: 3 And they sing the song of **M** the servant of *3475*

MOSES' (19) [MOSES]

Ex 17:12 **M** hands *were* heavy; and they took a 4872
18: 1 the priest of Midian, **M** father in law, 4872
18: 2 Jethro, **M** father in law, took Zipporah, 4872
18: 2 father in law, took Zipporah, **M** wife, 4872
18: 5 Jethro, **M** father in law, came with his sons 4872
18:12 Jethro, **M** father in law, took a burnt 4872
18:12 to eat bread with **M** father in law before 4872
18:14 when **M** father in law saw all that he did to 4872
18:17 **M** father in law said unto him, The thing 4872
32:19 **M** anger waxed hot, and he cast the tables 4872
34:29 the two tables of Testimony in **M** hand, 4872
34:35 of Moses, that the skin of **M** face shone: 4872
Lev 8:29 ram of consecration it was **M** part; 4872+3807.1
Nu 10:29 of Raguel the Midianite, **M** father in law, 4872
Jos 1: 1 Joshua the son of Nun, **M** minister, saying, 4872
Jdg 1:16 the children of the Kenite, **M** father in law, 4872
Mt 23: 2 The scribes and the Pharisees sit in **M** seat: *3475*
Jn 9:28 art his disciple; but we are **M** disciples. *3475*
Heb 10:28 He that despised **M** law died without mercy *3475*

MOST (135) [MUCH] See Index

MOTE (6)

Mt 7: 3 And why beholdest thou the **m** that is in thy *2595*
7: 4 Let me pull out the **m** out of thine eye; *2595*
7: 5 shalt thou see clearly to cast out the **m** out *2595*
Lk 6:41 And why beholdest thou the **m** that is in thy *2595*
6:42 let me pull out the **m** that is in thine eye, *2595*
6:42 shalt thou see clearly to pull out the **m** that *2595*

MOTH (9) [MOTHEATEN, MOTH-EATEN]

Job 4:19 the dust, which are crushed before the **m**? 6211
27:18 He buildeth his house as a **m**, and as a 6211
Ps 39:11 his beauty to consume away like a **m**: 6211
Isa 50: 9 old as a garment; the **m** shall eat them up. 6211
51: 8 For the **m** shall eat them up like a garment, 6211
Hos 5:12 Therefore *will* I *be* unto Ephraim as a **m**, 6211
Mt 6:19 where **m** and rust doth corrupt, and *4597*
6:20 where neither **m** nor rust doth corrupt, and *4597*
Lk 12:33 no thief approacheth, neither **m** corrupteth. *4597*

MOTHEATEN, MOTH-EATEN (2) [MOTH]

Job 13:28 consumeth, as a garment that is **m**. 398+6211
Jas 5: 2 are corrupted, and your garments are **m**. *4598*

MOTHER (245) [GRANDMOTHER, MOTHER'S, MOTHERS, MOTHERS']

Ge 2:24 shall a man leave his father and his **m**, 517
3:20 because she was the **m** of all living. 517

Ge 17:16 bless her, and she shall be *a* **m** of nations; NIH
20:12 of my father, but not the daughter of my **m**; 517
21:21 his **m** took him a wife out of the land of 517
24:53 to her brother and to her **m** precious things. 517
24:55 her brother and her **m** said, Let the damsel 517
24:60 be thou *the* **m** of thousands of millions, and NIH
24:67 Isaac brought her into his **m** Sarah's tent, 517
27:11 Jacob said to Rebekah his **m**, Behold, 517
27:13 his **m** said unto him, Upon me *be* thy curse, 517
27:14 and fetched, and brought *them* to his **m**: 517
27:14 his **m** made savoury meat, such as his father 517
28: 5 brother of Rebekah, Jacob's and Esau's **m**. 517
28: 7 And that Jacob obeyed his father and his **m**, 517
30:14 the field, and brought them unto his **m** Leah. 517
32:11 and smite me, *and* the **m** with the children. 517
37:10 Shall I and thy **m** and thy brethren indeed 517
44:20 he alone is left of his **m**, and his father 517
Ex 2: 8 And the maid went and called the child's **m**. 517
20:12 Honour thy father and thy **m**: that thy days 517
21:15 or his **m**, shall be surely put to death. 517
21:17 or his **m**, shall surely be put to death. 517
Lev 18: 7 or the nakedness of thy **m**, shalt thou not 517
18: 7 she *is* thy **m**; thou shalt not uncover her 517
18: 9 daughter of thy father, or daughter of thy **m**, 517
19: 3 Ye shall fear every man his **m**, and 517
20: 9 or his **m** shall be surely put to death: 517
20: 9 he hath cursed his father or his **m**; his blood 517
20:14 if a man take a wife and her **m**, it *is* 517
21: 2 *that is*, for his **m**, and for his father, and 517
21:11 nor defile himself for his father, or for his **m**; 517
Nu 6: 7 or for his **m**, for his brother, or for his sister, 517
26:59 of Levi, whom *her* **m** bare to Levi in Egypt: NIH
Dt 5:16 Honour thy father and thy **m**, as the LORD 517
13: 6 the son of thy **m**, or thy son, or thy daughter, 517
21:13 bewail her father and her **m** a full month: 517
21:18 or the voice of his **m**, and *that*, when they 517
21:19 shall his father and his **m** lay hold on him, 517
22:15 her **m**, take and bring forth *the tokens of* 517
27:16 *be* he that setteth light by his father or his **m**. 517
27:22 of his father, or the daughter of his **m**. 517
27:23 Cursed *be* he that lieth with his **m in law**. 2859
33: 9 Who said unto his father and to his **m**, I have 517
Jos 2:13 and my **m**, and my brethren, and my sisters, 517
2:18 thy **m**, and thy brethren, and all thy father's 517
6:23 her **m**, and her brethren, and all that she had; 517
Jdg 5: 7 I Deborah arose, that I arose a **m** in Israel. 517
5:28 The **m** of Sisera looked out at a window, and 517
8:19 *were* my brethren, *even* the sons of my **m**: 517
14: 2 and told his father and his **m**, and said, 517
14: 3 his father and his **m** said unto him, *Is there* 517
14: 4 his **m** knew not that it *was* of the LORD, 517
14: 5 his father and his **m**, *to* Timnath, and 517
14: 6 not his father or his **m** what he had done. 517
14: 9 came to his father and **m**, and he gave them, 517
14:16 I have not told *it* my father nor my **m**, and 517
17: 2 he said unto his **m**, The eleven hundred 517
17: 2 his **m** said, Blessed *be thou* of the LORD, 517
17: 3 eleven hundred *shekels* of silver to his **m**, 517
17: 3 his **m** said, I had wholly dedicated the silver 517
17: 4 Yet he restored the money unto his **m**; and 517
17: 4 his **m** took two hundred *shekels* of silver, 517
Ru 1:14 Orpah kissed her **m in law**; but Ruth clave 2545
2:11 all that thou hast done unto thy **m in law** 2545
2:11 and *how* thou hast left thy father and thy **m**, 517
2:18 her **m in law** saw what she had gleaned: 2545
2:19 her **m in law** said unto her, Where hast 2545
2:19 she shewed her **m in law** with whom she 2545
2:23 and dwelt with her **m in law**. 2545
3: 1 Naomi her **m in law** said unto her, 2545
3: 6 did according to all that her **m in law** bade 2545
3:16 when she came to her **m in law**, she said, 2545
3:17 to me, Go not empty unto thy **m in law**. 2545
1Sa 2:19 Moreover his **m** made him a little coat, and 517
15:33 so shall thy **m** be childless among women. 517
22: 3 Let my father and my **m**, I pray thee, 517
2Sa 17:25 of Nahash, sister to Zeruiah Joab's **m**. 517
19:37 by the grave of my father and of my **m**. 517
20:19 seekest to destroy a city and a **m** in Israel: 517
1Ki 1: 6 and *his* **m** bare him after Absalom. NIH
1:11 spake unto Bath-sheba the **m** of Solomon, 517
2:13 came to Bath-sheba the **m** of Solomon. 517
2:19 and caused a seat to be set for the king's **m**; 517
2:20 the king said unto her, Ask on, my **m**: for I 517
2:22 king Solomon answered and said unto his **m**, 517
3:27 and in no wise slay it: she *is* the **m** thereof. 517
15:13 also Maachah his **m**, even her he removed 517
17:23 the house, and delivered him unto his **m**: 517
19:20 kiss my father and my **m**, and *then* I will 517
22:52 in the way of his **m**, and in the way of 517
2Ki 3: 2 but not like his father, and like his **m**: 517
3:13 of thy father, and to the prophets of thy **m**. 517
4:19 And he said to a lad, Carry him to his **m**. 517
4:20 brought him to his **m**, he sat on her knees till 517
4:30 the **m** of the child said, *As* the LORD 517
9:22 so long as the whoredoms of thy **m** Jezebel 517
11: 1 when Athaliah the **m** of Ahaziah saw that 517
24:12 he, and his **m**, and his servants, and 517
24:15 the king's **m**, and the king's wives, and his 517
1Ch 2:26 name *was* Atarah; she *was* the **m** of Onam. 517
4: 9 his **m** called his name Jabez, saying, 517
2Ch 15:16 also *concerning* Maachah the **m** of Asa 517
22: 3 for his **m** was his counseller to do wickedly. 517
22:10 when Athaliah the **m** of Ahaziah saw that 517
Est 2: 7 for she had neither father nor **m**, and 517
2: 7 when her father and **m** were dead, 517
Job 17:14 to the worm, *Thou art* my **m**, and my sister. 517
Ps 27:10 When my father and my **m** forsake me, then 517
35:14 as one that mourneth for his **m**. 517
51: 5 and in sin did my **m** conceive me. 517
109:14 and let not the sin of his **m** be blotted out. 517
113: 9 to keep house, *to be* a joyful **m** of children. 517
131: 2 as a child that is weaned of his **m**: 517
Pr 1: 8 thy father, and forsake not the law of thy **m**: 517
4: 3 and only *beloved* in the sight of my **m**. 517
6:20 and forsake not the law of thy **m**: 517
10: 1 but a foolish son *is* the heaviness of his **m**. 517
15:20 but a foolish man despiseth his **m**. 517
19:26 wasteth *his* father, *and* chaseth away *his* **m**, 517
20:20 Whoso curseth his father or his **m**, his lamp 517
23:22 and despise not thy **m** when she is old. 517
23:25 Thy father and thy **m** shall be glad, and 517
28:24 Whoso robbeth his father or his **m**, and saith, 517
29:15 a child left *to himself* bringeth his **m** to 517
30:11 their father, and doth not bless their **m**. 517
30:17 at *his* father, and despiseth to obey *his* **m**, 517
31: 1 the prophecy that his **m** taught him. 517
SS 3:11 **m** crowned him in the day of his espousals, 517
6: 9 she *is* the *only* one of her **m**, she *is* 517
8: 1 my brother, that sucked the breasts of my **m**! 517
8: 5 there thy **m** brought thee forth: there she 517
Isa 8: 4 My father, and my **m**, the riches of 517
49: 1 from the bowels of my **m** hath he made 517
50: 1 for your transgressions *is* your **m** put away. 517
66:13 As one whom his **m** comforteth, so will I 517
Jer 15: 8 I have brought upon them against the **m** of 517
15:10 Woe is me, my **m**, that thou hast borne me a 517
16: 7 to drink for their father or for their **m**. 517
20:14 let not the day wherein my **m** bare me be 517
20:17 or that my **m** might have been my grave, and 517
22:26 thy **m** that bare thee, into another country, 517
50:12 Your **m** shall be sore confounded; she that 517
Eze 16: 3 father *was* an Amorite, and thy **m** a Hittite. 517
16:44 saying, As *is* the **m**, *so is* her daughter. 517
16:45 your **m** *was* a Hittite, and your father an 517
19: 2 say, What *is* thy **m**? A lioness: she lay down 517
19:10 Thy **m** *is* like a vine in thy blood, planted by 517
22: 7 In thee have they set light by father and **m**: 517
23: 2 were two women, the daughters of one **m**: 517
44:25 or for **m**, or for son, or for daughter, 517
Hos 2: 2 Plead with your **m**, plead: for she *is* not my 517
2: 5 For their **m** hath played the harlot: she that 517
4: 5 thee *in* the night, and I will destroy thy **m**. 517
10:14 the **m** was dashed in pieces upon *her* 517
Mic 7: 6 the daughter riseth up against her **m**, 517
7: 6 the daughter in law against her **m in law**; 2545
Zec 13: 3 and his **m** that begat him shall say unto him, 517
13: 3 his **m** that begat him shall thrust him through 517
Mt 1:18 When as his **m** Mary was espoused to *3384*
2:11 they saw the young child with Mary his **m**, *3384*
2:13 and take the young child and his **m**, and *3384*
2:14 he took the young child and his **m** by night, *3384*
2:20 and take the young child and his **m**, and *3384*
2:21 and took the young child and his **m**, and *3384*
8:14 he saw his **wife's m** laid, and sick of a *3994*
10:35 and the daughter against her **m**, and *3384*
10:35 the daughter in law against her **m in law**. *3994*
10:37 or **m** more than me is not worthy of me: *3384*
12:46 *his* **m** and his brethren stood without, *3384*

Mt 12:47 thy **m** and thy brethren stand without, *3384*
12:48 said unto him that told him, Who is my **m**? *3384*
12:49 and said, Behold my **m** and my brethren. *3384*
12:50 the same is my brother, and sister, and **m**. *3384*
13:55 is not his **m** called Mary? and his brethren, *3384*
14: 8 being before instructed of her **m**, said, *3384*
14:11 to the damsel: and she brought *it* to her **m**. *3384*
15: 4 saying, Honour thy father and **m**: *3384*
15: 4 and, He that curseth father or **m**, let him die *3384*
15: 5 Whosoever shall say to *his* father or *his* **m**, *3384*
15: 6 And honour not his father or his **m**, *he shall* *3384*
19: 5 this cause shall a man leave father and **m**, *3384*
19:19 Honour thy father and *thy* **m**: and, *3384*
19:29 father, or **m**, or wife, or children, or lands, *3384*
20:20 Then came to him the **m** of Zebedee's *3384*
27:56 and Mary the **m** of James and Joses, and *3384*
27:56 and Joses, and the **m** of Zebedee's children. *3384*
Mk 1:30 But Simon's **wife's m** lay sick of a fever, *3994*
3:31 There came then *his* brethren and his **m**, *3384*
3:32 thy **m** and thy brethren without seek for *3384*
3:33 saying, Who is my **m**, or my brethren? *3384*
3:34 and said, Behold my **m** and my brethren. *3384*
3:35 same is my brother, and my sister, and **m**. *3384*
5:40 taketh the father and the **m** of the damsel, *3384*
6:24 and said unto her **m**, What shall I ask? *3384*
6:28 and the damsel gave it to her **m**. *3384*
7:10 Moses said, Honour thy father and thy **m**; *3384*
7:10 and, Whoso curseth father or **m**, let him die *3384*
7:11 ye say, If a man shall say to *his* father or **m**, *3384*
7:12 no more to do ought for his father or his **m**; *3384*
10: 7 cause shall a man leave his father and **m**, *3384*
10:19 Defraud not, Honour thy father and **m**. *3384*
10:29 father, or **m**, or wife, or children, or lands, *3384*
15:40 and Mary the **m** of James the less and *3384*
15:47 Mary *the* **m** of Joses beheld where he was NIG
16: 1 and Mary the *m* of James, and Salome, NIG
Lk 1:43 that the **m** of my Lord should come to me? *3384*
1:60 And his **m** answered and said, Not *so;* but *3384*
2:33 his **m** marvelled at those *things* which were *3384*
2:34 and said unto Mary his **m**, Behold, *3384*
2:43 and Joseph and his **m** knew not *of it.* *3384*
2:48 and his **m** said unto him, Son, why hast *3384*
2:51 his **m** kept all these sayings in her heart. *3384*
4:38 And Simon's **wife's m** was taken with a *3994*
7:12 the only son of his **m**, and she was a *3384*
7:15 to speak. And he delivered him to his **m**. *3384*
8:19 Then came to him *his* **m** and his brethren, *3384*
8:20 Thy **m** and thy brethren stand without, *3384*
8:21 My **m** and my brethren are these which *3384*
8:51 and the father and the **m** of the maiden. *3384*
12:53 the **m** against the daughter, and *3384*
12:53 and the daughter against the **m**; *3384*
12:53 the **m in law** against her daughter in law, *3994*
12:53 the daughter in law against her **m in law**. *3994*
14:26 and **m**, and wife, and children, and *3384*
18:20 false witness, Honour thy father and thy **m**. *3384*
24:10 and Mary *the* **m** of James, and other *women* NIG
Jn 2: 1 of Galilee; and the **m** of Jesus was there: *3384*
2: 3 the **m** of Jesus saith unto him, They have *3384*
2: 5 His **m** saith unto the servants, *3384*
2:12 he, and his **m**, and his brethren, and *3384*
6:42 of Joseph, whose father and **m** we know? *3384*
19:25 there stood by the cross of Jesus his **m**, *3384*
19:26 When Jesus therefore saw *his* **m**, and *3384*
19:26 he saith unto his **m**, Woman, behold thy *3384*
19:27 Then saith he to the disciple, Behold thy **m**. *3384*
Ac 1:14 and Mary the **m** of Jesus, and with his *3384*
12:12 came to the house of Mary the **m** of John, *3384*
Ro 16:13 chosen in the Lord, and his **m** and mine. *3384*
Gal 4:26 is above is free, which is the **m** of us all. *3384*
Eph 5:31 cause shall a man leave his father and **m**, *3384*
6: 2 Honour thy father and **m**; (which is the first *3384*
2Ti 1: 5 in thy grandmother Lois, and thy **m** Eunice; *3384*
Heb 7: 3 Without father, **without m**, without descent, *282*
Rev 17: 5 THE **M** OF HARLOTS AND *3384*

MOTHER'S (75) [MOTHER]

Ge 24:28 and told *them of* her **m** house these things. 517
24:67 and Isaac was comforted after his **m** *death.* 517
27:29 and let thy **m** sons bow down to thee: 517
28: 2 to the house of Bethuel thy **m** father; 517
28: 2 of the daughters of Laban thy **m** brother. 517
29:10 Rachel the daughter of Laban his **m** brother, 517
29:10 the sheep of Laban his **m** brother, that Jacob 517
29:10 watered the flock of Laban his **m** brother. 517
43:29 his brother Benjamin, his **m** son, and said, 517
Ex 23:19 Thou shalt not seethe a kid in his **m** milk. 517
34:26 Thou shalt not seethe a kid in his **m** milk. 517
Lev 18:13 not uncover the nakedness of thy **m** sister: 517
18:13 for she *is* thy **m** near kinswoman. 517
20:17 or his **m** daughter, and see her nakedness, 517
20:19 not uncover the nakedness of thy **m** sister, 517
24:11 (and his **m** name *was* Shelomith, 517
Nu 12:12 when he cometh out of his **m** womb. 517
Dt 14:21 Thou shalt not seethe a kid in his **m** milk. 517
Jdg 9: 1 went to Shechem unto his **m** brethren, 517
9: 1 with all the family of the house of his **m** 517
9: 3 his **m** brethren spake of him in the ears of all 517
16:17 *been* a Nazarite unto God from my **m** womb: 517
Ru 1: 8 in law, Go, return each to her **m** house: 517
1Sa 20:30 and unto the confusion of thy **m** nakedness? 517
1Ki 11:26 whose **m** name *was* Zeruah, a widow 517
14:21 his **m** name *was* Naamah an Ammonitess. 517
14:31 his **m** name *was* Naamah an Ammonitess. 517
15: 2 his **m** name *was* Maachah, the daughter of 517
15:10 his **m** name *was* Maachah, the daughter of 517
22:42 his **m** name *was* Azubah the daughter of 517
2Ki 8:26 his **m** name *was* Athaliah, the daughter of 517
12: 1 And his **m** name *was* Zibiah of Beer-sheba. 517
14: 2 his **m** name *was* Jehoaddan of Jerusalem. 517
15: 2 And his **m** name *was* Jecholiah of Jerusalem. 517
15:33 his **m** name *was* Jerusha, the daughter of 517
18: 2 His **m** name also *was* Abi, the daughter of 517
21: 1 And his **m** name *was* Hephzi-bah. 517
21:19 his **m** name *was* Meshullemeth, the daughter 517
22: 1 his **m** name *was* Jedidah, the daughter of 517
23:31 his **m** name *was* Hamutal, the daughter of 517
23:36 his **m** name *was* Zebudah, the daughter of 517
24: 8 his **m** name *was* Nehushta, the daughter of 517
24:18 his **m** name *was* Hamutal, the daughter of 517
2Ch 12:13 his **m** name *was* Naamah an Ammonitess. 517
13: 2 His **m** name also *was* Michaiah the daughter 517
20:31 his **m** name *was* Azubah the daughter of 517
22: 2 His **m** name also *was* Athaliah the daughter 517
24: 1 His **m** name also *was* Zibiah of Beer-sheba. 517
25: 1 his **m** name *was* Jehoaddan of Jerusalem. 517
26: 3 His **m** name also *was* Jecoliah of Jerusalem. 517
27: 1 His **m** name also *was* Jerushah, the daughter 517
29: 1 his **m** name *was* Abijah, the daughter of 517
Job 1:21 Naked came I out of my **m** womb, and 517
3:10 Because it shut not up the doors of my *m* NIH
31:18 and I have guided her from my **m** womb;) 517
Ps 22: 9 me hope *when I was* upon my **m** breasts. 517
22:10 thou *art* my God from my **m** belly. 517
50:20 thou slanderest thine own **m** son. 517
69: 8 and an alien unto my **m** children. 517
71: 6 thou art he that took me out of my **m** 517
139:13 thou hast covered me in my **m** womb. 517
Ecc 5:15 As he came forth of his **m** womb, 517
SS 1: 6 my **m** children were angry with me; 517
3: 4 until I had brought him into my **m** house, 517
8: 2 lead thee, *and* bring thee into my **m** house, 517
Isa 50: 1 Where *is* the bill of your **m** divorcement, 517
Jer 52: 1 his **m** name *was* Hamutal the daughter of 517
Eze 16:45 Thou *art* thy **m** daughter, that lotheth her 517
Mt 19:12 which were so born from *their* **m** womb: *3384*
Lk 1:15 the Holy Ghost, even from his **m** womb. *3384*
Jn 3: 4 can he enter the second time into his **m** *3384*
19:25 and his **m** sister, Mary the *wife* of *3384*
Ac 3: 2 And a certain man lame from his **m** womb *3384*
14: 8 *his* feet, being a cripple from his **m** womb, *3384*
Gal 1:15 who separated me from my **m** womb, and *3384*

MOTHERS (7) [MOTHER]

Isa 49:23 and their queens thy **nursing m**: 3243
Jer 16: 3 concerning their **m** that bare them, and 517
La 2:12 They say to their **m**, Where *is* corn and 517
5: 3 and fatherless, our **m** *are* as widows. 517
Mk 10:30 and sisters, and **m**, and children, and lands, *3384*
1Ti 1: 9 murderers of fathers and **murderers of m**, *3389*
5: 2 The elder *women* as **m**; the younger as *3384*

MOTHERS' (1) [MOTHER]

La 2:12 when their soul was poured out into their **m** 517

MOTHS See MOTHEATEN

MOTIONS (1) [MOVE]
Ro 7: 5 the **m** of sins, which were by the law, *3804*

MOULDY (2)
Jos 9: 5 the bread of their provision was dry *and* **m**. 5350
9:12 but now, behold, it is dry, and it is **m**: 5350

MOUND; MOUNDS See EMINENT

MOUNT (263) [MOUNTAIN, MOUNTED, MOUNTING, MOUNTS]
Ge 10:30 as thou goest unto Sephar, a **m** of the east. 2022
14: 6 the Horites in their **m** Seir, unto El-paran, 2042
22:14 In the **m** of the LORD it shall be seen. 2022
31:21 and set his face *toward* the **m** Gilead. 2022
31:23 and they overtook him in the **m** Gilead. 2022
31:25 Now Jacob had pitched his tent in the **m**: 2022
31:25 Laban with his brethren pitched in the **m** of 2022
31:54 Jacob offered sacrifice upon the **m**, and 2022
31:54 did eat bread, and tarried all night in the **m**. 2022
36: 8 Thus dwelt Esau in **m** Seir: Esau *is* Edom. 2022
36: 9 Esau the father of the Edomites in **m** Seir: 2022
Ex 4:27 met him in the **m** of God, and kissed him. 2022
18: 5 where he encamped *at* the **m** of God: 2022
19: 2 and there Israel camped before the **m**. 2022
19:11 in the sight of all the people upon **m** Sinai. 2022
19:12 *that ye* go *not* up into the **m**, or touch 2022
19:12 whosoever toucheth the **m** shall be surely 2022
19:13 soundeth long, they shall come up to the **m**. 2022
19:14 Moses went down from the **m** unto 2022
19:16 a thick cloud upon the **m**, and the voice of 2022
19:17 and they stood at the nether part of the **m**. 2022
19:18 **m** Sinai was altogether on a smoke, 2022
19:18 a furnace, and the whole **m** quaked greatly. 2022
19:20 the LORD came down upon **m** Sinai, 2022
19:20 upon mount Sinai, on the top of the **m**: 2022
19:20 called Moses *up* to the top of the **m**; 2022
19:23 The people cannot come up to **m** Sinai: 2022
19:23 Set bounds about the **m**, and sanctify it. 2022
24:12 Come up to me into the **m**, and be there: 2022
24:13 and Moses went up into the **m** of God. 2022
24:15 Moses went up into the **m**, and a cloud 2022
24:15 into the mount, and a cloud covered the **m**. 2022
24:16 the glory of the LORD abode upon **m** 2022
24:17 the **m** in the eyes of the children of Israel. 2022
24:18 of the cloud, and gat him up into the **m**: 2022
24:18 Moses was in the **m** forty days and 2022
25:40 which was shewed thee in the **m**. 2022
26:30 thereof which was shewed thee in the **m**. 2022
27: 8 as it was shewed thee in the **m**, so 2022
31:18 end of communing with him upon **m** Sinai, 2022
32: 1 Moses delayed to come down out of the **m**, 2022
32:15 went down from the **m**, and the two tables 2022
32:19 his hands, and brake them beneath the **m**. 2022
33: 6 of their ornaments by the **m** Horeb. 2022
34: 2 come up in the morning unto **m** Sinai, and 2022
34: 2 thyself there to me in the top of the **m**. 2022
34: 3 let any man be seen throughout all the **m**; 2022
34: 3 let the flocks nor herds feed before that **m**. 2022
34: 4 in the morning, and went up unto **m** Sinai, 2022
34:29 when Moses came down from **m** Sinai with 2022
34:29 when he came down from the **m**, 2022
34:32 LORD had spoken with him in **m** Sinai. 2022
Lev 7:38 the LORD commanded Moses in **m** Sinai, 2022
25: 1 the LORD spake unto Moses in **m** Sinai, 2022
26:46 the children of Israel in **m** Sinai by 2022
27:34 Moses for the children of Israel in **m** Sinai. 2022
Nu 3: 1 the LORD spake with Moses in **m** Sinai. 2022
10:33 they departed from the **m** of the LORD 2022
20:22 from Kadesh, and came *unto* **m** Hor. 2022
20:23 spake unto Moses and Aaron in **m** Hor, 2022
20:25 his son, and bring them up *unto* **m** Hor: 2022
20:27 they went up into **m** Hor in the sight of all 2022
20:28 and Aaron died there in the top of the **m**: 2022
20:28 Moses and Eleazar came down from the **m**. 2022
21: 4 they journeyed from **m** Hor *by* the way of 2022
27:12 Get thee up into this **m** Abarim, and see 2022
28: 6 which was ordained in **m** Sinai for a sweet 2022
33:23 and pitched in **m** Shapher. 2022
33:24 they removed from **m** Shapher, and 2022
33:37 pitched in **m** Hor, in the edge of the land of 2022
33:38 Aaron the priest went up into **m** Hor at 2022
33:39 and three years old when he died in **m** Hor. 2022
33:41 they departed from **m** Hor, and pitched in 2022
34: 7 great sea you shall point out for you **m** Hor: 2022
34: 8 From **m** Hor ye shall point out *your border* 2022
Dt 1: 2 *by* the way of **m** Seir unto Kadesh-barnea.) 2022
1: 6 Ye have dwelt long enough in this **m**: 2022
1: 7 go *to* the **m** of the Amorites, and unto all 2022
2: 1 and we compassed **m** Seir many days. 2022
2: 5 I have given **m** Seir unto Esau *for* a 2022
3: 8 from the river of Arnon unto **m** Hermon; 2022
3:12 half **m** Gilead, and the cities thereof, gave I 2022
4:48 even unto **m** Sion, which *is* Hermon, 2022
5: 4 to face in the **m** out of the midst of the fire, 2022
5: 5 of the fire, and went not up into the **m**;) 2022
5:22 in the **m** out of the midst of the fire, 2022
9: 9 When I was gone up into the **m** to receive 2022
9: 9 I abode in the **m** forty days and 2022
9:10 which the LORD spake with you in the **m** 2022
9:15 So I turned and came down from the **m**, 2022
9:15 the mount, and the **m** burned with fire: 2022
9:21 into the brook that descended out of the **m**. 2022
10: 1 come up unto me into the **m**, and make thee 2022
10: 3 went up into the **m**, having the two tables 2022
10: 4 which the LORD spake unto you in the **m** 2022
10: 5 turned myself and came down from the **m**, 2022
10:10 I stayed in the **m**, according to the first 2022
11:29 that thou shalt put the blessing upon **m** 2022
11:29 mount Gerizim, and the curse upon **m** Ebal. 2022
27: 4 in **m** Ebal, and thou shalt plaister them with 2022
27:12 These shall stand upon **m** Gerizzim to bless 2022
27:13 these shall stand upon **m** Ebal to curse; 2022
32:49 *unto* **m** Nebo, which *is* in the land of Moab, 2022
32:50 die in the **m** whither thou goest up, and 2022
32:50 as Aaron thy brother died in **m** Hor, 2022
33: 2 he shined forth from **m** Paran, and he came 2022
Jos 8:30 unto the LORD God of Israel in **m** Ebal, 2022
8:33 half of them over against **m** Gerizim, and 2022
8:33 and half of them over against **m** Ebal; 2022
11:17 *Even* from the **m** Halak, that goeth up *to* 2022
11:17 in the valley of Lebanon under **m** Hermon: 2022
12: 1 from the river Arnon unto **m** Hermon, and 2022
12: 5 reigned in **m** Hermon, and in Salcah, and 2022
12: 7 valley of Lebanon even unto the **m** Halak, 2022
13: 5 from Baal-gad under **m** Hermon unto 2022
13:11 all **m** Hermon, and all Bashan unto Salcah; 2022
13:19 and Zareth-shahar in the **m** of the valley, 2022
15: 9 and went out to the cities of **m** Ephron; 2022
15:10 from Baalah westward unto **m** Seir, 2022
15:10 and passed along unto the side of **m** Jearim, 2022
15:11 passed along *to* **m** Baalah, and went out 2022
16: 1 up from Jericho throughout **m** Beth-el, 2022
17:15 if **m** Ephraim be too narrow for thee. 2022
19:50 *even* Timnath-serah in **m** Ephraim: 2022
20: 7 they appointed Kedesh in Galilee in **m** 2022
20: 7 Shechem in **m** Ephraim, and Kirjath-arba, 2022
21:21 Shechem with her suburbs in **m** Ephraim, 2022
24: 4 I gave unto Esau **m** Seir, to possess it; 2022
24:30 which *is* in **m** Ephraim, on the north side of 2022
24:33 which was given him in **m** Ephraim. 2022
Jdg 1:35 the Amorites would dwell in **m** Heres in 2022
2: 9 in the **m** of Ephraim, on the north side of 2022
3: 3 and the Hivites that dwelt in **m** Lebanon, 2022
3: 3 from **m** Baal-hermon unto the entering in 2022
3:27 of Israel went down with him from the **m**, 2022
4: 5 between Ramah and Beth-el in **m** Ephraim: 2022
4: 6 *saying,* Go and draw toward **m** Tabor, and 2022
4:12 son of Abinoam was gone up *to* **m** Tabor. 2022
4:14 So Barak went down from **m** Tabor, and 2022
7: 3 him return and depart early from **m** Gilead. 2022
7:24 Gideon sent messengers throughout all **m** 2022
9: 7 he went and stood in the top of **m** Gerizim, 2022
9:48 Abimelech gat him up *to* **m** Zalmon, he 2022
10: 1 and he dwelt in Shamir in **m** Ephraim. 2022
12:15 of Ephraim, in the **m** of the Amalekites. 2022
17: 1 there was a man of **m** Ephraim, whose 2022
17: 8 he came *to* **m** Ephraim to the house of 2022
18: 2 who when they came *to* **m** Ephraim, to 2022
18:13 they passed thence *unto* **m** Ephraim, and 2022
19: 1 sojourning on the side of **m** Ephraim, 2022
19:16 at even, which *was* also of **m** Ephraim; 2022
19:18 toward the side of **m** Ephraim; 2022
1Sa 1: 1 of **m** Ephraim, and his name *was* Elkanah, 2022
9: 4 he passed through **m** Ephraim, and 2022
13: 2 with Saul in Michmash and in **m** Beth-el, 2022
14:22 which had hid themselves in **m** Ephraim, 2022
31: 1 and fell down slain in **m** Gilboa. 2022

1Sa 31: 8 and his three sons fallen in **m** Gilboa. 2022
2Sa 1: 6 As I happened by chance upon **m** Gilboa, 2022
15:30 David went up by the ascent of *m* Olivet, NIH
15:32 the top *of the m*, where he worshipped God, NIH
20:21 a man of **m** Ephraim, Sheba the son of 2022
1Ki 4: 8 their names: The son of Hur, in **m** Ephraim: 2022
12:25 Jeroboam built Shechem in **m** Ephraim, 2022
18:19 *and* gather to me all Israel unto **m** Carmel, 2022
18:20 gathered the prophets together unto **m** 2022
19: 8 and forty nights unto Horeb the **m** of God. 2022
19:11 and stand upon the **m** before the LORD. 2022
2Ki 2:25 he went from thence to **m** Carmel, and 2022
4:25 came unto the man of God to **m** Carmel. 2022
5:22 even now there be come to me from **m** 2022
19:31 and they that escape out of **m** Zion: 2022
23:13 which *were* on the right hand of the **m** of 2022
23:16 the sepulchres that *were* there in the **m**, 2022
1Ch 4:42 five hundred men, went to **m** Seir, 2022
5:23 and Senir, and *unto* **m** Hermon. 2022
6:67 Shechem in **m** Ephraim with her suburbs; 2022
10: 1 and fell down slain in **m** Gilboa. 2022
10: 8 found Saul and his sons fallen in **m** Gilboa. 2022
2Ch 3: 1 of the LORD at Jerusalem in **m** Moriah, 2022
13: 4 Abijah stood up upon **m** Zemaraim, 2022
13: 4 which *is* in **m** Ephraim, and said, Hear me, 2022
15: 8 out of the cities which he had taken from **m** 2022
19: 4 the people from Beer-sheba to **m** Ephraim, 2022
20:10 children of Ammon and Moab and **m** Seir, 2022
20:22 Moab, and **m** Seir, which were come 2022
20:23 Moab stood up against the inhabitants of **m** 2022
33:15 all the altars that he had built in the **m** of 2022
Ne 8:15 Go forth *unto* the **m**, and fetch olive 2022
9:13 Thou camest down also upon **m** Sinai, and 2022
Job 20: 6 Though his excellency **m up** to 5927
39:27 Doth the eagle **m up** at thy command, and 1361
Ps 48: 2 *is* **m** Zion, *on* the sides of the north, the city 2022
48:11 Let **m** Zion rejoice, let the daughters of 2022
74: 2 this **m** Zion, wherein thou hast dwelt. 2022
78:68 tribe of Judah, the **m** Zion which he loved. 2022
107:26 They **m up** *to* the heaven, they go down 5927
125: 1 They that trust in the LORD *shall be* as **m** 2022
SS 4: 1 a flock of goats, that appear from **m** Gilead. 2022
Isa 4: 5 upon every dwelling place of **m** Zion, 2022
8:18 of hosts, which dwelleth in **m** Zion. 2022
9:18 they shall **m up** *like* the lifting up of smoke. 55
10:12 performed his whole work upon **m** Zion 2022
10:32 he shall shake his hand *against* the **m** of 2022
14:13 I will sit also upon the **m** of 2022
16: 1 unto the **m** of the daughter of Zion. 2022
18: 7 name of the LORD of hosts, the **m** Zion. 2022
24:23 when the LORD of hosts shall reign in **m** 2022
27:13 shall worship the LORD in the holy **m** at 2022
28:21 For the LORD shall rise up as *in* **m** 2022
29: 3 will lay siege against thee *with* a **m**, and 4674
29: 8 all the nations be, that fight against **m** Zion. 2022
31: 4 of hosts come down to fight for **m** Zion, 2022
37:32 and they that escape out of **m** Zion: 2022
40:31 they shall **m up** *with* wings as eagles; 5927
Jer 4:15 and publisheth affliction from **m** Ephraim. 2022
6: 6 down trees, and cast a **m** against Jerusalem: 5550
31: 6 *that* the watchmen upon the **m** Ephraim 2022
50:19 his soul shall be satisfied upon **m** Ephraim 2022
51:53 Though Babylon should **m up** *to* heaven, 5927
Eze 4: 2 a fort against it, and cast a **m** against it; 5550
10:16 lift up their wings to **m up** from the earth, 7311
21:22 the gates, to cast a **m**, *and* to build a fort. 5550
26: 8 cast a **m** against thee, and lift up 5550
35: 2 set thy face against **m** Seir, and 2022
35: 3 Behold, O **m** Seir, I *am* against thee, and 2022
35: 7 Thus will I make **m** Seir most desolate, 2022
35:15 O **m** Seir, and all Idumea, *even* all of it: 2022
Da 11:15 cast up a **m**, and take the most fenced 5550
Joel 2:32 for in **m** Zion and in Jerusalem shall be 2022
Ob 1: 8 and understanding out of the **m** of Esau? 2022
1: 9 to the end that every one of the **m** of Esau 2022
1:17 upon **m** Zion shall be deliverance, and 2022
1:19 *they of* the south shall possess the **m** of 2022
1:21 saviours shall come up on **m** Zion to judge 2022
1:21 up on mount Zion to judge the **m** of Esau; 2022
Mic 4: 7 the LORD shall reign over them in **m** 2022
Hab 3: 3 and the Holy One from **m** Paran. 2022
Zec 14: 4 his feet shall stand in that day upon the **m** 2022
14: 4 the **m** of Olives shall cleave in the midst 2022
Mt 21: 1 unto the **m** of Olives, then sent Jesus two *3735*
24: 3 And as he sat upon the **m** of Olives, *3735*
26:30 a hymn, they went out into the **m** of Olives. *3735*
Mk 11: 1 and Bethany, at the **m** of Olives, *3735*
13: 3 And as he sat upon the **m** of Olives over *3735*
14:26 a hymn, they went out into the **m** of Olives. *3735*
Lk 19:29 at the **m** called *the mount* of Olives, *3735*
19:29 at the mount called *the m* of Olives, NIG
19:37 *even* now at the descent of the **m** of Olives, *3735*
21:37 abode in the **m** that is called *the mount* of *3735*
21:37 abode in the mount that is called *the m* of NIG
22:39 went, as he was wont, to the **m** of Olives; *3735*
Jn 8: 1 Jesus went unto the **m** of Olives. *3735*
Ac 1:12 unto Jerusalem from the **m** called Olivet, *3735*
7:30 **m** Sina an angel of the Lord in a flame of *3735*
7:38 the angel which spake to him in the **m** Sina, *3735*
Gal 4:24 the one from the **m** Sinai, which gendereth *3735*
4:25 For *this* Agar is **m** Sinai in Arabia, and *3735*
Heb 8: 5 to the pattern shewed to thee in the **m**. *3735*
12:18 For ye are not come unto the **m** that might *3735*
12:22 But ye are come unto **m** Sion, and unto *3735*
2Pe 1:18 when we were with him in the holy **m**. *3735*
Rev 14: 1 and lo, a Lamb stood on the **m** Sion, and *3735*

MOUNTAIN (137) [MOUNT, MOUNTAINS]

Ge 12: 8 he removed from thence unto a **m** on 2022
14:10 and they that remained fled to the **m**. 2022
19:17 escape to the **m**, lest thou be consumed. 2022
19:19 I cannot escape to the **m**, lest *some* evil 2022
19:30 dwelt in the **m**, and his two daughters with 2022
Ex 3: 1 and came to the **m** of God, *even* to Horeb. 2022
3:12 of Egypt, ye shall serve God upon this **m**. 2022
15:17 plant them in the **m** of thine inheritance, 2022
19: 3 the LORD called unto him out of the **m**, 2022
20:18 noise of the trumpet, and the **m** smoking: 2022
Nu 13:17 this *way* southward, and go up into the **m**: 2022
14:40 gat them up into the top of the **m**, saying, 2022
Dt 1:19 which you saw *by* the way of the **m** of 2022
1:20 Ye are come unto the **m** of the Amorites, 2022
1:24 they turned and went up into the **m**, and 2022
1:44 the Amorites, which dwelt in that **m**, came 2022
2: 3 Ye have compassed this **m** long enough: 2022
3:25 that goodly **m**, and Lebanon. 2022
4:11 ye came near and stood under the **m**; and 2022
4:11 the **m** burnt with fire unto the midst of 2022
5:23 the darkness, (for the **m** did burn with fire,) 2022
32:49 Get thee up into this **m** Abarim, *unto* mount 2022
33:19 They shall call the people *unto* the **m**; 2022
34: 1 the plains of Moab unto the **m** of Nebo, 2022
Jos 2:16 she said unto them, Get you to the **m**, 2022
2:22 came unto the **m**, and abode there three 2022
2:23 descended from the **m**, and passed over, 2022
11:16 the **m** of Israel, and the valley of the same; 2022
14:12 Now therefore give me this **m**, whereof 2022
15: 8 the border went up to the top of the **m** that 2022
17:18 the **m** shall be thine; for it *is* a wood, 2022
18:16 the border came down to the end of the **m** 2022
20: 7 which *is* Hebron, in the **m** of Judah. 2022
Jdg 1: 9 that dwelt in the **m**, and in the south, and 2022
1:19 he drave out *the inhabitants of* the **m**; but 2022
1:34 forced the children of Dan into the **m**: 2022
3:27 that he blew a trumpet in the **m** of Ephraim, 2022
1Sa 17: 3 the Philistines stood on a **m** on the one 2022
17: 3 and Israel stood on a **m** on the other side: 2022
23:14 remained in a **m** in the wilderness of Ziph. 2022
23:26 Saul went on this side of the **m**, and David 2022
23:26 David and his men on that side of the **m**: 2022
2Ki 2:16 cast him upon some **m**, or into some valley. 2022
6:17 the **m** was full *of* horses and chariots of fire 2022
2Ch 2: 2 fourscore thousand to hew in the **m**, and 2022
2:18 fourscore thousand *to be* hewers in the **m**, 2022
Job 14:18 surely the **m** falling cometh to nought, and 2022
Ps 11: 1 say ye to my soul, Flee *as* a bird *to* your **m**? 2022
30: 7 by thy favour thou hast made my **m** to 2042
48: 1 city of our God, *in* the **m** of his holiness. 2022
78:54 *even to* this **m**, *which* his right hand had 2022
SS 4: 6 I will get me to the **m** of myrrh, and to 2022
Isa 2: 2 *that* the **m** of the LORD'S house shall be 2022
2: 3 and let us go up to the **m** of the LORD, 2022
11: 9 shall not hurt nor destroy in all my holy **m**: 2022
13: 2 Lift ye up a banner upon the high **m**, 2022
25: 6 in this **m** shall the LORD of hosts make 2022
25: 7 he will destroy in this **m** the face of 2022
25:10 For in this **m** shall the hand of the LORD 2022
30:17 ye be left as a beacon upon the top of a **m**, 2022

Isa 30:25 there shall be upon every high **m**, and 2022
30:29 a pipe to come into the **m** of the LORD, 2022
40: 4 and every **m** and hill shall be made low: 2022
40: 9 good tidings, get thee up into the high **m**; 2022
56: 7 Even them will I bring to my holy **m**, and 2022
57: 7 a lofty and high **m** hast thou set thy bed: 2022
57:13 the land, and shall inherit my holy **m**; 2022
65:11 that forget my holy **m**, that prepare a table 2022
65:25 shall not hurt nor destroy in all my holy **m**, 2022
66:20 to my holy **m** Jerusalem, saith the LORD, 2022
Jer 3: 6 she is gone up upon every high **m** and 2022
16:16 and they shall hunt them from every **m**, and 2022
17: 3 O my **m** in the field, I will give thy 2042
26:18 the **m** of the house as the high places of a 2022
31:23 O habitation of justice, *and* **m** of holiness. 2022
50: 6 they have gone from **m** to hill, they have 2022
51:25 Behold, I *am* against thee, O destroying **m**, 2022
51:25 the rocks, and will make thee a burnt **m**. 2022
La 5:18 Because of the **m** of Zion, which is 2022
Eze 11:23 stood upon the **m** which *is* on the east side 2022
17:22 will plant *it* upon a high **m** and eminent: 2022
17:23 In the **m** of the height of Israel will I plant 2022
20:40 For in mine holy **m**, in the mountain of 2022
20:40 in the **m** of the height of Israel, saith 2022
28:14 *so:* thou wast upon the holy **m** of God; 2022
28:16 I will cast thee as profane out of the **m** of 2022
40: 2 set me upon a very high **m**, by which *was* 2022
43:12 Upon the top of the **m** the whole limit 2022
Da 2:35 that smote the image became a great **m**, 2906
2:45 stone was cut out of the **m** without hands, 2906
9:16 away from thy city Jerusalem, thy holy **m**: 2022
9:20 LORD my God for the holy **m** of my God; 2022
11:45 between the seas in the glorious holy **m**; 2022
Joel 2: 1 in Zion, and sound an alarm in my holy **m**: 2022
3:17 your God dwelling in Zion, my holy **m**: 2022
Am 4: 1 of Bashan, that *are* in the **m** of Samaria, 2022
6: 1 ease in Zion, and trust in the **m** of Samaria, 2022
Ob 1:16 For as ye have drunk upon my holy **m**, *so* 2022
Mic 3:12 the **m** of the house as the high places of 2022
4: 1 *that* the **m** of the house of the LORD shall 2022
4: 2 let us go up to the **m** of the LORD, and 2022
7:12 from sea *to* sea, and *from* **m** *to* mountain. 2022
7:12 from sea *to* sea, and *from* mountain *to* **m**. 2022
Zep 3:11 no more be haughty because of my holy **m**. 2022
Hag 1: 8 Go up *to* the **m**, and bring wood, and 2022
Zec 4: 7 Who *art* thou, O great **m**? 2022
8: 3 the **m** of the LORD of hosts the holy 2022
8: 3 of the LORD of hosts the holy **m**. 2022
14: 4 half of the **m** shall remove toward 2022
Mt 4: 8 taketh him *up* into an exceeding high **m**, *3735*
5: 1 seeing the multitudes, he went up into a **m**: *3735*
8: 1 When he was come down from the **m**, *3735*
14:23 he went up into a **m** apart to pray: *3735*
15:29 and went up into a **m**, and sat down there. *3735*
17: 1 and bringeth them up into a high **m** apart, *3735*
17: 9 And as they came down from the **m**, Jesus *3735*
17:20 ye shall say unto this **m**, Remove hence to *3735*
21:21 but also if ye shall say unto this **m**, Be thou *3735*
28:16 into a **m** where Jesus had appointed them. *3735*
Mk 3:13 And he goeth up into a **m**, and calleth unto *3735*
6:46 them away, he departed into a **m** to pray. *3735*
9: 2 leadeth them up into a high **m** apart by *3735*
9: 9 And as they came down from the **m**, *3735*
11:23 That whosoever shall say unto this **m**, *3735*
Lk 3: 5 and every **m** and hill shall be brought low; *3735*
4: 5 And the devil, taking him up into a high **m**, *3735*
6:12 *that* he went out into a **m** to pray, and *3735*
8:32 a herd of many swine feeding on the **m**: *3735*
9:28 and James, and went up into a **m** to pray. *3735*
Jn 4:20 Our fathers worshipped in this **m**; and *3735*
4:21 when ye shall neither in this **m**, *3735*
6: 3 And Jesus went up into a **m**, and there he *3735*
6:15 he departed again into a **m** himself alone. *3735*
Heb 12:20 And if *so much as* a beast touch the **m**, *3735*
Rev 6:14 and every **m** and island were moved out of *3735*
8: 8 as *it were* a great **m** burning with fire was *3735*
21:10 me away in the spirit to a great and high **m**, *3735*

MOUNTAIN GOAT See HIND

MOUNTAIN SHEEP See CHAMOIS

MOUNTAINS (177) [MOUNTAIN]
Ge 7:20 the waters prevail; and the **m** were covered. 2022
8: 4 day of the month, upon the **m** of Ararat. 2022
8: 5 of the month, were the tops of the **m** seen. 2022
22: 2 upon one of the **m** which I will tell thee of. 2022
Ex 32:12 to slay them in the **m**, and to consume them 2022
Nu 13:29 and the Amorites, dwell in the **m**: 2022
23: 7 out of the **m** of the east, *saying,* Come, 2042
33:47 pitched in the **m** of Abarim, before Nebo. 2022
33:48 they departed from the **m** of Abarim, and 2022
Dt 2:37 river Jabbok, nor *unto* the cities in the **m**, 2022
12: 2 upon the high **m**, and upon the hills, and 2022
32:22 and set on fire the foundations of the **m**. 2022
33:15 for the chief things of the ancient **m**, and 2042
Jos 10: 6 in the **m** are gathered together against us. 2022
11: 2 to the kings that *were* on the north of the **m**, 2022
11: 3 the Jebusite in the **m**, and *to* the Hivite 2022
11:21 cut off the Anakims from the **m**, 2022
11:21 from all the **m** of Judah, and from all 2022
11:21 of Judah, and from all the **m** of Israel: 2022
12: 8 In the **m**, and in the valleys, and in 2022
15:48 in the **m**, Shamir, and Jattir, and Socoh, 2022
18:12 and went up through the **m** westward; 2022
Jdg 5: 5 The **m** melted from before the LORD, 2022
6: 2 made them the dens which *are* in the **m**, 2022
9:25 set liers in wait for him in the top of the **m**, 2022
9:36 come people down from the top of the **m**. 2022
9:36 Thou seest the shadow of the **m** as *if they* 2022
11:37 that I may go up and down upon the **m**, and 2022
11:38 and bewailed her virginity upon the **m**. 2022
1Sa 26:20 as when *one* doth hunt a partridge in the **m**. 2022
2Sa 1:21 Ye **m** of Gilboa, *let there be* no dew, 2022
1Ki 5:15 and fourscore thousand hewers in the **m**; 2022
19:11 a great and strong wind rent the **m**, and 2022
2Ki 19:23 I am come up *to* the height of the **m**, 2022
1Ch 12: 8 and *were* as swift as the roes upon the **m**: 2022
2Ch 18:16 I did see all Israel scattered upon the **m**, 2022
21:11 Moreover he made high places in the **m** of 2022
26:10 and vinedressers in the **m**, 2022
27: 4 Moreover he built cities in the **m** of Judah, 2022
Job 9: 5 Which removeth the **m**, and they know not: 2022
24: 8 They are wet with the showers of the **m**, 2022
28: 9 the rock; he overturneth the **m** by the roots. 2022
39: 8 The range of the **m** *is* his pasture, and 2022
40:20 Surely the **m** bring him forth food, 2022
Ps 36: 6 Thy righteousness *is* like the great **m**; 2042
46: 2 though the **m** be carried into the midst of 2022
46: 3 *though* the **m** shake with the swelling 2022
50:11 I know all the fowls of the **m**: and the wild 2022
65: 6 Which by his strength setteth fast the **m**; 2022
72: 3 The **m** shall bring peace to the people, and 2022
72:16 of corn in the earth upon the top of the **m**; 2022
76: 4 *and* excellent than the **m** of prey. 2042
83:14 and as the flame setteth the **m** on fire; 2022
87: 1 His foundation *is* in the holy **m**. 2042
90: 2 Before the **m** were brought forth, or 2022
104: 6 a garment: the waters stood above the **m**. 2022
104: 8 They go up *by* the **m**; they go down *by* 2022
114: 4 The **m** skipped like rams, *and* the little hills 2022
114: 6 Ye **m**, *that* ye skipped like rams; *and* 2022
125: 2 *As* the **m** *are* round about Jerusalem, so 2022
133: 3 *as the dew* that descended upon the **m** of 2042
144: 5 touch the **m**, and they shall smoke. 2022
147: 8 who maketh grass to grow *upon* the **m**. 2022
148: 9 **M**, and all hills; fruitful trees, and 2022
Pr 8:25 Before the **m** were settled, before the hills 2022
27:25 and herbs of the **m** are gathered. 2022
SS 2: 8 behold, he cometh leaping upon the **m**, 2022
2:17 a roe or a young hart upon the **m** of Bether. 2022
4: 8 the lions' dens, from the **m** of the leopards. 2042
8:14 or to a young hart upon the **m** of spices. 2022
Isa 2: 2 shall be established in the top of the **m**, 2022
2:14 upon all the high **m**, and upon all the hills 2022
13: 4 The noise of a multitude in the **m**, like as of 2022
14:25 and upon my **m** tread him under foot: 2022
17:13 shall be chased as the chaff of the **m** before 2022
18: 3 when *he* lifteth up an ensign *on* the **m**; 2022
18: 6 be left together unto the fowls of the **m**, 2022
22: 5 down the walls, and of crying to the **m**. 2022
34: 3 and the **m** shall be melted with their blood. 2022
37:24 am I come up *to* the height of the **m**, 2022
40:12 weighed the **m** in scales, and the hills in a 2022
41:15 thou shalt thresh the **m**, and beat *them* 2022
42:11 let them shout from the top of the **m**. 2022
42:15 I will make waste **m** and hills, and dry up 2022
44:23 ye **m**, O forest, and every tree therein: 2022

Isa 49:11 I will make all my **m** a way, and 2022
49:13 O earth; and break forth *into* singing, O **m**: 2022
52: 7 How beautiful upon the **m** are the feet of 2022
54:10 For the **m** shall depart, and the hills be 2022
55:12 the **m** and the hills shall break forth before 2022
64: 1 that the **m** might flow down at thy 2022
64: 3 the **m** flowed down at thy presence. 2022
65: 7 which have burnt incense upon the **m**, and 2022
65: 9 and out of Judah an inheritor of my **m**: 2022
Jer 3:23 from the hills, *and from* the multitude of **m**: 2022
4:24 I beheld the **m**, and lo, they trembled, and 2022
9:10 For the **m** will I take up a weeping and 2022
13:16 before your feet stumble upon the dark **m**, 2022
17:26 and from the **m**, and from the south, 2022
31: 5 Thou shalt yet plant vines upon the **m** of 2022
32:44 in the cities of the **m**, and in the cities of 2022
33:13 In the cities of the **m**, in the cities of 2022
46:18 Surely as Tabor *is* among the **m**, and 2022
50: 6 they have turned them away *on* the **m**: 2022
La 4:19 they pursued us upon the **m**, they laid wait 2022
Eze 6: 2 set thy face towards the **m** of Israel, and 2022
6: 3 say, Ye **m** of Israel, hear the word of 2022
6: 3 Thus saith the Lord GOD to the **m**, and 2022
6:13 in all the tops of the **m**, and under every 2022
7: 7 and not the sounding again of the **m**. 2022
7:16 shall be on the **m** like doves of the valleys, 2022
18: 6 *And* hath not eaten upon the **m**, 2022
18:11 but even hath eaten upon the **m**, 2022
18:15 *That* hath not eaten upon the **m**, 2022
19: 9 no more be heard upon the **m** of Israel. 2022
22: 9 in thee they eat upon the **m**: in the midst of 2022
31:12 upon the **m** and in all the valleys his 2022
32: 5 I will lay thy flesh upon the **m**, and fill 2022
32: 6 wherein thou swimmest, *even* to the **m**; 2022
33:28 the **m** of Israel shall be desolate, that none 2022
34: 6 My sheep wandered through all the **m**, and 2022
34:13 feed them upon the **m** of Israel by 2022
34:14 upon the high **m** of Israel shall their fold 2022
34:14 *in* a fat pasture shall they feed upon the **m** 2022
35: 8 I will fill his **m** *with* his slain *men*: in thy 2022
35:12 thou hast spoken against the **m** of Israel, 2022
36: 1 prophesy unto the **m** of Israel, and say, 2022
36: 1 say, Ye **m** of Israel, hear the word of 2022
36: 4 Therefore, ye **m** of Israel, hear the word of 2022
36: 4 Thus saith the Lord GOD to the **m**, and 2022
36: 6 say unto the **m**, and to the hills, to 2022
36: 8 ye, O **m** of Israel, ye shall shoot forth your 2022
37:22 one nation in the land upon the **m** of Israel; 2022
38: 8 against the **m** of Israel, which have been 2022
38:20 the **m** shall be thrown down, and the steep 2022
38:21 a sword against him throughout all my **m**, 2022
39: 2 and will bring thee upon the **m** of Israel: 2022
39: 4 Thou shalt fall upon the **m** of Israel, thou, 2022
39:17 *even* a great sacrifice upon the **m** of Israel, 2022
Hos 4:13 They sacrifice upon the tops of the **m**, and 2022
10: 8 they shall say to the **m**, Cover us; and to 2022
Joel 2: 2 as the morning spread upon the **m**: 2022
2: 5 Like the noise of chariots on the tops of **m** 2022
3:18 *that* the **m** shall drop down new wine, and 2022
Am 3: 9 Assemble yourselves upon the **m** of 2022
4:13 he that formeth the **m**, and createth 2022
9:13 the **m** shall drop sweet wine, and all 2022
Jnh 2: 6 I went down to the bottoms of the **m**; 2022
Mic 1: 4 the **m** shall be molten under him, and 2022
4: 1 shall be established in the top of the **m**, 2022
6: 1 contend thou before the **m**, and let the hills 2022
6: 2 Hear ye, O **m**, the LORD'S controversy, 2022
Na 1: 5 The **m** quake at him, and the hills melt, and 2022
1:15 Behold upon the **m** the feet of him that 2022
3:18 *dust:* thy people is scattered upon the **m**, 2022
Hab 3: 6 the everlasting **m** were scattered, 2042
3:10 The **m** saw thee, *and* they trembled: 2022
Hag 1:11 upon the **m**, and upon the corn, and 2022
Zec 6: 1 four chariots out from between two **m**; 2022
6: 1 and the **m** *were* mountains of brass. 2022
6: 1 and the mountains *were* **m** of brass. 2022
14: 5 ye shall flee *to* the valley of the **m**; for 2022
14: 5 for the valley of the **m** shall reach unto 2022
Mal 1: 3 laid his **m** and his heritage waste for 2022
Mt 18:12 and goeth into the **m**, and seeketh that *3735*
24:16 let them which be in Judea flee into the **m**: *3735*
Mk 5: 5 and day, he was in the **m**, and in the tombs, *3735*
5:11 Now there was there nigh unto the **m** a *3735*
13:14 then let them that be in Judea flee to the **m**: *3735*
Lk 21:21 let them which are in Judea flee to the **m**; *3735*
23:30 Then shall they begin to say to the **m**, *3735*
1Co 13: 2 so that *I* could remove **m**, and have no *3735*
Heb 11:38 and *in* **m**, and *in* dens and caves of *3735*
Rev 6:15 in the dens and in the rocks of the **m**; *3735*
6:16 And said to the **m** and rocks, Fall on us, *3735*
16:20 fled *away*, and the **m** were not found. *3735*
17: 9 The seven heads are seven **m**, on which *3735*

MOUNTED (1) [MOUNT]

Eze 10:19 and **m up** from the earth in my sight: 7426

MOUNTING (1) [MOUNT]

Isa 15: 5 for *by* the **m up** of Luhith with weeping 4608

MOUNTS (3) [MOUNT]

Jer 32:24 Behold the **m**, they are come *unto* the city 5550
33: 4 which are thrown down by the **m**, and 5550
Eze 17:17 by casting up **m**, and building forts, to cut 5550

MOURN (45) [MOURNED, MOURNER, MOURNERS, MOURNETH, MOURNFULLY, MOURNING]

Ge 23: 2 Abraham came to **m** for Sarah, and to weep 5594
1Sa 16: 1 unto Samuel, How long wilt thou **m** for Saul, 56
2Sa 3:31 you with sackcloth, and **m** before Abner. 5594
1Ki 13:29 came to the city, to **m** and to bury him. 5594
14:13 all Israel shall **m** for him, and bury him: 5594
Ne 8: 9 unto the LORD your God; **m** not, nor weep. 56
Job 2:11 together to come to **m** with him 5110
5:11 that those which **m** may be exalted *to* 6937
14:22 have pain, and his soul within him shall **m**. 56
Ps 55: 2 I **m** in my complaint, and make a noise; 7300
Pr 5:11 thou **m** at the last, when thy flesh and 5098
29: 2 when the wicked beareth rule, the people **m**. 584
Ecc 3: 4 to laugh; a time to **m**, and a time to dance; 5594
Isa 3:26 her gates shall lament and **m**; and she *being* 56
16: 7 the foundations of Kir-hareseth shall ye **m**; 1897
19: 8 The fishers also shall **m**, and all they that 578
38:14 I did **m** as a dove: mine eyes fail *with* 1897
59:11 all like bears, and **m sore** like doves: 1897+1897
61: 2 vengeance of our God; to comfort all that **m**; 57
61: 3 To appoint unto them that **m** in Zion, to give 57
66:10 rejoice for joy with her, all ye that **m** for her: 56
Jer 4:28 For this shall the earth **m**, and the heavens 56
12: 4 How long shall the land **m**, and the herbs of 56
48:31 *mine heart* shall **m** for the men of 1897
La 1: 4 The ways of Zion do **m**, because none come 57
Eze 7:12 let not the buyer rejoice, nor the seller **m**: 56
7:27 The king shall **m**, and the prince shall be 56
24:16 yet neither shalt thou **m** nor weep, 5594
24:23 ye shall not **m** nor weep; but ye shall pine 5594
24:23 your iniquities, and **m** one towards another. 5098
31:15 I **caused** Lebanon **to m** for him, and all 6937
Hos 4: 3 Therefore shall the land **m**, and every one that 56
10: 5 for the people thereof shall **m** over it, and 56
Joel 1: 9 the priests, the LORD'S ministers, **m**. 56
Am 1: 2 and the habitations of the shepherds shall **m**, 56
8: 8 and every one **m** that dwelleth therein? 56
9: 5 shall melt, and all that dwell therein shall **m**: 56
Zec 12:10 they shall **m** for him, as one mourneth for 5594
12:12 the land shall **m**, every family apart; 5594
Mt 5: 4 Blessed *are* they that **m**: for they shall be *3996*
9:15 Can the children of the bridechamber **m**, *3996*
24:30 and then shall all the tribes of the earth **m**, *2875*
Lk 6:25 that laugh now: for ye shall **m** and weep. *3996*
Jas 4: 9 Be afflicted, and **m**, and weep: let your *3996*
Rev 18:11 of the earth *shall* weep and **m** over her; *3996*

MOURNED (22) [MOURN]

Ge 37:34 upon his loins, and **m** for his son many days. 56
50: 3 and the Egyptians **m** for him threescore and 1058
50:10 there they **m** with a great and very sore 5594
Ex 33: 4 the people heard these evil tidings, they **m**: 56
Nu 14:39 children of Israel: and the people **m** greatly. 56
20:29 they **m** for Aaron thirty days, *even* all 1058
1Sa 15:35 nevertheless Samuel **m** for Saul: and 56
2Sa 1:12 they **m**, and wept, and fasted until even, 5594
11:26 husband was dead, she **m** for her husband. 5594
13:37 And *David* **m** for his son every day. 56
14: 2 be as a woman *that had* a long time **m** for 56
1Ki 13:30 they **m** over him, *saying*, Alas, my brother. 5594
14:18 all Israel **m** for him, according to the word 5594
1Ch 7:22 And Ephraim their father **m** many days, and 56
2Ch 35:24 And all Judah and Jerusalem **m** for Josiah. 56

Ezr 10: 6 for he **m** because of the transgression of them 56
Ne 1: 4 **m** *certain* days, and fasted, and prayed before 56
Zec 7: 5 When ye fasted and **m** in the fifth and 5594
Mt 11:17 we have **m** unto you, and ye have not *2354*
Mk 16:10 had been with him, as they **m** and wept. *3996*
Lk 7:32 we have **m** to you, and ye have not wept. *2354*
1Co 5: 2 ye are puffed up, and have not rather **m**, *3996*

MOURNER (1) [MOURN]

2Sa 14: 2 **feign** thyself **to be a m**, and put on now 56

MOURNERS (4) [MOURN]

Job 29:25 in the army, as *one that* comforteth the **m**. 57
Ecc 12: 5 long home, and the **m** go about the streets: 5594
Isa 57:18 and restore comforts unto him and to his **m**. 57
Hos 9: 4 *shall be* unto them as the bread of **m**; 205

MOURNETH (11) [MOURN]

2Sa 19: 1 Behold, the king weepeth and **m** for Absalom. 56
Ps 35:14 down heavily, as one that **m** for his mother. 57
88: 9 Mine eye **m** by reason of affliction: 1669
Isa 24: 4 The earth **m** *and* fadeth away, the world 56
24: 7 The new wine **m**, the vine languisheth, all 56
33: 9 The earth **m** *and* languisheth: Lebanon is 56
Jer 12:11 it desolate, *and being* desolate it **m** unto me; 56
14: 2 Judah **m**, and the gates thereof languish; 56
23:10 for because of swearing the land **m**; 56
Joel 1:10 The field is wasted, the land **m**; for the corn is 56
Zec 12:10 as one **m** for *his* only *son,* and shall be in 4553

MOURNFULLY (1) [MOURN]

Mal 3:14 that we have walked **m** before the LORD 6941

MOURNING (51) [MOURN]

Ge 27:41 The days of **m** for my father are at hand; 60
37:35 I will go down into the grave unto my son **m**. 57
50: 4 when the days of his **m** were past, 1068
50:10 and he made a **m** for his father seven days. 60
50:11 saw the **m** in the floor of Atad, they said, 60
50:11 This *is* a grievous **m** to the Egyptians: 60
Dt 26:14 I have not eaten thereof in my **m**, 205
34: 8 of weeping *and* **m** for Moses were ended. 60
2Sa 11:27 when the **m** was past, David sent and fet her 60
14: 2 put on now **m** apparel, and anoint not *thyself* 60
19: 2 the victory that day was *turned* into **m** unto all 60
Est 4: 3 *there was* great **m** among the Jews, and 60
6:12 Haman hasted to his house **m**, and having his 57
9:22 sorrow to joy, and from **m** into a good day: 60
Job 3: 8 the day, who are ready to raise up their **m**. 3882
30:28 I went **m** without the sun: I stood up, *and* 6937
30:31 My harp also is *turned* to **m**, and my organ 60
Ps 30:11 Thou hast turned for me my **m** into 4553
38: 6 down greatly; I go **m** all the day long. 6937
42: 9 why go I **m** because of the oppression of 6937
43: 2 why go I **m** because of the oppression of 6937
Ecc 7: 2 *It is* better to go to the house of **m**, than to go 60
7: 4 The heart of the wise *is* in the house of **m**; but 60
Isa 22:12 to **m**, and to baldness, and to girding with 4553
51:11 and joy; *and* sorrow and **m** shall flee away. 585
60:20 and the days of thy **m** shall be ended. 60
61: 3 them beauty for ashes, the oil of joy for **m**, 60
Jer 6:26 make thee **m**, *as* for an only *son,* most bitter 60
9:17 call for the **m** *women,* that they may come; 6969
16: 5 the LORD, Enter not *into* the house of **m**, 4798
16: 7 shall *men* tear *themselves* for them in **m**, 60
31:13 for I will turn their **m** into joy, and 60
La 2: 5 hath increased in the daughter of Judah **m** 8386
5:15 heart is ceased; our dance is turned into **m**. 60
Eze 2:10 therein lamentations, and **m**, and woe. 1899
7:16 all of them **m**, every one for his iniquity. 1993
24:17 Forbear to cry, make no **m** *for* the dead, 60
31:15 he went down to the grave I **caused a m**: 56
Da 10: 2 In those days I Daniel was **m** three full weeks. 56
Joel 2:12 and with weeping, and with **m**: 4553
Am 5:16 and they shall call the husbandman to **m**, and 60
8:10 I will turn your feasts into **m**, and all your 60
8:10 and I will make it as the **m** of an only *son,* and 60
Mic 1: 8 a wailing like the dragons, and **m** as the owls. 60
1:11 came not forth *in* the **m** of Beth-ezel; 4553
Zec 12:11 In that day shall there be a great **m** in 4553
12:11 as the **m** of Hadadrimmon in the valley of 4553
Mt 2:18 lamentation, and weeping, and great **m**, *3602*
2Co 7: 7 your **m**, your fervent mind toward me; *3602*
Jas 4: 9 let your laughter be turned to **m**, and *3997*

Rev 18: 8 come in one day, death, and **m**, and famine; *3997*

MOUSE (2) [MICE]

Lev 11:29 and the **m**, and the tortoise after his kind, 5909
Isa 66:17 and the abomination, and the **m**, 5909

MOUTH (424) [MOUTHS]

Ge 4:11 which hath opened her **m** to receive thy 6310
8:11 lo, in her **m** *was* an olive leaf pluckt off: 6310
24:57 will call the damsel, and inquire at her **m**. 6310
29: 2 and a great stone *was* upon the well's **m**. 6310
29: 3 and they rolled the stone from the well's **m**, 6310
29: 3 put the stone again upon the well's **m** in his 6310
29: 8 *till* they roll the stone from the well's **m**; 6310
29:10 rolled the stone from the well's **m**, and 6310
42:27 for behold, it *was* in his sack's **m**. 6310
43:12 the money that was brought again in the **m** 6310
43:21 every man's money *was* in the **m** of his 6310
44: 1 put every man's money in his sack's **m**. 6310
44: 2 in the sack's **m** of the youngest, and 6310
45:12 that *it is* my **m** that speaketh unto you. 6310
Ex 4:11 said unto him, Who hath made man's **m**? 6310
4:12 Now therefore go, and I will be with thy **m**, 6310
4:15 speak unto him, and put words in his **m**: 6310
4:15 I will be with thy **m**, and with his mouth, 6310
4:15 with his **m**, and will teach you what ye 6310
4:16 *even* he shall be to thee instead of a **m**, and 6310
13: 9 that the LORD'S law may be in thy **m**: 6310
23:13 neither let it be heard out of thy **m**. 6310
Nu 12: 8 With him will I speak **m** to mouth, 6310
12: 8 With him will I speak mouth to **m**, 6310
16:30 the earth open her **m**, and swallow them up, 6310
16:32 the earth opened her **m**, and 6310
22:28 the LORD opened the **m** of the ass, and 6310
22:38 the word that God putteth in my **m**, that 6310
23: 5 And the LORD put a word in Balaam's **m**, 6310
23:12 that which the LORD hath put in my **m**? 6310
23:16 put a word in his **m**, and said, Go again 6310
26:10 the earth opened her **m**, and 6310
30: 2 to all that proceedeth out of his **m**. 6310
32:24 that which hath proceeded out of your **m**. 6310
35:30 the murderer shall be put to death by the **m** 6310
Dt 8: 3 by every *word* that proceedeth out of the **m** 6310
11: 6 how the earth opened her **m**, and 6310
17: 6 At the **m** of two witnesses, or 6310
17: 6 at the **m** of one witness he shall not be put 6310
18:18 unto thee, and will put my words in his **m**; 6310
19:15 at the **m** of two witnesses, or at the mouth 6310
19:15 or at the **m** of three witnesses, shall 6310
23:23 which thou hast promised with thy **m**. 6310
30:14 in thy **m**, and in thy heart, that *thou* mayest 6310
32: 1 and hear, O earth, the words of my **m**. 6310
Jos 1: 8 of the law shall not depart out of thy **m**; 6310
6:10 shall *any* word proceed out of your **m**, 6310
9:14 asked not *counsel* at the **m** of the LORD. 6310
10:18 Roll great stones upon the **m** of the cave, 6310
10:22 Open the **m** of the cave, and bring out those 6310
10:27 laid great stones in the cave's **m**, 6310
Jdg 7: 6 putting their hand to their **m**, were three 6310
9:38 Where *is* now thy **m**, wherewith thou 6310
11:35 for I have opened my **m** unto the LORD, 6310
11:36 *if* thou hast opened thy **m** unto the LORD, 6310
11:36 to that which hath proceeded out of thy **m**; 6310
18:19 lay thine hand upon thy **m**, and go with us, 6310
1Sa 1:12 before the LORD, that Eli marked her **m**. 6310
2: 1 my **m** is enlarged over mine enemies; 6310
2: 3 let *not* arrogancy come out of your **m**: 6310
14:26 but no man put his hand to his **m**: 6310
14:27 in a honeycomb, and put his hand to his **m**; 6310
17:35 smote him, and delivered *it* out of his **m**: 6310
2Sa 1:16 for thy **m** hath testified against thee, saying, 6310
14: 3 unto him. So Joab put the words in her **m**. 6310
14:19 he put all these words in the **m** of thine 6310
17:19 and spread a covering over the well's **m**, 6440
18:25 If he *be* alone, *there is* tidings in his **m**. 6310
22: 9 his nostrils, and fire out of his **m** devoured: 6310
1Ki 7:31 the **m** of it within the chapiter and 6310
7:31 the **m** thereof *was* round *after* the work of 6310
7:31 also upon the **m** of it *were* gravings with 6310
8:15 which spake with his **m** unto David my 6310
8:24 thou spakest also with thy **m**, and 6310
13:21 Forasmuch as thou hast disobeyed the **m** of 6310
17:24 *that* the word of the LORD in thy **m** *is* 6310
19:18 and every **m** which hath not kissed him. 6310

1Ki	22:13	*declare* good unto the king *with* one **m**:	6310
	22:22	I will be a lying spirit in the **m** of all his	6310
	22:23	the LORD hath put a lying spirit in the **m**	6310
2Ki	4:34	put his **m** upon his mouth, and his eyes	6310
	4:34	put his mouth upon his **m**, and his eyes	6310
1Ch	16:12	his wonders, and the judgments of his **m**;	6310
2Ch	6: 4	he spake with his **m** to my father David,	6310
	6:15	spakest with thy **m**, and hast fulfilled *it*	6310
	18:21	be a lying spirit in the **m** of all his prophets.	6310
	18:22	the LORD hath put a lying spirit in the **m**	6310
	35:22	the words of Necho from the **m** of God,	6310
	36:12	*speaking* from the **m** of the LORD.	6310
	36:21	To fulfil the word of the LORD by the **m**	6310
	36:22	the **m** of Jeremiah might be accomplished,	6310
Ezr	1: 1	that the word of the LORD by the **m** of	6310
Ne	9:20	withheldest not thy manna from their **m**,	6310
Est	7: 8	As the word went out of the king's **m**,	6310
Job	3: 1	After this opened Job his **m**, and cursed his	6310
	5:15	from their **m**, and from the hand of	6310
	5:16	hath hope, and iniquity stoppeth her **m**.	6310
	7:11	Therefore I will not refrain my **m**; I will	6310
	8: 2	*how long shall* the words of thy **m** *be like* a	6310
	8:21	Till he fill thy **m** *with* laughing, and	6310
	9:20	mine own **m** shall condemn me:	6310
	12:11	the ear try words? and the **m** taste his meat?	2441
	15: 5	For thy **m** uttereth thine iniquity, and	6310
	15: 6	Thine own **m** condemneth thee, and not I;	6310
	15:13	and lettest *such* words go out of thy **m**?	6310
	15:30	by the breath of his **m** shall he go away.	6310
	16: 5	*But* I would strengthen you with my **m**, and	6310
	16:10	They have gaped upon me with their **m**;	6310
	19:16	*me* no answer; I intreated him with my **m**.	6310
	20:12	Though wickedness be sweet in his **m**,	6310
	20:13	forsake it not; but keep it still within his **m**:	2441
	21: 5	and lay *your* hand upon *your* **m**.	6310
	22:22	the law from his **m**, and lay up his words in	6310
	23: 4	before him, and fill my **m** *with* arguments.	6310
	23:12	I have esteemed the words of his **m** more	6310
	29: 9	and laid *their* hand on their **m**.	6310
	29:10	their tongue cleaved to the **roof of** their **m**.	2441
	29:23	they opened their **m** wide *as* for the latter	6310
	31:27	or my **m** hath kissed my hand:	6310
	31:30	(Neither have I suffered my **m** to sin by	2441
	32: 5	*was* no answer in the **m** of *these* three men,	6310
	33: 2	Behold now I have opened my **m**,	6310
	33: 2	my tongue hath spoken in my **m**.	2441
	34: 3	the ear trieth words, as the **m** tasteth meat.	2441
	35:16	Therefore doth Job open his **m** in vain;	6310
	37: 2	and the sound *that* goeth out of his **m**.	6310
	40: 4	I will lay my hand upon my **m**.	6310
	40:23	that he can draw up Jordan into his **m**.	6310
	41:19	Out of his **m** go burning lamps, *and*	6310
	41:21	and a flame goeth out of his **m**.	6310
Ps	5: 9	For *there is* no faithfulness in their **m**;	6310
	8: 2	Out of the **m** of babes and sucklings hast	6310
	10: 7	His **m** is full *of* cursing and deceit and	6310
	17: 3	I am purposed *that* my **m** shall not	6310
	17:10	own fat: *with* their **m** they speak proudly.	6310
	18: 8	his nostrils, and fire out of his **m** devoured:	6310
	19:14	Let the words of my **m**, and the meditation	6310
	22:21	Save me from the lion's **m**: for thou hast	6310
	32: 9	whose **m** must be held in with bit and	5716
	33: 6	all the host of them by the breath of his **m**.	6310
	34: 1	his praise *shall* continually *be* in my **m**.	6310
	35:21	they opened their **m** wide against me, *and*	6310
	36: 3	The words of his **m** *are* iniquity and deceit:	6310
	37:30	The **m** of the righteous speaketh wisdom,	6310
	38:13	*was* as a dumb *man that* openeth not his **m**.	6310
	38:14	and in whose **m** *are* no reproofs.	6310
	39: 1	I will keep my **m** with a bridle, while	6310
	39: 9	I was dumb, I opened not my **m**; because	6310
	40: 3	he hath put a new song in my **m**,	6310
	49: 3	My **m** shall speak of wisdom; and	6310
	50:16	thou shouldest take my covenant in thy **m**?	6310
	50:19	Thou givest thy **m** to evil, and thy tongue	6310
	51:15	and my **m** shall shew forth thy praise.	6310
	54: 2	O God; give ear to the words of my **m**.	6310
	55:21	*The words of* his **m** were smoother than	6310
	58: 6	Break their teeth, O God, in their **m**:	6310
	59: 7	Behold, they belch out with their **m**:	6310
	59:12	*For* the sin of their **m** *and* the words of their	6310
	62: 4	they bless with their **m**, but they curse	6310
	63: 5	and my **m** shall praise *thee with* joyful lips:	6310
	63:11	the **m** of them that speak lies shall be	6310
	66:14	my **m** hath spoken, when I was in trouble.	6310
	66:17	I cried unto him *with* my **m**, and *he was*	6310
	69:15	and let not the pit shut her **m** upon me.	6310
	71: 8	Let my **m** be filled *with* thy praise *and*	6310
	71:15	My **m** shall shew forth thy righteousness	6310
	73: 9	They set their **m** against the heavens, and	6310
	78: 1	incline your ears to the words of my **m**.	6310
	78: 2	I will open my **m** in a parable: I will utter	6310
	78:36	they did flatter him with their **m**,	6310
	81:10	of Egypt: open thy **m** wide, and I will fill it.	6310
	89: 1	with my **m** will I make known thy	6310
	103: 5	Who satisfieth thy **m** with good *things; so*	5716
	105: 5	his wonders, and the judgments of his **m**;	6310
	107:42	rejoice: and all iniquity shall stop her **m**.	6310
	109: 2	For the **m** of the wicked and the mouth of	6310
	109: 2	the **m** of the deceitful are opened against	6310
	109:30	will greatly praise the LORD with my **m**;	6310
	119:13	have I declared all the judgments of thy **m**.	6310
	119:43	not the word of truth utterly out of my **m**;	6310
	119:72	The law of thy **m** *is* better unto me than	6310
	119:88	so shall I keep the testimony of thy **m**.	6310
	119:103	my taste! *yea, sweeter* than honey to my **m**!	6310
	119:108	the freewill offerings of my **m**, O LORD,	6310
	119:131	I opened my **m**, and panted: for I longed	6310
	126: 2	was our **m** filled *with* laughter, and	6310
	137: 6	let my tongue cleave to the **roof of** my **m**;	2441
	138: 4	when they hear the words of thy **m**.	6310
	141: 3	Set a watch, O LORD, before my **m**;	6310
	141: 7	Our bones are scattered at the grave's **m**,	6310
	144: 8	Whose **m** speaketh vanity, and their right	6310
	144:11	whose **m** speaketh vanity, and their right	6310
	145:21	My **m** shall speak the praise of the LORD:	6310
	149: 6	*Let* the high *praises* of God *be* in their **m**,	1627
Pr	2: 6	out of his **m** *cometh* knowledge and	6310
	4: 5	neither decline from the words of my **m**.	6310
	4:24	Put away from thee a froward **m**, and	6310
	5: 3	and her **m** *is* smoother than oil:	2441
	5: 7	and depart not from the words of my **m**.	6310
	6: 2	Thou art snared with the words of thy **m**,	6310
	6: 2	thou art taken with the words of thy **m**,	6310
	6:12	a wicked man, walketh *with* a froward **m**.	6310
	7:24	and attend to the words of my **m**.	6310
	8: 7	For my **m** shall speak truth; and	2441
	8: 8	All the words of my **m** *are* in	6310
	8:13	the evil way, and the froward **m**, do I hate.	6310
	10: 6	but violence covereth the **m** of the wicked.	6310
	10:11	The **m** of a righteous *man is* a well of life:	6310
	10:11	but violence covereth the **m** of the wicked.	6310
	10:14	but the **m** of the foolish *is* near destruction.	6310
	10:31	The **m** of the just bringeth forth wisdom:	6310
	10:32	the **m** of the wicked *speaketh* frowardness.	6310
	11: 9	A hypocrite with *his* **m** destroyeth his	6310
	11:11	it is overthrown by the **m** of the wicked.	6310
	12: 6	but the **m** of the upright shall deliver them.	6310
	12:14	be satisfied *with* good by the fruit of *his* **m**:	6310
	13: 2	A man shall eat good by the fruit of *his* **m**:	6310
	13: 3	He that keepeth his **m** keepeth his life: *but*	6310
	14: 3	In the **m** of the foolish *is* a rod of pride: but	6310
	15: 2	but the **m** of fools poureth out foolishness.	6310
	15:14	but the **m** of fools feedeth on foolishness.	6310
	15:23	A man hath joy by the answer of his **m**: and	6310
	15:28	the **m** of the wicked poureth out evil	6310
	16:10	his **m** transgresseth not in judgment.	6310
	16:23	The heart of the wise teacheth his **m**, and	6310
	16:26	for himself; for his **m** craveth it of him.	6310
	18: 4	The words of a man's **m** *are as* deep	6310
	18: 6	and his **m** calleth for strokes.	6310
	18: 7	A fool's **m** *is* his destruction, and his lips	6310
	18:20	shall be satisfied with the fruit of his **m**;	6310
	19:24	will not so much as bring it to his **m** again.	6310
	19:28	and the **m** of the wicked devoureth iniquity.	6310
	20:17	afterwards his **m** shall be filled *with* gravel.	6310
	21:23	Whoso keepeth his **m** and his tongue	6310
	22:14	The **m** of strange *women is* a deep pit:	6310
	24: 7	for a fool: he openeth not his **m** in the gate.	6310
	26: 7	not equal: so *is* a parable in the **m** of fools.	6310
	26: 9	so *is* a parable in the **m** of fools.	6310
	26:15	it grieveth him to bring it again to his **m**.	6310
	26:28	by it; and a flattering **m** worketh ruin.	6310
	27: 2	*man* praise thee, and not thine own **m**;	6310
	30:20	she eateth, and wipeth her **m**, and saith,	6310
	30:32	thought evil, *lay thine* hand upon thy **m**.	6310
	31: 8	Open thy **m** for the dumb in the cause of all	6310
	31: 9	Open thy **m**, judge righteously, and	6310

Pr	31:26	She openeth her **m** with wisdom; and in her	6310
Ecc	5: 2	Be not rash with thy **m**, and let not thine	6310
	5: 6	Suffer not thy **m** to cause thy flesh to sin;	6310
	6: 7	All the labour of man *is* for his **m**, and	6310
	10:12	The words of a wise *man's* **m** *are* gracious;	6310
	10:13	The beginning of the words of his **m** *is*	6310
SS	1: 2	Let him kiss me with the kisses of his **m**:	6310
	5:16	His **m** *is* most sweet: yea, he *is* altogether	2441
	7: 9	the **roof of** thy **m** like the best wine, for my	2441
Isa	1:20	for the **m** of the LORD hath spoken *it*.	6310
	5:14	and opened her **m** without measure:	6310
	6: 7	he laid *it* upon my **m**, and said, Lo,	6310
	9:12	they shall devour Israel with open **m**.	6310
	9:17	an evildoer, and every **m** speaketh folly.	6310
	10:14	the wing, or opened the **m**, or peeped.	6310
	11: 4	shall smite the earth with the rod of his **m**,	6310
	19: 7	by the **m** of the brooks, and every thing	6310
	29:13	as this people draw near *me* with their **m**,	6310
	30: 2	*into* Egypt, and have not asked *at* my **m**;	6310
	34:16	for my **m** it hath commanded, and his spirit	6310
	40: 5	for the **m** of the LORD hath spoken *it*.	6310
	45:23	the word is gone out of my **m** *in*	6310
	48: 3	they went forth out of my **m**, and I shewed	6310
	49: 2	he hath made my **m** like a sharp sword;	6310
	51:16	I have put my words in thy **m**, and	6310
	53: 7	he was afflicted, yet he opened not his **m**:	6310
	53: 7	shearers is dumb, so he openeth not his **m**.	6310
	53: 9	neither *was any* deceit in his **m**.	6310
	55:11	my word be that goeth forth out of my **m**:	6310
	57: 4	against whom make ye a wide **m**, *and*	6310
	58:14	for the **m** of the LORD hath spoken *it*.	6310
	59:21	and my words which I have put in thy **m**,	6310
	59:21	shall not depart out of thy **m**, nor out of	6310
	59:21	of thy mouth, nor out of the **m** of thy seed,	6310
	59:21	nor out of the **m** of thy seed's seed,	6310
	62: 2	which the **m** of the LORD shall name.	6310
Jer	1: 9	put forth his hand, and touched my **m**.	6310
	1: 9	Behold, I have put my words in thy **m**.	6310
	5:14	I will make my words in thy **m** fire, and	6310
	7:28	is perished, and is cut off from their **m**.	6310
	9: 8	peaceably to his neighbour with his **m**,	6310
	9:12	*who is he* to whom the **m** of the LORD	6310
	9:20	let your ear receive the word of his **m**, and	6310
	12: 2	thou *art* near in their **m**, and far from their	6310
	15:19	from the vile, thou shalt be as my **m**:	6310
	23:16	*and* not out of the **m** of the LORD.	6310
	32: 4	shall speak with him **m** to mouth, and	6310
	32: 4	shall speak with him mouth to **m**, and	6310
	34: 3	he shall speak with thee **m** to mouth, and	6310
	34: 3	he shall speak with thee mouth to **m**, and	6310
	36: 4	Baruch wrote from the **m** of Jeremiah all	6310
	36: 6	which thou hast written from my **m**,	6310
	36:17	didst thou write all these words at his **m**?	6310
	36:18	all these words unto me with his **m**,	6310
	36:27	the words which Baruch wrote at the **m** of	6310
	36:32	who wrote therein from the **m** of Jeremiah	6310
	44:17	thing goeth forth out of our own **m**,	6310
	44:26	**m** of any man of Judah in all the land of	6310
	45: 1	these words in a book at the **m** of Jeremiah,	6310
	48:28	her nest in the sides of the hole's **m**.	6310
	51:44	I will bring forth out of his **m** that which he	6310
La	2:16	All thine enemies have opened their **m**	6310
	3:29	He putteth his **m** in the dust; if so be there	6310
	3:38	Out of the **m** of the most High proceedeth	6310
	4: 4	cleaveth to the **roof of** his **m** for thirst:	2441
Eze	2: 8	open thy **m**, and eat that I give thee.	6310
	3: 2	So I opened my **m**, and he caused me to eat	6310
	3: 3	and it was in my **m** as honey for sweetness.	6310
	3:17	therefore hear the word at my **m**, and	6310
	3:26	thy tongue cleave to the **roof of** thy **m**,	2441
	3:27	I will open thy **m**, and thou shalt say unto	6310
	4:14	came there abominable flesh into my **m**.	6310
	16:56	mentioned by thy **m** in the day of thy pride,	6310
	16:63	never open thy **m** any more, because of thy	6310
	21:22	to open the **m** in the slaughter,	6310
	24:27	In that day shall thy **m** be opened to him	6310
	29:21	I will give thee the opening of the **m** in	6310
	33: 7	therefore thou shalt hear the word at my **m**,	6310
	33:22	had opened my **m**, until *he* came to me in	6310
	33:22	my **m** was opened, and I was no more	6310
	33:31	for with their **m** they shew much love, *but*	6310
	34:10	for I will deliver my flock from their **m**,	6310
	35:13	Thus with your **m** ye have boasted against	6310
Da	3:26	Nebuchadnezzar came near to the **m** of	8651
	4:31	While the word *was* in the king's **m**,	6433
	6:17	and laid upon the **m** of the den;	6433
	7: 5	*it had* three ribs in the **m** of it between	6433
	7: 8	of man, and a **m** speaking great *things*.	6433
	7:20	a **m** that spake very great *things*, whose	6433
	10: 3	neither came flesh nor wine in my **m**,	6310
	10:16	I opened my **m**, and spake, and said unto	6310
Hos	2:17	away the names of Baalim out of her **m**,	6310
	6: 5	I have slain them by the words of my **m**:	6310
	8: 1	*Set* the trumpet to thy **m**. *He shall come* as	2441
Joel	1: 5	the new wine, for it is cut off from your **m**.	6310
Am	3:12	As the shepherd taketh out of the **m** of	6310
Mic	4: 4	for the **m** of the LORD of hosts hath	6310
	6:12	and their tongue *is* deceitful in their **m**.	6310
	7: 5	keep the doors of thy **m** from her that lieth	6310
	7:16	they shall lay *their* hand upon *their* **m**,	6310
Na	3:12	they shall even fall into the **m** of the eater.	6310
Zep	3:13	shall a deceitful tongue be found in their **m**:	6310
Zec	5: 8	he cast the weight of lead upon the **m**	6310
	8: 9	days these words by the **m** of the prophets,	6310
	9: 7	I will take away his blood out of his **m**,	6310
	14:12	their tongue shall consume away in their **m**.	6310
Mal	2: 6	The law of truth was in his **m**, and	6310
	2: 7	and they should seek the law at his **m**:	6310
Mt	4: 4	by every word that proceedeth out of the **m**	*4750*
	5: 2	And he opened his **m**, and taught them,	*4750*
	12:34	the abundance of the heart the **m** speaketh.	*4750*
	13:35	saying, I will open my **m** in parables;	*4750*
	15: 8	people draweth nigh unto me with their **m**,	*4750*
	15:11	Not that which goeth into the **m** defileth a	*4750*
	15:11	but that which cometh out of the **m**,	*4750*
	15:17	that whatsoever entereth in at the **m** goeth	*4750*
	15:18	out of the **m** come forth from the heart;	*4750*
	17:27	and when thou hast opened his **m**,	*4750*
	18:16	that in the **m** of two or three witnesses	*4750*
	21:16	Out of the **m** of babes and sucklings thou	*4750*
Lk	1:64	And his **m** was opened immediately, and	*4750*
	1:70	(As he spake by the **m** of his holy prophets,	*4750*
	4:22	words which proceeded out of his **m**.	*4750*
	6:45	for of the abundance of the heart his **m**	*4750*
	11:54	seeking to catch something out of his **m**,	*4750*
	19:22	Out of thine own **m** will I judge thee,	*4750*
	21:15	For I will give you a **m** and wisdom,	*4750*
	22:71	for we ourselves have heard of his own **m**.	*4750*
Jn	19:29	and put *it* upon hyssop, and put *it* to his **m**.	*4750*
Ac	1:16	which the Holy Ghost by the **m** of David	*4750*
	3:18	had shewed by the **m** of all his prophets,	*4750*
	3:21	**m** of all his holy prophets since the world	*4750*
	4:25	Who by the **m** of thy servant David hast	*4750*
	8:32	before his shearer, so opened he not his **m**:	*4750*
	8:35	Then Philip opened his **m**,	*4750*
	10:34	Then Peter opened *his* **m**, and said, Of a	*4750*
	11: 8	hath at any time entered into my **m**.	*4750*
	15: 7	that the Gentiles by my **m** should hear	*4750*
	15:27	shall also tell *you* the same *things* by **m**.	*3056*
	18:14	when Paul was *now* about to open *his* **m**,	*4750*
	22:14	and shouldest hear the voice of his **m**.	*4750*
	23: 2	that stood by him to smite him on the **m**.	*4750*
Ro	3:14	Whose **m** is full of cursing and bitterness:	*4750*
	3:19	that every **m** may be stopped, and all	*4750*
	10: 8	nigh thee, *even* in thy **m**, and in thy heart:	*4750*
	10: 9	That if thou shalt confess with thy **m**	*4750*
	10:10	with the **m** confession is made unto	*4750*
	15: 6	may with one mind *and* one **m** glorify God,	*4750*
1Co	9: 9	Thou shalt not muzzle the **m** of the ox that	NIG
2Co	6:11	O *ye* Corinthians, our **m** is open unto you,	*4750*
	13: 1	In the **m** of two or three witnesses shall	*4750*
Eph	4:29	communication proceed out of your **m**,	*4750*
	6:19	unto me, that *I* may open my **m** boldly,	*4750*
Col	3: 8	filthy communication out of your **m**.	*4750*
2Th	2: 8	Lord shall consume with the spirit of his **m**,	*4750*
2Ti	4:17	and I was delivered out of the **m** of the lion.	*4750*
Jas	3:10	Out of the same **m** proceedeth blessing and	*4750*
1Pe	2:22	no sin, neither was guile found in his **m**:	*4750*
Jude	1:16	their **m** speaketh great swelling *words*,	*4750*
Rev	1:16	out of his **m** went a sharp twoedged sword:	*4750*
	2:16	fight against them with the sword of my **m**.	*4750*
	3:16	cold nor hot, I will spue thee out of my **m**.	*4750*
	9:19	For their power is in their **m**, and in their	*4750*
	10: 9	but it shall be in thy **m** sweet as honey.	*4750*
	10:10	it up; and it was in my **m** sweet as honey:	*4750*
	11: 5	fire proceedeth out of their **m**, and	*4750*
	12:15	And the serpent cast out of his **m** water as a	*4750*
	12:16	and the earth opened her **m**, and	*4750*

Rev 12:16 flood which the dragon cast out of his **m**. *4750*
13: 2 of a bear, and his **m** as the mouth of a lion: *4750*
13: 2 of a bear, and his mouth as the **m** of a lion: *4750*
13: 5 And there was given unto him a **m** *4750*
13: 6 And he opened his **m** in blasphemy against *4750*
14: 5 And in their **m** was found no guile: for they *4750*
16:13 like frogs *come* out of the **m** of the dragon, *4750*
16:13 and out of the **m** of the beast, and out of *4750*
16:13 and out of the **m** of the false prophet. *4750*
19:15 And out of his **m** goeth a sharp sword, *4750*
19:21 which *sword* proceeded out of his **m**: *4750*

MOUTHS (18) [MOUTH]

Ge 44: 8 which we found in our sacks' **m**, 6310
Dt 31:19 put it in their **m**, that this song may be a 6310
31:21 for it shall not be forgotten out of the **m** of 6310
Ps 22:13 They gaped upon me *with* their **m**, *as* a 6310
78:30 But while their meat *was* yet in their **m**, 6310
115: 5 They have **m**, but they speak not: eyes have 6310
135:16 They have **m**, but they speak not; eyes have 6310
135:17 neither is there *any* breath in their **m**. 6310
Isa 52:15 the kings shall shut their **m** at him: 6310
Jer 44:25 your wives have both spoken with your **m**, 6310
La 3:46 All our enemies have opened their **m** 6310
Da 6:22 hath shut the lions' **m**, that they have not 6433
Mic 3: 5 he that putteth not into their **m**, they even 6310
Tit 1:11 Whose **m** must be **stopped**, who subvert *1993*
Heb 11:33 obtained promises, stopped the **m** of lions, *4750*
Jas 3: 3 Behold, we put bits in the horses' **m**, *4750*
Rev 9:17 and out of their **m** issued fire and smoke *4750*
9:18 the brimstone, which issued out of their **m**. *4750*

MOVE (13) [MOTIONS, MOVEABLE, MOVED, MOVEDST, MOVER, MOVETH, MOVING, UNMOVEABLE]

Ex 11: 7 of Israel shall not a dog **m** his tongue, 2782
Lev 11:10 of all that **m** in the waters, and of any living 8318
Dt 23:25 thou shalt not **m** a sickle unto thy 5130
32:21 I will **m** them **to jealousy** with *those which* 7065
Jdg 13:25 to **m** him **at times** in the camp of Dan, 6470
2Sa 7:10 in a place of their own, and **m** no more; 7264
2Ki 21: 8 Neither will I **make** the feet of Israel **m** any 5110
23:18 Let him alone; let no man **m** his bones. 5128
Jer 10: 4 with nails and with hammers, that it **m** not. 6328
Mic 7:17 they shall **m** out of their holes like worms 7264
Mt 23: 4 they *themselves* will not **m** them with *one* *2795*
Ac 17:28 in him we live, and **m**, and have our being; *2795*
20:24 But none of these *things* **m** me, *4160*

MOVEABLE (1) [MOVE]

Pr 5: 6 her ways are **m**, *that* thou canst not know 5128

MOVED (75) [MOVE]

Ge 1: 2 the Spirit of God **m** upon the face of 7363
7:21 all flesh died that **m** upon the earth, *both* of 7430
Dt 32:21 They have **m** me **to jealousy** with *that* 7065
Jos 10:21 none **m** his tongue against any of 2782
15:18 as she came *unto him,* that she **m** him to 5496
Jdg 1:14 when she came *to him,* that she **m** him to 5496
Ru 1:19 that all the city was **m** about them, and 1949
1Sa 1:13 only her lips **m**, but her voice was not 5128
2Sa 18:33 the king was **much m**, and went up to 7264
22: 8 the foundations of heaven **m** and shook, 7264
24: 1 he **m** David against them to say, Go, 5496
1Ch 16:30 world also shall be stable, that it be not **m**. 4131
17: 9 in their place, and shall be **m** no more; 7264
2Ch 18:31 and God **m** them *to depart* from him. 5496
Ezr 4:15 that they have **m** sedition within the same 5648
Est 5: 9 that he stood not up, nor **m** for him, he was 2111
Job 37: 1 heart trembleth, and is **m** out of his place. 5425
41:23 are firm in themselves; they cannot be **m**. 4131
Ps 10: 6 He hath said in his heart, I shall not be **m**: 4131
13: 4 those that trouble me rejoice when I am **m**. 4131
15: 5 He that doeth these *things* shall never be **m**. 4131
16: 8 *he is* at my right hand, I shall not be **m**. 4131
18: 7 the foundations also of the hills **m** and 7264
21: 7 mercy of the most High he shall not be **m**. 4131
30: 6 in my prosperity I said, I shall never be **m**. 4131
46: 5 *is* in the midst of her; she shall not be **m**: 4131
46: 6 The heathen raged, the kingdoms were **m**: 4131
55:22 he shall never suffer the righteous to be **m**. 4131
62: 2 *he is* my defence; I shall not be greatly **m**. 4131
62: 6 *he is* my defence; I shall not be **m**. 4131
66: 9 in life, and suffereth not our feet to be **m**. 4132
68: 8 *even* Sinai itself *was* **m** at the presence of NIH
78:58 **m** him **to jealousy** with their graven 7065
93: 1 also is stablished, *that* it cannot be **m**. 4131
96:10 shall be established *that* it shall not be **m**: 4131
99: 1 *between* the cherubims; let the earth be **m**. 5120
112: 6 Surely he shall not be **m** for ever: 4131
121: 3 He will not suffer thy foot to be **m**: he that 4132
Pr 12: 3 but the root of the righteous shall not be **m**. 4131
SS 5: 4 *the door,* and my bowels were **m** for him. 1993
Isa 6: 4 the posts of the door **m** at the voice of him 5128
7: 2 his heart was **m**, and the heart of his 5128
7: 2 as the trees of the wood are **m** with 5128
10:14 there was none that **m** the wing, or 5074
14: 9 Hell from beneath is **m** for thee to meet 7264
19: 1 the idols of Egypt shall be **m** at his 5128
24:19 the earth is **m exceedingly**. 4131+4131
40:20 prepare a graven image, *that* shall not be **m**. 4131
41: 7 it with nails, *that* it should not be **m**. 4131
Jer 4:24 they trembled, and all the hills **m lightly**. 7043
25:16 be **m**, and be mad, because of the sword 1607
46: 7 a flood, whose waters are **m** as the rivers? 1607
46: 8 and *his* waters are **m** like the rivers; 1607
49:21 The earth is **m** at the noise of their fall, 7493
50:46 of the taking of Babylon the earth is **m**, 7493
Da 8: 7 he was **m with choler** against him, and 4843
11:11 king of the south shall be **m with choler**, 4843
Mt 9:36 he was **m with compassion** on them, *4697*
14:14 and was **m with compassion** toward them, *4697*
18:27 of that servant was **m with compassion**, *4697*
20:24 **m with indignation** against the two brethren. *23*
21:10 all the city was **m**, saying, Who is this? *4579*
Mk 1:41 And Jesus, **m with compassion**, put forth *4697*
6:34 and was **m with compassion** toward them, *4697*
15:11 But the chief priests **m** the people, that he *383*
Ac 2:25 is on my right hand, that I should not be **m**: *4531*
7: 9 And the patriarchs, **m with envy**, *2206*
17: 5 the Jews which believed not, **m with envy**, *2206*
21:30 And all the city was **m**, and the people ran *2795*
Col 1:23 *be* not **m away** from the hope of the gospel, *3334*
1Th 3: 3 That no *man* should be **m** by these *4525*
Heb 11: 7 **m with fear**, prepared an ark to the saving *2125*
12:28 we receiving a kingdom which **cannot be m**, *761*
2Pe 1:21 holy men of God spake *as they were* **m** by *5342*
Rev 6:14 and island were **m** out of their places. *2795*

MOVEDST (1) [MOVE]

Job 2: 3 although thou **m** me against him, to destroy 5496

MOVER (1) [MOVE]

Ac 24: 5 a **m** of sedition among all the Jews *2795*

MOVETH (8) [MOVE]

Ge 1:21 and every living creature that **m**, 7430
1:28 over every living thing that **m** upon 7430
9: 2 upon all that **m** *upon* the earth, and upon all 7430
Lev 11:46 of every living creature that **m** in 7430
Job 40:17 He **m** his tail like a cedar: the sinews of his 2654
Ps 69:34 the seas, and every *thing* that **m** therein. 7430
Pr 23:31 colour in the cup, *when* it **m** itself aright. 1980
Eze 47: 9 *that* every thing that liveth, which **m**, 8317

MOVING (5) [MOVE]

Ge 1:20 abundantly the **m creature** that hath life, 5315
9: 3 Every **m thing** that liveth shall be meat for 7431
Job 16: 5 the **m** of my lips should asswage *your* 5205
Pr 16:30 **m** his lips he bringeth evil to pass. 7169
Jn 5: 3 withered, waiting for the **m** of the water. *2796*

MOWER (1) [MOWINGS, MOWN]

Ps 129: 7 Where*with* the **m** filleth not his hand; 7114

MOWINGS (1) [MOWER]

Am 7: 1 *it was* the latter growth after the king's **m**. 1488

MOWN (1) [MOWER]

Ps 72: 6 come down like rain upon the **m grass**: 1488

MOZA (5)

1Ch 2:46 bare Haran, and **M**, and Gazez: 4162
8:36 and Zimri; and Zimri begat **M**, 4162
8:37 **M** begat Binea: Rapha *was* his son, 4162
9:42 and Zimri; and Zimri begat **M**; 4162
9:43 **M** begat Binea; and Rephaiah his son, 4162

MOZAH (1)

Jos 18:26 And Mizpeh, and Chephirah, and **M**, 4681

MUCH (287) [FORASMUCH, FORSOMUCH, INASMUCH, INSOMUCH, MORE, MOST, OVERMUCH] See Index

MUDDY See FOUL

MUFFLERS (1)
Isa 3:19 The chains, and the bracelets, and the **m**, 7479

MULBERRY (4)
2Sa 5:23 come upon them over against the **m trees**. 1057
5:24 sound of a going in the tops of the **m trees**, 1057
1Ch 14:14 come upon them over against the **m trees**. 1057
14:15 a sound of going in the tops of the **m trees**, 1057

MULE (9) [MULES, MULES']
2Sa 13:29 every man gat him up upon his **m**, and fled. 6505
18: 9 Absalom rode upon a **m**, and the mule went 6505
18: 9 the **m** went under the thick boughs of a 6505
18: 9 and the **m** that *was* under him went away. 6505
1Ki 1:33 Solomon my son to ride upon mine own **m**, 6506
1:38 Solomon to ride upon king David's **m**, 6506
1:44 have caused him to ride upon the king's **m**: 6506
Ps 32: 9 Be ye not as the horse, *or* as the **m**, 6505
Zec 14:15 of the **m**, of the camel, and of the ass, and 6505

MULES (11) [MULE]
Ge 36:24 this *was that* Anah that found the **m** in 3222
1Ki 10:25 and armour, and spices, horses, and **m**, 6505
18: 5 find grass to save the horses and **m** alive, 6505
1Ch 12:40 and on **m**, and on oxen, *and* meat, meal, 6505
2Ch 9:24 raiment, harness, and spices, horses, and **m**, 6505
Ezr 2:66 six; their **m**, two hundred forty and five; 6505
Ne 7:68 six: their **m**, two hundred forty and five; 6505
Est 8:10 *and* riders on **m**, camels, *and* 7409
8:14 *So* the posts that rode upon **m** *and* 7409
Isa 66:20 and upon **m**, and upon swift beasts, 6505
Eze 27:14 thy fairs with horses and horsemen and **m**. 6505

MULES' (1) [MULE]
2Ki 5:17 be given to thy servant two **m** burden of 6505

MULTIPLIED (44) [MULTIPLY]
Ge 47:27 and grew, and **m** exceedingly. 7235
Ex 1: 7 and **m**, and waxed exceeding mighty; 7235
1:12 afflicted them, the more they **m** and grew. 7235
1:20 and the people **m**, and waxed very mighty. 7235
11: 9 that my wonders may be **m** in the land of 7235
Dt 1:10 The LORD your God hath **m** you, and 7235
8:13 thy silver and thy gold is **m**, and all that 7235
8:13 is multiplied, and all that thou hast is **m**; 7235
11:21 That your days may be **m**, and the days of 7235
Jos 24: 3 and **m** his seed, and gave him Isaac. 7235
1Ch 5: 9 their cattle were **m** in the land of Gilead. 7235
Job 27:14 If his children be **m**, *it is* for the sword: and 7235
35: 6 or *if* thy transgressions be **m**, what doest 7231
Ps 16: 4 Their sorrows shall be **m** *that* hasten *after* 7235
38:19 and they that hate me wrongfully are **m**. 7231
107:38 them also, so that they are **m** greatly; 7235
Pr 9:11 For by me thy days shall be **m**, and 7235
29:16 When the wicked are **m**, 7235
Isa 9: 3 Thou hast **m** the nation, *and* not increased 7235
59:12 For our transgressions are **m** before thee, 7231
Jer 3:16 when ye be **m** and increased in the land, 7235
Eze 5: 7 Because ye **m** more than the nations that 1995
11: 6 Ye have **m** your slain in this city, and 7235
16:25 one that passed by, and **m** thy whoredoms. 7235
16:29 Thou hast moreover **m** thy fornication in 7235
16:51 thou hast **m** thine abominations more than 7235
21:15 *their* heart may faint, and *their* ruins be **m**: 7235
23:19 Yet she **m** her whoredoms, in calling to 7235
31: 5 his boughs were **m**, and his branches 7235
35:13 and have **m** your words against me: 6280
Da 4: 1 dwell in all the earth; Peace be **m** unto you. 7680
6:25 dwell in all the earth; Peace be **m** unto you. 7680
Hos 2: 8 and oil, and **m** her silver and gold, 7235
8:14 and Judah hath **m** fenced cities: 7235
12:10 I have **m** visions, and used similitudes by 7235
Na 3:16 Thou hast **m** thy merchants above the stars 7235
Ac 6: 1 when the number of the disciples was **m**, *4129*
6: 7 the number of the disciples **m** in Jerusalem *4129*
7:17 the people grew and **m** in Egypt, *4129*
9:31 in the comfort of the Holy Ghost, were **m**. *4129*
12:24 But the word of God grew and **m**. *4129*
1Pe 1: 2 Grace unto you, and peace, be **m**. *4129*
2Pe 1: 2 peace be **m** unto you through *4129*
Jude 1: 2 Mercy unto you, and peace, and love, be **m**. *4129*

MULTIPLIEDST (1) [MULTIPLY]
Ne 9:23 Their children also **m** thou as the stars of 7235

MULTIPLIETH (3) [MULTIPLY]
Job 9:17 and **m** my wounds without cause. 7235
34:37 amongst us, and **m** his words against God. 7235
35:16 in vain; he **m** words without knowledge. 3527

MULTIPLY (46) [MULTIPLIED, MULTIPLIEDST, MULTIPLIETH, MULTIPLYING]
Ge 1:22 **m**, and fill the waters in the seas, and let 7235
1:22 in the seas, and let fowl **m** in the earth. 7235
1:28 **m**, and replenish the earth, and subdue it: 7235
3:16 I will **greatly m** thy sorrow and 7235+7235
6: 1 when men began to **m** on the face of 7231
8:17 and be fruitful, and **m** upon the earth. 7235
9: 1 Be fruitful, and **m**, and replenish the earth. 7235
9: 7 you, be ye fruitful, and **m**; bring forth 7235
9: 7 abundantly in the earth, and **m** therein. 7235
16:10 I will **m** thy seed **exceedingly**, that it 7235+7235
17: 2 and thee, and will **m** thee exceedingly. 7235
17:20 him fruitful, and will **m** him exceedingly; 7235
22:17 in multiplying I will **m** thy seed as the stars 7235
26: 4 I will **make** thy seed **to m** as the stars of 7235
26:24 **m** thy seed for my servant Abraham's sake. 7235
28: 3 and make thee fruitful, and **m** thee, 7235
35:11 be fruitful and **m**; a nation and a company 7235
48: 4 **m** thee, and I will make of thee a multitude 7235
Ex 1:10 lest they **m**, and it come to pass, that, 7235
7: 3 **m** my signs and my wonders in the land of 7235
23:29 and the beast of the field **m** against thee. 7227
32:13 I will **m** your seed as the stars of heaven, 7235
Lev 26: 9 **m** you, and establish my covenant with 7235
Dt 7:13 will love thee, and bless thee, and **m** thee: 7235
8: 1 **m**, and go in and possess the land which 7235
8:13 *when* thy herds and thy flocks **m**, and thy 7235
13:17 have compassion upon thee, and **m** thee, 7235
17:16 he shall not **m** horses to himself, nor cause 7235
17:16 to the end that he should **m** horses: 7235
17:17 Neither shall he **m** wives to himself, 7235
17:17 neither shall he greatly **m** to himself silver 7235
28:63 over you to do you good, and to **m** you; 7235
30: 5 do thee good, and **m** thee above thy fathers. 7235
30:16 his judgments, that thou mayest live and **m**: 7235
1Ch 4:27 neither did all their family **m**, like to 7235
Job 29:18 my nest, and I shall **m** *my* days as the sand. 7235
Jer 30:19 I will **m** them, and they shall not be few; 7235
33:22 so will I **m** the seed of David my servant, 7235
Eze 16: 7 I have caused thee to **m** as the bud of 7233
36:10 I will **m** men upon you, all the house of 7235
36:11 I will **m** upon you man and beast; and 7235
36:30 I will **m** the fruit of the tree, and 7235
37:26 **m** them, and will set my sanctuary in 7235
Am 4: 4 *at* Gilgal **m** transgression; and bring your 7235
2Co 9:10 and **m** your seed sown, and increase *4129*
Heb 6:14 bless thee, and multiplying I will **m** thee. *4129*

MULTIPLYING (2) [MULTIPLY]
Ge 22:17 in **m** I will multiply thy seed as the stars of 7235
Heb 6:14 I will bless thee, and **m** I will multiply thee. *4129*

MULTITUDE (243) [MULTITUDES]
Ge 16:10 that it shall not be numbered for **m**. 7230
28: 3 that thou mayest be a **m** of people; 6951
30:30 I *came,* and it is *now* increased unto a **m**; 7230
32:12 the sea, which cannot be numbered for **m**. 7230
48: 4 and I will make of thee a **m** of people; 6951
48:16 let them grow into a **m** in the midst of 7230
48:19 and his seed shall become a **m** of nations. 4393
Ex 12:38 a mixed **m** went up also with them; and 7227
23: 2 Thou shalt not follow a **m** to *do* evil; 7227
Lev 25:16 According to the **m** of years thou shalt 7230
Nu 11: 4 the **mixt m** that *was* among them fell a 628
32: 1 the children of Gad had a very great **m** of 7227
Dt 1:10 *are this* day as the stars of heaven for **m**. 7230
10:22 made thee as the stars of heaven for **m**. 7230
28:62 ye were as the stars of heaven for **m**; 7230
Jos 11: 4 as the sand that *is* upon the sea shore in **m**, 7230
Jdg 4: 7 Jabin's army, with his chariots and his **m**; 1995
6: 5 and they came as grasshoppers for **m**; 7230
7:12 along in the valley like grasshoppers for **m**; 7230
7:12 as the sand by the sea side for **m**. 7230

M

1Sa 13: 5 as the sand which *is* on the sea shore in **m**: 7230
14:16 the **m** melted away, and they went on 1995
2Sa 6:19 *even* among the whole **m** of Israel, as well 1995
17:11 as the sand that *is* by the sea for **m**; 7230
1Ki 3: 8 cannot be numbered nor counted for **m**. 7230
4:20 as the sand which *is* by the sea in **m**, eating 7230
8: 5 that could not be told nor numbered for **m**. 7230
20:13 Hast thou seen all this great **m**? 1995
20:28 will I deliver all this great **m** into thine 1995
2Ki 7:13 they *are* as all the **m** of Israel that are left in 1995
7:13 *I say,* they *are even* as all the **m** of 1995
19:23 With the **m** of my chariots I am come up *to* 7230
25:11 of Babylon, with the remnant of the **m**, 1995
2Ch 1: 9 a people like the dust of the earth **in m**. 7227
5: 6 could not be told nor numbered for **m**. 7230
13: 8 ye *be* a great **m**, and *there are* with you 1995
14:11 and in thy name we go against this **m**. 1995
20: 2 There cometh a great **m** against thee from 1995
20:15 nor dismayed by reason of this great **m**; 1995
20:24 they looked unto the **m**, and behold, 1995
28: 5 carried away a **great m** of them captives, 1419
30:18 For a **m** of the people, *even* many of 4768
32: 7 nor for all the **m** that *is* with him: 1995
Ne 13: 3 they separated from Israel all the **mixed m**. 6154
Est 5:11 the **m** of his children, and all *the things* 7230
10: 3 and accepted of the **m** of his brethren, 7230
Job 11: 2 Should not the **m** of words be answered? 7230
31:34 Did I fear a great **m**, or did the contempt of 1995
32: 7 and **m** of years should teach wisdom. 7230
33:19 and the **m** of his bones *with* strong *pain:* 7379
35: 9 By reason of the **m** of oppressions they 7230
39: 7 He scorneth the **m** of the city, 1995
Ps 5: 7 I will come *into* thy house in the **m** of thy 7230
5:10 cast them out in the **m** of their 7230
33:16 There is no king saved by the **m** of a host: 7230
42: 4 for I had gone with the **m**, I went with them 5519
42: 4 and praise, *with* a **m** that kept holyday. 1995
49: 6 boast themselves in the **m** of their riches; 7230
51: 1 according unto the **m** of thy tender mercies 7230
68:30 the **m** of the bulls, with the calves of 5712
69:13 O God, in the **m** of thy mercy hear me, 7230
69:16 turn unto me according to the **m** of thy 7230
74:19 **m** *of the wicked:* forget not 2416
94:19 In the **m** of my thoughts within me thy 7230
97: 1 let the **m** of isles be glad *thereof.* 7227
106: 7 they remembered not the **m** of thy mercies; 7230
106:45 repented according to the **m** of his mercies. 7230
109:30 yea, I will praise him among the **m**. 7227
Pr 10:19 In the **m** of words there wanteth not sin: but 7230
11:14 but in the **m** of counsellers *there is* safety. 7230
14:28 In the **m** of people *is* the king's honour: but 7230
15:22 in the **m** of counsellers *they* are established. 7230
20:15 There is gold, and a **m** of rubies: but 7230
24: 6 and in **m** of counsellers *there is* safety. 7230
Ecc 5: 3 For a dream cometh through the **m** of 7230
5: 3 and a fool's voice *is known* by **m** of words. 7230
5: 7 For in the **m** of dreams and many words 7230
Isa 1:11 To what purpose *is* the **m** of your sacrifices 7230
5:13 and their **m** dried up with thirst. 1995
5:14 their **m**, and their pomp, and he that 1995
13: 4 The noise of a **m** in the mountains, like as 1995
16:14 shall be contemned, with all *that* great **m**; 1995
17:12 Woe to the **m** of many people, *which* make 1995
29: 5 Moreover the **m** of thy strangers shall be 1995
29: 5 the **m** of the terrible ones *shall be* as chaff 1995
29: 7 the **m** of all the nations that fight against 1995
29: 8 so shall the **m** of all the nations be, 1995
31: 4 when a **m** of shepherds is called forth 4393
32:14 the **m** of the city shall be left; the forts and 1995
37:24 By the **m** of my chariots am I come up *to* 7230
47: 9 their perfection for the **m** of thy sorceries, 7230
47:12 and with the **m** of thy sorceries, 7230
47:13 Thou art wearied in the **m** of thy counsels. 7230
60: 6 The **m** of camels shall cover thee, 8229
63: 7 according to the **m** of his lovingkindnesses. 7230
Jer 3:23 the hills, *and from* the **m** of mountains: 1995
10:13 *there is* a **m** of waters in the heavens, and 1995
12: 6 yea, they have called a **m** after thee: 4392
30:14 of a cruel one, for the **m** of thine iniquity; 7230
30:15 thy sorrow *is* incurable for the **m** of thine 7230
44:15 all the women that stood *by,* a great **m**, 6951
46:25 I will punish the **m** of No, and Pharaoh, and 527
49:32 be a booty, and the **m** of their cattle a spoil: 1995
51:16 *there is* a **m** of waters in the heavens; 1995
51:42 she is covered with the **m** of the waves 1995
52:15 to the king of Babylon, and the rest of the **m**. 527
La 1: 5 for the LORD hath afflicted her for the **m** 7230
3:32 according to the **m** of his mercies. 7230
Eze 7:11 none of them *shall remain,* nor of their **m**, 1995
7:12 for wrath *is* upon all the **m** thereof. 1995
7:13 for the vision *is* touching the whole **m** 1995
7:14 for my wrath *is* upon all the **m** thereof. 1995
14: 4 that cometh according to the **m** of his idols; 7230
19:11 she appeared in her height with the **m** of 7230
23:42 a voice of a **m** being at ease *was* with her: 1995
27:12 by reason of the **m** of all *kind of* riches; 7230
27:16 Syria *was* thy merchant by reason of the **m** 7230
27:18 Damascus *was* thy merchant in the **m** of 7230
27:18 of thy making, for the **m** of all riches; 7230
27:33 kings of the earth with the **m** of thy riches 7230
28:16 By the **m** of thy merchandise they have 7230
28:18 Thou hast defiled thy sanctuaries by the **m** 7230
29:19 he shall take her **m**, and take her spoil, 1995
30: 4 they shall take *away* her **m**, and 1995
30:10 I will also make the **m** of Egypt to cease by 1995
30:15 of Egypt; and I will cut off the **m** of No. 1995
31: 2 unto Pharaoh king of Egypt, and to his **m**; 1995
31: 5 became long because of the **m** of waters, 7227
31: 9 I have made him fair by the **m** of his 7230
31:18 This *is* Pharaoh and all his **m**, saith 1995
32:12 of the mighty will I cause thy **m** to fall, 1995
32:12 and all the **m** thereof shall be destroyed. 1995
32:16 *even* for Egypt, and for all her **m**, saith 1995
32:18 wail for the **m** of Egypt, and cast them 1995
32:24 and all her **m** round about her grave, 1995
32:25 bed in the midst of the slain with all her **m**: 1995
32:26 There *is* Meshech, Tubal, and all her **m**: 1995
32:31 shall be comforted over all his **m**, 1995
32:32 *even* Pharaoh and all his **m**, saith the Lord 1995
39:11 and there shall they bury Gog and all his **m**: 1995
47: 9 there shall be a very **great m** of fish, 7227
Da 10: 6 the voice of his words like the voice of a **m**. 1995
11:10 and shall assemble a **m** of great forces: 1995
11:11 he shall set forth a great **m**; but 1995
11:11 but the **m** shall be given into his hand. 1995
11:12 *And* when he hath taken away the **m**, his 1995
11:13 shall set forth a **m** greater than the former, 1995
Hos 9: 7 for the **m** of thine iniquity, and the great 7230
10: 1 according to the **m** of his fruit he hath 7230
10:13 in thy way, in the **m** of thy mighty *men.* 7230
Mic 2:12 great noise by reason of *the* **m** *of* men. NIH
Na 3: 3 *there is* a **m** of slain, and a great number of 7230
3: 4 Because of the **m** of the whoredoms of 7230
Zec 2: 4 *as* towns without walls for the **m** of men 7230
Mt 13: 2 sat; and the whole **m** stood on the shore. *3793*
13:34 All these *things* spake Jesus unto the **m** in *3793*
13:36 Then Jesus sent the **m** away, and went into *3793*
14: 5 he feared the **m**, because they counted him *3793*
14:14 and saw a great **m**, and was moved with *3793*
14:15 send the **m** away, that they may go into *3793*
14:19 And he commanded the **m** to sit down on *3793*
14:19 to *his* disciples, and the disciples to the **m**. *3793*
15:10 And he called the **m**, and said unto them, *3793*
15:31 Insomuch that the **m** wondered, when they *3793*
15:32 and said, I have compassion on the **m**, *3793*
15:33 in the wilderness, as to fill so great a **m**? *3793*
15:35 And he commanded the **m** to sit down on *3793*
15:36 to his disciples, and the disciples to the **m**. *3793*
15:39 And he sent away the **m**, and took ship, and *3793*
17:14 And when they were come to the **m**, *3793*
20:29 from Jericho, a great **m** followed him. *3793*
20:31 And the **m** rebuked them, because *3793*
21: 8 And a very great **m** spread their garments *3793*
21:11 And the **m** said, This is Jesus the prophet of *3793*
21:46 they feared the **m**, because they took him *3793*
22:33 And when the **m** heard *this,* they were *3793*
23: 1 Then spake Jesus to the **m**, and to his *3793*
26:47 and with him a great **m** with swords and *3793*
27:20 elders persuaded the **m** that they should ask *3793*
27:24 and washed *his* hands before the **m**, saying, *3793*
Mk 2:13 and all the **m** resorted unto him, and *3793*
3: 7 and a great **m** from Galilee followed him, *4128*
3: 8 and they about Tyre and Sidon, a great **m**, *4128*
3: 9 ship should wait on him because of the **m**, *3793*
3:20 And *the* **m** cometh together again, so *3793*
3:32 And *the* **m** sat about him, and they said *3793*
4: 1 and there was gathered unto him a great **m**, *3793*
4: 1 the whole **m** was by the sea on the land. *3793*

Mk 4:36 And when they had sent away the **m**, 3793
5:31 Thou seest the **m** thronging thee, and 3793
7:33 And he took him aside from the **m**, and 3793
8: 1 In those days the **m** being very great, 3793
8: 2 I have compassion on the **m**, because 3793
9:14 he saw a great **m** about them, and 3793
9:17 And one of the **m** answered and said, 3793
14:43 and with him a great **m** with swords and 3793
15: 8 And the **m** crying aloud began to desire 3793
Lk 1:10 And the whole **m** of the people were 4128
2:13 And suddenly there was with the angel a **m** 4128
3: 7 Then said he to the **m** that came forth to be 3793
5: 6 this done, they inclosed a great **m** of fishes: 4128
5:19 they might bring him in because of the **m**, 3793
6:17 and a great **m** of people out of all Judea and 4128
6:19 And the whole **m** sought to touch him: 3793
8:37 Then the whole **m** of the country of 4128
8:45 the **m** throng thee and press *thee*, and 3793
9:12 and said unto him, Send the **m** away, 3793
9:16 gave to the disciples to set before the **m**. 3793
12: 1 together an **innumerable m** of people, 3461
18:36 And hearing the **m** pass by, he asked what 3793
19:37 the whole **m** of the disciples began to 4128
19:39 Pharisees from among the **m** said unto him, 3793
22: 6 him unto them in the absence of the **m**. 3793
22:47 behold a **m**, and he that was called Judas, 3793
23: 1 And the whole **m** of them arose, and 4128
Jn 5: 3 In these lay a great **m** of impotent *folk*, of 4128
5:13 himself away, a **m** being in *that* place. 3793
6: 2 And a great **m** followed him, because 3793
21: 6 now they were not able to draw it for the **m** 4128
Ac 2: 6 the **m** came together, and were confounded, 4128
4:32 And the **m** of them that believed were of 4128
5:16 There came also a **m** *out* of the cities round 4128
6: 2 Then the twelve called the **m** of 4128
6: 5 And the saying pleased the whole **m**: and 4128
14: 1 that a great **m** both of the Jews and *also* of 4128
14: 4 But the **m** of the city was divided: and 4128
15:12 Then all the **m** kept silence, and 4128
15:30 and when they had gathered the **m** together, 4128
16:22 And the **m** rose up together against them: 3793
17: 4 and of the devout Greeks a great **m**, and 4128
19: 9 but spake evil of *that* way before the **m**, 4128
19:33 And they drew Alexander out of the **m**, 3793
21:22 the **m** must needs come together: for they 4128
21:34 one *thing*, some another, among the **m**: 3793
21:36 For the **m** of the people followed *after*, 4128
23: 7 and the Sadducees: and the **m** was divided. 4128
24:18 the temple, neither with **m**, nor with tumult. 3793
25:24 ye see this *man*, about whom all the **m** of 4128
Heb 11:12 *so many* as the stars of the sky in **m**, and 4128
Jas 5:20 soul from death, and shall hide a **m** of sins. 4128
1Pe 4: 8 for charity shall cover the **m** of sins. 4128
Rev 7: 9 After this I beheld, and lo, a great **m**, 3793
19: 6 I heard as *it were* the voice of a great **m**, 3793

MULTITUDES (24) [MULTITUDE]
Eze 32:20 *to* the sword: draw her and all her **m**. 1995
Joel 3:14 **M**, multitudes in the valley of decision: 1995
3:14 Multitudes, **m** in the valley of decision: 1995
Mt 4:25 And there followed him great **m** *of people* 3793
5: 1 And seeing the **m**, he went up into a 3793
8: 1 from the mountain, great **m** followed him. 3793
8:18 Now when Jesus saw great **m** about him, 3793
9: 8 But when the **m** saw *it*, they marvelled, 3793
9:33 and the **m** marvelled, saying, It was never 3793
9:36 But when he saw the **m**, he was moved 3793
11: 7 Jesus began to say unto the **m** concerning 3793
12:15 and great **m** followed him, and he healed 3793
13: 2 And great **m** were gathered together unto 3793
14:22 the other side, while he sent the **m** away. 3793
14:23 And when he had sent the **m** away, he went 3793
15:30 And great **m** came unto him, having with 3793
19: 2 And great **m** followed him; and he healed 3793
21: 9 And the **m** that went before, 3793
26:55 In that *same* hour said Jesus to the **m**, 3793
Lk 5:15 and great **m** came together to hear, and 3793
14:25 And there went great **m** with him: and 3793
Ac 5:14 to the Lord, **m** both of men and women.) 4128
13:45 But when the Jews saw the **m**, they were 3793
Rev 17:15 and **m**, and nations, and tongues. 3793

MUNITION (2) [MUNITIONS]
Isa 29: 7 even all that fight against her and her **m**, 4685
Na 2: 1 keep the **m**, watch the way, make *thy* loins 4694

MUNITIONS (1) [MUNITION]
Isa 33:16 his place of defence *shall be* the **m** of 4679

MUPPIM (1)
Ge 46:21 Ehi, and Rosh, **M**, and Huppim, and Ard. 4649

MURDER (9) [MURDERER, MURDERERS, MURDERS]
Ps 10: 8 in the secret places doth he **m** the innocent: 2026
94: 6 and the stranger, and **m** the fatherless. 7523
Jer 7: 9 **m**, and commit adultery, and swear falsely, 7523
Hos 6: 9 the company of priests **m** *in* the way by 7523
Mt 19:18 Jesus said, Thou shalt do no **m**, Thou shalt 5407
Mk 15: 7 who had committed **m** in the insurrection. 5408
Lk 23:19 in the city, and *for* **m**, was cast into prison.) 5408
23:25 that for sedition and **m** was cast into prison, 5408
Ro 1:29 full of envy, **m**, debate, deceit, malignity; 5408

MURDERER (20) [MURDER]
Nu 35:16 instrument of iron, so that he die, he *is* a **m**: 7523
35:16 the **m** shall surely be put to death. 7523
35:17 he may die, and he die, he *is* a **m**: 7523
35:17 the **m** shall surely be put to death. 7523
35:18 he may die, and he die, he *is* a **m**: 7523
35:18 the **m** shall surely be put to death. 7523
35:19 revenger of blood himself shall slay the **m**: 7523
35:21 shall surely be put to death; *for* he *is* a **m**: 7523
35:21 the revenger of blood shall slay the **m**, 7523
35:30 the **m** shall be put to death by the mouth of 7523
35:31 shall take no satisfaction for the life of a **m**, 7523
2Ki 6:32 See ye how this son of a **m** hath sent to take 7523
Job 24:14 The **m** rising with the light killeth the poor 7523
Hos 9:13 *shall* bring forth his children to the **m**. 2026
Jn 8:44 He was a **m** from the beginning, and 443
Ac 3:14 desired a **m** to be granted unto you; 435+5406
28: 4 No doubt this man is a **m**, whom, 5406
1Pe 4:15 But let none of you suffer as a **m**, or *as* a 5406
1Jn 3:15 Whosoever hateth his brother is a **m**: and 443
3:15 ye know that no **m** hath eternal life abiding 443

MURDERERS (10) [MURDER]
2Ki 14: 6 the children of the **m** he slew not: 5221
Isa 1:21 righteousness lodged in it; but now **m**. 7523
Jer 4:31 for my soul is wearied because of **m**. 2026
Mt 22: 7 and destroyed those **m**, and burnt up their 5406
Ac 7:52 ye have been now the betrayers and **m**: 5406
21:38 wilderness four thousand men that were **m**? 4607
1Ti 1: 9 for **m of fathers** and murderers of mothers, 3964
1: 9 for murderers of fathers and **m of mothers**, 3389
Rev 21: 8 and **m**, and whoremongers, and sorcerers, 5406
22:15 and **m**, and idolaters, and whosoever loveth 5406

MURDERS (4) [MURDER]
Mt 15:19 **m**, adulteries, fornications, thefts, 5408
Mk 7:21 evil thoughts, adulteries, fornications, **m**, 5408
Gal 5:21 Envyings, **m**, drunkenness, revellings, and 5408
Rev 9:21 Neither repented they of their **m**, nor of 5408

MURMUR (9) [MURMURED, MURMURERS, MURMURING, MURMURINGS]
Ex 16: 7 and what *are* we, that ye **m** against us? 3885
16: 8 your murmurings which ye **m** against him: 3885
Nu 14:27 evil congregation, which **m** against me? 3885
14:27 of Israel, which they **m** against me. 3885
14:36 **made** all the congregation **to m** against 3885
16:11 and what *is* Aaron, that ye **m** against him? 3885
17: 5 of Israel, whereby they **m** against you. 3885
Jn 6:43 said unto them, **M** not among yourselves. 1111
1Co 10:10 Neither **m** ye, as some of them also 1111

MURMURED (19) [MURMUR]
Ex 15:24 the people **m** against Moses, saying, 3885
16: 2 of the children of Israel **m** against Moses 3885
17: 3 the people **m** against Moses, and said, 3885
Nu 14: 2 all the children of Israel **m** against Moses 3885
14:29 and upward, which have **m** against me, 3885
16:41 of the children of Israel **m** against Moses 3885
Dt 1:27 ye **m** in your tents, and said, Because 7279
Jos 9:18 all the congregation **m** against the princes. 3885
Ps 106:25 **m** in their tents, *and* hearkened not unto 7279
Isa 29:24 and they that **m** shall learn doctrine. 7279
Mt 20:11 And when they had received *it*, they **m** 1111
Mk 14: 5 given to the poor. And they **m against** her. 1690
Lk 5:30 and Pharisees **m** against his disciples, 1111

Lk 15: 2 And the Pharisees and scribes m, saying, *1234*
19: 7 And when they saw *it,* they all m, saying, *1234*
Jn 6:41 The Jews then m at him, because he said, *1111*
6:61 knew in himself that his disciples m at it, *1111*
7:32 The Pharisees heard that the people m such *1111*
1Co 10:10 as some of them also m, and *1111*

MURMURERS (1) [MURMUR]
Jude 1:16 These are m, complainers, walking after *1113*

MURMURING (2) [MURMUR]
Jn 7:12 And there was much m among the people *1112*
Ac 6: 1 there arose a m of the Grecians against *1112*

MURMURINGS (9) [MURMUR]
Ex 16: 7 for that he heareth your m against 8519
16: 8 for that the LORD heareth your m which 8519
16: 8 your m *are* not against us, but against 8519
16: 9 the LORD: for he hath heard your m. 8519
16:12 I have heard the m of the children of Israel: 8519
Nu 14:27 I have heard the m of the children of Israel, 8519
17: 5 I will make to cease from me the m of 8519
17:10 thou shalt quite take away their m from me, 8519
Php 2:14 Do all *things* without m and disputings: *1112*

MURRAIN (1)
Ex 9: 3 the sheep: *there shall be* a very grievous m. 1698

MUSE (1) [MUSED, MUSING]
Ps 143: 5 thy works; I m on the work of thy hands. 7878

MUSED (1) [MUSE]
Lk 3:15 and all *men* m in their hearts of John, *1260*

MUSHI (8) [MUSHITES]
Ex 6:19 the sons of Merari; Mahali and M: 4187
Nu 3:20 of Merari by their families; Mahli, and M. 4187
1Ch 6:19 The sons of Merari; Mahli, and M. 4187
6:47 the son of M, the son of Merari, the son of 4187
23:21 The sons of Merari; Mahli, and M. 4187
23:23 The sons of M; Mahli, and Eder, and 4187
24:26 The sons of Merari *were* Mahli and M: 4187
24:30 The sons also of M; Mahli, and Eder, and 4187

MUSHITES (2) [MUSHI]
Nu 3:33 of the Mahlites, and the family of the M: 4188
26:58 family of the Mahlites, the family of the M, 4188

MUSICAL (3) [MUSICK]
1Ch 16:42 a sound, and with m instruments of God. 7892
Ne 12:36 with the m instruments of David the man of 7892
Ecc 2: 8 m instruments, and that of all sorts. 7705+7705

MUSICIAN (55) [MUSICK]
Ps 4: T To the chief M on Neginoth, A Psalm of 5329
5: T To the chief M upon Nehiloth, A Psalm of 5329
6: T To the chief M on Neginoth upon 5329
8: T To the chief M upon Gittith, A Psalm of 5329
9: T To the chief M upon Muth-labben, A 5329
11: T To the chief M, *A Psalm* of David. 5329
12: T To the chief M upon Sheminith, A Psalm 5329
13: T To the chief M, A Psalm of David. 5329
14: T To the chief M, *A Psalm* of David. 5329
18: T To the chief M, *A Psalm* of David, 5329
19: T To the chief M, A Psalm of David. 5329
20: T To the chief M, A Psalm of David. 5329
21: T To the chief M, A Psalm of David. 5329
22: T To the chief M upon Aijeleth Shahar, 5329
31: T To the chief M, A Psalm of David. 5329
36: T To the chief M, *A Psalm* of David 5329
39: T To the chief M, *even* to Jeduthun, A Psalm 5329
40: T To the chief M, A Psalm of David. 5329
41: T To the chief M, A Psalm of David. 5329
42: T To the chief M, Maschil, for the sons of 5329
44: T To the chief M for the sons of Korah, 5329
45: T To the chief M upon Shoshannim, for 5329
46: T To the chief M for the sons of Korah, 5329
47: T To the chief M, A Psalm for the sons of 5329
49: T To the chief M, A Psalm for the sons of 5329
51: T To the chief M, A Psalm of David, 5329
52: T To the chief M, Maschil, *A Psalm* of 5329
53: T To the chief M upon Mahalath, Maschil, 5329
54: T To the chief M on Neginoth, Maschil, 5329
55: T To the chief M on Neginoth, Maschil, 5329
56: T To the chief M upon 5329
57: T To the chief M, Al-taschith, Michtam of 5329
58: T To the chief M, Al-taschith, Michtam of 5329
59: T To the chief M, Al-taschith, Michtam of 5329
60: T To the chief M upon Shushan-eduth, 5329
61: T To the chief M upon Neginah, *A Psalm* of 5329
62: T To the chief M, to Jeduthun, A Psalm of 5329
64: T To the chief M, A Psalm of David. 5329
65: T To the chief M, A Psalm *and* Song of 5329
66: T To the chief M, A Song *or* Psalm. 5329
67: T To the chief M on Neginoth, A Psalm *or* 5329
68: T To the chief M, A Psalm *or* Song of David. 5329
69: T To the chief M upon Shoshannim, *A Psalm* 5329
70: T To the chief M, *A Psalm* of David, to bring 5329
75: T To the chief M, Al-taschith, A Psalm *or* 5329
76: T To the chief M on Neginoth, A Psalm *or* 5329
77: T To the chief M, to Jeduthun, A Psalm of 5329
80: T To the chief M upon Shoshannim-Eduth, A 5329
81: T To the chief M upon Gittith, *A Psalm* of 5329
84: T To the chief M upon Gittith, A Psalm for 5329
85: T To the chief M, A Psalm for the sons of 5329
88: T To the chief M upon Mahalath Leannoth, 5329
109: T To the chief M, A Psalm of David. 5329
139: T To the chief M, A Psalm of David. 5329
140: T To the chief M, A Psalm of David. 5329

MUSICIANS (1) [MUSICK]
Rev 18:22 and m, and of pipers, and trumpeters, *3451*

MUSICK (16) [MUSICAL, MUSICIAN, MUSICIANS]
1Sa 18: 6 with joy, and with instruments of m. 7991
1Ch 15:16 *to be* the singers with instruments of m, 7892
2Ch 5:13 and cymbals and instruments of m, 7892
7: 6 the Levites also with instruments of m of 7892
23:13 also the singers with instruments of m, and 7892
34:12 all that could skill of instruments of m. 7892
Ecc 12: 4 all the daughters of m shall be brought low; 7892
La 3:63 and their rising up; I *am* their m. 4485
5:14 from the gate, the young men from their m. 5058
Da 3: 5 psaltery, dulcimer, and all kinds of m, 2170
3: 7 sackbut, psaltery, and all kinds of m, 2170
3:10 psaltery, and dulcimer, and all kinds of m, 2170
3:15 psaltery, and dulcimer, and all kinds of m, 2170
6:18 neither were instruments of m brought 1761
Am 6: 5 *and* invent to themselves instruments of m, 7892
Lk 15:25 nigh to the house, he heard m and dancing. *4858*

MUSING (1) [MUSE]
Ps 39: 3 within me, while I was m the fire burned: 1901

MUST (132) See Index

MUSTARD (5)
Mt 13:31 of heaven is like unto a grain of m seed, *4615*
17:20 If ye have faith as a grain of m seed, *4615*
Mk 4:31 *It is* like a grain of m seed, which, when it *4615*
Lk 13:19 It is like a grain of m seed, which a man *4615*
17: 6 If ye had faith as a grain of m seed, *4615*

MUSTERED (2) [MUSTERETH]
2Ki 25:19 which m the people of the land, and 6633
Jer 52:25 of the host, who m the people of the land; 6633

MUSTERETH (1) [MUSTERED]
Isa 13: 4 the LORD of hosts m the host of 6485

MUTE See DUMB

MUTH-LABBEN (1)
Ps 9: T Musician upon M, 1121+4192+1886.1+3807.1

MUTILATORS OF THE FLESH See CONCISION

MUTTER (1) [MUTTERED]
Isa 8:19 and unto wizards that peep, and that m: 1897

MUTTERED (1) [MUTTER]
Isa 59: 3 your tongue hath m perverseness. 1897

MUTUAL (1)
Ro 1:12 together with you by the m faith both of you *240*

MUZZLE (3)
Dt 25: 4 Thou shalt not m the ox when he treadeth 2629
1Co 9: 9 Thou shalt not m the mouth of the ox that *5392*
1Ti 5:18 Thou shalt not m the ox that treadeth out *5392*

MY (4370) [I] See Index

M

MYRA (1)
Ac 27: 5 of Cilicia and Pamphylia, we came to **M**, *3460*

MYRRH (17)
Ge 37:25 camels bearing spicery and balm and **m**, 3910
43:11 spices, and **m**, nuts, and almonds: 3910
Ex 30:23 of pure **m** five hundred *shekels,* and 4753
Est 2:12 *to wit,* six months with oil of **m**, and 4753
Ps 45: 8 All thy garments *smell of* **m**, and aloes, *and* 4753
Pr 7:17 I have perfumed my bed *with* **m**, aloes, and 4753
SS 1:13 A bundle of **m** *is* my well-beloved unto me; 4753
3: 6 perfumed *with* **m** and frankincense, with all 4753
4: 6 I will get me to the mountain of **m**, and 4753
4:14 **m** and aloes, with all the chief spices: 4753
5: 1 I have gathered my **m** with my spice; 4753
5: 5 my hands dropped *with* **m**, and my fingers 4753
5: 5 my fingers *with* sweet smelling **m**, 4753
5:13 lips *like* lilies, dropping sweet smelling **m**. 4753
Mt 2:11 him gifts; gold, and frankincense, and **m**. *4666*
Mk 15:23 gave him to drink wine **mingled with m**: *4669*
Jn 19:39 and brought a mixture of **m** and aloes, *4666*

MYRTLE (6)
Ne 8:15 **m** branches, and palm branches, and 1918
Isa 41:19 the shittah tree, and the **m**, and the oil tree; 1918
55:13 of the brier shall come up the **m tree**: 1918
Zec 1: 8 he stood among the **m trees** that *were* in 1918
1:10 the man that stood among the **m trees** 1918
1:11 the LORD that stood among the **m trees**, 1918

MYSELF (118) [I] See Index

MYSIA (2)
Ac 16: 7 After they were come to **M**, they assayed to *3465*
16: 8 And they passing by **M** came down to *3465*

MYSTERIES (5) [MYSTERY]
Mt 13:11 Because it is given unto you to know the **m** *3466*
Lk 8:10 Unto you it is given to know the **m** of *3466*
1Co 4: 1 of Christ, and stewards of the **m** of God. *3466*
13: 2 and understand all **m**, and all knowledge; *3466*
14: 2 *him;* howbeit in the spirit he speaketh **m**. *3466*

MYSTERY (22) [MYSTERIES]
Mk 4:11 Unto you it is given to know the **m** of *3466*
Ro 11:25 that ye should be ignorant of this **m**, *3466*
16:25 according to the revelation of the **m**, *3466*
1Co 2: 7 But we speak the wisdom of God in a **m**, *3466*
15:51 Behold, I shew you a **m**; We shall not all *3466*
Eph 1: 9 Having made known unto us the **m** of his *3466*
3: 3 revelation he made known unto me the **m**; *3466*
3: 4 ye may understand my knowledge in the **m** *3466*
3: 9 all *men* see what *is* the fellowship of the **m**, *3466*
5:32 This is a great **m**: but I speak concerning *3466*
6:19 to make known the **m** of the gospel, *3466*
Col 1:26 *Even* the **m** which hath been hid from ages *3466*
1:27 of the glory of this **m** among the Gentiles; *3466*
2: 2 to the acknowledgement of the **m** of God *3466*
4: 3 to speak the **m** of Christ, for which I am *3466*
2Th 2: 7 For the **m** of iniquity doth already work: *3466*
1Ti 3: 9 Holding the **m** of the faith in a pure *3466*
3:16 And without controversy great is the **m** of *3466*
Rev 1:20 The **m** of the seven stars which thou sawest *3466*
10: 7 to sound, the **m** of God should be finished, *3466*
17: 5 **M**, BABYLON THE GREAT, *3466*
17: 7 I will tell thee the **m** of the woman, and *3466*

MYTHS See FABLES

N

NAAM (1)
1Ch 4:15 the son of Jephunneh; Iru, Elah, and **N**: 5277

NAAMAH (5)
Ge 4:22 iron: and the sister of Tubal-cain *was* **N**. 5279
Jos 15:41 Beth-dagon, and **N**, and Makkedah; 5279
1Ki 14:21 his mother's name *was* **N** an Ammonitess. 5279
14:31 his mother's name *was* **N** an Ammonitess. 5279
2Ch 12:13 his mother's name *was* **N** an Ammonitess. 5279

NAAMAN (16) [NAAMAN'S, NAAMITES]
Ge 46:21 and Ashbel, Gera, and **N**, Ehi, and Rosh, 5283
Nu 26:40 the sons of Bela were Ard and **N**: *of Ard,* 5283
26:40 *and* of **N**, the family of the Naamites. 5283
2Ki 5: 1 Now **N**, captain of the host of the king of 5283
5: 6 I have *therewith* sent **N** my servant to thee, 5283
5: 9 So **N** came with his horses and with his 5283
5:11 **N** was wroth, and went away, and said, 5283
5:17 **N** said, Shall there not then, I pray thee, 5283
5:20 my master hath spared **N** this Syrian, 5283
5:21 So Gehazi followed after **N**. And when 5283
5:21 when **N** saw *him* running after him, he 5283
5:23 **N** said, Be content, take two talents. And he 5283
5:27 therefore of **N** shall cleave unto thee, 5283
1Ch 8: 4 And Abishua, and **N**, and Ahoah, 5283
8: 7 **N**, and Ahiah, and Gera, he removed them, 5283
Lk 4:27 of them was cleansed, saving **N** the Syrian. *3497*

NAAMAN'S (1) [NAAMAN]
2Ki 5: 2 a little maid; and she waited on **N** wife. 5283

NAAMATHITE (4)
Job 2:11 and Bildad the Shuhite, and Zophar the **N**: 5284
11: 1 Then answered Zophar the **N**, and said, 5284
20: 1 Then answered Zophar the **N**, and said, 5284
42: 9 Bildad the Shuhite *and* Zophar the **N** went, 5284

NAAMITES (1) [NAAMAN]
Nu 26:40 *and* of Naaman, the family of the **N**. 5280

NAARAH (3)
1Ch 4: 5 of Tekoa had two wives, Helah and **N**. 5292
4: 6 **N** bare him Ahuzam, and Hepher, and 5292
4: 6 and Haahashtari. These *were* the sons of **N**. 5292

NAARAI (1)
1Ch 11:37 Hezro the Carmelite, **N** the son of Ezbai, 5293

NAARAN (1)
1Ch 7:28 and eastward **N**, and westward Gezer, 5295

NAARATH (1)
Jos 16: 7 to **N**, and came to Jericho, and went out *at* 5292

NAASHON (1)
Ex 6:23 of Amminadab, sister of **N**, to wife; 5177

NAASSON (3)
Mt 1: 4 and Aminadab begat **N**; and Naasson begat *3476*
1: 4 begat Naasson; and **N** begat Salmon; *3476*
Lk 3:32 *the son* of Salmon, which was *the son* of **N**, *3476*

NABAL (18) [NABAL'S]
1Sa 25: 3 Now the name of the man *was* **N**; and 5037
25: 4 David heard in the wilderness that **N** did 5037
25: 5 go to **N**, and greet him in my name: 5037
25: 9 they spake to **N** according to all those 5037
25:10 **N** answered David's servants, and said, 5037
25:19 after you. But she told not her husband **N**. 5037
25:25 regard this man of Belial, even **N**: 5037
25:25 *is* he; **N** *is* his name, and folly *is* with him: 5037
25:26 and they that seek evil to my lord, be as **N**. 5037
25:34 surely there had not been left unto **N** by 5037
25:36 Abigail came to **N**; and behold, he held a 5037
25:37 when the wine was gone out of **N**, and 5037
25:38 ten days *after,* that the LORD smote **N**, 5037
25:39 when David heard that **N** was dead, he said, 5037
25:39 cause of my reproach from the hand of **N**, 5037
25:39 the wickedness of **N** upon his own head. 5037
30: 5 and Abigail the wife of **N** the Carmelite. 5037
2Sa 3: 3 of Abigail the wife of **N** the Carmelite; 5037

NABAL'S (4) [NABAL]
1Sa 25:14 men told Abigail, **N** wife, saying, Behold, 5037
25:36 **N** heart *was* merry within him, for he *was* 5037
27: 3 and Abigail the Carmelitess, **N** wife. 5037
2Sa 2: 2 and Abigail **N** wife the Carmelite. 5037

NABOTH (22) [NACHON'S]
1Ki 21: 1 *that* **N** the Jezreelite had a vineyard, 5022
21: 2 Ahab spake unto **N**, saying, Give me thy 5022
21: 3 **N** said to Ahab, The LORD forbid it me, 5022
21: 4 of the word which **N** the Jezreelite had 5022

1Ki 21: 6 Because I spake unto **N** the Jezreelite, and 5022
21: 7 I will give thee the vineyard of **N** 5022
21: 8 that *were* in his city, dwelling with **N**. 5022
21: 9 a fast, and set **N** on high among the people: 5022
21:12 a fast, and set **N** on high among the people. 5022
21:13 *even* against **N**, in the presence of 5022
21:13 **N** did blaspheme God and the king. 5022
21:14 to Jezebel, saying, **N** is stoned, and is dead. 5022
21:15 when Jezebel heard that **N** was stoned, and 5022
21:15 take possession of the vineyard of **N** 5022
21:15 thee for money: for **N** is not alive, but dead. 5022
21:16 to pass, when Ahab heard that **N** was dead, 5022
21:16 go down to the vineyard of **N** the Jezreelite, 5022
21:18 behold, *he is* in the vineyard of **N**, 5022
21:19 the blood of **N** shall dogs lick thy blood, 5022
2Ki 9:21 met him in the portion of **N** the Jezreelite. 5022
9:25 cast him in the portion of the field of **N** 5022
9:26 I have seen yesterday the blood of **N**, 5022

NACHON'S (1) [NABOTH]
2Sa 6: 6 when they came to **N** threshingfloor, 5225

NACHOR (2) [NAHOR]
Jos 24: 2 the father of Abraham, and the father of **N**: 5152
Lk 3:34 *the son* of Thara, which was *the son* of **N**, *3493*

NACON See NACHON'S

NADAB (20)
Ex 6:23 she bare him **N**, and Abihu, Eleazar, and 5070
24: 1 **N**, and Abihu, and seventy of the elders of 5070
24: 9 **N**, and Abihu, and seventy of the elders of 5070
28: 1 **N** and Abihu, Eleazar and Ithamar, 5070
Lev 10: 1 **N** and Abihu, the sons of Aaron, took either 5070
Nu 3: 2 **N** the firstborn, and Abihu, Eleazar, and 5070
3: 4 **N** and Abihu died before the LORD, 5070
26:60 unto Aaron was born **N**, and Abihu, 5070
26:61 **N** and Abihu died, when they offered 5070
1Ki 14:20 and **N** his son reigned in his stead. 5070
15:25 **N** the son of Jeroboam *began* to reign over 5070
15:27 for **N** and all Israel laid siege to Gibbethon. 5070
15:31 Now the rest of the acts of **N**, and all that 5070
1Ch 2:28 And the sons of Shammai; **N**, and Abishur. 5070
2:30 the sons of **N**; Seled, and Appaim: but 5070
6: 3 **N**, and Abihu, Eleazar, and Ithamar. 5070
8:30 and Zur, and Kish, and Baal, and **N**, 5070
9:36 Zur, and Kish, and Baal, and Ner, and **N**, 5070
24: 1 **N**, and Abihu, Eleazar, and Ithamar. 5070
24: 2 **N** and Abihu died before their father, and 5070

NAGGAI See NAGGE

NAGGE (1)
Lk 3:25 *the son* of Esli, which was *the son* of **N**, *3477*

NAHALAL (1)
Jos 21:35 with her suburbs, **N** with her suburbs; 5096

NAHALIEL (2)
Nu 21:19 from Mattanah *to* **N**: and from Nahaliel *to* 5160
21:19 *to* Nahaliel: and from **N** *to* Bamoth: 5160

NAHALLAL (1)
Jos 19:15 **N**, and Shimron, and Idalah, and 5096

NAHALOL (1)
Jdg 1:30 of Kitron, nor the inhabitants of **N**; 5096

NAHAM (1)
1Ch 4:19 the sons of *his* wife Hodiah the sister of **N**, 5163

NAHAMANI (1)
Ne 7: 7 Azariah, Raamiah, **N**, Mordecai, Bilshan, 5167

NAHARAI (2)
2Sa 23:37 Zelek the Ammonite, **N** the Beerothite, 5171
1Ch 11:39 Zelek the Ammonite, **N** the Berothite, 5171

NAHASH (9)
1Sa 11: 1 **N** the Ammonite came up, and 5176
11: 1 all the men of Jabesh said unto **N**, Make a 5176
11: 2 **N** the Ammonite answered them, On this 5176
12:12 when ye saw that **N** the king of the children 5176
2Sa 10: 2 shew kindness unto Hanun the son of **N**, 5176
17:25 that went in to Abigail the daughter of **N**, 5176
17:27 that Shobi the son of **N** of Rabbah of 5176
1Ch 19: 1 that **N** the king of the children of Ammon 5176
19: 2 shew kindness unto Hanun the son of **N**, 5176

NAHATH (5)
Ge 36:13 **N**, and Zerah, Shammah, and Mizzah: 5184
36:17 duke **N**, duke Zerah, duke Shammah, 5184
1Ch 1:37 of Reuel; **N**, Zerah, Shammah, and Mizzah. 5184
6:26 of Elkanah; Zophai his son, and **N** his son, 5184
2Ch 31:13 **N**, and Asahel, and Jerimoth, and Jozabad, 5184

NAHBI (1)
Nu 13:14 the tribe of Naphtali, **N** the son of Vophsi. 5147

NAHOR (15) [NACHOR, NAHOR'S]
Ge 11:22 And Serug lived thirty years, and begat **N**: 5152
11:23 Serug lived after he begat **N** two hundred 5152
11:24 **N** lived nine and twenty years, and 5152
11:25 **N** lived after he begat Terah an hundred 5152
11:26 and begat Abram, **N**, and Haran. 5152
11:27 Terah begat Abram, **N**, and Haran; and 5152
11:29 Abram and **N** took them wives: the name of 5152
22:20 hath also born children unto thy brother **N**; 5152
22:23 these eight Milcah did bear to **N**, 5152
24:10 went to Mesopotamia, unto the city of **N**. 5152
24:15 son of Milcah, the wife of **N**, 5152
24:24 the son of Milcah, which she bare unto **N**. 5152
29: 5 unto them, Know ye Laban the son of **N**? 5152
31:53 The God of Abraham, and the God of **N**, 5152
1Ch 1:26 Serug, **N**, Terah, 5152

NAHOR'S (2) [NAHOR]
Ge 11:29 the name of **N** wife, Milcah, the daughter 5152
24:47 she said, The daughter of Bethuel, **N** son, 5152

NAHSHON (9)
Nu 1: 7 Of Judah; **N** the son of Amminadab. 5177
2: 3 **N** the son of Amminadab *shall be* captain 5177
7:12 the first day was **N** the son of Amminadab, 5177
7:17 this *was* the offering of **N** the son of 5177
10:14 over his host *was* **N** the son of Amminadab. 5177
Ru 4:20 Amminadab begat **N**, and Nahshon begat 5177
4:20 begat Nahshon, and **N** begat Salmon, 5177
1Ch 2:10 Amminadab begat **N**, prince of the children 5177
2:11 And **N** begat Salma, and Salma begat Boaz, 5177

NAHUM (1)
Na 1: 1 The book of the vision of **N** the Elkoshite. 5151

NAIL (8) [NAILING, NAILS]
Jdg 4:21 Jael Heber's wife took a **n** of the tent, and 3489
4:21 smote the **n** into his temples, and fastened *it* 3489
4:22 lay dead, and the **n** *was* in his temples. 3489
5:26 She put her hand to the **n**, and her right 3489
Ezr 9: 8 and to give us a **n** in his holy place, 3489
Isa 22:23 I will fasten him *as* a **n** in a sure place; and 3489
22:25 shall the **n** that is fastened in the sure place 3489
Zec 10: 4 out of him the **n**, out of him the battle bow, 3489

NAILING (1) [NAIL]
Col 2:14 and took it out of the way, **n** it to *his* cross; *4338*

NAILS (10) [NAIL]
Dt 21:12 she shall shave her head, and pare her **n**; 6856
1Ch 22: 3 David prepared iron in abundance for the **n** 4548
2Ch 3: 9 the weight of the **n** *was* fifty shekels of 4548
Ecc 12:11 as **n** fastened *by* the masters of assemblies, 4930
Isa 41: 7 he fastened it with **n**, *that* it should not be 4548
Jer 10: 4 they fasten it with **n** and with hammers, 4548
Da 4:33 and his **n** like birds' *claws.* 2953
7:19 teeth *were of* iron, and his **n** *of* brass; 2953
Jn 20:25 I shall see in his hands the print of the **n**, *2247*
20:25 and put my finger into the print of the **n**, *2247*

NAIN (1)
Lk 7:11 *day* after, *that* he went into a city called **N**; *3484*

NAIOTH (6)
1Sa 19:18 And he and Samuel went and dwelt in **N**. 5121
19:19 Behold, David *is* at **N** in Ramah. 5121
19:22 *one* said, Behold, *they be* at **N** in Ramah. 5121
19:23 he went thither to **N** in Ramah: and 5121
19:23 prophesied, until he came to **N** in Ramah. 5121
20: 1 David fled from **N** in Ramah, and came 5121

NAKED (47) [NAKEDNESS]

Ge 2:25 they were both **n**, the man and his wife, 6174
3: 7 and they knew that they *were* **n**; 5903
3:10 and I was afraid, because I *was* **n**; 5903
3:11 he said, Who told thee that thou *wast* **n**? 5903
Ex 32:25 when Moses saw that the people *were* **n**; 6544
32:25 (for Aaron had **made** them **n** unto *their* 6544
1Sa 19:24 lay down **n** all that day and all *that* night. 6174
2Ch 28:15 with the spoil clothed all *that were* **n** 4636
28:19 for he **made** Judah **n**, and transgressed sore 6544
Job 1:21 **N** came I out of my mother's womb, and 6174
1:21 mother's womb, and **n** shall I return thither: 6174
22: 6 and stripped the **n** of their clothing. 6174
24: 7 They cause the **n** to lodge without clothing, 6174
24:10 They cause *him* to go **n** without clothing, 6174
26: 6 Hell *is* **n** before him, and destruction hath 6174
Ecc 5:15 **n** shall he return to go as he came, and 6174
Isa 20: 2 And he did so, walking **n** and barefoot. 6174
20: 3 Like as my servant Isaiah hath walked **n** 6174
20: 4 young and old, **n** and barefoot, 6174
58: 7 when thou seest the **n**, that thou cover him; 6174
La 4:21 shalt be drunken, and shalt **make** thyself **n**. 6168
Eze 16: 7 is grown, whereas thou *wast* **n** and bare. 5903
16:22 when thou wast **n** and bare, *and* 5903
16:39 thy fair jewels, and leave thee **n** and bare. 5903
18: 7 and hath covered the **n** with a garment; 5903
18:16 and hath covered the **n** with a garment, 5903
23:29 thy labour, and shall leave thee **n** and bare: 5903
Hos 2: 3 Lest I strip her **n**, and set her as *in* the day 6174
Am 2:16 the mighty shall flee away **n** in that day, 6174
Mic 1: 8 I will wail and howl, I will go stript and **n**: 6174
1:11 inhabitant of Saphir, having *thy* shame **n**: 6181
Hab 3: 9 Thy bow was **made quite n**, 5783+6181
Mt 25:36 **N**, and ye clothed me: I was sick, and *1131*
25:38 and took *thee* in? or **n**, and clothed *thee?* *1131*
25:43 **n**, and ye clothed me not: sick, and *1131*
25:44 or **n**, or sick, or in prison, and did not *1131*
Mk 14:51 having a linen cloth cast about *his* **n** *body;* *1131*
14:52 left the linen cloth, and fled from them **n**. *1131*
Jn 21: 7 *his* fisher's coat unto him, (for he was **n**,) *1131*
Ac 19:16 so that *they* fled out of that house **n** and *1131*
1Co 4:11 and are **n**, and are buffeted, and have no *1130*
2Co 5: 3 that being clothed we shall not be found **n**. *1131*
Heb 4:13 but all *things are* **n** and opened unto *1131*
Jas 2:15 If a brother or sister be **n**, and destitute of *1131*
Rev 3:17 and miserable, and poor, and blind, and **n**: *1131*
16:15 lest he walk **n**, and they see his shame. *1131*
17:16 and shall make her desolate and **n**, and *1131*

NAKEDNESS (57) [NAKED]

Ge 9:22 saw the **n** of his father, and told his two 6172
9:23 and covered the **n** of their father; 6172
9:23 and they saw not their father's **n**. 6172
42: 9 to see the **n** of the land you are come. 6172
42:12 but to see the **n** of the land you are come. 6172
Ex 20:26 that thy **n** be not discovered thereon. 6172
28:42 them linen breeches to cover *their* **n**; 1320+6172
Lev 18: 6 is near of kin to him, to uncover *their* **n**: 6172
18: 7 The **n** of thy father, or the nakedness of thy 6172
18: 7 or the **n** of thy mother, shalt thou not 6172
18: 7 *is* thy mother; thou shalt not uncover her **n**. 6172
18: 8 The **n** of thy father's wife shalt thou not 6172
18: 8 shalt thou not uncover: it *is* thy father's **n**. 6172
18: 9 The **n** of thy sister, the daughter of thy 6172
18: 9 *even* their **n** thou shalt not uncover. 6172
18:10 The **n** of thy son's daughter, or of thy 6172
18:10 *even* their **n** thou shalt not uncover: 6172
18:10 shalt not uncover: for theirs *is* thine own **n**. 6172
18:11 The **n** of thy father's wife's daughter, 6172
18:11 *is* thy sister, thou shalt not uncover her **n**. 6172
18:12 Thou shalt not uncover the **n** of thy father's 6172
18:13 Thou shalt not uncover the **n** of thy 6172
18:14 Thou shalt not uncover the **n** of thy father's 6172
18:15 Thou shalt not uncover the **n** of thy 6172
18:15 son's wife; thou shalt not uncover her **n**. 6172
18:16 Thou shalt not uncover the **n** of thy 6172
18:16 of thy brother's wife: it *is* thy brother's **n**. 6172
18:17 Thou shalt not uncover the **n** of a woman 6172
18:17 her daughter's daughter, to uncover her **n**; 6172
18:18 to vex *her,* to uncover her **n**, besides 6172
18:19 approach unto a woman to uncover her **n**, 6172
20:11 father's wife hath uncovered his father's **n**: 6172
20:17 and see her **n**, and she see his nakedness; 6172
20:17 and see her nakedness, and she see his **n**; 6172
20:17 he hath uncovered his sister's **n**; he shall 6172
20:18 her sickness, and shall uncover her **n**; 6172
20:19 thou shalt not uncover the **n** of thy 6172
20:20 he hath uncovered his uncle's **n**: 6172
20:21 he hath uncovered his brother's **n**; 6172
Dt 28:48 in **n**, and in want of all *things:* and he shall 5903
1Sa 20:30 and unto the confusion of thy mother's **n**? 6172
Isa 47: 3 Thy **n** shall be uncovered, yea, thy shame 6172
La 1: 8 despise her, because they have seen her **n**: 6172
Eze 16: 8 my skirt over thee, and covered thy **n**: 6172
16:36 thy **n** discovered through thy whoredoms 6172
16:37 will discover thy **n** unto them, that they 6172
16:37 unto them, that they may see all thy **n**. 6172
22:10 thee have they discovered their father's **n**: 6172
23:10 These discovered her **n**: they took her sons 6172
23:18 her whoredoms, and discovered her **n**: 6172
23:29 the **n** of thy whoredoms shall be 6172
Hos 2: 9 my wool and my flax *given* to cover her **n**. 6172
Na 3: 5 I will shew the nations thy **n**, and 4626
Hab 2:15 that thou mayest look on their **n**! 4589
Ro 8:35 or famine, or **n**, or peril, or sword? *1132*
2Co 11:27 and thirst, in fastings often, in cold and **n**. *1132*
Rev 3:18 and *that* the shame of thy **n** do not appear; *1132*

NAME (928) [NAME'S, NAMED, NAMELY, NAMES, NAMETH]

Ge 2:11 The **n** of the first *is* Pison: that *is it* which 8034
2:13 the **n** of the second river *is* Gihon: the same 8034
2:14 the **n** of the third river *is* Hiddekel: that *is it* 8034
2:19 living creature, that *was* the **n** thereof. 8034
3:20 And Adam called his wife's **n** Eve; because 8034
4:17 builded a city, and called the **n** of the city, 8034
4:17 of the city, after the **n** of his son, Enoch. 8034
4:19 the **n** of the one *was* Adah, and the name of 8034
4:19 *was* Adah, and the **n** of the other Zillah. 8034
4:21 his brother's **n** *was* Jubal: he was the father 8034
4:25 she bare a son, and called his **n** Seth: 8034
4:26 he called his **n** Enos; then began *men* to 8034
4:26 began *men* to call upon the **n** of 8034
5: 2 blessed them, and called their **n** Adam, 8034
5: 3 after his image; and called his **n** Seth: 8034
5:29 he called his **n** Noah, saying, This *same* 8034
10:25 the **n** of one *was* Peleg; for in his days was 8034
10:25 and his brother's **n** *was* Joktan. 8034
11: 4 let us make us a **n**, lest we be scattered 8034
11: 9 Therefore is the **n** of it called Babel; 8034
11:29 the **n** of Abram's wife *was* Sarai; and 8034
11:29 the **n** of Nahor's wife, Milcah, the daughter 8034
12: 2 and I will bless thee, and make thy **n** great; 8034
12: 8 and called upon the **n** of the LORD. 8034
13: 4 there Abram called on the **n** of the LORD. 8034
16: 1 an Egyptian, whose **n** *was* Hagar. 8034
16:11 bear a son, and shalt call his **n** Ishmael; 8034
16:13 she called the **n** of the LORD that spake 8034
16:15 Abram called his son's **n**, which Hagar 8034
17: 5 Neither shall thy **n** any more be called 8034
17: 5 called Abram, but thy **n** shall be Abraham; 8034
17:15 thou shalt not call her **n** Sarai, but 8034
17:15 her name Sarai, but Sarah *shall* her **n** *be.* 8034
17:19 son indeed; and thou shalt call his **n** Isaac: 8034
19:22 Therefore the **n** of the city was called Zoar. 8034
19:37 firstborn bare a son, and called his **n** Moab: 8034
19:38 also bare a son, and called his **n** Ben-ammi: 8034
21: 3 Abraham called the **n** of his son that was 8034
21:33 called there on the **n** of the LORD, 8034
22:14 Abraham called the **n** of that place 8034
22:24 his concubine, whose **n** *was* Reumah, she 8034
24:29 had a brother, and his **n** *was* Laban: 8034
25: 1 took a wife, and her **n** *was* Keturah. 8034
25:25 a hairy garment; and they called his **n** Esau. 8034
25:26 on Esau's heel; and his **n** was called Jacob: 8034
25:30 I *am* faint: therefore was his **n** called Edom. 8034
26:20 he called the **n** of the well Esek; because 8034
26:21 that also: and he called the **n** of it Sitnah. 8034
26:22 he called the **n** of it Rehoboth; and he said, 8034
26:25 called upon the **n** of the LORD, and 8034
26:33 the **n** of the city *is* Beer-sheba unto this 8034
28:19 he called the **n** of that place Beth-el: but 8034
28:19 the **n** of *that* city *was called* Luz at the first. 8034
29:16 the **n** of the elder *was* Leah, and the name 8034
29:16 and the **n** of the younger *was* Rachel. 8034
29:32 bare a son, and she called his **n** Reuben: 8034
29:33 this *son* also: and she called his **n** Simeon. 8034
29:34 three sons: therefore was his **n** called Levi. 8034

Ge	29:35	therefore she called his **n** Judah; and	8034
	30: 6	me a son: therefore called she his **n** Dan.	8034
	30: 8	and she called his **n** Naphtali.	8034
	30:11	A troop cometh: and she called his **n** Gad.	8034
	30:13	call me blessed: and she called his **n** Asher.	8034
	30:18	my husband: and she called his **n** Issachar.	8034
	30:20	him six sons: and she called his **n** Zebulun.	8034
	30:21	bare a daughter, and called her **n** Dinah.	8034
	30:24	she called his **n** Joseph; and said,	8034
	31:48	Therefore was the **n** of it called Galeed;	8034
	32: 2	and he called the **n** of that place Mahanaim.	8034
	32:27	he said unto him, What *is* thy **n**? And he	8034
	32:28	Thy **n** shall be called no more Jacob, but	8034
	32:29	and said, Tell *me,* I pray thee, thy **n**.	8034
	32:29	*is* it *that* thou dost ask after my **n**?	8034
	32:30	Jacob called the **n** of the place Peniel: for I	8034
	33:17	the **n** of the place is called Succoth.	8034
	35: 8	and the **n** of it was called Allon-bachuth.	8034
	35:10	God said unto him, Thy **n** *is* Jacob:	8034
	35:10	thy **n** shall not be called any more Jacob,	8034
	35:10	any more Jacob, but Israel shall be thy **n**:	8034
	35:10	be thy name: and he called his **n** Israel.	8034
	35:15	Jacob called the **n** of the place where God	8034
	35:18	(for she died) that she called his **n** Ben-oni:	8034
	36:32	and the **n** of his city *was* Dinhabah.	8034
	36:35	in his stead: and the **n** of his city *was* Avith.	8034
	36:39	the **n** of his city *was* Pau; and his wife's	8034
	36:39	his wife's **n** *was* Mehetabel, the daughter of	8034
	38: 1	a certain Adullamite, whose **n** *was* Hirah.	8034
	38: 2	of a certain Canaanite, whose **n** *was* Shuah;	8034
	38: 3	and bare a son; and he called his **n** Er.	8034
	38: 4	and bare a son; and she called his **n** Onan.	8034
	38: 5	and bare a son; and called his **n** Shelah:	8034
	38: 6	for Er his firstborn, whose **n** *was* Tamar.	8034
	38:29	therefore his **n** was called Pharez.	8034
	38:30	upon his hand: and his **n** was called Zarah.	8034
	41:45	Pharaoh called Joseph's **n**	8034
	41:51	Joseph called the **n** of the firstborn	8034
	41:52	the **n** of the second called he Ephraim:	8034
	48: 6	shall be called after the **n** of their brethren	8034
	48:16	let my **n** be named on them, and the name	8034
	48:16	and the **n** of my fathers Abraham and Isaac;	8034
	50:11	wherefore the **n** of it was called	8034
Ex	1:15	of which the **n** of the one *was* Shiphrah,	8034
	1:15	*was* Shiphrah, and the **n** of the other Puah:	8034
	2:10	she called his **n** Moses: and she said,	8034
	2:22	*him* a son, and he called his **n** Gershom:	8034
	3:13	and they shall say to me, What *is* his **n**?	8034
	3:15	this *is* my **n** for ever, and this *is* my	8034
	5:23	since I came to Pharaoh to speak in thy **n**,	8034
	6: 3	by *the* **n** *of* God Almighty, but *by* my name	NIH
	6: 3	*by* my **n** JEHOVAH was I not known to	8034
	9:16	that my **n** may be declared throughout all	8034
	15: 3	*is* a man of war: the LORD *is* his **n**.	8034
	15:23	the **n** of it was called Marah.	8034
	16:31	the house of Israel called the **n** thereof	8034
	17: 7	he called the **n** of the place Massah, and	8034
	17:15	and called the **n** of it Jehovah-nissi:	8034
	18: 3	of which the **n** of the one *was* Gershom;	8034
	18: 4	the **n** of the other *was* Eliezer; for the God	8034
	20: 7	Thou shalt not take the **n** of the LORD thy	8034
	20: 7	hold him guiltless that taketh his **n** in vain.	8034
	20:24	in all places where I record my **n** I will	8034
	23:13	make no mention of the **n** of other gods,	8034
	23:21	your transgressions: for my **n** *is* in him.	8034
	28:21	every one with his **n** shall they be	8034
	31: 2	I have called by **n** Bezaleel the son of Uri,	8034
	33:12	I know thee by **n**, and thou hast also found	8034
	33:17	grace in my sight, and I know thee by **n**.	8034
	33:19	I will proclaim the **n** of the LORD before	8034
	34: 5	and proclaimed the **n** of the LORD.	8034
	34:14	for the LORD, whose **n** *is* Jealous, *is* a	8034
	35:30	the LORD hath called by **n** Bezaleel	8034
	39:14	every one with his **n**, according to	8034
Lev	18:21	neither shalt thou profane the **n** of thy God:	8034
	19:12	ye shall not swear by my **n** falsely,	8034
	19:12	neither shalt thou profane the **n** of thy God:	8034
	20: 3	my sanctuary, and to profane my holy **n**.	8034
	21: 6	and not profane the **n** of their God:	8034
	22: 2	that they profane not my holy **n** *in those*	8034
	22:32	Neither shall ye profane my holy **n**; but	8034
	24:11	son blasphemed the **n** *of the LORD,*	8034
	24:11	(and his mother's **n** *was* Shelomith,	8034
	24:16	he that blasphemeth the **n** of the LORD,	8034
	24:16	when he blasphemeth the **n** *of the LORD,*	8034
Nu	4:32	by **n** ye shall reckon the instruments of	8034
	6:27	they shall put my **n** upon the children of	8034
	11: 3	he called the **n** of the place Taberah:	8034
	11:26	the **n** of the one *was* Eldad, and the name of	8034
	11:26	*was* Eldad, and the **n** of the other Medad:	8034
	11:34	he called the **n** of that place	8034
	17: 2	write thou every man's **n** upon his rod.	8034
	17: 3	thou shalt write Aaron's **n** upon the rod of	8034
	21: 3	and he called the **n** of the place Hormah.	8034
	25:14	Now the **n** of the Israelite that was slain,	8034
	25:15	the **n** of the Midianitish woman that was	8034
	26:46	the **n** of the daughter of Asher *was* Sarah.	8034
	26:59	the **n** of Amram's wife *was* Jochebed,	8034
	27: 4	Why should the **n** of our father be done	8034
	32:42	and called it Nobah, after his own **n**.	8034
Dt	3:14	called them after his own **n**,	8034
	5:11	Thou shalt not take the **n** of the LORD thy	8034
	5:11	hold *him* guiltless that taketh his **n** in vain.	8034
	6:13	and serve him, and shalt swear by his **n**.	8034
	7:24	thou shalt destroy their **n** from under	8034
	9:14	and blot out their **n** from under heaven:	8034
	10: 8	and to bless in his **n**, unto this day.	8034
	10:20	him shalt thou cleave, and swear by his **n**.	8034
	12: 5	out of all your tribes to put his **n** there,	8034
	12:11	shall choose to cause his **n** to dwell there;	8034
	12:21	to put his **n** there be too far from thee,	8034
	14:23	which he shall choose to place his **n** there,	8034
	14:24	thy God shall choose to set his **n** there,	8034
	16: 2	LORD shall choose to place his **n** there.	8034
	16: 6	**n** *in,* there thou shalt sacrifice the passover	8034
	16:11	thy God hath chosen to place his **n** there.	8034
	18: 5	to stand to minister in the **n** of the LORD,	8034
	18: 7	he shall minister in the **n** of the LORD his	8034
	18:19	my words which he shall speak in my **n**,	8034
	18:20	shall presume to speak a word in my **n**,	8034
	18:20	or that shall speak in the **n** of other gods,	8034
	18:22	When a prophet speaketh in the **n** of	8034
	21: 5	and to bless in the **n** of the LORD;	8034
	22:14	bring up an evil **n** upon her, and say, I took	8034
	22:19	he hath brought up an evil **n** upon a virgin	8034
	25: 6	in the **n** of his brother which is dead,	8034
	25: 6	is dead, that his **n** be not put out of Israel.	8034
	25: 7	to raise up unto his brother a **n** in Israel,	8034
	25:10	his **n** shall be called in Israel, The house of	8034
	26: 2	thy God shall choose to place his **n** there.	8034
	26:19	in praise, and in **n**, and in honour;	8034
	28:10	that thou art called by the **n** of the LORD;	8034
	28:58	*thou* mayest fear this glorious and fearful **n**,	8034
	29:20	the LORD shall blot out his **n** from under	8034
	32: 3	Because I will publish the **n** of the LORD:	8034
Jos	5: 9	Wherefore the **n** of the place is called	8034
	7: 9	us round, and cut off our **n** from the earth:	8034
	7: 9	and what wilt thou do unto thy great **n**?	8034
	7:26	Wherefore the **n** of that place was called,	8034
	9: 9	because of the **n** of the LORD thy God:	8034
	14:15	the **n** of Hebron before *was* Kirjath-arba;	8034
	15:15	the **n** of Debir before *was* Kirjath-sepher.	8034
	19:47	Dan, after the **n** of Dan their father.	8034
	21: 9	these cities which are *here* mentioned by **n**,	8034
	23: 7	neither make mention of the **n** of their	8034
Jdg	1:10	(now the **n** of Hebron before *was*	8034
	1:11	the **n** of Debir before *was* Kirjath-sepher.	8034
	1:17	and the **n** of the city was called Hormah.	8034
	1:23	(Now the **n** of the city before *was* Luz.)	8034
	1:26	built a city, and called the **n** thereof Luz:	8034
	1:26	which *is* the **n** thereof unto this day.	8034
	2: 5	And they called the **n** of that place Bochim:	8034
	8:31	him a son, whose **n** he called Abimelech.	8034
	13: 2	of the Danites, whose **n** *was* Manoah;	8034
	13: 6	whence he *was,* neither told he me his **n**:	8034
	13:17	the angel of the LORD, What *is* thy **n**,	8034
	13:18	Why askest thou thus after my **n**, seeing it	8034
	13:24	bare a son, and called his **n** Samson:	8034
	15:19	wherefore he called the **n** thereof	8034
	16: 4	the valley of Sorek, whose **n** *was* Delilah.	8034
	17: 1	of mount Ephraim, whose **n** *was* Micah.	8034
	18:29	they called the **n** of the city Dan, after	8034
	18:29	after the **n** of Dan their father, who was	8034
	18:29	howbeit the **n** of the city *was* Laish at	8034
Ru	1: 2	the **n** of the man *was* Elimelech, and	8034
	1: 2	the **n** of his wife Naomi, and the name of	8034
	1: 2	the **n** of his two sons Mahlon and Chilion,	8034
	1: 4	the **n** of the one *was* Orpah, and the name	8034

Ru 1: 4 one *was* Orpah, and the **n** of the other Ruth: 8034
2: 1 family of Elimelech; and his **n** *was* Boaz. 8034
2:19 The man's **n** with whom I wrought to day 8034
4: 5 to raise up the **n** of the dead upon his 8034
4:10 to raise up the **n** of the dead upon his 8034
4:10 that the **n** of the dead be not cut off from 8034
4:14 that his **n** may be famous in Israel. 8034
4:17 the *women her* neighbours gave it a **n**, 8034
4:17 born to Naomi; and they called his **n** Obed: 8034
1Sa 1: 1 of mount Ephraim, and his **n** *was* Elkanah, 8034
1: 2 the **n** of the one *was* Hannah, and the name 8034
1: 2 and the **n** of the other Peninnah: 8034
1:20 she bare a son, and called his **n** Samuel, 8034
7:12 and Shen, and called the **n** of it Eben-ezer, 8034
8: 2 Now the **n** of his firstborn was Joel; and 8034
8: 2 was Joel; and the **n** of his second, Abiah: 8034
9: 1 whose **n** *was* Kish, the son of Abiel, the son 8034
9: 2 he had a son, whose **n** *was* Saul, a choice 8034
14: 4 the **n** of the one *was* Bozez, and the name 8034
14: 4 *was* Bozez, and the **n** of the other Seneh. 8034
14:49 *were these;* the **n** of the firstborn Merab, 8034
14:49 and the **n** of the younger Michal: 8034
14:50 the **n** of Saul's wife *was* Ahinoam, 8034
14:50 the **n** of the captain of his host *was* Abner, 8034
16: 3 thou shalt anoint unto me *him* whom I **n** 559
17:12 of Beth-lehem-judah, whose **n** *was* Jesse; 8034
17:23 the Philistine of Gath, Goliath by **n**, 8034
17:45 I come to thee in the **n** of the LORD of 8034
18:30 of Saul; so that his **n** was much set by. 8034
20:42 sworn both of us in the **n** of the LORD, 8034
21: 7 his **n** *was* Doeg, an Edomite, the chiefest of 8034
24:21 that thou wilt not destroy my **n** out of my 8034
25: 3 Now the **n** of the man *was* Nabal; and 8034
25: 3 *was* Nabal; and the **n** of his wife Abigail: 8034
25: 5 go to Nabal, and greet him in my **n**: 8034
25: 9 to all those words in the **n** of David, 8034
25:25 for as his **n** *is,* so *is* he; Nabal *is* his name, 8034
25:25 *is* he; Nabal *is* his **n**, and folly *is* with him: 8034
28: 8 bring me *him* up, whom I shall **n** unto thee. 559
2Sa 3: 7 whose **n** *was* Rizpah, the daughter of Aiah: 8034
4: 2 the **n** of the one *was* Baanah, and the name 8034
4: 2 *was* Baanah, and the **n** of the other Rechab, 8034
4: 4 And his **n** *was* Mephibosheth. 8034
5:20 Therefore he called the **n** of that place 8034
6: 2 whose **n** is called *by* the name of 8034
6: 2 whose name is called *by* the **n** of 8034
6: 8 he called *the* **n** of the place Perez-uzzah to NIH
6:18 he blessed the people in the **n** of 8034
7: 9 of thy sight, and have made thee a great **n**, 8034
7: 9 like unto the **n** of the great *men* that *are* in 8034
7:13 He shall build a house for my **n**, and I will 8034
7:23 to make him a **n**, and to do for you great 8034
7:26 And let thy **n** be magnified for ever, saying, 8034
8:13 David gat *him* a **n** when he returned from 8034
9: 2 house of Saul a servant whose **n** *was* Ziba. 8034
9:12 had a young son, whose **n** *was* Micha. 8034
12:24 bare a son, and he called his **n** Solomon: 8034
12:25 he called his **n** Jedidiah, because of 8034
12:28 I take the city, and it be called after my **n**. 8034
13: 1 had a fair sister, whose **n** *was* Tamar; 8034
13: 3 Amnon had a friend, whose **n** *was* Jonadab, 8034
14: 7 shall not leave to my husband *neither* **n** nor 8034
14:27 and one daughter, whose **n** *was* Tamar: 8034
16: 5 whose **n** *was* Shimei, the son of Gera: 8034
17:25 a man's son, whose **n** *was* Ithra an Israelite, 8034
18:18 I have no son to keep my **n** in 8034
18:18 he called the pillar after his own **n**: and it is 8034
20: 1 whose **n** *was* Sheba, the son of Bichri, 8034
20:21 Sheba the son of Bichri by **n**, 8034
22:50 and I will sing praises unto thy **n**. 8034
23:18 and slew them, and had the **n** among three. 8034
23:22 and had the **n** among three mighty *men.* 8034
1Ki 1:47 God make the **n** of Solomon better than thy 8034
1:47 the name of Solomon better than thy **n**, 8034
3: 2 there was no house built unto the **n** of 8034
5: 3 **n** of the LORD his God for the wars 8034
5: 5 I purpose to build a house unto the **n** of 8034
5: 5 thy room, he shall build a house unto my **n**. 8034
7:21 right pillar, and called the **n** thereof Jachin: 8034
7:21 left pillar, and called the **n** thereof Boaz. 8034
8:16 build a house, that my **n** might be therein; 8034
8:17 for the **n** of the LORD God of Israel. 8034
8:18 in thine heart to build a house unto my **n**, 8034
8:19 he shall build the house unto my **n**. 8034
8:20 have built a house for the **n** of the LORD 8034
8:29 which thou hast said, My **n** shall be there: 8034
8:33 confess thy **n**, and pray, and 8034
8:35 confess thy **n**, and turn from their sin, 8034
8:42 (For they shall hear of thy great **n**, and of 8034
8:43 that all people of the earth may know thy **n**, 8034
8:43 which I have builded, is called by thy **n**. 8034
8:44 *toward* the house that I have built for thy **n**: 8034
8:48 and the house which I have built for thy **n**: 8034
9: 3 thou hast built, to put my **n** there for ever; 8034
9: 7 which I have hallowed for my **n**, 8034
10: 1 Solomon concerning the **n** of the LORD, 8034
11:26 whose mother's **n** *was* Zeruah, a widow 8034
11:36 which I have chosen me to put my **n** there. 8034
13: 2 born unto the house of David, Josiah by **n**; 8034
14:21 of all the tribes of Israel, to put his **n** there. 8034
14:21 his mother's **n** *was* Naamah an 8034
14:31 his mother's **n** *was* Naamah an 8034
15: 2 his mother's **n** *was* Maachah, the daughter 8034
15:10 his mother's **n** *was* Maachah, the daughter 8034
16:24 and called the **n** of the city which he built, 8034
16:24 after the **n** of Shemer, owner of the hill, 8034
18:24 call ye on the **n** of your gods, and I will call 8034
18:24 and I will call on the **n** of the LORD: 8034
18:25 call on the **n** of your gods, but put no fire 8034
18:26 called on the **n** of Baal from morning even 8034
18:31 LORD came, saying, Israel shall be thy **n**: 8034
18:32 *with* the stones he built an altar in the **n** of 8034
21: 8 So she wrote letters in Ahab's **n**, and 8034
22:16 *that which is* true in the **n** of the LORD? 8034
22:42 his mother's **n** *was* Azubah the daughter of 8034
2Ki 2:24 and cursed them in the **n** of the LORD. 8034
5:11 call on the **n** of the LORD his God, and 8034
8:26 his mother's **n** *was* Athaliah, the daughter 8034
12: 1 his mother's **n** *was* Zibiah of Beer-sheba. 8034
14: 2 his mother's **n** *was* Jehoaddan of 8034
14: 7 and called the **n** of it Joktheel unto this day. 8034
14:27 blot out the **n** of Israel from under heaven: 8034
15: 2 his mother's **n** *was* Jecholiah of Jerusalem. 8034
15:33 his mother's **n** *was* Jerusha, the daughter of 8034
18: 2 His mother's **n** also *was* Abi, the daughter 8034
21: 1 And his mother's **n** *was* Hephzi-bah. 8034
21: 4 LORD said, In Jerusalem will I put my **n**. 8034
21: 7 all tribes of Israel, will I put my **n** for ever: 8034
21:19 his mother's **n** *was* Meshullemeth, 8034
22: 1 his mother's **n** *was* Jedidah, the daughter of 8034
23:27 house of which I said, My **n** shall be there. 8034
23:31 his mother's **n** *was* Hamutal, the daughter 8034
23:34 turned his **n** *to* Jehoiakim, and took 8034
23:36 his mother's **n** *was* Zebudah, the daughter 8034
24: 8 his mother's **n** *was* Nehushta, the daughter 8034
24:17 in his stead, and changed his **n** *to* Zedekiah. 8034
24:18 his mother's **n** *was* Hamutal, the daughter 8034
1Ch 1:19 the **n** of the one *was* Peleg; because in his 8034
1:19 and his brother's **n** *was* Joktan. 8034
1:43 and the **n** of his city *was* Dinhabah. 8034
1:46 in his stead: and the **n** of his city *was* Avith. 8034
1:50 the **n** of his city *was* Pai; and his wife's 8034
1:50 his wife's **n** *was* Mehetabel, the daughter of 8034
2:26 had also another wife, whose **n** *was* Atarah; 8034
2:29 the **n** of the wife of Abishur *was* Abihail, 8034
2:34 a servant, an Egyptian, whose **n** *was* Jarha. 8034
4: 3 and the **n** of their sister *was* Hazelelponi: 8034
4: 9 his mother called his **n** Jabez, saying, 8034
4:41 these written by **n** came in the days of 8034
7:15 whose sister's **n** was Maachah;) 8034
7:15 and the **n** of the second *was* Zelophehad: 8034
7:16 bare a son, and she called his **n** Peresh; 8034
7:16 the **n** of his brother *was* Sheresh; and 8034
7:23 he called his **n** Beriah, because it went evil 8034
8:29 of Gibeon; whose wife's **n** *was* Maachah: 8034
9:35 Jehiel, whose wife's **n** *was* Maachah: 8034
11:20 he slew *them,* and had a **n** among the three. 8034
11:24 and had the **n** among the three mighties. 8034
12:31 which were expressed by **n**, to come and 8034
13: 6 the cherubims, whose **n** is called *on it.* 8034
14:11 they called the **n** of that place 8034
16: 2 he blessed the people in the **n** of 8034
16: 8 thanks unto the LORD, call upon his **n**, 8034
16:10 Glory ye in his holy **n**: let the heart of them 8034
16:29 unto the LORD the glory due unto his **n**: 8034
16:35 that *we* may give thanks to thy holy **n**, 8034
16:41 were chosen, who were expressed by **n**, 8034
17: 8 have made thee a **n** like the name of 8034

1Ch	17:8	have made thee a name like the **n** of	8034
	17:21	to make thee a **n** of greatness and	8034
	17:24	that thy **n** may be magnified for ever,	8034
	21:19	which he spake in the **n** of the LORD.	8034
	22:7	a house unto the **n** of the LORD my God:	8034
	22:8	thou shalt not build a house unto my **n**,	8034
	22:9	for his **n** shall be Solomon, and I will give	8034
	22:10	He shall build a house for my **n**; and	8034
	22:19	into the house that is *to be* built to the **n** of	8034
	23:13	unto him, and to bless in his **n** for ever.	8034
	28:3	Thou shalt not build a house for my **n**,	8034
	29:13	we thank thee, and praise thy glorious **n**.	8034
	29:16	for thine holy **n** *cometh* of thine hand,	8034
2Ch	2:1	to build a house for the **n** of the LORD,	8034
	2:4	I build a house to the **n** of the LORD my	8034
	3:17	called the **n** of *that on* the right hand	8034
	3:17	and the **n** of *that on* the left Boaz.	8034
	6:5	build a house *in,* that my **n** might be there;	8034
	6:6	that my **n** might be there;	8034
	6:7	for the **n** of the LORD God of Israel.	8034
	6:8	in thine heart to build a house for my **n**,	8034
	6:9	thy loins, he shall build the house for my **n**.	8034
	6:10	have built the house for the **n** of	8034
	6:20	hast said that *thou* wouldest put thy **n** there;	8034
	6:24	shall return and confess thy **n**, and pray and	8034
	6:26	confess thy **n**, *and* turn from their sin,	8034
	6:33	that all people of the earth may know thy **n**,	8034
	6:33	house which I have built is called by thy **n**.	8034
	6:34	the house which I have built for thy **n**;	8034
	6:38	the house which I have built for thy **n**:	8034
	7:14	If my people, which are called by my **n**,	8034
	7:16	this house, that my **n** may be there for ever:	8034
	7:20	which I have sanctified for my **n**,	8034
	12:13	of all the tribes of Israel, to put his **n** there.	8034
	12:13	his mother's **n** *was* Naamah an	8034
	13:2	His mother's **n** also *was* Michaiah	8034
	14:11	and in thy **n** we go against this multitude.	8034
	18:15	but the truth to me in the **n** of the LORD?	8034
	20:8	built thee a sanctuary therein for thy **n**,	8034
	20:9	in thy presence, (for thy **n** *is* in this house,)	8034
	20:26	the **n** of the same place was called,	8034
	20:31	his mother's **n** *was* Azubah the daughter of	8034
	22:2	His mother's **n** also *was* Athaliah	8034
	24:1	His mother's **n** also *was* Zibiah of	8034
	25:1	his mother's **n** *was* Jehoaddan of	8034
	26:3	His mother's **n** also *was* Jecoliah of	8034
	26:8	his **n** spread abroad even to the entering in	8034
	26:15	his **n** spread far abroad; for he was	8034
	27:1	His mother's **n** also *was* Jerushah,	8034
	28:9	the LORD was there, whose **n** *was* Oded:	8034
	28:15	the men which were expressed by **n** rose	8034
	29:1	his mother's **n** *was* Abijah, the daughter of	8034
	31:19	the men that were expressed by **n**,	8034
	33:4	In Jerusalem shall my **n** be for ever.	8034
	33:7	the tribes of Israel, will I put my **n** for ever:	8034
	33:18	him in the **n** of the LORD God of Israel,	8034
	36:4	Jerusalem, and turned his **n** *to* Jehoiakim.	8034
Ezr	2:61	the Gileadite, and was called after their **n**:	8034
	5:1	and Jerusalem in the **n** of the God of Israel,	8036
	5:14	they *were* delivered unto *one,* whose **n** *was*	8036
	6:12	the God that hath caused his **n** to dwell	8036
	8:20	all of them were expressed by **n**.	8034
Ne	1:9	place that I have chosen to set my **n** there.	8034
	1:11	of thy servants, who desire to fear thy **n**:	8034
	7:63	*to* wife, and was called after their **n**.	8034
	9:5	blessed be thy glorious **n**, which *is* exalted	8034
	9:7	and gavest him the **n** of Abraham;	8034
	9:10	So didst thou get thee a **n**, as *it is* this day.	8034
Est	2:5	whose **n** *was* Mordecai, the son of Jair,	8034
	2:14	in her, and *that* she were called by **n**.	8034
	2:22	certified the king *thereof* in Mordecai's **n**.	8034
	3:12	in the **n** of king Ahasuerus was it written,	8034
	8:8	in the king's **n**, and seal *it* with the king's	8034
	8:8	the writing which *is* written in the king's **n**,	8034
	8:10	And he wrote in the king Ahasuerus' **n**, and	8034
	9:26	called these days Purim after the **n** of Pur.	8034
Job	1:1	a man in the land of Uz, whose **n** *was* Job;	8034
	1:21	*away;* blessed be the **n** of the LORD.	8034
	18:17	and he shall have no **n** in the street.	8034
	42:14	he called the **n** of the first, Jemima; and	8034
	42:14	the **n** of the second, Kezia; and the name of	8034
	42:14	and the **n** of the third, Keren-happuch.	8034
Ps	5:11	let them also that love thy **n** be joyful in	8034
	7:17	will sing *praise* to the **n** of the LORD	8034
	8:1	how excellent *is* thy **n** in all the earth!	8034
	8:9	how excellent *is* thy **n** in all the earth!	8034
	9:2	I will sing *praise* to thy **n**, O thou most	8034
	9:5	thou hast put out their **n** for ever and ever.	8034
	9:10	they that know thy **n** will put their trust in	8034
	18:49	the heathen, and sing *praises* unto thy **n**.	8034
	20:1	the **n** of the God of Jacob defend thee;	8034
	20:5	in the **n** of our God we will set up *our*	8034
	20:7	we will remember the **n** of the LORD our	8034
	22:22	I will declare thy **n** unto my brethren: in	8034
	29:2	unto the LORD the glory due unto his **n**;	8034
	33:21	because we have trusted in his holy **n**.	8034
	34:3	with me, and let us exalt his **n** together.	8034
	41:5	of me, When shall he die, and his **n** perish?	8034
	44:5	through thy **n** will we tread them under that	8034
	44:8	all the day long, and praise thy **n** for ever.	8034
	44:20	If we have forgotten the **n** of our God, or	8034
	45:17	I will make thy **n** to be remembered in all	8034
	48:10	According to thy **n**, O God, so *is* thy praise	8034
	52:9	thou hast done *it:* and I will wait on thy **n**;	8034
	54:1	by thy **n**, and judge me by thy strength.	8034
	54:6	I will praise thy **n**, O LORD; for *it is*	8034
	61:5	*me* the heritage of those that fear thy **n**.	8034
	61:8	So will I sing *praise* unto thy **n** for ever,	8034
	63:4	I live: I will lift up my hands in thy **n**.	8034
	66:2	Sing forth the honour of his **n**: make his	8034
	66:4	sing unto thee; they shall sing *to* thy **n**.	8034
	68:4	Sing unto God, sing *praises to* his **n**:	8034
	68:4	that rideth upon the heavens by his **n** JAH,	8034
	69:30	I will praise the **n** of God with a song; and	8034
	69:36	and they that love his **n** shall dwell therein.	8034
	72:17	His **n** shall endure for ever: his name shall	8034
	72:17	his **n** shall be continued as long as the sun:	8034
	72:19	blessed *be* his glorious **n** for ever: and	8034
	74:7	the dwelling place of thy **n** to the ground.	8034
	74:10	shall the enemy blaspheme thy **n** for ever?	8034
	74:18	the foolish people have blasphemed thy **n**.	8034
	74:21	let the poor and needy praise thy **n**.	8034
	75:1	for *that* thy **n** *is* near thy wondrous works	8034
	76:1	*is* God known: his **n** *is* great in Israel.	8034
	79:6	kingdoms that have not called upon thy **n**.	8034
	79:9	God of our salvation, for the glory of thy **n**:	8034
	80:18	quicken us, and we will call upon thy **n**.	8034
	83:4	that the **n** of Israel may be no more in	8034
	83:16	that they may seek thy **n**, O LORD.	8034
	83:18	that thou, whose **n** alone *is* JEHOVAH,	8034
	86:9	before thee, O Lord; and shall glorify thy **n**.	8034
	86:11	in thy truth: unite my heart to fear thy **n**.	8034
	86:12	and I will glorify thy **n** for evermore.	8034
	89:12	Tabor and Hermon shall rejoice in thy **n**.	8034
	89:16	In thy **n** shall they rejoice all the day: and	8034
	89:24	and in my **n** shall his horn be exalted.	8034
	91:14	him on high, because he hath known my **n**.	8034
	92:1	to sing *praises* unto thy **n**, O most High:	8034
	96:2	Sing unto the LORD, bless his **n**;	8034
	96:8	unto the LORD the glory due unto his **n**:	8034
	99:3	Let them praise thy great and terrible **n**;	8034
	99:6	Samuel among them that call upon his **n**;	8034
	100:4	be thankful unto him, *and* bless his **n**.	8034
	102:15	So the heathen shall fear the **n** of	8034
	102:21	To declare the **n** of the LORD in Zion,	8034
	103:1	and all that is within me, *bless* his holy **n**.	8034
	105:1	thanks unto the LORD; call upon his **n**:	8034
	105:3	Glory ye in his holy **n**: let the heart of them	8034
	106:47	to give thanks unto thy holy **n**, *and*	8034
	109:13	in the generation following let their **n** be	8034
	111:9	for ever: holy and reverend *is* his **n**.	8034
	113:1	of the LORD, praise the **n** of the LORD.	8034
	113:2	Blessed be the **n** of the LORD from this	8034
	113:3	the same the LORD'S **n** *is* to be praised.	8034
	115:1	not unto us, but unto thy **n** give glory,	8034
	116:4	called I upon the **n** of the LORD;	8034
	116:13	and call upon the **n** of the LORD.	8034
	116:17	and will call upon the **n** of the LORD.	8034
	118:10	in the **n** of the LORD will I destroy them.	8034
	118:11	in the **n** of the LORD I will destroy them.	8034
	118:12	for in the **n** of the LORD I will destroy	8034
	118:26	Blessed *be* he that cometh in the **n** of	8034
	119:55	I have remembered thy **n**, O LORD, in	8034
	119:132	thou usest to do unto those that love thy **n**.	8034
	122:4	to give thanks unto the **n** of the LORD.	8034
	124:8	Our help *is* in the **n** of the LORD,	8034
	129:8	we bless you in the **n** of the LORD.	8034
	135:1	Praise ye the **n** of the LORD; praise *him,*	8034

Ps	135: 3	sing *praises* unto his **n**; for *it is* pleasant.	8034
	135:13	Thy **n**, O LORD, *endureth* for ever; *and*	8034
	138: 2	praise thy **n** for thy lovingkindness and	8034
	138: 2	hast magnified thy word above all thy **n**.	8034
	139:20	*and* thine enemies take *thy* **n** in vain.	NIH
	140:13	the righteous shall give thanks unto thy **n**:	8034
	142: 7	soul out of prison, that *I* may praise thy **n**:	8034
	145: 1	and I will bless thy **n** for ever and ever.	8034
	145: 2	and I will praise thy **n** for ever and ever.	8034
	145:21	let all flesh bless his holy **n** for ever and	8034
	148: 5	Let them praise the **n** of the LORD: for he	8034
	148:13	Let them praise the **n** of the LORD:	8034
	148:13	for his **n** alone *is* excellent; his glory *is*	8034
	149: 3	Let them praise his **n** in the dance: let them	8034
Pr	10: 7	*is* blessed: but the **n** of the wicked shall rot.	8034
	18:10	The **n** of the LORD *is* a strong tower:	8034
	21:24	Proud *and* haughty scorner *is* his **n**,	8034
	22: 1	A *good* **n** *is* rather to be chosen than great	8034
	30: 4	what *is* his **n**, and what *is* his son's name,	8034
	30: 4	and what *is* his son's **n**, if thou canst tell?	8034
	30: 9	steal, and take the **n** of my God *in vain*.	8034
Ecc	6: 4	and his **n** shall be covered with darkness.	8034
	7: 1	A *good* **n** *is* better than precious ointment;	8034
SS	1: 3	ointments thy **n** *is as* ointment poured forth,	8034
Isa	4: 1	only let us be called by thy **n**, to take away	8034
	7:14	bear a Son, and shall call his **n** Immanuel.	8034
	8: 3	to me, Call his **n** Maher-shalal-hash-baz.	8034
	9: 6	his **n** shall be called Wonderful,	8034
	12: 4	ye say, Praise the LORD, call upon his **n**,	8034
	12: 4	make mention that his **n** *is* exalted.	8034
	14:22	cut off from Babylon the **n**, and remnant,	8034
	18: 7	to the place of the **n** of the LORD of	8034
	24:15	*even* the **n** of the LORD God of Israel in	8034
	25: 1	I will exalt thee, I will praise thy **n**;	8034
	26: 8	the desire of *our* soul *is* to thy **n**, and to	8034
	26:13	thee only will we make mention of thy **n**.	8034
	29:23	they shall sanctify my **n**, and sanctify	8034
	30:27	the **n** of the LORD cometh from far,	8034
	41:25	rising of the sun shall he call upon my **n**:	8034
	42: 8	that *is* my **n**: and my glory will I not give to	8034
	43: 1	redeemed thee, I have called *thee* by thy **n**;	8034
	43: 7	*Even* every one that is called by my **n**: for I	8034
	44: 5	another shall call *himself* by the **n** of Jacob;	8034
	44: 5	and surname *himself* by the **n** of Israel.	8034
	45: 3	the LORD, which call *thee* by thy **n**,	8034
	45: 4	I have even called thee by thy **n**:	8034
	47: 4	our redeemer, the LORD of hosts *is* his **n**,	8034
	48: 1	which are called by the **n** of Israel, and	8034
	48: 1	which swear by the **n** of the LORD, and	8034
	48: 2	of Israel; The LORD of hosts *is* his **n**.	8034
	48:11	will I do *it*: for how should *my* **n** be	NIH
	48:19	his **n** should not have been cut off nor	8034
	49: 1	my mother hath he made mention of my **n**.	8034
	50:10	let him trust in the **n** of the LORD, and	8034
	51:15	The LORD of hosts *is* his **n**.	8034
	52: 5	my **n** continually every day *is* blasphemed.	8034
	52: 6	Therefore my people shall know my **n**:	8034
	54: 5	the LORD of hosts *is* his **n**; and	8034
	55:13	it shall be to the LORD for a **n**, for an	8034
	56: 5	a **n** better than *of* sons and *of* daughters:	8034
	56: 5	I will give them an everlasting **n**, that shall	8034
	56: 6	serve him, and to love the **n** of the LORD,	8034
	57:15	that inhabiteth eternity, whose **n** *is* Holy;	8034
	59:19	So shall they fear the **n** of the LORD from	8034
	60: 9	unto the **n** of the LORD thy God, and	8034
	62: 2	thou shalt be called by a new **n**, which	8034
	62: 2	which the mouth of the LORD shall **n**.	5344
	63:12	to make himself an everlasting **n**?	8034
	63:14	thy people, to make thyself a glorious **n**.	8034
	63:16	our redeemer; thy **n** *is* from everlasting.	8034
	63:19	over them; they were not called by thy **n**.	8034
	64: 2	to make thy **n** known to thine adversaries,	8034
	64: 7	*there is* none that calleth upon thy **n**,	8034
	65: 1	unto a nation *that* was not called by my **n**.	8034
	65:15	ye shall leave your **n** for a curse unto my	8034
	65:15	and call his servants by another **n**:	8034
	66:22	so shall your seed and your **n** remain.	8034
Jer	3:17	to the **n** of the LORD, to Jerusalem:	8034
	7:10	which is called by my **n**, and say,	8034
	7:11	Is this house, which is called by my **n**,	8034
	7:12	where I set my **n** at the first, and see what I	8034
	7:14	which is called by my **n**, wherein ye trust,	8034
	7:30	in the house which is called by my **n**,	8034
	10: 6	thou *art* great, and thy **n** *is* great in might.	8034
	10:16	The LORD of hosts *is* his **n**.	8034
	10:25	and upon the families that call not on thy **n**:	8034
	11:16	The LORD called thy **n**, A green olive	8034
	11:19	that his **n** may be no more remembered.	8034
	11:21	Prophesy not in the **n** of the LORD,	8034
	12:16	to swear by my **n**, The LORD liveth;	8034
	13:11	for a **n**, and for a praise, and for a glory:	8034
	14: 9	the midst of us, and we are called by thy **n**;	8034
	14:14	The prophets prophesy lies in my **n**:	8034
	14:15	the prophets that prophesy in my **n**,	8034
	15:16	for I am called by thy **n**, O LORD God of	8034
	16:21	they shall know that my **n** *is* The LORD.	8034
	20: 3	The LORD hath not called thy **n** Pashur,	8034
	20: 9	of him, nor speak any more in his **n**.	8034
	23: 6	this *is* his **n** whereby he shall be called,	8034
	23:25	that prophesy lies in my **n**, saying, I have	8034
	23:27	**n** by their dreams which they tell every	8034
	23:27	as their fathers have forgotten my **n** for	8034
	25:29	evil on the city which is called by my **n**,	8034
	26: 9	Why hast thou prophesied in the **n** of	8034
	26:16	for he hath spoken to us in the **n** of	8034
	26:20	that prophesied in the **n** of the LORD,	8034
	27:15	yet they prophesy a lie in my **n**;	8034
	29: 9	they prophesy falsely unto you in my **n**:	8034
	29:21	which prophesy a lie unto you in my **n**;	8034
	29:23	have spoken lying words in my **n**, which I	8034
	29:25	Because thou hast sent letters in thy **n** unto	8034
	31:35	thereof roar; The LORD of hosts *is* his **n**:	8034
	32:18	Mighty God, the LORD of hosts, *is* his **n**,	8034
	32:20	and hast made thee a **n**, as *at* this day;	8034
	32:34	which is called by my **n**, to defile it.	8034
	33: 2	to establish it; the LORD *is* his **n**;	8034
	33: 9	it shall be to me a **n** of joy, a praise and	8034
	33:16	this *is the* **n** wherewith she shall be called,	NIH
	34:15	me in the house which is called by my **n**.	8034
	34:16	ye turned and polluted my **n**, and	8034
	37:13	whose **n** *was* Irijah, the son of Shelemiah,	8034
	44:16	hast spoken unto us in the **n** of the LORD,	8034
	44:26	Behold, I have sworn by my great **n**,	8034
	44:26	that my **n** shall no more be named in	8034
	46:18	the King, whose **n** *is* the LORD of hosts,	8034
	48:15	the King, whose **n** *is* the LORD of hosts.	8034
	48:17	all ye that know his **n**, say, How is	8034
	50:34	*is* strong; the LORD of hosts *is* his **n**:	8034
	51:19	the LORD of hosts *is* his **n**.	8034
	51:57	the King, whose **n** *is* the LORD of hosts.	8034
	52: 1	his mother's **n** *was* Hamutal the daughter of	8034
La	3:55	I called upon thy **n**, O LORD, out of	8034
Eze	20:29	the **n** thereof is called Bamah unto this day.	8034
	20:39	pollute ye my holy **n** no more with your	8034
	24: 2	Son of man, write thee the **n** of the day,	8034
	36:20	they went, they profaned my holy **n**,	8034
	36:21	I had pity for mine holy **n**, which the house	8034
	36:23	I will sanctify my great **n**, which was	8034
	39: 7	So will I make my holy **n** known in	8034
	39: 7	I will not let *them* pollute my holy **n** any	8034
	39:16	also the **n** of the city *shall be* Hamonah.	8034
	39:25	of Israel, and will be jealous for my holy **n**;	8034
	43: 7	my holy **n**, shall the house of Israel no	8034
	43: 8	they have even defiled my holy **n** by their	8034
	48:35	the **n** of the city from *that* day *shall be*, The	8034
Da	1: 7	for he gave unto Daniel *the* **n** *of*	NIH
	2:20	Blessed be the **n** of God for ever and ever:	8036
	2:26	said to Daniel, whose **n** *was* Belteshazzar,	8036
	4: 8	whose **n** *was* Belteshazzar, according to	8036
	4: 8	according to the **n** of my god, and in whom	8036
	4:19	Daniel, whose **n** *was* Belteshazzar,	8036
	9: 6	which spake in thy **n** to our kings,	8034
	9:18	and the city which is called by thy **n**:	8034
	9:19	thy city and thy people are called by thy **n**.	8034
	10: 1	whose **n** was called Belteshazzar;	8034
Hos	1: 4	LORD said unto him, Call his **n** Jezreel;	8034
	1: 6	*God* said unto him, Call her **n** Lo-ruhamah:	8034
	1: 9	said *God*, Call his **n** Lo-ammi: for ye *are*	8034
	2:17	shall no more be remembered by their **n**.	8034
Joel	2:26	and praise the **n** of the LORD your God,	8034
	2:32	*that* whosoever shall call on the **n** of	8034
Am	2: 7	unto the *same* maid, to profane my holy **n**:	8034
	4:13	The LORD, The God of hosts, *is* his **n**.	8034
	5: 8	the face of the earth: The LORD *is* his **n**:	8034
	5:27	the LORD, whose **n** *is* The God of hosts.	8034
	6:10	for *we may* not make mention of the **n** of	8034
	9: 6	the face of the earth: The LORD *is* his **n**.	8034
	9:12	all the heathen, which are called by my **n**,	8034

Mic	4: 5	For all people will walk every one in the **n**	8034
	4: 5	we will walk in the **n** of the Lord our	8034
	5: 4	in the majesty of the **n** of the Lord his	8034
	6: 9	and *the man of* wisdom shall see thy **n**:	8034
Na	1:14	*that* no more of thy **n** be sown:	8034
Zep	1: 4	the **n** of the Chemarims with the priests;	8034
	3: 9	that they may all call upon the **n** of	8034
	3:12	and they shall trust in the **n** of the Lord.	8034
	3:20	for I will make you a **n** and a praise among	8034
Zec	5: 4	house of him that sweareth falsely by my **n**:	8034
	6:12	Behold the man whose **n** *is* The BRANCH;	8034
	10:12	they shall walk up and down in his **n**,	8034
	13: 3	for thou speakest lies in the **n** of	8034
	13: 9	they shall call on my **n**, and I will hear	8034
	14: 9	shall there be one Lord, and his **n** one.	8034
Mal	1: 6	unto you, O priests, that despise my **n**.	8034
	1: 6	ye say, Wherein have we despised thy **n**?	8034
	1:11	my **n** *shall be* great among the Gentiles;	8034
	1:11	place incense *shall be* offered unto my **n**,	8034
	1:11	for my **n** *shall be* great among the heathen,	8034
	1:14	and my **n** *is* dreadful among the heathen.	8034
	2: 2	to give glory unto my **n**, saith the Lord	8034
	2: 5	he feared me, and was afraid before my **n**.	8034
	3:16	the Lord, and that thought upon his **n**.	8034
	4: 2	unto you that fear my **n** shall the Sun of	8034
Mt	1:21	a son, and thou shalt call his **n** JESUS:	3686
	1:23	a son, and they shall call his **n** Emmanuel,	3686
	1:25	firstborn son: and *he* called his **n** JESUS.	3686
	6: 9	which art in heaven, Hallowed be thy **n**.	3686
	7:22	Lord, have we not prophesied in thy **n**?	3686
	7:22	and in thy **n** have cast out devils?	3686
	7:22	and in thy **n** done many wonderful works?	3686
	10:41	He that receiveth a prophet in the **n** of a	3686
	10:41	he that receiveth a righteous *man* in the **n**	3686
	10:42	of cold *water* only in the **n** of a disciple,	3686
	12:21	And in his **n** shall the Gentiles trust.	3686
	18: 5	one such little child in my **n** receiveth me.	3686
	18:20	or three are gathered together in my **n**,	3686
	21: 9	Blessed *is* he that cometh in the **n** of	3686
	23:39	Blessed is he that cometh in the **n** of	3686
	24: 5	For many shall come in my **n**, saying, I am	3686
	27:32	they found a man of Cyrene, Simon by **n**:	3686
	28:19	baptizing them in the **n** of the Father, and	3686
Mk	5: 9	And he asked him, What *is* thy **n**? And he	3686
	5: 9	And he answered, saying, My **n** *is* Legion:	3686
	5:22	of the rulers of the synagogue, Jairus by **n**;	3686
	6:14	And king Herod heard *of him;* (for his **n**	3686
	9:37	shall receive one of such children in my **n**,	3686
	9:38	we saw one casting out devils in thy **n**, and	3686
	9:39	is no *man* which shall do a miracle in my **n**,	3686
	9:41	give you a cup of water to drink in my **n**,	3686
	11: 9	Blessed *is* he that cometh in the **n** of	3686
	11:10	that cometh in the **n** of the Lord:	3686
	13: 6	For many shall come in my **n**, saying, I am	3686
	16:17	In my **n** shall they cast out devils;	3686
Lk	1: 5	of Aaron, and her **n** *was* Elisabeth.	3686
	1:13	thee a son, and thou shalt call his **n** John.	3686
	1:27	To a virgin espoused to a man whose **n** was	3686
	1:27	of David; and the virgin's **n** *was* Mary.	3686
	1:31	forth a son, and shalt call his **n** JESUS.	3686
	1:49	done to me great things; and holy *is* his **n**.	3686
	1:59	him Zacharias, after the **n** of his father.	3686
	1:61	none of thy kindred that is called by this **n**.	3686
	1:63	and wrote, saying, His **n** is John.	3686
	2:21	his **n** was called JESUS, which was *so*	3686
	2:25	a man in Jerusalem, whose **n** *was* Simeon;	3686
	6:22	reproach *you,* and cast out your **n** as evil,	3686
	8:30	Jesus asked him, saying, What is thy **n**?	3686
	9:48	Whosoever shall receive this child in my **n**	3686
	9:49	we saw one casting out devils in thy **n**;	3686
	10:17	the devils are subject unto us through thy **n**.	3686
	11: 2	which art in heaven, Hallowed be thy **n**.	3686
	13:35	Blessed *is* he that cometh in the **n** of	3686
	19:38	Blessed *be* the King that cometh in the **n** of	3686
	21: 8	for many shall come in my **n**, saying, I am	3686
	24:18	And the one *of them,* whose **n** *was*	3686
	24:47	be preached in his **n** among all nations,	3686
Jn	1: 6	a man sent from God, whose **n** *was* John.	3686
	1:12	of God, *even* to them that believe on his **n**:	3686
	2:23	in the feast *day,* many believed in his **n**,	3686
	3:18	he hath not believed in the **n** of the only	3686
	5:43	I am come in my Father's **n**, and ye receive	3686
	5:43	if another shall come in his own **n**, him ye	3686
	10: 3	and he calleth his own sheep by **n**, and	3686
	10:25	the works that I do in my Father's **n**,	3686
	12:13	of Israel that cometh in the **n** of the Lord.	3686
	12:28	Father, glorify thy **n**. Then came there a	3686
	14:13	And whatsoever ye shall ask in my **n**,	3686
	14:14	If ye shall ask any *thing* in my **n**, I will do	3686
	14:26	whom the Father will send in my **n**,	3686
	15:16	ye shall ask of the Father in my **n**,	3686
	16:23	Whatsoever ye shall ask the Father in my **n**,	3686
	16:24	Hitherto have ye asked nothing in my **n**:	3686
	16:26	At that day ye shall ask in my **n**: and I say	3686
	17: 6	I have manifested thy **n** unto the men	3686
	17:11	keep through thine own **n** those whom thou	3686
	17:12	them in the world, I kept them in thy **n**:	3686
	17:26	And I have declared unto them thy **n**, and	3686
	18:10	his right ear. The servant's **n** was Malchus.	3686
	20:31	believing ye might have life through his **n**.	3686
Ac	2:21	*that* whosoever shall call on the **n** of	3686
	2:38	be baptized every one of you in the **n** of	3686
	3: 6	In the **n** of Jesus Christ of Nazareth rise up	3686
	3:16	And his **n** through faith in his name hath	3686
	3:16	And his name through faith in his **n** hath	3686
	4: 7	they asked, By what power, or by what **n**,	3686
	4:10	that by the **n** of Jesus Christ of Nazareth,	3686
	4:12	for there is none other **n** under heaven	3686
	4:17	*they* speak henceforth to no man in this **n**.	3686
	4:18	to speak at all nor teach in the **n** of Jesus.	3686
	4:30	wonders may be done by the **n** of thy holy	3686
	5:28	you that *you* should not teach in this **n**?	3686
	5:40	that *they* should not speak in the **n** of Jesus,	3686
	5:41	counted worthy to suffer shame for his **n**.	3686
	7:58	at a young man's feet, whose **n** was Saul.	2564
	8:12	and the **n** of Jesus Christ, they were	3686
	8:16	only they were baptized in the **n** of	3686
	9:14	chief priests to bind all that call on thy **n**.	3686
	9:15	to bear my **n** before the Gentiles, and kings,	3686
	9:21	them which called on this **n** in Jerusalem,	3686
	9:27	boldly at Damascus in the **n** of Jesus.	3686
	9:29	And he spake boldly in the **n** of the Lord	3686
	10:43	that through his **n** whosoever believeth in	3686
	10:48	them to be baptized in the **n** of the Lord.	3686
	13: 6	a Jew, whose **n** *was* Bar-jesus:	3686
	13: 8	sorcerer (for so is his **n** by interpretation)	3686
	15:14	to take out of them a people for his **n**.	3686
	15:17	upon whom my **n** is called, saith the Lord,	3686
	15:26	Men that have hazarded their lives for the **n**	3686
	16:18	I command thee in the **n** of Jesus Christ to	3686
	19: 5	were baptized in the **n** of the Lord Jesus.	3686
	19:13	had evil spirits the **n** of the Lord Jesus,	3686
	19:17	and the **n** of the Lord Jesus was magnified.	3686
	21:13	also to die at Jerusalem for the **n** of	3686
	22:16	away thy sins, calling on the **n** of the Lord.	3686
	26: 9	contrary to the **n** of Jesus of Nazareth.	3686
	28: 7	*man* of the island, whose **n** was Publius;	3686
Ro	1: 5	to the faith among all nations, for his **n**:	3686
	2:24	For the **n** of God is blasphemed among	3686
	9:17	that my **n** might be declared throughout all	3686
	10:13	For whosoever shall call upon the **n** of	3686
	15: 9	among the Gentiles, and sing unto thy **n**.	3686
1Co	1: 2	with all that in every place call upon the **n**	3686
	1:10	brethren, by the **n** of our Lord Jesus Christ,	3686
	1:13	or were ye baptized in the **n** of Paul?	3686
	1:15	say that I had baptized in mine own **n**.	3686
	5: 4	In the **n** of our Lord Jesus Christ, when ye	3686
	6:11	ye are justified in the **n** of the Lord Jesus,	3686
Eph	1:21	and dominion, and every **n** that is named,	3686
	5:20	the Father in the **n** of our Lord Jesus Christ;	3686
Php	2: 9	given him a **n** which is above every name:	3686
	2: 9	given him a name which is above every **n**:	3686
	2:10	That at the **n** of Jesus every knee should	3686
Col	3:17	or deed, *do* all in the **n** of the Lord Jesus,	3686
2Th	1:12	That the **n** of our Lord Jesus Christ may be	3686
	3: 6	brethren, in the **n** of our Lord Jesus Christ,	3686
1Ti	6: 1	that the **n** of God and *his* doctrine be not	3686
2Ti	2:19	Let every one that nameth the **n** of Christ	3686
Heb	1: 4	obtained a more excellent **n** than they.	3686
	2:12	I will declare thy **n** unto my brethren,	3686
	6:10	which ye have shewed toward his **n**,	3686
	13:15	the fruit of *our* lips giving thanks to his **n**.	3686
Jas	2: 7	Do not they blaspheme *that* worthy **n** by	3686
	5:10	who have spoken in the **n** of the Lord,	3686
	5:14	anointing him with oil in the **n** of the Lord:	3686
1Pe	4:14	If ye be reproached for the **n** of Christ,	3686
1Jn	3:23	That we should believe on the **n** of his Son	3686
	5:13	that believe on the **n** of the Son of God;	3686

1Jn 5:13 that ye may believe on the **n** of the Son of 3686
3Jn 1:14 friends salute thee. Greet the friends by **n**. 3686
Rev 2:13 Satan's seat *is:* and thou holdest fast my **n**, 3686
2:17 and in the stone a new **n** written, 3686
3: 1 that thou hast a **n** that thou livest, and 3686
3: 5 I will not blot out his **n** out of the book of 3686
3: 5 but I will confess his **n** before my Father, 3686
3: 8 kept my word, and hast not denied my **n**. 3686
3:12 and I will write upon him the **n** of my God, 3686
3:12 and the **n** of the city of my God, *which is* 3686
3:12 and *I will write upon him* my new **n**. 3686
6: 8 and his **n** that sat on him *was* Death, and 3686
8:11 And the **n** of the star is called Wormwood: 3686
9:11 whose **n** in the Hebrew tongue *is* Abaddon, 3686
9:11 in the Greek *tongue* hath *his* **n** Apollyon. 3686
11:18 and them that fear thy **n**, small and great; 3686
13: 1 and upon his heads the **n** of blasphemy. 3686
13: 6 to blaspheme his **n**, and his tabernacle, and 3686
13:17 or the **n** of the beast, or the number of his 3686
13:17 name of the beast, or the number of his **n**. 3686
14: 1 having his Father's **n** written in their 3686
14:11 and whosoever receiveth the mark of his **n**. 3686
15: 2 his mark, *and* over the number of his **n**, 3686
15: 4 not fear thee, O Lord, and glorify thy **n**? 3686
16: 9 and blasphemed the **n** of God, which hath 3686
17: 5 And upon her forehead *was* a **n** written, 3686
19:12 and he had a **n** written, that no *man* knew, 3686
19:13 and his **n** is called The Word of God. 3686
19:16 on *his* vesture and on his thigh a **n** written, 3686
22: 4 and his **n** *shall be* in their foreheads. 3686

NAME'S (30) [NAME]

1Sa 12:22 not forsake his people for his great **n** sake: 8034
1Ki 8:41 cometh out of a far country for thy **n** sake; 8034
2Ch 6:32 is come from a far country for thy great **n** 8034
Ps 23: 3 in the paths of righteousness for his **n** sake. 8034
25:11 For thy **n** sake, O LORD, pardon mine 8034
31: 3 therefore for thy **n** sake lead me, and 8034
79: 9 and purge away our sins, for thy **n** sake. 8034
106: 8 Nevertheless he saved them for his **n** sake, 8034
109:21 for me, O GOD the Lord, for thy **n** sake: 8034
143:11 Quicken me, O LORD, for thy **n** sake: 8034
Isa 48: 9 For my **n** sake will I defer mine anger, and 8034
66: 5 that cast you out for my **n** sake, said, 8034
Jer 14: 7 testify against us, do thou *it* for thy **n** sake: 8034
14:21 Do not abhor *us,* for thy **n** sake, do not 8034
Eze 20: 9 I wrought for my **n** sake, that *it* should not 8034
20:14 I wrought for my **n** sake, that *it* should not 8034
20:22 mine hand, and wrought for my **n** sake, 8034
20:44 when I have wrought with you for my **n** 8034
36:22 O house of Israel, but for mine holy **n** sake, 8034
Mt 10:22 And ye shall be hated of all *men* for my **n** 3686
19:29 wife, or children, or lands, for my **n** sake, 3686
24: 9 ye shall be hated of all nations for my **n** 3686
Mk 13:13 And ye shall be hated of all *men* for my **n** 3686
Lk 21:12 before kings and rulers for my **n** sake. 3686
21:17 And ye shall be hated of all *men* for my **n** 3686
Jn 15:21 *things* will they do unto you for my **n** sake, 3686
Ac 9:16 great *things* he must suffer for my **n** sake. 3686
1Jn 2:12 *your* sins are forgiven you for his **n** sake. 3686
3Jn 1: 7 Because that for his **n** sake they went forth, 3686
Rev 2: 3 and for my **n** sake hast laboured, and 3686

NAMED (57) [NAME]

Ge 23:16 which he had **n** in the audience of the sons 1696
27:36 he said, Is not he rightly **n** Jacob? 7121+8034
48:16 let my name be **n** on them, and the name of 7121
Jos 2: 1 harlot's house, **n** Rahab, and lodged there. 8034
1Sa 4:21 she **n** the child Ichabod, saying, The glory 7121
17: 4 **n** Goliath, of Gath, whose height *was* six 8034
22:20 **n** Abiathar, escaped, and fled after David. 8034
2Ki 17:34 children of Jacob, whom he **n** Israel; 7760+8034
1Ch 23:14 of God, his sons were **n** of the tribe of Levi. 7121
Ecc 6:10 That which hath been is **n** already, 7121+8034
Isa 61: 6 ye shall be **n** the Priests of the LORD: 7121
Jer 44:26 that my name shall no more be **n** in 7121
Da 5:12 whom the king **n** Belteshazzar: 7761+8036
Am 6: 1 *which are* **n** chief of the nations, 5344
Mic 2: 7 O *thou that art* **n** the house of Jacob, is 559
Mt 9: 9 he saw a man, **n** Matthew, sitting at 3004
27:57 came a rich man of Arimathea, **n** Joseph, 5122
Mk 14:32 And they came to a place which was **n** 3686
15: 7 And there was *one* **n** Barabbas, *which lay* 3004
Lk 1: 5 king of Judea, a certain priest **n** Zacharias, 3686
1:26 God unto a city of Galilee, **n** Nazareth, 3686
2:21 **n** of the angel before he was conceived in 2564
5:27 and saw a publican, **n** Levi, sitting at 3686
6:13 he chose twelve, whom also he **n** apostles; 3687
6:14 Simon, (whom he also **n** Peter,) and 3687
8:41 there came a man **n** Jairus, and he was a 3686
10:38 a certain woman **n** Martha received him 3686
16:20 And there was a certain beggar **n** Lazarus, 3686
19: 2 And behold, *there was* a man **n** Zaccheus, 3686
23:50 And behold, *there was* a man **n** Joseph, 3686
Jn 3: 1 **n** Nicodemus, a ruler of the Jews: 3686
11: 1 *n* Lazarus, of Bethany, the town of Mary NIG
11:49 And one of them, *n* Caiaphas, being NIG
Ac 5: 1 But a certain man **n** Ananias, with Sapphira 3686
5:34 a Pharisee, **n** Gamaliel, a doctor of law, 3686
9:10 a certain disciple at Damascus, **n** Ananias; 3686
9:12 And hath seen in a vision a man **n** Ananias 3686
9:33 And there he found a certain man **n** 3686
9:36 Now there was at Joppa a certain disciple **n** 3686
11:28 And there stood up one of them **n** Agabus, 3686
12:13 a damsel came to hearken, **n** Rhoda. 3686
16: 1 **n** Timotheus, the son of a certain woman, 3686
16:14 And a certain woman **n** Lydia, a seller of 3686
17:34 and a woman **n** Damaris, and others with 3686
18: 2 And found a certain Jew **n** Aquila, born in 3686
18: 7 **n** Justus, one that worshipped God, 3686
18:24 And a certain Jew **n** Apollos, born at 3686
19:24 For a certain *man* **n** Demetrius, 3686
20: 9 a window a certain young man **n** Eutychus, 3686
21:10 from Judea a certain prophet, **n** Agabus. 3686
24: 1 and *with* a certain orator *n* Tertullus, NIG
27: 1 certain other prisoners unto *one* **n** Julius, 3686
Ro 15:20 preach the gospel, not where Christ was **n**, 3687
1Co 5: 1 is not so much as **n** amongst the Gentiles, 3687
Eph 1:21 and dominion, and every name that is **n**, 3687
3:15 the whole family in heaven and earth is **n**, 3687
5: 3 let it not be once **n** amongst you, 3687

NAMELY (23) [NAME] See Index

NAMES (97) [NAME]

Ge 2:20 Adam gave **n** to all cattle, and to the fowl 8034
25:13 these *are* the **n** of the sons of Ishmael, 8034
25:13 by their **n**, according to their generations: 8034
25:16 these *are* their **n**, by their towns, and 8034
26:18 he called their **n** after the names by which 8034
26:18 he called their names after the **n** by which 8034
36:10 These *are* the **n** of Esau's sons; Eliphaz 8034
36:40 these *are* the **n** of the dukes *that came* of 8034
36:40 their families, after their places, by their **n**; 8034
46: 8 these *are* the **n** of the children of Israel, 8034
Ex 1: 1 Now these *are* the **n** of the children of 8034
6:16 these *are* the **n** of the sons of Levi 8034
28: 9 grave on them the **n** of the children of 8034
28:10 Six of their **n** on one stone, and the *other* 8034
28:10 the *other* six **n** of the rest on the other 8034
28:11 stones with the **n** of the children of Israel: 8034
28:12 Aaron shall bear their **n** before the LORD 8034
28:21 the stones shall be with the **n** of 8034
28:21 twelve, according to their **n**, *like* 8034
28:29 Aaron shall bear the **n** of the children of 8034
39: 6 with the **n** of the children of Israel. 8034
39:14 the stones *were* according to the **n** of 8034
39:14 twelve, according to their **n**, *like* 8034
Nu 1: 2 with the number of *their* **n**, every male by 8034
1: 5 these *are* the **n** of the men that shall stand 8034
1:17 these men which are expressed by *their* **n**: 8034
1:18 according to the number of the **n**, 8034
1:20 according to the number of the **n**, by their 8034
1:22 according to the number of the **n**, by their 8034
1:24 according to the number of the **n**, 8034
1:26 according to the number of the **n**, 8034
1:28 according to the number of the **n**, 8034
1:30 according to the number of the **n**, 8034
1:32 according to the number of the **n**, 8034
1:34 according to the number of the **n**, 8034
1:36 according to the number of the **n**, 8034
1:38 according to the number of the **n**, 8034
1:40 according to the number of the **n**, 8034
1:42 according to the number of the **n**, 8034
3: 2 these *are* the **n** of the sons of Aaron; 8034
3: 3 These *are* the **n** of the sons of Aaron, 8034
3:17 these were the sons of Levi by their **n**; 8034
3:18 these *are* the **n** of the sons of Gershon by 8034

Nu	3:40	and upward, and take the number of their **n**.	8034
	3:43	all the firstborn males by the number of **n**,	8034
	13: 4	these *were* their **n**: of the tribe of Reuben,	8034
	13:16	These *are* the **n** of the men which Moses	8034
	26:33	the **n** of the daughters of Zelophehad *were*	8034
	26:53	inheritance according to the number of **n**.	8034
	26:55	according to the **n** of the tribes of their	8034
	27: 1	these *are* the **n** of his daughters; Mahlah,	8034
	32:38	and Baal-meon, (*their* **n** being changed,)	8034
	32:38	gave **other n** unto the cities which	8034+8034
	34:17	These *are* the **n** of the men which shall	8034
	34:19	the **n** of the men *are* these: Of the tribe of	8034
Dt	12: 3	and destroy the **n** of them out of that place.	8034
Jos	17: 3	these *are* the **n** of his daughters, Mahlah,	8034
1Sa	14:49	the **n** of his two daughters *were these;*	8034
	17:13	the **n** of his three sons that went to	8034
2Sa	5:14	these *be* the **n** of those that were born unto	8034
	23: 8	These *be* the **n** of the mighty *men* whom	8034
1Ki	4: 8	these *are* their **n**: The son of Hur, in mount	8034
1Ch	4:38	These mentioned by *their* **n** *were* princes in	8034
	6:17	these *be* the **n** of the sons of Gershom;	8034
	6:65	these cities, which are called by *their* **n**.	8034
	8:38	whose **n** *are* these, Azrikam, Bocheru, and	8034
	9:44	whose **n** *are* these, Azrikam, Bocheru, and	8034
	14: 4	Now these *are* the **n** of *his* children which	8034
	23:24	as they were counted by number of **n** by	8034
Ezr	5: 4	What are the **n** of the men that make this	8036
	5:10	We asked their **n** also, to certify thee,	8036
	5:10	that we might write the **n** of the men that	8036
	8:13	whose **n** *are* these, Eliphelet, Jeiel, and	8034
	10:16	all of them by *their* **n**, were separated, and	8034
Ps	16: 4	I not offer, nor take up their **n** into my lips.	8034
	49:11	they call *their* lands after their own **n**.	8034
	147: 4	of the stars; he calleth them all *by their* **n**.	8034
Isa	40:26	he calleth them all by **n** by the greatness of	8034
Eze	23: 4	the **n** of them *were* Aholah the elder, and	8034
	23: 4	Thus *were* their **n**; Samaria *is* Aholah, and	8034
	48: 1	Now these *are* the **n** of the tribes. From	8034
	48:31	the gates of the city *shall be* after the **n** of	8034
Da	1: 7	whom the prince of the eunuchs gave **n**:	8034
Hos	2:17	For I will take away the **n** of Baalim out of	8034
Zec	13: 2	*that* I will cut off the **n** of the idols out of	8034
Mt	10: 2	Now the **n** of the twelve apostles are these;	*3686*
Lk	10:20	because your **n** are written in heaven.	*3686*
Ac	1:15	(the number of **n** together were about an	*3686*
	18:15	But if it be a question of words and **n**, and	*3686*
Php	4: 3	whose **n** *are* in the book of life.	*3686*
Rev	3: 4	Thou hast a few **n** even in Sardis,	*3686*
	13: 8	whose **n** are not written in the book of life	*3686*
	17: 3	full of **n** of blasphemy, having seven heads	*3686*
	17: 8	whose **n** were not written in the book of life	*3686*
	21:12	gates twelve angels, and **n** written *there*on,	*3686*
	21:12	which are *the n* of the twelve tribes of	NIG
	21:14	in them the **n** of the twelve apostles of	*3686*

NAMETH (1) [NAME]

2Ti	2:19	Let every one that **n** the name of Christ	*3687*

NAOMI (20) [NAOMI'S]

Ru	1: 2	the name of his wife **N**, and the name of his	5281
	1: 8	**N** said unto her two daughters in law, Go,	5281
	1:11	**N** said, Turn again, my daughters: why will	5281
	1:19	moved about them, and they said, *Is* this **N**?	5281
	1:20	unto them, Call me not **N**, call me Mara:	5281
	1:21	why *then* call ye me **N**, seeing the LORD	5281
	1:22	So **N** returned, and Ruth the Moabitess,	5281
	2: 1	**N** had a kinsman of her husband's,	5281
	2: 2	Ruth the Moabitess said unto **N**, Let me	5281
	2: 6	back with **N** out of the country of Moab:	5281
	2:20	**N** said unto her daughter in law, Blessed *be*	5281
	2:20	**N** said unto her, The man *is* near of kin	5281
	2:22	**N** said unto Ruth her daughter in law, *It is*	5281
	3: 1	**N** her mother in law said unto her,	5281
	4: 3	he said unto the kinsman, **N**, that is come	5281
	4: 5	day thou buyest the field of the hand of **N**,	5281
	4: 9	and Mahlon's, of the hand of **N**.	5281
	4:14	the women said unto **N**, Blessed *be*	5281
	4:16	**N** took the child, and laid it in her bosom,	5281
	4:17	it a name, saying, There is a son born to **N**;	5281

NAOMI'S (1) [NAOMI]

Ru	1: 3	Elimelech **N** husband died; and she was	5281

NAPHISH (2)

Ge	25:15	Hadar, and Tema, Jetur, **N**, and Kedemah:	5305
1Ch	1:31	Jetur, **N**, and Kedemah. These *are* the sons	5305

NAPHTALI (50) [KEDESH-NAPHTALI, NEPHTHALIM]

Ge	30: 8	have prevailed: and she called his name **N**.	5321
	35:25	of Bilhah, Rachel's handmaid; Dan, and **N**:	5321
	46:24	the sons of **N**; Jahzeel, and Guni, and Jezer,	5321
	49:21	**N** *is* a hind let loose: he giveth goodly	5321
Ex	1: 4	Dan, and **N**, Gad, and Asher.	5321
Nu	1:15	Of **N**; Ahira the son of Enan.	5321
	1:42	*Of* the children of **N**, *throughout* their	5321
	1:43	*even* of the tribe of **N**, *were* fifty and	5321
	2:29	the tribe of **N**: and the captain of	5321
	2:29	the captain of the children of **N** *shall be*	5321
	7:78	prince of the children of **N**, *offered:*	5321
	10:27	children of **N** *was* Ahira the son of Enan.	5321
	13:14	Of the tribe of **N**, Nahbi the son of Vophsi.	5321
	26:48	*Of* the sons of **N** after their families:	5321
	26:50	These *are* the families of **N** according to	5321
	34:28	the prince of the tribe of the children of **N**,	5321
Dt	27:13	Gad, and Asher, and Zebulun, Dan, and **N**.	5321
	33:23	of **N** he said, O Naphtali, satisfied with	5321
	33:23	O **N**, satisfied with favour, and full *with*	5321
	34: 2	all **N**, and the land of Ephraim, and	5321
Jos	19:32	The sixth lot came out to the children of **N**,	5321
	19:32	*even* for the children of **N** according to	5321
	19:39	children of **N** according to their families,	5321
	20: 7	appointed Kedesh in Galilee in mount **N**,	5321
	21: 6	out of the tribe of **N**, and out of the half	5321
	21:32	out of the tribe of **N**, Kedesh in Galilee	5321
Jdg	1:33	Neither did **N** drive out the inhabitants of	5321
	4: 6	thee ten thousand men of the children of **N**	5321
	4:10	Barak called Zebulun and **N** to Kedesh;	5321
	5:18	**N** *were* a people *that* jeoparded their lives	5321
	6:35	unto Asher, and unto Zebulun, and unto **N**;	5321
	7:23	gathered themselves together out of **N**,	5321
1Ki	4:15	Ahimaaz *was* in **N**; he also took Basmath	5321
	7:14	He *was* a widow's son of the tribe of **N**,	5321
	15:20	and all Cinneroth, with all the land of **N**.	5321
2Ki	15:29	all the land of **N**, and carried them captive	5321
1Ch	2: 2	Joseph, and Benjamin, **N**, Gad, and Asher.	5321
	6:62	out of the tribe of **N**, and out of the tribe of	5321
	6:76	out of the tribe of **N**; Kedesh in Galilee	5321
	7:13	The sons of **N**; Jahziel, and Guni, and	5321
	12:34	of **N** a thousand captains, and with them	5321
	12:40	*even* unto Issachar and Zebulun and **N**,	5321
	27:19	of **N**, Jerimoth the son of Azriel:	5321
2Ch	16: 4	and all the store cities of **N**.	5321
	34: 6	and Ephraim, and Simeon, even unto **N**,	5321
Ps	68:27	princes of Zebulun, *and* the princes of **N**.	5321
Isa	9: 1	the land of Zebulun and the land of **N**,	5321
Eze	48: 3	even unto the west side, a *portion for* **N**.	5321
	48: 4	by the border of **N**, from the east side unto	5321
	48:34	of Gad, one gate of Asher, one gate of **N**.	5321

NAPHTUHIM (2)

Ge	10:13	and Anamim, and Lehabim, and **N**,	5320
1Ch	1:11	and Anamim, and Lehabim, and **N**,	5320

NAPHTUHITES See NAPHTUHIM

NAPKIN (3)

Lk	19:20	thy pound, which I have kept laid up in a **n**:	*4676*
Jn	11:44	and his face was bound about with a **n**.	*4676*
	20: 7	And the **n**, that was about his head,	*4676*

NARCISSUS (1)

Ro	16:11	Greet them that be of the *household* of **N**,	*3488*

NARD See SPIKENARD

NARROW (9) [NARROWED, NARROWER, NARROWLY]

Nu	22:26	went further, and stood in a **n** place,	6862
Jos	17:15	if mount Ephraim be too **n** for thee.	213
1Ki	6: 4	for the house he made windows of **n** lights.	331
Pr	23:27	deep ditch; and a strange *woman is* a **n** pit.	6862
Isa	49:19	shall even now be too **n** by reason of	3334
Eze	40:16	*there were* **n** windows to the little chambers,	331
	41:16	the **n** windows, and the galleries round about	331
	41:26	*there were* **n** windows and palm trees on	331
Mt	7:14	and **n** *is* the way, which leadeth unto life,	*2346*

NARROWED (1) [NARROW]

1Ki	6: 6	of the house he made **n rests** round about,	4052

N

NARROWER (1) [NARROW]
Isa 28:20 the covering **n** than that *he* can wrap 6887

NARROWLY (2) [NARROW]
Job 13:27 the stocks, and **lookest n** unto all my paths; 8104
Isa 14:16 They that see thee shall **n look** upon thee, 7688

NATHAN (43)
2Sa 5:14 and Shobab, and **N**, and Solomon, 5416
7: 2 That the king said unto **N** the prophet, 5416
7: 3 **N** said to the king, Go, do all that *is* in thine 5416
7: 4 that the word of the LORD came unto **N**, 5416
7:17 all this vision, so did **N** speak unto David. 5416
12: 1 the LORD sent **N** unto David. And he 5416
12: 5 he said to **N**, *As* the LORD liveth, the man 5416
12: 7 **N** said to David, Thou *art* the man. 5416
12:13 David said unto **N**, I have sinned against 5416
12:13 **N** said unto David, The LORD also hath 5416
12:15 **N** departed unto his house. And 5416
12:25 he sent by the hand of **N** the prophet; and 5416
23:36 Igal the son of **N** of Zobah, Bani 5416
1Ki 1: 8 **N** the prophet, and Shimei, and Rei, and 5416
1:10 **N** the prophet, and Benaiah, and the mighty 5416
1:11 Wherefore **N** spake unto Bath-sheba 5416
1:22 with the king, **N** the prophet also came in. 5416
1:23 told the king, saying, Behold **N** the prophet. 5416
1:24 And **N** said, My lord O king, hast thou said, 5416
1:32 **N** the prophet, and Benaiah the son of 5416
1:34 **N** the prophet anoint him there king over 5416
1:38 **N** the prophet, and Benaiah the son of 5416
1:44 **N** the prophet, and Benaiah the son of 5416
1:45 **N** the prophet have anointed him king in 5416
4: 5 Azariah the son of **N** *was* over the officers: 5416
4: 5 Zabud the son of **N** *was* principal officer, 5416
1Ch 2:36 Attai begat **N**, and Nathan begat Zabad, 5416
2:36 Attai begat Nathan, and **N** begat Zabad, 5416
3: 5 and Shobab, and **N**, and Solomon, four, 5416
11:38 Joel the brother of **N**, Mibhar the son of 5416
14: 4 Shammua, and Shobab, **N**, and Solomon, 5416
17: 1 that David said to **N** the prophet, Lo, 5416
17: 2 **N** said unto David, Do all that *is* in thine 5416
17: 3 that the word of God came to **N**, saying, 5416
17:15 all this vision, so did **N** speak unto David. 5416
29:29 in the book of **N** the prophet, and in 5416
2Ch 9:29 *are* they not written in the book of **N** 5416
29:25 of Gad the king's seer, and **N** the prophet: 5416
Ezr 8:16 for **N**, and for Zechariah, and 5416
10:39 And Shelemiah, and **N**, and Adaiah, 5416
Ps 51: T when **N** the prophet came unto him, 5416
Zec 12:12 the family of the house of **N** apart, and 5416
Lk 3:31 which was *the son* of **N**, which was *the son* *3481*

NATHANAEL (6)
Jn 1:45 Philip findeth **N**, and saith unto him, *3482*
1:46 And **N** said unto him, Can there any good *3482*
1:47 Jesus saw **N** coming to him, and saith of *3482*
1:48 **N** saith unto him, Whence knowest thou *3482*
1:49 **N** answered and saith unto him, Rabbi, *3482*
21: 2 and **N** of Cana in Galilee, and the *sons* of *3482*

NATHAN-MELECH (1)
2Ki 23:11 by the chamber of **N** the chamberlain, 5419

NATION (145) [NATIONS]
Ge 12: 2 I will make of thee a great **n**, and I will 1471
15:14 also that **n**, whom they shall serve, will I 1471
17:20 he beget, and I will make him a great **n**. 1471
18:18 shall surely become a great and mighty **n**, 1471
20: 4 Lord, wilt thou slay also a righteous **n**? 1471
21:13 the son of the bondwoman will I make a **n**, 1471
21:18 in thine hand; for I will make him a great **n**. 1471
35:11 a **n** and a company of nations shall be of 1471
46: 3 for I will there make of thee a great **n**. 1471
Ex 9:24 in all the land of Egypt since it became a **n**. 1471
19: 6 unto me a kingdom of priests, and a holy **n**. 1471
21: 8 to sell her unto a strange **n** he shall have no 5971
32:10 and I will make of thee a great **n**. 1471
33:13 and consider that this **n** *is* thy people. 1471
34:10 not been done in all the earth, nor in any **n**: 1471
Lev 18:26 *neither* any of **your own n**, nor any stranger 249
20:23 ye shall not walk in the manners of the **n**, 1471
Nu 14:12 will make of thee a greater **n** and 1471
Dt 4: 6 Surely this great **n** *is* a wise and 1471
4: 7 For what **n** *is there so* great, who hath God 1471
4: 8 what **n** *is there so* great, that hath statutes 1471
4:34 take him a **n** from the midst of *another* 1471
4:34 him a nation from the midst of *another* **n**, 1471
9:14 I will make of thee a **n** mightier and 1471
26: 5 became there a **n**, great, mighty, and 1471
28:33 shall a **n** which thou knowest not eat up; 5971
28:36 unto a **n** which neither thou nor thy fathers 1471
28:49 The LORD shall bring a **n** against thee 1471
28:49 a **n** whose tongue thou shalt not 1471
28:50 A **n** of fierce countenance, which shall not 1471
32:21 provoke them to anger with a foolish **n**. 1471
32:28 For they *are* a **n** void of counsel, neither *is* 1471
2Sa 7:23 what one **n** in the earth *is* like thy people, 1471
1Ki 18:10 thy God liveth, there is no **n** or kingdom, 1471
18:10 he took an oath of the kingdom and **n**, 1471
2Ki 17:29 Howbeit **every n** made gods of their 1471+1471
17:29 **every n** in their cities wherein they 1471+1471
1Ch 16:20 *when* they went from **n** to nation, and 1471
16:20 *when* they went from nation to **n**, and 1471
17:21 what one **n** in the earth *is* like thy people 1471
2Ch 15: 6 **n** was destroyed of nation, and city of city: 1471
15: 6 nation was destroyed of **n**, and city of city: 1471
32:15 for no god of any **n** or kingdom was able to 1471
Job 34:29 whether *it be done* against a **n**, or against a 1471
Ps 33:12 Blessed *is* the **n** whose God *is* the LORD; 1471
43: 1 and plead my cause against an ungodly **n**: 1471
83: 4 and let us cut them off from *being* a **n**; 1471
105:13 When they went from one **n** to another, 1471
106: 5 that *I* may rejoice in the gladness of thy **n**, 1471
147:20 He hath not dealt so with any **n**: and *as for* 1471
Pr 14:34 Righteousness exalteth a **n**: but sin *is* a 1471
Isa 1: 4 Ah sinful **n**, a people laden with iniquity, 1471
2: 4 **n** shall not lift up sword against nation, 1471
2: 4 nation shall not lift up sword against **n**, 1471
9: 3 Thou hast multiplied the **n**, *and* 1471
10: 6 I will send him against a hypocritical **n**, and 1471
14:32 then answer the messengers of the **n**? 1471
18: 2 to a **n** scattered and peeled, 1471
18: 2 a **n** meted out and trodden down, 1471
18: 7 a **n** meted out and trodden under foot, 1471
26: 2 that the righteous **n** which keepeth the truth 1471
26:15 Thou hast increased the **n**, O LORD, 1471
26:15 O LORD, thou hast increased the **n**: 1471
49: 7 to him whom the **n** abhorreth, to a servant 1471
51: 4 my people; and give ear unto me, O my **n**: 3816
55: 5 thou shalt call a **n** *that* thou knowest not, 1471
58: 2 as a **n** that did righteousness, and 1471
60:12 For the **n** and kingdom that will not serve 1471
60:22 a thousand, and a small one a strong **n**: 1471
65: 1 unto a **n** *that* was not called by my name. 1471
66: 8 *or* shall a **n** be born at once? for as soon as 1471
Jer 2:11 Hath a **n** changed *their* gods, which *are* yet 1471
5: 9 shall not my soul be avenged on such a **n** as 1471
5:15 Lo, I will bring a **n** upon you from far, 1471
5:15 it *is* a mighty **n**, it *is* an ancient nation, 1471
5:15 it *is* a mighty nation, it *is* an ancient **n**, 1471
5:15 a **n** whose language thou knowest not, 1471
5:29 shall not my soul be avenged on such a **n** as 1471
6:22 a great **n** shall be raised from the sides of 1471
7:28 This *is* a **n** that obeyeth not the voice of 1471
9: 9 shall not my soul be avenged on such a **n** as 1471
12:17 I will utterly pluck up and destroy that **n**, 1471
18: 7 *At what* instant I shall speak concerning a **n** 1471
18: 8 If that **n**, against whom I have pronounced, 1471
18: 9 *at what* instant I shall speak concerning a **n**, 1471
25:12 that **n**, saith the LORD, for their iniquity, 1471
25:32 evil *shall* go forth from **n** to nation, and 1471
25:32 evil *shall* go forth from nation to **n**, and 1471
27: 8 *that* the **n** and kingdom which will not 1471
27: 8 that **n** will I punish, saith the LORD, 1471
27:13 as the LORD hath spoken against the **n** 1471
31:36 cease from being a **n** before me for ever. 1471
33:24 that *they* should be no more a **n** before 1471
48: 2 come, and let us cut it off from *being* a **n**. 1471
49:31 Arise, get you up unto the wealthy **n**, 1471
49:36 there shall be no **n** whither the outcasts of 1471
50: 3 For out of the north there cometh up a **n** 1471
50:41 a great **n**, and many kings shall be raised up 1471
La 4:17 in our watching we have watched for a **n** 1471
Eze 2: 3 to a rebellious **n** that hath rebelled against 1471
37:22 I will make them one **n** in the land upon 1471
Da 3:29 That every people, **n**, and language, 524
8:22 four kingdoms shall stand up out of the **n**, 1471
12: 1 such as never was since there was a **n** *even* 1471

N

Joel 1: 6 For a **n** is come up upon my land, strong, 1471
Am 6:14 behold, I *will* raise up against you a **n**, 1471
Mic 4: 3 **n** shall not lift up a sword against nation, 1471
4: 3 nation shall not lift up a sword against **n**, 1471
4: 7 and her that was cast far off a strong **n**: 1471
Hab 1: 6 up the Chaldeans, *that* bitter and hasty **n**, 1471
Zep 2: 1 yea, gather together, O **n** not desired; 1471
2: 5 of the sea coast, the **n** of the Cherethites! 1471
Hag 2:14 *is* this people, and so *is* this **n** before me, 1471
Mal 3: 9 for ye *have* robbed me, *even* this whole **n**. 1471
Mt 21:43 given to a **n** bringing forth the fruits 1484
24: 7 For **n** shall rise against nation, and 1484
24: 7 For nation shall rise against **n**, and 1484
Mk 7:26 woman was a Greek, a Syrophenician by **n**; 1085
13: 8 For **n** shall rise against nation, and 1484
13: 8 For nation shall rise against **n**, and 1484
Lk 7: 5 For he loveth our **n**, and he hath built us a 1484
21:10 **N** shall rise against nation, and 1484
21:10 Nation shall rise against **n**, and 1484
23: 2 We found this *fellow* perverting the **n**, and 1484
Jn 11:48 and take away both our place and **n**. 1484
11:50 the people, and *that* the whole **n** perish not. 1484
11:51 prophesied that Jesus should die for *that* **n**; 1484
11:52 And not for *that* **n** only, but that also he 1484
18:35 Thine own **n** and the chief priests have 1484
Ac 2: 5 devout men, out of every **n** under heaven. 1484
7: 7 And the **n** to whom they shall be in 1484
10:22 of good report among all the **n** of the Jews, 1484
10:28 or come unto **one of another**; 246
10:35 But in every **n** he that feareth him, and 1484
24: 2 that very worthy deeds are done unto this **n** 1484
24:10 been of many years a judge unto this **n**, 1484
24:17 many years I came to bring alms to my **n**, 1484
26: 4 which was at the first among mine own **n** at 1484
28:19 not that I had ought to accuse my **n** of. 1484
Ro 10:19 *and* by a foolish **n** I will anger you. 1484
Gal 1:14 above many *my* equals in mine own **n**, 1085
Php 2:15 in the midst of a crooked and perverse **n**, 1074
1Pe 2: 9 a holy **n**, a peculiar people; 1484
Rev 5: 9 and tongue, and people, and **n**; 1484
14: 6 and to every **n**, and kindred, and tongue, 1484

NATIONS (336) [NATION]

Ge 10: 5 his tongue, after their families, in their **n**. 1471
10:20 in their countries, *and* in their **n**. 1471
10:31 their tongues, in their lands, after their **n**. 1471
10:32 of Noah, after their generations, in their **n**: 1471
10:32 by these were the **n** divided in the earth 1471
14: 1 king of Elam, and Tidal king of **n**; 1471
14: 9 *with* Tidal king of **n**, and Amraphel king of 1471
17: 4 and thou shalt be a father of many **n**. 1471
17: 5 for a father of many **n** have I made thee. 1471
17: 6 I will make **n** of thee, and kings shall come 1471
17:16 bless her, and she shall be *a mother* of **n**; 1471
18:18 all the **n** of the earth shall be blessed in 1471
22:18 in thy seed shall all the **n** of the earth be 1471
25:16 twelve princes according to their **n**. 523
25:23 Two **n** *are* in thy womb, and two manner of 1471
26: 4 in thy seed shall all the **n** of the earth be 1471
27:29 people serve thee, and **n** bow down to thee: 3816
35:11 and a company of **n** shall be of thee, 1471
48:19 and his seed shall become a multitude of **n**. 1471
Ex 34:24 For I will cast out the **n** before thee, and 1471
Lev 18:24 **n** are defiled which I cast out before you: 1471
18:28 as it spued out the **n** that *were* before you. 1471
Nu 14:15 the **n** which have heard the fame of thee 1471
23: 9 and shall not be reckoned among the **n**. 1471
24: 8 he shall eat up the **n** his enemies, and 1471
24:20 and said, Amalek *was* the first of the **n**; 1471
Dt 2:25 the fear of thee upon the **n** *that are* under 5971
4: 6 your understanding in the sight of the **n**, 5971
4:19 divided unto all **n** under the whole heaven. 5971
4:27 the LORD shall scatter you among the **n**, 5971
4:38 To drive out **n** from before thee greater and 1471
7: 1 hath cast out many **n** before thee, 1471
7: 1 seven **n** greater and mightier than thou; 1471
7:17 say in thine heart, These **n** *are* moe than I; 1471
7:22 the LORD thy God will put out those **n** 1471
8:20 As the **n** which the LORD destroyeth 1471
9: 1 to go in to possess **n** greater and 1471
9: 4 for the wickedness of these **n** the LORD 1471
9: 5 for the wickedness of these **n** the LORD 1471
11:23 will the LORD drive out all these **n** from 1471
11:23 ye shall possess greater **n** and mightier than 1471
12: 2 wherein the **n** which ye shall possess 1471
12:29 God shall cut off the **n** from before thee, 1471
12:30 How did these **n** serve their gods? 1471
14: 2 above all the **n** that *are* upon the earth. 5971
15: 6 thou shalt lend unto many **n**, but thou shalt 1471
15: 6 thou shalt reign over many **n**, but they shall 1471
17:14 over me, like as all the **n** that *are* about me; 1471
18: 9 to do after the abominations of those **n**. 1471
18:14 For these **n**, which thou shalt possess, 1471
19: 1 the LORD thy God hath cut off the **n**, 1471
20:15 which *are* not of the cities of these **n**. 1471
26:19 to make thee high above all **n** which he 1471
28: 1 set thee on high above all **n** of the earth: 1471
28:12 thou shalt lend unto many **n**, and thou shalt 1471
28:37 among all **n** whither the LORD shall lead 5971
28:65 among these **n** shalt thou find no ease, 1471
29:16 how we came through the **n** which ye 1471
29:18 to go *and* serve the gods of these **n**; 1471
29:24 Even all **n** shall say, Wherefore hath 1471
30: 1 shalt call *them* to mind among all the **n**, 1471
30: 3 will return and gather thee from all the **n**, 5971
31: 3 he will destroy these **n** from before thee, 1471
32: 8 When the most High divided to the **n** their 1471
32:43 Rejoice, O ye **n**, *with* his people: for he will 1471
Jos 12:23 one; the king of the **n** of Gilgal, one; 1471
23: 3 your God hath done unto all these **n** 1471
23: 4 I have divided unto you *by lot* these **n** that 1471
23: 4 with all the **n** that I have cut off, 1471
23: 7 That *ye* come not among these **n**, these that 1471
23: 9 hath driven out from before you great **n** 1471
23:12 cleave unto the remnant of these **n**, 1471
23:13 drive out *any of* these **n** from before you; 1471
Jdg 2:21 of the **n** which Joshua left when he died: 1471
2:23 Therefore the LORD left those **n**, without 1471
3: 1 Now these *are* the **n** which the LORD left, 1471
1Sa 8: 5 make us a king to judge us like all the **n**. 1471
8:20 That we also may be like all the **n**; and 1471
27: 8 for those **n** *were* of old the inhabitants of NIH
2Sa 7:23 thee from Egypt, *from* the **n** and their gods? 1471
8:11 gold that he had dedicated of all **n** which he 1471
1Ki 4:31 and his fame was in all **n** round about. 1471
11: 2 Of the **n** *concerning* which the LORD said 1471
14:24 **n** which the LORD cast out before 1471
2Ki 17:26 The **n** which thou hast removed, and 1471
17:33 after the manner of the **n** whom they 1471
17:41 So these **n** feared the LORD, and served 1471
18:33 Hath any of the gods of the **n** delivered at 1471
19:12 Have the gods of the **n** delivered them 1471
19:17 the kings of Assyria have destroyed the **n** 1471
21: 9 **n** whom the LORD destroyed before 1471
1Ch 14:17 LORD brought the fear of him upon all **n**. 1471
16:24 his marvellous works among all **n**. 5971
16:31 let *men* say among the **n**, The LORD 1471
17:21 by driving out **n** from before thy people, 1471
18:11 the gold that he brought from all *these* **n**; 1471
2Ch 7:20 to be a proverb and a byword among all **n**. 5971
13: 9 after the manner of the **n** of *other* lands? 5971
32:13 were the gods of the **n** of *those* lands any 1471
32:14 of those **n** that my fathers utterly destroyed, 1471
32:17 As the gods of the **n** of *other* lands have not 1471
32:23 that he was magnified in the sight of all **n** 1471
Ezr 4:10 the rest of the **n** whom the great and 524
Ne 1: 8 I will scatter you abroad among the **n**: 5971
9:22 thou gavest them kingdoms and **n**, 5971
13:26 among many **n** was there no king like him, 1471
Job 12:23 He increaseth the **n**, and destroyeth them: 1471
12:23 he enlargeth the **n**, and straiteneth them 1471
Ps 9:17 into hell, *and* all the **n** that forget God. 1471
9:20 *that* the **n** may know themselves *to be but* 1471
22:27 all the kindreds of the **n** shall worship 1471
22:28 and *he is* the governor among the **n**. 1471
47: 3 people under us, and the **n** under our feet. 3816
57: 9 I will sing unto thee among the **n**. 3816
66: 7 his power for ever; his eyes behold the **n**: 1471
67: 2 upon earth, thy saving health among all **n**. 1471
67: 4 O let the **n** be glad and sing for joy: 3816
67: 4 and govern the **n** upon earth. 3816
72:11 fall down before him: all **n** shall serve him. 1471
72:17 blessed in him: all **n** shall call him blessed. 1471
82: 8 judge the earth: for thou shalt inherit all **n**. 1471
86: 9 All **n** whom thou hast made shall come and 1471
96: 5 For all the gods of the **n** *are* idols: but 5971
106:27 To overthrow their seed also among the **n**, 1471
106:34 They did not destroy the **n**, 5971

N

Ps	108: 3	I will sing *praises* unto thee among the **n**.	3816
	113: 4	The LORD *is* high above all **n**, *and*	1471
	117: 1	O praise the LORD, all ye **n**: praise him,	1471
	118:10	All **n** compassed me about: but in the name	1471
	135:10	Who smote great **n**, and slew mighty kings;	1471
Pr	24:24	shall the people curse, **n** shall abhor him:	3816
Isa	2: 2	above the hills; and all **n** shall flow unto it.	1471
	2: 4	he shall judge among the **n**, and	1471
	5:26	he will lift up an ensign to the **n** from far,	1471
	9: 1	the sea, beyond Jordan, in Galilee of the **n**.	1471
	10: 7	his heart to destroy and cut off **n** not a few.	1471
	11:12	he shall set up an ensign for the **n**, and	1471
	13: 4	a tumultuous noise of the kingdoms of **n**	1471
	14: 6	he that ruled the **n** in anger, *is* persecuted,	1471
	14: 9	up from their thrones all the kings of the **n**.	1471
	14:12	to the ground, which didst weaken the **n**!	1471
	14:18	All the kings of the **n**, *even* all of them,	1471
	14:26	the hand that is stretched out upon all the **n**.	1471
	17:12	to the rushing of **n**, *that* make a rushing like	3816
	17:13	The **n** shall rush like the rushing of many	3816
	23: 3	*is* her revenue; and she is a mart of **n**.	1471
	25: 3	the city of the terrible **n** shall fear thee.	1471
	25: 7	and the vail that is spread over all **n**.	1471
	29: 7	the multitude of all the **n** that fight against	1471
	29: 8	so shall the multitude of all the **n** be,	1471
	30:28	to sift the **n** with the sieve of vanity:	1471
	33: 3	at the lifting up of thyself the **n** were	1471
	34: 1	Come near, ye **n**, to hear; and hearken,	1471
	34: 2	the indignation of the LORD *is* upon all **n**,	1471
	36:18	Hath any of the gods of the **n** delivered his	1471
	37:12	Have the gods of the **n** delivered them	1471
	37:18	kings of Assyria have laid waste all the **n**,	776
	40:15	the **n** *are* as a drop of a bucket, and	1471
	40:17	All **n** before him *are* as nothing; and	1471
	41: 2	gave the **n** before him, and made *him* rule	1471
	43: 9	Let all the **n** be gathered together, and	1471
	45: 1	I have holden, to subdue **n** before him;	1471
	45:20	near together, ye *that are* escaped of the **n**:	1471
	52:10	bare his holy arm in the eyes of all the **n**;	1471
	52:15	So shall he sprinkle many **n**; the kings shall	1471
	55: 5	and **n** *that* knew not thee shall run unto thee	1471
	60:12	yea, *those* **n** shall be utterly wasted.	1471
	61:11	and praise to spring forth before all the **n**.	1471
	64: 2	*that* the **n** may tremble at thy presence.	1471
	66:18	that *I* will gather all **n** and tongues;	1471
	66:19	send those that escape of them unto the **n**,	1471
	66:20	unto the LORD out of all **n** upon horses,	1471
Jer	1: 5	*and* I ordained thee a prophet unto the **n**.	1471
	1:10	I have this day set thee over the **n** and	1471
	3:17	all the **n** shall be gathered unto it, to	1471
	3:19	a goodly heritage of the hosts of **n**?	1471
	4: 2	and the **n** shall bless themselves in him, and	1471
	4:16	Make ye mention to the **n**; behold,	1471
	6:18	Therefore hear, ye **n**, and know,	1471
	9:26	for all *these* **n** *are* uncircumcised, and	1471
	10: 7	Who would not fear thee, O King of **n**?	1471
	10: 7	as among all the wise *men* of the **n**,	1471
	10:10	the **n** shall not be able to abide his	1471
	22: 8	many **n** shall pass by this city, and	1471
	25: 9	against all these **n** round about, and	1471
	25:11	these **n** shall serve the king of Babylon	1471
	25:13	Jeremiah hath prophesied against all the **n**.	1471
	25:14	For many **n** and great kings shall serve	1471
	25:15	cause all the **n**, to whom I send thee,	1471
	25:17	made all the **n** to drink, unto whom	1471
	25:31	the LORD hath a controversy with the **n**,	1471
	26: 6	will make this city a curse to all the **n** of	1471
	27: 7	all **n** shall serve him, and his son, and his	1471
	27: 7	*then* many **n** and great kings shall serve	1471
	27:11	the **n** that bring their neck under the yoke	1471
	28:11	of all **n** within the space of two full years.	1471
	28:14	a yoke of iron upon the neck of all these **n**,	1471
	29:14	I will gather you from all the **n**, and	1471
	29:18	among all the **n** whither I have driven	1471
	30:11	though I make a full end of all **n** whither I	1471
	31: 7	and shout among the chief of the **n**:	1471
	31:10	O ye **n**, and declare *it* in the isles afar off,	1471
	33: 9	and an honour before all the **n** of the earth,	1471
	36: 2	against Judah, and against all the **n**,	1471
	43: 5	that were returned from all **n**, whither they	1471
	44: 8	a reproach among all the **n** of the earth?	1471
	46:12	The **n** have heard *of* thy shame, and thy cry	1471
	46:28	for I will make a full end of all the **n**	1471
	50: 2	Declare ye among the **n**, and publish, and	1471
	50: 9	assembly of great **n** from the north country:	1471
	50:12	the hindermost of the **n** *shall be* a	1471
	50:23	Babylon become a desolation among the **n**!	1471
	50:46	is moved, and the cry is heard among the **n**.	1471
	51: 7	the **n** have drunken of her wine; therefore	1471
	51: 7	of her wine; therefore the **n** are mad.	1471
	51:20	for with thee will I break in pieces the **n**,	1471
	51:27	blow the trumpet among the **n**, prepare	1471
	51:27	the nations, prepare the **n** against her,	1471
	51:28	Prepare against her the **n** with the kings of	1471
	51:41	become an astonishment among the **n**!	1471
	51:44	the **n** shall not flow *together* any more unto	1471
La	1: 1	she *that was* great among the **n**, *and*	1471
Eze	5: 5	I have set it in the midst of the **n** and	1471
	5: 6	into wickedness more than the **n**,	1471
	5: 7	Because ye multiplied more than the **n** that	1471
	5: 7	of the **n** that *are* round about you;	1471
	5: 8	in the midst of thee in the sight of the **n**.	1471
	5:14	a reproach among the **n** that *are* round	1471
	5:15	an astonishment unto the **n** that *are* round	1471
	6: 8	that shall escape the sword among the **n**,	1471
	6: 9	the **n** whither they shall be carried captives,	1471
	12:15	when I shall scatter them among the **n**, and	1471
	19: 4	The **n** also heard of him; he was taken in	1471
	19: 8	the **n** set against him on every side from	1471
	25:10	may not be remembered among the **n**.	1471
	26: 3	will cause many **n** to come up against thee,	1471
	26: 5	and it shall become a spoil to the **n**.	1471
	28: 7	strangers upon thee, the terrible of the **n**:	1471
	29:12	I will scatter the Egyptians among the **n**,	1471
	29:15	shall it exalt itself any more above the **n**:	1471
	29:15	that *they* shall no more rule over the **n**.	1471
	30:11	his people with him, the terrible of the **n**,	1471
	30:23	I will scatter the Egyptians among the **n**,	1471
	30:26	I will scatter the Egyptians among the **n**,	1471
	31: 6	and under his shadow dwelt all great **n**.	1471
	31:12	strangers, the terrible of the **n**, have cut him	1471
	31:16	I made the **n** to shake at the sound of his	1471
	32: 2	Thou art like a young lion of the **n**, and	1471
	32: 9	I shall bring thy destruction among the **n**,	1471
	32:12	to fall, the terrible of the **n**, all of them:	1471
	32:16	the daughters of the **n** shall lament her:	1471
	32:18	and the daughters of the famous **n**,	1471
	35:10	These two **n** and these two countries shall	1471
	36:13	devourest up men, and hast bereaved thy **n**;	1471
	36:14	neither bereave thy **n** any more, saith	1471
	36:15	neither shalt thou cause thy **n** to fall any	1471
	37:22	they shall be no more two **n**, neither shall	1471
	38: 8	it is brought forth out of the **n**, and	5971
	38:12	the people *that are* gathered out of the **n**,	1471
	38:23	I will be known in the eyes of many **n**, and	1471
	39:27	sanctified in them in the sight of many **n**;	1471
Da	3: 4	is commanded, O people, **n**, and languages,	524
	3: 7	the **n**, and the languages, fell down *and*	524
	4: 1	unto all people, **n**, and languages, that dwell	524
	5:19	**n**, and languages, trembled and feared before	524
	6:25	**n**, and languages, that dwell in all the earth;	524
	7:14	a kingdom, that all people, **n**, and languages,	524
Hos	8:10	Yea, though they have hired among the **n**,	1471
	9:17	and they shall be wanderers among the **n**.	1471
Joel	3: 2	I will also gather all **n**, and will bring them	1471
	3: 2	whom they have scattered among the **n**,	1471
Am	6: 1	of Samaria, *which are* named chief of the **n**,	1471
	9: 9	I will sift the house of Israel among all **n**,	1471
Mic	4: 2	many **n** shall come, and say, Come, and	1471
	4: 3	many people, and rebuke strong **n** afar off;	1471
	4:11	Now also many **n** are gathered against thee,	1471
	7:16	The **n** shall see and be confounded at all	1471
Na	3: 4	that selleth **n** through her whoredoms, and	1471
	3: 5	I will shew the **n** thy nakedness, and	1471
Hab	1:17	and not spare continually to slay the **n**?	1471
	2: 5	gathereth unto him all **n**, and heapeth unto	1471
	2: 8	Because thou hast spoiled many **n**, all	1471
	3: 6	he beheld, and drove asunder the **n**; and	1471
Zep	2:14	in the midst of her, all the beasts of the **n**:	1471
	3: 6	I have cut off *the* **n**: their towers are	1471
	3: 8	for my determination *is* to gather the **n**,	1471
Hag	2: 7	I will shake all **n**, and the desire of all	1471
	2: 7	and the desire of all **n** shall come:	1471
Zec	2: 8	After the glory hath he sent me unto the **n**	1471
	2:11	many **n** shall be joined to the LORD in	1471
	7:14	among all the **n** whom they knew not:	1471
	8:22	strong **n** shall come to seek the LORD of	1471
	8:23	shall take hold out of all languages of the **n**,	1471

Zec 12: 9 *that* I will seek to destroy all the **n** that 1471
14: 2 For I will gather all **n** against Jerusalem to 1471
14: 3 LORD go forth, and fight against those **n**, 1471
14:16 *that* every one that is left of all the **n** which 1471
14:19 the punishment of all **n** that come not up to 1471
Mal 3:12 all **n** shall call you blessed: for ye shall be a 1471
Mt 24: 9 ye shall be hated of all **n** for my name's *1484*
24:14 in all the world for a witness unto all **n**; *1484*
25:32 And before him shall be gathered all **n**: and *1484*
28:19 Go ye therefore, and teach all **n**, *1484*
Mk 11:17 My house shall be called of all **n** the house *1484*
13:10 gospel must first be published among all **n**. *1484*
Lk 12:30 For all these *things* do the **n** of the world *1484*
21:24 and shall be led away captive into all **n**: *1484*
21:25 and upon the earth distress of **n**, *1484*
24:47 be preached in his name among all **n**, *1484*
Ac 13:19 And when he had destroyed seven **n** in *1484*
14:16 Who in times past suffered all **n** to walk in *1484*
17:26 And hath made of one blood all **n** of men *1484*
Ro 1: 5 for obedience to the faith among all **n**, *1484*
4:17 I have made thee a father of many **n**,) *1484*
4:18 that he might become the father of many **n**; *1484*
16:26 made known to all **n** for the obedience of *1484*
Gal 3: 8 *saying,* In thee shall all **n** be blessed. *1484*
Rev 2:26 to him will I give power over the **n**: *1484*
7: 9 of all **n**, and kindreds, and people, and *1484*
10:11 and **n**, and tongues, and kings. *1484*
11: 9 **n** shall see their dead bodies three days and *1484*
11:18 And the **n** were angry, and thy wrath is *1484*
12: 5 who was to rule all **n** with a rod of iron: *1484*
13: 7 him over all kindreds, and tongues, and **n**. *1484*
14: 8 she made all **n** drink of the wine of *1484*
15: 4 for all **n** shall come and worship before *1484*
16:19 into three parts, and the cities of the **n** fell: *1484*
17:15 and multitudes, and **n**, and tongues. *1484*
18: 3 For all **n** have drunk of the wine of *1484*
18:23 for by thy sorceries were all **n** deceived. *1484*
19:15 that with it he should smite the **n**: *1484*
20: 3 that he should deceive the **n** no more, *1484*
20: 8 And shall go out to deceive the **n** which are *1484*
21:24 And the **n** of them which are saved shall *1484*
21:26 bring the glory and honour of the **n** into it. *1484*
22: 2 of the tree *were* for the healing of the **n**. *1484*

N

NATIVE (1)
Jer 22:10 shall return no more, nor see his **n** country. 4138

NATIVITY (7)
Ge 11:28 before his father Terah in the land of his **n**, 4138
Ru 2:11 the land of thy **n**, and art come unto a 4138
Jer 46:16 to the land of our **n**, from the oppressing 4138
Eze 16: 3 and thy **n** *is* of the land of Canaan; 4138
16: 4 *as for* thy **n**, in the day thou wast born thy 4138
21:30 thou wast created, in the land of thy **n**. 4351
23:15 Babylonians of Chaldea, the land of their **n**: 4138

NATURAL (13) [NATURE]
Dt 34: 7 his eye was not dim, nor his **n force** abated. 3893
Ro 1:26 for even their women did change the **n** use *5446*
1:27 the men, leaving the **n** use of the woman, *5446*
1:31 **without n affection**, implacable, *794*
11:21 For if God spared not the **n** branches, *2596+5449*
11:24 which be the **n** *branches,* be graffed *2596+5449*
1Co 2:14 But the **n** man receiveth not the *things* of *5591*
15:44 It is sown a **n** body; it is raised a spiritual *5591*
15:44 There is a **n** body, and there is a spiritual *5591*
15:46 first *which is* spiritual, but *that which is* **n**; *5591*
2Ti 3: 3 **Without n affection**, trucebreakers, *794*
Jas 1:23 he is like unto a man beholding his **n** face *1078*
2Pe 2:12 But these, as **n** brute beasts, made to be *5446*

NATURALLY (2) [NATURE]
Php 2:20 who will **n** care for your state. *1104*
Jude 1:10 but what they know **n**, as brute beasts, *5447*

NATURE (12) [NATURAL, NATURALLY]
Ro 1:26 the natural use into that which is against **n**: *5449*
2:14 do by **n** the *things* contained in the law, *5449*
2:27 shall not uncircumcision which is by **n**, *5449*
11:24 cut out of the olive tree which is wild by **n**, *5449*
11:24 wert graffed contrary to **n** into a good olive *5449*
1Co 11:14 Doth not even **n** itself teach you, that, if a *5449*
Gal 2:15 We *who are* Jews by **n**, and not sinners of *5449*
4: 8 ye did service unto them which by **n** are no *5449*
Eph 2: 3 and were by **n** the children of wrath, *5449*
Heb 2:16 For verily he took not on *him the* **n** *of* NIG
Jas 3: 6 and setteth on fire the course of **n**; *1078*
2Pe 1: 4 you might be partakers of the divine **n**, *5449*

NAUGHT (3) [NOUGHT]
2Ki 2:19 but the water *is* **n**, and the ground barren. 7451
Pr 20:14 *It is* **n**, *it is* naught, saith the buyer: but 7451
20:14 *It is* naught, *it is* **n**, saith the buyer: but 7451

NAUGHTINESS (3) [NAUGHTY]
1Sa 17:28 I know thy pride, and the **n** of thine heart; 7455
Pr 11: 6 transgressors shall be taken in their own **n**. 1942
Jas 1:21 lay apart all filthiness and superfluity of **n**, *2549*

NAUGHTY (3) [NAUGHTINESS]
Pr 6:12 A **n** person, a wicked man, walketh *with* a 1100
17: 4 *and* a liar giveth ear to a **n** tongue. 1942
Jer 24: 2 the other basket *had* very **n** figs, 7451

NAUM (1)
Lk 3:25 which was *the son* of **N**, which was *the son* *3486*

NAVEL (4)
Job 40:16 and his force *is* in the **n** of his belly. 8306
Pr 3: 8 It shall be health to thy **n**, and marrow to 8270
SS 7: 2 Thy **n** *is like* a round goblet, *which* wanteth 8326
Eze 16: 4 in the day thou wast born thy **n** was not cut, 8270

NAVES (1)
1Ki 7:33 their **n**, and their felloes, and their spokes, 1354

NAVY (6)
1Ki 9:26 king Solomon made a **n** *of ships* in 590
9:27 Hiram sent in the **n** his servants, 590
10:11 the **n** also of Hiram, that brought gold from 590
10:22 For the king had at sea a **n** of Tharshish with 590
10:22 sea a navy of Tharshish with the **n** of Hiram: 590
10:22 once in three years came the **n** of Tharshish, 590

NAY (55) See Index

NAZARENE (1) [NAZARETH]
Mt 2:23 by the prophets, He shall be called a **N**. *3480*

NAZARENES (1) [NAZARETH]
Ac 24: 5 and a ringleader of the sect of the **N**: *3480*

NAZARETH (29) [NAZARENE, NAZARENES]
Mt 2:23 And he came and dwelt in a city called **N**: *3478*
4:13 And leaving **N**, he came and dwelt in *3478*
21:11 This is Jesus the prophet of **N** of Galilee. *3478*
26:71 This *fellow* was also with Jesus **of N**. *3480*
Mk 1: 9 *that* Jesus came from **N** of Galilee, and *3478*
1:24 have we to do with thee, *thou* Jesus **of N**? *3479*
10:47 And when he heard that it was Jesus **of N**, *3480*
14:67 said, *And* thou also wast with Jesus of **N**. *3479*
16: 6 Ye seek Jesus of **N**, which was crucified: *3479*
Lk 1:26 from God unto a city of Galilee, named **N**, *3478*
2: 4 out of the city of **N**, into Judea, unto *3478*
2:39 returned into Galilee, to their own city **N**. *3478*
2:51 and came to **N**, and was subject unto them: *3478*
4:16 And he came to **N**, where he had been *3478*
4:34 have we to do with thee, *thou* Jesus **of N**? *3479*
18:37 they told him, that Jesus **of N** passeth by. *3480*
24:19 Concerning Jesus **of N**, which was a *3480*
Jn 1:45 and the prophets, did write, Jesus of **N**, *3478*
1:46 Can there any good *thing* come out of **N**? *3478*
18: 5 They answered him, Jesus **of N**. Jesus saith *3480*
18: 7 Whom seek ye? And they said, Jesus **of N**. *3480*
19:19 JESUS **OF N** THE KING OF THE JEWS. *3480*
Ac 2:22 Jesus **of N**, a man approved of God among *3480*
3: 6 In the name of Jesus Christ **of N** rise up and *3480*
4:10 that by the name of Jesus Christ **of N**, *3480*
6:14 that this Jesus of **N** shall destroy this place, *3480*
10:38 How God anointed Jesus of **N** with *3478*
22: 8 And he said unto me, I am Jesus **of N**, *3480*
26: 9 *things* contrary to the name of Jesus **of N**. *3480*

NAZARITE (9) [NAZARITES]
Nu 6: 2 separate *themselves* to vow a vow of a **N**, 5139
6:13 this *is* the law of the **N**, when the days of 5139
6:18 the **N** shall shave the head of his separation 5139
6:19 and shall put *them* upon the hands of the **N**, 5139
6:20 and after *that* the **N** may drink wine. 5139
6:21 This *is* the law of the **N** who hath vowed, 5139

Jdg 13: 5 for the child shall be a **N** unto God from 5139
13: 7 **N** to God from the womb to the day of his 5139
16:17 for I *have been* a **N** unto God from my 5139

NAZARITES (3) [NAZARITE]

La 4: 7 Her **N** were purer than snow, they were 5139
Am 2:11 for prophets, and of your young men for **N**. 5139
2:12 ye gave the **N** wine to drink; 5139

NAZIRITE See NAZARITE

NEAH (1)

Jos 19:13 and goeth out *to* Remmon-methoar *to* **N**; 5269

NEAPOLIS (1)

Ac 16:11 to Samothracia, and the next *day* to **N**; *3496*

NEAR (211) [NEARER]

Ge 12:11 when he was **come n** to enter into Egypt, 7126
18:23 Abraham **drew n**, and said, Wilt thou also 5066
19: 9 *even* Lot, and **came n** to break the door. 5066
19:20 this city *is* **n** to flee unto, and it *is* a little 7138
20: 4 Abimelech had not **come n** her: and 7126
27:21 **Come n**, I pray thee, that I may feel thee, 5066
27:22 Jacob **went n** unto Isaac his father; and 5066
27:25 **Bring** *it* **n** to me, and I will eat of my son's 5066
27:25 he **brought** *it* **n** to him, and he did eat: and 5066
27:26 **Come n** now, and kiss me, my son. 5066
27:27 he **came n**, and kissed him: and he smelled 5066
29:10 that Jacob **went n**, and rolled the stone 5066
33: 3 seven times, until he **came n** to his brother. 5066
33: 6 the handmaidens **came n**, they and 5066
33: 7 Leah also with her children **came n**, and 5066
33: 7 after **came** Joseph **n** and Rachel, and 5066
37:18 afar off, even before he **came n** unto them, 7126
43:19 they **came n** to the steward of Joseph's 5066
44:18 Judah **came n** unto him, and said, O my 5066
45: 4 his brethren, **Come n** to me, I pray you. 5066
45: 4 they **came n**. And he said, I *am* Joseph 5066
45:10 thou shalt be **n** unto me, thou, and 7138
48:10 he **brought** them **n** unto him; and he kissed 5066
48:13 right hand, and **brought** *them* **n** unto him. 5066
Ex 12:48 and then let him **come n** and keep it; 7126
13:17 land of the Philistines, although that *was* **n**; 7138
14:20 that the one **came** not **n** the other all 7126
16: 9 of Israel, **Come n** before the LORD: 7126
19:22 which **come n** to the LORD, 5066
20:21 Moses **drew n** unto the thick darkness 5066
24: 2 Moses alone shall **come n** the LORD: 5066
28:43 when they **come n** unto the altar to minister 5066
30:20 when they **come n** to the altar to minister, 5066
40:32 when they **came n** unto the altar, 7126
Lev 9: 5 all the congregation **drew n** and 7126
10: 4 of Aaron, and said unto them, **Come n**, 7126
10: 5 So they **went n**, and carried them in their 7126
18: 6 None of you shall approach to any that is **n** 7607
18:12 she *is* thy father's **n kinswoman**. 7607
18:13 for she *is* thy mother's **n kinswoman**. 7607
18:17 *for* they *are* her **n kinswomen**: 7608
20:19 for he uncovereth his **n kin**: they shall bear 7607
21: 2 for his kin, that is **n** unto him, *that is,* for 7138
Nu 3: 6 **Bring** the tribe of Levi **n**, and present them 7126
5:16 the priest shall **bring** her **n**, and set her 7126
16: 5 and will **cause** *him* **to come n** unto him: 7126
16: 5 chosen will he **cause to come n** unto him. 7126
16: 9 to **bring** you **n** to himself to do the service 7126
16:10 he hath **brought** thee **n** *to him,* and all thy 7126
16:40 **come n** to offer incense before the LORD; 7126
17:13 Whosoever **cometh** any thing **n** unto 7131+7131
26: 3 in the plains of Moab by Jordan *n* Jericho, NIH
26:63 in the plains of Moab by Jordan *n* Jericho. NIH
31:12 of Moab, which *are* by Jordan *n* Jericho. NIH
31:48 captains of hundreds, **came n** unto Moses: 7126
32:16 they **came n** unto him, and said, We will 5066
33:48 pitched in the plains of Moab by Jordan *n* NIH
33:50 in the plains of Moab by Jordan *n* Jericho, NIH
34:15 on *this* side Jordan *n* Jericho eastward, NIH
35: 1 in the plains of Moab by Jordan *n* Jericho, NIH
36: 1 **came n**, and spake before Moses, and 7126
36:13 in the plains of Moab by Jordan *n* Jericho. NIH
Dt 1:22 ye **came n** unto me every one of you, and 7126
4:11 ye **came n** and stood under the mountain; 7126
5:23 that ye **came n** unto me, *even* all the heads 7126
5:27 **Go** thou **n**, and hear all that the LORD our 7126
16:21 **n unto** the altar of the LORD thy God, 681
21: 5 the priests the sons of Levi shall **come n**; 5066
25:11 the wife of the one **draweth n** for to deliver 7126
Jos 3: 4 **come** not **n** unto it, that ye may know 7126
10:24 **Come n**, put your feet upon the necks of 7126
10:24 they **came n**, and put their feet upon 7126
15:46 *lay* **n** Ashdod, with their villages: 3027+5921
17: 4 they **came n** before Eleazar the priest, and 7126
18:13 **n** the hill that *lieth* on the south side of 5921
21: 1 **came n** the heads of the fathers of 5066
Jdg 18:22 the men that *were* in the houses **n** to 5973
19:13 let us **draw n** to one of *these* places to 7126
20:24 the children of Israel **came n** against 7126
20:34 but they knew not that evil *was* **n** them. 5060
Ru 2:20 The man *is* **n of kin** unto us, one of our 7138
3: 9 thine handmaid; for thou *art* a **n kinsman**. 1350
3:12 And now it is true that I *am thy* **n kinsman**: 1350
1Sa 4:19 was with child, *n* to be delivered: NIH
7:10 the Philistines **drew n** to battle against 5066
9:18 Saul **drew n** to Samuel in the gate, and 5066
10:20 **caused** all the tribes of Israel **to come n**, 7126
10:21 **caused** the tribe of Benjamin **to come n** by 7126
14:36 the priest, Let us **draw n** hither unto God. 7126
14:38 Saul said, **Draw** ye **n** hither, all the chief of 5066
17:16 the Philistine **drew n** morning and evening, 5066
17:40 in his hand: and he **drew n** to the Philistine. 5066
17:41 Philistine came on and **drew n** unto David; 7131
30:21 when David **came n** to the people, he 5066
2Sa 1:15 and said, **Go n**, *and* fall upon him. 5066
14:30 Joab's field is **n** mine, and he hath 413+3027
18:25 And he came apace, and **drew n**. 7131
19:42 of Israel, Because the king *is* **n of kin** to us: 7138
20:16 say, I pray you, unto Joab, **Come n** hither, 7126
20:17 when he was **come n** unto her, the woman 7126
1Ki 8:46 unto the land of the enemy, far or **n**; 7138
18:30 said unto all the people, **Come n** unto me. 5066
18:30 all the people **came n** unto him. And he 5066
18:36 that Elijah the prophet **came n**, and said, 5066
21: 2 of herbs, because it *is* **n** unto my house: 7138
22:24 Zedekiah the son of Chenaanah **went n**, 5066
2Ki 4:27 Gehazi **came n** to thrust her away. And 5066
5:13 his servants **came n**, and spake unto him, 5066
2Ch 6:36 them away captives unto a land far off or **n**; 7138
18:23 Zedekiah the son of Chenaanah **came n**, 5066
21:16 that *were* **n** the Ethiopians: 3027+5921
29:31 **come n** and bring sacrifices and 5066
Est 5: 2 So Esther **drew n**, and touched the top of 7126
9: 1 his decree **drew n** to be put in execution, 5060
Job 31:37 as a prince would I **go n** unto him. 7126
33:22 his soul **draweth n** unto the grave, and 7126
41:16 One is so **n** to another, that no air can come 5066
Ps 22:11 Be not far from me; for trouble *is* **n**; 7138
32: 9 and bridle, lest *they* **come n** unto thee. 7126
73:28 *it is* good for me to **draw n** to God: I have 7132
75: 1 for *that* thy name *is* **n** thy wondrous works 7138
107:18 and they **draw n** unto the gates of death. 5060
119:151 Thou *art* **n**, O LORD; and all thy 7138
119:169 Let my cry **come n** before thee, O LORD: 7126
148:14 the children of Israel, a people **n unto** him. 7138
Pr 7: 8 Passing through the street **n** her corner; and 681
10:14 the mouth of the foolish *is* **n** destruction. 7138
27:10 *for* better *is* a neighbour *that is* **n** than a 7138
Isa 13:22 her time *is* **n** to come, and her days shall 7138
26:17 *that* **draweth n the time** of her delivery, 7126
29:13 Forasmuch as this people **draw n** *me* with 5066
33:13 and ye *that are* **n**, acknowledge my might. 7138
34: 1 **Come n**, ye nations, to hear; and hearken, 7126
41: 1 let them **come n**; then let them speak: let us 5066
41: 1 let us **come n** together to judgment. 7126
41: 5 of the earth were afraid, **drew n**, and came. 7126
45:20 **draw n** together, ye *that are* escaped of 5066
45:21 Tell ye, and **bring** *them* **n**; yea, let them 5066
46:13 I **bring n** my righteousness; it shall not be 7126
48:16 **Come** ye **n** unto me, hear ye this; I have 7126
50: 8 *He is* **n** that justifieth me; who will contend 7138
50: 8 *is* mine adversary? let him **come n** to me. 5066
51: 5 My righteousness *is* **n**; my salvation is gone 7138
54:14 from terror; for it shall not **come n** thee. 7126
55: 6 be found, call ye upon him while he is **n**: 7138
56: 1 for my salvation *is* **n** to come, and 7138
57: 3 But **draw n** hither, ye sons of the sorceress, 7126
57:19 and to *him that is* **n**, saith the LORD; 7138
65: 5 Stand by thyself, **come** not **n** to me; 5066
Jer 12: 2 thou *art* **n** in their mouth, and far from their 7138
25:26 far and **n**, one with another, and all 7138

Jer 30:21 I will **cause** him **to draw n**, and he shall 7126
42: 1 the least even **unto** the greatest, came **n**, 5704
46: 3 and shield, and **draw n** to battle. 5066
48:16 The calamity of Moab *is* **n** to come, and 7138
48:24 all the cities of the land of Moab, far or **n**. 7138
52:25 seven men of them that were **n** the king's 7200
La 3:57 Thou **drewest n** in the day *that* I called 7126
4:18 our end is **n**, our days are fulfilled; for our 7126
Eze 6:12 *he* that *is* **n** shall fall by the sword; and 7138
7: 7 the day of trouble *is* **n**, and not 7138
7:12 The time is come, the day **draweth n**: 5060
9: 1 **Cause** them that have charge over the city **to draw n**, 7126
9: 6 **come** not **n** any man upon whom *is* 5066
11: 3 Which say, *It is* not **n**; *let us* build 7138+871.1
18: 6 neither hath **come n** to a menstruous 7126
22: 4 thou hast **caused** thy days **to draw n**, and 7126
22: 5 *Those that be* **n**, and *those that be* far from 7138
30: 3 For the day *is* **n**, even the day of 7138
30: 3 even the day of the LORD *is* **n**, a cloudy 7138
40:46 which **come n** to the LORD to minister 7131
44:13 they shall not **come n** unto me, to do 5066
44:13 nor to **come n** to any of my holy *things*, in 5066
44:15 they shall **come n** to me to minister unto 7126
44:16 they shall **come n** to my table, to minister 7126
45: 4 which shall **come n** to minister unto 7131
Da 3: 8 at that time certain Chaldeans **came n**, 7127
3:26 Nebuchadnezzar **came n** to the mouth of 7127
6:12 they **came n**, and spake before the king 7127
7:13 and they **brought** him **n** before him. 7127
7:16 I **came n** unto one of them that stood *by*, 7127
8:17 So he came **n** where I stood: and when he 681
9: 7 all Israel, *that are* **n**, and *that are* far off, 7138
Joel 3: 9 mighty *men*, let all the men of war **draw n**; 5066
3:14 for the day of the LORD *is* **n** in the valley 7138
Am 6: 3 and **cause** the seat of violence **to come n**; 5066
Ob 1:15 For the day of the LORD *is* **n** upon all 7138
Zep 1:14 The great day of the LORD *is* **n**, *it is* near, 7138
1:14 LORD *is* near, *it is* **n**, and hasteth greatly, 7138
3: 2 in the LORD; she **drew** not **n** to her God. 7126
Mal 3: 5 I will **come n** to you to judgment; and 7126
Mt 21:34 And when the time of the fruit **drew n**, *1448*
24:33 shall see all these *things*, know that it is **n**, *1451*
Mk 13:28 forth leaves, ye know that summer is **n**: *1451*
Lk 15: 1 Then **drew n** unto him all the publicans *1448*
18:40 and when he was **come n**, he asked him, *1448*
19:41 And when he was **come n**, he beheld *1448*
21: 8 I am *Christ*; and the time **draweth n**: *1448*
22:47 and **drew n** unto Jesus to kiss him. *1448*
24:15 Jesus himself **drew n**, and went with them. *1448*
Jn 3:23 And John also was baptizing in Aenon **n** to *1451*
4: 5 **n** to the parcel of ground that Jacob gave to *4139*
11:54 went thence unto a country **n to** *1451*
Ac 7:31 as he **drew n** to behold *it*, the voice of *4334*
8:29 **Go n**, and join thyself to this chariot. *4334*
9: 3 as *he* journeyed, he **came n** Damascus: *1448*
10:24 called together his kinsmen and **n** friends. *316*
21:33 Then the chief captain **came n**, and *1448*
23:15 and we, or ever he **come n**, are ready to kill *1448*
27:27 deemed that they **drew n** to some country; *4317*
Heb 10:22 Let us **draw n** with a true heart in full *4334*

NEARER (2) [NEAR]
Ru 3:12 howbeit there is a kinsman **n** than I. 7138
Ro 13:11 for now *is* our salvation **n** than when we *1452*

NEARIAH (3)
1Ch 3:22 Igeal, and Bariah, and N, and Shaphat, six. 5294
3:23 the sons of N; Elioenai, and Hezekiah, and 5294
4:42 N, and Rephaiah, and Uzziel, the sons of 5294

NEBAI (1)
Ne 10:19 Hariph, Anathoth, N, 5109

NEBAIOTH See NEBAJOTH

NEBAJOTH (5)
Ge 25:13 the firstborn of Ishmael, N; and Kedar, and 5032
28: 9 the sister of N, to be his wife. 5032
36: 3 Bashemath Ishmael's daughter, sister of N. 5032
1Ch 1:29 The firstborn of Ishmael, N; then Kedar, 5032
Isa 60: 7 the rams of N shall minister unto thee: 5032

NEBALLAT (1)
Ne 11:34 Hadid, Zeboim, N, 5041

NEBAT (25)
1Ki 11:26 Jeroboam the son of N, an Ephrathite of 5028
12: 2 came to pass, when Jeroboam the son of N, 5028
12:15 the Shilonite unto Jeroboam the son of N. 5028
15: 1 the son of N reigned Abijam over Judah. 5028
16: 3 like the house of Jeroboam the son of N. 5028
16:26 in all the way of Jeroboam the son of N, 5028
16:31 walk in the sins of Jeroboam the son of N, 5028
21:22 like the house of Jeroboam the son of N, 5028
22:52 in the way of Jeroboam the son of N, 5028
2Ki 3: 3 unto the sins of Jeroboam the son of N, 5028
9: 9 like the house of Jeroboam the son of N, 5028
10:29 *from* the sins of Jeroboam the son of N, 5028
13: 2 followed the sins of Jeroboam the son of N, 5028
13:11 from all the sins of Jeroboam the son of N, 5028
14:24 from all the sins of Jeroboam the son of N, 5028
15: 9 not from the sins of Jeroboam the son of N, 5028
15:18 from the sins of Jeroboam the son of N, 5028
15:24 not from the sins of Jeroboam the son of N, 5028
15:28 not from the sins of Jeroboam the son of N, 5028
17:21 and they made Jeroboam the son of N king: 5028
23:15 high place which Jeroboam the son of N, 5028
2Ch 9:29 the seer against Jeroboam the son of N? 5028
10: 2 when Jeroboam the son of N, who *was* in 5028
10:15 the Shilonite to Jeroboam the son of N. 5028
13: 6 Yet Jeroboam the son of N, the servant of 5028

NEBO (13)
Nu 32: 3 and Elealeh, and Shebam, and N, and Beon, 5015
32:38 N, and Baal-meon, (*their* names being 5015
33:47 in the mountains of Abarim, before N. 5015
Dt 32:49 *unto* mount N, which *is* in the land of 5015
34: 1 the plains of Moab unto the mountain of N, 5015
1Ch 5: 8 in Aroer, even unto N and Baal-meon: 5015
Ezr 2:29 The children of N, fifty and two. 5015
10:43 Of the sons of N; Jeiel, Mattithiah, Zabad, 5015
Ne 7:33 The men of the other N, fifty and two. 5015
Isa 15: 2 Moab shall howl over N, and over Medeba: 5015
46: 1 Bel boweth down, N stoopeth, their idols 5015
Jer 48: 1 of hosts, the God of Israel; Woe unto N! 5015
48:22 and upon N, and upon Beth-diblathaim, 5015

NEBO-SARSEKIM See SARSECHIM

NEBUCHADNEZZAR (60) [NEBUCHADREZZAR]
2Ki 24: 1 In his days N king of Babylon came up, 5019
24:10 At that time the servants of N king of 5019
24:11 N king of Babylon came against the city, 5019
25: 1 *that* N king of Babylon came, he, and 5019
25: 8 which *is* the nineteenth year of king N king 5019
25:22 whom N king of Babylon had left, 5019
1Ch 6:15 and Jerusalem by the hand of N. 5019
2Ch 36: 6 Against him came up N king of Babylon, 5019
36: 7 N also carried of the vessels of the house of 5019
36:10 king N sent, and brought him to Babylon, 5019
36:13 he also rebelled against king N, who had 5019
Ezr 1: 7 which N had brought forth out of 5019
2: 1 whom N the king of Babylon had carried 5019
5:12 he gave them into the hand of N the king of 5020
5:14 which N took out of the temple that *was* in 5020
6: 5 which N took forth out of the temple which 5020
Ne 7: 6 whom N the king of Babylon had carried 5019
Est 2: 6 whom N the king of Babylon had carried 5019
Jer 27: 6 into the hand of N the king of Babylon, 5019
27: 8 kingdom which will not serve the same N 5019
27:20 Which N king of Babylon took not, 5019
28: 3 that N king of Babylon took away from this 5019
28:11 will I break the yoke of N king of Babylon 5019
28:14 that *they* may serve N king of Babylon; 5019
29: 1 to all the people whom N had carried away 5019
29: 3 sent unto Babylon to N king of Babylon, 5019
34: 1 when N king of Babylon, and all his army, 5019
39: 5 they brought him up to N king of Babylon 5019
Da 1: 1 came N king of Babylon *unto* Jerusalem, 5019
1:18 of the eunuchs brought them in before N. 5019
2: 1 in the second year of the reign of N, 5019
2: 1 N dreamed dreams, wherewith his spirit 5019
2:28 maketh known to the king N what shall be 5020
2:46 the king N fell upon his face, and 5020
3: 1 N the king made an image of gold, 5020
3: 2 N the king sent to gather together 5020
3: 2 of the image which N the king had set up. 5020
3: 3 of the image that N the king had set up; 5020
3: 3 they stood before the image that N had set 5020

Da 3: 5 worship the golden image that **N** the king 5020
3: 7 worshipped the golden image that **N** 5020
3: 9 They spake and said to the king **N**, O king, 5020
3:13 **N** in *his* rage and fury commanded to bring 5020
3:14 **N** spake and said unto them, *Is it* true, 5020
3:16 answered and said to the king, O **N**, 5020
3:19 was **N** full *of* fury, and the form of his 5020
3:24 **N** the king was astonied, and rose up in 5020
3:26 **N** came near to the mouth of the burning 5020
3:28 *Then* **N** spake, and said, Blessed *be* 5020
4: 1 **N** the king, unto all people, nations, 5020
4: 4 I **N** was at rest in mine house, and 5020
4:18 This dream I king **N** have seen. Now thou, 5020
4:28 All this came upon the king **N**. 5020
4:31 *saying*, O king **N**, to thee it is spoken; 5020
4:33 same hour was the thing fulfilled upon **N**: 5020
4:34 at the end of the days I **N** lift up mine eyes 5020
4:37 Now I **N** praise and extol and honour 5020
5: 2 silver vessels which his father **N** had taken 5020
5:11 whom the king **N** thy father, the king, *I say*, 5020
5:18 the most high God gave **N** thy father a 5020

NEBUCHADREZZAR (31) [NEBUCHADNEZZAR]

Jer 21: 2 for **N** king of Babylon maketh war against 5019
21: 7 into the hand of **N** king of Babylon, and 5019
22:25 even into the hand of **N** king of Babylon, 5019
24: 1 after that **N** king of Babylon had carried 5019
25: 1 that *was* the first year of **N** king of 5019
25: 9 and **N** the king of Babylon, my servant, and 5019
29:21 I will deliver them into the hand of **N** king 5019
32: 1 which *was* the eighteenth year of **N**. 5019
32:28 into the hand of **N** king of Babylon, and 5019
35:11 when **N** king of Babylon came up into 5019
37: 1 whom **N** king of Babylon made king in 5019
39: 1 came **N** king of Babylon and all his army 5019
39:11 Now **N** king of Babylon gave charge 5019
43:10 I *will* send and take **N** the king of Babylon, 5019
44:30 Judah into the hand of **N** king of Babylon, 5019
46: 2 which **N** king of Babylon smote in 5019
46:13 how **N** king of Babylon should come 5019
46:26 into the hand of **N** king of Babylon, and 5019
49:28 which **N** king of Babylon shall smite, 5019
49:30 for **N** king of Babylon hath taken counsel 5019
50:17 last this **N** king of Babylon hath broken his 5019
51:34 **N** the king of Babylon hath devoured me, 5019
52: 4 *that* **N** king of Babylon came, he and all his 5019
52:12 which *was* the nineteenth year of **N** king of 5019
52:28 This *is* the people whom **N** carried away 5019
52:29 In the eighteenth year of **N** he carried away 5019
52:30 twentieth year of **N** Nebuzar-adan 5019
Eze 26: 7 I *will* bring upon Tyrus **N** king of Babylon, 5019
29:18 **N** king of Babylon caused his army to serve 5019
29:19 I *will* give the land of Egypt unto **N** king of 5019
30:10 to cease by the hand of **N** king of Babylon. 5019

NEBUSHASBAN (1)

Jer 39:13 **N**, Rab-saris, and Nergal-sharezer, 5021

NEBUSHAZBAN See NEBUSHASBAN

NEBUZAR-ADAN (15)

2Ki 25: 8 came **N**, captain of the guard, a servant of 5018
25:11 did **N** the captain of the guard carry away. 5018
25:20 **N** captain of the guard took these, and 5018
Jer 39: 9 **N** the captain of the guard carried away 5018
39:10 **N** the captain of the guard left of the poor 5018
39:11 Jeremiah to **N** the captain of the guard, 5018
39:13 So **N** the captain of the guard sent, and 5018
40: 1 after that **N** the captain of the guard had let 5018
41:10 whom **N** the captain of the guard had 5018
43: 6 every person that **N** the captain of the guard 5018
52:12 came **N**, captain of the guard, *which* served 5018
52:15 **N** the captain of the guard carried away 5018
52:16 **N** the captain of the guard left *certain* of 5018
52:26 So **N** the captain of the guard took them, 5018
52:30 twentieth year of Nebuchadrezzar **N** 5018

NECESSARY (9) [NECESSITY]

Job 23:12 words of his mouth more than my **n** *food*. 2706
Ac 13:46 It was **n** that the word of God should first *316*
15:28 you no greater burden than these **n** *things*; *1876*
28:10 they laded *us* with such *things* as were **n**. *5532*
1Co 12:22 which seem to be more feeble, are **n**: *316*
2Co 9: 5 Therefore I thought it **n** to exhort *316*
Php 2:25 Yet I supposed it **n** to send to you *316*
Tit 3:14 also learn to maintain good works for **n** uses, *316*
Heb 9:23 **n** that the patterns of *things* in the heavens *318*

NECESSITIES (3) [NECESSITY]

Ac 20:34 these hands have ministered unto my **n**, *5532*
2Co 6: 4 in afflictions, in **n**, in distresses, *318*
12:10 in reproaches, in **n**, in persecutions, *318*

NECESSITY (10) [NECESSARY, NECESSITIES]

Lk 23:17 (For of **n** he must release one unto them at *318*
Ro 12:13 Distributing to the **n** of saints; given to *5532*
1Co 7:37 having no **n**, but hath power over his own *318*
9:16 for **n** is laid upon me; yea, woe is unto me, *318*
2Co 9: 7 *so let him give;* not grudgingly, or of **n**: *318*
Php 4:16 ye sent once and again unto my **n**. *5532*
Phm 1:14 that thy benefit should not be as *it were* of **n**, *318*
Heb 7:12 there is made of **n** a change also of the law. *318*
8: 3 wherefore *it is* of **n** that this *man* have *316*
9:16 must also of **n** be the death of the testator. *318*

NECHO (3)

2Ch 35:20 **N** king of Egypt came up to fight against 5224
35:22 hearkened not unto the words of **N** from 5224
36: 4 **N** took Jehoahaz his brother, and 5224

NECK (62) [NECKS, STIFFNECKED]

Ge 27:16 his hands, and upon the smooth of his **n**: 6677
27:40 thou shalt break his yoke from off thy **n**. 6677
33: 4 and fell on his **n**, and kissed him: 6677
41:42 fine linen, and put a gold chain about his **n**; 6677
45:14 he fell upon his brother Benjamin's **n**, and 6677
45:14 and wept; and Benjamin wept upon his **n**. 6677
46:29 he fell on his **n**, and wept on his neck a 6677
46:29 his neck, and wept on his **n** a good while. 6677
49: 8 thy hand *shall be* in the **n** of thine enemies; 6203
Ex 13:13 not redeem *it*, then thou shalt **break** his **n**: 6202
34:20 *him* not, then shalt thou **break** his **n**. 6202
Lev 5: 8 wring off his head from his **n**, but shall not 6203
Dt 21: 4 shall **strike off** the heifer's **n** there in 6202
28:48 and he shall put a yoke of iron upon thy **n**, 6677
31:27 For I know thy rebellion, and thy stiff **n**: 6203
1Sa 4:18 of the gate, and his **n** brake, and he died: 4665
2Ki 17:14 their necks, like to the **n** of their fathers, 6203
2Ch 36:13 he stiffened his **n**, and hardened his heart 6203
Ne 9:29 and hardened their **n**, and would not hear. 6203
Job 15:26 He runneth upon him, *even* on *his* **n**, 6677
16:12 he hath also taken *me* by my **n**, and 6203
39:19 hast thou clothed his **n** with thunder? 6677
41:22 In his **n** remaineth strength, and sorrow is 6677
Ps 75: 5 your horn on high: speak *not* with a stiff **n**. 6677
Pr 1: 9 unto thy head, and chains about thy **n**. 1621
3: 3 bind them about thy **n**; write them upon 1621
3:22 be life unto thy soul, and grace to thy **n**. 1621
6:21 upon thine heart, *and* tie them about thy **n**. 1621
29: 1 that being often reproved hardeneth *his* **n**, 6203
SS 1:10 rows *of jewels*, thy **n** with chains *of gold*. 6677
4: 4 Thy **n** *is* like the tower of David builded for 6677
4: 9 one of thine eyes, with one chain of thy **n**. 6677
7: 4 Thy **n** *is* as a tower of ivory; thine eyes *like* 6677
Isa 8: 8 and go over, he shall reach *even* to the **n**; 6677
10:27 his yoke from off thy **n**, and the yoke shall 6677
30:28 shall reach to the midst of the **n**, 6677
48: 4 thy **n** *is* an iron sinew, and thy brow brass: 6203
52: 2 loose thyself from the bands of thy **n**, 6677
66: 3 a lamb, *as if* he **cut off** a dog's **n**; 6202
Jer 7:26 nor inclined their ear, but hardened their **n**: 6203
17:23 made their **n** stiff, that *they* might not hear, 6203
27: 2 and yokes, and put them upon thy **n**, 6677
27: 8 that will not put their **n** under the yoke of 6677
27:11 the nations that bring their **n** under the yoke 6677
28:10 the yoke from off the prophet Jeremiah's **n**, 6677
28:11 **n** of all nations within the space of two full 6677
28:12 from off the **n** of the prophet Jeremiah, 6677
28:14 I have put a yoke of iron upon the **n** of all 6677
30: 8 *that* I will break his yoke from off thy **n**, 6677
La 1:14 they are wreathed, *and* come up upon my **n**: 6677
Eze 16:11 upon thine hands, and a chain on thy **n**. 1627
Da 5: 7 *have* a chain of gold about his **n**, and 6676
5:16 *have* a chain of gold about thy **n**, and 6676
5:29 *put* a chain of gold about his **n**, and made a 6676
Hos 10:11 *the corn;* but I passed over upon her fair **n**: 6677
Hab 3:13 by discovering the foundation unto the **n**. 6677
Mt 18: 6 that a millstone were hanged about his **n**, *5137*
Mk 9:42 that a millstone were hanged about his **n**, *5137*

Lk 15:20 and ran, and fell on his **n**, and kissed him. *5137*
17: 2 that a millstone were hanged about his **n**, *5137*
Ac 15:10 to put a yoke upon the **n** of the disciples, *5137*
20:37 and fell on Paul's **n**, and kissed him, *5137*

NECKLACES See TIRES

NECKS (18) [NECK]
Jos 10:24 put your feet upon the **n** of these kings. 6677
10:24 and put their feet upon the **n** of them. 6677
Jdg 5:30 *meet* for the **n** of *them that take* the spoil? 6677
8:21 the ornaments that *were* on their camels' **n**. 6677
8:26 the chains that *were* about their camels' **n**. 6677
2Sa 22:41 Thou hast also given me the **n** of mine 6203
2Ki 17:14 hardened their **n**, like to the neck of their 6203
Ne 3: 5 their nobles put not their **n** to the work of 6677
9:16 hardened their **n**, and hearkened not to thy 6203
9:17 hardened their **n**, and in their rebellion 6203
Ps 18:40 Thou hast also given me the **n** of mine 6203
Isa 3:16 walk with stretched forth **n** and 1627
Jer 19:15 because they have hardened their **n**, 6203
27:12 Bring your **n** under the yoke of the king of 6677
La 5: 5 Our **n** *are* under persecution: we labour, 6677
Eze 21:29 to bring thee upon the **n** of *them that are* 6677
Mic 2: 3 from which ye shall not remove your **n**; 6677
Ro 16: 4 have for my life laid down their own **n**: *5137*

NECO See NECHO

NECROMANCER (1)
Dt 18:11 or a wizard, or a **n**. 413+1875+1886.1

NEDABIAH (1)
1Ch 3:18 and Shenazar, Jecamiah, Hoshama, and **N**. 5072

NEED (49) [NEEDED, NEEDEST, NEEDETH, NEEDFUL, NEEDS, NEEDY]
Dt 15: 8 shalt surely lend him sufficient for his **n**, 4270
1Sa 21:15 *Have* I **n** of mad men, that ye have brought 2638
2Ch 2:16 out of Lebanon, as much as thou shalt **n**: 6878
20:17 Ye shall not **n** to fight in this *battle:* set NIH
Ezr 6: 9 that which *they* **have n of**, both young 2818
Pr 31:11 in her, so that he shall **have** no **n** of spoil. 2637
Mt 3:14 I have **n** to be baptized of thee, and *5532*
6: 8 Father knoweth what *things* ye have **n** of, *5532*
6:32 knoweth that ye **have n** of all these *things.* *5535*
9:12 They that be whole **n** not a *2192+5532*
14:16 said unto them, They **n** not depart; *2192+5532*
21: 3 ye shall say, The Lord hath **n** of them; *5532*
26:65 what further **n** have we of witnesses? *5532*
Mk 2:17 They that are whole have no **n** of *5532*
2:25 when he had **n**, and was a hungred, he, and *5532*
11: 3 say ye that the Lord hath **n** of him; and *5532*
14:63 What **n** we any further witnesses? *2192+5532*
Lk 5:31 that are whole **n** not a physician; *2192+5532*
9:11 and healed them that had **n** of healing. *5532*
12:30 your Father knoweth that ye **have n** of *5535*
15: 7 just *persons* which **n** no repentance. *2192+5532*
19:31 unto him, Because the Lord hath **n** of him. *5532*
19:34 And they said, The Lord hath **n** of him. *5532*
22:71 What **n** we any further witness? *2192+5532*
Jn 13:29 Buy *those things* that we have **n** of against *5532*
Ac 2:45 parted them to all *men,* as every *man* had **n**. *5532*
4:35 unto every man according as he had **n**. *5532*
Ro 16: 2 in whatsoever business she hath **n** of you: *5535*
1Co 7:36 and **n** so require, let him do what he will, *3784*
12:21 say unto the hand, I have no **n** of thee: *5532*
12:21 the head to the feet, I have no **n** of you. *5532*
12:24 For our comely *parts* have no **n**: *5532*
2Co 3: 1 or **n** we, as some *others,* epistles of *5535*
Php 4:12 be hungry, both to abound and to **suffer n**. *5302*
4:19 But my God shall supply all your **n** *5532*
1Th 1: 8 so that we **n** not to speak any *thing.* *2192+5532*
4: 9 But as touching brotherly love ye **n** *2192+5532*
5: 1 ye have no **n** that *I* write unto you. *5532*
Heb 4:16 and find grace to help in **time of n**. *2121*
5:12 ye have **n** that *one* teach you again which *5532*
5:12 and are become such as have **n** of milk, and *5532*
7:11 what further **n** *was there* that another priest *5532*
10:36 For ye have **n** of patience, that, after ye *5532*
1Pe 1: 6 though now for a season, if **n** be, *1163*
1Jn 2:27 and ye **n** not that any *man* teach you: *2192+5532*
3:17 and seeth his brother hath **n**, and *5532*
Rev 3:17 with goods, and have **n** of nothing; *5532*
21:23 And the city had no **n** of the sun, neither of *5532*
22: 5 and they **n** no candle, neither light of *2192+5532*

NEEDED (2) [NEED]
Jn 2:25 And **n** not that any should testify of *2192+5532*
Ac 17:25 as though he **n** any *thing,* seeing he giveth *4326*

NEEDEST (1) [NEED]
Jn 16:30 **n** not that any *man* should ask thee: *2192+5532*

NEEDETH (6) [NEED]
Ge 33:15 he said, What **n** it? let me find grace in NIH
Lk 11: 8 he will rise and give him as many as he **n**. *5535*
Jn 13:10 He that is washed **n** not save to wash *2192+5532*
Eph 4:28 he may have to give to him that **n**. *2192+5532*
2Ti 2:15 a workman that **n not to be ashamed**, *422*
Heb 7:27 Who **n** not daily, as *those* high priests, *318+2250*

NEEDFUL (6) [NEED]
Ezr 7:20 whatsoever more *shall be* **n** for the house of 2819
Lk 10:42 But one *thing* is **n**: and Mary hath chosen *5532*
Ac 15: 5 That it was **n** to circumcise them, and *1163*
Php 1:24 Nevertheless to abide in the flesh *is* **more n** *316*
Jas 2:16 not those *things which are* **n** to the body; *2006*
Jude 1: 3 it was **n** for me to write unto you, and *318+2192*

NEEDLE (2) [NEEDLE'S, NEEDLEWORK]
Mt 19:24 for a camel to go through the eye of a **n**, *4476*
Mk 10:25 for a camel to go through the eye of a **n**, *4476*

NEEDLE'S (1) [NEEDLE]
Lk 18:25 For it is easier for a camel to go through a **n** *4476*

NEEDLEWORK (9) [NEEDLE, WORK]
Ex 26:36 fine twined linen, **wrought with n**. 4639+7551
27:16 fine twined linen, wrought with **n**: 7551
28:39 and thou shalt make the girdle *of* **n**. 4639+7551
36:37 scarlet, and fine twined linen, *of* **n**; 4639+7551
38:18 for the gate of the court *was* **n**, 4639+7551
39:29 blue, and purple, and scarlet, *of* **n**; 4639+7551
Jdg 5:30 a prey of divers colours of **n**, 7553
5:30 of divers colours of **n** on both sides, 7553
Ps 45:14 be brought unto the king in **raiment of n**: 7553

NEEDS (16) [NEED]
Ge 17:13 thy money, **must n be circumcised**: 4135+4135
19: 9 to sojourn, and he will **n be a judge**: 8199+8199
24: 5 **must** I **n bring** thy son **again** unto 7725+7725
31:30 *though* thou wouldest **n be gone**, 1980+1980
2Sa 14:14 For we **must n die**, and *are* as water 4191+4191
Jer 10: 5 they **must n be borne**, because 5375+5375
Mt 18: 7 for it **must n** be that offences come; but *318*
Mk 13: 7 for *such things* **must n** be; but the end *shall* *1163*
Lk 14:18 a piece of ground, and I must **n** go and see it: *318*
Jn 4: 4 And he **must n** go through Samaria. *1163*
Ac 1:16 this scripture **must n** have been fulfilled, *1163*
17: 3 that Christ **must n** have suffered, and *1163*
21:22 the multitude **must n** come together: *1163+3843*
Ro 13: 5 Wherefore *ye* **must n** be subject, not only *318*
1Co 5:10 for then **must** ye **n** go out of the world. *3784*
2Co 11:30 If I **must n** glory, I will glory of the *things* *1163*

NEEDY (38) [NEED]
Dt 15:11 to thy poor, and to thy **n**, in thy land. 34
24:14 not oppress a hired servant *that is* poor and **n**, 34
Job 24: 4 They turn the **n** out of the way: the poor of 34
24:14 rising with the light killeth the poor and **n**, 34
Ps 9:18 For the **n** shall not alway be forgotten: 34
12: 5 for the sighing of the **n**, now will I arise, 34
35:10 and the **n** from him that spoileth him? 34
37:14 to cast down the poor and **n**, *and* to slay such 34
40:17 I *am* poor and **n**; *yet* the Lord thinketh upon 34
70: 5 I *am* poor and **n**: make haste unto me, O God: 34
72: 4 he shall save the children of the **n**, and 34
72:12 For he shall deliver the **n** when he crieth; 34
72:13 He shall spare the poor and **n**, and shall save 34
72:13 and needy, and shall save the souls of the **n**. 34
74:21 let the poor and **n** praise thy name. 34
82: 3 fatherless: do justice to the afflicted and **n**. 7326
82: 4 Deliver the poor and **n**: rid *them* out of 34
86: 1 O LORD, hear me: for I *am* poor and **n**. 34
109:16 persecuted the poor and **n** man, that *he* might 34
109:22 For I *am* poor and **n**, and my heart is wounded 34
113: 7 the dust, *and* lifteth the **n** out of the dunghill; 34
Pr 30:14 off the earth, and the **n** from *among* men. 34
31: 9 and plead the cause of the poor and **n**. 34

Pr 31:20 yea, she reacheth forth her hands to the **n**. 34
Isa 10: 2 To turn aside the **n** from judgment, and 1800
14:30 shall feed, and the **n** shall lie down in safety: 34
25: 4 a strength to the **n** in his distress, a refuge 34
26: 6 the feet of the poor, *and* the steps of the **n**. 1800
32: 7 lying words, even when the **n** speaketh right. 34
41:17 *When* the poor and **n** seek water, and *there is* 34
Jer 5:28 and the right of the **n** do they not judge. 34
22:16 He judged the cause of the poor and **n**; then 34
Eze 16:49 did she strengthen the hand of the poor and **n**. 34
18:12 Hath oppressed the poor and **n**, hath spoiled 34
22:29 and have vexed the poor and **n**: 34
Am 4: 1 which oppress the poor, which crush the **n**, 34
8: 4 Hear this, O ye that swallow up the **n**, even to 34
8: 6 poor for silver, and the **n** for a pair of shoes; 34

NEESED (1) [NEESINGS]
2Ki 4:35 the child **n** seven times, and the child 2237

NEESINGS (1) [NEESED]
Job 41:18 *By* his **n** a light doth shine, and his eyes *are* 5846

NEGINAH (1)
Ps 61: T To the chief Musician upon **N**, *A Psalm* of 5058

NEGINOTH (6)
Ps 4: T To the chief Musician on **N**, A Psalm of 5058
6: T To the chief Musician on **N** upon 5058
54: T To the chief Musician on **N**, Maschil, 5058
55: T To the chief Musician on **N**, Maschil, 5058
67: T To the chief Musician on **N**, A Psalm *or* 5058
76: T To the chief Musician on **N**, A Psalm *or* 5058

NEGLECT (4) [NEGLECTED, NEGLECTING, NEGLIGENT]
Mt 18:17 And if he shall **n to hear** them, tell *it* unto *3878*
18:17 but if he **n to hear** the church, let him be *3878*
1Ti 4:14 **N** not the gift that is in thee, which was *272*
Heb 2: 3 shall we escape, if we **n** so great salvation; *272*

NEGLECTED (1) [NEGLECT]
Ac 6: 1 their widows were **n** in the daily *3865*

NEGLECTING (1) [NEGLECT]
Col 2:23 and humility, and **n** of the body, not in any *857*

NEGLIGENT (2) [NEGLECT]
2Ch 29:11 My sons, be not now **n**: for the LORD 7952
2Pe 1:12 Wherefore I will not be **n** to put you always *272*

NEHELAMITE (3)
Jer 29:24 shalt thou also speak to Shemaiah the **N**, 5161
29:31 the LORD concerning Shemaiah the **N**; 5161
29:32 I will punish Shemaiah the **N**, and his seed: 5161

NEHEMIAH (8)
Ezr 2: 2 Jeshua, **N**, Seraiah, Reelaiah, Mordecai, 5166
Ne 1: 1 The words of **N** the son of Hachaliah. 5166
3:16 After him repaired **N** the son of Azbuk, 5166
7: 7 Jeshua, **N**, Azariah, Raamiah, Nahamani, 5166
8: 9 **N**, which *is* the Tirshatha, and Ezra 5166
10: 1 Now those that sealed *were*, **N**, 5166
12:26 in the days of **N** the governor, and of Ezra 5166
12:47 in the days of **N**, gave the portions of 5166

NEHILOTH (1)
Ps 5: T To the chief Musician upon **N**, A Psalm of 5155

NEHUM (1)
Ne 7: 7 Bilshan, Mispereth, Bigvai, **N**, Baanah. 5149

NEHUSHTA (1)
2Ki 24: 8 his mother's name *was* **N**, the daughter of 5179

NEHUSHTAN (1)
2Ki 18: 4 did burn incense to it: and he called it **N**. 5180

NEIEL (1)
Jos 19:27 **N**, and goeth out to Cabul on the left hand, 5272

NEIGHBOUR (106) [NEIGHBOUR'S, NEIGHBOURS, NEIGHBOURS']
Ex 3:22 every woman shall borrow of her **n**, and 7934
11: 2 let every man borrow of his **n**, and 7453
11: 2 every woman of her **n**, jewels of silver, and 7468
12: 4 his **n** next unto his house take *it* according 7934
20:16 shalt not bear false witness against thy **n**. 7453
21:14 if a man come presumptuously upon his **n**, 7453
22: 7 If a man shall deliver unto his **n** money or 7453
22: 9 he shall pay double unto his **n**. 7453
22:10 If a man deliver unto his **n** an ass, or an ox, 7453
22:14 if a man borrow *ought* of his **n**, and it be 7453
32:27 man his companion, and every man his **n**. 7138
Lev 6: 2 lie unto his **n** in that which was delivered 5997
6: 2 away by violence, or hath deceived his **n**; 5997
19:13 Thou shalt not defraud thy **n**, neither rob 7453
19:15 *but* in righteousness shalt thou judge thy **n**. 5997
19:16 shalt thou stand against the blood of thy **n**: 7453
19:17 thou shalt in any wise rebuke thy **n**, and 5997
19:18 but thou shalt love thy **n** as thyself: 7453
24:19 if a man cause a blemish in his **n**; as he 5997
25:14 if thou sell ought unto thy **n**, or 5997
25:15 after the jubile thou shalt buy of thy **n**, 5997
Dt 4:42 which should kill his **n** unawares, and 7453
5:20 shalt thou bear false witness against thy **n**. 7453
15: 2 Every creditor that lendeth *ought* unto his **n** 7453
15: 2 shall release *it*; he shall not exact *it* of his **n**, 7453
19: 4 Whoso killeth his **n** ignorantly, whom he 7453
19: 5 into the wood with his **n** to hew wood, 7453
19: 5 and lighteth upon his **n**, that he die; 7453
19:11 if any man hate his **n**, and lie in wait for 7453
22:26 for as when a man riseth against his **n**, and 7453
27:24 Cursed *be* he that smiteth his **n** secretly. 7453
Jos 20: 5 because he smote his **n** unwittingly, 7453
Ru 4: 7 plucked off his shoe, and gave *it* to his **n**: 7453
1Sa 15:28 hath given it to a **n** of thine, *that is* better 7453
28:17 and given it to thy **n**, *even* to David: 7453
2Sa 12:11 give *them* unto thy **n**, and he shall lie with 7453
1Ki 8:31 If any man trespass against his **n**, and 7453
20:35 said unto his **n** in the word of the LORD, 7453
2Ch 6:22 If a man sin against his **n**, and an oath be 7453
Job 12: 4 I am *as* one mocked of his **n**, who calleth 7453
16:21 man with God, as a man *pleadeth* for his **n**. 7453
Ps 12: 2 They speak vanity every one with his **n**: 7453
15: 3 not with his tongue, nor doeth evil to his **n**, 7453
15: 3 nor taketh up a reproach against his **n**. 7138
101: 5 Whoso privily slandereth his **n**, him will I 7453
Pr 3:28 Say not unto thy **n**, Go, and come again, 7453
3:29 Devise not evil against thy **n**, seeing he 7453
11: 9 hypocrite with *his* mouth destroyeth his **n**: 7453
11:12 He that is void of wisdom despiseth his **n**: 7453
12:26 The righteous *is* more excellent than his **n**: 7453
14:20 The poor is hated even of his own **n**: but 7453
14:21 He that despiseth his **n** sinneth: but he that 7453
16:29 A violent man enticeth his **n**, and 7453
18:17 but his **n** cometh and searcheth him. 7453
19: 4 but the poor is separated from his **n**. 7453
21:10 his **n** findeth no favour in his eyes. 7453
24:28 Be not a witness against thy **n** without 7453
25: 8 when thy **n** hath put thee to shame. 7453
25: 9 Debate thy cause with thy **n** *himself*; and 7453
25:18 false witness against his **n** *is* a maul, 7453
26:19 So *is* the man *that* deceiveth his **n**, and 7453
27:10 *for* better *is* a **n** *that is* near than a brother 7934
29: 5 A man that flattereth his **n** spreadeth a net 7453
Ecc 4: 4 that for this a man is envied of his **n**. 7453
Isa 3: 5 one by another, and every one by his **n**: 7453
19: 2 his brother, and every one against his **n**; 7453
41: 6 They helped every one his **n**; and *every one* 7453
Jer 6:21 the **n** and his friend shall perish. 7934
7: 5 execute judgment between a man and his **n**; 7453
9: 4 Take ye heed every one of his **n**, and trust 7453
9: 4 every **n** will walk *with* slanders. 7453
9: 5 they will deceive every one his **n**, and 7453
9: 8 *one* speaketh peaceably to his **n** with his 7453
9:20 and every one her **n** lamentation. 7468
22: 8 and they shall say every man to his **n**, 7453
23:27 dreams which they tell every man to his **n**, 7453
23:30 that steal my words every one from his **n**. 7453
23:35 Thus shall ye say every one to his **n**, and 7453
31:34 they shall teach no more every man his **n**, 7453
34:15 in proclaiming liberty every man to his **n**; 7453
34:17 one to his brother, and every man to his **n**: 7453
49:18 and Gomorrah and the **n** *cities* thereof, 7934
50:40 and Gomorrah and the **n** *cities* thereof, 7934
Hab 2:15 Woe unto him that giveth his **n** drink, 7453
Zec 3:10 shall ye call every man his **n**, under 7453
8:10 for I set all men every one against his **n**. 7453
8:16 Speak ye every man the truth to his **n**; 7453
8:17 imagine evil in your hearts against his **n**; 7453
14:13 lay hold every one on the hand of his **n**, 7453

N

Zec 14:13 hand shall rise up against the hand of his **n**. 7453
Mt 5:43 Thou shalt love thy **n**, and hate thine *4139*
19:19 and, Thou shalt love thy **n** as thyself. *4139*
22:39 unto it, Thou shalt love thy **n** as thyself. *4139*
Mk 12:31 Thou shalt love thy **n** as thyself. *4139*
12:33 the strength, and to love *his* **n** as himself, *4139*
Lk 10:27 and with all thy mind; and thy **n** as thyself. *4139*
10:29 said unto Jesus, And who is my **n**? *4139*
10:36 was **n** unto him that fell among the thieves? *4139*
Ac 7:27 But he that did his **n** wrong thrust him *4139*
Ro 13: 9 namely, Thou shalt love thy **n** as thyself. *4139*
13:10 Love worketh no ill to *his* **n**: therefore love *4139*
15: 2 Let every one of us please *his* **n** for *his* *4139*
Gal 5:14 *even* in *this;* Thou shalt love thy **n** as *4139*
Eph 4:25 speak every man truth with his **n**: *4139*
Heb 8:11 And they shall not teach every man his **n**, *4139*
Jas 2: 8 Thou shalt love thy **n** as thyself, ye do well: *4139*

NEIGHBOUR'S (29) [NEIGHBOUR]
Ex 20:17 Thou shalt not covet thy **n** house, thou shalt 7453
20:17 thou shalt not covet thy **n** wife, nor his 7453
20:17 nor his ass, nor any thing that *is* thy **n**. 7453
22: 8 he have put his hand unto his **n** goods. 7453
22:11 that he hath not put his hand unto his **n** 7453
22:26 If thou at all take thy **n** raiment to pledge, 7453
Lev 18:20 thou shalt not lie carnally with thy **n** wife, 5997
20:10 *even he* that committeth adultery with his **n** 7453
25:14 or buyest *ought* of thy **n** hand, ye shall not 5997
Dt 5:21 Neither shalt thou desire thy **n** wife, 7453
5:21 neither shalt thou covet thy **n** house, 7453
5:21 his ass, or any *thing* that *is* thy **n**. 7453+3807.1
19:14 Thou shalt not remove thy **n** landmark, 7453
22:24 because he hath humbled his **n** wife: 7453
23:24 When thou comest into thy **n** vineyard, 7453
23:25 thou comest into the standing corn of thy **n**, 7453
23:25 thou shalt not move a sickle unto thy **n** 7453
27:17 Cursed *be* he that removeth his **n** landmark. 7453
Job 31: 9 or *if* I have laid wait at my **n** door; 7453
Pr 6:29 So he that goeth in to his **n** wife; 7453
25:17 Withdraw thy foot from thy **n** house; 7453
Jer 5: 8 every one neighed after his **n** wife. 7453
22:13 *that* useth his **n** service without wages, and 7453
Eze 18: 6 neither hath defiled his **n** wife, neither hath 7453
18:11 upon the mountains, and defiled his **n** wife, 7453
18:15 house of Israel, hath not defiled his **n** wife, 7453
22:11 one hath committed abomination with his **n** 7453
33:26 and ye defile every one his **n** wife: 7453
Zec 11: 6 I *will* deliver the men every one into his **n** 7453

NEIGHBOURS (21) [NEIGHBOUR]
Jos 9:16 that they heard that they *were* their **n**, and 7138
Ru 4:17 the *women her* **n** gave it a name, saying, 7934
2Ki 4: 3 Go, borrow thee vessels abroad of all thy **n**, 7934
Ps 28: 3 which speak peace to their **n**, but 7453
31:11 especially among my **n**, and a fear to mine 7934
44:13 Thou makest us a reproach to our **n**, a scorn 7934
79: 4 We are become a reproach to our **n**, a scorn 7934
79:12 render unto our **n** sevenfold into their 7934
80: 6 Thou makest us a strife unto our **n**: and 7934
89:41 the way spoil him: he is a reproach to his **n**. 7934
Jer 12:14 saith the LORD against all mine evil **n**, 7934
49:10 and his brethren, and his **n**, and he *is* not. 7934
Eze 16:26 fornication with the Egyptians thy **n**, 7934
22:12 thou hast greedily gained of thy **n** by 7453
23: 5 doted on her lovers, on the Assyrians *her* **n**, 7138
23:12 She doted upon the Assyrians *her* **n**, 7138
Lk 1:58 And *her* **n** and her cousins heard how *4040*
14:12 neither thy kinsmen, nor *thy* rich **n**; *1069*
15: 6 he calleth together *his* friends and **n**, *1069*
15: 9 she calleth *her* friends and *her* **n** together, *1069*
Jn 9: 8 The **n** therefore, and they which before had *1069*

NEIGHBOURS' (1) [NEIGHBOUR]
Jer 29:23 have committed adultery with their **n** 7453

NEIGHED (1) [NEIGHING]
Jer 5: 8 every one **n** after his neighbour's wife. 6670

NEIGHING (1) [NEIGHED, NEIGHINGS]
Jer 8:16 at the sound of the **n** of his strong ones; 4684

NEIGHINGS (1) [NEIGHING]
Jer 13:27 I have seen thine adulteries, and thy **n**, 4684

NEITHER (879) See Index

NEKEB (1)
Jos 19:33 and Adami, **N**, and Jabneel, unto Lakum; 5346

NEKODA (4)
Ezr 2:48 The children of Rezin, the children of **N**, 5353
2:60 the children of **N**, six hundred fifty and 5353
Ne 7:50 the children of Rezin, the children of **N**, 5353
7:62 the children of **N**, six hundred forty and 5353

NEMUEL (3) [NEMUELITES]
Nu 26: 9 sons of Eliab; **N**, and Dathan, and Abiram. 5241
26:12 of **N**, the family of the Nemuelites: 5241
1Ch 4:24 The sons of Simeon *were*, **N**, and Jamin, 5241

NEMUELITE See NEMUELITES

NEMUELITES (1) [NEMUEL]
Nu 26:12 of Nemuel, the family of the **N**: of Jamin, 5242

NEPHEG (4)
Ex 6:21 the sons of Izhar; Korah, and **N**, and Zichri. 5298
2Sa 5:15 Ibhar also, and Elishua, and **N**, and Japhia, 5298
1Ch 3: 7 And Nogah, and **N**, and Japhia, 5298
14: 6 And Nogah, and **N**, and Japhia, 5298

NEPHEW (2) [NEPHEWS]
Job 18:19 He shall neither have son nor **n** among his 5220
Isa 14:22 remnant, and son, and **n**, saith the LORD. 5220

NEPHEWS (2) [NEPHEW]
Jdg 12:14 he had forty sons and thirty **n**, that 1121+1121
1Ti 5: 4 But if any widow have children or **n**, *1549*

NEPHISH (1)
1Ch 5:19 with Jetur, and **N**, and Nodab. 5305

NEPHISHESIM (1) [NEPHUSIM]
Ne 7:52 the children of Meunim, the children of **N**, 5300

NEPHTHALIM (3) [NAPHTALI]
Mt 4:13 sea coast, in the borders of Zabulon and **N**: *3508*
4:15 The land of Zabulon, and the land of **N**, *3508*
Rev 7: 6 Of the tribe of **N** *were* sealed twelve *3508*

NEPHTOAH (2)
Jos 15: 9 the hill unto the fountain of the water of **N**, 5318
18:15 and went out to the well of waters of **N**: 5318

NEPHUSIM (1) [NEPHISHESIM]
Ezr 2:50 the children of Mehunim, the children of **N**, 5300

NEPHUSSIM See NEPHISHESIM; NEPHUSIM

NER (16)
1Sa 14:50 host *was* Abner, the son of **N**, Saul's uncle. 5369
14:51 **N** the father of Abner *was* the son of Abiel. 5369
26: 5 Abner the son of **N**, the captain of his host: 5369
26:14 to Abner the son of **N**, saying, Answerest 5369
2Sa 2: 8 Abner the son of **N**, captain of Saul's host, 5369
2:12 Abner the son of **N**, and the servants of 5369
3:23 Abner the son of **N** came to the king, and 5369
3:25 Thou knowest Abner the son of **N**, that he 5369
3:28 ever from the blood of Abner the son of **N**: 5369
3:37 not of the king to slay Abner the son of **N**. 5369
1Ki 2: 5 unto Abner the son of **N**, and unto Amasa 5369
2:32 *thereof, to wit,* Abner the son of **N**, 5369
1Ch 8:33 **N** begat Kish, and Kish begat Saul, and 5369
9:36 Zur, and Kish, and Baal, and **N**, and Nadab, 5369
9:39 **N** begat Kish; and Kish begat Saul; and 5369
26:28 Abner the son of **N**, and Joab the son of 5369

NEREUS (1)
Ro 16:15 **N**, and his sister, and Olympas, and all *3517*

NERGAL (1)
2Ki 17:30 the men of Cuth made **N**, and the men of 5370

NERGAL-SHAREZER (3)
Jer 39: 3 *even* **N**, Samgar-nebo, Sarsechim, 5371
39: 3 Sarsechim, Rab-saris, **N**, Rab-mag, 5371
39:13 **N**, Rab-mag, and all the king of Babylon's 5371

NERI (1)
Lk 3:27 *son* of Salathiel, which was *the son* of **N**, *3518*

NERIAH (10)
Jer 32:12 of the purchase unto Baruch the son of **N**, 5374

Jer 32:16 of the purchase unto Baruch the son of N, 5374
36: 4 Jeremiah called Baruch the son of N: and 5374
36: 8 Baruch the son of N did according to all 5374
36:14 So Baruch the son of N took the roll in his 5374
36:32 gave it to Baruch the scribe, the son of N; 5374
43: 3 Baruch the son of N setteth thee on against 5374
43: 6 the prophet, and Baruch the son of N. 5374
45: 1 prophet spake unto Baruch the son of N, 5374
51:59 prophet commanded Seraiah the son of N, 5374

NERO (1)
2Ti 4: S when Paul was brought before N *3505*

NEST (15) [NESTS]
Nu 24:21 and thou puttest thy n in a rock. 7064
Dt 22: 6 If a bird's n chance to be before thee in 7064
32:11 As an eagle stirreth up her n, fluttereth over 7064
Job 29:18 I shall die in my n, and I shall multiply *my* 7064
39:27 at thy command, and make her n on high? 7064
Ps 84: 3 the swallow a n for herself, where she may 7064
Pr 27: 8 As a bird that wandereth from her n, so *is* a 7064
Isa 10:14 my hand hath found as a n the riches of 7064
16: 2 *that,* as a wandering bird cast out of the n, 7064
34:15 There shall the great owl **make** her n, and 7077
Jer 22:23 that **makest** thy n in the cedars, 7077
48:28 be like the dove *that* **maketh** her n in 7077
49:16 though thou shouldest make thy n as high 7064
Ob 1: 4 though *thou* set thy n among the stars, 7064
Hab 2: 9 that *he* may set his n on high, that *he* may 7064

NESTS (4) [NEST]
Ps 104:17 Where the birds **make** their n: *as for* 7077
Eze 31: 6 All the fowls of heaven **made** their n in his 7077
Mt 8:20 have holes, and the birds of the air *have* n; *2682*
Lk 9:58 have holes, and birds of the air *have* n; *2682*

NET (39) [NETS, NETWORK, NETWORKS]
Ex 27: 4 upon the n shalt thou make four brasen 7568
27: 5 that the n may be even to the midst of 7568
Job 18: 8 For he is cast into a n by his own feet, and 7568
19: 6 and hath compassed me with his n. 4686
Ps 9:15 in the n which they hid is their own foot 7568
10: 9 the poor, when he draweth him into his n. 7568
25:15 for he shall pluck my feet out of the n. 7568
31: 4 Pull me out of the n that they have laid 7568
35: 7 cause have they hid for me their n *in* a pit, 7568
35: 8 and let his n that he hath hid catch himself: 7568
57: 6 They have prepared a n for my steps; 7568
66:11 Thou broughtest us into the n; thou laidst 4686
140: 5 they have spread a n by the way side; 7568
Pr 1:17 Surely in vain the n *is* spread in the sight of 7568
12:12 The wicked desireth the n of evil *men:* but 4685
29: 5 his neighbour spreadeth a n for his feet. 7568
Ecc 9:12 as the fishes that are taken in an evil n, and 4685
Isa 51:20 head of all the streets, as a wild bull *in* a n: 4364
La 1:13 he hath spread a n for my feet, he hath 7568
Eze 12:13 My n also will I spread upon him, and 7568
17:20 I will spread my n upon him, and he shall 7568
19: 8 the provinces, and spread their n over him: 7568
32: 3 spread out my n over thee with a company 7568
32: 3 and they shall bring thee up in my n. 2764
Hos 5: 1 on Mizpah, and a n spread upon Tabor. 7568
7:12 shall go, I will spread my n upon them; 7568
Mic 7: 2 they hunt every man his brother *with* a n. 2764
Hab 1:15 they catch them in their n, and gather them 2764
1:16 Therefore they sacrifice unto their n, and 2764
1:17 Shall they therefore empty their n, and 2764
Mt 4:18 Andrew his brother, casting a n into the sea: *293*
13:47 the kingdom of heaven is like unto a n, *4522*
Mk 1:16 Andrew his brother casting a n into the sea: *293*
Lk 5: 5 at thy word I will let down the n. *1350*
5: 6 great multitude of fishes: and their n brake. *1350*
Jn 21: 6 Cast the n on the right side of the ship, and *1350*
21: 8 hundred cubits,) dragging the n with fishes. *1350*
21:11 and drew the n to land full of great fishes, *1350*
21:11 so many, *yet* was not the n broken. *1350*

NETHANEEL (14)
Nu 1: 8 Of Issachar; N the son of Zuar. 5417
2: 5 N the son of Zuar *shall be* captain of 5417
7:18 On the second day N the son of Zuar, 5417
7:23 this *was* the offering of N the son of Zuar. 5417
10:15 children of Issachar *was* N the son of Zuar. 5417
1Ch 2:14 N the fourth, Raddai the fifth, 5417
15:24 N, and Amasai, and Zechariah, and 5417
24: 6 Shemaiah the son of N the scribe, *one* of 5417
26: 4 and Sacar the fourth, and N the fifth, 5417
2Ch 17: 7 to Zechariah, and to N, and to Michaiah, 5417
35: 9 Shemaiah and N, his brethren, and 5417
Ezr 10:22 Maaseiah, Ishmael, N, Jozabad, and Elasah. 5417
Ne 12:21 Of Hilkiah, Hashabiah; of Jedaiah, N. 5417
12:36 Gilalai, Maai, N, and Judah, Hanani, 5417

NETHANEL See NETHANEEL

NETHANIAH (20)
2Ki 25:23 even Ishmael the son of N, and Johanan 5418
25:25 *that* Ishmael the son of N, the son of 5418
1Ch 25: 2 Zaccur, and Joseph, and N, and Asarelah, 5418
25:12 The fifth *to* N, *he,* his sons, and 5418
2Ch 17: 8 N, and Zebadiah, and Asahel, and 5418
Jer 36:14 all the princes sent Jehudi the son of N, 5418
40: 8 even Ishmael the son of N, and Johanan 5418
40:14 hath sent Ishmael the son of N to slay thee? 5418
40:15 I will slay Ishmael the son of N, and 5418
41: 1 *that* Ishmael the son of N the son of 5418
41: 2 arose Ishmael the son of N, and the ten men 5418
41: 6 Ishmael the son of N went forth from 5418
41: 7 that Ishmael the son of N slew them, *and* 5418
41: 9 Ishmael the son of N filled it *with them that* 5418
41:10 Ishmael the son of N carried them away 5418
41:11 the evil that Ishmael the son of N had done, 5418
41:12 went to fight with Ishmael the son of N, 5418
41:15 Ishmael the son of N escaped from Johanan 5418
41:16 had recovered from Ishmael the son of N, 5418
41:18 Ishmael the son of N had slain Gedaliah 5418

NETHER (15) [NETHERMOST]
Ex 19:17 and they stood at the n **part** of the mount. 8482
Dt 24: 6 No *man* shall take the n or the upper 7347
Jos 15:19 her the upper springs, and the n springs. 8482
16: 3 unto the coast of Beth-horon the n, and 8481
18:13 *lieth* on the south side of the n Beth-horon. 8481
Jdg 1:15 her the upper springs and the n springs. 8482
1Ki 9:17 built Gezer, and Beth-horon the n, 8481
1Ch 7:24 who built Beth-horon the n, and the upper, 8481
2Ch 8: 5 Beth-horon the n, fenced cities, *with* walls, 8481
Job 41:24 yea, as hard as a piece of the n *millstone.* 8482
Eze 31:14 to the n **parts** of the earth, in the midst of 8482
31:16 shall be comforted in the n **parts** of 8482
31:18 trees of Eden unto the n **parts** of the earth: 8482
32:18 unto the n **parts** of the earth, with them 8482
32:24 uncircumcised into the n **parts** of the earth, 8482

NETHERMOST (1) [NETHER]
1Ki 6: 6 The n chamber *was* five cubits broad, 8481

NETHINIMS (18)
1Ch 9: 2 the priests, Levites, and the N. 5411
Ezr 2:43 The N: the children of Ziha, the children of 5411
2:58 All the N, and the children of Solomon's 5411
2:70 and the singers, and the porters, and the N, 5411
7: 7 and the singers, and the porters, and the N, 5411
7:24 N, or ministers of this house of God, 5412
8:17 *and to* his brethren the N, at the place 5411
8:20 Also of the N, whom David and the princes 5411
8:20 of the Levites, two hundred and twenty N: 5411
Ne 3:26 Moreover the N dwelt in Ophel, unto 5411
3:31 the goldsmith's son unto the place of the N, 5411
7:46 The N: the children of Ziha, the children of 5411
7:60 All the N, and the children of Solomon's 5411
7:73 of the people, and the N, and all Israel, 5411
10:28 the N, and all they that had separated 5411
11: 3 the N, and the children of Solomon's 5411
11:21 the N dwelt in Ophel: and Ziha and 5411
11:21 and Ziha and Gispa *were* over the N. 5411

NETOPHAH (2)
Ezr 2:22 The men of N, fifty and six. 5199
Ne 7:26 The men of Beth-lehem and N, an hundred 5199

NETOPHATHI (1)
Ne 12:28 and from the villages of N; 5200

NETOPHATHITE (8)
2Sa 23:28 Zalmon the Ahohite, Maharai the N, 5200
23:29 Heleb the son of Baanah, a N, Ittai the son 5200
2Ki 25:23 Seraiah the son of Tanhumeth the N, and 5200
1Ch 11:30 Maharai the N, Heled the son of Baanah 5200

1Ch 11:30 Heled the son of Baanah the **N**, 5200
27:13 for the tenth month *was* Maharai the **N**, 5200
27:15 for the twelfth month *was* Heldai the **N**, 5200
Jer 40: 8 the sons of Ephai the **N**, and Jezaniah 5200

NETOPHATHITES (2)
1Ch 2:54 Beth-lehem, and the **N**, Ataroth, the house 5200
9:16 that dwelt in the villages of the **N**. 5200

NETS (13) [NET]
1Ki 7:17 *And* **n** of checker work, *and* wreaths of 7639
Ps 141:10 Let the wicked fall into their own **n**, 4364
Ecc 7:26 whose heart *is* snares and **n**, *and* her hands 2764
Isa 19: 8 they that spread **n** upon the waters shall 4365
Eze 26: 5 It shall be *a place for* the spreading of **n** in 2764
26:14 thou shalt be *a place* to spread **n** upon; 2764
47:10 they shall be a place to spread forth **n**; 2764
Mt 4:20 And they straightway left *their* **n**, and *1350*
4:21 with Zebedee their father, mending their **n**; *1350*
Mk 1:18 And straightway they forsook their **n**, and *1350*
1:19 who also *were* in the ship mending *their* **n**. *1350*
Lk 5: 2 out of them, and were washing *their* **n**. *1350*
5: 4 the deep, and let down your **n** for a draught. *1350*

NETTLES (5)
Job 30: 7 under the **n** they were gathered together. 2738
Pr 24:31 *and* **n** had covered the face thereof, and 2738
Isa 34:13 **n** and brambles in the fortresses thereof: 7057
Hos 9: 6 *places* for their silver, **n** shall possess them: 7057
Zep 2: 9 *even* the breeding of **n**, and saltpits, and 2738

NETWORK (7) [NET, WORK]
Ex 27: 4 thou shalt make for it a grate of **n** *of* 4639+7568
38: 4 **n** under the compass thereof beneath 4639+7568
1Ki 7:18 and two rows round about upon the one **n**, 7639
7:20 over against the belly which *was* by the **n**: 7639
7:42 *even* two rows *of* pomegranates for one **n**, 7639
Jer 52:22 with **n** and pomegranates upon 7639
52:23 all the pomegranates upon the **n** *were* an 7639

NETWORKS (3) [NET, WORK]
1Ki 7:41 the two **n**, to cover the two bowls of 7639
7:42 four hundred pomegranates for the two **n**, 7639
Isa 19: 9 and they that weave **n**, shall be confounded. 2355

NEVER (86) See Index

NEVERTHELESS (97) See Index

NEW (150) [NEWBORN, NEWLY, NEWNESS]
Ex 1: 8 Now there arose up a **n** king over Egypt, 2319
Lev 23:16 ye shall offer a **n** meat offering unto 2319
26:10 bring forth the old because of the **n**. 2319
Nu 16:30 if the LORD make a **n** thing, and 1278
28:26 when ye bring a **n** meat offering unto 2319
Dt 20: 5 What man *is there* that hath built a **n** house, 2319
22: 8 When thou buildest a **n** house, then 2319
24: 5 When a man hath taken a **n** wife, he shall 2319
32:17 knew not, *to* **n** *gods that* came newly up, 2319
Jos 9:13 bottles of wine, which we filled, *were* **n**; 2319
Jdg 5: 8 They chose **n** gods; then *was* war in 2319
15:13 they bound him with two **n** cords, and 2319
15:15 he found a **n** jawbone of an ass, and 2961
16:11 If they bind me fast with **n** ropes that never 2319
16:12 Delilah therefore took **n** ropes, and 2319
1Sa 6: 7 Now therefore make a **n** cart, and take two 2319
20: 5 to morrow *is* the **n moon**, and I should not 2320
20:18 said to *David,* To morrow *is* the **n moon**: 2320
20:24 when the **n moon** was come, the king sat 2320
2Sa 6: 3 they set the ark of God upon a **n** cart, and 2319
6: 3 the sons of Abinadab, drave the **n** cart. 2319
21:16 he being girded *with* a **n** *sword,* thought to 2319
1Ki 11:29 he had clad himself with a **n** garment; and 2319
11:30 Ahijah caught the **n** garment that *was* on 2319
2Ki 2:20 Bring me a **n** cruse, and put salt therein. 2319
4:23 *it is* neither **n moon**, nor sabbath. And she 2320
1Ch 13: 7 they carried the ark of God in a **n** cart out 2319
23:31 in the **n moons**, and on the set feasts, 2320
2Ch 2: 4 on the **n moons**, and on the solemn feasts 2320
8:13 on the **n moons**, and on the solemn feasts, 2320
20: 5 house of the LORD, before the **n** court, 2319
31: 3 and for the **n moons**, and for the set feasts, 2320
Ezr 3: 5 both of the **n moons**, and of all the set 2320
6: 4 rows of great stones, and a row of **n** timber: 2323
Ne 10:33 of the sabbaths, of the **n moons**, for the set 2320
10:39 of the **n wine**, and the oil, unto 8492
13: 5 tithes of the corn, the **n wine**, and the oil, 8492
13:12 the **n wine** and the oil unto the treasuries. 8492
Job 32:19 no vent; it is ready to burst like **n** bottles. 2319
Ps 33: 3 Sing unto him a **n** song; play skilfully with 2319
40: 3 he hath put a **n** song in my mouth, 2319
81: 3 Blow up the trumpet in the **n moon**, in 2320
96: 1 O sing unto the LORD a **n** song: sing unto 2319
98: 1 O sing unto the LORD a **n** song; for he 2319
144: 9 I will sing a **n** song unto thee, O God: 2319
149: 1 Sing unto the LORD a **n** song, *and* 2319
Pr 3:10 and thy presses shall burst out with **n wine**. 8492
Ecc 1: 9 and *there is* no **n** *thing* under the sun. 2319
1:10 thing whereof it may be said, See, this *is* **n**? 2319
SS 7:13 gates *are* all *manner of* pleasant *fruits,* **n** 2319
Isa 1:13 the **n moons** and sabbaths, the calling of 2320
1:14 Your **n moons** and your appointed feasts 2320
24: 7 The **n wine** mourneth, the vine languisheth, 8492
41:15 I will make thee a **n** sharp threshing 2319
42: 9 are come to pass, and **n** *things* do I declare: 2319
42:10 Sing unto the LORD a **n** song, *and* 2319
43:19 I will do a **n** *thing;* now it shall spring 2319
48: 6 will not ye declare *it?* I have shewed thee **n** 2319
62: 2 thou shalt be called by a **n** name, which 2319
65: 8 As the **n wine** is found in the cluster, and 8492
65:17 behold, I create **n** heavens and a new earth: 2319
65:17 behold, I create new heavens and a **n** earth: 2319
66:22 For as the **n** heavens and the new earth, 2319
66:22 For as the new heavens and the **n** earth, 2319
66:23 *that* from one **n moon** to another, and 2320
Jer 26:10 sat down in the entry of the **n** gate of 2319
31:22 for the LORD hath created a **n** *thing* in 2319
31:31 that I will make a **n** covenant with 2319
36:10 in the higher court *at* the entry of the **n** gate 2319
La 3:23 *They are* **n** every morning: great *is* thy 2319
Eze 11:19 and I will put a **n** spirit within you; 2319
18:31 and make you a **n** heart and a new spirit: 2319
18:31 and make you a new heart and a **n** spirit: 2319
36:26 A **n** heart also will I give you, and a new 2319
36:26 and a **n** spirit will I put within you: 2319
45:17 in the **n moons**, and in the sabbaths in all 2320
46: 1 in the day of the **n moon** it shall be opened. 2320
46: 3 in the sabbaths and in the **n moons**. 2320
46: 6 in the day of the **n moon** *it shall be* a young 2320
47:12 it shall **bring forth n fruit** according to his 1069
Hos 2:11 her feast *days,* her **n moons**, and 2320
4:11 and wine and **n wine** take *away* the heart. 8492
9: 2 feed them, and the **n wine** shall fail in her. 8492
Joel 1: 5 ye drinkers of wine, because of the **n wine**, 6071
1:10 the **n wine** is dried up, the oil languisheth. 8492
3:18 *that* the mountains shall drop down **n wine**, 6071
Am 8: 5 Saying, When will the **n moon** be gone, 2320
Hag 1:11 upon the **n wine**, and upon the oil, and 8492
Zec 9:17 young men cheerful, and **n wine** the maids. 8492
Mt 9:16 No *man* putteth a piece of **n** cloth unto an old *46*
9:17 Neither do *men* put **n** wine into old bottles: *3501*
9:17 but they put **n** wine into new bottles, and *3501*
9:17 but they put new wine into **n** bottles, and *2537*
13:52 bringeth forth out of his treasure *things* **n** *2537*
26:28 For this is my blood of the **n** testament, *2537*
26:29 until that day when I drink it **n** with you in *2537*
27:60 And laid it in his own **n** tomb, which he *2537*
Mk 1:27 what **n** doctrine *is* this? for with authority *2537*
2:21 No *man* also seweth a piece of **n** cloth on an *46*
2:21 else the **n** piece that filled it up taketh away *2537*
2:22 And no *man* putteth **n** wine into old bottles: *3501*
2:22 else the **n** wine doth burst the bottles, and *3501*
2:22 but **n** wine must be put into new bottles. *3501*
2:22 but new wine must be put into **n** bottles. *2537*
14:24 This is my blood of the **n** testament, *2537*
14:25 until that day that I drink it **n** in *2537*
16:17 out devils; they shall speak with **n** tongues; *2537*
Lk 5:36 No *man* putteth a piece of a **n** garment *2537*
5:36 *then* both the **n** maketh a rent, and the piece *2537*
5:36 the piece that was *taken* out of the **n** *2537*
5:37 And no *man* putteth **n** wine into old bottles; *3501*
5:37 else the **n** wine will burst the bottles, and *3501*
5:38 But **n** wine must be put into new bottles; *3501*
5:38 But new wine must be put into **n** bottles; *2537*
5:39 drunk old *wine* straightway desireth **n**: *3501*
22:20 This cup *is* the **n** testament in my blood, *2537*
Jn 13:34 A **n** commandment I give unto you, That ye *2537*
19:41 and in the garden a **n** sepulchre, *2537*
Ac 2:13 *These men* are full of **n wine**. *1098*

Ac 17:19 saying, May we know what this **n** doctrine, *2537*
17:21 but *either* to tell, or to hear some **n** *thing.*) *2537*
1Co 5: 7 the old leaven, that ye may be a **n** lump, *3501*
11:25 This cup is the **n** testament in my blood: *2537*
2Co 3: 6 made us able ministers of the **n** testament; *2537*
5:17 if any *man be* in Christ, *he is* a **n** creature: *2537*
5:17 past away; behold, all *things* are become **n**. *2537*
Gal 6:15 *thing,* nor uncircumcision, but a **n** creature. *2537*
Eph 2:15 for to make in himself of twain one **n** man, *2537*
4:24 And that *ye* put on the **n** man, which after *2537*
Col 2:16 or of the **n moon**, or of the sabbath days: *3561*
3:10 And have put on the **n** *man,* which is *3501*
Heb 8: 8 when I will make a **n** covenant with *2537*
8:13 A **n** *covenant,* he hath made the first old. *2537*
9:15 cause he is the mediator of the **n** testament, *2537*
10:20 *By* a **n** and living way, which he hath *4372*
12:24 And to Jesus the mediator of the **n** *3501*
2Pe 3:13 look for **n** heavens and a new earth, *2537*
3:13 look for new heavens and a **n** earth, *2537*
1Jn 2: 7 I write no **n** commandment unto you, but *2537*
2: 8 Again, a **n** commandment I write unto you, *2537*
2Jn 1: 5 not as though I wrote a **n** commandment *2537*
Rev 2:17 and in the stone a **n** name written, *2537*
3:12 the city of my God, *which is* **n** Jerusalem, *2537*
3:12 and *I will write upon him* my **n** name. *2537*
5: 9 And they sung a **n** song, saying, Thou art *2537*
14: 3 And they sung as *it were* a **n** song before *2537*
21: 1 And I saw a **n** heaven and a new earth: *2537*
21: 1 And I saw a new heaven and a **n** earth: *2537*
21: 2 And I John saw the holy city, **n** Jerusalem, *2537*
21: 5 the throne said, Behold, I make all *things* **n**. *2537*

NEWBORN (1) [BEAR, NEW]
1Pe 2: 2 As **n** babes, desire the sincere milk of *738*

NEWLY (2) [NEW]
Dt 32:17 *to* new *gods that* came **n** up, 4480+7138
Jdg 7:19 *and* they had but **n set** the watch: 6965+6965

NEWNESS (2) [NEW]
Ro 6: 4 *even* so we also should walk in **n** of life. *2538*
7: 6 that we should serve in **n** of spirit, and *2538*

NEWS (1)
Pr 25:25 so *is* good **n** from a far country. 8052

NEXT (60) See Index

NEZIAH (2)
Ezr 2:54 The children of **N**, the children of Hatipha. 5335
Ne 7:56 The children of **N**, the children of Hatipha. 5335

NEZIB (1)
Jos 15:43 And Jiphtah, and Ashnah, and **N**, 5334

NIBHAZ (1)
2Ki 17:31 the Avites made **N** and Tartak, and 5026

NIBSHAN (1)
Jos 15:62 **N**, and the city of salt, and En-gedi; 5044

NICANOR (1)
Ac 6: 5 and **N**, and Timon, and Parmenas, and *3527*

NICODEMUS (5)
Jn 3: 1 the Pharisees, named **N**, a ruler of the Jews: *3530*
3: 4 **N** saith unto him, How can a man be born *3530*
3: 9 **N** answered and said unto him, How can *3530*
7:50 **N** saith unto them, (he that came to *Jesus* *3530*
19:39 And there came also **N**, which at the first *3530*

NICOLAITANS (2)
Rev 2: 6 that thou hatest the deeds of the **N**, which I *3531*
2:15 also them that hold the doctrine of the **N**, *3531*

NICOLAS (1)
Ac 6: 5 Parmenas, and **N** a proselyte of Antioch: *3532*

NICOPOLIS (2)
Tit 3:12 be diligent to come unto me to **N**: *3533*
3: S of the Cretians, from **N** of Macedonia. *3533*

NIGER (1)
Ac 13: 1 and Simeon that was called **N**, and *3526*

NIGH (100)
Ge 47:29 the time **drew n** that Israel must die: and 7126
Ex 3: 5 he said, **Draw** not **n** hither: put off thy 7126
14:10 when Pharaoh **drew n**, the children of 7126
24: 2 they shall not **come n**; neither shall 5066
32:19 as soon as he **came n** unto the camp, 7126
34:30 and they were afraid to **come n** him. 5066
34:32 afterward all the children of Israel **came n**: 5066
Lev 10: 3 I will be sanctified in them that **come n** me, 7138
21: 3 for his sister a virgin, that is **n** unto him, 7138
21:21 shall **come n** to offer the offerings of 5066
21:21 he shall not **come n** to offer the bread of his 5066
21:23 nor **come n** unto the altar, because he hath 5066
25:49 *any* **that is n** of kin **unto** him of his family 7607
Nu 1:51 the stranger that **cometh n** shall be put to 7131
3:10 the stranger that **cometh n** shall be put to 7131
3:38 the stranger that **cometh n** shall be put to 7131
8:19 when the children of Israel **come n** unto 5066
18: 3 only they shall not **come n** the vessels of 7126
18: 4 and a stranger shall not **come n** unto you. 7126
18: 7 the stranger that **cometh n** shall be put to 7131
18:22 **come n** the tabernacle of the congregation, 7126
24:17 I shall behold him, but not **n**: there shall 7138
Dt 1: 7 unto all *the places* **n** thereunto, in the plain, 7934
2:19 *when* thou **comest n** over against 7126
4: 7 *so* great, who hath God *so* **n** unto them, 7138
13: 7 about you, **n** unto thee, or far off from thee, 7138
20: 2 when ye are **come n** unto the battle, 7126
20:10 When thou **comest n** unto a city to fight 7126
22: 2 if thy brother *be* not **n** unto thee, or *if* thou 7138
30:14 the word *is* very **n** unto thee, in thy mouth, 7138
Jos 8:11 **drew n**, and came before the city, and 5066
1Sa 17:48 came and **drew n** to meet David, 7126
2Sa 10:13 Joab **drew n**, and the people that *were* with 5066
11:20 Wherefore **approached** ye *so* **n** unto 5066
11:21 why **went** ye **n** the wall? 5066
15: 5 that when any man **came n** *to him* to do 7126
1Ki 2: 1 Now the days of David **drew n** that *he* 7126
8:59 be **n** unto the LORD our God day and 7138
1Ch 12:40 Moreover they *that were* **n** them, *even* unto 7138
19:14 the people that *were* with him **drew n** 5066
Est 9:20 of the king Ahasuerus, *both* **n** and far, 7138
Ps 32: 6 waters they shall not **come n** unto him. 5060
34:18 The LORD *is* **n** unto them that are of a 7138
69:18 **Draw n** unto my soul, *and* redeem it: 7126
73: 2 my steps had **well n** slipt. 369+3509.1
85: 9 Surely his salvation *is* **n** them that fear him; 7138
88: 3 and my life **draweth n** unto the grave. 5060
91: 7 thy right hand; *but* it shall not **come n** thee. 5066
91:10 neither shall *any* plague **come n** thy 7126
119:150 They **draw n** that follow after mischief: 7126
145:18 The LORD *is* **n** unto all them that call 7138
Pr 5: 8 and **come** not **n** the door of her house: 7126
Ecc 12: 1 nor the years **draw n**, when thou shalt say, 5060
Isa 5:19 counsel of the Holy One of Israel **draw n** 7126
Joel 2: 1 of the LORD cometh, for *it is* **n at hand**; 7138
Mt 15: 8 This people **draweth n** unto me with their *1448*
15:29 and came **n unto** the sea of Galilee; *3844*
21: 1 And when they **drew n** unto Jerusalem, and *1448*
24:32 forth leaves, ye know that summer *is* **n**: *1451*
Mk 2: 4 And when they could not **come n** unto him *4331*
5:11 Now there was there **n unto** the mountains *4314*
5:21 unto him: and he was **n unto** the sea. *3844*
11: 1 And when they **came n** to Jerusalem, *1448*
13:29 to pass, know that it is **n**, *even* at the doors. *1451*
Lk 7:12 Now when he **came n** to the gate of *1448*
10: 9 The kingdom of God is **come n** unto you. *1448*
10:11 that the kingdom of God is **come n** unto *1448*
15:25 and as he came and **drew n** to the house, *1448*
18:35 to pass, *that* as he was **come n** unto Jericho, *1448*
19:11 because he was **n to** Jerusalem, and *1451*
19:29 when he was **come n** to Bethphage and *1448*
19:37 And when he was **come n**, *even* now at *1448*
21:20 then know that the desolation thereof is **n**. *1448*
21:28 for your redemption **draweth n**. *1448*
21:30 own selves that summer is now **n at hand**. *1451*
21:31 ye that the kingdom of God is **n at hand**. *1451*
22: 1 Now the feast of unleavened bread **drew n**, *1448*
24:28 And they **drew n** unto the village, *1448*
Jn 6: 4 the passover, a feast of the Jews, was **n**. *1451*
6:19 on the sea, and drawing **n** unto the ship: *1451*
6:23 **n** unto the place where they did eat bread, *1451*
11:18 Now Bethany was **n** unto Jerusalem, *1451*

Jn 11:55 And the Jews' passover was **n at hand**: and *1451*
19:20 Jesus was crucified was **n to** the city: *1451*
19:42 *day;* for the sepulchre was **n at hand**. *1451*
Ac 7:17 But when the time of the promise **drew n**, *1448*
9:38 And forasmuch as Lydda was **n** to Joppa, *1451*
10: 9 on their journey, and **drew n** unto the city, *1448*
22: 6 was **come n** unto Damascus about noon, *1448*
27: 8 **n** whereunto was the city *of* Lasea. *1451*
Ro 10: 8 The word is **n** thee, *even* in thy mouth, and *1451*
Eph 2:13 far off are made **n** by the blood of Christ. *1451*
2:17 were afar off, and to them that were **n**; *1451*
Php 2:27 For indeed he was sick **n unto** death: but *3897*
2:30 Because for the work of Christ he was **n** *1448*
Heb 6: 8 and briers *is* rejected, and *is* **n** unto cursing; *1451*
7:19 *did;* by the which we **draw n** unto God. *1448*
Jas 4: 8 **Draw n** to God, and he will draw nigh to *1448*
4: 8 nigh to God, and he will **draw n** to you. *1448*
5: 8 for the coming of the Lord **draweth n**. *1448*

NIGHT (307) [MIDNIGHT, NIGHTS, YESTERNIGHT]

Ge 1: 5 the light Day, and the darkness he called **N**. 3915
1:14 of the heaven to divide the day from the **n**; 3915
1:16 the day, and the lesser light to rule the **n**: 3915
1:18 to rule over the day and over the **n**, and 3915
8:22 and winter, and day and **n** shall not cease. 3915
14:15 by **n**, and smote them, and pursued them 3915
19: 2 **tarry all n**, and wash your feet, and 3885
19: 2 Nay; but we will **abide** in the street **all n**. 3885
19: 5 *are* the men which came in to thee this **n**? 3915
19:33 they made their father drink wine that **n**: 3915
19:34 let us make him drink wine this **n** also; and 3915
19:35 they made their father drink wine that **n** 3915
20: 3 God came to Abimelech in a dream by **n**, 3915
24:54 men that *were* with him, and **tarried all n**; 3885
26:24 the LORD appeared unto him the same **n**, 3915
28:11 **tarried** there **all n**, because the sun was set; 3885
30:15 thee **to n** for thy son's mandrakes. 3915+1886.1
30:16 And he lay with her that **n**. 3915
31:24 came to Laban the Syrian in a dream by **n**, 3915
31:39 *whether* stolen by day, or stolen by **n**. 3915
31:40 drought consumed me, and the frost by **n**; 3915
31:54 eat bread, and **tarried all n** in the mount. 3885
32:13 he lodged there that *same* **n**; and took of 3915
32:21 and himself lodged that **n** in the company. 3915
32:22 he rose up that **n**, and took his two wives, 3915
40: 5 both of them, each man his dream in one **n**, 3915
41:11 we dreamed a dream in one **n**, I and he; 3915
46: 2 spake unto Israel in the visions of the **n**, 3915
49:27 the prey, and at **n** he shall divide the spoil. 6153
Ex 10:13 upon the land all that day, and all *that* **n**; 3915
12: 8 they shall eat the flesh in that **n**, roast with 3915
12:12 I will pass through the land of Egypt this **n**, 3915
12:30 Pharaoh rose up in the **n**, he, and all his 3915
12:31 he called for Moses and Aaron by **n**, and 3915
12:42 It *is* a **n** to be much observed unto 3915
12:42 this *is* that **n** of the LORD to be observed 3915
13:21 by **n** in a pillar of fire, to give them light; 3915
13:21 to give them light; to go by day and **n**: 3915
13:22 nor the pillar of fire by **n**, *from* before 3915
14:20 *to them,* but it gave light by **n** *to these:* so 3915
14:20 the one came not near the other all the **n**. 3915
14:21 to go *back* by a strong east wind all *that* **n**, 3915
40:38 fire was on it by **n**, in the sight of all 3915
Lev 6: 9 of the burning upon the altar all **n** unto 3915
6:20 of it in the morning, and half thereof at **n**. 6153
8:35 of the congregation day and **n** seven days, 3915
11:16 the **n hawk**, and the cuckow, and the hawk 8464
19:13 not **abide** with thee **all n** until the morning. 3885
Nu 9:16 it *by day,* and the appearance of fire by **n**. 3915
9:21 by day or by **n** that the cloud was taken up, 3915
11: 9 when the dew fell upon the camp in the **n**, 3915
11:32 all *that* **n**, and all the next day, and 3915
14: 1 and cried; and the people wept that **n**. 3915
14:14 pillar of a cloud, and in a pillar of fire by **n**. 3915
22: 8 Lodge here *this* **n**, and I will bring you 3915
22:19 I pray you, tarry ye also here *this* **n**, 3915
22:20 God came unto Balaam at **n**, and said unto 3915
Dt 1:33 a place to pitch your tents *in,* in fire by **n**, 3915
14:15 the **n hawk**, and the cuckow, and the hawk 8464
16: 1 God brought thee forth out of Egypt by **n**. 3915
16: 4 at even, **remain all n** until the morning. 3885
21:23 His body shall not **remain all n** upon 3885
23:10 of *uncleanness* that chanceth him by **n**, 3915
28:66 thou shalt fear day and **n**, and shalt have 3915

Jos 1: 8 thou shalt meditate therein day and **n**, that 3915
2: 2 there came men in hither **to n** of 3915
4: 3 lodging place, where you shall lodge *this* **n**. 3915
8: 3 *men* of valour, and sent them away by **n**. 3915
8: 9 but Joshua lodged that **n** among the people. 3915
8:13 Joshua went that **n** into the midst of 3915
10: 9 *and* went up from Gilgal all **n**. 3915
Jdg 6:25 it came to pass the same **n**, that the LORD 3915
6:27 could not do *it* by day, that he did *it* by **n**. 3915
6:40 God did so that **n**: for it was dry upon 3915
7: 9 it came to pass the same **n**, that the LORD 3915
9:32 Now therefore up by **n**, thou and the people 3915
9:34 by **n**, and they laid wait against Shechem *in* 3915
16: 2 laid wait for him all **n** in the gate of 3915
16: 2 were quiet all the **n**, saying, In the morning, 3915
19: 6 **tarry all n**, and let thine heart be merry. 3885
19: 9 towards evening, I pray you **tarry all n**: 3885
19:10 the man would not **tarry** *that* **n**, but he rose 3885
19:13 near to one of *these* places to **lodge all n**, 3885
19:25 and abused her all the **n** until the morning: 3915
20: 5 beset the house round about upon me by **n**, 3915
Ru 1:12 I should have a husband also **to n**, 3915+1886.1
3: 2 he winnoweth barley **to n** in 3915+1886.1
3:13 Tarry this **n**, and it shall be in the morning, 3915
1Sa 14:34 brought every man his ox with him *that* **n**, 3915
14:36 Let us go down after the Philistines by **n**, 3915
15:11 and he cried unto the LORD all **n**. 3915
15:16 what the LORD hath said to me *this* **n**. 3915
19:10 and David fled, and escaped that **n**. 3915
19:11 If thou save not thy life **to n**, 3915+1886.1
19:24 lay down naked all that day and all *that* **n**. 3915
25:16 They were a wall unto us both by **n** and 3915
26: 7 and Abishai came to the people by **n**: 3915
28: 8 and they came to the woman by **n**: 3915
28:20 had eaten no bread all the day, nor all the **n**. 3915
28:25 Then they arose up, and went away that **n**. 3915
31:12 went all **n**, and took the body of Saul and 3915
2Sa 2:29 his men walked all that **n** through the plain, 3915
2:32 Joab and his men went all **n**, and they came 3915
4: 7 and gat them away through the plain all **n**. 3915
7: 4 it came to pass that **n**, that the word of 3915
12:16 and went in, and lay **all n** upon the earth. 3885
17: 1 I will arise and pursue after David *this* **n**: 3915
17:16 Lodge not *this* **n** in the plains of 3915
19: 7 there will not tarry one with thee *this* **n**: 3915
21:10 by day, nor the beasts of the field by **n**. 3915
1Ki 3: 5 appeared to Solomon in a dream by **n**: 3915
3:19 this woman's child died in the **n**; because 3915
8:29 thine eyes may be open toward this house **n** 3915
8:59 nigh unto the LORD our God day and **n**, 3915
2Ki 6:14 they came by **n**, and compassed the city 3915
7:12 the king arose in the **n**, and said unto his 3915
8:21 he rose by **n**, and smote the Edomites 3915
19:35 it came to pass that **n**, that the angel of 3915
25: 4 all the men of war *fled* by **n** *by* the way of 3915
1Ch 9:33 were employed in *that* work day and **n**. 3915
17: 3 it came to pass the same **n**, that the word of 3915
2Ch 1: 7 In that **n** did God appear unto Solomon, 3915
6:20 may be open upon this house day and **n**, 3915
7:12 the LORD appeared to Solomon by **n**, 3915
21: 9 he rose up by **n**, and smote the Edomites 3915
35:14 of burnt offerings and the fat until **n**; 3915
Ne 1: 6 which I pray before thee now, day and **n**, 3915
2:12 I arose in the **n**, I and *some* few men with 3915
2:13 I went out by **n** by the gate of the valley, 3915
2:15 went I up in the **n** by the brook, and viewed 3915
4: 9 set a watch against them day and **n**, 3915
4:22 that in the **n** they may be a guard to us, and 3915
6:10 yea, in the **n** will they come to slay thee. 3915
9:12 in the **n** by a pillar of fire, to give them 3915
9:19 neither the pillar of fire by **n**, to shew them 3915
Est 4:16 neither eat nor drink three days, **n** or day; 3915
6: 1 On that **n** could not the king sleep, and 3915
Job 3: 3 the **n** *in which it was* said, There is a man 3915
3: 6 *As for* that **n**, let darkness seize upon it; 3915
3: 7 Lo, let that **n** be solitary, let no joyful voice 3915
4:13 In thoughts from the visions of the **n**, 3915
5:14 and grope in the noonday as **in the n**. 3915
7: 4 When shall I arise, and the **n** be gone? 6153
17:12 They change the **n** into day: the light *is* 3915
20: 8 shall be chased away as a vision of the **n**. 3915
24:14 and needy, and in the **n** is as a thief. 3915
26:10 until the day and **n** come to an end. 2822
27:20 a tempest stealeth him away in the **n**. 3915

Job	29:19	and the dew **lay all n** upon my branch.	3885
	30:17	bones are pierced in me in the **n season**:	3915
	33:15	In a dream, *in* a vision of the **n**, when deep	3915
	34:25	he overturneth *them* in the **n**, so that they	3915
	35:10	God my Maker, who giveth songs in the **n**;	3915
	36:20	Desire not the **n**, when people are cut off in	3915
Ps	1: 2	and in his law doth he meditate day and **n**.	3915
	6: 6	all the **n** make I my bed to swim;	3915
	16: 7	my reins also instruct me *in* the **n seasons**.	3915
	17: 3	thou hast visited *me* in the **n**; thou hast tried	3915
	19: 2	and **n** unto night sheweth knowledge.	3915
	19: 2	and night unto **n** sheweth knowledge.	3915
	22: 2	and in the **n season**, and am not silent.	3915
	30: 5	weeping may endure for a **n**, but	6153
	32: 4	and **n** thy hand was heavy upon me:	3915
	42: 3	My tears have been my meat day and **n**,	3915
	42: 8	in the **n** his song *shall be* with me, *and*	3915
	55:10	**n** they go about it upon the walls thereof:	3915
	63: 6	*and* meditate on thee in the **n** watches.	NIH
	74:16	The day *is* thine, the **n** also *is* thine:	3915
	77: 2	my sore ran in the **n**, and ceased not:	3915
	77: 6	I call to remembrance my song in the **n**:	3915
	78:14	a cloud, and all the **n** with a light of fire.	3915
	88: 1	I have cried day *and* **n** before thee:	3915
	90: 4	when it is past, and *as* a watch in the **n**.	3915
	91: 5	Thou shalt not be afraid for the terror by **n**;	3915
	92: 2	the morning, and thy faithfulness every **n**,	3915
	104:20	Thou makest darkness, and it is **n**:	3915
	105:39	a covering; and fire to give light in the **n**.	3915
	119:55	O LORD, in the **n**, and have kept thy law.	3915
	119:148	Mine eyes prevent the ***n*** watches, that *I*	NIH
	121: 6	not smite thee by day, nor the moon by **n**.	3915
	134: 1	which by **n** stand in the house of	3915
	136: 9	The moon and stars to rule by **n**: for his	3915
	139:11	even the **n** *shall be* light about me.	3915
	139:12	not from thee; but the **n** shineth as the day:	3915
Pr	7: 9	in the evening, in the black and dark **n**:	3915
	31:15	She riseth also while *it is* yet **n**, and	3915
	31:18	*is* good: her candle goeth not out by **n**.	3915
Ecc	2:23	yea, his heart taketh not rest in the **n**.	3915
	8:16	(for also *there is that* neither day nor **n**	3915
SS	1:13	he shall **lie all n** betwixt my breasts.	3885
	3: 1	By **n** on my bed I sought *him* whom my	3915
	3: 8	upon his thigh because of fear in the **n**.	3915
	5: 2	*and* my locks *with* the drops of the **n**.	3915
Isa	4: 5	and the shining of a flaming fire by **n**:	3915
	5:11	that continue until **n**, *till* wine inflame	5399
	15: 1	Because in the **n** Ar of Moab is laid waste,	3915
	15: 1	because in the **n** Kir of Moab is laid waste,	3915
	16: 3	make thy shadow as the **n** in the midst of	3915
	21: 4	the **n** of my pleasure hath he turned into	5399
	21:11	me out of Seir, Watchman, what of the **n**?	3915
	21:11	of the night? Watchman, what of the **n**?	3915
	21:12	The morning cometh, and also the **n**:	3915
	26: 9	*With* my soul have I desired thee in the **n**;	3915
	27: 3	lest *any* hurt it, I will keep it **n** and day.	3915
	28:19	morning shall it pass over, by day and by **n**:	3915
	29: 7	shall be as a dream of a **n** vision.	3915
	30:29	as *in* the **n** when a holy solemnity is kept;	3915
	34:10	It shall not be quenched **n** nor day;	3915
	38:12	from day *even* to **n** wilt thou make an end	3915
	38:13	from day *even* to **n** wilt thou make an end	3915
	59:10	we stumble at noonday as *in* the **n**; *we are*	5399
	60:11	they shall not be shut day nor **n**;	3915
	62: 6	shall never hold their peace day nor **n**:	3915
Jer	6: 5	let us go by **n**, and let us destroy her	3915
	9: 1	**n** for the slain of the daughter of my	3915
	14: 8	man *that* turneth aside to **tarry for a n**?	3885
	14:17	Let mine eyes run down *with* tears **n** and	3915
	16:13	there shall ye serve other gods day and **n**;	3915
	31:35	the moon and of the stars for a light by **n**,	3915
	33:20	my covenant of the **n**, and that there should	3915
	33:20	should not be day and **n** in their season;	3915
	33:25	If my covenant *be* not with day and **n**, *and*	3915
	36:30	the day to the heat, and in the **n** to the frost.	3915
	39: 4	and went forth out of the city by **n**,	3915
	49: 9	if thieves by **n**, they will destroy till they	3915
	52: 7	went forth out of the city by **n** *by* the way	3915
La	1: 2	She weepeth sore in the **n**, and her tears *are*	3915
	2:18	let tears run down like a river day and **n**:	3915
	2:19	Arise, cry out in the **n**: in the beginning of	3915
Da	2:19	*was* the secret revealed unto Daniel in a **n**	3916
	5:30	In that **n** *was* Belshazzar the king of	3916
	6:18	went to his palace, and **passed the n** fasting:	956
	7: 2	said, I saw in my vision by **n**, and behold,	3916
	7: 7	After this I saw in the **n** visions, and	3916
	7:13	I saw in the **n** visions, and behold, *one* like	3916
Hos	4: 5	prophet also shall fall with thee *in* the **n**,	3915
	7: 6	their baker sleepeth all the **n**; *in*	3915
Joel	1:13	come, **lie all n** in sackcloth, ye ministers of	3885
Am	5: 8	and maketh the day dark *with* **n**:	3915
Ob	1: 5	if robbers by **n**, (how art thou cut off!)	3915
Jnh	4:10	which came up **in a n**, and	1121+3915
	4:10	up in a night, and perished **in a n**:	1121+3915
Mic	3: 6	Therefore **n** *shall be* unto you, that *ye* shall	3915
Zec	1: 8	I saw by **n**, and behold a man riding upon a	3915
	14: 7	be known to the LORD, not day, nor **n**:	3915
Mt	2:14	took the young child and his mother by **n**,	*3571*
	14:25	And in the fourth watch of the **n** Jesus went	*3571*
	26:31	ye shall be offended because of me this **n**:	*3571*
	26:34	That this **n**, before *the* cock crow,	*3571*
	27:64	lest his disciples come by **n**, and steal him	*3571*
	28:13	His disciples came by **n**, and stole him	*3571*
Mk	4:27	and rise **n** and day, and the seed should	*3571*
	5: 5	And always, **n** and day, he was in	*3571*
	6:48	about the fourth watch of the **n** he cometh	*3571*
	14:27	ye shall be offended because of me this **n**:	*3571*
	14:30	say unto thee, That this day, *even* in this **n**,	*3571*
Lk	2: 8	keeping watch over their flock by **n**.	*3571*
	2:37	*God* with fastings and prayers **n** and day.	*3571*
	5: 5	we have toiled all the **n**, and have taken	*3571*
	6:12	and continued **all n** in prayer to God.	*1273*
	12:20	this **n** thy soul shall be required of thee:	*3571*
	17:34	in that **n** there shall be two *men* in one bed;	*3571*
	18: 7	which cry day and **n** unto him, though he	*3571*
	21:37	and at **n** he went out, and abode in	*3571*
Jn	3: 2	The same came to Jesus by **n**, and said unto	*3571*
	7:50	(he that came to *Jesus* by **n**, being one of	*3571*
	9: 4	the **n** cometh, when no *man* can work.	*3571*
	11:10	But if a man walk in the **n**, he stumbleth,	*3571*
	13:30	the sop went immediately out: and it was **n**.	*3571*
	19:39	which at the first came to Jesus by **n**, and	*3571*
	21: 3	and that **n** they caught nothing.	*3571*
Ac	5:19	But *the* angel of the Lord by **n** opened	*3571*
	9:24	watched the gates day and **n** to kill him.	*3571*
	9:25	Then the disciples took him by **n**, and	*3571*
	12: 6	the same **n** Peter was sleeping between two	*3571*
	16: 9	And a vision appeared to Paul in the **n**;	*3571*
	16:33	And he took them the same hour of the **n**,	*3571*
	17:10	sent away Paul and Silas by **n** unto Berea:	*3571*
	18: 9	Then spake the Lord to Paul in the **n** by a	*3571*
	20:31	years I ceased not to warn every one **n**	*3571*
	23:11	And the **n** following the Lord stood by him,	*3571*
	23:23	two hundred, at the third hour of the **n**;	*3571*
	23:31	and brought *him* by **n** to Antipatris.	*3571*
	26: 7	instantly serving *God* day and **n**, hope to	*3571*
	27:23	For there stood by me this **n** *the* angel of	*3571*
	27:27	But when the fourteenth **n** was come, as we	*3571*
Ro	13:12	The **n** is far spent, the day is at hand: let us	*3571*
1Co	11:23	That the Lord Jesus the *same* **n** in which he	*3571*
2Co	11:25	**a n and a day** I have been in the deep;	*3574*
1Th	2: 9	for labouring **n** and day, because *we* would	*3571*
	3:10	**N** and day praying exceedingly that *we*	*3571*
	5: 2	of the Lord so cometh as a thief in the **n**.	*3571*
	5: 5	we are not of the **n**, nor of darkness.	*3571*
	5: 7	For they that sleep sleep in the **n**; and	*3571*
	5: 7	they that be drunken are drunken in the **n**.	*3571*
2Th	3: 8	wrought with labour and travail **n** and day,	*3571*
1Ti	5: 5	in supplications and prayers **n** and day.	*3571*
2Ti	1: 3	have remembrance of thee in my prayers **n**	*3571*
2Pe	3:10	of the Lord will come as a thief in the **n**;	*3571*
Rev	4: 8	and they rest not day and **n**, saying, Holy,	*3571*
	7:15	and serve him day and **n** in his temple:	*3571*
	8:12	not for a third *part* of it, and the **n** likewise.	*3571*
	12:10	accused them before our God day and **n**.	*3571*
	14:11	and they have no rest day nor **n**,	*3571*
	20:10	be tormented day and **n** for ever and ever.	*3571*
	21:25	at all by day: for there shall be no **n** there.	*3571*
	22: 5	And there shall be no **n** there; and	*3571*

NIGHTS (18) [NIGHT]

Ge	7: 4	rain upon the earth forty days and forty **n**;	3915
	7:12	was upon the earth forty days and forty **n**.	3915
Ex	24:18	was in the mount forty days and forty **n**.	3915
	34:28	with the LORD forty days and forty **n**;	3915
Dt	9: 9	I abode in the mount forty days and forty **n**,	3915
	9:11	to pass at the end of forty days and forty **n**,	3915
	9:18	as at the first, forty days and forty **n**:	3915

N

Dt 9:25 before the LORD forty days and forty **n**, 3915
10:10 to the first time, forty days and forty **n**; 3915
1Sa 30:12 drunk *any* water, three days and three **n**. 3915
1Ki 19: 8 and forty **n** unto Horeb the mount of God. 3915
Job 2:13 upon the ground seven days and seven **n**, 3915
7: 3 and wearisome **n** are appointed to me. 3915
Isa 21: 8 and I *am* set in my ward whole **n**: 3915
Jnh 1:17 the belly of the fish three days and three **n**. 3915
Mt 4: 2 when he had fasted forty days and forty **n**, *3571*
12:40 three days and three **n** in the whale's belly; *3571*
12:40 and three **n** in the heart of the earth. *3571*

NIMRAH (1) [BETH-NIMRAH]
Nu 32: 3 **N**, and Heshbon, and Elealeh, and Shebam, 5247

NIMRIM (2)
Isa 15: 6 For the waters of **N** shall be desolate: 5249
Jer 48:34 for the waters also of **N** shall be desolate. 5249

NIMROD (4)
Ge 10: 8 Cush begat **N**: he began to be a mighty *one* 5248
10: 9 *Even* as **N** the mighty hunter before 5248
1Ch 1:10 Cush begat **N**: he began to be mighty upon 5248
Mic 5: 6 and the land of **N** in the entrances thereof: 5248

NIMSHI (5)
1Ki 19:16 Jehu the son of **N** shalt thou anoint to be 5250
2Ki 9: 2 Jehu the son of Jehoshaphat the son of **N**, 5250
9:14 the son of **N** conspired against Joram. 5250
9:20 *is* like the driving of Jehu the son of **N**; 5250
2Ch 22: 7 out with Jehoram against Jehu the son of **N**, 5250

NINE (50) [NINTH]
Ge 5: 5 all the days that Adam lived were **n** 8672
5: 8 all the days of Seth were **n** hundred 8672
5:11 all the days of Enos were **n** hundred 8672
5:14 all the days of Cainan were **n** hundred 8672
5:20 all the days of Jared were **n** hundred sixty 8672
5:27 all the days of Methuselah were **n** hundred 8672
5:27 were nine hundred sixty and **n** years: 8672
9:29 all the days of Noah were **n** hundred and 8672
11:19 he begat Reu two hundred and **n** years, 8672
11:24 Nahor lived **n** and twenty years, and 8672
17: 1 when Abram was ninety years old and **n**, 8672
17:24 Abraham *was* ninety years old and **n**, 8672
Ex 38:24 was twenty and **n** talents, and 8672
Lev 25: 8 years shall be unto thee forty and **n** years. 8672
Nu 1:23 *were* fifty and **n** thousand and 8672
2:13 *were* fifty and **n** thousand and 8672
29:26 on the fifth day **n** bullocks, two rams, *and* 8672
34:13 commanded to give unto the **n** tribes, 8672
Dt 3:11 **n** cubits *was* the length thereof, and 8672
Jos 13: 7 land for an inheritance unto the **n** tribes, 8672
14: 2 for the **n** tribes, and *for* the half tribe. 8672
15:32 all the cities *are* twenty and **n**, with their 8672
15:44 and Mareshah; **n** cities with their villages. 8672
15:54 and Zior; **n** cities with their villages. 8672
21:16 her suburbs; **n** cities out of those two tribes. 8672
Jdg 4: 3 for he had **n** hundred chariots of iron; and 8672
4:13 *even* **n** hundred chariots of iron, and all 8672
2Sa 24: 8 they came *to* Jerusalem at the end of **n** 8672
2Ki 14: 2 reigned twenty and **n** years in Jerusalem. 8672
15:13 the son of Jabesh *began* to reign in the **n** 8672
15:17 In the **n** and thirtieth year of Azariah king 8672
17: 1 to reign in Samaria over Israel **n** years. 8672
18: 2 he reigned twenty and **n** years in Jerusalem. 8672
1Ch 3: 8 And Elishama, and Eliada, and Eliphelet, **n**. 8672
9: 9 **n** hundred and fifty and six. 8672
2Ch 25: 1 he reigned twenty and **n** years in Jerusalem. 8672
29: 1 he reigned **n** and twenty years in Jerusalem. 8672
Ezr 1: 9 chargers of silver, **n** and twenty knives, 8672
2: 8 children of Zattu, **n** hundred forty and five. 8672
2:36 of Jeshua, **n** hundred seventy and three. 8672
2:42 of Shobai, *in* all an hundred thirty and **n**. 8672
Ne 7:38 three thousand **n** hundred and thirty. 8672
7:39 of Jeshua, **n** hundred seventy and three. 8672
11: 1 and **n** parts *to dwell* in *other* cities. 8672
11: 8 Sallai, **n** hundred twenty and eight. 8672
Mt 18:12 doth he not leave the ninety and **n**, and *1767*
18:13 of the ninety and **n** which went not astray. *1767*
Lk 15: 4 leave the ninety and **n** in the wilderness, *1767*
15: 7 **n** just *persons* which need no repentance. *1767*
17:17 there not ten cleansed? but where *are* the **n**? *1767*

NINETEEN (3) [NINETEENTH]
Ge 11:25 begat Terah an hundred and **n** years, 6240+8672
Jos 19:38 **n** cities with their villages. 6240+8672
2Sa 2:30 there lacked of David's servants **n** 6240+8672

NINETEENTH (4) [NINETEEN]
2Ki 25: 8 which *is* the **n** year of king 6240+8672
1Ch 24:16 The **n** to Pethahiah, the twentieth to 6240+8672
25:26 The **n** to Mallothi, *he,* his sons, and 6240+8672
Jer 52:12 which *was* the **n** year of 6240+8672

NINETY (24)
Ge 5: 9 And Enos lived **n** years, and begat Cainan: 8673
5:17 days of Mahalaleel were eight hundred **n** 8673
5:30 lived after he begat Noah five hundred **n** 8673
17: 1 And when Abram was **n** years old and nine, 8673
17:17 and shall Sarah, that is **n** years old, bear? 8673
17:24 Abraham *was* **n** years old and nine, 8673
1Sa 4:15 Now Eli *was* **n** and eight years old; and 8673
1Ch 9: 6 and their brethren, six hundred and **n**. 8673
Ezr 2:16 children of Ater of Hezekiah, **n** and eight. 8673
2:20 The children of Gibbar, **n** and five. 8673
2:58 *were* three hundred **n** and two. 8673
8:35 **n** and six rams, seventy and seven lambs, 8673
Ne 7:21 children of Ater of Hezekiah, **n** and eight. 8673
7:25 The children of Gibeon, **n** and five. 8673
7:60 *were* three hundred **n** and two. 8673
Jer 52:23 there were **n** and six pomegranates on a 8673
Eze 4: 5 of the days, three hundred and **n** days: 8673
4: 9 and **n** days shalt thou eat thereof. 8673
41:12 and the length thereof **n** cubits. 8673
Da 12:11 *be* a thousand two hundred and **n** days. 8673
Mt 18:12 doth he not leave the **n** and nine, and *1768*
18:13 rejoiceth more of that *sheep,* than of the **n** *1768*
Lk 15: 4 doth not leave the **n** and nine in *1768*
15: 7 *more* than over **n** and nine just *persons* *1768*

NINEVEH (19) [NINEVITES]
Ge 10:11 builded **N**, and the city Rehoboth, and 5210
10:12 Resen between **N** and Calah: the same *is* a 5210
2Ki 19:36 and went and returned, and dwelt at **N**. 5210
Isa 37:37 and went and returned, and dwelt at **N**. 5210
Jnh 1: 2 Arise, go to **N**, *that* great city, and 5210
3: 2 Arise, go unto **N**, *that* great city, and 5210
3: 3 So Jonah arose, and went unto **N**, 5210
3: 3 Now **N** was an exceeding great city of three 5210
3: 4 Yet forty days, and **N** *shall be* overthrown. 5210
3: 5 So the people of **N** believed God, and 5210
3: 6 For word came unto the king of **N**, and 5210
3: 7 published through **N** by the decree of 5210
4:11 should not I spare **N**, *that* great city, 5210
Na 1: 1 The burden of **N**. The book of the vision of 5210
2: 8 **N** *is* of old like a pool of water: yet they 5210
3: 7 flee from thee, and say, **N** is laid waste: 5210
Zep 2:13 will make **N** a desolation, *and* dry like a 5210
Mt 12:41 *The* men of **N** shall rise in judgment with *3536*
Lk 11:32 *The* men of **N** shall rise up in the judgment *3535*

NINEVITES (1) [NINEVEH]
Lk 11:30 For as Jonas was a sign unto the **N**, so *3536*

NINTH (34) [NINE]
Lev 23:32 in the **n** *day* of the month at even, 8672
25:22 and eat *yet* of old fruit until the **n** year; 8671
Nu 7:60 On the **n** day Abidan the son of Gideoni, 8671
2Ki 17: 6 In the **n** year of Hoshea, the king of Assyria 8671
18:10 that *is* the **n** year of Hoshea king of Israel, 8672
25: 1 it came to pass in the **n** year of his reign, 8671
25: 3 on the **n** *day* of the *fourth* month the famine 8672
1Ch 12:12 Johanan the eighth, Elzabad the **n**, 8671
24:11 The **n** to Jeshua, the tenth to Shecaniah, 8671
25:16 The **n** *to* Mattaniah, *he,* his sons, and 8671
27:12 The **n** *captain* for the ninth month *was* 8671
27:12 The ninth *captain* for the **n** month *was* 8671
2Ch 16:12 **n** year of his reign was diseased in his feet, 8672
Ezr 10: 9 It *was* the **n** month, on the twentieth *day* of 8671
Jer 36: 9 in the **n** month, *that* they proclaimed a fast 8671
36:22 king sat *in* the winterhouse in the **n** month: 8671
39: 1 In the **n** year of Zedekiah king of Judah, 8671
39: 2 in the fourth month, the **n** *day* of the month, 8672
52: 4 it came to pass in the **n** year of his reign, 8671
52: 6 the fourth month, in the **n** *day* of the month, 8672
Eze 24: 1 Again in the **n** year, in the tenth month, 8671
Hag 2:10 twentieth *day* of the **n** *month,* in the second 8671

Hag 2:18 twentieth day of the n *month, even* from 8671
Zec 7: 1 Zechariah in the fourth *day* of the n month, 8671
Mt 20: 5 he went out about the sixth and n hour, *1766*
27:45 darkness over all the land unto the n hour. *1766*
27:46 And about the n hour Jesus cried with a *1766*
Mk 15:33 over the whole land until the n hour. *1766*
15:34 And at the n hour Jesus cried with a loud *1766*
Lk 23:44 darkness over all the earth until the n hour. *1766*
Ac 3: 1 at the hour of prayer, *being* the n *hour.* *1766*
10: 3 about the n hour of the day, *1766*
10:30 and at the n hour I prayed in my house, and *1766*
Rev 21:20 the eighth, beryl; the n, a topaz; the tenth, *1766*

NISAN (2)
Ne 2: 1 it came to pass in the month N, *in* 5212
Est 3: 7 In the first month, that *is,* the month N, 5212

NISROCH (2)
2Ki 19:37 as he was worshipping *in* the house of N 5268
Isa 37:38 as he was worshipping *in* the house of N 5268

NITRE (2)
Pr 25:20 *and as* vinegar upon n, so *is* he that singeth 5427
Jer 2:22 For though thou wash thee with n, and 5427

NO (1393) [NONE, NOR, NOT] See Index

NOADIAH (2)
Ezr 8:33 of Jeshua, and N the son of Binnui, Levites; 5129
Ne 6:14 on the prophetess N, and the rest of 5129

NOAH (51) [NOAH'S, NOE]
Ge 5:29 he called his name N, saying, This *same* 5146
5:30 Lamech lived after he begat N five hundred 5146
5:32 N was five hundred years old: and 5146
5:32 and N begat Shem, Ham, and Japheth. 5146
6: 8 N found grace in the eyes of the LORD. 5146
6: 9 These *are* the generations of N: Noah was a 5146
6: 9 N was a just man *and* perfect in his 5146
6: 9 in his generations, *and* N walked with God. 5146
6:10 N begat three sons, Shem, Ham, and 5146
6:13 God said unto N, The end of all flesh is 5146
6:22 Thus did N; according to all that God 5146
7: 1 the LORD said unto N, Come thou and 5146
7: 5 N did according unto all that the LORD 5146
7: 6 N *was* six hundred years old when 5146
7: 7 N went in, and his sons, and his wife, and 5146
7: 9 went in two and two unto N into the ark, 5146
7: 9 and the female, as God had commanded N. 5146
7:13 In the selfsame day entered N, and Shem, 5146
7:13 the sons of N, and Noah's wife, and 5146
7:15 they went in unto N into the ark, two and 5146
7:23 N only remained *alive,* and *they* that *were* 5146
8: 1 God remembered N, and every living thing, 5146
8: 6 that N opened the window of the ark which 5146
8:11 N knew that the waters were abated from 5146
8:13 N removed the covering of the ark, and 5146
8:15 And God spake unto N, saying, 5146
8:18 N went forth, and his sons, and his wife, 5146
8:20 N builded an altar unto the LORD; and 5146
9: 1 God blessed N and his sons, and said unto 5146
9: 8 God spake unto N, and to his sons with 5146
9:17 God said unto N, This *is* the token of 5146
9:18 the sons of N, that went forth of the ark, 5146
9:19 These *are* the three sons of N: and of them 5146
9:20 N began *to be* a husbandman, and 5146
9:24 N awoke from his wine, and knew what his 5146
9:28 N lived after the flood three hundred and 5146
9:29 all the days of N were nine hundred and 5146
10: 1 these *are* the generations of the sons of N, 5146
10:32 These *are* the families of the sons of N, 5146
Nu 26:33 and N, Hoglah, Milcah, and Tirzah. 5270
27: 1 N, and Hoglah, and Milcah, and Tirzah. 5270
36:11 Tirzah, and Hoglah, and Milcah, and N, 5270
Jos 17: 3 and N, Hoglah, Milcah, and Tirzah. 5270
1Ch 1: 4 N, Shem, Ham, and Japheth. 5146
Isa 54: 9 For this *is as* the waters of N unto me: 5146
54: 9 for *as* I have sworn that the waters of N 5146
Eze 14:14 N, Daniel, and Job, were in it, they should 5146
14:20 Though N, Daniel, and Job, *were* in it, *as* I 5146
Heb 11: 7 By faith N, being warned of God of *things* *3575*
1Pe 3:20 of God waited in the days of N, *3575*
2Pe 2: 5 saved N the eighth *person,* a preacher of *3575*

NOAH'S (2) [NOAH]
Ge 7:11 In the six hundredth year of N life, in 5146
7:13 N wife, and the three wives of his sons with 5146

NOB (6)
1Sa 21: 1 came David to N to Ahimelech the priest: 5011
22: 9 said, I saw the son of Jesse coming to N, 5011
22:11 father's house, the priests that *were* in N: 5011
22:19 N, the city of the priests, smote he with 5011
Ne 11:32 *And at* Anathoth, N, Ananiah, 5011
Isa 10:32 As yet shall *he* remain at N *that* day: 5011

NOBAH (3)
Nu 32:42 N went and took Kenath, and the villages 5025
32:42 and called it N, after his own name. 5025
Jdg 8:11 of them that dwelt in tents on the east of N 5025

NOBLE (7) [NOBLEMAN, NOBLES]
Ezr 4:10 the great and n Asnappar brought over, 3358
Est 6: 9 hand of one of the king's **most** n princes, 6579
Jer 2:21 Yet I had planted thee a n vine, wholly a 8321
Ac 17:11 These were **more** n **than** those in *2104*
24: 3 *it* always, and in all places, **most** n Felix, *2903*
26:25 But he said, I am not mad, **most** n Festus; *2903*
1Co 1:26 not many mighty, not many n, *are called:* *2104*

NOBLEMAN (3) [MAN, NOBLE]
Lk 19:12 A certain n went into a far country to *444+2104*
Jn 4:46 And there was a certain n, whose son was *937*
4:49 The n saith unto him, Sir, come down ere *937*

NOBLES (30) [NOBLE]
Ex 24:11 upon the n of the children of Israel he laid 678
Nu 21:18 the well, the n of the people digged it, 5081
Jdg 5:13 have dominion over the n *among* the people: 117
1Ki 21: 8 the elders and to the n that *were* in his city, 2715
21:11 the n who *were* the inhabitants in his city, 2715
2Ch 23:20 the n, and the governors of the people, and 117
Ne 2:16 to the priests, nor to the n, nor to the rulers, 2715
3: 5 their n put not their necks to the work of 117
4:14 said unto the n, and to the rulers, and to 2715
4:19 I said unto the n, and to the rulers, and 2715
5: 7 I rebuked the n, and the rulers, and 2715
6:17 Moreover in those days the n of Judah sent 2715
7: 5 put into mine heart to gather together the n, 2715
10:29 their n, and entered into a curse, and into an 117
13:17 I contended with the n of Judah, and 2715
Est 1: 3 Media, the n and princes of the provinces, 6579
Job 29:10 The n held their peace, and their tongue 5057
Ps 83:11 Make their n like Oreb, and like Zeeb: yea, 5081
149: 8 with chains, and their n with fetters of iron; 3513
Pr 8:16 By me princes rule, and n, *even* all 5081
Ecc 10:17 when thy king *is* the son of n, and 2715
Isa 13: 2 that they may go *into* the gates of the n. 5081
34:12 They shall call the n thereof *to* 2715
43:14 have brought down all their n, and 1281
Jer 14: 3 their n have sent their little ones to 117
27:20 and all the n of Judah and Jerusalem; 2715
30:21 their n shall be of themselves, and 117
39: 6 also the king of Babylon slew all the n of 2715
Jnh 3: 7 by the decree of the king and his n, 1419
Na 3:18 thy n shall dwell *in the dust:* thy people is 117

NOD (1)
Ge 4:16 dwelt in the land of N, on the east of Eden. 5113

NODAB (1)
1Ch 5:19 with Jetur, and Nephish, and N. 5114

NOE (5) [NOAH]
Mt 24:37 But as the days of N *were,* so shall also *3575*
24:38 until the day that N entered into the ark, *3575*
Lk 3:36 *the son* of Sem, which was *the son* of N, *3575*
17:26 And as it was in the days of N, so shall it be *3575*
17:27 until the day that N entered into the ark, *3575*

NOGAH (2)
1Ch 3: 7 And N, and Nepheg, and Japhia, 5052
14: 6 And N, and Nepheg, and Japhia, 5052

NOHAH (1)
1Ch 8: 2 N the fourth, and Rapha the fifth. 5119

NOISE (88) [NOISED]
Ex 20:18 the n of the trumpet, and the mountain 6963

Ex 32:17 when Joshua heard the **n** of the people as 6963
32:17 *There is* a **n** of war in the camp. 6963
32:18 *but* the **n** of *them that* sing do I hear. 6963
Jos 6:10 not shout, nor **make** any **n** with your voice, 8085
Jdg 5:11 *They that are delivered* from the **n** of 6963
1Sa 4: 6 when the Philistines heard the **n** of 6963
4: 6 What *meaneth* the **n** of this great shout in 6963
4:14 when Eli heard the **n** of the crying, he said, 6963
4:14 he said, What *meaneth* the **n** of this tumult? 6963
14:19 that the **n** that *was* in the host of 1995
1Ki 1:41 Wherefore *is this* **n** of the city being in an 6963
1:45 rang again. This *is* the **n** that ye have heard. 6963
2Ki 7: 6 host of the Syrians to hear a **n** of chariots, 6963
7: 6 a **n** of horses, *even* the noise of a great host: 6963
7: 6 a noise of horses, *even* the **n** of a great host: 6963
11:13 when Athaliah heard the **n** of the guard 6963
1Ch 15:28 **making a n** with psalteries and harps. 8085
2Ch 23:12 Now when Athaliah heard the **n** of 6963
Ezr 3:13 So that the people could not discern the **n** 6963
3:13 from the **n** of the weeping of the people: 6963
3:13 a loud shout, and the **n** was heard afar off. 6963
Job 36:29 of the clouds, *or* the **n** of his tabernacle? 8663
36:33 The **n** thereof sheweth concerning it, 7452
37: 2 Hear attentively the **n** of his voice, and 7267
Ps 33: 3 a new song; play skilfully with a **loud n**. 8643
42: 7 Deep calleth unto deep at the **n** of thy 6963
55: 2 I mourn in my complaint, and **make a n**; 1949
59: 6 they **make a n** like a dog, and go round 1993
59:14 *and* let them **make a n** like a dog, and 1993
65: 7 Which stilleth the **n** of the seas, the noise of 7588
65: 7 the **n** of their waves, and the tumult of 7588
66: 1 **Make a joyful n** unto God, all ye lands: 7321
81: 1 **make a joyful n** unto the God of Jacob. 7321
93: 4 The LORD on high *is* mightier than the **n** 6963
95: 1 let us **make a joyful n** to the rock of our 7321
95: 2 *and* **make a joyful n** unto him with psalms. 7321
98: 4 **Make a joyful n** unto the LORD, all 7321
98: 4 **make a loud n**, and rejoice, and 6476
98: 6 sound of cornet **make a joyful n** before 7321
100: 1 **Make a joyful n** unto the LORD, all ye 7321
Isa 9: 5 battle of the warrior *is* with **confused n**, 7494
13: 4 The **n** of a multitude in the mountains, 6963
13: 4 a tumultuous **n** of the kingdoms of nations 6963
14:11 down *to* the grave, *and* the **n** of thy viols: 1998
17:12 *which* **make a n** like the noise of the seas; 1993
17:12 *which* make a noise like the **n** of the seas; 1993
24: 8 the **n** of them that rejoice endeth, the joy of 7588
24:18 *that* he who fleeth from the **n** of the fear 6963
25: 5 Thou shalt bring down the **n** of strangers, 7588
29: 6 great **n**, *with* storm and tempest, and 6963
31: 4 nor abase himself for the **n** of them: 1995
33: 3 At the **n** of the tumult the people fled; 6963
66: 6 A voice of **n** from the city, a voice from 7588
Jer 4:19 my heart **maketh a n** in me; I cannot hold 1993
4:29 The whole city shall flee for the **n** of 6963
10:22 the **n** of the bruit is come, and a great 6963
11:16 with the **n** of a great tumult he hath kindled 6963
25:31 A **n** shall come *even* to the ends of 7588
46:17 cry there, Pharaoh king of Egypt *is but* a **n**; 7588
47: 3 At the **n** of the stamping of the hoofs of his 6963
49:21 The earth is moved at the **n** of their fall, 6963
49:21 the **n** thereof was heard in the Red sea. 6963
50:46 At the **n** of the taking of Babylon the earth 6963
51:55 great waters, a **n** of their voice is uttered: 7588
La 2: 7 they have made a **n** in the house of 6963
Eze 1:24 they went, I heard the **n** of their wings, 6963
1:24 like the **n** of great waters, as the voice of 6963
1:24 the voice of speech, as the **n** of a host: 6963
3:13 *I heard* also the **n** of the wings of the living 6963
3:13 the **n** of the wheels over against them, and 6963
3:13 against them, and a **n** of a great rushing. 6963
19: 7 the fulness thereof, by the **n** of his roaring. 6963
26:10 thy walls shall shake at the **n** of 6963
26:13 I will cause the **n** of thy songs to cease; 1995
37: 7 there was a **n**, and behold a shaking, and 6963
43: 2 his voice *was* like a **n** of many waters: and 6963
Joel 2: 5 Like the **n** of chariots on the tops of 6963
2: 5 like the **n** of a flame of fire that devoureth 6963
Am 5:23 Take thou away from me the **n** of thy 1995
Mic 2:12 they shall **make great n** by reason of 1949
Na 3: 2 The **n** of a whip, and the noise of 6963
3: 2 the **n** of the rattling of the wheels, and 6963
Zep 1:10 *that there shall be* the **n** of a cry from 6963
Zec 9:15 shall drink, *and* **make a n** as *through* wine; 1993
Mt 9:23 the minstrels and the people **making** a **n**, *2350*
2Pe 3:10 the heavens shall pass away with a **great n**, *4500*
Rev 6: 1 and I heard, as *it were* the **n** of thunder, *5456*

NOISED (4) [NOISE]
Jos 6:27 his fame was *n* throughout all the country. NIH
Mk 2: 1 and it was **n** that he was in the house. *191*
Lk 1:65 all these sayings were **n abroad** throughout *1255*
Ac 2: 6 Now when this **was n abroad**, *1096+3588+5456*

NOISOME (4)
Ps 91: 3 of the fowler, *and* from the **n** pestilence. 1942
Eze 14:15 If I cause **n** beasts to pass through the land, 7451
14:21 and the **n** beast, and the pestilence, 7451
Rev 16: 2 and there fell a **n** and grievous sore upon *2556*

NOISY See CONCOUSE

NON (1)
1Ch 7:27 **N** his son, Jehoshua his son. 5126

NON-GREEKS See BARBARIANS

NONE (358) [NO] See Index

NOON (13) [NOONDAY, NOONDAYS, NOONTIDE]
Ge 43:16 for *these* men shall dine with me at **n**. 6672
43:25 ready the present against Joseph came at **n**: 6672
2Sa 4: 5 of Ish-bosheth, who lay on a bed at **n**. 6672
1Ki 18:26 name of Baal from morning even until **n**, 6672
18:27 it came to pass at **n**, that Elijah mocked 6672
20:16 they went out at **n**. But Ben-hadad *was* 6672
2Ki 4:20 he sat on her knees till **n**, and *then* died. 6672
Ps 55:17 Evening, and morning, and at **n**, will I pray, 6672
SS 1: 7 where thou makest *thy flock* to rest at **n**: 6672
Jer 6: 4 war against her; arise, and let us go up at **n**. 6672
Am 8: 9 that I will cause the sun to go down at **n**, 6672
Zep 2: 4 they shall drive out Ashdod at the **n day**, 6672
Ac 22: 6 was come nigh unto Damascus about **n**, *3314*

NOONDAY (8) [DAY, NOON]
Job 5:14 and grope in the **n** as in the night. 6672
11:17 *thine* age shall be clearer than the **n**; 6672
Ps 37: 6 as the light, and thy judgment as the **n**. 6672
91: 6 *nor* for the destruction *that* wasteth at **n**. 6672
Isa 16: 3 shadow as the night in the midst of the **n**; 6672
58:10 in obscurity, and thy darkness *be* as the **n**: 6672
59:10 we stumble at **n** as *in* the night; *we are* in 6672
Jer 15: 8 the mother of the young men a spoiler at **n**: 6672

NOONDAYS (1) [DAY, NOON]
Dt 28:29 thou shalt grope at **n**, as the blind gropeth 6672

NOONTIDE (1) [NOON]
Jer 20:16 the morning, and the shouting at **n**; 6256+6672

NOPH (7)
Isa 19:13 the princes of **N** are deceived; 5297
Jer 2:16 Also the children of **N** and Tahapanes have 5297
44: 1 at **N**, and in the country of Pathros, saying, 5297
46:14 and publish in **N** and in Tahpanhes: 5297
46:19 for **N** shall be waste and desolate without 5297
Eze 30:13 I will cause *their* images to cease out of **N**; 5297
30:16 and **N** *shall have* distresses daily. 5297

NOPHAH (1)
Nu 21:30 we have laid *them* waste even unto **N**, 5302

NOR (758) [NO] See Index

NORTH (132) [NORTHERN, NORTHWARD, NORTHWARDS]
Ge 28:14 to the east, and to the **n**, and to the south: 6828
Ex 26:20 on the **n** side *there shall be* twenty boards: 6828
26:35 and thou shalt put the table on the **n** side. 6828
27:11 likewise for the **n** side in length *there shall* 6828
36:25 *which is* toward the **n** corner, he made 6828
38:11 for the **n** side *the hangings were* an hundred 6828
Nu 2:25 Dan *shall be* on the **n side** by their armies: 6828
34: 7 this shall be your **n** border: from the great 6828
34: 9 at Hazar-enan: this shall be your **n** border. 6828
35: 5 and *on* the **n** side two thousand cubits; 6828
Jos 8:11 the city, and pitched on the **n side** of Ai: 6828
8:13 *even* all the host that *was* on the **n** of 6828
11: 2 to the kings that *were* on the **n** of 6828
15: 5 *their* border **in** the **n** quarter *was* 6828+1886.5
15: 6 and passed along by the **n** of Beth-arabah; 6828
15:10 on the **n side**, and went down *to* 6828+1886.5

Jos 16: 6 the sea *to* Michmethah on the **n side**; 6828
17: 9 also *was* on the **n side** of the river, 6828
17:10 they met together in Asher on the **n**, and 6828
18: 5 Joseph shall abide in their coasts on the **n**. 6828
18:12 their border on the **n** side was from Jordan; 6828
18:12 went up to the side of Jericho on the **n side**, 6828
18:16 which *is* in the valley of the giants on the **n**, 6828
18:17 was drawn from the **n**, and went forth *to* 6828
18:19 the outgoings of the border were at the **n** 6828
19:14 the border compasseth it on the **n side** *to* 6828
19:27 toward the **n side** *of* Beth-emek, 6828
24:30 on the **n side** of the hill of Gaash. 6828
Jdg 2: 9 of Ephraim, on the **n side** of the hill Gaash. 6828
7: 1 the Midianites were on the **n side** of them, 6828
21:19 which *is* on the **n side** of Beth-el, 4480+6828
1Ki 7:25 three looking toward the **n**, and 6828
2Ki 16:14 and put it on the **n** side of the altar. 6828+1886.5
1Ch 9:24 toward the east, west, **n**, and south. 6828
2Ch 4: 4 three looking toward the **n**, and 6828
Job 26: 7 He stretcheth out the **n** over the empty 6828
37: 9 the whirlwind: and cold out of the **n**. 4215
37:22 Fair weather cometh out of the **n**: with God 6828
Ps 48: 2 *is* mount Zion, *on* the sides of the **n**, 6828
89:12 The **n** and the south thou hast created them: 6828
107: 3 the west, from the **n**, and from the south. 6828
Pr 25:23 The **n** wind driveth away rain: so *doth* an 6828
Ecc 1: 6 the south, and turneth about unto the **n**; 6828
11: 3 tree fall toward the south, or toward the **n**, 6828
SS 4:16 Awake, O **n wind**; and come thou south; 6828
Isa 14:13 of the congregation, in the sides of the **n**: 6828
14:31 for there shall come from the **n** a smoke, 6828
41:25 I have raised up *one* from the **n**, and 6828
43: 6 I will say to the **n**, Give *up;* and to 6828
49:12 lo, these from the **n** and from the west; and 6828
Jer 1:13 the face thereof *is* towards the **n**. 6828+1886.5
1:14 Out of the **n** an evil shall break forth upon 6828
1:15 families of the kingdoms of the **n**, 6828+1886.5
3:12 Go and proclaim these words toward the **n**, 6828
3:18 **n** to the land that I have given for an 6828
4: 6 for I will bring evil from the **n**, and a great 6828
6: 1 for evil appeareth out of the **n**, and 6828
6:22 a people cometh from the **n** country, and 6828
10:22 a great commotion out of the **n** country, 6828
13:20 and behold them that come from the **n**: 6828
16:15 the children of Israel from the land of the **n**, 6828
23: 8 of Israel out of the **n** country, 6828+1886.5
25: 9 will send and take all the families of the **n**, 6828
25:26 all the kings of the **n**, far and near, one with 6828
31: 8 I *will* bring them from the **n** country, and 6828
46: 6 fall toward the **n** by the river Euphrates. 6828
46:10 in the **n** country by the river Euphrates. 6828
46:20 destruction cometh; it cometh out of the **n**. 6828
46:24 into the hand of the people of the **n**. 6828
47: 2 waters rise up out of the **n**, and shall be an 6828
50: 3 For out of the **n** there cometh up a nation 6828
50: 9 of great nations from the **n** country: 6828
50:41 a people shall come from the **n**, and a great 6828
51:48 the spoilers shall come unto her from the **n**, 6828
Eze 1: 4 behold, a whirlwind came out of the **n**, 6828
8: 3 of the inner gate that looketh toward the **n**; 6828
8: 5 up thine eyes now the way towards the **n**. 6828
8: 5 So I lift up mine eyes the way toward the **n**, 6828
8:14 LORD'S house which *was* towards the **n**; 6828
9: 2 which lieth toward the **n**, and every man a 6828
20:47 all faces from the south to the **n** shall be 6828
21: 4 against all flesh from the south *to* the **n**: 6828
26: 7 from the **n**, with horses, and with chariots, 6828
32:30 There *be* the princes of the **n**, all of them, 6828
38: 6 the house of Togarmah *of* the **n** quarters, 6828
38:15 thou shalt come from thy place out of the **n** 6828
39: 2 will cause thee to come up from the **n** parts, 6828
40:20 the outward court that looked toward the **n**, 6828
40:23 *was* over against the gate toward the **n**, 6828
40:35 he brought me to the **n** gate, and 6828
40:40 one goeth up to the entry of the **n** 6828+1886.5
40:44 which *was* at the side of the **n** gate; 6828
40:44 east gate *having* the prospect toward the **n**. 6828
40:46 the chamber whose prospect *is* toward the **n** 6828
41:11 one door toward the **n**, and another door 6828
42: 1 into the utter court, the way toward the **n**: 6828
42: 1 *was* before the building toward the **n**. 6828
42: 2 length of an hundred cubits *was* the **n** door, 6828
42: 4 of one cubit; and their doors toward the **n**. 6828
42:11 of the chambers which *were* toward the **n**, 6828
42:13 The **n** chambers *and* the south chambers, 6828
42:17 He measured the **n** side, five hundred reeds, 6828
44: 4 brought he me the way of the **n** gate before 6828
46: 9 he that entereth in *by* the way of the **n** gate 6828
46: 9 go forth *by* the way of the **n** gate: 6828+1886.5
46:19 which looked toward the **n**: 6828+1886.5
47:15 of the land toward the **n** side, 6828+1886.5
47:17 the **n** northward, and the border of Hamath. 6828
47:17 border of Hamath. And *this is* the **n** side. 6828
48: 1 From the **n** end to the coast of 6828+1886.5
48:10 toward the **n** five and twenty thousand *in* 6828
48:16 the **n** side four thousand and five hundred, 6828
48:17 the suburbs of the city shall be toward the **n** 6828
48:30 on the **n** side, four thousand and 6828
Da 11: 6 to the king of the **n** to make an agreement: 6828
11: 7 enter into the fortress of the king of the **n**, 6828
11: 8 continue *more* years than the king of the **n**. 6828
11:11 fight with him, *even* with the king of the **n**: 6828
11:13 For the king of the **n** shall return, and 6828
11:15 So the king of the **n** shall come, and cast up 6828
11:40 the king of the **n** shall come against him 6828
11:44 the east and out of the **n** shall trouble him: 6828
Am 8:12 from the **n** even to the east, they shall run 6828
Zep 2:13 he will stretch out his hand against the **n**, 6828
Zec 2: 6 *come forth,* and flee from the land of the **n**, 6828
6: 6 *are* therein go forth into the **n** country; 6828
6: 8 these that go toward the **n** country have 6828
6: 8 have quieted my spirit in the **n** country. 6828
14: 4 of the mountain shall remove toward the **n**, 6828
Lk 13:29 and from the **n**, and *from* the south, and *1005*
Ac 27:12 and lieth toward the south west and **n west**. 5566
Rev 21:13 the east three gates; on the **n** three gates; *1005*

NORTHEASTER See EUROCLYDON

NORTHERN (2) [NORTH]
Jer 15:12 Shall iron break the **n** iron and 4480+6828
Joel 2:20 I will remove far off from you the **n** *army,* 6830

NORTHWARD (23) [NORTH]
Ge 13:14 from the place where thou *art* **n**, 6828+1886.5
Ex 40:22 upon the side of the tabernacle **n**, 6828+1886.5
Lev 1:11 of the altar **n** before the LORD: 6828+1886.5
Dt 2: 3 mountain long enough: turn you **n**. 6828+1886.5
3:27 **n**, and southward, and eastward, 6828+1886.5
Jos 13: 3 even unto the borders of Ekron **n**, 6828+1886.5
15: 7 *so* **n**, looking toward Gilgal, that *is* 6828+1886.5
15: 8 end of the valley of the giants **n**: 6828+1886.5
15:11 went out unto the side of Ekron **n**: 6828+1886.5
17:10 **n** *it was* Manasseh's, and the sea is 6828+1886.5
18:18 the side over against Arabah **n**, 6828+1886.5
18:19 along to the side of Beth-hoglah **n**: 6828+1886.5
Jdg 12: 1 went **n**, and said unto Jephthah, 6828+1886.5
1Sa 14: 5 situate **n** over against Michmash, 4480+6828
1Ch 26:14 cast lots; and his lot came out **n**. 6828+1886.5
26:17 **n** four a day, southward four a day, 6828+1886.5
Eze 8: 5 behold, **n** at the gate of the altar this 4480+6828
40:19 an hundred cubits east*ward* and **n**. 6828
47: 2 he me out *of* the way of the gate **n**, 6828+1886.5
47:17 north **n**, and the border of Hamath. 6828+1886.5
48: 1 the border of Damascus **n**, 6828+1886.5
48:31 three gates **n**; one gate of Reuben, 6828+1886.5
Da 8: 4 and **n**, and southward; 6828+1886.5

NORTHWARDS (1) [NORTH]
Nu 3:35 on the side of the tabernacle **n**. 6828+1886.5

NOSE (12) [NOSES]
Lev 21:18 or he that hath a **flat n**, or any thing 2763
2Ki 19:28 therefore I will put my hook in thy **n**, and 639
Job 40:24 with his eyes: *his* **n** pierceth through snares. 639
41: 2 Canst thou put a hook into his **n**? or bore his 639
Pr 30:33 the wringing of the **n** bringeth forth blood: 639
SS 7: 4 thy **n** *is* as the tower of Lebanon which 639
7: 8 the vine, and the smell of thy **n** like apples; 639
Isa 3:21 The rings, and **n** jewels, 639
37:29 therefore will I put my hook in thy **n**, and 639
65: 5 These *are* a smoke in my **n**, a fire that 639
Eze 8:17 and lo, they put the branch to their **n**. 639
23:25 they shall take away thy **n** and thine ears; 639

NOSES (2) [NOSE]
Ps 115: 6 hear not: **n** have they, but they smell not: 639
Eze 39:11 and it *shall* stop the *n of the* passengers: and NIH

NOSTRILS (15)
Ge 2: 7 and breathed into his **n** the breath of life; 639
7:22 All in whose **n** *was* the breath of life, of all 639
Ex 15: 8 with the blast of thy **n** the waters were 639
Nu 11:20 until it come out at your **n**, and it be 639
2Sa 22: 9 There went up a smoke out of his **n**, and 639
22:16 at the blast of the breath of his **n**. 639
Job 4: 9 by the breath of his **n** are they consumed. 639
27: 3 *is* in me, and the spirit of God *is* in my **n**; 639
39:20 a grasshopper? the glory of his **n** *is* terrible. 5170
41:20 Out of his **n** goeth smoke, as *out of* a 5156
Ps 18: 8 There went up a smoke out of his **n**, and 639
18:15 O LORD, at the blast of the breath of thy **n**. 639
Isa 2:22 Cease ye from man, whose breath *is* in his **n**: 639
La 4:20 The breath of our **n**, the anointed of 639
Am 4:10 stink of your camps to come up unto your **n**: 639

NOT (6596) [NO] See Index

NOTABLE (5) [NOTE]
Da 8: 5 and the goat *had* a **n** horn between his eyes. 2380
8: 8 for it came up four **n ones** toward the four 2380
Mt 27:16 And they had then a **n** prisoner, *1978*
Ac 2:20 *that* great and **n** day of the Lord come: *2016*
4:16 for that indeed a **n** miracle hath been done *1110*

NOTE (3) [NOTABLE, NOTED]
Isa 30: 8 it before them in a table, and **n** it in a book, 2710
Ro 16: 7 who are of **n** among the apostles, *1978*
2Th 3:14 **n** that *man*, and have no company with *4593*

NOTED (1) [NOTE]
Da 10:21 I will shew thee that which is **n** in 7559

NOTHING (225) [THING] See Index

NOTICE (2)
2Sa 3:36 all the people **took n** *of it*, and it pleased 5234
2Co 9: 5 whereof *ye* **had n before**, that the same *4293*

NOTWITHSTANDING (36) See Index

NOUGHT (36) [NAUGHT] See Index

NOURISH (5) [NOURISHED, NOURISHER, NOURISHETH, NOURISHING, NOURISHMENT]
Ge 45:11 there will I **n** thee; for yet *there are* five 3557
50:21 I will **n** you and your little ones. And he 3557
Isa 7:21 *that* a man shall **n** a young cow, and 2421
23: 4 neither do I **n up** young men, *nor* bring up 1431
44:14 he planteth an ash, and the rain doth **n** *it*. 1431

NOURISHED (10) [NOURISH]
Ge 47:12 Joseph **n** his father, and his brethren, and 3557
2Sa 12: 3 ewe lamb, which he had bought and **n up**: 2421
Isa 1: 2 I have **n** and brought up children, and 1431
Eze 19: 2 she **n** her whelps among young lions. 7235
Ac 7:20 and **n up** in his father's house three months: *397*
7:21 took him up, and **n** him for her own son. *397*
12:20 their country was **n** by the king's *country*. *5142*
1Ti 4: 6 **n up** in the words of faith and of good *1789*
Jas 5: 5 ye have **n** your hearts, as in a day of *5142*
Rev 12:14 where she is **n** for a time, and times, and *5142*

NOURISHER (1) [NOURISH]
Ru 4:15 restorer of *thy* life, and a **n** of thine old age: 3557

NOURISHETH (1) [NOURISH]
Eph 5:29 but **n** and cherisheth it, even as the Lord *1625*

NOURISHING (1) [NOURISH]
Da 1: 5 so **n** them three years, that at the end 1431

NOURISHMENT (1) [NOURISH]
Col 2:19 by joints and bands having **n ministered**, *2023*

NOVICE (1)
1Ti 3: 6 Not a **n**, lest being lifted up with pride he *3504*

NOW (1356) See Index

NULLIFIES See VOID

NULLIFY See NOUGHT; VOID

NUMBER (178) [NUMBERED, NUMBEREST, NUMBERING, NUMBERS]
Ge 13:16 so that if a man can **n** the dust of the earth, 4487
15: 5 and tell the stars, if thou be able to **n** them: 5608
34:30 I *being* few in **n**, they shall gather 4557
41:49 he left numbering; for *it was* without **n**. 4557
Ex 12: 4 take *it* according to the **n** of the souls; 4373
16:16 *according to* the **n** of your persons; 4557
23:26 in thy land: the **n** of thy days I will fulfil. 4557
30:12 sum of the children of Israel after their **n**, 6485
Lev 15:13 he shall **n** to himself seven days for his 5608
15:28 she shall **n** to herself seven days, and 5608
23:16 the seventh sabbath shall ye **n** fifty days; 5608
25: 8 thou shalt **n** seven sabbaths of years unto 5608
25:15 According to the **n** of years after the jubile 4557
25:15 according unto the **n** of years of the fruits 4557
25:16 for *according to* the **n** *of the years* of 4557
25:50 sale shall be according unto the **n** of years, 4557
26:22 your cattle, and **make you few in n**; 4591
Nu 1: 2 with the **n** of *their* names, every male by 4557
1: 3 and Aaron shall **n** them by their armies. 6485
1:18 according to the **n** of the names, 4557
1:20 according to the **n** of the names, by their 4557
1:22 according to the **n** of the names, by their 4557
1:24 according to the **n** of the names, 4557
1:26 according to the **n** of the names, 4557
1:28 according to the **n** of the names, 4557
1:30 according to the **n** of the names, 4557
1:32 according to the **n** of the names, 4557
1:34 according to the **n** of the names, 4557
1:36 according to the **n** of the names, 4557
1:38 according to the **n** of the names, 4557
1:40 according to the **n** of the names, 4557
1:42 according to the **n** of the names, 4557
1:49 Only thou shalt not **n** the tribe of Levi, 6485
3:15 **N** the children of Levi after the house of 6485
3:15 a month old and upward shalt thou **n** them. 6485
3:22 according to the **n** of all the males, from a 4557
3:28 In the **n** of all the males, from a month old 4557
3:34 according to the **n** of all the males, from a 4557
3:40 **N** all the firstborn of the males of 6485
3:40 and upward, and take the **n** of their names. 4557
3:43 all the firstborn males by the **n** of names, 4557
3:48 wherewith the **odd n** of them is *to be* 5736
4:23 upward until fifty years old shalt thou **n** 6485
4:29 thou shalt **n** them after their families, 6485
4:30 even unto fifty years old shalt thou **n** them, 6485
4:37 Aaron did **n** according to 6485
4:41 Aaron did **n** according to 6485
14:29 according to your whole **n**, from twenty 4557
14:34 After the **n** of the days *in* which ye 4557
15:12 According to the **n** that ye shall prepare, so 4557
15:12 ye do to *every* one according to their **n**. 4557
23:10 and the **n** *of* the fourth part of Israel? 4557
26:53 an inheritance according to the **n** of names. 4557
29:18 for the lambs, *shall be* according to their **n**, 4557
29:21 for the lambs, *shall be* according to their **n**, 4557
29:24 for the lambs, *shall be* according to their **n**, 4557
29:27 for the lambs, *shall be* according to their **n**, 4557
29:30 for the lambs, *shall be* according to their **n**, 4557
29:33 for the lambs, *shall be* according to their **n**, 4557
29:37 for the lambs, *shall be* according to their **n**, 4557
31:36 was *in* **n** three hundred thousand and seven 4557
Dt 4:27 ye shall be left few in **n** among the heathen, 4557
7: 7 because ye were moe in **n** than any people; 7230
16: 9 Seven weeks shalt thou **n** unto thee: 5608
16: 9 begin to **n** the seven weeks from *such time* 5608
25: 2 according to his fault, by a *certain* **n**. 4557
28:62 ye shall be left few in **n**, whereas ye were 4962
32: 8 according to the **n** of the children of Israel. 4557
Jos 4: 5 according unto the **n** of the tribes of 4557
4: 8 according to the **n** of the tribes of 4557
Jdg 6: 5 both they and their camels were without **n**: 4557
7: 6 the **n** of them that lapped, putting their 4557
7:12 their camels *were* without **n**, as the sand by 4557
21:23 took *them* wives, according to their **n**, 4557
1Sa 6: 4 *according to* the **n** of the lords of 4557
6:18 *according to* the **n** of all the cities of 4557
14:17 **N** now, and see who is gone from us. 6485
2Sa 2:15 and went over by **n** twelve of Benjamin, 4557
21:20 on every foot six toes, four and twenty *in* **n**; 4557
24: 1 against them to say, Go, **n** Israel and Judah. 4487
24: 2 even to Beer-sheba, and **n** ye the people, 6485

2Sa	24: 2	that I may know the **n** of the people.	4557
	24: 4	of the king, to **n** the people *of* Israel.	6485
	24: 9	Joab gave *up* the sum of the **n** of the people	4662
1Ki	18:31	according to the **n** of the tribes of the sons	4557
	20:25	**n** thee an army, like the army that thou hast	4487
1Ch	7: 2	whose **n** *was* in the days of David two and	4557
	7: 9	the **n** of them, **after** their **genealogy** by	3187
	7:40	the **n** throughout the genealogy of them *that*	4557
	11:11	this *is* the **n** of the mighty *men* whom	4557
	21: 1	and provoked David to **n** Israel.	4487
	21: 2	Go, **n** Israel from Beer-sheba even to Dan;	5608
	21: 2	bring the **n** of them to me, that I may know	4557
	21: 5	Joab gave the sum of the **n** of the people	4662
	22:16	and the brass, and the iron, *there is* no **n**.	4557
	23: 3	their **n** by their polls, man by man,	4557
	23:24	as they were counted by **n** of names by	4557
	23:31	the new moons, and on the set feasts, by **n**,	4557
	25: 1	the **n** of the workmen according to their	4557
	25: 7	So the **n** of them, with their brethren *that*	4557
	27: 1	Now the children of Israel after their **n**,	4557
	27:23	David took not the **n** of them from twenty	4557
	27:24	Joab the son of Zeruiah began to **n**, but	4487
	27:24	neither was the **n** put in the account of	4557
2Ch	12: 3	the people *were* without **n** that came with	4557
	26:11	according to the **n** of their account by	4557
	26:12	The whole **n** of the chief of the fathers of	4557
	29:32	the **n** of the burnt offerings, which	4557
	30:24	**great n** of priests sanctified	7230+3807.1
	35: 7	to the **n** of thirty thousand, and	4557
Ezr	1: 9	this *is* the **n** of them: thirty chargers of	4557
	2: 2	The **n** of the men of the people of Israel:	4557
	3: 4	and *offered* the daily burnt offerings by **n**,	4557
	6:17	according to the **n** of the tribes of Israel.	4510
	8:34	By **n** *and* by weight of every one: and	4557
Ne	7: 7	The **n**, *I say*, of the men of the people of	4557
Est	9:11	On that day the **n** of those that were slain in	4557
Job	1: 5	offered burnt offerings *according to* the **n**	4557
	3: 6	let it not come into the **n** of the months.	4557
	5: 9	unsearchable; marvellous *things* without **n**:	4557
	9:10	finding out; yea, and wonders without **n**.	4557
	14: 5	the **n** of his months *are* with thee,	4557
	15:20	the **n** of years is hidden to the oppressor.	4557
	21:21	when the **n** of his months is cut off in	4557
	25: 3	Is there *any* **n** of his armies? and	4557
	31:37	I would declare unto him the **n** of my steps;	4557
	34:24	shall break in pieces mighty *men* without **n**,	2714
	36:26	neither can the **n** of his years be searched	4557
	38:21	born? or *because* the **n** of thy days *is* great?	4557
	38:37	Who can **n** the clouds in wisdom? or	5608
	39: 2	Canst thou **n** the months *that* they fulfil? or	5608
Ps	90:12	So teach *us* to **n** our days, that we may	4487
	105:12	When they were *but a few* men in **n**; yea,	4557
	105:34	and caterpillars, and that without **n**,	4557
	139:18	they are moe in **n** than the sand:	7235
	147: 4	He telleth the **n** of the stars; he calleth them	4557
SS	6: 8	and virgins without **n**.	4557
Isa	21:17	the residue of the **n** of archers, the mighty	4557
	40:26	*things*, that bringeth out their host by **n**:	4557
	65:11	that furnish the drink offering unto *that* **n**.	4507
	65:12	Therefore will I **n** you to the sword, and	4487
Jer	2:28	for *according* to the **n** of thy cities are thy	4557
	2:32	people have forgotten me days without **n**.	4557
	11:13	For *according to* the **n** of thy cities were thy	4557
	11:13	*according to* the **n** of the streets of	4557
	44:28	Yet a small **n** that escape the sword shall	4557
Eze	4: 4	*according to* the **n** of the days that thou	4557
	4: 5	according to the **n** of the days,	4557
	4: 9	*according to* the **n** of the days that thou	4557
	5: 3	Thou shalt also take thereof a few in **n**, and	4557
Da	9: 2	understood by books the **n** of the years,	4557
Hos	1:10	Yet the **n** of the children of Israel shall be	4557
Joel	1: 6	strong, and without **n**, whose teeth *are*	4557
Na	3: 3	of slain, and a **great n** of carcases;	3514
Mk	10:46	with his disciples and a **great n** of people,	*2425*
Lk	22: 3	being of the **n** of the twelve.	*706*
Jn	6:10	the men sat down, *in* **n** about five thousand.	*706*
Ac	1:15	(the **n** of names together were about an	*3793*
	4: 4	the **n** of the men was about five thousand.	*706*
	5:36	to whom a **n** of men, about four hundred,	*706*
	6: 1	when the **n** of the disciples was multiplied,	NIG
	6: 7	the **n** of the disciples multiplied in Jerusalem	*706*
	11:21	and a great **n** believed, and turned unto	*706*
	16: 5	in the faith, and increased in **n** daily.	*706*
Ro	9:27	Though the **n** of the children of Israel be as	*706*
2Co	10:12	For we dare not **make** *ourselves* **of the n**,	*1469*
1Ti	5: 9	Let not a widow be **taken into the n** under	*2639*
Rev	5:11	the **n** of them was ten thousand times ten	*706*
	7: 4	And I heard the **n** of them which were	*706*
	7: 9	which no *man* could **n**, of all nations, and	*705*
	9:16	And the **n** of the army of the horsemen *were*	*706*
	9:16	and I heard the **n** of them.	*706*
	13:17	the name of the beast, or the **n** of his name.	*706*
	13:18	Let him that hath understanding count the **n**	*706*
	13:18	for it is the **n** of a man; and his number *is*	*706*
	13:18	and his **n** *is* Six hundred threescore *and* six.	*706*
	15: 2	over his mark, *and* over the **n** of his name,	*706*
	20: 8	the **n** of whom *is* as the sand of the sea.	*706*

NUMBERED (128) [NUMBER]

Ge	13:16	of the earth, *then* shall thy seed also be **n**.	4487
	16:10	that it shall not be **n** for multitude.	5608
	32:12	of the sea, which cannot be **n** for multitude.	5608
Ex	30:13	one that passeth among them that are **n**,	6485
	30:14	one that passeth among them that are **n**,	6485
	38:25	the silver of them that were **n** of	6485
	38:26	for every one that went to be **n**,	6485
Nu	1:19	so he **n** them in the wilderness of Sinai.	6485
	1:21	Those that were **n** of them, *even* of the tribe	6485
	1:22	of their fathers, those that were **n** of them,	6485
	1:23	Those that were **n** of them, *even* of the tribe	6485
	1:25	Those that were **n** of them, *even* of the tribe	6485
	1:27	Those that were **n** of them, *even* of the tribe	6485
	1:29	Those that were **n** of them, *even* of the tribe	6485
	1:31	Those that were **n** of them, *even* of the tribe	6485
	1:33	Those that were **n** of them, *even* of the tribe	6485
	1:35	Those that were **n** of them, *even* of the tribe	6485
	1:37	Those that were **n** of them, *even* of the tribe	6485
	1:39	Those that were **n** of them, *even* of the tribe	6485
	1:41	Those that were **n** of them, *even* of the tribe	6485
	1:43	Those that were **n** of them, *even* of the tribe	6485
	1:44	These *are* those that were **n**, which Moses	6485
	1:44	which Moses and Aaron **n**, and the princes	6485
	1:45	So were all those that were **n** of	6485
	1:46	Even all they that were **n** were six hundred	6485
	1:47	of their fathers were not **n** among them.	6485
	2: 4	his host, and those that were **n** of them,	6485
	2: 6	those that were **n** thereof, *were* fifty and	6485
	2: 8	those that were **n** thereof, *were* fifty and	6485
	2: 9	All that were **n** in the camp of Judah *were*	6485
	2:11	those that were **n** thereof, *were* forty and	6485
	2:13	those that were **n** of them, *were* fifty and	6485
	2:15	those that were **n** of them, *were* forty and	6485
	2:16	All that were **n** in the camp of Reuben *were*	6485
	2:19	his host, and those that were **n** of them,	6485
	2:21	those that were **n** of them, *were* thirty and	6485
	2:23	those that were **n** of them, *were* thirty and	6485
	2:24	All that were **n** of the camp of Ephraim	6485
	2:26	his host, and those that were **n** of them,	6485
	2:28	those that were **n** of them, *were* forty and	6485
	2:30	those that were **n** of them, *were* fifty and	6485
	2:31	All they that were **n** in the camp of Dan	6485
	2:32	These *are* those which were **n** of	6485
	2:32	all those that were **n** of the camps	6485
	2:33	the Levites were not **n** among the children	6485
	3:16	Moses **n** them according to the word of	6485
	3:22	Those that were **n** of them, according to	6485
	3:22	*even* those that were **n** of them *were* seven	6485
	3:34	those that were **n** of them, according to	6485
	3:39	All that were **n** of the Levites, which Moses	6485
	3:39	Aaron **n** at the commandment of	6485
	3:42	Moses **n**, as the LORD commanded him,	6485
	3:43	and upward, of those that were **n** of them,	6485
	4:34	the chief of the congregation **n** the sons of	6485
	4:36	those that were **n** of them by their families	6485
	4:37	These *were* they that were **n** of the families	6485
	4:38	those that were **n** of the sons of Gershon,	6485
	4:40	Even those that were **n** of them,	6485
	4:41	These *are* they that were **n** of the families	6485
	4:42	those that were **n** of the families of the sons	6485
	4:44	Even those that were **n** of them after their	6485
	4:45	These *be* those that were **n** of the families	6485
	4:45	Aaron **n** according to the word of	6485
	4:46	All those that were **n** of the Levites,	6485
	4:46	and Aaron and the chief of Israel **n**,	6485
	4:48	Even those that were **n** of them, were eight	6485
	4:49	LORD they were **n** by the hand of Moses,	6485
	4:49	thus *were they* **n** of him, as the LORD	6485
	7: 2	and were over them that were **n**, offered:	6485

Nu 14:29 all that were **n** of you, according to your 6485
26: 7 and they that were **n** of them were forty and 6485
26:18 Gad according to those that were **n** of them, 6485
26:22 according to those that were **n** of them, 6485
26:25 according to those that were **n** of them, 6485
26:27 according to those that were **n** of them, 6485
26:34 those that were **n** of them, fifty and 6485
26:37 according to those that were **n** of them, 6485
26:41 and they that were **n** of them *were* forty and 6485
26:43 according to those that were **n** of them, 6485
26:47 according to those that were **n** of them; 6485
26:50 and they that were **n** of them *were* forty and 6485
26:51 These *were* the **n** of the children of Israel, 6485
26:54 according to those that were **n** of him. 6485
26:57 these *are* they that were **n** of the Levites 6485
26:62 those that were **n** of them were twenty and 6485
26:62 for they were not **n** among the children of 6485
26:63 These *are* they that were **n** by Moses and 6485
26:63 who **n** the children of Israel in the plains of 6485
26:64 them whom Moses and Aaron the priest **n**, 6485
26:64 when they **n** the children of Israel in 6485
Jos 8:10 **n** the people, and went up, he and the elders 6485
Jdg 20:15 the children of Benjamin were **n** at that 6485
20:15 *which* were **n** seven hundred chosen men. 6485
20:17 were **n** four hundred thousand men that 6485
21: 9 For the people were **n**, and behold, 6485
1Sa 11: 8 when he **n** them in Bezek, the children of 6485
13:15 Saul **n** the people that were present with 6485
14:17 when they had **n**, behold Jonathan and 6485
15: 4 **n** them in Telaim, two hundred thousand 6485
2Sa 18: 1 David **n** the people that *were* with him, 6485
24:10 David's heart smote him after that he had **n** 5608
1Ki 3: 8 that cannot be **n** nor counted for multitude. 4487
8: 5 that could not be told nor **n** for multitude. 4487
20:15 he **n** the young men of the princes of 6485
20:15 after them he **n** all the people, *even* all 6485
20:26 that Ben-hadad **n** the Syrians, and went up 6485
20:27 the children of Israel were **n**, and were all 6485
2Ki 3: 6 of Samaria the same time, and **n** all Israel. 6485
1Ch 21:17 *it* not I *that* commanded the people to be **n**? 4487
23: 3 Now the Levites were **n** from the age of 5608
23:27 the Levites *were* **n** from twenty years old 4557
2Ch 2:17 Solomon **n** all the strangers that *were* in 5608
2:17 where*with* David his father had **n** them; 5608
5: 6 which could not be told nor **n** for multitude. 4487
25: 5 he **n** them from twenty years old and 6485
Ezr 1: 8 **n** them unto Sheshbazzar, the prince of 5608
Ps 40: 5 speak *of them,* they are moe than can be **n**. 5608
Ecc 1:15 and that which is wanting cannot be **n**. 4487
Isa 22:10 And ye have **n** the houses of Jerusalem, and 5608
53:12 he was **n** with the transgressors; and 4487
Jer 33:22 As the host of heaven cannot be **n**, 5608
Da 5:26 God hath **n** thy kingdom, and finished it. 4483
Hos 1:10 the sea, which cannot be measured nor **n**; 5608
Mt 10:30 But the very hairs of your head are all **n**. *705*
Mk 15:28 And he was **n** with the transgressors. *3049*
Lk 12: 7 even the *very* hairs of your head are all **n**. *705*
Ac 1:17 For he was **n** with us, and had obtained part *2674*
1:26 and he was **n** with the eleven apostles. *4785*

NUMBEREST (3) [NUMBER]
Ex 30:12 soul unto the LORD, when *thou* **n** them; 6485
30:12 plague amongst them, when *thou* **n** them. 6485
Job 14:16 For now thou **n** my steps: dost thou not 5608

NUMBERING (2) [NUMBER]
Ge 41:49 sand of the sea, very much, until he left **n**; 5608
2Ch 2:17 after the **n** where*with* David his father had 5610

NUMBERS (3) [NUMBER]
1Ch 12:23 these *are* the **n** of the bands that were ready 4557
2Ch 17:14 these *are* the **n** of them according to 6486
Ps 71:15 all the day; for I know not the **n** *thereof.* 5615

NUMEROUS See POPULOUS

NUN (29)
Ex 33:11 servant Joshua, the son of **N**, a young man, 5126
Nu 11:28 Joshua the son of **N**, the servant of Moses, 5126
13: 8 the tribe of Ephraim, Oshea the son of **N**. 5126
13:16 Moses called Oshea the son of **N**, Jehoshua. 5126
14: 6 Joshua the son of **N**, and Caleb the son of 5126
14:30 son of Jephunneh, and Joshua the son of **N**. 5126
14:38 Joshua the son of **N**, and Caleb the son of 5126
26:65 son of Jephunneh, and Joshua the son of **N**. 5126
27:18 Take thee Joshua the son of **N**, a man in 5126
32:12 the Kenezite, and Joshua the son of **N**: 5126
32:28 Joshua the son of **N**, and the chief fathers 5126
34:17 Eleazar the priest, and Joshua the son of **N**. 5126
Dt 1:38 *But* Joshua the son of **N**, which standeth 5126
31:23 he gave Joshua the son of **N** a charge, 5126
32:44 of the people, he and Hoshea the son of **N**. 5126
34: 9 Joshua the son of **N** was full *of* the spirit of 5126
Jos 1: 1 LORD spake unto Joshua the son of **N**, 5126
2: 1 Joshua the son of **N** sent out of Shittim two 5126
2:23 came to Joshua the son of **N**, and told him 5126
6: 6 Joshua the son of **N** called the priests, and 5126
14: 1 Joshua the son of **N**, and the heads of 5126
17: 4 before Joshua the son of **N**, and before 5126
19:49 to Joshua the son of **N** among them: 5126
19:51 Joshua the son of **N**, and the heads of 5126
21: 1 unto Joshua the son of **N**, and unto 5126
24:29 that Joshua the son of **N**, the servant of 5126
Jdg 2: 8 Joshua the son of **N**, the servant of 5126
1Ki 16:34 which he spake by Joshua the son of **N**. 5126
Ne 8:17 for since the days of Jeshua the son of **N** 5126

NURSE (10) [NURSED, NURSING]
Ge 24:59 her **n**, and Abraham's servant, and his men. 3243
35: 8 Deborah Rebekah's **n** died, and she was 3243
Ex 2: 7 and call to thee a **n** of the Hebrew women, 3243
2: 7 that she may **n** the child for thee? 3243
2: 9 **n** it for me, and I will give *thee* thy wages. 3243
Ru 4:16 laid it in her bosom, and became **n** unto it. 539
2Sa 4: 4 of Jezreel, and his **n** took him up, and fled: 539
2Ki 11: 2 they hid him, *even* him and his **n**, in 3243
2Ch 22:11 and put him and his **n** in a bedchamber. 3243
1Th 2: 7 *even* as a **n** cherisheth her children: *5162*

NURSED (2) [NURSE]
Ex 2: 9 And the woman took the child, and **n** it. 5134
Isa 60: 4 and thy daughters shall be **n** at *thy* side. 539

NURSING (3) [NURSE]
Nu 11:12 as a **n father** beareth the sucking child, 539
Isa 49:23 kings shall be thy **n fathers**, and 539
49:23 and their queens thy **n mothers**: 3243

NURTURE (1)
Eph 6: 4 but bring them up in the **n** and *3809*

NUTS (2)
Ge 43:11 spices, and myrrh, **n**, and almonds: 992
SS 6:11 I went down into the garden of **n** to see 93

NYMPHA See NYMPHAS

NYMPHAS (1)
Col 4:15 and **N**, and the church which is in his *3564*

O

O (1086) [OH] See Index

OAK (15) [OAKS]
Ge 35: 4 Jacob hid them under the **o** which *was* by 424
35: 8 she was buried beneath Beth-el under an **o**: 437
Jos 24:26 a great stone, and set it up there under an **o**, 427
Jdg 6:11 sat under an **o** which *was* in Ophrah, 424
6:19 and brought *it* out unto him under the **o**, and 424
2Sa 18: 9 went under the thick boughs of a great **o**, 424
18: 9 his head caught hold of the **o**, and he was 424
18:10 said, Behold, I saw Absalom hanged in an **o**. 424
18:14 while he *was* yet alive in the midst of the **o**. 424
1Ki 13:14 of God, and found him sitting under an **o**: 424
1Ch 10:12 and buried their bones under the **o** in Jabesh, 424
Isa 1:30 For ye shall be as an **o** whose leaf fadeth, 424
6:13 as a teil tree, and as an **o**, whose substance *is* 437
44:14 and taketh the cypress and the **o**, 437
Eze 6:13 every green tree, and under every thick **o**, 424

OAKS (6) [OAK]
Isa 1:29 For they shall be ashamed of the **o** which ye 352

Isa 2:13 and lifted up, and upon all the **o** of Bashan, 437
Eze 27: 6 *Of* the **o** of Bashan have they made thine 437
Hos 4:13 under **o** and poplars and elms, because 437
Am 2: 9 of the cedars, and he *was* strong as the **o**; 437
Zec 11: 2 howl, O ye **o** of Bashan; for the forest of 437

OAR (1) [OARS]
Eze 27:29 all that handle the **o**, the mariners, *and* 4880

OARS (2) [OAR]
Isa 33:21 wherein shall go no galley with **o**, 7885
Eze 27: 6 the oaks of Bashan have they made thine **o**; 4880

OARSMEN See ROWERS

OATH (59) [OATHS, OATHS']
Ge 24: 8 then thou shalt be clear from this my **o**: 7621
24:41 shalt thou be clear from *this* my **o**, 423
24:41 not thee *one,* thou shalt be clear from my **o**. 423
26: 3 I will perform the **o** which I sware unto 7621
26:28 we said, Let there be now an **o** betwixt us, 423
50:25 Joseph **took an o** of the children of Israel, 7650
Ex 22:11 *Then* shall an **o** of the LORD be between 7621
Lev 5: 4 *it be* that a man shall pronounce with an **o**, 7621
Nu 5:19 the priest shall **charge** her **by an o**, 7650
5:21 **charge** the woman **with an o** 7621+7650+871.1
5:21 thee a curse and an **o** among thy people, 7621
30: 2 or swear an **o** to bind his soul with a bond; 7621
30:10 or bound her soul by a bond with an **o**; 7621
30:13 and every binding **o** to afflict the soul, 7621
Dt 7: 8 he would keep the **o** which he had sworn 7621
29:12 into his **o**, which the LORD thy God 423
29:14 you only do I make this covenant and this **o**; 423
Jos 2:17 We *will be* blameless of this thine **o** which 7621
2:20 we will be quit of thine **o** which thou hast 7621
9:20 of the **o** which we sware unto them. 7621
Jdg 21: 5 For *they* had made a great **o** concerning 7621
1Sa 14:26 to his mouth: for the people feared the **o**. 7621
14:27 his father **charged** the people **with the o**: 7650
14:28 **straitly charged** the people **with an o**, 7650+7650
2Sa 21: 7 of the LORD'S **o** that *was* between them, 7621
1Ki 2:43 hast thou not kept the **o** of the LORD, 7621
8:31 an **o** be laid upon him to cause him to swear, 423
8:31 the **o** come before thine altar in this house: 423
18:10 *He is* not *there;* he **took an o** of 7650
2Ki 11: 4 **took an o** of them in the house of 7650
1Ch 16:16 with Abraham, and of his **o** unto Isaac; 7621
2Ch 6:22 an **o** be laid upon him to make him swear, 423
6:22 the **o** come before thine altar in this house; 423
15:15 all Judah rejoiced at the **o**: for they had 7621
Ne 5:12 I called the priests, and **took an o** of them, 7650
10:29 and entered into a curse, and into an **o**, 7621
Ps 105: 9 made with Abraham, and his **o** unto Isaac; 7621
Ecc 8: 2 and *that* in regard of the **o** of God. 7621
9: 2 he that sweareth, as he that feareth an **o**. 7621
Jer 11: 5 That *I* may perform the **o** which I have 7621
Eze 16:59 which hast despised the **o** in breaking 423
17:13 with him, and hath taken an **o** of him: 423
17:16 whose **o** he despised, and whose covenant he 423
17:18 Seeing he despised the **o** by breaking 423
17:19 surely mine **o** that he hath despised, and 423
Da 9:11 the **o** that *is* written in the law of Moses 7621
Zec 8:17 against his neighbour; and love no false **o**: 7621
Mt 14: 7 Whereupon he promised with an **o** to give *3727*
26:72 And again he denied with an **o**, I do not *3727*
Lk 1:73 The **o** which he sware to our father *3727*
Ac 2:30 knowing that God had sworn with an **o** to *3727*
23:21 which have **bound** themselves **with an o**, *332*
Heb 6:16 an **o** for confirmation *is* to them an end of *3727*
6:17 of his counsel, confirmed *it* by an **o**: *3727*
7:20 And inasmuch as not without an **o** *he was* *3728*
7:21 (For those priests were made without an **o**; *3728*
7:21 this with an **o** by him that said unto him, *3728*
7:28 but the word of the **o**, which was since *3728*
Jas 5:12 neither by the earth, neither by any other **o**: *3727*

OATHS (3) [OATH]
Eze 21:23 in their sight, to them that have sworn **o**: 7621
Hab 3: 9 *according to* the **o** of the tribes, *even thy* 7621
Mt 5:33 but shalt perform unto the Lord thine **o**: *3727*

OATHS' (2) [OATH]
Mt 14: 9 nevertheless for the **o** sake, and them which *3727*
Mk 6:26 *yet* for his **o** sake, and for their sakes which *3727*

OBADIAH (20)
1Ki 18: 3 Ahab called **O**, which *was* the governor of 5662
18: 3 (Now **O** feared the LORD greatly: 5662
18: 4 that **O** took an hundred prophets, and 5662
18: 5 Ahab said unto **O**, Go into the land, unto all 5662
18: 6 **O** went another way by himself. 5662
18: 7 as **O** was in the way, behold Elijah met 5662
18:16 So **O** went to meet Ahab, and told him: and 5662
1Ch 3:21 the sons of Arnan, the sons of **O**, 5662
7: 3 Michael, and **O**, and Joel, Ishiah, five: 5662
8:38 Ishmael, and Sheariah, and **O**, and Hanan. 5662
9:16 **O** the son of Shemaiah, the son of Galal, 5662
9:44 Ishmael, and Sheariah, and **O**, and Hanan: 5662
12: 9 Ezer the first, **O** the second, Eliab the third, 5662
27:19 Of Zebulun, Ishmaiah the son of **O**: 5662
2Ch 17: 7 to **O**, and to Zechariah, and to Nethaneel, 5662
34:12 the overseers of them *were* Jahath and **O**, 5662
Ezr 8: 9 **O** the son of Jehiel, and with him two 5662
Ne 10: 5 Harim, Meremoth, **O**, 5662
12:25 Mattaniah, and Bakbukiah, **O**, Meshullam, 5662
Ob 1: 1 The vision of **O**. Thus saith the Lord GOD 5662

OBAL (1)
Ge 10:28 And **O**, and Abimael, and Sheba, 5745

OBED (13)
Ru 4:17 born to Naomi; and they called his name **O**: 5744
4:21 Salmon begat Boaz, and Boaz begat **O**, 5744
4:22 And **O** begat Jesse, and Jesse begat David. 5744
1Ch 2:12 And Boaz begat **O**, and Obed begat Jesse, 5744
2:12 And Boaz begat Obed, and **O** begat Jesse, 5744
2:37 Zabad begat Ephlal, and Ephlal begat **O**, 5744
2:38 And **O** begat Jehu, and Jehu begat Azariah, 5744
11:47 Eliel, and **O**, and Jasiel the Mesobaite. 5744
26: 7 Othni, and Rephael, and **O**, Elzabad, 5744
2Ch 23: 1 Azariah the son of **O**, and Maaseiah the son 5744
Mt 1: 5 and Booz begat **O** of Ruth; and Obed begat *5601*
1: 5 begat Obed of Ruth; and **O** begat Jesse; *5601*
Lk 3:32 which was *the son* of **O**, which was *the son* *5601*

OBED-EDOM (20)
2Sa 6:10 David carried it aside *into* the house of **O** 5654
6:11 *in* the house of **O** the Gittite three months: 5654
6:11 the LORD blessed **O**, and all his 5654
6:12 The LORD hath blessed the house of **O**, 5654
6:12 of **O** *into* the city of David with gladness. 5654
1Ch 13:13 carried it aside into the house of **O** 5654
13:14 the family of **O** in his house three months. 5654
13:14 the LORD blessed the house of **O**, and 5654
15:18 Elipheleh, and Mikneiah, and **O**, and Jeiel, 5654
15:21 Mikneiah, and **O**, and Jeiel, and Azaziah, 5654
15:24 **O** and Jehiah *were* doorkeepers for the ark. 5654
15:25 the LORD out of the house of **O** with joy. 5654
16: 5 Mattithiah, and Eliab, and Benaiah, and **O**: 5654
16:38 **O** with their brethren, threescore and eight; 5654
16:38 **O** also the son of Jeduthun and Hosah to be 5654
26: 4 Moreover the sons of **O** *were,* Shemaiah 5654
26: 8 All these of the sons of **O**: they and 5654
26: 8 the service, *were* threescore and two of **O**. 5654
26:15 To **O** southward; and to his sons the house 5654
2Ch 25:24 were found in the house of God with **O**, 5654

OBEDIENCE (12) [OBEY]
Ro 1: 5 for **o** to the faith among all nations, *5218*
5:19 by the **o** of one shall many be made *5218*
6:16 sin unto death, or of **o** unto righteousness? *5218*
16:19 For your **o** is come abroad unto all *men.* I *5218*
16:26 made known to all nations for the **o** of *5218*
1Co 14:34 but *they are commanded* to be **under o**, *5293*
2Co 7:15 whilst he remembereth the **o** of you all, *5218*
10: 5 captivity every thought to the **o** of Christ; *5218*
10: 6 all disobedience, when your **o** is fulfilled. *5218*
Phm 1:21 Having confidence in thy **o** I wrote unto *5218*
Heb 5: 8 *yet* learned he **o** by *the things* which he *5218*
1Pe 1: 2 unto **o** and sprinkling of the blood of Jesus *5218*

OBEDIENT (16) [OBEY]
Ex 24: 7 the LORD hath said will we do, and be **o**. 8085
Nu 27:20 of the children of Israel may be **o**. 8085
Dt 4:30 thy God, and shalt be **o** unto his voice; 8085
8:20 ye would not be **o** unto the voice of 8085
2Sa 22:45 soon as they hear, they shall be **o** unto me. 8085
Pr 25:12 *so is* a wise reprover upon an **o** ear. 8085
Isa 1:19 If ye be willing and **o**, ye shall eat the good 8085

Isa 42:24 his ways, neither were they **o** unto his law. 8085
Ac 6: 7 a great company of the priests were **o** to 5219
Ro 15:18 to make the Gentiles **o**, by word and deed, 5218
2Co 2: 9 proof of you, whether ye be **o** in all *things.* 5255
Eph 6: 5 be **o** to *them that are your* masters 5219
Php 2: 8 humbled himself, and became **o** unto death, 5255
Tit 2: 5 at home, good, **o** to their own husbands, 5293
2: 9 *Exhort* servants to be **o** unto their own 5293
1Pe 1:14 As **o** children, not fashioning yourselves 5218

OBEISANCE (9) [OBEY]
Ge 37: 7 round about, and **made o** to my sheaf. 7812
37: 9 and the eleven stars **made o** to me. 7812
43:28 they bowed down their heads, and **made o**. 7812
Ex 18: 7 his father in law, and **did o**, and kissed him; 7812
2Sa 1: 2 to David, that he fell to the earth, and did **o**. 7812
14: 4 and did **o**, and said, Help, O king. 7812
15: 5 any man came nigh *to him* to do him **o**, 7812
1Ki 1:16 Bath-sheba bowed, and **did o** unto the king. 7812
2Ch 24:17 princes of Judah, and **made o** to the king. 7812

OBEY (69) [OBEDIENCE, OBEDIENT, OBEISANCE, OBEYED, OBEYEDST, OBEYETH, OBEYING]
Ge 27: 8 **o** my voice according to *that* which I 8085+871.1
27:13 **o** my voice, and go fetch me *them.* 8085+871.1
27:43 Now therefore, my son, **o** my voice; 8085+871.1
Ex 5: 2 I should **o** his voice to let Israel go? 8085+871.1
19: 5 if ye will **o** my voice **indeed**, 8085+8085+871.1
23:21 Beware of him, and **o** his voice, 8085+871.1
23:22 if thou shalt **indeed o** his voice, and 8085+8085
Dt 11:27 if ye **o** the commandments of the LORD 8085
11:28 if ye will not **o** the commandments of 8085
13: 4 **o** his voice, and you shall serve him, and 8085
21:18 which will not **o** the voice of his 8085+871.1
21:20 rebellious, he will not **o** our voice; 8085+871.1
27:10 **o** the voice of the LORD thy God, 8085+871.1
28:62 thou wouldest not **o** the voice of 8085+871.1
30: 2 shalt **o** his voice according to all that 8085+871.1
30: 8 and **o** the voice of the LORD, 8085+871.1
30:20 *and* that thou mayest **o** his voice, 8085+871.1
Jos 24:24 God will we serve, and his voice will we **o**. 8085
1Sa 8:19 Nevertheless the people refused to **o** 8085+871.1
12:14 **o** his voice, and not rebel against 8085+871.1
12:15 if ye will not **o** the voice of 8085+871.1
15:19 thou not **o** the voice of the LORD, 8085+871.1
15:22 to **o** *is* better than sacrifice, *and* to hearken 8085
Ne 9:17 refused to **o**, neither were mindful of thy 8085
Job 36:11 If they **o** and serve *him,* they shall spend 8085
36:12 if they **o** not, they shall perish by the sword, 8085
Ps 18:44 As soon as they hear *of me,* they shall **o** 8085
Pr 30:17 at *his* father, and despiseth to **o** *his* mother, 3349
Isa 11:14 and the children of Ammon shall **o** them. 4928
Jer 7:23 **O** my voice, and I will be your God, 8085+871.1
11: 4 **O** my voice, and do them, 8085+871.1
11: 7 and protesting, saying, **O** my voice. 8085+871.1
12:17 But if they will not **o**, I will utterly pluck up 8085
18:10 that *it* **o** not my voice, then I will 8085+871.1
26:13 **o** the voice of the LORD your God; 8085+871.1
35:14 but **o** their father's commandment: 8085
38:20 They shall not deliver *thee.* **O**, I 8085+871.1
42: 6 **o** the voice of the LORD our God, 8085+871.1
42: 6 when we **o** the voice of the LORD 8085+871.1
42:13 neither **o** the voice of the LORD 8085+871.1
Da 7:27 and all dominions shall serve and **o** him. 8086
9:11 that *they* might not **o** thy voice; 8085+871.1
Zec 6:15 if ye will **diligently o** the voice of 8085+8085
Mt 8:27 that even the winds and the sea **o** him? *5219*
Mk 1:27 even the unclean spirits, and they do **o** him. *5219*
4:41 that even the wind and the sea **o** him? *5219*
Lk 8:25 even the winds and water, and they **o** him. *5219*
17: 6 thou planted in the sea; and it should **o** you. *5219*
Ac 5:29 said, We ought to **o** God rather than men. *3980*
5:32 whom God hath given to them that **o** him. *3980*
7:39 To whom our fathers would not **o**, *1096+5255*
Ro 2: 8 and do **not o** the truth, but *544*
2: 8 but **o** unrighteousness, indignation and *3982*
6:12 that *ye* should **o** it in the lusts thereof. *5219*
6:16 to whom ye yield yourselves servants to **o**, *5218*
6:16 to obey, *his* servants ye are to whom ye **o**; *5219*
Gal 3: 1 that *you* should not **o** the truth, *3982*
5: 7 who did hinder you that *ye* should not **o** *3982*
Eph 6: 1 Children, **o** your parents in the Lord: *5219*
Col 3:20 **o** *your* parents in all *things:* for this is well *5219*
3:22 **o** in all *things your* masters according to *5219*
2Th 1: 8 that **o** not the gospel of our Lord Jesus *5219*
3:14 And if any *man* **o** not our word by *this* *5219*
Tit 3: 1 and powers, to **o magistrates**, *3980*
Heb 5: 9 eternal salvation unto all them that **o** him; *5219*
13:17 **O** them that have the rule over you, and *3982*
Jas 3: 3 in the horses' mouths, that they may **o** us; *3982*
1Pe 3: 1 that, if any **o not** the word, they also may *544*
4:17 what *shall* the end *be* of them that **o not** *544*

OBEYED (41) [OBEY]
Ge 22:18 because thou hast **o** my voice. 8085+871.1
26: 5 Because that Abraham **o** my voice, 8085+871.1
28: 7 that Jacob **o** his father and his mother, and 8085
Jos 5: 6 they **o** not the voice of the LORD: 8085+871.1
22: 2 have **o** my voice in all that I commanded 8085
Jdg 2: 2 ye have not **o** my voice: why have ye done 8085
6:10 but ye have not **o** my voice. 8085+871.1
1Sa 15:20 I have **o** the voice of the LORD, 8085+871.1
15:24 feared the people, and **o** their voice. 8085+871.1
28:21 thine handmaid hath **o** thy voice, 8085+871.1
1Ki 20:36 Because thou hast not **o** the voice of 8085+871.1
2Ki 18:12 Because they **o** not the voice of 8085+871.1
1Ch 29:23 and prospered; and all Israel **o** him. 8085
2Ch 11: 4 they **o** the words of the LORD, and 8085
Pr 5:13 have not **o** the voice of my teachers, 8085+871.1
Jer 3:13 ye have not **o** my voice, saith the LORD. 8085
3:25 have not **o** the voice of the LORD 8085+871.1
9:13 have not **o** my voice, neither walked 8085+871.1
11: 8 Yet they **o** not, nor inclined their ear, but 8085
17:23 they **o** not, neither inclined their ear, but 8085
32:23 they **o** not thy voice, neither walked 8085+871.1
34:10 any more, then they **o**, and let *them* go. 8085
35: 8 Thus have we **o** the voice of 8085+871.1
35:10 have **o**, and done according to all that 8085
35:18 Because ye have **o** the commandment of 8085
40: 3 have not **o** his voice, therefore this 8085+871.1
42:21 ye have not **o** the voice of 8085+871.1
43: 4 the people, **o** not the voice of the LORD, 8085
43: 7 for they **o** not the voice of 8085+871.1
44:23 have not **o** the voice of the LORD, 8085+871.1
Da 9:10 Neither have we **o** the voice of 8085+871.1
9:14 he doeth: for we **o** not his voice. 8085+871.1
Zep 3: 2 She **o** not the voice; she received not 8085
Hag 1:12 **o** the voice of the LORD their God, and 8085
Ac 5:36 and all, as many as **o** him, were scattered, *3982*
5:37 and all, *even* as many as **o** him, *3982*
Ro 6:17 ye have **o** from the heart *that* form of *5219*
10:16 But they have not all **o** the gospel. *5219*
Php 2:12 my beloved, as ye have always **o**, *5219*
Heb 11: 8 should after receive for an inheritance, **o**; *5219*
1Pe 3: 6 *Even* as Sara **o** Abraham, calling him lord: *5219*

OBEYEDST (2) [OBEY]
1Sa 28:18 Because thou **o** not the voice of 8085+871.1
Jer 22:21 thy youth, that thou **o** not my voice. 8085+871.1

OBEYETH (3) [OBEY]
Isa 50:10 that **o** the voice of his servant, 8085+871.1
Jer 7:28 This *is* a nation that **o** not the voice 8085+871.1
11: 3 Cursed *be* the man that **o** not the words of 8085

OBEYING (3) [OBEY]
Jdg 2:17 **o** the commandments of the LORD; 8085
1Sa 15:22 as in **o** the voice of the LORD? 8085+871.1
1Pe 1:22 Seeing ye have purified your souls in **o** *5218*

OBIL (1)
1Ch 27:30 Over the camels also *was* **O** the Ishmaelite: 179

OBJECT (1)
Ac 24:19 and **o**, if they had ought against me. *2723*

OBLATION (35) [OBLATIONS]
Lev 2: 4 if thou bring an **o** of a meat offering baken 7133
2: 5 if thy **o** *be* a meat offering *baken* in a pan, 7133
2: 7 if thy **o** *be* a meat offering *baken* in 7133
2:12 *As for* the **o** of the firstfruits, ye shall offer 7133
2:13 every **o** of thy meat offering shalt thou 7133
3: 1 if his **o** *be* a sacrifice of peace offering, 7133
7:14 of it he shall offer one out of the whole **o** 7133
7:29 **o** unto the LORD of the sacrifice of his 7133
22:18 that will offer his **o** for all his vows, and 7133
Nu 18: 9 every **o** of theirs, every meat offering of 7133
31:50 therefore brought an **o** for the LORD, 7133
Isa 19:21 in that day, and shall do sacrifice and **o**; 4503

Isa 40:20 impoverished that he hath no **o** chooseth a 8641
66: 3 he that offereth an **o**, *as if he offered* 4503
Jer 14:12 when they offer burnt offering and an **o**, 4503
Eze 44:30 firstfruits of all *things,* and every **o** of all, 8641
45: 1 ye shall offer an **o** unto the LORD, a holy 8641
45: 6 over against the **o** of the holy *portion:* it 8641
45: 7 on the other side of the **o** of the holy 8641
45: 7 before the **o** of the holy *portion,* and 8641
45:13 This *is* the **o** that ye shall offer; the sixth 8641
45:16 All the people of the land shall give this **o** 8641
48: 9 The **o** that ye shall offer unto the LORD 8641
48:10 *even* for the priests, shall be *this* holy **o**; 8641
48:12 *this* **o** of the land that is offered shall be 8642
48:18 the residue in length over against the **o** of 8641
48:18 it shall be over against the **o** of the holy 8641
48:20 All the **o** *shall be* five and twenty thousand 8641
48:20 ye shall offer the holy **o** foursquare, 8641
48:21 the one side and on the other of the holy **o**, 8641
48:21 twenty thousand of the **o** toward the east 8641
48:21 it shall be the holy **o**; and the sanctuary of 8641
Da 2:46 commanded that *they* should offer an **o** and 4504
9:21 touched me about the time of the evening **o**. 4503
9:27 shall cause the sacrifice and the **o** to cease, 4503

OBLATIONS (5) [OBLATION]
Lev 7:38 of Israel to offer their **o** unto the LORD, 7133
2Ch 31:14 to distribute the **o** of the LORD, and 8641
Isa 1:13 Bring no more vain **o**; incense *is* an 4503
Eze 20:40 the firstfruits of your **o**, with all your holy 4864
44:30 of every *sort* of your **o**, shall be the priests': 8641

OBOTH (4)
Nu 21:10 of Israel set forward, and pitched in **O**. 88
21:11 they journeyed from **O**, and pitched at 88
33:43 they departed from Punon, and pitched in **O**. 88
33:44 they departed from **O**, and pitched in 88

OBSCURE (1) [OBSCURITY]
Pr 20:20 his lamp shall be put out in **o** darkness. 380

OBSCURITY (3) [OBSCURE]
Isa 29:18 the eyes of the blind shall see out of **o**, and 652
58:10 shall thy light rise in **o**, and thy darkness *be* 2822
59: 9 we wait for light, but behold **o**; 2822

OBSERVATION (1) [OBSERVE]
Lk 17:20 The kingdom of God cometh not with **o**: *3907*

OBSERVE (55) [OBSERVATION, OBSERVED, OBSERVER, OBSERVERS, OBSERVEST, OBSERVETH]
Ex 12:17 ye shall **o** the *feast of* unleavened bread; 8104
12:17 shall ye **o** this day in your generations by 8104
12:24 ye shall **o** this thing for an ordinance to thee 8104
31:16 to **o** the sabbath throughout their 6213
34:11 **O** thou that which I command thee *this* 8104
34:22 thou shalt **o** the feast of weeks, of 6213
Lev 19:26 shall ye use enchantment, nor **o times**. 6049
19:37 Therefore shall ye **o** all my statutes, and all 8104
Nu 28: 2 shall ye **o** to offer unto me in their due 8104
Dt 5:32 Ye shall **o** to do therefore as the LORD 8104
6: 3 **o** to do *it;* that it may be well with thee, and 8104
6:25 if we **o** to do all these commandments 8104
8: 1 I command thee *this* day shall ye **o** to do, 8104
11:32 ye shall **o** to do all the statutes and 8104
12: 1 which ye shall **o** to do in the land, 8104
12:28 **O** and hear all these words which I 8104
12:32 thing soever I command you, **o** to do it: 8104
15: 5 to **o** to do all these commandments which I 8104
16: 1 **O** the month of Abib, and keep 8104
16:12 and thou shalt **o** and do these statutes. 8104
16:13 Thou shalt **o** the feast of tabernacles seven 6213
17:10 thou shalt **o** to do according to all that they 8104
24: 8 that *thou* **o** diligently, and do according to 8104
24: 8 as I commanded them, *so* ye shall **o** to do. 8104
28: 1 to **o** *and* to do all his commandments which 8104
28:13 thee *this* day, to **o** and to do *them:* 8104
28:15 to **o** to do all his commandments and 8104
28:58 If thou wilt not **o** to do all the words of this 8104
31:12 and **o** to do all the words of this law: 8104
32:46 which ye shall command your children to **o** 8104
Jos 1: 7 that *thou* mayest **o** to do according to all 8104
1: 8 that thou mayest **o** to do according to all 8104
Jdg 13:14 *thing:* all that I commanded her let her **o**. 8104
1Ki 20:33 Now the men did **diligently** **o** whether *any* 5172
2Ki 17:37 for you, ye shall **o** to do for evermore; 8104
21: 8 only if they will **o** to do according to all 8104
2Ch 7:17 and shalt **o** my statutes and my judgments; 8104
Ne 1: 5 that love him and **o** his commandments: 8104
10:29 to **o** and do all the commandments of 8104
Ps 105:45 That they might **o** his statutes, and keep his 8104
107:43 will **o** these *things,* even they shall 8104
119:34 yea, I shall **o** it with *my* whole heart. 8104
Pr 23:26 thine heart, and let thine eyes **o** my ways. 5341
Jer 8: 7 and the swallow **o** the time of their coming; 8104
Eze 20:18 neither **o** their judgments, nor defile 8104
37:24 and **o** my statutes, and do them. 8104
Hos 13: 7 as a leopard by the way will I **o** *them:* 7789
Jnh 2: 8 They that **o** lying vanities forsake their own 8104
Mt 23: 3 All therefore whatsoever they bid you **o**, *5083*
23: 3 they bid you observe, *that* **o** and do; *5083*
28:20 Teaching them to **o** all *things* whatsoever I *5083*
Ac 16:21 us to receive, neither to **o**, being Romans. *4160*
21:25 concluded that they **o** no such *thing,* save *5083*
Gal 4:10 Ye **o** days, and months, and times, and *3906*
1Ti 5:21 that thou **o** these *things* without preferring *5442*

OBSERVED (11) [OBSERVE]
Ge 37:11 envied him; but his father **o** the saying. 8104
Ex 12:42 It *is* a night to be **much o** unto the LORD 8107
12:42 this *is* that night of the LORD to be **o** of 8107
Nu 15:22 and not **o** all these commandments, 6213
Dt 33: 9 for they have **o** thy word, and kept thy 8104
2Sa 11:16 it came to pass, when Joab **o** the city, 8104
2Ki 21: 6 **o times**, and used enchantments, and 6049
2Ch 33: 6 also he **o times**, and used enchantments, 6049
Hos 14: 8 I have heard *him,* and **o** him: I *am* like a 7789
Mk 6:20 he *was* a just man and a holy, and **o** him; *4933*
10:20 Master, all these have I **o** from my youth. *5442*

OBSERVER (1) [OBSERVE]
Dt 18:10 *or* an **o of times**, or an enchanter, or 6049

OBSERVERS (1) [OBSERVE]
Dt 18:14 hearkened unto **o of times**, and 6049

OBSERVEST (1) [OBSERVE]
Isa 42:20 Seeing many *things,* but thou **o** not; 8104

OBSERVETH (1) [OBSERVE]
Ecc 11: 4 He that **o** the wind shall not sow; and 8104

OBSTINATE (2)
Dt 2:30 **made** his heart **o**, that he might deliver him 553
Isa 48: 4 Because I knew that thou *art* **o**, and 7186

OBTAIN (15) [OBTAINED, OBTAINETH, OBTAINING]
Ge 16: 2 it may be that I may **o children** by her. 1129
Pr 8:35 and shall **o** favour of the LORD. 6329
Isa 35:10 they shall **o** joy and gladness, and sorrow 5381
51:11 they shall **o** gladness and joy; *and* sorrow 5381
Da 11:21 and **o** the kingdom by flatteries. 2388
Mt 5: 7 *are* the merciful: for they shall **o mercy**. *1653*
Lk 20:35 shall be accounted worthy to **o** that world, *5177*
Ro 11:31 your mercy they also may **o mercy**. *1653*
1Co 9:24 receiveth the prize? So run, that ye may **o**. *2638*
9:25 Now they *do it* to **o** a corruptible crown; *2983*
1Th 5: 9 but to **o** salvation by our Lord Jesus Christ, *4047*
2Ti 2:10 that they may also **o** the salvation which is *5177*
Heb 4:16 that we may **o** mercy, and find grace to *2983*
11:35 that they might **o** a better resurrection: *5177*
Jas 4: 2 ye kill, and desire *to have,* and cannot **o**: *2013*

OBTAINED (28) [OBTAIN]
Ne 13: 6 and after certain days **o** I *leave* of the king: 7592
Est 2: 9 pleased him, and she **o** kindness of him; 5375
2:15 Esther **o** favour in the sight of all them that 5375
2:17 she **o** grace and favour in his sight more 5375
5: 2 in the court, *that* she **o** favour in his sight: 5375
Hos 2:23 have mercy upon her that had not **o mercy**; 7355
Ac 1:17 with us, and had **o** part of this ministry. *2975*
22:28 With a great sum **o** I this freedom. *2932*
26:22 Having therefore **o** help of God, I continue *5177*
27:13 supposing that *they* had **o** *their* purpose, *2902*
Ro 11: 7 Israel hath not **o** that which he seeketh for; *2013*
11: 7 but the election hath **o** *it,* and the rest were *2013*
11:30 yet have now **o mercy** through their *1653*
1Co 7:25 as one that hath **o mercy of** the Lord to be *1653*
Eph 1:11 In whom also we have **o an inheritance**, *2820*
1Ti 1:13 but I **o mercy**, because I did *it* ignorantly in *1653*

1Ti 1:16 Howbeit for this cause I **o mercy**, that in *1653*
Heb 1: 4 as he hath by **inheritance o** a more *2816*
6:15 he had patiently endured, he **o** the promise. *2013*
8: 6 But now hath he **o** a more excellent *5177*
9:12 *place,* having **o** eternal redemption *for us.* *2147*
11: 2 For by it the elders **o a good report**. *3140*
11: 4 by which he **o witness** that he was *3140*
11:33 wrought righteousness, **o** promises, *2013*
11:39 having **o a good report** through faith, *3140*
1Pe 2:10 which had not **o mercy**, but now have *1653*
2:10 not obtained mercy, but now have **o mercy**. *1653*
2Pe 1: 1 to them that have **o** like precious faith with *2975*

OBTAINETH (2) [OBTAIN]
Pr 12: 2 A good *man* **o** favour of the LORD: but 6329
18:22 a good *thing,* and **o** favour of the LORD. 6329

OBTAINING (1) [OBTAIN]
2Th 2:14 to the **o** of the glory of our Lord Jesus *4047*

OCCASION (21) [OCCASIONED, OCCASIONS]
Ge 43:18 that he may **seek o** against us, and fall upon 1556
Jdg 9:33 thou do to them as thou shalt **find o**. 4672
14: 4 that he sought an **o** against the Philistines: 8385
1Sa 10: 7 *that* thou do as **o serve** thee; 3027+4672
2Sa 12:14 **given great o** to the enemies of the LORD **to blaspheme**, 5006+5006
Ezr 7:20 which thou shalt **have o** to bestow, 5308
Jer 2:24 *in* her **o** who can turn her away? 8385
Eze 18: 3 ye shall not have *o* any more to use this NIH
Da 6: 4 princes sought to find **o** against Daniel 5931
6: 4 they could find none **o** nor fault; 5931
6: 5 We shall not find any **o** against this Daniel, 5931
Ro 7: 8 But sin, taking **o** by the commandment, *874*
7:11 For sin, taking **o** by the commandment, *874*
14:13 or an **o to fall** in *his* brother's way. *4625*
2Co 5:12 but give you **o** to glory on our behalf, *874*
8: 8 but **by o** of the forwardness of others, and *1223*
11:12 that I may cut off **o** from them which desire *874*
11:12 cut off occasion from them which desire **o**; *874*
Gal 5:13 only *use* not liberty for an **o** to the flesh, but *874*
1Ti 5:14 give none **o** to the adversary to speak *874*
1Jn 2:10 and there is none **o of stumbling** in him. *4625*

OCCASIONED (1) [OCCASION]
1Sa 22:22 I have **o** *the death* of all the persons of thy 5437

OCCASIONS (3) [OCCASION]
Dt 22:14 give **o** of speech against her, and bring up 5949
22:17 he hath given **o** of speech *against her,* 5949
Job 33:10 Behold, he findeth **o** against me, 8569

OCCUPATION (5) [OCCUPY]
Ge 46:33 call you, and shall say, What *is* your **o**? 4639
47: 3 said unto his brethren, What *is* your **o**? 4639
Jnh 1: 8 cause this evil *is* upon us; What *is* thine **o**? 4399
Ac 18: 3 for *by* their **o** they were tentmakers. *5078*
19:25 called together with the workmen of **like o**, *5108*

OCCUPIED (7) [OCCUPY]
Ex 38:24 All the gold that was **o** for the work in all 6213
Jdg 16:11 with new ropes that never were **o**, 4399+6213
Eze 27:16 they **o** in thy fairs with emeralds, purple, 5414
27:19 and Javan going to and fro **o** in thy fairs: 5414
27:21 they **o** with thee in lambs, and rams, 3027+5503
27:22 they **o** in thy fairs with chief of all spices, 5414
Heb 13: 9 not profited them that have been **o therein**. *4043*

OCCUPIERS (1) [OCCUPY]
Eze 27:27 the **o** of thy merchandise, and all thy men 6148

OCCUPIETH (1) [OCCUPY]
1Co 14:16 how shall he that **o** the room of *378*

OCCUPY (2) [OCCUPATION, OCCUPIED, OCCUPIERS, OCCUPIETH, UNOCCUPIED]
Eze 27: 9 mariners were in thee to **o** thy merchandise. 6148
Lk 19:13 and said unto them, **O** till I come. *4231*

OCCURRENT (1)
1Ki 5: 4 *so that there is* neither adversary nor evil **o**. 6294

OCRAN (5)
Nu 1:13 Of Asher; Pagiel the son of **O**. 5918
2:27 of Asher *shall be* Pagiel the son of **O**. 5918
7:72 On the eleventh day Pagiel the son of **O**, 5918
7:77 this *was* the offering of Pagiel the son of **O**. 5918
10:26 children of Asher *was* Pagiel the son of **O**. 5918

ODD (1)
Nu 3:48 wherewith the **o number** of them is *to be* 5736

ODED (3)
2Ch 15: 1 of God came upon Azariah the son of **O**: 5752
15: 8 the prophecy *of* **O** the prophet, he took 5752
28: 9 the LORD was there, whose name *was* **O**: 5752

ODIOUS (2) [ODOUR]
1Ch 19: 6 that they had **made** themselves **o** to David, 887
Pr 30:23 For an **o** *woman* when she is married; and 8130

ODOUR (2) [ODIOUS, ODOURS]
Jn 12: 3 the house was filled with the **o** of *3744*
Php 4:18 an **o** of a sweet smell, a sacrifice *3744*

ODOURS (7) [ODOUR]
Lev 26:31 I will not smell the savour of your **sweet o**. 5207
2Ch 16:14 in the bed which was filled *with* **sweet o** 1314
Est 2:12 six months with **sweet o**, and with *other* 1314
Jer 34: 5 before thee, so shall they burn *o* for thee; NIH
Da 2:46 offer an oblation and **sweet o** unto him. 5208
Rev 5: 8 and golden vials full of **o**, which are *2368*
18:13 and **o**, and ointments, and frankincense, and *2368*

OF (34750) [HEREOF, THEREOF, WHEREOF] See Index

OFF (507) See Index

OFFENCE (19) [OFFEND]
1Sa 25:31 grief unto thee, nor **o** of heart unto my lord, 4383
Isa 8:14 for a rock of **o** to both the houses of Israel, 4383
Hos 5:15 till they **acknowledge** their **o**, and seek my 816
Mt 16:23 thou art an **o** unto me: for thou savourest *4625*
18: 7 woe to that man by whom the **o** cometh. *4625*
Ac 24:16 to have always a conscience **void of o** *677*
Ro 5:15 But not as the **o**, so also *is* the free gift. *3900*
5:15 For if through the **o** of one many be dead, *3900*
5:17 For if by one man's **o** death reigned by one; *3900*
5:18 Therefore as by the **o** of one *judgment* *3900*
5:20 the law entered, that the **o** might abound. *3900*
9:33 lay in Sion a stumblingstone and rock of **o**: *4625*
14:20 but *it is* evil for *that* man who eateth with **o**. *4348*
1Co 10:32 Give **none o**, neither to the Jews, nor to *677*
2Co 6: 3 Giving no **o** in any *thing,* that the ministry *4349*
11: 7 Have I committed an **o** in abasing myself *266*
Gal 5:11 then is the **o** of the cross ceased. *4625*
Php 1:10 and **without o** till the day of Christ; *677*
1Pe 2: 8 And a stone of stumbling, and a rock of **o**, *4625*

OFFENCES (7) [OFFEND]
Ecc 10: 4 not thy place; for yielding pacifieth great **o**. 2399
Mt 18: 7 Woe unto the world because of **o**: for it *4625*
18: 7 for it must needs be that **o** come; but woe to *4625*
Lk 17: 1 It is impossible but that **o** will come: *4625*
Ro 4:25 Who was delivered for our **o**, and *3900*
5:16 the free gift *is* of many **o** unto justification. *3900*
16:17 **o** contrary to the doctrine which ye have *4625*

OFFEND (25) [OFFENCE, OFFENCES, OFFENDED, OFFENDER, OFFENDERS]
Job 34:31 I have borne *chastisement,* I will not **o** *any* 2254
Ps 73:15 I should **o** *against* the generation of thy 898
119:165 love thy law: and nothing *shall* **o** them. 4383
Jer 2: 3 all that devour him shall **o**; evil shall come 816
50: 7 We **o** not, because they have sinned against 816
Hos 4:15 Israel, play the harlot, *yet* let not Judah **o**; 816
Hab 1:11 mind change, and he shall pass over, and **o**, 816
Mt 5:29 And if thy right eye **o** thee, pluck it out, and *4624*
5:30 And if thy right hand **o** thee, cut it off, and *4624*
13:41 gather out of his kingdom all **things that o**, *4625*
17:27 Notwithstanding, lest we should **o** them, *4624*
18: 6 But whoso shall **o** one of these little ones *4624*
18: 8 Wherefore if thy hand or thy foot **o** thee, *4624*
18: 9 And if thine eye **o** thee, pluck it out, and *4624*
Mk 9:42 And whosoever shall **o** one of *these* little *4624*
9:43 And if thy hand **o** thee, cut it off: it is better *4624*
9:45 And if thy foot **o** thee, cut it off: it is better *4624*
9:47 And if thine eye **o** thee, pluck it out: it is *4624*
Lk 17: 2 than that he should **o** one of these little *4624*
Jn 6:61 at it, he said unto them, Doth this **o** you? *4624*

1Co 8:13 Wherefore, if meat **make** my brother **to o**, 4624
8:13 lest I **make** my brother **to o**. 4624
Jas 2:10 and *yet* **o** in one *point,* he is guilty of all. 4417
3: 2 For *in* many *things* we **o** all. If any *man* 4417
3: 2 If any *man* **o** not in word, the same *is* a 4417

OFFENDED (25) [OFFEND]
Ge 20: 9 what have I **o** thee, that thou hast brought 2398
40: 1 *his* baker had **o** their lord the king of Egypt. 2398
2Ki 18:14 of Assyria to Lachish, saying, I have **o**; 2398
2Ch 28:13 for whereas we have **o** against the LORD 819
Pr 18:19 A brother **o** *is harder to be won* than a 6586
Jer 37:18 What have I **o** against thee, or against thy 2398
Eze 25:12 hath **greatly o**, and revenged himself 816+816
Hos 13: 1 in Israel; but when he **o** in Baal, he died. 816
Mt 11: 6 And blessed is *he,* whosoever shall not be **o** 4624
13:21 because of the word, by and by he is **o**. 4624
13:57 And they were **o** in him. But Jesus said 4624
15:12 Knowest thou that the Pharisees were **o**, 4624
24:10 And then shall many be **o**, and shall betray 4624
26:31 All ye shall be **o** because of me this night: 4624
26:33 Though all *men* shall be **o** because of thee, 4624
26:33 because of thee, *yet* will I never be **o**. 4624
Mk 4:17 the word's sake, immediately they are **o**. 4624
6: 3 here with us? And they were **o** at him. 4624
14:27 All ye shall be **o** because of me this night: 4624
14:29 Although all shall be **o**, yet *will* not I. 4624
Lk 7:23 And blessed is *he,* whosoever shall not be **o** 4624
Jn 16: 1 I spoken unto you, that ye should not be **o**. 4624
Ac 25: 8 *yet* against Cesar, have I **o** any *thing at all.* 264
Ro 14:21 brother stumbleth, or is **o**, or is *made* weak. 4624
2Co 11:29 I am not weak? who is **o**, and I burn not? 4624

OFFENDER (2) [OFFEND]
Isa 29:21 That **make** a man **an o** for a word, and 2398
Ac 25:11 For if I be an **o**, or have committed any *thing* 91

OFFENDERS (1) [OFFEND]
1Ki 1:21 and my son Solomon shall be *counted* **o**. 2400

OFFER (236) [OFFERED, OFFERETH, OFFERING, OFFERINGS]
Ge 22: 2 **o** him there for a burnt offering upon one of 5927
Ex 22:29 Thou shalt not delay *to o the first of* thy ripe NIH
23:18 Thou shalt not **o** the blood of my sacrifice 2076
29:36 thou shalt **o** every day a bullock *for* a sin 6213
29:38 Now this *is that* which thou shalt **o** upon 6213
29:39 The one lamb thou shalt **o** in the morning; 6213
29:39 and the other lamb thou shalt **o** at even: 6213
29:41 the other lamb thou shalt **o** at even, *and* 6213
30: 9 Ye shall **o** no strange incense thereon, nor 5927
34:25 Thou shalt not **o** the blood of my sacrifice 7819
35:24 Every one that did **o** an offering of silver 7311
Lev 1: 3 the herd, let him **o** a male without blemish: 7126
1: 3 he shall **o** it of his own voluntary will at 7126
2: 1 when any will **o** a meat offering unto 7126
2:12 ye shall **o** them unto the LORD: 7126
2:13 with all thine offerings thou shalt **o** salt. 7126
2:14 if thou **o** a meat offering of *thy* firstfruits 7126
2:14 thou shalt **o** for the meat offering of thy 7126
3: 1 of peace offering, if he **o** *it* of the herd; 7126
3: 1 he shall **o** it without blemish before 7126
3: 3 he shall **o** of the sacrifice of the peace 7126
3: 6 or female, he shall **o** it without blemish. 7126
3: 7 If he **o** a lamb for his offering, then shall he 7126
3: 7 then shall he **o** it before the LORD. 7126
3: 9 he shall **o** of the sacrifice of the peace 7126
3:12 a goat, then he shall **o** it before the LORD. 7126
3:14 he shall **o** thereof his offering, *even* an 7126
4:14 the congregation shall **o** a young bullock 7126
5: 8 who shall **o** *that* which *is* for the sin 7126
5:10 he shall **o** the second *for* a burnt offering, 6213
6:14 the sons of Aaron shall **o** it before 7126
6:20 which they shall **o** unto the LORD in 7126
6:21 thou **o** *for* a sweet savour unto the LORD. 7126
6:22 sons that is anointed in his stead shall **o** it: 6213
7: 3 he shall **o** of it all the fat thereof; the rump, 7126
7:11 which he shall **o** unto the LORD. 7126
7:12 If he **o** it for a thanksgiving, then he shall 7126
7:12 he shall **o** with the sacrifice of thanksgiving 7126
7:13 he shall **o** *for* his offering leavened bread 7126
7:14 of it he shall **o** one out of the whole 7126
7:25 of which *men* **o** an offering made by fire 7126
7:38 Israel to **o** their oblations unto the LORD, 7126
9: 2 and **o** *them* before the LORD. 7126
9: 7 **o** thy sin offering, and thy burnt offering, 6213
9: 7 **o** the offering of the people, and make an 6213
12: 7 Who shall **o** it before the LORD, and 7126
14:12 **o** him for a trespass offering, and the log of 7126
14:19 the priest shall **o** the sin offering, and 6213
14:20 And the priest shall **o** the burnt offering and 5927
14:30 And he shall **o** the one of the turtledoves, or 6213
15:15 the priest shall **o** them, the one *for* a sin 6213
15:30 the priest shall **o** the one *for* a sin offering, 6213
16: 6 Aaron shall **o** *his* bullock of the sin 7126
16: 9 lot fell, and **o** him *for* a sin offering. 6213
16:24 **o** his burnt offering, and the burnt offering 6213
17: 4 to **o** an offering unto the LORD before 7126
17: 5 which they **o** in the open field, even that 2076
17: 5 **o** them *for* peace offerings unto 2076
17: 7 they shall no more **o** their sacrifices unto 2076
17: 9 the congregation, to **o** it unto the LORD; 6213
19: 5 if ye **o a sacrifice** of peace offerings 2076+2077
19: 5 the LORD, ye shall **o** it at your own will. 2076
19: 6 It shall be eaten the *same* day ye **o** it, and 2077
21: 6 *and* the bread of their God, they do **o**: 7126
21:17 let him not approach to **o** the bread of his 7126
21:21 shall come nigh to **o** the offerings of 7126
21:21 he shall not come nigh to **o** the bread of his 7126
22:15 of Israel, which they **o** unto the LORD; 7311
22:18 that will **o** his oblation for all his vows, and 7126
22:18 which they will **o** unto the LORD for a 7126
22:19 *Ye shall o* at your own will a male without NIH
22:20 hath a blemish, *that* shall ye not **o**: 7126
22:22 ye shall not **o** these unto the LORD, 7126
22:23 that mayest thou **o** *for* a freewill offering; 6213
22:24 Ye shall not **o** unto the LORD that which 7126
22:25 Neither from a stranger's hand shall ye **o** 7126
22:29 when ye will **o** a sacrifice of thanksgiving 2076
22:29 unto the LORD, **o** *it* at your own will. 2076
23: 8 ye shall **o** an offering made by fire unto 7126
23:12 ye shall **o** that day when ye wave the sheaf 6213
23:16 ye shall **o** a new meat offering unto 7126
23:18 ye shall **o** with the bread seven lambs 7126
23:25 ye shall **o** an offering made by fire unto 7126
23:27 **o** an offering made by fire unto 7126
23:36 Seven days ye shall **o** an offering made by 7126
23:36 ye shall **o** an offering made by fire unto 7126
23:37 to **o** an offering made by fire unto 7126
27:11 of which they do not **o** a sacrifice unto 7126
Nu 5:25 before the LORD, and **o** it upon the altar: 7126
6:11 the priest shall **o** the one for a sin offering, 6213
6:14 he shall **o** his offering unto the LORD, 7126
6:16 shall **o** his sin offering, and his burnt 6213
6:17 he shall **o** the ram *for* a sacrifice of peace 6213
6:17 the priest shall **o** also his meat offering, and 6213
7:11 They shall **o** their offering, each prince on 7126
7:18 the son of Zuar, prince of Issachar, did **o**: 7126
7:24 prince of the children of Zebulun, *did o*: NIH
7:30 prince of the children of Reuben, *did o*: NIH
7:36 prince of the children of Simeon, *did o*: NIH
8:11 Aaron shall **o** the Levites before 5130
8:12 thou shalt **o** the one *for* a sin offering, and 6213
8:13 **o** them *for* an offering unto the LORD. 5130
8:15 cleanse them, and **o** them *for* an offering. 5130
9: 7 that *we* may not **o** an offering of 7126
15: 7 for a drink offering thou shalt **o** the third 7126
15:14 will **o** an offering made by fire, of a sweet 6213
15:19 ye shall **o up** a heave offering unto 7311
15:20 Ye shall **o up** a cake *of* the first of your 7311
15:24 that all the congregation shall **o** one young 6213
16:40 come near to **o** incense before the LORD; 6999
18:12 the firstfruits of them which they shall **o** 5414
18:19 the children of Israel **o** unto the LORD, 7311
18:24 which they **o** *as* a heave offering unto 7311
18:26 ye shall **o up** a heave offering of it for 7311
18:28 Thus you also shall **o** a heave offering unto 7311
18:29 Out of all your gifts ye shall **o** every heave 7311
28: 2 shall ye observe to **o** unto me in their due 7126
28: 3 by fire which ye shall **o** unto the LORD; 7126
28: 4 The one lamb shalt thou **o** in the morning, 6213
28: 4 and the other lamb shalt thou **o** at even; 6213
28: 8 the other lamb shalt thou **o** at even: as 6213
28: 8 thou shalt **o** *it,* a sacrifice made by fire, 6213
28:11 in the beginnings of your months ye shall **o** 7126
28:19 ye shall **o** a sacrifice made by fire *for* a 7126
28:20 three tenth deals shall ye **o** for a bullock, 6213
28:21 A several tenth deal shalt thou **o** for every 6213
28:23 Ye shall **o** these beside the burnt offering in 6213

Nu	28:24	After this manner ye shall **o** daily,	6213
	28:27	ye shall **o** the burnt offering for a sweet	7126
	28:31	Ye shall **o** *them* besides the continual burnt	6213
	29: 2	ye shall **o** a burnt offering for a sweet	6213
	29: 8	ye shall **o** a burnt offering unto the LORD	7126
	29:13	ye shall **o** a burnt offering, a sacrifice made	7126
	29:17	on the second day *ye shall o* twelve young	NIH
	29:36	ye shall **o** a burnt offering, a sacrifice made	7126
Dt	12:13	Take heed to thyself that thou **o** not thy	5927
	12:14	there thou shalt **o** thy burnt offerings, and	5927
	12:27	thou shalt **o** thy burnt offerings, the flesh	6213
	18: 3	from them that **o** a sacrifice, whether *it be*	2076
	27: 6	thou shalt **o** burnt offerings thereon unto	5927
	27: 7	thou shalt **o** peace offerings, and shalt eat	2076
	33:19	there they shall **o** sacrifices of	2076
Jos	22:23	or if to **o** thereon burnt offering or	5927
	22:23	or if to **o** peace offerings thereon,	6213
Jdg	3:18	when he had made an end to **o** the present,	7126
	6:26	**o** a burnt sacrifice with the wood of	5927
	11:31	and I will **o** it **up** *for* a burnt offering.	5927
	13:16	if thou wilt **o** a burnt offering, thou must	6213
	13:16	thou must **o** it unto the LORD.	5927
	16:23	to **o** a great sacrifice unto Dagon their god,	2076
1Sa	1:21	went up to **o** unto the LORD the yearly	2076
	2:19	when she came up with her husband to **o**	2076
	2:28	to **o** upon mine altar, to burn incense,	5927
	10: 8	to **o** burnt offerings, *and* to sacrifice	5927
2Sa	24:12	I **o** thee three *things;* choose thee one of	5190
	24:22	and **o** **up** what seemeth good unto him:	5927
	24:24	neither will I **o** burnt offerings unto	5927
1Ki	3: 4	thousand burnt offerings did Solomon **o** **up**	5927
	9:25	three times in a year did Solomon **o** burnt	5927
	13: 2	upon thee shall he **o** the priests of the high	2076
2Ki	5:17	for thy servant will henceforth **o** neither	6213
	10:24	when they went in to **o** sacrifices and	6213
1Ch	16:40	To **o** burnt offerings unto the LORD upon	5927
	21:10	I **o** thee three *things:* choose thee one of	5186
	21:24	nor **o** burnt offerings without cost.	5927
	23:31	to **o** all burnt sacrifices unto the LORD in	5927
	29:14	that we should be able to **o** *so* **willingly**	5068
	29:17	are present here, to **o** **willingly** unto thee.	5068
2Ch	23:18	to **o** the burnt offerings of the LORD, as it	5927
	24:14	to **o** *withal,* and spoons, and vessels of gold	5927
	29:21	Aaron to **o** *them* on the altar of the LORD.	5927
	29:27	Hezekiah commanded to **o** the burnt	5927
	35:12	to **o** unto the LORD, as it is written in	7126
	35:16	to **o** burnt offerings upon the altar of	5927
Ezr	3: 2	God of Israel, to **o** burnt offerings thereon,	5927
	3: 6	they to **o** burnt offerings unto the LORD.	5927
	6:10	That they may **o** sacrifices of sweet savours	1934
	7:17	**o** them upon the altar of the house of your	7127
Job	42: 8	and **o** **up** for yourselves a burnt offering;	5927
Ps	4: 5	**O** the sacrifices of righteousness, and	2076
	16: 4	their drink offerings of blood will I not **o**,	5258
	27: 6	will I **o** in his tabernacle sacrifices of joy;	2076
	50:14	**O** unto God thanksgiving; and pay thy	2076
	51:19	then shall they **o** bullocks upon thine altar.	5927
	66:15	I will **o** unto thee burnt sacrifices of	5927
	66:15	of rams; I will **o** bullocks with goats.	6213
	72:10	the kings of Sheba and Seba shall **o** gifts.	7126
	116:17	I will **o** to thee the sacrifice of	2076
Isa	57: 7	even thither wentest thou up to **o** sacrifice.	2076
Jer	11:12	unto the gods unto whom they **o** **incense**:	6999
	14:12	when they **o** burnt offering and an oblation,	5927
	33:18	want a man before me to **o** burnt offerings,	5927
Eze	6:13	the place where they did **o** sweet savour to	5414
	20:31	For when *ye* **o** your gifts, when *ye* make	5375
	43:18	to **o** burnt offerings thereon, and to sprinkle	5927
	43:22	on the second day thou shalt **o** a kid of	7126
	43:23	shalt **o** a young bullock without blemish,	7126
	43:24	thou shalt **o** them before the LORD, and	7126
	43:24	they shall **o** them **up** *for* a burnt offering	5927
	44: 7	when ye **o** my bread, the fat and the blood,	7126
	44:15	they shall stand before me to **o** unto me	7126
	44:27	he shall **o** his sin offering, saith the Lord	7126
	45: 1	ye shall **o** an oblation unto the LORD,	7311
	45:13	This *is* the oblation that ye shall **o**; the sixth	7311
	45:14	*ye shall o* the tenth part of a bath out of	NIH
	46: 4	the burnt offering that the prince shall **o**	7126
	48: 8	shall be the offering which ye shall **o** *of*	7311
	48: 9	The oblation that ye shall **o** unto	7311
	48:20	ye shall **o** the holy oblation foursquare,	7311
Da	2:46	commanded that *they* should **o** an oblation	5260
Hos	9: 4	They shall not **o** wine *offerings* to	5258
Am	4: 5	**o** a sacrifice of thanksgiving with leaven,	6999
	5:22	Though ye **o** me burnt offerings and	5927
Hag	2:14	and *that* which they **o** there *is* unclean.	7126
Mal	1: 7	*Ye* **o** polluted bread upon mine altar; and	5066
	1: 8	if ye **o** the blind for sacrifice, *is it* not evil?	5066
	1: 8	if ye **o** the lame and sick, *is it* not evil?	5066
	1: 8	**o** it now unto thy governor; will he be	7126
	3: 3	that they may **o** unto the LORD an	5066
Mt	5:24	thy brother, and then come and **o** thy gift.	*4374*
	8: 4	**o** the gift that Moses commanded for a	*4374*
Mk	1:44	**o** for thy cleansing *those things* which	*4374*
Lk	2:24	And to **o** a sacrifice according to that which	*1325*
	5:14	to the priest, and **o** for thy cleansing,	*4374*
	6:29	thee on the *one* cheek **o** also the other;	*3930*
	11:12	shall ask an egg, will he **o** him a scorpion?	*1929*
Heb	5: 1	that he may **o** both gifts and sacrifices for	*4374*
	5: 3	the people, so also for himself, to **o** for sins.	*4374*
	7:27	as *those* high priests, to **o** **up** sacrifice,	*399*
	8: 3	For every high priest is ordained to **o** gifts	*4374*
	8: 3	that this *man* have somewhat also to **o**.	*4374*
	8: 4	seeing that there are priests that **o** gifts	*4374*
	9:25	Nor yet that he should **o** himself often,	*4374*
	13:15	let us **o** the sacrifice of praise to God	*399*
1Pe	2: 5	holy priesthood, to **o** **up** spiritual sacrifices,	*399*
Rev	8: 3	that he should **o** *it* with the prayers of all	*1325*

OFFERED (143) [OFFER]

Ge	8:20	and **o** burnt offerings on the altar.	5927
	22:13	**o** him **up** for a burnt offering in the stead of	5927
	31:54	Jacob **o** sacrifice upon the mount, and	2076
	46: 1	**o** sacrifices unto the God of his father	2076
Ex	24: 5	which **o** burnt offerings, and	5927
	32: 6	**o** burnt offerings, and brought peace	5927
	35:22	every man that **o** *offered* an offering of	5130
	35:22	every man that offered *o* an offering of gold	NIH
	40:29	**o** upon it the burnt offering and the meat	5927
Lev	7: 8	skin of the burnt offering which he hath **o**.	7126
	7:15	shall be eaten the same day that it is **o**;	7133
	9:15	and slew it, and **o** it **for sin**, as the first.	2398
	9:16	and **o** it according to the manner.	6213
	10: 1	**o** strange fire before the LORD,	7126
	10:19	*this* day have they **o** their sin offering and	7126
	16: 1	when they **o** before the LORD, and died;	7126
Nu	3: 4	when they **o** strange fire before	7126
	7: 2	and were over them that were numbered, **o**:	7126
	7:10	the princes **o** *for* dedicating of the altar in	7126
	7:10	even the princes **o** their offering before	7126
	7:12	he that **o** his offering the first day was	7126
	7:19	He **o** *for* his offering one silver charger,	7126
	7:42	of Deuel, prince of the children of Gad, *o*:	NIH
	7:48	prince of the children of Ephraim, *o*:	NIH
	7:54	On the eighth day *o* Gamaliel the son of	NIH
	7:60	prince of the children of Benjamin, *o*:	NIH
	7:66	prince of the children of Dan, *o*:	NIH
	7:72	prince of the children of Asher, *o*:	NIH
	7:78	prince of the children of Naphtali, *o*:	NIH
	8:21	Aaron **o** them *as* an offering before	5130
	16:35	two hundred and fifty men that **o** incense.	7126
	16:38	for they **o** them before the LORD,	7126
	16:39	wherewith they that were burnt had **o**;	7126
	22:40	Balak **o** oxen and sheep, and sent to	2076
	23: 2	and Balaam **o** on *every* altar a bullock and	5927
	23: 4	I have **o** upon *every* altar a bullock and	5927
	23:14	and **o** a bullock and a ram on *every* altar.	5927
	23:30	and **o** a bullock and a ram on *every* altar.	5927
	26:61	when they **o** strange fire before	7126
	28:15	a sin offering unto the LORD shall be **o**,	6213
	28:24	it shall be **o** beside the continual burnt	6213
	31:52	all the gold of the offering that they **o** **up** to	7311
Jos	8:31	they **o** thereon burnt offerings unto	5927
Jdg	5: 2	when the people **willingly** **o** themselves.	5068
	5: 9	that **o** themselves **willingly** among	5068
	6:28	the second bullock was **o** upon the altar that	5927
	13:19	and **o** *it* upon a rock unto the LORD:	5927
	20:26	**o** burnt offerings and peace offerings	5927
	21: 4	and **o** burnt offerings and peace offerings.	5927
1Sa	1: 4	when the time was that Elkanah **o**, he gave	2076
	2:13	people *was, that* when any man **o** sacrifice,	2076
	6:14	**o** the kine a burnt offering unto	5927
	6:15	the men of Beth-shemesh **o** burnt offerings	5927
	7: 9	**o** it *for* a burnt offering wholly unto	5927
	13: 9	And he **o** the burnt offering.	5927
	13:12	myself therefore, and **o** a burnt offering.	5927
2Sa	6:17	David **o** burnt offerings and peace offerings	5927

2Sa	15:12	*even* from Giloh, while he **o** sacrifices.	2076
	24:25	and **o** burnt offerings and peace offerings.	5927
1Ki	3:15	**o up** burnt offerings, and offered peace	5927
	3:15	**o** peace offerings, and made a feast to all	6213
	8:62	with him, **o** sacrifice before the LORD.	2076
	8:63	Solomon **o** a sacrifice of peace offerings,	2076
	8:63	which he **o** unto the LORD, two and	2076
	8:64	for there he **o** burnt offerings, and meat	6213
	12:32	he **o** upon the altar (so did he in Beth-el,)	5927
	12:33	So he **o** upon the altar which he had made	5927
	12:33	and he **o** upon the altar, and burnt incense.	5927
	22:43	*for* the people **o** and burnt incense yet in	2076
2Ki	3:20	when the meat offering was **o**, that behold,	5927
	3:27	**o** him *for* a burnt offering upon the wall.	5927
	16:12	king approached to the altar, and **o** thereon.	5927
1Ch	6:49	his sons **o** upon the altar of the burnt	6999
	15:26	that they **o** seven bullocks and seven rams.	2076
	16: 1	they **o** burnt sacrifices and peace offerings	7126
	21:26	**o** burnt offerings and peace offerings, and	5927
	29: 6	the rulers over the king's work, **o willingly**,	5068
	29: 9	for that they **o willingly**, because	5068
	29: 9	with perfect heart they **o willingly** to	5068
	29:17	heart I have **willingly o** all these *things:*	5068
	29:21	**o** burnt offerings unto the LORD, on	5927
2Ch	1: 6	and **o** a thousand burnt offerings upon it.	5927
	4: 6	such **things** as they **o** for the burnt offering	4639
	7: 4	all the people **o** sacrifices before	2076
	7: 5	king Solomon **o** a sacrifice of twenty and	2076
	7: 7	for there he **o** burnt offerings, and the fat of	6213
	8:12	Solomon **o** burnt offerings unto the LORD	5927
	15:11	they **o** unto the LORD the same time,	2076
	17:16	who **willingly o** himself unto the LORD;	5068
	24:14	they **o** burnt offerings in the house of	5927
	29: 7	have not burnt incense nor **o** burnt offerings	5927
Ezr	1: 6	beside all *that* was **willingly o**.	5068
	2:68	**o freely** for the house of God to set it up in	5068
	3: 3	they **o** burnt offerings thereon unto	5927
	3: 4	and *o* the daily burnt offerings by number,	NIH
	3: 5	afterward *o* the continual burnt offering,	NIH
	3: 5	of every one that **willingly o** a freewill	5068
	6: 3	the place where they **o** sacrifices, and	1684
	6:17	**o** at the dedication of this house of God an	7127
	7:15	his counsellers have **freely o** unto the God	5069
	8:25	his lords, and all Israel *there* present, had **o**:	7311
	8:35	**o** burnt offerings unto the God of Israel,	7126
	10:19	*they o* a ram of the flock for their trespass.	NIH
Ne	11: 2	that **willingly o** themselves to dwell at	5068
	12:43	Also that day they **o** great sacrifices, and	2076
Job	1: 5	**o** burnt offerings *according to* the number	5927
Isa	57: 6	drink offering, thou hast **o** a meat offering.	5927
	66: 3	an oblation, *as if he o* swine's blood;	NIH
Jer	32:29	upon whose roofs they have **o incense** unto	6999
Eze	20:28	they **o** there their sacrifices, and there they	2076
	48:12	*this* oblation of the land that is **o** shall be	8641
Da	11:18	cause the reproach **o by** him to cease;	3807.1
Am	5:25	Have ye **o** unto me sacrifices and	5066
Jnh	1:16	**o** a sacrifice unto the LORD, and	2076
Mal	1:11	in every place incense *shall be* **o** unto my	5066
Ac	7:41	and **o** sacrifice unto the idol, and rejoiced in	*321*
	7:42	have ye **o** to me slain beasts and	*4374*
	8:18	Holy Ghost was given, he **o** them money,	*4374*
	15:29	That *ye* abstain from **meats o to idols**, and	*1494*
	21:25	keep themselves from **things o to idols**,	*1494*
	21:26	until that an offering should be **o** for every	*4374*
1Co	8: 1	Now as touching **things o unto idols**,	*1494*
	8: 4	**things** that are **o in sacrifice unto idols**,	*1494*
	8: 7	this hour, eat *it* as a **thing o unto an idol**;	*1494*
	8:10	to eat those **things** which are **o to idols**;	*1494*
	10:19	that which is **o in sacrifice to idols** is any	*1494*
	10:28	unto you, This is **o in sacrifice unto idols**,	*1494*
Php	2:17	and if I be **o** upon the sacrifice and	*4689*
2Ti	4: 6	For I am now ready to be **o**, and the time of	*4689*
Heb	5: 7	when he had **o up** prayers and	*4374*
	7:27	for this he did once, when he **o up** himself.	*399*
	9: 7	which he **o** for himself, and *for* the errors of	*4374*
	9: 9	in which were **o** both gifts and sacrifices,	*4374*
	9:14	who through the eternal Spirit **o** himself	*4374*
	9:28	So Christ was once **o** to bear the sins of	*4374*
	10: 1	never with those sacrifices which they **o**	*4374*
	10: 2	then would they not have ceased to be **o**?	*4374*
	10: 8	neither hadst pleasure *therein:* which are **o**	*4374*
	10:12	But this *man*, after he had **o** one sacrifice	*4374*
	11: 4	By faith Abel **o** unto God a more excellent	*4374*
	11:17	when he was tried, **o up** Isaac:	*4374*
	11:17	he that had received the promises **o up** *his*	*4374*
Jas	2:21	when he had **o** Isaac his son upon the altar?	*399*

OFFERETH (15) [OFFER]

Lev	6:26	The priest that **o** it **for sin** shall eat it: in	2398
	7: 8	the priest that **o** *any* man's burnt offering,	7126
	7: 9	and in the pan, shall be the priest's that **o** it.	7126
	7:16	it shall be eaten the *same* day that he **o** his	7126
	7:18	neither shall it be imputed unto him that **o**	7126
	7:29	He that **o** the sacrifice of his peace	7126
	7:33	that **o** the blood of the peace offerings, and	7126
	17: 8	that **o** a burnt offering or sacrifice,	5927
	21: 8	for he **o** the bread of thy God:	7126
	22:21	whosoever **o** a sacrifice of peace offerings	7126
Nu	15: 4	shall he that **o** his offering unto the LORD	7126
Ps	50:23	Whoso **o** praise glorifieth me: and to him	2076
Isa	66: 3	he that **o** an oblation, *as if he offered*	5927
Jer	48:35	him that **o** *in* the high places, and him that	5927
Mal	2:12	him that **o** an offering unto the LORD of	5066

OFFERING (724) [OFFER]

Ge	4: 3	fruit of the ground an **o** unto the LORD.	4503
	4: 4	LORD had respect unto Abel and to his **o**:	4503
	4: 5	unto Cain and to his **o** he had not respect.	4503
	22: 2	offer him there for a **burnt o** upon one of	5930
	22: 3	clave the wood for the **burnt o**, and	5930
	22: 6	Abraham took the wood of the **burnt o**,	5930
	22: 7	but where *is* the lamb for a **burnt o**?	5930
	22: 8	will provide himself a lamb for a **burnt o**:	5930
	22:13	offered him up for a **burnt o** in the stead of	5930
	35:14	he poured a **drink o** thereon, and he poured	5262
Ex	18:12	took a **burnt o** and sacrifices for God:	5930
	25: 2	children of Israel, that they bring me an **o**:	8641
	25: 2	willingly with his heart ye shall take my **o**.	8641
	25: 3	this *is* the **o** which ye shall take of them;	8641
	29:14	with fire without the camp: it *is* a **sin o**.	2403
	29:18	it *is* a **burnt o** unto the LORD: it *is* a	5930
	29:18	an **o made by fire** unto the LORD.	801
	29:24	shalt wave them *for* a **wave o** before	8573
	29:25	burn *them* upon the altar for a **burnt o**,	5930
	29:25	it *is* an **o made by fire** unto the LORD.	801
	29:26	wave it *for* a **wave o** before the LORD:	8573
	29:27	thou shalt sanctify the breast of the **wave o**,	8573
	29:27	the shoulder of the **heave o**, which is	8641
	29:28	for it *is* a **heave o**: and it shall be a heave	8641
	29:28	it shall be a **heave o** from the children of	8641
	29:28	*even* their **heave o** unto the LORD.	8641
	29:36	day a bullock *for* a **sin o** for atonement:	2403
	29:40	fourth *part* of a hin of wine *for* a **drink o**.	5262
	29:41	shalt do thereto according to the **meat o** of	4503
	29:41	according to the **drink o** thereof, for a	5262
	29:41	an **o made by fire** unto the LORD.	801
	29:42	*This shall be* a continual **burnt o**	5930
	30: 9	nor burnt sacrifice, nor **meat o**;	4503
	30: 9	neither shall ye pour **drink o** thereon.	5262
	30:10	with the blood of the **sin o** of atonements:	2403
	30:13	a half shekel *shall be* the **o** of the LORD.	8641
	30:14	above, shall give an **o** unto the LORD.	8641
	30:15	when *they* give an **o** unto the LORD,	8641
	30:20	to burn **o made by fire** unto the LORD:	801
	30:28	the altar of **burnt o** with all his vessels,	5930
	31: 9	the altar of **burnt o** with all his furniture,	5930
	35: 5	Take ye from amongst you an **o** unto	8641
	35: 5	let him bring it, an **o** of the LORD;	8641
	35:16	The altar of **burnt o** with his brasen grate,	5930
	35:21	they brought the LORD'S **o** to the work of	8641
	35:22	every man that offered *offered* an **o** of gold	8573
	35:24	Every one that did offer an **o** of silver and	8641
	35:24	of silver and brass brought the LORD'S **o**:	8641
	35:29	The children of Israel brought a **willing o**	5071
	36: 3	they received of Moses all the **o**, which	8641
	36: 6	any more work for the **o** of the sanctuary.	8641
	38: 1	he made the altar of **burnt o** *of* shittim	5930
	38:24	of the holy *place*, even the gold of the **o**,	8573
	38:29	the brass of the **o** *was* seventy talents, and	8573
	40: 6	thou shalt set the altar of the **burnt o** before	5930
	40:10	thou shalt anoint the altar of the **burnt o**,	5930
	40:29	he put the altar of **burnt o** *by* the door of	5930
	40:29	offered upon it the **burnt o** and the meat	5930
	40:29	upon it the burnt offering and the **meat o**;	4503
Lev	1: 2	If *any* man of you bring an **o** unto	7133
	1: 2	ye shall bring your **o** of the cattle, *even* of	7133
	1: 3	If his **o** *be* a burnt sacrifice of the herd,	7133
	1: 4	put his hand upon the head of the **burnt o**;	5930

Lev 1: 6 he shall flay the **burnt o**, and cut it into his 5930
1: 9 *to be* a burnt sacrifice, an **o made by fire**, 801
1:10 if his **o** *be* of the flocks, *namely,* of 7133
1:13 it *is* a burnt sacrifice, an **o made by fire**, of a 801
1:14 if the burnt sacrifice for his **o** to 7133
1:14 he shall bring his **o** of turtledoves, or 7133
1:17 it *is* a burnt sacrifice, an **o made by fire**, of a 801
2: 1 when any will offer a **meat o** unto 4503
2: 1 the LORD, his **o** shall be *of* fine flour; 7133
2: 2 *to be* an **o made by fire**, of a sweet savour 801
2: 3 the remnant of the **meat o** *shall be* Aaron's 4503
2: 4 if thou bring an oblation of a **meat o** baken 4503
2: 5 if thy oblation *be* a **meat o** *baken* in a pan, 4503
2: 6 and pour oil thereon: it *is* a **meat o**. 4503
2: 7 if thy oblation *be* a **meat o** *baken* in 4503
2: 8 thou shalt bring the **meat o** that is made of 4503
2: 9 the priest shall take from the **meat o** a 4503
2: 9 *it is* an **o made by fire**, of a sweet savour 801
2:10 that which is left of the **meat o** *shall be* 4503
2:11 No **meat o**, which ye shall bring unto 4503
2:11 *in* any **o** of the LORD **made by fire**. 801
2:13 every oblation of thy **meat o** shalt thou 4503
2:13 of thy God to be lacking from thy **meat o**: 4503
2:14 if thou offer a **meat o** of *thy* firstfruits unto 4503
2:14 thou shalt offer for the **meat o** of thy 4503
2:15 and lay frankincense thereon: it *is* a **meat o**. 4503
2:16 *it is* an **o made by fire** unto the LORD. 801
3: 1 if his oblation *be* a sacrifice of **peace o**, 8002
3: 2 he shall lay his hand upon the head of his **o**, 7133
3: 3 he shall offer of the sacrifice of the **peace o** 8002
3: 3 offering an **o made by fire** unto the LORD; 801
3: 5 *it is* an **o made by fire**, of a sweet savour 801
3: 6 if his **o** for a sacrifice of peace offering 7133
3: 6 if his offering for a sacrifice of **peace o** 8002
3: 7 If he offer a lamb for his **o**, then shall he 7133
3: 8 he shall lay his hand upon the head of his **o**, 7133
3: 9 he shall offer of the sacrifice of the **peace o** 8002
3: 9 offering an **o made by fire** unto the LORD; 801
3:11 *it is* the food of the **o made by fire** unto 801
3:12 if his **o** *be* a goat, then he shall offer it 7133
3:14 he shall offer thereof his **o**, *even* an offering 7133
3:14 *even* an **o made by fire** unto the LORD; 801
3:16 *it is* the food of the **o made by fire** for a 801
4: 3 blemish unto the LORD for a **sin o**. 2403
4: 7 at the bottom of the altar of the **burnt o**, 5930
4: 8 it all the fat of the bullock *for* the **sin o**; 2403
4:10 burn them upon the altar of the **burnt o**. 5930
4:18 at the bottom of the altar of the **burnt o**, 5930
4:20 as he did with the bullock for a **sin o**, 2403
4:21 it *is* a **sin o** for the congregation. 2403
4:23 he shall bring his **o**, a kid of the goats, 7133
4:24 they kill the **burnt o** before the LORD: 5930
4:24 offering before the LORD: it *is* a **sin o**. 2403
4:25 of the blood of the **sin o** with his finger, 2403
4:25 *it* upon the horns of the altar of **burnt o**, 5930
4:25 blood at the bottom of the altar of **burnt o**. 5930
4:28 he shall bring his **o**, a kid of the goats, 7133
4:29 lay his hand upon the head of the **sin o**, 2403
4:29 slay the **sin o** in the place of the burnt 2403
4:29 the sin offering in the place of the **burnt o**. 5930
4:30 *it* upon the horns of the altar of **burnt o**, 5930
4:32 if he bring a lamb for a sin **o**, he shall bring 7133
4:33 lay his hand upon the head of the **sin o**, 2403
4:33 slay it for a **sin o** in the place where they 2403
4:33 in the place where they kill the **burnt o**. 5930
4:34 of the blood of the **sin o** with his finger, 2403
4:34 *it* upon the horns of the altar of **burnt o**, 5930
5: 6 he shall bring his **trespass o** unto 817
5: 6 a lamb or a kid of the goats, for a **sin o**; 2403
5: 7 one for a **sin o**, and the other for a burnt 2403
5: 7 a sin offering, and the other for a **burnt o**. 5930
5: 8 who shall offer *that* which *is* for the **sin o** 2403
5: 9 he shall sprinkle of the blood of the **sin o** 2403
5: 9 out at the bottom of the altar: it *is* a **sin o**. 2403
5:10 And he shall offer the second *for* a **burnt o**, 5930
5:11 he that sinned shall bring for his **o** the tenth 7133
5:11 *part* of an ephah of fine flour for a **sin o**; 2403
5:11 *any* frankincense thereon: for it *is* a **sin o**. 2403
5:12 made by fire unto the LORD: it *is* a **sin o**. 2403
5:13 *remnant* shall be the priest's, as a **meat o**. 4503
5:15 the shekel of the sanctuary, for a **trespass o**: 817
5:16 for him with the ram of the **trespass o**, 817
5:18 for a **trespass o**, unto the priest: 817
5:19 It *is* a **trespass o**: he hath certainly 817
6: 5 it appertaineth, in the day of his **trespass o**. 819
6: 6 he shall bring his **trespass o** unto 817
6: 6 for a **trespass o**, unto the priest: 817
6: 9 saying, This *is* the law of the **burnt o**: 5930
6: 9 It *is* the **burnt o**, because of the burning 5930
6:10 consumed with the **burnt o** on the altar, 5930
6:12 lay the **burnt o** in order upon it; 5930
6:14 this *is* the law of the **meat o**: the sons of 4503
6:15 of the flour of the **meat o**, and of the oil 4503
6:15 the frankincense which *is* upon the **meat o**, 4503
6:17 as *is* the **sin o**, and as the trespass offering. 2403
6:17 as *is* the sin offering, and as the **trespass o**. 817
6:20 This *is* the **o** of Aaron and of his sons, 7133
6:20 ephah of fine flour *for* a **meat o** perpetual, 4503
6:21 the baken pieces of the **meat o** shalt thou 4503
6:23 For every **meat o** for the priest shall be 4503
6:25 saying, This *is* the law of the **sin o**: 2403
6:25 In the place where the **burnt o** is killed 5930
6:25 shall the **sin o** be killed before the LORD: 2403
6:30 no **sin o**, whereof *any* of the blood is 2403
7: 1 Likewise this *is* the law of the **trespass o**: 817
7: 2 In the place where they kill the **burnt o** 5930
7: 2 burnt offering shall they kill the **trespass o**: 817
7: 5 altar *for* an **o made by fire** unto the LORD: 801
7: 5 by fire unto the LORD: it *is* a **trespass o**. 817
7: 7 As the **sin o** *is,* so *is* the trespass offering: 2403
7: 7 As the sin offering *is,* so *is* the **trespass o**: 817
7: 8 the priest that offereth *any* man's **burnt o**, 5930
7: 8 skin of the **burnt o** which he hath offered. 5930
7: 9 all the **meat o** that is baken in the oven, 4503
7:10 every **meat o**, mingled with oil, and dry, 4503
7:13 he shall offer *for* his **o** leavened bread with 7133
7:14 oblation *for* a **heave o** unto the LORD, 8641
7:16 if the sacrifice of his **o** *be* a vow, or 7133
7:16 of his offering *be* a vow, or a **voluntary o**, 5071
7:25 of which *men* offer an **o made by fire** unto 801
7:30 that the breast may be waved *for* a **wave o** 8573
7:32 **heave o** of the sacrifices of your peace 8641
7:37 This *is* the law of the **burnt o**, of the meat 5930
7:37 of the **meat o**, and of the sin offering, and 4503
7:37 of the **sin o**, and of the trespass offering, 2403
7:37 of the **trespass o**, and of the consecrations, 817
8: 2 a bullock *for* the **sin o**, and two rams, and 2403
8:14 he brought the bullock *for* the **sin o**: and 2403
8:14 upon the head of the bullock *for* the **sin o**. 2403
8:18 he brought the ram for the **burnt o**: and 5930
8:21 *and* an **o made by fire** unto the LORD; 801
8:27 waved them *for* a **wave o** before 8573
8:28 burnt *them* on the altar upon the **burnt o**: 5930
8:28 it *is* an **o made by fire** unto the LORD. 801
8:29 waved it *for* a **wave o** before the LORD: 8573
9: 2 Take thee a young calf for a **sin o**, and 2403
9: 2 a ram for a **burnt o**, without blemish, and 5930
9: 3 Take ye a kid of the goats for a **sin o**; 2403
9: 3 first year, without blemish, for a **burnt o**; 5930
9: 4 and a **meat o** mingled with oil: 4503
9: 7 offer thy **sin o**, and thy burnt offering, and 2403
9: 7 thy **burnt o**, and make an atonement for 5930
9: 7 offer the **o** of the people, and make an 7133
9: 8 unto the altar, and slew the calf of the **sin o**, 2403
9:10 and the caul above the liver of the **sin o**, 2403
9:12 he slew the **burnt o**; and Aaron's sons 5930
9:13 they presented the **burnt o** unto him, 5930
9:14 burnt *them* upon the **burnt o** on the altar. 5930
9:15 he brought the people's **o**, and took 7133
9:15 which *was* the **sin o** for the people, and 2403
9:16 he brought the **burnt o**, and offered it 5930
9:17 he brought the **meat o**, and took a handful 4503
9:21 waved *for* a **wave o** before the LORD; 8573
9:22 came down from **o** of the sin offering, and 6213
9:22 came down from offering of the **sin o**, and 2403
9:22 and the **burnt o**, and peace offerings. 5930
9:24 consumed upon the altar the **burnt o** and 5930
10:12 Take the **meat o** that remaineth of 4503
10:15 to wave *it for* a **wave o** before the LORD; 8573
10:16 diligently sought the goat of the **sin o**, 2403
10:17 Wherefore have ye not eaten the **sin o** in 2403
10:19 *this* day have they offered their **sin o** 2403
10:19 and their **burnt o** before the LORD; 5930
10:19 *if* I had eaten the **sin o** to day, should it 2403
12: 6 bring a lamb of the first year for a **burnt o**, 5930
12: 6 a young pigeon, or a turtledove, for a **sin o**, 2403
12: 8 the one for the **burnt o**, and the other for a 5930
12: 8 the burnt offering, and the other for a **sin o**: 2403

Lev 14:10 three tenth deals of fine flour *for* a **meat o**, 4503
14:12 offer him for a **trespass o**, and the log of oil, 817
14:12 wave them *for* a **wave o** before 8573
14:13 in the place where he shall kill the **sin o** 2403
14:13 shall kill the sin offering and the **burnt o**, 5930
14:13 for as the **sin o** *is* the priest's, *so is* 2403
14:13 offering *is* the priest's, *so is* the **trespass o**: 817
14:14 take *some* of the blood of the **trespass o**, 817
14:17 right foot, upon the blood of the **trespass o**: 817
14:19 the priest shall offer the **sin o**, and make an 2403
14:19 and afterward he shall kill the **burnt o**: 5930
14:20 the priest shall offer the **burnt o** and 5930
14:20 and the **meat o** upon the altar: 4503
14:21 he shall take one lamb *for* a **trespass o** to be 817
14:21 of fine flour mingled with oil for a **meat o**, 4503
14:22 the one shall be a **sin o**, and the other a 2403
14:22 be a sin offering, and the other a **burnt o**. 5930
14:24 priest shall take the lamb of the **trespass o**, 817
14:24 the priest shall wave them *for* a **wave o** 8573
14:25 And he shall kill the lamb of the **trespass o**, 817
14:25 take *some* of the blood of the **trespass o**, 817
14:28 the place of the blood of the **trespass o**: 817
14:31 the one *for* a **sin o**, and the other *for* a burnt 2403
14:31 the other *for* a **burnt o**, with the meat 5930
14:31 other *for* a burnt offering, with the **meat o**: 4503
15:15 the one *for* a **sin o**, and the other *for* a burnt 2403
15:15 a sin offering, and the other *for* a **burnt o**; 5930
15:30 the priest shall offer the one *for* a **sin o**, 2403
15:30 a sin offering, and the other *for* a **burnt o**; 5930
16: 3 *place:* with a young bullock for a **sin o**, 2403
16: 3 for a sin offering, and a ram for a **burnt o**. 5930
16: 5 of Israel two kids of the goats for a **sin o**, 2403
16: 5 a sin offering, and one ram for a **burnt o**. 5930
16: 6 Aaron shall offer *his* bullock of the **sin o**, 2403
16: 9 LORD'S lot fell, and offer him *for* a **sin o**. 2403
16:11 Aaron shall bring the bullock of the **sin o**, 2403
16:11 shall kill the bullock of the **sin o** which *is* 2403
16:15 shall he kill the goat of the **sin o**, that *is* for 2403
16:24 offer his **burnt o**, and the burnt offering of 5930
16:24 the **burnt o** of the people, and make an 5930
16:25 the fat of the **sin o** shall he burn upon 2403
16:27 the bullock for the **sin o**, and the goat for 2403
16:27 the sin offering, and the goat for the **sin o**, 2403
17: 4 to offer an **o** unto the LORD before 7133
17: 8 that offereth a **burnt o** or sacrifice, 5930
19:21 he shall bring his **trespass o** unto 817
19:21 *even* a ram for a **trespass o**. 817
19:22 **trespass o** before the LORD for his sin 817
22:12 she may not eat of an **o** of the holy *things*. 8641
22:18 will offer unto the LORD for a **burnt o**; 5930
22:21 or a **freewill o** in beeves or sheep, it shall 5071
22:22 nor make an **o by fire** of them upon the altar 801
22:23 that mayest thou offer *for* a **freewill o**; 5071
22:24 neither shall you make *any* **o** *thereof* in your NIH
22:27 an **o made by fire** unto the LORD. 801+7133
23: 8 ye shall offer an **o made by fire** unto 801
23:12 first year for a **burnt o** unto the LORD. 5930
23:13 the **meat o** thereof *shall be* two tenth deals 4503
23:13 an **o made by fire** unto the LORD *for* a 801
23:13 the **drink o** thereof *shall be of* wine, 5262
23:14 that ye have brought an **o** unto your God: 7133
23:15 day that ye brought the sheaf of the **wave o**; 8573
23:16 ye shall offer a new **meat o** unto 4503
23:18 they shall be *for* a **burnt o** unto 5930
23:18 with their **meat o**, and their drink offerings, 4503
23:18 drink offerings, *even* an **o made by fire**, 801
23:19 sacrifice one kid of the goats for a **sin o**, 2403
23:20 firstfruits *for* a **wave o** before the LORD, 8573
23:25 ye shall offer an **o made by fire** unto 801
23:27 offer an **o made by fire** unto the LORD. 801
23:36 Seven days ye shall offer an **o made by fire** 801
23:36 ye shall offer an **o made by fire** unto 801
23:37 to offer an **o made by fire** unto the LORD, 801
23:37 a **burnt o**, and a meat offering, a sacrifice, 5930
23:37 a **meat o**, a sacrifice, and drink offerings, 4503
24: 7 *even* an **o made by fire** unto the LORD. 801
27: 9 whereof *men* bring an **o** unto the LORD, 7133
Nu 4:16 the daily **meat o**, and the anointing oil, *and* 4503
5: 9 every **o** of all the holy *things* of the children 8641
5:15 he shall bring her **o** for her, the tenth *part* of 7133
5:15 for it *is* an **o** of jealousy, an offering of 4503
5:15 an offering of jealousy, an **o** of memorial, 4503
5:18 and put the **o** of memorial in her hands, 4503
5:18 in her hands, which *is* the jealousy **o**: 4503
5:25 the priest shall take the jealousy **o** out of 4503
5:25 shall wave the **o** before the LORD, and 4503
5:26 the priest shall take a handful of the **o**, *even* 4503
6:11 the priest shall offer the one for a **sin o**, 2403
6:11 the other for a **burnt o**, and make an 5930
6:12 a lamb of the first year for a **trespass o**: 817
6:14 he shall offer his **o** unto the LORD, one he 7133
6:14 the first year without blemish for a **burnt o**, 5930
6:14 of the first year without blemish for a **sin o**, 2403
6:15 and their **meat o**, and their drink offerings. 4503
6:16 shall offer his **sin o**, and his burnt offering: 2403
6:16 shall offer his sin offering, and his **burnt o**: 5930
6:17 the priest shall offer also his **meat o**, and 4503
6:17 also his meat offering, and his **drink o**. 5262
6:20 the priest shall wave them *for* a **wave o** 8573
6:21 *of* his **o** unto the LORD for his separation, 7133
7: 3 they brought their **o** before the LORD, 7133
7:10 even the princes offered their **o** before 7133
7:11 They shall offer their **o**, each prince on *his* 7133
7:12 he that offered his **o** the first day was 7133
7:13 his **o** *was* one silver charger, the weight 7133
7:13 *of* fine flour mingled with oil for a **meat o**: 4503
7:15 one lamb of the first year, for a **burnt o**: 5930
7:16 One kid of the goats for a **sin o**: 2403
7:17 this *was* the **o** of Nahshon the son of 7133
7:19 He offered *for* his **o** one silver charger, 7133
7:19 *of* fine flour mingled with oil for a **meat o**: 4503
7:21 one lamb of the first year, for a **burnt o**: 5930
7:22 One kid of the goats for a **sin o**: 2403
7:23 this *was* the **o** of Nethaneel the son of Zuar. 7133
7:25 His **o** *was* one silver charger, the weight 7133
7:25 *of* fine flour mingled with oil for a **meat o**: 4503
7:27 one lamb of the first year, for a **burnt o**: 5930
7:28 One kid of the goats for a **sin o**: 2403
7:29 this *was* the **o** of Eliab the son of Helon. 7133
7:31 His **o** *was* one silver charger of the weight 7133
7:31 *of* fine flour mingled with oil for a **meat o**: 4503
7:33 one lamb of the first year, for a **burnt o**: 5930
7:34 One kid of the goats for a **sin o**: 2403
7:35 this *was* the **o** of Elizur the son of Shedeur. 7133
7:37 His **o** *was* one silver charger, the weight 7133
7:37 *of* fine flour mingled with oil for a **meat o**: 4503
7:39 one lamb of the first year, for a **burnt o**: 5930
7:40 One kid of the goats for a **sin o**: 2403
7:41 this *was* the **o** of Shelumiel the son of 7133
7:43 His **o** *was* one silver charger of the weight 7133
7:43 *of* fine flour mingled with oil for a **meat o**: 4503
7:45 one lamb of the first year, for a **burnt o**: 5930
7:46 One kid of the goats for a **sin o**: 2403
7:47 this *was* the **o** of Eliasaph the son of Deuel. 7133
7:49 His **o** *was* one silver charger, the weight 7133
7:49 *of* fine flour mingled with oil for a **meat o**: 4503
7:51 one lamb of the first year, for a **burnt o**: 5930
7:52 One kid of the goats for a **sin o**: 2403
7:53 this *was* the **o** of Elishama the son of 7133
7:55 His **o** *was* one silver charger of the weight 7133
7:55 *of* fine flour mingled with oil for a **meat o**: 4503
7:57 one lamb of the first year, for a **burnt o**: 5930
7:58 One kid of the goats for a **sin o**: 2403
7:59 this *was* the **o** of Gamaliel the son of 7133
7:61 His **o** *was* one silver charger, the weight 7133
7:61 *of* fine flour mingled with oil for a **meat o**: 4503
7:63 one lamb of the first year, for a **burnt o**: 5930
7:64 One kid of the goats for a **sin o**: 2403
7:65 this *was* the **o** of Abidan the son of 7133
7:67 His **o** *was* one silver charger, the weight 7133
7:67 *of* fine flour mingled with oil for a **meat o**: 4503
7:69 one lamb of the first year, for a **burnt o**: 5930
7:70 One kid of the goats for a **sin o**: 2403
7:71 this *was* the **o** of Ahiezer the son of 7133
7:73 His **o** *was* one silver charger, the weight 7133
7:73 *of* fine flour mingled with oil for a **meat o**: 4503
7:75 one lamb of the first year, for a **burnt o**: 5930
7:76 One kid of the goats for a **sin o**: 2403
7:77 this *was* the **o** of Pagiel the son of Ocran. 7133
7:79 His **o** *was* one silver charger, the weight 7133
7:79 *of* fine flour mingled with oil for a **meat o**: 4503
7:81 one lamb of the first year, for a **burnt o**: 5930
7:82 One kid of the goats for a **sin o**: 2403
7:83 this *was* the **o** of Ahira the son of Enan. 7133
7:87 All the oxen for the **burnt o** *were* twelve 5930
7:87 of the first year twelve, with their **meat o**: 4503
7:87 and the kids of the goats for **sin o** twelve. 2403
8: 8 them take a young bullock with his **meat o**, 4503

Nu 8: 8 young bullock shalt thou take for a **sin o**. 2403
8:11 LORD *for* an **o** of the children of Israel, 8573
8:12 thou shalt offer the one *for* a **sin o**, and 2403
8:12 the other *for* a **burnt o**, unto the LORD, 5930
8:13 and offer them *for* an **o** unto the LORD. 8573
8:15 shalt cleanse them, and offer them *for* an **o**. 8573
8:21 Aaron offered them *as* an **o** before 8573
9: 7 that *we* may not offer an **o** of the LORD 7133
9:13 he brought not the **o** of the LORD in his 7133
15: 3 will make an **o by fire** unto the LORD, 801
15: 3 a **burnt o**, or a sacrifice in performing a 5930
15: 3 or in a **freewill o**, or in your solemn feasts, 5071
15: 4 shall he that offereth his **o** unto the LORD 7133
15: 4 **meat o** of a tenth deal *of* flour mingled 4503
15: 5 **drink o** shalt thou prepare with the burnt 5262
15: 5 offering shalt thou prepare with the **burnt o** 5930
15: 6 thou shalt prepare *for* a **meat o** two tenth 4503
15: 7 for a **drink o** thou shalt offer the third *part* 5262
15: 8 thou preparest a bullock *for* a **burnt o**, 5930
15: 9 shall he bring with a bullock a **meat o** of 4503
15:10 thou shalt bring for a **drink o** half a hin *of* 5262
15:10 *for* an **o made by fire**, of a sweet savour 801
15:13 in **o** an offering made by fire, of a sweet 7126
15:13 in offering an **o made by fire**, of a sweet 801
15:14 will offer an **o made by fire**, of a sweet 801
15:19 ye shall offer up a **heave o** unto 8641
15:20 *of* the first of your dough *for* a **heave o**: 8641
15:20 as *ye do* the **heave o** of the threshingfloor, 8641
15:21 the LORD a **heave o** in your generations. 8641
15:24 shall offer one young bullock for a **burnt o**, 5930
15:24 with his **meat o**, and his drink offering, 4503
15:24 with his meat offering, and his **drink o**, 5262
15:24 and one kid of the goats for a **sin o**. 2403
15:25 they shall bring their **o**, a sacrifice made by 7133
15:25 their **sin o** before the LORD, for their 2403
15:27 bring a she goat of the first year for a **sin o**. 2403
16:15 unto the LORD, Respect not thou their **o**: 4503
18: 9 every **meat o** of theirs, and every sin 4503
18: 9 every **sin o** of theirs, and every trespass 2403
18: 9 of theirs, and every **trespass o** of theirs, 817
18:11 the **heave o** of their gift, with all the wave 8641
18:17 shalt burn their fat *for* an **o made by fire**, 801
18:24 which they offer *as* a **heave o** unto 8641
18:26 ye shall offer up a **heave o** of it for 8641
18:27 *this* your **heave o** shall be reckoned unto 8641
18:28 Thus you also shall offer a **heave o** unto 8641
18:28 ye shall give thereof the LORD'S **heave o** 8641
18:29 ye shall offer every **heave o** of the LORD, 8641
23: 3 Stand by thy **burnt o**, and I will go: 5930
23:15 said unto Balak, Stand here by thy **burnt o**, 5930
23:17 he stood by his **burnt o**, and the princes of 5930
28: 2 My **o**, *and* my bread for my sacrifices made 7133
28: 3 This *is* the **o made by fire** which ye shall 801
28: 3 spot day by day, *for* a continual **burnt o**. 5930
28: 5 tenth *part* of an ephah *of* flour for a **meat o**, 4503
28: 6 *It is* a continual **burnt o**, which was 5930
28: 7 the **drink o** thereof *shall be* the fourth *part* 5262
28: 7 be poured unto the LORD *for* a **drink o**. 5262
28: 8 as the **meat o** of the morning, and as 4503
28: 8 of the morning, and as the **drink o** thereof, 5262
28: 9 two tenth deals *of* flour *for* a **meat o**, 4503
28: 9 mingled with oil, and the **drink o** thereof: 5262
28:10 *This is* the **burnt o** of every sabbath, beside 5930
28:10 beside the continual **burnt o**, and his drink 5930
28:10 continual burnt offering, and his **drink o**. 5262
28:11 ye shall offer a **burnt o** unto the LORD; 5930
28:12 three tenth deals *of* flour *for* a **meat o**, 4503
28:12 two tenth deals *of* flour *for* a **meat o**, 4503
28:13 with oil *for* a **meat o** unto one lamb; 4503
28:13 *for* a **burnt o** *of* a sweet savour, a sacrifice 5930
28:14 this *is* the **burnt o** of every month 5930
28:15 one kid of the goats for a **sin o** unto 2403
28:15 besides the continual **burnt o**, and his drink 5930
28:15 continual burnt offering, and his **drink o**. 5262
28:19 by fire *for* a **burnt o** unto the LORD; 5930
28:20 their **meat o** *shall be of* flour mingled with 4503
28:22 one goat for a **sin o**, to make an atonement 2403
28:23 Ye shall offer these beside the **burnt o** in 5930
28:23 which *is* for a continual **burnt o**. 5930
28:24 be offered beside the continual **burnt o**, 5930
28:24 continual burnt offering, and his **drink o**. 5262
28:26 when ye bring a new **meat o** unto 4503
28:27 ye shall offer the **burnt o** for a sweet 5930
28:28 their **meat o** *of* flour mingled with oil, 4503
28:31 offer *them* besides the continual **burnt o**, 5930
28:31 his **meat o**, (they shall be unto you without 4503
29: 2 ye shall offer a **burnt o** for a sweet savour 5930
29: 3 their **meat o** *shall be of* flour mingled with 4503
29: 5 one kid of the goats for a **sin o**, to make an 2403
29: 6 Beside the **burnt o** of the month, and 5930
29: 6 his **meat o**, and the daily burnt offering, 4503
29: 6 the daily **burnt o**, and his meat offering, 5930
29: 6 and his **meat o**, and their drink offerings, 4503
29: 8 ye shall offer a **burnt o** unto the LORD 5930
29: 9 their **meat o** *shall be of* flour mingled with 4503
29:11 One kid of the goats *for* a **sin o**; beside 2403
29:11 beside the **sin o** of atonement, and 2403
29:11 the continual **burnt o**, and the meat 5930
29:11 the **meat o** of it, and their drink offerings. 4503
29:13 ye shall offer a **burnt o**, a sacrifice made 5930
29:14 their **meat o** *shall be of* flour mingled with 4503
29:16 one kid of the goats *for* a **sin o**; beside 2403
29:16 beside the continual **burnt o**, his meat 5930
29:16 his **meat o**, and his drink offering. 4503
29:16 his meat offering, and his **drink o**. 5262
29:18 their **meat o** and their drink offerings for 4503
29:19 one kid of the goats *for* a **sin o**; beside 2403
29:19 beside the continual **burnt o**, and the meat 5930
29:19 the **meat o** thereof, and their drink 4503
29:21 their **meat o** and their drink offerings for 4503
29:22 one goat for a **sin o**; beside the continual 2403
29:22 beside the continual **burnt o**, and his meat 5930
29:22 and his **meat o**, and his drink offering. 4503
29:22 and his meat offering, and his **drink o**. 5262
29:24 Their **meat o** and their drink offerings for 4503
29:25 one kid of the goats *for* a **sin o**; beside 2403
29:25 beside the continual **burnt o**, his meat 5930
29:25 his **meat o**, and his drink offering. 4503
29:25 his meat offering, and his **drink o**. 5262
29:27 their **meat o** and their drink offerings for 4503
29:28 one goat for a **sin o**; beside the continual 2403
29:28 beside the continual **burnt o**, and his meat 5930
29:28 and his **meat o**, and his drink offering. 4503
29:28 and his meat offering, and his **drink o**. 5262
29:30 their **meat o** and their drink offerings for 4503
29:31 one goat for a **sin o**; beside the continual 2403
29:31 beside the continual **burnt o**, his meat 5930
29:31 his **meat o**, and his drink offering. 4503
29:31 his meat offering, and his **drink o**. 5262
29:33 their **meat o** and their drink offerings for 4503
29:34 one goat for a **sin o**; beside the continual 2403
29:34 beside the continual **burnt o**, his meat 5930
29:34 his **meat o**, and his drink offering. 4503
29:34 his meat offering, and his **drink o**. 5262
29:36 ye shall offer a **burnt o**, a sacrifice made 5930
29:37 Their **meat o** and their drink offerings for 4503
29:38 one goat for a **sin o**; beside the continual 2403
29:38 beside the continual **burnt o**, and his meat 5930
29:38 and his **meat o**, and his drink offering. 4503
29:38 and his meat offering, and his **drink o**. 5262
31:29 the priest, *for* a **heave o** of the LORD. 8641
31:41 *which was* the LORD'S **heave o**, 8641
31:52 all the gold of the **o** that they offered up to 8641
Dt 12:11 the **heave o** of your hand, and all your 8641
12:17 freewill offerings, or **heave o** of thine hand: 8641
16:10 *with* a tribute of a **freewill o** of thine hand, 5071
23:23 *even* a **freewill o**, according as thou hast 5071
Jos 22:23 or if to offer thereon **burnt o** or 5930
22:23 if to offer thereon burnt offering or **meat o**, 4503
22:26 an altar, not for **burnt o**, nor for sacrifice: 5930
Jdg 11:31 and I will offer it up *for* a **burnt o**. 5930
13:16 if thou wilt offer a **burnt o**, thou must offer 5930
13:19 So Manoah took a kid with a **meat o**, and 4503
13:23 he would not have received a **burnt o** and 5930
13:23 a burnt offering and a **meat o** at our hands, 4503
1Sa 2:17 for men abhorred the **o** of the LORD. 4503
2:29 kick ye at my sacrifice and at mine **o**, 4503
3:14 not be purged with sacrifice nor **o** for ever. 4503
6: 3 but in any wise return him a **trespass o**: 817
6: 4 What *shall be* the **trespass o** which we shall 817
6: 8 which ye return him *for* a **trespass o**, 817
6:14 offered the kine a **burnt o** unto 5930
6:17 returned *for* a **trespass o** unto the LORD; 817
7: 9 offered it *for* a **burnt o** wholly unto 5930
7:10 And as Samuel was **o up** the burnt offering, 5927
7:10 as Samuel was offering up the **burnt o**, 5930
13: 9 Bring hither a **burnt o** to me, and peace 5930
13: 9 And he offered the **burnt o**. 5930

O

1Sa 13:10 that as soon as he had made an end of **o** 5927
13:10 had made an end of offering the **burnt o**, 5930
13:12 myself therefore, and offered a **burnt o**. 5930
26:19 thee up against me, let him accept an **o**: 4503
2Sa 6:18 as soon as David had made an end of **o** 5927
1Ki 18:29 they prophesied until *the time* of the **o** of 5927
18:36 it came to pass at *the time of* the **o** of 5927
2Ki 3:20 when the **meat o** was offered, that behold, 4503
3:27 offered him *for* a **burnt o** upon the wall. 5930
5:17 **burnt o** nor sacrifice unto other gods, 5930
10:25 as soon as he had made an end of **o** 6213
10:25 had made an end of offering the **burnt o**, 5930
16:13 he burnt his **burnt o** and his meat offering, 5930
16:13 he burnt his burnt offering and his **meat o**, 4503
16:13 poured his **drink o**, and sprinkled the blood 5262
16:15 the great altar burn the morning **burnt o**, 5930
16:15 the evening **meat o**, and the king's burnt 4503
16:15 the king's burnt sacrifice, and his **meat o**, 4503
16:15 with the **burnt o** of all the people of 5930
16:15 and their **meat o**, and their drink offerings; 4503
16:15 upon it all the blood of the **burnt o**, 5930
1Ch 6:49 sons offered upon the altar of the **burnt o**, 5930
16: 2 when David had made an end of **o** the burnt 5927
16:29 bring an **o**, and come before him: 4503
16:40 altar of the **burnt o** continually morning 5930
21:23 for wood, and the wheat for the **meat o**; 4503
21:26 heaven by fire upon the altar of **burnt o**. 5930
21:29 the wilderness, and the altar of the **burnt o**, 5930
22: 1 this *is* the altar of the **burnt o** for Israel. 5930
23:29 for the fine flour for **meat o**, and for 4503
2Ch 4: 6 such things as they offered for the **burnt o** 5930
7: 1 consumed the **burnt o** and the sacrifices; 5930
8:13 **o** according to the commandment of Moses, 5927
29:18 the altar of **burnt o**, with all the vessels 5930
29:21 for a **sin o** for the kingdom, and for 2403
29:23 they brought forth the he goats for the **sin o** 2403
29:24 for the king commanded *that* the **burnt o** 5930
29:24 and the **sin o** *should be made* for all Israel. 2403
29:27 Hezekiah commanded to offer the **burnt o** 5930
29:27 when the **burnt o** began, the song of 5930
29:28 all *this continued* until the **burnt o** was 5930
29:29 when *they* had made an end of **o**, the king 5927
29:32 all these *were* for a **burnt o** to the LORD. 5930
29:35 and the drink offerings for *every* **burnt o**. 5930
30:22 **o** peace offerings, and making confession 2076
35:14 Aaron *were busied* in **o** of burnt offerings 5927
Ezr 1: 4 besides the **freewill o** for the house of God 5071
3: 5 afterward *offered* the continual **burnt o**, 5930
3: 5 offered a **freewill o** unto the LORD. 5071
6:17 for a **sin o** for all Israel, twelve he goats, 2409
7:16 with the **freewill o** of the people, and of 5069
7:16 **o willingly** for the house of their God 5069
8:25 *even* the **o** of the house of our God, 8641
8:28 the gold *are* a **freewill o** unto the LORD 5071
8:35 seven lambs, twelve he goats *for* a **sin o**: 2403
8:35 all *this was* a **burnt o** unto the LORD. 5930
Ne 10:33 *for* the continual **meat o**, and for 4503
10:33 for the continual **burnt o**, of the sabbaths, 5930
10:34 the Levites, and the people, for the wood **o**, 7133
10:39 the children of Levi shall bring the **o** of 8641
13: 9 with the **meat o** and the frankincense. 4503
13:31 for the wood **o**, at times appointed, and 7133
Job 42: 8 and offer up for yourselves a **burnt o**; 5930
Ps 40: 6 Sacrifice and **o** thou didst not desire; mine 4503
40: 6 **burnt o** and sin offering hast thou not 5930
40: 6 and **sin o** hast thou not required. 2401
51:16 I give *it:* thou delightest not in **burnt o**. 5930
51:19 with **burnt o** and whole *burnt offering:* 5930
51:19 with burnt offering and whole *burnt o*: then NIH
96: 8 bring an **o**, and come into his courts. 4503
Isa 40:16 the beasts thereof sufficient *for* a **burnt o**. 5930
43:23 I have not caused thee to serve with an **o**, 4503
53:10 when thou shalt make his soul an **o for sin**, 817
57: 6 even to them hast thou poured a **drink o**, 5262
57: 6 drink offering, thou hast offered a **meat o**. 4503
61: 8 love judgment, I hate robbery for **burnt o**; 5930
65:11 that furnish the **drink o** unto *that* number. 4469
66:20 they shall bring all your brethren *for* an **o** 4503
66:20 as the children of Israel bring an **o** in a 4503
Jer 11:17 me to anger in **o incense** unto Baal. 6999
14:12 when they offer **burnt o** and an oblation, 5930
Eze 20:28 they presented the provocation of their **o**: 7133
40:38 the gates, where they washed the **burnt o**. 5930
40:39 to slay thereon the **burnt o** and the sin 5930
40:39 and the **sin o** and the trespass offering. 2403
40:39 and the sin offering and the **trespass o**. 817
40:42 tables *were* of hewn stone for the **burnt o**, 5930
40:42 wherewith they slew the **burnt o** 5930
40:43 upon the tables *was* the flesh of the **o**. 7133
42:13 lay the most holy *things,* and the **meat o**, 4503
42:13 and the **sin o**, and the trespass offering; 2403
42:13 and the sin offering, and the **trespass o**; 817
43:19 Lord GOD, a young bullock for a **sin o**. 2403
43:21 shalt take the bullock also of the **sin o**, 2403
43:22 kid of the goats without blemish for a **sin o**; 2403
43:24 they shall offer them up *for* a **burnt o** unto 5930
43:25 thou prepare every day a goat *for* a **sin o**: 2403
44:11 they shall slay the **burnt o** and the sacrifice 5930
44:27 he shall offer his **sin o**, saith the Lord 2403
44:29 They shall eat the **meat o**, and the sin 4503
44:29 and the **sin o**, and the trespass offering; 2403
44:29 and the sin offering, and the **trespass o**; 817
45:15 for a **meat o**, and for a burnt offering, and 4503
45:15 and for a **burnt o**, and for peace offerings, 5930
45:17 he shall prepare the **sin o**, and the meat 2403
45:17 the **meat o**, and the burnt offering, and 4503
45:17 and the **burnt o**, and the peace offerings, 5930
45:19 priest shall take of the blood of the **sin o**, 2403
45:22 the people of the land a bullock *for* a **sin o**. 2403
45:23 he shall prepare a **burnt o** to the LORD, 5930
45:23 and a kid of the goats daily *for* a **sin o**. 2403
45:24 he shall prepare a **meat o** *of* an ephah for a 4503
45:25 according to the **sin o**, according to 2403
45:25 according to the **burnt o**, and according to 5930
45:25 according to the **meat o**, and according to 4503
46: 2 the priests shall prepare his **burnt o** and 5930
46: 4 the **burnt o** that the prince shall offer unto 5930
46: 5 the **meat o** *shall be* an ephah for a ram, 4503
46: 5 the **meat o** for the lambs as he shall be able 4503
46: 7 he shall prepare a **meat o**, an ephah for a 4503
46:11 in the solemnities the **meat o** shall be an 4503
46:12 the prince shall prepare a voluntary **burnt o** 5930
46:12 he shall prepare his **burnt o** and his peace 5930
46:13 Thou shalt daily prepare a **burnt o** unto 5930
46:14 thou shalt prepare a **meat o** for it every 4503
46:14 a **meat o** continually *by* a perpetual 4503
46:15 the lamb, and the **meat o**, and the oil, 4503
46:15 every morning *for* a continual **burnt o**. 5930
46:20 where the priests shall boil the **trespass o** 817
46:20 boil the trespass offering and the **sin o**, 2403
46:20 where they shall bake the **meat o**; 4503
48: 8 shall be the **o** which ye shall offer *of* five 8641
Joel 1: 9 The **meat o** and the drink offering is cut off 4503
1: 9 the **drink o** is cut off from the house of 5262
1:13 for the **meat o** and the drink offering is 4503
1:13 the **drink o** is withholden from the house 5262
2:14 *even* a **meat o** and a drink offering unto 4503
2:14 and a **drink o** unto the LORD your God? 5262
Zep 3:10 of my dispersed, shall bring mine **o**. 4503
Mal 1:10 neither will I accept an **o** at your hand. 4503
1:11 *be* offered unto my name, and a pure **o**: 4503
1:13 and the sick; thus ye brought an **o**: 4503
2:12 him that offereth an **o** unto the LORD of 4503
2:13 insomuch that *he* regardeth not the **o** any 4503
3: 3 that they may offer unto the LORD an **o** in 4503
3: 4 shall the **o** of Judah and Jerusalem be 4503
Lk 23:36 coming to *him,* and **o** him vinegar, *4374*
Ac 21:26 until that an **o** should be offered for every *4376*
Ro 15:16 that the **o up** of the Gentiles might be *4376*
Eph 5: 2 and hath given himself for us an **o** and *4376*
Heb 10: 5 Sacrifice and **o** thou wouldest not, but *4376*
10: 8 Sacrifice and **o** and burnt offerings and *4376*
10: 8 and *o* for sin thou wouldest not, NIG
10:10 **o** of the body of Jesus Christ once for all. *4376*
10:11 and **o** oftentimes the same sacrifices, *4374*
10:14 For by one **o** he hath perfected for ever *4376*
10:18 of these *is, there is* no more **o** for sin. *4376*

OFFERINGS (265) [OFFER]

Ge 8:20 and offered **burnt o** on the altar. 5930
Ex 10:25 must give us also sacrifices and **burnt o**, 5930
20:24 shalt sacrifice thereon thy **burnt o**, and thy 5930
20:24 and thy **peace o**, thy sheep, and thine oxen: 8002
24: 5 which offered **burnt o**, and 5930
24: 5 sacrificed peace **o** *of* oxen unto 2077
29:28 of Israel of the sacrifice of their **peace o**, 8002
32: 6 offered **burnt o**, and brought peace 5930
32: 6 burnt offerings, and brought **peace o**; 8002

O

Ex	36: 3	brought yet unto him **free o** every morning.	5071
Lev	2: 3	holy of the **o** of the LORD **made by fire**.	801
	2:10	holy of the **o** of the LORD **made by fire**.	801
	2:13	with all thine **o** thou shalt offer salt.	7133
	4:10	the bullock of the sacrifice of **peace o**:	8002
	4:26	as the fat of the sacrifice of **peace o**:	8002
	4:31	away from off the sacrifice of **peace o**;	8002
	4:35	away from the sacrifice of the **peace o**;	8002
	4:35	according to the **o made by fire** unto	801
	5:12	according to the **o made by fire** unto	801
	6:12	he shall burn thereon the fat of the **peace o**.	8002
	6:17	*them for* their portion of my **o made by fire**;	801
	6:18	the **o** of the LORD **made by fire**:	801
	7:11	this *is* the law of the sacrifice of **peace o**,	8002
	7:13	the sacrifice of thanksgiving of his **peace o**.	8002
	7:14	that sprinkleth the blood of the **peace o**.	8002
	7:15	the flesh of the sacrifice of his **peace o** for	8002
	7:18	his **peace o** be eaten at all on the third day,	8002
	7:20	*of* the flesh of the sacrifice of **peace o**,	8002
	7:21	eat of the flesh of the sacrifice of **peace o**,	8002
	7:29	He that offereth the sacrifice of his **peace o**	8002
	7:29	the LORD of the sacrifice of his **peace o**.	8002
	7:30	bring the **o** of the LORD **made by fire**,	801
	7:32	offering of the sacrifices of your **peace o**.	8002
	7:33	that offereth the blood of the **peace o**, and	8002
	7:34	from off the sacrifices of their **peace o**,	8002
	7:35	out of the **o** of the LORD **made by fire**,	801
	7:37	and of the sacrifice of the **peace o**;	8002
	9: 4	Also a bullock and a ram for **peace o**,	8002
	9:18	and the ram *for* a sacrifice of **peace o**,	8002
	9:22	and the burnt offering, and **peace o**.	8002
	10:12	of the **o** of the LORD **made by fire**,	801
	10:14	of **peace o** of the children of Israel.	8002
	10:15	they bring with the **o made by fire** of the fat,	801
	17: 5	offer them *for* peace **o** unto the LORD.	2077
	19: 5	if ye offer a sacrifice of **peace o** unto	8002
	21: 6	for the **o** of the LORD **made by fire**, *and*	801
	21:21	to offer the **o** of the LORD **made by fire**:	801
	22:18	for all his vows, and for all his **freewill o**,	5071
	22:21	whosoever offereth a sacrifice of **peace o**	8002
	23:18	with their meat offering, and their **drink o**,	5262
	23:19	of the first year for a sacrifice of **peace o**.	8002
	23:37	a meat offering, a sacrifice, and **drink o**,	5262
	23:38	your vows, and beside all your **freewill o**,	5071
	24: 9	him of the **o** of the LORD **made by fire**,	801
Nu	6:14	and one ram without blemish for **peace o**,	8002
	6:15	and their meat offering, and their **drink o**.	5262
	6:17	*for* a sacrifice of **peace o** unto the LORD,	8002
	6:18	which *is* under the sacrifice of the **peace o**.	8002
	7:17	for a sacrifice of **peace o**, two oxen,	8002
	7:23	for a sacrifice of **peace o**, two oxen,	8002
	7:29	for a sacrifice of **peace o**, two oxen,	8002
	7:35	for a sacrifice of **peace o**, two oxen,	8002
	7:41	for a sacrifice of **peace o**, two oxen,	8002
	7:47	for a sacrifice of **peace o**, two oxen,	8002
	7:53	for a sacrifice of **peace o**, two oxen,	8002
	7:59	for a sacrifice of **peace o**, two oxen,	8002
	7:65	for a sacrifice of **peace o**, two oxen,	8002
	7:71	for a sacrifice of **peace o**, two oxen,	8002
	7:77	for a sacrifice of **peace o**, two oxen,	8002
	7:83	for a sacrifice of **peace o**, two oxen,	8002
	7:88	all the oxen for the sacrifice of the **peace o**	8002
	10:10	blow with the trumpets over your **burnt o**,	5930
	10:10	and over the sacrifices of your **peace o**;	8002
	15: 8	a vow, or **peace o** unto the LORD:	8002
	18: 8	**heave o** of all the hallowed *things* of	8641
	18:11	with all the **wave o** of the children of Israel:	8573
	18:19	All the **heave o** of the holy *things*, which	8641
	28:14	their **drink o** shall be half a hin of wine	5262
	28:31	you without blemish) and their **drink o**.	5262
	29: 6	and his meat offering, and their **drink o**,	5262
	29:11	the meat offering of it, and their **drink o**.	5262
	29:18	and their **drink o** for the bullocks,	5262
	29:19	meat offering thereof, and their **drink o**.	5262
	29:21	and their **drink o** for the bullocks,	5262
	29:24	and their **drink o** for the bullocks,	5262
	29:27	and their **drink o** for the bullocks,	5262
	29:30	and their **drink o** for the bullocks,	5262
	29:33	and their **drink o** for the bullocks,	5262
	29:37	and their **drink o** for the bullock,	5262
	29:39	besides your vows, and your **freewill o**,	5071
	29:39	for your **burnt o**, and for your meat	5930
	29:39	for your **meat o**, and for your drink	4503
	29:39	for your **drink o**, and for your peace	5262
	29:39	your drink offerings, and for your **peace o**.	8002
Dt	12: 6	thither ye shall bring your **burnt o**, and	5930
	12: 6	**heave o** of your hand, and your vows, and	8641
	12: 6	your **freewill o**, and the firstlings of your	5071
	12:11	your **burnt o**, and your sacrifices,	5930
	12:13	thy **burnt o** in every place that thou seest:	5930
	12:14	there thou shalt offer thy **burnt o**, and	5930
	12:17	nor thy **freewill o**, or heave offering of	5071
	12:27	thou shalt offer thy **burnt o**, the flesh and	5930
	18: 1	shall eat the **o** of the LORD **made by fire**,	801
	27: 6	thou shalt offer **burnt o** thereon unto	5930
	27: 7	thou shalt offer **peace o**, and shalt eat there,	8002
	32:38	*and* drank the wine of their **drink o**?	5257
Jos	8:31	they offered thereon **burnt o** unto	5930
	8:31	unto the LORD, and sacrificed **peace o**.	8002
	22:23	or if to offer peace **o** thereon,	2077
	22:27	the LORD before him with our **burnt o**,	5930
	22:27	with our sacrifices, and with our **peace o**;	8002
	22:28	not for **burnt o**, nor for sacrifices;	5930
	22:29	to build an altar for **burnt o**, for meat	5930
	22:29	for **meat o**, or for sacrifices,	4503
Jdg	20:26	offered **burnt o** and peace offerings before	5930
	20:26	and **peace o** before the LORD.	8002
	21: 4	and offered **burnt o** and peace offerings.	5930
	21: 4	and offered burnt offerings and **peace o**.	8002
1Sa	2:28	the **o made by fire** of the children of Israel?	801
	2:29	the chiefest of all the **o** of Israel my people?	4503
	6:15	the men of Beth-shemesh offered **burnt o**	5930
	10: 8	to offer **burnt o**, *and* to sacrifice sacrifices	5930
	10: 8	*and* to sacrifice sacrifices of **peace o**:	8002
	11:15	there they sacrificed sacrifices *of* **peace o**	8002
	13: 9	hither a burnt offering to me, and **peace o**.	8002
	15:22	the LORD *as great* delight in **burnt o**	5930
2Sa	1:21	*let there be* rain upon you, nor fields of **o**:	8641
	6:17	David offered **burnt o** and peace offerings	5930
	6:17	and **peace o** before the LORD.	8002
	6:18	David had made an end of offering **burnt o**	5930
	6:18	end of offering burnt offerings and **peace o**,	8002
	24:24	neither will I offer **burnt o** unto	5930
	24:25	and offered **burnt o** and peace offerings.	5930
	24:25	and offered burnt offerings and **peace o**.	8002
1Ki	3: 4	a thousand **burnt o** did Solomon offer up	5930
	3:15	offered up **burnt o**, and offered peace	5930
	3:15	offered **peace o**, and made a feast to all his	8002
	8:63	Solomon offered a sacrifice of **peace o**,	8002
	8:64	for there he offered **burnt o**, and meat	5930
	8:64	**meat o**, and the fat of the peace offerings:	4503
	8:64	meat offerings, and the fat of the **peace o**:	8002
	8:64	*was* too little to receive the **burnt o**,	5930
	8:64	**meat o**, and the fat of the peace offerings.	4503
	8:64	meat offerings, and the fat of the **peace o**.	8002
	9:25	times in a year did Solomon offer **burnt o**	5930
	9:25	**peace o** upon the altar which he built unto	8002
2Ki	10:24	they went in to offer sacrifices and **burnt o**,	5930
	16:13	sprinkled the blood of his **peace o**, upon	8002
	16:15	and their meat offering, and their **drink o**;	5262
1Ch	16: 1	burnt sacrifices and **peace o** before God.	8002
	16: 2	had made an end of offering the **burnt o**	5930
	16: 2	the burnt offerings and the **peace o**,	8002
	16:40	To offer **burnt o** unto the LORD upon	5930
	21:23	lo, I give *thee* the oxen *also* for **burnt o**,	5930
	21:24	the LORD, nor offer **burnt o** without cost.	5930
	21:26	offered **burnt o** and peace offerings, and	5930
	21:26	offered burnt offerings and **peace o**, and	8002
	29:21	offered **burnt o** unto the LORD, on	5930
	29:21	with their **drink o**, and sacrifices in	5262
2Ch	1: 6	and offered a thousand **burnt o** upon it.	5930
	2: 4	*for* the **burnt o** morning and evening,	5930
	7: 7	for there he offered **burnt o**, and the fat of	5930
	7: 7	the fat of the **peace o**, because the brasen	8002
	7: 7	made was not able to receive the **burnt o**,	5930
	7: 7	burnt offerings, and the **meat o**, and the fat.	4503
	8:12	Solomon offered **burnt o** unto the LORD	5930
	23:18	to offer the **burnt o** of the LORD, as it is	5930
	24:14	they offered **burnt o** in the house of	5930
	29: 7	have not burnt incense nor offered **burnt o**	5930
	29:31	and **thank o** into the house of the LORD.	8426
	29:31	brought in sacrifices and **thank o**;	8426
	29:31	as many as were of a free heart **burnt o**.	5930
	29:32	the number of the **burnt o**, which	5930
	29:34	so that they could not flay all the **burnt o**:	5930
	29:35	also the **burnt o** *were* in abundance,	5930
	29:35	with the fat of the **peace o**, and the drink	8002
	29:35	and the **drink o** for *every* burnt offering.	5262

2Ch 30:15 brought in the **burnt o** *into* the house of 5930
30:22 offering peace **o**, and making confession to 2077
31: 2 the priests and Levites for **burnt o** and 5930
31: 2 Levites for burnt offerings and for **peace o**, 8002
31: 3 portion of his substance for the **burnt o**, 5930
31: 3 *wit,* for the morning and evening **burnt o**, 5930
31: 3 the **burnt o** for the sabbaths, and for 5930
31:10 Since *the people* began to bring the **o** *into* 8641
31:12 brought in the **o** and the tithes and 8641
31:14 the east, *was* over the **freewill o** of God, 5071
33:16 sacrificed thereon peace **o** and 2077
33:16 thereon peace offerings and **thank o**, 8426
35: 7 all for the passover *o*, for all that were NIH
35: 8 gave unto the priests for the passover *o* two NIH
35: 9 gave unto the Levites for passover *o* five NIH
35:12 they removed the **burnt o**, that they might 5930
35:13 the *other* holy *o* sod they in pots, and NIH
35:14 Aaron *were busied* in offering of **burnt o** 5930
35:16 to offer **burnt o** upon the altar of 5930
Ezr 3: 2 God of Israel, to offer **burnt o** thereon, 5930
3: 3 they offered **burnt o** thereon unto 5930
3: 3 *even* **burnt o** morning and evening. 5930
3: 4 and *offered* the daily **burnt o** by number, 5930
3: 6 they to offer **burnt o** unto the LORD. 5930
6: 9 for the **burnt o** of the God of heaven, 5928
7:17 with their **meat o** and their drink offerings, 4504
7:17 with their meat offerings and their **drink o**, 5261
8:35 offered **burnt o** unto the God of Israel, 5930
Ne 10:33 for the **sin o** to make an atonement for 2403
10:37 our **o**, and the fruit of all *manner of* trees, 8641
12:44 for the **o**, for the firstfruits, and for 8641
13: 5 where aforetime they laid the **meat o**, 4503
13: 5 and the porters; and the **o** of the priests. 8641
Job 1: 5 offered **burnt o** *according to* the number of 5930
Ps 16: 4 *god:* their **drink o** of blood will I not offer, 5262
20: 3 Remember all thy **o**, and accept thy burnt 4503
50: 8 thee for thy sacrifices or thy **burnt o**, 5930
66:13 I will go *into* thy house with **burnt o**: I will 5930
119:108 the **freewill o** of my mouth, O LORD, and 5071
Pr 7:14 *I have* peace **o** with me; *this* day have I 2077
Isa 1:11 I am full *of* the **burnt o** of rams, and the fat 5930
43:23 brought me the small cattle of thy **burnt o**; 5930
56: 7 their **burnt o** and their sacrifices *shall be* 5930
Jer 6:20 your **burnt o** *are* not acceptable, nor your 5930
7:18 to pour out **drink o** unto other gods, that 5262
7:21 Put your **burnt o** unto your sacrifices, and 5930
7:22 of Egypt, concerning **burnt o** or sacrifices: 5930
17:26 bringing **burnt o**, and sacrifices, and 5930
17:26 **meat o**, and incense, and 4503
19: 5 to burn their sons with fire *for* **burnt o** unto 5930
19:13 have poured out **drink o** unto other gods. 5262
32:29 poured out **drink o** unto other gods, 5262
33:18 want a man before me to offer **burnt o**, 5930
33:18 to kindle **meat o**, and to do sacrifice 4503
41: 5 with **o** and incense in their hand, 4503
44:17 to pour out **drink o** unto her, as we have 5262
44:18 to pour out **drink o** unto her, we have 5262
44:19 poured out **drink o** unto her, did we make 5262
44:19 pour out **drink o** unto her, without our 5262
44:25 and to pour out **drink o** unto her: 5262
Eze 20:28 and poured out there their **drink o**. 5262
20:40 there will I require your **o**, and 8641
43:18 to offer **burnt o** thereon, and to sprinkle 5930
43:27 the priests shall make your **burnt o** upon 5930
43:27 offerings upon the altar, and your **peace o**; 8002
45:15 and for a burnt offering, and for **peace o**, 8002
45:17 it shall be the prince's part *to give* **burnt o**, 5930
45:17 **meat o**, and drink offerings, in the feasts, 4503
45:17 **drink o**, in the feasts, and in the new 5262
45:17 and the burnt offering, and the **peace o**, 8002
46: 2 prepare his burnt offering and his **peace o**, 8002
46:12 or **peace o** voluntarily unto the LORD, 8002
46:12 prepare his burnt offering and his **peace o**, 8002
Hos 6: 6 the knowledge of God more than **burnt o**. 5930
8:13 sacrifice flesh *for* the sacrifices of mine **o**, 1890
9: 4 They shall not offer wine *o* to the LORD, NIH
Am 4: 5 and proclaim *and* publish the **free o**: 5071
5:22 Though ye offer me **burnt o** and your meat 5930
5:22 offer me burnt offerings and your **meat o**, 4503
5:22 will I regard the **peace o** of your fat beasts. 8002
5:25 and **o** in the wilderness forty years, 4503
Mic 6: 6 shall I come before him with **burnt o**, 5930
Mal 3: 8 have we robbed thee? *In* tithes and **o**. 8641
Mk 12:33 is more than all **whole burnt o** and *3646*
Lk 21: 4 their abundance cast in unto the **o** of God: *1435*
Ac 24:17 I came to bring alms to my nation, and **o**. *4376*
Heb 10: 6 In **burnt o** and *sacrifices* for sin thou hast *3646*
10: 8 Sacrifice and offering and **burnt o** and *3646*

OFFICE (46) [OFFICER, OFFICERS, OFFICES]

Ge 41:13 me he restored unto mine **o**, and him he 3653
Ex 1:16 When ye **do the o of a midwife** to 3205
28: 1 he may **minister** unto me **in the priest's o**, 3547
28: 3 he may **minister** unto me **in the priest's o**. 3547
28: 4 he may **minister** unto me **in the priest's o**. 3547
28:41 may **minister** unto me **in the priest's o**. 3547
29: 1 to **minister** unto me **in the priest's o**: 3547
29: 9 the **priest's o** shall be theirs for a perpetual 3550
29:44 to **minister** to me **in the priest's o**. 3547
30:30 may **minister** unto me **in the priest's o**. 3547
31:10 of his sons, to **minister in the priest's o**, 3547
35:19 of his sons, to **minister in the priest's o**. 3547
39:41 to **minister in the priest's o**. 3547
40:13 he may **minister** unto me **in the priest's o**. 3547
40:15 may **minister** unto me **in the priest's o**: 3547
Lev 7:35 **minister** unto the LORD **in the priest's o**; 3547
16:32 **minister in the priest's o** in his father's 3547
Nu 3: 3 consecrated to **minister in the priest's o**. 3547
3: 4 Ithamar **ministered in the priest's o** in 3547
3:10 and they shall wait on their **priest's o**: 3550
4:16 *to* the **o** of Eleazar the son of Aaron 6486
18: 7 your **priest's o** for every thing of the altar, 3550
18: 7 I have given your **priest's o** *unto you as* a 3550
Dt 10: 6 **ministered in the priest's o** in his stead. 3547
1Ch 6:10 (he *it is* that **executed the priest's o** in 3547
6:32 they waited on their **o** according to their 5656
9:22 and Samuel the seer did ordain in their **set o**. 530
9:26 *were* in *their* **set o**, and were over 530
9:31 had the **set o** over the things that were made 530
23:28 Because their **o** *was* to wait on the sons of 4612
24: 2 and Ithamar **executed the priest's o**. 3547
2Ch 11:14 **executing the priest's o** unto the LORD: 3547
24:11 the king's **o** by the hand of the Levites, 6486
31:15 in the cities of the priests, in *their* **set o**, 530
31:18 for in their **set o** they sanctified themselves 530
Ne 13:13 their **o** *was* to distribute unto their brethren. 5921
Ps 109: 8 his days be few; *and* let another take his **o**. 6486
Eze 44:13 unto me, to **do the o of a priest** unto me, 3547
Lk 1: 8 *that* while he **executed the priest's o** *2407*
1: 9 According to the custom of the **priest's o**, *2405*
Ro 11:13 apostle of the Gentiles, I magnify mine **o**: *1248*
12: 4 and all members have not the same **o**: *4234*
1Ti 3: 1 If a man desire the **o of a bishop**, *1984*
3:10 then let them **use the o of a deacon**, *1247*
3:13 For they that have **used the o of a deacon** *1247*
Heb 7: 5 **o of** the **priesthood** have a commandment *2405*

OFFICER (12) [OFFICE]

Ge 37:36 an **o** of Pharaoh's, *and* captain of the guard. 5631
39: 1 Potiphar, an **o** of Pharaoh, captain of 5631
Jdg 9:28 Zebul his **o**? serve the men of Hamor 6496
1Ki 4: 5 Zabud the son of Nathan *was* **principal o**, 3548
4:19 *he was* the only **o** which *was* in the land. 5333
22: 9 the king of Israel called an **o**, and said, 5631
2Ki 8: 6 So the king appointed unto her a certain **o**, 5631
25:19 out of the city he took an **o** that was set 5631
2Ch 24:11 and the high priest's **o** came and 6496
Mt 5:25 and the judge deliver thee to the **o**, and *5257*
Lk 12:58 and the judge deliver thee to the **o**, and *4233*
12:58 the officer, and the **o** cast thee into prison. *4233*

OFFICERS (58) [OFFICE]

Ge 40: 2 Pharaoh was wroth against two *of* his **o**, 5631
40: 7 he asked Pharaoh's **o** that *were* with him in 5631
41:34 do *this,* and let him appoint **o** over the land, 6496
Ex 5: 6 of the people, and their **o**, saying, 7860
5:10 their **o**, and they spake to the people, 7860
5:14 the **o** of the children of Israel, 7860
5:15 the **o** of the children of Israel came and 7860
5:19 the **o** of the children of Israel did see *that* 7860
Nu 11:16 the elders of the people, and **o** over them; 7860
31:14 Moses was wroth with the **o** of the host, 6485
31:48 the **o** which *were* over thousands of 6485
Dt 1:15 over tens, and **o** among your tribes. 7860
16:18 and **o** shalt thou make thee in all thy gates, 7860
20: 5 the **o** shall speak unto the people, saying, 7860
20: 8 the **o** shall speak further unto the people, 7860
20: 9 when the **o** have made an end of speaking 7860

Dt 29:10 your elders, and your **o**, *with* all the men of 7860
31:28 your **o**, that I may speak these words in 7860
Jos 1:10 Joshua commanded the **o** of the people, 7860
3: 2 three days, that the **o** went through the host; 7860
8:33 and their elders, and **o**, and their judges, 7860
23: 2 for their **o**, and said unto them, I am old 7860
24: 1 and for their judges, and for their **o**; 7860
1Sa 8:15 and give to his **o**, and to his servants. 5631
1Ki 4: 5 Azariah the son of Nathan *was* over the **o**: 5324
4: 7 Solomon had twelve **o** over all Israel, 5324
4:27 those **o** provided victual for king Solomon, 5324
4:28 they unto the place where *the o* were, NIH
5:16 Besides the chief of Solomon's **o** which 5324
9:23 These *were* the chief of the **o** that *were* over 5324
2Ki 11:15 the **o** of the host, and said unto them, 6485
11:18 the priest appointed **o** over the house of 6485
24:12 and his servants, and his princes, and his **o**: 5631
24:15 and his **o**, and the mighty of the land, 5631
1Ch 23: 4 and six thousand *were* **o** and judges: 7860
26:29 business over Israel, for **o** and judges. 7860
26:30 *were* **o** among them of Israel on *this* side 6486
27: 1 their **o** that served the king in any matter of 7860
28: 1 with the **o**, and *with* the mighty *men*, and 5631
2Ch 8:10 these *were* the chief of king Solomon's **o**, 5324
18: 8 the king of Israel called for one *of his* **o**, 5631
19:11 also the Levites *shall be* **o** before you. 7860
34:13 *there were* scribes, and **o**, and porters. 7860
Est 1: 8 the king had appointed to all the **o** of his 7227
2: 3 let the king appoint **o** in all the provinces of 6496
9: 3 and **o** of the king, 4399+6213+1886.1
Isa 60:17 I will also make thy **o** peace, and 6486
Jer 29:26 that *ye* should be **o** in the house of 6496
Jn 7:32 and the chief priests sent **o** to take him. *5257*
7:45 Then came the **o** to the chief priests and *5257*
7:46 The **o** answered, Never man spake like this *5257*
18: 3 and **o** from the chief priests and Pharisees, *5257*
18:12 the captain and **o** of the Jews took Jesus, *5257*
18:18 **o** stood *there*, who had made a fire of coals; *5257*
18:22 one of the **o** which stood by stroke Jesus *5257*
19: 6 the chief priests therefore and **o** saw him, *5257*
Ac 5:22 But when the **o** came, and found them not *5257*
5:26 Then went the captain with the **o**, and *5257*

OFFICES (5) [OFFICE]
1Sa 2:36 I pray thee, into one of the **priests' o**, 3550
1Ch 24: 3 according to their **o** in their service. 6486
2Ch 7: 6 the priests waited on their **o**: the Levites 4931
23:18 Also Jehoiada appointed the **o** of the house 6486
Ne 13:14 the house of my God, and for the **o** thereof. 4929

OFFSCOURING (2)
La 3:45 Thou hast made us *as* the **o** and refuse in 5501
1Co 4:13 *and are* the **o** of all *things* unto this day. *4067*

OFFSPRING (12)
Job 5:25 and thine **o** as the grass of the earth. 6631
21: 8 with them, and their **o** before their eyes. 6631
27:14 and his **o** shall not be satisfied *with* bread. 6631
31: 8 let another eat; yea, let my **o** be rooted out. 6631
Isa 22:24 the **o** and the issue, all vessels of small 6631
44: 3 thy seed, and my blessing upon thine **o**: 6631
48:19 the **o** of thy bowels like the gravel thereof; 6631
61: 9 the Gentiles, and their **o** among the people: 6631
65:23 of the LORD, and their **o** with them. 6631
Ac 17:28 own poets have said, For we are also his **o**. *1085*
17:29 Forasmuch then as we are the **o** of God, *1085*
Rev 22:16 I am the root and the **o** of David, *and* *1085*

OFT (13) [OFTEN]
2Ki 4: 8 *so* it was, *that* **as o as** he passed by, 1767+4480
Job 21:17 **How o** is the candle of the wicked 4100+3509.1
21:17 *how o* cometh their destruction upon them! NIH
Ps 78:40 **How o** did they provoke him in 4100+3509.1
Mt 9:14 Why do we and the Pharisees fast **o**, but *4183*
17:15 he falleth into the fire, and **o** into the water. *4178*
18:21 **how o** shall my brother sin against me, and *4212*
Mk 7: 3 except they wash *their* hands **o**, eat not, *4435*
Ac 26:11 And I punished them **o** in every synagogue, *4178*
1Co 11:25 **as o as** ye drink *it*, in remembrance of *302+3740*
2Co 11:23 in prisons more frequent, in deaths **o**. *4178*
2Ti 1:16 for he **o** refreshed me, and was not ashamed *4178*
Heb 6: 7 drinketh *in* the rain that cometh **o** upon it, *4178*

OFTEN (15) [OFT, OFTENER, OFTENTIMES, OFTTIMES]
Pr 29: 1 that being **o** reproved hardeneth *his* neck, NIH
Mal 3:16 they that feared the LORD spake **o** one to NIH
Mt 23:37 **how o** would I have gathered thy children *4212*
Mk 5: 4 Because that he had been **o** bound with *4178*
Lk 5:33 Why do the disciples of John fast **o**, and *4437*
13:34 **how o** would I have gathered thy children *4212*
1Co 11:26 For **as o as** ye eat this bread, and *302+3740*
2Co 11:26 *In* journeyings **o**, *in* perils of waters, *4178*
11:27 in watchings **o**, in hunger and thirst, *4178*
11:27 in hunger and thirst, in fastings **o**, in cold *4178*
Php 3:18 of whom I have told you **o**, and now tell *4178*
1Ti 5:23 thy stomach's sake and thine **o** infirmities. *4437*
Heb 9:25 Nor yet that he should offer himself **o**, *4178*
9:26 must he **o** have suffered since *4178*
Rev 11: 6 with all plagues, **as o as** they will. *1437+3740*

OFTENER (1) [OFTEN]
Ac 24:26 wherefore he sent for him the **o**, and *4437*

OFTENTIMES (6) [OFTEN, TIME]
Job 33:29 *things* worketh God **o** with man, 6471+7969
Ecc 7:22 For **o** also thine own heart knoweth 6471+7227
Lk 8:29 For **o** it had caught him: and he was *4183+5550*
Ro 1:13 that **o** I purposed to come unto you, (but *4178*
2Co 8:22 whom we have **o** proved diligent in many *4178*
Heb 10:11 and offering **o** the same sacrifices, *4178*

OFTTIMES (3) [OFTEN, TIME]
Mt 17:15 for **o** he falleth into the fire, and oft into *4178*
Mk 9:22 And **o** it hath cast him into the fire, and *4178*
Jn 18: 2 for Jesus **o** resorted thither with his *4178*

OG (22)
Nu 21:33 **O** the king of Bashan went out against 5747
32:33 the kingdom of **O** king of Bashan, the land, 5747
Dt 1: 4 in Heshbon, and **O** the king of Bashan, 5747
3: 1 **O** the king of Bashan came out against us, 5747
3: 3 our God delivered into our hands **O** also, 5747
3: 4 of Argob, the kingdom of **O** in Bashan. 5747
3:10 cities of the kingdom of **O** in Bashan. 5747
3:11 For only **O** king of Bashan remained of 5747
3:13 and all Bashan, *being* the kingdom of **O**, 5747
4:47 the land of **O** king of Bashan, two kings of 5747
29: 7 of Heshbon, and **O** the king of Bashan, 5747
31: 4 do unto them as he did to Sihon and to **O**, 5747
Jos 2:10 and **O**, whom ye utterly destroyed. 5747
9:10 to **O** king of Bashan, which *was* at 5747
12: 4 the coast of **O** king of Bashan, *which was* 5747
13:12 All the kingdom of **O** in Bashan, 5747
13:30 all the kingdom of **O** king of Bashan, and 5747
13:31 cities of the kingdom of **O** in Bashan, 5747
1Ki 4:19 of the Amorites, and of **O** king of Bashan; 5747
Ne 9:22 and the land of **O** king of Bashan. 5747
Ps 135:11 **O** king of Bashan, and all the kingdoms of 5747
136:20 **O** the king of Bashan: for his mercy 5747

OH (17) [O] See Index

OHAD (2)
Ge 46:10 **O**, and Jachin, and Zohar, and Shaul the son 161
Ex 6:15 **O**, and Jachin, and Zohar, and Shaul the son 161

OHEL (1)
1Ch 3:20 **O**, and Berechiah, and Hasadiah, 169

OHOLAH See AHOLAH

OHOLIAB See AHOLIAB

OHOLIBAH See AHOLIBAH

OHOLIBAMAH See AHOLIBAMAH

OIL (202) [OILED]
Ge 28:18 *for* a pillar, and poured **o** upon the top of it. 8081
35:14 offering thereon, and he poured **o** thereon. 8081
Ex 25: 6 **O** for the light, spices for anointing oil, and 8081
25: 6 spices for anointing **o**, and for sweet 8081
27:20 that they bring thee pure **o** olive beaten for 8081
29: 2 cakes unleavened tempered with **o**, and 8081
29: 2 and wafers unleavened anointed with **o**: 8081
29: 7 shalt thou take the anointing **o**, and pour *it* 8081
29:21 of the anointing **o**, and sprinkle *it* upon 8081
29:40 with the fourth part of a hin of beaten **o**; 8081
30:24 of the sanctuary, and of **o** olive a hin: 8081

Ex	30:25	thou shalt make it an **o** of holy ointment,	8081
	30:25	it shall be a holy anointing **o**.	8081
	30:31	This shall be a holy anointing **o** unto me	8081
	31:11	the anointing **o**, and sweet incense for	8081
	35: 8	**o** for the light, and spices for anointing oil,	8081
	35: 8	spices for anointing **o**, and for the sweet	8081
	35:14	and his lamps, with the **o** for the light,	8081
	35:15	the anointing **o**, and the sweet incense, and	8081
	35:28	and **o** for the light, and for the anointing oil,	8081
	35:28	for the anointing **o**, and for the sweet	8081
	37:29	he made the holy anointing **o**, and the pure	8081
	39:37	all the vessels thereof, and the **o** for light,	8081
	39:38	the anointing **o**, and the sweet incense, and	8081
	40: 9	thou shalt take the anointing **o**, and	8081
Lev	2: 1	he shall pour **o** upon it, and	8081
	2: 2	of the **o** thereof, with all the frankincense	8081
	2: 4	cakes of fine flour mingled with **o**,	8081
	2: 4	or unleavened wafers anointed with **o**.	8081
	2: 5	*of* fine flour unleavened, mingled with **o**.	8081
	2: 6	shalt part it in pieces, and pour **o** thereon:	8081
	2: 7	it shall be made *of* fine flour with **o**.	8081
	2:15	thou shalt put **o** upon it, and	8081
	2:16	corn thereof, and *part* of the **o** thereof,	8081
	5:11	he shall put no **o** upon it, neither shall he	8081
	6:15	of the **o** thereof, and all the frankincense	8081
	6:21	In a pan it shall be made with **o**; *and*	8081
	7:10	meat offering, mingled with **o**, and dry,	8081
	7:12	unleavened cakes mingled with **o**,	8081
	7:12	and unleavened wafers anointed with **o**, and	8081
	7:12	cakes mingled with **o**, of fine flour, fried.	8081
	8: 2	the anointing **o**, and a bullock *for* the sin	8081
	8:10	Moses took the anointing **o**, and	8081
	8:12	he poured of the anointing **o** upon Aaron's	8081
	8:30	Moses took of the anointing **o**, and of	8081
	9: 4	and a meat offering mingled with **o**:	8081
	10: 7	for the anointing **o** of the LORD *is* upon	8081
	14:10	mingled with **o**, and one log of oil.	8081
	14:10	mingled with oil, and one log of **o**.	8081
	14:12	the log of **o**, and wave them *for* a wave	8081
	14:15	the priest shall take *some* of the log of **o**,	8081
	14:16	the priest shall dip his right finger in the **o**	8081
	14:16	shall sprinkle of the **o** with his finger seven	8081
	14:17	of the rest of the **o** that *is* in his hand shall	8081
	14:18	the remnant of the **o** that *is* in the priest's	8081
	14:21	one tenth deal of fine flour mingled with **o**	8081
	14:21	with oil for a meat offering, and a log of **o**;	8081
	14:24	the log of **o**, and the priest shall wave them	8081
	14:26	the priest shall pour of the **o** into the palm	8081
	14:27	**o** that *is* in his left hand seven times before	8081
	14:28	the priest shall put of the **o** that *is* in his	8081
	14:29	the rest of the **o** that *is* in the priest's hand	8081
	21:10	upon whose head the anointing **o** was	8081
	21:12	for the crown of the anointing **o** of his God	8081
	23:13	tenth deals *of* fine flour mingled with **o**,	8081
	24: 2	that they bring unto thee pure **o** olive	8081
Nu	4: 9	and all the **o** vessels thereof,	8081
	4:16	the priest *pertaineth* the **o** for the light,	8081
	4:16	the anointing **o**, *and* the oversight of all	8081
	5:15	he shall pour no **o** upon it, nor put	8081
	6:15	cakes *of* fine flour mingled with **o**, and	8081
	6:15	of unleavened bread anointed with **o**,	8081
	7:13	flour mingled with **o** for a meat offering:	8081
	7:19	flour mingled with **o** for a meat offering:	8081
	7:25	flour mingled with **o** for a meat offering:	8081
	7:31	flour mingled with **o** for a meat offering:	8081
	7:37	flour mingled with **o** for a meat offering:	8081
	7:43	flour mingled with **o** for a meat offering:	8081
	7:49	flour mingled with **o** for a meat offering:	8081
	7:55	flour mingled with **o** for a meat offering:	8081
	7:61	flour mingled with **o** for a meat offering:	8081
	7:67	flour mingled with **o** for a meat offering:	8081
	7:73	flour mingled with **o** for a meat offering:	8081
	7:79	flour mingled with **o** for a meat offering:	8081
	8: 8	*even* fine flour mingled with **o**, and	8081
	11: 8	the taste of it was as the taste of fresh **o**.	8081
	15: 4	mingled with the fourth *part* of a hin of **o**.	8081
	15: 6	mingled with the third *part* of a hin of **o**.	8081
	15: 9	deals *of* flour mingled with half a hin of **o**.	8081
	18:12	All the best of the **o**, and all the best of	3323
	28: 5	with the fourth *part* of a hin of beaten **o**.	8081
	28: 9	mingled with **o**, and the drink offering	8081
	28:12	mingled with **o**, for one bullock;	8081
	28:12	meat offering, mingled with **o**, for one ram;	8081
	28:13	a several tenth deal of flour mingled with **o**	8081
	28:20	offering *shall be of* flour mingled with **o**:	8081
	28:28	their meat offering *of* flour mingled with **o**,	8081
	29: 3	offering *shall be of* flour mingled with **o**,	8081
	29: 9	offering *shall be of* flour mingled with **o**,	8081
	29:14	offering *shall be of* flour mingled with **o**,	8081
	35:25	which was anointed with the holy **o**.	8081
Dt	7:13	thy corn, and thy wine, and thine **o**,	3323
	8: 8	pomegranates; a land of **o** olive, and honey;	8081
	11:14	in thy corn, and thy wine, and thine **o**.	3323
	12:17	or of thy **o**, or the firstlings of thy herds or	3323
	14:23	of thine **o**, and the firstlings of thy herds	3323
	18: 4	of thy **o**, and the first of the fleece of thy	3323
	28:40	but thou shalt not anoint *thyself with* the **o**;	8081
	28:51	or **o**, *or* the increase of thy kine, or	3323
	32:13	out of the rock, and **o** out of the flinty rock;	8081
	33:24	his brethren, and let him dip his foot in **o**.	8081
1Sa	10: 1	Samuel took a vial of **o**, and poured *it* upon	8081
	16: 1	fill thine horn *with* **o**, and go, I will send	8081
	16:13	Samuel took the horn of **o**, and	8081
2Sa	1:21	*as though he had* not *been* anointed with **o**.	8081
	14: 2	anoint not *thyself with* **o**, but be as a	8081
1Ki	1:39	Zadok the priest took a horn of **o** out of	8081
	5:11	and twenty measures of pure **o**:	8081
	17:12	of meal in a barrel, and a little **o** in a cruse:	8081
	17:14	not waste, neither shall the cruse of **o** fail,	8081
	17:16	wasted not, neither did the cruse of **o** fail,	8081
2Ki	4: 2	not any thing in the house, save a pot of **o**.	8081
	4: 6	*is* not a vessel more. And the **o** stayed.	8081
	4: 7	sell the **o**, and pay thy debt, and live thou	8081
	9: 1	take this box of **o** in thine hand, and go *to*	8081
	9: 3	take the box of **o**, and pour *it* on his head,	8081
	9: 6	he poured the **o** on his head, and said unto	8081
	18:32	vineyards, a land of **o** olive and of honey,	3323
1Ch	9:29	the **o**, and the frankincense, and the spices.	8081
	12:40	and **o**, and oxen, and sheep abundantly:	8081
	27:28	and over the cellars of **o** *was* Joash:	8081
2Ch	2:10	of wine, and twenty thousand baths of **o**.	8081
	2:15	and the barley, the **o**, and the wine,	8081
	11:11	and store of victual, and *of* **o** and wine.	8081
	31: 5	**o**, and honey, and of all the increase of	3323
	32:28	for the increase of corn, and wine, and **o**;	3323
Ezr	3: 7	meat, and drink, and **o**, unto them of Zidon,	8081
	6: 9	the God of heaven, wheat, salt, wine, and **o**,	4887
	7:22	to an hundred baths *of* **o**, and salt without	4887
Ne	5:11	*of* the corn, the wine, and the **o**, that ye	3323
	10:37	*of* trees, of wine and of **o**, unto the priests,	3323
	10:39	of the new wine, and the **o**, unto	3323
	13: 5	tithes of the corn, the new wine, and the **o**,	3323
	13:12	the new wine and the **o** unto the treasuries.	3323
Est	2:12	*to wit,* six months with **o** of myrrh, and	8081
Job	24:11	*Which* **make o** within their walls, *and*	6671
	29: 6	and the rock poured me out rivers of **o**;	8081
Ps	23: 5	thou anointest my head with **o**; my cup	8081
	45: 7	hath anointed thee *with* the **o** of gladness	8081
	55:21	his words were softer than **o**, yet *were* they	8081
	89:20	with my holy **o** have I anointed him:	8081
	92:10	an unicorn: I shall be anointed with fresh **o**.	8081
	104:15	*and* **o** to make *his* face to shine, and	8081
	109:18	bowels like water, and like **o** into his bones.	8081
	141: 5	*it shall be* an excellent **o**, *which* shall not	8081
Pr	5: 3	and her mouth *is* smoother than **o**:	8081
	21:17	he that loveth wine and **o** shall not be rich.	8081
	21:20	and **o** in the dwelling of the wise;	8081
Isa	41:19	shittah tree, and the myrtle, and the **o** tree;	8081
	61: 3	beauty for ashes, the **o** of joy for mourning,	8081
Jer	31:12	for **o**, and for the young of the flock and	3323
	40:10	**o**, and put *them* in your vessels, and	8081
	41: 8	and *of* barley, and *of* **o**, and *of* honey.	8081
Eze	16: 9	blood from thee, and I anointed thee with **o**.	8081
	16:13	thou didst eat fine flour, and honey, and **o**:	8081
	16:18	thou hast set mine **o** and mine incense	8081
	16:19	fine flour, and **o**, and honey, *wherewith* I	8081
	23:41	thou hast set mine incense and mine **o**.	8081
	27:17	and Pannag, and honey, and **o**, and balm.	8081
	32:14	cause their rivers to run like **o**, saith	8081
	45:14	Concerning the ordinance of **o**, the bath *of*	8081
	45:14	the ordinance of oil, the bath *of* **o**,	8081
	45:24	for a ram, and a hin of **o** for an ephah.	8081
	45:25	to the meat offering, and according to the **o**.	8081
	46: 5	be able to give, and a hin of **o** to an ephah.	8081
	46: 7	shall attain unto, and a hin of **o** to an ephah.	8081
	46:11	is able to give, and a hin of **o** to an ephah.	8081
	46:14	of an ephah, and the third *part* of a hin of **o**,	8081
	46:15	the lamb, and the meat offering, and the **o**,	8081

Hos 2: 5 and my flax, mine **o** and my drink. 8081
2: 8 and **o**, and multiplied her silver and gold, 3323
2:22 shall hear the corn, and the wine, and the **o**; 3323
12: 1 the Assyrians, and **o** is carried into Egypt. 8081
Joel 1:10 the new wine is dried up, the **o** languisheth. 3323
2:19 and **o**, and ye shall be satisfied therewith: 3323
2:24 and the fats shall overflow *with* wine and **o**. 3323
Mic 6: 7 *or* with ten thousands of rivers of **o**? 8081
6:15 but thou shalt not anoint *thee with* **o**; 8081
Hag 1:11 upon the **o**, and upon *that* which the ground 3323
2:12 or pottage, or wine, or **o**, or any meat, 8081
Zec 4:12 pipes empty the golden **o** out of themselves? NIH
Mt 25: 3 took their lamps, and took no **o** with them: *1637*
25: 4 But the wise took **o** in their vessels with *1637*
25: 8 said unto the wise, Give us of your **o**; *1637*
Mk 6:13 and anointed with **o** many *that were* sick, *1637*
Lk 7:46 Mine head with **o** thou didst not anoint: but *1637*
10:34 pouring in **o** and wine, and set him on his *1637*
16: 6 And he said, An hundred measures of **o**. *1637*
Heb 1: 9 hath anointed thee *with* the **o** of gladness *1637*
Jas 5:14 anointing him with **o** in the name of *1637*
Rev 6: 6 and *see* thou hurt not the **o** and the wine. *1637*
18:13 and **o**, and fine flour, and wheat, and *1637*

OILED (2) [OIL]
Ex 29:23 one cake of **o** bread, and one wafer out of 8081
Lev 8:26 a cake of **o** bread, and one wafer, and 8081

OINTMENT (27) [OINTMENTS]
Ex 30:25 thou shalt make it an oil of holy **o**, 4888
30:25 an **o** compound *after* the art of 7545
2Ki 20:13 the precious **o**, and all the house of his 8081
1Ch 9:30 *some* of the sons of the priests made the **o** 4842
Job 41:31 like a pot: he maketh the sea like a **pot of o**. 4841
Ps 133: 2 *It is* like the precious **o** upon the head, 8081
Pr 27: 9 **O** and perfume rejoice the heart: so 8081
27:16 hideth the wind, and the **o** of his right hand, 8081
Ecc 7: 1 A *good* name *is* better than precious **o**; and 8081
9: 8 be always white; and let thy head lack no **o**. 8081
10: 1 Dead flies cause the **o** of the apothecary to 8081
SS 1: 3 ointments thy name *is as* **o** poured forth, 8081
Isa 1: 6 neither bound up, neither mollified with **o**. 8081
39: 2 the precious **o**, and all the house of his 8081
57: 9 thou wentest to the king with **o**, and 8081
Mt 26: 7 having an alabaster box of very precious **o**, *3464*
26: 9 For this **o** might have been sold for much, *3464*
26:12 For in that she hath poured this **o** on my *3464*
Mk 14: 3 box of **o** of spikenard very precious; *3464*
14: 4 said, Why was this waste of the **o** made? *3464*
Lk 7:37 brought an alabaster box of **o**, *3464*
7:38 his feet, and anointed *them* with the **o**. *3464*
7:46 this *woman* hath anointed my feet with **o**. *3464*
Jn 11: 2 *that* Mary which anointed the Lord with **o**, *3464*
12: 3 Then took Mary a pound of **o** of spikenard, *3464*
12: 3 house was filled with the odour of the **o**. *3464*
12: 5 Why was not this **o** sold for three hundred *3464*

OINTMENTS (5) [OINTMENT]
SS 1: 3 Because of the savour of thy good **o** thy 8081
4:10 and the smell of thine **o** than all spices! 8081
Am 6: 6 and anoint themselves *with* the chief **o**: 8081
Lk 23:56 they returned, and prepared spices and **o**; *3464*
Rev 18:13 and **o**, and frankincense, and wine, and oil, *3464*

OLD (380) [ELDER, ELDERS, ELDEST, OLDNESS]
Ge 5:32 Noah was five hundred years **o**: and 1121
6: 4 same *became* mighty *men* which *were* of **o**, 5769
7: 6 Noah *was* six hundred years **o** when 1121
11:10 Shem *was* an hundred years **o**, and 1121
12: 4 five years **o** when he departed out of Haran. 1121
15: 9 Take me a heifer of **three years o**, and 8027
15: 9 a she goat of **three years o**, and a ram of 8027
15: 9 a ram of **three years o**, and a turtle-dove, 8027
15:15 thou shalt be buried in a good **o age**. 7872
16:16 Abram *was* fourscore and six years **o**, 1121
17: 1 when Abram was ninety years **o** and nine, 1121
17:12 he that is eight days **o** shall be circumcised 1121
17:17 born unto him that is an hundred years **o**? 1121
17:17 and shall Sarah, that is ninety years **o**, bear? 1323
17:24 Abraham *was* ninety years **o** and nine, 1121
17:25 Ishmael his son *was* thirteen years **o**, 1121
18:11 Now Abraham and Sarah *were* **o** *and* 2205
18:12 After I am **waxed o** shall I have pleasure, 1086
18:12 shall I have pleasure, my lord being **o** also? 2204
18:13 I of a surety bear *a child,* which am **o**? 2204
19: 4 the house round, both **o** and young, 2205
19:31 Our father *is* **o**, and *there is* not a man in 2204
21: 2 and bare Abraham a son in his **o age**, 2208
21: 4 his son Isaac being eight days **o**, 1121
21: 5 Abraham *was* an hundred years **o**, when his 1121
21: 7 for I have born *him* a son in his **o age**. 2208
23: 1 an hundred and seven and twenty **years o**: 8141
24: 1 Abraham was **o**, *and* well stricken in age: 2204
24:36 bare a son to my master when she was **o**: 2209
25: 8 died in a good **o age**, an old man, and 7872
25: 8 an **o man**, and full *of years;* and 2205
25:20 Isaac was forty years **o** when he took 1121
25:26 Isaac *was* threescore years **o** when she bare 1121
26:34 Esau was forty years **o** when he took to 1121
27: 1 that when Isaac was **o**, and his eyes were 2204
27: 2 he said, Behold now, I am **o**, I know not 2204
35:29 unto his people, *being* **o** and full of days: 2205
37: 2 Joseph, *being* seventeen years **o**, 1121
37: 3 because he *was* the son of his **o age**: 2208
41:46 Joseph *was* thirty years **o** when he stood 1121
43:27 father well, the **o man** of whom ye spake? 2205
44:20 an **o man**, and a child of *his* old age, a little 2205
44:20 and a child of *his* **o age**, a little one; 2208
47: 8 unto Jacob, How **o** *art* thou? 2416+3117+8141
49: 9 he couched as a lion, and as an **o lion**; 3833
50:26 *being* an hundred and ten years **o**: 1121
Ex 7: 7 Moses *was* fourscore years **o**, and 1121
7: 7 Aaron fourscore and three years **o**, 1121
10: 9 We will go with our young and with our **o**, 2205
30:14 from twenty years **o** and above, shall give 1121
38:26 from twenty years **o** and upward, for six 1121
Lev 13:11 It *is* an **o** leprosy in the skin of his flesh, 3462
19:32 honour the face of the **o man**, and fear thy 2205
25:22 and eat *yet* of **o** fruit until the ninth year; 3465
25:22 until her fruits come in ye shall eat *of* the **o** 3465
26:10 ye shall eat **o store**, and bring forth 3462+3465
26:10 bring forth the **o** because of the new. 3465
27: 3 of the male from twenty years **o** even unto 1121
27: 3 twenty years old even unto sixty years **o**, 1121
27: 5 if *it be* from five years **o** even unto twenty 1121
27: 5 five years old even unto twenty years **o**, 1121
27: 6 if *it be* from a month **o** even unto five years 1121
27: 6 *be* from a month old even unto five years **o**, 1121
27: 7 if *it be* from sixty years **o** and above; if *it be* 1121
Nu 1: 3 From twenty years **o** and upward, all that 1121
1:18 from twenty years **o** and upward, by their 1121
1:20 every male from twenty years **o** and 1121
1:22 every male from twenty years **o** and 1121
1:24 from twenty years **o** and upward, all that 1121
1:26 from twenty years **o** and upward, all that 1121
1:28 from twenty years **o** and upward, all that 1121
1:30 from twenty years **o** and upward, all that 1121
1:32 from twenty years **o** and upward, all that 1121
1:34 from twenty years **o** and upward, all that 1121
1:36 from twenty years **o** and upward, all that 1121
1:38 from twenty years **o** and upward, all that 1121
1:40 from twenty years **o** and upward, all that 1121
1:42 from twenty years **o** and upward, all that 1121
1:45 from twenty years **o** and upward, 1121
3:15 every male from a month **o** and 1121
3:22 all the males, from a month **o** and upward, 1121
3:28 from a month **o** and upward, *were* eight 1121
3:34 from a month **o** and upward, *were* six 1121
3:39 all the males from a month **o** and upward, 1121
3:40 of the children of Israel from a month **o** 1121
3:43 from a month **o** and upward, of those that 1121
4: 3 From thirty years **o** and upward even until 1121
4: 3 and upward even until fifty years **o**, 1121
4:23 From thirty years **o** and upward until fifty 1121
4:23 upward until fifty years **o** shalt thou 1121
4:30 From thirty years **o** and upward even unto 1121
4:30 upward even unto fifty years **o** shalt thou 1121
4:35 From thirty years **o** and upward even unto 1121
4:35 and upward even unto fifty years **o**, 1121
4:39 From thirty years **o** and upward even unto 1121
4:39 and upward even unto fifty years **o**, 1121
4:43 From thirty years **o** and upward even unto 1121
4:43 and upward even unto fifty years **o**, 1121
4:47 From thirty years **o** and upward even unto 1121
4:47 and upward even unto fifty years **o**, 1121
8:24 from twenty and five years **o** and 1121
14:29 from twenty years **o** and upward, 1121
18:16 from a month **o** shalt thou redeem, 1121

Nu 26: 2 from twenty years **o** and upward, 1121
26: 4 *the sum of the people,* from twenty years **o** 1121
26:62 all males from a month **o** and upward: 1121
32:11 from twenty years **o** and upward, shall see 1121
33:39 three years **o** when he died in mount Hor. 1121
Dt 2:20 giants dwelt therein **in o time**; and 6440+3807.1
8: 4 Thy raiment **waxed** not **o** upon thee, 1086
19:14 which they of **o time** have set in thine 7223
28:50 which shall not regard the person of the **o**, 2205
29: 5 your clothes are not **waxen o** upon you, and 1086
29: 5 and thy shoe is not **waxen o** upon thy foot. 1086
31: 2 *am* an hundred and twenty years **o** *this* day; 1121
32: 7 Remember the days **of o**, consider the years 5769
34: 7 and twenty years **o** when he died: 1121
Jos 5:11 they did eat of the **o corn** of the land on 5669
5:12 they had eaten of the **o corn** of the land; 5669
6:21 and **o**, and ox, and sheep, and ass, 2205
9: 4 took **o** sacks upon their asses, and 1087
9: 4 and wine bottles, **o**, and rent, and bound up; 1087
9: 5 **o** shoes and clouted upon their feet, and 1087
9: 5 upon their feet, and **o** garments upon them; 1087
9:13 our shoes are **become o** by reason of 1086
13: 1 Now Joshua was **o** *and* stricken in years; 2204
13: 1 Thou art **o** *and* stricken in years, and 2204
14: 7 Forty years **o** *was* I when Moses the servant 1121
14:10 I *am this* day fourscore and five years **o**. 1121
23: 1 that Joshua **waxed o** *and* stricken in age. 2204
23: 2 said unto them, I am **o** *and* stricken in age: 2204
24: 2 on the *other* side of the flood in **o time**, 5769
24:29 died, *being* an hundred and ten years **o**. 1121
Jdg 2: 8 died, *being* an hundred and ten years **o**. 1121
6:25 even the second bullock of seven **years o**, 8141
8:32 the son of Joash died in a good **o age**, 7872
19:16 there came an **o** man from his work out of 2205
19:17 the **o** man said, Whither goest thou? and 2205
19:20 the **o** man said, Peace *be* with thee; 2205
19:22 the master of the house, the **o man**, saying, 2205
Ru 1:12 go *your way;* for I am too **o** to have a 2204
4:15 of *thy* life, and a nourisher of thine **o age**: 7872
1Sa 2:22 Now Eli was very **o**, and heard all that his 2204
2:31 that there shall not be an **o man** in thine 2205
2:32 there shall not be an **o man** in thine house 2205
4:15 Now Eli *was* ninety and eight years **o**; and 1121
4:18 for he was an **o** man, and heavy. And he 2204
8: 1 it came to pass, when Samuel was **o**, that he 2204
8: 5 thou art **o**, and thy sons walk not in thy 2204
12: 2 I am **o** and grayheaded; and behold, 2204
17:12 the man went among men *for* an **o man** in 2204
27: 8 for those *nations were* of **o** the inhabitants 5769
28:14 she said, An **o** man cometh up; and he *is* 2205
2Sa 2:10 Ish-bosheth Saul's son *was* forty years **o** 1121
4: 4 was five years **o** when the tidings came of 1121
5: 4 David *was* thirty years **o** when he *began* to 1121
19:32 a very aged man, *even* fourscore years **o**: 1121
19:35 I *am this* day fourscore years **o**: *and* can I 1121
20:18 They were wont to speak in **o time**, saying, 7223
1Ki 1: 1 Now king David was **o** *and* stricken in 2204
1:15 the king was very **o**; and Abishag 2204
11: 4 For it came to pass, when Solomon was **o**, 2209
12: 6 king Rehoboam consulted with the **o men**, 2205
12: 8 he forsook the counsel of the **o men**, 2205
12:13 forsook the **o men's** counsel that they gave 2205
13:11 Now there dwelt an **o** prophet in Beth-el; 2205
13:25 told *it* in the city where the **o** prophet dwelt. 2205
13:29 the **o** prophet came to the city, to mourn 2205
14:21 and one years **o** when he *began* to reign, 1121
15:23 Nevertheless in the time of his **o age** he 2209
22:42 and five years **o** when he *began* to reign; 1121
2Ki 4:14 she hath no child, and her husband is **o**. 2204
8:17 two years **o** was he when he *began* to reign; 1121
8:26 twenty years **o** *was* Ahaziah when he *began* 1121
11:21 Seven years **o** *was* Jehoash when he *began* 1121
14: 2 and five years **o** when he *began* to reign, 1121
14:21 which *was* sixteen years **o**, and made him 1121
15: 2 Sixteen years **o** was he when he *began* to 1121
15:33 twenty years **o** was he when he *began* to 1121
16: 2 Twenty years **o** *was* Ahaz when he *began* 1121
18: 2 five years **o** was he when he *began* to reign; 1121
21: 1 Manasseh *was* twelve years **o** when he 1121
21:19 and two years **o** when he *began* to reign, 1121
22: 1 Josiah *was* eight years **o** when he *began* to 1121
23:31 and three years **o** when he *began* to reign; 1121
23:36 and five year **o** when he *began* to reign; 1121
24: 8 Jehoiachin *was* eighteen years **o** when he 1121
24:18 and one years **o** when he *began* to reign, 1121
1Ch 2:21 he married when he *was* threescore years **o**; 1121
4:40 *they* of Ham had dwelt there **of o**. 6440+3807.1
23: 1 So when David was **o** and full *of* days, 2204
23:27 *were* numbered from twenty years **o** 1121
27:23 the number of them from twenty years **o** 1121
29:28 he died in a good **o age**, full of days, riches, 7872
2Ch 10: 6 Rehoboam took counsel with the **o men** 2205
10: 8 he forsook the counsel which the **o men** 2205
10:13 forsook the counsel of the **o men**, 2205
12:13 and forty years **o** when he *began* to reign, 1121
20:31 and five years **o** when he *began* to reign, 1121
21: 5 and two years **o** when he *began* to reign, 1121
21:20 two *years* **o** was he when he *began* to reign, 1121
22: 2 two years **o** *was* Ahaziah when he *began* to 1121
24: 1 Joash *was* seven years **o** when he *began* to 1121
24:15 Jehoiada **waxed o**, and was full *of* days 2204
24:15 and thirty years **o** *was he* when he died. 1121
25: 1 and five years **o** *when* he *began* to reign, 1121
25: 5 he numbered them from twenty years **o** and 1121
26: 1 who *was* sixteen years **o**, and made him 1121
26: 3 Sixteen years **o** *was* Uzziah when he *began* 1121
27: 1 and five years **o** when he *began* to reign, 1121
27: 8 and twenty years **o** when he *began* to reign, 1121
28: 1 Ahaz *was* twenty years **o** when he *began* to 1121
29: 1 reign *when he was* five and twenty years **o**, 1121
31:16 of males, from three years **o** and upward, 1121
31:17 the Levites from twenty years **o** and 1121
33: 1 Manasseh *was* twelve years **o** when he 1121
33:21 and twenty years **o** when he *began* to reign, 1121
34: 1 Josiah *was* eight years **o** when he *began* to 1121
36: 2 and three years **o** when he *began* to reign, 1121
36: 5 and five years **o** when he *began* to reign, 1121
36: 9 Jehoiachin *was* eight years **o** when he 1121
36:11 and twenty years **o** when he *began* to reign, 1121
36:17 **o man**, or him that stooped for age: 2205
Ezr 3: 8 appointed the Levites from twenty years **o** 1121
4:15 moved sedition within the same of **o** time: 5957
4:19 it is found that this city of **o** time *hath* made 5957
Ne 3: 6 Moreover the **o** gate repaired Jehoiada 3465
9:21 their clothes **waxed** not **o**, and their feet 1086
12:39 above the **o** gate, and above the fish gate, 3465
12:46 Asaph of **o** *there were* chief of the singers, 6924
Est 3:13 all Jews, both young and **o**, little children 2205
Job 4:11 The **o lion** perisheth for lack of prey, and 3918
14: 8 Though the root thereof **wax o** in the earth, 2204
20: 4 Knowest thou *not* this of **o**, since man was 5703
21: 7 **become o**, yea, are mighty *in* power? 6275
22:15 Hast thou marked the **o** way which wicked 5769
30: 2 profit me, in whom **o age** was perished? 3624
32: 6 and said, I *am* young, and ye *are* **very o**; 3453
42:17 So Job died, *being* **o** and full of days. 2205
Ps 6: 7 it **waxeth o** because of all mine enemies. 6275
25: 6 for they *have been* **ever of o**. 4480+5769
32: 3 my bones **waxed o** through my roaring all 1086
37:25 I have been young, and *now* am **o**; yet have 2204
44: 1 thou didst in their days, in the times of **o**. 6924
55:19 and afflict them, even he that abideth of **o**. 6924
68:33 the heavens of heavens, *which were* **of o**; 6924
71: 9 Cast me not off in the time of **o age**; 2209
71:18 Now also when I am **o** and grayheaded, 2209
74: 2 *which* thou hast purchased **of o**; 6924
74:12 For God *is* my King of **o**, working salvation 6924
77: 5 I have considered the days of **o**, the years 6924
77:11 surely I will remember thy wonders of **o**. 6924
78: 2 in a parable: I will utter dark sayings of **o**: 6924
92:14 They shall still bring forth fruit in **o age**; 7872
93: 2 Thy throne is established of **o**: thou *art* from 227
102:25 **Of o** hast thou laid the foundation 6440+3807.1
102:26 yea, all of them shall **wax o** like a garment; 1086
119:52 I remembered thy judgments of **o**, 5769
119:152 I have known **of o** that thou hast founded 6924
143: 5 I remember the days of **o**; I meditate on all 6924
148:12 and maidens; **o men**, and children: 2205
Pr 8:22 beginning of his way, before his works of **o**. 227
17: 6 children *are* the crown of **o men**; 2205
20:29 and the beauty of **o men** *is* the gray head. 2205
22: 6 and when he is **o**, he will not depart from it. 2204
23:10 Remove not the **o** landmark; and enter not 5769
23:22 and despise not thy mother when she is **o**. 2204
Ecc 1:10 it hath been already **of o time**, 5769+3807.1
4:13 and a wise child than an **o** and foolish king, 2205
SS 7:13 *are* all *manner of* pleasant *fruits,* new and **o**, 3465
Isa 15: 5 *flee* unto Zoar, a heifer of **three years o**: 7992

Isa 20: 4 young and **o**, naked and barefoot, 2205
22:11 the two walls for the water of the **o** pool: 3465
25: 1 *thy* counsels of **o** *are* faithfulness *and* truth. 7350
30: 6 from whence *come* the young and **o lion**, 3918
30:33 For Tophet *is* ordained of **o**; yea, for the king 865
43:18 *things,* neither consider the *things* **of o**. 6931
46: 4 *even* to *your* **o age** I *am* he; and *even* to 2209
46: 9 Remember the former *things* of **o**: for I *am* 5769
50: 9 lo, they all shall **wax o** as a garment; 1086
51: 6 the earth shall **wax o** like a garment, and 1086
51: 9 *in* the ancient days, *in* the generations **of o**. 5769
57:11 have not I held my peace even of **o**, and 5769
58:12 *they that shall be* of thee shall build the **o** 5769
61: 4 they shall build the **o** wastes, they shall 5769
63: 9 and carried them all the days **of o**. 5769
63:11 he remembered the days **of o**, Moses, *and* 5769
65:20 nor an **o man** that hath not filled his days: 2205
65:20 for the child shall die an hundred years **o**; 1121
65:20 the sinner *being* an hundred years **o** shall be 1121
Jer 2:20 For **of o time** I have broken thy 4480+5769
6:16 the ways, and see, and ask for the **o** paths, 5769
28: 8 before thee of **o** prophesied both against 5769
31: 3 The LORD hath appeared of **o** unto me, 7350
31:13 the dance, both young men and **o** together: 2205
38:11 took thence **o** cast clouts and old rotten 1094
38:11 thence old cast clouts and **o** rotten rags, 1094
38:12 Put now *these* **o** cast clouts and rotten rags 1094
46:26 as *in* the days of **o**, saith the LORD. 6924
48:34 *as* a heifer of **three years o**: 7992
51:22 with thee will I break in pieces **o** and 2205
52: 1 and twenty year **o** when he *began* to reign, 1121
La 1: 7 things that she had in the days **of o**, 6924
2:17 that he had commanded in the days **of o**: 6924
2:21 and the **o** lie on the ground in the streets: 2205
3: 4 My flesh and my skin hath he **made o**; 1086
3: 6 me in dark places, as they that be dead of **o**. 5769
5:21 we shall be turned; renew our days as **of o**. 6924
Eze 9: 6 Slay utterly **o** *and* young, both maids, and 2205
23:43 said I unto *her that was* **o** *in* adulteries, 1087
25:15 to destroy *it for* the **o** hatred; 5769
26:20 with the people of **o time**, and shall set thee 5769
26:20 in places desolate of **o**, with them that go 5769
36:11 I will settle you after your **o estates**, and 6927
38:17 *Art* thou he of whom I have spoken in **o** 6931
Da 5:31 *being* about threescore and two year **o**. 1247
Joel 1: 2 Hear this, ye **o men**, and give ear, all ye 2205
2:28 your **o men** shall dream dreams, 2205
Am 9:11 and I will build it as *in* the days of **o**: 5769
Mic 5: 2 whose goings forth *have been* from **of o**, 6924
6: 6 burnt offerings, with calves of a year **o**? 1121
7:14 *in* Bashan and Gilead, as *in* the days of **o**. 5769
7:20 sworn unto our fathers from the days **of o**. 6924
Na 2: 8 Nineveh *is* of **o** like a pool of water: yet 3117
2:11 *even* the **o lion**, walked, *and* the lion's 3833
Zec 8: 4 There shall yet **o men** and old women 2205
8: 4 **o women** dwell in the streets of Jerusalem, 2205
Mal 3: 4 as *in* the days of **o**, and as *in* former years. 5769
Mt 2:16 coasts thereof, from **two years o** and under, *1332*
5:21 heard that it was said by them **of o time**, *744*
5:27 heard that it was said by them **of o time**, *744*
5:33 that it hath been said by them **of o time**, *744*
9:16 a piece of new cloth unto an **o** garment; *3820*
9:17 Neither do *men* put new wine into **o** *3820*
13:52 forth out of his treasure *things* new and **o**. *3820*
Mk 2:21 a piece of new cloth on an **o** garment: *3820*
2:21 that filled it up taketh away *from* the **o**, *3820*
2:22 And no *man* putteth new wine into **o** *3820*
Lk 1:18 for I am an **o man**, and my wife well *4246*
1:36 she hath also conceived a son in her **o age**: *1094*
2:42 And when he was twelve **years o**, *2094*
5:36 putteth a piece of a new garment upon an **o**; *3820*
5:36 *taken* out of the new agreeth not with the **o**. *3820*
5:37 And no *man* putteth new wine into **o** *3820*
5:39 No *man* also having drunk **o** *wine* *3820*
5:39 desireth new: for he saith, The **o** is better. *3820*
9: 8 that one of the **o** prophets was risen again. *744*
9:19 others *say,* that one of the **o** prophets is risen *744*
12:33 provide yourselves bags which **wax not o**, *3822*
Jn 3: 4 How can a man be born when he is **o**? *1088*
8:57 Thou art not yet fifty **years o**, and hast thou *2094*
21:18 but when thou shalt be **o**, thou shalt stretch *1095*
Ac 2:17 and your **o men** shall dream dreams: *4245*
4:22 For the man was above forty **years o**, *2094*
7:23 And when he was full forty years **o**, it came *5550*
15:21 For Moses of **o** time hath in every city them *744*
21:16 an **o** disciple, with whom we should lodge. *744*
Ro 4:19 when he was about an **hundred year o**, *1541*
6: 6 that our **o** man is crucified with *him,* that *3820*
1Co 5: 7 Purge out therefore the **o** leaven, that ye *3820*
5: 8 let us keep the feast, not with **o** leaven, *3820*
2Co 3:14 away in the reading of the **o** testament; *3820*
5:17 **o** *things* are past away; behold, all *things* are *744*
Eph 4:22 the former conversation the **o** man, *3820*
Col 3: 9 seeing that ye have put off the **o** man with *3820*
1Ti 4: 7 But refuse profane and **o wives'** fables, and *1126*
5: 9 into the number under threescore **years o**, *2094*
Heb 1:11 and they all shall **wax o** as *doth* a garment; *3822*
8:13 A new *covenant,* he hath **made** the first **o**. *3822*
8:13 and **waxeth o** *is* ready to vanish away. *1095*
1Pe 3: 5 For after this manner **in** the **o time** the holy *4218*
2Pe 1: 9 that *he* was purged from his **o** sins. *3819*
1:21 For the prophecy came not **in o time** by *4218*
2: 5 And spared not the **o** world, but saved Noah *744*
3: 5 by the word of God the heavens were **of o**, *1597*
1Jn 2: 7 an **o** commandment which ye had from *3820*
2: 7 The **o** commandment is the word which ye *3820*
Jude 1: 4 who were before **of o** ordained to this *3819*
Rev 12: 9 And the great dragon was cast *out, that* **o** *744*
20: 2 *that* **o** serpent, which is the devil, and Satan, *744*

OLDNESS (1) [OLD]

Ro 7: 6 of spirit, and not *in* the **o** of the letter. *3821*

OLIVE (38) [OLIVES, OLIVET, OLIVEYARD, OLIVEYARDS]

Ge 8:11 lo, in her mouth *was* an **o** leaf pluckt off: 2132
Ex 27:20 that they bring thee pure oil **o** beaten for 2132
30:24 shekel of the sanctuary, and of oil **o** a hin: 2132
Lev 24: 2 that they bring unto thee pure oil **o** beaten 2132
Dt 6:11 thou diggedst not, vineyards and **o trees**, 2132
8: 8 pomegranates; a land of oil **o**, and honey; 2132
24:20 When thou beatest thine **o tree**, thou shalt 2132
28:40 Thou shalt have **o trees** throughout all thy 2132
28:40 *with* the oil; for thine **o** shall cast *his fruit.* 2132
Jdg 9: 8 they said unto the **o tree**, Reign thou over 2132
9: 9 the **o tree** said unto them, Should I leave 2132
1Ki 6:23 the oracle he made two cherubims *of* **o** tree, 8081
6:31 of the oracle he made doors of **o** tree: 8081
6:32 The two doors also *were* of **o** tree; and 8081
6:33 he for the door of the temple posts of **o** tree, 8081
2Ki 18:32 and vineyards, a land of oil **o** and of honey, 2132
1Ch 27:28 over the **o trees** and the sycomore trees that 2132
Ne 8:15 fetch **o** branches, and pine branches, and 2132
Job 15:33 and shall cast off his flower as the **o**. 2132
Ps 52: 8 I *am* like a green **o tree** in the house of 2132
128: 3 thy children like **o** plants round about thy 2132
Isa 17: 6 as the shaking of an **o tree**, two *or* 2132
24:13 *there shall be* as the shaking of an **o tree**, 2132
Jer 11:16 A green **o tree**, fair, *and* of goodly fruit: 2132
Hos 14: 6 his beauty shall be as the **o tree**, and his 2132
Am 4: 9 your fig trees and your **o trees** increased, 2132
Hab 3:17 the labour of the **o** shall fail, and the fields 2132
Hag 2:19 and the pomegranate, and the **o** tree, 2132
Zec 4: 3 two **o trees** by it, one upon the right *side* of 2132
4:11 What *are* these two **o trees** upon the right 2132
4:12 What *be these* two **o** branches which 2132
Ro 11:17 and thou, being a **wild o tree**, wert graffed in *65*
11:17 of the root and fatness of the **o tree**; *1636*
11:24 cut out of the **o tree which is wild** by nature, *65*
11:24 contrary to nature into a **good o tree**: *2565*
11:24 *branches,* be graffed into their own **o tree**? *1636*
Jas 3:12 the fig tree, my brethren, bear **o berries**? *1636*
Rev 11: 4 These are the two **o trees**, and the two *1636*

OLIVE GROVES See OLIVEYARD

OLIVES (15) [OLIVE]

Jdg 15: 5 the standing corn, with the vineyards *and* **o**. 2132
Mic 6:15 thou shalt tread the **o**, but thou shalt not 2132
Zec 14: 4 stand in that day upon the mount of **O**, 2132
14: 4 the mount of **O** shall cleave in the midst 2132
Mt 21: 1 unto the mount of **O**, then sent Jesus two *1636*
24: 3 And as he sat upon the mount of **O**, *1636*
26:30 a hymn, they went out into the mount of **O**. *1636*
Mk 11: 1 and Bethany, at the mount of **O**, *1636*
13: 3 And as he sat upon the mount of **O** over *1636*
14:26 a hymn, they went out into the mount of **O**. *1636*
Lk 19:29 at the mount called *the mount* of **O**, *1636*
19:37 *even* now at the descent of the mount of **O**, *1636*

O

Lk 21:37 in the mount that is called *the mount* of **O**. *1636*
22:39 went, as he was wont, to the mount of **O**; *1636*
Jn 8: 1 Jesus went unto the mount of **O**. *1636*

OLIVET (2) [OLIVE]
2Sa 15:30 David went up by the ascent of *mount* **O**, 2132
Ac 1:12 unto Jerusalem from the mount called **O**, *1638*

OLIVEYARD (1) [OLIVE]
Ex 23:11 deal with thy vineyard, *and* with thy **o**. 2132

OLIVEYARDS (5) [OLIVE]
Jos 24:13 and **o** which ye planted not do ye eat. 2132
1Sa 8:14 your vineyards, and your **o**, *even* the best *of* 2132
2Ki 5:26 **o**, and vineyards, and sheep, and oxen, and 2132
Ne 5:11 their vineyards, their **o**, and their houses, 2132
9:25 and **o**, and fruit trees in abundance: 2132

OLYMPAS (1)
Ro 16:15 and **O**, and all the saints which are with *3652*

OMAR (3)
Ge 36:11 **O**, Zepho, and Gatam, and Kenaz. 201
36:15 duke **O**, duke Zepho, duke Kenaz, 201
1Ch 1:36 **O**, Zephi, and Gatam, Kenaz, and Timna, 201

OMEGA (4)
Rev 1: 8 I am Alpha and **O**, the beginning and *5598*
1:11 Saying, I am Alpha and **O**, the first and *5598*
21: 6 I am Alpha and **O**, the beginning and *5598*
22:13 I am Alpha and **O**, the beginning and *5598*

OMER (5) [OMERS]
Ex 16:16 an **o** for every man, *according to* 6016
16:18 when they did mete *it* with an **o**, he that 6016
16:32 Fill an **o** of it to be kept for your 6016
16:33 put an **o** full of manna therein, and lay it up 6016
16:36 Now an **o** *is* the tenth *part* of an ephah. 6016

OMERS (1) [OMER]
Ex 16:22 two **o** for one *man:* and all the rulers of 6016

OMITTED (1)
Mt 23:23 and have **o** the weightier *matters* of the law, *863*

OMNIPOTENT (1)
Rev 19: 6 Alleluia: for the Lord God **O** reigneth. *3841*

OMRI (18)
1Ki 16:16 wherefore all Israel made **O**, the captain of 6018
16:17 **O** went up from Gibbethon, and all Israel 6018
16:21 to make him king; and half followed **O**. 6018
16:22 the people that followed **O** prevailed 6018
16:22 of Ginath: so Tibni died, and **O** reigned. 6018
16:23 first year of Asa king of Judah *began* **O** to 6018
16:25 **O** wrought evil in the eyes of the LORD, 6018
16:27 Now the rest of the acts of **O** which he did, 6018
16:28 So **O** slept with his fathers, and was buried 6018
16:29 Ahab the son of **O** to reign over Israel: 6018
16:29 Ahab the son of **O** reigned over Israel in 6018
16:30 Ahab the son of **O** did evil in the sight of 6018
2Ki 8:26 the daughter of **O** king of Israel. 6018
1Ch 7: 8 **O**, and Jerimoth, and Abiah, and Anathoth, 6018
9: 4 the son of **O**, the son of Imri, the son of 6018
27:18 of Issachar, **O** the son of Michael: 6018
2Ch 22: 2 name also *was* Athaliah the daughter of **O**. 6018
Mic 6:16 For the statutes of **O** are kept, and all 6018

ON (2016) [THEREON, WHEREON] See Index

ONAM (4)
Ge 36:23 and Manahath, and Ebal, Shepho, and **O**. 208
1Ch 1:40 and Manahath, and Ebal, Shephi, and **O**. 208
2:26 name *was* Atarah; she *was* the mother of **O**. 208
2:28 And the sons of **O** were, Shammai, and Jada. 208

ONAN (8)
Ge 38: 4 and bare a son; and she called his name **O**. 209
38: 8 Judah said unto **O**, Go in unto thy brother's 209
38: 9 And **O** knew that the seed should not be his; 209
46:12 Er, and **O**, and Shelah, and Pharez, and 209
46:12 Er and **O** died in the land of Canaan. 209
Nu 26:19 The sons of Judah *were* Er and **O**: and Er 209
26:19 and Er and **O** died in the land of Canaan. 209
1Ch 2: 3 The sons of Judah; Er, and **O**, and Shelah: 209

ONCE (59) [ONE]
Ge 18:32 be angry, and I will speak yet but *this* **o**: 6471
Ex 10:17 my sin only *this* **o**, and intreat the LORD 6471
30:10 **o** in a year with the blood of the sin offering 259
30:10 **o** in the year shall he make atonement upon 259
Lev 16:34 children of Israel for all their sins **o** a year. 259
Nu 13:30 Let us **go up at o**, and possess it; 5927+5927
Dt 7:22 thou mayest not consume them **at o**, 4118
Jos 6: 3 of war, *and* go round about the city **o**. 259+6471
6:11 compassed the city, going about *it* **o**: 259+6471
6:14 second day they compassed the city **o**, 259+6471
Jdg 6:39 hot against me, and I will speak but *this* **o**: 6471
6:39 I pray thee, but *this* **o** with the fleece; 6471
16:18 saying, Come up *this* **o**, for he hath shewed 6471
16:28 I pray thee, only this **o**, O God, 6471
16:28 that I may be **at o** avenged of the Philistines 259
1Sa 26: 8 with the spear even to the earth **at o**, 259+6471
1Ki 10:22 **o** in three years came the navy of Tharshish, 259
2Ki 6:10 and saved himself there, not **o** nor twice. 259
2Ch 9:21 every three years **o** came the ships of 259
Ne 5:18 and **o in** ten days store of all *sorts of* wine: 996
13:20 all *kind of* ware lodged without Jerusalem **o** 6471
Job 33:14 For God speaketh **o**, yea twice, 259+871.1
40: 5 **O** have I spoken; but I will not answer: yea, 259
Ps 62:11 God hath spoken **o**; twice have I heard this; 259
74: 6 the carved work thereof **at o** with axes 3162
76: 7 who may stand in thy sight **when o** 227+4480
89:35 **O** have I sworn by my holiness that I will 259
Pr 28:18 *he that is* perverse in *his* ways shall fall at **o**. 259
Isa 42:14 I will destroy and devour **at o**. 3162
66: 8 *or* shall a nation be born **at o**? for as 259+6471
Jer 10:18 out the inhabitants of the land at this **o**, 6471
13:27 not be made clean? when *shall it* **o** *be?* 5750
16:21 this **o** cause them to know, 6471+871.1+1886.1
Hag 2: 6 Yet **o**, it *is* a little while, and I *will* shake 259
Lk 13:25 When **o** the master of the house *302+575+3739*
23:18 And they cried out **all at o**, saying, *3826*
Ro 6:10 For in that he died, he died unto sin **o**: but *2178*
7: 9 For I was alive without the law **o**: but *4218*
1Co 15: 6 seen of above five hundred brethren **at o**; *2178*
2Co 11:25 **o** was I stoned, thrice I suffered shipwrack, *530*
Gal 1:23 preacheth the faith which **o** he destroyed. *4218*
Eph 5: 3 let it **not** be **o** named amongst you, *3366*
Php 4:16 For even in Thessalonica ye sent **o** and again *530*
1Th 2:18 come unto you, even I Paul, **o** and again; *530*
Heb 6: 4 For *it is* impossible for those who were **o** *530*
7:27 for this he did **o**, when he offered up *2178*
9: 7 *went* the high priest alone **o** every year, *530*
9:12 by his own blood he entered in **o** into *2178*
9:26 now **o** in the end of the world hath he *530*
9:27 And as it is appointed unto men **o** to die, but *530*
9:28 So Christ was **o** offered to bear the sins of *530*
10: 2 that the worshippers **o** purged should have *530*
10:10 of the body of Jesus Christ **o for all**. *2178*
12:26 Yet **o** *more* I shake not the earth only, but *530*
12:27 And this *word,* Yet **o** *more,* signifieth *530*
1Pe 3:18 For Christ also hath **o** suffered for sins, *530*
3:20 when **o** the longsuffering of God waited in *530*
Jude 1: 3 faith which was **o** delivered unto the saints. *530*
1: 5 though ye **o** knew this, how that the Lord, *530*

ONE (1967) [ONCE, ONE'S, ONES] See Index

ONE'S (2) [ONE] See Index

ONES (77) [ONE] See Index

ONESIMUS (4)
Col 4: 9 With **O**, a faithful and beloved brother, *3682*
4: S to the Colossians by Tychicus and **O**. *3682*
Phm 1:10 I beseech thee for my son **O**, whom I have *3682*
1: S from Rome to Philemon, by **O** a servant. *3682*

ONESIPHORUS (2)
2Ti 1:16 The Lord give mercy unto the house of **O**; *3683*
4:19 and Aquila, and the household of **O**. *3683*

ONIONS (1)
Nu 11: 5 and the leeks, and the **o**, and the garlick: 1211

ONLY (253) See Index

ONO (5)
1Ch 8:12 Misham, and Shamed, who built **O**, and Lod, 207
Ezr 2:33 The children of Lod, Hadid, and **O**, 207

Ne 6: 2 in *some one of* the villages in the plain of O. 207
7:37 The children of Lod, Hadid, and O, 207
11:35 Lod, and O, the valley of craftsmen. 207

ONWARD (1)
Ex 40:36 the children of Israel **went** o in all their 5265

ONYCHA (1)
Ex 30:34 sweet spices, stacte, and o, and galbanum; 7827

ONYX (11)
Ge 2:12 *is* good: there *is* bdellium and the o stone. 7718
Ex 25: 7 O stones, and stones to be set in the ephod, 7718
28: 9 thou shalt take two o stones, and grave on 7718
28:20 fourth row a beryl, and an o, and a jasper: 7718
35: 9 o stones, and stones to be set for the ephod, 7718
35:27 the rulers brought o stones, and stones to be 7718
39: 6 they wrought o stones inclosed *in* ouches *of* 7718
39:13 the fourth row, a beryl, an o, and a jasper: 7718
1Ch 29: 2 o stones, and *stones* to be set, 7718
Job 28:16 with the precious o, or the sapphire. 7718
Eze 28:13 the beryl, the o, and the jasper, 7718

OPEN (124) [OPENED, OPENEST, OPENETH, OPENING, OPENINGS, OPENLY]
Ge 1:20 fowl *that* may fly above the earth in the o 6440
38:14 and sat in an o **place,** 5869+6607
Ex 21:33 if a man shall o a pit, or if a man shall dig a 6605
Lev 14: 7 shall let the living bird loose into the o 6440
14:53 living bird out of the city into the o fields, 6440
17: 5 which they offer in the o field, even that 6440
Nu 8:16 instead of such as o every womb, 6363
16:30 the earth o her mouth, and swallow them 6475
19:15 every o vessel, which hath no covering 6605
19:16 that is slain with a sword in the o fields, 6440
24: 3 and the man whose eyes are o hath said: 8365
24: 4 falling *into a trance,* but having his eyes o: 1540
24:15 and the man whose eyes are o hath said: 8365
24:16 falling *into a trance,* but having his eyes o: 1540
Dt 15: 8 thou shalt o thine hand **wide** unto 6605+6605
15:11 Thou shalt o thine hand **wide** unto 6605+6605
20:11 of peace, and o unto thee, then it shall be, 6605
28:12 The LORD shall o unto thee his good 6605
Jos 8:17 they left the city o, and pursued after Israel. 6605
10:22 O the mouth of the cave, and bring out 6605
1Sa 3: 1 in those days; *there was* no o vision. 6555
2Sa 11:11 of my lord, are encamped in the o fields; 6440
1Ki 6:18 *was* carved with knops and o flowers: 6358
6:29 of cherubims and palm trees and o flowers, 6358
6:32 of cherubims and palm trees and o flowers, 6358
6:35 and palm trees and o flowers: 6358
8:29 That thine eyes may be o toward this house 6605
8:52 That thine eyes may be o unto 6605
2Ki 6:17 said, LORD, I pray thee, o his eyes, 6491
6:20 o the eyes of these *men,* that they may see. 6491
9: 3 Then o the door, and flee, and tarry not. 6605
13:17 he said, O the window eastward. And he 6605
19:16 o, LORD, thine eyes, and see: and 6491
2Ch 6:20 That thine eyes may be o upon this house 6605
6:40 thine eyes be o, and *let* thine ears *be* attent 6605
7:15 Now mine eyes shall be o, and mine ears 6605
Ne 1: 6 thine ear now be attentive, and thine eyes o, 6605
6: 5 the fifth time with an o letter in his hand; 6605
Job 11: 5 would speak, and o his lips against thee; 6605
14: 3 dost thou o thine eyes upon such a one, 6491
32:20 be refreshed: I will o my lips and answer. 6605
34:26 He striketh them as wicked *men* in the o 4725
35:16 Therefore doth Job o his mouth in vain; 6475
41:14 Who can o the doors of his face? his teeth 6605
Ps 5: 9 their throat *is* an o sepulchre; they flatter 6605
34:15 and his ears *are* o unto their cry. NIH
49: 4 I will o my dark saying upon the harp. 6605
51:15 O Lord, o thou my lips; and my mouth 6605
78: 2 I will o my mouth in a parable: I will utter 6605
81:10 o thy mouth **wide,** and I will fill it. 7337
118:19 O to me the gates of righteousness: I will 6605
119:18 O thou mine eyes, that I may behold 1540
Pr 13:16 but a fool **layeth** o *his* folly. 6566
20:13 o thine eyes, *and* thou shalt be satisfied 6491
27: 5 O rebuke *is* better than secret love. 1540
31: 8 O thy mouth for the dumb in the cause of 6605
31: 9 O thy mouth, judge righteously, and 6605
SS 5: 2 my beloved that knocketh *saying,* O to me, 6605
5: 5 I rose up to o to my beloved; and my hands 6605

Isa 9:12 they shall devour Israel with o mouth. 3605
22:22 so he shall o, and none shall shut; and 6605
22:22 and he shall shut, and none shall o. 6605
24:18 for the windows from on high are o, and 6605
26: 2 O ye the gates, that the righteous nation 6605
28:24 doth he o and break the clods of his 6605
37:17 and hear; o thine eyes, O LORD, and see: 6491
41:18 I will o rivers in high places, and 6605
42: 7 To o the blind eyes, to bring out 6491
45: 1 to o before him the two leaved gates; 6605
45: 8 let the earth o, and let them bring forth 6605
60:11 Therefore thy gates shall be o continually; 6605
Jer 5:16 Their quiver *is* as an o sepulchre, they *are* 6605
9:22 of men shall fall as dung upon the o field, 6440
13:19 none shall o *them:* Judah shall be carried 6605
32:11 the law and custom, and that which was o: 1540
32:14 is sealed, and this evidence which is o; 1540
32:19 for thine eyes *are* o upon all the ways of 6491
50:26 from the utmost border, o her storehouses: 6605
Eze 2: 8 o thy mouth, and eat that I give thee. 6475
3:27 I will o thy mouth, and thou shalt say unto 6605
16: 5 thou wast cast out in the o field, to 6440
16:63 never o thy mouth any more, because of thy 6610
21:22 to o the mouth in the slaughter, 6605
25: 9 I *will* o the side of Moab from the cities, 6605
29: 5 thou shalt fall upon the o fields; thou shalt 6440
32: 4 I will cast thee forth upon the o field, and 6440
33:27 him that *is* in the o field will I give to 6440
37: 2 *there were* very many in the o valley; 6440
37:12 I *will* o your graves, and cause you to come 6605
39: 5 Thou shalt fall upon the o field: for I have 6440
46:12 o him the gate that looketh *toward* the east, 6605
Da 6:10 his windows being o in his chamber toward 6606
9:18 o thine eyes, and behold our desolations, 6491
Na 3:13 the gates of thy land shall be set wide o 6605
Zec 11: 1 O thy doors, O Lebanon, that the fire may 6605
12: 4 I will o mine eyes upon the house of Judah, 6491
Mal 3:10 if I will not o you the windows of heaven, 6605
Mt 13:35 saying, I will o my mouth in parables; *455*
25:11 the other virgins, saying, Lord, Lord, o to us. *455*
Lk 12:36 knocketh, they may o unto him immediately. *455*
13:25 at the door, saying, Lord, Lord, o unto us; *455*
Jn 1:51 Hereafter ye shall see heaven o, and *455*
10:21 a devil. Can a devil o the eyes of the blind? *455*
Ac 16:27 and seeing the prison doors o, he drew out *455*
18:14 And when Paul was *now* about to o *his* *455*
19:38 have a matter against any *man,* the law is o, *71*
26:18 To o their eyes, *and* to turn *them* from *455*
Ro 3:13 Their throat *is* an o sepulchre; with their *455*
2Co 3:18 with o face beholding as in a glass the glory *343*
6:11 O *ye* Corinthians, our mouth is o unto you, *455*
Eph 6:19 unto me, that *I* may o my mouth boldly, *457*
Col 4: 3 that God would o unto us a door of *455*
1Ti 5:24 Some men's sins are o **beforehand,** *4271*
Heb 6: 6 of God afresh, and **put** *him* **to** an o **shame.** *3856*
1Pe 3:12 and his ears *are* o unto their prayers: NIG
Rev 3: 8 I have set before thee an o door, and no *man* *455*
3:20 and o the door, I will come in to him, and *455*
5: 2 Who is worthy to o the book, and to loose *455*
5: 3 under the earth, was able to o the book, *455*
5: 4 because no *man* was found worthy to o and *455*
5: 5 hath prevailed to o the book, and to loose *455*
5: 9 to take the book, and to o the seals thereof: *455*
10: 2 And he had in his hand a little book o: and *455*
10: 8 take the little book which is o in the hand of *455*

OPENED (137) [OPEN]
Ge 3: 5 your eyes shall be o, and ye shall be as 6491
3: 7 the eyes of them both were o, and 6491
4:11 which hath o her mouth to receive thy 6475
7:11 and the windows of heaven were o. 6605
8: 6 that Noah o the window of the ark which he 6605
21:19 God o her eyes, and she saw a well of 6491
29:31 saw that Leah *was* hated, he o her womb: 6605
30:22 and God hearkened to her, and o her womb. 6605
41:56 Joseph o all the storehouses, and sold unto 6605
42:27 as one *of them* o his sack to give his ass 6605
43:21 to the inn, that we o our sacks, and behold, 6605
44:11 to the ground, and o every man his sack. 6605
Ex 2: 6 when she had o *it,* she saw the child: and 6605
Nu 16:32 the earth o her mouth, and swallowed them 6605
22:28 the LORD o the mouth of the ass, and 6605
22:31 Then the LORD o the eyes of Balaam, and 1540
26:10 the earth o her mouth, and swallowed them 6605

Dt 11: 6 how the earth **o** her mouth, and 6475
Jdg 3:25 behold, he **o** not the doors of the parlour; 6605
3:25 they took a key, and **o** *them:* and behold, 6605
4:19 she **o** a bottle of milk, and gave him drink, 6605
11:35 for I have **o** my mouth unto the LORD, 6475
11:36 *if* thou hast **o** thy mouth unto the LORD, 6475
19:27 **o** the doors of the house, and went out to go 6605
1Sa 3:15 and **o** the doors of the house of the LORD. 6605
2Ki 4:35 seven times, and the child **o** his eyes. 6491
6:17 the LORD **o** the eyes of the young man; 6491
6:20 And the LORD **o** their eyes, and they saw; 6491
9:10 *there shall be* none to bury *her.* And he **o** 6605
13:17 he **o** *it.* Then Elisha said, Shoot. And he 6605
15:16 because they **o** not *to him,* therefore 6605
2Ch 29: 3 **o** the doors of the house of the LORD, and 6605
Ne 7: 3 Let not the gates of Jerusalem be **o** until 6605
8: 5 Ezra **o** the book in the sight of all 6605
8: 5 and when he **o** *it,* all the people stood *up:* 6605
13:19 charged that they should not be **o** till after 6605
Job 3: 1 After this **o** Job his mouth, and cursed his 6605
29:23 they **o** their mouth **wide** *as* for the latter 6473
31:32 the street: *but* I **o** my doors to the traveller. 6605
33: 2 Behold now I have **o** my mouth, my tongue 6605
38:17 Have the gates of death been **o** unto thee? 1540
Ps 35:21 they **o** their mouth **wide** against me, *and* 7337
39: 9 I was dumb, I **o** not my mouth; because 6605
40: 6 thou didst not desire; mine ears hast thou **o**: 3738
78:23 from above, and **o** the doors of heaven, 6605
105:41 He **o** the rock, and the waters gushed out; 6605
106:17 The earth **o** and swallowed up Dathan, and 6605
109: 2 the mouth of the deceitful are **o** against me: 6605
119:131 I **o** my mouth, and panted: for I longed for 6473
SS 5: 6 I **o** to my beloved; but my beloved had 6605
Isa 5:14 and **o** her mouth without measure: 6473
10:14 moved the wing, or **o** the mouth, or peeped. 6475
14:17 *that* **o** not the house of his prisoners? 6605
35: 5 the eyes of the blind shall be **o**, and the ears 6491
48: 8 yea, from that time *that* thine ear was not **o**: 6605
50: 5 The Lord GOD hath **o** mine ear, and I was 6605
53: 7 he was afflicted, yet he **o** not his mouth: 6605
Jer 20:12 on them: for unto thee have I **o** my cause. 1540
50:25 The LORD hath **o** his armoury, and 6605
La 2:16 All thine enemies have **o** their mouth 6475
3:46 All our enemies have **o** their mouths 6475
Eze 1: 1 *that* the heavens were **o**, and I saw visions 6605
3: 2 So I **o** my mouth, and he caused me to eat 6605
16:25 hast **o** thy feet to every one that passed by, 6589
24:27 In that day shall thy mouth be **o** to him 6605
33:22 had **o** my mouth, until *he* came to me in 6605
33:22 my mouth was **o**, and I was no more dumb. 6605
37:13 when I have **o** your graves, O my people, 6605
44: 2 it shall not be **o**, and no man shall enter in 6605
46: 1 on the sabbath it shall be **o**, and in the day 6605
46: 1 in the day of the new moon it shall be **o**. 6605
Da 7:10 judgment was set, and the books were **o**. 6606
10:16 I **o** my mouth, and spake, and said unto him 6605
Na 2: 6 The gates of the rivers shall be **o**, and 6605
Zec 13: 1 In that day there shall be a fountain **o** to 6605
Mt 2:11 and when they had **o** their treasures, *455*
3:16 and lo, the heavens were **o** unto him, and *455*
5: 2 And he **o** his mouth, and taught them, *455*
7: 7 shall find; knock, and it shall be **o** unto you: *455*
7: 8 and to him that knocketh it shall be **o**. *455*
9:30 And their eyes were **o**; and Jesus straitly *455*
17:27 and when thou hast **o** his mouth, thou shalt *455*
20:33 say unto him, Lord, that our eyes may be **o**. *455*
27:52 And the graves were **o**; and many bodies of *455*
Mk 1:10 he saw the heavens **o**, and the Spirit like a *4977*
7:34 unto him, EPHPHATHA, that is, Be **o**. *1272*
7:35 And straightway his ears were **o**, *1272*
Lk 1:64 And his mouth was **o** immediately, and *455*
3:21 and praying, the heaven was **o**, *455*
4:17 And when he had **o** the book, he found *380*
11: 9 shall find; knock, and it shall be **o** unto you. *455*
11:10 and to him that knocketh it shall be **o**. *455*
24:31 And their eyes were **o**, and they knew him; *1272*
24:32 and while he **o** to us the scriptures? *1272*
24:45 Then **o** he their understanding, that *they* *1272*
Jn 9:10 said they unto him, How were thine eyes **o**? *455*
9:14 when Jesus made the clay, and **o** his eyes. *455*
9:17 sayest thou of him, that he hath **o** thine eyes? *455*
9:21 or who hath **o** his eyes, we know not: *455*
9:26 What did he to thee? how **o** he thine eyes? *455*
9:30 whence he is, and *yet* he hath **o** mine eyes. *455*
9:32 *man* **o** the eyes of one that was born blind. *455*
11:37 Could not this *man,* which **o** the eyes of *455*
Ac 5:19 But *the* angel of the Lord by night **o** *455*
5:23 but when we had **o**, we found no *man* within. *455*
7:56 And said, Behold, I see the heavens **o**, *455*
8:32 before his shearer, so **o** he not his mouth: *455*
8:35 Then Philip **o** his mouth, *455*
9: 8 and when his eyes were **o**, he saw no *man:* *455*
9:40 And she **o** her eyes: and when she saw Peter, *455*
10:11 And saw heaven **o**, and a certain vessel *455*
10:34 Then Peter **o** *his* mouth, and said, Of a truth *455*
12:10 the city; which **o** to them of his own accord: *455*
12:14 she **o** not the gate for gladness, but ran in, *455*
12:16 and when they had **o** *the door,* and saw him, *455*
14:27 how he had **o** *the* door of faith unto *455*
16:14 heard *us:* whose heart the Lord **o**, *1272*
16:26 and immediately all the doors were **o**, and *455*
1Co 16: 9 For a great door and effectual is **o** unto me, *455*
2Co 2:12 and a door was **o** unto me of the Lord, *455*
Heb 4:13 **o** unto the eyes of him with whom we have *5136*
Rev 4: 1 and behold, a door *was* **o** in heaven: *455*
6: 1 And I saw when the Lamb **o** one of the seals, *455*
6: 3 And when he had **o** the second seal, I heard *455*
6: 5 And when he had **o** the third seal, I heard *455*
6: 7 And when he had **o** the fourth seal, I heard *455*
6: 9 And when he had **o** the fifth seal, I saw *455*
6:12 And I beheld when he had **o** the sixth seal, *455*
8: 1 And when he had **o** the seventh seal, *455*
9: 2 And he **o** the bottomless pit; and there arose *455*
11:19 And the temple of God was **o** in heaven, and *455*
12:16 and the earth **o** her mouth, and swallowed up *455*
13: 6 And he **o** his mouth in blasphemy against *455*
15: 5 tabernacle of the testimony in heaven was **o**: *455*
19:11 And I saw heaven **o**, and behold a white *455*
20:12 stand before God; and the books were **o**: *455*
20:12 and another book was **o**, which is *the book* *455*

OPENEST (2) [OPEN]

Ps 104:28 thou **o** thine hand, they are filled *with* good. 6605
145:16 Thou **o** thine hand, and satisfiest the desire 6605

OPENETH (21) [OPEN]

Ex 13: 2 whatsoever **o** the womb among the children 6363
13:12 apart unto the LORD all that **o** the matrix, 6363
13:15 I sacrifice to the LORD all that **o** 6363
34:19 All that **o** the matrix *is* mine; and 6363
Nu 3:12 **o** the matrix among the children of Israel: 6363
18:15 Every thing **that** **o** the matrix in all flesh, 6363
Job 27:19 be gathered: he **o** his eyes, and he *is* not. 6491
33:16 he **o** the ears of men, and sealeth their 1540
36:10 He **o** also their ear to discipline, and 1540
36:15 his affliction, and **o** their ears in oppression. 1540
Ps 38:13 *I was* as a dumb *man that* **o** not his mouth. 6605
146: 8 The LORD **o** *the eyes of* the blind: 6491
Pr 13: 3 he that **o** **wide** his lips shall have 6589
24: 7 for a fool: he **o** not his mouth in the gate. 6605
31:26 She **o** her mouth with wisdom; and in her 6605
Isa 53: 7 her shearers is dumb, so he **o** not his mouth. 6605
Eze 20:26 pass through *the fire* all **that** **o** the womb, 6363
Lk 2:23 Every male that **o** the womb shall be called *1272*
Jn 10: 3 To him the porter **o**; and the sheep hear his *455*
Rev 3: 7 key of David, he that **o**, and no *man* shutteth; *455*
3: 7 no *man* shutteth; and shutteth, and no *man* **o**; *455*

OPENING (7) [OPEN]

1Ch 9:27 the **o** *thereof* every morning pertained to 4668
Job 12:14 he shutteth up a man, and there can be no **o**. 6605
Pr 8: 6 and the **o** of my lips *shall be* right things. 4669
Isa 42:20 **o** the ears, he heareth not. 6491
61: 1 the **o** **of the prison** to *them that are* bound; 6495
Eze 29:21 I will give thee the **o** of the mouth in 6610
Ac 17: 3 **O** and alleging, that Christ must needs have *1272*

OPENINGS (1) [OPEN]

Pr 1:21 place of concourse, in the **o** of the gates: 6607

OPENLY (15) [OPEN]

Ge 38:21 that *was* **o** by the way side? 5869+871.1+1886.1
Ps 98: 2 his righteousness hath he **o** **shewed** in 1540
Mt 6: 4 in secret himself shall reward thee **o**. *1722+5318*
6: 6 seeth in secret shall reward thee **o**. *1722+5318*
6:18 seeth in secret, shall reward thee **o**. *1722+5318*
Mk 1:45 insomuch that *Jesus* could no more **o** enter *5320*
8:32 And he spake *that* saying **o**. And Peter took *3954*

Jn 7: 4 he himself seeketh to be **known o**. *1722+3954*
7:10 the feast, not o, but as it were in secret. *5320*
7:13 Howbeit no *man* spake o of him for fear of *3954*
11:54 walked no more o among the Jews; *3954*
18:20 Jesus answered him, I spake o to the world; *3954*
Ac 10:40 raised up the third day, and shewed him o; *1717*
16:37 They have beaten us o uncondemned, *1219*
Col 2:15 he made a shew of *them* o, *1722+3954*

OPERATION (3) [OPERATIONS]
Ps 28: 5 nor the o of his hands, he shall destroy 4639
Isa 5:12 neither consider the o of his hands. 4639
Col 2:12 with *him* through the faith of the o of God, *1753*

OPERATIONS (1) [OPERATION]
1Co 12: 6 And there are diversities of o, but it is *1755*

OPHEL (5)
2Ch 27: 3 and on the wall of O he built much. 6077
33:14 compassed about O, and raised it up a very 6077
Ne 3:26 Moreover the Nethinims dwelt in O, 6077
3:27 that lieth out, even unto the wall of O. 6077
11:21 the Nethinims dwelt in O: and Ziha and 6077

OPHIR (13)
Ge 10:29 O, and Havilah, and Jobab: all these *were* 211
1Ki 9:28 they came to O, and fet from thence gold, 211
10:11 also of Hiram, that brought gold from O, 211
10:11 brought in from O great plenty of almug 211
22:48 made ships of Tharshish to go to O for gold: 211
1Ch 1:23 O, and Havilah, and Jobab. All these *were* 211
29: 4 of the gold of O, and seven thousand talents 211
2Ch 8:18 went with the servants of Solomon to O, 211
9:10 which brought gold from O, brought algum 211
Job 22:24 *the gold of* O as the stones of the brooks. 211
28:16 It cannot be valued with the gold of O, 211
Ps 45: 9 right hand did stand the queen in gold of O. 211
Isa 13:12 even a man than the golden wedge of O. 211

OPHNI (1)
Jos 18:24 and O, and Gaba; 6078

OPHRAH (8)
Jos 18:23 And Avim, and Parah, and O, 6084
Jdg 6:11 sat under an oak which *was* in O, 6084
6:24 unto this day it *is* yet in O of 6084
8:27 and put it in his city, *even* in O: 6084
8:32 of Joash his father, in O of the Abi-ezrites. 6084
9: 5 he went unto his father's house at O, and 6084
1Sa 13:17 turned unto the way that leadeth to O, 6084
1Ch 4:14 Meonothai begat O: and Seraiah begat 6084

OPINION (3) [OPINIONS]
Job 32: 6 was afraid, and durst not shew you mine o. 1843
32:10 Hearken to me; I also will shew mine o. 1843
32:17 also my part, I also will shew mine o. 1843

OPINIONS (1) [OPINION]
1Ki 18:21 and said, How long halt ye between two o? 5587

OPPORTUNITY (5)
Mt 26:16 And from that time he sought o to betray *2120*
Lk 22: 6 sought o to betray him unto them in *2120*
Gal 6:10 As we have therefore o, let us do good unto *2540*
Php 4:10 ye were also careful, but ye **lacked o**. *170*
Heb 11:15 they might have had o to have returned. *2540*

OPPOSE (1) [OPPOSED, OPPOSEST, OPPOSETH, OPPOSITIONS]
2Ti 2:25 instructing those that o **themselves**; *475*

OPPOSED (1) [OPPOSE]
Ac 18: 6 And when they o themselves, and *498*

OPPOSEST (1) [OPPOSE]
Job 30:21 with thy strong hand thou o thyself against 7852

OPPOSETH (1) [OPPOSE]
2Th 2: 4 Who o and exalteth himself above all that is *480*

OPPOSITIONS (1) [OPPOSE]
1Ti 6:20 and o of science falsely so called: *477*

OPPRESS (23) [OPPRESSED, OPPRESSETH, OPPRESSING, OPPRESSION, OPPRESSIONS, OPPRESSOR, OPPRESSORS]
Ex 3: 9 wherewith the Egyptians o them. 3905
22:21 shalt neither vex a stranger, nor o him: 3905
23: 9 Also thou shalt not o a stranger: for ye 3905
Lev 25:14 ye shall not o one another: 3238
25:17 Ye shall not therefore o one another; 3238
Dt 23:16 it liketh him best: thou shalt not o him. 3238
24:14 Thou shalt not o a hired servant *that is* poor 6231
Jdg 10:12 and the Maonites, did o you; 3905
Job 10: 3 *Is it* good unto thee that thou shouldest o, 6231
Ps 10:18 that the man of the earth may no more o. 6206
17: 9 From the wicked that o me, *from* my 7703
119:122 servant for good: let not the proud o me. 6231
Pr 22:22 *is* poor: neither o the afflicted in the gate: 1792
Isa 49:26 I will feed them that o thee with their own 3238
Jer 7: 6 *If* ye o not the stranger, the fatherless, and 6231
30:20 before me, and I will punish all that o them. 3905
Eze 45: 8 my princes shall no more o my people; and 3238
Hos 12: 7 of deceit *are* in his hand: he loveth to o. 6231
Am 4: 1 which o the poor, which crush the needy, 6231
Mic 2: 2 so they o a man and his house, even a man 6231
Zec 7:10 o not the widow, nor the fatherless, 6231
Mal 3: 5 against those that o the hireling in *his* 6231
Jas 2: 6 Do not rich *men* o you, and draw you *2616*

OPPRESSED (38) [OPPRESS]
Dt 28:29 thou shalt be only o and spoiled evermore, 6231
28:33 and thou shalt be only o and crushed alway: 6231
Jdg 2:18 of their groanings by reason of them that o 3905
4: 3 twenty years he mightily o the children of 3905
6: 9 out of the hand of all that o you, and 3905
10: 8 they vexed and o the children of Israel: 7533
1Sa 10:18 of all kingdoms, *and* of them that o you: 3905
12: 3 whom have I o? or of whose hand have I 7533
12: 4 Thou hast not defrauded us, nor o us, 7533
2Ki 13: 4 of Israel, because the king of Syria o them. 3905
13:22 Hazael king of Syria o Israel all the days of 3905
2Ch 16:10 of this *thing.* And Asa o *some* of the people 7533
Job 20:19 Because he hath o *and* hath forsaken 7533
35: 9 of oppressions they make *the* o to cry: NIH
Ps 9: 9 The LORD also will be a refuge for the o, 1790
10:18 To judge the fatherless and the o, that 1790
74:21 O let not the o return ashamed: let the poor 1790
103: 6 and judgment for all that are o. 6231
106:42 Their enemies also o them, and they were 3905
146: 7 Which executeth judgment for the o: 6231
Ecc 4: 1 the tears of such as were o, and they had no 6231
Isa 1:17 seek judgment, relieve the o, judge 2541
3: 5 the people shall be o, every one by another, 5065
23:12 O thou o virgin, daughter of Zidon: 6231
38:14 O LORD, I am o; undertake for me. 6234
52: 4 and the Assyrian o them without cause. 6231
53: 7 He was o, and he was afflicted, yet he 5065
58: 6 to let the o go free, and *that* ye break every 7533
Jer 50:33 and the children of Judah *were* o together: 6231
Eze 18: 7 hath not o any, *but* hath restored *to* 3238
18:12 Hath o the poor and needy, hath spoiled by 3238
18:16 Neither hath o any, hath not withholden 3238
18:18 *for* his father, because he **cruelly o**, 6231+6233
22:29 they have o the stranger wrongfully. 6231
Hos 5:11 Ephraim *is* o *and* broken in judgment, 6231
Am 3: 9 and the o in the midst thereof. 6217
Ac 7:24 defended *him,* and avenged him that was o, *2669*
10:38 and healing all that were o of the devil; *2616*

OPPRESSETH (5) [OPPRESS]
Nu 10: 9 in your land against the enemy that o you, 6887
Ps 56: 1 swallow me up; he fighting daily o me. 3905
Pr 14:31 He that o the poor reproacheth his Maker: 6231
22:16 He that o the poor to increase his *riches,* 6231
28: 3 A poor man that o the poor *is like* a 6231

OPPRESSING (3) [OPPRESS]
Jer 46:16 the land of our nativity, from the o sword. 3238
50:16 for fear of the o sword they shall turn every 3238
Zep 3: 1 her that is filthy and polluted, to the o city! 3238

OPPRESSION (24) [OPPRESS]
Ex 3: 9 I have also seen the o wherewith 3906
Dt 26: 7 on our affliction, and our labour, and our o: 3906
2Ki 13: 4 for he saw the o of Israel, because the king 3906
Job 36:15 in his affliction, and openeth their ears in o. 3906
Ps 12: 5 For the o of the poor, for the sighing of 7701
42: 9 I mourning because of the o of the enemy? 3906
43: 2 I mourning because of the o of the enemy? 3906
44:24 *and* forgettest our affliction and our o? 3906

Ps 55: 3 the enemy, because of the **o** of the wicked: 6125
62:10 Trust not in **o**, and become not vain in 6233
73: 8 and speak wickedly *concerning* **o**: 6233
107:39 are minished and brought low through **o**, 6115
119:134 Deliver me from the **o** of man: so will I 6233
Ecc 5: 8 If thou seest the **o** of the poor, and 6233
7: 7 Surely **o** maketh a wise *man* mad; and a gift 6233
Isa 5: 7 he looked for judgment, but behold **o**; 4939
30:12 trust in **o** and perverseness, and 6233
54:14 thou shalt be far from **o**; for thou shalt not 6233
59:13 speaking **o** and revolt, conceiving and 6233
Jer 6: 6 she *is* wholly **o** in the midst of her. 6233
22:17 and for **o**, and for violence, to do *it*. 6233
Eze 22: 7 in the midst of thee have they dealt by **o** 6233
22:29 The people of the land have **used o**, 6231+6233
46:18 by **o** to thrust them out of their possession; 3238

OPPRESSIONS (3) [OPPRESS]
Job 35: 9 By reason of the multitude of **o** they make 6217
Ecc 4: 1 considered all the **o** that *are* done under 6217
Isa 33:15 he that despiseth the gain of **o**, that shaketh 4642

OPPRESSOR (14) [OPPRESS]
Job 3:18 they hear not the voice of the **o**. 5065
15:20 and the number of years is hidden to the **o**. 6184
Ps 72: 4 the needy, and shall break in pieces the **o**. 6231
Pr 3:31 Envy thou not the **o**, and choose none 376+2555
28:16 that wanteth understanding *is* also a great **o**: 4642
Isa 9: 4 the rod of his **o**, as *in* the day of Midian. 5065
14: 4 and say, How hath the **o** ceased! 5065
51:13 every day because of the fury of the **o**, 6693
51:13 to destroy? and where *is* the fury of the **o**? 6693
Jer 21:12 *him that is* spoiled out of the hand of the **o**, 6231
22: 3 deliver the spoiled out of the hand of the **o**; 6216
25:38 because of the fierceness of the **o**, 3238
Zec 9: 8 no **o** shall pass through them any more: 5065
10: 4 the battle bow, out of him every **o** together. 5065

OPPRESSORS (8) [OPPRESS]
Job 27:13 the heritage of **o**, *which* they shall receive 6184
Ps 54: 3 up against me, and **o** seek after my soul: 6184
119:121 and justice: leave me not to mine **o**. 6231
Ecc 4: 1 on the side of their **o** *there was* power; but 6231
Isa 3:12 children *are* their **o**, and women rule over 5065
14: 2 they were; and they shall rule over their **o**. 5065
16: 4 the **o** are consumed out of the land. 7429
19:20 shall cry unto the LORD because of the **o**, 3905

OR (1130) See Index

ORACLE (17) [ORACLES]
2Sa 16:23 *was* as if a man had inquired at the **o** of 1697
1Ki 6: 5 *both* of the temple and of the **o**: 1687
6:16 *even* for the **o**, *even* for the most holy 1687
6:19 the **o** he prepared in the house within, to set 1687
6:20 the **o** in the forepart *was* twenty cubits in 1687
6:21 partition by the chains of gold before the **o**; 1687
6:22 also the whole altar that *was* by the **o** he 1687
6:23 within the **o** he made two cherubims *of* 1687
6:31 for the entering of the **o** he made doors of 1687
7:49 five on the left, before the **o**, with 1687
8: 6 into the **o** of the house, to the most holy 1687
8: 8 seen out in the holy *place* before the **o**, 1687
2Ch 3:16 *as* in the **o**, and put *them* on the heads of 1687
4:20 should burn after the manner before the **o**, 1687
5: 7 to the **o** of the house, into the most holy 1687
5: 9 staves were seen from the ark before the **o**; 1687
Ps 28: 2 when I lift up my hands toward thy holy **o**. 1687

ORACLES (4) [ORACLE]
Ac 7:38 who received *the* lively **o** to give unto us: *3051*
Ro 3: 2 that unto them were committed the **o** of *3051*
Heb 5:12 *be* the first principles of the **o** of God; *3051*
1Pe 4:11 *man* speak, *let him speak* as the **o** of God; *3051*

ORATION (1) [ORATOR]
Ac 12:21 upon his throne, and **made an o** unto them. *1215*

ORATOR (2) [ORATION]
Isa 3: 3 the cunning artificer, and the eloquent **o**. 3908
Ac 24: 1 and *with* a certain **o** *named* Tertullus, *4489*

ORCHARD (1) [ORCHARDS]
SS 4:13 Thy plants *are* an **o** of pomegranates, 6508

ORCHARDS (1) [ORCHARD]
Ecc 2: 5 I made me gardens and **o**, and I planted 6508

ORDAIN (5) [FOREORDAINED, ORDAINED, ORDAINETH]
1Ch 9:22 Samuel the seer did **o** in their set office. 3245
17: 9 Also I will **o** a place for my people Israel, 7760
Isa 26:12 LORD, thou wilt **o** peace for us: for thou 8239
1Co 7:17 so let him walk. And so **o** I in all churches. *1299*
Tit 1: 5 and **o** elders in every city, as I had *2525*

ORDAINED (37) [ORDAIN]
Nu 28: 6 which was **o** in mount Sinai for a sweet 6213
1Ki 12:32 Jeroboam **o** a feast in the eighth month, 6213
12:33 and **o** a feast unto the children of Israel: 6213
2Ki 23: 5 whom the kings of Judah had **o** to burn 5414
2Ch 11:15 he **o** him priests for the high places, and 5975
23:18 with singing, **as** it was **o by** David. 3027+5921
29:27 with the instruments **o by** David king 3027+5921
Est 9:27 The Jews **o**, and took upon them, and 6965
Ps 8: 2 sucklings hast thou **o** strength because 3245
8: 3 the moon and the stars, which thou hast **o**; 3559
81: 5 This he **o** in Joseph *for* a testimony, 7760
132:17 to bud: I have **o** a lamp for mine anointed. 6186
Isa 30:33 For Tophet *is* **o** of old; yea, for the king it is 6186
Jer 1: 5 *and* I **o** thee a prophet unto the nations. 5414
Da 2:24 whom the king had **o** to destroy the wise 4483
Hab 1:12 O LORD, thou hast **o** them for judgment; 7760
Mk 3:14 And he **o** twelve, that they should be with *4160*
Jn 15:16 and **o** you, that you should go and *5087*
Ac 1:22 must one be **o** *to be* a witness with us of his *1096*
10:42 to testify that it is he which was **o** of God *to* *3724*
13:48 as many as were **o** to eternal life believed. *5021*
14:23 And when they had **o** them elders in every *5500*
16: 4 that were **o** of the apostles and elders which *2919*
17:31 righteousness by *that* man whom he hath **o**; *3724*
Ro 7:10 And the commandment, which was **o** to life, NIG
13: 1 of God: the powers that be are **o** of God. *5021*
1Co 2: 7 *even* the hidden *wisdom,* which God **o** *4309*
9:14 hath the Lord **o** that they which preach *1299*
Gal 3:19 *it was* **o** by angels in the hand of a *1299*
Eph 2:10 which God hath **before o** that we should *4282*
1Ti 2: 7 Whereunto I am **o** a preacher, and *5087*
2Ti 4: S **o** the first bishop of the church of *5500*
Tit 3: S **o** the first bishop of the church of *5500*
Heb 5: 1 is **o** for men *in things* pertaining to God, *2525*
8: 3 For every high priest is **o** to offer gifts and *2525*
9: 6 Now when these *things* were thus **o**, *2680*
Jude 1: 4 who were **before** of old **o** to this *4270*

ORDAINETH (1) [ORDAIN]
Ps 7:13 he **o** his arrows against the persecutors. 6466

ORDER (61) [ORDERED, ORDERETH, ORDERINGS, ORDERLY]
Ge 22: 9 **laid** the wood **in o**, and bound Isaac his 6186
Ex 26:17 in one board, **set in o** one against another: 7947
27:21 his sons shall **o** it from evening to morning 6186
39:37 *even with* the lamps to be **set in o**, and all 4634
40: 4 **set in o** the things that are to be set in order 6186
40: 4 set in order the things that are to be **set in o** 6187
40:23 he **set** the bread **in o** upon it before 6186+6187
Lev 1: 7 and **lay** the wood **in o** upon the fire: 6186
1: 8 **lay** the parts, the head, and the fat, **in o** 6186
1:12 the priest shall **lay** them **in o** on the wood 6186
6:12 **lay** the burnt offering **in o** upon it; 6186
24: 3 shall Aaron **o** it from the evening unto 6186
24: 4 He shall **o** the lamps upon the pure 6186
24: 8 Every sabbath he shall **set** it **in o** before 6186
Jos 2: 6 which she had **laid in o** upon the roof. 6186
Jdg 13:12 How shall we **o** the child, and 1961+4941
2Sa 17:23 **put** his household **in o**, and 6680
1Ki 18:33 he **put** the wood **in o**, and cut the bullock in 6186
20:14 he said, Who shall **o** the battle? And he 631
2Ki 20: 1 saith the LORD, **Set** thine house **in o**; 6680
23: 4 high priest, and the priests of the **second o**; 4932
1Ch 6:32 waited on their office according to their **o**. 4941
15:13 for that we sought him not after the **due o**. 4941
23:31 according to the **o commanded** unto them, 4941
25: 2 which prophesied according to the **o** of 3027
25: 6 according to the king's **o** *to* Asaph, 3027
2Ch 8:14 according to the **o** of David his father, 4941
13:11 the *shew*bread also *set they* **in o** upon 4635
29:35 of the house of the LORD was **set in o**. 3559
Job 10:22 without any **o**, and *where* the light is as 5468
23: 4 I would **o** *my* cause before him, and fill my 6186

O

Job 33: 5 **set** *thy words* **in o** before me, stand up. 6186
37:19 *for* we cannot **o** *our speech* by reason of 6186
Ps 40: 5 they cannot be **reckoned up in o** unto thee: 6186
50:21 and **set** *them* **in o** before thine eyes. 6186
110: 4 Thou *art* a priest for ever after the **o** of 1700
119:133 **O** my steps in thy word: and let not any 3559
Ecc 12: 9 and sought out, *and* **set in o** many proverbs. 8626
Isa 9: 7 to **o** it, and to stablish it with judgment and 3559
38: 1 saith the LORD, **Set** thine house **in o**: 6680
44: 7 and shall declare it, and **set** it **in o** for me, 6186
Jer 46: 3 **O** ye the buckler and shield, and draw near 6186
Eze 41: 6 one over another, and thirty *in o*; 6471
Lk 1: 1 **set forth in o** a declaration of those things *392*
1: 3 to write unto thee **in o**, most excellent *2517*
1: 8 office before God in the **o** of his course, *5010*
Ac 11: 4 *and* expounded *it* **by o** unto them, saying, *2517*
18:23 *all* the country of Galatia and Phrygia **in o**, *2517*
1Co 11:34 And the rest will I **set in o** when I come. *1299*
14:40 Let all *things* be done decently and in **o**. *5010*
15:23 But every man in his own **o**: Christ *5001*
16: 1 as I have **given o** to the churches of *1299*
Col 2: 5 joying and beholding your **o**, and *5010*
Tit 1: 5 that thou shouldest **set in o** the *things* that *1930*
Heb 5: 6 a priest for ever after the **o** of Melchisedec. *5010*
5:10 Called of God a high priest after the **o** of *5010*
6:20 made a high priest for ever after the **o** of *5010*
7:11 should rise after the **o** of Melchisedec, *5010*
7:11 and not be called after the **o** of Aaron? *5010*
7:17 Thou *art* a priest for ever after the **o** of *5010*
7:21 Thou *art* a priest for ever after the **o** of *5010*

ORDERED (4) [ORDER]
Jdg 6:26 in the **o place**, and take the second bullock, 4634
2Sa 23: 5 **o** in all *things*, and sure: 6186
Job 13:18 Behold now, I have **o** *my* cause; I know 6186
Ps 37:23 The steps of a *good* man are **o** by 3559

ORDERETH (1) [ORDER]
Ps 50:23 to him that **o** *his* conversation *aright* will I 7760

ORDERINGS (1) [ORDER]
1Ch 24:19 These *were* the **o** of them in their service to 6486

ORDERLY (1) [ORDER]
Ac 21:24 but *that* thou thyself also **walkest o**, and *4748*

ORDINANCE (30) [ORDINANCES]
Ex 12:14 you shall keep it a feast by an **o** for ever. 2708
12:17 day in your generations by an **o** for ever. 2708
12:24 ye shall observe this thing for an **o** to thee 2706
12:43 and Aaron, This *is* the **o** of the passover: 2708
13:10 keep this **o** in his season from year to year. 2708
15:25 there he made for them a statute and an **o**, 4941
Lev 18:30 Therefore ye shall keep mine **o**, that *ye* 4931
22: 9 They shall therefore keep mine **o**, lest they 4931
Nu 9:14 according to the **o** of the passover, and 2708
9:14 ye shall have one **o**, both for the stranger, 2708
10: 8 they shall be to you for an **o** for ever 2708
15:15 One **o** *shall be both* for you *of* 2708
15:15 *with you*, an **o** for ever in your generations: 2708
18: 8 and to thy sons, by an **o** for ever. 2706
19: 2 This *is* the **o** of the law which the LORD 2708
31:21 This *is* the **o** of the law which the LORD 2708
Jos 24:25 and set them a statute and an **o** in Shechem. 4941
1Sa 30:25 it a statute and an **o** for Israel unto this day. 4941
2Ch 2: 4 our God. This *is an* **o** for ever to Israel. NIH
35:13 the passover with fire according to the **o**: 4941
35:25 to *this* day, and made them an **o** in Israel: 2706
Ezr 3:10 after the **o** of David king of Israel. 3027
Ps 99: 7 and the **o** *that* he gave them. 2706
Isa 24: 5 have transgressed the laws, changed the **o**, 2706
58: 2 and forsook not the **o** of their God: 4941
Eze 45:14 Concerning the **o** of oil, the bath *of* oil, 2706
46:14 a meat offering continually *by* a perpetual **o** 2708
Mal 3:14 and what profit *is it* that we have kept his **o**, 4931
Ro 13: 2 resisteth the power, resisteth the **o** of God: *1296*
1Pe 2:13 Submit yourselves to every **o** of man for *2937*

ORDINANCES (27) [ORDINANCE]
Ex 18:20 thou shalt teach them **o** and laws, and 2706
Lev 18: 3 ye not do: neither shall ye walk in their **o**. 2708
18: 4 and keep mine **o**, to walk therein: 2708
Nu 9:12 according to all the **o** of the passover they 2708
2Ki 17:34 or after their **o**, or after the law and 4941
17:37 the **o**, and the law, and the commandment, 4941
2Ch 33: 8 the statutes and the **o** by the hand of Moses. 4941
Ne 10:32 Also we made **o** for us, to charge ourselves 4687
Job 38:33 Knowest thou the **o** of heaven? canst thou 2708
Ps 119:91 continue *this* day according to thine **o**: 4941
Isa 58: 2 they ask of me the **o** of justice; they take 4941
Jer 31:35 *and* the **o** of the moon and of the stars for a 2708
31:36 If those **o** depart from before me, saith 2706
33:25 *if* I have not appointed the **o** of heaven and 2708
Eze 11:20 my statutes, and keep mine **o**, and do them: 4941
43:11 all the **o** thereof, and all the forms thereof, 2708
43:11 and all the **o** thereof, and do them. 2708
43:18 These *are* the **o** of the altar in the day when 2708
44: 5 all the **o** of the house of the LORD, 2708
Mal 3: 7 your fathers ye are gone away from mine **o**, 2706
Lk 1: 6 and **o** of the Lord blameless. *1345*
1Co 11: 2 remember me in all *things*, and keep the **o**, *3862*
Eph 2:15 the law of commandments *contained* in **o**; *1378*
Col 2:14 Blotting out the handwriting of **o** that was *1378*
2:20 living in the world, are ye **subject to o**, *1379*
Heb 9: 1 Then verily the first *covenant* had also **o** of *1345*
9:10 drinks, and divers washings, and carnal **o**, *1345*

ORDINARY (1)
Eze 16:27 have diminished thine **o** *food*, and 2706

OREB (7)
Jdg 7:25 two princes of the Midianites, **O** and Zeeb; 6159
7:25 they slew **O** upon the rock Oreb, and Zeeb 6159
7:25 they slew Oreb upon the rock **O**, and Zeeb 6159
7:25 brought the heads of **O** and Zeeb to Gideon 6159
8: 3 hands the princes of Midian, **O** and Zeeb: 6159
Ps 83:11 Make their nobles like **O**, and like Zeeb: 6159
Isa 10:26 to the slaughter of Midian at the rock **O**: 6159

OREN (1)
1Ch 2:25 and Bunah, and **O**, and Ozem, *and* Ahijah. 767

ORGAN (3) [ORGANS]
Ge 4:21 father of all such as handle the harp and **o**. 5748
Job 21:12 and harp, and rejoice at the sound of the **o**. 5748
30:31 and my **o** into the voice of them that weep. 5748

ORGANS (1) [ORGAN]
Ps 150: 4 praise him with stringed instruments and **o**. 5748

ORION (3)
Job 9: 9 **O**, and Pleiades, and the chambers of 3685
38:31 of Pleiades, or loose the bands of **O**? 3685
Am 5: 8 *him* that maketh the seven stars and **O**, 3685

ORNAMENT (7) [ORNAMENTS]
Pr 1: 9 For they *shall be* an **o** of grace unto thy 3880
4: 9 She shall give to thine head an **o** of grace: 3880
25:12 an **o** of fine gold, *so is* a wise reprover upon 2481
Isa 30:22 and the **o** of thy molten images of gold: 642
49:18 as with an **o**, and bind them *on thee*, as a 5716
Eze 7:20 As for the beauty of his **o**, he set it in 5716
1Pe 3: 4 *even the* **o** of a meek and quiet spirit, NIG

ORNAMENTS (14) [ORNAMENT]
Ex 33: 4 and no man did put on him his **o**. 5716
33: 5 therefore now put off thy **o** from thee, that I 5716
33: 6 themselves of their **o** by the mount Horeb. 5716
Jdg 8:21 took away the **o** that *were* on their camels' 7720
8:26 beside **o**, and collars, and purple raiment 7720
2Sa 1:24 who put on **o** of gold upon your apparel. 5716
Isa 3:18 bravery of *their* **tinkling o** *about their feet*, 5914
3:20 the **o of the legs**, and the headbands, and 6807
61:10 as a bridegroom decketh *himself* with **o**, 6287
Jer 2:32 Can a maid forget her **o**, *or* a bride her 5716
4:30 though thou deckest thee with **o** of gold, 5716
Eze 16: 7 and thou art come to **excellent o**: 5716+5716
16:11 I decked thee also *with* **o**, and I put 5716
23:40 and **deckedst** thyself **with o**, 5710+5716

ORNAN (12) [ARAUNAH]
1Ch 21:15 by the threshingfloor of **O** the Jebusite. 771
21:18 in the threshingfloor of **O** the Jebusite. 771
21:20 **O** turned back, and saw the angel; and 771
21:20 Now **O** was threshing wheat. 771
21:21 And as David came to **O**, Ornan looked and 771
21:21 **O** looked and saw David, and went out of 771
21:22 David said to **O**, Grant me the place of *this* 771
21:23 And **O** said unto David, Take *it* to thee, and 771
21:24 king David said to **O**, Nay; but I will verily 771

1Ch 21:25 So David gave to **O** for the place six 771
21:28 him in the threshingfloor of **O** the Jebusite, 771
2Ch 3: 1 in the threshingfloor of **O** the Jebusite. 771

ORPAH (2)
Ru 1: 4 the name of the one *was* **O**, and the name 6204
1:14 **O** kissed her mother in law; but Ruth clave 6204

ORPHANS (1)
La 5: 3 We are **o** and fatherless, our mothers *are* as 3490

OSEE (1) [HOSEA]
Ro 9:25 As he saith also in **O**, I will call *them* my *5617*

OSHEA (2) [JOSHUA]
Nu 13: 8 Of the tribe of Ephraim, **O** the son of Nun. 1954
13:16 Moses called **O** the son of Nun, Jehoshua. 1954

OSPRAY (2)
Lev 11:13 the eagle, and the ossifrage, and the **o**, 5822
Dt 14:12 the eagle, and the ossifrage, and the **o**, 5822

OSPREY See GIER

OSSIFRAGE (2)
Lev 11:13 the eagle, and the **o**, and the ospray, 6538
Dt 14:12 not eat: the eagle, and the **o**, and the ospray, 6538

OSTRICH (1) [OSTRICHES]
Job 39:13 or wings and feathers *unto* the **o**? 2624

OSTRICHES (1) [OSTRICH]
La 4: 3 become cruel, like the **o** in the wilderness. 3283

OTHER (465) [OTHER'S, OTHERS, OTHERWISE] See Index

OTHER'S (1) [OTHER] See Index

OTHERS (67) [OTHER] See Index

OTHERWISE (15) [OTHER] See Index

OTHNI (1)
1Ch 26: 7 **O**, and Rephael, and Obed, Elzabad, 6273

OTHNIEL (7)
Jos 15:17 **O** the son of Kenaz, the brother of Caleb, 6274
Jdg 1:13 **O** the son of Kenaz, Caleb's younger 6274
3: 9 delivered them, *even* **O** the son of Kenaz, 6274
3:11 forty years. And **O** the son of Kenaz died. 6274
1Ch 4:13 And the sons of Kenaz; **O**, and Seraiah: and 6274
4:13 and Seraiah: and the sons of **O**; Hathath. 6274
27:15 month *was* Heldai the Netophathite, of **O**: 6274

OUCHES (8)
Ex 28:11 thou shalt make them to be set *in* **o** *of* gold. 4865
28:13 And thou shalt make **o** *of* gold; 4865
28:14 and fasten the wreathen chains to the **o**. 4865
28:25 *chains* thou shalt fasten in the two **o**, 4865
39: 6 they wrought onyx stones inclosed *in* **o** *of* 4865
39:13 *they were* inclosed *in* **o** *of* gold in their 4865
39:16 they made two **o** *of* gold, and two gold 4865
39:18 wreathen *chains* they fastened in the two **o**, 4865

OUGHT (100) [OUGHTEST] See Index

OUGHTEST (4) [OUGHT] See Index

OUR (1165) [WE] See Index

OURS (12) [WE] See Index

OURSELVES (51) [WE] See Index

OUT (2777) [OUTER, OUTMOST, THEREOUT, WITHOUT] See Index

OUTCAST (1) [CAST, OUTCASTS]
Jer 30:17 because they called thee an **O**, *saying,* This 5080

OUTCASTS (7) [CAST, OUTCAST]
Ps 147: 2 he gathereth together the **o** of Israel. 1760
Isa 11:12 shall assemble the **o** of Israel, and 1760
16: 3 hide the **o**; bewray not him that wandereth. 5080
16: 4 Let mine **o** dwell with thee, Moab; be thou 5080
27:13 the **o** in the land of Egypt, and 5080
56: 8 The Lord GOD which gathereth the **o** of 1760
Jer 49:36 there shall be no nation whither the **o** of 5080

OUTER (3) [OUT]
Mt 8:12 kingdom shall be cast out into **o** darkness: *1857*
22:13 him away, and cast *him* into **o** darkness; *1857*
25:30 And cast ye the unprofitable servant into **o** *1857*

OUTGOINGS (8) [GO]
Jos 17: 9 of the river, and the **o** of it were at the sea: 8444
17:18 the **o** of it shall be thine: for thou shalt 8444
18:19 the **o** of the border were at the north bay of 8444
19:14 the **o** thereof are *in* the valley of 8444
19:22 and the **o** of their border were *at* Jordan: 8444
19:29 the **o** thereof are at the sea from the coast to 8444
19:33 and the **o** thereof were *at* Jordan: 8444
Ps 65: 8 thou makest the **o** of the morning and 4161

OUTLANDISH (1)
Ne 13:26 *nevertheless* even him did **o** women cause 5237

OUTLIVED (1) [LIVE]
Jdg 2: 7 all the days of the elders that **o** 310+748+3117

OUTMOST (4) [OUT]
Ex 26:10 of the one curtain *that is* **o** in the coupling, 7020
Nu 34: 3 the **o coast** of the salt sea eastward: 4480+7097
Dt 30: 4 be driven out unto the **o parts** of heaven, 7097
Isa 17: 6 *or* five **in** the **o** fruitful branches thereof, 871.1

OUTRAGEOUS (1)
Pr 27: 4 Wrath *is* cruel, and anger *is* **o**; but who is 7858

OUTRUN (1) [RUN]
Jn 20: 4 and the other disciple did **o** Peter, *4390+5030*

OUTSIDE (8)
Jdg 7:11 **o** of the armed *men* that *were* in the host. 7097
7:17 behold, when I come to the **o** of the camp, 7097
7:19 came unto the **o** of the camp *in* 7097
1Ki 7: 9 and *so* on the **o** toward the great court. 2351
Eze 40: 5 behold a wall on the **o** of the house round 2351
Mt 23:25 for ye make clean the **o** of the cup and *1855*
23:26 that the **o** of them may be clean also. *1622*
Lk 11:39 Now do ye Pharisees make clean the **o** of *1855*

OUTSTRETCHED (3) [STRETCH]
Dt 26: 8 with an **o** arm, and with great terribleness, 5186
Jer 21: 5 I myself will fight against you with an **o** 5186
27: 5 by my great power and by my **o** arm, and 5186

OUTWARD (14) [OUTWARDLY]
Nu 35: 4 **o** a thousand cubits round about. 2351+1886.5
1Sa 16: 7 for man looketh on the **o appearance**, but 5869
1Ch 26:29 his sons *were* for the **o** business over Israel, 2435
Ne 11:16 had the oversight of the **o** business of 2435
Est 6: 4 Now Haman was come into the **o** court of 2435
Eze 40:17 brought he me into the **o** court, and lo, 2435
40:20 the gate of the **o** court that looked toward 2435
40:34 the arches thereof *were* toward the **o** court; 2435
44: 1 **o** sanctuary which looketh *toward* the east; 2435
Mt 23:27 which indeed appear beautiful **o**, but *1855*
Ro 2:28 which is **o** in the flesh: *1722+3588+5318*
2Co 4:16 but though our **o** man perish, yet the inward *1854*
10: 7 ye look on *things* after the **o appearance**? *4383*
1Pe 3: 3 Whose adorning let it not be that **o** *1855*

OUTWARDLY (2) [OUTWARD]
Mt 23:28 so ye also **o** appear righteous unto men, *1855*
Ro 2:28 is not a Jew, which is one **o**; *1722+3588+5318*

OUTWENT (1) [GO]
Mk 6:33 and **o** them, and came together unto him. *4281*

OVEN (12) [OVENS]
Lev 2: 4 oblation of a meat offering baken in the **o**, 8574
7: 9 all the meat offering that is baken in the **o**, 8574
11:35 *whether it be* **o**, or ranges for pots, 8574
26:26 ten women shall bake your bread in one **o**, 8574
Ps 21: 9 Thou shalt make them as a fiery **o** in 8574
La 5:10 Our skin was black like an **o** because of 8574
Hos 7: 4 all adulterers, as an **o** heated by the baker, 8574
7: 6 they have made ready their heart like an **o**, 8574
7: 7 They are all hot as an **o**, and have devoured 8574
Mal 4: 1 the day cometh, that *shall* burn as an **o**; 8574
Mt 6:30 to day is, and to morrow is cast into the **o**, *2823*
Lk 12:28 the field, and to morrow is cast into the **o**; *2823*

OVENS (1) [OVEN]
Ex 8: 3 into thine **o**, and into thy kneadingtroughs: 8574

OVER (1009) See Index

OVERCAME (3) [OVERCOME]
Ac 19:16 and **o** them, and prevailed against them, so *2634*
Rev 3:21 *even* as I also **o**, and am set down with my *3528*
12:11 And they **o** him by the blood of the Lamb, *3528*

OVERCAST See LOWRING

OVERCHARGE (1) [CHARGE, OVERCHARGED]
2Co 2: 5 but in part: that I may not **o** you all. *1912*

OVERCHARGED (1) [OVERCHARGE]
Lk 21:34 lest at any time your hearts be **o** with *925*

OVERCOME (22) [OVERCAME, OVERCOMETH]
Ge 49:19 Gad, a troop shall **o** him: but he shall 1464
49:19 overcome him: but he shall **o** at the last. 1464
Ex 32:18 *is it* the voice of *them that* cry for being **o**: 2476
Nu 13:30 for we are **well able to o** it. 3201+3201
22:11 peradventure I shall be able to **o** them, and 3898
2Ki 16: 5 they besieged Ahaz, but could not **o** *him.* 3898
SS 6: 5 thine eyes from me, for they have **o** me: 7292
Isa 28: 1 the fat valleys of them that are **o** with wine. 1986
Jer 23: 9 like a man whom wine hath **o**, because of 5674
Lk 11:22 than he shall come upon *him,* and **o** him, *3528*
Jn 16:33 but be of good cheer; I have **o** the world. *3528*
Ro 3: 4 and mightest **o** when thou art judged. *3528*
12:21 Be not **o** of evil, but overcome evil with *3528*
12:21 not overcome of evil, but **o** evil with good. *3528*
2Pe 2:19 for of whom a man is **o**, of the same is he *2274*
2:20 they are again entangled therein, and **o**, *2274*
1Jn 2:13 because you have **o** the wicked one. *3528*
2:14 in you, and ye have **o** the wicked one. *3528*
4: 4 are of God, little children, and have **o** them: *3528*
Rev 11: 7 and shall **o** them, and kill them. *3528*
13: 7 to make war with the saints, and to **o** them: *3528*
17:14 with the Lamb, and the Lamb shall **o** them: *3528*

OVERCOMETH (11) [OVERCOME]
1Jn 5: 4 For whatsoever is born of God **o** the world: *3528*
5: 4 and this is the victory that **o** the world, *3528*
5: 5 Who is he that **o** the world, but he that *3528*
Rev 2: 7 To him that **o** will I give to eat of the tree *3528*
2:11 He that **o** shall not be hurt of the second *3528*
2:17 To him that **o** will I give to eat of *3528*
2:26 And he that **o**, and keepeth my works unto *3528*
3: 5 He that **o**, the same shall be clothed in *3528*
3:12 Him that **o** will I make a pillar in *3528*
3:21 To him that **o** will I grant to sit with me in *3528*
21: 7 He that **o** shall inherit all *things;* and I will *3528*

OVERDRIVE (1) [DRIVE]
Ge 33:13 if *men* should **o** them one day, all the flock 1849

OVERFLOW (13) [FLOW, OVERFLOWED, OVERFLOWETH, OVERFLOWING, OVERFLOWN]
Dt 11: 4 how he **made** the water of the Red sea **to o** 6687
Ps 69: 2 into deep waters, where the floods **o** me. 7857
69:15 Let not the waterflood **o** me, neither let 7857
Isa 8: 8 he shall **o** and go over, he shall reach *even* 7857
10:22 the consumption decreed shall **o** *with* 7857
28:17 and the waters shall **o** the hiding place. 7857
43: 2 through the rivers, they shall not **o** thee: 7857
Jer 47: 2 and shall **o** the land, and all that is therein; 7857
Da 11:10 certainly come, and **o**, and pass through: 7857
11:26 shall destroy him, and his army shall **o**: 7857
11:40 the countries, and shall **o** and pass over. 7857
Joel 2:24 and the fats shall **o** *with* wine and oil. 7783
3:13 you down; for the press is full, the fats **o**; 7783

OVERFLOWED (2) [OVERFLOW]
Ps 78:20 the waters gushed out, and the streams **o**; 7857
2Pe 3: 6 the world that then was, being **o** with water, *2626*

OVERFLOWETH (1) [OVERFLOW]
Jos 3:15 (for Jordan **o** all his banks all 4390+5921

OVERFLOWING (11) [OVERFLOW]
Job 28:11 He bindeth the floods from **o**; and the thing 1065
38:25 divided a watercourse for the **o of waters,** 7858
Isa 28: 2 as a flood of mighty waters **o**, 7857
28:15 when the **o** scourge shall pass through, 7857
28:18 when the **o** scourge shall pass through, then 7857
30:28 his breath, as an **o** stream, shall reach to 7857
Jer 47: 2 shall be an **o** flood, and shall overflow 7857
Eze 13:11 there shall be an **o** shower; and ye, O great 7857
13:13 there shall be an **o** shower in mine anger, 7857
38:22 an **o** rain, and great hailstones, fire, and 7857
Hab 3:10 the **o** of the water passed by: the deep 2230

OVERFLOWN (3) [OVERFLOW]
1Ch 12:15 when it had **o** all his banks; 4390+5921
Job 22:16 whose foundation was **o** *with* a flood: 3332
Da 11:22 *with* the arms of a flood shall they be **o** 7857

OVERLAID (35) [OVERLAY]
Ex 26:32 four pillars of shittim *wood* **o** with gold: 6823
36:34 he **o** the boards with gold, and made their 6823
36:34 for the bars, and **o** the bars with gold. 6823
36:36 of shittim *wood,* and **o** them with gold: 6823
36:38 he **o** their chapiters and their fillets with 6823
37: 2 he **o** it with pure gold within and without, 6823
37: 4 of shittim wood, and **o** them with gold. 6823
37:11 he **o** it with pure gold, and made thereunto 6823
37:15 and **o** them with gold, to bear the table. 6823
37:26 he **o** it with pure gold, *both* the top of it, 6823
37:28 *of* shittim wood, and **o** them with gold. 6823
38: 2 were of the same: and he **o** it with brass. 6823
38: 6 *of* shittim wood, and **o** them with brass. 6823
38:28 and **o** their chapiters, and filleted them. 6823
1Ki 3:19 died in the night; because she **o** it. 5921+7901
6:20 he **o** it with pure gold; and *so* covered 6823
6:21 So Solomon **o** the house within with pure 6823
6:21 before the oracle; and he **o** it with gold. 6823
6:22 the whole house he **o** with gold, until *he* 6823
6:22 altar that *was* by the oracle he **o** with gold. 6823
6:28 And he **o** the cherubims with gold. 6823
6:30 the floor of the house he **o** with gold, 6823
6:32 **o** *them* with gold, and spread gold upon 6823
10:18 throne of ivory, and **o** it with the best gold. 6823
2Ki 18:16 which Hezekiah king of Judah had **o**, 6823
2Ch 3: 4 twenty: and he **o** it within with pure gold. 6823
3: 5 which he **o** with fine gold, and set thereon 2645
3: 7 He **o** also the house, the beams, the posts, 2645
3: 8 he **o** it with fine gold, *amounting* to six 2645
3: 9 And he **o** the upper chambers with gold. 2645
3:10 of image work, and **o** them with gold. 6823
4: 9 and **o** the doors of them with brass. 6823
9:17 throne of ivory, and **o** it with pure gold. 6823
SS 5:14 his belly *is as* bright ivory **o** *with* sapphires. 5968
Heb 9: 4 the ark of the covenant **o** round about with *4028*

OVERLAY (13) [LAY, OVERLAID, OVERLAYING]
Ex 25:11 thou shalt **o** it with pure gold, within and 6823
25:11 within and without shalt thou **o** it, and 6823
25:13 of shittim wood, and **o** them with gold. 6823
25:24 thou shalt **o** it with pure gold, and 6823
25:28 **o** them with gold, that the table may be 6823
26:29 thou shalt **o** the boards with gold, and make 6823
26:29 and thou shalt **o** the bars with gold. 6823
26:37 of shittim *wood,* and **o** them with gold, 6823
27: 2 of the same: and thou shalt **o** it with brass. 6823
27: 6 of shittim wood, and **o** them with brass. 6823
30: 3 thou shalt **o** it with pure gold, the top 6823
30: 5 *of* shittim wood, and **o** them with gold. 6823
1Ch 29: 4 to **o** the walls of the houses *withal:* 2902

OVERLAYING (2) [OVERLAY]
Ex 38:17 the **o** of their chapiters *of* silver; and all 6826
38:19 the **o** of their chapiters and their fillets *of* 6826

OVERLIVED (1) [LIVE]
Jos 24:31 all the days of the elders that **o** 310+748+3117

OVERMUCH (1) [MUCH]
2Co 2: 7 one should be swallowed up with **o** sorrow. *4055*

OVERPASS (1) [OVERPAST]
Jer 5:28 yea, they **o** the deeds of the wicked: 5674

OVERPAST (2) [OVERPASS]
Ps 57: 1 my refuge, until *these* calamities be **o**. 5674
Isa 26:20 a little moment, until the indignation be **o**. 5674

OVERPLUS (1)
Lev 25:27 restore the **o** unto the man to whom he sold 5736

OVERRAN (1) [OVERRUNNING]
2Sa 18:23 ran *by* the way of the plain, and **o** Cushi. 5674

OVERRUNNING (1) [OVERRAN, RUN]
Na 1: 8 with an **o** flood he will make an utter end of 5674

OVERSEE (2) [OVERSEER, OVERSEERS, OVERSIGHT, SEE]
1Ch 9:29 *Some* of them also *were* appointed to **o** 5921
2Ch 2: 2 and six hundred to **o** them. 5329+5921

OVERSEER (7) [OVERSEE]
Ge 39: 4 he **made** him **o** over his house, and all *that* 6485
39: 5 time *that* he had **made** him **o** in his house, 6485
Ne 11: 9 Joel the son of Zichri *was* their **o**: 6496
11:14 their **o** *was* Zabdiel, the son of *one of* 6496
11:22 The **o** also of the Levites at Jerusalem *was* 6496
12:42 singers sang loud, with Jezrahiah *their* **o**. 6496
Pr 6: 7 Which having no guide, **o**, or ruler, 7860

OVERSEERS (6) [OVERSEE]
2Ch 2:18 and six hundred **o** to set the people a work. 5329
31:13 *were* **o** under the hand of Cononiah and 6496
34:12 and the **o** of them *were* Jahath and Obadiah, 6485
34:13 *were* **o** of all that wrought the work in any 5329
34:17 have delivered it into the hand of the **o**, and 6485
Ac 20:28 the which the Holy Ghost hath made you **o**, *1985*

OVERSHADOW (2) [OVERSHADOWED, SHADOW]
Lk 1:35 and the power of the Highest shall **o** thee: *1982*
Ac 5:15 of Peter passing by might **o** some of them. *1982*

OVERSHADOWED (3) [OVERSHADOW]
Mt 17: 5 he yet spake, behold, a bright cloud **o** them: *1982*
Mk 9: 7 And there was a cloud that **o** them: and *1982*
Lk 9:34 thus spake, there came a cloud, and **o** them: *1982*

OVERSIGHT (11) [OVERSEE]
Ge 43:12 in your hand; peradventure it *was* an **o**: 4870
Nu 3:32 *have* the **o** of them that keep the charge of 6486
4:16 *and* the **o** of all the tabernacle, and of all 6486
2Ki 12:11 that **had** the **o** *of* the house of the LORD: 6485
22: 5 that have the **o** of the house of the LORD: 6485
22: 9 that **have** the **o** *of* the house of the LORD. 6485
1Ch 9:23 their children had the **o of** the gates of 5921
2Ch 34:10 that had the **o** of the house of the LORD, 6485
Ne 11:16 **had the o** of the outward business of 5921
13: 4 **having the o** of the chamber of 5414+871.1
1Pe 5: 2 **taking the o** *thereof,* not by constraint, but *1983*

OVERSPREAD (1) [SPREAD, OVERSPREADING]
Ge 9:19 and of them was the whole earth **o**. 5310

OVERSPREADING (1) [OVERSPREAD]
Da 9:27 for the **o** of abominations he *shall* make *it* 3671

OVERTAKE (17) [OVERTAKEN, OVERTAKETH, OVERTOOK, TAKE]
Ge 44: 4 when thou dost **o** them, say unto them, 5381
Ex 15: 9 The enemy said, I will pursue, I will **o**, 5381
Dt 19: 6 **o** him, because the way is long, and 5381
28: 2 blessings shall come on thee, and **o** thee, 5381
28:15 curses shall come upon thee, and **o** thee: 5381
28:45 shall pursue thee, and **o** thee, till thou be 5381
Jos 2: 5 after them quickly; for ye shall **o** them. 5381
1Sa 30: 8 shall I **o** them? And he answered him, 5381
30: 8 for thou shalt **surely o** *them,* and 5381+5381
2Sa 15:14 lest he **o** us suddenly, and bring evil upon 5381
Isa 59: 9 far from us, neither doth justice **o** us: 5381
Jer 42:16 shall **o** you there in the land of Egypt, and 5381
Hos 2: 7 after her lovers, but she shall not **o** them; 5381
10: 9 the children of iniquity did not **o** them. 5381
Am 9:10 The evil shall not **o** nor prevent us. 5066
9:13 that the plowman shall **o** the reaper, and 5066
1Th 5: 4 that *that* day should **o** you as a thief. *2638*

OVERTAKEN (2) [OVERTAKE]
Ps 18:37 I have pursued mine enemies, and **o** them: 5381
Gal 6: 1 Brethren, if a man be **o** in a fault, ye which *4301*

OVERTAKETH (1) [OVERTAKE]
1Ch 21:12 while that the sword of thine enemies **o** 5381

OVERTHREW (12) [OVERTHROW]
Ge 19:25 he **o** those cities, and all the plain, and all 2015
19:29 when he **o** the cities in the which Lot dwelt. 2015
Ex 14:27 the LORD **o** the Egyptians in the midst of 5287
Dt 29:23 which the LORD **o** in his anger, and in his 2015
Ps 136:15 **o** Pharaoh and his host in the Red sea: 5287
Isa 13:19 shall be as when God **o** Sodom and 4114
Jer 20:16 man be as the cities which the LORD **o**, 2015
50:40 As God **o** Sodom and Gomorrah and 4114
Am 4:11 as God **o** Sodom and Gomorrah, and 4114
Mt 21:12 and **o** the tables of the moneychangers, and *2690*
Mk 11:15 and **o** the tables of the money-changers, *2690*
Jn 2:15 out the changers' money, and **o** the tables; *390*

OVERTHROW (19) [OVERTHREW, OVERTHROWETH, OVERTHROWN, THROW]
Ge 19:21 that I will not **o** *this* city, for the which thou 2015
19:29 and sent Lot out of the midst of the **o**, 2018
Ex 23:24 thou shalt **utterly o** them, and 2040+2040
Dt 12: 3 you shall **o** their altars, and break their 5422
29:23 like the **o** of Sodom, and Gomorrah, 4114
2Sa 10: 3 the city, and to spy it out, and to **o** it? 2015
11:25 battle *more* strong against the city, and **o** it: 2040
1Ch 19: 3 to search, and to **o**, and to spy out the land? 2015
Ps 106:26 against them, to **o** them in the wilderness: 5307
106:27 To **o** their seed also among the nations, and 5307
140: 4 who have purposed to **o** my goings. 1760
140:11 evil shall hunt the violent man to **o** *him.* 4073
Pr 18: 5 the wicked, to **o** the righteous in judgment. 5186
Jer 49:18 As *in* the **o** of Sodom and Gomorrah and 4114
Hag 2:22 I will **o** the throne of kingdoms, and I will 2015
2:22 I will **o** the chariots, and those that ride in 2015
Ac 5:39 But if it be of God, ye cannot **o** it; *2647*
2Ti 2:18 is past already; and **o** the faith of some. *396*
2Pe 2: 6 into ashes condemned *them* with an **o**, *2692*

OVERTHROWETH (5) [OVERTHROW]
Job 12:19 princes away spoiled, and **o** the mighty. 5557
Pr 13: 6 in the way: but wickedness **o** the sinner. 5557
21:12 *but God* **o** the wicked for *their* wickedness. 5557
22:12 and he **o** the words of the transgressor. 5557
29: 4 the land: but he that receiveth gifts **o** it. 2040

OVERTHROWN (16) [OVERTHROW]
Ex 15: 7 thou hast **o** them that rose up against thee: 2040
Jdg 9:40 before him, and many were **o** *and* wounded, 5307
2Sa 17: 9 when *some* of them be **o** at the first, 5307
2Ch 14:13 the Ethiopians were **o**, that they could not 5307
Job 19: 6 Know now that God hath **o** me, and 5791
Ps 141: 6 When their judges are **o** in stony places, 8058
Pr 11:11 but it is **o** by the mouth of the wicked. 2040
12: 7 The wicked *are* **o**, and *are* not: but 2015
14:11 The house of the wicked shall be **o**: but 8045
Isa 1: 7 and *it is* desolate, as **o** by strangers. 4114
Jer 18:23 thy sight, but let them be **o** before thee; 3782
La 4: 6 that was **o** as in a moment, and no hands 2015
Da 11:41 and many *countries* shall be **o**: 3782
Am 4:11 I have **o** *some* of you, as God overthrew 2015
Jnh 3: 4 Yet forty days, and Nineveh *shall be* **o**. 2015
1Co 10: 5 for they were **o** in the wilderness. *2693*

OVERTOOK (10) [OVERTAKE]
Ge 31:23 and they **o** him in the mount Gilead. 1692
31:25 Laban **o** Jacob. Now Jacob had pitched his 5381
44: 6 he **o** them, and he spake unto them these 5381
Ex 14: 9 **o** them encamping by the sea, 5381
Jdg 18:22 and **o** the children of Dan. 1692
20:42 the battle **o** them; and them which *came* out 1692
2Ki 25: 5 the king, and **o** him in the plains of Jericho: 5381
Jer 39: 5 and **o** Zedekiah in the plains of Jericho: 5381
52: 8 and **o** Zedekiah in the plains of Jericho; 5381
La 1: 3 all her persecutors **o** her between the straits. 5381

OVERTURN (4) [OVERTURNED, OVERTURNETH, TURN]
Job 12:15 he sendeth them out, and they **o** the earth. 2015
Eze 21:27 I will **o**, overturn, overturn it: and it shall be 5754
21:27 I will overturn, **o**, overturn it: and it shall be 5754
21:27 I will overturn, overturn, **o** it: and it shall be 5754

OVERTURNED (1) [OVERTURN]
Jdg 7:13 that it fell, and **o** it, 2015+4605+1886.5+3807.1

OVERTURNETH (3) [OVERTURN]
Job 9: 5 they know not: which **o** them in his anger. 2015
28: 9 the rock; he **o** the mountains by the roots. 2015
34:25 he **o** *them* in the night, so that they are 2015

O

OVERWHELM (1) [OVERWHELMED]
Job 6:27 Yea, ye **o** the fatherless, and you dig 5307+5921

OVERWHELMED (8) [OVERWHELM]
Ps 55: 5 are come upon me, and horror hath **o** me. 3680
61: 2 will I cry unto thee, when my heart is **o**: 5848
77: 3 I complained, and my spirit was **o**. Selah. 5848
78:53 they feared not: but the sea **o** their enemies. 3680
102: T when he is **o**, and poureth out his complaint 5848
124: 4 the waters had **o** us, the stream had gone 7857
142: 3 When my spirit was **o** within me, then 5848
143: 4 Therefore is my spirit **o** within me; 5848

OWE (1) [OWEST, OWETH]
Ro 13: 8 **O** no *man* any *thing*, but to love one *3784*

OWEST (4) [OWE]
Mt 18:28 by the throat, saying, Pay me that thou **o**. *3784*
Lk 16: 5 the first, How much **o** thou unto my lord? *3784*
16: 7 said he to another, And how much **o** thou? *3784*
Phm 1:19 **o** unto me even thine own self **besides**. *4359*

OWETH (2) [OWE]
Ac 21:11 at Jerusalem bind the man that **o** this girdle, *1510*
Phm 1:18 If he hath wronged thee, or **o** *thee* ought, *3784*

OWL (10) [OWLS]
Lev 11:16 the **o**, and the night hawk, and 1323+3284
11:17 the **little o**, and the cormorant, and 3563
11:17 and the cormorant, and the **great o**, 3244
Dt 14:15 the **o**, and the night hawk, and 1323+3284
14:16 The **little o**, and the great owl, and 3563
14:16 little owl, and the **great o**, and the swan, 3244
Ps 102: 6 the wilderness: I am like an **o** of the desert. 3563
Isa 34:11 the **o** also and the raven shall dwell in it: 3244
34:14 the **shrich o** also shall rest there, and 3917
34:15 There shall the **great o** make her nest, and 7091

OWLS (6) [OWL]
Job 30:29 to dragons, and a companion to **o**. 1323+3284
Isa 13:21 **o** shall dwell there, and satyrs shall 1323+3284
34:13 of dragons, *and* a court for **o**. 1323+3284
43:20 honour me, the dragons and the **o**: 1323+3284
Jer 50:39 and the **o** shall dwell therein: 1323+3284
Mic 1: 8 the dragons, and mourning as the **o**. 1323+3284

OWN (596) [OWNER, OWNERS, OWNETH]
Ge 1:27 So God created man in **his o** image, in 2050.2
5: 3 and begat *a son* in **his o** likeness, 2050.2
14:14 his trained *servants*, born in **his o** house, 2050.2
15: 4 he that shall come forth out of **thine o** 3509.2
30:25 that I may go unto **mine o** place, and 2967.1
30:30 now when shall I provide for **mine o** 2967.1
30:40 he put **his o** flocks by 2050.2+3807.1
47:24 four parts shall be **your o**, for seed of 3641.1
Ex 5:16 but the fault *is* in **thine o** people. 3509.2
18:27 and he went his way into **his o** land. 2050.2
21:36 and the dead shall be **his o**. 2050.2+3807.1
22: 5 of the best of **his o** field, and of the best 1930.2
22: 5 of the best of **his o** vineyard, shall he 2050.2
32:13 to whom thou swarest by **thine o self**, 3509.2
Lev 1: 3 he shall offer it of **his o** voluntary will at 2050.2
7:30 **His o** hands shall bring the offerings of 2050.2
14:15 *it* into the palm of **his o** left hand: 3548+1886.1
14:26 oil into the palm of **his o** left hand: 3548+1886.1
16:29 *at all, whether it be* one of **your o country**, 249
17:15 *beasts, whether it be* one of **your o country**, 249
18:10 for theirs *is* **thine o** nakedness. 3509.2
18:26 *neither* any of **your o nation**, nor any 249
19: 5 ye shall offer it at **your o** will. 3641.1
21:14 he shall take a virgin of **his o** people to 2050.2
22:19 *Ye shall offer* at **your o** will a male 3641.1
22:29 unto the LORD, offer *it* at **your o** will. 3641.1
24:22 the stranger, as for **one of** your **o country**: 249
25: 5 **That which groweth of it o accord** of thy 5599
25:41 shall return unto **his o** family, and 2050.2
Nu 1:52 every man by **his o** camp, and every man 1930.2
1:52 every man by **his o** standard, 2050.2
2: 2 of Israel shall pitch by **his o** standard, 2050.2
10:30 I will depart to **mine o** land, and to my 2967.1
13:33 we were in **our o** sight as grasshoppers, 5105.1
15:39 that ye seek not after **your o** heart and 3641.1
15:39 not after your own heart and **your o** eyes, 3641.1
16:28 for *I have* not *done them* of **mine o** mind. 2967.1
16:38 of these sinners against **their o** souls, 3963.1
24:13 to do *either* good or bad of **mine o** mind; 2967.1
27: 3 but died in **his o** sin, and had no sons. 2050.2
32:42 and called it Nobah, after **his o** name. 2050.2
36: 9 shall keep himself to **his o** inheritance. 2050.2
Dt 3:14 called them after **his o** name, 2050.2
12: 8 every man whatsoever *is* right in **his o** 2050.2
13: 6 or thy friend, which *is* as **thine o** soul, 3509.2
22: 2 thou shalt bring it unto **thine o** house, and 3509.2
23:24 thou mayest eat grapes thy fill at **thine o** 3509.2
24:13 that he may sleep in **his o** raiment, and 2050.2
24:16 every man shall be put to death for **his o** 2050.2
28:53 thou shalt eat the fruit of **thine o** body, 3509.2
33: 9 his brethren, nor knew **his o** children: 2050.2
Jos 7:11 have put *it* even amongst **their o** stuff. 1992.1
20: 6 come unto **his o** city, and unto his own 2050.2
20: 6 unto his own city, and unto **his o** house, 2050.2
Jdg 2:19 they ceased not from **their o** doings, 1992.1
7: 2 saying, **Mine o** hand hath saved me. 2967.1
8:29 of Joash went and dwelt in **his o** house. 2050.2
17: 6 did *that* which *was* right in **his o** eyes. 2050.2
21:25 did *that* which *was* right in **his o** eyes. 2050.2
Ru 4: 6 for myself, lest I mar **mine o** inheritance: 2967.1
1Sa 2:20 And they went unto **their o** home. 2050.2
5:11 let it go again to **his o** place, that it slay 2050.2
6: 9 if it goeth up *by* the way of **his o** coast *to* 2050.2
13:14 hath sought him a man after **his o** heart, 2050.2
14:46 and the Philistines went to **their o** place. 3963.1
15:17 When thou *wast* little in **thine o** sight, 3509.2
18: 1 and Jonathan loved him as **his o** soul. 2050.2
18: 3 because he loved him as **his o** soul. 2050.2
20:17 for he loved him as he loved **his o** soul. 2050.2
20:30 the son of Jesse to **thine o** confusion, 3509.2
25:26 *from* avenging thyself with **thine o** hand, 3509.2
25:33 *from* avenging myself with **mine o** hand. 2967.1
25:39 the wickedness of Nabal upon **his o** head. 2050.2
28: 3 buried him in Ramah, even in **his o** city. 2050.2
2Sa 4:11 person in **his o** house upon his bed? 2050.2
6:22 and will be base in **mine o** sight: 2967.1
7:10 that they may dwell in a place of **their o**, 2050.2
7:21 and according to **thine o** heart, 3509.2
12: 3 it did eat of **his o** meat, and drank of his 2050.2
12: 3 drank of **his o** cup, and lay in his bosom, 2050.2
12: 4 he spared to take of **his o** flock and of his 2050.2
12: 4 to take of his own flock and of **his o** herd, 2050.2
12:11 up evil against thee out of **thine o** house, 3509.2
12:20 he came to **his o** house; and when he 2050.2
14:24 Let him turn to **his o** house, and let him 2050.2
14:24 So Absalom returned to **his o** house, and 2050.2
17:11 *that* thou go to battle in **thine o** person. 3509.2
18:13 wrought falsehood against **mine o** life: 2967.1
18:18 he called the pillar after **his o** name: and 2050.2
19:28 among them that did eat at **thine o** table. 3509.2
19:30 is come *again* in peace unto **his o** house. 2050.2
19:37 that I may die in **mine o** city, *and* 2967.1
19:39 and he returned unto **his o** place. 2050.2
23:21 and slew him with **his o** spear. 2050.2
1Ki 1:12 that thou mayest save **thine o** life, and 3509.3
1:33 son to ride upon **mine o** mule, 2967.1+3807.1
2:23 not spoken this word against **his o** life. 2050.2
2:26 Get thee *to* Anathoth, unto **thine o** fields; 3509.2
2:32 shall return his blood upon **his o** head, 2050.2
2:34 he was buried in **his o** house in 2050.2
2:37 thy blood shall be upon **thine o** head. 3509.2
2:44 return thy wickedness upon **thine o** head; 3509.2
3: 1 had made an end of building **his o** house, 2050.2
7: 1 Solomon was building **his o** house 2050.2
8:38 every man the plague of **his o** heart, 2050.2
9:15 **his o** house, and Millo, and the wall of 2050.2
10: 6 It was a true report that I heard in **mine o** 2967.1
10:13 So she turned and went to **her o** country, 1886.3
11:19 that he gave him *to* wife the sister of **his o** 2050.2
11:21 that I may go to **mine o** country. 2967.1
11:22 thou seekest to go to **thine o** country? 3509.2
12:16 now see to **thine o** house, David. 3509.2
12:33 which he had devised of **his o** heart; 2050.2
13:30 he laid his carcase in **his o** grave; and 2050.2
14:12 thou therefore, get thee to **thine o** house: 3509.3
17:19 he abode, and laid him upon **his o** bed. 2050.2
22:36 his city, and every man to **his o** country. 2050.2
2Ki 2:12 he took hold of **his o** clothes, and 2050.2
3:27 from him, and returned to *their o* land. NIH
4:13 I dwell among **mine o** people. 2967.1
12:18 **his o** hallowed *things*, and all the gold 2050.2

2Ki	14: 6	every man shall be put to death for **his o**	2050.2
	17:23	So was Israel carried away out of **their o**	2050.2
	17:29	every nation made gods of **their o**,	2050.2
	17:33	the LORD, and served **their o** gods,	1992.1
	18:27	that *they* may eat **their o** dung, and drink	3963.1
	18:27	and drink **their o** piss with you?	1992.1
	18:31	*then* eat ye every man of **his o** vine, and	2050.2
	18:32	take you away to a land like **your o** land,	3641.1
	19: 7	a rumour, and shall return to **his o** land;	2050.2
	19: 7	him to fall by the sword in **his o** land.	2050.2
	19:34	for **mine o** sake, and for my servant	2967.1
	20: 6	I will defend this city for **mine o** sake,	2967.1
	21:18	was buried in the garden of **his o** house,	2050.2
	21:23	and slew the king in **his o** house.	2050.2
	23:30	and buried him in **his o** sepulchre.	2050.2
1Ch	11:23	and slew him with **his o** spear.	2050.2
	17:19	and according to **thine o** heart,	3509.2
	17:21	to redeem *to be* **his o** people,	2050.2+3807.1
	17:22	make **thine o** people for ever;	3509.2+3807.1
	29: 3	I have of **mine o** proper good,	2967.1+3807.1
	29:14	of thee, and of thine o have we given thee.	3027
	29:16	*cometh* of thine hand, and *is* all **thine o**.	3509.2
2Ch	6:23	recompensing his way upon **his o** head;	2050.2
	6:29	when every one shall know **his o** sore and	2050.2
	6:29	shall know his own sore and **his o** grief,	2050.2
	7:11	in **his o** house, he prosperously effected.	2050.2
	8: 1	the house of the LORD, and **his o** house,	2050.2
	9: 5	I heard in **mine o** land of thine acts,	2967.1
	9:12	went away to **her o** land, she and	1886.3
	10:16	*and* now, David, see to **thine o** house.	3509.2
	16:14	they buried him in **his o** sepulchres,	2050.2
	24:25	**his o** servants conspired against him for	2050.2
	25: 4	but every man shall die for **his o** sin.	2050.2
	25:15	which could not deliver **their o** people	3963.1
	31: 1	man to his possession, into **their o** cities.	1992.1
	32:21	returned with shame of face to **his o** land.	2050.2
	32:21	they that came forth of **his o** bowels slew	2050.2
	33:20	and they buried him *in* **his o** house:	2050.2
	33:24	against him, and slew him in **his o** house.	2050.2
Ezr	7:13	*which are* **minded of** their o **freewill** to go	5069
Ne	4: 4	turn their reproach upon **their o** head, and	3963.1
	6: 8	thou feignest them out of **thine o** heart.	3509.2
	6:16	were much cast down in **their o** eyes:	1992.1
Est	1:22	that every man should bear rule in **his o**	2050.2
	2: 7	were dead, took for **his o** daughter.	2050.2
	9:25	should return upon **his o** head, and that he	2050.2
Job	2:11	they came every one from **his o** place;	2050.2
	5:13	He taketh the wise in **their o** craftiness:	3963.1
	9:20	**mine o** mouth shall condemn me:	2967.1
	9:31	and **mine o** clothes shall abhor me.	2967.1
	13:15	I will maintain **mine o** ways before him.	2967.1
	15: 6	**Thine o** mouth condemneth thee, and	3509.2
	15: 6	yea, **thine o** lips testify against thee.	3509.2
	18: 7	and **his o** counsel shall cast him down.	1930.2
	18: 8	For he is cast into a net by **his o** feet, and	2050.2
	19:17	for the children's *sake* of mine *o* body.	NIH
	20: 7	*Yet* he shall perish for ever like **his o**	2050.2
	32: 1	because he *was* righteous in **his o** eyes.	2050.2
	40:14	will I also confess unto thee that **thine o**	3509.2
Ps	4: 4	commune with **your o** heart upon your	3641.1
	5:10	O God; let them fall by **their o** counsels;	1992.1
	7:16	His mischief shall return upon **his o** head,	2050.2
	7:16	dealing shall come down upon **his o** pate.	2050.2
	9:15	in the net which they hid is **their o** foot	3963.1
	9:16	the wicked is snared in the work of **his o**	2050.2
	12: 4	tongue will we prevail; our lips *are* our **o**:	854
	15: 4	*He that* sweareth to *his o* hurt, and	NIH
	17:10	They are inclosed *in* **their o** fat:	4123.1
	20: 4	Grant thee according to **thine o** heart, and	3509.2
	21:13	thou exalted, LORD, in **thine o** strength:	3509.2
	22:29	and none can keep alive **his o** soul.	2050.2
	33:12	the people *whom* he hath chosen for **his o**	2050.2
	35:13	my prayer returned into **mine o** bosom.	2967.1
	36: 2	For he flattereth himself in **his o** eyes,	2050.2
	37:15	Their sword shall enter into **their o** heart,	3963.1
	41: 9	Yea, **mine o** familiar friend, in whom I	2967.1
	44: 3	the land in possession by **their o** sword,	3963.1
	44: 3	neither did **their o** arm save them:	3963.1
	45:10	forget also **thine o** people, and	3509.3
	49:11	they call *their* lands after **their o** names.	3963.1
	50:20	thou slanderest **thine o** mother's son.	3509.2
	64: 8	So they shall make **their o** tongue to fall	3963.1
	67: 6	*and* God, *even* **our o** God, shall bless us.	5105.1
	74:22	Arise, O God, plead **thine o** cause:	3509.2
	77: 6	I commune with **mine o** heart: and	2967.1
	78:29	for he gave them **their o** desire;	3963.1
	78:52	made **his o** people to go forth like sheep,	2050.2
	81:12	So I gave them up unto **their o** heart's	3963.1
	81:12	*and* they walked in **their o** counsels.	1992.1
	94:23	he shall bring upon them **their o** iniquity,	3963.1
	94:23	shall cut them off in **their o** wickedness;	3963.1
	106:39	Thus were they defiled with **their o**	1992.1
	106:39	went a whoring with **their o** inventions.	1992.1
	106:40	insomuch that he abhorred **his o**	2050.2
	109:29	let them cover *themselves with* **their o**	3963.1
	138: 8	forsake not the works of **thine o** hands.	3509.2
	140: 9	the mischief of **their o** lips cover them.	4123.1
	141:10	Let the wicked fall into **their o** nets,	2050.2
Pr	1:18	they lay wait for **their o** blood; they lurk	3963.1
	1:18	they lurk privily for **their o** lives.	3963.1
	1:31	shall they eat of the fruit of **their o** way,	3963.1
	1:31	and be filled with **their o** devices.	1992.1
	3: 5	and lean not unto **thine o** understanding.	3509.2
	3: 7	Be not wise in **thine o** eyes: fear	3509.2
	5:15	Drink waters out of **thine o** cistern, and	3509.2
	5:15	and running waters out of **thine o** well.	3509.2
	5:17	Let them be only **thine o**, and	3509.2+3807.1
	5:22	**His o** iniquities shall take the wicked	2050.2
	6:32	he *that* doeth it destroyeth **his o** soul.	1931
	8:36	he that sinneth *against* me wrongeth **his o**	2050.2
	11: 5	the wicked shall fall by **his o** wickedness.	2050.2
	11: 6	transgressors shall be taken in their **o**	NIH
	11:17	The merciful man doeth good to **his o**	2050.2
	11:17	but *he that is* cruel troubleth **his o** flesh.	2050.2
	11:19	he that pursueth evil *pursueth it* to **his o**	2050.2
	11:29	He that troubleth **his o** house shall inherit	2050.2
	12:15	The way of a fool *is* right in **his o** eyes:	2050.2
	14:10	The heart knoweth **his o** bitterness;	5315+2050.2
	14:14	in heart shall be filled with **his o** ways:	2050.2
	14:20	The poor is hated even of **his o**	1930.2
	15:27	He that is greedy of gain troubleth **his o**	2050.2
	15:32	refuseth instruction despiseth **his o** soul:	2050.2
	16: 2	All the ways of a man *are* clean in **his o**	2050.2
	18:11	and as a high wall in **his o** conceit.	2050.2
	18:17	*He that is* first in **his o** cause *seemeth*	2050.2
	19: 8	He that getteth wisdom loveth **his o** soul:	2050.2
	19:16	the commandment keepeth **his o** soul;	2050.2
	20: 2	him to anger sinneth *against* **his o** soul.	2050.2
	20: 6	Most men will proclaim every one **his o**	2050.2
	20:24	can a man then understand **his o** way?	2050.2
	21: 2	Every way of a man *is* right in **his o** eyes:	2050.2
	23: 4	to be rich: cease from **thine o** wisdom.	3509.2
	25:27	*men* to search **their o** glory *is not* glory.	3963.1
	25:28	He that *hath* no rule over **his o** spirit *is*	2050.2
	26: 5	his folly, lest he be wise in **his o** conceit.	2050.2
	26:12	Seest thou a man wise in **his o** conceit?	2050.2
	26:16	The sluggard *is* wiser in **his o** conceit	2050.2
	27: 2	*man* praise thee, and not **thine o** mouth;	3509.2
	27: 2	a stranger, and not **thine o** lips.	3509.2
	27:10	**Thine o** friend, and thy father's friend,	3509.2
	28:10	he shall fall himself into **his o** pit:	2050.2
	28:11	The rich man *is* wise in **his o** conceit; but	2050.2
	28:26	He that trusteth in **his o** heart *is* a fool:	2050.2
	29:24	Whoso is partner with a thief hateth **his o**	2050.2
	30:12	a generation *that are* pure in **their o** eyes,	2050.2
	31:31	let **her o** works praise her in the gates.	1886.3
Ecc	1:16	I communed with **mine o** heart, saying,	2967.1
	3:22	than that a man should rejoice in **his o**	2050.2
	4: 5	his hands together, and eateth **his o** flesh.	2050.2
	7:22	For oftentimes also **thine o** heart knoweth	3509.2
	8: 9	ruleth over another to **his o** hurt.	2050.2+3807.1
SS	1: 6	*but* **mine o** vineyard have I not kept.	2967.1
Isa	2: 8	they worship the work of **their o** hands,	2050.2
	2: 8	*that* which **their o** fingers have made:	2050.2
	4: 1	We will eat **our o** bread, and wear our	5105.1
	4: 1	our own bread, and wear **our o** apparel:	5105.1
	5:21	Woe unto *them that are* wise in **their o**	1992.1
	5:21	own eyes, and prudent in **their o** sight!	1992.1
	9:20	they shall eat every man the flesh of **his o**	2050.2
	13:14	they shall every man turn to **his o** people,	2050.2
	13:14	and flee every one into **his o** land.	2050.2
	14: 1	and set them in **their o** land:	3963.1
	14:18	lie in glory, every one in **his o** house.	2050.2
	23: 7	**her o** feet shall carry her afar off to	1886.3
	31: 7	which **your o** hands have made unto you	3641.1
	36:12	that *they* may eat **their o** dung, and drink	3963.1
	36:12	and drink **their o** piss with you?	1992.1
	36:16	drink ye every one the waters of **his o**	2050.2

Isa 36:17 take you away to a land like **your o** land, 3641.1
37: 7 hear a rumour, and return to **his o** land; 2050.2
37: 7 him to fall by the sword in **his o** land. 2050.2
37:35 defend this city to save it for **mine o** sake, 2967.1
43:25 out thy transgressions for **mine o** sake, 2967.1
44: 9 they *are* **their o** witnesses; they see not, 1992.1
48:11 For **mine o** sake, *even* for mine own sake, 2967.1
48:11 For mine own sake, *even* for **mine o** sake, 2967.1
49:26 them that oppress thee with **their o** flesh; 3963.1
49:26 they shall be drunken with **their o** blood, 3963.1
53: 6 we have turned every one to **his o** way; 2050.2
56:11 they all look to **their o** way, every one for 3963.1
58: 7 that thou hide not thyself from **thine o** 3509.2
58:13 shalt honour him, not doing **thine o** ways, 3509.2
58:13 own ways, nor finding **thine o** pleasure, 3509.2
58:13 own pleasure, nor speaking *thine o* words: NIH
63: 5 **mine o** arm brought salvation unto me; 2967.1
65: 2 *that was* not good, after **their o** thoughts; 1992.1
66: 3 they have chosen **their o** ways, and 1992.1
Jer 1:16 worshipped the works of **their o** hands. 1992.1
2:19 **Thine o** wickedness shall correct thee, 3509.3
2:30 **your o** sword hath devoured your 3641.1
7:19 to the confusion of **their o** faces? 1992.1
9:14 after the imagination of **their o** heart, 3963.1
18:12 we will walk after **our o** devices, and 5105.1
23: 8 and they shall dwell in **their o** land. 3963.1
23:16 they speak a vision of **their o** heart, *and* 3963.1
23:17 after the imagination of **his o** heart, 2050.2
23:26 *they are* prophets of the deceit of **their o** 3963.1
25: 7 the works of your hands to **your o** hurt. 3641.1
25:14 according to the works of **their o** hands. 1992.1
27:11 those will I let remain still in **their o** land, 2050.2
30:18 the city shall be builded upon **her o** heap, 1886.3
31:17 shall come again to **their o** border. 3963.1
31:30 every one shall die for **his o** iniquity: 2050.2
37: 7 shall return *to* Egypt into **their o** land. 2050.2
42:12 and cause you to return to **your o** land. 3641.1
44: 9 **your o** wickedness, and the wickedness 3641.1
44:17 thing goeth forth out of **our o** mouth, 5105.1
46:16 let us go again to **our o** people, and to 5105.1
50:16 they shall flee every one to **his o** land. 2050.2
51: 9 let us go every one into **his o** country: 2050.2
52:27 carried away captive out of **his o** land. 2050.2
La 4:10 women have sodden **their o** children: 2006.1
Eze 11:21 I will recompense their way upon **their o** 3963.1
13: 2 them that prophesy out of **their o** hearts, 3963.1
13: 3 that follow **their o** spirit, and have seen 3963.1
13:17 which prophesy out of **their o** heart; 2006.1
14: 5 take the house of Israel in **their o** heart, 3963.1
14:14 *but* **their o** souls by their righteousness, 3963.1
14:20 **their o** souls by their righteousness. 3963.1
16: 6 and saw thee polluted in **thine o** blood, 3509.3
16:15 thou didst trust in **thine o** beauty, and 3509.3
16:52 bear **thine o** shame for thy sins that thou 3509.3
16:54 That thou mayest bear **thine o** shame, and 3509.3
17:19 it will I recompense upon **his o** head. 2050.2
20:26 I polluted them in **their o** gifts, in that 3963.1
20:43 ye shall lothe yourselves in **your o** sight 3641.1
22:31 **their o** way have I recompensed upon 3963.1
23:34 and pluck off **thine o** breasts: 3509.3
29: 3 My river *is* **mine o**, and I have 2967.1+3807.1
32:10 every man for **his o** life, in the day of thy 2050.2
33: 4 his blood shall be upon **his o** head. 2050.2
33:13 if he trust to **his o** righteousness, and 2050.2
34:13 will bring them to **their o** land, and 3963.1
36:17 when the house of Israel dwelt in **their o** 3963.1
36:17 they defiled it by **their o** way and by their 3963.1
36:24 and will bring you into **your o** land. 3641.1
36:31 shall ye remember **your o** evil ways, and 3641.1
36:31 shall lothe yourselves in **your o** sight for 3641.1
36:32 and confounded for **your o** ways, 3641.1
37:14 and I shall place you in **your o** land: 3641.1
37:21 and bring them into **their o** land: 3963.1
39:28 I have gathered them unto **their o** land, 3963.1
46:18 sons inheritance out of **his o** possession: 2050.2
Da 3:28 nor worship any god, except **their o** God. 1952.1
6:17 the king sealed it with **his o** signet, and 1886.8
8:24 shall be mighty, but not by **his o** power: 2050.2
9:19 defer not, for **thine o** sake, O my God: 3509.2
11: 9 and shall return into **his o** land. 2050.2
11:16 him shall do according to **his o** will, 2050.2
11:18 a prince for **his o** behalf shall cause 2050.2
11:18 without **his o** reproach he shall cause *it* to 2050.2
11:19 his face towards the fort of **his o** land: 2050.2
11:28 shall do *exploits,* and return to **his o** land. 2050.2
Hos 7: 2 now **their o** doings have beset them 1992.1
10: 6 Israel shall be ashamed of **his o** counsel. 2050.2
11: 6 devour *them,* because of **their o** counsels. 1992.1
13: 2 idols according to **their o** understanding, 3963.1
Joel 3: 4 your recompence upon **your o** head; 3641.1
3: 7 will return your recompence upon **your o** 3641.1
Am 6:13 Have we not taken to us horns by **our o** 5105.1
7:11 be led away captive out of **their o** land. 2050.2
Ob 1:15 reward shall return upon **thine o** head. 3509.2
Jnh 2: 8 lying vanities forsake **their o** mercy. 3963.1
Mic 7: 6 a man's enemies *are* the men of **his o** 2050.2
Hag 1: 9 and ye run every man unto **his o** house. 2050.2
Zec 5:11 and set there upon **her o** base. 1886.3
11: 5 and **their o** shepherds pity them not. 1992.1
12: 6 shall be inhabited again in **her o** place, 1886.3
Mal 3:17 a man spareth **his o** son that serveth him. 2050.2
Mt 2:12 they departed into **their o** country another *846*
7: 3 considerest not the beam that is in **thine o** *4674*
7: 4 and behold, a beam *is* in **thine o** eye? *4771*
7: 5 first cast out the beam out of **thine o** eye; *4771*
9: 1 and passed over, and came into **his o** city. *2398*
10:36 And a man's foes *shall be* they of **his o** *846*
13:54 And when he was come into **his o** country, *846*
13:57 save in **his o** country, and in his own house. *846*
13:57 save in his own country, and in **his o** house. *846*
16:26 gain the whole world, and lose **his o** soul? *846*
17:25 tribute? of **their o** children, or of strangers? *846*
20:15 for me to do what I will with **mine o**? *1699*
25:14 *who* called **his o** servants, and *2398*
25:27 I should have received **mine o** with usury. *1699*
27:31 and put **his o** raiment on him, and led him *846*
27:60 And laid it in **his o** new tomb, which he had *846*
Mk 6: 1 from thence, and came into **his o** country; *846*
6: 4 but in **his o** country, and among his own kin, *846*
6: 4 and among **his o** kin, and in his own house. *846*
6: 4 and among his own kin, and in **his o** house. *846*
7: 9 of God, that ye may keep **your o** tradition. *4771*
8: 3 And if I send them away fasting to **their o** *846*
8:36 gain the whole world, and lose **his o** soul? *846*
15:20 and put his **o** clothes on him, and led him *2398*
Lk 1:23 he departed to **his o** house. *846*
1:56 three months, and returned to **her o** house. *846*
2: 3 went to be taxed, every one into **his o** city. *2398*
2:35 a sword shall pierce through thy **o** soul also,) *846*
2:39 into Galilee, to **their o** city Nazareth. *846*
4:24 No prophet is accepted in **his o** country. *846*
5:25 and departed to **his o** house, glorifying God. *846*
5:29 And Levi made him a great feast in **his o** *846*
6:41 perceivest not the beam that is in **thine o** *2398*
6:42 not the beam that is in **thine o** eye? *4771*
6:42 cast out first the beam out of **thine o** eye, *4771*
6:44 For every tree is known by **his o** fruit. *2398*
8:39 Return to **thine o** house, and shew how *4771*
9:26 when he shall come in **his o** glory, and *in his* *846*
10:34 and set him on **his o** beast, and brought him *2398*
14:26 and sisters, yea, and **his o** life also, *1438*
16:12 who shall give you that which is **your o**? *5212*
18: 7 And shall not God avenge **his o** elect, *846*
19:22 Out of **thine o** mouth will I judge thee, *4771*
19:23 I might have required *mine o* with usury? NIG
21:30 know of **your o selves** that summer is now *1438*
22:71 for we ourselves have heard of **his o** mouth. *846*
Jn 1:11 He came unto **his o**, and his own received *2398*
1:11 unto his own, and **his o** received him not. *2398*
1:41 He first findeth **his o** brother Simon, and *2398*
4:41 many moe believed because of his **o** word; NIG
4:44 that a prophet hath no honour in **his o** *2398*
5:30 I can of **mine o self** do nothing: as I hear, *1683*
5:30 is just; because I seek not **mine o** will, *1699*
5:43 if another shall come in **his o** name, him ye *2398*
6:38 not to do **mine o** will, but the will of him *1699*
7:18 He that speaketh of himself seeketh **his o** *2398*
7:53 And every man went unto **his o** house. *846*
8: 9 *it,* being convicted by *their o* conscience, NIG
8:44 he speaketh a lie, he speaketh of **his o**: *2398*
8:50 And I seek not **mine o** glory: there is *one* *1473*
10: 3 and he calleth **his o** sheep by name, and *2398*
10: 4 And when he putteth forth **his o** sheep, he *2398*
10:12 the shepherd, whose **o** the sheep are not, *2398*
13: 1 having loved **his o** which were in *2398*
15:19 of the world, the world would love **his o**: *2398*
16:32 every man to **his o**, and shall leave me *2398*
17: 5 glorify thou me with **thine o self** with *4572*

Jn	17:11	keep through **thine o** name those whom	*4771*
	18:35	**Thine o** nation and the chief priests have	*4674*
	19:27	*that* disciple took her unto **his o** *home.*	*2398*
	20:10	went away again unto **their o home.**	*1438*
Ac	1: 7	which the Father hath put in **his o** power.	*2398*
	1:25	that *he* might go to **his o** place.	*2398*
	2: 6	that every man heard them speak in **his o**	*2398*
	2: 8	And how hear we every man in our **o**	*2398*
	3:12	as though by **our o** power or holiness we	*2398*
	4:23	they went to **their o** *company,* and	*2398*
	4:32	of the *things* which he possessed was **his o;**	*2398*
	5: 4	Whiles it remained, was it not **thine o**? and	*4771*
	5: 4	it was sold, was it not in **thine o** power?	*4674*
	7:21	him up, and nourished him for **her o** son.	*1438*
	7:41	and rejoiced in the works of **their o** hands.	*846*
	12:10	which opened to them **of** his **o accord:**	*844*
	13:22	a man after **mine o** heart, which shall fulfil	*1473*
	13:36	after he had served **his o** generation by	*2398*
	14:16	suffered all nations to walk in **their o** ways.	*846*
	15:22	to send chosen men of **their o company** to	*846*
	17:28	as certain also of **your o** poets have	*2596+4771*
	18: 6	Your blood *be* upon **your o** heads;	*4771*
	20:28	which he hath purchased with **his o** blood.	*2398*
	20:30	Also of your **o selves** shall men arise,	*846*
	21:11	and bound his *o* hands and feet, and said,	NIG
	25:19	against him of **their o** superstition,	*2398*
	26: 4	which was at the first among **mine o** nation	*1473*
	27:19	**with** our **o hands** the tackling of the ship.	*849*
	28:30	And Paul dwelt two whole years in **his o**	*2398*
Ro	1:24	through the lusts of **their o** hearts,	*846*
	1:24	to dishonour **their o** bodies between	*846*
	4:19	he considered not **his o** body now dead,	*1438*
	8: 3	God sending **his o** Son in the likeness of	*1438*
	8:32	He that spared not **his o** Son, but	*2398*
	10: 3	going about to establish **their o**	*2398*
	11:24	*branches,* be graffed into **their o** olive tree?	*2398*
	11:25	lest ye should be wise in **your o** conceits;	*1438*
	12:16	low estate. Be not wise in **your o** conceits.	*1438*
	14: 4	to **his o** master he standeth or falleth. Yea,	*2398*
	14: 5	man be fully persuaded in **his o** mind.	*2398*
	16: 4	Who have for my life laid down **their o**	*1438*
	16:18	not our Lord Jesus Christ, but **their o** belly;	*1438*
1Co	1:15	say that I had baptized in **mine o** name.	*1699*
	3: 8	every man shall receive **his o** reward	*2398*
	3: 8	his own reward according to **his o** labour.	*2398*
	3:19	He taketh the wise in **their o** craftiness.	*846*
	4: 3	yea, I judge not **mine o self**.	*1683*
	4:12	And labour, working with **our o** hands:	*2398*
	6:14	and will *also* raise up us by **his o** power.	*846*
	6:18	fornication sinneth against **his o** body.	*2398*
	6:19	ye have of God, and ye are not **your o**?	*1438*
	7: 2	let every man have **his o** wife, and let every	*1438*
	7: 2	and let every woman have **her o** husband.	*2398*
	7: 4	The wife hath not power of **her o** body, but	*2398*
	7: 4	the husband hath not power of **his o** body,	*2398*
	7:35	And this I speak for your **o** profit; not that I	*846*
	7:37	but hath power over **his o** will, and hath so	*2398*
	9: 7	Who goeth a warfare any time at **his o**	*2398*
	10:24	Let no *man* seek **his o**, but every man	*1438*
	10:29	I say, not **thine o**, but of the other's:	*1438*
	10:33	in all *things,* not seeking **mine o** profit,	*1683*
	11:21	every one taketh before *other* **his o** supper:	*2398*
	13: 5	seeketh not **her o**, is not easily provoked,	*1438*
	15:23	But every man in **his o** order: Christ	*2398*
	15:38	pleased him, and to every seed **his o** body.	*2398*
	16:21	The salutation of *me* Paul with **mine o**	*1699*
2Co	6:12	but ye are straitened in **your o** bowels.	*4771*
	8: 5	but first gave **their o selves** to the Lord,	*1438*
	8:17	**of** his **o accord** he went unto you.	*830*
	11:26	of robbers, *in* perils by *my o* countrymen,	NIG
	13: 5	ye be in the faith; prove **your o selves**.	*1438*
	13: 5	Know ye not **your o selves**, how that Jesus	*1438*
Gal	1:14	above many *my* equals in **mine o** nation,	*1473*
	4:15	ye would have plucked out **your o** eyes,	*4771*
	6: 4	But let every man prove **his o** work, and	*1438*
	6: 5	For every man shall bear **his o** burden.	*2398*
	6:11	I have written unto you with **mine o** hand.	*1699*
Eph	1:11	all *things* after the counsel of **his o** will:	*846*
	1:20	set *him* at **his o** right hand in the heavenly	*846*
	5:22	submit yourselves unto **your o** husbands,	*2398*
	5:24	*let* the wives *be* to their **o** husbands in	*2398*
	5:28	So ought men to love their wives as **their o**	*1438*
	5:29	For no *man* ever yet hated **his o** flesh; but	*1438*
Php	2: 4	Look not every man on **his o** *things,* but	*1438*
	2:12	work out **your o** salvation with fear and	*1438*
	2:21	For all seek **their o**, not the *things which*	*1438*
	3: 9	not having **mine o** righteousness, which is	*1699*
Col	3:18	submit yourselves unto **your o** husbands,	*2398*
1Th	2: 8	but also **our o** souls, because ye were dear	*1438*
	2:14	suffered like *things* of **your o** countrymen,	*2398*
	2:15	and their **o** prophets, and have persecuted	*2398*
	4:11	and to do **your o** *business,* and to work	*2398*
	4:11	and to work with your **o** hands,	*2398*
2Th	3:12	quietness they work, and eat **their o** bread.	*1438*
	3:17	The salutation of Paul with **mine o** hand,	*1699*
1Ti	1: 2	Unto Timothy, *my* **o** son in the faith:	*1103*
	3: 4	One that ruleth well **his o** house, having *his*	*2398*
	3: 5	(For if a man know not how to rule **his o**	*2398*
	3:12	*their* children and **their o** houses well.	*2398*
	5: 8	But if any provide not for **his o**, and	*2398*
	5: 8	and specially for those of his **o** house,	NIG
	6: 1	count **their o** masters worthy of all honour,	*2398*
2Ti	1: 9	but according to **his o** purpose and grace,	*2398*
	3: 2	For men shall be **lovers of** their **o selves,**	*5367*
	4: 3	after **their o** lusts shall they heap to	*2398*
Tit	1: 4	*mine* **o** son after the common faith:	*1103*
	1:12	*even* a prophet of **their o**, said,	*2398*
	2: 5	good, obedient to **their o** husbands,	*2398*
	2: 9	*Exhort* servants to be obedient unto **their o**	*2398*
Phm	1:12	receive him, that is, **mine o** bowels:	*1699*
	1:19	I Paul have written *it* with **mine o** hand,	*1699*
	1:19	owest unto me even **thine o self** besides.	*4572*
Heb	2: 4	of the Holy Ghost, according to **his o** will?	*846*
	3: 6	But Christ as a Son over **his o** house;	*846*
	4:10	he also hath ceased from **his o** works,	*846*
	7:27	first for **his o** sins, *and* then for	*2398*
	9:12	by **his o** blood he entered in once into	*2398*
	12:10	few days chastened *us* after **their o** pleasure;	*846*
	13:12	that he might sanctify the people with **his o**	*2398*
Jas	1:14	when he is drawn away of **his o** lust, and	*2398*
	1:18	**Of** his **o will** begat he us with the word of	*1014*
	1:22	not hearers only, deceiving **your o selves.**	*1438*
	1:26	not his tongue, but deceiveth **his o** heart,	*846*
1Pe	2:24	Who **his o self** bare our sins in his own body	*846*
	2:24	Who his own self bare our sins in **his o** body	*846*
	3: 1	*be* in subjection to **your o** husbands;	*2398*
	3: 5	being in subjection unto **their o** husbands:	*2398*
2Pe	2:12	and shall utterly perish in their **o** corruption;	*846*
	2:13	sporting themselves with **their o** deceivings	*846*
	2:22	The dog *is* turned to **his o** vomit again;	*2398*
	3: 3	days scoffers, walking after **their o** lusts,	*2398*
	3:16	other scriptures, unto **their o** destruction.	*2398*
	3:17	the wicked, fall from **your o** stedfastness.	*2398*
1Jn	3:12	Because **his o** works were evil, and his	*846*
Jude	1: 6	their first estate, but left **their o** habitation,	*2398*
	1:13	of the sea, foaming out **their o** shame;	*1438*
	1:16	complainers, walking after **their o** lusts;	*846*
	1:18	who should walk after **their o** ungodly	*1438*
Rev	1: 5	and washed us from our sins in **his o** blood,	*846*

OWNER (13) [OWN]

Ex	21:28	be eaten; but the **o** of the ox *shall be* quit.	1167
	21:29	it hath been testified to his **o**, and he hath	1167
	21:29	and his **o** also shall be put to death.	1167
	21:34	The **o** of the pit shall make *it* good, *and*	1167
	21:34	*it* good, *and* give money unto the **o** of them;	1167
	21:36	in time past, and his **o** hath not kept him in;	1167
	22:11	the **o** of it shall accept *thereof,* and he shall	1167
	22:12	he shall make restitution unto the **o** thereof.	1167
	22:14	or die, the **o** thereof *being* not with it,	1167
	22:15	*But* if the **o** thereof *be* with it, he shall not	1167
1Ki	16:24	the name of Shemer, **o** of the hill, Samaria.	113
Isa	1: 3	The ox knoweth his **o**, and the ass his	7069
Ac	27:11	believed the master and the **o of the ship,**	*3490*

OWNERS (5) [OWN]

Job	31:39	have caused the **o** thereof to lose their life:	1167
Pr	1:19	*which* taketh away the life of the **o** thereof.	1167
Ecc	5:11	what good *is there* to the **o** thereof,	1167
	5:13	*namely,* riches kept for the **o** thereof to	1167
Lk	19:33	the **o** thereof said unto them, Why loose ye	*2962*

OWNETH (1) [OWN]

Lev	14:35	he that **o** the house shall come and tell	3807.1

OX (64) [OXEN]

Ex	20:17	nor his maidservant, nor his **o**, nor his ass,	7794
	21:28	If an **o** gore a man or a woman, that they	7794

Ex 21:28 the **o** shall be surely stoned, and his flesh 7794
21:28 but the owner of the **o** *shall be* quit. 7794
21:29 if the **o** *were* wont to push with his horn in 7794
21:29 the **o** shall be stoned, and his owner also 7794
21:32 If the **o** shall push a manservant or 7794
21:32 shekels *of* silver, and the **o** shall be stoned. 7794
21:33 not cover it, and an **o** or an ass fall therein; 7794
21:35 if one man's **o** hurt another's, that he die; 7794
21:35 they shall sell the live **o**, and divide 7794
21:35 of it; and the dead *o* also they shall divide. NIH
21:36 Or *if* it be known that the **o** *hath* used to 7794
21:36 he shall surely pay **o** for ox; and the dead 7794
21:36 he shall surely pay ox for **o**; and the dead 7794
22: 1 If a man shall steal an **o**, or a sheep, and 7794
22: 1 he shall restore five oxen for an **o**, and 7794
22: 4 hand alive, whether it be **o**, or ass, or sheep; 7794
22: 9 *whether it be* for **o**, for ass, for sheep, 7794
22:10 or an **o**, or a sheep, or any beast, to keep; 7794
23: 4 If thou meet thine enemy's **o** or his ass 7794
23:12 that thine **o** and thine ass may rest, and 7794
34:19 thy cattle, *whether* **o** or sheep, *that* is male. 7794
Lev 7:23 no *manner* fat, of **o**, or of sheep, or of goat. 7794
17: 3 that killeth an **o**, or lamb, or goat, in 7794
27:26 shall sanctify it; whether *it be* **o**, or sheep: 7794
Nu 7: 3 two of the princes, and for *each* one an **o**: 7794
22: 4 as the **o** licketh up the grass of the field. 7794
Dt 5:14 thy maidservant, nor thine **o**, nor thine ass, 7794
5:21 his **o**, or his ass, or any *thing* that *is* thy 7794
14: 4 ye shall eat: the **o**, the sheep, and the goat, 7794
14: 5 and the **wild o**, and the chamois. 8377
18: 3 offer a sacrifice, whether *it be* **o** or sheep; 7794
22: 1 Thou shalt not see thy brother's **o** or his 7794
22: 4 brother's ass or his **o** fall down by the way, 7794
22:10 Thou shalt not plow with an **o** and an ass 7794
25: 4 Thou shalt not muzzle the **o** when he 7794
28:31 Thine **o** *shall be* slain before thine eyes, and 7794
Jos 6:21 and old, and **o**, and sheep, and ass, 7794
Jdg 3:31 Philistines six hundred men with an **o** goad: 1241
6: 4 for Israel, neither sheep, nor **o**, nor ass. 7794
1Sa 12: 3 whose **o** have I taken? or whose ass have I 7794
14:34 Bring me hither every man his **o**, and 7794
14:34 all the people brought every man his **o** with 7794
15: 3 and suckling, **o** and sheep, camel and ass. 7794
Ne 5:18 which was prepared *for me* daily *was* one **o** 7794
Job 6: 5 hath grass? or loweth the **o** over his fodder? 7794
24: 3 they take the widow's **o** for a pledge. 7794
40:15 I made with thee; he eateth grass as an **o**. 1241
Ps 69:31 shall please the LORD better than an **o** 7794
106:20 into the similitude of an **o** that eateth grass. 7794
Pr 7:22 as an **o** goeth to the slaughter, or as a fool 7794
14: 4 much increase *is* by the strength of the **o**. 7794
15:17 than a stalled **o** and hatred therewith. 7794
Isa 1: 3 The **o** knoweth his owner, and the ass his 7794
11: 7 and the lion shall eat straw like the **o**. 1241
32:20 that send forth *thither* the feet of the **o** and 7794
66: 3 He that killeth an **o** *is as if* he slew a man; 7794
Jer 11:19 *or an* **o** *that* is brought to the slaughter; 441
Eze 1:10 they four had the face of an **o** on the left 7794
Lk 13:15 each one of you on the sabbath loose his **o** *1016*
14: 5 shall have an ass or an **o** fallen into a pit, *1016*
1Co 9: 9 Thou shalt not muzzle the mouth of the **o** *1016*
1Ti 5:18 Thou shalt not muzzle the **o** that treadeth *1016*

OXEN (102) [OX]

Ge 12:16 **o**, and he asses, and menservants, and 1241
20:14 **o**, and menservants, and womenservants, 1241
21:27 Abraham took sheep and **o**, and gave *them* 1241
32: 5 I have **o**, and asses, flocks, and 7794
34:28 their **o**, and their asses, and that which *was* 1241
Ex 9: 3 the camels, upon the **o**, and upon the sheep: 1241
20:24 thy peace offerings, thy sheep, and thine **o**: 1241
22: 1 he shall restore five **o** for an ox, and 1241
22:30 Likewise shalt thou do with thine **o**, *and* 7794
24: 5 sacrificed peace offerings *of* **o** unto 6499
Nu 7: 3 six covered wagons, and twelve **o**; 1241
7: 6 Moses took the wagons and the **o**, and 1241
7: 7 four **o** he gave unto the sons of Gershon, 1241
7: 8 eight **o** he gave unto the sons of Merari, 1241
7:17 two **o**, five rams, five he goats, five lambs 1241
7:23 two **o**, five rams, five he goats, five lambs 1241
7:29 two **o**, five rams, five he goats, five lambs 1241
7:35 two **o**, five rams, five he goats, five lambs 1241
7:41 two **o**, five rams, five he goats, five lambs 1241
7:47 two **o**, five rams, five he goats, five lambs 1241
7:53 two **o**, five rams, five he goats, five lambs 1241
7:59 two **o**, five rams, five he goats, five lambs 1241
7:65 two **o**, five rams, five he goats, five lambs 1241
7:71 two **o**, five rams, five he goats, five lambs 1241
7:77 two **o**, five rams, five he goats, five lambs 1241
7:83 two **o**, five rams, five he goats, five lambs 1241
7:87 All the **o** for the burnt offering *were* twelve 1241
7:88 all the **o** for the sacrifice of the peace 1241
22:40 Balak offered **o** and sheep, and sent to 1241
23: 1 prepare me here seven **o** and seven rams. 6499
Dt 14:26 for **o**, or for sheep, or for wine, or 1241
Jos 7:24 his **o**, and his asses, and his sheep, and his 7794
1Sa 11: 7 he took a yoke of **o**, and hewed them in 1241
11: 7 after Samuel, so shall it be done unto his **o**. 1241
14:14 acre of land, *which* a yoke *of o might plow.* NIH
14:32 **o**, and calves, and slew *them* on the ground: 1241
15: 9 of the **o**, and of the fatlings, and the lambs, 1241
15:14 and the lowing of the **o** which I hear? 1241
15:15 spared the best of the sheep and of the **o**, 1241
15:21 the people took of the spoil, sheep and **o**, 1241
22:19 and sucklings, and **o**, and asses, and sheep, 7794
27: 9 the **o**, and the asses, and the camels, and 1241
2Sa 6: 6 and took hold of it; for the **o** shook *it.* 1241
6:13 gone six paces, he sacrificed **o** and fatlings. 7794
24:22 *here be* **o** for burnt sacrifice, and threshing 1241
24:22 and *other* instruments of the **o** for wood. 1241
24:24 and the **o** for fifty shekels of silver. 1241
1Ki 1: 9 Adonijah slew sheep and **o** and fat cattle by 1241
1:19 he hath slain **o** and fat cattle and sheep in 7794
1:25 hath slain **o** and fat cattle and sheep in 7794
4:23 Ten fat **o**, and twenty oxen out of 1241
4:23 twenty **o** out of the pastures, and 1241
7:25 It stood upon twelve **o**, three looking 1241
7:29 the ledges *were* lions, **o**, and cherubims: 1241
7:29 **o** *were certain* additions made of thin work. 1241
7:44 And one sea, and twelve **o** under the sea; 1241
8: 5 him before the ark, sacrificing sheep and **o**, 1241
8:63 two and twenty thousand **o**, and an hundred 1241
19:19 who *was* plowing *with* twelve yoke *of* **o** NIH
19:20 he left the **o**, and ran after Elijah, and said, 1241
19:21 took a yoke of **o**, and slew them, and boiled 1241
19:21 their flesh with the instruments of the **o**, 1241
2Ki 5:26 and **o**, and menservants, and maidservants? 1241
16:17 took down the sea from off the brasen **o** 1241
1Ch 12:40 and on mules, and on **o**, *and* meat, meal, 1241
12:40 wine, and oil, and **o**, and sheep abundantly: 1241
13: 9 his hand to hold the ark; for the **o** stumbled. 1241
21:23 lo, I give *thee* the **o** *also* for burnt offerings, 1241
2Ch 4: 3 under it *was* the similitude of **o**, which did 1241
4: 3 Two rows *of* **o** *were* cast, when it was cast. 1241
4: 4 It stood upon twelve **o**, three looking 1241
4:15 One sea, and twelve **o** under it. 1241
5: 6 sacrificed sheep and **o**, which could not be 1241
7: 5 a sacrifice of twenty and two thousand **o**, 1241
15:11 seven hundred **o** and seven thousand sheep. 1241
18: 2 killed sheep and **o** for him in abundance, 1241
29:33 the consecrated *things were* six hundred **o** 1241
31: 6 they also brought in the tithe of **o** and 1241
35: 8 hundred *small cattle,* and three hundred **o**. 1241
35: 9 thousand *small cattle,* and five hundred **o**. 1241
35:12 book of Moses. And so *did they* with the **o**. 1241
Job 1: 3 five hundred yoke of **o**, and five hundred 1241
1:14 The **o** were plowing, and the asses feeding 1241
42:12 a thousand yoke of **o**, and a thousand she 1241
Ps 8: 7 All sheep and **o**, yea, and the beasts of 504
144:14 *That* our **o** *may be* strong to labour; 441
Pr 14: 4 Where no **o** *are,* the crib *is* clean: but 504
Isa 7:25 it shall be for the sending forth of **o**, and 7794
22:13 and gladness, slaying **o**, and killing sheep, 1241
30:24 The **o** likewise and the young asses that ear 504
Jer 51:23 pieces the husbandman and his **yoke of o**; 6776
Da 4:25 they shall make thee to eat grass as **o**, 8450
4:32 they shall make thee to eat grass as **o**, and 8450
4:33 did eat grass as **o**, and his body was wet 8450
5:21 they fed him with grass like **o**, and his body 8450
Am 6:12 will *one* plow *there* with **o**? for ye have 1241
Mt 22: 4 my **o** and *my* fatlings *are* killed, and *5022*
Lk 14:19 I have bought five yoke of **o**, and I go to *1016*
Jn 2:14 And found in the temple those that sold **o** *1016*
2:15 out of the temple, and the sheep and the **o**; *1016*
Ac 14:13 brought **o** and garlands unto the gates, and *5022*
1Co 9: 9 out the corn. Doth God take care for **o**? *1016*

OXGOAD See GOAD

OZEM (2)
1Ch 2:15 **O** the sixth, David the seventh: 684
2:25 and Bunah, and Oren, and **O**, *and* Ahijah. 684

OZIAS (2) [AHAZIAH]
Mt 1: 8 Josaphat begat Joram; and Joram begat **O**; *3604*
1: 9 And **O** begat Joatham; and Joatham begat *3604*

OZNI (1) [OZNITES]
Nu 26:16 Of **O**, the family of the Oznites: of Eri, 244

OZNITES (1) [OZNI]
Nu 26:16 Of Ozni, the family of the **O**: of Eri, 244

P

PAARAI (1)
2Sa 23:35 Hezrai the Carmelite, **P** the Arbite, 6474

PACATIANA (1)
1Ti 6: S which is the chiefest city of Phrygia **P**. *3818*

PACES (1)
2Sa 6:13 ark of the LORD had **gone** six **p**, 6805+6806

PACIFIED (2) [PACIFY]
Est 7:10 for Mordecai. Then was the king's wrath **p**. 7918
Eze 16:63 when I am **p** toward thee for all that thou 3722

PACIFIETH (2) [PACIFY]
Pr 21:14 A gift in secret **p** anger: and a reward in 3711
Ecc 10: 4 not thy place; for yielding **p** great offences. 3240

PACIFY (1) [PACIFIED, PACIFIETH]
Pr 16:14 of death: but a wise man will **p** it. 3722

PADAN (1) [PADAN-ARAM]
Ge 48: 7 as for me, when I came from **P**, 6307

PADAN-ARAM (10) [ARAM, PADAN]
Ge 25:20 the daughter of Bethuel the Syrian of **P**, 6307
28: 2 Arise, go to **P**, to the house of Bethuel thy 6307
28: 5 he went to **P** unto Laban, son of Bethuel 6307
28: 6 sent him away to **P**, to take him a wife from 6307
28: 7 and his mother, and was gone to **P**; 6307
31:18 of his getting, which he had gotten in **P**, 6307
33:18 the land of Canaan, when he came from **P**; 6307
35: 9 when he came out of **P**, and blessed him. 6307
35:26 sons of Jacob, which were born to him in **P**. 6307
46:15 which she bare unto Jacob in **P**, with his 6307

PADDAN See PADAN

PADDAN ARAM See PADAN-ARAM

PADDLE (1)
Dt 23:13 thou shalt have a **p** upon thy weapon; and 3489

PADON (2)
Ezr 2:44 the children of Siaha, the children of **P**, 6303
Ne 7:47 the children of Sia, the children of **P**, 6303

PAGAN See CHEMARIMS

PAGANS See PUBLICAN

PAGIEL (5)
Nu 1:13 Of Asher; **P** the son of Ocran. 6295
2:27 of Asher *shall be* **P** the son of Ocran. 6295
7:72 On the eleventh day **P** the son of Ocran, 6295
7:77 this *was* the offering of **P** the son of Ocran. 6295
10:26 children of Asher *was* **P** the son of Ocran. 6295

PAHATH-MOAB (6)
Ezr 2: 6 The children of **P**, of the children of Jeshua 6355
8: 4 Of the sons of **P**; Elihoenai the son of 6355
10:30 of the sons of **P**; Adna, and Chelal, 6355
Ne 3:11 Hashub the son of **P**, repaired the other 6355
7:11 The children of **P**, of the children of Jeshua 6355
10:14 the people; Parosh, **P**, Elam, Zatthu, Bani, 6355

PAI (1)
1Ch 1:50 the name of his city *was* **P**; and his wife's 6464

PAID (4) [PAY]
Ezr 4:20 toll, tribute, and custom, *was* **p** unto them. 3052
Jnh 1: 3 so he **p** the fare thereof, and went down 5414
Mt 5:26 till thou hast **p** the uttermost farthing. *591*
Lk 12:59 till thou hast **p** the very last mite. *591*

PAIN (25) [PAINED, PAINFUL, PAINFULNESS, PAINS]
Job 14:22 his flesh upon him shall **have p**, and 3510
15:20 The wicked *man* **travaileth with p** all his 2342
33:19 He is chastened also with **p** upon his bed, 4341
33:19 the multitude of his bones *with* strong **p**: NIH
Ps 25:18 Look upon mine affliction and my **p**; and 5999
48: 6 them there, *and* **p**, as of a woman in travail. 2427
Isa 13: 8 shall be **in p** as a woman that travaileth: 2342
21: 3 Therefore are my loins filled *with* **p**: 2479
26:17 is **in p**, *and* crieth out in her pangs; 2342
26:18 have been with child, we have been **in p**, 2342
66: 7 before her **p** came, she was delivered of a 2256
Jer 6:24 hold of us, *and* **p**, as of a woman in travail. 2427
12:13 they have **put** themselves **to p**, *but* shall not 2470
15:18 Why is my **p** perpetual, and my wound 3511
22:23 upon thee, the **p** as of a woman in travail. 2427
30:23 it shall **fall with p** upon the head of 2342
51: 8 take balm for her **p**, if so be she may be 4341
Eze 30: 4 **great p** shall be in Ethiopia, when the slain 2479
30: 9 **great p** shall come upon them, as *in* 2479
30:16 Sin shall **have great p**, and No shall 2342+2342
Mic 4:10 Be **in p**, and labour to bring forth, 2342
Na 2:10 **much p** *is* in all loins, and the faces of them 2479
Ro 8:22 and **travaileth in p together** until now. *4944*
Rev 16:10 and they gnawed their tongues for **p**, *4192*
21: 4 neither shall there be any more **p**: *4192*

PAINED (5) [PAIN]
Ps 55: 4 My heart is **sore p** within me: and 2342
Isa 23: 5 shall they be **sorely p** *at* the report of Tyre. 2342
Jer 4:19 I am **p** *at* my very heart; my heart maketh a 2342
Joel 2: 6 their face *the* people shall be **much p**: 2342
Rev 12: 2 travailing in birth, and **p** to be delivered. *928*

PAINFUL (1) [PAIN]
Ps 73:16 I thought to know this, it *was* too **p** for me; 5999

PAINFULNESS (1) [PAIN]
2Co 11:27 In weariness and **p**, in watchings often, *3449*

PAINS (4) [PAIN]
1Sa 4:19 and travailed; for her **p** came upon her. 6735
Ps 116: 3 and the **p** of hell gat hold upon me: 4712
Ac 2:24 raised up, having loosed the **p** of death: *5604*
Rev 16:11 because of their **p** and their sores, *4192*

PAINTED (2) [PAINTEDST, PAINTING]
2Ki 9:30 heard *of it*; and she **p** 7760+7760+871.1+1886.1
Jer 22:14 *is* cieled with cedar, and **p** with vermilion. 4886

PAINTEDST (1) [PAINTED]
Eze 23:40 for whom thou didst wash *thyself*, **p** thy 3583

PAINTING (1) [PAINTED]
Jer 4:30 though thou rentest thy face with **p**, in vain 6320

PAIR (4)
Am 2: 6 for silver, and the poor for a **p** of shoes; NIH
8: 6 for silver, and the needy for a **p** of shoes; NIH
Lk 2:24 A **p** of turtledoves, or two young pigeons. *2201*
Rev 6: 5 he that sat on him had a **p of balances** in *2218*

PALACE (48) [PALACES]
1Ki 16:18 that he went into the **p** of the king's house, 759
21: 1 hard by the **p** of Ahab king of Samaria. 1964
2Ki 15:25 in the **p** of the king's house, with Argob and 759
20:18 they shall be eunuchs in the **p** of the king of 1964
1Ch 29: 1 for the **p** *is* not for man, but for the LORD 1002
29:19 to do all *these things*, and to build the **p**, 1002
2Ch 9:11 to the king's **p**, and harps and psalteries for 1004
Ezr 4:14 we have maintenance from *the king's* **p**, 1965
6: 2 in the **p** that *is* in the province of 1001
Ne 1: 1 twentieth year, as I was in Shushan the **p**, 1002
2: 8 of the **p** which *appertained* to the house, 1002
7: 2 Hananiah the ruler of the **p**, charge over 1002
Est 1: 2 his kingdom, which *was* in Shushan the **p**, 1002

Est 1: 5 people that were present in Shushan the **p**, 1002
1: 5 in the court of the garden of the king's **p**; 1055
2: 3 the fair young virgins unto Shushan the **p**, 1002
2: 5 *Now* in Shushan the **p** there was a certain 1002
2: 8 were gathered together unto Shushan the **p**, 1002
3:15 and the decree was given in Shushan the **p**. 1002
7: 7 of wine in his wrath *went* into the **p** garden: 1055
7: 8 the king returned out of the **p** garden into 1055
8:14 and the decree was given at Shushan the **p**. 1002
9: 6 in Shushan the **p** the Jews slew and 1002
9:11 Shushan the **p** was brought before the king. 1002
9:12 five hundred men in Shushan the **p**, 1002
Ps 45:15 they shall enter into the king's **p**. 1964
144:12 polished *after* the similitude of a **p**: 1964
SS 8: 9 a wall, we will build upon her a **p** of silver: 2918
Isa 25: 2 a **p** of strangers to be no city; it shall never 759
39: 7 they shall be eunuchs in the **p** of the king of 1964
Jer 30:18 the **p** shall remain after the manner thereof. 759
Da 1: 4 *had* ability in them to stand in the king's **p**, 1964
4: 4 rest in mine house, and flourishing in my **p**: 1965
4:29 walked in the **p** of the kingdom of Babylon. 1965
5: 5 upon the plaister of the wall of the king's **p**: 1965
6:18 the king went to his **p**, and passed the night 1965
8: 2 when I saw, that I *was* at Shushan *in* the **p**, 1002
11:45 he shall plant the tabernacles of his **p** 643
Am 4: 3 ye shall cast *them* into the **p**, saith 2038
Na 2: 6 be opened, and the **p** shall be dissolved. 1964
Mt 26: 3 of the people, unto the **p** of the high priest, *833*
26:58 him afar off unto the high priest's **p**, *833*
26:69 Now Peter sat without in the **p**: and a damsel *833*
Mk 14:54 afar off, even into the **p** of the high priest: *833*
14:66 And as Peter was beneath in the **p**, *833*
Lk 11:21 When a strong *man* armed keepeth his **p**, his *833*
Jn 18:15 went in with Jesus into the **p** of the high *833*
Php 1:13 bonds in Christ are manifest in all the **p**, *4232*

PALACES (33) [PALACE]
2Ch 36:19 burnt all the **p** thereof with fire, and 759
Ps 45: 8 and aloes, *and* cassia, out of the ivory **p**, 1964
48: 3 God is known in her **p** for a refuge. 759
48:13 Mark ye well her bulwarks, consider her **p**; 759
78:69 he built his sanctuary like high *p*, like NIH
122: 7 within thy walls, *and* prosperity within thy **p**. 759
Pr 30:28 hold with her hands, and *is* in kings' **p**. 1964
Isa 13:22 and dragons in *their* pleasant **p**: 1964
23:13 towers thereof, they raised up the **p** thereof; 759
32:14 Because the **p** shall be forsaken; 759
34:13 thorns shall come up *in* her **p**, nettles and 759
Jer 6: 5 let us go by night, and let us destroy her **p**. 759
9:21 *and* is entered into our **p**, to cut off 759
17:27 it shall devour the **p** of Jerusalem, and 759
49:27 and it shall consume the **p** of Ben-hadad. 759
La 2: 5 up Israel, he hath swallowed up all her **p**: 759
2: 7 the hand of the enemy the walls of her **p**; 759
Eze 19: 7 he knew their **desolate p**, and he laid waste 490
25: 4 they shall set their **p** in thee, and make their 2918
Hos 8:14 his cities, and it shall devour the **p** thereof. 759
Am 1: 4 which shall devour the **p** of Ben-hadad. 759
1: 7 of Gaza, which shall devour the **p** thereof: 759
1:10 of Tyrus, which shall devour the **p** thereof. 759
1:12 which shall devour the **p** of Bozrah. 759
1:14 it shall devour the **p** thereof, with shouting in 759
2: 2 and it shall devour the **p** of Kerioth: 759
2: 5 and it shall devour the **p** of Jerusalem. 759
3: 9 Publish in the **p** at Ashdod, and in 759
3: 9 and in the **p** in the land of Egypt, and say, 759
3:10 who store up violence and robbery in their **p**. 759
3:11 from thee, and thy **p** shall be spoiled. 759
6: 8 the excellency of Jacob, and hate his **p**: 759
Mic 5: 5 when he shall tread in our **p**, then shall we 759

PALAL (1)
Ne 3:25 **P** the son of Uzai, over against the turning 6420

PALE (2) [PALENESS]
Isa 29:22 neither shall his face now **wax p**. 2357
Rev 6: 8 And I looked, and behold a **p** horse: and *5515*

PALENESS (1) [PALE]
Jer 30: 6 in travail, and all faces are turned into **p**? 3420

PALESTINA (3) [PALESTINE]
Ex 15:14 shall take hold on the inhabitants of **P**. 6429
Isa 14:29 whole **P**, because the rod of him that smote 6429
14:31 cry, O city; thou, whole **P**, *art* dissolved: 6429

PALESTINE (1) [PALESTINA]
Joel 3: 4 O Tyre, and Zidon, and all the coasts of **P**? 6429

PALLU (4) [PALLUITES]
Ex 6:14 Hanoch, and **P**, Hezron, and Carmi: 6396
Nu 26: 5 of **P**, the family of the Palluites: 6396
26: 8 And the sons of **P**; Eliab. 6396
1Ch 5: 3 *were,* Hanoch, and **P**, Hezron, and Carmi. 6396

PALLUITES (1) [PALLU]
Nu 26: 5 of Pallu, the family of the **P**: 6384

PALM (37) [PALMS]
Ex 15:27 of water, and threescore and ten **p trees**: 8558
Lev 14:15 and pour *it* into the **p of** his own left **hand**: 3709
14:26 of the oil into the **p of** his own left **hand**: 3709
23:40 branches of **p trees**, and the boughs of 8558
Nu 33: 9 of water, and threescore and ten **p trees**; 8558
Dt 34: 3 of Jericho, the city of **p trees**, unto Zoar. 8558
Jdg 1:16 went up out of the city of **p trees** with 8558
3:13 and possessed the city of **p trees**. 8558
4: 5 she dwelt under the **p tree** of Deborah 8560
1Ki 6:29 of cherubims and **p trees** and open flowers, 8561
6:32 of cherubims and **p trees** and open flowers, 8561
6:32 upon the cherubims, and upon the **p trees**. 8561
6:35 and **p trees** and open flowers: 8561
7:36 he graved cherubims, lions, and **p trees**, 8561
2Ch 3: 5 and set thereon **p trees** and chains. 8561
28:15 the city of **p trees**, to their brethren: 8558
Ne 8:15 and **p** branches, and branches of thick trees, 8558
Ps 92:12 The righteous shall flourish like the **p tree**: 8558
SS 7: 7 This thy stature is like to a **p tree**, and 8558
7: 8 I said, I will go up to the **p tree**, I will take 8558
Jer 10: 5 They *are* upright as the **p tree**, but 8560
Eze 40:16 and upon *each* post *were* **p trees**. 8561
40:22 and their arches, and their **p trees**, 8561
40:26 it had **p trees**, one on this side, and 8561
40:31 and **p trees** *were* upon the posts thereof: 8561
40:34 **p trees** *were* upon the posts thereof, on this 8561
40:37 **p trees** *were* upon the posts thereof, on this 8561
41:18 *it was* made *with* cherubims and **p trees**, 8561
41:18 so that a **p tree** *was* between a cherub and a 8561
41:19 man *was* toward the **p tree** on the one side, 8561
41:19 the face of a young lion toward the **p tree** 8561
41:20 the door *were* cherubims and **p trees** made, 8561
41:25 doors of the temple, cherubims and **p trees**, 8561
41:26 **p trees** on the one side and on the other 8561
Joel 1:12 the **p tree** also, and the apple tree, 8558
Jn 12:13 Took branches of **p trees**, and went forth to *5404*
18:22 **stroke** Jesus **with the p of his hand**, *1325+4475*

PALMERWORM (3) [WORM]
Joel 1: 4 That which the **p** hath left hath the locust 1501
2:25 and the caterpillar, and the **p**, 1501
Am 4: 9 the **p** devoured *them:* yet have ye not 1501

PALMS (7) [PALM]
1Sa 5: 4 both the **p** of his hands *were* cut off upon 3709
2Ki 9:35 and the feet, and the **p** of *her* hands. 3709
Isa 49:16 I have graven thee upon the **p of** *my* **hands**; 3709
Da 10:10 my knees and *upon* the **p** of my hands. 3709
Mt 26:67 **smote** *him* **with the p of** their **hands**, *4474*
Mk 14:65 **strike** him **with the p of** their **hands**. *906+4475*
Rev 7: 9 with white robes, and **p** in their hands; *5404*

PALSIES (1) [PALSY]
Ac 8: 7 *with them:* and many **taken with p**, *3886*

PALSY (13) [PALSIES]
Mt 4:24 were lunatick, and those that **had the p**; *3885*
8: 6 my servant lieth at home **sick of the p**, *3885*
9: 2 they brought to him a **man sick of the p**, *3885*
9: 2 their faith said unto the **sick of the p**; *3885*
9: 6 (then saith he to the **sick of the p**,) *3885*
Mk 2: 3 bringing **one sick of the p**, *which was* *3885*
2: 4 down the bed wherein the **sick of the p** lay. *3885*
2: 5 he said unto the **sick of the p**, Son, thy sins *3885*
2: 9 is it easier to say to the **sick of the p**, *3885*
2:10 forgive sins, (he saith to the **sick of the p**,) *3885*
Lk 5:18 in a bed a man which was **taken with a p**: *3886*
5:24 (he said unto the **sick of the p**,) *3886*
Ac 9:33 his bed eight years, and was **sick of the p**. *3886*

PALTI (1)
Nu 13: 9 the tribe of Benjamin, **P** the son of Raphu. 6406

PALTIEL (1)
Nu 34:26 children of Issachar, **P** the son of Azzan. 6409

PALTITE (1)
2Sa 23:26 Helez the **P**, Ira the son of Ikkesh 6407

PAMPHYLIA (5)
Ac 2:10 Phrygia, and **P**, in Egypt, and in the parts of *3828*
13:13 from Paphos, they came to Perga in **P**: *3828*
14:24 passed throughout Pisidia, they came to **P**. *3828*
15:38 *them,* who departed from them from **P**, *3828*
27: 5 we had sailed over the sea of Cilicia and **P**, *3828*

PAN (7) [FIREPANS, FRYINGPAN, PANS]
Lev 2: 5 oblation *be* a meat offering *baken* in a **p**, 4227
6:21 In a **p** it shall be made with oil; *and when it* 4227
7: 9 is dressed in the fryingpan, and in the **p**, 4227
1Sa 2:14 he stroke *it* into the **p**, or kettle, or 3595
2Sa 13: 9 she took a **p**, and poured *them* out before 4958
1Ch 23:29 for *that which is baked in* the **p**, and for that 4227
Eze 4: 3 Moreover take thou unto thee an iron **p**, 4227

PANELED See CIELED

PANELS See CIELED

PANGS (9)
Isa 13: 8 **p** and sorrows shall take hold of *them;* they 6735
21: 3 **p** have taken hold upon me, as the pangs of 6735
21: 3 as the **p** of a woman that travaileth: 6735
26:17 is in pain, *and* crieth out in her **p**; 2256
Jer 22:23 how gracious shalt thou be when **p** come 2256
48:41 shall be as the heart of a woman **in** her **p**. 6887
49:22 Edom be as the heart of a woman **in** her **p**. 6887
50:43 hold of him, *and* **p** as of a woman in travail. 2427
Mic 4: 9 for **p** have taken thee as a woman in travail. 2427

PANIC See DISCOMFITED; DISCOMFITURE

PANNAG (1)
Eze 27:17 and **P**, and honey, and oil, and balm. 6436

PANS (4) [PAN]
Ex 27: 3 thou shalt make his **p** to receive his ashes, 5518
Nu 11: 8 and baked *it* in **p**, and made cakes *of* it: 6517
1Ch 9:31 over the things that were made in the **p**. 2281
2Ch 35:13 in **p**, and divided *them* speedily among all 6745

PANT (1) [PANTED, PANTETH]
Am 2: 7 That **p** after the dust of the earth on 7602

PANTED (2) [PANT]
Ps119:131 I opened my mouth, and **p**: for I longed for 7602
Isa 21: 4 My heart **p**, fearfulness affrighted me: 8582

PANTETH (3) [PANT]
Ps 38:10 My heart **p**, my strength faileth me: as for 5503
42: 1 As the hart **p** after the water brooks, so 6165
42: 1 so **p** my soul after thee, O God. 6165

PAPER (2)
Isa 19: 7 The **p reeds** by the brooks, by the mouth of 6169
2Jn 1:12 unto you, I would not *write* with **p** and ink: *5489*

PAPHOS (2)
Ac 13: 6 they had gone through the isle unto **P**, *3974*
13:13 when Paul and his company loosed from **P**, *3974*

PAPS (4)
Eze 23:21 by the Egyptians for the **p** of thy youth. 7699
Lk 11:27 and the **p** which thou hast sucked. *3149*
23:29 and the **p** which never gave suck. *3149*
Rev 1:13 and girt about the **p** with a golden girdle. *3149*

PAPYRUS See BULRUSH; BULRUSHES

PARABLE (49) [PARABLES]
Nu 23: 7 he took up his **p**, and said, Balak the king 4912
23:18 he took up his **p**, and said, Rise up, Balak, 4912
24: 3 he took up his **p**, and said, Balaam the son 4912
24:15 he took up his **p**, and said, Balaam the son 4912
24:20 on Amalek, he took up his **p**, and said, 4912
24:21 took up his **p**, and said, Strong *is* thy 4912
24:23 he took up his **p**, and said, Alas, who shall 4912
Job 27: 1 Moreover Job continued his **p**, and said, 4912
29: 1 Moreover Job continued his **p**, and said, 4912
Ps 49: 4 I will incline mine ear to a **p**: I will open 4912
78: 2 I will open my mouth in a **p**: I will utter 4912
Pr 26: 7 not equal: so *is* a **p** in the mouth of fools. 4912
26: 9 a drunkard, so *is* a **p** in the mouth of fools. 4912
Eze 17: 2 **speak a p** unto the house of Israel; 4911+4912
24: 3 And utter a **p** unto the rebellious house, and 4912
Mic 2: 4 In that day shall *one* take up a **p** against 4912
Hab 2: 6 Shall not all these take up a **p** against him, 4912
Mt 13:18 Hear ye therefore the **p** of the sower. *3850*
13:24 Another **p** put he forth unto them, saying, *3850*
13:31 Another **p** put he forth unto them, saying, *3850*
13:33 Another **p** spake he unto them; *3850*
13:34 and without a **p** spake he not unto them: *3850*
13:36 Declare unto us the **p** of the tares of *3850*
15:15 and said unto him, Declare unto us this **p**. *3850*
21:33 Hear another **p**: There was a certain *3850*
24:32 Now learn a **p** of the fig tree; When his *3850*
Mk 4:10 him with the twelve asked of him the **p**. *3850*
4:13 he said unto them, Know ye not this **p**? *3850*
4:34 But without a **p** spake he not unto them: *3850*
7:17 his disciples asked him concerning the **p**. *3850*
12:12 for they knew that he had spoken the **p** *3850*
13:28 Now learn a **p** of the fig tree; When her *3850*
Lk 5:36 And he spake also a **p** unto them; No *man* *3850*
6:39 And he spake a **p** unto them, Can the blind *3850*
8: 4 to him out of every city, he spake by a **p**: *3850*
8: 9 asked him, saying, What might this **p** be? *3850*
8:11 Now the **p** is this: The seed is the word of *3850*
12:16 And he spake a **p** unto them, saying, *3850*
12:41 speakest thou this **p** unto us, or even to all? *3850*
13: 6 He spake also this **p**; A certain *man* had a *3850*
14: 7 And he put forth a **p** to those which were *3850*
15: 3 And he spake this **p** unto them, saying, *3850*
18: 1 And he spake a **p** unto them *to this end,* *3850*
18: 9 And he spake this **p** unto certain which *3850*
19:11 heard these *things,* he added and spake a **p**, *3850*
20: 9 began he to speak to the people this **p**; *3850*
20:19 for they perceived that he had spoken this **p** *3850*
21:29 And he spake to them a **p**; Behold the fig *3850*
Jn 10: 6 This **p** spake Jesus unto them: but *3942*

PARABLES (16) [PARABLE]
Eze 20:49 they say of me, Doth he not speak **p**? 4912
Mt 13: 3 And he spake many *things* unto them in **p**, *3850*
13:10 Why speakest thou unto them in **p**? *3850*
13:13 Therefore speak I to them in **p**: because *3850*
13:34 *things* spake Jesus unto the multitude in **p**; *3850*
13:35 saying, I will open my mouth in **p**; *3850*
13:53 *that* when Jesus had finished these **p**, *3850*
21:45 chief priests and Pharisees had heard his **p**, *3850*
22: 1 and spake unto them again by **p**, *3850*
Mk 3:23 them unto *him,* and said unto them in **p**, *3850*
4: 2 And he taught them many *things* by **p**, and *3850*
4:11 are without, all *these things* are done in **p**: *3850*
4:13 and how *then* will ye know all **p**? *3850*
4:33 And with many such **p** spake he the word *3850*
12: 1 And he began to speak unto them by **p**. *3850*
Lk 8:10 but to others in **p**; that seeing they might *3850*

PARADISE (3)
Lk 23:43 To day shalt thou be with me in **p**. *3857*
2Co 12: 4 How that he was caught up into **p**, and *3857*
Rev 2: 7 which is in the midst of the **p** of God. *3857*

PARAH (1)
Jos 18:23 And Avim, and **P**, and Ophrah, 6511

PARALYTIC See PALSY

PARALYZED See PALSY

PARAMOURS (1)
Eze 23:20 For she doted upon their **p**, whose flesh *is* 6370

PARAN (11) [EL-PARAN]
Ge 21:21 he dwelt in the wilderness of **P**: and 6290
Nu 10:12 and the cloud rested in the wilderness of **P**. 6290
12:16 and pitched in the wilderness of **P**. 6290
13: 3 sent them from the wilderness of **P**: 6290
13:26 unto the wilderness of **P**, to Kadesh; 6290
Dt 1: 1 plain over against the Red *sea,* between **P**, 6290
33: 2 he shined forth from mount **P**, and he came 6290
1Sa 25: 1 and went down to the wilderness of **P**. 6290

1Ki 11:18 they arose out of Midian, and came *to* P: 6290
11:18 they took men with them out of P, and 6290
Hab 3: 3 and the Holy One from mount P. 6290

PARAPET See BATTLEMENT

PARBAR (2)
1Ch 26:18 At P westward, four at the causeway, *and* 6503
26:18 four at the causeway, *and* two at P. 6503

PARCEL (6)
Ge 33:19 he bought a p of a field, where he had 2513
Jos 24:32 in a p of ground which Jacob bought of 2513
Ru 4: 3 selleth a p of land, which *was* our brother 2513
1Ch 11:13 where was a p of ground full *of* barley; 2513
11:14 they set themselves in the midst of *that* p, 2513
Jn 4: 5 near to the p of ground that Jacob gave to *5564*

PARCHED (9)
Lev 23:14 neither bread, nor p *corn,* nor green ears, 7039
Jos 5:11 and p *corn* in the selfsame day. 7033
Ru 2:14 he reached her p *corn,* and she did eat, and 7039
1Sa 17:17 for thy brethren an ephah of this p *corn,* 7039
25:18 five measures of p *corn,* and an hundred 7039
2Sa 17:28 p *corn,* and beans, and lentiles, and 7039
17:28 and beans, and lentiles, and p *pulse,* 7039
Isa 35: 7 And the p ground shall become a pool, and 8273
Jer 17: 6 shall inhabit the p places in the wilderness, 2788

PARCHMENTS (1)
2Ti 4:13 and the books, *but* especially the p. *3200*

PARDON (16) [PARDONED, PARDONETH]
Ex 23:21 for he will not p your transgressions: 5375
34: 9 p our iniquity and our sin, and take us for 5545
Nu 14:19 P, I beseech thee, the iniquity of this people 5545
1Sa 15:25 p my sin, and turn again with me, 5375
2Ki 5:18 In this thing the LORD p thy servant, 5545
5:18 the LORD p thy servant in this thing. 5545
24: 4 which the LORD would not p. 5545
2Ch 30:18 The good LORD p every one 3722
Ne 9:17 thou *art* a God ready to p, gracious and 5547
Job 7:21 why dost thou not p my transgression, and 5375
Ps 25:11 name's sake, O LORD, p mine iniquity; 5545
Isa 55: 7 and to our God, for he will abundantly p. 5545
Jer 5: 1 that seeketh the truth; and I will p it. 5545
5: 7 How shall I p thee for this? thy children 5545
33: 8 I will p all their iniquities, whereby they 5545
50:20 be found: for I will p them whom I reserve. 5545

PARDONED (3) [PARDON]
Nu 14:20 I have p according to thy word: 5545
Isa 40: 2 is accomplished, that her iniquity is p: 7521
La 3:42 and have rebelled: thou hast not p. 5545

P

PARDONETH (1) [PARDON]
Mic 7:18 that p iniquity, and passeth by 5375

PARE (1)
Dt 21:12 she shall shave her head, and p her nails; 6213

PARENTS (21)
Mt 10:21 the children shall rise up against *their* p, *1118*
Mk 13:12 and children shall rise up against *their* p, *1118*
Lk 2:27 and when the p brought in the child Jesus, *1118*
2:41 Now his p went to Jerusalem every year at *1118*
8:56 And her p were astonished: but he charged *1118*
18:29 or p, or brethren, or wife, or children, *1118*
21:16 And ye shall be betrayed both by p, and *1118*
Jn 9: 2 Master, who did sin, this *man,* or his p, *1118*
9: 3 Neither hath this *man* sinned, nor his p: *1118*
9:18 until they called the p of him that had *1118*
9:20 His p answered them and said, We know *1118*
9:22 These *words* spake his p, because *1118*
9:23 Therefore said his p, He is of age; ask him. *1118*
Ro 1:30 inventors of evil *things,* disobedient to p, *1118*
2Co 12:14 the children ought not to lay up for the p, *1118*
12:14 for the parents, but the p for the children. *1118*
Eph 6: 1 Children, obey your p in the Lord: for this *1118*
Col 3:20 obey *your* p in all *things:* for this is well *1118*
1Ti 5: 4 shew piety at home, and to requite *their* p: *4269*
2Ti 3: 2 disobedient to p, unthankful, unholy, *1118*
Heb 11:23 was hid three months of his p, because *3962*

PARLOUR (5) [PARLOURS]
Jdg 3:20 he was sitting in a summer p, which he had 5944
3:23 shut the doors of the p upon him, and 5944
3:24 the doors of the p *were* locked, they said, 5944
3:25 behold, he opened not the doors of the p; 5944
1Sa 9:22 brought them into the p, and made them sit 3957

PARLOURS (1) [PARLOUR]
1Ch 28:11 of the inner p thereof, and of the place of 2315

PARMASHTA (1)
Est 9: 9 P, and Arisai, and Aridai, and Vajezatha, 6534

PARMENAS (1)
Ac 6: 5 and P, and Nicolas a proselyte of Antioch: *3937*

PARNACH (1)
Nu 34:25 of Zebulun, Elizaphan the son of P. 6535

PAROSH (5)
Ezr 2: 3 The children of P, two thousand an 6551
10:25 of the sons of P; Ramiah, and Jeziah, and 6551
Ne 3:25 the prison. After him Pedaiah the son of P. 6551
7: 8 The children of P, two thousand an 6551
10:14 P, Pahath-moab, Elam, Zatthu, Bani, 6551

PARSHANDATHA (1)
Est 9: 7 And P, and Dalphon, and Aspatha, 6577

PARSIN See UPHARSIN

PART (214) [APART, FOREPART, PARTED, PARTETH, PARTING, PARTITION, PARTLY, PARTS]
Ge 41:34 take up the fifth p of the land of Egypt in NIH
47:24 that you shall give the fifth p unto Pharaoh, NIH
47:26 *that* Pharaoh should have the fifth p; except NIH
Ex 16:36 Now an omer *is* the tenth p of an ephah. NIH
19:17 they stood at the nether p of the mount. 8482
29:26 before the LORD: and it shall be thy p. 4490
29:40 with the fourth p of a hin of beaten oil; 7253
29:40 the fourth p of a hin of wine *for* a drink NIH
Lev 1:16 cast it beside the altar on the east p, by 6924
2: 6 Thou shalt p it in pieces, and 6595+6626
2:16 p of the beaten corn thereof, and *part* of NIH
2:16 beaten corn thereof, and p of the oil thereof, NIH
5:11 p of an ephah of fine flour for a sin NIH
5:16 holy *thing,* and shall add the fifth p thereto, NIH
6: 5 shall add the fifth p more thereto, *and* NIH
6:20 the tenth p of an ephah of fine flour *for* a NIH
7:33 shall have the right shoulder for *his* p. 4490
8:29 of the ram of consecration it was Moses' p; 4490
11:35 every *thing* whereupon *any* p of their NIH
11:37 if *any* p of their carcase fall upon any NIH
11:38 *any* p of their carcase fall thereon, it *shall* NIH
13:41 he that hath his hair fallen off from the p of 6285
22:14 he shall put the fifth p thereof unto it, and NIH
23:13 *shall be of* wine, the fourth p of a hin. NIH
27:13 he shall add a fifth p thereof unto thy NIH
27:15 he shall add the fifth p of the money of thy NIH
27:16 LORD *some* p of a field of his possession, NIH
27:19 he shall add the fifth p of the money of thy NIH
27:27 and shall add a fifth p of it thereto: NIH
27:31 he shall add thereto the fifth p thereof. NIH
Nu 5: 7 add unto it the fifth p thereof, and give *it* NIH
5:15 the tenth p of an ephah of barley meal; NIH
15: 4 mingled with the fourth p of a hin of oil. NIH
15: 5 the fourth p of a hin *of* wine for a drink NIH
15: 6 mingled with the third p of a hin of oil. NIH
15: 7 thou shalt offer the third p of a hin *of* wine, NIH
18:20 neither shalt thou have any p among them: 2506
18:20 I *am* thy p and thine inheritance among 2506
18:26 for the LORD, *even* a tenth p of the tithe. NIH
18:29 *even* the hallowed p thereof out of it. NIH
22:41 that thence he might see the utmost p of 7097
23:10 and the number *of* the fourth p of Israel? 7255
23:13 thou shalt see but the utmost p of them, 7097
28: 5 a tenth p of an ephah *of* flour for a meat NIH
28: 5 mingled with the fourth p of a hin of beaten NIH
28: 7 *be* the fourth p of a hin for the one lamb: NIH
28:14 the third p of a hin unto a ram, and a fourth NIH
28:14 a ram, and a fourth p of a hin unto a lamb: NIH
Dt 10: 9 Wherefore Levi hath no p nor inheritance 2506
12:12 forasmuch as he hath no p nor inheritance 2506
14:27 for he hath no p nor inheritance with thee. 2506
14:29 he hath no p nor inheritance with thee,) 2506
18: 1 shall have no p nor inheritance with Israel: 2506
33:21 he provided the first p for himself, because NIH

Jos 14: 4 they gave no **p** unto the Levites in the land, 2506
15: 1 the **uttermost p** of the south *coast.* 4480+7097
15: 5 bay of the sea at the **uttermost p** of Jordan: 7097
15:13 he gave a **p** among the children of Judah, 2506
18: 7 the Levites have no **p** among you; for 2506
19: 9 for the **p** of the children of Judah was too 2506
22:25 of Gad; ye have no **p** in the LORD: 2506
22:27 time to come, Ye have no **p** in the LORD. 2506
Ru 1:17 *if ought* but death **p** thee and me. 6504
2: 3 her hap was to light on a **p** of the field 2513
3:13 **perform** unto thee **the p of a kinsman,** 1350
3:13 well; let him **do the kinsman's p**: 1350
3:13 if he will not **do the p of a kinsman** to 1350
3:13 will I **do the p of a kinsman** to thee, *as* 1350
1Sa 9: 8 I have here at hand the **fourth p** of a shekel 7253
14: 2 Saul tarried in the **uttermost p** of Gibeah 7097
23:20 our **p** *shall be* to deliver him into the king's NIH
30:24 as his **p** *is* that goeth down to the battle, so 2506
30:24 so *shall* his **p** *be* that tarrieth by the stuff: 2506
30:24 that tarrieth by the stuff: they shall **p** alike. 2505
2Sa 14: 6 *there was* none to **p** them, but the one 996+5337
18: 2 David sent forth a **third p** of the people 7992
18: 2 a **third p** under the hand of Abishai the son 7992
18: 2 a **third p** under the hand of Ittai the Gittite. 7992
20: 1 and said, We have no **p** in David, 2506
1Ki 6:24 from the **uttermost p** of the one wing unto 7098
6:24 **uttermost p** of the other *were* ten cubits. 7098
6:31 *and* side posts *were* a fifth *p of the wall.* NIH
6:33 posts of olive tree, a fourth *p of the wall.* NIH
2Ki 6:25 the **fourth p** of a kab of dove's dung for 7255
7: 5 when they were come to the **uttermost p** of 7097
7: 8 when these lepers came to the **uttermost p** 7097
11: 5 A third *p* of you that enter in on the sabbath NIH
11: 6 And a third *p shall be* at the gate of Sur; and NIH
11: 6 and a third *p* at the gate behind the guard: NIH
18:23 if thou be able **on** thy **p** to set riders upon 3807.1
1Ch 12:29 for hitherto the **greatest p** of them had kept 4768
2Ch 23: 4 A third *p* of you entering on the sabbath, NIH
23: 5 a third *p shall be* at the king's house; and NIH
23: 5 and a third *p* at the gate of the foundation: NIH
29:16 the priests went into the **inner p** *of* 6441
Ne 1: 9 out unto the **uttermost p** of the heaven, 7097
3: 9 of Hur, the ruler of the half **p** of Jerusalem. 6418
3:12 the ruler of the half **p** of Jerusalem, he and 6418
3:14 of Rechab, the ruler of **p** of Beth-haccerem; 6418
3:15 son of Col-hozeh, the ruler of **p** of Mizpah; 6418
3:16 the ruler of the half **p** of Beth-zur, 6418
3:17 the ruler of the half **p** of Keilah, in his part. 6418
3:17 the ruler of the half part of Keilah, in his **p**. 6418
3:18 the ruler of the half **p** of Keilah. 6418
5:11 also the hundredth *p* of the money, and NIH
9: 3 LORD their God *one* fourth *p* of the day; NIH
9: 3 *another* fourth *p* they confessed, and NIH
10:32 to charge ourselves yearly with the third *p* NIH
Job 32:17 *I said,* I will answer also my **p**, I also will 2506
41: 6 shall they **p** him among the merchants? 2673
Ps 5: 9 their inward *p is* very wickedness; NIH
22:18 They **p** my garments among them, and 2505
51: 6 in the hidden *p* thou shalt make me to know NIH
118: 7 The LORD **taketh** my **p** with them that 3807.1
Pr 8:26 nor the **highest p** of the dust of the world. 7218
8:31 Rejoicing in the **habitable p** of his earth; 8398
17: 2 shall **have p** of the inheritance among 2505
Isa 7:18 *is* in the **uttermost p** of the rivers of Egypt, 7097
24:16 From the **uttermost p** of the earth have we 3671
36: 8 if thou be able **on** thy **p** to set riders upon 3807.1
44:16 He burneth **p** thereof in the fire; with part 2677
44:16 with **p** thereof he eateth flesh; he roasteth 2677
44:19 to say, I have burnt **p** of it in the fire; 2677
Eze 4:11 also water by measure, the sixth *p* of a hin: NIH
5: 2 Thou shalt burn with fire a third *p* in NIH
5: 2 thou shalt take a third *p, and* smite about it NIH
5: 2 a third *p* thou shalt scatter in the wind; and NIH
5:12 A third *p* of thee shall die with NIH
5:12 a third *p* shall fall by the sword round about NIH
5:12 and I will scatter a third *p* into all the winds, NIH
39: 2 **leave** but **the sixth p** of thee, and 8338
45:11 that the bath may contain the **tenth p** of a 4643
45:11 and the ephah the tenth *p* of a homer: NIH
45:13 the sixth *p* of an ephah of a homer of wheat, NIH
45:13 ye shall **give the sixth p** of an ephah of a 8341
45:14 *ye shall offer* the **tenth p** of a bath out of 4643
45:17 it shall be the prince's **p** *to give* burnt 5921
46:14 the sixth *p* of an ephah, and the third *part* of NIH
46:14 of an ephah, and the third *p* of a hin of oil, NIH
Da 1: 2 **p** of the vessels of the house of God: 4480+7117
2:33 of iron, his feet **p** of iron and part of clay. 4481
2:33 of iron, his feet part of iron and **p** of clay. 4481
2:41 toes, **p** of potter's clay, and part of iron, 4481
2:41 toes, part of potter's clay, and **p** of iron, 4481
2:42 *as* the toes of the feet *were* **p** of iron, and 4481
2:42 **p** of clay, *so* the kingdom shall be partly 4481
5: 5 the king saw the **p** of the hand that wrote. 6447
5:24 *was* the **p** of the hand sent from him; and 6447
11:31 arms shall stand **on** his **p**, and they shall 4480
Joel 2:20 his **hinder p** towards the utmost sea, and 5490
Am 7: 4 devoured the great deep, and did eat up a **p**. 2506
Zec 13: 9 And I will bring the third *p* through the fire, NIH
Mk 4:38 And he was in the **hinder p of** the **ship,** *4403*
9:40 For he that is not against us is **on** our **p**. *5228*
13:27 from the **uttermost p** of the earth to *206*
13:27 of the earth to the **uttermost p** of heaven. *206*
Lk 10:42 and Mary hath chosen *that* good **p**, *3310*
11:36 therefore *be* full of light, having no **p** dark, *3313*
11:39 but your **inward p** is full of ravening and *2081*
17:24 that lighteneth out of the one *p* under NIG
17:24 shineth unto the other *p* under heaven; NIG
Jn 13: 8 If I wash thee not, thou hast no **p** with me. *3313*
19:23 and made four parts, to every soldier a **p**; *3313*
Ac 1: 8 and unto the **uttermost p** of the earth. *2078*
1:17 and had obtained **p** of this ministry. *2819*
1:25 That *he* may take **p** of this ministry and *2819*
5: 2 And kept back *p* of the price, his wife also NIG
5: 2 being privy *to it,* and brought a certain **p**, *3313*
5: 3 and to keep back *p* of the price of the land? NIG
8:21 Thou hast neither **p** nor lot in this matter: *3310*
14: 4 and **p** held with the Jews, and part *3303+3588*
14: 4 the Jews, **and p** with the apostles. *1161+3588*
16:12 which is the chief city of *that* **p** of *3310*
19:32 the **more p** knew not wherefore they were *4183*
23: 6 But when Paul perceived that the one **p** *3313*
23: 9 the scribes *that were* of the Pharisees' **p** *3313*
27:12 the **more p** advised to depart thence also, *4183*
27:41 the **hinder p** was broken with the violence *4403*
Ro 11:25 that blindness in **p** is happened to Israel, *3313*
1Co 12:24 abundant honour to that *p* which lacked: NIG
13: 9 For we know in **p**, and we prophesy in part. *3313*
13: 9 For we know in part, and we prophesy in **p**. *3313*
13:10 then that which is in **p** shall be done away. *3313*
13:12 now I know in **p**; but then shall I know *3313*
15: 6 of whom the **greater p** remain unto this *4183*
16:17 for that which was lacking **on your p** they *4771*
2Co 1:14 As also you have acknowledged us in **p**, *3313*
2: 5 he hath not grieved me, but in **p**: *3313*
6:15 what **p** hath he that believeth with an *3310*
Eph 4:16 working in the measure of every **p**, *3313*
Tit 2: 8 that he that is of the contrary *p* may be NIG
Heb 2:14 he also himself likewise **took p** of *3348*
7: 2 To whom also Abraham gave a tenth *p* of NIG
1Pe 4:14 **on** their **p** he is evil spoken of, but on your *2596*
4:14 spoken of, but **on** your **p** he is glorified. *2596*
Rev 6: 8 unto them over the fourth *p* of the earth, NIG
8: 7 and the third *p* of trees was burnt up, and all NIG
8: 8 and the third *p* of the sea became blood; NIG
8: 9 And the third *p* of the creatures which were NIG
8: 9 and the third *p* of the ships were destroyed. NIG
8:10 and it fell upon the third *p* of the rivers, and NIG
8:11 the third *p* of the waters became NIG
8:12 and the third *p* of the sun was smitten, and NIG
8:12 and the third *p* of the moon, and the third NIG
8:12 of the moon, and the third *p* of the stars; NIG
8:12 so as the third *p* of them was darkened and NIG
8:12 and the day shone not for a third *p* of it, NIG
9:15 and a year, for to slay the third *p* of men. NIG
9:18 By these three was the third *p* of men killed, NIG
11:13 and the tenth *p* of the city fell, and in NIG
12: 4 And his tail drew the third *p* of the stars of NIG
20: 6 holy *is* he that hath **p** in the first *3313*
21: 8 shall have their **p** in the lake which burneth *3313*
22:19 God shall take away his **p** out of the book *3313*

PARTAKER (9) [PARTAKERS, PARTAKEST]

Ps 50:18 with him, and hast been **p** with adulterers. 2506
1Co 9:10 that he that thresheth in hope should be **p** of *3348*
9:23 that I might be **p** thereof **with** *you.* *4791*
10:30 For if I by grace be a **p**, why am I evil *3348*
1Ti 5:22 no *man,* neither be **p** of other *men's* sins: *2841*
2Ti 1: 8 be thou **p** of the **afflictions** of the gospel *4777*

2Ti 2: 6 that laboureth must be first **p** of the fruits. *3335*
1Pe 5: 1 also a **p** of the glory that shall be revealed: *2844*
2Jn 1:11 For he that biddeth him God speed is **p** of *2841*

PARTAKERS (22) [PARTAKER]
Mt 23:30 we would not have been **p** with them in *2844*
Ro 15:27 For if the Gentiles have been **made p** of *2841*
1Co 9:12 If others be **p** of *this* power over you, *3348*
9:13 they which wait at the altar are **p with** *4829*
10:17 one body: for we are all **p** of *that* one bread. *3348*
10:18 are not they which eat *of* the sacrifices **p** of *2844*
10:21 ye cannot be **p** of the Lord's table, and *3348*
2Co 1: 7 that as you are **p** of the sufferings, so *2844*
Eph 3: 6 **p** of his promise in Christ by the gospel: *4830*
5: 7 Be not ye therefore **p with** them. *4830*
Php 1: 7 of the gospel, ye all are **p** of my grace. *4791*
Col 1:12 which hath made us meet to be **p** of *3310*
1Ti 6: 2 are faithful and beloved, **p** of the benefit. *482*
Heb 2:14 then as the children are **p** of flesh and *2841*
3: 1 holy brethren, **p** of the heavenly calling, *3353*
3:14 For we are made **p** of Christ, if we hold *3353*
6: 4 and were made **p** of the Holy Ghost, *3353*
12: 8 whereof all are **p**, then are ye bastards, and *3353*
12:10 that *we* might be **p** of his holiness. *3335*
1Pe 4:13 inasmuch as ye are **p** of Christ's sufferings; *2841*
2Pe 1: 4 that by these you might be **p** of the divine *2844*
Rev 18: 4 that ye be not **p** of her sins, and that ye *4790*

PARTAKEST (1) [PARTAKER]
Ro 11:17 and with *them* **p** of the root and *1096+4791*

PARTED (12) [PART]
Ge 2:10 from thence it was **p**, and became into four 6504
2Ki 2:11 horses of fire, and **p** them both asunder; 6504
2:14 the waters, they **p** hither and thither: 2673
Job 38:24 By what way is the light **p**, *which* scattereth 2505
Joel 3: 2 among the nations, and **p** my land. 2505
Mt 27:35 and **p** his garments, casting lots: *1266*
27:35 They **p** my garments among them, and *1266*
Mk 15:24 they **p** his garments, casting lots upon *1266*
Lk 23:34 And they **p** his raiment, and cast lots. *1266*
24:51 he was **p** from them, and carried up into *1339*
Jn 19:24 They **p** my raiment **among** them, and *1266*
Ac 2:45 **p** them to all *men,* as every *man* had need. *1266*

PARTETH (3) [PART]
Lev 11: 3 Whatsoever **p** the hoof, and 6536
Dt 14: 6 every beast that **p** the hoof, and 6536
Pr 18:18 to cease, and **p** between the mighty. 6504

PARTHIANS (1)
Ac 2: 9 **P**, and Medes, and Elamites, and *3934*

PARTIAL (2) [PARTIALITY]
Mal 2: 9 kept my ways, but have been **p** in the law. 6440
Jas 2: 4 Are ye not then **p** in yourselves, and *1252*

PARTIALITY (2) [PARTIAL]
1Ti 5:21 *one before another,* doing nothing by **p**. *4346*
Jas 3:17 **without p**, and without hypocrisy. *87*

PARTICIPATION See COMMUNION

PARTICULAR (2) [PARTICULARLY]
1Co 12:27 are the body of Christ, and members in **p**. *3313*
Eph 5:33 Nevertheless let every one of you in **p** so *2596*

PARTICULARLY (2) [PARTICULAR]
Ac 21:19 he declared **p** what *things* God *1520+1538+2596*
Heb 9: 5 of which *we* cannot now speak **p**. *2596+3313*

PARTIES (1)
Ex 22: 9 the cause of both **p**s shall come before 1992.1

PARTING (1) [PART]
Eze 21:21 For the king of Babylon stood at the **p** of 517

PARTITION (2) [PART]
1Ki 6:21 he **made a p** by the chains of gold before 5674
Eph 2:14 hath broken down the middle wall of **p** *5418*

PARTLY (5) [PART]
Da 2:42 *so* the kingdom shall be **p** strong, and 4481+7118
2:42 shall be partly strong, and **p** broken. 4481
1Co 11:18 among you; and I **p** believe *it.* *3313+5100*
Heb 10:33 **P**, whilst ye were made a *3303+3778*
10:33 **and p**, whilst ye became companions *1161+3778*

PARTNER (3) [PARTNERS]
Pr 29:24 Whoso is **p** with a thief hateth his own 2505
2Co 8:23 *he is* my **p** and fellowhelper concerning *2844*
Phm 1:17 If thou count me therefore a **p**, receive him *2844*

PARTNERS (2) [PARTNER]
Lk 5: 7 And they beckoned unto *their* **p**, *3353*
5:10 sons of Zebedee, which were **p** with Simon. *2844*

PARTRIDGE (2)
1Sa 26:20 as when *one* doth hunt a **p** in 7124
Jer 17:11 *As* the **p** sitteth *on eggs,* and hatcheth *them* 7124

PARTS (64) [PART]
Ge 47:24 four **p** shall be your own, for seed of 3027
Ex 33:23 mine hand, and thou shalt see my **back p**: 268
Lev 1: 8 shall lay the **p**, the head, and the fat, 5409
22:23 any thing superfluous or **lacking in** his **p**, 7038
Nu 10: 5 the camps that lie on the **east p** shall go 6924
11: 1 *that were* in the **uttermost p** of the camp. 7097
31:27 **divide** the prey **into two p**; between them 2673
Dt 19: 3 **divide** the coasts of thy land, which the LORD thy God giveth thee to inherit, **into three p**, 8027
30: 4 driven out unto the **outmost p** of heaven, 7097
Jos 18: 5 they shall divide it into seven **p**: Judah shall 2506
18: 6 therefore describe the land *into* seven **p**, 2506
18: 9 described it by cities into seven **p** in a 2506
1Sa 5: 9 and they had emerods in their **secret p**. 8368
2Sa 19:43 We have ten **p** in the king, and we have 3027
1Ki 6:38 was the house finished throughout all the **p** 1697
7:25 and all their **hinder p** *were* inward. 268
16:21 the people of Israel divided into **two p**: 2677
2Ki 11: 7 two **p** of all you that go forth on 3027
2Ch 4: 4 and all their **hinder p** *were* inward. 268
Ne 11: 1 and nine **p** *to dwell* in *other* cities. 3027
Job 26:14 Lo, these *are* **p** of his ways: but how little a 7098
38:36 Who hath put wisdom in the **inward p**? or 2910
41:12 I will not conceal his **p**, nor *his* power, 907
Ps 2: 8 the **uttermost p** of the earth *for* thy 657
51: 6 Behold, thou desirest truth in the **inward p**: 2910
63: 9 to destroy *it,* shall go into the **lower p** of 8482
65: 8 They also that dwell in the **uttermost p** are 7099
78:66 he smote his enemies in the **hinder p**: he put 268
136:13 To him which divided the Red sea into **p**: 1506
139: 9 *and* dwell in the **uttermost p** of the sea; 319
139:15 curiously wrought in the **lowest p** of 8482
Pr 18: 8 they go down *into* the **innermost p** of 2315
20:27 searching all the **inward p** of the belly. 2315
20:30 so *do* stripes the **inward p** of the belly. 2315
26:22 they go down *into* the **innermost p** of 2315
Isa 3:17 the LORD will discover their **secret p**. 6596
16:11 and mine **inward p** for Kir-haresh. 7130
44:23 hath done *it:* shout, ye **lower p** of the earth: 8482
Jer 31:33 I will put my law in their **inward p**, and 7130
34:18 in twain, and passed between the **p** thereof, 1335
34:19 which passed between the **p** of the calf; 1335
Eze 26:20 shall set thee **in the low p** of the earth, 8482
31:14 to the **nether p** of the earth, in the midst of 8482
31:16 shall be comforted in the **nether p** of 8482
31:18 of Eden unto the **nether p** of the earth: 8482
32:18 unto the **nether p** of the earth, with them 8482
32:24 into the **nether p** of the earth, 8482
37:11 our hope is lost: we are cut off **for** our **p**. 3807.1
38:15 come from thy place out of the **north p**, 3411
39: 2 cause thee to come up from the **north p**, 3411
48: 8 and *in* length as one of the *other* **p**, 2506
Zec 13: 8 two **p** therein shall be cut off *and* die; 6310
Mt 2:22 he turned aside into the **p** of Galilee: *3313*
12:42 for she came from the **uttermost p** of *4009*
Mk 8:10 and came into the **p** of Dalmanutha. *3313*
Lk 11:31 for she came from the **utmost p** of the earth *4009*
Jn 19:23 took his garments, and made four **p**, *3313*
Ac 2:10 and in the **p** of Libya about Cyrene, and *3313*
20: 2 And when he had gone over those **p**, and *3313*
Ro 15:23 But now having no more place in these **p**, *2824*
1Co 12:23 our uncomely *p* have more abundant NIG
12:24 For our comely *p* have no need: NIG
Eph 4: 9 that he also descended first into the lower **p** *3313*
Rev 16:19 And the great city was *divided* into three **p**, *3313*

PARUAH (1)
1Ki 4:17 Jehoshaphat the son of **P**, in Issachar: 6515

PARVAIM (1)
2Ch 3: 6 for beauty: and the gold *was* gold of **P**. 6516

PASACH (1)
1Ch 7:33 of Japhlet; **P**, and Bimhal, and Ashvath. 6457

PAS-DAMMIM (1)
1Ch 11:13 He was with David at **P**, and there 6450

PASEAH (3) [PHASEAH]
1Ch 4:12 and **P**, and Tehinnah the father of Irnahash. 6454
Ezr 2:49 the children of **P**, the children of Besai, 6454
Ne 3: 6 the old gate repaired Jehoiada the son of **P**, 6454

PASHHUR See PASHUR

PASHUR (14)
1Ch 9:12 the son of **P**, the son of Malchijah, and 6583
Ezr 2:38 The children of **P**, a thousand two hundred 6583
10:22 of the sons of **P**; Elioenai, Maaseiah, 6583
Ne 7:41 The children of **P**, a thousand two hundred 6583
10: 3 **P**, Amariah, Malchijah, 6583
11:12 the son of **P**, the son of Malchiah, 6583
Jer 20: 1 Now **P** the son of Immer the priest, 6583
20: 2 **P** smote Jeremiah the prophet, and put him 6583
20: 3 that **P** brought forth Jeremiah out of 6583
20: 3 The LORD hath not called thy name **P**, 6583
20: 6 **P**, and all that dwell in thine house shall go 6583
21: 1 when king Zedekiah sent unto him **P** 6583
38: 1 Gedaliah the son of **P**, and Jucal the son of 6583
38: 1 of Shelemiah, and **P** the son of Malchiah, 6583

PASS (830) [OVERPASS, PASSAGE, PASSAGES, PASSED, PASSEDST, PASSENGERS, PASSEST, PASSETH, PASSING, PAST] See Index

PASSAGE (4) [PASS]
Nu 20:21 Thus Edom refused to give Israel **p** through 5674
Jos 22:11 of Jordan, at the **p** of the children of Israel. 5676
1Sa 13:23 Philistines went out to the **p** of Michmash. 4569
Isa 10:29 They are gone over the **p**: they have taken 4569

PASSAGES (5) [PASS]
Jdg 12: 5 the Gileadites took the **p** of Jordan before 4569
12: 6 took him, and slew him at the **p** of Jordan: 4569
1Sa 14: 4 between the **p**, *by* which Jonathan sought to 4569
Jer 22:20 up thy voice in Bashan, and cry from the **p**: 5676
51:32 *that* the **p** are stopped, and the reeds they 4569

PASSED (161) [PASS] See Index

PASSEDST (1) [PASS] See Index

PASSENGERS (5) [PASS]
Pr 9:15 To call **p** who go right *on* their ways: 1870+5674
Eze 39:11 the valley of the **p** *on* the east of the sea: 5674
39:11 it *shall* stop the *noses of the* **p**: and 5674
39:14 passing through the land to bury with the **p** 5674
39:15 the **p** *that* pass through the land, when *any* 5674

PASSEST (5) [PASS] See Index

PASSETH (38) [PASS] See Index

PASSING (13) [PASS] See Index

PASSION (1) [PASSIONS]
Ac 1: 3 alive after his **p** by many infallible proofs, *3958*

PASSIONS (2) [PASSION]
Ac 14:15 We also are men **of like p with** you, *3663*
Jas 5:17 Elias was a man **subject to like p** as we *3663*

PASSOVER (76) [PASSOVERS]
Ex 12:11 ye shall eat it in haste: it *is* the LORD'S **p**. 6453
12:21 according to your families, and kill the **p**. 6453
12:27 It *is* the sacrifice of the LORD'S **p**, 6453
12:43 and Aaron, This *is* the ordinance of the **p**: 6453
12:48 will keep the **p** to the LORD, let all his 6453
34:25 the feast of the **p** be left unto the morning. 6453
Lev 23: 5 the first month at even *is* the LORD'S **p**. 6453
Nu 9: 2 Let the children of Israel also keep the **p** at 6453
9: 4 of Israel, that they should keep the **p**. 6453
9: 5 they kept the **p** on the fourteenth day of 6453
9: 6 that they could not keep the **p** on that day: 6453
9:10 yet he shall keep the **p** unto the LORD. 6453
9:12 according to all the ordinances of the **p** 6453
9:13 in a journey, and forbeareth to keep the **p**, 6453
9:14 and will keep the **p** unto the LORD; 6453
9:14 according to the ordinance of the **p**, and 6453
28:16 of the first month *is* the **p** of the LORD. 6453
33: 3 on the morrow after the **p** the children of 6453
Dt 16: 1 and keep the **p** unto the LORD thy God: 6453
16: 2 sacrifice the **p** unto the LORD thy God, 6453
16: 5 Thou mayest not sacrifice the **p** within any 6453
16: 6 *in*, there thou shalt sacrifice the **p** at even, 6453
Jos 5:10 kept the **p** on the fourteenth day of 6453
5:11 corn of the land on the morrow after the **p**, 6453
2Ki 23:21 Keep the **p** unto the LORD your God, 6453
23:22 Surely there was not holden such a **p** from 6453
23:23 *wherein* this **p** was holden to the LORD in 6453
2Ch 30: 1 to keep the **p** unto the LORD God of 6453
30: 2 to keep the **p** in the second month. 6453
30: 5 that *they* should come to keep the **p** unto 6453
30:15 they killed the **p** on the fourteenth *day* of 6453
30:18 yet did they eat the **p** otherwise than it was 6453
35: 1 Moreover Josiah kept a **p** unto the LORD 6453
35: 1 they killed the **p** on the fourteenth *day* of 6453
35: 6 So kill the **p**, and sanctify yourselves, and 6453
35: 7 all for the **p** *offerings*, for all that were 6453
35: 8 gave unto the priests for the **p** *offerings* two 6453
35: 9 gave unto the Levites for **p** *offerings* five 6453
35:11 they killed the **p**, and the priests sprinkled 6453
35:13 they roasted the **p** with fire according to 6453
35:16 to keep the **p**, and to offer burnt offerings 6453
35:17 that were present kept the **p** at that time, 6453
35:18 there was no **p** like to that, kept in Israel 6453
35:18 kings of Israel keep such a **p** as Josiah kept, 6453
35:19 year of the reign of Josiah was this **p** kept. 6453
Ezr 6:19 the children of the captivity kept the **p** upon 6453
6:20 killed the **p** for all the children of 6453
Eze 45:21 ye shall have the **p**, a feast of seven days; 6453
Mt 26: 2 that after two days is *the feast of* the **p**, *3957*
26:17 thou *that* we prepare for thee to eat the **p**? *3957*
26:18 I will keep the **p** at thy house with my *3957*
26:19 appointed them; and they made ready the **p**. *3957*
Mk 14: 1 After two days was *the feast of* the **p**, and *3957*
14:12 when they killed the **p**, his disciples said *3957*
14:12 and prepare that thou mayest eat the **p**? *3957*
14:14 where I shall eat the **p** with my disciples? *3957*
14:16 said unto them: and they made ready the **p**. *3957*
Lk 2:41 Jerusalem every year at the feast of the **P**. *3957*
22: 1 bread drew nigh, which is called the **P**. *3957*
22: 7 when the **p** must be killed. *3957*
22: 8 and John, saying, Go and prepare us the **p**, *3957*
22:11 where I shall eat the **p** with my disciples? *3957*
22:13 said unto them: and they made ready the **p**. *3957*
22:15 With desire I have desired to eat this **p** with *3957*
Jn 2:13 And the Jews' **p** was at hand, and *3957*
2:23 Now when he was in Jerusalem at the **p**, *3957*
6: 4 And the **p**, a feast of the Jews, was nigh. *3957*
11:55 And the Jews' **p** was nigh at hand: and *3957*
11:55 of the country up to Jerusalem before the **p**, *3957*
12: 1 Then Jesus six days before the **p** came to *3957*
13: 1 Now before the feast of the **p**, when Jesus *3957*
18:28 be defiled; but that they might eat the **p**. *3957*
18:39 that I should release unto you one at the **p**: *3957*
19:14 And it was the preparation of the **p**, and *3957*
1Co 5: 7 For even Christ our **p** is sacrificed for us: *3957*
Heb 11:28 Through faith he kept the **p**, and *3957*

PASSOVERS (1) [PASSOVER]
2Ch 30:17 of the **p** for every one *that was* not clean, 6453

PAST (51) [PASS]
Ge 50: 4 And when the days of his mourning were **p**, 5674
Ex 21:29 push with his horn **in time p**, 4480+8032+8543
21:36 *hath* used to push **in time p**, 4480+8032+8543
Nu 21:22 king's *high* way, until we be **p** thy borders. 5674
Dt 2:10 Emims dwelt therein **in times p**. 6440+3807.1
4:32 For ask now of the days that are **p**, 7223
4:42 hated him not **in times p**; 4480+8032+8543
19: 4 whom he hated not **in time p**; 4480+8032+8543
19: 6 as he hated him not **in time p**. 4480+8032+8543
1Sa 15:32 Surely the bitterness of death is **p**. 5493
19: 7 he was in his presence, as **in times p**. 865+8032
2Sa 3:17 **in times p** to be king 1571+1571+8032+8543
5: 2 Also **in time p**, when Saul was 865+1571+8032
11:27 when the mourning was **p**, David sent and 5674
16: 1 when David was a little **p** the top *of* 5674
1Ki 18:29 when midday was **p**, and they prophesied 5674

1Ch 9:20 was the ruler over them **in time p**, 6440+3807.1
11: 2 *And* moreover **in time p**, even when 8032+8543
Job 9:10 Which doeth great *things* **p** finding 369+5704
14:13 keep me secret, until thy wrath be **p**, 7725
17:11 My days are **p**, my purposes are broken off, 5674
29: 2 O that I were as *in* months **p**, as *in* the days 6924
Ps 90: 4 thy sight *are but* as yesterday when it is **p**, 5674
Ecc 3:15 and God requireth that which is **p**. 7291
SS 2:11 For lo, the winter is **p**, the rain is over *and* 5674
Jer 8:20 The harvest is **p**, the summer is ended, and 5674
Mt 14:15 is a desert place, and the time is now **p**; *3928*
Mk 16: 1 And when the sabbath was **p**, *1230*
Lk 9:36 And when the voice was **p**, Jesus was *1096*
Ac 12:10 When they were **p** the first and the second *1330*
14:16 Who in times **p** suffered all nations to walk *3944*
27: 9 because the fast was now already **p**, Paul *3928*
Ro 3:25 for the remission of sins that are **p**, *4266*
11:30 For as ye **in times p** have not believed *4218*
11:33 his judgments, and his ways **p finding out**! *421*
2Co 5:17 old *things* are **p away**; behold, all *things* *3928*
Gal 1:13 **in time p** in the Jews' religion, *4218*
1:23 That he which persecuted us **in times p** *4218*
5:21 as I have also **told** *you* **in time p**, *4302*
Eph 2: 2 Wherein **in time p** ye walked according to *4218*
2: 3 **in times p** in the lusts of our flesh, *4218*
4:19 Who being **p feeling** have given themselves *524*
2Ti 2:18 saying that the resurrection is **p** already; *1096*
Phm 1:11 Which **in time p** was to thee unprofitable, *4218*
Heb 1: 1 in divers manners spake in time **p** unto *3819*
11:11 was delivered of a child when *she* was **p** *3844*
1Pe 2:10 Which **in time p** *were* not a people, but *4218*
4: 3 For the time **p** of *our* life may suffice us to *3928*
1Jn 2: 8 because the darkness is **p**, and the true light *3855*
Rev 9:12 One woe is **p**; *and* behold, there come two *565*
11:14 The second woe is **p**; *and* behold, the third *565*

PASTOR (1) [PASTORS]
Jer 17:16 I have not hastened from *being* a **p** to 7462

PASTORS (8) [PASTOR]
Jer 2: 8 the **p** also transgressed against me, and 7462
3:15 I will give you **p** according to mine heart, 7462
10:21 For the **p** are become brutish, and have not 7462
12:10 Many **p** have destroyed my vineyard, 7462
22:22 The wind shall eat up all thy **p**, and 7462
23: 1 Woe be unto *the* **p** that destroy and 7462
23: 2 of Israel against the **p** that feed my people; 7462
Eph 4:11 evangelists; and some, **p** and teachers; *4166*

PASTURE (20) [PASTURES]
Ge 47: 4 for thy servants have no **p** for their flocks; 4829
1Ch 4:39 *side* of the valley, to seek **p** for their flocks. 4829
4:40 they found fat **p** and good, and the land *was* 4829
4:41 because *there was* **p** there for their flocks. 4829
Job 39: 8 The range of the mountains *is* his **p**, and 4829
Ps 74: 1 anger smoke against the sheep of thy **p**? 4830
79:13 sheep of thy **p** will give thee thanks for 4830
95: 7 we *are* the people of his **p**, and the sheep of 4830
100: 3 *we are* his people, and the sheep of his **p**. 4830
Isa 32:14 for ever, a joy of wild asses, a **p** of flocks; 4829
Jer 23: 1 that destroy and scatter the sheep of my **p**! 4830
25:36 *heard:* for the LORD *hath* spoiled their **p**. 4830
La 1: 6 princes are become like harts *that* find no **p**, 4829
Eze 34:14 I will feed them in a good **p**, and upon 4829
34:14 *in* a fat **p** shall they feed upon 4829
34:18 thing unto you to have eaten up the good **p**, 4829
34:31 the flock of my **p**, *are* men, *and* I *am* your 4830
Hos 13: 6 According to their **p**, so were they filled; 4830
Joel 1:18 are perplexed, because they have no **p**; 4829
Jn 10: 9 and shall go in and out, and find **p**. *3542*

PASTURELAND See SUBURBS

PASTURES (11) [PASTURE]
1Ki 4:23 twenty oxen out of the **p**, and an hundred 7471
Ps 23: 2 He maketh me to lie down in green **p**: 4999
65:12 They drop *upon* the **p** of the wilderness: 4999
65:13 The **p** are clothed with flocks; the valleys 3733
Isa 30:23 in that day shall thy cattle feed *in* large **p**. 3733
49: 9 and their **p** *shall be* in all high places. 4830
Eze 34:18 down with your feet the residue of your **p**? 4829
45:15 of two hundred, out of the **fat p** of Israel; 4945
Joel 1:19 for the fire hath devoured the **p** of 4999
1:20 the fire hath devoured the **p** of 4999
2:22 for the **p** of the wilderness do spring, 4999

PATARA (1)
Ac 21: 1 unto Rhodes, and from thence unto **P**: *3959*

PATE (1)
Ps 7:16 dealing shall come down upon his own **p**. 6936

PATH (23) [PATHS, PATHWAY]
Ge 49:17 an adder in the **p**, that biteth the horse heels, 734
Nu 22:24 the angel of the LORD stood in a **p** of 4934
Job 28: 7 *There is* a **p** which no fowl knoweth, and 5410
30:13 They mar my **p**, they set forward my 5410
41:32 He maketh a **p** to shine after him; 5410
Ps 16:11 Thou wilt shew me the **p** of life: in thy 734
27:11 lead me in a plain **p**, because of mine 734
77:19 thy **p** in the great waters, and thy footsteps 7635
119:35 Make me to go in the **p** of thy 5410
119:105 a lamp unto my feet, and a light unto my **p**. 5410
139: 3 Thou compassest my **p** and my lying down, 734
142: 3 within me, then thou knewest my **p**. 5410
Pr 1:15 with them; refrain thy foot from their **p**: 5410
2: 9 judgment, and equity; *yea,* every good **p**. 4570
4:14 Enter not into the **p** of the wicked, and 734
4:18 the **p** of the just *is* as the shining light, 734
4:26 Ponder the **p** of thy feet, and let all thy 4570
5: 6 Lest thou shouldest ponder the **p** of life, 734
Isa 26: 7 most upright, dost weigh the **p** of the just. 4570
30:11 ye out of the way, turn aside out of the **p**, 734
40:14 taught him in the **p** of judgment, and 734
43:16 in the sea, and a **p** in the mighty waters; 5410
Joel 2: 8 they shall walk every one in his **p**: 4546

PATHROS (5)
Isa 11:11 from **P**, and from Cush, and from Elam, 6624
Jer 44: 1 at Noph, and in the country of **P**, saying, 6624
44:15 of Egypt, in **P**, answered Jeremiah, saying, 6624
Eze 29:14 will cause them to return *into* the land of **P**, 6624
30:14 I will make **P** desolate, and will set fire in 6624

PATHRUSIM (2)
Ge 10:14 **P**, and Casluhim, (out of whom came 6625
1Ch 1:12 **P**, and Casluhim, (of whom came 6625

PATHRUSITES See PATHRUSIM

PATHS (42) [PATH]
Job 6:18 The **p** of their way are turned aside; they go 734
8:13 So *are* the **p** of all that forget God; and 734
13:27 and lookest narrowly unto all my **p**; 734
19: 8 and he hath set darkness in my **p**. 5410
24:13 the ways thereof, nor abide in the **p** thereof. 5410
33:11 my feet in the stocks, he marketh all my **p**. 734
38:20 that thou shouldest know the **p** to the house 5410
Ps 8: 8 *whatsoever* passeth *through* the **p** of 734
17: 4 I have kept *me from* the **p** of the destroyer. 734
17: 5 Hold up my goings in thy **p**, *that* my 4570
23: 3 he leadeth me in the **p** of righteousness for 4570
25: 4 me thy ways, O LORD; teach me thy **p**. 734
25:10 All the **p** of the LORD *are* mercy and 734
65:11 with thy goodness; and thy **p** drop fatness. 4570
Pr 2: 8 *He* keepeth the **p** of judgment, and 734
2:13 Who leave the **p** of uprightness, to walk in 734
2:15 *are* crooked, and *they* froward in their **p**: 4570
2:18 unto death, and her **p** unto the dead. 4570
2:19 *again,* neither take they hold of the **p** of life. 734
2:20 good *men,* and keep the **p** of the righteous. 734
3: 6 acknowledge him, and he shall direct thy **p**. 734
3:17 of pleasantness, and all her **p** *are* peace. 5410
4:11 way of wisdom; I have led thee in right **p**. 4570
7:25 decline to her ways, go not astray in her **p**. 5410
8: 2 places by the way, *in* the places of the **p**. 5410
8:20 in the midst of the **p** of judgment: 5410
Isa 2: 3 us of his ways, and we will walk in his **p**: 734
3:12 *thee* to err, and destroy the way of thy **p**. 734
42:16 I will lead them in **p** *that* they have not 5410
58:12 of the breach, The restorer of **p** to dwell in. 5410
59: 7 wasting and destruction are in their **p**. 4546
59: 8 they have made them crooked **p**: 5410
Jer 6:16 in the ways, and see, and ask for the old **p**, 5410
18:15 to stumble in their ways *from* the ancient **p**, 7635
18:15 to walk *in* **p**, *in* a way not cast up; 5410
La 3: 9 hewn stone, he hath made my **p** crooked. 5410
Hos 2: 6 make a wall, that she shall not find her **p**. 5410
Mic 4: 2 us of his ways, and we will walk in his **p**: 734
Mt 3: 3 ye the way of the Lord, make his **p** straight. *5147*

Mk 1: 3 ye the way of the Lord, make his **p** straight. *5147*
Lk 3: 4 ye the way of the Lord, make his **p** straight. *5147*
Heb 12:13 And make straight **p** for your feet, lest *that* *5163*

PATHWAY (1) [PATH]
Pr 12:28 and *in* the **p** *thereof there is* no death. 1870+5410

PATIENCE (34) [PATIENT, PATIENTLY]
Mt 18:26 **have p** with me, and I will pay thee all. *3114*
18:29 **Have p** with me, and I will pay thee all. *3114*
Lk 8:15 keep *it,* and bring forth fruit with **p**. *5281*
21:19 In your **p** possess ye your souls. *5281*
Ro 5: 3 knowing that tribulation worketh **p**; *5281*
5: 4 And **p**, experience; and experience, hope: *5281*
8:25 we see not, *then* do we with **p** wait for *it.* *5281*
15: 4 that we through **p** and comfort of *5281*
15: 5 Now the God of **p** and consolation grant *5281*
2Co 6: 4 in much **p**, in afflictions, in necessities, *5281*
12:12 apostle were wrought among you in all **p**, *5281*
Col 1:11 unto all **p** and longsuffering with *5281*
1Th 1: 3 and **p** of hope in our Lord Jesus Christ, *5281*
2Th 1: 4 in you in the churches of God for your **p** *5281*
1Ti 6:11 godliness, faith, love, **p**, meekness. *5281*
2Ti 3:10 faith, longsuffering, charity, **p**, *5281*
Tit 2: 2 temperate, sound in faith, in charity, in **p**. *5281*
Heb 6:12 through faith and **p** inherit the promises. *3115*
10:36 For ye have need of **p**, that, after ye have *5281*
12: 1 let us run with **p** the race that is set before *5281*
Jas 1: 3 *this,* that the trying of your faith worketh **p**. *5281*
1: 4 But let **p** have *her* perfect work, that ye *5281*
5: 7 and **hath long p** for it, until he receive *3114*
5:10 an example of suffering affliction, and of **p**. *3115*
5:11 Ye have heard of the **p** of Job, and *5281*
2Pe 1: 6 and to temperance **p**; and to patience *5281*
1: 6 to temperance patience; and to **p** godliness; *5281*
Rev 1: 9 and in the kingdom and **p** of Jesus Christ, *5281*
2: 2 and thy **p**, and how thou canst not bear *5281*
2: 3 and hast **p**, and for my name's sake hast *5281*
2:19 and faith, and thy **p**, and thy works; *5281*
3:10 Because thou hast kept the word of my **p**, *5281*
13:10 Here is the **p** and the faith of the saints. *5281*
14:12 Here is the **p** of the saints: here *are* they *5281*

PATIENT (9) [PATIENCE]
Ecc 7: 8 the **p** in spirit *is* better than the proud in 750
Ro 2: 7 To them who by **p continuance** in well *5281*
12:12 Rejoicing in hope; **p** in tribulation; *5278*
1Th 5:14 support the weak, be **p** toward all *men.* *3114*
2Th 3: 5 of God, and into the **p waiting** for Christ. *5281*
1Ti 3: 3 but **p**, not a brawler, not covetous; *1933*
2Ti 2:24 but be gentle unto all *men,* apt to teach, **p**, *420*
Jas 5: 7 Be **p** therefore, brethren, unto the coming *3114*
5: 8 Be ye also **p**; stablish your hearts: for *3114*

PATIENTLY (6) [PATIENCE]
Ps 37: 7 Rest in the LORD, and **wait p** for him: 2342
40: 1 I **waited p for** the LORD; and 6960+6960
Ac 26: 3 wherefore I beseech thee to hear me **p**. *3116*
Heb 6:15 And so, after he had **p endured**, *3114*
1Pe 2:20 buffeted for your faults, ye shall **take it p**? *5278*
2:20 ye do well, and suffer *for it,* ye **take it p**, *5278*

PATMOS (1)
Rev 1: 9 was in the isle that is called **P**, for the word *3963*

PATRIARCH (2) [PATRIARCHS]
Ac 2:29 let *me* freely speak unto you of the **p** *3966*
Heb 7: 4 the **p** Abraham gave the tenth of the spoils. *3966*

PATRIARCHS (2) [PATRIARCH]
Ac 7: 8 *begat* Jacob; and Jacob *begat* the twelve **p**. *3966*
7: 9 And the **p**, moved with envy, sold Joseph *3966*

PATRIMONY (1)
Dt 18: 8 beside that which cometh of the sale of his **p**. 1

PATROBAS (1)
Ro 16:14 **P**, Hermes, and the brethren which are with *3969*

PATTERN (14) [PATTERNS]
Ex 25: 9 *after* the **p** of the tabernacle, and the pattern 8403
25: 9 the **p** of all the instruments thereof, even 8403
25:40 look that thou make *them* after their **p**, 8403
Nu 8: 4 according unto the **p** which the LORD had 4758
Jos 22:28 that we may say *again,* Behold the **p** of 8403
2Ki 16:10 the **p** of it, according to all 8403
1Ch 28:11 David gave to Solomon his son the **p** of 8403
28:12 the **p** of all that he had by the spirit, of 8403
28:18 gold for the **p** of the chariot of 8403
28:19 hand upon me, *even* all the works of *this* **p**. 8403
Eze 43:10 their iniquities: and let them measure the **p**. 8508
1Ti 1:16 for a **p** to them which should hereafter *5296*
Tit 2: 7 In all *things* shewing thyself a **p** of good *5179*
Heb 8: 5 to the **p** shewed to thee in the mount. *5179*

PATTERNS (1) [PATTERN]
Heb 9:23 necessary that the **p** of *things* in *5262*

PAU (1)
Ge 36:39 the name of his city *was* **P**; and his wife's 6464

PAUL (157) [PAUL'S, SAUL]
Ac 13: 9 Then Saul, (who also *is called* **P**,) *3972*
13:13 Now when **P** and his company loosed from *3972*
13:16 Then **P** stood up, and beckoning with *his* *3972*
13:43 and religious proselytes followed **P** and *3972*
13:45 those *things* which were spoken by **P**, *3972*
13:46 Then **P** and Barnabas waxed bold, and said, *3972*
13:50 and raised persecution against **P** and *3972*
14: 9 The same heard **P** speak: who stedfastly *3972*
14:11 And when the people saw what **P** had done, *3972*
14:12 and **P**, Mercurius, because he was the chief *3972*
14:14 *Which* when the apostles, Barnabas and **P**, *3972*
14:19 and, having stoned **P**, drew *him* out of *3972*
15: 2 When therefore **P** and Barnabas had no *3972*
15: 2 they determined that **P** and Barnabas, and *3972*
15:12 and gave audience to Barnabas and **P**, *3972*
15:22 of their own company to Antioch with **P** *3972*
15:25 unto you with our beloved Barnabas and **P**, *3972*
15:35 **P** also and Barnabas continued in Antioch, *3972*
15:36 And some days after **P** said unto Barnabas, *3972*
15:38 But **P** thought not good to take him with *3972*
15:40 And **P** chose Silas, and departed, *3972*
16: 3 Him would **P** have to go forth with him; *3972*
16: 9 And a vision appeared to **P** in the night; *3972*
16:14 unto the *things* which were spoken of **P**. *3972*
16:17 The same followed **P** and us, and cried, *3972*
16:18 But **P**, being grieved, turned and said to *3972*
16:19 they caught **P** and Silas, and drew *them* *3972*
16:25 And at midnight **P** and Silas prayed, and *3972*
16:28 But **P** cried with a loud voice, saying, *3972*
16:29 and fell down before **P** and Silas, *3972*
16:36 keeper of the prison told this saying to **P**, *3972*
16:37 But **P** said unto them, They have beaten us *3972*
17: 2 And **P**, as his manner was, went in unto *3972*
17: 4 and consorted with **P** and Silas; *3972*
17:10 And the brethren immediately sent away **P** *3972*
17:13 word of God was preached of **P** at Berea, *3972*
17:14 immediately the brethren sent away **P** to go *3972*
17:15 And they that conducted **P** brought him *3972*
17:16 Now while **P** waited for them at Athens, his *3972*
17:22 Then **P** stood in the midst of Mars' hill, and *3972*
17:33 So **P** departed from among them. *3972*
18: 1 After these *things* **P** departed from Athens, *3972*
18: 5 **P** was pressed in spirit, and testified to *3972*
18: 9 Then spake the Lord to **P** in the night by a *3972*
18:12 insurrection with one accord against **P**, *3972*
18:14 And when **P** was *now* about to open *his* *3972*
18:18 And **P** *after this* tarried *there* yet a good *3972*
19: 1 **P** having passed through the upper coasts *3972*
19: 4 Then said **P**, John verily baptized *with* *3972*
19: 6 And when **P** had laid *his* hands upon them, *3972*
19:11 wrought special miracles by the hands of **P**: *3972*
19:13 We adjure you by Jesus whom **P** preacheth. *3972*
19:15 and said, Jesus I know, and **P** I know; *3972*
19:21 *things* were ended, **P** purposed in the spirit, *3972*
19:26 this **P** hath persuaded and turned away *3972*
19:30 And when **P** would have entered in unto *3972*
20: 1 **P** called unto *him* the disciples, and *3972*
20: 7 **P** preached unto them, ready to depart on *3972*
20: 9 and as **P** was long preaching, he sunk down *3972*
20:10 And **P** went down, and fell on him, and *3972*
20:13 unto Assos, there intending to take in **P**: *3972*
20:16 For **P** had determined to sail by Ephesus, *3972*
21: 4 who said to **P** through the Spirit, that *he* *3972*
21:13 Then **P** answered, What mean ye to weep *3972*
21:18 And the *day* following **P** went in with us *3972*
21:26 Then **P** took the men, and the next day *3972*
21:29 whom they supposed that **P** had brought *3972*

P

Ac 21:30 and they took **P**, and drew him out of 3972
21:32 and the soldiers, they left beating of **P**. 3972
21:37 And as **P** was to be led into the castle, 3972
21:39 But **P** said, I am a man *which am* a Jew of 3972
21:40 **P** stood on the stairs, and beckoned with 3972
22:25 **P** said unto the centurion that stood *by,* Is it 3972
22:28 And **P** said, But I was *free* born. 3972
22:30 and brought **P** down, and set *him* before 3972
23: 1 And **P**, earnestly beholding the council, 3972
23: 3 Then said **P** unto him, God shall smite thee, 3972
23: 5 Then said **P**, I wist not, brethren, that he 3972
23: 6 But when **P** perceived that the one part 3972
23:10 fearing lest **P** should have been pulled in 3972
23:11 by him, and said, Be of good cheer, **P**: 3972
23:12 neither eat nor drink till they had killed **P**. 3972
23:14 *we* will eat nothing until we have slain **P**. 3972
23:16 and entered into the castle, and told **P**. 3972
23:17 Then **P** called one of the centurions unto 3972
23:18 **P** the prisoner called me unto *him,* and 3972
23:20 bring down **P** to morrow into the council, 3972
23:24 that they may set **P** on, and bring *him* safe 3972
23:31 took **P**, and brought *him* by night to 3972
23:33 the governor, presented **P** also before him. 3972
24: 1 who informed the governor against **P**. 3972
24:10 Then **P**, after that the governor had 3972
24:23 And he commanded a centurion to keep **P**, 3972
24:24 he sent for **P**, and heard him concerning 3972
24:26 money should have been given him of **P**, 3972
24:27 to shew the Jews a pleasure, left **P** bound. 3972
25: 2 chief of the Jews informed him against **P**, 3972
25: 4 that **P** should be kept at Cesarea, and 3972
25: 6 commanded **P** to be brought. 3972
25: 7 and grievous complaints against **P**, 3972
25: 9 answered **P**, and said, Wilt thou go up to 3972
25:10 Then said **P**, I stand at Cesar's judgment 3972
25:19 *was* dead, whom **P** affirmed to be alive. 3972
25:21 But when **P** had appealed to be reserved 3972
25:23 at Festus' commandment **P** was brought 3972
26: 1 Then Agrippa said unto **P**, Thou art 3972
26: 1 Then **P** stretched forth the hand, and 3972
26:24 a loud voice, **P**, thou art beside thyself; 3972
26:28 Then Agrippa said unto **P**, Almost thou 3972
26:29 And **P** said, I would to God, that not only 3972
27: 1 they delivered **P** and certain other prisoners 3972
27: 3 And Julius courteously entreated **P**, and 3972
27: 9 was now already past, **P** admonished *them,* 3972
27:11 than those *things* which were spoken by **P**. 3972
27:21 But after long abstinence **P** stood *forth* in 3972
27:24 Saying, Fear not, **P**; thou must be brought 3972
27:31 **P** said to the centurion and to the soldiers, 3972
27:33 **P** besought *them* all to take meat, saying, 3972
27:43 But the centurion, willing to save **P**, 3972
28: 3 And when **P** had gathered a bundle of 3972
28: 8 to whom **P** entered in, and prayed, and 3972
28:15 whom when **P** saw, he thanked God, and 3972
28:16 **P** was suffered to dwell by himself with a 3972
28:17 that after three days **P** called the chief of 3972
28:25 after that **P** had spoken one word, 3972
28:30 And **P** dwelt two whole years in his own 3972
Ro 1: 1 **P**, a servant of Jesus Christ, called *to be* an 3972
1Co 1: 1 **P**, called *to be* an apostle of Jesus Christ 3972
1:12 I say, that every one of you saith, I am of **P**; 3972
1:13 was **P** crucified for you? or were ye 3972
1:13 or were ye baptized in the name of **P**? 3972
3: 4 For while one saith, I am of **P**; and another, 3972
3: 5 Who then is **P**, and who *is* Apollos, but 3972
3:22 Whether **P**, or Apollos, or Cephas, or 3972
16:21 The salutation of *me* **P** with mine own 3972
2Co 1: 1 **P**, an apostle of Jesus Christ by the will of 3972
10: 1 Now I **P** myself beseech you by 3972
Gal 1: 1 **P**, an apostle, (not of men, neither by man, 3972
5: 2 Behold, I **P** say unto you, that if ye be 3972
Eph 1: 1 **P**, an apostle of Jesus Christ by the will of 3972
3: 1 For this cause I **P**, the prisoner of Jesus 3972
Php 1: 1 **P** and Timotheus, the servants of Jesus 3972
Col 1: 1 **P**, an apostle of Jesus Christ by the will of 3972
1:23 whereof I **P** am made a minister; 3972
4:18 The salutation by the hand of me **P**. 3972
1Th 1: 1 **P**, and Silvanus, and Timotheus, unto 3972
2:18 come unto you, even I **P**, once and again; 3972
2Th 1: 1 **P**, and Silvanus, and Timotheus, unto 3972
3:17 The salutation of **P** with mine own hand, 3972
1Ti 1: 1 **P**, an apostle of Jesus Christ by 3972
2Ti 1: 1 **P**, an apostle of Jesus Christ by the will of 3972
4: 8 when **P** was brought before Nero 3972
Tit 1: 1 **P**, a servant of God, and an apostle of Jesus 3972
Phm 1: 1 **P**, a prisoner of Jesus Christ, and 3972
1: 9 *thee,* being such a one as **P** the aged, 3972
1:19 I **P** have written *it* with mine own hand, 3972
2Pe 3:15 even as our beloved brother **P** also 3972

PAUL'S (6) [PAUL]
Ac 19:29 men of Macedonia, **P** companions in travel, 3972
20:37 and fell on **P** neck, and kissed him, 3972
21: 8 And the next day we that were of **P** 3972
21:11 he took **P** girdle, and bound his *own* hands 3972
23:16 And when **P** sister's son heard of *their* 3972
25:14 Festus declared **P** cause unto the king, 3972

PAULUS (1)
Ac 13: 7 with the deputy *of the country,* Sergius **P**, 3972

PAVED (2) [PAVEMENT]
Ex 24:10 *there was* under his feet as it were a **p** work 3840
SS 3:10 the midst thereof being **p** *with* love, 7528

PAVEMENT (9) [PAVED]
2Ki 16:17 *were* under it, and put it upon a **p** of stones. 4837
2Ch 7: 3 *with their* faces to the ground upon the **p**, 7531
Est 1: 6 upon a **p** of red, and blue, and white, and 7531
Eze 40:17 and a **p** made for the court round about: 7531
40:17 thirty chambers *were* upon the **p**. 7531
40:18 the **p** by the side of the gates over against 7531
40:18 the length of the gates *was* the lower **p**. 7531
42: 3 over against the **p** which *was* for the utter 7531
Jn 19:13 judgment seat in a place *that is* called the **P**, 3038

PAVILION (4) [PAVILIONS]
Ps 18:11 his **p** round about him *were* dark waters 5521
27: 5 time of trouble he shall hide me in his **p**: 5520
31:20 thou shalt keep them secretly in a **p** from 5521
Jer 43:10 and he shall spread his **royal p** over them. 8237

PAVILIONS (3) [PAVILION]
2Sa 22:12 he made darkness **p** round about him, 5521
1Ki 20:12 he *was* drinking, he and the kings in the **p**, 5521
20:16 *was* drinking *himself* drunk in the **p**, 5521

PAW (2) [PAWETH, PAWS]
1Sa 17:37 The LORD that delivered me out of the **p** 3027
17:37 out of the **p** of the bear, he will deliver me 3027

PAWETH (1) [PAW]
Job 39:21 He **p** in the valley, and rejoiceth in *his* 2658

PAWS (1) [PAW]
Lev 11:27 whatsoever goeth upon his **p**, among all 3709

PAY (39) [PAID, PAYED, PAYETH, PAYMENT]
Ex 21:19 only he shall **p** *for* the loss of his time, and 5414
21:22 and he shall **p** as the judges determine. 5414
21:36 he shall **surely p** ox for ox; and 7999+7999
22: 7 if the thief be found, let him **p** double. 7999
22: 9 he shall **p** double unto his neighbour. 7999
22:17 he shall **p** money according to the dowry of 8254
Nu 20:19 *of* thy water, then I will **p** for it: 4377+5414
Dt 23:21 thy God, thou shalt not slack to **p** it: 7999
2Sa 15: 7 I pray thee, let me go and **p** my vow, 7999
1Ki 20:39 or else thou shalt **p** a talent of silver. 8254
2Ki 4: 7 **p** thy debt, and live thou and thy children 7999
2Ch 8: 8 them did Solomon **make to p** tribute until 5927
27: 5 So much did the children of Ammon **p** unto 7725
Ezr 4:13 walls set up *again, then* will they not **p** toll, 5415
Est 3: 9 I will **p** ten thousand talents of silver to 8254
4: 7 to **p** to the king's treasuries for the Jews, 8254
Job 22:27 shall hear thee, and thou shalt **p** thy vows. 7999
Ps 22:25 I will **p** my vows before them that fear him. 7999
50:14 and **p** thy vows unto the most High: 7999
66:13 with burnt offerings: I will **p** thee my vows, 7999
76:11 Vow, and **p** unto the LORD your God: 7999
116:14 I will **p** my vows unto the LORD now in 7999
116:18 I will **p** my vows unto the LORD now in 7999
Pr 19:17 which he hath given will he **p** him **again**. 7999
22:27 If thou hast nothing to **p**, why should he 7999
Ecc 5: 4 vowest a vow unto God, defer not to **p** it; 7999
5: 4 in fools: **p** that which thou hast vowed. 7999
5: 5 than that thou shouldest vow and not **p**. 7999
Jnh 2: 9 I will **p** *that* that I have vowed. 7999
Mt 17:24 and said, Doth not your master **p** tribute? 5055

Mt 18:25 But forasmuch as he had not to **p**, his lord *591*
18:26 have patience with me, and I will **p** thee all. *591*
18:28 by the throat, saying, **P** me that thou owest. *591*
18:29 Have patience with me, and I will **p** thee all. *591*
18:30 him into prison, till he should **p** the debt. *591*
18:34 till he should **p** all that was due unto him. *591*
23:23 for ye **p tithe of** mint and anise and cummin, *586*
Lk 7:42 And when they had nothing to **p**, he frankly *591*
Ro 13: 6 For for this cause **p** you tribute also: *5055*

PAYED (2) [PAY]
Pr 7:14 with me; *this* day have I **p** my vows. 7999
Heb 7: 9 who receiveth tithes, **p tithes** in Abraham. *1183*

PAYETH (1) [PAY]
Ps 37:21 The wicked borroweth, and **p** not **again**: 7999

PAYMENT (1) [PAY]
Mt 18:25 and all that he had, and **p** to be **made**. *591*

PEACE (429) [PEACEABLE, PEACEABLY, PEACEMAKERS]
Ge 15:15 thou shalt go to thy fathers in **p**; thou shalt 7965
24:21 the man wondering at her **held** his **p**, to wit 2790
26:29 but good, and have sent thee away in **p**: 7965
26:31 and they departed from him in **p**. 7965
28:21 that I come again to my father's house in **p**; 7965
34: 5 and Jacob **held** his **p** until they were come. 2790
41:16 God shall give Pharaoh an answer of **p**. 7965
43:23 he said, **P** *be* to you, fear not: your God, 7965
44:17 as for you, get you up in **p** unto your father. 7965
Ex 4:18 And Jethro said to Moses, Go in **p**. 7965
14:14 fight for you, and ye shall **hold** your **p**. 2790
18:23 this people shall also go to their place in **p**. 7965
20:24 thy **p offerings**, thy sheep, and thine oxen: 8002
24: 5 sacrificed **p** offerings *of* oxen unto 8002
29:28 Israel of the sacrifice of their **p offerings**, 8002
32: 6 burnt offerings, and brought **p offerings**; 8002
Lev 3: 1 if his oblation *be* a sacrifice of **p offering**, 8002
3: 3 **p offering** an offering made by fire unto 8002
3: 6 if his offering for a sacrifice of **p offering** 8002
3: 9 **p offering** an offering made by fire unto 8002
4:10 the bullock of the sacrifice of **p offerings**: 8002
4:26 as the fat of the sacrifice of **p offerings**: 8002
4:31 away from off the sacrifice of **p offerings**; 8002
4:35 away from the sacrifice of the **p offerings**; 8002
6:12 burn thereon the fat of the **p offerings**. 8002
7:11 *is* the law of the sacrifice of **p offerings**, 8002
7:13 sacrifice of thanksgiving of his **p offerings**. 8002
7:14 that sprinkleth the blood of the **p offerings**. 8002
7:15 the flesh of the sacrifice of his **p offerings** 8002
7:18 **p offerings** be eaten at all on the third day, 8002
7:20 *of* the flesh of the sacrifice of **p offerings**, 8002
7:21 of the flesh of the sacrifice of **p offerings**, 8002
7:29 **p offerings** unto the LORD shall bring his 8002
7:29 LORD of the sacrifice of his **p offerings**. 8002
7:32 of the sacrifices of your **p offerings**. 8002
7:33 that offereth the blood of the **p offerings**, 8002
7:34 from off the sacrifices of their **p offerings**, 8002
7:37 and of the sacrifice of the **p offerings**; 8002
9: 4 Also a bullock and a ram for **p offerings**, 8002
9:18 and the ram *for* a sacrifice of **p offerings**, 8002
9:22 and the burnt offering, and **p offerings**. 8002
10: 3 I will be glorified. And Aaron **held** his **p**. 1826
10:14 of **p offerings** of the children of Israel. 8002
17: 5 offer them *for* **p** offerings unto the LORD. 8002
19: 5 if ye offer a sacrifice of **p offerings** unto 8002
22:21 **p offerings** unto the LORD to accomplish 8002
23:19 the first year for a sacrifice of **p offerings**. 8002
26: 6 I will give **p** in the land, and ye shall lie 7965
Nu 6:14 one ram without blemish for **p offerings**, 8002
6:17 a sacrifice of **p offerings** unto the LORD, 8002
6:18 *is* under the sacrifice of the **p offerings**. 8002
6:26 his countenance upon thee, and give thee **p**. 7965
7:17 for a sacrifice of **p offerings**, two oxen, 8002
7:23 for a sacrifice of **p offerings**, two oxen, 8002
7:29 for a sacrifice of **p offerings**, two oxen, 8002
7:35 for a sacrifice of **p offerings**, two oxen, 8002
7:41 for a sacrifice of **p offerings**, two oxen, 8002
7:47 for a sacrifice of **p offerings**, two oxen, 8002
7:53 for a sacrifice of **p offerings**, two oxen, 8002
7:59 for a sacrifice of **p offerings**, two oxen, 8002
7:65 for a sacrifice of **p offerings**, two oxen, 8002
7:71 for a sacrifice of **p offerings**, two oxen, 8002
7:77 for a sacrifice of **p offerings**, two oxen, 8002
7:83 for a sacrifice of **p offerings**, two oxen, 8002
7:88 the sacrifice of the **p offerings** *were* twenty 8002
10:10 and over the sacrifices of your **p offerings**; 8002
15: 8 a vow, or **p offerings** unto the LORD: 8002
25:12 Behold, I give unto him my covenant of **p**: 7965
29:39 drink offerings, and for your **p offerings**. 8002
30: 4 and her father shall **hold** his **p** at her: 2790
30: 7 **held** his **p** at her in the day that he heard *it*: 2790
30:11 her husband heard *it*, and **held** his **p** at her, 2790
30:14 if her husband **altogether hold** his **p** 2790+2790
30:14 he **held** his **p** at her in the day that he 2790
Dt 2:26 Sihon king of Heshbon *with* words of **p**, 7965
20:10 to fight against it, then proclaim **p** unto it. 7965
20:11 if it make thee answer of **p**, and open unto 7965
20:12 if it will **make** no **p** with thee, but 7999
23: 6 Thou shalt not seek their **p** nor their 7965
27: 7 thou shalt offer **p offerings**, and shalt eat 8002
29:19 himself in his heart, saying, I shall have **p**, 7965
Jos 8:31 the LORD, and sacrificed **p offerings**. 8002
9:15 Joshua made **p** with them, and made a 7965
10: 1 how the inhabitants of Gibeon had **made p** 7999
10: 4 for it hath **made p** with Joshua and with 7999
10:21 to the camp to Joshua *at* Makkedah in **p**: 7965
11:19 There was not a city that **made p** with 7999
22:23 or if to offer **p** offerings thereon, 8002
22:27 our sacrifices, and with our **p offerings**; 8002
Jdg 4:17 for *there was* **p** between Jabin the king of 7965
6:23 the LORD said unto him, **P** *be* unto thee; 7965
8: 9 saying, When I come again in **p**, I will 7965
11:31 when I return in **p** from the children of 7965
18: 6 the priest said unto them, Go in **p**: 7965
18:19 they said unto him, **Hold** thy **p**, lay thine 2790
19:20 the old man said, **P** *be* with thee; 7965
20:26 and **p offerings** before the LORD. 8002
21: 4 and offered burnt offerings and **p offerings**. 8002
1Sa 1:17 Eli answered and said, Go in **p**: and 7965
7:14 there was **p** between Israel and 7965
10: 8 *and* to sacrifice sacrifices of **p offerings**: 8002
10:27 him no presents. But he **held** his **p**. 2790+3509.1
11:15 *of* **p offerings** before the LORD; 8002
13: 9 a burnt offering to me, and **p offerings**. 8002
20: 7 say thus, *It is* well; thy servant shall have **p**: 7965
20:13 send thee away, that thou mayest go in **p**: 7965
20:21 for *there is* **p** to thee, and no hurt; *as* 7965
20:42 Jonathan said to David, Go in **p**, 7965
25: 6 that liveth *in prosperity*, **P** *be* both *to* thee, 7965
25: 6 **p** *be to* thine house, and peace *be unto* all 7965
25: 6 and **p** *be unto* all that thou hast. 7965
25:35 said unto her, Go up in **p** to thine house; 7965
29: 7 Wherefore now return, and go in **p**, 7965
2Sa 3:21 David sent Abner away; and he went in **p**. 7965
3:22 had sent him away, and he was gone in **p**. 7965
3:23 he hath sent him away, and he is gone in **p**. 7965
6:17 and **p offerings** before the LORD. 8002
6:18 of offering burnt offerings and **p offerings**, 8002
10:19 they **made p** with Israel, and served them. 7999
13:20 **hold** now thy **p**, my sister: he *is* thy 2790
15: 9 the king said unto him, Go in **p**. So he 7965
15:27 return *into* the city in **p**, and your two sons 7965
17: 3 all returned: *so* all the people shall be *in* **p**. 7965
19:24 departed until the day he came *again* in **p**. 7965
19:30 is come *again* in **p** unto his own house. 7965
24:25 and offered burnt offerings and **p offerings**. 8002
1Ki 2: 5 shed the blood of war in **p**, and put 7965
2: 6 his hoar head go down *to* the grave in **p**. 7965
2:33 shall there be **p** for ever from the LORD. 7965
3:15 offered **p offerings**, and made a feast to all 8002
4:24 and he had **p** on all sides round about him. 7965
5:12 there was **p** between Hiram and Solomon; 7965
8:63 Solomon offered a sacrifice of **p offerings**, 8002
8:64 and the fat of the **p offerings**: 8002
8:64 and the fat of the **p offerings**. 8002
9:25 **p offerings** upon the altar which he built 8002
20:18 he said, Whether they be come out for **p**, 7965
22:17 let them return every man to his house in **p**. 7965
22:27 with water of affliction, until I come in **p**. 7965
22:28 Micaiah said, If thou return at all in **p**, 7965
22:44 Jehoshaphat **made p** with the king of 7999
2Ki 2: 3 he said, Yea, I know *it*; **hold** you your **p**. 2814
2: 5 Yea, I know *it*; **hold** you your **p**. 2814
5:19 he said unto him, Go in **p**. So he departed 7965
7: 9 *is* a day of good tidings, and we **hold** our **p**: 2814
9:17 send to meet them, and let him say, *Is it* **p**? 7965
9:18 and said, Thus saith the king, *Is it* **p**? 7965

2Ki 9:18 Jehu said, What hast thou to do with **p**? 7965
9:19 and said, Thus saith the king, *Is it* **p**? 7965
9:19 What hast thou to do with **p**? 7965
9:22 Joram saw Jehu, that he said, *Is it* **p**, Jehu? 7965
9:22 What **p**, so long as the whoredoms of thy 7965
9:31 she said, *Had* Zimri **p**, who slew his 7965
16:13 sprinkled the blood of his **p offerings**, 8002
18:36 the people **held** their **p**, and answered him 2790
20:19 *Is it* not *good,* if **p** and truth be in my days? 7965
22:20 thou shalt be gathered into thy grave in **p**; 7965
1Ch 12:18 **p**, peace *be* unto thee, and peace *be* to thine 7965
12:18 **p** *be* unto thee, and peace *be* to thine 7965
12:18 *be* unto thee, and **p** *be* to thine helpers; 7965
16: 1 and **p offerings** before God. 8002
16: 2 the burnt offerings and the **p offerings**, 8002
19:19 they **made p** with David, and became his 7999
21:26 and offered burnt offerings and **p offerings**, 8002
22: 9 I will give **p** and quietness unto Israel in his 7965
2Ch 7: 7 the fat of the **p offerings**, because 8002
15: 5 in those times *there was* no **p** to him that 7965
18:16 *therefore* every man to his house in **p**. 7965
18:26 with water of affliction, until I return in **p**. 7965
18:27 If thou certainly return in **p**, *then* hath not 7965
19: 1 returned to his house in **p** to Jerusalem. 7965
29:35 with the fat of the **p offerings**, and 8002
30:22 offering **p** offerings, and 8002
31: 2 for burnt offerings and for **p offerings**, 8002
33:16 sacrificed thereon **p** offerings and 8002
34:28 thou shalt be gathered to thy grave in **p**, 7965
Ezr 4:17 rest beyond the river: **P**, and at such a time. 8001
5: 7 written thus: Unto Darius the king, all **p**. 8001
7:12 of heaven, perfect *p*, and at such a time. NIH
9:12 nor seek their **p** or their wealth for ever: 7965
Ne 5: 8 **held** they their **p**, and found nothing *to* 2790
8:11 **Hold** your **p**, for the day *is* holy; 2013
Est 4:14 For if thou **altogether holdest** thy **p** 2790+2790
9:30 of Ahasuerus, *with* words of **p** and truth, 7965
10: 3 his people, and speaking **p** to all his seed. 7965
Job 5:23 the beasts of the field shall be **at p** with 7999
5:24 shalt know that thy tabernacle *shall be in* **p**; 7965
11: 3 Should thy lies **make** men **hold** their **p**? 2790
13: 5 you would **altogether hold** your **p**, 2790+2790
13:13 **Hold** your **p**, let me alone, that I may 2790
22:21 now thyself with him, and be **at p**: 7999
25: 2 with him, he maketh **p** in his high places. 7965
29:10 The nobles **held** their **p**, and 2244+6963
33:31 unto me: **hold** thy **p**, and I will speak. 2790
33:33 **hold** thy **p**, and I shall teach thee wisdom. 2790
Ps 4: 8 I will both lay me down in **p**, and sleep: 7965
7: 4 evil *unto* him that was **at p** with me; 7999
28: 3 which speak **p** to their neighbours, but 7965
29:11 the LORD will bless his people with **p**. 7965
34:14 and do good; seek **p**, and pursue it. 7965
35:20 For they speak not **p**: but they devise 7965
37:11 delight themselves in the abundance of **p**. 7965
37:37 the upright: for the end of *that* man *is* **p**. 7965
39: 2 *with* silence, I **held** my **p**, *even* from good; 2814
39:12 ear unto my cry; **hold** not thy **p** at my tears: 2790
55:18 He hath delivered my soul in **p** from 7965
55:20 his hands against such as be at **p** with him: 7965
72: 3 The mountains shall bring **p** to the people, 7965
72: 7 abundance of **p** so long as the moon 7965
83: 1 **hold** not thy **p**, and be not still, O God. 2790
85: 8 for he will speak **p** unto his people, and 7965
85:10 and **p** have kissed *each other.* 7965
109: 1 **Hold** not thy **p**, O God of my praise; 2790
119:165 Great **p** have they which love thy law: and 7965
120: 6 soul hath long dwelt with him that hateth **p**. 7965
120: 7 I *am for* **p**: but when I speak, they *are* for 7965
122: 6 Pray for the **p** of Jerusalem: they shall 7965
122: 7 **P** be within thy walls, *and* prosperity within 7965
122: 8 I will now say, **P** *be* within thee. 7965
125: 5 of iniquity: *but* **p** *shall be* upon Israel. 7965
128: 6 thy children's children, *and* **p** upon Israel. 7965
147:14 He maketh **p** *in* thy borders, *and* filleth thee 7965
Pr 3: 2 For length of days, and long life, and **p**, 7965
3:17 of pleasantness, and all her paths *are* **p**. 7965
7:14 *I have* **p** offerings with me; *this* day have I 8002
11:12 but a man of understanding **holdeth** his **p**. 2790
12:20 but to the counsellers of **p** *is* joy. 7965
16: 7 he **maketh** even his enemies **to be at p** 7999
17:28 Even a fool, when he **holdeth** his **p**, 2790
Ecc 3: 8 time to hate; a time of war, and a time of **p**. 7965
Isa 9: 6 The everlasting Father, The Prince of **P**. 7965
9: 7 *his* government and **p** *there shall be* no end, 7965
26: 3 Thou wilt keep *him in* **perfect p**, 7965+7965
26:12 LORD, thou wilt ordain **p** for us: for thou 7965
27: 5 my strength, *that* he may make **p** with me; 7965
27: 5 with me; *and* he shall make **p** with me. 7965
32:17 the work of righteousness shall be **p**; and 7965
33: 7 the ambassadors of **p** shall weep bitterly. 7965
36:21 they **held** their **p**, and answered him not a 2790
38:17 Behold, for **p** I had great bitterness: 7965
39: 8 For there shall be **p** and truth in my days. 7965
42:14 I have long time **holden** my **p**; I have been 2814
45: 7 I make **p**, and create evil: I the LORD do 7965
48:18 had thy **p** been as a river, and 7965
48:22 *There is* no **p**, saith the LORD, unto 7965
52: 7 bringeth good tidings, that publisheth **p**; 7965
53: 5 the chastisement of our **p** *was* upon him; 7965
54:10 neither shall the covenant of my **p** be 7965
54:13 and great *shall be* the **p** of thy children. 7965
55:12 go out with joy, and be led forth with **p**: 7965
57: 2 He shall enter *into* **p**: they shall rest in their 7965
57:11 have not I **held** my **p** even of old, and thou 2814
57:19 **P**, peace to *him that is* far off, and to *him* 7965
57:19 **p** to *him that is* far off, and to *him that is* 7965
57:21 *There is* no **p**, saith my God, to the wicked. 7965
59: 8 The way of **p** they know not; and *there is* 7965
59: 8 whosoever goeth therein shall not know **p**. 7965
60:17 I will also make thy officers **p**, and 7965
62: 1 For Zion's sake will I not **hold my p**, and 2814
62: 6 *which* shall never **hold** their **p** day nor 2814
64:12 wilt thou **hold** thy **p**, and afflict us very 2814
66:12 I will extend **p** to her like a river, and 7965
Jer 4:10 Jerusalem, saying, Ye shall have **p**; 7965
4:19 I cannot **hold** my **p**, because thou hast 2790
6:14 *of* my people slightly, saying, **P**, peace; 7965
6:14 *of* my people slightly, saying, Peace, **p**; 7965
6:14 Peace, peace; when *there is* no **p**. 7965
8:11 of my people slightly, saying, **P**, peace; 7965
8:11 of my people slightly, saying, Peace, **p**; 7965
8:11 Peace, peace; when *there is* no **p**. 7965
8:15 *We* looked for **p**, but no good *came; and* 7965
12: 5 *if* in the land of **p**, *wherein* thou trustedst, 7965
12:12 *other* end of the land: no flesh *shall* have **p**. 7965
14:13 but I will give you assured **p** in this place. 7965
14:19 *we* looked for **p**, and *there is* no good; and 7965
16: 5 for I have taken away my **p** from this 7965
23:17 The LORD hath said, Ye shall have **p**; 7965
28: 9 The prophet which prophesieth of **p**, 7965
29: 7 seek the **p** of the city whither I have caused 7965
29: 7 for in the **p** thereof shall ye have peace. 7965
29: 7 for in the peace thereof shall ye have **p**. 7965
29:11 the LORD, thoughts of **p**, and not of evil, 7965
30: 5 a voice of trembling, of fear, and not of **p**. 7965
33: 6 will reveal unto them the abundance of **p** 7965
34: 5 *But* thou shalt die in **p**: and with 7965
43:12 and he shall go forth from thence in **p**. 7965
La 3:17 thou hast removed my soul far off from **p**: 7965
Eze 7:25 they shall seek **p**, and *there shall be* none. 7965
13:10 they have seduced my people, saying, **P**; 7965
13:10 *there was* no **p**; and one built up a wall, and 7965
13:16 which see visions of **p** for her, and *there is* 7965
13:16 and *there is* no **p**, saith the Lord GOD. 7965
34:25 And I will make with them a covenant of **p**, 7965
37:26 Moreover I will make a covenant of **p** with 7965
43:27 upon the altar, and your **p offerings**; 8002
45:15 for a burnt offering, and for **p offerings**, 8002
45:17 and the burnt offering, and the **p offerings**, 8002
46: 2 his burnt offering and his **p offerings**, 8002
46:12 or **p offerings** voluntarily unto the LORD, 8002
46:12 his burnt offering and his **p offerings**, 8002
Da 4: 1 in all the earth; **P** be multiplied unto you. 8001
6:25 in all the earth; **P** be multiplied unto you. 8001
8:25 in his heart, and by **p** shall destroy many: 7962
10:19 **p** *be* unto thee, be strong, yea, be strong. 7965
Am 5:22 I regard the **p offerings** of your fat beasts. 8002
Ob 1: 7 the men that were at **p** with thee have 7965
Mic 3: 5 that bite with their teeth, and cry, **P**; 7965
5: 5 this *man* shall be *the* **p**, when the Assyrian 7965
Na 1:15 bringeth good tidings, that publisheth **p**. 7965
Zep 1: 7 **Hold** thy **p** at the presence of the Lord 2013
Hag 2: 9 in this place will I give **p**, saith the LORD 7965
Zec 6:13 the counsel of **p** shall be between them 7965
8:10 neither *was there any* **p** to him that went 7965
8:16 the judgment of truth and **p** in your gates: 7965
8:19 therefore love the truth and **p**. 7965

Zec 9:10 he shall speak **p** unto the heathen: and 7965
Mal 2: 5 My covenant was with him of life and **p**; 7965
2: 6 he walked with me in **p** and equity, and 7965
Mt 10:13 house be worthy, let your **p** come upon it: *1515*
10:13 if it be not worthy, let your **p** return to you. *1515*
10:34 Think not that I am come to send **p** on *1515*
10:34 on earth: I came not to send **p**, but a sword. *1515*
20:31 because they should **hold** their **p**: *4623*
26:63 But Jesus **held** his **p**. And the high priest *4623*
Mk 1:25 saying, **Hold** thy **p**, and come out of him. *5392*
3: 4 save life, or to kill? But they **held** their **p**. *4623*
4:39 the wind, and said unto the sea, **P**, be still. *4623*
5:34 go in **p**, and be whole of thy plague. *1515*
9:34 But they **held** their **p**: for by the way they *4623*
9:50 in yourselves, and **have p** one with another. *1514*
10:48 charged him that he should **hold** his **p**: *4623*
14:61 But he **held** his **p**, and answered nothing. *4623*
Lk 1:79 to guide our feet into the way of **p**. *1515*
2:14 and on earth **p**, good will towards men. *1515*
2:29 now lettest thou thy servant depart in **p**, *1515*
4:35 saying, **Hold** thy **p**, and come out of him. *5392*
7:50 Thy faith hath saved thee; go in **p**. *1515*
8:48 thy faith hath made thee whole; go in **p**.) *1515*
10: 5 house ye enter, first say, **P** *be* to this house. *1515*
10: 6 And if the son of **p** be there, your peace *1515*
10: 6 of peace be there, your **p** shall rest upon it: *1515*
11:21 keepeth his palace, his goods are in **p**: *1515*
12:51 Suppose ye that I am come to give **p** on *1515*
14: 4 And they **held** their **p**. And he took *him*, *2270*
14:32 an ambassage, and desireth conditions of **p**. *1515*
18:39 rebuked him, that he should **hold** his **p**: *4623*
19:38 **p** in heaven, and glory in the highest. *1515*
19:40 I tell you that, if these should **hold** their **p**, *4623*
19:42 the *things* which belong unto thy **p**! *1515*
20:26 marvelled at his answer, and **held** their **p**. *4601*
24:36 and saith unto them, **P** *be* unto you. *1515*
Jn 14:27 **P** I leave with you, my peace I give unto *1515*
14:27 I leave with you, my **p** I give unto you: *1515*
16:33 unto you, that in me ye might have **p**. *1515*
20:19 and saith unto them, **P** *be* unto you. *1515*
20:21 said Jesus to them again, **P** *be* unto you: *1515*
20:26 stood in the midst, and said, **P** *be* unto you. *1515*
Ac 10:36 of Israel, preaching **p** by Jesus Christ: *1515*
11:18 they heard these *things*, they **held** their **p**, *2270*
12:17 unto them with the hand to **hold** their **p**, *4601*
12:20 king's chamberlain their friend, desired **p**; *1515*
15:13 And after they had **held** their **p**, *4601*
15:33 they were let go in **p** from the brethren unto *1515*
16:36 you go: now therefore depart, and go in **p**. *1515*
18: 9 not afraid, but speak, and **hold** not thy **p**: *4623*
Ro 1: 7 Grace to you and **p** from God our Father, *1515*
2:10 But glory, honour, and **p**, to every *man* that *1515*
3:17 And the way of **p** have they not known: *1515*
5: 1 we have **p** with God through our Lord *1515*
8: 6 but to be spiritually minded *is* life and **p**. *1515*
10:15 the feet of them that preach the gospel of **p**, *1515*
14:17 and **p**, and joy in the Holy Ghost. *1515*
14:19 follow *after* the *things* which make for **p**, *1515*
15:13 fill you with all joy and **p** in believing, *1515*
15:33 Now the God of **p** *be* with you all. Amen. *1515*
16:20 And the God of **p** shall bruise Satan under *1515*
1Co 1: 3 Grace *be* unto you, and **p**, from God our *1515*
7:15 in such *cases*: but God hath called us to **p**. *1515*
14:30 that sitteth *by*, let the first **hold** his **p**. *4601*
14:33 but of **p**, as in all churches of the saints. *1515*
16:11 but conduct him forth in **p**, that he may *1515*
2Co 1: 2 *be* to you and **p** from God our Father, *1515*
13:11 of good comfort, be of one mind, **live in p**; *1514*
13:11 the God of love and **p** shall be with you. *1515*
Gal 1: 3 Grace *be* to you and **p** from God the Father, *1515*
5:22 joy, **p**, longsuffering, gentleness, goodness, *1515*
6:16 to this rule, **p** *be* on them, and mercy, *1515*
Eph 1: 2 Grace *be* to you, and **p**, from God our *1515*
2:14 For he is our **p**, who hath made both one, *1515*
2:15 of twain one new man, *so* making **p**; *1515*
2:17 and preached **p** to you which were afar off, *1515*
4: 3 keep the unity of the Spirit in the bond of **p**. *1515*
6:15 with the preparation of the gospel of **p**; *1515*
6:23 **P** *be* to the brethren, and love with faith, *1515*
Php 1: 2 Grace *be* unto you, and **p**, from God our *1515*
4: 7 And the **p** of God, which passeth all *1515*
4: 9 do: and the God of **p** shall be with you. *1515*
Col 1: 2 Grace *be* unto you, and **p**, from God our *1515*
1:20 having **made p** through the blood of his *1517*
3:15 And let the **p** of God rule in your hearts, *1515*
1Th 1: 1 Grace *be* unto you, and **p**, from God our *1515*
5: 3 For when they shall say, **P** and safety; then *1515*
5:13 *And* be at **p** among yourselves. *1514*
5:23 And the very God of **p** sanctify you wholly; *1515*
2Th 1: 2 Grace unto you, and **p**, from God our *1515*
3:16 Now the Lord of **p** himself give you peace *1515*
3:16 Now the Lord of peace himself give you **p** *1515*
1Ti 1: 2 Grace, mercy, *and* **p**, from God our Father *1515*
2Ti 1: 2 Grace, mercy, *and* **p**, from God the Father *1515*
2:22 but follow righteousness, faith, charity, **p**, *1515*
Tit 1: 4 Grace, mercy, *and* **p**, from God the Father *1515*
Phm 1: 3 Grace to you, and **p**, from God our Father *1515*
Heb 7: 2 also King of Salem, which is, King of **p**; *1515*
11:31 when she had received the spies with **p**. *1515*
12:14 Follow **p** with all *men*, and holiness, *1515*
13:20 Now the God of **p**, that brought again from *1515*
Jas 2:16 Depart in **p**, be you warmed and filled; *1515*
3:18 And the fruit of righteousness is sown in **p** *1515*
3:18 is sown in peace of them that make **p**. *1515*
1Pe 1: 2 Grace unto you, and **p**, be multiplied. *1515*
3:11 and do good; let him seek **p**, and ensue it. *1515*
5:14 **P** *be* with you all that are in Christ Jesus. *1515*
2Pe 1: 2 **p** be multiplied unto you through *1515*
3:14 diligent that ye may be found of him in **p**, *1515*
2Jn 1: 3 Grace be with you, mercy, *and* **p**, from God *1515*
3Jn 1:14 **P** *be* to thee. *Our* friends salute thee. *1515*
Jude 1: 2 unto you, and **p**, and love, be multiplied. *1515*
Rev 1: 4 Grace *be* unto you, and **p**, from him which *1515*
6: 4 that sat thereon to take **p** from the earth, *1515*

PEACEABLE (8) [PEACE]

Ge 34:21 These men *are* **p** with us; therefore let them 8003
2Sa 20:19 I *am one of them that are* **p** *and* faithful in 7999
1Ch 4:40 and the land *was* wide, and quiet, and **p**; 7961
Isa 32:18 my people shall dwell in a **p** habitation, 7965
Jer 25:37 the **p** habitations are cut down because of 7965
1Ti 2: 2 and **p** life in all godliness and honesty. *2272*
Heb 12:11 nevertheless afterward it yieldeth the **p** fruit *1516*
Jas 3:17 then **p**, gentle, *and* easy to be intreated, *1516*

PEACEABLY (12) [PEACE]

Ge 37: 4 hated him, and could not speak **p** unto him. 7965
Jdg 11:13 restore those *lands* again **p**. 7965+871.1
21:13 the rock Rimmon, and to call **p** unto them. 7965
1Sa 16: 4 at his coming, and said, Comest thou **p**? 7965
16: 5 he said, **P**: I am come to sacrifice unto 7965
1Ki 2:13 she said, Comest thou **p**? And he said, 7965
2:13 Comest thou peaceably? And he said, **P**. 7965
1Ch 12:17 ye be come **p** unto me to help me, 7965+3807.1
Jer 9: 8 *one* speaketh **p** to his neighbour with his 7965
Da 11:21 he shall come in **p**, and obtain the kingdom 7962
11:24 He shall enter **p** even upon 7962+871.1
Ro 12:18 as much as lieth in you, **live p** with all men. *1514*

PEACEMAKERS (1) [PEACE]

Mt 5: 9 Blessed *are* the **p**: for they shall be called *1518*

PEACOCKS (3)

1Ki 10:22 and silver, ivory, and apes, and **p**. 8500
2Ch 9:21 and silver, ivory, and apes, and **p**. 8500
Job 39:13 *Gavest thou* the goodly wings unto the **p**? 5965

PEARL (2) [PEARLS]

Mt 13:46 when he had found one **p** of great price, *3135*
Rev 21:21 every several gate was of one **p**: *3135*

PEARLS (8) [PEARL]

Job 28:18 No mention shall be made of coral, or of **p**: 1378
Mt 7: 6 neither cast ye your **p** before swine, *3135*
13:45 unto a merchant man, seeking goodly **p**: *3135*
1Ti 2: 9 broided hair, or gold, or **p**, or costly array; *3135*
Rev 17: 4 decked with gold and precious stone and **p**, *3135*
18:12 and of **p**, and fine linen, and purple, and *3135*
18:16 with gold, and precious stones, and **p**: *3135*
21:21 And the twelve gates *were* twelve **p**; *3135*

PECULIAR (7)

Ex 19: 5 ye shall be a **p treasure** unto me above all 5459
Dt 14: 2 the LORD hath chosen thee to be a **p** 5459
26:18 avouched thee *this* day to be his **p** people, 5459
Ps 135: 4 unto himself, *and* Israel for his **p treasure**. 5459
Ecc 2: 8 the **p treasure** of kings and of 5459
Tit 2:14 and purify unto himself a **p** people, *4041*
1Pe 2: 9 a holy nation, a **p** people; *1519+4047*

PEDAHEL (1)
Nu 34:28 of Naphtali, **P** the son of Ammihud. 6300

PEDAHZUR (5)
Nu 1:10 of Manasseh; Gamaliel the son of **P**. 6301
2:20 Manasseh *shall be* Gamaliel the son of **P**. 6301
7:54 eighth day *offered* Gamaliel the son of **P**, 6301
7:59 *was* the offering of Gamaliel the son of **P**. 6301
10:23 of Manasseh *was* Gamaliel the son of **P**. 6301

PEDAIAH (8)
2Ki 23:36 *was* Zebudah, the daughter of **P** of Rumah. 6305
1Ch 3:18 **P**, and Shenazar, Jecamiah, Hoshama, and 6305
3:19 the sons of **P** *were*, Zerubbabel, and 6305
27:20 half tribe of Manasseh, Joel the son of **P**: 6305
Ne 3:25 the prison. After him **P** the son of Parosh. 6305
8: 4 **P**, and Mishael, and Malchiah, and 6305
11: 7 the son of Joed, the son of **P**, the son of 6305
13:13 and Zadok the scribe, and of the Levites, **P**: 6305

PEDIGREES (1)
Nu 1:18 they **declared** their **p** after their families, 3205

PEELED (3)
Isa 18: 2 to a nation scattered and **p**, 4178
18: 7 of hosts *of* a people scattered and **p**, 4178
Eze 29:18 *was* made bald, and every shoulder *was* **p**: 4803

PEEP (1) [PEEPED]
Isa 8:19 and unto wizards that **p**, and that mutter: 6850

PEEPED (1) [PEEP]
Isa 10:14 moved the wing, or opened the mouth, or **p**. 6850

PEKAH (11)
2Ki 15:25 **P** the son of Remaliah, a captain of his, 6492
15:27 fiftieth year of Azariah king of Judah **P** 6492
15:29 In the days of **P** king of Israel came 6492
15:30 a conspiracy against **P** the son of Remaliah, 6492
15:31 the rest of the acts of **P**, and all that he did, 6492
15:32 In the second year of **P** the son of Remaliah 6492
15:37 king of Syria, and **P** the son of Remaliah. 6492
16: 1 In the seventeenth year of **P** the son of 6492
16: 5 **P** son of Remaliah king of Israel came up 6492
2Ch 28: 6 For **P** the son of Remaliah slew in Judah an 6492
Isa 7: 1 and **P** the son of Remaliah, king of Israel, 6492

PEKAHIAH (3)
2Ki 15:22 and **P** his son reigned in his stead. 6494
15:23 **P** the son of Menahem *began* to reign over 6494
15:26 the rest of the acts of **P**, and all that he did, 6494

PEKOD (2)
Jer 50:21 against it, and against the inhabitants of **P**: 6489
Eze 23:23 all the Chaldeans, **P**, and Shoa, and Koa, 6489

PELAIAH (3)
1Ch 3:24 **P**, and Akkub, and Johanan, and Dalaiah, 6411
Ne 8: 7 Jozabad, Hanan, **P**, and the Levites, 6411
10:10 Shebaniah, Hodijah, Kelita, **P**, Hanan, 6411

PELALIAH (1)
Ne 11:12 the son of **P**, the son of Amzi, the son of 6421

PELATIAH (5)
1Ch 3:21 the sons of Hananiah; **P**, and Jesaiah: 6410
4:42 having for their captains **P**, and Neariah, 6410
Ne 10:22 **P**, Hanan, Anaiah, 6410
Eze 11: 1 **P** the son of Benaiah, princes of the people. 6410
11:13 that **P** the son of Benaiah died. 6410

PELEG (7) [PHALEC]
Ge 10:25 the name of one *was* **P**; for in his days was 6389
11:16 lived four and thirty years, and begat **P**: 6389
11:17 Eber lived after he begat **P** four hundred 6389
11:18 And **P** lived thirty years, and begat Reu: 6389
11:19 **P** lived after he begat Reu two hundred 6389
1Ch 1:19 the name of the one *was* **P**; because in his 6389
1:25 Eber, **P**, Rehu, 6389

PELET (2)
1Ch 2:47 Geshan, and **P**, and Ephah, and Shaaph. 6404
12: 3 Jeziel, and **P**, the sons of Azmaveth; and 6404

PELETH (2) [PELETHITES]
Nu 16: 1 On, the son of **P**, sons of Reuben, 6431
1Ch 2:33 the sons of Jonathan; **P**, and Zaza. 6431

PELETHITES (7) [PELETH]
2Sa 8:18 *was over* both the Cherethites and the **P**; 6432
15:18 and all the **P**, and all the Gittites, 6432
20: 7 the **P**, and all the mighty *men:* and 6432
20:23 *was* over the Cherethites and over the **P**: 6432
1Ki 1:38 the **P**, went down, and caused Solomon to 6432
1:44 the **P**, and they have caused him to ride 6432
1Ch 18:17 *was* over the Cherethites and the **P**; 6432

PELICAN (3)
Lev 11:18 And the swan, and the **p**, and the gier eagle, 6893
Dt 14:17 the **p**, and the gier eagle, and 6893
Ps 102: 6 I am like a **p** of the wilderness: I am like an 6893

PELONITE (3)
1Ch 11:27 Shammoth the Harorite, Helez the **P**, 6397
11:36 Hepher the Mecherathite, Ahijah the **P**, 6397
27:10 for the seventh month *was* Helez the **P**, 6397

PEN (7)
Jdg 5:14 out of Zebulun they that handle the **p** of 7626
Job 19:24 That they were graven with an iron **p** and 5842
Ps 45: 1 my tongue *is* the **p** of a ready writer. 5842
Isa 8: 1 write in it with a man's **p** concerning 2747
Jer 8: 8 certainly in vain made he *it;* the **p** of 5842
17: 1 The sin of Judah *is* written with a **p** of iron, 5842
3Jn 1:13 I will not with ink and **p** write unto thee: *2563*

PENCE (5)
Mt 18:28 which ought him an hundred **p**: *1220*
Mk 14: 5 been sold for more than three hundred **p**, *1220*
Lk 7:41 the one ought five hundred **p**, and the other *1220*
10:35 he took out two **p**, and gave *them* to *1220*
Jn 12: 5 not this ointment sold for three hundred **p**, *1220*

PENIEL (1) [PENUEL]
Ge 32:30 Jacob called the name of the place **P**: for I 6439

PENINNAH (3)
1Sa 1: 2 *was* Hannah, and the name of the other **P**: 6444
1: 2 **P** had children, but Hannah had no 6444
1: 4 he gave to **P** his wife, and to all her sons 6444

PENKNIFE (1)
Jer 36:23 he cut it with the **p**, and 5608+8593+1886.1

PENNY (9) [PENNYWORTH]
Mt 20: 2 had agreed with the labourers for a **p** a day, *1220*
20: 9 eleventh hour, they received every man a **p**. *1220*
20:10 and they likewise received every man a **p**. *1220*
20:13 didst not thou agree with me for a **p**? *1220*
22:19 And they brought unto him a **p**. *1220*
Mk 12:15 ye me? bring me a **p**, that I may see *it.* *1220*
Lk 20:24 Shew me a **p**. Whose image and *1220*
Rev 6: 6 A measure of wheat for a **p**, and *1220*
6: 6 and three measures of barley for a **p**; *1220*

PENNYWORTH (2) [PENNY]
Mk 6:37 we go and buy two hundred **p** of bread, *1220*
Jn 6: 7 Two hundred **p** of bread is not sufficient *1220*

PENTECOST (3)
Ac 2: 1 And when the day of **P** was fully come, *4005*
20:16 for him, to be at Jerusalem the day of **P**. *4005*
1Co 16: 8 But I will tarry at Ephesus until **P**. *4005*

PENUEL (8) [PENIEL]
Ge 32:31 as he passed over **P** the sun rose upon him, 6439
Jdg 8: 8 he went up thence *to* **P**, and spake unto 6439
8: 8 the men of **P** answered him as the men of 6439
8: 9 he spake also unto the men of **P**, saying, 6439
8:17 he beat down the tower of **P**, and slew 6439
1Ki 12:25 went out from thence, and built **P**. 6439
1Ch 4: 4 **P** the father of Gedor, and Ezer the father 6439
8:25 And Iphedeiah, and **P**, the sons of Shashak; 6439

PENURY (2)
Pr 14:23 but the talk of the lips *tendeth* only to **p**. 4270
Lk 21: 4 she of her **p** hath cast in all the living that *5303*

PEOPLE (2139) [PEOPLE'S, PEOPLES]
Ge 11: 6 the **p** *is* one, and they have all one 5971
14:16 his goods, and the women also, and the **p**. 5971
17:14 that soul shall be cut off from his **p**; 5971

Ge 17:16 of nations; kings of **p** shall be of her. 5971
19: 4 and young, all the **p** from every quarter: 5971
23: 7 and bowed himself to the **p** of the land, 5971
23:11 in the presence of the sons of my **p** give I it 5971
23:12 Abraham bowed down himself before the **p** 5971
23:13 Ephron in the audience of the **p** of the land, 5971
25: 8 and full *of years;* and was gathered to his **p**. 5971
25:17 and died; and was gathered unto his **p**. 5971
25:23 two manner of **p** shall be separated from 3816
25:23 *the one* **p** shall be stronger than *the other* 3816
25:23 people shall be stronger than *the other* **p**; 3816
26:10 one of the **p** might lightly have lien with 5971
26:11 Abimelech charged all *his* **p**, saying, 5971
27:29 Let **p** serve thee, and nations bow down to 5971
28: 3 that thou mayest be a multitude of **p**; 5971
29: 1 came into the land of the **p** of the east. 1121
32: 7 and he divided the **p** that *was* with him, and 5971
34:16 dwell with you, and we will become one **p**. 5971
34:22 to be one **p**, if every male among us be 5971
35: 6 he and all the **p** that *were* with him. 5971
35:29 died, and was gathered unto his **p**, 5971
41:40 according unto thy word shall all my **p** be 5971
41:55 the **p** cried to Pharaoh for bread: 5971
42: 6 he *it was* that sold to all the **p** of the land: 5971
47:21 as for the **p**, he removed them to cities from 5971
47:23 Joseph said unto the **p**, Behold, I have 5971
48: 4 and I will make of thee a multitude of **p**; 5971
48:19 I know *it:* he also shall become a **p**, and 5971
49:10 unto him *shall* the gathering of the **p** *be.* 5971
49:16 Dan shall judge his **p**, as one of the tribes 5971
49:29 unto them, I *am to be* gathered unto my **p**: 5971
49:33 up the ghost, and was gathered unto his **p**. 5971
50:20 as *it is* this day, to save much **p** alive. 5971
Ex 1: 9 he said unto his **p**, Behold, the people of 5971
1: 9 the **p** of the children of Israel *are* moe and 5971
1:20 the **p** multiplied, and waxed very mighty. 5971
1:22 Pharaoh charged all his **p**, saying, 5971
3: 7 I have surely seen the affliction of my **p** 5971
3:10 that thou mayest bring forth my **p** 5971
3:12 When thou hast brought forth the **p** out of 5971
3:21 I will give this **p** favour in the sight of 5971
4:16 he shall be thy spokesman unto the **p**: and 5971
4:21 his heart, that he shall not let the **p** go. 5971
4:30 and did the signs in the sight of the **p**. 5971
4:31 the **p** believed: and when they heard that 5971
5: 1 the LORD God of Israel, Let my **p** go, 5971
5: 4 and Aaron, let the **p** from their works? 5971
5: 5 the **p** of the land now *are* many, and 5971
5: 6 the same day the taskmasters of the **p**, 5971
5: 7 Ye shall no more give the **p** straw to make 5971
5:10 the taskmasters of the **p** went out, and 5971
5:10 and they spake to the **p**, saying, 5971
5:12 So the **p** were scattered abroad throughout 5971
5:16 *are* beaten; but the fault *is* in thine own **p**. 5971
5:22 hast thou *so* evil entreated this **p**? 5971
5:23 in thy name, he hath done evil to this **p**; 5971
5:23 neither hast thou delivered thy **p** at all. 5971
6: 7 I will take you to me for a **p**, and I will be 5971
7: 4 *and* my **p** the children of Israel, 5971
7:14 *is* hardened, he refuseth to let the **p** go. 5971
7:16 saying, Let my **p** go, that they may serve 5971
8: 1 Thus saith the LORD, Let my **p** go, 5971
8: 3 upon thy **p**, and into thine ovens, and 5971
8: 4 and upon thy **p**, and upon all thy servants. 5971
8: 8 away the frogs from me, and from my **p**; 5971
8: 8 I will let the **p** go, that they may do 5971
8: 9 for thee, and for thy servants, and for thy **p**, 5971
8:11 and from thy servants, and from thy **p**; 5971
8:20 Thus saith the LORD, Let my **p** go, 5971
8:21 Else, if thou wilt not let my **p** go, behold, 5971
8:21 and upon thy **p**, and into thy houses: 5971
8:22 in which my **p** dwell, that no swarms *of* 5971
8:23 I will put a division between my **p** and thy 5971
8:23 a division between my people and thy **p**: 5971
8:29 his servants, and from his **p**, to morrow: 5971
8:29 letting the **p** go to sacrifice to the LORD. 5971
8:31 from his servants, and from his **p**; 5971
8:32 this time also, neither would he let the **p** go. 5971
9: 1 Let my **p** go, that they may serve me. 5971
9: 7 was hardened, and he did not let the **p** go. 5971
9:13 Let my **p** go, that they may serve me. 5971
9:14 and upon thy servants, and upon thy **p**; 5971
9:15 I may smite thee and thy **p** with pestilence; 5971
9:17 As yet exaltest thou thyself against my **p**, 5971
9:27 *is* righteous, and I and my **p** *are* wicked. 5971
10: 3 let my **p** go, that they may serve me. 5971
10: 4 Else, if thou refuse to let my **p** go, behold, 5971
11: 2 Speak now in the ears of the **p**, and 5971
11: 3 the LORD gave the **p** favour in the sight 5971
11: 3 and in the sight of the **p**.) 5971
11: 8 Get thee out, and all the **p** that follow thee: 5971
12:27 And the **p** bowed the head and worshipped. 5971
12:31 *and* get you forth from amongst my **p**, 5971
12:33 the Egyptians were urgent upon the **p**, that 5971
12:34 the **p** took their dough before it was 5971
12:36 the LORD gave the **p** favour in the sight 5971
13: 3 Moses said unto the **p**, Remember this day, 5971
13:17 to pass, when Pharaoh had let the **p** go, 5971
13:17 Lest peradventure the **p** repent when they 5971
13:18 God led the **p** about, *through* the way of 5971
13:22 pillar of fire by night, *from* before the **p**. 5971
14: 5 it was told the king of Egypt that the **p** fled: 5971
14: 5 of his servants was turned against the **p**, 5971
14: 6 ready his chariot, and took his **p** with him: 5971
14:13 Moses said unto the **p**, Fear ye not, 5971
14:31 the **p** feared the LORD, and believed 5971
15:13 Thou in thy mercy hast led forth the **p** 5971
15:14 The **p** shall hear, *and* be afraid: 5971
15:16 till thy **p** pass over, O LORD, till 5971
15:16 pass over, O LORD, till the **p** pass over, 5971
15:24 the **p** murmured against Moses, saying, 5971
16: 4 the **p** shall go out and gather a certain rate 5971
16:27 *that* there went out *some* of the **p** on 5971
16:30 So the **p** rested on the seventh day. 5971
17: 1 and *there was* no water for the **p** to drink. 5971
17: 2 Wherefore the **p** did chide with Moses, and 5971
17: 3 the **p** thirsted there for water; and 5971
17: 3 the **p** murmured against Moses, and said, 5971
17: 4 What shall I do unto this **p**? 5971
17: 5 Go on before the **p**, and take with thee of 5971
17: 6 come water out of it, that the **p** may drink. 5971
17:13 and his **p** with the edge of the sword. 5971
18: 1 for Israel his **p**, *and* that the LORD had 5971
18:10 who hath delivered the **p** from under 5971
18:13 the morrow, that Moses sat to judge the **p**: 5971
18:13 the **p** stood by Moses from the morning 5971
18:14 father in law saw all that he did to the **p**, 5971
18:14 What *is* this thing that thou doest to the **p**? 5971
18:14 all the **p** stand by thee from morning unto 5971
18:15 Because the **p** come unto me to inquire of 5971
18:18 both thou, and this **p** that *is* with thee: 5971
18:19 be thou for the **p** to God-ward, that thou 5971
18:21 Moreover thou shalt provide out of all the **p** 5971
18:22 let them judge the **p** at all seasons: and 5971
18:23 all this **p** shall also go to their place in 5971
18:25 made them heads over the **p**, rulers of 5971
18:26 they judged the **p** at all seasons: the hard 5971
19: 5 be a peculiar treasure unto me above all **p**: 5971
19: 7 and called for the elders of the **p**, 5971
19: 8 all the **p** answered together, and said, 5971
19: 8 Moses returned the words of the **p** unto 5971
19: 9 that the **p** may hear when I speak with thee, 5971
19: 9 Moses told the words of the **p** unto 5971
19:10 Go unto the **p**, and sanctify them to day and 5971
19:11 in the sight of all the **p** upon mount Sinai. 5971
19:12 thou shalt set bounds unto the **p** round 5971
19:14 went down from the mount unto the **p**, 5971
19:14 unto the people, and sanctified the **p**; 5971
19:15 he said unto the **p**, Be ready against 5971
19:16 that all the **p** that *was* in the camp trembled. 5971
19:17 Moses brought forth the **p** out of the camp 5971
19:21 said unto Moses, Go down, charge the **p**, 5971
19:23 The **p** cannot come up to mount Sinai: 5971
19:24 the **p** break through to come up unto 5971
19:25 So Moses went down unto the **p**, and 5971
20:18 all the **p** saw the thunderings, and 5971
20:18 when the **p** saw *it,* they removed, and 5971
20:20 Moses said unto the **p**, Fear not: for God is 5971
20:21 the **p** stood afar off, and Moses drew near 5971
22:25 If thou lend money to *any of* my **p** *that is* 5971
22:28 revile the gods, nor curse the ruler of thy **p**. 5971
23:11 and lie still; that the poor of thy **p** may eat: 5971
23:27 will destroy all the **p** to whom thou shalt 5971
24: 2 neither shall the **p** go up with him. 5971
24: 3 and told the **p** all the words of the LORD, 5971
24: 3 all the **p** answered *with* one voice, and said, 5971
24: 7 and read in the audience of the **p**: 5971
24: 8 and sprinkled *it* on the **p**, and said, 5971

Ex	30:33	a stranger, shall even be cut off from his **p**.	5971
	30:38	shall even be cut off from his **p**.	5971
	31:14	soul shall be cut off from amongst his **p**.	5971
	32: 1	when the **p** saw that Moses delayed to	5971
	32: 1	the **p** gathered themselves together unto	5971
	32: 3	all the **p** brake off the golden earrings	5971
	32: 6	the **p** sat down to eat and to drink, and	5971
	32: 7	for thy **p**, which thou broughtest out of	5971
	32: 9	I have seen this **p**, and behold, it *is* a	5971
	32: 9	and behold, it *is* a stiffnecked **p**:	5971
	32:11	why doth thy wrath wax hot against thy **p**,	5971
	32:12	and repent of *this* evil against thy **p**.	5971
	32:14	the evil which he thought to do unto his **p**.	5971
	32:17	when Joshua heard the noise of the **p** as	5971
	32:21	What did this **p** unto thee, that thou hast	5971
	32:22	thou knowest the **p**, that they *are set* on	5971
	32:25	when Moses saw that the **p** *were* naked;	5971
	32:28	there fell of the **p** that day about three	5971
	32:30	that Moses said unto the **p**, Ye have sinned	5971
	32:31	this **p** have sinned a great sin, and	5971
	32:34	lead the **p** unto *the place* of which I have	5971
	32:35	the LORD plagued the **p**, because they	5971
	33: 1	the **p** which thou hast brought up out of	5971
	33: 3	midst of thee; for thou *art* a stiffnecked **p**:	5971
	33: 4	when the **p** heard these evil tidings, they	5971
	33: 5	children of Israel, Ye *are* a stiffnecked **p**:	5971
	33: 8	*that* all the **p** rose up, and stood every man	5971
	33:10	all the **p** saw the cloudy pillar stand *at*	5971
	33:10	all the **p** rose up and worshipped,	5971
	33:12	See, thou sayest unto me, Bring up this **p**:	5971
	33:13	and consider that this nation *is* thy **p**.	5971
	33:16	and thy **p** have found grace in thy sight?	5971
	33:16	so shall we be separated, I and thy **p**,	5971
	33:16	from all the **p** that *are* upon the face of	5971
	34: 9	for it *is* a stiffnecked **p**; and pardon our	5971
	34:10	before all thy **p** I will do marvels, such as	5971
	34:10	all the **p** among which thou *art* shall see	5971
	36: 5	The **p** bring much more than enough for	5971
	36: 6	So the **p** were restrained from bringing.	5971
Lev	4: 3	do sin according to the sin of the **p**;	5971
	4:27	if any one of the common **p** sin through	5971
	7:20	even that soul shall be cut off from his **p**.	5971
	7:21	even that soul shall be cut off from his **p**.	5971
	7:25	that eateth *it* shall be cut off from his **p**.	5971
	7:27	even that soul shall be cut off from his **p**.	5971
	9: 7	an atonement for thyself, and for the **p**:	5971
	9: 7	offer the offering of the **p**, and make an	5971
	9:15	which *was* the sin offering for the **p**, and	5971
	9:18	of peace offerings, which *was* for the **p**:	5971
	9:22	Aaron lift up his hand towards the **p**, and	5971
	9:23	and came out, and blessed the **p**:	5971
	9:23	of the LORD appeared unto all the **p**.	5971
	9:24	*which* when all the **p** saw, they shouted,	5971
	10: 3	and before all the **p** I will be glorified.	5971
	10: 6	you die, and lest wrath come upon all the **p**:	5712
	16:15	that *is* for the **p**, and bring his blood within	5971
	16:24	the burnt offering of the **p**, and make an	5971
	16:24	an atonement for himself, and for the **p**.	5971
	16:33	and for all the **p** of the congregation.	5971
	17: 4	that man shall be cut off from among his **p**:	5971
	17: 9	that man shall be cut off from among his **p**.	5971
	17:10	and will cut him off from among his **p**.	5971
	18:29	*them* shall be cut off from among their **p**.	5971
	19: 8	that soul shall be cut off from among his **p**.	5971
	19:16	and down *as* a talebearer among thy **p**:	5971
	19:18	any grudge against the children of thy **p**,	5971
	20: 2	the **p** of the land shall stone him with	5971
	20: 3	and will cut him off from among his **p**;	5971
	20: 4	if the **p** of the land do any ways hide their	5971
	20: 5	with Molech, from among their **p**.	5971
	20: 6	and will cut him off from among his **p**.	5971
	20:17	shall be cut off in the sight of their **p**:	1121+5971
	20:18	them shall be cut off from among their **p**.	5971
	20:24	which have separated you from *other* **p**.	5971
	20:26	have severed you from *other* **p**, that *ye*	5971
	21: 1	none be defiled for the dead among his **p**:	5971
	21: 4	*being* a chief man among his **p**, to profane	5971
	21:14	he shall take a virgin of his own **p** to wife.	5971
	21:15	shall he profane his seed among his **p**:	5971
	23:29	he shall be cut off from among his **p**.	5971
	23:30	same soul will I destroy from among his **p**.	5971
	26:12	and will be your God, and ye shall be my **p**.	5971
Nu	5:21	make thee a curse and an oath among thy **p**,	5971
	5:27	the woman shall be a curse among her **p**.	5971
	9:13	soul shall be cut off from among his **p**:	5971
	11: 1	*when* the **p** complained, it displeased	5971
	11: 2	the **p** cried unto Moses; and when Moses	5971
	11: 8	*And* the **p** went about, and gathered *it,* and	5971
	11:10	Moses heard the **p** weep throughout their	5971
	11:11	that *thou* layest the burden of all this **p**	5971
	11:12	Have I conceived all this **p**? have I	5971
	11:13	should I have flesh to give unto all this **p**?	5971
	11:14	I am not able to bear all this **p** alone,	5971
	11:16	thou knowest to be the elders of the **p**,	5971
	11:17	they shall bear the burden of the **p** with	5971
	11:18	say thou unto the **p**, Sanctify yourselves	5971
	11:21	Moses said, The **p**, amongst whom I *am,*	5971
	11:24	told the **p** the words of the LORD, and	5971
	11:24	the seventy men of the elders of the **p**,	5971
	11:29	would God that all the LORD'S **p** were	5971
	11:32	the **p** stood up all that day, and all *that*	5971
	11:33	of the LORD was kindled against the **p**,	5971
	11:33	the LORD smote the **p** *with* a very great	5971
	11:34	because there they buried the **p** that lusted.	5971
	11:35	*And* the **p** journeyed from	5971
	12:15	the **p** journeyed not till Miriam was	5971
	12:16	afterward the **p** removed from Hazeroth,	5971
	13:18	what it *is;* and the **p** that dwelleth therein,	5971
	13:28	Nevertheless the **p** *be* strong that dwell in	5971
	13:30	Caleb stilled the **p** before Moses, and said,	5971
	13:31	We be not able to go up against the **p**;	5971
	13:32	all the **p** that we saw in it *are* men of a great	5971
	14: 1	and cried; and the **p** wept that night.	5971
	14: 9	neither fear ye the **p** of the land;	5971
	14:11	How long will this **p** provoke me?	5971
	14:13	up this **p** in thy might from among them;)	5971
	14:14	heard that thou LORD *art* among this **p**,	5971
	14:15	Now *if* thou shalt kill *all* this **p** as one man,	5971
	14:16	**p** into the land which he sware unto them,	5971
	14:19	the iniquity of this **p** according unto	5971
	14:19	as thou hast forgiven this **p**, from Egypt	5971
	14:39	of Israel: and the **p** mourned greatly.	5971
	15:26	seeing all the **p** were in ignorance.	5971
	15:30	that soul shall be cut off from among his **p**.	5971
	16:41	saying, Ye have killed the **p** of the LORD.	5971
	16:47	behold, the plague was begun among the **p**:	5971
	16:47	and made an atonement for the **p**.	5971
	20: 1	the **p** abode in Kadesh; and Miriam died	5971
	20: 3	the **p** chode with Moses, and spake, saying,	5971
	20:20	Edom came out against him with much **p**,	5971
	20:24	Aaron shall be gathered unto his **p**: for he	5971
	20:26	Aaron shall be gathered *unto his* **p**, and	NIH
	21: 2	If thou wilt indeed deliver this **p** into my	5971
	21: 4	and the soul of the **p** was much discouraged	5971
	21: 5	the **p** spake against God, and	5971
	21: 6	LORD sent fiery serpents among the **p**,	5971
	21: 6	among the people, and they bit the **p**;	5971
	21: 6	bit the people; and much **p** of Israel died.	5971
	21: 7	Therefore the **p** came to Moses, and said,	5971
	21: 7	from us. And Moses prayed for the **p**.	5971
	21:16	Gather the **p** together, and I will give them	5971
	21:18	the well, the nobles of the **p** digged it,	5971
	21:23	Sihon gathered all his **p** together, and	5971
	21:29	thou art undone, O **p** of Chemosh: he hath	5971
	21:33	he, and all his **p**, to the battle *at* Edrei.	5971
	21:34	into thy hand, and all his **p**, and his land;	5971
	21:35	they smote him, and his sons, and all his **p**,	5971
	22: 3	Moab was sore afraid of the **p**, because	5971
	22: 5	the river *of* the land of the children of his **p**,	5971
	22: 5	Behold, there is a **p** come out from Egypt:	5971
	22: 6	now therefore, I pray thee, curse me this **p**;	5971
	22:11	Behold, *there is* a **p** come out of Egypt,	5971
	22:12	go with them; thou shalt not curse the **p**:	5971
	22:17	I pray thee, curse me this **p**.	5971
	22:41	he might see the utmost part of the **p**.	5971
	23: 9	lo, the **p** shall dwell alone, and shall not be	5971
	23:24	the **p** shall rise up as a great lion, and lift up	5971
	24:14	now behold, I go unto my **p**: come	5971
	24:14	I will advertise thee what this **p** shall do to	5971
	24:14	people shall do to thy **p** in the latter days.	5971
	25: 1	the **p** begun to commit whoredom with	5971
	25: 2	they called the **p** unto the sacrifices of their	5971
	25: 2	the **p** did eat, and bowed down to their	5971
	25: 4	Take all the heads of the **p**, and hang them	5971
	25:15	he *was* head over a **p**, *and* of a chief house in	523
	26: 4	*Take the sum of the* **p**, from twenty years	NIH
	27:13	thou also shalt be gathered unto thy **p**,	5971
	31: 2	afterward shalt thou be gathered unto thy **p**.	5971

Nu 31: 3 Moses spake unto the **p**, saying, Arm some 5971
32:15 and ye shall destroy all this **p**. 5971
33:14 where was no water for the **p** to drink. 5971
Dt 1:28 The **p** *is* greater and taller than we; 5971
2: 4 command thou the **p**, saying, Ye are to pass 5971
2:10 a **p** great, and many, and tall, as 5971
2:16 and dead from among the **p**, 5971
2:21 A **p** great, and many, and tall, as 5971
2:32 he and all his **p**, to fight *at* Jahaz. 5971
2:33 we smote him, and his sons, and all his **p**. 5971
3: 1 he and all his **p**, to battle *at* Edrei. 5971
3: 2 and all his **p**, and his land, into thy hand; 5971
3: 3 Og also, the king of Bashan, and all his **p**: 5971
3:28 for he shall go over before this **p**, and 5971
4: 6 great nation *is* a wise and understanding **p**. 5971
4:10 Gather me the **p** together, and I will make 5971
4:20 to be unto him a **p** of inheritance, as *ye are* 5971
4:33 Did *ever* **p** hear the voice of God speaking 5971
5:28 have heard the voice of the words of this **p**, 5971
6:14 of the gods of the **p** which *are* round about 5971
7: 6 For thou *art* a holy **p** unto the LORD thy 5971
7: 6 chosen thee to be a special **p** unto himself, 5971
7: 6 above all **p** that *are* upon the face of 5971
7: 7 ye were moe in number than any **p**; 5971
7: 7 any people; for ye *were* the fewest of all **p**: 5971
7:14 Thou shalt be blessed above all **p**: 5971
7:16 thou shalt consume all the **p** which 5971
7:19 shall the LORD thy God do unto all the **p** 5971
9: 2 A **p** great and tall, the children of 5971
9: 6 for thou *art* a stiffnecked **p**. 5971
9:12 for thy **p** which thou hast brought forth out 5971
9:13 saying, I have seen this **p**, and behold, it *is* 5971
9:13 and behold, it *is* a stiffnecked **p**: 5971
9:26 destroy not thy **p** and thine inheritance, 5971
9:27 look not unto the stubbornness of this **p**, 5971
9:29 Yet they *are* thy **p** and thine inheritance, 5971
10:11 Arise, take thy journey before the **p**, 5971
10:15 *even* you above all **p**, as *it is* this day. 5971
13: 7 *Namely,* of the gods of the **p** which *are* 5971
13: 9 and afterwards the hand of all the **p**. 5971
14: 2 For thou *art* a holy **p** unto the LORD thy 5971
14: 2 chosen thee to be a peculiar **p** unto himself, 5971
14:21 for thou *art* a holy **p** unto the LORD thy 5971
16:18 they shall judge the **p** *with* just judgment. 5971
17: 7 and afterward the hands of all the **p**. 5971
17:13 all the **p** shall hear, and fear, and do no 5971
17:16 nor cause the **p** to return to Egypt, to 5971
18: 3 this shall be the priest's due from the **p**, 5971
20: 1 and chariots, *and* a **p** more than thou, 5971
20: 2 priest shall approach and speak unto the **p**, 5971
20: 5 the officers shall speak unto the **p**, saying, 5971
20: 8 the officers shall speak further unto the **p**, 5971
20: 9 have made an end of speaking unto the **p**, 5971
20: 9 make captains of the armies to lead the **p**. 5971
20:11 *that* all the **p** that is found therein shall be 5971
20:16 of the cities of these **p**, which the LORD 5971
21: 8 Be merciful, O LORD, unto thy **p** Israel, 5971
21: 8 lay not innocent blood unto thy **p** of 5971
26:15 bless thy **p** Israel, and the land which thou 5971
26:18 avouched thee *this* day to be his peculiar **p**, 5971
26:19 that thou mayest be a holy **p** unto 5971
27: 1 with the elders of Israel commanded the **p**, 5971
27: 9 this day thou art become the **p** of 5971
27:11 Moses charged the **p** the same day, saying, 5971
27:12 stand upon mount Gerizzim to bless the **p**, 5971
27:15 putteth *it* in *a* secret *place.* And all the **p** 5971
27:16 his mother. And all the **p** shall say, Amen. 5971
27:17 And all the **p** shall say, Amen. 5971
27:18 of the way. And all the **p** shall say, Amen. 5971
27:19 and widow. And all the **p** shall say, Amen. 5971
27:20 And all the **p** shall say, Amen. 5971
27:21 *of* beast. And all the **p** shall say, Amen. 5971
27:22 his mother. And all the **p** shall say, Amen. 5971
27:23 in law. And all the **p** shall say, Amen. 5971
27:24 And all the **p** shall say, Amen. 5971
27:25 And all the **p** shall say, Amen. 5971
27:26 to do them. And all the **p** shall say, Amen. 5971
28: 9 The LORD shall establish thee a holy **p** 5971
28:10 all **p** of the earth shall see that thou art 5971
28:32 thy daughters *shall be* given unto another **p**, 5971
28:64 the LORD shall scatter thee among all **p**, 5971
29:13 That he may establish thee to day for a **p** 5971
31: 7 for thou must go with this **p** unto the land 5971
31:12 Gather the **p** together, men, and women, 5971
31:16 this **p** will rise up, and go a whoring after 5971
32: 6 the LORD, O foolish **p** and unwise? 5971
32: 8 he set the bounds of the **p** according to 5971
32: 9 For the LORD'S portion *is* his **p**; Jacob *is* 5971
32:21 to jealousy with *those which are* not a **p**; 5971
32:36 For the LORD shall judge his **p**, and 5971
32:43 Rejoice, O ye nations, *with* his **p**: for he 5971
32:43 will be merciful *unto* his land, *and to* his **p**. 5971
32:44 the words of this song in the ears of the **p**, 5971
32:50 thou goest up, and be gathered unto thy **p**; 5971
32:50 in mount Hor, and was gathered unto his **p**: 5971
33: 3 Yea, he loved the **p**; all his saints *are* in thy 5971
33: 5 when the heads of the **p** *and* the tribes of 5971
33: 7 voice of Judah, and bring him unto his **p**: 5971
33:17 with them he shall push the **p** together *to* 5971
33:19 They shall call the **p** *unto* the mountain; 5971
33:21 he came *with* the heads of the **p**, 5971
33:29 *is* like unto thee, O **p** saved by the LORD, 5971
Jos 1: 2 go over this Jordan, thou, and all this **p**, 5971
1: 6 for unto this **p** shalt thou divide for an 5971
1:10 Joshua commanded the officers of the **p**, 5971
1:11 command the **p**, saying, Prepare you 5971
3: 3 they commanded the **p**, saying, When ye 5971
3: 5 Joshua said unto the **p**, Sanctify yourselves: 5971
3: 6 of the covenant, and pass over before the **p**. 5971
3: 6 ark of the covenant, and went before the **p**. 5971
3:14 when the **p** removed from their tents, 5971
3:14 the ark *of* the covenant before the **p**; 5971
3:16 and the **p** passed over right against Jericho. 5971
3:17 all the **p** were passed clean over Jordan. 1471
4: 1 when all the **p** were clean passed over 1471
4: 2 Take you twelve men out of the **p**, out of 5971
4:10 commanded Joshua to speak unto the **p**, 5971
4:10 and the **p** hasted and passed over. 5971
4:11 when all the **p** were clean passed over, 5971
4:11 and the priests, in the presence of the **p**. 5971
4:19 the **p** came up out of Jordan on the tenth 5971
4:24 That all the **p** of the earth might know 5971
5: 4 All the **p** that came out of Egypt, *that were* 5971
5: 5 Now all the **p** that came out were 5971
5: 5 all the **p** *that were* born in the wilderness by 5971
5: 6 till all the **p** *that were* men of war, 1471
5: 8 when they had done circumcising all the **p**, 1471
6: 5 all the **p** shall shout *with* a great shout; 5971
6: 5 the **p** shall ascend up every man straight 5971
6: 7 he said unto the **p**, Pass on, and 5971
6: 8 when Joshua had spoken unto the **p**, 5971
6:10 Joshua had commanded the **p**, saying, 5971
6:16 the trumpets, Joshua said unto the **p**, Shout; 5971
6:20 So the **p** shouted when *the priests* blew 5971
6:20 when the **p** heard the sound of the trumpet, 5971
6:20 the **p** shouted *with* a great shout, that 5971
6:20 so that the **p** went up into the city, 5971
7: 3 and said unto him, Let not all the **p** go up; 5971
7: 3 *and* make not all the **p** to labour thither; 5971
7: 4 So there went up thither of the **p** about 5971
7: 5 wherefore the hearts of the **p** melted, and 5971
7: 7 wherefore hast thou at all brought this **p** 5971
7:13 Up, sanctify the **p**, and say, 5971
8: 1 take all the **p** of war with thee, and arise, 5971
8: 1 of Ai, and his **p**, and his city, and his land: 5971
8: 3 So Joshua arose, and all the **p** of war, to go 5971
8: 5 I, and all the **p** that *are* with me, 5971
8: 9 but Joshua lodged that night among the **p**. 5971
8:10 numbered the **p**, and went up, he and 5971
8:10 and the elders of Israel, before the **p** *to* Ai. 5971
8:11 all the **p**, *even the people* of war that *were* 5971
8:11 *even the* **p** of war that *were* with him, NIH
8:13 when they had set the **p**, *even* all the host 5971
8:14 he and all his **p**, at a time appointed, before 5971
8:16 all the **p** that *were* in Ai were called 5971
8:20 the **p** that fled *to* the wilderness turned back 5971
8:33 that they should bless the **p** of Israel. 5971
10: 7 he, and all the **p** of war with him, and 5971
10:13 until the **p** had avenged themselves upon 1471
10:21 all the **p** returned to the camp to Joshua *at* 5971
10:33 Joshua smote him and his **p**, until *he* had 5971
11: 4 they and all their hosts with them, much **p**, 5971
11: 7 Joshua came, and all the **p** of war with him, 5971
14: 8 up with me made the heart of the **p** melt: 5971
17:14 one portion to inherit, seeing I *am* a great **p**, 5971
17:15 If thou *be* a great **p**, *then* get thee up to 5971
17:17 Thou *art* a great **p**, and hast great power: 5971
24: 2 Joshua said unto all the **p**, Thus saith 5971

Jos 24:16 the **p** answered and said, God forbid that 5971
24:17 among all the **p** through whom we passed: 5971
24:18 LORD drave out from before us all the **p**, 5971
24:19 Joshua said unto the **p**, Ye cannot serve 5971
24:21 the **p** said unto Joshua, Nay; but we will 5971
24:22 Joshua said unto the **p**, Ye *are* witnesses 5971
24:24 the **p** said unto Joshua, The LORD our 5971
24:25 So Joshua made a covenant with the **p** that 5971
24:27 Joshua said unto all the **p**, Behold, this 5971
24:28 So Joshua let the **p** depart, every man unto 5971
Jdg 1:16 and they went and dwelt among the **p**. 5971
2: 4 that the **p** lift up their voice, and wept. 5971
2: 6 when Joshua had let the **p** go, the children 5971
2: 7 the **p** served the LORD all the days of 5971
2:12 of the gods of the **p** that *were* round about 5971
2:20 Because that this **p** hath transgressed my 1471
3:18 he sent away the **p** that bare the present. 5971
4:13 of iron, and all the **p** that *were* with him, 5971
5: 2 when the **p** willingly offered themselves. 5971
5: 9 offered themselves willingly among the **p**. 5971
5:11 shall the **p** of the LORD go down to 5971
5:13 dominion over the nobles *among* the **p**: 5971
5:14 after thee, Benjamin, among thy **p**; out of 5971
5:18 Naphtali *were* a **p** *that* jeoparded their lives 5971
7: 1 all the **p** that *were* with him, rose up early, 5971
7: 2 The **p** that *are* with thee *are* too many for 5971
7: 3 go to, proclaim in the ears of the **p**, 5971
7: 3 there returned of the **p** twenty and 5971
7: 4 said unto Gideon, The **p** *are* yet *too* many; 5971
7: 5 So he brought down the **p** unto the water: 5971
7: 6 all the rest of the **p** bowed down upon their 5971
7: 7 let all the *other* **p** go every man unto his 5971
7: 8 So the **p** took victuals in their hand, and 5971
8: 5 loaves of bread unto the **p** that follow me; 5971
9:29 would to God this **p** were under my hand; 5971
9:32 thou and the **p** that *is* with thee, *and* lie in 5971
9:33 the **p** that *is* with him come out against 5971
9:34 all the **p** that *were* with him, by night, and 5971
9:35 the **p** that *were* with him, from lying in 5971
9:36 And when Gaal saw the **p**, he said to Zebul, 5971
9:36 there come **p** down from the top of 5971
9:37 See there come **p** down by the middle of 5971
9:38 *is* not this the **p** that thou hast despised? go 5971
9:42 that the **p** went out *into* the field; 5971
9:43 he took the **p**, and divided them into three 5971
9:43 the **p** *were* come forth out of the city; 5971
9:44 the two *other* companies ran upon all *the* **p** NIH
9:45 slew the **p** that *was* therein, and beat down 5971
9:48 he and all the **p** that *were* with him; 5971
9:48 and said unto the **p** that *were* with him, 5971
9:49 all the **p** likewise cut down every man his 5971
10:18 the **p** *and* princes of Gilead said one to 5971
11:11 the **p** made him head and captain over 5971
11:20 Sihon gathered all his **p** together, and 5971
11:21 and all his **p** into the hand of Israel, 5971
11:23 the Amorites from before his **p** Israel, 5971
12: 2 my **p** were at great strife with the children 5971
14: 3 of thy brethren, or among all my **p**, 5971
14:16 put forth a riddle unto the children of my **p**, 5971
14:17 she told the riddle to the children of her **p**. 5971
16:24 when the **p** saw him, they praised their god: 5971
16:30 and upon all the **p** that *were* therein. 5971
18: 7 to Laish, and saw the **p** that *were* therein, 5971
18:10 ye shall come unto a **p** secure, and to a 5971
18:20 and went in the midst of the **p**. 5971
18:27 unto a **p** *that were* at quiet and secure: 5971
20: 2 the chief of all the **p**, *even* of all the tribes 5971
20: 2 themselves in the assembly of the **p** of God, 5971
20: 8 all the **p** arose as one man, saying, We will 5971
20:10 to fetch victual for the **p**, that *they* may do, 5971
20:16 Among all this **p** *there were* seven hundred 5971
20:22 the **p** the men of Israel encouraged 5971
20:26 all the **p**, went up, and came *unto* the house 5971
20:31 of Benjamin went out against the **p**, 5971
20:31 they began to smite of the **p**, *and* kill, as at 5971
21: 2 the **p** came *to* the house of God, and 5971
21: 4 that the **p** rose early, and built there an 5971
21: 9 For the **p** were numbered, and behold, 5971
21:15 the **p** repented them for Benjamin, because 5971
Ru 1: 6 had visited his **p** in giving them bread. 5971
1:10 Surely we will return with thee unto thy **p**. 5971
1:15 thy sister in law is gone back unto her **p**, 5971
1:16 thy **p** *shall be* my people, and thy God my 5971
1:16 thy people *shall be* my **p**, and thy God my 5971
2:11 art come unto a **p** which thou knewest not 5971
3:11 for all the city of my **p** doth know that thou 5971
4: 4 and before the elders of my **p**. 5971
4: 9 *unto* all the **p**, Ye *are* witnesses *this* day, 5971
4:11 all the **p** that *were* in the gate, and 5971
1Sa 2:13 the priests' custom with the **p** *was, that* 5971
2:23 for I hear of your evil dealings by all this **p**. 5971
2:24 *ye* make the LORD'S **p** to transgress. 5971
2:29 chiefest of all the offerings of Israel my **p**? 5971
4: 3 when the **p** were come into the camp, 5971
4: 4 So the **p** sent *to* Shiloh, that they might 5971
4:17 been also a great slaughter among the **p**, 5971
5:10 the God of Israel to us, to slay us and our **p**. 5971
5:11 his own place, that it slay us not, and our **p**: 5971
6: 6 did they not let **the p** go, and 3963.1
6:19 even he smote of the **p** fifty thousand 5971
6:19 the **p** lamented, because the LORD had 5971
6:19 the LORD had smitten *many* of the **p** *with* 5971
8: 7 Hearken unto the voice of the **p** in all that 5971
8:10 unto the **p** that asked of him a king. 5971
8:19 Nevertheless the **p** refused to obey 5971
8:21 Samuel heard all the words of the **p**, and 5971
9: 2 upward *he was* higher than any of the **p**. 5971
9:12 for *there is* a sacrifice of the **p** to day in 5971
9:13 for the **p** will not eat until he come, because 5971
9:16 anoint him to be captain over my **p** Israel, 5971
9:16 that *he* may save my **p** out of the hand of 5971
9:16 for I have looked upon my **p**, because 5971
9:17 to thee of: this *same* shall reign over my **p**. 5971
9:24 for thee since *I* said, I have invited the **p**. 5971
10:11 the prophets, then the **p** said one to another, 5971
10:17 Samuel called the **p** together unto 5971
10:23 when he stood among the **p**, he was higher 5971
10:23 he was higher than any of the **p** from his 5971
10:24 Samuel said to all the **p**, See ye him whom 5971
10:24 that *there is* none like him among all the **p**? 5971
10:24 all the **p** shouted, and said, God save 5971
10:25 Samuel told the **p** the manner of 5971
10:25 Samuel sent all the **p** away, every man to 5971
11: 4 and told the tidings in the ears of the **p**: 5971
11: 4 and all the **p** lift up their voices, and wept. 5971
11: 5 Saul said, What aileth the **p** that they weep? 5971
11: 7 the fear of the LORD fell on the **p**, and 5971
11:11 that Saul put the **p** *in* three companies; 5971
11:12 the **p** said unto Samuel, Who *is* he that said, 5971
11:14 said Samuel to the **p**, Come, and let us go 5971
11:15 all the **p** went *to* Gilgal; and there they 5971
12: 6 Samuel said unto the **p**, *It is* the LORD 5971
12:18 all the **p** greatly feared the LORD and 5971
12:19 all the **p** said unto Samuel, Pray for thy 5971
12:20 Samuel said unto the **p**, Fear not: ye have 5971
12:22 For the LORD will not forsake his **p** for 5971
12:22 hath pleased the LORD to make you his **p**. 5971
13: 2 the rest of the **p** he sent every man to his 5971
13: 4 the **p** were called together after Saul *to* 5971
13: 5 **p** as the sand which *is* on the sea shore in 5971
13: 6 were in a strait, (for the **p** were distressed,) 5971
13: 6 the **p** did hide themselves in caves, and 5971
13: 7 and all the **p** followed him trembling. 5971
13: 8 and the **p** were scattered from him. 5971
13:11 Because I saw that the **p** were scattered 5971
13:14 commanded him to be captain over his **p**, 5971
13:15 Saul numbered the **p** that were present with 5971
13:16 and the **p** that were present with them, 5971
13:22 the hand of any of the **p** that *were* with Saul 5971
14: 2 the **p** that *were* with him *were* about six 5971
14: 3 the **p** knew not that Jonathan was gone. 5971
14:15 the host, in the field, and among all the **p**: 5971
14:17 said Saul unto the **p** that *were* with him, 5971
14:20 all the **p** that *were* with him assembled 5971
14:24 for Saul had adjured the **p**, saying, 5971
14:24 So none of the **p** tasted *any* food. 5971
14:26 when the **p** were come into the wood, 5971
14:26 to his mouth: for the **p** feared the oath. 5971
14:27 his father charged the **p** with the oath: 5971
14:28 answered one of the **p**, and said, Thy father 5971
14:28 Thy father straitly charged the **p** with an 5971
14:28 *any* food *this* day. And the **p** were faint. 5971
14:30 if haply the **p** had eaten freely to day of 5971
14:31 to Aijalon: and the **p** were very faint. 5971
14:32 the **p** flew upon the spoil, and took sheep, 5971
14:32 and the **p** did eat *them* with the blood. 5971
14:33 Behold, the **p** sin against the LORD, 5971
14:34 Disperse yourselves among the **p**, and 5971

1Sa 14:34 all the **p** brought every man his ox with him 5971
14:38 Draw ye near hither, all the chief of the **p**: 5971
14:39 *there was* not *a man* among all the **p** *that* 5971
14:40 the **p** said unto Saul, Do what seemeth 5971
14:41 Jonathan were taken: but the **p** escaped. 5971
14:45 the **p** said unto Saul, Shall Jonathan die, 5971
14:45 So the **p** rescued Jonathan, that he died not. 5971
15: 1 sent me to anoint thee to be king over his **p**, 5971
15: 4 Saul gathered the **p** together, and 5971
15: 8 utterly destroyed all the **p** with the edge of 5971
15: 9 Saul and the **p** spared Agag, and the best of 5971
15:15 for the **p** spared the best of the sheep and 5971
15:21 the **p** took of the spoil, sheep and oxen, 5971
15:24 because I feared the **p**, and obeyed their 5971
15:30 before the elders of my **p**, and before Israel, 5971
17:27 the **p** answered him after this manner, 5971
17:30 the **p** answered him again after the former 5971
18: 5 he was accepted in the sight of all the **p**, 5971
18:13 and he went out and came in before the **p**. 5971
23: 8 Saul called all the **p** together to war, to go 5971
26: 5 and the **p** pitched round about him. 5971
26: 7 and Abishai came to the **p** by night: 5971
26: 7 but Abner and the **p** lay round about him. 5971
26:14 David cried to the **p**, and to Abner the son 5971
26:15 for there came one of the **p** in to destroy 5971
27:12 He hath made his **p** Israel utterly to abhor 5971
30: 4 the **p** that *were* with him lift up their voice 5971
30: 6 for the **p** spake of stoning him, because 5971
30: 6 because the soul of all the **p** was grieved, 5971
30:21 and to meet the **p** that *were* with him: 5971
30:21 when David came near to the **p**, he saluted 5971
31: 9 the house of their idols, and among the **p**. 5971
2Sa 1: 4 That the **p** are fled from the battle, and 5971
1: 4 and many of the **p** also are fallen and dead; 5971
1:12 for the **p** of the LORD, and for the house 5971
2:26 ere thou bid the **p** return from following 5971
2:27 in the morning the **p** had gone up every one 5971
2:28 all the **p** stood still, and pursued after Israel 5971
2:30 when he had gathered all the **p** together, 5971
3:18 **p** Israel out of the hand of the Philistines, 5971
3:31 to all the **p** that *were* with him, Rent your 5971
3:32 at the grave of Abner; and all the **p** wept. 5971
3:34 And all the **p** wept again over him. 5971
3:35 when all the **p** came to cause David to eat 5971
3:36 all the **p** took notice *of it,* and it pleased 5971
3:36 whatsoever the king did, pleased all the **p**. 5971
3:37 For all the **p** and all Israel understood that 5971
5: 2 Thou shalt feed my **p** Israel, and thou shalt 5971
5:12 that he had exalted his kingdom for his **p** 5971
6: 2 went with all the **p** that *were* with him from 5971
6:18 he blessed the **p** in the name of the LORD 5971
6:19 he dealt among all the **p**, *even* among 5971
6:19 a flagon *of wine.* So all the **p** departed 5971
6:21 to appoint me ruler over the **p** of 5971
7: 7 whom I commanded to feed my **p** Israel, 5971
7: 8 to be ruler over my **p**, over Israel: 5971
7:10 Moreover I will appoint a place for my **p** 5971
7:11 commanded judges *to be* over my **p** Israel, 5971
7:23 what one nation in the earth *is* like thy **p**, 5971
7:23 whom God went to redeem for a **p** to 5971
7:23 and terrible, for thy land, before thy **p**, 5971
7:24 For thou hast confirmed to thyself thy **p** 5971
7:24 people Israel to be a **p** unto thee for ever; 5971
8:15 and justice unto all his **p**. 5971
10:10 the rest of the **p** he delivered into the hand 5971
10:12 let us play the men for our **p**, and for 5971
10:13 drew nigh, and the **p** that *were* with him, 5971
11: 7 how the **p** did, and how the war prospered. 5971
11:17 there fell *some* of the **p** of the servants of 5971
12:28 therefore gather the rest of the **p** together, 5971
12:29 David gathered all the **p** together, and 5971
12:31 he brought forth the **p** that *were* therein, 5971
12:31 and all the **p** returned *unto* Jerusalem. 5971
13:34 there came much **p** by the way of the hill 5971
14:13 hast thou thought such a thing against the **p** 5971
14:15 *it is* because the **p** have made me afraid: 5971
15:12 for the **p** increased continually with 5971
15:17 all the **p** after him, and tarried *in* a place 5971
15:23 a loud voice, and all the **p** passed over: 5971
15:23 all the **p** passed over, toward the way of 5971
15:24 until all the **p** had done passing out of 5971
15:30 all the **p** that *was* with him covered every 5971
16: 6 all the **p** and all the mighty *men were* on 5971
16:14 all the **p** that *were* with him, came weary, 5971
16:15 and all the **p** the men of Israel, 5971
16:18 this **p**, and all the men of Israel, choose, 5971
17: 2 all the **p** that *are* with him shall flee; and 5971
17: 3 I will bring back all the **p** unto thee: 5971
17: 3 if all returned: *so* all the **p** shall be *in* peace. 5971
17: 8 a man of war, and will not lodge with the **p**. 5971
17: 9 There is a slaughter among the **p** that 5971
17:16 and all the **p** that *are* with him. 5971
17:22 all the **p** that *were* with him, and 5971
17:29 and for the **p** that *were* with him, to eat: 5971
17:29 The **p** *is* hungry, and weary, and thirsty, 5971
18: 1 David numbered the **p** that *were* with him, 5971
18: 2 David sent forth a third part of the **p** under 5971
18: 2 the king said unto the **p**, I will surely go 5971
18: 3 the **p** answered, Thou shalt not go forth: 5971
18: 4 all the **p** came out by hundreds and 5971
18: 5 all the **p** heard when the king gave all 5971
18: 6 So the **p** went out *into* the field against 5971
18: 7 Where the **p** of Israel were slain before 5971
18: 8 the wood devoured more **p** that day than 5971
18:16 the **p** returned from pursuing after Israel: 5971
18:16 after Israel: for Joab held back the **p**. 5971
19: 2 was *turned* into mourning unto all the **p**: 5971
19: 2 for the **p** heard say that day *how* the king 5971
19: 3 the **p** gat them by stealth that day *into* 5971
19: 3 as **p** being ashamed steal away when they 5971
19: 8 they told unto all the **p**, saying, Behold, 5971
19: 8 all the **p** came before the king: for Israel 5971
19: 9 all the **p** were at strife throughout all 5971
19:39 all the **p** went over Jordan. And when 5971
19:40 all the **p** of Judah conducted the king, and 5971
19:40 the king, and also half the **p** of Israel. 5971
20:12 when the man saw that all the **p** stood still, 5971
20:13 all the **p** went on after Joab, to pursue after 376
20:15 all the **p** that *were* with Joab battered 5971
20:22 the woman went unto all the **p** in her 5971
22:28 the afflicted **p** thou wilt save: but thine eyes 5971
22:44 delivered me from the strivings of my **p**, 5971
22:44 a **p** *which* I knew not shall serve me. 5971
22:48 and that bringeth down the **p** under me, 5971
23:10 the **p** returned after him only to spoil. 5971
23:11 and the **p** fled from the Philistines. 5971
24: 2 even to Beer-sheba, and number ye the **p**, 5971
24: 2 that I may know the number of the **p**. 5971
24: 3 Now the LORD thy God add unto the **p**, 5971
24: 4 of the king, to number the **p** *of* Israel. 5971
24: 9 sum of the number of the **p** unto the king: 5971
24:10 him after that he had numbered the **p**. 5971
24:15 there died of the **p** from Dan even to 5971
24:16 said to the angel that destroyed the **p**, *It is* 5971
24:17 when he saw the angel that smote the **p**, 5971
24:21 that the plague may be stayed from the **p**. 5971
1Ki 1:39 and all the **p** said, God save king Solomon. 5971
1:40 all the **p** came up after him, and the people 5971
1:40 the **p** piped with pipes, and rejoiced *with* 5971
3: 2 Only the **p** sacrificed in high places, 5971
3: 8 thy servant *is* in the midst of thy **p** which 5971
3: 8 a great **p**, that cannot be numbered nor 5971
3: 9 an understanding heart to judge thy **p**, 5971
3: 9 who is able to judge this thy *so* great a **p**? 5971
4:34 there came of all **p** to hear the wisdom of 5971
5: 7 unto David a wise son over this great **p**. 5971
5:16 which ruled over the **p** that wrought in 5971
6:13 of Israel, and will not forsake my **p** Israel. 5971
8:16 Since the day that I brought forth my **p** 5971
8:16 but I chose David to be over my **p** Israel. 5971
8:30 of thy **p** Israel, when they shall pray 5971
8:33 When thy **p** Israel be smitten down before 5971
8:34 forgive the sin of thy **p** Israel, and 5971
8:36 the sin of thy servants, and of thy **p** Israel, 5971
8:36 which thou hast given to thy **p** for an 5971
8:38 be *made* by any man, *or* by all thy **p** Israel, 5971
8:41 that *is* not of thy **p** Israel, but cometh out of 5971
8:43 that all **p** of the earth may know thy name, 5971
8:43 thy name, to fear thee, as *do* thy **p** Israel; 5971
8:44 If thy **p** go out to battle against their 5971
8:50 forgive thy **p** that have sinned against thee, 5971
8:51 For they *be* thy **p**, and thine inheritance, 5971
8:52 unto the supplication of thy **p** Israel, 5971
8:53 them from among all the **p** of the earth, 5971
8:56 that hath given rest unto his **p** Israel, 5971
8:59 the cause of his **p** Israel at all times, as 5971
8:60 That all the **p** of the earth may know that 5971
8:66 On the eighth day he sent the **p** away: and 5971

1Ki	8:66	for David his servant, and for Israel his **p**.	5971
	9: 7	be a proverb and a byword among all **p**:	5971
	9:20	*And* all the **p** that were left of the Amorites,	5971
	9:23	which bare rule over the **p** that wrought in	5971
	12: 5	then come again to me. And the **p** departed.	5971
	12: 6	do you advise that *I* may answer this **p**?	5971
	12: 7	If thou wilt be a servant unto this **p** *this*	5971
	12: 9	counsel give ye that we may answer this **p**,	5971
	12:10	Thus shalt thou speak unto this **p** that spake	5971
	12:12	all the **p** came to Rehoboam the third day,	5971
	12:13	the king answered the **p** roughly, and	5971
	12:15	the king hearkened not unto the **p**;	5971
	12:16	the **p** answered the king, saying,	5971
	12:23	and *to* the remnant of the **p**, saying,	5971
	12:27	If this **p** go up to do sacrifice in the house	5971
	12:27	shall the heart of this **p** turn again unto their	5971
	12:30	for the **p** went *to worship* before the one,	5971
	12:31	made priests of the lowest of the **p**,	5971
	13:33	made again of the lowest of the **p** priests of	5971
	14: 2	told me that I should be king over this **p**.	5971
	14: 7	as I exalted thee from among the **p**,	5971
	14: 7	and made thee prince over my **p** Israel,	5971
	16: 2	and made thee prince over my **p** Israel;	5971
	16: 2	hast made my **p** Israel to sin, to provoke me	5971
	16:15	the **p** *were* encamped against Gibbethon,	5971
	16:16	the **p** that *were* encamped heard say,	5971
	16:21	were the **p** of Israel divided into two parts:	5971
	16:21	half of the **p** followed Tibni the son of	5971
	16:22	the **p** that followed Omri prevailed against	5971
	16:22	the **p** that followed Tibni the son of Ginath:	5971
	18:21	Elijah came unto all the **p**, and said, How	5971
	18:21	And the **p** answered him not a word.	5971
	18:22	said Elijah unto the **p**, I, *even* I only,	5971
	18:24	all the **p** answered and said, It is well	5971
	18:30	Elijah said unto all the **p**, Come near unto	5971
	18:30	all the **p** came near unto him. And he	5971
	18:37	that this **p** may know that thou *art*	5971
	18:39	when all the **p** saw *it,* they fell on their	5971
	19:21	and gave unto the **p**, and they did eat.	5971
	20: 8	all the elders and all the **p** said unto him,	5971
	20:10	for handfuls for all the **p** that follow me.	5971
	20:15	after them he numbered all the **p**, *even* all	5971
	20:42	go for his life, and thy **p** for his people.	5971
	20:42	go for his life, and thy people for his **p**.	5971
	21: 9	a fast, and set Naboth on high among the **p**:	5971
	21:12	a fast, and set Naboth on high among the **p**.	5971
	21:13	in the presence of the **p**, saying,	5971
	22: 4	I *am* as thou *art,* my **p** as thy people, my	5971
	22: 4	I *am* as thou *art,* my people as thy **p**, my	5971
	22:28	he said, Hearken, O **p**, every one of you.	5971
	22:43	*for* the **p** offered and burnt incense yet in	5971
2Ki	3: 7	I *am* as thou *art,* my **p** as thy people, *and*	5971
	3: 7	I *am* as thou *art,* my people as thy **p**, *and*	5971
	4:13	she answered, I dwell among mine own **p**.	5971
	4:41	he said, Pour out for the **p**, that they may	5971
	4:42	he said, Give unto the **p**, that they may eat.	5971
	4:43	He said again, Give the **p**, that they may	5971
	6:18	said, Smite this **p**, I pray thee,	1471
	6:30	the wall, and the **p** looked, and behold,	5971
	7:16	the **p** went out, and spoiled the tents of	5971
	7:17	the **p** trode upon him in the gate, and	5971
	7:20	for the **p** trode upon him in the gate, and	5971
	8:21	the chariots: and the **p** fled into their tents.	5971
	9: 6	I have anointed thee king over the **p** of	5971
	10: 9	stood, and said to all the **p**, Ye *be*	5971
	10:18	Jehu gathered all the **p** together, and	5971
	11:13	heard the noise of the guard *and* of the **p**,	5971
	11:13	she came to the **p** *into* the temple of	5971
	11:14	all the **p** of the land rejoiced, and blew with	5971
	11:17	the LORD and the king and the **p**,	5971
	11:17	that *they* should be the LORD'S **p**;	5971
	11:17	between the king also and the **p**.	5971
	11:18	all the **p** of the land went *into* the house of	5971
	11:19	and the guard, and all the **p** of the land;	5971
	11:20	all the **p** of the land rejoiced, and the city	5971
	12: 3	the **p** still sacrificed and burnt incense in	5971
	12: 8	to receive no *more* money of the **p**,	5971
	13: 7	Neither did he leave *of* the **p** to Jehoahaz	5971
	14: 4	as yet the **p** did sacrifice and burnt incense	5971
	14:21	all the **p** of Judah took Azariah, which *was*	5971
	15: 4	the **p** sacrificed and burnt incense still on	5971
	15: 5	over the house, judging the **p** of the land.	5971
	15:10	smote him before the **p**, and slew him, and	5971
	15:35	the **p** sacrificed and burnt incense still in	5971
	16: 9	carried *the p of* it captive to Kir, and slew	NIH
	16:15	with the burnt offering of all the **p** of	5971
	18:26	in the ears of the **p** that *are* on the wall.	5971
	18:36	the **p** held their peace, and answered him	5971
	20: 5	and tell Hezekiah the captain of my **p**,	5971
	21:24	the **p** of the land slew all them that had	5971
	21:24	the **p** of the land made Josiah his son king	5971
	22: 4	keepers of the door have gathered of the **p**:	5971
	22:13	for me, and for the **p**, and for all Judah,	5971
	23: 2	and all the **p**, both small and great:	5971
	23: 3	And all the **p** stood to the covenant.	5971
	23: 6	upon the graves of the children of the **p**.	5971
	23:21	the king commanded all the **p**, saying,	5971
	23:30	the **p** of the land took Jehoahaz the son of	5971
	23:35	the silver and the gold of the **p** of the land,	5971
	24:14	save the poorest sort of the **p** of the land.	5971
	25: 3	there was no bread for the **p** of the land.	5971
	25:11	Now the rest of the **p** that were left in	5971
	25:19	which mustered the **p** of the land, and	5971
	25:19	threescore men of the **p** of the land that	5971
	25:22	*as for* the **p** that remained in the land of	5971
	25:26	all the **p**, both small and great, and	5971
1Ch	5:25	went a whoring after the gods of the **p** of	5971
	10: 9	carry tidings unto their idols, and to the **p**.	5971
	11: 2	Thou shalt feed my **p** Israel, and thou shalt	5971
	11: 2	and thou shalt be ruler over my **p** Israel.	5971
	11:13	and the **p** fled from before the Philistines.	5971
	13: 4	the thing was right in the eyes of all the **p**.	5971
	14: 2	*was* lift up on high, because of his **p** Israel.	5971
	16: 2	he blessed the **p** in the name of	5971
	16: 8	make known his deeds among the **p**.	5971
	16:20	and from *one* kingdom to another **p**;	5971
	16:26	For all the gods of the **p** *are* idols: but	5971
	16:28	unto the LORD, ye kindreds of the **p**,	5971
	16:36	all the **p** said, Amen, and praised	5971
	16:43	all the **p** departed every man to his house:	5971
	17: 6	whom I commanded to feed my **p**, saying,	5971
	17: 7	that *thou* shouldest be ruler over my **p**	5971
	17: 9	Also I will ordain a place for my **p** Israel,	5971
	17:10	commanded judges *to be* over my **p** Israel.	5971
	17:21	what one nation in the earth *is* like thy **p**	5971
	17:21	whom God went to redeem *to be* his own **p**,	5971
	17:21	by driving out nations from before thy **p**,	5971
	17:22	For thy **p** Israel didst thou make thine own	5971
	17:22	Israel didst thou make thine own **p** for ever;	5971
	18:14	and justice among all his **p**.	5971
	19: 7	and the king of Maachah and his **p**;	5971
	19:11	the rest of the **p** he delivered unto the hand	5971
	19:13	let us behave ourselves valiantly for our **p**,	5971
	19:14	the **p** that *were* with him drew nigh before	5971
	20: 3	he brought out the **p** that *were* in it, and	5971
	20: 3	and all the **p** returned *to* Jerusalem.	5971
	21: 2	said to Joab and to the rulers of the **p**,	5971
	21: 3	The LORD make his **p** an hundred times	5971
	21: 5	Joab gave the sum of the number of the **p**	5971
	21:17	*Is it* not I *that* commanded the **p** to be	5971
	21:17	not on thy **p**, that *they* should be plagued.	5971
	21:22	that the plague may be stayed from the **p**.	5971
	22:18	before the LORD, and before his **p**.	5971
	23:25	God of Israel hath given rest unto his **p**,	5971
	28: 2	and said, Hear me, my brethren, and my **p**:	5971
	28:21	all the **p** *will be* wholly at thy	5971
	29: 9	the **p** rejoiced, for that they offered	5971
	29:14	who *am* I, and what *is* my **p**, that we should	5971
	29:17	and now have I seen with joy thy **p**,	5971
	29:18	of the thoughts of the heart of thy **p**,	5971
2Ch	1: 9	for thou hast made me king over a **p** like	5971
	1:10	that I may go out and come in before this **p**:	5971
	1:10	for who can judge this thy **p**, *that is so*	5971
	1:11	for thyself, that thou mayest judge my **p**,	5971
	2:11	Because the LORD hath loved his **p**,	5971
	2:18	six hundred overseers to set the **p** a work.	5971
	6: 5	Since the day that I brought forth my **p** out	5971
	6: 5	I any man to be a ruler over my **p** Israel:	5971
	6: 6	have chosen David to be over my **p** Israel.	5971
	6:21	of thy servant, and of thy **p** Israel,	5971
	6:24	if thy **p** Israel be put to the worse before	5971
	6:25	forgive the sin of thy **p** Israel, and	5971
	6:27	the sin of thy servants, and of thy **p** Israel,	5971
	6:27	which thou hast given unto thy **p** for an	5971
	6:29	or of all thy **p** Israel, when every one shall	5971
	6:32	which *is* not of thy **p** Israel, but is come	5971
	6:33	that all **p** of the earth may know thy name,	5971
	6:33	as *doth* thy **p** Israel, and may know that this	5971

2Ch 6:34 If thy **p** go out to war against their enemies 5971
6:39 forgive thy **p** which have sinned against 5971
7: 4 all the **p** offered sacrifices before 5971
7: 5 and all the **p** dedicated the house of God. 5971
7:10 month he sent the **p** away into their tents, 5971
7:10 and to Solomon, and to Israel his **p**. 5971
7:13 or if I send pestilence among my **p**; 5971
7:14 If my **p**, which are called by my name, 5971
8: 7 *As for* all the **p** that were left of the Hittites, 5971
8:10 and fifty, that bare rule over the **p**. 5971
10: 5 me after three days. And the **p** departed. 5971
10: 6 give ye *me* to return answer to this **p**? 5971
10: 7 If thou be kind to this **p**, and please them, 5971
10: 9 give ye that we may return answer to this **p**, 5971
10:10 Thus shalt thou answer the **p** that spake 5971
10:12 all the **p** came to Rehoboam on the third 5971
10:15 So the king hearkened not unto the **p**: 5971
10:16 the **p** answered the king, saying, 5971
12: 3 the **p** *were* without number that came with 5971
13:17 and his **p** slew them *with* a great slaughter: 5971
14:13 the **p** that *were* with him pursued them unto 5971
16:10 Asa oppressed *some* of the **p** the same time. 5971
17: 9 all the cities of Judah, and taught the **p**. 5971
18: 2 for the **p** that *he had* with him, and 5971
18: 3 I *am* as thou *art,* and my **p** as thy people; 5971
18: 3 I *am* as thou *art,* and my people as thy **p**; 5971
18:27 by me. And he said, Hearken, all ye **p**. 5971
19: 4 he went out again through the **p** from 5971
20: 7 inhabitants of this land before thy **p** Israel, 5971
20:21 when he had consulted with the **p**, he 5971
20:25 his **p** came to take away the spoil of them, 5971
20:33 for as yet the **p** had not prepared their 5971
21:14 a great plague will the LORD smite thy **p**, 5971
21:19 his **p** made no burning for him, like 5971
23: 5 all the **p** *shall be* in the courts of the house 5971
23: 6 all the **p** shall keep the watch of 5971
23:10 he set all the **p**, every man having his 5971
23:12 when Athaliah heard the noise of the **p** 5971
23:12 she came to the **p** *into* the house of 5971
23:13 all the **p** of the land rejoiced, and 5971
23:16 between all the **p**, and between the king, 5971
23:16 that *they* should be the LORD'S **p**. 5971
23:17 all the **p** went *to* the house of Baal, and 5971
23:20 the governors of the **p**, and all the people of 5971
23:20 all the **p** of the land, and brought down 5971
23:21 all the **p** of the land rejoiced: and the city 5971
24:10 all the princes and all the **p** rejoiced, and 5971
24:20 which stood above the **p**, and said unto 5971
24:23 destroyed all the princes of the **p** from 5971
24:23 the princes of the people from among the **p**, 5971
25:11 led forth his **p**, and went *to* the valley of 5971
25:15 hast thou sought after the gods of the **p**, 5971
25:15 which could not deliver their own **p** out of 5971
26: 1 all the **p** of Judah took Uzziah, who *was* 5971
26:21 the king's house, judging the **p** of the land. 5971
27: 2 of the LORD. And the **p** did yet corruptly. 5971
29:36 Hezekiah rejoiced, and all the **p**, that God 5971
29:36 all the people, that God had prepared the **p**: 5971
30: 3 neither had the **p** gathered themselves 5971
30:13 there assembled *at* Jerusalem much **p** to 5971
30:18 For a multitude of the **p**, *even* many of 5971
30:20 hearkened to Hezekiah, and healed the **p**. 5971
30:27 priests the Levites arose and blessed the **p**: 5971
31: 4 Moreover he commanded the **p** that dwelt 5971
31: 8 they blessed the LORD, and his **p** Israel. 5971
31:10 Since *the* **p** began to bring the offerings *into* NIH
31:10 for the LORD hath blessed his **p**; and 5971
32: 4 So there was gathered much **p** together, 5971
32: 6 he set captains of war over the **p**, and 5971
32: 8 the **p** rested themselves upon the words of 5971
32:13 my fathers have done unto all the **p** of *other* 5971
32:14 that could deliver his **p** out of mine hand, 5971
32:15 kingdom was able to deliver his **p** out of 5971
32:17 have not delivered their **p** out of mine hand, 5971
32:17 shall not the God of Hezekiah deliver his **p** 5971
32:18 the **p** of Jerusalem that *were* on the wall, 5971
32:19 as against the gods of the **p** of the earth, 5971
33:10 LORD spake to Manasseh, and to his **p**: 5971
33:17 Nevertheless the **p** did sacrifice still in 5971
33:25 the **p** of the land slew all them that had 5971
33:25 the **p** of the land made Josiah his son king 5971
34:30 the Levites, and all the **p**, great and small: 5971
35: 3 the LORD your God, and his **p** Israel, 5971
35: 5 of the fathers of your brethren the **p**, 1121+5971
35: 7 Josiah gave to the **p**, *of* the flock, 1121+5971
35: 8 his princes gave willingly unto the **p**, to 5971
35:12 the divisions of the families of the **p**, 1121+5971
35:13 *them* speedily among all the **p**. 1121+5971
36: 1 the **p** of the land took Jehoahaz the son of 5971
36:14 all the chief of the priests, and the **p**, 5971
36:15 because he had compassion on his **p**, and 5971
36:16 wrath of the LORD arose against his **p**, 5971
36:23 Who *is there* among you of all his **p**? 5971

Ezr 1: 3 Who *is there* among you of all his **p**? 5971
2: 2 The number of the men of the **p** of Israel: 5971
2:70 *some* of the **p**, and the singers, and 5971
3: 1 the **p** gathered themselves together as one 5971
3: 3 because of the **p** of *those* countries: 5971
3:11 all the **p** shouted *with* a great shout, 5971
3:13 So that the **p** could not discern the noise of 5971
3:13 joy from the noise of the weeping of the **p**: 5971
3:13 for the **p** shouted *with* a loud shout, and 5971
4: 4 the **p** of the land weakened the hands of 5971
4: 4 land weakened the hands of the **p** of Judah, 5971
5:12 carried the **p** away into Babylon. 5972
6:12 name to dwell there destroy all kings and **p**, 5972
7:13 that all they of the **p** of Israel, and *of* his 5972
7:16 with the freewill offering of the **p**, and 5972
7:25 which may judge all the **p** that *are* beyond 5972
8:15 I viewed the **p**, and the priests, and 5971
8:36 they furthered the **p**, and the house of God. 5971
9: 1 The **p** of Israel, and the priests, and 5971
9: 1 have not separated themselves from the **p** 5971
9: 2 themselves with the **p** of *those* lands: 5971
9:11 with the filthiness of the **p** of the lands, 5971
9:14 join in affinity with the **p** of these 5971
10: 1 and children: for the **p** wept very sore. 5971
10: 2 have taken strange wives of the **p** of 5971
10: 9 all the **p** sat in the street of the house of 5971
10:11 separate yourselves from the **p** of the land, 5971
10:13 the **p** *are* many, and *it is* a time of much 5971

Ne 1:10 Now these *are* thy servants and thy **p**, 5971
4: 6 half thereof: for the **p** had a mind to work. 5971
4:13 I even set the **p** after *their* families with 5971
4:14 and to the rulers, and to the rest of the **p**, 5971
4:19 to the rulers, and to the rest of the **p**, 5971
4:22 Likewise at the same time said I unto the **p**, 5971
5: 1 there was a great cry of the **p** and of their 5971
5:13 And the **p** did according to this promise. 5971
5:15 *been* before me were chargeable unto the **p**, 5971
5:15 even their servants bare rule over the **p**: 5971
5:18 the bondage was heavy upon this **p**. 5971
5:19 *according to* all that I have done for this **p**. 5971
7: 4 the **p** *were* few therein, and the houses *were* 5971
7: 5 the rulers, and the **p**, that *they* might be 5971
7: 7 *I say,* of the men of the **p** of Israel *was* 5971
7:72 *that* which the rest of the **p** gave *was* 5971
7:73 *some* of the **p**, and the Nethinims, and 5971
8: 1 all the **p** gathered themselves together as 5971
8: 3 the ears of all the **p** *were attentive* unto 5971
8: 5 opened the book in the sight of all the **p**; 5971
8: 5 (for he was above all the **p**;) and when he 5971
8: 5 and when he opened *it,* all the **p** stood *up:* 5971
8: 6 all the **p** answered, Amen, Amen, 5971
8: 7 caused the **p** to understand the law: 5971
8: 7 the law: and the **p** *stood* in their place. 5971
8: 9 the Levites that taught the **p**, said unto all 5971
8: 9 that taught the people, said unto all the **p**, 5971
8: 9 For all the **p** wept, when they heard 5971
8:11 So the Levites stilled all the **p**, saying, 5971
8:12 all the **p** went *their way* to eat, and to drink, 5971
8:13 together the chief of the fathers of all the **p**, 5971
8:16 So the **p** went forth, and brought *them,* and 5971
9:10 all his servants, and on all the **p** of his land: 5971
9:24 with their kings, and the **p** of the land, 5971
9:30 gavest thou them into the hand of the **p** of 5971
9:32 and on our fathers, and on all thy **p**, 5971
10:14 The chief of the **p**; Parosh, Pahath-moab, 5971
10:28 the rest of the **p**, the priests, the Levites, 5971
10:28 the **p** of the lands unto the law of God, 5971
10:30 give our daughters unto the **p** of the land, 5971
10:31 *if* the **p** of the land bring ware or 5971
10:34 the Levites, and the **p**, for the wood 5971
11: 1 the rulers of the **p** dwelt at Jerusalem: 5971
11: 1 the rest of the **p** also cast lots, to bring one 5971
11: 2 the **p** blessed all the men, that willingly 5971
11:24 king's hand in all matters concerning the **p**. 5971
12:30 purified the **p**, and the gates, and the wall. 5971

Ne 12:38	and the half of the **p** upon the wall,	5971
13: 1	the book of Moses in the audience of the **p**;	5971
13:24	to the language of **each p**.	5971+5971+2050.1
Est 1: 5	the king made a feast unto all the **p** that	5971
1:11	to shew the **p** and the princes her beauty:	5971
1:16	to all the **p** that *are* in all the provinces of	5971
1:22	to **every p** after their	5971+5971+2050.1
1:22	according to the language of every **p**.	5971
2:10	Esther had not shewed her **p** nor her	5971
2:20	had not *yet* shewed her kindred nor her **p**;	5971
3: 6	for they had shewed him the **p** of	5971
3: 6	of Ahasuerus, *even* the **p** of Mordecai.	5971
3: 8	There is a certain **p** scattered abroad and	5971
3: 8	dispersed among the **p** in all the provinces	5971
3: 8	their laws *are* diverse from all **p**;	5971
3:11	The silver *is* given to thee, the **p** also,	5971
3:12	to the rulers of **every p** of	5971+5971+2050.1
3:12	**every p** after their language;	5971+5971+2050.1
3:14	in every province *was* published unto all **p**,	5971
4: 8	and to make request before him for her **p**.	5971
4:11	the **p** of the king's provinces, do know,	5971
7: 3	me at my petition, and my **p** at my request:	5971
7: 4	I and my **p**, to be destroyed, to be slain, and	5971
8: 6	to see the evil that shall come unto my **p**?	5971
8: 9	*unto* **every p** after their	5971+5971+2050.1
8:11	all the power of the **p** and province that	5971
8:13	in every province *was* published unto all **p**,	5971
8:17	many of the **p** of the land became Jews;	5971
9: 2	for the fear of them fell upon all **p**.	5971
10: 3	seeking the wealth of his **p**, and	5971
Job 12: 2	No doubt but ye *are* the **p**, and	5971
12:24	the heart of the chief of the **p** of the earth,	5971
17: 6	He hath made me also a byword of the **p**;	5971
18:19	neither have son nor nephew among his **p**,	5971
34:20	the **p** shall be troubled at midnight,	5971
34:30	hypocrite reign not, lest the **p** be ensnared.	5971
36:20	the night, when **p** are cut off in their place.	5971
36:31	For by them judgeth he the **p**; he giveth	5971
Ps 2: 1	and the **p** imagine a vain *thing?*	3816
3: 6	I will not be afraid of ten thousands of **p**,	5971
3: 8	thy blessing *is* upon thy **p**. Selah.	5971
7: 7	So shall the congregation of the **p** compass	3816
7: 8	The LORD shall judge the **p**: judge me,	5971
9: 8	he shall minister judgment to the **p** in	3816
9:11	in Zion: declare among the **p** his doings.	5971
14: 4	who eat up my **p** *as* they eat bread, *and*	5971
14: 7	bringeth back the captivity of his **p**,	5971
18:27	For thou wilt save the afflicted **p**; but	5971
18:43	delivered me from the strivings of the **p**;	5971
18:43	a **p** *whom* I have not known shall serve me.	5971
18:47	avengeth me, and subdueth the **p** under me.	5971
22: 6	a reproach of men, and despised of the **p**.	5971
22:31	shall declare his righteousness unto a **p** that	5971
28: 9	Save thy **p**, and bless thine inheritance:	5971
29:11	The LORD will give strength unto his **p**;	5971
29:11	the LORD will bless his **p** with peace.	5971
33:10	he maketh the devices of the **p** of none	5971
33:12	the **p** *whom* he hath chosen for his own	5971
35:18	I will praise thee among much **p**.	5971
44: 2	*how* thou didst afflict the **p**, and cast them	3816
44:12	Thou sellest thy **p** for nought, and dost not	5971
44:14	a shaking of the head among the **p**.	3816
45: 5	*whereby* the **p** fall under thee.	5971
45:10	forget also thine own **p**, and thy father's	5971
45:12	*even* the rich among the **p** shall intreat thy	5971
45:17	shall the **p** praise thee for ever and ever.	5971
47: 1	O clap *your* hands, all ye **p**; shout unto God	5971
47: 3	He shall subdue the **p** under us, and	5971
47: 9	The princes of the **p** are gathered together,	5971
47: 9	*even* the **p** of the God of Abraham:	5971
49: 1	Hear this, all ye **p**; give ear, all ye	5971
50: 4	and to the earth, that *he* may judge his **p**.	5971
50: 7	Hear, O my **p**, and I will speak; O Israel,	5971
53: 4	who eat up my **p** *as* they eat bread:	5971
53: 6	God bringeth back the captivity of his **p**,	5971
56: 7	in *thine* anger cast down the **p**, O God.	5971
57: 9	I will praise thee, O Lord, among the **p**:	5971
59:11	Slay them not, lest my **p** forget:	5971
60: 3	Thou hast shewed thy **p** hard *things:* thou	5971
62: 8	ye **p**, pour out your heart before him:	5971
65: 7	of their waves, and the tumult of the **p**.	3816
66: 8	ye **p**, and make the voice of his praise to be	5971
67: 3	Let the **p** praise thee, O God; let all	5971
67: 3	praise thee, O God; let all the **p** praise thee.	5971
67: 4	for thou shalt judge the **p** righteously, and	5971
67: 5	Let the **p** praise thee, O God; let all	5971
67: 5	praise thee, O God; let all the **p** praise thee.	5971
68: 7	when thou wentest forth before thy **p**,	5971
68:22	I will bring *my* **p** again from the depths of	NIH
68:30	of the bulls, with the calves of the **p**,	5971
68:30	scatter thou the **p** *that* delight in war.	5971
68:35	that giveth strength and power unto *his* **p**.	5971
72: 2	He shall judge thy **p** with righteousness,	5971
72: 3	The mountains shall bring peace to the **p**,	5971
72: 4	He shall judge the poor of the **p**, he shall	5971
73:10	Therefore his **p** return hither: and waters of	5971
74:14	gavest him *to be* meat to the **p** inhabiting	5971
74:18	*that* the foolish **p** have blasphemed thy	5971
77:14	hast declared thy strength among the **p**.	5971
77:15	Thou hast with *thine* arm redeemed thy **p**,	5971
77:20	Thou leddest thy **p** like a flock by the hand	5971
78: 1	Give ear, O my **p**, to my law: incline your	5971
78:20	bread also? can he provide flesh for his **p**?	5971
78:52	made his own **p** to go forth like sheep, and	5971
78:62	He gave his **p** over also unto the sword; and	5971
78:71	young he brought him to feed Jacob his **p**,	5971
79:13	So we thy **p** and sheep of thy pasture will	5971
80: 4	thou be angry against the prayer of thy **p**?	5971
81: 8	Hear, O my **p**, and I will testify unto thee:	5971
81:11	my **p** would not hearken to my voice; and	5971
81:13	O that my **p** had hearkened unto me, *and*	5971
83: 3	have taken crafty counsel against thy **p**,	5971
85: 2	Thou hast forgiven the iniquity of thy **p**,	5971
85: 6	us again: that thy **p** may rejoice in thee?	5971
85: 8	for he will speak peace unto his **p**, and	5971
87: 6	shall count, when he writeth *up* the **p**,	5971
89:15	Blessed *is* the **p** that know the joyful sound:	5971
89:19	I have exalted *one* chosen out of the **p**.	5971
89:50	my bosom *the reproach of* all the mighty **p**;	5971
94: 5	They break in pieces thy **p**, O LORD, and	5971
94: 8	Understand, ye brutish among the **p**: and	5971
94:14	For the LORD will not cast off his **p**,	5971
95: 7	we *are* the **p** of his pasture, and the sheep of	5971
95:10	It *is* a **p** that do err in *their* heart, and	5971
96: 3	the heathen, his wonders among all **p**.	5971
96: 7	unto the LORD, O ye kindreds of the **p**,	5971
96:10	be moved: he shall judge the **p** righteously.	5971
96:13	with righteousness, and the **p** with his truth.	5971
97: 6	and all the **p** see his glory.	5971
98: 9	he judge the world, and the **p** with equity.	5971
99: 1	The LORD reigneth; let the **p** tremble:	5971
99: 2	in Zion; and he *is* high above all the **p**.	5971
100: 3	*we are* his **p**, and the sheep of his pasture.	5971
102:18	the **p** which *shall be* created shall praise	5971
102:22	When the **p** are gathered together, and	5971
105: 1	make known his deeds among the **p**.	5971
105:13	to another, from *one* kingdom to another **p**;	5971
105:20	*even* the ruler of the **p**, and let him go free.	5971
105:24	he increased his **p** greatly; and made them	5971
105:25	He turned their heart to hate his **p**, to deal	5971
105:40	*The* **p** asked, and he brought quails, and	NIH
105:43	he brought forth his **p** with joy, *and*	5971
105:44	and they inherited the labour of the **p**;	3816
106: 4	the favour *that thou bearest* unto thy **p**:	5971
106:40	wrath of the LORD kindled against his **p**,	5971
106:48	let all the **p** say, Amen. Praise ye	5971
107:32	exalt him also in the congregation of the **p**,	5971
108: 3	I will praise thee, O LORD, among the **p**:	5971
110: 3	Thy **p** *shall be* willing in the day of thy	5971
111: 6	He hath shewed his **p** the power of his	5971
111: 9	He sent redemption unto his **p**: he hath	5971
113: 8	with princes, *even* with the princes of his **p**.	5971
114: 1	the house of Jacob from a **p** of strange	5971
116:14	LORD now in the presence of all his **p**.	5971
116:18	LORD now in the presence of all his **p**,	5971
117: 1	all ye nations: praise him, all ye **p**.	523
125: 2	the LORD *is* round about his **p** from	5971
135:12	an heritage, an heritage unto Israel his **p**.	5971
135:14	For the LORD will judge his **p**, and	5971
136:16	To him which led his **p** through	5971
144: 2	I trust; who subdueth my **p** under me.	5971
144:15	Happy *is that* **p**, that is in such a case: *yea,*	5971
144:15	*yea,* happy *is that* **p**, whose God *is*	5971
148:11	Kings of the earth, and all **p**; princes, and	3816
148:14	He also exalteth the horn of his **p**,	5971
148:14	of the children of Israel, a **p** near unto him.	5971
149: 4	For the LORD taketh pleasure in his **p**:	5971
149: 7	the heathen, *and* punishments upon the **p**;	3816

Pr 11:14 Where no counsel *is,* the **p** fall: but in 5971
11:26 withholdeth corn, the **p** shall curse him: 3816
14:28 In the multitude of **p** *is* the king's honour: 5971
14:28 in the want of **p** *is* the destruction of 3816
14:34 a nation: but sin *is* a reproach to any **p**. 3816
24:24 him shall the **p** curse, nations shall abhor 5971
28:15 *so is* a wicked ruler over the poor **p**. 5971
29: 2 the righteous are in authority, the **p** rejoice: 5971
29: 2 when the wicked beareth rule, the **p** mourn. 5971
29:18 Where *there is* no vision, the **p** perish: but 5971
30:25 The ants *are* a **p** not strong, yet they 5971
Ecc 4:16 *There is* no end of all the **p**, *even* of all that 5971
12: 9 was wise, he still taught the **p** knowledge; 5971
Isa 1: 3 doth not know, my **p** doth not consider. 5971
1: 4 Ah sinful nation, a **p** laden with iniquity, 5971
1:10 unto the law of our God, ye **p** of Gomorrah. 5971
2: 3 many **p** shall go and say, Come ye, and 5971
2: 4 the nations, and shall rebuke many **p**: 5971
2: 6 Therefore thou hast forsaken thy **p** 5971
3: 5 the **p** shall be oppressed, every one by 5971
3: 7 nor clothing: make me not a ruler of the **p**. 5971
3:12 *As for* my **p**, children *are* their oppressors, 5971
3:12 O my **p**, they which lead thee cause *thee* to 5971
3:13 *up* to plead, and standeth to judge the **p**. 5971
3:14 into judgment with the ancients of his **p**, 5971
3:15 What mean ye *that* ye beat my **p** to pieces, 5971
5:13 Therefore my **p** are gone into captivity, 5971
5:25 anger of the LORD kindled against his **p**, 5971
6: 5 I dwell in the midst of a **p** of unclean lips: 5971
6: 9 he said, Go, and tell this **p**, Hear ye indeed, 5971
6:10 Make the heart of this **p** fat, and make their 5971
7: 2 his heart was moved, and the heart of his **p**, 5971
7: 8 shall Ephraim be broken, that *it be* not a **p**. 5971
7:17 upon thy **p**, and upon thy father's house, 5971
8: 6 Forsomuch as this **p** refuseth the waters of 5971
8: 9 O ye **p**, and ye shall be broken in pieces; 5971
8:11 that *I* should not walk in the way of this **p**, 5971
8:12 to all *them to* whom this **p** shall say, 5971
8:19 should not a **p** seek unto their God? for 5971
9: 2 The **p** that walked in darkness have seen a 5971
9: 9 all the **p** shall know, *even* Ephraim and 5971
9:13 For the **p** turneth not unto him that smiteth 5971
9:16 For the leaders of this **p** cause *them* to err; 5971
9:19 and the **p** shall be as the fuel of the fire: 5971
10: 2 take away the right from the poor of my **p**, 5971
10: 6 against the **p** of my wrath will I give him a 5971
10:13 I have removed the bounds of the **p**, and 5971
10:14 hath found as a nest the riches of the **p**: 5971
10:22 For though thy **p** Israel be as the sand of 5971
10:24 O my **p** that dwellest in Zion, be not afraid 5971
11:10 which shall stand for an ensign of the **p**; 5971
11:11 time to recover the remnant of his **p**, 5971
11:16 shall be a highway for the remnant of his **p**, 5971
12: 4 his name, declare his doings among the **p**, 5971
13: 4 in the mountains, like as of a great **p**; 5971
13:14 they shall every man turn to his own **p**, and 5971
14: 2 the **p** shall take them, and bring them to 5971
14: 6 He who smote the **p** in wrath *with* a 5971
14:20 hast destroyed thy land, *and* slain thy **p**: 5971
14:32 and the poor of his **p** shall trust in it. 5971
17:12 Woe to the multitude of many **p**, 5971
18: 2 to a **p** terrible from their beginning hitherto; 5971
18: 7 unto the LORD of hosts *of* a **p** scattered 5971
18: 7 from a **p** terrible from their beginning 5971
19:25 Blessed *be* Egypt my **p**, and Assyria 5971
22: 4 of the spoiling of the daughter of my **p**. 5971
23:13 this **p** was not, *till* the Assyrian founded it 5971
24: 2 it shall be, as *with* the **p**, so *with* the priest; 5971
24: 4 the haughty **p** of the earth do languish. 5971
24:13 be in the midst of the land among the **p**, 5971
25: 3 Therefore shall the strong **p** glorify thee, 5971
25: 6 hosts make unto all **p** a feast of fat things, 5971
25: 7 the face of the covering cast over all **p**, 5971
25: 8 the rebuke of his **p** shall he take away from 5971
26:11 and be ashamed for *their* envy at the **p**; 5971
26:20 Come, my **p**, enter thou into thy chambers, 5971
27:11 for it *is* a **p** of no understanding: therefore 5971
28: 5 diadem of beauty, unto the residue of his **p**, 5971
28:11 and another tongue will he speak to this **p**. 5971
28:14 that rule this **p** which *is* in Jerusalem. 5971
29:13 Forasmuch as this **p** draw near *me* with 5971
29:14 to do a marvellous work amongst this **p**, 5971
30: 5 They were all ashamed of a **p** *that* could not 5971
30: 6 of camels, to a **p** *that* shall not profit *them.* 5971
30: 9 That this *is* a rebellious **p**, lying children, 5971
30:19 For the **p** shall dwell in Zion at Jerusalem: 5971
30:26 the LORD bindeth up the breach of his **p**, 5971
30:28 *there shall be* a bridle in the jaws of the **p**, 5971
32:13 Upon the land of my **p** shall come up 5971
32:18 my **p** shall dwell in a peaceable habitation, 5971
33: 3 At the noise of the tumult the **p** fled; at 5971
33:12 the **p** shall be *as* the burnings of lime: 5971
33:19 Thou shalt not see a fierce **p**, a people of a 5971
33:19 a **p** of a deeper speech than *thou* canst 5971
33:24 the **p** that dwell therein *shall be* forgiven 5971
34: 1 ye nations, to hear; and hearken, ye **p**: 3816
34: 5 and upon the **p** of my curse, to judgment. 5971
36:11 in the ears of the **p** that *are* on the wall. 5971
40: 1 Comfort ye, comfort ye my **p**, saith your 5971
40: 7 bloweth upon it: surely the **p** *is* grass. 5971
41: 1 and let the **p** renew *their* strength: 3816
42: 5 he that giveth breath unto the **p** upon it, and 5971
42: 6 and give thee for a covenant of the **p**, 5971
42:22 this *is* a **p** robbed and spoiled; *they are* all 5971
43: 4 will I give men for thee, and **p** for thy life. 3816
43: 8 Bring forth the blind **p** that have eyes, and 5971
43: 9 and let the **p** be assembled: 3816
43:20 to give drink to my **p**, my chosen. 5971
43:21 This **p** have I formed for myself; they shall 5971
44: 7 for me, since I appointed the ancient **p**? 5971
47: 6 I was wroth with my **p**, I have polluted 5971
49: 1 unto me; and hearken, ye **p**, from afar; 3816
49: 8 and give thee for a covenant of the **p**, 5971
49:13 for the LORD hath comforted his **p**, and 5971
49:22 and set up my standard to the **p**: 5971
51: 4 Hearken unto me, my **p**; and give ear unto 5971
51: 4 my judgment to rest for a light of the **p**. 5971
51: 5 and mine arms shall judge the **p**; 5971
51: 7 the **p** in whose heart *is* my law; 5971
51:16 and say unto Zion, Thou *art* my **p**. 5971
51:22 thy God *that* pleadeth the cause of his **p**, 5971
52: 4 My **p** went down aforetime *into* Egypt to 5971
52: 5 that my **p** is taken away for nought? 5971
52: 6 Therefore my **p** shall know my name: 5971
52: 9 for the LORD hath comforted his **p**, 5971
53: 8 for the transgression of my **p** was he 5971
55: 4 I have given him *for* a witness to the **p**, 3816
55: 4 a leader and commander to the **p**. 3816
56: 3 hath utterly separated me from his **p**: 5971
56: 7 shall be called a house of prayer for all **p**. 5971
57:14 the stumblingblock out of the way of my **p**. 5971
58: 1 shew my **p** their transgression, and 5971
60: 2 cover the earth, and gross darkness the **p**: 3816
60:21 Thy **p** also *shall be* all righteous: they shall 5971
61: 9 and their offspring among the **p**: 5971
62:10 prepare you the way of the **p**; cast up, 5971
62:10 out the stones; lift up a standard for the **p**. 5971
62:12 they shall call them, The holy **p**, 5971
63: 3 and of the **p** *there was* none with me: 5971
63: 6 I will tread down the **p** in mine anger, and 5971
63: 8 For he said, Surely they *are* my **p**, 5971
63:11 the days of old, Moses, *and* his **p**, 5971
63:14 so didst thou lead thy **p**, to make thyself a 5971
63:18 The **p** of thy holiness have possessed *it* but 5971
64: 9 see, we beseech thee, we *are* all thy **p**. 5971
65: 2 mine hands all the day unto a rebellious **p**, 5971
65: 3 A **p** that provoketh me to anger continually 5971
65:10 lie down in, for my **p** that have sought me. 5971
65:18 Jerusalem a rejoicing, and her **p** a joy. 5971
65:19 I will rejoice in Jerusalem, and joy in my **p**: 5971
65:22 as the days of a tree *are* the days of my **p**, 5971
Jer 1:18 and against the **p** of the land. 5971
2:11 my **p** have changed their glory for *that* 5971
2:13 For my **p** have committed two evils; 5971
2:31 wherefore say my **p**, We are lords; we will 5971
2:32 yet my **p** have forgotten me days without 5971
4:10 surely thou hast greatly deceived this **p** 5971
4:11 At that time shall it be said to this **p** and 5971
4:11 wilderness toward the daughter of my **p**, 5971
4:22 For my **p** *is* foolish, they have not known 5971
5:14 and this **p** wood, and it shall devour them. 5971
5:21 O foolish **p**, and without understanding; 5971
5:23 this **p** hath a revolting and a rebellious 5971
5:26 For among my **p** are found wicked *men:* 5971
5:31 by their means; and my **p** love *to have it* so: 5971
6:14 the hurt of *the daughter of* my **p** slightly, 5971
6:19 behold, I will bring evil upon this **p**, 5971
6:21 I will lay stumblingblocks before this **p**, 5971

P

Jer	6:22	a **p** cometh from the north country, and	5971
	6:26	O daughter of my **p**, gird *thee* with	5971
	6:27	thee *for* a tower *and* a fortress among my **p**,	5971
	7:12	I did to it for the wickedness of my **p** Israel.	5971
	7:16	Therefore pray not thou for this **p**, neither	5971
	7:23	I will be your God, and ye shall be my **p**:	5971
	7:33	the carcases of this **p** shall be meat for	5971
	8: 5	is this **p** of Jerusalem slidden back *by* a	5971
	8: 7	my **p** know not the judgment of	5971
	8:11	the hurt of the daughter of my **p** slightly,	5971
	8:19	the voice of the cry of the daughter of my **p**	5971
	8:21	For the hurt of the daughter of my **p** am I	5971
	8:22	is not the health of the daughter of my **p**	5971
	9: 1	night for the slain of the daughter of my **p**!	5971
	9: 2	that I might leave my **p**, and go from them!	5971
	9: 7	how shall I do for the daughter of my **p**?	5971
	9:15	Behold, I *will* feed them, *even* this **p**, with	5971
	10: 3	For the customs of the **p** *are* vain: for *one*	5971
	11: 4	so shall ye be my **p**, and I will be your	5971
	11:14	Therefore pray not thou for this **p**, neither	5971
	12:14	which I have caused my **p** Israel to inherit;	5971
	12:16	they will diligently learn the ways of my **p**,	5971
	12:16	as they taught my **p** to swear by Baal; then	5971
	12:16	shall they be built in the midst of my **p**.	5971
	13:10	This evil **p**, which refuse to hear my words,	5971
	13:11	that *they* might be unto me for a **p**, and	5971
	14:10	Thus saith the LORD unto this **p**, Thus	5971
	14:11	unto me, Pray not for this **p** for *their* good.	5971
	14:16	the **p** to whom they prophesy shall be cast	5971
	14:17	for the virgin daughter of my **p** is broken	5971
	15: 1	*yet* my mind *could* not *be* toward this **p**:	5971
	15: 7	*them* of children, I will destroy my **p**,	5971
	15:20	I will make thee unto this **p** a fenced brasen	5971
	16: 5	I have taken away my peace from this **p**,	5971
	16:10	when thou shalt shew this **p** all these	5971
	17:19	stand in the gate of the children of the **p**,	5971
	18:15	Because my **p** hath forgotten me, they have	5971
	19: 1	*take* of the ancients of the **p**, and of	5971
	19:11	Even so will I break this **p** and this city, as	5971
	19:14	the LORD'S house; and said to all the **p**,	5971
	21: 7	the **p**, and such as are left in this city from	5971
	21: 8	unto this **p** thou shalt say, Thus saith	5971
	22: 2	and thy **p** that enter in by these gates:	5971
	22: 4	on horses, he, and his servants, and his **p**.	5971
	23: 2	of Israel against the pastors that feed my **p**;	5971
	23:13	in Baal, and caused my **p** Israel to err.	5971
	23:22	had caused my **p** to hear my words, then	5971
	23:27	Which think to cause my **p** to forget my	5971
	23:32	cause my **p** to err by their lies, and by their	5971
	23:32	therefore they shall not profit this **p** at all,	5971
	23:33	And when this **p**, or the prophet, or a priest,	5971
	23:34	and the priest, and the **p**, that shall say,	5971
	24: 7	they shall be my **p**, and I will be their God:	5971
	25: 1	**p** of Judah in the fourth year of Jehoiakim	5971
	25: 2	the prophet spake unto all the **p** of Judah,	5971
	25:19	his servants, and his princes, and all his **p**;	5971
	25:20	all the **mingled p**, and all the kings of	6153
	25:24	all the kings of the **mingled p** that dwell in	6153
	26: 7	all the **p** heard Jeremiah speaking these	5971
	26: 8	commanded *him* to speak unto all the **p**,	5971
	26: 8	and the prophets and all the **p** took him,	5971
	26: 9	all the **p** were gathered against Jeremiah in	5971
	26:11	prophets unto the princes and to all the **p**,	5971
	26:12	unto all the princes and to all the **p**,	5971
	26:16	all the **p** unto the priests and to	5971
	26:17	spake to all the assembly of the **p**, saying,	5971
	26:18	spake to all the **p** of Judah, saying,	5971
	26:23	body into the graves of the common **p**.	5971
	26:24	into the hand of the **p** to put him to death.	5971
	27:12	and serve him and his **p**, and live.	5971
	27:13	thou and thy **p**, by the sword, by	5971
	27:16	Also I spake to the priests and to all this **p**,	5971
	28: 1	the presence of the priests and of all the **p**,	5971
	28: 5	in the presence of all the **p** that stood in	5971
	28: 7	in thine ears, and in the ears of all the **p**.	5971
	28:11	Hananiah spake in the presence of all the **p**,	5971
	28:15	but thou makest this **p** to trust in a lie.	5971
	29: 1	to all the **p** whom Nebuchadnezzar had	5971
	29:16	of all the **p** that dwelleth in this city,	5971
	29:25	name unto all the **p** that *are* at Jerusalem,	5971
	29:32	shall not have a man to dwell among this **p**;	5971
	29:32	he behold the good that I will do for my **p**,	5971
	30: 3	that I will bring again the captivity of my **p**	5971
	30:22	ye shall be my **p**, and I will be your God.	5971
	31: 1	families of Israel, and they shall be my **p**.	5971
	31: 2	The **p** which were left of the sword found	5971
	31: 7	praise ye, and say, O LORD, save thy **p**,	5971
	31:14	my **p** shall be satisfied with my goodness,	5971
	31:33	will be their God, and they shall be my **p**.	5971
	32:21	hast brought forth thy **p** Israel out of	5971
	32:38	they shall be my **p**, and I will be their God:	5971
	32:42	have brought all this great evil upon this **p**,	5971
	33:24	Considerest thou not what this **p** have	5971
	33:24	thus they have despised my **p**, that *they*	5971
	34: 1	all the **p**, fought against Jerusalem, and	5971
	34: 8	with all the **p** which *were* at Jerusalem,	5971
	34:10	*Now* when all the princes, and all the **p**,	5971
	34:19	and the priests, and all the **p** of the land,	5971
	35:16	but this **p** hath not hearkened unto me:	5971
	36: 6	**p** *in* the LORD'S house upon the fasting	5971
	36: 7	the LORD hath pronounced against this **p**.	5971
	36: 9	before the LORD *to* all the **p** in Jerusalem,	5971
	36: 9	*to* all the **p** that came from the cities of	5971
	36:10	LORD'S house, in the ears of all the **p**.	5971
	36:13	Baruch read the book in the ears of the **p**.	5971
	36:14	wherein thou hast read in the ears of the **p**,	5971
	37: 2	nor his servants, nor the **p** of the land,	5971
	37: 4	came in and went out among the **p**:	5971
	37:12	himself thence in the midst of the **p**.	5971
	37:18	or against thy servants, or against this **p**,	5971
	38: 1	that Jeremiah had spoken unto all the **p**,	5971
	38: 4	the hands of all the **p**, in speaking such	5971
	38: 4	this man seeketh not the welfare of this **p**,	5971
	39: 8	the houses of the **p**, with fire, and brake	5971
	39: 9	remnant of the **p** that remained in the city,	5971
	39: 9	to him, with the rest of the **p** that remained.	5971
	39:10	of the guard left of the poor of the **p**,	5971
	39:14	carry him home: so he dwelt among the **p**.	5971
	40: 5	of Judah, and dwell with him among the **p**:	5971
	40: 6	dwelt with him among the **p** that were left	5971
	41:10	all the residue of the **p** that *were* in Mizpah,	5971
	41:10	and all the **p** that remained in Mizpah,	5971
	41:13	*that* when all the **p** which *were* with	5971
	41:14	So all the **p** that Ishmael had carried away	5971
	41:16	all the remnant of the **p** whom he had	5971
	42: 1	all the **p** from the least even unto	5971
	42: 8	all the **p** from the least even to the greatest,	5971
	43: 1	**p** all the words of the LORD their God,	5971
	43: 4	all the captains of the forces, and all the **p**,	5971
	44:15	even all the **p** that dwelt in the land of	5971
	44:20	Jeremiah said unto all the **p**, to the men,	5971
	44:20	to all the **p** which had given him *that*	5971
	44:21	and your princes, and the **p** of the land,	5971
	44:24	Moreover Jeremiah said unto all the **p**, and	5971
	46:16	let us go again to our own **p**, and to	5971
	46:24	she shall be delivered into the hand of the **p**	5971
	48:42	Moab shall be destroyed from *being* a **p**,	5971
	48:46	the **p** of Chemosh perisheth: for thy sons	5971
	49: 1	inherit Gad, and his **p** dwell in his cities?	5971
	50: 6	My **p** hath been lost sheep: their shepherds	5971
	50:16	sword they shall turn every one to his **p**,	5971
	50:37	upon all the mingled **p** that *are* in the midst	6153
	50:41	a **p** shall come from the north, and a great	5971
	51:45	My **p**, go ye out of the midst of her, and	5971
	51:58	the **p** shall labour in vain, and the folk in	5971
	52: 6	that there was no bread for the **p** of	5971
	52:15	away captive *certain* of the poor of the **p**,	5971
	52:15	the residue of the **p** that remained in	5971
	52:25	of the host, who mustered the **p** of the land;	5971
	52:25	threescore men of the **p** of the land,	5971
	52:28	This *is* the **p** whom Nebuchadrezzar carried	5971
La	1: 1	doth the city sit solitary, *that was* full of **p**!	5971
	1: 7	when her **p** fell into the hand of the enemy,	5971
	1:11	All her **p** sigh, they seek bread; they have	5971
	1:18	I pray you, all **p**, and behold my sorrow:	5971
	2:11	for the destruction of the daughter of my **p**;	5971
	3:14	I was a derision to all my **p**; *and* their song	5971
	3:45	and refuse in the midst of the **p**.	5971
	3:48	for the destruction of the daughter of my **p**.	5971
	4: 3	the daughter of my **p** *is* become cruel,	5971
	4: 6	**p** is greater than the punishment of the sin	5971
	4:10	in the destruction of the daughter of my **p**.	5971
Eze	3: 5	For thou *art* not sent to a **p** of a strange	5971
	3: 6	Not to many **p** of a strange speech and of a	5971
	3:11	unto the children of thy **p**, and speak unto	5971
	7:27	the hands of the **p** of the land shall be	5971
	11: 1	the son of Benaiah, princes of the **p**.	5971
	11:17	I will even gather you from the **p**, and	5971

Eze	11:20	they shall be my **p**, and I will be their God.	5971
	12:19	say unto the **p** of the land, Thus saith	5971
	13: 9	they shall not be in the assembly of my **p**,	5971
	13:10	even because they have seduced my **p**,	5971
	13:17	set thy face against the daughters of thy **p**,	5971
	13:18	Will ye hunt the souls of my **p**, and will ye	5971
	13:19	will ye pollute me among my **p** for	5971
	13:19	by your lying to my **p** that hear *your* lies?	5971
	13:21	deliver my **p** out of your hand, and	5971
	13:23	for I will deliver my **p** out of your hand:	5971
	14: 8	I will cut him off from the midst of my **p**;	5971
	14: 9	will destroy him from the midst of my **p**	5971
	14:11	that they may be my **p**, and I may be their	5971
	17: 9	many **p** to pluck it up by the roots thereof.	5971
	17:15	*they* might give him horses and much **p**.	5971
	18:18	and did *that* which *is* not good among his **p**,	5971
	20:34	I will bring you out from the **p**, and	5971
	20:35	will bring you into the wilderness of the **p**,	5971
	20:41	when I bring you out from the **p**, and	5971
	21:12	for it shall be upon my **p**, it *shall be* upon	5971
	21:12	by reason of the sword shall be upon my **p**:	5971
	22:29	The **p** of the land have used oppression,	5971
	23:24	and wheels, and with an assembly of **p**,	5971
	24:18	So I spake unto the **p** in the morning: and	5971
	24:19	the **p** said unto me, Wilt thou not tell us	5971
	25: 7	I will cut thee off from the **p**, and I will	5971
	25:14	upon Edom by the hand of my **p** Israel:	5971
	26: 2	she is broken *that was* the gates of the **p**:	5971
	26: 7	and companies, and much **p**.	5971
	26:11	he shall slay thy **p** by the sword, and	5971
	26:20	with the **p** of old time, and shall set thee in	5971
	27: 3	*which art* a merchant of the **p** for many	5971
	27:33	forth out of the seas, thou filledst many **p**;	5971
	27:36	The merchants among the **p** shall hiss at	5971
	28:19	All they that know thee among the **p** shall	5971
	28:25	from the **p** among whom they are scattered,	5971
	29:13	from the **p** whither they were scattered:	5971
	30: 5	all the **mingled p**, and Chub, and the men	6153
	30:11	He and his **p** with him, the terrible of	5971
	31:12	all the **p** of the earth are gone down from	5971
	32: 3	net over thee with a company of many **p**;	5971
	32: 9	I will also vex the hearts of many **p**, when I	5971
	32:10	I will make many **p** amazed at thee, and	5971
	33: 2	speak to the children of thy **p**, and say unto	5971
	33: 2	if the **p** of the land take a man of their	5971
	33: 3	he blow the trumpet, and warn the **p**;	5971
	33: 6	not the trumpet, and the **p** be not warned;	5971
	33:12	son of man, say unto the children of thy **p**,	5971
	33:17	Yet the children of thy **p** say, The way of	5971
	33:30	the children of thy **p** still are talking against	5971
	33:31	they come unto thee as the **p** cometh, and	5971
	33:31	they sit before thee *as* my **p**, and they hear	5971
	34:13	I will bring them out from the **p**, and	5971
	34:30	of Israel, *are* my **p**, saith the Lord GOD.	5971
	36: 3	lips of talkers, and *are* an infamy of the **p**:	5971
	36: 8	and yield your fruit to my **p** of Israel;	5971
	36:12	men to walk upon you, *even* my **p** Israel;	5971
	36:15	neither shalt thou bear the reproach of the **p**	5971
	36:20	These *are* the **p** of the LORD, and	5971
	36:28	ye shall be my **p**, and I will be your God.	5971
	37:12	Behold, O my **p**, I *will* open your graves,	5971
	37:13	O my **p**, and brought you up out of your	5971
	37:18	when the children of thy **p** shall speak unto	5971
	37:23	so shall they be my **p**, and I will be their	5971
	37:27	I will be their God, and they shall be my **p**.	5971
	38: 6	and all his bands: *and* many **p** with thee.	5971
	38: 8	*and is* gathered out of many **p**, against	5971
	38: 9	and all thy bands, and many **p** with thee.	5971
	38:12	upon the **p** *that are* gathered out of	5971
	38:14	In that day when my **p** of Israel dwelleth	5971
	38:15	thou, and many **p** with thee, all of them	5971
	38:16	thou shalt come up against my **p** of Israel,	5971
	38:22	and upon the many **p** that *are* with him,	5971
	39: 4	all thy bands, and the **p** that *is* with thee:	5971
	39: 7	name known in the midst of my **p** Israel;	5971
	39:13	all the **p** of the land shall bury *them;* and	5971
	39:27	I have brought them again from the **p**,	5971
	42:14	to *those things* which *are* for the **p**.	5971
	44:11	burnt offering and the sacrifice for the **p**,	5971
	44:19	*even* into the utter court to the **p**,	5971
	44:19	they shall not sanctify the **p** with their	5971
	44:23	they shall teach my **p** *the difference*	5971
	45: 8	my princes shall no more oppress my **p**;	5971
	45: 9	take away your exactions from my **p**,	5971
	45:16	All the **p** of the land shall give this oblation	5971
	45:22	for all the **p** of the land a bullock *for* a sin	5971
	46: 3	Likewise the **p** of the land shall worship *at*	5971
	46: 9	when the **p** of the land shall come before	5971
	46:18	that my **p** be not scattered every man from	5971
	46:20	out into the utter court, to sanctify the **p**.	5971
	46:24	of the house shall boil the sacrifice of the **p**.	5971
Da	2:44	and the kingdom shall not be left to other **p**,	5972
	3: 4	O **p**, nations, and languages,	5972
	3: 7	when all the **p** heard the sound of	5972
	3: 7	all the **p**, the nations, and the languages,	5972
	3:29	That every **p**, nation, and language,	5972
	4: 1	unto all **p**, nations, and languages, that	5972
	5:19	all **p**, nations, and languages, trembled	5972
	6:25	king Darius wrote unto all **p**, nations,	5972
	7:14	that all **p**, nations, and languages,	5972
	7:27	*shall be* given to the **p** of the saints of	5972
	8:24	and shall destroy the mighty and the holy **p**.	5971
	9: 6	and our fathers, and to all the **p** of the land.	5971
	9:15	that hast brought thy **p** forth out of the land	5971
	9:16	thy **p** *are become* a reproach to all *that are*	5971
	9:19	thy city and thy **p** are called by thy name.	5971
	9:20	my sin and the sin of my **p** Israel,	5971
	9:24	Seventy weeks are determined upon thy **p**	5971
	9:26	the **p** of the prince that *shall* come shall	5971
	10:14	what shall befall thy **p** in the latter days:	5971
	11:14	also the robbers of thy **p** shall exalt	5971
	11:15	shall not withstand, neither his chosen **p**,	5971
	11:23	and shall become strong with a small **p**.	1471
	11:32	the **p** that do know their God shall be	5971
	11:33	they that understand among the **p** shall	5971
	12: 1	which standeth for the children of thy **p**:	5971
	12: 1	at that time thy **p** shall be delivered,	5971
	12: 7	to scatter the power of the holy **p**,	5971
Hos	1: 9	for ye *are* not my **p**, and I will not be your	5971
	1:10	Ye *are* not my **p**, *there* it shall be said unto	5971
	2:23	I will say to *them which were* not my **p**,	5971
	2:23	*which were* not my people, Thou *art* my **p**;	5971
	4: 4	for thy **p** *are* as they that strive with	5971
	4: 6	My **p** are destroyed for lack of knowledge,	5971
	4: 8	They eat *up* the sin of my **p**, and they set	5971
	4: 9	there shall be, like **p**, like priest: and I will	5971
	4:12	My **p** ask *counsel* at their stocks, and	5971
	4:14	the **p** *that* doth not understand shall fall.	5971
	6:11	when I returned the captivity of my **p**.	5971
	7: 8	he hath mixed himself among the **p**;	5971
	9: 1	Rejoice not, O Israel, for joy, as *other* **p**:	5971
	10: 5	for the **p** thereof shall mourn over it, and	5971
	10:10	*the* **p** shall be gathered against them,	5971
	10:14	Therefore shall a tumult arise among thy **p**,	5971
	11: 7	my **p** are bent to backsliding from me:	5971
Joel	2: 2	a great **p** and a strong; there hath not been	5971
	2: 5	the stubble, as a strong **p** set in battle array.	5971
	2: 6	Before their face *the* **p** shall be much	5971
	2:16	Gather the **p**, sanctify the congregation,	5971
	2:17	Spare thy **p**, O LORD, and give not thine	5971
	2:17	wherefore should they say among the **p**,	5971
	2:18	be jealous for his land, and pity his **p**.	5971
	2:19	the LORD will answer and say unto his **p**,	5971
	2:26	and my **p** shall never be ashamed.	5971
	2:27	and my **p** shall never be ashamed.	5971
	3: 2	will plead with them there for my **p** and	5971
	3: 3	they have cast lots for my **p**; and	5971
	3: 8	sell them to the Sabeans, to a **p** far off:	1471
	3:16	the LORD *will be* the hope of his **p**, and	5971
Am	1: 5	the **p** of Syria shall go into captivity unto	5971
	3: 6	blown in the city, and the **p** not be afraid?	5971
	7: 8	I *will* set a plumbline in the midst of my **p**	5971
	7:15	unto me, Go, prophesy unto my **p** Israel.	5971
	8: 2	The end is come upon my **p** *of* Israel;	5971
	9:10	All the sinners of my **p** shall die by	5971
	9:14	I will bring again the captivity of my **p** of	5971
Ob	1:13	gate of my **p** in the day of their calamity:	5971
Jnh	1: 8	*is* thy country? and of what **p** *art* thou?	5971
	3: 5	So the **p** of Nineveh believed God, and	376
Mic	1: 2	Hear, all ye **p**; hearken, O earth, and all that	5971
	1: 9	he is come unto the gate of my **p**, *even* to	5971
	2: 4	he hath changed the portion of my **p**:	5971
	2: 8	Even of late my **p** is risen up as an enemy:	5971
	2: 9	The women of my **p** have ye cast out from	5971
	2:11	he shall even be the prophet of this **p**.	5971
	3: 3	Who also eat the flesh of my **p**, and	5971
	3: 5	the prophets that make my **p** err,	5971
	4: 1	above the hills; and **p** shall flow unto it.	5971

Mic 4: 3 he shall judge among many **p**, and 5971
4: 5 For all **p** will walk every one in the name 5971
4:13 thou shalt beat in pieces many **p**: and I will 5971
5: 7 of many **p** as a dew from the LORD, 5971
5: 8 **p** as a lion among the beasts of the forest, 5971
6: 2 the LORD hath a controversy with his **p**, 5971
6: 3 O my **p**, what have I done unto thee? and 5971
6: 5 O my **p**, remember now what Balak king of 5971
6:16 ye shall bear the reproach of my **p**. 5971
7:14 Feed thy **p** with thy rod, the flock of thine 5971
Na 3:13 thy **p** in the midst of thee *are* women: 5971
3:18 thy nobles shall dwell *in the dust*: thy **p** is 5971
Hab 2: 5 him all nations, and heapeth unto him all **p**: 5971
2: 8 all the remnant of the **p** shall spoil thee; 5971
2:10 shame to thy house by cutting off many **p**, 5971
2:13 *is it* not of the LORD of hosts that the **p** 5971
2:13 the **p** shall weary themselves for very 3816
3:13 wentest forth for the salvation of thy **p**, 5971
3:16 when *he* cometh up unto the **p**, he will 5971
Zep 1:11 for all the merchant **p** are cut down; 5971
2: 8 whereby they have reproached my **p**, and 5971
2: 9 the residue of my **p** shall spoil them, and 5971
2: 9 the remnant of my **p** shall possess them. 1471
2:10 magnified *themselves* against the **p** of 5971
3: 9 then will I turn to the **p** a pure language, 5971
3:12 in the midst of thee an afflicted and poor **p**, 5971
3:20 and a praise among all **p** of the earth, 5971
Hag 1: 2 This **p** say, The time is not come, 5971
1:12 high priest, with all the remnant of the **p**, 5971
1:12 and the **p** did fear before the LORD. 5971
1:13 in the LORD'S message unto the **p**, 5971
1:14 and the spirit of all the remnant of the **p**; 5971
2: 2 the high priest and to the residue of the **p**, 5971
2: 4 be strong, all ye **p** of the land, saith 5971
2:14 So *is* this **p**, and so *is* this nation before me, 5971
Zec 2:11 the LORD in that day, and shall be my **p**: 5971
7: 5 Speak unto all the **p** of the land, and to 5971
8: 6 eyes of the remnant of this **p** in these days, 5971
8: 7 I *will* save my **p** from the east country, and 5971
8: 8 they shall be my **p**, and I will be their God, 5971
8:11 now I *will* not *be* unto the residue of this **p** 5971
8:12 I will cause the remnant of this **p** to 5971
8:20 yet *come to pass,* that there shall come **p**, 5971
8:22 many **p** and strong nations shall come to 5971
9:16 save them in that day as the flock of his **p**: 5971
10: 9 I will sow them among the **p**: and they shall 5971
11:10 covenant which I had made with all the **p**. 5971
12: 2 cup of trembling unto all the **p** round about, 5971
12: 3 Jerusalem a burdensome stone for all **p**: 5971
12: 3 though all the **p** of the earth be gathered 1471
12: 4 will smite every horse of the **p** with 5971
12: 6 they shall devour all the **p** round about, 5971
13: 9 I will say, It *is* my **p**: and they shall say, 5971
14: 2 the residue of the **p** shall not be cut off 5971
14:12 the **p** that have fought against Jerusalem; 5971
Mal 1: 4 The **p** *against* whom the LORD hath 5971
2: 9 you contemptible and base before all the **p**, 5971
Mt 1:21 for he shall save his **p** from their sins. 2992
2: 4 chief priests and scribes of the **p** together, 2992
2: 6 a Governor, that shall rule my **p** Israel. 2992
4:16 The **p** which sat in darkness saw great 2992
4:23 and all *manner of* disease among the **p**. 2992
4:24 they brought unto him all **sick p** that 2192+2560
4:25 him great multitudes *of p* from Galilee, NIG
7:28 the **p** were astonished at his doctrine: 3793
9:23 saw the minstrels and the **p** making a noise, 3793
9:25 But when the **p** were put forth, he went in, 3793
9:35 and every disease among the **p**. 2992
12:23 And all the **p** were amazed, and said, Is this 3793
12:46 While he yet talked to the **p**, behold, 3793
14:13 when the **p** had heard *thereof,* they 3793
15: 8 This **p** draweth nigh unto me with their 2992
21:23 the elders of the **p** came unto him as he was 2992
21:26 But if we shall say, Of men; we fear the **p**; 3793
26: 3 and the scribes, and the elders of the **p**, 2992
26: 5 *day,* lest there be an uproar among the **p**. 2992
26:47 from the chief priests and elders of the **p**. 2992
27: 1 elders of the **p** took counsel against Jesus to 2992
27:15 was wont to release unto the **p** a prisoner, 3793
27:25 Then answered all the **p**, and said, 2992
27:64 and steal him *away,* and say unto the **p**, 2992
Mk 5:21 the other side, much **p** gathered unto him: 3793
5:24 and much **p** followed him, and 3793
6:33 And the **p** saw them departing, and 3793
6:34 saw much **p**, and was moved with 3793
6:45 unto Bethsaida, while he sent away the **p**. 3793
7: 6 This **p** honoureth me with *their* lips, but 2992
7:14 And when he had called all the **p** unto *him,* 3793
7:17 he was entered into *the* house from the **p**, 3793
8: 6 And he commanded the **p** to sit down on 3793
8: 6 and they did set *them* before the **p**. 3793
8:34 And when he had called the **p** unto *him* 3793
9:15 And straightway all the **p**, when they 3793
9:25 When Jesus saw that the **p** came running 3793
10: 1 and the **p** resort unto him again; and, as he 3793
10:46 with his disciples and a great number of **p**, 3793
11:18 all the **p** was astonished at his doctrine. 3793
11:32 if we shall say, Of men; they feared the **p**: 2992
12:12 sought to lay hold on him, but feared the **p**: 3793
12:37 And the common **p** heard him gladly. 3793
12:41 beheld how the **p** cast money into 3793
14: 2 feast *day,* lest there be an uproar of the **p**. 2992
15:11 But the chief priests moved the **p**, that he 3793
15:15 And *so* Pilate, willing to content the **p**, 3793
Lk 1:10 And the whole multitude of the **p** were 2992
1:17 to make ready a **p** prepared for the Lord. 2992
1:21 And the **p** waited for Zacharias, and 2992
1:68 for he hath visited and redeemed his **p**, 2992
1:77 To give knowledge of salvation unto his **p** 2992
2:10 tidings of great joy, which shall be to all **p**. 2992
2:31 thou hast prepared before the face of all **p**; 2992
2:32 the Gentiles, and the glory of thy **p** Israel. 2992
3:10 And the **p** asked him, saying, What shall 3793
3:15 And as the **p** were in expectation, and 2992
3:18 in his exhortation preached he unto the **p**. 2992
3:21 Now when all the **p** were baptized, it came 2992
4:42 and the **p** sought him, and came unto him, 3793
5: 1 as the **p** pressed upon him to hear the word 3793
5: 3 sat down, and taught the **p** out of the ship. 3793
6:17 a great multitude of **p** out of all Judea and 2992
7: 1 all his sayings in the audience of the **p**, 2992
7: 9 and said unto the **p** that followed him, 3793
7:11 of his disciples went with him, and much **p**. 3793
7:12 and much **p** of the city was with her. 3793
7:16 among us; and, That God hath visited his **p**. 2992
7:24 he began to speak unto the **p** concerning 3793
7:29 And all the **p** that heard *him,* and 2992
8: 4 And when much **p** were gathered together, 3793
8:40 was returned, the **p** gladly received him: 3793
8:42 (But as he went the **p** thronged him. 3793
8:47 she declared unto him before all the **p** for 2992
9:11 And the **p**, when they knew *it,* followed 3793
9:13 we should go and buy meat for all this **p**. 2992
9:18 saying, Whom say the **p** that I am? 3793
9:37 come down from the hill, much **p** met him. 3793
11:14 the dumb spake; and the **p** wondered. 3793
11:29 And when the **p** were gathered thick 3793
12: 1 together an innumerable multitude of **p**, 3793
12:54 And he said also to the **p**, When ye see a 3793
13:14 on the sabbath day, and said unto the **p**, 3793
13:17 all the **p** rejoiced for all the glorious *things* 3793
18:43 and all the **p**, when they saw *it,* gave praise 2992
19:47 the chief of the **p** sought to destroy him, 2992
19:48 for all the **p** were very attentive to hear 2992
20: 1 as he taught the **p** in the temple, and 2992
20: 6 if we say, Of men; all the **p** will stone us: 2992
20: 9 Then began he to speak to the **p** this 2992
20:19 to lay hands on him; and they feared the **p**: 2992
20:26 not take hold of his words before the **p**: 2992
20:45 Then in the audience of all the **p** he said 2992
21:23 distress in the land, and wrath upon this **p**. 2992
21:38 And all the **p** came early in the morning to 2992
22: 2 they might kill him; for they feared the **p**. 2992
22:66 the elders of the **p** and the chief priests and 2992
23: 4 said Pilate to the chief priests and *to* the **p**, 3793
23: 5 saying, He stirreth up the **p**, 2992
23:13 the chief priests and the rulers and the **p**, 2992
23:14 man unto me, as one that perverteth the **p**: 2992
23:27 there followed him a great company of **p**, 2992
23:35 And the **p** stood beholding. And the rulers 2992
23:48 And all the **p** that came together to that 3793
24:19 in deed and word before God and all the **p**: 2992
Jn 6:22 when the **p** which stood on the other side of 3793
6:24 When the **p** therefore saw that Jesus was 3793
7:12 murmuring among the **p** concerning him: 3793
7:12 others said, Nay; but he deceiveth the **p**. 3793
7:20 The **p** answered and said, Thou hast a 3793
7:31 And many of the **p** believed on him, and 3793

Jn 7:32 The Pharisees heard that the **p** murmured 3793
7:40 Many of the **p** therefore, when they heard 3793
7:43 So there was a division among the **p** 3793
7:49 But this **p** who knoweth not the law are 3793
8: 2 the temple, and all the **p** came unto him; 2992
11:42 of the **p** which stand by I said *it,* that they 3793
11:50 that one man should die for the **p**, and 2992
12: 9 Much **p** of the Jews therefore knew that he 3793
12:12 On the next day much **p** that were come to 3793
12:17 The **p** therefore that was with him when he 3793
12:18 For this cause the **p** also met him, for that 3793
12:29 The **p** therefore, that stood *by,* and heard *it,* 3793
12:34 The **p** answered him, We have heard out of 3793
18:14 that one man should die for the **p**. 2992
Ac 2:47 and having favour with all the **p**. 2992
3: 9 And all the **p** saw him walking and 2992
3:11 all the **p** ran together unto them in 2992
3:12 when Peter saw *it,* he answered unto the **p**, 2992
3:23 shall be destroyed from among the **p**. 2992
4: 1 And as they spake unto the **p**, the priests, 2992
4: 2 Being grieved that they taught the **p**, and 2992
4: 8 Ye rulers of the **p**, and elders of Israel, 2992
4:10 unto you all, and to all the **p** of Israel, 2992
4:17 But that it spread no further among the **p**, 2992
4:21 they might punish them, because of the **p**: 2992
4:25 and the **p** imagine vain *things?* 2992
4:27 with the Gentiles, and the **p** of Israel, 2992
5:12 and wonders wrought among the **p**; 2992
5:13 himself to them: but the **p** magnified them. 2992
5:20 speak in the temple to the **p** all the words of 2992
5:25 standing in the temple, and teaching the **p**. 2992
5:26 for they feared the **p**, lest they should have 2992
5:34 had in reputation among all the **p**, and 2992
5:37 and drew away much **p** after him: 2992
6: 8 great wonders and miracles among the **p**. 2992
6:12 And they stirred up the **p**, and the elders, 2992
7:17 the **p** grew and multiplied in Egypt, 2992
7:34 I have seen the affliction of my **p** which is 2992
8: 6 And the **p** with one accord gave heed unto 3793
8: 9 and bewitched the **p** of Samaria, giving out 1484
10: 2 which gave much alms to the **p**, and 2992
10:41 Not to all the **p**, but unto witnesses chosen 2992
10:42 he commanded us to preach unto the **p**, 2992
11:24 and much **p** was added unto the Lord. 3793
11:26 and taught much **p**, and the disciples were 3793
12: 4 after Easter to bring him forth to the **p**. 2992
12:11 *from* all the expectation of the **p** of 2992
12:22 And the **p** gave a shout, *saying, It is* 1218
13:15 ye have *any* word of exhortation for the **p**, 2992
13:17 The God of this **p** of Israel chose our 2992
13:17 exalted the **p** when *they* dwelt as strangers 2992
13:24 baptism of repentance to all the **p** of Israel. 2992
13:31 who are his witnesses unto the **p**. 2992
14:11 And when the **p** saw what Paul had done, 3793
14:13 and would have done sacrifice with the **p**. 3793
14:14 and ran in among the **p**, crying out, 3793
14:18 these sayings scarce restrained they the **p**, 3793
14:19 and Iconium, who persuaded the **p**, and, 3793
15:14 to take out of them a **p** for his name. 2992
17: 5 and sought to bring them out to the **p**. 1218
17: 8 And they troubled the **p** and the rulers of 3793
17:13 they came thither also, and stirred up the **p**. 3793
18:10 to hurt thee: for I have much **p** in this city. 2992
19: 4 baptism of repentance, saying unto the **p**, 2992
19:26 hath persuaded and turned away much **p**, 3793
19:30 Paul would have entered in unto the **p**, 1218
19:33 would have made *his* defence unto the **p**. 1218
19:35 when the townclerk had appeased the **p**, 3793
21:27 stirred up all the **p**, and laid hands on him, 3793
21:28 teacheth all *men* every where against the **p**, 2992
21:30 the city was moved, and the **p** ran together: 2992
21:35 of the soldiers for the violence of the **p**. 3793
21:36 For the multitude of the **p** followed *after,* 2992
21:39 beseech thee, suffer me to speak unto the **p**. 2992
21:40 and beckoned with the hand unto the **p**. 2992
23: 5 shalt not speak evil of the ruler of thy **p**. 2992
24:12 with any *man,* neither raising up the **p**, 3793
26:17 Delivering thee from the **p**, and *from* 2992
26:23 and should shew light unto the **p**, and to 2992
28: 2 And the **barbarous p** shewed us no little 915
28:17 I have committed nothing against the **p**, 2992
28:26 Saying, Go unto this **p**, and say, Hearing ye 2992
28:27 For the heart of this **p** is waxed gross, and 2992
Ro 9:25 he saith also in Osee, I will call *them* my **p**, 2992
9:25 call *them* my people, which were not my **p**; 2992
9:26 it was said unto them, Ye *are* not my **p**; 2992
10:19 you to jealousy by *them that are* no **p**, 1484
10:21 hands unto a disobedient and gainsaying **p**. 2992
11: 1 I say then, Hath God cast away his **p**? 2992
11: 2 God hath not cast away his **p** which he 2992
15:10 *he* saith, Rejoice, *ye* Gentiles, with his **p**. 2992
15:11 all ye Gentiles; and laud him, all ye **p**. 2992
1Co 10: 7 The **p** sat down to eat and drink, and 2992
14:21 and other lips will I speak unto this **p**; 2992
2Co 6:16 I will be their God, and they shall be my **p**. 2992
Tit 2:14 and purify unto himself a peculiar **p**, 2992
Heb 2:17 to make reconciliation for the sins of the **p**. 2992
4: 9 therefore a rest to the **p** of God. 2992
5: 3 as for the **p**, so also for himself, to offer for 2992
7: 5 to take tithes of the **p** according to the law, 2992
7:11 (for under it the **p** received the law,) 2992
8:10 to them a God, and they shall be to me a **p**: 2992
9: 7 for himself, and *for* the errors of the **p**: 2992
9:19 precept to all the **p** according to the law, 2992
9:19 and sprinkled both the book, and all the **p**, 2992
10:30 And again, The Lord shall judge his **p**. 2992
11:25 rather to suffer affliction with the **p** of God, 2992
13:12 that he might sanctify the **p** with his own 2992
1Pe 2: 9 a holy nation, a peculiar **p**; 2992
2:10 Which in time past *were* not a **p**, but 2992
2:10 not a people, but *are* now the **p** of God: 2992
2Pe 2: 1 there were false prophets also among the **p**, 2992
Jude 1: 5 having saved the **p** out of the land of Egypt, 2992
Rev 5: 9 and tongue, and **p**, and nation; 2992
7: 9 and kindreds, and **p**, and tongues, 2992
11: 9 And *they* of the **p** and kindreds and tongues 2992
14: 6 and kindred, and tongue, and **p**, 2992
18: 4 saying, Come out of her, my **p**, that ye be 2992
19: 1 I heard a great voice of much **p** in heaven, 3793
21: 3 and they shall be his **p**, and God himself 2992

PEOPLE'S (4) [PEOPLE]
Lev 9:15 he brought the **p** offering, and took 5971
Eze 46:18 Moreover the prince shall not take of the **p** 5971
Mt 13:15 For this **p** heart is waxed gross, and *their* 2992
Heb 7:27 first for his own sins, *and* then for the **p**: 2992

PEOPLES (2) [PEOPLE]
Rev 10:11 Thou must prophesy again before many **p**, 2992
17:15 are **p**, and multitudes, and nations, and 2992

PEOR (4) [BAAL-PEOR, BETH-PEOR, PEOR'S, PERADVENTURE]
Nu 23:28 Balak brought Balaam *unto* the top of **P**, 6465
25:18 they have beguiled you in the matter of **P**, 6465
31:16 against the LORD in the matter of **P**, 6465
Jos 22:17 *Is* the iniquity of **P** *too* little for us, from 6465

PEOR'S (1) [PEOR]
Nu 25:18 slain in the day of the plague for **P** sake. 6465

PERADVENTURE (32) [PEOR]
Ge 18:24 **P** there be fifty righteous within the city: 194
18:28 **P** there shall lack five of the fifty righteous: 194
18:29 said, **P** there shall be forty found there. 194
18:30 **P** there shall thirty be found there. And he 194
18:31 **P** there shall be twenty found there. And he 194
18:32 **P** ten shall be found there. And he said, 194
24: 5 **P** the woman will not be willing to follow 194
24:39 my master, **P** the woman will not follow me. 194
27:12 My father **p** will feel me, and I shall seem to 194
31:31 **P** thou wouldest take by force thy 6435
32:20 I will see his face; **p** he will accept of me. 194
38:11 for he said, **Lest p** he die also, as his 6435
42: 4 for he said, **Lest p** mischief befall him. 6435
43:12 *it* again in your hand; **p** it *was* an oversight: 194
44:34 **lest p** I see the evil that shall come on my 6435
50:15 Joseph will **p** hate us, and will certainly 3863
Ex 13:17 **Lest p** the people repent when they see 6435
32:30 **p** I shall make an atonement for your sin. 194
Nu 22: 6 **p** I shall prevail, *that* we may smite them, 194
22:11 **p** I shall be able to overcome them, and 194
23: 3 **p** the LORD will come to meet me: and 194
23:27 **p** it will please God that thou mayest curse 194
Jos 9: 7 said unto the Hivites, **P** ye dwell among us; 194
1Sa 6: 5 **p** he will lighten his hand from off you, and 194
9: 6 **p** he can shew us our way that we should go. 194
1Ki 18: 5 **p** we may find grass to save the horses and 194

1Ki 18:27 *or* **p** he sleepeth, and must be awaked. 194
20:31 to the king of Israel: **p** he will save thy life. 194
2Ki 2:16 **lest p** the spirit of the Lord hath taken 6435
Jer 20:10 *saying,* **P** he will be enticed, and we shall 194
Ro 5: 7 yet **p** for a good *man* some would even dare *5029*
2Ti 2:25 **if** God **p** will give them repentance to *3379*

PERAZIM (1) [BAAL-PERAZIM]
Isa 28:21 For the Lord shall rise up as *in* mount **P**, 6559

PERCEIVE (25) [PERCEIVED, PERCEIVEST, PERCEIVETH, PERCEIVING]
Dt 29: 4 the Lord hath not given you a heart to **p**, 3045
Jos 22:31 *This* day we **p** that the Lord *is* among 3045
1Sa 12:17 that ye may **p** and see that your wickedness 3045
2Sa 19: 6 for *this* day I **p**, that if Absalom had lived, 3045
2Ki 4: 9 I **p** that this *is* a holy man of God, 3045
Job 9:11 *him* not: he passeth on also, but I **p** him not. 995
23: 8 not *there;* and backward, but I cannot **p** him: 995
Pr 1: 2 instruction; to **p** the words of understanding; 995
Ecc 3:22 Wherefore I **p** that *there is* nothing better, 7200
Isa 6: 9 and see ye indeed, but **p** not. 3045
33:19 of a deeper speech than *thou* canst **p**; 8085
Mt 13:14 and seeing ye shall see, and shall not **p**: *1492*
Mk 4:12 That seeing they may see, and not **p**; and *1492*
7:18 Do ye not **p**, that whatsoever *thing* from *3539*
8:17 **p** ye not yet, neither understand? have ye *3539*
Lk 8:46 for I **p** that virtue is gone out of me. *1097*
Jn 4:19 unto him, Sir, I **p** that thou art a prophet. *2334*
12:19 **P** ye how ye prevail nothing? *2334*
Ac 8:23 For I **p** that thou art in the gall of bitterness, *3708*
10:34 Of a truth I **p** that God is no respecter of *2638*
17:22 I **p** that in all *things* ye are too *2334*
27:10 I **p** that *this* voyage will be with hurt and *2334*
28:26 and seeing ye shall see, and not **p**: *1492*
2Co 7: 8 for I **p** that the same epistle hath made you *991*
1Jn 3:16 Hereby **p** we the love *of God,* because *1097*

PERCEIVED (35) [PERCEIVE]
Ge 19:33 he **p** not when she lay down, nor when she 3045
19:35 he **p** not when she lay down, nor when she 3045
Jdg 6:22 when Gideon **p** that he *was* an angel of 7200
1Sa 3: 8 Eli **p** that the Lord had called the child. 995
28:14 Saul **p** that it *was* Samuel, and he stooped 3045
2Sa 5:12 David **p** that the Lord had established 3045
12:19 David **p** that the child was dead: 995
14: 1 Now Joab the son of Zeruiah **p** that 3045
1Ki 22:33 when the captains of the chariots **p** that it 7200
1Ch 14: 2 David **p** that the Lord had confirmed 3045
2Ch 18:32 that when the captains of the chariots **p** that 7200
Ne 6:12 lo, I **p** that God had not sent him; but 5234
6:16 for they **p** that this work was wrought of 3045
13:10 I **p** that the portions of the Levites had not 3045
Est 4: 1 When Mordecai **p** all that was done, 3045
Job 38:18 Hast thou **p** the breadth of the earth? 995
Ecc 1:17 folly: I **p** that this also *is* vexation of spirit. 3045
2:14 I myself **p** also that one event happeneth to 3045
Isa 64: 4 nor **p by the ear**, neither hath the eye seen, 238
Jer 23:18 and hath **p** and heard his word? 7200
38:27 with him; for the matter was not **p**. 8085
Mt 16: 8 *Which* when Jesus **p**, he said unto them, *1097*
21:45 his parables, they **p** that he spake of them. *1097*
22:18 But Jesus **p** their wickedness, and said, *1097*
Mk 2: 8 when Jesus **p** in his spirit that they so *1921*
Lk 1:22 they **p** that he had seen a vision in *1921*
5:22 But when Jesus **p** their thoughts, *1921*
9:45 and it was hid from them, that they **p** it not: *143*
20:19 for they **p** that he had spoken this parable *1097*
20:23 But he **p** their craftiness, and said unto *2657*
Jn 6:15 therefore **p** that they would come and *1097*
Ac 4:13 and **p** that they were unlearned and *2638*
23: 6 But when Paul **p** that the one part were *1097*
23:29 Whom I **p** to be accused of questions of *2147*
Gal 2: 9 **p** the grace that was given unto me, *1097*

PERCEIVEST (2) [PERCEIVE]
Pr 14: 7 when thou **p** not *in him* the lips of 3045
Lk 6:41 but **p** not the beam that is in thine own eye? *2657*

PERCEIVETH (3) [PERCEIVE]
Job 14:21 they are brought low, but he **p** *it* not of them. 995
33:14 speaketh once, yea twice, *yet man* **p** it not. 7789
Pr 31:18 She **p** that her merchandise *is* good: 2938

PERCEIVING (3) [PERCEIVE]
Mk 12:28 and **p** that he had answered them well, *1492*
Lk 9:47 And Jesus, **p** the thought of their heart, *1492*
Ac 14: 9 and **p** that he had faith to be healed, *1492*

PERDITION (8)
Jn 17:12 and none of them is lost, but the son of **p**; *684*
Php 1:28 which is to them an evident token of **p**, but *684*
2Th 2: 3 and *that* man of sin be revealed, the son of **p**; *684*
1Ti 6: 9 which drown men in destruction and **p**. *684*
Heb 10:39 we are not of *them* who draw back unto **p**; *684*
2Pe 3: 7 the day of judgment and **p** of ungodly men. *684*
Rev 17: 8 out of the bottomless *pit,* and go into **p**: *684*
17:11 and is of the seven, and goeth into **p**. *684*

PERES (1)
Da 5:28 **P**; Thy kingdom is divided, and given to 6537

PERESH (1)
1Ch 7:16 bare a son, and she called his name **P**; 6570

PEREZ (3)
1Ch 27: 3 Of the children of **P** *was* the chief of all 6557
Ne 11: 4 the son of Mahalaleel, of the children of **P**; 6557
11: 6 All the sons of **P** that dwelt at Jerusalem 6557

PEREZITE See PHARZITES

PEREZ-UZZA (1) [PEREZ-UZZAH, UZZAH]
1Ch 13:11 wherefore that place is called **P** to this day. 6560

PEREZ-UZZAH (1) [PEREZ-UZZA, UZZAH]
2Sa 6: 8 he called *the name* of the place **P** to this 6560

PERFECT (99) [PERFECTED, PERFECTING, PERFECTION, PERFECTLY, PERFECTNESS, UNPERFECT]
Ge 6: 9 was a just man *and* **p** in his generations, 8549
17: 1 walk before me, and be thou **p**. 8549
Lev 22:21 or sheep, it shall be **p** to be accepted; 8549
Dt 18:13 Thou shalt be **p** with the Lord thy God. 8549
25:15 *But* thou shalt have a **p** and just weight, 8003
25:15 a **p** and just measure shalt thou have: 8003
32: 4 *He is* the Rock, his work *is* **p**: for all his 8549
1Sa 14:41 Give a **p** *lot.* And Saul and Jonathan were 8549
2Sa 22:31 *As for* God, his way *is* **p**; the word of 8549
22:33 *and* power: and he maketh my way **p**. 8549
1Ki 8:61 therefore be **p** with the Lord our God, 8003
11: 4 his heart was not **p** with the Lord his 8003
15: 3 his heart was not **p** with the Lord his 8003
15:14 nevertheless Asa's heart was **p** with 8003
2Ki 20: 3 before thee in truth and with a **p** heart, 8003
1Ch 12:38 keep rank, came with a **p** heart to Hebron, 8003
28: 9 serve him with a **p** heart and with a willing 8003
29: 9 with **p** heart they offered willingly to 8003
29:19 give unto Solomon my son a **p** heart, 8003
2Ch 4:21 the tongs, *made he of* gold, *and* that **p** gold; 4357
15:17 nevertheless the heart of Asa was **p** all his 8003
16: 9 of *them* whose heart *is* **p** towards him. 8003
19: 9 the Lord, faithfully, and with a **p** heart. 8003
25: 2 sight of the Lord, but not with a **p** heart. 8003
Ezr 7:12 God of heaven, **p** *peace,* and at such a time. 1585
Job 1: 1 that man was **p** and upright, and one that 8535
1: 8 a **p** and an upright man, one that feareth 8535
2: 3 a **p** and an upright man, one that feareth 8535
8:20 God will not cast away a **p** *man,* neither 8535
9:20 *if I say, I am* **p**, it shall also prove me 8535
9:21 *Though* I *were* **p**, *yet* would I not know my 8535
9:22 therefore I said *it,* He destroyeth the **p** and 8535
22: 3 gain *to him,* that thou **makest** thy ways **p**? 8552
36: 4 *he that is* **p** in knowledge *is* with thee. 8549
37:16 the wondrous works of *him which is* **p** in 8549
Ps 18:30 *As for* God, his way *is* **p**: the word of 8549
18:32 me *with* strength, and maketh my way **p**. 8549
19: 7 The law of the Lord *is* **p**, converting 8549
37:37 Mark the **p** *man,* and behold the upright: 8535
64: 4 That *they* may shoot in secret at the **p**: 8535
101: 2 I will behave myself wisely in a **p** way. 8549
101: 2 I will walk within my house with a **p** heart. 8537
101: 6 he that walketh in a **p** way, he shall serve 8549
138: 8 The Lord will **p** that which concerneth 1584
139:22 I hate them *with* **p** hatred: I count them 8503
Pr 2:21 *in* the land, and the **p** shall remain in it. 8549
4:18 that shineth more and more unto the **p** day. 3559
11: 5 The righteousness of the **p** shall direct his 8549
Isa 18: 5 when the bud is **p**, and the sour grape is 8552

Isa 26: 3 Thou wilt keep him in p peace, 7965+7965
38: 3 before thee in truth and with a p heart, 8003
42:19 who is blind as he that is p, and blind as 7999
Eze 16:14 for it was p through my comeliness, 3632
27: 3 O Tyrus, thou hast said, I am of p beauty. 3632
27:11 round about; they have made thy beauty p. 3634
28:12 the sum, full of wisdom, and p in beauty. 3632
28:15 Thou wast p in thy ways from the day that 8549
Mt 5:48 Be ye therefore p, even as your Father 5046
5:48 even as your Father which is in heaven is p. 5046
19:21 If thou wilt be p, go and sell that thou hast, 5046
Lk 1: 3 having had p understanding of all things 199
6:40 every one that is p shall be as his master. 2675
Jn 17:23 in me, that they may be made p in one; 5048
Ac 3:16 this p soundness in the presence of you all. 3647
22: 3 taught according to the p manner of the law 195
24:22 having more p knowledge of that way, 197
Ro 12: 2 and acceptable, and p, will of God. 5046
1Co 2: 6 we speak wisdom among them that are p: 5046
13:10 But when that which is p is come, then 5046
2Co 12: 9 for my strength is made p in weakness. 5048
13:11 Be p, be of good comfort, be of one mind, 2675
Gal 3: 3 the Spirit, are ye now made p by the flesh? 2005
Eph 4:13 of the Son of God, unto a p man, 5046
Php 3:12 had already attained, either were already p: 5048
3:15 as many as be p, be thus minded: 5046
Col 1:28 that we may present every man p in Christ 5046
4:12 that ye may stand p and complete in all 5046
1Th 3:10 might p that which is lacking in your faith? 2675
2Ti 3:17 That the man of God may be p, 739
Heb 2:10 to make the captain of their salvation p 5048
5: 9 And being made p, he became the author 5048
7:19 For the law made nothing p, but 5048
9: 9 could not make him that did the service p, 5048
9:11 by a greater and more p tabernacle, 5046
10: 1 continually make the comers thereunto p. 5048
11:40 that they without us should not be made p. 5048
12:23 and to the spirits of just men made p, 5048
13:21 Make you p in every good work to do his 2675
Jas 1: 4 But let patience have her p work, that ye 5046
1: 4 that ye may be p and entire, 5046
1:17 good gift and every p gift is from above, 5046
1:25 But whoso looketh into the p law of liberty, 5046
2:22 his works, and by works was faith made p? 5048
3: 2 the same is a p man, and able also to bridle 5046
1Pe 5:10 make you p, stablish, strengthen, 2675
1Jn 4:17 Herein is our love made p, that we may 5048
4:18 no fear in love; but p love casteth out fear: 5046
4:18 He that feareth is not made p in love. 5048
Rev 3: 2 for I have not found thy works p before 4137

PERFECTED (8) [PERFECT]
2Ch 8:16 So the house of the LORD was p. 8003
24:13 the work was p by them, and they set 724+5927
Eze 27: 4 of the seas, thy builders have p thy beauty. 3634
Mt 21:16 of babes and sucklings thou hast p praise? 2675
Lk 13:32 to morrow, and the third day I shall be p. 5048
Heb 10:14 For by one offering he hath p for ever them 5048
1Jn 2: 5 in him verily is the love of God p: 5048
4:12 God dwelleth in us, and his love is p in us. 5048

PERFECTING (2) [PERFECT]
2Co 7: 1 and spirit, p holiness in the fear of God. 2005
Eph 4:12 For the p of the saints for the work of 2677

PERFECTION (11) [PERFECT]
Job 11: 7 canst thou find out the Almighty unto p? 8503
15:29 neither shall he prolong the p thereof upon 4512
28: 3 searcheth out all p, the stones of darkness, 8503
Ps 50: 2 Out of Zion, the p of beauty, God hath 4359
119:96 I have seen an end of all p: but 8502
Isa 47: 9 they shall come upon thee in their p for 8537
La 2:15 saying, Is this the city that men call The p 3632
Lk 8:14 of this life, and bring no fruit to p. 5052
2Co 13: 9 and this also we wish, even your p. 2676
Heb 6: 1 the doctrine of Christ, let us go on unto p; 5047
7:11 p were by the Levitical priesthood, 5050

PERFECTLY (7) [PERFECT]
Jer 23:20 in the latter days ye shall consider it p. 995+998
Mt 14:36 as many as touched were made p whole. 1295
Ac 18:26 unto him the way of God more p. 197
23:15 inquire something more p concerning him: 197
23:20 would inquire somewhat of him more p. 197
1Co 1:10 that ye be p joined together in the same 2675
1Th 5: 2 For yourselves know p that the day of 199

PERFECTNESS (1) [PERFECT]
Col 3:14 put on charity, which is the bond of p. 5047

PERFORM (42) [PERFORMANCE, PERFORMED, PERFORMETH, PERFORMING]
Ge 26: 3 I will p the oath which I sware unto 6965
Ex 18:18 thou art not able to p it thyself alone. 6213
Nu 4:23 all that enter in to p the service, to 6633+6635
Dt 4:13 which he commanded you to p, even ten 6213
9: 5 that he may p the word which the LORD 6965
23:23 gone out of thy lips thou shalt keep and p; 6213
25: 5 p the duty of a husband's brother unto 2992
25: 7 not p the duty of my husband's brother. 2992
Ru 3:13 he will p unto thee the part of a kinsman, 1350
1Sa 3:12 In that day I will p against Eli all things 6965
2Sa 14:15 it may be that the king will p the request of 6213
1Ki 6:12 will I p my word with thee, which I spake 6965
12:15 the LORD, that he might p his saying, 6965
2Ki 23: 3 to p the words of this covenant that were 6965
23:24 that he might p the words of the law which 6965
2Ch 10:15 of God, that the LORD might p his word, 6965
34:31 to p the words of the covenant which are 6213
Est 5: 8 to p my request, let the king and 6213
Job 5:12 so that their hands cannot p their enterprise. 6213
Ps 21:11 which they are not able to p. NIH
61: 8 name for ever, that I may daily p my vows. 7999
119:106 I will p it, that I will keep thy righteous 6965
119:112 I have inclined mine heart to p thy statutes 6213
Isa 9: 7 The zeal of the LORD of hosts will p this. 6213
19:21 shall vow a vow unto the LORD, and p it. 7999
44:28 is my shepherd, and shall p all my pleasure: 7999
Jer 1:12 well seen: for I will hasten my word to p it. 6213
11: 5 That I may p the oath which I have sworn 6965
28: 6 the LORD p thy words which thou hast 6965
29:10 p my good word towards you, in causing 6965
33:14 that I will p that good thing which I have 6965
44:25 We will surely p our vows that we have 6213
44:25 your vows, and surely p your vows. 6213+6213
Eze 12:25 will I say the word, and will p it, 6213
Mic 7:20 Thou wilt p the truth to Jacob, and 5414
Na 1:15 keep thy solemn feasts, p thy vows: 7999
Mt 5:33 but shalt p unto the Lord thine oaths: 591
Lk 1:72 To p the mercy promised to our fathers, 4160
Ro 4:21 he had promised, he was able also to p. 4160
7:18 but how to p that which is good I find not. 2716
2Co 8:11 p the doing of it; that as there was a 2005
Php 1: 6 you will p it until the day of Jesus Christ: 2005

PERFORMANCE (2) [PERFORM]
Lk 1:45 for there shall be a p of those things which 5050
2Co 8:11 there may be a p also out of that which you 2005

PERFORMED (21) [PERFORM]
1Sa 15:11 and hath not p my commandments. 6965
15:13 I have p the commandment of the LORD. 6965
2Sa 21:14 they p all that the king commanded. 6213
1Ki 8:20 the LORD hath p his word that he spake, 6965
2Ch 6:10 hath p his word that he hath spoken: 6965
Ne 9: 8 it, I say, to his seed, and hast p thy words; 6965
Est 1:15 she hath not p the commandment of 6213
5: 6 to the half of the kingdom it shall be p. 6213
7: 2 it shall be p, even to the half of 6213
Ps 65: 1 in Zion: and unto thee shall the vow be p. 7999
Isa 10:12 that when the Lord hath p his whole work 1214
Jer 23:20 and till he have p the thoughts of his heart: 6965
30:24 and until he have p the intents of his heart: 6965
34:18 which have not p the words of the covenant 6965
35:14 his sons not to drink wine, are p; 6965
35:16 have p the commandment of their father, 6965
51:29 for every purpose of the LORD shall be p 6965
Eze 37:14 have spoken it, and p it, saith the LORD. 6213
Lk 1:20 until the day that these things shall be p, 1096
2:39 And when they had p all things according 5055
Ro 15:28 When therefore I have p this, and 2005

PERFORMETH (4) [PERFORM]
Ne 5:13 from his labour, that p not this promise, 6965
Job 23:14 For he p the thing that is appointed for me: 7999
Ps 57: 2 unto God that p all things for me. 1584
Isa 44:26 and p the counsel of his messengers; 7999

PERFORMING (2) [PERFORM]
Nu 15: 3 or a sacrifice in **p** a vow, or in a freewill 6381
15: 8 or *for* a sacrifice in **p** a vow, or 6381

PERFUME (3) [PERFUMED, PERFUMES]
Ex 30:35 thou shalt make it a **p**, a confection *after* 7004
30:37 *as for* the **p** which thou shalt make, 7004
Pr 27: 9 Ointment and **p** rejoice the heart: so 7004

PERFUME-MAKERS See APOTHECARIES

PERFUMED (2) [PERFUME]
Pr 7:17 I have **p** my bed *with* myrrh, aloes, and 5130
SS 3: 6 **p** *with* myrrh and frankincense, with all 6999

PERFUMER See APOTHECARY

PERFUMERS See CONFECTIONARIES

PERFUMES (1) [PERFUME]
Isa 57: 9 didst increase thy **p**, and didst send thy 7547

PERGA (3)
Ac 13:13 from Paphos, they came to **P** in Pamphylia: *4011*
13:14 But when they departed from **P**, they came *4011*
14:25 And when they had preached the word in **P**, *4011*

PERGAMOS (2)
Rev 1:11 and unto **P**, and unto Thyatira, and *4010*
2:12 And to the angel of the church in **P** write; *4010*

PERGAMUM See PERGAMOS

PERHAPS (3)
Ac 8:22 if **p** the thought of thine heart may be *686*
2Co 2: 7 comfort *him*, **lest p** such a one should be *3381*
Phm 1:15 For **p** he therefore departed for a season, *5029*

PERIDA (1) [PERUDA]
Ne 7:57 the children of Sophereth, the children of **P**, 6514

PERIL (2) [PERILOUS, PERILS]
La 5: 9 We gat our bread with *the* **p** *of* our lives NIH
Ro 8:35 or famine, or nakedness, or **p**, or sword? *2794*

PERILOUS (1) [PERIL]
2Ti 3: 1 that in the last days **p** times shall come. *5467*

PERILS (8) [PERIL]
2Co 11:26 *in* **p** of waters, *in* perils of robbers, *2794*
11:26 *in* perils of waters, *in* **p** of robbers, *2794*
11:26 of robbers, *in* **p** by *my own* countrymen, *2794*
11:26 *in* **p** by the heathen, *in* perils in the city, *2794*
11:26 *in* perils by the heathen, *in* **p** in the city, *2794*
11:26 *in* **p** in the wilderness, *in* perils in the sea, *2794*
11:26 *in* perils in the wilderness, *in* **p** in the sea, *2794*
11:26 perils in the sea, *in* **p** among false brethren; *2794*

PERISH (120) [PERISHED, PERISHETH, PERISHING]
Ge 41:36 that the land **p** not through the famine. 3772
Ex 19:21 the LORD to gaze, and many of them **p**. 5307
21:26 his servant, or the eye of his maid, that it **p**; 7843
Lev 26:38 ye shall **p** among the heathen, and the land of 6
Nu 17:12 Behold, we die, we **p**, we all perish. 6
17:12 Behold, we die, we perish, we all **p**. 6
24:20 but his latter end *shall be* that he **p** for ever. 8
24:24 shall afflict Eber, and he also shall **p** for ever. 8
Dt 4:26 that ye shall soon **utterly p** from off the land 6+6
8:19 against you *this* day that ye shall **surely p**. 6+6
8:20 destroyeth before your face, so shall ye **p**; 6
11:17 *lest* ye **p** quickly from off the good land which 6
26: 5 A Syrian **ready to p** *was* my father, and 6
28:20 thou be destroyed, and until thou **p** quickly; 6
28:22 and they shall pursue thee until thou **p**. 6
30:18 that ye shall **surely p**, *and that* ye shall not 6+6
Jos 23:13 until ye **p** from off this good land which 6
23:16 ye shall **p** quickly from off the good land 6
Jdg 5:31 So let all thine enemies **p**, O LORD: but 6
1Sa 26:10 or he shall descend into battle, and **p**. 5595
27: 1 I shall now **p** one day by the hand of Saul: 5595
2Ki 9: 8 For the whole house of Ahab shall **p**: and I will 6
Est 3:13 to destroy, to kill, and to **cause to p**, all Jews, 6
4:16 *is* not according to the law: and if I **p**, I perish. 6
4:16 *is* not according to the law: and if I perish, I **p**. 6
7: 4 to be destroyed, to be slain, and to **p**. 6
8:11 their life, to destroy, to slay, and to **cause to p**, 6
9:28 nor the memorial of them **p** from their seed. 5486
Job 3: 3 Let the day **p** wherein I was born, and the night 6
4: 9 By the blast of God they **p**, and by the breath 6
4:20 they **p** for ever without *any* regarding *it*. 6
6:18 way are turned aside; they go to nothing, and **p**. 6
8:13 forget God; and the hypocrite's hope shall **p**: 6
18:17 His remembrance shall **p** from the earth, and 6
20: 7 *Yet* he shall **p** for ever like his own dung: 6
29:13 The blessing of him that was **ready to p** came 6
31:19 If I have seen *any* **p** for want of clothing, or 6
34:15 All flesh shall **p** together, and man shall 1478
36:12 they shall **p** by the sword, and they shall 5674
Ps 1: 6 but the way of the ungodly shall **p**. 6
2:12 lest he be angry, and ye **p** *from* the way, 6
9: 3 they shall fall and **p** at thy presence. 6
9:18 the expectation of the poor shall *not* **p** for ever. 6
37:20 the wicked shall **p**, and the enemies of 6
41: 5 evil of me, When shall he die, and his name **p**? 6
49:10 likewise the fool and the brutish person **p**, and 6
49:12 abideth not: he is like the beasts *that* **p**. 1820
49:20 understandeth not, is like the beasts *that* **p**. 1820
68: 2 *so* let the wicked **p** at the presence of God. 6
73:27 For lo, they that are far from thee shall **p**: 6
80:16 they **p** at the rebuke of thy countenance. 6
83:17 for ever; yea, let them be put to shame, and **p**: 6
92: 9 O LORD, for lo, thine enemies shall **p**; 6
102:26 They shall **p**, but thou shalt endure: yea, all of 6
112:10 melt away: the desire of the wicked shall **p**. 6
146: 4 to his earth; in that *very* day his thoughts **p**. 6
Pr 10:28 but the expectation of the wicked shall **p**. 6
11: 7 a wicked man dieth, *his* expectation shall **p**: 6
11:10 and when the wicked **p**, *there is* shouting. 6
19: 9 and *he that* speaketh lies shall **p**. 6
21:28 A false witness shall **p**: but the man that 6
28:28 but when they **p**, the righteous increase. 6
29:18 Where *there is* no vision, the people **p**: but 6544
31: 6 Give strong drink unto him that is **ready to p**, 6
Ecc 5:14 those riches **p** by evil travail: and he begetteth 6
Isa 26:14 and **made** all their memory **to p**. 6
27:13 they shall come which were ready to **p** in 6
29:14 for the wisdom of their wise *men* shall **p**, and 6
41:11 and they that strive with thee shall **p**. 6
60:12 and kingdom that will not serve thee shall **p**; 6
Jer 4: 9 *that* the heart of the king shall **p**, and the heart 6
6:21 the neighbour and his friend shall **p**. 6
10:11 *even* they shall **p** from the earth, and 7
10:15 in the time of their visitation they shall **p**. 6
18:18 for the law shall not **p** from the priest, 6
27:10 *that* I should drive you out, and ye should **p**. 6
27:15 that ye might **p**, ye, and the prophets that 6
40:15 be scattered, and the remnant in Judah **p**? 6
48: 8 the valley also shall **p**, and the plain shall be 6
51:18 in the time of their visitation they shall **p**. 6
Eze 7:26 the law shall **p** from the priest, and 6
25: 7 and I will **cause** thee **to p** out of the countries: 6
Da 2:18 his fellows should not **p** with the rest of 7
Am 1: 8 the remnant of the Philistines shall **p**, saith 6
2:14 Therefore the flight shall **p** from the swift, and 6
3:15 the houses of ivory shall **p**, and the great 6
Jnh 1: 6 be that God will think upon us, that we **p** not. 6
1:14 let us not **p** for this man's life, and lay not upon 6
3: 9 turn away from his fierce anger, that we **p** not? 6
Zec 9: 5 the king shall **p** from Gaza, and Ashkelon shall 6
Mt 5:29 for thee that one of thy members should **p**, *622*
5:30 for thee that one of thy members should **p**, *622*
8:25 and awoke him, saying, Lord, save us: we **p**. *622*
9:17 and the wine runneth out, and the bottles **p**: *622*
18:14 that one of these little ones should **p**. *622*
26:52 for all they that take the sword shall **p** with *622*
Mk 4:38 unto him, Master, carest thou not that we **p**? *622*
Lk 5:37 and be spilled, and the bottles shall **p**. *622*
8:24 awoke him, saying, Master, master, we **p**. *622*
13: 3 but, except ye repent, ye shall all likewise **p**. *622*
13: 5 but except ye repent, ye shall all likewise **p**. *622*
13:33 for it cannot be that a prophet **p** out of *622*
15:17 and to spare, and I **p** with hunger? *622*
21:18 But there shall not a hair of your head **p**. *622*
Jn 3:15 whosoever believeth in him should not **p**, *622*
3:16 whosoever believeth in him should not **p**, *622*
10:28 and they shall never **p**, neither shall any *man* *622*
11:50 the people, and *that* the whole nation **p** not. *622*
Ac 8:20 Thy money **p** with thee, *684+1510+1519*
13:41 Behold *ye* despisers, and wonder, and **p**: *853*
Ro 2:12 sinned without law shall also **p** without law: *622*

1Co 1:18 of the cross is to them that p foolishness; 622
8:11 thy knowledge shall the weak brother p, 622
2Co 2:15 in them that are saved, and in them that p: 622
4:16 but though our outward man p, yet 1311
Col 2:22 Which all are to p with the using;) after 5356
2Th 2:10 of unrighteousness in them that p; 622
Heb 1:11 They shall p; but thou remainest; and 622
2Pe 2:12 and shall utterly p in their own corruption; 2704
3: 9 not willing that any should p, but that all 622

PERISHED (26) [PERISH]
Nu 16:33 and they p from among the congregation. 6
21:30 Heshbon is p even unto Dibon, and we have 6
Jos 22:20 and that man p not alone in his iniquity. 1478
2Sa 1:27 the mighty fallen, and the weapons of war p! 6
Job 4: 7 Remember, I pray thee, who *ever* p, 6
30: 2 their hands profit me, in whom old age was p? 6
Ps 9: 6 destroyed cities; their memorial is p *with* them. 6
10:16 and ever: the heathen are p out of his land. 6
83:10 *Which* p at En-dor: they became *as* dung 8045
119:92 I should then have p in mine affliction. 6
Ecc 9: 6 and their hatred, and their envy, is now p; 6
Jer 7:28 truth is p, and is cut off from their mouth. 6
48:36 because the riches *that* he hath gotten are p. 6
49: 7 is counsel p from the prudent? is their wisdom 6
La 3:18 and my hope is p from the LORD: 6
Joel 1:11 the barley; because the harvest of the field is p. 6
Jnh 4:10 which came up in a night, and p in a night: 6
Mic 4: 9 is thy counseller p? for pangs have taken thee 6
7: 2 The good *man* is p out of the earth: and *there is* 6
Mt 8:32 steep place into the sea, and p in the waters. 599
Lk 11:51 which p between the altar and the temple: 622
Ac 5:37 he also p; and all, *even* as many as obeyed 622
1Co 15:18 also which are fallen asleep in Christ are p. 622
Heb 11:31 By faith the harlot Rahab p not with them 4881
2Pe 3: 6 then was, being overflowed with water, p: 622
Jude 1:11 for reward, and p in the gainsaying of Core. 622

PERISHETH (9) [PERISH]
Job 4:11 The old lion p for lack of prey, and the stout 6
Pr 11: 7 shall perish: and the hope of unjust *men* p. 6
Ecc 7:15 there is a just *man* that p in his righteousness, 6
Isa 57: 1 The righteous p, and no man layeth *it* to heart: 6
Jer 9:12 for what the land p *and* is burnt up like a 6
48:46 the people of Chemosh p: for thy sons are 6
Jn 6:27 Labour not for the meat which p, but for *that* 622
Jas 1:11 and the grace of the fashion of it p: 622
1Pe 1: 7 much more precious than of gold that p, 622

PERISHING (1) [PERISH]
Job 33:18 the pit, and his life from p by the sword. 5674

PERIZZITE (5) [PERIZZITES]
Ge 13: 7 and the P dwelled then in the land. 6522
Ex 33: 2 and the P, the Hivite, and the Jebusite: 6522
34:11 and the P, and the Hivite, and the Jebusite. 6522
Jos 9: 1 the P, the Hivite, and the Jebusite, 6522
11: 3 the P, and the Jebusite in the mountains, 6522

PERIZZITES (18) [PERIZZITE]
Ge 15:20 the Hittites, and the P, and the Rephaims, 6522
34:30 the land, amongst the Canaanites and the P: 6522
Ex 3: 8 the P, and the Hivites, and the Jebusites. 6522
3:17 the P, and the Hivites, and the Jebusites, 6522
23:23 the P, and the Canaanites, the Hivites, and 6522
Dt 7: 1 the P, and the Hivites, and the Jebusites, 6522
20:17 and the P, the Hivites, and the Jebusites; 6522
Jos 3:10 the P, and the Girgashites, and 6522
12: 8 the P, the Hivites, and the Jebusites: 6522
17:15 down for thyself there in the land of the P 6522
24:11 the P, and the Canaanites, and the Hittites, 6522
Jdg 1: 4 the Canaanites and the P into their hand: 6522
1: 5 and they slew the Canaanites and the P. 6522
3: 5 and P, and Hivites, and Jebusites: 6522
1Ki 9:20 Hittites, P, Hivites, and Jebusites, 6522
2Ch 8: 7 the P, and the Hivites, and the Jebusites, 6522
Ezr 9: 1 the Hittites, the P, the Jebusites, 6522
Ne 9: 8 the P, and the Jebusites, and 6522

PERJURED (1)
1Ti 1:10 for p *persons*, and if *there be* any other 1965

PERMISSION (1) [PERMIT]
1Co 7: 6 But I speak this by p, *and* not of 4774

PERMIT (2) [PERMISSION, PERMITTED]
1Co 16: 7 to tarry a while with you, if the Lord p. 2010
Heb 6: 3 And this will we do, if God p. 2010

PERMITTED (2) [PERMIT]
Ac 26: 1 unto Paul, Thou art p to speak for thyself. 2010
1Co 14:34 for it is not p unto them to speak; but 2010

PERNICIOUS (1)
2Pe 2: 2 And many shall follow their p ways; 684

PERPETUAL (28) [PERPETUALLY]
Ge 9:12 creature that *is* with you, for p generations: 5769
Ex 29: 9 the priest's office shall be theirs for a p 5769
30: 8 a p incense before the LORD throughout 8548
31:16 their generations, *for* a p covenant. 5769
Lev 3:17 *It shall be* a p statute for your generations 5769
6:20 an ephah of fine flour *for* a meat offering p, 8548
24: 9 of the LORD made by fire, *by* a p statute. 5769
25:34 may not be sold; for it *is* their p possession. 5769
Nu 19:21 it shall be a p statute unto them, that he that 5769
Ps 9: 6 destructions are come to a p end: 5331+3807.1
74: 3 Lift up thy feet unto the p desolations; 5331
78:66 hinder parts: he put them to a p reproach. 5769
Jer 5:22 sand *for* the bound of the sea *by* a p decree, 5769
8: 5 Jerusalem slidden back *by* a p backsliding? 5329
15:18 Why is my pain p, and my wound 5331
18:16 make their land desolate, *and* a p hissing; 5769
23:40 a p shame, which shall not be forgotten. 5769
25: 9 and a hissing, and p desolations. 5769
25:12 and will make it p desolations. 5769
49:13 and all the cities thereof shall be p wastes. 5769
50: 5 let us join ourselves to the LORD *in* a p 5769
51:39 sleep a p sleep, and not wake, saith 5769
51:57 mighty *men:* and they shall sleep a p sleep, 5769
Eze 35: 5 Because thou hast had a p hatred, and 5769
35: 9 I will make thee p desolations, and 5769
46:14 a meat offering continually *by* a p 5769
Hab 3: 6 were scattered, the p hills did bow: 5769
Zep 2: 9 and saltpits, and a p desolation: 5704+5769

PERPETUALLY (3) [PERPETUAL]
1Ki 9: 3 mine heart shall be there p. 3117+3605+1886.1
2Ch 7:16 mine heart shall be there p. 3117+3605+1886.1
Am 1:11 his anger did tear p, and he kept his 5703+3807.1

PERPLEXED (5) [PERPLEXITY]
Est 3:15 down to drink; but the city Shushan was p. 943
Joel 1:18 the herds of cattle are p, because they have 943
Lk 9: 7 and he was p, because that it was said of 1280
24: 4 as they were *much* p thereabout, behold, 1280
2Co 4: 8 not distressed; *we are* p, but not in despair; 639

P

PERPLEXITY (3) [PERPLEXED]
Isa 22: 5 of p by the Lord GOD of hosts in 3998
Mic 7: 4 thy visitation cometh; now shall be their p. 3998
Lk 21:25 upon the earth distress of nations, with p; 640

PERSECUTE (25) [PERSECUTED, PERSECUTEST, PERSECUTING, PERSECUTION, PERSECUTIONS, PERSECUTOR, PERSECUTORS]
Job 19:22 Why do ye p me as God, and are not 7291
19:28 ye should say, Why p we him? seeing 7291
Ps 7: 1 save me from all them that p me, and 7291
7: 5 Let the enemy p my soul, and take *it;* yea, 7291
10: 2 The wicked in *his* pride doth p the poor: 1814
31:15 of mine enemies, and from them that p me. 7291
35: 3 and stop *the way* against them that p me: 7291
35: 6 and let the angel of the LORD p them. 7291
69:26 For they p *him* whom thou hast smitten; 7291
71:11 p and take him; for *there is* none to deliver 7291
83:15 So p them with thy tempest, and 7291
119:84 thou execute judgment on them that p me? 7291
119:86 they p me wrongfully; help thou me. 7291
Jer 17:18 Let them be confounded that p me, but 7291
29:18 I will p them with the sword, with 7291
La 3:66 P and destroy them in anger from under 7291
Mt 5:11 and p *you,* and shall say all manner of evil 1377
5:44 which despitefully use you, and p you; 1377
10:23 But when they p you in this city, flee ye 1377
23:34 and p *them* from city to city: 1377
Lk 11:49 and *some* of them they shall slay and p: 1559
21:12 p *you,* delivering *you* up to *the* synagogues, 1377
Jn 5:16 And therefore did the Jews p Jesus, and 1377

Jn 15:20 have persecuted me, they will also **p** you; *1377*
Ro 12:14 Bless them which **p** you: bless, and *1377*

PERSECUTED (20) [PERSECUTE]
Dt 30: 7 and on them that hate thee, which **p** thee. 7291
Ps 109:16 **p** the poor and needy man, that *he* might 7291
119:161 Princes have **p** me without a cause: but 7291
143: 3 For the enemy hath **p** my soul; he hath 7291
Isa 14: 6 nations in anger, *is* **p**, *and* none hindereth. 4783
La 3:43 Thou hast covered with anger, and **p** us: 7291
Mt 5:10 Blessed *are* they which are **p** for *1377*
5:12 **p** they the prophets which were before you. *1377*
Jn 15:20 If they have **p** me, they will also persecute *1377*
Ac 7:52 of the prophets have not your fathers **p**? *1377*
22: 4 And I **p** this way unto the death, binding *1377*
26:11 I **p** *them* even unto strange cities. *1377*
1Co 4:12 we bless; being **p**, we suffer *it:* *1377*
15: 9 an apostle, because I **p** the church of God. *1377*
2Co 4: 9 **P**, but not forsaken; cast down, but *1377*
Gal 1:13 how that beyond measure I **p** the church of *1377*
1:23 That he which **p** us in times past now *1377*
4:29 he that was born after the flesh **p** him that *1377*
1Th 2:15 and their own prophets, and have **p** us; *1559*
Rev 12:13 he **p** the woman which brought forth *1377*

PERSECUTEST (6) [PERSECUTE]
Ac 9: 4 unto him, Saul, Saul, why **p** thou me? *1377*
9: 5 the Lord said, I am Jesus whom thou **p**: *1377*
22: 7 unto me, Saul, Saul, why **p** thou me? *1377*
22: 8 I am Jesus of Nazareth, whom thou **p**. *1377*
26:14 Saul, Saul, why **p** thou me? *1377*
26:15 And he said, I am Jesus whom thou **p**. *1377*

PERSECUTING (1) [PERSECUTE]
Php 3: 6 Concerning zeal, **p** the church; touching *1377*

PERSECUTION (10) [PERSECUTE]
La 5: 5 Our necks *are* under **p**: we labour, *and* 7291
Mt 13:21 or **p** ariseth because of the word, *1375*
Mk 4:17 or **p** ariseth for the word's sake, *1375*
Ac 8: 1 And at that time there was a great **p** against *1375*
11:19 **p** that arose about Stephen travelled as far *2347*
13:50 and raised **p** against Paul and Barnabas, *1375*
Ro 8:35 or **p**, or famine, or nakedness, or peril, or *1375*
Gal 5:11 why do I yet **suffer p**? *1377*
6:12 only lest they should **suffer p** for the cross *1377*
2Ti 3:12 live godly in Christ Jesus shall **suffer p**. *1377*

PERSECUTIONS (5) [PERSECUTE]
Mk 10:30 mothers, and children, and lands, with **p**; *1375*
2Co 12:10 in reproaches, in necessities, in **p**, *1375*
2Th 1: 4 and faith in all your **p** and tribulations that *1375*
2Ti 3:11 **P**, afflictions, which came unto me at *1375*
3:11 at Iconium, at Lystra; what **p** I endured: *1375*

PERSECUTOR (1) [PERSECUTE]
1Ti 1:13 before a blasphemer, and a **p**, and injurious: *1376*

PERSECUTORS (8) [PERSECUTE]
Ne 9:11 and their **p** thou threwest into the deeps, 7291
Ps 7:13 he ordaineth his arrows against the **p**. 1814
119:157 Many *are* my **p** and mine enemies; *yet* do I 7291
142: 6 deliver me from my **p**; for they are stronger 7291
Jer 15:15 and visit me, and revenge me of my **p**; 7291
20:11 therefore my **p** shall stumble, and they shall 7291
La 1: 3 all her **p** overtook her between the straits. 7291
4:19 Our **p** are swifter than the eagles of 7291

PERSEVERANCE (1)
Eph 6:18 and watching thereunto with all **p** and *4343*

PERSIA (29) [PERSIAN, PERSIANS]
2Ch 36:20 sons until the reign of the kingdom of **P**: 6539
36:22 Now in the first year of Cyrus king of **P**, 6539
36:22 stirred up the spirit of Cyrus king of **P**, 6539
36:23 Thus saith Cyrus king of **P**, All 6539
Ezr 1: 1 Now in the first year of Cyrus king of **P**, 6539
1: 1 stirred up the spirit of Cyrus king of **P**, 6539
1: 2 Thus saith Cyrus king of **P**, The LORD 6539
1: 8 Even those did Cyrus king of **P** bring forth 6539
3: 7 the grant that they had of Cyrus king of **P**. 6539
4: 3 as king Cyrus the king of **P** hath 6539
4: 5 all the days of Cyrus king of **P**, 6539
4: 5 even until the reign of Darius king of **P**. 6539
4: 7 unto Artaxerxes king of **P**; 6539
4:24 year of the reign of Darius king of **P**. 6540
6:14 and Darius, and Artaxerxes king of **P**. 6540
7: 1 in the reign of Artaxerxes king of **P**, 6539
9: 9 mercy unto us in the sight of the kings of **P**, 6539
Est 1: 3 the power of **P** and Media, the nobles and 6539
1:14 the seven princes of **P** and Media, 6539
1:18 Likewise shall the ladies of **P** and 6539
10: 2 the chronicles of the kings of Media and **P**? 6539
Eze 27:10 They of **P** and of Lud and of Phut were in 6539
38: 5 **P**, Ethiopia, and Libya with them; all of 6539
Da 8:20 two horns *are* the kings of Media and **P**. 6539
10: 1 In the third year of Cyrus king of **P** a thing 6539
10:13 the prince of the kingdom of **P** withstood 6539
10:13 and I remained there with the kings of **P**. 6539
10:20 will I return to fight with the prince of **P**: 6539
11: 2 there *shall* stand up yet three kings in **P**; 6539

PERSIAN (2) [PERSIA]
Ne 12:22 also the priests, to the reign of Darius the **P**. 6542
Da 6:28 of Darius, and in the reign of Cyrus the **P**. 6543

PERSIANS (5) [PERSIA]
Est 1:19 let it be written among the laws of the **P** 6539
Da 5:28 is divided, and given to the Medes and **P**. 6540
6: 8 according to the law of the Medes and **P**, 6540
6:12 according to the law of the Medes and **P**, 6540
6:15 **P** *is,* That no decree nor statute which 6540

PERSIS (1)
Ro 16:12 Salute the beloved **P**, which laboured much *4069*

PERSON (56) [PERSONS]
Ge 39: 6 Joseph was *a* goodly *p*, and well favoured. NIH
Ex 12:48 for no **uncircumcised p** shall eat thereof. 6189
Lev 19:15 thou shalt not respect the **p** of the poor, 6440
19:15 of the poor, nor honour the **p** of the mighty: 6440
Nu 5: 6 against the LORD, and that **p** be guilty; 5315
19:17 for an unclean *p* they shall take of the ashes NIH
19:18 a clean **p** shall take hyssop, and dip *it* in 376
19:19 the clean *p* shall sprinkle upon the unclean NIH
19:22 whatsoever the unclean *p* toucheth shall be NIH
31:19 whosoever hath killed *any* **p**, and 5315
35:11 which killeth *any* **p** at unawares. 5315
35:15 that every one that killeth *any* **p** unawares 5315
35:30 Whoso killeth *any* **p**, the murderer shall be 5315
35:30 one witness shall not testify against *any* **p** 5315
Dt 15:22 the unclean and the clean *p shall eat it* alike, NIH
27:25 that taketh reward to slay an innocent **p**s. 1818
28:50 which shall not regard the **p** of the old, 6440
Jos 20: 3 That the slayer that killeth *any* **p** unawares 5315
20: 9 that whosoever killeth *any* **p** at unawares 5315
1Sa 9: 2 the children of Israel a goodlier **p** than he: 376
16:18 and a comely **p**, and the LORD *is* with him. 376
25:35 to thy voice, and have accepted thy **p**. 6440
2Sa 4:11 when wicked men have slain a righteous **p** in 376
14:14 up *again;* neither doth God respect *any* **p**: 5315
17:11 and *that* thou go to battle in thine own **p**. 6440
Job 13: 8 Will ye accept his **p**? will ye contend for 6440
22:29 and he shall save the **humble p**. 5869+7807
32:21 Let me not, I pray you, accept *any* man's **p**, 6440
Ps 15: 4 In whose eyes a vile *p* is contemned; but he NIH
49:10 likewise the fool and the **brutish p** perish, 1198
101: 4 from me: I will not know a wicked *p*. NIH
105:37 *there was* not *one* feeble *p* among their NIH
Pr 6:12 A naughty **p**, a wicked man, walketh *with* a 120
18: 5 *It is* not good to accept the **p** of the wicked, 6440
24: 8 to do evil shall be called a mischievous **p**. 1167
28:17 to the blood of *any* **p** shall flee to the pit; 5315
Isa 32: 5 The **vile p** shall be no more called liberal, 5036
32: 6 For the **vile p** will speak villany, and 5036
Jer 43: 6 every **p** that Nebuzar-adan the captain of 5315
52:25 men of them that were near the king's **p**, 6440
Eze 16: 5 to the lothing of thy **p**, in the day that thou 5315
33: 6 and take *any* **p** from among them, 5315
44:25 they shall come at no dead **p** to defile 120
Da 11:21 in his estate shall stand up a **vile p**, to whom 959
Mal 1: 8 he be pleased with thee, or accept thy **p**? 6440
Mt 22:16 *man:* for thou regardest not the **p** of men. *4383*
27:24 I am innocent of the blood of this just **p**: NIG
Mk 12:14 *man:* for thou regardest not the **p** of men, *4383*
Lk 20:21 neither acceptest thou the **p** *of any,* but *4383*
1Co 5:13 from among yourselves *that* wicked **p**. NIG
2Co 2:10 your sakes *forgave I it* in the **p** of Christ; *4383*
Gal 2: 6 God accepteth no man's **p**:) for they who *4383*

P

Eph 5: 5 nor unclean *p*, nor covetous man who is an NIG
Heb 1: 3 and the express image of his **p**, and *5287*
12:16 *be* any fornicator, or profane *p*, as Esau, NIG
2Pe 2: 5 saved Noah the eighth *p*, a preacher of NIG

PERSONS (56) [PERSON]

Ge 14:21 Give me the **p**, and take the goods to 5315
36: 6 all the **p** of his house, and his cattle, and 5315
Ex 16:16 *according to* the number of your **p**; 5315
Lev 27: 2 the **p** *shall be* for the LORD by thy 5315
Nu 19:18 upon the **p** that were there, and upon him 5315
31:28 *both* of the **p**, and of the beeves, and of 120
31:30 of the **p**, of the beeves, of the asses, and 120
31:35 thirty and two thousand **p** in all, 120+5315
31:40 the **p** *were* sixteen thousand; of which 120+5315
31:40 the LORD'S tribute *was* thirty and two **p**. 5315
31:46 And sixteen thousand **p**;) 120+5315
Dt 1:17 Ye shall not respect **p** in judgment; *but* 6440
10:17 and a terrible, which regardeth not **p**, 6440
10:22 down into Egypt with threescore and ten **p**; 5315
16:19 thou shalt not respect **p**, neither take a gift: 6440
Jdg 9: 2 *which are* threescore and ten **p**, reign over 376
9: 4 wherewith Abimelech hired vain and light **p**, 376
9: 5 *being* threescore and ten **p**, upon one stone: 376
9:18 threescore and ten **p**, upon one stone, and 376
20:39 *and* kill of the men of Israel about thirty **p**: 376
1Sa 9:22 that were bidden, which *were* about thirty **p**. 376
22:18 and five **p** that did wear a linen ephod. 376
22:22 I have occasioned *the death* of all the **p** of 5315
2Ki 10: 6 Now the king's sons, *being* seventy **p**, 376
10: 7 slew seventy **p**, and put their heads in 376
2Ch 19: 7 nor respect of **p**, nor taking of gifts. 6440
Job 13:10 reprove you, if ye do secretly accept **p**. 6440
34:19 *to him* that accepteth not the **p** of princes, 6440
Ps 26: 4 I have not sat with vain **p**, neither will I go 4962
82: 2 and accept the **p** of the wicked? 6440
Pr 12:11 he that followeth vain *p is* void of NIH
24:23 *It is* not good to have respect of **p** in 6440
28:19 he that followeth after vain *p* shall have NIH
28:21 To have respect of **p** *is* not good: for for a 6440
Jer 52:29 Jerusalem eight hundred thirty and two **p**: 5315
52:30 *of* the Jews seven hundred forty and five **p**: 5315
52:30 all the **p** *were* four thousand and 5315
La 4:16 they respected not the **p** of the priests, 6440
Eze 17:17 and building forts, to cut off many **p**: 5315
27:13 they traded the **p** of men and vessels of 5315
Jnh 4:11 wherein are more than sixscore thousand **p** 120
Zep 3: 4 Her prophets *are* light *and* treacherous **p**: 376
Mal 1: 9 will he **regard** your **p**? 4480+5375+6440
Lk 15: 7 and nine just **p** which need no repentance. NIG
Ac 10:34 I perceive that God is no **respecter of p**: *4381*
17:17 and with the devout *p*, and in the market NIG
Ro 2:11 For there is no **respect of p** with God. *4382*
2Co 1:11 **p** thanks may be given by many on our *4383*
Eph 6: 9 neither is there **respect of p** with him. *4382*
Col 3:25 he hath done: and there is no **respect of p**. *4382*
1Ti 1:10 for perjured *p*, and if *there be* any other NIG
Jas 2: 1 *the Lord* of glory, with **respect of p**. *4382*
2: 9 But if ye **have respect to p**, ye commit sin, *4380*
1Pe 1:17 who **without respect of p** judgeth according *678*
2Pe 3:11 what manner *of p* ought ye to be in all holy NIG
Jude 1:16 *words,* having *men's* **p** in admiration NIG

PERSUADE (9) [PERSUADED, PERSUADEST, PERSUADETH, PERSUADING, PERSUASION]

1Ki 22:20 Who shall **p** Ahab, that he may go up and 6601
22:21 before the LORD, and said, I will **p** him. 6601
22:22 he said, Thou shalt **p** *him,* and prevail also: 6601
2Ch 32:11 Doth not Hezekiah **p** you to give over 5496
32:15 nor **p** you on this *manner,* neither yet 5496
Isa 36:18 *Beware* lest Hezekiah **p** you, saying, 5496
Mt 28:14 we will **p** him, and secure you. *3982*
2Co 5:11 therefore the terror of the Lord, we **p** men; *3982*
Gal 1:10 For do I now **p** men, or God? or do I seek *3982*

PERSUADED (20) [PERSUADE]

2Ch 18: 2 **p** him to go up *with him* to Ramoth-gilead. 5496
Pr 25:15 By long forbearing is a prince **p**, and a soft 6601
Mt 27:20 elders **p** the multitude that they should ask *3982*
Lk 16:31 and the prophets, neither will they be **p**, *3982*
20: 6 for they be **p** that John was a prophet. *3982*
Ac 13:43 **p** them to continue in the grace of God. *3982*
14:19 and Iconium, who **p** the people, and, *3982*
18: 4 and **p** *the* Jews and *the* Greeks. *3982*
19:26 this Paul hath **p** and turned away much *3982*
21:14 And when he would not be **p**, we ceased, *3982*
26:26 for I am **p** that none of these *things* are *3982*
Ro 4:21 And being **fully p** that, what he had *4135*
8:38 For I am **p**, that neither death, nor life, *3982*
14: 5 Let every man be **fully p** in his own mind. *4135*
14:14 I know, and am **p** by the Lord Jesus, *3982*
15:14 And I myself also am **p** of you, *3982*
2Ti 1: 5 mother Eunice; and I am **p** that in thee also. *3982*
1:12 I am **p** that he is able to keep that which I *3982*
Heb 6: 9 we are **p** better *things* of you, and *3982*
11:13 and were **p** of *them,* and embraced *them,* *3982*

PERSUADEST (1) [PERSUADE]

Ac 26:28 Almost thou **p** me to be a Christian. *3982*

PERSUADETH (2) [PERSUADE]

2Ki 18:32 not unto Hezekiah, when he **p** you, saying, 5496
Ac 18:13 This *fellow* **p** men to worship God contrary *374*

PERSUADING (2) [PERSUADE]

Ac 19: 8 **p** the *things* concerning the kingdom of *3982*
28:23 **p** them concerning Jesus, both out of *3982*

PERSUASION (1) [PERSUADE]

Gal 5: 8 *This* **p** *cometh* not of him that calleth you. *3988*

PERTAIN (6) [PERTAINED, PERTAINETH, PERTAINING]

Lev 7:20 that *p* unto the LORD, having his NIH
7:21 which *p* unto the LORD, even that soul NIH
1Sa 25:22 if I leave of all that *p* to him by the morning NIH
Ro 15:17 Christ *in those things* which **p to** God. *4314*
1Co 6: 3 how much more *things* **that p to** *this* **life**? *982*
2Pe 1: 3 hath given unto us all *things* that *p* unto life NIG

PERTAINED (17) [PERTAIN]

Nu 31:43 (Now the half that *p* unto the congregation NIH
Jos 24:33 they buried him in a hill that *p* to Phinehas NIH
Jdg 6:11 in Ophrah, that *p* unto Joash the Abi-ezrite: NIH
1Sa 25:21 that nothing was missed of all that *p* unto NIH
2Sa 2:15 which *p* to Ish-bosheth the son of Saul, and NIH
9: 9 I have given unto thy master's son all that **p** 1961
16: 4 thine *are* all that *p* unto Mephibosheth. NIH
1Ki 4:10 to him *p* Sochoh, and all the land of NIH
4:12 *to him* *p* Taanach and Megiddo, and NIH
4:13 to him *p* the towns of Jair the son of NIH
4:13 to him *also* *p* the region of Argob, which *is* NIH
7:48 Solomon made all the vessels that *p unto* NIH
2Ki 24: 7 Euphrates all that **p** to the king of Egypt. 1961
1Ch 9:27 the opening *thereof* every morning **p to** 5921
11:31 that *p* to the children of Benjamin, NIH
2Ch 12: 4 he took the fenced cities which *p* to Judah, NIH
34:33 the countries that *p* to the children of Israel, NIH

PERTAINETH (8) [PERTAIN]

Lev 14:32 whose hand is not able to get *that which p* NIH
Nu 4:16 of Aaron the priest *p* the oil for the light, NIH
Dt 22: 5 The woman shall not wear **that which p** 3627
1Sa 27: 6 wherefore Ziklag **p** unto the kings of Judah 1961
2Sa 6:12 all that *p* unto him, because of the ark of NIH
2Ch 26:18 said unto him, *It p* not unto thee, Uzziah, NIH
Ro 9: 4 to whom *p* the adoption, and the glory, and NIG
Heb 7:13 these *things* are spoken **p to** another tribe, *3348*

PERTAINING (8) [PERTAIN]

Jos 13:31 *were p* unto the children of Machir the son NIH
1Ch 26:32 for every matter *p* to God, and affairs of NIH
Ac 1: 3 speaking of the *things* **p** to the kingdom of *4012*
Ro 4: 1 our father, **as p to** the flesh, hath found? *2596*
1Co 6: 4 ye have judgments *of things* **p to** *this* **life**, *982*
Heb 2:17 and faithful high priest *in things* **p to** God, *4314*
5: 1 is ordained for men *in things* **p to** God, *4314*
9: 9 the service perfect, as **p to** the conscience; *2596*

PERUDA (1) [PERIDA]

Ezr 2:55 the children of Sophereth, the children of **P**, 6514

PERVERSE (20) [PERVERT]

Nu 22:32 because *thy* way is **p** before me: 3399
Dt 32: 5 *they are* a **p** and crooked generation. 6141
1Sa 20:30 Thou son of the **p** rebellious *woman*, do not 5753
Job 6:30 cannot my taste discern **p things**? 1942
9:20 *I say,* I *am* perfect, it shall also **prove** me **p**. 6140
Pr 4:24 and **p** lips put far from thee. 3891
8: 8 *there is* nothing froward or **p** in them. 6141

P

Pr 12: 8 but he that is of a **p** heart shall be despised. 5753
14: 2 but he that is **p** in his ways despiseth him. 3868
17:20 he that hath a **p** tongue falleth into 2015
19: 1 than *he that is* **p** in his lips, and *is* a fool. 6141
23:33 and thine heart shall utter **p things**. 8419
28: 6 than *he that is* **p** in *his* ways, though he *be* 6141
28:18 *he that is* **p** in *his* ways shall fall at once. 6140
Isa 19:14 The LORD hath mingled a **p** spirit in 5773
Mt 17:17 and said, O faithless and **p** generation, *1294*
Lk 9:41 O faithless and **p** generation, *1294*
Ac 20:30 speaking **p** *things,* to draw away disciples *1294*
Php 2:15 in the midst of a crooked and **p** nation, *1294*
1Ti 6: 5 **P disputings** of men of corrupt minds, and *3859*

PERVERSELY (3) [PERVERT]
2Sa 19:19 **did p** the day that my lord the king went 5753
1Ki 8:47 saying, We have sinned, and have **done p**, 5753
Ps 119:78 for they **dealt p with** me without a cause: 5791

PERVERSENESS (6) [PERVERT]
Nu 23:21 in Jacob, neither hath he seen **p** in Israel: 5999
Pr 11: 3 the **p** of transgressors shall destroy them. 5558
15: 4 but **p** therein *is* a breach in the spirit. 5558
Isa 30:12 trust in oppression and **p**, and stay thereon: 3868
59: 3 spoken lies, your tongue hath muttered **p**. 5766
Eze 9: 9 land is full *of* blood, and the city full *of* **p**: 4297

PERVERT (10) [PERVERSE, PERVERSELY, PERVERSENESS, PERVERTED, PERVERTETH, PERVERTING]
Dt 16:19 the wise, and **p** the words of the righteous. 5557
24:17 Thou shalt not **p** the judgment of 5186
Job 8: 3 Doth God **p** judgment? or doth 5791
8: 3 or doth the Almighty **p** justice? 5791
34:12 neither will the Almighty **p** judgment. 5791
Pr 17:23 of the bosom to **p** the ways of judgment. 5186
31: 5 and **p** the judgment of any of the afflicted. 8138
Mic 3: 9 that abhor judgment, and **p** all equity. 6140
Ac 13:10 wilt thou not cease to **p** the right ways of *1294*
Gal 1: 7 and would **p** the gospel of Christ. *3344*

PERVERTED (5) [PERVERT]
1Sa 8: 3 and took bribes, and **p** judgment. 5186
Job 33:27 **p** *that which was* right, and it profited me 5753
Isa 47:10 and thy knowledge, it hath **p** thee; 7725
Jer 3:21 for they have **p** their way, *and* they have 5753
23:36 for ye have **p** the words of the living God, 2015

PERVERTETH (5) [PERVERT]
Ex 23: 8 the wise, and **p** the words of the righteous. 5557
Dt 27:19 Cursed *be* he that **p** the judgment of 5186
Pr 10: 9 but he that **p** his ways shall be known. 6140
19: 3 The foolishness of man **p** his way: and 5557
Lk 23:14 this man unto me, as one that **p** the people: *654*

PERVERTING (2) [PERVERT]
Ecc 5: 8 **violent p** of judgment and justice in a 1499
Lk 23: 2 We found this *fellow* **p** the nation, and *1294*

PESTILENCE (47) [PESTILENCES, PESTILENT]
Ex 5: 3 lest he fall upon us with **p**, or with 1698
9:15 I may smite thee and thy people with **p**; 1698
Lev 26:25 your cities, I will send the **p** among you; 1698
Nu 14:12 I will smite them with the **p**, and 1698
Dt 28:21 The LORD shall make the **p** cleave unto 1698
2Sa 24:13 or that there be three days' **p** in thy land? 1698
24:15 So the LORD sent a **p** upon Israel from 1698
1Ki 8:37 if there be **p**, blasting, mildew, locust, *or* 1698
1Ch 21:12 even the **p**, in the land, and the angel of 1698
21:14 So the LORD sent **p** upon Israel: and 1698
2Ch 6:28 if there be **p**, if there be blasting, or 1698
7:13 the land, or if I send **p** among my people; 1698
20: 9 *as* the sword, judgment, or **p**, or famine, 1698
Ps 78:50 from death, but gave their life over to the **p**; 1698
91: 3 of the fowler, *and* from the noisome **p**. 1698
91: 6 *Nor* for the **p** *that* walketh in darkness; 1698
Jer 14:12 the sword, and by the famine, and by the **p**. 1698
21: 6 and beast: they shall die of a great **p**. 1698
21: 7 and such as are left in this city from the **p**, 1698
21: 9 the sword, and by the famine, and by the **p**: 1698
24:10 the famine, and the **p**, among them, 1698
27: 8 and with the famine, and with the **p**, 1698
27:13 by the sword, by the famine, and by the **p**, 1698
28: 8 of war, and of evil, and of **p**. 1698
29:17 the **p**, and will make them like vile figs, 1698
29:18 with the **p**, and will deliver them to be 1698
32:24 the sword, and *of* the famine, and *of* the **p**: 1698
32:36 the sword, and by the famine, and by the **p**; 1698
34:17 to the sword, to the **p**, and to the famine; 1698
38: 2 by the sword, by the famine, and by the **p**: 1698
42:17 by the sword, by the famine, and by the **p**: 1698
42:22 by the famine, and by the **p**, in the place 1698
44:13 by the sword, by the famine, and by the **p**: 1698
Eze 5:12 A third *part* of thee shall die with the **p**, and 1698
5:17 **p** and blood shall pass through thee; and 1698
6:11 by the sword, by the famine, and by the **p**. 1698
6:12 *He* that is far off shall die of the **p**; and 1698
7:15 *is* without, and the **p** and the famine within: 1698
7:15 in the city, famine and **p** shall devour him. 1698
12:16 the sword, from the famine, and from the **p**; 1698
14:19 Or *if* I send a **p** into that land, and pour out 1698
14:21 and the noisome beast, and the **p**, 1698
28:23 For I will send into her **p**, and blood into 1698
33:27 the forts and in the caves shall die of the **p**. 1698
38:22 I will plead against him with **p** and 1698
Am 4:10 I have sent among you the **p** after 1698
Hab 3: 5 Before him went the **p**, and burning coals 1698

PESTILENCES (2) [PESTILENCE]
Mt 24: 7 and **p**, and earthquakes in divers places. *3061*
Lk 21:11 be in divers places, and famines, and **p**; *3061*

PESTILENT (1) [PESTILENCE]
Ac 24: 5 For we have found this man a **p** *fellow,* and *3061*

PESTLE (1)
Pr 27:22 a fool in a mortar among wheat with a **p**, 5940

PETER (158) [CEPHAS, PETER'S, SIMON]
Mt 4:18 Simon called **P**, and Andrew his brother, *4074*
10: 2 who is called **P**, and Andrew his brother; *4074*
14:28 And **P** answered him and said, Lord, if it be *4074*
14:29 And when **P** was come down out of *4074*
15:15 Then answered **P** and said unto him, *4074*
16:16 And Simon **P** answered and said, Thou art *4074*
16:18 That thou art **P**, and upon this rock I will *4074*
16:22 Then **P** took him, and began to rebuke him, *4074*
16:23 But he turned, and said unto **P**, Get thee *4074*
17: 1 And after six days Jesus taketh **P**, James, *4074*
17: 4 Then answered **P**, and said unto Jesus, *4074*
17:24 they that received tribute money came to **P**, *4074*
17:26 **P** saith unto him, Of strangers. Jesus saith *4074*
18:21 Then came **P** to him, and said, Lord, *4074*
19:27 Then answered **P** and said unto him, *4074*
26:33 **P** answered and said unto him, Though all *4074*
26:35 **P** said unto him, Though I should die with *4074*
26:37 And he took with *him* **P** and the two sons *4074*
26:40 them asleep, and saith unto **P**, What, *4074*
26:58 But **P** followed him afar off unto the high *4074*
26:69 Now **P** sat without in the palace: and *4074*
26:73 unto *him* they that stood *by,* and said to **P**, *4074*
26:75 And **P** remembered the word of Jesus, *4074*
Mk 3:16 And Simon he surnamed **P**; *4074*
5:37 save **P**, and James, and John the brother of *4074*
8:29 And **P** answereth and saith unto him, *4074*
8:32 And **P** took him, and began to rebuke him. *4074*
8:33 he rebuked **P**, saying, Get thee behind me, *4074*
9: 2 And after six days Jesus taketh with *him* **P**, *4074*
9: 5 And **P** answered and said to Jesus, Master, *4074*
10:28 Then **P** began to say unto him, Lo, we have *4074*
11:21 And **P** calling to remembrance saith unto *4074*
13: 3 **P** and James and John and Andrew asked *4074*
14:29 But **P** said unto him, Although all shall be *4074*
14:33 And he taketh with him **P** and James and *4074*
14:37 and saith unto **P**, Simon, sleepest thou? *4074*
14:54 And **P** followed him afar off, even into *4074*
14:66 And as **P** was beneath in the palace, *4074*
14:67 And when she saw **P** warming himself, *4074*
14:70 they that stood by said again to **P**, *4074*
14:72 And **P** called to mind the word that Jesus *4074*
16: 7 and **P** that he goeth before you into Galilee: *4074*
Lk 5: 8 When Simon **P** saw *it,* he fell down at *4074*
6:14 Simon, (whom he also named **P**,) and *4074*
8:45 **P** and they that were with him said, Master, *4074*
8:51 he suffered no *man* to go in, save **P**, *4074*
9:20 I am? **P** answering said, The Christ of God. *4074*
9:28 he took **P** and John and James, and went up *4074*
9:32 But **P** and they that were with him were *4074*
9:33 from him, **P** said unto Jesus, Master, *4074*
12:41 Then **P** said unto him, Lord, speakest thou *4074*

Lk 18:28 Then **P** said, Lo, we have left all, *4074*
22: 8 And he sent **P** and John, saying, Go and *4074*
22:34 And he said, I tell thee, **P**, *the* cock shall *4074*
22:54 priest's house. And **P** followed afar off. *4074*
22:55 set down together, **P** sat down among them. *4074*
22:58 also of them. And **P** said, Man, I am not. *4074*
22:60 And **P** said, Man, I know not what thou *4074*
22:61 And the Lord turned, and looked upon **P**. *4074*
22:61 And **P** remembered the word of the Lord, *4074*
22:62 And **P** went out, *4074*
24:12 Then arose **P**, and ran unto the sepulchre; *4074*
Jn 1:44 of Bethsaida, the city of Andrew and **P**. *4074*
6:68 Then Simon **P** answered him, Lord, *4074*
13: 6 Then cometh he to Simon **P**: and *4074*
13: 6 and *P* saith unto him, Lord, dost thou wash NIG
13: 8 **P** saith unto him, Thou shalt never wash *4074*
13: 9 Simon **P** saith unto him, Lord, not my feet *4074*
13:24 Simon **P** therefore beckoned to him, that *he* *4074*
13:36 Simon **P** said unto him, Lord, whither goest *4074*
13:37 **P** said unto him, Lord, why cannot I follow *4074*
18:10 Then Simon **P** having a sword drew it, and *4074*
18:11 Then said Jesus unto **P**, Put up thy sword *4074*
18:15 And Simon **P** followed Jesus, and *so* *4074*
18:16 But **P** stood at the door without. Then went *4074*
18:16 her that kept the door, and brought in **P**. *4074*
18:17 saith the damsel that kept the door unto **P**, *4074*
18:18 and **P** stood with them, and *4074*
18:25 And Simon **P** stood and warmed himself. *4074*
18:26 being *his* kinsman whose ear **P** cut off, *4074*
18:27 **P** then denied again: and immediately *4074*
20: 2 and cometh to Simon **P**, and to the other *4074*
20: 3 **P** therefore went forth, and *that* other *4074*
20: 4 and the other disciple did outrun **P**, and *4074*
20: 6 Then cometh Simon **P** following him, and *4074*
21: 2 There were together Simon **P**, and *4074*
21: 3 Simon **P** saith unto them, I go a fishing. *4074*
21: 7 disciple whom Jesus loved saith unto **P**, *4074*
21: 7 Now when Simon **P** heard that it was *4074*
21:11 Simon **P** went up, and drew the net to land *4074*
21:15 Jesus saith to Simon **P**, Simon, *son* of *4074*
21:17 **P** was grieved because he said unto him *4074*
21:20 Then **P**, turning about, seeth the disciple *4074*
21:21 **P** seeing him saith to Jesus, Lord, and *4074*
Ac 1:13 where abode both **P**, and James, and John, *4074*
1:15 And in those days **P** stood up in the midst *4074*
2:14 But **P**, standing up with the eleven, lift up *4074*
2:37 and said unto **P** and *to* the rest of *4074*
2:38 Then **P** said unto them, Repent, and *4074*
3: 1 Now **P** and John went up together into *4074*
3: 3 Who seeing **P** and John about to go into *4074*
3: 4 And **P**, fastening his eyes upon him with *4074*
3: 6 Then **P** said, Silver and gold have I none; *4074*
3:11 as the lame *man* which was healed held **P** *4074*
3:12 And when **P** saw *it,* he answered unto *4074*
4: 8 Then **P**, filled with the Holy Ghost, *4074*
4:13 Now when they saw the boldness of **P** and *4074*
4:19 But **P** and John answered and said unto *4074*
5: 3 But **P** said, Ananias, why hath Satan filled *4074*
5: 8 And **P** answered unto her, Tell me whether *4074*
5: 9 Then **P** said unto her, How *is it* that ye have *4074*
5:15 that at the least the shadow of **P** passing by *4074*
5:29 Then **P** and the *other* apostles answered and *4074*
8:14 of God, they sent unto them **P** and John: *4074*
8:20 But **P** said unto him, Thy money perish *4074*
9:32 as **P** passed throughout all *quarters,* he *4074*
9:34 And **P** said unto him, Aeneas, Jesus Christ *4074*
9:38 the disciples had heard that **P** was there, *4074*
9:39 Then **P** arose and went with them. When he *4074*
9:40 But **P** put *them* all forth, *4074*
9:40 her eyes: and when she saw **P**, she sat up. *4074*
10: 5 call for *one* Simon, whose surname is **P**: *4074*
10: 9 **P** went up upon the house to pray about *4074*
10:13 And there came a voice to him, Rise, **P**; *4074*
10:14 But **P** said, Not so, Lord; for I have never *4074*
10:17 Now while **P** doubted in himself what *this* *4074*
10:18 which was surnamed **P**, were lodged there. *4074*
10:19 While **P** thought on the vision, the Spirit *4074*
10:21 Then **P** went down to the men which were *4074*
10:23 lodged *them.* And on the morrow **P** went *4074*
10:25 And as **P** was coming in, Cornelius met *4074*
10:26 But **P** took him up, saying, Stand up; *4074*
10:32 and call hither Simon, whose surname is **P**; *4074*
10:34 Then **P** opened *his* mouth, and said, Of a *4074*
10:44 While **P** yet spake these words, the Holy *4074*
10:45 as many as came with **P**, because that on *4074*
10:46 and magnify God. Then answered **P**, *4074*
11: 2 And when **P** was come up to Jerusalem, *4074*
11: 4 But **P** *rehearsed the matter* from *4074*
11: 7 I heard a voice saying unto me, Arise, **P**; *4074*
11:13 and call for Simon, whose surname is **P**; *4074*
12: 3 he proceeded further to take **P** also. *4074*
12: 5 **P** therefore was kept in prison: but *4074*
12: 6 the same night **P** was sleeping between two *4074*
12: 7 and he smote **P** on the side, and raised him *4074*
12:11 And when **P** was come to himself, he said, *4074*
12:13 And as **P** knocked at the door of the gate, *4074*
12:14 and told how **P** stood before the gate. *4074*
12:16 But **P** continued knocking: and when they *4074*
12:18 among the soldiers, what was become of **P**. *4074*
15: 7 **P** rose up, and said unto them, Men *and* *4074*
Gal 1:18 three years I went up to Jerusalem to see **P**, *4074*
2: 7 *the gospel* of the circumcision *was* unto **P**; *4074*
2: 8 (For he that wrought effectually in **P** to *4074*
2:11 But when **P** was come to Antioch, *4074*
2:14 I said unto **P** before *them* all, If thou, *4074*
1Pe 1: 1 **P**, an apostle of Jesus Christ, to *4074*
2Pe 1: 1 Simon **P**, a servant and an apostle of Jesus *4074*

PETER'S (4) [PETER]
Mt 8:14 And when Jesus was come into **P** house, *4074*
Jn 1:40 was Andrew, Simon **P** brother. *4074*
6: 8 Andrew, Simon **P** brother, saith unto him, *4074*
Ac 12:14 And when she knew **P** voice, she opened *4074*

PETHAHIAH (4)
1Ch 24:16 The nineteenth to **P**, the twentieth to 6611
Ezr 10:23 (the same *is* Kelita,) **P**, Judah, and Eliezer. 6611
Ne 9: 5 *and* **P**, said, Stand up *and* bless the LORD 6611
11:24 **P** the son of Meshezabeel, of the children 6611

PETHOR (2)
Nu 22: 5 therefore unto Balaam the son of Beor to **P**, 6604
Dt 23: 4 the son of Beor of **P** of Mesopotamia, 6604

PETHUEL (1)
Joel 1: 1 the LORD that came to Joel the son of **P**. 6602

PETITION (13) [PETITIONS]
1Sa 1:17 the God of Israel grant *thee* thy **p** that thou 7596
1:27 the LORD hath given me my **p** which I 7596
1Ki 2:16 now I **ask** one **p** of thee, deny me 7592+7596
2:20 she said, I desire one small **p** of thee; *I pray* 7596
Est 5: 6 at the banquet of wine, What *is* thy **p**? 7596
5: 7 and said, My **p** and my request *is;* 7596
5: 8 if it please the king to grant my **p**, and 7596
7: 2 of wine, What *is* thy **p**, queen Esther? 7596
7: 3 let my life be given me at my **p**, and 7596
9:12 now what *is* thy **p**? and it shall be granted 7596
Da 6: 7 that whosoever shall ask a **p** of any God or 1159
6:12 that every man that shall ask *a* **p** of any God NIH
6:13 but **maketh** his **p** three times a day. 1156+1159

PETITIONS (2) [PETITION]
Ps 20: 5 up *our* banners: the LORD fulfil all thy **p**. 4862
1Jn 5:15 we know that we have the **p** that we desired *155*

PEULLETHAI See PEULTHAI

PEULTHAI (1)
1Ch 26: 5 the sixth, Issachar the seventh, **P** the eighth: 6469

PHALEC (1) [PELEG]
Lk 3:35 which was *the son* of **P**, which was *the son* *5317*

PHALLU (1)
Ge 46: 9 Hanoch, and **P**, and Hezron, and Carmi. 6396

PHALTI (1) [PHALTIEL]
1Sa 25:44 David's wife, to **P** the son of Laish, 6406

PHALTIEL (1) [PHALTI]
2Sa 3:15 *her* husband, *even* from **P** the son of Laish. 6409

PHANUEL (1)
Lk 2:36 a prophetess, the daughter of **P**, of the tribe *5323*

PHARAOH (225) [PHARAOH'S, PHARAOH-HOPHRA, PHARAOH-NECHO, PHARAOH-NECHOH]
Ge 12:15 The princes also of **P** saw her, and 6547
12:15 saw her, and commended her before **P**: 6547

Ge 12:17 the LORD plagued **P** and his house with 6547
12:18 **P** called Abram, and said, What *is* this *that* 6547
12:20 **P** commanded *his* men concerning him: 6547
39: 1 Potiphar, an officer of **P**, captain of 6547
40: 2 **P** was wroth against two *of* his officers, 6547
40:13 Yet within three days shall **P** lift up thine 6547
40:14 make mention of me unto **P**, and bring me 6547
40:17 *there was* of all *manner of* bakemeats for **P**; 6547
40:19 Yet within three days shall **P** lift up thy 6547
41: 1 at the end of two full years, that **P** dreamed: 6547
41: 4 well favoured and fat kine. So **P** awoke. 6547
41: 7 And **P** awoke, and, behold, *it was* a dream. 6547
41: 8 **P** told them his dream; but *there was* none 6547
41: 8 *was* none that could interpret them unto **P**. 6547
41: 9 spake the chief butler unto **P**, saying, I do 6547
41:10 **P** was wroth with his servants, and put me 6547
41:14 **P** sent and called Joseph, and they brought 6547
41:14 changed his raiment, and came in unto **P**. 6547
41:15 **P** said unto Joseph, I have dreamed a 6547
41:16 Joseph answered **P**, saying, *It is* not in me: 6547
41:16 God shall give **P** an answer of peace. 6547
41:17 **P** said unto Joseph, In my dream, behold, 6547
41:25 Joseph said unto **P**, The dream of Pharaoh 6547
41:25 said unto Pharaoh, The dream of **P** *is* one: 6547
41:25 God hath shewed **P** what he *is* about to do. 6547
41:28 *is* the thing which I have spoken unto **P**: 6547
41:28 God *is* about to do he sheweth unto **P**. 6547
41:32 for that the dream was doubled unto **P** 6547
41:33 let **P** look out a man discreet and wise, 6547
41:34 Let **P** do *this,* and let him appoint officers 6547
41:35 lay up corn under the hand of **P**, and 6547
41:37 the thing was good in the eyes of **P**, and 6547
41:38 **P** said unto his servants, Can we find *such* 6547
41:39 **P** said unto Joseph, Forasmuch as God hath 6547
41:41 **P** said unto Joseph, See, I have set thee 6547
41:42 **P** took off his ring from his hand, and put it 6547
41:44 **P** said unto Joseph, I *am* Pharaoh, and 6547
41:44 I *am* **P**, and without thee shall no man lift 6547
41:45 **P** called Joseph's name Zaphnath-paaneah; 6547
41:46 old when he stood before **P** king of Egypt. 6547
41:46 Joseph went out from the presence of **P**, 6547
41:55 the people cried to **P** for bread: 6547
41:55 **P** said unto all the Egyptians, Go unto 6547
42:15 By the life of **P** ye shall not go forth hence, 6547
42:16 or else by the life of **P** surely ye *are* spies. 6547
44:18 against thy servant: for thou *art* even as **P**. 6547
45: 2 and the Egyptians and the house of **P** heard. 6547
45: 8 he hath made me a father to **P**, and lord of 6547
45:16 and it pleased **P** well, and his servants. 6547
45:17 **P** said unto Joseph, Say unto thy brethren, 6547
45:21 according to the commandment of **P**, and 6547
46: 5 in the wagons which **P** had sent to carry 6547
46:31 I will go up, and shew **P**, and say unto him, 6547
46:33 when **P** shall call you, and shall say, 6547
47: 1 Joseph came and told **P**, and said, 6547
47: 2 *even* five men, and presented them unto **P**. 6547
47: 3 **P** said unto his brethren, What *is* your 6547
47: 3 they said unto **P**, Thy servants *are* 6547
47: 4 They said moreover unto **P**, For to sojourn 6547
47: 5 **P** spake unto Joseph, saying, Thy father 6547
47: 7 in Jacob his father, and set him before **P**: 6547
47: 7 him before Pharaoh: and Jacob blessed **P**. 6547
47: 8 And **P** said unto Jacob, How old *art* thou? 6547
47: 9 Jacob said unto **P**, The days of the years of 6547
47:10 Jacob blessed **P**, and went out from before 6547
47:10 and went out from before **P**. 6547
47:11 the land of Rameses, as **P** had commanded. 6547
47:19 we and our land will be servants unto **P**: 6547
47:20 Joseph bought all the land of Egypt for **P**; 6547
47:22 priests had a portion assigned them of **P**, 6547
47:22 did eat their portion which **P** gave them: 6547
47:23 bought you *this* day and your land for **P**: 6547
47:24 that you shall give the fifth *part* unto **P**, and 6547
47:26 *that* **P** should have the fifth *part;* except 6547
50: 4 Joseph spake unto the house of **P**, saying, 6547
50: 4 speak, I pray you, in the ears of **P**, saying, 6547
50: 6 **P** said, Go up, and bury thy father, 6547
50: 7 with him went up all the servants of **P**, 6547
Ex 1:11 they built for **P** treasure cities, Pithom and 6547
1:19 the midwives said unto **P**, Because 6547
1:22 **P** charged all his people, saying, Every son 6547
2: 5 the daughter of **P** came down to wash 6547
2:15 Now when **P** heard this thing, he sought to 6547
2:15 Moses fled from the face of **P**, and dwelt in 6547
3:10 now therefore, and I will send thee unto **P**, 6547
3:11 that I should go unto **P**, and that I should 6547
4:21 see that thou do all *those* wonders before **P**, 6547
4:22 thou shalt say unto **P**, Thus saith 6547
5: 1 and Aaron went in, and told **P**, 6547
5: 2 **P** said, Who *is* the LORD, that I should 6547
5: 5 **P** said, Behold, the people of the land now 6547
5: 6 **P** commanded the same day 6547
5:10 spake to the people, saying, Thus saith **P**, 6547
5:15 children of Israel came and cried unto **P**, 6547
5:20 in the way, as they came forth from **P**: 6547
5:21 our savour to be abhorred in the eyes of **P**, 6547
5:23 For since I came to **P** to speak in thy name, 6547
6: 1 Now shalt thou see what I will do to **P**: 6547
6:11 Go in, speak unto **P** king of Egypt, that he 6547
6:12 how then shall **P** hear me, who *am* of 6547
6:13 of Israel, and unto **P** king of Egypt, 6547
6:27 *These are* they which spake to **P** king of 6547
6:29 speak thou unto **P** king of Egypt all that I 6547
6:30 and how shall **P** hearken unto me? 6547
7: 1 See, I have made thee a god to **P**: 6547
7: 2 Aaron thy brother shall speak unto **P**, 6547
7: 4 **P** shall not hearken unto you, that I may lay 6547
7: 7 three years old, when they spake unto **P**. 6547
7: 9 When **P** shall speak unto you, saying, 6547
7: 9 cast *it* before **P**, *and* it shall become a 6547
7:10 Moses and Aaron went in unto **P**, and 6547
7:10 Aaron cast down his rod before **P**, and 6547
7:11 **P** also called the wise men and 6547
7:15 Get thee unto **P** in the morning; lo, 6547
7:20 in the sight of **P**, and in the sight of his 6547
7:23 **P** turned and went into his house, 6547
8: 1 Go unto **P**, and say unto him, Thus saith 6547
8: 8 **P** called for Moses and Aaron, and said, 6547
8: 9 Moses said unto **P**, Glory over me: when 6547
8:12 Moses and Aaron went out from **P**: and 6547
8:12 the frogs which he had brought against **P**. 6547
8:15 when **P** saw that there was respite, he 6547
8:19 the magicians said unto **P**, This *is* the finger 6547
8:20 early in the morning, and stand before **P**; 6547
8:24 grievous swarm *of flies* into the house of **P**, 6547
8:25 **P** called for Moses and for Aaron, and said, 6547
8:28 **P** said, I will let you go, that ye may 6547
8:29 that the swarms *of flies* may depart from **P**, 6547
8:29 let not **P** deal deceitfully any more in not 6547
8:30 Moses went out from **P**, and intreated 6547
8:31 and he removed the swarms *of flies* from **P**, 6547
8:32 **P** hardened his heart at this time also, 6547
9: 1 unto Moses, Go in unto **P**, and tell him, 6547
9: 7 **P** sent, and behold, there was not one of 6547
9: 7 the heart of **P** was hardened, and he did not 6547
9: 8 it towards the heaven in the sight of **P**. 6547
9:10 ashes of the furnace, and stood before **P**; 6547
9:12 the LORD hardened the heart of **P**, and 6547
9:13 and stand before **P**, and say unto him, 6547
9:20 the servants of **P** made his servants 6547
9:27 **P** sent, and called for Moses and Aaron, 6547
9:33 Moses went out of the city from **P**, 6547
9:34 when **P** saw that the rain and the hail and 6547
9:35 the heart of **P** was hardened, neither would 6547
10: 1 the LORD said unto Moses, Go in unto **P**: 6547
10: 3 Moses and Aaron came in unto **P**, and 6547
10: 6 he turned himself, and went out from **P**. 6547
10: 8 and Aaron were brought again unto **P**: 6547
10:16 **P** called for Moses and Aaron in haste; 6547
10:18 he went out from **P**, and intreated 6547
10:24 **P** called unto Moses, and said, Go ye, 6547
10:28 **P** said unto him, Get thee from me, 6547
11: 1 Yet will I bring one plague *more* upon **P**, 6547
11: 5 from the firstborn of **P** that sitteth upon his 6547
11: 8 And he went out from **P** in a great anger. 6547
11: 9 unto Moses, **P** shall not hearken unto you; 6547
11:10 and Aaron did all these wonders before **P**: 6547
12:29 from the firstborn of **P** that sat on his 6547
12:30 **P** rose up in the night, he, and all his 6547
13:15 to pass, when **P** would hardly let us go, 6547
13:17 came to pass, when **P** had let the people go, 6547
14: 3 For **P** will say of the children of Israel, 6547
14: 4 I will be honoured upon **P**, and upon all his 6547
14: 5 the heart of **P** and of his servants was 6547
14: 8 the LORD hardened the heart of **P** king of 6547
14: 9 after them (all the horses *and* chariots of **P**, 6547
14:10 when **P** drew nigh, the children of Israel lift 6547
14:17 I will get me honour upon **P**, and upon all 6547

Ex 14:18 when I have gotten me honour upon **P**, 6547
14:28 all the host of **P** that came into the sea after 6547
15:19 For the horse of **P** went in with his chariots 6547
18: 4 and delivered me from the sword of **P**: 6547
18: 8 in law all the LORD had done unto **P** 6547
18:10 of the Egyptians, and out of the hand of **P**, 6547
Dt 6:22 upon **P**, and upon all his household, 6547
7: 8 from the hand of **P** king of Egypt. 6547
7:18 what the LORD thy God did unto **P**, 6547
11: 3 which he did in the midst of Egypt unto **P** 6547
29: 2 your eyes in the land of Egypt unto **P**, 6547
34:11 sent him to do in the land of Egypt to **P**, 6547
1Sa 6: 6 the Egyptians and **P** hardened their hearts? 6547
1Ki 3: 1 Solomon made affinity with **P** king of 6547
9:16 *For* **P** king of Egypt had gone up, and 6547
11: 1 together with the daughter of **P**, *women of* 6547
11:18 they came *to* Egypt, unto **P** king of Egypt; 6547
11:19 Hadad found great favour in the sight of **P**, 6547
11:20 Pharaoh's household among the sons of **P**. 6547
11:21 Hadad said to **P**, Let me depart, that I may 6547
11:22 **P** said unto him, But what *hast* thou lacked 6547
2Ki 17: 7 from under the hand of **P** king of Egypt, 6547
18:21 *is* **P** king of Egypt unto all that trust on 6547
23:35 Jehoiakim gave the silver and the gold to **P**; 6547
23:35 according to the commandment of **P**: 6547
1Ch 4:18 *are* the sons of Bithiah the daughter of **P**, 6547
2Ch 8:11 Solomon brought up the daughter of **P** out 6547
Ne 9:10 shewedst signs and wonders upon **P**, and 6547
Ps 135: 9 O Egypt, upon **P**, and upon all his servants. 6547
136:15 overthrew **P** and his host in the Red sea: 6547
Isa 19:11 the counsel of the wise counsellers of **P** is 6547
19:11 how say ye unto **P**, I *am* the son of 6547
30: 2 strengthen themselves in the strength of **P**, 6547
30: 3 Therefore shall the strength of **P** be your 6547
36: 6 so *is* **P** king of Egypt to all that trust in him. 6547
Jer 25:19 **P** king of Egypt, and his servants, and his 6547
46:17 cry there, **P** king of Egypt *is but* a noise; 6547
46:25 **P**, and Egypt, with their gods, and their 6547
46:25 even **P**, and *all* them that trust in him: 6547
47: 1 the Philistines, before that **P** smote Gaza. 6547
Eze 17:17 Neither shall **P** with *his* mighty army and 6547
29: 2 set thy face against **P** king of Egypt, and 6547
29: 3 Behold, I *am* against thee, **P** king of Egypt, 6547
30:21 I have broken the arm of **P** king of Egypt; 6547
30:22 I *am* against **P** king of Egypt, and 6547
30:25 and the arms of **P** shall fall down; 6547
31: 2 speak unto **P** king of Egypt, and to his 6547
31:18 This *is* **P** and all his multitude, saith 6547
32: 2 take up a lamentation for **P** king of Egypt, 6547
32:31 **P** shall see them, and shall be comforted 6547
32:31 *even* **P** and all his army slain by the sword, 6547
32:32 *even* **P** and all his multitude, saith the Lord 6547
Ac 7:10 and wisdom in the sight of **P** king of Egypt; *5328*
7:13 Joseph's kindred was made known unto **P**. *5328*
Ro 9:17 For the scripture saith unto **P**, Even for this *5328*

PHARAOH'S (48) [PHARAOH]
Ge 12:15 and the woman was taken into **P** house. 6547
37:36 an officer of **P**, *and* captain of the guard. 6547
40: 7 he asked **P** officers that *were* with him in 6547
40:11 **P** cup *was* in my hand: and I took 6547
40:11 pressed them into **P** cup, and I gave the cup 6547
40:11 and I gave the cup into **P** hand. 6547
40:13 thou shalt deliver **P** cup into his hand, 6547
40:20 to pass the third day, *which was* **P** birthday, 6547
40:21 and he gave the cup into **P** hand: 6547
45:16 And the fame *thereof* was heard *in* **P** house, 6547
47:14 Joseph brought the money into **P** house. 6547
47:20 over them: so the land became **P**. 6547+3807.1
47:25 my lord, and we will be **P** servants. 6547+3807.1
47:26 priests only, *which* became not **P**. 6547+3807.1
Ex 2: 7 said his sister to **P** daughter, Shall I go 6547
2: 8 **P** daughter said to her, Go. And the maid 6547
2: 9 **P** daughter said unto her, Take this child 6547
2:10 she brought him unto **P** daughter, and 6547
5:14 which **P** taskmasters had set over them, 6547
7: 3 I will harden **P** heart, and multiply my 6547
7:13 he hardened **P** heart, that he hearkened not 6547
7:14 **P** heart *is* hardened, he refuseth to let 6547
7:22 **P** heart was hardened, neither did he 6547
8:19 **P** heart was hardened, and he hearkened 6547
10: 7 **P** servants said unto him, How long shall 6547
10:11 And they were driven out from **P** presence. 6547
10:20 the LORD hardened **P** heart, so that he 6547
10:27 the LORD hardened **P** heart, and 6547
11: 3 in the sight of **P** servants, and in the sight 6547
11:10 the LORD hardened **P** heart, so that he 6547
14: 4 I will harden **P** heart, that he shall follow 6547
14:23 *even* all **P** horses, his chariots, and 6547
15: 4 **P** chariots and his host hath he cast into 6547
Dt 6:21 thy son, We were **P** bondmen in Egypt; 6547
1Sa 2:27 when they were in Egypt in **P** house? 6547
1Ki 3: 1 took **P** daughter, and brought her into 6547
7: 8 Solomon made also a house for **P** daughter, 6547
9:24 **P** daughter came up out of the city of David 6547
11:20 whom Tahpenes weaned in **P** house: 6547
11:20 Genubath was *in* **P** household among 6547
SS 1: 9 to a company of horses in **P** chariots. 6547
Jer 37: 5 **P** army was come forth out of Egypt: and 6547
37: 7 Behold, **P** army, which is come forth to 6547
37:11 up from Jerusalem for fear of **P** army, 6547
43: 9 which *is* at the entry of **P** house in 6547
Eze 30:24 I will break **P** arms, and he shall groan 6547
Ac 7:21 **P** daughter took him up, and nourished him *5328*
Heb 11:24 refused to be called the son of **P** daughter; *5328*

PHARAOH-HOPHRA (1) [PHARAOH]
Jer 44:30 I *will* give **P** king of Egypt into the hand of 6548

PHARAOH-NECHO (1) [PHARAOH]
Jer 46: 2 against the army of **P** king of Egypt, 6549

PHARAOH-NECHOH (4) [PHARAOH]
2Ki 23:29 In his days **P** king of Egypt went up against 6549
23:33 **P** put him in bands at Riblah in the land of 6549
23:34 **P** made Eliakim the son of Josiah king in 6549
23:35 according to his taxation, to give *it* unto **P**. 6549

PHARES (3) [PHAREZ]
Mt 1: 3 And Judas begat **P** and Zara of Thamar; *5329*
1: 3 and **P** begat Esrom; and Esrom begat *5329*
Lk 3:33 which was *the son* of **P**, which was *the son* *5329*

PHAREZ (12) [PHARES, PHARZITES]
Ge 38:29 upon thee: therefore his name was called **P**. 6557
46:12 and Onan, and Shelah, and **P**, and Zerah: 6557
46:12 and the sons of **P** were Hezron and Hamul. 6557
Nu 26:20 of **P**, the family of the Pharzites: of Zerah, 6557
26:21 the sons of **P** were; of Hezron, the family 6557
Ru 4:12 let thy house be like the house of **P**, 6557
4:18 Now these *are* the generations of **P**: 6557
4:18 the generations of Pharez: **P** begat Hezron, 6557
1Ch 2: 4 Tamar his daughter in law bare him **P** and 6557
2: 5 The sons of **P**; Hezron, and Hamul. 6557
4: 1 **P**, Hezron, and Carmi, and Hur, and 6557
9: 4 of the children of **P** the son of Judah. 6557

PHARISEE (11) [PHARISEE'S, PHARISEES, PHARISEES']
Mt 23:26 *Thou* blind **P**, cleanse first that *which is* *5330*
Lk 7:39 Now when the **P** which had bidden him *5330*
11:37 a certain **P** besought him to dine with him: *5330*
11:38 And when the **P** saw *it*, he marvelled that *5330*
18:10 the one a **P**, and the other a publican. *5330*
18:11 The **P** stood and prayed thus with himself, *5330*
Ac 5:34 a **P**, named Gamaliel, a doctor of law, *5330*
23: 6 Men *and* brethren, I am a **P**, the son of a *5330*
23: 6 brethren, I am a Pharisee, the son of a **P**: *5330*
26: 5 straitest sect of our religion I lived a **P**. *5330*
Php 3: 5 of the Hebrews; as touching the law, a **P**; *5330*

PHARISEE'S (2) [PHARISEE]
Lk 7:36 eat with him. And he went into the **P** house, *5330*
7:37 knew that *Jesus* sat at meat in the **P** house, *5330*

PHARISEES (86) [PHARISEE]
Mt 3: 7 But when he saw many of the **P** and *5330*
5:20 *the righteousness* of the scribes and **P**, *5330*
9:11 And when the **P** saw *it*, they said unto his *5330*
9:14 Why do we and the **P** fast oft, but *5330*
9:34 But the **P** said, He casteth out the devils *5330*
12: 2 But when the **P** saw *it*, they said unto him, *5330*
12:14 Then the **P** went out, and held a council *5330*
12:24 But when the **P** heard *it*, they said, *5330*
12:38 of the scribes and of the **P** answered, *5330*
15: 1 Then came to Jesus scribes and **P**, *5330*
15:12 Knowest thou that the **P** were offended, *5330*
16: 1 The **P** also with the Sadducees came, and *5330*
16: 6 and beware of the leaven of the **P** and *5330*
16:11 that *ye* should beware of the leaven of the **P** *5330*

Mt 16:12 but of the doctrine of the **P** and *of* 5330
19: 3 The **P** also came unto him, tempting him, 5330
21:45 chief priests and **P** had heard his parables, 5330
22:15 Then went the **P**, and took counsel how 5330
22:34 But when the **P** had heard that he had put 5330
22:41 While the **P** were gathered together, Jesus 5330
23: 2 The scribes and the **P** sit in Moses' seat: 5330
23:13 woe unto you, scribes and **P**, hypocrites! 5330
23:14 Woe unto you, scribes and **P**, hypocrites! 5330
23:15 Woe unto you, scribes and **P**, hypocrites! 5330
23:23 Woe unto you, scribes and **P**, hypocrites! 5330
23:25 Woe unto you, scribes and **P**, hypocrites! 5330
23:27 Woe unto you, scribes and **P**, hypocrites! 5330
23:29 Woe unto you, scribes and **P**, hypocrites! 5330
27:62 and **P** came together unto Pilate, 5330
Mk 2:16 and **P** saw him eat with publicans and 5330
2:18 disciples of John and of the **P** used to fast: 5330
2:18 do the disciples of John and of the **P** fast, 5330
2:24 And the **P** said unto him, Behold, why do 5330
3: 6 And the **P** went forth, and straightway took 5330
7: 1 Then came together unto him the **P**, and 5330
7: 3 For the **P**, and all the Jews, except they 5330
7: 5 Then the **P** and scribes asked him, 5330
8:11 And the **P** came forth, and began to 5330
8:15 beware of the leaven of the **P**, and *of* 5330
10: 2 And the **P** came to *him,* and asked him, Is it 5330
12:13 And they send unto him certain of the **P** 5330
Lk 5:17 that there were **P** and doctors of the law 5330
5:21 And the scribes and the **P** began to reason, 5330
5:30 and **P** murmured against his disciples, 5330
5:33 and likewise the *disciples* of the **P**; 5330
6: 2 And certain of the **P** said unto them, 5330
6: 7 And the scribes and **P** watched him, 5330
7:30 But the **P** and lawyers rejected the counsel 5330
7:36 And one of the **P** desired him that he would 5330
11:39 Now do ye **P** make clean the outside of 5330
11:42 But woe unto you, **P**! for ye tithe mint and 5330
11:43 Woe unto you, **P**! for ye love 5330
11:44 Woe unto you, scribes and **P**, hypocrites! 5330
11:53 and the **P** began to urge *him* vehemently, 5330
12: 1 *of all,* Beware ye of the leaven of the **P**, 5330
13:31 The same day there came certain *of the* **P**, 5330
14: 1 the chief **P** to eat bread on the sabbath day, 5330
14: 3 answering spake unto the lawyers and **P**, 5330
15: 2 And the **P** and scribes murmured, saying, 5330
16:14 And the **P** also, who were covetous, 5330
17:20 And when he was demanded of the **P**, 5330
19:39 And some of the **P** from among 5330
Jn 1:24 And they which were sent were of the **P**. 5330
3: 1 There was a man of the **P**, 5330
4: 1 the Lord knew how the **P** had heard that 5330
7:32 The **P** heard that the people murmured such 5330
7:32 and the **P** and the chief priests sent officers 5330
7:45 came the officers to the chief priests and **P**; 5330
7:47 Then answered them the **P**, Are ye also 5330
7:48 of the rulers or of the **P** believed on him? 5330
8: 3 **P** brought unto him a woman taken in 5330
8:13 The **P** therefore said unto him, 5330
9:13 They brought to the **P** him that aforetime 5330
9:15 Then again the **P** also asked him how he 5330
9:16 Therefore said some of the **P**, This man is 5330
9:40 And *some* of the **P** which were with him 5330
11:46 But some of them went their ways to the **P**, 5330
11:47 the chief priests and the **P** a council, 5330
11:57 and the **P** had given a commandment, 5330
12:19 The **P** therefore said among themselves, 5330
12:42 of the **P** they did not confess *him,* lest they 5330
18: 3 and officers from the chief priests and **P**, 5330
Ac 15: 5 certain of the sect of the **P** which believed, 5330
23: 6 and the other **P**, he cried out in the council, 5330
23: 7 there arose a dissension between the **P** and 5330
23: 8 angel nor spirit: but the **P** confess both. 5330

PHARISEES' (1) [PHARISEE]
Ac 23: 9 the scribes *that were* of the **P** part arose, 5330

PHAROSH (1)
Ezr 8: 3 Of the sons of Shechaniah, of the sons of **P**; 6551

PHARPAR (1)
2Ki 5:12 *Are* not Abana and **P**, rivers of Damascus, 6554

PHARZITES (1) [PHAREZ]
Nu 26:20 of Pharez, the family of the **P**: of Zerah, 6558

PHASEAH (1) [PASEAH]
Ne 7:51 the children of Uzza, the children of **P**, 6454

PHEBE (2)
Ro 16: 1 I commend unto you **P** our sister, which is 5402
16: S *sent* by **P** servant of the church at 5402

PHENICE (3) [PHENICIA]
Ac 11:19 arose about Stephen travelled as far as **P**, 5403
15: 3 they passed through **P** and Samaria, 5403
27:12 if by any means they might attain to **P**, *and* 5405

PHENICIA (1) [PHENICE, SYROPHENICIAN]
Ac 21: 2 And finding a ship sailing over unto **P**, 5403

PHI-BESETH (1)
Eze 30:17 of Aven and of **P** shall fall by the sword: 6364

PHICHOL (3)
Ge 21:22 **P** the chief captain of his host spake unto 6369
21:32 **P** the chief captain of his host, and 6369
26:26 and **P** the chief captain of his army. 6369

PHICOL See PHICHOL

PHILADELPHIA (2)
Rev 1:11 unto Sardis, and unto **P**, and unto Laodicea. 5359
3: 7 And to the angel of the church in **P** write; 5359

PHILEMON (2)
Phm 1: 1 unto **P** *our* dearly beloved, and 5371
1: S Written from Rome to **P**, by Onesimus a 5371

PHILETUS (1)
2Ti 2:17 a canker: of whom is Hymeneus and **P**; 5372

PHILIP (33) [PHILIP'S]
Mt 10: 3 **P**, and Bartholomew; Thomas, and 5376
Mk 3:18 and **P**, and Bartholomew, and Matthew, 5376
Lk 3: 1 and his brother **P** tetrarch of Iturea and 5376
6:14 and John, **P** and Bartholomew, 5376
Jn 1:43 and findeth **P**, and saith unto him, 5376
1:44 Now **P** was of Bethsaida, the city of 5376
1:45 **P** findeth Nathanael, and saith unto him, 5376
1:46 **P** saith unto him, Come and see. 5376
1:48 said unto him, Before that **P** called thee, 5376
6: 5 he saith unto **P**, Whence shall we buy 5376
6: 7 **P** answered him, Two hundred pennyworth 5376
12:21 The same came therefore to **P**, which was 5376
12:22 **P** cometh and telleth Andrew: and 5376
12:22 and again Andrew and **P** tell Jesus. 5376
14: 8 **P** saith unto him, Lord, shew us the Father, 5376
14: 9 and *yet* hast thou not known me, **P**? 5376
Ac 1:13 and John, and Andrew, **P**, and Thomas, 5376
6: 5 and **P**, and Prochorus, and Nicanor, and 5376
8: 5 Then **P** went down to the city of Samaria, 5376
8: 6 gave heed unto those *things* which **P** spake, 5376
8:12 But when they believed **P** preaching 5376
8:13 he continued with **P**, and wondered, 5376
8:26 And *the* angel of the Lord spake unto **P**, 5376
8:29 Then the Spirit said unto **P**, Go near, and 5376
8:30 And **P** ran *thither* to *him,* and heard him 5376
8:31 And he desired **P** that *he* would come up 5376
8:34 And the eunuch answered **P**, and said, 5376
8:35 Then **P** opened his mouth, 5376
8:37 And **P** said, If thou believest with all *thine* 5376
8:38 both into the water, both **P** and the eunuch; 5376
8:39 the Spirit of the Lord caught away **P**, 5376
8:40 But **P** was found at Azotus: and 5376
21: 8 we entered into the house of **P** 5376

PHILIP'S (3) [PHILIP]
Mt 14: 3 for Herodias' sake, his brother **P** wife. 5376
Mk 6:17 for Herodias' sake, his brother **P** wife: 5376
Lk 3:19 by him for Herodias his brother **P** wife, 5376

PHILIPPI (8) [PHILIPPIANS]
Mt 16:13 Jesus came into the coasts of Cesarea **P**, 5376
Mk 8:27 his disciples, into the towns of Cesarea **P**: 5376
Ac 16:12 And from thence to **P**, which is the chief 5375
20: 6 And we sailed away from **P** after the days 5375
1Co 16: S was written from **P** by Stephanas, 5375
2Co 13: S to the Corinthians was written from **P**, 5375
Php 1: 1 all the saints in Christ Jesus which are at **P**, 5375
1Th 2: 2 shamefully entreated, as ye know, at **P**, 5375

PHILIPPIANS (2) [PHILIPPI]

Php 4:15 Now ye **P** know also, that in the beginning *5374*
4: S It was written to the **P** from Rome by *5374*

PHILISTIA (3) [PHILISTIM, PHILISTIMS, PHILISTINE, PHILISTINES, PHILISTINES']

Ps 60: 8 my shoe: **P**, triumph thou because of me. 6429
87: 4 behold **P**, and Tyre, with Ethiopia; this *man* 6429
108: 9 I cast out my shoe; over **P** will I triumph. 6429

PHILISTIM (1) [PHILISTIA]

Ge 10:14 and Casluhim, (out of whom came **P**) 6430

PHILISTIMS (5) [PHILISTIA]

Ge 26: 1 Isaac went unto Abimelech king of the **P** 6430
26: 8 that Abimelech king of the **P** looked out at 6430
26:14 store of servants: and the **P** envied him. 6430
26:15 the **P** had stopped them, and filled them 6430
26:18 for the **P** had stopped them after the death 6430

PHILISTINE (33) [PHILISTIA]

1Sa 17: 8 *am* not I a **P**, and you servants to Saul? 6430
17:10 the **P** said, I defy the armies of Israel this 6430
17:11 and all Israel heard those words of the **P**, 6430
17:16 the **P** drew near morning and evening, and 6430
17:23 the **P** of Gath, Goliath by name, 6430
17:26 shall be done to the man that killeth this **P**, 6430
17:26 for who *is* this uncircumcised **P**, that he 6430
17:32 thy servant will go and fight with this **P**. 6430
17:33 Thou art not able to go against this **P** to 6430
17:36 this uncircumcised **P** shall be as one of 6430
17:37 he will deliver me out of the hand of this **P**. 6430
17:40 *was* in his hand: and he drew near to the **P**. 6430
17:41 the **P** came on and drew near unto David; 6430
17:42 when the **P** looked about, and saw David, 6430
17:43 the **P** said unto David, *Am* I a dog, 6430
17:43 And the **P** cursed David by his gods. 6430
17:44 the **P** said to David, Come to me, and I will 6430
17:45 said David to the **P**, Thou comest to me 6430
17:48 when the **P** arose, and came and drew nigh 6430
17:48 and ran *toward* the army to meet the **P**. 6430
17:49 slang *it,* and smote the **P** in his forehead, 6430
17:50 So David prevailed over the **P** with a sling 6430
17:50 a stone, and smote the **P**, and slew him; 6430
17:51 stood upon the **P**, and took his sword, and 6430
17:54 David took the head of the **P**, and 6430
17:55 Saul saw David go forth against the **P**, 6430
17:57 David returned from the slaughter of the **P**, 6430
17:57 Saul with the head of the **P** in his hand. 6430
18: 6 was returned from the slaughter of the **P**, 6430
19: 5 slew the **P**, and the LORD wrought a great 6430
21: 9 the priest said, The sword of Goliath the **P**, 6430
22:10 and gave him the sword of Goliath the **P**. 6430
2Sa 21:17 and smote the **P**, and killed him. 6430

PHILISTINES (246) [PHILISTIA]

Ge 21:32 and they returned into the land of the **P**. 6430
Ex 13:17 not *through* the way of the land of the **P**, 6430
23:31 the Red sea even unto the sea of the **P**, 6430
Jos 13: 2 all the borders of the **P**, and all Geshuri, 6430
13: 3 five lords of the **P**; the Gazathites, and 6430
Jdg 3: 3 *Namely,* five lords of the **P**, and all 6430
3:31 which slew *of* the **P** six hundred men with 6430
10: 6 the gods of the **P**, and forsook the LORD, 6430
10: 7 he sold them into the hands of the **P**, and 6430
10:11 the children of Ammon, and from the **P**? 6430
13: 1 them into the hand of the **P** forty years. 6430
13: 5 to deliver Israel out of the hand of the **P**. 6430
14: 1 in Timnath of the daughters of the **P**. 6430
14: 2 in Timnath of the daughters of the **P**: 6430
14: 3 to take a wife of the uncircumcised **P**? 6430
14: 4 that he sought an occasion against the **P**: 6430
14: 4 for at that time the **P** had dominion over 6430
15: 3 Now shall I be more blameless than the **P**, 6430
15: 5 let *them* go into the standing corn of the **P**, 6430
15: 6 the **P** said, Who hath done this? And they 6430
15: 6 the **P** came up, and burnt her and her father 6430
15: 9 the **P** went up, and pitched in Judah, and 6430
15:11 Knowest thou not that the **P** *are* rulers over 6430
15:12 we may deliver thee into the hand of the **P**. 6430
15:14 came unto Lehi, the **P** shouted against him: 6430
15:20 he judged Israel in the days of the **P** twenty 6430
16: 5 the lords of the **P** came up unto her, and 6430
16: 8 the lords of the **P** brought up to her seven 6430
16: 9 unto him, The **P** *be* upon thee, Samson. 6430
16:12 unto him, The **P** *be* upon thee, Samson. 6430
16:14 unto him, The **P** *be* upon thee, Samson. 6430
16:18 she sent and called for the lords of the **P**, 6430
16:18 the lords of the **P** came up unto her, and 6430
16:20 she said, The **P** *be* upon thee, Samson. 6430
16:21 the **P** took him, and put out his eyes, and 6430
16:23 the lords of the **P** gathered them together 6430
16:27 all the lords of the **P** *were* there; and 6430
16:28 that I may be at once avenged of the **P** for 6430
16:30 Samson said, Let me die with the **P**. And he 6430
1Sa 4: 1 Now Israel went out against the **P** to battle, 6430
4: 1 and the **P** pitched in Aphek. 6430
4: 2 the **P** put *themselves* in array against Israel: 6430
4: 2 Israel was smitten before the **P**: 6430
4: 3 the LORD smitten us to day before the **P**? 6430
4: 6 when the **P** heard the noise of the shout, 6430
4: 7 the **P** were afraid, for they said, God is 6430
4: 9 and quit yourselves like men, O ye **P**, 6430
4:10 the **P** fought, and Israel was smitten, and 6430
4:17 Israel is fled before the **P**, and there hath 6430
5: 1 the **P** took the ark of God, and brought it 6430
5: 2 When the **P** took the ark of God, they 6430
5: 8 gathered all the lords of the **P** unto them, 6430
5:11 and gathered together all the lords of the **P**, 6430
6: 1 was in the country of the **P** seven months. 6430
6: 2 the **P** called for the priests and the diviners, 6430
6: 4 *to* the number of the lords of the **P**: 6430
6:12 the lords of the **P** went after them unto 6430
6:16 when the five lords of the **P** had seen *it,* 6430
6:17 these *are* the golden emerods which the **P** 6430
6:18 cities of the **P** *belonging* to the five lords, 6430
6:21 The **P** have brought again the ark of 6430
7: 3 he will deliver you out of the hand of the **P**. 6430
7: 7 when the **P** heard that the children of Israel 6430
7: 7 the lords of the **P** went up against Israel. 6430
7: 7 of Israel heard *it,* they were afraid of the **P**. 6430
7: 8 he will save us out of the hand of the **P**. 6430
7:10 the **P** drew near to battle against Israel: 6430
7:10 with a great thunder on that day upon the **P**, 6430
7:11 pursued the **P**, and smote them, until *they* 6430
7:13 So the **P** were subdued, and they came no 6430
7:13 the hand of the LORD was against the **P** 6430
7:14 the cities which the **P** had taken from Israel 6430
7:14 did Israel deliver out of the hands of the **P**. 6430
9:16 save my people out of the hand of the **P**: 6430
10: 5 hill of God, where *is* the garrison of the **P**: 6430
12: 9 into the hand of the **P**, and into the hand of 6430
13: 3 Jonathan smote the garrison of the **P** that 6430
13: 3 the **P** heard *of it.* And Saul blew 6430
13: 4 *that* Saul had smitten a garrison of the **P**, 6430
13: 4 also was had in abomination with the **P**. 6430
13: 5 the **P** gathered themselves together to fight 6430
13:11 *that* the **P** gathered themselves together *at* 6430
13:12 The **P** will come down now upon me *to* 6430
13:16 but the **P** encamped in Michmash. 6430
13:17 the spoilers came out of the camp of the **P** 6430
13:19 for the **P** said, Lest the Hebrews make *them* 6430
13:20 all the Israelites went down *to* the **P**, 6430
13:23 the garrison of the **P** went out to 6430
14:11 themselves unto the garrison of the **P**: 6430
14:11 the **P** said, Behold, the Hebrews come forth 6430
14:19 that the noise that *was* in the host of the **P** 6430
14:21 Moreover the Hebrews *that* were with the **P** 6430
14:22 *when* they heard that the **P** fled, even they 6430
14:30 now a much greater slaughter among the **P**? 6430
14:31 they smote the **P** that day from Michmash 6430
14:36 Let us go down after the **P** by night, and 6430
14:37 of God, Shall I go down after the **P**? 6430
14:46 Saul went up from following the **P**: and 6430
14:46 and the **P** went to their own place. 6430
14:47 the kings of Zobah, and against the **P**: 6430
14:52 there was sore war against the **P** all 6430
17: 1 Now the **P** gathered together their armies to 6430
17: 2 and set the battle in array against the **P**. 6430
17: 3 the **P** stood on a mountain on the one side, 6430
17: 4 out a champion out of the camp of the **P**, 6430
17:19 in the valley of Elah, fighting with the **P**. 6430
17:21 and the **P** had put *the battle* in array, 6430
17:23 out of the armies of the **P**, and 6430
17:46 I will give the carcases of the host of the **P** 6430
17:51 when the **P** saw their champion was dead, 6430
17:52 and shouted, and pursued the **P**, 6430
17:52 the wounded of the **P** fell down by the way 6430

1Sa 17:53 of Israel returned from chasing after the **P**, 6430
18:17 but let the hand of the **P** be upon him. 6430
18:21 that the hand of the **P** may be against him. 6430
18:25 but an hundred foreskins of the **P**, 6430
18:25 to make David fall by the hand of the **P**. 6430
18:27 and slew of the **P** two hundred men; 6430
18:30 the princes of the **P** went forth: and it came 6430
19: 8 fought with the **P**, and slew them *with* a 6430
23: 1 the **P** fight against Keilah, and they rob 6430
23: 2 Shall I go and smite these **P**? 6430
23: 2 Go, and smite the **P**, and save Keilah. 6430
23: 3 come *to* Keilah against the armies of the **P**? 6430
23: 4 for I will deliver the **P** into thine hand. 6430
23: 5 fought with the **P**, and brought away their 6430
23:27 and come; for the **P** have invaded the land. 6430
23:28 after David, and went against the **P**: 6430
24: 1 Saul was returned from following the **P**, 6430
27: 1 speedily escape into the land of the **P**; 6430
27: 7 dwelt in the country of the **P** was a full year 6430
27:11 while he dwelleth in the country of the **P**. 6430
28: 1 that the **P** gathered their armies together for 6430
28: 4 the **P** gathered themselves together, and 6430
28: 5 when Saul saw the host of the **P**, he was 6430
28:15 for the **P** make war against me, and God is 6430
28:19 Israel with thee into the hand of the **P**: 6430
28:19 the host of Israel into the hand of the **P**. 6430
29: 1 Now the **P** gathered together all their 6430
29: 2 the lords of the **P** passed on by hundreds, 6430
29: 3 said the princes of the **P**, What *do* these 6430
29: 3 And Achish said unto the princes of the **P**, 6430
29: 4 the princes of the **P** were wroth with him; 6430
29: 4 the princes of the **P** said unto him, 6430
29: 7 that thou displease not the lords of the **P**. 6430
29: 9 notwithstanding the princes of the **P** have 6430
29:11 to return into the land of the **P**. 6430
29:11 And the **P** went up *to* Jezreel. 6430
30:16 that they had taken out of the land of the **P**, 6430
31: 1 Now the **P** fought against Israel: and 6430
31: 1 the men of Israel fled from before the **P**, 6430
31: 2 the **P** followed hard upon Saul and upon his 6430
31: 2 the **P** slew Jonathan, and Abinadab, and 6430
31: 7 fled; and the **P** came and dwelt in them. 6430
31: 8 when the **P** came to strip the slain, that they 6430
31: 9 and sent into the land of the **P** round about, 6430
31:11 heard of that which the **P** had done to Saul, 6430
2Sa 1:20 lest the daughters of the **P** rejoice, lest 6430
3:14 to me for an hundred foreskins of the **P**. 6430
3:18 my people Israel out of the hand of the **P**, 6430
5:17 when the **P** heard that they had anointed 6430
5:17 all the **P** came up to seek David; 6430
5:18 The **P** also came and spread themselves in 6430
5:19 the LORD, saying, Shall I go up to the **P**? 6430
5:19 for I will doubtless deliver the **P** into thine 6430
5:22 the **P** came up yet again, and 6430
5:24 out before thee, to smite the host of the **P**. 6430
5:25 smote the **P** from Geba until thou come *to* 6430
8: 1 that David smote the **P**, and subdued them: 6430
8: 1 Metheg-ammah out of the hand of the **P**. 6430
8:12 of the **P**, and of Amalek, and of the spoil of 6430
19: 9 he delivered us out of the hand of the **P**; 6430
21:12 where the **P** had hanged them, when 6430
21:12 when the **P** had slain Saul in Gilboa: 6430
21:15 Moreover the **P** had yet war again with 6430
21:15 with him, and fought against the **P**: 6430
21:18 that there was again a battle with the **P** at 6430
21:19 there was again a battle in Gob with the **P**, 6430
23: 9 when they defied the **P** *that* were there 6430
23:10 smote the **P** until his hand was weary, and 6430
23:11 the **P** were gathered together into a troop, 6430
23:11 *of* lentiles: and the people fled from the **P**. 6430
23:12 and defended it, and slew the **P**: 6430
23:13 the troop of the **P** pitched in the valley of 6430
23:14 the garrison of the **P** *was* then 6430
23:16 *men* brake through the host of the **P**, 6430
1Ki 4:21 from the river *unto* the land of the **P**, 6430
15:27 at Gibbethon, which *belongeth* to the **P**; 6430
16:15 which *belonged* to the **P**. 6430
2Ki 8: 2 sojourned in the land of the **P** seven years. 6430
8: 3 woman returned out of the land of the **P**: 6430
18: 8 He smote the **P**, *even* unto Gaza, and 6430
1Ch 1:12 and Casluhim, (of whom came the **P**,) 6430
10: 1 Now the **P** fought against Israel; and 6430
10: 1 the men of Israel fled from before the **P**, 6430
10: 2 the **P** followed hard after Saul, and after his 6430
10: 2 the **P** slew Jonathan, and Abinadab, and 6430
10: 7 fled: and the **P** came and dwelt in them. 6430
10: 8 when the **P** came to strip the slain, that they 6430
10: 9 and sent into the land of the **P** round about, 6430
10:11 when all Jabesh-gilead heard all that the **P** 6430
11:13 there the **P** were gathered together to battle, 6430
11:13 and the people fled from before the **P**. 6430
11:14 *that* parcel, and delivered it, and slew the **P**; 6430
11:15 the host of the **P** encamped in the valley of 6430
11:18 the three brake through the host of the **P**, 6430
12:19 when he came with the **P** against Saul to 6430
12:19 for the lords of the **P** upon advisement sent 6430
14: 8 when the **P** heard that David was anointed 6430
14: 8 all Israel, all the **P** went up to seek David. 6430
14: 9 the **P** came and spread themselves in 6430
14:10 of God, saying, Shall I go up against the **P**? 6430
14:13 the **P** yet again spread themselves abroad in 6430
14:15 forth before thee to smite the host of the **P**. 6430
14:16 they smote the host of the **P** from Gibeon 6430
18: 1 that David smote the **P**, and subdued them, 6430
18: 1 and her towns out of the hand of the **P**. 6430
18:11 and from the **P**, and from Amalek. 6430
20: 4 that there arose war at Gezer with the **P**; 6430
20: 5 there was war again with the **P**; and 6430
2Ch 9:26 from the river even unto the land of the **P**, 6430
17:11 Also *some* of the **P** brought Jehoshaphat 6430
21:16 up against Jehoram the spirit of the **P**, 6430
26: 6 he went forth and warred against the **P**, 6430
26: 6 built cities about Ashdod, and among the **P**. 6430
26: 7 God helped him against the **P**, and 6430
28:18 The **P** also had invaded the cities of the low 6430
Ps 56: T of David, when the **P** took him in Gath. 6430
83: 7 Amalek; the **P** with the inhabitants of Tyre; 6429
Isa 2: 6 *are* soothsayers like the **P**, and they please 6430
9:12 The Syrians before, and the **P** behind; 6430
11:14 they shall fly upon the shoulders of the **P** 6430
Jer 25:20 all the kings of the land of the **P**, and 6430
47: 1 came to Jeremiah the prophet against the **P**, 6430
47: 4 of the day that cometh to spoil all the **P**, 6430
47: 4 for the LORD *will* spoil the **P**, 6430
Eze 16:27 the daughters of the **P**, which are ashamed 6430
16:57 *are* round about her, the daughters of the **P**, 6430
25:15 Because the **P** have dealt by revenge, and 6430
25:16 I *will* stretch out mine hand upon the **P**, and 6430
Am 1: 8 the remnant of the **P** shall perish, saith 6430
6: 2 go down *to* Gath of the **P**: *be they* better 6430
9: 7 the **P** from Caphtor, and the Syrians from 6430
Ob 1:19 mount of Esau; and *they of* the plain the **P**: 6430
Zep 2: 5 O Canaan, the land of the **P**, I will even 6430
Zec 9: 6 and I will cut off the pride of the **P**. 6430

PHILISTINES' (4) [PHILISTIA]
Ge 21:34 Abraham sojourned in the **P** land many 6430
1Sa 14: 1 Come, and let us go over to the **P** garrison, 6430
14: 4 sought to go over unto the **P** garrison, 6430
1Ch 11:16 and the **P** garrison *was* then at Beth-lehem. 6430

PHILOLOGUS (1)
Ro 16:15 Salute **P**, and Julia, Nereus, and his sister, *5378*

PHILOSOPHERS (1) [PHILOSOPHY]
Ac 17:18 Then certain **p** of the Epicureans, and of *5386*

PHILOSOPHY (1) [PHILOSOPHERS]
Col 2: 8 Beware lest any *man* spoil you through **p** *5385*

PHINEHAS (24) [PHINEHAS']
Ex 6:25 of Putiel to wife; and she bare him **P**: 6372
Nu 25: 7 when **P**, the son of Eleazar, the son of 6372
25:11 **P**, the son of Eleazar, the son of Aaron 6372
31: 6 them and **P** the son of Eleazar the priest, 6372
Jos 22:13 of Gilead, **P** the son of Eleazar the priest, 6372
22:30 when **P** the priest, and the princes of 6372
22:31 **P** the son of Eleazar the priest said unto 6372
22:32 **P** the son of Eleazar the priest, and 6372
24:33 they buried him in a hill that pertained to **P** 6372
Jdg 20:28 **P**, the son of Eleazar, the son of Aaron, 6372
1Sa 1: 3 the two sons of Eli, Hophni and **P**, 6372
2:34 come upon thy two sons, on Hophni and **P**; 6372
4: 4 the two sons of Eli, Hophni and **P**, 6372
4:11 two sons of Eli, Hophni and **P**, were slain. 6372
4:17 Hophni and **P**, are dead, and the ark of God 6372
14: 3 the son of **P**, the son of Eli, 6372
1Ch 6: 4 Eleazar begat **P**, Phinehas begat Abishua, 6372

1Ch 6: 4 Eleazar begat Phinehas, **P** begat Abishua, 6372
6:50 Eleazar his son, **P** his son, Abishua his son, 6372
9:20 **P** the son of Eleazar was the ruler over 6372
Ezr 7: 5 the son of **P**, the son of Eleazar, 6372
8: 2 Of the sons of **P**; Gershom: of the sons of 6372
8:33 with him *was* Eleazar the son of **P**; and 6372
Ps 106:30 stood up **P**, and executed judgment: and 6372

PHINEHAS' (1) [PHINEHAS]
1Sa 4:19 **P** wife, was with child, *near* to be 6372

PHLEGON (1)
Ro 16:14 **P**, Hermas, Patrobas, Hermes, and *5393*

PHOEBE See PHEBE

PHOENICIA See PHENICE; PHENICIA

PHOENIX See PHENICE

PHRYGIA (4)
Ac 2:10 **P**, and Pamphylia, in Egypt, and in *5435*
16: 6 Now when they had gone throughout **P** and *5435*
18:23 *all* the country of Galatia and **P** in order, *5435*
1Ti 6: S which is the chiefest city of **P** Pacatiana. *5435*

PHURAH (2)
Jdg 7:10 go thou with **P** thy servant down to 6513
7:11 went he down with **P** his servant unto 6513

PHUT (2)
Ge 10: 6 Cush, and Mizraim, and **P**, and Canaan. 6316
Eze 27:10 and of Lud and of **P** were in thine army, 6316

PHUVAH (1) [PUAH]
Ge 46:13 Tola, and **P**, and Job, and Shimron. 6312

PHYGELLUS (1)
2Ti 1:15 from me; of whom are **P** and Hermogenes. *5436*

PHYGELUS See PHYGELLUS

PHYLACTERIES (1)
Mt 23: 5 they make broad their **p**, and enlarge *5440*

PHYSICIAN (6) [PHYSICIANS]
Jer 8:22 no balm in Gilead; *is there* no **p** there? 7495
Mt 9:12 They that be whole need not a **p**, but *2395*
Mk 2:17 They that are whole have no need of *the* **p**, *2395*
Lk 4:23 say unto me this proverb, **P**, heal thyself: *2395*
5:31 They that are whole need not a **p**; *2395*
Col 4:14 Luke, the beloved **p**, and Demas, greet you. *2395*

PHYSICIANS (6) [PHYSICIAN]
Ge 50: 2 Joseph commanded his servants the **p** to 7495
50: 2 his father: and the **p** embalmed Israel. 7495
2Ch 16:12 he sought not *to* the LORD, but to the **p**. 7495
Job 13: 4 *are* forgers of lies, ye *are* all **p** of no value. 7495
Mk 5:26 And had suffered many *things* of many **p**, *2395*
Lk 8:43 which had spent all *her* living upon **p**, *2395*

PICK (1)
Pr 30:17 the ravens of the valley shall **p** it **out**, and 5365

PICKED TROOPS See WORTHIES

PICTURES (3)
Nu 33:52 destroy all their **p**, and destroy all their 4906
Pr 25:11 spoken *is like* apples of gold in **p** of silver. 4906
Isa 2:16 ships of Tarshish, and upon all pleasant **p**. 7914

PIECE (43) [PIECES, SHOULDERPIECES]
Ge 15:10 and laid each **p** one against another: 1335
Ex 37: 7 **beaten out of one p** made he them, on 4749
Nu 10: 2 of a **whole p** thou shalt make them: 4749
Jdg 9:53 a certain woman cast a **p** of a millstone 6400
1Sa 2:36 crouch to him for a **p** of silver and a morsel of 95
2:36 priests' offices, that *I* may eat a **p** of bread. 6595
30:12 they gave him a **p** of a cake *of figs*, and 6400
2Sa 6:19 a **good p** *of flesh*, and a flagon *of wine*. So 829
11:21 did not a woman cast a **p** of a millstone 6400
23:11 where was a **p** of ground full *of* lentiles: 2513
2Ki 3:19 and mar every good **p of land** with stones. 2513
3:25 *on* every good **p of land** cast every man his 2513
1Ch 16: 3 and a **good p** *of flesh*, and a flagon *of wine*. 829
Ne 3:11 repaired the other **p**, and the tower of 4060
3:19 another **p** over against the going up to 4060
3:20 of Zabbai earnestly repaired the other **p**, 4060
3:21 the son of Urijah the son of Koz another **p**, 4060
3:24 Binnui the son of Henadad another **p**, 4060
3:27 After them the Tekoites repaired another **p**, 4060
3:30 Hanun the sixth son of Zalaph, another **p**. 4060
Job 41:24 yea, as hard as a **p** of the nether *millstone*. 6400
42:11 every man also gave him a **p of money**, 7192
Pr 6:26 woman *a man is brought* to a **p** of bread: 3603
28:21 for for a **p** of bread *that* man will 6595
SS 4: 3 thy temples *are* like a **p** of a pomegranate 6400
6: 7 As a **p** of a pomegranate *are* thy temples 6400
Jer 37:21 that *they* should give him daily a **p** of bread 3603
Eze 24: 4 *even* every good **p**, the thigh, and 5409
24: 6 bring it out **p** by piece; let no lot fall upon 5409
24: 6 bring it out piece by **p**; let no lot fall upon 5409
Am 3:12 mouth of the lion two legs, or a **p** of an ear; 915
4: 7 one **p** was rained upon, and the piece 2513
4: 7 and the **p** whereupon it rained not withered. 2513
Mt 9:16 No *man* putteth a **p** of new cloth unto an *1915*
17:27 his mouth, thou shalt find a **p of money**: *4715*
Mk 2:21 No *man* also seweth a **p** of new cloth on an *1915*
2:21 else the new **p that filled it up** taketh away *4138*
Lk 5:36 No *man* putteth a **p** of a new garment upon *1915*
5:36 the **p** that was *taken* out of the new agreeth *1915*
14:18 I have bought a **p of ground**, and I must *68*
15: 8 if she lose one **p**, doth not light a candle, *1406*
15: 9 for I have found the **p** which I had lost. *1406*
24:42 And they gave him a **p** of a broiled fish, *3313*

PIECES (121) [PIECE]
Ge 15:17 burning lamp that passed between those **p**. 1506
20:16 I have given thy brother a thousand *p* of NIH
33:19 for an hundred **p of money**. 7192
37:28 sold Joseph to the Ishmeelites for twenty *p* NIH
37:33 Joseph is **without doubt rent in p**. 2963+2963
44:28 and I said, Surely he is **torn in p**; 2963+2963
45:22 to Benjamin he gave three hundred *p* of NIH
Ex 15: 6 O LORD, hath **dashed in p** the enemy. 7492
22:13 If it be **torn in p**, *then* let him bring 2963+2963
29:17 thou shalt cut the ram in **p**, and wash 5409
29:17 and put *them* unto his **p**, and unto his head. 5409
Lev 1: 6 flay the burnt offering, and cut it into his **p**. 5409
1:12 he shall cut it into his **p**, with his head and 5409
2: 6 Thou shalt **part** it **in p**, and pour oil 6595+6626
6:21 the baken **p** of the meat offering shalt thou 6595
8:20 he cut the ram into **p**; and Moses burnt 5409
8:20 burnt the head, and the **p**, and the fat. 5409
9:13 unto him, with the **p** thereof, and the head: 5409
Jos 24:32 of Shechem for an hundred **p of silver**: 7192
Jdg 9: 4 ten *p* of silver out of the house of NIH
16: 5 every one *of us* eleven hundred *p* of silver. NIH
19:29 into twelve **p**, and sent her into all 5409
20: 6 **cut** her **in p**, and sent her throughout all 5408
1Sa 2:10 of the LORD shall be **broken to p**; 2865
11: 7 **hewed** them **in p**, and sent *them* throughout 5408
15:33 Samuel **hewed** Agag **in p** before 8158
1Ki 11:30 that *was* on him, and rent it *in* twelve **p**: 7168
11:31 he said to Jeroboam, Take thee ten **p**: 7168
18:23 **cut** it **in p**, and lay *it* on wood, and put no 5408
18:33 **cut** the bullock **in p**, and laid *him* on 5408
19:11 **brake in p** the rocks before the LORD; 7665
2Ki 2:12 own clothes, and **rent** them **in two p**. 7167+7168
5: 5 six thousand *p* of gold, and ten changes of NIH
6:25 until an ass's head was *sold* for fourscore *p* NIH
6:25 of a kab of dove's dung for five *p* of silver. NIH
11:18 and his images **brake** they **in p** throughly, 7665
18: 4 **brake in p** the brasen serpent that Moses 3807
23:14 he **brake in p** the images, and cut down 7665
24:13 **cut in p** all the vessels of gold which 7112
25:13 did the Chaldees break *in p*, and carried NIH
2Ch 23:17 **brake** his altars and his images **in p**, and 7665
25:12 of the rock, that they all were **broken in p**. 1234
28:24 **cut in p** the vessels of the house of God, 7112
31: 1 brake the images *in p*, and cut down NIH
34: 4 he brake *in p*, and made dust *of them*, and NIH
Job 16:12 **shaken** me **to p**, and set me up for his 6327
19: 2 my soul, and **break** me **in p** with words? 1792
34:24 He shall **break in p** mighty *men* without 7489
40:18 His bones *are as* **strong p** of brass; his bones 650
Ps 2: 9 thou shalt **dash** them **in p** like a potter's 5310
7: 2 **rending** *it* **in p**, while *there is* none to 6561
50:22 lest I **tear** *you* **in p**, and *there be* none to 2963
58: 7 *to shoot* his arrows, let them be as **cut in p**. 4135
68:30 *till every one* submit himself with **p** of 7518

P

Ps 72: 4 and shall **break in p** the oppressor. 1792
74:14 Thou **brakest** the heads of leviathan **in p**, 7533
89:10 Thou hast **broken** Rahab **in p**, as one that 1792
94: 5 They **break in p** thy people, O LORD, 1792
SS 8:11 thereof was to bring a thousand *p* of silver. NIH
Isa 3:15 What mean ye *that* ye **beat** my people **to p**, 1792
8: 9 O ye people, and ye shall be **broken in p**; 2865
8: 9 and ye shall be **broken in p**; 2865
8: 9 and ye shall be **broken in p**. 2865
13:16 Their children also shall be **dashed to p** 7376
13:18 bows also shall **dash** the young men **to p**; 7376
30:14 of the potters' vessel that is **broken in p**; 3807
45: 2 I will **break in p** the gates of brass, and 7665
Jer 5: 6 that goeth out thence shall be **torn in p**: 2963
23:29 like a hammer *that* **breaketh** the rock **in p**? 6327
50: 2 is confounded, Merodach is **broken in p**; 2865
50: 2 her images are **broken in p**. 2865
51:20 for with thee will I **break in p** the nations, 5310
51:21 with thee will I **break in p** the horse and 5310
51:21 with thee will I **break in p** the chariot and 5310
51:22 With thee also will I **break in p** man and 5310
51:22 with thee will I **break in p** old and young; 5310
51:22 with thee will I **break in p** the young man 5310
51:23 I will also **break in p** with thee 5310
51:23 with thee will I **break in p** the husbandman 5310
51:23 with thee will I **break in p** captains and 5310
La 3:11 turned aside my ways, and **pulled** me **in p**: 6582
Eze 4:14 *of* that which dieth of itself, or is **torn in p**; 2966
13:19 for handfuls of barley and for **p** of bread, 6595
24: 4 Gather the **p** thereof into it, *even* every 5409
Da 2: 5 ye shall be cut in **p**, and your houses shall 1917
2:34 *were* of iron and clay, and **brake** them **in p**. 1855
2:35 **broken to p** together, and became like 1855
2:40 forasmuch as iron **breaketh in p** and 1855
2:40 all these, shall it **break in p** and bruise. 1855
2:44 *but* it shall **break in p** and consume all 1855
2:45 *that* it **brake in p** the iron, the brass, 1855
3:29 shall be cut in **p**, and their houses shall be 1917
6:24 **brake** all their bones **in p** or ever they 1855
7: 7 it devoured and **brake in p**, and 1855
7:19 **brake in p**, and stamped the residue with 1855
7:23 and shall tread it down, and **break** it **in p**. 1855
Hos 3: 2 So I bought her to me for fifteen *p* of silver, NIH
8: 6 the calf of Samaria shall be **broken in p**. 7616
10:14 the mother was **dashed in p** upon *her* 7376
13:16 their infants shall be **dashed in p**, and 7376
Mic 1: 7 graven images thereof shall be **beaten to p**, 3807
3: 3 **chop** *them* **in p**, as for the pot, and as flesh 6566
4:13 thou shalt **beat in p** many people: and 1854
5: 8 and **teareth in p**, and none can deliver. 2963
Na 2: 1 He that **dasheth in p** is come up before thy 6327
2:12 The lion did **tear in p** enough for his 2963
3:10 her young children also were **dashed in p** 7376
Zec 11:12 So they weighed *for* my price thirty *p* of NIH
11:13 I took the thirty *p* of silver, and cast them to NIH
11:16 flesh of the fat, and **tear** their claws **in p**. 6561
12: 3 themselves with it shall be **cut in p**, 8295+8295
Mt 26:15 And they covenanted with him for thirty **p** NIG
27: 3 brought again the thirty **p** of silver to NIG
27: 5 And he cast down the **p** of silver in NIG
27: 6 And the chief priests took the silver **p**, and NIG
27: 9 saying, And they took the thirty **p** of silver, NIG
Mk 5: 4 by him, and the fetters **broken in p**: *4937*
Lk 15: 8 Either what woman having ten **p** of silver, NIG
Ac 19:19 and found *it* fifty thousand **p** of silver. NIG
23:10 Paul should have been **pulled in p** of them, *1288*
27:44 and some on **broken p** of the ship. *5100*

PIERCE (4) [PIERCED, PIERCETH, PIERCING, PIERCINGS]
Nu 24: 8 and **p** *them* **through** *with* his arrows. 4272
2Ki 18:21 man lean, it will go into his hand, and **p** it: 5344
Isa 36: 6 man lean, it will go into his hand, and **p** it: 5344
Lk 2:35 a sword shall **p through** thy own soul *1330*

PIERCED (8) [PIERCE]
Jdg 5:26 when she had **p** and stricken through his 4272
Job 30:17 My bones are **p** in me in the night season: 5365
Ps 22:16 inclosed me: they **p** my hands and my feet. 3738
Zec 12:10 they shall look upon me whom they have **p**, 1856
Jn 19:34 But one of the soldiers with a spear **p** his *3572*
19:37 They shall look on *him* whom they **p**. *1574*
1Ti 6:10 **p** themselves **through** with many sorrows. *4044*
Rev 1: 7 shall see him, and they *also* which **p** him: *1574*

PIERCETH (1) [PIERCE]
Job 40:24 it with his eyes: *his* nose **p** through snares. 5344

PIERCING (2) [PIERCE]
Isa 27: 1 strong sword shall punish leviathan the **p** 1281
Heb 4:12 **p** even to the dividing asunder of soul and *1338*

PIERCINGS (1) [PIERCE]
Pr 12:18 There is that speaketh like the **p** of a sword: 4094

PIETY (1)
1Ti 5: 4 let them learn first to **shew p** at home, and *2151*

PIG See SWINE

PIGEON (2) [PIGEONS]
Ge 15: 9 years old, and a turtle-dove, and a **young p**. 1469
Lev 12: 6 a young **p**, or a turtledove, for a sin 3123

PIGEONS (10) [PIGEON]
Lev 1:14 his offering of turtledoves, or of young **p**. 3123
5: 7 two turtledoves, or two young **p**, unto 3123
5:11 or two young **p**, then he that sinned shall 3123
12: 8 she shall bring two turtles, or two young **p**; 3123
14:22 two turtledoves, or two young **p**, such as he 3123
14:30 or of the young **p**, such as he can get; 3123
15:14 or two young **p**, and come before 3123
15:29 or two young **p**, and bring them unto 3123
Nu 6:10 two turtles, or two young **p**, to the priest, 3123
Lk 2:24 A pair of turtledoves, or two young **p**. *4058*

PI-HAHIROTH (4)
Ex 14: 2 that they turn and encamp before **P**, 6367
14: 9 by the sea, beside **P**, before Baal-zephon. 6367
Nu 33: 7 turned again unto **P**, which *is* before 6367
33: 8 they departed from before **P**hahiroth, and 6367

PILATE (56)
Mt 27: 2 delivered him to Pontius **P** the governor. *4091*
27:13 Then said **P** unto him, Hearest thou not *4091*
27:17 **P** said unto them, Whom will ye *that* I *4091*
27:22 **P** saith unto them, What shall I do then *4091*
27:24 When **P** saw that he could prevail nothing, *4091*
27:58 He went to **P**, and begged the body of *4091*
27:58 Then **P** commanded the body to be *4091*
27:62 and Pharisees came together unto **P**, *4091*
27:65 **P** said unto them, Ye have a watch: go your *4091*
Mk 15: 1 carried *him* away, and delivered *him* to **P**. *4091*
15: 2 And **P** asked him, Art thou the King of *4091*
15: 4 And **P** asked him again, saying, *4091*
15: 5 yet answered nothing; so that **P** marvelled. *4091*
15: 9 But **P** answered them, saying, Will ye *that* I *4091*
15:12 And **P** answered and said again unto them, *4091*
15:14 Then **P** said unto them, Why, what evil *4091*
15:15 And *so* **P**, willing to content the people, *4091*
15:43 and went in boldly unto **P**, and craved *4091*
15:44 And **P** marvelled if he were already dead: *4091*
Lk 3: 1 Pontius **P** being governor of Judea, and *4091*
13: 1 whose blood **P** had mingled with their *4091*
23: 1 of them arose, and led him unto **P**. *4091*
23: 3 And **P** asked him, saying, Art thou *4091*
23: 4 Then said **P** to the chief priests and *to* *4091*
23: 6 When **P** heard of Galilee, he asked whether *4091*
23:11 in a gorgeous robe, and sent him again to **P**. *4091*
23:12 And the same day **P** and Herod were made *4091*
23:13 And **P**, when he had called together *4091*
23:20 **P** therefore, willing to release Jesus, spake *4091*
23:24 And **P** gave sentence that it should be as *4091*
23:52 This *man* went unto **P**, and begged *4091*
Jn 18:29 **P** then went out unto them, and said, What *4091*
18:31 Then said **P** unto them, Take ye him, and *4091*
18:33 Then **P** entered into the judgment hall *4091*
18:35 **P** answered, Am I a Jew? Thine own *4091*
18:37 **P** therefore said unto him, Art thou a king *4091*
18:38 **P** saith unto him, What is truth? And when *4091*
19: 1 Then **P** therefore took Jesus, and *4091*
19: 4 **P** therefore went forth again, and *4091*
19: 5 And *P* saith unto them, Behold the man. NIG
19: 6 Crucify *him*, crucify *him*. **P** saith unto *4091*
19: 8 When **P** therefore heard that saying, he was *4091*
19:10 Then saith **P** unto him, Speakest thou not *4091*
19:12 *And* from thenceforth **P** sought to release *4091*
19:13 When **P** therefore heard that saying, *4091*
19:15 **P** saith unto them, Shall I crucify your *4091*
19:19 And **P** wrote a title, and put *it* on the cross. *4091*

Jn 19:21 Then said the chief priests of the Jews to **P**, *4091*
19:22 **P** answered, What I have written I have *4091*
19:31 besought **P** that their legs might be broken, *4091*
19:38 besought **P** that he might take away *4091*
19:38 and **P** gave *him* leave. He came therefore, *4091*
Ac 3:13 and denied him in the presence of **P**, *4091*
4:27 both Herod, and Pontius **P**, with *4091*
13:28 *yet* desired they **P** that he should be slain. *4091*
1Ti 6:13 who before Pontius **P** witnessed a good *4091*

PILDASH (1)
Ge 22:22 and Hazo, and **P**, and Jidlaph, and Bethuel. 6394

PILE (2)
Isa 30:33 the **p** thereof *is* fire and much wood; 4071
Eze 24: 9 I will even make the **p for fire** great. 4071

PILE OF RUBBLE See DUNGHILL

PILEHA (1)
Ne 10:24 Hallohesh, **P**, Shobek, 6401

PILGRIMAGE (4) [PILGRIMS]
Ge 47: 9 The days of the years of my **p** *are* an 4033
47: 9 the life of my fathers in the days of their **p**. 4033
Ex 6: 4 the land of their **p**, wherein they were 4033
Ps 119:54 have been my songs in the house of my **p**. 4033

PILGRIMS (2) [PILGRIMAGE]
Heb 11:13 that they were strangers and **p** on the earth. *3927*
1Pe 2:11 I beseech *you* as strangers and **p**, *3927*

PILHA See PILEHA

PILLAR (47) [PILLARS]
Ge 19:26 behind him, and she became a **p** of salt. 5333
28:18 set it up *for* a **p**, and poured oil upon 4676
28:22 this stone, which I have set *for* a **p**, shall be 4676
31:13 where thou anointedst the **p**, *and* 4676
31:45 Jacob took a stone, and set it up *for* a **p**. 4676
31:51 Behold this heap, and behold *this* **p**, 4676
31:52 This heap *be* witness, and *this* **p** *be* witness, 4676
31:52 not pass over this heap and this **p** unto me, 4676
35:14 Jacob set up a **p** in the place where he 4678
35:14 he talked with him, *even* a **p** of stone: 4678
35:20 Jacob set a **p** upon her grave: that *is* 4676
35:20 that *is* the **p** of Rachel's grave unto *this* 4678
Ex 13:21 the LORD went before them by day in a **p** 5982
13:21 by night in a **p** of fire, to give them light; 5982
13:22 He took not away the **p** of the cloud by day, 5982
13:22 nor the **p** of fire by night, *from* before 5982
14:19 the **p** of the cloud went from before their 5982
14:24 host of the Egyptians through the **p** of fire 5982
33: 9 the cloudy **p** descended, and stood *at* 5982
33:10 all the people saw the cloudy **p** stand *at* 5982
Nu 12: 5 the LORD came down in the **p** of 5982
14:14 by day time in a **p** of a cloud, and in a pillar 5982
14:14 pillar of a cloud, and in a **p** of fire by night. 5982
Dt 31:15 appeared in the tabernacle in a **p** of a cloud: 5982
31:15 the **p** of the cloud stood over the door of 5982
Jdg 9: 6 by the plain of the **p** that *was* in Shechem. 5324
20:40 arise up out of the city *with* a **p** of smoke, 5982
2Sa 18:18 had taken and reared up for himself a **p**, 4678
18:18 he called the **p** after his own name: and it is 4678
1Ki 7:21 he set up the right **p**, and called the name 5982
7:21 he set up the left **p**, and called the name 5982
2Ki 11:14 behold, the king stood by a **p**, as 5982
23: 3 the king stood by a **p**, and made a covenant 5982
25:17 The height of the one **p** *was* eighteen 5982
25:17 like unto these had the second **p** with 5982
2Ch 23:13 the king stood at his **p** at the entering in, 5982
Ne 9:12 thou leddest them in the day by a cloudy **p**; 5982
9:12 in the night by a **p** of fire, to give them 5982
9:19 the **p** of the cloud departed not from them 5982
9:19 neither the **p** of fire by night, to shew them 5982
Ps 99: 7 He spake unto them in the cloudy **p**: 5982
Isa 19:19 and a **p** at the border thereof to the LORD. 4676
Jer 1:18 an iron **p**, and brasen walls against 5982
52:21 the height of one **p** *was* eighteen cubits; 5982
52:22 The second **p** also and the pomegranates 5982
1Ti 3:15 living God, the **p** and ground of the truth. *4769*
Rev 3:12 Him that overcometh will I make a **p** in *4769*

PILLARS (89) [PILLAR]
Ex 24: 4 an altar under the hill, and twelve **p**, 4676
26:32 thou shalt hang it upon four **p** of shittim 5982
26:37 thou shalt make for the hanging five **p** of 5982
27:10 the twenty **p** thereof and their twenty 5982
27:10 the hooks of the **p** and their fillets *shall be* 5982
27:11 his twenty **p** and their twenty sockets *of* 5982
27:11 the hooks of the **p** and their fillets *of* silver. 5982
27:12 their **p** ten, and their sockets ten. 5982
27:14 their **p** three, and their sockets three. 5982
27:15 fifteen *cubits:* their **p** three, and 5982
27:16 *and* their **p** *shall be* four, and their sockets 5982
27:17 All the **p** round about the court *shall be* 5982
35:11 his boards, his bars, his **p**, and his sockets, 5982
35:17 his **p**, and their sockets, and the hanging for 5982
36:36 he made thereunto four **p** of shittim *wood,* 5982
36:38 the five **p** of it with their hooks: and 5982
38:10 Their **p** *were* twenty, and their brasen 5982
38:10 the hooks of the **p** and their fillets *were of* 5982
38:11 their **p** *were* twenty, and their sockets *of* 5982
38:11 the hooks of the **p** and their fillets *of* silver. 5982
38:12 their **p** ten, and their sockets ten; 5982
38:12 the hooks of the **p** and their fillets *of* silver. 5982
38:14 their **p** three, and their sockets three. 5982
38:15 their **p** three, and their sockets three. 5982
38:17 the sockets for the **p** *were of* brass; 5982
38:17 the hooks of the **p** and their fillets *of* silver; 5982
38:17 all the **p** of the court *were* filleted *with* 5982
38:19 their **p** *were* four, and their sockets *of* brass 5982
38:28 and five *shekels* he made hooks for the **p**, 5982
39:33 his bars, and his **p**, and his sockets, 5982
39:40 his **p**, and his sockets, and the hanging for 5982
40:18 put in the bars thereof, and reared up his **p**. 5982
Nu 3:36 the **p** thereof, and the sockets thereof, and 5982
3:37 the **p** of the court round about, and 5982
4:31 and the **p** thereof, and sockets thereof, 5982
4:32 the **p** of the court round about, and 5982
Dt 12: 3 break their **p**, and burn their groves with 4676
Jdg 16:25 them sport: and they set him between the **p**. 5982
16:26 Suffer me that I may feel the **p** whereupon 5982
16:29 Samson took hold of the two middle **p** 5982
1Sa 2: 8 for the **p** of the earth *are* the LORD's, and 4690
1Ki 7: 2 thirty cubits, upon four rows of cedar **p**, 5982
7: 2 cedar pillars, with cedar beams upon the **p**. 5982
7: 3 that *lay* on forty five **p**, fifteen *in* a row. 5982
7: 6 he made a porch of **p**; the length thereof 5982
7: 6 *the other* **p** and the thick beam *were* before 5982
7:15 For he cast two **p** *of* brass, of eighteen 5982
7:16 molten brass, to set upon the tops of the **p**: 5982
7:17 chapiters which *were* upon the top of the **p**; 5982
7:18 he made the **p**, and two rows round about 5982
7:19 top of the **p** *were* of lily work in the porch, 5982
7:20 the chapiters upon the two **p** *had* 5982
7:21 he set up the **p** in the porch of the temple: 5982
7:22 upon the top of the **p** *was* lily work: so 5982
7:22 so was the work of the **p** finished. 5982
7:41 The two **p**, and the two bowls of 5982
7:41 chapiters that *were* on the top of the *two* **p**; 5982
7:41 chapiters which *were* upon the top of the **p**; 5982
7:42 bowls of the chapiters that *were* upon the **p**; 5982
10:12 the king made *of* the almug trees **p** for 4552
2Ki 18:16 *from* the **p** which Hezekiah king of Judah 547
25:13 the **p** of brass that *were in* the house of 5982
25:16 The two **p**, one sea, and the bases which 5982
1Ch 18: 8 and the **p**, and the vessels of brass. 5982
2Ch 3:15 Also he made before the house two **p** of 5982
3:16 and put *them* on the heads of the **p**; 5982
3:17 he reared up the **p** before the temple, 5982
4:12 *To wit,* the two **p**, and the pommels, and 5982
4:12 *which were* on the top of the two **p**, 5982
4:12 chapiters which *were* on the top of the **p**; 5982
4:13 of the chapiters which *were* upon the **p**. 5982
Est 1: 6 and purple to silver rings and **p** of marble: 5982
Job 9: 6 out of her place, and the **p** thereof tremble. 5982
26:11 The **p** of heaven tremble and are astonished 5982
Ps 75: 3 *are* dissolved: I bear up the **p** of it. Selah. 5982
Pr 9: 1 her house, she hath hewn out her seven **p**: 5982
SS 3: 6 out of the wilderness like **p** of smoke, 8490
3:10 He made the **p** thereof *of* silver, the bottom 5982
5:15 His legs *are as* **p** of marble, set upon 5982
Jer 27:19 saith the LORD of hosts concerning the **p**, 5982
52:17 Also the **p** of brass that *were* in the house 5982
52:20 The two **p**, one sea, and twelve brasen bulls 5982
52:21 *concerning* the **p**, the height of one pillar 5982
Eze 40:49 *there were* **p** by the posts, one on this side, 5982
42: 6 but had not **p** as the pillars of the courts: 5982

P

Eze 42: 6 but had not pillars as the **p** of the courts: 5982
Joel 2:30 the earth, blood, and fire, and **p** of smoke. 8490
Gal 2: 9 Cephas, and John, who seemed to be **p**, *4769*
Rev 10: 1 as *it were* the sun, and his feet as **p** of fire: *4769*

PILLED (2)
Ge 30:37 **p** white strakes in them, and made 6478
30:38 he set the rods which he had **p** before 6478

PILLOW (3) [PILLOWS]
1Sa 19:13 put a **p** of goats' *hair for* his bolster, and 3523
19:16 with a **p** of goats' *hair for* his bolster. 3523
Mk 4:38 in the hinder part of the ship, asleep on a **p**: *4344*

PILLOWS (4) [PILLOW]
Ge 28:11 put *them for* his **p**, and lay down in that 4763
28:18 took the stone that he had put *for* his **p**, and 4763
Eze 13:18 Woe to *the women* that sew **p** to all 3704
13:20 Behold, I *am* against your **p**, where*with* ye 3704

PILOTS (4)
Eze 27: 8 O Tyrus, *that* were in thee, *were* thy **p**. 2259
27:27 thy **p**, thy calkers, and the occupiers of thy 2259
27:28 shall shake at the sound of the cry of thy **p**. 2259
27:29 the mariners, *and* all the **p** of the sea, 2259

PILTAI (1)
Ne 12:17 Zichri; of Miniamin, of Moadiah, **P**; 6408

PIN (3) [PINS]
Jdg 16:14 she fastened *it* with the **p**, and said unto 3489
16:14 went away with the **p** of the beam, and 3489
Eze 15: 3 will *men* take a **p** of it to hang any vessel 3489

PINE (8) [PINETH, PINING]
Lev 26:39 they that are left of you shall **p away** in 4743
26:39 their fathers shall they **p away** with them. 4743
Ne 8:15 **p** branches, and myrtle branches, and 8081
Isa 41:19 *and* the **p**, and the box tree together: 8410
60:13 the fir tree, the **p tree**, and the box together, 8410
La 4: 9 for these **p away**, stricken through for *want* 2100
Eze 24:23 ye shall **p away** for your iniquities, and 4743
33:10 we **p away** in them, how should we then 4743

PINETH (1) [PINE]
Mk 9:18 and gnasheth with his teeth, and **p away**: *3583*

PINING (1) [PINE]
Isa 38:12 he will cut me off with **p sickness**: 1803

PINNACLE (2)
Mt 4: 5 and setteth him on a **p** of the temple, *4419*
Lk 4: 9 and set him on a **p** of the temple, and *4419*

PINON (2)
Ge 36:41 Duke Aholibamah, duke Elah, duke **P**, 6373
1Ch 1:52 Duke Aholibamah, duke Elah, duke **P**, 6373

PINS (11) [PIN]
Ex 27:19 all the **p** thereof, and all the pins of 3489
27:19 and all the **p** of the court, *shall be of* brass. 3489
35:18 The **p** of the tabernacle, and the pins of 3489
35:18 and the **p** of the court, and their cords, 3489
38:20 all the **p** of the tabernacle, and of the court 3489
38:31 all the **p** of the tabernacle, and all the pins 3489
38:31 and all the **p** of the court round about. 3489
39:40 his **p**, and all the vessels of the service of 3489
Nu 3:37 their sockets, and their **p**, and their cords. 3489
4:32 their sockets, and their **p**, and their cords, 3489
Isa 3:22 and the wimples, and the **crisping p**, 2754

PIPE (4) [PIPED, PIPERS, PIPES]
1Sa 10: 5 a tabret, and a **p**, and a harp, before them; 2485
Isa 5:12 and the viol, the tabret, and **p**, and wine, 2485
30:29 as when one goeth with a **p** to come into 2485
1Co 14: 7 without life giving sound, whether **p** or harp, *836*

PIPED (4) [PIPE]
1Ki 1:40 the people **p** with pipes, and rejoiced *with* 2490
Mt 11:17 We have **p** unto you, and ye have not *832*
Lk 7:32 We have **p** unto you, and ye have not *832*
1Co 14: 7 how shall it be known what is **p** or harped? *832*

PIPERS (1) [PIPE]
Rev 18:22 and musicians, and of **p**, and trumpeters, *834*

PIPES (6) [PIPE]
1Ki 1:40 the people piped with **p**, and rejoiced *with* 2485
Jer 48:36 mine heart shall sound for Moab like **p**, 2485
48:36 mine heart shall sound like **p** for the men of 2485
Eze 28:13 of thy **p** was prepared in thee in the day 5345
Zec 4: 2 and seven **p** to the seven lamps, 4166
4:12 **p** empty the golden *oil* out of themselves? 6804

PIRAM (1)
Jos 10: 3 unto **P** king of Jarmuth, and unto Japhia 6502

PIRATHON (1) [PIRATHONITE]
Jdg 12:15 was buried in **P** in the land of Ephraim, 6552

PIRATHONITE (5) [PIRATHON]
Jdg 12:13 Abdon the son of Hillel, a **P**, judged Israel. 6553
12:15 Abdon the son of Hillel the **P** died, and 6553
2Sa 23:30 Benaiah the **P**, Hiddai of the brooks of 6553
1Ch 11:31 to the children of Benjamin, Benaiah the **P**, 6553
27:14 for the eleventh month *was* Benaiah the **P**, 6553

PISGAH (5)
Nu 21:20 *is* in the country of Moab, *to* the top of **P**, 6449
23:14 to the top of **P**, and built seven altars, and 6449
Dt 3:27 Get thee up *into* the top of **P**, and lift up 6449
4:49 the sea of the plain, under the springs of **P**. 6449
34: 1 *to* the top of **P**, that *is* over against Jericho. 6449

PISHON See PISON

PISIDIA (2)
Ac 13:14 they came to Antioch in **P**, and went into *4099*
14:24 And after they had passed throughout **P**, *4099*

PISON (1)
Ge 2:11 The name of the first *is* **P**: that *is it* which 6376

PISPAH (1)
1Ch 7:38 sons of Jether; Jephunneh, and **P**, and Ara. 6462

PISS (2) [PISSETH]
2Ki 18:27 and drink their own **p** with you? 4325+7272
Isa 36:12 and drink their own **p** with you? 4325+7272

PISSETH (6) [PISS]
1Sa 25:22 morning light *any that* **p** against the wall. 8366
25:34 morning light *any that* **p** against the wall. 8366
1Ki 14:10 will cut off from Jeroboam *him that* **p** 8366
16:11 he left him not *one that* **p** against a wall, 8366
21:21 will cut off from Ahab *him that* **p** against 8366
2Ki 9: 8 I will cut off from Ahab *him that* **p** against 8366

PIT (88) [PITS, SALTPITS, SLIMEPITS]
Ge 37:20 and cast him into some **p**, and we will say, 953
37:22 cast him into this **p** that *is* in the wilderness, 953
37:24 they took him, and cast him into a **p**: and 953
37:24 the **p** *was* empty, *there was* no water in it. 953
37:28 they drew and lift up Joseph out of the **p**, 953
37:29 Reuben returned unto the **p**; and behold, 953
37:29 behold, Joseph *was* not in the **p**; and he rent 953
Ex 21:33 if a man shall open a **p**, or if a man shall dig 953
21:33 or if a man shall dig a **p**, and not cover it, 953
21:34 The owner of the **p** shall make *it* good, *and* 953
Lev 11:36 Nevertheless a fountain or **p**, *wherein there* 953
Nu 16:30 and they go down quick into the **p**; 7585
16:33 went down alive into the **p**, and the earth 7585
2Sa 17: 9 he is hid now in some **p**, or in some *other* 6354
18:17 and cast him into a great **p** in the wood, and 6354
23:20 slew a lion in the midst of a **p** in time of 953
2Ki 10:14 and slew them at the **p** of the shearing house, 953
1Ch 11:22 and slew a lion in a **p** in a snowy day. 953
Job 6:27 and you dig *a p* for your friend. NIH
17:16 They shall go down *to* the bars of the **p**, 7585
33:18 He keepeth back his soul from the **p**, and 7845
33:24 Deliver him from going down *to* the **p**: 7845
33:28 will deliver his soul from going into the **p**, 7845
33:30 To bring back his soul from the **p**, to be 7845
Ps 7:15 He made a **p**, and digged it, and is fallen into 953
9:15 The heathen are sunk down in the **p** *that* 7845
28: 1 I become like them that go down into the **p**. 953
30: 3 me alive, that I should not go down *to* the **p**. 953
30: 9 in my blood, when I go down to the **p**? 7845
35: 7 cause have they hid for me their net *in* a **p**, 7845
40: 2 He brought me up also out of a horrible **p**, 953
55:23 shalt bring them down into the **p** of 875

Ps 57: 6 they have digged a **p** before me, into 7882
69:15 and let not the **p** shut her mouth upon me. 875
88: 4 counted with them that go down into the **p**: 953
88: 6 Thou hast laid me in the lowest **p**, 953
94:13 until the **p** be digged for the wicked. 7845
143: 7 I be like unto them that go down into the **p**. 953
Pr 1:12 and whole, as those that go down into the **p**: 953
22:14 The mouth of strange *women is* a deep **p**: 7745
23:27 and a strange *woman is* a narrow **p**. 875
26:27 Whoso diggeth a **p** shall fall therein: and 7845
28:10 he shall fall himself into his own **p**: 7816
28:17 to the blood of *any* person shall flee to the **p**; 953
Ecc 10: 8 He that diggeth a **p** shall fall into it; and 1475
Isa 14:15 brought down to hell, to the sides of the **p**. 953
14:19 a sword, that go down to the stones of the **p**; 953
24:17 Fear, and the **p**, and the snare, *are* upon 6354
24:18 the noise of the fear shall fall into the **p**; 6354
24:18 he that cometh up out of the midst of the **p** 6354
24:22 *as* prisoners are gathered in the **p**, and 953
30:14 or to take water *withal* out of the **p**. 1360
38:17 soul *delivered it* from the **p** of corruption: 7845
38:18 they that go down into the **p** cannot hope for 953
51: 1 to the hole of the **p** *whence* ye are digged. 953
51:14 that he should not die in the **p**, nor that his 7845
Jer 18:20 for they have digged a **p** for my soul. 7745
18:22 for they have digged a **p** to take me, and 7745
41: 7 *and cast them* into the midst of the **p**, he, and 953
41: 9 Now the **p** wherein Ishmael had cast all 953
48:43 Fear, and the **p**, and the snare, *shall be* 6354
48:44 that fleeth from the fear shall fall into the **p**; 6354
48:44 he that getteth up out of the **p** shall be taken 6354
Eze 19: 4 he was taken in their **p**, and they brought 7845
19: 8 their net over him: he was taken in their **p**. 7845
26:20 thee down with them that descend into the **p**, 953
26:20 of old, with them that go down to the **p**, 953
28: 8 They shall bring thee down to the **p**, and 7845
31:14 of men, with them that go down to the **p**. 953
31:16 to hell with them that descend into the **p**: 953
32:18 the earth, with them that go down into the **p**. 953
32:23 Whose graves are set in the sides of the **p**, 953
32:24 their shame with them that go down to the **p**. 953
32:25 their shame with them that go down to the **p**: 953
32:29 and with them that go down to the **p**. 953
32:30 their shame with them that go down to the **p**. 953
Zec 9:11 prisoners out of the **p** wherein *is* no water. 953
Mt 12:11 and if it fall into a **p** on the sabbath day, *999*
Lk 14: 5 shall have an ass or an ox fallen into a **p**, *5421*
Rev 9: 1 him was given the key of the bottomless **p**. *5421*
9: 2 And he opened the bottomless **p**; and *5421*
9: 2 and there arose a smoke out of the **p**, as *5421*
9: 2 darkened by reason of the smoke of the **p**. *5421*
9:11 *which is* the angel of the bottomless *p*, NIG
11: 7 bottomless *p* shall make war against them, NIG
17: 8 shall ascend out of the bottomless *p*, and NIG
20: 1 having the key of the bottomless *p* and NIG
20: 3 And cast him into the bottomless *p*, and NIG

PITCH (19) [PITCHED]

Ge 6:14 and shalt **p** it within and without with pitch. 3722
6:14 and shalt pitch it within and without with **p**. 3724
Ex 2: 3 daubed it with slime and with **p**, and 2203
Nu 1:52 the children of Israel shall **p** their **tents**, 2583
1:53 the Levites shall **p** round about 2583
2: 2 Every man of the children of Israel shall **p** 2583
2: 2 tabernacle of the congregation shall they **p**. 2583
2: 3 camp of Judah **p** throughout their armies: 2583
2: 5 those that do **p** next unto him *shall be* 2583
2:12 those which **p** by him *shall be* the tribe of 2583
3:23 The families of the Gershonites shall **p** 2583
3:29 The families of the sons of Kohath shall **p** 2583
3:35 *these* shall **p** on the side of the tabernacle 2583
Dt 1:33 to search you out a place to **p** your **tents** *in*, 2583
Jos 4:20 took out of Jordan, did Joshua **p** in Gilgal. 6965
Isa 13:20 neither shall the Arabian **p** **tent** there; 167
34: 9 the streams thereof shall be turned into **p**, 2203
34: 9 the land thereof shall become burning **p**. 2203
Jer 6: 3 they shall **p** *their* tents against her round 8628

PITCHED (82) [PITCH]

Ge 12: 8 **p** his tent, *having* Beth-el on the west, and 5186
13:12 of the plain, and **p** his **tent** toward Sodom. 167
26:17 **p** his **tent** in the valley of Gerar, and 2583
26:25 name of the LORD, and **p** his tent there: 5186
31:25 Now Jacob had **p** his tent in the mount: and 8628
31:25 Laban with his brethren **p** in the mount of 8628
33:18 and **p** his **tent** before the city. 2583
Ex 17: 1 of the LORD, and **p** in Rephidim: 2583
19: 2 desert of Sinai, and had **p** in the wilderness; 2583
33: 7 **p** it without the camp, afar off from 5186
Nu 1:51 when the tabernacle is to be **p**, the Levites 2583
2:34 so they **p** by their standards, and so they set 2583
9:17 there the children of Israel **p** their **tents**. 2583
9:18 at the commandment of the LORD they **p**: 2583
12:16 and **p** in the wilderness of Paran. 2583
21:10 of Israel set forward, and **p** in Oboth. 2583
21:11 journeyed from Oboth, and **p** at Ije-abarim, 2583
21:12 they removed, and **p** in the valley of Zared. 2583
21:13 and **p** on the *other* side of Arnon, 2583
22: 1 **p** in the plains of Moab on *this* side Jordan 2583
33: 5 removed from Rameses, and **p** in Succoth. 2583
33: 6 departed from Succoth, and **p** in Etham, 2583
33: 7 and they **p** before Migdol. 2583
33: 8 the wilderness of Etham, and **p** in Marah. 2583
33: 9 and ten palm trees; and they **p** there. 2583
33:15 and **p** in the wilderness of Sinai. 2583
33:16 desert of Sinai, and **p** at Kibroth-hattaavah. 2583
33:18 departed from Hazeroth, and **p** in Rithmah. 2583
33:19 from Rithmah, and **p** at Rimmon-parez. 2583
33:20 from Rimmon-parez, and **p** in Libnah. 2583
33:21 removed from Libnah, and **p** at Rissah. 2583
33:22 from Rissah, and **p** in Kehelathah. 2583
33:23 from Kehelathah, and **p** in mount Shapher. 2583
33:25 from Haradah, and **p** in Makheloth. 2583
33:27 they departed from Tahath, and **p** at Tarah. 2583
33:28 removed from Tarah, and **p** in Mithcah. 2583
33:29 went from Mithcah, and **p** in Hashmonah. 2583
33:31 from Moseroth, and **p** in Bene-jaakan. 2583
33:33 from Hor-hagidgad, and **p** in Jotbathah. 2583
33:36 **p** in the wilderness of Zin, which *is* 2583
33:37 **p** in mount Hor, in the edge of the land of 2583
33:41 from mount Hor, and **p** in Zalmonah. 2583
33:42 departed from Zalmonah, and **p** in Punon. 2583
33:43 they departed from Punon, and **p** in Oboth. 2583
33:44 and **p** in Ije-abarim, in the border of Moab. 2583
33:45 departed from Iim, and **p** in Dibon-gad. 2583
33:47 **p** in the mountains of Abarim, before Nebo. 2583
33:48 **p** in the plains of Moab by Jordan *near* 2583
33:49 they **p** by Jordan, from Beth-jesimoth *even* 2583
Jos 8:11 the city, and **p** on the north side of Ai: 2583
11: 5 and **p** together at the waters of Merom, 2583
Jdg 4:11 **p** his tent unto the plain of Zaanaim, 5186
6:33 went over, and **p** in the valley of Jezreel. 2583
7: 1 up early, and **p** beside the well of Harod: 2583
11:18 **p** on the *other* side of Arnon, but came not 2583
11:20 and **p** in Jahaz, and fought against Israel. 2583
15: 9 **p** in Judah, and spread themselves in Lehi. 2583
18:12 went up, and **p** in Kirjath-jearim, in Judah: 2583
1Sa 4: 1 to battle, and **p** beside Eben-ezer: 2583
4: 1 and the Philistines **p** in Aphek. 2583
13: 5 they came up, and **p** in Michmash, 2583
17: 1 **p** between Shochoh and Azekah, 2583
17: 2 **p** by the valley of Elah, and set the battle in 2583
26: 3 Saul **p** in the hill of Hachilah, which *is* 2583
26: 5 and came to the place where Saul had **p**: 2583
26: 5 and the people **p** round about him. 2583
28: 4 and came and **p** in Shunem: 2583
28: 4 all Israel together, and they **p** in Gilboa. 2583
29: 1 the Israelites **p** by a fountain which *is* in 2583
2Sa 6:17 of the tabernacle that David had **p** for it: 5186
17:26 and Absalom **p** *in* the land of Gilead. 2583
23:13 the troop of the Philistines **p** in the valley 2583
24: 5 they passed over Jordan, and **p** in Aroer, 2583
1Ki 20:27 the children of Israel **p** before them like 2583
20:29 they **p** one over against the other seven 2583
2Ki 25: 1 his host, against Jerusalem, and **p** against it; 2583
1Ch 15: 1 place for the ark of God, and **p** for it a tent. 5186
16: 1 the midst of the tent that David had **p** for it: 5186
19: 7 who came and **p** before Medeba. 2583
2Ch 1: 4 for it: for he had **p** a tent for it at Jerusalem. 5186
Jer 52: 4 **p** against it, and built forts against it round 2583
Heb 8: 2 which the Lord **p**, and not man. *4078*

PITCHER (12) [PITCHERS]

Ge 24:14 Let down thy **p**, I pray thee, that I may 3537
24:15 with her **p** upon her shoulder. 3537
24:16 to the well, and filled her **p**, and came up. 3537
24:17 I pray thee, drink a little water of thy **p**. 3537
24:18 let down her **p** upon her hand, and 3537

Ge 24:20 emptied her **p** into the trough, and ran again 3537
24:43 I pray thee, a little water of thy **p** to drink; 3537
24:45 Rebekah came forth with her **p** on her 3537
24:46 let down her **p** from her *shoulder,* and said, 3537
Ecc 12: 6 or the **p** be broken at the fountain, or 3537
Mk 14:13 there shall meet you a man bearing a **p** of *2765*
Lk 22:10 shall a man meet you, bearing a **p** of water; *2765*

PITCHERS (5) [PITCHER]
Jdg 7:16 with empty **p**, and lamps within 3537
7:16 empty pitchers, and lamps within the **p**. 3537
7:19 and brake the **p** that *were* in their hands. 3537
7:20 brake the **p**, and held the lamps in their left 3537
La 4: 2 how are they esteemed as earthen **p**, 5035

PITHOM (1)
Ex 1:11 for Pharaoh treasure cities, **P** and Raamses. 6619

PITHON (2)
1Ch 8:35 the sons of Micah *were,* **P**, and Melech, 6377
9:41 the sons of Micah *were,* **P**, and Melech, 6377

PITIED (6) [PITY]
Ps 106:46 He made them also to be **p** of all those that 7356
La 2: 2 all the habitations of Jacob, and hath not **p**: 2550
2:17 he hath thrown down, and hath not **p**: and 2550
2:21 of thine anger; thou hast killed, *and* not **p**. 2550
3:43 thou hast slain, thou hast not **p**. 2550
Eze 16: 5 None eye **p** thee, to do any of these unto 2347

PITIETH (3) [PITY]
Ps 103:13 Like as a father **p** *his* children, *so* 7355
103:13 *so* the LORD **p** them that fear him. 7355
Eze 24:21 of your eyes, and that which your soul **p**; 4263

PITIFUL (3) [PITY]
La 4:10 The hands of the **p** women have sodden 7362
Jas 5:11 that the Lord is **very p**, and of tender *4184*
1Pe 3: 8 love as brethren, *be* **p**, *be* courteous: *2155*

PITS (6) [PIT]
1Sa 13: 6 and in rocks, and in high places, and in **p**. 953
Ps 119:85 The proud have digged **p** for me, which *are* 7882
140:10 into **deep p**, *that* they rise not up again. 4113
Jer 2: 6 through a land of deserts and of **p**, 7745
14: 3 they came to the **p**, *and* found no water; 1356
La 4:20 was taken in their **p**, *of* whom we said, 7825

PITTANCE See NOUGHT

PITY (30) [PITIED, PITIETH, PITIFUL]
Dt 7:16 thine eye shall have no **p** upon them: 2347
13: 8 neither shall thine eye **p** him, neither shalt 2347
19:13 Thine eye shall not **p** him, but thou shalt 2347
19:21 thine eye shall not **p**; *but* life *shall go* for 2347
25:12 cut off her hand, thine eye shall not **p** *her.* 2347
2Sa 12: 6 he did this thing, and because he **had** no **p**. 2550
Job 6:14 To him that is afflicted **p** *should be shewed* 2617
19:21 **Have p** upon me, have pity upon me, O ye 2603
19:21 **have p** upon me, O ye my friends; 2603
Ps 69:20 I looked *for some* to **take p**, but *there was* 5110
Pr 19:17 He that **hath p** upon the poor lendeth unto 2603
28: 8 he shall gather it for him that will **p** 2603
Isa 13:18 they shall **have** no **p** on the fruit of 7355
63: 9 in his love and in his **p** he redeemed them; 2551
Jer 13:14 I will not **p**, nor spare, nor have mercy, but 2550
15: 5 For who shall **have p** upon thee, 2550
21: 7 neither **have p**, nor have mercy. 2550
Eze 5:11 mine eye spare, neither will I **have** any **p**. 2550
7: 4 shall not spare thee, neither will I **have p**: 2550
7: 9 eye shall not spare, neither will I **have p**: 2550
8:18 eye shall not spare, neither will I **have p**: 2550
9: 5 let not your eye spare, neither **have** ye **p**: 2550
9:10 neither will I **have p**, *but* I will recompense 2550
36:21 I **had p** for mine holy name, which 2550
Joel 2:18 be jealous for his land, and **p** his people. 2550
Am 1:11 did cast off all **p**, and his anger did tear 7356
Jnh 4:10 the LORD, Thou hast **had p** on the gourd, 2347
Zec 11: 5 and their own shepherds **p** them not. 2550
11: 6 For I will no more **p** the inhabitants of 2550
Mt 18:33 thy fellowservant, even as I **had p** on thee? *1653*

PLACE (721) [BURYINGPLACE, PLACED, PLACES, THRESHINGPLACE] See Index

PLACED (14) [PLACE] See Index

PLACES (220) [PLACE] See Index

PLAGUE (98) [PLAGUED, PLAGUES]
Ex 11: 1 Yet will I bring one **p** *more* upon Pharaoh, 5061
12:13 the **p** shall not be upon you to destroy *you,* 5063
30:12 that there be no **p** amongst them, when *thou* 5063
Lev 13: 2 it be in the skin of his flesh like the **p** of 5061
13: 3 the priest shall look on the **p** in the skin of 5061
13: 3 *when* the hair in the **p** is turned white, and 5061
13: 3 the **p** in sight *be* deeper than the skin of his 5061
13: 3 the skin of his flesh, it *is* a **p** of leprosy: 5061
13: 4 the priest shall shut up *him that hath* the **p** 5061
13: 5 *if* the **p** in his sight be at a stay, *and* 5061
13: 5 at a stay, *and* the **p** spread not in the skin; 5061
13: 6 *if* the **p** *be* somewhat dark, and the plague 5061
13: 6 and the **p** spread not in the skin, 5061
13: 9 When the **p** of leprosy is in a man, then 5061
13:12 *hath* the **p** from his head even to his foot, 5061
13:13 shall pronounce *him* clean *that hath* the **p**: 5061
13:17 behold, *if* the **p** be turned into white; then 5061
13:17 shall pronounce *him* clean *that hath* the **p**: 5061
13:20 it *is* a **p** of leprosy broken out of the boil. 5061
13:22 shall pronounce him unclean: it *is* a **p**. 5061
13:25 him unclean: it *is* the **p** of leprosy. 5061
13:27 him unclean: it *is* the **p** of leprosy. 5061
13:29 a man or woman hath a **p** upon the head or 5061
13:30 the priest shall see the **p**: and behold, *if* it 5061
13:31 if the priest look on the **p** of the scall, and 5061
13:31 the priest shall shut up *him that hath* the **p** 5061
13:32 seventh day the priest shall look on the **p**: 5061
13:44 him utterly unclean, his **p** *is* in his head. 5061
13:45 the leper in whom the **p** *is,* his clothes shall 5061
13:46 All the days wherein the **p** *shall be* in him 5061
13:47 The garment also that the **p** of leprosy is in, 5061
13:49 *if* the **p** be greenish or reddish in 5061
13:49 it *is* a **p** of leprosy, and shall be shewed 5061
13:50 the priest shall look upon the **p**, and shut up 5061
13:50 and shut up *it that hath* the **p** seven days: 5061
13:51 he shall look on the **p** on the seventh day: 5061
13:51 if the **p** be spread in the garment, either in 5061
13:51 the **p** *is* a fretting leprosy; it *is* unclean. 5061
13:52 or any thing of skin, wherein the **p** is: 5061
13:53 behold, the **p** be not spread in the garment, 5061
13:54 that they wash *the thing* wherein the **p** *is,* 5061
13:55 the priest shall look on the **p**, after *that* it is 5061
13:55 *if* the **p** have not changed his colour, and 5061
13:55 his colour, and the **p** be not spread; 5061
13:56 the **p** *be* somewhat dark after the washing 5061
13:57 it *is* a spreading **p**: thou shalt burn that NIH
13:57 shalt burn that wherein the **p** *is* with fire. 5061
13:58 if the **p** be departed from them, then it shall 5061
13:59 This *is* the law of the **p** of leprosy in a 5061
14: 3 *if* the **p** of leprosy be healed in the leper; 5061
14:32 This *is* the law *of him* in whom *is* the **p** of 5061
14:34 I put the **p** of leprosy in a house of the land 5061
14:35 It seemeth to me *there is* as it were a **p** in 5061
14:36 before the priest go *into it* to see the **p**, 5061
14:37 he shall look on the **p**, and behold, *if* 5061
14:37 *if* the **p** *be* in the walls of the house with 5061
14:39 *if* the **p** be spread in the walls of the house; 5061
14:40 they take away the stones in which the **p** *is,* 5061
14:43 if the **p** come again, and break out in 5061
14:44 and behold, *if* the **p** be spread in the house, 5061
14:48 behold, the **p** hath not spread in the house, 5061
14:48 the house clean, because the **p** is healed. 5061
14:54 This *is* the law for all *manner of* **p** of 5061
Nu 8:19 that there be no **p** among the children of 5063
11:33 smote the people *with* a very great **p**. 4347
14:37 the land, died by the **p** before the LORD. 4046
16:46 gone out from the LORD; the **p** is begun. 5063
16:47 behold, the **p** was begun among the people: 5063
16:48 and the living; and the **p** was stayed. 4046
16:49 Now they that died in the **p** were fourteen 4046
16:50 of the congregation: and the **p** was stayed. 4046
25: 8 So the **p** was stayed from the children of 4046
25: 9 those that died in the **p** were twenty and 4046
25:18 which was slain in the day of the **p** for 4046
26: 1 it came to pass after the **p**, that the LORD 4046
31:16 there was a **p** among the congregation of 4046
Dt 24: 8 Take heed in the **p** of leprosy, that *thou* 5061
28:61 Also every sickness, and every **p**, which *is* 4347
Jos 22:17 although there was a **p** in the congregation 5063
1Sa 6: 4 for one **p** *was* on you all, and on your lords. 4046
2Sa 24:21 that the **p** may be stayed from the people. 4046

2Sa 24:25 the land, and the **p** was stayed from Israel. 4046
1Ki 8:37 whatsoever **p**, whatsoever sickness *there* 5061
8:38 which shall know every man the **p** of his 5061
1Ch 21:22 that the **p** may be stayed from the people. 4046
2Ch 21:14 *with* a great **p** will the LORD smite thy 4046
Ps 89:23 before his face, and **p** them that hate him. 5062
91:10 neither shall *any* **p** come nigh thy dwelling. 5061
106:29 and the **p** brake in upon them. 4046
106:30 and *so* the **p** was stayed. 4046
Zec 14:12 this shall be the **p** where*with* the LORD 4046
14:15 so shall be the **p** of the horse, of the mule, 4046
14:15 beasts that shall be in these tents, as this **p**. 4046
14:18 that *have* no *rain;* there shall be the **p**, 4046
Mk 5:29 in *her* body that she was healed of *that* **p**. *3148*
5:34 go in peace, and be whole of thy **p**. *3148*
Rev 16:21 because of the **p** of the hail; *4127*
16:21 for the **p** thereof was exceeding great. *4127*

PLAGUED (6) [PLAGUE]
Ge 12:17 the LORD **p** Pharaoh and his house with 5060
Ex 32:35 the LORD **p** the people, because they 5062
Jos 24:5 I sent Moses also and Aaron, and I **p** Egypt, 5062
1Ch 21:17 not on thy people, that *they* should be **p**. 4046
Ps 73:5 neither are they **p** like *other* men. 5060
73:14 For all the day long have I been **p**, and 5060

PLAGUES (24) [PLAGUE]
Ge 12:17 his house with great **p** because of Sarai 5061
Ex 9:14 For I will at this time send all my **p** upon 4046
Lev 26:21 I will bring seven *times* moe **p** upon you 4347
Dt 28:59 the LORD will make thy **p** wonderful, 4347
28:59 the **p** of thy seed, *even* great plagues, and 4347
28:59 *even* great **p**, and of long continuance, and 4347
29:22 when they see the **p** of that land, and 4347
1Sa 4:8 Egyptians with all the **p** in the wilderness. 4347
Jer 19:8 and hiss because of all the **p** thereof. 4347
49:17 and shall hiss at all the **p** thereof. 4347
50:13 shall be astonished, and hiss at all her **p**. 4347
Hos 13:14 O death, I will be thy **p**; O grave, I will be 1698
Mk 3:10 him for to touch him, as many as had **p**. *3148*
Lk 7:21 he cured many of *their* infirmities and **p**, *3148*
Rev 9:20 **p** *yet* repented not of the works of their *4127*
11:6 and to smite the earth with all **p**, as often as *4127*
15:1 seven angels having the seven last **p**; *4127*
15:6 having the seven **p**, clothed in pure and *4127*
15:8 till the seven **p** of the seven angels were *4127*
16:9 of God, which hath power over these **p**: *4127*
18:4 of her sins, and that ye receive not of her **p**. *4127*
18:8 Therefore shall her **p** come in one day, *4127*
21:9 had the seven vials full of the seven last **p**, *4127*
22:18 unto him the **p** that are written in this book: *4127*

PLAIN (75) [PLAINLY, PLAINNESS, PLAINS]
Ge 11:2 that they found a **p** in the land of Shinar; 1237
12:6 the place of Sichem, unto the **p** of Moreh. 436
13:10 up his eyes, and beheld all the **p** of Jordan, 3603
13:11 Then Lot chose him all the **p** of Jordan; and 3603
13:12 Lot dwelled in the cities of the **p**, and 3603
13:18 came and dwelt in the **p** of Mamre, which *is* 436
14:13 for he dwelt in the **p** of Mamre the Amorite, 436
19:17 behind thee, neither stay thou in all the **p**; 3603
19:25 all the **p**, and all the inhabitants of 3603
19:28 toward all the land of the **p**, and beheld, 3603
19:29 when God destroyed the cities of the **p**, 3603
25:27 and Jacob *was* a **p** man, dwelling in tents. 8535
Dt 1:1 in the **p** over against the Red *sea,* between 6160
1:7 in the **p**, in the hills, and in the vale, and 6160
2:8 through the way of the **p** from Elath, and 6160
3:10 All the cities of the **p**, and all Gilead, and 4334
3:17 The **p** also, and Jordan, and the coast 6160
3:17 from Chinnereth even unto the sea of the **p**, 6160
4:43 in the **p** country, of the Reubenites; 4334
4:49 all the **p** on *this* side Jordan eastward, even 6160
4:49 even unto the sea of the **p**, under 6160
34:3 the south, and the **p** of the valley of Jericho, 3603
Jos 3:16 that came down toward the sea of the **p**, 6160
8:14 at a time appointed, before the **p**; 6160
11:16 the **p**, and the mountain of Israel, and 6160
12:1 mount Hermon, and all the **p** on the east: 6160
12:3 *from* the **p** to the sea of Cinneroth on 6160
12:3 unto the sea of the **p**, *even* the salt sea on 6160
13:9 and all the **p** of Medeba unto Dibon; 4334
13:16 midst of the river, and all the **p** by Medeba; 4334
13:17 Heshbon, and all her cities that *are* in the **p**; 4334
13:21 all the cities of the **p**, and all the kingdom 4334
20:8 upon the **p** out of the tribe of Reuben, 4334
Jdg 4:11 pitched his tent unto the **p** of Zaanaim, 436
9:6 by the **p** of the pillar that *was* in Shechem. 436
9:37 another company come along by the **p** of 436
11:33 twenty cities, and unto the **p** of the vineyards, 58
1Sa 10:3 thou shalt come to the **p** of Tabor, and 436
23:24 of Maon, in the **p** on the south of Jeshimon. 6160
2Sa 2:29 his men walked all that night through the **p**, 6160
4:7 and gat them away through the **p** all night. 6160
15:28 See, I will tarry in the **p** of the wilderness, 6160
18:23 Ahimaaz ran *by* the way of the **p**, and 3603
1Ki 7:46 In the **p** of Jordan did the king cast them, 3603
20:23 let us fight against them in the **p**, and 4334
20:25 we will fight against them in the **p**, *and* 4334
2Ki 14:25 entering of Hamath unto the sea of the **p**, 6160
25:4 and *the king* went the way toward the **p**. 6160
2Ch 4:17 In the **p** of Jordan did the king cast them, 3603
Ne 3:22 him repaired the priests, the men of the **p**. 3603
6:2 in *some one of* the villages in the **p** of Ono. 1237
12:28 both out of the **p country** round about 3603
Ps 27:11 lead me in a **p** path, because of mine 4334
Pr 8:9 They *are* all **p** to him that understandeth, 5228
15:19 but the way of the righteous *is* **made p**. 5549
Isa 28:25 When he hath **made p** the face thereof, 7737
40:4 be made straight, and the rough places **p**: 1237
Jer 17:26 from the **p**, and from the mountains, and 8219
21:13 *and* rock of the **p**, saith the LORD; 4334
39:4 and he went out the way of the **p**. 6160
48:8 shall perish, and the **p** shall be destroyed, 4334
48:21 judgment is come upon the **p** country; 4334
52:7 and they went *by* the way of the **p**. 6160
Eze 3:22 go forth into the **p**, and I will there talk 1237
3:23 I arose, and went forth into the **p**: and 1237
8:4 according to the vision that I saw in the **p**. 1237
Da 3:1 he set it up in the **p** of Dura, in the province 1236
Am 1:5 cut off the inhabitant from the **p** of Aven, 1237
Ob 1:19 of Esau; and *they of* the **p** the Philistines: 8219
Hab 2:2 Write the vision, and **make** *it* **p** upon tables, 874
Zec 4:7 before Zerubbabel *thou shalt* become a **p**: 4334
7:7 when *men* inhabited the south and the **p**? 8219
14:10 All the land shall be turned as a **p** from 6160
Mk 7:35 of his tongue was loosed, and he spake **p**. *3723*
Lk 6:17 and stood in the **p**, and the company *3977+5117*

PLAINLY (11) [PLAIN]
Ex 21:5 if the servant shall **p say**, I love my 559+559
Dt 27:8 the stones all the words of this law very **p**. 874
1Sa 2:27 Did I **p appear** unto the house of thy 1540+1540
10:16 **told** us **p** that the asses were found. 5046+5046
Ezr 4:18 ye sent unto us *hath been* **p** read before me. 6568
Isa 32:4 of the stammerers shall be ready to speak **p**. 6703
Jn 10:24 us to doubt? If thou be the Christ, tell us **p**. *3954*
11:14 Then said Jesus unto them **p**, Lazarus is *3954*
16:25 but I shall shew you **p** of the Father. *3954*
16:29 Lo, now speakest thou **p**, and *1722+3954*
Heb 11:14 For they that say such *things* **declare p** that *1718*

PLAINNESS (1) [PLAIN]
2Co 3:12 have such hope, we use great **p of speech**: *3954*

PLAINS (25) [PLAIN]
Ge 18:1 the LORD appeared unto him in the **p** of 436
Nu 22:1 pitched in the **p** of Moab on *this* side 6160
26:3 Eleazar the priest spake with them in the **p** 6160
26:63 in the **p** of Moab by Jordan *near* Jericho. 6160
31:12 unto the camp at the **p** of Moab, which *are* 6160
33:48 pitched in the **p** of Moab by Jordan *near* 6160
33:49 *even* unto Abel-shittim in the **p** of Moab. 6160
33:50 the LORD spake unto Moses in the **p** of 6160
35:1 the LORD spake unto Moses in the **p** of 6160
36:13 in the **p** of Moab by Jordan *near* Jericho. 6160
Dt 11:30 over against Gilgal, beside the **p** of Moreh? 436
34:1 Moses went up from the **p** of Moab unto 6160
34:8 for Moses in the **p** of Moab thirty days: 6160
Jos 4:13 the LORD unto battle, to the **p** of Jericho. 6160
5:10 of the month at even in the **p** of Jericho. 6160
11:2 of the **p** south of Cinneroth, and in 6160
12:8 in the **p**, and in the springs, and in 6160
13:32 distribute for inheritance in the **p** of Moab, 6160
2Sa 17:16 Lodge not *this* night in the **p** of 6160
2Ki 25:5 and overtook him in the **p** of Jericho: 6160
1Ch 27:28 the sycomore trees that *were* in the **low p** 8219
2Ch 9:27 trees that *are* in the **low p** in abundance. 8219

P

2Ch 26:10 both in the low country, and in the **p**: 4334
Jer 39: 5 and overtook Zedekiah in the **p** of Jericho: 6160
52: 8 and overtook Zedekiah in the **p** of Jericho; 6160

PLAISTER (7) [PLAISTERED]
Lev 14:42 take other morter, and shall **p** the house. 2902
Dt 27: 2 up great stones, and **p** them with plaister: 7874
27: 2 up great stones, and plaister them with **p**: 7875
27: 4 and thou shalt **p** them with plaister. 7874
27: 4 and thou shalt plaister them with **p**. 7875
Isa 38:21 **lay** *it* **for a p** upon the boil, and he shall 4799
Da 5: 5 upon the **p** of the wall of the king's palace: 1528

PLAISTERED (2) [PLAISTER]
Lev 14:43 he hath scraped the house, and after it is **p**; 2902
14:48 spread in the house, after the house was **p**: 2902

PLAITING (1) [PLATTED]
1Pe 3: 3 not be that outward *adorning* of **p** the hair, *1708*

PLANE See CHESNUT

PLANES (1)
Isa 44:13 he fitteth it with **p**, and he marketh it out 4741

PLANETS (1)
2Ki 23: 5 and to the **p**, and to all the host of heaven. 4208

PLANKS (3)
1Ki 6:15 covered the floor of the house with **p** of fir. 6763
Eze 41:25 *there were* thick **p** upon the face of 6086
41:26 side chambers of the house, and **thick p**. 5646

PLANT (42) [PLANTATION, PLANTED, PLANTEDST, PLANTERS, PLANTETH, PLANTING, PLANTINGS, PLANTS]
Ge 2: 5 every **p** of the field before it was in 7880
Ex 15:17 **p** them in the mountain of thine 5193
Dt 16:21 Thou shalt not **p** thee a grove *of* any trees 5193
28:30 thou shalt **p** a vineyard, and shalt not gather 5193
28:39 Thou shalt **p** vineyards, and dress *them,* but 5193
2Sa 7:10 will **p** them, that they may dwell in a place 5193
2Ki 19:29 and **p** vineyards, and eat the fruits thereof. 5193
1Ch 17: 9 will **p** them, and they shall dwell in their 5193
Job 14: 9 it will bud, and bring forth boughs like a **p**. 5194
Ps 107:37 sow the fields, and **p** vineyards, which may 5193
Ecc 3: 2 a time to **p**, and a time to pluck up *that* 5193
Isa 5: 7 and the men of Judah his pleasant **p**: 5194
17:10 therefore shalt thou **p** pleasant plants, and 5193
17:11 In the day shalt thou make thy **p** to grow, 5194
37:30 and **p** vineyards, and eat the fruit thereof. 5193
41:19 I will **p** in the wilderness the cedar, 5414
51:16 that I may **p** the heavens, and lay 5193
53: 2 he shall grow up before him as a **tender p**, 3126
65:21 inhabit *them;* and they shall **p** vineyards, 5193
65:22 they shall not **p**, and another eat: 5193
Jer 1:10 and to throw down, to build, and to **p**. 5193
2:21 the degenerate **p of** a strange **vine** unto me? 1612
18: 9 concerning a kingdom, to build and to **p** *it;* 5193
24: 6 and I will **p** them, and not pluck *them* up. 5193
29: 5 dwell *in them;* and **p** gardens, and eat 5193
29:28 dwell *in them;* and **p** gardens, and eat 5193
31: 5 Thou shalt yet **p** vines upon the mountains 5193
31: 5 the planters shall **p**, and shall eat *them* as 5193
31:28 to build, and to **p**, saith the LORD. 5193
32:41 I will **p** them in this land assuredly with my 5193
35: 7 nor **p** vineyard, nor have *any:* but all your 5193
42:10 and I will **p** you, and not pluck *you* up: 5193
Eze 17:22 will **p** *it* upon a high mountain and 8362
17:23 mountain of the height of Israel will I **p** it: 8362
28:26 shall build houses, and **p** vineyards; 5193
34:29 I will raise up for them a **p** of renown, and 4302
36:36 ruined *places, and* **p** that that was desolate: 5193
Da 11:45 he shall **p** the tabernacles of his palace 5193
Am 9:14 inhabit *them;* and they shall **p** vineyards, 5193
9:15 I will **p** them upon their land, and they shall 5193
Zep 1:13 inhabit *them;* and they shall **p** vineyards, 5193
Mt 15:13 But he answered and said, Every **p**, *5451*

PLANTATION (1) [PLANT]
Eze 17: 7 *he* might water it by the furrows of her **p**. 4302

PLANTED (39) [PLANT]
Ge 2: 8 the LORD God **p** a garden eastward in 5193
9:20 *to be* a husbandman, and he **p** a vineyard: 5193
21:33 *Abraham* **p** a grove in Beer-sheba, and 5193
Lev 19:23 shall have **p** all *manner of* trees for food, 5193
Nu 24: 6 of lign aloes *which* the LORD hath **p**, 5193
Dt 20: 6 what man *is he* that hath **p** a vineyard, and 5193
Jos 24:13 and oliveyards which ye **p** not do ye eat. 5193
Ps 1: 3 he shall be like a tree **p** by the rivers of 8362
80: 8 thou hast cast out the heathen, and **p** it. 5193
80:15 the vineyard which thy right hand hath **p**, 5193
92:13 Those that be **p** in the house of the LORD 8362
94: 9 He that **p** the ear, shall he not hear? he that 5193
104:16 the cedars of Lebanon, which he hath **p**; 5193
Ecc 2: 4 I builded me houses; I **p** me vineyards: 5193
2: 5 and I **p** trees in them of all *kind of* fruits: 5193
3: 2 and a time to pluck up *that which is* **p**; 5193
Isa 5: 2 **p** it *with* the choicest vine, and built a 5193
40:24 Yea, they shall not be **p**; yea, they shall not 5193
Jer 2:21 Yet I had **p** thee a noble vine, wholly a 5193
11:17 For the LORD of hosts, that **p** thee, 5193
12: 2 Thou hast **p** them, yea, they have taken 5193
17: 8 For he shall be as a tree **p** by the waters, 8362
45: 4 *that* which I have **p** I *will* pluck up, 5193
Eze 17: 5 seed of the land, and **p** it in a fruitful field; 5414
17: 8 It *was* **p** in a good soil by great waters, 8362
17:10 Yea behold, *being* **p**, shall it prosper? shall 8362
19:10 *is* like a vine in thy blood, **p** by the waters: 8362
19:13 And now she *is* **p** in the wilderness, in a dry 8362
Hos 9:13 as I saw Tyrus, *is* **p** in a pleasant place: 8362
Am 5:11 ye have **p** pleasant vineyards, but ye shall 5193
Mt 15:13 which my heavenly Father hath not **p**, *5452*
21:33 which **p** a vineyard, and hedged it round *5452*
Mk 12: 1 A *certain* man **p** a vineyard, and set a hedge *5452*
Lk 13: 6 A certain *man* had a fig tree **p** in his *5452*
17: 6 up by the root, and be thou **p** in the sea; *5452*
17:28 they drank, they bought, they sold, they **p**, *5452*
20: 9 A certain man **p** a vineyard, and let it forth *5452*
Ro 6: 5 For if we have been **p together** in *4854*
1Co 3: 6 I have **p**, Apollos watered; but God gave *5452*

PLANTEDST (2) [PLANT]
Dt 6:11 vineyards and olive trees, which thou **p** not; 5193
Ps 44: 2 out the heathen *with* thy hand, and **p** them; 5193

PLANTERS (1) [PLANT]
Jer 31: 5 the **p** shall plant, and shall eat *them* as 5193

PLANTETH (5) [PLANT]
Pr 31:16 with the fruit of her hands she **p** a vineyard. 5193
Isa 44:14 he **p** an ash, and the rain doth nourish *it.* 5193
1Co 3: 7 neither is he that **p** any *thing,* neither he *5452*
3: 8 Now he that **p** and he that watereth are one: *5452*
9: 7 who **p** a vineyard, and eateth not of *5452*

PLANTING (2) [PLANT]
Isa 60:21 the branch of my **p**, the work of my hands, 4302
61: 3 the **p** of the LORD, that *he* might be 4302

PLANTINGS (1) [PLANT]
Mic 1: 6 a heap of the field, *and* as **p** of a vineyard: 4302

PLANTS (8) [PLANT]
1Ch 4:23 and those that dwelt amongst **p** and hedges: 5196
Ps 128: 3 thy children like olive **p** round about thy 8363
144:12 That our sons *may be* as **p** grown up in 5195
SS 4:13 Thy **p** *are* an orchard of pomegranates, 7973
Isa 16: 8 have broken down the **principal p** thereof, 8291
17:10 therefore shalt thou plant pleasant **p**, and 5194
Jer 48:32 thy **p** are gone over the sea, they reach *even* 5189
Eze 31: 4 with her rivers running round about his **p**, 4302

PLASTER See MORTER

PLAT (2)
2Ki 9:26 I will requite thee in this **p**, saith 2513
9:26 cast him into the **p** *of ground,* according to 2513

PLATE (3) [BREASTPLATE, BREASTPLATES, PLATES]
Ex 28:36 thou shalt make a **p** *of* pure gold, and 6731
39:30 they made the **p** of the holy crown *of* pure 6731
Lev 8: 9 did he put the golden **p**, the holy crown; 6731

PLATES (6) [PLATE]
Ex 39: 3 they did beat the gold into **thin p**, and cut *it* 6341
Nu 16:38 let them make them broad **p** *for* a covering 6341
16:39 they were made broad ***p for*** a covering of NIH
1Ki 7:30 had four brasen wheels, and **p** of brass: 5633
7:36 For on the **p** of the ledges thereof, and 3871

Jer 10: 9 Silver **spread into p** is brought from 7554

PLATFORM See SCAFFOLD

PLATTED (3) [PLAITING]
Mt 27:29 And when they had **p** a crown of thorns, *4120*
Mk 15:17 and **p** a crown of thorns, and put *it* about *4120*
Jn 19: 2 And the soldiers **p** a crown of thorns, and *4120*

PLATTER (3)
Mt 23:25 clean the outside of the cup and of the **p**, *3953*
23:26 first that *which is* within the cup and **p**, *3953*
Lk 11:39 clean the outside of the cup and the **p**; *4094*

PLAY (17) [PLAYED, PLAYEDST, PLAYER, PLAYERS, PLAYETH, PLAYING]
Ex 32: 6 down to eat and to drink, and rose up to **p**. 6711
Dt 22:21 to **p the whore** *in* her father's house: 2181
1Sa 16:16 that he shall **p** with his hand, and thou shalt 5059
16:17 Provide me now a man that can **p** well, and 5059
21:15 *fellow* to **p the mad man** in my presence? 7696
2Sa 2:14 the young men now arise, and **p** before us. 7832
6:21 therefore will I **p** before the LORD. 7832
10:12 let us **p the men** for our people, and for 2388
Job 40:20 where all the beasts of the field **p**. 7832
41: 5 Wilt thou **p** with him as *with* a bird? or 7832
Ps 33: 3 a new song; **p** skilfully with a loud noise. 5059
104:26 *whom* thou hast made to **p** therein. 7832
Isa 11: 8 the sucking child shall **p** on the hole of 8173
Eze 33:32 and can **p** well **on an instrument**: 5059
Hos 3: 3 thou shalt not **p the harlot**, and thou shalt 2181
4:15 Though thou, Israel, **p the harlot**, *yet* let 2181
1Co 10: 7 sat down to eat and drink, and rose up to **p**. *3815*

PLAYED (18) [PLAY]
Ge 38:24 thy daughter in law hath **p the harlot**; 2181
Jdg 19: 2 his concubine **p the whore** against him, 2181
1Sa 16:23 David took a harp, and **p** with his hand: 5059
18: 7 the women answered *one another* as they **p**, 7832
18:10 David **p** with his hand, as at other times: 5059
19: 9 in his hand: and David **p** with *his* hand. 5059
26:21 I have **p the fool**, and have erred 5528
2Sa 6: 5 all the house of Israel **p** before the LORD 7832
2Ki 3:15 it came to pass, when the minstrel **p**, 5059
1Ch 13: 8 all Israel **p** before God with all *their* might, 7832
Jer 3: 1 thou hast **p the harlot** with many lovers; 2181
3: 6 green tree, and there hath **p the harlot**. 2181
3: 8 feared not, but went and **p the harlot** also. 2181
Eze 16:28 Thou hast **p the whore** also with 2181
16:28 thou hast **p the harlot** with them, and 2181
23: 5 Aholah **p the harlot** when she was mine; 2181
23:19 wherein she had **p the harlot** in the land of 2181
Hos 2: 5 For their mother hath **p the harlot**: that she 2181

PLAYEDST (2) [PLAY]
Eze 16:15 **p the harlot** because of thy renown, and 2181
16:16 divers colours, and **p the harlot** thereupon: 2181

PLAYER (1) [PLAY]
1Sa 16:16 out a man, *who is* a cunning **p** on a harp: 5059

PLAYERS (2) [PLAY]
Ps 68:25 the **p on instruments** *followed* after; 5059
87: 7 **p on instruments** *shall be there:* all my 2490

PLAYETH (1) [PLAY]
Eze 23:44 *they* go in unto a woman that **p the harlot**: 2181

PLAYING (7) [PLAY]
Lev 21: 9 if she profane herself by **p the whore**, she 2181
1Sa 16:18 *that is* cunning in **p**, and a mighty valiant 5059
1Ch 15:29 a window saw king David dancing and **p**: 7832
Ps 68:25 *them were* the damsels **p** with **timbrels**. 8608
Jer 2:20 green tree thou wanderest, **p the harlot**. 2181
Eze 16:41 will cause thee to cease from **p the harlot**, 2181
Zec 8: 5 *of* boys and girls **p** in the streets thereof. 7832

PLEA (2) [PLEAD]
Dt 17: 8 between **p** and plea, and between stroke 1779
17: 8 between plea and **p**, and between stroke 1779

PLEAD (39) [PLEA, PLEADED, PLEADETH, PLEADINGS]
Jdg 6:31 that stood against him, Will ye **p** for Baal? 7378
6:31 he that will **p** for him, let him be put to 7378
6:31 let him **p** for himself, because *one* hath cast 7378
6:32 saying, Let Baal **p** against him, because 7378
1Sa 24:15 **p** my cause, and deliver me out of thine 7378
Job 9:19 of judgment, who shall set me a time *to p*? NIH
13:19 Who *is* he *that* will **p** with me? for now, if I 7378
16:21 O that *one* might **p** for a man with God, 3198
19: 5 against me, and **p** against me my reproach: 3198
23: 6 Will he **p** against me with *his* great power? 7378
Ps 35: 1 **P** *my cause,* O LORD, with them that 7378
43: 1 and **p** my cause against an ungodly nation: 7378
74:22 Arise, O God, **p** thine own cause: 7378
119:154 **P** my cause, and deliver me: quicken me 7378
Pr 22:23 For the LORD will **p** their cause, and 7378
23:11 *is* mighty; he shall **p** their cause with thee. 7378
31: 9 and **p the cause** of the poor and needy. 1777
Isa 1:17 judge the fatherless, **p for** the widow. 7378
3:13 The LORD standeth *up* to **p**, and 7378
43:26 let us **p** together: declare thou, that thou 8199
66:16 by his sword will the LORD **p with** all 8199
Jer 2: 9 Wherefore I will yet **p** with you, saith 7378
2: 9 and with your children's children will I **p**. 7378
2:29 Wherefore will ye **p** with me? ye all have 7378
2:35 Behold, I *will* **p with** thee, because 8199
12: 1 *art* thou, O LORD, when I **p** with thee: 7378
25:31 with the nations, he *will* **p** with all flesh; 8199
30:13 *There is* none to **p** thy cause, that thou 1777
50:34 he shall **throughly p** their cause, that 7378+7378
51:36 I *will* **p** thy cause, and take vengeance for 7378
Eze 17:20 will **p** with him there *for* his trespass that 8199
20:35 and there will I **p** with you face to face. 8199
20:36 so will I **p** with you, saith the Lord GOD. 8199
38:22 I will **p** against him with pestilence and 8199
Hos 2: 2 **P** with your mother, plead: for she *is* not 7378
2: 2 Plead with your mother, **p**: for she *is* not 7378
Joel 3: 2 will **p** with them there for my people and 8199
Mic 6: 2 with his people, and he will **p** with Israel. 3198
7: 9 until he **p** my cause, and execute judgment 7378

PLEADED (3) [PLEAD]
1Sa 25:39 that hath **p** the cause of my reproach from 7378
La 3:58 O Lord, thou hast **p** the causes of my soul; 7378
Eze 20:36 Like as I **p** with your fathers in 8199

PLEADETH (3) [PLEAD]
Job 16:21 with God, as a man *p* for his neighbour. NIH
Isa 51:22 thy God *that* **p the cause** of his people, 7378
59: 4 None calleth for justice, nor any **p** for truth: 8199

PLEADINGS (1) [PLEAD]
Job 13: 6 and hearken to the **p** of my lips. 7379

PLEASANT (57) [PLEASE]
Ge 2: 9 to grow every tree that is **p** to the sight, 2530
3: 6 that it *was* **p** to the eyes, and a tree to be 8378
49:15 rest *was* good, and the land that *it was* **p**; 5276
2Sa 1:23 Jonathan *were* lovely and **p** in their lives, 5273
1:26 very **p** hast thou been unto me: thy love to 5276
1Ki 20: 6 shall be, *that* whatsoever *is* **p** in thine eyes, 4261
2Ki 2:19 I pray thee, the situation of *this* city *is* **p**, 2896
2Ch 32:27 for shields, and for all *manner of* **p** jewels; 2532
Ps 16: 6 The lines are fallen unto me in **p** *places;* 5273
81: 2 the timbrel, the **p** harp with the psaltery. 5273
106:24 Yea, they despised the **p** land, 2532
133: 1 how **p** *it is* for brethren to dwell together in 5273
135: 3 sing *praises* unto his name; for *it is* **p**. 5273
147: 1 our God; for *it is* **p**; *and* praise is comely. 5273
Pr 2:10 and knowledge is **p** unto thy soul; 5276
5:19 *Let her be as* the loving hind and **p** roe; 2580
9:17 are sweet, and bread *eaten* in secret is **p**. 5276
15:26 but *the words of* the pure *are* **p** words. 5278
16:24 **P** words *are as* a honeycomb, sweet to 5278
22:18 For *it is* a **p** *thing* if thou keep them within 5273
24: 4 be filled *with* all precious and **p** riches. 5273
Ecc 11: 7 a **p** *thing it is* for the eyes to behold the sun: 2896
SS 1:16 Behold, thou *art* fair, my beloved, yea, **p**: 5273
4:13 an orchard of pomegranates, with **p** fruits; 4022
4:16 come into his garden, and eat his **p** fruits. 4022
7: 6 How fair and how **p** art thou, O love, 5276
7:13 at our gates *are* all *manner of* **p** *fruits,* new 4022
Isa 2:16 ships of Tarshish, and upon all **p** pictures. 2532
5: 7 of Israel, and the men of Judah his **p** plant: 8191
13:22 and dragons in *their* **p** palaces: 6027
17:10 therefore shalt thou plant **p** plants, and 5282
32:12 for the **p** fields, for the fruitful vine. 2531
54:12 and all thy borders of **p** stones. 2656
64:11 and all our **p things** are laid waste. 4261

P

Jer 3:19 among the children, and give thee a **p** land, 2532
12:10 they have made my **p** portion a desolate 2532
23:10 the **p places** of the wilderness are dried up, 4999
25:34 And ye shall fall like a **p** vessel. 2532
31:20 *is he* a **p** child? for since I spake against 8191
La 1: 7 of her miseries all her **p things** that she had 4262
1:10 spread out his hand upon all her **p things**: 4261
1:11 they have given their **p things** for meat to 4261
2: 4 slew all *that were* **p** to the eye, in 4261
Eze 26:12 down thy walls, and destroy thy **p** houses: 2532
33:32 very lovely song *of* one that hath a **p** voice, 3303
Da 8: 9 and toward the east, and toward the **p** *land*. 6643
10: 3 I ate no **p** bread, neither came flesh nor 2532
11:38 and with precious stones, and **p things**. 2532
Hos 9: 6 the **p** *places* for their silver, nettles shall 4261
9:13 as I saw Tyrus, *is* planted in a **p place**: 5116
13:15 he shall spoil the treasure of all **p** vessels. 2532
Joel 3: 5 into your temples my goodly **p things**: 4261
Am 5:11 ye have planted **p** vineyards, but ye shall 2531
Mic 2: 9 have ye cast out from their **p** houses; 8588
Na 2: 9 *and* glory out of all the **p** furniture. 2532
Zec 7:14 for they laid the **p** land desolate. 2532
Mal 3: 4 and Jerusalem be **p** unto the LORD, 6149

PLEASANTNESS (1) [PLEASE]

Pr 3:17 Her ways *are* ways of **p**, and all her paths 5278

PLEASE (39) [MENPLEASERS, PLEASANT, PLEASANTNESS, PLEASED, PLEASETH, PLEASING, PLEASURE, PLEASURES]

Ex 21: 8 If she **p not** her master, 5869+7451+871.1
Nu 23:27 peradventure it will **p** God 3474+5869+871.1
1Sa 20:13 *but* if it **p** my father *to do* thee evil, 413+3190
2Sa 7:29 Therefore now let it **p** thee to bless 2974
1Ki 21: 6 or *else*, if it **p** thee, I will give thee *another* 2655
1Ch 17:27 let it **p** thee to bless the house of thy 2974
2Ch 10: 7 and **p** them, and speak good words to them, 7521
Ne 2: 5 If it **p** the king, and if thy servant 2895+5921
2: 7 I said unto the king, If it **p** the king, 2895+5921
Est 1:19 If it **p** the king, let there go a royal 2895
3: 9 If it **p** the king, let it be written that they 2895
5: 8 and if it **p** the king to grant my petition, and 2895
7: 3 in thy sight, O king, and if it **p** the king, 2895
8: 5 If it **p** the king, and if I have found favour 2896
9:13 said Esther, If it **p** the king, let it be granted 2896
Job 6: 9 Even *that* it would **p** God to destroy me: 2974
20:10 His children shall *seek to* **p** the poor, and 7521
Ps 69:31 *This* also shall **p** the LORD better than an 3190
Pr 16: 7 When a man's ways **p** the LORD, 7521
SS 2: 7 ye stir not up, nor awake *my* love, till he **p**. 2654
3: 5 ye stir not up, nor awake *my* love, till he **p**. 2654
8: 4 stir not up, nor awake *my* love, until he **p**. 2654
Isa 2: 6 they **p** themselves in the children of 5606
55:11 it shall accomplish that which I **p**, and 2654
56: 4 choose *the things* that **p** me, and take hold 2654
Jn 8:29 for I do always those *things* that **p** him. *701*
Ro 8: 8 then they that are in the flesh cannot **p** God. *700*
15: 1 of the weak, and not to **p** ourselves. *700*
15: 2 Let every one of us **p** *his* neighbour for *his* *700*
1Co 7:32 belong to the Lord, how he may **p** the Lord: *700*
7:33 *that are* of the world, how he may **p** *his* wife. *700*
7:34 of the world, how she may **p** *her* husband. *700*
10:33 Even as I **p** all *men* in all *things*, not seeking *700*
Gal 1:10 or do I seek to **p** men? for if I yet pleased *700*
1Th 2:15 and they **p** not God, and are contrary to all *700*
4: 1 of us how ye ought to walk and to **p** God, *700*
2Ti 2: 4 that he may **p** him who hath chosen *him* to *700*
Tit 2: 9 to **p** *them* **well** in all *things*; not *1510+2101*
Heb 11: 6 But without faith *it is* impossible to **p** *him*: *2100*

PLEASED (62) [PLEASE]

Ge 28: 8 daughters of Canaan **p not** Isaac 5869+7451+871.1
33:10 the face of God, and thou wast **p with** me. 7521
34:18 their words **p** Hamor, and 3190+5869+871.1
45:16 **p** Pharaoh **well**, and his 3190+5869+871.1
Nu 24: 1 when Balaam saw that it **p** 2896+5869+871.1
Dt 1:23 the saying **p** me **well**: and 3190+5869+871.1
Jos 22:30 of Manasseh spake, it **p** them. 3190+5869+871.1
22:33 the thing **p** the children of 3190+5869+871.1
Jdg 13:23 unto him, If the LORD were **p** to kill us, 2654
14: 7 and she **p** Samson **well**. 3474+5869+871.1
1Sa 12:22 it hath **p** the LORD to make you his 2974
18:20 told Saul, and the thing **p** him. 3474+5869+871.1
18:26 **p** David **well** to be the king's 3474+5869+871.1
2Sa 3:36 notice *of it*, and it **p** them: 3190+5869+871.1
3:36 the king did, **p** all the people. 2896+5869+871.1
17: 4 the saying **p** Absalom **well**, 3474+5869+871.1
19: 6 then it had **p** thee **well**. 3477+5869+871.1
1Ki 3:10 the speech **p** the Lord, 3190+5869+871.1
9: 1 all Solomon's desire which he was **p** to do, 2654
9:12 and they **p** him not. 3474+5869+871.1
2Ch 30: 4 the thing **p** the king and all 3474+5869+871.1
Ne 2: 6 So it **p** the king to send me; 3190+6440+3807.1
Est 1:21 the saying **p** the king and 3190+5869+871.1
2: 4 **p** the king; and he did so. 3190+5869+871.1
2: 9 the maiden **p** him, and 3190+5869+871.1
5:14 the thing **p** Haman; and he caused 3190
Ps 40:13 Be **p**, O LORD, to deliver me: O LORD, 7521
51:19 shalt thou be **p** with the sacrifices of 2654
115: 3 the heavens: he hath done whatsoever he **p**. 2654
135: 6 Whatsoever the LORD **p**, *that* did he in 2654
Isa 42:21 The LORD is **well p** for his righteousness' 2654
53:10 Yet it **p** the LORD to bruise him; he hath 2654
Da 6: 1 It **p** Darius to set over the kingdom an 8232
Jnh 1:14 for thou, O LORD, hast done as it **p** thee. 2654
Mic 6: 7 Will the LORD be **p** with thousands of 7521
Mal 1: 8 will he be **p with** thee, or accept thy 7521
Mt 3:17 is my beloved Son, in whom I am **well p**. *2106*
12:18 my beloved, in whom my soul is **well p**: *2106*
14: 6 Herodias danced before them, and **p** Herod. *700*
17: 5 is my beloved Son, in whom I am **well p**; *2106*
Mk 1:11 art my beloved Son, in whom I am **well p**. *2106*
6:22 and **p** Herod and them that sat with *him*, *700*
Lk 3:22 art my beloved Son; in thee I am **well p**. *2106*
Ac 6: 5 And the saying **p** the whole multitude: and *700*
12: 3 And because he saw it **p** the Jews, *701+1510*
15:22 Then **p** it the apostles and elders, with *1380*
15:34 Notwithstanding it **p** Silas to abide there *1380*
Ro 15: 3 For even Christ **p** not himself; but, as it is *700*
15:26 For it hath **p** *them of* Macedonia and *2106*
15:27 It hath **p** them verily; and their debtors they *2106*
1Co 1:21 it **p** God by the foolishness of preaching to *2106*
7:12 and she be **p** to dwell with him, let him not *4909*
7:13 and *if* he be **p** to dwell with her, let her not *4909*
10: 5 with many of them God was not **well p**: *2106*
12:18 one of them in the body, as **it hath p** him. *2309*
15:38 But God giveth it a body as it hath **p** him, *2309*
Gal 1:10 for if I yet **p** men, I should not be the servant *700*
1:15 But when it **p** God, who separated me from *2106*
Col 1:19 For it **p** *the Father* that in him should all *2106*
Heb 11: 5 he had this testimony, that *he* **p** God. *2100*
13:16 for with such sacrifices God is **well p**. *2100*
2Pe 1:17 is my beloved Son, in whom I am **well p**. *2106*

PLEASETH (6) [PLEASE]

Ge 16: 6 do to her as it **p** thee. 2896+5869+871.1
20:15 dwell where it **p** thee. 2896+5869+871.1
Jdg 14: 3 Get her for me; for she **p** me **well**. 3474+5869
Est 2: 4 let the maiden which **p** 3190+5869+871.1
Ecc 7:26 whoso **p** God shall escape 2896+6440+3807.1
8: 3 evil thing; for he doeth whatsoever **p** him. 2654

PLEASING (8) [PLEASE]

Est 8: 5 right before the king, and I *be* **p** in his eyes, 2896
Hos 9: 4 neither shall they be **p** unto him: 6149
Php 4:18 a sacrifice acceptable, **well p** to God. *2101*
Col 1:10 ye might walk worthy of the Lord unto all **p**, *699*
3:20 all *things*: for this is **well p** unto the Lord. *2101*
1Th 2: 4 not as **p** men, but God, which trieth our *700*
Heb 13:21 working in you *that which is* **well p** in his *2101*
1Jn 3:22 and do those *things* that are **p** in his sight. *701*

PLEASURE (61) [PLEASE]

Ge 18:12 saying, After I am waxed old shall I have **p**, 5730
Dt 23:24 mayest eat grapes thy fill at thine own **p**; 5315
1Ch 29:17 triest the heart, and **hast p** in uprightness. 7521
Ezr 5:17 let the king send his **p** to us concerning 7470
10:11 LORD God of your fathers, and do his **p**: 7522
Ne 9:37 at their **p**, and we *are* in great distress. 7522
Est 1: 8 *they* should do according to every man's **p**. 7522
Job 21:21 For what **p** hath he in his house after him, 2656
21:25 of his soul, and never eateth with **p**. 2896
22: 3 *Is it any* **p** to the Almighty, that thou art 2656
Ps 5: 4 For thou *art* not a God that hath **p** in 2655
35:27 which hath **p** in the prosperity of his 2655
51:18 Do good in thy **good p** unto Zion: 7522
102:14 For thy servants **take p** in her stones, and 7521
103:21 his hosts; ye ministers of his, that do his **p**. 7522
105:22 To bind his princes at his **p**; and teach his 5315

Ps 111: 2 sought out of all them that have **p** therein. 2656
147:10 he **taketh** not **p** in the legs of a man. 7521
147:11 The LORD **taketh p** in them that fear 7521
149: 4 For the LORD **taketh p** in his people: 7521
Pr 21:17 He that loveth **p** *shall be* a poor man: 8057
Ecc 2: 1 prove thee with mirth, therefore enjoy **p**: 2896
5: 4 defer not to pay it; for *he hath* no **p** in fools: 2656
12: 1 when thou shalt say, I have no **p** in them; 2656
Isa 21: 4 the night of my **p** hath he turned into fear 2837
44:28 *is* my shepherd, and shall perform all my **p**: 2656
46:10 counsel shall stand, and I will do all my **p**: 2656
48:14 he will do his **p** on Babylon, and his arm 2656
53:10 the **p** of the LORD shall prosper in his 2656
58: 3 in the day of your fast you find **p**, and 2656
58:13 *from* doing thy **p** on my holy day; 2656
58:13 thine own ways, nor finding thine own **p**, 2656
Jer 2:24 *that* snuffeth up the wind at her **p**; 185
22:28 *is he* a vessel wherein *is* no **p**? 2656
34:16 whom ye had set at liberty at their **p**, 5315
48:38 broken Moab like a vessel wherein *is* no **p**, 2656
Eze 16:37 with whom thou hast **taken p**, and all *them* 6149
18:23 Have I **any p at all** that the wicked 2654+2654
18:32 For I have no **p** in the death of him that 2654
33:11 I have no **p** in the death of the wicked; 2654
Hos 8: 8 the Gentiles as a vessel wherein *is* no **p**. 2656
Hag 1: 8 I will **take p** in it, and I will be glorified, 7521
Mal 1:10 I have no **p** in you, saith the LORD of 2656
Lk 12:32 for it is your Father's **good p** to give you *2106*
Ac 24:27 and Felix, willing to shew the Jews a **p**, *5485*
25: 9 But Festus, willing to do the Jews a **p**, *5485*
Ro 1:32 the same, but have **p** in them that do *them*. *4909*
2Co 12:10 Therefore I **take p** in infirmities, *2106*
Eph 1: 5 according to the **good p** of his will, *2107*
1: 9 according to his **good p** which he had *2107*
Php 2:13 in you both to will and to do of *his* **good p**. *2107*
2Th 1:11 and fulfil all the **good p** of *his* goodness, *2107*
2:12 not the truth, but had **p** in unrighteousness. *2106*
1Ti 5: 6 But she that **liveth in p** is dead while she *4684*
Heb 10: 6 and *sacrifices* for sin thou hast **had** no **p**. *2106*
10: 8 neither hadst **p** *therein:* which are offered *2106*
10:38 draw back, my soul shall **have** no **p** in him. *2106*
12:10 a few days chastened *us* after their own **p**; *1380*
Jas 5: 5 Ye have **lived in p** on the earth, and *5171*
2Pe 2:13 *as* they that count it **p** to riot in the day *2237*
Rev 4:11 and for thy **p** they are and were created. *2307*

PLEASURES (8) [PLEASE]
Job 36:11 days in prosperity, and their years in **p**. 5273
Ps 16:11 at thy right hand *there are* **p** for evermore. 5273
36: 8 shalt make them drink *of* the river of thy **p**. 5730
Isa 47: 8 *thou that art* **given to p**, that dwellest 5719
Lk 8:14 with cares and riches and **p** of *this* life, *2237*
2Ti 3: 4 **lovers of p** more than lovers of God; *5369*
Tit 3: 3 deceived, serving divers lusts and **p**, *2237*
Heb 11:25 than to enjoy the **p** of sin for a season; *619*

PLEDGE (22) [PLEDGES]
Ge 38:17 she said, Wilt thou give *me* a **p**, till thou 6162
38:18 he said, What **p** shall I give thee? And she 6162
38:20 to receive *his* **p** from the woman's hand: 6162
Ex 22:26 **at all take** thy neighbour's raiment **to p**, 2254+2254
Dt 24: 6 **take** the nether or the upper millstone **to p**: 2254
24: 6 to pledge: for he **taketh** *a man's* life **to p**. 2254
24:10 shalt not go into his house to fetch his **p**. 5667
24:11 lend shall bring out the **p** abroad unto thee. 5667
24:12 *be* poor, thou shalt not sleep with his **p**: 5667
24:13 In any case thou shalt deliver him the **p** 5667
24:17 nor **take** a widow's raiment **to p**: 2254
1Sa 17:18 how thy brethren fare, and take their **p**. 6161
Job 22: 6 For thou hast **taken a p** from thy brother 2254
24: 3 they **take** the widow's ox **for a p**. 2254
24: 9 from the breast, and **take a p** of the poor. 2254
Pr 20:16 and **take a p** of him for a strange *woman*. 2254
27:13 and **take a p** of him for a strange *woman*. 2254
Eze 18: 7 *but* hath restored *to* the debtor his **p**, 2258
18:12 hath not restored the **p**, and hath lift up his 2258
18:16 hath not **withholden the p**, 2254+2258
33:15 *If* the wicked restore the **p**, give again that 2258
Am 2: 8 down upon clothes **laid to p** by every altar, 2254

PLEDGES (2) [PLEDGE]
2Ki 18:23 **give p** to my lord the king of Assyria, and 6148
Isa 36: 8 Now therefore **give p**, I pray thee, to my 6148

PLEIADES (2)
Job 9: 9 and **P**, and the chambers of the south. 3598
38:31 Canst thou bind the sweet influences of **P**, 3598

PLENTEOUS (12) [PLENTY]
Ge 41:34 of the land of Egypt in the seven **p** years. 7647
41:47 in the seven **p** years the earth brought forth 7647
Dt 28:11 the LORD shall **make** thee **p** in goods, 3498
30: 9 the LORD thy God will **make** thee **p** in 3498
2Ch 1:15 and gold at Jerusalem *as* **p** as stones, NIH
Ps 86: 5 **p** in mercy unto all them that call upon 7227
86:15 longsuffering, and **p** in mercy and truth. 7227
103: 8 gracious, slow to anger, and **p** in mercy. 7227
130: 7 *is* mercy, and with him *is* **p** redemption. 7235
Isa 30:23 of the earth, and it shall be fat and **p**: 8082
Hab 1:16 them their portion *is* fat, and their meat **p**. 1277
Mt 9:37 The harvest truly is **p**, but the labourers *are* *4183*

PLENTEOUSNESS (2) [PLENTY]
Ge 41:53 the seven years of **p**, that was in the land of 7647
Pr 21: 5 The thoughts of the diligent *tend* only to **p**; 4195

PLENTIFUL (4) [PLENTY]
Ps 68: 9 Thou, O God, didst send a **p** rain, 5071
Isa 16:10 is taken away, and joy out of the **p field**; 3759
Jer 2: 7 I brought you into a **p** country, to eat 3759
48:33 and gladness is taken from the **p field**, 3759

PLENTIFULLY (3) [PLENTY]
Job 26: 3 thou **p** declared the thing as it is? 7230+3807.1
Ps 31:23 and **p** rewardeth the proud doer. 3499
Lk 12:16 of a certain rich man **brought forth p**: *2164*

PLENTY (13) [PLENTEOUS, PLENTEOUSNESS, PLENTIFUL, PLENTIFULLY]
Ge 27:28 of the earth, and **p** of corn and wine: 7230
41:29 there come seven years of great **p** 7647
41:30 all the **p** shall be forgotten in the land of 7647
41:31 the **p** shall not be known in the land by 7647
Lev 11:36 or pit, *wherein there is* **p** of water, 4723
1Ki 10:11 brought in from Ophir great **p** of almug 7235
2Ch 31:10 had enough to eat, and have left **p**: 7230+3807.1
Job 22:25 thy defence, and thou shalt have **p** of silver. 8443
37:23 and *in* judgment, and *in* **p** of justice: 7230
Pr 3:10 So shall thy barns be filled *with* **p**, and 7647
28:19 He that tilleth his land shall **have p** *of* 7646
Jer 44:17 for *then* **had** we **p** of victuals, and 7646
Joel 2:26 ye shall **eat in p**, and be satisfied, and 398+398

PLOT See FORECAST

PLOTTETH (1)
Ps 37:12 The wicked **p** against the just, and 2161

PLOUGH (1) [PLOW]
Lk 9:62 No *man* having put his hand to the **p**, and *723*

PLOW (8) [PLOUGH, PLOWED, PLOWERS, PLOWETH, PLOWING, PLOWMAN, PLOWMEN, PLOWSHARES]
Dt 22:10 Thou shalt not **p** with an ox and an ass 2790
1Sa 14:14 acre of land, *which* a yoke *of oxen might* **p**. NIH
Job 4: 8 they that **p** iniquity, and sow wickedness, 2790
Pr 20: 4 The sluggard will not **p** by reason of 2790
Isa 28:24 Doth the plowman **p** all day to sow? 2790
Hos 10:11 Judah shall **p**, *and* Jacob shall break his 2790
Am 6:12 will *one* **p** *there* with oxen? for ye have 2790
1Co 9:10 that he that ploweth should **p** in hope; and *722*

PLOWED (5) [PLOW]
Jdg 14:18 unto them, If ye had not **p** with my heifer, 2790
Ps 129: 3 The plowers **p** upon my back: they made 2790
Jer 26:18 Zion shall be **p** *like* a field, and 2790
Hos 10:13 Ye have **p** wickedness, ye have reaped 2790
Mic 3:12 Therefore shall Zion for your sake be **p** *as* a 2790

PLOWERS (1) [PLOW]
Ps 129: 3 The **p** plowed upon my back: they made 2790

PLOWETH (1) [PLOW]
1Co 9:10 that he that **p** should plow in hope; and *722*

PLOWING (4) [PLOW]
1Ki 19:19 who *was* **p** *with* twelve yoke *of oxen* before 2790
Job 1:14 The oxen were **p**, and the asses feeding 2790
Pr 21: 4 proud heart, *and* the **p** of the wicked, *is* sin. 5215

Lk 17: 7 of you, having a servant **p** or feeding cattle, *722*

PLOWMAN (2) [MAN, PLOW]
Isa 28:24 Doth the **p** plow all day to sow? doth he 2790
Am 9:13 that the **p** shall overtake the reaper, and 2790

PLOWMEN (2) [MAN, PLOW]
Isa 61: 5 and the sons of the alien *shall be* your **p** and 406
Jer 14: 4 the **p** were ashamed, they covered their 406

PLOWSHARES (3) [PLOW]
Isa 2: 4 they shall beat their swords into **p**, and 855
Joel 3:10 Beat your **p** into swords, and 855
Mic 4: 3 they shall beat their swords into **p**, and 855

PLUCK (30) [PLUCKED, PLUCKETH, PLUCKT]
Lev 1:16 he shall **p away** his crop with his feathers, 5493
Nu 33:52 and **quite p down** all their high places: 8045
Dt 23:25 thou mayest **p** the ears with thine hand; 6998
2Ch 7:20 will I **p** them **up by the roots** out of my 5428
Job 24: 9 They **p** the fatherless from the breast, and 1497
Ps 25:15 for he shall **p** my feet **out** of the net. 3318
52: 5 **p** thee out of *thy* dwelling place, and 5255
74:11 even thy right hand? **p** *it* out of thy bosom. 3615
80:12 that all they which pass by the way do **p** her? 717
Ecc 3: 2 and a time to **p up** *that which is* planted; 6131
Jer 12:14 I will **p** them out of their land, and pluck 5428
12:14 **p out** the house of Judah from among them. 5428
12:17 I will **utterly p up** and destroy that 5428+5428
18: 7 to **p up**, and to pull down, and to destroy 5428
22:24 my right hand, yet would I **p** thee thence; 5423
24: 6 and I will plant them, and not **p** *them* **up**. 5428
31:28 to **p up**, and to break down, and to throw 5428
42:10 and I will plant you, and not **p** *you* **up**: 5428
45: 4 *that* which I have planted I *will* **p up**, 5428
Eze 17: 9 many people to **p** it **up** by the roots thereof. 5375
23:34 and **p off** thine own breasts: 5423
Mic 3: 2 who **p off** their skin from off them, and 1497
5:14 I will **p up** thy groves out of the midst of 5428
Mt 5:29 offend thee, **p it out**, and cast *it* from thee: *1807*
12: 1 and began to **p** the ears of corn, and to eat. *5089*
18: 9 offend thee, **p it out**, and cast *it* from thee: *1807*
Mk 2:23 as they went, to **p** the ears of corn. *5089*
9:47 And if thine eye offend thee, **p it out**: it is *1544*
Jn 10:28 neither shall any *man* **p** them out of my *726*
10:29 no *man* is able to **p** *them* out of my Father's *726*

PLUCKED (14) [PLUCK]
Ex 4: 7 **p it out** of his bosom, and behold, it was 3318
Dt 28:63 ye shall be **p** from off the land whither thou 5255
Ru 4: 7 a man **p off** his shoe, and gave *it* to his 8025
2Sa 23:21 **p** the spear out of the Egyptian's hand, and 1497
Isa 50: 6 and my cheeks to them that **p off** the **hair**: 4803
Jer 6:29 in vain: for the wicked are not **p away**. 5423
12:15 after that I have **p** them **out**, I will return, 5428
31:40 it shall not be **p up**, nor thrown down any 5428
Eze 19:12 she was **p up** in fury, she was cast down to 5428
Mk 5: 4 and the chains had been **p asunder** by him, *1288*
Lk 6: 1 and his disciples **p** the ears of corn, and *5089*
17: 6 Be thou **p up by the root**, and be thou *1610*
Gal 4:15 ye would have **p out** your own eyes, and *1846*
Jude 1:12 twice dead, **p up by the roots**; *1610*

PLUCKETH (1) [PLUCK]
Pr 14: 1 but the foolish **p it down** with her hands. 2040

PLUCKT (10) [PLUCK]
Ge 8:11 and lo, in her mouth *was* an olive leaf **p off**: 2965
1Ch 11:23 **p** the spear out of the Egyptian's hand, and 1497
Ezr 9: 3 **p off** the hair of my head and of my beard, 4803
Ne 13:25 **p off** their **hair**, and made them swear by 4803
Job 29:17 the wicked, and **p** the spoil out of his teeth. 7993
Da 7: 4 I beheld till the wings thereof were **p**, and 4804
7: 8 three of the first horns **p up by the roots**: 6132
11: 4 for his kingdom shall be **p up**, even for 5428
Am 4:11 ye were as a firebrand **p** out of the burning: 5337
Zec 3: 2 *is* not this a brand **p** out of the fire? 5337

PLUMBLINE (4) [LINE]
Am 7: 7 the Lord stood upon a wall made by a **p**, 594
7: 7 made by a plumbline, with a **p** in his hand. 594
7: 8 And I said, A **p**. Then said the Lord, Behold, 594
7: 8 I *will* set a **p** in the midst of my people 594

PLUMMET (3)
2Ki 21:13 of Samaria, and the **p** of the house of Ahab: 4949
Isa 28:17 I lay to the line, and righteousness to the **p**: 4949
Zec 4:10 shall see the **p** in the hand of Zerubbabel 68+913

PLUNDER See BOOTY; PREY; SPOIL

PLUNGE (1)
Job 9:31 Yet shalt thou **p** me in the ditch, and 2881

POCHERETH OF ZEBAIM (1) [POCHERETH ZEBAIM]
Ezr 2:57 the children of **P**, the children 6380

POCHERETH ZEBAIM (1) [POCHERETH OF ZEBAIM]
Ne 7:59 of Hattil, the children of **P**, 6380

POETS (1)
Ac 17:28 as certain also of your own **p** have said, *4163*

POINT (9) [POINTED, POINTS]
Ge 25:32 Esau said, Behold, I *am* **at the p** to die: 1980
Nu 34: 7 from the great sea you shall **p out** for you 8376
34: 8 From mount Hor ye shall **p out** *your border* 8376
34:10 ye shall **p out** your east border from 184
Jer 17: 1 a pen of iron, *and* with the **p** of a diamond: 6856
Eze 21:15 I have set the **p** of the sword against all their 19
Mk 5:23 daughter **lieth at the p of death**: *2079+2192*
Jn 4:47 heal his son: for he was **at the p of** death. *3195*
Jas 2:10 and *yet* offend in one *p*, he is guilty of all. NIG

POINTED (1) [POINT]
Job 41:30 he spreadeth **sharp p** *things* upon the mire. 2742

POINTING See SIGNIFY

POINTS (2) [POINT]
Ecc 5:16 *that* in all **p** as he came, so shall he go: 5980
Heb 4:15 was in all *p* tempted like as *we are, yet* NIG

POISON (9)
Dt 32:24 with the **p** of serpents of the dust. 2534
32:33 Their wine *is* the **p** of dragons, and 2534
Job 6: 4 the **p** whereof drinketh up my spirit: 2534
20:16 He shall suck the **p** of asps: the viper's 7219
Ps 58: 4 Their **p** *is* like the poison of a serpent: 2534
58: 4 Their poison *is* like the **p** of a serpent: 2534
140: 3 like a serpent; adder's **p** *is* under their lips. 2534
Ro 3:13 used deceit; the **p** of asps *is* under their lips: *2447*
Jas 3: 8 *it is* an unruly evil, full of deadly **p**. *2447*

POISONOUS See HEMLOCK

POKERETH HAZZEBAIM See POCHERETH [OF] ZEBAIM

POLE (2)
Nu 21: 8 thee a fiery *serpent,* and set it upon a **p**: 5251
21: 9 put it upon a **p**, and it came to pass, that if a 5251

POLES See STAVES

POLICY (1)
Da 8:25 through his **p** also he shall cause craft to 7922

POLISHED (3) [POLISHING]
Ps 144:12 **p** *after* the similitude of a palace: 2404
Isa 49: 2 hath he hid me, and made me a **p** shaft; 1305
Da 10: 6 and his feet like in colour to **p** brass, 7044

POLISHING (1) [POLISHED]
La 4: 7 body than rubies, their **p** *was of* sapphire: 1508

POLL (3) [POLLED, POLLS]
Nu 3:47 shalt even take five shekels apiece by the **p**, 1538
Eze 44:20 they shall **only p** their heads. 3697+3697
Mic 1:16 and **p** thee for thy delicate children; 1494

POLLED (3) [POLL]
2Sa 14:26 when he **p** his head, (for it was at every 1548
14:26 (for it was at every year's end that he **p** *it*: 1548
14:26 *hair* was heavy on him, therefore he **p** it:) 1548

POLLS (6) [POLL]
Nu 1: 2 of *their* names, every male by their **p**; 1538
1:18 twenty years old and upward, by their **p**. 1538
1:20 by their **p**, every male from twenty years 1538
1:22 by their **p**, every male from twenty years 1538
1Ch 23: 3 their number by their **p**, man by man, 1538

1Ch 23:24 counted by number of names by their **p**, 1538

POLLUTE (11) [POLLUTED, POLLUTING, POLLUTION, POLLUTIONS]
Nu 18:32 neither shall ye **p** the holy *things* of 2490
35:33 So ye shall not **p** the land wherein ye *are:* 2610
Jer 7:30 house which is called by my name, to **p** it. 2930
Eze 7:21 of the earth for a spoil; and they shall **p** it. 2490
7:22 they shall **p** my secret *place:* for the robbers 2490
13:19 will ye **p** me among my people for handfuls 2490
20:31 ye **p** yourselves with all your idols, 2930
20:39 **p** ye my holy name no more with your 2490
39: 7 I will not let *them* **p** my holy name any 2490
44: 7 be in my sanctuary, to **p** it, *even* my house, 2490
Da 11:31 they shall **p** the sanctuary *of* strength, and 2490

POLLUTED (40) [POLLUTE]
Ex 20:25 thou lift up thy tool upon it, thou hast **p** it. 2490
2Ki 23:16 and burnt *them* upon the altar, and **p** it, 2930
2Ch 36:14 **p** the house of the LORD which he had 2930
Ezr 2:62 therefore were they, as **p**, put from 1351
Ne 7:64 therefore were they, as **p**, put from 1351
Ps 106:38 of Canaan: and the land was **p** with blood. 2610
Isa 47: 6 I have **p** mine inheritance, and given them 2490
48:11 will I do *it:* for how should *my name* be **p**? 2490
Jer 2:23 How canst thou say, I am not **p**, I have not 2930
3: 1 shall not that land be **greatly p**? 2610+2610
3: 2 thou hast **p** the land with thy whoredoms 2610
34:16 ye turned and **p** my name, and caused every 2490
La 2: 2 he hath **p** the kingdom and the princes 2490
4:14 they have **p** themselves with blood, so 1351
Eze 4:14 behold, my soul *hath* not *been* **p**: 2930
14:11 neither be **p** any more with all their 2930
16: 6 by thee, and saw thee **p** in thine own blood, 947
16:22 and bare, *and* wast **p** in thy blood. 947
20: 9 that *it* should not be **p** before the heathen, 2490
20:13 in them; and my sabbaths they greatly **p**: 2490
20:14 that *it* should not be **p** before the heathen, 2490
20:16 not in my statutes, but **p** my sabbaths: 2490
20:21 even live in them; they **p** my sabbaths: 2490
20:22 that *it* should not be **p** in the sight of 2490
20:24 had **p** my sabbaths, and their eyes were 2490
20:26 I **p** them in their own gifts, in that they 2930
20:30 Are ye **p** after the manner of your fathers? 2930
23:17 she was **p** with them, and her mind was 2930
23:30 *and* because thou art **p** with their idols. 2930
36:18 and for their idols *wherewith* they had **p** it: 2930
Hos 6: 8 that work iniquity, *and is* **p** with blood. 6121
9: 4 of mourners; all that eat thereof shall be **p**: 2930
Am 7:17 by line; and thou shalt die in a **p** land: 2931
Mic 2:10 because it is **p**, it shall destroy *you,* even 2930
Zep 3: 1 Woe to her that is filthy and **p**, to 1351
3: 4 her priests have **p** the sanctuary, they have 2490
Mal 1: 7 *Ye* offer **p** bread upon mine altar; and 1351
1: 7 and ye say, Wherein have we **p** thee? 1351
1:12 in that ye say, The table of the LORD *is* **p**; 1351
Ac 21:28 into the temple, and hath **p** this holy place. *2840*

POLLUTING (2) [POLLUTE]
Isa 56: 2 that keepeth the sabbath from **p** it, and 2490
56: 6 every one that keepeth the sabbath from **p** 2490

POLLUTION (1) [POLLUTE]
Eze 22:10 they humbled her that was set apart for **p**. 2931

POLLUTIONS (2) [POLLUTE]
Ac 15:20 that *they* abstain from **p** of idols, and *234*
2Pe 2:20 For if after they have escaped the **p** of *3393*

POLLUX (1)
Ac 28:11 in the isle, *whose* sign *was* **Castor and P**. *1359*

POMEGRANATE (10) [POMEGRANATES]
Ex 28:34 A golden bell and a **p**, a golden bell and 7416
28:34 and a pomegranate, a golden bell and a **p**, 7416
39:26 A bell and a **p**, a bell and a pomegranate, 7416
39:26 A bell and a pomegranate, a bell and a **p**, 7416
1Sa 14: 2 Gibeah under a **p tree** which *is* in Migron: 7416
SS 4: 3 thy temples *are* like a piece of a **p** within 7416
6: 7 As a piece of a **p** *are* thy temples within thy 7416
8: 2 drink of spiced wine, of the juice of my **p**. 7416
Joel 1:12 the **p tree**, the palm tree also, and the apple 7416
Hag 2:19 the fig tree, and the **p**, and the olive tree, 7416

POMEGRANATES (23) [POMEGRANATE]
Ex 28:33 the hem of it thou shalt make **p** of blue, 7416
39:24 they made upon the hems of the robe **p** of 7416
39:25 put the bells between the **p** upon the hem of 7416
39:25 of the robe, round about between the **p**; 7416
Nu 13:23 and *they brought* of the **p**, and of the figs. 7416
20: 5 place of seed, or of figs, or of vines, or of **p**; 7416
Dt 8: 8 and barley, and vines, and fig trees, and **p**; 7416
1Ki 7:18 chapiters that *were* upon the top, *with* **p**: 7416
7:20 the chapiters upon the two pillars *had* **p** also NIH
7:20 the **p** *were* two hundred *in* rows round 7416
7:42 four hundred **p** for the two networks, 7416
7:42 *even* two rows *of* **p** for one network, 7416
2Ki 25:17 **p** upon the chapiter round about, all *of* 7416
2Ch 3:16 made an hundred **p**, and put *them* on 7416
4:13 four hundred **p** on the two wreaths; 7416
4:13 two rows *of* **p** on each wreath, to cover 7416
SS 4:13 Thy plants *are* an orchard of **p**, 7416
6:11 the vine flourished, *and* the **p** budded. 7416
7:12 tender grape appear, *and* the **p** bud forth: 7416
Jer 52:22 and **p** upon the chapiters round about, 7416
52:22 pillar also and the **p** *were* like unto these. 7416
52:23 there were ninety and six **p** on a side; *and* 7416
52:23 all the **p** upon the network *were* an hundred 7416

POMMELS (3)
2Ch 4:12 the **p**, and the chapiters *which were* on 1543
4:12 the two wreaths to cover the two **p** of 1543
4:13 to cover the two **p** of the chapiters which 1543

POMP (7)
Isa 5:14 and their **p**, and he that rejoiceth, 7588
14:11 Thy **p** is brought down *to* the grave, *and* 1347
Eze 7:24 I will also make the **p** of the strong to 1347
30:18 the **p** of her strength shall cease in her: 1347
32:12 they shall spoil the **p** of Egypt, and all 1347
33:28 the **p** of her strength shall cease; 1347
Ac 25:23 with great **p**, and were entered into *5325*

PONDER (2) [PONDERED, PONDERETH]
Pr 4:26 **P** the path of thy feet, and let all thy ways 6424
5: 6 Lest thou shouldest **p** the path of life, 6424

PONDERED (1) [PONDER]
Lk 2:19 all these things, and **p** *them* in her heart. *4820*

PONDERETH (3) [PONDER]
Pr 5:21 eyes of the LORD, and he **p** all his goings. 6424
21: 2 his own eyes: but the LORD **p** the hearts. 8505
24:12 doth not he that **p** the heart consider *it?* and 8505

PONDS (3)
Ex 7:19 upon their **p**, and upon all their pools of 98
8: 5 over the **p**, and cause frogs to come up upon 98
Isa 19:10 all that make sluces *and* **p** for fish. 99

PONTIUS (4)
Mt 27: 2 and delivered him to **P** Pilate the governor. *4194*
Lk 3: 1 **P** Pilate being governor of Judea, and *4194*
Ac 4:27 both Herod, and **P** Pilate, with the Gentiles, *4194*
1Ti 6:13 who before **P** Pilate witnessed a good *4194*

PONTUS (3)
Ac 2: 9 in Judea, and Cappadocia, in **P**, and Asia, *4195*
18: 2 born in **P**, lately come from Italy, with his *4193*
1Pe 1: 1 to the strangers scattered throughout **P**, *4195*

POOL (22) [FISHPOOLS, POOLS]
2Sa 2:13 and met together by the **p** of Gibeon: 1295
2:13 the one on the one side of the **p**, and 1295
2:13 and the other on the other side of the **p**. 1295
4:12 and hanged *them* up over the **p** in Hebron. 1295
1Ki 22:38 *one* washed the chariot in the **p** of Samaria; 1295
2Ki 18:17 and stood by the conduit of the upper **p**, 1295
20:20 how he made a **p**, and a conduit, and 1295
Ne 2:14 the gate of the fountain, and to the king's **p**: 1295
3:15 the wall of the **p** of Siloah by the king's 1295
3:16 to the **p** that was made, and unto the house 1295
Isa 7: 3 at the end of the conduit of the upper **p** in 1295
22: 9 gathered together the waters of the lower **p**. 1295
22:11 the two walls for the water of the old **p**: 1295
35: 7 the parched ground shall become a **p**, and 98
36: 2 he stood by the conduit of the upper **p** in 1295
41:18 I will make the wilderness a **p** of water, and 98
Na 2: 8 Nineveh *is* of old like a **p** of water: yet they 1295

Jn 5: 2 is at Jerusalem by the sheep *market* a **p**, *2861*
5: 4 went down at a *certain* season into the **p**, *2861*
5: 7 the water is troubled, to put me into the **p**: *2861*
9: 7 said unto him, Go, wash in the **p** of Siloam, *2861*
9:11 unto me, Go to the **p** of Siloam, and wash: *2861*

POOLS (5) [POOL]
Ex 7:19 their ponds, and upon all their **p** of water, 4723
Ps 84: 6 make it a well; the rain also filleth the **p**. 1295
Ecc 2: 6 I made me **p** of water, to water therewith 1295
Isa 14:23 it a possession for the bittern, and **p** of water: 98
42:15 the rivers islands, and I will dry up the **p**. 98

POOR (205) [POVERTY]
Ge 41:19 **p** and very ill favoured and leanfleshed, 1803
Ex 22:25 to *any of* my people *that is* **p** by thee, 6041
23: 3 Neither shalt thou countenance a **p** *man* in 1800
23: 6 Thou shalt not wrest the judgment of thy **p** in 34
23:11 and lie still; that the **p** of thy people may eat: 34
30:15 the **p** shall not give less than half a shekel, 1800
Lev 14:21 if he *be* **p**, and cannot get *so much;* then 1800
19:10 thou shalt leave them for the **p** and 6041
19:15 thou shalt not respect the person of the **p**, 1800
23:22 thou shalt leave them unto the **p**, and to 6041
25:25 If thy brother be **waxen p**, and hath sold 4134
25:35 if thy brother be **waxen p**, and fallen in 4134
25:39 brother *that dwelleth* by thee be **waxen p**, 4134
25:47 thy brother *that dwelleth* by him **wax p**, 4134
Dt 15: 4 Save when there shall be no **p** among you; 34
15: 7 If there be among you a **p man** of one of thy 34
15: 7 nor shut thine hand from thy **p** brother: 34
15: 9 thine eye be evil against thy **p** brother, and 34
15:11 For the **p** shall never cease out of the land: 34
15:11 to thy **p**, and to thy needy, in thy land. 6041
24:12 if the man *be* **p**, thou shalt not sleep with 6041
24:14 shalt not oppress a hired servant *that is* **p** 6041
24:15 for he *is* **p**, and setteth his heart upon it: 6041
Jdg 6:15 my family *is* **p** in Manasseh, and I *am* 1800
Ru 3:10 not young men, whether **p** or rich. 1800
1Sa 2: 7 The LORD **maketh p**, and maketh rich: 3423
2: 8 He raiseth up the **p** out of the dust, *and* 1800
18:23 seeing that I *am* a **p** man, and 7326
2Sa 12: 1 in one city; the one rich, and the other **p**. 7326
12: 3 the **p** *man* had nothing, save one little ewe 7326
12: 4 took the **p** man's lamb, and dressed it for 7326
2Ki 25:12 the captain of the guard left of the **p** of 1803
Est 9:22 portions one to another, and gifts to the **p**. 34
Job 5:15 he saveth the **p** from the sword, from their 34
5:16 So the **p** hath hope, and iniquity stoppeth 1800
20:10 His children shall *seek to* please the **p**, and 1800
20:19 he hath oppressed *and* hath forsaken the **p**; 1800
24: 4 the **p** of the earth hide themselves together. 6041
24: 9 from the breast, and take a pledge of the **p**. 6041
24:14 murderer rising with the light killeth the **p** 6041
29:12 Because I delivered the **p** that cried, and 6041
29:16 I *was* a father to the **p**: and the cause *which* I 34
30:25 in trouble? was *not* my soul grieved for the **p**? 34
31:16 If I have withheld the **p** from *their* desire, 1800
31:19 want of clothing, or *any* **p** without covering; 34
34:19 nor regardeth the rich more than the **p**? 1800
34:28 So that *they* cause the cry of the **p** to come 1800
36: 6 life of the wicked: but giveth right to the **p**. 6041
36:15 He delivereth the **p** in his affliction, and 6041
Ps 9:18 the expectation of the **p** shall *not* perish for 6041
10: 2 wicked in *his* pride doth persecute the **p**: 6041
10: 8 his eyes are privily set against the **p**. 2489
10: 9 he lieth in wait to catch the **p**: he doth catch 6041
10: 9 he doth catch the **p**, when he draweth him 6041
10:10 that the **p** may fall by his strong *ones.* 2489
10:14 the **p** committeth *himself* unto thee; 2489
12: 5 For the oppression of the **p**, for the sighing 6041
14: 6 You have shamed the counsel of the **p**, 6041
34: 6 This **p** *man* cried, and the LORD heard 6041
35:10 which deliverest the **p** from him that is too 6041
35:10 the **p** and the needy from him that spoileth 6041
37:14 to cast down the **p** and needy, *and* to slay 6041
40:17 I *am* **p** and needy; *yet* the Lord thinketh 6041
41: 1 Blessed *is* he that considereth the **p**: 1800
49: 2 Both low and high, rich and **p**, together. 34
68:10 hast prepared of thy goodness for the **p**. 6041
69:29 I *am* **p** and sorrowful: let thy salvation, 6041
69:33 For the LORD heareth the **p**, and despiseth 34
70: 5 I *am* **p** and needy: make haste unto me, 6041
72: 2 and thy **p** with judgment. 6041
72: 4 He shall judge the **p** of the people, he shall 6041
72:12 the **p** also, and *him* that hath no helper. 6041
72:13 He shall spare the **p** and needy, and 1800
74:19 not the congregation of thy **p** for ever. 6041
74:21 let the **p** and needy praise thy name. 6041
82: 3 Defend the **p** and fatherless: do justice to 1800
82: 4 Deliver the **p** and needy: rid *them* out of 1800
86: 1 O LORD, hear me: for I *am* **p** and needy. 6041
107:41 Yet setteth he the **p** on high from affliction, 34
109:16 persecuted the **p** and needy man, that *he* 6041
109:22 For I *am* **p** and needy, and my heart is 6041
109:31 For he shall stand at the right hand of the **p**, 34
112: 9 He hath dispersed, he hath given to the **p**; 34
113: 7 He raiseth up the **p** out of the dust, *and* 1800
132:15 her provision: I will satisfy her **p** *with* bread. 34
140:12 cause of the afflicted, *and* the right of the **p**. 34
Pr 10: 4 *He becometh* **p** that dealeth *with* a slack 7326
10:15 the destruction of the **p** *is* their poverty. 1800
13: 7 *there is* that **maketh** himself **p**, yet *hath* 7326
13: 8 *are* his riches: but the **p** heareth not rebuke. 7326
13:23 Much food *is in* the tillage of the **p**: but 7326
14:20 The **p** is hated even of his own neighbour: 7326
14:21 he that hath mercy on the **p**, happy *is* he. 6035
14:31 He that oppresseth the **p** reproacheth his 1800
14:31 he that honoureth him hath mercy on the **p**. 34
17: 5 Whoso mocketh the **p** reproacheth his 7326
18:23 The **p** useth intreaties; but the rich 7326
19: 1 Better *is* the **p** that walketh in his integrity, 7326
19: 4 but the **p** is separated from his neighbour. 1800
19: 7 All the brethren of the **p** do hate him: 7326
19:17 He that hath pity upon the **p** lendeth unto 1800
19:22 and a **p** *man is* better than a liar. 7326
21:13 Whoso stoppeth his ears at the cry of the **p**, 1800
21:17 He that loveth pleasure *shall be* a **p** man: 4270
22: 2 The rich and **p** meet together: the LORD 7326
22: 7 The rich ruleth over the **p**, and the borrower 7326
22: 9 for he giveth of his bread to the **p**. 1800
22:16 He that oppresseth the **p** to increase his 1800
22:22 Rob not the **p**, because he *is* poor: 1800
22:22 Rob not the poor, because he *is* **p**: 1800
28: 3 A **p** man that oppresseth the poor *is like* a 7326
28: 3 A poor man that oppresseth the **p** *is like* a 1800
28: 6 Better *is* the **p** that walketh in his 7326
28: 8 shall gather it for him that will pity the **p**. 1800
28:11 the **p** that hath understanding searcheth him 1800
28:15 *so is* a wicked ruler over the **p** people. 1800
28:27 He that giveth unto the **p** *shall* not lack: but 7326
29: 7 righteous considereth the cause of the **p**: 1800
29:13 The **p** and the deceitful man meet together: 7326
29:14 The king that faithfully judgeth the **p**, 1800
30: 9 or lest I be **p**, and steal, and take the name 3423
30:14 to devour the **p** from off the earth, and 6041
31: 9 and plead the cause of the **p** and needy. 6041
31:20 She stretcheth out her hand to the **p**; yea, 6041
Ecc 4:13 Better *is* a **p** and a wise child than an old 4542
4:14 *he that is* born in his kingdom becometh **p**. 7326
5: 8 If thou seest the oppression of the **p**, and 7326
6: 8 what hath the **p**, that knoweth to walk 6041
9:15 Now there was found in it a **p** wise man, 4542
9:15 yet no man remembered that *same* **p** man. 4542
9:16 nevertheless the **p** *man's* wisdom *is* 4542
Isa 3:14 the spoil of the **p** *is* in your houses. 6041
3:15 to pieces, and grind the faces of the **p**? 6041
10: 2 to take away the right from the **p** of my 6041
10:30 *it* to be heard unto Laish, O **p** Anathoth. 6041
11: 4 But with righteousness shall he judge the **p**, 1800
14:30 the firstborn of the **p** shall feed, and 1800
14:32 and the **p** of his people shall trust in it. 6041
25: 4 For thou hast been a strength to the **p**, 1800
26: 6 *even* the feet of the **p**, *and* the steps of 6041
29:19 the **p** among men shall rejoice in the Holy 34
32: 7 he deviseth wicked devices to destroy the **p** 6041
41:17 *When* the **p** and needy seek water, and 6041
58: 7 that thou bring the **p** that are cast out *to thy* 6041
66: 2 *even to him that is* **p** and of a contrite spirit, 6041
Jer 2:34 the blood of the souls of the **p** innocents: 34
5: 4 Therefore I said, Surely these *are* **p**; 1800
20:13 for he hath delivered the soul of the **p** from 34
22:16 He judged the cause of the **p** and needy; 6041
39:10 of the guard left of the **p** of the people, 1800
40: 7 and children, and of the **p** of the land, 1803
52:15 away captive *certain* of the **p** of the people, 1803
52:16 *certain* of the **p** of the land for vinedressers 1803
Eze 16:49 neither did she strengthen the hand of the **p** 6041

Eze 18:12 Hath oppressed the **p** and needy, 6041
18:17 *That* hath taken off his hand from the **p**, 6041
22:29 and have vexed the **p** and needy: 6041
Da 4:27 thine iniquities by shewing mercy to the **p**; 6033
Am 2: 6 for silver, and the **p** for a pair of shoes; 34
2: 7 the dust of the earth on the head of the **p**, 1800
4: 1 which oppress the **p**, which crush 1800
5:11 as your treading *is* upon the **p**, 1800
5:12 they turn aside the **p** in the gate *from their* 34
8: 4 even to make the **p** of the land to fail, 6041
8: 6 That *we* may buy the **p** for silver, and 1800
Hab 3:14 their rejoicing *was* as to devour the **p** 6041
Zep 3:12 the midst of thee an afflicted and **p** people, 1800
Zec 7:10 nor the fatherless, the stranger, nor the **p**; 6041
11: 7 of slaughter, *even* you, O **p** of the flock. 6041
11:11 the **p** of the flock that waited upon me 6041
Mt 5: 3 Blessed *are* the **p** in spirit: for theirs is *4434*
11: 5 and the **p** have the gospel preached to them. *4434*
19:21 and give to the **p**, and thou shalt have *4434*
26: 9 been sold for much, and given to the **p**. *4434*
26:11 For ye have the **p** always with you; but *4434*
Mk 10:21 and give to the **p**, and thou shalt have *4434*
12:42 And there came a certain **p** widow, and *4434*
12:43 That this **p** widow hath cast more in, *4434*
14: 5 and have been given to the **p**. *4434*
14: 7 For ye have the **p** with you always, and *4434*
Lk 4:18 anointed me to preach the gospel to the **p**; *4434*
6:20 on his disciples, and said, Blessed *be ye* **p**: *4434*
7:22 are raised, to the **p** the gospel is preached. *4434*
14:13 call the **p**, the maimed, the lame, the blind: *4434*
14:21 and bring in hither the **p**, and the maimed, *4434*
18:22 and distribute unto the **p**, and thou shalt *4434*
19: 8 Lord, the half of my goods I give to the **p**; *4434*
21: 2 And he saw also a certain **p** widow casting *3998*
21: 3 that this **p** widow hath cast in more than *4434*
Jn 12: 5 three hundred pence, and given to the **p**? *4434*
12: 6 This he said, not that he cared for the **p**; but *4434*
12: 8 For the **p** always ye have with you; but *4434*
13:29 or that he should give something to the **p**. *4434*
Ro 15:26 for the **p** saints which are at Jerusalem. *4434*
1Co 13: 3 though I bestow all my goods to feed *the* **p**, NIG
2Co 6:10 as **p**, yet making many rich; as having *4434*
8: 9 was rich, *yet* for your sakes he became **p**, *4433*
9: 9 dispersed abroad; he hath given to the **p**: *3993*
Gal 2:10 *they would* that we should remember the **p**; *4434*
Jas 2: 2 there come in also a **p** *man* in vile raiment; *4434*
2: 3 and say to the **p**, Stand thou there, or *4434*
2: 5 Hath not God chosen the **p** of this world *4434*
2: 6 But ye have despised the **p**. Do not rich *4434*
Rev 3:17 and miserable, and **p**, and blind, and naked: *4434*
13:16 and great, rich and **p**, free and bond, *4434*

POORER (1) [POVERTY]
Lev 27: 8 if he be **p** than thy estimation, then he shall 4134

POOREST (1) [POVERTY]
2Ki 24:14 save the **p sort** of the people of the land. 1803

POPLAR (1) [POPLARS]
Ge 30:37 Jacob took him rods of green **p**, and of 3839

POPLARS (1) [POPLAR]
Hos 4:13 under oaks and **p** and elms, because 3839

POPULOUS (2)
Dt 26: 5 there a nation, great, mighty, and **p**: 7227
Na 3: 8 Art thou better than **p** No, that was situate 527

PORATHA (1)
Est 9: 8 And **P**, and Adalia, and Aridatha, 6334

PORCH (39) [PORCHES]
Jdg 3:23 Ehud went forth through the **p**, and shut 4528
1Ki 6: 3 the **p** before the temple of the house, 197
7: 6 he made a **p** of pillars; the length thereof *was* 197
7: 6 the **p** *was* before them: and *the other* pillars 197
7: 7 he made a **p** for the throne where he might 197
7: 7 he might judge, *even* the **p** of judgment: 197
7: 8 he dwelt *had* another court within the **p**, 197
7: 8 whom he had taken *to wife*, like unto this **p**. 197
7:12 of the LORD, and for the **p** of the house. 197
7:19 top of the pillars *were* of lily work in the **p**, 197
7:21 he set up the pillars in the **p** of the temple: 197
1Ch 28:11 gave to Solomon his son the pattern of the **p**, 197
2Ch 3: 4 the **p** that *was* in the front *of the house*, 197
8:12 the LORD, which he had built before the **p**, 197
15: 8 that *was* before the **p** of the LORD. 197
29: 7 Also they have shut up the doors of the **p**, 197
29:17 the month came they to the **p** of the LORD: 197
Eze 8:16 between the **p** and the altar, *were* about five 197
40: 7 the threshold of the gate by the **p** of the gate 197
40: 8 He measured also the **p** of the gate within, 197
40: 9 measured he the **p** of the gate, eight cubits; 197
40: 9 two cubits; and the **p** of the gate *was* inward. 197
40:15 of the **p** of the inner gate *were* fifty cubits. 197
40:39 in the **p** of the gate *were* two tables on this 197
40:40 which *was* at the **p** of the gate, *were* two 197
40:48 he brought me to the **p** of the house, and 197
40:48 measured *each* post of the **p**, five cubits on 197
40:49 The length of the **p** *was* twenty cubits, and 197
41:25 thick planks upon the face of the **p** without. 197
41:26 on the sides of the **p**, and *upon* the side 197
44: 3 he shall enter by the way of the **p** of *that* 197
46: 2 the prince shall enter by the way of the **p** of 197
46: 8 he shall go in *by* the way of the **p** of *that* 197
Joel 2:17 weep between the **p** and the altar, and 197
Mt 26:71 And when he was gone out into the **p**, *4440*
Mk 14:68 And he went out into the **p**; and *the* cock *4259*
Jn 10:23 Jesus walked in the temple in Solomon's **p**. *4745*
Ac 3:11 unto them in the **p** that is called Solomon's, *4745*
5:12 were all with one accord in Solomon's **p**. *4745*

PORCHES (2) [PORCH]
Eze 41:15 with the inner temple, and the **p** of the court; 197
Jn 5: 2 Hebrew tongue Bethesda, having five **p**. *4745*

PORCIUS (1)
Ac 24:27 But after two years **P** Festus came into *4201*

PORT (1)
Ne 2:13 to the dung **p**, and viewed the walls of 8179

PORTER (6) [PORTERS]
2Sa 18:26 the watchman called unto the **p**, and said, 7778
2Ki 7:10 they came and called unto the **p** of the city: 7778
1Ch 9:21 **p** of the door of the tabernacle of 7778
2Ch 31:14 of Imnah the Levite, the **p** toward the east, 7778
Mk 13:34 his work, and commanded the **p** to watch. *2377*
Jn 10: 3 To him the **p** openeth; and the sheep hear *2377*

PORTERS (33) [PORTER]
2Ki 7:11 he called the **p**; and they told *it to* 7778
1Ch 9:17 the **p** *were*, Shallum, and Akkub, and 7778
9:18 they *were* **p** in the companies of 7778
9:22 All these which were chosen to be **p** in 7778
9:24 In four quarters were the **p**, toward the east, 7778
9:26 For these Levites, the four chief **p**, *were* in 7778
15:18 Mikneiah, and Obed-edom, and Jeiel, the **p**. 7778
16:38 also the son of Jeduthun and Hosah to be **p**: 7778
16:42 of God. And the sons of Jeduthun *were* **p**. 8179
23: 5 Moreover four thousand *were* **p**; and 7778
26: 1 Concerning the divisions of the **p**: Of 7778
26:12 Among these *were* the divisions of the **p**, 7778
26:19 These *are* the divisions of the **p** among 7778
2Ch 8:14 the **p** also by their courses at every gate: for 7778
23: 4 and of the Levites, *shall be* **p** of the doors; 7778
23:19 he set the **p** at the gates of the house of 7778
34:13 *there were* scribes, and officers, and **p**. 7778
35:15 king's seer; and the **p** *waited* at every gate; 7778
Ezr 2:42 The children of the **p**: the children of 7778
2:70 the singers, and the **p**, and the Nethinims, 7778
7: 7 the singers, and the **p**, and the Nethinims, 7778
7:24 any of the priests and Levites, singers, **p**, 8652
10:24 and of the **p**; Shallum, and Telem, and Uri. 7778
Ne 7: 1 the **p** and the singers and the Levites were 7778
7:45 The **p**: the children of Shallum, the children 7778
7:73 the **p**, and the singers, and *some* of 7778
10:28 the priests, the Levites, the **p**, the singers, 7778
10:39 that minister, and the **p**, and the singers: 7778
11:19 Moreover the **p**, Akkub, Talmon, and 7778
12:25 *were* **p** keeping the ward at the thresholds 7778
12:45 and the **p** kept the ward of their God, 7778
12:47 gave the portions of the singers and the **p**, 7778
13: 5 to the Levites, and the singers, and the **p**; 7778

PORTICO See ARCHES

PORTION (100) [PORTIONS]
Ge 14:24 the **p** of the men which went with me, 2506
14:24 Eshcol, and Mamre; let them take their **p**. 2506

Ge 31:14 *Is there* yet any **p** or inheritance for us in 2506
47:22 for the priests had a **p** assigned them of 2706
47:22 did eat their **p** which Pharaoh gave them: 2706
48:22 Moreover I have given to thee one **p** above 7926
Lev 6:17 I have given it *unto them for* their **p** of my 2506
7:35 This *is the* **p** of the anointing of Aaron, and NIH
Nu 31:30 thou shalt take one **p** of fifty, of the persons, 270
31:36 *which was* the **p** of them that went out to 2506
31:47 Moses took one **p** of fifty, *both* of man and 270
Dt 21:17 by giving him a double **p** of all that he 6310
32: 9 For the LORD'S **p** *is* his people; Jacob *is* 2506
33:21 because there, *in* a **p** of the lawgiver, 2513
Jos 17:14 given me *but* one lot and one **p** to inherit, 2256
19: 9 Out of the **p** of the children of Judah *was* 2256
1Sa 1: 5 unto Hannah he gave a worthy **p**; for he 4490
9:23 Bring the **p** which I gave thee, of which I 4490
1Ki 12:16 the king, saying, What **p** have we in David? 2506
2Ki 2: 9 let a double **p** of thy spirit be upon me. 6310
9:10 the dogs shall eat Jezebel in the **p** of 2506
9:21 met him in the **p** of Naboth the Jezreelite. 2513
9:25 cast him in the **p** of the field of Naboth 2513
9:36 In the **p** of Jezreel shall dogs eat the flesh 2506
9:37 the face of the field in the **p** of Jezreel; 2506
2Ch 10:16 the king, saying, What **p** have we in David? 2506
28:21 For Ahaz **took away a p** *out* of the house 2505
31: 3 *He appointed* also the king's **p** of his 4521
31: 4 in Jerusalem to give the **p** of the priests 4521
31:16 *his* daily **p** for their service in their charges 1697
Ezr 4:16 by this means thou shalt have no **p** on *this* 2508
Ne 2:20 you have no **p**, nor right, nor memorial, 2506
11:23 that a **certain p** *should be* for the singers, 548
12:47 the singers and the porters, every day his **p**: 1697
Job 20:29 This *is* the **p** of a wicked man from God, 2506
24:18 as the waters; their **p** is cursed in the earth: 2513
26:14 how little a **p** is heard of him? but 1697
27:13 This *is* the **p** of a wicked man with God, 2506
31: 2 For what **p** of God *is there* from above? and 2506
Ps 11: 6 *this shall be* the **p** of their cup. 4521
16: 5 The LORD *is* the **p** of mine inheritance 4490
17:14 *which have* their **p** in *this* life, and 2506
63:10 by the sword: they shall be a **p** for foxes. 4521
73:26 the strength of my heart, and my **p** for ever. 2506
119:57 *Thou art* my **p**, O LORD: I have said that 2506
142: 5 *and* my **p** in the land of the living. 2506
Pr 31:15 to her household, and a **p** to her maidens. 2706
Ecc 2:10 and this was my **p** of all my labour. 2506
2:21 laboured therein shall he leave it *for* his **p**. 2506
3:22 rejoice in his own works; for that *is* his **p**: 2506
5:18 which God giveth him: for it *is* his **p**. 2506
5:19 to take his **p**, and to rejoice in his labour; 2506
9: 6 neither have they any more a **p** for ever in 2506
9: 9 for that *is* thy **p** in *this* life, and in thy 2506
11: 2 Give a **p** to seven, and also to eight; 2506
Isa 17:14 This *is* the **p** of them that spoil us, and 2506
53:12 Therefore will I divide him *a p* with NIH
57: 6 the smooth *stones* of the stream *is* thy **p**; 2506
61: 7 *for* confusion they shall rejoice in their **p**: 2506
Jer 10:16 The **p** of Jacob *is* not like them: for he *is* 2506
12:10 they have trodden my **p** under foot, 2513
12:10 they have made my pleasant **p** a desolate 2513
13:25 *is* thy lot, the **p** of thy measures from me, 4490
51:19 The **p** of Jacob *is* not like them; for he *is* 2506
52:34 every day a **p** until the day of his death, 1697
La 3:24 The LORD *is* my **p**, saith my soul; 2506
Eze 45: 1 unto the LORD, a holy *p* of the land: NIH
45: 4 The holy *p* of the land shall be for NIH
45: 6 over against the oblation of the holy *p*: it NIH
45: 7 *a p shall be* for the prince on the one side NIH
45: 7 the other side of the oblation of the holy *p*, NIH
45: 7 before the oblation of the holy *p*, and NIH
48: 1 are his sides east *and* west; a *p for* Dan. NIH
48: 2 east side unto the west side, a *p for* Asher. NIH
48: 3 even unto the west side, a *p for* Naphtali. NIH
48: 4 side unto the west side, a *p for* Manasseh. NIH
48: 5 side unto the west side, a *p for* Ephraim. NIH
48: 6 even unto the west side, a *p for* Reuben. NIH
48: 7 east side unto the west side, a *p for* Judah. NIH
48:18 the holy *p shall be* ten thousand eastward, NIH
48:18 be over against the oblation of the holy *p*; NIH
48:23 the west side, Benjamin *shall have* a *p*. NIH
48:24 unto the west side, Simeon *shall have* a *p*. NIH
48:25 east side unto the west side, Issachar a *p*. NIH
48:26 east side unto the west side, Zebulun a *p*. NIH
48:27 the east side unto the west side, Gad a *p*. NIH
Da 1: 8 himself with the **p of** the king's **meat**, 6598
1:13 that eat *of* the **p of** the king's **meat**: 6598
1:15 which did eat the **p of** the king's **meat**. 6598
1:16 Thus Melzar took away the **p of** their **meat**, 6598
4:15 *let* his **p** *be* with the beasts in the grass of 2508
4:23 *let* his **p** *be* with the beasts of the field, 2508
11:26 they that feed of the **p of** his **meat** shall 6598
Mic 2: 4 he hath changed the **p** of my people: 2506
Hab 1:16 because by them their **p** *is* fat, and 2506
Zec 2:12 the LORD shall inherit Judah his **p** in 2506
Mt 24:51 and appoint *him* his **p** with the hypocrites: *3313*
Lk 12:42 to give *them their* **p of meat** in due season? *4620*
12:46 will appoint *him* his **p** with the unbelievers. *3313*
15:12 give me the **p** of goods that falleth to *me*. *3313*

PORTIONS (16) [PORTION]

Dt 18: 8 They shall have like **p** to eat, beside that 2506
Jos 17: 5 there fell ten **p** to Manasseh, beside 2256
1Sa 1: 4 and to all her sons and her daughters, **p**: 4490
2Ch 31:19 to give **p** to all the males among the priests, 4490
Ne 8:10 send **p** unto *them* for whom nothing is 4490
8:12 to send **p**, and to make great mirth, because 4490
12:44 of the cities the **p** of the law for the priests 4521
12:47 gave the **p** of the singers and the porters, 4521
13:10 I perceived that the **p** of the Levites had not 4521
Est 9:19 good day, and *of* sending **p** one to another. 4490
9:22 of sending **p** one to another, and gifts to 4490
Eze 45: 7 length *shall be* over against one of the **p**, 2506
47:13 tribes of Israel: Joseph *shall have two* **p**. 2256
48:21 over against the **p** for the prince: 2506
48:29 and these *are* their **p**, saith the Lord GOD. 4256
Hos 5: 7 shall a month devour them with their **p**. 2506

POSSESS (106) [POSSESSED, POSSESSEST, POSSESSETH, POSSESSING, POSSESSION, POSSESSIONS, POSSESSOR, POSSESSORS]

Ge 22:17 thy seed shall **p** the gate of his enemies; 3423
24:60 let thy seed **p** the gate of those which hate 3423
Lev 20:24 their land, and I will give it unto you to **p** it, 3423
Nu 13:30 and said, Let us go up at once, and **p** it; 3423
14:24 whereinto he went; and his seed shall **p** it. 3423
27:11 next to him of his family, and he shall **p** it: 3423
33:53 for I have given you the land to **p** it. 3423
Dt 1: 8 **p** the land which the LORD sware unto 3423
1:21 **p** *it*, as the LORD God of thy fathers hath 3423
1:39 unto them will I give it, and they shall **p** it. 3423
2:24 begin to **p** *it*, and contend with him *in* 3423
2:31 begin to **p**, that *thou* mayest inherit his 3423
3:18 your God hath given you this land to **p** it: 3423
3:20 *until* they also **p** the land which the LORD 3423
4: 1 **p** the land which the LORD God of your 3423
4: 5 so in the land whither ye go to **p** it. 3423
4:14 them in the land whither ye go over to **p** it. 3423
4:22 but ye *shall* go over, and **p** that good land. 3423
4:26 land whereunto you go over Jordan to **p** it; 3423
5:31 *them* in the land which I give them to **p** it. 3423
5:33 *your* days in the land which ye shall **p**. 3423
6: 1 do *them* in the land whither ye go to **p** it: 3423
6:18 **p** the good land which the LORD sware 3423
7: 1 thee into the land whither thou goest to **p** it, 3423
8: 1 **p** the land which the LORD sware unto 3423
9: 1 to go in to **p** nations greater and 3423
9: 4 LORD hath brought me in to **p** this land: 3423
9: 5 of thine heart, dost thou go to **p** their land: 3423
9: 6 this good land to **p** it for thy righteousness; 3423
9:23 and **p** the land which I have given you; 3423
10:11 that they may go in and **p** the land, 3423
11: 8 ye may be strong, and go in and **p** the land, 3423
11: 8 and possess the land, whither ye go to **p** it; 3423
11:10 For the land, whither thou goest in to **p** it, 3423
11:11 the land, whither ye go to **p** it, *is* a land of 3423
11:23 ye shall **p** greater nations and mightier than 3423
11:29 in unto the land whither thou goest to **p** it, 3423
11:31 For ye shall pass over Jordan to go in to **p** 3423
11:31 and ye shall **p** it, and dwell therein. 3423
12: 1 God of thy fathers giveth thee to **p** it, 3423
12: 2 wherein the nations which ye shall **p** served 3423
12:29 whither thou goest to **p** them, and 3423
15: 4 God giveth thee *for* an inheritance to **p** it: 3423
17:14 shalt **p** it, and shalt dwell therein, and 3423
18:14 For these nations, which thou shalt **p**, 3423
19: 2 which the LORD thy God giveth thee to **p** 3423
19:14 that the LORD thy God giveth thee to **p** it. 3423
21: 1 the LORD thy God giveth thee to **p** it, 3423

Dt 23:20 to in the land whither thou goest to **p** it. 3423
25:19 God giveth thee *for* an inheritance to **p** it, 3423
28:21 off the land, whither thou goest to **p** it. 3423
28:63 from off the land whither thou goest to **p** it. 3423
30: 5 thy fathers possessed, and thou shalt **p** it; 3423
30:16 thee in the land whither thou goest to **p** it. 3423
30:18 whither thou passest over Jordan to go to **p** 3423
31: 3 from before thee, and thou shalt **p** them: 3423
31:13 the land whither ye go over Jordan to **p** it. 3423
32:47 the land, whither ye go over Jordan to **p** it. 3423
33:23 the LORD: **p** thou the west and the south. 3423
Jos 1:11 pass over this Jordan, to go in to **p** the land, 3423
1:11 the LORD your God giveth you to **p** it. 3423
18: 3 How long *are* you slack to go to **p** the land, 3423
23: 5 ye shall **p** their land, as the LORD your 3423
24: 4 I gave unto Esau mount Seir, to **p** it; 3423
24: 8 into your hand, that ye might **p** their land; 3423
Jdg 2: 6 man unto his inheritance to **p** the land. 3423
11:23 his people Israel, and shouldest thou **p** it? 3423
11:24 Wilt not thou **p** that which Chemosh thy 3423
11:24 which Chemosh thy god **giveth** thee **to p**? 3423
11:24 drive out from before us, them will we **p**. 3423
18: 9 slothful to go, *and* to enter to **p** the land. 3423
1Ki 21:18 of Naboth, whither he is gone down to **p** it. 3423
1Ch 28: 8 that ye may **p** *this* good land, and leave *it* 3423
Ezr 9:11 The land, *unto* which ye go to **p** it, 3423
Ne 9:15 promisedst them that *they* should go in to **p** 3423
9:23 their fathers, that *they* should go in to **p** *it*. 3423
Job 7: 3 So am I **made to p** months of vanity, and 5157
13:26 **makest** me **to p** the iniquities of my youth. 3423
Isa 14: 2 the house of Israel shall **p** them in the land 5157
14:21 *that* they do not rise, nor **p** the land, nor fill 3423
34:11 the cormorant and the bittern shall **p** it; 3423
34:17 they shall **p** it for ever, from generation to 3423
57:13 he that putteth his trust in me shall **p** 5157
61: 7 in their land they shall **p** the double: 3423
Jer 30: 3 I gave to their fathers, and they shall **p** it. 3423
Eze 7:24 the heathen, and they shall **p** their houses: 3423
33:25 and shed blood: and shall ye **p** the land? 3423
33:26 neighbour's wife: and shall ye **p** the land? 3423
35:10 countries shall be mine, and we will **p** it; 3423
36:12 they shall **p** thee, and thou shalt be their 3423
Da 7:18 **p** the kingdom for ever, even for ever and 2631
Hos 9: 6 *places* for their silver, nettles shall **p** them: 3423
Am 2:10 to **p** the land of the Amorite. 3423
9:12 That they may **p** the remnant of Edom, and 3423
Ob 1:17 the house of Jacob shall **p** their 3423
1:19 *they of* the south shall **p** the mount of Esau; 3423
1:19 they shall **p** the fields of Ephraim, and 3423
1:19 of Samaria: and Benjamin *shall* **p** Gilead. NIH
1:20 of Israel *shall* **p** that of the Canaanites, NIH
1:20 in Sepharad, shall **p** the cities of the south. 3423
Hab 1: 6 to **p** the dwelling places *that are* not theirs. 3423
Zep 2: 9 and the remnant of my people shall **p** them. 5157
Zec 8:12 I will **cause** the remnant of this people **to p** 5157
Lk 18:12 in the week, I give tithes of all that I **p**. *2932*
21:19 In your patience **p** ye your souls. *2932*
1Th 4: 4 know how to **p** his vessel in sanctification *2932*

POSSESSED (39) [POSSESS]
Nu 21:24 **p** his land from Arnon unto Jabbok, 3423
21:35 none left him alive: and they **p** his land. 3423
Dt 3:12 *which* we **p** at that time, from Aroer, 3423
4:47 they **p** his land, and the land of Og king of 3423
30: 5 bring thee into the land which thy fathers **p**, 3423
Jos 1:15 they also have **p** the land which 3423
12: 1 **p** their land on the *other* side Jordan toward 3423
13: 1 there remaineth *yet* very much land to be **p**. 3423
19:47 **p** it, and dwelt therein, and called Leshem, 3423
21:43 and they **p** it, and dwelt therein. 3423
22: 9 of their possession, whereof they were **p**, 270
Jdg 3:13 smote Israel, and **p** the city of palm trees. 3423
11:21 so Israel **p** all the land of the Amorites, 3423
11:22 they **p** all the coasts of the Amorites, 3423
2Ki 17:24 they **p** Samaria, and dwelt in the cities 3423
Ne 9:22 so they **p** the land of Sihon, and the land of 3423
9:24 So the children went in and **p** the land, and 3423
9:25 a fat land, and **p** houses full *of* all goods, 3423
Ps 139:13 For thou hast **p** my reins: thou hast covered 7069
Pr 8:22 The LORD **p** me *in* the beginning of his 7069
Isa 63:18 The people of thy holiness have **p** *it* but 3423
Jer 32:15 and vineyards shall be **p** again in this land. 7069
32:23 they came in, and **p** it; but they obeyed not 3423
Da 7:22 the time came that the saints **p** 2631
Mt 4:24 and those which were **p with devils**, and *1139*
8:16 unto him many *that were* **p with devils**: *1139*
8:28 there met him two **p with devils**, *1139*
8:33 what was befallen to the **p of the devils**. *1139*
9:32 brought to him a dumb man **p with a devil**. *1139*
12:22 was brought unto him **one p with a devil**, *1139*
Mk 1:32 and them that were **p with devils**. *1139*
5:15 and see him that was **p with the devil**, and *1139*
5:16 it befell to him that was **p with the devil**, *1139*
5:18 he that had been **p with the devil** prayed *1139*
Lk 8:36 he that was **p of the devils** was healed. *1139*
Ac 4:32 of the *things* which he **p** was his own; *5225*
8: 7 came out of many that were **p** *with them*: *2192*
16:16 a certain damsel **p with** a spirit of *2192*
1Co 7:30 and they that buy, as though they **p** not; *2722*

POSSESSEST (1) [POSSESS]
Dt 26: 1 and **p** it, and dwellest therein; 3423

POSSESSETH (2) [POSSESS]
Nu 36: 8 that **p** an inheritance in any tribe of 3423
Lk 12:15 in the abundance of the *things* which he **p**. *5225*

POSSESSING (1) [POSSESS]
2Co 6:10 as having nothing, and *yet* **p** all *things*. *2722*

POSSESSION (105) [POSSESS]
Ge 17: 8 all the land of Canaan, for an everlasting **p**; 272
23: 4 give me a **p** of a buryingplace with you, 272
23: 9 it me for a **p** of a buryingplace amongst you. 272
23:18 Unto Abraham for a **p** in the presence of 4736
23:20 were made sure unto Abraham for a **p** of a 272
26:14 For he had **p** of flocks, and possession of 4735
26:14 and **p** of herds, and great store of servants: 4735
36:43 to their habitations in the land of their **p**: 272
47:11 and gave them a **p** in the land of Egypt, 272
47:27 they **had p** therein, and grew, and 270
48: 4 to thy seed after thee *for* an everlasting **p**. 272
49:30 Ephron the Hittite for a **p** of a buryingplace. 272
50:13 which Abraham bought with the field for a **p** 272
Lev 14:34 which I give to you for a **p**, and I put 272
14:34 of leprosy in a house of the land of your **p**; 272
25:10 and ye shall return every man unto his **p**, and 272
25:13 jubile ye shall return every man unto his **p**. 272
25:24 in all the land of your **p** ye shall grant a 272
25:25 hath sold away *some* of his **p**, and *if any of* 272
25:27 he sold it; that he may return unto his **p**. 272
25:28 it shall go out, and he shall return unto his **p**. 272
25:32 *and* the houses of the cities of their **p**, 272
25:33 the house that was sold, and the city of his **p**, 272
25:33 *are* their **p** among the children of Israel. 272
25:34 may not be sold; for it *is* their perpetual **p**. 272
25:41 and unto the **p** of his fathers shall he return. 272
25:45 begat in your land: and they shall be your **p**. 272
25:46 children after you, to inherit *them for* a **p**; 272
27:16 the LORD *some part* of a field of his **p**, 272
27:21 the **p** thereof shall be the priest's. 272
27:22 which *is* not of the fields of his **p**; 272
27:24 *even* to him to whom the **p** of the land *did* 272
27:28 of man and beast, and of the field of his **p**, 272
Nu 24:18 Edom shall be a **p**, Seir also shall be a 3424
24:18 Seir also shall be a **p** for his enemies; 3424
26:56 According to the lot shall the **p** thereof be 5159
27: 4 a **p** among the brethren of our father. 272
27: 7 thou shalt surely give them a **p** of an 272
32: 5 this land be given unto thy servants for a **p**, 272
32:22 this land shall be your **p** before the LORD. 272
32:29 ye shall give them the land of Gilead for a **p**: 272
32:32 that the **p** of our inheritance on *this* side 272
35: 2 the inheritance of their **p** cities to dwell in; 272
35: 8 *shall be* of the **p** of the children of Israel: 272
35:28 the slayer shall return into the land of his **p**. 272
Dt 2: 5 I have given mount Seir unto Esau *for* a **p**. 3425
2: 9 for I will not give thee of their land *for* a **p**; 3425
2: 9 given Ar unto the children of Lot *for* a **p**. 3425
2:12 as Israel did unto the land of his **p**, 3425
2:19 the land of the children of Ammon *any* **p**; 3425
2:19 given it unto the children of Lot *for* a **p**. 3425
3:20 *then* shall ye return every man unto his **p**, 3425
11: 6 and all the substance that *was* in their **p**, 7272
32:49 I give unto the children of Israel for a **p**: 272
Jos 1:15 ye shall return unto the land of your **p**, and 3425
12: 6 LORD gave it *for* a **p** unto the Reubenites, 3425
12: 7 Israel *for* a **p** according to their divisions; 3425

P

Jos 13:29 *this* was *the p* of the half tribe of NIH
21:12 they to Caleb the son of Jephunneh for his **p**. 272
21:41 All the cities of the Levites within the **p** of 272
22: 4 unto your tents, *and* unto the land of your **p**, 272
22: 7 of Manasseh Moses had given *p* in Bashan: NIH
22: 9 to the land of their **p**, whereof they were 272
22:19 if the land of your **p** *be* unclean, *then* pass ye 272
22:19 pass ye over unto the land of the **p** of 272
22:19 tabernacle dwelleth, and **take p** among us: 270
1Ki 21:15 **take p** of the vineyard of Naboth 3423
21:16 of Naboth the Jezreelite, to **take p** of it. 3423
21:19 Hast thou killed, and also **taken p**? 3423
1Ch 28: 1 over all the substance and **p** of the king, 4735
2Ch 11:14 For the Levites left their suburbs and their **p**, 272
20:11 reward us, to come to cast us out of thy **p**, 3425
31: 1 every man to his **p**, into their own cities. 272
Ne 11: 3 Judah dwelt every one in his **p** in their cities, 272
Ps 2: 8 and the uttermost parts of the earth *for* thy **p**. 272
44: 3 For they **got** not the land **in p** by their own 3423
69:35 that they may dwell there, and **have** it **in p**. 3423
83:12 **take** to ourselves the houses of God **in p**. 3423
Pr 28:10 but the upright shall have good *things* in **p**. 5157
Isa 14:23 I will also make it a **p** for the bittern, and 4180
Eze 11:15 the LORD: unto us is this land given in **p**. 4181
25: 4 deliver thee to the men of the east for a **p**, 4181
25:10 the Ammonites, and will give them in **p**, 4181
36: 2 even the ancient high places are ours in **p**: 4181
36: 3 that ye might be a **p** unto the residue of 4181
36: 5 which have appointed my land into their **p** 4181
44:28 ye shall give them no **p** in Israel: I *am* their 272
44:28 them no possession in Israel: I *am* their **p**. 272
45: 5 for themselves, for a **p** *for* twenty chambers. 272
45: 6 ye shall appoint the **p** of the city five 272
45: 7 of the holy *portion,* and of the **p** of the city, 272
45: 7 the holy *portion,* and before the **p** of the city, 272
45: 8 In the land shall be his **p** in Israel: and 272
46:16 his sons'; it *shall be* their **p** by inheritance. 272
46:18 by oppression to thrust them out of their **p**; 272
46:18 give his sons inheritance out of his own **p**: 272
46:18 be not scattered every man from his **p**. 272
48:20 oblation foursquare, with the **p** of the city. 272
48:21 and of the **p** of the city, over against the five 272
48:22 Moreover from the **p** of the Levites, *and* 272
48:22 of the Levites, *and* from the **p** of the city, 272
Ac 5: 1 with Sapphira his wife, sold a **p**, *2933*
7: 5 that *he* would give it to him for a **p**, *2697*
7:45 in with Jesus into the **p** of the Gentiles, *2697*
Eph 1:14 until the redemption of the **purchased p**, *4047*

POSSESSIONS (12) [POSSESS]

Ge 34:10 and trade you therein, and **get** you **p** therein. 270
Nu 32:30 they shall **have p** among you in the land of 270
1Sa 25: 2 a man in Maon, whose **p** *were* in Carmel; 4639
1Ch 7:28 their **p** and habitations *were,* Beth-el and 272
9: 2 Now the first inhabitants that *dwelt* in their **p** 272
2Ch 32:29 and **p** of flocks and herds in abundance: 4735
Ecc 2: 7 also I had great **p** of great and small cattle 4735
Ob 1:17 the house of Jacob shall possess their **p**. 4180
Mt 19:22 he went away sorrowful: for he had great **p**. *2933*
Mk 10:22 and went away grieved: for he had great **p**. *2933*
Ac 2:45 And sold their **p** and goods, and *2933*
28: 7 In the same quarters were **p** of the chief *5564*

POSSESSOR (2) [POSSESS]

Ge 14:19 the most high God, **p** of heaven and earth: 7069
14:22 most high God, the **p** of heaven and earth, 7069

POSSESSORS (2) [POSSESS]

Zec 11: 5 Whose **p** slay them, and hold themselves 7069
Ac 4:34 for as many as were **p** of lands or *2935*

POSSIBLE (15) [IMPOSSIBLE, UNPOSSIBLE]

Mt 19:26 is unpossible; but with God all *things* are **p**. *1415*
24:24 insomuch that, if *it were* **p**, *they shall* *1415*
26:39 and prayed, saying, O my Father, if it be **p**, *1415*
Mk 9:23 all *things are* **p** to him that believeth. *1415*
10:27 not with God: for with God all *things* are **p**. *1415*
13:22 and wonders, to seduce, if *it were* **p**, *1415*
14:35 on the ground, and prayed that, if it were **p**, *1415*
14:36 Abba, Father, all *things are* **p** unto thee; *1415*
Lk 18:27 *are* unpossible with men are **p** with God. *1415*
Ac 2:24 it was not **p** that he should be holden of it. *1415*
20:16 for he hasted, if it were **p** for him, to be at *1415*
27:39 if it were **p**, to thrust in the ship. *1410*
Ro 12:18 If *it be* **p**, as much as lieth in you, *1415*
Gal 4:15 for I bear you record, that if *it had been* **p**, *1415*
Heb 10: 4 For *it is* **not p** that the blood of bulls and *102*

POST (11) [POSTS]

Ex 12: 7 and on the **upper door p** of the houses, 4947
21: 6 bring him to the door, or unto the **door p**; 4201
1Sa 1: 9 Now Eli the priest sat upon a seat by a **p** of 4201
Job 9:25 Now my days are swifter than a **p**: they flee 7323
Jer 51:31 One **p** shall run to meet another, and 7323
Eze 40:14 even unto the **p** of the court round about 352
40:16 and upon *each* **p** *were* palm trees. 352
40:48 measured *each* **p** of the porch, five cubits on 352
41: 3 measured the **p** of the door, two cubits; 352
43: 8 their **p** by my posts, and the wall between 4201
46: 2 shall stand by the **p** of the gate, and 4201

POSTERITY (9)

Ge 45: 7 God sent me before you to preserve you a **p** 7611
Nu 9:10 of your **p** shall be unclean by reason of a 1755
1Ki 16: 3 I will take away the **p** of Baasha, and 310
16: 3 posterity of Baasha, and the **p** of his house; 310
21:21 will take away thy **p**, and will cut off from 310
Ps 49:13 yet their **p** approve their sayings. Selah. 310
109:13 Let his **p** be cut off; *and* in the generation 319
Da 11: 4 not to his **p**, nor according to his dominion 319
Am 4: 2 away with hooks, and your **p** with fishhooks. 319

POSTS (42) [POST]

Ex 12: 7 strike *it* on the two **side p** and on the upper 4201
12:22 the two **side p** with the blood that *is* in 4201
12:23 on the two **side p**, the LORD will pass 4201
Dt 6: 9 thou shalt write them upon the **p** of thy 4201
11:20 thou shalt write them upon the **door p** of 4201
Jdg 16: 3 the two **p**, and went away with them, bar 4201
1Ki 6:31 *and* **side p** *were* a fifth *part of the wall.* 4201
6:33 he for the door of the temple **p** of olive tree, 4201
7: 5 all the doors and **p** *were* square, *with* 4201
2Ch 3: 7 the **p**, and the walls thereof, and the doors 5592
30: 6 So the **p** went with the letters from the king 7323
30:10 So the **p** passed from city to city through 7323
Est 3:13 the letters were sent by **p** into all the king's 7323
3:15 The **p** went out, being hastened by 7323
8:10 sent letters by **p** on horseback, *and* 7323
8:14 *So* the **p** that rode upon mules *and* 7323
Pr 8:34 at my gates, waiting at the **p** of my doors. 4201
Isa 6: 4 the **p** of the door moved at the voice of him 520
57: 8 the **p** hast thou set up thy remembrance: 4201
Eze 40: 9 the **p** thereof, two cubits; and the porch of 352
40:10 the **p** had one measure on this side and 352
40:14 He made also **p** *of* threescore cubits, 352
40:16 to their **p** within the gate round about, 352
40:21 the **p** thereof and the arches thereof were 352
40:24 he measured the **p** thereof and the arches 352
40:26 and another on that side, upon the **p** thereof. 352
40:29 the **p** thereof, and the arches thereof, 352
40:31 and palm trees *were* upon the **p** thereof: 352
40:33 and the **p** thereof, and the arches thereof, 352
40:34 palm trees *were* upon the **p** thereof, on this 352
40:36 the **p** thereof, and the arches thereof, and 352
40:37 the **p** thereof *were* toward the utter court; 352
40:37 palm trees *were* upon the **p** thereof, on this 352
40:38 the entries thereof *were* by the **p** of the gates, 352
40:49 *there were* pillars by the **p**, one on this side, 352
41: 1 measured the **p**, six cubits broad on the one 352
41:16 The **door p**, and the narrow windows, and 5592
41:21 The **p** of the temple *were* squared, *and* 4201
43: 8 their post by my **p**, and the wall between 4201
45:19 put *it* upon the **p** of the house, and upon 4201
45:19 upon the **p** of the gate of the inner court. 4201
Am 9: 1 the lintel of the door, that the **p** may shake: 5592

POT (22) [POTS, POTSHERD, POTSHERDS, POTTER, POTTER'S, POTTERS, POTTERS', WASHPOT, WATERPOT, WATERPOTS]

Ex 16:33 Take a **p**, and put an omer full of manna 6803
Lev 6:28 if it be sodden in a brasen **p**, it shall be both 3627
Jdg 6:19 he put the broth in a **p**, and brought *it* out 6517
1Sa 2:14 *it* into the pan, or kettle, or caldron, or **p**; 6517
2Ki 4: 2 not any thing in the house, save a **p** of oil. 610
4:38 Set on the great **p**, and seethe pottage for 5518
4:39 came and shred *them* into the **p** of pottage: 5518
4:40 O thou man of God, *there is* death in the **p**. 5518
4:41 he cast *it* into the **p**; and he said, Pour out 5518

2Ki 4:41 may eat. And there was no harm in the **p**. 5518
Job 41:20 as *out of* a seething **p** or caldron. 1731
41:31 He maketh the deep to boil like a **p**: 5518
41:31 he maketh the sea like a **p of ointment**. 4841
Pr 17: 3 The **fining p** *is* for silver, and the furnace 4715
27:21 *As* the **fining p** for silver, and the furnace 4715
Ecc 7: 6 For as the crackling of thorns under a **p**, so 5518
Jer 1:13 I said, I see a seething **p**; and the face 5518
Eze 24: 3 Set on a **p**, set *it* on, and also pour water 5518
24: 6 to the **p** whose scum *is* therein, and 5518
Mic 3: 3 as for the **p**, and as flesh within the caldron. 5518
Zec 14:21 every **p** in Jerusalem and in Judah shall be 5518
Heb 9: 4 wherein *was* the golden **p** that had manna, *4713*

POTENTATE (1)
1Ti 6:15 *who is* the blessed and only **P**, the King of *1413*

POTIPHAR (2)
Ge 37:36 the Medanites sold him into Egypt unto **P**, 6318
39: 1 **P**, an officer of Pharaoh, captain of 6318

POTI-PHERAH (3)
Ge 41:45 Asenath the daughter of **P** priest of On. 6319
41:50 which Asenath the daughter of **P** priest of 6319
46:20 which Asenath the daughter of **P** priest of 6319

POTS (15) [POT]
Ex 16: 3 when we sat by the flesh **p**, *and* when we 5518
38: 3 the **p**, and the shovels, and the basons, 5518
Lev 11:35 *whether it be* oven, or **ranges for p**, 3600
1Ki 7:45 the **p**, and the shovels, and the basons: and 5518
2Ki 25:14 the **p**, and the shovels, and the snuffers, 5518
2Ch 4:11 Huram made the **p**, and the shovels, and 5518
4:16 The **p** also, and the shovels, and 5518
35:13 the *other* holy *offerings* sod they in **p**, and 5518
Ps 58: 9 Before your **p** can feel the thorns, he shall 5518
68:13 Though ye have lien among the **p**, *yet shall* 8240
81: 6 his hands were delivered from the **p**. 1731
Jer 35: 5 the house of the Rechabites **p** full *of* wine, 1375
Zec 14:20 the **p** in the LORD'S house shall be like 5518
Mk 7: 4 and **p**, brasen vessels, and of tables. *3582*
7: 8 of men, *as* the washing of **p** and cups: *3582*

POTSHERD (4) [POT]
Job 2: 8 he took him a **p** to scrape himself withal; 2789
Ps 22:15 My strength is dried up like a **p**; and 2789
Pr 26:23 a wicked heart *are like* a **p** covered with 2789
Isa 45: 9 *Let* the **p** *strive* with the potsherds of 2789

POTSHERDS (1) [POT]
Isa 45: 9 *Let* the potsherd *strive* with the **p** of 2789

POTTAGE (7)
Ge 25:29 Jacob sod **p**: and Esau came from the field, 5138
25:30 with that same red **p**; for I *am* faint: NIH
25:34 Jacob gave Esau bread and **p** of lentiles; 5138
2Ki 4:38 and seethe **p** for the sons of the prophets. 5138
4:39 and came and shred *them* into the pot of **p**: 5138
4:40 as they were eating of the **p**, that they cried 5138
Hag 2:12 or **p**, or wine, or oil, or any meat, shall it be 5138

POTTER (10) [POT]
Isa 41:25 as *upon* morter, and as the **p** treadeth clay. 3335
64: 8 we *are* the clay, and thou our **p**; and we all 3335
Jer 18: 4 of clay was marred in the hand of the **p**: 3335
18: 4 as seemed good to the **p** to make *it*. 3335
18: 6 of Israel, cannot I do with you as this **p**? 3335
La 4: 2 the work of the hands of the **p**! 3335
Zec 11:13 LORD said unto me, Cast it unto the **p**: 3335
11:13 cast them to the **p** *in* the house of 3335
Ro 9:21 Hath not the **p** power over the clay, of *2763*
Rev 2:27 as the vessels of a **p** *shall* they be broken to *2764*

POTTER'S (10) [POT]
Ps 2: 9 thou shalt dash them in pieces like a **p** 3335
Isa 29:16 down shall be esteemed as the **p** clay: 3335
Jer 18: 2 go down *to* the **p** house, and there I will 3335
18: 3 I went down *to* the **p** house, and behold, 3335
18: 6 as the clay *is* in the **p** hand, so *are* ye in 3335
19: 1 Go and get a **p** earthen bottle, and *take* of 3335
19:11 this city, as *one* breaketh a **p** vessel, 3335
Da 2:41 and toes, part of **p** clay, and part of iron, 6353
Mt 27: 7 and bought with them the **p** field, to bury *2763*
27:10 And gave them for the **p** field, as the Lord *2763*

POTTERS (1) [POT]
1Ch 4:23 These *were* the **p**, and those that dwelt 3335

POTTERS' (1) [POT]
Isa 30:14 he shall break it as the breaking of the **p** 3335

POUND (10) [POUNDS]
1Ki 10:17 three **p** *of* gold went to one shield: 4488
Ezr 2:69 five thousand **p** *of* silver, and one hundred 4488
Ne 7:71 two thousand and two hundred **p** *of* silver. 4488
7:72 two thousand **p** *of* silver, and threescore 4488
Lk 19:16 saying, Lord, thy **p** hath gained ten pounds. *3414*
19:18 Lord, thy **p** hath gained five pounds. *3414*
19:20 saying, Lord, behold, *here is* thy **p**, *3414*
19:24 Take from him the **p**, and give *it* to him that *3414*
Jn 12: 3 Then took Mary a **p** of ointment of *3046*
19:39 and aloes, about an hundred **p** *weight*. *3046*

POUNDS (5) [POUND]
Lk 19:13 and delivered them ten **p**, and said unto *3414*
19:16 saying, Lord, thy pound hath gained ten **p**. *3414*
19:18 saying, Lord, thy pound hath gained five **p**. *3414*
19:24 and give *it* to him that hath ten **p**. *3414*
19:25 they said unto him, Lord, he hath ten **p**.) *3414*

POUR (63) [POURED, POUREDST, POURETH, POURING]
Ex 4: 9 **p** *it upon* the dry *land*: and the water which 8210
29: 7 and **p** *it* upon his head, and anoint him. 3332
29:12 **p** all the blood beside the bottom of 8210
30: 9 neither shall ye **p** drink offering thereon. 5258
Lev 2: 1 he shall **p** oil upon it, and put frankincense 3332
2: 6 shalt part it in pieces, and **p** oil thereon: 3332
4: 7 shall **p** all the blood of the bullock at 8210
4:18 shall **p out** all the blood at the bottom of 8210
4:25 shall **p out** his blood at the bottom of 8210
4:30 shall **p out** all the blood thereof at 8210
4:34 shall **p out** all the blood thereof at 8210
14:15 and **p** *it* into the palm of his own left hand: 3332
14:18 **p** upon the head of him that is to be 5414
14:26 the priest shall **p** of the oil into the palm of 3332
14:41 they shall **p out** the dust that they scrape 8210
17:13 he shall even **p out** the blood thereof, and 8210
Nu 5:15 he shall **p** no oil upon it, nor put 3332
24: 7 He shall **p** the water out of his buckets, and 5140
Dt 12:16 ye shall **p** it upon the earth as water. 8210
12:24 thou shalt **p** it upon the earth as water. 8210
15:23 thou shalt **p** it upon the ground as water. 8210
Jdg 6:20 *them* upon this rock, and **p out** the broth. 8210
1Ki 18:33 **p** *it* on the burnt sacrifice, and on the wood. 3332
2Ki 4: 4 shalt **p out** into all those vessels, and 3332
4:41 he said, **P out** for the people, that they may 3332
9: 3 **p** *it* on his head, and say, Thus saith 3332
Job 36:27 they **p down** rain according to the vapour 2212
Ps 42: 4 When I remember these *things*, I **p out** my 8210
62: 8 ye people, **p out** your heart before him: 8210
69:24 **P out** thine indignation upon them, and 8210
79: 6 **P out** thy wrath upon the heathen that have 8210
Pr 1:23 behold, I will **p out** my spirit unto you, 5042
Isa 44: 3 For I will **p** water upon *him that is* thirsty, 3332
44: 3 floods upon the dry *ground*: I will **p** my 3332
45: 8 and let the skies **p down** righteousness: 5140
Jer 6:11 I *will* **p** *it* **out** upon the children abroad, and 8210
7:18 to **p out** drink offerings unto other gods, 5258
10:25 **P out** thy fury upon the heathen that know 8210
14:16 for I will **p** their wickedness upon them. 8210
18:21 **p out** their *blood* by the force of the sword; 5064
44:17 to **p out** drink offerings unto her, as we 5258
44:18 to **p out** drink offerings unto her, we have 5258
44:19 **p out** drink offerings unto her, without our 5258
44:25 and to **p out** drink offerings unto her: 5258
La 2:19 **p out** thine heart like water before the face 8210
Eze 7: 8 Now will I shortly **p out** my fury upon 8210
14:19 **p out** my fury upon it in blood, to cut off 8210
20: 8 I said, *I* will **p out** my fury upon them, 8210
20:13 *I* would **p out** my fury upon them in 8210
20:21 I said, *I* would **p out** my fury upon them, 8210
21:31 I will **p out** mine indignation upon thee, 8210
24: 3 on a pot, set *it* on, and also **p** water into it: 3332
30:15 I will **p** my fury upon Sin, the strength of 8210
Hos 5:10 I will **p out** my wrath upon them like 8210
Joel 2:28 that I will **p out** my spirit upon all flesh; 8210
2:29 in those days will I **p out** my spirit. 8210
Mic 1: 6 I will **p down** the stones thereof into 5064
Zep 3: 8 to **p** upon them mine indignation, *even* all 8210

Zec 12:10 I will **p** upon the house of David, and 8210
Mal 3:10 and **p** you **out** a blessing, 7324
Ac 2:17 I will **p out** of my Spirit upon all flesh: *1632*
2:18 on my handmaidens I will **p out** in those *1632*
Rev 16: 1 **p out** the vials of the wrath of God upon *1632*
16: 2 and **p out** his vial upon the earth; *1632*
16: 3 And the second angel **p out** his vial upon *1632*
16: 4 And the third angel **p out** his vial upon *1632*
16: 8 And the fourth angel **p out** his vial upon *1632*
16:10 And the fifth angel **p out** his vial upon *1632*
16:12 And the sixth angel **p out** his vial upon *1632*
16:17 And the seventh angel **p out** his vial into *1632*

POURED (84) [POUR]

Ge 28:18 up *for* a pillar, and **p** oil upon the top of it. 3332
35:14 he **p** a drink offering thereon, and 5258
35:14 drink offering thereon, and he **p** oil thereon. 3332
Ex 9:33 and the rain was not **p** upon the earth. 5413
30:32 Upon man's flesh shall it not be **p**, 3251
Lev 4:12 where the ashes are **p out**, and burn him on 8211
4:12 where the ashes are **p out** shall he be burnt. 8211
8:12 he **p** of the anointing oil upon Aaron's 3332
8:15 **p** the blood at the bottom of the altar, and 3332
9: 9 **p out** the blood at the bottom of the altar: 3332
21:10 upon whose head the anointing oil was **p**, 3332
Nu 28: 7 **cause** the strong wine **to be p** unto 5258
Dt 12:27 the blood of thy sacrifices shall be **p out** 8210
1Sa 1:15 but have **p out** my soul before the LORD. 8210
7: 6 **p** *it* **out** before the LORD, and fasted on 8210
10: 1 **p** *it* upon his head, and kissed him, and 3332
2Sa 13: 9 she took a pan, and **p** *them* **out** before him; 3332
23:16 drink thereof, but **p** it **out** unto the LORD. 5258
1Ki 13: 3 the ashes that *are* upon it shall be **p out**. 8210
13: 5 *was* rent, and the ashes **p out** from the altar, 8210
2Ki 3:11 which **p** water on the hands of Elijah. 3332
4: 5 brought *the vessels* to her; and she **p out**. 3332
4:40 So they **p out** for the men to eat. And it 3332
9: 6 he **p** the oil on his head, and said unto him, 3332
16:13 **p** his drink offering, and sprinkled 5258
1Ch 11:18 not drink *of* it, but **p** it **out** to the LORD, 5258
2Ch 12: 7 my wrath shall not be **p out** upon 5413
34:21 wrath of the LORD that is **p out** upon us, 5413
34:25 my wrath shall be **p out** upon this place, 5413
Job 3:24 and my roarings are **p out** like the waters. 5413
10:10 Hast thou not **p** me **out** as milk, and 5413
29: 6 and the rock **p** me **out** rivers of oil; 6694
30:16 now my soul is **p out** upon me; the days of 8210
Ps 22:14 I am **p out** like water, and all my bones are 8210
45: 2 grace is **p** into thy lips: therefore God hath 3332
77:17 The clouds **p out** water: the skies sent out a 2229
142: 2 I **p out** my complaint before him; I shewed 8210
SS 1: 3 ointments thy name *is as* ointment **p forth**, 7324
Isa 26:16 they **p out** a prayer *when* thy chastening 6694
29:10 For the LORD hath **p out** upon you 5258
32:15 Until the spirit be **p** upon us from on high, 6168
42:25 Therefore he hath **p** upon him the fury of 8210
53:12 because he hath **p out** his soul unto death: 6168
57: 6 even to them hast thou **p** a drink offering, 8210
Jer 7:20 and my fury *shall be* **p out** upon this place, 5413
19:13 have **p out** drink offerings unto other gods. 5258
32:29 **p out** drink offerings unto other gods, 5258
42:18 my fury hath been **p forth** upon 5413
42:18 so shall my fury be **p forth** upon you, 5413
44: 6 my fury and mine anger was **p forth**, 5413
44:19 **p out** drink offerings unto her, did we make 5258
La 2: 4 of Zion: he **p out** his fury like fire. 8210
2:11 are troubled, my liver is **p** upon the earth, 8210
2:12 when their soul was **p out** into their 8210
4: 1 the stones of the sanctuary are **p out** in 8210
4:11 he hath **p out** his fierce anger, and 8210
Eze 16:36 Because thy filthiness was **p out**, and 8210
20:28 and **p out** there their drink offerings. 5258
20:33 and with fury **p out**, will I rule over you: 8210
20:34 a stretched out arm, and with fury **p out**. 8210
22:22 ye shall know that I the LORD have **p out** 8210
22:31 Therefore have I **p out** mine indignation 8210
23: 8 and **p** their whoredom upon her. 8210
24: 7 she **p** it not upon the ground, to cover it 8210
36:18 Wherefore I **p** my fury upon them for 8210
39:29 for I have **p out** my spirit upon the house of 8210
Da 9:11 therefore the curse is **p** upon us, and 5413
9:27 that determined shall be **p** upon 5413
Mic 1: 4 as the waters *that are* **p** down a steep place. 5064
Na 1: 6 his fury is **p out** like fire, and the rocks are 5413
Zep 1:17 their blood shall be **p out** as dust, and 8210
Mt 26: 7 and **p** *it* on his head, as he sat at meat. *2708*
26:12 For in that she hath **p** this ointment on my *906*
Mk 14: 3 and she brake the box, and **p** *it* on his head. *2708*
Jn 2:15 and **p out** the changers' money, and *1632*
Ac 10:45 that on the Gentiles also was **p out** the gift *1632*
Rev 14:10 which is **p out** without mixture into the cup *2767*

POUREDST (1) [POUR]

Eze 16:15 **p out** thy fornications on every one that 8210

POURETH (11) [POUR]

Job 12:21 He **p** contempt upon princes, and 8210
16:13 he **p out** my gall upon the ground. 8210
16:20 *but* mine eye **p out** *tears* unto God. 1811
Ps 75: 8 is full *of* mixture; and he **p out** of the same: 5064
102: T and **p out** his complaint before the LORD. 8210
107:40 He **p** contempt upon princes, and 8210
Pr 15: 2 but the mouth of fools **p out** foolishness. 5042
15:28 the mouth of the wicked **p out** evil *things.* 5042
Am 5: 8 and **p** them **out** upon the face of the earth: 8210
9: 6 and **p** them **out** upon the face of the earth: 8210
Jn 13: 5 he **p** water into a bason, and began to wash *906*

POURING (2) [POUR]

Eze 9: 8 in thy **p out** of thy fury upon Jerusalem? 8210
Lk 10:34 **p in** oil and wine, and set him on his own *2022*

POURTRAY (1) [POURTRAYED]

Eze 4: 1 and **p** upon it *the* city, *even* Jerusalem: 2710

POURTRAYED (3) [POURTRAY]

Eze 8:10 of Israel, **p** upon the wall round about. 2707
23:14 for when she saw men **p** upon the wall, 2707
23:14 the images of the Chaldeans **p** with 2710

POVERTY (15) [IMPOVERISH, IMPOVERISHED, POOR, POORER, POOREST]

Ge 45:11 and all that thou hast, **come to p**. 3423
Pr 6:11 So shall thy **p** come as one that travelleth, 7389
10:15 the destruction of the poor *is* their **p**. 7389
11:24 more than is meet, but *it tendeth* to **p**. 4270
13:18 **P** and shame *shall be to* him that refuseth 7389
20:13 Love not sleep, lest thou **come to p**; 3423
23:21 and the glutton shall **come to p**: 3423
24:34 So shall thy **p** come *as* one that travelleth; 7389
28:19 after vain *persons* shall have **p** enough. 7389
28:22 considereth not that **p** shall come *upon* him. 2639
30: 8 give me neither **p** nor riches; feed me with 7389
31: 7 forget his **p**, and remember his misery no 7389
2Co 8: 2 their deep **p** abounded unto the riches of *4432*
8: 9 that ye through his **p** might be rich. *4432*
Rev 2: 9 and tribulation, and **p**, (but thou art rich) *4432*

POWDER (8) [POWDERS]

Ex 32:20 ground *it* to **p**, and strawed *it* upon 1854
Dt 28:24 The LORD shall make the rain of thy land **p** 80
2Ki 23: 6 stampt *it* small to **p**, and cast the powder 6083
23: 6 cast the **p** thereof upon the graves of 6083
23:15 *and* stampt *it* small to **p**, and burnt 6083
2Ch 34: 7 had beaten the graven images into **p**, and 1854
Mt 21:44 it shall fall, it will **grind** him **to p**. *3039*
Lk 20:18 it shall fall, it will **grind** him **to p**. *3039*

POWDERS (1) [POWDER]

SS 3: 6 and frankincense, with all **p** of the merchant? 81

POWER (272) [POWERFUL, POWERS]

Ge 31: 6 ye know that with all my **p** I have served 3581
31:29 It is in the **p** of my hand to do you hurt: but 410
32:28 for **as a prince hast** thou **p** with God and 8280
49: 3 of dignity, and the excellency of **p**: 5794
Ex 9:16 I raised thee up, for to shew *in* thee my **p**; 3581
15: 6 O LORD, is become glorious in **p**: 3581
21: 8 unto a strange nation he shall **have** no **p**, 4910
32:11 forth out of the land of Egypt with great **p**, 3581
Lev 26:19 I will break the pride of your **p**; and I will 5797
26:37 ye shall have no **p to stand** before your 8617
Nu 14:17 beseech thee, let the **p** of my Lord be great, 3581
22:38 have I now **any p at all** to say any 3201+3201
Dt 4:37 in his sight with his mighty **p** out of Egypt; 3581
8:17 My **p** and the might of mine hand hath 3581
8:18 for *it is* he that giveth thee **p** to get wealth, 3581
9:29 which thou broughtest out by thy mighty **p** 3581
32:36 when he seeth that *their* **p** is gone, and 3027

Jos	8:20	they had no **p** to flee this way or	3027+871.1
	17:17	Thou *art* a great people, and hast great **p**:	3581
1Sa	9: 1	of Aphiah, a Benjamite, a mighty *man* of **p**.	2428
	30: 4	wept, until they had no more **p** to weep.	3581
2Sa	22:33	God *is* my strength *and* **p**: and he maketh	2428
2Ki	17:36	up out of the land of Egypt with great **p**	3581
	19:26	Therefore their inhabitants *were* of small **p**,	3027
1Ch	20: 1	*to battle,* Joab led forth the **p** of the army,	2428
	29:11	the **p**, and the glory, and the victory, and	1369
	29:12	in thine hand *is* **p** and might; and in thine	3581
2Ch	14:11	with many, *or* with *them that have* no **p**:	3581
	20: 6	in thine hand *is there not* **p** and might, so	3581
	22: 9	So the house of Ahaziah had no **p** to keep	3581
	25: 8	for God hath **p** to help, and to cast down.	3581
	26:13	five hundred, that made war with mighty **p**,	3581
	32: 9	against Lachish, and all his **p** with him,)	4475
Ezr	4:23	and made them to cease by force and **p**.	2429
	8:22	his **p** and his wrath *is* against all them that	5797
Ne	1:10	whom thou hast redeemed by thy great **p**,	3581
	5: 5	**p** *to redeem them;* for other men have	410+3027
Est	1: 3	the **p** of Persia and Media, the nobles and	2428
	8:11	all the **p** of the people and province that	2428
	9: 1	of the Jews hoped to **have p** over them,	7980
	10: 2	all the acts of his **p** and of his might, and	8633
Job	1:12	Behold, all that he hath *is* in thy **p**;	3027
	5:20	and in war from the **p** of the sword.	3027
	21: 7	become old, yea, are mighty *in* **p**?	2428
	23: 6	Will he plead against me with *his* great **p**?	3581
	24:22	He draweth also the mighty with his **p**:	3581
	26: 2	hast thou helped *him that is* without **p**?	3581
	26:12	He divideth the sea with his **p**, and by his	3581
	26:14	the thunder of his **p** who can understand?	1369
	36:22	Behold, God exalteth by his **p**:	3581
	37:23	*he is* excellent in **p**, and *in* judgment, and	3581
	41:12	nor *his* **p**, nor his comely proportion.	1369
Ps	21:13	*so* will we sing and praise thy **p**.	1369
	22:20	my darling from the **p** of the dog.	3027
	37:35	I have seen the wicked in **great p**, and	6184
	49:15	God will redeem my soul from the **p** of	3027
	59:11	scatter them by thy **p**; and bring them	2428
	59:16	I will sing of thy **p**; yea, I will sing aloud of	5797
	62:11	I heard this; that **p** *belongeth* unto God.	5797
	63: 2	To see thy **p** and thy glory, so *as* I have	5797
	65: 6	fast the mountains; *being* girded with **p**:	1369
	66: 3	through the greatness of thy **p** shall thine	5797
	66: 7	He ruleth by his **p** for ever; his eyes behold	1369
	68:35	that giveth strength and **p** unto *his* people.	8592
	71:18	*and* thy **p** to every one *that* is to come.	1369
	78:26	and by his **p** he brought in the south wind.	5797
	79:11	according to the greatness of thy **p**:	2220
	90:11	Who knoweth the **p** of thine anger?	5797
	106: 8	that *he* might make his **mighty p** to be	1369
	110: 3	people *shall be* willing in the day of thy **p**,	2428
	111: 6	He hath shewed his people the **p** of his	3581
	145:11	the glory of thy kingdom, and talk of thy **p**;	1369
	147: 5	Great *is* our Lord, and of great **p**:	3581
	150: 1	praise him in the firmament of his **p**.	5797
Pr	3:27	when it is in the **p** of thine hand to do *it.*	410
	18:21	Death and life *are* in the **p** of the tongue:	3027
Ecc	4: 1	on the side of their oppressors *there was* **p**;	3581
	5:19	hath **given** him **p** to eat thereof, and to take	7980
	6: 2	yet God **giveth** him not **p** to eat thereof, but	7980
	8: 4	Where the word of a king *is, there is* **p**: and	7983
	8: 8	*There is* no man that hath **p** over the spirit	7989
	8: 8	neither *hath* he **p** in the day of death:	7983
Isa	37:27	Therefore their inhabitants *were* of small **p**,	3027
	40:26	of *his* might, for that *he is* strong in **p**;	3581
	40:29	He giveth **p** to the faint; and to *them that*	3581
	43:17	the chariot and horse, the army and the **p**;	5808
	47:14	they shall not deliver themselves from the **p**	3027
	50: 2	or have I no **p** to deliver? behold, at my	3581
Jer	10:12	He hath made the earth by his **p**, he hath	3581
	27: 5	by my great **p** and by my outstretched arm,	3581
	32:17	the earth by thy great **p** and stretched out	3581
	51:15	He hath made the earth by his **p**, he hath	3581
Eze	17: 9	even without great **p** or many people to	2220
	22: 6	every one were in thee to their **p** to shed	2220
	30: 6	and the pride of her **p** shall come down:	5797
Da	2:37	thee a kingdom, **p**, and strength, and glory.	2632
	3:27	upon whose bodies the fire had no **p**,	7981
	4:30	of the kingdom by the might of my **p**,	2632
	6:27	who hath delivered Daniel from the **p** of	3028
	8: 6	and ran unto him in the fury of his **p**.	3581
	8: 7	there was no **p** in the ram to stand before	3581
	8:22	stand up out of the nation, but not in his **p**.	3581
	8:24	his **p** shall be mighty, but not by his own	3581
	8:24	shall be mighty, but not by his own **p**:	3581
	11: 6	she shall not retain the **p** of the arm;	3581
	11:25	he shall stir up his **p** and his courage	3581
	11:43	he shall **have p** over the treasures of gold	4910
	12: 7	to scatter the **p** of the holy people,	3027
Hos	12: 3	and by his strength he **had p** with God:	8280
	12: 4	he **had p** over *the* angel, and prevailed:	7786
	13:14	I will ransom them from the **p** of the grave;	3027
Mic	2: 1	because it is in the **p** of their hand.	410
	3: 8	truly I am full *of* **p** by the spirit of	3581
Na	1: 3	great in **p**, and will not at all acquit	3581
	2: 1	*thy* loins strong, fortify *thy* **p** mightily.	3581
Hab	1:11	offend, *imputing* this his **p** unto his god.	3581
	2: 9	that *he* may be delivered from the **p** of evil!	3709
	3: 4	his hand: and there *was* the hiding of his **p**.	5797
Zec	4: 6	Not by might, nor by **p**, but by my spirit,	3581
	9: 4	her out, and he will smite her **p** in the sea;	2428
Mt	6:13	and the **p**, and the glory, for ever.	*1411*
	9: 6	Son of man hath **p** on earth to forgive sins,	*1849*
	9: 8	which had given such **p** unto men.	*1849*
	10: 1	he gave them **p** against unclean spirits,	*1849*
	22:29	knowing the scriptures, nor the **p** of God.	*1411*
	24:30	man coming in the clouds of heaven with **p**	*1411*
	26:64	Son of man sitting on the right hand of **p**,	*1411*
	28:18	All **p** is given unto me in heaven and	*1849*
Mk	2:10	Son of man hath **p** on earth to forgive sins,	*1849*
	3:15	And to have **p** to heal sicknesses, and to	*1849*
	6: 7	two; and gave them **p over** unclean spirits;	*1849*
	9: 1	seen the kingdom of God come with **p**.	*1411*
	12:24	not the scriptures, neither the **p** of God?	*1411*
	13:26	of man coming in *the* clouds with great **p**	*1411*
	14:62	Son of man sitting on the right hand of **p**,	*1411*
Lk	1:17	go before him in the spirit and **p** of Elias,	*1411*
	1:35	the **p** of the Highest shall overshadow thee:	*1411*
	4: 6	All this **p** will I give thee, and the glory of	*1849*
	4:14	And Jesus returned in the **p** of the Spirit	*1411*
	4:32	at his doctrine: for his word was with **p**.	*1849*
	4:36	and **p** he commandeth the unclean spirits,	*1411*
	5:17	the **p** of the Lord was *present* to heal them.	*1411*
	5:24	of man hath **p** upon earth to forgive sins,	*1849*
	9: 1	and gave them **p** and authority over all	*1411*
	9:43	And they were all amazed at the **mighty p**	*3168*
	10:19	I give unto you **p** to tread on serpents and	*1849*
	10:19	scorpions, and over all the **p** of the enemy:	*1411*
	12: 5	which after *he* hath killed hath **p** to cast	*1849*
	20:20	*so they* might deliver him unto the **p** and	*746*
	21:27	the Son of man coming in a cloud with **p**	*1411*
	22:53	but this is your hour, and the **p** of darkness.	*1849*
	22:69	man sit on the right hand of the **p** of God.	*1411*
	24:49	until ye be endued with **p** from on high.	*1411*
Jn	1:12	to them gave he **p** to become the sons of	*1849*
	10:18	I have **p** to lay it down, and I have power to	*1849*
	10:18	to lay it down, and I have **p** to take it again.	*1849*
	17: 2	As thou hast given him **p over** all flesh,	*1849*
	19:10	knowest thou not that I have **p** to crucify	*1849*
	19:10	to crucify thee, and have **p** to release thee?	*1849*
	19:11	Thou couldest have no **p** *at all* against me,	*1849*
Ac	1: 7	which the Father hath put in his own **p**.	*1849*
	1: 8	But ye shall receive **p**, after that the Holy	*1411*
	3:12	as though by our own **p** or holiness we had	*1411*
	4: 7	they asked, By what **p**, or by what name,	*1411*
	4:33	And with great **p** gave the apostles witness	*1411*
	5: 4	after it was sold, was it not in thine own **p**?	*1849*
	6: 8	And Stephen, full of faith and **p**, did great	*1411*
	8:10	saying, This *man* is the great **p** of God.	*1411*
	8:19	Saying, Give me also this **p**, that on	*1849*
	10:38	Nazareth with the Holy Ghost and with **p**:	*1411*
	26:18	to light, and *from* the **p** of Satan unto God,	*1849*
Ro	1: 4	*And* declared *to be* the Son of God with **p**,	*1411*
	1:16	for it is the **p** of God unto salvation to	*1411*
	1:20	are made, *even* his eternal **p** and Godhead;	*1411*
	9:17	that I might shew my **p** in thee, and that my	*1411*
	9:21	Hath not the potter **p over** the clay, of	*1849*
	9:22	shew *his* wrath, and to make his **p** known,	*1415*
	13: 1	For there is no **p** but of God: the powers	*1849*
	13: 2	Whosoever therefore resisteth the **p**,	*1849*
	13: 3	Wilt thou then not be afraid of the **p**?	*1849*
	15:13	in hope, through the **p** of the Holy Ghost.	*1411*
	15:19	and wonders, by the **p** of the Spirit of God;	*1411*
	16:25	Now to him that is of **p** to stablish you	*1410*
1Co	1:18	unto us which are saved it is the **p** of God.	*1411*
	1:24	Christ the **p** of God, and the wisdom of	*1411*

1Co 2: 4 but in demonstration of the Spirit and of **p**: *1411*
2: 5 in the wisdom of men, but in the **p** of God. *1411*
4:19 of them which are puffed up, but the **p**. *1411*
4:20 kingdom of God *is* not in word, but in **p**. *1411*
5: 4 with the **p** of our Lord Jesus Christ, *1411*
6:12 I will not be **brought under** the **p** of any. *1850*
6:14 and will *also* raise up us by his own **p**. *1411*
7: 4 The wife **hath** not **p** of her own body, but *1850*
7: 4 likewise also the husband **hath** not **p** of his *1850*
7:37 but hath **p** over his own will, and hath so *1849*
9: 4 Have we not **p** to eat and to drink? *1849*
9: 5 Have we not **p** to lead about a sister, a wife, *1849*
9: 6 have not we **p** to forbear working? *1849*
9:12 If others be partakers of *this* **p over** you, *1849*
9:12 Nevertheless we have not used this **p**; but *1849*
9:18 that *I* abuse not my **p** in the gospel. *1849*
11:10 For this cause ought the woman to have **p** *1849*
15:24 put down all rule and all authority and **p**. *1411*
15:43 it is sown in weakness; it is raised in **p**: *1411*
2Co 4: 7 that the excellency of the **p** may be of God, *1411*
6: 7 By the word of truth, by the **p** of God, *1411*
8: 3 For to *their* **p**, I bear record, *yea,* and *1411*
8: 3 beyond *their* **p** *they were* willing of *1411*
12: 9 that the **p** of Christ may rest upon me. *1411*
13: 4 yet he liveth by the **p** of God. *1411*
13: 4 we shall live with him by the **p** of God *1411*
13:10 according to the **p** which the Lord hath *1849*
Eph 1:19 greatness of his **p** to us-ward who believe, *1411*
1:19 according to the working of his mighty **p**, *2479*
1:21 and **p**, and might, and dominion, and *1849*
2: 2 according to the prince of the **p** of the air, *1849*
3: 7 unto me by the effectual working of his **p**. *1411*
3:20 think, according to the **p** that worketh in us, *1411*
6:10 in the Lord, and in the **p** of his might. *2904*
Php 3:10 and the **p** of his resurrection, and *1411*
Col 1:11 according to his glorious **p**, unto all *2904*
1:13 Who hath delivered us from the **p** of *1849*
2:10 which is the head of all principality and **p**: *1849*
1Th 1: 5 but also in **p**, and in the Holy Ghost, and *1411*
2Th 1: 9 of the Lord, and from the glory of his **p**; *2479*
1:11 *his* goodness, and the work of faith with **p**: *1411*
2: 9 is after the working of Satan with all **p** *1411*
3: 9 Not because we have not **p**, but to make *1849*
1Ti 6:16 to whom *be* honour and **p** everlasting. *2904*
2Ti 1: 7 but of **p**, and of love, and of a sound mind. *1411*
1: 8 of the gospel according to the **p** of God; *1411*
3: 5 of godliness, but denying the **p** thereof: *1411*
Heb 1: 3 upholding all *things* by the word of his **p**, *1411*
2:14 might destroy him that had the **p** of death, *2904*
7:16 but after the **p** of an endless life. *1411*
1Pe 1: 5 Who are kept by the **p** of God through faith *1411*
2Pe 1: 3 According as his divine **p** hath given unto *1411*
1:16 when we made known unto you the **p** and *1411*
2:11 which are greater in **p** and might, *2479*
Jude 1:25 *be* glory and majesty, dominion and **p**, *1849*
Rev 2:26 to him will I give **p** over the nations: *1849*
4:11 O Lord, to receive glory and honour and **p**: *1411*
5:12 is the Lamb that was slain to receive **p**, *1411*
5:13 Blessing, and honour, and glory, and **p**, *2904*
6: 4 ***p*** was given to him that sat thereon to take NIG
6: 8 And **p** was given unto them over the fourth *1849*
7:12 and honour, and **p**, and might, *1411*
9: 3 and unto them was given **p**, as *1849*
9: 3 as the scorpions of the earth have **p**. *1849*
9:10 and their **p** *was* to hurt men five months. *1849*
9:19 For their **p** is in their mouth, and in their *1849*
11: 3 And I will give ***p*** unto my two witnesses, NIG
11: 6 These have **p** to shut heaven, that it rain not *1849*
11: 6 have **p** over waters to turn them to blood, *1849*
11:17 because thou hast taken *to thee* thy great **p**, *1411*
12:10 of our God, and the **p** of his Christ: *1849*
13: 2 and the dragon gave him his **p**, and his seat, *1411*
13: 4 the dragon which gave **p** unto the beast: *1849*
13: 5 **p** was given unto him to continue forty *and* *1849*
13: 7 and **p** was given him over all kindreds, and *1849*
13:12 And he exerciseth all the **p** of the first beast *1849*
13:14 he **had p** to do in the sight of the beast; *1325*
13:15 And he **had p** to give life unto the image of *1325*
14:18 out from the altar, which had **p** over fire; *1849*
15: 8 from the glory of God, and from his **p**; *1411*
16: 8 ***p*** was given unto him to scorch men with NIG
16: 9 of God, which hath **p** over these plagues: *1849*
17:12 receive **p** as kings one hour with the beast. *1849*
17:13 and shall give their **p** and strength unto *1411*
18: 1 come down from heaven, having great **p**; *1849*
19: 1 Salvation, and glory, and honour, and **p**, *1411*
20: 6 on such the second death hath no **p**, but *1849*

POWERFUL (3) [POWER]
Ps 29: 4 The voice of the LORD *is* **p**; the voice of 3581
2Co 10:10 For *his* letters, say they, *are* weighty and **p**; *2478*
Heb 4:12 and **p**, and sharper than any twoedged *1756*

POWERS (14) [POWER]
Mt 24:29 and the **p** of the heavens shall be shaken: *1411*
Mk 13:25 the **p** that are in heaven shall be shaken. *1411*
Lk 12:11 and *unto* magistrates, and **p**, take ye no *1849*
21:26 for the **p** of heaven shall be shaken. *1411*
Ro 8:38 nor angels, nor principalities, nor **p**, *1411*
13: 1 Let every soul be subject unto the higher **p**. *1849*
13: 1 of God: the **p** that be are ordained of God. *1849*
Eph 3:10 **p** in heavenly *places* might be known by *1849*
6:12 blood, but against principalities, against **p**, *1849*
Col 1:16 or dominions, or principalities, or **p**: *1849*
2:15 *And* having spoiled principalities and **p**, *1849*
Tit 3: 1 mind to be subject to principalities and **p**, *1849*
Heb 6: 5 of God, and the **p** of the world to come, *1411*
1Pe 3:22 and **p** being made subject unto him. *1411*

PRACTICES (1) [PRACTISE]
2Pe 2:14 heart they have exercised with **covetous p**; *4124*

PRACTISE (4) [PRACTICES, PRACTISED]
Ps 141: 4 to **p** wicked works with men that work 5953
Isa 32: 6 to **p** hypocrisy, and to utter error against 6213
Da 8:24 **p**, and shall destroy the mighty and the holy 6213
Mic 2: 1 they **p** it, because it is in the power of their 6213

PRACTISED (2) [PRACTISE]
1Sa 23: 9 David knew that Saul **secretly p** mischief 2790
Da 8:12 truth to the ground; and it **p**, and prospered. 6213

PRAISE (248) [PRAISED, PRAISES, PRAISETH, PRAISING]
Ge 29:35 she said, Now will I **p** the LORD: 3034
49: 8 thou *art he* whom thy brethren shall **p**: 3034
Lev 19:24 shall be holy to **p** the LORD *withal.* 1974
Dt 10:21 He *is* thy **p**, and he *is* thy God, that hath 8416
26:19 in **p**, and in name, and in honour; 8416
Jdg 5: 2 **P** ye the LORD for the avenging of Israel, 1288
5: 3 I will sing ***p*** to the LORD God of Israel. NIH
1Ch 16: 4 to thank and **p** the LORD God of Israel: 1984
16:35 thanks to thy holy name, *and* glory in thy **p**. 8416
23: 5 which I made, *said David,* to **p** *therewith.* 1984
23:30 every morning to thank and **p** the LORD, 1984
25: 3 a harp, to give thanks and to **p** the LORD. 1984
29:13 we thank thee, and **p** thy glorious name. 1984
2Ch 7: 6 which David the king had made to **p** 3034
8:14 to **p** and minister before the priests, 1984
20:19 stood up to **p** the LORD God of Israel 1984
20:21 that should **p** the beauty of holiness, as *they* 1984
20:21 before the army, and to say, **P** the LORD; 3034
20:22 when they began to sing and to **p**, 8416
23:13 of musick, and such as taught to *sing* **p**. 1984
29:30 **p** unto the LORD with the words of 1984
31: 2 to **p** in the gates of the tents of the LORD. 1984
Ezr 3:10 to **p** the LORD, after the ordinance of 1984
Ne 9: 5 which *is* exalted above all blessing and **p**. 8416
12:24 over against them, to **p** *and* to give thanks, 1984
12:46 and songs of **p** and thanksgiving unto God. 8416
Ps 7:17 I will **p** the LORD according to his 3034
7:17 will sing ***p*** to the name of the LORD most NIH
9: 1 I will **p** *thee,* O LORD, with my whole 3034
9: 2 I will sing ***p*** to thy name, O thou most High. NIH
9:14 That I may shew forth all thy **p** in the gates 8416
21:13 *so* will we sing and **p** thy power. 2167
22:22 in the midst of the congregation will I **p** 1984
22:23 Ye that fear the LORD, **p** him; all ye 1984
22:25 My **p** *shall be* of thee in the great 8416
22:26 they shall **p** the LORD that seek him: 1984
28: 7 and with my song will I **p** him. 3034
30: 9 Shall the dust **p** thee? shall it declare thy 3034
30:12 To the end that *my* glory may sing ***p*** to thee, NIH
33: 1 *for* **p** is comely for the upright. 8416
33: 2 **P** the LORD with harp: sing unto him 3034
34: 1 his **p** *shall* continually *be* in my mouth. 8416
35:18 I will **p** thee among much people. 1984
35:28 *and* of thy **p** all the day long. 8416
40: 3 song in my mouth, *even* **p** unto our God: 8416
42: 4 with the voice of joy and **p**, *with* a 8426

P

Ps 42: 5 for I shall yet **p** him *for* the help of his 3034
42:11 for I shall yet **p** him, *who is* the health of 3034
43: 4 yea, upon the harp will I **p** thee, O God my 3034
43: 5 for I shall yet **p** him, *who is* the health of 3034
44: 8 all the day long, and **p** thy name for ever. 3034
45:17 shall the people **p** thee for ever and ever. 3034
48:10 so *is* thy **p** unto the ends of the earth: 8416
49:18 *men* will **p** thee, when thou doest well to 3034
50:23 Whoso offereth **p** glorifieth me: and to him 8426
51:15 and my mouth shall shew forth thy **p**. 8416
52: 9 I will **p** thee for ever, because thou hast 3034
54: 6 I will **p** thy name, O LORD; for *it is* good. 3034
56: 4 In God I will **p** his word, in God I have put 1984
56:10 In God will I **p** *his* word: in the LORD 1984
56:10 *his* word: in the LORD will I **p** *his* word. 1984
57: 7 my heart is fixed: I will sing and **give p**. 2167
57: 9 I will **p** thee, O Lord, among the people: 3034
61: 8 So will I sing ***p*** unto thy name for ever, NIH
63: 3 *is* better than life, my lips shall **p** thee. 7623
63: 5 and my mouth shall **p** *thee with* joyful lips: 1984
65: 1 **P** waiteth for thee, O God, in Zion: and 8416
66: 2 honour of his name: make his **p** glorious. 8416
66: 8 and make the voice of his **p** to be heard: 8416
67: 3 Let the people **p** thee, O God; let all 3034
67: 3 O God; let all the people **p** thee. 3034
67: 5 Let the people **p** thee, O God; let all 3034
67: 5 O God; let all the people **p** thee. 3034
69:30 I will **p** the name of God with a song; and 1984
69:34 Let the heaven and earth **p** him, the seas, 1984
71: 6 my **p** *shall be* continually of thee. 8416
71: 8 Let my mouth be filled *with* thy **p** *and* 8416
71:14 and will yet **p** thee more and more. 8416
71:22 I will also **p** thee with the psaltery, *even* thy 3034
74:21 let the poor and needy **p** thy name. 1984
76:10 Surely the wrath of man shall **p** thee: 3034
79:13 we will shew forth thy **p** to all generations. 8416
86:12 I will **p** thee, O Lord my God, with all my 3034
88:10 shall the dead arise *and* **p** thee? Selah. 3034
89: 5 the heavens shall **p** thy wonders, 3034
98: 4 make a loud noise, and rejoice, and sing ***p***. NIH
99: 3 Let them **p** thy great and terrible name; 3034
100: T A Psalm of **p**. 8426
100: 4 *and* into his courts with **p**: 8416
102:18 the people which *shall be* created shall **p** 1984
102:21 the LORD in Zion, and his **p** in Jerusalem; 8416
104:33 I will sing ***p*** to my God while I have my NIH
104:35 the LORD, O my soul. **P** ye the LORD. 1984
105:45 and keep his laws. **P** ye the LORD. 1984
106: 1 **P** ye the LORD. O give thanks unto 1984
106: 2 the LORD? *who* can shew forth all his **p**? 8416
106:12 believed they his words; they sang his **p**. 8416
106:47 thy holy name, *and* to triumph in thy **p**. 8416
106:48 all the people say, Amen. **P** ye the LORD. 1984
107: 8 Oh that *men* would **p** the LORD *for* his 3034
107:15 Oh that *men* would **p** the LORD *for* his 3034
107:21 Oh that *men* would **p** the LORD *for* his 3034
107:31 Oh that *men* would **p** the LORD *for* his 3034
107:32 and **p** him in the assembly of the elders. 1984
108: 1 I will sing and **give p**, even *with* my glory. 2167
108: 3 I will **p** thee, O LORD, among the people: 3034
109: 1 Hold not thy peace, O God of my **p**; 8416
109:30 I will greatly **p** the LORD with my mouth; 3034
109:30 yea, I will **p** him among the multitude. 1984
111: 1 **P** ye the LORD. I will praise the LORD 1984
111: 1 I will **p** the LORD with *my* whole heart, 3034
111:10 *commandments:* his **p** endureth for ever. 8416
112: 1 **P** ye the LORD. Blessed *is* the man *that* 1984
113: 1 **P** ye the LORD. Praise, O ye servants of 1984
113: 1 **P**, O ye servants of the LORD, praise 1984
113: 1 of the LORD, **p** the name of the LORD. 1984
113: 9 joyful mother of children. **P** ye the LORD. 1984
115:17 The dead **p** not the LORD, neither any 1984
115:18 time forth and for evermore. **P** the LORD. 1984
116:19 of thee, O Jerusalem. **P** ye the LORD. 1984
117: 1 O **p** the LORD, all ye nations: praise him, 1984
117: 1 all ye nations: **p** him, all ye people. 7623
117: 2 *endureth* for ever. **P** ye the LORD. 1984
118:19 will go into them, *and* I will **p** the LORD: 3034
118:21 I will **p** thee: for thou hast heard me, and 3034
118:28 Thou *art* my God, and I will **p** thee: *thou art* 3034
119: 7 I will **p** thee with uprightness of heart, 3034
119:164 Seven *times* a day do I **p** thee because 1984
119:171 My lips shall utter **p**, when thou hast taught 8416
119:175 Let my soul live, and it shall **p** thee; and 1984
135: 1 **P** ye the LORD. Praise ye the name of 1984
135: 1 **P** ye the name of the LORD; praise *him,* 1984
135: 1 **p** *him,* O ye servants of the LORD. 1984
135: 3 **P** the LORD; for the LORD *is* good: 1984
135:21 dwelleth *at* Jerusalem. **P** ye the LORD. 1984
138: 1 I will **p** thee with my whole heart: 3034
138: 1 before the gods will I sing ***p*** unto thee. NIH
138: 2 **p** thy name for thy lovingkindness and 3034
138: 4 All the kings of the earth shall **p** thee, 3034
139:14 I will **p** thee; for I am fearfully and 3034
142: 7 soul out of prison, that *I* may **p** thy name: 3034
145: T David's *Psalm of* **p**. 8416
145: 2 and I will **p** thy name for ever and ever. 1984
145: 4 One generation shall **p** thy works to 7623
145:10 All thy works shall **p** thee, O LORD; and 3034
145:21 My mouth shall speak the **p** of the LORD: 8416
146: 1 **P** ye the LORD. Praise the LORD, O my 1984
146: 1 ye the LORD. **P** the LORD, O my soul. 1984
146: 2 While I live will I **p** the LORD: I will sing 1984
146:10 unto all generations. **P** ye the LORD. 1984
147: 1 **P** ye the LORD: for *it is* good to sing 1984
147: 1 our God; for *it is* pleasant; *and* **p** is comely. 8416
147: 7 sing ***p*** upon the harp unto our God: NIH
147:12 **P** the LORD, O Jerusalem; praise thy 7623
147:12 O Jerusalem; **p** thy God, O Zion. 1984
147:20 have not known them. **P** ye the LORD. 1984
148: 1 **P** ye the LORD. Praise ye the LORD 1984
148: 1 **P** ye the LORD from the heavens: 1984
148: 1 from the heavens: **p** him in the heights. 1984
148: 2 **P** ye him, all his angels: praise ye him, 1984
148: 2 all his angels: **p** ye him, all his hosts. 1984
148: 3 **P** ye him, sun and moon: praise him, all ye 1984
148: 3 sun and moon: **p** him, all ye stars of light. 1984
148: 4 **P** him, ye heavens of heavens, and 1984
148: 5 Let them **p** the name of the LORD: for he 1984
148: 7 **P** the LORD from the earth, ye dragons, 1984
148:13 Let them **p** the name of the LORD: for his 1984
148:14 horn of his people, the **p** of all his saints; 8416
148:14 a people near unto him. **P** ye the LORD. 1984
149: 1 **P** ye the LORD. Sing unto the LORD a 1984
149: 1 *and* his **p** in the congregation of saints. 8416
149: 3 Let them **p** his name in the dance: let them 1984
149: 9 have all his saints. **P** ye the LORD. 1984
150: 1 **P** ye the LORD. Praise God in his 1984
150: 1 **P** God in his sanctuary: praise him in 1984
150: 1 **p** him in the firmament of his power. 1984
150: 2 **P** him for his mighty acts: praise him 1984
150: 2 **p** him according to his excellent greatness. 1984
150: 3 **P** him with the sound of the trumpet: 1984
150: 3 **p** him with the psaltery and harp. 1984
150: 4 **P** him with the timbrel and dance: 1984
150: 4 **p** him with stringed instruments and 1984
150: 5 **P** him upon the loud cymbals: praise him 1984
150: 5 **p** him upon the high sounding cymbals. 1984
150: 6 Let every *thing that hath* breath **p** 1984
150: 6 breath praise the LORD. **P** ye the LORD. 1984
Pr 27: 2 Let another *man* **p** thee, and not thine own 1984
27:21 the furnace for gold; so *is* a man to his **p**. 4110
28: 4 They that forsake the law **p** the wicked: but 1984
31:31 and let her own works **p** her in the gates. 1984
Isa 12: 1 day thou shalt say, O LORD, I will **p** thee: 3034
12: 4 ye say, **P** the LORD, call upon his name, 3034
25: 1 I will exalt thee, I will **p** thy name; 3034
38:18 For the grave cannot **p** thee, death can *not* 3034
38:19 The living, the living, he shall **p** thee, as I 3034
42: 8 to another, neither my **p** to graven images. 8416
42:10 *and* his **p** from the end of the earth, ye that 8416
42:12 and declare his **p** in the islands. 8416
43:21 for myself; they shall shew forth my **p**. 8416
48: 9 *for* my **p** will I refrain for thee, that *I* cut 8416
60:18 call thy walls Salvation, and thy gates **P**. 8416
61: 3 the garment of **p** for the spirit of heaviness; 8416
61:11 and **p** to spring forth before all the nations. 8416
62: 7 and till he make Jerusalem a **p** in the earth. 8416
62: 9 gathered it shall eat it, and **p** the LORD; 1984
Jer 13:11 and for a name, and for a **p**, and for a glory: 8416
17:14 and I shall be saved: for thou *art* my **p**. 8416
17:26 and incense, and bringing *sacrifices of* **p**, 8426
20:13 Sing unto the LORD, **p** ye the LORD: 1984
31: 7 publish ye, **p** ye, and say, O LORD, save 1984
33: 9 a **p** and an honour before all the nations of 8416
33:11 them that shall say, **P** the LORD of hosts: 3034
33:11 of them that shall bring the **sacrifice of p** 8426
48: 2 *There shall be* no more **p** of Moab: 8416

Jer 49:25 How is the city of **p** not left, the city of my 8416
51:41 *how* is the **p** of the whole earth surprised! 8416
Da 2:23 I thank thee, and **p** thee, O thou God of my 7624
4:37 Now I Nebuchadnezzar **p** and extol and 7624
Joel 2:26 and **p** the name of the LORD your God, 1984
Hab 3: 3 the heavens, and the earth was full *of* his **p**. 8416
Zep 3:19 I will get them **p** and fame in every land 8416
3:20 and a **p** among all people of the earth, 8416
Mt 21:16 and sucklings thou hast perfected **p**? *136*
Lk 18:43 when they saw *it,* gave **p** unto God. *136*
19:37 **p** God with a loud voice for all the mighty *134*
Jn 9:24 and said unto him, Give God the **p**: *1391*
12:43 For they loved the **p** of men more than *1391*
12:43 the praise of men more than the **p** of God. *1391*
Ro 2:29 whose **p** *is* not of men, but of God. *1868*
13: 3 *is* good, and thou shalt have **p** of the same: *1868*
15:11 And again, **P** the Lord, all ye Gentiles; and *134*
1Co 4: 5 and then shall every man have **p** of God. *1868*
11: 2 Now I **p** you, brethren, that you remember *1867*
11:17 Now in this that I declare *unto you* I **p** *you* *1867*
11:22 shall I **p** you in this? I praise *you* not. *1867*
11:22 shall I praise you in this? I **p** *you* not. *1867*
2Co 8:18 whose **p** *is* in the gospel throughout all *1868*
Eph 1: 6 To the **p** of the glory of his grace, *1868*
1:12 That we should be to the **p** of his glory, *1868*
1:14 unto the **p** of his glory. *1868*
Php 1:11 Jesus Christ unto the glory and **p** of God. *1868*
4: 8 if *there be* any virtue, and if *there be* any **p**, *1868*
Heb 2:12 in the midst of the church will I **sing p** unto *5214*
13:15 let us offer the sacrifice of **p** to God *133*
1Pe 1: 7 might be found unto **p** and honour and *1868*
2:14 and *for* the **p** of them that do well. *1868*
4:11 to whom be **p** and dominion for ever and *1391*
Rev 19: 5 saying, **P** our God, all ye his servants, and *134*

PRAISED (26) [PRAISE]

Jdg 16:24 when the people saw him, they **p** their god: 1984
2Sa 14:25 to be so much **p** as Absalom for his beauty: 1984
22: 4 call on the LORD, who is *worthy* to be **p**: 1984
1Ch 16:25 great *is* the LORD, and greatly to be **p**: 1984
16:36 the people said, Amen, and **p** the LORD. 1984
23: 5 four thousand **p** the LORD with 1984
2Ch 5:13 and **p** the LORD, *saying,* For *he is* good; 1984
7: 3 worshipped, and **p** the LORD, *saying,* For 3034
7: 6 for ever, when David **p** by their ministry; 1984
30:21 and the priests **p** the LORD day by day, 1984
Ezr 3:11 when they **p** the LORD, because 1984
Ne 5:13 Amen, and **p** the LORD. 1984
Ps 18: 3 upon the LORD, who is *worthy* to be **p**: 1984
48: 1 and greatly to be **p** in the city of our God, 1984
72:15 for him continually; *and* daily shall he be **p**. 1288
96: 4 the LORD *is* great, and greatly to be **p**: 1984
113: 3 of the same the LORD'S name *is* to be **p**. 1984
145: 3 Great *is* the LORD, and greatly to be **p**; 1984
Pr 31:30 that feareth the LORD, she shall be **p**. 1984
Ecc 4: 2 Wherefore I **p** the dead which are already 7623
SS 6: 9 and the concubines, and they **p** her. 1984
Isa 64:11 beautiful house, where our fathers **p** thee, 1984
Da 4:34 I **p** and honoured him that liveth for ever, 7624
5: 4 **p** the gods of gold, and of silver, of brass, 7624
5:23 and thou hast **p** the gods of silver, and gold, 7624
Lk 1:64 tongue *loosed,* and he spake, and **p** God. *2127*

PRAISES (29) [PRAISE]

Ex 15:11 in holiness, fearful *in* **p**, doing wonders? 8416
2Sa 22:50 and I will **sing p** unto thy name. 2167
2Ch 29:30 they *sang* **p** with gladness, and they bowed 1984
Ps 9:11 Sing *p* to the LORD, which dwelleth in NIH
18:49 the heathen, and sing *p* unto thy name. NIH
22: 3 O thou that inhabitest the **p** of Israel. 8416
27: 6 yea, I will sing *p* unto the LORD. NIH
47: 6 Sing *p* to God, sing *praises:* sing *praises* NIH
47: 6 sing *p*: sing *praises* unto our King, NIH
47: 6 sing *praises:* sing **p** unto our King, NIH
47: 6 *praises:* sing *praises* unto our King, sing *p*. NIH
47: 7 all the earth: sing ye *p* with understanding. NIH
56:12 upon me, O God: I will render **p** unto thee. 8426
68: 4 Sing unto God, sing *p to* his name: NIH
68:32 of the earth; O sing *p unto* the Lord; Selah. NIH
75: 9 for ever; I will sing *p* to the God of Jacob. NIH
78: 4 shewing to the generation to come the **p** of 8416
92: 1 and to sing *p* unto thy name, O most High: NIH
108: 3 I will sing *p* unto thee among the nations. NIH
135: 3 sing *p* unto his name; for *it is* pleasant. NIH
144: 9 an instrument of ten strings will I sing *p* NIH
146: 2 I will sing *p* unto my God while I have *any* NIH
147: 1 for *it is* good to sing *p* unto our God; for *it* NIH
149: 3 let them sing *p* unto him with the timbrel NIH
149: 6 *Let* the high *p* of God *be* in their mouth, and NIH
Isa 60: 6 they shall shew forth the **p** of the LORD. 8416
63: 7 of the LORD, *and* the **p** of the LORD, 8416
Ac 16:25 and Silas prayed, and **sang p** unto God: *5214*
1Pe 2: 9 that ye should shew forth the **p** of him who *703*

PRAISETH (1) [PRAISE]

Pr 31:28 her blessed; her husband *also,* and he **p** her. 1984

PRAISING (10) [PRAISE]

2Ch 5:13 to make one sound to be heard in **p** and 1984
23:12 noise of the people running and **p** the king, 1984
Ezr 3:11 they sung together by course in **p** and 1984
Ps 84: 4 in thy house: they will be still **p** thee. Selah. 1984
Lk 2:13 a multitude of the heavenly host **p** God, *134*
2:20 **p** God for all *the things* that they had heard *134*
24:53 in the temple, **p** and blessing God. *134*
Ac 2:47 **P** God, and having favour with all *134*
3: 8 the temple, walking, and leaping, and **p** God. *134*
3: 9 all the people saw him walking and **p** God: *134*

PRANSING (1) [PRANSINGS]

Na 3: 2 of the **p** horses, and of the jumping 1725

PRANSINGS (2) [PRANSING]

Jdg 5:22 horsehoofs broken by the means of the **p**, 1726
5:22 the pransings, the **p** of their mighty *ones.* 1726

PRATING (3)

Pr 10: 8 but a **p** fool shall fall. 8193
10:10 eye causeth sorrow: but a **p** fool shall fall. 8193
3Jn 1:10 **p against** us with malicious words: *5396*

PRAY (313) [PRAYED, PRAYER, PRAYERS, PRAYEST, PRAYETH, PRAYING]

Ge 12:13 Say, **I p thee**, thou *art* my sister: that it may 4994
13: 8 **I p thee**, between me and thee, and 4994
13: 9 separate thyself, **I p thee**, from me: if *thou* 4994
16: 2 **I p thee**, go in unto my maid; it may be that 4994
18: 3 pass not away, **I p thee**, from thy servant: 4994
18: 4 **I p you**, be fetched, and wash your feet, 4994
19: 2 Behold now, my lords, turn in, **I p you**, 4994
19: 7 **I p you**, brethren, do not *so* wickedly. 4994
19: 8 let me, **I p you**, bring them out unto you, 4994
20: 7 and he shall **p** for thee, and thou shalt live: 6419
23:13 saying, But if thou *wilt give it,* **I p thee**, 3863
24: 2 Put, **I p thee**, thy hand under my thigh: 4994
24:12 **I p thee**, send me good speed *this* day, and 4994
24:14 thy pitcher, **I p thee**, that I may drink; 4994
24:17 ran to meet her, and said, Let me, **I p thee**, 4994
24:23 tell me, **I p thee**: is there room *in* thy 4994
24:43 and I say to her, Give me, **I p thee**, 4994
24:45 and I said unto her, Let me drink, **I p thee**. 4994
25:30 Esau said to Jacob, Feed me, **I p thee**, 4994
27: 3 Now therefore take, **I p thee**, thy weapons, 4994
27:19 arise, **I p thee**, sit and eat of my venison, 4994
27:21 Come near, **I p thee**, that I may feel thee, 4994
30:14 Give me, **I p thee**, of thy son's mandrakes. 4994
30:27 Laban said unto him, **I p thee**, if I have 4994
32:11 Deliver me, **I p thee**, from the hand of my 4994
32:29 asked *him,* and said, Tell *me,* **I p thee**, 4994
33:10 Jacob said, Nay, **I p thee**, if now I have 4994
33:11 Take, **I p thee**, my blessing that is brought 4994
33:14 Let my lord, **I p thee**, pass over before his 4994
34: 8 **I p you** give her him to wife. 4994
37: 6 he said unto them, Hear, **I p you**, this 4994
37:14 he said to him, Go, **I p thee**, see whether it 4994
37:16 tell me, **I p thee**, where they feed *their* 4994
38:16 said, Go to, **I p thee**, let me come in unto 4994
38:25 she said, Discern, **I p thee**, whose *are* 4994
40: 8 *belong* to God? tell me *them,* **I p you**. 4994
40:14 **I p thee**, unto me, and make mention of me 4994
44:18 said, O my lord, let thy servant, **I p thee**, 4994
44:33 Now therefore, **I p thee**, let thy servant 4994
45: 4 his brethren, Come near to me, **I p you**. 4994
47: 4 now therefore, **we p thee**, let thy servants 4994
47:29 put, **I p thee**, thy hand under my thigh, and 4994
47:29 with me; bury me not, **I p thee**, in Egypt: 4994
48: 9 **I p thee**, unto me, and I will bless them. 4994
50: 4 speak, **I p you**, in the ears of Pharaoh, 4994

Ge 50: 5 **I p thee**, and bury my father, and I will 4994
50:17 Forgive, **I p** thee now, the trespass of thy 577
50:17 now, **we p thee**, forgive the trespass of 4994
Ex 4:13 he said, O my Lord, send, **I p thee**, by 4994
4:18 **I p thee**, and return unto my brethren 4994
5: 3 let us go, **we p thee**, three days' journey 4994
10:17 Now therefore forgive, **I p thee**, my sin 4994
32:32 if not, blot me, **I p thee**, out of thy book 4994
33:13 Now therefore, **I p thee**, if I have found 4994
34: 9 O Lord, let my Lord, **I p thee**, go amongst 4994
Nu 10:31 he said, Leave us not, **I p thee**; 4994
11:15 thus with me, kill me, **I p thee**, out of hand, 4994
16: 8 unto Korah, Hear, **I p you**, ye sons of Levi: 4994
16:26 saying, Depart, **I p you**, from the tents of 4994
20:17 Let us pass, **I p thee**, through thy country: 4994
21: 7 **p** unto the LORD, that he take away 6419
22: 6 Come now therefore, **I p thee**, curse me 4994
22:16 Let nothing, **I p thee**, hinder thee from 4994
22:17 come therefore, **I p thee**, curse me this 4994
22:19 Now therefore, **I p you**, tarry ye also here 4994
23:13 Balak said unto him, Come, **I p thee**, 4994
23:27 Balak said unto Balaam, Come, **I p thee**, 4994
Dt 3:25 **I p thee**, let me go over, and see the good 4994
Jos 2:12 Now therefore, **I p you**, swear unto me by 4994
7:19 said unto Achan, My son, give, **I p thee**, 4994
Jdg 1:24 they said unto him, Shew us, **we p thee**, 4994
4:19 he said unto her, Give me, **I p thee**, a little 4994
6:18 Depart not hence, **I p thee**, until I come 4994
6:39 **I p thee**, but *this* once with the fleece; 4994
8: 5 unto the men of Succoth, Give, **I p you**, 4994
9: 2 Speak, **I p you**, in the ears of all the men of 4994
9:38 go out, **I p** now, and fight with them. 4994
10:15 deliver us only, **we p thee**, this day. 4994
11:17 saying, Let me, **I p thee**, pass through thy 4994
11:19 said unto him, Let us pass, **we p thee**, 4994
13: 4 **I p thee**, and drink not wine nor strong 4994
13:15 **I p thee**, let us detain thee, until we shall 4994
15: 2 than she? take her, I p thee, instead of her. 4994
16: 6 Delilah said to Samson, Tell me, **I p thee**, 4994
16:10 now tell me, **I p thee**, wherewith thou 4994
16:28 **I p thee**, and strengthen me, I pray thee, 4994
16:28 **I p thee**, only this once, O God, 4994
18: 5 unto him, Ask *counsel,* **we p thee**, of God, 4994
19: 6 **I p thee**, and tarry all night, and let thine 4994
19: 8 father said, Comfort thine heart, **I p thee**. 4994
19: 9 towards evening, **I p you** tarry all night: 4994
19:11 **I p thee**, and let us turn in into this city of 4994
19:23 *nay,* **I p you**, do not *so* wickedly; 4994
Ru 2: 7 **I p you**, let me glean and gather after 4994
1Sa 2:36 of bread, and shall say, Put me, **I p thee**, 4994
3:17 **I p thee** hide *it* not from me: God do so 4994
7: 5 and I will **p** for you unto the LORD. 6419
9:18 said, Tell me, **I p thee**, where the seer's 4994
10:15 Saul's uncle said, Tell me, **I p thee**, 4994
12:19 **P** for thy servants unto the LORD thy 6419
12:23 against the LORD in ceasing to **p** for you: 6419
14:29 see, **I p you**, how mine eyes have been 4994
15:25 **I p thee**, pardon my sin, and turn again 4994
15:30 *yet* honour me now, **I p thee,** 4994
16:22 saying, Let David, **I p thee**, stand before 4994
19: 2 now therefore, **I p thee**, take heed to 4994
20:29 he said, Let me go, **I p thee**; for our family 4994
20:29 get away, **I p thee**, and see my brethren. 4994
22: 3 **I p thee**, come forth, *and be* with you, 4994
23:22 Go, **I p you**, prepare yet, and know and 4994
25: 8 give, **I p thee**, whatsoever cometh to thine 4994
25:24 and let thine handmaid, **I p thee,** 4994
25:25 Let not my lord, **I p thee**, regard this man 4994
25:28 **I p thee**, forgive the trespass of thine 4994
26: 8 now therefore let me smite him, **I p thee**, 4994
26:11 but, **I p thee**, take thou now the spear that 6258
26:19 Now therefore, **I p thee**, let my lord 4994
28: 8 he said, **I p thee**, divine unto me by 4994
28:22 Now therefore, **I p thee**, hearken thou also 4994
30: 7 Ahimelech's son, **I p thee**, bring me hither 4994
2Sa 1: 4 **I p thee**, tell me. And he answered, 4994
1: 9 Stand, **I p thee**, upon me, and slay me: 4994
7:27 hath thy servant found in his heart to **p** this 6419
13: 5 say unto him, **I p thee**, let my sister Tamar 4994
13: 6 **I p thee**, let Tamar my sister come, and 4994
13:13 Now therefore, **I p thee**, speak unto 4994
13:26 said Absalom, If not, **I p thee**, let my 4994
14: 2 a wise woman, and said unto her, **I p thee**, 4994
14:11 said she, **I p thee**, let the king remember 4994
14:12 woman said, Let thine handmaid, **I p thee**, 4994
14:18 the woman, Hide not from me, **I p thee**, 4994
15: 7 **I p thee**, let me go and pay my vow, 4994
15:31 David said, O LORD, **I p thee**, turn 4994
16: 9 me go over, **I p thee**, and take off his head. 4994
18:22 howsoever, let me, **I p thee**, also run after 4994
19:37 Let thy servant, **I p thee**, turn back again, 4994
20:16 say, **I p you**, unto Joab, Come near hither, 4994
24:17 let thine hand, **I p thee**, be against me, and 4994
1Ki 1:12 Now therefore come, let me, **I p thee**, 4994
2:17 he said, Speak, **I p thee**, unto Solomon 4994
2:20 petition of thee; *I p thee,* say me not nay. NIH
8:26 of Israel, let thy word, **I p thee**, be verified, 4994
8:30 when they shall **p** towards this place: 6419
8:33 **p**, and make supplication unto thee in this 6419
8:35 if they **p** towards this place, and confess thy 6419
8:42 he shall come and **p** towards this house; 6419
8:44 shall **p** unto the LORD toward the city 6419
8:48 and **p** unto thee toward their land, 6419
13: 6 **p** for me, that my hand may be restored me 6419
14: 2 Arise, **I p thee**, and disguise thyself, 4994
17:10 called to her, and said, Fetch me, **I p thee**, 4994
17:11 said, Bring me, **I p thee**, a morsel of bread 4994
17:21 and said, O LORD my God, **I p thee**, 4994
19:20 said, Let me, **I p thee**, kiss my father and 4994
20: 7 **I p you**, and see how this *man* seeketh 4994
20:31 let us, **I p thee**, put sackcloth on our loins, 4994
20:32 Ben-hadad saith, **I p thee**, let me live. 4994
20:35 word of the LORD, Smite me, **I p thee**. 4994
20:37 another man, and said, Smite me, **I p thee**. 4994
22: 5 Inquire, **I p thee**, at the word of 4994
22:13 let thy word, **I p thee**, be like the word of 4994
2Ki 1:13 **I p thee**, let my life, and the life of these 4994
2: 2 said unto Elisha, Tarry here, **I p thee**; 4994
2: 4 said unto him, Elisha, tarry here, **I p thee**; 4994
2: 6 Elijah said unto him, Tarry, **I p thee**, here; 4994
2: 9 Elisha said, **I p thee**, let a double portion of 4994
2:16 them go, **we p thee**, and seek thy master: 4994
2:19 Behold, **I p thee**, the situation of *this* city *is* 4994
4:10 make a little chamber, **I p thee**, on the wall; 4994
4:22 said, Send me, **I p thee**, one of the young 4994
4:26 Run now, **I p thee**, to meet her, and 4994
5: 7 **I p you**, and see how he seeketh a quarrel 4994
5:15 now therefore, **I p thee**, take a blessing of 4994
5:17 Naaman said, Shall there not then, **I p thee**, 4994
5:22 give them, **I p thee**, a talent of silver, and 4994
6: 2 Let us go, **we p thee**, unto Jordan, and 4994
6: 3 **I p thee**, and go with thy servants. 4994
6:17 said, LORD, **I p thee**, open his eyes, 4994
6:18 Smite this people, **I p thee**, with blindness. 4994
7:13 and said, Let *some* take, **I p thee**, 4994
8: 4 saying, Tell me, **I p thee**, all the great 4994
18:23 Now therefore, **I p thee**, give pledges to 4994
18:26 Joah, unto Rab-shakeh, Speak, **I p thee**, 4994
1Ch 17:25 thy servant hath found *in his heart* to **p** 6419
21:17 let thine hand, **I p thee**, O LORD my 4994
2Ch 6:24 **p** and make supplication before thee in this 6419
6:26 *yet* if they **p** towards this place, and 6419
6:32 out arm; if they come and **p** in this house; 6419
6:34 they **p** unto thee toward this city which 6419
6:37 **p** unto thee in the land of their captivity, 2603
6:38 **p** toward their land, which thou gavest unto 6419
7:14 **p**, and seek my face, and turn from their 6419
18: 4 Inquire, **I p thee**, at the word of 4994
18:12 **I p thee**, be like one of theirs, and 4994
Ezr 6:10 **p** for the life of the king, and of his sons. 6739
Ne 1: 6 which **I p** before thee now, day and night, 6419
1:11 prosper, **I p thee**, thy servant *this* day, and 4994
5:10 corn: **I p you**, let us leave off this usury. 4994
5:11 Restore, **I p you**, to them, even *this* day, 4994
Job 4: 7 Remember, **I p thee**, who *ever* perished, 4994
6:29 Return, **I p you**, let it not be iniquity; yea, 4994
8: 8 For inquire, **I p thee**, of the former age, and 4994
21:15 profit should we have, if we **p** unto him? 6293
22:22 Receive, **I p thee**, the law from his mouth, 4994
32:21 Let me not, **I p you**, accept *any* man's 4994
33: 1 Wherefore, Job, **I p thee**, hear my 4994
33:26 He shall **p** unto God, and he will be 6279
42: 8 and my servant Job shall **p** for you: 6419
Ps 5: 2 and my God: for unto thee will **I p**. 6419
32: 6 For this shall every one *that is* godly **p** unto 6419
55:17 and at noon, will **I p**, and cry aloud: 7878
119:76 Let, **I p thee**, thy merciful kindness be for 4994
122: 6 **P** for the peace of Jerusalem: they shall 7592

Isa	5: 3	judge, **I p you**, betwixt me and my	4994
	16:12	that he shall come to his sanctuary to **p**;	6419
	29:11	that is learned, saying, Read this, **I p thee**:	4994
	29:12	is not learned, saying, Read this, **I p thee**:	4994
	36: 8	Now therefore give pledges, **I p thee**,	4994
	36:11	and Joah unto Rabshakeh, Speak, **I p thee**,	4994
	45:20	and **p** unto a god *that* cannot save.	6419
Jer	7:16	Therefore **p** not thou for this people,	6419
	11:14	Therefore **p** not thou for this people,	6419
	14:11	**P** not for this people for *their* good.	6419
	21: 2	Inquire, **I p thee**, of the LORD for us; for	4994
	29: 7	and **p** unto the LORD for it:	6419
	29:12	ye shall go and **p** unto me, and I will	6419
	32: 8	said unto me, Buy my field, **I p thee**, that *is*	4994
	37: 3	**P** now unto the LORD our God for us.	6419
	37:20	hear now, **I p thee**, O my lord the king:	4994
	37:20	let my supplication, **I p thee**, be accepted	4994
	40:15	**I p thee**, and I will slay Ishmael the son of	4994
	42: 2	**p** for us unto the LORD thy God, *even* for	6419
	42: 4	I *will* **p** unto the LORD your God	6419
	42:20	**P** for us unto the LORD our God;	6419
La	1:18	hear, **I p you**, all people, and behold my	4994
Eze	33:30	**I p you**, and hear what *is* the word that	4994
Jnh	1: 8	said they unto him, Tell us, **we p thee**,	4994
	4: 2	said, **I p thee**, O LORD, *was* not this my	577
Mic	3: 1	I said, Hear, **I p you**, O heads of Jacob,	4994
	3: 9	Hear this, **I p you**, ye heads of the house of	4994
Hag	2:15	now, **I p you**, consider from this day and	4994
Zec	7: 2	and their men, to **p** before the LORD,	2470
	8:21	Let us go speedily to **p** before the LORD,	2470
	8:22	in Jerusalem, and to **p** before the LORD.	2470
Mal	1: 9	now, **I p you**, beseech God that he will be	4994
Mt	5:44	and **p** for them which despitefully use you,	*4336*
	6: 5	they love to **p** standing in the synagogues	*4336*
	6: 6	thy door, **p** to thy Father which is in secret;	*4336*
	6: 7	But when ye **p**, use not vain repetitions,	*4336*
	6: 9	After this manner therefore **p** ye:	*4336*
	9:38	**P** ye therefore the Lord of the harvest,	*1189*
	14:23	he went up into a mountain apart to **p**:	*4336*
	19:13	he should put *his* hands on them, and **p**:	*4336*
	24:20	But **p** ye that your flight be not in	*4336*
	26:36	Sit ye here, while I go and **p** yonder.	*4336*
	26:41	Watch and **p**, that ye enter not into	*4336*
	26:53	Thinkest thou that I cannot now **p** to my	*3870*
Mk	5:17	And they began to **p** him to depart out of	*3870*
	5:23	*I p thee,* come and lay *thy* hands on her,	NIG
	6:46	he departed into a mountain to **p**.	*4336*
	11:24	when ye **p**, believe that ye receive *them,*	*4336*
	13:18	And **p** ye that your flight be not in	*4336*
	13:33	Take ye heed, watch and **p**: for ye know	*4336*
	14:32	to his disciples, Sit ye here, while I shall **p**.	*4336*
	14:38	Watch ye and **p**, lest ye enter into	*4336*
Lk	6:12	*that* he went out into a mountain to **p**, and	*4336*
	6:28	and **p** for them which despitefully use you.	*4336*
	9:28	James, and went up into a mountain to **p**.	*4336*
	10: 2	**p** ye therefore the Lord of the harvest,	*1189*
	11: 1	Lord, teach us to **p**, as John also taught his	*4336*
	11: 2	And he said unto them, When ye **p**, say,	*4336*
	14:18	and see it: I **p** thee have me excused.	*2065*
	14:19	to prove them: I **p** thee have me excused.	*2065*
	16:27	Then he said, I **p** thee therefore, father,	*2065*
	18: 1	*to this end,* that *men* ought always to **p**,	*4336*
	18:10	Two men went up into the temple to **p**;	*4336*
	21:36	Watch ye therefore, and **p** always, that ye	*1189*
	22:40	**P** that *ye* enter not into temptation.	*4336*
	22:46	rise and **p**, lest ye enter into temptation.	*4336*
Jn	14:16	And I will **p** the Father, and he shall give	*2065*
	16:26	unto you, that I will **p** the Father for you:	*2065*
	17: 9	I **p** for them: I pray not for the world, but	*2065*
	17: 9	I **p** not for the world, but for *them* which	*2065*
	17:15	I **p** not that thou shouldest take them out of	*2065*
	17:20	Neither **p** I for these alone, but for them	*2065*
Ac	8:22	of this thy wickedness, and **p** God,	*1189*
	8:24	and said, **P** ye to the Lord for me,	*1189*
	8:34	eunuch answered Philip, and said, I **p** thee,	*1189*
	10: 9	Peter went up upon the house to **p** about	*4336*
	24: 4	I **p** *thee* that thou wouldest hear us of thy	*3870*
	27:34	Wherefore I **p** you to take *some* meat:	*3870*
Ro	8:26	for we know not what we should **p** for as	*4336*
1Co	11:13	is it comely that a woman **p** unto God	*4336*
	14:13	an *unknown* tongue **p** that he may interpret.	*4336*
	14:14	For if I **p** in an *unknown* tongue, my spirit	*4336*
	14:15	I will **p** with the spirit, and will pray with	*4336*
	14:15	and will **p** with the understanding also:	*4336*
2Co	5:20	we **p** *you* in Christ's stead, be ye reconciled	*1189*
	13: 7	Now I **p** to God that ye do no evil; not that	*2172*
Php	1: 9	And this I **p**, that your love may abound yet	*4336*
Col	1: 9	since the day we heard *it,* do not cease to **p**	*4336*
1Th	5:17	**P** without ceasing.	*4336*
	5:23	and *I p God* your whole spirit and soul and	NIG
	5:25	Brethren, **p** for us.	*4336*
2Th	1:11	Wherefore also we **p** always for you,	*4336*
	3: 1	Finally, brethren, **p** for us, that the word of	*4336*
1Ti	2: 8	I will therefore that men **p** every where,	*4336*
2Ti	4:16	*I p God* that it may not be laid to their	NIG
Heb	13:18	**P** for us: for we trust we have a good	*4336*
Jas	5:13	let him **p**. Is any merry? let him sing	*4336*
	5:14	and let them **p** over him, anointing him	*4336*
	5:16	and **p** one for another, that ye may be	*2172*
1Jn	5:16	I do not say that he shall **p** for it.	*2065*

PRAYED (65) [PRAY]

Ge	20:17	So Abraham **p** unto God: and God healed	6419
Nu	11: 2	when Moses **p** unto the LORD, the fire	6419
	21: 7	from us. And Moses **p** for the people.	6419
Dt	9:20	and I **p** for Aaron also the same time.	6419
	9:26	I **p** therefore unto the LORD, and said,	6419
1Sa	1:10	and **p** unto the LORD, and wept sore.	6419
	1:27	For this child I **p**; and the LORD hath	6419
	2: 1	Hannah **p**, and said, My heart rejoiceth in	6419
	8: 6	judge us. And Samuel **p** unto the LORD.	6419
2Ki	4:33	upon them twain, and **p** unto the LORD.	6419
	6:17	Elisha **p**, and said, LORD, I pray thee,	6419
	6:18	Elisha **p** unto the LORD, and said,	6419
	19:15	Hezekiah **p** before the LORD, and said,	6419
	19:20	*That* which thou hast **p** to me against	6419
	20: 2	to the wall, and **p** unto the LORD, saying,	6419
2Ch	30:18	Hezekiah **p** for them, saying, The good	6419
	32:20	the son of Amoz, **p** and cried *to* heaven.	6419
	32:24	sick to the death, and **p** unto the LORD:	6419
	33:13	**p** unto him: and he was intreated of him,	6419
Ezr	10: 1	Now when Ezra had **p**, and when he had	6419
Ne	1: 4	and fasted, and **p** before the God of heaven,	6419
	2: 4	make request? So I **p** to the God of heaven.	6419
Job	42:10	captivity of Job, when he **p** for his friends:	6419
Isa	37:15	And Hezekiah **p** unto the LORD, saying,	6419
	37:21	Whereas thou hast **p** to me against	6419
	38: 2	toward the wall, and **p** unto the LORD,	6419
Jer	32:16	son of Neriah, I **p** unto the LORD, saying,	6419
Da	6:10	**p**, and gave thanks before his God, as he	6739
	9: 4	I **p** unto the LORD my God, and made my	6419
Jnh	2: 1	Jonah **p** unto the LORD his God out of	6419
	4: 2	he **p** unto the LORD, and said, I pray thee,	6419
Mt	26:39	fell on his face, and **p**, saying, O my Father,	*4336*
	26:42	second time, and **p**, saying, O my Father,	*4336*
	26:44	and went away again, and **p** the third time,	*4336*
Mk	1:35	departed into a solitary place, and there **p**.	*4336*
	5:18	he that had been possessed with the devil **p**	*3870*
	14:35	the ground, and **p** that, if it were possible,	*4336*
	14:39	and **p**, and spake the same words.	*4336*
Lk	5: 3	**p** him that *he* would thrust out a little from	*2065*
	5:16	himself into the wilderness, and **p**.	*4336*
	9:29	And as he **p**, the fashion of his countenance	*4336*
	18:11	The Pharisee stood and **p** thus with himself,	*4336*
	22:32	But I have **p** for thee, that thy faith fail not:	*1189*
	22:41	a stone's cast, and kneeled down, and **p**,	*4336*
	22:44	And being in an agony he **p** more earnestly:	*4336*
Jn	4:31	In the mean while *his* disciples **p** him,	*2065*
Ac	1:24	And they **p**, and said, Thou, Lord,	*4336*
	4:31	And when they had **p**, the place was shaken	*1189*
	6: 6	and when they had **p**, they laid *their* hands	*4336*
	8:15	when they were come down, **p** for them,	*4336*
	9:40	*them* all forth, and kneeled down, and **p**;	*4336*
	10: 2	alms to the people, and **p to** God alway.	*1189*
	10:30	and at the ninth hour I **p** in my house, and	*4336*
	10:48	Then **p** they him to tarry certain days.	*2065*
	13: 3	And when they had fasted and **p**, and	*4336*
	14:23	and had **p** with fasting, they commended	*4336*
	16: 9	and **p** him, saying, Come over into	*3870*
	16:25	And at midnight Paul and Silas **p**, and	*4336*
	20:36	he kneeled down, and **p** with them all.	*4336*
	21: 5	and we kneeled down on the shore, and **p**.	*4336*
	22:17	even while I **p** in the temple, I was in a	*4336*
	23:18	**p** *me* to bring this young man unto thee,	*2065*
	28: 8	and **p**, and laid *his* hands on him, and	*4336*
Jas	5:17	he **p earnestly** that it might not rain:	*4335+4336*
	5:18	And he **p** again, and the heaven gave rain,	*4336*

P

PRAYER (114) [PRAY]

2Sa 7:27 found in his heart to pray this **p** unto thee. 8605
1Ki 8:28 Yet have thou respect unto the **p** of thy 8605
8:28 to hearken unto the cry and to the **p**, 8605
8:29 **p** which thy servant shall **make** 6419+8605
8:38 What **p** and supplication soever be *made* by 8605
8:45 hear thou *in* heaven their **p** and their 8605
8:49 hear thou their **p** and their supplication *in* 8605
8:54 had made an end of praying all this **p** 8605
9: 3 I have heard thy **p** and thy supplication, 8605
2Ki 19: 4 wherefore lift up *thy* **p** for the remnant that 8605
20: 5 I have heard thy **p**, I have seen thy tears: 8605
2Ch 6:19 therefore to the **p** of thy servant, 8605
6:19 the **p** which thy servant prayeth before 8605
6:20 to hearken unto the **p** which thy servant 8605
6:29 *Then* what **p** *or* what supplication soever 8605
6:35 hear thou from the heavens their **p** and 8605
6:39 their **p** and their supplications, and 8605
6:40 *let* thine ears *be* attent unto the **p** *that is* 8605
7:12 I have heard thy **p**, and have chosen this 8605
7:15 mine ears attent unto the **p** *that is made* in 8605
30:27 their **p** came *up* to his holy dwelling place, 8605
33:18 his **p** unto his God, and the words of 8605
33:19 His **p** also, and *how God* was intreated of 8605
Ne 1: 6 that *thou* mayest hear the **p** of thy servant, 8605
1:11 let now thine ear be attentive to the **p** of thy 8605
1:11 to the **p** of thy servants, who desire to fear 8605
4: 9 Nevertheless we **made** our **p** unto our God, 6419
11:17 the principal to begin the thanksgiving in **p**: 8605
Job 15: 4 off fear, and restrainest **p** before God. 7881
16:17 injustice in mine hands: also my **p** is pure. 8605
22:27 Thou shalt **make** thy **p** unto him, and 6279
Ps 4: 1 have mercy upon me, and hear my **p**. 8605
5: 3 *in* the morning will I direct *my* **p** unto thee, NIH
6: 9 the LORD will receive my **p**. 8605
17: T A **P** of David. 8605
17: 1 attend unto my cry, give ear unto my **p**, 8605
35:13 and my **p** returned into mine own bosom. 8605
39:12 Hear my **p**, O LORD, and give ear unto 8605
42: 8 with me, *and my* **p** unto the God of my life. 8605
54: 2 Hear my **p**, O God; give ear to the words of 8605
55: 1 Give ear to my **p**, O God; and hide not 8605
61: 1 Hear my cry, O God; attend unto my **p**. 8605
64: 1 Hear my voice, O God, in my **p**: 7879
65: 2 O thou that hearest **p**, unto thee shall all 8605
66:19 *me;* he hath attended to the voice of my **p**. 8605
66:20 *be* God, which hath not turned away my **p**, 8605
69:13 *as for* me, my **p** *is* unto thee, O LORD, 8605
72:15 **p** also shall be **made** for him continually; 6419
80: 4 how long wilt thou be angry against the **p** 8605
84: 8 O LORD God *of* hosts, hear my **p**: 8605
86: T A **P** of David. 8605
86: 6 Give ear, O LORD, unto my **p**; and 8605
88: 2 Let my **p** come before thee: incline thine 8605
88:13 and in the morning shall my **p** prevent thee. 8605
90: T A **P** of Moses the man of God. 8605
102: T A **P** of the afflicted, when he is 8605
102: 1 Hear my **p**, O LORD, and let my cry 8605
102:17 He will regard the **p** of the destitute, and 8605
102:17 of the destitute, and not despise their **p**. 8605
109: 4 my adversaries: but I *give myself unto* **p**. 8605
109: 7 be condemned: and let his **p** become sin. 8605
141: 2 Let my **p** be set forth before thee *as* 8605
141: 5 for yet my **p** also *shall be* in their 8605
142: T of David; A **P** when he was in the cave. 8605
143: 1 Hear my **p**, O LORD, give ear to my 8605
Pr 15: 8 but the **p** of the upright *is* his delight. 8605
15:29 but he heareth the **p** of the righteous. 8605
28: 9 the law, even his **p** *shall be* abomination. 8605
Isa 26:16 they poured out a **p** *when* thy chastening 3908
37: 4 wherefore lift up *thy* **p** for the remnant that 8605
38: 5 I have heard thy **p**, I have seen thy tears: 8605
56: 7 and make them joyful in my house of **p**: 8605
56: 7 for mine house shall be called a house of **p** 8605
Jer 7:16 neither lift up cry nor **p** for them, 8605
11:14 neither lift up a cry or **p** for them: 8605
La 3: 8 when I cry and shout, he shutteth out my **p**. 8605
3:44 a cloud, that *our* **p** should not pass through. 8605
Da 9: 3 to seek *by* **p** and supplications, with fasting, 8605
9:13 yet **made** we not our **p** before the LORD 2470
9:17 hear the **p** of thy servant, and 8605
9:21 Yea, whiles I *was* speaking in **p**, even 8605
Jnh 2: 7 my **p** came in unto thee, into thine holy 8605
Hab 3: 1 A **p** of Habakkuk the prophet upon 8605
Mt 17:21 this kind goeth not out but by **p** and fasting. *4335*
21:13 My house shall be called the house of **p**; *4335*
21:22 all *things,* whatsoever ye shall ask in **p**, *4335*
23:14 and for a pretence **make** long **p**: *4336*
Mk 9:29 forth by nothing, but by **p** and fasting. *4335*
11:17 shall be called of all nations the house of **p**? *4335*
Lk 1:13 for thy **p** is heard; and thy wife Elisabeth *1162*
6:12 to pray, and continued all night in **p** to God. *4335*
19:46 It is written, My house is the house of **p**: *4335*
22:45 And when he rose up from **p**, and *4335*
Ac 1:14 These all continued with one accord in **p** *4335*
3: 1 up together into the temple at the hour of **p**, *4335*
6: 4 But we will give ourselves continually to **p**, *4335*
10:31 thy **p** is heard, and thine alms are had in *4335*
12: 5 **p** was made without ceasing of the church *4335*
16:13 a river side, where **p** was wont to be made; *4335*
16:16 And it came to pass, as we went to **p**, *4335*
Ro 10: 1 my heart's desire and **p** to God for Israel is, *1162*
12:12 in tribulation; continuing instant in **p**; *4335*
1Co 7: 5 ye may give yourselves to fasting and **p**, *4335*
2Co 1:11 You also helping together by **p** for us, *1162*
9:14 And by their **p** for you, which long after *1162*
Eph 6:18 Praying always with all **p** and *4335*
Php 1: 4 Always in every **p** of mine for you all *1162*
1:19 shall turn to my salvation through your **p**, *1162*
4: 6 but in every *thing* by **p** and supplication *4335*
Col 4: 2 Continue in **p**, and watch in the same with *4335*
1Ti 4: 5 it is sanctified by the word of God and **p**. *1783*
Jas 5:15 And the **p** of faith shall save the sick, and *2171*
5:16 The effectual fervent **p** of a righteous *man* *1162*
1Pe 4: 7 be ye therefore sober, and watch unto **p**. *4335*

PRAYERS (24) [PRAY]

Ps 72:20 The **p** of David the son of Jesse are ended. 8605
Isa 1:15 yea, when ye make many **p**, I will not hear: 8605
Mk 12:40 and for a pretence **make** long **p**: *4336*
Lk 2:37 *God* with fastings and **p** night and day. *1162*
5:33 and make **p**, and likewise the *disciples* of *1162*
20:47 and for a shew **make** long **p**: *4336*
Ac 2:42 and in breaking of bread, and in **p**. *4335*
10: 4 Thy **p** and thine alms are come up for a *4335*
Ro 1: 9 I make mention of you, always in my **p**, *4335*
15:30 that *ye* strive together with me in *your* **p** to *4335*
Eph 1:16 for you, making mention of you in my **p**; *4335*
Col 4:12 always labouring fervently for you in **p**, *4335*
1Th 1: 2 you all, making mention of you in our **p**; *4335*
1Ti 2: 1 **p**, intercessions, *and* giving of thanks, *4335*
5: 5 in supplications and **p** night and day. *4335*
2Ti 1: 3 I have remembrance of thee in my **p** night *1162*
Phm 1: 4 making mention of thee always in my **p**, *4335*
1:22 for I trust that through your **p** I shall be *4335*
Heb 5: 7 when he had offered up **p** and *1162*
1Pe 3: 7 grace of life; that your **p** be not hindered. *4335*
3:12 and his ears *are open* unto their **p**: *1162*
Rev 5: 8 full of odours, which are the **p** of saints. *4335*
8: 3 that he should offer *it* with the **p** of all *4335*
8: 4 *which came* with the **p** of the saints, *4335*

PRAYEST (2) [PRAY]

Mt 6: 5 And when thou **p**, thou shalt not be as *4336*
6: 6 But thou, when thou **p**, enter into thy *4336*

PRAYETH (7) [PRAY]

1Ki 8:28 which thy servant **p** before thee to day: 6419
2Ch 6:19 the prayer which thy servant **p** before thee: 6419
6:20 which thy servant **p** towards this place. 6419
Isa 44:17 worshippeth *it,* and **p** unto it, and saith, 6419
Ac 9:11 *one* called Saul, of Tarsus: for behold, he **p**, *4336*
1Co 11: 5 But every woman that **p** or *4336*
14:14 my spirit **p**, but my understanding is *4336*

PRAYING (20) [PRAY]

1Sa 1:12 as she continued **p** before the LORD, 6419
1:26 that stood by thee here, **p** unto the LORD. 6419
1Ki 8:54 *that* when Solomon had made an end of **p** 6419
2Ch 7: 1 Now when Solomon had made an end of **p**, 6419
Da 6:11 found Daniel **p** and making supplication 1156
9:20 **p**, and confessing my sin and the sin of my 6419
Mk 11:25 And when ye stand **p**, forgive, if ye have *4336*
Lk 1:10 were **p** without at the time of incense. *4336*
3:21 and **p**, the heaven was opened, *4336*
9:18 And it came to pass, as he was alone **p**, *4336*
11: 1 And it came to pass *that,* as he was **p** in a *4336*

Ac 11: 5 I was in the city of Joppa **p**: and in a trance *4336*
12:12 where many were gathered together **p**. *4336*
1Co 11: 4 Every man **p** or prophesying, having *his* *4336*
2Co 8: 4 **P** us with much intreaty that we would *1189*
Eph 6:18 **P** always with all prayer and supplication in *4336*
Col 1: 3 of our Lord Jesus Christ, **p** always for you, *4336*
4: 3 Withal **p** also for us, that God would open *4336*
1Th 3:10 day **p** exceedingly that *we* might see your *1189*
Jude 1:20 your most holy faith, **p** in the Holy Ghost, *4336*

PREACH (50) [PREACHED, PREACHER, PREACHEST, PREACHETH, PREACHING]

Ne 6: 7 thou hast also appointed prophets to **p** of 7121
Isa 61: 1 me to **p good tidings unto** the meek; 1319
Jnh 3: 2 and **p** unto it the preaching that I bid thee. 7121
Mt 4:17 From that time Jesus began to **p**, and to say, *2784*
10: 7 And as ye go, **p**, saying, The kingdom of *2784*
10:27 in the ear, *that* **p** ye upon the housetops. *2784*
11: 1 thence to teach and to **p** in their cities. *2784*
Mk 1: 4 **p** the baptism of repentance for *2784*
1:38 into the next towns, that I may **p** there also: *2784*
3:14 and that he might send them forth to **p**, *2784*
16:15 and **p** the gospel to every creature. *2784*
Lk 4:18 he hath anointed me to **p the gospel** to *2097*
4:18 to **p** deliverance to the captives, and *2784*
4:19 To **p** the acceptable year of the Lord. *2784*
4:43 I must **p** the kingdom of God to other cities *2097*
9: 2 And he sent them to **p** the kingdom of God, *2784*
9:60 but go thou and **p** the kingdom of God. *1229*
Ac 5:42 they ceased not to teach and **p** Jesus Christ. *2097*
10:42 And he commanded us to **p** unto *2784*
14:15 **p** unto you that *ye* should turn from these *2097*
15:21 old time hath in every city them that **p** him, *2784*
16: 6 were forbidden of the Holy Ghost to **p** *2980*
16:10 had called us for to **p the gospel** unto them. *2097*
17: 3 this Jesus, whom I **p** unto you, is Christ. *2605*
Ro 1:15 I am ready to **p the gospel** to you that are at *2097*
10: 8 that is, the word of faith, which we **p**; *2784*
10:15 And how shall they **p**, except they be sent? *2784*
10:15 the feet of them that **p the gospel** of peace, *2097*
15:20 Yea, so have I strived to **p the gospel**, *2097*
1Co 1:17 sent me not to baptize, but to **p the gospel**: *2097*
1:23 But we **p** Christ crucified, unto the Jews a *2784*
9:14 hath the Lord ordained that they which **p** *2605*
9:16 For though I **p the gospel**, I have nothing *2097*
9:16 yea, woe is unto me, if I **p** not **the gospel**! *2097*
9:18 *Verily* that, when I **p the gospel**, I may *2097*
15:11 *were* I or they, so we **p**, and so ye believed. *2784*
2Co 2:12 when I came to Troas to ***p*** Christ's gospel, NIG
4: 5 For we **p** not ourselves, but Christ Jesus *2784*
10:16 To **p the gospel** in the *regions* beyond you, *2097*
Gal 1: 8 **p** any other **gospel** unto you than *that* *2097*
1: 9 If any *man* **p** any other **gospel** unto you *2097*
1:16 that I might **p** him among the heathen; *2097*
2: 2 *that* gospel which I **p** among the Gentiles, *2784*
5:11 And I, brethren, if I yet **p** circumcision, *2784*
Eph 3: 8 that *I* should **p** among the Gentiles *2097*
Php 1:15 Some indeed **p** Christ even of envy and *2784*
1:16 The one **p** Christ of contention, *2605*
Col 1:28 Whom we **p**, warning every man, and *2605*
2Ti 4: 2 **P** the word; be instant in season, out of *2784*
Rev 14: 6 having the everlasting gospel to **p** unto *2097*

PREACHED (61) [PREACH]

Ps 40: 9 I have **p** righteousness in the great 1319
Mt 11: 5 and the poor have **the gospel p** to them. *2097*
24:14 And this gospel of the kingdom shall be **p** *2784*
26:13 Wheresoever this gospel shall be **p** in *2784*
Mk 1: 7 And **p**, saying, There cometh one mightier *2784*
1:39 And he **p** in their synagogues throughout *2784*
2: 2 the door: and he **p** the word unto them. *2980*
6:12 went out, and **p** that *men* should repent. *2784*
14: 9 Wheresoever this gospel shall be **p** *2784*
16:20 And they went forth, and **p** every where, *2784*
Lk 3:18 And many other *things* in his exhortation **p** *2097*
4:44 And he **p** in the synagogues of Galilee. *2784*
7:22 dead are raised, to the poor **the gospel** is **p**. *2097*
16:16 since that time the kingdom of God is **p**, *2097*
20: 1 and **p the gospel**, the chief priests and *2097*
24:47 remission of sins should be **p** in his name *2784*
Ac 3:20 Jesus Christ, which **before** was **p** unto you: *4296*
4: 2 **p** through Jesus the resurrection from *2605*
8: 5 the city of Samaria, and **p** Christ unto them. *2784*
8:25 had testified and **p** the word of the Lord, *2980*
8:25 **p the gospel** in many villages of *2097*
8:35 at the same scripture, and **p** unto him Jesus. *2097*
8:40 and passing through he **p** in all the cities, *2097*
9:20 And straightway he **p** Christ in *2784*
9:27 how he had **p boldly** at Damascus in *3955*
10:37 after the baptism which John **p**; *2784*
13: 5 they **p** the word of God in the synagogues *2605*
13:24 When John had **first p** before his coming *4296*
13:38 that through this *man* is **p** unto you *2605*
13:42 words might be **p** to them the next sabbath. *2980*
14: 7 And there they **p the gospel**. *2097*
14:21 And when they had **p the gospel** to that *2097*
14:25 And when they had **p** the word in Perga, *2980*
15:36 city where we have **p** the word of the Lord, *2605*
17:13 the word of God was **p** of Paul at Berea, *2605*
17:18 because he **p** unto them Jesus, and *2097*
20: 7 Paul **p** unto them, ready to depart on *1256*
Ro 15:19 I have fully **p** the gospel of Christ. NIG
1Co 9:27 that by any means, when I have **p** to others, *2784*
15: 1 I declare unto you the gospel which I **p** *2097*
15: 2 if ye keep in memory what I **p** unto you, *2097*
15:12 Now if Christ be **p** that he rose from *2784*
2Co 1:19 who was **p** among you by us, *even* by me *2784*
11: 4 whom we have not **p**, or *if* ye receive *2784*
11: 7 I have **p** to you the gospel of God freely? *2097*
Gal 1: 8 you than *that* which we have **p** unto you, *2097*
1:11 that the gospel which was **p** of me is not *2097*
3: 8 **p before the gospel** unto Abraham, *4283*
4:13 flesh I **p the gospel** unto you at the first. *2097*
Eph 2:17 and **p** peace to you which were afar off, *2097*
Php 1:18 whether in pretence, or in truth, Christ is **p**; *2605*
Col 1:23 which was **p** to every creature which is *2784*
1Th 2: 9 of you, we **p** unto you the gospel of God. *2784*
1Ti 3:16 seen of angels, **p** unto the Gentiles, *2784*
Heb 4: 2 For unto us was **the gospel p**, as well as *2097*
4: 2 but the word **p** did not profit them, *189*
4: 6 they to whom it was first **p** entered not in *2097*
1Pe 1:12 **p the gospel** unto you with the Holy Ghost *2097*
1:25 word which by the **gospel** is **p** unto you. *2097*
3:19 he went and **p** unto the spirits in prison; *2784*
4: 6 For for this cause was the **gospel p** also to *2097*

PREACHER (11) [PREACH]

Ecc 1: 1 The words of the **P**, the son of David, 6953
1: 2 of vanities, saith the **P**, vanity of vanities; 6953
1:12 I the **P** was king over Israel in Jerusalem. 6953
7:27 Behold, this have I found, saith the **P**, 6953
12: 8 Vanity of vanities, saith the **P**; all *is* vanity. 6953
12: 9 moreover, because the **P** was wise, he still 6953
12:10 The **P** sought to find out acceptable words: 6953
Ro 10:14 and how shall they hear without a **p**? *2784*
1Ti 2: 7 Whereunto I am ordained a **p**, and *2783*
2Ti 1:11 Whereunto I am appointed a **p**, and *2783*
2Pe 2: 5 saved Noah the eighth *person,* a **p** of *2783*

PREACHEST (1) [PREACH]

Ro 2:21 thou that **p** *a man* should not steal, *2784*

PREACHETH (3) [PREACH]

Ac 19:13 We adjure you by Jesus whom Paul **p**. *2784*
2Co 11: 4 For if he that cometh **p** another Jesus, *2784*
Gal 1:23 now **p** the faith which once he destroyed. *2097*

PREACHING (27) [PREACH]

Jnh 3: 2 and preach unto it the **p** that I bid thee. 7150
Mt 3: 1 the Baptist, **p** in the wilderness of Judea, *2784*
4:23 and **p** the gospel of the kingdom, *2784*
9:35 and **p** the gospel of the kingdom, and *2784*
12:41 because they repented at the **p** of Jonas; *2782*
Mk 1:14 **p** the gospel of the kingdom of God, *2784*
Lk 3: 3 **p** the baptism of repentance for *2784*
8: 1 **p** and shewing the glad tidings of *2784*
9: 6 **p the gospel**, and healing every where. *2097*
11:32 for they repented at the **p** of Jonas; and *2782*
Ac 8: 4 abroad went every where **p** the word. *2097*
8:12 But when they believed Philip **p** the *things* *2097*
10:36 children of Israel, **p** peace by Jesus Christ: *2097*
11:19 **p** the word to none but unto *the* Jews only. *2980*
11:20 spake unto the Grecians, **p** the Lord Jesus. *2097*
15:35 teaching and **p** the word of the Lord, *2097*
20: 9 and as Paul was long **p**, he sunk down with *1256*
20:25 among whom I have gone **p** the kingdom of *2784*
28:31 **P** the kingdom of God, and teaching those *2784*
Ro 16:25 and the **p** of Jesus Christ, according to *2782*

1Co 1:18 For the **p** of the cross is to them that perish *3056*
1:21 it pleased God by the foolishness of **p** to *2782*
2: 4 my **p** *was* not with enticing words of man's *2782*
15:14 then *is* our **p** vain, and your faith *is* also *2782*
2Co 10:14 for we are come as far as to you also in **p** NIG
2Ti 4:17 that by me the **p** might be fully known, and *2782*
Tit 1: 3 due times manifested his word through **p**, *2782*

PRECEPT (11) [PRECEPTS]
Isa 28:10 For **p** *must be* upon precept, precept upon 6673
28:10 For precept *must be* upon **p**, precept upon 6673
28:10 *must be* upon precept, **p** upon precept; 6673
28:10 *must be* upon precept, precept upon **p**; 6673
28:13 the word of the LORD was unto them **p** 6673
28:13 the LORD was unto them precept upon **p**, 6673
28:13 them precept upon precept, **p** upon precept; 6673
28:13 them precept upon precept, precept upon **p**; 6673
29:13 their fear towards me is taught *by* the **p** of 4687
Mk 10: 5 hardness of your heart he wrote you this **p**. *1785*
Heb 9:19 For when Moses had spoken every **p** to all *1785*

PRECEPTS (24) [PRECEPT]
Ne 9:14 commandedst them **p**, statutes, and laws, 4687
Ps 119: 4 Thou hast commanded *us* to keep thy **p** 6490
119:15 I will meditate in thy **p**, and have respect 6490
119:27 Make me to understand the way of thy **p**: 6490
119:40 Behold, I have longed after thy **p**: 6490
119:45 And I will walk at liberty: for I seek thy **p**. 6490
119:56 This I had, because I kept thy **p**. 6490
119:63 that fear thee, and of them that keep thy **p**. 6490
119:69 *but* I will keep thy **p** with *my* whole heart. 6490
119:78 a cause: *but* I will meditate in thy **p**. 6490
119:87 me upon earth; but I forsook not thy **p**. 6490
119:93 I will never forget thy **p**: for with them thou 6490
119:94 *am* thine, save me; for I have sought thy **p**. 6490
119:100 than the ancients, because I keep thy **p**. 6490
119:104 Through thy **p** I get understanding: 6490
119:110 a snare for me: yet I erred not from thy **p**. 6490
119:128 Therefore I esteem all *thy* **p** concerning all 6490
119:134 the oppression of man: so will I keep thy **p**. 6490
119:141 and despised: *yet* do not I forget thy **p**. 6490
119:159 Consider how I love thy **p**: quicken me, 6490
119:168 I have kept thy **p** and thy testimonies: 6490
119:173 hand help me; for I have chosen thy **p**. 6490
Jer 35:18 kept all his **p**, and done according unto all 4687
Da 9: 5 even by departing from thy **p** and from thy 4687

PRECIOUS (76)
Ge 24:53 to her brother and to her mother **p things**. 4030
Dt 33:13 for the **p things** of heaven, for the dew, and 4022
33:14 for the **p** fruits brought forth by the sun, 4022
33:14 and for the **p things** put forth by the moon, 4022
33:15 and for the **p things** of the lasting hills, 4022
33:16 for the **p things** of the earth and 4022
1Sa 3: 1 the word of the LORD was **p** in those 3368
26:21 my soul was **p** in thine eyes this day: 3365
2Sa 12:30 *was* a talent of gold with the **p** stones: 3368
1Ki 10: 2 and very much gold, and **p** stones: 3368
10:10 and of spices very great store, and **p** stones: 3368
10:11 great plenty of almug trees, and **p** stones. 3368
2Ki 1:13 of these fifty thy servants, be **p** in thy sight. 3365
1:14 therefore let my life now be **p** in thy sight. 3365
20:13 shewed them all the house of his **p things**, 5238
20:13 the **p** ointment, and all the house of his 2896
1Ch 20: 2 talent of gold, and *there were* **p** stones in it; 3368
29: 2 all *manner of* **p** stones, and marble stones 3368
29: 8 they with whom *p* stones were found gave NIH
2Ch 3: 6 he garnished the house with **p** stones for 3368
9: 1 and gold in abundance, and **p** stones: 3368
9: 9 of spices great abundance, and **p** stones: 3368
9:10 brought algum trees and **p** stones. 3368
20:25 **p** jewels, which they stript off for 2532
21: 3 of gold, and of **p things**, with fenced cities 4030
32:27 for **p** stones, and for spices, and for shields, 3368
Ezr 1: 6 and with beasts, and with **p things**, 4030
8:27 and two vessels of fine copper, **p** as gold. 2532
Job 28:10 the rocks; and his eye seeth every **p thing**. 3366
28:16 of Ophir, with the **p** onyx, or the sapphire. 3368
Ps 49: 8 (For the redemption of their soul is **p**, and 3365
72:14 and **p** shall their blood be in his sight. 3365
116:15 **P** in the sight of the LORD *is* the death of 3368
126: 6 goeth forth and weepeth, bearing **p** seed, 4901
133: 2 *It is* like the **p** ointment upon the head, 2896
139:17 How **p** also are thy thoughts unto me, 3365
Pr 1:13 We shall find all **p** substance, we shall fill 3368
3:15 She *is* more **p** than rubies: and all the things 3368
6:26 and the adulteress will hunt for the **p** life. 3368
12:27 but the substance of a diligent man *is* **p**. 3368
17: 8 A gift *is as* a **p** stone in the eyes of him that 2580
20:15 but the lips of knowledge *are* a **p** jewel. 3366
24: 4 shall the chambers be filled *with* all **p** 3368
Ecc 7: 1 A *good* name *is* better than **p** ointment; and 2896
Isa 13:12 I will **make** a man more **p** than fine gold; 3365
28:16 a **p** corner *stone,* a sure foundation: 3368
39: 2 shewed them the house of his **p things**, 5238
39: 2 the **p** ointment, and all the house of his 2896
43: 4 Since thou wast **p** in my sight, thou hast 3365
Jer 15:19 if thou take forth the **p** from the vile, 3368
20: 5 all the **p things** thereof, and all 3366
La 4: 2 The **p** sons of Zion, comparable to fine 3368
Eze 22:25 they have taken the treasure and **p things**; 3366
27:20 Dedan *was* thy merchant in **p** clothes for 2667
27:22 all spices, and with all **p** stones, and gold. 3368
28:13 every **p** stone *was* thy covering, the sardius, 3368
Da 11: 8 *and* with their **p** vessels of silver and 2532
11:38 and with **p** stones, and pleasant things. 3368
11:43 of silver, and over all the **p** *things* of Egypt: 2532
Mt 26: 7 having an alabaster box of **very p** ointment, *927*
Mk 14: 3 box of ointment of spikenard **very p**; *4185*
1Co 3:12 silver, **p** stones, wood, hay, stubble; *5093*
Jas 5: 7 the husbandman waiteth for the **p** fruit of *5093*
1Pe 1: 7 *being* much **more p** than of gold that *5093*
1:19 But with the **p** blood of Christ, as of a lamb *5093*
2: 4 indeed of men, but chosen of God, *and* **p**, *1784*
2: 6 I lay in Sion a chief corner stone, elect, **p**: *1784*
2: 7 Unto you therefore which believe *he is* **p**: *5092*
2Pe 1: 1 to them that have obtained **like p** faith with *2472*
1: 4 unto us exceeding great and **p** promises: *5093*
Rev 17: 4 decked with gold and **p** stone and pearls, *5093*
18:12 and **p** stones, and of pearls, and fine linen, *5093*
18:12 and all *manner* vessels of **most p** wood, *5093*
18:16 decked with gold, and **p** stones, and pearls: *5093*
21:11 and her light *was* like unto a stone **most p**, *5093*
21:19 *were* garnished with all *manner of* **p** stones. *5093*

PREDESTINATE (2) [PREDESTINATED]
Ro 8:29 he also did **p** *to be* conformed to the image *4309*
8:30 Moreover whom he did **p**, them he also *4309*

PREDESTINATED (2) [PREDESTINATE]
Eph 1: 5 Having **p** us unto the adoption of children *4309*
1:11 being **p** according to the purpose of him *4309*

PREDESTINED See PREDESTINATE; PREDESTINATED

PREEMINENCE (3) [EMINENT]
Ecc 3:19 so that a man **hath** no **p** above a beast: 4195
Col 1:18 that in all *things* he might have the **p**. *4409*
3Jn 1: 9 who **loveth to have** the **p among** them, *5383*

PREFER (1) [PREFERRED, PREFERRING]
Ps 137: 6 if I **p** not Jerusalem above my chief joy. 5927

PREFERRED (5) [PREFER]
Est 2: 9 he **p** her and her maids unto the best *place* 8138
Da 6: 3 this Daniel was **p** above the presidents 5330
Jn 1:15 that cometh after me is **p before** me: *1096+1715*
1:27 it is, who coming after me is **p** before me, *1096*
1:30 cometh a man which is **p before** me: *1096+1715*

PREFERRING (2) [PREFER]
Ro 12:10 brotherly love; in honour **p** one another; *4285*
1Ti 5:21 that thou observe these *things* without **p** *4299*

PREMEDITATE (1)
Mk 13:11 what ye shall speak, neither do ye **p**: *3191*

PREPARATION (9) [PREPARE]
1Ch 22: 5 I will *therefore* now **make p** for it. 3559
Na 2: 3 *be* with flaming torches in the day of his **p**, 3559
Mt 27:62 that followed the *day of the* **p**, the chief *3904*
Mk 15:42 because it was the **p**, that is, the day before *3904*
Lk 23:54 And *that* day was the **p**, and the sabbath *3904*
Jn 19:14 And it was the **p** of the passover, and *3904*
19:31 The Jews therefore, because it was the **p**, *3904*
19:42 of the Jews' **p** *day;* for the sepulchre was *3904*
Eph 6:15 And *your* feet shod with the **p** of the gospel *2091*

P

PREPARATIONS (1) [PREPARE]
Pr 16: 1 The **p** of the heart in man, and the answer 4633

PREPARE (81) [PREPARATION, PREPARATIONS, PREPARED, PREPAREDST, PREPAREST, PREPARETH, PREPARING, UNPREPARED]
Ex 15: 2 *is* my God, and I will **p** him **a habitation**; 5115
16: 5 that on the sixth day they shall **p** *that* which 3559
Nu 15: 5 offering shalt thou **p** with the burnt offering 6213
15: 6 thou shalt **p** *for* a meat offering two tenth 6213
15:12 According to the number that ye shall **p**, so 6213
23: 1 and **p** me here seven oxen and seven rams. 3559
23:29 **p** me here seven bullocks and seven rams. 3559
Dt 19: 3 Thou shalt **p** thee a way, and divide 3559
Jos 1:11 the people, saying, **P** you victuals; 3559
22:26 we said, Let us now **p** to build us an altar, 6213
1Sa 7: 3 **p** your hearts unto the LORD, and 3559
23:22 **p** yet, and know and see his place where his 3559
1Ki 18:44 unto Ahab, **P** *thy chariot,* and get thee down, 631
1Ch 9:32 over the shewbread, to **p** *it* every sabbath. 3559
29:18 of thy people, and **p** their heart unto thee: 3559
2Ch 2: 9 Even to **p** me timber in abundance: for 3559
31:11 Hezekiah commanded to **p** chambers in 3559
35: 4 **p** *yourselves* by the houses of your fathers, 3559
35: 6 sanctify yourselves, and **p** your brethren, 3559
Est 5: 8 Haman come to the banquet that I shall **p** 6213
Job 8: 8 and **p** *thyself* to the search of their fathers: 3559
11:13 If thou **p** thine heart, and stretch out thine 3559
27:16 silver as the dust, and **p** raiment as the clay; 3559
27:17 He may **p** *it,* but the just shall put *it* on, and 3559
Ps 10:17 thou wilt **p** their heart, thou wilt cause thine 3559
59: 4 and **p** themselves without *my* fault: 3559
61: 7 O **p** mercy and truth, *which* may preserve 4487
107:36 that they may **p** a city for habitation; 3559
Pr 24:27 **P** thy work without, and make it fit for 3559
30:25 yet they **p** their meat in the summer; 3559
Isa 14:21 **P** slaughter for his children for the iniquity 3559
21: 5 **P** the table, watch *in* the watchtower, eat, 6186
40: 3 **P** ye the way of the LORD, 6437
40:20 a cunning workman to **p** a graven image, 3559
57:14 shall say, Cast ye up, cast ye up, **p** the way, 6437
62:10 **p** you the way of the people; cast up, 6437
65:11 that **p** a table for *that* troop, and that furnish 6186
Jer 6: 4 **P** ye war against her; arise, and let us go up 6942
12: 3 and **p** them for the day of slaughter. 6942
22: 7 I will **p** destroyers against thee, every one 6942
46:14 say ye, Stand fast, and **p** thee; for the sword 3559
51:12 set up the watchmen, **p** the ambushes: 3559
51:27 the nations, **p** the nations against her, 6942
51:28 **P** against her the nations with the kings of 6942
Eze 4:15 and thou shalt **p** thy bread therewith. 6213
12: 3 **p** thee stuff for removing, and remove by 6213
35: 6 I will **p** thee unto blood, and blood shall 6213
38: 7 **p** for thyself, thou, and all thy company 3559
43:25 Seven days shalt thou **p** every day a goat 6213
43:25 they shall also **p** a young bullock, and 6213
45:17 he shall **p** the sin offering, and the meat 6213
45:22 upon that day shall the prince **p** for himself 6213
45:23 seven days of the feast he shall **p** a burnt 6213
45:24 he shall **p** a meat offering *of* an ephah for a 6213
46: 2 the priests shall **p** his burnt offering and 6213
46: 7 he shall **p** a meat offering, an ephah for a 6213
46:12 Now when the prince shall **p** a voluntary 6213
46:12 he shall **p** his burnt offering and his peace 6213
46:13 Thou shalt daily **p** a burnt offering unto 6213
46:13 thou shalt **p** it every morning. 6213
46:14 thou shalt **p** a meat offering for it every 6213
46:15 Thus shall they **p** the lamb, and the meat 6213
Joel 3: 9 **P** war, wake up the mighty *men,* let all 6942
Am 4:12 this unto thee, **p** to meet thy God, O Israel. 3559
Mic 3: 5 their mouths, they even **p** war against him. 6942
Mal 3: 1 and he shall **p** the way before me: 6437
Mt 3: 3 **P** ye the way of the Lord, make his paths *2090*
11:10 thy face, which shall **p** thy way before thee. *2680*
26:17 Where wilt thou *that* we **p** for thee to eat *2090*
Mk 1: 2 thy face, which shall **p** thy way before thee. *2680*
1: 3 **P** ye the way of the Lord, make his paths *2090*
14:12 and **p** that thou mayest eat the passover? *2090*
Lk 1:76 before the face of the Lord to **p** his ways; *2090*
3: 4 **P** ye the way of the Lord, make his paths *2090*
7:27 thy face, which shall **p** thy way before thee. *2680*
22: 8 and John, saying, Go and **p** us the passover, *2090*
22: 9 said unto him, Where wilt thou *that* we **p**? *2090*
Jn 14: 2 have told you. I go to **p** a place for you. *2090*
14: 3 And if I go and **p** a place for you, I will *2090*
1Co 14: 8 who shall **p** himself to the battle? *3903*
Phm 1:22 But withal **p** me also a lodging: for I trust *2090*

PREPARED (101) [PREPARE]
Ge 24:31 for I have **p** the house, and room for 6437
27:17 and the bread, which she had **p**, 6213
Ex 12:39 neither had they **p** for themselves *any* 6213
23:20 to bring thee into the place which I have **p**. 3559
Nu 21:27 let the city of Sihon be built and **p**: 3559
23: 4 I have **p** seven altars, and I have offered 6186
Jos 4: 4 whom he had **p** of the children of Israel, 3559
4:13 About forty thousand **p** for war passed over 2502
2Sa 15: 1 that Absalom **p** him chariots and horses, 6213
1Ki 1: 5 he **p** him chariots and horsemen, and 6213
5:18 so they **p** timber and stones to build 3559
6:19 the oracle he **p** in the house within, to set 3559
2Ki 6:23 he **p** great provision for them: and 3739
1Ch 12:39 drinking: for their brethren had **p** for them. 3559
15: 1 **p** a place for the ark of God, and 3559
15: 3 unto his place, which he had **p** for it. 3559
15:12 of Israel unto *the place that* I have **p** for it. 3559
22: 3 David **p** iron in abundance for the nails for 3559
22: 5 So David **p** abundantly before his death. 3559
22:14 in my trouble I have **p** for the house of 3559
22:14 timber also and stone have I **p**; and 3559
29: 2 Now I have **p** with all my might for 3559
29: 3 above all *that* I have **p** for the holy house, 3559
29:16 all this store that we have **p** to build thee a 3559
2Ch 1: 4 to *the place which* David had **p** for it: 3559
3: 1 in the place that David had **p** in 3559
8:16 Now all the work of Solomon was **p** unto 3559
12:14 he **p** not his heart to seek the LORD. 3559
16:14 divers kinds *of spices* **p** by 7543
17:18 fourscore thousand **ready p for** the war. 2502
19: 3 the land, and hast **p** thine heart to seek God. 3559
20:33 for as yet the people had not **p** their hearts 3559
26:14 Uzziah **p** for them throughout all the host 3559
27: 6 he **p** his ways before the LORD his God. 3559
29:19 have we **p** and sanctified, and behold, 3559
29:36 all the people, that God had **p** the people: 3559
31:11 the house of the LORD; and they **p** *them,* 3559
35:10 So the service was **p**, and the priests stood 3559
35:14 therefore the Levites **p** for themselves, and 3559
35:15 for their brethren the Levites **p** for them. 3559
35:16 So all the service of the LORD was **p** 3559
35:20 all this, when Josiah had **p** the temple, 3559
Ezr 7:10 For Ezra had **p** his heart to seek the law of 3559
Ne 5:18 Now *that* which was **p** *for me* daily *was* 6213
5:18 also fowls were **p** for me, and once in ten 6213
8:10 portions unto *them* for whom nothing is **p**: 3559
13: 5 he had **p** for him a great chamber, where 6213
Est 5: 4 day unto the banquet that I have **p** for him. 6213
5: 5 came to the banquet that Esther had **p**. 6213
5:12 the king unto the banquet that she had **p** 6213
6: 4 on the gallows that he had **p** for him. 3559
6:14 Haman unto the banquet that Esther had **p**. 6213
7:10 on the gallows that he had **p** for Mordecai. 3559
Job 28:27 declare it; he **p** it, yea, and searched it out. 3559
29: 7 the city, *when* I **p** my seat in the street; 3559
Ps 7:13 He hath also **p** for him the instruments of 3559
9: 7 for ever: he hath **p** his throne for judgment. 3559
57: 6 They have **p** a net for my steps; my soul is 3559
68:10 O God, hast **p** of thy goodness for the poor. 3559
74:16 *is* thine: thou hast **p** the light and the sun. 3559
103:19 The LORD hath **p** his throne in 3559
Pr 8:27 When he **p** the heavens, I *was* there: 3559
19:29 Judgments are **p** for scorners, and 3559
21:31 The horse *is* **p** against the day of battle: but 3559
Isa 30:33 yea, for the king it is **p**; he hath made *it* 3559
64: 4 *what* he hath **p** for him that waiteth for him. 6213
Eze 23:41 upon a stately bed, and a table **p** before it, 6186
28:13 of thy pipes was **p** in thee in the day that 3559
38: 7 Be thou **p**, and prepare for thyself, thou, 3559
Da 2: 9 for ye have **p** lying and corrupt words to 2164
Hos 2: 8 her silver and gold, *which* they **p** for Baal. 6213
6: 3 his going forth *is* **p** as the morning; and 3559
Jnh 1:17 Now the LORD had **p** a great fish to 4487
4: 6 the LORD God **p** a gourd, and made *it* to 4487
4: 7 God **p** a worm when the morning rose 4487
4: 8 did arise, that God **p** a vehement east wind; 4487

Na 2: 5 the wall thereof, and the defence shall be **p**. 3559
Zep 1: 7 for the LORD hath **p** a sacrifice, he hath 3559
Mt 20:23 *it shall be given to them* for whom it is **p** of *2090*
22: 4 are bidden, Behold, I have **p** my dinner: *2090*
25:34 inherit the kingdom **p** for you from *2090*
25:41 **p** for the devil and his angels: *2090*
Mk 10:40 *it shall be given to them* for whom it is **p**. *2090*
14:15 you a large upper room furnished *and* **p**: *2092*
Lk 1:17 to make ready a people **p** for the Lord. *2680*
2:31 Which thou hast **p** before the face of all *2090*
12:47 **p** not *himself,* neither did according to his *2090*
23:56 they returned, and **p** spices and ointments; *2090*
24: 1 bringing the spices which they had **p**, and *2090*
Ro 9:23 of mercy, which he had **afore p** unto glory, *4282*
1Co 2: 9 *the things* which God hath **p** for them that *2090*
2Ti 2:21 master's use, *and* **p** unto every good work. *2090*
Heb 10: 5 wouldest not, but a body hast thou **p** me: *2675*
11: 7 **p** an ark to the saving of his house; *2680*
11:16 their God: for he hath **p** for them a city. *2090*
Rev 8: 6 the seven trumpets **p** themselves to sound. *2090*
9: 7 locusts *were* like unto horses **p** unto battle; *2090*
9:15 which were **p** for an hour, and a day, and *2090*
12: 6 where she hath a place **p** of God, *2090*
16:12 the way of the kings of the east might be **p**. *2090*
21: 2 **p** as a bride adorned for her husband. *2090*

PREPAREDST (1) [PREPARE]
Ps 80: 9 Thou **p** *room* before it, and didst cause it to 6437

PREPAREST (3) [PREPARE]
Nu 15: 8 when thou **p** a bullock *for* a burnt offering, 6213
Ps 23: 5 Thou **p** a table before me in the presence of 6186
65: 9 thou **p** them corn, when thou hast so 3559

PREPARETH (3) [PREPARE]
2Ch 30:19 *That* **p** his heart to seek God, the LORD 3559
Job 15:35 bring forth vanity, and their belly **p** deceit. 3559
Ps 147: 8 with clouds, who **p** rain for the earth, 3559

PREPARING (2) [PREPARE]
Ne 13: 7 in **p** him a chamber in the courts of 6213
1Pe 3:20 while the ark was a **p**, wherein few, that is, *2680*

PRESBYTERY (1)
1Ti 4:14 with the laying on of the hands of the **p**. *4244*

PRESCRIBED (1) [PRESCRIBING]
Isa 10: 1 that write grievousness *which* they have **p**; 3789

PRESCRIBING (1) [PRESCRIBED]
Ezr 7:22 baths *of* oil, and salt without **p** *how much.* 3792

PRESENCE (116) [PRESENT]
Ge 3: 8 his wife hid themselves from the **p** of 6440
4:16 Cain went out from the **p** of 6440+3807.1
16:12 he shall dwell in the **p** of all his brethren. 6440
23:11 in the **p** of the sons of my people give I it 5869
23:18 Unto Abraham for a possession in the **p** of 5869
25:18 *and* he died in the **p** of all his brethren. 6440
27:30 Jacob was yet scarce gone out from the **p** of 6440
41:46 Joseph went out from the **p** of Pharaoh, 6440
45: 3 answer him; for they were troubled at his **p**. 6440
47:15 for why should we die **in** thy **p**? for 5048
Ex 10:11 they were driven out from Pharaoh's **p**. 6440
33:14 My **p** shall go *with thee,* and I will give 6440
33:15 If thy **p** go not *with me,* carry us not up 6440
35:20 of Israel departed from the **p** of Moses. 6440
Lev 22: 3 that soul shall be cut off from my **p**: 6440
Nu 20: 6 Aaron went from the **p** of the assembly 6440
Dt 25: 9 wife come unto him in the **p** of the elders, 5869
Jos 4:11 and the priests, in the **p** of the people. 6440
8:32 which he wrote in the **p** of the children of 6440
1Sa 18:11 *it.* And David avoided out of his **p** twice. 6440
19: 7 and he was in his **p**, as in times past. 6440
19:10 he slipt away out of Saul's **p**, and he smote 6440
21:15 this *fellow* to play the mad man **in** my **p**? 5921
2Sa 16:19 *should I* not *serve* in the **p** of his son? as I 6440
16:19 as I have served in thy father's **p**, so will I 6440
16:19 thy father's presence, so will I be in thy **p**. 6440
24: 4 the captains of the host went out from the **p** 6440
1Ki 1:28 she came into the king's **p**, and 6440
8:22 **in the p** of all the congregation of Israel, 5048
12: 2 heard *of it,* (for he was fled from the **p** of 6440
21:13 **in the p** of the people, saying, 5048
2Ki 3:14 were it not that I regard the **p** of 6440
5:27 he went out from his **p** a leper *as white* as 6440
13:23 neither cast he them from his **p** as yet. 6440
24:20 until he had cast them out from his **p**, 6440
25:19 of them that were **in** the king's **p**, 6440+7200
1Ch 16:27 Glory and honour *are* in his **p**; strength and 6440
16:33 shall the trees of the wood sing out at the **p** 6440
24:31 sons of Aaron in the **p** of David the king, 6440
2Ch 6:12 **in the p** of all the congregation of Israel, 5048
9:23 all the kings of the earth sought the **p** of 6440
10: 2 whither he had fled from the **p** of Solomon 6440
20: 9 we stand before this house, and in thy **p**, 6440
34: 4 brake down the altars of Baalim in his **p**; 6440
Ne 2: 1 Now I had not been *beforetime* sad in his **p**. 6440
Est 1:10 the seven chamberlains that served **in the p** 6440
8:15 Mordecai went out from the **p** of the king 6440
Job 1:12 So Satan went forth from the **p** of 6440
2: 7 So went Satan forth from the **p** of 6440
23:15 Therefore am I troubled at his **p**: when I 6440
Ps 9: 3 they shall fall and perish at thy **p**. 6440
16:11 in thy **p** *is* fulness of joy; at thy right hand 6440
17: 2 Let my sentence come forth from thy **p**; 6440
23: 5 Thou preparest a table before me **in the p** 5048
31:20 Thou shalt hide them in the secret of thy **p** 6440
51:11 Cast me not away from thy **p**; and take not 6440
68: 2 *so* let the wicked perish at the **p** of God. 6440
68: 8 the heavens also dropped at the **p** of God: 6440
68: 8 *even* Sinai itself *was moved* at the **p** of 6440
95: 2 Let us come before his **p** with 6440
97: 5 The hills melted like wax at the **p** of 6440
97: 5 at the **p** of the Lord of the whole earth. 6440
100: 2 come before his **p** with singing. 6440
114: 7 Tremble, thou earth, at the **p** of the Lord, 6440
114: 7 at the **p** of the God of Jacob; 6440+3807.1
116:14 the LORD now in the **p** of all his people. 5048
116:18 the LORD now in the **p** of all his people, 5048
139: 7 or whither shall I flee from thy **p**? 6440
140:13 thy name: the upright shall dwell in thy **p**. 6440
Pr 14: 7 Go from the **p** of a foolish man, when thou 5048
17:18 *and* becometh surety in the **p** of his friend. 6440
25: 6 Put not forth thyself in the **p** of the king, 6440
25: 7 **p** of the prince whom thine eyes have seen. 6440
Isa 1: 7 strangers devour it in your **p**, and *it is* 5048
19: 1 the idols of Egypt shall be moved at his **p**, 6440
63: 9 and the angel of his **p** saved them: 6440
64: 1 the mountains might flow down at thy **p**, 6440
64: 2 *that* the nations may tremble at thy **p**. 6440
64: 3 the mountains flowed down at thy **p**. 6440
Jer 4:26 were broken down at the **p** of the LORD, 6440
5:22 will ye not tremble at my **p**, which have 6440
23:39 and your fathers, *and cast you* out of my **p**: 6440
28: 1 in the **p** of the priests and of all the people, 5869
28: 5 the prophet Hananiah in the **p** of the priests, 5869
28: 5 in the **p** of all the people that stood in 5869
28:11 Hananiah spake in the **p** of all the people, 5869
32:12 in the **p** of the witnesses that subscribed 5869
52: 3 Judah, till he had cast them out from his **p**, 6440
Eze 38:20 shall shake at my **p**, and the mountains 6440
Da 2:27 Daniel answered **in the p** of the king, and 6925
Jnh 1: 3 Tarshish from the **p** of the LORD, 6440+3807.1
1: 3 Tarshish from the **p** of the LORD. 6440+3807.1
1:10 For the men knew that he fled from the **p** of 6440
Na 1: 5 the earth is burnt at his **p**, yea, the world, 6440
Zep 1: 7 Hold thy peace at the **p** of the Lord GOD: 6440
Lk 1:19 I am Gabriel, that stand **in the p** of God; *1799*
13:26 We have eaten and drunk **in** thy **p**, and *1799*
14:10 shalt thou have worship **in the p** of them *1799*
15:10 there is joy **in the p** of the angels of God *1799*
Jn 20:30 truly did Jesus **in the p** of his disciples, *1799*
Ac 3:13 and denied him **in the p** of Pilate, *2596+4383*
3:16 this perfect soundness **in the p** of you all. *561*
3:19 shall come from the **p** of the Lord; *4383*
5:41 And they departed from the **p** of *4383*
27:35 and gave thanks to God **in p** of *them* all: *1799*
1Co 1:29 That no flesh should glory in his **p**. *1799*
2Co 10: 1 who in **p** *am* base among you, but *4383*
10:10 but *his* bodily **p** *is* weak, and *his* speech *3952*
Php 2:12 not as in my **p** only, but now much more in *3952*
1Th 2:17 being taken from you for a short time **in p**, *4383*
2:19 *Are* not even ye **in the p** of our Lord Jesus *1715*
2Th 1: 9 destruction from the **p** of the Lord, *4383*
Heb 9:24 now to appear in the **p** of God for us: *4383*
Jude 1:24 to present *you* faultless **before the p** of his *2714*
Rev 14:10 and brimstone **in the p** of the holy angels, *1799*
14:10 the holy angels, and **in the p** of the Lamb: *1799*

PRESENT (106) [PRESENCE, PRESENTED, PRESENTING, PRESENTLY, PRESENTS]

Ge 32:13 took of that which came to his hand a **p** for 4503
32:18 it *is* a **p** sent unto my lord Esau: 4503
32:20 I will appease him with the **p** that goeth 4503
32:21 So went the **p** over before him: and 4503
33:10 in thy sight, then receive my **p** at my hand: 4503
43:11 carry down the man a **p**, a little balm, and 4503
43:15 the men took that **p**, and they took double 4503
43:25 they made ready the **p** against Joseph came 4503
43:26 they brought him the **p** which *was* in their 4503
Ex 34: 2 **p** thyself there to me in the top of 5324
Lev 14:11 the priest that maketh *him* clean shall **p** 5975
16: 7 **p** them before the LORD *at* the door of 5975
27: 8 he shall **p** himself before the priest, and 5975
27:11 then he shall **p** the beast before the priest: 5975
Nu 3: 6 and **p** them before Aaron the priest, 5975
Dt 31:14 **p** yourselves in the tabernacle of 3320
Jdg 3:15 by him the children of Israel sent a **p** unto 4503
3:17 he brought the **p** unto Eglon king of Moab: 4503
3:18 when he had made an end to offer the **p**, 4503
3:18 he sent away the people that bare the **p**. 4503
6:18 and bring forth my **p**, and set *it* before thee. 4503
1Sa 9: 7 *there is* not a **p** to bring to the man of God: 8670
10:19 **p** yourselves before the LORD by your 3320
13:15 Saul numbered the people that were **p** with 4672
13:16 and the people that were **p** with them, 4672
21: 3 *of* bread in mine hand, or what there is **p**. 4672
30:26 Behold a **p** for you of the spoil of 1293
2Sa 20: 4 *within* three days, and be thou here **p**. 5975
1Ki 9:16 given it *for* a **p** unto his daughter, 7964
10:25 they brought every man his **p**, vessels of 4503
15:19 I have sent unto thee a **p** of silver and gold; 7810
20:27 and were all **p**, and went against them: 3557
2Ki 8: 8 Take a **p** in thine hand, and go, meet 4503
8: 9 went to meet him, and took a **p** with him, 4503
16: 8 and sent *it for* a **p** to the king of Assyria. 7810
17: 4 brought no **p** to the king of Assyria, as *he* 4503
18:31 Make *an agreement* with me *by* a **p**, and 1293
20:12 sent letters and a **p** unto Hezekiah: 4503
1Ch 29:17 which are **p** here, to offer willingly unto 4672
2Ch 5:11 all the priests that were **p** were sanctified, 4672
9:24 they brought every man his **p**, vessels of 4503
29:29 all that were **p** with him bowed themselves, 4672
30:21 the children of Israel that were **p** at 4672
31: 1 all Israel that were **p** went out to the cities 4672
34:32 he caused all that were **p** in Jerusalem and 4672
34:33 made all that were **p** in Israel to serve, 4672
35: 7 the passover *offerings,* for all that were **p**, 4672
35:17 the children of Israel that were **p** kept 4672
35:18 all Judah and Israel that were **p**, and 4672
Ezr 8:25 his lords, and all Israel *there* **p**, had offered: 4672
Est 1: 5 people that were **p** in Shushan the palace, 4672
4:16 gather together all the Jews that are **p** in 4672
Job 1: 6 came to **p** themselves before the LORD, 3320
2: 1 came to **p** themselves before the LORD, 3320
2: 1 Satan came also among them to **p** himself 3320
Ps 46: 1 and strength, a very **p** help in trouble. 4672
Isa 18: 7 In that time shall the **p** be brought unto 7862
36:16 Make *an agreement* with me *by* a **p**, and 1293
39: 1 sent letters and a **p** to Hezekiah: 4503
Jer 36: 7 It may be they will **p** their supplication 5307
42: 9 unto whom ye sent me to **p** your 5307
Eze 27:15 they brought thee *for* a **p** horns of ivory and 814
Da 9:18 for we do not **p** our supplications before 5307
Hos 10: 6 It shall be also carried unto Assyria *for* a **p** 4503
Lk 2:22 him to Jerusalem, to **p** *him* to the Lord; *3936*
5:17 the power of the Lord was *p* to heal them. NIG
13: 1 There were **p** at that season some that told *3918*
18:30 not receive manifold more in this *p* time, NIG
Jn 14:25 I spoken unto you, being *yet* **p** with you. *3306*
Ac 10:33 therefore are we all **here p** before God, *3918*
21:18 us unto James; and all the elders were **p**. *3854*
25:24 and all men which are **here p with** us, *4840*
28: 2 because of the **p** rain, and because of *2186*
Ro 7:18 dwelleth no good *thing:* for to will is **p** with *3873*
7:21 when I would do good, evil is **p** with me. *3873*
8:18 For I reckon that the sufferings of *this* **p** *3568*
8:38 nor principalities, nor powers, nor *things* **p**, *1764*
11: 5 at *this* **p** time also there is a remnant *3568*
12: 1 that *ye* **p** your bodies a living sacrifice, *3936*
1Co 3:22 or death, or *things* **p**, or *things* to come; *1764*
4:11 Even unto this **p** hour we both hunger, and *737*
5: 3 I verily, as absent in body, but **p** in spirit, *3918*
5: 3 have judged already, as though I were **p**, *3918*
7:26 therefore that this is good for the **p** distress, *1764*
15: 6 of whom the greater part remain unto **this p**, *737*
2Co 4:14 us also by Jesus, and shall **p** *us* with you. *3936*
5: 8 from the body, and to be **p** with the Lord. *1736*
5: 9 we labour, that, whether **p** or absent, *1736*
10: 2 be bold when I am **p** with *that* confidence, *3918*
10:11 *will we be* also in deed when we are **p**. *3918*
11: 2 that *I* may **p** *you as* a chaste virgin to *3936*
11: 9 And when I was **p** with you, and wanted, *3918*
13: 2 foretell *you,* as if I were **p** the second *time;* *3918*
13:10 lest being **p** I should use sharpness, *3918*
Gal 1: 4 that he might deliver us from *this* **p** evil *1764*
4:18 and not only when I am **p** with you. *3918*
4:20 I desire to be **p** with you now, and *3918*
Eph 5:27 That he might **p** it to himself a glorious *3936*
Col 1:22 to **p** you holy and unblameable and *3936*
1:28 that we may **p** every man perfect in Christ *3936*
2Ti 4:10 having loved *this* **p** world, and is departed *3568*
Tit 2:12 and godly, in *this* **p** world; *3568*
Heb 9: 9 Which *was* a figure for the time *then* **p**, *1764*
12:11 Now no chastening for the **p** seemeth to be *3918*
2Pe 1:12 know *them,* and be stablished in the **p** truth. *3918*
Jude 1:24 to **p** *you* faultless before the presence of his *2476*

PRESENTED (18) [PRESENT]

Ge 46:29 to Goshen, and **p** himself unto him; 7200
47: 2 *even* five men, and **p** them unto Pharaoh. 3322
Lev 2: 8 when it is **p** unto the priest, he shall bring it 7126
7:35 in the day *when* he **p** them to minister unto 7126
9:12 Aaron's sons **p** unto him the blood, 4672
9:13 they **p** the burnt offering unto him, with 4672
9:18 Aaron's sons **p** unto him the blood, 4672
16:10 shall be **p** alive before the LORD, to make 5975
Dt 31:14 **p** themselves in the tabernacle of 3320
Jos 24: 1 and they **p** themselves before God. 3320
Jdg 6:19 *it* out unto him under the oak, and **p** *it.* 5066
20: 2 **p** themselves in the assembly of the people 3320
1Sa 17:16 and evening, and **p** himself forty days. 3320
Jer 38:26 I **p** my supplication before the king, 5307
Eze 20:28 there they **p** the provocation of their 5414
Mt 2:11 their treasures, they **p** unto him gifts; *4374*
Ac 9:41 called the saints and widows, **p** her alive. *3936*
23:33 to the governor, **p** Paul also **before** him. *3936*

PRESENTING (1) [PRESENT]

Da 9:20 **p** my supplication before the LORD my 5307

PRESENTLY (5) [PRESENT]

1Sa 2:16 not fail to burn the fat **p**, 3117+1886.1+3509.1
Pr 12:16 A fool's wrath is **p** known: 3117+871.1+1886.1
Mt 21:19 for ever. And **p** the fig tree withered away. *3916*
26:53 he shall **p** give me more than twelve legions *737*
Php 2:23 Him therefore I hope to send **p**, so soon as *1824*

PRESENTS (10) [PRESENT]

1Sa 10:27 they despised him, and brought him no **p**. 4503
1Ki 4:21 they brought **p**, and served Solomon all 4503
2Ki 17: 3 became his servant, and gave him **p**. 4503
2Ch 17: 5 and all Judah brought to Jehoshaphat **p**; and 4503
17:11 of the Philistines brought Jehoshaphat **p**, 4503
32:23 and **p** to Hezekiah king of Judah: 4030
Ps 68:29 at Jerusalem shall kings bring **p** unto thee. 7862
72:10 of Tarshish and *of* the isles shall bring **p**: 4503
76:11 let all that be round about him bring **p** unto 7862
Mic 1:14 Therefore shalt thou give **p** to 7964

PRESERVE (30) [PRESERVED, PRESERVER, PRESERVEST, PRESERVETH]

Ge 19:32 with him, that we may **p** seed of our father. 2421
19:34 with him, that we may **p** seed of our father. 2421
45: 5 for God did send me before you to **p life**. 4241
45: 7 God sent me before you to **p** you a 7760
Dt 6:24 that he might **p** us **alive**, as *it is at* this day. 2421
Ps 12: 7 thou shalt **p** them from this generation for 5341
16: 1 **P** me, O God: for in thee do I put my trust. 8104
25:21 Let integrity and uprightness **p** me; for I 5341
32: 7 hiding place; thou shalt **p** me from trouble; 5341
40:11 and thy truth continually **p** me. 5341
41: 2 The LORD will **p** him, and keep him 8104
61: 7 prepare mercy and truth, *which* may **p** him. 5341
64: 1 **p** my life from fear of the enemy. 5341
79:11 **p** thou those that are appointed to die; 3498

P

Ps 86: 2 **P** my soul; for I *am* holy: O thou my God, 8104
121: 7 The LORD shall **p** thee from all evil: 8104
121: 7 thee from all evil: he shall **p** thy soul. 8104
121: 8 The LORD shall **p** thy going out and 8104
140: 1 the evil man: **p** me from the violent man; 5341
140: 4 of the wicked; **p** me from the violent man; 5341
Pr 2:11 Discretion shall **p** thee, understanding shall 8104
4: 6 Forsake her not, and she shall **p** thee: 8104
14: 3 but the lips of the wise shall **p** them. 8104
20:28 Mercy and truth **p** the king: and his throne 5341
22:12 The eyes of the LORD **p** knowledge, and 5341
Isa 31: 5 deliver *it;* and passing over he will **p** *it.* 4422
49: 8 I will **p** thee, and give thee for a covenant 5341
Jer 49:11 thy fatherless children, I will **p** *them* **alive**; 2421
Lk 17:33 and whosoever shall lose *his life* shall **p** it. *2225*
2Ti 4:18 and will **p** *me* unto his heavenly kingdom: *4982*

PRESERVED (16) [PRESERVE]
Ge 32:30 seen God face to face, and my life is **p**. 5337
Jos 24:17 **p** us in all the way wherein we went, and 8104
1Sa 30:23 who hath **p** us, and delivered the company 8104
2Sa 8: 6 the LORD **p** David whithersoever he 3467
8:14 the LORD **p** David whithersoever he 3467
1Ch 18: 6 Thus the LORD **p** David whithersoever he 3467
18:13 Thus the LORD **p** David whithersoever he 3467
Job 10:12 favour, and thy visitation hath **p** my spirit. 8104
29: 2 as *in* the days *when* God **p** me; 8104
Ps 37:28 forsaketh not his saints; they are **p** for ever: 8104
Isa 49: 6 of Jacob, and to restore the **p** of Israel: 5341
Hos 12:13 out of Egypt, and by a prophet was he **p**. 8104
Mt 9:17 new wine into new bottles, and both are **p**. *4933*
Lk 5:38 be put into new bottles; and both are **p**. *4933*
1Th 5:23 body be **p** blameless unto the coming of *5083*
Jude 1: 1 and **p** *in* Jesus Christ, *and* called: *5083*

PRESERVER (1) [PRESERVE]
Job 7:20 what shall I do unto thee, O thou **p** of men? 5341

PRESERVEST (2) [PRESERVE]
Ne 9: 6 and all that *is* therein, and thou **p** them all; 2421
Ps 36: 6 O LORD, thou **p** man and beast. 3467

PRESERVETH (8) [PRESERVE]
Job 36: 6 He **p** not the **life** of the wicked: but 2421
Ps 31:23 *for the* LORD **p** the faithful, and 5341
97:10 he **p** the souls of his saints; he delivereth 8104
116: 6 The LORD **p** the simple: I was brought 8104
145:20 The LORD **p** all them that love him: but 8104
146: 9 The LORD **p** the strangers; he relieveth 8104
Pr 2: 8 of judgment, and **p** the way of his saints. 8104
16:17 he that keepeth his way **p** his soul. 8104

PRESIDENTS (5)
Da 6: 2 over these three **p**; of whom Daniel *was* 5632
6: 3 this Daniel was preferred above the **p** and 5632
6: 4 the **p** and princes sought to find occasion 5632
6: 6 these **p** and princes assembled *together* to 5632
6: 7 All the **p** of the kingdom, the governors, 5632

PRESS (9) [PRESSED, PRESSES, PRESSETH, PRESSFAT, WINEPRESS, WINEPRESSES]
Joel 3:13 for the **p** is full, the fats overflow; 1660
Hag 2:16 for to draw out fifty *vessels out of* the **p**, 6333
Mk 2: 4 could not come nigh unto him for the **p**, *3793*
5:27 came in the **p** behind, and touched his *3793*
5:30 turned him about in the **p**, and said, *3793*
Lk 8:19 and could not come at him for the **p**. *3793*
8:45 throng thee and **p** *thee,* and sayest thou, *598*
19: 3 and could not for the **p**, because he was *3793*
Php 3:14 I **p** toward the mark for the prize of *1377*

PRESS CHARGES See ACCUSE; IMPLEAD

PRESSED (15) [PRESS]
Ge 19: 3 he **p** upon them greatly; and they turned in 6484
19: 9 they **p** sore upon the man, *even* Lot, and 6484
40:11 **p** them into Pharaoh's cup, and I gave 7818
Jdg 16:16 when she **p** him daily with her words, and 6693
2Sa 13:25 he **p** him: howbeit he would not go, but 6555
13:27 Absalom **p** him, that he let Amnon and all 6555
Est 8:14 and **p on** by the king's commandment, 1765
Eze 23: 3 there were their breasts **p**, and there they 4600
Am 2:13 Behold, I am **p** under you, as a cart is 5781
2:13 as a cart is **p** *that is* full *of* sheaves. 5781
Mk 3:10 insomuch that *they* **p upon** him for to touch *1968*
Lk 5: 1 as the people **p upon** him to hear the word *1945*
6:38 **p down**, and shaken *together,* and *4085*
Ac 18: 5 Paul was **p** in spirit, and testified to *4912*
2Co 1: 8 that we were **p** out of measure, above *916*

PRESSES (4) [PRESS]
Ne 13:15 Judah *some* treading **wine p** on the sabbath, 1660
Pr 3:10 and thy **p** shall burst out with new wine. 3342
Isa 16:10 treaders shall tread out no wine in *their* **p**; 3342
Jer 48:33 I have caused wine to fail from the **wine p**: 3342

PRESSETH (2) [PRESS]
Ps 38: 2 fast in me, and thy hand **p** me **sore**. 5181+5921
Lk 16:16 of God is preached, and every *man* **p** into it. *971*

PRESSFAT (1) [PRESS]
Hag 2:16 when *one* came to the **p** for to draw out 3342

PRESUME (2) [PRESUMED, PRESUMPTUOUS, PRESUMPTUOUSLY]
Dt 18:20 which shall **p** to speak a word in my name, 2102
Est 7: 5 *is* he, that **durst p** in his heart to do so? 4390

PRESUMED (1) [PRESUME]
Nu 14:44 they **p** to go up unto the hill top: 6075

PRESUMPTUOUS (2) [PRESUME]
Ps 19:13 Keep back thy servant also from **p** *sins;* let 2086
2Pe 2:10 **P** *are they,* selfwilled, they are not afraid to *5113*

PRESUMPTUOUSLY (6) [PRESUME]
Ex 21:14 if a man **come p** upon his neighbour, 2102
Nu 15:30 the soul that doeth *ought* **p**, 3027+7311+871.1
Dt 1:43 of the LORD, and went **p** up into the hill. 2102
17:12 the man that will do **p**, and will not 2087+871.1
17:13 shall hear, and fear, and do no more **p**. 2102
18:22 the prophet hath spoken it **p**: 2087+871.1

PRETENCE (3)
Mt 23:14 and for a **p** make long prayer: *4392*
Mk 12:40 and for a **p** make long prayers: *4392*
Php 1:18 every way, whether in **p**, or in truth, *4392*

PRETORIUM (1)
Mk 15:16 led him away into the hall, called **P**; *4232*

PREVAIL (29) [PREVAILED, PREVAILEST, PREVAILETH]
Ge 7:20 Fifteen cubits upward did the waters **p**; and 1396
Nu 22: 6 peradventure I shall **p**, *that* we may smite 3201
Jdg 16: 5 and by what *means* we may **p** against him, 3201
1Sa 2: 9 in darkness; for by strength shall no man **p**. 1396
17: 9 if I **p** against him, and kill him, then 3201
26:25 do great things, and also shalt **still p**. 3201+3201
1Ki 22:22 Thou shalt persuade *him,* and **p** also: 3201
2Ch 14:11 *art* our God; let not man **p** against thee. 6113
18:21 shalt entice *him,* and thou shalt also **p**: 3201
Est 6:13 thou shalt not **p** against him, but 3201
Job 15:24 *they* shall **p against** him, as a king ready to 8630
18: 9 the heel, *and* the robber shall **p** against him. 2388
Ps 9:19 Arise, O LORD; let not man **p**: let 5810
12: 4 Who have said, With our tongue will we **p**; 1396
65: 3 Iniquities **p** against me: *as for* our 1396
Ecc 4:12 if one **p against** him, two shall withstand 8630
Isa 7: 1 to war against it, but could not **p** against it. 3898
16:12 to his sanctuary to pray; but he shall not **p**. 3201
42:13 yea, roar; he shall **p** against his enemies. 1396
47:12 be able to profit, if so be thou mayest **p**. 6206
Jer 1:19 they shall not **p** against thee; for I *am* with 3201
5:22 thereof toss themselves, yet can they not **p**; 3201
15:20 but they shall not **p** against thee: 3201
20:10 we shall **p** against him, and we shall take 3201
20:11 shall stumble, and they shall not **p**: 3201
Da 11: 7 and shall deal against them, and shall **p**: 2388
Mt 16:18 and the gates of hell shall not **p against** it. *2729*
27:24 When Pilate saw that he could **p** nothing, *5623*
Jn 12:19 Perceive ye how ye **p** nothing? *5623*

PREVAILED (37) [PREVAIL]
Ge 7:18 the waters **p**, and were increased greatly 1396
7:19 the waters **p** exceedingly upon the earth; 1396
7:24 And the waters **p** upon the earth an hundred 1396
30: 8 I wrestled with my sister, and I have **p**: 3201
32:25 And when he saw that he **p** not against him, 3201
32:28 power with God and with men, and hast **p**. 3201
47:20 his field, because the famine **p** over them: 2388

Ge 49:26 The blessings of thy father have **p** above 1396
Ex 17:11 when Moses held up his hand, that Israel **p**: 1396
17:11 and when he let down his hand, Amalek **p**. 1396
Jdg 1:35 yet the hand of the house of Joseph **p**, so 3513
3:10 and his hand **p** against Chushan-rishathaim. 5810
4:24 **p** against Jabin the king of Canaan, 7186
6: 2 the hand of Midian **p** against Israel: *and* 5810
1Sa 17:50 So David **p** over the Philistine with a sling 2388
2Sa 11:23 Surely the men **p** against us, and came out 1396
24: 4 Notwithstanding the king's word **p** against 2388
1Ki 16:22 the people that followed Omri **p** against 2388
2Ki 25: 3 the *fourth* month the famine **p** in the city, 2388
1Ch 5: 2 For Judah **p** above his brethren, and of him 1396
21: 4 Nevertheless the king's word **p** against 2388
2Ch 8: 3 went *to* Hamath-zobah, and **p** against it. 2388
13:18 the children of Judah **p**, because they relied 553
27: 5 king of the Ammonites, and **p** against them. 2388
Ps 13: 4 mine enemy say, I have **p against** him; 3201
129: 2 my youth: yet they have not **p** against me. 3201
Jer 20: 7 thou art stronger than I, and hast **p**: I am in 3201
38:22 have set thee on, and have **p** against thee: 3201
La 1:16 children are desolate, because the enemy **p**. 1396
Da 7:21 war with the saints, and **p** against them; 3202
Hos 12: 4 Yea, he had power over *the* angel, and **p**: 3201
Ob 1: 7 thee have deceived thee, *and* **p** against thee; 3201
Lk 23:23 voices of them and of the chief priests **p**. *2729*
Ac 19:16 and **p** against them, so that *they* fled out of *2480*
19:20 So mightily grew the word of God and **p**. *2480*
Rev 5: 5 hath **p** to open the book, and to loose *3528*
12: 8 And **p** not; neither was their place found *2480*

PREVAILEST (1) [PREVAIL]
Job 14:20 Thou **p** for ever **against** him, and 8630

PREVAILETH (1) [PREVAIL]
La 1:13 fire into my bones, and it **p** against them: 7287

PREVALENT See SUPERFLUITY; SUPERFLUOUS

PREVENT (7) [PREVENTED, PREVENTEST]
Job 3:12 Why did the knees **p** me? or why 6923
Ps 59:10 The God of my mercy shall **p** me: 6923
79: 8 let thy tender mercies speedily **p** us: for we 6923
88:13 and in the morning shall my prayer **p** thee. 6923
119:148 Mine eyes **p** the *night* watches, that *I* might 6923
Am 9:10 The evil shall not overtake nor **p** us. 6923
1Th 4:15 the Lord shall not **p** them which are asleep. *5348*

PREVENTED (9) [PREVENT]
2Sa 22: 6 me about; the snares of death **p** me: 6923
22:19 They **p** me in the day of my calamity: but 6923
Job 30:27 and rested not: the days of affliction **p** me. 6923
41:11 Who hath **p** me, that I should repay *him?* 6923
Ps 18: 5 me about: the snares of death **p** me. 6923
18:18 They **p** me in the day of my calamity: but 6923
119:147 I **p** the dawning of the morning, and cried: 6923
Isa 21:14 they **p** with their bread him that fled. 6923
Mt 17:25 Jesus **p** him, saying, What thinkest thou, *4399*

PREVENTEST (1) [PREVENT]
Ps 21: 3 For thou **p** him *with* the blessings of 6923

PREY (73)
Ge 49: 9 from the **p**, my son, thou art gone up: 2964
49:27 in the morning he shall devour the **p**, and 5706
Nu 14: 3 our wives and our children should be a **p**? 957
14:31 your little ones, which ye said should be a **p**, 957
23:24 he shall not lie down until he eat *of* the **p**, 2964
31:11 and all the **p**, *both* of men and of beasts. 4455
31:12 the **p**, and the spoil, unto Moses, and 4455
31:26 Take the sum of the **p** that was taken, *both* 4455
31:27 divide the **p** into two parts; between them 4455
31:32 *being* the rest of the **p** which the men of war 957
Dt 1:39 which ye said should be a **p**, and 957
2:35 Only the cattle we **took for a p** unto 962
3: 7 of the cities, we **took for a p** to ourselves. 962
Jos 8: 2 shall ye **take for a p** unto yourselves: 962
8:27 the spoil of that city Israel **took for a p** unto 962
11:14 the children of Israel **took for a p** unto 962
Jdg 5:30 have they *not* divided the **p**; to every man a 7998
5:30 to Sisera a **p** of divers colours, a prey of 7998
5:30 a **p** of divers colours of needlework, 7998
8:24 give me every man the earrings of his **p**. 7998
8:25 cast therein every man the earrings of his **p**. 7998
2Ki 21:14 they shall become a **p** and a spoil to all their 957
Ne 4: 4 give them for a **p** in the land of captivity: 961
Est 3:13 and *to take* the spoil of them for a **p**. 962
8:11 women, and *to take* the spoil of them for a **p**, 962
9:15 but on the **p** they laid not their hand. 961
9:16 but they laid not their hands on the **p**, 961
Job 4:11 The old lion perisheth for lack of **p**, and 2964
9:26 swift ships: as the eagle *that* hasteth to the **p**. 400
24: 5 forth to their work; rising betimes for a **p**: 2964
38:39 Wilt thou hunt the **p** for the lion? or fill 2964
39:29 From thence she seeketh the **p**, *and* her eyes 400
Ps 17:12 Like as a lion *that* is greedy of his **p**, and 2963
76: 4 *and* excellent than the mountains of **p**. 2964
104:21 The young lions roar after *their* **p**, and seek 2964
124: 6 who hath not given us *as* a **p** to their teeth. 2964
Pr 23:28 She also lieth in wait as *for* a **p**, and 2863
Isa 5:29 lay hold of the **p**, and shall carry *it* away 2964
10: 2 that widows may be their **p**, and *that* they 7998
10: 6 to take the **p**, and to tread them down like 957
31: 4 and the young lion roaring on his **p**, 2964
33:23 is the **p** of a great spoil divided; the lame 5706
33:23 of a great spoil divided; the lame take the **p**. 957
42:22 they are for a **p**, and none delivereth; *for* a 957
49:24 Shall the **p** be taken from the mighty, or 4455
49:25 and the **p** of the terrible shall be delivered: 4455
59:15 departeth from evil **maketh** himself a **p**: 7997
Jer 21: 9 and his life shall be unto him for a **p**. 7998
30:16 all that **p upon** thee will I give for a prey. 962
30:16 all that prey upon thee will I give for a **p**. 957
38: 2 for he shall have his life for a **p**, and 7998
39:18 but thy life shall be for a **p** unto thee: 7998
45: 5 thy life will I give unto thee for a **p** in all 7998
Eze 7:21 give it into the hands of the strangers for a **p**, 957
19: 3 a young lion, and it learned to catch the **p**; 2964
19: 6 learned to catch the **p**, *and* devoured men. 2964
22:25 like a roaring lion ravening the **p**; 2964
22:27 thereof *are* like wolves ravening the **p**, 2964
26:12 and **make a p** of thy merchandise: 962
29:19 and take her spoil, and **take** her **p**; 957+962
34: 8 surely because my flock became a **p**, and 957
34:22 my flock, and they shall no more be a **p**; 957
34:28 they shall no more be a **p** to the heathen, 957
36: 4 which became a **p** and derision to the residue 957
36: 5 with despiteful minds, to cast it out for a **p**. 957
38:12 To take a spoil, and to **take a p**; to turn 957+962
38:13 gathered thy company to **take a p**? 957+962
Da 11:24 he shall scatter among them the **p**, and spoil, 961
Am 3: 4 a lion roar in the forest, when he hath no **p**? 2964
Na 2:12 filled his holes *with* **p**, and his dens *with* 2964
2:13 I will cut off thy **p** from the earth, and 2964
3: 1 full *of* lies *and* robbery; the **p** departeth not; 2964
Zep 3: 8 until the day that I rise up to the **p**: 5706

PRICE (33) [PRICES, PRISED]
Lev 25:16 of years thou shalt increase the **p** thereof, 4736
25:16 of years thou shalt diminish the **p** of it: 4736
25:50 the **p** of his sale shall be according unto 3701
25:51 **p of** his **redemption** out of the money that 1353
25:52 he give *him* again the **p of** his **redemption**. 1353
Dt 23:18 bring the hire of a whore, or the **p** of a dog, 4242
2Sa 24:24 Nay; but I will surely buy *it* of thee at a **p**: 4242
1Ki 10:28 merchants received the linen yarn at a **p**. 4242
1Ch 21:22 thou shalt grant it me for the full **p**: that 3701
21:24 Nay; but I will verily buy *it* for the full **p**: 3701
2Ch 1:16 merchants received the linen yarn at a **p**. 4242
Job 28:13 Man knoweth not the **p** thereof; neither is it 6187
28:15 neither shall silver be weighed *for* the **p** 4242
28:18 for the **p** of wisdom *is* above rubies. 4901
Ps 44:12 and dost not increase *thy wealth* by their **p**. 4242
Pr 17:16 Wherefore *is there* a **p** in the hand of a fool 4242
27:26 and the goats *are* the **p** of the field. 4242
31:10 for her **p** *is* far above rubies. 4377
Isa 45:13 not for **p** nor reward, saith the LORD of 4242
55: 1 and milk without money and without **p**. 4242
Jer 15:13 treasures will I give to the spoil without **p**, 4242
Zec 11:12 unto them, If ye think good, give *me* my **p**; 7939
11:12 So they weighed *for* my **p** thirty *pieces* of 7939
11:13 a goodly **p** that I was prised at of them. 3366
Mt 13:46 when he had found one pearl of **great p**, *4186*
27: 6 the treasury, because it is the **p** of blood. *5092*
27: 9 of silver, the **p** of him that was valued, *5092*
Ac 5: 2 And kept back *part* of the **p**, his wife also *5092*
5: 3 and to keep back *part* of the **p** of the land? *5092*
19:19 all *men:* and they counted the **p** of them, *5092*
1Co 6:20 For ye are bought with a **p**: therefore *5092*

P

1Co 7:23 Ye are bought with a **p**; be not ye *5092*
1Pe 3: 4 which is in the sight of God of **great p**. *4185*

PRICES (1) [PRICE]
Ac 4:34 brought the **p** of the *things* that were sold, *5092*

PRICKED (2) [PRICKING]
Ps 73:21 heart was grieved, and I was **p** *in* my reins. 8150
Ac 2:37 Now when they heard *this,* they were **p** in *2660*

PRICKING (1) [PRICKED, PRICKS]
Eze 28:24 there shall be no more a **p** brier unto 3992

PRICKS (3) [PRICKING]
Nu 33:55 let remain of them *shall be* **p** in your eyes, 7899
Ac 9: 5 *it is* hard for thee to kick against the **p**. *2759*
26:14 *it is* hard for thee to kick against the **p**. *2759*

PRIDE (49) [PROUD, PROUDLY]
Lev 26:19 I will break the **p** of your power; and I will 1347
1Sa 17:28 I know thy **p**, and the naughtiness of thine 2087
2Ch 32:26 humbled himself for the **p** of his heart, 1363
Job 33:17 *from his* purpose, and hide **p** from man. 1466
35:12 because of the **p** of evil men. 1347
41:15 *His* scales *are his* **p**, shut up *together as* 1346
41:34 he *is* a king over all the children of **p**. 7830
Ps 10: 2 The wicked in *his* **p** doth persecute 1346
10: 4 through the **p** of his countenance, 1363
31:20 secret of thy presence from the **p** of man: 7407
36:11 Let not the foot of **p** come against me, and 1346
59:12 their lips let them even be taken in their **p**: 1347
73: 6 Therefore **p** compasseth them about as a 1346
Pr 8:13 **p**, and arrogancy, and the evil way, and 1344
11: 2 *When* **p** cometh, then cometh shame: but 2087
13:10 Only by **p** cometh contention: but with 2087
14: 3 In the mouth of the foolish *is* a rod of **p**: but 1346
16:18 **P** *goeth* before destruction, and a haughty 1347
29:23 A man's **p** shall bring him low: but 1346
Isa 9: 9 that say in the **p** and stoutness of heart, 1346
16: 6 We have heard of the **p** of Moab; *he is* very 1347
16: 6 of his haughtiness, and his **p**, and his wrath: 1347
23: 9 to stain the **p** of all glory, *and* to bring into 1347
25:11 he shall bring down their **p** together with 1346
28: 1 Woe to the crown of **p**, to the drunkards of 1348
28: 3 The crown of **p**, the drunkards of Ephraim, 1348
Jer 13: 9 After this manner will I mar the **p** of Judah, 1347
13: 9 of Judah, and the great **p** of Jerusalem. 1347
13:17 soul shall weep in secret places for *your* **p**; 1466
48:29 We have heard the **p** of Moab; *he is* 1347
48:29 and his **p**, and the haughtiness of his heart. 1346
49:16 hath deceived thee, *and* the **p** of thine heart, 2087
Eze 7:10 the rod hath blossomed, **p** hath budded. 2087
16:49 **p**, fulness of bread, and abundance of 1347
16:56 by thy mouth in the day of thy **p**, 1347
30: 6 and the **p** of her power shall come down: 1347
Da 4:37 and those that walk in **p** he *is* able to abase. 1467
5:20 was lifted up, and his mind hardened in **p**, 2103
Hos 5: 5 the **p** of Israel doth testify to his face: 1347
7:10 the **p** of Israel testifieth to his face: and 1347
Ob 1: 3 The **p** of thine heart hath deceived thee, 2087
Zep 2:10 This shall they have for their **p**, because 1347
3:11 the midst of thee them that rejoice in thy **p**, 1346
Zec 9: 6 and I will cut off the **p** of the Philistines. 1347
10:11 and the **p** of Assyria shall be brought down, 1347
11: 3 young lions; for the **p** of Jordan is spoiled. 1347
Mk 7:22 an evil eye, blasphemy, **p**, foolishness: *5243*
1Ti 3: 6 lest being **lifted up with p** he fall into *5187*
1Jn 2:16 and the lust of the eyes, and the **p** of life, *212*

PRIEST (496) [PRIEST'S, PRIESTHOOD, PRIESTS, PRIESTS']
Ge 14:18 and he *was* the **p** of the most high God. 3548
41:45 the daughter of Poti-pherah **p** of On. 3548
41:50 of Poti-pherah **p** of On bare unto him. 3548
46:20 of Poti-pherah **p** of On bare unto him. 3548
Ex 2:16 Now the **p** of Midian had seven daughters: 3548
3: 1 of Jethro his father in law, the **p** of Midian: 3548
18: 1 When Jethro, the **p** of Midian, 3548
29:30 *And* that son that is **p** in his stead shall put 3548
31:10 the holy garments for Aaron the **p**, and 3548
35:19 *place,* the holy garments for Aaron the **p**, 3548
38:21 by the hand of Ithamar, son to Aaron the **p**. 3548
39:41 and the holy garments for Aaron the **p**, 3548
Lev 1: 7 the sons of Aaron the **p** shall put fire upon 3548
1: 9 the **p** shall burn all on the altar, *to be* a 3548
1:12 the **p** shall lay them in order on the wood 3548
1:13 the **p** shall bring *it* all, and burn *it* upon 3548
1:15 the **p** shall bring it unto the altar, and 3548
1:17 the **p** shall burn it upon the altar, upon 3548
2: 2 the **p** shall burn the memorial of it upon 3548
2: 8 when it is presented unto the **p**, he shall 3548
2: 9 the **p** shall take from the meat offering a 3548
2:16 the **p** shall burn the memorial of it, *part* of 3548
3:11 the **p** shall burn it upon the altar: *it is* 3548
3:16 the **p** shall burn them upon the altar: *it is* 3548
4: 3 If the **p** that is anointed do sin according to 3548
4: 5 the **p** that is anointed shall take of 3548
4: 6 the **p** shall dip his finger in the blood, and 3548
4: 7 the **p** shall put *some* of the blood upon 3548
4:10 the **p** shall burn them upon the altar of 3548
4:16 the **p** that is anointed shall bring of 3548
4:17 the **p** shall dip his finger *in some* of 3548
4:20 the **p** shall make an atonement for them, 3548
4:25 the **p** shall take of the blood of the sin 3548
4:26 the **p** shall make an atonement for him as 3548
4:30 the **p** shall take of the blood thereof with 3548
4:31 the **p** shall burn *it* upon the altar for a sweet 3548
4:31 the **p** shall make an atonement for him, and 3548
4:34 the **p** shall take of the blood of the sin 3548
4:35 the **p** shall burn them upon the altar, 3548
4:35 the **p** shall make an atonement for his sin 3548
5: 6 the **p** shall make an atonement for him 3548
5: 8 he shall bring them unto the **p**, who shall 3548
5:10 the **p** shall make an atonement for him for 3548
5:12 shall he bring it to the **p**, and the priest shall 3548
5:12 the **p** shall take his handful of it, *even* a 3548
5:13 the **p** shall make an atonement for him as 3548
5:16 the fifth *part* thereto, and give it unto the **p**: 3548
5:16 the **p** shall make an atonement for him with 3548
5:18 for a trespass offering, unto the **p**: 3548
5:18 the **p** shall make an atonement for him 3548
6: 6 for a trespass offering, unto the **p**: 3548
6: 7 the **p** shall make an atonement for him 3548
6:10 the **p** shall put on his linen garment, and 3548
6:12 the **p** shall burn wood on it every morning, 3548
6:22 the **p** of his sons that is anointed in his 3548
6:23 For every meat offering for the **p** shall be 3548
6:26 The **p** that offereth it for sin shall eat it: 3548
7: 5 the **p** shall burn them upon the altar *for* an 3548
7: 7 the **p** that maketh atonement therewith 3548
7: 8 the **p** that offereth *any* man's burnt 3548
7: 8 *even* the **p** shall have to himself the skin of 3548
7:31 the **p** shall burn the fat upon the altar: but 3548
7:32 the right shoulder shall ye give unto the **p** 3548
7:34 have given them unto Aaron the **p** and 3548
12: 6 tabernacle of the congregation, unto the **p**: 3548
12: 8 the **p** shall make an atonement for her, and 3548
13: 2 he shall be brought unto Aaron the **p**, or 3548
13: 3 the **p** shall look on the plague in the skin of 3548
13: 3 the **p** shall look on him, and pronounce him 3548
13: 4 the **p** shall shut up *him that hath* the plague 3548
13: 5 the **p** shall look on him the seventh day: 3548
13: 5 the **p** shall shut him up seven days more: 3548
13: 6 the **p** shall look on him again the seventh 3548
13: 6 the skin, the **p** shall pronounce him clean: 3548
13: 7 after that he hath been seen of the **p** for his 3548
13: 7 he shall be seen of the **p** again: 3548
13: 8 *if* the **p** see that behold, the scab spreadeth 3548
13: 8 then the **p** shall pronounce him unclean: 3548
13: 9 a man, then he shall be brought unto the **p**; 3548
13:10 the **p** shall see *him:* and behold, *if* the rising 3548
13:11 the **p** shall pronounce him unclean, *and* 3548
13:12 even to his foot, wheresoever the **p** looketh; 3548
13:13 the **p** shall consider: and behold, *if* 3548
13:15 the **p** shall see the raw flesh, and 3548
13:16 unto white, he shall come unto the **p**; 3548
13:17 the **p** shall see him: and behold, *if* 3548
13:17 the **p** shall pronounce *him* clean *that hath* 3548
13:19 and it be shewed to the **p**; 3548
13:20 if, when the **p** seeth it, behold, it *be* in sight 3548
13:20 the **p** shall pronounce him unclean: 3548
13:21 if the **p** look on it, and behold, *there be* no 3548
13:21 then the **p** shall shut him up seven days: 3548
13:22 then the **p** shall pronounce him unclean: 3548
13:23 and the **p** shall pronounce him clean. 3548
13:25 the **p** shall look upon it: and behold, *if* 3548
13:25 wherefore the **p** shall pronounce him 3548
13:26 if the **p** look on it, and behold, *there be* no 3548
13:26 then the **p** shall shut him up seven days: 3548
13:27 the **p** shall look upon him the seventh day: 3548

Lev 13:27 then the **p** shall pronounce him unclean: 3548
13:28 and the **p** shall pronounce him clean: 3548
13:30 Then the **p** shall see the plague: and behold, 3548
13:30 then the **p** shall pronounce him unclean: 3548
13:31 if the **p** look on the plague of the scall, and 3548
13:31 the **p** shall shut up *him that hath* the plague 3548
13:32 in the seventh day the **p** shall look on 3548
13:33 the **p** shall shut up *him that hath* the scall 3548
13:34 in the seventh day the **p** shall look on 3548
13:34 then the **p** shall pronounce him clean: 3548
13:36 the **p** shall look on him: and behold, *if* 3548
13:36 the **p** shall not seek for yellow hair: 3548
13:37 and the **p** shall pronounce him clean. 3548
13:39 the **p** shall look: and behold, *if* the bright 3548
13:43 the **p** shall look upon it: and behold, *if* 3548
13:44 the **p** shall pronounce him utterly unclean, 3548
13:49 of leprosy, and shall be shewed unto the **p**: 3548
13:50 the **p** shall look upon the plague, and 3548
13:53 if the **p** shall look, and behold, the plague 3548
13:54 the **p** shall command that they wash 3548
13:55 the **p** shall look on the plague, after *that* it 3548
13:56 if the **p** look, and behold, the plague *be* 3548
14: 2 He shall be brought unto the **p**: 3548
14: 3 the **p** shall go forth out of the camp; and 3548
14: 3 the **p** shall look, and behold, *if* the plague 3548
14: 4 shall the **p** command to take for him that is 3548
14: 5 the **p** shall command that one of the birds 3548
14:11 the **p** that maketh *him* clean shall present 3548
14:12 the **p** shall take one he lamb, and offer him 3548
14:14 the **p** shall take *some* of the blood of 3548
14:14 the **p** shall put *it* upon the tip of the right 3548
14:15 the **p** shall take *some* of the log of oil, and 3548
14:16 the **p** shall dip his right finger in the oil that 3548
14:17 **p** put upon the tip of the right ear of him 3548
14:18 the **p** shall make an atonement for him 3548
14:19 the **p** shall offer the sin offering, and 3548
14:20 the **p** shall offer the burnt offering and 3548
14:20 the **p** shall make an atonement for him, and 3548
14:23 the eighth day for his cleansing unto the **p**, 3548
14:24 the **p** shall take the lamb of the trespass 3548
14:24 the **p** shall wave them *for* a wave offering 3548
14:25 the **p** shall take *some* of the blood of 3548
14:26 the **p** shall pour of the oil into the palm of 3548
14:27 the **p** shall sprinkle with his right finger 3548
14:28 the **p** shall put of the oil that *is* in his hand 3548
14:31 the **p** shall make an atonement for him that 3548
14:35 owneth the house shall come and tell the **p**, 3548
14:36 the **p** shall command that they empty 3548
14:36 before the **p** go *into it* to see the plague, 3548
14:36 afterward the **p** shall go in to see the house: 3548
14:38 the **p** shall go out of the house to the door 3548
14:39 the **p** shall come again the seventh day, 3548
14:40 the **p** shall command that they take away 3548
14:44 the **p** shall come and look, and behold, 3548
14:48 if the **p** shall come in, and look *upon it,* 3548
14:48 the **p** shall pronounce the house clean, 3548
15:14 the congregation, and give them unto the **p**: 3548
15:15 the **p** shall offer them, the one *for* a sin 3548
15:15 the **p** shall make an atonement for him 3548
15:29 young pigeons, and bring them unto the **p**, 3548
15:30 the **p** shall offer the one *for* a sin offering, 3548
15:30 the **p** shall make an atonement for her 3548
16:30 For on that day shall *the* **p** make an NIH
16:32 the **p**, whom he shall anoint, and whom he 3548
17: 5 unto the **p**, and offer them *for* peace 3548
17: 6 the **p** shall sprinkle the blood upon the altar 3548
19:22 the **p** shall make an atonement for him with 3548
21: 9 the daughter of any **p**, if she profane herself 3548
21:10 *he that is* the high **p** among his brethren, 3548
21:21 hath a blemish, of the seed of Aaron the **p**, 3548
22:11 if the **p** buy *any* soul with his money, 3548
22:14 shall give *it* unto the **p** with the holy *thing.* 3548
23:10 of the firstfruits of your harvest unto the **p**: 3548
23:11 on the morrow after the sabbath the **p** shall 3548
23:20 the **p** shall wave them with the bread of 3548
23:20 they shall be holy to the LORD for the **p**. 3548
27: 8 he shall present himself before the **p**, and 3548
27: 8 before the priest, and the **p** shall value him; 3548
27: 8 his ability that vowed shall the **p** value him. 3548
27:11 then he shall present the beast before the **p**: 3548
27:12 the **p** shall value it, whether it be good or 3548
27:12 thou valuest it, *who art* the **p**, so shall it be. 3548
27:14 the **p** shall estimate it, whether it be good 3548
27:14 as the **p** shall estimate it, so shall it stand. 3548
27:18 the **p** shall reckon unto him the money 3548
27:23 the **p** shall reckon unto him the worth of 3548
Nu 3: 6 and present them before Aaron the **p**, 3548
3:32 Eleazar the son of Aaron the **p** *shall be* 3548
4:16 Aaron the **p** *pertaineth* the oil for the light, 3548
4:28 the hand of Ithamar the son of Aaron the **p**. 3548
4:33 the hand of Ithamar the son of Aaron the **p**. 3548
5: 8 unto the LORD, *even* to the **p**; 3548
5: 9 which they bring unto the **p**, shall be his. 3548
5:10 whatsoever any man giveth the **p**, it shall 3548
5:15 shall the man bring his wife unto the **p**, 3548
5:16 the **p** shall bring her near, and set her 3548
5:17 the **p** shall take holy water in an earthen 3548
5:17 the floor of the tabernacle the **p** shall take, 3548
5:18 the **p** shall set the woman before 3548
5:18 the **p** shall have in his hand the bitter water 3548
5:19 the **p** shall charge her by an oath, and 3548
5:21 the **p** shall charge the woman with an oath 3548
5:21 the **p** shall say unto the woman, 3548
5:23 the **p** shall write these curses in a book, 3548
5:25 the **p** shall take the jealousy offering out of 3548
5:26 the **p** shall take a handful of the offering, 3548
5:30 the **p** shall execute upon her all this law. 3548
6:10 two turtles, or two young pigeons, to the **p**, 3548
6:11 the **p** shall offer the one for a sin offering, 3548
6:16 the **p** shall bring *them* before the LORD, 3548
6:17 the **p** shall offer also his meat offering, and 3548
6:19 the **p** shall take the sodden shoulder of 3548
6:20 the **p** shall wave them *for* a wave offering 3548
6:20 this *is* holy for the **p**, with the wave breast 3548
7: 8 the hand of Ithamar the son of Aaron the **p**. 3548
15:25 the **p** shall make an atonement for all 3548
15:28 the **p** shall make an atonement for the soul 3548
16:37 Speak unto Eleazar the son of Aaron the **p**, 3548
16:39 Eleazar the **p** took the brasen censers, 3548
18:28 LORD'S heave offering to Aaron the **p**. 3548
19: 3 ye shall give her unto Eleazar the **p**, that he 3548
19: 4 Eleazar the **p** shall take of her blood with 3548
19: 6 the **p** shall take cedar wood, and hyssop, 3548
19: 7 the **p** shall wash his clothes, and he shall 3548
19: 7 and the **p** shall be unclean until the even. 3548
25: 7 the son of Eleazar, the son of Aaron the **p**, 3548
25:11 the son of Eleazar, the son of Aaron the **p**, 3548
26: 1 and unto Eleazar the son of Aaron the **p**, 3548
26: 3 Eleazar the **p** spake with them in the plains 3548
26:63 numbered by Moses and Eleazar the **p**, 3548
26:64 whom Moses and Aaron the **p** numbered, 3548
27: 2 before Eleazar the **p**, and before the princes 3548
27:19 set him before Eleazar the **p**, and before all 3548
27:21 he shall stand before Eleazar the **p**, 3548
27:22 set him before Eleazar the **p**, and before all 3548
31: 6 them and Phinehas the son of Eleazar the **p**, 3548
31:12 Eleazar the **p**, and unto the congregation of 3548
31:13 Eleazar the **p**, and all the princes of 3548
31:21 Eleazar the **p** said unto the men of war 3548
31:26 Eleazar the **p**, and the chief fathers of 3548
31:29 of their half, and give *it* unto Eleazar the **p**, 3548
31:31 Eleazar the **p** did as the LORD 3548
31:41 unto Eleazar the **p**, as the LORD 3548
31:51 and Eleazar the **p** took the gold of them, 3548
31:54 Eleazar the **p** took the gold of the captains 3548
32: 2 to Eleazar the **p**, and unto the princes of 3548
32:28 them Moses commanded Eleazar the **p**, 3548
33:38 Aaron the **p** went up into mount Hor at 3548
34:17 Eleazar the **p**, and Joshua the son of Nun. 3548
35:25 abide in it unto the death of the high **p**, 3548
35:28 of his refuge until the death of the high **p**: 3548
35:28 after the death of the high **p** the slayer shall 3548
35:32 to dwell in the land, until the death of the **p**. 3548
Dt 17:12 will not hearken unto the **p** that standeth to 3548
18: 3 they shall give unto the **p** the shoulder, and 3548
20: 2 that the **p** shall approach and speak unto 3548
26: 3 thou shalt go unto the **p** that shall be in 3548
26: 4 the **p** shall take the basket out of thine 3548
Jos 14: 1 which Eleazar the **p**, and Joshua the son of 3548
17: 4 they came near before Eleazar the **p**, and 3548
19:51 which Eleazar the **p**, and Joshua the son of 3548
20: 6 until the death of the high **p** that shall be in 3548
21: 1 fathers of the Levites unto Eleazar the **p**, 3548
21: 4 the children of Aaron the **p**, *which were* of 3548
21:13 of Aaron the **p** Hebron with her suburbs, 3548
22:13 Phinehas the son of Eleazar the **p**, 3548
22:30 when Phinehas the **p**, and the princes of 3548
22:31 Phinehas the son of Eleazar the **p** said unto 3548

P

Jos	22:32	Phinehas the son of Eleazar the **p**, and	3548
Jdg	17: 5	one of his sons, who became his **p**.	3548
	17:10	be unto me a father and a **p**, and I will give	3548
	17:12	the young man became his **p**, and was in	3548
	17:13	me good, seeing I have a Levite to *my* **p**.	3548
	18: 4	with me, and hath hired me, and I am his **p**.	3548
	18: 6	the **p** said unto them, Go in peace:	3548
	18:17	the **p** stood *in* the entering of the gate with	3548
	18:18	Then said the **p** unto them, What do ye?	3548
	18:19	go with us, and be to us a father and a **p**:	3548
	18:19	*is it* better for thee to be a **p** unto the house	3548
	18:19	or that thou be a **p** unto a tribe and a family	3548
	18:24	I made, and the **p**, and ye are gone away:	3548
	18:27	the **p** which he had, and came unto Laish,	3548
1Sa	1: 9	Now Eli the **p** sat upon a seat by a post of	3548
	2:11	minister unto the LORD before Eli the **p**.	3548
	2:14	all that the fleshhook brought up the **p** took	3548
	2:15	that sacrificed, Give flesh to roast for the **p**;	3548
	2:28	out of all the tribes of Israel to be my **p**,	3548
	2:35	I will raise me up a faithful **p**, *that* shall do	3548
	14: 3	the son of Eli, the LORD'S **p** in Shiloh,	3548
	14:19	came to pass, while Saul talked unto the **p**,	3548
	14:19	Saul said unto the **p**, Withdraw thine hand.	3548
	14:36	said the **p**, Let us draw near hither unto	3548
	21: 1	came David to Nob to Ahimelech the **p**:	3548
	21: 2	David said unto Ahimelech the **p**, The king	3548
	21: 4	the **p** answered David, and said, *There is* no	3548
	21: 5	David answered the **p**, and said unto him,	3548
	21: 6	So the **p** gave him hallowed *bread*: for	3548
	21: 9	the **p** said, The sword of Goliath	3548
	22:11	the king sent to call Ahimelech the **p**,	3548
	23: 9	he said to Abiathar the **p**, Bring hither	3548
	30: 7	David said to Abiathar the **p**,	3548
2Sa	15:27	The king said also unto Zadok the **p**, *Art*	3548
1Ki	1: 7	the son of Zeruiah, and with Abiathar the **p**:	3548
	1: 8	Zadok the **p**, and Benaiah the son of	3548
	1:19	Abiathar the **p**, and Joab the captain of	3548
	1:25	the captains of the host, and Abiathar the **p**;	3548
	1:26	Zadok the **p**, and Benaiah the son of	3548
	1:32	Call me Zadok the **p**, and Nathan	3548
	1:34	let Zadok the **p** and Nathan the prophet	3548
	1:38	So Zadok the **p**, and Nathan the prophet,	3548
	1:39	Zadok the **p** took a horn of oil out of	3548
	1:42	Jonathan the son of Abiathar the **p** came:	3548
	1:44	the king hath sent with him Zadok the **p**,	3548
	1:45	Zadok the **p** and Nathan the prophet have	3548
	2:22	for Abiathar the **p**, and for Joab the son of	3548
	2:26	unto Abiathar the **p** said the king, Get thee	3548
	2:27	Abiathar from being **p** unto the LORD;	3548
	2:35	Zadok the **p** did the king put in the room of	3548
	4: 2	he had; Azariah the son of Zadok the **p**,	3548
2Ki	11: 9	all *things* that Jehoiada the **p** commanded:	3548
	11: 9	on the sabbath, and came to Jehoiada the **p**.	3548
	11:10	to the captains over hundreds did the **p** give	3548
	11:15	Jehoiada the **p** commanded the captains of	3548
	11:15	For the **p** had said, Let her not be slain *in*	3548
	11:18	slew Mattan the **p** of Baal before the altars.	3548
	11:18	the **p** appointed officers over the house of	3548
	12: 2	days where*in* Jehoiada the **p** instructed him.	3548
	12: 7	king Jehoash called for Jehoiada the **p**,	3548
	12: 9	Jehoiada the **p** took a chest, and bored a	3548
	12:10	the king's scribe and the high **p** came up,	3548
	16:10	king Ahaz sent to Urijah the **p** the fashion	3548
	16:11	Urijah the **p** built an altar according to all	3548
	16:11	Urijah the **p** made *it* against king Ahaz	3548
	16:15	king Ahaz commanded Urijah the **p**,	3548
	16:16	Thus did Urijah the **p**, according to all that	3548
	22: 4	Go up to Hilkiah the high **p**, that he may	3548
	22: 8	Hilkiah the high **p** said unto Shaphan	3548
	22:10	Hilkiah the **p** hath delivered me a book.	3548
	22:12	the king commanded Hilkiah the **p**, and	3548
	22:14	So Hilkiah the **p**, and Ahikam, and Achbor,	3548
	23: 4	the king commanded Hilkiah the high **p**,	3548
	23:24	the **p** found *in* the house of the LORD.	3548
	25:18	of the guard took Seraiah the chief **p**,	3548
	25:18	Zephaniah the second **p**, and the three	3548
1Ch	16:39	Zadok the **p**, and his brethren the priests,	3548
	24: 6	Zadok the **p**, and Ahimelech the son of	3548
	27: 5	*was* Benaiah the son of Jehoiada, a chief **p**:	3548
	29:22	to be the chief governor, and Zadok to be **p**.	3548
2Ch	13: 9	*the same* may be a **p** of *them that are* no	3548
	15: 3	and without a teaching **p**, and without law.	3548
	19:11	Amariah the chief **p** *is* over you in all	3548
	22:11	king Jehoram, the wife of Jehoiada the **p**,	3548
	23: 8	*things* that Jehoiada the **p** had commanded,	3548
	23: 8	for Jehoiada the **p** dismissed not	3548
	23: 9	Moreover Jehoiada the **p** delivered to	3548
	23:14	Jehoiada the **p** brought out the captains of	3548
	23:14	For the **p** said, Slay her not *in* the house of	3548
	23:17	slew Mattan the **p** of Baal before the altars.	3548
	24: 2	the LORD all the days of Jehoiada the **p**.	3548
	24:20	upon Zechariah the son of Jehoiada the **p**,	3548
	24:25	for the blood of the sons of Jehoiada the **p**,	3548
	26:17	Azariah the **p** went in after him, and	3548
	26:20	Azariah the chief **p**, and all the priests,	3548
	31:10	Azariah the chief **p** of the house of Zadok	3548
	34: 9	when they came to Hilkiah the high **p**,	3548
	34:14	Hilkiah the **p** found a book of the law of	3548
	34:18	saying, Hilkiah the **p** hath given me a book.	3548
Ezr	2:63	*things* till there stood *up* a **p** with Urim	3548
	7: 5	of Eleazar, the son of Aaron the chief **p**:	3548
	7:11	the king Artaxerxes gave unto Ezra the **p**,	3548
	7:12	Artaxerxes, king of kings, unto Ezra the **p**,	3549
	7:21	that whatsoever Ezra the **p**, the scribe of	3549
	8:33	hand of Meremoth the son of Uriah the **p**;	3548
	10:10	Ezra the **p** stood up, and said unto them,	3548
	10:16	Ezra the **p**, *with* certain chief of the fathers,	3548
Ne	3: 1	Eliashib the high **p** rose up with his	3548
	3:20	door of the house of Eliashib the high **p**.	3548
	7:65	*things*, till there stood *up* a **p** with Urim	3548
	8: 2	Ezra the **p** brought the law before	3548
	8: 9	Ezra the **p** the scribe, and the Levites that	3548
	10:38	the **p** the son of Aaron shall be with	3548
	12:26	the governor, and of Ezra the **p**, the scribe.	3548
	13: 4	before this, Eliashib the **p**, having	3548
	13:13	Shelemiah the **p**, and Zadok the scribe, and	3548
	13:28	of Joiada, the son of Eliashib the high **p**,	3548
Ps	110: 4	Thou *art* a **p** for ever after the order of	3548
Isa	8: 2	Uriah the **p**, and Zechariah the son of	3548
	24: 2	shall be, as *with* the people, so *with* the **p**;	3548
	28: 7	the **p** and the prophet have erred through	3548
Jer	6:13	from the prophet even unto the **p** every one	3548
	8:10	from the prophet even unto the **p** every one	3548
	14:18	the **p** go about into a land that they know	3548
	18:18	for the law shall not perish from the **p**,	3548
	20: 1	Now Pashur the son of Immer the **p**,	3548
	21: 1	Zephaniah the son of Maaseiah the **p**,	3548
	23:11	For both prophet and **p** are profane; yea,	3548
	23:33	or the prophet, or a **p**, shall ask thee,	3548
	23:34	and the **p**, and the people, that shall say,	3548
	29:25	to Zephaniah the son of Maaseiah the **p**,	3548
	29:26	The LORD hath made thee **p** in the stead	3548
	29:26	thee priest in the stead of Jehoiada the **p**,	3548
	29:29	Zephaniah the **p** read this letter in the ears	3548
	37: 3	Zephaniah the son of Maaseiah the **p** to	3548
	52:24	of the guard took Seraiah the chief **p**,	3548
	52:24	Zephaniah the second **p**, and the three	3548
La	2: 6	indignation of his anger the king and the **p**.	3548
	2:20	shall the **p** and the prophet be slain in	3548
Eze	1: 3	LORD came expressly unto Ezekiel the **p**,	3548
	7:26	the law shall perish from the **p**, and	3548
	44:13	unto me, to **do the office of a p** unto me,	3547
	44:21	Neither shall any **p** drink wine, when they	3548
	44:22	of Israel, or a widow that had a **p** before.	3548
	44:30	ye shall also give unto the **p** the first of	3548
	45:19	the **p** shall take of the blood of the sin	3548
Hos	4: 4	thy people *are* as they that strive with the **p**.	3548
	4: 6	reject thee, that *thou* shalt be no **p** to me:	3547
	4: 9	there shall be, like people, like **p**: and I will	3548
Am	7:10	Amaziah *the* **p** of Beth-el sent to Jeroboam	3548
Hag	1: 1	to Joshua the son of Josedech the high **p**,	3548
	1:12	Joshua the son of Josedech the high **p**,	3548
	1:14	of Joshua the son of Josedech the high **p**,	3548
	2: 2	to Joshua the son of Josedech the high **p**	3548
	2: 4	O Joshua, son of Josedech, the high **p**;	3548
Zec	3: 1	he shewed me Joshua the high **p** standing	3548
	3: 8	O Joshua the high **p**, thou, and thy fellows	3548
	6:11	of Joshua the son of Josedech the high **p**;	3548
	6:13	he shall be a **p** upon his throne: and	3548
Mt	8: 4	shew thyself to the **p**, and offer the gift that	*2409*
	26: 3	of the people, unto the palace of the **high p**,	*749*
	26:57	Jesus led *him* away to Caiaphas the **high p**,	*749*
	26:62	And the **high p** arose, and said unto him,	*749*
	26:63	And the **high p** answered and said unto him,	*749*
	26:65	Then the **high p** rent his clothes, saying,	*749*
Mk	1:44	shew thyself to the **p**, and offer for thy	*2409*
	2:26	of God in the days of Abiathar the **high p**,	*749*
	14:47	and smote a servant of the **high p**, and	*749*

Mk 14:53 And they led Jesus away to the **high p**: and 749
14:54 afar off, even into the palace of the **high p**: 749
14:60 And the **high p** stood up in the midst, and 749
14:61 Again the **high p** asked him, and said unto 749
14:63 Then the **high p** rent his clothes, and saith, 749
14:66 there cometh one of the maids of the **high p**: 749
Lk 1: 5 king of Judea, a certain **p** named Zacharias, *2409*
5:14 no *man:* but go, and shew thyself to the **p**, *2409*
10:31 And by chance there came down a certain **p** *2409*
22:50 one of them smote the servant of the **high p**, 749
Jn 11:49 being the **high p** that *same* year, said unto 749
11:51 but being **high p** that year, he prophesied 749
18:13 which was the **high p** that *same* year. 749
18:15 that disciple was known unto the **high p**, and 749
18:15 in with Jesus into the palace of the **high p**. 749
18:16 which was known unto the **high p**, and 749
18:19 The **high p** then asked Jesus of his disciples, 749
18:22 saying, Answerest thou the **high p** so? 749
18:24 sent him bound unto Caiaphas the **high p**. 749
18:26 One of the servants of the **high p**, being *his* 749
Ac 4: 6 And Annas the **high p**, and Caiaphas, and 749
4: 6 many as were of the kindred of the **high p**, 748
5:17 Then the **high p** rose up, and all they that 749
5:21 But the **high p** came, and they that were 749
5:24 Now when the *high* **p** and the captain of *2409*
5:27 the council: and the **high p** asked them, 749
7: 1 Then said the **high p**, Are these *things* so? 749
9: 1 disciples of the Lord, went unto the **high p**, 749
14:13 Then the **p** of Jupiter, which was before *2409*
22: 5 As also the **high p** doth bear me witness, and 749
23: 2 And the **high p** Ananias commanded them 749
23: 4 stood by said, Revilest thou God's **high p**? 749
23: 5 I wist not, brethren, that he was the **high p**: 749
24: 1 And after five days Ananias the **high p** 749
25: 2 Then the **high p** and the chief of the Jews 749
Heb 2:17 faithful **high p** *in things* pertaining to God, 749
3: 1 the Apostle and **High P** of our profession, 749
4:14 Seeing then that we have a great **high p**, 749
4:15 For we have not a **high p** which cannot be 749
5: 1 For every **high p** taken from among men is 749
5: 5 glorified not himself to be made a **high p**; 749
5: 6 a **p** for ever after the order of Melchisedec. *2409*
5:10 Called of God a **high p** after the order of 749
6:20 made a **high p** for ever after the order of 749
7: 1 king of Salem, **p** of the most high God, *2409*
7: 3 the Son of God; abideth a **p** continually. *2409*
7:11 what further need *was there* that another **p** *2409*
7:15 of Melchisedec there ariseth another **p**, *2409*
7:17 Thou *art* a **p** for ever after the order of *2409*
7:20 as not without an oath *he was made* **p**: NIG
7:21 Thou *art* a **p** for ever after the order of *2409*
7:26 For such a **high p** became us, *who is* holy, 749
8: 1 We have such a **high p**, who is set on 749
8: 3 For every **high p** is ordained to offer gifts 749
8: 4 if he were on earth, he should not be a **p**, *2409*
9: 7 But into the second *went* the **high p** alone 749
9:11 But Christ being come a **high p** of good 749
9:25 as the **high p** entereth into the holy *place* 749
10:11 And every **p** standeth daily ministering and *2409*
10:21 And *having* a high **p** over the house of *2409*
13:11 into the sanctuary by the **high p** for sin, 749

PRIEST'S (46) [PRIEST]

Ex 28: 1 he may **minister** unto me **in the p office**, 3547
28: 3 he may **minister** unto me **in the p office**. 3547
28: 4 he may **minister** unto me **in the p office**. 3547
28:41 they may **minister** unto me **in the p office**. 3547
29: 1 to **minister** unto me **in the p office**: 3547
29: 9 the **p office** shall be theirs for a perpetual 3550
29:44 his sons, to **minister** to me **in the p office**. 3547
30:30 *they* may **minister** unto me **in the p office**. 3547
31:10 of his sons, to **minister in the p office**, 3547
35:19 of his sons, to **minister in the p office**. 3547
39:41 sons' garments, to **minister in the p office**. 3547
40:13 he may **minister** unto me **in the p office**. 3547
40:15 they may **minister** unto me **in the p office**: 3547
Lev 5:13 *the remnant* shall be the **p**, as a 3548+3807.1
7: 9 in the pan, shall be the **p** that offereth it. 3548
7:14 it shall be the **p** that sprinkleth 3548+3807.1
7:35 **minister** unto the LORD **in the p office**; 3547
14:13 for as the sin offering *is* the **p**, *so is* 3548
14:18 the remnant of the oil that *is* in the **p** hand 3548
14:29 the rest of the oil that *is* in the **p** hand he 3548
16:32 **minister in the p office** in his father's 3547
22:10 eat *of* the holy *thing:* a sojourner of the **p**, 3548
22:12 If the **p** daughter also be *married* unto a 3548
22:13 if the **p** daughter be a widow, or divorced, 3548
27:21 the possession thereof shall be the **p**. 3548
Nu 3: 3 he consecrated to **minister in the p office**. 3547
3: 4 Ithamar **ministered in the p office** in 3547
3:10 and they shall wait on their **p office**: 3550
18: 7 thy sons with thee shall keep your **p office** 3550
18: 7 I have given your **p office** *unto you as* a 3550
Dt 10: 6 Eleazar his son **ministered in the p office** 3547
18: 3 And this shall be the **p** due from the people, 3548
Jdg 18:20 the **p** heart was glad, and he took 3548
1Sa 2:13 the **p** servant came, while the flesh was in 3548
2:15 the **p** servant came, and said to the man that 3548
1Ch 6:10 (he *it is* that **executed the p office** in 3547
24: 2 Eleazar and Ithamar **executed the p office**. 3547
2Ch 11:14 **executing the p office** unto the LORD: 3547
24:11 and the high **p** officer came and 3548
Mal 2: 7 For the **p** lips should keep knowledge, and 3548
Mt 26:51 and stroke a servant of the **high p**, and *749*
26:58 followed him afar off unto the **high p** palace, *749*
Lk 1: 8 *that* while he **executed the p office** before *2407*
1: 9 According to the custom of the **p office**, *2405*
22:54 and brought him into the **high p** house. *749*
Jn 18:10 and smote the **high p** servant, and cut off his *749*

PRIESTHOOD (16) [PRIEST]

Ex 40:15 everlasting **p** throughout their generations. 3550
Nu 16:10 of Levi with thee: and seek ye the **p** also? 3550
18: 1 with thee shall bear the iniquity of your **p**. 3550
25:13 *even* the covenant of an everlasting **p**; 3550
Jos 18: 7 for the **p** of the LORD *is* their inheritance: 3550
Ezr 2:62 were they, as polluted, put from the **p**. 3550
Ne 7:64 were they, as polluted, put from the **p**. 3550
13:29 because they have defiled the **p**, and 3550
13:29 the covenant of the **p**, and of the Levites. 3550
Heb 7: 5 **office of** the **p** have a commandment to *2405*
7:11 perfection were by the Levitical **p**, *2420*
7:12 For the **p** being changed, there is made of *2420*
7:14 tribe Moses spake nothing concerning **p**. *2420*
7:24 continueth ever, hath an unchangeable **p**. *2420*
1Pe 2: 5 are built *up* a spiritual house, a holy **p**, *2406*
2: 9 a royal **p**, a holy nation, a peculiar people; *2406*

PRIESTS (392) [PRIEST]

Ge 47:22 Only the land of the **p** bought he not; 3548
47:22 for the **p** had a portion assigned them of 3548
47:26 the fifth *part;* except the land of the **p** only, 3548
Ex 19: 6 ye shall be unto me a kingdom of **p**, and 3548
19:22 let the **p** also, which come near to 3548
19:24 let not the **p** and the people break through 3548
Lev 1: 5 the **p**, Aaron's sons, shall bring the blood, 3548
1: 8 And the **p**, Aaron's sons, shall lay the parts, 3548
1:11 the **p**, Aaron's sons, shall sprinkle his blood 3548
2: 2 he shall bring it to Aaron's sons the **p**: and 3548
3: 2 Aaron's sons the **p** shall sprinkle the blood 3548
6:29 All the males among the **p** shall eat thereof: 3548
7: 6 Every male among the **p** shall eat thereof: 3548
13: 2 the priest, or unto one of his sons the **p**: 3548
16:33 he shall make an atonement for the **p**, and 3548
21: 1 Speak unto the **p** the sons of Aaron, and 3548
Nu 3: 3 sons of Aaron, the **p** which were anointed, 3548
10: 8 the sons of Aaron, the **p**, shall blow with 3548
Dt 17: 9 And thou shalt come unto the **p** the Levites, 3548
17:18 of *that which is* before the **p** the Levites: 3548
18: 1 The **p** the Levites, *and* all the tribe of Levi, 3548
19:17 before the **p** and the judges, which shall be 3548
21: 5 the **p** the sons of Levi shall come near; 3548
24: 8 do according to all that the **p** the Levites 3548
27: 9 and the **p** the Levites spake unto all Israel, 3548
31: 9 delivered it unto the **p** the sons of Levi, 3548
Jos 3: 3 the **p** the Levites bearing it, then ye shall 3548
3: 6 Joshua spake unto the **p**, saying, Take up 3548
3: 8 thou shalt command the **p** that bear the ark 3548
3:13 as soon as the soles of the feet of the **p** that 3548
3:14 the **p** bearing the ark *of* the covenant before 3548
3:15 the feet of the **p** that bare the ark were 3548
3:17 the **p** that bare the ark *of* the covenant of 3548
4: 9 in the place where the feet of the **p** which 3548
4:10 For the **p** which bare the ark stood in 3548
4:11 and the **p**, in the presence of the people. 3548
4:16 Command the **p** that bear the ark of 3548
4:17 Joshua therefore commanded the **p**, saying, 3548
4:18 when the **p** that bare the ark of the covenant 3548

Jos	6: 4	seven **p** shall bear before the ark seven	3548
	6: 4	and the **p** shall blow with the trumpets.	3548
	6: 6	Joshua the son of Nun called the **p**, and	3548
	6: 6	let seven **p** bear seven trumpets of rams'	3548
	6: 8	that the seven **p** bearing the seven trumpets	3548
	6: 9	the armed men went before the **p** that blew	3548
	6: 9	*the* **p** going on, and blowing with	NIH
	6:12	and the **p** took up the ark of the LORD.	3548
	6:13	seven **p** bearing seven trumpets of rams'	3548
	6:13	*the* **p** going on, and blowing with	NIH
	6:16	when the **p** blew with the trumpets, Joshua	3548
	6:20	So the people shouted when *the* **p** blew with	NIH
	8:33	and on that side before the **p** the Levites,	3548
	21:19	the cities of the children of Aaron, the **p**,	3548
Jdg	18:30	his sons were **p** to the tribe of Dan until	3548
1Sa	1: 3	Hophni and Phinehas, the **p** of the LORD,	3548
	5: 5	Therefore neither the **p** of Dagon, nor any	3548
	6: 2	the Philistines called for the **p** and	3548
	22:11	his father's house, the **p** that *were* in Nob:	3548
	22:17	Turn, and slay the **p** of the LORD;	3548
	22:17	their hand to fall upon the **p** of the LORD.	3548
	22:18	to Doeg, Turn thou, and fall upon the **p**.	3548
	22:18	he fell upon the **p**, and slew on that day	3548
	22:19	Nob, the city of the **p**, smote he with	3548
	22:21	David that Saul had slain the LORD'S **p**.	3548
2Sa	8:17	Ahimelech the son of Abiathar, *were* the **p**;	3548
	15:35	there with thee Zadok and Abiathar the **p**?	3548
	15:35	shalt tell *it* to Zadok and Abiathar the **p**.	3548
	17:15	Hushai unto Zadok and to Abiathar the **p**,	3548
	19:11	David sent to Zadok and to Abiathar the **p**,	3548
	20:25	and Zadok and Abiathar *were* the **p**:	3548
1Ki	4: 4	and Zadok and Abiathar *were* the **p**:	3548
	8: 3	of Israel came, and the **p** took up the ark.	3548
	8: 4	even those did the **p** and the Levites bring	3548
	8: 6	the **p** brought in the ark of the covenant of	3548
	8:10	when the **p** were come out of the holy	3548
	8:11	So that the **p** could not stand to minister	3548
	12:31	made **p** of the lowest of the people,	3548
	12:32	he placed in Beth-el the **p** of the high	3548
	13: 2	upon thee shall he offer the **p** of the high	3548
	13:33	made again of the lowest of the people **p** of	3548
	13:33	he became *one of* the **p** of the high places.	3548
2Ki	10:11	his great *men*, and his kinsfolks, and his **p**,	3548
	10:19	of Baal, all his servants, and all his **p**;	3548
	12: 4	Jehoash said to the **p**, All the money of	3548
	12: 5	Let the **p** take *it* to them, every man of his	3548
	12: 6	twentieth year of king Jehoash the **p** had	3548
	12: 7	the *other* **p**, and said unto them, Why repair	3548
	12: 8	the **p** consented to receive no *more* money	3548
	12: 9	the **p** that kept the door put therein all	3548
	17:27	Carry thither one of the **p** whom ye brought	3548
	17:28	one of the **p** whom they had carried away	3548
	17:32	of the lowest of them **p** of the high places,	3548
	19: 2	Shebna the scribe, and the elders of the **p**,	3548
	23: 2	the **p**, and the prophets, and all the people,	3548
	23: 4	high priest, and the **p** of the second order;	3548
	23: 5	he put down the **idolatrous p**, whom	3649
	23: 8	he brought all the **p** out of the cities of	3548
	23: 8	defiled the high places where the **p** had	3548
	23: 9	Nevertheless the **p** of the high places came	3548
	23:20	he slew all the **p** of the high places that	3548
1Ch	9: 2	the **p**, Levites, and the Nethinims.	3548
	9:10	of the **p**; Jedaiah, and Jehoiarib, and Jachin,	3548
	9:30	*some* of the sons of the **p** made	3548
	13: 2	with them *also to* the **p** and Levites *which*	3548
	15:11	David called for Zadok and Abiathar the **p**,	3548
	15:14	So the **p** and the Levites sanctified	3548
	15:24	Zechariah, and Benaiah, and Eliezer, the **p**,	3548
	16: 6	Jahaziel the **p** with trumpets continually	3548
	16:39	Zadok the priest, and his brethren the **p**,	3548
	18:16	Abimelech the son of Abiathar, *were* the **p**;	3548
	23: 2	of Israel, with the **p** and the Levites.	3548
	24: 6	*before* the chief of the fathers of the **p** and	3548
	24:31	the chief of the fathers of the **p** and Levites,	3548
	28:13	Also for the courses of the **p** and	3548
	28:21	the courses of the **p** and the Levites,	3548
2Ch	4: 6	but the sea *was* for the **p** to wash in.	3548
	4: 9	Furthermore he made the court of the **p**,	3548
	5: 5	these did the **p** *and* the Levites bring up.	3548
	5: 7	the **p** brought in the ark of the covenant of	3548
	5:11	when the **p** were come out of the holy	3548
	5:11	all the **p** that were present were sanctified,	3548
	5:12	and twenty **p** sounding with trumpets:)	3548
	5:14	So that the **p** could not stand to minister by	3548

	6:41	let thy **p**, O LORD God, be clothed *with*	3548
	7: 2	the **p** could not enter into the house of	3548
	7: 6	the **p** waited on their offices: the Levites	3548
	7: 6	the **p** sounded trumpets before them, and	3548
	8:14	the courses of the **p** to their service, and	3548
	8:14	to praise and minister before the **p**,	3548
	8:15	the commandment of the king unto the **p**	3548
	11:13	the **p** and the Levites that *were* in all Israel	3548
	11:15	he ordained him **p** for the high places, and	3548
	13: 9	Have ye not cast out the **p** of the LORD,	3548
	13: 9	have made you **p** after the manner of	3548
	13:10	the **p**, which minister unto the LORD,	3548
	13:12	his **p** with sounding trumpets to cry alarm	3548
	13:14	and the **p** sounded with the trumpets.	3548
	17: 8	and with them Elishama and Jehoram, **p**.	3548
	19: 8	*of* the **p**, and of the chief of the fathers of	3548
	23: 4	of the **p** and of the Levites, *shall be* porters	3548
	23: 6	save the **p**, and they that minister of	3548
	23:18	LORD by the hand of the **p** the Levites,	3548
	24: 5	he gathered together the **p** and the Levites,	3548
	26:17	with him fourscore **p** of the LORD,	3548
	26:18	the LORD, but to the **p** the sons of Aaron,	3548
	26:19	while he was wroth with the **p**, the leprosy	3548
	26:19	before the **p** in the house of the LORD,	3548
	26:20	and all the **p**, looked upon him, and behold,	3548
	29: 4	he brought in the **p** and the Levites, and	3548
	29:16	the **p** went into the inner part *of* the house	3548
	29:21	he commanded the **p** the sons of Aaron to	3548
	29:22	the **p** received the blood, and sprinkled *it*	3548
	29:24	the **p** killed them, and they made	3548
	29:26	of David, and the **p** with the trumpets.	3548
	29:34	the **p** were *too* few, so that they could not	3548
	29:34	until the *other* **p** had sanctified themselves:	3548
	29:34	in heart to sanctify themselves than the **p**.	3548
	30: 3	the **p** had not sanctified themselves	3548
	30:15	the **p** and the Levites were ashamed, and	3548
	30:16	the **p** sprinkled the blood, *which they*	3548
	30:21	and the **p** praised the LORD day by day,	3548
	30:24	a great number of **p** sanctified themselves.	3548
	30:25	with the **p** and the Levites, and all	3548
	30:27	the **p** the Levites arose and blessed	3548
	31: 2	Hezekiah appointed the courses of the **p**	3548
	31: 2	the **p** and Levites for burnt offerings and	3548
	31: 4	in Jerusalem to give the portion of the **p**	3548
	31: 9	Hezekiah questioned with the **p** and	3548
	31:15	and Shecaniah, in the cities of the **p**,	3548
	31:17	Both *to* the genealogy of the **p** by the house	3548
	31:19	Also of the sons of Aaron the **p**,	3548
	31:19	give portions to all the males among the **p**,	3548
	34: 5	he burnt the bones of the **p** upon their	3548
	34:30	the **p**, and the Levites, and all the people,	3548
	35: 2	he set the **p** in their charges, and	3548
	35: 8	the people, to the **p**, and to the Levites:	3548
	35: 8	gave unto the **p** for the passover *offerings*	3548
	35:10	the **p** stood in their place, and the Levites in	3548
	35:11	the **p** sprinkled *the blood* from their hands,	3548
	35:14	made ready for themselves, and for the **p**:	3548
	35:14	the **p** the sons of Aaron *were busied* in	3548
	35:14	and for the **p** the sons of Aaron.	3548
	35:18	the **p**, and the Levites, and all Judah and	3548
	36:14	Moreover all the chief of the **p**, and	3548
Ezr	1: 5	and Benjamin, and the **p**, and the Levites,	3548
	2:36	The **p**: the children of Jedaiah, of the house	3548
	2:61	of the children of the **p**: the children of	3548
	2:70	So the **p**, and the Levites, and *some* of	3548
	3: 2	his brethren the **p**, and Zerubbabel the son	3548
	3: 8	the remnant of their brethren the **p** and	3548
	3:10	they set the **p** in their apparel with	3548
	3:12	many of the **p** and Levites and chief of	3548
	6: 9	according to the appointment of the **p**	3549
	6:16	the **p**, and the Levites, and the rest of	3549
	6:18	they set the **p** in their divisions, and	3549
	6:20	For the **p** and the Levites were purified	3548
	6:20	for their brethren the **p**, and for themselves.	3548
	7: 7	of the **p**, and the Levites, and the singers,	3548
	7:13	and *of* his **p** and Levites, in my realm,	3549
	7:16	offering of the people, and of the **p**,	3549
	7:24	that *touching* any of the **p** and Levites,	3549
	8:15	the **p**, and found there none of the sons of	3548
	8:24	I separated twelve of the chief of the **p**,	3548
	8:29	ye weigh *them* before the chief of the **p**	3548
	8:30	So took the **p** and the Levites the weight of	3548
	9: 1	people of Israel, and the **p**, and the Levites,	3548
	9: 7	iniquities have we, our kings, *and* our **p**,	3548

Ezr 10: 5 made the chief **p**, the Levites, and all Israel, 3548
10:18 among the sons of the **p** there were found 3548
Ne 2:16 nor to the **p**, nor to the nobles, nor to 3548
3: 1 high priest rose up with his brethren the **p**, 3548
3:22 after him repaired the **p**, the men of 3548
3:28 From above the horse gate repaired the **p**, 3548
5:12 I called the **p**, and took an oath of them, 3548
7:39 The **p**: the children of Jedaiah, of the house 3548
7:63 of the **p**: the children of Habaiah, 3548
7:73 So the **p**, and the Levites, and the porters, 3548
8:13 the **p**, and the Levites, unto Ezra the scribe, 3548
9:32 on our **p**, and on our prophets, and on our 3548
9:34 our princes, our **p**, nor our fathers, kept thy 3548
9:38 write *it;* and our princes, Levites, *and* **p**, 3548
10: 8 Bilgai, Shemaiah: these *were* the **p**. 3548
10:28 the **p**, the Levites, the porters, the singers, 3548
10:34 we cast the lots *among* the **p**, the Levites, 3548
10:36 unto the **p** that minister in the house of our 3548
10:37 *of* trees, of wine and of oil, unto the **p**, 3548
10:39 the **p** that minister, and the porters, and 3548
11: 3 the **p**, and the Levites, and the Nethinims, 3548
11:10 Of the **p**: Jedaiah the son of Joiarib, Jachin, 3548
11:20 residue of Israel, of the **p**, *and* the Levites, 3548
12: 1 Now these *are* the **p** and the Levites that 3548
12: 7 These *were* the chief of the **p** and of their 3548
12:12 in the days of Joiakim were **p**, the chief of 3548
12:22 also the **p**, to the reign of Darius 3548
12:30 the **p** and the Levites purified themselves, 3548
12:41 the **p**; Eliakim, Maaseiah, Miniamin, 3548
12:44 the cities the portions of the law for the **p** 3548
12:44 for Judah rejoiced for the **p** and for 3548
13: 5 and the porters; and the offerings of the **p**. 3548
13:30 appointed the wards of the **p** and 3548
Ps 78:64 Their **p** fell by the sword; and their widows 3548
99: 6 Moses and Aaron among his **p**, and 3548
132: 9 Let thy **p** be clothed *with* righteousness; 3548
132:16 I will also clothe her **p** with salvation: and 3548
Isa 37: 2 the elders of the **p** covered with sackcloth, 3548
61: 6 But ye shall be named the **P** of the LORD: 3548
66:21 I will also take of them for **p** *and* 3548
Jer 1: 1 of the **p** that *were* in Anathoth in the land 3548
1:18 against the **p** thereof, and against 3548
2: 8 The **p** said not, Where *is* the LORD? and 3548
2:26 and their **p**, and their prophets, 3548
4: 9 the **p** shall be astonished, and the prophets 3548
5:31 and the **p** bear rule by their means; 3548
8: 1 the bones of the **p**, and the bones of 3548
13:13 the **p**, and the prophets, and all 3548
19: 1 of the people, and of the ancients of the **p**; 3548
26: 7 So the **p** and the prophets and all the people 3548
26: 8 that the **p** and the prophets and all 3548
26:11 spake the **p** and the prophets unto 3548
26:16 all the people unto the **p** and to 3548
27:16 Also I spake to the **p** and to all this people, 3548
28: 1 in the presence of the **p** and of all 3548
28: 5 prophet Hananiah in the presence of the **p**, 3548
29: 1 to the **p**, and to the prophets, and to all 3548
29:25 the priest, and to all the **p**, saying, 3548
31:14 I will satiate the soul of the **p** with fatness, 3548
32:32 their **p**, and their prophets, and the men of 3548
33:18 Neither shall the **p** the Levites want a man 3548
33:21 and with the Levites the **p**, my ministers. 3548
34:19 and the **p**, and all the people of the land, 3548
48: 7 shall go forth into captivity *with* his **p** 3548
49: 3 *and* his **p** and his princes together. 3548
La 1: 4 her **p** sigh: her virgins *are* afflicted, and 3548
1:19 my **p** and mine elders gave up the ghost in 3548
4:13 of her prophets, *and* the iniquities of her **p**, 3548
4:16 they respected not the persons of the **p**, 3548
Eze 22:26 Her **p** have violated my law, and 3548
40:45 prospect *is* toward the south, *is* for the **p**, 3548
40:46 prospect *is* toward the north *is* for the **p**, 3548
42:13 where the **p** that approach unto the LORD 3548
42:14 When the **p** enter *therein,* then shall they 3548
43:19 thou shalt give to the **p** the Levites that *be* 3548
43:24 the **p** shall cast salt upon them, and 3548
43:27 the **p** shall make your burnt offerings upon 3548
44:15 the **p** the Levites, the sons of Zadok, 3548
44:31 The **p** shall not eat *of* any thing that is dead 3548
45: 4 be for the **p** the ministers of the sanctuary, 3548
46: 2 the **p** shall prepare his burnt offering and 3548
46:19 into the holy chambers of the **p**, 3548
46:20 This *is* the place where the **p** shall boil 3548
48:10 for them, *even* for the **p**, shall be *this* holy 3548
48:11 *It shall be* for the **p** that are sanctified of 3548
48:13 over against the border of the **p**, the Levites 3548
Hos 5: 1 Hear ye this, O **p**; and hearken, ye house of 3548
6: 9 the company of **p** murder *in* the way by 3548
10: 5 the **p** thereof *that* rejoiced on it, for 3649
Joel 1: 9 the **p**, the LORD'S ministers, mourn. 3548
1:13 Gird yourselves, and lament, ye **p**: howl, 3548
2:17 Let the **p**, the ministers of the LORD, 3548
Mic 3:11 the **p** thereof teach for hire, and 3548
Zep 1: 4 *and* the name of the Chemarims with the **p**; 3548
3: 4 her **p** have polluted the sanctuary, 3548
Hag 2:11 Ask now the **p** *concerning* the law, saying, 3548
2:12 be holy? And the **p** answered and said, No. 3548
2:13 the **p** answered and said, It shall be 3548
Zec 7: 3 *And* to speak unto the **p** which *were* in 3548
7: 5 to the **p**, saying, When ye fasted and 3548
Mal 1: 6 hosts unto you, O **p**, that despise my name. 3548
2: 1 now, O ye **p**, this commandment *is* for you. 3548
Mt 2: 4 And when he had gathered all the **chief p** *749*
12: 4 which were with him, but only for the **p**? *2409*
12: 5 how that on the sabbath days the **p** in *2409*
16:21 *things* of the elders and **chief p** and scribes, *749*
20:18 of man shall be betrayed unto the **chief p** *749*
21:15 And when the **chief p** and scribes saw *749*
21:23 the **chief p** and the elders of the people came *749*
21:45 And when the **chief p** and Pharisees had *749*
26: 3 Then assembled together the **chief p**, and *749*
26:14 called Judas Iscariot, went unto the **chief p**, *749*
26:47 from the **chief p** and elders of the people. *749*
26:59 Now the **chief p**, and elders, and all *749*
27: 1 all the **chief p** and elders of the people took *749*
27: 3 again the thirty pieces of silver to the **chief p** *749*
27: 6 And the **chief p** took the silver pieces, and *749*
27:12 And when he was accused of the **chief p** and *749*
27:20 But the **chief p** and elders persuaded *749*
27:41 Likewise also the **chief p** mocking *him,* with *749*
27:62 the **chief p** and Pharisees came together unto *749*
28:11 shewed unto the **chief p** all the *things* that *749*
Mk 2:26 which is not lawful to eat but for the **p**, and *2409*
8:31 of the elders, and *of* the **chief p**, and scribes, *749*
10:33 of man shall be delivered unto the **chief p**, *749*
11:18 And the scribes and **chief p** heard *it,* and *749*
11:27 there come to him the **chief p**, and *749*
14: 1 and the **chief p** and the scribes sought how *749*
14:10 one of the twelve, went unto the **chief p**, *749*
14:43 from the **chief p** and the scribes and *749*
14:53 with him were assembled all the **chief p** and *749*
14:55 And the **chief p** and all the council sought *749*
15: 1 And straightway in the morning the **chief p** *749*
15: 3 And the **chief p** accused him of many *things:* *749*
15:10 For he knew that the **chief p** had delivered *749*
15:11 But the **chief p** moved the people, that he *749*
15:31 Likewise also the **chief p** mocking said *749*
Lk 3: 2 Annas and Caiaphas being the **high p**, *749*
6: 4 it is not lawful to eat but for the **p** alone? *2409*
9:22 of the elders and **chief p** and scribes, *749*
17:14 unto them, Go shew yourselves unto the **p**. *2409*
19:47 But the **chief p** and the scribes and the chief *749*
20: 1 the **chief p** and the scribes came upon *him* *749*
20:19 And the **chief p** and the scribes the same *749*
22: 2 And the **chief p** and scribes sought how they *749*
22: 4 and communed with the **chief p** and *749*
22:52 Then Jesus said unto the **chief p**, and *749*
22:66 the elders of the people and the **chief p** and *749*
23: 4 Then said Pilate to the **chief p** and *to* *749*
23:10 And the **chief p** and scribes stood and *749*
23:13 when he had called together the **chief p** and *749*
23:23 voices of them and of the **chief p** prevailed. *749*
24:20 And how the **chief p** and our rulers delivered *749*
Jn 1:19 when the Jews sent **p** and Levites from *2409*
7:32 and the **chief p** sent officers to take him. *749*
7:45 Then came the officers to the **chief p** and *749*
11:47 Then gathered the **chief p** and the Pharisees *749*
11:57 Now both the chief **p** and the Pharisees had *749*
12:10 But the **chief p** consulted that they might put *749*
18: 3 and officers from the **chief p** and Pharisees, *749*
18:35 and the **chief p** have delivered thee unto me: *749*
19: 6 When the **chief p** therefore and officers saw *749*
19:15 The **chief p** answered, We have no king but *749*
19:21 Then said the **chief p** of the Jews to Pilate, *749*
Ac 4: 1 the **p**, and the captain of the temple, and *2409*
4:23 and reported all that the **chief p** and elders *749*
5:24 and the **chief p** heard these things, *749*
6: 7 a great company of the **p** were obedient to *2409*

Ac 9:14 And here he hath authority from the **chief p** *749*
9:21 he might bring them bound unto the **chief p**? *749*
19:14 a Jew, *and* **chief of the p**, which did so. *749*
22:30 and commanded the **chief p** and all their *749*
23:14 And they came to the **chief p** and elders, and *749*
25:15 the **chief p** and the elders of the Jews *749*
26:10 having received authority from the **chief p**; *749*
26:12 and commission from the **chief p**, *749*
Heb 7:21 (For those **p** were made without an oath; *2409*
7:23 And they truly were many **p**, because *2409*
7:27 as *those* **high p**, to offer up sacrifice, first for *749*
7:28 For the law maketh men **high p** which have *749*
8: 4 seeing that there are **p** that offer gifts *2409*
9: 6 the **p** went always into the first tabernacle, *2409*
Rev 1: 6 us kings and **p** unto God and his Father; *2409*
5:10 hast made us unto our God kings and **p**: *2409*
20: 6 but they shall be **p** of God and of Christ, *2409*

PRIESTS' (10) [PRIEST]

Jos 4: 3 out of the place where the **p** feet stood firm, 3548
4:18 the soles of the **p** feet were lift up unto 3548
1Sa 2:13 the **p** custom with the people *was, that* 3548
2:36 I pray thee, into one of the **p offices**, 3550
2Ki 12:16 *into* the house of the LORD: it was the **p**. 3548
Ezr 2:69 *of* silver, and one hundred **p** garments. 3548
Ne 7:70 five hundred and thirty **p** garments. 3548
7:72 and threescore and seven **p** garments. 3548
12:35 *certain* of the **p** sons with trumpets; 3548
Eze 44:30 of your oblations, shall be the **p**: 3548+3807.1

PRINCE (102) [PRINCE'S, PRINCES, PRINCESS, PRINCESSES]

Ge 23: 6 thou *art* a mighty **p** among us: in the choice 5387
32:28 for **as a p hast** thou **power** with God and 8280
34: 2 **p** of the country, saw her, he took her, and 5387
Ex 2:14 Who made thee a **p** and a judge over us? 8269
Nu 7:11 each **p** on *his* day, for the dedicating of 5387
7:18 the son of Zuar, **p** of Issachar, did offer: 5387
7:24 **p** of the children of Zebulun, *did offer:* 5387
7:30 **p** of the children of Reuben, *did offer:* 5387
7:36 **p** of the children of Simeon, *did offer:* 5387
7:42 of Deuel, **p** of the children of Gad, *offered:* 5387
7:48 **p** of the children of Ephraim, *offered:* 5387
7:54 of Pedahzur, **p** of the children of Manasseh: 5387
7:60 **p** of the children of Benjamin, *offered:* 5387
7:66 **p** of the children of Dan, *offered:* 5387
7:72 **p** of the children of Asher, *offered:* 5387
7:78 **p** of the children of Naphtali, *offered:* 5387
16:13 **make** thyself **altogether a p** over 8323+8323
17: 6 for each **p** one, according to their fathers' 5387
25:14 a **p** of a chief house among the Simeonites. 5387
25:18 the daughter of a **p** of Midian, their sister, 5387
34:18 ye shall take one **p** of every tribe, to divide 5387
34:22 the **p** of the tribe of the children of Dan, 5387
34:23 The **p** of the children of Joseph, for 5387
34:24 the **p** of the tribe of the children of 5387
34:25 the **p** of the tribe of the children of 5387
34:26 the **p** of the tribe of the children of 5387
34:27 the **p** of the tribe of the children of Asher, 5387
34:28 the **p** of the tribe of the children of 5387
Jos 22:14 of each chief house a **p** throughout all the tribes 1
2Sa 3:38 Know ye not that there is a **p** and a great 8269
1Ki 11:34 I will make him **p** all the days of his life for 5387
14: 7 and made thee **p** over my people Israel, 5057
16: 2 and made thee **p** over my people Israel; 5057
1Ch 2:10 begat Nahshon, **p** of the children of Judah; 5387
5: 6 away captive: he *was* **p** of the Reubenites. 5387
Ezr 1: 8 them unto Sheshbazzar, the **p** of Judah. 5387
Job 21:28 For ye say, Where *is* the house of the **p**? 5081
31:37 my steps; as a **p** would I go near unto him. 5057
Pr 14:28 want of people *is* the destruction of the **p**. 7333
17: 7 not a fool: much less do lying lips a **p**. 5081
19: 6 Many will intreat the favour of the **p**: and 5081
25: 7 of the **p** whom thine eyes have seen. 5081
25:15 By long forbearing is a **p** persuaded, and 7101
28:16 The **p** that wanteth understanding *is* also a 5057
Isa 9: 6 The everlasting Father, The **P** of Peace. 8269
Jer 51:59 of his reign. And *this* Seraiah *was* a quiet **p**. 8269
Eze 7:27 the **p** shall be clothed with desolation, and 5387
12:10 This burden *concerneth* the **p** in Jerusalem, 5387
12:12 the **p** that *is* among them shall bear upon 5387
21:25 thou, profane wicked **p** of Israel, whose day 5387
28: 2 Son of man, say unto the **p** of Tyrus, 5057
30:13 there shall be no more a **p** of the land of 5387
34:24 and my servant David a **p** among them; 5387
37:25 my servant David *shall be* their **p** for ever. 5387
38: 2 the chief **p** of Meshech and Tubal, and 5387
38: 3 O Gog, the chief **p** of Meshech and Tubal: 5387
39: 1 O Gog, the chief **p** of Meshech and Tubal: 5387
44: 3 *It is* for the **p**; the prince, he shall sit in it to 5387
44: 3 the **p**, he shall sit in it to eat bread before 5387
45: 7 *a portion shall be* for the **p** on the one side 5387
45:16 shall give this oblation for the **p** in Israel. 5387
45:22 upon that day shall the **p** prepare for 5387
46: 2 the **p** shall enter by the way of the porch of 5387
46: 4 the burnt offering that the **p** shall offer unto 5387
46: 8 when the **p** shall enter, he shall go in *by* 5387
46:10 the **p** in the midst of them, when they go in, 5387
46:12 Now when the **p** shall prepare a voluntary 5387
46:16 If the **p** give a gift unto any of his sons, 5387
46:17 year of liberty; after, it shall return to the **p**: 5387
46:18 Moreover the **p** shall not take of 5387
48:21 the residue *shall be* for the **p**, on the one 5387
48:21 over against the portions for the **p**: 5387
48:22 the border of Benjamin, shall be for the **p**. 5387
Da 1: 7 Unto whom the **p** of the eunuchs gave 8269
1: 8 he requested of the **p** of the eunuchs that he 8269
1: 9 and tender love with the **p** of the eunuchs. 8269
1:10 the **p** of the eunuchs said unto Daniel, I fear 8269
1:11 whom the **p** of the eunuchs had set over 8269
1:18 the **p** of the eunuchs brought them in before 8269
8:11 he magnified *himself even* to the **p** of 8269
8:25 he shall also stand up against the **P** of 8269
9:25 to build Jerusalem unto the Messiah the **P** 5057
9:26 the people of the **p** that *shall* come shall 5057
10:13 the **p** of the kingdom of Persia withstood 8269
10:20 now will I return to fight with the **p** of 8269
10:20 gone forth, lo, the **p** of Grecia shall come. 8269
10:21 me in these *things,* but Michael your **p**. 8269
11:18 a **p** for his own behalf shall cause 7101
11:22 be broken; yea also, the **p** of the covenant. 5057
12: 1 the great **p** which standeth for the children 8269
Hos 3: 4 without a **p**, and without a sacrifice, and 8269
Mic 7: 3 the **p** asketh, and the judge *asketh* for a 8269
Mt 9:34 He casteth out the devils through the **p** of *758*
12:24 but by Beelzebub the **p** of the devils. *758*
Mk 3:22 by the **p** of the devils casteth he out devils. *758*
Jn 12:31 now shall the **p** of this world be cast out. *758*
14:30 for the **p** of this world cometh, and *758*
16:11 because the **p** of this world is judged. *758*
Ac 3:15 And killed the **P** of life, whom God hath *747*
5:31 God exalted with his right hand *to be* a **P** *747*
Eph 2: 2 according to the **p** of the power of the air, *758*
Rev 1: 5 the dead, and the **p** of the kings of the earth. *758*

PRINCE'S (3) [PRINCE]

SS 7: 1 are thy feet with shoes, O **p** daughter! 5081
Eze 45:17 it shall be the **p** part *to give* burnt offerings, 5387
48:22 in the midst *of that* which is the **p**, 5387+3807.1

PRINCES (273) [PRINCE]

Ge 12:15 The **p** also of Pharaoh saw her, and 8269
17:20 twelve **p** shall he beget, and I will make 5387
25:16 twelve **p** according to their nations. 5387
Nu 1:16 **p** of the tribes of their fathers, heads of 5387
1:44 and Aaron numbered, and the **p** of Israel, 5387
7: 2 That the **p** of Israel, heads of the house of 5387
7: 2 who *were* the **p** of the tribes, and were over 5387
7: 3 a wagon for two of the **p**, and for *each* one 5387
7:10 the **p** offered *for* dedicating of the altar in 5387
7:10 even the **p** offered their offering before 5387
7:84 when it was anointed, by the **p** of Israel: 5387
10: 4 they blow *but* with one *trumpet,* then the **p**, 5387
16: 2 two hundred and fifty **p** of the assembly, 5387
17: 2 of all their **p** according to the house of their 5387
17: 6 every one of their **p** gave him a rod apiece, 5387
21:18 The **p** digged the well, the nobles of 8269
22: 8 and the **p** of Moab abode with Balaam. 8269
22:13 said unto the **p** of Balak, Get you into your 8269
22:14 the **p** of Moab rose up, and they went unto 8269
22:15 Balak sent yet again **p**, more, and 8269
22:21 his ass, and went with the **p** of Moab. 8269
22:35 So Balaam went with the **p** of Balak. 8269
22:40 to Balaam, and to the **p** that *were* with him. 8269
23: 6 burnt sacrifice, he, and all the **p** of Moab. 8269
23:17 burnt offering, and the **p** of Moab with him. 8269
27: 2 and before the **p** and all the congregation, 5387
31:13 the priest, and all the **p** of the congregation, 5387
32: 2 and unto the **p** of the congregation, saying, 5387

P

Nu 36: 1 and spake before Moses, and before the **p**, 5387
Jos 9:15 the **p** of the congregation sware unto them. 5387
9:18 the **p** of the congregation had sworn unto 5387
9:18 the congregation murmured against the **p**. 5387
9:19 all the **p** said unto all the congregation, 5387
9:21 the **p** said unto them, Let them live; but 5387
9:21 as the **p** had promised them. 5387
13:21 whom Moses smote with the **p** of Midian, 5387
17: 4 the son of Nun, and before the **p**, saying, 5387
22:14 with him ten **p**, of each chief house a prince 5387
22:30 the **p** of the congregation and heads of 5387
22:32 the **p**, returned from the children of 5387
Jdg 5: 3 give ear, O ye **p**; I, *even* I, will sing unto 7336
5:15 the **p** of Issachar *were* with Deborah; 8269
7:25 they took two **p** of the Midianites, Oreb 8269
8: 3 God hath delivered into your hands the **p** of 8269
8: 6 the **p** of Succoth said, *Are* the hands of 8269
8:14 he described unto him the **p** of Succoth, 8269
10:18 *and* **p** of Gilead said one to another, 8269
1Sa 2: 8 to set *them* among **p**, and to make them 5081
18:30 the **p** of the Philistines went forth: and 8269
29: 3 said the **p** of the Philistines, What *do* these 8269
29: 3 Achish said unto the **p** of the Philistines, 8269
29: 4 the **p** of the Philistines were wroth with 8269
29: 4 the **p** of the Philistines said unto him, 8269
29: 9 notwithstanding the **p** of the Philistines 8269
2Sa 10: 3 the **p** of the children of Ammon said unto 8269
19: 6 that thou regardest neither **p** nor servants: 8269
1Ki 4: 2 these *were* the **p** which he had; Azariah 8269
9:22 his **p**, and his captains, and rulers of his 8269
20:14 *Even* by the young men of the **p** of 8269
20:15 he numbered the young men of the **p** of 8269
20:17 the young men of the **p** of the provinces 8269
20:19 So these young men of the **p** of 8269
2Ki 11:14 as the manner *was*, and the **p** and 8269
24:12 and his servants, and his **p**, and his officers: 8269
24:14 all the **p**, and all the mighty *men* of valour, 8269
1Ch 4:38 These mentioned by *their* names *were* **p** in 5387
7:40 *and* mighty *men* of valour, chief of the **p**. 5387
19: 3 the **p** of the children of Ammon said to 8269
22:17 David also commanded all the **p** of Israel to 8269
23: 2 he gathered together all the **p** of Israel, 8269
24: 6 the **p**, and Zadok the priest, and 8269
27:22 These *were* the **p** of the tribes of Israel. 8269
28: 1 David assembled all the **p** of Israel, 8269
28: 1 the **p** of the tribes, and the captains of 8269
28:21 also the **p** and all the people *will be* wholly 8269
29: 6 of the fathers and **p** of the tribes of Israel, 8269
29:24 all the **p**, and the mighty *men*, and all 8269
2Ch 12: 5 *to* the **p** of Judah, that were gathered 8269
12: 6 Whereupon the **p** of Israel and the king 8269
17: 7 the third year of his reign he sent to his **p**, 8269
21: 4 the sword, and *divers* also of the **p** of Israel. 8269
21: 9 Jehoram went forth with his **p**, and all *his* 8269
22: 8 found the **p** of Judah, and the sons of 8269
23:13 and the **p** and the trumpets by the king: 8269
24:10 all the **p** and all the people rejoiced, and 8269
24:17 Now after the death of Jehoiada came the **p** 8269
24:23 destroyed all the **p** of the people from 8269
28:14 the spoil before the **p** and all 8269
28:21 of the **p**, and gave *it* unto the king of 8269
29:30 the **p** commanded the Levites to *sing* praise 8269
30: 2 his **p**, and all the congregation in 8269
30: 6 and his **p** throughout all Israel and Judah, 8269
30:12 the commandment of the king and of the **p**, 8269
30:24 the **p** gave to the congregation a thousand 8269
31: 8 and the **p** came and saw the heaps, 8269
32: 3 He took counsel with his **p** and his mighty 8269
32:31 *of* the ambassadors of the **p** of Babylon, 8269
35: 8 his **p** gave willingly unto the people, to 8269
36:18 and the treasures of the king, and of his **p**; 8269
Ezr 7:28 and before all the king's mighty **p**. 8269
8:20 the **p** had appointed for the service of 8269
9: 1 the **p** came to me, saying, The people of 8269
9: 2 the hand of the **p** and rulers hath been chief 8269
10: 8 according to the counsel of the **p** and 8269
Ne 9:32 on our **p**, and on our priests, and on our 8269
9:34 our **p**, our priests, nor our fathers, kept thy 8269
9:38 write *it*; and our **p**, Levites, *and* priests, 8269
12:31 I brought up the **p** of Judah upon the wall, 8269
12:32 went Hoshaiah, and half of the **p** of Judah, 8269
Est 1: 3 he made a feast unto all his **p** and 8269
1: 3 Media, the nobles and **p** of the provinces, 8269
1:11 to shew the people and the **p** her beauty: 8269
1:14 Memucan, the seven **p** of Persia and Media, 8269
1:16 answered before the king and the **p**, 8269
1:16 *also* to all the **p**, and to all the people that 8269
1:18 Media say this day unto all the king's **p**, 8269
1:21 the saying pleased the king and the **p**; and 8269
2:18 the king made a great feast unto all his **p** 8269
3: 1 set his seat above all the **p** that *were* with 8269
5:11 how he had advanced him above the **p** and 8269
6: 9 the hand of one of the king's most noble **p**, 8269
Job 3:15 Or with **p** that had gold, who filled their 8269
12:19 He leadeth **p** away spoiled, and 3548
12:21 He poureth contempt upon **p**, and 5081
29: 9 The **p** refrained talking, and laid *their* hand 8269
34:18 *art* wicked? *and to* **p**, *Ye are* ungodly? 5081
34:19 *to him* that accepteth not the persons of **p**, 8269
Ps 45:16 whom thou mayest make **p** in all the earth. 8269
47: 9 The **p** of the people are gathered together, 5081
68:27 the **p** of Judah *and* their council, the princes 8269
68:27 the **p** of Zebulun, *and* the princes of 8269
68:27 princes of Zebulun, *and* the **p** of Naphtali. 8269
68:31 **P** shall come out of Egypt; Ethiopia shall 2831
76:12 He shall cut off the spirit of **p**: *he is* terrible 5057
82: 7 die like men, and fall like one of the **p**. 8269
83:11 yea, all their **p** as Zebah, and as Zalmunna: 5257
105:22 To bind his **p** at his pleasure; and teach his 8269
107:40 He poureth contempt upon **p**, and 5081
113: 8 That *he* may set *him* with **p**, *even* with 5081
113: 8 with princes, *even* with the **p** of his people. 5081
118: 9 in the LORD than to put confidence in **p**. 5081
119:23 **P** also did sit *and* speak against me: *but* 8269
119:161 **P** have persecuted me without a cause: but 8269
146: 3 Put not your trust in **p**, *nor* in the son of 5081
148:11 all people; **p**, and all judges of the earth: 8269
Pr 8:15 By me kings reign, and **p** decree justice. 7336
8:16 By me **p** rule, and nobles, *even* all 8269
17:26 just *is* not good, *nor* to strike **p** for equity. 5081
19:10 much less for a servant to have rule over **p**. 8269
28: 2 of a land many *are* the **p** thereof: 8269
31: 4 kings to drink wine; nor for **p** strong drink: 7336
Ecc 10: 7 and **p** walking as servants upon the earth. 8269
10:16 *is* a child, and thy **p** eat in the morning. 8269
10:17 thy **p** eat in due season, for strength, and 8269
Isa 1:23 Thy **p** *are* rebellious, and companions of 8269
3: 4 I will give children *to be* their **p**, and 8269
3:14 ancients of his people, and the **p** thereof: 8269
10: 8 he saith, *Are* not my **p** altogether kings? 8269
19:11 Surely the **p** of Zoan *are* fools, the counsel 8269
19:13 The **p** of Zoan are become fools, 8269
19:13 become fools, the **p** of Noph are deceived; 8269
21: 5 eat, drink: arise, ye **p**, *and* anoint the shield. 8269
23: 8 the crowning *city*, whose merchants *are* **p**, 8269
30: 4 For his **p** were at Zoan, and 8269
31: 9 his **p** shall be afraid of the ensign, saith 8269
32: 1 and **p** shall rule in judgment. 8269
34:12 *be* there, and all her **p** shall be nothing. 8269
40:23 That bringeth the **p** to nothing; he maketh 7336
41:25 he shall come *upon* **p** as *upon* morter, and 5461
43:28 Therefore I have profaned the **p** of 8269
49: 7 shall see and arise, **p** also shall worship, 8269
Jer 1:18 against the **p** thereof, against the priests 8269
2:26 their **p**, and their priests, and their prophets, 8269
4: 9 the king shall perish, and the heart of the **p**; 8269
8: 1 the bones of his **p**, and the bones of 8269
17:25 and **p** sitting upon the throne of David, 8269
17:25 in chariots and on horses, they, and their **p**, 8269
24: 1 the **p** of Judah, with the carpenters and 8269
24: 8 his **p**, and the residue of Jerusalem, 8269
25:18 and the kings thereof, *and* the **p** thereof, 8269
25:19 his servants, and his **p**, and all his people; 8269
26:10 When the **p** of Judah heard these things, 8269
26:11 the prophets unto the **p** and to all 8269
26:12 spake Jeremiah unto all the **p** and to all 8269
26:16 said the **p** and all the people unto the priests 8269
26:21 with all his mighty *men*, and all the **p**, 8269
29: 2 the **p** of Judah and Jerusalem, and 8269
32:32 they, their kings, their **p**, their priests, and 8269
34:10 *Now* when all the **p**, and all the people, 8269
34:19 The **p** of Judah, and the princes of 8269
34:19 the **p** of Jerusalem, the eunuchs, and 8269
34:21 his **p** will I give into the hand of their 8269
35: 4 of God, which *was* by the chamber of the **p**, 8269
36:12 lo, all the **p** sat there, *even* Elishama 8269
36:12 the son of Hananiah, and all the **p**. 8269
36:14 Therefore all the **p** sent Jehudi the son of 8269

Jer 36:19 said the **p** unto Baruch, Go, hide thee, thou 8269
36:21 in the ears of all the **p** which stood beside 8269
37:14 took Jeremiah, and brought him to the **p**. 8269
37:15 Wherefore the **p** were wroth with Jeremiah, 8269
38: 4 Therefore the **p** said unto the king, 8269
38:17 go forth unto the king of Babylon's **p**, 8269
38:18 wilt not go forth to the king of Babylon's **p**, 8269
38:22 *be* brought forth to the king of Babylon's **p**, 8269
38:25 if the **p** hear that I have talked with thee, 8269
38:27 came all the **p** unto Jeremiah, and 8269
39: 3 all the **p** of the king of Babylon came in, 8269
39: 3 with all the residue of the **p** of the king of 8269
39:13 Rab-mag, and all the king of Babylon's **p**; 7227
41: 1 of the seed royal, and the **p** of the king, 7227
44:17 we, and our fathers, our kings, and our **p**, 8269
44:21 and your **p**, and the people of the land, 8269
48: 7 captivity *with* his priests and his **p** together. 8269
49: 3 *and* his priests and his **p** together. 8269
49:38 will destroy from thence the king and the **p**, 8269
50:35 and upon her **p**, and upon her wise *men*. 8269
51:57 I will make drunk her **p**, and her wise *men*, 8269
52:10 he slew also all the **p** of Judah in Riblah. 8269
La 1: 6 her **p** are become like harts *that* find no 8269
2: 2 polluted the kingdom and the **p** thereof. 8269
2: 9 her king and her **p** *are* among the Gentiles: 8269
5:12 **P** are hanged up by their hand: the faces of 8269
Eze 11: 1 the son of Benaiah, **p** of the people. 8269
17:12 the **p** thereof, and led them with him to 8269
19: 1 thou up a lamentation for the **p** of Israel, 5387
21:12 it *shall be* upon all the **p** of Israel: 5387
22: 6 Behold, the **p** of Israel, every one were in 5387
22:27 Her **p** in the midst thereof *are* like wolves 8269
23:15 upon their heads, all of them **p** to look to, 7991
26:16 all the **p** of the sea shall come down from 5387
27:21 Arabia, and all the **p** of Kedar, 5387
32:29 There *is* Edom, her kings, and all her **p**, 5387
32:30 There *be* the **p** of the north, all of them, and 5257
39:18 drink the blood of the **p** of the earth, 5387
45: 8 and my **p** shall no more oppress my people; 5387
45: 9 Let it suffice you, O **p** of Israel: 5387
Da 1: 3 and of the king's seed, and of the **p**; 6579
3: 2 the king sent to gather together the **p**, 324
3: 3 the **p**, the governors and captains, the judges, 324
3:27 the **p**, governors, and captains, and 324
5: 2 and his **p**, his wives, and his concubines, 7261
5: 3 the king, and his **p**, his wives, and 7261
6: 1 over the kingdom an hundred and twenty **p**, 324
6: 2 that the **p** might give accounts unto them, 324
6: 3 was preferred above the presidents and **p**, 324
6: 4 **p** sought to find occasion against Daniel 324
6: 6 **p** assembled *together* to the king, 324
6: 7 the governors, and the **p**, the counsellers and 324
8:25 shall also stand up against the Prince of **p**; 8269
9: 6 our **p**, and our fathers, and to all the people 8269
9: 8 to our **p**, and to our fathers, because 8269
10:13 lo, Michael, one of the chief **p**, came to 8269
11: 5 the south shall be strong, and *one* of his **p**; 8269
11: 8 with their **p**, *and* with their precious vessels 5257
Hos 5:10 The **p** of Judah were like them that remove 8269
7: 3 their wickedness, and the **p** with their lies. 8269
7: 5 *In* the day of our king the **p** have made *him* 8269
7:16 their **p** shall fall by the sword for the rage 8269
8: 4 they have **made p**, and I knew *it* not: 7786
8:10 a little for the burden of the king of **p**. 8269
9:15 love them no more: all their **p** *are* revolters. 8269
13:10 whom thou saidst, Give me a king and **p**? 8269
Am 1:15 he and his **p** together, saith the LORD. 8269
2: 3 will slay all the **p** thereof with him, 8269
Mic 3: 1 of Jacob, and ye **p** of the house of Israel; 7101
3: 9 **p** of the house of Israel, that abhor 7101
Hab 1:10 and the **p** *shall be* a scorn unto them: 7336
Zep 1: 8 that I will punish the **p**, and the king's 8269
3: 3 Her **p** within her *are* roaring lions; 8269
Mt 2: 6 art not the least among the **p** of Juda: 2232
20:25 Ye know that the **p** of the Gentiles exercise *758*
1Co 2: 6 nor of the **p** of this world, that come to *758*
2: 8 Which none of the **p** of this world knew: *758*

PRINCESS (1) [PRINCE]
La 1: 1 *and* **p** among the provinces, *how* is she 8282

PRINCESSES (1) [PRINCE]
1Ki 11: 3 **p**, and three hundred concubines: 8282

PRINCIPAL (17) [PRINCIPALITIES, PRINCIPALITY]
Ex 30:23 Take thou also unto thee **p** spices, of pure 7218
Lev 6: 5 he shall even restore it in the **p**, and 7218
Nu 5: 7 he shall recompense his trespass with the **p** 7218
1Ki 4: 5 Zabud the son of Nathan *was* **p officer**, *and* 3548
2Ki 25:19 in the city, and the **p** scribe of the host, 8269
1Ch 24: 6 one **p** household being taken for Eleazar, and 1
24:31 *even* the **p** fathers over against their 7218
Ne 11:17 *was* the **p** to begin the thanksgiving in 7218
Pr 4: 7 Wisdom *is* the **p thing**; *therefore* 7225
Isa 16: 8 have broken down the **p plants** thereof, 8291
28:25 cast in the **p** wheat and the appointed 7795
Jer 25:34 wallow yourselves *in the ashes*, ye **p** of 117
25:35 way to flee, nor the **p** of the flock to escape. 117
25:36 and a howling of the **p** of the flock, 117
52:25 the **p** scribe of the host, who mustered 8269
Mic 5: 5 him seven shepherds, and eight **p** men. 5257
Ac 25:23 the chief captains, and **p** men of the city, *1851*

PRINCIPALITIES (7) [PRINCIPAL]
Jer 13:18 for your **p** shall come down, *even* 4761
Ro 8:38 nor life, nor angels, nor **p**, nor powers, *746*
Eph 3:10 To the intent that now unto the **p** and *746*
6:12 not against flesh and blood, but against **p**, *746*
Col 1:16 *be* thrones, or dominions, or **p**, or powers: *746*
2:15 *And* having spoiled **p** and powers, he made a *746*
Tit 3: 1 Put them in mind to be subject to **p** and *746*

PRINCIPALITY (2) [PRINCIPAL]
Eph 1:21 Far above all **p**, and power, and might, and *746*
Col 2:10 in him, which is the head of all **p** and power: *746*

PRINCIPLES (2)
Heb 5:12 which *be* the first **p** of the oracles of God; *4747*
6: 1 Therefore leaving the **p** of the doctrine of *746*

PRINT (4) [PRINTED]
Lev 19:28 for the dead, nor **p** any marks upon you: 5414
Job 13:27 thou **settest a p** upon the heels of my feet. 2707
Jn 20:25 Except I shall see in his hands the **p** of *5179*
20:25 and put my finger into the **p** of the nails, *5179*

PRINTED (1) [PRINT]
Job 19:23 now written! O that they were **p** in a book! 2710

PRISCA (1) [PRISCILLA]
2Ti 4:19 Salute **P** and Aquila, and the household of *4251*

PRISCILLA (5) [PRISCA]
Ac 18: 2 lately come from Italy, with his wife **P**; *4252*
18:18 into Syria, and with him **P** and Aquila: *4252*
18:26 whom when Aquila and **P** had heard, *4252*
Ro 16: 3 Greet **P** and Aquila my helpers in Christ *4252*
1Co 16:19 Aquila and **P** salute you much in the Lord, *4252*

PRISED (1) [PRICE]
Zec 11:13 a goodly price that I was **p** at of them. 3365

PRISON (90) [FELLOWPRISONER, FELLOWPRISONERS, IMPRISONED, IMPRISONMENT, IMPRISONMENTS, PRISONER, PRISONERS, PRISONS]
Ge 39:20 and put him into the **p**, 1004+5470+1886.1
39:20 and he was there in the **p**. 1004+5470+1886.1
39:21 sight of the keeper of the **p**. 1004+5470+1886.1
39:22 the keeper of the **p** 1004+5470+1886.1
39:22 prisoners that *were* in the **p**; 1004+5470+1886.1
39:23 The keeper of the **p** looked 1004+5470+1886.1
40: 3 into the **p**, the place where 1004+5470+1886.1
40: 5 which *were* bound in the **p**. 1004+5470+1886.1
42:16 fetch your brother, and ye shall be **kept in p**, 631
42:19 brethren be bound in the house of your **p**: 4929
Jdg 16:21 of brass; and he did grind in the **p** house. 631
16:25 they called for Samson out of the **p** house; 631
1Ki 22:27 Put this *fellow in* the **p**, 1004+3608+1886.1
2Ki 17: 4 shut him up, and bound him *in* **p**. 1004+3608
25:27 of Jehoiachin king of Judah out of **p**; 1004+3608
25:29 changed his **p** garments: and he did eat 3608
2Ch 16:10 with the seer, and put him *in* a **p** house; 4115
18:26 Put this *fellow in* the **p**, 1004+3608+1886.1
Ne 3:25 high house, that *was* by the court of the **p**. 4307
12:39 and they stood still in the **p** gate. 4307
Ps 142: 7 Bring my soul out of **p**, that *I* may praise 4525
Ecc 4:14 For out of **p** he cometh to 631+1004+1886.1
Isa 24:22 shall be shut up in the **p**, and after many 4525

Isa 42: 7 to bring out the prisoners from the **p**, *and* 4525
42: 7 them that sit in darkness out of the **p** house. 3608
42:22 in holes, and they are hid in **p** houses: 3608
53: 8 He was taken from **p** and from judgment: 6115
61: 1 the **opening of the p** to *them that are* 6495
Jer 29:26 that thou shouldest put him in **p**, and in 4115
32: 2 prophet was shut up in the court of the **p**, 4307
32: 8 the **p** according to the word of the LORD, 4307
32:12 all the Jews that sat in the court of the **p**. 4307
33: 1 he was yet shut up in the court of the **p**, 4307
37: 4 they had not put him *into* **p**. 1004+3628+1886.1
37:15 put him *in* **p** *in* the house of 612+1004+1886.1
37:15 for they had made that the **p**. 1004+3608+1886.1
37:18 that ye have put me in **p**? 1004+3608+1886.1
37:21 commit Jeremiah into the court of the **p**, 4307
37:21 Jeremiah remained in the court of the **p**. 4307
38: 6 that *was* in the court of the **p**: 4307
38:13 Jeremiah remained in the court of the **p**. 4307
38:28 So Jeremiah abode in the court of the **p** 4307
39:14 took Jeremiah out of the court of the **p**, and 4307
39:15 while he was shut up in the court of the **p**, 4307
52:11 in **p** till the day of his death. 1004+6486+1886.1
52:31 brought him forth out of **p**; 1004+3628+1886.1
52:33 changed his **p** garments: and he did 3608
Mt 4:12 Jesus had heard that John was **cast into p**, *3860*
5:25 thee to the officer, and thou be cast into **p**. *5438*
11: 2 Now when John had heard in the **p** *1201*
14: 3 and put *him* in **p** for Herodias' sake, *5438*
14:10 And he sent, and beheaded John in the **p**. *5438*
18:30 but went and cast him into **p**, till he should *5438*
25:36 I was in **p**, and ye came unto me. *5438*
25:39 we thee sick, or in **p**, and came unto thee? *5438*
25:43 sick, and in **p**, and ye visited me not. *5438*
25:44 or in **p**, and did not minister unto thee? *5438*
Mk 1:14 Now after that John was **put in p**, Jesus *3860*
6:17 and bound him in **p** for Herodias' sake, *5438*
6:27 and he went and beheaded him in the **p**, *5438*
Lk 3:20 yet this above all, that he shut up John in **p**. *5438*
12:58 the officer, and the officer cast thee into **p**. *5438*
22:33 to go with thee, both into **p**, and to death. *5438*
23:19 in the city, and *for* murder, was cast into **p**.) *5438*
23:25 for sedition and murder was cast into **p**, *5438*
Jn 3:24 For John was not yet cast into **p**. *5438*
Ac 5:18 and put them in the common **p**. *5084*
5:19 of the Lord by night opened the **p** doors, *5438*
5:21 and sent to the **p** to have them brought. *1201*
5:22 and found them not in the **p**, they returned, *5438*
5:23 The **p** truly found we shut with all safety, *1201*
5:25 the men whom ye put in **p** are standing in *5438*
8: 3 and women committed *them* to **p**. *5438*
12: 4 he put *him* in **p**, and delivered *him* to four *5438*
12: 5 Peter therefore was kept in **p**: but *5438*
12: 6 and *the* keepers before the door kept the **p**. *5438*
12: 7 came upon *him*, and a light shined in the **p**: *3612*
12:17 how the Lord had brought him out of the **p**. *5438*
16:23 they cast *them* into **p**, charging the jailor to *5438*
16:24 thrust them into the inner **p**, and made their *5438*
16:26 that the foundations of the **p** were shaken: *1201*
16:27 And the **keeper of the p** awaking out of his *1200*
16:27 and seeing the **p** doors open, he drew out *5438*
16:36 And the **keeper of the p** told this saying to *1200*
16:37 being Romans, and have cast *us* into **p**; *5438*
16:40 And they went out of the **p**, and *5438*
26:10 and many of the saints did I shut up in **p**, *5438*
1Pe 3:19 he went and preached unto the spirits in **p**; *5438*
Rev 2:10 the devil shall cast *some* of you into **p**, *5438*
20: 7 Satan shall be loosed out of his **p**, *5438*

PRISONER (13) [PRISON]

Ps 79:11 Let the sighing of the **p** come before thee, 615
102:20 To hear the groaning of the **p**; to loose those 615
Mt 27:15 was wont to release unto the people a **p**, *1198*
27:16 And they had then a notable **p**, *1198*
Mk 15: 6 at *that* feast he released unto them one **p**, *1198*
Ac 23:18 Paul the **p** called me unto *him*, and *1198*
25:27 it seemeth to me unreasonable to send a **p**, *1198*
28:17 *yet* was I delivered **p** from Jerusalem into *1198*
Eph 3: 1 the **p** of Jesus Christ for you Gentiles, *1198*
4: 1 I therefore, the **p** of the Lord, beseech you *1198*
2Ti 1: 8 the testimony of our Lord, nor of me his **p**: *1198*
Phm 1: 1 a **p** of Jesus Christ, and Timothy *our* *1198*
1: 9 the aged, and now also a **p** of Jesus Christ. *1198*

PRISONERS (20) [PRISON]

Ge 39:20 a place where the king's **p** *were* bound: 615
39:22 hand all the **p** that *were* in the prison; 615
Nu 21: 1 and **took** *some* of them **p**. 7617+7628
Job 3:18 *There* the **p** rest together; they hear not 615
Ps 69:33 heareth the poor, and despiseth not his **p**. 615
146: 7 to the hungry. The LORD looseth the **p**: 631
Isa 10: 4 me they shall bow down under the **p**, 616
14:17 *that* opened not the house of his **p**? 615
20: 4 king of Assyria lead away the Egyptians **p**, 7628
24:22 *as* **p** are gathered in the pit, and shall be shut 616
42: 7 to bring out the **p** from the prison, *and* 616
49: 9 That *thou* mayest say to the **p**, Go forth; 631
La 3:34 To crush under his feet all the **p** of the earth, 615
Zec 9:11 forth thy **p** out of the pit wherein *is* no water. 615
9:12 Turn ye to the strong hold, ye **p** of hope: 615
Ac 16:25 praises unto God: and the **p** heard them. *1198*
16:27 supposing that the **p** had been fled. *1198*
27: 1 and certain other **p** unto *one* named Julius, *1202*
27:42 And the soldiers' counsel was to kill the **p**, *1202*
28:16 the centurion delivered the **p** to the captain *1198*

PRISONS (3) [PRISON]

Lk 21:12 and into **p**, being brought before kings and *5438*
Ac 22: 4 binding and delivering into **p** both men and *5438*
2Co 11:23 in **p** more frequent, in deaths oft. *5438*

PRIVATE (1) [PRIVATELY, PRIVILY, PRIVY]

2Pe 1:20 that no prophecy of the scripture is of *any* **p** *2398*

PRIVATELY (8) [PRIVATE]

Mt 24: 3 the disciples came unto him **p**, *2398+2596*
Mk 6:32 into a desert place by ship **p**. *2398+2596*
9:28 his disciples asked him **p**, Why could *2398+2596*
13: 3 and John and Andrew asked him **p**, *2398+2596*
Lk 9:10 went aside **p** into a desert place *2398+2596*
10:23 him unto *his* disciples, and said **p**, *2398+2596*
Ac 23:19 the hand, and went *with him* aside **p**, *2398+2596*
Gal 2: 2 but **p** to them which were of *2398+2596*

PRIVILY (15) [PRIVATE]

Jdg 9:31 sent messengers unto Abimelech **p**, 8649+871.1
1Sa 24: 4 the skirt of Saul's robe **p**. 3909+871.1+1886.1
Ps 10: 8 his eyes are **p set** against the poor. 6845
11: 2 that *they* may **p** shoot at the upright in 652+1119
31: 4 Pull me out of the net that they have **laid p** 2934
64: 5 they commune of **laying** snares **p**; they say, 2934
101: 5 Whoso **p** slandereth his neighbour, him will 5643
142: 3 I walked have they **p laid** a snare for me. 2934
Pr 1:11 let us **lurk p** for the innocent without 6845
1:18 own blood; they **lurk p** for their own lives. 6845
Mt 1:19 was minded to put her away **p**. *2977*
2: 7 when he had **p** called the wise men, *2977*
Ac 16:37 and now do they thrust us out **p**? *2977*
Gal 2: 4 who **came in p** to spy out our liberty which *3922*
2Pe 2: 1 who **p** shall **bring in** damnable heresies, *3919*

PRIVY (4) [PRIVATE]

Dt 23: 1 in the stones, or hath *his* **p member** cut off, 8212
1Ki 2:44 all the wickedness which thine heart is **p** to, 3045
Eze 21:14 which **entereth into** their **p chambers**. 2314
Ac 5: 2 his wife also being **p** *to it*, and brought a *4894*

PRIZE (2)

1Co 9:24 in a race run all, but one receiveth the **p**? *1017*
Php 3:14 I press toward the mark for the **p** of *1017*

PROCEED (15) [PROCEEDED, PROCEEDETH, PROCEEDING]

Ex 25:35 according to the six branches that **p out** of 3318
Jos 6:10 neither shall *any* word **p** out of your mouth, 3318
2Sa 7:12 which shall **p** out of thy bowels, and I will 3318
Job 40: 5 yea, twice; but I will **p** no **further**. 3254
Isa 29:14 I will **p** to do a marvellous work amongst 3254
51: 4 for a law shall **p** from me, and I will make 3318
Jer 9: 3 for they **p** from evil to evil, and they know 3318
30:19 out of them shall **p** thanksgiving and 3318
30:21 their governor shall **p** from the midst of 3318
Hab 1: 7 and their dignity shall **p** of themselves. 3318
Mt 15:18 But those *things* which **p** out of the mouth *1607*
15:19 For out of the heart **p** evil thoughts, *1831*
Mk 7:21 **p** evil thoughts, adulteries, fornications, *1607*
Eph 4:29 Let no corrupt communication **p out** of *1607*
2Ti 3: 9 But they shall **p** no further: for their folly *4298*

PROCEEDED (9) [PROCEED]
Nu 30:12 whatsoever **p** **out** of her lips concerning her 4161
32:24 do that which hath **p** out of your mouth. 3318
Jdg 11:36 do to me according to that which hath **p** out 3318
Job 36: 1 Elihu also **p**, and said, 3254
Lk 4:22 gracious words which **p** **out** of his mouth. *1607*
Jn 8:42 for I **p** **forth** and came from God; *1831*
Ac 12: 3 the Jews, he **p** **further** to take Peter also. *4369*
Rev 4: 5 And out of the throne **p** lightnings and *1607*
19:21 the horse, which *sword* **p** out of his mouth: *1607*

PROCEEDETH (11) [PROCEED]
Ge 24:50 and said, The thing **p** from the LORD: 3318
Nu 30: 2 he shall do according to all that **p** out of his 3318
Dt 8: 3 by every *word* **that p out** of the mouth of 4161
1Sa 24:13 Wickedness **p** from the wicked: 3318
Ecc 10: 5 the sun, as an error *which* **p** from the ruler: 3318
La 3:38 Out of the mouth of the most High **p** not 3318
Hab 1: 4 the righteous; therefore wrong judgment **p**. 3318
Mt 4: 4 by every word that **p** out of the mouth of *1607*
Jn 15:26 which **p** from the Father, he shall testify of *1607*
Jas 3:10 Out of the same mouth **p** blessing and *1831*
Rev 11: 5 fire **p** **out** of their mouth, and *1607*

PROCEEDING (1) [PROCEED]
Rev 22: 1 **p** **out** of the throne of God and of *1607*

PROCESS (5)
Ge 4: 3 in **p** of time it came to pass, that Cain 7093
38:12 **in p of time** the daughter of 3117+7235+1886.1
Ex 2:23 to pass in **p of time**, 3117+7227+1886.1+1886.1
Jdg 11: 4 it came to pass **in p of time**, that 3117+4480
2Ch 21:19 that **in p of time**, 3117+3117+4480+3807.1

PROCHORUS (1)
Ac 6: 5 and **P**, and Nicanor, and Timon, and *4402*

PROCLAIM (23) [PROCLAIMED, PROCLAIMETH, PROCLAIMING, PROCLAMATION]
Ex 33:19 I will **p** the name of the LORD 7121+871.1
Lev 23: 2 which ye shall **p** *to be* holy convocations, 7121
23: 4 which ye shall **p** in their seasons. 7121
23:21 ye shall **p** on the selfsame day, *that* it may 7121
23:37 which ye shall **p** *to be* holy convocations, 7121
25:10 **p** liberty throughout *all* the land unto all 7121
Dt 20:10 city to fight against it, then **p** peace unto it. 7121
Jdg 7: 3 therefore go to, **p** in the ears of the people, 7121
1Ki 21: 9 **P** a fast, and set Naboth on high among 7121
2Ki 10:20 Jehu said, **P** a solemn assembly for Baal. 6942
Ne 8:15 and **p** in all their cities, 5674+6963
Est 6: 9 the street of the city, and **p** before him, 7121
Pr 20: 6 Most men will **p** every one his own 7121
Isa 61: 1 to **p** liberty to the captives, and the opening 7121
61: 2 To **p** the acceptable year of the LORD, 7121
Jer 3:12 Go and **p** these words toward the north, and 7121
7: 2 **p** there this word, and say, Hear the word 7121
11: 6 **P** all these words in the cities of Judah, and 7121
19: 2 and **p** there the words that I shall tell thee, 7121
34: 8 *were* at Jerusalem, to **p** liberty unto them; 7121
34:17 behold, I **p** a liberty for you, saith 7121
Joel 3: 9 **P** ye this among the Gentiles; Prepare war, 7121
Am 4: 5 and **p** *and* publish the free offerings: 7121

PROCLAIMED (16) [PROCLAIM]
Ex 34: 5 and **p** the name of the LORD. 7121+871.1
34: 6 **p**, The LORD, The LORD God, merciful 7121
36: 6 they **caused it to be p** throughout 5674+6963
1Ki 21:12 They **p** a fast, and set Naboth on high 7121
2Ki 10:20 a solemn assembly for Baal. And they **p** *it*. 7121
23:16 of the LORD which the man of God **p**, 7121
23:16 of God proclaimed, who **p** these words. 7121
23:17 **p** these things that thou hast done against 7121
2Ch 20: 3 and **p** a fast throughout all Judah. 7121
Ezr 8:21 I **p** a fast there, at the river Ahava, that *we* 7121
Est 6:11 the street of the city, and **p** before him, 7121
Isa 62:11 the LORD hath **p** unto the end of 8085
Jer 36: 9 *that* they **p** a fast before the LORD *to* all 7121
Jnh 3: 5 and **p** a fast, and put on sackcloth, 7121
3: 7 he **caused** *it* **to be p** and published through 2199
Lk 12: 3 ear in closets shall be **p** upon the housetops. *2784*

PROCLAIMETH (1) [PROCLAIM]
Pr 12:23 but the heart of fools **p** foolishness. 7121

PROCLAIMING (3) [PROCLAIM]
Jer 34:15 in **p** liberty every man to his neighbour; 7121
34:17 in **p** liberty, every one to his brother, and 7121
Rev 5: 2 And I saw a strong angel **p** with a loud *2784*

PROCLAMATION (9) [PROCLAIM]
Ex 32: 5 Aaron **made p**, and said, To morrow *is* a 7121
1Ki 15:22 king Asa **made** a **p** throughout all Judah; 8085
22:36 there went a **p** throughout the host about 7440
2Ch 24: 9 they made a **p** through Judah and 6963
30: 5 to **make p** throughout all Israel, 5674+6963
36:22 that he **made a p** throughout all his 5674+6963
Ezr 1: 1 that he **made a p** throughout all his 5674+6963
10: 7 they **made p** throughout Judah and 5674+6963
Da 5:29 his neck, and **made a p** concerning him, 3745

PROCORUS See PROCHORUS

PROCURE (2) [PROCURED, PROCURETH]
Jer 26:19 Thus *might* we **p** great evil against our 6213
33: 9 and for all the prosperity that I **p** unto it. 6213

PROCURED (2) [PROCURE]
Jer 2:17 Hast thou not **p** this unto thyself, in that 6213
4:18 thy doings have **p** these *things* unto thee; 6213

PROCURETH (1) [PROCURE]
Pr 11:27 He that diligently seeketh good **p** favour: 1245

PRODUCE (1)
Isa 41:21 **P** your cause, saith the LORD; bring forth 7126

PROFANE (33) [PROFANED, PROFANENESS, PROFANETH, PROFANING]
Lev 18:21 neither shalt thou **p** the name of thy God: 2490
19:12 neither shalt thou **p** the name of thy God: 2490
20: 3 my sanctuary, and to **p** my holy name. 2490
21: 4 a chief man among his people, to **p** himself. 2490
21: 6 their God, and not **p** the name of their God: 2490
21: 7 shall not take a wife *that is* a whore, or **p**; 2491
21: 9 if she **p** herself by playing the whore, she 2490
21:12 nor **p** the sanctuary of his God; 2490
21:14 or a divorced *woman*, or **p**, *or* a harlot, 2491
21:15 Neither shall he **p** his seed among his 2490
21:23 a blemish; that he **p** not my sanctuaries: 2490
22: 2 that they **p** not my holy name *in those* 2490
22: 9 sin for it, and die therefore, if they **p** it: 2490
22:15 they shall not **p** the holy *things* of 2490
22:32 Neither shall ye **p** my holy name; but I will 2490
Ne 13:17 *is* this that ye do, and **p** the sabbath day? 2490
Jer 23:11 For both prophet and priest are **p**; yea, 2610
Eze 21:25 thou, **p** wicked prince of Israel, whose day 2491
22:26 put no difference between the holy and **p**, 2455
23:39 the same day into my sanctuary to **p** it; 2490
24:21 Behold, I *will* **p** my sanctuary, 2490
28:16 I will **cast** thee **as p** out of the mountain of 2490
42:20 between the sanctuary and the **p** *place*. 2455
44:23 *the difference* between the holy and **p**, 2455
48:15 *shall be* a **p** *place* for the city, for dwelling, 2455
Am 2: 7 in unto the *same* maid, to **p** my holy name: 2490
Mt 12: 5 days the priests in the temple **p** the sabbath, *953*
Ac 24: 6 Who also hath gone about to **p** the temple: *953*
1Ti 1: 9 and for sinners, for unholy and **p**, *952*
4: 7 But refuse **p** and old wives' fables, and *952*
6:20 avoiding **p** *and* vain babblings, and *952*
2Ti 2:16 But shun **p** *and* vain babblings: for they will *952*
Heb 12:16 there *be* any fornicator, or **p** *person*, as Esau, *952*

PROFANED (15) [PROFANE]
Lev 19: 8 he hath **p** the hallowed *thing* of 2490
Ps 89:39 thou hast **p** his crown *by casting it* to 2490
Isa 43:28 Therefore I have **p** the princes of 2490
Eze 22: 8 mine holy *things*, and hast **p** my sabbaths. 2490
22:26 have **p** mine holy *things:* they have put no 2490
22:26 from my sabbaths, and I am **p** among them. 2490
23:38 in the same day, and have **p** my sabbaths. 2490
25: 3 Aha, against my sanctuary, when it was **p**; 2490
36:20 whither they went, they **p** my holy name, 2490
36:21 which the house of Israel had **p** among 2490
36:22 which ye have **p** among the heathen, 2490
36:23 which was **p** among the heathen, 2490
36:23 which ye have **p** in the midst of them; 2490
Mal 1:12 ye *have* **p** it, in that ye say, The table of 2490
2:11 for Judah hath **p** the holiness of the LORD 2490

PROFANENESS (1) [PROFANE]
Jer 23:15 for from the prophets of Jerusalem is **p** 2613

PROFANETH (1) [PROFANE]
Lev 21: 9 by playing the whore, she **p** her father: 2490

PROFANING (2) [PROFANE]
Ne 13:18 yet ye bring more wrath upon Israel by **p** 2490
Mal 2:10 by **p** the covenant of our fathers? 2490

PROFESS (3) [PROFESSED, PROFESSING, PROFESSION]
Dt 26: 3 I **p** *this* day unto the LORD thy God, 5046
Mt 7:23 And then will I **p** unto them, I never knew *3670*
Tit 1:16 They **p** that *they* know God; but in works *3670*

PROFESSED (2) [PROFESS]
2Co 9:13 your **p** subjection unto the gospel of Christ, *3671*
1Ti 6:12 hast **p** a good profession before many *3670*

PROFESSING (3) [PROFESS]
Ro 1:22 **P** *themselves* to be wise, they became *5335*
1Ti 2:10 But (which becometh women **p** godliness) *1861*
6:21 Which some **p** have erred concerning *1861*

PROFESSION (4) [PROFESS]
1Ti 6:12 hast professed a good **p** before many *3671*
Heb 3: 1 the Apostle and High Priest of our **p**, *3671*
4:14 Jesus the Son of God, let us hold fast *our* **p**. *3671*
10:23 Let us hold fast the **p** of *our* hope without *3671*

PROFIT (45) [PROFITABLE, PROFITED, PROFITETH, PROFITING, UNPROFITABLE]
Ge 25:32 **what p** shall this birthright do to 4100+3807.1
37:26 What **p** *is it* if we slay our brother, and 1215
1Sa 12:21 vain *things,* which cannot **p** nor deliver; 3276
Est 3: 8 it *is* not for the king's **p** to suffer them. 7737
Job 21:15 what **p** should we have, if we pray unto 3276
30: 2 *might* the strength of their hands **p** me, 3807.1
35: 3 *and,* What **p** shall I have, *if I be cleansed* 3276
35: 8 thy righteousness *may* **p** the son of man. NIH
Ps 30: 9 What **p** *is there* in my blood, when I go 1215
Pr 10: 2 Treasures of wickedness **p** nothing: but 3276
11: 4 Riches **p** not in the day of wrath: but 3276
14:23 In all labour there is **p**: but the talk of 4195
Ecc 1: 3 What **p** hath a man of all his labour which 3504
2:11 of spirit, and *there was* no **p** under the sun. 3504
3: 9 What **p** *hath* he that worketh in *that* 3504
5: 9 Moreover the **p** of the earth *is* for all: 3504
5:16 what **p** hath he that hath laboured for 3504
7:11 and *by it there is* **p** to them that see the sun. 3148
Isa 30: 5 ashamed of a people *that* could not **p** them, 3276
30: 5 nor be a help nor **p**, but a shame, and also a 3276
30: 6 to a people *that* shall not **p** *them.* 3276
44: 9 their delectable *things* shall not **p**; and 3276
47:12 if so be thou shalt be able to **p**, if so be thou 3276
48:17 LORD thy God which teacheth thee to **p**, 3276
57:12 and thy works; for they shall not **p** thee. 3276
Jer 2: 8 and walked after *things that* do not **p**. 3276
2:11 their glory for *that which* doth not **p**. 3276
7: 8 ye trust in lying words, *that* cannot **p**. 3276
12:13 put themselves to pain, *but* shall not **p**: 3276
16:19 vanity, and *things* wherein *there is* no **p**. 3276
23:32 they shall not **p** this people **at all**, 3276+3276
Mal 3:14 what **p** *is it* that we have kept his 1215
Mk 8:36 For what shall it **p** a man, if he shall gain *5623*
Ro 3: 1 or what **p** *is there* of circumcision? *5622*
1Co 7:35 And this I speak for your own **p**; not that I *4851*
10:33 *men* in all *things,* not seeking mine own **p**, *4851*
10:33 but the *p* of many, that they may be saved. NIG
12: 7 the Spirit is given to every man to **p withal**. *4851*
14: 6 speaking with tongues, what shall I **p** you, *5623*
Gal 5: 2 be circumcised, Christ shall **p** you nothing. *5623*
2Ti 2:14 that *they* strive not about words to no **p**, *5539*
Heb 4: 2 but the word preached did not **p** them, *5623*
12:10 but he for *our* **p**, that *we* might be partakers *4851*
Jas 2:14 What *doth it* **p**, my brethren, though a man *3786*
2:16 *are* needful to the body; what *doth it* **p**? *3786*

PROFITABLE (13) [PROFIT]
Job 22: 2 Can a man be **p** unto God, as he that is wise 5532
22: 2 as he that is wise may be **p** unto himself? 5532
Ecc 10:10 to more strength: but wisdom *is* **p** to direct. 3504
Isa 44:10 molten a graven image *that* is **p** for 3276
Jer 13: 7 the girdle was marred, it was **p** for nothing. 6743
Mt 5:29 for it is **p** for thee that one of thy members *4851*
5:30 for it is **p** for thee that one of thy members *4851*
Ac 20:20 *And* how I kept back nothing that was **p** *4851*
1Ti 4: 8 godliness is **p** unto all *things,* having *5624*
2Ti 3:16 and *is* **p** for doctrine, for reproof, *5624*
4:11 with thee: for he is **p** to me for the ministry. *2173*
Tit 3: 8 These *things* are good and **p** unto men. *5624*
Phm 1:11 but now **p** to thee and to me: *2173*

PROFITED (6) [PROFIT]
Job 33:27 *that which was* right, and it **p** me not; 7737
Mt 15: 5 *by* whatsoever thou mightest be **p** by me; *5623*
16:26 For what is a man **p**, if he shall gain *5623*
Mk 7:11 *by* whatsoever thou mightest be **p** by me; *5623*
Gal 1:14 And **p** in the Jews' religion above many *my* *4298*
Heb 13: 9 which have not **p** them that have been *5623*

PROFITETH (6) [PROFIT]
Job 34: 9 It **p** a man nothing that he should delight 5532
Hab 2:18 What **p** the graven image that the maker 3276
Jn 6:63 spirit that quickeneth; the flesh **p** nothing: *5623*
Ro 2:25 For circumcision verily **p**, if thou keep *5623*
1Co 13: 3 and have not charity, it **p** me nothing. *5623*
1Ti 4: 8 For bodily exercise **p** little: *1510+5624*

PROFITING (1) [PROFIT]
1Ti 4:15 to them; that thy **p** may appear to all. *4297*

PROFOUND (1)
Hos 5: 2 the revolters are **p to make** slaughter, 6009

PROGENITORS (1)
Ge 49:26 **p** unto the utmost bound of the everlasting 2029

PROGNOSTICATORS (1)
Isa 47:13 the monthly **p**, stand *up,* and save thee from 3045

PROJECTIONS See TENONS

PROLONG (14) [PROLONGED, PROLONGETH]
Dt 4:26 ye shall not **p** *your* days upon it, but 748
4:40 that thou mayest **p** *thy* days upon the earth, 748
5:33 *that* ye may **p** *your* days in the land which ye 748
11: 9 that ye may **p** *your* days in the land, 748
17:20 to the end that he may **p** *his* days in his 748
22: 7 with thee, and *that* thou mayest **p** *thy* days. 748
30:18 *that* ye shall not **p** *your* days upon the land, 748
32:47 through this thing ye shall **p** *your* days in 748
Job 6:11 what *is* mine end, that I should **p** my life? 748
15:29 neither shall he **p** the perfection thereof 5186
Ps 61: 6 Thou wilt **p** the king's **life**: 3117+3117+5921
Pr 28:16 he that hateth covetousness shall **p** *his* days. 748
Ecc 8:13 neither shall he **p** *his* days, *which are* as a 748
Isa 53:10 he shall **p** *his* days, and the pleasure of 748

PROLONGED (9) [PROLONG]
Dt 5:16 that thy days may be **p**, and that it may go 748
6: 2 days of thy life; and that thy days may be **p**. 748
Pr 28: 2 *and* knowledge the state *thereof* shall be **p**. 748
Ecc 8:12 do evil an hundred *times,* and his *days* be **p**, 748
Isa 13:22 *is* near to come, and her days shall not be **p**. 4900
Eze 12:22 The days are **p**, and every vision faileth? 748
12:25 shall come to pass; it shall be no more **p**: 4900
12:28 There shall none of my words be **p** any 4900
Da 7:12 yet their lives were **p** for a season and time. 754

PROLONGETH (2) [PROLONG]
Pr 10:27 The fear of the LORD **p** days: but 3254
Ecc 7:15 there is a wicked *man* that **p** *his life* in his 748

PROMISCUOUS See WHORE; WHORE'S; WHORES

PROMISE (53) [PROMISED, PROMISEDST, PROMISES, PROMISING]
Nu 14:34 and ye shall know my **breach of p**. 8569
1Ki 8:56 hath not failed one word of all his good **p**, 1697
2Ch 1: 9 let thy **p** unto David my father be 1697
Ne 5:12 that *they* should do according to this **p**. 1697
5:13 from his labour, that performeth not this **p**, 1697
5:13 And the people did according to this **p**. 1697
Ps 77: 8 gone for evermore? doth *his* **p** fail for evermore? 562
105:42 For he remembered his holy **p**, 1697
Lk 24:49 I send the **p** of my Father upon you: *1860*
Ac 1: 4 but wait for the **p** of the Father, which, *1860*
2:33 having received of the Father the **p** of *1860*
2:39 For the **p** is unto you, and to your children, *1860*

Ac 7:17 But when the time of the **p** drew nigh, *1860*
13:23 to *his* **p** raised unto Israel a Saviour, *1860*
13:32 how that the **p** which was made unto *1860*
23:21 are they ready, looking for a **p** from thee. *1860*
26: 6 am judged for the hope of the **p** made of *1860*
26: 7 Unto which *p* our twelve tribes, NIG
Ro 4:13 For the **p**, that he should be the heir of *1860*
4:14 made void, and the **p** made of none effect: *1860*
4:16 to the end the **p** might be sure to all *1860*
4:20 He staggered not at the **p** of God through *1860*
9: 8 the children of the **p** are counted for *1860*
9: 9 For this *is* the word of **p**, At this time will I *1860*
Gal 3:14 that we might receive the **p** of the Spirit *1860*
3:17 that *it* should make the **p** of none effect. *1860*
3:18 inheritance *be* of the law, *it is* no more of **p**: *1860*
3:18 but God gave *it* to Abraham by **p**. *1860*
3:19 should come to whom the **p** was **made**; *1861*
3:22 that the **p** by faith of Jesus Christ might be *1860*
3:29 and heirs according to the **p**. *1860*
4:23 but he of the freewoman *was* by **p**. *1860*
4:28 as Isaac was, are the children of **p**. *1860*
Eph 1:13 ye were sealed with *that* holy Spirit of **p**, *1860*
2:12 and strangers from the covenants of **p**, *1860*
3: 6 partakers of his **p** in Christ by the gospel: *1860*
6: 2 (which is the first commandment with **p**;) *1860*
1Ti 4: 8 all *things,* having **p** of the life that now is, *1860*
2Ti 1: 1 according to the **p** of life which is in Christ *1860*
Heb 4: 1 a **p** being left *us* of entering into his rest, *1860*
6:13 For when God **made p** to Abraham, *1861*
6:15 he had patiently endured, he obtained the **p**. *1860*
6:17 heirs of **p** the immutability of his counsel, *1860*
9:15 they which are called might receive the **p** *1860*
10:36 the will of God, ye might receive the **p**. *1860*
11: 9 By faith he sojourned in the land of **p**, as *in* *1860*
11: 9 Jacob, the heirs with *him* of the same **p**: *1860*
11:39 report through faith, received not the **p**: *1860*
2Pe 2:19 While they **p** them liberty, they themselves *1861*
3: 4 And saying, Where is the **p** of his coming? *1860*
3: 9 The Lord is not slack concerning *his* **p**, *1860*
3:13 Nevertheless we, according to his **p**, *1862*
1Jn 2:25 And this is the **p** that he hath promised us, *1860*

PROMISED (48) [PROMISE]
Ex 12:25 according as he hath **p**, that ye shall keep 1696
Nu 14:40 up unto the place which the LORD hath **p**: 559
Dt 1:11 as ye *are,* and bless you, as he hath **p** you!) 1696
6: 3 as the LORD God of thy fathers hath **p** 1696
9:28 bring them into the land which he **p** them, 1696
10: 9 according as the LORD thy God **p** him. 1696
12:20 as he hath **p** thee, and thou shalt say, I will 1696
15: 6 thy God blesseth thee, as he **p** thee: 1696
19: 8 give thee all the land which he **p** to give 1696
23:23 thy God, which thou hast **p** with thy mouth. 1696
26:18 as he hath **p** thee, and that *thou* shouldest 1696
27: 3 as the LORD God of thy fathers hath **p** 1696
Jos 9:21 as the princes had **p** them. 1696
22: 4 given rest unto your brethren, as he **p** them: 1696
23: 5 as the LORD your God hath **p** unto you. 1696
23:10 *it is* that fighteth for you, as he hath **p** you. 1696
23:15 which the LORD your God **p** you; 1696
2Sa 7:28 thou hast **p** this goodness unto thy servant: 1696
1Ki 2:24 who hath made me a house, as he **p**, 1696
5:12 gave Solomon wisdom, as he **p** him: 1696
8:20 as the LORD **p**, and have built a house for 1696
8:56 his people Israel, according to all that he **p**: 1696
8:56 which he **p** by the hand of Moses his 1696
9: 5 as I **p** to David thy father, saying, 1696
2Ki 8:19 as he **p** him to give to him alway a light, *and* 559
1Ch 17:26 and hast **p** this goodness unto thy servant: 1696
2Ch 6:10 as the LORD **p**, and have built the house 1696
6:15 my father *that* which thou hast **p** him; 1696
6:16 my father *that* which thou hast **p** him, 1696
21: 7 as he **p** to give a light to him and to his sons 559
Ne 9:23 *concerning* which thou hadst **p** to their 559
Est 4: 7 of the sum of the money that Haman had **p** 559
Jer 32:42 upon them all the good that I have **p** them. 1696
33:14 which I have **p** unto the house of Israel 1696
Mt 14: 7 Whereupon he **p** with an oath to give her *3670*
Mk 14:11 they were glad, and **p** to give him money. *1861*
Lk 1:72 To perform the mercy *p* to our fathers, and NIG
22: 6 And he **p**, and sought opportunity to betray *1843*
Ac 7: 5 yet he **p** that *he* would give it to him for a *1861*
Ro 1: 2 (Which he had **p afore** by his prophets in *4279*
4:21 what he had **p**, he was able also to perform. *1861*
Tit 1: 2 that cannot lie, **p** before the world began; *1861*
Heb 10:23 without wavering; (for he *is* faithful that **p**;) *1861*
11:11 she judged him faithful who had **p**. *1861*
12:26 but now he hath **p**, saying, Yet once *more* I *1861*
Jas 1:12 which the Lord hath **p** to them that love *1861*
2: 5 heirs of the kingdom which he hath **p** to *1861*
1Jn 2:25 And this is the promise that he hath **p** us, *1861*

PROMISEDST (3) [PROMISE]
1Ki 8:24 servant David my father that thou **p** him: 1696
8:25 servant David my father that thou **p** him, 1696
Ne 9:15 **p** them that *they* should go in to possess 559

PROMISES (13) [PROMISE]
Ro 9: 4 the law, and the service *of God,* and the **p**; *1860*
15: 8 to confirm the **p** made unto the fathers: *1860*
2Co 1:20 For all the **p** of God in him *are* yea, and *1860*
7: 1 Having therefore these **p**, dearly beloved, *1860*
Gal 3:16 to Abraham and his seed were the **p** made. *1860*
3:21 *Is* the law then against the **p** of God? *1860*
Heb 6:12 through faith and patience inherit the **p**. *1860*
7: 6 and blessed him that had the **p**. *1860*
8: 6 which was established upon better **p**. *1860*
11:13 not having received the **p**, but having seen *1860*
11:17 he that had received the **p** offered up *his* *1860*
11:33 wrought righteousness, obtained **p**, *1860*
2Pe 1: 4 unto us exceeding great and precious **p**: *1862*

PROMISING (1) [PROMISE]
Eze 13:22 return from his wicked way, by **p** him **life**: 2421

PROMOTE (5) [PROMOTED, PROMOTION]
Nu 22:17 I will **p** thee **unto** very great **honour**, 3513+3513
22:37 am I not able indeed to **p** thee **to honour**? 3513
24:11 to **p** thee **unto great honour**; 3513+3513
Est 3: 1 After these things did king Ahasuerus **p** 1431
Pr 4: 8 Exalt her, and she shall **p** thee: she shall 7311

PROMOTED (5) [PROMOTE]
Jdg 9: 9 and man, and go to be **p** over the trees? 5128
9:11 good fruit, and go to be **p** over the trees? 5128
9:13 and man, and go to be **p** over the trees? 5128
Est 5:11 all *the things* where*in* the king had **p** him, 1431
Da 3:30 the king **p** Shadrach, Meshach, and 6744

PROMOTION (2) [PROMOTE]
Ps 75: 6 For **p** *cometh* neither from the east, 7311
Pr 3:35 but shame shall be the **p** of fools. 7311

PRONOUNCE (23) [PRONOUNCED, PRONOUNCING]
Lev 5: 4 whatsoever *it be* that a man shall **p** with an 981
13: 3 shall look on him, and **p** him **unclean**. 2930
13: 6 not in the skin, the priest shall **p** him **clean**: 2891
13: 8 then the priest shall **p** him **unclean**: 2930
13:11 the priest shall **p** him **unclean**, *and* 2930
13:13 he shall **p** *him* **clean** *that hath* the plague: 2891
13:15 see the raw flesh, and **p** him to be **unclean**: 2930
13:17 the priest shall **p** *him* **clean** *that hath* 2891
13:20 the priest shall **p** him **unclean**: 2930
13:22 then the priest shall **p** him **unclean**: 2930
13:23 and the priest shall **p** him **clean**. 2891
13:25 wherefore the priest shall **p** him **unclean**: it 2930
13:27 then the priest shall **p** him **unclean**: 2930
13:28 and the priest shall **p** him **clean**: 2891
13:30 then the priest shall **p** him **unclean**: 2930
13:34 the skin; then the priest shall **p** him **clean**: 2891
13:37 *is* clean: and the priest shall **p** him **clean**. 2891
13:44 priest shall **p** him **utterly unclean**, 2930+2930
13:59 to **p** it **clean**, or to pronounce it unclean. 2891
13:59 to pronounce it clean, or to **p** it **unclean**. 2930
14: 7 shall **p** him **clean**, and shall let the living 2891
14:48 the priest shall **p** the house **clean**, because 2891
Jdg 12: 6 for he could not frame to **p** *it* right. 1696

PRONOUNCED (14) [PRONOUNCE]
Ne 6:12 but *that* he **p** *this* prophecy against me: 1696
Jer 11:17 that planted thee, hath **p** evil against thee, 1696
16:10 Wherefore hath the LORD **p** all this great 1696
18: 8 If that nation, against whom I have **p**, turn 1696
19:15 upon all her towns all the evil that I have **p** 1696
25:13 land all my words which I have **p** against it, 1696
26:13 him of the evil that he hath **p** against you. 1696
26:19 of the evil which he had **p** against them? 1696
34: 5 for I have **p** the word, saith the LORD. 1696
35:17 all the evil that I have **p** against them: 1696

Jer 36: 7 the fury that the LORD hath **p** against this 1696
36:18 He **p** all these words unto me with his 7121
36:31 all the evil that I have **p** against them; 1696
40: 2 The LORD thy God hath **p** this evil upon 1696

PRONOUNCING (1) [PRONOUNCE]
Lev 5: 4 **p** with *his* lips to do evil, or to do good, 981

PROOF (5) [PROVE]
2Co 2: 9 did I write, that I might know the **p** of you, *1382*
8:24 the **p** of your love, and of our boasting on *1732*
13: 3 Since ye seek a **p** of Christ speaking in me, *1382*
Php 2:22 But ye know the **p** of him, that, as a son *1382*
2Ti 4: 5 an evangelist, **make full p** of thy ministry. *4135*

PROOFS (1) [PROVE]
Ac 1: 3 alive after his passion by many **infallible p**, *5039*

PROPER (4)
1Ch 29: 3 I have of mine own **p good**, *of* gold and 5459
Ac 1:19 insomuch as that field is called in their **p** *2398*
1Co 7: 7 But every man hath **his p** gift of God, *2398*
Heb 11:23 because they saw *he was* a **p** child; *791*

PROPERTY See HABITATION

PROPHECIES (2) [PROPHESY]
1Co 13: 8 but whether *there be* **p**, they shall fail; *4394*
1Ti 1:18 according to the **p** which went before on *4394*

PROPHECY (21) [PROPHESY]
2Ch 9:29 in the **p** of Ahijah the Shilonite, and in 5016
15: 8 the **p** *of* Oded the prophet, he took courage, 5016
Ne 6:12 but *that* he pronounced *this* **p** against me: 5016
Pr 30: 1 words of Agur the son of Jakeh, *even* the **p**: 4853
31: 1 the **p** that his mother taught him. 4853
Da 9:24 to seal up the vision and **p**, and to anoint 5030
Mt 13:14 And in them is fulfilled the **p** of Esaias, *4394*
Ro 12: 6 whether **p**, *let us prophesy* according to *4394*
1Co 12:10 to another **p**; to another discerning of *4394*
13: 2 And though I have *the gift of* **p**, and *4394*
1Ti 4:14 that is in thee, which was given thee by **p**, *4394*
2Pe 1:19 We have also a more sure word **of p**; *4397*
1:20 that no **p** of the scripture is of *any* private *4394*
1:21 For the **p** came not in old time by the will *4394*
Rev 1: 3 and they that hear the words of *this* **p**, and *4394*
11: 6 that it rain not in the days of their **p**: *4394*
19:10 for the testimony of Jesus is the spirit of **p**. *4394*
22: 7 keepeth the sayings of the **p** of this book. *4394*
22:10 Seal not the sayings of the **p** of this book: *4394*
22:18 that heareth the words of the **p** of this book, *4394*
22:19 away from the words of the book of this **p**, *4394*

PROPHESIED (50) [PROPHESY]
Nu 11:25 rested upon them, they **p**, and did not cease. 5012
11:26 unto the tabernacle: and they **p** in the camp. 5012
1Sa 10:10 God came upon him, and he **p** among them. 5012
10:11 he **p** among the prophets, then the people 5012
18:10 and he **p** in the midst of the house: 5012
19:20 the messengers of Saul, and they also **p**. 5012
19:21 sent other messengers, and they **p** likewise. 5012
19:21 again the third time, and they **p** also. 5012
19:23 he went on, and **p**, until he came to Naioth 5012
19:24 **p** before Samuel in like manner, and 5012
1Ki 18:29 they **p** until *the time* of the offering of 5012
22:10 and all the prophets **p** before them. 5012
22:12 all the prophets **p** so, saying, Go up *to* 5012
1Ch 25: 2 which **p** according to the order of the king. 5012
25: 3 who **p** with a harp, to give thanks and 5012
2Ch 18: 7 for he never **p** good unto me, but 5012
18: 9 and all the prophets **p** before them. 5012
18:11 all the prophets **p** so, saying, Go up *to* 5012
20:37 Eliezer the son of Dodavah of Mareshah **p** 5012
Ezr 5: 1 **p** unto the Jews that *were* in Judah and 5013
Jer 2: 8 the prophets **p** by Baal, and walked after 5012
20: 1 heard *that* Jeremiah **p** these things. 5012
20: 6 all thy friends, to whom thou hast **p** lies. 5012
23:13 they **p** in Baal, and caused my people Israel 5012
23:21 I have not spoken to them, yet they **p**. 5012
25:13 which Jeremiah hath **p** against all 5012
26: 9 Why hast thou **p** in the name of 5012
26:11 for he hath **p** against this city, as ye have 5012
26:18 Micah the Morasthite **p** in the days of 5012
26:20 there was also a man that **p** in the name of 5012
26:20 who **p** against this city and against this land 5012
28: 6 perform thy words which thou hast **p**, 5012
28: 8 before thee of old **p** both against many 5012
29:31 Because that Shemaiah hath **p** unto you, 5012
37:19 Where *are* now your prophets which **p** unto 5012
Eze 11:13 it came to pass, when I **p**, that Pelatiah 5012
37: 7 So I **p** as I was commanded: and as I 5012
37: 7 as I **p**, there was a noise, and behold a 5012
37:10 So I **p** as he commanded me, and the breath 5012
38:17 which **p** in those days *many* years, that *I* 5012
Zec 13: 4 every one of his vision, when he hath **p**; 5012
Mt 7:22 Lord, Lord, have we not **p** in thy name? *4395*
11:13 all the prophets and the law **p** until John. *4395*
Mk 7: 6 Well hath Esaias **p** of you hypocrites, as it *4395*
Lk 1:67 filled with the Holy Ghost, and **p**, saying, *4395*
Jn 11:51 he **p** that Jesus should die for *that* nation; *4395*
Ac 19: 6 and they spake with tongues, and **p**. *4395*
1Co 14: 5 all spake with tongues, but rather that ye **p**: *4395*
1Pe 1:10 who **p** of the grace *that should come* unto *4395*
Jude 1:14 from Adam, **p** of these, saying, Behold, *4395*

PROPHESIETH (7) [PROPHESY]
Jer 28: 9 The prophet which **p** of peace, when 5012
Eze 12:27 and he **p** of the times *that are* far off. 5012
Zec 13: 3 him shall thrust him through when he **p**. 5012
1Co 11: 5 **p** with *her* head uncovered dishonoureth *4395*
14: 3 But he that **p** speaketh unto men *to* *4395*
14: 4 but he that **p** edifieth *the* church. *4395*
14: 5 for greater *is* he that **p** than he that speaketh *4395*

PROPHESY (90) [PROPHECIES, PROPHECY, PROPHESIED, PROPHESIETH, PROPHESYING, PROPHESYINGS, PROPHET, PROPHET'S, PROPHETESS, PROPHETS]
Nu 11:27 said, Eldad and Medad do **p** in the camp. 5012
1Sa 10: 5 and a harp, before them; and they shall **p**: 5012
10: 6 thou shalt **p** with them, and shalt be turned 5012
1Ki 22: 8 for he doth not **p** good concerning me, but 5012
22:18 Did I not tell thee that he would **p** no good 5012
1Ch 25: 1 and of Jeduthun, who should **p** with harps, 5012
2Ch 18:17 Did I not tell thee *that* he would not **p** good 5012
Isa 30:10 **P** not unto us right *things*, speak unto us 2372
30:10 speak unto us smooth *things*, **p** deceits: 2372
Jer 5:31 The prophets **p** falsely, and the priests bear 5012
11:21 **P** not in the name of the LORD, 5012
14:14 unto me, The prophets **p** lies in my name: 5012
14:14 they **p** unto you a false vision and 5012
14:15 concerning the prophets that **p** in my name, 5012
14:16 the people to whom they **p** shall be cast out 5012
19:14 whither the LORD had sent him to **p**; 5012
23:16 the words of the prophets that **p** unto you: 5012
23:25 that **p** lies in my name, saying, I have 5012
23:26 be in the heart of the prophets that **p** lies? 5012
23:32 I *am* against them that **p** false dreams, 5012
25:30 Therefore **p** thou against them all these 5012
26:12 The LORD sent me to **p** against this house 5012
27:10 For they **p** a lie unto you, to remove you far 5012
27:14 king of Babylon: for they **p** a lie unto you. 5012
27:15 the LORD, yet they **p** a lie in my name; 5012
27:15 ye, and the prophets that **p** unto you. 5012
27:16 the words of your prophets that **p** unto you, 5012
27:16 from Babylon: for they **p** a lie unto you. 5012
29: 9 For they **p** falsely unto you in my name: 5012
29:21 which **p** a lie unto you in my name; 5012
32: 3 saying, Wherefore dost thou **p**, and say, 5012
Eze 4: 7 *be* uncovered, and thou shalt **p** against it. 5012
6: 2 the mountains of Israel, and **p** against them, 5012
11: 4 Therefore **p** against them, prophesy, O son 5012
11: 4 prophesy against them, **p**, O son of man. 5012
13: 2 **p** against the prophets of Israel that 5012
13: 2 against the prophets of Israel that **p**, 5012
13: 2 say thou unto them that **p** out of their own 5030
13:16 *To wit,* the prophets of Israel which **p** 5012
13:17 thy people, which **p** out of their own heart; 5012
13:17 of their own heart; and **p** thou against them, 5012
20:46 and **p** against the forest of the south field; 5012
21: 2 and **p** against the land of Israel, 5012
21: 9 Son of man, **p**, and say, Thus saith 5012
21:14 **p**, and smite *thine* hands together, and 5012
21:28 thou, son of man, **p** and say, Thus saith 5012
25: 2 against the Ammonites, and **p** against them; 5012
28:21 set thy face against Zidon, and **p** against it, 5012
29: 2 and **p** against him, and against all Egypt: 5012
30: 2 Son of man, **p** and say, Thus saith the Lord 5012
34: 2 **p** against the shepherds of Israel, prophesy, 5012
34: 2 shepherds of Israel, **p**, and say unto them, 5012

Eze 35: 2 face against mount Seir, and **p** against it, 5012
36: 1 **p** unto the mountains of Israel, and say, 5012
36: 3 Therefore **p** and say, Thus saith the Lord 5012
36: 6 **P** therefore concerning the land of Israel, 5012
37: 4 **P** upon these bones, and say unto them, 5012
37: 9 **P** unto the wind, prophesy, son of man, and 5012
37: 9 **p**, son of man, and say to the wind, 5012
37:12 Therefore **p** and say unto them, Thus saith 5012
38: 2 of Meshech and Tubal, and **p** against him, 5012
38:14 Therefore, son of man, **p** and say unto Gog, 5012
39: 1 thou son of man, **p** against Gog, and say, 5012
Joel 2:28 your sons and your daughters shall **p**, 5012
Am 2:12 commanded the prophets, saying, **P** not. 5012
3: 8 Lord GOD hath spoken, who can but **p**? 5012
7:12 of Judah, and there eat bread, and **p** there: 5012
7:13 **p** not again any more *at* Beth-el: for it *is* 5012
7:15 said unto me, Go, **p** unto my people Israel. 5012
7:16 **P** not against Israel, and drop not *thy word* 5012
Mic 2: 6 **P** ye not, *say they to them that* prophesy: 5197
2: 6 Prophesy ye not, *say they to them that* **p**: 5197
2: 6 they shall not **p** to them, *that* they shall not 5197
2:11 *saying,* I will **p** unto thee of wine and 5197
Zec 13: 3 *that* when any shall yet **p**, then his father 5012
Mt 15: 7 well did Esaias **p** of you, saying, *4395*
26:68 Saying, **P** unto us, *thou* Christ, Who is he *4395*
Mk 14:65 and to buffet him, and to say unto him, **P**: *4395*
Lk 22:64 and asked him, saying, **P**, who is it that *4395*
Ac 2:17 and your sons and your daughters shall **p**, *4395*
2:18 in those days of my Spirit; and they shall **p**: *4395*
21: 9 had four daughters, virgins, which did **p**. *4395*
Ro 12: 6 *let us* **p** according to the proportion of faith; NIG
1Co 13: 9 For we know in part, and we **p** in part. *4395*
14: 1 spiritual *gifts,* but rather that ye may **p**. *4395*
14:24 But if all **p**, and there come in one that *4395*
14:31 For ye may all **p** one by one, that all may *4395*
14:39 covet to **p**, and forbid not to speak with *4395*
Rev 10:11 Thou must **p** again before many peoples, *4395*
11: 3 they shall **p** a thousand two hundred *and* *4395*

PROPHESYING (6) [PROPHESY]

1Sa 10:13 when he had made an end of **p**, he came *to* 5012
19:20 they saw the company of the prophets **p**, 5012
Ezr 6:14 they prospered through the **p** of Haggai 5017
1Co 11: 4 Every man praying or **p**, having *his* head *4395*
14: 6 or by knowledge, or by **p**, or by doctrine? *4394*
14:22 but **p** *serveth* not for them that believe not, *4394*

PROPHESYINGS (1) [PROPHESY]

1Th 5:20 Despise not **p**. *4394*

PROPHET (242) [PROPHESY]

Ge 20: 7 for he *is* a **p**, and he shall pray for thee, and 5030
Ex 7: 1 and Aaron thy brother shall be thy **p**. 5030
Nu 12: 6 If there be a **p** among you, *I* the LORD 5030
Dt 13: 1 If there arise among you a **p**, or a dreamer 5030
13: 3 shalt not hearken unto the words of that **p**, 5030
13: 5 that **p**, or that dreamer of dreams, shall be 5030
18:15 up unto thee a **P** from the midst of thee, 5030
18:18 I will raise them up a **P** from among their 5030
18:20 the **p**, which shall presume to speak a word 5030
18:20 name of other gods, even that **p** shall die. 5030
18:22 When a **p** speaketh in the name of 5030
18:22 the **p** hath spoken it presumptuously: 5030
34:10 there arose not a **p** since in Israel like unto 5030
Jdg 6: 8 That the LORD sent a **p** unto the children 5030
1Sa 3:20 *was* established to be a **p** of the LORD. 5030
9: 9 for *he that is* now *called* a **P** was beforetime 5030
22: 5 the **p** Gad said unto David, Abide not in 5030
2Sa 7: 2 That the king said unto Nathan the **p**, 5030
12:25 he sent by the hand of Nathan the **p**; and 5030
24:11 the word of the LORD came unto the **p** 5030
1Ki 1: 8 Nathan the **p**, and Shimei, and Rei, and 5030
1:10 Nathan the **p**, and Benaiah, and the mighty 5030
1:22 with the king, Nathan the **p** also came in. 5030
1:23 told the king, saying, Behold Nathan the **p**. 5030
1:32 Nathan the **p**, and Benaiah the son of 5030
1:34 Nathan the **p** anoint him there king over 5030
1:38 Nathan the **p**, and Benaiah the son of 5030
1:44 Nathan the **p**, and Benaiah the son of 5030
1:45 Nathan the **p** have anointed him king in 5030
11:29 that the **p** Ahijah the Shilonite found him in 5030
13:11 Now there dwelt an old **p** in Beth-el; and 5030
13:18 I *am* a **p** also as thou *art;* and an angel 5030
13:20 came unto the **p** that brought him back: 5030
13:23 *to wit,* for the **p** whom he had brought 5030
13:25 and told *it* in the city where the old **p** dwelt. 5030
13:26 when the **p** that brought him back from 5030
13:29 the **p** took up the carcase of the man of 5030
13:29 the old **p** came to the city, to mourn and 5030
14: 2 behold, there *is* Ahijah the **p**, which told 5030
14:18 by the hand of his servant Ahijah the **p**. 5030
16: 7 also by the hand of the **p** Jehu the son of 5030
16:12 he spake against Baasha by Jehu the **p**, 5030
18:22 I, *even* I only, remain a **p** of the LORD; 5030
18:36 that Elijah the **p** came near, and said, 5030
19:16 shalt thou anoint to be **p** in thy room. 5030
20:13 there came a **p** unto Ahab king of Israel, 5030
20:22 the **p** came to the king of Israel, and 5030
20:38 So the **p** departed, and waited for the king 5030
22: 7 *Is there* not here a **p** of the LORD besides, 5030
2Ki 3:11 *Is there* not here a **p** of the LORD, 5030
5: 3 Would God my lord *were* with the **p** that *is* 5030
5: 8 and he shall know that there is a **p** in Israel. 5030
5:13 *if* the **p** had bid thee *do some* great thing, 5030
6:12 Elisha, the **p** that *is* in Israel, telleth 5030
9: 1 Elisha the **p** called one of the children of 5030
9: 4 the young man, *even* the young man the **p**, 5030
14:25 the son of Amittai, the **p**, which *was* of 5030
19: 2 to Esai the **p** the son of Amoz. 5030
20: 1 the **p** Isaiah the son of Amoz came to him, 5030
20:11 Isaiah the **p** cried unto the LORD: and 5030
20:14 came Isaiah the **p** unto king Hezekiah, 5030
23:18 with the bones of the **p** that came out of 5030
1Ch 17: 1 that David said to Nathan the **p**, Lo, 5030
29:29 in the book of Nathan the **p**, and in 5030
2Ch 9:29 not written in the book of Nathan the **p**, 5030
12: 5 came Shemaiah the **p** to Rehoboam, and 5030
12:15 not written in the book of Shemaiah the **p**, 5030
13:22 *are* written in the story of the **p** Iddo. 5030
15: 8 the prophecy *of* Oded the **p**, he took 5030
18: 6 *Is there* not here a **p** of the LORD besides, 5030
21:12 came a writing to him from Elijah the **p**, 5030
25:15 he sent unto him a **p**, which said unto him, 5030
25:16 the **p** forbare, and said, I know that God 5030
26:22 first and last, did Isaiah the **p**, the son of 5030
28: 9 a **p** of the LORD was there, whose name 5030
29:25 of Gad the king's seer, and Nathan the **p**: 5030
32:20 the **p** Isaiah the son of Amoz, prayed and 5030
32:32 *are* written in the vision of Isaiah the **p**, 5030
35:18 in Israel from the days of Samuel the **p**; 5030
36:12 humbled not himself before Jeremiah the **p** 5030
Ezr 5: 1 Haggai the **p**, and Zechariah the son of 5029
6:14 through the prophesying of Haggai the **p** 5029
Ps 51: T when Nathan the **p** came unto him, 5030
74: 9 *there is* no more any **p**: neither *is there* 5030
Isa 3: 2 and the **p**, and the prudent, and the ancient, 5030
9:15 and the **p** that teacheth lies, he *is* the tail. 5030
28: 7 and the **p** have erred through strong drink, 5030
37: 2 unto Isaiah the **p** the son of Amoz. 5030
38: 1 Isaiah the **p** the son of Amoz came unto 5030
39: 3 came Isaiah the **p** unto king Hezekiah, 5030
Jer 1: 5 *and* I ordained thee a **p** unto the nations. 5030
6:13 from the **p** even unto the priest every one 5030
8:10 from the **p** even unto the priest every one 5030
14:18 both the **p** and the priest go about into a 5030
18:18 from the wise, nor the word from the **p**. 5030
20: 2 Pashur smote Jeremiah the **p**, and put him 5030
23:11 For both **p** and priest are profane; yea, 5030
23:28 The **p** that hath a dream, let him tell a 5030
23:33 or the **p**, or a priest, shall ask thee, saying, 5030
23:34 *as for* the **p**, and the priest, and the people, 5030
23:37 Thus shalt thou say to the **p**, What hath 5030
25: 2 The which Jeremiah the **p** spake unto all 5030
28: 1 *that* Hananiah the son of Azur the **p**, 5030
28: 5 the **p** Jeremiah said unto the prophet 5030
28: 5 the prophet Jeremiah said unto the **p** 5030
28: 6 Even the **p** Jeremiah said, Amen: 5030
28: 9 The **p** which prophesieth of peace, 5030
28: 9 when the word of the **p** shall come to pass, 5030
28: 9 *then* shall the **p** be known, that the LORD 5030
28:10 Hananiah the **p** took the yoke from off 5030
28:10 the yoke from off the **p** Jeremiah's neck, 5030
28:11 And the **p** Jeremiah went his way. 5030
28:12 *p*, after that Hananiah the prophet had NIH
28:12 **p** had broken the yoke from off the neck of 5030
28:12 yoke from off the neck of the **p** Jeremiah, 5030
28:15 said the **p** Jeremiah unto Hananiah 5030
28:15 the prophet Jeremiah unto Hananiah the **p**, 5030

Jer 28:17 So Hananiah the **p** died the same year in 5030
29: 1 **p** sent from Jerusalem unto the residue of 5030
29:26 man *that is* mad, and **maketh** himself **a p**, 5012
29:27 which **maketh** himself **a p** to you? 5012
29:29 read this letter in the ears of Jeremiah the **p**. 5030
32: 2 Jeremiah the **p** was shut up in the court of 5030
34: 6 Jeremiah the **p** spake all these words unto 5030
36: 8 to all that Jeremiah the **p** commanded him, 5030
36:26 take Baruch the scribe and Jeremiah the **p**: 5030
37: 2 which he spake by the **p** Jeremiah. 5030
37: 3 of Maaseiah the priest to the **p** Jeremiah, 5030
37: 6 came the word of the LORD unto the **p** 5030
37:13 he took Jeremiah the **p**, saying, Thou fallest 5030
38: 9 in all that they have done to Jeremiah the **p**, 5030
38:10 take up Jeremiah the **p** out of the dungeon, 5030
38:14 took Jeremiah the **p** unto him into the third 5030
42: 2 said unto Jeremiah the **p**, Let, we beseech 5030
42: 4 Jeremiah the **p** said unto them, I have heard 5030
43: 6 Jeremiah the **p**, and Baruch the son of 5030
45: 1 The word that Jeremiah the **p** spake unto 5030
46: 1 to Jeremiah the **p** against the Gentiles; 5030
46:13 that the LORD spake to Jeremiah the **p**, 5030
47: 1 to Jeremiah the **p** against the Philistines, 5030
49:34 **p** against Elam in the beginning of 5030
50: 1 land of the Chaldeans by Jeremiah the **p**. 5030
51:59 The word which Jeremiah the **p** 5030
La 2:20 the **p** be slain in the sanctuary of the Lord? 5030
Eze 2: 5 yet shall know that there hath been a **p** 5030
7:26 shall they seek a vision of the **p**; but 5030
14: 4 before his face, and cometh to the **p**; 5030
14: 7 cometh to a **p** to inquire of him concerning 5030
14: 9 if the **p** be deceived when he hath spoken a 5030
14: 9 I the LORD have deceived that **p**, and 5030
14:10 the punishment of the **p** shall be even as 5030
33:33 shall they know that a **p** hath been among 5030
Da 9: 2 of the LORD came to Jeremiah the **p**, 5030
Hos 4: 5 the **p** also shall fall with thee *in* the night, 5030
9: 7 Israel shall know *it:* the **p** *is* a fool, 5030
9: 8 the **p** *is* a snare of a fowler in all his ways, 5030
12:13 by a **p** the LORD brought Israel out of 5030
12:13 out of Egypt, and by a **p** was he preserved. 5030
Am 7:14 and said to Amaziah, I *was* no **p**, 5030
Mic 2:11 he shall even be the **p** of this people. 5197
Hab 1: 1 The burden which Habakkuk the **p** did see. 5030
3: 1 A prayer of Habakkuk the **p** upon 5030
Hag 1: 1 the **p** unto Zerubbabel the son of Shealtiel, 5030
1: 3 the word of the LORD by Haggai the **p**, 5030
1:12 the words of Haggai the **p**, as the LORD 5030
2: 1 came the word of the LORD by the **p** 5030
2:10 the word of the LORD by Haggai the **p**, 5030
Zec 1: 1 of Berechiah, the son of Iddo the **p**, saying, 5030
1: 7 of Berechiah, the son of Iddo the **p**, saying, 5030
13: 5 he shall say, I *am* no **p**, I *am* a 5030
Mal 4: 5 I *will* send you Elijah the **p** before 5030
Mt 1:22 which was spoken of the Lord by the **p**, *4396*
2: 5 of Judea: for thus it is written by the **p**, *4396*
2:15 spoken of the Lord by the **p**, saying, *4396*
2:17 that which was spoken by Jeremie the **p**, *4396*
3: 3 For this is he that was spoken of by the **p** *4396*
4:14 fulfilled which was spoken by Esaias the **p**, *4396*
8:17 fulfilled which was spoken by Esaias the **p**, *4396*
10:41 He that receiveth a **p** in the name of a *4396*
10:41 of a **p** shall receive a prophet's reward; *4396*
11: 9 A **p**? yea, I say unto you, and more than a *4396*
11: 9 yea, I say unto you, and more than a **p**. *4396*
12:17 fulfilled which was spoken by Esaias the **p**, *4396*
12:39 be given to it, but the sign of the **p** Jonas: *4396*
13:35 be fulfilled which was spoken by the **p**, *4396*
13:57 A **p** is not without honour, save in his own *4396*
14: 5 because they counted him as a **p**. *4396*
16: 4 be given unto it, but the sign of the **p** Jonas. *4396*
21: 4 be fulfilled which was spoken by the **p**, *4396*
21:11 This is Jesus the **p** of Nazareth of Galilee. *4396*
21:26 we fear the people; for all hold John as a **p**. *4396*
21:46 because they took him for a **p**. *4396*
24:15 spoken of by Daniel the **p**, stand in the holy *4396*
27: 9 that which was spoken by Jeremie the **p**, *4396*
27:35 be fulfilled which was spoken by the **p**, *4396*
Mk 6: 4 A **p** is not without honour, but in his own *4396*
6:15 That it is a **p**, or as one of the prophets. *4396*
11:32 *men* counted John, that he was a **p** indeed. *4396*
13:14 spoken of by Daniel the **p**, standing where *4396*
Lk 1:76 child, shalt be called the **p** of the Highest: *4396*
3: 4 in the book of the words of Esaias the **p**, *4396*
4:17 unto him the book of the **p** Esaias. *4396*
4:24 No **p** is accepted in his own country. *4396*
4:27 were in Israel in the time of Eliseus the **p**; *4396*
7:16 saying, That a great **p** is risen up among us; *4396*
7:26 A **p**? Yea, I say unto you, and much more *4396*
7:26 I say unto you, and much more than a **p**. *4396*
7:28 is not a greater **p** than John the Baptist: *4396*
7:39 saying, This *man,* if he were a **p**, *4396*
11:29 sign be given it, but the sign of Jonas the **p**. *4396*
13:33 for it cannot be that a **p** perish out of *4396*
20: 6 for they be persuaded that John was a **p**. *4396*
24:19 which was a **p** mighty in deed and *4396*
Jn 1:21 Art thou *that* **p**? And he answered, No. *4396*
1:23 the way of the Lord, as said the **p** Esaias. *4396*
1:25 be not *that* Christ, nor Elias, neither *that* **p**? *4396*
4:19 unto him, Sir, I perceive that thou art a **p**. *4396*
4:44 that a **p** hath no honour in his own country. *4396*
6:14 This is of a truth *that* **p** that should come *4396*
7:40 *this* saying, said, Of a truth this is the **P**. *4396*
7:52 and look: for out of Galilee ariseth no **p**. *4396*
9:17 hath opened thine eyes? He said, He is a **p**. *4396*
12:38 That the saying of Esaias the **p** might be *4396*
Ac 2:16 But this is that which was spoken by the **p** *4396*
2:30 Therefore being a **p**, and knowing that God *4396*
3:22 A **p** shall the Lord your God raise up unto *4396*
3:23 *that* every soul, which will not hear that **p**, *4396*
7:37 A **p** shall the Lord your God raise up unto *4396*
7:48 in temples made with hands; as saith the **p**, *4396*
8:28 and sitting in his chariot read Esaias the **p**. *4396*
8:30 to *him,* and heard him read the **p** Esaias, *4396*
8:34 I pray thee, of whom speaketh the **p** this? *4396*
13: 6 a **false p**, a Jew, whose name *was* *5578*
13:20 and fifty years, until Samuel the **p**. *4396*
21:10 there came down from Judea a certain **p**, *4396*
28:25 Well spake the Holy Ghost by Esaias the **p** *4396*
1Co 14:37 If any *man* think himself to be a **p**, or *4396*
Tit 1:12 of themselves, *even* a **p** of their own, said, *4396*
2Pe 2:16 man's voice forbad the madness of the **p**. *4396*
Rev 16:13 and out of the mouth of the **false p**. *5578*
19:20 with him the **false p** that wrought miracles *5578*
20:10 where the beast and the **false p** *are,* and *5578*

PROPHET'S (2) [PROPHESY]

Am 7:14 I *was* no prophet, neither *was* I a **p** son; 5030
Mt 10:41 name of a prophet shall receive a **p** reward; *4396*

PROPHETESS (8) [PROPHESY]

Ex 15:20 Miriam the **p**, the sister of Aaron, took a 5031
Jdg 4: 4 Deborah, a **p**, the wife of Lapidoth, 5031
2Ki 22:14 and Asahiah, went unto Huldah the **p**, 5031
2Ch 34:22 king *had appointed,* went to Huldah the **p**, 5031
Ne 6:14 on the **p** Noadiah, and the rest of 5031
Isa 8: 3 I went unto the **p**; and she conceived, and 5031
Lk 2:36 a **p**, the daughter of Phanuel, of the tribe of *4398*
Rev 2:20 which calleth herself a **p**, to teach and *4398*

PROPHETS (239) [PROPHESY]

Nu 11:29 God that all the LORD'S people were **p**, 5030
1Sa 10: 5 that thou shalt meet a company of **p** 5030
10:10 the hill, behold, a company of **p** met him; 5030
10:11 he prophesied among the **p**, then the people 5030
10:11 the son of Kish? *Is* Saul also among the **p**? 5030
10:12 a proverb, *Is* Saul also among the **p**? 5030
19:20 when they saw the company of the **p** 5030
19:24 they say, *Is* Saul also among the **p**? 5030
28: 6 neither by dreams, nor by Urim, nor by **p**. 5030
28:15 me no more, neither by **p**, nor by dreams: 5030
1Ki 18: 4 when Jezebel cut off the **p** of the LORD, 5030
18: 4 that Obadiah took an hundred **p**, and 5030
18:13 did when Jezebel slew the **p** of the LORD, 5030
18:13 men of the LORD'S **p** by fifty in a cave, 5030
18:19 the **p** of Baal four hundred and fifty, and 5030
18:19 fifty, and the **p** of the groves four hundred, 5030
18:20 gathered the **p** together unto mount Carmel. 5030
18:22 Baal's **p** *are* four hundred and fifty men. 5030
18:25 Elijah said unto the **p** of Baal, Choose you 5030
18:40 Elijah said unto them, Take the **p** of Baal; 5030
19: 1 withal how he had slain all the **p** with 5030
19:10 thine altars, and slain thy **p** with the sword; 5030
19:14 thine altars, and slain thy **p** with the sword; 5030
20:35 a certain man of the sons of the **p** said unto 5030
20:41 of Israel discerned him that he *was* of the **p**. 5030
22: 6 the king of Israel gathered the **p** together, 5030
22:10 and all the **p** prophesied before them. 5030

1Ki 22:12 all the **p** prophesied so, saying, Go up *to* 5030
22:13 the words of the **p** *declare* good unto 5030
22:22 be a lying spirit in the mouth of all his **p**. 5030
22:23 a lying spirit in the mouth of all these thy **p**, 5030
2Ki 2: 3 the sons of the **p** that *were at* Beth-el came 5030
2: 5 the sons of the **p** that *were* at Jericho came 5030
2: 7 fifty men of the sons of the **p** went, and 5030
2:15 when the sons of the **p** which *were* to view 5030
3:13 get thee to the **p** of thy father, and to 5030
3:13 of thy father, and to the **p** of thy mother. 5030
4: 1 the wives of the sons of the **p** unto Elisha, 5030
4:38 the sons of the **p** *were* sitting before him: 5030
4:38 and seethe pottage for the sons of the **p**. 5030
5:22 two young men of the sons of the **p**: 5030
6: 1 the sons of the **p** said unto Elisha, 5030
9: 1 prophet called one of the children of the **p**, 5030
9: 7 may avenge the blood of my servants the **p**, 5030
10:19 therefore call unto me all the **p** of Baal, 5030
17:13 by all the **p**, *and by* all the seers, saying, 5030
17:13 which I sent to you by my servants the **p**. 5030
17:23 as he had said by all his servants the **p**. 5030
21:10 the LORD spake by his servants the **p**, 5030
23: 2 the **p**, and all the people, both small and 5030
24: 2 which he spake by his servants the **p**. 5030
1Ch 16:22 not mine anointed, and do my **p** no harm. 5030
2Ch 18: 5 gathered together *of* **p** four hundred men, 5030
18: 9 and all the **p** prophesied before them. 5030
18:11 all the **p** prophesied so, saying, Go up *to* 5030
18:12 the words of the **p** *declare* good to the king 5030
18:21 be a lying spirit in the mouth of all his **p**. 5030
18:22 a lying spirit in the mouth of these thy **p**, 5030
20:20 believe his **p**, so shall ye prosper. 5030
24:19 Yet he sent **p** to them, to bring them again 5030
29:25 the commandment of the LORD by his **p**. 5030
36:16 and despised his words, and misused his **p**, 5030
Ezr 5: 1 the **p**, Haggai the prophet, and 5029
5: 2 with them *were* the **p** of God helping them. 5029
9:11 hast commanded by thy servants the **p**, 5030
Ne 6: 7 thou hast also appointed **p** to preach of thee 5030
6:14 prophetess Noadiah, and the rest of the **p**, 5030
9:26 slew thy **p** which testified against them to 5030
9:30 against them by thy spirit in thy **p**: 5030
9:32 on our **p**, and on our fathers, and on all thy 5030
Ps 105:15 not mine anointed, and do my **p** no harm. 5030
Isa 29:10 the **p** and your rulers, the seers hath he 5030
30:10 to the **p**, Prophesy not unto us right *things*, 2374
Jer 2: 8 the **p** prophesied by Baal, and walked after 5030
2:26 their princes, and their priests, and their **p**, 5030
2:30 your own sword hath devoured your **p**, 5030
4: 9 shall be astonished, and the **p** shall wonder. 5030
5:13 the **p** shall become wind, and the word *is* 5030
5:31 The **p** prophesy falsely, and the priests bear 5030
7:25 even sent unto you all my servants the **p**, 5030
8: 1 the bones of the **p**, and the bones of 5030
13:13 the **p**, and all the inhabitants of Jerusalem, 5030
14:13 behold, the **p** say unto them, Ye shall not 5030
14:14 unto me, The **p** prophesy lies in my name: 5030
14:15 the **p** that prophesy in my name, 5030
14:15 and famine shall those **p** be consumed. 5030
23: 9 heart within me is broken because of the **p**; 5030
23:13 I have seen folly in the **p** of Samaria; 5030
23:14 I have seen also in the **p** of Jerusalem a 5030
23:15 saith the LORD of hosts concerning the **p**; 5030
23:15 for from the **p** of Jerusalem is profaneness 5030
23:16 Hearken not unto the words of the **p** that 5030
23:21 I have not sent *these* **p**, yet they ran: I have 5030
23:25 I have heard what the **p** said, that prophesy 5030
23:26 How long shall *this* be in the heart of the **p** 5030
23:26 *they are* **p** of the deceit of their own heart; 5030
23:30 I *am* against the **p**, saith the LORD, 5030
23:31 Behold, I *am* against the **p**, saith 5030
25: 4 hath sent unto you all his servants the **p**, 5030
26: 5 hearken to the words of my servants the **p**, 5030
26: 7 So the priests and the **p** and all the people 5030
26: 8 that the priests and the **p** and all the people 5030
26:11 the **p** unto the princes and to all the people, 5030
26:16 all the people unto the priests and to the **p**; 5030
27: 9 Therefore hearken not ye to your **p**, nor to 5030
27:14 the words of the **p** that speak unto you, 5030
27:15 ye, and the **p** that prophesy unto you. 5030
27:16 Hearken not to the words of your **p** that 5030
27:18 if they *be* **p**, and if the word of the LORD 5030
28: 8 The **p** that have been before me and before 5030
29: 1 to the **p**, and to all the people whom 5030
29: 8 Let not your **p** and your diviners, that *be* in 5030
29:15 The LORD hath raised us up **p** in 5030
29:19 I sent unto them by my servants the **p**, 5030
32:32 their **p**, and the men of Judah, and 5030
35:15 sent also unto you all my servants the **p**, 5030
37:19 Where *are* now your **p** which prophesied 5030
44: 4 I sent unto you all my servants the **p**, 5030
La 2: 9 the law *is* no *more;* her **p** also find no 5030
2:14 Thy **p** have seen vain and foolish things for 5030
4:13 For the sins of her **p**, *and* the iniquities of 5030
Eze 13: 2 prophesy against the **p** of Israel that 5030
13: 3 Woe unto the foolish **p**, that follow their 5030
13: 4 thy **p** are like the foxes in the deserts. 5030
13: 9 mine hand shall be upon the **p** that see 5030
13:16 *To wit,* the **p** of Israel which prophesy 5030
22:25 *There is* a conspiracy of her **p** in the midst 5030
22:28 her **p** have daubed them *with* untempered 5030
38:17 in old time by my servants the **p** of Israel, 5030
Da 9: 6 have we hearkened unto thy servants the **p**, 5030
9:10 he set before us by his servants the **p**. 5030
Hos 6: 5 Therefore have I hewed *them* by the **p**; 5030
12:10 I have also spoken by the **p**, and I have 5030
12:10 used similitudes by the ministry of the **p**. 5030
Am 2:11 I raised up of your sons for **p**, and of your 5030
2:12 commanded the **p**, saying, Prophesy not. 5030
3: 7 revealeth his secret unto his servants the **p**. 5030
Mic 3: 5 Thus saith the LORD concerning the **p** 5030
3: 6 the sun shall go down over the **p**, and 5030
3:11 and the **p** thereof divine for money: 5030
Zep 3: 4 Her **p** *are* light *and* treacherous persons: 5030
Zec 1: 4 unto whom the former **p** have cried, saying, 5030
1: 5 *are* they? and the **p**, do they live for ever? 5030
1: 6 which I commanded my servants the **p**, 5030
7: 3 to the **p**, saying, Should I weep in the fifth 5030
7: 7 the LORD hath cried by the former **p**, 5030
7:12 hosts hath sent in his spirit by the former **p**: 5030
8: 9 days these words by the mouth of the **p**, 5030
13: 2 also I will cause the **p** and the unclean spirit 5030
13: 4 *that* the **p** shall be ashamed every one of his 5030
Mt 2:23 be fulfilled which was spoken by the **p**, *4396*
5:12 persecuted they the **p** which were before *4396*
5:17 that I am come to destroy the law, or the **p**: *4396*
7:12 so to them: for this is the law and the **p**. *4396*
7:15 Beware of **false p**, which come to you in *5578*
11:13 For all the **p** and the law prophesied until *4396*
13:17 That many **p** and righteous *men* have *4396*
16:14 Elias; and others, Jeremias, or one of the **p**. *4396*
22:40 commandments hang all the law and the **p**. *4396*
23:29 because ye build the tombs of the **p**, and *4396*
23:30 partakers with them in the blood of the **p**. *4396*
23:31 are the children of them which killed the **p**. *4396*
23:34 I send unto you **p**, and wise *men*, and *4396*
23:37 *thou* that killest the **p**, and stonest them *4396*
24:11 And many **false p** shall rise, and *5578*
24:24 and **false p**, and shall shew great signs and *5578*
26:56 that the scriptures of the **p** might be *4396*
Mk 1: 2 As it is written in the **p**, Behold, I send my *4396*
6:15 That it is a prophet, or as one of the **p**. *4396*
8:28 some *say,* Elias; and others, One of the **p**. *4396*
13:22 For false Christs and **false p** shall rise, and *5578*
Lk 1:70 (As he spake by the mouth of his holy **p**, *4396*
6:23 the like manner did their fathers unto the **p**. *4396*
6:26 for so did their fathers to the **false p**. *5578*
9: 8 that one of the old **p** was risen again. *4396*
9:19 others *say,* that one of the old **p** is risen *4396*
10:24 that many **p** and kings have desired to see *4396*
11:47 for ye build the sepulchres of the **p**, and *4396*
11:49 I will send them **p** and apostles, and *4396*
11:50 That the blood of all the **p**, which was shed *4396*
13:28 and Isaac, and Jacob, and all the **p**, in *4396*
13:34 which killest the **p**, and stonest them that *4396*
16:16 The law and the **p** *were* until John: *4396*
16:29 saith unto him, They have Moses and the **p**; *4396*
16:31 unto him, If they hear not Moses and the **p**, *4396*
18:31 all *things* that are written by the **p** *4396*
24:25 slow of heart to believe all that the **p** have *4396*
24:27 And beginning at Moses and all the **p**, *4396*
24:44 and *in* the **p**, and *in* the psalms, *4396*
Jn 1:45 and the **p**, did write, Jesus of Nazareth, *4396*
6:45 It is written in the **p**, And they shall be all *4396*
8:52 Abraham is dead, and the **p**; and *4396*
8:53 and the **p** are dead: whom makest thou *4396*
Ac 3:18 had shewed by the mouth of all his **p**, *4396*
3:21 of all his holy **p** since the world began. *4396*

Ac 3:24 and all the **p** from Samuel and those that *4396*
3:25 Ye are the children of the **p**, and of *4396*
7:42 as it is written in the book of the **p**, O *ye* *4396*
7:52 Which of the **p** have not your fathers *4396*
10:43 To him give all the **p** witness, that through *4396*
11:27 And in these days came **p** from Jerusalem *4396*
13: 1 in the church that was at Antioch certain **p** *4396*
13:15 the **p** the rulers of the synagogue sent unto *4396*
13:27 nor *yet* the voices of the **p** which are read *4396*
13:40 upon you, which is spoken of in the **p**; *4396*
15:15 And to this agree the words of the **p**; as it is *4396*
15:32 and Silas, being **p** also themselves, *4396*
24:14 which are written in the law and the **p**: *4396*
26:22 none other *things* than those which the **p** *4396*
26:27 King Agrippa, believest thou the **p**? I know *4396*
28:23 and *out of* the **p**, from morning till evening. *4396*
Ro 1: 2 (Which he had promised afore by his **p** in *4396*
3:21 being witnessed by the law and the **p**; *4396*
11: 3 they have killed thy **p**, and digged down *4396*
16:26 and by the scriptures of the **p**, *4397*
1Co 12:28 first apostles, secondarily **p**, *4396*
12:29 *are* all **p**? *are* all teachers? *are* all workers *4396*
14:29 Let the **p** speak two or three, and let *4396*
14:32 And the spirits of the **p** are subject to *4396*
14:32 spirits of the prophets are subject to the **p**: *4396*
Eph 2:20 upon the foundation of the apostles and **p**, *4396*
3: 5 unto his holy apostles and **p** by the Spirit; *4396*
4:11 and some, **p**; and some, evangelists; and *4396*
1Th 2:15 and their own **p**, and have persecuted us; *4396*
Heb 1: 1 spake in time past unto the fathers by the **p**, *4396*
11:32 *of* David also, and Samuel, and *of* the **p**: *4396*
Jas 5:10 Take, my brethren, the **p**, who have spoken *4396*
1Pe 1:10 Of which salvation the **p** have inquired and *4396*
2Pe 2: 1 But there were **false p** also among *5578*
3: 2 which were spoken before by the holy **p**, *4396*
1Jn 4: 1 many **false p** are gone out into the world. *5578*
Rev 10: 7 as he hath declared to his servants the **p**. *4396*
11:10 these two **p** tormented them that dwelt on *4396*
11:18 give reward unto thy servants the **p**, *4396*
16: 6 they have shed the blood of saints and **p**, *4396*
18:20 *thou* heaven, and ye holy apostles and **p**; *4396*
18:24 And in her was found the blood of **p**, and *4396*
22: 6 the Lord God of the holy **p** sent his angel to *4396*
22: 9 and of thy brethren the **p**, and of them *4396*

PROPITIATION (3)

Ro 3:25 Whom God hath set forth *to be* a **p** through *2435*
1Jn 2: 2 And he is the **p** for our sins: and not for *2434*
4:10 and sent his Son *to be* the **p** for our sins. *2434*

PROPORTION (3)

1Ki 7:36 according to the **p** of every one, and 4626
Job 41:12 his parts, nor *his* power, nor his comely **p**. 6187
Ro 12: 6 *let us prophesy* according to the **p** of faith; *356*

PROPRIETY See SOBRIETY

PROSELYTE (2) [PROSELYTES]

Mt 23:15 ye compass sea and land to make one **p**, *4339*
Ac 6: 5 and Parmenas, and Nicolas a **p** of Antioch: *4339*

PROSELYTES (2) [PROSELYTE]

Ac 2:10 and strangers of Rome, Jews and **p**, *4339*
13:43 and religious **p** followed Paul and *4339*

PROSPECT (6)

Eze 40:44 and their **p** *was* toward the south: 6440
40:44 one at the side of the east gate *having* the **p** 6440
40:45 This chamber, whose **p** *is* toward the south, 6440
40:46 the chamber whose **p** *is* toward the north *is* 6440
42:15 toward the gate whose **p** *is* toward the east, 6440
43: 4 way of the gate whose **p** *is* toward the east. 6440

PROSPER (49) [PROSPERED, PROSPERETH, PROSPERITY, PROSPEROUS, PROSPEROUSLY]

Ge 24:40 send his angel with thee, and **p** thy way; 6743
24:42 if now thou do **p** my way which I go: 6743
39: 3 *that* the LORD **made** all that he did **to p** 6743
39:23 which he did, the LORD **made** *it* **to p**. 6743
Nu 14:41 of the LORD? but it shall not **p**. 6743
Dt 28:29 and thou shalt not **p** in thy ways: 6743
29: 9 do them, that ye may **p** *in* all that ye do. 7919
Jos 1: 7 that thou mayest **p** whithersoever thou 7919
1Ki 2: 3 that thou mayest **p** *in* all that thou doest, 7919
22:12 saying, Go up *to* Ramoth-gilead, and **p**: 6743
22:15 he answered him, Go, and **p**: for 6743
1Ch 22:11 **p** thou, and build the house of the LORD 6743
22:13 shalt thou **p**, if thou takest heed to fulfil 6743
2Ch 13:12 God of your fathers; for you shall not **p**. 6743
18:11 saying, Go up *to* Ramoth-gilead, and **p**: 6743
18:14 **p**, and they shall be delivered into your 6743
20:20 believe his prophets, so shall ye **p**. 6743
24:20 of the LORD, that ye cannot **p**? 6743
26: 5 he sought the LORD, God **made** him **to p**. 6743
Ne 1:11 **p**, I pray thee, thy servant *this* day, and 6743
2:20 The God of heaven, he will **p** us; 6743
Job 12: 6 The tabernacles of robbers **p**, and they that 7951
Ps 1: 3 and whatsoever he doeth shall **p**. 6743
73:12 these *are* the ungodly, who **p** in the world; 7961
122: 6 of Jerusalem: they shall **p** that love thee. 7951
Pr 28:13 He that covereth his sins shall not **p**: but 6743
Ecc 11: 6 for thou knowest not whether shall **p**, 3787
Isa 53:10 the pleasure of the LORD shall **p** in his 6743
54:17 weapon *that* is formed against thee shall **p**; 6743
55:11 and it shall **p** *in the thing* whereto I sent it. 6743
Jer 2:37 and thou shalt not **p** in them. 6743
5:28 the cause of the fatherless, yet they **p**; 6743
10:21 therefore they shall not **p**; and all their 7919
12: 1 Wherefore doth the way of the wicked **p**? 6743
20:11 for they shall not **p**: *their* everlasting 7919
22:30 a man *that* shall not **p** in his days: 6743
22:30 for no man of his seed shall **p**, sitting upon 6743
23: 5 a King shall reign and **p**, and shall execute 7919
32: 5 ye fight with the Chaldeans, ye shall not **p**. 6743
La 1: 5 adversaries are the chief, her enemies **p**; 7951
Eze 16:13 and thou didst **p** into a kingdom. 6743
17: 9 Thus saith the Lord GOD; Shall it **p**? 6743
17:10 Yea behold, *being* planted, shall it **p**? shall 6743
17:15 Shall he **p**? shall he escape that doeth such 6743
Da 8:24 shall **p**, and practise, and shall destroy 6743
8:25 also he shall **cause** craft **to p** in his hand; 6743
11:27 speak lies at one table; but it shall not **p**: 6743
11:36 shall **p** till the indignation be accomplished: 6743
3Jn 1: 2 I wish above all *things* that thou mayest **p** *2137*

PROSPERED (13) [PROSPER]

Ge 24:56 me not, seeing the LORD hath **p** my way; 6743
Jdg 4:24 the hand of the children of Israel **p**, 1980
2Sa 11: 7 the people did, and **how** the war **p**. 7965+3807.1
2Ki 18: 7 *and* he **p** whithersoever he went forth: 7919
1Ch 29:23 as king instead of David his father, and **p**; 6743
2Ch 14: 7 us rest on every side. So they built and **p**. 6743
31:21 his God, he did *it* with all his heart, and **p**. 6743
32:30 of David. And Hezekiah **p** in all his works. 6743
Ezr 6:14 they **p** through the prophesying of Haggai 6744
Job 9: 4 hardened *himself* against him, and hath **p**? 7999
Da 6:28 So this Daniel **p** in the reign of Darius, and 6744
8:12 truth to the ground; and it practised, and **p**. 6743
1Co 16: 2 as *God* hath **p** him, that there be no *2137*

PROSPERETH (4) [PROSPER]

Ezr 5: 8 work goeth fast on, and **p** in their hands. 6744
Ps 37: 7 because of him who **p** *in* his way, 6743
Pr 17: 8 that hath it: whithersoever it turneth, it **p**. 7919
3Jn 1: 2 and be in health, even as thy soul **p**. *2137*

PROSPERITY (17) [PROSPER]

Dt 23: 6 Thou shalt not seek their peace nor their **p** 2896
1Sa 25: 6 thus shall ye say to him that liveth *in p*, NIH
1Ki 10: 7 and **p** exceedeth the fame which I heard. 2896
Job 15:21 in **p** the destroyer shall come *upon* him. 7965
36:11 serve *him,* they shall spend their days in **p**, 2896
Ps 30: 6 And in my **p** I said, I shall never be moved. 7959
35:27 which hath pleasure in the **p** of his servant. 7965
73: 3 the foolish, *when* I saw the **p** of the wicked. 7965
118:25 O LORD, I beseech thee, **send** now **p**. 6743
122: 7 within thy walls, *and* **p** within thy palaces. 7962
Pr 1:32 and the **p** of fools shall destroy them. 7962
Ecc 7:14 In the day of **p** be joyful, but in the day of 2896
Jer 22:21 I spake unto thee in thy **p**; *but* thou saidst, 7962
33: 9 and for all the **p** that I procure unto it. 7965
La 3:17 my soul far off from peace: I forgat **p**. 2896
Zec 1:17 My cities through **p** shall yet be spread 2896
7: 7 when Jerusalem was inhabited and in **p**, 7961

PROSPEROUS (8) [PROSPER]

Ge 24:21 the LORD had **made** his journey **p** 6743
39: 2 was with Joseph, and he was a **p** man; 6743
Jos 1: 8 for then thou shalt **make** thy way **p**, and 6743

Jdg 18: 5 whether our way which we go shall be p. 6743
Job 8: 6 make the habitation of thy righteousness p. 7999
Isa 48:15 brought him, and he shall make his way p. 6743
Zec 8:12 For the seed *shall be* p; the vine shall give 7965
Ro 1:10 have a p journey by the will of God to *2137*

PROSPEROUSLY (2) [PROSPER]
2Ch 7:11 and in his own house, he p effected. 6743
Ps 45: 4 *in* thy majesty ride p because of truth and 6743

PROSTITUTE (1)
Lev 19:29 Do not p thy daughter, to cause her to be a 2490

PROSTITUTES See HARLOTS; SODOMITES; WHORE; WHORE'S; WHORES

PROSTITUTION See WHORE; WHORE'S; WHORES; WHOREDOM

PROTECTION (1)
Dt 32:38 them rise up and help you, *and* be your p. 5643

PROTEST (3) [PROTESTED, PROTESTING]
Ge 43: 3 man did solemnly p unto us, saying, 5749+5749
1Sa 8: 9 howbeit yet p solemnly unto them, 5749+5749
1Co 15:31 I p by your rejoicing which I have in Christ *3513*

PROTESTED (3) [PROTEST]
1Ki 2:42 and p unto thee, saying, Know for a certain, 5749
Jer 11: 7 For I earnestly p unto your fathers 5749+5749
Zec 3: 6 the angel of the LORD p unto Joshua, 5749

PROTESTING (1) [PROTEST]
Jer 11: 7 rising early and p, saying, Obey my voice. 5749

PROUD (48) [PRIDE]
Job 9:13 his anger, the p helpers do stoop under him. 7293
26:12 his understanding he smiteth through the p. 7293
38:11 and here shall thy p waves be stayed? 1347
40:11 behold every one *that is* p, and abase him. 1343
40:12 Look on every one *that is* p, *and* bring him 1343
Ps 12: 3 *and* the tongue that speaketh p *things:* 1419
31:23 and plentifully rewardeth the p doer. 1346
40: 4 respecteth not the p, nor such as turn aside 7295
86:14 the p are risen against me, and 2086
94: 2 judge of the earth: render a reward to the p. 1343
101: 5 a high look and a p heart will not I suffer. 7342
119:21 Thou hast rebuked the p *that are* cursed, 2086
119:51 The p have had me greatly in derision: 2086
119:69 The p have forged a lie against me: *but* 2086
119:78 Let the p be ashamed; for they dealt 2086
119:85 The p have digged pits for me, which *are* 2086
119:122 servant for good: let not the p oppress me. 2086
123: 4 are at ease, *and with* the contempt of the p. 1349
124: 5 Then the p waters had gone over our soul. 2121
138: 6 the lowly: but the p he knoweth afar off. 1364
140: 5 The p have hid a snare for me, and cords; 1343
Pr 6:17 A p look, a lying tongue, and hands that 7311
15:25 LORD will destroy the house of the p: 1343
16: 5 Every one *that is* p in heart *is* an 1362
16:19 than to divide the spoil with the p. 1343
21: 4 a p heart, *and* the plowing of the wicked, 7342
21:24 P *and* haughty scorner *is* his name, 2086
21:24 *is* his name, who dealeth in p wrath. 2087
28:25 He that is of a p heart stirreth up strife: but 7342
Ecc 7: 8 the patient in spirit *is* better than the p in 1362
Isa 2:12 of hosts *shall be* upon every one *that is* p 1343
13:11 I will cause the arrogancy of the p to cease, 2086
16: 6 heard of the pride of Moab; *he is* very p: 1341
Jer 13:15 Hear ye, and give ear; be not p: for 1361
43: 2 all the p men, saying unto Jeremiah, 2086
48:29 heard the pride of Moab; *he is* exceeding p: 1343
50:29 for she hath been p against the LORD, 2102
50:31 Behold, I *am* against thee, *O thou* most p, 2087
50:32 the most p shall stumble and fall, and 2087
Hab 2: 5 *he is* a p man, neither keepeth at home, 3093
Mal 3:15 now we call the p happy; yea, they that 2086
4: 1 all the p, yea, and all that do wickedly, 2086
Lk 1:51 he hath scattered the p in the imagination *5244*
Ro 1:30 haters of God, despiteful, p, boasters, *5244*
1Ti 6: 4 He is p, knowing nothing, but doting about *5187*
2Ti 3: 2 covetous, boasters, p, blasphemers, *5244*
Jas 4: 6 God resisteth the p, but giveth grace unto *5244*
1Pe 5: 5 for God resisteth the p, and giveth grace to *5244*

PROUDLY (9) [PRIDE]
Ex 18:11 for in the thing wherein they dealt p *he was* 2102
1Sa 2: 3 Talk no more *so* exceeding p; let *not* 1364+1364
Ne 9:10 for thou knewest that they dealt p against 2102
9:16 they and our fathers dealt p, and 2102
9:29 yet they dealt p, and hearkened not unto 2102
Ps 17:10 *with* their mouth they speak p. 1348+871.1
31:18 which speak grievous things p and 1346+871.1
Isa 3: 5 the child shall behave himself p against 7292
Ob 1:12 neither shouldest thou have spoken p in 1431

PROVE (25) [PROOF, PROOFS, PROVED, PROVETH, PROVING]
Ex 16: 4 a certain rate every day, that I may p them, 5254
20:20 for God is come to p you, and that his fear 5254
Dt 8: 2 to humble thee, *and* to p thee, to know what 5254
8:16 humble thee, and that he might p thee, 5254
33: 8 whom thou didst p at Massah, *and* 5254
Jdg 2:22 That through them I may p Israel, 5254
3: 1 which the LORD left, to p Israel by them, 5254
3: 4 they were to p Israel by them, to know 5254
6:39 let me p, I pray thee, but *this* once with 5254
1Ki 10: 1 she came to p him with hard questions. 5254
2Ch 9: 1 she came to p Solomon with hard questions 5254
Job 9:20 I *am* perfect, it shall also p me perverse. 6140
Ps 26: 2 Examine me, O LORD, and p me; try my 5254
Ecc 2: 1 I will p thee with mirth, therefore 5254
Da 1:12 P thy servants, I beseech thee, ten days; 5254
Mal 3:10 p me now herewith, saith the LORD of 974
Lk 14:19 five yoke of oxen, and I go to p them: *1381*
Jn 6: 6 And this he said to p him: for he himself *3985*
Ac 24:13 Neither can they p *the things* whereof they *3936*
25: 7 against Paul, which they could not p. *584*
Ro 12: 2 that ye may p what *is that* good, and *1381*
2Co 8: 8 and to p the sincerity of your love. *1381*
13: 5 ye be in the faith; p your own selves. *1381*
Gal 6: 4 But let every man p his own work, and then *1381*
1Th 5:21 P all *things;* hold fast *that which is* good. *1381*

PROVED (15) [PROVE]
Ge 42:15 Hereby ye shall be p: By the life of Pharaoh 974
42:16 be kept in prison, that your words may be p, 974
Ex 15:25 and an ordinance, and there he p them, 5254
1Sa 17:39 for he had not p *it.* And David said unto 5254
17:39 for I have not p *them.* And David put them 5254
Ps 17: 3 Thou hast p mine heart; thou hast visited *me* 974
66:10 For thou, O God, hast p us: thou hast tried 974
81: 7 I p thee at the waters of Meribah. Selah. 974
95: 9 fathers tempted me, p me, and saw my work. 974
Ecc 7:23 All this have I p by wisdom: I said, I will 5254
Da 1:14 to them in this matter, and p them ten days. 5254
Ro 3: 9 for we have before p both Jews and *4256*
2Co 8:22 whom we have oftentimes p diligent in *1381*
1Ti 3:10 And let these also first be p; then let them *1381*
Heb 3: 9 p me, and saw my works forty years. *1381*

PROVENDER (7)
Ge 24:25 We have both straw and p enough, and 4554
24:32 gave straw and p for the camels, and 4554
42:27 opened his sack to give his ass p in the inn, 4554
43:24 washed their feet; and he gave their asses p. 4554
Jdg 19:19 Yet there is both straw and p for our asses; 4554
19:21 into his house, and gave p unto the asses: 1101
Isa 30:24 asses that ear the ground shall eat clean p, 1098

PROVERB (20) [PROVERBS]
Dt 28:37 an astonishment, a p, and a byword, 4912
1Sa 10:12 Therefore it became a p, *Is* Saul also 4912
24:13 As saith the p of the ancients, 4912
1Ki 9: 7 Israel shall be a p and a byword among all 4912
2Ch 7:20 will make it to be a p and a byword among 4912
Ps 69:11 also my garment; and I became a p to them. 4912
Pr 1: 6 To understand a p, and the interpretation; 4912
Isa 14: 4 That thou shalt take up this p against 4912
Jer 24: 9 to be a reproach and a p, a taunt and a 4912
Eze 12:22 what *is* that p *that* ye have in the land of 4912
12:23 I will make this p to cease, and they shall 4912
12:23 they shall no more use it as a p in Israel; 4911
14: 8 will make him a sign and a p, and I will cut 4912
16:44 useth proverbs shall use *this* p against thee, 4911
18: 2 that ye use this p concerning the land 4911+4912
18: 3 any more to use this p in Israel. 4911+4912
Hab 2: 6 and a taunting p against him, and say, 2420
Lk 4:23 Ye will surely say unto me this p, *3850*

Jn 16:29 speakest thou plainly, and speakest no **p**. *3942*
2Pe 2:22 unto them according to the true **p**, *3942*

PROVERBS (9) [PROVERB]
Nu 21:27 Wherefore they that **speak in p** say, 4911
1Ki 4:32 he spake three thousand **p**: and his songs 4912
Pr 1: 1 The **p** of Solomon the son of David, king of 4912
10: 1 The **p** of Solomon. A wise son maketh a 4912
25: 1 These *are* also **p** of Solomon, which 4912
Ecc 12: 9 and sought out, *and* set in order many **p**. 4912
Eze 16:44 every one that **useth p** shall use *this* 4911
Jn 16:25 These *things* have I spoken unto you in **p**: *3942*
16:25 when I shall no more speak unto you in **p**, *3942*

PROVETH (1) [PROVE]
Dt 13: 3 for the LORD your God **p** you, to know 5254

PROVIDE (11) [PROVIDED, PROVIDENCE, PROVIDETH, PROVIDING, PROVISION]
Ge 22: 8 God will **p** himself a lamb for a burnt 7200
30:30 now when shall I **p** for mine own house 6213
Ex 18:21 Moreover thou shalt **p** out of all the people 2372
1Sa 16:17 **P** me now a man that can play well, and 7200
2Ch 2: 7 in Jerusalem, whom David my father did **p**. 3559
Ps 78:20 bread also? can he **p** flesh for his people? 3559
Mt 10: 9 **P** neither gold, nor silver, nor brass in your *2932*
Lk 12:33 **p** yourselves bags which wax not old, *4160*
Ac 23:24 And **p** *them* beasts, that they may set Paul *3936*
Ro 12:17 **P** *things* honest in the sight of all men. *4306*
1Ti 5: 8 But if any **p** not **for** his own, and *4306*

PROVIDED (9) [PROVIDE]
Dt 33:21 he **p** the first *part* for himself, because 7200
1Sa 16: 1 for I have **p** me a king among his sons. 7200
2Sa 19:32 he had **p** the king **of sustenance** while he 3557
1Ki 4: 7 which **p victuals** for the king and his 3557
4:27 those officers **p victual** for king Solomon, 3557
2Ch 32:29 Moreover he **p** him cities, and 6213
Ps 65: 9 them corn, when thou hast so **p for** it. 3559
Lk 12:20 shall *those things* be, which thou hast **p**? *2090*
Heb 11:40 God having **p** some better *thing* for us, *4265*

PROVIDENCE (1) [PROVIDE]
Ac 24: 2 deeds are done unto this nation by thy **p**, *4307*

PROVIDETH (2) [PROVIDE]
Job 38:41 Who **p** for the raven his food? when his 3559
Pr 6: 8 **P** her meat in the summer, *and* 3559

PROVIDING (1) [PROVIDE]
2Co 8:21 **P** *for* honest *things*, not only in the sight of *4306*

PROVINCE (27) [PROVINCES]
Ezr 2: 1 Now these *are* the children of the **p** that 4082
5: 8 the king, that we went into the **p** of Judea, 4083
6: 2 in the palace that *is* in the **p** of the Medes, 4083
7:16 gold that thou canst find in all the **p** of 4083
Ne 1: 3 there in the **p** *are* in great affliction 4082
7: 6 These *are* the children of the **p**, that went 4082
11: 3 Now these *are* the chief of the **p** that dwelt 4082
Est 1:22 into **every p** according to 4082+4082+2050.1
3:12 that *were* over **every p**, 4082+4082+2050.1
3:12 **every p** according to 4082+4082+2050.1
3:14 **every p** *was* published 3605+4082+4082+2050.1
4: 3 in **every p**, 3605+4082+4082+2050.1
8: 9 *unto* **every p** according to 4082+4082+2050.1
8:11 the people and **p** that would assault them, 4082
8:13 **every p** *was* published 3605+4082+2050.1
8:17 in **every p**, and 3605+4082+4082+2050.1
9:28 **every p**, and every city; 4082+4082+2050.1
Ecc 5: 8 perverting of judgment and justice in a **p**, 4082
Da 2:48 made him ruler over the whole **p** of 4083
2:49 over the affairs of the **p** of Babylon: 4083
3: 1 in the plain of Dura, in the **p** of Babylon. 4083
3:12 set over the affairs of the **p** of Babylon, 4083
3:30 and Abed-nego, in the **p** of Babylon. 4083
8: 2 *in* the palace, which *is* in the **p** of Elam; 4082
11:24 even upon the fattest places of the **p**; 4082
Ac 23:34 read *the letter*, he asked of what **p** he was: *1885*
25: 1 Now when Festus was come into the **p**, *1885*

PROVINCES (30) [PROVINCE]
1Ki 20:14 by the young men of the princes of the **p**. 4082
20:15 the young men of the princes of the **p**, 4082
20:17 the young men of the princes of the **p** went 4082
20:19 So these young men of the princes of the **p** 4082
Ezr 4:15 hurtful unto kings and **p**, and that they have 4083
Est 1: 1 *over* an hundred and seven and twenty **p**:) 4082
1: 3 and Media, the nobles and princes of the **p**, 4082
1:16 to all the people that *are* in all the **p** of 4082
1:22 For he sent letters into all the king's **p**, 4082
2: 3 let the king appoint officers in all the **p** of 4082
2:18 he made a release to the **p**, and gave gifts, 4082
3: 8 dispersed among the people in all the **p** of 4082
3:13 were sent by posts into all the king's **p**, 4082
4:11 the people of the king's **p**, do know, 4082
8: 5 the Jews which *are* in all the king's **p**: 4082
8: 9 rulers of the **p** which *are* from India unto 4082
8: 9 an hundred twenty and seven **p**, *unto* every 4082
8:12 Upon one day in all the **p** of king 4082
9: 2 throughout all the **p** of the king Ahasuerus, 4082
9: 3 all the rulers of the **p**, and the lieutenants, 4082
9: 4 and his fame went out throughout all the **p**: 4082
9:12 have they done in the rest of the king's **p**? 4082
9:16 the other Jews that *were* in the king's **p** 4082
9:20 that *were* in all the **p** of the king Ahasuerus, 4082
9:30 and seven **p** of the kingdom of Ahasuerus, 4082
Ecc 2: 8 the peculiar treasure of kings and of the **p**: 4082
La 1: 1 *and* princess among the **p**, *how* is she 4082
Eze 19: 8 set against him on every side from the **p**, 4082
Da 3: 2 the sheriffs, and all the rulers of the **p**, 4083
3: 3 the sheriffs, and all the rulers of the **p**, 4083

PROVING (2) [PROVE]
Ac 9:22 at Damascus, **p** that this is *very* Christ. *4822*
Eph 5:10 **P** what is acceptable unto the Lord. *1381*

PROVISION (11) [PROVIDE]
Ge 42:25 his sack, and to give them **p** for the way: 6720
45:21 of Pharaoh, and gave them **p** for the way. 6720
Jos 9: 5 all the bread of their **p** was dry *and* mouldy. 6718
9:12 This our bread we **took** hot for our **p** out of 6679
1Ki 4: 7 each man *his* month in a year **made p**. 3557
4:22 Solomon's **p** for one day was thirty 3899
2Ki 6:23 he prepared great **p** for them: and 3740
1Ch 29:19 the palace, *for* the which I have **made p**. 3559
Ps 132:15 I will abundantly bless her **p**: I will satisfy 6718
Da 1: 5 the king appointed them a daily **p** of 1697
Ro 13:14 and make not **p for** the flesh, to *fulfil* *4307*

PROVOCATION (8) [PROVOKE]
1Ki 15:30 by his **p** where*with* he provoked 3708
21:22 for the **p** wherewith thou hast provoked *me* 3708
Job 17: 2 and *doth not* mine eye continue in their **p**? 4784
Ps 95: 8 as *in* the **p**, *and* as *in* the day of temptation 4808
Jer 32:31 city hath been to me *as* a **p of** mine **anger** 639
Eze 20:28 there they presented the **p** of their offering: 3708
Heb 3: 8 Harden not your hearts, as in the **p**, in *3894*
3:15 harden not your hearts, as in the **p**. *3894*

PROVOCATIONS (3) [PROVOKE]
2Ki 23:26 of all the **p** that Manasseh had provoked 3708
Ne 9:18 up out of Egypt, and had wrought great **p**; 5007
9:26 them to thee, and they wrought great **p**. 5007

PROVOKE (42) [PROVOCATION, PROVOCATIONS, PROVOKED, PROVOKEDST, PROVOKETH, PROVOKING]
Ex 23:21 of him, and obey his voice, **p** him not; 4843
Nu 14:11 How long will this people **p** me? 5006
Dt 4:25 of the LORD thy God, to **p** him **to anger**: 3707
9:18 the sight of the LORD, to **p** him **to anger**. 3707
31:20 and **p** me, and break my covenant. 5006
31:29 to **p** him **to anger** through the work of your 3707
32:21 I will **p** them **to anger** with a foolish 3707
1Ki 14: 9 to **p** me **to anger**, and hast cast me behind 3707
16: 2 to sin, to **p** me **to anger** with their sins; 3707
16:26 to **p** the LORD God of Israel **to anger** 3707
16:33 **p** the LORD God of Israel **to anger** than 3707
2Ki 17:11 wicked things to **p** the LORD **to anger**: 3707
17:17 the sight of the LORD, to **p** him **to anger**. 3707
21: 6 the sight of the LORD, to **p** *him* **to anger**. 3707
22:17 that they might **p** me **to anger** with all 3707
23:19 Israel had made to **p** *the LORD* **to anger**, 3707
2Ch 33: 6 the sight of the LORD, to **p** him **to anger**. 3707
34:25 that *they* might **p** me **to anger** with all 3707
Job 12: 6 and they that **p** God are secure; 7264
Ps 78:40 How oft did they **p** him in the wilderness, 4784
Isa 3: 8 the LORD, to **p** the eyes of his glory. 4784
Jer 7:18 other gods, that *they* may **p** me **to anger**. 3707

Jer 7:19 Do they p me to anger? saith the LORD: 3707
7:19 do they not p themselves to the confusion of NIH
11:17 p me to anger in offering incense unto 3707
25: 6 p me not to anger with the works of your 3707
25: 7 that ye might p me to anger with the works 3707
32:29 unto other gods, to p me to anger. 3707
32:32 which they have done to p me to anger, 3707
44: 3 they have committed to p me to anger, 3707
44: 8 In that ye p me unto wrath with the works 3707
Eze 8:17 with violence, and have returned to p me 3707
16:26 thy whoredoms, to p me to anger. 3707
Lk 11:53 and to p him to speak of many things: 653
Ro 10:19 I will p you to jealousy by them that are no 3863
11:11 the Gentiles, for to p them to jealousy. 3863
11:14 If by any means I may p to emulation 3863
1Co 10:22 Do we p the Lord to jealousy? are we 3863
Eph 6: 4 ye fathers, p not your children to wrath: 3949
Col 3:21 p not your children to anger, lest they be 2042
Heb 3:16 For some, when they had heard, did p: 3893
10:24 And let us consider one another to p unto 3948

PROVOKED (33) [PROVOKE]
Nu 14:23 neither shall any of them that p me see it: 5006
16:30 ye shall understand that these men have p 5006
Dt 9: 8 Also in Horeb ye p the LORD to wrath, 7107
9:22 ye p the LORD to wrath. 7107
32:16 They p him to jealousy with strange gods, 7065
32:16 with abominations p they him to anger. 3707
32:21 they have p me to anger with their 3707
Jdg 2:12 unto them, and p the LORD to anger. 3707
1Sa 1: 6 her adversary also p her sore, for to 3707+3708
1: 7 to the house of the LORD, so she p her; 3707
1Ki 14:22 they p him to jealousy with their sins 7065
15:30 he p the LORD God of Israel to anger. 3707
21:22 wherewith thou hast p me to anger, 3707
22:53 and p to anger the LORD God of Israel, 3707
2Ki 21:15 have p me to anger, since the day their 3707
23:26 of all the provocations that Manasseh had p 3707
1Ch 21: 1 and p David to number Israel. 5496
2Ch 28:25 p to anger the LORD God of his fathers. 3707
Ezr 5:12 had p the God of heaven unto wrath, 7265
Ne 4: 5 for they have p thee to anger before 3707
Ps 78:56 Yet they tempted and p the most high God, 4784
78:58 For they p him to anger with their high 3707
106: 7 but p him at the sea, even at the Red sea. 4784
106:29 Thus they p him to anger with their 3707
106:33 Because they p his spirit, so that he spake 4784
106:43 they p him with their counsel, and 4784
Isa 1: 4 have p the Holy One of Israel unto anger, 5006
Jer 8:19 Why have they p me to anger with their 3707
32:30 p me to anger with the work of their 3707
Hos 12:14 Ephraim p him to anger most bitterly: 3707
Zec 8:14 when your fathers p me to wrath, saith 7107
1Co 13: 5 her own, is not easily p, thinketh no evil; 3947
2Co 9: 2 a year ago; and your zeal hath p very many. 2042

PROVOKEDST (1) [PROVOKE]
Dt 9: 7 how thou p the LORD thy God to wrath 7107

PROVOKETH (3) [PROVOKE]
Pr 20: 2 whoso p him to anger sinneth against his 5674
Isa 65: 3 A people that p me to anger continually to 3707
Eze 8: 3 the image of jealousy, which p to jealousy. 7069

PROVOKING (6) [PROVOKE]
Dt 32:19 because of the p of his sons, 3708
1Ki 14:15 made their groves, p the LORD to anger. 3707
16: 7 in p him to anger with the work of his 3707
16:13 in p the LORD God of Israel to anger 3707
Ps 78:17 they sinned yet more against him by p 4784
Gal 5:26 p one another, envying one another. 4292

PRUDENCE (3) [PRUDENT, PRUDENTLY]
2Ch 2:12 endued with p and understanding, 7922
Pr 8:12 I wisdom dwell with p, and find out 6195
Eph 1: 8 abounded toward us in all wisdom and p; 5428

PRUDENT (24) [PRUDENCE]
1Sa 16:18 p in matters, and a comely person, and 995
Pr 12:16 but a p man covereth shame. 6175
12:23 A p man concealeth knowledge: but 6175
13:16 Every p man dealeth with knowledge: but 6175
14: 8 The wisdom of the p is to understand his 6175
14:15 but the p man looketh well to his going. 6175
14:18 but the p are crowned with knowledge. 6175
15: 5 but he that regardeth reproof is p. 6191
16:21 The wise in heart shall be called p: and 995
18:15 The heart of the p getteth knowledge; and 995
19:14 and a p wife is from the LORD. 7919
22: 3 A p man foreseeth the evil, and 6175
27:12 A p man foreseeth the evil, and 6175
Isa 3: 2 and the prophet, and the p, and the ancient, 7080
5:21 in their own eyes, and p in their own sight! 995
10:13 have done it, and by my wisdom; for I am p: 995
29:14 the understanding of their p men shall be 995
Jer 49: 7 is counsel perished from the p? is their 995
Hos 14: 9 and he shall understand these things? p, and 995
Am 5:13 Therefore the p shall keep silence in that 7919
Mt 11:25 hast hid these things from the wise and p, 4908
Lk 10:21 hast hid these things from the wise and p, 4908
Ac 13: 7 of the country, Sergius Paulus, a p man; 4908
1Co 1:19 bring to nothing the understanding of the p. 4908

PRUDENTLY (1) [PRUDENCE]
Isa 52:13 Behold, my servant shall deal p, he shall be 7919

PRUNE (2) [PRUNED, PRUNING, PRUNINGHOOKS]
Lev 25: 3 six years thou shalt p thy vineyard, and 2168
25: 4 neither sow thy field, nor p thy vineyard. 2168

PRUNED (1) [PRUNE]
Isa 5: 6 it shall not be p, nor digged; but there shall 2168

PRUNING (1) [PRUNE]
Isa 18: 5 shall both cut off the sprigs with p hooks, 4211

PRUNINGHOOKS (3) [HOOK, PRUNE]
Isa 2: 4 into plowshares, and their spears into p: 4211
Joel 3:10 into swords, and your p into spears: 4211
Mic 4: 3 into plowshares, and their spears into p: 4211

PSALM (88) [PSALMIST, PSALMS]
1Ch 16: 7 on that day David delivered first this p to NIH
Ps 3: T A P of David, when he fled from Absalom 4210
4: T chief Musician on Neginoth, A P of David. 4210
5: T Musician upon Nehiloth, A P of David. 4210
6: T Neginoth upon Sheminith, A P of David. 4210
8: T chief Musician upon Gittith, A P of David. 4210
9: T Musician upon Muth-labben, A P of David. 4210
11: T To the chief Musician, A P of David. NIH
12: T Musician upon Sheminith, A P of David. 4210
13: T To the chief Musician, A P of David. 4210
14: T To the chief Musician, A P of David. NIH
15: T A P of David. 4210
18: T To the chief Musician, A P of David, NIH
19: T To the chief Musician, A P of David. 4210
20: T To the chief Musician, A P of David. 4210
21: T To the chief Musician, A P of David. 4210
22: T upon Aijeleth Shahar, A P of David. 4210
23: T A P of David. 4210
24: T A P of David. 4210
25: T A P of David. NIH
26: T A P of David. NIH
27: T A P of David. NIH
28: T A P of David. NIH
29: T A P of David. 4210
30: T A P and Song at the dedication of the house 4210
31: T To the chief Musician, A P of David. 4210
32: T A P of David, Maschil. NIH
34: T A P of David, when he changed his NIH
35: T A P of David. NIH
36: T A P of David the servant of the LORD. NIH
37: T A P of David. NIH
38: T A P of David, to bring to remembrance. 4210
39: T even to Jeduthun, A P of David. 4210
40: T To the chief Musician, A P of David. 4210
41: T To the chief Musician, A P of David. 4210
47: T chief Musician, A P for the sons of Korah. 4210
48: T A Song and P for the sons of Korah. 4210
49: T chief Musician, A P for the sons of Korah. 4210
50: T A P of Asaph. 4210
51: T To the chief Musician, A P of David, 4210
52: T the chief Musician, Maschil, A P of David, NIH
53: T upon Mahalath, Maschil, A P of David. NIH
54: T Maschil, A P of David, when the Ziphims NIH
55: T on Neginoth, Maschil, A P of David. NIH
61: T Musician upon Neginah, A P of David. NIH
62: T chief Musician, to Jeduthun, A P of David. 4210
63: T A P of David, when he was in 4210
64: T To the chief Musician, A P of David. 4210

Ps 65: T the chief Musician, A **P** *and* Song of David. 4210
66: T To the chief Musician, A Song *or* **P**. 4210
67: T chief Musician on Neginoth, A **P** *or* Song. 4210
68: T the chief Musician, A **P** *or* Song of David. 4210
69: T Musician upon Shoshannim, *A P* of David. NIH
70: T To the chief Musician, *A P* of David, NIH
72: T *A P* for Solomon. NIH
73: T A **P** of Asaph. 4210
75: T Al-taschith, A **P** *or* Song of Asaph. 4210
76: T on Neginoth, A **P** *or* Song of Asaph. 4210
77: T chief Musician, to Jeduthun, A **P** of Asaph. 4210
79: T A **P** of Asaph. 4210
80: T upon Shoshannim-Eduth, A **P** of Asaph. 4210
81: T chief Musician upon Gittith, *A P* of Asaph. NIH
81: 2 Take a **p**, and bring hither the timbrel, 2172
82: T A **P** of Asaph. 4210
83: T A Song *or* **P** of Asaph. 4210
84: T upon Gittith, A **P** for the sons of Korah. 4210
85: T chief Musician, A **P** for the sons of Korah. 4210
87: T A **P** *or* Song for the sons of Korah. 4210
88: T A Song *or* **P** for the sons of Korah. To 4210
92: T A **P** *or* Song for the sabbath day. 4210
98: T A **P**. 4210
98: 5 with the harp, and the voice of a **p**. 2172
100: T A **P** of praise. 4210
101: T A **P** of David. 4210
103: T *A P* of David. NIH
108: T A Song *or* **P** of David. 4210
109: T To the chief Musician, A **P** of David. 4210
110: T A **P** of David. 4210
138: T *A P* of David. NIH
139: T To the chief Musician, A **P** of David. 4210
140: T To the chief Musician, A **P** of David. 4210
141: T A **P** of David. 4210
143: T A **P** of David. 4210
144: T *A P* of David. NIH
145: T David's *P of* praise. NIH
Ac 13:33 as it is also written in the second **p**, *5568*
13:35 Wherefore he saith also in another *p*, Thou NIG
1Co 14:26 every one of you hath a **p**, hath a doctrine, *5568*

PSALMIST (1) [PSALM]
2Sa 23: 1 of Jacob, and the sweet **p** of Israel, said, 2158

PSALMS (9) [PSALM]
1Ch 16: 9 Sing unto him, **sing p** unto him, talk you of 2167
Ps 95: 2 *and* make a joyful noise unto him with **p**. 2158
105: 2 Sing unto him, **sing p** unto him: talk ye of 2167
Lk 20:42 And David himself saith in the book of **P**, *5568*
24:44 the prophets, and *in* the **p**, concerning me. *5568*
Ac 1:20 For it is written in the book of **P**, Let his *5568*
Eph 5:19 Speaking to yourselves in **p** and hymns and *5568*
Col 3:16 and admonishing one another in **p** and *5568*
Jas 5:13 let him pray. Is any merry? let him **sing p**. *5567*

PSALTERIES (14) [PSALTERY]
2Sa 6: 5 on **p**, and on timbrels, and on cornets, and 5035
1Ki 10:12 king's house, harps also and **p** for singers: 5035
1Ch 13: 8 with **p**, and with timbrels, and 5035
15:16 **p** and harps and cymbals, sounding, 5035
15:20 and Benaiah, with **p** on Alamoth; 5035
15:28 making a noise with **p** and harps. 5035
16: 5 Jeiel with **p** and with harps; but 5035
25: 1 with harps, with **p**, and with cymbals: 5035
25: 6 with cymbals, **p**, and harps, for the service 5035
2Ch 5:12 having cymbals and **p** and harps, 5035
9:11 king's palace, and harps and **p** for singers: 5035
20:28 they came *to* Jerusalem with **p** and harps 5035
29:25 with **p**, and with harps, according to 5035
Ne 12:27 *with* cymbals, **p**, and with harps. 5035

PSALTERY (13) [PSALTERIES]
1Sa 10: 5 coming down from the high place with a **p**, 5035
Ps 33: 2 sing unto him with the **p** *and* an instrument 5035
57: 8 Awake up, my glory; awake, **p** and harp: 5035
71:22 I will also praise thee with the **p**, 3627+5035
81: 2 the timbrel, the pleasant harp with the **p**. 5035
92: 3 instrument of ten strings, and upon the **p**; 5035
108: 2 Awake, **p** and harp: I *myself* will awake 5035
144: 9 upon a **p** *and* an instrument of ten strings 5035
150: 3 the trumpet: praise him with the **p** and harp. 5035
Da 3: 5 flute, harp, sackbut, **p**, dulcimer, and 6460
3: 7 sackbut, **p**, and all kinds of musick, 6460
3:10 **p**, and dulcimer, and all kinds of musick, 6460
3:15 **p**, and dulcimer, and all kinds of musick, 6460

PTOLEMAIS (1)
Ac 21: 7 we came to **P**, and saluted the brethren, and *4424*

PUA (1) [PUAH]
Nu 26:23 the Tolaites: of **P**, the family of the Punites: 6312

PUAH (3) [PHUVAH, PUA, PUNITES]
Ex 1:15 *was* Shiphrah, and the name of the other **P**: 6326
Jdg 10: 1 arose to defend Israel Tola the son of **P**, 6312
1Ch 7: 1 and **P**, Jashub, and Shimron, four. 6312

PUBLIC See OPEN; OPENLY; PUBLICK; PUBLICKLY

PUBLICAN (6) [PUBLICANS]
Mt 10: 3 Bartholomew; Thomas, and Matthew the **p**; *5057*
18:17 him be unto thee as a heathen *man* and a **p**. *5057*
Lk 5:27 and saw a **p**, named Levi, sitting at *5057*
18:10 the one a Pharisee, and the other a **p**. *5057*
18:11 unjust, adulterers, or even as this **p**. *5057*
18:13 And the **p**, standing afar off, would not lift *5057*

PUBLICANS (17) [PUBLICAN]
Mt 5:46 have ye? do not even the **p** the same? *5057*
5:47 ye more *than others?* do not even the **p** so? *5057*
9:10 many **p** and sinners came and sat down *5057*
9:11 Why eateth your Master with **p** and *5057*
11:19 and a winebibber, a friend of **p** and sinners. *5057*
21:31 That the **p** and the harlots go into *5057*
21:32 but the **p** and the harlots believed him: and *5057*
Mk 2:15 many **p** and sinners sat also together with *5057*
2:16 and Pharisees saw him eat with **p** and *5057*
2:16 he eateth and drinketh with **p** and sinners? *5057*
Lk 3:12 Then came also **p** to be baptized, and *5057*
5:29 and there was a great company of **p** and *5057*
5:30 do ye eat and drink with **p** and sinners? *5057*
7:29 all the people that heard *him,* and the **p**, *5057*
7:34 and a winebibber, a friend of **p** and sinners. *5057*
15: 1 Then drew near unto him all the **p** and *5057*
19: 2 which was *the* **chief among** the **p**, and *754*

PUBLICK (1) [PUBLICKLY]
Mt 1:19 and not willing to **make her a p example**, *3856*

PUBLICKLY (2) [PUBLICK]
Ac 18:28 he mightily convinced the Jews, *and that* **p**, *1219*
20:20 and have taught you **p**, and from house to *1219*

PUBLISH (17) [PUBLISHED, PUBLISHETH]
Dt 32: 3 Because I will **p** the name of the LORD: 7121
1Sa 31: 9 to **p** *it in* the house of their idols, and 1319
2Sa 1:20 in Gath, **p** *it* not in the streets of Askelon; 1319
Ne 8:15 that they should **p** and proclaim in all their 8085
Ps 26: 7 That *I* may **p** with the voice of 8085
Jer 4: 5 Declare ye in Judah, and **p** in Jerusalem; 8085
4:16 behold, **p** against Jerusalem, *that* watchers 8085
5:20 house of Jacob, and **p** it in Judah, saying, 8085
31: 7 **p** ye, praise ye, and say, O LORD, save 8085
46:14 **p** in Migdol, and publish in Noph and 8085
46:14 and **p** in Noph and in Tahpanhes: 8085
50: 2 the nations, and **p**, and set up a standard; 8085
50: 2 and set up a standard; **p**, *and* conceal not: 8085
Am 3: 9 **P** in the palaces at Ashdod, and in 8085
4: 5 and proclaim *and* **p** the free offerings: 8085
Mk 1:45 and began to **p** *it* much, and to blaze abroad *2784*
5:20 began to **p** in Decapolis how great *things* *2784*

PUBLISHED (11) [PUBLISH]
Est 1:20 make shall be **p** throughout all his empire, 8085
1:22 that it should be **p** according to 1696
3:14 in every province *was* **p** unto all people, 1540
8:13 in every province *was* **p** unto all people, 1540
Ps 68:11 great *was* the company of those that **p** *it.* 1319
Jnh 3: 7 **p** through Nineveh by the decree of the king 559
Mk 7:36 *so* much the more a great deal they **p** *it;* *2784*
13:10 And the gospel must first be **p** among all *2784*
Lk 8:39 **p** throughout the whole city how great *2784*
Ac 10:37 which was **p** throughout all Judea, and *1096*
13:49 And the word of the Lord was **p** throughout *1308*

PUBLISHETH (4) [PUBLISH]
Isa 52: 7 that bringeth good tidings, that **p** peace; 8085
52: 7 good tidings of good, that **p** salvation; 8085
Jer 4:15 and **p** affliction from mount Ephraim. 8085
Na 1:15 that bringeth good tidings, that **p** peace. 8085

PUBLIUS (2)
Ac 28: 7 chief *man* of the island, whose name was **P**; *4196*
28: 8 that the father of **P** lay sick of a fever and *4196*

PUDENS (1)
2Ti 4:21 and **P**, and Linus, and Claudia, and all *4227*

PUFFED (5) [PUFFETH]
1Co 4: 6 that no one of you be **p up** for one against *5448*
4:18 Now some are **p up**, as though I would not *5448*
4:19 not the speech of them which are **p up**, but *5448*
5: 2 And ye are **p up**, and have not rather *5448*
13: 4 charity vaunteth not itself, is not **p up**, *5448*

PUFFETH (3) [PUFFED, PUFT]
Ps 10: 5 *as for* all his enemies, he **p** at them. 6315
12: 5 I will set *him* in safety *from him that* **p** at 6315
1Co 8: 1 Knowledge **p up**, but charity edifieth. *5448*

PUFT (1) [PUFFETH]
Col 2:18 not seen, vainly **p up** by his fleshly mind, *5448*

PUHITES (1)
1Ch 2:53 the **P**, and the Shumathites, and 6336

PUITES See PUNITES

PUL (4) [TIGLATH-PILESER]
2Ki 15:19 *And* **P** the king of Assyria came against 6322
15:19 Menahem gave **P** a thousand talents of 6322
1Ch 5:26 the God of Israel stirred up the spirit of **P** 6322
Isa 66:19 *to* Tarshish, **P**, and Lud, that draw the bow, 6322

PULL (15) [PULLED, PULLING]
1Ki 13: 4 so that he could not **p** it **in again** to him. 7725
Ps 31: 4 **P** me **out** of the net that they have laid 3318
Isa 22:19 and from thy state shall he **p** thee **down**. 2040
Jer 1:10 to **p down**, and to destroy, and to throw 5422
12: 3 **p** them **out** like sheep for the slaughter, and 5423
18: 7 pluck up, and to **p down**, and to destroy *it*; 5422
24: 6 I will build them, and not **p** *them* **down**; 2040
42:10 not **p** *you* **down**, and I will plant you, and 2040
Eze 17: 9 shall he not **p up** the roots thereof, and cut 5423
Mic 2: 8 ye **p** off the robe with the garment from 6584
Mt 7: 4 Let me **p out** the mote out of thine eye; *1544*
Lk 6:42 let me **p out** the mote that is in thine eye, *1544*
6:42 shalt thou see clearly to **p out** the mote that *1544*
12:18 I will **p down** my barns, and build greater; *2507*
14: 5 will not straightway **p** him **out** on *385*

PULLED (7) [PULL]
Ge 8: 9 took her, and **p** her **in** unto him into the ark. 935
19:10 **p** Lot into the house to them, and shut to 935
Ezr 6:11 let timber be **p down** from his house, and 5256
La 3:11 turned aside my ways, and **p** me **in pieces**: 6582
Am 9:15 they shall no more be **p up** out of their land 5428
Zec 7:11 **p** away the shoulder, and stopped their ears, 5414
Ac 23:10 Paul should have been **p in pieces** of them, *1288*

PULLING (2) [PULL]
2Co 10: 4 mighty through God to the **p down** of *2506*
Jude 1:23 others save with fear, **p** *them* out of the fire; *726*

PULPIT (1)
Ne 8: 4 Ezra the scribe stood upon a **p** of wood, 4026

PULSE (3)
2Sa 17:28 and beans, and lentiles, and parched *p*, NIH
Da 1:12 let them give us **p** to eat, and water to 2235
1:16 that they should drink; and gave them **p**. 2235

PUNISH (32) [PUNISHED, PUNISHMENT, PUNISHMENTS, UNPUNISHED]
Lev 26:18 I will **p** you seven *times* more for your sins. 3256
26:24 will **p** you yet seven *times* for your sins. 5221
Pr 17:26 Also to **p** the just *is* not good, *nor* to strike 6064
Isa 10:12 I will **p** the fruit of the stout heart of 6485
13:11 I will **p** the world for *their* evil, and 6485
24:21 *that* the LORD shall **p** the host of the high 6485
26:21 the LORD cometh out of his place to **p** 6485
27: 1 strong sword shall **p** leviathan the piercing 6485
Jer 9:25 that I will **p** all *them which are* circumcised 6485
11:22 the LORD of hosts, Behold, I will **p** them: 6485
13:21 What wilt thou say when he shall **p** thee? 6485
21:14 I will **p** you according to the fruit of your 6485
23:34 I will even **p** that man and his house. 6485
25:12 *that* I will **p** the king of Babylon, and that 6485
27: 8 that nation will I **p**, saith the LORD, 6485
29:32 I will **p** Shemaiah the Nehelamite, and his 6485
30:20 and I will **p** all that oppress them. 6485
36:31 I will **p** him and his seed and his servants 6485
44:13 For I will **p** them that dwell in the land of 6485
44:29 the LORD, that I will **p** you in this place, 6485
46:25 I will **p** the multitude of No, and Pharaoh, 6485
50:18 I *will* **p** the king of Babylon and his land, 6485
51:44 I will **p** Bel in Babylon, and I will bring 6485
Hos 4: 9 I will **p** them for their ways, and 6485
4:14 I will not **p** your daughters when they 6485
12: 2 and *will* **p** Jacob according to his ways; 6485
Am 3: 2 therefore I will **p** you for all your iniquities. 6485
Zep 1: 8 that I will **p** the princes, and the king's 6485
1: 9 In the same day also will I **p** all those that 6485
1:12 and **p** the men that are settled on their lees: 6485
Zec 8:14 As I thought to **p** you, when your fathers 7489
Ac 4:21 finding nothing how they might **p** them, *2849*

PUNISHED (17) [PUNISH]
Ex 21:20 under his hand; he shall be **surely p**. 5358+5358
21:21 he continue a day or two, he shall not be **p**: 5358
21:22 he shall be **surely p**, according as 6064+6064
Ezr 9:13 seeing that thou our God hast **p** us less than 2820
Job 31:11 yea, it *is* an iniquity *to be* **p** *by* the judges. NIH
31:28 This also *were* an iniquity *to be* **p** *by* NIH
Pr 21:11 When the scorner is **p**, the simple is made 6064
22: 3 but the simple pass on, and are **p**. 6064
27:12 *but* the simple pass on, *and* are **p**. 6064
Jer 44:13 as I have **p** Jerusalem, by the sword, by 6485
50:18 his land, as I have **p** the king of Assyria. 6485
Zep 3: 7 should not be cut off, howsoever I **p** them: 6485
Zec 10: 3 against the shepherds, and I **p** the goats: 6485
Ac 22: 5 bound unto Jerusalem, for to be **p**. *5097*
26:11 And I **p** them oft in every synagogue, and *5097*
2Th 1: 9 Who shall be **p** *with* everlasting *1349+5099*
2Pe 2: 9 the unjust unto the day of judgment *to be* **p**: *2849*

PUNISHMENT (27) [PUNISH]
Ge 4:13 My **p** *is* greater than *I* can bear. 5771
Lev 26:41 they then accept of the **p of** their **iniquity**: 5771
26:43 they shall accept of the **p of** their **iniquity**: 5771
1Sa 28:10 there shall no **p** happen to thee for this 5771
Job 31: 3 and a **strange p** to the workers of iniquity? 5235
Pr 19:19 *A man* of great wrath *shall* suffer **p**: for if 6066
La 3:39 man complain, a man for the **p of** his **sins**? 2399
4: 6 For the **p of** the **iniquity** of the daughter of 5771
4: 6 is greater than the **p of** the **sin** of Sodom, 2403
4:22 The **p of** thine **iniquity** is accomplished, 5771
Eze 14:10 they shall bear the **p of** their **iniquity**: 5771
14:10 the **p** of the prophet shall be even as 5771
14:10 even as the **p** of him that seeketh *unto him;* 5771
Am 1: 3 for four, I will not turn away *the* **p** thereof; NIH
1: 6 for four, I will not turn away *the* **p** thereof; NIH
1: 9 for four, I will not turn away *the* **p** thereof; NIH
1:11 for four, I will not turn away *the* **p** thereof; NIH
1:13 for four, I will not turn away *the* **p** thereof; NIH
2: 1 for four, I will not turn away *the* **p** thereof; NIH
2: 4 for four, I will not turn away *the* **p** thereof; NIH
2: 6 for four, I will not turn away *the* **p** thereof; NIH
Zec 14:19 This shall be the **p** of Egypt, and 2403
14:19 the **p** of all nations that come not up to 2403
Mt 25:46 And these shall go away into everlasting **p**: *2851*
2Co 2: 6 Sufficient to such *a man is* this **p**, *2009*
Heb 10:29 Of how much sorer **p**, suppose ye, shall he *5098*
1Pe 2:14 as unto them that are sent by him for the **p** *1557*

PUNISHMENTS (2) [PUNISH]
Job 19:29 for wrath *bringeth* the **p** of the sword, 5771
Ps 149: 7 upon the heathen, *and* **p** upon the people; 8433

PUNITES (1) [PUAH]
Nu 26:23 of the Tolaites: of Pua, the family of the **P**: 6324

PUNON (2)
Nu 33:42 departed from Zalmonah, and pitched in **P**. 6325
33:43 they departed from **P**, and pitched in 6325

PUR (3) [PURIM]
Est 3: 7 they cast **P**, that *is*, the lot, before Haman 6332
9:24 had cast **P**, that *is*, the lot, to consume 6332
9:26 these days Purim after the name of **P**. 6332

PURAH See PHURAH

PURCHASE (8) [PURCHASED]

Ge 49:32 The **p** of the field and of the cave that *is* 4735
Lev 25:33 if a man **p** of the Levites, then the house 1350
Jer 32:11 So I took the evidence of the **p**, *both* that 4736
32:12 I gave the evidence of the **p** unto Baruch 4736
32:12 witnesses that subscribed the book of the **p**, 4736
32:14 this evidence of the **p**, both which is sealed, 4736
32:16 of the **p** unto Baruch the son of Neriah, 4736
1Ti 3:13 deacon well **p** to themselves a good degree, *4046*

PURCHASED (9) [PURCHASE]

Ge 25:10 The field which Abraham **p** of the sons of 7069
Ex 15:16 till the people pass over, *which* thou hast **p**. 7069
Ru 4:10 the wife of Mahlon, have I **p** to be my wife, 7069
Ps 74: 2 thy congregation, *which* thou hast **p** of old; 7069
78:54 this mountain, *which* his right hand had **p**. 7069
Ac 1:18 Now this *man* **p** a field with the reward of *2932*
8:20 that the gift of God may be **p** with money. *2932*
20:28 which he hath **p** with his own blood. *4046*
Eph 1:14 until the redemption of the **p** **possession**, *4047*

PURE (97) [PURIFY]

Ex 25:11 thou shalt overlay it with **p** gold, within 2889
25:17 thou shalt make a mercy seat *of* **p** gold: 2889
25:24 thou shalt overlay it with **p** gold, and 2889
25:29 *of* **p** gold shalt thou make them. 2889
25:31 thou shalt make a candlestick of **p** gold: 2889
25:36 all it *shall be* one beaten work *of* **p** gold. 2889
25:38 the snuffdishes thereof, *shall be of* **p** gold. 2889
25:39 *Of* a talent of **p** gold shall he make it, 2889
27:20 that they bring thee **p** oil olive beaten for 2134
28:14 two chains *of* **p** gold at the ends; 2889
28:22 at the ends *of* wreathen work *of* **p** gold. 2889
28:36 thou shalt make a plate *of* **p** gold, and 2889
30: 3 thou shalt overlay it with **p** gold, the top 2889
30:23 of **p** myrrh five hundred *shekels*, and 1865
30:34 *these* sweet spices with **p** frankincense: 2134
30:35 tempered together, **p** *and* holy: 2889
31: 8 the **p** candlestick with all his furniture, and 2889
37: 2 he overlaid it with **p** gold within 2889
37: 6 he made the mercy seat *of* **p** gold: 2889
37:11 he overlaid it with **p** gold, and 2889
37:16 and *his* covers to cover withal, *of* **p** gold. 2889
37:17 he made the candlestick *of* **p** gold: 2889
37:22 all of it *was* one beaten work *of* **p** gold. 2889
37:23 his snuffers, and his snuffdishes, *of* **p** gold. 2889
37:24 *Of* a talent *of* **p** gold made he it, and all 2889
37:26 he overlaid it with **p** gold, *both* the top of it, 2889
37:29 and the **p** incense of sweet spices, 2889
39:15 at the ends, *of* wreathen work *of* **p** gold. 2889
39:25 they made bells of **p** gold, and put the bells 2889
39:30 they made the plate of the holy crown *of* **p** 2889
39:37 The **p** candlestick, *with* the lamps thereof, 2889
Lev 24: 2 that they bring unto thee **p** oil olive beaten 2134
24: 4 He shall order the lamps upon the **p** 2889
24: 6 a row, upon the **p** table before the LORD. 2889
24: 7 thou shalt put **p** frankincense upon *each* 2134
Dt 32:14 thou didst drink the **p** blood of the grape. 2561
2Sa 22:27 With the **p** thou wilt shew thyself pure; and 1305
22:27 With the pure thou wilt **shew** thyself **p**; and 1305
1Ki 5:11 and twenty measures of **p** oil: 3795
6:20 he overlaid it with **p** gold; and *so* 5462
6:21 overlaid the house within with **p** gold: 5462
7:49 the candlesticks *of* **p** gold, five on the right 5462
7:50 and the spoons, and the censers *of* **p** gold; 5462
10:21 of the forest of Lebanon *were of* **p** gold: 5462
1Ch 28:17 Also **p** gold *for* the fleshhooks, and 2889
2Ch 3: 4 and he overlaid it within with **p** gold. 2889
4:20 the manner before the oracle, *of* **p** gold; 5462
4:22 and the spoons, and the censers, of **p** gold: 5462
9:17 throne of ivory, and overlaid it with **p** gold. 2889
9:20 of the forest of Lebanon *were of* **p** gold: 5462
13:11 also *set they* in order upon the **p** table; 2889
Ezr 6:20 all of them *were* **p**, and killed the passover 2889
Job 4:17 shall a man be more **p** than his Maker? 2891
8: 6 If thou *wert* **p** and upright; surely now he 2134
11: 4 My doctrine *is* **p**, and I am clean in thine 2134
16:17 in mine hands: also my prayer is **p**. 2134
25: 5 yea, the stars are not **p** in his sight. 2141
28:19 neither shall it be valued with **p** gold. 2889
Ps 12: 6 The words of the LORD *are* **p** words: 2889
18:26 With the **p** thou wilt shew thyself pure; and 1305
18:26 With the pure thou wilt **shew** thyself **p**; and 1305
19: 8 the commandment of the LORD *is* **p**, 1249
21: 3 thou settest a crown of **p** **gold** on his head. 6337
24: 4 He that hath clean hands, and a **p** heart; 1249
119:140 Thy word *is* very **p**: therefore thy servant 6884
Pr 15:26 but *the words of* the **p** *are* pleasant words. 2889
20: 9 made my heart clean, I am **p** from my sin? 2891
20:11 whether his work *be* **p**, and whether *it be* 2134
21: 8 strange: but *as for* the **p**, his work *is* right. 2134
30: 5 Every word of God *is* **p**: he *is* a shield unto 6884
30:12 *There is* a generation *that are* **p** in their own 2889
Da 7: 9 and the hair of his head like the **p** wool: 5343
Mic 6:11 Shall I **count** *them* **p** with the wicked 2135
Zep 3: 9 then will I turn to the people a **p** language, 1305
Mal 1:11 *be* offered unto my name, and a **p** offering: 2889
Mt 5: 8 Blessed *are* the **p** in heart: for they shall see *2513*
Ac 20:26 that I *am* **p** from the blood of all *men*. *2513*
Ro 14:20 All *things* indeed *are* **p**; but *it is* evil for *2513*
Php 4: 8 *things are* just, whatsoever *things are* **p**, *53*
1Ti 1: 5 commandment is charity out of a **p** heart, *2513*
3: 9 Holding the mystery of the faith in a **p** *2513*
5:22 partaker of other *men's* sins: keep thyself **p**. *53*
2Ti 1: 3 whom I serve from *my* forefathers with **p** *2513*
2:22 with them that call on the Lord out of a **p** *2513*
Tit 1:15 Unto the **p** all *things are* pure: but *2513*
1:15 Unto the pure all *things are* **p**: but *2513*
1:15 are defiled and unbelieving *is* nothing **p**; *2513*
Heb 10:22 and *our* bodies washed with **p** water. *2513*
Jas 1:27 **P** religion and undefiled before God and *2513*
3:17 But the wisdom that is from above is first **p**, *53*
1Pe 1:22 *see that ye* love one another with a **p** heart *2513*
2Pe 3: 1 in both which I stir up your **p** minds by *1506*
1Jn 3: 3 hope in him purifieth himself, even as he is **p**. *53*
Rev 15: 6 clothed in **p** and white linen, and *2513*
21:18 and the city *was* **p** gold, like unto clear *2513*
21:21 and the street of the city *was* **p** gold, as *it* *2513*
22: 1 And he shewed me a **p** river of water of *2513*

PURELY (1) [PURIFY]

Isa 1:25 **p** purge away thy dross, 1253+1886.1+3509.1

PURENESS (3) [PURIFY]

Job 22:30 and it is delivered by the **p** of thine hands. 1252
Pr 22:11 He that loveth **p** of heart, *for* the grace of 2889
2Co 6: 6 By **p**, by knowledge, by longsuffering, *54*

PURER (2) [PURIFY]

La 4: 7 Her Nazarites were **p** than snow, they were 2141
Hab 1:13 *Thou art* of **p** eyes than to behold evil, and 2889

PURGE (15) [PURGED, PURGETH, PURGING]

2Ch 34: 3 in the twelfth year he began to **p** Judah and 2891
Ps 51: 7 **P** me with hyssop, and I shall be clean: 2398
65: 3 our transgressions, thou shalt **p** them **away**. 3722
79: 9 deliver us, and **p** **away** our sins, for thy 3722
Isa 1:25 purely **p** **away** thy dross, and take away all 6884
Eze 20:38 I will **p** **out** from among you the rebels, 1305
43:20 thus shalt thou cleanse and **p** it. 3722
43:26 Seven days shall they **p** the altar and 3722
Da 11:35 try them, and to **p**, and to make *them* white, 1305
Mal 3: 3 sons of Levi, and **p** them as gold and silver, 2212
Mt 3:12 and he will **throughly** **p** his floor, and *1245*
Lk 3:17 and he will **throughly** **p** his floor, and *1245*
1Co 5: 7 **P** **out** therefore the old leaven, that ye may *1571*
2Ti 2:21 If a man therefore **p** himself from these, *1571*
Heb 9:14 **p** your conscience from dead works to *2511*

PURGED (14) [PURGE]

1Sa 3:14 the iniquity of Eli's house shall not be **p** 3722
2Ch 34: 8 when he had **p** the land, and the house, 2891
Pr 16: 6 By mercy and truth iniquity is **p**: and by 3722
Isa 4: 4 shall have **p** the blood of Jerusalem from 1740
6: 7 thine iniquity is taken away, and thy sin **p**. 3722
22:14 Surely this iniquity shall not be **p** from you 3722
27: 9 shall the iniquity of Jacob be **p**; 3722
Eze 24:13 because I have **p** thee, and thou wast not 2891
24:13 I have purged thee, and thou wast not **p**, 2891
24:13 thou shalt not be **p** from thy filthiness any 2891
Heb 1: 3 when he had by himself **p** our sins, *2512+4160*
9:22 And almost all *things* are by the law **p** with *2511*
10: 2 that the worshippers once **p** should have *2508*
2Pe 1: 9 hath forgotten that *he* was **p** from his old *2512*

PURGETH (1) [PURGE]

Jn 15: 2 and every *branch* that beareth fruit, he **p** it, *2508*

PURGING (1) [PURGE]
Mk 7:19 goeth out into the draught, **p** all meats? *2511*

PURIFICATION (8) [PURIFY]
Nu 19: 9 for a water of separation: it *is* a **p for sin.** 2403
19:17 of the ashes of the burnt *heifer* of **p for sin,** 2403
2Ch 30:19 according to the **p** of the sanctuary. 2893
Ne 12:45 ward of their God, and the ward of the **p,** 2893
Est 2: 3 and let their **things for p** be given *them:* 8562
2: 9 he speedily gave her her **things for p,** 8562
Lk 2:22 And when the days of her **p** according to *2512*
Ac 21:26 signify the accomplishment of the days of **p,** *49*

PURIFICATIONS (1) [PURIFY]
Est 2:12 so were the days of their **p** accomplished, 4795

PURIFIED (12) [PURIFY]
Lev 8:15 **p** the altar, and poured the blood at 2398
Nu 8:21 the Levites were **p,** and they washed their 2398
31:23 nevertheless it shall be **p** with the water of 2398
2Sa 11: 4 for she was **p** from her uncleanness: 6942
Ezr 6:20 the priests and the Levites were **p** together, 2891
Ne 12:30 the priests and the Levites **p** themselves, 2891
12:30 **p** the people, and the gates, and the wall. 2891
Ps 12: 6 tried in a furnace of earth, **p** seven times. 2212
Da 12:10 Many shall be **p,** and made white, and 1305
Ac 24:18 Jews from Asia found me **p** in the temple, *48*
Heb 9:23 in the heavens should be **p** with these; *2511*
1Pe 1:22 Seeing ye have **p** your souls in obeying *48*

PURIFIER (1) [PURIFY]
Mal 3: 3 he shall sit *as* a refiner and **p** of silver: and 2891

PURIFIETH (2) [PURIFY]
Nu 19:13 **p** not himself, defileth the tabernacle of 2398
1Jn 3: 3 And every *man* that hath this hope in him **p** *48*

PURIFY (14) [PURE, PURELY, PURENESS, PURER, PURIFICATION, PURIFICATIONS, PURIFIED, PURIFIER, PURIFIETH, PURIFYING, PURITY]
Nu 19:12 He shall **p** himself with it on the third day, 2398
19:12 if he **p** not himself the third day, then 2398
19:19 on the seventh day he shall **p** *himself,* and 2398
19:20 shall be unclean, and shall not **p** himself, 2398
31:19 **p** *both* yourselves and your captives on 2398
31:20 **p** all *your* raiment, and all that is made of 2398
Job 41:25 by reason of breakings they **p** themselves. 2398
Isa 66:17 **p** themselves in the gardens behind one *tree* 2891
Eze 43:26 days shall they purge the altar and **p** it; 2891
Mal 3: 3 he shall **p** the sons of Levi, and purge them 2891
Jn 11:55 before the passover, to **p** themselves. *48*
Ac 21:24 and **p** thyself with them, and be at charges *48*
Tit 2:14 and **p** unto himself a peculiar people, *2511*
Jas 4: 8 and **p** *your* hearts, *ye* double minded. *48*

PURIFYING (12) [PURIFY]
Lev 12: 4 continue in the blood of her **p** three and 2893
12: 4 until the days of her **p** be fulfilled. 2892
12: 5 she shall continue in the blood of her **p** 2893
12: 6 when the days of her **p** are fulfilled, for a 2892
Nu 8: 7 Sprinkle water of **p** upon them, and 2403
1Ch 23:28 in the **p** of all holy *things,* and the work of 2893
Est 2:12 with *other* **things for the p** of the women;) 8562
Jn 2: 6 after the manner of the **p** of the Jews, *2512*
3:25 of John's disciples and the Jews about **p.** *2512*
Ac 15: 9 and them, **p** their hearts by faith. *2511*
21:26 the next day **p** himself with them entered into *48*
Heb 9:13 the unclean, sanctifieth to the **p** of the flesh: *2514*

PURIM (5) [PUR]
Est 9:26 Wherefore they called these days **P** after 6332
9:28 *that* these days of **P** should not fail from 6332
9:29 to confirm this second letter of **P.** 6332
9:31 To confirm these days of **P** in their times 6332
9:32 of Esther confirmed these matters of **P;** 6332

PURITY (2) [PURIFY]
1Ti 4:12 in charity, in spirit, in faith, in **p.** *47*
5: 2 as mothers; the younger as sisters, with all **p.** *47*

PURLOINING (1)
Tit 2:10 Not **p,** but shewing all good fidelity; *3557*

PURPLE (48)
Ex 25: 4 **p,** and scarlet, and fine linen, and 713
26: 1 twined linen, and blue, and **p,** and scarlet: 713
26:31 **p,** and scarlet, and fine twined linen *of* 713
26:36 and **p,** and scarlet, and fine twined linen, 713
27:16 and **p,** and scarlet, and fine twined linen, 713
28: 5 and blue, and **p,** and scarlet, and fine linen. 713
28: 6 *of* blue, and *of* **p,** *of* scarlet, and fine twined 713
28: 8 and **p,** and scarlet, and fine twined linen. 713
28:15 *of* **p,** and *of* scarlet, and *of* fine twined linen, 713
28:33 of **p,** and of scarlet, round about the hem 713
35: 6 **p,** and scarlet, and fine linen, and 713
35:23 **p,** and scarlet, and fine linen, and goats' *hair,* 713
35:25 and of **p,** *and* of scarlet, and of fine linen. 713
35:35 in blue, and in **p,** in scarlet, and in fine linen, 713
36: 8 twined linen, and blue, and **p,** and scarlet: 713
36:35 and **p,** and scarlet, and fine twined linen: 713
36:37 **p,** and scarlet, and fine twined linen, 713
38:18 and **p,** and scarlet, and fine twined linen: 713
38:23 and in **p,** and in scarlet, and fine linen. 713
39: 1 of the blue, and **p,** and scarlet, they made 713
39: 2 and **p,** and scarlet, and fine twined linen. 713
39: 3 in the **p,** and in the scarlet, and in the fine 713
39: 5 and **p,** and scarlet, and fine twined linen; 713
39: 8 and **p,** and scarlet, and fine twined linen. 713
39:24 of blue, and **p,** and scarlet, *and* twined *linen.* 713
39:29 and blue, and **p,** and scarlet, *of* needlework; 713
Nu 4:13 from the altar, and spread a **p** cloth thereon: 713
Jdg 8:26 **p** raiment that *was* on the kings of Midian, 713
2Ch 2: 7 in **p,** and crimson, and blue, and that can 710
2:14 in **p,** in blue, and in fine linen, and 713
3:14 **p,** and crimson, and fine linen, and 713
Est 1: 6 and **p** to silver rings and pillars of marble: 713
8:15 and *with* a garment of fine linen and **p:** 713
Pr 31:22 of tapestry; her clothing *is* silk and **p.** 713
SS 3:10 thereof *of* gold, the covering of it *of* **p,** 713
7: 5 and the hair of thine head like **p;** 713
Jer 10: 9 blue and **p** *is* their clothing: they *are* all 713
Eze 27: 7 **p** from the isles of Elishah was that which 713
27:16 **p,** and broidered work, and fine linen, and 713
Mk 15:17 And they clothed him with **p,** and platted a *4209*
15:20 they took off the **p** from him, and put his *4209*
Lk 16:19 which was clothed in **p** and fine linen, and *4209*
Jn 19: 2 on his head, and they put on him a **p** robe, *4210*
19: 5 the crown of thorns, and the **p** robe. *4210*
Ac 16:14 a **seller of p,** of the city of Thyatira, *4211*
Rev 17: 4 And the woman was arrayed in **p** and *4209*
18:12 and **p,** and silk, and scarlet, and all thyine *4209*
18:16 and **p,** and scarlet, and decked with gold, *4210*

PURPOSE (36) [PURPOSED, PURPOSES, PURPOSETH, PURPOSING]
Ru 2:16 **let fall** also *some* of the handfuls **of p** 7997+7997
1Ki 5: 5 I **p** to build a house unto the name of 559
2Ch 28:10 now ye **p** to keep under the children of Judah 559
Ezr 4: 5 to frustrate their **p,** all the days of Cyrus 6098
Ne 8: 4 of wood, which they had made for the **p;** 1697
Job 33:17 That *he* may withdraw man *from his* **p,** and 4639
Pr 20:18 Every **p** is established by counsel: and 4284
Ecc 3: 1 and a time to every **p** under the heaven: 2656
3:17 for *there is* a time there for every **p** and 2656
8: 6 Because to every **p** there is time and 2656
Isa 1:11 **To** what **p** *is* the multitude of your 3807.1
14:26 This *is* the **p** that is purposed upon 6098
30: 7 Egyptians shall help in vain, and to **no p:** 7385
Jer 6:20 To what **p** cometh there to me incense 2088
26: 3 which I **p** to do unto them because of 2803
36: 3 hear all the evil which I **p** to do unto them; 2803
49:30 and hath conceived a **p** against you. 4284
51:29 for every **p** of the LORD shall be 4284
Da 6:17 that the **p** might not be changed concerning 6640
Mt 26: 8 saying, To **what p** *is* this waste? *5101*
Ac 11:23 that with **p** of heart *they* would cleave unto *4286*
26:16 for I have appeared unto thee for this **p,** to NIG
27:13 supposing that *they* had obtained *their* **p,** *4286*
27:43 to save Paul, kept them from *their* **p;** *1013*
Ro 8:28 them who are *the* called according to *his* **p.** *4286*
9:11 that the **p** of God according to election *4286*
9:17 Even for this same **p** have I raised thee up, NIG
2Co 1:17 or *the things* that I **p,** do I purpose *1011*
1:17 that I purpose, do I **p** according to the flesh, *1011*
Eph 1:11 being predestinated according to the **p** of *4286*
3:11 According to the eternal **p** which he *4286*
6:22 Whom I have sent unto you **for** the same **p,** *1519*
Col 4: 8 Whom I have sent unto you **for** the same **p,** *1519*
2Ti 1: 9 but according to his own **p** and grace, *4286*

2Ti 3:10 **p**, faith, longsuffering, charity, patience, *4286*
1Jn 3: 8 For this **p** the Son of God was manifested, NIG

PURPOSED (19) [PURPOSE]
2Ch 32: 2 that he was **p** to fight against Jerusalem, 6440
Ps 17: 3 I am **p** *that* my mouth shall not transgress. 2161
140: 4 who have **p** to overthrow my goings. 2803
Isa 14:24 to pass; and as I have **p**, *so* shall it stand: 3289
14:26 This *is* the purpose that is **p** upon the whole 3289
14:27 For the LORD of hosts hath **p**, and 3289
19:12 the LORD of hosts hath **p** upon Egypt. 3289
23: 9 The LORD of hosts hath **p** it, to stain 3289
46:11 bring it to pass; I have **p** *it,* I will also do it. 3335
Jer 4:28 because I have spoken *it,* I have **p** *it,* and 2161
49:20 that he hath **p** against the inhabitants of 2803
50:45 that he hath **p** against the land of 2803
La 2: 8 The LORD hath **p** to destroy the wall of 2803
Da 1: 8 Daniel **p** in his heart that he would not 7760
Ac 19:21 *things* were ended, Paul **p** in the spirit, *5087*
20: 3 he **p** to return through Macedonia. *1096+1106*
Ro 1:13 that oftentimes I **p** to come unto you, (but *4388*
Eph 1: 9 good pleasure which he had **p** in himself: *4388*
3:11 to the eternal purpose which he **p** *4160*

PURPOSES (5) [PURPOSE]
Job 17:11 My days are past, my **p** are broken off, 2154
Pr 15:22 Without counsel **p** *are* disappointed: but 4284
Isa 19:10 they shall be broken *in* the **p** thereof, 8356
Jer 49:20 his **p**, that he hath purposed against 4284
50:45 his **p**, that he hath purposed against the land 4284

PURPOSETH (1) [PURPOSE]
2Co 9: 7 Every man according as he **p** in *his* heart, *4255*

PURPOSING (1) [PURPOSE]
Ge 27:42 doth comfort himself, *p* to kill thee. NIH

PURSE (5) [PURSES]
Pr 1:14 in thy lot among us; let us all have one **p**: 3599
Mk 6: 8 no scrip, no bread, no money in *their* **p**: *2223*
Lk 10: 4 Carry neither **p**, nor scrip, nor shoes: and *905*
22:35 When I sent you without **p**, and scrip, and *905*
22:36 But now, he that hath a **p**, let him take *it,* and *905*

PURSES (1) [PURSE]
Mt 10: 9 neither gold, nor silver, nor brass in your **p**; *2223*

PURSUE (29) [PURSUED, PURSUER, PURSUERS, PURSUETH, PURSUING]
Ge 35: 5 and they did not **p** after the sons of Jacob. 7291
Ex 15: 9 The enemy said, I will **p**, I will overtake, 7291
Dt 19: 6 Lest the avenger of the blood **p** the slayer, 7291
28:22 and they shall **p** thee until thou perish. 7291
28:45 shall **p** thee, and overtake thee, till thou be 7291
Jos 2: 5 **p** after them quickly; for ye shall overtake 7291
8:16 in Ai were called *together* to **p** after them: 7291
10:19 *but* **p** after your enemies, and smite 7291
20: 5 if the avenger of blood **p** after him, then 7291
1Sa 24:14 after whom dost thou **p**? after a dead dog, 7291
25:29 Yet a man is risen to **p** thee, and to seek thy 7291
26:18 Wherefore doth my lord thus **p** after his 7291
30: 8 saying, Shall I **p** after this troop? 7291
30: 8 he answered him, **P**: for thou shalt surely 7291
2Sa 17: 1 and I will arise and **p** after David *this* night: 7291
20: 6 **p** after him, lest he get him fenced cities, 7291
20: 7 to **p** after Sheba the son of Bichri. 7291
20:13 to **p** after Sheba the son of Bichri. 7291
24:13 before thine enemies, while they **p** thee? 7291
Job 13:25 and fro? and wilt thou **p** the dry stubble? 7291
30:15 they **p** my soul as the wind: and my welfare 7291
Ps 34:14 and do good; seek peace, and **p** it. 7291
Isa 30:16 therefore shall they that **p** you be swift. 7291
Jer 48: 2 O Madmen; the sword shall **p** thee. 310+1980
Eze 35: 6 thee unto blood, and blood shall **p** thee: 7291
35: 6 not hated blood, even blood shall **p** thee. 7291
Hos 8: 3 *thing that is* good: the enemy shall **p** him. 7291
Am 1:11 he did **p** his brother with the sword, 7291
Na 1: 8 and darkness shall **p** his enemies. 7291

PURSUED (38) [PURSUE]
Ge 14:14 and eighteen, and **p** *them* unto Dan. 7291
14:15 and smote them, and **p** them unto Hobah, 7291
31:23 and **p** after him seven days' journey; 7291
31:36 my sin, that thou hast *so* **hotly p** after me? 1814
Ex 14: 8 and he **p** after the children of Israel: 7291
14: 9 the Egyptians **p** after them (all the horses 7291
14:23 the Egyptians **p**, and went in after them to 7291
Dt 11: 4 sea to overflow them as they **p** after you, 7291
Jos 2: 7 the men **p** after them the way to Jordan 7291
2: 7 as soon as they which **p** after them were 7291
8:16 they **p** after Joshua, and were drawn away 7291
8:17 they left the city open, and **p** after Israel. 7291
24: 6 the Egyptians **p** after your fathers with 7291
Jdg 1: 6 they **p** after him, and caught him, and 7291
4:16 Barak **p** after the chariots, and after 7291
4:22 behold, as Barak **p** Sisera, Jael came out to 7291
7:23 of all Manasseh, and **p** after the Midianites. 7291
7:25 **p** Midian, and brought the heads of Oreb 7291
8:12 he **p** after them, and took the two kings of 7291
20:45 **p hard** after them unto Gidom, and 1692
1Sa 7:11 **p** the Philistines, and smote them, 7291
17:52 and shouted, and **p** the Philistines, 7291
23:25 when Saul heard *that,* he **p** after David *in* 7291
30:10 David **p**, he and four hundred men: for two 7291
2Sa 2:19 Asahel **p** after Abner; and in going he 7291
2:24 Joab also and Abishai **p** after Abner: and 7291
2:28 stood still, and **p** after Israel no more, 7291
20:10 Abishai his brother **p** after Sheba the son of 7291
22:38 I have **p** mine enemies, and 7291
1Ki 20:20 the Syrians fled; and Israel **p** them: and 7291
2Ki 25: 5 the army of the Chaldees **p** after the king, 7291
2Ch 13:19 Abijah **p** after Jeroboam, and took cities 7291
14:13 the people that *were* with him **p** them unto 7291
Ps 18:37 I have **p** mine enemies, and 7291
Isa 41: 3 He **p** them, *and* passed safely; *even by* 7291
Jer 39: 5 the Chaldeans' army **p** after them, and 7291
52: 8 the army of the Chaldeans **p** after the king, 7291
La 4:19 they **p** us upon the mountains, they laid 1814

PURSUER (1) [PURSUE]
La 1: 6 they are gone without strength before the **p**. 7291

PURSUERS (5) [PURSUE]
Jos 2:16 you to the mountain, lest the **p** meet you; 7291
2:16 there three days, until the **p** be returned: 7291
2:22 there three days, until the **p** were returned: 7291
2:22 the **p** sought *them* throughout all the way, 7291
8:20 *to* the wilderness turned back upon the **p**. 7291

PURSUETH (8) [PURSUE]
Lev 26:17 and ye shall flee when none **p** you. 7291
26:36 a sword; and they shall fall when none **p**. 7291
26:37 as it were before a sword, when none **p**: 7291
Pr 11:19 he that **p** evil *pursueth it* to his own death. 7291
11:19 he that pursueth evil *p it* to his own death. NIH
13:21 Evil **p** sinners: but to the righteous good 7291
19: 7 he **p** *them with* words, *yet* they *are* 7291
28: 1 The wicked flee when no man **p**: but 7291

PURSUING (8) [PURSUE]
Jdg 8: 4 men that *were* with him, faint, yet **p** *them.* 7291
8: 5 I am **p** after Zebah and Zalmunna, kings of 7291
1Sa 23:28 Wherefore Saul returned from **p** after 7291
2Sa 3:22 of David and Joab came from *p* a troop, NIH
18:16 and the people returned from **p** after Israel: 7291
1Ki 18:27 or he is **p**, or he is in a journey, *or* 7873
22:33 of Israel, that they turned back from **p** him. 310
2Ch 18:32 of Israel, they turned back *again* from **p** him. 310

PURTENANCE (1)
Ex 12: 9 head with his legs, and with the **p** thereof. 7130

PUSH (9) [PUSHING, PUSHT]
Ex 21:29 if the ox *were* **wont to p with his horn** in 5056
21:32 If the ox shall **p** a manservant or 5055
21:36 Or *if* it be known that the ox *hath* **used to p** 5056
Dt 33:17 with them he shall **p** the people together *to* 5055
1Ki 22:11 With these shalt thou **p** the Syrians, 5055
2Ch 18:10 With these thou shalt **p** Syria until they be 5055
Job 30:12 they **p away** my feet, and they raise up 7971
Ps 44: 5 Through thee will we **p down** our enemies: 5055
Da 11:40 the end shall the king of the south **p** at him: 5055

PUSHING (1) [PUSH]
Da 8: 4 I saw the ram **p** westward, and northward, 5055

PUSHT (1) [PUSH]
Eze 34:21 and **p** all the diseased with your horns, 5055

PUT (911) [PUTTEST, PUTTETH, PUTTING] See Index

PUTEOLI (1)
Ac 28:13 wind blew, and we came the next day to **P**: *4223*

PUTHITES See PUHITES

PUTIEL (1)
Ex 6:25 took him *one* of the daughters of **P** to wife; 6317

PUTRIFYING (1)
Isa 1: 6 in it; *but* wounds, and bruises, and **p** sores: 2961

PUTTEST (7) [PUT] See Index

PUTTETH (30) [PUT] See Index

PUTTING (17) [PUT] See Index

PYGARG (1)
Dt 14: 5 the **p**, and the wild ox, and the chamois. 1788

Q

QUAILS (4)
Ex 16:13 that at even the **q** came up, and covered 7958
Nu 11:31 brought **q** from the sea, and let *them* fall by 7958
11:32 all the next day, and they gathered the **q**: 7958
Ps 105:40 he brought **q**, and satisfied them *with* 7958

QUAKE (4) [EARTHQUAKE, EARTHQUAKES, QUAKED, QUAKING]
Joel 2:10 The earth shall **q** before them; the heavens 7264
Na 1: 5 The mountains **q** at him, and the hills melt, 7493
Mt 27:51 and the earth did **q**, and the rocks rent; *4579*
Heb 12:21 *that* Moses said, I exceedingly fear and **q**;) *1790*

QUAKED (2) [QUAKE]
Ex 19:18 a furnace, and the whole mount **q** greatly. 2729
1Sa 14:15 they also trembled, and the earth **q**: 7264

QUAKING (2) [QUAKE]
Eze 12:18 eat thy bread with **q**, and drink thy water 7494
Da 10: 7 a great **q** fell upon them, so that they fled to 2731

QUANTITY (1)
Isa 22:24 and the issue, all vessels of **small q**, 6996

QUARREL (4)
Lev 26:25 shall **avenge the q** of *my* covenant: 5358+5359
2Ki 5: 7 and see how he **seeketh a q** against me. 579
Mk 6:19 Therefore Herodias **had a q against** him, *1758*
Col 3:13 if any *man* have a **q** against any: *3437*

QUARRIES (2)
Jdg 3:19 he himself turned again from the **q** that 6456
3:26 passed beyond the **q**, and escaped unto 6456

QUARTER (8) [QUARTERS]
Ge 19: 4 and young, all the people from **every q**: 7097
Nu 34: 3 your south **q** shall be from the wilderness 6285
Jos 15: 5 *their* border in the north **q** *was* 6285+3807.1
18:14 the children of Judah: this *was* the west **q**. 6285
18:15 the south **q** *was* from the end of 6285
Isa 47:15 they shall wander every one to his **q**; 5676
56:11 every one for his gain, from his **q**. 7097
Mk 1:45 and they came to him **from every q**. *3836*

QUARTERS (9) [QUARTER]
Ex 13: 7 there be leaven seen with thee in all thy **q**. 1366
Dt 22:12 thee fringes upon the four **q** of thy vesture, 3671
1Ch 9:24 In four **q** were the porters, toward the east, 7307
Jer 49:36 the four winds from the four **q** of heaven, 7098
Eze 38: 6 the house of Togarmah *of* the north **q**, and 3411
Ac 9:32 as Peter passed throughout all *q*, he came NIG
16: 3 because of the Jews which were in those **q**: *5117*
28: 7 In the same **q** were possessions of the chief *5117*
Rev 20: 8 nations which are in the four **q** of the earth, *1137*

QUARTUS (1)
Ro 16:23 of the city saluteth you, and **Q** a brother. *2890*

QUATERNIONS (1)
Ac 12: 4 delivered *him* to four **q** of soldiers to keep *5069*

QUEEN (54) [QUEENS]
1Ki 10: 1 when the **q** of Sheba heard of the fame of 4436
10: 4 when the **q** of Sheba had seen all 4436
10:10 the **q** of Sheba gave to king Solomon. 4436
10:13 king Solomon gave unto the **q** of Sheba all 4436
11:19 his own wife, the sister of Tahpenes the **q**. 1377
15:13 even her he removed from *being* **q**, because 1377
2Ki 10:13 of the king and the children of the **q**. 1377
2Ch 9: 1 when the **q** of Sheba heard of the fame of 4436
9: 3 when the **q** of Sheba had seen the wisdom 4436
9: 9 neither was there any such spice as the **q** of 4436
9:12 king Solomon gave to the **q** of Sheba all 4436
15:16 he removed her from *being* **q**, because 1377
Ne 2: 6 said unto me, (the **q** also sitting by him,) 7694
Est 1: 9 Also Vashti the **q** made a feast for 4436
1:11 To bring Vashti the **q** before the king with 4436
1:12 the **q** Vashti refused to come at the king's 4436
1:15 What shall *we* do unto the **q** Vashti 4436
1:16 Vashti the **q** hath not done wrong to 4436
1:17 For *this* deed of the **q** shall come abroad 4436
1:17 Vashti the **q** to be brought in before him, 4436
1:18 which have heard of the deed of the **q**. 4436
2: 4 let the maiden which pleaseth the king be **q** 4427
2:17 her head, and **made** her **q** instead of Vashti. 4427
2:22 to Mordecai, who told *it* unto Esther the **q**; 4436
4: 4 was the **q** exceedingly grieved; and she sent 4436
5: 2 when the king saw Esther the **q** standing in 4436
5: 3 king unto her, What wilt thou, **q** Esther? 4436
5:12 Esther the **q** did let no *man* come in with 4436
7: 1 Haman came to banquet with Esther the **q**. 4436
7: 2 of wine, What *is* thy petition, **q** Esther? 4436
7: 3 Esther the **q** answered and said, If I have 4436
7: 5 and said unto Esther the **q**, 4436
7: 6 was afraid before the king and the **q**. 4436
7: 7 to make request for his life to Esther the **q**; 4436
7: 8 Will he force the **q** also before me in 4436
8: 1 Haman the Jews' enemy unto Esther the **q**. 4436
8: 7 the king Ahasuerus said unto Esther the **q** 4436
9:12 the king said unto Esther the **q**, The Jews 4436
9:29 Esther the **q**, the daughter of Abihail, and 4436
9:31 and Esther the **q** had enjoined them, 4436
Ps 45: 9 right hand did stand the **q** in gold of Ophir. 7694
Jer 7:18 to make cakes to the **q** of heaven, and 4446
13:18 Say unto the king and to the **q**, 1377
29: 2 the **q**, and the eunuchs, the princes of Judah 1377
44:17 to burn incense unto the **q** of heaven, and 4446
44:18 since we left off to burn incense to the **q** of 4446
44:19 when we burnt incense to the **q** of heaven, 4446
44:25 to burn incense to the **q** of heaven, and 4446
Da 5:10 *Now* the **q**, by reason of the words of 4433
5:10 *and* the **q** spake and said, O king, live for 4433
Mt 12:42 *The* **q** of the south shall rise up in *938*
Lk 11:31 *The* **q** of the south shall rise up in *938*
Ac 8:27 authority under Candace **q** of the Ethiopians, *938*
Rev 18: 7 I sit a **q**, and am no widow, and shall see no *938*

QUEENS (3) [QUEEN]
SS 6: 8 There *are* threescore **q**, and 4436
6: 9 *yea*, the **q** and the concubines, and 4436
Isa 49:23 and their **q** thy nursing mothers: 8282

QUENCH (12) [QUENCHED, UNQUENCHABLE]
2Sa 14: 7 *so* they shall **q** my coal which is left, and 3518
21:17 to battle, that thou **q** not the light of Israel. 3518
Ps 104:11 of the field: the wild asses **q** their thirst. 7665
SS 8: 7 Many waters cannot **q** love, neither can 3518
Isa 1:31 both burn together, and none shall **q** *them*. 3518
42: 3 and the smoking flax shall he not **q**: 3518
Jer 4: 4 burn that none can **q** *it*, because of the evil 3518
21:12 burn that none can **q** *it*, because of the evil 3518
Am 5: 6 and *there be* none to **q** *it* in Beth-el. 3518
Mt 12:20 not break, and smoking flax shall he not **q**, *4570*
Eph 6:16 wherewith ye shall be able to **q** all the fiery *4570*
1Th 5:19 **Q** not the Spirit. *4570*

QUENCHED (17) [QUENCH]
Nu 11: 2 prayed unto the LORD, the fire was **q**. 8257
2Ki 22:17 against this place, and shall not be **q**. 3518
2Ch 34:25 out upon this place, and shall not be **q**. 3518
Ps 118:12 like bees; they are **q** as the fire of thorns: 1846
Isa 34:10 It shall not be **q** night nor day; the smoke 3518

Isa 43:17 not rise: they are extinct, they are **q** as tow. 3518
66:24 shall not die, neither shall their fire be **q**; 3518
Jer 7:20 and it shall burn, and shall not be **q**. 3518
17:27 palaces of Jerusalem, and it shall not be **q**. 3518
Eze 20:47 the flaming flame shall not be **q**, and 3518
20:48 LORD have kindled it: it shall not be **q**. 3518
Mk 9:43 into hell, into the fire that **never** shall **be q**: *762*
9:44 their worm dieth not, and the fire is not **q**. *4570*
9:45 into hell, into the fire that **never** shall **be q**: *762*
9:46 their worm dieth not, and the fire is not **q**. *4570*
9:48 their worm dieth not, and the fire is not **q**. *4570*
Heb 11:34 **Q** the violence of fire, escaped the edge of *4570*

QUESTION (14) [QUESTIONED, QUESTIONING, QUESTIONS]
Mt 22:35 asked *him a* **q**, tempting him, and saying, NIG
Mk 8:11 came forth, and began to **q with** him, *4802*
9:16 he asked the scribes, What **q** ye with them? *4802*
11:29 I will also ask of you one **q**, and *3056*
12:34 And no *man* after that durst ask him *any* **q**. NIG
Lk 20:40 And after that they durst not ask him any **q** NIG
Jn 3:25 Then there arose a **q** between *some* of *2214*
Ac 15: 2 unto the apostles and elders about this **q**. *2213*
18:15 But if it be a **q** of words and names, and *2213*
19:40 For we are in danger to be **called in q** for *1458*
23: 6 resurrection of the dead I am **called in q**. *2919*
24:21 the dead I am **called in q** by you this day. *2919*
1Co 10:25 *that* eat, **asking** no **q** for conscience sake: *350*
10:27 eat, **asking** no **q** for conscience sake. *350*

QUESTIONED (3) [QUESTION]
2Ch 31: 9 Hezekiah **q** with the priests and the Levites 1875
Mk 1:27 insomuch that *they* **q** among themselves, *4802*
Lk 23: 9 Then he **q** *with* him in many words; but *1905*

QUESTIONING (2) [QUESTION]
Mk 9:10 **q** *one* **with** *another* what the rising from *4802*
9:14 about them, and *the* scribes **q** with them. *4802*

QUESTIONS (14) [QUESTION]
1Ki 10: 1 she came to prove him with **hard q**. 2420
10: 3 Solomon told her all her **q**: there was not 1697
2Ch 9: 1 she came to prove Solomon with **hard q** at 2420
9: 2 Solomon told her all her **q**: and there was 1697
Mt 22:46 from that day forth ask him any moe **q**. NIG
Lk 2:46 both hearing them, and asking them **q**. NIG
Ac 23:29 Whom I perceived to be accused of **q** of *2213*
25:19 But had certain **q** against him of their own *2213*
25:20 because I doubted of such *manner of* **q**, *2214*
26: 3 customs and **q** which are among the Jews: *2213*
1Ti 1: 4 and endless genealogies, which minister **q**, *2214*
6: 4 but doting about **q** and strifes of words, *2214*
2Ti 2:23 But foolish and unlearned **q** avoid, *2214*
Tit 3: 9 But avoid foolish **q**, and genealogies, and *2214*

QUICK (10) [QUICKEN, QUICKENED, QUICKENETH, QUICKENING, QUICKLY, QUICKSANDS]
Lev 13:10 *there be* **q raw** flesh in the rising; 2416+4241
13:24 the **q** *flesh* that burneth have a white bright 4241
Nu 16:30 unto them, and they go down **q** into the pit; 2416
Ps 55:15 *and* let them go down **q** *into* hell: 2416
124: 3 they had swallowed us up **q**, when their 2416
Isa 11: 3 shall **make him of q understanding** in 7306
Ac 10:42 was ordained of God *to be* the Judge of **q** *2198*
2Ti 4: 1 who shall judge the **q** and the dead at his *2198*
Heb 4:12 For the word of God *is* **q**, and powerful, *2198*
1Pe 4: 5 account to him that is ready to judge the **q** *2198*

QUICKEN (13) [QUICK]
Ps 71:20 shalt **q** me again, and shalt bring me up 2421
80:18 **q** us, and we will call upon thy name. 2421
119:25 the dust: **q** thou me according to thy word. 2421
119:37 *and* **q** thou me in thy way. 2421
119:40 thy precepts: **q** me in thy righteousness. 2421
119:88 **Q** me after thy lovingkindness; so shall I 2421
119:107 **q** me, O LORD, according unto thy word. 2421
119:149 **q** me according to thy judgment. 2421
119:154 deliver me: **q** me according to thy word. 2421
119:156 **q** me according to thy judgments. 2421
119:159 **q** me, O LORD, according to thy 2421
143:11 **Q** me, O LORD, for thy name's sake: 2421
Ro 8:11 **q** your mortal bodies by his Spirit that *2227*

QUICKENED (7) [QUICK]
Ps 119:50 in my affliction: for thy word hath **q** me. 2421
119:93 thy precepts: for with them thou hast **q** me. 2421
1Co 15:36 *Thou* fool, *that* which thou sowest is not **q**, *2227*
Eph 2: 1 And you *hath he* **q**, who were dead in NIG
2: 5 hath **q** *us* **together with** Christ, (by grace *4806*
Col 2:13 of your flesh, hath he **q together** with him, *4806*
1Pe 3:18 put to death in the flesh, but **q** by the Spirit: *2227*

QUICKENETH (5) [QUICK]
Jn 5:21 and **q** *them;* even so the Son quickeneth *2227*
5:21 *them;* even so the Son **q** whom he will. *2227*
6:63 It is the spirit that **q**; the flesh profiteth *2227*
Ro 4:17 who **q** the dead, and calleth those *things* *2227*
1Ti 6:13 who **q** all *things,* and *before* Christ Jesus, *2227*

QUICKENING (1) [QUICK]
1Co 15:45 the last Adam *was made* a **q** spirit. *2227*

QUICKLY (39) [QUICK]
Ge 18: 6 **Make ready q** three measures of fine meal, 4116
27:20 How *is it that* thou hast found *it so* **q**, my 4116
Ex 32: 8 They have turned aside **q** out of the way 4118
Nu 16:46 go **q** unto the congregation, and make an 4120
Dt 9: 3 thou drive them out, and destroy them **q**, 4118
9:12 Arise, get thee down **q** from hence; 4118
9:12 **q** turned aside out of the way which I 4118
9:16 ye had turned aside **q** out of the way which 4118
11:17 *lest* ye perish **q** from off the good land 4120
28:20 thou be destroyed, and until thou perish **q**; 4118
Jos 2: 5 pursue after them **q**; for ye shall overtake 4118
8:19 the ambush arose **q** out of their place, and 4120
10: 6 come up to us **q**, and save us, and help us: 4120
23:16 ye shall perish **q** from off the good land 4120
Jdg 2:17 they turned **q** out of the way which their 4118
1Sa 20:19 *then* thou shalt go down **q**, and come to 3966
2Sa 17:16 Now therefore send **q**, and tell David, 4120
17:18 they went both of them away **q**, and 4120
17:21 Arise, and **pass q** over the water: 4120
2Ki 1:11 thus hath the king said, Come down **q**. 4120
2Ch 18: 8 and said, **Fetch q** Micaiah the son of Imla. 4116
Ecc 4:12 and a threefold cord is not **q** broken. 4120+871.1
Mt 5:25 Agree with thine adversary **q**, whiles thou *5036*
28: 7 And go **q**, and tell his disciples that he is *5036*
28: 8 And they departed **q** from the sepulchre *5036*
Mk 16: 8 And they went out **q**, and fled from *5036*
Lk 14:21 Go out **q** into the streets and lanes of *5030*
16: 6 thy bill, and sit down **q**, and write fifty. *5030*
Jn 11:29 As soon as she heard *that,* she arose **q**, and *5036*
13:27 said Jesus unto him, That thou doest, do **q**. *5030*
Ac 12: 7 raised him up, saying, Arise up **q**. *1722+5034*
22:18 and get *thee* **q** out of Jerusalem: *1722+5034*
Rev 2: 5 or else I *will* come unto thee **q**, and *5034*
2:16 or else I *will* come unto thee **q**, and *5036*
3:11 Behold, I come **q**: hold *that* fast which thou *5036*
11:14 is past; *and* behold, the third woe cometh **q**. *5036*
22: 7 Behold, I come **q**: blessed *is* he that *5036*
22:12 And behold, I come **q**; and my reward *is* *5036*
22:20 these *things* saith, Surely I come **q**. *5036*

QUICKSANDS (1) [QUICK, SAND]
Ac 27:17 and fearing lest they should fall into the **q**, *4950*

QUIET (31) [QUIETED, QUIETETH, QUIETLY, QUIETNESS]
Jdg 16: 2 were **q** all the night, saying, In the morning, 2790
18: 7 the manner of the Zidonians, **q** and secure; 8252
18:27 unto a people *that were* at **q** and secure: 8252
2Ki 11:20 of the land rejoiced, and the city was **in q**: 8252
1Ch 4:40 the land *was* wide, and **q**, and peaceable; 8252
2Ch 14: 1 In his days the land was **q** ten years. 8252
14: 5 and the kingdom was **q** before him. 8252
20:30 So the realm of Jehoshaphat was **q**: for his 8252
23:21 the city was **q**, after that they had slain 8252
Job 3:13 For now should I have lien *still* and been **q**, 8252
3:26 in safety, neither had I rest, neither was I **q**; 5117
21:23 full strength, *being* wholly at ease and **q**. 7961
Ps 35:20 matters against *them that are* **q** in the land. 7282
107:30 are they glad because they be **q**; so 8367
Pr 1:33 and shall be **q** from fear of evil. 7599
Ecc 9:17 The words of wise *men are* heard in **q**, 5183
Isa 7: 4 say unto him, Take heed, and be **q**; 8252
14: 7 The whole earth is at rest, *and* is **q**: 8252
32:18 in sure dwellings, and in **q** resting places; 7600
33:20 thine eyes shall see Jerusalem a **q** 7600

Jer 30:10 and be **q**, and none shall make *him* afraid. 7599
47: 6 how long *will it be* ere thou be **q**? 8252
47: 7 How can it be **q**, seeing the LORD hath 8252
49:23 *there is* sorrow on the sea; it cannot be **q**. 8252
51:59 his reign. And *this* Seraiah *was* a **q** prince. 4496
Eze 16:42 and I will be **q**, and will be no more angry. 8252
Na 1:12 Though *they be* **q**, and likewise many, 8003
Ac 19:36 ye ought to be **q**, and to do nothing rashly. *2687*
1Th 4:11 And that *ye* study to be **q**, and to do your *2270*
1Ti 2: 2 that we may lead a **q** and peaceable life in *2263*
1Pe 3: 4 *even the ornament* of a meek and **q** spirit, *2272*

QUIETED (2) [QUIET]
Ps 131: 2 Surely I have behaved and **q** myself, as a 1826
Zec 6: 8 have **q** my spirit in the north country. 5117

QUIETETH (1) [QUIET]
Job 37:17 when he **q** the earth by the south *wind?* 8252

QUIETLY (2) [QUIET]
2Sa 3:27 gate to speak with him **q**, 7987+871.1+1886.1
La 3:26 and **q** **wait** for the salvation of the LORD. 1748

QUIETNESS (10) [QUIET]
Jdg 8:28 the country was **in q** forty years in the days 8252
1Ch 22: 9 give peace and **q** unto Israel in his days. 8253
Job 20:20 Surely he shall not feel **q** in his belly, 7961
34:29 When he **giveth q**, who then can make 8252
Pr 17: 1 Better *is* a dry morsel, and **q** therewith, 7962
Ecc 4: 6 Better *is* a handful *with* **q**, than both 5183
Isa 30:15 in **q** and in confidence shall be your 8252
32:17 the effect of righteousness **q** and 8252
Ac 24: 2 Seeing that by thee we enjoy great **q**, and *1515*
2Th 3:12 that with **q** they work, and eat their own *2271*

QUIRINIUS See CYRENIUS

QUIT (6)
Ex 21:19 his staff, then shall he that smote *him* be **q**: 5352
21:28 be eaten; but the owner of the ox *shall be* **q**. 5355
Jos 2:20 we will be **q** of thine oath which thou hast 5355
1Sa 4: 9 Be strong, and **q** yourselves like men, O ye 1961
4: 9 to you: **q** yourselves like men, and fight. 1961
1Co 16:13 fast in the faith, **q** you **like men**, be strong. *407*

QUITE (7)
Ge 31:15 and hath **q** **devoured** also our money. 398+398
Ex 23:24 and **q** **break down** their images. 7665+7665
Nu 17:10 thou shalt **q** **take away** their murmurings 3615
33:52 and **q** **pluck down** all their high places: 8045
2Sa 3:24 sent him away, and he is **q** **gone**? 1980+1980
Job 6:13 in me? and is wisdom driven *q* from me? NIH
Hab 3: 9 Thy bow was **made q naked**, 5783+6181

QUIVER (7)
Ge 27: 3 thy **q** and thy bow, and go out to the field, 8522
Job 39:23 The **q** rattleth against him, the glittering 827
Ps 127: 5 Happy *is* the man that hath his **q** full of 827
Isa 22: 6 Elam bare the **q** with chariots of men *and* 827
49: 2 me a polished shaft; in his **q** hath he hid me; 827
Jer 5:16 Their **q** *is* as an open sepulchre, they *are* all 827
La 3:13 He hath caused the arrows of his **q** to enter 827

QUIVERED (1)
Hab 3:16 my belly trembled; my lips **q** at the voice: 6750

R

RAAMAH (5)
Ge 10: 7 Havilah, and Sabtah, and **R**, and Sabtecha: 7484
10: 7 and the sons of **R**; Sheba, and Dedan. 7484
1Ch 1: 9 Havilah, and Sabta, and **R**, and Sabtecha. 7484
1: 9 And the sons of **R**; Sheba, and Dedan. 7484
Eze 27:22 The merchants of Sheba and **R**, they *were* 7484

RAAMIAH (1)
Ne 7: 7 Azariah, **R**, Nahamani, Mordecai, Bilshan, 7485

RAAMSES (1) [RAMESES]
Ex 1:11 for Pharaoh treasure cities, Pithom and **R**. 7486

RABBAH (13) [RABBATH]
Jos 13:25 of Ammon, unto Aroer that *is* before **R**; 7237
15:60 which *is* Kirjath-jearim, and **R**; 7237
2Sa 11: 1 the children of Ammon, and besieged **R**. 7237
12:26 Joab fought against **R** of the children of 7237
12:27 I have fought against **R**, and have taken 7237
12:29 went to **R**, and fought against it, and 7237
17:27 that Shobi the son of Nahash of **R** of 7237
1Ch 20: 1 of Ammon, and came and besieged **R**. 7237
20: 1 And Joab smote **R**, and destroyed it. 7237
Jer 49: 2 of war to be heard in **R** of the Ammonites; 7237
49: 3 cry, ye daughters of **R**, gird ye with 7237
Eze 25: 5 I will make **R** a stable for camels, and 7237
Am 1:14 I will kindle a fire in the wall of **R**, and 7237

RABBATH (2) [RABBAH]
Dt 3:11 *is* it not in **R** of the children of Ammon? 7237
Eze 21:20 that the sword may come to **R** of 7237

RABBI (8) [RABBONI]
Mt 23: 7 and to be called of men, **R**, Rabbi. *4461*
23: 7 and to be called of men, Rabbi, **R**. *4461*
23: 8 But be not ye called **R**: for one is your *4461*
Jn 1:38 **R**, (which is to say, being interpreted, *4461*
1:49 Nathanael answered and saith unto him, **R**, *4461*
3: 2 to Jesus by night, and said unto him, **R**, *4461*
3:26 they came unto John, and said unto him, **R**, *4461*
6:25 they said unto him, **R**, when camest thou *4461*

RABBIT See HARE

RABBITH (1)
Jos 19:20 And **R**, and Kishion, and Abez, 7245

RABBONI (1) [RABBI]
Jn 20:16 She turned herself, and saith unto him, **R**; *4462*

RAB-MAG (2)
Jer 39: 3 Sarsechim, Rab-saris, Nergal-sharezer, **R**, 7248
39:13 **R**, and all the king of Babylon's princes; 7248

RABSARIS, RAB-SARIS (3) [RABSARIS]
2Ki 18:17 the king of Assyria sent Tartan and **R** and 7249
Jer 39: 3 Samgar-nebo, Sarsechim, **R**, 7249
39:13 **R**, and Nergal-sharezer, Rab-mag, and 7249

RABSHAKEH, RAB-SHAKEH (16) [RAB-SHAKEH]
2Ki 18:17 **R** from Lachish to king Hezekiah with a 7262
18:19 **R** said unto them, Speak ye now to 7262
18:26 Shebna, and Joah, unto **R**, Speak, I pray 7262
18:27 **R** said unto them, Hath my master sent me 7262
18:28 **R** stood and cried with a loud voice in 7262
18:37 clothes rent, and told him the words of **R**. 7262
19: 4 thy God will hear all the words of **R**, 7262
19: 8 So **R** returned, and found the king of 7262
Isa 36: 2 the king of Assyria sent **R** from Lachish to 7262
36: 4 **R** said unto them, Say ye now to Hezekiah, 7262
36:11 said Eliakim and Shebna and Joah unto **R**, 7262
36:12 **R** said, Hath my master sent me to thy 7262
36:13 **R** stood, and cried with a loud voice in 7262
36:22 clothes rent, and told him the words of **R**. 7262
37: 4 LORD thy God will hear the words of **R**, 7262
37: 8 So **R** returned, and found the king of 7262

RACA (1)
Mt 5:22 **R**, shall be in danger of the council: *4469*

RACAL See RACHAL

RACE (4)
Ps 19: 5 *and* rejoiceth as a strong *man* to run a **r**. 734
Ecc 9:11 under the sun, that the **r** *is* not to the swift, 4793
1Co 9:24 Know ye not that they which run in a **r** run *4712*
Heb 12: 1 let us run with patience the **r** that is set before *73*

RACHAB (1) [RAHAB]
Mt 1: 5 And Salmon begat Booz of **R**; and *4477*

RACHAL (1)
1Sa 30:29 to *them* which *were* in **R**, and to *them* 7403

RACHEL (42) [RACHEL'S, RAHEL]
Ge 29: 6 **R** his daughter cometh with the sheep. 7354

R

Ge 29: 9 with them, **R** came with her father's sheep: 7354
29:10 when Jacob saw **R** the daughter of Laban 7354
29:11 Jacob kissed **R**, and lifted up his voice, 7354
29:12 Jacob told **R** that he *was* her father's 7354
29:16 and the name of the younger *was* **R**. 7354
29:17 but **R** was beautiful and well favoured. 7354
29:18 Jacob loved **R**; and said, I will serve thee 7354
29:18 I will serve thee seven years for **R** thy 7354
29:20 Jacob served seven years for **R**; and 7354
29:25 did not I serve with thee for **R**? wherefore 7354
29:28 he gave him **R** his daughter to wife *also.* 7354
29:29 Laban gave to **R** his daughter Bilhah his 7354
29:30 he went in also unto **R**, and he loved also 7354
29:30 he loved also **R** more than Leah, and 7354
29:31 he opened her womb: but **R** *was* barren. 7354
30: 1 when **R** saw that she bare Jacob no 7354
30: 1 bare Jacob no *children,* **R** envied her sister; 7354
30: 2 Jacob's anger was kindled against **R**: and 7354
30: 6 **R** said, God hath judged me, and hath also 7354
30: 8 **R** said, With great wrestlings have I 7354
30:14 **R** said to Leah, Give me, I pray thee, of thy 7354
30:15 **R** said, Therefore he shall lie with thee to 7354
30:22 God remembered **R**, and God hearkened to 7354
30:25 it came to pass, when **R** had born Joseph, 7354
31: 4 Jacob sent and called **R** and Leah to 7354
31:14 **R** and Leah answered and said unto him, 7354
31:19 **R** had stolen the images that *were* her 7354
31:32 For Jacob knew not that **R** had stolen them. 7354
31:34 Now **R** had taken the images, and put them 7354
33: 1 and unto **R**, and unto the two handmaids. 7354
33: 2 and **R** and Joseph hindermost. 7354
33: 7 after came Joseph near and **R**, and 7354
35:16 and **R** travailed, and she had hard labour. 7354
35:19 **R** died, and was buried in the way to 7354
35:24 The sons of **R**; Joseph, and Benjamin: 7354
46:19 The sons of **R** Jacob's wife; Joseph, and 7354
46:22 These *are* the sons of **R**, which were born 7354
46:25 which Laban gave unto **R** his daughter, and 7354
48: 7 **R** died by me in the land of Canaan in 7354
Ru 4:11 woman that is come into thine house like **R** 7354
Mt 2:18 **R** weeping for her children, and would not *4478*

RACHEL'S (5) [RACHEL]
Ge 30: 7 Bilhah **R** maid conceived again, and 7354
31:33 out of Leah's tent, and entered into **R** tent. 7354
35:20 that *is* the pillar of **R** grave unto *this* day. 7354
35:25 the sons of Bilhah, **R** handmaid; Dan, and 7354
1Sa 10: 2 thou shalt find two men by **R** sepulchre in 7354

RADDAI (1)
1Ch 2:14 Nethaneel the fourth, **R** the fifth, 7288

RAFTERS (1)
SS 1:17 of our house *are* cedar, *and* our **r** of fir. 7351

RAGAU (1)
Lk 3:35 which was *the son* of **R**, which was *the son* *4466*

RAGE (18) [RAGED, RAGETH, RAGING]
2Ki 5:12 So he turned and went away in a **r**. 2534
19:27 and thy coming in, and thy **r** against me. 7264
19:28 Because thy **r** against me and thy tumult is 7264
2Ch 16:10 for *he was* in a **r** with him because of this 2197
28: 9 ye have slain them in a **r** *that* reacheth up 2197
Job 39:24 the ground with fierceness and **r**: 7267
40:11 Cast abroad the **r** of thy wrath: and 5678
Ps 2: 1 Why do the heathen **r**, and the people 7283
7: 6 because of the **r** of mine enemies: 5678
Pr 6:34 For jealousy *is* the **r** of a man: therefore 2534
29: 9 whether he **r** or laugh, *there is* no rest. 7264
Isa 37:28 and thy coming in, and thy **r** against me. 7264
37:29 Because thy **r** against me, and thy tumult, 7264
Jer 46: 9 **r**, ye chariots; and let the mighty *men* come 1984
Da 3:13 Nebuchadnezzar in *his* **r** and 7266
Hos 7:16 fall by the sword for the **r** of their tongue: 2195
Na 2: 4 The chariots shall **r** in the streets, they shall 1984
Ac 4:25 Why did the heathen **r**, and the people *5433*

RAGED (1) [RAGE]
Ps 46: 6 The heathen **r**, the kingdoms were moved: 1993

RAGETH (1) [RAGE]
Pr 14:16 from evil: but the fool **r**, and *is* confident. 5674

RAGGED (1)
Isa 2:21 into the tops of the **r rocks**, for fear of 5553

RAGING (5) [RAGE]
Ps 89: 9 Thou rulest the **r** of the sea: when 1348
Pr 20: 1 Wine *is* a mocker, strong drink *is* **r**: and 1993
Jnh 1:15 into the sea: and the sea ceased from her **r**. 2197
Lk 8:24 rebuked the wind and the **r** of the water: *2830*
Jude 1:13 **R** waves of the sea, foaming out their own *66*

RAGS (4)
Pr 23:21 and drowsiness shall clothe *a man* with **r**. 7168
Isa 64: 6 and all our righteousnesses *are* as filthy **r**; 899
Jer 38:11 thence old cast clouts and old **rotten r**, 4418
38:12 **rotten r** under thine armholes under 4418

RAGUEL (1)
Nu 10:29 the son of **R** the Midianite, Moses' father in 7467

RAHAB (10) [RACHAB]
Jos 2: 1 harlot's house, named **R**, and lodged there. 7343
2: 3 the king of Jericho sent unto **R**, saying, 7343
6:17 only **R** the harlot shall live, she and all that 7343
6:23 brought out **R**, and her father, and 7343
6:25 Joshua saved **R** the harlot alive, and her 7343
Ps 87: 4 I will make mention of **R** and Babylon to 7294
89:10 Thou hast broken **R** in pieces, as one that is 7294
Isa 51: 9 *Art* thou not it that hath cut **R**, *and* 7294
Heb 11:31 By faith the harlot **R** perished not with *4460*
Jas 2:25 Likewise also was not **R** the harlot justified *4460*

RAHAM (1)
1Ch 2:44 Shema begat **R**, the father of Jorkoam: and 7357

RAHEL (1) [RACHEL]
Jer 31:15 **R** weeping for her children refused to be 7354

RAIDING See ROVERS

RAIL (1) [RAILED, RAILER, RAILING, RAILINGS]
2Ch 32:17 He wrote also letters to **r** on the LORD 2778

RAILED (3) [RAIL]
1Sa 25:14 to salute our master; and he **r** on them. 5860
Mk 15:29 And they that passed by **r on** him, *987*
Lk 23:39 malefactors which were hanged **r** on him, *987*

RAILER (1) [RAIL]
1Co 5:11 or a **r**, or a drunkard, or an extortioner; *3060*

RAILING (4) [RAIL]
1Pe 3: 9 Not rendering evil for evil, or **r** for railing: *3059*
3: 9 Not rendering evil for evil, or railing for **r**: *3059*
2Pe 2:11 bring not **r** accusation against them before *989*
Jude 1: 9 durst not bring against *him* a **r** accusation, *988*

RAILINGS (1) [RAIL]
1Ti 6: 4 cometh envy, strife, **r**, evil surmisings, *988*

RAIMENT (57)
Ge 24:53 of gold, and **r**, and gave *them* to Rebekah: 899
27:15 Rebekah took goodly **r** of her eldest son 899
27:27 he smelled the smell of his **r**, and 899
28:20 will give me bread to eat, and **r** to put on, 899
41:14 he shaved *himself,* and changed his **r**, and 8071
45:22 all of them he gave each man changes of **r**; 8071
45:22 *pieces* of silver, and five changes of **r**. 8071
Ex 3:22 jewels of silver, and jewels of gold, and **r**: 8071
12:35 jewels of silver, and jewels of gold, and **r**: 8071
21:10 her **r**, and her duty of marriage, shall he not 3682
22: 9 for **r**, *or* for any manner of lost *thing,* which 8008
22:26 If thou at all take thy neighbour's **r** to 8008
22:27 *is* his covering only, it *is* his **r** for his skin: 8071
Lev 11:32 *be* any vessel of wood, or **r**, or skin, or sack, 899
Nu 31:20 purify all *your* **r**, and all that is made of 899
Dt 8: 4 Thy **r** waxed not old upon thee, neither did 8071
10:18 the stranger, in giving him food and **r**. 8071
21:13 she shall put the **r** of her captivity from off 8071
22: 3 so shalt thou do with his **r**; and with all lost 8071
24:13 that he may sleep in his own **r**, and 8008
24:17 nor take a widow's **r** to pledge: 899
Jos 22: 8 and with iron, and with very much **r**: 8008
Jdg 3:16 he did gird it under his **r** upon his right 4055
8:26 purple **r** that *was* on the kings of Midian, 899
Ru 3: 3 put thy **r** upon thee, and get thee down *to* 8071
1Sa 28: 8 put on other **r**, and he went, and two men 899

2Ki 5: 5 *pieces* of gold, and ten changes of **r**. 899
7: 8 **r**, and went and hid *it;* and came again, and 899
2Ch 9:24 **r**, harness, and spices, horses, and mules, 8008
Est 4: 4 she sent **r** to clothe Mordecai, and to take 899
Job 27:16 silver as the dust, and prepare **r** as the clay; 4403
Ps 45:14 brought unto the king in **r of needlework**: 7553
Isa 14:19 *and as* the **r** of those that are slain, 3830
63: 3 my garments, and I will stain all my **r**. 4403
Eze 16:13 thy **r** *was of* fine linen, and silk, and 4403
Zec 3: 4 and *I will* clothe thee with **change of r**. 4254
Mt 3: 4 And the same John had his **r** of camel's *1742*
6:25 life more than meat, and the body than **r**? *1742*
6:28 And why take ye thought for **r**? *1742*
11: 8 A man clothed in soft **r**? behold, they that *2440*
17: 2 as the sun, and his **r** was white as the light. *2440*
27:31 and put his own **r** on him, and led him *2440*
28: 3 was like lightning, and his **r** white as snow: *1742*
Mk 9: 3 And his **r** became shining, exceeding white *2440*
Lk 7:25 A man clothed in soft **r**? Behold, *2440*
9:29 and his **r** *was* white *and* glistering. *2441*
10:30 which **stripped** him **of** his **r**, and *1562*
12:23 than meat, and the body *is more* than **r**. *1742*
23:34 And they parted his **r**, and cast lots. *2440*
Jn 19:24 They parted my **r** among them, and for my *2440*
Ac 18: 6 he shook *his* **r**, and said unto them, *2440*
22:20 and kept the **r** of them that slew him. *2440*
1Ti 6: 8 and **r** let us be therewith content. *4629*
Jas 2: 2 and there come in also a poor *man* in vile **r**; *2066*
Rev 3: 5 the same shall be clothed in white **r**; *2440*
3:18 and white **r**, that thou mayest be clothed, *2440*
4: 4 twenty elders sitting, clothed in white **r**; *2440*

RAIN (102) [RAINBOW, RAINED, RAINY]
Ge 2: 5 for the LORD God had not **caused** it **to r** 4305
7: 4 I will **cause** it **to r** upon the earth forty days 4305
7:12 the **r** was upon the earth forty days and 1653
8: 2 and the **r** from heaven was restrained; 1653
Ex 9:18 I will **cause** it **to r** a very grievous hail, 4305
9:33 and the **r** was not poured upon the earth. 4306
9:34 when Pharaoh saw that the **r** and the hail 4306
16: 4 Behold, I will **r** bread from heaven for you; 4305
Lev 26: 4 I will give you **r** in due season, and the land 1653
Dt 11:11 *and* drinketh water of the **r** of heaven: 4306
11:14 That I will give *you* the **r** of your land in 4306
11:14 the **first r** and the latter rain, that thou 3138
11:14 the first rain and the **latter r**, that thou 4456
11:17 that there be no **r**, and *that* the land yield 4306
28:12 the heaven to give the **r** unto thy land in his 4306
28:24 The LORD shall make the **r** of thy land 4306
32: 2 My doctrine shall drop as the **r**, my speech 4306
32: 2 as the **small r** upon the tender herb, and 8164
1Sa 12:17 and he shall send thunder and **r**; 4306
12:18 the LORD sent thunder and **r** that day: 4306
2Sa 1:21 *be* no dew, neither *let there be* **r** upon you, 4306
23: 4 out of the earth by clear shining after **r**. 4306
1Ki 8:35 there is no **r**, because they have sinned 4306
8:36 give **r** upon thy land, which thou hast given 4306
17: 1 there shall not be dew nor **r** these years, but 4306
17: 7 because there had been no **r** in the land. 1653
17:14 until the day *that* the LORD sendeth **r** 1653
18: 1 unto Ahab; and I will send **r** upon the earth. 4306
18:41 for *there is* a sound of abundance of **r**. 1653
18:44 and get thee down, that the **r** stop thee not. 1653
18:45 and wind, and there was a great **r**. 1653
2Ki 3:17 shall not see wind, neither shall ye see **r**; 1653
2Ch 6:26 there is no **r**, because they have sinned 4306
6:27 send **r** upon thy land, which thou hast given 4306
7:13 If I shut up heaven that there be no **r**, or if I 4306
Ezr 10: 9 because of *this* matter, and for the **great r**. 1653
10:13 *it is* a time of **much r**, and *we are* not able 1653
Job 5:10 Who giveth **r** upon the earth, and 4306
20:23 and shall **r** *it* upon him while he is eating. 4305
28:26 When he made a decree for the **r**, and 4306
29:23 they waited for me as for the **r**; and 4306
29:23 opened their mouth wide *as* for the **latter r**. 4456
36:27 they pour down **r** according to the vapour 4306
37: 6 likewise *to* the small **r**, and *to* the great rain 1653
37: 6 small rain, and *to* the great **r** of his strength. 1653
38:26 To **cause** it **to r** on the earth, *where* no man 4305
38:28 Hath the **r** a father? or who hath begotten 4306
Ps 11: 6 Upon the wicked he shall **r** snares, fire and 4305
68: 9 Thou, O God, didst send a plentiful **r**, 1653
72: 6 He shall come down like **r** upon the mown 4306
84: 6 make it a well; the **r** also filleth the pools. 4175
105:32 He gave them hail *for* **r**, *and* flaming fire in 1653
135: 7 he maketh lightnings for the **r**; he bringeth 4306
147: 8 with clouds, who prepareth **r** for the earth, 4306
Pr 16:15 and his favour *is* as a cloud of the **latter r**. 4456
25:14 false gift *is like* clouds and wind without **r**. 1653
25:23 The north wind driveth away **r**: so *doth* an 1653
26: 1 as **r** in harvest, so honour *is* not seemly for 4306
28: 3 *is like* a sweeping **r** which leaveth no food. 4306
Ecc 11: 3 If the clouds be full *of* **r**, they empty 1653
12: 2 nor the clouds return after the **r**: 1653
SS 2:11 the winter is past, the **r** is over *and* gone; 1653
Isa 4: 6 and for a covert from storm and from **r**. 4306
5: 6 I will also command the clouds that they **r** 4305
5: 6 the clouds that they rain no **r** upon it. 4306
30:23 shall he give the **r** of thy seed, that thou 4306
44:14 planteth an ash, and the **r** doth nourish *it*. 1653
55:10 For as the **r** cometh down, and the snow 1653
Jer 3: 3 and there hath been no **latter r**; 4456
5:24 that giveth **r**, both the former and the latter, 1653
10:13 he maketh lightnings with **r**, and 4306
14: 4 for there was no **r** in the earth, 1653
14:22 vanities of the Gentiles that can **cause r**? 1652
51:16 he maketh lightnings with **r**, and 4306
Eze 1:28 the bow that is in the cloud in the day of **r**, 1653
38:22 I will **r** upon him, and upon his bands, and 4305
38:22 an overflowing **r**, and great hailstones, fire, 1653
Hos 6: 3 he shall come unto us as the **r**, as the latter 1653
6: 3 as the latter *and* **former r** *unto* the earth. 3384
10:12 till he come and **r** righteousness upon you. 3384
Joel 2:23 for he hath given you the **former r** 4175
2:23 he will cause to come down for you the **r**, 1653
2:23 the **former r**, and the latter rain in the first 4175
2:23 and the **latter r** in the first *month*. 4456
Am 4: 7 also I have withholden the **r** from you, 1653
4: 7 I **caused** it **to r** upon one city, and caused it 4305
4: 7 and **caused** it not **to r** upon another city: 4305
Zec 10: 1 Ask ye of the LORD **r** in the time of 4306
10: 1 the LORD rain in the time of the **latter r**; 4456
10: 1 give them showers of **r**, to every one grass 1653
14:17 of hosts, even upon them shall be no **r**. 1653
14:18 that *have* no **r**; there shall be the plague, NIH
Mt 5:45 and **sendeth r** on the just and *on* the unjust. *1026*
7:25 And the **r** descended, and the floods came, *1028*
7:27 And the **r** descended, and the floods came, *1028*
Ac 14:17 and gave us **r** from heaven, and *5205*
28: 2 because of the present **r**, and because of *5205*
Heb 6: 7 For the earth which drinketh *in* the **r** that *5205*
Jas 5: 7 for it, until he receive the early and latter **r**. *5205*
5:17 and he prayed earnestly that it might not **r**: *1026*
5:18 and the heaven gave **r**, and the earth *5205*
Rev 11: 6 it **r** not in the days of their prophecy: *1026+5205*

RAINBOW (2) [BOW, RAIN]
Rev 4: 3 and *there was* a **r** round about the throne, *2463*
10: 1 and a **r** *was* upon *his* head, and his face *was* *2463*

RAINED (9) [RAIN]
Ge 19:24 the LORD **r** upon Sodom and 4305
Ex 9:23 the LORD **r** hail upon the land of Egypt. 4305
Ps 78:24 had **r down** manna upon them to eat, and 4305
78:27 He **r** flesh also upon them as dust, and 4305
Eze 22:24 nor **r upon** in the day of indignation. 1656
Am 4: 7 one piece was **r** upon, and the piece 4305
4: 7 and the piece whereupon it **r** not withered. 4305
Lk 17:29 day that Lot went out of Sodom it **r** fire *1026*
Jas 5:17 it **r** not on the earth *by the space of* three *1026*

RAINY (1) [RAIN]
Pr 27:15 A continual dropping in a **very r** day and 5464

RAISE (59) [RAISED, RAISER, RAISETH, RAISING]
Ge 38: 8 and marry her, and **r up** seed to thy brother. 6965
Ex 23: 1 Thou shalt not **r** a false report: put not thine 5375
Dt 18:15 The LORD thy God will **r up** unto thee a 6965
18:18 I will **r** them **up** a Prophet from among 6965
25: 7 My husband's brother refuseth to **r up** unto 6965
Jos 8:29 **r** thereon a great heap of stones, 6965
Ru 4: 5 to **r up** the name of the dead upon his 6965
4:10 to **r up** the name of the dead upon his 6965
1Sa 2:35 I will **r** me **up** a faithful priest, *that* shall do 6965
2Sa 12:11 I will **r up** evil against thee out of thine 6965
12:17 *went* to him, to **r** him **up** from the earth: 6965
1Ki 14:14 Moreover the LORD shall **r** him **up** a 6965
1Ch 17:11 that I will **r up** thy seed after thee, 6965

R

Job 3: 8 who are ready to r up their mourning. 5782
19:12 r up their way against me, and 5549
30:12 they r up against me the ways of their 5549
Ps 41:10 be merciful unto me, and r me up, 6965
Isa 15: 5 for in the way of Horonaim they shall r up 5782
29: 3 a mount, and I will r forts against thee. 6965
44:26 and I will r up the decayed places thereof: 6965
49: 6 be my servant to r up the tribes of Jacob, 6965
58:12 thou shalt r up the foundations of many 6965
61: 4 they shall r up the former desolations, and 6965
Jer 23: 5 that I will r unto David a righteous Branch, 6965
30: 9 their king, whom I will r up unto them. 6965
50: 9 I will r and cause to come up against 5782
50:32 and fall, and none shall r him up: 6965
51: 1 I will r up against Babylon, and 5782
Eze 23:22 Behold, I will r up thy lovers against thee, 5782
34:29 I will r up for them a plant of renown, and 6965
Hos 6: 2 in the third day he will r us up, and 6965
Joel 3: 7 I will r them out of the place whither ye 5782
Am 5: 2 upon her land; there is none to r her up. 6965
6:14 I will r up against you a nation, 6965
9:11 In that day will I r up the tabernacle of 6965
9:11 I will r up his ruins, and I will build it as in 6965
Mic 5: 5 shall we r against him seven shepherds, 6965
Hab 1: 3 there are that r up strife and contention. 5375
1: 6 For lo, I r up the Chaldeans, that bitter and 6965
Zec 11:16 For lo, I will r up a shepherd in the land, 6965
Mt 3: 9 that God is able of these stones to r up 1453
10: 8 the lepers, r the dead, cast out devils: 1453
22:24 his wife, and r up seed unto his brother. 450
Mk 12:19 his wife, and r up seed unto his brother. 1817
Lk 3: 8 That God is able of these stones to r up 1453
20:28 his wife, and r up seed unto his brother. 1817
Jn 2:19 this temple, and in three days I will r it up. 1453
6:39 but should r it up again at the last day. 450
6:40 and I will r him up at the last day. 450
6:44 draw him: and I will r him up at the last day. 450
6:54 and I will r him up at the last day. 450
Ac 2:30 he would r up Christ to sit on his throne; 450
3:22 A prophet shall the Lord your God r up unto 450
7:37 A prophet shall the Lord your God r up unto 450
26: 8 with you, that God should r the dead? 1453
1Co 6:14 and will also r up us by his own power. 1825
2Co 4:14 the Lord Jesus shall r up us also by Jesus, 1453
Heb 11:19 Accounting that God was able to r him up, 1453
Jas 5:15 save the sick, and the Lord shall r him up; 1453

RAISED (85) [RAISE]

Ex 9:16 in very deed for this cause have I r thee up, 5975
Jos 5: 7 their children, whom he r up in their stead, 6965
7:26 they r over him a great heap of stones unto 6965
Jdg 2:16 Nevertheless the LORD r up judges, 6965
2:18 when the LORD r them up judges, then 6965
3: 9 the LORD r up a deliverer to the children 6965
3:15 the LORD r them up a deliverer, Ehud 6965
2Sa 23: 1 and the man who was r up on high, 6965
1Ki 5:13 And king Solomon r a levy out of all Israel; 5927
9:15 reason of the levy which king Solomon r; 5927
2Ch 32: 5 r it up to the towers, and another wall 5927
33:14 r it up a very great height, and 1361
Ezr 1: 5 with all them whose spirit God had r, 5782
Job 14:12 shall not awake, nor be r out of their sleep. 5782
SS 8: 5 I r thee up under the apple tree: there thy 5782
Isa 14: 9 it hath r up from their thrones all the kings 6965
23:13 they r up the palaces thereof; 6209
41: 2 Who r up the righteous man from the east, 5782
41:25 I have r up one from the north, and he shall 5782
45:13 I have r him up in righteousness, and I will 5782
Jer 6:22 a great nation shall be r from the sides of 5782
25:32 a great whirlwind shall be r up from 5782
29:15 The LORD hath r us up prophets in 6965
50:41 many kings shall be r up from the coasts of 5782
51:11 the LORD hath r up the spirit of the kings 5782
Da 7: 5 it r up itself on one side, and it had three 6966
Am 2:11 I r up of your sons for prophets, and 6965
Zec 2:13 for he is r up out of his holy habitation. 5782
9:13 and r up thy sons, O Zion, against thy sons, 5782
Mt 1:24 Then Joseph being r from sleep did as 1326
11: 5 the dead are r up, and the poor have 1453
16:21 and be killed, and be r again the third day. 1453
17:23 the third day he shall be r again. And they 1453
Lk 1:69 And hath r up a horn of salvation for us in 1453
7:22 are cleansed, the deaf hear, the dead are r, 1453
9:22 scribes, and be slain, and be r the third day. 1453
20:37 Now that the dead are r, even Moses 1453
Jn 12: 1 had been dead, whom he r from the dead. 1453
12: 9 whom he had r from the dead. 1453
12:17 and r him from the dead, bare record. 1453
Ac 2:24 Whom God hath r up, having loosed 450
2:32 This Jesus hath God r up, whereof we all are 450
3:15 of life, whom God hath r from the dead; 1453
3:26 you first God, having r up his Son Jesus, 450
4:10 ye crucified, whom God r from the dead, 1453
5:30 The God of our fathers r up Jesus, 1453
10:40 Him God r up the third day, and 1453
12: 7 and r him up, saying, Arise up quickly. 1453
13:22 he r up unto them David to be their king; 1453
13:23 to his promise r unto Israel a Saviour, 1453
13:30 But God r him from the dead: 1453
13:33 in that he hath r up Jesus again; 450
13:34 And as concerning that he r him up from 450
13:37 whom God r again, saw no corruption. 1453
13:50 and r persecution against Paul and 1892
17:31 all men, in that he hath r him from the dead. 450
Ro 4:24 if we believe on him that r up Jesus our 1453
4:25 and was r again for our justification. 1453
6: 4 that like as Christ was r up from the dead 1453
6: 9 Knowing that Christ being r from the dead 1453
7: 4 even to him who is r from the dead, 1453
8:11 But if the Spirit of him that r up Jesus from 1453
8:11 he that r up Christ from the dead shall also 1453
9:17 for this same purpose have I r thee up, 1825
10: 9 shalt believe in thine heart that God hath r 1453
1Co 6:14 And God hath both r up the Lord, and 1453
15:15 we have testified of God that he r up 1453
15:15 whom he r not up, if so be that the dead 1453
15:16 For if the dead rise not, then is not Christ r: 1453
15:17 And if Christ be not r, your faith is vain; 1453
15:35 some man will say, How are the dead r up? 1453
15:42 sown in corruption; it is r in incorruption: 1453
15:43 It is sown in dishonour; it is r in glory: it is 1453
15:43 it is sown in weakness; it is r in power: 1453
15:44 sown a natural body; it is r a spiritual body. 1453
15:52 and the dead shall be r incorruptible, and 1453
2Co 4:14 Knowing that he which r up the Lord Jesus 1453
Gal 1: 1 God the Father, who r him from the dead;) 1453
Eph 1:20 when he r him from the dead, and set him 1453
2: 6 And hath r us up together, and made us sit 4891
Col 2:12 of God, who hath r him from the dead. 1453
1Th 1:10 whom he r from the dead, even Jesus, 1453
2Ti 2: 8 r from the dead according to my gospel: 1453
Heb 11:35 received their dead r to life again: 386+1537
1Pe 1:21 that r him up from the dead, and gave him 1453

RAISER (1) [RAISE]

Da 11:20 shall stand up in his estate a r of taxes in 5674

RAISETH (8) [RAISE]

1Sa 2: 8 He r up the poor out of the dust, and 6965
Job 41:25 When he r up himself, the mighty are 7613
Ps 107:25 he commandeth, and r the stormy wind, 5975
113: 7 He r up the poor out of the dust, and 6965
145:14 and r up all those that be bowed down. 2210
146: 8 the LORD r them that are bowed down: 2210
Jn 5:21 For as the Father r up the dead, and 1453
2Co 1: 9 in ourselves, but in God which r the dead: 1453

RAISING (2) [RAISE]

Hos 7: 4 who ceaseth from r after he hath kneaded 5782
Ac 24:12 any man, neither r up the people, 1999+4160

RAISINS (4)

1Sa 25:18 parched corn, and an hundred clusters of r, 6778
30:12 of a cake of figs, and two clusters of r: 6778
2Sa 16: 1 an hundred bunches of r, and an hundred 6778
1Ch 12:40 cakes of figs, and bunches of r, and wine, 6778

RAKEM (1)

1Ch 7:16 and his sons were Ulam and R. 7552

RAKKATH (1)

Jos 19:35 Zer, and Hammath, R, and Chinnereth, 7557

RAKKON (1)

Jos 19:46 Me-jarkon, and R, with the border before 7542

RAM (97) [RAM'S, RAMS, RAMS']

Ge 15: 9 and a r of three years old, and a turtle-dove, 352
22:13 behold behind him a r caught in a thicket by 352

Ge 22:13 Abraham went and took the **r**, and 352
Ex 29:15 Thou shalt also take one **r**; and Aaron and 352
29:15 shall put their hands upon the head of the **r**. 352
29:16 thou shalt slay the **r**, and thou shalt take his 352
29:17 thou shalt cut the **r** in pieces, and wash 352
29:18 thou shalt burn the whole **r** upon the altar: 352
29:19 thou shalt take the other **r**; and Aaron and 352
29:19 shall put their hands upon the head of the **r**. 352
29:20 shalt thou kill the **r**, and take of his blood, 352
29:22 Also thou shalt take of the **r** the fat and 352
29:22 right shoulder; for it *is* a **r** of consecration: 352
29:26 thou shalt take the breast of the **r** of Aaron's 352
29:27 is heaved up, of the **r** of the consecration, 352
29:31 And thou shalt take the **r** of the consecration, 352
29:32 and his sons shall eat the flesh of the **r**, 352
Lev 5:15 a **r** without blemish out of the flocks, 352
5:16 for him with the **r** of the trespass offering, 352
5:18 he shall bring a **r** without blemish out of 352
6: 6 a **r** without blemish out of the flock, with thy 352
8:18 he brought the **r** for the burnt offering: and 352
8:18 sons laid their hands upon the head of the **r**. 352
8:20 he cut the **r** into pieces; and Moses burnt 352
8:21 and Moses burnt the whole **r** upon the altar: 352
8:22 he brought the other **r**, the ram of 352
8:22 brought the other ram, the **r** of consecration: 352
8:22 sons laid their hands upon the head of the **r**. 352
8:29 *for* of the **r** of consecration it was Moses' 352
9: 2 and a **r** for a burnt offering, without blemish, 352
9: 4 Also a bullock and a **r** for peace offerings, 352
9:18 and the **r** *for* a sacrifice of peace offerings, 352
9:19 the fat of the bullock and of the **r**, the rump, 352
16: 3 a sin offering, and a **r** for a burnt offering. 352
16: 5 a sin offering, and one **r** for a burnt offering. 352
19:21 *even* a **r** for a trespass offering. 352
19:22 **r** of the trespass offering before the LORD 352
Nu 5: 8 beside the **r** of the atonement, whereby an 352
6:14 one **r** without blemish for peace offerings, 352
6:17 he shall offer the **r** *for* a sacrifice of peace 352
6:19 priest shall take the sodden shoulder of the **r**, 352
7:15 One young bullock, one **r**, one lamb of 352
7:21 One young bullock, one **r**, one lamb of 352
7:27 One young bullock, one **r**, one lamb of 352
7:33 One young bullock, one **r**, one lamb of 352
7:39 One young bullock, one **r**, one lamb of 352
7:45 One young bullock, one **r**, one lamb of 352
7:51 One young bullock, one **r**, one lamb of 352
7:57 One young bullock, one **r**, one lamb of 352
7:63 One young bullock, one **r**, one lamb of 352
7:69 One young bullock, one **r**, one lamb of 352
7:75 One young bullock, one **r**, one lamb of 352
7:81 One young bullock, one **r**, one lamb of 352
15: 6 Or for a **r**, thou shalt prepare *for* a meat 352
15:11 or for one **r**, or for a lamb, or a kid. 352
23: 2 offered on *every* altar a bullock and a **r**. 352
23: 4 offered upon *every* altar a bullock and a **r**. 352
23:14 and offered a bullock and a **r** on *every* altar. 352
23:30 and offered a bullock and a **r** on *every* altar. 352
28:11 two young bullocks, and one **r**, seven lambs 352
28:12 a meat offering, mingled with oil, for one **r**; 352
28:14 the third *part* of a hin unto a **r**, and a fourth 352
28:19 and one **r**, and seven lambs of the first year: 352
28:20 for a bullock, and two tenth deals for a **r**; 352
28:27 two young bullocks, one **r**, seven lambs of 352
28:28 unto one bullock, two tenth deals unto one **r**, 352
29: 2 one **r**, *and* seven lambs of the first year 352
29: 3 for a bullock, *and* two tenth deals for a **r**, 352
29: 8 one **r**, *and* seven lambs of the first year; 352
29: 9 to a bullock, *and* two tenth deals to one **r**, 352
29:14 two tenth deals to each **r** of the two rams, 352
29:36 one bullock, one **r**, seven lambs of the first 352
29:37 for the **r**, and for the lambs, *shall be* 352
Ru 4:19 Hezron begat **R**, and Ram begat 7410
4:19 begat Ram, and **R** begat Amminadab, 7410
1Ch 2: 9 unto him; Jerahmeel, and **R**, and Chelubai. 7410
2:10 **R** begat Amminadab; and 7410
2:25 **R** the firstborn, and Bunah, and Oren, and 7410
2:27 the sons of **R** the firstborn of Jerahmeel 7410
Ezr 10:19 *they offered* a **r** of the flock for their 352
Job 32: 2 of Barachel the Buzite, of the kindred of **R**: 7410
Eze 43:23 and a **r** out of the flock without blemish. 352
43:25 and a **r** out of the flock, without blemish. 352
45:24 an ephah for a **r**, and a hin of oil for an 352
46: 4 without blemish, and a **r** without blemish. 352
46: 5 the meat offering *shall be* an ephah for a **r**, 352
46: 6 without blemish, and six lambs, and a **r**: 352
46: 7 an ephah for a **r**, and for the lambs according 352
46:11 an ephah to a **r**, and to the lambs as he is 352
Da 8: 3 there stood before the river a **r** which had 352
8: 4 I saw the **r** pushing westward, 352
8: 6 he came to the **r** that had two horns, which I 352
8: 7 I saw him come close unto the **r**, and he was 352
8: 7 and smote the **r**, and brake his two horns: 352
8: 7 there was no power in the **r** to stand before 352
8: 7 there was none that could deliver the **r** out of 352
8:20 The **r** which thou sawest having two horns 352

RAM'S (1) [RAM]
Jos 6: 5 *that* when *they* make a long blast with the **r** 3104

RAMA (1) [RAMAH]
Mt 2:18 In **R** was there a voice heard, lamentation, *4471*

RAMAH (36) [RAMA, RAMATHITE]
Jos 18:25 Gibeon, and **R**, and Beeroth, 7414
19:29 *then* the coast turneth *to* **R**, and to 7414
19:36 And Adamah, and **R**, and Hazor, 7414
Jdg 4: 5 under the palm tree of Deborah between **R** 7414
19:13 places to lodge all night, in Gibeah, or in **R**. 7414
1Sa 1:19 and returned, and came to their house to **R**: 7414
2:11 Elkanah went to **R** to his house. And 7414
7:17 his return *was* to **R**; for there *was* his 7414
8: 4 and came to Samuel unto **R**, 7414
15:34 Samuel went to **R**; and Saul went up to his 7414
16:13 So Samuel rose up, and went to **R**. 7414
19:18 came to Samuel to **R**, and told him all that 7414
19:19 Behold, David *is* at Naioth in **R**. 7414
19:22 went he also to **R**, and came to a great well 7414
19:22 *one* said, Behold, *they be* at Naioth in **R**. 7414
19:23 he went thither to Naioth in **R**: and 7414
19:23 prophesied, until he came to Naioth in **R**. 7414
20: 1 David fled from Naioth in **R**, and came 7414
22: 6 Saul abode in Gibeah under a tree in **R**, 7414
25: 1 and buried him in his house at **R**. 7414
28: 3 and buried him in **R**, even in his own city. 7414
1Ki 15:17 built **R**, that *he* might not suffer *any* to go 7414
15:21 heard *thereof,* that he left off building of **R**, 7414
15:22 they took away the stones of **R**, and 7414
2Ki 8:29 which the Syrians had given him at **R**, 7414
2Ch 16: 1 built **R**, to the intent that *he* might let none 7414
16: 5 heard *it,* that he left off building of **R**, 7414
16: 6 they carried away the stones of **R**, and 7414
22: 6 of the wounds which were given him at **R**, 7414
Ezr 2:26 The children of **R** and Gaba, six hundred 7414
Ne 7:30 The men of **R** and Geba, six hundred 7414
11:33 Hazor, **R**, Gittaim, 7414
Isa 10:29 at Geba; **R** is afraid; Gibeah of Saul is fled. 7414
Jer 31:15 A voice was heard in **R**, lamentation, *and* 7414
40: 1 captain of the guard had let him go from **R**, 7414
Hos 5: 8 the cornet in Gibeah, *and* the trumpet in **R**: 7414

RAMATH (1)
Jos 19: 8 these cities to Baalath-beer, **R** of the south. 7414

RAMATH MIZPAH See RAMATH-MIZPEH

RAMATHAIM See RAMATHAIM-ZOPHIM

RAMATHAIM-ZOPHIM (1) [ZOPHIM]
1Sa 1: 1 Now there was a certain man of **R**, 7436

RAMATHITE (1) [RAMAH]
1Ch 27:27 over the vineyards *was* Shimei the **R**: over 7435

RAMATH-LEHI (1) [LEHI]
Jdg 15:17 out of his hand, and called that place **R**. 7437

RAMATH-MIZPEH (1) [MIZPEH]
Jos 13:26 from Heshbon unto **R**, and Betonim; and 7434

RAMESES (4) [RAAMSES]
Ge 47:11 in the best of the land, in the land of **R**, 7486
Ex 12:37 the children of Israel journeyed from **R** to 7486
Nu 33: 3 they departed from **R** in the first month, 7486
33: 5 the children of Israel removed from **R**, and 7486

RAMIAH (1)
Ezr 10:25 **R**, and Jeziah, and Malchiah, and Miamin, 7422

RAMOTH (8) [RAMOTH-GILEAD]
Dt 4:43 **R** in Gilead, of the Gadites; and Golan in 7216

Jos 20: 8 **R** in Gilead out of the tribe of Gad, and 7216
21:38 tribe of Gad, **R** in Gilead with her suburbs, 7433
1Sa 30:27 to *them* which *were* in south **R**, and to *them* 7418
1Ki 22: 3 Know ye that **R** in Gilead *is* ours, and 7433
1Ch 6:73 **R** with her suburbs, and Anem with her 7216
6:80 **R** in Gilead with her suburbs, and 7216
Ezr 10:29 and Adaiah, Jashub, and Sheal, and **R**. 7433

RAMOTH-GILEAD (19) [GILEAD, RAMOTH]

1Ki 4:13 The son of Geber, in **R**; to him *pertained* 1568
22: 4 Wilt thou go with me to battle *to* **R**? 7433
22: 6 Shall I go against **R** to battle, or shall I 7433
22:12 saying, Go up *to* **R**, and prosper: 7433
22:15 shall we go against **R** to battle, or shall we 7433
22:20 that he may go up and fall at **R**? 7433
22:29 the king of Judah went up *to* **R**. 7433
2Ki 8:28 the war against Hazael king of Syria in **R**; 7433
9: 1 this box of oil in thine hand, and go *to* **R**: 7433
9: 4 *even* the young man the prophet, went *to* **R**. 7433
9:14 (Now Joram had kept **R**, he and all Israel, 7433
2Ch 18: 2 and persuaded him to go up *with him* to **R**. 7433
18: 3 king of Judah, Wilt thou go with me *to* **R**? 7433
18: 5 Shall we go to **R** to battle, or shall I 7433
18:11 saying, Go up *to* **R**, and prosper: 7433
18:14 shall we go to **R** to battle, or shall I 7433
18:19 of Israel, that he may go up and fall at **R**? 7433
18:28 the king of Judah went up to **R**. 7433
22: 5 to war against Hazael king of Syria at **R**: 7433

RAMPART (2)

La 2: 8 therefore he made the **r** and the wall to 2426
Na 3: 8 whose **r** *was* the sea, *and* her wall *was* from 2426

RAMS (68) [RAM]

Ge 31:10 the **r** which leaped upon the cattle *were* 6260
31:12 all the **r** which leap upon the cattle *are* 6260
31:38 and the **r** of thy flock have I not eaten. 352
32:14 he goats, two hundred ewes, and twenty **r**, 352
Ex 29: 1 young bullock, and two **r** without blemish, 352
29: 3 in the basket, with the bullock and the two **r**. 352
35:23 goats' *hair*, and red skins of **r**, and 352
Lev 8: 2 and two **r**, and a basket of unleavened bread; 352
23:18 first year, and one young bullock, and two **r**: 352
Nu 7:17 two oxen, five **r**, five he goats, five lambs of 352
7:23 two oxen, five **r**, five he goats, five lambs of 352
7:29 two oxen, five **r**, five he goats, five lambs of 352
7:35 two oxen, five **r**, five he goats, five lambs of 352
7:41 two oxen, five **r**, five he goats, five lambs of 352
7:47 two oxen, five **r**, five he goats, five lambs of 352
7:53 two oxen, five **r**, five he goats, five lambs of 352
7:59 two oxen, five **r**, five he goats, five lambs of 352
7:65 two oxen, five **r**, five he goats, five lambs of 352
7:71 two oxen, five **r**, five he goats, five lambs of 352
7:77 two oxen, five **r**, five he goats, five lambs of 352
7:83 two oxen, five **r**, five he goats, five lambs of 352
7:87 the **r** twelve, the lambs of the first year 352
7:88 *were* twenty and four bullocks, the **r** sixty, 352
23: 1 and prepare me here seven oxen and seven **r**. 352
23:29 prepare me here seven bullocks and seven **r**. 352
29:13 two **r**, *and* fourteen lambs of the first year; 352
29:14 two tenth deals to each ram of the two **r**, 352
29:17 two **r**, fourteen lambs of the first year 352
29:18 for the **r**, and for the lambs, *shall be* 352
29:20 And on the third day eleven bullocks, two **r**, 352
29:21 for the **r**, and for the lambs, *shall be* 352
29:23 two **r**, *and* fourteen lambs of the first year 352
29:24 for the **r**, and for the lambs, *shall be* 352
29:26 two **r**, *and* fourteen lambs of the first year 352
29:27 for the **r**, and for the lambs, *shall be* 352
29:29 two **r**, *and* fourteen lambs of the first year 352
29:30 for the **r**, and for the lambs, *shall be* 352
29:32 two **r**, *and* fourteen lambs of the first year 352
29:33 for the **r**, and for the lambs, *shall be* 352
Dt 32:14 and **r** of the breed of Bashan, and goats, 352
1Sa 15:22 *and* to hearken than the fat of **r**. 352
2Ki 3: 4 and an hundred thousand **r**, *with* the wool. 352
1Ch 15:26 that they offered seven bullocks and seven **r**. 352
29:21 a thousand **r**, *and* a thousand lambs, 352
2Ch 13: 9 himself with a young bullock and seven **r**, 352
17:11 seven thousand and seven hundred **r**, and 352
29:21 seven **r**, and seven lambs, and seven he 352
29:22 likewise, when they had killed the **r**, they 352
29:32 an hundred **r**, *and* two hundred lambs: 352
Ezr 6: 9 both young bullocks, and **r**, and lambs, 1798
6:17 two hundred **r**, four hundred lambs; 1798
7:17 **r**, lambs, with their meat offerings and 1798
8:35 ninety and six **r**, seventy and seven lambs, 352
Job 42: 8 unto you now seven bullocks and seven **r**, 352
Ps 66:15 sacrifices of fatlings, with the incense of **r**; 352
114: 4 The mountains skipped like **r**, *and* the little 352
114: 6 Ye mountains, *that* ye skipped like **r**; *and* 352
Isa 1:11 I am full *of* the burnt offerings of **r**, and 352
34: 6 and goats, with the fat of the kidneys of **r**: 352
60: 7 the **r** of Nebajoth shall minister unto thee: 352
Jer 51:40 lambs to the slaughter, like **r** with he goats. 352
Eze 4: 2 and set *battering* **r** against it round about. 3733
21:22 to appoint *battering* **r** against the gates, 3733
27:21 with thee in lambs, and **r**, and goats: 352
34:17 and cattle, between the **r** and the he goats. 352
39:18 of **r**, of lambs, and of goats, of bullocks, 352
45:23 seven **r** without blemish daily the seven 352
Mic 6: 7 the LORD be pleased with thousands of **r**, 352

RAMS' (9) [RAM]

Ex 25: 5 **r** skins dyed red, and badgers' skins, and 352
26:14 thou shalt make a covering for the tent *of* **r** 352
35: 7 **r** skins dyed red, and badgers' skins, and 352
36:19 he made a covering for the tent *of* **r** skins 352
39:34 the covering of **r** skins dyed red, and 352
Jos 6: 4 before the ark seven trumpets of **r horns**: 3104
6: 6 of **r horns** before the ark of the LORD. 3104
6: 8 of **r horns** passed on before the LORD, 3104
6:13 **r horns** before the ark of the LORD went 3104

RAN (61) [RUN]

Ge 18: 2 when he saw *them*, he **r** to meet them from 7323
18: 7 Abraham **r** unto the herd, and fetcht a calf 7323
24:17 the servant **r** to meet her, and said, Let me, 7323
24:20 **r** again unto the well to draw *water*, and 7323
24:28 the damsel **r**, and told *them of* her mother's 7323
24:29 Laban **r** out unto the man, unto the well. 7323
29:12 and she **r** and told her father. 7323
29:13 that he **r** to meet him, and embraced him, 7323
33: 4 Esau **r** to meet him, and embraced him, 7323
Ex 9:23 hail, and the fire **r along** upon the ground; 1980
Nu 11:27 there **r** a young man, and told Moses, and 7323
16:47 and **r** into the midst of the congregation; 7323
Jos 7:22 sent messengers, and they **r** unto the tent; 7323
8:19 they **r** as soon as *he* had stretched out his 7323
Jdg 7:21 and all the host **r**, and cried, and fled. 7323
9:21 Jotham **r away**, and fled, and went to Beer, 5127
9:44 the two *other* companies **r** upon all 6584
13:10 **r**, and shewed her husband, and said unto 7323
1Sa 3: 5 he **r** unto Eli, and said, Here *am* I; for thou 7323
4:12 there **r** a man of Benjamin out of the army, 7323
10:23 they **r** and fetched him thence: and when he 7323
17:22 **r** *into* the army, and came and saluted his 7323
17:48 **r** *toward* the army to meet the Philistine. 7323
17:51 Therefore David **r**, and stood upon 7323
20:36 *And* as the lad **r**, he shot an arrow beyond 7323
2Sa 18:21 And Cushi bowed himself unto Joab, and **r**. 7323
18:23 Ahimaaz **r** *by* the way of the plain, and 7323
1Ki 2:39 that two of the servants of Shimei **r away** 1272
18:35 the water **r** round about the altar; and 1980
18:46 **r** before Ahab to the entrance of Jezreel. 7323
19:20 **r** after Elijah, and said, Let me, I pray thee, 7323
22:35 the blood **r out** of the wound into the midst 3332
2Ch 32: 4 the brook that **r** through the midst of 7857
Ps 77: 2 my sore **r** in the night, and ceased not: 5064
105:41 they **r** in the dry *places like* a river. 1980
133: 2 that **r down** upon the beard, *even* Aaron's 3381
Jer 23:21 I have not sent *these* prophets, yet they **r**: 7323
Eze 1:14 the living creatures **r** and returned as 7519
47: 2 behold, there **r out** waters on the right side. 6379
Da 8: 6 and **r** unto him in the fury of his power. 7323
Mt 8:32 the whole herd of swine **r violently** down a *3729*
27:48 And straightway one of them **r**, and took a *5143*
Mk 5: 6 Jesus afar off, he **r** and worshipped him, *5143*
5:13 the herd **r violently** down a steep place into *3729*
6:33 and **r** afoot thither out of all cities, and *4936*
6:55 And **r through** that whole region round *4063*
15:36 And one **r** and filled a spunge *full* of *5143*
Lk 8:33 the herd **r violently** down a steep place into *3729*
15:20 and **r**, and fell on his neck, and kissed him. *5143*
19: 4 And he **r before**, *4390*
24:12 Then arose Peter, and **r** unto the sepulchre; *5143*
Jn 20: 4 So they **r** both together: and the other *5143*
Ac 3:11 all the people **r together** unto them in *4936*

Ac 7:57 their ears, and r upon him with one accord, *3729*
8:30 And Philip r *thither* **to** *him,* and heard him *4370*
12:14 but r **in**, and told how Peter stood before *1532*
14:14 and r **in** among the people, crying out, *1530*
21:30 and the people r **together**: *1096+4890*
21:32 and centurions, and r **down** unto them: *2701*
27:41 two seas met, they r the ship **aground**; *2027*
Jude 1:11 r **greedily after** the error of Balaam for *1632*

RANG (2) [RING]
1Sa 4: 5 *with* a great shout, so that the earth r **again**. 1949
1Ki 1:45 thence rejoicing, so that the city r **again**. 1949

RANGE (1) [RANGES, RANGING]
Job 39: 8 The r of the mountains *is* his pasture, and 3491

RANGES (4) [RANGE]
Lev 11:35 *whether it be* oven, or r **for pots**, they shall 3600
2Ki 11: 8 he that cometh within the r, let him be 7713
11:15 unto them, Have her forth without the r: 7713
2Ch 23:14 and said unto them, Have her forth of the r: 7713

RANGING (1) [RANGE]
Pr 28:15 *As* a roaring lion, and a r bear; *so is* a 8264

RANK (6) [RANKS]
Ge 41: 5 corn came up upon one stalk, r and good. 1277
41: 7 the seven thin ears devoured the seven r 1277
Nu 2:16 And they shall set forth in the **second** r. 8145
2:24 And they shall go forward in the **third** r. 7992
1Ch 12:33 of war, fifty thousand, which could **keep** r: 5737
12:38 All these men of war, that could keep r, 4634

RANKS (4) [RANK]
1Ki 7: 4 and light *was* against light *in* three r. 6471
7: 5 and light *was* against light *in* three r. 6471
Joel 2: 7 on his ways, and they shall not break their r: 734
Mk 6:40 And they sat down **in** r, by hundreds, *4237+4237*

RANSACKED See RIFLED

RANSOM (13) [RANSOMED]
Ex 21:30 he shall give *for* the r of his life whatsoever 6306
30:12 shall they give every man a r for his soul 3724
Job 33:24 going down *to* the pit: I have found a r. 3724
36:18 then a great r cannot deliver thee. 3724
Ps 49: 7 *his* brother, nor give to God a r for him: 3724
Pr 6:35 He will not regard any r; neither will he 3724
13: 8 The r of a man's life *are* his riches: but 3724
21:18 The wicked *shall be* a r for the righteous, 3724
Isa 43: 3 I gave Egypt *for* thy r, Ethiopia and 3724
Hos 13:14 I will r them from the power of the grave; 6299
Mt 20:28 and to give his life a r for many. *3083*
Mk 10:45 and to give his life a r for many. *3083*
1Ti 2: 6 Who gave himself a r for all, to be testified *487*

RANSOMED (3) [RANSOM]
Isa 35:10 the r of the LORD shall return, and 6299
51:10 of the sea a way for the r to pass over? 1350
Jer 31:11 r him from the hand of *him that was* 1350

RAPHA (2) [BETH-RAPHA]
1Ch 8: 2 Nohah the fourth, and **R** the fifth. 7498
8:37 **R** *was* his son, Eleasah his son, Azel his 7498

RAPHU (1)
Nu 13: 9 Of the tribe of Benjamin, Palti the son of **R**. 7505

RARE (1)
Da 2:11 *it is* a r thing that the king requireth, and 3358

RASE (2)
Ps 137: 7 **R** *it,* rase *it, even* to the foundation thereof. 6168
137: 7 Rase *it,* r *it, even* to the foundation thereof. 6168

RASH (2) [RASHLY]
Ecc 5: 2 Be not r with thy mouth, and let not thine 926
Isa 32: 4 The heart also of the r shall understand 4116

RASHLY (1) [RASH]
Ac 19:36 ye ought to be quiet, and to do nothing r. *4312*

RASOR (7)
Nu 6: 5 there shall no r come upon his head. 8593
Jdg 13: 5 a son; and no r shall come on his head: 4177
16:17 There hath not come a r upon mine head; 4177
1Sa 1:11 and there shall no r come upon his head. 4177
Ps 52: 2 like a sharp r, working deceitfully. 8593
Isa 7:20 shall the Lord shave with a r that is hired, 8593
Eze 5: 1 take thee a barber's r, and cause *it* to pass 8593

RAT See MOUSE

RATE (5)
Ex 16: 4 go out and gather a **certain** r every day, 1697
1Ki 10:25 spices, horses, and mules, a r year by year. 1697
2Ki 25:30 a daily r for every day, all the days of his 1697
2Ch 8:13 Even after a **certain** r every day, offering 1697
9:24 spices, horses, and mules, a r year by year. 1697

RATHER (62) See Index

RATS See MICE

RATTLETH (1) [RATTLING]
Job 39:23 The quiver r against him, the glittering 7439

RATTLING (1) [RATTLETH]
Na 3: 2 the noise of the r of the wheels, and of 7494

RAVEN (6) [RAVENS]
Ge 8: 7 he sent forth a r, which went forth to and 6158
Lev 11:15 Every r after his kind; 6158
Dt 14:14 And every r after his kind, 6158
Job 38:41 Who provideth for the r his food? when his 6158
SS 5:11 his locks *are* bushy, *and* black as a r. 6158
Isa 34:11 the owl also and the r shall dwell in it: 6158

RAVENING (5) [RAVENOUS]
Ps 22:13 *with* their mouths, *as* a r and a roaring lion. 2963
Eze 22:25 midst thereof, like a roaring lion r the prey; 2963
22:27 the midst thereof *are* like wolves r the prey, 2963
Mt 7:15 but inwardly they are r wolves. *727*
Lk 11:39 but your inward part is full of r and *724*

RAVENOUS (3) [RAVENING]
Isa 35: 9 nor *any* r beast shall go up thereon, 6530
46:11 Calling a r **bird** from the east, the man that 5861
Eze 39: 4 I will give thee unto the r birds of every 5861

RAVENS (5) [RAVEN]
1Ki 17: 4 I have commanded the r to feed thee there. 6158
17: 6 the r brought him bread and flesh in 6158
Ps 147: 9 his food, *and* to the young r which cry. 6158
Pr 30:17 the r of the valley shall pick it out, and 6158
Lk 12:24 Consider the r: for they neither sow nor *2876*

RAVIN (2)
Ge 49:27 Benjamin shall r *as* a wolf: in the morning 2963
Na 2:12 his holes *with* prey, and his dens *with* r. 2966

RAVINES See BROOKS

RAVISHED (5) [RAVISHT]
SS 4: 9 Thou hast r my **heart**, my sister, 3823
4: 9 thou hast r my **heart** with one of thine 3823
Isa 13:16 houses shall be spoiled, and their wives r. 7901
La 5:11 They r the women in Zion, *and* the maids 6031
Zec 14: 2 and the houses rifled, and the women r; 7901

RAVISHT (2) [RAVISHED]
Pr 5:19 and be thou r always with her love. 7686
5:20 be r with a strange *woman,* and 7686

RAW (7)
Ex 12: 9 Eat not of it r, nor sodden at all with water, 4995
Lev 13:10 *there be* **quick** r flesh in the rising; 2416+4241
13:14 when r flesh appeareth in him, he shall be 2416
13:15 the priest shall see the r flesh, 2416
13:15 *for* the r flesh *is* unclean: it *is* a leprosy. 2416
13:16 Or if the r flesh turn again, and be changed 2416
1Sa 2:15 he will not have sodden flesh of thee, but r. 2416

RAZOR See RASOR

REACH (15) [REACHED, REACHETH, REACHING]
Ge 11: 4 and a tower, whose top *may* r unto heaven; NIH
Ex 26:28 midst of the boards shall r from end to end. 1272
28:42 the loins even unto the thighs they shall r: 1961
Lev 26: 5 your threshing shall r **unto** the vintage, 5381
26: 5 the vintage shall r **unto** the sowing time: 5381
Nu 34:11 shall r unto the side of the sea of 4229
35: 4 *shall* r from the wall of the city and NIH

Job 20: 6 the heavens, and his head r unto the clouds; 5060
Isa 8: 8 and go over, he shall r *even* to the neck; 5060
30:28 shall r **to** the midst of the neck, 5704
Jer 48:32 over the sea, they r *even* to the sea of Jazer: 5060
Zec 14: 5 for the valley of the mountains shall r unto 5060
Jn 20:27 **R** hither thy finger, and behold my hands; *5342*
20:27 and r *hither* thy hand, and thrust *it* into my *5342*
2Co 10:13 to us, a measure to r even unto you. *2185*

REACHED (8) [REACH]
Ge 28:12 on the earth, and the top of it r to heaven: 5060
Jos 19:11 r to Dabbasheth, and reached to the river 6293
19:11 and r to the river that *is* before Jokneam; 6293
Ru 2:14 he r her parched *corn,* and she did eat, and 6642
Da 4:11 the height thereof r unto heaven, and 4291
4:20 whose height r unto the heaven, and 4291
2Co 10:14 *our measure,* as though we r not unto you: *2185*
Rev 18: 5 For her sins have r unto heaven, and God *190*

REACHETH (14) [REACH]
Nu 21:30 even unto Nophah, which *r* unto Medeba. NIH
Jos 19:22 the coast r to Tabor, and Shahazimah, and 6293
19:26 r to Carmel westward, and 6293
19:27 r to Zebulun, and to the valley of 6293
19:34 r to Zebulun on the south side, and 6293
19:34 r to Asher on the west side, and to Judah 6293
2Ch 28: 9 ye have slain them in a rage *that* r up unto 5060
Ps 36: 5 *and* thy faithfulness *r* unto the clouds. NIH
108: 4 the heavens: and thy truth *r* unto the clouds. NIH
Pr 31:20 yea, she r **forth** her hands to the needy. 7971
Jer 4:10 whereas the sword r unto the soul). 5060
4:18 *it is* bitter, because it r unto thine heart. 5060
51: 9 for her judgment r unto heaven, and 5060
Da 4:22 r unto heaven, and thy dominion to the end 4291

REACHING (4) [REACH]
2Ch 3:11 *was* five cubits, r to the wall of the house: 5060
3:11 r to the wing of the other cherub. 5060
3:12 *was* five cubits, r to the wall of the house: 5060
Php 3:13 r **forth** unto those *things which are* before, *1901*

READ (70) [READEST, READETH, READING]
Ex 24: 7 and r in the audience of the people: 7121
Dt 17:19 he shall r therein all the days of his life: 7121
31:11 thou shalt r this law before all Israel in 7121
Jos 8:34 afterward he r all the words of the law, 7121
8:35 which Joshua r not before all 7121
2Ki 5: 7 when the king of Israel had r the letter, 7121
19:14 of the hand of the messengers, and r it: 7121
22: 8 gave the book to Shaphan, and he r it. 7121
22:10 a book. And Shaphan r it before the king. 7121
22:16 of the book which the king of Judah hath r: 7121
23: 2 he r in their ears all the words of the book 7121
2Ch 34:18 a book. And Shaphan r it before the king. 7121
34:24 which they have r before the king of Judah: 7121
34:30 he r in their ears all the words of the book 7121
Ezr 4:18 sent unto us *hath been* plainly r before me. 7123
4:23 Artaxerxes' letter *was* r before Rehum, 7123
Ne 8: 3 he r therein before the street that *was* 7121
8: 8 So they r in the book in the law of God 7121
8:18 last day, he r in the book of the law of God. 7121
9: 3 r in the book of the law of the LORD their 7121
13: 1 On that day they r in the book of Moses in 7121
Est 6: 1 and they were r before the king. 7121
Isa 29:11 that is learned, saying, **R** this, I pray thee: 7121
29:12 is not learned, saying, **R** this, I pray thee: 7121
34:16 ye out of the book of the LORD, and r: 7121
37:14 from the hand of the messengers, and r it: 7121
Jer 29:29 Zephaniah the priest r this letter in the ears 7121
36: 6 Therefore go thou, and r in the roll, 7121
36: 6 also thou shalt r them in the ears of all 7121
36:10 r Baruch in the book the words of Jeremiah 7121
36:13 when Baruch r the book in the ears of 7121
36:14 thou hast r in the ears of the people, 7121
36:15 Sit down now, and r it in our ears. 7121
36:15 it in our ears. So Baruch r *it* in their ears. 7121
36:21 Jehudi r it in the ears of the king, and in 7121
36:23 *that* when Jehudi had r three or four leaves, 7121
51:61 and shalt see, and shalt r all these words; 7121
Da 5: 7 Whosoever shall r this writing, and 7123
5: 8 wise *men:* but they could not r the writing, 7123
5:15 that they should r this writing, and 7123
5:16 now if thou canst r the writing, and 7123
5:17 yet I will r the writing unto the king, and 7123

Mt 12: 3 unto them, Have ye not r what David did, *314*
12: 5 Or have ye not r in the law, how that on *314*
19: 4 and said unto them, Have ye not r, *314*
21:16 have ye never r, Out of the mouth of babes *314*
21:42 unto them, Did ye never r in the scriptures, *314*
22:31 have ye not r that which was spoken unto *314*
Mk 2:25 Have ye never r what David did, when he *314*
12:10 And have ye not r this scripture; The stone *314*
12:26 have ye not r in the book of Moses, how in *314*
Lk 4:16 on the sabbath day, and stood up for to r. *314*
6: 3 Have ye not r so much as this, what David *314*
Jn 19:20 This title then r many of the Jews: for *314*
Ac 8:28 sitting in his chariot r Esaias the prophet. *314*
8:30 to *him,* and heard him r the prophet Esaias, *314*
8:32 The place of the scripture which he r was *314*
13:27 *yet* the voices of the prophets which are r *314*
15:21 being r in the synagogues every sabbath day. *314*
15:31 *Which* when they had r, they rejoiced for *314*
23:34 And when the governor had r *the letter,* he *314*
2Co 1:13 unto you, than what you r or acknowledge; *314*
3: 2 in our hearts, known and r of all men: *314*
3:15 But *even* unto this day, when Moses is r, *314*
Eph 3: 4 Whereby, when ye r, ye may understand my *314*
Col 4:16 And when *this* epistle is r amongst you, *314*
4:16 cause that it be r also in the church of *314*
4:16 that ye likewise r the *epistle* from Laodicea. *314*
1Th 5:27 *this* epistle be r unto all the holy brethren. *314*
Rev 5: 4 was found worthy to open and to r the book, *314*

READEST (2) [READ]
Lk 10:26 What is written in the law? how r thou? *314*
Ac 8:30 and said, Understandest thou what thou r? *314*

READETH (4) [READ]
Hab 2: 2 plain upon tables, that he may run that r it. 7121
Mt 24:15 holy place, (whoso r, let him understand:) *314*
Mk 13:14 it ought not, (let him that r understand,) *314*
Rev 1: 3 Blessed *is* he that r, and they that hear *314*

READINESS (3) [READY]
Ac 17:11 they received the word with all r **of mind,** *4288*
2Co 8:11 the doing *of it;* that as *there was* a r *4288*
10: 6 And having in a r to revenge all *2092*

READING (6) [READ]
Ne 8: 8 and caused *them* to understand the r. 4744
Jer 36: 8 r in the book the words of the LORD *in* 7121
51:63 when thou hast made an end of r this book, 7121
Ac 13:15 And after the r of the law and the prophets *320*
2Co 3:14 untaken away in the r of the old testament; *320*
1Ti 4:13 Till I come, give attendance to r, *320*

READY (100) [ALREADY, READINESS]
Ge 18: 6 **Make** r **quickly** three measures of fine 4116
43:16 *these* men home, and slay, and **make** r; 3559
43:25 they **made** r the present against Joseph 3559
46:29 Joseph **made** r his chariot, and went up to 631
Ex 14: 6 he **made** r his chariot, and took his people 631
17: 4 this people? they be almost r to stone me. NIH
19:11 be r against the third day: for the third day 3559
19:15 unto the people, Be r against the third day: 3559
34: 2 be r in the morning, and come up in 3559
Nu 32:17 we ourselves will go r armed before 2363
Dt 1:41 of war, ye were r to go up into the hill. 1951
26: 5 A Syrian r **to perish** *was* my father, and 6
Jos 8: 4 not very far from the city, but be ye all r: 3559
Jdg 6:19 **made** r a kid, and unleavened *cakes of* an 6213
13:15 until we shall have **made** r a kid for thee. 6213
1Sa 25:18 five sheep r **dressed**, and five measures of 6213
2Sa 15:15 thy servants *are r to do* whatsoever my lord NIH
18:22 my son, seeing that thou hast no tidings r? 4672
1Ki 6: 7 was built *of* stone **made** r *before it was* 8003
2Ki 9:21 Joram said, **Make** r. And his chariot was 631
9:21 his chariot was **made** r. And Joram king of 631
1Ch 12:23 of the bands that were r **armed** to the war, 2502
12:24 and eight hundred, r **armed** to the war. 2502
28: 2 our God, and had **made** r for the building: 3559
2Ch 17:18 fourscore thousand r **prepared for** the war. 2502
35:14 afterward they **made** r for themselves, and 3559
Ezr 7: 6 he *was* a r scribe in the law of Moses, 4106
Ne 9:17 thou *art* a God r **to pardon**, gracious and 5547
Est 3:14 that *they* should be r against that day. 6264
8:13 that the Jews should be r against that day to 6264
Job 3: 8 who are r to raise up their mourning. 6264

Job 12: 5 He that is **r** to slip with *his* feet *is as* a lamp 3559
15:23 that the day of darkness is **r** at his hand. 3559
15:24 against him, as a king **r** to the battle. 6264
15:28 which are **r to become** heaps. 6257
17: 1 my days are extinct, the graves *are* **r** for me. NIH
18:12 and destruction *shall be* **r** at his side. 3559
29:13 The blessing of him that was **r to perish** came 6
32:19 no vent; it is **r to burst** like new bottles. 1234
Ps 7:12 he hath bent his bow, and **made** it **r**. 3559
11: 2 they **make r** their arrow upon the string, 3559
21:12 *when* thou shalt **make r** *thine arrows* upon 3559
38:17 For I *am* **r** to halt, and my sorrow *is* 3559
45: 1 *the* king: my tongue *is* the pen of a **r** writer. 4106
86: 5 For thou, Lord, *art* good, and **r to forgive**; 5546
88:15 **r to die** from *my* youth *up: while* I suffer 1478
Pr 24:11 unto death, and *those that are* **r** to be slain; 4131
31: 6 Give strong drink unto him that is **r to perish**, 6
Ecc 5: 1 *be* more **r** to hear, than to give the sacrifice 7138
Isa 27:13 they shall come which were **r** to perish in NIH
30:13 iniquity shall be to you as a breach **r** to fall, NIH
32: 4 the tongue of the stammerers shall be **r** to 4116
38:20 The LORD *was* **r** to save me: therefore NIH
41: 7 the anvil, saying, It *is* **r** for the sodering: 2896
51:13 of the oppressor, as if he were **r** to destroy? 3559
Eze 7:14 blown the trumpet, even to **make** all **r**; 3559
Da 3:15 Now if ye be **r** that at what time ye hear 6263
Hos 7: 6 For they have **made r** their heart like an 7126
Mt 22: 4 *my* fatlings *are* killed, and all *things are* **r**: *2092*
22: 8 The wedding is **r**, but they which were *2092*
24:44 Therefore be ye also **r**: for in such an hour *2092*
25:10 they *that were* **r** went in with him to *2092*
26:19 and they **made r** the passover. *2090*
Mk 14:15 *and* prepared: there **make r** for us. *2090*
14:16 unto them: and they **made r** the passover. *2090*
14:38 The spirit truly *is* **r**, but the flesh *is* weak. *4289*
Lk 1:17 to **make r** a people prepared for the Lord. *2090*
7: 2 was dear unto him, was sick, and **r** to die. *3195*
9:52 of the Samaritans, to **make r** for him. *2090*
12:40 Be ye therefore **r** also: for the Son of man *2092*
14:17 Come; for all *things* are now **r**. *2092*
17: 8 **Make r** wherewith I may sup, and *2090*
22:12 large upper room furnished: there **make r**. *2090*
22:13 unto them: and they **made r** the passover. *2090*
22:33 Lord, I am **r** to go with thee, both into *2092*
Jn 7: 6 is not yet come: but your time is alway **r**. *2092*
Ac 10:10 but while they **made r**, he fell into a trance, *3903*
20: 7 unto them, **r to** depart on the morrow; *3195*
21:13 for I am **r** not to be bound only, but also to *2093*
23:15 we, or ever he come near, are **r** to kill him. *2092*
23:21 and now are they **r**, looking for a promise *2092*
23:23 **Make r** two hundred soldiers to go to *2090*
Ro 1:15 I am **r** to preach the gospel to you that are *4289*
2Co 8:19 same Lord, and *declaration of* your **r mind**: *4288*
9: 2 that Achaia was **r** a year ago; *3903*
9: 3 in this behalf; that, as I said, ye may be **r**: *3903*
9: 5 that the same might be **r**, as *a matter of* *2092*
10:16 line of *things* **made r to** our **hand**. *1519+2092*
12:14 the third *time* I am **r** to come to you; *2093*
1Ti 6:18 **r to distribute**, willing to communicate; *2130*
2Ti 4: 6 For I am **now r** to be offered, and the time *2235*
Tit 3: 1 to be **r** to every good work, *2092*
Heb 8:13 and waxeth old *is* **r** to vanish away. *1451*
1Pe 1: 5 salvation **r** to be revealed in the last time. *2092*
3:15 *be* **r** always to *give* an answer to every *man* *2092*
4: 5 Who shall give account to him that is **r** to *2093*
5: 2 not for filthy lucre, but **of a r mind**; *4290*
Rev 3: 2 the *things* which remain, that are **r to** die: *3195*
12: 4 the woman which was **r to** be delivered, *3195*
19: 7 is come, and his wife hath **made** herself **r**. *2090*

REAIA (1)
1Ch 5: 5 Micah his son, **R** his son, Baal his son, 7211

REAIAH (3)
1Ch 4: 2 **R** the son of Shobal begat Jahath; and 7211
Ezr 2:47 the children of Gahar, the children of **R**, 7211
Ne 7:50 The children of **R**, the children of Rezin, 7211

REALIZE See WIST

REALLY See SURETY; THROUGHLY

REALM (7)
2Ch 20:30 So the **r** of Jehoshaphat was quiet: for his 4438
Ezr 7:13 and *of* his priests and Levites, in my **r**, 4437
7:23 for why should there be wrath against the **r** 4437
Da 1:20 *and* astrologers that *were* in all his **r**. 4438
6: 3 king thought to set him over the whole **r**. 4437
9: 1 which was made king over the **r** of 4438
11: 2 he shall stir up all against the **r** of Grecia. 4438

REAP (32) [REAPED, REAPER, REAPERS, REAPEST, REAPETH, REAPING]
Lev 19: 9 when ye **r** the harvest of your land, 7114
19: 9 thou shalt not **wholly r** the corners 3615+3807.1
23:10 shall **r** the harvest thereof, then ye shall 7114
23:22 when ye **r** the harvest of your land, 7114
25: 5 own accord of thy harvest thou shalt not **r**, 7114
25:11 neither **r** that which groweth of itself in it, 7114
Ru 2: 9 *Let* thine eyes *be* on the field that they do **r**, 7114
1Sa 8:12 to **r** his harvest, and to make his 7114
2Ki 19:29 **r**, and plant vineyards, and eat the fruits 7114
Job 4: 8 and sow wickedness, **r** the same. 7114
24: 6 They **r** *every one* his corn in the field: and 7114
Ps 126: 5 They that sow in tears shall **r** in joy. 7114
Pr 22: 8 He that soweth iniquity shall **r** vanity: and 7114
Ecc 11: 4 and he that regardeth the clouds shall not **r**. 7114
Isa 37:30 **r**, and plant vineyards, and eat the fruit 7114
Jer 12:13 They have sown wheat, but shall **r** thorns: 7114
Hos 8: 7 the wind, and they shall **r** the whirlwind: 7114
10:12 to yourselves in righteousness, **r** in mercy; 7114
Mic 6:15 Thou shalt sow, but thou shalt not **r**; 7114
Mt 6:26 for they sow not, neither do they **r**, *2325*
25:26 thou knewest that I **r** where I sowed not, *2325*
Lk 12:24 for they neither sow nor **r**; which neither *2325*
Jn 4:38 I sent you to **r** *that* whereon ye bestowed no *2325*
1Co 9:11 great *thing* if we shall **r** your carnal *things?* *2325*
2Co 9: 6 soweth sparingly shall **r** also sparingly; *2325*
9: 6 he which soweth bountifully shall **r** also *2325*
Gal 6: 7 a man soweth, that shall he also **r**. *2325*
6: 8 to his flesh shall of the flesh **r** corruption; *2325*
6: 8 Spirit shall of the Spirit **r** life everlasting. *2325*
6: 9 for in due season we shall **r**, if we faint not. *2325*
Rev 14:15 sat on the cloud, Thrust in thy sickle, and **r**: *2325*
14:15 for the time is come for thee to **r**; for *2325*

REAPED (4) [REAP]
Hos 10:13 plowed wickedness, ye have **r** iniquity; 7114
Jas 5: 4 the hire of the labourers which have **r** *down* *270*
5: 4 the cries of them which have **r** are entered *2325*
Rev 14:16 his sickle on the earth; and the earth was **r**. *2325*

REAPER (1) [REAP]
Am 9:13 that the plowman shall overtake the **r**, and 7114

REAPERS (9) [REAP]
Ru 2: 3 came, and gleaned in the field after the **r**: 7114
2: 4 said unto the **r**, The LORD *be* with you. 7114
2: 5 unto his servant that was set over the **r**, 7114
2: 6 the servant that was set over the **r** answered 7114
2: 7 and gather after the **r** amongst the sheaves: 7114
2:14 she sat beside the **r**: and he reached her 7114
2Ki 4:18 a day, that he went out to his father to the **r**. 7114
Mt 13:30 in the time of harvest I will say to the **r**, *2327*
13:39 end of the world; and the **r** are *the* angels. *2327*

REAPEST (2) [REAP]
Lev 23:22 of the corners of thy field when thou **r**, 7114
Lk 19:21 not down, and **r** that thou didst not sow. *2325*

REAPETH (4) [REAP]
Isa 17: 5 the corn, and **r** the ears *with* his arm; 7114
Jn 4:36 And he that **r** receiveth wages, and *2325*
4:36 and he that **r** may rejoice together. *2325*
4:37 saying true, One soweth, and another **r**. *2325*

REAPING (3) [REAP]
1Sa 6:13 *they of* Beth-shemesh *were* **r** *their* wheat 7114
Mt 25:24 **r** where thou hast not sown, and *2325*
Lk 19:22 I laid not down, and **r** that I did not sow: *2325*

REAR (4) [REARED]
Ex 26:30 thou shalt **r up** the tabernacle according to 6965
Lev 26: 1 neither **r** you **up** a standing image, 6965
2Sa 24:18 **r** an altar unto the LORD in 6965
Jn 2:20 and wilt thou **r** it **up** in three days? *1453*

REAR GUARD See REREWARD

R

REARED (10) [REAR]
Ex 40:17 of the month, *that* the tabernacle was **r up**. 6965
40:18 Moses **r up** the tabernacle, and fastened his 6965
40:18 put in the bars thereof, and **r up** his pillars. 6965
40:33 he **r up** the court round about 6965
Nu 9:15 on the day that the tabernacle was **r up**, 6965
2Sa 18:18 had taken and **r up** for himself a pillar, 5324
1Ki 16:32 he **r up** an altar for Baal *in* the house of 6965
2Ki 21: 3 he **r up** altars for Baal, and made a grove, 6965
2Ch 3:17 he **r up** the pillars before the temple, 6965
33: 3 he **r up** altars for Baalim, and made groves, 6965

REASON (71) [REASONABLE, REASONED, REASONING, REASONS, UNREASONABLE]
Ge 41:31 land **by r of** that famine following; 4480+6440
47:13 *all* the land of Canaan fainted **by r of** 4480+6440
Ex 2:23 the children of Israel sighed **by r of** 4480
2:23 their cry came up unto God **by r of** 4480
3: 7 have heard their cry **by r of** their 4480+6440
8:24 the land was corrupted **by r of** 4480+6440
Nu 9:10 of your posterity shall be unclean **by r of** 3807.1
18: 8 unto thee have I given them **by r of** 3807.1
18:32 ye shall bear no sin **by r of** it, when ye 5921
Dt 5: 5 for ye were afraid **by r of** the fire, 4480+6440
23:10 that is not clean **by r of** *uncleanness* that 4480
Jos 9:13 our shoes are become old **by r of** the very 4480
Jdg 2:18 of their groanings **by r of** them that 4480
1Sa 12: 7 that I may **r** with you before the LORD of 8199
1Ki 9:15 this *is* the **r** of the levy which king 1697
14: 4 for his eyes were set **by r of** his age. 4480
2Ch 5:14 stand to minister **by r of** the cloud: 4480+6440
20:15 Be not afraid nor dismayed **by r of** 4480+6440
21:15 until thy bowels fall out **by r of** 4480
21:19 his bowels fell out **by r of** his sickness: 5973
Job 6:16 Which are blackish **by r of** the ice, *and* 4480
9:14 *and* choose out my words *to* **r** with him? NIH
13: 3 to the Almighty, and I desire to **r** with God. 3198
15: 3 Should he **r** *with* unprofitable talk? or 3198
17: 7 Mine eye also is dim **by r of** sorrow, and 4480
31:23 and **by r of** his highness I could not endure. 4480
35: 9 **By r of** the multitude of oppressions they 4480
35: 9 they cry out **by r of** the arm of the mighty. 4480
37:19 order *our speech* **by r of** darkness. 4480+6440
41:25 **by r of** breakings they purify themselves. 4480
Ps 38: 8 I have roared **by r of** the disquietness of my 4480
44:16 blasphemeth; **by r of** the enemy and 4480+6440
78:65 like a mighty *man* that shouteth **by r of** 4480
88: 9 Mine eye mourneth **by r of** affliction: 4480
90:10 if **by r of** strength *they be* fourscore years, 871.1
102: 5 **By r of** the voice of my groaning my bones 4480
Pr 20: 4 The sluggard will not plow **by r of** 4480
26:16 conceit than seven *men* that can render a **r**. 2940
Ecc 7:25 the **r** *of things,* and to know the wickedness 2808
Isa 1:18 Come now, and let us **r together**, saith 3198
49:19 shall even now be too narrow **by r of** 4480
Eze 19:10 and full of branches **by r of** many waters. 4480
21:12 terrors **by r of** the sword shall be upon my 413
26:10 **By r of** the abundance of his horses their 4480
27:12 Tarshish *was* thy merchant **by r of** 4480
27:16 Syria *was* thy merchant **by r of** 4480
28:17 thou hast corrupted thy wisdom **by r of** thy 5921
Da 4:36 At the same time my **r** returned unto me; 4486
5:10 by **r** of the words of the king and his lords, 6903
8:12 the daily *sacrifice* **by r of** transgression, 871.1
Jnh 2: 2 I cried **by r of** mine affliction unto 4480
Mic 2:12 they shall make great noise **by r of** 4480
Mt 16: 8 why **r** ye among yourselves, because *1260*
Mk 2: 8 Why **r** ye these *things* in your hearts? *1260*
8:17 Why **r** ye, because ye have no bread? *1260*
Lk 5:21 the scribes and the Pharisees began to **r**, *1260*
5:22 said unto them, What **r** ye in your hearts? *1260*
Jn 6:18 And the sea arose by **r** of a great wind that NIG
12:11 **Because** that **by r of** him many of the Jews *1223*
Ac 6: 2 It is not **r** that we should leave the word of *701*
18:14 **r** would that I should bear with you: *2596+3056*
Ro 8:20 **by r of** him who hath subjected *the same,* *1223*
2Co 3:10 this respect, **by r of** the glory that excelleth. *1752*
Heb 5: 3 And **by r hereof** he ought, as for *1223+3778*
5:14 *even* those who **by r of** use have their *1223*
7:23 suffered to continue **by r of** death: *1223+3588*
1Pe 3:15 a **r** of the hope that is in you with meekness *3056*
2Pe 2: 2 **by r of** whom the way of truth shall be evil *1223*
Rev 8:13 to the inhabiters of the earth **by r of** *1537*
9: 2 the air were darkened **by r of** the smoke of *1537*
18:19 had ships in the sea **by r of** her costliness: *1537*

REASONABLE (1) [REASON]
Ro 12: 1 unto God, *which is* your **r** service. *3050*

REASONED (12) [REASON]
Mt 16: 7 And they **r** among themselves, saying, *It is* *1260*
21:25 And they **r** with themselves, saying, If we *1260*
Mk 2: 8 his spirit that they so **r** within themselves, *1260*
8:16 And they **r** among themselves, saying, *It is* *1260*
11:31 And they **r** with themselves, saying, If we *3049*
Lk 20: 5 And they **r** with themselves, saying, If we *4817*
20:14 they **r** among themselves, saying, This is *1260*
24:15 that while they communed *together* and **r**, *4802*
Ac 17: 2 three sabbath days **r** with them out of *1256*
18: 4 And he **r** in the synagogue every sabbath, *1256*
18:19 into the synagogue, and **r** with the Jews. *1256*
24:25 And as he **r** of righteousness, temperance, *1256*

REASONING (5) [REASON]
Job 13: 6 Hear now my **r**, and hearken to 8433
Mk 2: 6 scribes sitting there, and **r** in their hearts, *1260*
12:28 and having heard them **r together**, and *4802*
Lk 9:46 Then there arose a **r** among them, which of *1261*
Ac 28:29 and had great **r** among themselves. *4803*

REASONS (2) [REASON]
Job 32:11 I gave ear to your **r**, whilst you searched 8394
Isa 41:21 bring forth your strong *r*, saith the King of NIH

REBA (2)
Nu 31: 8 and Rekem, and Zur, and Hur, and **R**, 7254
Jos 13:21 Evi, and Rekem, and Zur, and Hur, and **R**, 7254

REBECCA (1) [REBEKAH]
Ro 9:10 but when **R** also had conceived by one, *4479*

REBEKAH (28) [REBECCA, REBEKAH'S]
Ge 22:23 Bethuel begat **R**: these eight Milcah did 7259
24:15 that behold, **R** came out, who was born to 7259
24:29 **R** had a brother, and his name *was* Laban: 7259
24:30 when he heard the words of **R** his sister, 7259
24:45 **R** came forth with her pitcher on her 7259
24:51 Behold, **R** *is* before thee, take *her,* and go, 7259
24:53 of gold, and raiment, and gave *them* to **R**: 7259
24:58 they called **R**, and said unto her, Wilt thou 7259
24:59 they sent away **R** their sister, and her nurse, 7259
24:60 they blessed **R**, and said unto her, Thou *art* 7259
24:61 **R** arose, and her damsels, and they rode 7259
24:61 and the servant took **R**, and went his way. 7259
24:64 **R** lift up her eyes, and when she saw Isaac, 7259
24:67 and took **R**, and she became his wife; 7259
25:20 Isaac was forty years old when he took **R** to 7259
25:21 intreated of him, and **R** his wife conceived. 7259
25:28 did eat of *his* venison: but **R** loved Jacob. 7259
26: 7 the men of the place should kill me for **R**; 7259
26: 8 behold, Isaac *was* sporting with **R** his wife. 7259
26:35 were a grief of mind unto Isaac and to **R**. 7259
27: 5 **R** heard when Isaac spake to Esau his son. 7259
27: 6 **R** spake unto Jacob her son, saying, 7259
27:11 Jacob said to **R** his mother, Behold, 7259
27:15 **R** took goodly raiment of her eldest son 7259
27:42 words of Esau her elder son were told to **R**: 7259
27:46 **R** said to Isaac, I am weary of my life 7259
28: 5 the brother of **R**, Jacob's and 7259
49:31 there they buried Isaac and **R** his wife; and 7259

REBEKAH'S (2) [REBEKAH]
Ge 29:12 her father's brother, and that he *was* **R** son: 7259
35: 8 Deborah **R** nurse died, and she was buried 7259

REBEL (14) [REBELLED, REBELLEST, REBELLION, REBELLIOUS, REBELS]
Nu 14: 9 Only **r** not ye against the LORD, 4775
Jos 1:18 Whosoever *he be* that doth **r** against thy 4784
22:16 that ye might **r** *this* day against 4775
22:18 *seeing* ye **r** to day against the LORD, 4775
22:19 **r** not against the LORD, nor rebel against 4775
22:19 not against the LORD, nor **r** against us, 4775
22:29 God forbid that we should **r** against 4775
1Sa 12:14 not **r** against the commandment of 4784
12:15 **r** against the commandment of the LORD, 4784
Ne 2:19 thing that ye do? will ye **r** against the king? 4775
6: 6 saith *it, that* thou and the Jews think to **r**: 4775

Job 24:13 They are of those that r **against** the light; 4775
Isa 1:20 if ye refuse and r, ye shall be devoured 4784
Hos 7:14 for corn and wine, *and* they r against me. 5493

REBELLED (34) [REBEL]
Ge 14: 4 and *in* the thirteenth year they r. 4775
Nu 20:24 ye r against my word at the water of 4784
27:14 For ye r **against** my commandment in 4784
Dt 1:26 r against the commandment of the LORD 4784
1:43 r against the commandment of the LORD, 4784
9:23 you r against the commandment of 4784
1Ki 12:19 So Israel r against the house of David unto 6586
2Ki 1: 1 Moab r against Israel after the death of 6586
3: 5 that the king of Moab r against the king of 6586
3: 7 The king of Moab hath r against me: 6586
18: 7 he r against the king of Assyria, and 4775
24: 1 then he turned and r against him. 4775
24:20 that Zedekiah r against the king of 4775
2Ch 10:19 Israel r against the house of David unto this 6586
13: 6 is risen up, and hath r against his lord. 4775
36:13 he also r against king Nebuchadnezzar, 4775
Ne 9:26 r against thee, and cast thy law behind their 4775
Ps 5:10 for they have r against thee. 4784
105:28 it dark; and they r not against his word. 4784
107:11 Because they r against the words of God, 4784
Isa 1: 2 up children, and they have r against me. 6586
63:10 they r, and vexed his holy Spirit: therefore 4784
Jer 52: 3 that Zedekiah r against the king of 4775
La 1:18 for I have r against his commandment: 4784
1:20 within me; for I have **grievously** r: 4784+4784
3:42 We have transgressed and have r: thou hast 4784
Eze 2: 3 to a rebellious nation that hath r against 4775
17:15 he r against him in sending his 4775
20: 8 they r against me, and would not hearken 4784
20:13 the house of Israel r against me in 4784
20:21 Notwithstanding the children r against me: 4784
Da 9: 5 and have done wickedly, and have r, 4775
9: 9 though we have r against him; 4775
Hos 13:16 for she hath r against her God: 4784

REBELLEST (2) [REBEL]
2Ki 18:20 dost thou trust, that thou r against me? 4775
Isa 36: 5 dost thou trust, that thou r against me? 4775

REBELLION (9) [REBEL]
Dt 31:27 For I know thy r, and thy stiff neck: 4805
Jos 22:22 if *it be* in r, or if in transgression against 4777
1Sa 15:23 For r *is as* the sin of witchcraft, and 4805
Ezr 4:19 *that* r and sedition *have been* made therein. 4776
Ne 9:17 in their r appointed a captain to return to 4805
Job 34:37 For he addeth r unto his sin, he clappeth *his* 6588
Pr 17:11 An evil *man* seeketh only r: therefore 4805
Jer 28:16 thou hast taught r against the LORD. 5627
29:32 he hath taught r against the LORD. 5627

REBELLIOUS (36) [REBEL]
Dt 9: 7 ye have been r against the LORD. 4784
9:24 You have been r against the LORD from 4784
21:18 If a man have a stubborn and r son, 4784
21:20 This our son *is* stubborn and r, he will not 4784
31:27 ye have been r against the LORD; 4784
1Sa 20:30 Thou son of the perverse r *woman,* do not I 4780
Ezr 4:12 building the r and the bad city, and have set 4779
4:15 know that this city *is* a r city, and 4779
Ps 66: 7 let not the r exalt themselves. Selah. 5637
68: 6 with chains: but the r dwell *in* a dry *land.* 5637
68:18 yea, *for* the r also, that the LORD God 5637
78: 8 their fathers, a stubborn and r generation; 4784
Isa 1:23 Thy princes *are* r, and companions of 5637
30: 1 Woe to the r children, saith the LORD, 5637
30: 9 That this *is* a r people, lying children, 4805
50: 5 and I was not r, neither turned away back. 4784
65: 2 out mine hands all the day unto a r people, 5637
Jer 4:17 because she hath been r against me, 4784
5:23 this people hath a revolting and a r heart; 4784
Eze 2: 3 to a r nation that hath rebelled against me: 4775
2: 5 they will forbear, (for they *are* a r house,) 4805
2: 6 at their looks, though they *be* a r house. 4805
2: 7 they will forbear: for they *are* most r. 4805
2: 8 Be not thou r like *that* rebellious house: 4805
2: 8 Be not thou rebellious like *that* r house: 4805
3: 9 at their looks, though they *be* a r house. 4805
3:26 to them a reprover: for they *are* a r house. 4805
3:27 let him forbear: for they *are* a r house. 4805
12: 2 thou dwellest in the midst of a r house, 4805
12: 2 to hear, and hear not: for they *are* a r house. 4805
12: 3 will consider, though they *be* a r house. 4805
12: 9 the r house, said unto thee, What doest 4805
12:25 for in your days, O r house, will I say 4805
17:12 Say now to the r house, Know ye not what 4805
24: 3 utter a parable unto the r house, and 4805
44: 6 thou shalt say to the r, *even* to the house of 4805

REBELS (3) [REBEL]
Nu 17:10 to be kept for a token against the r; 1121+4805
20:10 and he said unto them, Hear now, ye r; 4784
Eze 20:38 And I will purge out from among you the r, 4775

REBIRTH See REGENERATION

REBUKE (46) [REBUKED, REBUKER, REBUKES, REBUKETH, REBUKING, UNREBUKEABLE]
Lev 19:17 thou shalt **in any wise** r thy 3198+3198
Dt 28:20 send upon thee cursing, vexation, and r, 4045
Ru 2:16 that she may glean *them,* and r her not. 1605
2Ki 19: 3 a day of trouble, and of r, and blasphemy: 8433
1Ch 12:17 God of our fathers look *thereon,* and r *it.* 3198
Ps 6: 1 O LORD, r me not in thine anger, 3198
18:15 of the world were discovered at thy r, 1606
38: 1 O LORD, r me not in thy wrath: 3198
68:30 **R** the company of spearmen, the multitude 1605
76: 6 At thy r, O God of Jacob, both the chariot 1606
80:16 they perish at the r of thy countenance. 1606
104: 7 At thy r they fled; at the voice of thy 1606
Pr 9: 8 r a wise *man,* and he will love thee. 3198
13: 1 but a scorner heareth not r. 1606
13: 8 *are* his riches: but the poor heareth not r. 1606
24:25 to them that r *him* shall be delight, and 3198
27: 5 Open r *is* better than secret love. 8433
Ecc 7: 5 *It is* better to hear the r of the wise, than for 1606
Isa 2: 4 the nations, and shall r many people: 3198
17:13 *God* shall r them, and they shall flee far 1605
25: 8 the r of his people shall he take away from 2781
30:17 One thousand *shall flee* at the r of one; 1606
30:17 rebuke of one; at the r of five shall ye flee: 1606
37: 3 day of trouble, and of r, and of blasphemy: 8433
50: 2 behold, at my r I dry up the sea, I make 1606
51:20 *of* the fury of the LORD, the r of thy God. 1606
54: 9 *I* would not be wroth with thee, nor r thee. 1605
66:15 with fury, and his r with flames of fire. 1606
Jer 15:15 know that for thy sake I have suffered r. 2781
Hos 5: 9 Ephraim shall be desolate in the day of r: 8433
Mic 4: 3 many people, and r strong nations afar off; 3198
Zec 3: 2 unto Satan, The LORD r thee, O Satan; 1605
3: 2 LORD that hath chosen Jerusalem r thee: 1605
Mal 3:11 I will r the devourer for your sakes, and 1605
Mt 16:22 and began to r him, saying, Be it far from *2008*
Mk 8:32 And Peter took him, and began to r him. *2008*
Lk 17: 3 If thy brother trespass against thee, r him; *2008*
19:39 said unto him, Master, r thy disciples. *2008*
Php 2:15 and harmless, the sons of God **without** r, *298*
1Ti 5: 1 **R** not an elder, but intreat *him* as a father; *1969*
5:20 Them that sin r before all, that others also *1651*
2Ti 4: 2 reprove, r, exhort with all longsuffering *2008*
Tit 1:13 Wherefore r them sharply, that they may be *1651*
2:15 and exhort, and r with all authority. *1651*
Jude 1: 9 but said, The Lord r thee. *2008*
Rev 3:19 As many as I love, I r and chasten: *1651*

REBUKED (25) [REBUKE]
Ge 31:42 labour of my hands, and r *thee* yesternight. 3198
37:10 his father r him, and said unto him, What *is* 1605
Ne 5: 7 I r the nobles, and the rulers, and said unto 7378
Ps 9: 5 Thou hast r the heathen, thou hast 1605
106: 9 He r the Red sea also, and it was dried up: 1605
119:21 Thou hast r the proud *that are* cursed, 1605
Mt 8:26 Then he arose, and r the winds and the sea; *2008*
17:18 And Jesus r the devil; and he departed out *2008*
19:13 and pray: and the disciples r them. *2008*
20:31 And the multitude r them, because *2008*
Mk 1:25 And Jesus r him, saying, Hold thy peace, *2008*
4:39 and r the wind, and said unto the sea, *2008*
8:33 he r Peter, saying, Get thee behind me, *2008*
9:25 he r the foul spirit, saying unto him, *2008*
10:13 and *his* disciples r those that brought *them.* *2008*
Lk 4:35 And Jesus r him, saying, Hold thy peace, *2008*
4:39 And he stood over her, and r the fever; and *2008*
8:24 and r the wind and the raging of the water: *2008*

Lk 9:42 tare *him.* And Jesus **r** the unclean spirit, *2008*
9:55 But he turned, and **r** them, and said, *2008*
18:15 but when *his* disciples saw *it,* they **r** them. *2008*
18:39 And they which went before **r** him, that he *2008*
23:40 But the other answering **r** him, saying, Dost *2008*
Heb 12: 5 the Lord, nor faint when thou art **r** of him: *1651*
2Pe 2:16 But was **r** for his iniquity: the dumb ass *1649*

REBUKER (1) [REBUKE]
Hos 5: 2 though I *have been* a **r** of them all. 4148

REBUKES (3) [REBUKE]
Ps 39:11 When thou with **r** dost correct man for 8433
Eze 5:15 in thee in anger and in fury and in furious **r**. 8433
25:17 great vengeance upon them with furious **r**, 8433

REBUKETH (4) [REBUKE]
Pr 9: 7 he that **r** a wicked *man getteth* himself a 3198
28:23 He that **r** a man, afterwards shall find more 3198
Am 5:10 They hate him that **r** in the gate, and 3198
Na 1: 4 He **r** the sea, and maketh it dry, and 1605

REBUKING (2) [REBUKE]
2Sa 22:16 at the **r** of the LORD, at the blast of 1606
Lk 4:41 And he **r** *them* suffered them not to speak: *2008*

RECAB See RECHAB

RECABITE See RECHABITES

RECAH See RECHAH

RECALL (1)
La 3:21 This I **r** to my mind, therefore have I hope. 7725

RECEDED See ABATED

RECEIPT (3) [RECEIVE]
Mt 9: 9 named Matthew, sitting at the **r of custom**: *5058*
Mk 2:14 *son* of Alpheus sitting at the **r of custom**, *5058*
Lk 5:27 named Levi, sitting at the **r of custom**: *5058*

RECEIVE (176) [RECEIPT, RECEIVED, RECEIVEDST, RECEIVER, RECEIVETH, RECEIVING]
Ge 4:11 which hath opened her mouth to **r** thy 3947
33:10 in thy sight, then **r** my present at my hand: 3947
38:20 to **r** *his* pledge from the woman's hand: 3947
Ex 27: 3 thou shalt make his pans to **r** his **ashes**, 1878
29:25 thou shalt **r** them of their hands, and 3947
Nu 18:28 which ye **r** of the children of Israel; 3947
Dt 9: 9 When I was gone up into the mount to **r** 3947
33: 3 at thy feet; *every one* shall **r** of thy words. 5375
1Sa 10: 4 of bread; which thou shalt **r** of their hands. 3947
2Sa 18:12 Though I should **r** a thousand *shekels of* 8254
1Ki 5: 9 thou shalt **r** *them:* and thou shalt 5375
8:64 *was* too little to **r** the burnt offerings, 3557
2Ki 5:16 before whom I stand, I will **r** none. 3947
5:26 *Is it* a time to **r** money, and to receive 3947
5:26 to **r** garments, and oliveyards, and 3947
12: 7 **r** no *more* money of your acquaintance, 3947
12: 8 the priests consented to **r** no *more* money 3947
2Ch 7: 7 made was not able to **r** the burnt offerings, 3557
Job 2:10 shall we **r** good at the hand of God, and 6901
2:10 at the hand of God, and shall we not **r** evil? 6901
22:22 **R**, I pray thee, the law from his mouth, and 3947
27:13 *which* they shall **r** of the Almighty. 3947
Ps 6: 9 the LORD will **r** my prayer. 3947
24: 5 He shall **r** the blessing from the LORD, 5375
49:15 of the grave: for he shall **r** me. Selah. 3947
73:24 thy counsel, and afterward **r** me *to* glory. 3947
75: 2 When I shall **r** the congregation I will 3947
Pr 1: 3 To **r** the instruction of wisdom, justice, and 3947
2: 1 if thou wilt **r** my words, and hide my 3947
4:10 Hear, O my son, and **r** my sayings; and 3947
8:10 **R** my instruction, and not silver; and 3947
10: 8 The wise in heart will **r** commandments: 3947
19:20 Hear counsel, and **r** instruction, that thou 6901
Isa 57: 6 meat offering. Should I **r comfort** in these? 5162
Jer 5: 3 *but* they have refused to **r** correction: 3947
9:20 let your ear **r** the word of his mouth, and 3947
17:23 that *they* might not hear, nor **r** instruction. 3947
32:33 they have not hearkened to **r** instruction. 3947
35:13 Will ye not **r** instruction to hearken to my 3947
Eze 3:10 all my words that I shall speak unto thee **r** 3947
16:61 when thou shalt **r** thy sisters, thine elder 3947
36:30 that ye shall **r** no more reproach of famine 3947
Da 2: 6 ye shall **r** of me gifts and rewards and 6902
Hos 10: 6 Ephraim shall **r** shame, and Israel shall be 3947
14: 2 Take away all iniquity, and **r** *us* graciously: 3947
Mic 1:11 of Beth-ezel; he shall **r** of you his standing. 3947
Zep 3: 7 thou wilt fear me, thou wilt **r** instruction; 3947
Mal 3:10 that *there shall* not *be room* enough *to* **r** *it.* NIH
Mt 10:14 And whosoever shall not **r** you, nor hear *1209*
10:41 of a prophet shall **r** a prophet's reward; *2983*
10:41 *man* shall **r** a righteous *man's* reward. *2983*
11: 5 The blind **r** their **sight**, and the lame walk, *308*
11:14 And if ye will **r** *it,* this is Elias, which was *1209*
18: 5 And whoso shall **r** one such little child in *1209*
19:11 unto them, All *men* cannot **r** this saying, *5562*
19:12 He that is able to **r** *it,* let him receive *it.* *5562*
19:12 He that is able to receive *it,* let him **r** *it.* *5562*
19:29 shall **r** an hundredfold, and shall inherit *2983*
20: 7 and whatsoever is right, *that* shall ye **r**. *2983*
21:22 ye shall ask in prayer, believing, ye shall **r**. *2983*
21:34 that *they* might **r** the fruits of it. *2983*
23:14 therefore ye shall **r** the greater damnation. *2983*
Mk 2: 2 insomuch that there was no room to **r** *them,* NIG
4:16 the word, immediately **r** it with gladness; *2983*
4:20 the word, and **r** *it,* and bring forth fruit, *3858*
6:11 And whosoever shall not **r** you, nor hear *1209*
9:37 Whosoever shall **r** one of such children in *1209*
9:37 and whosoever shall **r** me, receiveth not *1209*
10:15 Whosoever shall not **r** the kingdom of God *1209*
10:30 But he shall **r** an hundredfold now in this *2983*
10:51 said unto him, Lord, that I might **r** my **sight**. *308*
11:24 believe that ye **r** *them,* and ye shall have *2983*
12: 2 that he might **r** from the husbandmen of *2983*
12:40 these shall **r** greater damnation. *2983*
Lk 6:34 if ye lend *to them* of whom ye hope to **r**, *618*
6:34 also lend to sinners, to **r** as much **again**. *618*
8:13 when they hear, **r** the word with joy; *1209*
9: 5 And whosoever will not **r** you, when ye go *1209*
9:48 Whosoever shall **r** this child in my name *1209*
9:48 whosoever shall **r** me receiveth him that *1209*
9:53 And they did not **r** him, because his face *1209*
10: 8 whatsoever city ye enter, and they **r** you, *1209*
10:10 city ye enter, and they **r** you not, *1209*
16: 4 they may **r** me into their houses. *1209*
16: 9 they may **r** you into everlasting habitations. *1209*
18:17 Whosoever shall not **r** the kingdom of God *1209*
18:30 Who shall not **r** manifold more in this *618*
18:41 And he said, Lord, that I may **r** my **sight**. *308*
18:42 And Jesus said unto him, **R** thy **sight**: *308*
19:12 a far country to **r** for himself a kingdom, *2983*
20:47 the same shall **r** greater damnation. *2983*
23:41 for we **r** the due reward of our deeds: *618*
Jn 3:11 that we have seen; and ye **r** not our witness. *2983*
3:27 and said, A man can **r** nothing, *2983*
5:34 But I **r** not testimony from man: *2983*
5:41 I **r** not honour from men. *2983*
5:43 in my Father's name, and ye **r** me not: *2983*
5:43 shall come in his own name, him ye will **r**. *2983*
5:44 which **r** honour one of another, and *2983*
7:23 If a man on the sabbath day **r** circumcision, *2983*
7:39 which they that believe on him should **r**: *2983*
14: 3 I will come again, and **r** you unto myself; *3880*
14:17 whom the world cannot **r**, because it seeth *2983*
16:14 for he shall **r** of mine, and shall shew *it* *2983*
16:24 ask, and ye shall **r**, that your joy may be *2983*
20:22 and saith unto them, **R** ye the Holy Ghost: *2983*
Ac 1: 8 But ye shall **r** power, after that the Holy *2983*
2:38 and ye shall **r** the gift of the Holy Ghost. *2983*
3: 5 expecting to **r** something of them. *2983*
3:21 Whom the heaven must **r** until the times of *1209*
7:59 and saying, Lord Jesus, **r** my spirit. *1209*
8:15 for them, that they might **r** the Holy Ghost: *2983*
8:19 I lay hands, he may **r** the Holy Ghost. *2983*
9:12 *his* hand on him, that he might **r** his **sight**. *308*
9:17 that thou mightest **r** thy **sight**, and be filled *308*
10:43 believeth in him shall **r** remission of sins. *2983*
16:21 which are not lawful for us to **r**, neither to *3858*
18:27 exhorting the disciples to **r** him: *588*
20:35 he said, It is more blessed to give than to **r**. *2983*
22:13 and said unto me, Brother Saul, **r** thy **sight**. *308*
22:18 for they will not **r** thy testimony concerning *3858*
26:18 that they may **r** forgiveness of sins, and *2983*
Ro 5:17 much more they which **r** abundance of *2983*
13: 2 they that resist shall **r** to themselves *2983*
14: 1 Him that is weak in the faith **r** you, *but* *4355*
15: 7 Wherefore **r** ye one another, as Christ also *4355*

Ro 16: 2 That ye **r** her in the Lord, as becometh *4327*
1Co 3: 8 every man shall **r** his own reward *2983*
3:14 he hath built thereupon, he shall **r** a reward. *2983*
4: 7 and what hast thou that thou didst not **r**? *2983*
4: 7 now if thou didst **r** *it,* why dost thou glory, *2983*
14: 5 he interpret, that the church may **r** edifying. *2983*
2Co 5:10 that every one may **r** the *things done* in *his* *2865*
6: 1 also that ye **r** not the grace of God in vain. *1209*
6:17 not the unclean *thing;* and I will **r** you, *1523*
7: 2 **R** us; we have wronged no *man,* we have *5562*
7: 9 that ye might **r** **damage** by us in nothing. *2210*
8: 4 with much intreaty that we would **r** the gift, *1209*
11: 4 or *if* ye **r** another spirit, which ye have not *2983*
11:16 if otherwise, yet as a fool **r** me, that I may *1209*
Gal 3:14 that we might **r** the promise of the Spirit *2983*
4: 5 that we might **r** the adoption of sons. *618*
Eph 6: 8 the same shall he **r** of the Lord, whether *he* *2865*
Php 2:29 **R** him therefore in the Lord with all *4327*
Col 3:24 Knowing that of the Lord ye shall **r** *618*
3:25 But he that doeth wrong shall **r** *for* *2865*
4:10 if he come unto you, **r** him;) *1209*
1Ti 5:19 Against an elder **r** not an accusation, but *3858*
Phm 1:12 thou therefore **r** him, that is, mine own *4355*
1:15 a season, that thou shouldest **r** him for ever; *568*
1:17 therefore a partner, **r** him as myself. *4355*
Heb 7: 5 **r** the office of the priesthood have a *2983*
7: 8 And here men that die **r** tithes; but there he *2983*
9:15 they which are called might **r** the promise *2983*
10:36 the will of God, ye might **r** the promise. *2865*
11: 8 which he should after **r** for an inheritance, *2983*
Jas 1: 7 For let not that man think that he shall **r** *2983*
1:12 he is tried, he shall **r** the crown of life, *2983*
1:21 and **r** with meekness the engrafted word, *1209*
3: 1 knowing that we shall **r** the greater *2983*
4: 3 Ye ask, and **r** not, because ye ask amiss, *2983*
5: 7 for it, until he **r** the early and latter rain. *2983*
1Pe 5: 4 ye shall **r** a crown of glory that fadeth not *2865*
2Pe 2:13 And shall **r** the reward of unrighteousness, *2865*
1Jn 3:22 we **r** of him, because we keep his *2983*
5: 9 If we **r** the witness of men, the witness of *2983*
2Jn 1: 8 have wrought, but *that* we **r** a full reward. *618*
1:10 not this doctrine, **r** him not into *your* house, *2983*
3Jn 1: 8 We therefore ought to **r** such, that we might *618*
1:10 neither doth he himself **r** the brethren, and *1926*
Rev 4:11 O Lord, to **r** glory and honour and power: *2983*
5:12 Worthy is the Lamb that was slain to **r** *2983*
13:16 to **r** a mark in their right hand, or in their *1325*
14: 9 and **r** *his* mark in his forehead, or in his *2983*
17:12 **r** power as kings one hour with the beast. *2983*
18: 4 of her sins, and that ye **r** not of her plagues. *2983*

RECEIVED (160) [RECEIVE]

Ge 26:12 **r** in the same year an hundredfold: 4672
Ex 32: 4 he **r** *them* at their hand, and fashioned it 3947
36: 3 they **r** of Moses all the offering, which 3947
Nu 12:14 and after *that* let her be **r** **in** *again.* 622
23:20 Behold, I have **r** *commandment* to bless: 3947
34:14 have **r** *their inheritance;* and half the tribe 3947
34:14 half the tribe of Manasseh have **r** their 3947
34:15 the half tribe have **r** their inheritance on 3947
36: 3 of the tribe whereinto they are **r**: 1961+3807.1
36: 4 of the tribe whereunto they are **r**: 1961+3807.1
Jos 13: 8 and the Gadites have **r** their inheritance, 3947
18: 2 which had not *yet* **r** their inheritance. 2505
18: 7 have **r** their inheritance beyond Jordan on 3947
Jdg 13:23 he would not have **r** a burnt offering and 3947
1Sa 12: 3 of whose hand have I **r** *any* bribe to blind 3947
25:35 So David **r** of her hand *that* which she had 3947
1Ki 10:28 the king's merchants **r** the linen yarn at a 3947
2Ki 19:14 Hezekiah **r** the letter of the hand of 3947
1Ch 12:18 David **r** them, and made them captains of 6901
2Ch 1:16 the king's merchants **r** the linen yarn at a 3947
4: 5 *and* it **r** and held three thousand baths. 2388
29:22 the priests **r** the blood, and sprinkled *it* on 6901
30:16 *which they* **r** of the hand of the Levites. NIH
Est 4: 4 his sackcloth from him: but he **r** *it* not. 6901
Job 4:12 to me, and mine ear **r** a little thereof. 3947
Ps 68:18 thou hast **r** gifts for men; yea, *for* 3947
Pr 24:32 *it* well: I looked upon *it, and* **r** instruction. 3947
Isa 37:14 Hezekiah **r** the letter from the hand of 3947
40: 2 for she hath **r** of the LORD's hand double 3947
Jer 2:30 smitten your children; they **r** no correction: 3947
Eze 18:17 *that* hath not **r** usury nor increase, 3947
Zep 3: 2 obeyed not the voice; she **r** not correction; 3947

Mt 10: 8 out devils: freely ye have **r**, freely give. *2983*
13:19 This is he which **r** **seed** by the way side. *4687*
13:20 But he that **r** the **seed** into stony *places,* *4687*
13:22 He also that **r** **seed** among the thorns is he *4687*
13:23 But he that **r** **seed** into the good ground is *4687*
17:24 they that **r** tribute money came to Peter, *2983*
20: 9 eleventh hour, they **r** every man a penny. *2983*
20:10 they supposed that they should have **r** *2983*
20:10 and they likewise **r** every man a penny. *2983*
20:11 And when they had **r** *it,* they murmured *2983*
20:34 and immediately their eyes **r** **sight**, and *308*
25:16 Then he that had **r** the five talents went *2983*
25:17 And likewise he that *had* **r** two, he also NIG
25:18 But he that had **r** one went and digged in *2983*
25:20 And *so* he that had **r** five talents came and *2983*
25:22 He also that had **r** two talents came and *2983*
25:24 Then he which had **r** the one talent came *2983*
25:27 at my coming I should have **r** mine own *2865*
Mk 7: 4 which they have **r** to hold, *as* the washing *3880*
10:52 And immediately he **r** his **sight**, and *308*
15:23 wine mingled with myrrh: but he **r** *it* not. *2983*
16:19 he was **r** **up** into heaven, and sat on the right *353*
Lk 6:24 that are rich: for ye have **r** your consolation. *568*
8:40 Jesus was returned, the people **gladly** **r** him: *588*
9:11 and he **r** them, and spake unto them of *1209*
9:51 the time was come that he should be **r** **up**, *354*
10:38 a certain woman named Martha **r** him into *5264*
15:27 because he hath **r** him *safe and* sound. *618*
18:43 And immediately he **r** his **sight**, and *308*
19: 6 and came down, and **r** him joyfully. *5264*
19:15 having **r** the kingdom, then he commanded *2983*
Jn 1:11 came unto his own, and his own **r** him not. *3880*
1:12 But as many as **r** him, to them gave he *2983*
1:16 And of his fulness have all we **r**, and *2983*
3:33 He that hath **r** his testimony hath set to *his* *2983*
4:45 was come into Galilee, the Galileans **r** him, *1209*
6:21 Then they willingly **r** him into the ship: and *2983*
9:11 wash: and I went and washed, and I **r** **sight**. *308*
9:15 also asked him how he had **r** his **sight**. *308*
9:18 that he had been blind, and **r** his **sight**, *308*
9:18 called the parents of him that had **r** his **sight**. *308*
10:18 This commandment have I **r** of my Father. *2983*
13:30 having **r** the sop went immediately out: *2983*
17: 8 and they have **r** *them,* and have known *2983*
18: 3 having **r** a band *of men,* and officers from *2983*
19:30 When Jesus therefore had **r** the vinegar, *2983*
Ac 1: 9 and a cloud **r** him out of their sight. *5274*
2:33 having **r** of the Father the promise of *2983*
2:41 Then they that gladly **r** his word were *588*
3: 7 his feet and ankle bones **r** **strength**, *4732*
7:38 who **r** *the* lively oracles to give unto us: *1209*
7:53 Who have **r** the law by the disposition of *2983*
8:14 heard that Samaria had **r** the word of God, *1209*
8:17 hands on them, and they **r** the Holy Ghost. *2983*
9:18 and he **r** **sight** forthwith, and arose, and *308*
9:19 And when he had **r** meat, he was *2983*
10:16 and the vessel was **r** **up** again into heaven. *353*
10:47 which have **r** the Holy Ghost as well as *2983*
11: 1 the Gentiles had also **r** the word of God. *1209*
15: 4 they were **r** of the church, and *of* *588*
16:24 Who, having **r** such a charge, thrust them *2983*
17: 7 Whom Jason hath **r**: and these all do *5264*
17:11 in that they **r** the word with all readiness of *1209*
19: 2 Have ye **r** the Holy Ghost since ye *2983*
20:24 which I have **r** of the Lord Jesus, *2983*
21:17 come to Jerusalem, the brethren **r** us gladly. *1209*
22: 5 from whom also I **r** letters unto *1209*
26:10 having **r** authority from the chief priests; *2983*
28: 2 and **r** us every one, because of the present *4355*
28: 7 who **r** us, and lodged *us* three days *324*
28:21 We neither **r** letters out of Judea *1209*
28:30 hired house, and **r** all that came in unto him, *588*
Ro 1: 5 By whom we have **r** grace and apostleship, *2983*
4:11 And he **r** the sign of circumcision, a seal of *2983*
5:11 by whom we have now **r** the atonement. *2983*
8:15 For ye have not **r** the spirit of bondage *2983*
8:15 but ye have **r** the Spirit of adoption, *2983*
14: 3 judge him that eateth: for God hath **r** him. *4355*
15: 7 as Christ also **r** us, to the glory of God. *4355*
1Co 2:12 Now we have **r**, not the spirit of the world, *2983*
4: 7 dost thou glory, as if thou hadst not **r** *it?* *2983*
11:23 For I have **r** of the Lord *that* which also I *3880*
15: 1 which also you have **r**, and wherein ye *3880*
15: 3 unto you first *of all* that which I also **r**, *3880*

2Co 4: 1 as we have **r mercy**, we faint not; *1653*
7:15 how with fear and trembling you **r** him. *1209*
11: 4 which ye have not **r**, or another gospel, *2983*
11:24 Of the Jews five times **r** I forty *stripes* save *2983*
Gal 1: 9 other gospel unto you than that ye have **r**, *3880*
1:12 For I neither **r** it of man, neither was I *3880*
3: 2 **R** ye the Spirit by the works of the law, or *2983*
4:14 but **r** me as an angel of God, *even* as *1209*
Php 4: 9 and **r**, and heard, and seen in me, do: *3880*
4:18 having **r** of Epaphroditus the *things which* *1209*
Col 2: 6 ye have therefore **r** Christ Jesus the Lord, *3880*
4:10 (touching whom ye **r** commandments: *2983*
4:17 Take heed to the ministry which thou hast **r** *3880*
1Th 1: 6 having **r** the word in much affliction, *1209*
2:13 when ye **r** the word of God which *ye* heard *3880*
2:13 ye **r** *it* not as the word of men, but as it is in *1209*
4: 1 that as ye have **r** of us how ye ought to *3880*
2Th 2:10 because they **r** not the love of the truth, *1209*
3: 6 and not after the tradition which he **r** of us. *3880*
1Ti 3:16 believed on in the world, **r up** into glory. *353*
4: 3 which God hath created to be **r** with *3336*
4: 4 to be refused, if it be **r** with thanksgiving: *2983*
Heb 2: 2 disobedience **r** a just recompence of *2983*
7: 6 counted from them **r tithes** of Abraham, *1183*
7:11 (for under it the people **r** the **law**,) *3549*
10:26 For if we sin wilfully after that *we* have **r** *2983*
11:11 Through faith also Sara herself **r** strength to *2983*
11:13 not having **r** the promises, but having seen *2983*
11:17 he that had **r** the promises offered up *his* *324*
11:19 from whence also he **r** him in a figure. *2865*
11:31 when she had **r** the spies with peace. *1209*
11:35 Women **r** their dead raised to life again: *2983*
11:39 report through faith, **r** not the promise: *2865*
Jas 2:25 when she had **r** the messengers, and *5264*
1Pe 1:18 **r by tradition from** your **fathers**; *3970*
4:10 As every man hath **r** *the* gift, *even so* *2983*
2Pe 1:17 For he **r** from God the Father honour and *2983*
1Jn 2:27 But the anointing which ye have **r** of him *2983*
2Jn 1: 4 as we have **r** a commandment from *2983*
Rev 2:27 broken to shivers: even as I **r** of my Father. *2983*
3: 3 therefore how thou hast **r** and heard, *2983*
17:12 ten kings, which have **r** no kingdom as yet; *2983*
19:20 with which he deceived them that had **r** *2983*
20: 4 neither had **r** *his* mark upon their *2983*

RECEIVEDST (1) [RECEIVE]
Lk 16:25 remember that thou in thy lifetime **r** thy *618*

RECEIVER (1) [RECEIVE]
Isa 33:18 where *is* the **r**? where *is* he that counted 8254

RECEIVETH (37) [RECEIVE]
Jdg 19:18 and there *is* no man that **r** me to house. 622
Job 35: 7 thou him? or what **r** he of thine hand? 3947
Pr 21:11 the wise is instructed, he **r** knowledge. 3947
29: 4 the land: but he that **r** gifts overthroweth it. NIH
Jer 7:28 of the LORD their God, nor **r** correction: 3947
Mal 2:13 or **r** *it with* good will at your hand. 3947
Mt 7: 8 For every one that asketh **r**; and he that *2983*
10:40 He that **r** you receiveth me, and he that *1209*
10:40 He that receiveth you **r** me, and he that *1209*
10:40 he that **r** me receiveth him that sent me. *1209*
10:40 he that receiveth me **r** him that sent me. *1209*
10:41 He that **r** a prophet in the name of a *1209*
10:41 he that **r** a righteous *man* in the name of a *2983*
13:20 heareth the word, and anon with joy **r** it; *2983*
18: 5 one such little child in my name **r** me. *1209*
Mk 9:37 one of such children in my name, **r** me: *1209*
9:37 receive me, **r** not me, but him that sent me. *1209*
Lk 9:48 shall receive this child in my name **r** me: *1209*
9:48 whosoever shall receive me **r** him that sent *1209*
11:10 For every one that asketh **r**; and he that *2983*
15: 2 This *man* **r** sinners, and eateth with them. *4327*
Jn 3:32 he testifieth; and no *man* **r** his testimony. *2983*
4:36 And he that reapeth **r** wages, and *2983*
12:48 He that rejecteth me, and **r** not my words, *2983*
13:20 He that **r** whomsoever I send receiveth me; *2983*
13:20 He that receiveth whomsoever I send **r** me; *2983*
13:20 he that **r** me receiveth him that sent me. *2983*
13:20 he that receiveth me **r** him that sent me. *2983*
1Co 2:14 But the natural man **r** not the *things* of *1209*
9:24 run in a race run all, but one **r** the prize? *2983*
Heb 6: 7 whom it is dressed, **r** blessing from God: *3335*
7: 8 there he *r them,* of whom it is witnessed NIG
7: 9 as *I* may so say, Levi also, who **r** tithes, *2983*
12: 6 and scourgeth every son whom he **r**. *3858*
3Jn 1: 9 the preeminence among them, **r** us not. *1926*
Rev 2:17 which no *man* knoweth saving he that **r** *it.* *2983*
14:11 and whosoever **r** the mark of his name. *2983*

RECEIVING (7) [RECEIVE]
2Ki 5:20 in not **r** at his hands *that* which he brought: 3947
Ac 17:15 and **r** a commandment unto Silas and *2983*
Ro 1:27 **r** in themselves *that* recompence of their *618*
11:15 what *shall* the **r** *of them be,* but life from *4356*
Php 4:15 with me as concerning giving and **r**, *3028*
Heb 12:28 Wherefore we **r** a kingdom which cannot *3880*
1Pe 1: 9 **R** the end of your faith, *even* the salvation *2865*

RECENT CONVERT See NOVICE

RECHAB (13) [RECHABITES]
2Sa 4: 2 *was* Baanah, and the name of the other **R**, 7394
4: 5 **R** and Baanah, went, and came about 7394
4: 6 and **R** and Baanah his brother escaped. 7394
4: 9 David answered **R** and Baanah his brother, 7394
2Ki 10:15 he lighted on Jehonadab the son of **R** 7394
10:23 Jehu went, and Jehonadab the son of **R**, 7394
1Ch 2:55 of Hemath, the father of the house of **R**. 7394
Ne 3:14 dung gate repaired Malchiah the son of **R**, 7394
Jer 35: 6 for Jonadab the son of **R** our father 7394
35: 8 **R** our father in all that he hath charged us, 7394
35:14 The words of Jonadab the son of **R**, that he 7394
35:16 Because the sons of Jonadab the son of **R** 7394
35:19 Jonadab the son of **R** shall not want a man 7394

RECHABITES (4) [RECHAB]
Jer 35: 2 Go unto the house of the **R**, and speak unto 7397
35: 3 all his sons, and the whole house of the **R**; 7397
35: 5 I set before the sons of the house of the **R** 7397
35:18 Jeremiah said unto the house of the **R**, 7397

RECHAH (1)
1Ch 4:12 father of Irnahash. These *are* the men of **R**. 7397

RECITE See REHEARSE

RECKON (8) [RECKONED, RECKONETH, RECKONING]
Lev 25:50 he shall **r** with him that bought him from 2803
27:18 the priest shall **r** unto him the money 2803
27:23 the priest shall **r** unto him the worth of thy 2803
Nu 4:32 by name ye shall **r** the instruments of 6485
Eze 44:26 they shall **r** unto him seven days. 5608
Mt 18:24 And when he had begun to **r**, one was *4868*
Ro 6:11 Likewise **r** ye also yourselves to be dead *3049*
8:18 For I **r** that the sufferings of *this* present *3049*

RECKONED (22) [RECKON]
Nu 18:27 *this* your heave offering shall be **r** unto 2803
23: 9 and shall not be **r** among the nations. 2803
2Sa 4: 2 (for Beeroth also was **r** to Benjamin: 2803
2Ki 12:15 Moreover they **r** not with the men, 2803
1Ch 5: 1 the **genealogy** is not to be **r** after 3187
5: 7 the **genealogy** of their generations was **r**, 3187
5:17 All these were **r by genealogies** in the days 3187
7: 5 **r** in all **by** their **genealogies** fourscore and 3187
7: 7 were **r by** their **genealogies** twenty and 3187
9: 1 So all Israel were **r by genealogies**; and 3187
9:22 These were **r by** their **genealogy** in their 3187
2Ch 31:19 to all that were **r by genealogies** among 3187
Ezr 2:62 *among* those that were **r by genealogy**, 3187
8: 3 with him were **r by genealogy** of the males 3187
Ne 7: 5 that *they* might be **r by genealogy**. 3187
7:64 *among* those that were **r by genealogy**, 3187
Ps 40: 5 they cannot be **r up in order** unto thee: *if* I 6186
Isa 38:13 I **r** till morning, *that,* as a lion, so will he 7737
Lk 22:37 And he was **r** among the transgressors: *3049*
Ro 4: 4 that worketh is the reward not **r** of grace, *3049*
4: 9 for we say that faith was **r** to Abraham for *3049*
4:10 How was it then **r**? when he was in *3049*

RECKONETH (1) [RECKON]
Mt 25:19 servants cometh, and **r** with them. *3056+4868*

RECKONING (2) [RECKON]
2Ki 22: 7 Howbeit there was no **r made** with them of 2803
1Ch 23:11 therefore they were in one **r**, according to 6486

RECOMMENDED (2)
Ac 14:26 from whence they had been **r** to the grace *3860*

R

Ac 15:40 being r by the brethren unto the grace of 3860

RECOMPENCE (20) [RECOMPENSE]

Dt 32:35 To me belongeth vengeance, and r; 8005
Job 15:31 trust in vanity: for vanity shall be his r. 8545
Pr 12:14 the r of a man's hands shall be rendered 1576
Isa 35: 4 come with vengeance, even God with a r; 1576
59:18 fury to his adversaries, r to his enemies; 1576
59:18 his enemies; to the islands he will repay r. 1576
66: 6 a voice of the LORD that rendereth r to 1576
Jer 51: 6 he will render unto her a r. 1576
La 3:64 Render unto them a r, O LORD, 1576
Hos 9: 7 visitation are come, the days of r are come; 7966
Joel 3: 4 will ye render me a r? and if ye 1576
3: 4 speedily will I return your r upon your own 1576
3: 7 and will return your r upon your own head: 1576
Lk 14:12 also bid thee again, and a r be made thee. 468
Ro 1:27 receiving in themselves that r of their error 489
11: 9 and a stumblingblock, and a r unto them: 468
2Co 6:13 Now for a r in the same, (I speak as unto my 489
Heb 2: 2 disobedience received a just r of reward; 1738
10:35 which hath great r of reward. 3405
11:26 for he had respect unto the r of the reward. 3405

RECOMPENCES (2) [RECOMPENSE]

Isa 34: 8 the year of r for the controversy of Zion. 7966
Jer 51:56 for the LORD God of r shall surely 1578

RECOMPENSE (26) [RECOMPENCE, RECOMPENCES, RECOMPENSED, RECOMPENSEST, RECOMPENSING]

Nu 5: 7 he shall r his trespass with the principal 7725
5: 8 if the man have no kinsman to r 7725
Ru 2:12 The LORD r thy work, and a full reward 7999
2Sa 19:36 why should the king r it me with such a 1580
Job 34:33 he will r it, whether thou refuse, or 7999
Pr 20:22 Say not thou, I will r evil; but wait on 7999
Isa 65: 6 I will not keep silence, but will r, 7999
65: 6 will recompense, even r into their bosom, 7999
Jer 16:18 first I will r their iniquity and their sin 7999
25:14 I will r them according to their deeds, and 7999
50:29 r her according to her work; according to 7999
Eze 7: 3 and will r upon thee all thine abominations. 5414
7: 4 I will r thy ways upon thee, and 5414
7: 8 and will r thee for all thine abominations. 5414
7: 9 I will r thee according to thy ways and 5414
9:10 but I will r their way upon their head. 5414
11:21 I will r their way upon their own heads, 5414
16:43 I also will r thy way upon thine head, 5414
17:19 even it will I r upon his own head. 5414
23:49 they shall r your lewdness upon you, and 5414
Hos 12: 2 according to his doings will he r him. 7725
Joel 3: 4 if ye r me, swiftly and speedily will I return 1580
Lk 14:14 thou shalt be blessed; for they cannot r thee: 467
Ro 12:17 R to no man evil for evil. Provide things 591
2Th 1: 6 Seeing it is a righteous thing with God to r 467
Heb 10:30 belongeth unto me, I will r, saith the Lord. 467

RECOMPENSED (10) [RECOMPENSE]

Nu 5: 8 let the trespass be r unto the LORD, 7725
2Sa 22:21 to the cleanness of my hands hath he r me. 7725
22:25 Therefore the LORD hath r me according 7725
Ps 18:20 to the cleanness of my hands hath he r me. 7725
18:24 Therefore hath the LORD r me according 7725
Pr 11:31 the righteous shall be r in the earth: 7999
Jer 18:20 Shall evil be r for good? for they have 7999
Eze 22:31 their own way have I r upon their heads, 5414
Lk 14:14 for thou shalt be r at the resurrection of 467
Ro 11:35 to him, and it shall be r unto him again? 467

RECOMPENSEST (1) [RECOMPENSE]

Jer 32:18 r the iniquity of the fathers into the bosom 7999

RECOMPENSING (1) [RECOMPENSE]

2Ch 6:23 by r his way upon his own head; 5414

RECONCILE (5) [RECONCILED, RECONCILIATION, RECONCILING]

Lev 6:30 to r withal in the holy place, shall be eaten: 3722
1Sa 29: 4 for wherewith should he r himself unto his 7521
Eze 45:20 him that is simple: so shall ye r the house. 3722
Eph 2:16 And that he might r both unto God in one 604
Col 1:20 his cross, by him to r all things unto himself; 604

RECONCILED (7) [RECONCILE]

Mt 5:24 first be r to thy brother, and then come and 1259
Ro 5:10 we were r to God by the death of his Son, 2644
5:10 much more, being r, we shall be saved by 2644
1Co 7:11 remain unmarried, or be r to her husband: 2644
2Co 5:18 who hath r us to himself by Jesus Christ, 2644
5:20 pray you in Christ's stead, be ye r to God. 2644
Col 1:21 mind by wicked works, yet now hath he r 604

RECONCILIATION (8) [RECONCILE]

Lev 8:15 and sanctified it, to make r upon it. 3722
2Ch 29:24 they made r with their blood upon 2398
Eze 45:15 for peace offerings, to make r for them, 3722
45:17 to make r for the house of Israel. 3722
Da 9:24 to make r for iniquity, and to bring in 3722
2Co 5:18 and hath given to us the ministry of r; 2643
5:19 and hath committed unto us the word of r. 2643
Heb 2:17 to make r for the sins of the people. 2433

RECONCILING (3) [RECONCILE]

Lev 16:20 when he hath made an end of r the holy 3722
Ro 11:15 For if the casting away of them be the r of 2643
2Co 5:19 that God was in Christ r the world unto 2644

RECORD (30) [RECORDED, RECORDER, RECORDS]

Ex 20:24 in all places where I r my name I will come 2142
Dt 30:19 I call heaven and earth to r this day against 5749
31:28 and call heaven and earth to r against them. 5749
1Ch 16: 4 to r, and to thank and praise the LORD 2142
Ezr 6: 2 a roll, and therein was a r thus written: 1799
Job 16:19 witness is in heaven, and my r is on high. 7717
Isa 8: 2 I took unto me faithful witnesses to r, 5749
Jn 1:19 And this is the r of John, when the Jews 3141
1:32 And John bare r, saying, I saw the Spirit 3140
1:34 and bare r that this is the Son of God. 3140
8:13 said unto him, Thou bearest r of thyself; 3140
8:13 bearest record of thyself; thy r is not true. 3141
8:14 said unto them, Though I bear r of myself, 3140
8:14 I bear record of myself, yet my r is true: 3141
12:17 and raised him from the dead, bare r. 3140
19:35 And he that saw it bare r, and his record is 3140
19:35 he that saw it bare record, and his r is true: 3141
Ac 20:26 Wherefore I take you to r this day, that I 3143
Ro 10: 2 For I bear them r that they have a zeal of 3140
2Co 1:23 Moreover I call God for a r upon my soul, 3144
8: 3 I bear r, yea, and beyond their power they 3140
Gal 4:15 for I bear you r, that if it had been 3140
Php 1: 8 For God is my r, how greatly I long after 3144
Col 4:13 For I bear him r, that he hath a great zeal 3140
1Jn 5: 7 For there are three that bear r in heaven, 3140
5:10 he believeth not the r that God gave of his 3141
5:11 And this is the r, that God hath given to us 3141
3Jn 1:12 yea, and we also bear r; and ye know that 3140
1:12 bear record; and ye know that our r is true. 3141
Rev 1: 2 Who bare r of the word of God, and of 3140

RECORDED (1) [RECORD]

Ne 12:22 and Jaddua, were r chief of the fathers: 3789

RECORDER (9) [RECORD]

2Sa 8:16 and Jehoshaphat the son of Ahilud was r; 2142
20:24 and Jehoshaphat the son of Ahilud was r: 2142
1Ki 4: 3 Jehoshaphat the son of Ahilud, the r. 2142
2Ki 18:18 the scribe, and Joah the son of Asaph the r. 2142
18:37 the scribe, and Joah the son of Asaph the r, 2142
1Ch 18:15 and Jehoshaphat the son of Ahilud, r. 2142
2Ch 34: 8 the city, and Joah the son of Joahaz the r, 2142
Isa 36: 3 the scribe, and Joah, Asaph's son, the r. 2142
36:22 and Joah, the son of Asaph, the r, 2142

RECORDS (3) [RECORD]

Ezr 4:15 be made in the book of the r of thy fathers: 1799
4:15 so shalt thou find in the book of the r, and 1799
Est 6: 1 he commanded to bring the book of r of 2146

RECOUNT (1)

Na 2: 5 He shall r his worthies: they shall stumble 2142

RECOVER (21) [RECOVERED, RECOVERING]

Jdg 11:26 did ye not r them within that time? 5337
1Sa 30: 8 and without fail r all. 5337+5337
2Sa 8: 3 as he went to r his border at the river 7725
2Ki 1: 2 of Ekron whether I shall r of this disease. 2421
5: 3 for he would r him of his leprosy. 622
5: 6 that thou mayest r him of his leprosy. 622
5: 7 that this man doth send unto me to r a man 622
5:11 his hand over the place, and r the leper. 622

R

2Ki 8: 8 by him, saying, Shall I **r** of this disease? 2421
8: 9 me to thee, saying, Shall I **r** of this disease? 2421
8:10 unto him, Thou mayest **certainly r**: 2421+2421
8:14 told me *that* thou shouldest **surely r**. 2421+2421
2Ch 13:20 Neither did Jeroboam **r** strength again in 6113
14:13 that they could not **r** themselves; 4241
Ps 39:13 O spare me, that I may **r strength**, before I 1082
Isa 11:11 second time to **r** the remnant of his people, 7069
38:16 so wilt thou **r** me, and make me to live. 2492
38:21 for a plaister upon the boil, and he shall **r**. 2421
Hos 2: 9 will **r** my wool and my flax *given* to cover 5337
Mk 16:18 hands on the sick, and they shall **r**. *2192+2573*
2Ti 2:26 And *that* they may **r** themselves out of *366*

RECOVERED (11) [RECOVER]
1Sa 30:18 David **r** all that the Amalekites had carried 5337
30:19 that they had taken to them: David **r** all. 7725
30:22 give them *ought* of the spoil that we have **r**, 5337
2Ki 13:25 Joash beat him, and **r** the cities of Israel. 7725
14:28 and how he **r** Damascus, and Hamath, 7725
16: 6 At that time Rezin king of Syria **r** Elath to 7725
20: 7 they took and laid *it* on the boil, and he **r**. 2421
Isa 38: 9 he had been sick, and was **r** of his sickness: 2421
39: 1 had heard that he had been sick, and was **r**. 2388
Jer 8:22 the health of the daughter of my people **r**? 5927
41:16 the remnant of the people whom he had **r** 7725

RECOVERING (1) [RECOVER]
Lk 4:18 to the captives, and **r of sight** to the blind, *309*

RED (53) [REDDISH, REDNESS]
Ge 25:25 the first came out **r**, all over like a hairy 132
25:30 with that same **r** *pottage;* for I *am* faint: 122
49:12 *His eyes shall be* **r** with wine, and *his* teeth 2447
Ex 10:19 the locusts, and cast them into the **R** sea; 5488
13:18 *through* the way of the wilderness of the **R** 5488
15: 4 captains also are drowned in the **R** sea. 5488
15:22 So Moses brought Israel from the **R** sea, 5488
23:31 I will set thy bounds from the **R** sea even 5488
25: 5 And rams' skins **dyed r**, and badgers' skins, 119
26:14 a covering for the tent *of* rams' skins **dyed r**, 119
35: 7 And rams' skins **dyed r**, and badgers' skins, 119
35:23 goats' *hair,* and **r** skins of rams, and 119
36:19 a covering for the tent *of* rams' skins **dyed r**, 119
39:34 And the covering of rams' skins **dyed r**, and 119
Nu 14:25 *into* the wilderness *by* the way of the **R** sea. 5488
19: 2 that they bring thee a **r** heifer without spot, 122
21: 4 from mount Hor *by* the way of the **R** sea, 5488
21:14 What he did in the **R sea**, and *in* the brooks 5492
33:10 from Elim, and encamped by the **R** sea. 5488
33:11 they removed from the **R** sea, and 5488
Dt 1: 1 in the plain over against the **R** *sea,* between 5489
1:40 into the wilderness *by* the way of the **R** sea. 5488
2: 1 into the wilderness *by* the way of the **R** sea, 5488
11: 4 how he made the water of the **R** sea to 5488
Jos 2:10 dried up the water of the **R** sea for you, 5488
4:23 as the LORD your God did to the **R** sea, 5488
24: 6 with chariots and horsemen *unto* the **R** sea. 5488
Jdg 11:16 walked through the wilderness unto the **R** 5488
1Ki 9:26 on the shore of the **R** sea, in the land of 5488
2Ki 3:22 saw the water on the other side *as* **r** as blood: 122
Ne 9: 9 and heardest their cry by the **R** sea; 5488
Est 1: 6 upon a pavement of **r**, and blue, and white, 923
Ps 75: 8 LORD *there is* a cup, and the wine is **r**; 2560
106: 7 provoked *him* at the sea, *even* at the **R** sea. 5488
106: 9 He rebuked the **R** sea also, and it was dried 5488
106:22 of Ham, *and* terrible *things* by the **R** sea. 5488
136:13 To him which divided the **R** sea into parts: 5488
136:15 and his host in the **R** sea: 5488
Pr 23:31 Look not thou upon the wine when it is **r**, 119
Isa 1:18 though they be **r** like crimson, they shall be 119
27: 2 day sing ye unto her, A vineyard of **r wine**. 2561
63: 2 Wherefore *art thou* **r** in thine apparel, and 122
Jer 49:21 the noise thereof was heard in the **R** sea. 5488
Na 2: 3 The shield of his mighty *men is* **made r**, 119
Zec 1: 8 and behold a man riding upon a **r** horse, and 122
1: 8 behind him *were there* **r** horses, speckled, 122
6: 2 In the first chariot *were* **r** horses; and in 122
Mt 16: 2 *It will be* fair weather: for the sky is **r**. *4449*
16: 3 for the sky is **r** and lowring. O *ye* *4449*
Ac 7:36 and in the **R** sea, and in the wilderness *2063*
Heb 11:29 By faith they passed through the **R** sea as *2063*
Rev 6: 4 there went out another horse *that was* **r**: *4450*
12: 3 and behold a great **r** dragon, having seven *4450*

REDDISH (6) [RED]
Lev 13:19 *and* **somewhat r**, and it be shewed to 125
13:24 a white bright spot, **somewhat r**, or white; 125
13:42 bald head, or bald forehead, a white **r** sore; 125
13:43 *if* the rising of the sore *be* white **r** in his bald 125
13:49 *if* the plague be greenish or **r** in the garment, 125
14:37 greenish or **r**, which in sight *are* lower than 125

REDEEM (56) [REDEEMED, REDEEMEDST, REDEEMER, REDEEMETH, REDEEMING, REDEMPTION]
Ex 6: 6 I will **r** you with a stretched out arm, and 1350
13:13 every firstling of an ass thou shalt **r** with a 6299
13:13 if thou wilt not **r** *it,* then thou shalt break 6299
13:13 of man amongst thy children shalt thou **r**. 6299
13:15 but all the firstborn of my children I **r**. 6299
34:20 the firstling of an ass thou shalt **r** with a 6299
34:20 if thou **r** *him* not, then shalt thou break his 6299
34:20 All the firstborn of thy sons thou shalt **r**: 6299
Lev 25:25 *if any of* his kin come to **r** it, then shall he 1350
25:25 then shall he **r** that which his brother sold. 1350
25:26 if the man have none to **r** *it,* and himself be 1350
25:26 redeem *it,* and himself be able to **r** it; 1353+4672
25:29 he may **r** it within a whole year after 1353+1961
25:29 is sold; *within* a full year may he **r** it. 1353+1961
25:32 may the Levites **r** at any time. 1353
25:48 one of his brethren may **r** him: 1350
25:49 may **r** him, or *any* that is nigh of kin unto 1350
25:49 of kin unto him of his family may **r** him; 1350
25:49 or if he be able, he may **r** himself. 1350
27:13 if he will **at all r** it, then he shall add 1350+1350
27:15 if he that sanctified *it* will **r** his house, then 1350
27:19 the field will **in any wise r** it, 1350+1350
27:20 if he will not **r** the field, or if he have sold 1350
27:27 he shall **r** *it* according to thine estimation, 6299
27:31 if a man will **at all r** *ought* of his 1350+1350
Nu 18:15 firstborn of man shalt thou **surely r**, 6299+6299
18:15 the firstling of unclean beasts shalt thou **r**. 6299
18:16 *be* redeemed from a month old shalt thou **r**, 6299
18:17 or the firstling of a goat, thou shalt not **r**; 6299
Ru 4: 4 If thou wilt **r** *it,* redeem *it:* but if thou wilt 1350
4: 4 If thou wilt redeem *it,* **r** *it:* but if thou wilt 1350
4: 4 but if thou wilt not **r** *it, then* tell me, 1350
4: 4 for *there is* none to **r** *it* besides thee; and 1350
4: 4 and I *am* after thee. And he said, I will **r** *it.* 1350
4: 6 the kinsman said, I cannot **r** *it* for myself, 1350
4: 6 **r** thou my right to thyself; for I cannot 1350
4: 6 thou my right to thyself; for I cannot **r** *it.* 1350
2Sa 7:23 whom God went to **r** for a people to 6299
1Ch 17:21 whom God went to **r** *to be* his own people, 6299
Ne 5: 5 *to* **r** *them;* for other men have our lands NIH
Job 5:20 In famine he shall **r** thee from death: and 6299
6:23 or, **R** me from the hand of the mighty? 6299
Ps 25:22 **R** Israel, O God, out of all his troubles. 6299
26:11 **r** me, and be merciful unto me. 6299
44:26 for our help, and **r** us for thy mercy's sake. 6299
49: 7 None *of them* can **by any means r** 6299+6299
49:15 God will **r** my soul from the power of 6299
69:18 Draw nigh unto my soul, *and* **r** it: 1350
72:14 He shall **r** their soul from deceit and 1350
130: 8 And he shall **r** Israel from all his iniquities. 6299
Isa 50: 2 my hand shortened at all, that *it* cannot **r**? 6304
Jer 15:21 I will **r** thee out of the hand of the terrible. 6299
Hos 13:14 of the grave; I will **r** them from death: 1350
Mic 4:10 there the LORD shall **r** thee from the hand 1350
Gal 4: 5 To **r** them that were under the law, that we *1805*
Tit 2:14 that he might **r** us from all iniquity, and *3084*

REDEEMED (62) [REDEEM]
Ge 48:16 The Angel which **r** me from all evil, 1350
Ex 15:13 hast led forth the people *which* thou hast **r**: 1350
21: 8 her to himself, then shall he let her be **r**: 6299
Lev 19:20 not **at all r**, nor freedom given her; 6299+6299
25:30 if it be not **r** within the space of a full year, 1350
25:31 they may be **r**, and they shall go out 1353+1961
25:48 After *that* he is sold he may be **r** again; 1353
25:54 if he be not **r** in these *years,* then he shall 1350
27:20 to another man, it shall not be **r** any more. 1350
27:27 or if it be not **r**, then it shall be sold 1350
27:28 field of his possession, shall be sold or **r**: 1350
27:29 which shall be devoted of men, shall be **r**; 6299
27:33 thereof shall be holy; it shall not be **r**. 1350
Nu 3:46 for **those that are** *to be* **r** of the two 6302
3:48 the odd number of them is *to be* **r**, 6302
3:49 and above them that were **r** by the Levites: 6302

Nu 3:51 the money of them that were r unto Aaron 6302
18:16 those that are *to be* r from a month old 6299
Dt 7: 8 r you out of the house of bondmen, 6299
9:26 which thou hast r through thy greatness, 6299
13: 5 and r you out of the house of bondage, 6299
15:15 of Egypt, and the LORD thy God r thee: 6299
21: 8 whom thou hast r, and lay not innocent 6299
24:18 and the LORD thy God r thee thence: 6299
2Sa 4: 9 who hath r my soul out of all adversity, 6299
1Ki 1:29 that hath r my soul out of all distress, 6299
1Ch 17:21 thy people, whom thou hast r out of Egypt? 6299
Ne 1:10 whom thou hast r by thy great power, and 6299
5: 8 We after our ability have r our brethren 7069
Ps 31: 5 thou hast r me, O LORD God of truth. 6299
71:23 unto thee; and my soul, which thou hast r. 6299
74: 2 rod of thine inheritance, *which* thou hast r; 1350
77:15 Thou hast with *thine* arm r thy people, 1350
106:10 and r them from the hand of the enemy. 1350
107: 2 Let the r of the LORD say *so,* whom he 1350
107: 2 whom he hath r from the hand of 1350
136:24 hath r us from our enemies: for his mercy 6561
Isa 1:27 Zion shall be r with judgment, and 6299
29:22 who r Abraham, concerning the house of 6299
35: 9 be found there; but the r shall walk *there:* 1350
43: 1 for I have r thee, I have called *thee* by thy 1350
44:22 thy sins: return unto me; for I have r thee. 1350
44:23 for the LORD hath r Jacob, and 1350
48:20 The LORD hath r his servant Jacob. 1350
51:11 Therefore the r of the LORD shall return, 6299
52: 3 and ye shall be r without money. 1350
52: 9 comforted his people, he hath r Jerusalem. 1350
62:12 The holy people, The r of the LORD: 1350
63: 4 in mine heart, and the year of my r is come. 1350
63: 9 in his love and in his pity he r them; and 1350
Jer 31:11 For the LORD hath r Jacob, and 6299
La 3:58 the causes of my soul; thou hast r my life. 1350
Hos 7:13 though I have r them, yet they have spoken 6299
Mic 6: 4 and r thee out of the house of servants; 6299
Zec 10: 8 and gather them; for I have r them: 6299
Lk 1:68 for he hath visited and r his people, *3085+4160*
24:21 it had been he which should have r Israel: *3084*
Gal 3:13 Christ hath r us from the curse of the law, *1805*
1Pe 1:18 Forasmuch as ye know that ye were not r *3084*
Rev 5: 9 hast r us to God by thy blood out of every *59*
14: 3 four thousand, which were r from the earth. *59*
14: 4 These were r from among men, *being* *59*

REDEEMEDST (1) [REDEEM]
2Sa 7:23 which thou r to thee from Egypt, *from* 6299

REDEEMER (18) [REDEEM]
Job 19:25 For I know *that* my R liveth, and *that* he 1350
Ps 19:14 O LORD, my strength, and my r. 1350
78:35 *was* their rock, and the high God their r. 1350
Pr 23:11 For their R *is* mighty; he shall plead their 1350
Isa 41:14 will help thee, saith the LORD, and thy r, 1350
43:14 the LORD, your r, the Holy One of Israel; 1350
44: 6 of Israel, and his r the LORD of hosts; 1350
44:24 thy r, and he that formed thee from 1350
47: 4 *As for* our r, the LORD of hosts *is* his 1350
48:17 the LORD, thy r, the Holy One of Israel; 1350
49: 7 the r of Israel, *and* his Holy One, 1350
49:26 that I the LORD *am* thy Saviour and thy r, 1350
54: 5 his name; and thy r the Holy One of Israel; 1350
54: 8 mercy on thee, saith the LORD thy r. 1350
59:20 the r shall come to Zion, and unto them 1350
60:16 that I the LORD *am* thy Saviour and thy r, 1350
63:16 thou, O LORD, *art* our father, our r; 1350
Jer 50:34 Their r *is* strong; the LORD of hosts *is* his 1350

REDEEMETH (2) [REDEEM]
Ps 34:22 The LORD r the soul of his servants: and 6299
103: 4 Who r thy life from destruction; 1350

REDEEMING (3) [REDEEM]
Ru 4: 7 in former time in Israel concerning r 1353
Eph 5:16 R the time, because the days are evil. *1805*
Col 4: 5 toward them that are without, r the time. *1805*

REDEMPTION (20) [REDEEM]
Lev 25:24 possession ye shall grant a r for the land. 1353
25:51 price of his r out of the money that he was 1353
25:52 shall he give *him* again the price of his r. 1353
Nu 3:49 Moses took the r money of them that were 6306
Ps 49: 8 (For the r of their soul is precious, and 6306
111: 9 He sent r unto his people: he hath 6304
130: 7 *there is* mercy, and with him *is* plenteous r. 6304
Jer 32: 7 for the right of r *is* thine to buy *it.* 1353
32: 8 of inheritance *is* thine, and the r *is* thine; 1353
Lk 2:38 spake of him to all them that looked for r in *3085*
21:28 lift up your heads; for your r draweth nigh. *629*
Ro 3:24 grace through the r that is in Christ Jesus: *629*
8:23 for the adoption, *to wit,* the r of our body. *629*
1Co 1:30 and righteousness, and sanctification, and r: *629*
Eph 1: 7 In whom we have r through his blood, *629*
1:14 until the r of the purchased possession, *629*
4:30 whereby ye are sealed unto the day of r. *629*
Col 1:14 In whom we have r through his blood, *629*
Heb 9:12 *place,* having obtained eternal r *for us.* *3085*
9:15 for the r of the transgressions that were *629*

REDNESS (1) [RED]
Pr 23:29 wounds without cause? who hath r of eyes? 2448

REDOUND (1)
2Co 4:15 thanksgiving of many r to the glory of God. *4052*

REDUCE See MINISH; MINISHED

REED (33) [REEDS]
1Ki 14:15 as a r is shaken in the water, and he shall 7070
2Ki 18:21 thou trustest upon the staff of this bruised r, 7070
Job 40:21 shady trees, in the covert of the r, and fens. 7070
Isa 36: 6 thou trustest in the staff of this broken r, 7070
42: 3 A bruised r shall he not break, and 7070
Eze 29: 6 they have been a staff of r to the house of 7070
40: 3 line of flax in his hand, and a measuring r; 7070
40: 5 in the man's hand a measuring r of six 7070
40: 5 the breadth of the building, one r; 7070
40: 5 one reed; and the height, one r. 7070
40: 6 of the gate, *which was* one r broad; 7070
40: 6 *of the gate, which was* one r broad. 7070
40: 7 *every* little chamber *was* one r long, and 7070
40: 7 *was* one reed long, and one r broad; 7070
40: 7 by the porch of the gate within *was* one r. 7070
40: 8 also the porch of the gate within, one r. 7070
41: 8 chambers *were* a full r of six great cubits. 7070
42:16 the east side with the measuring r, 7070
42:16 with the measuring r round about. 7070
42:17 with the measuring r round about. 7070
42:18 five hundred reeds, with the measuring r. 7070
42:19 five hundred reeds with the measuring r. 7070
Mt 11: 7 to see? A r shaken with the wind? *2563*
12:20 A bruised r shall he not break, and *2563*
27:29 *it* upon his head, and a r in his right hand: *2563*
27:30 and took the r, and smote him on the head. *2563*
27:48 and put *it* on a r, and gave him to drink. *2563*
Mk 15:19 And they smote him on the head with a r, *2563*
15:36 and put *it* on a r, and gave him to drink, *2563*
Lk 7:24 for to see? A r shaken with the wind? *2563*
Rev 11: 1 And there was given me a r like unto a rod: *2563*
21:15 And he that talked with me had a golden r *2563*
21:16 and he measured the city with the r, *2563*

REEDS (11) [REED]
Isa 19: 6 and dried up: the r and flags shall wither. 7070
19: 7 The paper r by the brooks, by the mouth of 6169
35: 7 each lay, *shall be* grass with r and rushes. 7070
Jer 51:32 the r they have burnt with fire, and the men of 98
Eze 42:16 five hundred r, with the measuring reed 7070
42:17 He measured the north side, five hundred r, 7070
42:18 five hundred r, with the measuring reed. 7070
42:19 measured five hundred r with 7070
42:20 five hundred r long, and five hundred NIH
45: 1 twenty thousand r, and the breadth *shall be* NIH
48: 8 *of* five and twenty thousand r *in* breadth, NIH

REEL (2)
Ps 107:27 They r to and fro, and stagger like a 2287
Isa 24:20 The earth shall r to and fro like a 5128+5128

REELAIAH (1)
Ezr 2: 2 Seraiah, R, Mordecai, Bilshan, Mizpar, 7480

REFINE (1) [REFINED, REFINER, REFINER'S]
Zec 13: 9 will r them as silver is refined, and will try 6884

REFINED (5) [REFINE]
1Ch 28:18 for the altar of incense r gold by weight; 2212

1Ch 29: 4 and seven thousand talents of r silver, 2212
Isa 25: 6 full of marrow, of wines on the lees **well** r. 2212
48:10 Behold, I have r thee, but not with silver; 6884
Zec 13: 9 will refine them as silver is r, and will try 6884

REFINER (1) [REFINE]
Mal 3: 3 And he shall sit *as* a r and purifier of silver: 6884

REFINER'S (1) [REFINE]
Mal 3: 2 for he *is* like a r fire, and like fullers' sope: 6884

REFORMATION (1) [REFORMED]
Heb 9:10 imposed *on them* until the time of r. *1357*

REFORMED (1) [REFORMATION]
Lev 26:23 if ye will not be r by me by these *things,* 3256

REFRAIN (9) [REFRAINED, REFRAINETH]
Ge 45: 1 Joseph could not r himself before all them 662
Job 7:11 Therefore I will not r my mouth; I will 2820
Pr 1:15 way with them; r thy foot from their path: 4513
Ecc 3: 5 and a time to r from embracing; 7368
Isa 48: 9 *for* my praise will I r for thee, that *I* cut 2413
64:12 Wilt thou r thyself for these *things,* O 662
Jer 31:16 **R** thy voice from weeping, and thine eyes 4513
Ac 5:38 **R** from these men, and let them alone: *868*
1Pe 3:10 let him r his tongue from evil, and his lips *3973*

REFRAINED (7) [REFRAIN]
Ge 43:31 went out, and r himself, and said, Set on 662
Est 5:10 Nevertheless Haman r himself: and when he 662
Job 29: 9 The princes r talking, and laid *their* hand 6113
Ps 40: 9 lo, I have not r my lips, O LORD, 3607
119:101 I have r my feet from every evil way, that I 3607
Isa 42:14 my peace; I have been still, *and* r myself: 662
Jer 14:10 they have not r their feet, therefore 2820

REFRAINETH (1) [REFRAIN]
Pr 10:19 not sin: but he that r his lips *is* wise. 2820

REFRESH (3) [REFRESHED, REFRESHETH, REFRESHING]
1Ki 13: 7 and r *thyself,* and I will give thee a reward. 5582
Ac 27: 3 to go unto *his* friends to r himself. *1958+5177*
Phm 1:20 of thee in the Lord: r my bowels in the Lord. *373*

REFRESHED (10) [REFRESH]
Ex 23:12 thy handmaid, and the stranger, may be r. 5314
31:17 on the seventh day he rested, and was r. 5314
1Sa 16:23 so Saul was r, and was well, and the evil 7304
2Sa 16:14 came weary, and r themselves there. 5314
Job 32:20 I will speak, that I may be r: I will open my 7304
Ro 15:32 by the will of God, and may **with** you be r. *4875*
1Co 16:18 For they have r my spirit and yours: *373*
2Co 7:13 of Titus, because his spirit was r by you all. *373*
2Ti 1:16 for he oft r me, and was not ashamed of my *404*
Phm 1: 7 the bowels of the saints are r by thee, *373*

REFRESHETH (1) [REFRESH]
Pr 25:13 send him: for he r the soul of his masters. 7725

REFRESHING (2) [REFRESH]
Isa 28:12 cause the weary to rest; and this *is* the r: 4774
Ac 3:19 when *the* times of r shall come from *403*

REFUGE (47)
Nu 35: 6 the Levites *there shall be* six cities for r, 4733
35:11 ye shall appoint you cities to be cities of r 4733
35:12 they shall be unto you cities for r from 4733
35:13 ye shall give six cities shall ye have for r. 4733
35:14 land of Canaan, *which* shall be cities of r. 4733
35:15 These six cities shall be a r, *both* for 4733
35:25 shall restore him to the city of his r, 4733
35:26 come *without* the border of the city of his r, 4733
35:27 him without the borders of the city of his r, 4733
35:28 of his r until the death of the high priest: 4733
35:32 for him that is fled to the city of his r, 4733
Dt 33:27 The eternal God *is thy* r, and underneath 4585
Jos 20: 2 Appoint out for you cities of r, 4733
20: 3 they shall be your r from the avenger of 4733
21:13 her suburbs, *to be* a city of r for the slayer; 4733
21:21 *to be* a city of r for the slayer; 4733
21:27 her suburbs, *to be* a city of r for the slayer; 4733
21:32 her suburbs, *to be* a city of r for the slayer; 4733
21:38 her suburbs, *to be* a city of r for the slayer; 4733
2Sa 22: 3 my high tower, and my r, my saviour; 4498
1Ch 6:57 *the city* of r, and Libnah with her suburbs, 4733
6:67 they gave unto them, *of* the cities of r, 4733
Ps 9: 9 The LORD also will be a r for 4869
9: 9 for the oppressed, a r in times of trouble. 4869
14: 6 of the poor, because the LORD *is* his r. 4268
46: 1 God *is* our r and strength, a very present 4268
46: 7 hosts *is* with us; the God of Jacob *is* our r. 4869
46:11 hosts *is* with us; the God of Jacob *is* our r. 4869
48: 3 God is known in her palaces for a r. 4869
57: 1 the shadow of thy wings will I **make** my r, 2620
59:16 my defence and r in the day of my trouble. 4498
62: 7 rock of my strength, *and* my r, *is* in God. 4268
62: 8 heart before him: God *is* a r for us. Selah. 4268
71: 7 unto many; but thou *art* my strong r. 4268
91: 2 of the LORD, *He is* my r and my fortress: 4268
91: 9 *which is* my r, *even* the most High, 4268
94:22 and my God *is* the rock of my r. 4268
104:18 The high hills *are* a r for the wild goats; 4268
142: 4 r failed me; no man cared for my soul. 4498
142: 5 Thou *art* my r *and* my portion in the land of 4268
Pr 14:26 and his children shall have a **place of** r. 4268
Isa 4: 6 for a **place of** r, and for a covert from 4268
25: 4 a r from the storm, a shadow from the heat, 4268
28:15 for we have made lies our r, and 4268
28:17 the hail shall sweep away the r of lies, and 4268
Jer 16:19 and my r in the day of affliction, 4498
Heb 6:18 who have **fled for** r to lay hold upon *2703*

REFUSE (26) [REFUSED, REFUSEDST, REFUSETH]
Ex 4:23 *if* thou r to let him go, behold, I will slay 3985
8: 2 if thou r to let *them* go, behold, I will smite 3986
9: 2 For if thou r to let *them* go, and wilt hold 3986
10: 3 How long wilt thou r to humble thyself 3985
10: 4 Else, if thou r to let my people go, behold, 3986
16:28 How long r ye to keep my commandments 3985
22:17 If her father **utterly** r to give her 3985+3985
1Sa 15: 9 every thing *that was* vile and r, that they 4549
Job 34:33 whether thou r, or whether thou choose; 3988
Pr 8:33 Hear instruction, and be wise, and r *it* not. 6544
21: 7 because they r to do judgment. 3985
21:25 killeth him; for his hands r to labour. 3985
Isa 1:20 if ye r and rebel, ye shall be devoured *with* 3985
7:15 that he may know to r the evil, and 3988
7:16 For before the child shall know to r 3988
Jer 8: 5 they hold fast deceit, they r to return. 3985
9: 6 through deceit they r to know me, saith 3985
13:10 This evil people, which r to hear my words, 3987
25:28 if they r to take the cup at thine hand to 3985
38:21 if thou r to go forth, this *is* the word that 3986
La 3:45 and r in the midst of the people. 3973
Am 8: 6 of shoes; *yea,* and sell the r of the wheat? 4651
Ac 25:11 any *thing* worthy of death, I r not to die: *3868*
1Ti 4: 7 But r profane and old wives' fables, and *3868*
5:11 But the younger widows r: for when they *3868*
Heb 12:25 See *that* ye r not him that speaketh: for if *3868*

REFUSED (33) [REFUSE]
Ge 37:35 he r to be comforted; and he said, For I will 3985
39: 8 he r, and said unto his master's wife, 3985
48:19 his father r, and said, I know *it,* my son, 3985
Nu 20:21 Thus Edom r to give Israel passage through 3985
1Sa 8:19 Nevertheless the people r to obey the voice 3985
16: 7 height of his stature; because I have r him: 3988
28:23 he r, and said, I will not eat. But his 3985
2Sa 2:23 Howbeit he r to turn aside: 3985
13: 9 poured *them* out before him; but he r to eat. 3985
1Ki 20:35 I pray thee. And the man r to smite him. 3985
21:15 which he r to give thee for money: 3985
2Ki 5:16 And he urged him to take *it;* but he r. 3985
Ne 9:17 r to obey, neither were mindful of thy 3985
Est 1:12 the queen Vashti r to come at the king's 3985
Job 6: 7 The things *that* my soul r to touch *are* as 3985
Ps 77: 2 and ceased not: my soul r to be comforted. 3985
78:10 covenant of God, and r to walk in his law; 3985
78:67 Moreover he r the tabernacle of Joseph, 3988
118:22 The stone *which* the builders r is become 3988
Pr 1:24 Because I have called, and ye r; I have 3985
Isa 54: 6 of youth, when thou wast r, saith thy God. 3988
Jer 5: 3 *but* they have r to receive correction: 3985
5: 3 harder than a rock; they have r to return. 3985
11:10 their forefathers, which r to hear my words; 3985
31:15 Rahel weeping for her children r to be 3985
50:33 held them fast; they r to let them go. 3985
Eze 5: 6 for they have r my judgments, and 3988

Hos 11: 5 shall be his king, because they **r** to return. 3985
Zec 7:11 they **r** to hearken, and pulled away 3985
Ac 7:35 This Moses whom they **r**, saying, Who made *720*
1Ti 4: 4 creature of God *is* good, and nothing to be **r**, *579*
Heb 11:24 **r** to be called the son of Pharaoh's daughter; *720*
12:25 for if they escaped not who **r** him that *3868*

REFUSEDST (1) [REFUSE]
Jer 3: 3 a whore's forehead, thou **r** to be ashamed. 3985

REFUSETH (9) [REFUSE]
Ex 7:14 heart *is* hardened, he **r** to let the people go. 3985
Nu 22:13 for the LORD **r** to give me leave to go 3985
22:14 and said, Balaam **r** to come with us. 3985
Dt 25: 7 My husband's brother **r** to raise up unto his 3985
Pr 10:17 but he that **r** reproof erreth. 5800
13:18 shame *shall be to* him that **r** instruction: 6544
15:32 He that **r** instruction despiseth his own 6544
Isa 8: 6 Forsomuch as this people **r** the waters of 3988
Jer 15:18 my wound incurable, *which* **r** to be healed? 3985

REGARD (30) [REGARDED, REGARDEST, REGARDETH, REGARDING]
Ge 45:20 Also **r** not your stuff; for the good of 2347+5869
Ex 5: 9 and let them not **r** vain words. 8159
Lev 19:31 **R** not them that have familiar spirits, 413+6437
Dt 28:50 which shall not **r** the person of the old, 5375
1Sa 4:20 answered not, neither did she **r** *it.* 3820+7896
25:25 I pray thee, **r** this man of Belial, 3820+7760
2Sa 13:20 he *is* thy brother; **r** not this thing. So 3820+7896
2Ki 3:14 were it not that I **r** the presence of 5375
Job 3: 4 let not God **r** it from above, neither let 1875
35:13 hear vanity, neither will the Almighty **r** it. 7789
36:21 Take heed, **r** not iniquity: for this hast 413+6437
Ps 28: 5 Because they **r** not the works of the LORD, 995
31: 6 I have hated them that **r** lying vanities: but 8104
66:18 If I **r** iniquity in my heart, the Lord will 7200
94: 7 not see, neither shall the God of Jacob **r** *it.* 995
102:17 He will **r** the prayer of the destitute, and 6437
Pr 5: 2 That *thou* mayest **r** discretion, and *that* thy 8104
6:35 He will not **r** any ransom; 5375+6440
Ecc 8: 2 and *that* in **r** of the oath of God. 1700
Isa 5:12 they **r** not the work of the LORD, 5027
13:17 against them, which shall not **r** silver; 2803
La 4:16 hath divided them; he will no more **r** them: 5027
Da 11:37 Neither shall he **r** the God of his fathers, 995
11:37 nor the desire of women, nor **r** any god: 995
Am 5:22 I will not accept *them:* neither will I **r** 5027
Hab 1: 5 and **r**, and wonder marvellously: 5027
Mal 1: 9 will he **r** your **persons**? 4480+5375+6440
Lk 18: 4 Though I fear not God, nor **r** man; *1788*
Ac 8:11 And to him they **had r**, because that of *4337*
Ro 14: 6 to the Lord he doth not **r** *it.* He that eateth, *5426*
14: 6 He that **r** the day, regardeth *it* unto *5426*
14: 6 that regardeth the day, **r** *it* unto the Lord; *5426*
14: 6 and he that **r** not the day, to the Lord he *5426*

REGARDED (9) [REGARD]
Ex 9:21 he that **r** not the word of the LORD 3820+7760
1Ki 18:29 nor any to answer, nor any that **r**. 7182
1Ch 17:17 hast **r** me according to the estate of a man 7200
Ps 106:44 Nevertheless he **r** their affliction, when he 7200
Pr 1:24 have stretched out my hand, and no man **r**; 7181
Da 3:12 these men, O king, have not **r** thee: 2942+7761
Lk 1:48 For he hath **r** the low estate of his *1914*
18: 2 which feared not God, neither **r** man: *1788*
Heb 8: 9 and I **r** them **not**, saith the Lord. *272*

REGARDEST (4) [REGARD]
2Sa 19: 6 that thou **r** neither princes nor servants: 3807.1
Job 30:20 not hear me: I stand *up,* and thou **r** me *not.* 995
Mt 22:16 neither carest thou for any *man:* for thou **r** *991*
Mk 12:14 carest for no *man:* for thou **r** not *991+1519*

REGARDETH (15) [REGARD]
Dt 10:17 and a terrible, which **r** not persons, 5375
Job 34:19 nor **r** the rich more than the poor? 5234
39: 7 neither **r** he the crying of the driver. 8085
Pr 12:10 A righteous *man* **r** the life of his beast: but 3045
13:18 but he that **r** reproof shall be honoured. 8104
15: 5 but he that **r** reproof is prudent. 8104
29: 7 of the poor: *but* the wicked **r** not to know *it.* 995
Ecc 5: 8 for *he that is* higher than the highest **r**; and 8104
11: 4 and he that **r** the clouds shall not reap. 7200
Isa 33: 8 he hath despised the cities, he **r** no man. 2803
Da 6:13 **r** not thee, O king, nor the decree that thou 7761
Mal 2:13 insomuch that *he* **r** not the offering 413+6437

REGARDING (2) [REGARD]
Job 4:20 they perish for ever without *any* **r** *it.* 7760
Php 2:30 **not r** *his* life, to supply your lack of service *3851*

REGEM (1)
1Ch 2:47 **R**, and Jotham, and Geshan, and Pelet, and 7276

REGEMMELECH (1)
Zec 7: 2 sent *unto* the house of God Sherezer and **R**, 7278

REGENERATION (2)
Mt 19:28 That ye which have followed me, in the **r**, *3824*
Tit 3: 5 by the washing of **r**, and renewing of *3824*

REGION (15) [REGIONS]
Dt 3: 4 threescore cities, all the **r** of Argob, 2256
3:13 all the **r** of Argob, with all Bashan, which 2256
1Ki 4:11 The son of Abinadab, *in* all the **r** of Dor; 5299
4:13 to him *also pertained* the **r** of Argob, 2256
4:24 For he had dominion over all *the* **r** on *this* NIH
Mt 3: 5 and all the **r round about** Jordan, *4066*
4:16 and to them which sat in the **r** and *5561*
Mk 1:28 throughout all the **r round about** Galilee. *4066*
6:55 And ran through that whole **r round about**, *4066*
Lk 3: 1 of Iturea and of the **r** of Trachonitis, *5561*
4:14 fame of him through all the **r round about**. *4066*
7:17 and throughout all the **r round about**. *4066*
Ac 13:49 Lord was published throughout all the **r**. *5561*
14: 6 and *unto* the **r that lieth round about**: *4066*
16: 6 throughout Phrygia and the **r** of Galatia, *5561*

REGIONS (4) [REGION]
Ac 8: 1 scattered abroad throughout the **r** of Judea *5561*
2Co 10:16 To preach the gospel in the *r* beyond you, NIG
11:10 stop me of this boasting in the **r** of Achaia. *2824*
Gal 1:21 Afterwards I came into the **r** of Syria and *2824*

REGISTER (3)
Ezr 2:62 These sought their **r** *among* those that were 3791
Ne 7: 5 I found a **r** of the genealogy of them which 5612
7:64 These sought their **r** *among* those that were 3791

REGULAR See SERVILE

REHABIAH (5)
1Ch 23:17 the sons of Eliezer *were,* **R** the chief. 7345
23:17 but the sons of **R** were very many. 7345
24:21 Concerning **R**: of the sons of Rehabiah, 7345
24:21 of the sons of **R**, the first *was* Isshiah. 7345
26:25 **R** his son, and Jeshaiah his son, and 7345

REHEARSE (2) [REHEARSED]
Ex 17:14 in a book, and **r** *it* in the ears of Joshua: 7760
Jdg 5:11 they **r** the righteous acts of the LORD, 8567

REHEARSED (4) [REHEARSE]
1Sa 8:21 and he **r** them in the ears of the LORD. 1696
17:31 David spake, they **r** *them* before Saul: 5046
Ac 11: 4 But Peter *r the matter* from the beginning, NIG
14:27 they **r** all that God had done with them, and *312*

REHOB (10) [BETH-REHOB]
Nu 13:21 the land from the wilderness of Zin unto **R**, 7340
Jos 19:28 and **R**, and Hammon, and Kanah, 7340
19:30 Ummah also, and Aphek, and **R**: twenty 7340
21:31 with her suburbs, and **R** with her suburbs; 7340
Jdg 1:31 nor of Helbah, nor of Aphik, nor of **R**: 7340
2Sa 8: 3 the son of **R**, king of Zobah, 7340
8:12 of Hadadezer, son of **R**, king of Zobah. 7340
10: 8 and of **R**, and Ish-tob, and Maacah, 7340
1Ch 6:75 with her suburbs, and **R** with her suburbs: 7340
Ne 10:11 Micha, **R**, Hashabiah, 7340

REHOBOAM (50) [ROBOAM]
1Ki 11:43 and **R** his son reigned in his stead. 7346
12: 1 **R** went *to* Shechem: for all Israel were 7346
12: 3 of Israel came, and spake unto **R**, saying, 7346
12: 6 king **R** consulted with the old men, 7346
12:12 and all the people came to **R** the third day, 7346
12:17 in the cities of Judah, **R** reigned over them. 7346
12:18 king **R** sent Adoram, who *was* over 7346
12:18 Therefore king **R** made speed to get *him* up 7346

1Ki 12:21 when **R** was come *to* Jerusalem, he 7346
12:21 to bring the kingdom again to **R** the son of 7346
12:23 Speak unto **R**, the son of Solomon, king of 7346
12:27 *even* unto **R** king of Judah, and they shall 7346
12:27 kill me, and go again to **R** king of Judah. 7346
14:21 **R** the son of Solomon reigned in Judah. 7346
14:21 **R** *was* forty and one years old when he 7346
14:25 it came to pass in the fifth year of king **R**, 7346
14:27 king **R** made in their stead brasen shields, 7346
14:29 Now the rest of the acts of **R**, and all that 7346
14:30 there was war between **R** and Jeroboam all 7346
14:31 **R** slept with his fathers, and was buried 7346
15: 6 there was war between **R** and Jeroboam all 7346
1Ch 3:10 Solomon's son *was* **R**, Abia his son, 7346
2Ch 9:31 and **R** his son reigned in his stead. 7346
10: 1 **R** went to Shechem: for *to* Shechem were 7346
10: 3 and all Israel came and spake to **R**, 7346
10: 6 king **R** took counsel with the old men that 7346
10:12 all the people came to **R** on the third day, 7346
10:13 king **R** forsook the counsel of the old men, 7346
10:17 in the cities of Judah, **R** reigned over them. 7346
10:18 king **R** sent Hadoram that *was* over 7346
10:18 king **R** made speed to get *him* up to *his* 7346
11: 1 when **R** was come *to* Jerusalem, he 7346
11: 1 that *he* might bring the kingdom again to **R**. 7346
11: 3 Speak unto **R** the son of Solomon, king of 7346
11: 5 **R** dwelt in Jerusalem, and built cities for 7346
11:17 made **R** the son of Solomon strong, 7346
11:18 **R** took him Mahalath the daughter of 7346
11:21 **R** loved Maachah the daughter of Absalom 7346
11:22 **R** made Abijah the son of Maachah 7346
12: 1 when **R** had established the kingdom, and 7346
12: 2 *that* in the fifth year of king **R** Shishak king 7346
12: 5 came Shemaiah the prophet to **R**, and *to* 7346
12:10 Instead of which king **R** made shields of 7346
12:13 So king **R** strengthened himself in 7346
12:13 for **R** *was* one and forty years old when he 7346
12:15 Now the acts of **R**, first and last, *are* they 7346
12:15 *there were* wars between **R** and 7346
12:16 **R** slept with his fathers, and was buried in 7346
13: 7 have strengthened themselves against **R** 7346
13: 7 when **R** was young and tender hearted, and 7346

REHOBOTH (4)
Ge 10:11 builded Nineveh, and the city **R**, and Calah, 7344
26:22 he called the name of it **R**; and he said, 7344
36:37 Saul of **R** *by* the river reigned in his stead. 7344
1Ch 1:48 Shaul of **R** *by* the river reigned in his stead. 7344

REHU (1)
1Ch 1:25 Eber, Peleg, **R**, 7466

REHUM (8)
Ezr 2: 2 Bilshan, Mizpar, Bigvai, **R**, Baanah. 7348
4: 8 **R** the chancellor and Shimshai the scribe 7348
4: 9 *wrote* **R** the chancellor, and Shimshai 7348
4:17 *Then* sent the king an answer unto **R** 7348
4:23 king Artaxerxes' letter *was* read before **R**, 7348
Ne 3:17 him repaired the Levites, **R** the son of Bani. 7348
10:25 **R**, Hashabnah, Maaseiah, 7348
12: 3 Shechaniah, **R**, Meremoth, 7348

REI (1)
1Ki 1: 8 **R**, and the mighty *men* which *belonged* to 7472

REIGN (168) [REIGNED, REIGNEST, REIGNETH, REIGNING]
Ge 37: 8 to him, Shalt thou **indeed** r over us? 4427+4427
Ex 15:18 The LORD shall r for ever and ever. 4427
Lev 26:17 they that hate you shall r over you; and 7287
Dt 15: 6 thou shalt r over many nations, but 4910
15: 6 but they shall not r over thee. 4910
Jdg 9: 2 r over you, or that one reign over you? 4910
9: 2 reign over you, or that one r over you? 4910
9: 8 said unto the olive tree, **R** thou over us. 4427
9:10 to the fig tree, Come thou, *and* r over us. 4427
9:12 unto the vine, Come thou, *and* r over us. 4427
9:14 the bramble, Come thou, *and* r over us. 4427
1Sa 8: 7 rejected me, that *I* should not r over them. 4427
8: 9 manner of the king that shall r over them. 4427
8:11 manner of the king that shall r over you: 4427
9:17 thee of: this *same* shall r over my people. 6113
11:12 Who *is* he that said, Shall Saul r over us? 4427
12:12 unto me, Nay; but a king shall r over us: 4427
2Sa 2:10 years old when he *began* to r over Israel, 4427
3:21 that thou mayest r over all that thine heart 4427
5: 4 *was* thirty years old when he *began* to r, 4427
1Ki 1:11 that Adonijah the son of Haggith doth r, 4427
1:13 Assuredly Solomon thy son shall r after 4427
1:13 my throne? why then doth Adonijah r? 4427
1:17 *saying,* Assuredly Solomon thy son shall r 4427
1:24 Adonijah shall r after me, and he shall sit 4427
1:30 Assuredly Solomon thy son shall r after 4427
2:15 Israel set their faces on me, that *I* should r: 4427
6: 1 in the fourth year of Solomon's r over 4427
11:37 thou shalt r according to all that thy soul 4427
14:21 and one years old when he *began* to r, 4427
15:25 Nadab the son of Jeroboam *began* to r over 4427
15:33 son of Ahijah to r over all Israel in Tirzah, 4427
16: 8 the son of Baasha to r over Israel in Tirzah, 4427
16:11 it came to pass, when he *began* to r, 4427
16:15 of Judah did Zimri r seven days in Tirzah. 4427
16:23 king of Judah *began* Omri to r over Israel, 4427
16:29 Ahab the son of Omri to r over Israel: 4427
22:41 Jehoshaphat the son of Asa *began* to r over 4427
22:42 and five years old when he *began* to r; 4427
22:51 Ahaziah the son of Ahab *began* to r over 4427
2Ki 3: 1 Now Jehoram the son of Ahab *began* to r 4427
8:16 of Jehoshaphat king of Judah *began* to r. 4427
8:17 two years old was he when he *began* to r; 4427
8:25 son of Jehoram king of Judah *begin* to r. 4427
8:26 years old *was* Ahaziah when he *began* to r; 4427
9:29 of Ahab *began* Ahaziah to r over Judah. 4427
11: 3 six years. And Athaliah *did* r over the land. 4427
11:21 years old *was* Jehoash when he *began* to r. 4427
12: 1 seventh year of Jehu Jehoash *began* to r; 4427
13: 1 of Jehu *began* to r over Israel in Samaria, 4427
13:10 son of Jehoahaz to r over Israel in Samaria, 4427
14: 2 and five years old when he *began* to r, 4427
14:23 Joash king of Israel *began* to r in Samaria, 4427
15: 1 Azariah son of Amaziah king of Judah to r. 4427
15: 2 years old was he when he *began* to r, 4427
15: 8 r over Israel in Samaria six months. 4427
15:13 Shallum the son of Jabesh *began* to r in 4427
15:17 Menahem the son of Gadi to r over Israel, 4427
15:23 *began* to r over Israel in Samaria, 4427
15:27 Remaliah *began* to r over Israel in Samaria, 4427
15:32 the son of Uzziah king of Judah to r. 4427
15:33 years old was he when he *began* to r, 4427
16: 1 the son of Jotham king of Judah *began* to r. 4427
16: 2 years old *was* Ahaz when he *began* to r, 4427
17: 1 Elah to r in Samaria over Israel nine years. 4427
18: 1 the son of Ahaz king of Judah *began* to r. 4427
18: 2 five years old was he when he *began* to r; 4427
21: 1 *was* twelve years old when he *began* to r, 4427
21:19 and two years old when he *began* to r, 4427
22: 1 *was* eight years old when he *began* to r, 4427
23:31 and three years old when he *began* to r; 4427
23:33 that *he* might not r in Jerusalem; 4427
23:36 and five year old when he *began* to r; 4427
24: 8 *was* eighteen years old when he *began* to r, 4427
24:12 took him in the eighth year of his r. 4427
24:18 and one years old when he *began* to r, 4427
25: 1 it came to pass in the ninth year of his r, 4427
25:27 of Babylon, in the year that he *began* to r, 4427
1Ch 4:31 These *were* their cities unto the r of David. 4427
26:31 In the fortieth year of the r of David they 4438
29:30 With all his r and his might, and the times 4438
2Ch 1: 8 and hast **made** me **to** r in his stead. 4427
3: 2 second month, in the fourth year of his r. 4438
12:13 and forty years old when he *began* to r, 4427
13: 1 Jeroboam *began* Abijah to r over Judah. 4427
15:10 in the fifteenth year of the r of Asa. 4438
15:19 the five and thirtieth year of the r of Asa. 4438
16: 1 thirtieth year of the r of Asa Baasha king of 4438
16:12 ninth year of his r was diseased in his feet, 4438
16:13 died in the one and fortieth year of his r. 4427
17: 7 Also in the third year of his r he sent to his 4427
20:31 and five years old when he *began* to r, 4427
21: 5 and two years old when he *began* to r, 4427
21:20 two *years* old was he when he *began* to r, 4427
22: 2 years old *was* Ahaziah when he *began* to r, 4427
23: 3 unto them, Behold, the king's son shall r, 4427
24: 1 *was* seven years old when he *began* to r, 4427
25: 1 and five years old *when* he *began* to r, 4427
26: 3 years old *was* Uzziah when he *began* to r, 4427
27: 1 and five years old when he *began* to r, 4427
27: 8 and twenty years old when he *began* to r, 4427
28: 1 *was* twenty years old when he *began* to r, 4427

2Ch 29: 1 Hezekiah *began* to r *when he was* five and 4427
29: 3 He in the first year of his r, in the first 4427
29:19 which king Ahaz in his r did cast away in 4438
33: 1 *was* twelve years old when he *began* to r, 4427
33:21 and twenty years old when he *began* to r, 4427
34: 1 *was* eight years old when he *began* to r, 4427
34: 3 For in the eighth year of his r, while he was 4427
34: 8 Now in the eighteenth year of his r, 4427
35:19 In the eighteenth year of the r of Josiah was 4438
36: 2 and three years old when he *began* to r, 4427
36: 5 and five years old when he *began* to r, 4427
36: 9 *was* eight years old when he *began* to r, 4427
36:11 and twenty years old when he *began* to r, 4427
36:20 his sons until the r of the kingdom of 4427
Ezr 4: 5 even until the r of Darius king of Persia. 4438
4: 6 in the r of Ahasuerus, in the beginning of 4438
4: 6 of Ahasuerus, in the beginning of his r, 4438
4:24 So it ceased unto the second year of the r 4437
6:15 which *was in* the sixth year of the r of 4437
7: 1 in the r of Artaxerxes king of Persia, 4438
8: 1 in the r of Artaxerxes the king. 4438
Ne 12:22 the priests, to the r of Darius the Persian. 4438
Est 1: 3 In the third year of his r, he made a feast 4427
2:16 month Tebeth, in the seventh year of his r. 4438
Job 34:30 That the hypocrite r not, lest the people be 4427
Ps 146:10 The LORD shall r for ever, *even* thy God, 4427
Pr 8:15 By me kings r, and princes decree justice. 4427
Ecc 4:14 For out of prison he cometh to r; 4427
Isa 24:23 when the LORD of hosts shall r in mount 4427
32: 1 a king shall r in righteousness, and princes 4427
Jer 1: 2 of Judah, in the thirteenth year of his r. 4427
22:15 Shalt thou r, because thou closest *thyself* in 4427
23: 5 a King shall r and prosper, and 4427
26: 1 In the beginning of the r of Jehoiakim 4468
27: 1 In the beginning of the r of Jehoiakim 4467
28: 1 in the beginning of the r of Zedekiah king 4467
33:21 that he should not have a son to r upon his 4427
49:34 of the r of Zedekiah king of Judah, 4438
51:59 *into* Babylon in the fourth year of his r. 4427
52: 1 and twenty year old when he *began* to r, 4427
52: 4 it came to pass in the ninth year of his r, 4427
52:31 r lifted up the head of Jehoiachin king of 4438
Da 1: 1 In the third year of the r of Jehoiakim king 4438
2: 1 in the second year of the r of 4438
6:28 So this Daniel prospered in the r of Darius, 4437
6:28 of Darius, and in the r of Cyrus the Persian. 4437
8: 1 In the third year of the r of king Belshazzar 4438
9: 2 In the first year of his r I Daniel understood 4427
Mic 4: 7 the LORD shall r over them in mount 4427
Mt 2:22 But when he heard that Archelaus did r in *936*
Lk 1:33 And he shall r over the house of Jacob for *936*
3: 1 Now in the fifteenth year of the r of *2231*
19:14 We will not have this *man* to r over us. *936*
19:27 which would not that I should r over them, *936*
Ro 5:17 of the gift of righteousness shall r in life by *936*
5:21 might grace r through righteousness unto *936*
6:12 Let not sin therefore r in your mortal body, *936*
15:12 and he that *shall* rise to r **over** the Gentiles; *757*
1Co 4: 8 and I would *to God* ye did r, that we also *936*
4: 8 ye did reign, that we also might r **with** you. *4821*
15:25 For he must r, till he hath put all enemies *936*
2Ti 2:12 we shall also r **with** *him:* if we deny *him,* *4821*
Rev 5:10 and priests: and we shall r on the earth. *936*
11:15 his Christ; and he shall r for ever and ever. *936*
20: 6 and shall r with him a thousand years. *936*
22: 5 and they shall r for ever and ever. *936*

REIGNED (176) [REIGN]

Ge 36:31 these *are* the kings that r in the land of 4427
36:31 before there r *any* king over the children of 4427
36:32 Bela the son of Beor r in Edom: and 4427
36:33 Jobab the son of Zerah of Bozrah r in his 4427
36:34 Husham of the land of Temani r in his 4427
36:35 Midian in the field of Moab, r in his stead: 4427
36:36 and Samlah of Masrekah r in his stead. 4427
36:37 Saul of Rehoboth *by* the river r in his stead. 4427
36:38 Baal-hanan the son of Achbor r in his 4427
36:39 of Achbor died, and Hadar r in his stead: 4427
Jos 12: 5 r in mount Hermon, and in Salcah, and 4910
13:10 which r in Heshbon, unto the border of 4427
13:12 which r in Ashtaroth and in Edrei, 4427
13:21 king of the Amorites, which r in Heshbon, 4427
Jdg 4: 2 of Jabin king of Canaan, that r in Hazor; 4427
9:22 When Abimelech had r three years over 7786
1Sa 13: 1 Saul r one year; and when he had reigned 4427
13: 1 and when he had r two years over Israel, 4427
2Sa 2:10 *began* to reign over Israel, and r two years. 4427
5: 4 he *began* to reign, *and* he r forty years. 4427
5: 5 In Hebron he r over Judah seven years and 4427
5: 5 in Jerusalem he r thirty and three years 4427
8:15 David r over all Israel; and David executed 4427
10: 1 and Hanun his son r in his stead. 4427
16: 8 house of Saul, in whose stead thou hast r; 4427
1Ki 2:11 the days that David r over Israel *were* forty 4427
2:11 seven years r he in Hebron, and thirty and 4427
2:11 and thirty and three years r he in Jerusalem. 4427
4:21 Solomon r over all kingdoms from the river 4910
11:24 and dwelt therein, and r in Damascus. 4427
11:25 and he abhorred Israel, and r over Syria. 4427
11:42 the time that Solomon r in Jerusalem over 4427
11:43 and Rehoboam his son r in his stead. 4427
12:17 the cities of Judah, Rehoboam r over them. 4427
14:19 of Jeroboam, how he warred, and how he r, 4427
14:20 the days which Jeroboam r *were* two and 4427
14:20 and Nadab his son r in his stead. 4427
14:21 Rehoboam the son of Solomon r in Judah. 4427
14:21 and he r seventeen years in Jerusalem, 4427
14:31 And Abijam his son r in his stead. 4427
15: 1 the son of Nebat r Abijam over Judah. 4427
15: 2 Three years r he in Jerusalem. And his 4427
15: 8 of David: and Asa his son r in his stead. 4427
15: 9 king of Israel r Asa **over** Judah. 4427+4428
15:10 forty and one years r he in Jerusalem. 4427
15:24 and Jehoshaphat his son r in his stead. 4427
15:25 king of Judah, and r over Israel two years. 4427
15:28 did Baasha slay him, and r in his stead. 4427
15:29 it came to pass, when he r, *that* he smote all 4427
16: 6 in Tirzah: and Elah his son r in his stead. 4427
16:10 of Asa king of Judah, and r in his stead. 4427
16:22 son of Ginath: so Tibni died, and Omri r. 4427
16:23 twelve years: six years r he in Tirzah. 4427
16:28 in Samaria: and Ahab his son r in his stead. 4427
16:29 Ahab the son of Omri r over Israel in 4427
22:40 and Ahaziah his son r in his stead. 4427
22:42 he r twenty and five years in Jerusalem. 4427
22:50 and Jehoram his son r in his stead. 4427
22:51 king of Judah, and r two years over Israel. 4427
2Ki 1:17 Jehoram r in his stead in the second year of 4427
3: 1 king of Judah, and r twelve years. 4427
3:27 he took his eldest son that should have r in 4427
8:15 so that he died: and Hazael r in his stead. 4427
8:17 to reign; and he r eight years in Jerusalem. 4427
8:24 and Ahaziah his son r in his stead. 4427
8:26 to reign; and he r one year in Jerusalem. 4427
10:35 And Jehoahaz his son r in his stead. 4427
10:36 the time that Jehu r over Israel in Samaria 4427
12: 1 to reign; and forty years r he in Jerusalem. 4427
12:21 and Amaziah his son r in his stead. 4427
13: 1 Israel in Samaria, *and* r seventeen years. NIH
13: 9 in Samaria: and Joash his son r in his stead. 4427
13:10 over Israel in Samaria, *and* r sixteen years. NIH
13:24 and Ben-hadad his son r in his stead. 4427
14: 1 r Amaziah the son of Joash king of Judah. 4427
14: 2 and r twenty and nine years in Jerusalem. 4427
14:16 and Jeroboam his son r in his stead. 4427
14:23 reign in Samaria, *and* r forty and one years. NIH
14:29 and Zachariah his son r in his stead. 4427
15: 2 and he r two and fifty years in Jerusalem. 4427
15: 7 of David: and Jotham his son r in his stead. 4427
15:10 and slew him, and r in his stead. 4427
15:13 of Judah; and he r a full month in Samaria. 4427
15:14 and slew him, and r in his stead. 4427
15:17 over Israel, *and* r ten years in Samaria. NIH
15:22 and Pekahiah his son r in his stead. 4427
15:23 over Israel in Samaria, *and* r two years. NIH
15:25 he killed him, and r in his room. 4427
15:27 over Israel in Samaria, *and* r twenty years. NIH
15:30 and slew him, and r in his stead, 4427
15:33 and he r sixteen years in Jerusalem. 4427
15:38 his father: and Ahaz his son r in his stead. 4427
16: 2 r sixteen years in Jerusalem, and did not 4427
16:20 and Hezekiah his son r in his stead. 4427
18: 2 he r twenty and nine years in Jerusalem. 4427
19:37 And Esarhaddon his son r in his stead. 4427
20:21 and Manasseh his son r in his stead. 4427
21: 1 and r fifty and five years in Jerusalem. 4427
21:18 of Uzza: and Amon his son r in his stead. 4427
21:19 to reign, and he r two years in Jerusalem. 4427

2Ki 21:26 of Uzza: and Josiah his son **r** in his stead. 4427
22: 1 and he **r** thirty and one years in Jerusalem. 4427
23:31 and he **r** three months in Jerusalem. 4427
23:36 and he **r** eleven years in Jerusalem. 4427
24: 6 and Jehoiachin his son **r** in his stead. 4427
24: 8 and he **r** in Jerusalem three months. 4427
24:18 and he **r** eleven years in Jerusalem. 4427
1Ch 1:43 Now these *are* the kings that **r** in the land 4427
1:43 *any* king **r** over the children of Israel; 4427
1:44 Jobab the son of Zerah of Bozrah **r** in his 4427
1:45 Husham of the land of the Temanites **r** in 4427
1:46 Midian in the field of Moab, **r** in his stead: 4427
1:47 Samlah of Masrekah **r** in his stead. 4427
1:48 Shaul of Rehoboth *by* the river **r** in his 4427
1:49 Baal-hanan the son of Achbor **r** in his 4427
1:50 Baal-hanan was dead, Hadad **r** in his stead: 4427
3: 4 and there he **r** seven years and six months: 4427
3: 4 and in Jerusalem he **r** thirty and three years. 4427
18:14 So David **r** over all Israel, and executed 4427
19: 1 of Ammon died, and his son **r** in his stead. 4427
29:26 Thus David the son of Jesse **r** over all 4427
29:27 the time that he **r** over Israel *was* forty 4427
29:27 seven years **r** he in Hebron, and thirty and 4427
29:27 and thirty and three *years* **r** he in Jerusalem. 4427
29:28 honour: and Solomon his son **r** in his stead. 4427
2Ch 1:13 of the congregation, and **r** over Israel. 4427
9:26 he **r** over all the kings from the river even 4910
9:30 Solomon **r** in Jerusalem over all Israel forty 4427
9:31 and Rehoboam his son **r** in his stead. 4427
10:17 the cities of Judah, Rehoboam **r** over them. 4427
12:13 strengthened himself in Jerusalem, and **r**: 4427
12:13 and he **r** seventeen years in Jerusalem, 4427
12:16 of David: and Abijah his son **r** in his stead. 4427
13: 2 He **r** three years in Jerusalem. His mother's 4427
14: 1 Asa his son **r** in his stead. In his days 4427
17: 1 Jehoshaphat his son **r** in his stead, and 4427
20:31 Jehoshaphat **r** over Judah: *he was* thirty 4427
20:31 he **r** twenty and five years in Jerusalem. 4427
21: 1 And Jehoram his son **r** in his stead. 4427
21: 5 to reign, and he **r** eight years in Jerusalem. 4427
21:20 he **r** in Jerusalem eight years, and 4427
22: 1 the son of Jehoram king of Judah **r**. 4427
22: 2 to reign, and he **r** one year in Jerusalem. 4427
22:12 God six years: and Athaliah **r** over the land. 4427
24: 1 to reign, and he **r** forty years in Jerusalem. 4427
24:27 And Amaziah his son **r** in his stead. 4427
25: 1 he **r** twenty and nine years in Jerusalem. 4427
26: 3 and he **r** fifty and two years in Jerusalem. 4427
26:23 *is* a leper: and Jotham his son **r** in his stead. 4427
27: 1 and he **r** sixteen years in Jerusalem. 4427
27: 8 to reign, and **r** sixteen years in Jerusalem. 4427
27: 9 of David: and Ahaz his son **r** in his stead. 4427
28: 1 and he **r** sixteen years in Jerusalem: 4427
28:27 and Hezekiah his son **r** in his stead. 4427
29: 1 he **r** nine and twenty years in Jerusalem. 4427
32:33 And Manasseh his son **r** in his stead. 4427
33: 1 and he **r** fifty and five years in Jerusalem: 4427
33:20 and Amon his son **r** in his stead. 4427
33:21 to reign, and **r** two years in Jerusalem. 4427
34: 1 and he **r** in Jerusalem one and thirty years. 4427
36: 2 and he **r** three months in Jerusalem. 4427
36: 5 and he **r** eleven years in Jerusalem: 4427
36: 8 Judah: and Jehoiachin his son **r** in his stead. 4427
36: 9 he **r** three months and ten days in 4427
36:11 to reign, and **r** eleven years in Jerusalem. 4427
Est 1: 1 (this *is* Ahasuerus which **r**, from India even 4427
Isa 37:38 and Esar-haddon his son **r** in his stead. 4427
Jer 22:11 which **r** instead of Josiah his father, 4427
37: 1 king Zedekiah the son of Josiah **r** instead of 4427
52: 1 and he **r** eleven years in Jerusalem. 4427
Ro 5:14 Nevertheless death **r** from Adam to Moses, *936*
5:17 For if by one man's offence death **r** by one; *936*
5:21 That as sin hath **r** unto death, even so might *936*
1Co 4: 8 ye are rich, ye have **r as kings** without us: *936*
Rev 11:17 taken *to thee* thy great power, and hast **r**. *936*
20: 4 and **r** with Christ a thousand years. *936*

REIGNEST (1) [REIGN]
1Ch 29:12 honour *come* of thee, and thou **r** over all; 4910

REIGNETH (13) [REIGN]
1Sa 12:14 also the king that **r** over you continue 4427
2Sa 15:10 then ye shall say, Absalom **r** in Hebron. 4427
1Ki 1:18 now behold, Adonijah **r**; and now, my lord 4427
1Ch 16:31 *men* say among the nations, The LORD **r**. 4427
Ps 47: 8 God **r** over the heathen: God sitteth upon 4427
93: 1 The LORD **r**, he is clothed with majesty; 4427
96:10 Say among the heathen *that* the LORD **r**: 4427
97: 1 The LORD **r**; let the earth rejoice; let 4427
99: 1 The LORD **r**; let the people tremble: 4427
Pr 30:22 For a servant when he **r**; and a fool when 4427
Isa 52: 7 that saith unto Zion, Thy God **r**! 4427
Rev 17:18 which **r** over the kings of the earth. *932+2192*
19: 6 Alleluia: for the Lord God Omnipotent **r**. *936*

REIGNING (1) [REIGN]
1Sa 16: 1 seeing I have rejected him from **r** over 4427

REINS (15)
Job 16:13 he cleaveth my **r** asunder, and doth not 3629
19:27 *though* my **r** be consumed within me. 3629
Ps 7: 9 the righteous God trieth the hearts and **r**. 3629
16: 7 my **r** also instruct me *in* the night seasons. 3629
26: 2 and prove me; try my **r** and my heart. 3629
73:21 was grieved, and I was pricked *in* my **r**. 3629
139:13 For thou hast possessed my **r**: thou hast 3629
Pr 23:16 Yea, my **r** shall rejoice, when thy lips 3629
Isa 11: 5 and faithfulness the girdle of his **r**. 2504
Jer 11:20 that triest the **r** and the heart, 3629
12: 2 *art* near in their mouth, and far from their **r**. 3629
17:10 I the LORD search the heart, *I* try the **r**, 3629
20:12 the righteous, *and* seest the **r** and the heart, 3629
La 3:13 the arrows of his quiver to enter into my **r**. 3629
Rev 2:23 know that I am he which searcheth the **r** *3510*

REJECT (4) [REJECTED, REJECTETH]
Hos 4: 6 hast rejected knowledge, I will also **r** thee, 3988
Mk 6:26 which sat with *him,* he would not **r** her. *114*
7: 9 Full well ye **r** the commandment of God, *114*
Tit 3:10 after the first and second admonition, **r**; *3868*

REJECTED (29) [REJECT]
1Sa 8: 7 for they have not **r** thee, but they have 3988
8: 7 have not rejected thee, but they have **r** me, 3988
10:19 ye have *this* day **r** your God, who himself 3988
15:23 Because thou hast **r** the word of 3988
15:23 he hath also **r** thee from *being* king. 3988
15:26 for thou hast **r** the word of the LORD, and 3988
15:26 the LORD hath **r** thee from being king 3988
16: 1 seeing I have **r** him from reigning over 3988
2Ki 17:15 they **r** his statutes, and his covenant that he 3988
17:20 the LORD **r** all the seed of Israel, and 3988
Isa 53: 3 He is despised and **r** of men; a man of 2310
Jer 2:37 for the LORD hath **r** thy confidences, and 3988
6:19 unto my words, nor *to* my law, but **r** it. 3988
6:30 call them, because the LORD hath **r** them. 3988
7:29 for the LORD hath **r** and forsaken 3988
8: 9 lo, they have **r** the word of the LORD; 3988
14:19 Hast thou **utterly r** Judah? hath thy 3988+3988
La 5:22 thou hast **utterly r** us; thou art very 3988+3988
Hos 4: 6 because thou hast **r** knowledge, I will also 3988
Mt 21:42 The stone which the builders **r**, *593*
Mk 8:31 suffer many *things,* and be **r** of the elders, *593*
12:10 The stone which the builders **r** is become *593*
Lk 7:30 lawyers **r** the counsel of God against *114*
9:22 and be **r** of the elders and chief priests and *593*
17:25 many *things,* and be **r** of this generation. *593*
20:17 is written, The stone which the builders **r**, *593*
Gal 4:14 was in my flesh ye despised not, nor **r**; *1609*
Heb 6: 8 But that which beareth thorns and briers *is* **r**, *96*
12:17 would have inherited the blessing, he was **r**: *593*

REJECTETH (1) [REJECT]
Jn 12:48 He that **r** me, and receiveth not my words, *114*

REJOICE (192) [REJOICED, REJOICEST, REJOICETH, REJOICING]
Lev 23:40 ye shall **r** before the LORD your God 8055
Dt 12: 7 ye shall **r** in all that you put your hand 8055
12:12 ye shall **r** before the LORD your God, 8055
12:18 thou shalt **r** before the LORD thy God in 8055
14:26 and thou shalt **r**, thou and thine household, 8055
16:11 thou shalt **r** before the LORD thy God, 8055
16:14 thou shalt **r** in thy feast, thou, and thy son, 8055
16:15 therefore thou shalt surely **r**. 1961+8056
26:11 thou shalt **r** in every good *thing* which 8055
27: 7 eat there, and **r** before the LORD thy God. 8055
28:63 the LORD will **r** over you to destroy you, 7797

Dt 30: 9 for the LORD will again **r** over thee for 7797
32:43 **R**, O ye nations, *with* his people: for he will 7442
33:18 he said, **R**, Zebulun, in thy going out; 8055
Jdg 9:19 *then* **r** ye in Abimelech, and let him also 8055
9:19 ye in Abimelech, and let him also **r** in you: 8055
16:23 sacrifice unto Dagon their god, and to **r**: 8057
1Sa 2: 1 mine enemies; because I **r** in thy salvation. 8055
19: 5 thou sawest *it*, and didst **r**: wherefore then 8055
2Sa 1:20 lest the daughters of the Philistines **r**, 8055
1Ch 16:10 let the heart of them **r** that seek 8055
16:31 Let the heavens be glad, and let the earth **r**: 1523
16:32 let the fields **r**, and all that *is* therein. 5970
2Ch 6:41 and let thy saints **r** in goodness. 8055
20:27 for the LORD had **made** them **to r** over 8055
Ne 12:43 for God had **made** them **r** *with* great joy: 8055
Job 3:22 Which **r exceedingly**, *and* 413+1524+8056
20:18 restitution *be*, and he shall not **r** *therein*. 5965
21:12 and harp, and **r** at the sound of the organ. 8055
Ps 2:11 the LORD with fear, and **r** with trembling. 1523
5:11 let all those that put their trust in thee **r**: 8055
9: 2 I will be glad and **r** in thee: I will sing 5970
9:14 daughter of Zion: I will **r** in thy salvation. 1523
13: 4 those that trouble me **r** when I am moved. 1523
13: 5 thy mercy; my heart shall **r** in thy salvation. 1523
14: 7 Jacob shall **r**, *and* Israel shall be glad. 1523
20: 5 We will **r** in thy salvation, and in the name 7442
21: 1 and in thy salvation how greatly shall he **r**! 1523
30: 1 and hast not **made** my foes **to r** over me. 8055
31: 7 I will be glad and **r** in thy mercy: for thou 8055
32:11 Be glad in the LORD, and **r**, ye righteous: 1523
33: 1 **R** in the LORD, O ye righteous: *for* praise 7442
33:21 For our heart shall **r** in him, because 8055
35: 9 in the LORD: it shall **r** in his salvation. 7797
35:19 are mine enemies wrongfully **r** over me: 8055
35:24 and let them not **r** over me. 8055
35:26 brought to confusion together that **r** at mine 8056
38:16 *Hear me*, lest *otherwise* they should **r** over 8055
40:16 Let all those that seek thee **r** and be glad in 7797
48:11 Let mount Zion **r**, let the daughters of 8055
51: 8 the bones *which* thou hast broken may **r**. 1523
53: 6 Jacob shall **r**, *and* Israel shall be glad. 1523
58:10 The righteous shall **r** when he seeth 8055
60: 6 I will **r**, I will divide Shechem, and 5937
63: 7 in the shadow of thy wings will I **r**. 7442
63:11 the king shall **r** in God; every one that 8055
65: 8 **makest** the outgoings of the morning and evening **to r**. 7442
65:12 and the little hills **r** on every side. 1524
66: 6 the flood on foot: there did we **r** in him. 8055
68: 3 righteous be glad; let them **r** before God: 5970
68: 3 yea, let them **exceedingly r**. 7797+8057+871.1
68: 4 by his name JAH, and **r** before him. 5937
70: 4 Let all those that seek thee **r** and be glad in 7797
71:23 My lips shall **greatly r** when I sing unto 7442
85: 6 us again: that thy people may **r** in thee? 8055
86: 4 **R** the soul of thy servant: for unto thee, 8055
89:12 Tabor and Hermon shall **r** in thy name. 7442
89:16 In thy name shall they **r** all the day: and 1523
89:42 thou hast **made** all his enemies **to r**. 8055
90:14 that we may **r** and be glad all our days. 7442
96:11 Let the heavens **r**, and let the earth be glad; 8055
96:12 shall all the trees of the wood **r** 7442
97: 1 The LORD reigneth; let the earth **r**; 1523
97:12 **R** in the LORD, ye righteous; and 8055
98: 4 make a loud noise, and **r**, and sing *praise*. 7442
104:31 for ever: the LORD shall **r** in his works. 8055
105: 3 let the heart of them **r** that seek 8055
106: 5 that *I* may **r** in the gladness of thy nation, 8055
107:42 The righteous shall see *it*, and **r**: and 8055
108: 7 I will **r**, I will divide Shechem, and 5937
109:28 let them be ashamed; but let thy servant **r**. 8055
118:24 hath made; we will **r** and be glad in it. 1523
119:162 I **r** at thy word, as one that findeth great 7797
149: 2 Let Israel **r** in him that made him: let 8055
Pr 2:14 Who **r** to do evil, *and* delight in 8056
5:18 and **r** with the wife of thy youth. 8055
23:15 heart be wise, my heart shall **r**, even mine. 8055
23:16 Yea, my reins shall **r**, when thy lips speak 5937
23:24 of the righteous shall **greatly r**: 1523+1524
23:25 shall be glad, and she that bare thee shall **r**. 1523
24:17 **R** not when thine enemy falleth, and let not 8055
27: 9 Ointment and perfume **r** the heart: so 8055
28:12 When righteous *men* do **r**, *there is* great 5970
29: 2 the righteous are in authority, the people **r**: 8055
29: 6 *is* a snare: but the righteous doth sing and **r**. 8056
31:25 and she shall **r** in time to come. 7832
Ecc 3:12 for *a man* to **r**, and to do good in his life. 8055
3:22 than that a man should **r** in his own works; 8055
4:16 they also that come after shall not **r** in him. 8055
5:19 to take his portion, and to **r** in his labour; 8055
11: 8 if a man live many years, *and* **r** in them all; 8055
11: 9 **R**, O young man, in thy youth; and let thy 8055
SS 1: 4 we will be glad and **r** in thee, we will 8055
Isa 8: 6 and **r** in Rezin and Remaliah's son; 4885
9: 3 *and* as *men* **r** when they divide the spoil. 1523
13: 3 *even* them that **r** in my highness. 5947
14: 8 the fir trees **r** at thee, *and* the cedars of 8055
14:29 **R** not thou, whole Palestina, because 8055
23:12 he said, Thou shalt no more **r**, O thou 5937
24: 8 the noise of them that **r** endeth, the joy of 5947
25: 9 we will be glad and **r** in his salvation. 8055
29:19 the poor among men shall **r** in the Holy 1523
35: 1 the desert shall **r**, and blossom as the rose. 1523
35: 2 **r** even *with* joy and singing: 1523
41:16 thou shalt **r** in the LORD, *and* shalt glory 1523
61: 7 *for* confusion they shall **r** in their portion: 7442
61:10 I will **greatly r** in the LORD, 7797+7797
62: 5 over the bride, *so* shall thy God **r** over thee. 7797
65:13 my servants shall **r**, but ye shall be 8055
65:18 and **r** for ever *in that* which I create: 1523
65:19 I will **r** in Jerusalem, and joy in my people: 1523
66:10 **R** ye with Jerusalem, and be glad with her, 8055
66:10 **r** for joy with her, all ye that mourn for her: 7797
66:14 when ye see *this*, your heart shall **r**, and 7797
Jer 31:13 shall the virgin **r** in the dance, both young 8055
31:13 and **make** them **r** from their sorrow. 8055
32:41 I will **r** over them to do them good, and 7797
51:39 that they may **r**, and sleep a perpetual 5937
La 2:17 he hath **caused** *thine* enemy **to r** over thee, 8055
4:21 **R** and be glad, O daughter of Edom, 7797
Eze 7:12 let not the buyer **r**, nor the seller mourn: 8055
35:15 As thou didst **r** at the inheritance of 8057
Hos 9: 1 **R** not, O Israel, for joy, as *other* people: 8055
Joel 2:21 Fear not, O land; be glad and **r**: for 8055
2:23 of Zion, and **r** in the LORD your God: 8055
Am 6:13 *Ye* which **r** in a thing of nought, which say, 8056
Mic 7: 8 **R** not against me, O mine enemy: when I 8055
Hab 1:15 in their drag: therefore they **r** and are glad. 8055
3:18 Yet I will **r** in the LORD, I will joy in 5937
Zep 3:11 of the midst of thee them that **r** in thy pride, 5947
3:14 be glad and **r** with all the heart, O daughter 5937
3:17 he will save, he will **r** over thee with joy; 7797
Zec 2:10 Sing and **r**, O daughter of Zion: for lo, 8055
4:10 the day of small *things?* for they shall **r**, 8055
9: 9 **R** greatly, O daughter of Zion; shout, 1523
10: 7 and their heart shall **r** as *through* wine: 8055
10: 7 be glad; their heart shall **r** in the LORD. 1523
Mt 5:12 **R**, and be exceeding glad: for great *is* your *5463*
Lk 1:14 and gladness; and many shall **r** at his birth. *5463*
6:23 **R** ye in that day, and leap *for joy*: for *5463*
10:20 Notwithstanding in this **r** not, that *5463*
10:20 but rather **r**, because your names are *5463*
15: 6 saying unto them, **R with** me; *4796*
15: 9 neighbours together, saying, **R with** me; *4796*
19:37 whole multitude of the disciples began to **r** *5463*
Jn 4:36 and he that reapeth may **r** together. *5463*
5:35 ye were willing for a season to **r** in his light. *21*
14:28 If ye loved me, ye would **r**, because I said, *5463*
16:20 and lament, but the world shall **r**: *5463*
16:22 and your heart shall **r**, and your joy no *man* *5463*
Ac 2:26 Therefore did my heart **r**, and my tongue *2165*
Ro 5: 2 and **r** in hope of the glory of God. *2744*
12:15 **R** with them that do rejoice, and weep with *5463*
12:15 Rejoice with them that do **r**, and weep with *5463*
15:10 *he* saith, **R**, *ye* Gentiles, with his people. *2165*
1Co 7:30 and they that **r**, as though they rejoiced not; *5463*
12:26 be honoured, all the members **r with** *it*. *4796*
2Co 2: 3 sorrow from *them of* whom I ought to **r**; *5463*
7: 9 Now I **r**, not that ye were made sorry, but *5463*
7:16 I **r** therefore that I have confidence in you *5463*
Gal 4:27 For it is written, **R**, *thou* barren that bearest *2165*
Php 1:18 and I therein do **r**, yea, and will rejoice. *5463*
1:18 and I therein do rejoice, yea, and will **r**. *5463*
2:16 that I may **r** in the day of Christ, that I have *2745*
2:17 of your faith, I joy, and **r with** you all. *4796*
2:18 same *cause* also do ye joy, and **r with** me. *4796*
2:28 ye may **r**, and *that* I may be the less *5463*
3: 1 Finally, my brethren, **r** in the Lord. *5463*

Php 3: 3 and r in Christ Jesus, and have no 2744
4: 4 R in the Lord alway: *and* again I say, 5463
4: 4 in the Lord alway: *and* again I say, R. 5463
Col 1:24 Who now r in my sufferings for you, and 5463
1Th 5:16 R evermore. 5463
Jas 1: 9 Let the brother of low degree r in that he is 2744
4:16 But now ye r in your boastings: all such 2744
1Pe 1: 6 Wherein ye greatly r, though now for a 21
1: 8 ye r with joy unspeakable and full of glory: 21
4:13 But r, inasmuch as ye are partakers of 5463
Rev 11:10 And they that dwell upon the earth shall r 5463
12:12 Therefore r, ye heavens, and ye that dwell 2165
18:20 R over her, *thou* heaven, and ye holy 2165
19: 7 Let us be glad and r, and give honour to him: 21

REJOICED (47) [REJOICE]

Ex 18: 9 Jethro r for all the goodness which 2302
Dt 28:63 *that* as the LORD r over you to do you 7797
30: 9 over thee for good, as he r over thy fathers: 7797
Jdg 19: 3 of the damsel saw him, he r to meet him. 8055
1Sa 6:13 their eyes, and saw the ark, and r to see *it.* 8055
11:15 and all the men of Israel r greatly. 8055
1Ki 1:40 r *with* great joy, so that the earth rent with 8056
5: 7 that he r greatly, and said, Blessed *be* 8055
2Ki 11:14 all the people of the land r, and blew with 8056
11:20 all the people of the land r, and the city was 8055
1Ch 29: 9 the people r, for that they offered willingly, 8055
29: 9 and David the king also r *with* great joy. 8055
2Ch 15:15 all Judah r at the oath: for they had sworn 8055
23:13 all the people of the land r, and 8056
23:21 all the people of the land r: and the city 8055
24:10 And all the princes and all the people r, and 8055
29:36 Hezekiah r, and all the people, that God 8055
30:25 land of Israel, and that dwelt in Judah, r. 8055
Ne 12:43 that day they offered great sacrifices, and r: 8055
12:43 the wives also and the children r: so 8055
12:44 for Judah r for the priests and for 8057
Est 8:15 and the city of Shushan r and was glad. 6670
Job 31:25 If I r because my wealth *was* great, and 8055
31:29 If I r at the destruction of him that hated 8055
Ps 35:15 in mine adversity they r, and 8055
97: 8 the daughters of Judah r, because of thy 1523
119:14 I have r in the way of thy testimonies, 7797
Ecc 2:10 any joy; for my heart r in all my labour: 8056
Jer 15:17 not in the assembly of the mockers, nor r; 5937
50:11 Because ye were glad, because ye r, O ye 5937
Eze 25: 6 r in heart with all thy despite against 8055
Hos 10: 5 the priests thereof *that* r on it, for the glory 1523
Ob 1:12 neither shouldest thou have r over 8055
Mt 2:10 the star, they r *with* exceeding great joy. 5463
Lk 1:47 And my spirit hath r in God my Saviour. 21
1:58 great mercy upon her; and they r with her. 4796
10:21 In that hour Jesus r in spirit, and said, I thank 21
13:17 all the people r for all the glorious *things* 5463
Jn 8:56 Your father Abraham r to see my day: and 21
Ac 7:41 and r in the works of their own hands. 2165
15:31 they had read, they r for the consolation. 5463
16:34 he set meat before *them,* and r, believing in 21
1Co 7:30 and they that rejoice, as though they r not; 5463
2Co 7: 7 mind toward me; so that I r the more. 5463
Php 4:10 But I r in the Lord greatly, that now at 5463
2Jn 1: 4 I r greatly that I found of thy children 5463
3Jn 1: 3 For I r greatly, when *the* brethren came and 5463

REJOICEST (1) [REJOICE]

Jer 11:15 when thou doest evil, then thou r. 5937

REJOICETH (18) [REJOICE]

1Sa 2: 1 and said, My heart r in the LORD, 5970
Job 39:21 paweth in the valley, and r in *his* strength. 7797
Ps 16: 9 Therefore my heart is glad, and my glory r: 1523
19: 5 *and* r as a strong *man* to run a race. 7797
28: 7 therefore my heart greatly r; and with my 5937
Pr 11:10 it goeth well with the righteous, the city r: 5970
13: 9 The light of the righteous r: but the lamp of 8055
15:30 The light of the eyes r the heart: *and* a good 8055
29: 3 Whoso loveth wisdom r his father: but 8055
Isa 5:14 and their pomp, and he that r, 5938
62: 5 *as* the bridegroom r over the bride, *so* 4885
64: 5 Thou meetest him that r and 7797
Eze 35:14 When the whole earth r, I will make thee 8055
Mt 18:13 he r more of that *sheep,* than of the ninety 5463
Jn 3:29 r greatly because of 5463+5479
1Co 13: 6 R not in iniquity, but rejoiceth in the truth; 5463
13: 6 Rejoiceth not in iniquity, but r in the truth; 4796
Jas 2:13 no mercy; and mercy r against judgment. 2620

REJOICING (28) [REJOICE]

1Ki 1:45 they are come up from thence r, so that 8056
2Ch 23:18 with r and with singing, as it was ordained 8057
Job 8:21 mouth *with* laughing, and thy lips *with* r. 8643
Ps 19: 8 statutes of the LORD *are* right, r the heart: 8055
45:15 With gladness and r shall they be brought: 1524
107:22 and declare his works with r. 7440
118:15 The voice of r and salvation *is* in 7440
119:111 for ever: for they *are* the r of my heart. 8342
126: 6 shall doubtless come again with r, 7440
Pr 8:30 was daily *his* delight, r always before him; 7832
8:31 R in the habitable part of his earth; and 7832
Isa 65:18 I create Jerusalem a r, and her people a joy. 1525
Jer 15:16 was unto me the joy and r of mine heart: 8057
Hab 3:14 their r *was* as to devour the poor secretly. 5951
Zep 2:15 This *is* the r city that dwelt carelessly, 5947
Lk 15: 5 found *it,* he layeth *it* on his shoulders, r. 5463
Ac 5:41 r that they were counted worthy to suffer 5463
8:39 him no more: and he went *on* his way r. 5463
Ro 12:12 R in hope; patient in tribulation; 5463
1Co 15:31 I protest by your r which I have in Christ 2746
2Co 1:12 For our r is this, the testimony of our 2746
1:14 us in part, that we are your r, 2745
6:10 As sorrowful, yet alway r; as poor, 5463
Gal 6: 4 and then shall he have r in himself alone, 2745
Php 1:26 That your r may be *more* abundant in Jesus 2745
1Th 2:19 For what *is* our hope, or joy, or crown of r? 2746
Heb 3: 6 and the r of the hope firm unto the end. 2745
Jas 4:16 rejoice in your boastings: all such r is evil. 2746

REKEM (5)

Nu 31: 8 and R, and Zur, and Hur, and Reba, 7552
Jos 13:21 Evi, and R, and Zur, and Hur, and Reba, 7552
18:27 And R, and Irpeel, and Taralah, 7552
1Ch 2:43 Korah, and Tappuah, and R, and Shema. 7552
2:44 father of Jorkoam: and R begat Shammai. 7552

RELATIVES See KINDRED; KINDREDS

RELEASE (21) [RELEASED]

Dt 15: 1 of *every* seven years thou shalt make a r. 8059
15: 2 this *is* the manner of the r: Every creditor 8059
15: 2 r *it;* he shall not exact *it* of his neighbour, 8058
15: 2 because it is called the LORD'S r. 8059
15: 3 is thine with thy brother thine hand shall r; 8058
15: 9 The seventh year, the year of r, is at hand; 8059
31:10 in the solemnity of the year of r, in 8059
Est 2:18 he made a r to the provinces, and 2010
Mt 27:15 Now at *that* feast the governor was wont to r 630
27:17 unto them, Whom will ye *that* I r unto you? 630
27:21 Whether of the twain will ye *that* I r unto 630
Mk 15: 9 Will ye *that* I r unto you the King of 630
15:11 that he should rather r Barabbas unto them. 630
Lk 23:16 I will therefore chastise him, and r *him.* 630
23:17 (For of necessity he must r one unto them at 630
23:18 with this *man,* and r unto us Barabbas: 630
23:20 Pilate therefore, willing to r Jesus, spake 630
Jn 18:39 that I should r unto you one at the passover: 630
18:39 *that* I r unto you the King of the Jews? 630
19:10 to crucify thee, and have power to r thee? 630
19:12 *And* from thenceforth Pilate sought to r him: 630

RELEASED (4) [RELEASE]

Mt 27:26 Then r he Barabbas unto them: 630
Mk 15: 6 Now at *that* feast he r unto them one 630
15:15 r Barabbas unto them, and delivered Jesus, 630
Lk 23:25 And he r unto them him that for sedition and 630

RELIED (3) [RELY]

2Ch 13:18 they r upon the LORD God of their 8172
16: 7 Because thou hast r on the king of Syria, 8172
16: 7 not r on the LORD thy God, therefore is 8172

RELIEF (1) [RELIEVE, RELIEVED, RELIEVETH]

Ac 11:29 determined to send r unto 1248+1519

RELIEVE (7) [RELIEF]

Lev 25:35 in decay with thee; then thou shalt r him: 2388
Isa 1:17 seek judgment, r the oppressed, judge 833
La 1:11 their pleasant things for meat to r the soul: 7725
1:16 the comforter that *should* r my soul is far 7725
1:19 they sought their meat, to r their souls. 7725

1Ti 5:16 let them r them, and let not the church be *1884*
5:16 that it may r them that are widows indeed. *1884*

RELIEVED (1) [RELIEF]
1Ti 5:10 the saints' feet, if she have r the afflicted, *1884*

RELIEVETH (1) [RELIEF]
Ps 146: 9 he r the fatherless and widow: 5749

RELIGION (5) [RELIGIOUS]
Ac 26: 5 that after the most straitest sect of our r I *2356*
Gal 1:13 conversation in time past in the **Jews'** r, *2454*
1:14 And profited in the **Jews'** r above many *2454*
Jas 1:26 his own heart, this *man's* r *is* vain. *2356*
1:27 Pure r and undefiled before God and *2356*

RELIGIOUS (2) [RELIGION]
Ac 13:43 and r proselytes followed Paul and *4576*
Jas 1:26 If any *man* among you seem to be r, and *2357*

RELY (1) [RELIED]
2Ch 16: 8 yet, because thou didst r on the LORD, 8172

REMAIN (79) [REMAINDER, REMAINED, REMAINEST, REMAINETH, REMAINING, REMNANT]
Ge 38:11 **R** a widow *at* thy father's house, till Shelah 3427
Ex 8: 9 *that* they may r in the river only? 7604
8:11 thy people; they shall r in the river only. 7604
12:10 ye shall let nothing of it r until 3498
23:18 neither shall the fat of my sacrifice r until 3885
29:34 r unto the morning, then thou shalt burn 3498
Lev 19: 6 if ought r until the third day, it shall be 3498
25:28 that which is sold shall r in the hand of him 1961
25:52 if there r but few years unto the year of 7604
27:18 the money according to the years that r, 3498
Nu 33:55 **come to** pass, *that those* which ye let r 3498
Dt 2:34 little ones, of every city, we left none to r: 8300
16: 4 day at even, r **all night** until the morning. 3885
19:20 those which r shall hear, and fear, and 7604
21:13 shall r in thine house, and bewail her father 3427
21:23 His body shall not r **all night** upon the tree, 3885
Jos 1:14 shall r in the land which Moses gave you 3427
2:11 neither did there r any more courage in any 6965
8:22 so that *they* let none of them r or escape. 8300
10:27 cave's mouth, *which* r until this very day. NIH
10:28 the souls that *were* therein; he let none r: 8300
10:30 he let none r in it; but did unto the king 8300
23: 4 divided unto you *by lot* these nations that r, 7604
23: 7 these nations, these that r amongst you; 7604
23:12 *even* these that r among you, and 7604
Jdg 5:17 why did Dan r *in* ships? Asher continued 1481
21: 7 How shall we do for wives for them that r, 3498
21:16 How shall we do for wives for them that r, 3498
1Sa 20:19 was *in hand,* and shalt r by the stone Ezel. 3427
1Ki 11:16 (For six months did Joab r there with all 3427
18:22 I, *even* I only, r a prophet of the LORD; 3498
2Ki 7:13 I pray thee, five of the horses that r, 7604
Ezr 9:15 for we r *yet* escaped, as *it is* this day: 7604
Job 21:32 to the grave, and shall r in the tomb. 8245
27:15 Those that r of him shall be buried in 8300
37: 8 beasts go into dens, and r in their places. 7931
Ps 55: 7 I wander far off, *and* r in the wilderness. 3885
Pr 2:21 *in* the land, and the perfect shall r in it. 3498
21:16 shall r in the congregation of the dead. 5117
Isa 10:32 As yet shall *he* r at Nob *that* day: he shall 5975
32:16 and righteousness r in the fruitful field. 3427
44:13 beauty of a man; that it may r *in* the house. 3427
65: 4 Which r among the graves, and lodge in 3427
66:22 *shall* r before me, saith the LORD, so 5975
66:22 so shall your seed and your name r. 5975
Jer 8: 3 residue of them that r of this evil family, 7604
8: 3 which r in all the places whither I have 7604
17:25 of Jerusalem: and this city shall r for ever. 3427
24: 8 that r in this land, and them that dwell in 7604
27:11 those will I let r **still** in their own land, 3240
27:19 concerning the residue of the vessels that r 3498
27:21 concerning the vessels that r *in* the house 3498
30:18 the palace shall r after the manner thereof. 3427
38: 4 hands of the men of war that r in this city, 7604
42:17 none of them shall r or escape from the evil 8300
44: 7 out of Judah, to leave you none to r; 7611
44:14 shall escape or r, that *they* should return 8300
51:62 to cut it off, that none shall r in it, 3427
Eze 7:11 none of them *shall* r, nor of their multitude, NIH
17:21 they that r shall be scattered towards all 7604
31:13 his ruin shall all the fowls of the heaven r, 7931
32: 4 will **cause** all the fowls of the heaven **to** r 7931
39:14 those that r upon the face of the earth, 3498
Am 6: 9 if there r ten men in one house, that they 3498
Ob 1:14 those of his that did r in the day of distress. 8300
Zec 5: 4 it shall r in the midst of his house, and 3885
12:14 All the families that r, every family apart, 7604
Lk 10: 7 And in the same house r, eating and *3306*
Jn 6:12 Gather up the fragments that r, that nothing *4052*
15:11 that my joy might r in you, and *that* your *3306*
15:16 forth fruit, and *that* your fruit should r: *3306*
19:31 that the bodies should not r upon the cross *3306*
1Co 7:11 let her r unmarried, or be reconciled to *her* *3306*
15: 6 of whom the greater part r unto this *3306*
1Th 4:15 r unto the coming of the Lord shall not *4035*
4:17 r shall be caught up together with them in *4035*
Heb 12:27 those *things* which cannot be shaken may r. *3306*
1Jn 2:24 heard from the beginning shall r in you, *3306*
Rev 3: 2 and strengthen the *things* which r, *3062*

REMAINDER (6) [REMAIN]
Ex 29:34 then thou shalt burn the r with fire: 3498
Lev 6:16 the r thereof shall Aaron and his sons eat: 3498
7:16 on the morrow also the r of it shall be 3498
7:17 the r of the flesh of the sacrifice on 3498
2Sa 14: 7 husband *neither* name nor r upon the earth. 7611
Ps 76:10 the r of wrath shalt thou restrain. 7611

REMAINED (53) [REMAIN]
Ge 7:23 Noah only r *alive,* and *they* that *were* with 7604
14:10 and they that r fled to the mountain. 7604
Ex 8:31 and from his people; there r not one. 7604
10:15 there r not any green thing in the trees, or 3498
10:19 there r not one locust in all the coasts of 7604
14:28 there r not so much as one of them. 7604
Nu 11:26 there r two *of the* men in the camp, 7604
35:28 Because he should have r in the city of his 3427
36:12 their inheritance r in the tribe of the family 1961
Dt 3:11 For only Og king of Bashan r of 7604
4:25 ye shall have r **long** in the land, and 3462
Jos 10:20 that the rest *which* r of them entered into 8277
11:22 in Gaza, in Gath, and in Ashdod, there r. 7604
13:12 who r of the remnant of the giants: 7604
18: 2 there r among the children of Israel seven 3498
21:20 the Levites which r of the children of 3498
21:26 families of the children of Kohath that r. 3498
Jdg 7: 3 and two thousand; and there r ten thousand. 7604
1Sa 11:11 that they which r were scattered, so 7604
23:14 r in a mountain in the wilderness of Ziph. 3427
24: 3 and his men r in the sides of the cave. 3427
2Sa 13:20 So Tamar r desolate *in* her brother 3427
1Ki 22:46 which r in the days of his father Asa, 7604
2Ki 10:11 So Jehu slew all that r of the house of Ahab 7604
10:17 he slew all that r unto Ahab in Samaria, 7604
13: 6 there r the grove also in Samaria.) 5975
24:14 none r, save the poorest sort of the people 7604
25:22 *as for* the people that r in the land of Judah, 7604
1Ch 13:14 the ark of God r with the family of 3427
Ecc 2: 9 in Jerusalem: also my wisdom r with me. 5975
Jer 34: 7 for these defenced cities r of the cities of 7604
37:10 there r *but* wounded men among them, 7604
37:16 and Jeremiah had r there many days; 3427
37:21 Thus Jeremiah r in the court of the prison. 3427
38:13 and Jeremiah r in the court of the prison. 3427
39: 9 the remnant of the people that r in the city, 7604
39: 9 to him, with the rest of the people that r. 7604
41:10 and all the people that r in Mizpah, 7604
48:11 therefore his taste r in him, and his sent is 5975
51:30 forborn to fight, they have r in *their* holds: 3427
52:15 the residue of the people that r in the city, 7604
La 2:22 of the LORD'S anger none escaped nor r: 8300
Eze 3:15 r there astonished among them seven days. 3427
Da 10: 8 great vision, and there r no strength in me: 7604
10:13 and I r there with the kings of Persia. 3498
10:17 straightway there r no strength in me, 5975
Mt 11:23 in Sodom, it would have r until this day. *3306*
14:20 they took up of the fragments that r twelve *4052*
Lk 1:22 he beckoned unto them, and r speechless. *1265*
9:17 there was taken up of fragments that r to *4052*
Jn 6:13 which r **over and above** unto them that *4052*
Ac 5: 4 Whiles it r, was it not thine own? and *3306*
27:41 and r unmoveable, but the hinder part was *3306*

R

REMAINEST (2) [REMAIN]

La 5:19 Thou, O LORD, **r** for ever; thy throne 3427
Heb 1:11 but thou **r**; and they all shall wax old as *1265*

REMAINETH (37) [REMAIN]

Ge 8:22 While the earth **r**, seedtime and harvest, 3117
Ex 10: 5 is escaped which **r** unto you from the hail, 7604
12:10 that which **r** of it until the morning ye shall 3498
16:23 that which **r over** lay up for you to be kept 5736
26:12 the remnant that **r** of the curtains of 5736
26:12 the half curtain that **r**, shall hang over 5736
26:13 a cubit on the other side of that which **r** in 5736
Lev 8:32 that which **r** of the flesh and of the bread 3498
10:12 Take the meat offering that **r** of 3498
16:16 that **r** among them in the midst of their 7931
Nu 24:19 and shall destroy him that **r** of the city. 8300
Jos 8:29 a great heap of stones, *that* **r** unto this day. NIH
13: 1 there **r** *yet* very much land to be possessed. 7604
13: 2 This is the land that *yet* **r**: all the borders of 7604
Jdg 5:13 he made him that **r** have dominion over 8300
1Sa 6:18 *which stone* **r** unto this day in the field of NIH
16:11 There **r** yet the youngest, and behold, 7604
1Ch 17: 1 the ark of the covenant of the LORD **r** NIH
Ezr 1: 4 whosoever **r** in any place where he 7604
Job 19: 4 *that* I have erred, mine error **r** with myself. 3885
21:34 seeing *in* your answers there **r** falsehood? 7604
41:22 In his neck **r** strength, and sorrow is turned 3885
Isa 4: 3 he that **r** in Jerusalem, shall be called holy, 3498
Jer 38: 2 He that **r** in this city shall die by the sword, 3427
47: 4 from Tyrus and Zidon every helper that **r**: 8300
Eze 6:12 he that **r** and is besieged shall die by 7604
Hag 2: 5 out of Egypt, so my spirit **r** among you: 5975
Zec 9: 7 he that **r**, even he, *shall be* for our God, and 7604
Jn 9:41 now ye say, We see; therefore your sin **r**. *3306*
1Co 7:29 it **r**, that both they that have *1510+3062+3588*
2Co 3:11 much more that which **r** *is* glorious. *3306*
3:14 for until this day **r** the same vail untaken *3306*
9: 9 to the poor: his righteousness **r** for ever. *3306*
Heb 4: 6 therefore it **r** that some *must* enter therein, *620*
4: 9 There **r** therefore a rest to the people of God. *620*
10:26 the truth, there **r** no more sacrifice for sins, *620*
1Jn 3: 9 doth not commit sin; for his seed **r** in him: *3306*

REMAINING (14) [REMAIN]

Nu 9:22 **r** thereon, the children of Israel abode in 7931
Dt 3: 3 we smote him until none was left to him **r**. 8300
Jos 10:33 and his people, until *he* had left him none **r**. 8300
10:37 he left none **r**, according to all that he had 8300
10:39 the souls that *were* therein; he left none **r**: 8300
10:40 he left none **r**, but utterly destroyed all that 8300
11: 8 smote them, until *they* left them none **r**. 8300
21:40 which were **r** of the families of the Levites, 3498
2Sa 21: 5 from **r** in any of the coasts of Israel, 3320
2Ki 10:11 and his priests, until *he* left him none **r**. 8300
1Ch 9:33 *who* **r** in the chambers *were* free: NIH
Job 18:19 his people, nor *any* **r** in his dwellings. 8300
Ob 1:18 there shall not be *any* **r** of the house of 8300
Jn 1:33 see the Spirit descending, and **r** on him, *3306*

REMALIAH (11) [REMALIAH'S]

2Ki 15:25 Pekah the son of **R**, a captain of his, 7425
15:27 of **R** *began* to reign over Israel in Samaria, 7425
15:30 a conspiracy against Pekah the son of **R**, 7425
15:32 In the second year of Pekah the son of **R** 7425
15:37 the king of Syria, and Pekah the son of **R**. 7425
16: 1 **R** Ahaz the son of Jotham king of Judah 7425
16: 5 Pekah son of **R** king of Israel came up *to* 7425
2Ch 28: 6 For Pekah the son of **R** slew in Judah an 7425
Isa 7: 1 and Pekah the son of **R**, king of Israel, 7425
7: 4 of Rezin with Syria, and of the son of **R**. 7425
7: 5 Because Syria, Ephraim, and the son of **R**, 7425

REMALIAH'S (2) [REMALIAH]

Isa 7: 9 and the head of Samaria *is* **R** son. 7425
8: 6 go softly, and rejoice in Rezin and **R** son; 7425

REMEDY (3)

2Ch 36:16 arose against his people, till *there was* no **r**. 4832
Pr 6:15 suddenly shall he be broken without **r**. 4832
29: 1 suddenly be destroyed, and that without **r**. 4832

REMEMBER (148) [REMEMBERED, REMEMBEREST, REMEMBERETH, REMEMBERING, REMEMBRANCE, REMEMBRANCES]

Ge 9:15 I will **r** my covenant, which *is* between me 2142
9:16 that I may **r** the everlasting covenant 2142
40:23 Yet did not the chief butler **r** Joseph, but 2142
41: 9 saying, I do **r** my faults *this* day: 2142
Ex 13: 3 Moses said unto the people, **R** this day, 2142
20: 8 **R** the sabbath day, to keep it holy. 2142
32:13 **R** Abraham, Isaac, and Israel, thy servants, 2142
Lev 26:42 will I **r** my covenant with Jacob, and 2142
26:42 also my covenant with Abraham will I **r**; 2142
26:42 will I remember; and I will **r** the land. 2142
26:45 I will for their sakes **r** the covenant of their 2142
Nu 11: 5 We **r** the fish, which we did eat in Egypt 2142
15:39 **r** all the commandments of the LORD, 2142
15:40 That ye may **r**, and do all my 2142
Dt 5:15 **r** that thou wast a servant in the land of 2142
7:18 shalt **well r** what the LORD thy 2142+2142
8: 2 thou shalt **r** all the way which the LORD 2142
8:18 thou shalt **r** the LORD thy God: for *it is* 2142
9: 7 **R**, *and* forget not, how thou provokedst 2142
9:27 **R** thy servants, Abraham, Isaac, and Jacob; 2142
15:15 thou shalt **r** that thou wast a bondman in 2142
16: 3 that thou mayest **r** the day when thou 2142
16:12 thou shalt **r** that thou wast a bondman in 2142
24: 9 **R** what the LORD thy God did unto 2142
24:18 thou shalt **r** that thou wast a bondman in 2142
24:22 thou shalt **r** that thou wast a bondman in 2142
25:17 **R** what Amalek did unto thee by the way, 2142
32: 7 **R** the days of old, consider the years of 2142
Jos 1:13 **R** the word which Moses the servant of 2142
Jdg 9: 2 **r** also that I *am* your bone and your flesh. 2142
16:28 **r** me, I pray thee, and strengthen me, I pray 2142
1Sa 1:11 **r** me, and not forget thine handmaid, but 2142
15: 2 I **r** *that* which Amalek did to Israel, 6485
25:31 well with my lord, then **r** thine handmaid. 2142
2Sa 14:11 let the king **r** the LORD thy God, 2142
19:19 neither do thou **r** *that* which thy servant did 2142
2Ki 9:25 for **r** how that, when I and thou rode 2142
20: 3 **r** now how I have walked before thee in 2142
1Ch 16:12 **R** his marvellous works that he hath done, 2142
2Ch 6:42 **r** the mercies of David thy servant. 2142
Ne 1: 8 **R**, I beseech thee, the word that thou 2142
4:14 **r** the Lord, *which is* great and terrible, and 2142
13:14 **R** me, O my God, concerning this, and 2142
13:22 **R** me, O my God, *concerning* this also, and 2142
13:29 **R** them, O my God, because they have 2142
13:31 the firstfruits. **R** me, O my God, for good. 2142
Job 4: 7 **R**, I pray thee, who *ever* perished, 2142
7: 7 O **r** that my life *is* wind: mine eye shall no 2142
10: 9 **R**, I beseech thee, that thou hast made me 2142
11:16 *and* **r** *it* as waters *that* pass away: 2142
14:13 wouldest appoint me a set time, and **r** me. 2142
21: 6 Even when I **r** I am afraid, and 2142
36:24 **R** that thou magnify his work, which men 2142
41: 8 hand upon him, **r** the battle, do no more. 2142
Ps 20: 3 **R** all thy offerings, and accept thy burnt 2142
20: 7 we will **r** the name of the LORD our God. 2142
22:27 All the ends of the world shall **r** and 2142
25: 6 **R**, O LORD, thy tender mercies and 2142
25: 7 **R** not the sins of my youth, nor my 2142
25: 7 according to thy mercy **r** thou me for thy 2142
42: 4 When I **r** these *things*, I pour out my soul in 2142
42: 6 will I **r** thee from the land of Jordan, 2142
63: 6 When I **r** thee upon my bed, *and* 2142
74: 2 **R** thy congregation, *which* thou hast 2142
74:18 **R** this, *that* the enemy hath reproached, 2142
74:22 **r** how the foolish *man* reproacheth thee 2142
77:10 *I will* **r** the years of the right hand of NIH
77:11 I will **r** the works of the LORD: surely I 2142
77:11 surely I will **r** thy wonders of old. 2142
79: 8 O **r** not against us former iniquities: let thy 2142
89:47 **R** how short my time is: wherefore hast 2142
89:50 **R**, Lord, the reproach of thy servants; 2142
103:18 to those that **r** his commandments to do 2142
105: 5 **R** his marvellous works that he hath done; 2142
106: 4 **R** me, O LORD, with the favour *that thou* 2142
119:49 **R** the word unto thy servant, upon which 2142
132: 1 LORD, **r** David, *and* all his afflictions: 2142
137: 6 If I do not **r** thee, let my tongue cleave to 2142
137: 7 **R**, O LORD, the children of Edom *in* 2142
143: 5 I **r** the days of old; I meditate on all thy 2142

Pr 31: 7 his poverty, and r his misery no more. 2142
Ecc 5:20 For he shall not much r the days of his life; 2142
11: 8 them all; yet let him r the days of darkness; 2142
12: 1 R now thy Creator in the days of thy youth, 2142
SS 1: 4 in thee, we will r thy love more than wine: 2142
Isa 38: 3 said, R now, O LORD, I beseech thee, 2142
43:18 R ye not the former *things,* neither consider 2142
43:25 for mine own sake, and will not r thy sins. 2142
44:21 R these, O Jacob and Israel; for thou *art* my 2142
46: 8 R this, and shew yourselves men: bring *it* 2142
46: 9 R the former *things* of old: for I *am* God, 2142
47: 7 thy heart, neither didst r the latter end of it. 2142
54: 4 shalt not r the reproach of thy widowhood 2142
64: 5 *those that* r thee in thy ways: 2142
64: 9 O LORD, neither r iniquity for ever: 2142
Jer 2: 2 I r thee, the kindness of thy youth, the love 2142
3:16 neither shall they r it; neither shall they 2142
14:10 he will now r their iniquity, and visit their 2142
14:21 r, break not thy covenant with us. 2142
15:15 r me, and visit me, and revenge me of my 2142
17: 2 Whilst their children r their altars and 2142
18:20 R that I stood before thee to speak good for 2142
31:20 I do **earnestly** r him still: 2142+2142
31:34 their iniquity, and I will r their sin no more. 2142
44:21 did not the LORD r them, and came it *not* 2142
51:50 r the LORD afar off, and let Jerusalem 2142
La 5: 1 R, O LORD, what is come upon us: 2142
Eze 6: 9 they that escape of you shall r me among 2142
16:60 Nevertheless I will r my covenant with thee 2142
16:61 thou shalt r thy ways, and be ashamed, 2142
16:63 That thou mayest r, and be confounded, 2142
20:43 there shall ye r your ways, and all your 2142
23:27 eyes unto them, nor r Egypt any more. 2142
36:31 shall ye r your own evil ways, and 2142
Hos 7: 2 they consider not in their hearts *that* I r all 2142
8:13 now will he r their iniquity, and visit their 2142
9: 9 *therefore* he will r their iniquity, he will 2142
Mic 6: 5 r now what Balak king of Moab consulted, 2142
Hab 3: 2 of the years make known; in wrath r mercy. 2142
Zec 10: 9 they shall r me in far countries; and 2142
Mal 4: 4 R ye the law of Moses my servant, which I 2142
Mt 16: 9 neither r the five loaves of the five *3421*
27:63 Saying, Sir, we r that that deceiver said, *3415*
Mk 8:18 having ears, hear ye not? and do ye not r? *3421*
Lk 1:72 to our fathers, and to r his holy covenant; *3415*
16:25 r that thou in thy lifetime receivedst thy *3415*
17:32 R Lot's wife. *3421*
23:42 r me when thou comest into thy kingdom. *3415*
24: 6 r how he spake unto you when he was yet *3415*
Jn 15:20 R the word that I said unto you, *3421*
16: 4 ye may r that I told you of them. *3421*
Ac 20:31 Therefore watch, and r, that *by the space of* *3421*
20:35 and to r the words of the Lord Jesus, *3421*
1Co 11: 2 that you r me in all *things,* and keep *3415*
Gal 2:10 Only *they would* that we should r the poor; *3421*
Eph 2:11 Wherefore r, that ye *being* in time passed *3421*
Col 4:18 R my bonds. Grace *be* with you. Amen. *3421*
1Th 2: 9 For ye r, brethren, our labour and travail: *3421*
2Th 2: 5 R ye not, that, when I was yet with you, *3421*
2Ti 2: 8 R that Jesus Christ of the seed of David *3421*
Heb 8:12 and their iniquities will I r no more. *3415*
10:17 their sins and iniquities will I r no more. *3415*
13: 3 R *them that are* in bonds, as bound with *3403*
13: 7 R them which have the rule over you, *3421*
3Jn 1:10 if I come, I will r his deeds which he doeth, *5279*
Jude 1:17 r ye the words which were spoken before *3415*
Rev 2: 5 R therefore from whence thou art fallen, *3421*
3: 3 R therefore how thou hast received and *3421*

REMEMBERED (57) [REMEMBER]

Ge 8: 1 God r Noah, and every living thing, and 2142
19:29 that God r Abraham, and sent Lot out of 2142
30:22 God r Rachel, and God hearkened to her, 2142
42: 9 Joseph r the dreams which he dreamed of 2142
Ex 2:24 God r his covenant with Abraham, 2142
6: 5 keep in bondage; and I have r my covenant. 2142
Nu 10: 9 ye shall be r before the LORD your God, 2142
Jdg 8:34 the children of Israel r not the LORD their 2142
1Sa 1:19 Hannah his wife; and the LORD r her. 2142
2Ch 24:22 Thus Joash the king r not the kindness 2142
Est 2: 1 he r Vashti, and what she had done, and 2142
9:28 *that* these days *should be* r and 2142
Job 24:20 he shall be no more r; and wickedness shall 2142
Ps 45:17 I will **make** thy name **to be** r in all 2142
77: 3 I r God, and was troubled: I complained, 2142
78:35 they r that God *was* their rock, and the high 2142
78:39 For he r that they *were but* flesh; a wind 2142
78:42 They r not his hand: *nor* the day when he 2142
98: 3 He hath r his mercy and his truth toward 2142
105: 8 He hath r his covenant for ever, the word 2142
105:42 For he r his holy promise, *and* Abraham his 2142
106: 7 they r not the multitude of thy mercies; but 2142
106:45 he r for them his covenant, and 2142
109:14 Let the iniquity of his fathers be r with 2142
109:16 Because that he r not to shew mercy, but 2142
111: 4 He hath made his wonderful works to be r: 2143
119:52 I r thy judgments of old, O LORD; and 2142
119:55 I have r thy name, O LORD, in the night, 2142
136:23 Who r us in our low estate: for his mercy 2142
137: 1 sat down, yea, we wept, when we r Zion. 2142
Ecc 9:15 the city; yet no man r that *same* poor man. 2142
Isa 23:16 sing many songs, that thou mayest be r. 2142
57:11 that thou hast lied, and hast not r me, 2142
63:11 he r the days of old, Moses, *and* his people, 2142
65:17 the former shall not be r, nor come into 2142
Jer 11:19 the living, that his name may be no more r. 2142
La 1: 7 Jerusalem r in the days of her affliction and 2142
2: 1 r not his footstool in the day of his anger! 2142
Eze 3:20 which he hath done shall not be r; 2142
16:22 thy whoredoms thou hast not r the days of 2142
16:43 Because thou hast not r the days of thy 2142
21:24 ye have **made** your iniquity **to be** r, 2142
21:32 midst of the land; thou shalt be no *more* r: 2142
25:10 that the Ammonites may not be r among 2142
33:13 all his righteousnesses shall not be r; 2142
Hos 2:17 and they shall no more be r by their name. 2142
Am 1: 9 to Edom, and r not the brotherly covenant: 2142
Jnh 2: 7 When my soul fainted within me I r 2142
Zec 13: 2 out of the land, and they shall no more be r: 2142
Mt 26:75 And Peter r the word of Jesus, which said *3415*
Lk 22:61 And Peter r the word of the Lord, how he *5279*
24: 8 And they r his words, *3415*
Jn 2:17 And his disciples r that it was written, *3415*
2:22 his disciples r that he had said this unto *3415*
12:16 r they that these *things* were written of him, *3415*
Ac 11:16 Then r I the word of the Lord, how that he *3415*
Rev 18: 5 unto heaven, and God hath r her iniquities. *3421*

REMEMBEREST (2) [REMEMBER]

Ps 88: 5 that lie in the grave, whom thou r no more: 2142
Mt 5:23 there r that thy brother hath ought against *3415*

REMEMBERETH (5) [REMEMBER]

Ps 9:12 he maketh inquisition for blood, he r them: 2142
103:14 knoweth our frame; he r that we *are* dust. 2142
La 1: 9 she r not her last end; therefore she came 2142
Jn 16:21 of the child, she r no more the anguish, *3421*
2Co 7:15 whilst he r the obedience of you all, *363*

REMEMBERING (2) [REMEMBER]

La 3:19 R mine affliction and my misery, 2142
1Th 1: 3 R without ceasing your work of faith, and *3421*

REMEMBRANCE (53) [REMEMBER]

Ex 17:14 for I will utterly put out the r of Amalek 2143
Nu 5:15 of memorial, **bringing** iniquity **to** r. 2142
Dt 25:19 *that* thou shalt blot out the r of Amalek 2143
32:26 I would make the r of them to cease from 2143
2Sa 18:18 I have no son to **keep** my name **in** r: 2142
1Ki 17:18 art thou come unto me to **call** my sin **to** r, 2142
Job 18:17 His r shall perish from the earth, and 2143
Ps 6: 5 For in death *there is* no r of thee: in 2143
30: 4 and give thanks at the r of his holiness. 2143
34:16 to cut off the r of them from the earth. 2143
38: T A Psalm of David, to **bring to** r. 2142
70: T *A Psalm* of David, to **bring to** r. 2142
77: 6 I **call to** r my song in the night: I commune 2142
83: 4 the name of Israel may be no more **in** r. 2142
97:12 and give thanks at the r of his holiness. 2143
102:12 for ever; and thy r unto all generations. 2143
112: 6 the righteous shall be in everlasting r. 2143
Ecc 1:11 *There is* no r of former *things;* neither shall 2146
1:11 r of *things* that are to come with *those* that 2146
2:16 For *there is* no r of the wise more than of 2146
Isa 26: 8 *our* soul *is* to thy name, and to the r of thee. 2143
43:26 **Put** me **in** r: let us plead together: 2142
57: 8 and the posts hast thou set up thy r: 2146
La 3:20 My soul hath *them* **still in** r, and 2142+2142

R

Eze 21:23 he will **call to** r the iniquity, that *they* may 2142
21:24 because, *I say,* that ye are **come to** r, 2142
23:19 in **calling to** r the days of her youth, 2142
23:21 Thus thou **calledst to** r the lewdness of thy 6485
29:16 which **bringeth** *their* iniquity **to** r, 2142
Mal 3:16 a book of r was written before him for 2146
Mk 11:21 And Peter **calling to** r saith unto him, *363*
Lk 1:54 holpen his servant Israel, in r of *his* mercy, *3415*
22:19 which is given for you: this do in r of me. *364*
Jn 14:26 all *things,* and **bring** all *things* **to** your r, *5279*
Ac 10:31 thine alms are had in r in the sight of God. *3415*
1Co 4:17 who shall **bring** you **into** r of my ways *363*
11:24 which is broken for you: this do in r of me. *364*
11:25 this do ye, as oft as ye drink *it,* in r of me. *364*
Php 1: 3 I thank my God upon every r of you, *3417*
1Th 3: 6 and that ye have good r of us always, *3417*
1Ti 4: 6 If thou **put** the brethren **in** r of these *things,* *5294*
2Ti 1: 3 that without ceasing I have r of thee in my *3417*
1: 5 When I call to r the unfeigned faith that is *5280*
1: 6 Wherefore I **put** thee **in** r that *thou* stir up *363*
2:14 Of these *things* **put** *them* **in** r, *5279*
Heb 10: 3 But in those *sacrifices there is* a r *again* *364*
10:32 But **call to** r the former days, in which, *363*
2Pe 1:12 **put** you always **in** r of these *things,* though *5279*
1:13 to stir you up by **putting** *you* **in** r; *5280*
1:15 decease to have these *things* always in r. *3420*
3: 1 I stir up your pure minds by way of r: *5280*
Jude 1: 5 I will therefore **put** you **in** r, though ye *5279*
Rev 16:19 and great Babylon **came in** r before God, *3415*

REMEMBRANCES (1) [REMEMBER]
Job 13:12 Your r *are* like unto ashes, your bodies to 2146

REMETH (1)
Jos 19:21 **R**, and En-gannim, and En-haddah, and 7432

REMISSION (10) [REMIT]
Mt 26:28 which is shed for many for the r of sins. *859*
Mk 1: 4 preach the baptism of repentance for the r of *859*
Lk 1:77 unto his people by the r of their sins, *859*
3: 3 preaching the baptism of repentance for the r *859*
24:47 r of sins should be preached in his name *859*
Ac 2:38 in the name of Jesus Christ for the r of sins, *859*
10:43 believeth in him shall receive r of sins. *859*
Ro 3:25 to declare his righteousness for the r of sins *3929*
Heb 9:22 and without shedding of blood is no r. *859*
10:18 Now where r of these *is, there is* no more *859*

REMIT (1) [REMISSION, REMITTED]
Jn 20:23 Whose soever sins ye r, they are remitted *863*

REMITTED (1) [REMIT]
Jn 20:23 soever sins ye remit, they are r unto them; *863*

REMMON (1)
Jos 19: 7 Ain, **R**, and Ether, and Ashan; four cities 7417

REMMON-METHOAR (1)
Jos 19:13 and goeth out *to* **R** *to* Neah; 7417+8388+1886.1

REMNANT (92) [REMAIN]
Ex 26:12 the r that remaineth of the curtains of 5629
Lev 2: 3 the r of the meat offering *shall be* Aaron's 3498
5:13 *the* r shall be the priest's, as a meat NIH
14:18 the r of the oil that *is* in the priest's hand he 3498
Dt 3:11 king of Bashan remained of the r of giants; 3499
28:54 towards the r of his children which he shall 3499
Jos 12: 4 *which was* of the r of the giants, that dwelt 3499
13:12 who remained of the r of the giants: 3499
23:12 cleave unto the r of these nations, 3499
2Sa 21: 2 of Israel, but of the r of the Amorites; 3499
1Ki 12:23 and *to* the r of the people, saying, 3499
14:10 will take away the r of the house of 310
22:46 the r of the sodomites, which remained in 3499
2Ki 19: 4 wherefore lift up *thy* prayer for the r that 7611
19:30 the r that is escaped of the house of Judah 7604
19:31 For out of Jerusalem shall go forth a r, and 7611
21:14 I will forsake the r of mine inheritance, 7611
25:11 of Babylon, with the r of the multitude, 3499
1Ch 6:70 for the family of the r of the sons of 3498
2Ch 30: 6 Israel, and he will return to the r of you, 7604
34: 9 of all the r of Israel, and of all Judah and 7611
Ezr 3: 8 the r of their brethren the priests and 7605
9: 8 to leave us a **r to escape**, and to give us a 6413
9:14 so that *there should be* no r nor escaping? 7611
Ne 1: 3 The r that are left of the captivity there in 7604
Job 22:20 but the r of them the fire consumeth. 3499
Isa 1: 9 of hosts had left unto us a very small r, 8300
10:20 *that* the r of Israel, and such as are escaped 7605
10:21 The r shall return, *even* the remnant of 7605
10:21 *even* the r of Jacob, unto the mighty God. 7605
10:22 sand of the sea, *yet* a r of them shall return: 7605
11:11 second time to recover the r of his people, 7605
11:16 there shall be a highway for the r of his 7605
14:22 r, and son, and nephew, saith the LORD. 7605
14:30 root with famine, and he shall slay thy **r**. 7611
15: 9 of Moab, and upon the r of the land. 7611
16:14 the r *shall be* very small *and* feeble. 7605
17: 3 from Damascus, and the r of Syria: 7605
37: 4 wherefore lift up *thy* prayer for the r that is 7611
37:31 the r that is escaped of the house of Judah 7604
37:32 For out of Jerusalem shall go forth a r, and 7611
46: 3 and all the r of the house of Israel, 7611
Jer 6: 9 They shall throughly glean the r of Israel as 7611
11:23 there shall be no r of them: for I will bring 7611
15:11 Verily it shall be well with thy r; 8281
23: 3 I will gather the r of my flock out of all 7611
25:20 and Ekron, and the r of Ashdod: 7611
31: 7 O LORD, save thy people, the r of Israel. 7611
39: 9 r of the people that remained in the city, 3499
40:11 heard that the king of Babylon had left a r 7611
40:15 be scattered, and the r in Judah perish? 7611
41:16 all the r of the people whom he had 7611
42: 2 the LORD thy God, *even* for all this r; 7611
42:15 the word of the LORD, ye r of Judah; 7611
42:19 hath said concerning you, O ye r of Judah; 7611
43: 5 of the forces, took all the r of Judah, 7611
44:12 I will take the r of Judah, that have set their 7611
44:14 So that none of the r of Judah, which are 7611
44:28 all the r of Judah, that are gone into 7611
47: 4 the r of the country of Caphtor. 7611
47: 5 Ashkelon is cut off *with* the r of their 7611
Eze 5:10 the whole r of thee will I scatter into all 7611
6: 8 Yet will I **leave a r**, that ye may have *some* 3498
11:13 *wilt* thou make a full end of the r of Israel? 7611
14:22 therein shall be left a r that shall be brought 6413
23:25 thine ears; and thy r shall fall by the sword: 319
25:16 and destroy the r of the sea coast. 7611
Joel 2:32 and in the r whom the LORD *shall* call. 8300
Am 1: 8 the r of the Philistines shall perish, saith 7611
5:15 hosts will be gracious unto the r of Joseph. 7611
9:12 That they may possess the r of Edom, and 7611
Mic 2:12 of thee; I will surely gather the r of Israel; 7611
4: 7 I will make her that halted a r, and her that 7611
5: 3 the r of his brethren shall return unto 3499
5: 7 the r of Jacob shall be in the midst of many 7611
5: 8 the r of Jacob shall be among the Gentiles 7611
7:18 passeth by the transgression of the r of his 7611
Hab 2: 8 all the r of the people shall spoil thee; 3499
Zep 1: 4 I will cut off the r of Baal from this place, 7605
2: 7 the coast shall be for the r of the house of 7611
2: 9 and the r of my people shall possess them. 3499
3:13 The r of Israel shall not do iniquity, 7611
Hag 1:12 the high priest, with all the r of the people, 7611
1:14 and the spirit of all the r of the people; 7611
Zec 8: 6 If it be marvellous in the eyes of the r of 7611
8:12 I will cause the r of this people to possess 7611
Mt 22: 6 And the r took his servants, and *3062*
Ro 9:27 be as the sand of the sea, a r shall be saved: *2640*
11: 5 at *this* present time also there is a r *3005*
Rev 11:13 and the r were affrighted, and gave glory to *3062*
12:17 went to make war with the r of her seed, *3062*
19:21 And the r were slain with the sword of him *3062*

REMOVE (45) [REMOVED, REMOVETH, REMOVING]
Ge 48:17 to r it from Ephraim's head unto 5493
Nu 36: 7 the children of Israel r from tribe to tribe: 5437
36: 9 Neither shall the inheritance r from *one* 5437
Dt 19:14 Thou shalt not r thy neighbour's landmark, 5253
Jos 3: 3 ye shall r from your place, and go after it. 5265
Jdg 9:29 under my hand; then would I r Abimelech. 5493
2Sa 6:10 So David would not r the ark of 5493
2Ki 23:27 I will r Judah also out of my sight, 5493
24: 3 to r *them* out of his sight, for the sins of 5493
2Ch 33: 8 Neither will I any more r the foot of Israel 5493
Job 24: 2 *Some* r the landmarks; they violently take 5381
27: 5 till I die I will not r my integrity from me. 5493
Ps 36:11 and let not the hand of the wicked r me. 5110
39:10 **R** thy stroke away from me: I am 5493

Ps 119:22 **R** from me reproach and contempt; for I 1556
119:29 **R** from me the way of lying: and grant me 5493
Pr 4:27 hand nor *to* the left: **r** thy foot from evil. 5493
5: 8 **R** thy way **far** from her, and come not nigh 7368
22:28 **R** not the ancient landmark, which thy 5253
23:10 **R** not the old landmark; and enter not into 5253
30: 8 **R far** from me vanity and lies: give me 7368
Ecc 11:10 Therefore **r** sorrow from thy heart, and 5493
Isa 13:13 and the earth shall **r** out of her place, 7493
46: 7 he standeth; from his place shall he not **r**: 4185
Jer 4: 1 out of my sight, then shalt thou not **r**. 5110
27:10 a lie unto you, to **r** you **far** from your land; 7368
32:31 that *I* should **r** it from before my face, 5493
50: 3 they shall **r**, they shall depart, both man 5110
50: 8 **R** out of the midst of Babylon, and go forth 5110
Eze 12: 3 for removing, and **r** by day in their sight; 1540
12: 3 thou shalt **r** from thy place to another place 1540
12:11 they shall **r** *and* go into captivity. 1473
21:26 **R** the diadem, and take off the crown: 5493
45: 9 **r** violence and spoil, and execute judgment 5493
Hos 5:10 The princes of Judah were like them that **r** 5253
Joel 2:20 I will **r far off** from you the northern *army,* 7368
3: 6 that *ye* might **r** them **far** from their border. 7368
Mic 2: 3 from which ye shall not **r** your necks; 4185
Zec 3: 9 I will **r** the iniquity of that land in one day. 4185
14: 4 half of the mountain shall **r** toward 4185
Mt 17:20 this mountain, **R** hence to yonder place; *3327*
17:20 and it shall **r**; and nothing shall be *3327*
Lk 22:42 if thou be willing, **r** this cup from me: *3911*
1Co 13: 2 so that *I* could **r** mountains, and have no *3179*
Rev 2: 5 and will **r** thy candlestick out of his place, *2795*

REMOVED (91) [REMOVE]

Ge 8:13 Noah **r** the covering of the ark, and looked, 5493
12: 8 he **r** from thence unto a mountain on 6275
13:18 Abram **r** his **tent**, and came and dwelt in 167
26:22 he **r** from thence, and digged another well; 6275
30:35 he **r** that day the he goats that were 5493
47:21 he **r** them to cities from *one* end of 5674
Ex 8:31 he **r** the swarms *of flies* from Pharaoh, 5493
14:19 the camp of Israel, **r** and went behind them; 5265
20:18 when the people saw *it,* they **r**, and 5128
Nu 12:16 afterward the people **r** from Hazeroth, and 5265
21:12 From thence they **r**, and pitched in 5265
21:13 From thence they **r**, and pitched on 5265
33: 5 the children of Israel **r** from Rameses, and 5265
33: 7 they **r** from Etham, and turned again unto 5265
33: 9 they **r** from Marah, and came unto Elim: 5265
33:10 they **r** from Elim, and encamped by 5265
33:11 they **r** from the Red sea, and encamped in 5265
33:14 they **r** from Alush, and encamped at 5265
33:16 they **r** from the desert of Sinai, and 5265
33:21 they **r** from Libnah, and pitched at Rissah. 5265
33:24 they **r** from mount Shapher, and 5265
33:25 they **r** from Haradah, and pitched in 5265
33:26 they **r** from Makheloth, and encamped at 5265
33:28 they **r** from Tarah, and pitched in Mithcah. 5265
33:32 they **r** from Bene-jaakan, and encamped at 5265
33:34 they **r** from Jotbathah, and encamped at 5265
33:36 they **r** from Ezion-gaber, and pitched in 5265
33:37 they **r** from Kadesh, and pitched in mount 5265
33:46 they **r** from Dibon-gad, and encamped in 5265
33:47 they **r** from Almon-diblathaim, and 5265
Dt 28:25 shalt be **r** into all the kingdoms of the earth. 2189
Jos 3: 1 they **r** from Shittim, and came to Jordan, 5265
3:14 when the people **r** from their tents, to pass 5265
1Sa 6: 3 to you why his hand is not **r** from you. 5493
18:13 Therefore Saul **r** him from him, and 5493
2Sa 20:12 he **r** Amasa out of the highway *into* 5437
20:13 When he was **r** out of the highway, all 3014
1Ki 15:12 and **r** all the idols that his fathers had made. 5493
15:13 even her he **r** from *being* queen, because 5493
15:14 the high places were not **r**: 5493
2Ki 15: 4 Save that the high places were not **r**: 5493
15:35 Howbeit the high places were not **r**: 5493
16:17 of the bases, and **r** the laver from off them; 5493
17:18 with Israel, and **r** them out of his sight: 5493
17:23 Until the LORD **r** Israel out of his sight, 5493
17:26 The nations which thou hast **r**, and 1540
18: 4 He **r** the high places, and brake the images, 5493
23:27 as I have **r** Israel, and will cast off this city 5493
1Ch 8: 6 of Geba, and they **r** them to Manahath: 1540
8: 7 he **r** them, and begat Uzza, and Ahihud. 1540
2Ch 15:16 he **r** her from *being* queen, because she had 5493
35:12 they **r** the burnt offerings, that they might 5493
Job 14:18 to nought, and the rock is **r** out of his place. 6275
18: 4 and shall the rock be **r** out of his place? 6275
19:10 and mine hope hath he **r** like a tree. 5265
36:16 would he have **r** thee out of the strait *into* a 5496
Ps 46: 2 though the earth be **r**, and though 4171
81: 6 I **r** his shoulder from the burden: his hands 5493
103:12 *so* **far** hath he **r** our transgressions from us. 7368
104: 5 of the earth, *that* it should not be **r** for ever. 4131
125: 1 *which* cannot be **r**, *but* abideth for ever. 4131
Pr 10:30 The righteous shall never be **r**: but 4131
Isa 6:12 the LORD have **r** men **far away**, and 7368
10:13 I have **r** the bounds of the people, and 5493
10:31 Madmenah is **r**; the inhabitants of Gebim 5074
22:25 nail that is fastened in the sure place be **r**, 4185
24:20 a drunkard, and shall be **r** like a cottage; 5110
26:15 thou hadst **r** *it* **far** *unto* all the ends of 7368
29:13 have **r** their heart **far** from me, and 7368
30:20 yet shall not thy teachers be **r into a corner** 3670
33:20 not one of the stakes thereof shall ever be **r**, 5265
38:12 and is **r** from me as a shepherd's tent: 1540
54:10 mountains shall depart, and the hills be **r**; 4131
54:10 neither shall the covenant of my peace be **r**, 4131
Jer 15: 4 I will cause them to be **r** into all kingdoms 2189
24: 9 I will deliver them to be **r** into all 2189
29:18 will deliver them to be **r** to all 2189
34:17 I will make you to be **r** into all 2189
La 1: 8 hath grievously sinned; therefore she is **r**: 5206
3:17 thou hast **r** my soul **far off** from peace: 2186
Eze 7:19 in the streets, and their gold shall be **r**: 5079
23:46 and *will* give them to be **r** and spoiled. 2189
36:17 me as the uncleanness of a **r woman**. 5079
Am 6: 7 them that stretched themselves shall be **r**. 5493
Mic 2: 4 how hath he **r** *it* from me! turning away he 4185
7:11 *in* that day shall the decree be **far r**. 7368
Mt 21:21 Be thou **r**, and be thou cast into the sea; *142*
Mk 11:23 Be thou **r**, and be thou cast into the sea; *142*
Ac 7: 4 he **r** him into this land, wherein ye now *3351*
13:22 And when he had **r** him, he raised up unto *3179*
Gal 1: 6 soon **r** from him that called you into *3346*

REMOVETH (5) [REMOVE]

Dt 27:17 Cursed *be* he that **r** his neighbour's 5253
Job 9: 5 Which **r** the mountains, and they know not: 6275
12:20 He **r away** the speech of the trusty, and 5493
Ecc 10: 9 Whoso **r** stones shall be hurt therewith; 5265
Da 2:21 he **r** kings, and setteth up kings: he giveth 5709

REMOVING (5) [REMOVE]

Ge 30:32 **r** from thence all the speckled and 5493
Isa 49:21 *am* desolate, a captive, and **r to and fro**? 5493
Eze 12: 3 prepare thee stuff for **r**, and remove by day 1473
12: 4 thy stuff by day in their sight, as stuff for **r**: 1473
Heb 12:27 the **r** of those *things* that are shaken, *3331*

REMPHAN (1)

Ac 7:43 of Moloch, and the star of your god **R**, *4481*

REND (9) [RENDER, RENDERED, RENDEREST, RENDERETH, RENDERING, RENDING, RENT, RENTEST]

Ex 39:23 round about the hole, *that* it should not **r**. 7167
Lev 10: 6 not your heads, neither **r** your clothes; 6533
13:56 he shall **r** it out of the garment, or out of 7167
21:10 not uncover his head, nor **r** his clothes; 6533
1Ki 11:11 I will **surely** **r** the kingdom from 7167+7167
11:12 *but* I will **r** it out of the hand of thy son. 7167
11:13 Howbeit I will not **r away** all the kingdom; 7167
2Ch 34:27 didst **r** thy clothes, and weep before me; 7167
Isa 64: 1 O that thou wouldest **r** the heavens, 7167

RENDER (33) [REND]

Nu 18: 9 which they shall **r** unto me, *shall be* most 7725
Dt 32:41 I will **r** vengeance to mine enemies, and 7725
32:43 and will **r** vengeance to his adversaries, and 7725
Jdg 9:57 of Shechem did God **r** upon their heads: 7725
1Sa 26:23 The LORD **r** to every man his 7725
2Ch 6:30 **r** unto every man according unto all his 5414
Job 33:26 for he will **r** unto man his righteousness. 7725
34:11 For the work of a man shall he **r** unto him, 7999
Ps 28: 4 work of their hands; **r** to them their desert. 7725
38:20 They also that **r** evil for good are mine 7999
56:12 upon me, O God: I will **r** praises unto thee. 7999
79:12 **r** unto our neighbours sevenfold into their 7725
94: 2 judge of the earth: **r** a reward to the proud. 7725

Ps 116:12 What shall I r unto the LORD *for* all his 7725
Pr 24:12 shall *not* he r to *every* man according to his 7725
24:29 I will r to the man according to his work. 7725
26:16 conceit than seven *men* that can r a reason. 7725
Isa 66:15 to r his anger with fury, and his rebuke 7725
Jer 51: 6 he *will* r unto her a recompence. 7999
51:24 I will r unto Babylon and to all 7999
La 3:64 R unto them a recompence, O LORD, 7725
Hos 14: 2 so will we r the calves of our lips. 7999
Joel 3: 4 will ye r me a recompence? and if ye 7999
Zec 9:12 even to day do I declare *that* I will r double 7725
Mt 21:41 which shall r him the fruits in their seasons. *591*
22:21 R therefore unto Cesar the *things* which are *591*
Mk 12:17 R to Cesar the *things* that are Cesar's, and *591*
Lk 20:25 R therefore unto Cesar the *things* which be *591*
Ro 2: 6 Who will r to every *man* according to his *591*
13: 7 R therefore to all *their* dues: tribute to whom *591*
1Co 7: 3 Let the husband r unto the wife due *591*
1Th 3: 9 For what thanks can we r to God **again** for *467*
5:15 See that none r evil for evil unto any *man*; *591*

RENDERED (4) [REND]
Jdg 9:56 Thus God r the wickedness of Abimelech, 7725
2Ki 3: 4 r unto the king of Israel an hundred 7725
2Ch 32:25 Hezekiah r not **again** according to 7725
Pr 12:14 the recompence of a man's hands shall be r 7725

RENDEREST (1) [REND]
Ps 62:12 for thou r to *every* man according to his 7999

RENDERETH (1) [REND]
Isa 66: 6 a voice of the LORD that r recompence to 7999

RENDERING (1) [REND]
1Pe 3: 9 Not r evil for evil, or railing for railing: but *591*

RENDING (1) [REND]
Ps 7: 2 r *it* **in pieces**, while *there is* none to deliver. 6561

RENEW (6) [RENEWED, RENEWEST, RENEWING]
1Sa 11:14 let us go *to* Gilgal, and r the kingdom there. 2318
Ps 51:10 O God; and r a right spirit within me. 2318
Isa 40:31 they that wait upon the LORD shall r *their* 2498
41: 1 and let the people r *their* strength: 2498
La 5:21 and we shall be turned; r our days as of old. 2318
Heb 6: 6 fall away, to r *them* again unto repentance; *340*

RENEWED (6) [RENEW]
2Ch 15: 8 r the altar of the LORD, that *was* before 2318
Job 29:20 fresh in me, and my bow was r in my hand. 2498
Ps 103: 5 *so that* thy youth is r like the eagle's. 2318
2Co 4:16 yet the inward *man* is r day by day. *341*
Eph 4:23 And be r in the spirit of your mind; *365*
Col 3:10 And have put on the new *man*, which is r in *341*

RENEWEST (2) [RENEW]
Job 10:17 Thou r thy witnesses against me, and 2318
Ps 104:30 are created: and thou r the face of the earth. 2318

RENEWING (2) [RENEW]
Ro 12: 2 but be ye transformed by the r of your mind, *342*
Tit 3: 5 of regeneration, and r of the Holy Ghost; *342*

RENOUNCED (1)
2Co 4: 2 But have r the hidden *things* of dishonesty, *550*

RENOWN (7) [RENOWNED]
Ge 6: 4 mighty *men* which *were* of old, men of r. 8034
Nu 16: 2 famous in the congregation, men of r: 8034
Eze 16:14 thy r went forth among the heathen for thy 8034
16:15 playedst the harlot because of thy r, and 8034
34:29 I will raise up for them a plant of r, and 8034
39:13 it shall be to them a r the day that I shall be 8034
Da 9:15 and hast gotten thee r, as *at* this day; 8034

RENOWNED (4) [RENOWN]
Nu 1:16 These *were* the r of the congregation, 7121
Isa 14:20 the seed of evildoers shall never be r. 7121
Eze 23:23 captains and rulers, great lords and r, all of 7121
26:17 the r city, which wast strong in the sea, she 1984

RENT (76) [REND]
Ge 37:29 *was* not in the pit; and he r his clothes. 7167
37:33 Joseph is **without doubt** r **in pieces**. 2963+2963
37:34 Jacob r his clothes, and put sackcloth upon 7167
44:13 they r their clothes, and laded every man 7167
Ex 28:32 the hole of an habergeon, *that* it be not r. 7167
Lev 13:45 whom the plague *is*, his clothes shall be r, 6533
Nu 14: 6 them that searched the land, r their clothes: 7167
Jos 7: 6 Joshua r his clothes, and fell to the earth 7167
9: 4 and wine bottles, old, and r, and bound up; 1234
9:13 we filled, *were* new; and behold, they be r: 1234
Jdg 11:35 that he r his clothes, and said, Alas, 7167
14: 6 he r him as *he* would have rent a kid, and 8156
14: 6 he rent him as *he* would have r a kid, and 8156
1Sa 4:12 *to* Shiloh the same day with his clothes r, 7167
15:27 hold upon the skirt of his mantle, and it r. 7167
15:28 The LORD hath r the kingdom of Israel 7167
28:17 for the LORD hath r the kingdom out of 7167
2Sa 1: 2 of the camp from Saul with his clothes r, 7167
1:11 David took hold on his clothes, and r them; 7167
3:31 R your clothes, and gird you with 7167
13:19 r her garment of divers colours that *was* on 7167
13:31 his servants stood *by* with their clothes r. 7167
15:32 Archite *came* to meet him with his coat r, 7167
1Ki 1:40 so that the earth r with the sound of them. 1234
11:30 that *was* on him, and r it *in* twelve pieces: 7167
11:31 I will r the kingdom out of the hand of 7167
13: 3 the altar *shall be* r, and the ashes that *are* 7167
13: 5 The altar also *was* r, and the ashes poured 7167
14: 8 r the kingdom **away** from the house of 7167
19:11 a great and strong wind r the mountains, 6561
21:27 that he r his clothes, and put sackcloth 7167
2Ki 2:12 and r them **in** two **pieces**. 7167+7168
5: 7 that he r his clothes, and said, *Am* I God, 7167
5: 8 that the king of Israel had r his clothes, 7167
5: 8 Wherefore hast thou r thy clothes? 7167
6:30 words of the woman, that he r his clothes; 7167
11:14 Athaliah r her clothes, and cried, Treason, 7167
17:21 For he r Israel from the house of David; 7167
18:37 to Hezekiah with *their* clothes r, and 7167
19: 1 when king Hezekiah heard *it*, that he r his 7167
22:11 of the book of the law, that he r his clothes. 7167
22:19 and hast r thy clothes, and wept before me; 7167
2Ch 23:13 Athaliah r her clothes, and said, Treason, 7167
34:19 the words of the law, that he r his clothes. 7167
Ezr 9: 3 I r my garment and my mantle, and 7167
9: 5 having r my garment and my mantle, I fell 7167
Est 4: 1 Mordecai r his clothes, and put on 7167
Job 1:20 r his mantle, and shaved his head, and 7167
2:12 they r every one his mantle, and 7167
26: 8 and the cloud is not r under them. 1234
Ecc 3: 7 A time to r, and a time to sew; a time to 7167
Isa 3:24 instead of a girdle a r; and instead of well 5364
36:22 to Hezekiah with *their* clothes r, and 7167
37: 1 when king Hezekiah heard *it*, that he r his 7167
Jer 36:24 nor r their garments, *neither* the king, 7167
41: 5 their clothes r, and having cut themselves, 7167
Eze 13:11 shall fall; and a stormy wind shall r *it*. 1234
13:13 I will even r *it with* a stormy wind in my 1234
29: 7 thou didst break, and r all their shoulder: 1234
30:16 No shall be r **asunder**, and Noph *shall* 1234
Hos 13: 8 will r the caul of their heart, and there will 7167
Joel 2:13 r your heart, and not your garments, and 7167
Mt 7: 6 under their feet, and turn *again* and r you. *4486*
9:16 from the garment, and the r is made worse. *4978*
26:65 Then the high priest r his clothes, saying, *1284*
27:51 the vail of the temple was r in twain from *4977*
27:51 and the earth did quake, and the rocks r; *4977*
Mk 2:21 *from* the old, and the r is made worse. *4978*
9:26 and r him sore, and came out of *him*: and *4682*
14:63 Then the high priest r his clothes, and saith, *1284*
15:38 And the vail of the temple was r in twain *4977*
Lk 5:36 *then* both the new **maketh a** r, and *4977*
23:45 the vail of the temple was r in the midst. *4977*
Jn 19:24 Let us not r it, but cast lots for it, whose it *4977*
Ac 14:14 heard *of*, they r their clothes, and ran in *1284*
16:22 and the magistrates r **off** their clothes, and *4048*

RENTEST (1) [REND]
Jer 4:30 though thou r thy face with painting, 7167

REPAIR (14) [REPAIRED, REPAIRER, REPAIRING]
2Ki 12: 5 let them r the breaches of the house, 2388
12: 7 Why r ye not the breaches of the house? 2388
12: 8 neither to r the breaches of the house. 2388
12:12 hewed stone to r the breaches of the house 2388
12:12 for all that was laid out for the house to r 2394
22: 5 the LORD, to r the breaches of the house, 2388
22: 6 buy timber and hewn stone to r the house. 2388

2Ch 24: 4 *that* Joash was minded to **r** the house of 2318
24: 5 gather of all Israel money to **r** the house of 2388
24:12 carpenters to **r** the house of the LORD, 2318
34: 8 to **r** the house of the LORD his God. 2388
34:10 of the LORD, to **r** and mend the house: 918
Ezr 9: 9 to **r** the desolations thereof, and to give us a 5975
Isa 61: 4 they shall **r** the waste cities, the desolations 2318

REPAIRED (44) [REPAIR]
Jdg 21:23 and **r** the cities, and dwelt in them. 1129
1Ki 11:27 **r** the breaches of the city of David his 5462
18:30 he **r** the altar of the LORD that was 7495
2Ki 12: 6 priests had not **r** the breaches of the house. 2388
12:14 **r** therewith the house of the LORD. 2388
1Ch 11: 8 round about: and Joab **r** the rest of the city. 2421
2Ch 29: 3 of the house of the LORD, and **r** them. 2388
32: 5 **r** Millo *in* the city of David, and made darts 2388
33:16 he **r** the altar of the LORD, and 1129
Ne 3: 4 next unto them **r** Meremoth the son of 2388
3: 4 next unto them **r** Meshullam the son of 2388
3: 4 next unto them **r** Zadok the son of Baana. 2388
3: 5 next unto them the Tekoites **r**; but 2388
3: 6 Moreover the old gate **r** Jehoiada the son of 2388
3: 7 next unto them **r** Melatiah the Gibeonite, 2388
3: 8 Next unto him **r** Uzziel the son of 2388
3: 8 Next unto him also **r** Hananiah the son of 2388
3: 9 next unto them **r** Rephaiah the son of Hur, 2388
3:10 next unto them **r** Jedaiah the son of 2388
3:10 next unto him **r** Hattush the son of 2388
3:11 **r** the other piece, and the tower of 2388
3:12 next unto him **r** Shallum the son of 2388
3:13 The valley gate **r** Hanun, and 2388
3:14 the dung gate **r** Malchiah the son of 2388
3:15 the gate of the fountain **r** Shallun the son of 2388
3:16 After him **r** Nehemiah the son of Azbuk, 2388
3:17 After him **r** the Levites, Rehum the son of 2388
3:17 Next unto him **r** Hashabiah, the ruler of 2388
3:18 After him **r** their brethren, Bavai the son of 2388
3:19 next to him **r** Ezer the son of Jeshua, 2388
3:20 son of Zabbai earnestly **r** the other piece, 2388
3:21 After him **r** Meremoth the son of Urijah 2388
3:22 after him **r** the priests, the men of the plain. 2388
3:23 After him **r** Benjamin and Hashub over 2388
3:23 After him **r** Azariah the son of Maaseiah 2388
3:24 After him **r** Binnui the son of Henadad 2388
3:27 After them the Tekoites **r** another piece, 2388
3:28 From above the horse gate **r** the priests, 2388
3:29 After them **r** Zadok the son of Immer over 2388
3:29 After him **r** also Shemaiah the son of 2388
3:30 After him **r** Hananiah the son of 2388
3:30 After him **r** Meshullam the son of 2388
3:31 After him **r** Malchiah the goldsmith's son 2388
3:32 corner unto the sheep gate **r** the goldsmiths 2388

REPAIRER (1) [REPAIR]
Isa 58:12 thou shalt be called, The **r** of the breach, 1443

REPAIRING (1) [REPAIR]
2Ch 24:27 upon him, and the **r** of the house of God, 3247

REPAY (8) [REPAYED, REPAYETH]
Dt 7:10 that hateth him, he will **r** him to his face. 7999
Job 21:31 and who shall **r** him *what* he hath done? 7999
41:11 that I should **r** *him? whatsoever is* under 7999
Isa 59:18 accordingly he will **r**, fury to his 7999
59:18 to the islands he will **r** recompence. 7999
Lk 10:35 when I come again, I will **r** thee. *591*
Ro 12:19 Vengeance *is* mine; I will **r**, saith the Lord. *467*
Phm 1:19 I will **r** *it:* albeit I do not say to thee how *661*

REPAYED (1) [REPAY]
Pr 13:21 but to the righteous good shall be **r**. 7999

REPAYETH (1) [REPAY]
Dt 7:10 **r** them that hate him to their face, 7999

REPAYING See REQUITE; REQUITED; REQUITING

REPEATETH (1) [REPETITIONS]
Pr 17: 9 he that **r** a matter separateth very friends. 8138

REPENT (46) [REPENTANCE, REPENTED, REPENTEST, REPENTETH, REPENTING, REPENTINGS]
Ex 13:17 Lest peradventure the people **r** when they 5162
32:12 and **r** of *this* evil against thy people. 5162
Nu 23:19 neither the son of man, that he should **r**: 5162
Dt 32:36 his people, and **r** himself for his servants, 5162
1Sa 15:29 also the Strength of Israel will not lie nor **r**: 5162
15:29 for he *is* not a man, that *he* should **r**. 5162
1Ki 8:47 **r**, and make supplication unto thee in 7725
Job 42: 6 I abhor *myself,* and **r** in dust and ashes. 5162
Ps 90:13 and let it **r** thee concerning thy servants. 5162
110: 4 The LORD hath sworn, and will not **r**, 5162
135:14 he will **r** himself concerning his servants. 5162
Jer 4:28 spoken *it,* I have purposed *it,* and will not **r**, 5162
18: 8 I will **r** of the evil that I thought to do unto 5162
18:10 not my voice, then I will **r** of the good, 5162
26: 3 that I may **r** me of the evil, which I purpose 5162
26:13 the LORD will **r** him of the evil that he 5162
42:10 for I **r** me of the evil that I have done unto 5162
Eze 14: 6 **R**, and turn *yourselves* from your idols; and 7725
18:30 **R**, and turn *yourselves* from all your 7725
24:14 neither will I spare, neither will I **r**; 5162
Joel 2:14 Who knoweth *if* he will return and **r**, and 5162
Jnh 3: 9 Who can tell *if* God will turn and **r**, and 5162
Mt 3: 2 And saying, **R** ye: for the kingdom of *3340*
4:17 time Jesus began to preach, and to say, **R**: *3340*
Mk 1:15 is at hand: **r** ye, and believe the gospel. *3340*
6:12 went out, and preached that *men* should **r**. *3340*
Lk 13: 3 but, except ye **r**, ye shall all likewise *3340*
13: 5 but except ye **r**, ye shall all likewise perish. *3340*
16:30 went unto them from the dead, they will **r**. *3340*
17: 3 rebuke him; and if he **r**, forgive him. *3340*
17: 4 in a day turn again to thee, saying, I **r**; *3340*
Ac 2:38 **R**, and be baptized every one of you in *3340*
3:19 **R** ye therefore, and be converted, that your *3340*
8:22 **R** therefore of this thy wickedness, and *3340*
17:30 now commandeth all men every where to **r**: *3340*
26:20 that *they* should **r** and turn to God, and *3340*
2Co 7: 8 with a letter, I do not **r**, though I did repent: *3338*
7: 8 with a letter, I do not repent, though I did **r**: *3338*
Heb 7:21 unto him, The Lord sware and will not **r**, *3338*
Rev 2: 5 art fallen, and **r**, and do the first works; *3340*
2: 5 candlestick out of his place, except thou **r**. *3340*
2:16 **R**; or else I *will* come unto thee quickly, and will fight against them with the sword of my mouth *3340*
2:21 And I gave her space to **r** of her *3340*
2:22 except they **r** of their deeds. *3340*
3: 3 and heard, and hold fast, and **r**. *3340*
3:19 and chasten: be zealous therefore, and **r**. *3340*

REPENTANCE (26) [REPENT]
Hos 13:14 **r** shall be hid from mine eyes. 5164
Mt 3: 8 Bring forth therefore fruits meet for **r**: *3341*
3:11 I indeed baptize you with water unto **r**: but *3341*
9:13 come to call *the* righteous, but sinners to **r**. *3341*
Mk 1: 4 preach the baptism of **r** for the remission of *3341*
2:17 not to call *the* righteous, but sinners to **r**. *3341*
Lk 3: 3 preaching the baptism of **r** for *3341*
3: 8 Bring forth therefore fruits worthy of **r**, and *3341*
5:32 not to call *the* righteous, but sinners to **r**. *3341*
15: 7 and nine just *persons* which need no **r**. *3341*
24:47 And that **r** and remission of sins should be *3341*
Ac 5:31 for to give **r** to Israel, and forgiveness of *3341*
11:18 God also to the Gentiles granted **r** unto life. *3341*
13:24 the baptism of **r** to all the people of Israel. *3341*
19: 4 John verily baptized *with* the baptism of **r**, *3341*
20:21 **r** toward God, and faith toward our Lord *3341*
26:20 and turn to God, and do works meet for **r**. *3341*
Ro 2: 4 that the goodness of God leadeth thee to **r**? *3341*
11:29 the gifts and calling of God *are* **without r**. *278*
2Co 7: 9 were made sorry, but that ye sorrowed to **r**: *3341*
7:10 For godly sorrow worketh **r** to salvation not *3341*
2Ti 2:25 if God peradventure will give them **r** to *3341*
Heb 6: 1 not laying again the foundation of **r** from *3341*
6: 6 shall fall away, to renew *them* again unto **r**; *3341*
12:17 for he found no place of **r**, though he *3341*
2Pe 3: 9 should perish, but that all should come to **r**. *3341*

REPENTED (32) [REPENT]
Ge 6: 6 it **r** the LORD that he had made man on 5162
Ex 32:14 the LORD **r** of the evil which he thought 5162
Jdg 2:18 for it **r** the LORD because of their 5162
21: 6 the children of Israel **r** them for Benjamin 5162
21:15 the people **r** them for Benjamin, because 5162
1Sa 15:35 the LORD **r** that he had made Saul king 5162
2Sa 24:16 the LORD **r** him of the evil, and said to 5162
1Ch 21:15 he **r** him of the evil, and said to the angel 5162
Ps 106:45 **r** according to the multitude of his mercies. 5162

R

Jer 8: 6 no man r him of his wickedness, saying, 5162
20:16 which the LORD overthrew, and r not: 5162
26:19 the LORD r him of the evil which he had 5162
31:19 Surely after that I was turned, I r; and 5162
Am 7: 3 The LORD r for this: It shall not be, 5162
7: 6 The LORD r for this: This also shall not 5162
Jnh 3:10 God r of the evil, that he had said that he 5162
Zec 8:14 saith the LORD of hosts, and I r not: 5162
Mt 11:20 works were done, because they r not. *3340*
11:21 Sidon they would have r long ago in *3340*
12:41 because they r at the preaching of Jonas; *3340*
21:29 I will not: but afterward he r, and went. *3338*
21:32 ye, when ye had seen *it,* r not afterward, *3338*
27: 3 r himself, and brought again the thirty *3338*
Lk 10:13 they had a great while ago r, sitting in *3340*
11:32 for they r at the preaching of Jonas; and *3340*
2Co 7:10 repentance to salvation **not** to be **r of**: *278*
12:21 and have not r of the uncleanness and *3340*
Rev 2:21 to repent of her fornication; and she r not. *3340*
9:20 *yet* r not of the works of their hands, *3340*
9:21 Neither r they of their murders, nor of their *3340*
16: 9 and they r not to give him glory. *3340*
16:11 and their sores, and r not of their deeds. *3340*

REPENTEST (1) [REPENT]
Jnh 4: 2 of great kindness, and r thee of the evil. 5162

REPENTETH (5) [REPENT]
Ge 6: 7 the air; for it r me that I have made them. 5162
1Sa 15:11 It r me that I have set up Saul to be king: 5162
Joel 2:13 and of great kindness, and r him of the evil. 5162
Lk 15: 7 shall be in heaven over one sinner that r, *3340*
15:10 of the angels of God over one sinner that r. *3340*

REPENTING (1) [REPENT]
Jer 15: 6 and destroy thee; I am weary with r. 5162

REPENTINGS (1) [REPENT]
Hos 11: 8 within me, my r are kindled together. 5150

REPETITIONS (1) [REPEATETH]
Mt 6: 7 But when ye pray, **use not vain** r, as *945*

REPHAEL (1)
1Ch 26: 7 Othni, and **R**, and Obed, Elzabad, 7501

REPHAH (1)
1Ch 7:25 **R** *was* his son, also Resheph, and Telah his 7506

REPHAIAH (5)
1Ch 3:21 the sons of **R**, the sons of Arnan, the sons 7509
4:42 Neariah, and **R**, and Uzziel, the sons of 7509
7: 2 **R**, and Jeriel, and Jahmai, and Jibsam, and 7509
9:43 **R** his son, Eleasah his son, Azel his son. 7509
Ne 3: 9 next unto them repaired **R** the son of Hur, 7509

REPHAIM (6) [REPHAIMS]
2Sa 5:18 and spread themselves in the valley of **R**. 7497
5:22 and spread themselves in the valley of **R**. 7497
23:13 of the Philistines pitched in the valley of **R**. 7497
1Ch 11:15 the Philistines encamped in the valley of **R**. 7497
14: 9 and spread themselves in the valley of **R**. 7497
Isa 17: 5 as he that gathereth ears in the valley of **R**. 7497

REPHAIMS (2) [REPHAIM]
Ge 14: 5 smote the **R** in Ashteroth Karnaim, and 7497
15:20 the Hittites, and the Perizzites, and the **R**, 7497

REPHAITES See GIANT; REPHAIMS

REPHAN See REMPHAN

REPHIDIM (5)
Ex 17: 1 of the LORD, and pitched in **R**: 7508
17: 8 came Amalek, and fought with Israel in **R**. 7508
19: 2 For they were departed from **R**, and 7508
Nu 33:14 removed from Alush, and encamped at **R**, 7508
33:15 they departed from **R**, and pitched in 7508

REPLENISH (2) [REPLENISHED]
Ge 1:28 and multiply, and r the earth, and subdue it: 4390
9: 1 Be fruitful, and multiply, and r the earth. 4390

REPLENISHED (5) [REPLENISH]
Isa 2: 6 because they be r from the east, and 4390
23: 2 of Zidon, that pass over the sea, have r. 4390
Jer 31:25 and I have r every sorrowful soul. 4390
Eze 26: 2 unto me: I shall be r, *now* she is laid waste: 4390
27:25 thou wast r, and made very glorious in 4390

REPLIEST (1)
Ro 9:20 O man, who art thou that **r against** God? *470*

REPORT (30) [REPORTED]
Ge 37: 2 Joseph brought unto his father their evil **r**. 1681
Ex 23: 1 Thou shalt not raise a false r: put not thine 8088
Nu 13:32 they brought up an **evil r** of the land which 1681
14:37 Even *those* men that did bring up the evil r 1681
Dt 2:25 who shall hear r of thee, and shall tremble, 8088
1Sa 2:24 my sons; for *it is* no good r that I hear: 8052
1Ki 10: 6 It was a true r that I heard in mine own 1697
2Ch 9: 5 *It was* a true r which I heard in mine own 1697
Ne 6:13 *that* they might have *matter* for an evil r, 8034
Pr 15:30 *and* a good r maketh the bones fat. 8052
Isa 23: 5 As *at* the r concerning Egypt, so shall they 8088
23: 5 shall they be sorely pained *at* the r of Tyre. 8088
28:19 shall be a vexation only *to* understand the r. 8052
53: 1 Who hath believed our r? and to whom is 8052
Jer 20:10 **R**, *say they,* and we will report it. All my 5046
20:10 Report, *say they,* and we will r it. All my 5046
50:43 The king of Babylon hath heard the r of 8088
Jn 12:38 he spake, Lord, who hath believed our r? *189*
Ac 6: 3 ye out among you seven men **of honest r**, *3140*
10:22 of **good r** among all the nation of the Jews, *3140*
22:12 **having a good r** of all the Jews which *3140*
Ro 10:16 Esaias saith, Lord, who hath believed our **r**? *189*
1Co 14:25 and r that God is in you of a truth. *518*
2Co 6: 8 and dishonour, by **evil r** and good report: *1426*
6: 8 and dishonour, by evil report and **good r**: *2162*
Php 4: 8 *are* lovely, whatsoever *things are* of **good r**; *2163*
1Ti 3: 7 Moreover he must have a good r of them *3141*
Heb 11: 2 For by it the elders **obtained a good r**. *3140*
11:39 having **obtained a good r** through faith, *3140*
3Jn 1:12 Demetrius **hath good r** of all *men,* and *3140*

REPORTED (12) [REPORT]
Ne 6: 6 *It is* r among the heathen, and 8085
6: 7 now shall it be r to the king according to 8085
6:19 Also they r his good deeds before me, and 559
Est 1:17 husbands in their eyes, when it shall be r, 559
Eze 9:11 inkhorn by his side, r the matter, saying, 7725
Mt 28:15 this saying is **commonly r** among the Jews *1310*
Ac 4:23 and r all that the chief priests and elders had *518*
16: 2 Which was **well r of** by the brethren that *3140*
Ro 3: 8 And not *rather,* (as we be **slanderously r**, *987*
1Co 5: 1 It is r commonly *that there is* fornication *191*
1Ti 5:10 **Well r** of for good works; if she have *3140*
1Pe 1:12 which are now r unto you by them that have *312*

REPRESENTATIVE See DEPUTED

REPROACH (88) [REPROACHED, REPROACHES, REPROACHEST, REPROACHETH, REPROACHFULLY]
Ge 30:23 a son; and said, God hath taken away my r: 2781
34:14 is uncircumcised; for that *were* a r unto us: 2781
Jos 5: 9 *This* day have I rolled away the r of Egypt 2781
Ru 2:15 even among the sheaves, and r her not: 3637
1Sa 11: 2 right eyes, and lay it *for* a r upon all Israel. 2781
17:26 and taketh away the r from Israel? 2781
25:39 that hath pleaded the cause of my r from 2781
2Ki 19: 4 his master hath sent to r the living God; 2778
19:16 which hath sent him to r the living God. 2778
Ne 1: 3 in the province *are* in great affliction and r: 2781
2:17 wall of Jerusalem, that we be no more a r. 2781
4: 4 turn their r upon their own head, and 2781
5: 9 of the r of the heathen our enemies? 2781
6:13 for an evil report, that they might r me. 2778
Job 19: 5 against me, and plead against me my r: 2781
20: 3 I have heard the check of my r, and 3639
27: 6 my heart shall not r *me* so long as I live. 2778
Ps 15: 3 nor taketh up a r against his neighbour. 2781
22: 6 a r of men, and despised of the people. 2781
31:11 I was a r among all mine enemies, but 2781
39: 8 make me not the r of the foolish. 2781
42:10 a sword in my bones, mine enemies r me; 2778
44:13 Thou makest us a r to our neighbours, 2781
57: 3 save me *from* the r of him that would 2778
69: 7 Because for thy sake I have borne r; 2781
69:10 my soul with fasting, that was to my **r**. 2781
69:19 Thou hast known my r, and my shame, and 2781

Ps 69:20 **R** hath broken my heart; and I am full of 2781
71:13 let them be covered *with* r and 2781
74:10 O God, how long shall the adversary r? 2778
78:66 hinder parts: he put them to a perpetual r. 2781
79: 4 We are become a r to our neighbours, 2781
79:12 sevenfold into their bosom their r, 2781
89:41 way spoil him: he is a r to his neighbours. 2781
89:50 Remember, Lord, the r of thy servants; 2781
89:50 *how* I do bear in my bosom *the r of* all NIH
102: 8 Mine enemies r me all the day; *and* 2778
109:25 I became also a r unto them: *when* they 2781
119:22 Remove from me r and contempt; for I 2781
119:39 Turn away my r which I fear: for thy 2781
Pr 6:33 he get; and his r shall not be wiped away. 2781
14:34 a nation: but sin *is* a r to any people. 2617
18: 3 also contempt, and with ignominy r. 2781
19:26 a son that causeth shame, and **bringeth** r. 2659
22:10 shall go out; yea, strife and r shall cease. 7036
Isa 4: 1 be called by thy name, to take away our r. 2781
30: 5 a help nor profit, but a shame, and also a r. 2781
37: 4 his master hath sent to r the living God, 2778
37:17 which hath sent to r the living God. 2778
51: 7 fear ye not the r of men, neither be ye 2781
54: 4 shalt not remember the r of thy widowhood 2781
Jer 6:10 the word of the LORD is unto them a r; 2781
20: 8 the word of the LORD was made a r unto 2781
23:40 I will bring an everlasting r upon you, and 2781
24: 9 to be a r and a proverb, a taunt and a curse, 2781
29:18 and an astonishment, and a hissing, and a r, 2781
31:19 because I did bear the r of my youth. 2781
42:18 and an astonishment, and a curse, and a r; 2781
44: 8 and a r among all the nations of the earth? 2781
44:12 an astonishment, and a curse, and a r. 2781
49:13 a desolation, a r, a waste, and a curse; 2781
51:51 are confounded, because we have heard r: 2781
La 3:30 that smiteth him: he is filled full with r. 2781
3:61 Thou hast heard their r, O LORD, *and* 2781
5: 1 come upon us: consider, and behold our r. 2781
Eze 5:14 a r among the nations that *are* round about 2781
5:15 So it shall be a r and a taunt, an instruction 2781
16:57 as *at* the time of *thy* r of the daughters of 2781
21:28 the Ammonites, and concerning their r; 2781
22: 4 have I made thee a r unto the heathen, 2781
36:15 neither shalt thou bear the r of the people 2781
36:30 that ye shall receive no more r of famine 2781
Da 9:16 thy people *are become* a r to all *that are* 2781
11:18 a prince for his own behalf shall cause the r 2781
11:18 without his own r he shall cause *it* to turn 2781
Hos 12:14 and his r shall his Lord return unto him. 2781
Joel 2:17 O LORD, and give not thine heritage to r, 2781
2:19 I will no more make you a r among 2781
Mic 6:16 therefore ye shall bear the r of my people. 2781
Zep 2: 8 I have heard the r of Moab, and 2781
3:18 of thee, *to whom* the r of it *was* a burden. 2781
Lk 1:25 on *me,* to take away my r among men. *3681*
6:22 and shall r *you,* and cast out your name as *3679*
2Co 11:21 I speak as concerning r, as though we had *819*
1Ti 3: 7 lest he fall into r and the snare of the devil. *3680*
4:10 For therefore we both labour and **suffer** r, *3679*
Heb 11:26 Esteeming the r of Christ greater riches *3680*
13:13 unto him without the camp, bearing his r. *3680*

REPROACHED (15) [REPROACH]
2Ki 19:22 Whom hast thou r and blasphemed? and 2778
19:23 By thy messengers thou hast r the Lord, 2778
Job 19: 3 These ten times have ye r me: you are not 3637
Ps 55:12 For *it was* not an enemy *that* r me; then 2778
69: 9 the reproaches of them that r thee are fallen 2778
74:18 *that* the enemy hath r, O LORD, and 2778
79:12 wherewith they have r thee, O Lord. 2778
89:51 Wherewith thine enemies have r, 2778
89:51 wherewith they have r the footsteps of 2778
Isa 37:23 Whom hast thou r and blasphemed? and 2778
37:24 By thy servants hast thou r the Lord, and 2778
Zep 2: 8 whereby they have r my people, and 2778
2:10 because they have r and 2778
Ro 15: 3 The reproaches of them that r thee fell on *3679*
1Pe 4:14 If ye be r for the name of Christ, happy *are* *3679*

REPROACHES (5) [REPROACH]
Ps 69: 9 the r of them that reproached thee are 2781
Isa 43:28 given Jacob to the curse, and Israel to r. 1421
Ro 15: 3 The r of them that reproached thee fell on *3680*
2Co 12:10 in r, in necessities, in persecutions, *5196*

Heb 10:33 ye were made a gazingstock both by r *3680*

REPROACHEST (1) [REPROACH]
Lk 11:45 Master, thus saying thou r us also. *5195*

REPROACHETH (7) [REPROACH]
Nu 15:30 or a stranger, the same r the LORD; 1442
Ps 44:16 For the voice of him that r and 2778
74:22 remember how the foolish *man* r thee 2781
119:42 I have wherewith to answer him that r me: 2778
Pr 14:31 He that oppresseth the poor r his Maker: 2778
17: 5 Whoso mocketh the poor r his Maker: *and* 2778
27:11 heart glad, that I may answer him that r me. 2778

REPROACHFULLY (2) [REPROACH]
Job 16:10 have smitten me upon the cheek r; 2781+871.1
1Ti 5:14 none occasion to the adversary to **speak** r. *3059*

REPROBATE (4) [REPROBATES]
Jer 6:30 **R** silver shall *men* call them, because 3988
Ro 1:28 God gave them over to a r mind, to do those *96*
2Ti 3: 8 men of corrupt minds, r concerning the faith. *96*
Tit 1:16 and disobedient, and unto every good work r. *96*

REPROBATES (3) [REPROBATE]
2Co 13: 5 that Jesus Christ is in you, except ye be r? *96*
13: 6 I trust that ye shall know that we are not r. *96*
13: 7 do *that which is* honest, though we be as r. *96*

REPROOF (15) [REPROVE]
Job 26:11 heaven tremble and are astonished at his r. 1606
Pr 1:23 Turn you at my r: behold, I will pour out 8433
1:25 all my counsel, and would none of my r: 8433
1:30 none of my counsel: they despised all my r. 8433
5:12 hated instruction, and my heart despised r; 8433
10:17 but he that refuseth r erreth. 8433
12: 1 but he that hateth r *is* brutish. 8433
13:18 but he that regardeth r shall be honoured. 8433
15: 5 but he that regardeth r is prudent. 8433
15:10 the way: *and* he that hateth r shall die. 8433
15:31 The ear that heareth the r of life abideth 8433
15:32 but he that heareth r getteth understanding. 8433
17:10 A r entereth more into a wise *man* than an 1606
29:15 The rod and r give wisdom: but a child left 8433
2Ti 3:16 profitable for doctrine, for r, for correction, *1650*

REPROOFS (2) [REPROVE]
Ps 38:14 heareth not, and in whose mouth *are* no r. 8433
Pr 6:23 and r of instruction *are* the way of life: 8433

REPROVE (19) [REPROOF, REPROOFS, REPROVED, REPROVER, REPROVETH, UNREPROVEABLE]
2Ki 19: 4 will r the words which the LORD thy God 3198
Job 6:25 right words! but what doth your arguing r? 3198
6:26 Do ye imagine to r words, and the speeches 3198
13:10 He will **surely** r you, if ye do 3198+3198
22: 4 Will he r thee for fear of thee? will he enter 3198
Ps 50: 8 I will not r thee for thy sacrifices or 3198
50:21 *but* I will r thee, and set *them* in order 3198
141: 5 let him r me; *it shall be* an excellent oil, 3198
Pr 9: 8 **R** not a scorner, lest he hate thee: rebuke a 3198
19:25 r one that hath understanding, *and* he will 3198
30: 6 lest he r thee, and thou be found a liar. 3198
Isa 11: 3 neither r after the hearing of his ears: 3198
11: 4 and r with equity for the meek of the earth: 3198
37: 4 will r the words which the LORD thy God 3198
Jer 2:19 and thy backslidings shall r thee: 3198
Hos 4: 4 Yet let no man strive, nor r another: for thy 3198
Jn 16: 8 he will r the world of sin, and *1651*
Eph 5:11 works of darkness, but rather r *them.* *1651*
2Ti 4: 2 r, rebuke, exhort with all longsuffering and *1651*

REPROVED (10) [REPROVE]
Ge 20:16 and with all *other:* thus she was r. 3198
21:25 Abraham r Abimelech because of a well of 3198
1Ch 16:21 them wrong: yea, he r kings for their sakes, 3198
Ps 105:14 them wrong: yea, he r kings for their sakes; 3198
Pr 29: 1 He, that being often r hardeneth *his* neck, 8433
Jer 29:27 why hast thou not r Jeremiah of Anathoth, 1605
Hab 2: 1 and what I shall answer when I am r. 8433
Lk 3:19 being r by him for Herodias his brother *1651*
Jn 3:20 to the light, lest his deeds should be r. *1651*
Eph 5:13 But all *things* that are r are made manifest *1651*

REPROVER (2) [REPROVE]
Pr 25:12 *so is* a wise r upon an obedient ear. 3198
Eze 3:26 shalt be dumb, and shalt not be to them a r: 376

REPROVETH (4) [REPROVE]
Job 40: 2 the Almighty instruct *him?* he that r God, 3198
Pr 9: 7 He that r a scorner getteth to himself 3256
15:12 A scorner loveth not one that r him: 3198
Isa 29:21 lay a snare for him that r in the gate, and 3198

REPUTATION (5) [REPUTED]
Ecc 10: 1 *doth* a little folly *him that is* in r for 3368
Ac 5:34 had in r among all the people, and *5093*
Gal 2: 2 but privately to them which were **of** r, *1380*
Php 2: 7 But **made** himself **of no** r, and took *upon* *2758*
2:29 Lord with all gladness; and hold such in r: *1784*

REPUTED (2) [REPUTATION]
Job 18: 3 counted as beasts, *and* r **vile** in your sight? 2933
Da 4:35 all the inhabitants of the earth *are* r as 2804

REQUEST (19) [REQUESTED, REQUESTS]
Jdg 8:24 unto them, I would **desire a** r of you, 7592+7596
2Sa 14:15 it may be that the king will perform the r of 1697
14:22 in that the king hath fulfilled the r of his 1697
Ezr 7: 6 the king granted him all his r, according to 1246
Ne 2: 4 said unto me, For what dost thou **make** r? 1245
Est 4: 8 and to **make** r before him for her people. 1245
5: 3 what *is* thy r? it shall be even given thee to 1246
5: 6 what *is* thy r? even to the half of 1246
5: 7 and said, My petition and my r *is;* 1246
5: 8 to perform my r, let the king and 1246
7: 2 what *is* thy r? and it shall be performed, 1246
7: 3 me at my petition, and my people at my r: 1246
7: 7 Haman stood *up* to **make** r for his life to 1245
9:12 or what *is* thy r further? and it shall be 1246
Job 6: 8 O that I might have my r; and *that* God 7596
Ps 21: 2 and hast not withholden the r of his lips. 782
106:15 he gave them their r; but sent leanness into 7596
Ro 1:10 **Making** r, if by any means now at length I *1189*
Php 1: 4 of mine for you all making r with joy, *1162*

REQUESTED (5) [REQUEST]
Jdg 8:26 the weight of the golden earrings that he r 7592
1Ki 19: 4 he r for himself that he might die; and said, 7592
1Ch 4:10 And God granted *him that* which he r. 7592
Da 1: 8 he r of the prince of the eunuchs that he 1245
2:49 Daniel r of the king, and he set Shadrach, 1156

REQUESTS (1) [REQUEST]
Php 4: 6 supplication with thanksgiving let your r be *155*

REQUIRE (29) [REQUIRED, REQUIREST, REQUIRETH, REQUIRING]
Ge 9: 5 surely your blood of your lives will I r; 1875
9: 5 at the hand of every beast will I r it, and 1875
9: 5 at the hand of every man's brother will I r 1875
31:39 of my hand didst thou r it, *whether* stolen 1245
43: 9 for him; of my hand shalt thou r him: 1245
Dt 10:12 what doth the LORD thy God r of thee, 7592
18:19 shall speak in my name, I will r *it* of him. 1875
23:21 for the LORD thy God will **surely** r 1875+1875
Jos 22:23 let the LORD himself r *it;* 1245
1Sa 20:16 *saying,* Let the LORD even r *it* at 1245
2Sa 3:13 one thing I r of thee, that is, Thou shalt not 7592
4:11 therefore now r his blood of your hand, 1245
19:38 whatsoever thou shalt r of me, *that* will I do 977
1Ki 8:59 Israel at all times, **as the matter** shall r: 1697
1Ch 21: 3 doth my lord r this *thing?* why will he be a 1245
2Ch 24:22 he said, The LORD look upon *it,* and r *it.* 1875
Ezr 7:21 shall r of you, *it* be done speedily, 7593
8:22 For I was ashamed to r of the king a band 7592
Ne 5:12 restore *them,* and will r nothing of them; 1245
Ps 10:13 he hath said in his heart, Thou wilt not r *it.* 1875
Eze 3:18 but his blood will I r at thine hand. 1245
3:20 but his blood will I r at thine hand. 1245
20:40 there will I r your offerings, and 1875
33: 6 his blood will I r at the watchman's hand. 1875
33: 8 but his blood will I r at thine hand. 1245
34:10 I will r my flock at their hand, and 1875
Mic 6: 8 what doth the LORD r of thee, but to do 1875
1Co 1:22 For the Jews r a sign, and the Greeks seek *154*
7:36 and need so r, let him do what he will, *1096*

REQUIRED (22) [REQUIRE]
Ge 42:22 therefore, behold, also his blood is r. 1875
Ex 12:36 *as they* r. And they spoiled the Egyptians. NIH
1Sa 21: 8 because the king's business r haste. 1961
2Sa 12:20 when he r, they set bread before him, and 7592
1Ch 16:37 the ark continually, as every day's **work** r: 1697
2Ch 8:14 the priests, as the **duty** of every day r: 1697
24: 6 Why hast thou not r of the Levites to bring 1875
Ezr 3: 4 to the custom, **as** the duty of every day r; 4941
Ne 5:18 yet for *all* this r not I the bread of 1245
Est 2:15 she r nothing but what Hegai the king's 1245
Ps 40: 6 and sin offering hast thou not r. 7592
137: 3 that carried us away captive r of us a song; 7592
137: 3 they that wasted us r *of us* mirth, NIH
Pr 30: 7 Two *things* have I r of thee; deny me *them* 7592
Isa 1:12 who hath r this at your hand, to tread my 1245
Lk 11:50 of the world, may be r of this generation; *1567*
11:51 unto you, It shall be r of this generation. *1567*
12:20 this night thy soul shall be r of thee: *523*
12:48 much is given, of him shall be much r: *2212*
19:23 that at my coming I might have r *mine own* *4238*
23:24 gave sentence that it should be as they r. *155*
1Co 4: 2 Moreover it is r in stewards, that a man be *2212*

REQUIREST (1) [REQUIRE]
Ru 3:11 fear not; I will do to thee all that thou r: 559

REQUIRETH (2) [REQUIRE]
Ecc 3:15 already been; and God r that which is past. 1245
Da 2:11 *it is* a rare thing that the king r, and there is 7593

REQUIRING (1) [REQUIRE]
Lk 23:23 loud voices, r that he might be crucified. *154*

REQUITE (9) [REQUITED, REQUITING]
Ge 50:15 will **certainly** r us all the evil which 7725+7725
Dt 32: 6 Do ye thus r the LORD, O foolish people 1580
2Sa 2: 6 I also will r you this kindness, 854+6213
16:12 that the LORD will r me good for his 7725
2Ki 9:26 I will r thee in this plat, saith the LORD. 7999
Ps 10:14 and spite, to r *it* with thy hand: 5414
41:10 and raise me up, that I may r them. 7999
Jer 51:56 God of recompences shall **surely** r. 7999+7999
1Ti 5: 4 piety at home, and to r *their* parents: *287+591*

REQUITED (2) [REQUITE]
Jdg 1: 7 as I have done, so God hath r me. And they 7999
1Sa 25:21 unto him: and he hath r me evil for good. 7725

REQUITING (1) [REQUITE]
2Ch 6:23 do, and judge thy servants, by r the wicked, 7725

REREWARD (6)
Nu 10:25 *which was* the r of all the camps throughout 622
Jos 6: 9 the r came after the ark, *the priests* going on, 622
6:13 the r came after the ark of the LORD, 622
1Sa 29: 2 and his men passed on in the r with Achish. 314
Isa 52:12 and the God of Israel *will be* your r. 622
58: 8 the glory of the LORD shall be thy r. 622

RESCUE (3) [RESCUED, RESCUETH]
Dt 28:31 and thou shalt have none to r *them.* 3467
Ps 35:17 r my soul from their destructions, 7725
Hos 5:14 I will take away, and none shall r *him.* 5337

RESCUED (3) [RESCUE]
1Sa 14:45 So the people r Jonathan, that he died not. 6299
30:18 carried away: and David r his two wives. 5337
Ac 23:27 then came I with an army, and r him, *1807*

RESCUETH (1) [RESCUE]
Da 6:27 He delivereth and r, and he worketh signs 5338

RESEMBLANCE (1) [RESEMBLE]
Zec 5: 6 This *is* their r through all the earth. 5869

RESEMBLE (1) [RESEMBLANCE, RESEMBLED]
Lk 13:18 of God like? and whereunto shall I r it? *3666*

RESEMBLED (1) [RESEMBLE]
Jdg 8:18 *each* one r the children of a king. 8389+3509.1

RESEN (1)
Ge 10:12 **R** between Nineveh and Calah: the same *is* 7449

RESERVE (3) [RESERVED, RESERVETH]

Jer 3: 5 Will he r *his anger* for ever? will he keep *it* 5201
50:20 be found: for I will pardon them whom I r. 7604
2Pe 2: 9 to r the unjust unto the day of judgment *to* *5083*

RESERVED (16) [RESERVE]

Ge 27:36 he said, Hast thou not r a blessing for me? 680
Nu 18: 9 This shall be thine of the most holy *things,* r NIH
Jdg 21:22 we r not to each man his wife in the war: 3947
Ru 2:18 gave to her that she **had** r after she was 3498
2Sa 8: 4 but r of them *for* an hundred chariots. 3498
1Ch 18: 4 but r of them an hundred chariots. 3498
Job 21:30 That the wicked is r to the day of 2820
38:23 Which I have r against the time of trouble, 2820
Ac 25:21 But when Paul had appealed to be r unto *5083*
Ro 11: 4 I have r to myself seven thousand men, *2641*
1Pe 1: 4 that fadeth not away, r in heaven for you, *5083*
2Pe 2: 4 chains of darkness, *to be* r unto judgment; *5083*
2:17 to whom the mist of darkness is r for ever. *5083*
3: 7 r unto fire against the day of judgment and *5083*
Jude 1: 6 he hath r in everlasting chains under *5083*
1:13 to whom is r the blackness of darkness for *5083*

RESERVETH (2) [RESERVE]

Jer 5:24 he r unto us the appointed weeks of 8104
Na 1: 2 and he r *wrath* for his enemies. 5201

RESHEPH (1)

1Ch 7:25 also **R**, and Telah his son, and Tahan his 7566

RESIDUE (34)

Ex 10: 5 they shall eat the r of that which is escaped 3499
1Ch 6:66 *the* r of the families of the sons of Kohath NIH
Ne 11:20 the r of Israel, of the priests, *and* 7605
Isa 21:17 the r of the number of archers, the mighty 7605
28: 5 diadem of beauty, unto the r of his people, 7605
38:10 I am deprived of the r of my years. 3499
44:17 the r thereof he maketh a god, *even* his 7611
44:19 shall I make the r thereof an abomination? 3499
Jer 8: 3 r of them that remain of this evil family, 7611
15: 9 the r of them will I deliver to the sword 7611
24: 8 his princes, and the r of Jerusalem, 7611
27:19 concerning the r of the vessels that remain 3499
29: 1 r of the elders which were carried away 3499
39: 3 with all the r of the princes of the king of 7611
41:10 Ishmael carried away captive all the r of 7611
52:15 the r of the people that remained in 3499
Eze 9: 8 *wilt* thou destroy all the r of Israel in thy 7611
23:25 and thy r shall be devoured by the fire. 319
34:18 ye must tread down with your feet the r of 3499
34:18 but ye must foul the r with your feet? 3498
36: 3 that ye might be a possession unto the r of 7611
36: 4 derision to the r of the heathen that *are* 7611
36: 5 have I spoken against the r of the heathen, 7611
48:18 the r in length over against the oblation of 3498
48:21 the r *shall be* for the prince, on the one side 3498
Da 7: 7 and stamped the r with the feet of it: 7606
7:19 in pieces, and stamped the r with his feet; 7606
Zep 2: 9 the r of my people shall spoil them, and 7611
Hag 2: 2 the high priest and to the r of the people, 7611
Zec 8:11 now I *will* not *be* unto the r of this people 7611
14: 2 the r of the people shall not be cut off from 3499
Mal 2:15 Yet had he the r of the spirit. And 7605
Mk 16:13 And they went and told *it* unto the r: *3062*
Ac 15:17 That the r of men might seek after *2645*

RESIN See BDELLIUM

RESIST (10) [RESISTED, RESISTETH]

Zec 3: 1 Satan standing at his right hand to r him. 7853
Mt 5:39 But I say unto you, That *ye* r not evil: but *436*
Lk 21:15 shall not be able to gainsay nor r. *436*
Ac 6:10 And they were not able to r the wisdom and *436*
7:51 and ears, ye do always r the Holy Ghost: *496*
Ro 13: 2 they that r shall receive to themselves *436*
2Ti 3: 8 so do these also r the truth: *436*
Jas 4: 7 **R** the devil, and he will flee from you. *436*
5: 6 *and* killed the just; *and* he doth not r you. *498*
1Pe 5: 9 Whom r stedfast in the faith, knowing that *436*

RESISTED (2) [RESIST]

Ro 9:19 he yet find fault? For who hath r his will? *436*
Heb 12: 4 Ye have not yet r unto blood, *478*

RESISTETH (4) [RESIST]

Ro 13: 2 Whosoever therefore r the power, *498*
13: 2 resisteth the power, r the ordinance of God: *436*
Jas 4: 6 God r the proud, but giveth grace unto *498*
1Pe 5: 5 for God r the proud, and giveth grace to *498*

RESOLVED (1)

Lk 16: 4 I am r what to do, that, when I am put out *1097*

RESORT (4) [RESORTED]

Ne 4:20 sound of the trumpet, r ye thither unto us: 6908
Ps 71: 3 whereunto *I* may continually r: 935
Mk 10: 1 and the people r unto him again; and, as he *4848*
Jn 18:20 in the temple, whither the Jews always r; *4905*

RESORTED (5) [RESORT]

2Ch 11:13 the Levites that *were* in all Israel r to him 3320
Mk 2:13 and all the multitude r unto him, and *2064*
Jn 10:41 And many r unto him, and said, John did *2064*
18: 2 for Jesus ofttimes r thither with his *4863*
Ac 16:13 and spake unto the women which r *thither.* *4905*

RESPECT (34) [RESPECTED, RESPECTER, RESPECTETH]

Ge 4: 4 the LORD had r unto Abel and to his 8159
4: 5 unto Cain and to his offering he had not r. 8159
Ex 2:25 of Israel, and God **had** r **unto** *them.* 3045
Lev 19:15 thou shalt not r the person of the poor, 5375
26: 9 For I will have r unto you, and make you 6437
Nu 16:15 unto the LORD, **R** not thou their offering: 6437
Dt 1:17 Ye shall not r persons in judgment; *but* 5234
16:19 thou shalt not r persons, neither take a gift: 5234
2Sa 14:14 up *again;* neither doth God r *any* person: 5375
1Ki 8:28 Yet **have** thou r unto the prayer of thy 6437
2Ki 13:23 had r unto them, because of his covenant 6437
2Ch 6:19 **Have** r therefore to the prayer of thy 6437
19: 7 nor r of persons, nor taking of gifts. 4856
Ps 74:20 **Have** r unto the covenant: for the dark 5027
119: 6 when I have r unto all thy commandments. 5027
119:15 in thy precepts, and **have** r unto thy ways. 5027
119:117 I will **have** r unto thy statutes continually. 8159
138: 6 *be* high, yet **hath** he r unto the lowly: 7200
Pr 24:23 *It is* not good to have r of persons in 5234
28:21 To have r of persons *is* not good: for for a 5234
Isa 17: 7 his eyes shall have r to the Holy One of 7200
17: 8 neither shall r *that* which his fingers have 7200
22:11 neither had r unto him that fashioned it 7200
Ro 2:11 For there is no **r of persons** with God. *4382*
2Co 3:10 was made glorious had no glory in this r, *3313*
Eph 6: 9 neither is there **r of persons** with him. *4382*
Php 4:11 Not that I speak **in** r **of** want: for I have *2596*
Col 2:16 or in r of a holyday, or of the new moon, or *3313*
3:25 he hath done: and there is no **r of persons**. *4382*
Heb 11:26 for he had r unto the recompence of *578*
Jas 2: 1 *the Lord* of glory, with **r of persons**. *4382*
2: 3 And ye have r to him that weareth the gay *1914*
2: 9 But if ye **have r to persons**, ye commit sin, *4380*
1Pe 1:17 who **without r of persons** judgeth according *678*

RESPECTED (1) [RESPECT]

La 4:16 they r not the persons of the priests, 5375

RESPECTER (1) [RESPECT]

Ac 10:34 truth I perceive that God is no **r of persons**: *4381*

RESPECTETH (2) [RESPECT]

Job 37:24 he r not any *that are* wise of heart. 7200
Ps 40: 4 r not the proud, nor such as turn aside 413+6437

RESPITE (2)

Ex 8:15 when Pharaoh saw that there was r, he 7309
1Sa 11: 3 said unto him, **Give** us seven days' r, 7503

RESPONSIBLE See OCCASIONED

REST (275) [RESTED, RESTEST, RESTETH, RESTING, RESTS]

Ge 8: 9 the dove found no r for the sole of her foot, 4494
18: 4 your feet, and r yourselves under the tree: 8172
30:36 and Jacob fed the r of Laban's flocks. 3498
49:15 he saw that r *was* good, and the land that *it* 4496
Ex 5: 5 and you **make** them r from their burdens. 7673
16:23 To morrow *is* the r of the holy sabbath unto 7677
23:11 the seventh *year* thou shalt let it r and 8058
23:12 and on the seventh day thou shalt r: 7673
23:12 that thine ox and thine ass may r, and 5117
28:10 the *other* six names of the r on the other 3498

R

Ex 31:15 in the seventh *is* the sabbath of **r**, holy to 7677
33:14 shall go *with thee,* and I will **give** thee **r**. 5117
34:21 but on the seventh day thou shalt **r**: 7673
34:21 in earing time and in harvest thou shalt **r**. 7673
35: 2 a holy *day,* a sabbath of **r** to the LORD: 7677
Lev 5: 9 the **r** of the blood shall be wrung out at 7604
14:17 of the **r** of the oil that *is* in his hand shall 3499
14:29 the **r** of the oil that *is* in the priest's hand he 3498
16:31 It *shall be* a sabbath of **r** unto you, and 7677
23: 3 the seventh day *is* the sabbath of **r**, a holy 7677
23:32 It *shall be* unto you a sabbath of **r**, and 7677
25: 4 in the seventh year shall be a sabbath of **r** 7677
25: 5 *for* it is a year of **r** unto the land. 7677
26:34 *even* then shall the land **r**, and enjoy her 7673
26:35 As long as it lieth desolate it shall **r**; 7673
26:35 because it did not **r** in your sabbaths, 7673
Nu 31: 8 beside *the* **r** *of* them that were slain; NIH
31:32 *being* the **r** of the prey which the men of 3499
Dt 3:13 the **r** of Gilead, and all Bashan, *being* 3499
3:20 Until the LORD have **given r** unto your 5117
5:14 and thy maidservant may **r** as well as thou. 5117
12: 9 For ye are not as yet come to the **r** and 4496
12:10 *when* he **giveth** you **r** from all your 5117
25:19 the LORD thy God hath **given** thee **r** 5117
28:65 neither shall the sole of thy foot have **r**: 4494
Jos 1:13 The LORD your God hath **given** you **r**, 5117
1:15 the LORD have **given** your brethren **r**, 5117
3:13 all the earth, shall **r** in the waters of Jordan, 5117
10:20 that the **r** *which* remained of them entered 8300
13:27 the **r** of the kingdom of Sihon king of 3499
14:15 the Anakims. And the land **had r** from war. 8252
17: 2 There was also *a lot* for the **r** of 3498
17: 6 the **r** of Manasseh's sons had the land of 3498
21: 5 the **r** of the children of Kohath had by lot 3498
21:34 the **r** of the Levites, out of the tribe of 3498
21:44 the LORD **gave** them **r** round about, 5117
22: 4 now the LORD your God hath **given r** 5117
23: 1 **given r** unto Israel from all their enemies 5117
Jdg 3:11 the land **had r** forty years. And Othniel 8252
3:30 And the land **had r** fourscore years. 8252
5:31 his might. And the land **had r** forty years. 8252
7: 6 all the **r** of the people bowed down upon 3499
7: 8 he sent all *the* **r** *of* Israel every man unto his NIH
Ru 1: 9 The LORD grant you that you may find **r**, 4496
3: 1 My daughter, shall I not seek **r** for thee, 4494
3:18 for the man will not be in **r**, until he have 8252
1Sa 13: 2 the **r** of the people he sent every man to his 3499
15:15 and the **r** we have utterly destroyed. 3498
2Sa 3:29 Let it **r** on the head of Joab, and on all his 2342
7: 1 the LORD had **given** him **r** round about 5117
7:11 have **caused** thee **to r** from all thine 5117
10:10 the **r** of the people he delivered into 3499
12:28 gather the **r** of the people together, 3499
21:10 suffered neither the birds of the air to **r** on 5117
1Ki 5: 4 now the LORD my God hath **given** me **r** 5117
8:56 that hath given **r** unto his people Israel, 4496
11:41 the **r** of the acts of Solomon, and all that he 3499
14:19 the **r** of the acts of Jeroboam, how he 3499
14:29 Now the **r** of the acts of Rehoboam, and 3499
15: 7 Now the **r** of the acts of Abijam, and 3499
15:23 The **r** of all the acts of Asa, and all his 3499
15:31 Now the **r** of the acts of Nadab, and all that 3499
16: 5 Now the **r** of the acts of Baasha, and 3499
16:14 Now the **r** of the acts of Elah, and all that 3499
16:20 Now the **r** of the acts of Zimri, and 3499
16:27 Now the **r** of the acts of Omri which he did, 3499
20:30 the **r** fled to Aphek, into the city; and 3498
22:39 Now the **r** of the acts of Ahab, and all that 3499
22:45 Now the **r** of the acts of Jehoshaphat, and 3499
2Ki 1:18 Now the **r** of the acts of Ahaziah which he 3499
2:15 The spirit of Elijah doth **r** on Elisha. 5117
4: 7 and live thou and thy children of the **r**. 3498
8:23 the **r** of the acts of Joram, and all that he 3499
10:34 Now the **r** of the acts of Jehu, and all that 3499
12:19 the **r** of the acts of Joash, and all that he 3499
13: 8 Now the **r** of the acts of Jehoahaz, and 3499
13:12 the **r** of the acts of Joash, and all that he 3499
14:15 Now the **r** of the acts of Jehoash which he 3499
14:18 the **r** of the acts of Amaziah, *are* they not 3499
14:28 Now the **r** of the acts of Jeroboam, and 3499
15: 6 the **r** of the acts of Azariah, and all that he 3499
15:11 the **r** of the acts of Zachariah, behold, 3499
15:15 the **r** of the acts of Shallum, and 3499
15:21 the **r** of the acts of Menahem, and all that 3499
15:26 the **r** of the acts of Pekahiah, and all that he 3499
15:31 the **r** of the acts of Pekah, and all that he 3499
15:36 Now the **r** of the acts of Jotham, and 3499
16:19 Now the **r** of the acts of Ahaz which he did, 3499
20:20 the **r** of the acts of Hezekiah, and all his 3499
21:17 Now the **r** of the acts of Manasseh, and 3499
21:25 Now the **r** of the acts of Amon which he 3499
23:28 Now the **r** of the acts of Josiah, and all that 3499
24: 5 Now the **r** of the acts of Jehoiakim, and 3499
25:11 Now the **r** of the people that were left in 3499
1Ch 4:43 they smote the **r** of the Amalekites that 7611
6:31 of the LORD, after that the ark had **r**. 4494
6:77 Unto the **r** of the children of Merari *were* 3498
11: 8 and Joab repaired the **r** of the city. 7605
12:38 all the **r** also of Israel *were of* one heart to 7611
16:41 and Jeduthun, and the **r** that were chosen, 7605
19:11 the **r** of the people he delivered unto 3499
22: 9 *be* born to thee, who shall be a man of **r**; 4496
22: 9 I will **give** him **r** from all his enemies round 5117
22:18 hath he *not* **given** you **r** on every side? 5117
23:25 The LORD God of Israel hath **given r** 5117
24:20 the **r** of the sons of Levi *were these:* Of 3498
28: 2 **r** for the ark of the covenant of the LORD, 4496
2Ch 9:29 Now the **r** of the acts of Solomon, first and 7605
13:22 the **r** of the acts of Abijah, and his ways, 3499
14: 6 for the land had **r**, and he had no war in 8252
14: 6 because the LORD had **given** him **r**. 5117
14: 7 and he hath **given** us **r** on every side. 5117
14:11 for we **r** on thee, and in thy name we go 8172
15:15 and the LORD **gave** them **r** round about. 5117
20:30 for his God **gave** him **r** round about. 5117
20:34 Now the **r** of the acts of Jehoshaphat, first 3499
24:14 they had finished *it,* they brought the **r** 7605
25:26 Now the **r** of the acts of Amaziah, first and 3499
26:22 Now the **r** of the acts of Uzziah, first and 3499
27: 7 Now the **r** of the acts of Jotham, and all his 3499
28:26 Now the **r** of his acts and of all his ways, 3499
32:32 Now the **r** of the acts of Hezekiah, and 3499
33:18 Now the **r** of the acts of Manasseh, and 3499
35:26 Now the **r** of the acts of Josiah, and 3499
36: 8 Now the **r** of the acts of Jehoiakim, and 3499
Ezr 4: 3 the **r** of the chief of the fathers of Israel, 7605
4: 7 Tabeel, and the **r** of their companions, 7605
4: 9 the scribe, and the **r** of their companions; 7606
4:10 the **r** of the nations whom the great and 7606
4:10 the **r** *that are on this* side the river, and 7606
4:17 *to* the **r** of their companions that dwell in 7606
4:17 in Samaria, and *unto* the **r** beyond the river: 7606
6:16 and the **r** of the children of the captivity, 7606
7:18 to do with the **r** of the silver and gold, 7606
Ne 2:16 to the rulers, nor to the **r** that did the work. 3499
4:14 and to the rulers, and to the **r** of the people, 3499
4:19 to the rulers, and to the **r** of the people, 3499
6: 1 the Arabian, and the **r** of our enemies, 3499
6:14 and the **r** of the prophets, 3499
7:72 *that* which the **r** of the people gave *was* 7611
9:28 after they had **r**, they did evil again before 5117
10:28 the **r** of the people, the priests, the Levites, 7605
11: 1 the **r** of the people also cast lots, to bring 7605
Est 9:12 what have they done in the **r** of the king's 7605
9:16 had **r** from their enemies, and slew of their 5118
Job 3:13 I should have slept: then had I been **at r**, 5117
3:17 *from* troubling; and there the weary be **at r**. 5117
3:18 *There* the prisoners **r** together; they hear 7599
3:26 I was not in safety, neither had I **r**, 8252
11:18 *and* thou shalt **take** thy **r** in safety. 7901
14: 6 Turn from him, that he may **r**, till he shall 2308
17:16 the pit, when *our* **r** together *is* in the dust. 5183
30:17 the night season: and my sinews **take** no **r**. 7901
Ps 16: 9 my flesh also shall **r** in hope. 7931
17:14 leave the **r** of their *substance* to their babes. 3499
37: 7 **R** in the LORD, and wait patiently for 1826
38: 3 neither *is there any* **r** in my bones because 7965
55: 6 *for then* would I fly away, and be **at r**. 7931
94:13 That *thou* mayest **give** him **r** from the days 8252
95:11 wrath that they should not enter into my **r**. 4496
116: 7 Return unto thy **r**, O my soul; for 4494
125: 3 For the rod of the wicked shall not **r** upon 5117
132: 8 Arise, O LORD, into thy **r**; thou, and 4496
132:14 This *is* my **r** for ever: here will I dwell; 4496
Pr 6:35 neither will he **r content**, though thou givest 14
29: 9 whether he rage or laugh, *there is* no **r**. 5183
29:17 Correct thy son, and he shall **give** thee **r**; 5117
Ecc 2:23 yea, his heart **taketh** not **r** in the night. 7901

Ecc 6: 5 nor known *any thing:* this hath more **r** than 5183
SS 1: 7 where thou **makest** *thy flock* **to** r at noon: 7257
Isa 7:19 shall **r** all of them in the desolate valleys, 5117
10:19 the **r** of the trees of his forest shall be few, 7605
11: 2 the Spirit of the LORD shall **r** upon him, 5117
11:10 Gentiles seek: and his **r** shall be glorious. 4496
14: 3 LORD shall **give** thee **r** from thy sorrow, 5117
14: 7 The whole earth is **at r**, *and* is quiet: 5117
18: 4 I will **take** my **r**, and I will consider in my 8252
23:12 *to* Chittim; there also shalt thou have no **r**. 5117
25:10 mountain shall the hand of the LORD **r**, 5117
28:12 This *is* the **r** *wherewith* ye may cause 4496
28:12 *wherewith* ye may **cause** the weary **to r**; 5117
30:15 In returning and **r** shall ye be saved; 5183
34:14 the shrich owl also shall **r** there, and 7280
34:14 rest there, and find for herself a **place of r**. 4494
51: 4 I will **make** my judgment **to r** for a light of 7280
57: 2 they shall **r** in their beds, *each one* walking 5117
57:20 when it cannot **r**, whose waters cast up 8252
62: 1 and for Jerusalem's sake I will not **r**, 8252
62: 7 give him no **r**, till he establish, and till he 1824
63:14 the Spirit of the LORD **caused** him **to r**: 5117
66: 1 unto me? and where *is* the place of my **r**? 4496
Jer 6:16 and ye shall find **r** for your souls. 4771
30:10 shall be **in r**, and be quiet, and none shall 8252
31: 2 *even* Israel when *I* went to **cause** him **to r**. 7280
39: 9 with the **r** of the people that remained. 3499
45: 3 I fainted in my sighing, and I find no **r**. 4496
46:27 be **in r** and at ease, and none shall make 8252
47: 6 up thyself into thy scabbard, **r**, and be still. 7280
50:34 that he may **give r** to the land, and 7280
52:15 king of Babylon, and the **r** of the multitude. 3499
La 1: 3 among the heathen, she findeth no **r**: 4494
2:18 give thyself no **r**; let not the apple of thine 6314
5: 5 we labour, *and* have no **r**. 5117
Eze 5:13 I will **cause** my fury **to r** upon them, and 5117
16:42 So will I **make** my fury towards thee **to r**, 5117
21:17 and I will **cause** my fury **to r**: 5117
24:13 till I have **caused** my fury **to r** upon thee. 5117
38:11 I will go *to* them that are **at r**, that dwell 8252
44:30 that he may **cause** the blessing **to r** in thine 5117
45: 8 *the r of* the land shall they give to the house NIH
48:23 As for the **r** of the tribes, from the east side 3499
Da 2:18 his fellows should not perish with the **r** of 7606
4: 4 I Nebuchadnezzar was at **r** in mine house, 7954
7:12 As concerning the **r** of the beasts, they had 7606
12:13 thy way till the end *be:* for thou shalt **r**, 5117
Mic 2:10 Arise ye, and depart; for this *is* not *your* **r**: 4496
Hab 3:16 that I might **r** in the day of trouble: 5117
Zep 3:17 he will **r** in his love, he will joy over thee 2790
Zec 1:11 behold, all the earth sitteth still, and is **at r**. 8252
9: 1 and Damascus *shall be* the **r** thereof: 4496
11: 9 let the **r** eat every one the flesh of another. 7604
Mt 11:28 and are heavy laden, and I will **give** you **r**. *373*
11:29 in heart: and ye shall find **r** unto your souls. *372*
12:43 dry places, seeking **r**, and findeth none. *372*
26:45 unto them, Sleep on now, and **take** your **r**: *373*
27:49 The **r** said, Let be, let us see whether Elias *3062*
Mk 6:31 apart into a desert place, and **r** a while: *373*
14:41 unto them, Sleep on now, and **take** your **r**: *373*
Lk 10: 6 peace be there, your peace shall **r** upon it: *1879*
11:24 he walketh through dry places, seeking **r**; *372*
12:26 *is* least, why take ye thought for the **r**? *3062*
24: 9 *things* unto the eleven, and *to* all the **r**. *3062*
Jn 11:13 that he had spoken of **taking of r** in sleep. *2838*
Ac 2:26 moreover also my flesh shall **r** in hope: *2681*
2:37 said unto Peter and *to* the **r** of the apostles, *3062*
5:13 And of the **r** durst no *man* join himself to *3062*
7:49 the Lord: or what *is* the place of my **r**? *2663*
9:31 Then had the churches **r** throughout all *1515*
27:44 And the **r**, some on boards, and some on *3062*
Ro 11: 7 hath obtained *it*, and the **r** were blinded, *3062*
1Co 7:12 But to the **r** speak I, not the Lord: If any *3062*
11:34 And the **r** will I set in order when I come. *3062*
2Co 2:13 I had no **r** in my spirit, because I found not *425*
7: 5 our flesh had no **r**, but *we were* troubled on *425*
12: 9 that the power of Christ may **r** upon me. *1981*
2Th 1: 7 And to you who are troubled **r** with us, *425*
Heb 3:11 in my wrath, They shall not enter into my **r**. *2663*
3:18 he that *they* should not enter into his **r**, *2663*
4: 1 promise being left *us* of entering into his **r**, *2663*
4: 3 For we which have believed do enter into **r**, *2663*
4: 3 in my wrath, if they shall enter into my **r**: *2663*
4: 4 And God did **r** the seventh day from all his *2664*
4: 5 *place* again, If they shall enter into my **r**. *2663*
4: 8 For if Jesus had **given** them **r**, *then* *2664*
4: 9 therefore a **r** to the people of God. *4520*
4:10 For he that is entered into his **r**, he also *2663*
4:11 Let us labour therefore to enter into that **r**, *2663*
1Pe 4: 2 That *he* no longer should live the **r** of *his* *1954*
Rev 2:24 unto you I say, and unto the **r** in Thyatira, *3062*
4: 8 and they **r** not day and night, saying, *372+2192*
6:11 that they should **r** yet for a little season, *373*
9:20 And the **r** of the men which were not killed *3062*
14:11 and they have no **r** day nor night, *372*
14:13 the Spirit, that they may **r** from their labours; *373*
20: 5 But the **r** of the dead lived not again until *3062*

RESTED (21) [REST]

Ge 2: 2 he **r** on the seventh day from all his work 7673
2: 3 that in it he had **r** from all his work which 7673
8: 4 the ark **r** in the seventh month, on 5117
Ex 10:14 of Egypt, and **r** in all the coasts of Egypt: 5117
16:30 So the people **r** on the seventh day. 7673
20:11 all that in them *is*, and **r** the seventh day: 5117
31:17 on the seventh day he **r**, and was refreshed. 7673
Nu 9:18 upon the tabernacle they **r in** the **tents**. 2583
9:23 of the LORD they **r in** the **tents**, 2583
10:12 and the cloud **r** in the wilderness of Paran. 7931
10:36 when it **r**, he said, Return, O LORD, 5117
11:25 to pass, that when the spirit **r** upon them, 5117
11:26 the spirit **r** upon them; and they *were* of 5117
Jos 11:23 by their tribes. And the land **r** from war. 8252
1Ki 6:10 and they **r** on the house with timber of cedar. 270
2Ch 32: 8 the people **r** themselves upon the words of 5564
Est 9:17 on the fourteenth day of the same **r** they, 5118
9:18 on the fifteenth *day* of the same they **r**, and 5118
9:22 As the days wherein the Jews **r** from their 5117
Job 30:27 My bowels boiled, and **r** not: the days of 1826
Lk 23:56 **r** the sabbath day according to *2270*

RESTEST (1) [REST]

Ro 2:17 and **r** in the law, and makest thy boast of *1879*

RESTETH (4) [REST]

Job 24:23 be given him *to be* in safety, whereon he **r**; 8172
Pr 14:33 Wisdom **r** in the heart of him that hath 5117
Ecc 7: 9 be angry: for anger **r** in the bosom of fools. 5117
1Pe 4:14 the spirit of glory and of God **r** upon you: *373*

RESTING (5) [REST]

Nu 10:33 to search out a **r place** for them. 4496
2Ch 6:41 into thy **r place**, thou, and the ark of thy 5118
Pr 24:15 of the righteous; spoil not his **r place**: 7258
Isa 32:18 and in sure dwellings, and in quiet **r places**; 4496
Jer 50: 6 to hill, they have forgotten their **r place**. 7258

RESTITUTION (6)

Ex 22: 3 *for* he should **make full** r; if he have 7999+7999
22: 5 best of his own vineyard, shall he **make r**. 7999
22: 6 kindled the fire shall **surely make r**. 7999+7999
22:12 he shall **make r** unto the owner thereof. 7999
Job 20:18 according to *his* substance *shall* the **r** *be*, 8545
Ac 3:21 **r** of all *things*, which God hath spoken by *605*

RESTORE (40) [RESTORED, RESTORER, RESTORETH]

Ge 20: 7 Now therefore **r** the man *his* wife; for he *is* 7725
20: 7 if thou **r** *her* not, know thou that thou shalt 7725
40:13 lift up thine head, and **r** thee unto thy place: 7725
42:25 to **r** every man's money into his sack, and 7725
Ex 22: 1 he shall **r** five oxen for an ox, and 7999
22: 4 it be ox, or ass, or sheep; he shall **r** double. 7999
Lev 6: 4 that he shall **r** that which he took violently 7725
6: 5 he shall even **r** it in the principal, and 7999
24:21 And he that killeth a beast, he shall **r** it: and 7999
25:27 **r** the overplus unto the man to whom he 7725
25:28 if he be not able to **r** *it* to him, then 7725
Nu 35:25 the congregation shall **r** him to the city of 7725
Dt 22: 2 after it, and thou shalt **r** it to him **again**. 7725
Jdg 11:13 therefore **r** those *lands* **again** peaceably. 7725
17: 3 now therefore I will **r** it unto thee. 7725
1Sa 12: 3 mine eyes therewith? and I will **r** *it* you. 7725
2Sa 9: 7 will **r** thee all the land of Saul thy father; 7725
12: 6 he shall **r** the lamb fourfold, because he did 7999
16: 3 To day shall the house of Israel **r** me 7725
1Ki 20:34 my father took from thy father, I will **r**; 7725
2Ki 8: 6 **R** all that *was* hers, and all the fruits of 7725
Ne 5:11 **R**, I pray you, to them, even *this* day, 7725
5:12 We will **r** *them*, and will require nothing of 7725

Job 20:10 the poor, and his hands shall r their goods. 7725
20:18 That which he laboured for shall he r, and 7725
Ps 51:12 R unto me the joy of thy salvation; and 7725
Pr 6:31 *if* he be found, he shall r sevenfold; he 7999
Isa 1:26 I will r thy judges as at the first, and 7725
42:22 *for* a spoil, and none saith, R. 7725
49: 6 of Jacob, and to r the preserved of Israel: 7725
57:18 r comforts unto him and to his mourners. 7999
Jer 27:22 I bring them up, and r them to this place. 7725
30:17 For I will r health unto thee, and I will heal 5927
Eze 33:15 *If* the wicked r the pledge, give again that 7725
Da 9:25 the going forth of the commandment to r 7725
Joel 2:25 I will r to you the years that the locust hath 7999
Mt 17:11 Elias truly shall first come, and r all *things.* *600*
Lk 19: 8 *man* by false accusation, I r *him* fourfold. *591*
Ac 1: 6 wilt thou at this time r **again** the kingdom to *600*
Gal 6: 1 r such a one in the spirit of meekness; *2675*

RESTORED (27) [RESTORE]
Ge 20:14 unto Abraham, and r him Sarah his wife. 7725
40:21 r the chief butler unto his butlership **again**; 7725
41:13 me he r unto mine office, and him he 7725
42:28 he said unto his brethren, My money is r; 7725
Dt 28:31 before thy face, and shall not be r to thee: 7725
Jdg 17: 3 when he had r the eleven hundred *shekels* 7725
17: 4 Yet he r the money unto his mother; and 7725
1Sa 7:14 had taken from Israel were r to Israel, 7725
1Ki 13: 6 for me, that my hand may be r me **again**. 7725
13: 6 the king's hand was r him **again**, and 7725
2Ki 8: 1 whose son he had r **to life**, saying, Arise, 2421
8: 5 the king how he had r a dead *body* **to life**, 2421
8: 5 the woman, whose son he had r **to life**, 2421
8: 5 and this *is* her son, whom Elisha r **to life**. 2421
14:22 He built Elath, and r it to Judah, after that 7725
14:25 He r the coast of Israel from the entering of 7725
2Ch 8: 2 That the cities which Huram had r to 5414
26: 2 He built Eloth, and r it to Judah, after that 7725
Ezr 6: 5 be r, and brought *again* unto the temple 8421
Ps 69: 4 then I r *that* which I took not away. 7725
Eze 18: 7 *but* hath r *to* the debtor his pledge, 7725
18:12 hath not r the pledge, and hath lift up his 7725
Mt 12:13 *it* forth; and it was r whole, *like* as the other. *600*
Mk 3: 5 *it* out: and his hand was r whole as the other. *600*
8:25 and he was r, and saw every *man* clearly. *600*
Lk 6:10 and his hand was r whole as the other. *600*
Heb 13:19 to do this, that I may be r to you the sooner. *600*

RESTORER (2) [RESTORE]
Ru 4:15 he shall be unto thee a r of *thy* life, and 7725
Isa 58:12 of the breach, The r of paths to dwell in. 7725

RESTORETH (2) [RESTORE]
Ps 23: 3 He r my soul: he leadeth me in the paths of 7725
Mk 9:12 and r all *things;* and how it is written of *600*

RESTRAIN (2) [RESTRAINED, RESTRAINEST, RESTRAINT]
Job 15: 8 of God? and dost thou r wisdom to thyself? 1639
Ps 76:10 the remainder of wrath shalt thou r. 2296

RESTRAINED (8) [RESTRAIN]
Ge 8: 2 and the rain from heaven was r; 3607
11: 6 now nothing will be r from them, 1219
16: 2 the LORD hath r me from bearing: 6113
Ex 36: 6 So the people were r from bringing. 3607
1Sa 3:13 made themselves vile, and he r them not. 3543
Isa 63:15 and of thy mercies towards me? are they r? 662
Eze 31:15 I r the floods thereof, and the great waters 4513
Ac 14:18 And with these sayings scarce r they *2664*

RESTRAINEST (1) [RESTRAIN]
Job 15: 4 castest off fear, and r prayer before God. 1639

RESTRAINT (1) [RESTRAIN]
1Sa 14: 6 for *there is* no r to the LORD to save by 4622

RESTS (1) [REST]
1Ki 6: 6 house he made **narrowed** r round about, 4052

RESURRECTION (41)
Mt 22:23 which say that there is no r, and asked him, *386*
22:28 Therefore in the r whose wife shall she be of *386*
22:30 For in the r they neither marry, nor are given *386*
22:31 But as touching the r of the dead, have ye *386*
27:53 And came out of the graves after his r, and *1454*
Mk 12:18 him *the* Sadducees, which say there is no r; *386*
12:23 In the r therefore, when they shall rise, *386*
Lk 14:14 for thou shalt be recompensed at the r of *386*
20:27 which deny that there is any r; *386*
20:33 Therefore in the r whose wife of them is *386*
20:35 and the r from the dead, neither marry, *386*
20:36 children of God, being the children of the r. *386*
Jn 5:29 they that have done good, unto the r of life; *386*
5:29 that have done evil, unto the r of damnation. *386*
11:24 I know that he shall rise again in the r at *386*
11:25 Jesus said unto her, I am the r, and the life: *386*
Ac 1:22 be ordained *to be* a witness with us of his r. *386*
2:31 seeing *this* before, spake of the r of Christ, *386*
4: 2 preached through Jesus the r from the dead. *386*
4:33 apostles witness of the r of the Lord Jesus: *386*
17:18 he preached unto them Jesus, and the r. *386*
17:32 And when they heard of the r of the dead, *386*
23: 6 and r of the dead I am called in question. *386*
23: 8 For the Sadducees say that there is no r, *386*
24:15 that there shall be a r of the dead, both of *386*
24:21 Touching the r of the dead I am called in *386*
Ro 1: 4 the Spirit of holiness, by the r from the dead: *386*
6: 5 we shall be also *in the likeness* of *his* r: *386*
1Co 15:12 how say some among you that there is no r *386*
15:13 But if there be no r of the dead, then *386*
15:21 by man *came* also the r of the dead. *386*
15:42 So also *is* the r of the dead. It is sown in *386*
Php 3:10 and the power of his r, and the fellowship of *386*
3:11 If by any means I might attain unto the r of *1815*
2Ti 2:18 have erred, saying that the r is past already; *386*
Heb 6: 2 and of r of the dead, and of eternal *386*
11:35 that they might obtain a better r: *386*
1Pe 1: 3 hope by the r of Jesus Christ from the dead, *386*
3:21 toward God,) by the r of Jesus Christ: *386*
Rev 20: 5 years were finished. This *is* the first r. *386*
20: 6 and holy *is* he that hath part in the first r: *386*

RETAIN (7) [RETAINED, RETAINETH]
Job 2: 9 unto him, Dost thou still r thine integrity? 2388
Pr 4: 4 said unto me, Let thine heart r my words: 8551
11:16 retaineth honour: and strong *men* r riches. 8551
Ecc 8: 8 hath power over the spirit to r the spirit; 3607
Da 11: 6 she shall not r the power of the arm; 6113
Jn 20:23 *and* whose soever *sins* ye r, they are *2902*
Ro 1:28 And even as they did not like to r God in *2192*

RETAINED (6) [RETAIN]
Jdg 7: 8 his tent, and r *those* three hundred men: 2388
19: 4 in law, the damsel's father, r him; 2388+871.1
Da 10: 8 in me into corruption, and I r no strength. 6113
10:16 turned upon me, and I have r no strength. 6113
Jn 20:23 *and* whose soever *sins* ye retain, they are r. *2902*
Phm 1:13 Whom I would have r with me, that in thy *2722*

RETAINETH (3) [RETAIN]
Pr 3:18 upon her: and happy *is* every one that r her. 8551
11:16 A gracious woman r honour: and 8551
Mic 7:18 he r not his anger for ever, because 2388

RETIRE (2) [RETIRED]
2Sa 11:15 r ye from him, that he may be smitten, and 7725
Jer 4: 6 r, stay not: for I will bring evil from 5756

RETIRED (2) [RETIRE]
Jdg 20:39 when the men of Israel r in the battle, 2015
2Sa 20:22 they r from the city, every man to his tent. 6327

RETURN (263) [RETURNED, RETURNETH, RETURNING]
Ge 3:19 thou eat bread, till thou r unto the ground; 7725
3:19 for dust thou *art,* and unto dust shalt thou r. 7725
14:17 his r from the slaughter of Chedorlaomer, 7725
16: 9 R to thy mistress, and submit thyself under 7725
18:10 I will **certainly** r unto thee according 7725+7725
18:14 At the time appointed I will r unto thee, 7725
31: 3 R unto the land of thy fathers, and to thy 7725
31:13 and r unto the land of thy kindred. 7725
32: 9 R unto thy country, and to thy kindred, and 7725
Ex 4:18 r unto my brethren which *are* in Egypt, and 7725
4:19 unto Moses in Midian, Go, r *into* Egypt: 7725
4:21 When thou goest to r into Egypt, 7725
13:17 when they see war, and they r to Egypt: 7725
Lev 25:10 ye shall r every man unto his possession, 7725
25:10 and ye shall r every man unto his family. 7725
25:13 In the year of this jubile ye shall r every 7725
25:27 sold it; that he may r unto his possession. 7725
25:28 go out, and he shall r unto his possession. 7725

R

Lev 25:41 shall r unto his own family, and unto 7725
25:41 unto the possession of his fathers shall he r. 7725
27:24 In the year of the jubile the field shall r 7725
Nu 10:36 when it rested, he said, R, O Lord, 7725
14: 3 were it not better for us to r into Egypt? 7725
14: 4 us make a captain, and let us r into Egypt. 7725
23: 5 R unto Balak, and thus thou shalt speak. 7725
32:18 We will not r unto our houses, until 7725
32:22 afterward ye shall r, and be guiltless before 7725
35:28 shall r into the land of his possession. 7725
Dt 3:20 shall ye r every man unto his possession, 7725
17:16 nor **cause** the people **to** r to Egypt, to 7725
17:16 Ye shall henceforth r no more that way. 7725
20: 5 let him go and r to his house, lest he die in 7725
20: 6 let him *also* go and r unto his house, lest he 7725
20: 7 let him go and r unto his house, lest he die 7725
20: 8 let him go and r unto his house, lest his 7725
30: 2 shalt r unto the Lord thy God, and 7725
30: 3 will r and gather thee from all the nations, 7725
30: 8 thou shalt r and obey the voice of 7725
Jos 1:15 ye shall r unto the land of your possession, 7725
20: 6 shall the slayer r, and come unto his own 7725
22: 4 therefore now r ye, and get ye unto your 6437
22: 8 R with much riches unto your tents, and 7725
Jdg 7: 3 let him r and depart early from mount 7725
11:31 when I r in peace from the children of 7725
Ru 1: 6 that she might r from the country of Moab: 7725
1: 7 they went on the way to r unto the land of 7725
1: 8 in law, Go, r each to her mother's house: 7725
1:10 Surely we will r with thee unto thy people. 7725
1:15 unto her gods: r thou after thy sister in law. 7725
1:16 *or* to r from following after thee: 7725
1Sa 6: 3 **in any wise** r him a trespass 7725+7725
6: 4 trespass offering which we shall r to him? 7725
6: 8 which ye r him *for* a trespass offering, 7725
7: 3 If ye do r unto the Lord with all your 7725
7:17 his r *was* to Ramah; for there *was* his 8666
9: 5 that *was* with him, Come, and let us r; 7725
15:26 said unto Saul, I will not r with thee: 7725
26:21 r, my son David: for I will no more do thee 7725
29: 4 **Make** *this* fellow r, that he may go again to 7725
29: 7 Wherefore now r, and go in peace, 7725
29:11 to r into the land of the Philistines. 7725
2Sa 2:26 ere thou bid the people r from following 7725
3:16 said Abner unto him, Go, r. And he 7725
10: 5 until your beards be grown, and *then* r. 7725
12:23 I shall go to him, but he shall not r to me. 7725
15:19 r to thy place, and abide with the king: 7725
15:20 I may, r thou, and take back thy brethren: 7725
15:27 r *into* the city in peace, and your two sons 7725
15:34 if thou r *to* the city, and say unto Absalom, 7725
19:14 unto the king, R thou, and all thy servants. 7725
24:13 see what answer I shall r *to* him that sent 7725
1Ki 2:32 the Lord shall r his blood upon his own 7725
2:33 therefore r upon the head of Joab, 7725
2:44 the Lord shall r thy wickedness upon 7725
8:48 *so* r unto thee with all their heart, and 7725
12:24 r every man to his house; for this thing is 7725
12:26 Now shall the kingdom r to the house of 7725
13:16 he said, I may not r with thee, nor go in 7725
19:15 r on thy way to the wilderness of 7725
20:22 for at the r of the year the king of Syria will 8666
20:26 it came to pass at the r of the year, 8666
22:17 let them r every man to his house in peace. 7725
22:28 Micaiah said, If thou r **at all** in 7725+7725
2Ki 18:14 I have offended; r from me: 7725
19: 7 hear a rumour, and shall r to his own land; 7725
19:33 *by the same* shall he r, and shall not come 7725
20:10 but let the shadow r backward ten degrees. 7725
1Ch 19: 5 until your beards be grown, and *then* r. 7725
2Ch 6:24 shall r and confess thy name, and pray and 7725
6:38 If they r to thee with all their heart and 7725
10: 6 What counsel give ye *me* to r answer to 7725
10: 9 What advice give ye that we may r answer 7725
11: 4 r every man to his house, for this thing is 7725
18:16 let them r *therefore* every man to his house 7725
18:26 with water of affliction, until I r in peace. 7725
18:27 If thou **certainly** r in peace, *then* 7725+7725
30: 6 Israel, and he will r to the remnant of you, 7725
30: 9 away *his* face from you, if ye r unto him. 7725
Ne 2: 6 when wilt thou r? So it pleased the king to 7725
4:12 From all places whence ye shall r unto us 7725
9:17 in their rebellion appointed a captain to r to 7725
Est 4:15 Esther bade *them* r Mordecai *this answer:* 7725
9:25 should r upon his own head, and that he 7725
Job 1:21 mother's womb, and naked shall I r thither: 7725
6:29 R, I pray you, let it not be iniquity; yea, 7725
6:29 yea, r again, my righteousness *is* in it. 7725
7:10 He shall r no more to his house, 7725
10:21 Before I go whence I shall not r, *even* to 7725
15:22 He believeth not that *he* shall r out of 7725
16:22 then I shall go the way *whence* I shall not r. 7725
17:10 But *as for* you all, do you r, and come now: 7725
22:23 If thou r to the Almighty, thou shalt be 7725
33:25 he shall r to the days of his youth: 7725
36:10 and commandeth that they r from iniquity. 7725
39: 4 they go forth, and r not unto them. 7725
Ps 6: 4 R, O Lord, deliver my soul: O save me 7725
6:10 let them r *and* be ashamed suddenly. 7725
7: 7 for their sakes therefore r thou on high. 7725
7:16 His mischief shall r upon his own head, 7725
59: 6 They r at evening: they make a noise like a 7725
59:14 at evening let them r; *and* let them make a 7725
73:10 Therefore his people r hither: and waters of 7725
74:21 O let not the oppressed r ashamed: let 7725
80:14 R, we beseech thee, O God *of* hosts: 7725
90: 3 and sayest, R, ye children of men. 7725
90:13 R, O Lord, how long? and let it repent 7725
94:15 judgment shall r unto righteousness: and 7725
104:29 their breath, they die, and r to their dust. 7725
116: 7 R unto thy rest, O my soul; for the Lord 7725
Pr 2:19 None that go *unto* her r *again,* neither take 7725
26:27 he that rolleth a stone, it will r upon him. 7725
Ecc 1: 7 the rivers come, thither they r **again**. 1980+7725
5:15 naked shall he r to go as he came, and 7725
12: 2 nor the clouds r after the rain: 7725
12: 7 shall the dust r to the earth as it was: and 7725
12: 7 and the spirit shall r unto God who gave it. 7725
SS 6:13 R, return, O Shulamite; return, return, 7725
6:13 Return, r, O Shulamite; return, return, 7725
6:13 r, return, that we may look upon thee. 7725
6:13 return, r, that we may look upon thee. 7725
Isa 6:13 *be* a tenth, and *it* shall r, and shall be eaten: 7725
10:21 The remnant shall r, *even* the remnant of 7725
10:22 of the sea, *yet* a remnant of them shall r: 7725
19:22 and they shall r *even* to the Lord, 7725
21:12 if ye will inquire, inquire ye: r, come. 7725
35:10 the ransomed of the Lord shall r, and 7725
37: 7 shall hear a rumour, and r to his own land; 7725
37:34 *by the same* shall he r, and shall not come 7725
44:22 r unto me; for I have redeemed thee. 7725
45:23 shall not r, That unto me every knee shall 7725
51:11 the redeemed of the Lord shall r, 7725
55: 7 let him r unto the Lord, and he will have 7725
55:11 it shall not r unto me void, but it shall 7725
63:17 R for thy servants' sake, the tribes of thine 7725
Jer 3: 1 another man's, shall he r unto her again? 7725
3: 1 yet r **again** to me, saith the Lord. 7725
3:12 say, R, thou backsliding Israel, saith 7725
3:22 R, ye backsliding children, *and* I will heal 7725
4: 1 If thou wilt r, O Israel, saith the Lord, 7725
4: 1 O Israel, saith the Lord, r unto me: 7725
5: 3 harder than a rock; they have refused to r. 7725
8: 4 not arise? shall he turn away, and not r? 7725
8: 5 they hold fast deceit, they refuse to r. 7725
12:15 I will r, and have compassion on them, and 7725
15: 7 my people, *sith* they r not from their ways. 7725
15:19 If thou r, then will I bring thee again, *and* 7725
15:19 let them r unto thee; but return not thou 7725
15:19 return unto thee; but r not thou unto them. 7725
18:11 r ye now every one from his evil way, and 7725
22:10 for he shall r no more, nor see his native 7725
22:11 this place; He shall not r thither any more: 7725
22:27 to the land whereunto they desire to r, 7725
22:27 desire to return, thither shall they not r. 7725
23:14 that none doth r from his wickedness: 7725
23:20 The anger of the Lord shall not r, 7725
24: 7 for they shall r unto me with their whole 7725
29:10 in **causing** you **to** r to this place. 7725
30: 3 I will **cause** them **to** r to the land that I 7725
30:10 Jacob shall r, and shall be in rest, and 7725
30:24 The fierce anger of the Lord shall not r, 7725
31: 8 a great company shall r thither. 7725
32:44 for I will **cause** their captivity **to** r, 7725
33: 7 **cause** the captivity of Judah and the captivity
of Israel **to** r, 7725
33:11 For I will **cause to** r the captivity of 7725
33:26 for I will **cause** their captivity **to** r, 7725

R

Jer 34:11 **caused** the servants and the handmaids, whom they had let go free, **to r**, 7725
34:16 **caused** every man his servant, . . . **to r**, 7725
34:22 and **cause** them **to r** to this city; 7725
35:15 **R** ye now every man from his evil way, and 7725
36: 3 that they may **r** every man from his evil 7725
36: 7 and will **r** every one from his evil way: 7725
37: 7 shall **r** *to* Egypt into their own land. 7725
37:20 that thou **cause** me not **to r** *to* the house of 7725
38:26 that *he* would not **cause** me **to r** *to* 7725
42:12 and **cause** you **to r** to your own land. 7725
44:14 that *they* should **r** *into* the land of Judah, 7725
44:14 to the which they have a desire to **r** to 7725
44:14 for none shall **r** but such as shall escape. 7725
44:28 **r** out of the land of Egypt *into* the land of 7725
46:27 and Jacob shall **r**, and be in rest and at ease, 7725
50: 9 a mighty expert *man;* none shall **r** in vain. 7725
Eze 7:13 For the seller shall not **r** to that which is 7725
7:13 whole multitude thereof, *which* shall not **r**; 7725
13:22 that *he* should not **r** from his wicked way, 7725
16:55 shall **r** to their former estate, and Samaria 7725
16:55 her daughters shall **r** to their former estate, 7725
16:55 thy daughters shall **r** to your former estate. 7725
18:23 *and* not that he should **r** from his ways, and 7725
21: 5 out of his sheath: it shall not **r** any more. 7725
21:30 Shall I **cause** *it* **to r** into his sheath? I will 7725
29:14 will **cause** them **to r** *into* the land of 7725
35: 9 and thy cities shall not **r**: 7725
46: 9 he shall not **r** *by* the way of the gate 7725
46:17 year of liberty; after, it shall **r** to the prince: 7725
47: 6 **caused** me **to r** to the brink of the river. 7725
Da 10:20 now will I **r** to fight with the prince of 7725
11: 9 *his* kingdom, and shall **r** into his own land. 7725
11:10 shall he **r**, and be stirred up, *even* to his 7725
11:13 For the king of the north shall **r**, and 7725
11:28 shall he **r** *into* his land with great riches; 7725
11:28 he shall do *exploits,* and **r** to his own land. 7725
11:29 At the time appointed he shall **r**, and 7725
11:30 **r**, and have indignation against the holy 7725
11:30 he shall even **r**, and have intelligence with 7725
Hos 2: 7 she say, I will go and **r** to my first husband; 7725
2: 9 Therefore will I **r**, and take *away* my corn 7725
3: 5 Afterward shall the children of Israel **r**, and 7725
5:15 I will go *and* **r** to my place, till they 7725
6: 1 Come and let us **r** unto the LORD: for he 7725
7:10 they do not **r** to the LORD their God, 7725
7:16 They **r**, *but* not *to* the most High: they are 7725
8:13 and visit their sins: they shall **r** *to* Egypt. 7725
9: 3 Ephraim shall **r** *to* Egypt, and they shall eat 7725
11: 5 He shall not **r** into the land of Egypt, but 7725
11: 5 shall be his king, because they refused to **r**. 7725
11: 9 mine anger, I will not **r** to destroy Ephraim: 7725
12:14 and his reproach shall his Lord **r** unto him. 7725
14: 1 O Israel, **r** unto the LORD thy God; 7725
14: 7 They that dwell under his shadow shall **r**; 7725
Joel 2:14 Who knoweth *if* he will **r** and repent, and 7725
3: 4 speedily will I **r** your recompence upon 7725
3: 7 will **r** your recompence upon your own 7725
Ob 1:15 thy reward shall **r** upon thine own head. 7725
Mic 1: 7 and they shall **r** to the hire of a harlot. 7725
5: 3 the remnant of his brethren shall **r** unto 7725
Mal 1: 4 but we will **r** and build the desolate places; 7725
3: 7 have not kept *them.* **R** unto me, and I will 7725
3: 7 I will **r** unto you, saith the LORD of hosts. 7725
3: 7 of hosts. But ye said, Wherein shall we **r**? 7725
3:18 shall ye **r**, and discern between 7725
Mt 2:12 in a dream that *they* should not **r** to Herod, *344*
10:13 if it be not worthy, let your peace **r** to you. *1994*
12:44 I will **r** into my house from whence I came *1994*
24:18 Neither let him which is in the field **r** back *1994*
Lk 8:39 **R** to thine own house, and shew how great *5290*
11:24 I will **r** unto my house whence I came out. *5290*
12:36 their lord, when he will **r** from the wedding; *360*
17:31 is in the field, let him likewise not **r** back. *1994*
19:12 to receive for himself a kingdom, and to **r**. *5290*
Ac 13:34 *now* no more to **r** to corruption, he said on *5290*
15:16 After this I will **r**, and will build again *390*
18:21 but I will **r** again unto you, if God will. *344*
20: 3 he purposed to **r** through Macedonia. *5290*

RETURNED (185) [RETURN]

Ge 8: 3 the waters **r** from off the earth continually: 7725
8: 9 she **r** unto him into the ark, for the waters 7725
8:12 which **r** not again unto him any more. 7725
14: 7 they **r**, and came to En-mishpat, which *is* 7725
18:33 and Abraham **r** unto his place. 7725
21:32 and they **r** into the land of the Philistines. 7725
22:19 So Abraham **r** unto his young men, and 7725
31:55 and Laban departed, and **r** unto his place. 7725
32: 6 the messengers **r** to Jacob, saying, 7725
33:16 So Esau **r** that day on his way unto Seir. 7725
37:29 Reuben **r** unto the pit; and behold, 7725
37:30 he **r** unto his brethren, and said, The child 7725
38:22 he **r** to Judah, and said, I cannot find her; 7725
42:24 **r** to them *again,* and communed with them, 7725
43:10 surely now we had **r** this second time. 7725
43:18 Because of the money that was **r** in our 7725
44:13 laded every man his ass, and **r** to the city. 7725
50:14 Joseph **r** into Egypt, he, and his brethren, 7725
Ex 4:18 and **r** to Jethro his father in law, 7725
4:20 upon an ass, and he **r** to the land of Egypt: 7725
5:22 Moses **r** unto the LORD, and said, Lord, 7725
14:27 the sea **r** to his strength when the morning 7725
14:28 the waters **r**, and covered the chariots, and 7725
19: 8 Moses **r** the words of the people unto 7725
32:31 Moses **r** unto the LORD, and said, Oh, 7725
34:31 all the rulers of the congregation **r** unto 7725
Lev 22:13 no child, and is **r** unto her father's house, 7725
Nu 13:25 they **r** from searching of the land after forty 7725
14:36 who **r**, and made all the congregation to 7725
16:50 Aaron **r** unto Moses unto the door of 7725
23: 6 he **r** unto him, and lo, *he* stood by his burnt 7725
24:25 rose up, and went and **r** to his place: 7725
Dt 1:45 ye **r** and wept before the LORD; but 7725
Jos 2:16 there three days, until the pursuers be **r**: 7725
2:22 there three days, until the pursuers were **r**: 7725
2:23 So the two men **r**, and descended from 7725
4:18 that the waters of Jordan **r** unto their place, 7725
6:14 the city once, and **r** *into* the camp: 7725
7: 3 they **r** to Joshua, and said unto him, Let not 7725
8:24 that all the Israelites **r** *unto* Ai, and smote it 7725
10:15 Joshua **r**, and all Israel with him, unto 7725
10:21 all the people **r** to the camp to Joshua *at* 7725
10:38 Joshua **r**, and all Israel with him, to Debir; 7725
10:43 Joshua **r**, and all Israel with him, unto 7725
22: 9 of Gad and the half tribe of Manasseh **r**, 7725
22:32 **r** from the children of Reuben, and 7725
Jdg 2:19 *that* they **r**, and corrupted *themselves* more 7725
5:29 answered *her,* yea, she **r** answer to herself, 7725
7: 3 there **r** of the people twenty and 7725
7:15 **r** into the host of Israel, and said, Arise; 7725
8:13 Gideon the son of Joash **r** from battle 7725
11:39 of two months, that she **r** unto her father, 7725
14: 8 after a time he **r** to take her, and he turned 7725
21:23 they went and **r** unto their inheritance, and 7725
Ru 1:22 So Naomi **r**, and Ruth the Moabitess, 7725
1:22 which **r** out of the country of Moab: 7725
1Sa 1:19 and **r**, and came to their house to Ramah: 7725
6:16 had seen *it,* they **r** *to* Ekron the same day. 7725
6:17 **r** *for* a trespass offering unto the LORD; 7725
17:15 **r** from Saul to feed his father's sheep *at* 7725
17:53 the children of Israel **r** from chasing after 7725
17:57 as David **r** from the slaughter of 7725
18: 6 when David was **r** from the slaughter of 7725
23:28 Wherefore Saul **r** from pursuing after 7725
24: 1 when Saul was **r** from following 7725
25:39 for the LORD hath **r** the wickedness of 7725
26:25 went on his way, and Saul **r** to his place. 7725
27: 9 and the apparel, and **r**, and came to Achish. 7725
2Sa 1: 1 when David was **r** from the slaughter of 7725
1:22 and the sword of Saul **r** not empty. 7725
2:30 Joab **r** from following Abner: and when he 7725
3:16 said Abner unto him, Go, return. And he **r**. 7725
3:27 when Abner was **r** *to* Hebron, Joab took 7725
6:20 David **r** to bless his household. And Michal 7725
8:13 David gat *him* a name when he **r** from 7725
10:14 So Joab **r** from the children of Ammon, and 7725
11: 4 her uncleanness: and she **r** unto her house. 7725
12:31 and all the people **r** *unto* Jerusalem. 7725
14:24 So Absalom **r** to his own house, and 5437
16: 8 The LORD hath **r** upon thee all the blood 7725
17: 3 the man whom thou seekest *is* as if all **r**: *so* 7725
17:20 could not find *them,* they **r** *to* Jerusalem. 7725
18:16 and the people **r** from pursuing after Israel: 7725
19:15 So the king **r**, and came to Jordan. 7725
19:39 blessed him; and he **r** unto his own place. 7725
20:22 And Joab **r** *to* Jerusalem unto the king. 7725
23:10 the people **r** after him only to spoil. 7725

1Ki 12:24 to the word of the LORD, and r to depart, 7725
13:10 r not by the way that he came to Beth-el. 7725
13:33 After this thing Jeroboam r not from his 7725
19:21 he r **back** from him, and took a yoke of 7725
2Ki 2:25 and from thence he r *to* Samaria. 7725
3:27 departed from him, and r to *their own* land. 7725
4:35 he r, and walked in the house to and fro; 7725
5:15 he r to the man of God, he and all his 7725
7:15 And the messengers r, and told the king. 7725
8: 3 that the woman r out of the land of 7725
9:15 king Joram was r to be healed in Jezreel of 7725
14:14 and hostages, and r to Samaria. 7725
19: 8 So Rab-shakeh r, and found the king of 7725
19:36 and went and r, and dwelt at Nineveh. 7725
23:20 bones upon them, and r *to* Jerusalem. 7725
1Ch 16:43 his house: and David r to bless his house. 5437
20: 3 and all the people r *to* Jerusalem. 7725
2Ch 10: 2 heard *it,* that Jeroboam r out of Egypt. 7725
11: 4 and r from going against Jeroboam. 7725
14:15 camels in abundance, and r *to* Jerusalem. 7725
19: 1 Jehoshaphat the king of Judah r to his 7725
19: 8 when they r *to* Jerusalem. 7725
20:27 they r, every man of Judah and Jerusalem, 7725
22: 6 he r to be healed in Jezreel because of 7725
25:10 and they r home in great anger. 7725
25:24 the hostages also, and r *to* Samaria. 7725
28:15 to their brethren: then they r *to* Samaria. 7725
31: 1 *them all.* Then all the children of Israel r, 7725
32:21 So he r with shame of face to his own land. 7725
34: 7 all the land of Israel, he r to Jerusalem. 7725
34: 9 and Benjamin; and they r *to* Jerusalem. 7725
Ezr 5: 5 they r **answer** by letter concerning this 8421
5:11 thus they r us answer, saying, We are 8421
Ne 2:15 entered by the gate of the valley, and *so* r. 7725
4:15 that we r all of us to the wall, every one 7725
9:28 yet when they r, and cried unto thee, thou 7725
Est 2:14 on the morrow she r into the second house 7725
7: 8 the king r out of the palace garden into 7725
Ps 35:13 and my prayer r into mine own bosom. 7725
60: T when Joab r, and smote of Edom in 7725
78:34 and they r and inquired early after God. 7725
Ecc 4: 1 So I r, and considered all the oppressions 7725
4: 7 Then I r, and I saw vanity under the sun. 7725
9:11 I r, and saw under the sun, that the race *is* 7725
Isa 37: 8 So Rabshakeh r, and found the king of 7725
37:37 and went and r, and dwelt at Nineveh. 7725
38: 8 So the sun r ten degrees, by which degrees 7725
Jer 3: 7 she r not. And her treacherous sister Judah 7725
14: 3 no water; they r *with* their vessels empty; 7725
40:12 Even all the Jews r out of all places whither 7725
41:14 captive from Mizpah cast about and r, 7725
43: 5 that were r from all nations, whither they 7725
Eze 1:14 r as the appearance of a flash of lightning. 7725
8:17 and have r to provoke me to anger: 7725
47: 7 Now when I had r, behold, at the bank of 7725
Da 4:34 mine understanding r unto me, and 8421
4:36 At the same time my reason r unto me; and 8421
4:36 mine honour and brightness r unto me; 8421
Hos 6:11 when I r the captivity of my people. 7725
Am 4: 6 yet have ye not r unto me, saith 7725
4: 8 yet have ye not r unto me, saith 7725
4: 9 devoured *them:* yet have ye not r unto me, 7725
4:10 yet have ye not r unto me, saith 7725
4:11 yet have ye not r unto me, saith 7725
Zec 1: 6 they r and said, Like as the LORD of 7725
1:16 I am r to Jerusalem with mercies: 7725
7:14 that no man passed through nor r: 7725
8: 3 I am r unto Zion, and will dwell in 7725
Mt 21:18 Now in the morning as he r into the city, *1877*
Mk 14:40 And when he r, he found them asleep *5290*
Lk 1:56 three months, and r to her own house. *5290*
2:20 And the shepherds r, glorifying and *1994*
2:39 they r into Galilee, to their own city *5290*
2:43 when they had fulfilled the days, as they r, *5290*
4: 1 And Jesus being full of the Holy Ghost r *5290*
4:14 And Jesus r in the power of the Spirit into *5290*
8:37 he went *up* into the ship, and r *back again.* *5290*
8:40 And it came to pass, that when Jesus was r, *5290*
9:10 And the apostles, when they were r, *5290*
10:17 And the seventy r *again* with joy, saying, *5290*
17:18 There are not found that r to give glory to *5290*
19:15 And it came to pass, that when he was r, *1880*
23:48 were done, smote their breasts, and r. *5290*
23:56 And they r, and prepared spices and *5290*
24: 9 And r from the sepulchre, and told all these *5290*
24:33 and r to Jerusalem, and found the eleven *5290*
24:52 and r to Jerusalem with great joy: *5290*
Ac 1:12 Then r they unto Jerusalem from the mount *5290*
5:22 them not in the prison, they r, and told, *390*
8:25 r to Jerusalem, and preached the gospel in *5290*
12:25 And Barnabas and Saul r from Jerusalem, *5290*
13:13 John departing from them r to Jerusalem. *5290*
14:21 they r *again* to Lystra, and *to* Iconium, and *5290*
21: 6 we took ship; and they r home *again.* *5290*
23:32 to go with him, and r to the castle: *5290*
Gal 1:17 into Arabia, and r again unto Damascus. *5290*
Heb 11:15 they might have had opportunity to have r. *344*
1Pe 2:25 but are now r unto the Shepherd and *1994*

RETURNETH (7) [RETURN]
Ps 146: 4 His breath goeth forth, he r to his earth; 7725
Pr 26:11 As a dog r to his vomit, *so* a fool returneth 7725
26:11 to his vomit, *so* a fool r to his folly. 8138
Ecc 1: 6 the wind r *again* according to his circuits. 7725
Isa 55:10 r not thither, but watereth the earth, and 7725
Eze 35: 7 from it him that passeth out and him that r. 7725
Zec 9: 8 that passeth by, and because of him that r: 7725

RETURNING (4) [RETURN]
Isa 30:15 In r and rest shall ye be saved; in quietness 7729
Lk 7:10 And they that were sent, r to the house, *5290*
Ac 8:28 Was r, and sitting in his chariot read Esaias *5290*
Heb 7: 1 who met Abraham r from the slaughter of *5290*

REU (4)
Ge 11:18 And Peleg lived thirty years, and begat **R**: 7466
11:19 Peleg lived after he begat **R** two hundred 7466
11:20 **R** lived two and thirty years, and 7466
11:21 **R** lived after he begat Serug two hundred 7466

REUBEN (74) [REUBENITE, REUBENITES]
Ge 29:32 and bare a son, and she called his name **R**: 7205
30:14 **R** went in the days of wheat harvest, and 7205
35:22 that **R** went and lay with Bilhah his father's 7205
35:23 **R**, Jacob's firstborn, and Simeon, and Levi, 7205
37:21 **R** heard *it,* and he delivered him out of 7205
37:22 **R** said unto them, Shed no blood, *but* 7205
37:29 **R** returned unto the pit; and behold, 7205
42:22 **R** answered them, saying, Spake I not unto 7205
42:37 **R** spake unto his father, saying, Slay my 7205
46: 8 Jacob and his sons: **R**, Jacob's firstborn. 7205
46: 9 the sons of **R**; Hanoch, and Phallu, and 7205
48: 5 as **R** and Simeon, they shall be mine. 7205
49: 3 **R**, thou *art* my firstborn, my might, and 7205
Ex 1: 2 **R**, Simeon, Levi, and Judah, 7205
6:14 The sons of **R** the firstborn of Israel; 7205
6:14 and Carmi: these *be* the families of **R**. 7205
Nu 1: 5 of *the tribe of* **R**; Elizur the son of Shedeur. 7205
1:20 the children of **R**, Israel's eldest son, 7205
1:21 *even* of the tribe of **R**, *were* forty and 7205
2:10 of the camp of **R** according to their armies: 7205
2:10 the captain of the children of **R** *shall be* 7205
2:16 All that were numbered in the camp of **R** 7205
7:30 prince of the children of **R**, *did offer:* 7205
10:18 the standard of the camp of **R** set forward 7205
13: 4 of the tribe of **R**, Shammua the son of 7205
16: 1 On, the son of Peleth, sons of **R**, took *men:* 7205
26: 5 **R**, the eldest son of Israel: the children of 7205
26: 5 the children of **R**; Hanoch, *of whom* 7205
32: 1 Now the children of **R** and the children of 7205
32: 2 the children of **R** came and spake unto 7205
32: 6 children of Gad and to the children of **R**, 7205
32:25 and the children of **R** spake unto Moses, 7205
32:29 the children of **R** will pass with you over 7205
32:31 of Gad and the children of **R** answered, 7205
32:33 to the children of **R**, and unto half the tribe 7205
32:37 the children of **R** built Heshbon, and 7205
34:14 For the tribe of the children of **R** according 7206
Dt 11: 6 the sons of Eliab, the son of **R**: 7205
27:13 **R**, Gad, and Asher, and Zebulun, Dan, and 7205
33: 6 Let **R** live, and not die; and let *not* his men 7205
Jos 4:12 the children of **R**, and the children of Gad, 7205
13:15 of **R** *inheritance* according to their families. 7205
13:23 the border of the children of **R** was Jordan, 7205
13:23 of the children of **R** after their families, 7205
15: 6 went up *to* the stone of Bohan the son of **R**: 7205
18: 7 Gad, and **R**, and half the tribe of Manasseh, 7205
18:17 *to* the stone of Bohan the son of **R**, 7205

Jos 20: 8 upon the plain out of the tribe of **R**, 7205
21: 7 by their families *had* out of the tribe of **R**, 7205
21:36 out of the tribe of **R**, Bezer with her 7205
22: 9 the children of **R** and the children of Gad 7205
22:10 the children of **R** and the children of Gad 7205
22:11 the children of **R** and the children of Gad 7205
22:13 of Israel sent unto the children of **R**, 7205
22:15 they came unto the children of **R**, and 7205
22:21 the children of **R** and the children of Gad 7205
22:25 ye children of **R** and children of Gad; 7205
22:30 heard the words that the children of **R** and 7205
22:31 the priest said unto the children of **R**, 7205
22:32 returned from the children of **R**, and 7205
22:33 destroy the land wherein the children of **R** 7205
22:34 the children of **R** and the children of Gad 7205
Jdg 5:15 For the divisions of **R** *there were* great 7205
5:16 For the divisions of **R** *there were* great 7205
1Ch 2: 1 **R**, Simeon, Levi, and Judah, Issachar, and 7205
5: 1 Now the sons of **R** the firstborn of Israel, 7205
5: 3 *I say,* of **R** the firstborn of Israel *were,* 7205
5:18 The sons of **R**, and the Gadites, and half 7205
6:63 out of the tribe of **R**, and out of the tribe of 7205
6:78 *were given them* out of the tribe of **R**, 7205
Eze 48: 6 even unto the west side, a *portion for* **R**. 7205
48: 7 by the border of **R**, from the east side unto 7205
48:31 one gate of **R**, one gate of Judah, one gate 7205
Rev 7: 5 Of the tribe of **R** *were* sealed twelve *4502*

REUBENITE (1) [REUBEN]
1Ch 11:42 Adina the son of Shiza the **R**, a captain of 7206

REUBENITES (16) [REUBEN]
Nu 26: 7 These *are* the families of the **R**: and 7206
Dt 3:12 gave I unto the **R** and to the Gadites. 7206
3:16 unto the **R** and unto the Gadites I gave 7206
4:43 in the plain country, of the **R**; 7206
29: 8 gave it for an inheritance unto the **R**, and 7206
Jos 1:12 to the **R**, and to the Gadites, and to half 7206
12: 6 LORD gave it *for* a possession unto the **R**, 7206
13: 8 With whom the **R** and the Gadites have 7206
22: 1 Joshua called the **R**, and the Gadites, and 7206
2Ki 10:33 and the **R**, and the Manassites, from Aroer, 7206
1Ch 5: 6 away captive: he *was* prince of the **R**. 7206
5:26 even the **R**, and the Gadites, and the half 7206
11:42 a captain of the **R**, and thirty with him, 7206
12:37 of the **R**, and the Gadites, and of the half 7206
26:32 whom king David made rulers over the **R**, 7206
27:16 the ruler of the **R** *was* Eliezer the son of 7206

REUEL (10) [DEUEL]
Ge 36: 4 to Esau Eliphaz; and Bashemath bare **R**; 7467
36:10 **R** the son of Bashemath the wife of Esau. 7467
36:13 these *are* the sons of **R**; Nahath, and Zerah, 7467
36:17 these *are* the sons of **R** Esau's son; 7467
36:17 these *are* the dukes *that came* of **R** in 7467
Ex 2:18 when they came to **R** their father, he said, 7467
Nu 2:14 sons of Gad *shall be* Eliasaph the son of **R**. 7467
1Ch 1:35 **R**, and Jeush, and Jaalam, and Korah. 7467
1:37 The sons of **R**; Nahath, Zerah, Shammah, 7467
9: 8 the son of **R**, the son of Ibnijah; 7467

REUMAH (1)
Ge 22:24 his concubine, whose name *was* **R**, she bare 7208

REVEAL (7) [REVEALED, REVEALER, REVEALETH, REVELATION, REVELATIONS]
Job 20:27 The heaven shall **r** his iniquity; and 1540
Jer 33: 6 will **r** unto them the abundance of peace 1540
Da 2:47 seeing thou couldest **r** this secret. 1541
Mt 11:27 and *he* to whomsoever the Son will **r** *him.* *601*
Lk 10:22 the Son, and *he* to whom the Son will **r** *him.* *601*
Gal 1:16 To **r** his Son in me, that I might preach him *601*
Php 3:15 God shall **r** even this unto you. *601*

REVEALED (38) [REVEAL]
Dt 29:29 *those things* which are **r** *belong* unto us and 1540
1Sa 3: 7 neither was the word of the LORD yet **r** 1540
3:21 for the LORD **r** himself to Samuel in 1540
2Sa 7:27 of Israel, hast **r** to thy servant, saying, 241+1540
Isa 22:14 it was **r** in mine ears *by* the LORD of 1540
23: 1 from the land of Chittim it is **r** to them. 1540
40: 5 And the glory of the LORD shall be **r**, and 1540
53: 1 and to whom is the arm of the LORD **r**? 1540
56: 1 near to come, and my righteousness to be **r**. 1540
Jer 11:20 on them: for unto thee have I **r** my cause. 1540
Da 2:19 *was* the secret **r** unto Daniel in a night 1541
2:30 this secret *is* not **r** to me for *any* wisdom 1541
10: 1 king of Persia a thing was **r** unto Daniel, 1540
Mt 10:26 there is nothing covered, that shall not be **r**; *601*
11:25 and prudent, and hast **r** them unto babes. *601*
16:17 for flesh and blood hath not **r** *it* unto thee, *601*
Lk 2:26 And it was **r** unto him by the Holy Ghost, *5537*
2:35 that the thoughts of many hearts may be **r**. *601*
10:21 and prudent, and hast **r** them unto babes: *601*
12: 2 there is nothing covered, that shall not be **r**; *601*
17:30 it be in the day when the Son of man is **r**. *601*
Jn 12:38 to whom hath the arm of the Lord been **r**? *601*
Ro 1:17 For therein is the righteousness of God **r** *601*
1:18 For the wrath of God is **r** from heaven *601*
8:18 with the glory which shall be **r** in us. *601*
1Co 2:10 But God hath **r** *them* unto us by his Spirit: *601*
3:13 shall declare *it,* because it shall be **r** by fire; *601*
14:30 If *any thing* be **r** to another that sitteth *by,* let *601*
Gal 3:23 unto the faith which should afterwards be **r**. *601*
Eph 3: 5 as it is now **r** unto his holy apostles and *601*
2Th 1: 7 when the Lord Jesus shall be **r** from heaven *602*
2: 3 and *that* man of sin be **r**, the son of *601*
2: 6 withholdeth that he might be **r** in his time. *601*
2: 8 And then shall *that* Wicked be **r**, whom *601*
1Pe 1: 5 unto salvation ready to be **r** in the last time. *601*
1:12 Unto whom it was **r**, that not unto *601*
4:13 that, when his glory shall be **r**, ye may be *602*
5: 1 also a partaker of the glory that shall be **r**: *601*

REVEALER (1) [REVEAL]
Da 2:47 a Lord of kings, and a **r** of secrets, 1541

REVEALETH (6) [REVEAL]
Pr 11:13 A talebearer **r** secrets: but he that is of a 1540
20:19 He that goeth about *as* a talebearer **r** 1540
Da 2:22 He **r** the deep and secret *things:* he 1541
2:28 there is a God in heaven that **r** secrets, and 1541
2:29 he that **r** secrets maketh known to thee 1541
Am 3: 7 he **r** his secret unto his servants 1540

REVELATION (10) [REVEAL]
Ro 2: 5 and **r** of the righteous judgment of God; *602*
16:25 according to the **r** of the mystery, *602*
1Co 14: 6 except I shall speak to you either by **r**, or *602*
14:26 hath a doctrine, hath a tongue, hath a **r**, *602*
Gal 1:12 was I taught *it,* but by the **r** of Jesus Christ. *602*
2: 2 And I went up by **r**, and communicated unto *602*
Eph 1:17 of wisdom and **r** in the knowledge of him: *602*
3: 3 How that by **r** he made known unto me *602*
1Pe 1:13 *be* brought unto you at the **r** of Jesus Christ; *602*
Rev 1: 1 The **R** of Jesus Christ, which God gave unto *602*

REVELATIONS (2) [REVEAL]
2Co 12: 1 I will come to visions and **r** of the Lord. *602*
12: 7 measure through the abundance of the **r**, *602*

REVELING See SPORTING

REVELLINGS (2)
Gal 5:21 murders, drunkenness, **r**, and such like: *2970*
1Pe 4: 3 **r**, banquetings, and abominable idolatries: *2970*

REVENGE (5) [VENGEANCE]
Jer 15:15 and visit me, and **r** me of my persecutors; 5358
20:10 and we shall take our **r** on him. 5360
Eze 25:15 Because the Philistines have dealt by **r**, and 5360
2Co 7:11 yea, *what* zeal, yea, *what* **r**! *1557*
10: 6 And having in a readiness to **r** all *1556*

REVENGED (1) [VENGEANCE]
Eze 25:12 greatly offended, and **r** himself upon them; 5358

REVENGER (7) [VENGEANCE]
Nu 35:19 The **r** of blood himself shall slay 1350
35:21 the **r** of blood shall slay the murderer, 1350
35:24 the **r** of blood according to these 1350
35:25 the slayer out of the hand of the **r** of blood, 1350
35:27 the **r** of blood find him without the borders 1350
35:27 and the **r** of blood kill the slayer; 1350
Ro 13: 4 a **r** to *execute* wrath upon him that doeth *1558*

REVENGERS (1) [VENGEANCE]
2Sa 14:11 that thou wouldest not suffer the **r** of blood 1350

R

REVENGES (1) [VENGEANCE]
Dt 32:42 from the beginning of **r** upon the enemy. 6546

REVENGETH (2) [VENGEANCE]
Na 1: 2 God *is* jealous, and the LORD **r**; 5358
1: 2 the LORD **r**, and *is* furious; 5358

REVENGING (1) [VENGEANCE]
Ps 79:10 **r** of the blood of thy servants which is 5360

REVENUE (3) [REVENUES]
Ezr 4:13 *so* thou shalt endamage the **r** of the kings. 674
Pr 8:19 than fine gold; and my **r** than choice silver. 8393
Isa 23: 3 of Sihor, the harvest of the river, *is* her **r**; 8393

REVENUES (3) [REVENUE]
Pr 15: 6 but in the **r** of the wicked *is* trouble. 8393
16: 8 righteousness than great **r** without right. 8393
Jer 12:13 they shall be ashamed of your **r** because 8393

REVERENCE (13) [REVERENCED, REVEREND]
Lev 19:30 keep my sabbaths, and **r** my sanctuary: 3372
26: 2 keep my sabbaths, and **r** my sanctuary: 3372
2Sa 9: 6 unto David, he fell on his face, and did **r**. 7812
1Ki 1:31 **did r** to the king, and said, Let my lord 7812
Est 3: 2 But Mordecai bowed not, nor did *him* **r**. 7812
3: 5 nor did him **r**, *then* was Haman full *of* 7812
Ps 89: 7 to be **had in r** of all them that are about 3372
Mt 21:37 them his son, saying, They will **r** my son. *1788*
Mk 12: 6 last unto them, saying, They will **r** my son. *1788*
Lk 20:13 it may be they will **r** *him* when they see *1788*
Eph 5:33 and the wife *see* that she **r** *her* husband. *5399*
Heb 12: 9 which corrected *us*, and we **gave** *them* **r**: *1788*
12:28 we may serve God acceptably with **r** *127*

REVERENCED (1) [REVERENCE]
Est 3: 2 in the king's gate, bowed, and **r** Haman: 7812

REVEREND (1) [REVERENCE]
Ps 111: 9 covenant for ever: holy and **r** *is* his name. 3372

REVERSE (3)
Nu 23:20 and he hath blessed; and I cannot **r** it. 7725
Est 8: 5 let it be written to **r** the letters devised by 7725
8: 8 sealed with the king's ring, may no man **r**. 7725

REVILE (2) [REVILED, REVILERS, REVILEST, REVILINGS]
Ex 22:28 Thou shalt not **r** the gods, nor curse 7043
Mt 5:11 when *men* shall **r** you, and persecute *you*, *3679*

REVILED (6) [REVILE]
Mt 27:39 that passed by, **r** him, wagging their heads, *987*
Mk 15:32 And they that were crucified with him **r** *3679*
Jn 9:28 Then they **r** him, and said, Thou art his *3058*
1Co 4:12 being **r**, we bless; being persecuted, *3058*
1Pe 2:23 Who, when he was **r**, reviled not again; *3058*
2:23 Who, when he was reviled, **r** not **again**; *486*

REVILERS (1) [REVILE]
1Co 6:10 nor covetous, nor drunkards, nor **r**, *3060*

REVILEST (1) [REVILE]
Ac 23: 4 stood by said, **R** thou God's high priest? *3058*

REVILINGS (2) [REVILE]
Isa 51: 7 of men, neither be ye afraid of their **r**. 1421
Zep 2: 8 and the **r** of the children of Ammon, 1421

REVIVE (8) [REVIVED, REVIVING]
Ne 4: 2 will they **r** the stones out of the heaps of 2421
Ps 85: 6 Wilt thou not **r** us again: that thy people 2421
138: 7 in the midst of trouble, thou wilt **r** me: 2421
Isa 57:15 to **r** the spirit of the humble, and to revive 2421
57:15 and to **r** the heart of the contrite ones. 2421
Hos 6: 2 After two days will he **r** us: in the third day 2421
14: 7 they shall **r** *as* the corn, and grow as 2421
Hab 3: 2 **r** thy work in the midst of the years, 2421

REVIVED (6) [REVIVE]
Ge 45:27 carry him, the spirit of Jacob their father **r**: 2421
Jdg 15:19 had drunk, his spirit came again, and he **r**: 2421
1Ki 17:22 of the child came into him again, and he **r**. 2421
2Ki 13:21 of Elisha, he **r**, and stood up on his feet. 2421
Ro 7: 9 the commandment came, sin **r**, and I died. *326*
14: 9 to this end Christ both died, and rose, and **r**, *326*

REVIVING (2) [REVIVE]
Ezr 9: 8 and give us a little **r** in our bondage. 4241
9: 9 to give us a **r**, to set up the house of our 4241

REVOLT (3) [REVOLTED, REVOLTERS, REVOLTING]
2Ch 21:10 The same time also did Libnah **r** from 6586
Isa 1: 5 ye will **r** more and more: the whole head *is* 5627
59:13 speaking oppression and **r**, conceiving and 5627

REVOLTED (7) [REVOLT]
2Ki 8:20 In his days Edom **r** from under the hand of 6586
8:22 Yet Edom **r** from under the hand of Judah 6586
8:22 this day. Then Libnah **r** at the same time. 6586
2Ch 21: 8 In his days the Edomites **r** from under 6586
21:10 So the Edomites **r** from under the hand of 6586
Isa 31: 6 whom the children of Israel have deeply **r**. 5627
Jer 5:23 and a rebellious heart; they are **r** and gone. 5493

REVOLTERS (3) [REVOLT]
Jer 6:28 They *are* all grievous **r**, walking with 5637
Hos 5: 2 the **r** are profound to make slaughter, 7846
9:15 love them no more: all their princes *are* **r**. 5637

REVOLTING (1) [REVOLT]
Jer 5:23 this people hath a **r** and a rebellious heart; 5637

REWARD (80) [REWARDED, REWARDER, REWARDETH, REWARDS]
Ge 15: 1 I *am* thy shield, *and* thy exceeding great **r**. 7939
Nu 18:31 for it *is* your **r** for your service in 7939
Dt 10:17 which regardeth not persons, nor taketh **r**: 7810
27:25 Cursed *be* he that taketh **r** to slay an 7810
32:41 and will **r** them that hate me. 7999
Ru 2:12 a full **r** be given thee of the LORD God of 4909
1Sa 24:19 wherefore the LORD **r** thee good for that 7999
2Sa 3:39 the LORD shall **r** the doer of evil 7999
4:10 I would have given him a **r for** *his* **tidings**: 1309
19:36 the king recompense *it* me *with* such a **r**? 1578
1Ki 13: 7 and refresh *thyself*, and I will give thee a **r**. 4991
2Ch 20:11 Behold, I say, *how* they **r** us, to come to 1580
Job 6:22 or, **Give a r** for me of your substance? 7809
7: 2 as a hireling looketh for the **r of** his **work**: 6467
Ps 15: 5 to usury, nor taketh **r** against the innocent. 7810
19:11 *and* in keeping of them *there is* great **r**. 6118
40:15 Let them be desolate for a **r** of their shame 6118
54: 5 He shall **r** evil unto mine enemies: cut them 7725
58:11 Verily *there is* a **r** for the righteous: 6529
70: 3 Let them be turned back for a **r** of their 6118
91: 8 thou behold and see the **r** of the wicked. 8011
94: 2 judge of the earth: render a **r** to the proud. 1576
109:20 *Let* this *be* the **r** of mine adversaries from 6468
127: 3 *and* the fruit of the womb *is his* **r**. 7939
Pr 11:18 that soweth righteousness *shall be* a sure **r**. 7938
21:14 and a **r** in the bosom strong wrath. 7810
24:14 thou hast found *it*, then there shall be a **r**, 319
24:20 For there shall be no **r** to the evil *man*; 319
25:22 upon his head, and the LORD shall **r** thee. 7999
Ecc 4: 9 because they have a good **r** for their labour. 7939
9: 5 any thing, neither have they any more a **r**; 7939
Isa 3:11 *it shall be* ill *with him*: for the **r** of his 1576
5:23 Which justify the wicked for **r**, and 7810
40:10 his **r** *is* with him, and his work before him. 7939
45:13 not for price nor **r**, saith the LORD of 7810
62:11 his **r** *is* with him, and his work before him. 7939
Jer 40: 5 of the guard gave him victuals and a **r**, 4864
Eze 16:34 in that thou givest a **r**, and no reward is 868
16:34 no **r** is given unto thee, therefore thou art 868
Hos 4: 9 for their ways, and **r** them their doings. 7725
9: 1 thou hast loved a **r** upon every cornfloor. 868
Ob 1:15 thy **r** shall return upon thine own head. 1576
Mic 3:11 The heads thereof judge for **r**, and 7810
7: 3 prince asketh, and the judge *asketh* for a **r**; 7966
Mt 5:12 for great *is* your **r** in heaven: for so *3408*
5:46 love them which love you, what **r** have ye? *3408*
6: 1 otherwise ye have no **r** of your Father *3408*
6: 2 Verily I say unto you, They have their **r**. *3408*
6: 4 seeth in secret himself shall **r** thee openly. *591*
6: 5 Verily I say unto you, They have their **r**. *3408*
6: 6 thy Father which seeth in secret shall **r** thee *591*
6:16 Verily I say unto you, They have their **r**. *3408*
6:18 which seeth in secret, shall **r** thee openly. *591*
10:41 of a prophet shall receive a prophet's **r**; *3408*
10:41 *man* shall receive a righteous *man's* **r**. *3408*
10:42 say unto you, he shall in no wise lose his **r**. *3408*

R

Mt 16:27 he shall **r** every man according to his works. *591*
Mk 9:41 I say unto you, he shall not lose his **r**. *3408*
Lk 6:23 *joy:* for behold, your **r** *is* great in heaven: *3408*
6:35 and your **r** shall be great, and ye shall be *3408*
23:41 for we receive the **due r** of our deeds: *514*
Ac 1:18 Now this *man* purchased a field with the **r** *3408*
Ro 4: 4 Now to him that worketh is the **r** not *3408*
1Co 3: 8 every man shall receive his own **r** *3408*
3:14 hath built thereupon, he shall receive a **r**. *3408*
9:17 For if I do this *thing* willingly, I have a **r**: *3408*
9:18 What is my **r** then? *Verily* that, when I *3408*
Col 2:18 Let no *man* **beguile** you **of** your **r** in a *2603*
3:24 ye shall receive the **r** of the inheritance: *469*
1Ti 5:18 And, The labourer *is* worthy of his **r**. *3408*
2Ti 4:14 the Lord **r** him according to his works: *591*
Heb 2: 2 received a just recompence of **r**; *3405*
10:35 which hath great **recompence of r**. *3405*
11:26 had respect unto the **recompence of** the **r**. *3405*
2Pe 2:13 And shall receive the **r** of unrighteousness, *3408*
2Jn 1: 8 have wrought, but *that* we receive a full **r**. *3408*
Jude 1:11 ran greedily after the error of Balaam for **r**, *3408*
Rev 11:18 that *thou* shouldest give **r** unto thy servants *3408*
18: 6 **R** her even as she rewarded you, and *591*
22:12 and my **r** *is* with me, to give every man *3408*

REWARDED (14) [REWARD]
Ge 44: 4 Wherefore have ye **r** evil for good? 7999
1Sa 24:17 for thou hast **r** me good, whereas I have 1580
24:17 me good, whereas I have **r** thee evil. 1580
2Sa 22:21 The LORD **r** me according to my 1580
2Ch 15: 7 hands be weak: for your work shall be **r**. 7939
Ps 7: 4 If I have **r** evil *unto* him that was at peace 1580
18:20 The LORD **r** me according to my 1580
35:12 They **r** me evil for good *to* the spoiling of 7999
103:10 nor **r** us according to our iniquities. 1580
109: 5 they have **r** me evil for good, and hatred for 7760
Pr 13:13 that feareth the commandment shall be **r**. 7999
Isa 3: 9 for they have **r** evil unto themselves. 1580
Jer 31:16 for thy work shall be **r**, saith the LORD; 7939
Rev 18: 6 Reward her even as she **r** you, and *591*

REWARDER (1) [REWARD]
Heb 11: 6 *that* he is a **r** of them that diligently seek *3406*

REWARDETH (6) [REWARD]
Job 21:19 he **r** him, and he shall know *it.* 7999
Ps 31:23 and plentifully **r** the proud doer. 7999
137: 8 happy *shall he be,* that **r** thee as thou hast 7999
Pr 17:13 Whoso **r** evil for good, evil shall not depart 7725
26:10 The great *God* that formed all *things* both **r** 7936
26:10 rewardeth the fool, and **r** transgressors. 7936

REWARDS (5) [REWARD]
Nu 22: 7 with the **r of divination** in their hand; 7081
Isa 1:23 one loveth gifts, and followeth after **r**: 8021
Da 2: 6 receive of me gifts and **r** and great honour: 5023
5:17 be to thyself, and give thy **r** to another; 5023
Hos 2:12 These *are* my **r** that my lovers have given 866

REZEPH (2)
2Ki 19:12 **R**, and the children of Eden which *were* in 7530
Isa 37:12 **R**, and the children of Eden which *were* in 7530

REZIA (1)
1Ch 7:39 the sons of Ulla; Arah, and Haniel, and **R**. 7525

REZIN (11)
2Ki 15:37 to send against Judah **R** the king of Syria, 7526
16: 5 **R** king of Syria and Pekah son of Remaliah 7526
16: 6 At that time **R** king of Syria recovered 7526
16: 9 *the people of* it captive to Kir, and slew **R**. 7526
Ezr 2:48 The children of **R**, the children of Nekoda, 7526
Ne 7:50 the children of **R**, the children of Nekoda, 7526
Isa 7: 1 *that* **R** the king of Syria, and Pekah the son 7526
7: 4 for the fierce anger of **R** with Syria, and 7526
7: 8 and the head of Damascus *is* **R**; 7526
8: 6 and rejoice in **R** and Remaliah's son; 7526
9:11 set up the adversaries of **R** against him, 7526

REZON (1)
1Ki 11:23 up *another* adversary, **R** the son of Eliadah, 7331

RHEGIUM (1)
Ac 28:13 thence we fet a compass, and came to **R**: *4484*

RHESA (1)
Lk 3:27 *the son* of Joanna, which was *the son* of **R**, *4488*

RHODA (1)
Ac 12:13 a damsel came to hearken, named **R**. *4498*

RHODES (1)
Ac 21: 1 and the *day* following unto **R**, and from *4499*

RIB (5) [RIBS]
Ge 2:22 the **r**, which the LORD God had taken 6763
2Sa 2:23 fifth *r*, that the spear came out behind him; NIH
3:27 smote him there *under* the fifth *r*, that he NIH
4: 6 they smote him under the fifth *r:* and NIH
20:10 so he smote him therewith in the fifth *r*, and NIH

RIBAI (2)
2Sa 23:29 Ittai the son of **R** out of Gibeah of 7380
1Ch 11:31 Ithai the son of **R** of Gibeah, that pertained 7380

RIBBAND (1)
Nu 15:38 upon the fringe of the borders a **r** of blue: 6616

RIBLAH (11)
Nu 34:11 coast shall go down from Shepham *to* **R**, 7247
2Ki 23:33 Pharaoh-nechoh put him in bands at **R** in 7247
25: 6 him up to the king of Babylon to **R**; 7247
25:20 brought them to the king of Babylon to **R**: 7247
25:21 and slew them at **R** in the land of Hamath. 7247
Jer 39: 5 of Babylon to **R** in the land of Hamath, 7247
39: 6 the sons of Zedekiah in **R** before his eyes: 7247
52: 9 of Babylon to **R** in the land of Hamath; 7247
52:10 he slew also all the princes of Judah in **R**. 7247
52:26 brought them to the king of Babylon to **R**. 7247
52:27 put them to death in **R** in the land of 7247

RIBS (2) [RIB]
Ge 2:21 he took one of his **r**, and closed up the flesh 6763
Da 7: 5 *it had* three **r** in the mouth of it between 5967

RICH (81) [ENRICH, ENRICHED, ENRICHEST, RICHER, RICHES, RICHLY]
Ge 13: 2 Abram *was* very **r** in cattle, in silver, and 3513
14:23 thou shouldest say, I have **made** Abram **r**: 6238
Ex 30:15 The **r** shall not give more, and the poor 6223
Lev 25:47 or stranger **wax r** by thee, 3027+5381
Ru 3:10 not young men, whether poor or **r**. 6223
1Sa 2: 7 The LORD maketh poor, and **maketh r**: 6238
2Sa 12: 1 in one city; the one **r**, and the other poor. 6223
12: 2 The **r** *man* had exceeding many flocks and 6223
12: 4 there came a traveller unto the **r** man, and 6223
Job 15:29 He shall not be **r**, neither shall his 6238
27:19 The **r** *man* shall lie down, but he shall not 6223
34:19 nor regardeth the **r** more than the poor? 7771
Ps 45:12 *even* the **r** among the people shall intreat 6223
49: 2 Both low and high, **r** and poor, together. 6223
49:16 Be not thou afraid when one is **made r**, 6238
Pr 10: 4 but the hand of the diligent **maketh r**. 6238
10:15 The **r** *man's* wealth *is* his strong city: 6223
10:22 it **maketh r**, and he addeth no sorrow with 6238
13: 7 There is that maketh himself **r**, yet *hath* 6238
14:20 but the **r** *hath* many friends. 6223
18:11 The **r** *man's* wealth *is* his strong city, and 6223
18:23 but the **r** answereth roughly. 6223
21:17 he that loveth wine and oil shall not be **r**. 6238
22: 2 The **r** and poor meet together: the LORD 6223
22: 7 The **r** ruleth over the poor, and 6223
22:16 his *riches, and* he that giveth to the **r**, 6223
23: 4 Labour not to be **r**: cease from thine own 6238
28: 6 *that is* perverse in *his* ways, though he *be* **r**. 6223
28:11 The **r** man *is* wise in his own conceit; but 6223
28:20 he that maketh haste to be **r** shall not be 6238
28:22 He that hasteth to be **r** *hath* an evil eye, and 1952
Ecc 5:12 the abundance of the **r** will not suffer him 6223
10: 6 in great dignity, and the **r** sit in low place. 6223
10:20 and curse not the **r** in thy bedchamber: 6223
Isa 53: 9 the wicked, and with the **r** in his death; 6223
Jer 5:27 they are become great, and **waxen r**. 6238
9:23 let not the **r** *man* glory in his riches: 6223
Eze 27:24 broidered work, and in chests of **r apparel**, 1264
Hos 12: 8 Ephraim said, Yet I am **become r**, I have 6238
Mic 6:12 For the **r** *men* thereof are full *of* violence, 6223
Zec 11: 5 Blessed *be* the LORD; for I am **r**: 6238
Mt 19:23 That a **r** *man* shall hardly enter into *4145*

Mt 19:24 than for a r *man* to enter into the kingdom 4145
27:57 there came a r man of Arimathea, 4145
Mk 10:25 than for a r man to enter into the kingdom 4145
12:41 and many *that were* r cast in much. 4145
Lk 1:53 and the r he hath sent empty away. 4147
6:24 But woe unto you that are r: for ye have 4145
12:16 The ground of a certain r man brought 4145
12:21 for himself, and is not r towards God. 4147
14:12 neither thy kinsmen, nor *thy* r neighbours; 4145
16: 1 There was a certain r man, which had a 4145
16:19 There was a certain r man, which was 4145
16:21 crumbs which fell from the r *man's* table: 4145
16:22 the r *man* also died, and was buried; 4145
18:23 he was very sorrowful: for he was very r. 4145
18:25 than for a r *man* to enter into the kingdom 4145
19: 2 chief among the publicans, and he was r. 4145
21: 1 saw the r *men* casting their gifts into 4145
Ro 10:12 for the same Lord over all *is* r unto all that 4147
1Co 4: 8 Now ye are full, now ye are r, ye have 4147
2Co 6:10 as poor, yet **making** many r; as having 4148
8: 9 that, though he was r, *yet* for your sakes he 4145
8: 9 that ye through his poverty might be r. 4147
Eph 2: 4 But God, who is r in mercy, for his great 4145
1Ti 6: 9 But they that will be r fall into temptation 4147
6:17 Charge *them that are* r in this world, 4145
6:18 that *they* be r in good works, ready to 4147
Jas 1:10 But the r, in that he is made low: because 4145
1:11 also shall the r *man* fade away in his ways. 4145
2: 5 chosen the poor of this world r in faith, 4145
2: 6 Do not r *men* oppress you, and draw you 4145
5: 1 ye r *men,* weep and howl for your miseries 4145
Rev 2: 9 and tribulation, and poverty, (but thou art r) 4145
3:17 I am r, and increased with goods, and 4145
3:18 gold tried in the fire, that thou mayest be r; 4147
6:15 and the r *men,* and the chief captains, and 4145
13:16 and great, r and poor, free and bond, 4145
18: 3 the merchants of the earth are **waxed** r 4147
18:15 of these *things,* which were **made** r by her, 4147
18:19 wherein were **made** r all that had ships in 4147

RICHER (1) [RICH]
Da 11: 2 the fourth shall be far r than *they* all: 6238+6239

RICHES (98) [RICH]
Ge 31:16 For all the r which God hath taken from 6239
36: 7 For their r were more than that they might 7399
Jos 22: 8 Return with much r unto your tents, and 5233
1Sa 17:25 the king will enrich him *with* great r, and 6239
1Ki 3:11 neither hast asked r for thyself, nor hast 6239
3:13 thou hast not asked, both r, and honour: 6239
10:23 exceeded all the kings of the earth for r 6239
1Ch 29:12 Both r and honour *come* of thee, and 6239
29:28 a good old age, full of days, r, and honour: 6239
2Ch 1:11 thou hast not asked r, wealth, or honour, 6239
1:12 I will give thee r, and wealth, and honour, 6239
9:22 passed all the kings of the earth in r 6239
17: 5 and he had r and honour in abundance. 6239
18: 1 Now Jehoshaphat had r and honour in 6239
20:25 in abundance both r with the dead bodies, 7399
32:27 Hezekiah had exceeding much r and 6239
Est 1: 4 When he shewed the r of his glorious 6239
5:11 Haman told them of the glory of his r, and 6239
Job 20:15 He hath swallowed down r, and he shall 2428
36:19 Will he esteem thy r? *no,* not gold, nor all 7769
Ps 37:16 hath *is* better than the r of many wicked. 1995
39: 6 he heapeth up *r,* and knoweth not who shall NIH
49: 6 boast themselves in the multitude of their r; 6239
52: 7 trusted in the abundance of his r, *and* 6239
62:10 if r increase, set not *your* heart *upon them.* 2428
73:12 prosper in the world; they increase *in* r. 2428
104:24 made them all: the earth is full *of* thy r. 7075
112: 3 Wealth and r *shall be* in his house: and 6239
119:14 way of thy testimonies, as *much as* in all r. 1952
Pr 3:16 and in her left hand r and honour. 6239
8:18 **R** and honour *are* with me; *yea,* durable 6239
8:18 with me; *yea,* durable r and righteousness. 1952
11: 4 **R** profit not in the day of wrath: but 1952
11:16 retaineth honour: and strong *men* retain r. 6239
11:28 He that trusteth in his r shall fall: but 6239
13: 7 that maketh himself poor, yet *hath* great r. 1952
13: 8 The ransom of a man's life *are* his r: but 6239
14:24 The crown of the wise *is* their r: *but* 6239
19:14 House and r *are* the inheritance of fathers: 1952
22: 1 name *is* rather to be chosen than great r, 6239
22: 4 *and* the fear of the LORD *are* r, 6239
22:16 that oppresseth the poor to increase his *r,* NIH
23: 5 for *r* certainly make themselves wings; NIH
24: 4 be filled *with* all precious and pleasant r. 1952
27:24 For r *are* not for ever: and doth the crown 2633
30: 8 give me neither poverty nor r; feed me with 6239
Ecc 4: 8 neither is his eye satisfied *with* r; 6239
5:13 *namely,* r kept for the owners thereof to 6239
5:14 those r perish by evil travail: and 6239
5:19 Every man also to whom God hath given r 6239
6: 2 A man to whom God hath given r, wealth, 6239
9:11 the wise, nor yet r to men of understanding, 6239
Isa 8: 4 the r of Damascus and the spoil of Samaria 2428
10:14 my hand hath found as a nest the r of 2428
30: 6 they will carry their r upon the shoulders of 2428
45: 3 **hidden** r of secret places, that thou mayest 4301
61: 6 ye shall eat the r of the Gentiles, and 2428
Jer 9:23 let not the rich *man* glory in his r: 6239
17:11 *so* he that getteth r, and not by right, 6239
48:36 the r *that* he hath gotten are perished. 3502
Eze 26:12 they shall make a spoil of thy r, and make a 2428
27:12 by reason of the multitude of all *kind of* r; 1952
27:18 of thy making, for the multitude of all r; 1952
27:27 Thy r, and thy fairs, thy merchandise, 1952
27:33 of the earth with the multitude of thy r 1952
28: 4 thine understanding thou hast gotten thee r, 2428
28: 5 by thy traffick hast thou increased thy r, 2428
28: 5 and thine heart is lifted up because of thy r: 2428
Da 11: 2 by his strength through his r he shall stir up 6239
11:13 years with a great army and with much r. 7399
11:24 among them the prey, and spoil, and r: 7399
11:28 shall he return *into* his land with great r; 7399
Mt 13:22 and the deceitfulness of r, choke the word, 4149
Mk 4:19 and the deceitfulness of r, and the lusts of 4149
10:23 How hardly shall they that have r enter into 5536
10:24 how hard is it for them that trust in r to 5536
Lk 8:14 with cares and r and pleasures of *this* life, 4149
16:11 who will commit to your trust the true *r?* NIG
18:24 How hardly shall they that have r enter into 5536
Ro 2: 4 Or despisest thou the r of his goodness and 4149
9:23 And that he might make known the r of his 4149
11:12 Now if the fall of them *be* the r of 4149
11:12 the diminishing of them the r of 4149
11:33 O the depth of the r both of the wisdom 4149
2Co 8: 2 their deep poverty abounded unto the r of 4149
Eph 1: 7 of sins, according to the r of his grace; 4149
1:18 what the r of the glory of his inheritance in 4149
2: 7 r of his grace in *his* kindness towards us 4149
3: 8 the Gentiles the unsearchable r of Christ; 4149
3:16 grant you, according to the r of his glory, 4149
Php 4:19 according to his r in glory by Christ Jesus. 4149
Col 1:27 r of the glory of this mystery among 4149
2: 2 unto all r of the full assurance of 4149
1Ti 6:17 nor trust in uncertain r, but in the living 4149
Heb 11:26 Esteeming the reproach of Christ greater r 4149
Jas 5: 2 Your r are corrupted, and your garments 4149
Rev 5:12 and r, and wisdom, and strength, and 4149
18:17 in one hour so great r is come to nought. 4149

RICHLY (2) [RICH]
Col 3:16 Let the word of Christ dwell in you r in all 4146
1Ti 6:17 who giveth us r all *things* to enjoy; 4146

RICHLY ORNAMENTED ROBE See COAT OF MANY COLOURS; DIVERS; DIVERSE

RID (6) [RIDDANCE]
Ge 37:22 that he might r him out of their hands, 5337
Ex 6: 6 I will r you out of their bondage, and I will 5337
Lev 26: 6 I will r evil beasts out of the land, 7673
Ps 82: 4 r *them* out of the hand of the wicked. 5337
144: 7 r me, and deliver me out of great waters, 6475
144:11 **R** me, and deliver me from the hand of 6475

RIDDANCE (2) [RID]
Lev 23:22 thou shalt not **make clean** r of the corners 3615
Zep 1:18 for he shall make even a speedy r of all 3617

RIDDEN (1) [RIDE]
Nu 22:30 upon which thou hast r ever since *I was* 7392

RIDDLE (9)
Jdg 14:12 I will now put forth a r unto you: 2420
14:13 Put forth thy r, that we may hear it. 2420
14:14 they could not *in* three days expound the r. 2420

Jdg 14:15 that he may declare unto us the **r**, lest we 2420
14:16 thou hast put forth a **r** unto the children of 2420
14:17 she told the **r** to the children of her people. 2420
14:18 with my heifer, ye had not found out my **r**. 2420
14:19 unto them which expounded the **r**. 2420
Eze 17: 2 **put forth a r**, and speak a parable 2330+2420

RIDDLES See DARK SAYINGS; DARK SPEECHES; HARD SENTENCES

RIDE (20) [RIDDEN, RIDER, RIDERS, RIDETH, RIDING, RODE]
Ge 41:43 he **made** him **to r** in the second chariot 7392
Dt 32:13 He **made** him **r** on the high places of 7392
Jdg 5:10 Speak, ye that **r on** white asses, ye that sit 7392
2Sa 16: 2 asses *be* for the king's household to **r on**; 7392
19:26 that I may **r** thereon, and go to the king; 7392
1Ki 1:33 **cause** Solomon my son **to r** upon mine 7392
1:38 **caused** Solomon **to r** upon king David's 7392
1:44 they have **caused** him **to r** upon the king's 7392
2Ki 10:16 So they **made** him **r** in his chariot. 7392
Job 30:22 thou **causest** me **to r** *upon it,* and 7392
Ps 45: 4 *in* thy majesty **r** prosperously because 7392
66:12 Thou hast **caused** men **to r** over our heads; 7392
Isa 30:16 and, We will **r** upon the swift; therefore 7392
58:14 I will **cause** thee **to r** upon the high places 7392
Jer 6:23 they **r** upon horses, set in array as men for 7392
50:42 they shall **r** upon horses, *every one* put in 7392
Hos 10:11 I will **make** Ephraim **to r**; Judah shall 7392
14: 3 we will not **r** upon horses: neither will we 7392
Hab 3: 8 that thou didst **r** upon thine horses *and* 7392
Hag 2:22 the chariots, and those that **r** in them; 7392

RIDER (7) [RIDE]
Ge 49:17 so that his **r** shall fall backward. 7392
Ex 15: 1 and his **r** hath he thrown into the sea. 7392
15:21 and his **r** hath he thrown into the sea. 7392
Job 39:18 on high, she scorneth the horse and his **r**. 7392
Jer 51:21 will I break in pieces the horse and his **r**; 7392
51:21 will I break in pieces the chariot and his **r**; 7392
Zec 12: 4 with astonishment, and his **r** with madness: 7392

RIDERS (5) [RIDE]
2Ki 18:23 if thou be able on thy part to set **r** upon 7392
Est 8:10 *and* **r** on mules, camels, *and* 7392
Isa 36: 8 if thou be able on thy part to set **r** upon 7392
Hag 2:22 the horses and their **r** shall come down, 7392
Zec 10: 5 and the **r** on horses shall be confounded. 7392

RIDETH (7) [RIDE]
Lev 15: 9 what saddle soever he **r** upon that hath 7392
Dt 33:26 *who* **r** *upon* the heaven in thy help, and 7392
Est 6: 8 the horse that the king **r** upon, and 7392
Ps 68: 4 extol him that **r** upon the heavens by his 7392
68:33 To him that **r** upon the heavens of heavens, 7392
Isa 19: 1 the LORD **r** upon a swift cloud, and 7392
Am 2:15 shall he that **r** the horse deliver himself. 7392

RIDGES (1)
Ps 65:10 *Thou* waterest the **r** thereof abundantly: 8525

RIDING (10) [RIDE]
Nu 22:22 Now he was **r** upon his ass, and his two 7392
2Ki 4:24 and go *forward;* slack not *thy* **r** for me, 7392
Jer 17:25 **r** in chariots and on horses, they, and 7392
22: 4 **r** in chariots and on horses, he, and 7392
Eze 23: 6 young men, horsemen **r** upon horses. 7392
23:12 most gorgeously, horsemen **r** upon horses, 7392
23:23 and renowned, all of them **r** upon horses. 7392
38:15 all of them **r** upon horses, a great company, 7392
Zec 1: 8 behold a man **r** upon a red horse, and 7392
9: 9 **r** upon an ass, and upon a colt the foal of an 7392

RIFLED (1)
Zec 14: 2 and the houses **r**, and the women ravished; 8155

RIGHT (359) [ARIGHT, BIRTHRIGHT, RIGHTEOUS, RIGHTEOUSLY, RIGHTEOUSNESS, RIGHTEOUSNESS', RIGHTEOUSNESSES, RIGHTLY, UNRIGHTEOUS]
Ge 13: 9 *take* the left hand, then I will **go to the r**; 3231
13: 9 or if *thou depart to* the **r hand**, then I will 3225
18:25 Shall not the Judge of all the earth do **r**? 4941
24:48 which had led me in the **r** way to take my 571
24:49 that I may turn to the **r hand**, or to the left. 3225
48:13 Ephraim in his **r hand** toward Israel's left 3225
48:13 in his left hand towards Israel's **r hand**, 3225
48:14 Israel stretched out his **r hand**, and laid *it* 3225
48:17 when Joseph saw that his father laid his **r** 3225
48:18 the firstborn; put thy **r hand** upon his head. 3225
Ex 14:22 *were* a wall unto them on their **r hand**, 3225
14:29 *were* a wall unto them on their **r hand**, 3225
15: 6 Thy **r hand**, O LORD, is become glorious 3225
15: 6 thy **r hand**, O LORD, hath dashed in 3225
15:12 Thou stretchedst out thy **r hand**, the earth 3225
15:26 wilt do that which is **r** in his sight, and 3477
29:20 and put *it* upon the tip of the **r** ear of Aaron, NIH
29:20 upon the tip of the **r** ear of his sons, and 3233
29:20 upon the thumb of their **r** hand, and 3233
29:20 upon the great toe of their **r** foot, and 3233
29:22 fat that *is* upon them, and the **r** shoulder; 3225
Lev 7:32 the **r** shoulder shall ye give unto the priest 3225
7:33 shall have the **r** shoulder for *his* part. 3225
8:23 put *it* upon the tip of Aaron's **r** ear, and 3233
8:23 upon the thumb of his **r** hand, and upon 3233
8:23 and upon the great toe of his **r** foot. 3233
8:24 put of the blood upon the tip of their **r** ear, 3233
8:24 upon the thumbs of their **r** hands, and 3233
8:24 and upon the great toes of their **r** feet: 3233
8:25 and their fat, and the **r** shoulder: 3225
8:26 *them* on the fat, and upon the **r** shoulder: 3225
9:21 the **r** shoulder Aaron waved *for* a wave 3225
14:14 the priest shall put *it* upon the tip of the **r** 3233
14:14 upon the thumb of his **r** hand, and upon 3233
14:14 and upon the great toe of his **r** foot: 3233
14:16 the priest shall dip his **r** finger in the oil 3225
14:17 tip of the **r** ear of him that is to be cleansed, 3233
14:17 upon the thumb of his **r** hand, and upon 3233
14:17 and upon the great toe of his **r** foot, 3233
14:25 put *it* upon the tip of the **r** ear of him that is 3233
14:25 upon the thumb of his **r** hand, and upon 3233
14:25 and upon the great toe of his **r** foot: 3233
14:27 the priest shall sprinkle with his **r** finger 3233
14:28 tip of the **r** ear of him that is to be cleansed, 3233
14:28 upon the thumb of his **r** hand, and upon 3233
14:28 and upon the great toe of his **r** foot, 3233
Nu 18:18 wave breast and as the **r** shoulder are thine. 3225
20:17 we will not turn *to* the **r hand** nor *to* 3225
22:26 *was* no way to turn *either to* the **r hand** 3225
27: 7 The daughters of Zelophehad speak **r**: 3651
Dt 2:27 I will neither turn *unto* the **r hand** nor *to* 3225
5:32 ye shall not turn aside *to* the **r hand** or 3225
6:18 thou shalt do *that which is* **r** and good in 3477
12: 8 every man whatsoever *is* **r** in his own eyes. 3477
12:25 when thou shalt do *that which is* **r** in 3477
12:28 and **r** in the sight of the LORD thy God. 3477
13:18 to do *that which is* **r** in the eyes of 3477
17:11 shew thee, *to* the **r hand**, nor *to* the left. 3225
17:20 *to* the **r hand**, or *to* the left: 3225
21: 9 when thou shalt do *that which is* **r** in 3477
21:17 of his strength; the **r** of the firstborn *is* his. 4941
28:14 *to* the **r hand**, or *to* the left, to go after 3225
32: 4 and without iniquity, just and **r** *is* he. 3477
33: 2 from his **r hand** *went* a fiery law for them. 3225
Jos 1: 7 turn not from it *to* the **r hand** or *to* the left, 3225
3:16 the people passed over **r against** Jericho. 5048
9:25 seemeth good and **r** unto thee to do unto us, 3477
17: 7 the border went *along* on the **r hand** unto 3225
23: 6 *ye* turn not aside therefrom *to* the **r hand** 3225
Jdg 3:16 he did gird it under his raiment upon his **r** 3225
3:21 took the dagger from his **r** thigh, and 3225
5:26 and her **r hand** to the workmen's hammer; 3225
7:20 the trumpets in their **r** hands to blow 3225
12: 6 for he could not frame to pronounce *it* **r**. 3651
16:29 of the one with his **r hand**, and of the other 3225
17: 6 every man did *that* which *was* **r** in his own 3477
21:25 every man did *that* which *was* **r** in his own 3477
Ru 4: 6 redeem thou my **r** to thyself; for I cannot 1353
1Sa 6:12 turned not aside *to* the **r hand** or *to* the left; 3225
11: 2 that *I* may thrust out all your **r** eyes, and 3225
12:23 but I will teach you the good and the **r** way: 3477
2Sa 2:19 in going he turned not to the **r hand** nor to 3225
2:21 Turn thee aside to thy **r hand** or to thy left, 3225
14:19 none can **turn to the r hand** or to the left 3231
15: 3 unto him, See, thy matters *are* good and **r**; 5228
16: 6 all the mighty *men were* on his **r hand** and 3225
19:28 What **r** therefore have I yet to cry any more 6666
19:43 and we have also more *r* in David than ye: NIH
20: 9 Joab took Amasa by the beard with the **r** 3225
24: 5 *on* the **r side** of the city that *lieth* in 3225
1Ki 2:19 king's mother; and she sat on his **r hand**. 3225

1Ki	6: 8	chamber *was* in the **r** side of the house:	3233
	7:21	he set up the **r** pillar, and called the name	3233
	7:39	he put five bases on the **r** side of the house,	3225
	7:39	he set the sea on the **r** side of the house	3233
	7:49	five on the **r side**, and five on the left,	3225
	11:33	to do *that* which *is* **r** in mine eyes, and	3477
	11:38	do that *is* **r** in my sight, to keep my statutes	3477
	14: 8	to do *that* only which *was* **r** in mine eyes;	3477
	15: 5	Because David did *that* which *was* **r** in	3477
	15:11	Asa did *that* which *was* **r** in the eyes of	3477
	22:19	of heaven standing by him on his **r hand**	3225
	22:43	doing *that* which *was* **r** in the eyes of	3477
2Ki	10:15	and said to him, Is thine heart **r**,	3477
	10:30	in executing *that* which *is* **r** in mine eyes,	3477
	11:11	from the **r** corner of the temple to the left	3233
	12: 2	Jehoash did *that* which *was* **r** in the sight of	3477
	12: 9	on the **r side** as one cometh *into* the house	3225
	14: 3	he did *that* which *was* **r** in the sight of	3477
	15: 3	he did *that* which *was* **r** in the sight of	3477
	15:34	he did *that* which *was* **r** in the sight of	3477
	16: 2	did not *that* which *was* **r** in the sight of	3477
	17: 9	*were* not **r** against the LORD their God,	3651
	18: 3	he did *that* which *was* **r** in the sight of	3477
	22: 2	he did *that* which *was* **r** in the sight of	3477
	22: 2	turned not aside *to* the **r hand** or *to* the left.	3225
	23:13	which *were* on the **r hand** of the mount of	3225
1Ch	6:39	brother Asaph, who stood on his **r hand**,	3225
	12: 2	could **use** both **the r hand** and the left in	3231
	13: 4	for the thing was **r** in the eyes of all	3474
2Ch	3:17	one on the **r hand**, and the other on the left;	3225
	3:17	called the name of *that on* the **r hand**	3233
	4: 6	put five on the **r hand**, and five on the left,	3225
	4: 7	five on the **r hand**, and five on the left.	3225
	4: 8	five on the **r side**, and five on the left.	3225
	4:10	he set the sea on the **r** side of the east end,	3233
	14: 2	and **r** in the eyes of the LORD his God:	3477
	18:18	the host of heaven standing on his **r hand**	3225
	20:32	doing *that* which *was* **r** in the sight of	3477
	23:10	from the **r** side of the temple to the left side	3233
	24: 2	Joash did *that* which *was* **r** in the sight of	3477
	25: 2	he did *that* which *was* **r** in the sight of	3477
	26: 4	he did *that* which *was* **r** in the sight of	3477
	27: 2	he did *that* which *was* **r** in the sight of	3477
	28: 1	he did not *that* which *was* **r** in the sight of	3477
	29: 2	he did *that* which *was* **r** in the sight of	3477
	31:20	wrought *that* which *was* good and **r** and	3477
	34: 2	he did *that* which *was* **r** in the sight of	3477
	34: 2	declined neither *to* the **r hand**, nor *to*	3225
Ezr	8:21	to seek of him a **r** way for us, and for our	3477
Ne	2:20	nor **r**, nor memorial, in Jerusalem.	6666
	8: 4	and Hilkiah, and Maaseiah, on his **r hand**;	3225
	9:13	gavest them **r** judgments, and true laws,	3477
	9:33	for thou hast done **r**, but we have done	571
	12:31	whereof *one* went on the **r hand** upon	3225
Est	8: 5	the thing **seem r** before the king, and I *be*	3787
Job	6:25	How forcible are **r** words! but what doth	3476
	23: 9	*him:* he hideth *himself* on the **r hand**,	3225
	30:12	Upon *my* **r hand** rise the youth; they push	3225
	33:27	perverted *that which was* **r**, and it profited	3477
	34: 6	Should I lie against my **r**? my wound *is*	4941
	34:17	Shall even he that hateth **r** govern? and wilt	4941
	34:23	For he will not lay upon man more *than* **r**;	NIH
	35: 2	Thinkest thou this to be **r**, *that* thou saidst,	4941
	36: 6	life of the wicked: but giveth **r** to the poor.	4941
	40:14	thee that thine own **r hand** can save thee.	3225
	42: 7	have not spoken of me *the thing that is* **r**,	3559
	42: 8	have not spoken of me *the thing which is* **r**,	3559
Ps	9: 4	For thou hast maintained my **r** and	4941
	9: 4	thou satest in the throne judging **r**.	6664
	16: 8	because *he is* at my **r hand**, I shall not be	3225
	16:11	at thy **r hand** *there are* pleasures for	3225
	17: 1	Hear the **r**, O LORD, attend unto my cry,	6664
	17: 7	O thou that savest by thy **r hand** them	3225
	18:35	thy **r hand** hath holden me up, and	3225
	19: 8	The statutes of the LORD *are* **r**,	3477
	20: 6	with the saving strength of his **r hand**.	3225
	21: 8	thy **r hand** shall find out those that hate	3225
	26:10	and their **r hand** is full *of* bribes.	3225
	33: 4	For the word of the LORD *is* **r**; and all his	3477
	44: 3	thy **r hand**, and thine arm, and the light of	3225
	45: 4	thy **r hand** shall teach thee terrible *things.*	3225
	45: 6	the sceptre of thy kingdom *is* a **r** sceptre.	4334
	45: 9	**r hand** did stand the queen in gold of	3225
	46: 5	God shall help her, *and that* **r** early.	6437
	48:10	thy **r hand** is full *of* righteousness.	3225
	51:10	O God; and renew a **r** spirit within me.	3559
	60: 5	save *with* thy **r hand**, and hear me.	3225
	63: 8	hard after thee: thy **r hand** upholdeth me.	3225
	73:23	thou hast holden *me* by my **r** hand.	3225
	74:11	thou thy hand, even thy **r hand**?	3225
	77:10	*I will remember* the years of the **r hand** of	3225
	78:37	For their heart was not **r** with him,	3559
	78:54	*which* his **r hand** had purchased.	3225
	80:15	the vineyard which thy **r hand** hath	3225
	80:17	thy hand be upon the man of thy **r hand**,	3225
	89:13	strong is thy hand, *and* high is thy **r hand**.	3225
	89:25	also in the sea, and his **r hand** in the rivers.	3225
	89:42	Thou hast set up the **r hand** of his	3225
	91: 7	at thy side, and ten thousand at thy **r hand**;	3225
	98: 1	he hath done marvellous *things:* his **r hand**,	3225
	107: 7	he led them forth by the **r** way, that *they*	3477
	108: 6	save *with* thy **r hand**, and answer me.	3225
	109: 6	over him: and let Satan stand at his **r hand**.	3225
	109:31	For he shall stand at the **r hand** of the poor,	3225
	110: 1	said unto my Lord, Sit thou at my **r hand**,	3225
	110: 5	The Lord at thy **r hand** shall strike through	3225
	118:15	the **r hand** of the LORD doeth valiantly.	3225
	118:16	The **r hand** of the LORD is exalted:	3225
	118:16	the **r hand** of the LORD doeth valiantly.	3225
	119:75	that thy judgments *are* **r**, and *that* thou *in*	6664
	119:128	**esteem** all *thy* precepts concerning all *things* **to be r**;	3474
	121: 5	the LORD *is* thy shade upon thy **r** hand.	3225
	137: 5	let my **r hand** forget *her cunning.*	3225
	138: 7	and thy **r hand** shall save me.	3225
	139:10	lead me, and thy **r hand** shall hold me.	3225
	139:14	and *that* my soul knoweth **r well**.	3966
	140:12	cause of the afflicted, *and* the **r** of the poor.	4941
	142: 4	I looked *on my* **r hand**, and beheld, but	3225
	144: 8	their **r hand** *is* a right hand of falsehood.	3225
	144: 8	their right hand *is* a **r hand** of falsehood.	3225
	144:11	their **r hand** *is* a right hand of falsehood:	3225
	144:11	their right hand *is* a **r hand** of falsehood:	3225
Pr	3:16	Length of days *is* in her **r hand**; and in her	3225
	4:11	way of wisdom; I have led thee in **r** paths.	3476
	4:25	Let thine eyes look **r on**, and	5227+3807.1
	4:27	Turn not *to* the **r hand** nor *to* the left:	3225
	8: 6	the opening of my lips *shall be* **r things**.	4339
	8: 9	and **r** to them that find knowledge.	3477
	9:15	To call passengers who **go r** *on* their ways:	3474
	12: 5	The thoughts of the righteous *are* **r**: *but*	4941
	12:15	The way of a fool *is* **r** in his own eyes: but	3477
	14:12	There is a way which seemeth **r** unto a	3477
	16: 8	than great revenues without **r**.	4941
	16:13	of kings; and *they* love him that speaketh **r**.	3477
	16:25	There is a way that seemeth **r** unto a man,	3477
	20:11	his work *be* pure, and whether *it be* **r**.	3477
	21: 2	Every way of a man *is* **r** in his own eyes:	3477
	21: 8	strange: but *as for* the pure, his work *is* **r**.	3477
	23:16	shall rejoice, when thy lips speak **r things**.	4339
	24:26	*Every man* shall kiss *his* lips that giveth a **r**	5228
	27:16	the wind, and the ointment of his **r hand**,	3225
Ecc	4: 4	I considered all travail, and every **r** work,	3788
	10: 2	A wise *man's* heart *is* at his **r hand**; but	3225
SS	2: 6	my head, and his **r hand** doth embrace me.	3225
	8: 3	and his **r hand** should embrace me.	3225
Isa	9:20	he shall snatch on the **r hand**, and	3225
	10: 2	to take away the **r** from the poor of my	4941
	30:10	Prophesy not unto us **r** *things,* speak unto	5229
	30:21	when ye **turn to the r hand**, and when ye	541
	32: 7	even when the needy speaketh **r**.	4941
	41:10	I will uphold thee with the **r hand** of my	3225
	41:13	I the LORD thy God will hold thy **r hand**,	3225
	44:20	nor say, *Is there* not a lie in my **r hand**?	3225
	45: 1	to Cyrus, whose **r hand** I have holden, to	3225
	45:19	I declare **things that are r**.	4339
	48:13	and my **r hand** hath spanned the heavens:	3225
	54: 3	For thou shalt break forth *on* the **r hand**	3225
	62: 8	The LORD hath sworn by his **r hand**, and	3225
	63:12	That led *them* by the **r hand** of Moses *with*	3225
Jer	2:21	planted thee a noble vine, wholly a **r** seed:	571
	5:28	and the **r** of the needy do they not judge.	4941
	17:11	*so* he that getteth riches, and not by **r**,	4941
	17:16	out of my lips was **r before** thee.	5227+6440
	22:24	of Judah were the signet upon my **r** hand,	3225
	23:10	their course is evil, and their force *is* not **r**.	3651
	32: 7	for the **r** of redemption *is* thine to buy *it.*	4941
	32: 8	for the **r** of inheritance *is* thine, and	4941

Jer 34:15 now turned, and had done **r** in my sight, 3477
49: 5 be driven out every man **r forth**; 6440+3807.1
La 2: 3 he hath drawn back his **r hand** from before 3225
2: 4 *he* stood *with* his **r hand** as an adversary, 3225
3:35 To turn aside the **r** of a man before the face 4941
Eze 1:10 a man, and the face of a lion, on the **r side**: 3225
4: 6 lie again on thy **r** side, and thou shalt bear 3233
10: 3 Now the cherubims stood on the **r side** of 3225
16:46 that dwelleth at thy **r hand**, *is* Sodom and 3225
18: 5 be just, and do that which is lawful and **r**, 6666
18:19 son hath done that which is lawful and **r**, 6666
18:21 do that which is lawful and **r**, he shall 6666
18:27 doeth that which is lawful and **r**, he shall 6666
21:16 other, *either* **on the r hand**, *or* on the left, 3231
21:22 At his **r hand** was the divination for 3225
21:27 it shall be no *more,* until he come whose **r** 4941
33:14 his sin, and do that which is lawful and **r**; 6666
33:16 he hath done that which is lawful and **r**; 6666
33:19 do that which is lawful and **r**, he shall live 6666
39: 3 will cause thine arrows to fall out of thy **r** 3225
47: 1 from under from the **r** side of the house, 3233
47: 2 behold, there ran out waters on the **r** side. 3233
Da 12: 7 when he held up his **r hand** and his left 3225
Hos 14: 9 for the ways of the LORD *are* **r**, and 3477
Am 3:10 For they know not to do **r**, saith 5229
5:12 turn aside the poor in the gate *from their* **r**. NIH
Jnh 4:11 that cannot discern between their **r hand** 3225
Hab 2:16 the cup of the LORD'S **r hand** shall be 3225
Zec 3: 1 Satan standing at his **r hand** to resist him. 3225
4: 3 one upon the **r** *side* of the bowl, and 3225
4:11 What *are* these two olive trees upon the **r** 3225
11:17 *shall be* upon his arm, and upon his **r** eye: 3225
11:17 and his **r** eye shall be utterly darkened. 3225
12: 6 round about, on the **r hand** and on the left: 3225
Mal 3: 5 that turn aside the stranger *from his* **r**, and NIH
Mt 5:29 And if thy **r** eye offend thee, pluck it out, *1188*
5:30 And if thy **r** hand offend thee, cut it off, *1188*
5:39 whosoever shall smite thee on thy **r** cheek, *1188*
6: 3 let not thy left hand know what thy **r hand** *1188*
20: 4 and whatsoever is **r** I will give you. *1342*
20: 7 and whatsoever is **r**, *that* shall ye receive. *1342*
20:21 the one on thy **r hand**, and the other on *1188*
20:23 am baptized *with:* but to sit on my **r hand**, *1188*
22:44 said unto my Lord, Sit thou on my **r hand**, *1188*
25:33 And he shall set the sheep on his **r hand**, *1188*
25:34 shall the King say unto them on his **r hand**, *1188*
26:64 Son of man sitting on the **r hand** of power, *1188*
27:29 *it* upon his head, and a reed in his **r hand**: *1188*
27:38 one on the **r hand**, and another on the left. *1188*
Mk 5:15 sitting, and clothed, and **in** his **r mind**: *4993*
10:37 one on thy **r hand**, and the other on thy left *1188*
10:40 But to sit on my **r hand** and on my left *1188*
12:36 said to my Lord, Sit thou on my **r hand**, *1188*
14:62 Son of man sitting on the **r hand** of power, *1188*
15:27 the one on *his* **r hand**, and the other on his *1188*
16: 5 they saw a young man sitting on the **r side**, *1188*
16:19 into heaven, and sat on the **r hand** of God. *1188*
Lk 1:11 on the **r side** of the altar of incense. *1188*
6: 6 there was a man whose **r** hand was *1188*
8:35 feet of Jesus, clothed, and **in** his **r mind**: *4993*
10:28 he said unto him, Thou hast answered **r**: *3723*
12:57 even of yourselves judge ye not what *is* **r**? *1342*
20:42 said to my Lord, Sit thou on my **r hand**, *1188*
22:50 of the high priest, and cut off his **r** ear. *1188*
22:69 man sit on the **r hand** of the power of God. *1188*
23:33 one on the **r hand**, and the other on the left. *1188*
Jn 18:10 high priest's servant, and cut off his **r** ear. *1188*
21: 6 Cast the net on the **r** side of the ship, and *1188*
Ac 2:25 for he is on my **r hand**, that I should not be *1188*
2:33 Therefore being by the **r hand** of God *1188*
2:34 said unto my Lord, Sit thou on my **r hand**, *1188*
3: 7 And he took him by the **r** hand, and lift *him* *1188*
4:19 Whether it be **r** in the sight of God to *1342*
5:31 Him hath God exalted with his **r hand** *to* *1188*
7:55 and Jesus standing on the **r hand** of God, *1188*
7:56 the Son of man standing on the **r hand** of *1188*
8:21 for thy heart is not **r** in the sight of God. *2117*
13:10 wilt thou not cease to pervert the **r** ways of *2117*
Ro 8:34 *again,* who is even at the **r hand** of God, *1188*
2Co 6: 7 the armour of righteousness on the **r hand** *1188*
Gal 2: 9 and Barnabas the **r hands** of fellowship; *1188*
Eph 1:20 set *him* at his own **r hand** in the heavenly *1188*
6: 1 obey your parents in the Lord: for this is **r**. *1342*
Col 3: 1 where Christ sitteth on the **r hand** of God. *1188*
Heb 1: 3 sat down on the **r hand** of the Majesty on *1188*
1:13 Sit on my **r hand**, until I make thine *1188*
8: 1 who is set on the **r hand** of the throne of *1188*
10:12 for ever, sat down on the **r hand** of God; *1188*
12: 2 is set down at the **r hand** of the throne of *1188*
13:10 whereof they have no **r** to eat which serve *1849*
1Pe 3:22 into heaven, and is on the **r hand** of God; *1188*
2Pe 2:15 Which have forsaken the **r** way, and *2117*
Rev 1:16 And he had in his **r** hand seven stars: and *1188*
1:17 And he laid his **r** hand upon me, *1188*
1:20 stars which thou sawest in my **r hand**, *1188*
2: 1 that holdeth the seven stars in his **r hand**, *1188*
5: 1 And I saw in the **r hand** of him that sat on *1188*
5: 7 took the book out of the **r hand** of him that *1188*
10: 2 and he set his **r** foot upon the sea, and *1188*
13:16 to receive a mark in their **r** hand, or in their *1188*
22:14 that they may have **r** to the tree of life, and *1849*

RIGHTEOUS (238) [RIGHT]

Ge 7: 1 for thee have I seen **r** before me in this 6662
18:23 Wilt thou also destroy the **r** with 6662
18:24 Peradventure there be fifty **r** within 6662
18:24 not spare the place for the fifty **r** that *are* 6662
18:25 this manner, to slay the **r** with the wicked: 6662
18:25 that the **r** should be as the wicked, that be 6662
18:26 If I find in Sodom fifty **r** within the city, 6662
18:28 there shall lack five of the fifty **r**: 6662
20: 4 Lord, wilt thou slay also a **r** nation? 6662
38:26 and said, She hath been more **r** than I; 6663
Ex 9:27 the LORD *is* **r**, and I and my people *are* 6662
23: 7 and the innocent and **r** slay thou not: 6662
23: 8 the wise, and perverteth the words of the **r**. 6662
Nu 23:10 Let me die the death of the **r**, and let my 3477
Dt 4: 8 and judgments *so* **r** as all this law, 6662
16:19 of the wise, and pervert the words of the **r**. 6662
25: 1 they shall justify the **r**, and condemn 6662
Jdg 5:11 they rehearse the **r acts** of the LORD, 6666
5:11 *even* the **r acts** *towards the inhabitants* of 6666
1Sa 12: 7 the LORD of all the **r acts** of the LORD, 6666
24:17 he said to David, Thou *art* more **r** than I: 6662
2Sa 4:11 when wicked men have slain a **r** person in 6662
1Ki 2:32 who fell upon two men more **r** and 6662
8:32 justifying the **r**, to give him according to 6662
2Ki 10: 9 stood, and said to all the people, Ye *be* **r**: 6662
2Ch 6:23 by justifying the **r**, by giving him according 6662
12: 6 and they said, The LORD *is* **r**. 6662
Ezr 9:15 O LORD God of Israel, thou *art* **r**: for we 6662
Ne 9: 8 hast performed thy words; for thou *art* **r**: 6662
Job 4: 7 or where were the **r** cut off? 3477
9:15 Whom, though I were **r**, *yet* would I not 6663
10:15 and *if* I be **r**, *yet* will I not lift up my head. 6663
15:14 *is* born of a woman, that he should be **r**? 6663
17: 9 The **r** also shall hold on his way, and 6662
22: 3 pleasure to the Almighty, that thou art **r**? 6663
22:19 The **r** see *it*, and are glad: and the innocent 6662
23: 7 There the **r** *might* dispute with him; so 3477
32: 1 because he *was* **r** in his own eyes. 6662
34: 5 For Job hath said, I am **r**: and God hath 6663
35: 7 If thou be **r**, what givest thou him? or 6663
36: 7 He withdraweth not his eyes from the **r**: but 6662
40: 8 thou condemn me, that thou mayest be **r**? 6663
Ps 1: 5 nor sinners in the congregation of the **r**. 6662
1: 6 For the LORD knoweth the way of the **r**: 6662
5:12 For thou, LORD, wilt bless the **r**; 6662
7: 9 for the **r** God trieth the hearts and reins. 6662
7:11 God judgeth the **r**, and God is angry *with* 6662
11: 3 be destroyed, what can the **r** do? 6662
11: 5 The LORD trieth the **r**: but the wicked 6662
11: 7 For the **r** LORD loveth righteousness; 6662
14: 5 for God *is* in the generation of the **r**. 6662
19: 9 of the LORD *are* true *and* **r** altogether. 6663
31:18 and contemptuously against the **r**. 6662
32:11 Be glad in the LORD, and rejoice, ye **r**: 6662
33: 1 Rejoice in the LORD, O ye **r**: *for* praise is 6662
34:15 The eyes of the LORD *are* upon the **r**, and 6662
34:17 *The* **r** cry, and the LORD heareth, and NIH
34:19 Many *are* the afflictions of the **r**: but 6662
34:21 and they that hate the **r** shall be desolate. 6662
35:27 and be glad, that favour my **r cause**: 6664
37:16 A little that a **r** *man* hath *is* better than 6662
37:17 be broken: but the LORD upholdeth the **r**. 6662
37:21 but the **r** sheweth mercy, and giveth. 6662
37:25 yet have I not seen the **r** forsaken, nor his 6662
37:29 The **r** shall inherit the land, and 6662

Ps 37:30 The mouth of the r speaketh wisdom, and 6662
37:32 The wicked watcheth the r, and seeketh to 6662
37:39 the salvation of the r is of the LORD: 6662
52: 6 The r also shall see, and fear, and 6662
55:22 he shall never suffer the r to be moved. 6662
58:10 The r shall rejoice when he seeth 6662
58:11 shall say, Verily there is a reward for the r: 6662
64:10 The r shall be glad in the LORD, and 6662
68: 3 let the r be glad; let them rejoice before 6662
69:28 of the living, and not be written with the r. 6662
72: 7 In his days shall the r flourish; and 6662
75:10 but the horns of the r shall be exalted. 6662
92:12 The r shall flourish like the palm tree: 6662
94:21 together against the soul of the r, 6662
97:11 Light is sown for the r, and gladness for 6662
97:12 Rejoice in the LORD, ye r; and 6662
107:42 The r shall see it, and rejoice: and 3477
112: 4 is gracious, and full of compassion, and r. 6662
112: 6 the r shall be in everlasting remembrance. 6662
116: 5 Gracious is the LORD, and r; yea, 6662
118:15 and salvation is in the tabernacles of the r: 6662
118:20 of the LORD, into which the r shall enter. 6662
119: 7 when I shall have learned thy r judgments. 6664
119:62 unto thee because of thy r judgments. 6664
119:106 I will perform it, that I will keep thy r 6664
119:137 R art thou, O LORD, and upright are thy 6662
119:138 testimonies that thou hast commanded are r 6664
119:160 every one of thy r judgments endureth for 6664
119:164 do I praise thee because of thy r judgments. 6664
125: 3 wicked shall not rest upon the lot of the r; 6662
125: 3 lest the r put forth their hands unto iniquity. 6662
129: 4 The LORD is r: he hath cut asunder 6662
140:13 Surely the r shall give thanks unto thy 6662
141: 5 Let the r smite me; it shall be a kindness: 6662
142: 7 the r shall compass me about; for thou shalt 6662
145:17 The LORD is r in all his ways, and 6662
146: 8 are bowed down: the LORD loveth the r: 6662
Pr 2: 7 He layeth up sound wisdom for the r: he is 3477
2:20 of good men, and keep the paths of the r. 6662
3:32 to the LORD: but his secret is with the r. 3477
10: 3 The LORD will not suffer the soul of the r 6662
10:11 The mouth of a r man is a well of life: but 6662
10:16 The labour of the r tendeth to life: the fruit 6662
10:21 The lips of the r feed many: but fools die 6662
10:24 but the desire of the r shall be granted. 6662
10:25 but the r is an everlasting foundation. 6662
10:28 The hope of the r shall be gladness: but 6662
10:30 The r shall never be removed: but 6662
10:32 The lips of the r know what is acceptable: 6662
11: 8 The r is delivered out of trouble, and 6662
11:10 When it goeth well with the r, the city 6662
11:21 but the seed of the r shall be delivered. 6662
11:23 The desire of the r is only good: but 6662
11:28 but the r shall flourish as a branch. 6662
11:30 The fruit of the r is a tree of life; and 6662
11:31 the r shall be recompensed in the earth: 6662
12: 3 but the root of the r shall not be moved. 6662
12: 5 The thoughts of the r are right: but 6662
12: 7 are not: but the house of the r shall stand. 6662
12:10 A r man regardeth the life of his beast: but 6662
12:12 but the root of the r yieldeth fruit. 6662
12:26 The r is more excellent than his neighbour: 6662
13: 5 A r man hateth lying: but a wicked man is 6662
13: 9 The light of the r rejoiceth: but the lamp of 6662
13:21 but to the r good shall be repayed. 6662
13:25 The r eateth to the satisfying of his soul: 6662
14: 9 at sin: but among the r there is favour. 3477
14:19 and the wicked at the gates of the r. 6662
14:32 but the r hath hope in his death. 6662
15: 6 In the house of the r is much treasure: but 6662
15:19 but the way of the r is made plain. 3477
15:28 The heart of the r studieth to answer: but 6662
15:29 but he heareth the prayer of the r. 6662
16:13 R lips are the delight of kings; and 6664
18: 5 the wicked, to overthrow the r in judgment. 6662
18:10 the r runneth into it, and is safe. 6662
21:12 The r man wisely considereth the house of 6662
21:18 The wicked shall be a ransom for the r, and 6662
21:26 day long: but the r giveth and spareth not. 6662
23:24 The father of the r shall greatly rejoice: 6662
24:15 wicked man, against the dwelling of the r; 6662
24:24 He that saith unto the wicked, Thou art r; 6662
25:26 A r man falling down before the wicked is 6662
28: 1 man pursueth: but the r are bold as a lion. 6662
28:10 Whoso causeth the r to go astray in an evil 3477
28:12 When r men do rejoice, there is great glory: 6662
28:28 but when they perish, the r increase. 6662
29: 2 When the r are in authority, the people 6662
29: 6 is a snare: but the r doth sing and rejoice. 6662
29: 7 The r considereth the cause of the poor: but 6662
29:16 but the r shall see their fall. 6662
Ecc 3:17 God shall judge the r and the wicked: 6662
7:16 Be not r over much; neither make thyself 6662
8:14 it happeneth according to the work of the r: 6662
9: 1 that the r, and the wise, and their works, 6662
9: 2 there is one event to the r, and to 6662
Isa 3:10 Say ye to the r, that it shall be well with 6662
5:23 take away the righteousness of the r from 6662
24:16 have we heard songs, even glory to the r. 6662
26: 2 that the r nation which keepeth the truth 6662
41: 2 Who raised up the r man from the east, 6664
41:26 beforetime, that we may say, He is r? yea, 6662
53:11 by his knowledge shall my r servant justify 6662
57: 1 The r perisheth, and no man layeth it to 6662
57: 1 none considering that the r is taken away 6662
60:21 Thy people also shall be all r: they shall 6662
Jer 12: 1 R art thou, O LORD, when I plead with 6662
20:12 that triest the r, and seest the reins and 6662
23: 5 that I will raise unto David a r Branch, and 6662
La 1:18 The LORD is r; for I have rebelled 6662
Eze 3:20 When a r man doth turn from his 6662
3:21 Nevertheless if thou warn the r man, that 6662
3:21 warn the righteous man, that the r sin not, 6662
13:22 lies ye have made the heart of the r sad, 6662
16:52 they are more r than thou: yea, be thou 6663
18:20 the righteousness of the r shall be upon 6662
18:24 when the r turneth away from his 6662
18:26 When a r man turneth away from his 6662
21: 3 will cut off from thee the r and the wicked. 6662
21: 4 then that I will cut off from thee the r and 6662
23:45 the r men, they shall judge them after 6662
33:12 The righteousness of the r shall not deliver 6662
33:12 neither shall the r be able to live for his 6662
33:13 When I shall say to the r, that he shall 6662
33:18 When the r turneth from his righteousness, 6662
Da 9:14 for the LORD our God is r in all his 6662
Am 2: 6 because they sold the r for silver, and 6662
Hab 1: 4 for the wicked doth compass about the r; 6662
1:13 devoureth the man that is more r than he? 6662
Mal 3:18 and discern between the r and the wicked, 6662
Mt 9:13 for I am not come to call the r, but 1342
10:41 he that receiveth a r man in the name of a 1342
10:41 r man shall receive a righteous man's 1342
10:41 man shall receive a r man's reward. 1342
13:17 r men have desired to see those things 1342
13:43 Then shall the r shine forth as the sun in 1342
23:28 so ye also outwardly appear r unto men, 1342
23:29 and garnish the sepulchres of the r, 1342
23:35 That upon you may come all the r blood 1342
23:35 from the blood of r Abel unto the blood of 1342
25:37 Then shall the r answer him, saying, Lord, 1342
25:46 but the r into life eternal. 1342
Mk 2:17 I came not to call the r, but sinners to 1342
Lk 1: 6 And they were both r before God, 1342
5:32 I came not to call the r, but sinners to 1342
18: 9 trusted in themselves that they were r, 1342
23:47 saying, Certainly this was a r man. 1342
Jn 7:24 to the appearance, but judge r judgment. 1342
17:25 O r Father, the world hath not known thee: 1342
Ro 2: 5 and revelation of the r judgment of God; 1341
3:10 it is written, There is none r, no, not one: 1342
5: 7 For scarcely for a r man will one die: 1342
5:19 the obedience of one shall many be made r. 1342
2Th 1: 5 Which is a manifest token of the r 1342
1: 6 Seeing it is a r thing with God to 1342
1Ti 1: 9 that the law is not made for a r man, but 1342
2Ti 4: 8 which the Lord, the r judge, shall give me 1342
Heb 11: 4 by which he obtained witness that he was r, 1342
Jas 5:16 The effectual fervent prayer of a r man 1342
1Pe 3:12 For the eyes of the Lord are over the r, and 1342
4:18 And if the r scarcely be saved, where shall 1342
2Pe 2: 8 (For that r man dwelling among them, 1342
2: 8 vexed his r soul from day to day with their 1342
1Jn 2: 1 with the Father, Jesus Christ the r: 1342
2:29 If ye know that he is r, ye know that every 1342
3: 7 he that doeth righteousness is r, even as he 1342
3: 7 righteousness is righteous, even as he is r. 1342
3:12 own works were evil, and his brother's r. 1342

R

Rev 16: 5 Thou art **r**, O Lord, which art, and wast, *1342*
16: 7 true and **r** *are* thy judgments. *1342*
19: 2 For true and **r** *are* his judgments: for he *1342*
22:11 and *he that is* **r**, let him be righteous still: *1342*
22:11 and *he that is* righteous, let him be **r** still: *1344*

RIGHTEOUSLY (8) [RIGHT]

Dt 1:16 judge **r** between every man and his brother, 6664
Ps 67: 4 for thou shalt judge the people **r**, and 4334
96:10 he shall judge the people **r**. 4339+871.1
Pr 31: 9 judge **r**, and plead the cause of the poor and 6664
Isa 33:15 He that walketh **r**, and speaketh uprightly; 6666
Jer 11:20 that judgest **r**, that triest the reins and 6664
Tit 2:12 **r**, and godly, in *this* present world; *1346*
1Pe 2:23 committed *himself* to him that judgeth **r**: *1346*

RIGHTEOUSNESS (302) [RIGHT]

Ge 15: 6 the LORD; and he counted it to him *for* **r**. 6666
30:33 So shall my **r** answer for me in time to 6666
Lev 19:15 *but* in **r** shalt thou judge thy neighbour. 6664
Dt 6:25 it shall be our **r**, if we observe to do all 6666
9: 4 For my **r** the LORD hath brought me in to 6666
9: 5 Not for thy **r**, or for the uprightness of thine 6666
9: 6 not this good land to possess it for thy **r**; 6666
24:13 it shall be **r** unto thee before the LORD 6666
33:19 there they shall offer sacrifices of **r**: 6664
1Sa 26:23 The LORD render to every man his **r** and 6666
2Sa 22:21 LORD rewarded me according to my **r**: 6666
22:25 hath recompensed me according to my **r**; 6666
1Ki 3: 6 in **r**, and in uprightness of heart with thee; 6666
8:32 to give him according to his **r**. 6666
2Ch 6:23 by giving him according to his **r**. 6666
Job 6:29 be iniquity; yea, return again, my **r** *is* in it. 6664
8: 6 make the habitation of thy **r** prosperous. 6664
27: 6 My **r** I hold fast, and will not let it go: 6666
29:14 I put on **r**, and it clothed me: my judgment 6664
33:26 with joy: for he will render unto man his **r**. 6666
35: 2 *that* thou saidst, My **r** *is* more than God's? 6664
35: 8 and thy **r** *may profit* the son of man. 6666
36: 3 from afar, and will ascribe **r** to my Maker. 6664
Ps 4: 1 Hear me when I call, O God of my **r**: 6664
4: 5 Offer the sacrifices of **r**, and put your trust 6664
5: 8 in thy **r** because of mine enemies; 6666
7: 8 according to my **r**, and according to mine 6664
7:17 I will praise the LORD according to his **r**: 6664
9: 8 he shall judge the world in **r**, he shall 6664
11: 7 For the righteous LORD loveth **r**; 6666
15: 2 worketh **r**, and speaketh the truth in his 6664
17:15 *As for* me, I will behold thy face in **r**: 6664
18:20 LORD rewarded me according to my **r**; 6664
18:24 recompensed me according to my **r**, 6664
22:31 shall declare his **r** unto a people that *shall* 6666
23: 3 he leadeth me in the paths of **r** for his 6664
24: 5 and **r** from the God of his salvation. 6666
31: 1 me never be ashamed: deliver me in thy **r**. 6666
33: 5 He loveth **r** and judgment: the earth is full 6666
35:24 O LORD my God, according to thy **r**; 6664
35:28 my tongue shall speak of thy **r** *and* of thy 6664
36: 6 Thy **r** *is* like the great mountains; 6666
36:10 know thee; and thy **r** to the upright in heart. 6666
37: 6 he shall bring forth thy **r** as the light, and 6664
40: 9 I have preached **r** in the great congregation: 6664
40:10 I have not hid thy **r** within my heart; I have 6666
45: 4 of truth and meekness *and* **r**; 6664
45: 7 Thou lovest **r**, and hatest wickedness: 6664
48:10 ends of the earth: thy right hand is full *of* **r**. 6664
50: 6 the heavens shall declare his **r**: for God *is* 6664
51:14 *and* my tongue shall sing aloud of thy **r**. 6666
51:19 thou be pleased with the sacrifices of **r**, 6664
52: 3 than good; *and* lying rather than to speak **r**. 6664
58: 1 Do ye indeed speak **r**, O congregation? 6664
65: 5 *By* terrible *things* in **r** wilt thou answer us, 6664
69:27 and let them not come into thy **r**. 6666
71: 2 Deliver me in thy **r**, and cause me to 6666
71:15 My mouth shall shew forth thy **r** *and* 6666
71:16 I will make mention of thy **r**, *even* of thine 6666
71:19 Thy **r** also, O God, *is* very high, who hast 6666
71:24 My tongue also shall talk of thy **r** all 6666
72: 1 O God, and thy **r** unto the king's son. 6666
72: 2 He shall judge thy people with **r**, and 6664
72: 3 to the people, and the little hills, by **r**. 6666
85:10 **r** and peace have kissed *each other.* 6664
85:11 and **r** shall look down from heaven. 6664
85:13 **R** shall go before him; and shall set *us* in 6664
88:12 and thy **r** in the land of forgetfulness? 6666
89:16 the day: and in thy **r** shall they be exalted. 6666
94:15 judgment shall return unto **r**: and all 6664
96:13 he shall judge the world with **r**, and 6664
97: 2 **r** and judgment *are* the habitation of his 6664
97: 6 The heavens declare his **r**, and all 6664
98: 2 his **r** hath he openly shewed in the sight of 6666
98: 9 with **r** shall he judge the world, and 6664
99: 4 thou executest judgment and **r** in Jacob. 6666
103: 6 The LORD executeth **r** and judgment for 6666
103:17 fear him, and his **r** unto children's children; 6666
106: 3 *and* he that doeth **r** at all times. 6666
106:31 *that* was counted unto him for **r** unto all 6666
111: 3 and glorious: and his **r** endureth for ever. 6666
112: 3 *be* in his house: and his **r** endureth for ever. 6666
112: 9 given to the poor; his **r** endureth for ever; 6666
118:19 Open to me the gates of **r**: I will go into 6664
119:40 after thy precepts: quicken me in thy **r**. 6666
119:123 for thy salvation, and for the word of thy **r**. 6664
119:142 Thy **r** *is* an everlasting righteousness, and 6666
119:142 Thy righteousness *is* an everlasting **r**, and 6664
119:144 The **r** of thy testimonies *is* everlasting: give 6664
119:172 thy word: for all thy commandments *are* **r**. 6664
132: 9 Let thy priests be clothed *with* **r**; and let thy 6664
143: 1 in thy faithfulness answer me, *and* in thy **r**. 6666
145: 7 thy great goodness, and shall sing of thy **r**. 6666
Pr 2: 9 shalt thou understand **r**, and judgment, 6664
8: 8 All the words of my mouth *are* in **r**; *there is* 6664
8:18 *are* with me; *yea,* durable riches and **r**. 6666
8:20 I lead in the way of **r**, in the midst of 6666
10: 2 profit nothing: but **r** delivereth from death. 6666
11: 4 day of wrath: but **r** delivereth from death. 6666
11: 5 The **r** of the perfect shall direct his way: 6666
11: 6 The **r** of the upright shall deliver them: but 6666
11:18 *to* him that soweth **r** *shall be* a sure reward. 6666
11:19 As **r** *tendeth* to life: so he that pursueth evil 6666
12:17 *He that* speaketh truth sheweth forth **r**: but 6664
12:28 In the way of **r** *is* life; and *in* the pathway 6666
13: 6 **R** keepeth *him that is* upright in the way: 6666
14:34 **R** exalteth a nation: but sin *is* a reproach to 6666
15: 9 but he loveth him that followeth after **r**. 6666
16: 8 Better *is* a little with **r** than great revenues 6666
16:12 for the throne is established by **r**. 6666
16:31 of glory, *if* it be found in the way of **r**. 6666
21:21 He that followeth after **r** and mercy findeth 6666
21:21 and mercy findeth life, **r**, and honour. 6666
25: 5 and his throne shall be established in **r**. 6664
Ecc 3:16 the place of **r**, *that* iniquity *was* there. 6664
7:15 there is a just *man* that perisheth in his **r**, 6664
Isa 1:21 **r** lodged in it; but now murderers. 6664
1:26 be called, The city of **r**, the faithful city. 6664
1:27 with judgment, and her converts with **r**. 6666
5: 7 behold oppression; for **r**, but behold a cry. 6666
5:16 and God that is holy shall be sanctified in **r**. 6666
5:23 take away the **r** of the righteous from him. 6666
10:22 consumption decreed shall overflow *with* **r**. 6666
11: 4 with **r** shall he judge the poor, and 6664
11: 5 **r** shall be the girdle of his loins, and 6664
16: 5 and seeking judgment, and hasting **r**. 6664
26: 9 the inhabitants of the world will learn **r**. 6664
26:10 to the wicked, *yet* will he not learn **r**: 6664
28:17 will I lay to the line, and **r** to the plummet: 6666
32: 1 a king shall reign in **r**, and princes shall 6664
32:16 and **r** remain in the fruitful field. 6666
32:17 the work of **r** shall be peace; and the effect 6666
32:17 the effect of **r** quietness and assurance for 6666
33: 5 he hath filled Zion *with* judgment and **r**. 6666
41:10 uphold thee with the right hand of my **r**. 6664
42: 6 I the LORD have called thee in **r**, and 6664
45: 8 from above, and let the skies pour down **r**: 6664
45: 8 forth salvation, and let **r** spring up together; 6666
45:13 I have raised him up in **r**, and I will direct 6664
45:19 I the LORD speak **r**, I declare things that 6664
45:23 the word is gone out of my mouth *in* **r**, and 6666
45:24 in the LORD have I **r** and strength: 6666
46:12 ye stouthearted, that *are* far from **r**: 6666
46:13 I bring near my **r**; it shall not be far off, and 6666
48: 1 the God of Israel, *but* not in truth, nor in **r**. 6666
48:18 as a river, and thy **r** as the waves of the sea: 6666
51: 1 Hearken to me, ye that follow after **r**, 6664
51: 5 My **r** *is* near; my salvation is gone forth, 6664
51: 6 for ever, and my **r** shall not be abolished. 6666
51: 7 Hearken unto me, ye that know **r**, 6664
51: 8 my **r** shall be for ever, and my salvation 6666

Isa 54:14 In r shalt thou be established: thou shalt be 6666
54:17 and their r *is* of me, saith the LORD. 6666
56: 1 *is* near to come, and my r to be revealed. 6666
57:12 I will declare thy r, and thy works; for they 6666
58: 2 as a nation that did r, and forsook not 6666
58: 8 thy r shall go before thee; the glory of 6664
59:16 unto him; and his r, it sustained him. 6666
59:17 For he put on r as a breastplate, and 6666
60:17 thy officers peace, and thine exactors r. 6666
61: 3 that they might be called trees of r, 6664
61:10 he hath covered me with the robe of r, as a 6666
61:11 so the Lord GOD will cause r and 6666
62: 1 until the r thereof go forth as brightness, 6664
62: 2 the Gentiles shall see thy r, and all kings 6664
63: 1 I that speak in r, mighty to save. 6666
64: 5 meetest him that rejoiceth and worketh r, 6664
Jer 4: 2 in truth, in judgment, and in r; 6666
9:24 judgment, and r, in the earth: 6666
22: 3 Execute ye judgment and r, and deliver 6666
23: 6 he shall be called, THE LORD OUR R. 6664
33:15 will I cause the Branch of r to grow up 6666
33:15 he shall execute judgment and r in the land. 6666
33:16 she shall be called, The LORD our r. 6664
51:10 The LORD hath brought forth our r: 6666
Eze 3:20 When a righteous *man* doth turn from his r, 6664
3:20 his r which he hath done shall not be 6666
14:14 *but* their own souls by their r, 6666
14:20 *but* deliver their own souls by their r. 6666
18:20 the r of the righteous shall be upon him, 6666
18:22 in his r that he hath done he shall live. 6666
18:24 the righteous turneth away from his r, 6666
18:24 All his r that he hath done shall not be 6666
18:26 a righteous *man* turneth away from his r, 6666
33:12 The r of the righteous shall not deliver him 6666
33:12 to live for his *r* in the day that he sinneth. NIH
33:13 if he trust to his own r, and 6666
33:18 When the righteous turneth from his r, and 6666
Da 4:27 break off thy sins by r, and thine iniquities 6665
9: 7 r *belongeth* unto thee, but unto us 6666
9:16 O Lord, according to all thy r, I beseech 6666
9:24 to bring in everlasting r, and to seal up 6664
12: 3 they that **turn** many **to** r as the stars for 6663
Hos 2:19 I will betroth thee unto me in r, and 6664
10:12 Sow to yourselves in r, reap in mercy; 6666
10:12 till he come and rain r upon you. 6664
Am 5: 7 to wormwood, and leave off r in the earth, 6666
5:24 down as waters, and r as a mighty stream. 6666
6:12 into gall, and the fruit of r into hemlock: 6666
Mic 6: 5 that *ye* may know the r of the LORD. 6666
7: 9 forth to the light, *and* I shall behold his r. 6666
Zep 2: 3 his judgment; seek r, seek meekness: 6664
Zec 8: 8 and I will be their God, in truth and in r. 6666
Mal 3: 3 may offer unto the LORD an offering in r. 6666
4: 2 the Sun of r arise with healing in his wings; 6666
Mt 3:15 for thus it becometh us to fulfil all r. 1343
5: 6 *are* they which do hunger and thirst after r: 1343
5:20 That except your r shall exceed 1343
5:20 shall exceed *the* r of the scribes NIG
6:33 seek ye first the kingdom of God, and his r; 1343
21:32 For John came unto you in the way of r, 1343
Lk 1:75 In holiness and r before him, all the days of 1343
Jn 16: 8 the world of sin, and of r, and of judgment: 1343
16:10 Of r, because I go to my Father, and ye see 1343
Ac 10:35 and worketh r, is accepted with him. 1343
13:10 *thou* child of the devil, *thou* enemy of all r, 1343
17:31 in the which he will judge the world in r by 1343
24:25 And as he reasoned of r, temperance, and 1343
Ro 1:17 For therein is the r of God revealed from 1343
2:26 Therefore if the uncircumcision keep the r 1345
3: 5 But if our unrighteousness commend the r 1343
3:21 But now the r of God without the law is 1343
3:22 Even the r of God *which is* by faith of 1343
3:25 to declare his r for the remission of sins 1343
3:26 To declare, *I say,* at this time his r: that he 1343
4: 3 and it was counted unto him for r. 1343
4: 5 the ungodly, his faith is counted for r. 1343
4: 6 unto whom God imputeth r without works, 1343
4: 9 that faith was reckoned to Abraham for r. 1343
4:11 a seal of the r of the faith which he had *yet* 1343
4:11 that r might be imputed unto them also: 1343
4:13 through the law, but through the r of faith. 1343
4:22 And therefore it was imputed to him for r. 1343
5:17 of the gift of r shall reign in life by one, 1343
5:18 by the r of one *the free gift came* upon all 1345
5:21 might grace reign through r unto eternal 1343
6:13 your members *as* instruments of r unto 1343
6:16 of sin unto death, or of obedience unto r? 1343
6:18 free from sin, ye became the servants of r. 1343
6:19 now yield your members servants to r unto 1343
6:20 the servants of sin, ye were free from r. 1343
8: 4 That the r of the law might be fulfilled in 1345
8:10 of sin; but the Spirit *is* life because of r. 1343
9:28 he will finish the work, and cut *it* short in r: 1343
9:30 the Gentiles, which followed not *after* r, 1343
9:30 not *after* righteousness, have attained to r, 1343
9:30 even the r which is of faith. 1343
9:31 which followed *after* the law of r, 1343
9:31 hath not attained to the law of r. 1343
10: 3 For they being ignorant of God's r, and 1343
10: 3 and going about to establish their own r, 1343
10: 3 have not submitted themselves unto the r of 1343
10: 4 For Christ *is* the end of the law for r to 1343
10: 5 For Moses describeth the r which is of 1343
10: 6 But the r which is of faith speaketh on this 1343
10:10 For with the heart *man* believeth unto r; 1343
14:17 but r, and peace, and joy in the Holy Ghost. 1343
1Co 1:30 and r, and sanctification, and redemption: 1343
15:34 Awake to r, and sin not: for some have not 1346
2Co 3: 9 much more doth the ministration of r 1343
5:21 that we might be made the r of God in him. 1343
6: 7 by the armour of r on the right hand and 1343
6:14 for what fellowship hath r with 1343
9: 9 given to the poor: his r remaineth for ever. 1343
9:10 and increase the fruits of your r;) 1343
11:15 also be transformed as the ministers of r; 1343
Gal 2:21 for if r *come* by the law, then Christ is dead 1343
3: 6 and it was accounted to him for r. 1343
3:21 verily r should have been by the law. 1343
5: 5 the Spirit wait for the hope of r by faith. 1343
Eph 4:24 which after God is created in r and 1343
5: 9 Spirit *is* in all goodness and r and truth;) 1343
6:14 and having on the breastplate of r; 1343
Php 1:11 Being filled with the fruits of r, which are 1343
3: 6 touching the r which is in the law, 1343
3: 9 not having mine own r, which is of the law, 1343
3: 9 of Christ, the r which is of God by faith: 1343
1Ti 6:11 flee these *things;* and follow *after* r, 1343
2Ti 2:22 but follow r, faith, charity, peace, 1343
3:16 for correction, for instruction in r: 1343
4: 8 there is laid up for me a crown of r, 1343
Tit 3: 5 Not by works of r which we have done, but 1343
Heb 1: 8 a sceptre of r *is* the sceptre of thy kingdom. 2118
1: 9 Thou hast loved r, and hated iniquity; 1343
5:13 that useth milk *is* unskilful in the word of r: 1343
7: 2 first being by interpretation King of r, and 1343
11: 7 and became heir of the r which is by faith. 1343
11:33 wrought r, obtained promises, stopped 1343
12:11 of r unto them which are exercised thereby. 1343
Jas 1:20 For the wrath of man worketh not the r of 1343
2:23 and it was imputed unto him for r: 1343
3:18 And the fruit of r is sown in peace of them 1343
1Pe 2:24 being dead to sins, should live unto r: 1343
2Pe 1: 1 precious faith with us through the r of God 1343
2: 5 Noah the eighth *person,* a preacher of r, 1343
2:21 for them not to have known the way of r, 1343
3:13 and a new earth, wherein dwelleth r. 1343
1Jn 2:29 ye know that every one which doeth r is 1343
3: 7 he that doeth r is righteous, even as he is 1343
3:10 whosoever doeth not r is not of God, 1343
Rev 19: 8 white: for the fine linen is the r of saints. 1345
19:11 True, and in r he doth judge and make war. 1343

RIGHTEOUSNESS' (4) [RIGHT]

Ps 143:11 for thy r sake bring my soul out of trouble. 6666
Isa 42:21 The LORD is well pleased for his r sake; 6664
Mt 5:10 Blessed *are* they which are persecuted for r 1343
1Pe 3:14 But and if ye suffer for r sake, happy *are* 1343

RIGHTEOUSNESSES (3) [RIGHT]

Isa 64: 6 and all our r *are* as filthy rags; 6666
Eze 33:13 all his r shall not be remembered; 6666
Da 9:18 our supplications before thee for our r, 6666

RIGHTLY (4) [RIGHT]

Ge 27:36 he said, Is not he r named Jacob? for he 3588
Lk 7:43 And he said unto him, Thou hast r judged. 3723
20:21 we know that thou sayest and teachest r, 3723
2Ti 2:15 be ashamed, r **dividing** the word of truth. 3718

RIGOUR (5)
Ex 1:13 made the children of Israel to serve with r: 6531
1:14 wherein they made them serve, *was* with r. 6531
Lev 25:43 Thou shalt not rule over him with r; but 6531
25:46 ye shall not rule one over another with r. 6531
25:53 *the other* shall not rule with r over him in 6531

RIMMON (14) [GATH-RIMMON, HADADRIMMON, RIMMON-PAREZ]
Jos 15:32 And Lebaoth, and Shilhim, and Ain, and R: 7417
Jdg 20:45 toward the wilderness unto the rock of R: 7417
20:47 and fled to the wilderness unto the rock R, 7417
20:47 and abode in the rock R four months. 7417
21:13 of Benjamin that *were* in the rock R, 7417
2Sa 4: 2 the sons of R a Beerothite, of the children 7417
4: 5 the sons of R the Beerothite, Rechab and 7417
4: 9 the sons of R the Beerothite, and said unto 7417
2Ki 5:18 goeth *into* the house of R to worship there, 7417
5:18 and I bow myself *in* the house of R: 7417
5:18 when I bow down myself *in* the house of R, 7417
1Ch 4:32 Ain, R, and Tochen, and Ashan, five cities: 7417
6:77 R with her suburbs, Tabor with her 7417
Zec 14:10 a plain from Geba to R south of Jerusalem: 7417

RIMMON PEREZ See RIMMON-PAREZ

RIMMON-PAREZ (2) [RIMMON]
Nu 33:19 departed from Rithmah, and pitched at R. 7428
33:20 they departed from R, and pitched in 7428

RING (11) [EARRING, EARRINGS, RANG, RINGLEADER, RINGS, RINGSTRAKED]
Ge 41:42 Pharaoh took off his r from his hand, and 2885
Ex 26:24 together above the head of it unto one r: 2885
36:29 together at the head thereof, to one r: 2885
Est 3:10 the king took his r from his hand, and 2885
3:12 was it written, and sealed with the king's r. 2885
8: 2 the king took off his r, which he had taken 2885
8: 8 king's name, and seal *it* with the king's r: 2885
8: 8 sealed with the king's r, may no man 2885
8:10 sealed *it* with the king's r, and sent letters 2885
Lk 15:22 and put *it* on him; and put a r on his hand, *1146*
Jas 2: 2 unto your assembly a man **with a gold** r, *5554*

RINGLEADER (1) [LEAD, RING]
Ac 24: 5 and a r of the sect of the Nazarenes: *4414*

RINGS (44) [RING]
Ex 25:12 And thou shalt cast four r of gold for it, and 2885
25:12 two r *shall be* in the one side of it, and 2885
25:12 side of it, and two r in the other side of it. 2885
25:14 thou shalt put the staves into the r by 2885
25:15 The staves shall be in the r of the ark: 2885
25:26 thou shalt make for it four r of gold, and 2885
25:26 put the r in the four corners that *are* on 2885
25:27 Over against the border shall the r be for 2885
26:29 make their r *of* gold *for* places for the bars: 2885
27: 4 upon the net shalt thou make four brasen r 2885
27: 7 the staves shall be put into the r, and 2885
28:23 thou shalt make upon the breastplate two r 2885
28:23 shalt put the two r on the two ends of 2885
28:24 r *which are* on the ends of the breastplate. 2885
28:26 thou shalt make two r of gold, and 2885
28:27 two *other* r of gold thou shalt make, and 2885
28:28 they shall bind the breastplate by the r 2885
28:28 unto the r of the ephod with a lace of blue, 2885
30: 4 two golden r shalt thou make to it under 2885
35:22 and earrings, and r, and tablets, 2885
36:34 made their r *of* gold *to be* places for 2885
37: 3 he cast for it four r of gold, *to be set* by 2885
37: 3 even two r upon the one side of it, and 2885
37: 3 of it, and two r upon the other side of it. 2885
37: 5 he put the staves into the r by the sides of 2885
37:13 he cast for it four r of gold, and put 2885
37:13 put the r upon the four corners that *were* in 2885
37:14 Over against the border were the r, 2885
37:27 he made two r of gold for it under 2885
38: 5 he cast four r for the four ends of the grate 2885
38: 7 he put the staves into the r on the sides of 2885
39:16 made two ouches *of* gold, and two gold r; 2885
39:16 put the two r in the two ends of 2885
39:17 in the two r on the ends of the breastplate. 2885
39:19 they made two r of gold, and put *them* on 2885
39:20 they made two *other* golden r, and put them 2885
39:21 they did bind the breastplate by his r unto 2885
39:21 unto the r of the ephod with a lace of blue, 2885
Nu 31:50 and bracelets, r, earrings, and tablets, 2885
Est 1: 6 and purple to silver r and pillars of marble: 1550
SS 5:14 His hands *are as* gold r set with the beryl: 1550
Isa 3:21 The r, and nose jewels, 2885
Eze 1:18 As for their r, they were so high that they 1354
1:18 their r *were* full *of* eyes round about them 1354

RINGSTRAKED (7) [RING]
Ge 30:35 removed that day the he goats that were r 6124
30:39 brought forth cattle r, speckled, and 6124
30:40 set the faces of the flocks toward the r, and 6124
31: 8 if he said thus, The r shall be thy hire; then 6124
31: 8 shall be thy hire; then bare all the cattle r. 6124
31:10 rams which leaped upon the cattle *were* r, 6124
31:12 the rams which leap upon the cattle *are* r, 6124

RINNAH (1)
1Ch 4:20 and R, Ben-hanan, and Tilon. 7441

RINSED (3)
Lev 6:28 it shall be both scoured, and r in water. 7857
15:11 hath not r his hands in water, he shall wash 7857
15:12 every vessel of wood shall be r in water. 7857

RIOT (3) [RIOTING, RIOTOUS]
Tit 1: 6 having faithful children not accused of r or *810*
1Pe 4: 4 run not with *them* to the same excess of r, *810*
2Pe 2:13 *as* they that count it pleasure to r in the day *5172*

RIOTING (1) [RIOT]
Ro 13:13 not in r and drunkenness, not in *2970*

RIOTOUS (3) [RIOT]
Pr 23:20 amongst r **eaters** of flesh: 2151
28: 7 he that is a companion of r *men* shameth 2151
Lk 15:13 and there wasted his substance with r living. *811*

RIP (1) [RIPT]
2Ki 8:12 and r **up** their women with child. 1234

RIPE (8) [FIRSTRIPE, RIPENING, UNRIPE]
Ge 40:10 the clusters thereof **brought forth** r grapes: 1310
Ex 22:29 not delay *to offer the first of* thy r **fruits**, 4395
Nu 13:20 Now the time *was* the time of the **first** r 1061
18:13 *And* whatsoever is **first** r in the land, 1061
Jer 24: 2 good figs, *even* like the figs *that are* **first** r: 1073
Joel 3:13 Put ye in the sickle, for the harvest is r: 1310
Rev 14:15 to reap; for the harvest of the earth is r. *3583*
14:18 vine of the earth; for her grapes are **fully** r. *187*

RIPENING (1) [RIPE]
Isa 18: 5 and the sour grape is r in the flower, 1580

RIPHATH (2)
Ge 10: 3 Ashkenaz, and R, and Togarmah. 7384
1Ch 1: 6 Ashchenaz, and R, and Togarmah. 7384

RIPT (3) [RIP]
2Ki 15:16 therein that were with child he r **up**. 1234
Hos 13:16 and their women with child shall be r **up**. 1234
Am 1:13 they have r **up** the women with child at 1234

RISE (142) [ARISE, ARISETH, ARISING, AROSE, RISEN, RISEST, RISETH, RISING, ROSE, SUNRISING]
Ge 19: 2 ye shall r **up early**, and go on your ways. 7925
31:35 my lord that I cannot r **up** before thee; 6965
Ex 8:20 R **up early** in the morning, and 7925
9:13 R **up early** in the morning, and 7925
12:31 R **up**, *and* get you forth from amongst my 6965
21:19 If he r **again**, and walk abroad upon his 6965
Lev 19:32 Thou shalt r **up** before the hoary head, and 6965
Nu 10:35 R **up**, LORD, and let thine enemies be 6965
22:20 come to call thee, r **up**, *and* go with them; 6965
23:18 and said, R **up**, Balak, and hear; 6965
23:24 the people shall r **up** as a great lion, and 6965
24:17 a Sceptre shall r out of Israel, and 6965
Dt 2:13 Now r **up**, *said I,* and get you over 6965
2:24 R ye **up**, take your journey, and pass over 6965
19:11 r **up** against him, and smite him mortally 6965
19:15 One witness shall not r **up** against a man 6965
19:16 If a false witness r **up** against any man to 6965
28: 7 r **up** against thee *to be* smitten before thy 6965
29:22 of your children that shall r **up** after you, 6965

Dt 31:16 this people will **r up**, and go a whoring 6965
32:38 let them **r up** and help you, *and* be your 6965
33:11 smite through the loins of them that **r** 6965
33:11 of them that hate him, that they **r** not again. 6965
Jos 8: 7 ye shall **r up** from the ambush, and 6965
18: 4 they shall **r**, and go through the land, and 6965
Jdg 8:21 Zalmunna said, **R** thou, and fall upon us: 6965
9:33 thou shalt **r early**, and set upon the city: 7925
20:38 **make** a great flame with smoke **r up** out of 5927
1Sa 22:13 that *he* should **r** against me, to lie in wait, 6965
24: 7 and suffered them not to **r** against Saul. 6965
29:10 Wherefore now **r up early** in the morning 7925
2Sa 12:21 child was dead, thou didst **r** and eat bread. 6965
18:32 all that **r** against thee to do *thee* hurt, be as 6965
2Ki 16: 7 the king of Israel, which **r up** against me. 6965
Ne 2:18 they said, Let us **r up** and build. So they 6965
Job 20:27 and the earth shall **r up** against him. 6965
30:12 Upon *my* right hand **r** the youth; they push 6965
Ps 3: 1 many *are* they that **r up** against me. 6965
17: 7 *in thee* from those that **r up** *against them.* 6965
18:38 wounded them that they were not able to **r**: 6965
18:48 thou liftest me up above those that **r up** 6965
27: 3 though war should **r** against me, in this *will* 6965
35:11 False witnesses did **r up**; they laid to my 6965
36:12 are cast down, and shall not be able to **r**. 6965
41: 8 and *now* that he lieth he shall **r up** no more. 6965
44: 5 we tread them under that **r up** against us. 6965
59: 1 defend me from them that **r up** against me. 6965
74:23 the tumult of those that **r up** against thee 6965
92:11 *desire* of the wicked that **r up** against me. 6965
94:16 Who will **r up** for me against 6965
119:62 At midnight I will **r** to give thanks unto 6965
127: 2 *It is* vain for you to **r up** early, to sit up 6965
139:21 am not I grieved with those that **r up** 8618
140:10 into deep pits, *that* they **r** not **up again**. 6965
Pr 24:22 For their calamity shall **r** suddenly; and 6965
28:12 but when the wicked **r**, a man is hidden. 6965
28:28 When the wicked **r**, men hide themselves: 6965
Ecc 10: 4 If the spirit of the ruler **r up** against thee, 5927
12: 4 he shall **r up** at the voice of the bird, and 6965
SS 2:10 **R up**, my love, my fair one, and 6965
3: 2 I will **r** now, and go about the city in 6965
Isa 5:11 Woe unto them that **r up early** in 7925
14:21 *that* they do not **r**, nor possess the land, 6965
14:22 For I will **r up** against them, saith 6965
24:20 upon it; and it shall fall, and not **r** again. 6965
26:14 not live; *they are* deceased, they shall not **r**: 6965
28:21 For the LORD shall **r up** as *in* mount 6965
32: 9 **R up**, ye women that are at ease, hear my 6965
33:10 Now will I **r**, saith the LORD; now will I 6965
43:17 shall lie down together, they shall not **r**: 6965
54:17 every tongue *that* shall **r** against thee in 6965
58:10 shall thy light **r** in obscurity, and 2224
Jer 25:27 spue, and fall, and **r** no more, because 6965
37:10 *yet* should they **r up** every man in his tent, 6965
47: 2 waters **r up** out of the north, and shall be an 5927
49:14 come against her, and **r up** to the battle. 6965
51: 1 in the midst of them that **r up** against me, 6965
51:64 shall not **r** from the evil that I *will* bring 6965
La 1:14 *from whom* I am not able to **r up**. 6965
Da 7:24 another shall **r** after them; and he shall be 6966
Am 5: 2 of Israel is fallen; she shall no more **r**: 6965
7: 9 I will **r** against the house of Jeroboam with 6965
8: 8 it shall **r up** wholly as a flood; and it shall 5927
8:14 even they shall fall, and never **r up** again. 6965
9: 5 it shall **r up** wholly like a flood; and 5927
Ob 1: 1 and let us **r up** against her in battle. 6965
Na 1: 9 affliction shall not **r up** the second time. 6965
Hab 2: 7 Shall they not **r up** suddenly that *shall* bite 6965
Zep 3: 8 until the day that I **r up** to the prey: 6965
Zec 14:13 his hand shall **r up** against the hand of his 5927
Mt 5:45 for he **maketh** his sun **to r** on the evil and *393*
10:21 the children shall **r up against** *their* *1881*
12:41 *The* men of Nineveh shall **r** in judgment *450*
12:42 *The* queen of the south shall **r up** in *1453*
20:19 and the third day he shall **r again**. *450*
24: 7 For nation shall **r** against nation, and *1453*
24:11 And many false prophets shall **r**, and *1453*
26:46 **R**, let us be going: behold, he is at hand *1453*
27:63 yet alive, After three days I will **r** *again.* *1453*
Mk 3:26 And if Satan **r up** against himself, and *450*
4:27 and **r** night and day, and the seed should *1453*
8:31 and be killed, and after three days **r again**. *450*
9:31 after that he is killed, he shall **r** the third day. *450*
10:34 kill him: and the third day he shall **r again**. *450*
10:49 saying unto him, Be of good comfort, **r**; *1453*
12:23 the resurrection therefore, when they shall **r**, *450*
12:25 For when they shall **r** from the dead, *450*
12:26 And as touching the dead, that they **r**: *1453*
13: 8 For nation shall **r** against nation, and *1453*
13:12 children shall **r up** against *their* parents, *1881*
13:22 For false Christs and false prophets shall **r**, *1453*
14:42 **R up**, let us go; lo, he that betrayeth me is *1453*
Lk 5:23 be forgiven thee; or to say, **R up** and walk? *1453*
6: 8 **R up**, and stand *forth* in the midst. *1453*
11: 7 are with me in bed; I cannot **r** and give thee? *450*
11: 8 Though he will not **r** and give him, because *450*
11: 8 yet because of his importunity he will **r** and *450*
11:31 *The* queen of the south shall **r up** in *1453*
11:32 *The* men of Nineveh shall **r up** in *450*
12:54 When ye see a cloud **r out** of the west, *393*
18:33 to death: and the third day he shall **r again**. *450*
21:10 Nation shall **r** against nation, and *1453*
22:46 **r** and pray, lest ye enter into temptation. *450*
24: 7 and be crucified, and the third day **r again**. *450*
24:46 and to **r** from the dead the third day: *450*
Jn 5: 8 unto him, **R**, take up thy bed, and walk. *1453*
11:23 saith unto her, Thy brother shall **r again**. *450*
11:24 I know that he shall **r again** in *450*
20: 9 that he must **r again** from the dead. *450*
Ac 3: 6 the name of Jesus Christ of Nazareth **r up** *1453*
10:13 And there came a voice to him, **R**, Peter; *450*
26:16 But **r**, and stand upon thy feet: for I have *450*
26:23 that he *should be* the first *that* should **r** from *386*
Ro 15:12 and he that *shall* **r** to reign over the Gentiles; *450*
1Co 15:15 raised not up, if so be that the dead **r** not. *1453*
15:16 For if the dead **r** not, then is not Christ *1453*
15:29 for the dead, if the dead **r** not at all? *1453*
15:32 what advantageth it me, if the dead **r** not? *1453*
1Th 4:16 of God: and the dead in Christ shall **r** first: *450*
Heb 7:11 should **r** after the order of Melchisedec, *450*
Rev 11: 1 **R**, and measure the temple of God, and *1453*
13: 1 and saw a beast **r up** out of the sea, *305*

RISEN (51) [RISE]

Ge 19:23 The sun was **r** upon the earth when Lot 3318
Ex 22: 3 If the sun be **r** upon him, *there shall be* 2224
Nu 32:14 ye are **r up** in your fathers' stead, 6965
Jdg 9:18 ye are **r up** against my father's house *this* 6965
Ru 2:15 when she was **r up** to glean, Boaz 6965
1Sa 25:29 Yet a man is **r** to pursue thee, and to seek 6965
2Sa 14: 7 the whole family is **r** against thine 6965
1Ki 8:20 I am **r up** in the room of David my father, 6965
2Ki 6:15 when the servant of the man of God was **r** 6965
2Ch 6:10 for I am **r up** in the room of David my 6965
13: 6 is **r up**, and hath rebelled against his lord. 6965
21: 4 Now when Jehoram was **r up** to 6965
Ps 20: 8 and fallen: but we are **r**, and stand upright. 6965
27:12 for false witnesses are **r up** against me, and 6965
54: 3 For strangers are **r up** against me, and 6965
86:14 the proud are **r** against me, and 6965
Isa 60: 1 and the glory of the LORD is **r** upon thee. 2224
Eze 7:11 Violence is **r up** into a rod of wickedness: 6965
47: 5 for the waters were **r**, waters to swim in, 1342
Mic 2: 8 Even of late my people is **r up** as an 6965
Mt 11:11 hath not **r** a greater than John the Baptist: *1453*
14: 2 he is **r** from the dead; and therefore mighty *1453*
17: 9 the Son of man be **r again** from the dead. *450*
26:32 But after I am **r** *again,* I will go before you *1453*
27:64 say unto the people, He is **r** from the dead: *1453*
28: 6 for he is **r**, as he said. Come, see the place *1453*
28: 7 tell his disciples that he is **r** from the dead; *1453*
Mk 6:14 That John the Baptist was **r** from the dead, *1453*
6:16 whom I beheaded: he is **r** from the dead. *1453*
9: 9 till the Son of man were **r** from the dead. *450*
14:28 But after that I am **r**, I will go before you *1453*
16: 6 he is **r**; he is not here: behold the place *1453*
16: 9 Now when *Jesus* was **r** early the first *day* of *450*
16:14 them which had seen him after he was **r**. *1453*
Lk 7:16 That a great prophet is **r up** among us; *1453*
9: 7 of some, that John was **r** from the dead; *1453*
9: 8 that one of the old prophets was **r again**. *450*
9:19 *say,* that one of the old prophets is **r again**. *450*
13:25 When once the master of the house is **r up**, *1453*
24: 6 He is not here, but is **r**: remember how he *1453*
24:34 The Lord is **r** indeed, and hath appeared to *1453*
Jn 2:22 When therefore he was **r** from the dead, *1453*
21:14 after that he was **r** from the dead. *1453*

Ac 17: 3 have suffered, and **r again** from the dead; *450*
Ro 8:34 that is **r** *again,* who is even at the right hand *1453*
1Co 15:13 of the dead, then is Christ not **r**: *1453*
15:14 And if Christ be not **r**, then *is* our *1453*
15:20 But now is Christ **r** from the dead, *and* *1453*
Col 2:12 wherein also you are **r with** *him* through *4891*
3: 1 If ye then be **r with** Christ, seek those *4891*
Jas 1:11 For the sun is no sooner **r** with a burning *393*

RISEST (2) [RISE]
Dt 6: 7 when thou liest down, and when thou **r up**. 6965
11:19 when thou liest down, and when thou **r up**. 6965

RISETH (14) [RISE]
Dt 22:26 for as when a man **r** against his neighbour, 6965
Jos 6:26 that **r up** and buildeth this city Jericho: 6965
2Sa 23: 4 *when* the sun **r**, *even* a morning without 2224
Job 9: 7 Which commandeth the sun, and it **r** not; 2224
14:12 So man lieth down, and **r** not: till 6965
24:22 he **r up**, and no *man* is sure of life. 6965
27: 7 he that **r up** against me as the unrighteous. 6965
31:14 What then shall I do when God **r up**? and 6965
Pr 24:16 falleth seven *times,* and **r up** *again:* but 6965
31:15 She **r** also while *it is* yet night, and 6965
Isa 47:11 thou shalt not know from whence it **r**: 7837
Jer 46: 8 Egypt **r up** like a flood, and *his* waters are 5927
Mic 7: 6 the daughter **r up** against her mother, 6965
Jn 13: 4 He **r** from supper, and laid aside *his* *1453*

RISING (39) [RISE]
Lev 13: 2 a man shall have in the skin of his flesh a **r**, 7613
13:10 *if* the **r** *be* white in the skin, and it have 7613
13:10 and *there be* quick raw flesh in the **r**; 7613
13:19 in the place of the boil there be a white **r**, 7613
13:28 it *is* a **r** of the burning, and the priest shall 7613
13:43 *if* the **r** of the sore *be* white reddish in his 7613
14:56 for a **r**, and for a scab, and for a bright spot: 7613
Nu 2: 3 on the east side toward the **r of the sun** 4217
Jos 12: 1 *other* side Jordan toward the **r** of the sun, 4217
2Ch 36:15 his messengers, **r up betimes**, and sending; 7925
Ne 4:21 half of them held the spears from the **r** of 5927
Job 16: 8 my leanness **r up** in me beareth witness to 6965
24: 5 forth to their work; **r betimes** for a prey: 7836
24:14 The murderer **r** with the light killeth 6965
Ps 50: 1 called the earth from the **r** of the sun unto 4217
113: 3 From the **r** of the sun unto the going down 4217
Pr 27:14 **r early** in the morning, it shall be counted a 7925
30:31 and a king, against whom *there is* **no r up**. 510
Isa 41:25 from the **r** of the sun shall he call upon my 4217
45: 6 That they may know from the **r** of the sun, 4217
59:19 and his glory from the **r** of the sun. 4217
60: 3 and kings to the brightness of thy **r**. 2225
Jer 7:13 **r up early** and speaking, but ye heard not; 7925
7:25 daily **r up early** and sending *them:* 7925
11: 7 **r early** and protesting, saying, Obey my 7925
25: 3 spoken unto you, **r early** and speaking; 7925
25: 4 **r early** and sending *them;* but ye have not 7925
26: 5 both **r up early**, and sending *them,* but 7925
29:19 **r up early** and sending *them;* but ye would 7925
32:33 **r up early** and teaching *them,* yet they 7925
35:14 spoken unto you, **r early** and speaking; 7925
35:15 **r up early** and sending *them,* saying, 7925
44: 4 **r early** and sending *them,* saying, Oh, 7925
La 3:63 Behold their sitting down, and their **r up**; 7012
Mal 1:11 For from the **r** of the sun even unto 4217
Mk 1:35 **r up** a great while before day, he went out, *450*
9:10 questioning *one* with *another* what the **r** *450*
16: 2 they came unto the sepulchre at the **r** of *393*
Lk 2:34 set for the fall and **r again** of many in Israel; *386*

RISKED See HAZARDED; JEOPARDED

RISSAH (2)
Nu 33:21 removed from Libnah, and pitched at **R**. 7446
33:22 they journeyed from **R**, and pitched in 7446

RITES (1)
Nu 9: 3 according to all the **r** of it, and according to 2708

RITHMAH (2)
Nu 33:18 departed from Hazeroth, and pitched in **R**. 7575
33:19 they departed from **R**, and pitched at 7575

RIVAL See VEX; VEXATION; VEXED

RIVER (176) [RIVER'S, RIVERS]
Ge 2:10 a **r** went out of Eden to water the garden; 5104
2:13 the name of the second **r** *is* Gihon: 5104
2:14 the name of the third **r** *is* Hiddekel: that *is* 5104
2:14 of Assyria. And the fourth **r** *is* Euphrates. 5104
15:18 from the **r** of Egypt unto the great river, 5104
15:18 from the river of Egypt unto the great **r**, 5104
15:18 Egypt unto the great river, the **r** Euphrates: 5104
31:21 passed over the **r**, and set his face *toward* 5104
36:37 Saul of Rehoboth *by* the **r** reigned in his 5104
41: 1 and behold, he stood by the **r**. 2975
41: 2 there came up out of the **r** seven well 2975
41: 3 other kine came up after them out of the **r**, 2975
41: 3 by the *other* kine upon the brink of the **r**. 2975
41:17 behold, I stood upon the bank of the **r**: 2975
41:18 there came up out of the **r** seven kine, 2975
Ex 1:22 son that is born ye shall cast into the **r**, 2975
2: 5 came down to wash *herself* at the **r**; 2975
4: 9 that thou shalt take of the water of the **r**, 2975
4: 9 the water which thou takest out of the **r** 2975
7:17 hand upon the waters which *are* in the **r**, 2975
7:18 the fish that *is* in the **r** shall die, and 2975
7:18 in the river shall die, and the **r** shall stink; 2975
7:18 shall lothe to drink of the water of the **r**. 2975
7:20 and smote the waters that *were* in the **r**, 2975
7:20 all the waters that *were* in the **r** were turned 2975
7:21 the fish that *was* in the **r** died; and the river 2975
7:21 the **r** stunk, and the Egyptians could not 2975
7:21 could not drink of the water of the **r**; 2975
7:24 all the Egyptians digged round about the **r** 2975
7:24 they could not drink of the water of the **r**. 2975
7:25 after *that* the LORD had smitten the **r**. 2975
8: 3 the **r** shall bring forth frogs abundantly, 2975
8: 9 *that* they may remain in the **r** only? 2975
8:11 thy people; they shall remain in the **r** only. 2975
17: 5 thy rod, wherewith thou smotest the **r**, 2975
23:31 and from the desert unto the **r**: 5104
Nu 22: 5 which *is* by the **r** *of* the land of the children 5104
24: 6 they spread forth, as gardens by the **r side**, 5104
34: 5 compass from Azmon unto the **r** of Egypt, 5158
Dt 1: 7 *unto* Lebanon, unto the great **r**, the river 5104
1: 7 unto the great river, the **r** Euphrates. 5104
2:24 your journey, and pass over the **r** Arnon: 5158
2:36 which *is* by the brink of the **r** of Arnon, and 5158
2:36 *from* the city that *is* by the **r**, even unto 5158
2:37 *nor unto* any place of the **r** Jabbok, 5158
3: 8 from the **r** of Arnon unto mount Hermon; 5158
3:12 which *is* by the **r** Arnon, and half mount 5158
3:16 I gave from Gilead even unto the **r** Arnon, 5158
3:16 and the border, even unto the **r** Jabbok, 5158
4:48 which *is* by the bank of the **r** Arnon, 5158
11:24 the wilderness and Lebanon, from the **r**, 5104
11:24 from the river, the **r** Euphrates, 5104
Jos 1: 4 and this Lebanon even unto the great **r**, 5104
1: 4 the **r** Euphrates, all the land of the Hittites, 5104
12: 1 from the **r** Arnon unto mount Hermon, and 5158
12: 2 which *is* upon the bank of the **r** of Arnon, 5158
12: 2 *from* the middle of the **r**, and *from* half 5158
12: 2 *from* half Gilead, even unto the **r** Jabbok, 5158
13: 9 that *is* upon the bank of the **r** Arnon, and 5158
13: 9 and the city that *is* in the midst of the **r**, and 5158
13:16 that *is* on the bank of the **r** Arnon, and 5158
13:16 and the city that *is* in the midst of the **r**, and 5158
15: 4 and went out *unto* the **r** of Egypt; 5158
15: 7 which *is* on the south side of the **r**: 5158
15:47 unto the **r** of Egypt, and the great sea, and 5158
16: 8 from Tappuah westward *unto* the **r** Kanah; 5158
17: 9 the coast descended *unto* the **r** Kanah, 5158
17: 9 *unto* the river Kanah, southward of the **r**: 5158
17: 9 also *was* on the north side of the **r**, 5158
19:11 and reached to the **r** that *is* before Jokneam; 5158
Jdg 4: 7 I will draw unto thee to the **r** Kishon 5158
4:13 from Harosheth of the Gentiles unto the **r** 5158
5:21 The **r** of Kishon swept them away, 5158
5:21 them away, *that* ancient **r**, the river Kishon. 5158
5:21 them away, *that* ancient river, the **r** Kishon. 5158
2Sa 8: 3 as he went to recover his border at the **r** 5104
10:16 out the Syrians that *were* beyond the **r**: 5104
17:13 to that city, and we will draw it into the **r**, 5158
24: 5 city that *lieth* in the midst of the **r** of Gad, 5158
1Ki 4:21 from the **r** *unto* the land of the Philistines, 5104
4:24 over all *the region* on *this* side the **r**, 5104
4:24 over all the kings on *this* side the **r**: 5104

R

1Ki 8:65 from the entering in of Hamath unto the **r** 5158
14:15 shall scatter them beyond the **r**, because 5104
2Ki 10:33 from Aroer, which *is* by the **r** Arnon, 5158
17: 6 in Halah and in Habor *by* the **r** of Gozan, 5104
18:11 in Halah and in Habor *by* the **r** of Gozan, 5104
23:29 the king of Assyria to the **r** Euphrates: 5104
24: 7 **r** of Egypt unto the river Euphrates all that 5158
24: 7 **r** Euphrates all that pertained to the king of 5104
1Ch 1:48 Shaul of Rehoboth *by* the **r** reigned in his 5104
5: 9 in of the wilderness from the **r** Euphrates: 5104
5:26 Habor, and Hara, and to the **r** Gozan, 5104
18: 3 as he went to stablish his dominion by the **r** 5104
19:16 forth the Syrians that *were* beyond the **r**: 5104
2Ch 7: 8 from the entering in of Hamath unto the **r** 5158
9:26 he reigned over all the kings from the **r** 5104
Ezr 4:10 the rest *that are on this* side the **r**, and 5103
4:11 Thy servants the men *on this* side the **r**, and 5103
4:16 shalt have no portion on *this* side the **r**. 5103
4:17 in Samaria, and *unto* the rest beyond the **r**: 5103
4:20 have ruled over all *countries* beyond the **r**; 5103
5: 3 governor on *this* side the **r**, and 5103
5: 6 governor on *this* side the **r**, and 5103
5: 6 which *were* on *this* side the **r**, sent unto 5103
6: 6 *therefore,* Tatnai, governor beyond the **r**, 5103
6: 6 which *are* beyond the **r**, be ye far from 5103
6: 8 *even* of the tribute beyond the **r**, 5103
6:13 Tatnai, governor on *this* side the **r**, 5103
7:21 to all the treasurers which *are* beyond the **r**, 5103
7:25 judge all the people that *are* beyond the **r**, 5103
8:15 I gathered them together to the **r** that 5104
8:21 I proclaimed a fast there, at the **r** Ahava, 5104
8:31 we departed from the **r** of Ahava on 5104
8:36 and *to* the governors on *this* side the **r**: 5104
Ne 2: 7 be given me to the governors beyond the **r**, 5104
2: 9 I came to the governors beyond the **r**, and 5104
3: 7 throne of the governor on *this* side the **r**. 5104
Job 40:23 Behold, he drinketh up a **r**, *and* hasteth not: 5104
Ps 36: 8 thou shalt make them drink *of* the **r** of thy 5158
46: 4 *There is* a **r**, the streams whereof shall 5104
65: 9 thou greatly enrichest it *with* the **r** of God, 6388
72: 8 and from the **r** unto the ends of the earth. 5104
80:11 unto the sea, and her branches unto the **r**. 5104
105:41 they ran in the dry *places like* a **r**. 5104
Isa 7:20 *namely,* by them beyond the **r**, by the king 5104
8: 7 bringeth up upon them the waters of the **r**, 5104
11:15 wind shall he shake his hand over the **r**, 5104
19: 5 and the **r** shall be wasted and dried up. 5104
23: 3 the harvest of the **r**, *is* her revenue; 2975
23:10 Pass through thy land as a **r**, O daughter of 2975
27:12 channel of the **r** unto the stream of Egypt, 5104
48:18 had thy peace been as a **r**, and 5104
66:12 I will extend peace to her like a **r**, and 5104
Jer 2:18 of Assyria, to drink the waters of the **r**? 5104
17: 8 *that* spreadeth out her roots by the **r**, and 3105
46: 2 which was by the **r** Euphrates in 5104
46: 6 fall toward the north by the **r** Euphrates. 5104
46:10 in the north country by the **r** Euphrates. 5104
La 2:18 let tears run down like a **r** day and night: 5158
Eze 1: 1 as I *was* among the captives by the **r** of 5104
1: 3 in the land of the Chaldeans by the **r** 5104
3:15 that dwelt by the **r** of Chebar, and I sat 5104
3:23 as the glory which I saw by the **r** of 5104
10:15 creature that I saw by the **r** of Chebar. 5104
10:20 under the God of Israel by the **r** of Chebar; 5104
10:22 same faces which I saw by the **r** of Chebar, 5104
29: 3 My **r** *is* mine own, and I have made *it for* 2975
29: 9 The **r** *is* mine, and I have made *it.* 2975
43: 3 like the vision that I saw by the **r** Chebar; 5104
47: 5 *and it was* a **r** that I could not pass over: 5158
47: 5 swim in, a **r** that could not be passed over. 5158
47: 6 caused me to return to the brink of the **r**. 5158
47: 7 at the bank of the **r** *were* very many trees 5158
47: 9 every *thing* shall live whither the **r** cometh. 5158
47:12 by the **r** upon the bank thereof, on this side 5158
47:19 of strife *in* Kadesh, *the* **r** to the great sea. 5159
48:28 *and to the* **r** toward the great sea. 5159
Da 8: 2 I saw in a vision, and I was by the **r** of Ulai. 180
8: 3 there stood before the **r** a ram which had two 180
8: 6 which I had seen standing before the **r**, and 180
10: 4 as I was by the side of the great **r**, which *is* 5104
12: 5 the one on this side of the bank of the **r**, 2975
12: 5 the other on that side of the bank of the **r**. 2975
12: 6 which *was* upon the waters of the **r**, 2975
12: 7 which *was* upon the waters of the **r**, 2975
Am 6:14 in of Hemath unto the **r** of the wilderness. 5158
Mic 7:12 from the fortress even to the **r**, and 5104
Zec 9:10 and from the **r** *even* to the ends of the earth. 5104
10:11 and all the deeps of the **r** shall dry up: 2975
Mk 1: 5 were all baptized of him in the **r** *of* Jordan, *4215*
Ac 16:13 sabbath we went out of the city by a **r** side, *4215*
Rev 9:14 which are bound in the great **r** Euphrates. *4215*
16:12 out his vial upon the great **r** Euphrates; *4215*
22: 1 And he shewed me a pure **r** of water of life, *4215*
22: 2 and of either side of the **r**, *was there* *4215*

RIVER'S (3) [RIVER]

Ex 2: 3 she laid *it* in the flags by the **r** brink. 2975
2: 5 her maidens walked along by the **r** side; 2975
7:15 thou shalt stand by the **r** brink against he 2975

RIVERS (77) [RIVER]

Ex 7:19 upon their **r**, and upon their ponds, and 2975
8: 5 over the **r**, and over the ponds, and 2975
Lev 11: 9 in the seas, and in the **r**, them shall ye eat. 5158
11:10 in the **r**, of all that move in the waters, and 5158
Dt 10: 7 Gudgodah to Jotbath, a land of **r** of waters. 5158
2Ki 5:12 *Are* not Abana and Pharpar, **r** of Damascus, 5104
19:24 have I dried up all the **r** of besieged *places.* 2975
Job 20:17 He shall not see the **r**, the floods, 6390
28:10 He cutteth out **r** among the rocks; and 2975
29: 6 and the rock poured me out **r** of oil; 6388
Ps 1: 3 he shall be like a tree planted by the **r** of 6388
74:15 and the flood: thou driedst up mighty **r**. 5104
78:16 and caused waters to run down like **r**. 5104
78:44 had turned their **r** into blood; and 2975
89:25 also in the sea, and his right hand in the **r**. 5104
107:33 He turneth **r** into a wilderness, and 5104
119:136 **R** of waters run down mine eyes, because 6388
137: 1 By the **r** of Babylon, there we sat down, 5104
Pr 5:16 *and* **r** of waters in the streets. 6388
21: 1 the hand of the LORD, *as* the **r** of water: 6388
Ecc 1: 7 All the **r** run into the sea; yet the sea *is* not 5158
1: 7 unto the place from whence the **r** come, 5158
SS 5:12 His eyes *are* as *the eyes of* doves by the **r** of 650
Isa 7:18 *is* in the uttermost part of the **r** of Egypt, 2975
18: 1 which *is* beyond the **r** of Ethiopia: 5104
18: 2 whose land the **r** have spoiled. 5104
18: 7 under foot, whose land the **r** have spoiled, 5104
19: 6 they shall turn the **r** far away; *and* 5104
30:25 **r** *and* streams of waters in the day of 6388
32: 2 as **r** of water in a dry place, as the shadow 6388
33:21 LORD *will be* unto us a place of broad **r** 5104
37:25 I dried up all the **r** of the besieged *places.* 2975
41:18 I will open **r** in high places, and 5104
42:15 I will make the **r** islands, and I will dry up 5104
43: 2 through the **r**, they shall not overflow thee: 5104
43:19 a way in the wilderness, *and* **r** in the desert. 5104
43:20 *and* **r** in the desert, to give drink to my 5104
44:27 to the deep, Be dry, and I will dry up thy **r**: 5104
47: 2 the leg, uncover the thigh, pass over the **r**. 5104
50: 2 I dry up the sea, I make the **r** a wilderness: 5104
Jer 31: 9 I will cause them to walk by the **r** of waters 5158
46: 7 a flood, whose waters are moved as the **r**? 5104
46: 8 and *his* waters are moved like the **r**; 5104
La 3:48 Mine eye runneth down *with* **r** of water for 6388
Eze 6: 3 and to the hills, to the **r**, and to the valleys; 650
29: 3 great dragon that lieth in the midst of his **r**, 2975
29: 4 I will cause the fish of thy **r** to stick unto 2975
29: 4 will bring thee up out of the midst of thy **r**, 2975
29: 4 all the fish of thy **r** shall stick unto thy 2975
29: 5 thee and all the fish of thy **r**: 2975
29:10 against thy **r**, and I will make the land of 2975
30:12 I will make the **r** dry, and sell the land into 2975
31: 4 the deep set him up on high with her **r** 5104
31: 4 sent out her **little r** unto all the trees of 8585
31:12 his boughs are broken by all the **r** of 650
32: 2 thou camest forth with thy **r**, and 5104
32: 2 waters with thy feet, and fouledst their **r**. 5104
32: 6 the mountains; and the **r** shall be full of thee. 650
32:14 cause their **r** to run like oil, saith the Lord 5104
34:13 them upon the mountains of Israel by the **r**, 650
35: 8 in thy valleys, and in all thy **r**, shall they fall 650
36: 4 to the hills, to the **r**, and to the valleys, to 650
36: 6 and to the hills, to the **r**, and to the valleys, 650
47: 9 whithersoever the **r** shall come, shall live: 5158
Joel 1:20 for the **r** of waters are dried up, and the fire 650
3:18 and all the **r** of Judah shall flow *with* waters, 650
Mic 6: 7 of rams, *or* with ten thousands of **r** of oil? 5158

R

Na 1: 4 and maketh it dry, and drieth up all the r: 5104
2: 6 The gates of the r shall be opened, and 5104
3: 8 populous No, that was situate among the r, 2975
Hab 3: 8 Was the LORD displeased against the r? 5104
3: 8 *was* thine anger against the r? *was* thy 5104
3: 9 Selah. Thou didst cleave the earth *with* r. 5104
Zep 3:10 From beyond the r of Ethiopia my 5104
Jn 7:38 out of his belly shall flow r of living water. *4215*
Rev 8:10 and it fell upon the third *part* of the r, and *4215*
16: 4 third angel poured out his vial upon the r *4215*

RIZIA See REZIA

RIZPAH (4)
2Sa 3: 7 whose name *was* **R**, the daughter of Aiah: 7532
21: 8 the king took the two sons of **R** 7532
21:10 And **R** the daughter of Aiah took sackcloth, 7532
21:11 it was told David what **R** the daughter of 7532

ROAD (1)
1Sa 27:10 Whither have ye **made a r** to day? 6584

ROAR (23) [ROARED, ROARETH, ROARING, ROARINGS]
1Ch 16:32 Let the sea r, and the fulness thereof: 7481
Ps 46: 3 *Though* the waters thereof r *and* 1993
74: 4 Thine enemies r in the midst of thy 7580
96:11 let the sea r, and the fulness thereof. 7481
98: 7 Let the sea r, and the fulness thereof; 7481
104:21 The young lions r after *their* prey, and seek 7580
Isa 5:29 *be* like a lion, they shall r like young lions: 7580
5:29 they shall r, and lay hold of the prey, and 5098
5:30 in that day they shall r against them like 5098
42:13 he shall cry, yea, r; he shall prevail against 6873
59:11 We r all like bears, and mourn sore like 1993
Jer 5:22 though they r, yet can they not pass over it? 1993
25:30 The LORD shall r from on high, and 7580
25:30 he shall **mightily** r upon his 7580+7580
31:35 divideth the sea when the waves thereof r; 1993
50:42 their voice shall r like the sea, and 1993
51:38 They shall r together like lions: they shall 7580
51:55 when her waves do r like great waters, 1993
Hos 11:10 he shall r like a lion: when he shall roar, 7580
11:10 when he shall r, then the children shall 7580
Joel 3:16 The LORD also shall r out of Zion, and 7580
Am 1: 2 The LORD will r from Zion, and utter his 7580
3: 4 Will a lion r in the forest, when he hath no 7580

ROARED (5) [ROAR]
Jdg 14: 5 behold, a young lion r against him. 7580
Ps 38: 8 I have r by reason of the disquietness of my 7580
Isa 51:15 that divided the sea, whose waves r: 1993
Jer 2:15 The young lions r upon him, *and* yelled, 7580
Am 3: 8 The lion hath r, who will not fear? the Lord 7580

ROARETH (3) [ROAR]
Job 37: 4 After it a voice r: he thundereth with 7580
Jer 6:23 their voice r like the sea; and they ride 1993
Rev 10: 3 cried with a loud voice, as *when* a lion r: *3455*

ROARING (16) [ROAR]
Job 4:10 The r of the lion, and the voice of the fierce 7581
Ps 22: 1 helping me, *and from* the words of my r? 7581
22:13 their mouths, *as* a ravening and a r lion. 7580
32: 3 my bones waxed old through my r all 7581
Pr 19:12 The king's wrath *is* as the r of a lion; but 5099
20: 2 The fear of a king *is* as the r of a lion: 5099
28:15 *As* a r lion, and a ranging bear; *so is* a 5098
Isa 5:29 Their r *shall be* like a lion, they shall roar 7581
5:30 shall roar against them like the r of the sea: 5100
31: 4 as the lion and the young lion r on his prey, 1897
Eze 19: 7 the fulness thereof, by the noise of his r. 7581
22:25 like a r lion ravening the prey; 7580
Zep 3: 3 Her princes within her *are* r lions; 7580
Zec 11: 3 a voice of the r of young lions; for 7581
Lk 21:25 with perplexity; the sea and the waves r; *2278*
1Pe 5: 8 the devil, as a r lion, walketh about, *5612*

ROARINGS (1) [ROAR]
Job 3:24 and my r are poured out like the waters. 7581

ROAST (5) [ROASTED, ROASTETH]
Ex 12: 8 r with fire, and unleavened bread; 6748
12: 9 nor sodden at all with water, but r with fire; 6748
Dt 16: 7 thou shalt r and eat *it* in the place which 1310
1Sa 2:15 Give flesh to r for the priest; 6740
Isa 44:16 eateth flesh; he roasteth r, and is satisfied: 6748

ROASTED (3) [ROAST]
2Ch 35:13 they r the passover with fire according to 1310
Isa 44:19 I have r flesh, and eaten *it:* and shall I make 6740
Jer 29:22 whom the king of Babylon r in the fire; 7033

ROASTETH (2) [ROAST]
Pr 12:27 The slothful *man* r not that which he took 2760
Isa 44:16 he eateth flesh; he r roast, and is satisfied: 6740

ROB (8) [ROBBED, ROBBER, ROBBERS, ROBBERY, ROBBETH]
Lev 19:13 neither r *him:* the wages of him that is 1497
26:22 which shall r you **of** your **children**, and 7921
1Sa 23: 1 and they r the threshingfloors. 8154
Pr 22:22 **R** not the poor, because he *is* poor: 1497
Isa 10: 2 their prey, and *that* they may r the fatherless. 962
17:14 that spoil us, and the lot of them that r us. 962
Eze 39:10 r those that robbed them, saith the Lord 962
Mal 3: 8 Will a man r God? Yet ye *have* robbed me. 6906

ROBBED (13) [ROB]
Jdg 9:25 they r all that came along *that* way by 1497
2Sa 17: 8 as a bear **r of** her **whelps** in the field: 7909
Ps 119:61 The bands of the wicked have r me: *but* 5749
Pr 17:12 *Let* a bear r of her whelps meet a man, 7909
Isa 10:13 have r their treasures, and I have put down 8154
42:22 this *is* a people r and spoiled; *they are* all of 962
Jer 50:37 *is* upon her treasures; and they shall be r. 962
Eze 33:15 give again that he had r, walk in 1500
39:10 rob those that r them, saith the Lord GOD. 962
Mal 3: 8 Yet ye *have* r me. But ye say, Wherein 6906
3: 8 ye say, Wherein have we r thee? *In* tithes 6906
3: 9 for ye *have* r me, *even* this whole nation. 6906
2Co 11: 8 I r other churches, taking wages *of them,* to *4813*

ROBBER (5) [ROB]
Job 5: 5 and the r swalloweth up their substance. 6782
18: 9 the heel, *and* the r shall prevail against him. 6782
Eze 18:10 If he beget a son *that is* a r, a shedder of 6530
Jn 10: 1 some other way, the same is a thief and a r. *3027*
18:40 but Barabbas. Now Barabbas was a r. *3027*

ROBBERS (11) [ROB]
Job 12: 6 The tabernacles of r prosper, and they that 7703
Isa 42:24 gave Jacob for a spoil, and Israel to the r? 962
Jer 7:11 my name, become a den of r in your eyes? 6530
Eze 7:22 they shall pollute my secret *place:* for the r 6530
Da 11:14 also the r of thy people shall exalt 1121+6530
Hos 6: 9 as troops *of* r wait for a man, *so* NIH
7: 1 *and* the troop *of* r spoileth without. NIH
Ob 1: 5 to thee, if r by night, (how art thou cut off!) 7703
Jn 10: 8 that ever came before me are thieves and r: *3027*
Ac 19:37 *which are* neither **r of churches**, nor yet *2417*
2Co 11:26 *in* perils of waters, *in* perils of r, *3027*

ROBBERY (7) [ROB]
Ps 62:10 in oppression, and become not vain in r: 1498
Pr 21: 7 The r of the wicked shall destroy them; 7701
Isa 61: 8 love judgment, I hate r for burnt offering; 1498
Eze 22:29 **exercised** r, and have vexed the poor 1497+1498
Am 3:10 store up violence and r in their palaces. 7701
Na 3: 1 it *is* all full *of* lies *and* r; the prey departeth 6563
Php 2: 6 thought it not r to be equal with God: *725*

ROBBETH (1) [ROB]
Pr 28:24 Whoso r his father or his mother, and saith, 1497

ROBE (26) [ROBES]
Ex 28: 4 a r, and a broidered coat, a mitre, and 4598
28:31 thou shalt make the r of the ephod all of 4598
28:34 upon the hem of the r round about. 4598
29: 5 the r of the ephod, and the ephod, and 4598
39:22 he made the r of the ephod *of* woven work, 4598
39:23 *there was* a hole in the midst of the r, as 4598
39:24 they made upon the hems of the r 4598
39:25 the pomegranates upon the hem of the r, 4598
39:26 round about the hem of the r to minister *in;* 4598
Lev 8: 7 clothed him with the r, and put the ephod 4598
1Sa 18: 4 Jonathan stript himself of the r that *was* 4598
24: 4 and cut off the skirt of Saul's r privily. 4598
24:11 see, yea see the skirt of thy r in my hand: 4598
24:11 for in that I cut off the skirt of thy r, and 4598
1Ch 15:27 David *was* clothed with a r of fine linen, 4598
Job 29:14 my judgment *was* as a r and a diadem. 4598

R

Isa 22:21 I will clothe him with thy r, and 3801
61:10 he hath covered me with the r of 4598
Jnh 3: 6 he laid his r from him, and covered *him* with 155
Mic 2: 8 ye pull off the r with the garment from them 145
Mt 27:28 stripped him, and put on him a scarlet r. *5511*
27:31 they took the r off from him, and put his *5511*
Lk 15:22 Bring forth the best r, and put *it* on him; *4749*
23:11 and arrayed him in a gorgeous r, *2066*
Jn 19: 2 on his head, and they put on him a purple r, *2440*
19: 5 the crown of thorns, and the purple r. *2440*

ROBES (11) [ROBE]
2Sa 13:18 for with such r were the king's daughters 4598
1Ki 22:10 sat each on his throne, having put on *their* r, 899
22:30 enter into the battle; but put thou on thy r. 899
2Ch 18: 9 clothed in *their* r, and they sat in a void 899
18:29 will go to the battle; but put thou on thy r. 899
Eze 26:16 lay away their r, and put off their broidered 4598
Lk 20:46 which desire to walk in **long** r, and *4749*
Rev 6:11 And white r were given unto every one of *4749*
7: 9 clothed with white r, and palms in their *4749*
7:13 are these which are arrayed in white r? *4749*
7:14 and have washed their r, and made them *4749*

ROBOAM (2) [REHOBOAM]
Mt 1: 7 And Solomon begat R; and Roboam begat *4497*
1: 7 and R begat Abia; and Abia begat Asa; *4497*

ROCK (119) [ROCKS]
Ex 17: 6 I will stand before thee there upon the r in 6697
17: 6 thou shalt smite the r, and there shall come 6697
33:21 place by me, and thou shalt stand upon a r: 6697
33:22 that I will put thee in a clift of the r, and 6697
Nu 20: 8 and speak ye unto the r before their eyes; 5553
20: 8 shalt bring forth to them water out of the r: 5553
20:10 the congregation together before the r, 5553
20:10 must we fetch you water out of this r? 5553
20:11 and with his rod he smote the r twice: 5553
24:21 and thou puttest thy nest in a r. 5553
Dt 8:15 who brought thee forth water out of the r of 6697
32: 4 *He is* the R, his work *is* perfect: for all his 6697
32:13 he made him to suck honey out of the r, 5553
32:13 out of the rock, and oil out of the flinty r; 6697
32:15 and lightly esteemed the R of his salvation. 6697
32:18 Of the R *that* begat thee thou art unmindful, 6697
32:30 except their R had sold them, and 6697
32:31 For their r *is* not as our Rock, even our 6697
32:31 For their rock *is* not as our R, even our 6697
32:37 *are* their gods, *their* r in whom they trusted, 6697
Jdg 1:36 up to Akrabbim, from the r, and upward. 5553
6:20 unleavened *cakes,* and lay *them* upon this r, 5553
6:21 and there rose up fire out of the r, 6697
6:26 the LORD thy God upon the top of this r, 4581
7:25 they slew Oreb upon the r Oreb, and Zeeb 6697
13:19 and offered *it* upon a r unto the LORD: 6697
15: 8 and dwelt in the top of the r Etam. 5553
15:11 men of Judah went to the top of the r Etam, 5553
15:13 new cords, and brought him up from the r. 5553
20:45 fled toward the wilderness unto the r of 5553
20:47 fled to the wilderness unto the r Rimmon, 5553
20:47 and abode in the r Rimmon four months. 5553
21:13 of Benjamin that *were* in the r Rimmon, 5553
1Sa 2: 2 neither *is there* any r like our God. 6697
14: 4 *there was* a sharp r on the one side, and 5553
14: 4 one side, and a sharp r on the other side: 5553
23:25 wherefore he came down *into* a r, and 5553
2Sa 21:10 and spread it for her upon the r, 6697
22: 2 The LORD *is* my r, and my fortress, and 5553
22: 3 The God of my r; in him will I trust: *he is* 6697
22:32 the LORD? and who *is* a r, save our God? 6697
22:47 blessed *be* my r; and exalted be the God of 6697
22:47 exalted be the God of the r of my salvation. 6697
23: 3 of Israel said, the R of Israel spake to me, 6697
1Ch 11:15 thirty captains went down to the r to David, 6697
2Ch 25:12 brought them unto the top of the r, and 5553
25:12 cast them down from the top of the r, 5553
Ne 9:15 broughtest forth water for them out of the r 5553
Job 14:18 and the r is removed out of his place. 6697
18: 4 and shall the r be removed out of his place? 6697
19:24 with an iron pen and lead in the r for ever! 6697
24: 8 and embrace the r for want of a shelter. 6697
28: 9 He putteth forth his hand upon the r; 2496
29: 6 and the r poured me out rivers of oil; 6697
39: 1 when the wild goats of the r bring forth? 5553
39:28 She dwelleth and abideth on the r, upon 5553
39:28 upon the crag of the r, and the strong place. 5553
Ps 18: 2 The LORD *is* my r, and my fortress, and 5553
18:31 the LORD? or who *is* a r save our God? 6697
18:46 blessed *be* my r; and let the God of my 6697
27: 5 he hide me; he shall set me up upon a r. 6697
28: 1 Unto thee will I cry, O LORD, my r; 6697
31: 2 be thou my strong r, for a house of defence 6697
31: 3 For thou *art* my r and my fortress; therefore 5553
40: 2 set my feet upon a r, *and* established my 5553
42: 9 I will say unto God my r, Why hast thou 5553
61: 2 lead me to the r *that* is higher than I. 6697
62: 2 He only *is* my r and my salvation; *he is* my 6697
62: 6 He only *is* my r and my salvation: *he is* my 6697
62: 7 the r of my strength, *and* my refuge, is in 6697
71: 3 save me; for thou *art* my r and my fortress. 5553
78:16 He brought streams also out of the r, and 5553
78:20 Behold, he smote the r, that the waters 6697
78:35 And they remembered that God *was* their r, 6697
81:16 *with* honey out of the r should I have 6697
89:26 my God, and the r of my salvation. 6697
92:15 *he is* my r, and *there is* no unrighteousness 6697
94:22 and my God *is* the r of my refuge. 6697
95: 1 let us make a joyful noise to the r of our 6697
105:41 He opened the r, and the waters gushed 6697
114: 8 Which turned the r *into* a standing water, 6697
Pr 30:19 in the air; the way of a serpent upon a r; 6697
SS 2:14 O my dove, *that art* in the clefts of the r, 5553
Isa 2:10 Enter into the r, and hide thee in the dust, 6697
8:14 for a r of offence to both the houses of 6697
10:26 to the slaughter of Midian at the r Oreb: 6697
17:10 hast not been mindful of the r of thy 6697
22:16 that graveth a habitation for himself in a r? 5553
32: 2 as the shadow of a great r in a weary land. 5553
42:11 let the inhabitants of the r sing, let them 5553
48:21 he caused the waters to flow out of the r for 6697
48:21 he clave the r also, and the waters gushed 6697
51: 1 look unto the r *whence* ye are hewn, and 6697
Jer 5: 3 they have made their faces harder than a r; 5553
13: 4 and hide it there in a hole of the r. 5553
18:14 *which cometh* from the r of the field? 6697
21:13 *and* r of the plain, saith the LORD; 6697
23:29 like a hammer *that* breaketh the r in pieces? 5553
48:28 dwell in the r, and be like the dove *that* 5553
49:16 O thou that dwellest in the clefts of the r, 5553
Eze 24: 7 she set it upon the top of a r; she poured it 5553
24: 8 I have set her blood upon the top of a r, 5553
26: 4 from her, and make her like the top of a r. 5553
26:14 I will make thee like the top of a r: 5553
Am 6:12 Shall horses run upon the r? will *one* plow 5553
Ob 1: 3 thou that dwellest in the clefts of the r, 5553
Mt 7:24 a wise man, which built his house upon a r: *4073*
7:25 and it fell not: for it was founded upon a r. *4073*
16:18 and upon this r I will build my church; *4073*
27:60 new tomb, which he had hewn out in the r: *4073*
Mk 15:46 in a sepulchre which was hewn out of a r, *4073*
Lk 6:48 digged deep, and laid the foundation on a r: *4073*
6:48 not shake it: for it was founded upon a r. *4073*
8: 6 And some fell upon a r; and as soon as it *4073*
8:13 They on the r *are they,* which, when they *4073*
Ro 9:33 in Sion a stumblingstone and r of offence: *4073*
1Co 10: 4 for they drank of *that* spiritual R that *4073*
10: 4 that followed *them:* and *that* R was Christ. *4073*
1Pe 2: 8 a stone of stumbling, and a r of offence, *4073*

ROCKS (23) [ROCK]
Nu 23: 9 For from the top of the r I see him, and 6697
1Sa 13: 6 and in r, and in high places, and in pits. 5553
24: 2 and his men upon the r of the wild goats. 6697
1Ki 19:11 brake in pieces the r before the LORD; 5553
Job 28:10 He cutteth out rivers among the r; and 6697
30: 6 *in* caves of the earth, and *in* the r. 3710
Ps 78:15 He clave the r in the wilderness, and 6697
104:18 for the wild goats; *and* the r for the conies. 5553
Pr 30:26 yet make they their houses in the r; 5553
Isa 2:19 they shall go into the holes of the r, and 6697
2:21 To go into the clifts of the r, and into 6697
2:21 into the tops of the **ragged** r, for fear of 5553
7:19 in the holes of the r, and upon all thorns, 5553
33:16 of defence *shall be* the munitions of r: 5553
57: 5 in the valleys under the clifts of the r? 5553
Jer 4:29 go into thickets, and climb up upon the r: 3710
16:16 every hill, and out of the holes of the r. 5553
51:25 roll thee down from the r, and will make 5553

Na 1: 6 like fire, and the r are thrown down by him. 6697
Mt 27:51 and the earth did quake, and the r rent; *4073*
Ac 27:29 lest we should have fallen upon r, *5117+5138*
Rev 6:15 in the dens and in the r of the mountains; *4073*
6:16 And said to the mountains and r, Fall on us, *4073*

ROD (86) [RODS]
Ex 4: 2 *is* that in thine hand? And he said, A r. 4294
4: 4 and caught it, and it became a r in his hand: 4294
4:17 thou shalt take this r in thine hand, 4294
4:20 and Moses took the r of God in his hand. 4294
7: 9 Take thy r, and cast *it* before Pharaoh, *and* 4294
7:10 Aaron cast down his r before Pharaoh, and 4294
7:12 For they cast down every man his r, and 4294
7:12 but Aaron's r swallowed up their rods. 4294
7:15 the r which was turned to a serpent shalt 4294
7:17 I will smite with the r that *is* in mine hand 4294
7:19 Take thy r, and stretch out thine hand upon 4294
7:20 he lift up the r, and smote the waters that 4294
8: 5 Stretch forth thine hand with thy r over 4294
8:16 Stretch out thy r, and smite the dust of 4294
8:17 for Aaron stretched out his hand with his r, 4294
9:23 Moses stretched forth his r toward heaven: 4294
10:13 Moses stretched forth his r over the land of 4294
14:16 lift thou up thy r, and stretch out thine hand 4294
17: 5 and thy r, wherewith thou smotest the river, 4294
17: 9 of the hill with the r of God in mine hand. 4294
21:20 with a r, and he die under his hand; 7626
Lev 27:32 *even of* whatsoever passeth under the r, 7626
Nu 17: 2 take of every one of them a r according to 4294
17: 2 write thou every man's name upon his r. 4294
17: 3 thou shalt write Aaron's name upon the r 4294
17: 3 for one r *shall be* for the head of the house 4294
17: 5 *that* the man's r, whom I shall choose, shall 4294
17: 6 every one of their princes gave him a r 4294
17: 6 and the r of Aaron *was* among their rods. 4294
17: 8 the r of Aaron for the house of Levi was 4294
17: 9 and they looked, and took every man his r. 4294
17:10 Bring Aaron's r again before 4294
20: 8 Take the r, and gather thou the assembly 4294
20: 9 Moses took the r from before the LORD, 4294
20:11 and with his r he smote the rock twice: 4294
1Sa 14:27 wherefore he put forth the end of the r that 4294
14:43 taste a little honey with the end of the r that 4294
2Sa 7:14 I will chasten him with the r of men, and 7626
Job 9:34 Let him take his r away from me, and 7626
21: 9 neither *is* the r of God upon them. 7626
Ps 2: 9 Thou shalt break them with a r of iron; 7626
23: 4 thy r and thy staff they comfort me. 7626
74: 2 the r of thine inheritance, *which* thou hast 7626
89:32 will I visit their transgression with the r, 7626
110: 2 The LORD shall send the r of thy strength 4294
125: 3 For the r of the wicked shall not rest upon 7626
Pr 10:13 a r *is* for the back of him that is void of 7626
13:24 He that spareth his r hateth his son: but 7626
14: 3 In the mouth of the foolish *is* a r of pride: 2415
22: 8 reap vanity: and the r of his anger shall fail. 7626
22:15 the r of correction shall drive it far from 7626
23:13 for *if* thou beatest him with the r, he shall 7626
23:14 Thou shalt beat him with the r, and 7626
26: 3 for the ass, and a r for the fools' back. 7626
29:15 The r and reproof give wisdom: but a child 7626
Isa 9: 4 the r of his oppressor, as *in* the day of 7626
10: 5 the r of mine anger, and the staff in their 7626
10:15 as if the r should shake *itself against* them 7626
10:24 he shall smite thee with a r, and shall lift up 7626
10:26 *as* his r *was* upon the sea, so shall he lift it 4294
11: 1 there shall come forth a r out of the stem of 2415
11: 4 he shall smite the earth with the r of his 7626
14:29 the r of him that smote thee is broken: 7626
28:27 out with a staff, and the cummin with a r. 7626
30:31 be beaten down, *which* smote with a r. 7626
Jer 1:11 And I said, I see a r of an almond tree. 4731
10:16 and Israel *is* the r of his inheritance: 7626
48:17 the strong staff broken, *and* the beautiful r! 4731
51:19 and *Israel is* the r of his inheritance: 7626
La 3: 1 hath seen affliction by the r of his wrath. 7626
Eze 7:10 the r hath blossomed, pride hath budded. 4294
7:11 Violence is risen up into a r of wickedness: 4294
19:14 fire is gone out of a r of her branches, 4294
19:14 that she hath no strong r *to be* a sceptre to 4294
20:37 I will cause you to pass under the r, and 7626
21:10 it contemneth the r of my son, *as* every 7626
21:13 and what if *the sword* contemn even the r? 7626
Mic 5: 1 they shall smite the judge of Israel with a r 7626
6: 9 hear ye the r, and who hath appointed it. 4294
7:14 Feed thy people with thy r, the flock of 7626
1Co 4:21 shall I come unto you with a r, or in love, *4464*
Heb 9: 4 and Aaron's r that budded, and the tables *4464*
Rev 2:27 And he shall rule them with a r of iron; *4464*
11: 1 there was given me a reed like unto a r: *4464*
12: 5 who was to rule all nations with a r of iron: *4464*
19:15 and he shall rule them with a r of iron: and *4464*

RODE (15) [RIDE]
Ge 24:61 they r upon the camels, and followed 7392
Jdg 10: 4 he had thirty sons that r on thirty ass colts, 7392
12:14 that r on threescore and ten ass colts: 7392
1Sa 25:20 it was *so, as* she r on the ass, that she came 7392
25:42 Abigail hasted, and rose, and r upon an ass, 7392
30:17 young men, which r upon camels, and fled. 7392
2Sa 18: 9 Absalom r upon a mule, and the mule went 7392
22:11 he r upon a cherub, and did fly: and he was 7392
1Ki 13:13 they saddled him the ass: and he r thereon, 7392
18:45 great rain. And Ahab r, and went to Jezreel. 7392
2Ki 9:16 So Jehu r *in a chariot,* and went to Jezreel; 7392
9:25 and thou r together after Ahab his father, 7392
Ne 2:12 beast with me, save the beast that I r upon. 7392
Est 8:14 *So* the posts that r upon mules *and* 7392
Ps 18:10 he r upon a cherub, and did fly: yea, he did 7392

RODENTS See MOLE; MOLES

RODS (15) [ROD]
Ge 30:37 Jacob took him r of green poplar, and 4731
30:37 made the white appear which *was* in the r. 4731
30:38 he set the r which he had pilled before 4731
30:39 the flocks conceived before the r, and 4731
30:41 that Jacob laid the r before the eyes of 4731
30:41 that they might conceive among the r. 4731
Ex 7:12 but Aaron's rod swallowed up their r. 4294
Nu 17: 2 to the house of their fathers twelve r: 4294
17: 6 to their fathers' houses, *even* twelve r: 4294
17: 6 and the rod of Aaron *was* among their r. 4294
17: 7 Moses laid up the r before the LORD in 4294
17: 9 Moses brought out all the r from before 4294
Eze 19:11 she had strong r for the sceptres of them 4294
19:12 her strong r were broken and withered; 4294
2Co 11:25 Thrice was I **beaten with** r, once was I *4463*

ROE (7) [ROEBUCK, ROEBUCKS, ROES]
2Sa 2:18 and Asahel *was as* light of foot as a wild r. 6643
Pr 5:19 *her be as* the loving hind and pleasant r; 3280
6: 5 Deliver thyself as a r from the hand *of* 6643
SS 2: 9 My beloved *is* like a r or a young hart: 6643
2:17 be thou like a r or a young hart upon 6643
8:14 be thou like to a r or to a young hart upon 6643
Isa 13:14 it shall be as the chased r, and as a sheep 6643

ROEBUCK (4) [ROE]
Dt 12:15 eat thereof, as of the r, and as of the hart. 6643
12:22 Even as the r and the hart is eaten, so 6643
14: 5 the r, and the fallow deer, and the wild 6643
15:22 *shall eat it* alike, as the r, and as the hart. 6643

ROEBUCKS (1) [ROE]
1Ki 4:23 and r, and fallowdeer, and fatted fowl. 6643

ROES (5) [ROE]
1Ch 12: 8 *were* as swift as the r upon the mountains: 6643
SS 2: 7 by the r, and by the hinds of the field, 6643
3: 5 by the r, and by the hinds of the field, 6643
4: 5 Thy two breasts *are* like two young r *that* 6646
7: 3 Thy two breasts *are* like two young r *that* 6646

ROGELIM (2)
2Sa 17:27 and Barzillai the Gileadite of R, 7274
19:31 Barzillai the Gileadite came down from R, 7274

ROHGAH (1)
1Ch 7:34 Ahi, and R, Jehubbah, and Aram. 7303

ROLL (28) [ROLLED, ROLLER, ROLLETH, ROLLING, ROLLS]
Ge 29: 8 *till* they r the stone from the well's mouth; 1556
Jos 10:18 R great stones upon the mouth of the cave, 1556
1Sa 14:33 r a great stone unto me *this* day. 1556
Ezr 6: 2 a r, and therein *was* a record thus written: 4040
Isa 8: 1 Take thee a great r, and write in it with a 1549
Jer 36: 2 Take thee a r of a book, and write therein 4039

Jer 36: 4 had spoken unto him, upon a **r** of a book. 4039
36: 6 Therefore go thou, and read in the **r**, 4039
36:14 Take in thine hand the **r** wherein thou hast 4039
36:14 So Baruch the son of Neriah took the **r** in 4039
36:20 they laid up the **r** in the chamber of 4039
36:21 So the king sent Jehudi to fet the **r**: and 4039
36:23 until all the **r** was consumed in the fire that 4039
36:25 to the king that *he* would not burn the **r**: 4039
36:27 after that the king had burnt the **r**, and 4039
36:28 Take thee again another **r**, and write in it 4039
36:28 all the former words that were in the first **r**, 4039
36:29 Thou hast burnt this **r**, saying, Why hast 4039
36:32 took Jeremiah another **r**, and gave it to 4039
51:25 **r** thee **down** from the rocks, and will make 1556
Eze 2: 9 unto me; and lo, a **r** of a book *was* therein; 4039
3: 1 eat this **r**, and go speak unto the house of 4039
3: 2 my mouth, and he caused me to eat that **r**. 4039
3: 3 fill thy bowels with this **r** that I give thee. 4039
Mic 1:10 in the house of Aphrah **r** thyself *in* the dust. 6428
Zec 5: 1 and looked, and behold, a flying **r**. 4039
5: 2 I answered, I see a flying **r**; the length 4039
Mk 16: 3 Who shall **r** us **away** the stone from the door *617*

ROLLED (12) [ROLL]

Ge 29: 3 they **r** the stone from the well's mouth, and 1556
29:10 **r** the stone from the well's mouth, and 1556
Jos 5: 9 *This* day have I **r** **away** the reproach of 1556
Job 30:14 the desolation they **r** themselves *upon me*. 1556
Isa 9: 5 confused noise, and garments **r** in blood; 1556
34: 4 the heavens shall be **r** **together** as a scrole: 1556
Mt 27:60 he **r** a great stone to the door of *4351*
28: 2 came and **r** **back** the stone from the door, *617*
Mk 15:46 **r** a stone unto the door of the sepulchre. *4351*
16: 4 they saw that the stone was **r** **away**: *617*
Lk 24: 2 And they found the stone **r** **away** from *617*
Rev 6:14 departed as a scrole when it is **r** **together**; *1507*

ROLLER (1) [ROLL]

Eze 30:21 to put a **r** to bind it, to make it strong to 2848

ROLLETH (1) [ROLL]

Pr 26:27 he that **r** a stone, it will return upon him. 1556

ROLLING (1) [ROLL]

Isa 17:13 and like a **r** **thing** before the whirlwind. 1534

ROLLS (1) [ROLL]

Ezr 6: 1 and search was made in the house of the **r**, 5609

ROMAMTI-EZER (2)

1Ch 25: 4 Hanani, Eliathah, Giddalti, and **R**, 7320
25:31 The four and twentieth to **R**, *he*, his sons, 7320

ROMAN (5) [ROME]

Ac 22:25 lawful for you to scourge a man *that is* a **R**, *4514*
22:26 heed what thou doest: for this man is a **R**. *4514*
22:27 and said unto him, Tell me, art thou a **R**? *4514*
22:29 after he knew that he was a **R**, and because *4514*
23:27 having understood that he was a **R**. *4514*

ROMANS (7) [ROME]

Jn 11:48 and the **R** shall come and take away both *4514*
Ac 16:21 us to receive, neither to observe, being **R**. *4514*
16:37 being **R**, and have cast *us* into prison; *444+4514*
16:38 when they heard that they were **R**, *4514*
25:16 It is not the manner of the **R** to deliver any *4514*
28:17 from Jerusalem into the hands of the **R**. *4514*
Ro 16: S Written to the **R** from Corinthus, *and* *4514*

ROME (15) [ROMAN, ROMANS]

Ac 2:10 and strangers **of** **R**, Jews and proselytes, *4514*
18: 2 had commanded all Jews to depart from **R**:) *4516*
19:21 After I have been there, I must also see **R**. *4516*
23:11 so must thou bear witness also at **R**. *4516*
28:14 them seven days: and so we went toward **R**. *4516*
28:16 And when we came to **R**, the centurion *4516*
Ro 1: 7 To all that be in **R**, beloved of God, *4516*
1:15 preach the gospel to you that are at **R** also. *4516*
Gal 6: S Unto the Galatians written from **R**. *4516*
Eph 6: S Written from **R** unto the Ephesians by *4516*
Php 4: S It was written to the Philippians from **R** by *4516*
Col 4: S Written from **R** to the Colossians by *4516*
2Ti 1:17 But, when he was in **R**, he sought me out *4516*
4: S was written from **R**, when Paul was *4516*
Phm 1: S Written from **R** to Philemon, by Onesimus *4516*

ROOF (20) [ROOFS]

Ge 19: 8 came they under the shadow of my **r**. 6982
Dt 22: 8 then thou shalt make a battlement for thy **r**, 1406
Jos 2: 6 had brought them up to the **r** **of the house**, 1406
2: 6 which she had laid in order upon the **r**. 1406
2: 8 she came up unto them upon the **r**; 1406
Jdg 16:27 *there were* upon the **r** about three thousand 1406
2Sa 11: 2 and walked upon the **r** of the king's house: 1406
11: 2 from the **r** he saw a woman washing 1406
18:24 the watchman went *up* to the **r** over 1406
Ne 8:16 every one upon the **r** **of** his **house**, and 1406
Job 29:10 tongue cleaved to the **r** **of** their **mouth**. 2441
Ps 137: 6 let my tongue cleave to the **r** **of** my **mouth**; 2441
SS 7: 9 the **r** **of** thy **mouth** like the best wine, 2441
La 4: 4 cleaveth to the **r** **of** his **mouth** for thirst: 2441
Eze 3:26 thy tongue cleave to the **r** **of** thy **mouth**, 2441
40:13 the gate from the **r** of *one* little chamber to 1406
40:13 of *one* little chamber to the **r** of another: 1406
Mt 8: 8 that thou shouldest come under my **r**: *4721*
Mk 2: 4 they uncovered the **r** where he was: *4721*
Lk 7: 6 that thou shouldest enter under my **r**: *4721*

ROOFS (2) [ROOF]

Jer 19:13 of all the houses upon whose **r** they have 1406
32:29 upon whose **r** they have offered incense 1406

ROOM (32) [ROOMS]

Ge 24:23 is there **r** *in* thy father's house for us to 4725
24:25 and provender enough, and **r** to lodge in. 4725
24:31 prepared the house, and **r** for the camels. 4725
26:22 For now the LORD hath **made** **r** for us, 7337
2Sa 19:13 host before me continually in the **r** of Joab. 8478
1Ki 2:35 the son of Jehoiada **in** his **r** over the host: 8478
2:35 Zadok the priest did the king put **in** the **r** of 8478
5: 1 anointed him king **in the r of** his father: 8478
5: 5 whom I will set upon thy throne **in** thy **r**, 8478
8:20 I am risen up **in the r of** David my father, 8478
19:16 shalt thou anoint to be prophet **in** thy **r**. 8478
2Ki 15:25 he killed him, and reigned **in** his **r**. 8478
23:34 of Josiah king **in the r of** Josiah his father, 8478
2Ch 6:10 for I am risen up **in the r of** David my 8478
26: 1 made him king **in the r of** his father 8478
Ps 31: 8 thou hast set my feet in a **large** **r**. 4800
80: 9 Thou preparedst *r* before it, and didst cause NIH
Pr 18:16 A man's gift **maketh** **r** for him, and 7337
Mal 3:10 that *there shall* not *be* **r** enough *to receive* NIH
Mt 2:22 reign in Judea **in the r of** his father Herod, *473*
Mk 2: 2 insomuch that there was no **r** to receive *5562*
14:15 And he will shew you a large **upper** **r** *508*
Lk 2: 7 because there was no **r** for them in the inn. *5117*
12:17 I have no **r** where to bestow my fruits? NIG
14: 8 to a wedding, sit not down in the **highest** **r**; *4411*
14: 9 thou begin with shame to take the lowest **r**. *5117*
14:10 art bidden, go and sit down in the lowest **r**; *5117*
14:22 as thou hast commanded, and yet there is **r**. *5117*
22:12 And he shall shew you a large **upper** **r** *508*
Ac 1:13 they went up into an **upper** **r**, where abode *5253*
24:27 Porcius Festus **came into** Felix' **r**: *1240+2983*
1Co 14:16 how shall he that occupieth the **r** of *5117*

ROOMS (7) [ROOM]

Ge 6:14 **r** shalt thou make *in* the ark, and shalt pitch 7064
1Ki 20:24 out of his place, and put captains **in** their **r**: 8478
1Ch 4:41 utterly unto this day, and dwelt **in** their **r**: 8478
Mt 23: 6 And love the **uppermost** **r** at feasts, and *4411*
Mk 12:39 and the **uppermost** **r** at feasts: *4411*
Lk 14: 7 he marked how they chose out the **chief** **r**; *4411*
20:46 in the synagogues, and the **chief** **r** at feasts; *4411*

ROOSTER See COCK; COCKCROWING; GREYHOUND

ROOT (44) [ROOTED, ROOTS]

Dt 29:18 lest there should be among you a **r** that 8328
Jdg 5:14 Out of Ephraim *was there* a **r** of them 8328
1Ki 14:15 he shall **r** **up** Israel out of this good land, 5428
2Ki 19:30 of Judah shall *yet* again **take** **r** downward, 8328
Job 5: 3 I have seen the foolish **taking** **r**: but 8327
14: 8 Though the **r** thereof wax old in the earth, 8328
19:28 seeing the **r** of the matter is found in me; 8328
29:19 My **r** *was* spread out by the waters, and 8328
31:12 and would **r** **out** all mine increase. 8327
Ps 52: 5 and **r** thee **out** of the land of the living. 8327
80: 9 didst **cause** **it to take deep** **r**, and 8327+8328
Pr 12: 3 the **r** of the righteous shall not be moved. 8328

R

Pr 12:12 but the **r** of the righteous yieldeth *fruit.* 8328
Isa 5:24 *so* their **r** shall be as rottenness, and 8328
11:10 in that day there shall be a **r** of Jesse, 8328
14:29 for out of the serpent's **r** shall come forth a 8328
14:30 I will kill thy **r** with famine, and he shall 8328
27: 6 **cause** them that come of Jacob **to take r**: 8327
37:31 of Judah shall again take **r** downward, 8328
40:24 yea, their stock shall not **take r** in the earth: 8327
53: 2 tender plant, and as a **r** out of a dry ground: 8328
Jer 1:10 to **r out**, and to pull down, and to destroy, 5428
12: 2 hast planted them, yea, they have **taken r**: 8327
Eze 31: 7 his branches: for his **r** was by great waters. 8328
Hos 9:16 Ephraim is smitten, their **r** is dried up, 8328
Mal 4: 1 that it shall leave them neither **r** nor branch. 8328
Mt 3:10 And now also the axe is laid unto the **r** of *4491*
13: 6 and because *they* had not **r**, they withered *4491*
13:21 Yet hath he not **r** in himself, but dureth for *4491*
13:29 the tares, ye **r up** also the wheat with them. *1610*
Mk 4: 6 and because *it* had no **r**, it withered away. *4491*
4:17 And have no **r** in themselves, and so endure *4491*
Lk 3: 9 And now also the axe is laid unto the **r** of *4491*
8:13 and these have no **r**, which for a while *4491*
17: 6 Be thou **plucked up by the r**, and be thou *1610*
Ro 11:16 the lump *is* also *holy:* and if the **r** *be* holy, *4491*
11:17 and with *them* partakest of the **r** and *4491*
11:18 thou bearest not the **r**, but the root thee. *4491*
11:18 thou bearest not the root, but the **r** thee. *4491*
15:12 There shall be a **r** of Jesse, and he that *shall* *4491*
1Ti 6:10 For the love of money is the **r** of all evil: *4491*
Heb 12:15 lest any **r** of bitterness springing up trouble *4491*
Rev 5: 5 Lion of the tribe of Juda, the **r** of David, *4491*
22:16 I am the **r** and the offspring of David, *and* *4491*

ROOTED (8) [ROOT]
Dt 29:28 the LORD **r** them **out** of their land in 5428
Job 18:14 His confidence shall be **r out** of his 5423
31: 8 another eat; yea, let my offspring be **r out**. 8327
Pr 2:22 and the transgressors shall be **r** out of it. 5255
Zep 2: 4 at the noon day, and Ekron shall be **r up**. 6131
Mt 15:13 Father hath not planted, shall be **r up**. *1610*
Eph 3:17 that ye, being **r** and grounded in love, *4492*
Col 2: 7 **R** and built up in him, and stablished in *4492*

ROOTS (20) [ROOT]
2Ch 7:20 will I **pluck** them **up by the r** out of my 5428
Job 8:17 His **r** are wrapped about the heap, *and* 8328
18:16 His **r** shall be dried up beneath, and 8328
28: 9 he overturneth the mountains by the **r**. 8328
30: 4 by the bushes, and juniper **r** *for* their meat. 8328
Isa 11: 1 and a Branch shall grow out of his **r**: 8328
Jer 17: 8 *that* spreadeth out her **r** by the river, and 8328
Eze 17: 6 and the **r** thereof were under him: 8328
17: 7 this vine did bend her **r** toward him, and 8328
17: 9 shall he not pull up the **r** thereof, and cut 8328
17: 9 many people to pluck it up by the **r** thereof. 8328
Da 4:15 Nevertheless leave the stump of his **r** in 8330
4:23 yet leave the stump of the **r** thereof in 8330
4:26 to leave the stump of the tree **r**; 8330
7: 8 three of the first horns **pluckt up by** the **r**: 6132
11: 7 out of a branch of her **r** shall *one* stand up 8328
Hos 14: 5 as the lily, and cast forth his **r** as Lebanon. 8328
Am 2: 9 fruit from above, and his **r** from beneath. 8328
Mk 11:20 they saw the fig tree dried up from the **r**. *4491*
Jude 1:12 twice dead, **plucked up by the r**; *1610*

ROPE (1) [ROPES]
Isa 5:18 of vanity, and sin as it were with a cart **r**: 5688

ROPES (6) [ROPE]
Jdg 16:11 If they bind me fast with new **r** that never 5688
16:12 Delilah therefore took new **r**, and 5688
2Sa 17:13 shall all Israel bring **r** to that city, and 2256
1Ki 20:31 **r** upon our heads, and go out to the king of 2256
20:32 *put* **r** on their heads, and came to the king 2256
Ac 27:32 Then the soldiers cut off the **r** of the boat, *4979*

ROSE (136) [RISE]
Ge 4: 8 that Cain **r up** against Abel his brother, and 6965
18:16 the men **r up** from thence, and 6965
19: 1 Lot seeing *them* **r up** to meet them; and 6965
20: 8 Therefore Abimelech **r early** in 7925
21:14 Abraham **r up early** in the morning, and 7925
21:32 Abimelech **r up**, and Phichol the chief 6965
22: 3 Abraham **r up early** in the morning, and 7925
22: 3 **r up**, and went unto the place of which God 6965
22:19 they **r up** and went together to Beer-sheba; 6965
24:54 they **r up** in the morning, and he said, 6965
25:34 and drink, and **r up**, and went his way: 6965
26:31 they **r up betimes** in the morning, and 7925
28:18 Jacob **r up early** in the morning, and 7925
31:17 Jacob **r up**, and set his sons and his wives 6965
31:21 he **r up**, and passed over the river, and 6965
31:55 **early** in the morning Laban **r up**, and 7925
32:22 he **r up** that night, and took his two wives, 6965
32:31 as he passed over Penuel the sun **r** upon 2224
37:35 and all his daughters **r up** to comfort him; 6965
43:15 **r up**, and went down *to* Egypt, and 6965
46: 5 Jacob **r up** from Beer-sheba: and the sons 6965
Ex 10:23 neither **r** any from his place for three days: 6965
12:30 Pharaoh **r up** in the night, he, and all his 6965
15: 7 overthrown them that **r up against** thee: 6965
24: 4 **r up early** in the morning, and builded an 7925
24:13 Moses **r up**, and his minister Joshua: and 6965
32: 6 they **r up early** on the morrow, and 7925
32: 6 down to eat and to drink, and **r up** to play. 6965
33: 8 *that* all the people **r up**, and stood every 6965
33:10 all the people **r up** and worshipped, 6965
34: 4 Moses **r up early** in the morning, and 7925
Nu 14:40 they **r up early** in the morning, and 7925
16: 2 they **r up** before Moses, with certain of 6965
16:25 Moses **r up** and went unto Dathan and 6965
22:13 Balaam **r up** in the morning, and said unto 6965
22:14 the princes of Moab **r up**, and they went 6965
22:21 Balaam **r up** in the morning, and 6965
24:25 Balaam **r up**, and went and returned to his 6965
25: 7 saw *it,* he **r up** from amongst 6965
Dt 33: 2 from Sinai, and **r up** from Seir unto them; 2224
Jos 3: 1 Joshua **r early** in the morning; and 7925
3:16 above stood *and* **r up** *upon* a heap very far, 6965
6:12 Joshua **r early** in the morning, and 7925
6:15 that they **r early** about the dawning of 7925
7:16 So Joshua **r up early** in the morning, and 7925
8:10 Joshua **r up early** in the morning, and 7925
8:14 Ai saw *it,* that they hasted and **r up early**, 7925
Jdg 6:21 and there **r up** fire out of the rock, 5927
6:38 for he **r up early** on the morrow, and 7925
7: 1 **r up early**, and pitched beside the well of 7925
9:34 Abimelech **r up**, and all the people that 6965
9:35 Abimelech **r up**, and the people that *were* 6965
9:43 and he **r up** against them, and smote them. 6965
19: 5 early in the morning, that he **r up** to depart: 6965
19: 7 when the man **r up** to depart, his father in 6965
19: 9 when the man **r up** to depart, he, and 6965
19:10 he **r up** and departed, and came over 6965
19:27 her lord **r up** in the morning, and 6965
19:28 the man **r up**, and gat him unto his place. 6965
20: 5 the men of Gibeah **r** against me, and 6965
20:19 the children of Israel **r up** in the morning, 6965
20:33 all the men of Israel **r up** out of their place, 6965
21: 4 that the people **r early**, and built there an 7925
Ru 3:14 she **r up** before one could know another. 6965
1Sa 1: 9 So Hannah **r up** after *they* had eaten in 6965
1:19 they **r up** in the morning **early**, and 7925
15:12 when Samuel **r early** to meet Saul in 7925
16:13 So Samuel **r up**, and went to Ramah. 6965
17:20 David **r up early** in the morning, and 7925
24: 7 Saul **r up** out of the cave, and went on *his* 6965
24: 8 David also **r** afterward, and went out of 6965
25:42 Abigail hasted, and **r**, and rode upon an ass, 6965
29:11 his men **r up early** to depart in 7925
2Sa 15: 2 Absalom **r up early**, and stood beside 7925
18:31 *this* day of all them that **r up** against thee. 6965
19: 8 the king **r**, and sat in the gate. And they 6965
22:40 them that **r up** against me hast thou 6965
22:49 on high above them that **r up** against me: 6965
1Ki 1:49 and **r up**, and went every man his way. 6965
2:19 the king **r up** to meet her, and 6965
3:20 she **r** at midnight, and took my son from 6965
3:21 when I **r** in the morning to give my child 6965
21:16 that Ahab **r up** to go down to the vineyard 6965
2Ki 3:22 they **r up early** in the morning, and the sun 7925
3:24 the Israelites **r up** and smote the Moabites, 6965
7: 5 they **r up** in the twilight, to go unto 6965
8:21 he **r** by night, and smote the Edomites 6965
2Ch 20:20 they **r early** in the morning, and went forth 7925
21: 9 he **r up** by night, and smote the Edomites 6965
26:19 the leprosy even **r up** in his forehead 2224
28:15 men which were expressed by name **r up**, 6965

2Ch 29:20 Hezekiah the king **r early**, and gathered 7925
Ezr 1: 5 **r up** the chief of the fathers of Judah and 6965
5: 2 **r up** Zerubbabel the son of Shealtiel, and 6966
10: 6 Ezra **r up** from before the house of God, 6965
Ne 3: 1 Eliashib the high priest **r up** with his 6965
4:14 **r up**, and said unto the nobles, and to 6965
Job 1: 5 **r up early** in the morning, and 7925
Ps 18:39 under me those that **r up against** me. 6965
124: 2 was on our side, when men **r up** against us: 6965
SS 2: 1 I am the **r** of Sharon, *and* the lily of 2261
5: 5 I **r up** to open to my beloved; and 6965
Isa 35: 1 desert shall rejoice, and blossom as the **r**. 2261
Jer 26:17 **r up** certain of the elders of the land, and 6965
La 3:62 The lips of those that **r up** against me, and 6965
Da 3:24 **r up** in haste, *and* spake, and said unto his 6966
8:27 afterward I **r up**, and did the king's 6965
Jnh 1: 3 Jonah **r up** to flee unto Tarshish from 6965
4: 7 God prepared a worm when the morning **r** 5927
Zep 3: 7 they **r early**, *and* corrupted all their doings. 7925
Mk 10: 1 And he **r** from thence, *450*
10:50 away his garment, **r**, and came to Jesus. *450*
Lk 4:29 And **r up**, and thrust him out of the city, and *450*
5:25 And immediately he **r up** before them, and *450*
5:28 And he left all, **r up**, and followed him. *450*
8:24 Master, master, we perish. Then he **r**, *1453*
16:31 be persuaded, though one **r** from the dead. *450*
22:45 And when he **r up** from prayer, and *450*
24:33 And they **r up** the same hour, and *450*
Jn 11:31 that she **r up** hastily and went out, *450*
Ac 5:17 Then the high priest **r up**, and all they that *450*
5:36 For before these days **r up** Theudas, *450*
5:37 After this *man* **r up** Judas of Galilee in *450*
10:41 and drink with him after he **r** from the dead. *450*
14:20 about him, he **r up**, and came into the city: *450*
15: 5 But there **r up** certain of the sect of *1817*
15: 7 Peter **r up**, and said unto them, Men *and* *450*
16:22 And the multitude **r up together** against *4911*
26:30 thus spoken, the king **r up**, and the governor, *450*
Ro 14: 9 For to this end Christ both died, and **r**, *450*
1Co 10: 7 sat down to eat and drink, and **r up** to play. *450*
15: 4 that he **r** *again* the third day according to *1453*
15:12 Now if Christ be preached that he **r** from *1453*
2Co 5:15 unto him which died for them, and **r** *again*. *1453*
1Th 4:14 if we believe that Jesus died and **r again**, *450*
Rev 19: 3 And her smoke **r up** for ever and ever. *305*

ROSH (1)
Ge 46:21 and Ashbel, Gera, and Naaman, Ehi, and **R**, 7220

ROT (5) [ROTTEN, ROTTENNESS]
Nu 5:21 when the LORD doth make thy thigh to **r**, 5307
5:22 make *thy* belly to swell, and *thy* thigh to **r**: 5307
5:27 her belly shall swell, and her thigh shall **r**: 5307
Pr 10: 7 but the name of the wicked shall **r**. 7537
Isa 40:20 no oblation chooseth a tree *that* will not **r**; 7537

ROTTEN (5) [ROT]
Job 13:28 he, as a **r thing**, consumeth, as a garment 7538
41:27 iron as straw, *and* brass as **r** wood. 7539
Jer 38:11 took thence old cast clouts and old **r rags**, 4418
38:12 **r rags** under thine armholes under 4418
Joel 1:17 The seed is **r** under their clods, the garners 5685

ROTTENNESS (5) [ROT]
Pr 12: 4 she that maketh ashamed *is* as **r** in his 7538
14:30 of the flesh: but envy the **r** of the bones. 7538
Isa 5:24 *so* their root shall be as **r**, and their blossom 4716
Hos 5:12 as a moth, and to the house of Judah as **r**. 7538
Hab 3:16 **r** entered into my bones, and I trembled in 7538

ROUGH (7) [ROUGHLY]
Dt 21: 4 shall bring down the heifer unto a **r** valley, 386
Isa 27: 8 he stayeth his **r** wind in the day of the east 7186
40: 4 be made straight, and the **r places** plain: 7406
Jer 51:27 cause the horses to come up as the **r** 5569
Da 8:21 the **r** goat *is* the king of Grecia: and 8163
Zec 13: 4 neither shall they wear a **r** garment to 8181
Lk 3: 5 and the **r** ways *shall be* made smooth; *5138*

ROUGHLY (6) [ROUGH]
Ge 42: 7 strange unto them, and spake **r** unto them; 7186
42:30 spake **r** to us, and took us for spies of 7186
1Sa 20:10 tell me? or what *if* thy father answer thee **r**? 7186
1Ki 12:13 the king answered the people **r**, and 7186
2Ch 10:13 the king answered them **r**; and king 7186
Pr 18:23 useth intreaties; but the rich answereth **r**. 5794

ROUND (320)
Ge 19: 4 **compassed** the house **r**, both old and 5437
23:17 that *were* in all the borders **r about**, 5439
35: 5 was upon the cities that *were* **r about** them, 5439
37: 7 your sheaves **stood r about**, and 5437
41:48 of the field, which *was* **r about** every city, 5439
Ex 7:24 all the Egyptians digged **r about** the river 5439
16:13 in the morning the dew lay **r about** 5439
16:14 of the wilderness *there lay* a small **r thing**, 2636
19:12 shalt set bounds unto the people **r about**, 5439
25:11 shalt make upon it a crown *of* gold **r about**. 5439
25:24 and make thereto a crown *of* gold **r about**. 5439
25:25 unto it a border of a handbreadth **r about**, 5439
25:25 golden crown to the border thereof **r about**. 5439
27:17 All the pillars **r about** the court *shall be* 5439
28:32 of woven work **r about** the hole of it, 5439
28:33 and of scarlet, **r about** the hem thereof; 5439
28:33 and bells of gold between them **r about**: 5439
28:34 upon the hem of the robe **r about**. 5439
29:16 and sprinkle *it* **r about** upon the altar. 5439
29:20 sprinkle the blood upon the altar **r about**. 5439
30: 3 the sides thereof **r about**, and the horns 5439
30: 3 shalt make unto it a crown *of* gold **r about**. 5439
37: 2 and made a crown *of* gold to it **r about**. 5439
37:11 made thereunto a crown *of* gold **r about**. 5439
37:12 a border of a handbreadth **r about**; 5439
37:12 of gold for the border thereof **r about**. 5439
37:26 the sides thereof **r about**, and the horns of 5439
37:26 he made unto it a crown *of* gold **r about**. 5439
38:16 All the hangings of the court **r about** *were* 5439
38:20 and of the court **r about**, *were of* brass. 5439
38:31 the sockets of the court **r about**, and 5439
38:31 and all the pins of the court **r about**. 5439
39:23 *with* a band **r about** the hole, *that* it should 5439
39:25 **r about** between the pomegranates; 5439
39:26 **r about** the hem of the robe to minister *in*; 5439
40: 8 thou shalt set up the court **r about**, and 5439
40:33 he reared up the court **r about** 5439
Lev 1: 5 sprinkle the blood **r about** upon the altar 5439
1:11 shall sprinkle his blood **r about** upon 5439
3: 2 sprinkle the blood upon the altar **r about**. 5439
3: 8 the blood thereof **r about** upon the altar. 5439
3:13 the blood thereof upon the altar **r about**. 5439
7: 2 the blood thereof shall he sprinkle **r about** 5439
8:15 put *it* upon the horns of the altar **r about** 5439
8:19 sprinkled the blood upon the altar **r about**. 5439
8:24 sprinkled the blood upon the altar **r about**. 5439
9:12 which he sprinkled **r about** upon the altar. 5439
9:18 which he sprinkled upon the altar **r about**, 5439
14:41 the house to be scraped within **r about**, 5439
16:18 put *it* upon the horns of the altar **r about**. 5439
19:27 Ye shall not **r** the corners of your heads, 5362
25:31 **r about** them shall be counted as the fields 5439
25:44 *shall be* of the heathen that *are* **r about** 5439
Nu 1:50 and shall encamp **r about** the tabernacle. 5439
1:53 the Levites shall pitch **r about** 5439
3:26 by the altar **r about**, and the cords of it for 5439
3:37 the pillars of the court **r about**, and 5439
4:26 by the tabernacle and by the altar **r about**, 5439
4:32 the pillars of the court **r about**, and 5439
11:24 and set them **r about** the tabernacle. 5439
11:31 **r about** the camp, and as it were two cubits 5439
11:32 abroad for themselves **r about** the camp. 5439
16:34 all Israel that *were* **r about** them fled at 5439
22: 4 company lick up all *that are* **r about** us, 5439
32:33 *even* the cities of the country **r about**. 5439
34:12 your land with the coasts thereof **r about**. 5439
35: 2 Levites suburbs for the cities **r about** them. 5439
35: 4 and outward a thousand cubits **r about**. 5439
Dt 6:14 of the gods of the people which *are* **r about** 5439
12:10 rest from all your enemies **r about**, 4480+5439
13: 7 gods of the people which *are* **r about** you, 5439
21: 2 cities which *are* **r about** him that is slain: 5439
25:19 rest from all thine enemies **r about**, 4480+5439
Jos 6: 3 men of war, *and* **go r about** the city once. 5362
7: 9 land shall hear *of it*, and shall **environ** us **r**, 5437
15:12 Judah **r about** according to their families. 5439
18:20 by the coasts thereof **r about**, according to 5439
19: 8 all the villages that *were* **r about** these 5439
21:11 with the suburbs thereof **r about** it. 5439
21:42 every one with their suburbs **r about** them: 5439
21:44 the LORD gave them rest **r about**, 5439

R

Jos 23: 1 Israel from all their enemies **r about,** 4480+5439
Jdg 2:12 of the gods of the people that *were* **r about** 5439
2:14 the hands of their enemies **r about,** 4480+5439
7:21 they stood every man in his place **r about** 5439
19:22 **beset** the house **r about,** *and* beat at 5437
20: 5 **beset** the house **r about** upon me by night, 5437
20:29 And Israel set liers in wait **r about** Gibeah. 5439
20:43 *Thus* they **inclosed** the Benjamites **r about,** 3803
1Sa 14:21 into the camp *from the country* **r about,** 5439
23:26 **compassed** David and his men **r about** 5849
26: 5 and the people pitched **r about** him. 5439
26: 7 but Abner and the people lay **r about** him. 5439
31: 9 sent into the land of the Philistines **r about,** 5439
2Sa 5: 9 David built **r about** from Millo and inward. 5439
7: 1 rest **r about** from all his enemies; 4480+5439
22:12 he made darkness pavilions **r about** him, 5439
1Ki 3: 1 and the wall of Jerusalem **r about.** 5439
4:24 had peace on all sides **r about** him. 4480+5439
4:31 and his fame was in all nations **r about.** 5439
6: 5 of the house he built chambers **r about,** 5439
6: 5 *against* the walls of the house **r about,** 5439
6: 5 the oracle: and he made chambers **r about:** 5439
6: 6 the house he made narrowed rests **r about,** 5439
6:29 he carved all the walls of the house **r about** 4524
7:12 the great court **r about** *was with* three rows 5439
7:18 two rows **r about** upon the one network, 5439
7:20 *in* rows **r about** upon the other chapiter. 5439
7:23 *it was* **r** all about, and his height *was* five 5696
7:23 thirty cubits did **compass** it **r about.** 5437+5439
7:24 **r about** *there were* knops **compassing** 5437+5439
7:24 ten in a cubit, compassing the sea **r about:** 5439
7:31 the mouth thereof *was* **r** *after* the work of 5696
7:31 with their borders, foursquare, not **r.** 5696
7:35 in the top of the base *was there* a **r** compass 5696
7:36 of every one, and additions **r about.** 5439
10:19 and the top of the throne *was* **r** behind: 5696
18:35 the water ran **r about** the altar; and 5439
2Ki 6:17 and chariots of fire **r about** Elisha. 5439
11: 8 ye shall compass the king **r about,** 5439
11:11 his weapons in his hand, **r about** the king, 5439
17:15 *went* after the heathen that *were* **r about** 5439
23: 5 and in the **places r about** Jerusalem; 4524
25: 1 and they built forts against it **r about.** 5439
25: 4 Chaldees *were* against the city **r about:**) 5439
25:10 brake down the walls of Jerusalem **r about.** 5439
25:17 pomegranates upon the chapiter **r about,** 5439
1Ch 4:33 all their villages that *were* **r about** the same 5439
6:55 and the suburbs thereof **r about** it. 5439
9:27 they lodged **r about** the house of God, 5439
10: 9 sent into the land of the Philistines **r about,** 5439
11: 8 he built the city **r about,** even from Millo 5439
11: 8 city round about, even from Millo **r about:** 5439
22: 9 rest from all his enemies **r about:** 4480+5439
28:12 of all the chambers **r about,** of 5439
2Ch 4: 2 **r** in compass, and five cubits the height 5696
4: 2 line of thirty cubits did compass it **r about.** 5439
4: 3 which did compass it **r about:** 5439+5439
4: 3 ten in a cubit, compassing the sea **r about.** 5439
14:14 they smote all the cities **r about** Gerar; 5439
15:15 the LORD gave them rest **r about.** 4480+5439
17:10 of the lands that *were* **r about** Judah, 5439
20:30 for his God gave him rest **r about.** 4480+5439
23: 7 the Levites shall compass the king **r about,** 5439
23:10 and the temple, by the king **r about.** 5439
34: 6 unto Naphtali, with their mattocks **r about.** 5439
Ne 12:28 both out of the plain country **r about** 5439
12:29 builded them villages **r about** Jerusalem. 5439
Job 10: 8 and fashioned me together **r about;** 5439
16:13 His archers **compass** me **r about,** he 5437
19:12 and encamp **r about** my tabernacle. 5439
22:10 Therefore snares *are* **r about** thee, and 5439
37:12 it is turned **r about** by his counsels: 4524
41:14 of his face? his teeth *are* terrible **r about.** 5439
Ps 3: 6 have set *themselves* against me **r about.** 5439
18:11 his pavilion **r about** him *were* dark waters 5439
22:12 strong *bulls* of Bashan have **beset** me **r.** 3803
27: 6 lifted up above mine enemies **r about** me: 5439
34: 7 encampeth **r about** them that fear him, 5439
44:13 and a derision to them that are **r about** us. 5439
48:12 Walk about Zion, and **go r about** her: 5362
50: 3 it shall be very tempestuous **r about** him. 5439
59: 6 a noise like a dog, and **go r about** the city. 5437
59:14 a noise like a dog, and **go r about** the city. 5437
76:11 let all that be **r about** him bring presents 5439
78:28 of their camp, **r about** their habitations. 5439
79: 3 they shed like water **r about** Jerusalem; 5439
79: 4 and derision to them that are **r about** us. 5439
88:17 They **came r about** me daily like water; 5437
89: 8 or *to* thy faithfulness **r about** thee? 5439
97: 2 Clouds and darkness *are* **r about** him: 5439
97: 3 and burneth up his enemies **r about.** 5439
125: 2 *As* the mountains *are* **r about** Jerusalem, so 5439
125: 2 the LORD *is* **r about** his people from 5439
128: 3 thy children like olive plants **r about** thy 5439
SS 7: 2 Thy navel *is like* a **r** goblet, *which* wanteth 5469
Isa 3:18 *their* cauls, and *their* **r tires like the moon,** 7720
15: 8 For the cry is **gone r about** the borders of 5362
29: 3 camp against thee **r about,** 1754+1886.1+3509.1
42:25 it hath set him on fire **r about,** yet he 4480+5439
49:18 Lift up thine eyes **r about,** and behold: 5439
60: 4 Lift up thine eyes **r about,** and see: all they 5439
Jer 1:15 against all the walls thereof **r about,** and 5439
4:17 a field, are they against her **r about;** 4480+5439
6: 3 shall pitch *their* tents against her **r about;** 5439
12: 9 the birds **r about** *are* against her; 5439
21:14 and it shall devour all things **r about** it. 5439
25: 9 against all these nations **r about,** and 5439
46: 5 fear *was* **r about,** saith the LORD. 4480+5439
46:14 for the sword shall devour **r about** thee. 5439
50:14 in array against Babylon **r about:** 5439
50:15 Shout against her **r about:** she hath given 5439
50:29 that bend the bow, camp against it **r about;** 5439
50:32 and it shall devour all **r about** him. 5439
51: 2 they shall be against her **r about.** 4480+5439
52: 4 against it, and built forts against it **r about.** 5439
52: 7 the Chaldeans *were* by the city **r about:**) 5439
52:14 down all the walls of Jerusalem **r about.** 5439
52:22 pomegranates upon the chapiters **r about,** 5439
52:23 upon the network *were* an hundred **r about.** 5439
La 1:17 *that* his adversaries *should be* **r about** him: 5439
2: 3 a flaming fire, *which* devoureth **r about.** 5439
2:22 *in* a solemn day my terrors **r about,** 4480+5439
Eze 1:18 their rings *were* full *of* eyes **r about** them 5439
1:27 as the appearance of fire **r about** within it, 5439
1:27 of fire, and it had brightness **r about.** 5439
1:28 the appearance of the brightness **r about.** 5439
4: 2 and set *battering* rams against it **r about.** 5439
5: 5 and countries *that are* **r about** her. 5439
5: 6 than the countries that *are* **r about** her: 5439
5: 7 more than the nations that *are* **r about** you, 5439
5: 7 of the nations that *are* **r about** you; 5439
5:12 a third *part* shall fall by the sword **r about** 5439
5:14 among the nations that *are* **r about** thee, 5439
5:15 unto the nations that *are* **r about** thee, 5439
6: 5 I will scatter your bones **r about** your 5439
6:13 be among their idols **r about** their altars, 5439
8:10 pourtrayed upon the wall **r about.** 5439+5439
10:12 and the wheels, *were* full *of* eyes **r about,** 5439
11:12 of the heathen that *are* **r about** you. 5439
16:37 I will even gather them **r about** 4480+5439
16:57 all *that are* **r about** her, the daughters of 5439
16:57 which despise thee **r about.** 4480+5439
23:24 thee buckler and shield and helmet **r about:** 5439
27:11 thine army *were* upon thy walls **r about,** 5439
27:11 their shields upon thy walls **r about;** 5439
28:24 grieving thorn of all *that are* **r about** them, 5439
28:26 that despise them **r about** them; 4480+5439
31: 4 with her rivers running **r about** his plants, 5439
32:23 and her company is **r about** her grave: 5439
32:24 and all her multitude **r about** her grave, 5439
32:25 her graves *are* **r about** him: all of them 5439
32:26 her graves *are* **r about** him: all of them 5439
34:26 and the **places r about** my hill a blessing; 5439
36: 4 of the heathen that *are* **r about;** 4480+5439
36:36 the heathen that are left **r about** you shall 5439
37: 2 caused me to pass by them **r about:** 5439+5439
40: 5 on the outside of the house **r about,** 5439+5439
40:14 post of the court **r about** the gate. 5439+5439
40:16 to their posts within the gate **r about,** 5439+5439
40:16 windows *were* **r about** inward: 5439+5439
40:17 made for the court **r about:** 5439+5439
40:25 and in the arches thereof **r about,** 5439+5439
40:29 and in the arches thereof **r about:** 5439+5439
40:30 the arches **r about** *were* five and 5439+5439
40:33 in the arches thereof **r about:** 5439+5439
40:36 and the windows to it **r about:** 5439+5439
40:43 a hand broad, fastened **r about:** 5439+5439
41: 5 **r about** the house on every side. 5439+5439

Eze 41: 6 house for the side chambers **r about**, 5439+5439
41: 7 *went* still upward **r about** the house: 5439+5439
41: 8 also the height of the house **r about**: 5439+5439
41:10 cubits **r about** the house on every side. 5439
41:11 that was left *was* five cubits **r about**. 5439+5439
41:12 *was* five cubits thick **r about**, 5439+5439
41:16 the galleries **r about** on their three *stories,* 5439
41:16 cieled with wood **r about**, and 5439+5439
41:17 by all the wall **r about** within 5439+5439
41:19 made through all the house **r about**. 5439+5439
42:15 the east, and measured it **r about**. 5439+5439
42:16 with the measuring reed **r about**. 5439
42:17 with the measuring reed **r about**. 5439
42:20 it had a wall **r about**, five hundred 5439+5439
43:12 thereof **r about** *shall be* most holy. 5439+5439
43:13 by the edge thereof **r about** *shall be* a span: 5439
43:20 of the settle, and upon the border **r about**: 5439
45: 1 *be* holy in all the borders thereof **r about**. 5439
45: 2 five hundred *in breadth,* square **r about**; 5439
45: 2 fifty cubits **r about** *for* the suburbs thereof. 5439
46:23 *there was* a row *of building* **r about** in 5439
46:23 **r about** them four, and *it was* made *with* 5439
46:23 *with* boiling places under the rows **r about**. 5439
48:35 *It was* **r about** eighteen thousand *measures:* 5439
Joel 3:11 gather yourselves together **r about**: 4480+5439
3:12 I sit to judge all the heathen **r about**. 4480+5439
Am 3:11 An adversary *there shall be* even **r about** 5439
Jnh 2: 5 the depth **closed** me **r about**, the weeds 5437
Na 3: 8 *that had* the waters **r about** it, 5439
Zec 2: 5 will be unto her a wall of fire **r about**, and 5439
7: 7 and the cities thereof **r about** her, 5439
12: 2 of trembling unto all the people **r about**, 5439
12: 6 they shall devour all the people **r about**, 5439
14:14 the wealth of all the heathen **r about** shall 5439
Mt 3: 5 and all the **region r about** Jordan, *4066*
14:35 they sent out into all that **country r about**, *4066*
21:33 and hedged it **r about**, and digged a *4060*
Mk 1:28 throughout all the **region r about** Galilee. *4066*
3: 5 And when he had **looked r about** on them *4017*
3:34 And he looked **r about** on them which sat *2945*
5:32 And he **looked r about** to see her that had *4017*
6: 6 And he went **r about** the villages, teaching. *2945*
6:36 that they may go into the country **r about**, *2945*
6:55 ran through that whole **region r about**, *4066*
9: 8 when they had **looked r about**, *4017*
10:23 And Jesus **looked r about**, and saith unto *4017*
11:11 when he had **looked r about** upon all *4017*
Lk 1:65 And fear came on all that **dwelt r about** *4039*
2: 9 the glory of the Lord **shone r about** them: *4034*
4:14 fame of him through all the **region r about**. *4066*
4:37 into every place of the **country r about**. *4066*
6:10 And **looking r about** upon them all, he said *4017*
7:17 and throughout all the **region r about**. *4066*
8:37 **country** of the Gadarenes **r about** *4066*
9:12 may go into the towns and country **r about**, *2945*
19:43 and **compass** thee **r**, and keep thee in on *4033*
Jn 10:24 Then **came** the Jews **r about** him, and *2944*
Ac 5:16 *out* of the cities **r about** unto Jerusalem, *4038*
9: 3 suddenly there **shined r about** him a light *4015*
14: 6 and *unto* the **region that lieth r about**: *4066*
14:20 as the disciples **stood r about** him, *2944*
22: 6 from heaven a great light **r about** me. *4012*
25: 7 came down from Jerusalem **stood r about**, *4026*
26:13 **shining r about** me and them which *4034*
Ro 15:19 and **r about** unto Illyricum, *2945*
Heb 9: 4 the ark of the covenant overlaid **r about** *3840*
Rev 4: 3 *there was* a rainbow **r about** the throne, *2943*
4: 4 And **r about** the throne *were* four and *2943*
4: 6 midst of the throne, and **r about** the throne, *2945*
5:11 I heard the voice of many angels **r about** *2943*
7:11 And all the angels stood **r about** the throne, *2945*

ROUSE (1)
Ge 49: 9 and as an old lion; who shall **r** him **up**? 6965

ROUTED See DISCOMFITED; DISCOMFITURE

ROUTING See DISCOMFITED; DISCOMFITURE

ROVERS (1)
1Ch 12:21 they helped David against the band *of the* **r**: NIH

ROW (17) [ROWED, ROWERS, ROWING, ROWS]
Ex 28:17 *the first* **r** *shall be* a sardius, a topaz, and 2905
28:17 and a carbuncle: this *shall be* the first **r**. 2905
28:18 the second **r** *shall be* an emerald, 2905
28:19 the third **r** a ligure, an agate, and 2905
28:20 the fourth **r** a beryl, and an onyx, and 2905
39:10 *the first* **r** *was* a sardius, a topaz, and 2905
39:10 and a carbuncle: *this was* the first **r**. 2905
39:11 the second **r**, an emerald, a sapphire, and 2905
39:12 the third **r**, a ligure, an agate, and 2905
39:13 the fourth **r**, a beryl, an onyx, and a jasper: 2905
Lev 24: 6 thou shalt set them *in* two rows, six on a **r**, 4635
24: 7 shalt put pure frankincense upon *each* **r**, 4635
1Ki 6:36 of hewed stone, and a **r** of cedar beams. 2905
7: 3 that *lay* on forty five pillars, fifteen *in* a **r**. 2905
7:12 a **r** of cedar beams, both for the inner court 2905
Ezr 6: 4 rows of great stones, and a **r** of new timber: 5073
Eze 46:23 *there was* a **r** *of building* round about in 2905

ROWED (2) [ROW]
Jnh 1:13 Nevertheless the men **r hard** to bring *it* to 2864
Jn 6:19 So when they had **r** about five and twenty *1643*

ROWERS (1) [ROW]
Eze 27:26 Thy **r** have brought thee into great waters: 7751

ROWING (1) [ROW]
Mk 6:48 And he saw them toiling in **r**; for the wind *1643*

ROWS (16) [ROW]
Ex 28:17 it settings of stones, *even* four **r** of stones: 2905
39:10 they set in it four **r** of stones: *the first* row 2905
Lev 24: 6 thou shalt set them *in* two **r**, six on a row, 4634
1Ki 6:36 he built the inner court *with* three **r** of 2905
7: 2 thirty cubits, upon four **r** of cedar pillars, 2905
7: 4 *there were* windows *in* three **r**, and 2905
7:12 about *was with* three **r** *of* hewed stones, 2905
7:18 two **r** round about upon the one network, 2905
7:20 the pomegranates *were* two hundred *in* **r** 2905
7:24 the knops *were* cast *in* two **r**, when it was 2905
7:42 *even* two **r** *of* pomegranates for one 2905
2Ch 4: 3 Two **r** *of* oxen *were* cast, when it was cast. 2905
4:13 two **r** *of* pomegranates on each wreath, to 2905
Ezr 6: 4 *With* three **r** of great stones, and a row of 5073
SS 1:10 Thy cheeks are comely with **r** *of jewels,* 8447
Eze 46:23 *it was* made *with* boiling places under the **r** 2918

ROYAL (29)
Ge 49:20 *shall be* fat, and he shall yield **r** dainties. 4428
Jos 10: 2 as one of the **r** cities, and because it *was* 4467
1Sa 27: 5 for why should thy servant dwell in the **r** 4467
2Sa 12:26 the children of Ammon, and took the **r** city. 4410
1Ki 10:13 which Solomon gave her of his **r** bounty. 4428
2Ki 11: 1 she arose and destroyed all the seed **r**. 4467
25:25 of the seed **r**, came, and ten men with him, 4410
1Ch 29:25 bestowed upon him *such* **r** majesty as had 4438
2Ch 22:10 destroyed all the seed **r** of the house of 4467
Est 1: 7 **r** wine in abundance, according to the state 4438
1: 9 **r** house which *belonged* to king Ahasuerus. 4438
1:11 the queen before the king with the crown **r**, 4438
1:19 let there go a **r** commandment from him, 4438
1:19 let the king give her **r estate** unto another 4438
2:16 into his house **r** in the tenth month, 4438
2:17 so that he set the **r** crown upon her head, 4438
5: 1 that Esther put on *her* **r** *apparel,* and 4438
5: 1 the king sat upon his **r** throne in the royal 4438
5: 1 the king sat upon his royal throne in the **r** 4438
6: 8 Let the **r** apparel be brought which the king 4438
6: 8 the crown **r** which is set upon his head: 4438
8:15 the presence of the king in **r** apparel *of* blue 4438
Isa 62: 3 and a **r** diadem in the hand of thy God. 4410
Jer 41: 1 of the seed **r**, and the princes of the king, 4410
43:10 he shall spread his **r pavilion** over them. 8237
Da 6: 7 have consulted together to establish a **r** 4430
Ac 12:21 arrayed in **r** apparel, sat upon his throne, and *937*
Jas 2: 8 If ye fulfil the **r** law according to *937*
1Pe 2: 9 a **r** priesthood, a holy nation, a peculiar *934*

RUBBING (1)
Lk 6: 1 of corn, and did eat, **r** *them* in *their* hands. *5597*

RUBBISH (2)
Ne 4: 2 out of the heaps of the **r** which are burnt? 6083
4:10 of burdens is decayed, and *there is* much **r**; 6083

RUBIES (6)
Job 28:18 for the price of wisdom *is* above **r**. 6443
Pr 3:15 She *is* more precious than **r**: and all 6443

R

Pr 8:11 For wisdom *is* better than r; and all 6443
20:15 There is gold, and a multitude of r: but 6443
31:10 for her price *is* far above r. 6443
La 4: 7 they were more ruddy *in* body than r, 6443

RUBY See AGATES; SARDIUS

RUDDER (1)
Ac 27:40 and loosed the r bands, and hoised up *4079*

RUDDY (4)
1Sa 16:12 Now he *was* r, *and* withal of a beautiful 132
17:42 *but* a youth, and r, and of a fair countenance. 132
SS 5:10 My beloved *is* white and r, the chiefest 122
La 4: 7 they were more r *in* body than rubies, 119

RUDE (1)
2Co 11: 6 But though *I be* r in speech, yet not in *2399*

RUDIMENTS (2)
Col 2: 8 after the r of the world, and not after *4747*
2:20 be dead with Christ from the r of the world, *4747*

RUE (1)
Lk 11:42 for ye tithe mint and r and all *manner of* *4076*

RUFUS (2)
Mk 15:21 the father of Alexander and **R**, to bear his *4504*
Ro 16:13 Salute **R** chosen in the Lord, and *4504*

RUHAMAH (1) [LO-RUHAMAH]
Hos 2: 1 Ammi; and to your sisters, **R**. 7355

RUIN (11) [RUINED, RUINOUS, RUINS]
2Ch 28:23 they were the r of him, and of all Israel. 3782
Ps 89:40 thou hast brought his strong holds to r. 4288
Pr 24:22 and who knoweth the r of them both? 6365
26:28 by it; and a flattering mouth worketh r. 4072
Isa 3: 6 our ruler, and *let* this r *be* under thy hand: 4384
23:13 the palaces thereof; *and* he brought it to r. 4654
25: 2 of a city a heap; *of* a defenced city a r: 4654
Eze 18:30 so iniquity shall not be your r. 4383
27:27 the midst of the seas in the day of thy r. 4658
31:13 Upon his r shall all the fowls of the heaven 4658
Lk 6:49 it fell; and the r of that house was great. *4485*

RUINED (3) [RUIN]
Isa 3: 8 For Jerusalem is r, and Judah is fallen: 3782
Eze 36:35 and r cities *are become* fenced, 2040
36:36 know that I the LORD build the r *places,* 2040

RUINOUS (3) [RUIN]
2Ki 19:25 be to lay waste fenced cities *into* r heaps. 5327
Isa 17: 1 from *being* a city, and it shall be a r heap. 4654
37:26 be to lay waste defenced cities *into* r heaps. 5327

RUINS (3) [RUIN]
Eze 21:15 heart may faint, and *their* r be multiplied: 4383
Am 9:11 I will raise up his r, and I will build it as *in* 2034
Ac 15:16 and I will build again the r thereof, and *2679*

R

RULE (66) [RULED, RULER, RULER'S, RULERS, RULEST, RULETH, RULING]
Ge 1:16 the greater light to r the day, and the lesser 4475
1:16 the day, and the lesser light to r the night: 4475
1:18 to r over the day and over the night, and 4910
3:16 *be* to thy husband, and he shall r over thee. 4910
4: 7 *be* his desire, and thou shalt r over him. 4910
Lev 25:43 Thou shalt not r over him with rigour; but 7287
25:46 ye shall not r one over another with rigour. 7287
25:53 *the other* shall not r with rigour **over** him in 7287
Jdg 8:22 **R** thou over us, both thou, and thy son, and 4910
8:23 said unto them, I will not r over you, 4910
8:23 over you, neither shall my son r over you: 4910
8:23 rule over you: the LORD shall r over you. 4910
1Ki 9:23 which **bare** r over the people that wrought 7287
22:31 two captains that had r over *his* chariots, NIH
2Ch 8:10 and fifty, that **bare** r over the people. 7287
Ne 5:15 *yea,* even their servants **bare** r over 7980
Est 1:22 that every man should **bear** r in his own 8323
9: 1 the Jews had r over them that hated them;) 7980
Ps 110: 2 r thou in the midst of thine enemies. 7287
136: 8 The sun to r by day: for his mercy *endureth* 4475
136: 9 The moon and stars to r by night: for his 4475
Pr 8:16 By me princes r, and nobles, *even* all 8323
12:24 The hand of the diligent shall **bear** r: but 4910
17: 2 A wise servant shall **have** r over a son that 4910
19:10 much less for a servant to **have** r over 4910
25:28 He that *hath* no r over his own spirit *is like* 4623
29: 2 when the wicked **beareth** r, the people 4910
Ecc 2:19 yet shall he **have** r over all my labour 7980
Isa 3: 4 their princes, and babes shall r over them. 4910
3:12 their oppressors, and women r over them. 4910
14: 2 and they shall r over their oppressors. 7287
19: 4 a fierce king shall r over them, saith 4910
28:14 that r this people which *is* in Jerusalem. 4910
32: 1 and princes shall r in judgment. 8323
40:10 strong *hand,* and his arm *shall* r for him: 4910
41: 2 before him, and **made** *him* r **over** kings? 7287
44:13 The carpenter stretcheth out *his* r; 6957
52: 5 they that r **over** them make *them* to howl, 4910
63:19 We are *thine:* thou never **barest** r over 4910
Jer 5:31 and the priests **bear** r by their means; 7287
Eze 19:11 rods for the sceptres of them that **bare** r, 4910
19:14 she hath no strong rod *to be* a sceptre to r. 4910
20:33 and with fury poured out, will I r over you: 4427
29:15 that *they* shall no more r over the nations. 7287
Da 2:39 which shall **bear** r over all the earth. 7981
4:26 shalt have known that the heavens do r. 7990
11: 3 that shall r *with* great dominion, and 4910
11:39 he shall **cause** them **to** r **over** many, and 4910
Joel 2:17 that the heathen should r **over** them: 4910
Zec 6:13 and shall sit and r upon his throne: 4910
Mt 2: 6 a Governor, that shall r my people Israel. *4165*
Mk 10:42 r **over** the Gentiles exercise lordship over *757*
1Co 15:24 when he shall have put down all r and *746*
2Co 10:13 according to the measure of the r which *2583*
10:15 by you according to our r abundantly, *2583*
Gal 6:16 And as many as walk according to this r, *2583*
Php 3:16 *let us* walk by the same r, *let us* mind *2583*
Col 3:15 And let the peace of God r in your hearts, *1018*
1Ti 3: 5 (For if a man know not how to r his own *4291*
5:17 Let the elders that r well be counted worthy *4291*
Heb 13: 7 Remember them which **have the** r **over** *2233*
13:17 Obey them that **have the** r **over** you, and *2233*
13:24 Salute all them that **have the** r **over** you, *2233*
Rev 2:27 And he shall r them with a rod of iron; *4165*
12: 5 who was to r all nations with a rod of iron: *4165*
19:15 and he shall r them with a rod of iron: and *4165*

RULED (13) [RULE]
Ge 24: 2 of his house that r over all that he had, 4910
41:40 unto thy word shall all my people be r: 5401
Jos 12: 2 who dwelt in Heshbon, *and* r from Aroer, 4910
Ru 1: 1 came to pass in the days when the judges r, 8199
1Ki 5:16 which r over the people that wrought in 7287
1Ch 26: 6 that r throughout the house of their father: 4474
Ezr 4:20 which have r over all *countries* beyond 7990
Ps 106:41 and they that hated them r over them. 4910
Isa 14: 6 he that r the nations in anger, *is* persecuted, 7287
La 5: 8 Servants have r over us: *there is* none that 4910
Eze 34: 4 with force and with cruelty have ye r them. 7287
Da 5:21 till he knew that the most high God r in 7990
11: 4 nor according to his dominion which he r: 4910

RULER (84) [RULE]
Ge 41:43 he made him *r* over all the land of Egypt. NIH
43:16 he said to **the** r of his house, 834+5921
45: 8 and a r throughout all the land of Egypt. 4910
Ex 22:28 the gods, nor curse the r of thy people. 5387
Lev 4:22 When a r hath sinned, and done somewhat 5387
Nu 13: 2 ye send a man, every one a r among them. 5387
Jdg 9:30 when Zebul the r of the city heard 8269
1Sa 25:30 and shall have appointed thee r over Israel; 5057
2Sa 6:21 to appoint me r over the people of 5057
7: 8 to be r over my people, over Israel: 5057
20:26 Ira also the Jairite was a **chief** r about 3548
1Ki 1:35 I have appointed him to be r over Israel and 5057
11:28 he **made** him r over all the charge of 6485
2Ki 25:22 **made** Gedaliah the son of Ahikam, the son of Shaphan, r. 6485
1Ch 5: 2 his brethren, and of him *came* the **chief**; 5057
9:11 son of Ahitub, the r of the house of God; 5057
9:20 Phinehas the son of Eleazar was the r over 5057
11: 2 and thou shalt be r over my people Israel. 5057
17: 7 that *thou* shouldest be r over my people 5057
26:24 the son of Moses, *was* r of the treasures. 5057
27: 4 and *of* his course *was* Mikloth also the r: 5057
27:16 the r of the Reubenites *was* Eliezer the son 5057
28: 4 for he hath chosen Judah to be the r; and 5057

2Ch 6: 5 neither chose I any man to be a r over my 5057
7:18 There shall not fail thee a man *to be* r in 4910
11:22 the chief, to be r among his brethren: 5057
19:11 the r of the house of Judah, for all 5057
26:11 hand of Jeiel the scribe and Maaseiah the r, 7860
31:12 over which Cononiah the Levite *was* r, and 5057
31:13 and Azariah the r of the house of God. 5057
Ne 3: 9 of Hur, the r of the half part of Jerusalem. 8269
3:12 the r of the half part of Jerusalem, he and 8269
3:14 of Rechab, the r of part of Beth-haccerem; 8269
3:15 son of Col-hozeh, the r of part of Mizpah; 8269
3:16 of Azbuk, the r of the half part of Beth-zur, 8269
3:17 the r of the half part of Keilah, in his part. 8269
3:18 of Henadad, the r of the half part of Keilah. 8269
3:19 Ezer the son of Jeshua, the r of Mizpah, 8269
7: 2 Hananiah the r of the palace, charge over 8269
11:11 of Ahitub, *was* the r of the house of God. 5057
Ps 68:27 There *is* little Benjamin *with* their r, 7287
105:20 *even* the r of the people, and let him go 4910
105:21 lord of his house, and r of all his substance: 4910
Pr 6: 7 Which having no guide, overseer, or r, 4910
23: 1 When thou sittest to eat with a r, 4910
28:15 *so is* a wicked r over the poor people. 4910
29:12 If a r hearken to lies, all his servants *are* 4910
Ecc 10: 4 If the spirit of the r rise up against thee, 4910
10: 5 as an error *which* proceedeth from the r: 7989
Isa 3: 6 be thou our r, and *let* this ruin *be* under thy 7101
3: 7 make me not a r of the people. 7101
16: 1 Send ye the lamb *to* the r of the land from 4910
Jer 51:46 and violence in the land, r against ruler. 4910
51:46 and violence in the land, ruler against r. 4910
Da 2:10 therefore *there is* no king, lord, nor r, 7990
2:38 and hath **made** thee r over them all. 7981
2:48 **made** him r over the whole province of 7981
5: 7 and shall be the third r in the kingdom. 7981
5:16 and shalt be the third r in the kingdom. 7981
5:29 that *he* should be the third r in 7990
Mic 5: 2 come forth unto me *that is* to be r in Israel; 4910
Hab 1:14 creeping things, *that have* no r over them? 4910
Mt 9:18 there came a *certain* r, and worshipped him, *758*
24:45 whom his lord hath **made** r over his *2525*
24:47 That he shall **make** him r over all his *2525*
25:21 **make** thee r over many *things:* enter thou *2525*
25:23 **make** thee r over many *things:* enter thou *2525*
Mk 5:35 there came from the **r of the synagogue's** *752*
5:36 he saith unto the **r of the synagogue**, Be not *752*
5:38 to the house of the **r of the synagogue**, *752*
Lk 8:41 and he was a r of the synagogue: *758*
8:49 **r of the synagogue's** *house,* saying to him, *752*
12:42 whom *his* lord shall **make** r over his *2525*
12:44 that he will **make** him r over all that he *2525*
13:14 And the **r of the synagogue** answered with *752*
18:18 And a certain r asked him, saying, *758*
Jn 2: 9 When the **r of the feast** had tasted the water *755*
3: 1 named Nicodemus, a r of the Jews: *758*
Ac 7:27 Who made thee a r and a judge over us? *758*
7:35 saying, Who made thee a r and a judge? *758*
7:35 the same did God send *to be* a r and *758*
18: 8 And Crispus, the *chief* **r of the synagogue**, *752*
18:17 the *chief* **r of the synagogue**, and beat *him* *752*
23: 5 Thou shalt not speak evil of the r of thy *758*

RULER'S (2) [RULE]

Pr 29:26 Many seek the r favour; but *every* man's 4910
Mt 9:23 And when Jesus came into the r house, and *758*

RULERS (78) [RULE]

Ge 47: 6 then make them r over my cattle. 8269
Ex 16:22 all the r of the congregation came and 5387
18:21 *to be* r of thousands, *and* rulers of 8269
18:21 *and* r of hundreds, rulers of fifties, and 8269
18:21 of hundreds, r of fifties, and rulers of tens: 8269
18:21 of hundreds, rulers of fifties, and r of tens: 8269
18:25 r of thousands, rulers of hundreds, rulers of 8269
18:25 r of hundreds, rulers of fifties, and rulers of 8269
18:25 of hundreds, r of fifties, and rulers of tens. 8269
18:25 of hundreds, rulers of fifties, and r of tens. 8269
34:31 all the r of the congregation returned unto 5387
35:27 the r brought onyx stones, and stones to be 5387
Dt 1:13 and I will make them r over you. 7218
Jdg 15:11 Knowest thou not that the Philistines *are* r 4910
2Sa 8:18 and David's sons were **chief** r. 3548
1Ki 9:22 and r of his chariots, and his horsemen. 8269
2Ki 10: 1 unto the r of Jezreel, to the elders, and 8269
11: 4 Jehoiada sent and fet the r over hundreds, 8269
11:19 he took the r over hundreds, and 8269
1Ch 21: 2 said to Joab and to the r of the people, 8269
26:32 whom king David **made** r over 6485
27:31 All these *were* the r of the substance which 8269
29: 6 with the r over the king's work, 8269
2Ch 29:20 gathered the r of the city, and went up *to* 8269
35: 8 and Jehiel, r of the house of God, 5057
Ezr 9: 2 and r hath been chief in this trespass. 5461
10:14 Let now our r of all the congregation stand, 8269
Ne 2:16 the r knew not whither I went, or what I 5461
2:16 to the priests, nor to the nobles, nor to the r, 5461
4:14 and to the r, and to the rest of the people, 5461
4:16 the r *were* behind all the house of Judah. 8269
4:19 to the r, and to the rest of the people, 5461
5: 7 the r, and said unto them, You exact usury, 5461
5:17 an hundred and fifty of the Jews and r, 5461
7: 5 the r, and the people, that *they* might be 5461
11: 1 the r of the people dwelt at Jerusalem: 8269
12:40 of God, and I, and the half of the r with me: 5461
13:11 contended I with the r, and said, Why is 5461
Est 3:12 to the r of every people of every province 8269
8: 9 r of the provinces which *are* from India 8269
9: 3 all the r of the provinces, and 8269
Ps 2: 2 the r take counsel together, against 7336
Isa 1:10 the word of the LORD, ye r of Sodom; 7101
14: 5 staff of the wicked, *and* the sceptre of the r. 4910
22: 3 All thy r are fled together, they are bound 7101
29:10 the prophets and your r, the seers hath he 7218
49: 7 to a servant of r, Kings shall see and arise, 4910
Jer 33:26 that *I* will not take *any* of his seed *to be* r 4910
51:23 thee will I break in pieces captains and r. 5461
51:28 all the r thereof, and all the land of his 5461
51:57 her r, and her mighty *men:* and they shall 5461
Eze 23: 6 *were* clothed with blue, captains and r, 5461
23:12 captains and r clothed most gorgeously, 5461
23:23 captains and r, great lords and renowned, 5461
Da 3: 2 the sheriffs, and all the r of the provinces, 7984
3: 3 the sheriffs, and all the r of the provinces, 7984
Hos 4:18 her r *with* shame do love, Give ye. 4043
Mk 5:22 there cometh one of the **r of the synagogue**, *752*
13: 9 and ye shall be brought before r and *2232*
Lk 21:12 before kings and r for my name's sake. *2232*
23:13 the chief priests and the r and the people, *758*
23:35 And the r also with them derided *him,* *758*
24:20 our r delivered him to be condemned to *758*
Jn 7:26 Do the r know indeed that this is the very *758*
7:48 Have any of the r or of the Pharisees *758*
12:42 Nevertheless among the *chief* r also many *758*
Ac 3:17 ignorance ye did *it,* as *did* also your r. *758*
4: 5 that their r, and elders, and scribes, *758*
4: 8 Ye r of the people, and elders of Israel, *758*
4:26 the r were gathered together against *758*
13:15 the prophets the **r of the synagogue** sent *752*
13:27 and their r, because they knew him not, *758*
14: 5 and *also* of the Jews with their r, to use *them* *758*
16:19 drew *them* into the market-place unto the r, *758*
17: 6 and certain brethren unto the **r of the city**, *4173*
17: 8 troubled the people and the **r of the city**, *4173*
Ro 13: 3 For r are not a terror to good works, but *758*
Eph 6:12 against the r of the darkness of this world, *2888*

RULEST (2) [RULE]

2Ch 20: 6 r *not* thou over all the kingdoms of 4910
Ps 89: 9 Thou r the raging of the sea: when 4910

RULETH (14) [RULE]

2Sa 23: 3 He that r over men *must be* just, ruling *in* 4910
Ps 59:13 let them know that God r in Jacob unto 4910
66: 7 He r by his power for ever; his eyes behold 4910
103:19 in the heavens; and his kingdom r over all. 4910
Pr 16:32 he that r his spirit than he that taketh a city. 4910
22: 7 The rich r over the poor, and the borrower 4910
Ecc 8: 9 *there is* a time wherein one man r over 7980
9:17 more than the cry of him that r among 4910
Da 4:17 the most High r in the kingdom of men, 7990
4:25 till thou know that the most High r in 7990
4:32 until thou know that the most High r in 7990
Hos 11:12 Judah yet r with God, and is faithful with 7300
Ro 12: 8 he that r, with diligence; he that sheweth *4291*
1Ti 3: 4 One that r well his own house, having *his* *4291*

RULING (3) [RULE]

2Sa 23: 3 over men *must be* just, r *in* the fear of God. 4910

Jer 22:30 throne of David, and r any more in Judah. 4910
1Ti 3:12 r *their* children and their own houses well. *4291*

RUMAH (1)
2Ki 23:36 *was* Zebudah, the daughter of Pedaiah of R. 7316

RUMBLING (1)
Jer 47: 3 *and at* the r of his wheels, the fathers shall 1995

RUMOUR (10) [RUMOURS]
2Ki 19: 7 he shall hear a r, and shall return to his own 8052
Isa 37: 7 he shall hear a r, and return to his own 8052
Jer 49:14 I have heard a r from the LORD, and 8052
51:46 ye fear for the r that shall be heard in 8052
51:46 a r shall both come *one* year, and after that 8052
51:46 after that in *another* year *shall come* a r, 8052
Eze 7:26 upon mischief, and r shall be upon rumour; 8052
7:26 upon mischief, and rumour shall be upon r; 8052
Ob 1: 1 We have heard a r from the LORD, and 8052
Lk 7:17 And this r of him went forth throughout all *3056*

RUMOURS (2) [RUMOUR]
Mt 24: 6 And ye shall hear of wars and r of wars: *189*
Mk 13: 7 when ye shall hear of wars and r of wars, *189*

RUMP (5)
Ex 29:22 thou shalt take of the ram the fat and the r, 451
Lev 3: 9 the fat thereof, *and* the whole r, it shall he 451
7: 3 the r, and the fat that covereth the inwards, 451
8:25 the r, and all the fat that *was* upon 451
9:19 the r, and that which covereth *the inwards,* 451

RUN (71) [FORERUNNER, OUTRUN, OVERRUNNING, RAN, RUNNEST, RUNNETH, RUNNING]
Ge 49:22 by a well; *whose* branches r over the wall. 6805
Lev 15: 3 *whether* his flesh r with his issue, or 7325
15:25 or if it r beyond the time of her separation; 2100
Jdg 18:25 lest angry fellows r upon thee, and 6293
1Sa 8:11 and *some* shall r before his chariots. 7323
17:17 and r *to* the camp to thy brethren; 7323
20: 6 me that *he* might r *to* Beth-lehem his city: 7323
20:36 he said unto his lad, R, find out now 7323
2Sa 15: 1 and horses, and fifty men to r before him. 7323
18:19 Let me now r, and bear the king tidings, 7323
18:22 let me, I pray thee, also r after Cushi. 7323
18:22 Joab said, Wherefore wilt thou r, my son, 7323
18:23 howsoever, *said he,* let me r. And he said 7323
18:23 he said unto him, R. Then Ahimaaz ran *by* 7323
22:30 For by thee I have r *through* a troop: by my 7323
1Ki 1: 5 horsemen, and fifty men to r before him. 7323
2Ki 4:22 that I may r to the man of God, and 7323
4:26 R now, I pray thee, to meet her, and 7323
5:20 I will r after him, and take somewhat of 7323
2Ch 16: 9 For the eyes of the LORD r to and fro 7751
Ps 18:29 For by thee I have r *through* a troop; and 7323
19: 5 *and* rejoiceth as a strong *man* to r a race. 7323
58: 7 melt away as waters *which* r continually: 1980
59: 4 They r and prepare themselves without *my* 7323
78:16 and caused waters to r down like rivers. 3381
104:10 into the valleys, *which* r among the hills. 1980
119:32 I will r the way of thy commandments, 7323
119:136 Rivers of waters r down mine eyes, 3381
Pr 1:16 For their feet r to evil, and make haste to 7323
Ecc 1: 7 All the rivers r into the sea; yet the sea *is* 1980
SS 1: 4 Draw me, we will r after thee: the king 7323
Isa 33: 4 and fro of locusts shall he r upon them. 8264
40:31 they shall r, and not be weary; *and* 7323
55: 5 nations *that* knew not thee shall r unto thee 7323
59: 7 Their feet r to evil, and they make haste to 7323
Jer 5: 1 R ye to and fro through the streets of 7751
9:18 that our eyes may r down *with* tears, and 3381
12: 5 If thou hast r with the footmen, and 7323
13:17 r down *with* tears, because the LORD'S 3381
14:17 Let mine eyes r down *with* tears night and 3381
49: 3 lament, and r to and fro by the hedges; 7751
49:19 I will suddenly make him r away from her: 7323
50:44 I will make them suddenly r away from 7323
51:31 One post shall r to meet another, and 7323
La 2:18 let tears r down like a river day and night: 3381
Eze 24:16 nor weep, neither shall thy tears r down. 935
32:14 cause their rivers to r like oil, saith 1980
Da 12: 4 many shall r to and fro, and knowledge 7751
Joel 2: 4 of horses; and as horsemen, so shall they r. 7323
2: 7 They shall r like mighty *men;* they shall 7323
2: 9 They shall r to and fro in the city; 8264
2: 9 they shall r upon the wall, they shall climb 7323
Am 5:24 let judgment r down as waters, and 1556
6:12 Shall horses r upon the rock? will *one* plow 7323
8:12 they shall r to and fro to seek the word of 7751
Na 2: 4 like torches, they shall r like the lightnings. 7323
Hab 2: 2 upon tables, that he may r that readeth it. 7323
Hag 1: 9 and ye r every man unto his own house. 7323
Zec 2: 4 said unto him, R, speak to this young man, 7323
4:10 which r to and fro through the whole 7751
Mt 28: 8 and did r to bring his disciples word. *5143*
1Co 9:24 Know ye not that they which r in a race run *5143*
9:24 Know ye not that they which run in a race r *5143*
9:24 the prize? So r, that ye may obtain. *5143*
9:26 I therefore so r, not as uncertainly; so *5143*
Gal 2: 2 lest by any means I should r, or had run, *5143*
2: 2 any means I should run, or had r, in vain. *5143*
5: 7 Ye did r well; who did hinder you that *ye* *5143*
Php 2:16 that I have not r in vain, neither laboured in *5143*
Heb 12: 1 let us r with patience the race that is set *5143*
1Pe 4: 4 r not with *them* to the same excess of riot, *4936*

RUNNEST (1) [RUN]
Pr 4:12 and when thou r, thou shalt not stumble. 7323

RUNNETH (11) [RUN]
Ezr 8:15 I gathered them together to the river that r to 935
Job 15:26 He r upon him, *even* on *his* neck, upon 7323
16:14 upon breach, he r upon me like a giant. 7323
Ps 23: 5 anointest my head with oil; my cup r over. 7310
147:15 *upon* earth: his word r very swiftly. 7323
Pr 18:10 the righteous r into it, and is safe. 7323
La 1:16 mine eye r down *with* water, because 3381
3:48 Mine eye r down *with* rivers of water for 3381
Mt 9:17 and the wine r out, and the bottles perish: *1632*
Jn 20: 2 Then she r, and cometh to Simon Peter, *5143*
Ro 9:16 nor of him that r, but of God that sheweth *5143*

RUNNING (26) [RUN]
Lev 14: 5 be killed in an earthen vessel over r water: 2416
14: 6 of the bird *that was* killed over the r water: 2416
14:50 the birds in an earthen vessel over r water: 2416
14:51 in the r water, and sprinkle the house seven 2416
14:52 with the r water, and with the living bird, 2416
15: 2 When any man hath a r issue out of his 2100
15:13 bathe his flesh in r water, and shall be 2416
22: 4 seed of Aaron *is* a leper, or hath a r issue; 2100
Nu 19:17 and r water shall be put thereto in a vessel: 2416
2Sa 18:24 and looked, and behold a man r alone. 7323
18:26 the watchman saw another man r: and 7323
18:26 and said, Behold *another* man r alone. 7323
18:27 Me thinketh the r of the foremost *is* like 4794
18:27 *is* like the r of Ahimaaz the son of Zadok. 4794
2Ki 5:21 when Naaman saw *him* r after him, he 7323
2Ch 23:12 Athaliah heard the noise of the people r 7323
Pr 5:15 and r waters out of thine own well. 5140
6:18 feet that be swift in r to mischief, 7323
Isa 33: 4 as the r to and fro of locusts shall he run 4944
Eze 31: 4 with her rivers r round about his plants, 1980
Mk 9:15 greatly amazed, and r to *him* saluted him. *4370*
9:25 Jesus saw that the people came r together, *1998*
10:17 there came one r, and kneeled to him, and *4370*
Lk 6:38 and shaken *together,* and r over, *5240*
Ac 27:16 And r under a certain island *which is* *5295*
Rev 9: 9 of chariots of many horses r to battle. *5143*

RUSE See WILILY

RUSH (4) [BULRUSH, BULRUSHES, RUSHED, RUSHES, RUSHETH, RUSHING]
Job 8:11 Can the r grow up without mire? can 1573
Isa 9:14 off from Israel head and tail, branch and r, 100
17:13 The nations shall r like the rushing of many 7582
19:15 which the head or tail, branch or r, may do. 100

RUSHED (3) [RUSH]
Jdg 9:44 r forward, and stood *in* the entering of 6584
20:37 the liers in wait hasted, and r upon Gibeah; 6584
Ac 19:29 they r with one accord into the theatre. *3729*

RUSHES (1) [RUSH]
Isa 35: 7 each lay, *shall be* grass with reeds and r. 1573

RUSHETH (1) [RUSH]
Jer 8: 6 to his course, as the horse r into the battle. 7857

RUSHING (8) [RUSH]
Isa 17:12 to the **r** of nations, *that* make a rushing like 7588
17:12 *that* **make a r** like the rushing of mighty 7582
17:12 *that* make a rushing like the **r** of mighty 7588
17:13 The nations shall rush like the **r** of many 7588
Jer 47: 3 of his strong *horses,* at the **r** of his chariots, 7494
Eze 3:12 and I heard behind me a voice of a great **r**, 7494
3:13 over against them, and a noise of a great **r**. 7494
Ac 2: 2 a sound from heaven as of a **r** mighty wind, *5342*

RUST (3)
Mt 6:19 where moth and **r** doth corrupt, and *1035*
6:20 where neither moth nor **r** doth corrupt, and *1035*
Jas 5: 3 the **r** of them shall be a witness against *2447*

RUTH (13)
Ru 1: 4 *was* Orpah, and the name of the other **R**: 7327
1:14 her mother in law; but **R** clave unto her. 7327
1:16 **R** said, Intreat me not to leave thee, *or* 7327
1:22 So Naomi returned, and **R** the Moabitess, 7327
2: 2 **R** the Moabitess said unto Naomi, Let me 7327
2: 8 said Boaz unto **R**, Hearest thou not, 7327
2:21 **R** the Moabitess said, He said unto me also, 7327
2:22 Naomi said unto **R** her daughter in law, 7327
3: 9 she answered, I *am* **R** thine handmaid: 7327
4: 5 thou must buy *it* also of **R** the Moabitess, 7327
4:10 Moreover **R** the Moabitess, the wife of 7327
4:13 So Boaz took **R**, and she was his wife: and 7327
Mt 1: 5 and Booz begat Obed of **R**; and Obed begat *4503*

RUTHLESS See IMPLACABLE

RUTHLESSLY See RIGOUR

RYE (2)
Ex 9:32 the wheat and the **r** were not smitten: 3698
Isa 28:25 appointed barley and the **r** *in* their place? 3698

S

SABACHTHANI (2)
Mt 27:46 a loud voice, saying, ELI, ELI, LAMA **S**? *4518*
Mk 15:34 loud voice, saying, ELOI, ELOI, LAMA **S**? *4518*

SABAOTH (2)
Ro 9:29 Except the Lord of **s** had left us a seed, *4519*
Jas 5: 4 are entered into the ears of the Lord of **s**. *4519*

SABBATH (137) [SABBATHS]
Ex 16:23 To morrow *is* the rest of the holy **s** unto 7676
16:25 to day; for to day *is* a **s** unto the LORD: 7676
16:26 on the seventh day, *which is* the **s**, in it 7676
16:29 for that the LORD hath given you the **s**, 7676
20: 8 Remember the **s** day, to keep it holy. 7676
20:10 the seventh day *is* the **s** of the LORD thy 7676
20:11 wherefore the LORD blessed the **s** day, 7676
31:14 Ye shall keep the **s** therefore; for it *is* holy 7676
31:15 in the seventh *is* the **s** of rest, holy to 7676
31:15 whosoever doeth *any* work in the **s** day, 7676
31:16 the children of Israel shall keep the **s**, 7676
31:16 to observe the **s** throughout their 7676
35: 2 to you a holy *day,* a **s** of rest to the LORD: 7676
35: 3 throughout your habitations upon the **s** day. 7676
Lev 16:31 It *shall be* a **s** of rest unto you, and ye shall 7676
23: 3 the seventh day *is* the **s** of rest, a holy 7676
23: 3 ye shall do no work *therein:* it *is* the **s** of 7676
23:11 on the morrow after the **s** the priest shall 7676
23:15 count unto you from the morrow after the **s**, 7676
23:16 Even unto the morrow after the seventh **s** 7676
23:24 the first *day* of the month, shall ye have a **s**, 7677
23:32 It *shall be* unto you a **s** of rest, and ye shall 7676
23:32 unto even, shall ye **celebrate** your **s**. 7673+7676
23:39 on the first day *shall be* a **s**, and on 7677
23:39 and on the eighth day *shall be* a **s**. 7677
24: 8 **Every s** he shall set it in order
3117+3117+7676+7676
+871.1+871.1+1886.1+1886.1
25: 2 the land **keep a s** unto the LORD. 7673+7676
25: 4 in the seventh year shall be a **s** of rest unto 7676
25: 4 of rest unto the land, a **s** for the LORD: 7676
25: 6 the **s** of the land shall be meat for you; 7676
Nu 15:32 a man that gathered sticks upon the **s** day. 7676
28: 9 on the **s** day two lambs of the first year 7676
28:10 the burnt offering of **every s**, 7676+7676+871.1
Dt 5:12 Keep the **s** day to sanctify it, as the LORD 7676
5:14 the seventh day *is* the **s** of the LORD thy 7676
5:15 thy God commanded thee to keep the **s** day. 7676
2Ki 4:23 *it is* neither new moon, nor **s**. And she said, 7676
11: 5 A third *part* of you that enter in on the **s** 7676
11: 7 two parts of all you that go forth on the **s**, 7676
11: 9 man his men that were to come in on the **s**, 7676
11: 9 with them that should go out on the **s**, and 7676
16:18 the covert for the **s** that they had built in 7676
1Ch 9:32 the shewbread, to prepare *it* **every s**. 7676+7676
2Ch 23: 4 A third *part* of you entering on the **s**, of 7676
23: 8 man his men that were to come in on the **s**, 7676
23: 8 with them that were to go out on the **s**: 7676
36:21 *for* as long as *she* lay desolate she **kept s**, 7673
Ne 9:14 madest known unto them thy holy **s**, and 7676
10:31 or any victuals on the **s** day to sell, 7676
10:31 *that* we would not buy *it* of them on the **s**, 7676
13:15 Judah *some* treading wine presses on the **s**, 7676
13:15 which they brought *into* Jerusalem on the **s** 7676
13:16 sold on the **s** unto the children of Judah, 7676
13:17 *is* this that ye do, and profane the **s** day? 7676
13:18 more wrath upon Israel by profaning the **s**. 7676
13:19 of Jerusalem began to be dark before the **s**, 7676
13:19 they should not be opened till after the **s**: 7676
13:19 no burden be brought in on the **s** day. 7676
13:21 that time forth came they no *more* on the **s**. 7676
13:22 *and* keep the gates, to sanctify the **s** day. 7676
Ps 92: T A Psalm *or* Song for the **s** day. 7676
Isa 56: 2 that keepeth the **s** from polluting it, and 7676
56: 6 every one that keepeth the **s** from polluting 7676
58:13 If thou turn away thy foot from the **s**, 7676
58:13 call the **s** a delight, the holy of the LORD, 7676
66:23 moon to another, and from one **s** to another, 7676
Jer 17:21 bear no burden on the **s** day, 7676
17:22 a burden out of your houses on the **s** day, 7676
17:22 do ye any work, but hallow ye the **s** day, 7676
17:24 through the gates of this city on the **s** day, 7676
17:24 but hallow the **s** day, to do no work therein; 7676
17:27 not hearken unto me to hallow the **s** day, 7676
17:27 in at the gates of Jerusalem on the **s** day; 7676
Eze 46: 1 on the **s** it shall be opened, and in 3117+7676
46: 4 **s** day *shall be* six lambs without blemish, 7676
46:12 his peace offerings, as he did on the **s** day: 7676
Am 8: 5 the **s**, that we may set forth wheat, 7676
Mt 12: 1 At that time Jesus went on the **s** day *4521*
12: 2 which is not lawful to do upon the **s** day. *4521*
12: 5 how that on the **s** days the priests in *4521*
12: 5 days the priests in the temple profane the **s**, *4521*
12: 8 For the Son of man is Lord even of the **s** *4521*
12:10 saying, Is it lawful to heal on the **s** days? *4521*
12:11 and if it fall into a pit on the **s** day, will he *4521*
12:12 Wherefore it is lawful to do well on the **s** *4521*
24:20 be not in the winter, neither on the **s** day: *4521*
28: 1 In the end of the **s**, as it began to dawn *4521*
Mk 1:21 straightway on the **s** day he entered into *4521*
2:23 that he went through the corn fields on the **s** *4521*
2:24 why do they on the **s** day *that* which is not *4521*
2:27 The **s** was made for man, *and* not man for *4521*
2:27 was made for man, *and* not man for the **s**: *4521*
2:28 the Son of man is Lord also of the **s**. *4521*
3: 2 whether he would heal him on the **s** day; *4521*
3: 4 Is it lawful to do good on the **s** days, or *4521*
6: 2 And when the **s** day was come, he began to *4521*
15:42 that is, the **day before the s**, *4315*
16: 1 And when the **s** was past, Mary Magdalene, *4521*
Lk 4:16 he went into the synagogue on the **s** day, *4521*
4:31 of Galilee, and taught them on the **s** days. *4521*
6: 1 And it came to pass on the second **s** after *4521*
6: 2 which is not lawful to do on the **s** days? *4521*
6: 5 That the Son of man is Lord also of the **s**. *4521*
6: 6 And it came to pass also on another **s**, *4521*
6: 7 whether he would heal on the **s** day; *4521*
6: 9 *thing;* Is it lawful on the **s** days to do good, *4521*
13:10 teaching in one of the synagogues on the **s**. *4521*
13:14 because that Jesus had healed on the **s** day, *4521*
13:14 come and be healed, and not on the **s** day. *4521*
13:15 doth not each one of you on the **s** loose his *4521*
13:16 be loosed from this bond on the **s** day? *4521*

S

Lk 14: 1 chief Pharisees to eat bread on the s day, *4521*
14: 3 saying, Is it lawful to heal on the s day? *4521*
14: 5 will not straightway pull him out on the s *4521*
23:54 day was the preparation, and the s drew on. *4521*
23:56 rested the s day according to *4521*
Jn 5: 9 and walked: and on the same day was the s. *4521*
5:10 said unto him that was cured, It is the s day: *4521*
5:16 he had done these *things* on the s day. *4521*
5:18 because he not only had broken the s, but *4521*
7:22 and ye on the s day circumcise a man. *4521*
7:23 If a man on the s day receive circumcision, *4521*
7:23 made a man every whit whole on the s day? *4521*
9:14 And it was the s day when Jesus made *4521*
9:16 of God, because he keepeth not the s day. *4521*
19:31 not remain upon the cross on the s day, *4521*
19:31 (for that s day was a high day,) *4521*
Ac 1:12 Jerusalem a **s day's journey**. *2192+3598+4521*
13:14 and went into the synagogue on the s day, *4521*
13:27 of the prophets which are read every s day, *4521*
13:42 might be preached to them the next s. *4521*
13:44 And the next s day came almost the whole *4521*
15:21 being read in the synagogues every s day. *4521*
16:13 And on the s we went out of the city by a *4521*
17: 2 three s days reasoned with them out of *4521*
18: 4 And he reasoned in the synagogue every s, *4521*
Col 2:16 or of the new moon, or of the **s days**: *4521*

SABBATHS (35) [SABBATH]
Ex 31:13 of Israel, saying, Verily my s ye shall keep: 7676
Lev 19: 3 his mother, and his father, and keep my s: 7676
19:30 Ye shall keep my s, and reverence my 7676
23:15 wave offering; seven s shall be complete: 7676
23:38 Beside the s of the LORD, and 7676
25: 8 thou shalt number seven s of years unto 7676
25: 8 the space of the seven s of years shall be 7676
26: 2 Ye shall keep my s, and reverence my 7676
26:34 shall the land enjoy her s, as long as it lieth 7676
26:34 then shall the land rest, and enjoy her s. 7676
26:35 because it did not rest in your s, when ye 7676
26:43 shall be left of them, and shall enjoy her s, 7676
1Ch 23:31 burnt sacrifices unto the LORD in the s, 7676
2Ch 2: 4 on the s, and on the new moons, and on 7676
8:13 on the s, and on the new moons, and on 7676
31: 3 the burnt offerings for the s, and for 7676
36:21 until the land had enjoyed her s: 7676
Ne 10:33 of the s, of the new moons, for the set 7676
Isa 1:13 the new moons and s, the calling of 7676
56: 4 LORD unto the eunuchs that keep my s, 7676
La 1: 7 adversaries saw her, *and* did mock at her s. 4868
2: 6 solemn feasts and s to be forgotten in Zion, 7676
Eze 20:12 Moreover also I gave them my s, to be a 7676
20:13 in them; and my s they greatly polluted: 7676
20:16 not in my statutes, but polluted my s: 7676
20:20 hallow my s; and they shall be a sign 7676
20:21 shall even live in them; they polluted my s: 7676
20:24 had polluted my s, and their eyes were after 7676
22: 8 mine holy *things,* and hast profaned my s. 7676
22:26 have hid their eyes from my s, and I am 7676
23:38 in the same day, and have profaned my s. 7676
44:24 and they shall hallow my s. 7676
45:17 in the s in all solemnities of the house of 7676
46: 3 door of this gate before the LORD in the s 7676
Hos 2:11 and her s, and all her solemn feasts. 7676

SABEANS (4)
Job 1:15 the S fell *upon them,* and took them away; 7614
Isa 45:14 merchandise of Ethiopia and of the S, 5436
Eze 23:42 sort *were* brought S from the wilderness, 5436
Joel 3: 8 they shall sell them to the S, to a people far 7615

SABTA (1) [SABTAH]
1Ch 1: 9 Havilah, and S, and Raamah, and Sabtecha. 5454

SABTAH (1) [SABTA]
Ge 10: 7 Havilah, and S, and Raamah, and Sabtecha: 5454

SABTECA See SABTECHA

SABTECHA (2)
Ge 10: 7 Havilah, and Sabtah, and Raamah, and S: 5455
1Ch 1: 9 Havilah, and Sabta, and Raamah, and S. 5455

SACAR (2)
1Ch 11:35 Ahiam the son of S the Hararite, Eliphal 7940
26: 4 and S the fourth, and Nethaneel the fifth, 7940

SACK (9) [SACK'S, SACKBUT, SACKCLOTH, SACKCLOTHES, SACKS, SACKS']
Ge 42:25 to restore every man's money into his s, 8242
42:27 as one *of them* opened his s to give his ass 8242
42:28 money is restored; and lo, *it is* even in my s: 572
42:35 every man's bundle of money *was* in his s: 8242
43:21 man's money *was* in the mouth of his s, 572
44:11 they speedily took down every man his s to 572
44:11 to the ground, and opened every man his s. 572
44:12 and the cup was found in Benjamin's s. 572
Lev 11:32 vessel of wood, or raiment, or skin, or s, 8242

SACK'S (3) [SACK]
Ge 42:27 his money; for behold, it *was* in his s mouth. 572
44: 1 and put every man's money in his s mouth. 572
44: 2 in the s mouth of the youngest, and his corn 572

SACKBUT (4) [SACK]
Da 3: 5 flute, harp, s, psaltery, dulcimer, and 5443
3: 7 flute, harp, s, psaltery, and all kinds of 5443
3:10 flute, harp, s, psaltery, and dulcimer, and 5443
3:15 flute, harp, s, psaltery, and dulcimer, and 5443

SACKCLOTH (46) [CLOTH, SACK]
Ge 37:34 put s upon his loins, and mourned for his 8242
2Sa 3:31 gird you with s, and mourn before Abner. 8242
21:10 Rizpah the daughter of Aiah took s, and 8242
1Ki 20:31 put s on our loins, and ropes upon our 8242
20:32 So they girded s on their loins, and 8242
21:27 put s upon his flesh, and fasted, and lay in 8242
21:27 and fasted, and lay in s, and went softly. 8242
2Ki 6:30 and behold, *he had* s within upon his flesh. 8242
19: 1 covered himself with s, and went *into* 8242
19: 2 and the elders of the priests, covered with s, 8242
1Ch 21:16 the elders *of Israel, who were* clothed in s, 8242
Est 4: 1 put on s with ashes, and went out into 8242
4: 2 enter into the king's gate clothed with s. 8242
4: 3 and wailing; *and* many lay in s and ashes. 8242
4: 4 and to take away his s from him: 8242
Job 16:15 I have sewed s upon my skin, and 8242
Ps 30:11 thou hast put off my s, and girded me *with* 8242
35:13 when they were sick, my clothing *was* s: 8242
69:11 I made s also my garment; and I became a 8242
Isa 3:24 instead of a stomacher a girding of s; *and* 8242
15: 3 streets they shall gird themselves with s: 8242
20: 2 Go and loose the s from off thy loins, and 8242
22:12 and to baldness, and to girding with s: 8242
32:11 make ye bare, and gird *s* upon *your* loins. NIH
37: 1 covered himself with s, and went *into* 8242
37: 2 and the elders of the priests covered with s, 8242
50: 3 with blackness, and I make s their covering. 8242
58: 5 to spread s and ashes *under him?* wilt thou 8242
Jer 4: 8 For this gird you with s, lament and howl: 8242
6:26 gird *thee* with s, and wallow thyself in 8242
48:37 *shall be* cuttings, and upon the loins s. 8242
49: 3 cry, ye daughters of Rabbah, gird ye with s; 8242
La 2:10 they have girded themselves with s: 8242
Eze 7:18 They shall also gird *themselves* with s, and 8242
27:31 gird them with s, and they shall weep for 8242
Da 9: 3 with fasting, and s, and ashes: 8242
Joel 1: 8 Lament like a virgin girded with s for 8242
1:13 come, lie all night in s, ye ministers of my 8242
Am 8:10 I will bring up s upon all loins, and 8242
Jnh 3: 5 and proclaimed a fast, and put on s, 8242
3: 6 and covered *him* with s, and sat in ashes. 8242
3: 8 let man and beast be covered with s, and 8242
Mt 11:21 they would have repented long ago in s *4526*
Lk 10:13 while ago repented, sitting in s and ashes. *4526*
Rev 6:12 and the sun became black as s of hair, and *4526*
11: 3 *and* threescore days, clothed in s. *4526*

SACKCLOTHES (1) [CLOTH, SACK]
Ne 9: 1 and with s, and earth upon them. 8242

SACKS (9) [SACK]
Ge 42:25 Joseph commanded to fill their s *with* corn, 3627
42:35 it came to pass as they emptied their s, 8242
43:12 was brought again in the mouth of your s, 572
43:18 in our s at the first time *are* we brought in; 572
43:21 to the inn, that we opened our s, and behold, 572
43:22 we cannot tell who put our money in our s. 572
43:23 hath given you treasure in your s: 572
44: 1 saying, Fill the men's s *with* food, as much 572
Jos 9: 4 took old s upon their asses, and 8242

SACKS' (1) [SACK]
Ge 44: 8 the money, which we found in our **s** mouths, 572

SACRED See HALLOW; HALLOWED

SACRIFICE (218) [SACRIFICED, SACRIFICEDST, SACRIFICES, SACRIFICETH, SACRIFICING]
Ge 31:54 Jacob offered **s** upon the mount, and 2077
Ex 3:18 that we may **s** to the LORD our God. 2076
5: 3 the desert, and **s** unto the LORD our God; 2076
5: 8 saying, Let us go *and* **s** to our God. 2076
5:17 ye say, Let us go *and* **do s** to the LORD. 2076
8: 8 that they may **do s** unto the LORD. 2076
8:25 and said, Go ye, **s** to your God in the land. 2076
8:26 for we shall **s** the abomination of 2076
8:26 shall we **s** the abomination of the Egyptians 2076
8:27 **s** to the LORD our God, as he shall 2076
8:28 that ye may **s** to the LORD your God in 2076
8:29 letting the people go to **s** to the LORD. 2076
10:25 that we may **s** unto the LORD our God. 6213
12:27 It *is* the **s** of the LORD's passover, 2077
13:15 I **s** to the LORD all that openeth 2076
20:24 shalt **s** thereon thy burnt offerings, and thy 2076
23:18 Thou shalt not offer the blood of my **s** with 2077
23:18 neither shall the fat of my **s** remain until 2282
29:28 of Israel of the **s** of their peace offerings, 2077
30: 9 nor **burnt s**, nor meat offering; 5930
34:15 do **s** unto their gods, and *one* call thee, and 2076
34:15 and *one* call thee, and thou eat of his **s**; 2077
34:25 Thou shalt not offer the blood of my **s** with 2077
34:25 neither shall the **s** of the feast of 2077
Lev 1: 3 If his offering *be* a **burnt s** of the herd, 5930
1: 9 *to be* a **burnt s**, an offering made by fire, 5930
1:10 of the sheep, or of the goats, for a **burnt s**; 5930
1:13 it *is* a **burnt s**, an offering made by fire, 5930
1:14 if the **burnt s** for his offering to 5930
1:17 it *is* a **burnt s**, an offering made by fire, 5930
3: 1 if his oblation *be* a **s** of peace offering, if he 2077
3: 3 he shall offer of the **s** of the peace offering 2077
3: 5 shall burn it on the altar upon the **burnt s**, 5930
3: 6 if his offering for a **s** of peace offering unto 2077
3: 9 he shall offer of the **s** of the peace offering 2077
4:10 the bullock of the **s** of peace offerings: 2077
4:26 as the fat of the **s** of peace offerings: 2077
4:31 as the fat is taken away from off the **s** of 2077
4:35 away from the **s** of the peace offerings; 2077
7:11 this *is* the law of the **s** of peace offerings, 2077
7:12 he shall offer with the **s** of thanksgiving 2077
7:13 the **s** of thanksgiving of his peace offerings. 2077
7:15 the flesh of the **s** of his peace offerings for 2077
7:16 if the **s** of his offering *be* a vow, or 2077
7:16 be eaten the *same* day that he offereth his **s**: 2077
7:17 the remainder of the flesh of the **s** on 2077
7:18 if *any* of the flesh of the **s** of his peace 2077
7:20 the soul that eateth *of* the flesh of the **s** of 2077
7:21 eat of the flesh of the **s** of peace offerings, 2077
7:29 He that offereth the **s** of his peace offerings 2077
7:29 the LORD of the **s** of his peace offerings. 2077
7:37 and of the **s** of the peace offerings; 2077
8:21 it *was* a **burnt s** for a sweet savour, *and* 5930
9: 4 for peace offerings, to **s** before the LORD; 2076
9:17 the altar, beside the **burnt s** of the morning. 5930
9:18 and the ram *for* a **s** of peace offerings, 2077
17: 8 that offereth a burnt offering or **s**, 2077
19: 5 if ye **offer** a **s** of peace offerings unto 2076+2077
22:21 whosoever offereth a **s** of peace offerings 2077
22:29 when ye will offer a **s** of thanksgiving unto 2077
23:19 ye shall **s** one kid of the goats for a sin 6213
23:19 two lambs of the first year for a **s** of peace 2077
23:37 a meat offering, a **s**, and drink offerings, 2077
27:11 of which they do not offer a **s** unto 7133
Nu 6:17 he shall offer the ram *for* a **s** of peace 2077
6:18 put *it* in the fire which *is* under the **s** of 2077
7:17 for a **s** of peace offerings, two oxen, 2077
7:23 for a **s** of peace offerings, two oxen, 2077
7:29 for a **s** of peace offerings, two oxen, 2077
7:35 for a **s** of peace offerings, two oxen, 2077
7:41 for a **s** of peace offerings, two oxen, 2077
7:47 for a **s** of peace offerings, two oxen, 2077
7:53 for a **s** of peace offerings, two oxen, 2077
7:59 for a **s** of peace offerings, two oxen, 2077
7:65 for a **s** of peace offerings, two oxen, 2077
7:71 for a **s** of peace offerings, two oxen, 2077
7:77 for a **s** of peace offerings, two oxen, 2077
7:83 for a **s** of peace offerings, two oxen, 2077
7:88 all the oxen for the **s** of the peace offerings 2077
15: 3 or a **s** in performing a vow, or in a freewill 2077
15: 5 thou prepare with the burnt offering or **s**, 2077
15: 8 or *for* a **s** in performing a vow, or 2077
15:25 a **s made by fire** unto the LORD, and 801
23: 6 lo, *he* stood by his **burnt s**, he, and all 5930
28: 6 a **s made by fire** unto the LORD. 801
28: 8 thou shalt offer *it*, a **s made by fire**, 801
28:13 a **s made by fire** unto the LORD. 801
28:19 ye shall offer a **s made by fire** *for* a burnt 801
28:24 seven days, the meat of the **s made by fire**, 801
29: 6 a **s made by fire** unto the LORD. 801
29:13 shall offer a burnt offering, a **s made by fire**, 801
29:36 shall offer a burnt offering, a **s made by fire**, 801
Dt 15:21 thou shalt not **s** it unto the LORD thy 2076
16: 2 **s** the passover unto the LORD thy God, 2076
16: 5 Thou mayest not **s** the passover within any 2076
16: 6 *in*, there thou shalt **s** the passover at even, 2076
17: 1 Thou shalt not **s** unto the LORD thy God 2076
18: 3 from them that offer a **s**, whether *it be* ox or 2077
33:10 and whole *burnt s* upon thine altar. NIH
Jos 22:26 us an altar, not for burnt offering, nor for **s**: 2077
Jdg 6:26 offer a **burnt s** with the wood of the grove 5930
16:23 for to offer a great **s** unto Dagon their god, 2077
1Sa 1: 3 to **s** unto the LORD of hosts in Shiloh. 2076
1:21 up to offer unto the LORD the yearly **s**, 2077
2:13 people *was, that* when any man offered **s**, 2077
2:19 up with her husband to offer the yearly **s**. 2077
2:29 Wherefore kick ye at my **s** and at mine 2077
3:14 not be purged with **s** nor offering for ever. 2077
9:12 for *there is* a **s** of the people to day in 2077
9:13 until he come, because he doth bless the **s**; 2077
10: 8 *and* to **s** sacrifices of peace offerings: 2076
15:15 of the oxen, to **s** unto the LORD thy God; 2076
15:21 to **s** unto the LORD thy God in Gilgal. 2076
15:22 to obey *is* better than **s**, *and* to hearken than 2077
16: 2 say, I am come to **s** to the LORD. 2076
16: 3 call Jesse to the **s**, and I will shew thee 2077
16: 5 I am come to **s** unto the LORD: 2076
16: 5 and come with me to the **s**. 2077
16: 5 and his sons, and called them to the **s**. 2077
20: 6 for *there is* a yearly **s** there for all 2077
20:29 for our family hath a **s** in the city; and 2077
2Sa 24:22 *here be* oxen for **burnt s**, and threshing 5930
1Ki 3: 4 the king went to Gibeon to **s** there; for that 2076
8:62 with him, offered **s** before the LORD. 2077
8:63 Solomon offered a **s** of peace offerings, 2077
12:27 If this people go up to do **s** in the house of 2077
18:29 *the time* of the offering of the *evening* **s**, 4503
18:33 pour *it* on the **burnt s**, and on the wood. 5930
18:36 at *the time of* the offering of the *evening* **s**, 4503
18:38 consumed the **burnt s**, and the wood, and 5930
2Ki 5:17 neither burnt offering nor **s** unto other gods, 2077
10:19 for I have a great **s** *to do* to Baal; 2077
14: 4 as yet the people did **s** and burnt incense on 2076
16:15 the king's **burnt s**, and his meat offering, 5930
16:15 burnt offering, and all the blood of the **s**: 2077
17:35 to them, nor serve them, nor **s** to them: 2076
17:36 shall ye worship, and to him shall ye do **s**. 2076
2Ch 2: 6 a house, save only to **burn s** before him? 6999
7: 5 king Solomon offered a **s** of twenty and 2077
7:12 chosen this place to myself for a house of **s**. 2077
11:16 to **s** unto the LORD God of their fathers. 2076
28:23 *therefore* will I **s** to them, that they may 2076
33:17 Nevertheless the people did **s** still in 2076
Ezr 4: 2 we **do s** unto him since the days of 2076
9: 4 and I sat astonied until the evening **s**. 4503
9: 5 at the evening **s** I arose up from my 4503
Ne 4: 2 will they **s**? will they make an end in a day? 2076
Ps 20: 3 all thy offerings, and accept thy **burnt s**. 5930
40: 6 **S** and offering thou didst not desire; mine 2077
50: 5 that have made a covenant with me by **s**. 2077
51:16 For thou desirest not **s**; else would I give *it*: 2077
54: 6 I will freely **s** unto thee: I will praise thy 2076
107:22 let them **s** the sacrifices of thanksgiving, 2076
116:17 I will offer to thee the **s** of thanksgiving, 2077
118:27 bind the **s** with cords, *even* unto the horns 2282
141: 2 the lifting up of my hands *as* the evening **s**. 4503
Pr 15: 8 The **s** of the wicked *is* an abomination to 2077
21: 3 *is* more acceptable to the LORD than **s**. 2077
21:27 The **s** of the wicked *is* abomination: 2077
Ecc 5: 1 ready to hear, than to give the **s** of fools: 2077
Isa 19:21 in that day, and shall do **s** and oblation; 2077

Isa 34: 6 for the LORD hath a **s** in Bozrah, and 2077
57: 7 even thither wentest thou up to offer **s**. 2077
Jer 33:11 of them that shall bring the **s of praise** *into* 8426
33:18 meat offerings, and to do **s** continually. 2077
46:10 for the Lord GOD of hosts hath a **s** in 2077
Eze 39:17 gather yourselves on every side to my **s** that 2077
39:17 side to my sacrifice that I do **s** for you, 2076
39:17 *even* a great **s** upon the mountains of Israel, 2077
39:19 of my **s** which I have sacrificed for you. 2077
40:42 they slew the burnt offering and the **s**. 2077
44:11 the burnt offering and the **s** for the people, 2077
46:24 of the house shall boil the **s** of the people. 2077
Da 8:11 by him the daily *s* was taken away, and NIH
8:12 a host was given *him* against the daily *s* by NIH
8:13 *shall be* the vision *concerning* the daily *s*, NIH
9:27 *in* the midst of the week he shall cause the **s** 2077
11:31 shall take away the daily *s*, and they shall NIH
12:11 from the time *that* the daily *s* shall be taken NIH
Hos 3: 4 without a **s**, and without an image, and 2077
4:13 They **s** upon the tops of the mountains, and 2076
4:14 with whores, and they **s** with harlots: 2076
6: 6 For I desired mercy, and not **s**; and 2077
8:13 They **s** flesh *for* the sacrifices of mine 2076
12:11 they **s** bullocks in Gilgal; yea, their altars 2076
13: 2 of them, Let the men that **s** kiss the calves. 2076
Am 4: 5 offer a **s of thanksgiving** with leaven, and 8426
Jnh 1:16 offered a **s** unto the LORD, and 2077
2: 9 I will **s** unto thee with the voice of 2076
Hab 1:16 Therefore they **s** unto their net, and 2076
Zep 1: 7 for the LORD hath prepared a **s**, he hath 2077
1: 8 come to pass in the day of the LORD'S **s**, 2077
Zec 14:21 all they that **s** shall come and take of them, 2076
Mal 1: 8 And if ye offer the blind for **s**, *is it* not evil? 2076
Mt 9:13 *that* meaneth, I will have mercy, and not **s**: *2378*
12: 7 *this* meaneth, I will have mercy, and not **s**, *2378*
Mk 9:49 and every **s** shall be salted with salt. *2378*
Lk 2:24 And to offer a **s** according to that which is *2378*
Ac 7:41 and offered **s** unto the idol, and rejoiced in *2378*
14:13 and would have done **s** with the people. *2380*
14:18 that *they* had not **done s** unto them. *2380*
Ro 12: 1 that *ye* present your bodies a living **s**, holy, *2378*
1Co 8: 4 **things** that are **offered in s unto idols**, *1494*
10:19 that which is **offered in s to idols** is any *1494*
10:20 *I say,* that *the things* which the Gentiles **s**, *2380*
10:20 they **s** to devils, and not to God: *2380*
10:28 unto you, This is **offered in s unto idols**, *1494*
Eph 5: 2 and a **s** to God for a sweetsmelling savour. *2378*
Php 2:17 and if I be offered upon the **s** and service of *2378*
4:18 a **s** acceptable, well pleasing to God. *2378*
Heb 7:27 as *those* high priests, to offer up **s**, first for *2378*
9:26 to put away sin by the **s** of himself. *2378*
10: 5 **S** and offering thou wouldest not, but *2378*
10: 8 **S** and offering and burnt offerings and *2378*
10:12 But this *man,* after he had offered one **s** for *2378*
10:26 there remaineth no more **s** for sins, *2378*
11: 4 unto God a more excellent **s** than Cain, *2378*
13:15 let us offer the **s** of praise to God *2378*

SACRIFICED (33) [SACRIFICE]

Ex 24: 5 **s** peace offerings *of* oxen unto the LORD. 2076
32: 8 have **s** thereunto, and said, These *be* thy 2076
Dt 32:17 They **s** unto devils, not *to* God; *to* gods 2076
Jos 8:31 unto the LORD, and **s** peace offerings. 2076
Jdg 2: 5 and they **s** there unto the LORD. 2076
1Sa 2:15 servant came, and said to the man that **s**, 2076
6:15 **s** sacrifices the same day unto the LORD. 2076
11:15 there they **s** sacrifices *of* peace offerings 2076
2Sa 6:13 had gone six paces, he **s** oxen and fatlings. 2076
1Ki 3: 2 Only the people **s** in high places, because 2076
3: 3 only he **s** and burnt incense in high places. 2076
11: 8 which burnt incense and **s** unto their gods. 2076
2Ki 12: 3 the people still **s** and burnt incense in 2076
15: 4 the people **s** and burnt incense still on 2076
15:35 the people **s** and burnt incense still in 2076
16: 4 he **s** and burnt incense in the high places, 2076
17:32 which **s** for them in the houses of the high 6213
1Ch 21:28 of Ornan the Jebusite, then he **s** there. 2076
29:21 they **s** sacrifices unto the LORD, and 2076
2Ch 5: 6 **s** sheep and oxen, which could not be told 2076
28: 4 He **s** also and burnt incense in the high 2076
28:23 For he **s** unto the gods of Damascus, 2076
33:16 **s** thereon peace offerings and 2076
33:22 for Amon **s** unto all the carved images 2076
34: 4 the graves of them that had **s** unto them. 2076

Ps 106:37 they **s** their sons and their daughters unto 2076
106:38 whom they **s** unto the idols of Canaan: 2076
Eze 16:20 these hast thou **s** unto them to be devoured. 2076
39:19 of my sacrifice which I have **s** for you. 2076
Hos 11: 2 they **s** unto Baalim, and burned incense to 2076
1Co 5: 7 For even Christ our passover is **s** for us: *2380*
Rev 2:14 to eat **things s unto idols**, and to commit *1494*
2:20 and to eat **things s unto idols**. *1494*

SACRIFICEDST (1) [SACRIFICE]

Dt 16: 4 which thou **s** the first day at even, 2076

SACRIFICES (79) [SACRIFICE]

Ge 46: 1 offered **s** unto the God of his father Isaac. 2077
Ex 10:25 Thou must give us also **s** and 2077
18:12 in law, took a burnt offering and **s** for God: 2077
Lev 7:32 offering of the **s** of your peace offerings. 2077
7:34 from off the **s** of their peace offerings, 2077
10:13 of the **s** of the LORD **made by fire**: 801
10:14 *which* are given out of the **s** of peace 2077
17: 5 that the children of Israel may bring their **s**, 2077
17: 7 they shall no more offer their **s** unto devils, 2077
Nu 10:10 and over the **s** of your peace offerings; 2077
25: 2 they called the people unto the **s** of their 2077
28: 2 *and* my bread for my **s made by fire**, 801
Dt 12: 6 your **s**, and your tithes, and heave offerings 2077
12:11 your **s**, your tithes, and the heave offering 2077
12:27 the blood of thy **s** shall be poured out upon 2077
32:38 Which did eat the fat of their **s**, *and* 2077
33:19 there they shall offer **s** of righteousness: 2077
Jos 13:14 **s** of the LORD God of Israel **made by fire** 801
22:27 with our **s**, and with our peace offerings; 2077
22:28 not for burnt offerings, nor for **s**; 2077
22:29 burnt offerings, for meat offerings, or for **s**, 2077
1Sa 6:15 sacrificed **s** the same day unto the LORD. 2077
10: 8 *and* to sacrifice **s** of peace offerings: 2077
11:15 there they sacrificed **s** *of* peace offerings 2077
15:22 *as great* delight in burnt offerings and **s**, 2077
2Sa 15:12 *even* from Giloh, while he offered **s**. 2077
2Ki 10:24 when they went in to offer **s** and 2077
1Ch 16: 1 they offered **burnt s** and peace offerings 5930
23:31 to offer all **burnt s** unto the LORD in 5930
29:21 they sacrificed **s** unto the LORD, and 2077
29:21 and **s** in abundance for all Israel: 2077
2Ch 7: 1 and consumed the burnt offering and the **s**; 2077
7: 4 all the people offered **s** before the LORD. 2077
13:11 every evening **burnt s** and sweet incense: 5930
29:31 come near and bring **s** and thank offerings 2077
29:31 the congregation brought in **s** and 2077
Ezr 6: 3 the place where they offered **s**, and *let* 1685
6:10 That they may offer **s** of sweet savours unto 7127
Ne 12:43 Also that day they offered great **s**, and 2077
Ps 4: 5 Offer the **s** of righteousness, and put your 2077
27: 6 will I offer in his tabernacle **s** of joy; 2077
50: 8 I will not reprove thee for thy **s** or thy burnt 2077
51:17 The **s** of God *are* a broken spirit: a broken 2077
51:19 shalt thou be pleased with the **s** of 2077
66:15 I will offer unto thee **burnt s** of fatlings, 5930
106:28 unto Baal-peor, and ate the **s** of the dead. 2077
107:22 let them sacrifice the **s** of thanksgiving, 2077
Pr 17: 1 than a house full *of* **s** with strife. 2077
Isa 1:11 To what purpose *is* the multitude of your **s** 2077
29: 1 add ye year to year; let them kill **s**. 2282
43:23 neither hast thou honoured me *with* thy **s**. 2077
43:24 hast thou filled me *with* the fat of thy **s**: 2077
56: 7 their **s** *shall be* accepted upon mine altar; 2077
Jer 6:20 not acceptable, nor your **s** sweet unto me. 2077
7:21 Put your burnt offerings unto your **s**, and 2077
7:22 of Egypt, concerning burnt offerings or **s**: 2077
17:26 **s**, and meat offerings, and incense, and 2077
17:26 and incense, and bringing *s of* praise, NIH
Eze 20:28 they offered there their **s**, and there they 2077
40:41 eight tables, whereupon they slew *their s*. NIH
Hos 4:19 they shall be ashamed because of their **s**. 2077
8:13 They sacrifice flesh *for* the **s** of mine 2077
9: 4 their **s** *shall be* unto them as the bread of 2077
Am 4: 4 bring your **s** *every* morning, *and* your tithes 2077
5:25 Have ye offered unto me **s** and offerings in 2077
Mk 12:33 more than all whole burnt offerings and **s**. *2378*
Lk 13: 1 blood Pilate had mingled with their **s**. *2378*
Ac 7:42 **s** *by the space of* forty years in *2378*
1Co 10:18 are not they which eat *of* the **s** partakers of *2378*
Heb 5: 1 that he may offer both gifts and **s** for sins: *2378*
8: 3 high priest is ordained to offer gifts and **s**: *2378*

Heb 9: 9 in which were offered both gifts and **s**, *2378*
9:23 *things* themselves with better **s** than these. *2378*
10: 1 can never with those **s** which they offered *2378*
10: 3 But in those **s** *there is* a remembrance *again* NIG
10: 6 and **s** for sin thou hast had no pleasure. NIG
10:11 and offering oftentimes the same **s**, *2378*
13:16 for with such **s** God is well pleased. *2378*
1Pe 2: 5 a holy priesthood, to offer up spiritual **s**, *2378*

SACRIFICETH (6) [SACRIFICE]
Ex 22:20 He that **s** unto *any* god, save unto 2076
Ecc 9: 2 to him that **s**, and to him that sacrificeth 2076
9: 2 him that sacrificeth, and to him that **s** not: 2076
Isa 65: 3 that **s** in gardens, and burneth incense upon 2076
66: 3 he that **s** a lamb, *as if* he cut off a dog's 2076
Mal 1:14 **s** unto the Lord a corrupt *thing*: for I *am* a 2076

SACRIFICING (2) [SACRIFICE]
1Ki 8: 5 with him before the ark, **s** sheep and oxen, 2076
12:32 **s** unto the calves that he had made: 2076

SACRILEGE (1)
Ro 2:22 that abhorrest idols, dost thou **commit s**? *2416*

SAD (11) [SADLY, SADNESS]
Ge 40: 6 looked upon them, and behold, they *were* **s**. 2196
1Sa 1:18 and her countenance was no more *s*. NIH
1Ki 21: 5 said unto him, Why is thy spirit **so s**, 5620
Ne 2: 1 Now I had not been *beforetime* **s** in his 7451
2: 2 Why *is* thy countenance **s**, seeing thou *art* 7451
2: 3 why should not my countenance be **s**, 3415
Eze 13:22 *ye* have **made** the heart of the righteous **s**, 3512
13:22 the righteous sad, whom I have not **made s**; 3510
Mt 6:16 not as the hypocrites, of a **s countenance**: *4659*
Mk 10:22 And he was **s** at *that* saying, and went away *4768*
Lk 24:17 have one to another, as ye walk, and are **s**? *4659*

SADDLE (4) [SADDLED]
Lev 15: 9 what **s** soever he rideth upon that hath 4817
2Sa 19:26 for thy servant said, I will **s** me an ass, 2280
1Ki 13:13 he said unto his sons, **S** me the ass. So they 2280
13:27 he spake to his sons, saying, **S** me the ass. 2280

SADDLED (10) [SADDLE]
Ge 22: 3 **s** his ass, and took two of his young men 2280
Nu 22:21 **s** his ass, and went with the princes of 2280
Jdg 19:10 *there were* with him two asses **s**, 2280
2Sa 16: 1 with a couple of asses **s**, and upon them 2280
17:23 he **s** *his* ass, and arose, and gat him *home* to 2280
1Ki 2:40 **s** his ass, and went to Gath to Achish to 2280
13:13 So they **s** him the ass: and he rode thereon, 2280
13:23 after he had drunk, that he **s** for him the ass, 2280
13:27 Saddle me the ass. And they **s** *him*. 2280
2Ki 4:24 she **s** an ass, and said to her servant, Drive, 2280

SADDLES See FURNITURE

SADDUCEES (14)
Mt 3: 7 of the Pharisees and **S** come to his baptism, *4523*
16: 1 The Pharisees also with the **S** came, and *4523*
16: 6 of the leaven of the Pharisees and *of the* **S**. *4523*
16:11 of the leaven of the Pharisees and *of the* **S**? *4523*
16:12 the doctrine of the Pharisees and *of the* **S**. *4523*
22:23 The same day came to him *the* **S**, which say *4523*
22:34 had heard that he had put the **S** to silence, *4523*
Mk 12:18 Then come unto him *the* **S**, which say there *4523*
Lk 20:27 Then came to *him* certain of the **S**, *4523*
Ac 4: 1 of the temple, and the **S**, came upon them, *4523*
5:17 were with him, (which is the sect of the **S**,) *4523*
23: 6 Paul perceived that the one part were **S**, *4523*
23: 7 dissension between the Pharisees and the **S**: *4523*
23: 8 For the **S** say that there is no resurrection, *4523*

SADLY (1) [SAD]
Ge 40: 7 Wherefore look ye *so* **s** to day? 7451

SADNESS (1) [SAD]
Ecc 7: 3 for by the **s** of the countenance the heart is 7455

SADOC (2)
Mt 1:14 And Azor begat **S**; and Sadoc begat Achim; *4524*
1:14 and **S** begat Achim; and Achim begat *4524*

SAFE (13) [SAVE]
1Sa 12:11 enemies on every side, and ye dwelled **s**. 983
2Sa 18:29 the king said, *Is* the young man Absalom **s**? 7965
18:32 unto Cushi, *Is* the young man Absalom **s**? 7965
Job 21: 9 Their houses *are* **s** from fear, neither *is* 7965
Ps119:117 Hold thou me up, and I shall be **s**: and 3467
Pr 18:10 the righteous runneth into it, and is **s**. 7682
29:25 putteth his trust in the LORD shall be **s**. 7682
Isa 5:29 shall **carry** *it* **away s**, and none shall 6403
Eze 34:27 they shall be **s** in their land, and shall know 983
Lk 15:27 because he hath received him *s and* sound. NIG
Ac 23:24 and **bring** *him* **s** unto Felix the governor. *1295*
27:44 to pass, that *they* **escaped** all **s** to land. *1295*
Php 3: 1 me indeed *is* not grievous, but for you *it is* **s**. *804*

SAFEGUARD (1) [GUARD, SAVE]
1Sa 22:23 thy life: but with me thou *shalt be* **in s**. 4931

SAFELY (21) [SAVE]
Lev 26: 5 to the full, and dwell in your land **s**. 983+3807.1
1Ki 4:25 Judah and Israel dwelt **s**, every man 983+3807.1
Ps 78:53 he led them on **s**, so that they feared 983+3807.1
Pr 1:33 But whoso hearkeneth unto me shall dwell **s**, 983
3:23 shalt thou walk *in* thy way **s**, and 983+3807.1
31:11 The heart of her husband doth **s** trust in her, NIH
Isa 41: 3 He pursued them, *and* passed **s**; *even by* 7965
Jer 23: 6 be saved, and Israel shall dwell **s**: 983+3807.1
32:37 I will cause them to dwell **s**: 983+3807.1
33:16 and Jerusalem shall dwell **s**: 983+3807.1
Eze 28:26 they shall dwell **s** therein, and 983+3807.1
34:25 they shall dwell **s** in the wilderness, 983+3807.1
34:28 they shall dwell **s**, and none shall 983+3807.1
38: 8 and they shall dwell **s** all of them. 983+3807.1
38:11 *to* them that are at rest, that dwell **s**, 983+3807.1
38:14 when my people of Israel dwelleth **s**, 983+3807.1
39:26 when they dwelt **s** in their land, and 983+3807.1
Hos 2:18 the earth, and will make them to lie down **s**. 983
Zec 14:11 but Jerusalem shall be **s** inhabited. 983
Mk 14:44 same is he; take him, and lead *him* away **s**. *806*
Ac 16:23 charging the jailor to keep them **s**: *806*

SAFETY (19) [SAVE]
Lev 25:18 do them; and ye shall dwell in the land in **s**. 983
25:19 ye shall eat *your* fill, and dwell therein in **s**. 983
Dt 12:10 enemies round about, so that ye dwell **in s**; 983
33:12 The beloved of the LORD shall dwell in **s** 983
33:28 Israel then shall dwell *in* **s** alone: 983
Job 3:26 I was not **in s**, neither had I rest, 7951
5: 4 His children are far from **s**, and they are 3468
5:11 those which mourn may be exalted *to* **s**. 3468
11:18 *about thee, and* thou shalt take thy rest in **s**. 983
24:23 *Though* it be given him *to be* in **s**, 983
Ps 4: 8 LORD, only makest me dwell in **s**. 983
12: 5 I will set *him* in **s** *from him that* puffeth at 3468
33:17 A horse *is* a vain thing for **s**: neither shall 8668
Pr 11:14 in the multitude of counsellers *there is* **s**. 8668
21:31 the day of battle: but **s** *is* of the LORD. 8668
24: 6 and in multitude of counsellers *there is* **s**. 8668
Isa 14:30 shall feed, and the needy shall lie down in **s**: 983
Ac 5:23 The prison truly found we shut with all **s**, *803*
1Th 5: 3 For when they shall say, Peace and **s**; then *803*

SAFFRON (1)
SS 4:14 Spikenard and **s**; calamus and cinnamon, 3750

SAID (4001) [SAY] See Index

SAIDST (22) [SAY] See Index

SAIL (8) [SAILED, SAILERS, SAILING]
Isa 33:23 their mast, they could not spread the **s**: 5251
Eze 27: 7 that which thou spreadest forth to be thy **s**; 5251
Ac 20: 3 wait for him, as he was about to **s** into Syria, *321*
20:16 For Paul had determined to **s by** Ephesus, *3896*
27: 1 when it was determined that we should **s** *636*
27: 2 meaning to **s** by the coasts of Asia; *4126*
27:17 strake **s**, and so were driven. *4632*
27:24 God hath given thee all them that **s** with *4126*

SAILED (15) [SAIL]
Lk 8:23 But as they **s** he fell asleep: and there came *4126*
Ac 13: 4 and from thence they **s** to Cyprus. *636*
14:26 And thence **s** to Antioch, from whence they *636*
15:39 *so* Barnabas took Mark, and **s** unto Cyprus; *1602*
18:18 and **s thence** into Syria, and with him *1602*
18:21 if God will. And he **s** from Ephesus. *321*
20: 6 And we **s away** from Philippi after the days *1602*
20:13 we went before to ship, and **s** unto Assos, *321*

Ac 20:15 And we s thence, and came the next day 636
21: 3 and s into Syria, and landed at Tyre: 4126
27: 4 we s under Cyprus, because the winds 5284
27: 5 And when we had s over the sea of Cilicia 1277
27: 7 And when we had s slowly many days, and 1020
27: 7 we s under Crete, over against Salmone; 5284
27:13 loosing thence, they s close by Crete. 3881

SAILERS (1) [SAIL]

Rev 18:17 and s, and as many as trade by sea, 3492

SAILING (3) [SAIL]

Ac 21: 2 And finding a ship s over unto Phenicia, 1276
27: 6 found a ship of Alexandria s into Italy; 4126
27: 9 and when s was now dangerous, because 4144

SAILORS See SHIPMEN

SAINT (5) [SAINTS, SAINTS']

Ps 106:16 the camp, and Aaron the s of the LORD. 6918
Da 8:13 I heard one s speaking, and another saint 6918
8:13 another s said unto that certain saint which 6918
8:13 another saint said unto that certain s which NIH
Php 4:21 Salute every s in Christ Jesus. The brethren 40

SAINTS (95) [SAINT]

Dt 33: 2 and he came with ten thousands of s: 6944
33: 3 loved the people; all his s are in thy hand: 6918
1Sa 2: 9 He will keep the feet of his s, and 2623
2Ch 6:41 and let thy s rejoice in goodness. 2623
Job 5: 1 and to which of the s wilt thou turn? 6918
15:15 Behold, he putteth no trust in his s; yea, 6918
Ps 16: 3 But to the s that are in the earth, and to 6918
30: 4 O ye s of his, and give thanks at 2623
31:23 O love the LORD, all ye his s: for 2623
34: 9 O fear the LORD, ye his s: for there is no 6918
37:28 loveth judgment, and forsaketh not his s; 2623
50: 5 Gather my s together unto me; those that 2623
52: 9 on thy name; for it is good before thy s. 2623
79: 2 the flesh of thy s unto the beasts of 2623
85: 8 speak peace unto his people, and to his s: 2623
89: 5 also in the congregation of the s. 6918
89: 7 to be feared in the assembly of the s, 6918
97:10 he preserveth the souls of his s; 2623
116:15 sight of the LORD is the death of his s. 2623
132: 9 and let thy s shout for joy. 2623
132:16 and her s shall shout aloud for joy. 2623
145:10 O LORD; and thy s shall bless thee. 2623
148:14 horn of his people, the praise of all his s; 2623
149: 1 and his praise in the congregation of s. 2623
149: 5 Let the s be joyful in glory: let them sing 2623
149: 9 this honour have all his s. Praise ye 2623
Pr 2: 8 and preserveth the way of his s. 2623
Da 7:18 the s of the most High shall take 6922
7:21 and the same horn made war with the s, and 6922
7:22 judgment was given to the s of the most 6922
7:22 the time came that the s possessed 6922
7:25 shall wear out the s of the most High, and 6922
7:27 shall be given to the people of the s of 6922
Hos 11:12 ruleth with God, and is faithful with the s. 6918
Zec 14: 5 my God shall come, and all the s with thee. 6918
Mt 27:52 and many bodies of s which slept arose, 40
Ac 9:13 how much evil he hath done to thy s at 40
9:32 down also to the s which dwelt at Lydda. 40
9:41 and when he had called the s and widows, 40
26:10 and many of the s did I shut up in prison, 40
Ro 1: 7 be in Rome, beloved of God, called to be s: 40
8:27 he maketh intercession for the s according to 40
12:13 Distributing to the necessity of s; given to 40
15:25 I go unto Jerusalem to minister unto the s. 40
15:26 for the poor s which are at Jerusalem. 40
15:31 I have for Jerusalem may be accepted of the s; 40
16: 2 as becometh s, and that ye assist her in 40
16:15 Olympas, and all the s which are with them. 40
1Co 1: 2 are sanctified in Christ Jesus, called to be s, 40
6: 1 to law before the unjust, and not before the s? 40
6: 2 Do ye not know that the s shall judge 40
14:33 but of peace, as in all churches of the s. 40
16: 1 Now concerning the collection for the s, as I 40
16:15 addicted themselves to the ministry of the s,) 40
2Co 1: 1 with all the s which are in all Achaia: 40
8: 4 us the fellowship of the ministering to the s. 40
9: 1 For as touching the ministering to the s, it is 40
9:12 service not only supplieth the want of the s, 40
13:13 All the s salute you. 40
Eph 1: 1 to the s which are at Ephesus, and to 40
1:15 faith in the Lord Jesus, and love unto all the s, 40
1:18 riches of the glory of his inheritance in the s, 40
2:19 but fellowcitizens with the s, and of 40
3: 8 Unto me, who am less than the least of all s, 40
3:18 May be able to comprehend with all s what is 40
4:12 For the perfecting of the s for the work of 40
5: 3 be once named amongst you, as becometh s; 40
6:18 all perseverance and supplication for all s; 40
Php 1: 1 to all the s in Christ Jesus which are at 40
4:22 All the s salute you, chiefly they that are of 40
Col 1: 2 To the s and faithful brethren in Christ which 40
1: 4 and of the love which ye have to all the s, 40
1:12 partakers of the inheritance of the s in light: 40
1:26 but now is made manifest to his s: 40
1Th 3:13 coming of our Lord Jesus Christ with all his s. 40
2Th 1:10 When he shall come to be glorified in his s, 40
Phm 1: 5 hast toward the Lord Jesus, and toward all s; 40
1: 7 the bowels of the s are refreshed by thee, 40
Heb 6:10 in that ye have ministered to the s, and 40
13:24 them that have the rule over you, and all the s. 40
Jude 1: 3 the faith which was once delivered unto the s. 40
1:14 the Lord cometh with ten thousands of his s, 40
Rev 5: 8 full of odours, which are the prayers of s. 40
8: 3 that he should offer it with the prayers of all s 40
8: 4 which came with the prayers of the s, 40
11:18 and to the s, and them that fear thy name, 40
13: 7 it was given unto him to make war with the s, 40
13:10 Here is the patience and the faith of the s. 40
14:12 Here is the patience of the s: here are they that 40
15: 3 just and true are thy ways, thou King of s. 40
16: 6 For they have shed the blood of s and 40
17: 6 the woman drunken with the blood of the s, 40
18:24 and of s, and of all that were slain upon 40
19: 8 for the fine linen is the righteousness of s. 40
20: 9 and compassed the camp of the s about, and 40

SAINTS' (1) [SAINT]

1Ti 5:10 if she have washed the s feet, 40

SAITH (1262) [SAY] See Index

SAKE (145) [SAKES]

Ge 3:17 cursed is the ground for thy s; in sorrow 5668
8:21 curse the ground any more for man's s; 5668
12:13 it may be well with me for thy s; 5668+871.1
12:16 he entreated Abram well for her s: 5668+871.1
18:29 he said, I will not do it for forty's s. 5668+871.1
18:31 I will not destroy it for twenty's s. 5668+871.1
18:32 I will not destroy it for ten's s. 5668+871.1
20:11 they will slay me for my wife's s. 1697+5921
26:24 seed for my servant Abraham's s. 5668+871.1
30:27 that the LORD hath blessed me for thy s. 1558
39: 5 the Egyptian's house for Joseph's s; 1558
Ex 18: 8 and to the Egyptians for Israel's s, 182
21:26 he shall let him go free for his eye's s. 8478
21:27 he shall let him go free for his tooth's s. 8478
Nu 11:29 said unto him, Enviest thou for my s? 3807.1
25:11 while he was zealous for my s among 2967.1
25:18 slain in the day of the plague for Peor's s. 1697
1Sa 12:22 his people for his great name's s: 5668+871.1
23:10 to destroy the city for my s. 5668+871.1
2Sa 5:12 kingdom for his people Israel's s. 5668+871.1
7:21 For thy word's s, and according to 5668+871.1
9: 1 shew him kindness for Jonathan's s? 5668+871.1
9: 7 kindness for Jonathan thy father's s, 5668+871.1
18: 5 Deal gently for my s with the young man, 3807.1
1Ki 8:41 of a far country for thy name's s; 4616+3807.1
11:12 not do it for David thy father's s: 4616+3807.1
11:13 thy son for David my servant's s, 4616+3807.1
11:13 for Jerusalem's s, which I have 4616+3807.1
11:32 one tribe for my servant David's s, 4616+3807.1
11:32 and for Jerusalem's s, 4616+3807.1
11:34 his life for David my servant's s, 4616+3807.1
15: 4 Nevertheless for David's s did 4616+3807.1
2Ki 8:19 Judah for David his servant's s, 4616+3807.1
19:34 to save it, for mine own s, and for 4616+3807.1
19:34 and for my servant David's s. 4616+3807.1
20: 6 defend this city for mine own s, 4616+3807.1
20: 6 and for my servant David's s. 4616+3807.1
1Ch 17:19 O LORD, for thy servant's s, and 5668+871.1
2Ch 6:32 far country for thy great name's s, 4616+3807.1
Ne 9:31 Nevertheless for thy great mercies' s thou 871.1
Job 19:17 though I intreated for the children's s of NIH

Ps 6: 4 O save me for thy mercy's s. 4616+3807.1
23: 3 of righteousness for his name's s. 4616+3807.1
25: 7 thou me for thy goodness' s, 4616+3807.1
25:11 For thy name's s, O LORD, 4616+3807.1
31: 3 therefore for thy name's s lead me, 4616+3807.1
31:16 thy servant: save me for thy mercy's s. 871.1
44:22 for thy s are we killed all the day long; 5921
44:26 and redeem us for thy mercy's s. 4616+3807.1
69: 6 GOD of hosts, be ashamed for my s: 871.1
69: 6 that seek thee be confounded for my s, 871.1
69: 7 Because for thy s I have borne reproach; 5921
79: 9 away our sins, for thy name's s. 4616+3807.1
106: 8 he saved them for his name's s, 4616+3807.1
109:21 GOD the Lord, for thy name's s: 4616+3807.1
115: 1 for thy mercy, *and* for thy truth's s. 5921
132:10 For thy servant David's s turn not 5668+871.1
143:11 O LORD, for thy name's s: 4616+3807.1
143:11 for thy righteousness' s bring my soul out 871.1
Isa 37:35 this city to save it for mine own s, 4616+3807.1
37:35 and for my servant David's s. 4616+3807.1
42:21 pleased for his righteousness' s; 4616+3807.1
43:14 the Holy One of Israel; For your s 4616+3807.1
43:25 thy transgressions for mine own s, 4616+3807.1
45: 4 For Jacob my servant's s, and 4616+3807.1
48: 9 For my name's s will I defer mine 4616+3807.1
48:11 For mine own s, *even* for mine 4616+3807.1
48:11 own sake, *even* for mine own s, 4616+3807.1
54:15 together against thee shall fall for thy s. 5921
62: 1 For Zion's s will I not hold my 4616+3807.1
62: 1 for Jerusalem's s I will not rest, 4616+3807.1
63:17 Return for thy servants' s, 4616+3807.1
66: 5 that cast you out for my name's s, 4616+3807.1
Jer 14: 7 do thou *it* for thy name's s: 4616+3807.1
14:21 Do not abhor *us,* for thy name's s, 4616+3807.1
15:15 know that for thy s I have suffered rebuke. 5921
Eze 20: 9 I wrought for my name's s, that *it* 4616+3807.1
20:14 I wrought for my name's s, that *it* 4616+3807.1
20:22 and wrought for my name's s, 4616+3807.1
20:44 wrought with you for my name's s, 4616+3807.1
36:22 of Israel, but for mine holy name's s, 3807.1
Da 9:17 that is desolate, for the Lord's s. 4616+3807.1
9:19 for thine own s, O my God: 4616+3807.1
Jnh 1:12 for I know that for my s this great 7945+871.1
Mic 3:12 Therefore shall Zion for your s be 1558+871.1
Mt 5:10 which are persecuted for righteousness' s: *1752*
5:11 of evil against you falsely, for my s. *1752*
10:18 before governors and kings for my s, *1752*
10:22 shall be hated of all *men* for my name's s: *1223*
10:39 he that loseth his life for my s shall find it. *1752*
14: 3 and put *him* in prison for Herodias' s, *1223*
14: 9 nevertheless for the oaths' s, and *1223*
16:25 whosoever will lose his life for my s shall *1752*
19:12 eunuchs for the kingdom of heaven's s. *1223*
19:29 or children, or lands, for my name's s, *1752*
24: 9 be hated of all nations for my name's s. *1223*
24:22 for the elect's s those days shall be *1223*
Mk 4:17 or persecution ariseth for the word's s, *1223*
6:17 and bound him in prison for Herodias' s, *1223*
6:26 *yet* for his oaths' s, and for their sakes *1223*
8:35 but whosoever shall lose his life for my s *1752*
10:29 or wife, or children, or lands, for my s, *1752*
13: 9 be brought before rulers and kings for my s, *1752*
13:13 shall be hated of all *men* for my name's s: *1223*
13:20 but for the elect's s, whom he hath chosen, *1223*
Lk 6:22 your name as evil, for the Son of man's s. *1752*
9:24 but whosoever will lose his life for my s, *1752*
18:29 or children, for the kingdom of God's s, *1752*
21:12 before kings and rulers for my name's s. *1752*
21:17 shall be hated of all *men* for my name's s. *1223*
Jn 12: 9 and they came not for Jesus' s only, *1223*
13:37 thee now? I will lay down my life for thy s. *5228*
13:38 Wilt thou lay down thy life for my s? *5228*
14:11 or else believe me for the very works' s. *1223*
15:21 will they do unto you for my name's s, *1223*
Ac 9:16 *things* he must suffer for my name's s. *5228*
26: 7 For which hope's s, king Agrippa, I am *4012*
Ro 4:23 Now it was not written for his s alone, *1223*
8:36 For thy s we are killed all the day long; *1752*
13: 5 only for wrath, but also for conscience s. *1223*
15:30 for the Lord Jesus Christ's s, and for *1223*
1Co 4:10 We *are* fools for Christ's s, but ye *are* wise *1223*
9:23 And this I do for the gospel's s, that I *1223*
10:25 asking no question for conscience s: *1223*
10:27 eat, asking no question for conscience s. *1223*
10:28 eat not for his s that shewed *it,* and *1223*
10:28 *for* conscience s: for the earth *is* the Lord's, NIG
2Co 4: 5 and ourselves your servants for Jesus' s. *1223*
4:11 are alway delivered unto death for Jesus' s, *1223*
12:10 in persecutions, in distresses for Christ's s: *5228*
Eph 4:32 even as God for Christ's s hath forgiven *1722*
Php 1:29 believe on him, but also to suffer for his s; *5228*
Col 1:24 of Christ in my flesh for his body's s, *5228*
3: 6 For which *things'* s the wrath of God *1223*
1Th 1: 5 of *men* we were among you for your s. *1223*
5:13 them very highly in love for their work's s. *1223*
1Ti 5:23 but use a little wine for thy stomach's s *1223*
Tit 1:11 which *they* ought not, for filthy lucre's s. *5484*
Phm 1: 9 *Yet* for love's s I rather beseech *thee,* being *1223*
1Pe 2:13 to every ordinance of man for the Lord's s: *1223*
3:14 But and if ye suffer for righteousness' s, *1223*
1Jn 2:12 *your* sins are forgiven you for his name's s. *1223*
2Jn 1: 2 For the truth's s, which dwelleth in us, and *1223*
3Jn 1: 7 Because that for his name's s they went *5228*
Rev 2: 3 and for my name's s hast laboured, and *1223*

SAKES (31) [SAKE]
Ge 18:26 I will spare all the place for their s. 5668+871.1
Lev 26:45 I will for their s remember the covenant 3807.1
Dt 1:37 the LORD was angry with me for your s, 1558
3:26 was wroth with me for your s, 4616+3807.1
4:21 the LORD was angry with me for your s, 1697
Jdg 21:22 Be favourable unto them for our s: NIH
Ru 1:13 for it grieveth me much for your s that 4480
1Ch 16:21 yea, he reproved kings for their s, 5921
Ps 7: 7 for their s therefore return thou on high. 5921
105:14 yea, he reproved kings for their s; 5921
106:32 it went ill with Moses for their s: 5668+871.1
122: 8 For my brethren and companions' s, 4616+3807.1
Isa 65: 8 so will I do for my servants' s, 4616+3807.1
Eze 36:22 I do not *this* for your s, O house of 4616+3807.1
36:32 Not for your s do I *this,* saith 4616+3807.1
Da 2:30 for *their* s that shall make known 1701
Mal 3:11 I will rebuke the devourer for your s, and 3807.1
Mk 6:26 for their s which sat with *him,* he would not NIG
Jn 11:15 And I am glad for your s that I was not *1223*
12:30 came not because of me, but for your s. *1223*
17:19 And for their s I sanctify myself, that they *5228*
Ro 11:28 the gospel, *they are* enemies for your s: *1223*
11:28 *they are* beloved for the fathers' s. *1223*
1Co 4: 6 to myself and *to* Apollos for your s; *1223*
9:10 Or saith he *it* altogether for our s? For our *1223*
9:10 For our s, no doubt, *this* is written: that he *1223*
2Co 2:10 for your s *forgave I it* in the person of *1223*
4:15 For all *things are* for your s, that *1223*
8: 9 he was rich, *yet* for your s he became poor, *1223*
1Th 3: 9 for all the joy wherewith we joy for your s *1223*
2Ti 2:10 I endure all *things* for the elects' s, *1223*

SAKIA See SHACHIA

SALA (1) [SALAH]
Lk 3:35 *the son* of Heber, which was *the son* of S, *4527*

SALAH (6) [SALA]
Ge 10:24 Arphaxad begat S; and Salah begat Eber. 7974
10:24 Arphaxad begat Salah; and S begat Eber. 7974
11:12 lived five and thirty years, and begat S: 7974
11:13 Arphaxad lived after he begat S four 7974
11:14 And S lived thirty years, and begat Eber: 7974
11:15 S lived after he begat Eber four hundred 7974

SALAMIS (1)
Ac 13: 5 And when they were at S, they preached *4529*

SALATHIEL (4)
1Ch 3:17 And the sons of Jeconiah; Assir, S his son, 7597
Mt 1:12 brought to Babylon, Jechonias begat S; *4528*
1:12 begat Salathiel; and S begat Zorobabel; *4528*
Lk 3:27 which was *the son* of S, which was *the son* *4528*

SALCAH (2) [SALCHAH]
Jos 12: 5 mount Hermon, and in S, and in all Bashan, 5548
13:11 all mount Hermon, and all Bashan unto S; 5548

SALCHAH (2) [SALCAH]
Dt 3:10 and all Bashan, unto S and Edrei, 5548
1Ch 5:11 against them, in the land of Bashan unto S: 5548

SALE (3) [SELL]
Lev 25:27 let him count the years of the **s** thereof, 4465
25:50 the price of his **s** shall be according unto 4465
Dt 18: 8 beside **that which cometh of** the **s** of his 4465

SALECAH See SALCAH; SALCHAH

SALEM (4) [JERUSALEM]
Ge 14:18 Melchizedek king of **S** brought forth bread 8004
Ps 76: 2 In **S** also is his tabernacle, and his dwelling 8004
Heb 7: 1 For this Melchisedec, king of **S**, priest of *4532*
7: 2 and after that also King of **S**, which is, *4532*

SALIM (1)
Jn 3:23 John also was baptizing in Aenon near to **S**, *4530*

SALLAI (2)
Ne 11: 8 **S**, nine hundred twenty and eight. 5543
12:20 Of **S**, Kallai; of Amok, Eber; 5543

SALLU (3)
1Ch 9: 7 **S** the son of Meshullam, the son of 5543
Ne 11: 7 **S** the son of Meshullam, the son of Joed, 5543
12: 7 **S**, Amok, Hilkiah, Jedaiah. These *were* 5543

SALMA (4)
1Ch 2:11 Nahshon begat **S**, and Salma begat Boaz, 8007
2:11 Nahshon begat Salma, and **S** begat Boaz, 8007
2:51 **S** the father of Beth-lehem, Hareph 8007
2:54 The sons of **S**; Beth-lehem, and 8007

SALMON (6)
Ru 4:20 begat Nahshon, and Nahshon begat **S**, 8009
4:21 And **S** begat Boaz, and Boaz begat Obed, 8012
Ps 68:14 kings in it, it was *white as* snow in **S**. 6756
Mt 1: 4 begat Naasson; and Naasson begat **S**; *4533*
1: 5 And **S** begat Booz of Rachab; and *4533*
Lk 3:32 *the son* of Booz, which was *the son* of **S**, *4533*

SALMONE (1)
Ac 27: 7 we sailed under Crete, over against **S**; *4534*

SALOME (2)
Mk 15:40 of James the less and of Joses, and **S**; *4539*
16: 1 and **S**, had bought *sweet* spices, that they *4539*

SALT (41) [SALTED, SALTNESS, SALTPITS]
Ge 14: 3 in the vale of Siddim, which *is* the **s** sea. 4417
19:26 behind him, and she became a pillar of **s**. 4417
Lev 2:13 thy meat offering shalt thou season with **s**; 4417
2:13 neither shalt thou suffer the **s** of 4417
2:13 with all thine offerings thou shalt offer **s**. 4417
Nu 18:19 it *is* a covenant of **s** for ever before 4417
34: 3 be the outmost coast of the **s** sea eastward: 4417
34:12 and the goings out of it shall be *at* the **s** sea: 4417
Dt 3:17 *even* the **s** sea, under Ashdoth-pisgah 4417
29:23 **s**, *and* burning, *that* it is not sown, 4417
Jos 3:16 *even* the **s** sea, failed, *and* were cut off: 4417
12: 3 sea of the plain, *even* the **s** sea on the east, 4417
15: 2 border was from the shore of the **s** sea, 4417
15: 5 the east border *was* the **s** sea, *even* unto 4417
15:62 and the city of **s**, and En-gedi; 4417
18:19 bay of the **s** sea at the south end of Jordan: 4417
Jdg 9:45 and beat down the city, and sowed it *with* **s**. 4417
2Sa 8:13 smiting of the Syrians in the valley of **s**, 4417
2Ki 2:20 Bring me a new cruse, and put **s** therein. 4417
2:21 cast the **s** in there, and said, Thus saith 4417
14: 7 He slew *of* Edom in the valley of **s** ten 4417
1Ch 18:12 in the valley of **s** eighteen thousand. 4417
2Ch 13: 5 to him and to his sons *by* a covenant of **s**? 4417
25:11 went *to* the valley of **s**, and smote *of* 4417
Ezr 6: 9 the God of heaven, wheat, **s**, wine, and oil, 4416
7:22 and **s** without prescribing *how much*. 4416
Job 6: 6 that which is unsavoury be eaten without **s**? 4417
Ps 60: T smote of Edom in the valley of **s** twelve 4417
Jer 17: 6 *in* a **s** land and not inhabited. 4420
Eze 43:24 the priests shall cast **s** upon them, and 4417
47:11 shall not be healed; they shall be given to **s**. 4417
Mt 5:13 Ye are the **s** of the earth: but if the salt have *217*
5:13 but if the **s** have lost his savour, *217*
Mk 9:49 and every sacrifice shall be salted with **s**. *251*
9:50 **S** *is* good: but if the salt have lost his *217*
9:50 but if the **s** have lost his saltness, *217*
9:50 Have **s** in yourselves, and have peace one *217*
Lk 14:34 **S** *is* good: but if the salt have lost his savour, *217*
14:34 but if the **s** have lost his savour, *217*
Col 4: 6 speech *be* alway with grace, seasoned with **s**, *217*
Jas 3:12 so *can* no fountain *both* yield **s** water and *252*

SALTED (4) [SALT]
Eze 16: 4 to supple *thee;* thou wast not **s at all**, 4414+4414
Mt 5:13 have lost his savour, wherewith shall it be **s**? *233*
Mk 9:49 For every one shall be **s** with fire, and *233*
9:49 and every sacrifice shall be **s** with salt. *233*

SALTNESS (1) [SALT]
Mk 9:50 but if the salt have **lost** his **s**, wherewith will *358*

SALTPITS (1) [PIT, SALT]
Zep 2: 9 and **s**, and a perpetual desolation: 4379+4417

SALU (1)
Nu 25:14 *was* Zimri, the son of **S**, a prince of a chief 5543

SALUTATION (6) [SALUTE]
Lk 1:29 cast in her mind what manner of **s** this *783*
1:41 *that,* when Elisabeth heard the **s** of Mary, *783*
1:44 as soon as the voice of thy **s** sounded in mine *783*
1Co 16:21 The **s** of *me* Paul with mine own hand. *783*
Col 4:18 The **s** by the hand of me Paul. *783*
2Th 3:17 The **s** of Paul with mine own hand, which is *783*

SALUTATIONS (1) [SALUTE]
Mk 12:38 and *love* **s** in the marketplaces, *783*

SALUTE (39) [SALUTATION, SALUTATIONS, SALUTED, SALUTETH]
1Sa 10: 4 they will **s** thee, and 7592+7965+3807.1
13:10 went out to meet him, that he might **s** him. 1288
25:14 out of the wilderness to **s** our master; 1288
2Sa 8:10 to **s** him, and to bless him, 7592+7965+3807.1
2Ki 4:29 *thy way:* if thou meet any man, **s** him not; 1288
4:29 if any **s** thee, answer him not *again:* and 1288
10:13 we go down to **s** the children of the king 7965
Mt 5:47 And if ye **s** your brethren only, what do ye *782*
10:12 And when ye come into a house **s** it. *782*
Mk 15:18 And began to **s** him, Hail, King of the Jews. *782*
Lk 10: 4 nor shoes: and **s** no *man* by the way. *782*
Ac 25:13 and Bernice came unto Cesarea to **s** Festus. *782*
Ro 16: 5 **S** my wellbeloved Epenetus, who is *782*
16: 7 **S** Andronicus and Junia, my kinsmen, and *782*
16: 9 **S** Urban our helper in Christ, and *782*
16:10 **S** Apelles approved in Christ. Salute them *782*
16:10 **S** them which are of Aristobulus' *782*
16:11 **S** Herodion my kinsman. Greet them that be *782*
16:12 **S** Tryphena and Tryphosa, who labour in *782*
16:12 **S** the beloved Persis, which laboured much *782*
16:13 **S** Rufus chosen in the Lord, and his mother *782*
16:14 **S** Asyncritus, Phlegon, Hermas, Patrobas, *782*
16:15 **S** Philologus, and Julia, Nereus, and *782*
16:16 **S** one another with a holy kiss. The churches *782*
16:16 a holy kiss. The churches of Christ **s** you. *782*
16:21 Jason, and Sosipater, my kinsmen, **s** you. *782*
16:22 who wrote *this* epistle, **s** you in the Lord. *782*
1Co 16:19 The churches of Asia **s** you. Aquila and *782*
16:19 Aquila and Priscilla **s** you much in the Lord, *782*
2Co 13:13 All the saints **s** you. *782*
Php 4:21 **S** every saint in Christ Jesus. The brethren *782*
4:22 All the saints **s** you, chiefly they that are of *782*
Col 4:15 **S** the brethren which are in Laodicea, and *782*
2Ti 4:19 **S** Prisca and Aquila, and the household of *782*
Tit 3:15 All that are with me **s** thee. Greet them that *782*
Phm 1:23 There **s** thee Epaphras, my fellowprisoner in *782*
Heb 13:24 **S** all them that have the rule over you, and *782*
13:24 and all the saints. They of Italy **s** you. *782*
3Jn 1:14 *Our* friends **s** thee. Greet the friends by *782*

SALUTED (9) [SALUTE]
Jdg 18:15 house of Micah, and **s** him. 7592+7965+3807.1
1Sa 17:22 and came and **s** his brethren. 7592+7965+3807.1
30:21 to the people, he **s** them. 7592+7965+3807.1
2Ki 10:15 he **s** him, and said to him, Is thine heart 1288
Mk 9:15 greatly amazed, and running to *him* **s** him. *782*
Lk 1:40 into the house of Zacharias, and **s** Elisabeth. *782*
Ac 18:22 and gone up, and **s** the church, he went down *782*
21: 7 and **s** the brethren, and abode with them one *782*
21:19 And when he had **s** them, he declared *782*

SALUTETH (5) [SALUTE]
Ro 16:23 mine host, and of the whole church, **s** you. *782*

S

Ro 16:23 Erastus the chamberlain of the city s you, 782
Col 4:10 Aristarchus my fellowprisoner s you, and 782
4:12 who is *one* of you, a servant of Christ, s you, 782
1Pe 5:13 at Babylon, elected together with *you,* s you; 782

SALVATION (164) [SAVE]

Ge 49:18 I have waited for thy s, O LORD. 3444
Ex 14:13 stand still, and see the s of the LORD, 3444
15: 2 and song, and he is become my s: 3444
Dt 32:15 and lightly esteemed the Rock of his s. 3444
1Sa 2: 1 mine enemies; because I rejoice in thy s. 3444
11:13 for to day the LORD hath wrought s in 8668
14:45 who hath wrought this great s in Israel? 3444
19: 5 the LORD wrought a great s for all Israel: 8668
2Sa 22: 3 the horn of my s, my high tower, and 3468
22:36 Thou hast also given me the shield of thy s: 3468
22:47 and exalted be the God of the rock of my s. 3468
22:51 *He is* the tower of s for his king: and 3444
23: 5 for *this is* all my s, and all *my* desire, 3468
1Ch 16:23 the earth; shew forth from day to day his s. 3444
16:35 O God of our s, and gather us together, and 3468
2Ch 6:41 be clothed *with* s, and let thy saints rejoice 8668
20:17 and see the s of the LORD with you, 3444
Job 13:16 He also *shall be* my s: for a hypocrite shall 3444
Ps 3: 8 S *belongeth* unto the LORD: thy blessing 3444
9:14 the daughter of Zion: I will rejoice in thy s. 3444
13: 5 thy mercy; my heart shall rejoice in thy s. 3444
14: 7 O that the s of Israel *were come* out of 3444
18: 2 and the horn of my s, *and* my high tower. 3468
18:35 Thou hast also given me the shield of thy s: 3468
18:46 and let the God of my s be exalted. 3468
20: 5 We will rejoice in thy s, and in the name of 3444
21: 1 and in thy s how greatly shall he rejoice! 3444
21: 5 His glory *is* great in thy s: honour and 3444
24: 5 and righteousness from the God of his s. 3468
25: 5 for thou *art* the God of my s; on thee do I 3468
27: 1 The LORD *is* my light and my s; whom 3468
27: 9 me not, neither forsake me, O God of my s. 3468
35: 3 persecute me: say unto my soul, I *am* thy s. 3444
35: 9 in the LORD: it shall rejoice in his s. 3444
37:39 the s of the righteous *is* of the LORD: 8668
38:22 Make haste to help me, O Lord my s. 8668
40:10 I have declared thy faithfulness and thy s: 8668
40:16 let such as love thy s say continually, 8668
50:23 *aright* will I shew the s of God. 3468
51:12 Restore unto me the joy of thy s; and 3468
51:14 O God, thou God of my s: 8668
53: 6 O that the s of Israel *were come* out of 3444
62: 1 waiteth upon God: from him *cometh* my s. 3444
62: 2 He only *is* my rock and my s; *he is* my 3444
62: 6 He only *is* my rock and my s: *he is* my 3444
62: 7 In God *is* my s and my glory: the rock of 3468
65: 5 wilt thou answer us, O God of our s; 3468
68:19 us *with benefits, even* the God of our s. 3444
68:20 *He that is* our God *is* the God of s; and 4190
69:13 of thy mercy hear me, in the truth of thy s. 3468
69:29 let thy s, O God, set me up on high. 3444
70: 4 let such as love thy s say continually, 3444
71:15 thy righteousness *and* thy s all the day; 8668
74:12 of old, working s in the midst of the earth. 3444
78:22 not in God, and trusted not in his s: 3444
79: 9 Help us, O God of our s, for the glory of 3468
85: 4 O God of our s, and cause thine anger 3468
85: 7 thy mercy, O LORD, and grant us thy s. 3468
85: 9 Surely his s *is* nigh them that fear him; 3468
88: 1 O LORD God of my s, I have cried day 3444
89:26 my Father, my God, and the rock of my s. 3444
91:16 life will I satisfy him, and shew him my s. 3444
95: 1 us make a joyful noise to the rock of our s. 3468
96: 2 his name; shew forth his s from day to day. 3444
98: 2 The LORD hath made known his s: 3444
98: 3 all the ends of the earth have seen the s of 3444
106: 4 unto thy people: O visit me with thy s; 3444
116:13 I will take the cup of s, and call upon 3444
118:14 my strength and song, and is become my s. 3444
118:15 and s *is* in the tabernacles of the righteous: 3444
118:21 thou hast heard me, and art become my s. 3444
119:41 O LORD, *even* thy s, according to thy 8668
119:81 My soul fainteth for thy s: *but* I hope in thy 8668
119:123 Mine eyes fail for thy s, and for the word of 3444
119:155 S *is* far from the wicked: for they seek not 3444
119:166 I have hoped for thy s, and done thy 3444
119:174 I have longed for thy s, O LORD; and 3444
132:16 I will also clothe her priests with s: and 3468
140: 7 O GOD the Lord, the strength of my s, 3444
144:10 *It is he* that giveth s unto kings: 8668
149: 4 he will beautify the meek with s. 3444
Isa 12: 2 Behold, God *is* my s; I will trust, and not be 3444
12: 2 and *my* song; he also is become my s. 3444
12: 3 shall ye draw water out of the wells of s. 3444
17:10 thou hast forgotten the God of thy s, 3468
25: 9 we will be glad and rejoice in his s. 3444
26: 1 s will *God* appoint *for* walls and bulwarks. 3444
33: 2 our s also in the time of trouble. 3444
33: 6 the stability of thy times, *and* strength of s: 3444
45: 8 let them bring forth s, and let righteousness 3468
45:17 saved in the LORD *with* an everlasting s: 8668
46:13 shall not be far off, and my s shall not tarry: 8668
46:13 I will place s in Zion for Israel my glory. 8668
49: 6 that *thou* mayest be my s unto the end of 3444
49: 8 and in a day of s have I helped thee: 3444
51: 5 my s is gone forth, and mine arms shall 3468
51: 6 my s shall be for ever, and 3444
51: 8 and my s from generation to generation. 3444
52: 7 good tidings of good, that publisheth s; 3444
52:10 all the ends of the earth shall see the s of 3444
56: 1 for my s *is* near to come, and 3444
59:11 *there is* none; for s, *but* it is far off from us. 3444
59:16 therefore his arm **brought** s unto him; and 3467
59:17 and a helmet of s upon his head; 3444
60:18 thou shalt call thy walls S, and thy gates 3444
61:10 he hath clothed me with the garments of s, 3468
62: 1 and the s thereof as a lamp *that* burneth. 3444
62:11 the daughter of Zion, Behold, thy s cometh; 3468
63: 5 mine own arm **brought** s unto me; 3467
Jer 3:23 Truly in vain *is s hoped for* from the hills, NIH
3:23 truly in the LORD our God *is* the s of 8668
La 3:26 and quietly wait for the s of the LORD. 8668
Jnh 2: 9 *that* that I have vowed. S *is* of the LORD. 3444
Mic 7: 7 I will wait for the God of my s: 3468
Hab 3: 8 upon thine horses *and* thy chariots of s? 3444
3:13 Thou wentest forth for the s of thy people, 3468
3:13 thy people, *even* for s with thine anointed; 3468
3:18 the LORD, I will joy in the God of my s. 3468
Zec 9: 9 he *is* just, and **having** s; lowly, and 3467
Lk 1:69 And hath raised up a horn of s for us in *4991*
1:77 To give knowledge of s unto his people by *4991*
2:30 For mine eyes have seen thy s, *4992*
3: 6 And all flesh shall see the s of God. *4992*
19: 9 unto him, This day is s come to this house, *4991*
Jn 4:22 know what we worship: for s is of the Jews. *4991*
Ac 4:12 Neither is there s in any other: for there is *4991*
13:26 to you is the word of this s sent. *4991*
13:47 that thou shouldest be for s unto the ends of *4991*
16:17 high God, which shew unto us the way of s. *4991*
28:28 that the s of God is sent unto the Gentiles, *4992*
Ro 1:16 for it is the power of God unto s to every *4991*
10:10 with the mouth confession is made unto s. *4991*
11:11 *rather* through their fall s *is come* unto *4991*
13:11 for now *is* our s nearer than when we *4991*
2Co 1: 6 be afflicted, *it is* for your consolation and s, *4991*
1: 6 *it is* for your consolation and s. *4991*
6: 2 and in the day of s have I succoured thee: *4991*
6: 2 accepted time; behold, now *is* the day of s.) *4991*
7:10 For godly sorrow worketh repentance to s *4991*
Eph 1:13 the word of truth, the gospel of your s: *4991*
6:17 And take the helmet of s, and the sword of *4992*
Php 1:19 For I know that this shall turn to my s *4991*
1:28 but to you of s, and that of God. *4991*
2:12 work out your own s with fear and *4991*
1Th 5: 8 and love; and for a helmet, the hope of s. *4991*
5: 9 but to obtain s by our Lord Jesus Christ, *4991*
2Th 2:13 you to s through sanctification of the Spirit *4991*
2Ti 2:10 that they may also obtain the s which is in *4991*
3:15 which are able to make thee wise unto s *4991*
Tit 2:11 For the grace of God that bringeth s hath *4992*
Heb 1:14 minister for them who shall be heirs of s? *4991*
2: 3 shall we escape, if we neglect so great s; *4991*
2:10 to make the captain of their s perfect *4991*
5: 9 he became the author of eternal s unto all *4991*
6: 9 and *things* that accompany s, though we *4991*
9:28 appear the second time without sin unto s. *4991*
1Pe 1: 5 unto s ready to be revealed in the last time. *4991*
1: 9 end of your faith, *even* the s of *your* souls. *4991*
1:10 Of which s the prophets have inquired and *4991*
2Pe 3:15 *that* the longsuffering of our Lord *is* s; *4991*
Jude 1: 3 to write unto you of the common s, *4991*
Rev 7:10 S to our God which sitteth upon the throne, *4991*

S

Rev 12:10 Now is come **s**, and strength, and *4991*
19: 1 saying, Alleluia; **S**, and glory, and honour, *4991*

SAMARIA (124) [SAMARITAN, SAMARITANS]
1Ki 13:32 the high places which *are* in the cities of **S**, 8111
16:24 he bought the hill **S** of Shemer for two 8111
16:24 the name of Shemer, owner of the hill, **S**. 8111
16:28 slept with his fathers, and was buried in **S**: 8111
16:29 son of Omri reigned over Israel in **S** twenty 8111
16:32 the house of Baal, which he had built in **S**. 8111
18: 2 And *there was* a sore famine in **S**. 8111
20: 1 he went up and besieged **S**, and 8111
20:10 if the dust of **S** shall suffice for handfuls for 8111
20:17 saying, There are men come out of **S**. 8111
20:34 thee in Damascus, as my father made in **S**. 8111
20:43 house heavy and displeased, and came to **S**. 8111
21: 1 hard by the palace of Ahab king of **S**. 8111
21:18 to meet Ahab king of Israel, which *is* in **S**: 8111
22:10 void place *in* the entrance of the gate of **S**; 8111
22:37 So the king died, and was brought *to* **S**; and 8111
22:37 *to* Samaria; and they buried the king in **S**. 8111
22:38 *one* washed the chariot in the pool of **S**; 8111
22:51 **S** the seventeenth year of Jehoshaphat king 8111
2Ki 1: 2 a lattice in his upper chamber that *was* in **S**, 8111
1: 3 up to meet the messengers of the king of **S**, 8111
2:25 and from thence he returned *to* **S**. 8111
3: 1 **S** the eighteenth year of Jehoshaphat king 8111
3: 6 king Jehoram went out of **S** the same time, 8111
5: 3 my lord *were* with the prophet that *is* in **S**; 8111
6:19 man whom ye seek. But he led them to **S**. 8111
6:20 when they were come *into* **S**, that Elisha 8111
6:20 and behold, *they were* in the midst of **S**. 8111
6:24 all his host, and went up, and besieged **S**. 8111
6:25 there was a great famine in **S**: and behold, 8111
7: 1 of barley for a shekel, in the gate of **S**. 8111
7:18 to morrow about *this* time in the gate of **S**: 8111
10: 1 Ahab had seventy sons in **S**. And Jehu 8111
10: 1 Jehu wrote letters, and sent *to* **S**, unto 8111
10:12 he arose and departed, and came *to* **S**. 8111
10:17 when he came *to* **S**, he slew all that 8111
10:17 he slew all that remained unto Ahab in **S**, 8111
10:35 they buried him in **S**. And Jehoahaz his son 8111
10:36 the time that Jehu reigned over Israel in **S** 8111
13: 1 son of Jehu *began* to reign over Israel in **S**, 8111
13: 6 there remained the grove also in **S**.) 8111
13: 9 with his fathers; and they buried him in **S**: 8111
13:10 son of Jehoahaz to reign over Israel in **S**, 8111
13:13 Joash was buried in **S** with the kings of 8111
14:14 and hostages, and returned to **S**. 8111
14:16 was buried in **S** with the kings of Israel; 8111
14:23 of Joash king of Israel *began* to reign in **S**, 8111
15: 8 Jeroboam reign over Israel in **S** six months. 8111
15:13 of Judah; and he reigned a full month in **S**. 8111
15:14 came *to* **S**, and smote Shallum the son of 8111
15:14 smote Shallum the son of Jabesh in **S**, and 8111
15:17 over Israel, *and reigned* ten years in **S**. 8111
15:23 Menahem *began* to reign over Israel in **S**, 8111
15:25 conspired against him, and smote him in **S**, 8111
15:27 of Remaliah *began* to reign over Israel in **S**, 8111
17: 1 of Elah to reign in **S** over Israel nine years. 8111
17: 5 went up *to* **S**, and besieged it three years. 8111
17: 6 the king of Assyria took **S**, and 8111
17:24 placed *them* in the cities of **S** instead of 8111
17:24 they possessed **S**, and dwelt in the cities 8111
17:26 hast removed, and placed in the cities of **S**, 8111
17:28 whom they had carried away from **S** came 8111
18: 9 king of Assyria came up against **S**, 8111
18:10 year of Hoshea king of Israel, **S** was taken. 8111
18:34 have they delivered **S** out of mine hand? 8111
21:13 I will stretch over Jerusalem the line of **S**, 8111
23:18 the bones of the prophet that came out of **S**. 8111
23:19 the high places that *were* in the cities of **S**, 8111
2Ch 18: 2 *certain* years he went down to Ahab to **S**. 8111
18: 9 place *at* the entering in of the gate of **S**; 8111
22: 9 they caught him, (for he *was* hid in **S**,) and 8111
25:13 from **S** even unto Beth-horon, and 8111
25:24 the hostages also, and returned *to* **S**. 8111
28: 8 spoil from them, and brought the spoil to **S**. 8111
28: 9 he went out before the host that came to **S**, 8111
28:15 to their brethren: then they returned *to* **S**. 8111
Ezr 4:10 set in the cities of **S**, and the rest *that are* on 8115
4:17 the rest of their companions that dwell in **S**, 8115
Ne 4: 2 before his brethren and the army of **S**, 8111
Isa 7: 9 the head of Ephraim *is* **S**, and the head of 8111
7: 9 and the head of **S** *is* Remaliah's son. 8111
8: 4 the spoil of **S** shall be taken away before 8111
9: 9 *even* Ephraim and the inhabitant of **S**, 8111
10: 9 Hamath as Arpad? *is* not **S** as Damascus? 8111
10:10 did excel *them of* Jerusalem and *of* **S**; 8111
10:11 as I have done unto **S** and her idols, so 8111
36:19 and have they delivered **S** out of my hand? 8111
Jer 23:13 I have seen folly in the prophets of **S**; 8111
31: 5 yet plant vines upon the mountains of **S**: 8111
41: 5 from Shiloh, and from **S**, *even* fourscore 8111
Eze 16:46 thine elder sister *is* **S**, she and her daughters 8111
16:51 Neither hath **S** committed half of thy sins; 8111
16:53 the captivity of **S** and her daughters, then 8111
16:55 **S** and her daughters shall return to their 8111
23: 4 **S** *is* Aholah, and Jerusalem Aholibah. 8111
23:33 and desolation, *with* the cup of thy sister **S**. 8111
Hos 7: 1 was discovered, and the wickedness of **S**: 8111
8: 5 Thy calf, O **S**, hath cast *thee* off; 8111
8: 6 but the calf of **S** shall be broken in pieces. 8111
10: 5 The inhabitants of **S** shall fear because 8111
10: 7 *As for* **S**, her king is cut off as the foam 8111
13:16 **S** shall become desolate; for she hath 8111
Am 3: 9 yourselves upon the mountains of **S**, 8111
3:12 out that dwell in **S** in the corner of a bed, 8111
4: 1 of Bashan, that *are* in the mountain of **S**, 8111
6: 1 ease in Zion, and trust in the mountain of **S**, 8111
8:14 They that swear by the sin of **S**, and say, 8111
Ob 1:19 the fields of Ephraim, and the fields of **S**: 8111
Mic 1: 1 which he saw concerning **S** and Jerusalem. 8111
1: 5 *is it* not **S**? and what *are* the high places of 8111
1: 6 Therefore I will make **S** as a heap of 8111
Lk 17:11 that he passed through the midst of **S** and *4540*
Jn 4: 4 And he must needs go through **S**. *4540*
4: 5 Then cometh he to a city of **S**, which is *4540*
4: 7 There cometh a woman of **S** to draw water: *4540*
4: 9 Then saith the woman of **S** unto him, *4542*
4: 9 drink of me, which am a woman of **S**? *4542*
Ac 1: 8 and in **S**, and unto the uttermost part of *4540*
8: 1 throughout the regions of Judea and **S**, *4540*
8: 5 Then Philip went down to the city of **S**, and *4540*
8: 9 and bewitched the people of **S**, giving out *4540*
8:14 heard that **S** had received the word of God, *4540*
9:31 rest throughout all Judea and Galilee and **S**, *4540*
15: 3 they passed through Phenice and **S**, *4540*

SAMARITAN (3) [SAMARIA]
Lk 10:33 But a certain **S**, as he journeyed, *4541*
17:16 his feet, giving him thanks: and he was a **S**. *4541*
Jn 8:48 Say we not well that thou art a **S**, and hast a *4541*

SAMARITANS (7) [SAMARIA]
2Ki 17:29 of the high places which the **S** had made, 8118
Mt 10: 5 and into *any* city of the **S** enter ye not: *4541*
Lk 9:52 and entered into a village of the **S**, *4541*
Jn 4: 9 For the Jews have no dealings with the **S**. *4541*
4:39 And many of the **S** of that city believed on *4541*
4:40 So when the **S** were come unto him, *4541*
Ac 8:25 the gospel in many villages of the **S**. *4541*

SAME (332) [SELFSAME] See Index

SAMGAR See SAMGAR-NEBO

SAMGAR-NEBO (1)
Jer 39: 3 **S**, Sarsechim, Rab-saris, Nergal-sharezer, 5562

SAMLAH (4)
Ge 36:36 and **S** of Masrekah reigned in his stead. 8072
36:37 **S** died, and Saul of Rehoboth *by* the river 8072
1Ch 1:47 **S** of Masrekah reigned in his stead. 8072
1:48 when **S** was dead, Shaul of Rehoboth *by* 8072

SAMOS (1)
Ac 20:15 and the next *day* we arrived at **S**, and *4544*

SAMOTHRACE See SAMOTHRACIA

SAMOTHRACIA (1)
Ac 16:11 we came with a straight course to **S**, and *4543*

SAMSON (36) [SAMSON'S]
Jdg 13:24 woman bare a son, and called his name **S**: 8123
14: 1 **S** went down *to* Timnath, and saw a woman 8123
14: 3 **S** said unto his father, Get her for me; 8123
14: 5 went **S** down, and his father and 8123
14: 7 with the woman; and she pleased **S** well. 8123

Jdg 14:10 **S** made there a feast; for so used the young 8123
14:12 **S** said unto them, I will now put forth a 8123
15: 1 that **S** visited his wife with a kid; 8123
15: 3 **S** said concerning them, Now shall I be 8123
15: 4 **S** went and caught three hundred foxes, 8123
15: 6 they answered, **S**, the son in law of 8123
15: 7 **S** said unto them, Though ye have done 8123
15:10 they answered, To bind **S** are we come up, 8123
15:11 said to **S**, Knowest thou not that 8123
15:12 **S** said unto them, Swear unto me, that ye 8123
15:16 **S** said, With the jawbone of an ass, 8123
16: 1 went **S** to Gaza, and saw there a harlot, 8123
16: 2 *told* the Gazites, saying, **S** is come hither. 8123
16: 3 **S** lay till midnight, and arose at midnight, 8123
16: 6 Delilah said to **S**, Tell me, I pray thee, 8123
16: 7 **S** said unto her, If they bind me with seven 8123
16: 9 unto him, The Philistines *be* upon thee, **S**. 8123
16:10 Delilah said unto **S**, Behold, thou hast 8123
16:12 unto him, The Philistines *be* upon thee, **S**. 8123
16:13 Delilah said unto **S**, Hitherto thou hast 8123
16:14 unto him, The Philistines *be* upon thee, **S**. 8123
16:20 she said, The Philistines *be* upon thee, **S**. 8123
16:23 Our god hath delivered **S** our enemy into 8123
16:25 that they said, Call for **S**, that he may make 8123
16:25 they called for **S** out of the prison house; 8123
16:26 **S** said unto the lad that held him by 8123
16:27 women, that beheld while **S** made sport. 8123
16:28 **S** called unto the LORD, and said, O Lord 8123
16:29 **S** took hold of the two middle pillars upon 8123
16:30 **S** said, Let me die with the Philistines. 8123
Heb 11:32 and *of* Barak, and *of* **S**, and *of* Jephthae; *4546*

SAMSON'S (3) [SAMSON]

Jdg 14:15 that they said unto **S** wife, Entice thy 8123
14:16 **S** wife wept before him, and said, 8123
14:20 **S** wife was *given* to his companion, 8123

SAMUEL (142)

1Sa 1:20 that she bare a son, and called his name **S**, 8050
2:18 **S** ministered before the LORD, *being* a 8050
2:21 And the child **S** grew before the LORD. 8050
2:26 the child **S** grew on, and was in favour both 8050
3: 1 the child **S** ministered unto the LORD 8050
3: 3 of God *was*, and **S** was laid down *to sleep;* 8050
3: 4 That the LORD called **S**: and 8050
3: 6 the LORD called yet again, **S**. 8050
3: 6 **S** arose and went to Eli, and said, Here *am* 8050
3: 7 Now **S** did not yet know the LORD, 8050
3: 8 the LORD called **S** again the third time. 8050
3: 9 Therefore Eli said unto **S**, Go, lie down: 8050
3: 9 So **S** went and lay down in his place. 8050
3:10 and called as at other times, **S**, Samuel. 8050
3:10 and called as at other times, Samuel, **S**. 8050
3:10 **S** answered, Speak; for thy servant heareth. 8050
3:11 the LORD said to **S**, Behold, I will do a 8050
3:15 **S** lay until the morning, and opened 8050
3:15 And **S** feared to shew Eli the vision. 8050
3:16 Eli called **S**, and said, Samuel, my son. 8050
3:16 Eli called Samuel, and said, **S**, my son. 8050
3:18 **S** told him every whit, and hid nothing 8050
3:19 And **S** grew, and the LORD was with him, 8050
3:20 **S** *was* established to be a prophet of 8050
3:21 for the LORD revealed himself to **S** in 8050
4: 1 the word of **S** came to all Israel. Now Israel 8050
7: 3 **S** spake unto all the house of Israel, saying, 8050
7: 5 **S** said, Gather all Israel to Mizpeh, and 8050
7: 6 **S** judged the children of Israel in Mizpeh. 8050
7: 8 the children of Israel said to **S**, Cease not to 8050
7: 9 **S** took a sucking lamb, and offered *it for* a 8050
7: 9 **S** cried unto the LORD for Israel; and 8050
7:10 as **S** was offering up the burnt offering, 8050
7:12 **S** took a stone, and set *it* between Mizpeh 8050
7:13 was against the Philistines all the days of **S**. 8050
7:15 And **S** judged Israel all the days of his life. 8050
8: 1 it came to pass, when **S** was old, that he 8050
8: 4 and came to **S** unto Ramah, 8050
8: 6 the thing displeased **S**, when they said, 8050
8: 6 judge us. And **S** prayed unto the LORD. 8050
8: 7 the LORD said unto **S**, Hearken unto 8050
8:10 **S** told all the words of the LORD unto 8050
8:19 the people refused to obey the voice of **S**; 8050
8:21 **S** heard all the words of the people, and 8050
8:22 the LORD said to **S**, Hearken unto their 8050
8:22 **S** said unto the men of Israel, Go ye every 8050
9:14 behold, **S** came out against them, for to go 8050
9:15 Now the LORD had told **S** in his ear a day 8050
9:17 when **S** saw Saul, the LORD said unto 8050
9:18 Saul drew near to **S** in the gate, and said, 8050
9:19 **S** answered Saul, and said, I *am* the seer: 8050
9:22 **S** took Saul and his servant, and 8050
9:23 **S** said unto the cook, Bring the portion 8050
9:24 *S* said, Behold that which is left; set *it* NIH
9:24 the people. So Saul did eat with **S** that day. 8050
9:25 *S* communed with Saul upon the top of NIH
9:26 that **S** called Saul to the top of the house, 8050
9:26 went out both of them, he and **S**, abroad. 8050
9:27 **S** said to Saul, Bid the servant pass on 8050
10: 1 **S** took a vial of oil, and poured *it* upon his 8050
10: 9 when he had turned his back to go from **S**, 8050
10:14 saw that *they were* no where, we came to **S**. 8050
10:15 Tell me, I pray thee, what **S** said unto you. 8050
10:16 whereof **S** spake, he told him not. 8050
10:17 **S** called the people together unto 8050
10:20 when **S** had caused all the tribes of Israel to 8050
10:24 **S** said to all the people, See ye him whom 8050
10:25 **S** told the people the manner of 8050
10:25 **S** sent all the people away, every man to his 8050
11: 7 cometh not forth after Saul and after **S**, 8050
11:12 the people said unto **S**, Who *is* he that said, 8050
11:14 said **S** to the people, Come, and let us go *to* 8050
12: 1 **S** said unto all Israel, Behold, I have 8050
12: 6 **S** said unto the people, *It is* the LORD that 8050
12:11 **S**, and delivered you out of the hand of 8050
12:18 So **S** called unto the LORD; and 8050
12:18 people greatly feared the LORD and **S**. 8050
12:19 all the people said unto **S**, Pray for thy 8050
12:20 **S** said unto the people, Fear not: ye have 8050
13: 8 according to the set time that **S** *had* 8050
13: 8 *had appointed:* but **S** came not *to* Gilgal; 8050
13:10 offering the burnt offering, behold, **S** came; 8050
13:11 **S** said, What hast thou done? And Saul 8050
13:13 **S** said to Saul, Thou hast done foolishly: 8050
13:15 **S** arose, and gat him up from Gilgal *unto* 8050
15: 1 **S** also said unto Saul, The LORD sent me 8050
15:10 came the word of the LORD unto **S**, 8050
15:11 it grieved **S**; and he cried unto the LORD 8050
15:12 when **S** rose early to meet Saul in 8050
15:12 it was told **S**, saying, Saul came to Carmel, 8050
15:13 **S** came to Saul: and Saul said unto him, 8050
15:14 **S** said, What *meaneth* then this bleating of 8050
15:16 **S** said unto Saul, Stay, and I will tell thee 8050
15:17 **S** said, When thou *wast* little in thine own 8050
15:20 Saul said unto **S**, Yea, I have obeyed 8050
15:22 **S** said, Hath the LORD *as great* delight in 8050
15:24 Saul said unto **S**, I have sinned: for I have 8050
15:26 **S** said unto Saul, I will not return with thee: 8050
15:27 as **S** turned about to go away, he laid hold 8050
15:28 **S** said unto him, The LORD hath rent 8050
15:31 So **S** turned again after Saul; and 8050
15:32 said **S**, Bring you hither to me Agag 8050
15:33 **S** said, As thy sword hath made women 8050
15:33 **S** hewed Agag in pieces before the LORD 8050
15:34 **S** went to Ramah; and Saul went up to his 8050
15:35 **S** came no more to see Saul until the day of 8050
15:35 nevertheless **S** mourned for Saul: and 8050
16: 1 the LORD said unto **S**, How long wilt 8050
16: 2 **S** said, How can I go? if Saul hear *it*, he 8050
16: 4 **S** did *that* which the LORD spake, and 8050
16: 7 the LORD said unto **S**, Look not on his 8050
16: 8 and made him pass before **S**. 8050
16:10 made seven of his sons to pass before **S**. 8050
16:10 **S** said unto Jesse, The LORD hath not 8050
16:11 **S** said unto Jesse, Are here all *thy* children? 8050
16:11 **S** said unto Jesse, Send and fetch him: 8050
16:13 **S** took the horn of oil, and anointed him in 8050
16:13 So **S** rose up, and went to Ramah. 8050
19:18 came to **S** to Ramah, and told him all that 8050
19:18 And he and **S** went and dwelt in Naioth. 8050
19:20 **S** standing *as* appointed over them, 8050
19:22 he asked and said, Where *are* **S** and David? 8050
19:24 prophesied before **S** in like manner, and 8050
25: 1 **S** died; and all the Israelites were gathered 8050
28: 3 Now **S** was dead, and all Israel had 8050
28:11 up unto thee? And he said, Bring me up **S**. 8050
28:12 when the woman saw **S**, she cried with a 8050
28:14 Saul perceived that it *was* **S**, and he stooped 8050
28:15 **S** said to Saul, Why hast thou disquieted 8050
28:16 said **S**, Wherefore then dost thou ask of me, 8050

1Sa 28:20 was sore afraid, because of the words of **S**: 8050
1Ch 6:28 And the sons of **S**; the firstborn Vashni, and 8050
9:22 and **S** the seer did ordain in their set office. 8050
11: 3 according to the word of the LORD by **S**. 8050
26:28 all that **S** the seer, and Saul the son of Kish, 8050
29:29 they *are* written in the book of **S** the seer, 8050
2Ch 35:18 kept in Israel from the days of **S** 8050
Ps 99: 6 and **S** among them that call upon his name; 8050
Jer 15: 1 Though Moses and **S** stood before me, 8050
Ac 3:24 and all the prophets from **S** and those that *4545*
13:20 and fifty years, until **S** the prophet. *4545*
Heb 11:32 *of* David also, and **S**, and *of* the prophets: *4545*

SANBALLAT (10)
Ne 2:10 When **S** the Horonite, and Tobiah 5571
2:19 when **S** the Horonite, and Tobiah 5571
4: 1 that when **S** heard that we builded the wall, 5571
4: 7 *that* when **S**, and Tobiah, and the Arabians, 5571
6: 1 when **S**, and Tobiah, and Geshem 5571
6: 2 That **S** and Geshem sent unto me, saying, 5571
6: 5 sent **S** his servant unto me in like manner 5571
6:12 for Tobiah and **S** had hired him. 5571
6:14 and **S** according to these their works, 5571
13:28 *was* son in law to **S** the Horonite: 5571

SANCTIFICATION (5) [SANCTIFY]
1Co 1:30 and righteousness, and **s**, and redemption: *38*
1Th 4: 3 For this is the will of God, *even* your **s**, *38*
4: 4 should know how to possess his vessel in **s** *38*
2Th 2:13 chosen you to salvation through **s** of the Spirit *38*
1Pe 1: 2 through **s** of the Spirit, unto obedience and *38*

SANCTIFIED (62) [SANCTIFY]
Ge 2: 3 God blessed the seventh day, and **s** it: 6942
Ex 19:14 mount unto the people, and **s** the people; 6942
29:43 and *the tabernacle* shall be **s** by my glory. 6942
Lev 8:10 and all that *was* therein, and **s** them. 6942
8:15 and **s** it, to make reconciliation upon it. 6942
8:30 **s** Aaron, *and* his garments, and his sons, 6942
10: 3 I will be **s** in them that come nigh me, and 6942
27:15 if he that **s** *it* will redeem his house, then 6942
27:19 if he that **s** the field will in any wise redeem 6942
Nu 7: 1 **s** it, and all the instruments thereof, 6942
7: 1 and had anointed them, and **s** them; 6942
8:17 in the land of Egypt, I **s** them for myself. 6942
20:13 with the LORD, and he was **s** in them. 6942
Dt 32:51 ye **s** me not in the midst of the children of 6942
1Sa 7: 1 **s** Eleazar his son to keep the ark of 6942
16: 5 he **s** Jesse and his sons, and called them to 6942
21: 5 yea, though it were **s** *this* day in the vessel. 6942
1Ch 15:14 the Levites **s** themselves to bring up the ark 6942
2Ch 5:11 (for all the priests that were present were **s**, 6942
7:16 For now have I chosen and **s** this house, 6942
7:20 this house, which I have **s** for my name, 6942
29:15 their brethren, and **s** themselves, and came, 6942
29:17 they **s** the house of the LORD in eight 6942
29:19 have we prepared and **s**, and behold, 6942
29:34 and until the *other* priests had **s** themselves: 6942
30: 3 the priests had not **s** themselves 6942
30: 8 into his sanctuary, which he hath **s** for ever: 6942
30:15 **s** themselves, and brought in the burnt 6942
30:17 many in the congregation that were not **s**: 6942
30:24 and a great number of priests **s** themselves. 6942
31:18 for in their set office they **s** themselves *in* 6942
Ne 3: 1 they **s** it, and set up the doors of it; 6942
3: 1 even unto the tower of Meah they **s** it, 6942
12:47 they **s** *holy things* unto the Levites; and 6942
12:47 the Levites **s** *them* unto the children of 6942
Job 1: 5 that Job sent and **s** them, and rose up early 6942
Isa 5:16 God that is holy shall be **s** in righteousness. 6942
13: 3 I have commanded my **s ones**, I have also 6942
Jer 1: 5 thou camest forth out of the womb I **s** thee, 6942
Eze 20:41 and I will be **s** in you before the heathen. 6942
28:22 judgments in her, and shall be **s** in her. 6942
28:25 shall be **s** in them in the sight of 6942
36:23 when I shall be **s** in you before their eyes. 6942
38:16 when I shall be **s** in thee, O Gog, 6942
39:27 am **s** in them in the sight of many nations; 6942
48:11 *It shall be* for the priests that are **s** of 6942
Jn 10:36 Say ye *of him,* whom the Father hath **s**, and *37*
17:19 that they also might be **s** through the truth. *37*
Ac 20:32 an inheritance among all them which are **s**. *37*
26:18 inheritance among them which are **s** by faith *37*
Ro 15:16 be acceptable, being **s** by the Holy Ghost. *37*
1Co 1: 2 to them that are **s** in Christ Jesus, called *to be* *37*
6:11 but ye are **s**, but ye are justified in the name of *37*
7:14 For the unbelieving husband is **s** by the wife, *37*
7:14 and the unbelieving wife is **s** by the husband: *37*
1Ti 4: 5 For it is **s** by the word of God and prayer. *37*
2Ti 2:21 **s**, and meet for the master's use, *and* *37*
Heb 2:11 and they who are **s** *are* all of one: *37*
10:10 By the which will we are **s** through *37*
10:14 he hath perfected for ever them that are **s**. *37*
10:29 wherewith he was **s**, an unholy *thing,* and *37*
Jude 1: 1 to them that are **s** by God the Father, and *37*

SANCTIFIETH (4) [SANCTIFY]
Mt 23:17 the gold, or the temple that **s** the gold? *37*
23:19 *is* greater, the gift, or the altar that **s** the gift? *37*
Heb 2:11 For both he that **s** and they who are sanctified *37*
9:13 the unclean, **s** to the purifying of the flesh: *37*

SANCTIFY (70) [SANCTIFICATION, SANCTIFIED, SANCTIFIETH]
Ex 13: 2 **S** unto me all the firstborn, 6942
19:10 **s** them to day and to morrow, and let them 6942
19:22 come near to the LORD, **s** themselves, 6942
19:23 Set bounds about the mount, and **s** it. 6942
28:41 and consecrate them, and **s** them, 6942
29:27 thou shalt **s** the breast of the wave offering, 6942
29:33 was made, to consecrate *and* to **s** them: 6942
29:36 for it, and thou shalt anoint it, to **s** it. 6942
29:37 make an atonement for the altar, and **s** it; 6942
29:44 I will **s** the tabernacle of the congregation, 6942
29:44 I will **s** also both Aaron and his sons, 6942
30:29 thou shalt **s** them, that they may be most 6942
31:13 know that I *am* the LORD that doth **s** you. 6942
40:10 and all his vessels, and **s** the altar: 6942
40:11 shalt anoint the laver and his foot, and **s** it. 6942
40:13 holy garments, and anoint him, and **s** him; 6942
Lev 8:11 both the laver and his foot, to **s** them. 6942
8:12 Aaron's head, and anointed him, to **s** him. 6942
11:44 ye shall therefore **s** yourselves, and ye shall 6942
20: 7 **S** yourselves therefore, and be ye holy: for I 6942
20: 8 and do them: I *am* the LORD which **s** you. 6942
21: 8 Thou shalt **s** him therefore; for he offereth 6942
21: 8 for I the LORD, which **s** you, *am* holy. 6942
21:15 his people: for I the LORD do **s** him. 6942
21:23 my sanctuaries: for I the LORD do **s** them. 6942
22: 9 if they profane it: I the LORD do **s** them. 6942
22:16 holy *things:* for I the LORD do **s** them. 6942
27:14 when a man shall **s** his house *to be* holy 6942
27:16 if a man shall **s** unto the LORD *some part* 6942
27:17 If he **s** his field from the year of jubile, 6942
27:18 if he **s** his field after the jubile, then 6942
27:22 if *a man* **s** unto the LORD a field which he 6942
27:26 be the LORD's firstling, no man shall **s** it; 6942
Nu 11:18 **S** yourselves against to morrow, and 6942
20:12 to **s** me in the eyes of the children of Israel, 6942
27:14 to **s** me at the water before their eyes: 6942
Dt 5:12 Keep the sabbath day to **s** it, as the LORD 6942
15:19 of thy flock thou shalt **s** unto the LORD 6942
Jos 3: 5 Joshua said unto the people, **S** yourselves: 6942
7:13 Up, **s** the people, and say, 6942
7:13 and say, **S** yourselves against to morrow: 6942
1Sa 16: 5 **s** yourselves, and come with me to 6942
1Ch 15:12 **s** yourselves, *both* ye and your brethren, 6942
23:13 that he should **s** the most holy *things,* he 6942
2Ch 29: 5 **s** now yourselves, and sanctify the house of 6942
29: 5 **s** the house of the LORD God of your 6942
29:17 on the first *day* of the first month to **s**, 6942
29:34 in heart to **s** themselves than the priests. 6942
30:17 *was* not clean, to **s** *them* unto the LORD. 6942
35: 6 **s** yourselves, and prepare your brethren, 6942
Ne 13:22 *and* keep the gates, to **s** the sabbath day. 6942
Isa 8:13 **S** the LORD of hosts himself; and *let* him 6942
29:23 they shall **s** my name, and sanctify the Holy 6942
29:23 **s** the Holy One of Jacob, and shall fear 6942
66:17 They that **s** themselves, and purify 6942
Eze 20:12 know that I *am* the LORD that **s** them. 6942
36:23 I will **s** my great name, which was profaned 6942
37:28 shall know that I the LORD do **s** Israel, 6942
38:23 Thus will I magnify myself, and **s** myself; 6942
44:19 they shall not **s** the people with their 6942
46:20 not out into the utter court, to **s** the people. 6942
Joel 1:14 **S** ye a fast, call a solemn assembly, 6942
2:15 in Zion, **s** a fast, call a solemn assembly: 6942
2:16 Gather the people, **s** the congregation, 6942

Jn 17:17 **S** them through thy truth: thy word is truth. *37*
17:19 And for their sakes I **s** myself, that they also *37*
Eph 5:26 That he might **s** and cleanse *it* with *37*
1Th 5:23 And the very God of peace **s** you wholly; and *37*
Heb 13:12 that he might **s** the people with his own blood, *37*
1Pe 3:15 But **s** the Lord God in your hearts: and *37*

SANCTUARIES (5) [SANCTUARY]
Lev 21:23 he hath a blemish; that he profane not my **s**: 4720
26:31 bring your **s** unto desolation, and I will not 4720
Jer 51:51 for strangers are come into the **s** of 4720
Eze 28:18 Thou hast defiled thy **s** by the multitude of 4720
Am 7: 9 and the **s** of Israel shall be laid waste; 4720

SANCTUARY (137) [SANCTUARIES]
Ex 15:17 *in* the **S**, O Lord, *which* thy hands have 4720
25: 8 let them make me a **s**; that I may dwell 4720
30:13 half a shekel after the shekel of the **s**: 6944
30:24 hundred *shekels,* after the shekel of the **s**, 6944
36: 1 all *manner of* work for the service of the **s**, 6944
36: 3 brought for the work of the service of the **s**, 6944
36: 4 *men,* that wrought all the work of the **s**, 6944
36: 6 any more work for the offering of the **s**. 6944
38:24 and thirty shekels, after the shekel of the **s**. 6944
38:25 and fifteen shekels, after the shekel of the **s**: 6944
38:26 *is,* half a shekel, after the shekel of the **s**, 6944
38:27 of silver were cast the sockets of the **s**, 6944
Lev 4: 6 before the LORD, before the vail of the **s**. 6944
5:15 after the shekel of the **s**, for a trespass 6944
10: 4 carry your brethren from before the **s** out of 6944
12: 4 no hallowed *thing,* nor come into the **s**, 4720
16:33 he shall make an atonement for the holy **s**, 4720
19:30 keep my sabbaths, and reverence my **s**: 4720
20: 3 to defile my **s**, and to profane my holy 4720
21:12 Neither shall he go out of the **s**, nor profane 4720
21:12 the sanctuary, nor profane the **s** of his God; 4720
26: 2 keep my sabbaths, and reverence my **s**: 4720
27: 3 shekels of silver, after the shekel of the **s**. 6944
27:25 shall be according to the shekel of the **s**: 6944
Nu 3:28 six hundred, keeping the charge of the **s**. 6944
3:31 the vessels of the **s** wherewith they 6944
3:32 of them that keep the charge of the **s**. 6944
3:38 keeping the charge of the **s** for the charge 4720
3:47 after the shekel of the **s** shalt thou take 6944
3:50 and five *shekels,* after the shekel of the **s**: 6944
4:12 wherewith they minister in the **s**, and 6944
4:15 sons have made an end of covering the **s**, 6944
4:15 all the vessels of the **s**, as the camp is to set 6944
4:16 of all that therein *is,* in the **s**, and in 6944
7: 9 the service of the **s** belonging unto them 6944
7:13 of seventy shekels, after the shekel of the **s**; 6944
7:19 of seventy shekels, after the shekel of the **s**; 6944
7:25 of seventy shekels, after the shekel of the **s**; 6944
7:31 of seventy shekels, after the shekel of the **s**; 6944
7:37 of seventy shekels, after the shekel of the **s**; 6944
7:43 of seventy shekels, after the shekel of the **s**; 6944
7:49 of seventy shekels, after the shekel of the **s**; 6944
7:55 of seventy shekels, after the shekel of the **s**; 6944
7:61 of seventy shekels, after the shekel of the **s**; 6944
7:67 of seventy shekels, after the shekel of the **s**; 6944
7:73 of seventy shekels, after the shekel of the **s**; 6944
7:79 of seventy shekels, after the shekel of the **s**; 6944
7:85 hundred *shekels,* after the shekel of the **s**: 6944
7:86 ten *shekels* apiece, after the shekel of the **s**: 6944
8:19 the children of Israel come nigh unto the **s**. 6944
10:21 the Kohathites set forward, bearing the **s**: 4720
18: 1 with thee shall bear the iniquity of the **s**: 4720
18: 3 they shall not come nigh the vessels of the **s** 6944
18: 5 ye shall keep the charge of the **s**, and 6944
18:16 after the shekel of the **s**, which *is* twenty 6944
19:20 he hath defiled the **s** of the LORD: 4720
Jos 24:26 an oak, that *was* by the **s** of the LORD. 4720
1Ch 9:29 all the instruments of the **s**, and the fine 6944
22:19 and build ye the **s** of the LORD God, 4720
24: 5 for the governors of the **s**, and governors *of* 6944
28:10 hath chosen thee to build a house for the **s**: 4720
2Ch 20: 8 and have built thee a **s** therein for thy name, 4720
26:18 go out of the **s**; for thou hast trespassed; 4720
29:21 the kingdom, and for the **s**, and for Judah. 4720
30: 8 enter into his **s**, which he hath sanctified for 4720
30:19 according to the purification of the **s**. 6944
36:17 men with the sword in the house of their **s**, 4720
Ne 10:39 where *are* the vessels of the **s**, and 4720
Ps 20: 2 Send thee help from the **s**, and 6944
63: 2 thy glory, so *as* I have seen thee in the **s**. 6944
68:24 the goings of my God, my King, in the **s**. 6944
73:17 Until I went into the **s** of God; *then* 4720
74: 3 *that* the enemy hath done wickedly in the **s**. 6944
74: 7 They have cast fire into thy **s**, they have 4720
77:13 Thy way, O God, *is* in the **s**: who *is so* 6944
78:54 he brought them to the border of his **s**, 6944
78:69 he built his **s** like high *palaces,* like 4720
96: 6 before him: strength and beauty *are* in his **s**. 4720
102:19 hath looked down from the height of his **s**; 6944
114: 2 Judah was his **s**, *and* Israel his dominion. 6944
134: 2 Lift up your hands *in* the **s**, and bless 6944
150: 1 Praise God in his **s**: praise him in 6944
Isa 8:14 he shall be for a **s**; but for a stone of 4720
16:12 that he shall come to his **s** to pray; 4720
43:28 I have profaned the princes of the **s**, 6944
60:13 box together, to beautify the place of my **s**; 4720
63:18 our adversaries have trodden down thy **s**. 4720
Jer 17:12 from the beginning *is* the place of our **s**. 4720
La 1:10 seen *that* the heathen entered into her **s**, 4720
2: 7 cast off his altar, he hath abhorred his **s**, 4720
2:20 the prophet be slain in the **s** of the Lord? 4720
4: 1 the stones of the **s** are poured out in the top 6944
Eze 5:11 thou hast defiled my **s** with all thy 4720
8: 6 that *I* should go far off from my **s**? 4720
9: 6 upon whom *is* the mark; and begin at my **s**. 4720
11:16 yet will I be to them as a little **s** in 4720
23:38 they have defiled my **s** in the same day, and 4720
23:39 they came the same day into my **s** to 4720
24:21 Behold, I *will* profane my **s**, the excellency 4720
25: 3 Because thou saidst, Aha, against my **s**, 4720
37:26 will set my **s** in the midst of them for 4720
37:28 when my **s** shall be in the midst of them for 4720
41:21 temple *were* squared, *and* the face of the **s**; 6944
41:23 And the temple and the **s** had two doors. 6944
42:20 to make a separation between the **s** and 6944
43:21 appointed place of the house, without the **s**. 4720
44: 1 outward **s** which looketh *toward* the east; 4720
44: 5 the house, with every going forth of the **s**. 4720
44: 7 In that ye have brought *into my* **s** strangers, NIH
44: 7 to be in my **s**, to pollute it, *even* my house, 4720
44: 8 ye have set keepers of my charge in my **s** 4720
44: 9 in flesh, shall enter into my **s**, 4720
44:11 Yet they shall be ministers in my **s**, 4720
44:15 that kept the charge of my **s** when 4720
44:16 They shall enter into my **s**, and they shall 4720
44:27 in the day that he goeth into the **s**, unto 6944
44:27 unto the inner court, to minister in the **s**, 6944
45: 2 Of this there shall be for the **s** five hundred 6944
45: 3 in it shall be the **s** *and* the most holy *place.* 4720
45: 4 be for the priests the ministers of the **s**, 4720
45: 4 for their houses, and a holy place for the **s**. 4720
45:18 bullock without blemish, and cleanse the **s**: 4720
47:12 their waters they issued out of the **s**: 4720
48: 8 and the **s** shall be in the midst of it. 4720
48:10 the **s** of the LORD shall be in the midst 4720
48:21 the **s** of the house *shall be* in the midst 4720
Da 8:11 and the place of his **s** was cast down. 4720
8:13 to give both the **s** and the host to be trodden 6944
8:14 hundred days; then shall the **s** be cleansed. 6944
9:17 cause thy face to shine upon thy **s** that is 4720
9:26 *shall* come shall destroy the city and the **s**; 6944
11:31 they shall pollute the **s** *of* strength, and 4720
Zep 3: 4 her priests have polluted the **s**, they have 6944
Heb 8: 2 A minister of the **s**, and of the true tabernacle, *40*
9: 1 ordinances of divine service, and a worldly **s**. *40*
9: 2 and the shewbread; which is called the **s**. *40*
13:11 whose blood is brought into the **s** by the high *40*

SAND (28) [QUICKSANDS]
Ge 22:17 and as the **s** which *is* upon the sea shore; 2344
32:12 and make thy seed as the **s** of the sea, 2344
41:49 Joseph gathered corn as the **s** of the sea, 2344
Ex 2:12 he slew the Egyptian, and hid him in the **s**. 2344
Dt 33:19 of the seas, and *of* treasures hid in the **s**. 2344
Jos 11: 4 *even* as the **s** that *is* upon the sea shore in 2344
Jdg 7:12 as the **s** by the sea side for multitude. 2344
1Sa 13: 5 people as the **s** which *is* on the sea shore in 2344
2Sa 17:11 as the **s** that *is* by the sea for multitude; 2344
1Ki 4:20 as the **s** which *is* by the sea in multitude, 2344
4:29 *even* as the **s** that *is* on the sea shore. 2344
Job 6: 3 For now it would be heavier than the **s** of 2344
29:18 and I shall multiply *my* days as the **s**. 2344
Ps 78:27 and feathered fowls like as the **s** of the sea: 2344

S

Ps 139:18 they are moe in number than the **s**: 2344
Pr 27: 3 A stone *is* heavy, and the **s** weighty; but 2344
Isa 10:22 For though thy people Israel be as the **s** of 2344
48:19 Thy seed also had been as the **s**, and 2344
Jer 5:22 which have placed the **s** *for* the bound of 2344
15: 8 are increased to me above the **s** of the seas: 2344
33:22 neither the **s** of the sea measured: 2344
Hos 1:10 of Israel shall be as the **s** of the sea, 2344
Hab 1: 9 and they shall gather the captivity as the **s**. 2344
Mt 7:26 which built his house upon the **s**: *285*
Ro 9:27 the children of Israel be as the **s** of the sea, *285*
Heb 11:12 as the **s** which is by the sea shore *285*
Rev 13: 1 And I stood upon the **s** of the sea, and saw a *285*
20: 8 the number of whom *is* as the **s** of the sea. *285*

SANDAL See SHOE; SHOE'S; SHOES

SANDALS (2)
Mk 6: 9 But *be* shod with **s**; and not put on two *4547*
Ac 12: 8 unto him, Gird thyself, and bind on thy **s**. *4547*

SANG (11) [SING]
Ex 15: 1 **s** Moses and the children of Israel this song 7891
Nu 21:17 Israel **s** this song, Spring up, O well; 7891
Jdg 5: 1 **s** Deborah and Barak the son of Abinoam 7891
1Sa 29: 5 of whom they **s** one to another in dances, 6030
2Ch 29:28 the singers **s**, and the trumpeters sounded: 7891
29:30 they *s* praises with gladness, and NIH
Ne 12:42 the singers **s loud**, with Jezrahiah *their* 8085
Job 38: 7 When the morning stars **s** together, and 7442
Ps 7: T of David, which he **s** unto the LORD, 7891
106:12 believed they his words; they **s** his praise. 7891
Ac 16:25 and Silas prayed, and **s praises** unto God: *5214*

SANK (2) [SINK]
Ex 15: 5 they **s** into the bottom as a stone. 3381
15:10 they **s** as lead in the mighty waters. 6749

SANSANNAH (1)
Jos 15:31 And Ziklag, and Madmannah, and **S**, 5578

SAP (1)
Ps 104:16 The trees of the LORD are full *of s*; NIH

SAPH (1)
2Sa 21:18 Sibbechai the Hushathite slew **S**, 5593

SAPHIR (1)
Mic 1:11 Pass ye away, thou inhabitant of **S**, 8208

SAPPHIRA (1)
Ac 5: 1 with **S** his wife, sold a possession, *4551*

SAPPHIRE (9) [SAPPHIRES]
Ex 24:10 feet as it were a paved work of a **s stone**, 5601
28:18 *shall be* an emerald, a **s**, and a diamond. 5601
39:11 an emerald, a **s**, and a diamond. 5601
Job 28:16 of Ophir, with the precious onyx, or the **s**. 5601
La 4: 7 body than rubies, their polishing *was of* **s**: 5601
Eze 1:26 of a throne, as the appearance of a **s** stone: 5601
10: 1 appeared over them as it were a **s** stone, 5601
28:13 the beryl, the onyx, and the jasper, the **s**, 5601
Rev 21:19 the second, **s**; the third, a chalcedony; *4552*

SAPPHIRES (3) [SAPPHIRE]
Job 28: 6 The stones of it *are* the place of **s**: and 5601
SS 5:14 his belly *is as* bright ivory overlaid *with* **s**. 5601
Isa 54:11 fair colours, and lay thy foundations with **s**. 5601

SARA (3) [SARAH]
Ro 9: 9 time will I come, and **S** shall have a son. *4564*
Heb 11:11 Through faith also **S** herself received *4564*
1Pe 3: 6 *Even* as **S** obeyed Abraham, calling him *4564*

SARA'S (1) [SARAH]
Ro 4:19 neither *yet* the deadness of **S** womb: *4564*

SARAH (37) [SARA, SARA'S, SARAH'S, SARAI, SARAI'S]
Ge 17:15 her name Sarai, but **S** *shall* her name *be*. 8283
17:17 and shall **S**, that is ninety years old, bear? 8283
17:19 **S** thy wife shall bear thee a son indeed; 8283
17:21 which **S** shall bear unto thee at this set time 8283
18: 6 And Abraham hastened into the tent unto **S**, 8283
18: 9 they said unto him, Where *is* **S** thy wife? 8283
18:10 of life; and lo, **S** thy wife shall have a son. 8283
18:10 **S** heard *it in* the tent door, which *was* 8283
18:11 Now Abraham and **S** *were* old *and* 8283
18:11 it ceased to be with **S** after the manner of 8283
18:12 Therefore **S** laughed within herself, saying, 8283
18:13 Wherefore did **S** laugh, saying, 8283
18:14 to the time of life, and **S** shall have a son. 8283
18:15 **S** denied, saying, I laughed not; for she was 8283
20: 2 Abraham said of **S** his wife, She *is* my 8283
20: 2 Abimelech king of Gerar sent, and took **S**. 8283
20:14 unto Abraham, and restored him **S** his wife. 8283
20:16 unto **S** he said, Behold, I have given thy 8283
20:18 because of **S** Abraham's wife. 8283
21: 1 the LORD visited **S** as he had said, and 8283
21: 1 the LORD did unto **S** as he had spoken. 8283
21: 2 For **S** conceived, and bare Abraham a son 8283
21: 3 born unto him, whom **S** bare to him, Isaac. 8283
21: 6 **S** said, God hath made me to laugh, *so* 8283
21: 7 that **S** should have given children suck? 8283
21: 9 **S** saw the son of Hagar the Egyptian, 8283
21:12 in all that **S** hath said unto thee, 8283
23: 1 **S** was an hundred and seven and 8283
23: 1 *these were* the years of the life of **S**. 8283
23: 2 **S** died in Kirjath-arba; the same *is* Hebron 8283
23: 2 Abraham came to mourn for **S**, and to weep 8283
23:19 Abraham buried **S** his wife in the cave of 8283
24:36 **S** my master's wife bare a son to my master 8283
25:10 there was Abraham buried, and **S** his wife. 8283
49:31 There they buried Abraham and **S** his wife; 8283
Nu 26:46 the name of the daughter of Asher *was* **S**. 8294
Isa 51: 2 your father, and unto **S** *that* bare you: 8283

SARAH'S (2) [SARAH]
Ge 24:67 Isaac brought her into his mother **S** tent, 8283
25:12 **S** handmaid, bare unto Abraham: 8283

SARAI (16) [SARAH]
Ge 11:29 the name of Abram's wife *was* **S**; and 8297
11:30 But **S** was barren; she had no child. 8297
11:31 **S** his daughter in law, his son Abram's 8297
12: 5 Abram took **S** his wife, and Lot his 8297
12:11 that he said unto **S** his wife, Behold now, 8297
12:17 great plagues because of **S** Abram's wife. 8297
16: 1 Now **S** Abram's wife bare him no *children*: 8297
16: 2 **S** said unto Abram, Behold now, 8297
16: 2 And Abram hearkened to the voice of **S**. 8297
16: 3 **S** Abram's wife took Hagar her maid 8297
16: 5 **S** said unto Abram, My wrong *be* upon 8297
16: 6 Abram said unto **S**, Behold, thy maid *is* in 8297
16: 6 when **S** dealt hardly with her, she fled from 8297
16: 8 I flee from the face of my mistress **S**. 8297
17:15 God said unto Abraham, *As for* **S** thy wife, 8297
17:15 thou shalt not call her name **S**, but 8297

SARAI'S (1) [SARAH]
Ge 16: 8 he said, Hagar, **S** maid, whence camest 8297

SARAPH (1)
1Ch 4:22 and the men of Chozeba, and Joash, and **S**, 8315

SARDINE (1)
Rev 4: 3 to look upon like a jasper and a **s** stone: *4555*

SARDIS (3)
Rev 1:11 and unto **S**, and unto Philadelphia, and *4554*
3: 1 And unto the angel of the church in **S** write; *4554*
3: 4 Thou hast a few names even in **S**, *4554*

SARDITES (1)
Nu 26:26 of Sered, the family of the **S**: of Elon, 5625

SARDIUS (4)
Ex 28:17 *the first* row *shall be* a **s**, a topaz, and 124
39:10 *the first* row *was* a **s**, a topaz, and 124
Eze 28:13 the **s**, topaz, and the diamond, the beryl, 124
Rev 21:20 The fifth, sardonyx; the sixth, **s**; *4556*

SARDONYX (1)
Rev 21:20 The fifth, **s**; the sixth, sardius; the seventh, *4557*

SAREPTA (1) [ZAREPHATH]
Lk 4:26 save unto **S**, *a city* of Sidon, unto a woman *4558*

SARGON (1)
Isa 20: 1 (when **S** the king of Assyria sent him,) 5623

SARID (2)
Jos 19:10 the border of their inheritance was unto **S**: 8301
19:12 turned from **S** eastward *toward* 8301

SARON (1)
Ac 9:35 And all that dwelt at Lydda and **S** saw him, *4565*

SARSECHIM (1)
Jer 39: 3 Samgar-nebo, **S**, Rab-saris, 8310

SARUCH (1)
Lk 3:35 Which was *the son* of **S**, which was *the son* *4562*

SAT (192) [SIT]
Ge 18: 1 he **s** *in* the tent door in the heat of the day; 3427
19: 1 at even; and Lot **s** in the gate of Sodom: 3427
21:16 **s** her **down** over against *him* a good way 3427
21:16 she **s** over against *him*, and lift up her 3427
31:34 in the camel's furniture, and **s** upon them. 3427
37:25 they **s down** to eat bread: and they lift up 3427
38:14 wrapped herself, and **s** in an open place, 3427
43:33 they **s** before him, the firstborn according 3427
48: 2 strengthened himself, and **s** upon the bed. 3427
Ex 2:15 land of Midian: and he **s down** by a well. 3427
12:29 from the firstborn of Pharaoh that **s** on his 3427
16: 3 when we **s** by the flesh pots, *and* when we 3427
17:12 and put *it* under him, and he **s** thereon; 3427
18:13 that Moses **s** to judge the people: 3427
32: 6 the people **s down** to eat and to drink, and 3427
Lev 15: 6 he that sitteth on *any* thing whereon he **s** 3427
15:22 whosoever toucheth any thing that she **s** 3427
Dt 33: 3 they **s down** at thy feet; *every one* shall 8497
Jdg 6:11 **s** under an oak which *was* in Ophrah, 3427
13: 9 again unto the woman as she **s** in the field: 3427
19: 6 they **s down**, and did eat and drink both of 3427
19:15 he **s** him **down** in a street of the city: 3427
20:26 **s** there before the LORD, and fasted that 3427
Ru 2:14 she **s** beside the reapers: and he reached her 3427
4: 1 Boaz up *to* the gate, and **s** him **down** there: 3427
4: 1 And he turned aside, and **s down**. 3427
4: 2 said, Sit ye down here. And they **s down**. 3427
1Sa 1: 9 Now Eli the priest **s** upon a seat by a post 3427
4:13 Eli **s** upon a seat *by* the wayside watching: 3427
19: 9 as he **s** in his house with his javelin in his 3427
20:24 the king **s** him **down** to eat meat. 3427
20:25 the king **s** upon his seat, as at other times, 3427
20:25 Abner **s** by Saul's side, and David's place 3427
28:23 he arose from the earth, and **s** upon the bed. 3427
2Sa 2:13 they **s down**, the one on the one side of 3427
7: 1 when the king **s** in his house, and 3427
7:18 **s** before the LORD, and he said, Who *am* 3427
18:24 David **s** between the two gates: and 3427
19: 8 the king rose, and **s** in the gate. And they 3427
23: 8 The Tachmonite that **s** in the seat, 3427
1Ki 2:12 **s** Solomon upon the throne of David his 3427
2:19 **s down** on his throne, and caused a seat to 3427
2:19 king's mother; and she **s** on his right hand. 3427
13:20 it came to pass, as they **s** at the table, 3427
16:11 to reign, as soon as he **s** on his throne, 3427
19: 4 and came and **s down** under a juniper tree: 3427
21:13 children of Belial, and **s** before him: 3427
22:10 Jehoshaphat the king of Judah **s** each on his 3427
2Ki 1: 9 behold, he **s** on the top of a hill. And he 3427
4:20 he **s** on her knees till noon, and *then* died. 3427
6:32 Elisha **s** in his house, and the elders sat 3427
6:32 sat in his house, and the elders **s** with him; 3427
11:19 And he **s** on the throne of the kings. 3427
13:13 and Jeroboam **s** upon his throne: 3427
1Ch 17: 1 it came to pass, as David **s** in his house, 3427
17:16 the king came and **s** before the LORD, 3427
29:23 Solomon **s** on the throne of the LORD as 3427
2Ch 18: 9 Jehoshaphat king of Judah **s** either of them 3427
18: 9 they **s** in a void place *at* the entering in of 3427
Ezr 9: 3 and of my beard, and **s down** astonied. 3427
9: 4 and I **s** astonied until the evening sacrifice. 3427
10: 9 all the people **s** in the street of the house of 3427
10:16 **s down** in the first day of the tenth month 3427
Ne 1: 4 *that* I **s down** and wept, and 3427
8:17 made booths, and **s** under the booths: 3427
Est 1: 2 when the king Ahasuerus **s** on the throne of 3427
1:14 *and* which **s** the first in the kingdom;) 3427
2:19 then Mordecai **s** in the king's gate. 3427
2:21 while Mordecai **s** in the king's gate, 3427
3:15 the king and Haman **s down** to drink; but 3427
5: 1 the king **s** upon his royal throne in the royal 3427
Job 2: 8 and he **s down** among the ashes. 3427
2:13 So they **s down** with him upon the ground 3427
29:25 **s** chief, and dwelt as a king in the army, 3427
Ps 26: 4 I have not **s** with vain persons, neither will 3427
137: 1 there we **s down**, yea, we wept, 3427
SS 2: 3 I **s down** under his shadow with great 3427
Jer 3: 2 In the ways hast thou **s** for them, as 3427
15:17 I **s** not in the assembly of the mockers, 3427
15:17 nor rejoiced; I **s** alone because of thy hand: 3427
26:10 **s down** in the entry of the new gate of 3427
32:12 before all the Jews that **s** in the court of 3427
36:12 lo, all the princes **s** there, *even* Elishama 3427
36:22 Now the king **s** *in* the winterhouse in 3427
39: 3 **s** in the middle gate, *even* Nergal-sharezer, 3427
Eze 3:15 I **s** where they sat, and remained there 3427
3:15 I sat where they **s**, and remained there 3427
8: 1 as I **s** in mine house, and the elders of 3427
8: 1 and the elders of Judah **s** before me, 3427
8:14 there **s** women weeping for Tammuz. 3427
14: 1 elders of Israel unto me, and **s** before me. 3427
20: 1 to inquire of the LORD, and **s** before me. 3427
Da 2:49 but Daniel **s** in the gate of the king. NIH
Jnh 3: 6 covered *him* with sackcloth, and **s** in ashes. 3427
4: 5 **s** on the east side of the city, and 3427
4: 5 him a booth, and **s** under it in the shadow, 3427
Mt 4:16 The people which **s** in darkness saw great *2521*
4:16 and to them which **s** in the region and *2521*
9:10 as Jesus **s at meat** in the house, behold, *345*
9:10 and **s down with** him and his disciples. *4873*
13: 1 out of the house, and **s** by the sea side. *2521*
13: 2 unto him, so that he went into a ship, and **s**; *2521*
13:48 and **s down**, and gathered the good into *2523*
14: 9 and them which **s with** him **at meat**, *4873*
15:29 went up into a mountain, and **s down** there. *2521*
24: 3 And as he **s** upon the mount of Olives, *2521*
26: 7 and poured *it* on his head, as he **s at meat**. *345*
26:20 even was come, he **s down** with the twelve. *345*
26:55 I **s** daily with you teaching in the temple, *2516*
26:58 and went in, and **s** with the servants, to see *2521*
26:69 Now Peter **s** without in the palace: and *2521*
28: 2 back the stone from the door, and **s** upon it. *2521*
Mk 2:15 that as *Jesus* **s at meat** in his house, *2621*
2:15 and sinners **s also together with** Jesus and *4873*
3:32 And *the* multitude **s** about him, and they *2521*
3:34 round about on them which **s** about him, *2521*
4: 1 that he entered into a ship, and **s** in the sea; *2521*
6:22 them that **s with** *him*, the king said unto *4873*
6:26 for their sakes which **s with** *him*, he would *4873*
6:40 And they **s down** in ranks, by hundreds, and *377*
9:35 And he **s down**, and called the twelve, and *2523*
10:46 of Timeus, **s** by the *high*way side begging. *2521*
11: 2 shall find a colt tied, whereon never man **s**; *2523*
11: 7 their garments on him; and he **s** upon him. *2523*
12:41 And Jesus **s** over against the treasury, and *2523*
13: 3 And as he **s** upon the mount of Olives over *2521*
14: 3 house of Simon the leper, as he **s at meat**, *2621*
14:18 And as they **s** and did eat, Jesus said, *345*
14:54 and he **s** with the servants, and *4775*
16:14 appeared unto the eleven as they **s at meat**, *345*
16:19 into heaven, and **s** on the right hand of God. *2523*
Lk 4:20 gave *it* again to the minister, and **s down**. *2523*
5: 3 And he **s down**, and taught the people out *2523*
5:29 and of others that **s** down with them. *2621*
7:15 And he that was dead **s up**, and began to *339*
7:36 the Pharisee's house, and **s down to meat**. *347*
7:37 when she knew that *Jesus* **s at meat** in *345*
7:49 And they that **s at meat with** *him* began to *4873*
10:39 which also **s** at Jesus' feet, and heard his *3869*
11:37 and he went in, and **s down to meat**. *377*
14:15 And when one of them that **s at meat with** *4873*
18:35 a certain blind man **s** by the way side *2521*
19:30 find a colt tied, whereon yet never man **s**: *2523*
22:14 he **s down**, and the twelve apostles with him. *377*
22:55 down together, Peter **s down** among them. *2521*
22:56 But a certain maid beheld him as he **s** by *2521*
24:30 as he **s at meat** with them, he took bread, *2625*
Jn 4: 6 with *his* journey, **s** thus on the well: *2516*
6: 3 and there he **s** with his disciples. *2521*
6:10 So the men **s down**, *in* number about five *377*
8: 2 unto him; and he **s down**, and taught them. *2523*
9: 8 said, Is not this he that **s** and begged? *2521*
11:20 and met him: but Mary **s** *still* in the house. *2516*
12: 2 of them that **s at the table with** him. *4873*

S

Jn 12:14 when he had found a young ass, **s** thereon; 2523
19:13 **s down** in the judgment seat in a place *that* 2523
Ac 2: 3 like as of fire, and it **s** upon each of them. 2523
3:10 And they knew that it was he which **s** for 2521
6:15 And all that **s** in the council, 2516
9:40 her eyes: and when she saw Peter, she **s up**. 339
12:21 **s** upon his throne, and made an oration unto 2523
13:14 synagogue on the sabbath day, and **s down**. 2523
14: 8 And there **s** a certain man at Lystra, 2521
16:13 and we **s down**, and spake unto the women 2523
20: 9 And there **s** in a window a certain young 2521
25:17 on the morrow I **s** on the judgment seat, 2523
26:30 and Bernice, and they that **s with** them: 4775
1Co 10: 7 The people **s down** to eat and drink, and 2523
Heb 1: 3 **s down** on the right hand of the Majesty on 2523
10:12 for ever, **s down** on the right hand of God; 2523
Rev 4: 2 was set in heaven, and one **s** on the throne. 2521
4: 3 And he that **s** was to look upon like a jasper 2521
4: 9 and thanks to him that **s** on the throne, 2521
4:10 twenty elders fall down before him that **s** 2521
5: 1 And I saw in the right hand of him that **s** on 2521
5: 7 right hand of him that **s** upon the throne. 2521
6: 2 and he that **s** on him had a bow; and 2521
6: 4 *power* was given to him that **s** thereon to 2521
6: 5 he that **s** on him had a pair of balances in 2521
6: 8 and his name that **s** on him *was* Death, and 2521
9:17 and them that **s** on them, 2521
11:16 which **s** before God on their seats, 2521
14:14 upon the cloud one **s** like unto the Son of 2521
14:15 crying with a loud voice to him that **s** on 2521
14:16 And he that **s** on the cloud thrust in his 2521
19: 4 and worshipped God that **s** on the throne, 2521
19:11 he that **s** upon him *was* called Faithful and 2521
19:19 make war against him that **s** on the horse, 2521
19:21 the sword of him that **s** upon the horse, 2521
20: 4 and they **s** upon them, and judgment was 2523
20:11 and him that **s** on it, from whose face 2521
21: 5 And he that **s** upon the throne said, Behold, 2521

SATAN (55) [SATAN'S]
1Ch 21: 1 **S** stood *up* against Israel, and 7854
Job 1: 6 the LORD, and **S** came also among them. 7854
1: 7 the LORD said unto **S**, Whence comest 7854
1: 7 **S** answered the LORD, and said, 7854
1: 8 the LORD said unto **S**, Hast thou 7854
1: 9 **S** answered the LORD, and said, Doth Job 7854
1:12 the LORD said unto **S**, Behold, all that he 7854
1:12 So **S** went forth from the presence of 7854
2: 1 **S** came also among them to present himself 7854
2: 2 the LORD said unto **S**, From whence 7854
2: 2 **S** answered the LORD, and said, 7854
2: 3 the LORD said unto **S**, Hast thou 7854
2: 4 **S** answered the LORD, and said, Skin for 7854
2: 6 the LORD said unto **S**, Behold, he *is* in 7854
2: 7 So went **S** forth from the presence of 7854
Ps 109: 6 over him: and let **S** stand at his right hand. 7854
Zec 3: 1 **S** standing at his right hand to resist him. 7854
3: 2 the LORD said unto **S**, The LORD 7854
3: 2 unto Satan, The LORD rebuke thee, O **S**; 7854
Mt 4:10 saith Jesus unto him, Get thee hence, **S**: 4567
12:26 And if **S** cast out Satan, he is divided 4567
12:26 And if Satan cast out **S**, he is divided 4567
16:23 and said unto Peter, Get thee behind me, **S**: 4567
Mk 1:13 in the wilderness forty days, tempted of **S**; 4567
3:23 in parables, How can **S** cast out Satan? 4567
3:23 in parables, How can Satan cast out **S**? 4567
3:26 And if **S** rise up against himself, and 4567
4:15 **S** cometh immediately, and taketh away 4567
8:33 saying, Get thee behind me, **S**: 4567
Lk 4: 8 and said unto him, Get thee behind me, **S**: 4567
10:18 I beheld **S** as lightning fall from heaven. 4567
11:18 If **S** also be divided against himself, 4567
13:16 whom **S** hath bound, lo *these* eighteen 4567
22: 3 Then entered **S** into Judas surnamed 4567
22:31 Simon, behold, **S** hath desired *to have* you, 4567
Jn 13:27 And after the sop **S** entered into him. 4567
Ac 5: 3 why hath **S** filled thine heart to lie to 4567
26:18 to light, and *from* the power of **S** unto God, 4567
Ro 16:20 And the God of peace shall bruise **S** under 4567
1Co 5: 5 To deliver such a one unto **S** for 4567
7: 5 that **S** tempt you not for your incontinency. 4567
2Co 2:11 Lest **S** should get an advantage of us: 4567
11:14 for **S** himself is transformed into an angel 4567
12: 7 the messenger of **S** to buffet me, lest I 4566
1Th 2:18 I Paul, once and again; but **S** hindered us. 4567
2Th 2: 9 is after the working of **S** with all power 4567
1Ti 1:20 whom I have delivered unto **S**, that they 4567
5:15 For some are already turned aside after **S**. 4567
Rev 2: 9 and are not, but *are* the synagogue of **S**. 4567
2:13 was slain among you, where **S** dwelleth. 4567
2:24 and which have not known the depths of **S**, 4567
3: 9 I *will* make *them* of the synagogue of **S**, 4567
12: 9 called the devil, and **S**, which deceiveth 4567
20: 2 and **S**, and bound him a thousand years, 4567
20: 7 **S** shall be loosed out of his prison, 4567

SATAN'S (1) [SATAN]
Rev 2:13 *even* where **S** seat *is*: and thou holdest fast 4567

SATEST (2) [SIT]
Ps 9: 4 thou **s** in the throne judging right. 3427
Eze 23:41 **s** upon a stately bed, and a table prepared 3427

SATIATE (2) [SATIATED, UNSATIABLE]
Jer 31:14 I will **s** the soul of the priests with fatness, 7301
46:10 it shall be **s** and made drunk with their 7646

SATIATED (1) [SATIATE]
Jer 31:25 For I have **s** the weary soul, and I have 7301

SATISFACTION (2) [SATISFY]
Nu 35:31 Moreover ye shall take no **s** for the life of a 3724
35:32 ye shall take no **s** for him that is fled to 3724

SATISFIED (43) [SATISFY]
Ex 15: 9 the spoil; my lust shall be **s** upon them; 4390
Lev 26:26 by weight: and ye shall eat, and not be **s**. 7646
Dt 14:29 shall come, and shall eat and be **s**; 7646
33:23 **s** with favour, and full *with* the blessing of 7649
Job 19:22 me as God, and are not **s** with my flesh? 7646
27:14 and his offspring shall not be **s** *with* bread. 7646
31:31 O that we had of his flesh! we cannot be **s**. 7646
Ps 17:15 I shall be **s**, when *I* awake, *with* thy 7646
22:26 The meek shall eat and be **s**: they shall 7646
36: 8 They shall be **abundantly s** with 7301
37:19 and in the days of famine they shall be **s**. 7646
59:15 down for meat, and grudge if they be not **s**. 7646
63: 5 My soul shall be **s** as *with* marrow and 7646
65: 4 we shall be **s** with the goodness of thy 7646
81:16 *with* honey out of the rock should I have **s** 7646
104:13 the earth is **s** with the fruit of thy works. 7646
105:40 and **s** them *with* the bread of heaven. 7646
Pr 12:11 He that tilleth his land shall be **s** *with* 7646
12:14 A man shall be **s** *with* good by the fruit of 7646
14:14 and a good man *shall be* **s** from himself. NIH
18:20 A man's belly shall be **s** with the fruit of 7646
19:23 *he that hath it* shall abide **s**; he shall not be 7649
20:13 thine eyes, *and* thou shalt be **s** *with* bread. 7646
27:20 never full; so the eyes of man are never **s**. 7646
30:15 There are three *things that* are never **s**, 7646
Ecc 1: 8 man cannot utter *it*: the eye is not **s** with 7646
4: 8 his labour; neither is his eye **s** *with* riches; 7646
5:10 He that loveth silver shall not be **s** *with* 7646
Isa 9:20 eat on the left hand, and they shall not be **s**: 7646
44:16 he eateth flesh; he roasteth roast, and is **s**: 7646
53:11 see of the travail of his soul, *and* shall be **s**: 7646
66:11 be **s** with the breasts of her consolations; 7646
Jer 31:14 my people shall be **s** with my goodness, 7646
50:10 all that spoil her shall be **s**, saith 7646
50:19 his soul shall be **s** upon mount Ephraim and 7646
La 5: 6 *and to* the Assyrians, to be **s** *with* bread. 7646
Eze 16:28 harlot with them, and yet couldest not be **s**. 7646
16:29 and yet thou wast not **s** herewith. 7646
Joel 2:19 and oil, and ye shall be **s** therewith: 7646
2:26 be **s**, and praise the name of the LORD 7646
Am 4: 8 to drink water; but they were not **s**: 7646
Mic 6:14 Thou shalt eat, but not be **s**; and thy casting 7646
Hab 2: 5 cannot be **s**, but gathereth unto him all 7646

SATISFIEST (1) [SATISFY]
Ps 145:16 and **s** the desire of every living thing. 7646

SATISFIETH (3) [SATISFY]
Ps 103: 5 Who **s** thy mouth with good *things*; so 7646
107: 9 For he **s** the longing soul, and filleth 7646
Isa 55: 2 your labour for *that which* **s** not? hearken 7654

S

SATISFY (10) [SATISFACTION, SATISFIED, SATISFIEST, SATISFIETH, SATISFYING]

Job 38:27 To **s** the desolate and waste *ground;* and 7646
Ps 90:14 O **s** us early *with* thy mercy; that we may 7646
91:16 *With* long life will I **s** him, and shew him 7646
132:15 her provision: I will **s** her poor *with* bread. 7646
Pr 5:19 let her breasts **s** thee at all times; and 7301
6:30 if he steal to **s** his soul when he is hungry; 4390
Isa 58:10 soul to the hungry, and **s** the afflicted soul; 7646
58:11 **s** thy soul in drought, and make fat thy 7646
Eze 7:19 they shall not **s** their souls, neither fill their 7646
Mk 8: 4 From whence can a man **s** these *men* with *5526*

SATISFYING (2) [SATISFY]

Pr 13:25 The righteous eateth to the **s** of his soul: but 7648
Col 2:23 not in any honour to the **s** of the flesh. *4140*

SATRAP See LIEUTENANTS

SATYR (1) [SATYRS]

Isa 34:14 the island, and the **s** shall cry to his fellow; 8163

SATYRS (1) [SATYR]

Isa 13:21 shall dwell there, and **s** shall dance there. 8163

SAUL (394) [PAUL, SAUL'S]

Ge 36:37 **S** of Rehoboth *by* the river reigned in his 7586
36:38 **S** died, and Baal-hanan the son of Achbor 7586
1Sa 9: 2 he had a son, whose name *was* **S**, a choice 7586
9: 3 Kish said to **S** his son, Take now one of 7586
9: 5 **S** said to his servant that *was* with him, 7586
9: 7 said **S** to his servant, But behold, *if* we go, 7586
9: 8 the servant answered **S** again, and said, 7586
9:10 Then said **S** to his servant, Well said; come, 7586
9:15 told Samuel in his ear a day before **S** came, 7586
9:17 when Samuel saw **S**, the LORD said unto 7586
9:18 **S** drew near to Samuel in the gate, and 7586
9:19 Samuel answered **S**, and said, I *am* the seer: 7586
9:21 **S** answered and said, *Am* not I a Benjamite, 7586
9:22 Samuel took **S** and his servant, and 7586
9:24 *that* which *was* upon it, and set *it* before **S**. 7586
9:24 So **S** did eat with Samuel that day. 7586
9:25 *Samuel* communed with **S** upon the top of 7586
9:26 that Samuel called **S** to the top of 7586
9:26 **S** arose, and they went out both of them, 7586
9:27 Samuel said to **S**, Bid the servant pass on 7586
10:11 son of Kish? *Is* **S** also among the prophets? 7586
10:12 a proverb, *Is* **S** also among the prophets? 7586
10:16 **S** said unto his uncle, He told us plainly 7586
10:21 was taken, and **S** the son of Kish was taken: 7586
10:26 **S** also went home to Gibeah; and 7586
11: 4 came the messengers *to* Gibeah of **S**, and 7586
11: 5 **S** came after the herd out of the field; 7586
11: 5 **S** said, What aileth the people that they 7586
11: 6 the spirit of God came upon **S** when he 7586
11: 7 Whosoever cometh not forth after **S** and 7586
11:11 that **S** put the people *in* three companies; 7586
11:12 Who *is* he that said, Shall **S** reign over us? 7586
11:13 **S** said, There shall not a man be put to 7586
11:15 there they made **S** king before the LORD 7586
11:15 there **S** and all the men of Israel rejoiced 7586
13: 1 **S** reigned one year; and when he had 7586
13: 2 **S** chose him three thousand *men* of Israel; 7586
13: 2 *whereof* two thousand were with **S** in 7586
13: 3 the Philistines heard *of it.* And **S** blew 7586
13: 4 all Israel heard say *that* **S** had smitten a 7586
13: 4 the people were called together after **S** *to* 7586
13: 7 As for **S**, he *was* yet in Gilgal, and all 7586
13: 9 **S** said, Bring hither a burnt offering to me, 7586
13:10 **S** went out to meet him, that he might 7586
13:11 **S** said, Because I saw that the people were 7586
13:13 Samuel said to **S**, Thou hast done foolishly: 7586
13:15 **S** numbered the people that were present 7586
13:16 **S**, and Jonathan his son, and the people that 7586
13:22 hand of any of the people that *were* with **S** 7586
13:22 with **S** and with Jonathan his son was there 7586
14: 1 that Jonathan the son of **S** said unto 7586
14: 2 **S** tarried in the uttermost part of Gibeah 7586
14:16 the watchmen of **S** in Gibeah of Benjamin 7586
14:17 said **S** unto the people that *were* with him, 7586
14:18 **S** said unto Ahiah, Bring hither the ark of 7586
14:19 came to pass, while **S** talked unto the priest, 7586
14:19 **S** said unto the priest, Withdraw thine hand. 7586
14:20 **S** and all the people that *were* with him 7586
14:21 to be with the Israelites that *were* with **S** 7586
14:24 for **S** had adjured the people, saying, 7586
14:33 they told **S**, saying, Behold, the people sin 7586
14:34 **S** said, Disperse yourselves among 7586
14:35 **S** built an altar unto the LORD: the same 7586
14:36 **S** said, Let us go down after the Philistines 7586
14:37 **S** asked *counsel* of God, Shall I go down 7586
14:38 **S** said, Draw ye near hither, all the chief of 7586
14:40 the people said unto **S**, Do what seemeth 7586
14:41 Therefore **S** said unto the LORD God of 7586
14:41 Give a perfect *lot.* And **S** and 7586
14:42 **S** said, Cast *lots* between me and Jonathan 7586
14:43 **S** said to Jonathan, Tell me what thou hast 7586
14:44 **S** answered, God do so and more also: 7586
14:45 the people said unto **S**, Shall Jonathan die, 7586
14:46 **S** went up from following the Philistines: 7586
14:47 So **S** took the kingdom over Israel, and 7586
14:49 Now the sons of **S** were Jonathan, and 7586
14:51 Kish *was* the father of **S**; and Ner the father 7586
14:52 war against the Philistines all the days of **S**: 7586
14:52 when **S** saw any strong man, or any valiant 7586
15: 1 Samuel also said unto **S**, The LORD sent 7586
15: 4 **S** gathered the people together, and 7586
15: 5 **S** came to a city of Amalek, and laid wait in 7586
15: 6 **S** said unto the Kenites, Go, depart, get you 7586
15: 7 **S** smote the Amalekites from Havilah *until* 7586
15: 9 **S** and the people spared Agag, and the best 7586
15:11 It repenteth me that I have set up **S** to be 7586
15:12 when Samuel rose early to meet **S** in 7586
15:12 **S** came to Carmel, and behold, 7586
15:13 Samuel came to **S**: and Saul said unto him, 7586
15:13 **S** said unto him, Blessed *be* thou of 7586
15:15 **S** said, They have brought them from 7586
15:16 Samuel said unto **S**, Stay, and I will tell 7586
15:20 **S** said unto Samuel, Yea, I have obeyed 7586
15:24 **S** said unto Samuel, I have sinned: for I 7586
15:26 Samuel said unto **S**, I will not return with 7586
15:31 So Samuel turned again after **S**; and 7586
15:31 after Saul; and **S** worshipped the LORD. 7586
15:34 **S** went up to his house *to* Gibeah of Saul. 7586
15:34 Saul went up to his house *to* Gibeah of **S**. 7586
15:35 Samuel came no more to see **S** until the day 7586
15:35 nevertheless Samuel mourned for **S**: and 7586
15:35 the LORD repented that he had made **S** 7586
16: 1 How long wilt thou mourn for **S**, 7586
16: 2 if **S** hear *it,* he will kill me. And 7586
16:14 the spirit of the LORD departed from **S**, 7586
16:17 **S** said unto his servants, Provide me now a 7586
16:19 Wherefore **S** sent messengers unto Jesse, 7586
16:20 and sent *them* by David his son unto **S**. 7586
16:21 David came to **S**, and stood before him: 7586
16:22 **S** sent to Jesse, saying, Let David, I pray 7586
16:23 when the *evil* spirit from God was upon **S**, 7586
16:23 so **S** was refreshed, and was well, and 7586
17: 2 **S** and the men of Israel were gathered 7586
17: 8 *am* not I a Philistine, and you servants to **S**? 7586
17:11 When **S** and all Israel heard those words of 7586
17:12 among men *for* an old man in the days of **S**. 7586
17:13 of Jesse went *and* followed **S** to the battle: 7586
17:14 and the three eldest followed **S**. 7586
17:15 returned from **S** to feed his father's sheep *at* 7586
17:19 Now **S**, and they, and all the men of Israel, 7586
17:31 David spake, they rehearsed *them* before **S**: 7586
17:32 David said to **S**, Let no man's heart fail 7586
17:33 **S** said to David, Thou art not able to go 7586
17:34 David said unto **S**, Thy servant kept his 7586
17:37 **S** said unto David, Go, and the LORD be 7586
17:38 **S** armed David with his armour, and he put 7586
17:39 had not proved *it.* And David said unto **S**, 7586
17:55 when **S** saw David go forth against 7586
17:57 brought him before **S** with the head of 7586
17:58 **S** said to him, Whose son *art* thou, *thou* 7586
18: 1 when he made an end of speaking unto **S**, 7586
18: 2 **S** took him that day, and would let him go 7586
18: 5 David went out whithersoever **S** sent him, 7586
18: 5 **S** set him over the men of war, and he was 7586
18: 6 singing and dancing, to meet king **S**, 7586
18: 7 **S** hath slain his thousands, and David his 7586
18: 8 **S** was very wroth, and the saying 7586
18: 9 **S** eyed David from that day and forward. 7586
18:10 that the evil spirit from God came upon **S**, 7586
18:11 **S** cast the javelin; for he said, I will smite 7586
18:12 **S** was afraid of David, because the LORD 7586
18:12 was with him, and was departed from **S**. 7586

1Sa 18:13	Therefore **S** removed him from him, and	7586
18:15	Wherefore when **S** saw that he behaved	7586
18:17	**S** said to David, Behold my elder daughter	7586
18:17	For **S** said, Let not mine hand be upon him,	7586
18:18	David said unto **S**, Who *am* I? and what *is*	7586
18:20	and they told **S**, and the thing pleased him.	7586
18:21	**S** said, I will give him her, that she may be	7586
18:21	Wherefore **S** said to David, Thou shalt *this*	7586
18:22	**S** commanded his servants,	7586
18:24	the servants of **S** told him, saying, On this	7586
18:25	**S** said, Thus shall ye say to David, The	7586
18:25	**S** thought to make David fall by the hand of	7586
18:27	**S** gave him Michal his daughter to wife.	7586
18:28	**S** saw and knew that the LORD *was* with	7586
18:29	**S** was yet the more afraid of David; and	7586
18:29	and **S** became David's enemy continually.	7586
18:30	more wisely than all the servants of **S**;	7586
19: 1	**S** spake to Jonathan his son, and to all his	7586
19: 2	**S** my father seeketh to kill thee:	7586
19: 4	Jonathan spake good of David unto **S** his	7586
19: 6	**S** hearkened unto the voice of Jonathan:	7586
19: 6	**S** sware, *As* the LORD liveth, he shall not	7586
19: 7	Jonathan brought David to **S**, and he was in	7586
19: 9	the evil spirit from the LORD was upon **S**,	7586
19:10	**S** sought to smite David even to the wall	7586
19:11	**S** also sent messengers unto David's house,	7586
19:14	And when **S** sent messengers to take David,	7586
19:15	**S** sent the messengers *again* to see David,	7586
19:17	**S** said unto Michal, Why hast thou	7586
19:17	Michal answered **S**, He said unto me,	7586
19:18	and told him all that **S** had done to him.	7586
19:19	it was told **S**, saying, Behold, David *is* at	7586
19:20	**S** sent messengers to take David: and	7586
19:20	of God was upon the messengers of **S**,	7586
19:21	when it was told **S**, he sent other	7586
19:21	And **S** sent messengers again the third time,	7586
19:24	they say, *Is* **S** also among the prophets?	7586
20:26	Nevertheless **S** spake not any thing that	7586
20:27	**S** said unto Jonathan his son,	7586
20:28	Jonathan answered **S**, David earnestly	7586
20:32	Jonathan answered **S** his father, and	7586
20:33	**S** cast a javelin at him to smite him:	7586
21: 7	Now a *certain* man of the servants of **S** *was*	7586
21: 7	chiefest of the herdmen that *belonged* to **S**.	7586
21:10	fled that day for fear of **S**, and went to	7586
21:11	**S** hath slain his thousands, and David his	7586
22: 6	When **S** heard that David was discovered,	7586
22: 6	(now **S** abode in Gibeah under a tree in	7586
22: 7	**S** said unto his servants that stood about	7586
22: 9	which *was* set over the servants of **S**, and	7586
22:12	**S** said, Hear now, thou son of Ahitub.	7586
22:13	**S** said unto him, Why have ye conspired	7586
22:21	Abiathar shewed David that **S** had slain	7586
22:22	*was* there, that he would surely tell **S**:	7586
23: 7	it was told **S** that David was come *to*	7586
23: 7	**S** said, God hath delivered him into mine	7586
23: 8	**S** called all the people together to war,	7586
23: 9	David knew that **S** secretly practised	7586
23:10	thy servant hath certainly heard that **S**	7586
23:11	Will **S** come down, as thy servant hath	7586
23:12	deliver me and my men into the hand of **S**?	7586
23:13	it was told **S** that David was escaped from	7586
23:14	**S** sought him every day, but God delivered	7586
23:15	David saw that **S** was come out to seek his	7586
23:17	for the hand of **S** my father shall not find	7586
23:17	and that also **S** my father knoweth.	7586
23:19	came up the Ziphites to **S** to Gibeah,	7586
23:21	**S** said, Blessed *be* ye of the LORD; for ye	7586
23:24	they arose, and went to Ziph before **S**: but	7586
23:25	**S** also and his men went to seek *him*. And	7586
23:25	when **S** heard *that*, he pursued after David	7586
23:26	**S** went on this side of the mountain, and	7586
23:26	David made haste to get away for fear of **S**;	7586
23:26	for **S** and his men compassed David and his	7586
23:27	there came a messenger unto **S**, saying,	7586
23:28	Wherefore **S** returned from pursuing after	7586
24: 1	when **S** was returned from following	7586
24: 2	**S** took three thousand chosen men out of all	7586
24: 3	*was* a cave; and **S** went in to cover his feet:	7586
24: 7	and suffered them not to rise against **S**.	7586
24: 7	**S** rose up out of the cave, and went on *his*	7586
24: 8	and cried after **S**, saying, My lord the king.	7586
24: 8	when **S** looked behind him, David stooped	7586
24: 9	David said to **S**, Wherefore hearest thou	7586
24:16	an end of speaking these words unto **S**,	7586
24:16	that **S** said, *Is* this thy voice, my son David?	7586
24:16	And **S** lift up his voice, and wept.	7586
24:22	David sware unto **S**. And Saul went home;	7586
24:22	**S** went home; but David and his men gat	7586
25:44	**S** had given Michal his daughter,	7586
26: 1	the Ziphites came unto **S** to Gibeah, saying,	7586
26: 2	**S** arose, and went down to the wilderness	7586
26: 3	**S** pitched in the hill of Hachilah, which *is*	7586
26: 3	he saw that **S** came after him into	7586
26: 4	understood that **S** was come in very deed.	7586
26: 5	and came to the place where **S** had pitched:	7586
26: 5	David beheld the place where **S** lay, and	7586
26: 5	**S** lay in the trench, and the people pitched	7586
26: 6	Who will go down with me to **S** to	7586
26: 7	**S** lay sleeping within the trench, and	7586
26:17	**S** knew David's voice, and said, *Is* this thy	7586
26:21	said **S**, I have sinned: return, my son David:	7586
26:25	**S** said to David, Blessed *be* thou, my son	7586
26:25	on his way, and **S** returned to his place.	7586
27: 1	shall now perish one day by the hand of **S**:	7586
27: 1	**S** shall despair of me, to seek me any more	7586
27: 4	it was told **S** that David was fled *to* Gath:	7586
28: 3	**S** had put away those that had familiar	7586
28: 4	**S** gathered all Israel together, and	7586
28: 5	when **S** saw the host of the Philistines, he	7586
28: 6	when **S** inquired of the LORD,	7586
28: 7	said **S** unto his servants, Seek me a woman	7586
28: 8	**S** disguised himself, and put on other	7586
28: 9	Behold, thou knowest what **S** hath done,	7586
28:10	**S** sware to her by the LORD, saying,	7586
28:12	the woman spake to **S**, saying, Why hast	7586
28:12	Why hast thou deceived me? for thou *art* **S**.	7586
28:13	the woman said unto **S**, I saw gods	7586
28:14	**S** perceived that it *was* Samuel, and	7586
28:15	Samuel said to **S**, Why hast thou disquieted	7586
28:15	**S** answered, I am sore distressed; for	7586
28:20	**S** fell straightway all along on the earth,	7586
28:21	the woman came unto **S**, and saw that he	7586
28:25	she brought *it* before **S**, and before his	7586
29: 3	the servant of **S** the king of Israel,	7586
29: 5	**S** slew his thousands, and David his ten	7586
31: 2	the Philistines followed hard upon **S** and	7586
31: 3	the battle went sore against **S**, and	7586
31: 4	said **S** unto his armourbearer, Draw thy	7586
31: 4	therefore **S** took a sword, and fell upon it.	7586
31: 5	when his armourbearer saw that **S** was	7586
31: 6	So **S** died, and his three sons, and	7586
31: 7	that **S** and his sons were dead, they forsook	7586
31: 8	that they found **S** and his three sons fallen	7586
31:11	of that which the Philistines had done to **S**,	7586
31:12	took the body of **S** and the bodies of his	7586
2Sa 1: 1	Now it came to pass after the death of **S**,	7586
1: 2	a man came out of the camp from **S** with	7586
1: 4	and **S** and Jonathan his son are dead also.	7586
1: 5	How knowest thou that **S** and Jonathan his	7586
1: 6	behold, **S** leaned upon his spear;	7586
1:12	for **S**, and for Jonathan his son, and for	7586
1:17	lamented with this lamentation over **S**	7586
1:21	the shield of **S**, *as though he had* not *been*	7586
1:22	and the sword of **S** returned not empty.	7586
1:23	**S** and Jonathan *were* lovely and pleasant in	7586
1:24	Ye daughters of Israel, weep over **S**,	7586
2: 4	of Jabesh-gilead *were they* that buried **S**.	7586
2: 5	*even* unto **S**, and have buried him.	7586
2: 7	for your master **S** is dead, and also	7586
2: 8	took Ish-bosheth the son of **S**, and	7586
2:12	the servants of Ish-bosheth the son of **S**,	7586
2:15	*pertained* to Ish-bosheth the son of **S**,	7586
3: 1	there was long war between the house of **S**	7586
3: 1	the house of **S** waxed weaker and weaker.	7586
3: 6	while there was war between the house of **S**	7586
3: 6	made himself strong for the house of **S**.	7586
3: 7	**S** had a concubine, whose name *was*	7586
3: 8	*this* day unto the house of **S** thy father,	7586
3:10	translate the kingdom from the house of **S**,	7586
4: 4	five years old when the tidings came of **S**	7586
4: 8	Behold the head of Ish-bosheth the son of **S**	7586
4: 8	avenged my lord the king this day of **S**,	7586
4:10	one told me, saying, Behold, **S** is dead,	7586
5: 2	Also in time past, when **S** was king over us,	7586
6:20	Michal the daughter of **S** came out to meet	7586
6:23	Therefore Michal the daughter of **S** had no	7586
7:15	as I took *it* from **S**, whom I put away before	7586

S

2Sa 9: 1 there yet *any* that is left of the house of **S**, 7586
9: 2 *there was* of the house of **S** a servant whose 7586
9: 3 *Is there* not yet any of the house of **S**, 7586
9: 6 the son of Jonathan, the son of **S**, was come 7586
9: 7 will restore thee all the land of **S** thy father; 7586
9: 9 unto thy master's son all that pertained to **S** 7586
12: 7 and I delivered thee out of the hand of **S**; 7586
16: 5 out a man of the family of the house of **S**, 7586
16: 8 upon thee all the blood of the house of **S**, 7586
19:17 Ziba the servant of the house of **S**, and 7586
19:24 Mephibosheth the son of **S** came down to 7586
21: 1 *It is* for **S**, and for *his* bloody house, 7586
21: 2 **S** sought to slay them in his zeal to 7586
21: 4 We will have no silver nor gold of **S**, nor of 7586
21: 6 them up unto the LORD in Gibeah of **S**, 7586
21: 7 the son of Jonathan the son of **S**, because 7586
21: 7 between David and Jonathan the son of **S**. 7586
21: 8 whom she bare unto **S**, Armoni and 7586
21: 8 the five sons of Michal the daughter of **S**, 7586
21:11 of Aiah, the concubine of **S**, had done. 7586
21:12 David went and took the bones of **S** and 7586
21:12 when the Philistines had slain **S** in Gilboa: 7586
21:13 he brought up from thence the bones of **S** 7586
21:14 the bones of **S** and Jonathan his son buried 7586
22: 1 of all his enemies, and out of the hand of **S**: 7586
1Ch 5:10 in the days of **S** they made war with 7586
8:33 Kish begat **S**, and Saul begat Jonathan, and 7586
8:33 **S** begat Jonathan, and Malchishua, and 7586
9:39 Kish begat **S**; and Saul begat Jonathan, and 7586
9:39 **S** begat Jonathan, and Malchishua, and 7586
10: 2 the Philistines followed hard after **S**, and 7586
10: 2 and Malchishua, the sons of **S**. 7586
10: 3 the battle went sore against **S**, and 7586
10: 4 said **S** to his armourbearer, Draw thy 7586
10: 4 So **S** took a sword, and fell upon it. 7586
10: 5 when his armourbearer saw that **S** was 7586
10: 6 So **S** died, and his three sons, and all his 7586
10: 7 that **S** and his sons were dead, then 7586
10: 8 that they found **S** and his sons fallen in 7586
10:11 heard all that the Philistines had done to **S**, 7586
10:12 took away the body of **S**, and the bodies of 7586
10:13 So **S** died for his transgression which he 7586
11: 2 in time past, even when **S** was king, 7586
12: 1 himself close because of **S** the son of Kish: 7586
12:19 when he came with the Philistines against **S** 7586
12:19 He will fall to his master **S** to *the jeopardy* 7586
12:23 to Hebron, to turn the kingdom of **S** to him, 7586
12:29 the kindred of **S**, three thousand: 7586
12:29 them had kept the ward of the house of **S**. 7586
13: 3 for we inquired not *at* it in the days of **S**. 7586
15:29 that Michal the daughter of **S** looking out at 7586
26:28 **S** the son of Kish, and Abner the son of 7586
Ps 18: T of all his enemies, and from the hand of **S**: 7586
52: T when Doeg the Edomite came and told **S**, 7586
54: T when the Ziphims came and said to **S**, 7586
57: T of David, when he fled from **S** in the cave. 7586
59: T when **S** sent, and they watcht the house to 7586
Isa 10:29 Ramah is afraid; Gibeah of **S** is fled. 7586
Ac 7:58 at a young man's feet, whose name was **S**. *4569*
8: 1 And **S** was consenting unto his death. *4569*
8: 3 As for **S**, he made havock of the church, *4569*
9: 1 And **S**, yet breathing out threatenings and *4569*
9: 4 **S**, Saul, why persecutest thou me? *4549*
9: 4 Saul, **S**, why persecutest thou me? *4549*
9: 8 And **S** arose from the earth; and when his *4569*
9:11 in the house of Judas for *one* called **S**, *4569*
9:17 him said, Brother **S**, the Lord, *even* Jesus, *4549*
9:19 Then was **S** certain days with the disciples *4569*
9:22 But **S** increased the more in strength, and *4569*
9:24 But their laying await was known of **S**. *4569*
9:26 And when **S** was come to Jerusalem, *4569*
11:25 departed Barnabas to Tarsus, for to seek **S**: *4569*
11:30 the elders by the hands of Barnabas and **S**. *4569*
12:25 and **S** returned from Jerusalem, *4569*
13: 1 brought up with Herod the tetrarch, and **S**. *4569*
13: 2 **S** for the work whereunto I have called *4569*
13: 7 who called for Barnabas and **S**, and *4569*
13: 9 Then **S**, (who also *is called* Paul,) *4569*
13:21 and God gave unto them **S** the son of Cis, *4549*
22: 7 unto me, **S**, Saul, why persecutest thou me? *4549*
22: 7 unto me, Saul, **S**, why persecutest thou me? *4549*
22:13 and stood, and said unto me, Brother **S**, *4549*
26:14 **S**, Saul, why persecutest thou me? *4549*
26:14 Saul, **S**, why persecutest thou me? *4549*

SAUL'S (31) [SAUL]
1Sa 9: 3 the asses of Kish **S** father were lost. 7586
10:14 **S** uncle said unto him and to his servant, 7586
10:15 **S** uncle said, Tell me, I pray thee, 7586
14:50 the name of **S** wife *was* Ahinoam, 7586
14:50 his host *was* Abner, the son of Ner, **S** uncle. 7586
16:15 **S** servants said unto him, Behold now, 7586
18: 5 and also in the sight of **S** servants. 7586
18:10 and *there was* a javelin in **S** hand. 7586
18:19 it came to pass at the time when Merab **S** 7586
18:20 Michal **S** daughter loved David: and 7586
18:23 **S** servants spake those words in the ears of 7586
18:28 and *that* Michal **S** daughter loved him. 7586
19: 2 Jonathan **S** son delighted much in David: 7586
19:10 he slipt away out of **S** presence, and 7586
20:25 Abner sat by **S** side, and David's place was 7586
20:30 Then **S** anger was kindled against Jonathan, 7586
23:16 Jonathan **S** son arose, and went to David 7586
24: 4 cut off the skirt of **S** robe privily. 7586+3807.1
24: 5 because he had cut off **S** skirt. 7586+3807.1
26:12 and the cruse of water from **S** bolster; 7586
31: 2 and Abinadab, and Malchishua, **S** sons. 7586
2Sa 2: 8 the son of Ner, captain of **S** host, 7586+3807.1
2:10 Ish-bosheth **S** son *was* forty years old when 7586
3:13 except thou first bring Michal **S** daughter, 7586
3:14 David sent messengers to Ish-bosheth **S** 7586
4: 1 when **S** son heard that Abner was dead in 7586
4: 2 **S** son had two men *that were* captains of 7586
4: 4 Jonathan, **S** son, had a son *that was* lame of 7586
6:16 Michal **S** daughter looked through a 7586
9: 9 called to Ziba, **S** servant, and said unto him, 7586
1Ch 12: 2 of a bow, *even* of **S** brethren of Benjamin. 7586

SAVE (233) [SAFE, SAFEGUARD, SAFELY, SAFETY, SALVATION, SAVED, SAVEST, SAVETH, SAVING, SAVIOUR, SAVIOURS]
Ge 12:12 they will kill me, but they will **s** thee **alive**. 2421
14:24 **S** only that which the young men have 1107
39: 6 he had, **s** the bread which he did eat. 518+3588
45: 7 and to **s** your **lives** by a great deliverance. 2421
50:20 as *it is* this day, to **s** much people **alive**. 2421
Ex 1:22 and every daughter ye shall **s** **alive**. 2421
12:16 **s** *that* which every man must eat, that only 389
22:20 **s** unto the LORD only, he shall be utterly 1115
Nu 14:30 **s** Caleb the son of Jephunneh, and 518+3588
26:65 **s** Caleb the son of Jephunneh, and 518+3588
32:12 **S** Caleb the son of Jephunneh the Kenezite, 1115
Dt 1:36 **S** Caleb the son of Jephunneh, he shall see 2108
15: 4 **S** when there shall be no poor among you; 657
20: 4 for you against your enemies, to **s** you. 3467
20:16 thou shalt **s** **alive** nothing that breatheth: 2421
22:27 damsel cried, and *there was* none to **s** her. 3467
28:29 spoiled evermore, and no man shall **s** *thee*. 3467
Jos 2:13 *that* ye will **s** **alive** my father, and 2421
10: 6 up to us quickly, and **s** us, and help us: 3467
11:13 Israel burned none of them, **s** Hazor only; 2108
11:19 **s** the Hivites the inhabitants of Gibeon: 1115
14: 4 **s** cities to dwell *in*, with their suburbs 518+3588
22:22 against the LORD, (**s** us not this day,) 3467
Jdg 6:14 thou shalt **s** Israel from the hand of 3467
6:15 O my Lord, wherewith shall I **s** Israel? 3467
6:31 will ye **s** him? he that will plead for him, 3467
6:36 If thou wilt **s** Israel by mine hand, as thou 3467
6:37 shall I know that thou wilt **s** Israel by mine 3467
7: 7 three hundred men that lapped will I **s** you, 3467
7:14 This *is* nothing else **s** the sword of Gideon 518
1Sa 4: 3 it may **s** us out of the hand of our enemies. 3467
7: 8 that he will **s** us out of the hand of 3467
9:16 that *he* may **s** my people out of the hand of 3467
10:24 people shouted, and said, **God s** the king. 2421
10:27 of Belial said, How shall this *man* **s** us? 3467
11: 3 then, if *there be* no man to **s** us, we will 3467
14: 6 for *there is* no restraint to the LORD to **s** 3467
19:11 saying, If thou **s** not thy life to night, 4422
21: 9 take *it*: for *there is* no other **s** that here. 2108
23: 2 Go, and smite the Philistines, and **s** Keilah. 3467
30:17 **s** four hundred young men, 518+3588
30:22 **s** *to* every man his wife and his 518+3588
2Sa 3:18 By the hand of my servant David I will **s** 3467
12: 3 **s** one little ewe lamb, which he had 518+3588
16:16 **God s** the king, God save the king. 2421
16:16 God save the king, **God s** the king. 2421
22:28 the afflicted people thou wilt **s**: but 3467

S

2Sa 22:32 For who *is* God, s the LORD? and 1107+4480
22:32 and who *is* a rock, s our God? 1107+4480
22:42 They looked, but *there was* none to s; 3467
1Ki 1:12 that thou mayest s thine own life, and 4422
1:25 before him, and say, God s king Adonijah. 2421
1:34 the trumpet, and say, God s king Solomon. 2421
1:39 all the people said, God s king Solomon. 2421
3:18 with us in the house, s we two in the house. 2108
8: 9 *There was* nothing in the ark s the two 7535
15: 5 s only in the matter of Urijah the Hittite. 7535
18: 5 find grass to s the horses and mules alive, 2421
20:31 of Israel: peradventure he will s thy life. 2421
22:31 s only with the king of Israel. 518+3588
2Ki 4: 2 any thing in the house, s a pot of oil. 518+3588
7: 4 if they s us alive, we shall live; and if they 2421
11:12 clapt their hands, and said, God s the king. 2421
15: 4 S that the high places were not removed: 7535
16: 7 s me out of the hand of the king of Syria, 3467
19:19 I beseech thee, s *thou* us out of his hand, 3467
19:34 to s it, for mine own sake, and for my 3467
24:14 s the poorest sort of the people of the land. 2108
1Ch 16:35 say ye, S us, O God of our salvation, and 3467
2Ch 2: 6 s only to burn sacrifice before him? 518+3588
5:10 *There was* nothing in the ark s the two 7535
18:30 or great, s only with the king of Israel. 518+3588
21:17 s Jehoahaz, the youngest of his sons. 518+3588
23: 6 s the priests, and they that minister of 518+3588
23:11 anointed him, and said, God s the king. 2421
Ne 2:12 with me, s the beast that I rode upon. 518+3588
6:11 I *am,* would go into the temple to s his life? 2421
Job 2: 6 Behold, he *is* in thine hand; but s his life. 8104
20:20 he shall not s of that which he desired. 4422
22:29 lifting up; and he shall s the humble person. 3467
40:14 thee that thine own right hand can s thee. 3467
Ps 3: 7 Arise, O LORD; s me, O my God: 3467
6: 4 my soul: O s me for thy mercy's sake. 3467
7: 1 s me from all them that persecute me, and 3467
18:27 For thou wilt s the afflicted people; but 3467
18:31 For who *is* God s the LORD? or 1107+4480
18:31 the LORD? or who *is* a rock s our God? 2108
18:41 *there was* none to s *them: even* unto 3467
20: 9 S, LORD: let the king hear us when we 3467
22:21 S me from the lion's mouth: for thou hast 3467
28: 9 S thy people, and bless thine inheritance: 3467
31: 2 strong rock, for a house of defence to s me. 3467
31:16 thy servant: s me for thy mercy's sake. 3467
37:40 and s them, because they trust in him. 3467
44: 3 neither did their own arm s them: 3467
44: 6 in my bow, neither shall my sword s me. 3467
54: 1 S me, O God, by thy name, and judge me 3467
55:16 call upon God; and the LORD shall s me. 3467
57: 3 s me *from* the reproach of him that would 3467
59: 2 of iniquity, and s me from bloody men. 3467
60: 5 s *with* thy right hand, and hear me. 3467
69: 1 S me, O God; for the waters are come in 3467
69:35 For God will s Zion, and will build 3467
71: 2 incline thine ear unto me, and s me. 3467
71: 3 thou hast given commandment to s me; 3467
72: 4 he shall s the children of the needy, and 3467
72:13 needy, and shall s the souls of the needy. 3467
76: 9 to judgment, to s all the meek of the earth. 3467
80: 2 stir up thy strength, and come and s us. 3444
86: 2 my God, s thy servant that trusteth in thee. 3467
86:16 and s the son of thine handmaid. 3467
106:47 S us, O LORD our God, and gather us 3467
108: 6 s *with* thy right hand, and answer me. 3467
109:26 my God: O s me according to thy mercy: 3467
109:31 to s *him* from those that condemn his soul. 3467
118:25 S now, I beseech thee, O LORD: 3467
119:94 I *am* thine, s me; for I have sought thy 3467
119:146 s me, and I shall keep thy testimonies. 3467
138: 7 and thy right hand shall s me. 3467
145:19 he also will hear their cry, and will s them. 3467
Pr 20:22 *but* wait on the LORD, and he shall s thee. 3467
Isa 25: 9 we have waited for him, and he will s us: 3467
33:22 the LORD *is* our king; he will s us. 3467
35: 4 *with* a recompence; he will come and s you. 3467
37:20 O LORD our God, s us from his hand, 3467
37:35 For I will defend this city to s it for mine 3467
38:20 The LORD *was ready* to s me: therefore 3467
45:20 and pray unto a god *that* cannot s. 3467
46: 7 he not answer, nor s him out of his trouble. 3467
47:13 s thee from *these things* that shall come 3467
47:15 every one to his quarter; none shall s thee. 3467
49:25 with thee, and I will s thy children. 3467
59: 1 hand is not shortened, that *it* cannot s; 3467
63: 1 I that speak in righteousness, mighty to s. 3467
Jer 2:27 their trouble they will say, Arise, and s us. 3467
2:28 if they can s thee in the time of thy trouble: 3467
11:12 they shall not s them at all in 3467+3467
14: 9 as a mighty *man that* cannot s? 3467
15:20 for I *am* with thee to s thee and to deliver 3467
17:14 I shall be healed; s me, and I shall be saved: 3467
30:10 I *will* s thee from afar, and thy seed from 3467
30:11 I *am* with thee, saith the LORD, to s thee: 3467
31: 7 praise ye, and say, O LORD, s thy people, 3467
42:11 for I *am* with you to s you, and to deliver 3467
46:27 I *will* s thee from afar off, and thy seed 3467
48: 6 s your lives, and be like the heath in 4422
La 4:17 watched for a nation *that* could not s *us.* 3467
Eze 3:18 wicked from his wicked way, to s his life; 2421
13:18 will ye s the souls alive *that come* unto 2421
13:19 and to s the souls alive that should not live, 2421
18:27 is lawful and right, he shall s his soul alive. 2421
34:22 Therefore will I s my flock, and they shall 3467
36:29 I will also s you from all your 3467
37:23 I will s them out of all their dwelling 3467
Da 6: 7 or man for thirty days, s of thee, O king, 3861
6:12 or man within thirty days, s of thee, O king, 3861
Hos 1: 7 will s them by the LORD their God, and 3467
1: 7 will not s them by bow, nor by sword, 3467
13:10 where *is any other* that may s thee in all thy 3467
14: 3 Asshur shall not s us: we will not ride upon 3467
Hab 1: 2 unto thee *of* violence, and thou wilt not s? 3467
Zep 3:17 he will s, he will rejoice over thee with joy; 3467
3:19 I will s her that halteth, and gather her that 3467
Zec 8: 7 I *will* s my people from the east country, 3467
8:13 so will I s you, and ye shall be a blessing: 3467
9:16 the LORD their God shall s them in that 3467
10: 6 I will s the house of Joseph, and I will bring 3467
12: 7 The LORD also shall s the tents of Judah 3467
Mt 1:21 for he shall s his people from their sins. *4982*
8:25 to *him,* and awoke him, saying, Lord, s us: *4982*
11:27 s the Son, and *he* to whomsoever the Son *1508*
13:57 s in his own country, and in his own house. *1508*
14:30 to sink, he cried, saying, Lord, s me. *4982*
16:25 For whosoever will s his life shall lose it: *4982*
17: 8 their eyes, they saw no *man,* s Jesus only. *1508*
18:11 For the Son of man is come to s that which *4982*
19:11 this saying, s *they* to whom it is given. *235*
27:40 and buildest *it* in three days, s thyself. *4982*
27:42 He saved others; himself he cannot s. If he *4982*
27:49 let us see whether Elias will come to s him. *4982*
Mk 3: 4 to s life, or to kill? But they held their *4982*
5:37 s Peter, and James, and John the brother of *1508*
6: 5 s that he laid *his* hands upon a few sick *1508*
6: 8 nothing for *their* journey, s a staff only; *1508*
8:35 For whosoever will s his life shall lose it; *4982*
8:35 and the gospel's, the same shall s it. *4982*
9: 8 *man* any more, s Jesus only with themselves. *235*
15:30 S thyself, and come down from the cross. *4982*
15:31 He saved others; himself he cannot s. *4982*
Lk 4:26 s unto Sarepta, *a city* of Sidon, unto a *1508*
6: 9 or to do evil? to s life, or to destroy *it? 4982*
8:51 he suffered no *man* to go in, s Peter, *1508*
9:24 For whosoever will s his life shall lose it: *4982*
9:24 lose his life for my sake, the same shall s it. *4982*
9:56 to s *them.* And they went to another village. *4982*
17:18 to give glory to God, s this stranger. *1508*
17:33 Whosoever shall seek to s his life shall lose *4982*
18:19 me good? none *is* good, s one, *that is,* God. *1508*
19:10 come to seek and to s that which was lost. *4982*
23:35 let him s himself, if he be Christ, *4982*
23:37 If thou be the King of the Jews, s thyself. *4982*
23:39 saying, If thou be Christ, s thyself and us. *4982*
Jn 6:22 s that one whereinto his disciples were *1508*
6:46 s he which is of God, he hath seen *1508*
12:27 Father, s me from this hour: but for this *4982*
12:47 not to judge the world, but to s the world. *4982*
13:10 He that is washed needeth not s to wash *his 2228*
Ac 2:40 S yourselves from this untoward *4982*
20:23 S that the Holy Ghost witnesseth in every *4133*
21:25 s only that they keep themselves from *1508*
27:43 But the centurion, willing to s Paul, *1295*
Ro 11:14 *are* my flesh, and might s some of them. *4982*
1Co 1:21 of preaching to s them that believe. *4982*
2: 2 s Jesus Christ, and him crucified. *1508*
2:11 a man, s the spirit of man which is in him? *1508*

S

Lk 2:11 is born this day in the city of David a **S**, *4990*
Jn 4:42 this is indeed the Christ, the **S** of the world. *4990*
Ac 5:31 with his right hand *to be* a Prince and a **S**, *4990*
13:23 to *his* promise raised unto Israel a **S**, *4990*
Eph 5:23 of the church: and he is the **S** of the body. *4990*
Php 3:20 from whence also we look for the **S**, *4990*
1Ti 1: 1 Christ by the commandment of God our **S**, *4990*
2: 3 and acceptable in the sight of God our **S**; *4990*
4:10 in the living God, who is the **S** of all men, *4990*
2Ti 1:10 by the appearing of our **S** Jesus Christ, *4990*
Tit 1: 3 to the commandment of God our **S**; *4990*
1: 4 the Father and the Lord Jesus Christ our **S**. *4990*
2:10 the doctrine of God our **S** in all *things.* *4990*
2:13 of the great God and our **S** Jesus Christ; *4990*
3: 4 love of God our **S** toward man appeared, *4990*
3: 6 us abundantly through Jesus Christ our **S**; *4990*
2Pe 1: 1 of God and our **S** Jesus Christ: *4990*
1:11 kingdom of our Lord and **S** Jesus Christ. *4990*
2:20 knowledge of the Lord and **S** Jesus Christ, *4990*
3: 2 of us the apostles of the Lord and **S**: *4990*
3:18 knowledge of our Lord and **S** Jesus Christ. *4990*
1Jn 4:14 Father sent the Son *to be* the **S** of the world. *4990*
Jude 1:25 To the only wise God our **S**, *be* glory and *4990*

SAVIOURS (2) [SAVE]
Ne 9:27 to thy manifold mercies thou gavest them **s**, 3467
Ob 1:21 **s** shall come up on mount Zion to judge 3467

SAVOUR (54) [SAVOUREST, SAVOURS, SAVOURY, UNSAVOURY]
Ge 8:21 the LORD smelled a sweet **s**; and 7381
Ex 5:21 you have made our **s** to be abhorred in 7381
29:18 it *is* a sweet **s**, an offering made by fire unto 7381
29:25 for a sweet **s** before the LORD: 7381
29:41 to the drink offering thereof, for a sweet **s**, 7381
Lev 1: 9 made by fire, of a sweet **s** unto the LORD. 7381
1:13 made by fire, of a sweet **s** unto the LORD. 7381
1:17 made by fire, of a sweet **s** unto the LORD. 7381
2: 2 made by fire, of a sweet **s** unto the LORD: 7381
2: 9 made by fire, of a sweet **s** unto the LORD. 7381
2:12 shall not be burnt on the altar for a sweet **s**. 7381
3: 5 made by fire, of a sweet **s** unto the LORD. 7381
3:16 of the offering made by fire for a sweet **s**: 7381
4:31 the altar for a sweet **s** unto the LORD; 7381
6:15 shall burn *it upon* the altar *for* a sweet **s**, 7381
6:21 thou offer *for* a sweet **s** unto the LORD. 7381
8:21 it *was* a burnt sacrifice for a sweet **s**, *and* 7381
8:28 they *were* consecrations for a sweet **s**: it *is* 7381
17: 6 burn the fat for a sweet **s** unto the LORD. 7381
23:13 made by fire unto the LORD *for* a sweet **s**: 7381
23:18 made by fire, of sweet **s** unto the LORD. 7381
26:31 I will not smell the **s** of your sweet odours. 7381
Nu 15: 3 to make a sweet **s** unto the LORD, of 7381
15: 7 hin *of* wine, *for* a sweet **s** unto the LORD. 7381
15:10 made by fire, of a sweet **s** unto the LORD. 7381
15:13 made by fire, of a sweet **s** unto the LORD. 7381
15:14 made by fire, of a sweet **s** unto the LORD; 7381
15:24 for a sweet **s** unto the LORD, with his 7381
18:17 by fire, for a sweet **s** unto the LORD. 7381
28: 2 made by fire, *for* a sweet **s** unto me, 7381
28: 6 was ordained in mount Sinai for a sweet **s**, 7381
28: 8 made by fire, *of* a sweet **s** unto the LORD. 7381
28:13 *for* a burnt offering *of* a sweet **s**, a sacrifice 7381
28:24 made by fire, *of* a sweet **s** unto the LORD: 7381
28:27 offering for a sweet **s** unto the LORD; 7381
29: 2 ye shall offer a burnt offering for a sweet **s** 7381
29: 6 according unto their manner, for a sweet **s**, 7381
29: 8 offering unto the LORD *for* a sweet **s**; 7381
29:13 made by fire, *of* a sweet **s** unto the LORD; 7381
29:36 made by fire, *of* a sweet **s** unto the LORD: 7381
Ecc 10: 1 of the apothecary to send forth a **stinking s**: 887
SS 1: 3 Because of the **s** of thy good ointments thy 7381
Eze 6:13 the place where they did offer sweet **s** to all 7381
16:19 hast even set it before them for a sweet **s**: 7381
20:28 there also they made their sweet **s**, and 7381
20:41 I will accept you with *your* sweet **s**, when I 7381
Joel 2:20 his **ill s** shall come up, because he hath 6709
Mt 5:13 but if the salt have **lost** his **s**, *3471*
Lk 14:34 but if the salt have **lost** his **s**, *3471*
2Co 2:14 maketh manifest the **s** of his knowledge by *3744*
2:15 For we are unto God a **sweet s** of Christ, *2175*
2:16 To the one *we are* the **s** of death unto death; *3744*
2:16 and to the other the **s** of life unto life. *3744*
Eph 5: 2 a sacrifice to God for a sweetsmelling **s**. *3744*

SAVOUREST (2) [SAVOUR]
Mt 16:23 for thou **s** not the *things* that be of God, but *5426*
Mk 8:33 for thou **s** not the *things* that be of God, but *5426*

SAVOURS (1) [SAVOUR]
Ezr 6:10 That they may offer sacrifices of **sweet s** 5208

SAVOURY (6) [SAVOUR]
Ge 27: 4 make me **s meat**, such as I love, and 4303
27: 7 make me **s meat**, that I may eat, and 4303
27: 9 I will make them **s meat** for thy father, 4303
27:14 his mother made **s meat**, such as his father 4303
27:17 she gave the **s meat** and the bread, 4303
27:31 he also had made **s meat**, and brought *it* 4303

SAW (548) [SEE, SAWED, SAWN, SAWS] See Index

SAWED (1) [SAW]
1Ki 7: 9 **s** with saws, within and without, even from 1641

SAWEST (21) [SEE] See Index

SAWN (1) [SAW]
Heb 11:37 they were **s asunder**, were tempted, *4249*

SAWS (3) [SAW]
2Sa 12:31 put *them* under **s**, and under harrows of 4050
1Ki 7: 9 sawed with **s**, within and without, even 4050
1Ch 20: 3 cut *them* with **s**, and with harrows of iron, 4050

SAY (1057) [GAINSAY, SAID, SAIDST, SAITH, SAYEST, SAYING, SAYINGS] See Index

SAYEST (40) [SAY] See Index

SAYING (1445) [SAY] See Index

SAYINGS (31) [SAY] See Index

SCAB (7) [SCABBED]
Lev 13: 2 a **s**, or bright spot, and it be in the skin of 5597
13: 6 it *is but* a **s**: and he shall wash his clothes, 4556
13: 7 if the **s** spread much abroad in the skin, 4556
13: 8 the **s** spreadeth in the skin, then the priest 4556
14:56 a rising, and for a **s**, and for a bright spot: 5597
Dt 28:27 and with the **s**, and with the itch, 1618
Isa 3:17 Therefore the Lord will **smite with a s** 5596

SCABBARD (1)
Jer 47: 6 put up thyself into thy **s**, rest, and be still. 8593

SCABBED (2) [SCAB]
Lev 21:20 be scurvy, or **s**, or hath his stones broken; 3217
22:22 maimed, or having a wen, or scurvy, or **s**, 3217

SCAFFOLD (1)
2Ch 6:13 For Solomon had made a brasen **s**, of five 3595

SCALE ARMOR See MAIL

SCALES (10)
Lev 11: 9 whatsoever hath fins and **s** in the waters, 7193
11:10 all that have not fins nor **s** in the seas, and 7193
11:12 Whatsoever hath no fins nor **s** in the waters, 7193
Dt 14: 9 all that have fins and **s** shall ye eat: 7193
14:10 hath not fins and **s** ye may not eat; 7193
Job 41:15 *His* **s** *are his* pride, shut up *together as* 650+4043
Isa 40:12 weighed the mountains in **s**, and the hills in 6425
Eze 29: 4 the fish of thy rivers to stick unto thy **s**, 7193
29: 4 the fish of thy rivers shall stick unto thy **s**. 7193
Ac 9:18 there fell from his eyes as it had been **s**: *3013*

SCALETH (1)
Pr 21:22 A wise *man* **s** the city of the mighty, and 5927

SCALL (14)
Lev 13:30 it *is* a **dry s**, *even* a leprosy upon the head 5424
13:31 if the priest look on the plague of the **s**, 5424
13:31 *that hath* the plague of the **s** seven days: 5424
13:32 *if* the **s** spread not, and there be in it no 5424
13:32 the **s** *be* not in sight deeper than the skin; 5424
13:33 be shaven, but the **s** shall he not shave; 5424
13:33 the priest shall shut up *him that hath* the **s** 5424
13:34 seventh day the priest shall look on the **s**: 5424
13:34 behold, *if* the **s** be not spread in the skin, 5424
13:35 if the **s** spread much in the skin after his 5424
13:36 behold, *if* the **s** be spread in the skin, 5424
13:37 if the **s** be in his sight at a stay, and 5424

Lev 13:37 up therein; the s is healed, he *is* clean: 5424
14:54 for all *manner of* plague of leprosy, and s, 5424

SCALP (1)
Ps 68:21 the hairy s of such a one as goeth on still in 6936

SCANT (1)
Mic 6:10 and the s measure *that is* abominable? 7332

SCAPEGOAT (4) [GOAT]
Lev 16: 8 for the LORD, and the other lot for the s. 5799
16:10 the goat, on which the lot fell to be the s, 5799
16:10 *and* to let him go for a s into the wilderness. 5799
16:26 he that let go the goat for the s shall wash 5799

SCARCE (3) [SCARCELY, SCARCENESS, SCAREST]
Ge 27:30 Jacob was yet **s gone out** from 3318+3318
Ac 14:18 And with these sayings s restrained they *3433*
27: 7 and s were come over against Cnidus, *3433*

SCARCELY (2) [SCARCE]
Ro 5: 7 For s for a righteous *man* will one die: *3433*
1Pe 4:18 And if the righteous s be saved, where shall *3433*

SCARCENESS (1) [SCARCE]
Dt 8: 9 land wherein thou shalt eat bread without s, 4544

SCAREST (1) [SCARCE]
Job 7:14 thou s me with dreams, and terrifiest me 2865

SCARLET (52)
Ge 38:28 and bound upon his hand a **s thread**, 8144
38:30 that had the **s thread** upon his hand: 8144
Ex 25: 4 s, and fine linen, and goats' *hair*, 8144+8438
26: 1 and blue, and purple, and s: 8144+8438
26:31 s, and fine twined linen *of* cunning 8144+8438
26:36 purple, and s, and fine twined linen, 8144+8438
27:16 purple, and s, and fine twined linen, 8144+8438
28: 5 and purple, and s, and fine linen. 8144+8438
28: 6 *of* purple, *of* s, and fine twined linen, 8144+8438
28: 8 purple, and s, and fine twined linen. 8144+8438
28:15 and *of* s, and *of* fine twined linen, 8144+8438
28:33 of purple, and of s, round about 8144+8438
35: 6 s, and fine linen, and goats' *hair*, 8144+8438
35:23 s, and fine linen, and goats' *hair*, and 8144+8438
35:25 of purple, *and* of s, and of fine linen. 8144+8438
35:35 s, and in fine linen, and of 8144+8438
36: 8 and blue, and purple, and s: 8144+8438
36:35 purple, and s, and fine twined linen: 8144+8438
36:37 purple, and s, and fine twined linen, 8144+8438
38:18 purple, and s, and fine twined linen: 8144+8438
38:23 and in s, and fine linen. 8144+8438+1886.1
39: 1 the blue, and purple, and s, 8144+8438+1886.1
39: 2 purple, and s, and fine twined linen. 8144+8438
39: 3 and in the s, and in the fine linen, 8144+8438
39: 5 purple, and s, and fine twined linen; 8144+8438
39: 8 purple, and s, and fine twined linen. 8144+8438
39:24 and purple, and s, *and* twined *linen*. 8144+8438
39:29 and purple, and s, *of* needlework; 8144+8438
Lev 14: 4 and cedar wood, and s, and hyssop: 8144+8438
14: 6 the s, and the hyssop, and shall dip 8144+8438
14:49 and cedar wood, and s, and hyssop: 8144+8438
14:51 the s, and the living bird, and 8144+8438
14:52 and with the hyssop, and with the s: 8144+8438
Nu 4: 8 shall spread upon them a cloth of s, 8144+8438
19: 6 s, and cast *it* into the midst of 8144+8438
Jos 2:18 thou shalt bind this line of s thread in 8144
2:21 and she bound the s line in the window. 8144
2Sa 1:24 weep over Saul, who clothed you in s, 8144
Pr 31:21 for all her household *are* clothed with s. 8144
SS 4: 3 Thy lips *are* like a thread of s, and 8144
Isa 1:18 though your sins be as s, they shall be as 8144
La 4: 5 they that were brought up in s embrace 8438
Da 5: 7 shall be clothed with s, and *have* a chain of 711
5:16 thou shalt be clothed with s, and *have* a 711
5:29 they clothed Daniel with s, and *put* a chain 711
Na 2: 3 *men is* made red, the valiant men *are* **in s**: 8529
Mt 27:28 they stripped him, and put on him a **s** robe. *2847*
Heb 9:19 and s wool, and hyssop, and sprinkled both *2847*
Rev 17: 3 I saw a woman sit upon a **s coloured** beast, *2847*
17: 4 woman was arrayed in purple and **s colour**, *2847*
18:12 and s, and all thyine wood, and all *manner* *2847*
18:16 and s, and decked with gold, and *2847*

SCATTER (38) [SCATTERED, SCATTERETH, SCATTERING]
Ge 11: 9 from thence did the LORD s them **abroad** 6327
49: 7 divide them in Jacob, and s them in Israel. 6327
Lev 26:33 I will s you among the heathen, and 2219
Nu 16:37 of the burning, and s thou the fire yonder; 2219
Dt 4:27 the LORD shall s you among the nations, 6327
28:64 the LORD shall s thee among all people, 6327
32:26 I said, I would s them **into corners**, 6284
1Ki 14:15 shall s them beyond the river, because they 2219
Ne 1: 8 I will s you **abroad** among the nations: 6327
Ps 59:11 s them by thy power; and bring them down, 5128
68:30 s thou the people *that* delight in war. 967
106:27 the nations, and to s them in the lands. 2219
144: 6 Cast forth lightning, and s them: shoot out 6327
Isa 28:25 s the cummin, and cast in the principal 2236
41:16 them away, and the whirlwind shall s them: 6327
Jer 9:16 I will s them also among the heathen, 6327
13:24 Therefore will I s them as the stubble that 6327
18:17 I will s them as *with* an east wind before 6327
23: 1 that destroy and s the sheep of my pasture! 6327
49:32 I will s into all winds them *that are* in 2219
49:36 and will s them towards all those winds; 2219
Eze 5: 2 a third *part* thou shalt s in the wind; and 2219
5:10 the whole remnant of thee will I s into all 2219
5:12 I will s a third *part* into all the winds, and 2219
6: 5 I will s your bones round about your altars. 2219
10: 2 the cherubims, and s *them* over the city. 2236
12:14 I will s toward every wind all that *are* about 2219
12:15 when I shall s them among the nations, and 6327
20:23 that *I* would s them among the heathen, and 6327
22:15 I will s thee among the heathen, and 6327
29:12 I will s the Egyptians among the nations, 6327
30:23 I will s the Egyptians among the nations, 6327
30:26 I will s the Egyptians among the nations, 6327
Da 4:14 shake off his leaves, and s his fruit: 921
11:24 he shall s among them the prey, and spoil, 967
12: 7 when *he* shall have accomplished to s 5310
Hab 3:14 they came out as a whirlwind to s me: 6327
Zec 1:21 up *their* horn over the land of Judah to s it. 2219

SCATTERED (71) [SCATTER]
Ge 11: 4 lest we be **s abroad** upon the face of 6327
11: 8 So the LORD s them **abroad** from thence 6327
Ex 5:12 So the people were **s abroad** throughout all 6327
Nu 10:35 LORD, and let thine enemies be s; 6327
Dt 30: 3 whither the LORD thy God hath s thee. 6327
1Sa 11:11 that they which remained were s, so 6327
13: 8 *to* Gilgal; and the people were s from him. 6327
13:11 Because I saw that the people were s from 5310
2Sa 18: 8 For the battle was there s over the face of 6327
22:15 he sent out arrows, and s them; lightning, 6327
1Ki 22:17 he said, I saw all Israel s upon the hills, 6327
2Ki 25: 5 and all his army were s from him. 6327
2Ch 18:16 I did see all Israel s upon the mountains, 6327
Est 3: 8 There is a certain people **s abroad** and 6340
Job 4:11 and the stout lion's whelps are **s abroad**. 6504
18:15 brimstone shall be s upon his habitation. 2219
Ps 18:14 Yea, he sent out his arrows, and s them; 6327
44:11 for meat; and hast s us among the heathen. 2219
53: 5 for God hath s the bones of him that 6340
60: 1 O God, thou hast cast us off, thou hast s us, 6555
68: 1 Let God arise, let his enemies be s: let them 6327
68:14 When the Almighty s kings in it, it was 6566
89:10 thou hast s thine enemies with thy strong 6340
92: 9 all the workers of iniquity shall be s. 6504
141: 7 Our bones are s at the grave's mouth, 6340
Isa 18: 2 swift messengers, to a nation s and peeled, 4900
18: 7 unto the LORD of hosts *of* a people s 4900
33: 3 the lifting up of thyself the nations were s. 5310
Jer 3:13 hast s thy ways to the strangers under every 6340
10:21 not prosper; and all their flocks shall be s. 6327
23: 2 Ye have s my flock, and driven them away, 6327
30:11 full end of all nations whither I have s thee, 6327
31:10 He that s Israel will gather him, and 2219
40:15 which are gathered unto thee should be s, 6327
50:17 Israel *is* a s sheep; the lions have driven 6340
52: 8 and all his army was s from him. 6327
Eze 6: 8 when ye shall be s through the countries. 2219
11:16 although I have s them among 6327
11:17 out of the countries where ye have been s, 6327
17:21 they that remain shall be s towards all 6566
20:34 you out of the countries wherein ye are s, 6327
20:41 of the countries wherein ye have been s; 6327

S

Eze 28:25 from the people among whom they are **s**, 6327
29:13 from the people whither they were **s**: 6327
34: 5 they were **s**, because *there is* no shepherd: 6327
34: 5 all the beasts of the field, when they were **s**. 6327
34: 6 my flock was **s** upon all the face of 6327
34:12 day that he is among his sheep *that are* **s**; 6567
34:12 places where they have been **s** in the cloudy 6327
34:21 with your horns, till ye have **s** them abroad; 6327
36:19 I **s** them among the heathen, and they were 6327
46:18 that my people be not **s** every man from his 6327
Joel 3: 2 whom they have **s** among the nations, and 6340
Na 3:18 *dust:* thy people is **s** upon the mountains, 6335
Hab 3: 6 the everlasting mountains were **s**, 6327
Zec 1:19 These *are* the horns which have **s** Judah, 2219
1:21 These *are* the horns which have **s** Judah, so 2219
7:14 I **s** them **with a whirlwind** among all 5590
13: 7 the shepherd, and the sheep shall be **s**: 6327
Mt 9:36 because they fainted, and were **s abroad**, *4496*
26:31 the sheep of the flock shall be **s abroad**. *1287*
Mk 14:27 the shepherd, and the sheep shall be **s**. *1287*
Lk 1:51 he hath **s** the proud in the imagination of *1287*
Jn 11:52 the children of God that were **s abroad**. *1287*
16:32 yea, is now come, that ye shall be **s**, *4650*
Ac 5:36 obeyed him, were **s**, and brought to nought. *1262*
8: 1 they were all **s abroad** throughout *1289*
8: 4 Therefore they that were **s abroad** went *1289*
11:19 Now they which were **s abroad** upon *1289*
Jas 1: 1 tribes which are **s abroad**, *1290+1722+3588*
1Pe 1: 1 to the strangers **s throughout** Pontus, *1290*

SCATTERETH (10) [SCATTER]

Job 37:11 the thick cloud: he **s** his bright cloud: 6327
38:24 *which* **s** the east wind upon the earth? 6327
Ps 147:16 like wool: he **s** the hoarfrost like ashes. 6340
Pr 11:24 There is that **s**, and yet increaseth; and 6340
20: 8 of judgment **s** *away* all evil with his eyes. 2219
20:26 A wise king **s** the wicked, and bringeth 2219
Isa 24: 1 and **s abroad** the inhabitants thereof. 6327
Mt 12:30 and he that gathereth not with me **s abroad**. *4650*
Lk 11:23 and he that gathereth not with me **s**. *4650*
Jn 10:12 the wolf catcheth them, and **s** the sheep. *4650*

SCATTERING (1) [SCATTER]

Isa 30:30 *with* **s**, and tempest, and hailstones. 5311

SCEPTRE (15) [SCEPTRES]

Ge 49:10 The **s** shall not depart from Judah, nor a 7626
Nu 24:17 a **S** shall rise out of Israel, and shall smite 7626
Est 4:11 whom the king shall hold out the golden **s**, 8275
5: 2 the king held out to Esther the golden **s** that 8275
5: 2 drew near, and touched the top of the **s**. 8275
8: 4 the king held out the golden **s** toward 8275
Ps 45: 6 the **s** of thy kingdom *is* a right sceptre. 7626
45: 6 the sceptre of thy kingdom *is* a right **s**. 7626
Isa 14: 5 staff of the wicked, *and* the **s** of the rulers. 7626
Eze 19:14 that she hath no strong rod *to be* a **s** to rule. 7626
Am 1: 5 him that holdeth the **s** from the house of 7626
1: 8 him that holdeth the **s** from Ashkelon, and 7626
Zec 10:11 and the **s** of Egypt shall depart away. 7626
Heb 1: 8 a **s** of righteousness *is* the sceptre of thy *4464*
1: 8 a sceptre of righteousness *is* the **s** of thy *4464*

SCEPTRES (1) [SCEPTRE]

Eze 19:11 she had strong rods for the **s** of them that 7626

SCEVA (1)

Ac 19:14 And there were seven sons of *one* **S**, a Jew, *4630*

SCHEMES See MISCHIEF; MISCHIEFS

SCHEMING See SLEIGHT

SCHISM (1)

1Co 12:25 That there should be no **s** in the body; but *4978*

SCHOLAR (2)

1Ch 25: 8 the small as the great, the teacher as the **s**. 8527
Mal 2:12 the master and the **s**, out of the tabernacles 6030

SCHOOL (1) [SCHOOLMASTER]

Ac 19: 9 disputing daily in the **s** of one Tyrannus. *4981*

SCHOOLMASTER (2) [MASTER, SCHOOL]

Gal 3:24 Wherefore the law was our **s** *to bring us* *3807*
3:25 faith is come, we are no longer under a **s**. *3807*

SCIENCE (2)

Da 1: 4 understanding **s**, and such as *had* ability in 4093
1Ti 6:20 and oppositions of **s** falsely so called: *1108*

SCOFF (1) [SCOFFERS]

Hab 1:10 they shall **s** at the kings, and the princes 7046

SCOFFERS (1) [SCOFF]

2Pe 3: 3 that there shall come in the last days **s**, *1703*

SCORCH (1) [SCORCHED]

Rev 16: 8 *power* was given unto him to **s** men with *2739*

SCORCHED (3) [SCORCH]

Mt 13: 6 And when the sun was up, they were **s**; and *2739*
Mk 4: 6 But when the sun was up, it was **s**; and *2739*
Rev 16: 9 And men were **s** *with* great heat, and *2739*

SCORCHING See VEHEMENT

SCORN (16) [SCORNER, SCORNERS, SCORNEST, SCORNETH, SCORNFUL, SCORNING]

2Ki 19:21 hath despised thee, *and* **laughed** thee **to s**; 3932
2Ch 30:10 they **laughed** them **to s**, and mocked them. 7832
Ne 2:19 heard *it,* they **laughed** us **to s**, and 3932
Est 3: 6 he thought **s** to lay hands on Mordecai alone; 959
Job 12: 4 the just upright *man is* **laughed to s**. 7814
16:20 My friends **s** me: *but* mine eye poureth out 3887
22:19 are glad: and the innocent **laugh** them **to s**. 3932
Ps 22: 7 All they that see me **laugh** me **to s**: 3932
44:13 a **s** and a derision to them that are round 3933
79: 4 a **s** and derision to them that are round 3933
Isa 37:22 hath despised thee, *and* **laughed** thee **to s**; 3932
Eze 23:32 thou shalt be **laughed to s** and had in 6712
Hab 1:10 and the princes *shall be* a **s** unto them: 4890
Mt 9:24 but sleepeth. And they **laughed him to s**. *2606*
Mk 5:40 And they **laughed** him **to s**. But when he *2606*
Lk 8:53 And they **laughed** him **to s**, knowing that *2606*

SCORNER (11) [SCORN]

Pr 9: 7 He that reproveth a **s** getteth to himself 3887
9: 8 Reprove not a **s**, lest he hate thee: rebuke a 3887
13: 1 but a **s** heareth not rebuke. 3887
14: 6 A **s** seeketh wisdom, and *findeth it* not: but 3887
15:12 A **s** loveth not one that reproveth him: 3887
19:25 Smite a **s**, and the simple will beware: and 3887
21:11 When the **s** is punished, the simple is made 3887
21:24 Proud *and* haughty **s** *is* his name, 3887
22:10 Cast out the **s**, and contention shall go out; 3887
24: 9 *is* sin: and the **s** *is* an abomination to men. 3887
Isa 29:20 the **s** is consumed, and all that watch for 3887

SCORNERS (4) [SCORN]

Pr 1:22 the **s** delight in their scorning, and 3887
3:34 Surely he scorneth the **s**: but he giveth 3887
19:29 Judgments are prepared for **s**, and 3887
Hos 7: 5 of wine; he stretched out his hand with **s**. 3945

SCORNEST (2) [SCORN]

Pr 9:12 but *if* thou **s**, thou alone shalt bear *it.* 3887
Eze 16:31 hast not been as a harlot, in that *thou* **s** hire; 7046

SCORNETH (4) [SCORN]

Job 39: 7 He **s** the multitude of the city, 7832
39:18 on high, she **s** the horse and his rider. 7832
Pr 3:34 Surely he **s** the scorners: but he giveth 3887
19:28 An ungodly witness **s** judgment: and 3887

SCORNFUL (3) [SCORN]

Ps 1: 1 of sinners, nor sitteth in the seat of the **s**. 3887
Pr 29: 8 **S** men bring a city into a snare: but 3944
Isa 28:14 hear the word of the LORD, ye **s** men, 3944

SCORNING (3) [SCORN]

Job 34: 7 *is* like Job, *who* drinketh up **s** like water? 3933
Ps 123: 4 Our soul is exceedingly filled *with* the **s** of 3933
Pr 1:22 the scorners delight in their **s**, and 3944

SCORPION (2) [SCORPIONS]

Lk 11:12 if he shall ask an egg, will he offer him a **s**? *4651*
Rev 9: 5 and their torment *was* as the torment of a **s**, *4651*

SCORPION PASS See MAALEH-ACRABBIM

SCORPIONS (9) [SCORPION]

Dt 8:15 **s**, and drought, where *there was* no water; 6137

1Ki 12:11 with whips, but I will chastise you with **s**. 6137
12:14 with whips, but I will chastise you with **s**. 6137
2Ch 10:11 with whips, but I *will chastise you* with **s**. 6137
10:14 with whips, but I *will chastise you* with **s**. 6137
Eze 2: 6 *be* with thee, and thou dost dwell among **s**: 6137
Lk 10:19 unto you power to tread on serpents and **s**, *4651*
Rev 9: 3 as the **s** of the earth have power. *4651*
9:10 And they had tails like unto **s**, and *4651*

SCOUNDREL See NAUGHTINESS; NAUGHTY

SCOURED (1)
Lev 6:28 it shall be both **s**, and rinsed in water. 4838

SCOURGE (12) [SCOURGED, SCOURGES, SCOURGETH, SCOURGING, SCOURGINGS]
Job 5:21 Thou shalt be hid from the **s** of the tongue: 7752
9:23 If the **s** slay suddenly, he will laugh at 7752
Isa 10:26 the LORD of hosts shall stir up a **s** for him 7752
28:15 when the overflowing **s** shall pass through, 7752
28:18 when the overflowing **s** shall pass through, 7752
Mt 10:17 and they will **s** you in their synagogues; *3146*
20:19 and to **s**, and to crucify *him:* and the third *3146*
23:34 *some* of them shall ye **s** in your *3146*
Mk 10:34 and shall **s** him, and shall spit upon him, *3146*
Lk 18:33 And they shall **s** *him,* and put him to death: *3146*
Jn 2:15 And when he had made a **s** of small cords, *5416*
Ac 22:25 lawful for you to **s** a man *that is* a Roman, *3147*

SCOURGED (4) [SCOURGE]
Lev 19:20 she shall be **s**, they shall not be put to 1244
Mt 27:26 and when he had **s** Jesus, he delivered *him* *5417*
Mk 15:15 when he had **s** *him,* to be crucified. *5417*
Jn 19: 1 therefore took Jesus, and **s** *him.* *3146*

SCOURGES (1) [SCOURGE]
Jos 23:13 and **s** in your sides, and thorns in your eyes, 7850

SCOURGETH (1) [SCOURGE]
Heb 12: 6 and **s** every son whom he receiveth. *3146*

SCOURGING (1) [SCOURGE]
Ac 22:24 and bade that he should be examined by **s**; *3148*

SCOURGINGS (1) [SCOURGE]
Heb 11:36 others had trial of *cruel* mockings and **s**, *3148*

SCRABLED (1)
1Sa 21:13 **s** on the doors of the gate, and let his spittle 8427

SCRAPE (3) [SCRAPED]
Lev 14:41 they shall pour out the dust that they **s off** 7096
Job 2: 8 he took him a potsherd to **s** himself withal; 1623
Eze 26: 4 I will also **s** her dust from her, and 5500

SCRAPED (2) [SCRAPE]
Lev 14:41 he shall **cause** the house **to be s** within 7106
14:43 after he hath **s** the house, and after it is 7096

SCRIBE (52) [SCRIBE'S, SCRIBES]
2Sa 8:17 *were* the priests; and Seraiah *was* the **s**; 5608
20:25 Sheva *was* **s**: and Zadok and Abiathar *were* 5608
2Ki 12:10 that the king's **s** and the high priest came 5608
18:18 Shebna the **s**, and Joah the son of Asaph 5608
18:37 Shebna the **s**, and Joah the son of Asaph 5608
19: 2 Shebna the **s**, and the elders of the priests, 5608
22: 3 the son of Meshullam, the **s**, *to* the house of 5608
22: 8 the high priest said unto Shaphan the **s**, 5608
22: 9 Shaphan the **s** came to the king, and 5608
22:10 Shaphan the **s** shewed the king, saying, 5608
22:12 Shaphan the **s**, and Asahiah a servant of 5608
25:19 in the city, and the principal **s** of the host, 5608
1Ch 18:16 *were* the priests; and Shavsha *was* **s**; 5608
24: 6 Shemaiah the son of Nethaneel the **s**, *one* of 5608
27:32 uncle *was* a counseller, a wise man, and a **s**: 5608
2Ch 24:11 the king's **s** and the high priest's officer 5608
26:11 of their account by the hand of Jeiel the **s** 5608
34:15 and said to Shaphan the **s**, 5608
34:18 Shaphan the **s** told the king, saying, 5608
34:20 Shaphan the **s**, and Asaiah a servant of 5608
Ezr 4: 8 Shimshai the **s** wrote a letter against 5613
4: 9 Shimshai the **s**, and the rest of their 5613
4:17 *to* Shimshai the **s**, and *to* the rest of their 5613
4:23 Shimshai the **s**, and their companions, 5613
7: 6 he *was* a ready **s** in the law of Moses, 5608
7:11 the **s**, *even* a scribe of the words of 5608
7:11 *even* a **s** of the words of 5608
7:12 a **s** of the law of the God of heaven, 5613
7:21 the **s** of the law of the God of heaven, 5613
Ne 8: 1 they spake unto Ezra the **s** to bring the book 5608
8: 4 Ezra the **s** stood upon a pulpit of wood, 5608
8: 9 Ezra the priest the **s**, and the Levites that 5608
8:13 the priests, and the Levites, unto Ezra the **s**, 5608
12:26 the governor, and of Ezra the priest, the **s**. 5608
12:36 man of God, and Ezra the **s** before them. 5608
13:13 Zadok the **s**, and of the Levites, Pedaiah: 5608
Isa 33:18 Where *is* the **s**? where *is* the receiver? 5608
36: 3 Shebna the **s**, and Joah, Asaph's son, 5608
36:22 Shebna the **s**, and Joah, the son of Asaph, 5608
37: 2 Shebna the **s**, and the elders of the priests 5608
Jer 36:10 of Gemariah the son of Shaphan the **s**, 5608
36:12 *even* Elishama the **s**, and Delaiah the son of 5608
36:20 the roll in the chamber of Elishama the **s**, 5608
36:26 to take Baruch the **s** and Jeremiah 5608
36:32 gave it to Baruch the **s**, the son of Neriah; 5608
37:15 *in* prison *in* the house of Jonathan the **s**: 5608
37:20 not to return *to* the house of Jonathan the **s**, 5608
52:25 the principal **s** of the host, who mustered 5608
Mt 8:19 And a certain **s** came, and said unto him, *1122*
13:52 Therefore every **s** *which is* instructed unto *1122*
Mk 12:32 And the **s** said unto him, Well, Master, *1122*
1Co 1:20 where *is* the **s**? where *is* the disputer of this *1122*

SCRIBE'S (2) [SCRIBE]
Jer 36:12 *into* the king's house, into the **s** chamber: 5608
36:21 he took it out of Elishama the **s** chamber. 5608

SCRIBES (68) [SCRIBE]
1Ki 4: 3 Elihoreph and Ahiah, the sons of Shisha, **s**; 5608
1Ch 2:55 the families of the **s** which dwelt at Jabez; 5608
2Ch 34:13 of the Levites *there were* **s**, and officers, 5608
Est 3:12 were the king's **s** called on the thirteenth 5608
8: 9 were the king's **s** called at that time in 5608
Jer 8: 8 certainly in vain made he *it;* the pen of the **s** 5608
Mt 2: 4 chief priests and **s** of the people together, *1122*
5:20 shall exceed *the righteousness* of the **s** *1122*
7:29 as *one* having authority, and not as the **s**. *1122*
9: 3 certain of the **s** said within themselves, *1122*
12:38 Then certain of the **s** and of the Pharisees *1122*
15: 1 Then came to Jesus **s** and Pharisees, *1122*
16:21 *things* of the elders and chief priests and **s**, *1122*
17:10 then say the **s** that Elias must first come? *1122*
20:18 unto the chief priests and *unto the* **s**, *1122*
21:15 and **s** saw the wonderful *things* that he did, *1122*
23: 2 The **s** and the Pharisees sit in Moses' seat: *1122*
23:13 woe unto you, **s** and Pharisees, hypocrites! *1122*
23:14 Woe unto you, **s** and Pharisees, hypocrites! *1122*
23:15 Woe unto you, **s** and Pharisees, hypocrites! *1122*
23:23 Woe unto you, **s** and Pharisees, hypocrites! *1122*
23:25 Woe unto you, **s** and Pharisees, hypocrites! *1122*
23:27 Woe unto you, **s** and Pharisees, hypocrites! *1122*
23:29 Woe unto you, **s** and Pharisees, hypocrites! *1122*
23:34 unto you prophets, and wise *men,* and **s**: *1122*
26: 3 and the **s**, and the elders of the people, *1122*
26:57 where the **s** and the elders were assembled. *1122*
27:41 the chief priests mocking *him,* with the **s** *1122*
Mk 1:22 as *one* that had authority, and not as the **s**. *1122*
2: 6 But there were certain of the **s** sitting there, *1122*
2:16 And when the **s** and Pharisees saw him eat *1122*
3:22 And the **s** which came down from *1122*
7: 1 and certain of the **s**, which came from *1122*
7: 5 Then the Pharisees and **s** asked him, *1122*
8:31 of the elders, and *of* the chief priests, and **s**, *1122*
9:11 Why say the **s** that Elias must first come? *1122*
9:14 and *the* **s** questioning with them. *1122*
9:16 And he asked the **s**, What question ye with *1122*
10:33 unto the chief priests, and unto the **s**; *1122*
11:18 And the **s** and chief priests heard *it,* and *1122*
11:27 the chief priests, and the **s**, and the elders, *1122*
12:28 And one of the **s** came, and having heard *1122*
12:35 How say the **s** that Christ is the Son of *1122*
12:38 Beware of the **s**, which love to go in long *1122*
14: 1 the **s** sought how they might take him by *1122*
14:43 the chief priests and the **s** and the elders. *1122*
14:53 all the chief priests and the elders and the **s**. *1122*
15: 1 with the elders and **s** and the whole council, *1122*
15:31 mocking said among themselves with the **s**, *1122*
Lk 5:21 And the **s** and the Pharisees began to *1122*
5:30 But their **s** and Pharisees murmured against *1122*
6: 7 And the **s** and Pharisees watched him, *1122*

Lk 9:22 of the elders and chief priests and s, 1122
11:44 Woe unto you, s and Pharisees, hypocrites! 1122
11:53 the s and the Pharisees began to urge *him* 1122
15: 2 And the Pharisees and s murmured, saying, 1122
19:47 But the chief priests and the s and the chief 1122
20: 1 and the s came upon *him* with the elders, 1122
20:19 the s the same hour sought to lay hands on 1122
20:39 Then certain of the s answering said, 1122
20:46 Beware of the s, which desire to walk in 1122
22: 2 and s sought how they might kill him; 1122
22:66 the chief priests and the s came together, 1122
23:10 And the chief priests and s stood and 1122
Jn 8: 3 And the s and Pharisees brought unto him a 1122
Ac 4: 5 that their rulers, and elders, and s, 1122
6:12 and the s, and came upon *him,* and 1122
23: 9 the s *that were* of the Pharisees' part arose, 1122

SCRIP (7)
1Sa 17:40 a shepherd's bag which he had, even in a s; 3219
Mt 10:10 Nor s for *your* journey, neither two coats, *4082*
Mk 6: 8 no s, no bread, no money in *their* purse: *4082*
Lk 9: 3 neither staves, nor s, neither bread, *4082*
10: 4 Carry neither purse, nor s, nor shoes: and *4082*
22:35 I sent you without purse, and s, and shoes, *4082*
22:36 a purse, let him take *it,* and likewise *his* s: *4082*

SCRIPTURE (32) [SCRIPTURES]
Da 10:21 I will shew thee that which is noted in the s 3791
Mk 12:10 And have ye not read this s; The stone *1124*
15:28 And the s was fulfilled, which saith, *1124*
Lk 4:21 This day is this s fulfilled in your ears. *1124*
Jn 2:22 and they believed the s, and the word which *1124*
7:38 He that believeth on me, as the s hath said, *1124*
7:42 Hath not the s said, That Christ cometh of *1124*
10:35 of God came, and the s cannot be broken; *1124*
13:18 but that the s may be fulfilled, He that *1124*
17:12 of perdition; that the s might be fulfilled. *1124*
19:24 that the s might be fulfilled, which saith, *1124*
19:28 that the s might be fulfilled, saith, I thirst. *1124*
19:36 were done, that the s should be fulfilled, *1124*
19:37 And again another s saith, They shall look *1124*
20: 9 For as yet they knew not the s, that he must *1124*
Ac 1:16 this s must needs have been fulfilled, *1124*
8:32 The place of the s which he read was this, *1124*
8:35 and began at the same s, and preached unto *1124*
Ro 4: 3 For what saith the s? Abraham believed *1124*
9:17 For the s saith unto Pharaoh, Even for this *1124*
10:11 For the s saith, Whosoever believeth on *1124*
11: 2 Wot ye not what the s saith of Elias? how *1124*
Gal 3: 8 And the s, foreseeing that God would *1124*
3:22 But the s hath concluded all under sin, *1124*
4:30 Nevertheless what saith the s? Cast out *1124*
1Ti 5:18 For the s saith, Thou shalt not muzzle *1124*
2Ti 3:16 All s *is* given by inspiration of God, and *1124*
Jas 2: 8 If ye fulfil the royal law according to the s, *1124*
2:23 And the s was fulfilled which saith, *1124*
4: 5 Do ye think that the s saith in vain, *1124*
1Pe 2: 6 Wherefore also it is contained in the s, *1124*
2Pe 1:20 that no prophecy of the s is of *any* private *1124*

SCRIPTURES (21) [SCRIPTURE]
Mt 21:42 saith unto them, Did ye never read in the s, *1124*
22:29 unto them, Ye do err, not knowing the s, *1124*
26:54 *But* how then shall the s be fulfilled, *1124*
26:56 that the s of the prophets might be fulfilled. *1124*
Mk 12:24 therefore err, because ye know not the s, *1124*
14:49 ye took me not: but the s must be fulfilled. *1124*
Lk 24:27 he expounded unto them in all the s *1124*
24:32 the way, and while he opened to us the s? *1124*
24:45 that *they* might understand the s, *1124*
Jn 5:39 Search the S; for in them ye think ye have *1124*
Ac 17: 2 days reasoned with them out of the s, *1124*
17:11 and searched the s daily, whether those *1124*
18:24 an eloquent man, *and* mighty in the s, *1124*
18:28 shewing by the s that Jesus was Christ. *1124*
Ro 1: 2 afore by his prophets in the holy s,) *1124*
15: 4 and comfort of the s might have hope. *1124*
16:26 and by the s of the prophets, *1124*
1Co 15: 3 Christ died for our sins according to the s; *1124*
15: 4 rose *again* the third day according to the s: *1124*
2Ti 3:15 from a child thou hast known the holy s, *1121*
2Pe 3:16 unstable wrest, as *they do* also the other s, *1124*

SCROLE (2)
Isa 34: 4 the heavens shall be rolled together as a s: 5612
Rev 6:14 And the heaven departed as a s when it is *975*

SCROLL See BOOK; SCROLE; VOLUME

SCUM (5)
Eze 24: 6 to the pot whose s *is* therein, and 2457
24: 6 *is* therein, and whose s is not gone out of it! 2457
24:11 in it, *that* the s of it may be consumed. 2457
24:12 and her great s went not forth out of her: 2457
24:12 forth out of her: her s *shall be* in the fire. 2457

SCURVY (2)
Lev 21:20 or be s, or scabbed, or hath his stones 1618
22:22 maimed, or having a wen, or s, or scabbed, 1618

SCYTHIAN (1)
Col 3:11 barbarian, S, bond *nor* free: *4658*

SEA (400) [SEAFARING, SEAS]
Ge 1:26 them have dominion over the fish of the s, 3220
1:28 have dominion over the fish of the s, and 3220
9: 2 the earth, and upon all the fishes of the s; 3220
14: 3 in the vale of Siddim, which *is* the salt s. 3220
22:17 and as the sand which *is* upon the s shore; 3220
32:12 make thy seed as the sand of the s, 3220
41:49 Joseph gathered corn as the sand of the s, 3220
49:13 Zebulun shall dwell at the haven of the s; 3220
Ex 10:19 the locusts, and cast them into the Red s; 3220
13:18 the way of the wilderness of the Red s: 3220
14: 2 between Migdol and the s, over against 3220
14: 2 before it shall ye encamp by the s. 3220
14: 9 overtook them encamping by the s, 3220
14:16 stretch out thine hand over the s, and 3220
14:16 on dry *ground* through the midst of the s. 3220
14:21 Moses stretched out his hand over the s; 3220
14:21 the LORD caused the s to go *back* by a 3220
14:21 made the s dry *land,* and the waters were 3220
14:22 into the midst of the s upon the dry *ground:* 3220
14:23 went in after them to the midst of the s, 3220
14:26 Stretch out thine hand over the s, 3220
14:27 Moses stretched forth his hand over the s, 3220
14:27 the s returned to his strength when 3220
14:27 the Egyptians in the midst of the s. 3220
14:28 all the host of Pharaoh that came into the s 3220
14:29 walked upon dry *land* in the midst of the s; 3220
14:30 Israel saw the Egyptians dead upon the s 3220
15: 1 and his rider hath he thrown into the s. 3220
15: 4 and his host hath he cast into the s: 3220
15: 4 captains also are drowned in the Red s. 3220
15: 8 depths were congealed in the heart of the s. 3220
15:10 blow with thy wind, the s covered them: 3220
15:19 and with his horsemen into the s, 3220
15:19 again the waters of the s upon them; 3220
15:19 went on dry *land* in the midst of the s. 3220
15:21 and his rider hath he thrown into the s. 3220
15:22 So Moses brought Israel from the Red s, 3220
20:11 the s, and all that in them *is,* and rested 3220
23:31 I will set thy bounds from the Red s even 3220
23:31 Red sea even unto the s of the Philistines, 3220
Nu 11:22 shall all the fish of the s be gathered 3220
11:31 brought quails from the s, and let *them* fall 3220
13:29 the Canaanites dwell by the s, and by 3220
14:25 *into* the wilderness *by* the way of the Red s. 3220
21: 4 from mount Hor *by* the way of the Red s, 3220
21:14 What he did in the **Red** s, and *in* the brooks 5492
33: 8 passed through the midst of the s into 3220
33:10 from Elim, and encamped by the Red s. 3220
33:11 they removed from the Red s, and 3220
34: 3 be the outmost coast of the salt s eastward: 3220
34: 5 and the goings out of it shall be at the s. 3220
34: 6 you shall even have the great s for a border: 3220
34: 7 from the great s you shall point out for you 3220
34:11 shall reach unto the side of the s of 3220
34:12 and the goings out of it shall be *at* the salt s: 3220
Dt 1: 1 in the plain over against the Red *s,* between NIH
1: 7 the vale, and in the south, and by the s side, 3220
1:40 into the wilderness *by* the way of the Red s. 3220
2: 1 into the wilderness *by* the way of the Red s, 3220
3:17 Chinnereth even unto the s of the plain, 3220
3:17 *even* the salt s, under Ashdoth-pisgah 3220
4:49 even unto the s of the plain, under 3220
11: 4 how he made the water of the Red s to 3220

Dt 11:24 even unto the uttermost **s** shall your coast 3220
30:13 Neither *is* it beyond the **s**, that *thou* 3220
30:13 Who shall go over the **s** for us, and bring it 3220
34: 2 and all the land of Judah, unto the utmost **s**, 3220
Jos 1: 4 unto the great **s** *toward* the going down of 3220
2:10 dried up the water of the Red **s** for you, 3220
3:16 those that came down toward the **s** of 3220
3:16 *even* the salt **s**, failed, *and* were cut off: 3220
4:23 as the LORD your God did to the Red **s**, 3220
5: 1 of the Canaanites, which *were* by the **s**, 3220
9: 1 in all the coasts of the great **s** over against 3220
11: 4 *even* as the sand that *is* upon the **s** shore in 3220
12: 3 *from* the plain to the **s** of Cinneroth on 3220
12: 3 unto the **s** of the plain, *even* the salt sea on 3220
12: 3 sea of the plain, *even* the salt **s** on the east, 3220
13:27 *even* unto the edge of the **s** of Cinnereth on 3220
15: 2 border was from the shore of the salt **s**, 3220
15: 4 the goings out of that coast were at the **s**: 3220
15: 5 the east border *was* the salt **s**, *even* unto 3220
15: 5 bay of the **s** at the uttermost part of Jordan: 3220
15:11 the goings out of the border were at the **s**. 3220
15:12 the west border *was* to the great **s**, and 3220
15:46 From Ekron even unto the **s**, all that *lay* 3220
15:47 and the great **s**, and the border *thereof*. 3220
16: 3 and the goings out thereof are at the **s**. 3220
16: 6 the border went out toward the **s** *to* 3220
16: 8 and the goings out thereof were at the **s**. 3220
17: 9 and the outgoings of it were at the **s**: 3220
17:10 *it was* Manasseh's, and the **s** is his border; 3220
18:14 compassed the corner of the **s** southward, 3220
18:19 bay of the salt **s** at the south end of Jordan: 3220
19:11 their border went up toward the **s**, and 3220
19:29 the outgoings thereof are at the **s** from 3220
23: 4 cut off, even *unto* the great **s** westward. 3220
24: 6 you came unto the **s**; and the Egyptians 3220
24: 6 with chariots and horsemen *unto* the Red **s**. 3220
24: 7 brought the **s** upon them, and 3220
Jdg 5:17 Asher continued on the **s** shore, and 3220
7:12 as the sand by the **s** side for multitude. 3220
11:16 through the wilderness unto the Red **s**, 3220
1Sa 13: 5 people as the sand which *is* on the **s** shore 3220
2Sa 17:11 as the sand that *is* by the **s** for multitude; 3220
22:16 the channels of the **s** appeared, 3220
1Ki 4:20 as the sand which *is* by the **s** in multitude, 3220
4:29 *even* as the sand that *is* on the **s** shore. 3220
5: 9 bring *them* down from Lebanon unto the **s**: 3220
5: 9 I will convey them by **s** *in* flotes unto 3220
7:23 he made a molten **s**, ten cubits from the one 3220
7:24 in a cubit, compassing the **s** round about: 3220
7:25 the **s** *was set* above upon them, and all their 3220
7:39 he set the **s** on the right side of the house 3220
7:44 And one **s**, and twelve oxen under the sea; 3220
7:44 And one sea, and twelve oxen under the **s**; 3220
9:26 on the shore of the Red **s**, in the land of 3220
9:27 shipmen that had knowledge of the **s**, 3220
10:22 For the king had at **s** a navy of Tharshish 3220
18:43 his servant, Go up now, look toward the **s**. 3220
18:44 there ariseth a little cloud out of the **s**, 3220
2Ki 14:25 entering of Hamath unto the **s** of the plain, 3220
16:17 took down the **s** from off the brasen oxen 3220
25:13 the brasen **s** that *was* in the house of 3220
25:16 one **s**, and the bases which Solomon had 3220
1Ch 16:32 Let the **s** roar, and the fulness thereof: 3220
18: 8 wherewith Solomon made the brasen **s**, and 3220
2Ch 2:16 we will bring it to thee *in* flotes by **s** *to* 3220
4: 2 Also he made a molten **s** of ten cubits from 3220
4: 3 in a cubit, compassing the **s** round about. 3220
4: 4 the **s** *was set* above upon them, and all their 3220
4: 6 but the **s** *was* for the priests to wash in. 3220
4:10 he set the **s** on the right side of the east end, 3220
4:15 One **s**, and twelve oxen under it. 3220
8:17 to Eloth, at the **s** side in the land of Edom. 3220
8:18 and servants that had knowledge of the **s**; 3220
20: 2 thee from beyond the **s** on this side Syria; 3220
Ezr 3: 7 to bring cedar trees from Lebanon to the **s** 3220
Ne 9: 9 and heardest their cry by the Red **s**; 3220
9:11 thou didst divide the **s** before them, so 3220
9:11 that they went through the midst of the **s** on 3220
Est 10: 1 upon the land, and *upon* the isles of the **s**. 3220
Job 6: 3 it would be heavier than the sand of the **s**: 3220
7:12 *Am* I a **s**, or a whale, that thou settest a 3220
9: 8 and treadeth upon the waves of the **s**. 3220
11: 9 than the earth, and broader than the **s**. 3220
12: 8 the fishes of the **s** shall declare unto thee. 3220
14:11 *As* the waters fail from the **s**, and the flood 3220
26:12 He divideth the **s** with his power, and 3220
28:14 not in me: and the **s** saith, *It is* not with me. 3220
36:30 upon it, and covereth the bottom of the **s**. 3220
38: 8 Or *who* shut up the **s** with doors, when it 3220
38:16 Hast thou entered into the springs of the **s**? 3220
41:31 he maketh the **s** like a pot of ointment. 3220
Ps 8: 8 the fish of the **s**, *and whatsoever* passeth 3220
33: 7 He gathereth the waters of the **s** together as 3220
46: 2 be carried into the midst of the **s**; 3220
65: 5 and of them that are afar off *upon* the **s**: 3220
66: 6 He turned the **s** into dry *land*: they went 3220
68:22 *my people* again from the depths of the **s**: 3220
72: 8 He shall have dominion also from **s** to sea, 3220
72: 8 He shall have dominion also from sea to **s**, 3220
74:13 Thou didst divide the **s** by thy strength: 3220
77:19 Thy way *is* in the **s**, and thy path in 3220
78:13 He divided the **s**, and caused them to pass 3220
78:27 feathered fowls like as the sand of the **s**: 3220
78:53 but the **s** overwhelmed their enemies. 3220
80:11 She sent out her boughs unto the **s**, and 3220
89: 9 Thou rulest the raging of the **s**: when 3220
89:25 I will set his hand also in the **s**, and 3220
93: 4 *yea, than* the mighty waves of the **s**. 3220
95: 5 The **s** *is* his, and he made it: and his hands 3220
96:11 let the **s** roar, and the fulness thereof. 3220
98: 7 Let the **s** roar, and the fulness thereof; 3220
104:25 *So is* this great and wide **s**, wherein *are* 3220
106: 7 provoked *him* at the **s**, *even* at the Red sea. 3220
106: 7 provoked *him* at the sea, *even* at the Red **s**. 3220
106: 9 He rebuked the Red **s** also, and it was dried 3220
106:22 of Ham, *and* terrible *things* by the Red **s**. 3220
107:23 They that go down to the **s** in ships, that do 3220
114: 3 The **s** saw *it*, and fled: Jordan was driven 3220
114: 5 What ailed thee, O thou **s**, that thou 3220
136:13 To him which divided the Red **s** into parts: 3220
136:15 and his host in the Red **s**: 3220
139: 9 *and* dwell in the uttermost parts of the **s**; 3220
146: 6 and earth, the **s**, and all that therein is: 3220
Pr 8:29 When he gave to the **s** his decree, that 3220
23:34 as he that lieth down in the midst of the **s**, 3220
30:19 the way of a ship in the midst of the **s**; and 3220
Ecc 1: 7 All the rivers run into the **s**; yet the sea *is* 3220
1: 7 rivers run into the sea; yet the **s** *is* not full; 3220
Isa 5:30 roar against them like the roaring of the **s**: 3220
9: 1 grievously afflict *her by* the way of the **s**, 3220
10:22 thy people Israel be as the sand of the **s**, 3220
10:26 *as* his rod *was* upon the **s**, so shall he lift it 3220
11: 9 of the LORD, as the waters cover the **s**. 3220
11:11 from Hamath, and from the islands of the **s**. 3220
11:15 utterly destroy the tongue of the Egyptian **s**; 3220
16: 8 are stretched out, they are gone over the **s**. 3220
18: 2 That sendeth ambassadors by the **s**, even in 3220
19: 5 the waters shall fail from the **s**, and 3220
21: 1 The burden of the desert of the **s**. 3220
23: 2 that pass over the **s**, have replenished. 3220
23: 4 for the **s** hath spoken, *even* the strength of 3220
23: 4 *even* the strength of the **s**, saying, I travail 3220
23:11 He stretched out his hand over the **s**, 3220
24:14 they shall cry aloud from the **s**. 3220
24:15 LORD God of Israel in the isles of the **s**. 3220
27: 1 and he shall slay the dragon that *is* in the **s**. 3220
42:10 ye that go down to the **s**, and all that is 3220
43:16 which maketh a way in the **s**, and a path in 3220
48:18 and thy righteousness as the waves of the **s**: 3220
50: 2 behold, at my rebuke I dry up the **s**, I make 3220
51:10 *Art* thou not it which hath dried the **s**, 3220
51:10 that hath made the depths of the **s** a way for 3220
51:15 that divided the **s**, whose waves roared: 3220
57:20 the wicked *are* like the troubled **s**, when it 3220
60: 5 the abundance of the **s** shall be converted 3220
63:11 out of the **s** with the shepherd of his flock? 3220
Jer 5:22 the bound of the **s** *by* a perpetual decree, 3220
6:23 their voice roareth like the **s**; and they ride 3220
25:22 kings of the isles which *are* beyond the **s**, 3220
27:19 concerning the **s**, and concerning the bases, 3220
31:35 which divideth the **s** when the waves 3220
33:22 neither the sand of the **s** measured: 3220
46:18 and as Carmel by the **s**, *so* shall he come. 3220
47: 7 against Ashkelon, and against the **s** shore? 3220
48:32 thy plants are gone over the **s**, they reach 3220
48:32 the sea, they reach *even* to the **s** of Jazer: 3220
49:21 the noise thereof was heard in the Red **s**. 3220
49:23 *there is* sorrow on the **s**; it cannot be quiet. 3220

Jer 50:42 their voice shall roar like the **s**, and 3220
51:36 I will dry up her **s**, and make her springs 3220
51:42 The **s** is come up upon Babylon: she is 3220
52:17 the brasen **s** that *was* in the house of 3220
52:20 one **s**, and twelve brasen bulls that *were* 3220
La 2:13 for thy breach *is* great like the **s**: who can 3220
4: 3 Even the **s monsters** draw out the breast, 8577
Eze 25:16 and destroy the remnant of the **s** coast. 3220
26: 3 as the **s** causeth his waves to come up. 3220
26: 5 the spreading of nets in the midst of the **s**: 3220
26:16 all the princes of the **s** shall come down 3220
26:17 which wast strong in the **s**, she and 3220
26:18 the isles that *are* in the **s** shall be troubled at 3220
27: 3 O thou that art situate at the entry of the **s**, 3220
27: 9 all the ships of the **s** with their mariners 3220
27:29 the mariners, *and* all the pilots of the **s**, 3220
27:32 like the destroyed in the midst of the **s**? 3220
38:20 So that the fishes of the **s**, and the fowls of 3220
39:11 valley of the passengers *on* the east of the **s**: 3220
47: 8 go down into the desert, and go into the **s**: 3220
47: 8 *which* being brought forth into the **s**, 3220
47:10 as the fish of the great **s**, exceeding many. 3220
47:15 from the great **s**, the way of Hethlon, as 3220
47:17 the border from the **s** shall be Hazar-enan, 3220
47:18 *by* Jordan, from the border unto the east **s**. 3220
47:19 of strife *in* Kadesh, *the* river to the great **s**. 3220
47:20 The west side also *shall be* the great **s** from 3220
48:28 *and to the* river toward the great **s**. 3220
Da 7: 2 winds of the heaven strove upon the great **s**. 3221
7: 3 four great beasts came up from the **s**, 3221
Hos 1:10 of Israel shall be as the sand of the **s**, 3220
4: 3 the fishes of the **s** also shall be taken away. 3220
Joel 2:20 with his face toward the east **s**, and 3220
2:20 his hinder part towards the utmost **s**, and 3220
Am 5: 8 that calleth for the waters of the **s**, and 3220
8:12 they shall wander from **s** to sea, and 3220
8:12 they shall wander from sea to **s**, and 3220
9: 3 be hid from my sight in the bottom of the **s**, 3220
9: 6 he that calleth for the waters of the **s**, and 3220
Jnh 1: 4 the LORD sent out a great wind into the **s**, 3220
1: 4 there was a mighty tempest in the **s**, so 3220
1: 5 the wares that *were* in the ship into the **s**, 3220
1: 9 which hath made the **s** and the dry *land*. 3220
1:11 unto thee, that the **s** may be calm unto us? 3220
1:11 for the **s** wrought, and was tempestuous. 3220
1:12 Take me up, and cast me forth into the **s**; 3220
1:12 the sea; so shall the **s** be calm unto you: 3220
1:13 for the **s** wrought, and was tempestuous 3220
1:15 took up Jonah, and cast him forth into the **s**: 3220
1:15 the sea: and the **s** ceased from her raging. 3220
Mic 7:12 from **s** *to* sea, and *from* mountain *to* 3220
7:12 from sea *to* **s**, and *from* mountain *to* 3220
7:19 cast all their sins into the depths of the **s**. 3220
Na 1: 4 He rebuketh the **s**, and maketh it dry, and 3220
3: 8 whose rampart *was* the **s**, *and* her wall *was* 3220
3: 8 *was* the sea, *and* her wall *was* from the **s**? 3220
Hab 1:14 makest men as the fishes of the **s**, as 3220
2:14 of the LORD, as the waters cover the **s**. 3220
3: 8 *was* thy wrath against the **s**, that thou didst 3220
3:15 Thou didst walk through the **s** *with* thine 3220
Zep 1: 3 the fishes of the **s**, and the stumblingblocks 3220
2: 5 Woe unto the inhabitants of the **s** coast, 3220
2: 6 the **s** coast shall be dwellings *and* 3220
Hag 2: 6 and the earth, and the **s**, and the dry *land*; 3220
Zec 9: 4 and he will smite her power in the **s**; 3220
9:10 his dominion *shall be* from **s** *even* to sea, 3220
9:10 his dominion *shall be* from sea *even* to **s**, 3220
10:11 he shall pass through the **s** *with* affliction, 3220
10:11 shall smite the waves in the **s**, and all 3220
14: 8 half of them toward the former **s**, and 3220
14: 8 and half of them toward the hinder **s**: 3220
Mt 4:13 in Capernaum, which is **upon the s coast**, *3864*
4:15 *by* the way of the **s**, beyond Jordan, *2281*
4:18 And Jesus, walking by the **s** of Galilee, *2281*
4:18 Andrew his brother, casting a net into the **s**: *2281*
8:24 there arose a great tempest in the **s**, *2281*
8:26 he arose, and rebuked the winds and the **s**; *2281*
8:27 that even the winds and the **s** obey him? *2281*
8:32 ran violently down a steep place into the **s**, *2281*
13: 1 Jesus out of the house, and sat by the **s** side. *2281*
13:47 *that was* cast into the **s**, and gathered of *2281*
14:24 But the ship was now in the midst of the **s**, *2281*
14:25 Jesus went unto them, walking on the **s**. *2281*
14:26 the disciples saw him walking on the **s**, *2281*
15:29 and came nigh unto the **s** of Galilee; *2281*
17:27 go thou to the **s**, and cast a hook, and *2281*
18: 6 *that* he were drowned in the depth of the **s**. *2281*
21:21 thou removed, and be thou cast into the **s**; *2281*
23:15 for ye compass **s** and land to make one *2281*
Mk 1:16 Now as he walked by the **s** of Galilee, *2281*
1:16 Andrew his brother casting a net into the **s**: *2281*
2:13 And he went forth again by the **s** side; and *2281*
3: 7 himself with his disciples to the **s**: *2281*
4: 1 And he began again to teach by the **s** side: *2281*
4: 1 that he entered into a ship, and sat in the **s**; *2281*
4: 1 the whole multitude was by the **s** on *2281*
4:39 and said unto the **s**, Peace, be still. *2281*
4:41 that even the wind and the **s** obey him? *2281*
5: 1 they came over unto the other side of the **s**, *2281*
5:13 ran violently down a steep place into the **s**, *2281*
5:13 two thousand,) and were choked in the **s**. *2281*
5:21 unto him: and he was nigh unto the **s**. *2281*
6:47 the ship was in the midst of the **s**, and *2281*
6:48 walking upon the **s**, and would have passed *2281*
6:49 But when they saw him walking upon the **s**, *2281*
7:31 and Sidon, he came unto the **s** of Galilee, *2281*
9:42 about his neck, and he were cast into the **s**. *2281*
11:23 thou removed, and be thou cast into the **s**; *2281*
Lk 6:17 and *from* the **s coast** of Tyre and Sidon, *3882*
17: 2 and he cast into the **s**, than that he should *2281*
17: 6 up by the root, and be thou planted in the **s**; *2281*
21:25 the **s** and the waves roaring; *2281*
Jn 6: 1 After these *things* Jesus went over the **s** of *2281*
6: 1 the sea of Galilee, *which is* the **s** of Tiberias. NIG
6:16 his disciples went down unto the **s**, *2281*
6:17 and went over the **s** towards Capernaum. *2281*
6:18 And the **s** arose by reason of a great wind *2281*
6:19 they see Jesus walking on the **s**, and *2281*
6:22 **s** saw that there was none other boat there, *2281*
6:25 had found him on the other side of the **s**, *2281*
21: 1 again to the disciples at the **s** of Tiberias; *2281*
21: 7 was naked,) and did cast himself into the **s**. *2281*
Ac 4:24 and earth, and the **s**, and all that in them is: *2281*
7:36 and in the Red **s**, and in the wilderness *2281*
10: 6 a tanner, whose house is by the **s** side: *2281*
10:32 house of *one* Simon a tanner by the **s** side: *2281*
14:15 and the **s**, and all *things* that are therein: *2281*
17:14 sent away Paul to go as *it were* to the **s**: *2281*
27: 5 And when we had sailed over the **s** of *3989*
27:30 when they had let down the boat into the **s**, *2281*
27:38 the ship, and cast out the wheat into the **s**. *2281*
27:40 they committed *themselves* unto the **s**, and *2281*
27:43 swim should cast *themselves* first into *the* **s**, NIG
28: 4 whom, though he hath escaped the **s**, *2281*
Ro 9:27 the children of Israel be as the sand of the **s**, *2281*
1Co 10: 1 the cloud, and all passed through the **s**; *2281*
10: 2 unto Moses in the cloud and in the **s**; *2281*
2Co 11:26 *in* perils in the wilderness, *in* perils in the **s**, *2281*
Heb 11:12 as the sand which is by the **s** shore *2281*
11:29 By faith they passed through the Red **s** as *2281*
Jas 1: 6 for he that wavereth is like a wave of the **s** *2281*
3: 7 and of *things* **in the s**, is tamed, and *1724*
Jude 1:13 Raging waves of the **s**, foaming out their *2281*
Rev 4: 6 And before the throne *there was* a **s** of glass *2281*
5:13 and such as are in the **s**, and all that are in *2281*
7: 1 on the earth, nor on the **s**, nor on any tree. *2281*
7: 2 it was given to hurt the earth and the **s**, *2281*
7: 3 not the earth, neither the **s**, nor the trees, *2281*
8: 8 burning with fire was cast into the **s**: *2281*
8: 8 and the third *part* of the **s** became blood; *2281*
8: 9 *part* of the creatures which were in the **s**, *2281*
10: 2 and he set his right foot upon the **s**, and *2281*
10: 5 And the angel which I saw stand upon the **s** *2281*
10: 6 and the **s**, and the *things* which are therein, *2281*
10: 8 hand of the angel which standeth upon the **s** *2281*
12:12 to the inhabiters of the earth and of the **s**! *2281*
13: 1 And I stood upon the sand of the **s**, and *2281*
13: 1 and saw a beast rise up out of the **s**, *2281*
14: 7 and the **s**, and the fountains of waters. *2281*
15: 2 And I saw as *it were* a **s** of glass mingled *2281*
15: 2 stand on the **s** of glass, having *the* harps of *2281*
16: 3 second angel poured out his vial upon the **s**; *2281*
16: 3 and every living soul died in the **s**. *2281*
18:17 and sailers, and as many as trade by **s**, *2281*
18:19 ships in the **s** by reason of her costliness: *2281*
18:21 and cast *it* into the **s**, saying, *2281*
20: 8 the number of whom *is* as the sand of the **s**. *2281*
20:13 And the **s** gave up the dead which were in *2281*

Rev 21: 1 passed away; and there was no more **s**. *2281*

SEA COWS See BADGERS'

SEAFARING (1) [FARE, SEA]
Eze 26:17 *that wast* inhabited of **s** men, the renowned 3220

SEAL (26) [SEALED, SEALEST, SEALETH, SEALING, SEALS]
1Ki 21: 8 sealed *them* with his **s**, and sent the letters 2368
Ne 9:38 our princes, Levites, *and* priests, **s** *unto it.* 2856
Est 8: 8 king's name, and **s** *it* with the king's ring: 2856
Job 38:14 It is turned as clay *to* the **s**; and they stand 2368
41:15 *his* pride, shut up *together as with* a close **s**. 2368
SS 8: 6 Set me as a **s** upon thine heart, as a seal 2368
8: 6 seal upon thine heart, as a **s** upon thine arm: 2368
Isa 8:16 **s** the law among my disciples. 2856
Jer 32:44 **s** *them,* and take witnesses in the land of 2856
Da 9:24 to **s up** the vision and prophecy, and 2856
12: 4 shut up the words, and **s** the book, 2856
Jn 3:33 testimony hath **set to** *his* **s** that God is true. *4972*
Ro 4:11 a **s** of the righteousness of the faith which *4973*
1Co 9: 2 for the **s** of mine apostleship are ye in *4973*
2Ti 2:19 having this **s**, The Lord knoweth them that *4973*
Rev 6: 3 And when he had opened the second **s**, *4973*
6: 5 And when he had opened the third **s**, *4973*
6: 7 And when he had opened the fourth **s**, *4973*
6: 9 And when he had opened the fifth **s**, I saw *4973*
6:12 I beheld when he had opened the sixth **s**, *4973*
7: 2 the east, having the **s** of the living God: *4973*
8: 1 And when he had opened the seventh **s**, *4973*
9: 4 only *those* men which have not the **s** of *4973*
10: 4 **S** *up those things* which the seven thunders *4972*
20: 3 and shut him up, and **set a s** upon him, *4972*
22:10 **S** not the sayings of the prophecy of this *4972*

SEALED (36) [SEAL]
Dt 32:34 with me, *and* **s up** among my treasures? 2856
1Ki 21: 8 **s** *them* with his seal, and sent the letters 2856
Ne 10: 1 Now those that **s** *were,* Nehemiah, 2856
Est 3:12 was it written, and **s** with the king's ring. 2856
8: 8 **s** with the king's ring, may no man reverse. 2856
8:10 **s** *it* with the king's ring, and sent letters by 2856
Job 14:17 My transgression *is* **s up** in a bag, and 2856
SS 4:12 *my* spouse; a spring shut up, a fountain **s**. 2856
Isa 29:11 unto you as the words of a book that is **s**, 2856
29:11 pray thee: and he saith, I cannot; for it *is* **s**: 2856
Jer 32:10 **s** *it,* and took witnesses, and weighed *him* 2856
32:11 *both* that which was **s** *according to* the law 2856
32:14 both which is **s**, and this evidence which is 2856
Da 6:17 the king **s** it with his own signet, and 2857
12: 9 *are* closed up and **s** till the time of the end. 2856
Jn 6:27 unto you: for him hath God the Father **s**. *4972*
Ro 15:28 and have **s** to them this fruit, *4972*
2Co 1:22 Who hath also **s** us, and given the earnest *4972*
Eph 1:13 ye were **s** with *that* holy Spirit of promise, *4972*
4:30 whereby ye are **s** unto the day of *4972*
Rev 5: 1 and on the backside, **s** with seven seals. *2696*
7: 3 till we have **s** the servants of our God in *4972*
7: 4 I heard the number of them which were **s**: *4972*
7: 4 *and there were* **s** an hundred *and* forty *and* *4972*
7: 5 Of the tribe of Juda *were* **s** twelve *4972*
7: 5 Of the tribe of Reuben *were* **s** twelve *4972*
7: 5 Of the tribe of Gad *were* **s** twelve thousand. *4972*
7: 6 Of the tribe of Aser *were* **s** twelve *4972*
7: 6 Of the tribe of Nephthalim *were* **s** twelve *4972*
7: 6 Of the tribe of Manasses *were* **s** twelve *4972*
7: 7 Of the tribe of Simeon *were* **s** twelve *4972*
7: 7 Of the tribe of Levi *were* **s** twelve *4972*
7: 7 Of the tribe of Isachar *were* **s** twelve *4972*
7: 8 Of the tribe of Zabulon *were* **s** twelve *4972*
7: 8 Of the tribe of Joseph *were* **s** twelve *4972*
7: 8 Of the tribe of Benjamin *were* **s** twelve *4972*

SEALEST (1) [SEAL]
Eze 28:12 Thou **s up** the sum, full *of* wisdom, and 2856

SEALETH (3) [SEAL]
Job 9: 7 and it riseth not; and **s up** the stars. 1157+2856
33:16 the ears of men, and **s** their instruction. 2856
37: 7 He **s up** the hand of every man; that all 2856

SEALING (1) [SEAL]
Mt 27:66 **s** the stone, and setting a watch. *4972*

SEALS (5) [SEAL]
Rev 5: 1 and on the backside, sealed with seven **s**. *4973*
5: 2 open the book, and to loose the **s** thereof? *4973*
5: 5 the book, and to loose the seven **s** thereof. *4973*
5: 9 to take the book, and to open the **s** thereof: *4973*
6: 1 I saw when the Lamb opened one of the **s**, *4973*

SEAM (1)
Jn 19:23 now the coat was **without s**, woven from *729*

SEARCH (48) [SEARCHED, SEARCHEST, SEARCHETH, SEARCHING, SEARCHINGS, UNSEARCHABLE]
Lev 27:33 He shall not **s** whether it be good or bad, 1239
Nu 10:33 to **s out** a resting place for them. 8446
13: 2 that they may **s** the land of Canaan, 8446
13:32 through which we have gone to **s** it, 8446
14: 7 The land, which we passed through to **s** it, 8446
14:36 the men, which Moses sent to **s** the land, 8446
14:38 *which were* of the men that went to **s** 8446
Dt 1:22 they shall **s** us **out** the land, and bring us 2658
1:33 to **s** you **out** a place to pitch your tents *in,* 8446
13:14 and **make s**, and ask diligently; 2713
Jos 2: 2 the children of Israel to **s out** the country. 2658
2: 3 for they be come to **s out** all the country. 2658
Jdg 18: 2 to spy out the land, and to **s** it; 2713
18: 2 and they said unto them, Go, **s** the land: 2713
1Sa 23:23 that I will **s** him **out** throughout all 2664
2Sa 10: 3 to **s** the city, and to spy it out, and 2713
1Ki 20: 6 they shall **s** thine house, and the houses of 2664
2Ki 10:23 **S**, and look that there be here with you 2664
1Ch 19: 3 are not his servants come unto thee for to **s**, 2713
Ezr 4:15 That **s** may be **made** in the book of 1240
4:19 **s** hath been **made**, and it is found that this 1240
5:17 let there be **s made** in the king's treasure 1240
6: 1 and **s** was **made** in the house of the rolls, 1240
Job 8: 8 and prepare *thyself* to the **s** of their fathers: 2714
13: 9 *Is it* good that he should **s** you **out**? or 2713
38:16 or hast thou walked in the **s** of the depth? 2714
Ps 44:21 Shall not God **s** this **out**? for he knoweth 2713
64: 6 They **s out** iniquities; they accomplish a 2664
64: 6 out iniquities; they accomplish a diligent **s**: 2665
77: 6 own heart: and my spirit **made diligent s**. 2664
139:23 **S** me, O God, and know my heart: try me, 2713
Pr 25: 2 but the honour of kings *is* to **s out** a matter. 2713
25:27 so *for men* to **s** their own glory *is not* glory. 2714
Ecc 1:13 **s out** by wisdom concerning all *things* that 8446
7:25 to **s**, and to seek out wisdom, and 8446
Jer 2:34 I have not found it by **secret s**, but upon all 4290
17:10 I the LORD **s** the heart, *I* try the reins, 2713
29:13 find *me,* when ye shall **s for** me with all 1875
La 3:40 Let us **s** and try our ways, and turn again to 2664
Eze 34: 6 and none did **s** or seek *after them.* 1875
34: 8 neither did my shepherds **s** for my flock, 1875
34:11 will both **s** my sheep, and seek them out. 1875
39:14 after the end of seven months shall they **s**. 2713
Am 9: 3 I will **s** and take them out thence; 2664
Zep 1:12 *that* I will **s** Jerusalem with candles, and 2664
Mt 2: 8 Go and **s** diligently for the young child; *1833*
Jn 5:39 **S** the Scriptures; for in them ye think ye *2045*
7:52 **S**, and look: for out of Galilee ariseth no *2045*

SEARCHED (20) [SEARCH]
Ge 31:34 Laban **s** all the tent, but found *them* not. 4959
31:35 And he **s**, but found not the images. 2664
31:37 Whereas thou hast **s** all my stuff, what hast 4959
44:12 he **s**, *and* began at the eldest, and left at 2664
Nu 13:21 **s** the land from the wilderness of Zin unto 8446
13:32 which they had **s** unto the children of Israel, 8446
14: 6 *which were* of them that **s** the land, 8446
14:34 After the number of the days *in* which ye **s** 8446
Dt 1:24 unto the valley of Eshcol, and **s** it **out**. 7270
Job 5:27 we have **s** it, so it *is;* hear it, and know thou 2713
28:27 declare it; he prepared it, yea, and **s** it **out**. 2713
29:16 and the cause *which* I knew not I **s out**. 2713
32:11 your reasons, whilst you **s out** what to say. 2713
36:26 can the number of his years be **s out**. 2714
Ps 139: 1 O LORD, thou hast **s** me, and known *me.* 2713
Jer 31:37 the foundations of the earth **s out** beneath, 2713
46:23 saith the LORD, though it cannot be **s**; 2713
Ob 1: 6 How are *the things of* Esau **s out**! *how* are 2664
Ac 17:11 and **s** the scriptures daily, whether those *350*
1Pe 1:10 the prophets have inquired and **s diligently**, *1830*

SEARCHEST (2) [SEARCH]
Job 10: 6 after mine iniquity, and **s** after my sin? 1875
Pr 2: 4 as silver, and **s for** her as *for* hid treasures; 2664

SEARCHETH (8) [SEARCH]
1Ch 28: 9 for the LORD **s** all hearts, and 1875
Job 28: 3 **s out** all perfection, the stones of darkness, 2713
39: 8 and he **s** after every green thing. 1875
Pr 18:17 but his neighbour cometh and **s** him. 2713
28:11 the poor that hath understanding **s** him **out**. 2713
Ro 8:27 And he that **s** the hearts knoweth what *is* *2045*
1Co 2:10 for the Spirit **s** all *things*, yea, the deep *2045*
Rev 2:23 shall know that I am he which **s** the reins *2045*

SEARCHING (5) [SEARCH]
Nu 13:25 they returned from **s** of the land after forty 8446
Job 11: 7 Canst thou *by* **s** find out God? canst thou 2714
Pr 20:27 **s** all the inward parts of the belly. 2664
Isa 40:28 is weary? *there is* no **s** of his understanding. 2714
1Pe 1:11 **S** what, or what manner of time the Spirit *2045*

SEARCHINGS (1) [SEARCH]
Jdg 5:16 of Reuben *there were* great **s** of heart. 2714

SEARED (1)
1Ti 4: 2 having their conscience **s with a hot iron**; *2743*

SEAS (25) [SEA]
Ge 1:10 together of the waters called he **S**: 3220
1:22 fill the waters in the **s**, and let fowl multiply 3220
Lev 11: 9 in the **s**, and in the rivers, them shall ye eat. 3220
11:10 all that have not fins nor scales in the **s**, 3220
Dt 33:19 they shall suck *of* the abundance of the **s**, 3220
Ne 9: 6 the **s**, and all that *is* therein, and 3220
Ps 8: 8 passeth *through* the paths of the **s**. 3220
24: 2 For he hath founded it upon the **s**, and 3220
65: 7 Which stilleth the noise of the **s**, the noise 3220
69:34 the **s**, and every *thing* that moveth therein. 3220
135: 6 and in earth, in the **s**, and all deep places. 3220
Isa 17:12 *which* make a noise like the noise of the **s**; 3220
Jer 15: 8 are increased to me above the sand of the **s**: 3220
Eze 27: 4 Thy borders *are* in the midst of the **s**, 3220
27:25 made very glorious in the midst of the **s**. 3220
27:26 wind hath broken thee in the midst of the **s**. 3220
27:27 shall fall into the midst of the **s** in the day 3220
27:33 When thy wares went forth out of the **s**, 3220
27:34 broken by the **s** in the depths of the waters, 3220
28: 2 I sit *in* the seat of God, in the midst of the **s**; 3220
28: 8 of *them that are* slain in the midst of the **s**. 3220
32: 2 the nations, and thou *art* as a whale in the **s**: 3220
Da 11:45 the **s** in the glorious holy mountain; 3220
Jnh 2: 3 cast me *into* the deep, in the midst of the **s**; 3220
Ac 27:41 And falling into a place **where two s met**, *1337*

SEASON (56) [SEASONED, SEASONS]
Ge 40: 4 and they continued a **s** in ward. 3117
Ex 13:10 keep this ordinance in his **s** from year to 4150
Lev 2:13 of thy meat offering shalt thou **s** with salt; 4414
26: 4 I will give you rain in **due s**, and the land 6256
Nu 9: 2 also keep the passover at his **appointed s**. 4150
9: 3 at even, ye shall keep it in his **appointed s**: 4150
9: 7 **appointed s** among the children of Israel? 4150
9:13 offering of the LORD in his **appointed s**, 4150
28: 2 ye observe to offer unto me in their **due s**. 4150
Dt 11:14 give *you* the rain of your land in his **due s**, 6256
16: 6 *at* the **s** that thou camest forth out of Egypt. 4150
28:12 to give the rain unto thy land in his **s**, 6256
Jos 24: 7 and ye dwelt in the wilderness a long **s**. 3117
2Ki 4:16 he said, About this **s**, according to the time 4150
4:17 bare a son at that **s** that Elisha had said unto 4150
1Ch 21:29 *were* at that **s** in the high place at Gibeon. 6256
2Ch 15: 3 Now for a long **s** Israel *hath been* without 3117
Job 5:26 like as a shock of corn cometh in in his **s**. 6256
30:17 My bones are pierced in me in the **night s**: 3915
38:32 Canst thou bring forth Mazzaroth in his **s**? 6256
Ps 1: 3 that bringeth forth his fruit in his **s**; 6256
22: 2 and in the **night s**, and am not silent. 3915
104:27 *thou* mayest give *them* their meat in **due s**. 6256
145:15 and thou givest them their meat in **due s**. 6256
Pr 15:23 a word *spoken* in **due s**, how good 6256+2050.2
Ecc 3: 1 To every *thing there is* a **s**, and a time to 2165
10:17 thy princes eat in **due s**, for strength, and 6256
Isa 50: 4 to **speak** a word **in s** to *him that is* weary: 5790
Jer 5:24 both the former and the latter, in his **s**: 6256
33:20 there should not be day and night in their **s**; 6256
Eze 34:26 cause the shower to come down in his **s**; 6256
Da 7:12 yet their lives were prolonged for a **s** and 2166
Hos 2: 9 my wine in the **s** thereof, and will recover 4150
Mt 24:45 his household, to give them meat in **due s**? *2540*
Mk 9:50 lost his saltness, wherewith will you **s** it? *741*
12: 2 And at the **s** he sent to the husbandmen a *2540*
Lk 1:20 which shall be fulfilled in their **s**. *2540*
4:13 he departed from him for a **s**. *2540*
12:42 to give *them their* portion of meat in **due s**? *2540*
13: 1 There were present at that **s** some that told *2540*
20:10 And at the **s** he sent a servant to *2540*
23: 8 for he was desirous to see him of a long **s**, NIG
Jn 5: 4 For an angel went down at a *certain* **s** into *2540*
5:35 ye were willing for a **s** to rejoice in his *5610*
Ac 13:11 shalt be blind, not seeing the sun for a **s**. *2540*
19:22 but he himself stayed in Asia for a **s**. *5550*
24:25 when I have a **convenient s**, I will call for *2540*
2Co 7: 8 made you sorry, though *it were* but for a **s**. *5610*
Gal 6: 9 for in due **s** we shall reap, if we faint not. *2540*
2Ti 4: 2 be instant **in s**, out of season; reprove, *2122*
4: 2 be instant in season, **out of s**; reprove, *171*
Phm 1:15 For perhaps he therefore departed for a **s**, *5610*
Heb 11:25 than to enjoy the pleasures of sin for a **s**; *4340*
1Pe 1: 6 though now for a **s**, if need be, *3641*
Rev 6:11 that they should rest yet for a little **s**, *5550*
20: 3 and after that he must be loosed a little **s**. *5550*

SEASONED (2) [SEASON]
Lk 14:34 have lost his savour, wherewith shall it be **s**? *741*
Col 4: 6 your speech *be* alway with grace, **s** with salt, *741*

SEASONS (12) [SEASON]
Ge 1:14 for signs, and for **s**, and for days, and years: 4150
Ex 18:22 let them judge the people at all **s**: and 6256
18:26 they judged the people at all **s**: the hard 6256
Lev 23: 4 which ye shall proclaim in their **s**. 4150
Ps 16: 7 my reins also instruct me *in* the **night s**. 3915
104:19 He appointed the moon for **s**: the sun 4150
Da 2:21 he changeth the times and the **s**: 2166
Mt 21:41 which shall render him the fruits in their **s**. *2540*
Ac 1: 7 It is not for you to know *the* times or *the* **s**, *2540*
14:17 gave us rain from heaven, and fruitful **s**, *2540*
20:18 what manner I have been with you at all **s**, *5550*
1Th 5: 1 But of the times and the **s**, brethren, *2540*

SEAT (59) [SIT]
Ex 25:17 thou shalt make a **mercy s** *of* pure gold: 3727
25:18 make them, in the two ends of the **mercy s**. 3727
25:19 *even* of the **mercy s** shall ye make 3727
25:20 covering the **mercy s** with their wings, 3727
25:20 toward the **mercy s** shall the faces of 3727
25:21 thou shalt put the **mercy s** above upon 3727
25:22 with thee from above the **mercy s**, 3727
26:34 thou shalt put the **mercy s** upon the ark of 3727
30: 6 before the **mercy s** that *is* over 3727
31: 7 the **mercy s** that *is* thereupon, and all 3727
35:12 *with* the **mercy s**, and the vail of 3727
37: 6 he made the **mercy s** *of* pure gold: 3727
37: 7 he them, on the two ends of the **mercy s**; 3727
37: 8 out of the **mercy s** made he the cherubims 3727
37: 9 covered with their wings over the **mercy s**, 3727
39:35 and the staves thereof, and the **mercy s**, 3727
40:20 and put the **mercy s** above upon the ark: 3727
Lev 16: 2 *place* within the vail before the **mercy s**, 3727
16: 2 I will appear in the cloud upon the **mercy s**. 3727
16:13 the **mercy s** that *is* upon the Testimony, 3727
16:14 sprinkle *it* with his finger upon the **mercy s** 3727
16:14 before the **mercy s** shall he sprinkle of 3727
16:15 sprinkle it upon the **mercy s**, and before 3727
16:15 the mercy seat, and before the **mercy s**: 3727
Nu 7:89 **mercy s** that *was* upon the ark of 3727
Jdg 3:20 God unto thee. And he arose out of *his* **s**. 3678
1Sa 1: 9 Now Eli the priest sat upon a **s** by a post of 3678
4:13 Eli sat upon a **s** *by* the wayside watching: 3678
4:18 that he fell from off the **s** backward by 3678
20:18 be missed, because thy **s** will be empty. 4186
20:25 the king sat upon his **s**, as at other times, 4186
20:25 as at other times, *even* upon a **s** by the wall: 4186
2Sa 23: 8 The Tachmonite that sat in the **s**, 7675
1Ki 2:19 caused a **s** to be set for the king's mother; 3678
10:19 stays on either side on the place of the **s**, 7675
1Ch 28:11 and of the place of the **mercy s**, 3727
Est 3: 1 set his **s** above all the princes that *were* 3678

S

Job 23: 3 find him! *that* I might come *even* to his **s**! 8499
29: 7 the city, *when* I prepared my **s** in the street; 4186
Ps 1: 1 nor sitteth in the **s** of the scornful. 4186
Pr 9:14 on a **s** in the high places of the city, 3678
Eze 8: 3 where *was* the **s** of the image of jealousy, 4186
28: 2 hast said, I *am* a God, I sit *in* the **s** of God, 4186
Am 6: 3 and cause the **s** of violence to come near; 7675
Mt 23: 2 and the Pharisees sit in Moses' **s**: *2515*
27:19 When he was set down on the **judgment s**, *968*
Jn 19:13 sat down in the **judgment s** in a place *that is* *968*
Ac 18:12 and brought him to the **judgment s**, *968*
18:16 And he drave them from the **judgment s**. *968*
18:17 and beat *him* before the **judgment s**. *968*
25: 6 and the next day sitting in the **judgment s**, *968*
25:10 said Paul, I stand at Cesar's **judgment s**, *968*
25:17 on the morrow I sat on the **judgment s**, and *968*
Ro 14:10 for we shall all stand before the **judgment s** *968*
2Co 5:10 all appear before the **judgment s** of Christ; *968*
Heb 9: 5 cherubims of glory shadowing the **mercy s**; *2435*
Rev 2:13 *even* where Satan's **s** *is:* and thou holdest *2362*
13: 2 his power, and his **s**, and great authority. *2362*
16:10 poured out his vial upon the **s** of the beast; *2362*

SEATED (1) [SIT]
Dt 33:21 there, *in* a portion of the lawgiver, *was he* **s**; 5603

SEATS (11) [SIT]
Mt 21:12 and the **s** of them that sold doves, *2515*
23: 6 at feasts, and the **chief s** in the synagogues, *4410*
Mk 11:15 and the **s** of them that sold doves; *2515*
12:39 And the **chief s** in the synagogues, and *4410*
Lk 1:52 He hath put down the mighty from *their* **s**, *2362*
11:43 for ye love the **uppermost s** in *4410*
20:46 and the **highest s** in the synagogues, and *4410*
Jas 2: 6 and draw you before the **judgment s**? *2922*
Rev 4: 4 about the throne *were* four and twenty **s**: *2362*
4: 4 and upon the **s** I saw four and twenty elders *2362*
11:16 which sat before God on their **s**, *2362*

SEATWARD (1) [SIT]
Ex 37: 9 *even* to the **mercy s** were the faces of 3727

SEBA (4)
Ge 10: 7 **S**, and Havilah, and Sabtah, and Raamah, 5434
1Ch 1: 9 **S**, and Havilah, and Sabta, and Raamah, 5434
Ps 72:10 the kings of Sheba and **S** shall offer gifts. 5434
Isa 43: 3 *for* thy ransom, Ethiopia and **S** for thee. 5434

SEBAM See SHEBAM

SEBAT (1)
Zec 1: 7 which *is* the month **S**, in the second year of 7627

SECACAH (1)
Jos 15:61 the wilderness, Beth-arabah, Middin, and **S**, 5527

SECHU (1)
1Sa 19:22 and came to a great well that *is* in **S**: 7906

SECOND (173) [SECONDARILY, TWO]
Ge 1: 8 and the morning were the **s** day. 8145
2:13 the name of the **s** river *is* Gihon: the same 8145
6:16 **s**, and third *stories* shalt thou make it. 8145
7:11 in the **s** month, the seventeenth day of 8145
8:14 in the **s** month, on the seven and 8145
22:15 unto Abraham out of heaven the **s time**, 8145
30: 7 conceived again, and bare Jacob a **s** son. 8145
30:12 And Zilpah Leah's maid bare Jacob a **s** son. 8145
32:19 so commanded he the **s**, and the third, and 8145
41: 5 he slept and dreamed the **s time**: and 8145
41:43 he made him to ride in the **s** chariot which 4932
41:52 the name of the **s** called he Ephraim: 8145
43:10 surely now we had returned this **s time**. 6471
47:18 they came unto him the **s** year, and 8145
Ex 2:13 when he went out the **s** day, behold, 8145
16: 1 on the fifteenth day of the **s** month after 8145
26: 4 of *another* curtain, in the coupling of the **s**. 8145
26: 5 the curtain that *is* in the coupling of the **s**; 8145
26:10 edge of the curtain which coupleth the **s**. 8145
26:20 for the **s** side of the tabernacle on the north 8145
28:18 the **s** row *shall be* an emerald, a sapphire, 8145
36:11 of *another* curtain, in the coupling of the **s**. 8145
36:12 curtain which *was* in the coupling of the **s**: 8145
36:17 edge of the curtain which coupleth the **s**. 8145
39:11 the **s** row, an emerald, a sapphire, and 8145
40:17 it came to pass in the first month in the **s** 8145
Lev 5:10 And he shall offer the **s** *for* a burnt offering, 8145
13:58 it shall be washed the **s time**, and shall be 8145
Nu 1: 1 on the first *day* of the **s** month, 8145
1: 1 in the **s** year after they were come out of 8145
1:18 together on the first *day* of the **s** month, 8145
2:16 And they shall set forth in the **s rank**. 8145
7:18 On the **s** day Nethaneel the son of Zuar, 8145
9: 1 in the first month of the **s** year after they 8145
9:11 The fourteenth day of the **s** month at even 8145
10: 6 When you blow an alarm the **s time**, then 8145
10:11 it came to pass on the twentieth *day* of the **s** 8145
10:11 *day* of the second month, in the **s** year, 8145
29:17 on the **s** day *ye shall offer* twelve young 8145
Jos 5: 2 again the children of Israel the **s time**. 8145
6:14 the **s** day they compassed the city once, 8145
10:32 which took it on the **s** day, and smote it 8145
19: 1 the **s** lot came forth to Simeon, *even* for 8145
Jdg 6:25 even the **s** bullock of seven years old, and 8145
6:26 take the **s** bullock, and offer a burnt 8145
6:28 the **s** bullock was offered upon the altar that 8145
20:24 against the children of Benjamin the **s** day. 8145
20:25 forth against them out of Gibeah the **s** day, 8145
1Sa 8: 2 was Joel; and the name of his **s**, Abiah: 4932
20:27 *which was* the **s** *day* of the month, 8145
20:34 and did eat no meat the **s** day of the month: 8145
26: 8 at once, and I will not *smite* him the **s time**. 8138
2Sa 3: 3 his **s**, Chileab, of Abigail the wife of Nabal 4932
14:29 when he sent again the **s time**, he would 8145
1Ki 6: 1 in the month Zif, which *is* the **s** month, 8145
9: 2 LORD appeared to Solomon the **s time**, 8145
15:25 Israel in the **s** year of Asa king of Judah, 8147
18:34 he said, **Do** *it* **the s time**. And they did *it* 8138
18:34 they **did** *it* **the s time**. And he said, Do *it* 8138
19: 7 angel of the LORD came again the **s time**, 8145
2Ki 1:17 Jehoram reigned in his stead in the **s** year of 8147
9:19 he sent *out* a **s** on horseback, which came to 8145
10: 6 he wrote a letter the **s time** to them, saying, 8145
14: 1 In the **s** year of Joash son of Jehoahaz king 8147
15:32 In the **s** year of Pekah the son of Remaliah 8147
19:29 in the **s** year that which springeth of 8145
23: 4 high priest, and the priests of the **s order**; 4932
25:17 like unto these had the **s** pillar with 8145
25:18 Zephaniah the **s** priest, and the three 4932
1Ch 2:13 and Abinadab the **s**, and Shimma the third, 8145
3: 1 the **s** Daniel, of Abigail the Carmelitess: 8145
3:15 the **s** Jehoiakim, the third Zedekiah, 8145
7:15 and the name of the **s** *was* Zelophehad: 8145
8: 1 Ashbel the **s**, and Aharah the third, 8145
8:39 Jehush the **s**, and Eliphelet the third. 8145
12: 9 Ezer the first, Obadiah the **s**, Eliab 8145
15:18 with them their brethren of the **s degree**, 4932
23:11 Jahath was the chief, and Zizah the **s**: but 8145
23:19 Jeriah the first, Amariah the **s**, Jahaziel 8145
23:20 Michah the first, and Jesiah the **s**. 8145
24: 7 lot came forth to Jehoiarib, the **s** to Jedaiah, 8145
24:23 *of Hebron;* Jeriah *the first,* Amariah the **s**, 8145
25: 9 the **s** *to* Gedaliah, who with his brethren 8145
26: 2 Jediael the **s**, Zebadiah the third, 8145
26: 4 Jehozabad the **s**, Joah the third, and 8145
26:11 Hilkiah the **s**, Tebaliah the third, 8145
27: 4 over the course of the **s** month *was* Dodai 8145
29:22 Solomon the son of David king the **s time**, 8145
2Ch 3: 2 he began to build in the **s** *day* of the second 8145
3: 2 he began to build in the second *day* of the **s** 8145
27: 5 pay unto him, both the **s** year, and the third. 8145
30: 2 to keep the passover in the **s** month. 8145
30:13 feast of unleavened bread in the **s** month, 8145
30:15 on the fourteenth *day* of the **s** month: 8145
35:24 and put him in the **s** chariot that he had; 4932
Ezr 1:10 silver basons of a **s sort** four hundred and 4932
3: 8 Now in the **s** year of their coming unto 8145
3: 8 in the **s** month, began Zerubbabel the son of 8145
4:24 So it ceased unto the **s** year of the reign of 8648
Ne 8:13 on the **s** day were gathered together 8145
11: 9 Judah the son of Senuah *was* **s** over 4932
11:17 Bakbukiah the **s** among his brethren, and 4932
Est 2:14 on the morrow she returned into the **s** house 8145
2:19 virgins were gathered together the **s time**, 8145
7: 2 the king said again unto Esther on the **s** day 8145
9:29 to confirm this **s** letter of Purim. 8145
Job 42:14 the name of the **s**, Kezia; and the name of 8145
Ecc 4: 8 There is one *alone,* and *there is* not a **s**; yea, 8145
4:15 with the **s** child that shall stand *up* in his 8145

Isa 11:11 **s time** to recover the remnant of his people, 8145
37:30 the **s** year that which springeth of the same: 8145
Jer 1:13 of the LORD came unto me the **s time**, 8145
13: 3 of the LORD came unto me the **s time**, 8145
33: 1 the LORD came unto Jeremiah the **s time**, 8145
41: 4 it came to pass the **s** day after *he* had slain 8145
52:22 The **s** pillar also and the pomegranates *were* 8145
52:24 Zephaniah the **s** priest, and the three 4932
Eze 10:14 the **s** face *was* the face of a man, and 8145
43:22 on the **s** day thou shalt offer a kid of 8145
Da 2: 1 in the **s** year of the reign of 8147
7: 5 a **s**, like to a bear, and it raised up itself on 8578
Jnh 3: 1 of the LORD came unto Jonah the **s time**, 8145
Na 1: 9 affliction shall not rise up the **s time**. 6471
Zep 1:10 a howling from the **s**, and a great crashing 4932
Hag 1: 1 In the **s** year of Darius the king, in the sixth 8147
1:15 in the **s** year of Darius the king. 8147
2:10 twentieth *day* of the ninth *month,* in the **s** 8147
Zec 1: 1 In the eighth month, in the **s** year of Darius, 8147
1: 7 *is* the month Sebat, in the **s** year of Darius, 8147
6: 2 and in the **s** chariot black horses; 8145
Mt 21:30 And he came to the **s**, *1208*
22:26 Likewise the **s** also, and the third, unto *1208*
22:39 And the **s** *is* like unto it, Thou shalt love thy *1208*
26:42 He went away again the **s time**, and *1208+1537*
Mk 12:21 And the **s** took her, and died, neither left he *1208*
12:31 And the **s** *is* like, *namely* this, Thou shalt *1208*
14:72 And the **s time** *the* cock crew. *1208+1537*
Lk 6: 1 to pass on the **s** sabbath **after the first**, *1207*
12:38 And if he shall come in the **s** watch, or *1208*
19:18 And the **s** came, saying, Lord, thy pound *1208*
20:30 And the **s** took her to wife, and he died *1208*
Jn 3: 4 can he enter the **s time** into his mother's *1208*
4:54 This *is* again the **s** miracle *that* Jesus did, *1208*
21:16 He saith to him again the **s time**, Simon, *1208*
Ac 7:13 And at the **s** time Joseph was made known *1208*
10:15 *spake* unto him again the **s time**, *1208+1537*
12:10 they were past the first and the **s** ward, *1208*
13:33 as it is also written in the **s** psalm, Thou art *1208*
1Co 15:47 earthy: the **s** man *is* the Lord from heaven. *1208*
2Co 1:15 you before, that you might have a **s** benefit; *1208*
13: 2 foretell *you,* as if I were present the **s** *time;* *1208*
13: S The **s** *epistle* to the Corinthians was written *1208*
2Th 3: S The **s** *epistle* to the Thessalonians was *1208*
2Ti 4: S The **s** *epistle* unto Timotheus, ordained *1208*
4: S when Paul was brought before Nero the **s** *1208*
Tit 3:10 a heretick after the first and **s** admonition, *1208*
Heb 8: 7 should no place have been sought for the **s**. *1208*
9: 3 And after the **s** vail, the tabernacle which is *1208*
9: 7 But into the **s** *went* the high priest alone *1208*
9:28 the **s time** without sin unto salvation. *1208+1537*
10: 9 away the first, that he may establish the **s**. *1208*
2Pe 3: 1 This **s** epistle, beloved, I now write unto *1208*
Rev 2:11 that overcometh shall not be hurt of the **s** *1208*
4: 7 and the **s** beast like a calf, and the third *1208*
6: 3 And when he had opened the **s** seal, I heard *1208*
6: 3 I heard the **s** beast say, Come and see. *1208*
8: 8 And the **s** angel sounded, and as *it were* a *1208*
11:14 The **s** woe is past; *and* behold, the third *1208*
16: 3 And the **s** angel poured out his vial upon *1208*
20: 6 on such the **s** death hath no power, but *1208*
20:14 cast into the lake of fire. This is the **s** death. *1208*
21: 8 and brimstone: which is the **s** death. *1208*
21:19 the **s**, sapphire; the third, a chalcedony; *1208*

SECONDARILY (1) [SECOND]

1Co 12:28 first apostles, **s** prophets, thirdly teachers, *1208*

SECRET (68) [SECRETLY, SECRETS]

Ge 49: 6 O my soul, come not thou into their **s**; 5475
Dt 27:15 putteth *it* in *a* **s** *place.* And all the people 5643
29:29 The **s** *things belong* unto the LORD our 5641
Jdg 3:19 said, I have a **s** errand unto thee, O king: 5643
13:18 thou thus after my name, seeing it *is* **s**? 6383
1Sa 5: 9 and they had emerods in their **s parts**. 8368
19: 2 and abide in a **s place**, and hide thyself: 5643
Job 14:13 that thou wouldest **keep** me **s**, until thy 5641
15: 8 Hast thou heard the **s** of God? and dost thou 5475
15:11 with thee? is there *any* **s** thing with thee? 328
20:26 All darkness *shall be* hid in his **s places**: 6845
29: 4 when the **s** of God *was* upon my tabernacle; 5475
40:13 the dust together; *and* bind their faces in **s**. 2934
Ps 10: 8 in the **s places** doth he murder the innocent: 4565
17:12 as it were a young lion lurking in **s places**. 4565
18:11 He made darkness his **s place**; his pavilion 5643
19:12 *his* errors? cleanse thou me from **s** *faults.* 5641
25:14 The **s** of the LORD *is* with them that fear 5475
27: 5 in the **s** of his tabernacle shall he hide me; 5643
31:20 Thou shalt hide them in the **s** of thy 5643
64: 2 Hide me from the **s counsel** of the wicked; 5475
64: 4 That *they* may shoot in **s** at the perfect: 4565
81: 7 I answered thee in the **s place** of thunder: 5643
90: 8 our **s** *sins* in the light of thy countenance. 5956
91: 1 He that dwelleth in the **s place** of the most 5643
139:15 when I was made in **s**, *and* 5643
Pr 3:32 the LORD: but his **s** *is* with the righteous. 5475
9:17 are sweet, and bread *eaten* in **s** is pleasant. 5643
21:14 A gift in **s** pacifieth anger: and a reward in 5643
25: 9 and discover not a **s** *to* another: 5475
27: 5 Open rebuke *is* better than **s** love. 5641
Ecc 12:14 with every **s** *thing,* whether *it be* good, or 5956
SS 2:14 in the **s places** of the stairs, let me see thy 5643
Isa 3:17 and the LORD will discover their **s parts**. 6596
45: 3 hidden riches of **s places**, that thou mayest 4565
45:19 I have not spoken in **s**, in a dark place of 5643
48:16 I have not spoken in **s** from the beginning; 5643
Jer 2:34 I have not found it by **s search**, but upon all 4290
13:17 my soul shall weep in **s places** for *your* 4565
23:24 Can any hide himself in **s places** that I shall 4565
49:10 I have uncovered his **s places**, and he shall 4565
La 3:10 bear lying in wait, *and as* a lion in **s places**. 4565
Eze 7:22 they shall pollute my **s** *place:* for 6845
28: 3 *there is* no **s** *that* they can hide *from* thee: 5640
Da 2:18 of the God of heaven concerning this **s**; 7328
2:19 *was* the **s** revealed unto Daniel in a night 7328
2:22 **s** *things:* he knoweth what *is* in 5642
2:27 The **s** which the king hath demanded 7328
2:30 this **s** *is* not revealed to me for *any* wisdom 7328
2:47 seeing thou couldest reveal this **s**. 7328
4: 9 gods *is* in thee, and no **s** troubleth thee, 7328
Am 3: 7 he revealeth his **s** unto his servants 5475
Mt 6: 4 That thine alms may be in **s**: and thy Father *2927*
6: 4 thy Father which seeth in **s** himself shall *2927*
6: 6 thy door, pray to thy Father which is in **s**; *2927*
6: 6 thy Father which seeth in **s** shall reward *2927*
6:18 to fast, but unto thy Father which is in **s**: *2927*
6:18 and thy Father, which seeth in **s**, *2927*
13:35 I will utter *things which have been* **kept s** *2928*
24:26 behold, *he is* in the **s chambers**; believe *it* *5009*
Mk 4:22 neither was *any thing* **kept s**, but that it *614*
Lk 8:17 For nothing is **s**, that shall not be made *2927*
11:33 putteth *it* in a **s place**, neither under a *2927*
Jn 7: 4 *there is* no *man that* doeth any *thing* in **s**, *2927*
7:10 the feast, not openly, but as it were in **s**. *2927*
18:20 always resort; and in **s** have I said nothing. *2927*
Ro 16:25 which was **kept s** since the world began, *4601*
Eph 5:12 of those *things* which are done of them in **s**. *2931*

SECRETLY (20) [SECRET]

Ge 31:27 Wherefore didst thou flee away **s**, and 2244
Dt 13: 6 entice thee **s**, saying, Let us 5643+871.1+1886.1
27:24 that smiteth his neighbour **s**. 5643+871.1+1886.1
28:57 of all *things* **s** in the siege 5643+871.1+1886.1
Jos 2: 1 Nun sent out of Shittim two men to spy **s**, 2791
1Sa 18:22 Commune with David **s**, 3909+871.1+1886.1
23: 9 David knew that Saul **s practised** mischief 2790
2Sa 12:12 For thou didst *it* **s**: but I will 5643+871.1+1886.1
2Ki 17: 9 the children of Israel did **s** *those* things that 2644
Job 4:12 Now a thing was **s brought** to me, and 1589
13:10 if ye do **s** accept persons. 5643+871.1+1886.1
31:27 my heart hath been **s** 5643+871.1+1886.1
Ps 10: 9 He lieth in wait **s** as a lion in 4565+871.1+1886.1
31:20 thou shalt **keep** them **s** in a pavilion from 6845
Jer 37:17 asked him **s** in his house, 5643+871.1+1886.1
38:16 king sware **s** unto Jeremiah, 5643+871.1+1886.1
40:15 to Gedaliah in Mizpah **s**, 5643+871.1+1886.1
Hab 3:14 *was* as to devour the poor **s**. 4565+871.1+1886.1
Jn 11:28 and called Mary her sister **s**, saying, *2977*
19:38 disciple of Jesus, but **s** for fear of the Jews, *2928*

SECRETS (10) [SECRET]

Dt 25:11 forth her hand, and taketh him by the **s**: 4016
Job 11: 6 that he would shew thee the **s** of wisdom, 8587
Ps 44:21 this out? for he knoweth the **s** of the heart. 8587
Pr 11:13 A talebearer revealeth **s**: but he that is of a 5475
20:19 that goeth about *as* a talebearer revealeth **s**: 5475
Da 2:28 there is a God in heaven that revealeth **s**, 7328
2:29 he that revealeth **s** maketh known to thee 7328

Da 2:47 a Lord of kings, and a revealer of **s**, 7328
Ro 2:16 In the day when God shall judge the **s** of *2927*
1Co 14:25 And thus are the **s** of his heart made *2927*

SECT (5)
Ac 5:17 with him, (which is the **s** of the Sadducees,) *139*
15: 5 But there rose up certain of the **s** of *139*
24: 5 and a ringleader of the **s** of the Nazarenes: *139*
26: 5 that after the most straitest **s** of our religion I *139*
28:22 for as concerning this **s**, we know that every *139*

SECU See SECHU

SECUNDUS (1)
Ac 20: 4 of the Thessalonians, Aristarchus and **S**; *4580*

SECURE (7) [SECURELY, SECURITY]
Jdg 8:11 and smote the host: for the host was **s**. 983
18: 7 the manner of the Zidonians, quiet and **s**; 982
18:10 ye shall come unto a people **s**, and to a large 982
18:27 unto a people *that were* at quiet and **s**: 982
Job 11:18 thou shalt be **s**, because there is hope; yea, 982
12: 6 and they that provoke God are **s**; 987
Mt 28:14 we will persuade him, and **s** you. *275+4160*

SECURELY (2) [SECURE]
Pr 3:29 seeing he dwelleth **s** by thee. 983+3807.1
Mic 2: 8 them that pass by **s** *as men* averse from war. 983

SECURITY (1) [SECURE]
Ac 17: 9 And when they had taken **s** of Jason, and *2425*

SEDITION (5) [SEDITIONS]
Ezr 4:15 that they have moved **s** within the same of 849
4:19 *that* rebellion and **s** *have been* made therein. 849
Lk 23:19 (Who for a certain **s** made in the city, and *4714*
23:25 And he released unto them him that for **s** *4714*
Ac 24: 5 a mover of **s** among all the Jews throughout *4714*

SEDITIONS (1) [SEDITION]
Gal 5:20 emulations, wrath, strife, **s**, heresies, *1370*

SEDUCE (3) [SEDUCED, SEDUCERS, SEDUCETH, SEDUCING]
Mk 13:22 and shall shew signs and wonders, to **s**, if *it* *635*
1Jn 2:26 unto you concerning them that **s** you. *4105*
Rev 2:20 and to **s** my servants to commit fornication, *4105*

SEDUCED (3) [SEDUCE]
2Ki 21: 9 Manasseh **s** them to do more evil than did 8582
Isa 19:13 they have also **s** Egypt, *even they that are* 8582
Eze 13:10 even because they have **s** my people, 2937

SEDUCERS (1) [SEDUCE]
2Ti 3:13 evil men and **s** shall wax worse and worse, *1114*

SEDUCETH (1) [SEDUCE]
Pr 12:26 but the way of the wicked **s** them. 8582

SEDUCING (1) [SEDUCE]
1Ti 4: 1 giving heed to **s** spirits, and doctrines of *4108*

SEE (597) [EYESIGHT, FORESAW, FORESEEING, FORESEETH, OVERSEE, SAW, SAWEST, SEEING, SEEN, SEER, SEER'S, SEERS, SEEST, SEETH, SIGHT, SIGHTS] See Index

SEED (279) [SEED'S, SEEDS, SEEDTIME]
Ge 1:11 the herb yielding **s**, *and* the fruit tree 2233
1:11 his kind, whose **s** *is* in itself, upon the earth: 2233
1:12 *and* herb yielding **s** after his kind, and 2233
1:12 whose **s** *was* in itself, after his kind: 2233
1:29 I have given you every herb bearing **s**, 2233
1:29 in the which *is* the fruit of a tree yielding **s**; 2233
3:15 and between thy **s** and her seed; 2233
3:15 and between thy seed and her **s**; 2233
4:25 *said she,* hath appointed me another **s** 2233
7: 3 to keep **s** alive upon the face of all 2233
9: 9 with you and with your **s** after you; 2233
12: 7 and said, Unto thy **s** will I give this land: 2233
13:15 to thee will I give it, and to thy **s** for ever. 2233
13:16 I will make thy **s** as the dust of the earth: 2233
13:16 the earth, *then* shall thy **s** also be numbered. 2233
15: 3 Behold, to me thou hast given no **s**: 2233
15: 5 and he said unto him, So shall thy **s** be. 2233
15:13 Know of a surety that thy **s** shall be a 2233
15:18 saying, Unto thy **s** have I given this land, 2233
16:10 I will multiply thy **s** exceedingly, that it 2233
17: 7 thy **s** after thee in their generations for an 2233
17: 7 be a God unto thee, and to thy **s** after thee. 2233
17: 8 I will give unto thee, and to thy **s** after thee, 2233
17: 9 and thy **s** after thee in their generations. 2233
17:10 between me and you and thy **s** after thee; 2233
17:12 of any stranger, which *is* not of thy **s**. 2233
17:19 *and* with his **s** after him. 2233
19:32 that we may preserve **s** of our father. 2233
19:34 that we may preserve **s** of our father. 2233
21:12 her voice; for in Isaac shall thy **s** be called. 2233
21:13 will I make a nation, because he *is* thy **s**. 2233
22:17 in multiplying I will multiply thy **s** as 2233
22:17 thy **s** shall possess the gate of his enemies; 2233
22:18 in thy **s** shall all the nations of the earth be 2233
24: 7 saying, Unto thy **s** will I give this land; 2233
24:60 let thy **s** possess the gate of those which 2233
26: 3 for unto thee, and unto thy **s**, I will give all 2233
26: 4 I will make thy **s** to multiply as the stars of 2233
26: 4 and will give unto thy **s** all these countries; 2233
26: 4 in thy **s** shall all the nations of the earth be 2233
26:24 multiply thy **s** for my servant Abraham's 2233
28: 4 of Abraham, to thee, and to thy **s** with thee; 2233
28:13 thou liest, to thee will I give it, and to thy **s**; 2233
28:14 thy **s** shall be as the dust of the earth, and 2233
28:14 in thy **s** shall all the families of the earth be 2233
32:12 and make thy **s** as the sand of the sea, 2233
35:12 and to thy **s** after thee will I give the land. 2233
38: 8 and marry her, and raise up **s** to thy brother. 2233
38: 9 Onan knew that the **s** should not be his; 2233
38: 9 lest that he should give **s** to his brother. 2233
46: 6 into Egypt, Jacob, and all his **s** with him: 2233
46: 7 all his **s** brought he with him into Egypt. 2233
47:19 and give *us* **s**, that we may live, and not die, 2233
47:23 lo, *here is* **s** for you, and ye shall sow 2233
47:24 for **s** of the field, and for your food, and 2233
48: 4 will give this land to thy **s** after thee *for* an 2233
48:11 and lo, God hath shewed me also thy **s**. 2233
48:19 his **s** shall become a multitude of nations. 2233
Ex 16:31 it *was* like coriander **s**, white; and the taste 2233
28:43 for ever unto him and his **s** after him. 2233
30:21 and to his **s** throughout their generations. 2233
32:13 I will multiply your **s** as the stars of heaven, 2233
32:13 I have spoken of will I give unto your **s**, 2233
33: 1 to Jacob, saying, Unto thy **s** will I give it: 2233
Lev 11:37 fall upon any sowing **s** which is to be sown, 2233
11:38 if *any* water be put upon the **s**, and *any part* 2233
12: 2 If a woman have **conceived s**, and born a 2232
15:16 if any man's **s** of copulation go out from 2233
15:17 every skin, whereon is the **s** of copulation, 2233
15:18 whom man shall lie *with* **s** of copulation, 2233
15:32 *of him* whose **s** goeth from him, and is 2233
18:21 thou shalt not let *any* of thy **s** pass through 2233
19:19 thou shalt not **sow** thy field **with** mingled **s**: 2232
20: 2 that giveth *any* of his **s** unto Molech; 2233
20: 3 because he hath given of his **s** unto Molech, 2233
20: 4 when he giveth of his **s** unto Molech, and 2233
21:15 Neither shall he profane his **s** among his 2233
21:17 Whosoever *he be* of thy **s** in their 2233
21:21 hath a blemish, of the **s** of Aaron the priest, 2233
22: 3 Whosoever *he be* of all your **s** among your 2233
22: 4 What man soever of the **s** of Aaron *is* a 2233
22: 4 or a man whose **s** goeth from him; 2233+7902
26:16 ye shall sow your **s** in vain, for your 2233
27:16 thy estimation shall be according to the **s** 2233
27:16 a homer of barley **s** *shall be valued* at fifty 2233
27:30 *whether* of the **s** of the land, *or* of the fruit 2233
Nu 5:28 shall be free, and shall **conceive s**. 2232+2233
11: 7 the manna *was* as coriander **s**, and 2233
14:24 he went; and his **s** shall possess it. 2233
16:40 no stranger, which *is* not of the **s** of Aaron, 2233
18:19 LORD unto thee and to thy **s** with thee. 2233
20: 5 it *is* no place of **s**, or of figs, or vines, or 2233
24: 7 his **s** *shall be* in many waters, and his king 2233
25:13 he shall have it, and his **s** after him, 2233
Dt 1: 8 to give unto them and to their **s** after them. 2233
4:37 therefore he chose their **s** after them, and 2233
10:15 he chose their **s** after them, *even* you above 2233
11: 9 fathers to give unto them and to their **s**, 2233
11:10 where thou sowedst thy **s**, and wateredst *it* 2233
14:22 shalt truly tithe all the increase of thy **s**, 2233
22: 9 lest the fruit of *thy* **s** which thou hast sown, 2233
28:38 Thou shalt carry much **s** out *into* the field, 2233
28:46 and for a wonder, and upon thy **s** for ever. 2233
28:59 the plagues of thy **s**, *even* great plagues, 2233

S

Dt	30: 6	the heart of thy **s**, to love the LORD thy	2233
	30:19	that *both* thou and thy **s** may live:	2233
	31:21	be forgotten out of the mouths of their **s**:	2233
	34: 4	unto Jacob, saying, I will give it unto thy **s**:	2233
Jos	24: 3	and multiplied his **s**, and gave him Isaac.	2233
Ru	4:12	of the **s** which the LORD shall give thee	2233
1Sa	2:20	The LORD give thee **s** of this woman for	2233
	8:15	he will take the tenth of your **s**, and of your	2233
	20:42	and between my **s** and thy seed for ever.	2233
	20:42	and between my seed and thy **s** for ever.	2233
	24:21	that thou wilt not cut off my **s** after me, and	2233
2Sa	4: 8	lord the king this day of Saul, and of his **s**.	2233
	7:12	thy fathers, I will set up thy **s** after thee,	2233
	22:51	unto David, and to his **s** for evermore.	2233
1Ki	2:33	of Joab, and upon the head of his **s** for ever:	2233
	2:33	upon his **s**, and upon his house, and	2233
	11:14	he *was* of the king's **s** in Edom.	2233
	11:39	And I will for this afflict the **s** of David, but	2233
	18:32	great as would contain two measures of **s**.	2233
2Ki	5:27	cleave unto thee, and unto thy **s** for ever.	2233
	11: 1	she arose and destroyed all the **s** royal.	2233
	17:20	the LORD rejected all the **s** of Israel, and	2233
	25:25	of the **s** royal, came, and ten men with him,	2233
1Ch	16:13	O ye **s** of Israel his servant, ye children of	2233
	17:11	that I will raise up thy **s** after thee,	2233
2Ch	20: 7	gavest it to the **s** of Abraham thy friend for	2233
	22:10	destroyed all the **s** royal of the house of	2233
Ezr	2:59	and their **s**, whether they *were* of Israel:	2233
	9: 2	that the holy **s** have mingled themselves	2233
Ne	7:61	nor their **s**, whether they *were* of Israel.	2233
	9: 2	the **s** of Israel separated themselves from all	2233
	9: 8	to give *it, I say,* to his **s**, and hast performed	2233
Est	6:13	If Mordecai *be* of the **s** of the Jews,	2233
	9:27	upon their **s**, and upon all such as joined	2233
	9:28	the memorial of them perish from their **s**.	2233
	9:31	had decreed for themselves and for their **s**,	2233
	10: 3	his people, and speaking peace to all his **s**.	2233
Job	5:25	Thou shalt know also that thy **s** *shall be*	2233
	21: 8	Their **s** is established in their sight with	2233
	39:12	that he will bring home thy **s**, and gather *it*	2233
Ps	18:50	to David, and to his **s** for evermore.	2233
	21:10	their **s** from among the children of men.	2233
	22:23	all ye the **s** of Jacob, glorify him; and	2233
	22:23	and fear him, all ye the **s** of Israel.	2233
	22:30	A **s** shall serve him; it shall be accounted to	2233
	25:13	at ease; and his **s** shall inherit the earth.	2233
	37:25	righteous forsaken, nor his **s** begging bread.	2233
	37:26	and lendeth; and his **s** *is* blessed.	2233
	37:28	but the **s** of the wicked shall be cut off.	2233
	69:36	The **s** also of his servants shall inherit it:	2233
	89: 4	Thy **s** will I stablish for ever, and build up	2233
	89:29	His **s** also will I make *to endure* for ever,	2233
	89:36	His **s** shall endure for ever, and his throne	2233
	102:28	and their **s** shall be established before thee.	2233
	105: 6	O ye **s** of Abraham his servant, ye children	2233
	106:27	To overthrow their **s** also among	2233
	112: 2	His **s** shall be mighty upon earth:	2233
	126: 6	and weepeth, bearing precious **s**,	2233
Pr	11:21	but the **s** of the righteous shall be delivered.	2233
Ecc	11: 6	In the morning sow thy **s**, and in	2233
Isa	1: 4	a **s** of evildoers, children that are	2233
	5:10	and the **s** of a homer shall yield an ephah.	2233
	6:13	*so* the holy **s** *shall be* the substance thereof.	2233
	14:20	the **s** of evildoers shall never be renowned.	2233
	17:11	in the morning shalt thou make thy **s** to	2233
	23: 3	by great waters the **s** of Sihor, the harvest	2233
	30:23	shall he give the rain of thy **s**, that thou	2233
	41: 8	I have chosen, the **s** of Abraham my friend.	2233
	43: 5	I will bring thy **s** from the east, and	2233
	44: 3	*ground:* I will pour my spirit upon thy **s**,	2233
	45:19	I said not unto the **s** of Jacob, Seek ye me	2233
	45:25	In the LORD shall all the **s** of Israel be	2233
	48:19	Thy **s** also had been as the sand, and	2233
	53:10	he shall see *his* **s**, he shall prolong *his* days,	2233
	54: 3	thy **s** shall inherit the Gentiles, and	2233
	55:10	that it may give **s** to the sower, and bread to	2233
	57: 3	the **s** of the adulterer and the whore.	2233
	57: 4	children of transgression, a **s** of falsehood,	2233
	59:21	of thy mouth, nor out of the mouth of thy **s**,	2233
	59:21	nor out of the mouth of thy seed's **s**,	2233
	61: 9	their **s** shall be known among the Gentiles,	2233
	61: 9	that they *are* the **s** *which* the LORD hath	2233
	65: 9	I will bring forth a **s** out of Jacob, and	2233
	65:23	for they *are* the **s** of the blessed of	2233
	66:22	so shall your **s** and your name remain.	2233
Jer	2:21	planted thee a noble vine, wholly a right **s**:	2233
	7:15	*even* the whole **s** of Ephraim.	2233
	22:28	he and his **s**, and are cast into a land which	2233
	22:30	for no man of his **s** shall prosper,	2233
	23: 8	which led the **s** of the house of Israel out of	2233
	29:32	punish Shemaiah the Nehelamite, and his **s**:	2233
	30:10	and thy **s** from the land of their captivity;	2233
	31:27	and the house of Judah *with* the **s** of man,	2233
	31:27	the seed of man, and *with* the **s** of beast.	2233
	31:36	the **s** of Israel also shall cease from being a	2233
	31:37	I will also cast off all the **s** of Israel for all	2233
	33:22	will I multiply the **s** of David my servant,	2233
	33:26	will I cast away the **s** of Jacob, and	2233
	33:26	that *I* will not take *any* of his **s** *to be* rulers	2233
	33:26	his seed *to be* rulers over the **s** of Abraham,	2233
	35: 7	nor sow **s**, nor plant vineyard, nor have	2233
	35: 9	neither have we vineyard, nor field, nor **s**:	2233
	36:31	I will punish him and his **s** and his servants	2233
	41: 1	of the **s** royal, and the princes of the king,	2233
	46:27	and thy **s** from the land of their captivity;	2233
	49:10	his **s** is spoiled, and his brethren, and	2233
Eze	17: 5	He took also of the **s** of the land, and	2233
	17:13	hath taken of the king's **s**, and made a	2233
	20: 5	lifted up mine hand unto the **s** of the house	2233
	43:19	priests the Levites that *be* of the **s** of Zadok,	2233
	44:22	they shall take maidens of the **s** of	2233
Da	1: 3	and of the king's **s**, and of the princes;	2233
	2:43	they shall mingle themselves with the **s** of	2234
	9: 1	the son of Ahasuerus, of the **s** of the Medes,	2233
Joel	1:17	The **s** is rotten under their clods, the garners	6507
Am	9:13	and the treader of grapes him that soweth **s**;	2233
Hag	2:19	*Is* the **s** yet in the barn? yea, as yet the vine,	2233
Zec	8:12	For the **s** *shall be* prosperous; the vine shall	2233
Mal	2: 3	I *will* corrupt your **s**, and spread dung upon	2233
	2:15	That he might seek a godly **s**.	2233
Mt	13:19	This is he which **received** **s** by the way	*4687*
	13:20	But he that **received** the **s** into stony *places,*	*4687*
	13:22	He also that **received** **s** among the thorns is	*4687*
	13:23	But he that **received** **s** into the good ground	*4687*
	13:24	a man which sowed good **s** in his field:	*4690*
	13:27	Sir, didst not thou sow good **s** in thy field?	*4690*
	13:31	of heaven is like unto a **grain of** mustard **s**,	*2848*
	13:37	He that soweth the good **s** is the Son of	*4690*
	13:38	the good **s** are the children of the kingdom;	*4690*
	17:20	If ye have faith as a **grain of** mustard **s**,	*2848*
	22:24	his wife, and raise up **s** unto his brother.	*4690*
Mk	4:26	as if a man should cast **s** into the ground,	*4703*
	4:27	day, and the **s** should spring and grow up,	*4703*
	4:31	*It is* like a **grain of** mustard **s**, which,	*2848*
	12:19	his wife, and raise up **s** unto his brother.	*4690*
	12:20	the first took a wife, and dying left no **s**.	*4690*
	12:21	took her, and died, neither left he *any* **s**:	*4690*
	12:22	And the seven had her, and left no **s**: last of	*4690*
Lk	1:55	to Abraham, and to his **s** for ever.	*4690*
	8: 5	A sower went out to sow his **s**: and as he	*4703*
	8:11	parable is this: The **s** is the word of God.	*4703*
	13:19	It is like a **grain of** mustard **s**, which a man	*2848*
	17: 6	If ye had faith as a **grain of** mustard **s**,	*2848*
	20:28	*his* wife, and raise up **s** unto his brother.	*4690*
Jn	7:42	That Christ cometh of the **s** of David, and	*4690*
	8:33	We be Abraham's **s**, and were never in	*4690*
	8:37	I know that ye are Abraham's **s**; but ye seek	*4690*
Ac	3:25	And in thy **s** shall all the kindreds of	*4690*
	7: 5	and to his **s** after him, when *as yet* he had	*4690*
	7: 6	That his **s** should sojourn in a strange land;	*4690*
	13:23	Of this *man's* **s** hath God according to *his*	*4690*
Ro	1: 3	which was made of the **s** of David	*4690*
	4:13	or to his **s**, through the law, but through	*4690*
	4:16	end the promise might be sure to all the **s**;	*4690*
	4:18	to that which was spoken, So shall thy **s** be.	*4690*
	9: 7	Neither, because they are the **s** of Abraham,	*4690*
	9: 7	but, In Isaac shall thy **s** be called.	*4690*
	9: 8	of the promise are counted for the **s**.	*4690*
	9:29	Except the Lord of sabaoth had left us a **s**,	*4690*
	11: 1	of the **s** of Abraham, *of* the tribe of	*4690*
1Co	15:38	pleased him, and to every **s** his own body.	*4690*
2Co	9:10	Now he that ministereth **s** to the sower both	*4690*
	9:10	and multiply your **s** **sown**, and increase	*4703*
	11:22	*am* I. Are they the **s** of Abraham? so *am* I.	*4690*
Gal	3:16	and his **s** were the promises made.	*4690*
	3:16	but as of one, And to thy **s**, which is Christ.	*4690*
	3:19	till the **s** should come to whom the promise	*4690*
	3:29	then are ye Abraham's **s**, and	*4690*

2Ti 2: 8 Remember that Jesus Christ of the **s** of 4690
Heb 2:16 but he took on *him* the **s** of Abraham. 4690
11:11 Sara herself received strength to conceive **s**, 4690
11:18 was said, That in Isaac shall thy **s** be called: 4690
1Pe 1:23 not of corruptible **s**, but *of* incorruptible, 4701
1Jn 3: 9 not commit sin; for his **s** remaineth in him: 4690
Rev 12:17 to make war with the remnant of her **s**, 4690

SEED'S (1) [SEED]
Isa 59:21 nor out of the mouth of thy **s** seed, saith 2233

SEEDS (5) [SEED]
Dt 22: 9 shalt not **sow** thy vineyard with divers **s**: 2232
Mt 13: 4 some *s* fell by the way side, and the fowls NIG
13:32 Which indeed is the least of all **s**: but 4690
Mk 4:31 is less than all the **s** that be in the earth: 4690
Gal 3:16 *He* saith not, And to **s**, as of many; but as of 4690

SEEDTIME (1) [SEED, TIME]
Ge 8:22 **s** and harvest, and cold and heat, and 2233

SEEING (116) [SEE] See Index

SEEK (244) [SEEKEST, SEEKETH, SEEKING, SOUGHT]
Ge 37:16 he said, I **s** my brethren: tell me, I pray 1245
43:18 that he may **s occasion** against us, and fall 1556
Lev 13:36 the priest shall not **s** for yellow hair: 1239
19:31 neither **s** after wizards, to be defiled by 1245
Nu 15:39 that ye **s** not after your own heart and 8446
16:10 with thee: and **s** ye the priesthood also? 1245
24: 1 to **s** for enchantments, but he set his face 7125
Dt 4:29 if from thence thou shalt **s** the LORD thy 1245
4:29 thou shalt find *him*, if thou **s** him with all 1875
12: 5 *even* unto his habitation shall ye **s**, and 1875
22: 2 it shall be with thee until thy brother **s after** 1875
23: 6 Thou shalt not **s** their peace nor their 1875
Ru 3: 1 My daughter, shall I not **s** rest for thee, 1245
1Sa 9: 3 servants with thee, and arise, go **s** the asses. 1245
10: 2 The asses which thou wentest to **s** are 1245
10:14 he said, To **s** the asses: and when we saw 1245
16:16 to **s out** a man, *who is* a cunning player on 1245
23:15 David saw that Saul was come out to **s** his 1245
23:25 his men went to **s** *him*. And they told 1245
24: 2 went to **s** David and his men upon the rocks 1245
25:26 and they that **s** evil to my lord, be as Nabal. 1245
25:29 is risen to pursue thee, and to **s** thy soul: 1245
26: 2 to **s** David in the wilderness of Ziph. 1245
26:20 for the king of Israel is come out to **s** a flea, 1245
27: 1 to **s** me any more in any coast of Israel: 1245
28: 7 **S** me a woman that hath a familiar spirit, 1245
2Sa 5:17 all the Philistines came up to **s** David; 1245
1Ki 2:40 went to Gath to Achish to **s** his servants: 1245
18:10 whither my lord hath not sent to **s** thee: 1245
19:10 am left; and they **s** my life, to take it away. 1245
19:14 am left; and they **s** my life, to take it away. 1245
2Ki 2:16 let them go, we pray thee, and **s** thy master: 1245
6:19 and I will bring you to the man whom ye **s**. 1245
1Ch 4:39 of the valley, to **s** pasture for their flocks. 1245
14: 8 all the Philistines went up to **s** David. 1245
16:10 let the heart of them rejoice that **s** 1245
16:11 **S** the LORD and his strength, seek his 1875
16:11 and his strength, **s** his face continually. 1245
22:19 and your soul to **s** the LORD your God; 1875
28: 8 **s** for all the commandments of the LORD 1875
28: 9 if thou **s** him, he will be found of thee; but 1875
2Ch 7:14 **s** my face, and turn from their wicked 1245
11:16 **s** the LORD God of Israel came *to* 1245
12:14 he prepared not his heart to **s** the LORD. 1875
14: 4 commanded Judah to **s** the LORD God of 1875
15: 2 if ye **s** him, he will be found of you; but 1875
15:12 they entered into a covenant to **s** 1875
15:13 That whosoever would not **s** the LORD 1875
19: 3 and hast prepared thine heart to **s** God. 1875
20: 3 set himself to **s** the LORD, and 1875
20: 4 cities of Judah they came to **s** the LORD. 1245
30:19 *That* prepareth his heart to **s** God, 1875
31:21 and in the commandments, to **s** his God, 1875
34: 3 he began to **s** after the God of David his 1875
Ezr 4: 2 for we **s** your God, as ye *do*; and we do 1875
6:21 to **s** the LORD God of Israel, did eat, 1875
7:10 For Ezra had prepared his heart to **s** the law 1875
8:21 to **s** of him a right way for us, and for our 1245
8:22 God *is* upon all them for good that **s** him; 1245
9:12 nor **s** their peace or their wealth for ever: 1875
Ne 2:10 to **s** the welfare of the children of Israel. 1245

Job 5: 8 I would **s** unto God, and unto God would I 1875
7:21 thou shalt **s** me **in the morning**, but I *shall* 7836
8: 5 If thou wouldest **s** unto God **betimes**, and 7836
20:10 His children shall *s to* please the poor, and NIH
Ps 4: 2 will ye love vanity, *and* **s after** leasing? 1245
9:10 LORD, hast not forsaken them that **s** thee. 1875
10: 4 will not **s** *after God:* God *is* not *in* all his 1875
10:15 the evil *man:* **s out** his wickedness *till* thou 1875
14: 2 were *any* that did understand, *and* **s** God. 1875
22:26 they shall praise the LORD that **s** him: 1875
24: 6 This *is* the generation of them that **s** him, 1875
24: 6 that seek him, that **s** thy face, O Jacob. 1245
27: 4 I desired of the LORD, that will I **s after**; 1245
27: 8 *When thou saidst,* **S** ye my face; my heart 1245
27: 8 said unto thee, Thy face, LORD, will I **s**. 1245
34:10 they that **s** the LORD shall not want any 1875
34:14 and do good; **s** peace, and pursue it. 1245
35: 4 and put to shame that **s after** my soul: 1245
38:12 They also that **s after** my life lay snares *for* 1245
38:12 they that **s** my hurt speak mischievous 1875
40:14 confounded together that **s after** my soul to 1245
40:16 Let all those that **s** thee rejoice and be glad 1245
53: 2 *any* that did understand, that did **s** God. 1875
54: 3 against me, and oppressors **s after** my soul: 1245
63: 1 thou *art* my God; **early** will I **s** thee: 7836
63: 9 those *that* **s** my soul, to destroy *it*, shall go 1245
69: 6 let not those that **s** thee be confounded for 1245
69:32 and your heart shall live that **s** God. 1875
70: 2 and confounded that **s after** my soul: 1245
70: 4 Let all those that **s** thee rejoice and be glad 1245
71:13 *with* reproach and dishonour that **s** my hurt. 1245
71:24 are brought unto shame, that **s** my hurt. 1245
83:16 that they may **s** thy name, O LORD. 1245
104:21 after *their* prey, and **s** their meat from God. 1245
105: 3 let the heart of them rejoice that **s** 1245
105: 4 **S** the LORD, and his strength: seek his 1875
105: 4 and his strength: **s** his face evermore. 1245
109:10 let them **s** *their bread* also out of their 1875
119: 2 *and that* **s** him with the whole heart. 1875
119:45 I will walk at liberty: for I **s** thy precepts. 1875
119:155 from the wicked: for they **s** not thy statutes. 1875
119:176 gone astray like a lost sheep; **s** thy servant; 1245
122: 9 of the LORD our God I will **s** thy good. 1245
Pr 1:28 they shall **s** me **early**, but they shall not 7836
7:15 **diligently** to **s** thy face, and I have found 7836
8:17 and those that **s** me **early** shall find me. 7836
21: 6 tossed to and fro of them that **s** death. 1245
23:30 at the wine; they that go to **s** mixt wine. 2713
23:35 when shall I awake? I will **s** it yet again. 1245
28: 5 they that **s** the LORD understand all 1245
29:10 hate the upright: but the just **s** his soul. 1245
29:26 Many **s** the ruler's favour; but *every* man's 1245
Ecc 1:13 I gave my heart to **s** and search out by 1875
7:25 to **s out** wisdom, and the reason *of things,* 1245
8:17 because though a man labour to **s** *it* **out**, 1245
SS 3: 2 I will **s** *him* whom my soul loveth: 1245
6: 1 turned aside? that we may **s** him with thee. 1245
Isa 1:17 **s** judgment, relieve the oppressed, judge 1875
8:19 **S** unto them that have familiar spirits, and 1875
8:19 should not a people **s** unto their God? 1875
9:13 neither do they **s** the LORD of hosts. 1875
11:10 of the people; to it shall the Gentiles **s**: 1875
19: 3 they shall **s** to the idols, and to 1875
26: 9 *with* my spirit within me will I **s** thee **early**: 7836
29:15 Woe unto them that **s deep** to hide *their* 6009
31: 1 Holy One of Israel, neither **s** the LORD. 1875
34:16 **S** ye out of the book of the LORD, and 1875
41:12 Thou shalt **s** them, and shalt not find them, 1245
41:17 *When* the poor and needy **s** water, and 1245
45:19 not unto the seed of Jacob, **S** ye me in vain: 1245
51: 1 after righteousness, ye that **s** the LORD: 1245
55: 6 **S** ye the LORD while he may be found, 1875
58: 2 Yet they **s** me daily, and delight to know 1875
Jer 2:24 all they that **s** her will not weary 1245
2:33 Why trimmest thou thy way to **s** love? 1245
4:30 lovers will despise thee, they will **s** thy life. 1245
5: 1 know, and **s** in the broad places thereof, 1245
11:21 that **s** thy life, saying, Prophesy not in 1245
19: 7 and by the hands of them that **s** their lives: 1245
19: 9 they that **s** their lives, shall straiten them. 1245
21: 7 and into the hand of those that **s** their life: 1245
22:25 I will give thee into the hand of them that **s** 1245
29: 7 **s** the peace of the city whither I have 1875
29:13 ye shall **s** me, and find *me*, when ye shall 1245

Jer 30:14 lovers have forgotten thee; they **s** thee not; 1875
34:20 and into the hand of them that **s** their life: 1245
34:21 into the hand of them that **s** their life, and 1245
38:16 into the hand of these men that **s** thy life. 1245
44:30 and into the hand of them that **s** his life; 1245
45: 5 **s** *them* not: for behold, I *will* bring evil 1245
46:26 into the hand of those that **s** their lives, 1245
49:37 and before them that **s** their life: 1245
50: 4 they shall go, and **s** the LORD their God. 1245
La 1:11 All her people sigh, they **s** bread; they have 1245
Eze 7:25 they shall **s** peace, and *there shall be* none. 1245
7:26 then shall they **s** a vision of the prophet; but 1245
34: 6 and none did search or **s** *after them.* 1245
34:11 will both search my sheep, and **s** them **out**. 1239
34:12 so will I **s out** my sheep, and will deliver 1239
34:16 I will **s** that which was lost, and bring again 1245
Da 9: 3 to **s** *by* prayer and supplications, 1245
Hos 2: 7 she shall **s** them, but shall not find *them:* 1245
3: 5 **s** the LORD their God, and David their 1245
5: 6 and with their herds to **s** the LORD; 1245
5:15 acknowledge their offence, and **s** my face: 1245
5:15 in their affliction they will **s** me **early**. 7836
7:10 LORD their God, nor **s** him for all this. 1245
10:12 for *it is* time to **s** the LORD, till he come 1875
Am 5: 4 house of Israel, **S** ye me, and ye shall live: 1875
5: 5 **s** not Beth-el, nor enter *into* Gilgal, and 1875
5: 6 **S** the LORD, and ye shall live; lest he 1875
5: 8 ***S*** *him* that maketh the seven stars and NIH
5:14 **S** good, and not evil, that ye may live: and 1875
8:12 run to and fro to **s** the word of the LORD, 1245
Na 3: 7 whence shall I **s** comforters for thee? 1245
3:11 thou also shalt **s** strength because of 1245
Zep 2: 3 **S** ye the LORD, all ye meek of the earth, 1245
2: 3 **s** righteousness, seek meekness: 1245
2: 3 seek righteousness, **s** meekness: 1245
Zec 8:21 the LORD, and to **s** the LORD of hosts: 1245
8:22 strong nations shall come to **s** the LORD 1245
11:16 neither shall **s** the young one, nor heal that 1245
12: 9 *that* I will **s** to destroy all the nations that 1245
Mal 2: 7 and they should **s** the law at his mouth: 1245
2:15 That he might **s** a godly seed. 1245
3: 1 the LORD, whom ye **s**, shall suddenly 1245
Mt 2:13 for Herod will **s** the young child to destroy *2212*
6:32 **after** all these *things* do the Gentiles **s**): *1934*
6:33 But **s** ye first the kingdom of God, and *2212*
7: 7 **s**, and ye shall find; knock, and it shall be *2212*
28: 5 for I know that ye **s** Jesus, which was *2212*
Mk 1:37 they said unto him, All *men* **s for** thee. *2212*
3:32 and thy brethren without **s for** thee. *2212*
8:12 Why doth this generation **s after** a sign? *1934*
16: 6 Ye **s** Jesus of Nazareth, which was *2212*
Lk 11: 9 **s**, and ye shall find; knock, and it shall be *2212*
11:29 they **s** a sign; and there shall no sign be *1934*
12:29 And **s** not ye what ye shall eat, or what ye *2212*
12:30 *things* do the nations of the world **s after**: *1934*
12:31 But rather **s** ye the kingdom of God; *2212*
13:24 will **s** to enter in, and shall not be able. *2212*
15: 8 the house, and **s** diligently till she find *it?* *2212*
17:33 Whosoever shall **s** to save his life shall lose *2212*
19:10 For the Son of man is come to **s** and to save *2212*
24: 5 Why **s** ye the living among the dead? *2212*
Jn 1:38 and saith unto them, What **s** ye? *2212*
5:30 is just; because I **s** not mine own will, *2212*
5:44 **s** not the honour that *cometh* from God *2212*
6:26 Ye **s** me, not because ye saw *the* miracles, *2212*
7:25 Is not this he, whom they **s** to kill? *2212*
7:34 Ye shall **s** me, and shall not find *me:* and *2212*
7:36 Ye shall **s** me, and shall not find *me:* and *2212*
8:21 and ye shall **s** me, and shall die in your *2212*
8:37 but ye **s** to kill me, because my word hath *2212*
8:40 But now ye **s** to kill me, a man that hath *2212*
8:50 And I **s** not mine own glory: there is *one* *2212*
13:33 Ye shall **s** me: and as I said unto the Jews, *2212*
18: 4 and said unto them, Whom **s** ye? *2212*
18: 7 Then asked he them again, Whom **s** ye? *2212*
18: 8 told you that I am *he:* if therefore ye **s** me, *2212*
Ac 10:19 said unto him, Behold, three men **s** thee: *2212*
10:21 and said, Behold, I am he whom ye **s**: *2212*
11:25 departed Barnabas to Tarsus, for to **s** Saul: *327*
15:17 That the residue of men might **s after** *1567*
17:27 That *they* should **s** the Lord, if haply they *2212*
Ro 2: 7 continuance in well doing **s for** glory *2212*
11: 3 and I am left alone, and they **s** my life. *2212*
1Co 1:22 a sign, and the Greeks **s after** wisdom: *2212*
7:27 **s** not to be loosed. Art thou loosed from a *2212*
7:27 Art thou loosed from a wife? **s** not a wife. *2212*
10:24 Let no *man* **s** his own, but every man *2212*
14:12 **s** that ye may excel to the edifying of *2212*
2Co 12:14 not be burdensome to you: for I **s** not yours, *2212*
13: 3 Since ye **s** a proof of Christ speaking in me, *2212*
Gal 1:10 or do I **s** to please men? for if I yet pleased *2212*
2:17 But if, while we **s** to be justified by Christ, *2212*
Php 2:21 For all **s** their own, not the *things which are* *2212*
Col 3: 1 with Christ, **s** those *things* which are above, *2212*
Heb 11: 6 is a rewarder of them that **diligently s** him. *1567*
11:14 *things* declare plainly that they **s** a country. *1934*
13:14 no continuing city, but we **s** one to come. *1934*
1Pe 3:11 and do good; let him **s** peace, and ensue it. *2212*
Rev 9: 6 And in those days shall men **s** death, and *2212*

SEEKEST (9) [SEEK]

Ge 37:15 the man asked him, saying, What **s** thou? 1245
Jdg 4:22 and I will shew thee the man whom thou **s**. 1245
2Sa 17: 3 the man whom thou **s** *is* as if all returned: 1245
20:19 thou **s** to destroy a city and a mother in 1245
1Ki 11:22 thou **s** to go to thine own country? 1245
Pr 2: 4 If thou **s** her as silver, and searchest for her 1245
Jer 45: 5 **s** thou great *things* for thyself? seek *them* 1245
Jn 4:27 yet no *man* said, What **s** thou? or, *2212*
20:15 whom **s** thou? She, supposing him to be *2212*

SEEKETH (42) [SEEK]

1Sa 19: 2 saying, Saul my father **s** to kill thee: 1245
20: 1 my sin before thy father, that he **s** my life? 1245
22:23 for he that **s** my life seeketh thy life: but 1245
22:23 for he that seeketh my life **s** thy life: but 1245
23:10 thy servant hath certainly heard that Saul **s** 1245
24: 9 saying, Behold, David **s** thy hurt? 1245
2Sa 16:11 which came forth of my bowels, **s** my life: 1245
1Ki 20: 7 pray you, and see how this *man* **s** mischief: 1245
2Ki 5: 7 and see how he **s a quarrel** against me. 579
Job 39:29 From thence she **s** the prey, *and* her eyes 2658
Ps 37:32 watcheth the righteous, and **s** to slay him. 1245
Pr 11:27 He that **diligently s** good procureth favour: 7836
11:27 he that **s** mischief, it shall come *unto* him. 1875
14: 6 A scorner **s** wisdom, and *findeth it* not: but 1245
15:14 The heart of him that hath understanding **s** 1245
17: 9 He that covereth a transgression **s** love; but 1245
17:11 An evil *man* **s** only rebellion: therefore 1245
17:19 *and* he that exalteth his gate **s** destruction. 1245
18: 1 **s** *and* intermeddleth with all wisdom. 1245
18:15 and the ear of the wise **s** knowledge. 1245
31:13 She **s** wool, and flax, and worketh willingly 1875
Ecc 7:28 Which yet my soul **s**, but I find not: 1245
Isa 40:20 he **s** unto him a cunning workman to 1245
Jer 5: 1 that executeth judgment, that **s** the truth; 1245
30:17 *saying,* This *is* Zion, whom no man **s after**. 1875
38: 4 for this man **s** not the welfare of this 1875
La 3:25 that wait for him, to the soul *that* **s** him. 1875
Eze 14:10 as the punishment of him that **s** *unto him;* 1875
34:12 As a shepherd **s out** his flock in the day 1243
Mt 7: 8 that asketh receiveth; and he that **s** findeth: *2212*
12:39 and adulterous generation **s after** a sign; *1934*
16: 4 and adulterous generation **s after** a sign; *1934*
18:12 and **s** that which is gone astray? *2212*
Lk 11:10 and he that **s** findeth; and to him that *2212*
Jn 4:23 for the Father **s** such to worship him. *2212*
7: 4 and he himself **s** to be known openly. *2212*
7:18 He that speaketh of himself **s** his own *2212*
7:18 but he that **s** his glory that sent him, *2212*
8:50 own glory: there is *one* that **s** and judgeth. *2212*
Ro 3:11 there is none that **s** after God. NIG
11: 7 Israel hath not obtained that which he **s for**; *1934*
1Co 13: 5 **s** not her own, is not easily provoked, *2212*

SEEKING (14) [SEEK]

Est 10: 3 **s** the wealth of his people, and 1875
Isa 16: 5 and **s** judgment, and hasting righteousness. 1875
Mt 12:43 through dry places, **s** rest, and findeth none. *2212*
13:45 like unto a merchant man, **s** goodly pearls: *2212*
Mk 8:11 **s** of him a sign from heaven, tempting him. *2212*
Lk 2:45 they turned back again to Jerusalem, **s** him. *2212*
11:24 he walketh through dry places, **s** rest; *2212*
11:54 and **s** to catch something out of his mouth, *2212*
13: 7 *these* three years I come **s** fruit on this fig *2212*
Jn 6:24 and came to Capernaum, **s for** Jesus. *2212*
Ac 13: 8 **s** to turn away the deputy from the faith. *2212*
13:11 he went about **s** *some* to lead him by *2212*

S

1Co 10:33 Even as I please all *men* in all *things,* not s 2212
1Pe 5: 8 walketh about, s whom he may devour: 2212

SEEM (22) [SEEMED, SEEMETH, SEEMLY, UNSEEMLY]
Ge 27:12 I shall s to him as a deceiver; 1961+5869+871.1
Dt 15:18 It shall not s hard unto thee, 5869+871.1
25: 3 thy brother should s vile **unto** thee. 5869+3807.1
Jos 24:15 if it s evil **unto** you to serve 5869+871.1
1Sa 24: 4 to him as it shall s good **unto** thee. 5869+871.1
2Sa 19:37 to him what shall s good **unto** thee. 5869+871.1
19:38 *that* which shall s good **unto** thee: 5869+871.1
1Ki 21: 2 *or,* if it s good to thee, I will give 5869+871.1
1Ch 13: 2 If *it* s good unto you, and *that it be* of NIH
Ezr 5:17 Now therefore, if *it* s good to the king, NIH
7:18 whatsoever shall s **good** to thee, and to thy 3191
Ne 9:32 let not all the trouble s little before thee, NIH
Est 5: 4 If *it* s good unto the king, let the king and NIH
8: 5 the thing s **right** before the king, and I *be* 3787
Jer 40: 4 If it s good **unto** thee to come with 5869+871.1
40: 4 if it s ill **unto** thee to come with me 5869+871.1
Na 2: 4 they shall s like torches, they shall run like 4758
1Co 11:16 But if any *man* s to be contentious, we have *1380*
12:22 which s to be more feeble, are necessary: *1380*
2Co 10: 9 That I may not s as if *I* would terrify you by *1380*
Heb 4: 1 any of you should s to come short *of it.* *1380*
Jas 1:26 If any *man* among you s to be religious, *1380*

SEEMED (16) [SEEM]
Ge 19:14 he s as one that mocked unto 1961+5869+871.1
29:20 they s unto him *but* a few 1961+5869+871.1
2Sa 3:19 in Hebron all that s good **to** Israel, 5869+871.1
3:19 that s *good* **to** the whole house of 5869+871.1
Ecc 9:13 also under the sun, and it *s* great unto me: NIH
Jer 18: 4 as s good **to** the potter to make *it.* 5869+871.1
27: 5 it unto whom it s meet **unto** me. 5869+871.1
Mt 11:26 Father: for so it s good in thy sight. *1096*
Lk 1: 3 It s **good** to me also, having had perfect *1380*
10:21 Father; for so it s good in thy sight. *1096*
24:11 And their words s to them as idle tales, and *5316*
Ac 15:25 It s **good** unto us, being assembled with one *1380*
15:28 For it s **good** to the Holy Ghost, and to us, *1380*
Gal 2: 6 But of these who s to be somewhat, *1380*
2: 6 for they who s *to be somewhat* in *1380*
2: 9 Cephas, and John, who s to be pillars, *1380*

SEEMETH (28) [SEEM]
Lev 14:35 It s to me *there is* as it were a plague in 7200
Nu 16: 9 *S it but* a small thing unto you, that the God NIH
Jos 9:25 as it s good and right unto thee to do 5869+871.1
Jdg 10:15 us whatsoever s good **unto** thee; 5869+871.1
19:24 do with them what s good **unto** you: 5869+871.1
1Sa 1:23 said unto her, Do what s thee good; 5869+871.1
3:18 let him do what s him good. 5869+871.1
11:10 do with us all that s good **unto** you. 5869+871.1
14:36 Do whatsoever s good **unto** thee. 5869+871.1
14:40 Do what s good **unto** thee. 5869+871.1
18:23 David said, **S** it to you a light *thing* 5869+871.1
2Sa 10:12 LORD do that which s him good. 5869+871.1
15:26 him do to me as s good **unto** him. 5869+871.1
18: 4 What s you best I will do. 5869+871.1
24:22 and offer up what s good **unto** him: 5869+871.1
Est 3:11 to do with them as it s good **to** thee. 5869+871.1
Pr 14:12 There is a way which s right **unto** a 6440+3807.1
16:25 There is a way that s right **unto** a 6440+3807.1
18:17 *He that is* first in his own cause *s* just; but NIH
Jer 26:14 me as s good and meet **unto** you. 5869+871.1
40: 4 whither it s good and convenient for 5869+871.1
40: 5 go wheresoever it s convenient **unto** 5869+871.1
Eze 34:18 *S it* a small thing unto you to have eaten up NIH
Lk 8:18 shall be taken even *that* which he s to have. *1380*
Ac 17:18 other *some,* He s to be a setter forth of *1380*
25:27 For it s to me unreasonable to send a *1380*
1Co 3:18 If any *man* among you s to be wise in this *1380*
Heb 12:11 Now no chastening for the present s to be *1380*

SEEMLY (2) [SEEM]
Pr 19:10 Delight *is* not s for a fool; much less for a 5000
26: 1 rain in harvest, so honour *is* not s for a fool. 5000

SEEN (277) [SEE] See Index

SEER (21) [SEE]
1Sa 9: 9 thus he spake, Come, and let us go to the s: 7200
9: 9 *called* a Prophet was beforetime called a **S.**) 7200
9:11 and said unto them, Is the s here? 7200
9:19 Samuel answered Saul, and said, I *am* the s: 7200
2Sa 15:27 also unto Zadok the priest, *Art not* thou a s? 7200
24:11 unto the prophet Gad, David's s, saying, 2374
1Ch 9:22 Samuel the s did ordain in their set office. 7200
21: 9 LORD spake unto Gad, David's s, saying, 2374
25: 5 of Heman the king's s in the words of God, 2374
26:28 all that Samuel the s, and Saul the son of 7200
29:29 *are* written in the book of Samuel the s, 7200
29:29 the prophet, and in the book of Gad the s, 2374
2Ch 9:29 in the visions of Iddo the s against 2374
12:15 and of Iddo the s concerning genealogies? 2374
16: 7 at that time Hanani the s came to Asa king 7200
16:10 Asa was wroth with the s, and put him *in* a 7200
19: 2 Jehu the son of Hanani the s went out to 2374
29:25 of Gad the king's s, and Nathan 2374
29:30 the words of David, and of Asaph the s. 2374
35:15 and Heman, and Jeduthun the king's s; 2374
Am 7:12 Amaziah said unto Amos, O thou s, go, 2374

SEER'S (1) [SEE]
1Sa 9:18 Tell me, I pray thee, where the s house *is.* 7200

SEERS (6) [SEE]
2Ki 17:13 by all the prophets, *and by* all the s, saying, 2374
2Ch 33:18 the words of the s that spake to him in 2374
33:19 they *are* written among the sayings of the s. 2374
Isa 29:10 and your rulers, the s hath he covered. 2374
30:10 Which say to the s, See not; and to 7203
Mic 3: 7 shall the s be ashamed, and the diviners 2374

SEEST (36) [SEE] See Index

SEETH (54) [SEE] See Index

SEETHE (9) [SEETHING]
Ex 16:23 will bake *to day,* and s that ye will seethe; 1310
16:23 will bake *to day,* and seethe that ye will s; 1310
23:19 Thou shalt not s a kid in his mother's milk. 1310
29:31 and s his flesh in the holy place. 1310
34:26 Thou shalt not s a kid in his mother's milk. 1310
Dt 14:21 Thou shalt not s a kid in his mother's milk. 1310
2Ki 4:38 and s pottage for the sons of the prophets. 1310
Eze 24: 5 and let them s the bones of it therein. 1310
Zec 14:21 shall come and take of them, and s therein: 1310

SEETHING (3) [SEETHE]
1Sa 2:13 servant came, while the flesh was in s, 1310
Job 41:20 goeth smoke, as *out of* a s pot or caldron. 5301
Jer 1:13 I said, I see a s pot; and the face thereof *is* 5301

SEGUB (3)
1Ki 16:34 up the gates thereof in his youngest *son* **S,** 7687
1Ch 2:21 threescore years old; and she bare him **S.** 7687
2:22 **S** begat Jair, who had three and 7687

SEIR (39)
Ge 14: 6 the Horites in their mount **S,** unto El-paran, 8165
32: 3 him to Esau his brother unto the land of **S,** 8165
33:14 to endure, until I come unto my lord unto **S.** 8165
33:16 Esau returned that day on his way unto **S.** 8165
36: 8 Thus dwelt Esau in mount **S**: Esau *is* Edom. 8165
36: 9 Esau the father of the Edomites in mount **S**: 8165
36:20 These *are* the sons of **S** the Horite, 8165
36:21 the children of **S** in the land of Edom. 8165
36:30 of Hori, among their dukes in the land of **S.** 8165
Nu 24:18 **S** also shall be a possession for his 8165
Dt 1: 2 the way of mount **S** unto Kadesh-barnea.) 8165
1:44 as bees do, and destroyed you in **S,** 8165
2: 1 and we compassed mount **S** many days. 8165
2: 4 the children of Esau, which dwell in **S**; 8165
2: 5 I have given mount **S** unto Esau *for* a 8165
2: 8 which dwelt in **S,** through the way of 8165
2:12 The Horims also dwelt in **S** beforetime; but 8165
2:22 to the children of Esau, which dwelt in **S,** 8165
2:29 (As the children of Esau which dwell in **S,** 8165
33: 2 from Sinai, and rose up from **S** unto them; 8165
Jos 11:17 from the mount Halak, that goeth up *to* **S,** 8165
12: 7 unto the mount Halak, that goeth up to **S**; 8165
15:10 from Baalah westward unto mount **S,** 8165
24: 4 I gave unto Esau mount **S,** to possess it; 8165
Jdg 5: 4 LORD, when thou wentest out of **S,** 8165
1Ch 1:38 the sons of **S**; Lotan, and Shobal, and 8165
4:42 five hundred men, went to mount **S,** 8165
2Ch 20:10 of Ammon and Moab and mount **S,** 8165
20:22 Moab, and mount **S,** which were come 8165

2Ch 20:23 stood up against the inhabitants of mount **S**, 8165
20:23 had made an end of the inhabitants of **S**, 8165
25:11 smote *of* the children of **S** ten thousand. 8165
25:14 he brought the gods of the children of **S**, 8165
Isa 21:11 He calleth to me out of **S**, Watchman, 8165
Eze 25: 8 Because that Moab and **S** do say, Behold, 8165
35: 2 set thy face against mount **S**, and 8165
35: 3 Behold, O mount **S**, I *am* against thee, and 8165
35: 7 Thus will I make mount **S** most desolate, 8165
35:15 O mount **S**, and all Idumea, *even* all of it: 8165

SEIRAH See SEIRATH

SEIRATH (1)
Jdg 3:26 beyond the quarries, and escaped unto **S**. 8167

SEIZE (4) [SEIZED]
Jos 8: 7 up from the ambush, and **s upon** the city: 3423
Job 3: 6 *As for* that night, let darkness **s** upon it; 3947
Ps 55:15 Let death **s** upon them, *and* let them go 5377
Mt 21:38 us kill him, and let us **s** on his inheritance. *2722*

SEIZED (1) [SEIZE]
Jer 49:24 fear hath **s** on *her:* anguish and 2388

SELA (1) [SELA-HAMMAHLEKOTH]
Isa 16: 1 ruler of the land from **S** to the wilderness, 5554

SELAH (75)
2Ki 14: 7 took **S** by war, and called the name of it 5554
Ps 3: 2 *There is* no help for him in God. **S**. 5542
3: 4 and he heard me out of his holy hill. **S**. 5542
3: 8 thy blessing *is* upon thy people. **S**. 5542
4: 2 ye love vanity, *and* seek after leasing? **S**. 5542
4: 4 own heart upon your bed, and be still. **S**. 5542
7: 5 and lay mine honour in the dust. **S**. 5542
9:16 in the work of his own hands. Higgaion. **S**. 5542
9:20 may know themselves *to be but* men. **S**. 5542
20: 3 and accept thy burnt sacrifice. **S**. 5542
21: 2 not withholden the request of his lips. **S**. 5542
24: 6 seek him, that seek thy face, O Jacob. **S**. 5542
24:10 LORD of hosts, he *is* the King of glory. **S**. 5542
32: 4 is turned into the drought of summer. **S**. 5542
32: 5 thou forgavest the iniquity of my sin. **S**. 5542
32: 7 me about *with* songs of deliverance. **S**. 5542
39: 5 man at his best state *is* altogether vanity. **S**. 5542
39:11 like a moth: surely every man *is* vanity. **S**. 5542
44: 8 day long, and praise thy name for ever. **S**. 5542
46: 3 shake with the swelling thereof. **S**. 5542
46: 7 with us; the God of Jacob *is* our refuge. **S**. 5542
46:11 with us; the God of Jacob *is* our refuge. **S**. 5542
47: 4 the excellency of Jacob whom he loved. **S**. 5542
48: 8 our God: God will establish it for ever. **S**. 5542
49:13 yet their posterity approve their sayings. **S**. 5542
49:15 of the grave: for he shall receive me. **S**. 5542
50: 6 for God *is* judge himself. **S**. 5542
52: 3 lying rather than to speak righteousness. **S**. 5542
52: 5 root thee out of the land of the living. **S**. 5542
54: 3 they have not set God before them. **S**. 5542
55: 7 far off, *and* remain in the wilderness. **S**. 5542
55:19 **S**. Because they have no changes, therefore 5542
57: 3 **S**. God shall send forth his mercy and 5542
57: 6 whereof they are fallen *themselves.* **S**. 5542
59: 5 not merciful to any wicked transgressors. **S**. 5542
59:13 ruleth in Jacob unto the ends of the earth. **S**. 5542
60: 4 *it* may be displayed because of the truth. **S**. 5542
61: 4 I will trust in the covert of thy wings. **S**. 5542
62: 4 their mouth, but they curse inwardly. **S**. 5542
62: 8 heart before him: God *is* a refuge for us. **S**. 5542
66: 4 unto thee; they shall sing *to* thy name. **S**. 5542
66: 7 let not the rebellious exalt themselves. **S**. 5542
66:15 of rams; I will offer bullocks with goats. **S**. 5542
67: 1 *and* cause his face to shine upon us; **S**. 5542
67: 4 and govern the nations upon earth. **S**. 5542
68: 7 thou didst march through the wilderness; **S**. 5542
68:19 *benefits, even* the God of our salvation. **S**. 5542
68:32 the earth; O sing *praises unto* the Lord; **S**. 5542
75: 3 *are* dissolved: I bear up the pillars of it. **S**. 5542
76: 3 the shield, and the sword, and the battle. **S**. 5542
76: 9 to save all the meek of the earth. **S**. 5542
77: 3 and my spirit was overwhelmed. **S**. 5542
77: 9 he in anger shut up his tender mercies? **S**. 5542
77:15 thy people, the sons of Jacob and Joseph. **S**. 5542
81: 7 I proved thee at the waters of Meribah. **S**. 5542
82: 2 and accept the persons of the wicked? **S**. 5542
83: 8 they have holpen the children of Lot. **S**. 5542
84: 4 thy house: they will be still praising thee. **S**. 5542
84: 8 my prayer: give ear, O God of Jacob. **S**. 5542
85: 2 thou hast covered all their sin. **S**. 5542
87: 3 *things* are spoken of thee, O city of God. **S**. 5542
87: 6 the people, *that* this *man* was born there. **S**. 5542
88: 7 thou hast afflicted *me with* all thy waves. **S**. 5542
88:10 shall the dead arise *and* praise thee? **S**. 5542
89: 4 build up thy throne to all generations. **S**. 5542
89:37 and *as* a faithful witness in heaven. **S**. 5542
89:45 thou hast covered him with shame. **S**. 5542
89:48 his soul from the hand of the grave? **S**. 5542
140: 3 adder's poison *is* under their lips. **S**. 5542
140: 5 the way side; they have set grins for me. **S**. 5542
140: 8 *lest* they exalt themselves. **S**. 5542
143: 6 soul *thirsteth* after thee, as a thirsty land. **S**. 5542
Hab 3: 3 **S**. His glory covered the heavens, and 5542
3: 9 **S**. Thou didst cleave the earth *with* rivers. 5542
3:13 the foundation unto the neck. **S**. 5542

SELA-HAMMAHLEKOTH (1) [SELA]
1Sa 23:28 they called that place **S**. 5555

SELED (2)
1Ch 2:30 the sons of Nadab; **S**, and Appaim: but 5540
2:30 and Appaim: but **S** died without children. 5540

SELEUCIA (1)
Ac 13: 4 forth by the Holy Ghost, departed unto **S**; *4581*

SELF (6) [HERSELF, HIMSELF, ITSELF, SELFSAME, SELFWILL, SELFWILLED, SELVES, THEMSELVES, THYSELF, YOURSELVES]
Ex 32:13 to whom thou swarest by **thine own s**, 3509.2
Jn 5:30 I can of **mine own s** do nothing: as I hear, *1683*
17: 5 glorify thou me with **thine own s** with *4572*
1Co 4: 3 yea, I judge not **mine own s**. *1683*
Phm 1:19 owest unto me even **thine own s** besides. *4572*
1Pe 2:24 Who **his own s** bare our sins in his own *846*

SELF-CONTROL See TEMPERANCE

SELFSAME (15) [SAME, SELF]
Ge 7:13 In the **s** day entered Noah, and Shem, and 6106
17:23 the flesh of their foreskin in the **s** day, 6106
17:26 In the **s** day was Abraham circumcised, and 6106
Ex 12:17 for in this **s** day have I brought your armies 6106
12:41 thirty years, even the **s** day it came to pass, 6106
12:51 it came to pass the **s** day, *that* the LORD 6106
Lev 23:14 until the **s** day that ye have brought an 6106
23:21 ye shall proclaim on the **s** day, *that* it may 6106
Dt 32:48 the LORD spake unto Moses that **s** day, 6106
Jos 5:11 and parched *corn* in the **s** day. 6106
Eze 40: 1 in the **s** day the hand of the LORD was 6106
Mt 8:13 And his servant was healed in the **s** hour. *1565*
1Co 12:11 all these worketh *that* one and the **s** Spirit, *846*
2Co 5: 5 Now he that hath wrought us for the **s** *thing* *846*
7:11 For behold this **s** *thing,* that ye sorrowed *846*

SELFWILL (1) [SELF, WILL]
Ge 49: 6 and in their **s** they digged down a wall. 7522

SELFWILLED (2) [SELF, WILL]
Tit 1: 7 not **s**, not soon angry, not given to wine, *829*
2Pe 2:10 Presumptuous *are they,* **s**, they are not afraid *829*

SELL (35) [SALE, SELLER, SELLERS, SELLEST, SELLETH, SOLD]
Ge 25:31 Jacob said, **S** me *this* day thy birthright. 4376
37:27 let us **s** him to the Ishmeelites, and let not 4376
Ex 21: 7 if a man **s** his daughter to be a maidservant, 4376
21: 8 to **s** her unto a strange nation he shall have 4376
21:35 they shall **s** the live ox, and divide 4376
22: 1 steal an ox, or a sheep, and kill it, or **s** it; 4376
Lev 25:14 if thou **s ought** unto thy neighbour, 4376+4465
25:15 of years of the fruits he shall **s** unto thee: 4376
25:16 *the years* of the fruits doth he **s** unto thee. 4376
25:29 if a man **s** a dwelling house in a walled city, 4376
25:47 **s** himself unto the stranger *or* sojourner by 4376
Dt 2:28 Thou shalt **s** me meat for money, that I may 7666
14:21 may eat it; or thou mayest **s** *it* unto an alien: 4376
21:14 thou shalt not **s** her **at all** for money, 4376+4376
Jdg 4: 9 for the LORD shall **s** Sisera into the hand 4376
1Ki 21:25 which did **s** himself to work wickedness in 4376
2Ki 4: 7 **s** the oil, and pay thy debt, and live thou 4376
Ne 5: 8 and will you even **s** your brethren? 4376

S

Ne 10:31 or any victuals on the sabbath day to **s**, 4376
Pr 23:23 Buy the truth, and **s** *it* not; *also* wisdom, 4376
Eze 30:12 and **s** the land into the hand of the wicked: 4376
48:14 they shall not **s** of it, neither exchange, 4376
Joel 3: 8 I will **s** your sons and your daughters into 4376
3: 8 they shall **s** them to the Sabeans, to a 4376
Am 8: 5 the new moon be gone, that we may **s** corn? 7666
8: 6 *yea,* and **s** the refuse of the wheat? 7666
Zec 11: 5 they that **s** them say, Blessed *be* 4376
Mt 19:21 go *and* **s** that thou hast, and give to *4453*
25: 9 but go ye rather to them that **s**, and buy for *4453*
Mk 10:21 **s** whatsoever thou hast, and give to *4453*
Lk 12:33 **S** that ye have, and give alms; *4453*
18:22 Yet lackest thou one *thing:* **s** all that thou *4453*
22:36 let him **s** his garment, and buy one. *4453*
Jas 4:13 there a year, and **buy and s**, and get gain: *1710*
Rev 13:17 And that no *man* might buy or **s**, save he *4453*

SELLER (4) [SELL]
Isa 24: 2 as *with* the buyer, so *with* the **s**; 4376
Eze 7:12 let not the buyer rejoice, nor the **s** mourn: 4376
7:13 For the **s** shall not return to that which is 4376
Ac 16:14 a **s of purple**, of the city of Thyatira, *4211*

SELLERS (1) [SELL]
Ne 13:20 **s** of all *kind of* ware lodged without 4376

SELLEST (1) [SELL]
Ps 44:12 Thou **s** thy people for nought, and dost not 4376

SELLETH (7) [SELL]
Ex 21:16 and **s** him, or if he be found in his hand, 4376
Dt 24: 7 and maketh merchandise of him, or **s** him; 4376
Ru 4: 3 **s** a parcel of land, which *was* our brother 4376
Pr 11:26 *shall be* upon the head of him that **s** *it.* 7666
31:24 **s** *it;* and delivereth girdles unto 4376
Na 3: 4 that **s** nations through her whoredoms, and 4376
Mt 13:44 for joy thereof goeth and **s** all that he hath, *4453*

SELVEDGE (2)
Ex 26: 4 the one curtain from the **s** in the coupling; 7098
36:11 of one curtain from the **s** in the coupling: 7098

SELVES (7) [SELF]
Lk 21:30 know of **your own s** that summer is now *1438*
Ac 20:30 Also of your **own s** shall men arise, *846*
2Co 8: 5 but first gave **their own s** to the Lord, and *1438*
13: 5 ye be in the faith; prove **your own s**. *1438*
13: 5 Know ye not **your own s**, how that Jesus *1438*
2Ti 3: 2 For men shall be **lovers of** their **own s**, *5367*
Jas 1:22 not hearers only, deceiving **your own s**. *1438*

SEM (1) [SHEM]
Lk 3:36 which was *the son* of **S**, which was *the son* *4590*

SEMACHIAH (1)
1Ch 26: 7 brethren *were* strong men, Elihu, and **S**. 5565

SEMAKIAH See SEMACHIAH

SEMEI (1)
Lk 3:26 which was *the son* of **S**, which was *the son* *4584*

SEMEIN See SEMEI

SENAAH (2)
Ezr 2:35 The children of **S**, three thousand and 5570
Ne 7:38 The children of **S**, three thousand nine 5570

SENATE (1) [SENATORS]
Ac 5:21 and all the **s** of the children of Israel, and *1087*

SENATORS (1) [SENATE]
Ps 105:22 at his pleasure; and teach his **s** wisdom. 2205

SEND (234) [SENDEST, SENDETH, SENDING, SENT, SENTEST] See Index

SENDEST (6) [SEND] See Index

SENDETH (15) [SEND] See Index

SENDING (14) [SEND] See Index

SENEH (1)
1Sa 14: 4 *was* Bozez, and the name of the other **S**. 5573

SENIR (2)
1Ch 5:23 from Bashan unto Baal-hermon and **S**, 8149
Eze 27: 5 made all thy *ship* boards of fir trees of **S**: 8149

SENNACHERIB (13)
2Ki 18:13 **S** king of Assyria come up against all 5576
19:16 hear the words of **S**, which hath sent him to 5576
19:20 me against **S** king of Assyria I have heard. 5576
19:36 So **S** king of Assyria departed, and went 5576
2Ch 32: 1 the establishment *thereof,* **S** king of Assyria 5576
32: 2 when Hezekiah saw that **S** was come, and 5576
32: 9 After this did **S** king of Assyria send his 5576
32:10 Thus saith **S** king of Assyria, Whereon do 5576
32:22 from the hand of **S** the king of Assyria, 5576
Isa 36: 1 *that* **S** king of Assyria came up against all 5576
37:17 hear all the words of **S**, which hath sent to 5576
37:21 Whereas thou hast prayed to me against **S** 5576
37:37 So **S** king of Assyria departed, and went 5576

SENSE (1) [SENSES, SENSUAL]
Ne 8: 8 gave the **s**, and caused *them* to understand 7922

SENSELESS See SILLY; SOTTISH

SENSES (1) [SENSE]
Heb 5:14 *even* those who by reason of use have their **s** *145*

SENSUAL (2) [SENSE]
Jas 3:15 not from above, but *is* earthly, **s**, devilish. *5591*
Jude 1:19 **s**, having not the Spirit. *5591*

SENSUALITY See LASCIVIOUSNESS

SENT (690) [SEND] See Index

SENTENCE (11) [SENTENCES]
Dt 17: 9 and they shall shew thee the **s** of judgment: 1697
17:10 thou shalt do according to the **s**, which *they* 1697
17:11 According to the **s** of the law which they NIH
17:11 thou shalt not decline from the **s** which they 1697
Ps 17: 2 Let my **s** come forth from thy presence; 4941
Pr 16:10 A **divine s** *is* in the lips of the king: 7081
Ecc 8:11 Because **s** *against* an evil work is not 6599
Jer 4:12 now also will I give **s** against them. 4941
Lk 23:24 And Pilate **gave s** that it should be as they *1948*
Ac 15:19 Wherefore my **s** is, that *we* trouble not *2919*
2Co 1: 9 But we had the **s** of death in ourselves, *610*

SENTENCES (2) [SENTENCE]
Da 5:12 shewing of **hard s**, and dissolving of doubts, 280
8:23 and understanding **dark s**, shall stand up. 2420

SENTEST (4) [SEND] See Index

SENUAH (1)
Ne 11: 9 Judah the son of **S** *was* second over 5574

SEORIM (1)
1Ch 24: 8 The third to Harim, the fourth to **S**, 8188

SEPARATE (32) [SEPARATED, SEPARATETH, SEPARATING, SEPARATION]
Ge 13: 9 **s** thyself, I pray thee, from me: if *thou wilt* 6504
30:40 Jacob did **s** the lambs, and set the faces of 6504
49:26 head of him *that was* **s from** his brethren. 5139
Lev 15:31 Thus shall ye **s** the children of Israel from 5144
22: 2 that they **s** themselves from the holy *things* 5144
Nu 6: 2 woman shall **s** *themselves* to vow a vow of 6381
6: 2 to **s** *themselves* unto the LORD: 5144
6: 3 He shall **s** *himself* from wine and 5144
8:14 Thus shalt thou **s** the Levites from among 914
16:21 **S** yourselves from among this congregation, 914
Dt 19: 2 Thou shalt **s** three cities for thee in the midst 914
19: 7 Thou shalt **s** three cities for thee. 914
29:21 the LORD shall **s** him unto evil out of all 914
Jos 16: 9 the **s** cities for the children of Ephraim 3995
1Ki 8:53 For thou didst **s** them from among all 914
Ezr 10:11 and **s** yourselves from the people of the land, 914
Jer 37:12 to **s** himself thence in the midst of 2505
Eze 41:12 **s place** *at* the end toward the west *was* 1508
41:13 the **s place**, and the building, with the walls 1508
41:14 of the **s place** toward the east, an hundred 1508
41:15 against the **s place** which *was* behind it, 1508
42: 1 chamber that *was* over against the **s place**, 1508
42:10 over against the **s place**, and over against 1508
42:13 which *are* before the **s place**, 1508

Mt 25:32 and he shall s them one from another, as a *873*
Lk 6:22 when they shall s you *from their company,* *873*
Ac 13: 2 S me Barnabas and Saul for the work *873*
Ro 8:35 Who shall s us from the love of Christ? *5563*
8:39 shall be able to s us from the love of God, *5563*
2Co 6:17 and be ye s, saith the Lord, and touch not *873*
Heb 7:26 s from sinners, and made higher than *5563*
Jude 1:19 These be they who s themselves, sensual, *592*

SEPARATED (33) [SEPARATE]
Ge 13:11 they s themselves the one from the other. 6504
13:14 after that Lot was s from him, Lift up now 6504
25:23 two manner of people shall be s from thy 6504
Ex 33:16 so shall we be s, I and thy people, from all 6395
Lev 20:24 which have s you from *other* people. 914
20:25 which I have s from you as unclean. 914
Nu 16: 9 that the God of Israel hath s you from 914
Dt 10: 8 At that time the LORD s the tribe of Levi, 914
32: 8 when he s the sons of Adam, 6504
33:16 head of him *that was* s **from** his brethren. 5139
1Ch 12: 8 of the Gadites there s themselves unto David 914
23:13 Aaron was s, that he should sanctify 914
25: 1 the captains of the host s to the service of 914
2Ch 25:10 Amaziah s them, to wit, the army that was 914
Ezr 6:21 all such as had s themselves unto them from 914
8:24 I s twelve of the chief of the priests, 914
9: 1 have not s themselves from the people of 914
10: 8 himself s from the congregation of those that 914
10:16 were s, and sat down in the first day of 914
Ne 4:19 and large, and we *are* s upon the wall, 6504
9: 2 the seed of Israel s themselves from all 914
10:28 all they that had s themselves from 914
13: 3 that they s from Israel all the mixed 914
Pr 18: 1 having s himself, seeketh *and* 6504
19: 4 but the poor is s from his neighbour. 6504
Isa 56: 3 The LORD hath **utterly** s me from his 914+914
59: 2 your iniquities have s between you and your 914
Hos 4:14 for themselves are s with whores, and 6504
9:10 and s themselves unto *that* shame; 5144
Ac 19: 9 he departed from them, and s the disciples, *873*
Ro 1: 1 *to be* an apostle, s unto the gospel of God, *873*
Gal 1:15 who s me from my mother's womb, and *873*
2:12 they were come, he withdrew and s himself, *873*

SEPARATETH (5) [SEPARATE]
Nu 6: 5 *in* the which he s *himself* unto the LORD, 5144
6: 6 All the days that he s *himself* unto 5144
Pr 16:28 and a whisperer s chief friends. 6504
17: 9 but he that repeateth a matter s very friends. 6504
Eze 14: 7 which s himself from me, and setteth up his 5144

SEPARATING (1) [SEPARATE]
Zec 7: 3 s myself, as I have done these so 5144

SEPARATION (26) [SEPARATE]
Lev 12: 2 according to the days of the s for her 5079
12: 5 she shall be unclean two weeks, as *in* her s: 5079
15:20 every *thing* that she lieth upon in her s shall 5079
15:25 blood many days out of the time of her s, 5079
15:25 or if it run beyond the time of her s; 5079
15:25 uncleanness shall be as the days of her s: 5079
15:26 issue shall be unto her as the bed of her s: 5079
15:26 be unclean, as the uncleanness of her s. 5079
Nu 6: 4 All the days of his s shall he eat nothing 5145
6: 5 All the days of the vow of his s there shall 5145
6: 8 All the days of his s he *is* holy unto 5145
6:12 unto the LORD the days of his s, 5145
6:12 shall be lost, because his s was defiled. 5145
6:13 when the days of his s are fulfilled: 5145
6:18 the Nazarite shall shave the head of his s *at* 5145
6:18 shall take the hair of the head of his s, and 5145
6:19 after *the hair of* his s is shaven: 5145
6:21 *of* his offering unto the LORD for his s, 5145
6:21 so he must do after the law of his s. 5145
19: 9 of the children of Israel for a water of s: 5079
19:13 the water of s was not sprinkled upon him, 5079
19:20 the water of s hath not been sprinkled upon 5079
19:21 that he that sprinkleth the water of s shall 5079
19:21 he that toucheth the water of s shall be 5079
31:23 it shall be purified with the water of s: 5079
Eze 42:20 to **make a** s between the sanctuary and 914

SEPHAR (1)
Ge 10:30 as thou goest unto S, a mount of the east. 5611

SEPHARAD (1)
Ob 1:20 the captivity of Jerusalem, which *is* in S, 5614

SEPHARVAIM (6) [SEPHARVITES]
2Ki 17:24 from S, and placed *them* in the cities of 5617
17:31 and Anammelech, the gods of S. 5617
18:34 where *are* the gods of S, Hena, and Ivah? 5617
19:13 the king of the city of S, *of* Hena, and Ivah? 5617
Isa 36:19 where *are* the gods of S? and have they 5617
37:13 the king of the city of S, Hena, and Ivah? 5617

SEPHARVITES (1) [SEPHARVAIM]
2Ki 17:31 the S burnt their children in fire to 5616

SEPULCHRE (54) [SEPULCHRES]
Ge 23: 6 none of us shall withhold from thee his s, 6913
Dt 34: 6 but no man knoweth of his s unto this day. 6900
Jdg 8:32 was buried in the s of Joash his father, in 6913
1Sa 10: 2 thou shalt find two men by Rachel's s in 6900
2Sa 2:32 and buried him in the s of his father, 6913
4:12 and buried *it* in the s of Abner in Hebron. 6913
17:23 died, and was buried in the s of his father. 6913
21:14 in Zelah, in the s of Kish his father: 6913
1Ki 13:22 thy carcase shall not come unto the s of thy 6913
13:31 bury me in the s wherein the man of God *is* 6913
2Ki 9:28 buried him in his s with his fathers in 6900
13:21 and they cast the man into the s of Elisha: 6913
21:26 he was buried in his s in the garden of 6900
23:17 *It is* the s of the man of God, which came 6913
23:30 *to* Jerusalem, and buried him in his own s. 6900
Ps 5: 9 their throat *is* an open s; they flatter with 6913
Isa 22:16 that thou hast hewed thee out a s here, 6913
22:16 *as* he that heweth him out a s on high, *and* 6913
Jer 5:16 Their quiver *is* as an open s, they *are* all 6913
Mt 27:60 he rolled a great stone to the door of the s, *3419*
27:61 the other Mary, sitting over against the s. *5028*
27:64 that the s be made sure until the third day, *5028*
27:66 So they went, and made the s sure, *5028*
28: 1 and the other Mary to see the s. *5028*
28: 8 And they departed quickly from the s with *3419*
Mk 15:46 laid him in a s which was hewn out of a *3419*
15:46 and rolled a stone unto the door of the s. *3419*
16: 2 they came unto the s at the rising of *3419*
16: 3 us away the stone from the door of the s? *3419*
16: 5 And entering into the s, they saw a young *3419*
16: 8 they went out quickly, and fled from the s; *3419*
Lk 23:53 and laid it in a s *that was* hewn in stone, *3418*
23:55 and beheld the s, and how his body was *3419*
24: 1 early in the morning, they came unto the s, *3418*
24: 2 found the stone rolled away from the s. *3419*
24: 9 And returned from the s, and told all these *3419*
24:12 Then arose Peter, and ran unto the s; and *3419*
24:22 us astonished, which were early at the s; *3419*
24:24 of them which were with us went to the s, *3419*
Jn 19:41 and in the garden a new s, wherein was *3419*
19:42 of the Jews' preparation *day;* for the s was *3419*
20: 1 unto the s, and seeth the stone taken away *3419*
20: 1 and seeth the stone taken away from the s. *3419*
20: 2 have taken away the Lord out of the s, *3419*
20: 3 and *that* other disciple, and came to the s. *3419*
20: 4 did outrun Peter, and came first to the s. *3419*
20: 6 and went into the s, and seeth the linen *3419*
20: 8 which came first to the s, and he saw, and *3419*
20:11 But Mary stood without at the s weeping: *3419*
20:11 she stooped down, and looked into the s, *3419*
Ac 2:29 buried, and his s is with us unto this day. *3418*
7:16 laid in the s that Abraham bought for a sum *3418*
13:29 *him* down from the tree, and laid *him* in a s. *3419*
Ro 3:13 Their throat *is* an open s; with their tongues *5028*

SEPULCHRES (16) [SEPULCHRE]
Ge 23: 6 in the choice of our s bury thy dead; 6913
2Ki 23:16 he spied the s that *were* there in the mount, 6913
23:16 took the bones out of the s, and burnt *them* 6913
2Ch 16:14 they buried him in his own s, which he had 6913
21:20 city of David, but not in the s of the kings. 6913
24:25 they buried him not in the s of the kings. 6913
28:27 they brought him not into the s of the kings 6913
32:33 they buried him in the chiefest of the s of 6913
35:24 was buried in *one of the* s of his fathers. 6913
Ne 2: 3 the place of my fathers' s, *lieth* waste, and 6913
2: 5 unto the city of my fathers' s, that I may 6913
3:16 unto *the place* over against the s of David, 6913
Mt 23:27 for ye are like unto whited s, which indeed *5028*

Mt 23:29 and garnish the **s** of the righteous, *3419*
Lk 11:47 for ye build the **s** of the prophets, and *3419*
11:48 indeed killed them, and ye build their **s**. *3419*

SERAH (2)
Ge 46:17 and Ishui, and Beriah, and **S** their sister: 8294
1Ch 7:30 and Ishuai, and Beriah, and **S** their sister. 8294

SERAIAH (20)
2Sa 8:17 *were* the priests; and **S** *was* the scribe; 8304
2Ki 25:18 the captain of the guard took **S** the chief 8304
25:23 **S** the son of Tanhumeth the Netophathite, 8304
1Ch 4:13 the sons of Kenaz; Othniel, and **S**: and 8304
4:14 **S** begat Joab, the father of the valley of 8304
4:35 of Josibiah, the son of **S**, the son of Asiel, 8304
6:14 Azariah begat **S**, and Seraiah begat 8304
6:14 begat Seraiah, and **S** begat Jehozadak, 8304
Ezr 2: 2 **S**, Reelaiah, Mordecai, Bilshan, Mizpar, 8304
7: 1 Ezra the son of **S**, the son of Azariah, 8304
Ne 10: 2 **S**, Azariah, Jeremiah, 8304
11:11 **S** the son of Hilkiah, the son of Meshullam, 8304
12: 1 of Shealtiel, and Jeshua: **S**, Jeremiah, Ezra, 8304
12:12 of **S**, Meraiah; of Jeremiah, Hananiah; 8304
Jer 36:26 **S** the son of Azriel, and Shelemiah the son 8304
40: 8 **S** the son of Tanhumeth, and the sons of 8304
51:59 prophet commanded **S** the son of Neriah, 8304
51:59 of his reign. And *this* **S** *was* a quiet prince. 8304
51:61 Jeremiah said to **S**, When thou comest *to* 8304
52:24 the captain of the guard took **S** the chief 8304

SERAPHIMS (2)
Isa 6: 2 Above it stood the **s**: each one had six 8314
6: 6 flew one of the **s** unto me, having a live 8314

SERAPHS See SERAPHIMS

SERED (2)
Ge 46:14 sons of Zebulun; **S**, and Elon, and Jahleel. 5624
Nu 26:26 of **S**, the family of the Sardites: of Elon, 5624

SEREDITE See SARDITES

SERGEANTS (2)
Ac 16:35 the magistrates sent the **s**, saying, Let those *4465*
16:38 And the **s** told these words unto *4465*

SERGIUS (1)
Ac 13: 7 with the deputy *of the country*, **S** Paulus, *4588*

SERIOUSNESS See GRAVITY

SERPENT (38) [SERPENT'S, SERPENTS]
Ge 3: 1 Now the **s** was more subtil than any beast 5175
3: 2 the woman said unto the **s**, We may eat of 5175
3: 4 the **s** said unto the woman, Ye shall not 5175
3:13 The **s** beguiled me, and I did eat. 5175
3:14 the LORD God said unto the **s**, 5175
49:17 Dan shall be a **s** by the way, an adder in 5175
Ex 4: 3 he cast it on the ground, and it became a **s**; 5175
7: 9 *it* before Pharaoh, *and* it shall become a **s**. 8577
7:10 and before his servants, and it became a **s**. 8577
7:15 the rod which was turned to a **s** shalt thou 5175
Nu 21: 8 Make thee a fiery *s*, and set it upon a pole: NIH
21: 9 Moses made a **s** of brass, and put it upon a 5175
21: 9 came to pass, that if a **s** had bitten *any* man, 5175
21: 9 when he beheld the **s** of brass, he lived. 5175
2Ki 18: 4 brake in pieces the brasen **s** that Moses had 5175
Job 26:13 his hand hath formed the crooked **s**. 5175
Ps 58: 4 Their poison *is* like the poison of a **s**: 5175
140: 3 They have sharpened their tongues like a **s**; 5175
Pr 23:32 At the last it biteth like a **s**, and 5175
30:19 eagle in the air; the way of a **s** upon a rock; 5175
Ecc 10: 8 whoso breaketh a hedge, a **s** shall bite him. 5175
10:11 Surely the **s** will bite without enchantment; 5175
Isa 14:29 and his fruit *shall be* a **fiery** flying **s**. 8314
27: 1 sword shall punish leviathan the piercing **s**, 5175
27: 1 even leviathan *that* crooked **s**; 5175
30: 6 and old lion, the viper and **fiery** flying **s**, 8314
Jer 46:22 The voice thereof shall go like a **s**; for they 5175
Am 5:19 leaned his hand on the wall, and a **s** bit him. 5175
9: 3 thence will I command the **s**, and he shall 5175
Mic 7:17 They shall lick the dust like a **s**, they shall 5175
Mt 7:10 Or if he ask a fish, will he give him a **s**? *3789*
Lk 11:11 *ask* a fish, will he for a fish give him a **s**? *3789*
Jn 3:14 And as Moses lifted up the **s** in *3789*
2Co 11: 3 as the **s** beguiled Eve through his subtilty, *3789*
Rev 12: 9 the great dragon was cast *out, that* old **s**, *3789*
12:14 and half a time, from the face of the **s**. *3789*
12:15 And the **s** cast out of his mouth water as a *3789*
20: 2 *that* old **s**, which is the devil, and Satan, *3789*

SERPENT'S (2) [SERPENT]
Isa 14:29 for out of the **s** root shall come forth a 5175
65:25 dust *shall be* the **s** meat. They shall not hurt 5175

SERPENTS (13) [SERPENT]
Ex 7:12 every man his rod, and they became **s**: 8577
Nu 21: 6 the LORD sent fiery **s** among the people, 5175
21: 7 that he take away the **s** from us. 5175
Dt 8:15 *wherein were* fiery **s**, and scorpions, and 5175
32:24 upon them, with the poison of **s** of the dust. 2119
Jer 8:17 For behold, I will send **s**, cockatrices, 5175
Mt 10:16 be ye therefore wise as **s**, and harmless as *3789*
23:33 *Ye* **s**, *ye* generation of vipers, how can ye *3789*
Mk 16:18 They shall take up **s**; and if they drink any *3789*
Lk 10:19 I give unto you power to tread on **s** and *3789*
1Co 10: 9 them also tempted, and were destroyed of **s**. *3789*
Jas 3: 7 of birds, and of **s**, and of *things* in the sea, *2062*
Rev 9:19 for their tails *were* like unto **s**, and *3789*

SERUG (5)
Ge 11:20 Reu lived two and thirty years, and begat **S**: 8286
11:21 Reu lived after he begat **S** two hundred 8286
11:22 And **S** lived thirty years, and begat Nahor: 8286
11:23 **S** lived after he begat Nahor two hundred 8286
1Ch 1:26 **S**, Nahor, Terah, 8286

SERVANT (493) [SERVE]
Ge 9:25 a **s** of servants shall he be unto his brethren. 5650
9:26 God of Shem; and Canaan shall be his **s**. 5650
9:27 tents of Shem; and Canaan shall be his **s**. 5650
18: 3 pass not away, I pray thee, from thy **s**: 5650
18: 5 for therefore are you come to your **s**. 5650
19:19 thy **s** hath found grace in thy sight, and 5650
24: 2 Abraham said unto his eldest **s** of his house 5650
24: 5 the **s** said unto him, Peradventure 5650
24: 9 the **s** put his hand under the thigh of 5650
24:10 the **s** took ten camels of the camels of his 5650
24:14 she *that* thou hast appointed for thy **s** Isaac; 5650
24:17 the **s** ran to meet her, and said, Let me, 5650
24:34 And he said, I *am* Abraham's **s**. 5650
24:52 that, when Abraham's **s** heard their words, 5650
24:53 the **s** brought forth jewels of silver, and 5650
24:59 her nurse, and Abraham's **s**, and his men. 5650
24:61 and the **s** took Rebekah, and went his way. 5650
24:65 For she had said unto the **s**, What man *is* 5650
24:65 the **s** had said, It *is* my master: therefore 5650
24:66 the **s** told Isaac all things that he had done. 5650
26:24 multiply thy seed for my **s** Abraham's sake. 5650
32: 4 Thy **s** Jacob saith thus, I have sojourned 5650
32:10 which thou hast shewed unto thy **s**; 5650
32:18 thou shalt say, *They be* thy **s** Jacob's; it *is* a 5650
32:20 Behold, thy **s** Jacob *is* behind us. 5650
33: 5 which God hath graciously given thy **s**. 5650
33:14 my lord, I pray thee, pass over before his **s**: 5650
39:17 saying, The Hebrew **s**, which thou hast 5650
39:19 After this manner did thy **s** to me; 5650
41:12 a Hebrew, **s** to the captain of the guard; 5650
43:28 Thy **s** our father *is* in good health, he *is* yet 5650
44:10 he with whom it is found shall be my **s**; and 5650
44:17 hand the cup is found, he shall be my **s**; 5650
44:18 said, O my lord, let thy **s**, I pray thee, 5650
44:18 and let not thine anger burn against thy **s**: 5650
44:24 it came to pass when we came up unto thy **s** 5650
44:27 thy **s** my father said unto us, Ye know that 5650
44:30 therefore when I come to thy **s** my father, 5650
44:31 of thy **s** our father with sorrow to the grave. 5650
44:32 For thy **s** became surety for the lad unto my 5650
44:33 let thy **s** abide instead of the lad a bondman 5650
49:15 to bear, and became a **s** unto tribute. 5647
Ex 4:10 nor since thou hast spoken unto thy **s**: 5650
12:44 But every man's **s** that is bought for money, 5650
12:45 and a **hired** **s** shall not eat thereof. 7916
14:31 and believed the LORD, and his **s** Moses. 5650
21: 2 If thou buy a Hebrew **s**, six years he shall 5650
21: 5 if the **s** shall plainly say, I love my master, 5650
21:20 if a man smite his **s**, or his maid, with a rod, 5650
21:26 if a man smite the eye of his **s**, or the eye of 5650
33:11 his **s** Joshua, the son of Nun, a young man, 8334
Lev 22:10 or a **hired** **s**, shall not eat *of* the holy *thing*. 7916

S

Lev	25: 6	for thy **s**, and for thy maid, and for thy	5650
	25: 6	for thy **hired s**, and for thy stranger that	7916
	25:40	*But* as a **hired s**, *and* as a sojourner,	7916
	25:50	according to the time of a **hired s** shall it be	7916
	25:53	*And* as a yearly **hired s** shall he be with	7916
Nu	11:11	Wherefore hast thou afflicted thy **s**?	5650
	11:28	the **s** of Moses, *one* of his young men,	8334
	12: 7	My **s** Moses *is* not so, who *is* faithful in all	5650
	12: 8	were ye not afraid to speak against my **s**	5650
	14:24	my **s** Caleb, because he had another spirit	5650
Dt	3:24	thou hast begun to shew thy **s** thy greatness,	5650
	5:15	remember that thou wast a **s** in the land of	5650
	15:17	the door, and he shall be thy **s** for ever.	5650
	15:18	for he hath been worth a double **hired s** *to*	7916
	23:15	Thou shalt not deliver unto his master the **s**	5650
	24:14	Thou shalt not oppress a **hired s** *that is*	7916
	34: 5	So Moses the **s** of the LORD died there in	5650
Jos	1: 1	Now after the death of Moses the **s** of	5650
	1: 2	Moses my **s** is dead; now therefore arise,	5650
	1: 7	which Moses my **s** commanded thee:	5650
	1:13	Remember the word which Moses the **s** of	5650
	1:15	which Moses the LORD'S **s** gave you on	5650
	5:14	unto him, What saith my lord unto his **s**?	5650
	8:31	As Moses the **s** of the LORD commanded	5650
	8:33	as Moses the **s** of the LORD had	5650
	9:24	his **s** Moses to give you all the land,	5650
	11:12	as Moses the **s** of the LORD commanded.	5650
	11:15	As the LORD commanded Moses his **s**, so	5650
	12: 6	Them did Moses the **s** of the LORD and	5650
	12: 6	Moses the **s** of the LORD gave it *for* a	5650
	13: 8	*even* as Moses the **s** of the LORD gave	5650
	14: 7	Forty years old *was* I when Moses the **s** of	5650
	18: 7	which Moses the **s** of the LORD gave	5650
	22: 2	Ye have kept all that Moses the **s** of	5650
	22: 4	which Moses the **s** of the LORD gave you	5650
	22: 5	which Moses the **s** of the LORD charged	5650
	24:29	the **s** of the LORD, died, *being* an hundred	5650
Jdg	2: 8	the **s** of the LORD, died, *being* an hundred	5650
	7:10	go thou with Phurah thy **s** down to the host:	5288
	7:11	went he down with Phurah his **s** unto	5288
	15:18	this great deliverance into the hand of thy **s**:	5650
	19: 3	having his **s** with him, and a couple of	5288
	19: 9	he, and his concubine, and his **s**, his father	5288
	19:11	the **s** said unto his master, Come, I pray	5288
	19:13	he said unto his **s**, Come, and let us draw	5288
Ru	2: 5	said Boaz unto his **s** that was set over	5288
	2: 6	the **s** that was set over the reapers answered	5288
1Sa	2:13	the priest's **s** came, while the flesh was in	5288
	2:15	the priest's **s** came, and said to the man that	5288
	3: 9	shalt say, Speak, LORD; for thy **s** heareth.	5650
	3:10	Samuel answered, Speak; for thy **s** heareth.	5650
	9: 5	Saul said to his **s** that *was* with him, Come,	5288
	9: 7	said Saul to his **s**, But behold, *if* we go,	5288
	9: 8	the **s** answered Saul again, and said,	5288
	9:10	said Saul to his **s**, Well said; come, let us	5288
	9:22	Samuel took Saul and his **s**, and	5288
	9:27	Bid the **s** pass on before us, (and he passed	5288
	10:14	Saul's uncle said unto him and to his **s**,	5288
	17:32	thy **s** will go and fight with this Philistine.	5650
	17:34	Thy **s** kept his father's sheep, and	5650
	17:36	Thy **s** slew both the lion and the bear: and	5650
	17:58	*I am* the son of thy **s** Jesse	5650
	19: 4	unto him, Let not the king sin against his **s**,	5650
	20: 7	say thus, *It is* well; thy **s** shall have peace:	5650
	20: 8	Therefore thou shalt deal kindly with thy **s**;	5650
	20: 8	for thou hast brought thy **s** into a covenant	5650
	22: 8	my son hath stirred up my **s** against me,	5650
	22:15	let not the king impute *any* thing unto his **s**,	5650
	22:15	for thy **s** knew nothing of all this, less or	5650
	23:10	thy **s** hath certainly heard that Saul seeketh	5650
	23:11	Will Saul come down, as thy **s** hath heard?	5650
	23:11	God of Israel, I beseech thee, tell thy **s**.	5650
	25:39	of Nabal, and hath kept his **s** from evil:	5650
	25:41	*let* thine handmaid *be* a **s** to wash the feet	8198
	26:18	doth my lord thus pursue after his **s**?	5650
	26:19	let my lord the king hear the words of his **s**.	5650
	27: 5	for why should thy **s** dwell in the royal city	5650
	27:12	therefore he shall be my **s** for ever.	5650
	28: 2	Surely thou shalt know what thy **s** can do.	5650
	29: 3	this David, the **s** of Saul the king of Israel,	5650
	29: 8	what hast thou found in thy **s** so long as I	5650
	30:13	a young man of Egypt, **s** to an Amalekite;	5650
2Sa	3:18	By the hand of my **s** David I will save my	5650
	7: 5	Go and tell my **s** David, Thus saith	5650
	7: 8	so shalt thou say unto my **s** David,	5650
	7:20	for thou, Lord GOD, knowest thy **s**.	5650
	7:21	great things, to make thy **s** know *them*.	5650
	7:25	that thou hast spoken concerning thy **s**,	5650
	7:26	let the house of thy **s** David be established	5650
	7:27	God of Israel, hast revealed to thy **s**, saying,	5650
	7:27	hath thy **s** found in his heart to pray this	5650
	7:28	hast promised this goodness unto thy **s**:	5650
	7:29	let it please thee to bless the house of thy **s**,	5650
	7:29	with thy blessing let the house of thy **s** be	5650
	9: 2	*there was* of the house of Saul a **s** whose	5650
	9: 2	*Art* thou Ziba? And he said, Thy **s** *is he*.	5650
	9: 6	And he answered, Behold thy **s**.	5650
	9: 8	he bowed himself, and said, What *is* thy **s**,	5650
	9: 9	called to Ziba, Saul's **s**, and said unto him,	5288
	9:11	my lord the king hath commanded his **s**,	5650
	9:11	commanded his servant, so shall thy **s** do.	5650
	11:21	Thy **s** Uriah the Hittite is dead also.	5650
	11:24	and thy **s** Uriah the Hittite is dead also.	5650
	13:17	he called his **s** that ministered unto him,	5288
	13:18	his **s** brought her out, and bolted the door	8334
	13:24	said, Behold now, thy **s** hath sheepshearers;	5650
	13:24	and his servants go with thy **s**.	5650
	13:35	the king's sons come: as thy **s** said, so it is.	5650
	14:19	for thy **s** Joab, he bade me, and he put all	5650
	14:20	fetch about *this* form of speech hath thy **s**	5650
	14:22	To day thy **s** knoweth that I have found	5650
	14:22	the king hath fulfilled the request of his **s**.	5650
	15: 2	Thy **s** *is* of one of the tribes of Israel.	5650
	15: 8	For thy **s** vowed a vow while I abode at	5650
	15:21	or life, even there *also* will thy **s** be.	5650
	15:34	say unto Absalom, I will be thy **s**, O king;	5650
	15:34	as I *have been* thy father's **s** hitherto, so	5650
	15:34	servant hitherto, so *will* I now also *be* thy **s**:	5650
	16: 1	Ziba the **s** of Mephibosheth met him, with a	5288
	18:29	When Joab sent the king's **s**, and *me* thy	5650
	18:29	*me* thy **s**, I saw a great tumult, but I knew	5650
	19:17	Ziba the **s** of the house of Saul, and	5288
	19:19	neither do thou remember *that* which thy **s**	5650
	19:20	For thy **s** doth know that I have sinned:	5650
	19:26	My lord, O king, my **s** deceived me:	5650
	19:26	for thy **s** said, I will saddle me an ass, that I	5650
	19:26	go to the king; because thy **s** *is* lame.	5650
	19:27	he hath slandered thy **s** unto my lord	5650
	19:28	yet didst thou set thy **s** among them that did	5650
	19:35	can thy **s** taste what I eat or what I drink?	5650
	19:35	should thy **s** be yet a burden unto my lord	5650
	19:36	Thy **s** will go a little *way* over Jordan with	5650
	19:37	Let thy **s**, I pray thee, turn back again, that I	5650
	19:37	behold thy **s** Chimham; let him go over	5650
	24:10	O LORD, take away the iniquity of thy **s**;	5650
	24:21	is my lord the king come to his **s**?	5650
1Ki	1:19	but Solomon thy **s** hath he not called.	5650
	1:26	*even* me thy **s**, and Zadok the priest, and	5650
	1:26	and thy **s** Solomon, hath he not called.	5650
	1:27	and thou hast not shewed *it* unto thy **s**,	5650
	1:51	that he will not slay his **s** with the sword.	5650
	2:38	my lord the king hath said, so will thy **s** do.	5650
	3: 6	Thou hast shewed unto thy **s** David my	5650
	3: 7	thou hast made thy **s** king instead of David	5650
	3: 8	thy **s** *is* in the midst of thy people which	5650
	3: 9	thy **s** an understanding heart to judge thy	5650
	8:24	Who hast kept with thy **s** David my father	5650
	8:25	keep with thy **s** David my father that thou	5650
	8:26	which thou spakest unto thy **s** David my	5650
	8:28	have thou respect unto the prayer of thy **s**,	5650
	8:28	which thy **s** prayeth before thee to day:	5650
	8:29	which thy **s** shall make towards this place.	5650
	8:30	hearken thou to the supplication of thy **s**,	5650
	8:52	may be open unto the supplication of thy **s**,	5650
	8:53	as thou spakest by the hand of Moses thy **s**,	5650
	8:56	he promised by the hand of Moses his **s**.	5650
	8:59	that *he* maintain the cause of his **s**, and	5650
	8:66	that the LORD had done for David his **s**,	5650
	11:11	from thee, and will give it to thy **s**.	5650
	11:26	an Ephrathite of Zereda, Solomon's **s**,	5650
	11:32	(But he shall have one tribe for my **s**	5650
	11:36	that David my **s** may have a light alway	5650
	11:38	and my commandments, as David my **s** did;	5650
	12: 7	If thou wilt be a **s** unto this people *this* day,	5650
	14: 8	*yet* thou hast not been as my **s** David,	5650
	14:18	which he spake by the hand of his **s** Ahijah	5650
	15:29	which he spake by his **s** Ahijah	5650
	16: 9	his **s** Zimri, captain of half *his* chariots,	5650

1Ki	18: 9	that thou wouldest deliver thy **s** into	5650
	18:12	but *I* thy **s** fear the LORD from my youth.	5650
	18:36	*that* I *am* thy **s**, and *that* I have done all	5650
	18:43	said to his **s**, Go up now, look toward	5288
	19: 3	*belongeth* to Judah, and left his **s** there.	5288
	20: 9	All that thou didst send for to thy **s** at	5650
	20:32	said, Thy **s** Ben-hadad saith, I pray thee,	5650
	20:39	Thy **s** went out into the midst of the battle;	5650
	20:40	as thy **s** was busy here and there, he was	5650
2Ki	4: 1	saying, Thy **s** my husband is dead;	5650
	4: 1	thou knowest that thy **s** did fear	5650
	4:12	he said to Gehazi his **s**, Call this	5288
	4:24	said to her **s**, Drive, and go *forward;* slack	5288
	4:25	that he said to Gehazi his **s**, Behold,	5288
	4:38	he said unto his **s**, Set on the great pot, and	5288
	5: 6	I have *therewith* sent Naaman my **s** to thee,	5650
	5:15	I pray thee, take a blessing of thy **s**.	5650
	5:17	be given to thy **s** two mules' burden of	5650
	5:17	for thy **s** will henceforth offer neither burnt	5650
	5:18	In this thing the LORD pardon thy **s**,	5650
	5:18	the LORD pardon thy **s** in this thing.	5650
	5:20	the **s** of Elisha the man of God, said,	5288
	5:25	And he said, Thy **s** went no whither.	5650
	6:15	when the **s** of the man of God was risen	8334
	6:15	his **s** said unto him, Alas, my master,	5288
	8: 4	the king talked with Gehazi the **s** of	5288
	8:13	Hazael said, But what, *is* thy **s** a dog,	5650
	9:36	which he spake by his **s** Elijah the Tishbite,	5650
	10:10	done *that* which he spake by his **s** Elijah.	5650
	14:25	which he spake by the hand of his **s** Jonah,	5650
	16: 7	of Assyria, saying, I *am* thy **s** and thy son:	5650
	17: 3	Hoshea became his **s**, and gave him	5650
	18:12	all that Moses the **s** of the LORD	5650
	19:34	mine own sake, and for my **s** David's sake.	5650
	20: 6	mine own sake, and for my **s** David's sake.	5650
	21: 8	according to all the law that my **s** Moses	5650
	22:12	and Asahiah a **s** of the king's, saying,	5650
	24: 1	and Jehoiakim became his **s** three years:	5650
	25: 8	a **s** of the king of Babylon, *unto* Jerusalem:	5650
1Ch	2:34	Sheshan had a **s**, an Egyptian, whose name	5650
	2:35	Sheshan gave his daughter to Jarha his **s** to	5650
	6:49	according to all that Moses the **s** of God	5650
	16:13	O ye seed of Israel his **s**, ye children of	5650
	17: 4	Go and tell David my **s**, Thus saith	5650
	17: 7	thus shalt thou say unto my **s** David,	5650
	17:18	*speak* more to thee for the honour of thy **s**?	5650
	17:18	of thy servant? for thou knowest thy **s**.	5650
	17:23	that thou hast spoken concerning thy **s**	5650
	17:24	*let* the house of David thy **s** *be* established	5650
	17:25	hast told thy **s** that *thou* wilt build him a	5650
	17:25	thy **s** hath found *in his heart* to pray before	5650
	17:26	and hast promised this goodness unto thy **s**:	5650
	17:27	let it please thee to bless the house of thy **s**,	5650
	21: 8	beseech thee, do away the iniquity of thy **s**;	5650
2Ch	1: 3	which Moses the **s** of the LORD had made	5650
	6:15	Thou which hast kept with thy **s** David my	5650
	6:16	keep with thy **s** David my father *that* which	5650
	6:17	which thou hast spoken unto thy **s** David.	5650
	6:19	therefore to the prayer of thy **s**,	5650
	6:19	the prayer which thy **s** prayeth before thee:	5650
	6:20	to hearken unto the prayer which thy **s**	5650
	6:21	therefore unto the supplications of thy **s**,	5650
	6:42	remember the mercies of David thy **s**.	5650
	13: 6	the **s** of Solomon the son of David, is risen	5650
	24: 6	of Moses the **s** of the LORD,	5650
	24: 9	**s** of God laid upon Israel in the wilderness.	5650
	32:16	LORD God, and against his **s** Hezekiah.	5650
	34:20	and Asaiah a **s** of the king's, saying,	5650
Ne	1: 6	that *thou* mayest hear the prayer of thy **s**,	5650
	1: 7	which thou commandedst thy **s** Moses.	5650
	1: 8	the word that thou commandedst thy **s**	5650
	1:11	thine ear be attentive to the prayer of thy **s**,	5650
	1:11	thy **s** *this* day, and grant him mercy in	5650
	2: 5	and if thy **s** have found favour in thy sight,	5650
	2:10	and Tobiah the **s**, the Ammonite,	5650
	2:19	Tobiah the **s**, the Ammonite, and	5650
	4:22	Let every one with his **s** lodge within	5288
	6: 5	sent Sanballat his **s** unto me in like manner	5288
	9:14	and laws, by the hand of Moses thy **s**:	5650
	10:29	which was given by Moses the **s** of God,	5650
Job	1: 8	unto Satan, Hast thou considered my **s** Job,	5650
	2: 3	unto Satan, Hast thou considered my **s** Job,	5650
	3:19	*are* there; and the **s** *is* free from his master.	5650
	7: 2	As a **s** earnestly desireth the shadow, and	5650
	19:16	I called my **s**, and he gave *me* no answer;	5650
	41: 4	wilt thou take him for a **s** for ever?	5650
	42: 7	me *the thing that is* right, as my **s** Job *hath.*	5650
	42: 8	go to my **s** Job, and offer up for yourselves	5650
	42: 8	and my **s** Job shall pray for you:	5650
	42: 8	me *the thing which is* right, like my **s** Job.	5650
Ps	18: T	*A Psalm* of David, the **s** of the LORD,	5650
	19:11	Moreover by them *is* thy **s** warned: *and*	5650
	19:13	Keep back thy **s** also from presumptuous	5650
	27: 9	*far* from me; put not thy **s** away in anger:	5650
	31:16	Make thy face to shine upon thy **s**: save me	5650
	35:27	hath pleasure in the prosperity of his **s**.	5650
	36: T	*A Psalm* of David the **s** of the LORD.	5650
	69:17	hide not thy face from thy **s**; for I am in	5650
	78:70	He chose David also his **s**, and took him	5650
	86: 2	my God, save thy **s** that trusteth in thee.	5650
	86: 4	Rejoice the soul of thy **s**: for unto thee,	5650
	86:16	give thy strength unto thy **s**, and save	5650
	89: 3	my chosen, I have sworn unto David my **s**,	5650
	89:20	I have found David my **s**; with my holy oil	5650
	89:39	Thou hast made void the covenant of thy **s**:	5650
	105: 6	O ye seed of Abraham his **s**, ye children of	5650
	105:17	*even* Joseph, *who* was sold for a **s**:	5650
	105:26	He sent Moses his **s**; *and* Aaron whom he	5650
	105:42	his holy promise, *and* Abraham his **s**.	5650
	109:28	let them be ashamed; but let thy **s** rejoice.	5650
	116:16	Oh LORD, truly I *am* thy **s**; I *am* thy	5650
	116:16	I *am* thy **s**, *and* the son of thy handmaid:	5650
	119:17	Deal bountifully with thy **s**, *that* I may live,	5650
	119:23	*but* thy **s** did meditate in thy statutes.	5650
	119:38	Stablish thy word unto thy **s**, who *is*	5650
	119:49	Remember the word unto thy **s**, upon which	5650
	119:65	Thou hast dealt well with thy **s**, O LORD,	5650
	119:76	according to thy word unto thy **s**.	5650
	119:84	How many *are* the days of thy **s**? when wilt	5650
	119:122	Be surety for thy **s** for good: let not	5650
	119:124	Deal with thy **s** according unto thy mercy,	5650
	119:125	I *am* thy **s**; give me understanding, that I	5650
	119:135	Make thy face to shine upon thy **s**; and	5650
	119:140	word *is* very pure: therefore thy **s** loveth it.	5650
	119:176	gone astray like a lost sheep; seek thy **s**;	5650
	132:10	For thy **s** David's sake turn not away	5650
	136:22	*Even* an heritage unto Israel his **s**: for his	5650
	143: 2	enter not into judgment with thy **s**: for in	5650
	143:12	all them that afflict my soul: for I *am* thy **s**.	5650
	144:10	who delivereth David his **s** from the hurtful	5650
Pr	11:29	and the fool *shall be* **s** to the wise of heart.	5650
	12: 9	*He that is* despised, and hath a **s**, *is* better	5650
	14:35	The king's favour *is* toward a wise **s**: but	5650
	17: 2	A wise **s** shall have rule over a son that	5650
	19:10	much less for a **s** to have rule over princes.	5650
	22: 7	and the borrower *is* **s** to the lender.	5650
	29:19	A **s** will not be corrected by words:	5650
	29:21	He that delicately bringeth up his **s** from a	5650
	30:10	Accuse not a **s** unto his master, lest he	5650
	30:22	For a **s** when he reigneth; and a fool when	5650
Ecc	7:21	are spoken; lest thou hear thy **s** curse thee:	5650
Isa	20: 3	Like as my **s** Isaiah hath walked naked and	5650
	22:20	that I will call my **s** Eliakim the son of	5650
	24: 2	the priest; as *with* the **s**, so *with* his master;	5650
	37:35	mine own sake, and for my **s** David's sake.	5650
	41: 8	thou, Israel, *art* my **s**, Jacob whom I have	5650
	41: 9	and said unto thee, Thou *art* my **s**;	5650
	42: 1	Behold my **s**, whom I uphold; mine elect,	5650
	42:19	Who *is* blind, but my **s**? or deaf, as my	5650
	42:19	is perfect, and blind as the LORD'S **s**?	5650
	43:10	the LORD, and my **s** whom I have chosen:	5650
	44: 1	Yet now hear, O Jacob my **s**; and Israel,	5650
	44: 2	Fear not, O Jacob, my **s**; and	5650
	44:21	O Jacob and Israel; for thou *art* my **s**:	5650
	44:21	I have formed thee; thou *art* my **s**: O Israel,	5650
	44:26	That confirmeth the word of his **s**, and	5650
	48:20	The LORD hath redeemed his **s** Jacob.	5650
	49: 3	said unto me, Thou *art* my **s**, O Israel,	5650
	49: 5	that formed me from the womb *to be* his **s**,	5650
	49: 6	is a light thing that thou shouldest be my **s**	5650
	49: 7	to a **s** of rulers, Kings shall see and arise,	5650
	50:10	that obeyeth the voice of his **s**, that walketh	5650
	52:13	Behold, my **s** shall deal prudently, he shall	5650
	53:11	by his knowledge shall my righteous **s**	5650
Jer	2:14	*Is* Israel a **s**? *is* he a homeborn *slave?* why	5650
	25: 9	my **s**, and will bring them against this land,	5650
	27: 6	Nebuchadnezzar the king of Babylon, my **s**;	5650
	30:10	thou not, O my **s** Jacob, saith the LORD;	5650

Jer 33:21 my covenant be broken with David my s, 5650
33:22 so will I multiply the seed of David my s, 5650
33:26 David my s, *so* that *I* will not take *any* of 5650
34:16 caused every man his s, and every man his 5650
43:10 my s, and will set his throne upon these 5650
46:27 O my s Jacob, and be not dismayed, 5650
46:28 Fear thou not, O Jacob my s, saith 5650
Eze 28:25 their land that I have given to my s Jacob. 5650
34:23 and he shall feed them, *even* my s David; 5650
34:24 and my s David a prince among them; 5650
37:24 David my s *shall be* king over them; and 5650
37:25 the land that I have given unto Jacob my s, 5650
37:25 my s David *shall be* their prince for ever. 5650
Da 6:20 O Daniel, s of the living God, is thy God, 5649
9:11 *is* written in the law of Moses the s of God, 5650
9:17 hear the prayer of thy s, and 5650
10:17 For how can the s of this my lord talk with 5650
Hag 2:23 will I take thee, O Zerubbabel, my s, 5650
Zec 3: 8 I *will* bring forth my s the BRANCH. 5650
Mal 1: 6 son honoureth *his* father, and a s his master: 5650
4: 4 Remember ye the law of Moses my s, 5650
Mt 8: 6 Lord, my s lieth at home sick of the palsy, *3816*
8: 8 the word only, and my s shall be healed. *3816*
8: 9 and to my s, Do this, and he doeth *it.* *1401*
8:13 And his s was healed in the selfsame hour. *3816*
10:24 above *his* master, nor the s above his lord. *1401*
10:25 he be as his master, and the s as his lord. *1401*
12:18 Behold my s, whom I have chosen; my *3816*
18:26 The s therefore fell down, and *1401*
18:27 Then the lord of that s was moved with *1401*
18:28 But the same s went out, and found one of *1401*
18:32 said unto him, O *thou* wicked s, I forgave *1401*
20:27 will be chief among you, let him be your s: *1401*
23:11 that is greatest among you shall be your s. *1249*
24:45 Who then is a faithful and wise s, whom his *1401*
24:46 Blessed *is* that s, whom his lord when he *1401*
24:48 But *and* if that evil s shall say in his heart, *1401*
24:50 The lord of that s shall come in a day when *1401*
25:21 Well *done, thou* good and faithful s: *1401*
25:23 unto him, Well *done,* good and faithful s; *1401*
25:26 said unto him, *Thou* wicked and slothful s, *1401*
25:30 And cast ye the unprofitable s into outer *1401*
26:51 and stroke a s of the high priest's, and *1401*
Mk 9:35 *the same* shall be last of all, and s of all. *1249*
10:44 of you will be the chiefest, shall be s of all. *1401*
12: 2 at the season he sent to the husbandmen a s, *1401*
12: 4 And again he sent unto them another s; and *1401*
14:47 and smote a s of the high priest, and cut off *1401*
Lk 1:54 He hath holpen his s Israel, *3816*
1:69 salvation for us in the house of his s David; *3816*
2:29 Lord, now lettest thou thy s depart in peace, *1401*
7: 2 And a certain centurion's s, who was dear *1401*
7: 3 him that he would come and heal his s. *1401*
7: 7 but say in a word, and my s shall be healed. *3816*
7: 8 and to my s, Do this, and he doeth *it.* *1401*
7:10 found the s whole that had been sick. *1401*
12:43 Blessed *is* that s, whom his lord when he *1401*
12:45 But and if that s say in his heart, My lord *1401*
12:46 The lord of that s will come in a day when *1401*
12:47 And that s, which knew his lord's will, and *1401*
14:17 And sent his s at supper time to say to them *1401*
14:21 So that s came, and shewed his lord these *1401*
14:21 master of the house being angry said to his s, *1401*
14:22 And the s said, Lord, it is done as thou hast *1401*
14:23 And the lord said unto the s, Go out into *1401*
16:13 No s can serve two masters: for either he *3610*
17: 7 having a s plowing or feeding cattle, *1401*
17: 9 Doth he thank that s because he did *1401*
19:17 And he said unto him, Well, *thou* good s: *1401*
19:22 mouth will I judge thee, *thou* wicked s. *1401*
20:10 And at the season he sent a s to *1401*
20:11 And again he sent another s: and they beat *1401*
22:50 And one of them smote the s of the high *1401*
Jn 8:34 Whosoever committeth sin is the s of sin. *1401*
8:35 And the s abideth not in the house for ever: *1401*
12:26 and where I am, there shall also my s be: *1249*
13:16 unto you, The s is not greater than his lord; *1401*
15:15 for the s knoweth not what his lord doeth: *1401*
15:20 unto you, The s is not greater than his lord. *1401*
18:10 and smote the high priest's s, and cut off *1401*
Ac 4:25 Who by the mouth of thy s David hast said, *3816*
Ro 1: 1 Paul, a s of Jesus Christ, called *to be* an *1401*
14: 4 Who art thou that judgest another *man's* s? *3610*
16: 1 which is a s of the church which is at *1249*
16: S *sent* by Phebe s of the church at Cenchrea. *1249*
1Co 7:21 Art thou called *being* a s? care not for it: *1401*
7:22 the Lord, *being* a s, is the Lord's freeman: *1401*
7:22 he that is called, *being* free, is Christ's s. *1401*
9:19 all *men,* yet have I **made** myself s unto all, *1402*
Gal 1:10 pleased men, I should not be the s of Christ. *1401*
4: 1 as he is a child, differeth nothing from a s, *1401*
4: 7 Wherefore thou art no more a s, but a son; *1401*
Php 2: 7 and took *upon him* the form of a s, and *1401*
Col 4:12 is *one* of you, a s of Christ, saluteth you, *1401*
2Ti 2:24 And the s of the Lord must not strive; but *1401*
Tit 1: 1 a s of God, and an apostle of Jesus Christ, *1401*
Phm 1:16 Not now as a s, but above a servant, *1401*
1:16 but above a s, a brother beloved, *1401*
1: S from Rome to Philemon, by Onesimus a s. *3610*
Heb 3: 5 verily *was* faithful in all his house, as a s, *2324*
Jas 1: 1 a s of God and of the Lord Jesus Christ, *1401*
2Pe 1: 1 a s and an apostle of Jesus Christ, *1401*
Jude 1: 1 the s of Jesus Christ, and brother of James, *1401*
Rev 1: 1 and signified *it* by his angel unto his s John: *1401*
15: 3 And they sing the song of Moses the s of *1401*

SERVANT'S (9) [SERVE]

Ge 19: 2 into your s house, and tarry all night, and 5650
2Sa 7:19 thou hast spoken also of thy s house for a 5650
1Ki 11:13 one tribe to thy son for David my s sake, 5650
11:34 all the days of his life for David my s sake, 5650
2Ki 8:19 not destroy Judah for David his s sake, 5650
1Ch 17:17 for thou hast *also* spoken of thy s house for 5650
17:19 for thy s sake, and according to thine own 5650
Isa 45: 4 For Jacob my s sake, and Israel mine elect, 5650
Jn 18:10 off his right ear. The s name was Malchus. *1401*

SERVANTS (476) [SERVE]

Ge 9:25 a servant of s shall he be unto his brethren. 5650
14:14 he armed his trained *s,* born in his own NIH
14:15 he and his s, by night, and smote them, and 5650
20: 8 called all his s, and told all these things in 5650
21:25 which Abimelech's s had violently taken 5650
26:14 possession of herds, and great store of s: 5657
26:15 For all the wells which his father's s had 5650
26:19 Isaac's s digged in the valley, and 5650
26:25 tent there: and there Isaac's s digged a well. 5650
26:32 that Isaac's s came, and told him 5650
27:37 all his brethren have I given to him for s; 5650
32:16 he delivered *them* into the hand of his s, 5650
32:16 said unto his s, Pass over before me, and 5650
40:20 that he made a feast unto all his s: 5650
40:20 and of the chief baker among his s. 5650
41:10 Pharaoh was wroth with his s, and put me 5650
41:37 eyes of Pharaoh, and in the eyes of all his s. 5650
41:38 Pharaoh said unto his s, Can we find *such* 5650
42:10 my lord, but to buy food are thy s come. 5650
42:11 we *are* true *men,* thy s are no spies. 5650
42:13 they said, Thy s *are* twelve brethren, 5650
44: 7 God forbid that thy s should do according 5650
44: 9 With whom*soever* of thy s it be found, 5650
44:16 God hath found out the iniquity of thy s: 5650
44:16 behold, we *are* my lord's s, both we, and 5650
44:19 My lord asked his s, saying, Have ye a 5650
44:21 thou saidst unto thy s, Bring him down 5650
44:23 thou saidst unto thy s, Except your 5650
44:31 thy s shall bring down the gray hairs of thy 5650
45:16 and it pleased Pharaoh well, and his s. 5650
47: 3 Thy s *are* shepherds, both we, *and* also our 5650
47: 4 for thy s have no pasture for their flocks; 5650
47: 4 let thy s dwell in the land of Goshen. 5650
47:19 and we and our land will be s unto Pharaoh: 5650
47:25 of my lord, and we will be Pharaoh's s. 5650
50: 2 Joseph commanded his s the physicians to 5650
50: 7 with him went up all the s of Pharaoh, 5650
50:17 forgive the trespass of the s of the God of 5650
50:18 his face; and they said, Behold, we *be* thy s. 5650
Ex 5:15 Wherefore dealest thou thus with thy s? 5650
5:16 *There is* no straw given unto thy s, and 5650
5:16 behold, thy s *are* beaten; but the fault *is* in 5650
5:21 in the eyes of his s, to put a sword in their 5650
7:10 and before his s, and it became a serpent. 5650
7:20 sight of Pharaoh, and in the sight of his s; 5650
8: 3 into the house of thy s, and upon thy 5650
8: 4 and upon thy people, and upon all thy s. 5650
8: 9 for thee, and for thy s, and for thy people, 5650
8:11 and from thy s, and from thy people; 5650
8:21 upon thy s, and upon thy people, and 5650

Ex 8:29 from his s, and from his people, to morrow: 5650
8:31 from his s, and from his people; 5650
9:14 and upon thy s, and upon thy people; 5650
9:20 amongst the s of Pharaoh made his servants 5650
9:20 amongst the servants of Pharaoh made his s 5650
9:21 not the word of the LORD left his s 5650
9:30 as for thee and thy s, I know that ye will 5650
9:34 and hardened his heart, he and his s. 5650
10: 1 hardened his heart, and the heart of his s, 5650
10: 6 the houses of all thy s, and the houses of all 5650
10: 7 Pharaoh's s said unto him, How long shall 5650
11: 3 in the sight of Pharaoh's s, and in the sight 5650
11: 8 all these thy s shall come down unto me, 5650
12:30 he, and all his s, and all the Egyptians; 5650
14: 5 and of his s was turned against the people, 5650
32:13 Isaac, and Israel, thy s, 5650
Lev 25:42 For they *are* my s, which I brought forth 5650
25:55 For unto me the children of Israel *are* s; 5650
25:55 they *are* my s whom I brought forth out of 5650
Nu 22:18 and said unto the s of Balak, 5650
22:22 upon his ass, and his two s *were* with him. 5288
31:49 Thy s have taken the sum of the men of war 5650
32: 4 *is* a land for cattle, and thy s have cattle: 5650
32: 5 let this land be given unto thy s for a 5650
32:25 Thy s will do as my lord commandeth. 5650
32:27 thy s will pass over, every man armed for 5650
32:31 As the LORD hath said unto thy s, so 5650
Dt 9:27 Remember thy s, Abraham, Isaac, and 5650
29: 2 and unto all his s, and unto all his land; 5650
32:36 his people, and repent himself for his s, 5650
32:43 for he will avenge the blood of his s, and 5650
34:11 and to all his s, and to all his land, 5650
Jos 9: 8 they said unto Joshua, We *are* thy s. 5650
9: 9 From a very far country thy s are come 5650
9:11 and say unto them, We *are* your s: 5650
9:24 said, Because it was certainly told thy s, 5650
10: 6 Slack not thy hand from thy s; 5650
Jdg 3:24 When he was gone out, his s came; and 5650
6:27 Gideon took ten men of his s, and did as 5650
19:19 and for the young man *which is* with thy s: 5650
1Sa 4: 9 that ye be not s unto the Hebrews, 5647
8:14 the best *of them,* and give *them* to his s. 5650
8:15 and give to his officers, and to his s. 5650
8:17 tenth of your sheep: and ye shall be his s. 5650
9: 3 Take now one of the s with thee, and arise, 5288
12:19 Pray for thy s unto the LORD thy God, 5650
16:15 Saul's s said unto him, Behold now, an evil 5650
16:16 Let our lord now command thy s *which are* 5650
16:17 Saul said unto his s, Provide me now a man 5650
16:18 answered one of the s, and said, Behold, 5288
17: 8 *am* not I a Philistine, and you s to Saul? 5650
17: 9 and *to* kill me, then will we be your s: 5650
17: 9 then shall ye be our s, and serve us. 5650
18: 5 the people, and also in the sight of Saul's s. 5650
18:22 Saul commanded his s, *saying,* Commune 5650
18:22 hath delight in thee, and all his s love thee: 5650
18:23 Saul's s spake those words in the ears of 5650
18:24 the s of Saul told him, saying, On this 5650
18:26 when his s told David these words, 5650
18:30 himself more wisely than all the s of Saul; 5650
19: 1 and to all his s, that they should kill David. 5650
21: 2 I have appointed *my* s to such and such a 5288
21: 7 Now a *certain* man of the s of Saul *was* 5650
21:11 the s of Achish said unto him, *Is* not this 5650
21:14 said Achish unto his s, Lo, you see the man 5650
22: 6 and all his s *were* standing about him;) 5650
22: 7 Saul said unto his s that stood about him, 5650
22: 9 which *was* set over the s of Saul, and said, 5650
22:14 who *is so* faithful among all thy s as David, 5650
22:17 the s of the king would not put forth their 5650
24: 7 So David stayed his s with *these* words, and 376
25: 8 cometh to thine hand unto thy s, 5650
25:10 Nabal answered David's s, and said, 5650
25:10 there be many s now a days that break 5650
25:19 she said unto her s, Go on before me; 5288
25:40 when the s of David were come to Abigail 5650
25:41 servant to wash the feet of the s of my lord. 5650
28: 7 said Saul unto his s, Seek me a woman that 5650
28: 7 his s said to him, Behold, *there is* a woman 5650
28:23 his s, together with the woman, 5650
28:25 she brought *it* before Saul, and before his s; 5650
29:10 with thy master's s that are come with thee: 5650
2Sa 2:12 and the s of Ish-bosheth the son of Saul, 5650
2:13 the s of David, went out, and met together 5650
2:15 son of Saul, and twelve of the s of David. 5650
2:17 the men of Israel, before the s of David. 5650
2:30 there lacked of David's s nineteen men and 5650
2:31 the s of David had smitten of Benjamin, 5650
3:22 the s of David and Joab came from 5650
3:38 the king said unto his s, Know ye not that 5650
6:20 to day in the eyes of the handmaids of his s, 5650
8: 2 *so* the Moabites became David's s, and 5650
8: 6 the Syrians became s to David, and 5650
8: 7 of gold that were on the s of Hadadezer, 5650
8:14 and all they of Edom became David's s. 5650
9:10 Thou therefore, and thy sons, and thy s, 5650
9:10 Now Ziba had fifteen sons and twenty s. 5650
9:12 all that dwelt in the house of Ziba *were* s 5650
10: 2 him by the hand of his s for his father. 5650
10: 2 David's s came *into* the land of the children 5650
10: 3 hath not David *rather* sent his s unto thee, 5650
10: 4 Wherefore Hanun took David's s, and 5650
10:19 when all the kings *that were* s to Hadarezer 5650
11: 1 sent Joab, and his s with him, and all Israel; 5650
11: 9 the king's house with all the s of his lord, 5650
11:11 my lord Joab, and the s of my lord, 5650
11:13 out to lie on his bed with the s of his lord, 5650
11:17 there fell *some* of the people of the s of 5650
11:24 shooters shot from off the wall upon thy s; 5650
11:24 *some* of the king's s be dead, and 5650
12:18 the s of David feared to tell him that 5650
12:19 when David saw that his s whispered, 5650
12:19 therefore David said unto his s, Is the child 5650
12:21 said his s unto him, What thing *is* this that 5650
13:24 beseech thee, and his s go with thy servant. 5650
13:28 Now Absalom had commanded his s, 5288
13:29 the s of Absalom did unto Amnon as 5288
13:31 all his s stood *by* with their clothes rent. 5650
13:36 the king also and all his s wept very sore. 5650
14:30 Therefore he said unto his s, See, 5650
14:30 And Absalom's s set the field on fire. 5650
14:31 Wherefore have thy s set my field on fire? 5650
15:14 David said unto all his s that *were* with him 5650
15:15 the king's s said unto the king, Behold, 5650
15:15 thy s *are ready to do* whatsoever my lord 5650
15:18 all his s passed on beside him; and all 5650
16: 6 at David, and at all the s of king David: 5650
16:11 to Abishai, and to all his s, Behold, my son, 5650
17:20 when Absalom's s came to the woman to 5650
18: 7 of Israel were slain before the s of David, 5650
18: 9 Absalom met the s of David. And Absalom 5650
19: 5 hast shamed *this* day the faces of all thy s, 5650
19: 6 that thou regardest neither princes nor s: 5650
19: 7 go forth, and speak comfortably unto thy s: 5650
19:14 unto the king, Return thou, and all thy s. 5650
19:17 his fifteen sons and his twenty s with him; 5650
20: 6 take thou thy lord's s, and pursue after him, 5650
21:15 his s with him, and fought against 5650
21:22 the hand of David, and by the hand of his s. 5650
24:20 the king and his s coming on toward him: 5650
1Ki 1: 2 Wherefore his s said unto him, Let there be 5650
1: 9 and all the men of Judah the king's s: 5650
1:33 Take with you the s of your lord, and 5650
1:47 moreover the king's s came to bless our 5650
2:39 that two of the s of Shimei ran away unto 5650
2:39 saying, Behold, thy s *be* in Gath. 5650
2:40 and went to Gath to Achish to seek his s: 5650
2:40 Shimei went, and brought his s from Gath. 5650
3:15 and made a feast to all his s. 5650
5: 1 Hiram king of Tyre sent his s unto 5650
5: 6 and my s shall be with thy servants: 5650
5: 6 and my servants shall be with thy s: 5650
5: 6 unto thee will I give hire for thy s 5650
5: 9 My s shall bring *them* down from Lebanon 5650
8:23 mercy with thy s that walk before thee with 5650
8:32 do, and judge thy s, condemning 5650
8:36 forgive the sin of thy s, and of thy people 5650
9:22 his s, and his princes, and his captains, and 5650
9:27 Hiram sent in the navy his s, shipmen that 5650
9:27 of the sea, with the s of Solomon. 5650
10: 5 the sitting of his s, and the attendance of his 5650
10: 8 Happy *are* thy men, happy *are* these thy s, 5650
10:13 and went to her own country, she and her s. 5650
11:17 certain Edomites of his father's s with him, 5650
12: 7 to them, then they will be thy s for ever. 5650
15:18 and delivered them into the hand of his s: 5650
20: 6 Yet I will send my s unto thee to morrow 5650
20: 6 search thine house, and the houses of thy s; 5650

1Ki	20:12	in the pavilions, that he said unto his **s**,	5650
	20:23	the **s** of the king of Syria said unto him,	5650
	20:31	his **s** said unto him, Behold now, we have	5650
	22: 3	the king of Israel said unto his **s**, Know ye	5650
	22:49	Let my **s** go with thy servants in the ships.	5650
	22:49	Let my servants go with thy **s** in the ships.	5650
2Ki	1:13	let my life, and the life of these fifty thy **s**,	5650
	2:16	there be with thy **s** fifty strong men;	5650
	3:11	one of the king of Israel's **s** answered and	5650
	5:13	his **s** came near, and spake unto him, and	5650
	5:23	and laid *them* upon two of his **s**;	5288
	6: 3	Be content, I pray thee, and go with thy **s**.	5650
	6: 8	took counsel with his **s**, saying, In such and	5650
	6:11	he called his **s**, and said unto them, Will ye	5650
	6:12	one of his **s** said, None, my lord, O king:	5650
	7:12	king arose in the night, and said unto his **s**,	5650
	7:13	one of his **s** answered and said, Let *some*	5650
	9: 7	that I may avenge the blood of my **s**	5650
	9: 7	the blood of all the **s** of the LORD, at	5650
	9:11	Jehu came forth to the **s** of his lord: and	5650
	9:28	his **s** carried him *in a chariot* to Jerusalem,	5650
	10: 5	We *are* thy **s**, and will do all that thou shalt	5650
	10:19	of Baal, all his **s**, and all his priests;	5647
	10:23	here with you none of the **s** of the LORD,	5650
	12:20	his **s** arose, and made a conspiracy,	5650
	12:21	of Shomer, his **s**, smote him, and he died;	5650
	14: 5	that he slew his **s** which had slain the king	5650
	17:13	which I sent to you by my **s** the prophets.	5650
	17:23	as he had said by all his **s** the prophets.	5650
	18:24	of one captain of the least of my master's **s**,	5650
	18:26	I pray thee, to thy **s** in the Syrian language;	5650
	19: 5	So the **s** of king Hezekiah came to Isaiah.	5650
	19: 6	*with* which the **s** of the king of Assyria	5288
	21:10	the LORD spake by his **s** the prophets,	5650
	21:23	the **s** of Amon conspired against him, and	5650
	22: 9	Thy **s** have gathered the money that was	5650
	23:30	his **s** carried him *in a chariot* dead from	5650
	24: 2	which he spake by his **s** the prophets.	5650
	24:10	At that time the **s** of Nebuchadnezzar king	5650
	24:11	against the city, and his **s** *did* besiege it.	5650
	24:12	and his **s**, and his princes, and his officers:	5650
	25:24	Fear not to be the **s** of the Chaldees:	5650
1Ch	18: 2	the Moabites became David's **s**, and	5650
	18: 6	the Syrians became David's **s**, and	5650
	18: 7	of gold that were on the **s** of Hadarezer,	5650
	18:13	and all the Edomites became David's **s**.	5650
	19: 2	So the **s** of David came into the land of	5650
	19: 3	are not his **s** come unto thee for to search,	5650
	19: 4	Wherefore Hanun took David's **s**, and	5650
	19:19	when the **s** of Hadarezer saw that they were	5650
	19:19	made peace with David, and became his **s**:	5647
	20: 8	the hand of David, and by the hand of his **s**.	5650
	21: 3	lord the king, *are* they not all my lord's **s**?	5650
2Ch	2: 8	for I know that thy **s** can skill to cut timber	5650
	2: 8	and behold, my **s** *shall be* with thy servants,	5650
	2: 8	and behold, my servants *shall be* with thy **s**,	5650
	2:10	behold, I will give to thy **s**, the hewers that	5650
	2:15	lord hath spoken of, let him send unto his **s**:	5650
	6:14	and *shewest* mercy unto thy **s**,	5650
	6:23	do, and judge thy **s**, by requiting	5650
	6:27	forgive the sin of thy **s**, and of thy people	5650
	8: 9	Israel did Solomon make no **s** for his work;	5650
	8:18	Huram sent him by the hands of his **s** ships,	5650
	8:18	and **s** that had knowledge of the sea;	5650
	8:18	they went with the **s** of Solomon to Ophir,	5650
	9: 4	the sitting of his **s**, and the attendance of his	5650
	9: 7	*are* thy men, and happy *are* these thy **s**,	5650
	9:10	the **s** also of Huram, and the servants of	5650
	9:10	the **s** of Solomon, which brought gold from	5650
	9:12	went away to her own land, she and her **s**.	5650
	9:21	ships went *to* Tarshish with the **s** of Huram:	5650
	10: 7	words to them, they will be thy **s** for ever.	5650
	12: 8	Nevertheless they shall be his **s**; that they	5650
	24:25	his own **s** conspired against him for	5650
	25: 3	that he slew his **s** that had killed the king	5650
	32: 9	king of Assyria send his **s** to Jerusalem,	5650
	32:16	his **s** spake yet *more* against the LORD	5650
	33:24	his **s** conspired against him, and slew him	5650
	34:16	saying, All that was committed to thy **s**,	5650
	35:23	the king said to his **s**, Have me away; for I	5650
	35:24	His **s** therefore took him out of *that* chariot,	5650
	36:20	where they were **s** to him and his sons until	5650
Ezr	2:55	The children of Solomon's **s**: the children	5650
	2:58	and the children of Solomon's **s**,	5650
	2:65	Beside their **s** and their maids, of whom	5650
	4:11	Thy **s** the men *on this* side the river, and	5649
	5:11	We are the **s** of the God of heaven and	5649
	9:11	Which thou hast commanded by thy **s**	5650
Ne	1: 6	for the children of Israel thy **s**, and	5650
	1:10	Now these *are* thy **s** and thy people,	5650
	1:11	to the prayer of thy **s**, who desire to fear thy	5650
	2:20	therefore we his **s** will arise and build:	5650
	4:16	*that* the half of my **s** wrought in the work,	5288
	4:23	So neither I, nor my brethren, nor my **s**,	5288
	5: 5	bondage our sons and our daughters to be **s**,	5650
	5:10	I likewise, *and* my brethren, and my **s**,	5288
	5:15	*yea,* even their **s** bare rule over the people:	5288
	5:16	all my **s** *were* gathered thither unto	5288
	7:57	The children of Solomon's **s**: the children	5650
	7:60	and the children of Solomon's **s**,	5650
	9:10	on all his **s**, and on all the people of his	5650
	9:36	we *are* **s** *this* day, and *for* the land that thou	5650
	9:36	and the good thereof, behold, we *are* **s** in it:	5650
	11: 3	and the children of Solomon's **s**.	5650
	13:19	*some* of my **s** set I at the gates, *that* there	5288
Est	1: 3	made a feast unto all his princes and his **s**;	5650
	2: 2	said the king's **s** that ministered unto him,	5288
	2:18	a great feast unto all his princes and his **s**,	5650
	3: 2	all the king's **s**, that *were* in the king's gate,	5650
	3: 3	the king's **s**, which *were* in the king's gate,	5650
	4:11	All the king's **s**, and the people of	5650
	5:11	him above the princes and **s** of the king.	5650
	6: 3	said the king's **s** that ministered unto him,	5288
	6: 5	the king's **s** said unto him, Behold,	5288
Job	1:15	they have slain the **s** with the edge of	5288
	1:16	the sheep, and the **s**, and consumed them;	5288
	1:17	slain the **s** with the edge of the sword;	5288
	4:18	Behold, he put no trust in his **s**; and his	5650
Ps	34:22	The LORD redeemeth the soul of his **s**:	5650
	69:36	The seed also of his **s** shall inherit it: and	5650
	79: 2	The dead bodies of thy **s** have they given *to*	5650
	79:10	of the blood of thy **s** which is shed.	5650
	89:50	Remember, Lord, the reproach of thy **s**;	5650
	90:13	and let it repent thee concerning thy **s**.	5650
	90:16	Let thy work appear unto thy **s**, and	5650
	102:14	For thy **s** take pleasure in her stones, and	5650
	102:28	The children of thy **s** shall continue, and	5650
	105:25	hate his people, to deal subtilly with his **s**.	5650
	113: 1	Praise, O ye **s** of the LORD, praise	5650
	119:91	to thine ordinances: for all *are* thy **s**.	5650
	123: 2	as the eyes of **s** *look* unto the hand of their	5650
	134: 1	ye the LORD, all ye **s** of the LORD,	5650
	135: 1	praise *him,* O ye **s** of the LORD.	5650
	135: 9	O Egypt, upon Pharaoh, and upon all his **s**.	5650
	135:14	and he will repent himself concerning his **s**.	5650
Pr	29:12	a ruler hearken to lies, all his **s** *are* wicked.	8334
Ecc	2: 7	I got *me* **s** and maidens, and had servants	5650
	2: 7	and maidens, and had **s** born in *my* house;	NIH
	10: 7	I have seen **s** upon horses, and	5650
	10: 7	and princes walking as **s** upon the earth.	5650
Isa	14: 2	them in the land of the LORD for **s**	5650
	36: 9	of one captain of the least of my master's **s**,	5650
	36:11	unto thy **s** in the Syrian language;	5650
	37: 5	So the **s** of king Hezekiah came to Isaiah.	5650
	37: 6	where*with* the **s** of the king of Assyria have	5288
	37:24	By thy **s** hast thou reproached the Lord, and	5650
	54:17	This *is* the heritage of the **s** of the LORD,	5650
	56: 6	to love the name of the LORD, to be his **s**,	5650
	65: 9	shall inherit it, and my **s** shall dwell there.	5650
	65:13	my **s** shall eat, but ye shall be hungry:	5650
	65:13	my **s** shall drink, but ye shall be thirsty:	5650
	65:13	my **s** shall rejoice, but ye shall be ashamed:	5650
	65:14	my **s** shall sing for joy of heart, but ye shall	5650
	65:15	slay thee, and call his **s** by another name:	5650
	66:14	the LORD shall be known towards his **s**,	5650
Jer	7:25	I have even sent unto you all my **s**	5650
	21: 7	his **s**, and the people, and such as are left in	5650
	22: 2	thy **s**, and thy people that enter in by these	5650
	22: 4	and on horses, he, and his **s**, and his people.	5650
	25: 4	the LORD hath sent unto you all his **s**	5650
	25:19	his **s**, and his princes, and all his people;	5650
	26: 5	To hearken to the words of my **s**	5650
	29:19	which I sent unto them by my **s**	5650
	34:11	caused the **s** and the handmaids, whom they	5650
	34:11	brought them into subjection for **s** and	5650
	34:16	to be unto you for **s** and for handmaids.	5650
	35:15	I have sent also unto you all my **s**	5650
	36:24	nor any of his **s** that heard all these words.	5650

Jer 36:31 and his seed and his **s** for their iniquity; 5650
37: 2 neither he, nor his **s**, nor the people of 5650
37:18 or against thy **s**, or against this people, 5650
44: 4 Howbeit I sent unto you all my **s** 5650
46:26 king of Babylon, and into the hand of his **s**: 5650
La 5: 8 **S** have ruled over us: *there is* none that doth 5650
Eze 38:17 in old time by my **s** the prophets of Israel, 5650
46:17 give a gift of his inheritance to one of his **s**, 5650
Da 1:12 Prove thy **s**, I beseech thee, ten days; and 5650
1:13 and as thou seest, deal with thy **s**. 5650
2: 4 tell thy **s** the dream, and we will shew 5649
2: 7 Let the king tell his **s** the dream, and 5649
3:26 ye **s** of the most high God, come forth, and 5649
3:28 delivered his **s** that trusted in him, and 5649
9: 6 Neither have we hearkened unto thy **s** 5650
9:10 which he set before us by his **s** 5650
Joel 2:29 also upon the **s** and upon the handmaids in 5650
Am 3: 7 he revealeth his secret unto his **s** 5650
Mic 6: 4 and redeemed thee out of the house of **s**; 5650
Zec 1: 6 which I commanded my **s** the prophets, 5650
2: 9 and they shall be a spoil to their **s**: 5647
Mt 13:27 So the **s** of the householder came and *1401*
13:28 The **s** said unto him, Wilt thou then *that* we *1401*
14: 2 And said unto his **s**, This is John *3816*
18:23 which would take account of his **s**. *1401*
21:34 he sent his **s** to the husbandmen, that *they* *1401*
21:35 And the husbandmen took his **s**, and *1401*
21:36 Again, he sent other **s** moe than the first: *1401*
22: 3 And sent forth his **s** to call them that were *1401*
22: 4 Again, he sent forth other **s**, saying, *1401*
22: 6 And the remnant took his **s**, and *1401*
22: 8 Then saith he to his **s**, The wedding is *1401*
22:10 So those **s** went out into the *high*ways, and *1401*
22:13 Then said the king to the **s**, Bind him hand *1249*
25:14 *who* called his own **s**, and delivered unto *1401*
25:19 After a long time the lord of those **s** *1401*
26:58 and went in, and sat with the **s**, to see *5257*
Mk 1:20 father Zebedee in the ship with the **hired s**, *3411*
13:34 and gave authority to his **s**, and to every *1401*
14:54 and he sat with the **s**, and warmed himself *5257*
14:65 the **s** did strike him with the palms of their *5257*
Lk 12:37 Blessed *are* those **s**, whom the lord when he *1401*
12:38 and find *them* so, blessed are those **s**. *1401*
15:17 How many hired *s* of my father's have NIG
15:19 thy son: make me as one of thy hired *s*. NIG
15:22 But the father said to his **s**, Bring forth *1401*
15:26 And he called one of the **s**, and asked what *3816*
17:10 say, We are unprofitable **s**: *1401*
19:13 And he called his ten **s**, and delivered them *1401*
19:15 he commanded these **s** to be called unto *1401*
Jn 2: 5 His mother saith unto the **s**, Whatsoever he *1249*
2: 9 (but the **s** which drew the water knew;) *1249*
4:51 his **s** met him, and told *him*, saying, *1401*
15:15 Henceforth I call you not **s**; for the servant *1401*
18:18 And the **s** and officers stood *there*, who had *1401*
18:26 One of the **s** of the high priest, being *his* *1401*
18:36 were of this world, then would my **s** fight, *5257*
Ac 2:18 And on my **s** and on my handmaidens I *1401*
4:29 and grant unto thy **s**, that with all boldness *1401*
10: 7 he called two of his **household s**, and *3610*
16:17 These men are the **s** of the most high God, *1401*
Ro 6:16 that to whom ye yield yourselves **s** to obey, *1401*
6:16 to obey, *his* **s** ye are to whom ye obey; *1401*
6:17 that ye were the **s** of sin, but ye have *1401*
6:18 from sin, ye became the **s** of righteousness. *1402*
6:19 for as ye have yielded your members **s** to *1401*
6:19 now yield your members **s** to righteousness *1401*
6:20 For when ye were the **s** of sin, ye were free *1401*
6:22 and become **s** to God, ye have your fruit *1402*
1Co 7:23 bought with a price; be not ye the **s** of men. *1401*
2Co 4: 5 and ourselves your **s** for Jesus' sake. *1401*
Eph 6: 5 **S**, be obedient to *them that are your* masters *1401*
6: 6 but as the **s** of Christ, doing the will of God *1401*
Php 1: 1 Paul and Timotheus, the **s** of Jesus Christ, *1401*
Col 3:22 **S**, obey in all *things your* masters according *1401*
4: 1 give unto *your* **s** that which is just and *1401*
1Ti 6: 1 Let as many **s** as are under the yoke count *1401*
Tit 2: 9 *Exhort* **s** to be obedient unto their own *1401*
1Pe 2:16 cloke of maliciousness, but as the **s** of God. *1401*
2:18 **S**, *be* subject to *your* masters with all fear; *3610*
2Pe 2:19 they themselves are the **s** of corruption: *1401*
Rev 1: 1 to shew unto his **s** *things* which must *1401*
2:20 and to seduce my **s** to commit fornication, *1401*
7: 3 till we have sealed the **s** of our God in their *1401*
10: 7 as he hath declared to his **s** the prophets. *1401*
11:18 that *thou* shouldest give reward unto thy **s** *1401*
19: 2 hath avenged the blood of his **s** at her hand. *1401*
19: 5 all ye his **s**, and ye that fear him, both *1401*
22: 3 shall be in it; and his **s** shall serve him: *1401*
22: 6 his **s** *the things* which must shortly be done. *1401*

SERVANTS' (4) [SERVE]

Ge 46:34 Thy **s** trade hath been about cattle from our 5650
Ex 8:24 *into* his **s** houses, and into all the land of 5650
Isa 63:17 Return for thy **s** sake, the tribes of thine 5650
65: 8 so will I do for my **s** sakes, that *I* may not 5650

SERVE (209) [BONDSERVANT, BONDSERVICE, EYESERVICE, FELLOWSERVANT, FELLOWSERVANTS, MAIDSERVANT, MAIDSERVANT'S, MAIDSERVANTS, MAIDSERVANTS', MANSERVANT, MANSERVANT'S, MANSERVANTS, MENSERVANTS, SERVANT, SERVANT'S, SERVANTS, SERVANTS', SERVED, SERVEDST, SERVEST, SERVETH, SERVICE, SERVILE, SERVING, SERVITOR, SERVITUDE, WOMENSERVANTS]

Ge 15:13 in a land *that is* not theirs, and shall **s** them; 5647
15:14 that nation, whom they shall **s**, will I judge: 5647
25:23 and the elder shall **s** the younger. 5647
27:29 Let people **s** thee, and nations bow down to 5647
27:40 shalt thou live, and shalt **s** thy brother; 5647
29:15 shouldest thou therefore **s** me for nought? 5647
29:18 I will **s** thee seven years for Rachel thy 5647
29:25 did not I **s** with thee for Rachel? wherefore 5647
29:27 thou shalt **s** with me yet seven other years. 5647
Ex 1:13 **made** the children of Israel **to s** with 5647
1:14 all their service, wherein they **made** them **s**, 5647
3:12 ye shall **s** God upon this mountain. 5647
4:23 unto thee, Let my son go, that he may **s** me: 5647
7:16 that they may **s** me in the wilderness: 5647
8: 1 Let my people go, that they may **s** me. 5647
8:20 Let my people go, that they may **s** me. 5647
9: 1 Let my people go, that they may **s** me. 5647
9:13 Let my people go, that they may **s** me. 5647
10: 3 let my people go, that they may **s** me. 5647
10: 7 that they may **s** the LORD their God: 5647
10: 8 unto them, Go, **s** the LORD your God: 5647
10:11 go now ye *that are* men, and **s** the LORD; 5647
10:24 unto Moses, and said, Go ye, **s** the LORD; 5647
10:26 for thereof must we take to **s** the LORD 5647
10:26 we know not with what we must **s** 5647
12:31 and go, **s** the LORD, as ye have said. 5647
14:12 Let us alone, that we may **s** the Egyptians? 5647
14:12 For *it had been* better for us to **s** 5647
20: 5 not bow down thyself to them, nor **s** them: 5647
21: 2 buy a Hebrew servant, six years he shall **s**: 5647
21: 6 with an aul; and he shall **s** him for ever. 5647
23:24 nor **s** them, nor do after their works: 5647
23:25 ye shall **s** the LORD your God, and 5647
23:33 for if thou **s** their gods, it will surely be a 5647
Lev 25:39 thou shalt not **compel** him **to s** as a 5647+5656
25:40 *and* shall **s** thee unto the year of jubile: 5647
Nu 4:24 of the Gershonites, to **s**, and for burdens: 5647
4:26 all that is made for them: so shall they **s**. 5647
8:25 the service *thereof*, and shall **s** no more: 5647
18: 7 the altar, and within the vail; and ye shall **s**: 5647
18:21 for their service which they **s**, *even* 5647
Dt 4:19 be driven to worship them, and **s** them, 5647
4:28 there ye shall **s** gods, the work of men's 5647
5: 9 bow down thyself unto them, nor **s** them: 5647
6:13 and **s** him, and shalt swear by his name. 5647
7: 4 following me, that they may **s** other gods: 5647
7:16 neither shalt thou **s** their gods; for that *will* 5647
8:19 other gods, and **s** them, and worship them, 5647
10:12 to **s** the LORD thy God with all thy heart 5647
10:20 him shalt thou **s**, and to him shalt thou 5647
11:13 to **s** him with all your heart and with all 5647
11:16 and **s** other gods, and worship them; 5647
12:30 How did these nations **s** their gods? 5647
13: 2 thou hast not known, and let us **s** them; 5647
13: 4 and you shall **s** him, and cleave unto him. 5647
13: 6 saying, Let us go and **s** other gods, 5647
13:13 saying, Let us go and **s** other gods, 5647
15:12 be sold unto thee, and **s** thee six years; 5647
20:11 tributaries unto thee, and they shall **s** thee. 5647
28:14 *to* the left, to go after other gods to **s** them. 5647
28:36 there shalt thou **s** other gods, wood and 5647
28:48 Therefore shalt thou **s** thine enemies which 5647

S

Dt 28:64 there thou shalt **s** other gods, which neither 5647
29:18 to go *and* **s** the gods of these nations; 5647
30:17 and worship other gods, and **s** them; 5647
31:20 **s** them, and provoke me, and break my 5647
Jos 16:10 unto this day, and **s** under tribute. 5647
22: 5 to **s** him with all your heart and with all 5647
23: 7 nor cause to swear *by them,* neither **s** them, 5647
24:14 and **s** him in sincerity and in truth: 5647
24:14 and in Egypt; and **s** ye the LORD. 5647
24:15 if it seem evil unto you to **s** the LORD, 5647
24:15 choose you *this* day whom you will **s**; 5647
24:15 and my house, we will **s** the LORD. 5647
24:16 should forsake the LORD, to **s** other gods; 5647
24:18 *therefore* will we also **s** the LORD; for he 5647
24:19 unto the people, Ye cannot **s** the LORD: 5647
24:20 **s** strange gods, then he will turn and do you 5647
24:21 Nay; but we will **s** the LORD. 5647
24:22 ye have chosen you the LORD, to **s** him. 5647
24:24 The LORD our God will we **s**, and his 5647
Jdg 2:19 in following other gods to **s** them, and 5647
9:28 and who *is* Shechem, that we should **s** him? 5647
9:28 **s** the men of Hamor the father of Shechem: 5647
9:28 of Shechem: for why should we **s** him? 5647
9:38 Who *is* Abimelech, that we should **s** him? 5647
1Sa 7: 3 hearts unto the LORD, and **s** him only: 5647
10: 7 *that* thou do as **occasion s** thee; 3027+4672
11: 1 a covenant with us, and we will **s** thee. 5647
12:10 the hand of our enemies, and we will **s** thee. 5647
12:14 **s** him, and obey his voice, and not rebel 5647
12:20 but **s** the LORD with all your heart; 5647
12:24 and **s** him in truth with all your heart: 5647
17: 9 then shall ye be our servants, and **s** us. 5647
26:19 of the LORD, saying, Go, **s** other gods. 5647
2Sa 15: 8 *to* Jerusalem, then I will **s** the LORD. 5647
16:19 again, whom should I **s**? *should I* not *serve* 5647
16:19 *should I* not **s** in the presence of his son? NIH
22:44 a people *which* I knew not shall **s** me. 5647
1Ki 9: 6 but go and **s** other gods, and worship them: 5647
12: 4 he put upon us, lighter, and we will **s** thee. 5647
12: 7 wilt **s** them, and answer them, and 5647
2Ki 10:18 Baal a little; *but* Jehu shall **s** him much. 5647
17:35 to them, nor **s** them, nor sacrifice to them: 5647
25:24 in the land, and **s** the king of Babylon; 5647
1Ch 28: 9 **s** him with a perfect heart and with a 5647
2Ch 7:19 shall go and **s** other gods, and 5647
10: 4 that he put upon us, and we will **s** thee. 5647
29:11 to **s** him, and that *you* should minister unto 8334
30: 8 **s** the LORD your God, that the fierceness 5647
33:16 commanded Judah to **s** the LORD God of 5647
34:33 **made** all that were present in Israel **to s**, 5975
34:33 to serve, *even* to **s** the LORD their God. 5647
35: 3 **s** now the LORD your God, and his 5647
Job 21:15 *is* the Almighty, that we should **s** him? 5647
36:11 **s** *him,* they shall spend their days in 5647
39: 9 Will the unicorn be willing to **s** thee, or 5647
Ps 2:11 **S** the LORD with fear, and rejoice with 5647
18:43 a people *whom* I have not known shall **s** 5647
22:30 A seed shall **s** him; it shall be accounted to 5647
72:11 down before him: all nations shall **s** him. 5647
97: 7 Confounded be all they that **s** graven 5647
100: 2 **S** the LORD with gladness: come before 5647
101: 6 that walketh in a perfect way, he shall **s** me. 8334
102:22 and the kingdoms, to **s** the LORD. 5647
Isa 14: 3 hard bondage wherein thou wast **made to s**, 5647
19:23 the Egyptians shall **s** *with* the Assyrians. 5647
43:23 I have not **caused** thee **to s** with an 5647
43:24 thou hast **made** me **to s** with thy sins, 5647
56: 6 to **s** him, and to love the name of 8334
60:12 kingdom that will not **s** thee shall perish; 5647
Jer 5:19 shall ye **s** strangers in a land *that is* not 5647
11:10 and they went after other gods to **s** them: 5647
13:10 other gods, to **s** them, and to worship them, 5647
16:13 there shall ye **s** other gods day and night; 5647
17: 4 I will **cause** thee **to s** thine enemies in 5647
25: 6 go not after other gods to **s** them, and 5647
25:11 these nations shall **s** the king of Babylon 5647
25:14 great kings shall **s** themselves of them also: 5647
27: 6 of the field have I given him also to **s** him. 5647
27: 7 all nations shall **s** him, and his son, and 5647
27: 7 and great kings shall **s** themselves of him. 5647
27: 8 kingdom which will not **s** the same 5647
27: 9 Ye shall not **s** the king of Babylon: 5647
27:11 **s** him, those will I let remain still in their 5647
27:12 and **s** him and his people, and live. 5647
27:13 nation that will not **s** the king of Babylon? 5647
27:14 Ye shall not **s** the king of Babylon: 5647
27:17 unto them; **s** the king of Babylon, and live: 5647
28:14 that *they* may **s** Nebuchadnezzar king of 5647
28:14 king of Babylon; and they shall **s** him: 5647
30: 8 strangers shall no more **s** themselves of 5647
30: 9 they shall **s** the LORD their God, and 5647
34: 9 that none should **s** himself of them, *to wit,* 5647
34:10 that none should **s** themselves of them any 5647
35:15 go not after other gods to **s** them, and 5647
40: 9 saying, Fear not to **s** the Chaldeans: 5647
40: 9 dwell in the land and **s** the king of Babylon, 5647
40:10 I *will* dwell at Mizpah to **s** the Chaldeans, 5975
44: 3 *and* to **s** other gods, whom they knew not, 5647
Eze 20:32 of the countries, to **s** wood and stone. 8334
20:39 **s** ye every one his idols, and hereafter *also,* 5647
20:40 of Israel, all of them in the land, **s** me: 5647
29:18 **caused** his army **to s** a great service against 5647
48:18 shall be for food unto them that **s** the city. 5647
48:19 they that **s** the city shall serve it out of all 5647
48:19 they that serve the city shall **s** it out of all 5647
Da 3:12 they **s** not thy gods, nor worship the golden 6399
3:14 and Abed-nego, do not ye **s** my gods, 6399
3:17 our God whom we **s** *is* able to deliver us 6399
3:18 O king, that we will not **s** thy gods, 6399
3:28 that they might not **s** nor worship any god, 6399
7:14 and languages, should **s** him: 6399
7:27 and all dominions shall **s** and obey him. 6399
Zep 3: 9 of the LORD, to **s** him *with* one consent. 5647
Mal 3:14 Ye have said, It *is* vain to **s** God: and 5647
Mt 4:10 Lord thy God, and him only shalt thou **s**. *3000*
6:24 No *man* can **s** two masters: for either he *1398*
6:24 the other. Ye cannot **s** God and mammon. *1398*
Lk 1:74 of our enemies might **s** him without fear, *3000*
4: 8 Lord thy God, and him only shalt thou **s**. *3000*
10:40 care that my sister hath left me to **s** alone? *1247*
12:37 to meat, and will come forth and **s** them. *1247*
15:29 *his* father, Lo, these many years do I **s** thee, *1398*
16:13 No servant can **s** two masters: for either he *1398*
16:13 the other. Ye cannot **s** God and mammon. *1398*
17: 8 and gird thyself, and **s** me, till I have eaten *1247*
22:26 and he that is chief, as he that doth **s**. *1247*
Jn 12:26 If any *man* **s** me, let him follow me; and *1247*
12:26 if any *man* **s** me, him will *my* Father *1247*
Ac 6: 2 should leave the word of God, and **s** tables. *1247*
7: 7 they come forth, and **s** me in this place. *3000*
27:23 angel of God, whose I am, and whom I **s**, *3000*
Ro 1: 9 whom I **s** with my spirit in the gospel of his *3000*
6: 6 that henceforth we should not **s** sin. *1398*
7: 6 that we should **s** in newness of spirit, and *1398*
7:25 with the mind I myself **s** the law of God; *1398*
9:12 said unto her, The elder shall **s** the younger. *1398*
16:18 For *they that are* such **s** not our Lord Jesus *1398*
Gal 5:13 to the flesh, but by love **s** one another. *1398*
Col 3:24 of the inheritance: for ye **s** the Lord Christ. *1398*
1Th 1: 9 how ye turned to God from idols to **s** *1398*
2Ti 1: 3 whom I **s** from *my* forefathers with pure *3000*
Heb 8: 5 Who **s** unto the example and shadow of *3000*
9:14 from dead works to **s** the living God? *3000*
12:28 whereby we may **s** God acceptably with *3000*
13:10 whereof they have no right to eat which **s** *3000*
Rev 7:15 and **s** him day and night in his temple: *3000*
22: 3 shall be in it; and his servants shall **s** him: *3000*

SERVED (74) [SERVE]

Ge 14: 4 Twelve years they **s** Chedorlaomer, and 5647
29:20 Jacob **s** seven years for Rachel; and 5647
29:30 and **s** with him yet seven other years. 5647
30:26 for whom I have **s** thee, and let me go: 5647
30:29 Thou knowest how I have **s** thee, and how 5647
31: 6 ye know that with all my power I have **s** 5647
31:41 I **s** thee fourteen years for thy two 5647
39: 4 found grace in his sight, and he **s** him: 8334
40: 4 charged Joseph with them, and he **s** them: 8334
Dt 12: 2 nations which ye shall possess **s** their gods, 5647
17: 3 hath gone and **s** other gods, and 5647
29:26 For they went and **s** other gods, and 5647
Jos 23:16 have gone and **s** other gods, and 5647
24: 2 the father of Nachor: and they **s** other gods. 5647
24:14 put away the gods which your fathers **s** on 5647
24:15 whether the gods which your fathers **s** that 5647
24:31 Israel **s** the LORD all the days of Joshua, 5647
Jdg 2: 7 the people **s** the LORD all the days of 5647
2:11 in the sight of the LORD, and **s** Baalim: 5647

Jdg 2:13 the LORD, and **s** Baal and Ashtaroth. 5647
3: 6 daughters to their sons, and **s** their gods. 5647
3: 7 their God, and **s** Baalim and the groves. 5647
3: 8 the children of Israel **s** Chushan-rishathaim 5647
3:14 So the children of Israel **s** Eglon the king of 5647
8: 1 Why hast thou **s** us thus, that *thou* calledst 6213
10: 6 **s** Baalim, and Ashtaroth, and the gods of 5647
10: 6 and forsook the LORD, and **s** not him. 5647
10:10 have forsaken our God, and *also* **s** Baalim. 5647
10:13 Yet ye have forsaken me, and **s** other gods: 5647
10:16 gods from among them, and **s** the LORD: 5647
1Sa 7: 4 and Ashtaroth, and **s** the LORD only. 5647
8: 8 and **s** other gods, so do they also unto thee. 5647
12:10 and have **s** Baalim and Ashtaroth: 5647
2Sa 10:19 they made peace with Israel, and **s** them. 5647
16:19 as I have **s** in thy father's presence, so will I 5647
1Ki 4:21 and **s** Solomon all the days of his life. 5647
9: 9 and have worshipped them, and **s** them: 5647
16:31 and went and **s** Baal, and worshipped him. 5647
22:53 For he **s** Baal, and worshipped him, and 5647
2Ki 10:18 and said unto them, Ahab **s** Baal a little; 5647
17:12 For they **s** idols, whereof the LORD had 5647
17:16 all the host of heaven, and **s** Baal. 5647
17:33 feared the LORD, and **s** their own gods, 5647
17:41 **s** their graven images, both their children, 5647
18: 7 against the king of Assyria, and **s** him not. 5647
21: 3 all the host of heaven, and **s** them. 5647
21:21 and **s** the idols that his father served, 5647
21:21 and served the idols that his father **s**, 5647
1Ch 19: 5 and told David how the men were **s**. NIH
27: 1 their officers that **s** the king in any matter 8334
2Ch 7:22 and worshipped them, and **s** them: 5647
24:18 God of their fathers, and **s** groves and idols: 5647
33: 3 all the host of heaven, and **s** them. 5647
33:22 Manasseh his father had made, and **s** them; 5647
Ne 9:35 For they have not **s** thee in their kingdom, 5647
Est 1:10 the seven chamberlains that **s** in 8334
Ps 106:36 they **s** their idols: which were a snare unto 5647
137: 8 *he be,* that rewardeth thee as thou hast **s** us. 1580
Ecc 5: 9 *is* for all: the king *himself* is **s** by the field. 5647
Jer 5:19 **s** strange gods in your land, so shall ye 5647
8: 2 whom they have **s**, and after whom they 5647
16:11 have **s** them, and have worshipped them, 5647
22: 9 and worshipped other gods, and **s** them. 5647
34:14 when he hath **s** thee six years, thou shalt let 5647
52:12 *which* **s** the king of Babylon, 5975+6440+3807.1
Eze 29:18 for the service that he had **s** against it: 5647
29:20 *for* his labour wherewith he **s** against it, 5647
34:27 the hand of those that **s** themselves of them. 5647
Hos 12:12 Israel **s** for a wife, and for a wife he kept 5647
Lk 2:37 but **s** *God* with fastings and prayers night *3000*
Jn 12: 2 they made him a supper; and Martha **s**: *1247*
Ac 13:36 after he had **s** his own generation by *5256*
Ro 1:25 and **s** the creature more than the Creator, *3000*
Php 2:22 *the* father, he hath **s** with me in the gospel. *1398*

SERVEDST (1) [SERVE]

Dt 28:47 Because thou **s** not the LORD thy God 5647

SERVEST (2) [SERVE]

Da 6:16 Thy God whom thou **s** continually, 6399
6:20 is thy God, whom thou **s** continually, 6399

SERVETH (9) [SERVE]

Nu 3:36 all the vessels thereof, and all that **s** thereto, 5656
Mal 3:17 as a man spareth his own son that **s** him. 5647
3:18 between him that **s** God and *him* that 5647
3:18 that serveth God and *him* that **s** him not. 5647
Lk 22:27 he that sitteth at meat, or he that **s**? *1247*
22:27 at meat? but I am among you as he that **s**. *1247*
Ro 14:18 For he that in these *things* **s** Christ *is* *1398*
1Co 14:22 prophesying *s* not for them that believe not, NIG
Gal 3:19 Wherefore then *s* the law? It was added NIG

SERVICE (132) [SERVE]

Ge 29:27 we will give thee this also for the **s** which 5656
30:26 for thou knowest my **s** which I have done 5656
Ex 1:14 in brick, and in all manner of **s** in the field: 5656
1:14 all their **s**, wherein they made them serve, 5656
12:25 he hath promised, that ye shall keep this **s**. 5656
12:26 say unto you, What mean you by this **s**? 5656
13: 5 that thou shalt keep this **s** in this month. 5656
27:19 All the vessels of the tabernacle in all the **s** 5656
30:16 shalt appoint it for the **s** of the tabernacle of 5656
31:10 the clothes of **s**, and the holy garments for 8278
35:19 The clothes of **s**, to do service in the holy 8278
35:19 to **do s** in the holy *place,* the holy garments 8334
35:21 and for all his **s**, and for the holy garments. 5656
35:24 found shittim wood for any work of the **s**, 5656
36: 1 *manner of* work for the **s** of the sanctuary, 5656
36: 3 for the work of the **s** of the sanctuary, 5656
36: 5 more than enough for the **s** of the work, 5656
38:21 *for* the **s** of the Levites, by the hand of 5656
39: 1 and scarlet, they made clothes of **s**, 8278
39: 1 to do **s** in the holy *place,* and made the holy 8334
39:40 all the vessels of the **s** of the tabernacle, 5656
39:41 The clothes of **s** to do service in the holy 8278
39:41 The clothes of service to do **s** in the holy 8334
Nu 3: 7 to do the **s** of the tabernacle. 5656
3: 8 of Israel, to do the **s** of the tabernacle. 5656
3:26 and the cords of it for all the **s** thereof. 5656
3:31 and the hanging, and all the **s** thereof. 5656
4: 4 This *shall be* the **s** of the sons of Kohath in 5656
4:19 appoint them every one to his **s** and to his 5656
4:23 all that enter in to **perform** the **s**, to 6633+6635
4:24 This *is* the **s** of the families of 5656
4:26 all the instruments of their **s**, and all that is 5656
4:27 his sons shall be all the **s** of the sons of 5656
4:27 in all their burdens, and in all their **s**: 5656
4:28 This *is* the **s** of the families of the sons of 5656
4:30 every one that entereth into the **s**, to do 6635
4:31 according to all their **s** in the tabernacle of 5656
4:32 all their instruments, and with all their **s**: 5656
4:33 This *is* the **s** of the families of the sons of 5656
4:33 according to all their **s**, in the tabernacle of 5656
4:35 years old, every one that entereth into the **s**, 6635
4:37 all that *might* **do s** in the tabernacle of 5647
4:39 years old, every one that entereth into the **s**, 6635
4:41 of all that *might* **do s** in the tabernacle of 5647
4:43 years old, every one that entereth into the **s**, 6635
4:47 every one that came to do the **s** of 5656
4:47 the **s** of the burden in the tabernacle of 5656
4:49 every one according to his **s**, and 5656
7: 5 that they may be to do the **s** of 5656
7: 5 to every man according to his **s**. 5656
7: 7 the sons of Gershon, according to their **s**: 5656
7: 8 the sons of Merari, according unto their **s**, 5656
7: 9 the **s** of the sanctuary belonging unto them 5656
8:11 that they may execute the **s** of the LORD. 5656
8:15 after that shall the Levites go in to **do** the **s** 5647
8:19 to do the **s** of the children of Israel in 5656
8:22 after that went the Levites in to do their **s** in 5656
8:24 upward they shall go in to wait upon the **s** 5656
8:25 they shall cease waiting upon the **s** *thereof,* 5656
8:26 to keep the charge, and shall do no **s**. 5656
16: 9 to bring you near to himself to do the **s** of 5656
18: 4 for all the **s** of the tabernacle: 5656
18: 6 to do the **s** of the tabernacle of 5656
18: 7 your priest's office *unto you as* a **s** of gift: 5656
18:21 for their **s** which they serve, *even* 5656
18:21 *even* the **s** of the tabernacle of 5656
18:23 the Levites shall do the **s** of the tabernacle 5656
18:31 for it *is* your reward for your **s** in 5656
Jos 22:27 that *we* might do the **s** of the LORD 5656
1Ki 12: 4 make thou the grievous **s** of thy father, 5656
1Ch 6:31 these *are they* whom David set over the **s** of 3027
6:48 *of* **s** of the tabernacle of the house of God. 5656
9:13 very able men *for* the work of the **s** of 5656
9:19 the Korahites, *were* over the work of the **s**, 5656
23:24 that did the work for the **s** of the house of 5656
23:26 nor any vessels of it for the **s** thereof. 5656
23:28 Aaron for the **s** of the house of the LORD, 5656
23:28 and the work of the **s** of the house of God; 5656
23:32 in the **s** of the house of the LORD. 5656
24: 3 according to their offices in their **s**. 5656
24:19 These *were* the orderings of them in their **s** 5656
25: 1 the captains of the host separated to the **s** of 5656
25: 1 of the workmen according to their **s** was: 5656
25: 6 and harps, for the **s** of the house of God, 5656
26: 8 able men for strength for the **s**, 5656
26:30 of the LORD, and in the **s** of the king. 5656
28:13 for all the work of the **s** of the house of 5656
28:13 for all the vessels of **s** in the house of 5656
28:14 of **all manner of s**; 5656+5656+2050.1
28:14 of **every kind of s**: 5656+5656+2050.1
28:20 work for the **s** of the house of the LORD. 5656
28:21 *even they shall be with thee* for all the **s** of 5656
28:21 willing skilful *man,* for any *manner of* **s**: 5656

S

1Ch 29: 5 is willing to consecrate his s *this* day unto 3027
29: 7 gave for the s of the house of God *of* gold 5656
2Ch 8:14 the courses of the priests to their s, and 5656
12: 8 that they may know my s, and the service 5656
12: 8 and the s of the kingdoms of the countries. 5656
24:12 work of the s of the house of the LORD, 5656
29:35 So the s of the house of the LORD was set 5656
31: 2 every man according to his s, the priests 5656
31:16 *his* daily portion for their s in their charges 5656
31:21 in every work that he began in the s of 5656
34:13 work in **any manner of** s: 5656+5656+2050.1
35: 2 encouraged them to the s of the house of 5656
35:10 So the s was prepared, and the priests stood 5656
35:15 they might not depart from their s; 5656
35:16 So all the s of the LORD was prepared 5656
Ezr 6:18 for the s of God, which *is* at Jerusalem; 5673
7:19 thee for the s of the house of thy God, 6402
8:20 the princes had appointed for the s of 5656
Ne 10:32 a shekel for the s of the house of our God; 5656
Ps 104:14 for the cattle, and herb for the s of man: 5656
Jer 22:13 *that* **useth** his neighbour's s without wages, 5647
Eze 29:18 his army to serve a great s against Tyrus: 5656
29:18 for the s that he had served against it: 5656
44:14 for all the s thereof, and for all that shall be 5656
Jn 16: 2 killeth you will think that he doeth God s. *2999*
Ro 9: 4 the law, and the s *of God,* and the promises; *2999*
12: 1 unto God, *which is* your reasonable s. *2999*
15:31 that my s which I have for Jerusalem may *1248*
2Co 9:12 For the administration of this s not only *3009*
11: 8 taking wages *of them,* to do you s. *1248*
Gal 4: 8 ye did s unto them which by nature are no *1398*
Eph 6: 7 With good will **doing** s, as to the Lord, and *1398*
Php 2:17 upon the sacrifice and s of your faith, *3009*
2:30 *his* life, to supply your lack of s toward me. *3009*
1Ti 6: 2 but rather **do** *them* s, because they are *1398*
Heb 9: 1 *covenant* had also ordinances of **divine** s, *2999*
9: 6 accomplishing the s *of God.* *2999*
9: 9 that could not make him that did the s *3000*
Rev 2:19 I know thy works, and charity, and s, *1248*

SERVILE (12) [SERVE]
Lev 23: 7 ye shall do no s work *therein.* 5656
23: 8 ye shall do no s work *therein.* 5656
23:21 ye shall do no s work *therein: it shall be* a 5656
23:25 Ye shall do no s work *therein:* but ye shall 5656
23:35 ye shall do no s work *therein.* 5656
23:36 *and* ye shall do no s work *therein.* 5656
Nu 28:18 ye shall do no *manner of* s work *therein:* 5656
28:25 a holy convocation; ye shall do no s work. 5656
28:26 a holy convocation; ye shall do no s work: 5656
29: 1 a holy convocation; ye shall do no s work: 5656
29:12 ye shall do no s work, and ye shall keep a 5656
29:35 ye shall do no s work *therein:* 5656

SERVING (7) [SERVE]
Ex 14: 5 that we have let Israel go from s us? 5647
Dt 15:18 hired servant *to thee,* in s thee six years: 5647
Lk 10:40 But Martha was cumbered about much s, *1248*
Ac 20:19 S the Lord with all humility of mind, and *1398*
26: 7 instantly s *God* day and night, hope to *3000*
Ro 12:11 in business; fervent in spirit; s the Lord; *1398*
Tit 3: 3 deceived, s divers lusts and pleasures, *1398*

SERVITOR (1) [SERVE]
2Ki 4:43 his s said, What, should I set this before an 8334

SERVITUDE (2) [SERVE]
2Ch 10: 4 ease thou somewhat the grievous s of thy 5656
La 1: 3 of affliction, and because of great s: 5656

SET (695) [SETTER, SETTEST, SETTETH, SETTING, SETTINGS]
See Index

SETH (8) [SHETH]
Ge 4:25 she bare a son, and called his name S: 8352
4:26 to S, *to* him also there was born a son; and 8352
5: 3 after his image; and called his name S: 8352
5: 4 the days of Adam after he had begotten S 8352
5: 6 S lived an hundred and five years, and 8352
5: 7 S lived after he begat Enos eight hundred 8352
5: 8 all the days of S were nine hundred 8352
Lk 3:38 *the son* of Enos, which was *the son* of S, *4589*

SETHUR (1)
Nu 13:13 Of the tribe of Asher, S the son of Michael. 5639

SETTER (1) [SET]
Ac 17:18 other *some,* He seemeth to be a **s forth** of *2604*

SETTEST (7) [SET] See Index

SETTETH (22) [SET] See Index

SETTING (3) [SET] See Index

SETTINGS (1) [SET]
Ex 28:17 thou shalt set in it s of stones, *even* four 4396

SETTLE (10) [SETTLED, SETTLEST]
1Ch 17:14 I will s him in mine house and in my 5975
Eze 36:11 I will s you after your old estates, and 3427
43:14 *even* to the lower s *shall be* two cubits, 5835
43:14 from the lesser s *even* to the greater settle 5835
43:14 from the lesser settle *even* to the greater s 5835
43:17 the s *shall be* fourteen *cubits* long and 5835
43:20 on the four corners of the s, and upon 5835
45:19 upon the four corners of the s of the altar, 5835
Lk 21:14 S *it* therefore in your hearts, not to meditate *5087*
1Pe 5:10 you perfect, stablish, strengthen, s *you.* *2311*

SETTLED (7) [SETTLE]
1Ki 8:13 a **s place** for thee to abide in for ever. 4349
2Ki 8:11 he s his countenance stedfastly, until *he* 5975
Ps 119:89 O LORD, thy word *is* s in heaven. 5324
Pr 8:25 Before the mountains were s, before 2883
Jer 48:11 he *hath* s on his lees, and hath not been 8252
Zep 1:12 and punish the men that are s on their lees: 7087
Col 1:23 If ye continue in the faith grounded and s, *1476*

SETTLEMENT See HABITATION

SETTLEST (1) [SETTLE]
Ps 65:10 *thou* s the furrows thereof: thou makest it 5181

SEVEN (463) [SEVENFOLD, SEVENS, SEVENTH]
Ge 5: 7 he begat Enos eight hundred and s years, 7651
5:25 lived an hundred eighty and s years, 7651
5:26 Methuselah lived after he begat Lamech s 7651
5:31 all the days of Lamech were s hundred 7651
5:31 were seven hundred seventy and s years: 7651
7: 4 For yet s days, *and* I will cause it to rain 7651
7:10 it came to pass after s days, that the waters 7651
8:10 he stayed yet other s days; and again he 7651
8:12 he stayed yet other s days; and sent forth 7651
8:14 on the s and twentieth day of the month, 7651
11:21 he begat Serug two hundred and s years, 7651
21:28 Abraham set s ewe lambs of the flock by 7651
21:29 What *mean* these s ewe lambs which thou 7651
21:30 For *these* s ewe lambs shalt thou take of my 7651
23: 1 was an hundred and s and twenty years old: 7651
25:17 an hundred and thirty and s years: 7651
29:18 I will serve thee s years for Rachel thy 7651
29:20 Jacob served s years for Rachel; and 7651
29:27 thou shalt serve with me yet s other years. 7651
29:30 and served with him yet s other years. 7651
31:23 and pursued after him s days' journey; 7651
33: 3 and bowed himself to the ground s times, 7651
41: 2 there came up out of the river s well 7651
41: 3 s other kine came up after them out of 7651
41: 4 leanfleshed kine did eat up the s well 7651
41: 5 s ears of corn came up upon one stalk, rank 7651
41: 6 s thin ears and blasted with the east wind 7651
41: 7 And the s thin ears devoured the seven rank NIH
41: 7 And the seven thin ears devoured the s rank 7651
41:18 there came up out of the river s kine, 7651
41:19 s other kine came up after them, poor and 7651
41:20 the ill favoured kine did eat up the first s fat 7651
41:22 s ears came up in one stalk, full and good: 7651
41:23 s ears, withered, thin, *and* blasted with 7651
41:24 the thin ears devoured the s good ears: 7651
41:26 The s good kine *are* seven years; and 7651
41:26 The seven good kine *are* s years; and 7651
41:26 and the s good ears *are* seven years: 7651
41:26 and the seven good ears *are* s years: 7651
41:27 the s thin and ill favoured kine that came up 7651
41:27 kine that came up after them *are* s years; 7651
41:27 the s empty ears blasted with the east wind 7651
41:27 the east wind shall be s years of famine. 7651
41:29 there come s years of great plenty 7651
41:30 there shall arise after them s years of 7651
41:34 the land of Egypt in the s plenteous years. 7651

Ge	41:36	to the land against the **s** years of famine,	7651
	41:47	in the **s** plenteous years the earth brought	7651
	41:48	he gathered up all the food of the **s** years,	7651
	41:53	the **s** years of plenteousness, that was in	7651
	41:54	the **s** years of dearth began to come,	7651
	46:25	bare these unto Jacob: all the souls *were* **s**.	7651
	47:28	of Jacob was an hundred forty and **s** years.	7651
	50:10	he made a mourning for his father **s** days.	7651
Ex	2:16	Now the priest of Midian had **s** daughters:	7651
	6:16	of Levi *were* an hundred thirty and **s** years.	7651
	6:20	*were* an hundred and thirty and **s** years.	7651
	7:25	**s** days were fulfilled, after *that* the LORD	7651
	12:15	**S** days shall ye eat unleavened bread;	7651
	12:19	**S** days shall there be no leaven found in	7651
	13: 6	**S** days thou shalt eat unleavened bread, and	7651
	13: 7	Unleavened bread shall be eaten **s** days;	7651
	22:30	**s** days it shall be with his dam; on	7651
	23:15	thou shalt eat unleavened bread **s** days, as I	7651
	25:37	thou shalt make the **s** lamps thereof: and	7651
	29:30	priest in his stead shall put them on **s** days,	7651
	29:35	**s** days shalt thou consecrate them.	7651
	29:37	**S** days thou shalt make an atonement for	7651
	34:18	**s** days thou shalt eat unleavened bread, as I	7651
	37:23	he made his **s** lamps, and his snuffers, and	7651
	38:24	and **s** hundred and thirty shekels,	7651
	38:25	a thousand **s** hundred and threescore and	7651
	38:28	of the thousand **s** hundred seventy and	7651
Lev	4: 6	sprinkle of the blood **s** times before	7651
	4:17	sprinkle *it* **s** times before the LORD,	7651
	8:11	he sprinkled thereof upon the altar **s** times,	7651
	8:33	tabernacle of the congregation *in* **s** days,	7651
	8:33	an end: for **s** days shall he consecrate you.	7651
	8:35	of the congregation day and night **s** days,	7651
	12: 2	she shall be unclean **s** days; according to	7651
	13: 4	shut up *him that hath* the plague **s** days:	7651
	13: 5	the priest shall shut him up **s** days more:	7651
	13:21	then the priest shall shut him up **s** days:	7651
	13:26	then the priest shall shut him up **s** days:	7651
	13:31	*him that hath* the plague of the scall **s** days:	7651
	13:33	shut up *him that hath* the scall **s** days more:	7651
	13:50	and shut up *it that hath* the plague **s** days:	7651
	13:54	and he shall shut it up **s** days more:	7651
	14: 7	is to be cleansed from the leprosy **s** times,	7651
	14: 8	and shall tarry abroad out of his tent **s** days.	7651
	14:16	shall sprinkle of the oil with his finger **s**	7651
	14:27	in his left hand **s** times before the LORD:	7651
	14:38	of the house, and shut up the house **s** days:	7651
	14:51	and sprinkle the house **s** times:	7651
	15:13	he shall number to himself **s** days for his	7651
	15:19	be blood, she shall be put apart **s** days:	7651
	15:24	be upon him, he shall be unclean **s** days;	7651
	15:28	she shall number to herself **s** days, and	7651
	16:14	of the blood with his finger **s** times.	7651
	16:19	of the blood upon it with his finger **s** times,	7651
	22:27	then it shall be **s** days under the dam;	7651
	23: 6	**s** days ye must eat unleavened bread.	7651
	23: 8	made by fire unto the LORD **s** days:	7651
	23:15	**s** sabbaths shall be complete:	7651
	23:18	ye shall offer with the bread **s** lambs	7651
	23:34	of tabernacles *for* **s** days unto the LORD.	7651
	23:36	**S** days ye shall offer an offering made by	7651
	23:39	ye shall keep a feast unto the LORD **s**	7651
	23:40	rejoice before the LORD your God **s** days.	7651
	23:41	ye shall keep it a feast unto the LORD **s**	7651
	23:42	Ye shall dwell in booths **s** days; all that are	7651
	25: 8	thou shalt number **s** sabbaths of years unto	7651
	25: 8	of years unto thee, **s** times seven years;	7651
	25: 8	of years unto thee, seven times **s** years;	7651
	25: 8	the space of the **s** sabbaths of years shall be	7651
	26:18	I will punish you **s** *times* more for your	7651
	26:21	I will bring **s** *times* moe plagues upon you	7651
	26:24	will punish you yet **s** *times* for your sins.	7651
	26:28	will chastise you **s** *times* for your sins.	7651
Nu	1:31	*were* fifty and **s** thousand and four hundred.	7651
	1:39	and two thousand and **s** hundred.	7651
	2: 8	*were* fifty and **s** thousand and four hundred.	7651
	2:26	and two thousand and **s** hundred.	7651
	2:31	and fifty and **s** thousand and six hundred.	7651
	3:22	were numbered of them *were* **s** thousand	7651
	4:36	their families were two thousand **s** hundred	7651
	8: 2	the **s** lamps shall give light over against	7651
	12:14	her face, should she not be ashamed **s** days?	7651
	12:14	let her be shut out from the camp **s** days,	7651
	12:15	Miriam was shut out from the camp **s** days:	7651
	13:22	*were.* (Now Hebron was built **s** years	7651
	16:49	were fourteen thousand and **s** hundred,	7651
	19: 4	the tabernacle of the congregation **s** times:	7651
	19:11	*body* of any man shall be unclean **s** days.	7651
	19:14	that *is* in the tent, shall be unclean **s** days.	7651
	19:16	a man, or a grave, shall be unclean **s** days.	7651
	23: 1	Build me here **s** altars, and prepare me here	7651
	23: 1	prepare me here **s** oxen and seven rams.	7651
	23: 1	prepare me here seven oxen and **s** rams.	7651
	23: 4	I have prepared **s** altars, and I have offered	7651
	23:14	built **s** altars, and offered a bullock and	7651
	23:29	Build me here **s** altars, and prepare me here	7651
	23:29	prepare me here **s** bullocks and seven rams.	7651
	23:29	prepare me here seven bullocks and **s** rams.	7651
	26: 7	three thousand and **s** hundred and thirty.	7651
	26:34	fifty and two thousand and **s** hundred.	7651
	26:51	and a thousand **s** hundred and thirty.	7651
	28:11	**s** lambs of the first year without spot;	7651
	28:17	**s** days shall unleavened bread be eaten.	7651
	28:19	and one ram, and **s** lambs of the first year:	7651
	28:21	for every lamb, throughout the **s** lambs;	7651
	28:24	ye shall offer daily, *throughout* the **s** days,	7651
	28:27	one ram, **s** lambs of the first year;	7651
	28:29	deal unto one lamb, throughout the **s** lambs;	7651
	29: 2	**s** lambs of the first year without blemish:	7651
	29: 4	deal for one lamb, throughout the **s** lambs:	7651
	29: 8	one ram, *and* **s** lambs of the first year;	7651
	29:10	deal for one lamb, throughout the **s** lambs:	7651
	29:12	ye shall keep a feast unto the LORD **s**	7651
	29:32	on the seventh day **s** bullocks, two rams,	7651
	29:36	**s** lambs of the first year without blemish:	7651
	31:19	do ye abide without the camp **s** days:	7651
	31:36	**s** and thirty thousand and five hundred	7651
	31:43	thirty thousand *and* **s** thousand and	7651
	31:52	was sixteen thousand **s** hundred and	7651
Dt	7: 1	**s** nations greater and mightier than thou;	7651
	15: 1	At the end of *every* **s** years thou shalt make	7651
	16: 3	**s** days shalt thou eat unleavened bread	7651
	16: 4	bread seen with thee in all thy coast **s** days;	7651
	16: 9	**S** weeks shalt thou number unto thee:	7651
	16: 9	begin to number the **s** weeks from *such*	7651
	16:13	observe the feast of tabernacles **s** days,	7651
	16:15	**S** days shalt thou keep a solemn feast unto	7651
	28: 7	thee one way, and flee before thee **s** ways.	7651
	28:25	against them, and flee **s** ways before them:	7651
	31:10	saying, At the end of *every* **s** years,	7651
Jos	6: 4	**s** priests shall bear before the ark seven	7651
	6: 4	seven priests shall bear before the ark **s**	7651
	6: 4	the seventh day ye shall compass the city **s**	7651
	6: 6	let **s** priests bear seven trumpets of rams'	7651
	6: 6	let seven priests bear **s** trumpets of rams'	7651
	6: 8	that the **s** priests bearing the seven trumpets	7651
	6: 8	that the seven priests bearing the **s** trumpets	7651
	6:13	**s** priests bearing seven trumpets of rams'	7651
	6:13	seven priests bearing **s** trumpets of rams'	7651
	6:15	compassed the city after the same manner **s**	7651
	6:15	only on that day they compassed the city **s**	7651
	18: 2	among the children of Israel **s** tribes,	7651
	18: 5	they shall divide it into **s** parts: Judah shall	7651
	18: 6	therefore describe the land *into* **s** parts,	7651
	18: 9	described it by cities into **s** parts in a book,	7651
Jdg	6: 1	them into the hand of Midian **s** years.	7651
	6:25	even the second bullock of **s** years old, and	7651
	8:26	a thousand and **s** hundred *shekels* of gold;	7651
	12: 9	for his sons. And he judged Israel **s** years.	7651
	14:12	declare it me *within* the **s** days of the feast,	7651
	14:17	she wept before him the **s** days, while their	7651
	16: 7	If they bind me with **s** green withs that	7651
	16: 8	her **s** green withs which had not been dried,	7651
	16:13	If thou weavest the **s** locks of my head with	7651
	16:19	she caused *him* to shave off the **s** locks of	7651
	20:15	*which* were numbered **s** hundred chosen	7651
	20:16	Among all this people *there were* **s** hundred	7651
Ru	4:15	which *is* better to thee than **s** sons,	7651
1Sa	2: 5	so that the barren hath born **s**; and she that	7651
	6: 1	in the country of the Philistines **s** months.	7651
	10: 8	**s** days shalt thou tarry, till I come to thee,	7651
	11: 3	said unto him, Give us **s** days' respite,	7651
	13: 8	he tarried **s** days, according to the set time	7651
	16:10	Jesse made **s** of his sons to pass before	7651
	31:13	under a tree at Jabesh, and fasted **s** days.	7651
2Sa	2:11	Hebron over the house of Judah was **s** years	7651
	5: 5	In Hebron he reigned over Judah **s** years	7651
	8: 4	thousand *chariots,* and **s** hundred horsemen,	7651

2Sa 10:18 David slew *the men of* **s** hundred chariots 7651
21: 6 Let **s** men of his sons be delivered unto us, 7651
21: 9 they fell *all* **s** together, and were put to 7651
23:39 Uriah the Hittite: thirty and **s** *in* all. 7651
24:13 Shall **s** years of famine come unto thee in 7651
1Ki 2:11 **s** years reigned he in Hebron, and thirty and 7651
6: 6 and the third *was* **s** cubits broad: 7651
6:38 of it. So was he **s** years in building it. 7651
7:17 **s** for the one chapiter, and seven for 7651
7:17 one chapiter, and **s** for the other chapiter. 7651
8:65 **s** days and seven days, *even* fourteen days. 7651
8:65 seven days and **s** days, *even* fourteen days. 7651
11: 3 he had **s** hundred wives, princesses, and 7651
16:15 of Judah did Zimri reign **s** days in Tirzah. 7651
18:43 *is* nothing. And he said, Go again **s** times. 7651
19:18 Yet I have left *me* **s** thousand in Israel, 7651
20:15 all the children of Israel, *being* **s** thousand. 7651
20:29 they pitched one over against the other **s** 7651
20:30 and **s** thousand of the men that were left. 7651
2Ki 3: 9 they fetcht a compass of **s** days' journey: 7651
3:26 he took with him **s** hundred men that drew 7651
4:35 the child neesed **s** times, and the child 7651
5:10 Go and wash in Jordan **s** times, and 7651
5:14 and dipped *himself* **s** times in Jordan, 7651
8: 1 it shall also come upon the land **s** years. 7651
8: 2 sojourned in the land of the Philistines **s** 7651
8: 3 it came to pass at the **s** years' end, that 7651
11:21 **S** years old *was* Jehoash when he *began* to 7651
24:16 *even* **s** thousand, and craftsmen and smiths 7651
25:27 it came to pass in the **s** and thirtieth year of 7651
25:27 on the **s** and twentieth *day* of the month, 7651
1Ch 3: 4 there he reigned **s** years and six months: 7651
3:24 and Johanan, and Dalaiah, and Anani, **s**. 7651
5:13 Jorai, and Jachan, and Zia, and Heber, **s**. 7651
5:18 *were* four and forty thousand **s** hundred and 7651
7: 5 their genealogies fourscore and **s** thousand. 7651
9:13 a thousand and **s** hundred and threescore; 7651
9:25 *were* to come after **s** days from time to time 7651
10:12 under the oak in Jabesh, and fasted **s** days. 7651
12:25 for the war, **s** thousand and one hundred. 7651
12:27 him *were* three thousand and **s** hundred; 7651
12:34 with shield and spear thirty and **s** thousand. 7651
15:26 that they offered **s** bullocks and seven rams. 7651
15:26 that they offered seven bullocks and **s** rams. 7651
18: 4 **s** thousand horsemen, and twenty thousand 7651
19:18 David slew of the Syrians **s** thousand *men* 7651
26:30 men of valour, a thousand and **s** hundred, 7651
26:32 two thousand and **s** hundred chief fathers, 7651
29: 4 and **s** thousand talents of refined silver, 7651
29:27 **s** years reigned he in Hebron, and thirty and 7651
2Ch 7: 8 same time Solomon kept the feast **s** days, 7651
7: 9 for they kept the dedication of the altar **s** 7651
7: 9 of the altar seven days, and the feast **s** days. 7651
13: 9 himself with a young bullock and **s** rams, 7651
15:11 **s** hundred oxen and seven thousand sheep. 7651
15:11 seven hundred oxen and **s** thousand sheep. 7651
17:11 **s** thousand and seven hundred rams, and 7651
17:11 seven thousand and **s** hundred rams, and 7651
17:11 and **s** thousand and seven hundred he goats. 7651
17:11 and seven thousand and **s** hundred he goats. 7651
24: 1 Joash *was* **s** years old when he *began* to 7651
26:13 and **s** thousand and five hundred, 7651
29:21 they brought **s** bullocks, and seven rams, 7651
29:21 **s** rams, and seven lambs, and seven he 7651
29:21 and **s** lambs, and seven he goats, 7651
29:21 and seven lambs, and **s** he goats, 7651
30:21 bread **s** days with great gladness: 7651
30:22 and they did eat throughout the feast **s** days, 7651
30:23 assembly took counsel to keep other **s** days: 7651
30:23 and they kept *other* **s** days *with* gladness. 7651
30:24 a thousand bullocks and **s** thousand sheep; 7651
35:17 the feast of unleavened bread **s** days. 7651
Ezr 2: 5 of Arah, **s** hundred seventy and five. 7651
2: 9 of Zaccai, **s** hundred and threescore. 7651
2:25 and Beeroth, **s** hundred and forty and three. 7651
2:33 Hadid, and Ono, **s** hundred twenty and five. 7651
2:38 a thousand two hundred forty and **s**. 7651
2:65 of whom *there were* **s** thousand three 7651
2:65 seven thousand three hundred thirty and **s**: 7651
2:66 Their horses *were* **s** hundred thirty and six; 7651
2:67 six thousand **s** hundred and twenty. 7651
6:22 kept the feast of unleavened bread **s** days 7651
7:14 of his **s** counsellers, to inquire concerning 7655
8:35 ninety and six rams, seventy and **s** lambs, 7657

Ne 7:14 of Zaccai, **s** hundred and threescore. 7651
7:18 of Adonikam, six hundred threescore and **s**. 7651
7:19 of Bigvai, two thousand threescore and **s**. 7651
7:29 and Beeroth, **s** hundred forty and three. 7651
7:37 Hadid, and Ono, **s** hundred twenty and one. 7651
7:41 a thousand two hundred forty and **s**. 7651
7:67 of whom *there were* **s** thousand three 7651
7:67 seven thousand three hundred thirty and **s**: 7651
7:68 Their horses, **s** hundred thirty and six: 7651
7:69 six thousand **s** hundred and twenty asses. 7651
7:72 and threescore and **s** priests' garments. 7651
8:18 they kept the feast **s** days; and on the eighth 7651
Est 1: 1 *over* an hundred and **s** and 7651
1: 5 both unto great and small, **s** days, in 7651
1:10 the **s** chamberlains that served in 7651
1:14 the **s** princes of Persia and Media, 7651
2: 9 **s** maidens, *which were* meet to be given 7651
8: 9 an hundred twenty and **s** provinces, 7651
9:30 **s** provinces of the kingdom of Ahasuerus, 7651
Job 1: 2 there were born unto him **s** sons and 7651
1: 3 His substance also was **s** thousand sheep, 7651
2:13 sat down with him upon the ground **s** days 7651
2:13 upon the ground seven days and **s** nights, 7651
5:19 yea, in **s** there shall no evil touch thee. 7651
42: 8 Therefore take unto you now **s** bullocks and 7651
42: 8 unto you now seven bullocks and **s** rams, 7651
42:13 He had also **s** sons and three daughters. 7658
Ps 12: 6 tried in a furnace of earth, purified **s times**. 7659
119:164 **S** *times* a day do I praise thee because 7651
Pr 6:16 yea, **s** *are* an abomination unto him: 7651
9: 1 her house, she hath hewn out her **s** pillars: 7651
24:16 For a just *man* falleth **s** *times*, and riseth up 7651
26:16 conceit than **s** *men* that can render a reason. 7651
26:25 for *there are* **s** abominations in his heart. 7651
Ecc 11: 2 Give a portion to **s**, and also to eight; 7651
Isa 4: 1 in that day **s** women shall take hold of one 7651
11:15 shall smite it in *the* **s** streams, and 7651
30:26 shall be sevenfold, as the light of **s** days, 7651
Jer 15: 9 She that hath borne **s** languisheth: she hath 7651
34:14 At the end of **s** years let ye go every man 7651
52:25 **s** men of them that were near the king's 7651
52:30 away captive *of* the Jews **s** hundred forty 7651
52:31 it came to pass in the **s** and thirtieth year of 7651
Eze 3:15 remained there astonished among them **s** 7651
3:16 it came to pass at the end of **s** days, that 7651
29:17 it came to pass in the **s** and twentieth year, 7651
39: 9 and they shall burn them with fire **s** years: 7651
39:12 **s** months shall the house of Israel be 7651
39:14 after the end of **s** months shall they search. 7651
40:22 they went up unto it by **s** steps; and 7651
40:26 *there were* **s** steps to go up to it, and 7651
41: 3 and the breadth of the door, **s** cubits. 7651
43:25 **S** days shalt thou prepare every day a goat 7651
43:26 **S** days shall they purge the altar and 7651
44:26 they shall reckon unto him **s** days. 7651
45:21 shall have the passover, a feast of **s** days; 7620
45:23 **s** days of the feast he shall prepare a burnt 7651
45:23 **s** bullocks and seven rams without blemish 7651
45:23 **s** rams without blemish daily the seven 7651
45:23 seven rams without blemish daily the **s** 7651
45:25 shall he do the like in the feast *of* the **s** 7651
Da 3:19 **s** *times* more than *it was* wont to be heat. 7655
4:16 unto him; and let **s** times pass over him. 7655
4:23 of the field, till **s** times pass over him; 7655
4:25 of heaven, and **s** times shall pass over thee, 7655
4:32 as oxen, and **s** times shall pass over thee, 7655
9:25 the Messiah the Prince *shall be* **s** weeks, 7651
Am 5: 8 *Seek him* that maketh the **s stars** and 3598
Mic 5: 5 shall we raise against him **s** shepherds, and 7651
Zec 3: 9 upon one stone *shall be* **s** eyes: 7651
4: 2 his **s** lamps thereon, and seven pipes to 7651
4: 2 and **s** pipes to the seven lamps, 7651
4: 2 and seven pipes to the **s** lamps, 7651
4:10 in the hand of Zerubbabel *with* those **s**; 7651
Mt 12:45 taketh with himself **s** other spirits more *2033*
15:34 And they said, **S**, and a few little fishes. *2033*
15:36 And he took the **s** loaves and the fishes, and *2033*
15:37 the broken *meat* that was left **s** baskets full. *2033*
16:10 Neither the **s** loaves of the four thousand, *2033*
18:21 against me, and I forgive him? till **s times**? *2034*
18:22 unto him, I say not unto thee, Until **s times**: *2034*
18:22 seven times: but, Until seventy times **s**. *2033*
22:25 Now there were with us **s** brethren: and *2033*
22:28 whose wife shall she be of the **s**? *2033*

Mk 8: 5 many loaves have ye? And they said, **S.** 2033
8: 6 and he took the **s** loaves, and gave thanks, 2033
8: 8 of the broken *meat* that was left **s** baskets. 2033
8:20 And when the **s** among four thousand, 2033
8:20 of fragments took ye up? And they said, **S.** 2033
12:20 Now there were **s** brethren: and the first 2033
12:22 And the **s** had her, and left no seed: last of 2033
12:23 she be of them? for the **s** had her to wife. 2033
16: 9 out of whom he had cast **s** devils. 2033
Lk 2:36 had lived with a husband **s** years from her 2033
8: 2 out of whom went **s** devils, 2033
11:26 taketh to *him* **s** other spirits more wicked 2033
17: 4 And if he trespass against thee **s times** in a 2034
17: 4 and **s times** in a day turn again to thee, 2034
20:29 There were therefore **s** brethren: and 2033
20:31 took her; and in like manner the **s** also: 2033
20:33 wife of them is she? for **s** had her to wife. 2033
Ac 6: 3 look ye out among you **s** men of honest 2033
13:19 And when he had destroyed **s** nations in 2033
19:14 And there were sons of *one* Sceva, a Jew, 2033
20: 6 Troas in five days; where we abode **s** days. 2033
21: 4 finding disciples, we tarried there **s** days: 2033
21: 8 the evangelist, which was *one* of the **s**; 2033
21:27 And when the **s** days were almost ended, 2033
28:14 and were desired to tarry with them **s** days: 2033
Ro 11: 4 I have reserved to myself **s thousand** men, 2035
Heb 11:30 after they were compassed about **s** days. 2033
Rev 1: 4 John to the **s** churches which are in Asia: 2033
1: 4 from the **s** spirits which are before his 2033
1:11 send *it* unto the **s** churches which are in 2033
1:12 being turned, I saw **s** golden candlesticks; 2033
1:13 And in the midst of the **s** candlesticks one 2033
1:16 And he had in his right hand **s** stars: and 2033
1:20 The mystery of the **s** stars which thou 2033
1:20 right hand, and the **s** golden candlesticks. 2033
1:20 The **s** stars are the angels of the seven 2033
1:20 The seven stars are the angels of the **s** 2033
1:20 the **s** candlesticks which thou sawest are 2033
1:20 which thou sawest are the **s** churches. 2033
2: 1 These *things* saith he that holdeth the **s** 2033
2: 1 who walketh in the midst of the **s** golden 2033
3: 1 These *things* saith he that hath the **s** spirits 2033
3: 1 the seven spirits of God, and the **s** stars; 2033
4: 5 *there were* **s** lamps of fire burning before 2033
4: 5 the throne, which are the **s** spirits of God. 2033
5: 1 and on the backside, sealed with **s** seals. 2033
5: 5 the book, and to loose the **s** seals thereof. 2033
5: 6 *been* slain, having **s** horns and seven eyes, 2033
5: 6 *been* slain, having seven horns and **s** eyes, 2033
5: 6 which are the **s** spirits of God sent forth 2033
8: 2 And I saw the **s** angels which stood before 2033
8: 2 and to them were given **s** trumpets. 2033
8: 6 And the **s** angels which had the seven 2033
8: 6 And the seven angels which had the **s** 2033
10: 3 had cried, **s** thunders uttered their voices. 2033
10: 4 And when the **s** thunders had uttered their 2033
10: 4 Seal *up those things* which the **s** thunders 2033
11:13 in the earthquake were slain of men **s** 2033
12: 3 having **s** heads and ten horns, and 2033
12: 3 and ten horns, and **s** crowns upon his heads. 2033
13: 1 having **s** heads and ten horns, and upon his 2033
15: 1 **s** angels having the seven last plagues; 2033
15: 1 seven angels having the **s** last plagues; 2033
15: 6 And the **s** angels came out of the temple, 2033
15: 6 having the **s** plagues, clothed in pure and 2033
15: 7 And one of the four beasts gave unto the **s** 2033
15: 7 **s** golden vials full of the wrath of God, 2033
15: 8 till the **s** plagues of the seven angels were 2033
15: 8 till the seven plagues of the **s** angels were 2033
16: 1 out of the temple saying to the **s** angels, 2033
17: 1 And there came one of the **s** angels which 2033
17: 1 of the seven angels which had the **s** vials, 2033
17: 3 having **s** heads and ten horns. 2033
17: 7 which hath the **s** heads and ten horns. 2033
17: 9 The **s** heads are seven mountains, on which 2033
17: 9 The seven heads are **s** mountains, on which 2033
17:10 And there are **s** kings: five are fallen, and 2033
17:11 and is of the **s**, and goeth into perdition. 2033
21: 9 And there came unto me one of the **s** angels 2033
21: 9 the **s** vials full of the seven last plagues, 2033
21: 9 the seven vials full of the **s** last plagues, 2033

SEVENFOLD (6) [SEVEN]
Ge 4:15 vengeance shall be taken on him **s**. 7659
4:24 If Cain shall be avenged **s**, truly Lamech 7659
4:24 truly Lamech seventy and **s**. 7651
Ps 79:12 render unto our neighbours **s** into their 7659
Pr 6:31 *if* he be found, he shall restore **s**; he shall 7659
Isa 30:26 the light of the sun shall be **s**, as the light of 7659

SEVENS (2) [SEVEN]
Ge 7: 2 beast thou shalt take to thee **by s**, 7651+7651
7: 3 Of fowls also of the air **by s**, 7651+7651

SEVENTEEN (10) [SEVENTEENTH]
Ge 37: 2 Joseph, *being* **s** years old, 6240+7651
47:28 Jacob lived in the land of Egypt **s** 6240+7651
Jdg 8:14 *even* **threescore and s** men. 7651+7657+2050.1
1Ki 14:21 and he reigned **s** years in Jerusalem, 6240+7651
2Ki 13: 1 in Samaria, *and reigned* **s** years. 6240+7651
1Ch 7:11 *were* **s** thousand and two hundred 6240+7651
2Ch 12:13 and he reigned **s** years in Jerusalem, 6240+7651
Ezr 2:39 children of Harim, a thousand and **s**. 6240+7651
Ne 7:42 children of Harim, a thousand *and* **s**. 6240+7651
Jer 32: 9 *even* **s** shekels of silver. 6235+7651+2050.1

SEVENTEENTH (6) [SEVENTEEN]
Ge 7:11 the **s** day of the month, 6240+7651
8: 4 on the **s** day of the month, upon 6240+7651
1Ki 22:51 **s** year of Jehoshaphat king of Judah, 6240+7651
2Ki 16: 1 In the **s** year of Pekah the son of 6240+7651
1Ch 24:15 The **s** to Hezir, the eighteenth to 6240+7651
25:24 The **s** to Joshbekashah, *he,* his sons, 6240+7651

SEVENTH (120) [SEVEN]
Ge 2: 2 on the **s** day God ended his work which he 7637
2: 2 he rested on the **s** day from all his work 7637
2: 3 God blessed the **s** day, and sanctified it: 7637
8: 4 the ark rested in the **s** month, on 7637
Ex 12:15 bread from the first day until the **s** day, 7637
12:16 in the **s** day there shall be a holy 7637
13: 6 in the **s** day *shall be* a feast to the LORD. 7637
16:26 on the **s** day, *which is* the sabbath, in it 7637
16:27 of the people on the **s** day for to gather, 7637
16:29 let no man go out of his place on the **s** day. 7637
16:30 So the people rested on the **s** day. 7637
20:10 the **s** day *is* the sabbath of the LORD thy 7637
20:11 and all that in them *is,* and rested the **s** day: 7637
21: 2 and in the **s** he shall go out free for nothing. 7637
23:11 the **s** *year* thou shalt let it rest and lie still; 7637
23:12 thy work, and on the **s** day thou shalt rest: 7637
24:16 the **s** day he called unto Moses out of 7637
31:15 in the **s** *is* the sabbath of rest, holy to 7637
31:17 on the **s** day he rested, and was refreshed. 7637
34:21 shalt work, but on the **s** day thou shalt rest: 7637
35: 2 on the **s** day there shall be to you a holy 7637
Lev 13: 5 the priest shall look on him the **s** day: 7637
13: 6 the priest shall look on him again the **s** day: 7637
13:27 the priest shall look upon him the **s** day: 7637
13:32 in the **s** day the priest shall look on 7637
13:34 in the **s** day the priest shall look on 7637
13:51 he shall look on the plague on the **s** day: 7637
14: 9 it shall be on the **s** day, *that* he shall shave 7637
14:39 the priest shall come again the **s** day, 7637
16:29 *that* in the **s** month, on the tenth *day* of 7637
23: 3 the **s** day *is* the sabbath of rest, a holy 7637
23: 8 in the **s** day *is* a holy convocation: ye shall 7637
23:16 Even unto the morrow after the **s** sabbath 7637
23:24 saying, In the **s** month, in the first *day* of 7637
23:27 Also on the tenth *day* of this **s** month *there* 7637
23:34 The fifteenth day of this **s** month *shall be* 7637
23:39 Also in the fifteenth day of the **s** month, 7637
23:41 ye shall celebrate it in the **s** month. 7637
25: 4 in the **s** year shall be a sabbath of rest unto 7637
25: 9 to sound on the tenth *day* of the **s** month, 7637
25:20 ye shall say, What shall we eat the **s** year? 7637
Nu 6: 9 his cleansing, on the **s** day shall he shave it. 7637
7:48 On the **s** day Elishama the son of 7637
19:12 and on the **s** day he shall be clean: 7637
19:12 then the **s** day he shall not be clean. 7637
19:19 unclean on the third day, and on the **s** day: 7637
19:19 on the **s** day he shall purify him*self,* and 7637
28:25 on the **s** day ye shall have a holy 7637
29: 1 in the **s** month, on the first *day* of 7637
29: 7 ye shall have on the tenth *day* of this **s** 7637
29:12 on the fifteenth day of the **s** month ye shall 7637
29:32 on the **s** day seven bullocks, two rams, *and* 7637
31:19 captives on the third day, and on the **s** day. 7637

Nu 31:24 ye shall wash your clothes on the **s** day, 7637
Dt 5:14 the **s** day *is* the sabbath of the LORD thy 7637
15: 9 saying, The **s** year, the year of release, is at 7651
15:12 in the **s** year thou shalt let him go free from 7637
16: 8 on the **s** day *shall be* a solemn assembly to 7637
Jos 6: 4 the **s** day ye shall compass the city seven 7637
6:15 it came to pass on the **s** day, that they rose 7637
6:16 it came to pass at the **s** time, when 7637
19:40 *And* the **s** lot came out for the tribe of 7637
Jdg 14:15 it came to pass on the **s** day, that they said 7637
14:17 it came to pass on the **s** day, that he told 7637
14:18 the men of the city said unto him on the **s** 7637
2Sa 12:18 it came to pass on the **s** day, that the child 7637
1Ki 8: 2 the month Ethanim, which *is* the **s** month. 7637
16:10 the twenty and **s** year of Asa king of Judah, 7651
16:15 **s** year of Asa king of Judah did Zimri reign 7651
18:44 it came to pass at the **s** *time,* that he said, 7637
20:29 that in the **s** day the battle was joined: 7637
2Ki 11: 4 the **s** year Jehoiada sent and fet the rulers 7637
12: 1 In the **s** year of Jehu Jehoash *began to* 7651
13:10 **s** year of Joash king of Judah *began* 7651
15: 1 **s** year of Jeroboam king of Israel *began* 7651
18: 9 which *was* the **s** year of Hoshea son of Elah 7637
25: 8 the fifth month, on the **s** *day* of the month, 7651
25:25 it came to pass in the **s** month, *that* Ishmael 7637
1Ch 2:15 Ozem the sixth, David the **s**: 7637
12:11 Attai the sixth, Eliel the **s**, 7637
24:10 The **s** to Hakkoz, the eighth to Abijah, 7637
25:14 The **s** *to* Jesharelah, *he,* his sons, and 7637
26: 3 Jehohanan the sixth, Elioenai the **s**. 7637
26: 5 Ammiel the sixth, Issachar the **s**, 7637
27:10 The **s** *captain* for the seventh month *was* 7637
27:10 The seventh *captain* for the **s** month *was* 7637
2Ch 5: 3 king in the feast which *was in* the **s** month. 7637
7:10 twentieth day of the **s** month he sent 7637
23: 1 in the **s** year Jehoiada strengthened himself, 7637
31: 7 and finished *them* in the **s** month. 7637
Ezr 3: 1 when the **s** month was come, and 7637
3: 6 From the first day of the **s** month began 7637
7: 7 in the **s** year of Artaxerxes the king. 7651
7: 8 which *was in* the **s** year of the king. 7637
Ne 7:73 when the **s** month came, the children of 7637
8: 2 upon the first day of the **s** month. 7637
8:14 dwell in booths in the feast of the **s** month: 7637
10:31 *that* we would leave the **s** year, and 7637
Est 1:10 On the **s** day, when the heart of the king 7637
2:16 the month Tebeth, in the **s** year of his reign. 7651
Jer 28:17 prophet died the same year in the **s** month. 7637
41: 1 Now it came to pass in the **s** month, 7637
52:28 in the **s** year three thousand Jews and three 7651
Eze 20: 1 it came to pass in the **s** year, in the fifth 7637
30:20 in the first *month,* in the **s** *day* of 7651
45:20 thou shalt do the **s** *day* of the month for 7651
45:25 In the **s** *month,* in the fifteenth day of 7637
Hag 2: 1 In the **s** *month,* in the one and twentieth *day* 7637
Zec 7: 5 and **s** *month,* even those seventy years, 7637
8:19 the fast of the **s**, and the fast of the tenth, 7637
Mt 22:26 the second also, and the third, unto the **s**. *2033*
Jn 4:52 Yesterday at the **s** hour the fever left him. *1442*
Heb 4: 4 For *he* spake in a certain place of the **s** *day* *1442*
4: 4 And God did rest the **s** day from all his *1442*
Jude 1:14 And Enoch also, the **s** from Adam, *1442*
Rev 8: 1 And when he had opened the **s** seal, *1442*
10: 7 But in the days of the voice of the **s** angel, *1442*
11:15 And the **s** angel sounded; and there were *1442*
16:17 And the **s** angel poured out his vial into *1442*
21:20 the sixth, sardius; the **s**, chrysolite; *1442*

SEVENTY (61)

Ge 4:24 truly Lamech **s** and sevenfold. 7657
5:12 Cainan lived **s** years, and begat Mahalaleel: 7657
5:31 the days of Lamech were seven hundred **s** 7657
11:26 Terah lived **s** years, and begat Abram, 7657
12: 4 Abram *was* **s** and five years old when he 7657
Ex 1: 5 came *out of* the loins of Jacob were **s** souls: 7657
24: 1 and Abihu, and **s** of the elders of Israel; 7657
24: 9 and Abihu, and **s** of the elders of Israel: 7657
38:28 of the thousand seven hundred **s** and 7657
38:29 the brass of the offering *was* **s** talents, and 7657
Nu 7:13 thirty *shekels,* one silver bowl of **s** shekels, 7657
7:19 thirty *shekels,* one silver bowl of **s** shekels, 7657
7:25 thirty *shekels,* one silver bowl of **s** shekels, 7657
7:31 thirty *shekels,* one silver bowl of **s** shekels, 7657
7:37 thirty *shekels,* one silver bowl of **s** shekels, 7657
7:43 thirty *shekels,* a silver bowl of **s** shekels, 7657
7:49 thirty *shekels,* one silver bowl of **s** shekels, 7657
7:55 thirty *shekels,* one silver bowl of **s** shekels, 7657
7:61 thirty *shekels,* one silver bowl of **s** shekels, 7657
7:67 thirty *shekels,* one silver bowl of **s** shekels, 7657
7:73 thirty *shekels,* one silver bowl of **s** shekels, 7657
7:79 thirty *shekels,* one silver bowl of **s** shekels, 7657
7:85 an hundred and thirty *shekels,* each bowl **s**: 7657
11:16 Gather unto me **s** men of the elders of 7657
11:24 gathered the **s** men of the elders of 7657
11:25 *was* upon him, and gave *it* unto the **s** elders: 7657
31:32 and **s** thousand and five thousand sheep, 7657
Jdg 9:56 unto his father, in slaying his **s** brethren: 7657
2Sa 24:15 Dan even to Beer-sheba **s** thousand men. 7657
2Ki 10: 1 Ahab had **s** sons in Samaria. And Jehu 7657
10: 6 Now the king's sons, *being* **s** persons, 7657
10: 7 slew **s** persons, and put their heads in 7657
1Ch 21:14 and there fell of Israel **s** thousand men. 7657
Ezr 2: 3 two thousand an hundred **s** and two. 7657
2: 4 of Shephatiah, three hundred **s** and two. 7657
2: 5 children of Arah, seven hundred **s** and five. 7657
2:36 house of Jeshua, nine hundred **s** and three. 7657
2:40 of the children of Hodaviah, **s** and four. 7657
8: 7 the son of Athaliah, and with him **s** males. 7657
8:14 Uthai, and Zabbud, and with them **s** males. 7657
8:35 ninety and six rams, **s** and seven lambs, 7651
Ne 7: 8 two thousand an hundred **s** and two. 7657
7: 9 of Shephatiah, three hundred **s** and two. 7657
7:39 house of Jeshua, nine hundred **s** and three. 7657
7:43 *and* of the children of Hodevah, **s** and four. 7657
11:19 kept the gates, *were* an hundred **s** and two. 7657
Est 9:16 slew of their foes **s** and five thousand, but 7657
Isa 23:15 that Tyre shall be forgotten **s** years, 7657
23:15 after the end of **s** years shall Tyre sing as a 7657
23:17 it shall come to pass after the end of **s** 7657
Jer 25:11 shall serve the king of Babylon **s** years. 7657
25:12 to pass, when **s** years are accomplished, 7657
29:10 That after **s** years be accomplished at 7657
Eze 8:11 there stood before them **s** men of 7657
41:12 the end toward the west *was* **s** cubits broad; 7657
Da 9: 2 that *he* would accomplish **s** years in 7657
9:24 **S** weeks are determined upon thy people 7657
Zec 7: 5 and seventh *month,* even those **s** years, 7657
Mt 18:22 **Until seven times: but, Until s times seven.** *1441*
Lk 10: 1 *things* the Lord appointed other **s** also, *1440*
10:17 And the **s** returned *again* with joy, saying, *1440*

SEVER (4) [SEVERED]

Ex 8:22 I will **s** in that day the land of Goshen, 6395
9: 4 the LORD shall **s** between the cattle of 6395
Eze 39:14 they shall **s out** men of continual 914
Mt 13:49 **and s the wicked from among the just,** *873*

SEVERAL (12) [SEVERALLY]

Nu 28:13 a **s tenth deal** of flour mingled with 6241+6241
28:21 A **s tenth deal** shalt thou offer for 6241+6241
28:29 A **s tenth deal** unto one lamb, 6241+6241
29:10 A **s tenth deal** for one lamb, 6241+6241
29:15 a **s tenth deal** to each lamb of 6241+6241
2Ki 15: 5 the day of his death, and dwelt in a **s** house. 2669
2Ch 11:12 in every **s city** *he put* shields 5892+5892+2050.1
26:21 and dwelt *in* a **s** house, *being* a leper; 2669
28:25 in every **s city** of Judah he 5892+5892+2050.1
31:19 in every **s city**, the men that 5892+5892+2050.1
Mt 25:15 **to every man according to his s ability; and** *2398*
Rev 21:21 every **s** gate was of one pearl: *303+1520*

SEVERALLY (1) [SEVERAL]

1Co 12:11 dividing to every man **s** as he will. *2398*

SEVERED (3) [SEVER]

Lev 20:26 have **s** you from *other* people, that *ye* should 914
Dt 4:41 Moses **s** three cities on *this* side Jordan 914
Jdg 4:11 had **s** himself from the Kenites, and 6504

SEVERITY (2)

Ro 11:22 Behold therefore the goodness and **s** of God: *663*
11:22 on them which fell, **s**; but toward thee, *663*

SEW (2) [SEWED, SEWEST, SEWETH, SOW]

Ecc 3: 7 A time to rent, and a time to **s**; a time to 8609
Eze 13:18 Woe to *the women* that **s** pillows to all 8609

SEWED (2) [SEW]

Ge 3: 7 they **s** fig leaves **together,** and 8609

Job 16:15 I have s sackcloth upon my skin, and 8609

SEWEST (1) [SEW]
Job 14:17 up in a bag, and thou s up mine iniquity. 2950

SEWETH (1) [SEW]
Mk 2:21 No *man* also s a piece of new cloth on an *1976*

SEXUAL IMMORALITY See FORNICATION

SEXUALLY IMMORAL See WHOREMONGER; WHOREMONGERS

SHAALABBIN (1)
Jos 19:42 And S, and Aijalon, and Jethlah, 8169

SHAALBIM (2)
Jdg 1:35 dwell in mount Heres in Aijalon, and in S: 8169
1Ki 4: 9 in S, and Beth-shemesh, and 8169

SHAALBONITE (2)
2Sa 23:32 Eliahba the S, *of* the sons of Jashen, 8170
1Ch 11:33 Azmaveth the Baharumite, Eliahba the S, 8170

SHAALIM See SHALIM

SHAAPH (2)
1Ch 2:47 and Geshan, and Pelet, and Ephah, and S. 8174
2:49 She bare also S the father of Madmannah, 8174

SHAARAIM (2)
1Sa 17:52 of the Philistines fell down by the way to S, 8189
1Ch 4:31 and at Beth-birei, and at S. 8189

SHAASHGAZ (1)
Est 2:14 to the custody of S, the king's chamberlain, 8190

SHABBETHAI (3)
Ezr 10:15 Meshullam and S the Levite helped them. 7678
Ne 8: 7 Jamin, Akkub, S, Hodijah, Maaseiah, 7678
11:16 S and Jozabad, of the chief of the Levites, 7678

SHACHIA (1)
1Ch 8:10 Jeuz, and S, and Mirma. These *were* his 7634

SHADE (1) [SHADY]
Ps 121: 5 the LORD *is* thy s upon thy right hand. 6738

SHADOW (73) [OVERSHADOW, SHADOWING, SHADOWS]
Ge 19: 8 therefore came they under the s of my roof. 6738
Jdg 9:15 *then come and* put your trust in my s: 6738
9:36 Thou seest the s of the mountains as *if they* 6738
2Ki 20: 9 shall the s go forward ten degrees, or 6738
20:10 It is a light thing for the s to go down ten 6738
20:10 but let the s return backward ten degrees. 6738
20:11 he brought the s ten degrees backward, 6738
1Ch 29:15 our days on the earth *are* as a s, and *there is* 6738
Job 3: 5 Let darkness and the **s of death** stain it; 6757
7: 2 As a servant earnestly desireth the s, and 6738
8: 9 because our days upon earth *are* a s:) 6738
10:21 to the land of darkness and the **s of death**; 6757
10:22 *and of* the **s of death**, without any order, 6757
12:22 and bringeth out to light the **s of death**. 6757
14: 2 he fleeth also as a s, and continueth not. 6738
16:16 and on mine eyelids *is* the **s of death**; 6757
17: 7 of sorrow, and all my members *are* as a s. 6738
24:17 morning *is* to them even as the **s of death**: 6757
24:17 *they are in* the terrors of the **s of death**. 6757
28: 3 the stones of darkness, and the **s of death**. 6757
34:22 *There is* no darkness, nor **s of death**, 6757
38:17 hast thou seen the doors of the **s of death**? 6757
40:22 The shady trees cover him *with* their s; 6752
Ps 17: 8 the eye, hide me under the s of thy wings, 6738
23: 4 I walk through the valley of the **s of death**, 6757
36: 7 men put their trust under the s of thy wings. 6738
44:19 and covered us with the **s of death**. 6757
57: 1 in the s of thy wings will I make my refuge, 6738
63: 7 in the s of thy wings will I rejoice. 6738
80:10 The hills were covered *with* the s of it, and 6738
91: 1 shall abide under the s of the Almighty. 6738
102:11 My days *are* like a s that declineth; and 6738
107:10 as sit in darkness and in the **s of death**, 6757
107:14 them out of darkness and the **s of death**, 6757
109:23 I am gone like the s when it declineth: I am 6738
144: 4 his days *are* as a s that passeth away. 6738
Ecc 6:12 of his vain life which he spendeth as a s? 6738
8:13 shall he prolong *his* days, *which are* as a s; 6738
SS 2: 3 I sat down under his s with great delight, 6738
Isa 4: 6 there shall be a tabernacle for a s in 6738
9: 2 they that dwell in the land of the **s of death**, 6757
16: 3 make thy s as the night in the midst of 6738
25: 4 a refuge from the storm, a s from the heat, 6738
25: 5 *even* the heat with the s of a cloud: 6738
30: 2 of Pharaoh, and to trust in the s of Egypt. 6738
30: 3 the trust in the s of Egypt *your* confusion. 6738
32: 2 as the s of a great rock in a weary land. 6738
34:15 and lay, and hatch, and gather under her s: 6738
38: 8 I will bring again the s of the degrees, 6738
49: 2 in the s of his hand hath he hid me, and 6738
51:16 have covered thee in the s of mine hand, 6738
Jer 2: 6 a land of drought, and of the **s of death**, 6757
13:16 he turn it into the **s of death**, *and* make *it* 6757
48:45 They that fled stood under the s of Heshbon 6738
La 4:20 Under his s we shall live among 6738
Eze 17:23 in the s of the branches thereof shall they 6738
31: 6 and under his s dwelt all great nations. 6738
31:12 of the earth are gone down from his s, 6738
31:17 *that* dwelt under his s in the midst of 6738
Da 4:12 the beasts of the field had s under it, and 2927
Hos 4:13 and elms, because the s thereof *is* good: 6738
14: 7 They that dwell under his s shall return; 6738
Am 5: 8 and turneth the **s of death** into the morning, 6757
Jnh 4: 5 made him a booth, and sat under it in the s, 6738
4: 6 that *it* might be a s over his head, to deliver 6738
Mt 4:16 the region and s of death light is sprung up. *4639*
Mk 4:32 fowls of the air may lodge under the s of it. *4639*
Lk 1:79 that sit in darkness and *in* the s of death, *4639*
Ac 5:15 that at the least the s of Peter passing by *4639*
Col 2:17 Which are a s of *things* to come; but *4639*
Heb 8: 5 s of heavenly *things,* as Moses was *4639*
10: 1 For the law having a s of good *things* to *4639*
Jas 1:17 is no variableness, neither s of turning. *644*

SHADOWING (3) [SHADOW]
Isa 18: 1 Woe to the land s with wings, which *is* 6767
Eze 31: 3 and with a s shrowd, and of a high stature; 6751
Heb 9: 5 And over it the cherubims of glory s *2683*

SHADOWS (3) [SHADOW]
SS 2:17 the s flee away, turn, my beloved, and be 6752
4: 6 Until the day break, and the s flee away, 6752
Jer 6: 4 for the s of the evening are stretched out. 6752

SHADRACH (15)
Da 1: 7 to Hananiah, of S; and to Mishael, 7714
2:49 and he set S, Meshach, and Abed-nego, 7715
3:12 of Babylon, S, Meshach, and Abed-nego; 7715
3:13 in *his* rage and fury commanded to bring S, 7715
3:14 *Is it* true, O S, Meshach, and Abed-nego, 7715
3:16 S, Meshach, and Abed-nego, answered and 7715
3:19 form of his visage was changed against S, 7715
3:20 men that *were* in his army to bind S, 7715
3:22 of the fire slew those men that took up S, 7715
3:23 three men, S, Meshach, and Abed-nego, 7715
3:26 *and* spake, and said, S, Meshach, and 7715
3:26 come *hither.* Then S, Meshach, and 7715
3:28 said, Blessed *be* the God of S, Meshach, 7715
3:29 speak any thing amiss against the God of S, 7715
3:30 the king promoted S, Meshach, and 7715

SHADY (2) [SHADE]
Job 40:21 He lieth under the **s trees**, in the covert of 6628
40:22 The **s trees** cover him *with* their shadow; 6628

SHAFT (4)
Ex 25:31 his s, and his branches, his bowls, 3409
37:17 his s, and his branch, his bowls, his knops, 3409
Nu 8: 4 unto the s thereof, unto the flowers thereof, 3409
Isa 49: 2 hath he hid me, and made me a polished s; 2671

SHAGE (1)
1Ch 11:34 Jonathan the son of S the Hararite, 7681

SHAGEE See SHAGE

SHAHAR (1)
Ps 22: T To the chief Musician upon Aijeleth S, 7837

SHAHARAIM (1)
1Ch 8: 8 S begat *children* in the country of Moab, 7842

SHAHAZIMAH (1)
Jos 19:22 to Tabor, and **S**, and Beth-shemesh; 7831

SHAHAZUMAH See SHAHAZIMAH

SHAKE (39) [SHAKED, SHAKEN, SHAKETH, SHAKING, SHOOK]
Jdg 16:20 out as at other times *before,* and **s** myself. 5287
Ne 5:13 So God **s out** every man from his house, 5287
Job 4:14 trembling, which **made** all my bones **to s**. 6342
15:33 He shall **s off** his unripe grape as the vine, 2554
16: 4 words against you, and **s** mine head at you. 5128
Ps 22: 7 shoot out the lip, they **s** the head, *saying,* 5128
46: 3 *though* the mountains **s** with the swelling 7493
69:23 and **make** their loins continually **to s**. 4571
72:16 the fruit thereof shall **s** like Lebanon: 7493
Isa 2:19 when he ariseth to **s terribly** the earth. 6206
2:21 when he ariseth to **s terribly** the earth. 6206
10:15 as if the rod should **s** *itself against* them 5130
10:32 he shall **s** his hand *against* the mount of 5130
11:15 with his mighty wind shall he **s** his hand 5130
13: 2 exalt the voice unto them, **s** the hand, 5130
13:13 Therefore I will **s** the heavens, and the earth 7264
14:16 the earth to tremble, that did **s** kingdoms; 7493
24:18 and the foundations of the earth do **s**. 7493
33: 9 and Bashan and Carmel **s off** *their fruits.* 5287
52: 2 **S** thyself from the dust; arise, *and* sit down, 5287
Jer 23: 9 because of the prophets; all my bones **s**; 7363
Eze 26:10 thy walls shall **s** at the noise of 7493
26:15 Shall not the isles **s** at the sound of thy fall, 7493
27:28 The suburbs shall **s** at the sound of the cry 7493
31:16 I **made** the nations **to s** at the sound of his 7493
38:20 shall **s** at my presence, and the mountains 7493
Da 4:14 **s off** his leaves, and scatter his fruit: 5426
Joel 3:16 and the heavens and the earth shall **s**: 7493
Am 9: 1 the lintel of the door, that the posts may **s**: 7493
Hag 2: 6 I *will* **s** the heavens, and the earth, and 7493
2: 7 I will **s** all nations, and the desire of all 7493
2:21 I *will* **s** the heavens and the earth; 7493
Zec 2: 9 I *will* **s** mine hand upon them, and 5130
Mt 10:14 or city, **s off** the dust of your feet. *1621*
28: 4 And for fear of him the keepers did **s**, and *4579*
Mk 6:11 **s off** the dust under your feet for a *1621*
Lk 6:48 upon that house, and could not **s** it: *4531*
9: 5 **s off** the very dust from your feet for a *660*
Heb 12:26 Yet once *more* I **s** not the earth only, but *4579*

SHAKED (1) [SHAKE]
Ps 109:25 *when* they looked upon me they **s** their 5128

SHAKEN (22) [SHAKE]
Lev 26:36 the sound of a **s** leaf shall chase them; and 5086
1Ki 14:15 as a reed is **s** in the water, and he shall root 5110
2Ki 19:21 the daughter of Jerusalem hath **s** her head at 5128
Ne 5:13 even thus be he **s out**, and emptied. 5287
Job 16:12 **s** me **to pieces**, and set me up for his mark. 6327
38:13 that the wicked might be **s** out of it? 5287
Ps 18: 7 also of the hills moved and were **s**, 1607
Isa 37:22 the daughter of Jerusalem hath **s** her head at 5128
Na 2: 3 and the fir trees shall be **terribly s**. 7477
3:12 if they be **s**, they shall even fall into 5128
Mt 11: 7 wilderness to see? A reed **s** with the wind? *4531*
24:29 and the powers of the heavens shall be **s**: *4531*
Mk 13:25 the powers that are in heaven shall be **s**. *4531*
Lk 6:38 and **s** *together,* and running over, *4531*
7:24 for to see? A reed **s** with the wind? *4531*
21:26 for the powers of heaven shall be **s**. *4531*
Ac 4:31 the place was **s** where they were assembled *4531*
16:26 so that the foundations of the prison were **s**: *4531*
2Th 2: 2 That ye be not soon **s** in mind, or *4531*
Heb 12:27 the removing of those *things* that are **s**, *4531*
12:27 that those *things* which cannot be **s** may *4531*
Rev 6:13 when she is **s** of a mighty wind. *4579*

SHAKETH (7) [SHAKE]
Job 9: 6 Which **s** the earth out of her place, and 7264
Ps 29: 8 The voice of the LORD **s** the wilderness; 2342
29: 8 the LORD **s** the wilderness of Kadesh. 2342
60: 2 broken it: heal the breaches thereof; for it **s**. 4131
Isa 10:15 the saw magnify itself against him that **s** it? 5130
19:16 of the LORD of hosts, which he **s** over it. 5130
33:15 that **s** his hands from holding of bribes, 5287

SHAKING (8) [SHAKE]
Job 41:29 as stubble: he laugheth at the **s** of a spear. 7494
Ps 44:14 a **s** of the head among the people. 4493
Isa 17: 6 as the **s** of an olive tree, two *or* three berries 5363
19:16 of the **s** of the hand of the LORD of hosts, 8573
24:13 *there shall be* as the **s** of an olive tree, *and* 5363
30:32 and in battles of **s** will he fight with it. 8573
Eze 37: 7 behold a **s**, and the bones came together, 7494
38:19 Surely in that day there shall be a great **s** in 7494

SHALEM (1)
Ge 33:18 Jacob came to **S**, a city of Shechem, 8004

SHALIM (1)
1Sa 9: 4 they passed through the land of **S**, and 8171

SHALISHA (1) [BAAL-SHALISHA]
1Sa 9: 4 passed through the land of **S**, but 8031

SHALL (9838) [SHALT] See Index

SHALLECHETH (1)
1Ch 26:16 with the gate **S**, by the causeway of 7996

SHALLEKETH See SHALLECHETH

SHALLUM (27)
2Ki 15:10 **S** the son of Jabesh conspired against him, 7967
15:13 **S** the son of Jabesh *began* to reign in 7967
15:14 smote **S** the son of Jabesh in Samaria, and 7967
15:15 the rest of the acts of **S**, and his conspiracy 7967
22:14 the wife of **S** the son of Tikvah, the son of 7967
1Ch 2:40 begat Sisamai, and Sisamai begat **S**, 7967
2:41 **S** begat Jekamiah, and Jekamiah begat 7967
3:15 the third Zedekiah, the fourth **S**. 7967
4:25 **S** his son, Mibsam his son, Mishma his son. 7967
6:12 Ahitub begat Zadok, and Zadok begat **S**, 7967
6:13 **S** begat Hilkiah, and Hilkiah begat Azariah, 7967
7:13 Jahziel, and Guni, and Jezer, and **S**, 7967
9:17 the porters *were,* **S**, and Akkub, and 7967
9:17 and their brethren: **S** *was* the chief; 7967
9:19 And **S** the son of Kore, the son of Ebiasaph, 7967
9:31 who *was* the firstborn of **S** the Korahite, 7967
2Ch 28:12 Jehizkiah the son of **S**, and Amasa the son 7967
34:22 the wife of **S** the son of Tikvath, the son of 7967
Ezr 2:42 the children of **S**, the children of Ater, 7967
7: 2 The son of **S**, the son of Zadok, the son of 7967
10:24 and of the porters; **S**, and Telem, and Uri. 7967
10:42 **S**, Amariah, *and* Joseph. 7967
Ne 3:12 next unto him repaired **S** the son of 7967
7:45 the children of **S**, the children of Ater, 7967
Jer 22:11 For thus saith the LORD touching **S** 7967
32: 7 Hanameel the son of **S** thine uncle *shall* 7967
35: 4 the chamber of Maaseiah the son of **S**, 7967

SHALLUN (1)
Ne 3:15 the gate of the fountain repaired **S** the son 7968

SHALMAI (2)
Ezr 2:46 the children of **S**, the children of Hanan, 8073
Ne 7:48 the children of Hagaba, the children of **S**, 8014

SHALMAN (1) [SHALMANESER]
Hos 10:14 as **S** spoiled Beth-arbel in the day of battle: 8020

SHALMANESER (2) [SHALMAN]
2Ki 17: 3 Against him came up **S** king of Assyria; 8022
18: 9 *that* **S** king of Assyria came up against 8022

SHALT (1616) [SHALL] See Index

SHAMA (1)
1Ch 11:44 **S** and Jehiel the sons of Hothan 8091

SHAMARIAH (1)
2Ch 11:19 him children; Jeush, and **S**, and Zaham. 8114

SHAMBLES (1)
1Co 10:25 Whatsoever is sold in the **s**, *that* eat, *3111*

SHAME (100) [ASHAMED, SHAMED, SHAMEFASTNESS, SHAMEFUL, SHAMEFULLY, SHAMELESSLY, SHAMETH]
Ex 32:25 naked unto *their* **s** amongst their enemies:) 8103
Jdg 18: 7 that might **put** *them* **to s** in *any* thing; 3637
1Sa 20:34 because his father had **done** him **s**. 3637
2Sa 13:13 I, whither shall I cause my **s** to go? 2781

S

2Ch 32:21 So he returned with **s** of face to his own 1322
Job 8:22 They that hate thee shall be clothed with **s**; 1322
Ps 4: 2 how long *will ye turn* my glory into **s**? 3639
35: 4 and **put to s** that seek after my soul: 3637
35:26 let them be clothed with **s** and 1322
40:14 and **put to s** that wish me evil. 3637
40:15 Let them be desolate for a reward of their **s** 1322
44: 7 and hast **put** them **to s** that hated us. 954
44: 9 thou hast cast off, and **put** us **to s**; and 3637
44:15 and the **s** of my face hath covered me, 1322
53: 5 thou hast **put** *them* **to s**, because God hath 954
69: 7 borne reproach; **s** hath covered my face. 3639
69:19 my reproach, and my **s**, and my dishonour: 1322
70: 3 turned back for a reward of their **s** that say, 1322
71:24 for they are **brought unto s**, that seek my 2659
83:16 Fill their faces *with* **s**; that they may seek 7036
83:17 yea, let them be put to **s**, and perish: 2659
89:45 thou hast covered him with **s**. Selah. 955
109:29 Let mine adversaries be clothed with **s**, and 3639
119:31 thy testimonies: O LORD, **put** me not **to s**. 954
132:18 His enemies will I clothe with **s**: but 1322
Pr 3:35 but **s** shall be the promotion of fools. 7036
9: 7 reproveth a scorner getteth to himself **s**: 7036
10: 5 sleepeth in harvest *is* a son that **causeth s**. 954
11: 2 *When* pride cometh, then cometh **s**: but 7036
12:16 but a prudent *man* covereth **s**. 7036
13: 5 wicked *man* is loathsome, and **cometh to s**. 2659
13:18 **s** *shall be to* him that refuseth instruction: 7036
14:35 but his wrath is *against* him that **causeth s**. 954
17: 2 shall have rule over a son that **causeth s**, 954
18:13 he heareth *it*, it *is* folly and **s** unto him. 3639
19:26 *is* a son that **causeth s**, and 954
25: 8 when thy neighbour hath **put** thee **to s**. 3637
25:10 Lest he that heareth *it* **put** thee **to s**, and 2616
29:15 left *to himself* **bringeth** his mother **to s**. 954
Isa 20: 4 *their* buttocks uncovered, *to* the **s** of Egypt. 6172
22:18 there the chariots of thy glory *shall be* the **s** 7036
30: 3 shall the strength of Pharaoh be your **s**, 1322
30: 5 help nor profit, but a **s**, and also a reproach. 1322
47: 3 shall be uncovered, yea, thy **s** shall be seen: 2781
50: 6 I hid not my face from **s** and spitting. 3639
54: 4 for thou shalt not be **put to s**: 2659
54: 4 for thou shalt forget the **s** of thy youth, and 1322
61: 7 For your **s** *you shall have* double; and 1322
Jer 3:24 For **s** hath devoured the labour of our 1322
3:25 We lie down in our **s**, and our confusion 1322
13:26 skirts upon thy face, that thy **s** may appear. 7036
20:18 that my days should be consumed with **s**? 1322
23:40 a perpetual **s**, which shall not be forgotten. 3640
46:12 The nations have heard *of* thy **s**, and thy cry 7036
48:39 how hath Moab turned the back with **s**! so 954
51:51 **s** hath covered our faces: for strangers are 3639
Eze 7:18 **s** *shall be* upon all faces, and baldness upon 955
16:52 bear thine own **s** for thy sins that thou hast 3639
16:52 be thou confounded also, and bear thy **s**, 3639
16:54 That thou mayest bear thine own **s**, and 3639
16:63 open thy mouth any more, because of thy **s**, 3639
32:24 yet have they borne their **s** with them that 3639
32:25 yet have they borne their **s** with them that 3639
32:30 bear their **s** with them that go down to 3639
34:29 neither bear the **s** of the heathen any more. 3639
36: 6 because ye have borne the **s** of the heathen: 3639
36: 7 that *are* about you, they shall bear their **s**. 3639
36:15 hear in thee the **s** of the heathen any more, 3639
39:26 After that they have borne their **s**, and all 3639
44:13 most holy *place:* but they shall bear their **s**, 3639
Da 12: 2 and some to **s** *and* everlasting contempt. 2781
Hos 4: 7 *therefore* will I change their glory into **s**. 7036
4:18 her rulers *with* **s** do love, Give ye. 7036
9:10 and separated themselves unto *that* **s**; 1322
10: 6 Ephraim shall receive **s**, and Israel shall be 1317
Ob 1:10 For *thy* violence against thy brother Jacob **s** 955
Mic 1:11 inhabitant of Saphir, having *thy* **s** naked: 1322
2: 6 prophesy to them, *that* they shall not take **s**. 3639
7:10 and **s** shall cover her which said unto me, 955
Na 3: 5 thy nakedness, and the kingdoms thy **s**. 7036
Hab 2:10 Thou hast consulted **s** to thy house by 1322
2:16 Thou art filled *with* **s** for glory: drink thou 7036
Zep 3: 5 he faileth not; but the unjust knoweth no **s**. 1322
3:19 every land where they have been put to **s**. 1322
Lk 14: 9 thou begin with **s** to take the lowest room. *152*
Ac 5:41 counted worthy to **suffer s** for his name. *818*
1Co 4:14 I write not these *things* to **s** you, but as my *1788*
6: 5 I speak to your **s**. Is it so, that there is not a *1791*
11: 6 but *if it* be a **s** for a woman to be shorn or *149*
11:14 if a man have long hair, it is a **s** unto him? *819*
11:22 church of God, and **s** them that have not? *2617*
14:35 for it is a **s** for women to speak in *149*
15:34 knowledge of God: I speak *this* to your **s**. *1791*
Eph 5:12 For it is a **s** even to speak of those *things* *149*
Php 3:19 *is their* belly, and *whose* glory *is* in their **s**, *152*
Heb 6: 6 of God afresh, and **put** *him* **to** an **open s**. *3856*
12: 2 despising the **s**, and is set down at the right *152*
Jude 1:13 waves of the sea, foaming out their own **s**; *152*
Rev 3:18 *that* the **s** of thy nakedness do not appear; *152*
16:15 lest he walk naked, and they see his **s**. *808*

SHAMED (4) [SHAME]
Ge 38:23 Let her take *it* to her, lest we be **s**: 937
2Sa 19: 5 Thou hast **s** *this* day the faces of all thy 954
1Ch 8:12 Eber, and Misham, and **S**, who built Ono, 8106
Ps 14: 6 You have **s** the counsel of the poor, because 954

SHAMEFASTNESS (1) [SHAME]
1Ti 2: 9 in modest apparel, with **s** and sobriety; *127*

SHAMEFUL (2) [SHAME]
Jer 11:13 have ye set up altars to *that* **s thing**, 1322
Hab 2:16 and **s spuing** *shall be* on thy glory. 7022

SHAMEFULLY (4) [SHAME]
Hos 2: 5 she that conceived them hath **done s**: for she 954
Mk 12: 4 in the head, and sent *him* away **s handled**. *821*
Lk 20:11 and **entreated** *him* **s**, and sent *him* away *818*
1Th 2: 2 and were **s entreated**, as ye know, *5195*

SHAMELESSLY (1) [SHAME]
2Sa 6:20 as one of the vain *fellows* **s uncovereth** 1540

SHAMER (2)
1Ch 6:46 son of Amzi, the son of Bani, the son of **S**, 8106
7:34 the sons of **S**; Ahi, and Rohgah, Jehubbah, 8106

SHAMETH (1) [SHAME]
Pr 28: 7 he that is a companion of riotous *men* **s** his 3637

SHAMGAR (2)
Jdg 3:31 after him was **S** the son of Anath, 8044
5: 6 In the days of **S** the son of Anath, in 8044

SHAMHUTH (1)
1Ch 27: 8 The fifth captain for the fifth month *was* **S** 8049

SHAMIR (4)
Jos 15:48 in the mountains, **S**, and Jattir, and Socoh, 8069
Jdg 10: 1 and he dwelt in **S** in mount Ephraim. 8069
10: 2 three years, and died, and was buried in **S**. 8069
1Ch 24:24 Michah: of the sons of Michah; **S**. 8069

SHAMMA (1)
1Ch 7:37 and **S**, and Shilshah, and Ithran, and Beera. 8037

SHAMMAH (8)
Ge 36:13 Nahath, and Zerah, **S**, and Mizzah: 8048
36:17 duke Nahath, duke Zerah, duke **S**, 8048
1Sa 16: 9 Jesse made **S** to pass by. And he said, 8048
17:13 next unto him Abinadab, and the third **S**. 8048
2Sa 23:11 after him *was* **S** the son of Agee 8048
23:25 **S** the Harodite, Elika the Harodite, 8048
23:33 **S** the Hararite, Ahiam the son of Sharar 8048
1Ch 1:37 of Reuel; Nahath, Zerah, **S**, and Mizzah. 8048

SHAMMAI (6)
1Ch 2:28 the sons of Onam were, **S**, and Jada. 8060
2:28 And the sons of **S**; Nadab, and Abishur. 8060
2:32 the sons of Jada the brother of **S**; Jether, 8060
2:44 the father of Jorkoam: and Rekem begat **S**. 8060
2:45 the son of **S** *was* Maon: and Maon *was* 8060
4:17 and **S**, and Ishbah the father of Eshtemoa. 8060

SHAMMOTH (1)
1Ch 11:27 **S** the Harorite, Helez the Pelonite, 8054

SHAMMUA (5)
Nu 13: 4 of the tribe of Reuben, **S** the son of Zaccur. 8051
2Sa 5:14 **S**, and Shobab, and Nathan, and Solomon, 8051
1Ch 14: 4 **S**, and Shobab, Nathan, and Solomon, 8051
Ne 11:17 Abda the son of **S**, the son of Galal, the son 8051
12:18 Of Bilgah, **S**; of Shemaiah, Jehonathan; 8051

SHAMSHERAI (1)
1Ch 8:26 And **S**, and Shehariah, and Athaliah, 8125

SHAPE (2) [SHAPEN, SHAPES]
Lk 3:22 the Holy Ghost descended in a bodily **s** *1491*
Jn 5:37 heard his voice at any time, nor seen his **s**. *1491*

SHAPEN (1) [SHAPE]
Ps 51: 5 Behold, I was **s** in iniquity; and in sin did 2342

SHAPES (1) [SHAPE]
Rev 9: 7 And the **s** of the locusts *were* like unto *3667*

SHAPHAM (1)
1Ch 5:12 **S** the next, and Jaanai, and Shaphat in 8223

SHAPHAN (30)
2Ki 22: 3 *that* the king sent **S** the son of Azaliah, 8227
22: 8 Hilkiah the high priest said unto **S** 8227
22: 8 Hilkiah gave the book to **S**, and he read it. 8227
22: 9 **S** the scribe came to the king, and 8227
22:10 **S** the scribe shewed the king, saying, 8227
22:10 me a book. And **S** read it before the king. 8227
22:12 Ahikam the son of **S**, and Achbor the son 8227
22:12 **S** the scribe, and Asahiah a servant of 8227
22:14 Ahikam, and Achbor, and **S**, and Asahiah, 8227
25:22 the son of Ahikam, the son of **S**, ruler. 8227
2Ch 34: 8 he sent **S** the son of Azaliah, and Maaseiah 8227
34:15 Hilkiah answered and said to **S** the scribe, 8227
34:15 And Hilkiah delivered the book to **S**. 8227
34:16 **S** carried the book to the king, and 8227
34:18 **S** the scribe told the king, saying, 8227
34:18 me a book. And **S** read it before the king. 8227
34:20 Ahikam the son of **S**, and Abdon the son of 8227
34:20 **S** the scribe, and Asaiah a servant of 8227
Jer 26:24 of Ahikam the son of **S** was with Jeremiah, 8227
29: 3 By the hand of Elasah the son of **S**, and 8227
36:10 in the chamber of Gemariah the son of **S** 8227
36:11 the son of Gemariah, the son of **S**, 8227
36:12 Gemariah the son of **S**, and Zedekiah 8227
39:14 Gedaliah the son of Ahikam the son of **S**, 8227
40: 5 to Gedaliah the son of Ahikam the son of **S**, 8227
40: 9 Gedaliah the son of Ahikam the son of **S** 8227
40:11 Gedaliah the son of Ahikam the son of **S**; 8227
41: 2 son of Ahikam the son of **S** with the sword, 8227
43: 6 Gedaliah the son of Ahikam the son of **S**, 8227
Eze 8:11 midst of them stood Jaazaniah the son of **S**, 8227

SHAPHAT (8)
Nu 13: 5 Of the tribe of Simeon, **S** the son of Hori. 8202
1Ki 19:16 Elisha the son of **S** of Abel-meholah shalt 8202
19:19 and found Elisha the son of **S**, 8202
2Ki 3:11 and said, Here *is* Elisha the son of **S**, 8202
6:31 if the head of Elisha the son of **S** shall stand 8202
1Ch 3:22 Igeal, and Bariah, and Neariah, and **S**, six. 8202
5:12 the next, and Jaanai, and **S** in Bashan. 8202
27:29 *were* in the valleys *was* **S** the son of Adlai: 8202

SHAPHER (2)
Nu 33:23 from Kehelathah, and pitched in mount **S**. 8234
33:24 they removed from mount **S**, and 8234

SHAPHIR See SAPHIR

SHARAI (1)
Ezr 10:40 Machnadebai, Shashai, **S**, 8298

SHARAIM (1)
Jos 15:36 **S**, and Adithaim, and Gederah, and 8189

SHARAR (1)
2Sa 23:33 Ahiam the son of **S** the Hararite, 8325

SHARE (1)
1Sa 13:20 to sharpen every man his **s**, and his coulter, 4282

SHAREZER (2)
2Ki 19:37 and **S** *his sons* smote him with the sword: 8272
Isa 37:38 and **S** his sons smote him with the sword; 8272

SHARON (6) [SHARONITE]
1Ch 5:16 in her towns, and in all the suburbs of **S**, 8289
27:29 over the herds that fed in **S** *was* Shitrai 8289
SS 2: 1 I am the rose of **S**, *and* the lily of 8289
Isa 33: 9 **S** is like a wilderness; and Bashan and 8289
35: 2 the excellency of Carmel and **S**, they shall 8289
65:10 **S** shall be a fold of flocks, and the valley of 8289

SHARONITE (1) [SHARON]
1Ch 27:29 herds that fed in Sharon *was* Shitrai the **S**: 8290

SHARP (25) [SHARPEN, SHARPENED, SHARPENETH, SHARPER, SHARPLY, SHARPNESS]
Ex 4:25 Zipporah took a **s stone**, and cut off 6864
Jos 5: 2 Make thee **s** knives, and circumcise again 6697
5: 3 Joshua made him **s** knives, and 6697
1Sa 14: 4 *there was* a **s** rock on the one side, and 8127
14: 4 the one side, and a **s** rock on the other side: 8127
Job 41:30 **S** stones *are* under him: he spreadeth sharp 2303
41:30 he spreadeth **s pointed** *things* upon 2742
Ps 45: 5 Thine arrows *are* **s** in the heart of the king's 8150
52: 2 like a **s** rasor, working deceitfully. 3913
57: 4 and arrows, and their tongue a **s** sword. 2299
120: 4 **S** arrows of the mighty, with coals of 8150
Pr 5: 4 as wormwood, **s** as a twoedged sword. 2299
25:18 *is* a maul, and a sword, and a **s** arrow. 8150
Isa 5:28 Whose arrows *are* **s**, and all their bows 8150
41:15 I will make thee a new **s** threshing 2742
49: 2 he hath made my mouth like a **s** sword; 2299
Eze 5: 1 thou, son of man, take thee a **s** knife, 2299
Ac 15:39 And the **contention** was so **s** *between* *3948*
Rev 1:16 out of his mouth went a **s** twoedged sword: *3691*
2:12 These *things* saith he which hath the **s** *3691*
14:14 a golden crown, and in his hand a **s** sickle. *3691*
14:17 is in heaven, he also having a **s** sickle. *3691*
14:18 cried with a loud cry to him that had the **s** *3691*
14:18 Thrust in thy **s** sickle, and gather *3691*
19:15 And out of his mouth goeth a **s** sword, *3691*

SHARPEN (2) [SHARP]
1Sa 13:20 to **s** every man his share, and his coulter, 3913
13:21 and for the axes, and to **s** the goads. 5324

SHARPENED (4) [SHARP]
Ps 140: 3 They have **s** their tongues like a serpent; 8150
Eze 21: 9 A sword, a sword is **s**, and also furbished: 2300
21:10 It is **s** to make a sore slaughter; *it is* 2300
21:11 this sword is **s**, and it *is* furbished, to give it 2300

SHARPENETH (3) [SHARP]
Job 16: 9 his teeth; mine enemy **s** his eyes upon me. 3913
Pr 27:17 Iron **s** iron; so a man sharpeneth 2300
27:17 so a man **s** the countenance of his friend. 2300

SHARPER (2) [SHARP]
Mic 7: 4 the *most* upright *is* **s** than a thorn hedge: NIH
Heb 4:12 powerful, and **s** than any twoedged sword, *5114*

SHARPLY (2) [SHARP]
Jdg 8: 1 And they did chide with him **s**. 2394+871.1
Tit 1:13 Wherefore rebuke them **s**, that they may be *664*

SHARPNESS (1) [SHARP]
2Co 13:10 lest being present I should use **s**, *664*

SHARUHEN (1)
Jos 19: 6 And Beth-lebaoth, and **S**; thirteen cities and 8287

SHASHAI (1)
Ezr 10:40 Machnadebai, **S**, Sharai, 8343

SHASHAK (2)
1Ch 8:14 And Ahio, **S**, and Jeremoth, 8349
8:25 And Iphedeiah, and Penuel, the sons of **S**; 8349

SHATTERED See VEX; VEXATION; VEXED

SHATTERS See SUNDER

SHAUL (7) [SHAULITES]
Ge 46:10 and **S** the son of a Canaanitish woman. 7586
Ex 6:15 and **S** the son of a Canaanitish woman: 7586
Nu 26:13 of **S**, the family of the Shaulites. 7586
1Ch 1:48 **S** of Rehoboth *by* the river reigned in his 7586
1:49 when **S** was dead, Baal-hanan the son of 7586
4:24 and Jamin, Jarib, Zerah, *and* **S**: 7586
6:24 Uriel his son, Uzziah his son, and **S** his son. 7586

SHAULITES (1) [SHAUL]
Nu 26:13 the Zarhites: of Shaul, the family of the **S**. 7587

SHAVE (14) [SHAVED, SHAVEN]
Lev 13:33 shall be shaven, but the scall shall he not **s**; 1548
14: 8 **s off** all his hair, and wash *himself* in water, 1548
14: 9 *that* he shall **s** all his hair **off** his head and 1548
14: 9 even all his hair he shall **s off**: 1548
21: 5 neither shall they **s off** the corner of their 1548
Nu 6: 9 he shall **s** his head in the day of his 1548
6: 9 on the seventh day shall he **s** it. 1548
6:18 the Nazarite shall **s** the head of his 1548
8: 7 let them **s** all their flesh, and let them 5674+8593
Dt 21:12 and she shall **s** her head, and pare her nails; 1548
Jdg 16:19 she **caused** *him* **to s off** the seven locks of 1548
Isa 7:20 In the same day shall the Lord **s** with a 1548
Eze 44:20 Neither shall they **s** their heads, nor suffer 1548
Ac 21:24 with them, that they may **s** *their* heads: *3587*

SHAVED (4) [SHAVE]
Ge 41:14 he **s** *himself,* and changed his raiment, and 1548
2Sa 10: 4 **s off** the *one* half of their beards, and 1548
1Ch 19: 4 **s** them, and cut off their garments in 1548
Job 1:20 **s** his head, and fell down upon the ground, 1494

SHAVEH (1) [SHAVEH KIRIATHAIM]
Ge 14:17 at the valley of **S**, which *is* the king's dale. 7740

SHAVEH KIRIATHAIM (1)
Ge 14: 5 in Ham, and the Emims in **S**, 7741

SHAVEN (7) [SHAVE]
Lev 13:33 He shall be **s**, but the scall shall he not 1548
Nu 6:19 after *the hair of* his separation is **s**: 1548
Jdg 16:17 if I be **s**, then my strength will go from me, 1548
16:22 head began to grow *again* after he was **s**. 1548
Jer 41: 5 having their beards **s**, and their clothes rent, 1548
1Co 11: 5 for *that* is even all one as if she were **s**. *3587*
11: 6 *it* be a shame for a woman to be shorn or **s**, *3587*

SHAVSHA (1)
1Ch 18:16 *were* the priests; and **S** *was* scribe; 7798

SHE (981) [HER, HERS, HERSELF] See Index

SHEAF (9) [SHEAVES]
Ge 37: 7 and lo, my **s** arose, and also stood upright; 485
37: 7 round about, and made obeisance to my **s**. 485
Lev 23:10 ye shall bring a **s** of the firstfruits of your 6016
23:11 And he shall wave the **s** before the LORD, 6016
23:12 ye shall offer that day when ye wave the **s** a 6016
23:15 from the day that ye brought the **s** of 6016
Dt 24:19 hast forgot a **s** in the field, thou shalt not go 6016
Job 24:10 and they take away the **s** *from* the hungry; 6016
Zec 12: 6 the wood, and like a torch of fire in a **s**; 5995

SHEAL (1)
Ezr 10:29 and Adaiah, Jashub, and **S**, and Ramoth. 7594

SHEALTIEL (9)
Ezr 3: 2 Zerubbabel the son of **S**, and his brethren, 7597
3: 8 began Zerubbabel the son of **S**, and 7597
5: 2 rose up Zerubbabel the son of **S**, and 7598
Ne 12: 1 that went up with Zerubbabel the son of **S**, 7597
Hag 1: 1 the prophet unto Zerubbabel the son of **S**, 7597
1:12 Zerubbabel the son of **S**, and Joshua the son 7597
1:14 up the spirit of Zerubbabel the son of **S**, 7597
2: 2 Speak now to Zerubbabel the son of **S**, 7597
2:23 O Zerubbabel, my servant, the son of **S**, 7597

SHEAR (4) [SHEARER, SHEARERS, SHEARING, SHEEPSHEARERS, SHORN]
Ge 31:19 Laban went to **s** his sheep: and Rachel had 1494
38:13 in law goeth up to Timnath to **s** his sheep. 1494
Dt 15:19 thy bullock, nor **s** the firstling of thy sheep. 1494
1Sa 25: 4 in the wilderness that Nabal did **s** his sheep. 1494

SHEARD (1) [SHEARDS]
Isa 30:14 of it a **s** to take fire from the hearth, 2789

SHEARDS (1) [SHEARD]
Eze 23:34 thou shalt break the **s** thereof, and pluck off 2789

SHEARER (1) [SHEAR]
Ac 8:32 and like a lamb dumb before his **s**, so *2751*

SHEARERS (3) [SHEAR]
1Sa 25: 7 now I have heard that thou hast **s**: now thy 1494
25:11 my flesh that I have killed for my **s**, and 1494
Isa 53: 7 as a sheep before her **s** is dumb, so 1494

SHEARIAH (2)
1Ch 8:38 Ishmael, and **S**, and Obadiah, and Hanan. 8187
9:44 Ishmael, and **S**, and Obadiah, and Hanan: 8187

SHEARING (3) [SHEAR]
1Sa 25: 2 and he was **s** his sheep in Carmel. 1494
2Ki 10:12 *And* as he *was at* the **s** house in the way, 1044
10:14 slew them at the pit of the **s** house, 1044

SHEAR-JASHUB (1)
Isa 7: 3 now to meet Ahaz, thou, and **S** thy son, 7610

SHEATH (8)
1Sa 17:51 drew it out of the **s** thereof, and slew him, 8593
2Sa 20: 8 fastened upon his loins in the **s** thereof; 8593
1Ch 21:27 he put up his sword again into the **s** thereof. 5084
Eze 21: 3 will draw forth my sword out of his **s**, and 8593
21: 4 shall my sword go forth out of his **s** against 8593
21: 5 have drawn forth my sword out of his **s**: 8593
21:30 Shall I cause *it* to return into his **s**? I will 8593
Jn 18:11 unto Peter, Put up thy sword into the **s**: *2336*

SHEAVES (9) [SHEAF]
Ge 37: 7 we *were* binding **s** in the field, and lo, 485
37: 7 your **s** stood round about, and 485
Ru 2: 7 and gather after the reapers amongst the **s**: 6016
2:15 Let her glean even among the **s**, and 6016
Ne 13:15 and bringing in **s**, and lading asses; 6194
Ps 126: 6 with rejoicing, bringing his **s** *with him.* 485
129: 7 his hand; nor he that **bindeth s** his bosom. 6014
Am 2:13 as a cart is pressed *that is* full *of* **s**. 5995
Mic 4:12 for he shall gather them as the **s** into 5995

SHEBA (32) [BEER-SHEBA]
Ge 10: 7 and the sons of Raamah; **S**, and Dedan. 7614
10:28 And Obal, and Abimael, and **S**, 7614
25: 3 Jokshan begat **S**, and Dedan. And the sons 7614
Jos 19: 2 inheritance Beer-sheba, or **S**, and Moladah, 7652
2Sa 20: 1 whose name *was* **S**, the son of Bichri, 7652
20: 2 *and* followed **S** the son of Bichri: 7652
20: 6 Now shall **S** the son of Bichri do us more 7652
20: 7 to pursue after **S** the son of Bichri. 7652
20:10 Abishai his brother pursued after **S** the son 7652
20:13 to pursue after **S** the son of Bichri. 7652
20:21 **S** the son of Bichri by name, 7652
20:22 they cut off the head of **S** the son of Bichri, 7652
1Ki 10: 1 when the queen of **S** heard of the fame of 7614
10: 4 when the queen of **S** had seen all 7614
10:10 the queen of **S** gave to king Solomon. 7614
10:13 king Solomon gave unto the queen of **S** all 7614
1Ch 1: 9 And the sons of Raamah; **S**, and Dedan. 7614
1:22 And Ebal, and Abimael, and **S**, 7614
1:32 And the sons of Jokshan; **S**, and Dedan. 7614
5:13 **S**, and Jorai, and Jachan, and Zia, and 7652
2Ch 9: 1 when the queen of **S** heard of the fame of 7614
9: 3 when the queen of **S** had seen the wisdom 7614
9: 9 spice as the queen of **S** gave king Solomon. 7614
9:12 king Solomon gave to the queen of **S** all her 7614
Job 6:19 the companies of **S** waited for them. 7614
Ps 72:10 the kings of **S** and Seba shall offer gifts. 7614
72:15 and to him shall be given of the gold of **S**: 7614
Isa 60: 6 and Ephah; all they from **S** shall come: 7614
Jer 6:20 cometh there to me incense from **S**, 7614
Eze 27:22 The merchants of **S** and Raamah, they *were* 7614
27:23 Eden, the merchants of **S**, Asshur, *and* 7614
38:13 **S**, and Dedan, and the merchants of 7614

SHEBAH (1) [BEER-SHEBA]
Ge 26:33 he called it **S**: therefore the name of the city 7656

SHEBAM (1)
Nu 32: 3 and Elealeh, and **S**, and Nebo, and Beon, 7643

SHEBANIAH (7)
1Ch 15:24 **S**, and Jehoshaphat, and Nethaneel, and 7645
Ne 9: 4 Jeshua, and Bani, Kadmiel, **S**, Bunni, 7645
9: 5 Hodijah, **S**, *and* Pethahiah, said, Stand up 7645
10: 4 Hattush, **S**, Malluch, 7645
10:10 **S**, Hodijah, Kelita, Pelaiah, Hanan, 7645
10:12 Zaccur, Sherebiah, **S**, 7645
12:14 Of Melicu, Jonathan; of **S**, Joseph; 7645

SHEBARIM (1)
Jos 7: 5 them *from* before the gate *even* unto **S**, 7671

SHEBAT See SEBAT

SHEBER (1)
1Ch 2:48 Caleb's concubine, bare **S**, and Tirhanah. 7669

SHEBNA (9)
2Ki 18:18 **S** the scribe, and Joah the son of Asaph 7644
18:26 **S**, and Joah, unto Rab-shakeh, Speak, 7644
18:37 **S** the scribe, and Joah the son of Asaph 7644
19: 2 **S** the scribe, and the elders of the priests, 7644
Isa 22:15 *even* unto **S**, which *is* over the house, *and* 7644
36: 3 **S** the scribe, and Joah, Asaph's son, 7644
36:11 said Eliakim and **S** and Joah unto 7644
36:22 **S** the scribe, and Joah, the son of Asaph, 7644
37: 2 **S** the scribe, and the elders of the priests 7644

SHEBUEL (3)
1Ch 23:16 *Of* the sons of Gershom, **S** *was* the chief. 7619
25: 4 Uzziel, **S**, and Jerimoth, Hananiah, Hanani, 7619
26:24 **S** the son of Gershom, the son of Moses, 7619

SHECANIAH (2)
1Ch 24:11 The ninth to Jeshua, the tenth to **S**, 7935
2Ch 31:15 and Jeshua, and Shemaiah, Amariah, and **S**, 7935

SHECHANIAH (8)
1Ch 3:21 the sons of Obadiah, the sons of **S**. 7935
3:22 the sons of **S**; Shemaiah: and the sons of 7935
Ezr 8: 3 Of the sons of **S**, of the sons of Pharosh; 7935
8: 5 Of the sons of **S**; the son of Jahaziel, and 7935
10: 2 **S** the son of Jehiel, *one* of the sons of Elam, 7935
Ne 3:29 him repaired also Shemaiah the son of **S**, 7935
6:18 he *was* the son in law of **S** the son of Arah; 7935
12: 3 **S**, Rehum, Meremoth, 7935

SHECHEM (62) [SHECHEM'S, SHECHEMITES, SYCHEM]
Ge 33:18 Jacob came to Shalem, a city of **S**, which *is* 7927
34: 2 when **S** the son of Hamor the Hivite, 7928
34: 3 **S** spake unto his father Hamor, saying, 7928
34: 6 Hamor the father of **S** went out unto Jacob 7928
34: 8 The soul of my son **S** longeth for your 7928
34:11 **S** said unto her father and unto her 7928
34:13 the sons of Jacob answered **S** and Hamor 7928
34:18 words pleased Hamor, and **S** Hamor's son. 7928
34:20 **S** his son came unto the gate of their city, 7928
34:24 unto **S** his son hearkened all that went out 7928
34:26 and **S** his son with the edge of the sword, 7928
35: 4 hid them under the oak which *was* by **S**. 7927
37:12 went to feed their father's flock in **S**. 7927
37:13 Do not thy brethren feed *the flock* in **S**? 7927
37:14 of the vale of Hebron, and he came to **S**. 7927
Nu 26:31 and *of* **S**, the family of the Shechemites: 7928
Jos 17: 2 for the children of **S**, and for the children of 7928
17: 7 Asher *to* Michmethah, that *lieth* before **S**; 7927
20: 7 **S** in mount Ephraim, and Kirjath-arba, 7927
21:21 For they gave them **S** with her suburbs in 7927
24: 1 Joshua gathered all the tribes of Israel to **S**, 7927
24:25 set them a statute and an ordinance in **S**. 7927
24:32 brought up out of Egypt, buried they in **S**, 7927
24:32 father of **S** for an hundred pieces of silver: 7927
Jdg 8:31 his concubine that *was* in **S**, she also bare 7927
9: 1 Abimelech the son of Jerubbaal went to **S** 7927
9: 2 I pray you, in the ears of all the men of **S**, 7927
9: 3 the ears of all the men of **S** all these words: 7927
9: 6 all the men of **S** gathered together, and 7927
9: 6 by the plain of the pillar that *was* in **S**. 7927
9: 7 unto them, Hearken unto me, you men of **S**, 7927
9:18 king over the men of **S**, because he *is* your 7927
9:20 devour the men of **S**, and the house of 7927
9:20 let fire come out from the men of **S**, and 7927
9:23 spirit between Abimelech and the men of **S**; 7927
9:23 the men of **S** dealt treacherously with 7927
9:24 upon the men of **S**, which aided him in 7927
9:25 the men of **S** set liers in wait for him in 7927
9:26 came with his brethren, and went over to **S**: 7927
9:26 the men of **S** put their confidence in him. 7927
9:28 Who *is* Abimelech, and who *is* **S**, that we 7927
9:28 serve the men of Hamor the father of **S**: 7927
9:31 son of Ebed and his brethren be come to **S**; 7927
9:34 they laid wait against **S** *in* four companies. 7927
9:39 Gaal went out before the men of **S**, and 7927
9:41 that *they* should not dwell in **S**. 7927
9:46 when all the men of the tower of **S** heard 7927
9:47 that all the men of the tower of **S** were 7927
9:49 that all the men of the tower of **S** died also, 7927
9:57 all the evil of the men of **S** did God render 7927
21:19 highway that goeth up from Beth-el to **S**, 7927
1Ki 12: 1 Rehoboam went *to* **S**: for all Israel were 7927
12: 1 for all Israel were come *to* **S** to make him 7927
12:25 Jeroboam built **S** in mount Ephraim, and 7927
1Ch 6:67 **S** in mount Ephraim with her suburbs; 7927
7:19 Ahian, and **S**, and Likhi, and Aniam. 7928
7:28 **S** also and the towns thereof, unto Gaza and 7927
2Ch 10: 1 Rehoboam went to **S**: for *to* Shechem were 7927
10: 1 for *to* **S** were all Israel come to make him 7927
Ps 60: 6 I will divide **S**, and mete out the valley of 7927
108: 7 I will divide **S**, and mete out the valley of 7927
Jer 41: 5 That there came certain from **S**, 7927

SHECHEM'S (2) [SHECHEM]
Ge 33:19 **S** father, for an hundred pieces of money. 7928
34:26 took Dinah out of **S** house, and went out. 7928

SHECHEMITES (1) [SHECHEM]
Nu 26:31 and *of* Shechem, the family of the **S**: 7930

SHED (52) [SHEDDER, SHEDDETH, SHEDDING]
Ge 9: 6 man's blood, by man shall his blood be **s**: 8210
37:22 **S** no blood, *but* cast him into this pit that *is* 8210
Ex 22: 2 he die, *there shall* no blood *be* **s** for him. NIH
22: 3 upon him, *there shall be* blood **s** for him; NIH
Lev 17: 4 he hath **s** blood; and that man shall be cut 8210
Nu 35:33 be cleansed of the blood that is **s** therein, 8210
35:33 but by the blood of him that **s** it. 8210
Dt 19:10 That innocent blood be not **s** in thy land, 8210
21: 7 and say, Our hands have not **s** this blood, 8210
1Sa 25:26 withholden thee from coming to **s** blood, NIH
25:31 either that thou hast **s** blood causeless, or 8210
25:33 kept me this day from coming to **s** blood, NIH
2Sa 20:10 and **s out** his bowels to the ground, 8210
1Ki 2: 5 **s** the blood of war in peace, and put 7760
2:31 which Joab **s**, from me, and from the house 8210
2Ki 21:16 Moreover Manasseh **s** innocent blood very 8210
24: 4 also *for* the innocent blood that he **s**: for he 8210
1Ch 22: 8 Thou hast **s** blood abundantly, and 8210
22: 8 thou hast **s** much blood upon the earth in 8210
28: 3 *hast been* a man of war, and hast **s** blood. 8210
Ps 79: 3 Their blood have they **s** like water round 8210
79:10 of the blood of thy servants which is **s**. 8210
106:38 **s** innocent blood, *even* the blood of their 8210
Pr 1:16 feet run to evil, and make haste to **s** blood. 8210
6:17 and hands that **s** innocent blood, 8210
Isa 59: 7 and they make haste to **s** innocent blood: 8210
Jer 7: 6 and **s** not innocent blood in this place, 8210
22: 3 neither **s** innocent blood in this place. 8210
22:17 for to **s** innocent blood, and for oppression, 8210
La 4:13 that *have* **s** the blood of the just in the midst 8210
Eze 16:38 that break wedlock and **s** blood are judged; 8210
22: 4 become guilty in thy blood that thou hast **s**; 8210
22: 6 every one were in thee to their power to **s** 8210
22: 9 In thee are men that carry tales to **s** blood: 8210
22:12 In thee have they taken gifts to **s** blood; 8210
22:27 to **s** blood, *and* to destroy souls, to get 8210
23:45 after the manner of *women* that **s** blood; 8210
33:25 your eyes toward your idols, and **s** blood: 8210
35: 5 hast **s** *the blood of* the children of Israel by 5064
36:18 for the blood that they had **s** upon the land, 8210
Joel 3:19 they have **s** innocent blood in their land. 8210
Mt 23:35 all the righteous blood **s** upon the earth, *1632*
26:28 which is **s** for many for the remission of *1632*
Mk 14:24 of the new testament, which is **s** for many. *1632*
Lk 11:50 which was **s** from the foundation of *1632*
22:20 testament in my blood, which is **s** for you. *1632*
Ac 2:33 he hath **s forth** this, which ye now see and *1632*
22:20 the blood of thy martyr Stephen was **s**, *1632*
Ro 3:15 Their feet *are* swift to **s** blood: *1632*
5: 5 the love of God is **s abroad** in our hearts *1632*
Tit 3: 6 Which he **s** on us abundantly through Jesus *1632*
Rev 16: 6 For they have **s** the blood of saints and *1632*

SHEDDER (1) [SHED]
Eze 18:10 a **s** of blood, and *that* doeth the like to *any* 8210

SHEDDETH (2) [SHED]
Ge 9: 6 Whoso **s** man's blood, by man shall his 8210
Eze 22: 3 The city **s** blood in the midst of it, that her 8210

SHEDDING (1) [SHED]
Heb 9:22 and without **s of blood** is no remission. *130*

SHEDEUR (5)
Nu 1: 5 of *the tribe of* Reuben; Elizur the son of **S**. 7707
2:10 of Reuben *shall be* Elizur the son of **S**. 7707
7:30 On the fourth day Elizur the son of **S**, 7707
7:35 this *was* the offering of Elizur the son of **S**. 7707
10:18 and over his host *was* Elizur the son of **S**. 7707

SHEEP (187) [SHEEP'S, SHEEPCOTE, SHEEPCOTES, SHEEPFOLD, SHEEPFOLDS, SHEEPMASTER, SHEEPSHEARERS, SHEEPSKINS, SHEPHERD, SHEPHERD'S, SHEPHERDS, SHEPHERDS']
Ge 4: 2 Abel was a keeper of **s**, but Cain was a 6629
12:16 he had **s**, and oxen, and he asses, and 6629
20:14 Abimelech took **s**, and oxen, and 6629
21:27 Abraham took **s** and oxen, and gave *them* 6629
29: 2 lo, there *were* three flocks of **s** lying by it; 6629
29: 3 watered the **s**, and put the stone again upon 6629
29: 6 Rachel his daughter cometh with the **s**. 6629
29: 7 water ye the **s**, and go *and* feed *them*. 6629
29: 8 from the well's mouth; then we water the **s**. 6629
29: 9 with them, Rachel came with her father's **s**: 6629
29:10 the **s** of Laban his mother's brother, 6629
30:32 all the brown cattle among the **s**, and 3775
30:33 the goats, and brown amongst the **s**, 3775
30:35 all the brown amongst the **s**, and gave *them* 3775
31:19 Laban went to shear his **s**: and Rachel had 6629
34:28 They took their **s**, and their oxen, and their 6629
38:13 in law goeth up to Timnath to shear his **s**. 6629
Ex 9: 3 the camels, upon the oxen, and upon the **s**: 6629
12: 5 ye shall take *it* out from the **s**, or from 3532
20:24 thy peace offerings, thy **s**, and thine oxen: 6629
22: 1 shall steal an ox, or a **s**, and kill it, or sell it; 7716
22: 1 five oxen for an ox, and four **s** for a sheep. 6629
22: 1 five oxen for an ox, and four sheep for a **s**. 7716
22: 4 his hand alive, whether it be ox, or ass, or **s**; 7716
22: 9 for ass, for **s**, for raiment, *or* for any 7716
22:10 or an ox, or a **s**, or any beast, to keep; 7716
22:30 thou do with thine oxen, *and* with thy **s**: 6629
34:19 thy cattle, *whether* ox or **s**, *that* is male. 7716
Lev 1:10 *namely,* of the **s**, or of the goats, for a burnt 3775
7:23 eat no *manner* fat, of ox, or of **s**, or of goat. 3775
22:19 of the beeves, of the **s**, or of the goats. 3775
22:21 or a freewill offering in beeves or **s**, it shall 6629
22:27 or a **s**, or a goat, is brought forth, then 3775
27:26 man shall sanctify it; whether *it be* ox, or **s**: 7716
Nu 18:17 or the firstling of a **s**, or the firstling of a 3775
22:40 Balak offered oxen and **s**, and sent to 6629
27:17 be not as **s** which have no shepherd. 6629
31:28 of the beeves, and of the asses, and of the **s**: 6629
31:32 and seventy thousand and five thousand **s**, 6629
31:36 and thirty thousand and five hundred **s**: 6629
31:37 the LORD'S tribute of the **s** was six 6629
31:43 *and* seven thousand and five hundred **s**, 6629
32:24 for your little ones, and folds for your **s**; 6792
32:36 fenced cities: and folds for **s**. 6629
Dt 7:13 increase of thy kine, and the flocks of thy **s**, 6629
14: 4 shall eat: the ox, the **s**, and the goat, 3775+7716
14:26 or for **s**, or for wine, or for strong drink, or 6629
15:19 thy bullock, nor shear the firstling of thy **s**. 6629
17: 1 or **s**, wherein is blemish, *or* any evil 7716
18: 3 that offer a sacrifice, whether *it be* ox or **s**; 7716
18: 4 thy oil, and the first of the fleece of thy **s**, 6629
22: 1 not see thy brother's ox or his **s** go astray, 7716
28: 4 increase of thy kine, and the flocks of thy **s**. 6629
28:18 increase of thy kine, and the flocks of thy **s**. 6629
28:31 thy **s** *shall be* given unto thine enemies, 6629
28:51 the increase of thy kine, or flocks of thy **s**, 6629
32:14 Butter of kine, and milk of **s**, with fat of 6629
Jos 6:21 and old, and ox, and **s**, and ass, 7716
7:24 and his **s**, and his tent, and all that he had: 6629
Jdg 6: 4 for Israel, neither **s**, nor ox, nor ass. 7716
1Sa 8:17 He will take the tenth of your **s**: and 6629
14:32 took **s**, and oxen, and calves, and slew *them* 6629
14:34 every man his **s**, and slay *them* here, and 7716
15: 3 and suckling, ox and **s**, camel and ass. 7716
15: 9 the best of the **s**, and of the oxen, and of 6629
15:14 then this bleating of the **s** in mine ears, 6629
15:15 for the people spared the best of the **s** and 6629
15:21 the people took of the spoil, **s** and oxen, 6629
16:11 the youngest, and behold, he keepeth the **s**. 6629
16:19 Send me David thy son, which *is* with the **s**. 6629
17:15 returned from Saul to feed his father's **s** *at* 6629
17:20 left the **s** with a keeper, and took, and went, 6629
17:28 with whom hast thou left those few **s** in 6629
17:34 Thy servant kept his father's **s**, and 6629
22:19 and sucklings, and oxen, and asses, and **s**, 7716
25: 2 he had three thousand **s**, and a thousand 6629
25: 2 and he was shearing his **s** in Carmel. 6629
25: 4 in the wilderness that Nabal did shear his **s**. 6629
25:16 the while we were with them keeping the **s**. 6629
25:18 five **s** ready dressed, and five measures of 6629
27: 9 took away the **s**, and the oxen, and 6629
2Sa 7: 8 from following the **s**, to be ruler over my 6629
17:29 butter, and **s**, and cheese of kine, for David, 6629
24:17 these **s**, what have they done? let thine 6629
1Ki 1: 9 Adonijah slew **s** and oxen and fat cattle by 6629
1:19 and fat cattle and **s** in abundance, 6629
1:25 and fat cattle and **s** in abundance, 6629
4:23 an hundred **s**, beside harts, and roebucks, 6629
8: 5 him before the ark, sacrificing **s** and oxen, 6629
8:63 and an hundred and twenty thousand **s**. 6629
22:17 the hills, as **s** that have not a shepherd: 6629
2Ki 5:26 **s**, and oxen, and menservants, and 6629
1Ch 5:21 *of* **s** two hundred and fifty thousand, and 6629
12:40 wine, and oil, and oxen, and **s** abundantly: 6629
17: 7 the sheepcote, *even* from following the **s**, 6629
21:17 *as for* these **s**, what have they done? 6629
2Ch 5: 6 sacrificed **s** and oxen, which could not be 6629
7: 5 and an hundred and twenty thousand **s**: 6629
14:15 carried away **s** and camels in abundance, 6629
15:11 seven hundred oxen and seven thousand **s**. 6629
18: 2 Ahab killed **s** and oxen for him in 6629
18:16 the mountains, as **s** that have no shepherd: 6629
29:33 six hundred oxen and three thousand **s**. 6629
30:24 a thousand bullocks and seven thousand **s**; 6629
30:24 a thousand bullocks and ten thousand **s**: 6629
31: 6 they also brought in the tithe of oxen and **s**, 6629
Ne 3: 1 the priests, and they built the **s** gate; 6629
3:32 unto the **s** gate repaired the goldsmiths 6629
5:18 *for me* daily *was* one ox *and* six choice **s**; 6629
12:39 the tower of Meah, even unto the **s** gate: 6629
Job 1: 3 His substance also was seven thousand **s**, 6629
1:16 hath burnt up the **s**, and the servants, and 6629
31:20 were *not* warmed with the fleece of my **s**; 3532
42:12 for he had fourteen thousand **s**, and 6629
Ps 8: 7 All **s** and oxen, yea, and the beasts of 6792
44:11 Thou hast given us like **s** appointed for 6629
44:22 we are counted as **s** for the slaughter. 6629
49:14 Like **s** they are laid in the grave; death shall 6629
74: 1 *why* doth thine anger smoke against the **s** 6629
78:52 made his own people to go forth like **s**, and 6629
79:13 **s** of thy pasture will give thee thanks for 6629
95: 7 people of his pasture, and the **s** of his hand. 6629
100: 3 *we are* his people, and the **s** of his pasture. 6629
119:176 I have gone astray like a lost **s**; seek thy 7716
144:13 *that* our **s** may bring forth thousands and 6629
SS 4: 2 Thy teeth *are* like a flock of **s** *that are* even NIH
6: 6 Thy teeth *are* as a flock of **s** which go up 7353
Isa 7:21 man shall nourish a young cow, and two **s**; 6629
13:14 and as a **s** that no *man* taketh up: 6629
22:13 killing **s**, eating flesh, and drinking wine: 6629
53: 6 All we like **s** have gone astray; we have 6629
53: 7 as a **s** before her shearers is dumb, so 7353
Jer 12: 3 pull them out like **s** for the slaughter, and 6629
23: 1 that destroy and scatter the **s** of my pasture! 6629
50: 6 My people hath been lost **s**: their shepherds 6629
50:17 Israel *is* a scattered **s**; the lions have driven 7716
Eze 34: 6 My **s** wandered through all the mountains, 6629
34:11 will both search my **s**, and seek them out. 6629
34:12 that he is among his **s** *that are* scattered; 6629
34:12 so will I seek out my **s**, and will deliver 6629
Hos 12:12 served for a wife, and for a wife he kept *s*. NIH
Joel 1:18 yea, the flocks of **s** are made desolate. 6629
Mic 2:12 I will put them together as the **s** of Bozrah, 6629
5: 8 as a young lion among the flocks of **s**: 6629
Zec 13: 7 the shepherd, and the **s** shall be scattered: 6629
Mt 9:36 scattered abroad, as **s** having no shepherd. *4263*
10: 6 But go rather to the lost **s** of the house of *4263*
10:16 I send you forth as **s** in the midst of wolves: *4263*
12:11 that shall have one **s**, and if it fall into a pit *4263*
12:12 How much then is a man better than a **s**? *4263*
15:24 but unto the lost **s** of the house of Israel. *4263*
18:12 if a man have an hundred **s**, and one of *4263*
18:13 he rejoiceth more of that *s*, than of NIG

S

Mt 25:32 as a shepherd divideth *his* s from the goats: *4263*
25:33 And he shall set the s on his right hand, but *4263*
26:31 the s of the flock shall be scattered abroad. *4263*
Mk 6:34 they were as s not having a shepherd: *4263*
14:27 the shepherd, and the s shall be scattered. *4263*
Lk 15: 4 What man of you, having an hundred s, *4263*
15: 6 for I have found my s which was lost. *4263*
Jn 2:14 those that sold oxen and s and doves, *4263*
2:15 out of the temple, and the s and the oxen; *4263*
5: 2 Now there is at Jerusalem by the s *market* a *4262*
10: 2 in by the door is the shepherd of the s. *4263*
10: 3 the porter openeth; and the s hear his voice: *4263*
10: 3 and he calleth his own s by name, and *4263*
10: 4 And when he putteth forth his own s, he *4263*
10: 4 he goeth before them, and the s follow him: *4263*
10: 7 I say unto you, I am the door of the s. *4263*
10: 8 and robbers: but the s did not hear them. *4263*
10:11 the good shepherd giveth his life for the s. *4263*
10:12 not the shepherd, whose own the s are not, *4263*
10:12 wolf coming, and leaveth the s, and fleeth: *4263*
10:12 the wolf catcheth them, and scattereth the s. *4263*
10:13 he is a hireling, and careth not for the s. *4263*
10:14 and know my *s,* and am known of mine. NIG
10:15 the Father: and I lay down my life for the s. *4263*
10:16 And other s I have, which are not of this *4263*
10:26 because ye are not of my s, as I said unto *4263*
10:27 My s hear my voice, and I know them, and *4263*
21:16 I love thee. He saith unto him, Feed my s. *4263*
21:17 love thee. Jesus saith unto him, Feed my s. *4263*
Ac 8:32 was this, He was led as a s to the slaughter; *4263*
Ro 8:36 we are accounted as s for the slaughter. *4263*
Heb 13:20 *that* great shepherd of the s, through *4263*
1Pe 2:25 For ye were as s going astray; but are now *4263*
Rev 18:13 and s, and horses, and chariots, and slaves, *4263*

SHEEP'S (1) [SHEEP]
Mt 7:15 which come to you in s clothing, but *4263*

SHEEPCOTE (2) [SHEEP]
2Sa 7: 8 I took thee from the s, from following 5116
1Ch 17: 7 I took thee from the s, *even* from following 5116

SHEEPCOTES (1) [SHEEP]
1Sa 24: 3 he came to the s by the way, where 1448+6629

SHEEPFOLD (1) [FOLD, SHEEP]
Jn 10: 1 not by the door into the s, *833+3588+4263*

SHEEPFOLDS (3) [FOLD, SHEEP]
Nu 32:16 We will build s here for our cattle, 1448+6629
Jdg 5:16 Why abodest thou among the s, to hear 4942
Ps 78:70 his servant, and took him from the s: 4356+6629

SHEEPMASTER (1) [MASTER, SHEEP]
2Ki 3: 4 Mesha king of Moab was a s, and 5349

SHEEPSHEARERS (3) [SHEAR, SHEEP]
Ge 38:12 went up unto his s to Timnath, he 1494+6629
2Sa 13:23 that Absalom had s in Baal-hazor, which *is* 1494
13:24 and said, Behold now, thy servant hath s; 1494

SHEEPSKINS (1) [SHEEP, SKIN]
Heb 11:37 they wandered about in s and goatskins; *3374*

SHEERAH See SHERAH

SHEET (2) [SHEETS]
Ac 10:11 as *it had been* a great s knit at the four *3607*
11: 5 vessel descend, as *it had been* a great s, *3607*

SHEETS (2) [SHEET]
Jdg 14:12 I will give you thirty s and thirty change of 5466
14:13 shall ye give me thirty s and thirty change 5466

SHEHARIAH (1)
1Ch 8:26 And Shamsherai, and S, and Athaliah, 7841

SHEKEL (43) [SHEKELS]
Ge 24:22 took a golden earring of half a s weight, 1235
Ex 30:13 half a s after the shekel of the sanctuary: 8255
30:13 half a shekel after the s of the sanctuary: 8255
30:13 (a s *is* twenty gerahs:) a half shekel *shall be* 8255
30:13 a half s *shall be* the offering of the LORD. 8255
30:15 the poor shall not give less than half a s, 8255
30:24 of cassia five hundred *shekels,* after the s of 8255
38:24 thirty shekels, after the s of the sanctuary. 8255
38:25 fifteen shekels, after the s of the sanctuary: 8255
38:26 A bekah for every man, *that is,* half a s, 8255
38:26 *is,* half a shekel, after the s of the sanctuary, 8255
Lev 5:15 after the s of the sanctuary, for a trespass 8255
27: 3 of silver, after the s of the sanctuary. 8255
27:25 shall be according to the s of the sanctuary: 8255
27:25 the sanctuary: twenty gerahs shall be the s. 8255
Nu 3:47 after the s of the sanctuary shalt thou take 8255
3:47 thou take *them:* (the s *is* twenty gerahs:) 8255
3:50 five *shekels,* after the s of the sanctuary: 8255
7:13 after the s of the sanctuary; 8255
7:19 after the s of the sanctuary; 8255
7:25 after the s of the sanctuary; 8255
7:31 after the s of the sanctuary; 8255
7:37 after the s of the sanctuary; 8255
7:43 after the s of the sanctuary; 8255
7:49 after the s of the sanctuary; 8255
7:55 after the s of the sanctuary; 8255
7:61 after the s of the sanctuary; 8255
7:67 after the s of the sanctuary; 8255
7:73 after the s of the sanctuary; 8255
7:79 after the s of the sanctuary; 8255
7:85 four hundred *shekels,* after the s of 8255
7:86 *shekels* apiece, after the s of the sanctuary: 8255
18:16 after the s of the sanctuary, which *is* twenty 8255
1Sa 9: 8 I have here at hand the fourth part of a s of 8255
2Ki 7: 1 *shall* a measure of fine flour *be sold* for a s, 8255
7: 1 two measures of barley for a s, in the gate 8255
7:16 So a measure of fine flour was *sold* for a s, 8255
7:16 two measures of barley for a s, according to 8255
7:18 Two measures of barley for a s, and 8255
7:18 a shekel, and a measure of fine flour for a s, 8255
Ne 10:32 a s for the service of the house of our God; 8255
Eze 45:12 the s *shall be* twenty gerahs: 8255
Am 8: 5 the s great, and falsifying the balances by 8255

SHEKELS (96) [SHEKEL]
Ge 23:15 the land *is worth* four hundred s of silver; 8255
23:16 four hundred s of silver, current *money* 8255
24:22 two bracelets for her hands of ten *s* weight NIH
Ex 21:32 he shall give unto their master thirty s *of* 8255
30:23 of pure myrrh five hundred *s,* and of sweet NIH
30:23 *even* two hundred and fifty *s,* and of sweet NIH
30:23 of sweet calamus two hundred and fifty *s,* NIH
30:24 of cassia five hundred *s,* after the shekel of NIH
38:24 nine talents, and seven hundred and thirty s, 8255
38:25 seven hundred and threescore and fifteen s, 8255
38:28 and five *s* he made hooks for the pillars, NIH
38:29 and two thousand and four hundred s. 8255
Lev 5:15 with thy estimation *by* s of silver, after 8255
27: 3 even thy estimation shall be fifty s of silver, 8255
27: 4 then thy estimation shall be thirty s. 8255
27: 5 estimation shall be of the male twenty s, 8255
27: 5 twenty shekels, and for the female ten s. 8255
27: 6 thy estimation shall be of the male five s of 8255
27: 6 thy estimation *shall be* three s of silver. 8255
27: 7 thy estimation shall be fifteen s, and for 8255
27: 7 be fifteen shekels, and for the female ten s. 8255
27:16 seed *shall be valued* at fifty s of silver. 8255
Nu 3:47 Thou shalt even take five s apiece by 8255
3:50 and five *s,* after the shekel of the sanctuary: NIH
7:13 thirty *s,* one silver bowl of seventy shekels, NIH
7:13 thirty *shekels,* one silver bowl of seventy s, 8255
7:14 One spoon of ten *s* of gold, full *of* incense: NIH
7:19 thirty *s,* one silver bowl of seventy shekels, NIH
7:19 thirty *shekels,* one silver bowl of seventy s, 8255
7:20 One spoon of gold of ten *s,* full *of* incense: NIH
7:25 thirty *s,* one silver bowl of seventy shekels, NIH
7:25 thirty *shekels,* one silver bowl of seventy s, 8255
7:26 One golden spoon of ten *s,* full *of* incense: NIH
7:31 thirty *s,* one silver bowl of seventy shekels, NIH
7:31 thirty *shekels,* one silver bowl of seventy s, 8255
7:32 One golden spoon *of* ten *s,* full *of* incense: NIH
7:37 thirty *s,* one silver bowl of seventy shekels, NIH
7:37 thirty *shekels,* one silver bowl of seventy s, 8255
7:38 One golden spoon of ten *s,* full *of* incense: NIH
7:43 thirty *s,* a silver bowl of seventy shekels, NIH
7:43 thirty *shekels,* a silver bowl of seventy s, 8255
7:44 One golden spoon of ten *s,* full *of* incense: NIH
7:49 thirty *s,* one silver bowl of seventy shekels, NIH
7:49 thirty *shekels,* one silver bowl of seventy s, 8255
7:50 One golden spoon of ten *s,* full *of* incense: NIH
7:55 thirty *s,* one silver bowl of seventy shekels, NIH
7:55 thirty *shekels,* one silver bowl of seventy s, 8255

Nu 7:56 One golden spoon of ten *s*, full *of* incense: NIH
7:61 thirty *s*, one silver bowl of seventy shekels, NIH
7:61 thirty *shekels,* one silver bowl of seventy **s**, 8255
7:62 One golden spoon of ten *s*, full *of* incense: NIH
7:67 thirty *s*, one silver bowl of seventy shekels, NIH
7:67 thirty *shekels,* one silver bowl of seventy **s**, 8255
7:68 One golden spoon of ten *s*, full *of* incense: NIH
7:73 thirty *s*, one silver bowl of seventy shekels, NIH
7:73 thirty *shekels,* one silver bowl of seventy **s**, 8255
7:74 One golden spoon of ten *s*, full *of* incense: NIH
7:79 thirty *s*, one silver bowl of seventy shekels, NIH
7:79 thirty *shekels,* one silver bowl of seventy **s**, 8255
7:80 One golden spoon of ten *s*, full *of* incense: NIH
7:85 an hundred and thirty *s*, each bowl seventy: NIH
7:85 four hundred *s*, after the shekel of NIH
7:86 full *of* incense, *weighing* ten *s* apiece, NIH
7:86 of the spoons *was* an hundred and twenty *s*. NIH
18:16 to thine estimation, *for* the money of five **s**, 8255
31:52 sixteen thousand seven hundred and fifty **s**. 8255
Dt 22:19 they shall amerce him in an hundred *s* of NIH
22:29 unto the damsel's father fifty *s* of silver, NIH
Jos 7:21 two hundred **s** *of* silver, and a wedge of 8255
7:21 a wedge of gold of fifty **s** weight, then 8255
Jdg 8:26 a thousand and seven hundred *s* of gold; NIH
17: 2 The eleven hundred *s* of silver that were NIH
17: 3 when he had restored the eleven hundred *s* NIH
17: 4 and his mother took two hundred *s* of silver, NIH
17:10 I will give thee ten *s* of silver by the year, NIH
1Sa 17: 5 the weight of the coat *was* five thousand **s** 8255
17: 7 his spear's head *weighed* six hundred **s** *of* 8255
2Sa 14:26 *at* two hundred **s** after the king's weight. 8255
18:11 I would have given thee ten *s of* silver, and NIH
18:12 Though I should receive a thousand *s of* NIH
21:16 *weighed* three hundred *s* of brass *in* weight, NIH
24:24 and the oxen for fifty **s** of silver. 8255
1Ki 10:16 six hundred *s* of gold went to one target. NIH
10:29 went out of Egypt for six hundred *s* of NIH
2Ki 15:20 of each man fifty **s** *of* silver, to give to 8255
1Ch 21:25 the place six hundred **s** of gold *by* weight. 8255
2Ch 1:17 Egypt a chariot for six hundred *s* of silver, NIH
3: 9 the weight of the nails *was* fifty **s** of gold. 8255
9:15 six hundred *s* of beaten gold went to one NIH
9:16 three hundred *s* of gold went to one shield. NIH
Ne 5:15 and wine, beside forty **s** of silver; 8255
Jer 32: 9 him the money, *even* seventeen **s** of silver. 8255
Eze 4:10 shalt eat *shall be* by weight, twenty **s** a day: 8255
45:12 twenty **s**, five and twenty shekels, 8255
45:12 five and twenty **s**, fifteen shekels, 8255
45:12 five and twenty shekels, fifteen **s**, 8255

SHELAH (11) [SHELANITES]

Ge 38: 5 and bare a son; and called his name **S**: 7956
38:11 thy father's house, till **S** my son be grown: 7956
38:14 for she saw that **S** was grown, and she was 7956
38:26 because that I gave her not to **S** my son. 7956
46:12 and Onan, and **S**, and Pharez, and Zerah: 7956
Nu 26:20 of **S**, the family of the Shelanites: 7956
1Ch 1:18 Arphaxad begat **S**, and Shelah begat Eber. 7974
1:18 Arphaxad begat Shelah, and **S** begat Eber. 7974
1:24 Shem, Arphaxad, **S**, 7974
2: 3 The sons of Judah; Er, and Onan, and **S**: 7956
4:21 The sons of **S** the son of Judah *were,* Er 7956

SHELANITES (1) [SHELAH]

Nu 26:20 of Shelah, the family of the **S**: 8024

SHELEMIAH (10)

1Ch 26:14 the lot eastward fell to **S**. Then *for* 8018
Ezr 10:39 And **S**, and Nathan, and Adaiah, 8018
10:41 Azareel, and **S**, Shemariah, 8018
Ne 3:30 After him repaired Hananiah the son of **S**, 8018
13:13 **S** the priest, and Zadok the scribe, and 8018
Jer 36:14 the son of **S**, the son of Cushi, unto Baruch, 8018
36:26 **S** the son of Abdeel, to take Baruch 8018
37: 3 Zedekiah the king sent Jehucal the son of **S** 8018
37:13 the son of **S**, the son of Hananiah; 8018
38: 1 Jucal the son of **S**, and Pashur the son of 8018

SHELEPH (2)

Ge 10:26 and **S**, and Hazarmaveth, and Jerah, 8026
1Ch 1:20 and **S**, and Hazarmaveth, and Jerah, 8026

SHELESH (1)

1Ch 7:35 Zophah, and Imna, and **S**, and Amal. 8028

SHELOMI (1)

Nu 34:27 the children of Asher, Ahihud the son of **S**. 8015

SHELOMITH (9) [SHELOMOTH]

Lev 24:11 (and his mother's name *was* **S**, the daughter 8019
1Ch 3:19 and Hananiah, and **S** their sister: 8019
23: 9 of Shimei; **S**, and Haziel, and Haran, three. 8019
23:18 *Of* the sons of Izhar; **S** the chief. 8019
26:25 his son, and Zichri his son, and **S** his son. 8019
26:26 Which **S** and his brethren *were* over all 8019
26:28 *anything, it was* under the hand of **S**, 8019
2Ch 11:20 him Abijah, and Attai, and Ziza, and **S**. 8019
Ezr 8:10 of the sons of **S**; the son of Josiphiah, and 8019

SHELOMOTH (2) [SHELOMITH]

1Ch 24:22 Of the Izharites; **S**: of the sons of 8013
24:22 Shelomoth: of the sons of **S**; Jahath. 8013

SHELTER (2)

Job 24: 8 and embrace the rock for want of a **s**. 4268
Ps 61: 3 For thou hast been a **s** for me, *and* a strong 4268

SHELUMIEL (5)

Nu 1: 6 Of Simeon; **S** the son of Zurishaddai. 8017
2:12 Simeon *shall be* **S** the son of Zurishaddai. 8017
7:36 On the fifth day **S** the son of Zurishaddai, 8017
7:41 this *was* the offering of **S** the son of 8017
10:19 of Simeon *was* **S** the son of Zurishaddai. 8017

SHEM (17) [SEM]

Ge 5:32 and Noah begat **S**, Ham, and Japheth. 8035
6:10 begat three sons, **S**, Ham, and Japheth. 8035
7:13 **S**, and Ham, and Japheth, the sons of Noah, 8035
9:18 of the ark, were **S**, and Ham, and Japheth: 8035
9:23 **S** and Japheth took a garment, and laid *it* 8035
9:26 he said, Blessed *be* the LORD God of **S**; 8035
9:27 and he shall dwell in the tents of **S**; 8035
10: 1 of the sons of Noah, **S**, Ham, and Japheth: 8035
10:21 Unto **S** also, the father of all the children of 8035
10:22 The children of **S**; Elam, and Asshur, and 8035
10:31 These *are* the sons of **S**, after their families, 8035
11:10 These *are* the generations of **S**: Shem *was* 8035
11:10 **S** *was* an hundred years old, and 8035
11:11 **S** lived after he begat Arphaxad five 8035
1Ch 1: 4 Noah, **S**, Ham, and Japheth. 8035
1:17 The sons of **S**; Elam, and Asshur, and 8035
1:24 **S**, Arphaxad, Shelah, 8035

SHEMA (6)

Jos 15:26 Amam, and **S**, and Moladah, 8090
1Ch 2:43 Korah, and Tappuah, and Rekem, and **S**. 8087
2:44 **S** begat Raham, the father of Jorkoam: and 8087
5: 8 the son of **S**, the son of Joel, who dwelt in 8087
8:13 Beriah also, and **S**, who *were* heads of 8087
Ne 8: 4 and **S**, and Anaiah, and Urijah, and Hilkiah, 8087

SHEMAAH (1)

1Ch 12: 3 then Joash, the sons of **S** the Gibeathite; 8094

SHEMAIAH (41)

1Ki 12:22 the word of God came unto **S** the man of 8098
1Ch 3:22 the sons of Shechaniah; **S**: and the sons of 8098
3:22 the sons of **S**; Hattush, and Igeal, and 8098
4:37 of Jedaiah, the son of Shimri, the son of **S**; 8098
5: 4 **S** his son, Gog his son, Shimei his son, 8098
9:14 **S** the son of Hasshub, the son of Azrikam, 8098
9:16 Obadiah the son of **S**, the son of Galal, 8098
15: 8 **S** the chief, and his brethren two hundred: 8098
15:11 and Joel, **S**, and Eliel, and Amminadab, 8098
24: 6 **S** the son of Nethaneel the scribe, *one* of 8098
26: 4 Moreover the sons of Obed-edom *were,* **S** 8098
26: 6 Also unto **S** his son were sons born, 8098
26: 7 The sons of **S**; Othni, and Rephael, and 8098
2Ch 11: 2 the word of the LORD came to **S** the man 8098
12: 5 Then came **S** the prophet to Rehoboam, and 8098
12: 7 the word of the LORD came to **S**, saying, 8098
12:15 *are* they not written in the book of **S** 8098
17: 8 *even* **S**, and Nethaniah, and Zebadiah, and 8098
29:14 and of the sons of Jeduthun; **S**, and Uzziel. 8098
31:15 Jeshua, and **S**, Amariah, and Shecaniah, 8098
35: 9 **S** and Nethaneel, his brethren, and 8098
Ezr 8:13 and **S**, and with them threescore males. 8098
8:16 for **S**, and for Elnathan, and for Jarib, and 8098
10:21 and Elijah, and **S**, and Jehiel, and Uzziah. 8098
10:31 Eliezer, Ishijah, Malchiah, **S**, Shimeon, 8098

Ne 3:29 After him repaired also **S** the son of 8098
6:10 Afterward I came *unto* the house of **S** 8098
10: 8 Maaziah, Bilgai, **S**: these *were* the priests. 8098
11:15 **S** the son of Hashub, the son of Azrikam, 8098
12: 6 **S**, and Joiarib, Jedaiah, 8098
12:18 Of Bilgah, Shammua; of **S**, Jehonathan; 8098
12:34 Judah, and Benjamin, and **S**, and Jeremiah, 8098
12:35 the son of **S**, the son of Mattaniah, the son 8098
12:36 **S**, and Azarael, Milalai, Gilalai, Maai, 8098
12:42 **S**, and Eleazar, and Uzzi, and Jehohanan, 8098
Jer 26:20 Urijah the son of **S** of Kirjath-jearim, 8098
29:24 *Thus* shalt thou also speak to **S** 8098
29:31 Thus saith the LORD concerning **S** 8098
29:31 Because that **S** hath prophesied unto you, 8098
29:32 I will punish **S** the Nehelamite, and his 8098
36:12 Delaiah the son of **S**, and Elnathan the son 8098

SHEMARIAH (3)
1Ch 12: 5 and **S**, and Shephatiah the Haruphite, 8114
Ezr 10:32 Benjamin, Malluch, *and* **S**. 8114
10:41 Azareel, and Shelemiah, **S**, 8114

SHEMEBER (1)
Ge 14: 2 **S** king of Zeboiim, and the king of Bela, 8038

SHEMER (2)
1Ki 16:24 he bought the hill Samaria of **S** for two 8106
16:24 after the name of **S**, owner of the hill, 8106

SHEMIDA (3) [SHEMIDAITES]
Nu 26:32 *of* **S**, the family of the Shemidaites: and 8061
Jos 17: 2 of Hepher, and for the children of **S**: 8061
1Ch 7:19 the sons of **S** were, Ahian, and Shechem, 8061

SHEMIDAITES (1) [SHEMIDA]
Nu 26:32 *of* Shemida, the family of the **S**: and 8062

SHEMINITH (3)
1Ch 15:21 and Azaziah, with harps on the **S** to excel. 8067
Ps 6: T To the chief Musician on Neginoth upon **S**, 8067
12: T To the chief Musician upon **S**, A Psalm of 8067

SHEMIRAMOTH (4)
1Ch 15:18 **S**, and Jehiel, and Unni, Eliab, and 8070
15:20 **S**, and Jehiel, and Unni, and Eliab, and 8070
16: 5 **S**, and Jehiel, and Mattithiah, and Eliab, 8070
2Ch 17: 8 **S**, and Jehonathan, and Adonijah, and 8070

SHEMUEL (3)
Nu 34:20 children of Simeon, **S** the son of Ammihud. 8050
1Ch 6:33 a singer, the son of Joel, the son of **S**, 8050
7: 2 and Jeriel, and Jahmai, and Jibsam, and **S**, 8050

SHEN (1)
1Sa 7:12 set *it* between Mizpeh and **S**, and called 8129

SHENAZAR (1)
1Ch 3:18 Pedaiah, and **S**, Jecamiah, Hoshama, and 8137

SHENAZZAR See SHENAZAR

SHENIR (2)
Dt 3: 9 call Sirion; and the Amorites call it **S**;) 8149
SS 4: 8 from the top of **S** and Hermon, from 8149

SHEPHAM (2)
Nu 34:10 out your east border from Hazar-enan to **S**: 8221
34:11 the coast shall go down from **S** *to* Riblah, 8221

SHEPHATHIAH (1)
1Ch 9: 8 Meshullam the son of **S**, the son of Reuel, 8203

SHEPHATIAH (12)
2Sa 3: 4 and the fifth, **S** the son of Abital; 8203
1Ch 3: 3 The fifth, **S** of Abital: the sixth, Ithream by 8203
12: 5 and Shemariah, and **S** the Haruphite, 8203
27:16 of the Simeonites, **S** the son of Maachah: 8203
2Ch 21: 2 and Azariah, and Michael, and **S**: 8203
Ezr 2: 4 The children of **S**, three hundred seventy 8203
2:57 The children of **S**, the children of Hattil, 8203
8: 8 of the sons of **S**; Zebadiah the son of 8203
Ne 7: 9 The children of **S**, three hundred seventy 8203
7:59 The children of **S**, the children of Hattil, 8203
11: 4 the son of Amariah, the son of **S**, 8203
Jer 38: 1 **S** the son of Mattan, and Gedaliah the son 8203

SHEPHER See SHAPHER

SHEPHERD (43) [HERD, SHEEP]
Ge 46:34 for every **s** *is* an abomination unto 6629+7462
49:24 (from thence *is* the **s**, the stone of Israel:) 7462
Nu 27:17 LORD be not as sheep which have no **s**. 7462
1Ki 22:17 upon the hills, as sheep that have not a **s**: 7462
2Ch 18:16 the mountains, as sheep that have no **s**: 7462
Ps 23: 1 The LORD *is* my **s**; I shall not want. 7462
80: 1 Give ear, O **S** of Israel, thou that leadest 7462
Ecc 12:11 of assemblies, *which* are given from one **s**. 7462
Isa 40:11 He shall feed his flock like a **s**: he shall 7462
44:28 *He is* my **s**, and shall perform all my 7462
63:11 up out of the sea with the **s** of his flock? 7462
Jer 31:10 and keep him as a **s** *doth* his flock. 7462
43:12 of Egypt, as a **s** putteth on his garment; 7462
49:19 and who *is* that **s** that will stand before me? 7462
50:44 and who *is* that **s** that will stand before me? 7462
51:23 I will also break in pieces with thee the **s** 7462
Eze 34: 5 they were scattered, because *there is* no **s**: 7462
34: 8 because *there was* no **s**, neither did my 7462
34:12 As a **s** seeketh out his flock in the day that 7462
34:23 I will set up one **s** over them, and he shall 7462
34:23 he shall feed them, and he shall be their **s**. 7462
37:24 over them; and they all shall have one **s**: 7462
Am 3:12 As the **s** taketh out of the mouth of the lion 7462
Zec 10: 2 they were troubled, because *there was* no **s**. 7462
11:15 unto thee yet the instruments of a foolish **s**. 7462
11:16 For lo, I *will* raise up a **s** in the land, 7462
11:17 Woe to the idol **s** that leaveth the flock! 7473
13: 7 against my **s**, and against the man *that is* 7462
13: 7 smite the **s**, and the sheep shall be 7462
Mt 9:36 scattered abroad, as sheep having no **s**. *4166*
25:32 as a **s** divideth *his* sheep from the goats: *4166*
26:31 I will smite the **s**, and the sheep of the flock *4166*
Mk 6:34 because they were as sheep not having a **s**: *4166*
14:27 I will smite the **s**, and the sheep shall be *4166*
Jn 10: 2 But he that entereth in by the door is the **s** *4166*
10:11 I am the good **s**: the good shepherd giveth *4166*
10:11 the good **s** giveth his life for the sheep. *4166*
10:12 But *he that is* a hireling, and not the **s**, *4166*
10:14 I am the good **s**, and know my *sheep*, and *4166*
10:16 and there shall be one fold, *and* one **s**. *4166*
Heb 13:20 *that* great **s** of the sheep, through the blood *4166*
1Pe 2:25 but are now returned unto the **S** and *4166*
5: 4 And when the **chief S** shall appear, ye shall *750*

SHEPHERD'S (2) [HERD, SHEEP]
1Sa 17:40 put them in a **s** bag which he had, even in a 7462
Isa 38:12 and is removed from me as a **s** tent: 7473

SHEPHERDS (37) [HERD, SHEEP]
Ge 46:32 the men *are* **s**, for their trade hath 6629+7462
47: 3 Thy servants *are* **s**, both we, *and* 6629+7462
Ex 2:17 the **s** came and drove them away: but 7462
2:19 delivered us out of the hand of the **s**, 7462
1Sa 25: 7 now thy **s** which were with us, we hurt 7462
Isa 13:20 neither shall the **s** make their fold there. 7462
31: 4 when a multitude of **s** is called forth against 7462
56:11 and they *are* **s** *that* cannot understand: 7462
Jer 6: 3 The **s** with their flocks shall come unto her; 7462
23: 4 I will set up **s** over them which shall feed 7462
25:34 Howl, ye **s**, and cry; and wallow yourselves 7462
25:35 the **s** shall have no way to flee, nor 7462
25:36 A voice of the cry of the **s**, and a howling 7462
33:12 shall be a habitation of **s** causing *their* 7462
50: 6 their **s** have caused them to go astray, 7462
Eze 34: 2 prophesy against the **s** of Israel, prophesy, 7462
34: 2 Thus saith the Lord GOD unto the **s**; 7462
34: 2 Woe *be* to the **s** of Israel that do feed 7462
34: 2 should not the **s** feed the flocks? 7462
34: 7 Therefore, ye **s**, hear the word of 7462
34: 8 neither did my **s** search for my flock, but 7462
34: 8 the **s** fed themselves, and fed not my flock; 7462
34: 9 Therefore, O ye **s**, hear the word of 7462
34:10 Behold, I *am* against the **s**; and I will 7462
34:10 neither shall the **s** feed themselves any 7462
Am 1: 2 the habitations of the **s** shall mourn, and 7462
Mic 5: 5 shall we raise against him seven **s**, and 7462
Na 3:18 Thy **s** slumber, O king of Assyria: 7462
Zep 2: 6 coast shall be dwellings *and* cottages for **s**, 7462
Zec 10: 3 Mine anger was kindled against the **s**, and I 7462
11: 3 *There is* a voice of the howling of the **s**; 7462
11: 5 for I am rich: and their own **s** pity them not. 7462
11: 8 Three **s** also I cut off in one month; and 7462
Lk 2: 8 And there were in the same country **s** *4166*

S

Lk 2:15 the **s** said one to another, Let us now go *4166*
2:18 those *things* which were told them by the **s**. *4166*
2:20 And the **s** returned, glorifying and *4166*

SHEPHERDS' (1) [HERD, SHEEP]
SS 1: 8 and feed thy kids beside the **s** tents. 7462

SHEPHI (1) [SHEPHO]
1Ch 1:40 and Manahath, and Ebal, **S**, and Onam. 8195

SHEPHO (1) [SHEPHI]
Ge 36:23 and Manahath, and Ebal, **S**, and Onam. 8195

SHEPHUPHAN (1)
1Ch 8: 5 And Gera, and **S**, and Huram. 8197

SHERAH (1)
1Ch 7:24 (And his daughter *was* **S**, who built 7609

SHEREBIAH (8)
Ezr 8:18 **S**, with his sons and his brethren, eighteen; 8274
8:24 **S**, Hashabiah, and ten of their brethren with 8274
Ne 8: 7 Bani, and **S**, Jamin, Akkub, Shabbethai, 8274
9: 4 **S**, Bani, *and* Chenani, and cried with a loud 8274
9: 5 **S**, Hodijah, Shebaniah, *and* Pethahiah, said, 8274
10:12 Zaccur, **S**, Shebaniah, 8274
12: 8 Binnui, Kadmiel, **S**, Judah, *and* Mattaniah, 8274
12:24 **S**, and Jeshua the son of Kadmiel, 8274

SHERESH (1)
1Ch 7:16 the name of his brother *was* **S**; and his sons 8329

SHEREZER (1)
Zec 7: 2 they had sent *unto* the house of God **S** 8272

SHERIFFS (2)
Da 3: 2 the **s**, and all the rulers of the provinces, 8614
3: 3 the **s**, and all the rulers of the provinces, 8614

SHESHACH (2)
Jer 25:26 and the king of **S** shall drink after them. 8347
51:41 How is **S** taken! and *how* is the praise of 8347

SHESHAI (3)
Nu 13:22 where Ahiman, **S**, and Talmai, the children 8344
Jos 15:14 **S**, and Ahiman, and Talmai, the children of 8344
Jdg 1:10 and they slew **S**, and Ahiman, and Talmai. 8344

SHESHAN (5)
1Ch 2:31 the sons of Ishi; **S**. And the children of 8348
2:31 Sheshan. And the children of **S**; Ahlai. 8348
2:34 Now **S** had no sons, but daughters. 8348
2:34 **S** had a servant, an Egyptian, whose name 8348
2:35 **S** gave his daughter to Jarha his servant to 8348

SHESHBAZZAR (4)
Ezr 1: 8 numbered them unto **S**, the prince of Judah. 8339
1:11 All *these* did **S** bring up with *them of* 8339
5:14 delivered unto *one,* whose name *was* **S**, 8340
5:16 came the same **S**, *and* laid the foundation of 8340

SHETH (2) [SETH]
Nu 24:17 of Moab, and destroy all the children of **S**. 8352
1Ch 1: 1 Adam, **S**, Enosh, 8352

SHETHAR (1)
Est 1:14 **S**, Admatha, Tarshish, Meres, Marsena, *and* 8369

SHETHAR-BOZENAI See SHETHAR-BOZNAI

SHETHAR-BOZNAI (4)
Ezr 5: 3 **S**, and their companions, and said thus unto 8370
5: 6 **S**, and his companions the Apharsachites, 8370
6: 6 **S**, and your companions the Apharsachites, 8370
6:13 *this* side the river, **S**, and their companions, 8370

SHEVA (2)
2Sa 20:25 **S** *was* scribe: and Zadok and Abiathar *were* 7724
1Ch 2:49 **S** the father of Machbenah, and the father 7724

SHEW (228) [SHEWBREAD, SHEWED, SHEWEDST, SHEWEST, SHEWETH, SHEWING]
Ge 12: 1 father's house, unto a land that I will **s** thee: 7200
20:13 This *is* thy kindness which thou shalt **s** unto 6213
24:12 and **s** kindness unto my master Abraham. 6213
40:14 **s** kindness, I pray thee, unto me, and 6213
46:31 go up, and **s** Pharaoh, and say unto him, 5046
Ex 7: 9 unto you, saying, **S** a miracle for you: 5414
9:16 I raised thee up, for to **s** *in* thee my power; 7200
10: 1 that I might **s** these my signs before him: 7896
13: 8 And thou shalt **s** thy son in that day, saying, 5046
14:13 the LORD, which he will **s** to you to day: 6213
18:20 shalt **s** them the way *wherein* they must 3045
25: 9 According to all that I **s** thee, *after* 7200
33:13 **s** me now thy way, that I may know thee, 3045
33:18 And he said, I beseech thee, **s** me thy glory. 7200
33:19 will **s** **mercy** on whom I will shew mercy. 7355
33:19 will shew mercy on whom I will **s** **mercy**. 7355
Nu 16: 5 Even to morrow the LORD will **s** who *are* 3045
Dt 1:33 to **s** you by what way ye should go, and in a 7200
3:24 thou hast begun to **s** thy servant thy 7200
5: 5 that time, to **s** you the word of the LORD: 5046
7: 2 with them, nor **s** **mercy** unto them: 2603
13:17 **s** thee mercy, and have compassion upon 5414
17: 9 they shall **s** thee the sentence of judgment: 5046
17:10 which the LORD shall choose shall **s** thee; 5046
17:11 from the sentence which they shall **s** thee, 5046
28:50 of the old, nor **s** **favour** to the young: 2603
32: 7 ask thy father, and he will **s** thee; 5046
Jos 2:12 that ye will also **s** kindness unto my 6213
5: 6 sware that *he* would not **s** them the land, 7200
Jdg 1:24 they said unto him, **S** us, we pray thee, 7200
1:24 the city, and we will **s** thee mercy. 5973+6213
4:22 I will **s** thee the man whom thou seekest. 7200
6:17 then **s** me a sign that thou talkest with me. 6213
1Sa 3:15 And Samuel feared to **s** Eli the vision. 5046
8: 9 **s** them the manner of the king that shall 5046
9: 6 peradventure he can **s** us our way that we 5046
9:27 a while, that I may **s** thee the word of God. 8085
10: 8 come to thee, and **s** thee what thou shalt do. 3045
14:12 Come up to us, and we will **s** you a thing. 3045
16: 3 and I will **s** thee what thou shalt do: 3045
20: 2 or small, but that he will **s** it me: 241+1540
20:12 I then send not unto thee, and **s** it thee; 241+1540
20:13 I will **s** it thee, and send thee away, 241+1540
20:14 thou shalt not only while yet I live **s** me 6213
22:17 when he fled, and did not **s** it to me. 241+1540
25: 8 Ask thy young men, and they will **s** thee. 5046
2Sa 2: 6 now the LORD **s** kindness and truth unto 6213
3: 8 which against Judah do **s** kindness *this* day 6213
9: 1 that I may **s** him kindness for Jonathan's 6213
9: 3 that I may **s** the kindness of God unto him? 6213
9: 7 for I will **surely** **s** thee kindness for 6213+6213
10: 2 I will **s** kindness unto Hanun the son of 6213
15:25 and **s** me *both* it, and his habitation: 7200
22:26 the merciful thou wilt **s** thyself **merciful**, 2616
22:26 the upright man thou wilt **s** thyself **upright**. 8552
22:27 With the pure thou wilt **s** thyself **pure**; and 1305
22:27 the froward thou wilt **s** thyself **unsavoury**. 6617
1Ki 1:52 If he will **s** himself a worthy man, 1961+3807.1
2: 2 and **s** thyself a man; 1961+3807.1
2: 7 **s** kindness unto the sons of Barzillai 6213
18: 1 third year, saying, Go, **s** thyself unto Ahab; 7200
18: 2 Elijah went to **s** himself unto Ahab. 7200
18:15 I will surely **s** myself unto him to day. 7200
2Ki 6:11 Will ye not **s** me which of us *is* for the king 5046
7:12 I will now **s** you what the Syrians have 5046
1Ch 16:23 **s** **forth** from day to day his salvation. 1319
19: 2 I will **s** kindness unto Hanun the son of 6213
2Ch 16: 9 to **s** himself **strong** in the behalf of *them* 2388
Ezr 2:59 they could not **s** their fathers' house, and 5046
Ne 7:61 they could not **s** their fathers' house, 5046
9:19 to **s** them **light**, and the way wherein they 215
Est 1:11 to **s** the people and the princes her beauty: 7200
2:10 had charged her that she should not **s** *it.* 5046
4: 8 to **s** *it* unto Esther, and to declare *it* unto 7200
Job 10: 2 **s** me wherefore thou contendest with me. 3045
11: 6 that he would **s** thee the secrets of wisdom, 5046
15:17 I will **s** thee, hear me; and that which I have 2331
32: 6 and durst not **s** you mine opinion. 2331
32:10 Hearken to me; I also will **s** mine opinion. 2331
32:17 also my part, I also will **s** mine opinion. 2331
33:23 a thousand, to **s** unto man his uprightness: 5046
36: 2 I will **s** thee that *I have* yet to speak on 2331
Ps 4: 6 *be* many that say, Who will **s** us *any* good? 7200
9: 1 I will **s** **forth** all thy marvellous works. 5608
9:14 That I may **s** **forth** all thy praise in 5608
16:11 Thou wilt **s** me the path of life: in thy 3045
17: 7 **S** thy **marvellous** lovingkindness, O thou 6395
18:25 the merciful thou wilt **s** thyself **merciful**; 2616
18:25 an upright man thou wilt **s** thyself **upright**; 8552

Ps	18:26	With the pure thou wilt **s** thyself **pure**; and	1305
	18:26	the froward thou wilt **s** thyself **froward**.	6617
	25: 4	**S** me thy ways, O LORD; teach me thy	3045
	25:14	fear him; and he will **s** them his covenant.	3045
	39: 6	Surely every man walketh **in a vain s**:	6754
	50:23	*aright* will I **s** the salvation of God.	7200
	51:15	and my mouth shall **s forth** thy praise.	5046
	71:15	My mouth shall **s forth** thy righteousness	5608
	79:13	we will **s forth** thy praise to all generations.	5608
	85: 7	**S** us thy mercy, O LORD, and grant us thy	7200
	86:17	**S** me a token for good; that they which hate	6213
	88:10	Wilt thou **s** wonders to the dead? shall	6213
	91:16	will I satisfy him, and **s** him my salvation.	7200
	92: 2	To **s forth** thy lovingkindness in	5046
	92:15	To **s** that the LORD *is* upright: *he is* my	5046
	94: 1	to whom vengeance belongeth, **s** thyself.	3313
	96: 2	**s forth** his salvation from day to day.	1319
	106: 2	the LORD? *who* can **s forth** all his praise?	8085
	109:16	Because that he remembered not to **s**	6213
Pr	18:24	that hath friends must **s** himself **friendly**:	7462
Isa	3: 9	The **s** of their countenance doth witness	1971
	27:11	he that formed them will **s** them no **favour**.	2603
	30:30	shall **s** the lighting down of his arm,	7200
	41:22	*them* forth, and **s** us what shall happen:	5046
	41:22	let them **s** the former *things,* what they *be,*	5046
	41:23	**S** the *things* that are to come hereafter,	5046
	43: 9	**s** us former *things?* let them bring forth	8085
	43:21	for myself; they shall **s forth** my praise.	5608
	44: 7	and shall come, let them **s** unto them.	5046
	46: 8	Remember this, and **s yourselves men**:	377
	47: 6	thou didst **s** them no mercy; upon	7760
	49: 9	to *them* that *are* in darkness, **S** yourselves.	1540
	58: 1	**s** my people their transgression, and	5046
	60: 6	they shall **s forth** the praises of	1319
Jer	16:10	when thou shalt **s** this people all these	5046
	16:13	and night; where I will not **s** you favour.	5414
	18:17	I will **s** them the back, and not the face,	7200
	33: 3	**s** thee great and mighty *things,* which thou	5046
	42: 3	That the LORD thy God may **s** us the way	5046
	42:12	I will **s** mercies unto you, that he may have	5414
	50:42	they *are* cruel, and will not **s mercy**:	7355
	51:31	to **s** the king of Babylon that his city is	5046
Eze	22: 2	yea, thou shalt **s** her all her abominations.	3045
	33:31	for with their mouth they **s** much love, *but*	6213
	37:18	Wilt thou not **s** us what thou meanest by	5046
	40: 4	set thine heart upon all that I shall **s** thee;	7200
	40: 4	for to the intent that *I* might **s** *them* unto	7200
	43:10	of man, **s** the house to the house of Israel,	5046
	43:11	**s** them the form of the house, and	3045
Da	2: 2	the Chaldeans, for to **s** the king his dreams.	5046
	2: 4	the dream, and we will **s** the interpretation.	2324
	2: 6	if ye **s** the dream, and the interpretation	2324
	2: 6	therefore **s** me the dream, and	2324
	2: 7	and we will **s** the interpretation of it.	2324
	2: 9	I shall know that ye can **s** me	2324
	2:10	There is not a man upon the earth that can **s**	2324
	2:11	there is none other that can **s** it before	2324
	2:16	that *he* would **s** the king the interpretation.	2324
	2:24	and I will **s** unto the king the interpretation.	2324
	2:27	the soothsayers, **s** unto the king;	2324
	4: 2	I thought it good to **s** the signs and	2324
	5: 7	**s** me the interpretation thereof, shall be	2324
	5:12	be called, and he will **s** the interpretation.	2324
	5:15	they could not **s** the interpretation of	2324
	9:23	I am come to **s** *thee;* for thou *art* greatly	5046
	10:21	I will **s** thee that which is noted in	5046
	11: 2	now will I **s** thee the truth. Behold,	5046
Joel	2:30	I will **s** wonders in the heavens and in	5414
Mic	7:15	Egypt will I **s** unto him marvellous *things.*	7200
Na	3: 5	I will **s** the nations thy nakedness, and	7200
Hab	1: 3	Why dost thou **s** me iniquity, and cause *me*	7200
Zec	1: 9	said unto me, I will **s** thee what these *be.*	7200
	7: 9	**s** mercy and compassions every man to his	6213
Mt	8: 4	**s** thyself to the priest, and offer the gift that	*1166*
	11: 4	**s** John **again** *those things* which ye do hear	*518*
	12:18	and he shall **s** judgment to the Gentiles.	*518*
	14: 2	works do **s forth** themselves **in** him.	*1754*
	16: 1	tempting desired him that *he* would **s** them	*1925*
	16:21	From that time forth began Jesus to **s** unto	*1166*
	22:19	**S** me the tribute money. And they brought	*1925*
	24: 1	his disciples came to *him* for to **s** him	*1925*
	24:24	and shall **s** great signs and wonders;	*1325*
Mk	1:44	**s** thyself to the priest, and offer for thy	*1166*
	6:14	mighty works do **s forth** themselves in	*1754*
	13:22	and shall **s** signs and wonders, to seduce,	*1325*
	14:15	And he will **s** you a large upper room	*1166*
Lk	1:19	unto thee, and to **s** thee these **glad tidings**.	*2097*
	5:14	no *man:* but go, and **s** thyself to the priest,	*1166*
	6:47	doeth them, I will **s** you to whom he is like:	*5263*
	8:39	**s** how great *things* God hath done unto	*1334*
	17:14	unto them, Go **s** yourselves unto the priests.	*1925*
	20:24	**S** me a penny. Whose image and	*1925*
	20:47	and for a **s** make long prayers:	*4392*
	22:12	And he shall **s** you a large upper room	*1166*
Jn	5:20	and he will **s** him greater works than these,	*1166*
	7: 4	If thou do these *things,* **s** thyself to	*5319*
	11:57	he should **s** *it,* that they might take him.	*3377*
	14: 8	Lord, **s** us the Father, and it sufficeth us.	*1166*
	14: 9	and how sayest thou *then,* **S** us the Father?	*1166*
	16:13	he speak: and he will **s** you *things* to come.	*312*
	16:14	shall receive of mine, and shall **s** *it* unto you.	*312*
	16:15	he shall take of mine, and shall **s** *it* unto you.	*312*
	16:25	but I shall **s** you plainly of the Father.	*312*
Ac	1:24	which knowest the hearts of all *men,* **s**	*322*
	2:19	And I will **s** wonders in heaven above, and	*1325*
	7: 3	and come into the land which I shall **s** thee.	*1166*
	9:16	For I will **s** him how great *things* he must	*5263*
	12:17	*Go* **s** these *things* unto James, and to	*518*
	16:17	which **s** unto us the way of salvation.	*2605*
	24:27	and Felix, willing to **s** the Jews a pleasure,	*2698*
	26:23	and should **s** light unto the people, and	*2605*
Ro	2:15	Which **s** the work of the law written in their	*1731*
	9:17	that I might **s** my power in thee, and	*1731*
	9:22	willing to **s** *his* wrath, and to make his	*1731*
1Co	11:26	ye do **s** the Lord's death till he come.	*2605*
	12:31	and yet **s** I unto you a more excellent way.	*1166*
	15:51	Behold, I **s** you a mystery; We shall not all	*3004*
2Co	8:24	Wherefore **s** ye to them, and before	*1731*
Gal	6:12	As many as desire to **make a fair s** in	*2146*
Eph	2: 7	That in the ages to come he might **s**	*1731*
Col	2:15	and powers, he **made a s** of *them* openly,	*1165*
	2:23	Which *things* have indeed a **s** of wisdom in	*3056*
1Th	1: 9	For they themselves **s** of us what manner of	*518*
1Ti	1:16	that in me first Jesus Christ might **s forth**	*1731*
	5: 4	let them learn first to **s piety** at home, and	*2151*
	6:15	Which in his times he shall **s**, *who is*	*1166*
2Ti	2:15	Study to **s** thyself approved unto God,	*3936*
Heb	6:11	And we desire that every one of you do **s**	*1731*
	6:17	willing more abundantly to **s** unto the heirs	*1925*
Jas	2:18	**s** me thy faith without thy works, and I will	*1166*
	2:18	and I will **s** thee my faith by my works.	*1166*
	3:13	let him **s** out of a good conversation his	*1166*
1Pe	2: 9	that ye should **s forth** the praises of him	*1804*
1Jn	1: 2	bear witness, and **s** unto you *that* eternal life,	*518*
Rev	1: 1	to **s** unto his servants *things* which must	*1166*
	4: 1	I will **s** thee *things* which must be hereafter.	*1166*
	17: 1	I will **s** unto thee the judgment of the great	*1166*
	21: 9	saying, *Come* hither, I will **s** thee the bride,	*1166*
	22: 6	**s** unto his servants *the things* which must	*1166*

SHEWBREAD (18) [BREAD, SHEW]

Ex	25:30	thou shalt set upon the table **s** before	3899+6440
	35:13	and all his vessels, and the **s**,	3899+6440
	39:36	all the vessels thereof, and the **s**,	3899+6440
Nu	4: 7	upon the table of **s** they shall spread a cloth	6440
1Sa	21: 6	was no bread there but the **s**,	3899+6440+1886.1
1Ki	7:48	whereupon the **s** *was,*	3899+6440+1886.1
1Ch	9:32	**s**, to prepare *it* every	3899+4635+1886.1
	23:29	Both for the **s**, and for	3899+4635+1886.1
	28:16	*by* weight *he gave* gold for the tables of **s**,	4635
2Ch	2: 4	*for* the continual **s**, and *for* the burnt	4635
	4:19	whereon the **s** *was set;*	3899+6440+1886.1
	13:11	the **s**bread also *set they* in order upon	3899
	29:18	and the **s** table, with all the vessels thereof.	4635
Ne	10:33	For the **s**, and *for* the continual meat	3899+4635
Mt	12: 4	and did eat the **s**, which was not	*740+3588+4286*
Mk	2:26	and did eat the **s**, which is not	*740+3588+4286*
Lk	6: 4	and did take and eat the **s**,	*740+3588+4286*
Heb	9: 2	and the table, and the **s**;	*740+4286*

SHEWED (135) [SHEW]

Ge	19:19	which thou hast **s** unto me in saving my	6213
	24:14	thereby shall I know that thou hast **s**	6213
	32:10	which thou hast **s** unto thy servant;	6213
	39:21	**s** him mercy, and gave him favour in	5186
	41:25	God hath **s** Pharaoh what he *is* about to do.	5046
	41:39	Forasmuch as God hath **s** thee all this,	3045
	48:11	and lo, God hath **s** me also thy seed.	7200

S

Ex 15:25 the LORD **s** him a tree, *which* when he 3384
25:40 which was **s** thee in the mount. 7200
26:30 thereof which was **s** thee in the mount. 7200
27: 8 as it was **s** thee in the mount, so shall they 7200
Lev 13:19 somewhat reddish, and it be **s** to the priest; 7200
13:49 of leprosy, and shall be **s** unto the priest: 7200
24:12 that the mind of the LORD might be **s** 6567
Nu 8: 4 the pattern which the LORD had **s** Moses, 7200
13:26 and **s** them the fruit of the land. 7200
14:11 for all the signs which I have **s** among 6213
Dt 4:35 Unto thee it was **s**, that thou mightest know 7200
4:36 upon earth he **s** thee his great fire; and 7200
5:24 the LORD our God hath **s** us his glory and 7200
6:22 the LORD **s** signs and wonders, great and 5414
34: 1 the LORD **s** him all the land of Gilead, 7200
34:12 in all the great terror which Moses **s** in 6213
Jos 2:12 the LORD, since I have **s** you kindness, 6213
Jdg 1:25 when he **s** them the entrance into the city, 7200
4:12 they **s** Sisera that Barak the son of 5046
8:35 Neither **s** they kindness to the house of 6213
8:35 all the goodness which he had **s** unto Israel. 6213
13:10 ran, and **s** her husband, and said unto him, 5046
13:23 neither would he have **s** us all these *things,* 7200
16:18 up *this* once, for he hath **s** me all his heart. 5046
Ru 2:11 unto her, It hath **fully been s** me, 5046+5046
2:19 she **s** her mother in law with whom she had 5046
3:10 *for* thou hast **s more** kindness in the latter 3190
1Sa 11: 9 and **s** *it* to the men of Jabesh; 5046
15: 6 for ye **s** kindness to all the children of 6213
19: 7 and Jonathan **s** him all those things. 5046
22:21 Abiathar **s** David that Saul had slain 5046
24:18 thou hast **s** *this* day how that thou hast dealt 5046
2Sa 2: 5 that ye have **s** this kindness unto your lord, 6213
10: 2 of Nahash, as his father **s** kindness unto me. 6213
11:22 and **s** David all that Joab had sent him for. 5046
1Ki 1:27 and thou hast not **s** *it* unto thy servant, 3045
3: 6 Thou hast **s** unto thy servant David my 6213
16:27 Omri which he did, and his might that he **s**, 6213
22:45 and his might that he **s**, and how he warred, 6213
2Ki 6: 6 he **s** him the place. And he cut down a 7200
8:10 howbeit the LORD hath **s** me that he shall 7200
8:13 The LORD hath **s** me *that* thou *shalt be* 7200
11: 4 of the LORD, and **s** them the king's son. 7200
20:13 **s** them all the house of his precious things, 7200
20:13 all his dominion, that Hezekiah **s** them not. 7200
20:15 among my treasures that I have not **s** them. 7200
22:10 Shaphan the scribe **s** the king, saying, 5046
1Ch 19: 2 because his father **s** kindness to me. 6213
2Ch 1: 8 Thou hast **s** great mercy unto David my 6213
7:10 that the LORD had **s** unto David, 6213
Ezr 9: 8 now for a little space grace hath been **s** from NIH
Est 1: 4 When he **s** the riches of his glorious 7200
2:10 Esther had not **s** her people nor her kindred: 5046
2:20 Esther had not *yet* **s** her kindred nor her 5046
3: 6 for they had **s** him the people of Mordecai: 5046
Job 6:14 To him that is afflicted pity *should be* **s** NIH
Ps 31:21 for he hath **s** me his **marvellous** kindness 6381
60: 3 Thou hast **s** thy people hard *things:* thou 7200
71:18 until I have **s** thy strength unto *this* 5046
71:20 *Thou,* which hast **s** me great and 7200
78:11 and his wonders that he had **s** them. 7200
98: 2 his righteousness hath he **openly s** in 1540
105:27 They **s** his signs among them, and 7760
111: 6 He hath **s** his people the power of his 5046
118:27 God *is* the LORD, which hath **s** us **light**: 215
142: 2 before him; I **s** before him my trouble. 5046
Pr 26:26 his wickedness shall be **s** before the *whole* 1540
Ecc 2:19 where*in* I have **s** myself **wise** under the sun. 2449
Isa 26:10 Let **favour** be **s** to the wicked, *yet* will he 2603
39: 2 **s** them the house of his precious things, 7200
39: 2 all his dominion, that Hezekiah **s** them not. 7200
39: 4 among my treasures that I have not **s** them. 7200
40:14 and **s** to him the way of understanding? 3045
43:12 and have saved, and I have **s**, 8085
48: 3 went forth out of my mouth, and I **s** them; 8085
48: 5 *it* to thee; before it came to pass I **s** *it* thee: 8085
48: 6 will not ye declare *it?* I have **s** thee new 8085
Jer 24: 1 The LORD **s** me, and behold, two baskets 7200
38:21 this *is* the word that the LORD hath **s** me: 7200
Eze 11:25 all the things that the LORD had **s** me. 7200
20:11 **s** them my judgments, which *if* a man do, 3045
22:26 neither have they **s** *difference* between 3045
Am 7: 1 Thus hath the Lord GOD **s** unto me; and 7200
7: 4 Thus hath the Lord GOD **s** unto me: and 7200
7: 7 Thus he **s** me: and behold, the Lord stood 7200
8: 1 Thus hath the Lord GOD **s** unto me: and 7200
Mic 6: 8 He hath **s** thee, O man, what *is* good; and 5046
Zec 1:20 And the LORD **s** me four carpenters. 7200
3: 1 he **s** me Joshua the high priest standing 7200
Mt 28:11 **s** unto the chief priests all the *things* that *518*
Lk 1:51 He hath **s** strength with his arm; he hath *4160*
1:58 her cousins heard how the Lord had **s great** *3170*
4: 5 **s** unto him all the kingdoms of the world in *1166*
7:18 And the disciples of John **s** him of all these *518*
10:37 And he said, He that **s** mercy on him. Then *4160*
14:21 **s** his lord these *things.* Then the master of *518*
20:37 dead are raised, even Moses **s** at the bush, *3377*
24:40 he **s** them *his* hands and *his* feet. *1925*
Jn 10:32 Many good works have I **s** you from my *1166*
20:20 said, he **s** unto them *his* hands and his side. *1166*
21: 1 After these *things* Jesus **s** himself again to *5319*
21: 1 of Tiberias; and on this wise **s** he *himself.* *5319*
21:14 This *is* now the third time *that* Jesus **s** *5319*
Ac 1: 3 To whom also he **s** himself alive after his *3936*
3:18 But *those things,* which God **before** had **s** *4293*
4:22 on whom this miracle of healing was **s**. *1096*
7:26 And the next day he **s** himself unto them as *3700*
7:36 after that he had **s** wonders and signs in *4160*
7:52 they have slain them which **s before** of *4293*
10:28 God hath **s** me that *I* should not call any *1166*
10:40 raised up the third day, and **s** him openly; *1325*
11:13 And he **s** us how he had seen an angel in his *518*
19:18 and confessed, and **s** their deeds. *312*
20:20 that was profitable *unto you,* but have **s** you, *312*
20:35 I have **s** you all *things,* how that so *5263*
23:22 no *man* that thou hast **s** these *things* to me. *1718*
26:20 But **s** first unto them of Damascus, *518*
28: 2 And the barbarous people **s** us no little *3930*
28:21 neither any of the brethren that came **s** or *518*
Ro 1:19 in them; for God hath **s** *it* unto them. *5319*
1Co 10:28 eat not for his sake that **s** *it,* and *3377*
Heb 6:10 of love, which ye have **s** toward his name, *1731*
8: 5 to the pattern **s** to thee in the mount. *1166*
Jas 2:13 without mercy, that hath **s** no mercy; *4160*
2Pe 1:14 even as our Lord Jesus Christ hath **s** me. *1213*
Rev 21:10 and high mountain, and **s** me *that* great city, *1166*
22: 1 And he **s** me a pure river of water of life, *1166*
22: 8 feet of the angel which **s** me these *things.* *1166*

SHEWEDST (2) [SHEW]

Ne 9:10 **s** signs and wonders upon Pharaoh, and 5414
Jer 11:18 and I know *it:* then thou **s** me their doings. 7200

SHEWEST (5) [SHEW]

2Ch 6:14 and **s** mercy unto thy servants, NIH
Job 10:16 again thou **s** thyself **marvellous** upon me. 6381
Jer 32:18 Thou **s** lovingkindness unto thousands, and 6213
Jn 2:18 said unto him, What sign **s** thou unto us, *1166*
6:30 therefore unto him, What sign **s** thou then, *4160*

SHEWETH (20) [SHEW]

Ge 41:28 What God *is* about to do he **s** unto Pharaoh. 7200
Nu 23: 3 whatsoever he **s** me I will tell thee. And he 7200
1Sa 22: 8 *there is* none that **s** me that my son 241+1540
22: 8 **s unto** me that my son hath stirred up 241+1540
2Sa 22:51 **s** mercy to his anointed, unto David, and 6213
Job 36: 9 he **s** them their work, and 5046
36:33 The noise thereof **s** concerning it, the cattle 5046
Ps 18:50 **s** mercy to his anointed, to David, and 6213
19: 1 and the firmament **s** his handywork. 5046
19: 2 and night unto night **s** knowledge. 2331
37:21 but the righteous **s mercy**, and giveth. 2603
112: 5 A good man **s favour**, and lendeth: he will 2603
147:19 He **s** his word unto Jacob, his statutes and 5046
Pr 12:17 *He that* speaketh truth **s forth** 5046
27:25 the tender grass **s** itself, and herbs of 7200
Isa 41:26 yea, *there is* none that **s**, yea, *there is* none 5046
Mt 4: 8 and **s** him all the kingdoms of the world, *1166*
Jn 5:20 and **s** him all *things* that himself doeth: *1166*
Ro 9:16 him that runneth, but of God that **s mercy**. *1653*
12: 8 he that **s mercy**, with cheerfulness. *1653*

SHEWING (15) [SHEW]

Ex 20: 6 **s** mercy unto thousands of them that love 6213
Dt 5:10 **s** mercy unto thousands of them that love 6213
Ps 78: 4 **s** to the generation to come the praises of 5608
SS 2: 9 the windows, **s** himself through the lattice. 6692
Da 4:27 and thine iniquities by **s mercy** to the poor; 2604

Da 5:12 **s** of hard sentences, and dissolving of 263
Lk 1:80 was in the deserts till the day of his **s** unto *323*
8: 1 **s the glad tidings** of the kingdom of God: *2097*
Ac 9:39 and **s** the coats and garments which Dorcas *1925*
18:28 **s** by the scriptures that Jesus was Christ. *1925*
2Th 2: 4 the temple of God, **s** himself that he is God. *584*
Tit 2: 7 In all *things* **s** thyself a pattern of good *3930*
2: 7 in doctrine *s* uncorruptness, gravity, NIG
2:10 Not purloining, but **s** all good fidelity; *1731*
3: 2 *but* gentle, **s** all meekness unto all men. *1731*

SHIBAH See SHEBAH

SHIBBOLETH (1) [SIBBOLETH]
Jdg 12: 6 said they unto him, Say now **S**: and he said 7641

SHIBMAH (1)
Nu 32:38 (*their* names being changed,) and **S**: 7643

SHICRON (1)
Jos 15:11 the border was drawn to **S**, and 7942

SHIELD (45) [SHIELDS]
Ge 15: 1 I *am* thy **s**, *and* thy exceeding great reward. 4043
Dt 33:29 the **s** of thy help, and who *is* the sword of 4043
Jdg 5: 8 was there a **s** or spear seen among forty 4043
1Sa 17: 7 and one bearing a **s** went before him. 6793
17:41 the man that bare the **s** *went* before him. 6793
17:45 a sword, and with a spear, and with a **s**: 3591
2Sa 1:21 for there the **s** of the mighty is vilely cast 4043
1:21 the **s** of Saul, *as though he had* not *been* 4043
22: 3 *he is* my **s**, and the horn of my salvation, 4043
22:36 Thou hast also given me the **s** of thy 4043
1Ki 10:17 three pound *of* gold went to one **s**: 4043
2Ki 19:32 an arrow there, nor come before it *with* **s**, 4043
1Ch 12: 8 the battle, that could handle **s** and buckler, 6793
12:24 The children of Judah that bare **s** and 6793
12:34 with them with **s** and spear thirty and 6793
2Ch 9:16 hundred *shekels* of gold went to one **s**. 4043
17:17 *men* with bow and **s** two hundred thousand. 4043
25: 5 forth *to* war, that could handle spear and **s**. 6793
Job 39:23 against him, the glittering spear and the **s**. 3591
Ps 3: 3 thou, O LORD, *art* a **s** for me; my glory, 4043
5:12 favour wilt thou compass him as *with* a **s**. 6793
18:35 Thou hast also given me the **s** of thy 4043
28: 7 The LORD *is* my strength and my **s**; 4043
33:20 for the LORD: he *is* our help and our **s**. 4043
35: 2 Take hold of **s** and buckler, and stand up 4043
59:11 and bring them down, O Lord our **s**. 4043
76: 3 the **s**, and the sword, and the battle. 4043
84: 9 O God our **s**, and look upon the face of 4043
84:11 For the LORD God *is* a sun and **s**: 4043
91: 4 his truth *shall be thy* **s** and buckler. 6793
115: 9 in the LORD: he *is* their help and their **s**. 4043
115:10 in the LORD: he *is* their help and their **s**. 4043
115:11 in the LORD: he *is* their help and their **s**. 4043
119:114 Thou *art* my hiding place and my **s**: I hope 4043
144: 2 my deliverer; my **s**, and *he* in whom I trust; 4043
Pr 30: 5 he *is* a **s** unto them that put their trust in 4043
Isa 21: 5 drink: arise, ye princes, *and* anoint the **s**. 4043
22: 6 *and* horsemen, and Kir uncovered the **s**. 4043
Jer 46: 3 Order ye the buckler and **s**, and draw near 6793
46: 9 and the Libyans, that handle the **s**; 4043
Eze 23:24 thee buckler and **s** and helmet round about: 4043
27:10 they hanged the **s** and helmet in thee; 4043
38: 5 with them; all of them *with* **s** and helmet: 4043
Na 2: 3 The **s** of his mighty *men is* made red, 4043
Eph 6:16 Above all, taking the **s** of faith, *2375*

SHIELDS (23) [SHIELD]
2Sa 8: 7 David took the **s** of gold that were on 7982
1Ki 10:17 *he made* three hundred **s** *of* beaten gold; 4043
14:26 he took away all the **s** of gold which 4043
14:27 Rehoboam made in their stead brasen **s**, 4043
2Ki 11:10 the priest give king David's spears and **s**, 7982
1Ch 18: 7 David took the **s** of gold that were on 7982
2Ch 9:16 three hundred **s** *made he of* beaten gold: 4043
11:12 in every several city *he put* **s** and spears, 6793
12: 9 he carried away also the **s** of gold which 4043
12:10 Instead of which king Rehoboam made **s** of 4043
14: 8 that bare **s** and drew bows, two hundred 4043
23: 9 bucklers, and **s**, that *had been* king David's, 7982
26:14 prepared for them throughout all the host **s**, 4043
32: 5 and made darts and **s** in abundance. 4043
32:27 for **s**, and for all *manner of* pleasant jewels; 4043
Ne 4:16 the **s**, and the bows, and the habergeons; 4043
Ps 47: 9 for the **s** of the earth *belong* unto God: he is 4043
SS 4: 4 a thousand bucklers, all **s** of mighty *men*. 7982
Isa 37:33 an arrow there, nor come before it *with* **s**, 4043
Jer 51:11 gather the **s**: the LORD hath raised up 7982
Eze 27:11 they hanged their **s** upon thy walls round 7982
38: 4 *even* a great company *with* bucklers and **s**, 4043
39: 9 both the **s** and the bucklers, the bows and 4043

SHIGGAION (1)
Ps 7: T **S** of David, which he sang unto 7692

SHIGIONOTH (1)
Hab 3: 1 A prayer of Habakkuk the prophet upon **S**. 7692

SHIHOR (1)
1Ch 13: 5 from **S** of Egypt even unto the entering of 7883

SHIHOR-LIBNATH (1)
Jos 19:26 and reacheth to Carmel westward, and to **S**; 7884

SHIKKERON See SHICRON

SHILHI (2)
1Ki 22:42 name *was* Azubah the daughter of **S**. 7977
2Ch 20:31 name *was* Azubah the daughter of **S**. 7977

SHILHIM (1)
Jos 15:32 and **S**, and Ain, and Rimmon: 7978

SHILLEM (2) [SHILLEMITES]
Ge 46:24 Jahzeel, and Guni, and Jezer, and **S**. 8006
Nu 26:49 of **S**, the family of the Shillemites. 8006

SHILLEMITES (1) [SHILLEM]
Nu 26:49 of Shillem, the family of the **S**. 8016

SHILOAH (1)
Isa 8: 6 refuseth the waters of **S** that go softly, 7975

SHILOH (33) [SHILONITE, SHILONITES, TAANATH-SHILOH]
Ge 49:10 from between his feet, until **S** come; 7886
Jos 18: 1 children of Israel assembled together *at* **S**, 7887
18: 8 cast lots for you before the LORD in **S**. 7887
18: 9 and came *again* to Joshua to the host *at* **S**. 7887
18:10 Joshua cast lots for them in **S** before 7887
19:51 divided for an inheritance by lot in **S** before 7887
21: 2 they spake unto them at **S** in the land of 7887
22: 9 from the children of Israel out of **S**, 7887
22:12 of Israel gathered themselves together *at* **S**, 7887
Jdg 18:31 all the time that the house of God was in **S**. 7887
21:12 they brought them unto the camp *to* **S**, 7887
21:19 *there is* a feast of the LORD in **S** yearly *in* 7887
21:21 if the daughters of **S** come out to dance in 7887
21:21 every man his wife of the daughters of **S**, 7887
1Sa 1: 3 to sacrifice unto the LORD of hosts in **S**. 7887
1: 9 Hannah rose up after *they* had eaten in **S**, 7887
1:24 him *unto* the house of the LORD *in* **S**: 7887
2:14 So they did in **S** unto all the Israelites that 7887
3:21 the LORD appeared again in **S**: for 7887
3:21 to Samuel in **S** by the word of the LORD. 7887
4: 3 covenant of the LORD out of **S** unto us, 7887
4: 4 So the people sent *to* **S**, that they might 7887
4:12 came *to* **S** the same day with his clothes 7887
14: 3 the son of Eli, the LORD'S priest in **S**, 7887
1Ki 2:27 he spake concerning the house of Eli in **S**. 7887
14: 2 be the wife of Jeroboam; and get thee *to* **S**: 7887
14: 4 went *to* **S**, and came *to* the house of Ahijah. 7887
Ps 78:60 So that he forsook the tabernacle of **S**, 7887
Jer 7:12 go ye now unto my place which *was* in **S**, 7887
7:14 and to your fathers, as I have done to **S**. 7887
26: 6 will I make this house like **S**, and will make 7887
26: 9 This house shall be like **S**, and this city 7887
41: 5 from **S**, and from Samaria, *even* fourscore 7887

SHILONI (1)
Ne 11: 5 the son of Zechariah, the son of **S**. 8023

SHILONITE (5) [SHILOH]
1Ki 11:29 that the prophet Ahijah the **S** found him in 7888
12:15 which the LORD spake by Ahijah the **S** 7888
15:29 which he spake by his servant Ahijah the **S**: 7888
2Ch 9:29 in the prophecy of Ahijah the **S**, and in 7888
10:15 which he spake by the hand of Ahijah the **S** 7888

S

SHILONITES (1) [SHILOH]
1Ch 9: 5 of the **S**; Asaiah the firstborn, and his sons. 7888

SHILSHAH (1)
1Ch 7:37 and Shamma, and **S**, and Ithran, and Beera. 8030

SHIMEA (5) [SHIMEAH]
2Sa 21:21 Jonathan the son of **S** the brother of David 8092
1Ch 3: 5 **S**, and Shobab, and Nathan, and Solomon, 8092
6:30 **S** his son, Haggiah his son, Asaiah his son. 8092
6:39 Asaph the son of Berachiah, the son of **S**, 8092
20: 7 Jonathan the son of **S** David's brother slew 8092

SHIMEAH (3) [SHIMEA]
2Sa 13: 3 *was* Jonadab, the son of **S** David's brother: 8093
13:32 the son of **S** David's brother, answered and 8093
1Ch 8:32 Mikloth begat **S**. And these also dwelt with 8039

SHIMEAM (1)
1Ch 9:38 Mikloth begat **S**. And they also dwelt with 8043

SHIMEATH (2) [SHIMEATHITES]
2Ki 12:21 For Jozachar the son of **S**, and 8100
2Ch 24:26 Zabad the son of **S** an Ammonitess, and 8100

SHIMEATHITES (1) [SHIMEATH]
1Ch 2:55 the Tirathites, the **S**, *and* Suchathites. 8101

SHIMEI (42)
Nu 3:18 of Gershon by their families; Libni, and **S**. 8096
2Sa 16: 5 whose name *was* **S**, the son of Gera: 8096
16: 7 thus said **S** when he cursed, Come out, 8096
16:13 **S** went along on the hill's side over against 8096
19:16 **S** the son of Gera, a Benjamite, which *was* 8096
19:18 **S** the son of Gera fell down before the king, 8096
19:21 said, Shall not **S** be put to death for this, 8096
19:23 Therefore the king said unto **S**, Thou shalt 8096
1Ki 1: 8 **S**, and Rei, and the mighty *men* which 8096
2: 8 *thou hast* with thee **S** the son of Gera, 8096
2:36 the king sent and called for **S**, and said unto 8096
2:38 **S** said unto the king, The saying *is* good: 8096
2:38 And **S** dwelt in Jerusalem many days. 8096
2:39 that two of the servants of **S** ran away unto 8096
2:39 they told **S**, saying, Behold, thy servants *be* 8096
2:40 **S** arose, and saddled his ass, and went to 8096
2:40 **S** went, and brought his servants from 8096
2:41 it was told Solomon that **S** had gone from 8096
2:42 the king sent and called for **S**, and said unto 8096
2:44 The king said moreover to **S**, Thou knowest 8096
4:18 **S** the son of Elah, in Benjamin: 8096
1Ch 3:19 sons of Pedaiah *were*, Zerubbabel, and **S**: 8096
4:26 Hamuel his son, Zacchur his son, **S** his son. 8096
4:27 **S** had sixteen sons and six daughters; but 8096
5: 4 Shemaiah his son, Gog his son, **S** his son, 8096
6:17 of the sons of Gershom; Libni, and **S**. 8096
6:29 Libni his son, **S** his son, Uzza his son, 8096
6:42 of Ethan, the son of Zimmah, the son of **S**, 8096
23: 7 Of the Gershonites *were*, Laadan, and **S**. 8096
23: 9 The sons of **S**; Shelomith, and Haziel, and 8096
23:10 the sons of **S** *were*, Jahath, Zina, and Jeush, 8096
23:10 and Beriah. These four *were* the sons of **S**. 8096
25:17 The tenth *to* **S**, *he*, his sons, and 8096
27:27 over the vineyards *was* **S** the Ramathite: 8096
2Ch 29:14 of the sons of Heman; Jehiel, and **S**: and 8096
31:12 *was* ruler, and **S** his brother *was* the next. 8096
31:13 the hand of Cononiah and **S** his brother, 8096
Ezr 10:23 Jozabad, and **S**, and Kelaiah, (the same *is* 8096
10:33 Eliphelet, Jeremai, Manasseh, *and* **S**. 8096
10:38 And Bani, and Binnui, **S**, 8096
Est 2: 5 the son of Jair, the son of **S**, the son of 8096
Zec 12:13 the family of **S** apart, and their wives apart; 8097

SHIMEITES See SHIMITES

SHIMEON (1)
Ezr 10:31 Eliezer, Ishijah, Malchiah, Shemaiah, **S**, 8095

SHIMHI (1)
1Ch 8:21 and Beraiah, and Shimrath, the sons of **S**; 8096

SHIMI (1) [SHIMITES]
Ex 6:17 Libni, and **S**, according to their families. 8096

SHIMITES (1) [SHIMI]
Nu 3:21 of the Libnites, and the family of the **S**: 8097

SHIMMA (1)
1Ch 2:13 and Abinadab the second, and **S** the third, 8092

SHIMON (1)
1Ch 4:20 the sons of **S** *were*, Amnon, and Rinnah, 7889

SHIMRATH (1)
1Ch 8:21 Adaiah, and Beraiah, and **S**, the sons of 8119

SHIMRI (3)
1Ch 4:37 of Allon, the son of Jedaiah, the son of **S**, 8113
11:45 Jediael the son of **S**, and Joha his brother, 8113
2Ch 29:13 of the sons of Elizaphan; **S**, and Jeiel: and 8113

SHIMRITH (1)
2Ch 24:26 and Jehozabad the son of **S** a Moabitess. 8116

SHIMRON (5) [SHIMRONITES]
Ge 46:13 Tola, and Phuvah, and Job, and **S**. 8110
Nu 26:24 of **S**, the family of the Shimronites. 8110
Jos 11: 1 to the king of **S**, and to the king of 8110
19:15 and **S**, and Idalah, and Beth-lehem: 8110
1Ch 7: 1 *were*, Tola, and Puah, Jashub, and **S**, four. 8110

SHIMRONITES (1) [SHIMRON]
Nu 26:24 of Shimron, the family of the **S**. 8117

SHIMRON-MERON (1)
Jos 12:20 The king of **S**, one; the king of Achshaph, 8112

SHIMSHAI (4)
Ezr 4: 8 **S** the scribe wrote a letter against Jerusalem 8124
4: 9 **S** the scribe, and the rest of their 8124
4:17 *to* **S** the scribe, and *to* the rest of their 8124
4:23 **S** the scribe, and their companions, 8124

SHINAB (1)
Ge 14: 2 **S** king of Admah, and Shemeber king of 8134

SHINAR (7)
Ge 10:10 and Accad, and Calneh, in the land of **S**. 8152
11: 2 that they found a plain in the land of **S**; 8152
14: 1 to pass in the days of Amraphel king of **S**, 8152
14: 9 Amraphel king of **S**, and Arioch king of 8152
Isa 11:11 from **S**, and from Hamath, and from 8152
Da 1: 2 which he carried *into* the land of **S** *to* 8152
Zec 5:11 To build it a house in the land of **S**: 8152

SHINE (32) [SHINED, SHINETH, SHINING, SHONE]
Nu 6:25 The LORD **make** his face **s** upon thee, and 215
Job 3: 4 it from above, neither let the light **s** upon it. 3313
10: 3 and **s** upon the counsel of the wicked? 3313
11:17 thou shalt **s forth**, thou shalt be as 5774
18: 5 put out, and the spark of his fire shall not **s**. 5050
22:28 and the light shall **s** upon thy ways. 5050
36:32 commandeth it *not to* **s** by *the cloud* that NIH
37:15 and **caused** the light of his cloud **to s**? 3313
41:18 *By* his neesings a light doth **s**, and his eyes 1984
41:32 He **maketh** a path **to s** after him; *one* would 215
Ps 31:16 **Make** thy face **to s** upon thy servant: 215
67: *and* **cause** his face **to s** upon us; Selah. 215
80: 1 dwellest *between* the cherubims, **s forth**. 3313
80: 3 us again, O God, and **cause** thy face **to s**; 215
80: 7 O God *of* hosts, and **cause** thy face **to s**; 215
80:19 O LORD God *of* hosts, **cause** thy face **to s**; 215
104:15 *and* oil to **make** *his* face **to s**, and 6670
119:135 **Make** thy face **to s** upon thy servant; and 215
Ecc 8: 1 a man's wisdom **maketh** his face **to s**, and 215
Isa 13:10 and the moon shall not **cause** her light **to s**. 5050
60: 1 Arise, **s**; for thy light is come, and the glory 215
Jer 5:28 They are waxen fat, they **s**: yea, 6245
Da 9:17 **cause** thy face **to s** upon thy sanctuary that is 215
12: 3 they that be wise shall **s** as the brightness of 2094
Mt 5:16 Let your light so **s** before men, that they *2989*
13:43 Then shall the righteous **s forth** as the sun *1584*
17: 2 and his face did **s** as the sun, and *2989*
2Co 4: 4 is the image of God, should **s** unto them. *826*
4: 6 who commanded the light to **s** out of *2989*
Php 2:15 among whom ye **s** as lights in the world; *5316*
Rev 18:23 And the light of a candle shall **s** no more at *5316*
21:23 of the sun, neither of the moon, to **s** in it: *5316*

SHINED (9) [SHINE]
Dt 33: 2 he **s forth** from mount Paran, and he came 3313
Job 29: 3 When his candle **s** upon my head, *and* 1984

Job 31:26 If I beheld the sun when it **s**, or the moon 1984
Ps 50: 2 the perfection of beauty, God hath **s**. 3313
Isa 9: 2 of death, upon them hath the light **s**. 5050
Eze 43: 2 many waters: and the earth **s** with his glory. 215
Ac 9: 3 suddenly there **s round about** him a light *4015*
12: 7 came upon *him*, and a light **s** in the prison: *2989*
2Co 4: 6 shine out of darkness, hath **s** in our hearts, *2989*

SHINETH (9) [SHINE]
Job 25: 5 Behold *even* to the moon, and it **s** not; yea, 166
Ps 139:12 not from thee; but the night **s** as the day: 215
Pr 4:18 that **s more and more** unto the perfect day. 1980
Mt 24:27 out of the east, and **s** *even* unto the west; *5316*
Lk 17:24 **s** unto the other *part* under heaven; *2989*
Jn 1: 5 And the light **s** in darkness; and *5316*
2Pe 1:19 as unto a light that **s** in a dark place, *5316*
1Jn 2: 8 darkness is past, and the true light now **s**. *5316*
Rev 1:16 his countenance *was* as the sun **s** in his *5316*

SHINING (11) [SHINE]
2Sa 23: 4 out of the earth by **clear s** after rain. 5051
Pr 4:18 the path of the just *is* as the **s** light, 5051
Isa 4: 5 by day, and the **s** of a flaming fire by night: 5051
Joel 2:10 and the stars shall withdraw their **s**: 5051
3:15 and the stars shall withdraw their **s**. 5051
Hab 3:11 *and* at the **s** of thy glittering spear. 5051
Mk 9: 3 And his raiment became **s**, exceeding white *4744*
Lk 11:36 as when the **bright s** of a candle doth give *796*
24: 4 two men stood by them in **s** garments: *797*
Jn 5:35 He was a burning and a **s** light: and ye were *5316*
Ac 26:13 **s round about** me and them which *4034*

SHION (1)
Jos 19:19 And Hapharaim, and **S**, and Anaharath, 7866

SHIP (71) [FORESHIP, SHIPMASTER, SHIPMEN, SHIPPING, SHIPS, SHIPWRACK]
Pr 30:19 the way of a **s** in the midst of the sea; and 591
Isa 33:21 neither shall gallant **s** pass thereby. 6716
Eze 27: 5 They have made all thy **s** boards of fir trees NIH
Jnh 1: 3 *to* Joppa; and he found a **s** going *to* Tarshish: 591
1: 4 in the sea, so that the **s** was like to be broken. 591
1: 5 cast forth the wares that *were* in the **s** into 591
1: 5 was gone down into the sides of the **s**; 5600
Mt 4:21 his brother, in a **s** with Zebedee their father, *4143*
4:22 And they immediately left the **s** and *4143*
8:23 And when he was entered into a **s**, *4143*
8:24 insomuch that the **s** was covered with *4143*
9: 1 And he entered into a **s**, and passed over, *4143*
13: 2 unto him, so that he went into a **s**, and sat; *4143*
14:13 thence by **s** into a desert place apart: *4143*
14:22 constrained his disciples to get into a **s**, *4143*
14:24 But the **s** was now in the midst of the sea, *4143*
14:29 when Peter was come down out of the **s**, *4143*
14:32 And when they were come into the **s**, *4143*
14:33 Then they that were in the **s** came and *4143*
15:39 and took **s**, and came into the coasts of *4143*
Mk 1:19 who also *were* in the **s** mending *their* nets. *4143*
1:20 they left their father Zebedee in the **s** with *4143*
3: 9 that a **small s** should wait on him because *4142*
4: 1 so that he entered into a **s**, and sat in *4143*
4:36 they took him *even* as he was in the **s**. *4143*
4:37 and the waves beat into the **s**, so that it was *4143*
4:38 And he was in the **hinder part of** the **s**, *4403*
5: 2 And when he was come out of the **s**, *4143*
5:18 And when he was come into the **s**, he that *4143*
5:21 And when Jesus was passed over again by **s** *4143*
6:32 And they departed into a desert place by **s** *4143*
6:45 constrained his disciples to get into the **s**, *4143*
6:47 the **s** was in the midst of the sea, and *4143*
6:51 And he went up unto them into the **s**; and *4143*
6:54 And when they were come out of the **s**, *4143*
8:10 And straightway he entered into a **s** with *4143*
8:13 entering into the **s** again departed to *4143*
8:14 neither had they in the **s** with them more *4143*
Lk 5: 3 and taught the people out of the **s**. *4143*
5: 7 which were in the other **s**, that *they* should *4143*
8:22 that he went into a **s** with his disciples: *4143*
8:37 and he went *up* into the **s**, and *4143*
Jn 6:17 And entered into a **s**, and went over the sea *4143*
6:19 on the sea, and drawing nigh unto the **s**: *4143*
6:21 Then they willingly received him into the **s**: *4143*
6:21 immediately the **s** was at the land whither *4143*
21: 3 and entered into a **s** immediately; *4143*
21: 6 Cast the net on the right side of the **s**, and *4143*
21: 8 And the other disciples came in a **little s**; *4142*
Ac 20:13 And we went before to **s**, and sailed unto *4143*
20:38 And they accompanied him unto the **s**. *4143*
21: 2 And finding a **s** sailing over unto Phenicia, *4143*
21: 3 for there the **s** was to unlade *her* burden. *4143*
21: 6 taken our leave one of another, we took **s**; *4143*
27: 2 And entering into a **s** of Adramyttium, *4143*
27: 6 And there the centurion found a **s** of *4143*
27:10 not only of the lading and **s**, but also of our *4143*
27:11 believed the master and the **owner of the s**, *3490*
27:15 And when the **s** was caught, and could not *4143*
27:17 they used helps, undergirding the **s**; *4143*
27:18 the next *day* they **lightened the s**; *1546+4160*
27:19 with our own hands the tackling of the **s**. *4143*
27:22 of *any man's* life among you, but of the **s**. *4143*
27:30 the shipmen were about to flee out of the **s**, *4143*
27:31 to the soldiers, Except these abide in the **s**, *4143*
27:37 And we were in all in the **s** two hundred *4143*
27:38 they lightened the **s**, and cast out the wheat *4143*
27:39 if it were possible, to thrust in the **s**. *4143*
27:41 where two seas met, they ran the **s** aground; *3491*
27:44 and some on broken pieces of the **s**. *4143*
28:11 And after three months we departed in a **s** *4143*

SHIPHI (1)
1Ch 4:37 Ziza the son of **S**, the son of Allon, the son 8230

SHIPHMITE (1)
1Ch 27:27 for the wine cellars *was* Zabdi the **S**: 8225

SHIPHRAH (1)
Ex 1:15 of which the name of the one *was* **S**, and 8236

SHIPHTAN (1)
Nu 34:24 children of Ephraim, Kemuel the son of **S**. 8204

SHIPMASTER (2) [MASTER, SHIP]
Jnh 1: 6 So the **s** came to him, and 2259+7227+1886.1
Rev 18:17 And every **s**, and all the company in ships, *2942*

SHIPMEN (3) [MAN, SHIP]
1Ki 9:27 **s** that had knowledge of the sea, 376+591
Ac 27:27 about midnight the **s** deemed that they drew *3492*
27:30 And as the **s** were about to flee out of *3492*

SHIPPING (1) [SHIP]
Jn 6:24 they also **took s**, *1519+1684+3588+4143*

SHIPS (39) [SHIP]
Ge 49:13 he *shall be* for a haven of **s**; and his border 591
Nu 24:24 And **s** *shall come* from the coast of Chittim, 6716
Dt 28:68 shall bring thee *into* Egypt again with **s**, 591
Jdg 5:17 why did Dan remain *in* **s**? Asher continued 591
1Ki 9:26 king Solomon made a navy *of* **s** in NIH
22:48 Jehoshaphat made **s** of Tharshish to go to 591
22:48 for the **s** were broken at Ezion-geber. 591
22:49 my servants go with thy servants in the **s**. 591
2Ch 8:18 sent him by the hands of his servants **s**, 591
9:21 For the king's **s** went *to* Tarshish with 591
9:21 every three years once came the **s** of 591
20:36 he joined himself with him to make **s** to go 591
20:36 and they made the **s** in Ezion-geber. 591
20:37 the **s** were broken, that they were not able to 591
Job 9:26 They are passed away as the swift **s**: as 591
Ps 48: 7 Thou breakest the **s** of Tarshish with an east 591
104:26 There go the **s**: *there is* that leviathan, 591
107:23 They that go down to the sea in **s**, that do 591
Pr 31:14 She is like the merchant's **s**; she bringeth her 591
Isa 2:16 upon all the **s** of Tarshish, and upon all 591
23: 1 Howl, ye **s** of Tarshish; for it is laid waste, 591
23:14 Howl, ye **s** of Tarshish: for your strength is 591
43:14 and the Chaldeans, whose cry *is* in the **s**. 591
60: 9 the **s** of Tarshish first, to bring thy sons from 591
Eze 27: 9 all the **s** of the sea with their mariners were 591
27:25 The **s** of Tarshish did sing of thee *in* thy 591
27:29 of the sea, shall come down from their **s**, 591
30: 9 in **s** to make the careless Ethiopians afraid, 6716
Da 11:30 For *the* **s** of Chittim shall come against 6716
11:40 and with horsemen, and with many **s**; 591
Mk 4:36 And there were also with him other **little s**. *4142*
Lk 5: 2 And saw two **s** standing by the lake: but *4143*
5: 3 And he entered into one of the **s**, which was *4143*
5: 7 and filled both the **s**, so that they began to *4143*
5:11 And when they had brought *their* **s** to land, *4143*

Jas 3: 4 Behold also the **s**, which though they be so 4143
Rev 8: 9 and the third *part* of the **s** were destroyed. 4143
18:17 every shipmaster, and all the company in **s**, 4143
18:19 wherein were made rich all that had **s** in 4143

SHIPWRACK (2) [SHIP]
2Co 11:25 thrice I **suffered s**, a night and a day I have 3489
1Ti 1:19 put away, concerning faith have **made s**: 3489

SHISHA (1)
1Ki 4: 3 Elihoreph and Ahiah, the sons of **S**, scribes; 7894

SHISHAK (7)
1Ki 11:40 unto **S** king of Egypt, and was in Egypt 7895
14:25 *that* **S** king of Egypt came up against 7895
2Ch 12: 2 *that* in the fifth year of king Rehoboam **S** 7895
12: 5 together to Jerusalem because of **S**, 7895
12: 5 have I also left you in the hand of **S**. 7895
12: 7 out upon Jerusalem by the hand of **S**. 7895
12: 9 So **S** king of Egypt came up against 7895

SHITRAI (1)
1Ch 27:29 over the herds that fed in Sharon *was* **S** 7861

SHITTAH (1)
Isa 41:19 the **s tree**, and the myrtle, and the oil tree; 7848

SHITTIM (32) [ABEL-SHITTIM]
Ex 25: 5 dyed red, and badgers' skins, and **s** wood, 7848
25:10 they shall make an ark of **s** wood: 7848
25:13 thou shalt make staves of **s** wood, and 7848
25:23 Thou shalt also make a table *of* **s** wood: 7848
25:28 thou shalt make the staves *of* **s** wood, and 7848
26:15 for the tabernacle *of* **s** wood standing up. 7848
26:26 thou shalt make bars *of* **s** wood; five for 7848
26:32 thou shalt hang it upon four pillars of **s** 7848
26:37 make for the hanging five pillars of **s** *wood,* 7848
27: 1 thou shalt make an altar *of* **s** wood, 7848
27: 6 staves of **s** wood, and overlay them with 7848
30: 1 incense upon: *of* **s** wood shalt thou make it. 7848
30: 5 thou shalt make the staves *of* **s** wood, and 7848
35: 7 dyed red, and badgers' skins, and **s** wood, 7848
35:24 with whom was found **s** wood for any work 7848
36:20 he made boards for the tabernacle *of* **s** 7848
36:31 he made bars of **s** wood; five for the boards 7848
36:36 he made thereunto four pillars of **s** *wood,* 7848
37: 1 Bezaleel made the ark *of* **s** wood: 7848
37: 4 he made staves of **s** wood, and 7848
37:10 he made the table *of* **s** wood: two cubits 7848
37:15 he made the staves *of* **s** wood, and 7848
37:25 he made the incense altar *of* **s** wood: 7848
37:28 he made the staves of **s** wood, and 7848
38: 1 he made the altar of burnt offering *of* **s** 7848
38: 6 he made the staves *of* **s** wood, and 7848
Nu 25: 1 Israel abode in **S**, and the people begun to 7851
Dt 10: 3 I made an ark of **s** wood, and hewed two 7848
Jos 2: 1 Joshua the son of Nun sent out of **S** two 7851
3: 1 they removed from **S**, and came to Jordan, 7851
Joel 3:18 the LORD, and shall water the valley of **S**. 7851
Mic 6: 5 of Beor answered him; from **S** unto Gilgal; 7851

SHIVERS (1)
Rev 2:27 of a potter *shall* they be **broken to s**: 4937

SHIZA (1)
1Ch 11:42 Adina the son of **S** the Reubenite, a captain 7877

SHOA (1)
Eze 23:23 all the Chaldeans, Pekod, and **S**, and Koa, 7772

SHOBAB (4)
2Sa 5:14 and **S**, and Nathan, and Solomon, 7727
1Ch 2:18 sons *are* these; Jesher, and **S**, and Ardon. 7727
3: 5 and **S**, and Nathan, and Solomon, four, 7727
14: 4 Shammua, and **S**, Nathan, and Solomon, 7727

SHOBACH (2)
2Sa 10:16 **S** the captain of the host of Hadarezer *went* 7731
10:18 smote **S** the captain of their host, who died 7731

SHOBAI (2)
Ezr 2:42 the children of Hatita, the children of **S**, 7630
Ne 7:45 the children of **S**, an hundred thirty and 7630

SHOBAL (9)
Ge 36:20 Lotan, and **S**, and Zibeon, and Anah, 7732
36:23 the children of **S** *were* these; Alvan, and 7732
36:29 duke Lotan, duke **S**, duke Zibeon, 7732
1Ch 1:38 **S**, and Zibeon, and Anah, and Dishon, and 7732
1:40 The sons of **S**; Alian, and Manahath, and 7732
2:50 of Ephratah; **S** the father of Kirjath-jearim, 7732
2:52 **S** the father of Kirjath-jearim had sons; 7732
4: 1 Hezron, and Carmi, and Hur, and **S**. 7732
4: 2 Reaiah the son of **S** begat Jahath; and 7732

SHOBEK (1)
Ne 10:24 Hallohesh, Pileha, **S**, 7733

SHOBI (1)
2Sa 17:27 that **S** the son of Nahash of Rabbah of 7629

SHOCHO (1)
2Ch 28:18 **S** with the villages thereof, and Timnah 7755

SHOCHOH (2)
1Sa 17: 1 were gathered together *at* **S**, 7755
17: 1 pitched between **S** and Azekah, 7755

SHOCK (1)
Job 5:26 like as a **s of corn** cometh in in his season. 1430

SHOCKS (1)
Jdg 15: 5 burnt up both the **s**, and also the standing 1430

SHOCO (1)
2Ch 11: 7 And Beth-zur, and **S**, and Adullam, 7755

SHOD (4) [UNSHOD]
2Ch 28:15 **s** them, and gave them to eat and to drink, 5274
Eze 16:10 **s** thee *with* badgers' *skin,* and I girded thee 5274
Mk 6: 9 But *be* **s** with sandals; and not put on two 5265
Eph 6:15 And *your* feet **s** with the preparation of 5265

SHOE (9) [SHOE'S, SHOELATCHET, SHOES]
Dt 25: 9 loose his **s** from off his foot, and spit in his 5275
25:10 The house of him that hath his **s** loosed. 5275
29: 5 and thy **s** is not waxen old upon thy foot. 5275
Jos 5:15 unto Joshua, Loose thy **s** from off thy foot; 5275
Ru 4: 7 a man plucked off his **s**, and gave *it* to his 5275
4: 8 Buy *it* for thee. So he drew off his **s**. 5275
Ps 60: 8 over Edom will I cast out my **s**: 5275
108: 9 over Edom will I cast out my **s**; 5275
Isa 20: 2 thy loins, and put off thy **s** from thy foot. 5275

SHOE'S (1) [SHOE]
Jn 1:27 whose **s** latchet I am not worthy to unloose. 5266

SHOELATCHET (1) [LATCHET, SHOE]
Ge 14:23 not *take* from a thread even to a **s**, 5275+8288

SHOES (21) [SHOE]
Ex 3: 5 put off thy **s** from off thy feet, for the place 5275
12:11 your **s** on your feet, and your staff in your 5275
Dt 33:25 Thy **s** *shall be* iron and brass; and as thy 4515
Jos 9: 5 old **s** and clouted upon their feet, and 5275
9:13 our **s** are become old by reason of the very 5275
1Ki 2: 5 his loins, and in his **s** that *were* on his feet. 5275
SS 7: 1 How beautiful are thy feet with **s**, 5275
Isa 5:27 nor the latchet of their **s** be broken: 5275
Eze 24:17 put on thy **s** upon thy feet, and cover not 5275
24:23 your heads, and your **s** upon your feet: 5275
Am 2: 6 for silver, and the poor for a pair of **s**; 5275
8: 6 for silver, and the needy for a pair of **s**; 5275
Mt 3:11 than I, whose **s** I am not worthy to bear: 5266
10:10 neither two coats, neither **s**, nor yet staves: 5266
Mk 1: 7 the latchet of whose **s** I am not worthy to 5266
Lk 3:16 the latchet of whose **s** I am not worthy to 5266
10: 4 Carry neither purse, nor scrip, nor **s**: and 5266
15:22 put a ring on his hand, and **s** on *his* feet: 5266
22:35 I sent you without purse, and scrip, and **s**, 5266
Ac 7:33 the Lord to him, Put off *thy* **s** from thy feet: 5266
13:25 whose **s** of *his* feet I am not worthy to 5266

SHOHAM (1)
1Ch 24:27 Beno, and **S**, and Zaccur, and Ibri. 7719

SHOMER (2)
2Ki 12:21 Jehozabad the son of **S**, his servants, 7763
1Ch 7:32 and **S**, and Hotham, and Shua their sister. 7763

SHONE (7) [SHINE]
Ex 34:29 skin of his face **s** while he talked with him. 7160

S

Ex 34:30 saw Moses, behold, the skin of his face **s**; 7160
34:35 of Moses, that the skin of Moses' face **s**: 7160
2Ki 3:22 the sun **s** upon the water, and the Moabites 2224
Lk 2: 9 the glory of the Lord **s round about** them: *4034*
Ac 22: 6 suddenly there **s** from heaven a great light *4015*
Rev 8:12 and the day **s** not for a third *part* of it, *5316*

SHOOK (12) [SHAKE]
2Sa 6: 6 and took hold of it; for the oxen **s** *it.* 8058
22: 8 the earth **s** and trembled; the foundations of 1607
22: 8 the foundations of heaven moved and **s**, 1607
Ne 5:13 Also I **s** my lap, and said, So God shake out 5287
Ps 18: 7 the earth **s** and trembled; the foundations 1607
68: 8 The earth **s**, the heavens also dropped at 7493
77:18 the world: the earth trembled and **s**. 7493
Isa 23:11 his hand over the sea, he **s** the kingdoms: 7264
Ac 13:51 But they **s off** the dust of their feet against *1621*
18: 6 he **s** *his* raiment, and said unto them, *1621*
28: 5 And he **s off** the beast into the fire, and *660*
Heb 12:26 Whose voice then **s** the earth: but now he *4531*

SHOOT (21) [BOWSHOT, SHOOTERS, SHOOTETH, SHOOTING, SHOT]
Ex 36:33 he made the middle bar to **s** through 1272
1Sa 20:20 I will **s** three arrows on the side *thereof,* as 3384
20:36 Run, find out now the arrows which I **s**. 3384
2Sa 11:20 knew ye not that they would **s** from 3384
2Ki 13:17 he opened *it.* Then Elisha said, **S**. And he 3384
19:32 nor **s** an arrow there, nor come before it 3384
1Ch 5:18 and to **s** with bow, and skilful in war, 1869
2Ch 26:15 to **s** arrows and great stones withal. 3384
Ps 11: 2 that *they* may privily **s** at the upright in 3384
22: 7 they **s out** the lip, they shake the head, 6362
58: 7 *when* he bendeth *his bow to* **s** his arrows, NIH
64: 3 and bend *their bows to* **s** their arrows, NIH
64: 4 That *they* may **s** in secret at the perfect: 3384
64: 4 suddenly do they **s** at him, and fear not. 3384
64: 7 God shall **s** at them *with* an arrow; 3384
144: 6 **s out** thine arrows, and destroy them. 7971
Isa 37:33 nor **s** an arrow there, nor come before it 3384
Jer 50:14 bend the bow, **s** at her, spare no arrows: 3034
Eze 31:14 neither **s up** their top among the thick 5414
36: 8 ye shall **s forth** your branches, and 5414
Lk 21:30 When they now **s forth**, ye see and *4261*

SHOOTERS (1) [SHOOT]
2Sa 11:24 the **s** shot from off the wall upon thy 4175

SHOOTETH (3) [SHOOT]
Job 8:16 and his branch **s forth** in his garden, 3318
Isa 27: 8 In measure, when it **s forth**, thou wilt 7971
Mk 4:32 than all herbs, and **s out** great branches; *4160*

SHOOTING (2) [SHOOT]
1Ch 12: 2 in *hurling* stones and *s* arrows out of a bow, NIH
Am 7: 1 beginning of the **s up** of the latter growth; 5927

SHOPHACH (2)
1Ch 19:16 **S** the captain of the host of Hadarezer *went* 7780
19:18 killed **S** the captain of the host. 7780

S

SHOPHAN See ATROTH SHOPHAN

SHORE (17)
Ge 22:17 and as the sand which *is* upon the sea **s**; 8193
Ex 14:30 saw the Egyptians dead upon the sea **s**. 8193
Jos 11: 4 *even* as the sand that *is* upon the sea **s** in 8193
15: 2 their south border was from the **s** of the salt 7097
Jdg 5:17 Asher continued on the sea **s**, and abode in 2348
1Sa 13: 5 people as the sand which *is* on the sea **s** in 8193
1Ki 4:29 *even* as the sand that *is* on the sea **s**. 8193
9:26 on the **s** of the Red sea, in the land of 8193
Jer 47: 7 against Ashkelon, and against the sea **s**? 2348
Mt 13: 2 sat; and the whole multitude stood on the **s**. *123*
13:48 they drew to **s**, and sat down, and *123*
Mk 6:53 the land of Genesaret, and **drew to** the **s**. *4358*
Jn 21: 4 was now come, Jesus stood on the **s**: *123*
Ac 21: 5 and we kneeled down on the **s**, and prayed. *123*
27:39 but they discovered a certain creek with a **s**, *123*
27:40 the mainsail to the wind, and made toward **s**. *123*
Heb 11:12 as the sand which is by the sea **s** *5491*

SHORELANDS See SUBURBS

SHORN (4) [SHEAR]
SS 4: 2 *are* like a flock of *sheep that are* **even s**, 7094
Ac 18:18 having **s** *his* head in Cenchrea: for he had a *2751*
1Co 11: 6 the woman be not covered, let her also be **s**: *2751*
11: 6 but *if it* be a shame for a woman to be **s** or *2751*

SHORT (13) [SHORTENED, SHORTER, SHORTLY]
Nu 11:23 Is the LORD'S hand **waxed s**? 7114
2Ki 10:32 days the LORD began to **cut** Israel **s**: 7096
Job 17:12 into day: the light *is* **s**, because of darkness. 7138
20: 5 the triumphing of the wicked *is* **s**, 4480+7138
Ps 89:47 Remember how **s** my **time** is: 2465
Ro 3:23 and **come s** of the glory of God; *5302*
9:28 the work, and **cut** *it* **s** in righteousness: *4932*
9:28 a **s** work will the Lord make upon the earth. *4932*
1Co 7:29 But this I say, brethren, the time *is* **s**: *4958*
1Th 2:17 being taken from you for a **s** time in *5610*
Heb 4: 1 any of you should seem to **come s** *of it.* *5302*
Rev 12:12 he knoweth that he hath *but* a **s** time. *3641*
17:10 he cometh, he must continue a **s** *space.* *3641*

SHORTENED (9) [SHORT]
Ps 89:45 The days of his youth hast thou **s**: thou hast 7114
102:23 my strength in the way; he **s** my days. 7114
Pr 10:27 but the years of the wicked shall be **s**. 7114
Isa 50: 2 Is my hand **s at all**, that *it* cannot 7114+7114
59: 1 Behold, the LORD'S hand is not **s**, that *it* 7114
Mt 24:22 And except those days should be **s**, *2856*
24:22 for the elect's sake those days shall be **s**. *2856*
Mk 13:20 And except that the Lord had **s** *those* days, *2856*
13:20 whom he hath chosen, he hath **s** the days. *2856*

SHORTER (2) [SHORT]
Isa 28:20 For the bed is **s** than that *a man* can stretch 7114
Eze 42: 5 Now the upper chambers *were* **s**: for 7114

SHORTLY (15) [SHORT]
Ge 41:32 by God, and God will **s** bring it to pass. 4116
Jer 27:16 *shall* now **s** be brought again from Babylon: 4120
Eze 7: 8 Now will I **s** pour out my fury upon 4480+7138
Ac 25: 4 he himself would depart **s** *thither.* *1722+5034*
Ro 16:20 shall bruise Satan under your feet **s**. *1722+5034*
1Co 4:19 But I will come to you **s**, if the Lord will, *5030*
Php 2:19 Lord Jesus to send Timotheus **s** unto you, *5030*
2:24 in the Lord that I also myself shall come **s**. *5030*
1Ti 3:14 I unto thee, hoping to come unto thee **s**: *5030*
2Ti 4: 9 Do thy diligence to come **s** unto me: *5030*
Heb 13:23 with whom, if he come **s**, I will see you. *5030*
2Pe 1:14 Knowing that **s** *I* must put off *this* my *5031*
3Jn 1:14 But I trust *I* shall **s** see thee, and we shall *2112*
Rev 1: 1 *things* which must **s** come to pass; *1722+5034*
22: 6 *the things* which must **s** be done. *1722+5034*

SHOSHANNIM (2)
Ps 45: T To the chief Musician upon **S**, for the sons 7799
69: T To the chief Musician upon **S**, *A Psalm* of 7799

SHOSHANNIM-EDUTH (1)
Ps 80: T To the chief Musician upon **S**, A 5715+7799

SHOT (16) [SHOOT]
Ge 40:10 though it budded, *and* her blossoms **s forth**; 5927
49:23 grieved him, and **s** *at him,* and hated him: 7232
Ex 19:13 shall surely be stoned, or **s through**; 3384+3384
Nu 21:30 We have **s** at them; Heshbon is perished 3384
1Sa 20:20 on the side *thereof,* as *though* I **s** at a mark. 7971
20:36 as the lad ran, he **s** an arrow beyond him. 3384
20:37 place of the arrow which Jonathan had **s**, 3384
2Sa 11:24 the shooters **s** from off the wall upon thy 3384
2Ki 13:17 he **s**. And he said, The arrow of 3384
2Ch 35:23 the archers **s** at king Josiah; and the king 3384
Ps 18:14 he **s out** lightnings, and discomfited them. 7232
Jer 9: 8 Their tongue *is as* an arrow **s out**; 7819
Eze 17: 6 brought forth branches, and **s forth** sprigs. 7971
17: 7 and **s forth** her branches toward him, 7971
31: 5 of the multitude of waters, when he **s forth**. 7971
31:10 he hath **s up** his top among the thick 5414

SHOULD (783) [SHOULDEST] See Index

SHOULDER (38) [SHOULDERPIECES, SHOULDERS]
Ge 21:14 putting *it* on her **s**, and the child, and 7926
24:15 with her pitcher upon her **s**. 7926
24:45 came forth with her pitcher on her **s**; 7926
24:46 let down her pitcher from her *s*, and said, NIH

Ge 49:15 bowed his s to bear, and became a servant 7926
Ex 29:22 the fat that *is* upon them, and the right s; 7785
29:27 the s of the heave offering, which is waved, 7785
Lev 7:32 the right s shall ye give unto the priest *for* a 7785
7:33 the fat, shall have the right s for *his* part. 7785
7:34 the heave s have I taken of the children of 7785
8:25 two kidneys, and their fat, and the right s: 7785
8:26 put *them* on the fat, and upon the right s: 7785
9:21 the right s Aaron waved *for* a wave offering 7785
10:14 and heave s shall ye eat in a clean place; 7785
10:15 The heave s and the wave breast shall they 7785
Nu 6:19 the priest shall take the sodden s of the ram, 2220
6:20 with the wave breast and heave s: 7785
18:18 the wave breast and as the right s are thine. 7785
Dt 18: 3 and they shall give unto the priest the s, and 2220
Jos 4: 5 ye up every man of you a stone upon his s, 7926
Jdg 9:48 laid *it* on his s, and said unto the people that 7926
1Sa 9:24 the cook took up the s, and *that* which *was* 7785
Ne 9:29 withdrew the s, and hardened their neck, 3802
Job 31:22 *Then* let mine arm fall from *my* s **blade**, 7929
31:36 Surely I would take it upon my s, *and* 7926
Ps 81: 6 I removed his s from the burden: his hands 7926
Isa 9: 4 the staff of his s, the rod of his oppressor, 7926
9: 6 and the government shall be upon his s: and 7926
10:27 burden shall be taken away from off thy s, 7926
22:22 of the house of David will I lay upon his s; 7926
46: 7 They bear him upon the s, they carry him, 3802
Eze 12: 7 *and* I bare *it* upon *my* s in their sight. 3802
12:12 them shall bear upon *his* s in the twilight, 3802
24: 4 *even* every good piece, the thigh, and the s; 3802
29: 7 thou didst break, and rent all their s: 3802
29:18 *was* made bald, and every s *was* peeled: 3802
34:21 ye have thrust with side and with s, 3802
Zec 7:11 pulled away the s, and stopped their ears, 3802

SHOULDERPIECES (4) [PIECE, SHOULDER]
Ex 28: 7 It shall have the two s *thereof* joined at 3802
28:25 put *them* on the s of the ephod before it. 3802
39: 4 They made s for it, to couple *it* together: 3802
39:18 put them on the s of the ephod, before it. 3802

SHOULDERS (20) [SHOULDER]
Ge 9:23 laid *it* upon both their s, and 7926
Ex 12:34 bound up in their clothes upon their s. 7926
28:12 thou shalt put the two stones upon the s of 3802
28:12 the LORD upon his two s for a memorial. 3802
39: 7 he put them on the s of the ephod, *that they* 3802
Nu 7: 9 *was that* they should bear upon *their* s. 3802
Dt 33:12 day long, and he shall dwell between his s. 3802
Jdg 16: 3 bar and all, and put *them* upon his s, and 3802
1Sa 9: 2 from his s and upward *he was* higher than 7926
10:23 higher than any of the people from his s 7926
17: 6 his legs, and a target of brass between his s. 3802
1Ch 15:15 of God upon their s with the staves thereon, 3802
2Ch 35: 3 *it shall* not *be* a burden upon your s: 3802
Isa 11:14 they shall fly upon the s of the Philistines 3802
14:25 and his burden depart from off their s. 7926
30: 6 they will carry their riches upon the s of 3802
49:22 thy daughters shall be carried upon *their* s. 3802
Eze 12: 6 In their sight shalt thou bear *it* upon *thy* s, 3802
Mt 23: 4 to be borne, and lay *them* on men's s; *5606*
Lk 15: 5 when he hath found *it,* he layeth *it* on his s, *5606*

SHOULDEST (73) [SHOULD] See Index

SHOUT (36) [SHOUTED, SHOUTETH, SHOUTING, SHOUTINGS]
Ex 32:18 *It is* not the voice of *them that* s for 6030
Nu 23:21 and the s of a king *is* among them. 8643
Jos 6: 5 all the people shall s *with* a great shout; 7321
6: 5 all the people shall shout *with* a great s; 8643
6:10 saying, Ye shall not s, nor make any noise 7321
6:10 out of your mouth, until the day I bid you s; 7321
6:10 the day I bid you shout; then shall ye s. 7321
6:16 Joshua said unto the people, S; 7321
6:20 the people shouted *with* a great s, that 8643
1Sa 4: 5 all Israel shouted *with* a great s, so that 8643
4: 6 the Philistines heard the noise of the s, 8643
4: 6 What *meaneth* the noise of this great s in 8643
2Ch 13:15 the men of Judah **gave a** s: and as the men 7321
Ezr 3:11 all the people shouted *with* a great s, 8643
3:13 s of joy from the noise of the weeping of 8643
3:13 for the people shouted *with* a loud s, and 8643
Ps 5:11 let them ever s **for joy**, because 7442
32:11 s **for joy**, all *ye that are* upright in heart. 7442
35:27 Let them s **for joy**, and be glad, that favour 7442
47: 1 s unto God with the voice of triumph. 7321
47: 5 God is gone up with a s, the LORD with 8643
65:13 with corn; they s **for joy**, they also sing. 7321
132: 9 and let thy saints s **for joy**. 7442
132:16 and her saints shall s **aloud for joy**. 7442+7444
Isa 12: 6 Cry out and s, thou inhabitant of Zion: 7442
42:11 let them s from the top of the mountains. 6681
44:23 for the LORD hath done *it:* s, ye lower 7321
Jer 25:30 he shall **give a** s, as they that tread 1959+6030
31: 7 and s among the chief of the nations: 6670
50:15 S against her round about: she hath given 7321
51:14 and they shall lift up a s against thee. 1959
La 3: 8 Also when I cry and s, he shutteth out my 7768
Zep 3:14 s, O Israel; be glad and rejoice with all 7321
Zec 9: 9 of Zion; s, O daughter of Jerusalem: 7321
Ac 12:22 And the people **gave a** s, *saying, It is* *2019*
1Th 4:16 himself shall descend from heaven with a s, *2752*

SHOUTED (14) [SHOUT]
Ex 32:17 heard the noise of the people as they s, 7452
Lev 9:24 people saw, they s, and fell on their faces. 7442
Jos 6:20 So the people s when *the priests* blew with 7321
6:20 the people s *with* a great shout, that 7321
Jdg 15:14 unto Lehi, the Philistines s against him: 7321
1Sa 4: 5 all Israel s *with* a great shout, so that 7321
10:24 all the people s, and said, God save 7321
17:20 going forth to the fight, and s for the battle. 7321
17:52 and s, and pursued the Philistines, 7321
2Ch 13:15 as the men of Judah s, it came to pass, 7321
Ezr 3:11 all the people s *with* a great shout, 7321
3:12 s **aloud** for joy: 6963+7311+8643+871.1+3807.1
3:13 for the people s *with* a loud shout, and 7321
Job 38: 7 and all the sons of God s **for joy**? 7321

SHOUTETH (1) [SHOUT]
Ps 78:65 like a mighty *man* that s by reason of wine. 7442

SHOUTING (15) [SHOUT]
2Sa 6:15 brought up the ark of the LORD with s, 8643
1Ch 15:28 ark of the covenant of the LORD with s, 8643
2Ch 15:14 with s, and with trumpets, and with cornets. 8643
Job 39:25 the thunder of the captains, and the s. 8643
Pr 11:10 and when the wicked perish, *there is* s. 7440
Isa 16: 9 for the s for thy summer fruits and for thy 1959
16:10 shall be no singing, neither shall there be s: 7321
16:10 I have made *their vintage* s to cease. 1959
Jer 20:16 cry in the morning, and the s at noontide; 8643
48:33 none shall tread *with* s; *their* shouting *shall* 1959
48:33 *with* shouting; *their* s *shall be* no shouting. 1959
48:33 *with* shouting; *their* shouting *shall be* no s. 1959
Eze 21:22 in the slaughter, to lift up the voice with s, 8643
Am 1:14 palaces thereof, with s in the day of battle, 8643
2: 2 with s, *and* with the sound of the trumpet: 8643

SHOUTINGS (1) [SHOUT]
Zec 4: 7 bring forth the headstone *thereof with* s, 8663

SHOVEL (1) [SHOVELS]
Isa 30:24 which hath been winnowed with the s and 7371

SHOVELS (9) [SHOVEL]
Ex 27: 3 his s, and his basons, and his fleshhooks, 3257
38: 3 the s, and the basons, *and* the fleshhooks, 3257
Nu 4:14 the fleshhooks, and the s, and the basons, 3257
1Ki 7:40 made the lavers, and the s, and the basons. 3257
7:45 And the pots, and the s, and the basons: and 3257
2Ki 25:14 the s, and the snuffers, and the spoons, and 3257
2Ch 4:11 made the pots, and the s, and the basons. 3257
4:16 the s, and the fleshhooks, and all their 3257
Jer 52:18 the s, and the snuffers, and the bowls, and 3257

SHOW See FOREWARN; SHEW

SHOW SYMPATHY See BEMOAN; BEMOANED; BEMOANING

SHOW THE SAME FAVOR See REQUITE; REQUITED; REQUITING

SHOWER (4) [SHOWERS]
Eze 13:11 there shall be an overflowing s; and ye, 1653
13:13 there shall be an overflowing s in mine 1653
34:26 I will cause the s to come down in his 1653
Lk 12:54 straightway ye say, There cometh a s; *3655*

SHOWERS (9) [SHOWER]
Dt 32: 2 the tender herb, and as the **s** upon the grass: 7241
Job 24: 8 They are wet with the **s** of the mountains, 2230
Ps 65:10 thou makest it soft with **s**: thou blessest 7241
72: 6 the mown grass: as **s** that water the earth. 7241
Jer 3: 3 Therefore the **s** have been withholden, and 7241
14:22 or can the heavens give **s**? *art* not thou he, 7241
Eze 34:26 in his season; there shall be **s** of blessing. 1653
Mic 5: 7 as the **s** upon the grass, that tarrieth not for 7241
Zec 10: 1 give them **s** of rain, to every one grass in 4306

SHRANK (2)
Ge 32:32 of Israel eat not *of* the sinew which **s**, 5384
32:32 hollow of Jacob's thigh in the sinew that **s**. 5384

SHRED (1)
2Ki 4:39 came and **s** *them* into the pot of pottage: 6398

SHREWD See UNSAVOURY

SHRICH (1)
Isa 34:14 the **s owl** also shall rest there, and find for 3917

SHRINE PROSTITUTE See SODOMITE; SODOMITES

SHRINES (1)
Ac 19:24 which made silver **s** for Diana, *3485*

SHROWD (1)
Eze 31: 3 with a shadowing **s**, and of a high stature; 2793

SHRUBS (1)
Ge 21:15 and she cast the child under one of the **s**. 7880

SHUA (2) [SHUAH]
1Ch 2: 3 him of the daughter of **S** the Canaanitess. 7770
7:32 and Hotham, and **S** their sister. 7774

SHUAH (5) [SHUA]
Ge 25: 2 and Medan, and Midian, and Ishbak, and **S**. 7744
38: 2 of a certain Canaanite, whose name *was* **S**; 7770
38:12 in process of time the daughter of **S** Judah's 7770
1Ch 1:32 and Medan, and Midian, and Ishbak, and **S**. 7744
4:11 Chelub the brother of **S** begat Mehir, 7746

SHUAL (2) [HAZAR-SHUAL]
1Sa 13:17 that leadeth to Ophrah, unto the land of **S**: 7777
1Ch 7:36 and Harnepher, and **S**, and Beri, and Imrah, 7777

SHUBAEL (3)
1Ch 24:20 Levi *were these:* Of the sons of Amram; **S**: 7619
24:20 Shubael: of the sons of **S**; Jehdeiah. 7619
25:20 The thirteenth *to* **S**, *he,* his sons, and 7619

SHUHAM (1) [SHUHAMITES]
Nu 26:42 of **S**, the family of the Shuhamites. 7748

SHUHAMITES (2) [SHUHAM]
Nu 26:42 of Shuham, the family of the **S**. These *are* 7749
26:43 All the families of the **S**, according to those 7749

SHUHITE (5)
Job 2:11 Bildad the **S**, and Zophar the Naamathite: 7747
8: 1 Then answered Bildad the **S**, and said, 7747
18: 1 Then answered Bildad the **S**, and said, 7747
25: 1 Then answered Bildad the **S**, and said, 7747
42: 9 Eliphaz the Temanite and Bildad the **S** *and* 7747

SHULAMITE (2)
SS 6:13 Return, return, O **S**; return, return, that we 7759
6:13 What will ye see in the **S**? As it were 7759

SHULAMMITE See SHULAMITE

SHUMATHITES (1)
1Ch 2:53 the Puhites, and the **S**, and the Mishraites; 8126

SHUN (1) [SHUNNED]
2Ti 2:16 But **s** profane *and* vain babblings: for they *4026*

SHUNAMMITE (8)
1Ki 1: 3 found Abishag a **S**, and brought her to 7767
1:15 and Abishag the **S** ministered unto the king. 7767
2:17 that he give me Abishag the **S** to wife. 7767
2:21 Let Abishag the **S** be given to Adonijah thy 7767
2:22 why dost thou ask Abishag the **S** for 7767
2Ki 4:12 he said to Gehazi his servant, Call this **S**. 7767
4:25 his servant, Behold, *yonder is* that **S**: 7767
4:36 he called Gehazi, and said, Call this **S**. 7767

SHUNEM (3)
Jos 19:18 was toward Jezreel, and Chesulloth, and **S**, 7766
1Sa 28: 4 and came and pitched in **S**: 7766
2Ki 4: 8 And it fell on a day, that Elisha passed to **S**, 7766

SHUNI (2) [SHUNITES]
Ge 46:16 **S**, and Ezbon, Eri, and Arodi, and Areli. 7764
Nu 26:15 of **S**, the family of the Shunites: 7764

SHUNITES (1) [SHUNI]
Nu 26:15 the Haggites: of Shuni, the family of the **S**: 7765

SHUNNED (1) [SHUN]
Ac 20:27 For I have not **s** to declare unto you all *5288*

SHUPHAM (1) [SHUPHAMITES]
Nu 26:39 Of **S**, the family of the Shuphamites: 8197

SHUPHAMITES (1) [SHUPHAM]
Nu 26:39 Of Shupham, the family of the **S**: 7781

SHUPPIM (3)
1Ch 7:12 **S** also, and Huppim, the children of Ir, *and* 8206
7:15 took to wife *the sister* of Huppim and **S**, 8206
26:16 To **S** and Hosah *the lot came forth* 8206

SHUR (6)
Ge 16: 7 by the fountain in the way to **S**. 7793
20: 1 dwelled between Kadesh and **S**, and 7793
25:18 they dwelt from Havilah unto **S**, that *is* 7793
Ex 15:22 and they went out into the wilderness of **S**; 7793
1Sa 15: 7 from Havilah *until* thou comest *to* **S**, 7793
27: 8 inhabitants of the land as thou goest to **S**, 7793

SHUSHAN (21)
Ne 1: 1 the twentieth year, as I was in **S** the palace, 7800
Est 1: 2 of his kingdom, which *was* in **S** the palace, 7800
1: 5 the people that were present in **S** the palace, 7800
2: 3 all the fair young virgins unto **S** the palace, 7800
2: 5 *Now* in **S** the palace there was a certain 7800
2: 8 were gathered together unto **S** the palace, 7800
3:15 and the decree was given in **S** the palace. 7800
3:15 to drink; but the city **S** was perplexed. 7800
4: 8 decree that was given at **S** to destroy them, 7800
4:16 together all the Jews that are present in **S**, 7800
8:14 and the decree was given at **S** the palace. 7800
8:15 and the city of **S** rejoiced and was glad. 7800
9: 6 in **S** the palace the Jews slew and 7800
9:11 in **S** the palace was brought before the king. 7800
9:12 destroyed five hundred men in **S** the palace, 7800
9:13 let it be granted to the Jews which *are* in **S** 7800
9:14 the decree was given at **S**; and they hanged 7800
9:15 For the Jews that *were* in **S** gathered 7800
9:15 and slew three hundred men at **S**; 7800
9:18 the Jews that *were* at **S** assembled together 7800
Da 8: 2 when I saw, that I *was* at **S** *in* the palace, 7800

SHUSHAN-EDUTH (1)
Ps 60: T To the chief Musician upon **S**, Michtam of 7802

SHUT (105) [SHUTTETH, SHUTTING]
Ge 7:16 commanded him: and the LORD **s** him in. 5462
19: 6 door unto them, and **s** the door after him, 5462
19:10 into the house to them, and **s** to the door. 5462
Ex 14: 3 in the land, the wilderness hath **s** them in. 5462
Lev 13: 4 the priest shall **s up** *him that hath* 5462
13: 5 the priest shall **s** him **up** seven days more: 5462
13:11 him unclean, *and* shall not **s** him **up**: 5462
13:21 then the priest shall **s** him **up** seven days: 5462
13:26 then the priest shall **s** him **up** seven days: 5462
13:31 the priest shall **s up** *him that hath* 5462
13:33 the priest shall **s up** *him that hath* the scall 5462
13:50 and **s up** *it that hath* the plague seven days: 5462
13:54 and he shall **s** it **up** seven days more: 5462
14:38 the house, and **s up** the house seven days: 5462
14:46 it is **s up** shall be unclean until the even. 5462
Nu 12:14 let her be **s** out from the camp seven days, 5462
12:15 Miriam was **s** out from the camp seven 5462
Dt 11:17 he **s up** the heaven, that there be no rain, 6113
15: 7 nor **s** thine hand from thy poor brother: 7092
32:30 sold them, and the LORD had **s** them **up**? 5462
32:36 is gone, and *there is* none **s up**, or left. 6113

S

Jos 2: 7 after them were gone out, they **s** the gate. 5462
6: 1 Jericho was **straitly s up** 5462+5462+2050.1
Jdg 3:23 **s** the doors of the parlour upon him, and 5462
9:51 **s** *it* to them, and gat them up to the top of 5462
1Sa 1: 5 but the LORD had **s up** her womb. 5462
1: 6 because the LORD had **s up** her womb. 5462
6:10 to the cart, and **s up** their calves at home: 3607
23: 7 for he is **s in**, by entering into a town that 5462
2Sa 20: 3 So they were **s up** unto the day of their 6887
1Ki 8:35 When heaven is **s up**, and there is no rain, 6113
14:10 *and him that is* **s up** and left in Israel, and 6113
21:21 and *him that is* **s up** and left in Israel, 6113
2Ki 4: 4 thou shalt **s** the door upon thee and 5462
4: 5 and **s** the door upon her and upon her sons, 5462
4:21 and **s** *the door* upon him, and went out. 5462
4:33 **s** the door upon them twain, and 5462
6:32 **s** the door, and hold him fast at the door: 5462
9: 8 and *him that is* **s up** and left in Israel: 6113
14:26 for *there was* not any **s up**, nor any left, 6113
17: 4 therefore the king of Assyria **s** him **up**, and 6113
2Ch 6:26 When the heaven is **s up**, and there is no 6113
7:13 If I **s up** heaven that there be no rain, or if I 6113
28:24 **s up** the doors of the house of the LORD, 5462
29: 7 Also they have **s up** the doors of the porch, 5462
Ne 6:10 the son of Mehetabeel, who *was* **s up**; 6113
6:10 and let us **s** the doors of the temple: 5462
7: 3 let them **s** the doors, and bar *them:* and 1479
13:19 I commanded that the gates should be **s**, 5462
Job 3:10 Because it **s** not **up** the doors of my 5462
11:10 **s up**, or gather together, then who can 5462
38: 8 Or *who* **s up** the sea with doors, when it 5526
41:15 *his* pride, **s up** *together as with* a close seal. 5462
Ps 31: 8 hast not **s** me **up** into the hand of 5462
69:15 and let not the pit **s** her mouth upon me. 332
77: 9 hath he in anger **s up** his tender mercies? 7092
88: 8 *I am* **s up**, and I cannot come forth. 3607
Ecc 12: 4 the doors shall be **s** in the streets, when 5462
SS 4:12 *my* spouse; a spring **s up**, a fountain sealed. 5274
Isa 6:10 and make their ears heavy, and **s** their eyes; 8173
22:22 so he shall open, and none shall **s**; and 5462
22:22 and he shall **s**, and none shall open. 5462
24:10 every house is **s up**, that no *man may* come 5462
24:22 shall be **s up** in the prison, and after many 5462
26:20 thy chambers, and **s** thy doors about thee: 5462
44:18 for he hath **s** their eyes, that *they* cannot 2902
45: 1 leaved gates; and the gates shall not be **s**; 5462
52:15 the kings shall **s** their mouths at him: 7092
60:11 they shall not be **s** day nor night; 5462
66: 9 bring forth, and **s** *the womb?* saith thy God. 6113
Jer 13:19 The cities of the south shall be **s up**, and 5462
20: 9 heart as a burning fire **s up** in my bones, 6113
32: 2 Jeremiah the prophet was **s up** in the court 3607
32: 3 For Zedekiah king of Judah had **s** him **up**, 3607
33: 1 while he was yet **s up** in the court of 6113
36: 5 commanded Baruch, saying, I *am* **s up**; 6113
39:15 while he was **s up** in the court of the prison, 6113
Eze 3:24 unto me, Go, **s** thyself within thine house. 5462
44: 1 which looketh *toward* the east; and it *was* **s**. 5462
44: 2 This gate shall be **s**, it shall not be opened, 5462
44: 2 hath entered in by it, therefore it shall be **s**. 5462
46: 1 the east shall be **s** the six working days; 5462
46: 2 but the gate shall not be **s** until the evening. 5462
46:12 after his going forth *one* shall **s** the gate. 5462
Da 6:22 hath **s** the lions' mouths, that they have not 5463
8:26 wherefore **s** thou **up** the vision; for *it shall* 5640
12: 4 **s up** the words, and seal the book, 5640
Mal 1:10 Who *is there* even among you that would **s** 5462
Mt 6: 6 thy closet, and when thou hast **s** thy door, *2808*
23:13 for ye **s up** the kingdom of heaven against *2808*
25:10 him to the marriage: and the door was **s**. *2808*
Lk 3:20 this above all, that he **s up** John in prison. *2623*
4:25 when the heaven was **s up** three years and *2808*
11: 7 the door is now **s**, and my children are with *2808*
13:25 and hath **s** to the door, and ye begin to stand *608*
Jn 20:19 when the doors were **s** where the disciples *2808*
20:26 *then* came Jesus, the doors being **s**, *2808*
Ac 5:23 The prison truly found we **s** with all safety, *2808*
21:30 the temple: and forthwith the doors were **s**. *2808*
26:10 and many of the saints did I **s up** in prison, *2623*
Gal 3:23 **s up** unto the faith which should afterwards *4788*
Rev 3: 8 thee an open door, and no *man* can **s** it: *2808*
11: 6 These have power to **s** heaven, that it rain *2808*
20: 3 him into the bottomless *pit*, and **s** him **up**, *2808*
21:25 And the gates of it shall not be **s** at all by *2808*

SHUTHALHITES (1) [SHUTHELAH]
Nu 26:35 of Shuthelah, the family of the **S**: 8364

SHUTHELAH (4) [SHUTHALHITES]
Nu 26:35 of **S**, the family of the Shuthalhites: 7803
26:36 these *are* the sons of **S**: of Eran, the family 7803
1Ch 7:20 **S**, and Bered his son, and Tahath his son, 7803
7:21 his son, and **S** his son, and Ezer, and Elead, 7803

SHUTHELAHITE See SHUTHALHITES

SHUTTETH (8) [SHUT]
Job 12:14 it cannot be built *again:* he **s up** a man, and 5462
Pr 16:30 He **s** his eyes to devise froward things: 6095
17:28 he that **s** his lips *is esteemed a man* of 331
Isa 33:15 of blood, and **s** his eyes from seeing evil; 6105
La 3: 8 when I cry and shout, he **s out** my prayer. 5640
1Jn 3:17 **s up** his bowels *of compassion* from him, *2808*
Rev 3: 7 of David, he that openeth, and no *man* **s**; *2808*
3: 7 *man* shutteth; and **s**, and no *man* openeth; *2808*

SHUTTING (1) [SHUT]
Jos 2: 5 it came to pass *about the time* of **s** of 5462

SHUTTLE (1)
Job 7: 6 My days are swifter than a **weaver's s**, and 708

SIA (1) [SIAHA]
Ne 7:47 the children of **S**, the children of Padon, 5517

SIAHA (1) [SIA]
Ezr 2:44 the children of **S**, the children of Padon, 5517

SIBBECAI (2) [SIBBECHAI]
1Ch 11:29 **S** the Hushathite, Ilai the Ahohite, 5444
27:11 for the eighth month *was* **S** the Hushathite, 5444

SIBBECHAI (2) [SIBBECAI]
2Sa 21:18 **S** the Hushathite slew Saph, which *was* of 5444
1Ch 20: 4 at which time **S** the Hushathite slew Sippai, 5444

SIBBOLETH (1) [SHIBBOLETH]
Jdg 12: 6 he said **S**: for he could not frame to 5451

SIBMAH (4)
Jos 13:19 **S**, and Zareth-shahar in the mount of 7643
Isa 16: 8 of Heshbon languish, *and* the vine of **S**: 7643
16: 9 with the weeping of Jazer the vine of **S**: 7643
Jer 48:32 O vine of **S**, I will weep for thee with 7643

SIBRAIM (1)
Eze 47:16 Hamath, Berothah, **S**, which *is* between 5453

SICHEM (1)
Ge 12: 6 passed through the land unto the place of **S**, 7927

SICK (88) [SICKLY, SICKNESS, SICKNESSES]
Ge 48: 1 that *one* told Joseph, Behold, thy father *is* **s**: 2470
Lev 15:33 of her that is **s** of her flowers, and of him 1739
1Sa 19:14 messengers to take David, she said, He *is* **s**. 2470
30:13 left me, because three days agone I **fell s**. 2470
2Sa 12:15 wife bare unto David, and it was **very s**. 605
13: 2 *so* vexed, that he **fell s** for his sister Tamar; 2470
13: 5 down on thy bed, and **make** thyself **s**: 2470
13: 6 So Amnon lay down, and **made** himself **s**: 2470
1Ki 14: 1 that time Abijah the son of Jeroboam **fell s**. 2470
14: 5 ask a thing of thee for her son; for he *is* **s**: 2470
17:17 the woman, the mistress of the house, **fell s**; 2470
2Ki 1: 2 chamber that *was* in Samaria, and was **s**: 2470
8: 7 Ben-hadad the king of Syria was **s**; and 2470
8:29 son of Ahab in Jezreel, because he was **s**. 2470
13:14 Now Elisha was **fallen s** of his sickness 2470
20: 1 In those days was Hezekiah **s** unto death. 2470
20:12 for he had heard that Hezekiah had been **s**. 2470
2Ch 22: 6 son of Ahab at Jezreel, because he was **s**. 2470
32:24 In those days Hezekiah was **s** to the death, 2470
Ne 2: 2 thy countenance sad, seeing thou *art* not **s**? 2470
Ps 35:13 *as for* me, when they were **s**, my clothing 2470
Pr 13:12 Hope deferred **maketh** the heart **s**: but 2470
23:35 stricken me, *shalt thou say, and* I was not **s**; 2470
SS 2: 5 comfort me with apples: for I *am* **s** of love. 2470
5: 8 that ye tell him, that I *am* **s** of love. 2470
Isa 1: 5 the whole head *is* **s**, and the whole heart 2483
33:24 the inhabitant shall not say, I am **s**: 2470
38: 1 In those days was Hezekiah **s** unto death. 2470
38: 9 when he had been **s**, and was recovered of 2470

S

Isa 39: 1 for he had heard that he had been **s**, and 2470
Jer 14:18 then behold **them that are s** with famine: 8463
Eze 34: 4 neither have ye healed that which was **s**, 2470
34:16 and will strengthen that which was **s**: 2470
Da 8:27 I Daniel fainted, and was **s** *certain* days; 2470
Hos 7: 5 have **made** *him* **s** *with* bottles of wine; 2470
Mic 6:13 Therefore also will I **make** *thee* **s** in 2470
Mal 1: 8 if ye offer the lame and **s**, *is it* not evil? 2470
1:13 *which was* torn, and the lame, and the **s**; 2470
Mt 4:24 they brought unto him all **s people** 2192+2560
8: 6 my servant lieth at home **s of the palsy**, *3885*
8:14 his wife's mother laid, and **s of a fever**. *4445*
8:16 with *his* word, and healed all that were **s**: *2560*
9: 2 they brought to him a **man s of the palsy**, *3885*
9: 2 their faith said unto the **s of the palsy**; *3885*
9: 6 (then saith he to the **s of the palsy**,) *3885*
9:12 not a physician, but they that are **s**. *2192+2560*
10: 8 Heal the **s**, cleanse the lepers, raise the dead, *770*
14:14 toward them, and he healed their **s**. *732*
25:36 I was **s**, and ye visited me: I was in prison, *770*
25:39 Or when saw we thee **s**, *772*
25:43 **s**, and in prison, and ye visited me not. *772*
25:44 or **s**, or in prison, and did not minister unto *772*
Mk 1:30 But Simon's wife's mother lay **s of a fever**, *4445*
1:34 And he healed many *that were* **s** of *2192+2560*
2: 3 bringing **one s of the palsy**, *which was* *3885*
2: 4 the bed wherein the **s of the palsy** lay. *3885*
2: 5 he said unto the **s of the palsy**, Son, *3885*
2: 9 is it easier to say to the **s of the palsy**, *3885*
2:10 forgive sins, (he saith to the **s of the palsy**,) *3885*
2:17 need of *the* physician, but they that are **s**: *2560*
6: 5 save that he laid *his* hands upon a few **s** *folk*, *732*
6:13 and anointed with oil many *that were* **s**, and *732*
6:55 to carry about in beds those that were **s**, *2560*
6:56 they laid the **s** in the streets, and *770*
16:18 they shall lay hands on the **s**, and they shall *732*
Lk 4:40 all they that had *any* **s** with divers diseases *770*
5:24 (he said unto the **s of the palsy**,) *3886*
5:31 not a physician; but they that are **s**. *2192+2560*
7: 2 unto him, was **s**, and ready to die. *2192+2560*
7:10 found the servant whole that had been **s**. *770*
9: 2 the kingdom of God, and to heal the **s**. *770*
10: 9 And heal the **s** that are therein, *772*
Jn 4:46 whose son was **s** at Capernaum. *770*
11: 1 Now a certain *man* was **s**, *named* Lazarus, *770*
11: 2 with her hair, whose brother Lazarus was **s**.) *770*
11: 3 Lord, behold, he whom thou lovest is **s**. *770*
11: 6 When he had heard therefore that he was **s**, *770*
Ac 5:15 Insomuch that *they* brought forth the **s** into *772*
5:16 bringing **s** *folks*, and *them which were* vexed *772*
9:33 his bed eight years, and was **s of the palsy**. *3886*
9:37 pass in those days, that she was **s**, and died: *770*
19:12 body were brought unto the **s** handkerchiefs *770*
28: 8 that the father of Publius lay **s of** a fever *4912*
Php 2:26 because that ye had heard that he had been **s**. *770*
2:27 For indeed he was **s** nigh unto death: but *770*
2Ti 4:20 but Trophimus have I left at Miletum **s**. *770*
Jas 5:14 Is any **s** among you? let him call for *770*
5:15 And the prayer of faith shall save the **s**, and *2577*

SICKLE (12)

Dt 16: 9 *as thou* beginnest *to put* the **s** to the corn. 2770
23:25 thou shalt not move a **s** unto thy 2770
Jer 50:16 him that handleth the **s** in the time of 4038
Joel 3:13 Put ye in the **s**, for the harvest is ripe: 4038
Mk 4:29 immediately he putteth in the **s**, because *1407*
Rev 14:14 a golden crown, and in his hand a sharp **s**. *1407*
14:15 sat on the cloud, Thrust in thy **s**, and reap: *1407*
14:16 And he that sat on the cloud thrust in his **s** *1407*
14:17 is in heaven, he also having a sharp **s**. *1407*
14:18 with a loud cry to him that had the sharp **s**, *1407*
14:18 Thrust in thy sharp **s**, and gather *1407*
14:19 And the angel thrust in his **s** into the earth, *1407*

SICKLY (1) [SICK]

1Co 11:30 this cause many *are* weak and **s** among you, *732*

SICKNESS (20) [SICK]

Ex 23:25 I will take **s** away from the midst of thee. 4245
Lev 20:18 a man shall lie with a woman **having** her **s**, 1739
Dt 7:15 the LORD will take away from thee all **s**, 2483
28:61 Also every **s**, and every plague, which *is* 2483
1Ki 8:37 whatsoever plague, whatsoever **s** *there be*; 4245
17:17 his **s** was so sore, that there was no breath 2483
2Ki 13:14 Now Elisha was fallen sick of his **s** whereof 2483
2Ch 6:28 whatsoever sore or whatsoever **s** *there be*: 4245
21:15 thou *shalt* have great **s** by disease of thy 2483
21:15 until thy bowels fall out by reason of the **s** 2483
21:19 his bowels fell out by reason of his **s**: 2483
Ps 41: 3 thou wilt make all his bed in his **s**. 2483
Ecc 5:17 *he hath* much sorrow and wrath with his **s**. 2483
Isa 38: 9 had been sick, and was recovered of his **s**: 2483
38:12 he will cut me off with **pining s**: from day 1803
Hos 5:13 When Ephraim saw his **s**, and Judah *saw* 2483
Mt 4:23 and healing all *manner of* **s** and all *manner* *3554*
9:35 and healing every **s** and every disease *3554*
10: 1 and to heal all *manner of* **s** and all *manner* *3554*
Jn 11: 4 This **s** is not unto death, but for the glory of *769*

SICKNESSES (4) [SICK]

Dt 28:59 and sore **s**, and of long continuance. 2483
29:22 the **s** which the LORD hath laid upon it; 8463
Mt 8:17 took our infirmities, and bare our **s**. *3554*
Mk 3:15 And to have power to heal **s**, and to cast out *3554*

SIDDIM (3)

Ge 14: 3 these were joined together in the vale of **S**, 7708
14: 8 joined battle with them in the vale of **S**; 7708
14:10 the vale of **S** *was* full of slimepits; and 7708

SIDE (444) [ASIDE, BACKSIDE, SIDES, WAYSIDE]

Ge 6:16 the door of the ark shalt thou set in the **s** 6654
38:21 *is* the harlot, that *was* openly by the **way s**? 1870
Ex 2: 5 her maidens walked along **by** the river's **s**; 3027
12: 7 strike *it* on the two **s posts** and on the upper 4201
12:22 the two **s posts** with the blood that *is* in 4201
12:23 on the two **s posts**, the LORD will pass 4201
17:12 the one on the **one s**, and the other on 2088
17:12 the one side, and the other on the **other s**; 2088
25:12 two rings *shall be* in the one **s** of it, and 6763
25:12 side of it, and two rings in the other **s** of it. 6763
25:32 branches of the candlestick out of the one **s**, 6654
25:32 of the candlestick out of the other **s**: 6654
26:13 a cubit on the **one s**, and a cubit on 2088
26:13 a cubit on the **other s** of that which 2088
26:13 over the sides of the tabernacle on **this s** 2088
26:13 of the tabernacle on this side and on **that s**, 2088
26:18 twenty boards on the south **s** southward. 6285
26:20 for the second **s** of the tabernacle on 6763
26:20 on the north **s** *there shall be* twenty boards: 6285
26:26 five for the boards of the one **s** of 6763
26:27 five bars for the boards of the other **s** of 6763
26:27 five bars for the boards of the **s** of 6763
26:35 on the **s** of the tabernacle toward the south: 6763
26:35 and thou shalt put the table on the north **s**. 6763
27: 9 for the south **s** southward *there shall be* 6285
27: 9 linen of an hundred cubits long for one **s**: 6285
27:11 likewise for the north **s** in length *there shall* 6285
27:12 *for* the breadth of the court on the west **s** 6285
27:13 the breadth of the court on the east **s** 6285
27:14 The hangings of *one* **s** *of the gate shall be* 3802
27:15 on the other **s** *shall be* hangings, 3802
28:26 which *is* in the **s** of the ephod inward. 5676
32:15 on **the one s** and on the other *were* they 2088
32:26 and said, Who *is* **on** the LORD'S **s**? 3807.1
32:27 Put every man his sword by his **s**, *and* go in 3409
36:11 likewise he made in the uttermost **s** of 8193
36:23 twenty boards for the south **s** southward: 6285
36:25 for the other **s** of the tabernacle, *which is* 6763
36:31 five for the boards of the one **s** of 6763
36:32 five bars for the boards of the other **s** of 6763
37: 3 even two rings upon the one **s** of it, and 6763
37: 3 of it, and two rings upon the other **s** of it. 6763
37: 8 One cherub on the end on **this s**, and 2088
37: 8 another cherub on the *other* end on **that s**: 2088
37:18 of the candlestick out of the one **s** thereof, 6654
37:18 of the candlestick out of the other **s** thereof: 6654
38: 9 on the south **s** southward the hangings of 6285
38:11 for the north **s** *the hangings were* an 6285
38:12 for the west **s** *were* hangings of fifty cubits, 6285
38:13 And for the east **s** eastward fifty cubits. 6285
38:14 The hangings of the *one* **s** *of the gate were* 3802
38:15 for the other **s** of the court gate, on this 3802
39:19 which *was* on the **s** of the ephod inward. 5676
40:22 upon the **s** of the tabernacle northward, 3409
40:24 on the **s** of the tabernacle southward. 3409
Lev 1:11 he shall kill it on the **s** of the altar 3409
1:15 the blood thereof shall be wrung out at the **s** 7023

S

Lev	5: 9	of the sin offering upon the **s** of the altar;	7023
Nu	2: 3	on the **east s** toward the rising of the sun	6924
	2:10	On the **south s** *shall be* the standard of	8486
	2:18	On the **west s** *shall be* the standard of	3220
	2:25	Dan *shall be* on the **north s** by their armies:	6828
	3:29	pitch on the **s** of the tabernacle southward.	3409
	3:35	*these* shall pitch on the **s** of the tabernacle	3409
	10: 6	the camps that lie on the **south s** shall take	8486
	11:31	as it were a day's journey **on this s**, and	3541
	11:31	as it were a day's journey **on the other s**,	3541
	16:27	of Korah, Dathan, and Abiram, on **every s**:	5439
	21:13	and pitched on the *other* **s** of Arnon,	5676
	22: 1	pitched in the plains of Moab on *this* **s**	5676
	22:24	a wall *being* on **this s**, and a wall on that	2088
	22:24	*being* on this side, and a wall on **that s**.	2088
	24: 6	they spread forth, as gardens by the **river s**,	5104
	32:19	not inherit with them on *yonder* **s** Jordan,	5676
	32:19	our inheritance is fallen to us on *this* **s**	5676
	32:32	inheritance on *this* **s** Jordan *may be* ours.	5676
	34:11	Shepham *to* Riblah, on the **east s** of Ain;	6924
	34:11	shall reach unto the **s** of the sea of	3802
	34:15	on *this* **s** Jordan *near* Jericho eastward,	5676
	35: 5	the city *on* the east **s** two thousand cubits,	6285
	35: 5	*on* the south **s** two thousand cubits, and	6285
	35: 5	*on* the west **s** two thousand cubits, and	6285
	35: 5	and *on* the north **s** two thousand cubits;	6285
	35:14	Ye shall give three cities on *this* **s** Jordan,	5676
Dt	1: 1	all Israel on *this* **s** Jordan in the wilderness,	5676
	1: 5	On *this* **s** Jordan, in the land of Moab,	5676
	1: 7	the vale, and in the south, and by the sea **s**,	2348
	3: 8	Amorites the land that *was* on *this* **s** Jordan,	5676
	4:32	*ask* from the one **s** of heaven unto the other,	7097
	4:41	Moses severed three cities on *this* **s** Jordan	5676
	4:46	On *this* **s** Jordan, in the valley over against	5676
	4:47	which *were* on *this* **s** Jordan *toward*	5676
	4:49	all the plain on *this* **s** Jordan eastward, even	5676
	11:30	*Are* they not on the *other* **s** Jordan, by	5676
	31:26	put it in the **s** of the ark of the covenant of	6654
Jos	1:14	which Moses gave you on *this* **s** Jordan;	5676
	1:15	you on *this* **s** Jordan *toward* the sunrising.	5676
	2:10	that *were* on the *other* **s** Jordan, Sihon and	5676
	5: 1	which *were* on the **s** of Jordan westward,	5676
	7: 2	on the **east s** of Beth-el, and spake unto	6924
	7: 7	and dwelt on the *other* **s** Jordan!	5676
	8: 9	and Ai, on the **west s** of Ai:	3220
	8:11	the city, and pitched on the **north s** of Ai:	6828
	8:12	and Ai, on the **west s** of the city.	3220
	8:22	some **on** this **s**, and some on that side:	4480
	8:22	some on this side, and some **on** that **s**:	4480
	8:33	stood **on** this **s** the ark and on that side	4480
	8:33	and on **that s** before the priests the Levites,	2088
	9: 1	when all the kings which *were* on *this* **s**	5676
	12: 1	possessed their land on the *other* **s** Jordan	5676
	12: 7	the children of Israel smote on *this* **s** Jordan	5676
	13:27	Cinnereth on the *other* **s** Jordan eastward.	5676
	13:32	on the *other* **s** Jordan, *by* Jericho, eastward.	5676
	14: 3	and a half tribe on the *other* **s** Jordan:	5676
	15: 3	it went out to the **south s** to	5045
	15: 3	ascended up on the **south s** unto	5045
	15: 7	which *is* on the **south s** of the river:	5045
	15: 8	of Hinnom unto the south **s** of the Jebusite;	3802
	15:10	passed along unto the **s** of mount Jearim,	3802
	15:10	on the **north s**, and went down *to*	6828+1886.5
	15:11	the border went out unto the **s** of Ekron	3802
	16: 5	on the **east s** was Ataroth-addar,	4217
	16: 6	the sea *to* Michmethah on the **north s**;	6828
	17: 5	which *were* on the *other* **s** Jordan;	5676
	17: 9	also *was* on the **north s** of the river,	6828
	18:12	their border on the north **s** was from	6285
	18:12	the border went up to the **s** of Jericho on	3802
	18:12	up to the side of Jericho on the **north s**,	6828
	18:13	to the **s** of Luz, which *is* Beth-el,	3802
	18:13	near the hill that *lieth* on the **south s** of	5045
	18:16	to the **s** of Jebusi on the south, and	3802
	18:18	passed along toward the **s** over against	3802
	18:19	the border passed along to the **s** of	3802
	18:20	Jordan was the border of it on the east **s**.	6285
	19:14	the border compasseth it on the **north s** *to*	6828
	19:27	toward the **north s** *of* Beth-emek,	6828
	19:34	and reacheth to Zebulun on the **south s**, and	5045
	19:34	reacheth to Asher on the west **s**, and	NIH
	20: 8	on the *other* **s** Jordan *by* Jericho eastward,	5676
	22: 4	the LORD gave you on the *other* **s** Jordan.	5676
	22: 7	their brethren on *this* **s** Jordan westward.	5676
	24: 2	Your fathers dwelt on the *other* **s** of	5676
	24: 3	Abraham from the *other* **s** of the flood,	5676
	24: 8	which dwelt on the *other* **s** Jordan;	5676
	24:14	fathers served on the *other* **s** of the flood,	5676
	24:15	served that *were* on the *other* **s** of the flood,	5676
	24:30	on the **north s** of the hill of Gaash.	6828
Jdg	2: 9	on the **north s** of the hill Gaash.	6828
	7: 1	the Midianites were on the **north s** of them,	6828
	7:12	as the sand by the sea **s** for multitude.	8193
	7:18	blow ye the trumpets also **on every s** of all	5439
	7:25	and Zeeb to Gideon on the *other* **s** Jordan.	5676
	8:34	of all their enemies **on every s**:	4480+5439
	10: 8	*other* **s** Jordan in the land of the Amorites,	5676
	11:18	by the **east s** of the land of Moab,	4217+8121
	11:18	pitched on the *other* **s** of Arnon, but	5676
	19: 1	sojourning on the **s** of mount Ephraim,	3411
	19:18	toward the **s** of mount Ephraim;	3411
	21:19	which *is* on the **north s** of Beth-el,	4480+6828
	21:19	on **the east s** of the highway	4217+8121+1886.1
1Sa	4:18	off the seat backward by the **s** of the gate,	3027
	6: 8	in a coffer by the **s** thereof;	6654
	12:11	out of the hand of your enemies on **every s**,	5439
	14: 1	Philistines' garrison, that *is* on the other **s**.	5676
	14: 4	*there was* a sharp rock on the one **s**, and	5676
	14: 4	one side, and a sharp rock on the other **s**:	5676
	14:40	Be ye on one **s**, and I and Jonathan my son	5676
	14:40	and Jonathan my son will be on the other **s**.	5676
	14:47	fought against all his enemies **on every s**,	5439
	17: 3	stood on a mountain on the **one s**,	2088
	17: 3	Israel stood on a mountain on the **other s**:	2088
	20:20	I will shoot three arrows on the **s** *thereof*, as	6654
	20:21	Behold, the arrows *are* **on this s** of thee,	2008
	20:25	Abner sat by Saul's **s**, and David's place	6654
	23:26	Saul went on this **s** of the mountain, and	6654
	23:26	and his men on that **s** of the mountain:	6654
	26:13	David went over *to* the *other* **s**, and	5676
	31: 7	Israel that *were* on the *other* **s** of the valley,	5676
	31: 7	*they* that *were* on the *other* **s** Jordan,	5676
2Sa	2:13	the one on the **one s** of the pool, and	2088+4480
	2:13	the other on the **other s** of the pool.	2088+4480
	2:16	and *thrust* his sword in his fellow's **s**;	6654
	13:34	people by the way of the hill **s** behind him.	6654
	16:13	Shimei went along on the hill's **s** over	6763
	18: 4	the king stood by the gate **s**, and all	3027
	24: 5	*on* the **right s** of the city that *lieth* in	3225
1Ki	4:24	over all *the region* on *this* **s** the river,	5676
	4:24	over all the kings on *this* **s** the river:	5676
	5: 3	the wars which were **about** him **on every s**,	5437
	5: 4	my God hath given me rest on **every s**,	5439
	6: 8	chamber *was* in the right **s** of the house:	3802
	6:31	*and* **s posts** *were* a fifth *part of the wall*.	4201
	7: 7	*it was* covered with cedar **from one s** of	4480
	7:30	at the **s** of every addition.	5676
	7:39	he put five bases on the right **s** of the house,	3802
	7:39	and five on the left **s** of the house:	3802
	7:39	he set the sea on the right **s** of the house	3802
	7:49	five on the **right s**, and five on the left,	3225
	10:19	**on either s** on	2088+2088+4480+4480+2050.1
	10:20	twelve lions stood there on **the one s** and	2088
2Ki	3:22	water **on the other s** *as* red as blood:	4480+5048
	9:32	to the window, and said, Who *is* **on** my **s**?	854
	12: 9	on the **right s** as one cometh *into* the house	3225
	16:14	and put it on the north **s** of the altar.	3409
1Ch	4:39	*even* unto the east *s* of the valley, to seek	NIH
	6:78	on the *other* **s** Jordan *by* Jericho, on the east	5676
	6:78	Jordan *by* Jericho, on the east **s** of Jordan,	NIH
	12:18	*we*, David, and **on** thy **s**, thou son of Jesse:	5973
	12:37	on the *other* **s** of Jordan, of the Reubenites,	5676
	22:18	he *not* given you rest **on every s**?	4480+5439
	26:30	officers among them of Israel on *this* **s**	5676
2Ch	4: 8	five on the **right s**, and five on the left.	3225
	4:10	he set the sea on the right **s** of the east end,	3802
	8:17	to Eloth, at the sea **s** in the land of Edom.	8193
	9:18	stays **on each s**	2088+2088+4480+4480+2050.1
	9:19	twelve lions stood there on the **one s**	2088+4480
	11:12	having Judah and Benjamin **on** his **s**.	3807.1
	14: 7	and he hath given us rest **on every s**.	4480+5439
	20: 2	thee from beyond the sea on this **s** Syria;	NIH
	23:10	from the right **s** of the temple to the left	3802
	23:10	of the temple to the left **s** of the temple,	3802
	32:22	and guided them **on every s**.	4480+5439
	32:30	brought it straight down to the west *s* of	NIH
	33:14	on the west *s* of Gihon, in the valley,	NIH
Ezr	4:10	the rest *that are* on *this* **s** the river, and	5675

Ezr	4:11	Thy servants the men *on this* **s** the river,	5675
	4:16	shalt have no portion on *this* **s** the river.	5675
	5: 3	governor on *this* **s** the river, and	5675
	5: 6	governor on *this* **s** the river, and	5675
	5: 6	which *were* on *this* **s** the river, sent unto	5675
	6:13	Tatnai, governor on *this* **s** the river,	5675
	8:36	and *to* the governors on *this* **s** the river:	5676
Ne	3: 7	unto the throne of the governor on *this* **s**	5676
	4:18	every one had his sword girded by his **s**,	4975
Job	1:10	about all that he hath **on every s**?	4480+5439
	18:11	Terrors shall make him afraid **on every s**,	5439
	18:12	and destruction *shall be* ready at his **s**.	6763
	19:10	He hath destroyed me **on every s**, and I am	5439
Ps	12: 8	The wicked walk **on every s**, when	5439
	31:13	fear *was* **on every s**: while they took	4480+5439
	65:12	and the little hills rejoice **on every s**.	2296
	71:21	my greatness, and comfort me **on every s**.	5437
	91: 7	A thousand shall fall at thy **s**, and	6654
	118: 6	The LORD *is* **on** my **s**; I will not fear:	3807.1
	124: 1	not *been* the LORD who was **on** our **s**,	3807.1
	124: 2	not *been* the LORD who was **on** our **s**,	3807.1
	140: 5	they have spread a net by the **way s**;	3027+4570
Ecc	4: 1	on the **s** of their oppressors *there was*	3027
Isa	60: 4	and thy daughters shall be nursed at *thy* **s**.	6654
Jer	6:25	of the enemy *and* fear *is* **on every s**.	4480+5439
	20:10	defaming of many, fear **on every s**.	4480+5439
	49:29	cry unto them, Fear *is* **on every s**.	4480+5439
	52:23	were ninety and six pomegranates on a **s**;	7307
Eze	1:10	a man, and the face of a lion, on the **right s**:	3225
	1:10	they four had the face of an ox on the **left s**;	8040
	1:23	which covered on this *s*, and every one had	NIH
	1:23	which covered on that *s*, their bodies.	NIH
	4: 4	Lie thou also upon thy left **s**, and lay	6654
	4: 6	lie again on thy right **s**, and thou shalt bear	6654
	4: 8	thou shalt not turn thee from one **s** to	6654
	4: 9	of the days that thou shalt lie upon thy **s**,	6654
	9: 2	*with* linen, with a writer's inkhorn by his **s**:	4975
	9: 3	which *had* the writer's inkhorn by his **s**;	4975
	9:11	which *had* the inkhorn by his **s**, reported	4975
	10: 3	Now the cherubims stood on the **right s** of	3225
	11:23	mountain which *is* on the **east s** of the city.	6924
	16:33	thee **on every s** for thy whoredom.	4480+5439
	19: 8	the nations set against him **on every s** from	5439
	23:22	bring them against thee **on every s**;	4480+5439
	25: 9	I *will* open the **s** of Moab from the cities,	3802
	28:23	by the sword upon her **on every s**;	4480+5439
	34:21	Because ye have thrust with **s** and	6654
	36: 3	and swallowed you up **on every s**,	4480+5439
	37:21	will gather them **on every s**, and	4480+5439
	39:17	gather yourselves **on every s** to my	4480+5439
	40:10	of the gate eastward *were* three on **this s**,	6311
	40:10	*were* three on this side, and three on **that s**;	6311
	40:10	and the posts had one measure on **this s** and	6311
	40:10	had one measure on this side and on **that s**.	6311
	40:12	the little chambers *was* one cubit *on this s*,	NIH
	40:12	and the space *was* one cubit on **that s**:	6311
	40:12	the little chambers *were* six cubits on **this s**,	6311
	40:12	cubits on this side, and six cubits on **that s**.	6311
	40:18	the pavement by the **s** of the gates over	3802
	40:21	little chambers thereof *were* three on **this s**	6311
	40:21	*were* three on this side and three on **that s**;	6311
	40:26	one on **this s**, and another on that side,	6311
	40:26	one on this side, and another on **that s**,	6311
	40:34	posts thereof, on **this s**, and on that side:	6311
	40:34	posts thereof, on this side, and on **that s**:	6311
	40:37	posts thereof, on **this s**, and on that side:	6311
	40:37	posts thereof, on this side, and on **that s**:	6311
	40:39	porch of the gate *were* two tables on **this s**,	6311
	40:39	two tables on **that s**, to slay thereon	6311
	40:40	at the **s** without, as one goeth up to	3802
	40:40	on the other **s**, which *was* at the porch of	3802
	40:41	Four tables *were* on **this s**, and four tables	6311
	40:41	four tables on **that s**, by the side of	6311
	40:41	four tables on that side, by the **s** of the gate;	3802
	40:44	which *was* at the **s** of the north gate;	3802
	40:44	one at the **s** of the east gate *having*	3802
	40:48	five cubits on **this s**, and five cubits on that	6311
	40:48	on this side, and five cubits on **that s**:	6311
	40:48	of the gate *was* three cubits on **this s**,	6311
	40:48	on this side, and three cubits on **that s**.	6311
	40:49	one on **this s**, and another on that side.	6311
	40:49	one on this side, and another on **that s**.	6311
	41: 1	six cubits broad on the **one s**, and six cubits	6311
	41: 1	and six cubits broad on the **other s**,	6311
	41: 2	of the door *were* five cubits on the **one s**,	6311
	41: 2	the one side, and five cubits on the **other s**:	6311
	41: 5	the breadth of *every* **s chamber**,	6763
	41: 5	round about the house **on every s**.	5439
	41: 6	the **s chambers** *were* three, one over	6763
	41: 6	the house for the **s chambers** round about,	6763
	41: 7	about still upward to the **s chambers**:	6763
	41: 8	the foundations of the **s chambers** *were* a	6763
	41: 9	which *was* for the **s chamber** without, *was*	6763
	41: 9	place of the **s chambers** that *were* within.	6763
	41:10	round about the house **on every s**.	5439+5439
	41:11	the doors of the **s chambers** *were* toward	6763
	41:15	the galleries thereof on the **one s** and on	6311
	41:15	thereof on the one side and on the **other s**,	6311
	41:19	man *was* toward the palm tree on the **one s**,	6311
	41:19	lion toward the palm tree on the **other s**:	6311
	41:26	palm trees on the **one s** and on the other	6311
	41:26	trees on the one side and on the **other s**,	6311
	41:26	*upon* the **s chambers** of the house, and	6763
	42: 9	these chambers *was* the entry on the **east s**,	6921
	42:16	He measured the east **s** with the measuring	7307
	42:17	He measured the north **s**, five hundred	7307
	42:18	He measured the south **s**, five hundred	7307
	42:19	He turned about to the west **s**, *and*	7307
	45: 7	for the prince on the **one s**	2088
	45: 7	on the **other s** of the oblation of the holy	2088
	45: 7	from the west **s** westward, and from	6285
	45: 7	and from the east **s** eastward:	6285
	46:19	the entry, which *was* at the **s** of the gate,	3802
	47: 1	from under from the right **s** of the house,	3802
	47: 1	side of the house, at the south *s* of the altar.	NIH
	47: 2	behold, there ran out waters on the right **s**.	3802
	47: 7	the river *were* very many trees on the **one s**	2088
	47:12	on **this s** and on that side, shall grow all	2088
	47:12	on this side and on **that s**, shall grow all	2088
	47:15	*be* the border of the land toward the north **s**,	6285
	47:17	border of Hamath. And *this is* the north **s**.	6285
	47:18	the east **s** ye shall measure from Hauran,	6285
	47:18	unto the east sea. And *this is* the east **s**.	6285
	47:19	the south **s** southward, from Tamar *even* to	6285
	47:19	great sea. And *this is* the south **s** southward.	6285
	47:20	The west **s** also *shall be* the great sea from	6285
	47:20	over against Hamath. This *is* the west **s**.	6285
	48: 2	from the east **s** unto the west side, a *portion*	6285
	48: 2	from the east side unto the west **s**, a *portion*	6285
	48: 3	from the east **s** even unto the west side,	6285
	48: 3	from the east side even unto the west **s**,	6285
	48: 4	from the east **s** unto the west side, a *portion*	6285
	48: 4	from the east side unto the west **s**, a *portion*	6285
	48: 5	from the east **s** unto the west side, a *portion*	6285
	48: 5	from the east side unto the west **s**, a *portion*	6285
	48: 6	from the east **s** even unto the west side,	6285
	48: 6	from the east side even unto the west **s**,	6285
	48: 7	from the east **s** unto the west side, a *portion*	6285
	48: 7	from the east side unto the west **s**, a *portion*	6285
	48: 8	of Judah, from the east **s** unto the west side,	6285
	48: 8	of Judah, from the east side unto the west **s**,	6285
	48: 8	from the east **s** unto the west side:	6285
	48: 8	from the east side unto the west **s**:	6285
	48:16	the north **s** four thousand and five hundred,	6285
	48:16	the south **s** four thousand and five hundred,	6285
	48:16	on the east **s** four thousand and	6285
	48:16	the west **s** four thousand and five hundred.	6285
	48:21	on the **one s** and on the other of the holy	2088
	48:23	from the east **s** unto the west side,	6285
	48:23	from the east side unto the west **s**,	6285
	48:24	from the east **s** unto the west side,	6285
	48:24	from the east side unto the west **s**,	6285
	48:25	from the east **s** unto the west side,	6285
	48:25	from the east side unto the west **s**,	6285
	48:26	from the east **s** unto the west side,	6285
	48:26	from the east side unto the west **s**,	6285
	48:27	from the east **s** unto the west side, Gad a	6285
	48:27	from the east side unto the west **s**, Gad a	6285
	48:28	the border of Gad, at the south **s** southward,	6285
	48:30	on the north **s**, four thousand and	6285
	48:32	at the east **s** four thousand and	6285
	48:33	*at* the south **s** four thousand and	6285
	48:34	*At* the west **s** four thousand and	6285
Da	7: 5	it raised up itself on one **s**, and *it had* three	7859
	10: 4	as I was by the **s** of the great river, which *is*	3027
	11:17	she shall not stand *on his s*, neither be for	NIH
	12: 5	the one on **this s** of the bank of the river,	2008
	12: 5	the other on that **s** of the bank of the river.	2008

Ob 1:11 In the day that thou stoodest on the **other s**, 5048
Jnh 4: 5 sat on the **east s** of the city, and there made 6924
Zec 4: 3 one upon the right *s* of the bowl, and NIH
4: 3 and the other upon the left *s* thereof. NIH
4:11 trees upon the right *s* of the candlestick NIH
4:11 the candlestick and upon the left *s* thereof? NIH
5: 3 shall be cut off *as* on this *s* according to it; NIH
5: 3 shall be cut off *as* on that *s* according to it. NIH
Mt 8:18 commandment to depart unto the **other s**. *4008*
8:28 And when he was come to the **other s** into *4008*
13: 1 Jesus out of the house, and sat **by** the sea **s**. *3844*
13: 4 some *seeds* fell **by** the way **s**, and the fowls *3844*
13:19 is he which received seed **by** the way **s**. *3844*
14:22 and to go before him unto the **other s**, *4008*
16: 5 his disciples were come to the **other s**, *4008*
20:30 two blind men sitting **by** the way **s**, *3844*
Mk 2:13 And he went forth again **by** the sea **s**; and *3844*
4: 1 And he began again to teach **by** the sea **s**: *3844*
4: 4 some fell by the **way s**, and the fowls of *3598*
4:15 And these are they by the **way s**, where *3598*
4:35 Let us pass over unto the **other s**. *4008*
5: 1 And they came over unto the **other s** of *4008*
5:21 passed over again by ship unto the **other s**, *4008*
6:45 to go to the **other s** before unto Bethsaida, *4008*
8:13 into the ship again departed to the **other s**. *4008*
10: 1 coasts of Judea by the **farther s** of Jordan: *4008*
10:46 of Timeus, sat by the ***high*way s** begging. *3598*
16: 5 saw a young man sitting on the **right s**, *1188*
Lk 1:11 on the **right s** of the altar of incense. *1188*
8: 5 and as he sowed, some fell by the **way s**; *3598*
8:12 Those by the **way s** are they that hear; then *3598*
8:22 Let us go over unto the **other s** of the lake. *4008*
10:31 he saw him, he **passed by on the other s**. *492*
10:32 *on him,* and **passed by on the other s**. *492*
18:35 a certain blind man sat by the **way s** *3598*
19:43 thee round, and keep thee in **on every s**, *3840*
Jn 6:22 **on the other s** of the sea saw that there was *4008*
6:25 had found him **on the other s** of the sea, *4008*
19:18 with him, **on either s one**, *1782+1782+2532*
19:34 of the soldiers with a spear pierced his **s**, *4125*
20:20 he shewed unto them *his* hands and his **s**. *4125*
20:25 and thrust my hand into his **s**, I will not *4125*
20:27 *hither* thy hand, and thrust *it* into my **s**: *4125*
21: 6 Cast the net on the right **s** of the ship, and *3313*
Ac 10: 6 a tanner, whose house is **by** the sea **s**: *3844*
10:32 house of *one* Simon a tanner **by** the sea **s**: *3844*
12: 7 and he smote Peter on the **s**, and raised him *4125*
16:13 sabbath we went out of the city **by** a river **s**, *3844*
2Co 4: 8 *We are* troubled on every *s*, yet not NIG
7: 5 *we were* troubled on every *s*; without *were* NIG
Rev 22: 2 and **of either s** of the river, *1782+1782+2532*

SIDES (48) [SIDE]
Ex 25:14 the staves into the rings by the **s** of the ark, 6763
25:32 six branches shall come out of the **s** of it; 6654
26:13 it shall hang over the **s** of the tabernacle on 6654
26:22 for the **s** of the tabernacle westward thou 3411
26:23 the corners of the tabernacle in the **two s**. 3411
26:27 of the tabernacle, for the **two s** westward. 3411
27: 7 the staves shall be upon the two **s** of 6763
28:27 shalt put them on the two **s** of the ephod 3802
30: 3 the **s** thereof round about, and the horns 7023
30: 4 upon the two **s** of it shalt thou make *it;* and 6654
32:15 the tables *were* written on both their **s**; 5676
36:27 for the **s** of the tabernacle westward he 3411
36:28 the corners of the tabernacle in the **two s**. 3411
36:32 boards of the tabernacle for the **s** westward. 3411
37: 5 he put the staves into the rings by the **s** of 6763
37:18 And six branches going out of the **s** thereof; 6654
37:26 the **s** thereof round about, and the horns of 7023
37:27 two corners of it, upon the two **s** thereof, 6654
38: 7 he put the staves into the rings on the **s** of 6763
39:20 put them on the two **s** of the ephod 3802
Nu 33:55 thorns in your **s**, and shall vex you in 6654
Jos 23:13 scourges in your **s**, and thorns in your eyes, 6654
Jdg 2: 3 they shall be *as thorns* in your **s**, and 6654
5:30 of divers colours of needlework on both **s**, NIH
1Sa 24: 3 and his men remained in the **s** of the cave. 3411
1Ki 4:24 and he had peace on all **s** round about him. 5676
6:16 he built twenty cubits on the **s** of the house, 3411
2Ki 19:23 *to* the **s** of Lebanon, and will cut down 3411
Ps 48: 2 *is* mount Zion, *on* the **s** of the north, 3411
128: 3 Thy wife *shall be* as a fruitful vine by the **s** 3411
Isa 14:13 of the congregation, in the **s** of the north: 3411
14:15 be brought down to hell, to the **s** of the pit. 3411
37:24 of the mountains, *to* the **s** of Lebanon; 3411
66:12 ye shall be borne upon *her* **s**, and 6654
Jer 6:22 a great nation shall be raised from the **s** of 3411
48:28 her nest in the **s** of the hole's mouth. 5676
49:32 I will bring their calamity from all **s** 5676
Eze 1: 8 of a man under their wings on their four **s**; 7253
1:17 they went, they went upon their four **s**: 7253
10:11 they went, they went upon their four **s**; 7253
32:23 Whose graves are set in the **s** of the pit, and 3411
41: 2 the **s** of the door *were* five cubits on the one 3802
41:26 on the **s** of the porch, and *upon* the side 3802
42:20 He measured it by the four **s**: it had a wall 7307
46:19 there *was* a place on the **two s** westward. 3411
48: 1 for these are his **s** east *and* west; a *portion* 6285
Am 6:10 shall say unto *him* that *is* by the **s** of 3411
Jnh 1: 5 But Jonah was gone down into the **s** of 3411

SIDON (14) [SIDONIANS, ZIDON]
Ge 10:15 Canaan begat **S** his firstborn, and Heth, 6721
10:19 the border of the Canaanites was from **S**, 6721
Mt 11:21 **S** they would have repented long ago in *4605*
11:22 for Tyre and **S** at the day of judgment, *4605*
15:21 and departed into the coasts of Tyre and **S**. *4605*
Mk 3: 8 and they about Tyre and **S**, a great *4605*
7:24 and went into the borders of Tyre and **S**, *4605*
7:31 departing from the coasts of Tyre and **S**, *4605*
Lk 4:26 save unto Sarepta, *a city* of **S**, unto a *4605*
6:17 and *from* the sea coast of Tyre and **S**, *4605*
10:13 mighty works had been done in Tyre and **S**, *4605*
10:14 tolerable for Tyre and **S** at the judgment, *4605*
Ac 12:20 highly displeased with them of Tyre and **S**: *4606*
27: 3 And the next *day* we touched at **S**. *4605*

SIDONIANS (5) [SIDON]
Dt 3: 9 (*Which* Hermon the **S** call Sirion; and 6722
Jos 13: 4 Mearah that *is* beside the **S**, unto Aphek, 6722
13: 6 *and* all the **S**, them will I drive out from 6722
Jdg 3: 3 the **S**, and the Hivites that dwelt in mount 6722
1Ki 5: 6 *that* can skill to hew timber like unto the **S**. 6722

SIEGE (17) [BESIEGE]
Dt 20:19 field *is* man's *life*) to employ *them* in the **s**: 4692
28:53 given thee, in the **s**, and in the straitness, 4692
28:55 because he hath nothing left him in the **s**, 4692
28:57 them for want of all *things* secretly in the **s** 4692
1Ki 15:27 and all Israel **laid s** to Gibbethon. 6696
2Ch 32: 9 (but he *himself laid* **s** against Lachish, and NIH
32:10 ye trust, that ye abide in the **s** in Jerusalem? 4692
Isa 29: 3 will **lay s** against thee *with* a mount, and 6696
Jer 19: 9 eat every one the flesh of his friend in the **s** 4692
Eze 4: 2 lay **s** against it, and build a fort against it, 4692
4: 3 be besieged, and thou shalt **lay s** against it. 6696
4: 7 shalt set thy face toward the **s** of Jerusalem, 4692
4: 8 till thou hast ended the days of thy **s**. 4692
5: 2 when the days of the **s** are fulfilled: 4692
Mic 5: 1 he hath laid **s** against us: they shall smite 4692
Na 3:14 Draw thee waters for the **s**, fortify thy 4692
Zec 12: 2 when they shall be in the **s** both against 4692

SIEGEWORKS See BULWARKS

SIEVE (2)
Isa 30:28 to sift the nations with the **s** of vanity: 5299
Am 9: 9 like as *corn* is sifted in a **s**, yet shall not 3531

SIFT (3) [SIFTED]
Isa 30:28 to **s** the nations with the sieve of vanity: 5130
Am 9: 9 I will **s** the house of Israel among all 5128
Lk 22:31 *to have* you, that *he* may **s** *you* as wheat: *4617*

SIFTED (1) [SIFT]
Am 9: 9 like as *corn* is **s** in a sieve, yet shall not 5128

SIGH (7) [SIGHED, SIGHEST, SIGHETH, SIGHING, SIGHS]
Isa 24: 7 vine languisheth, all the merryhearted do **s**. 584
La 1: 4 her priests **s**: her virgins *are* afflicted, and 584
1:11 All her people **s**, they seek bread; they have 584
1:21 They have heard that I **s**; *there is* none to 584
Eze 9: 4 a mark upon the foreheads of the men that **s** 584
21: 6 **S** therefore, thou son of man, with 584
21: 6 and with bitterness **s** before their eyes. 584

SIGHED (3) [SIGH]
Ex 2:23 the children of Israel **s** by reason of 584

S

Mk 7:34 he **s**, and saith unto him, EPHPHATHA, *4727*
8:12 And he **s deeply** in his spirit, and saith, *389*

SIGHEST (1) [SIGH]
Eze 21: 7 when they say unto thee, Wherefore **s** thou? 584

SIGHETH (1) [SIGH]
La 1: 8 yea, she **s**, and turneth backward. 584

SIGHING (7) [SIGH]
Job 3:24 For my **s** cometh before I eat, and 585
Ps 12: 5 for the **s** of the needy, now will I arise, 603
31:10 life is spent with grief, and my years with **s**: 585
79:11 Let the **s** of the prisoner come before thee, 603
Isa 21: 2 all the **s** thereof have I made to cease. 585
35:10 gladness, and sorrow and **s** shall flee away. 585
Jer 45: 3 I fainted in my **s**, and I find no rest. 585

SIGHS (1) [SIGH]
La 1:22 for my **s** *are* many, and my heart *is* faint. 585

SIGHT (333) [SEE]
Ge 2: 9 to grow every tree that is pleasant to the **s**, 4758
18: 3 if now I have found favour in thy **s**, 5869
19:19 thy servant hath found grace in thy **s**, and 5869
21:11 the thing was very grievous in Abraham's **s** 5869
21:12 Let it not be grievous in thy **s** because 5869
23: 4 I may bury my dead out of my **s**. 6440+3807.1
23: 8 I should bury my dead out of my **s**; 6440+3807.1
32: 5 tell my lord, that I may find grace in thy **s**. 5869
33: 8 *These are* to find grace in the **s** of my lord. 5869
33:10 if now I have found grace in thy **s**, then 5869
33:15 let me find grace in the **s** of my lord. 5869
38: 7 was wicked in the **s** of the LORD; 5869
39: 4 Joseph found grace in his **s**, and he served 5869
39:21 gave him favour in the **s** of the keeper of 5869
47:18 there is not ought left in the **s** of my lord, 6440
47:25 let us find grace in the **s** of my lord, and 5869
47:29 If now I have found grace in thy **s**, put, 5869
Ex 3: 3 I will now turn aside, and see this great **s**, 4758
3:21 I will give this people favour in the **s** of 5869
4:30 and did the signs in the **s** of the people. 5869
7:20 in the **s** of Pharaoh, and in the sight of his 5869
7:20 of Pharaoh, and in the **s** of his servants; 5869
9: 8 it towards the heaven in the **s** of Pharaoh. 5869
11: 3 the LORD gave the people favour in the **s** 5869
11: 3 in the **s** of Pharaoh's servants, and in 5869
11: 3 and in the **s** of the people.) 5869
12:36 the LORD gave the people favour in the **s** 5869
15:26 wilt do that which is right in his **s**, and 5869
17: 6 Moses did so in the **s** of the elders of Israel. 5869
19:11 in the **s** of all the people upon mount Sinai. 5869
24:17 the **s** of the glory of the LORD *was* like 4758
33:12 and thou hast also found grace in my **s**. 5869
33:13 I pray thee, if I have found grace in thy **s**, 5869
33:13 know thee, that I may find grace in thy **s**: 5869
33:16 and thy people have found grace in thy **s**? 5869
33:17 for thou hast found grace in my **s**, and 5869
34: 9 If now I have found grace in thy **s**, O Lord, 5869
40:38 by night, in the **s** of all the house of Israel, 5869
Lev 10:19 should it have been accepted in the **s** of 5869
13: 3 the plague **in s** *be* deeper than the skin of 4758
13: 4 **in s** *be* not deeper than the skin, and 4758
13: 5 *if* the plague in his **s** be at a stay, *and* 5869
13:20 it *be* **in s** lower than the skin, and the hair 4758
13:25 and it *be* **in s** deeper than the skin; 4758
13:30 behold, *if* it *be* **in s** deeper than the skin; 4758
13:31 it *be* not **in s** deeper than the skin, and 4758
13:32 the scall *be* not **in s** deeper than the skin; 4758
13:34 in the skin, nor *be* **in s** deeper than the skin; 4758
13:37 if the scall be in his **s** at a stay, and 5869
14:37 reddish, which **in s** *are* lower than the wall; 4758
20:17 they shall be cut off in the **s** of their people: 5869
25:53 shall not rule with rigour over him in thy **s**. 5869
26:45 of the land of Egypt in the **s** of the heathen, 5869
Nu 3: 4 priest's office in the **s** of Aaron their father. 6440
11:11 wherefore have I not found favour in thy **s**, 5869
11:15 out of hand, if I have found favour in thy **s**; 5869
13:33 we were in our own **s** as grasshoppers, and 5869
13:33 as grasshoppers, and so we were in their **s**. 5869
19: 5 *one* shall burn the heifer in his **s**; her skin, 5869
20:27 they went up into mount Hor in the **s** of all 5869
25: 6 a Midianitish *woman* in the **s** of Moses, 5869
25: 6 in the **s** of all the congregation of 5869
27:19 and give him a charge in their **s**. 5869
32: 5 said they, if we have found grace in thy **s**, 5869
32:13 that had done evil in the **s** of the LORD, 5869
33: 3 a high hand in the **s** of all the Egyptians. 5869
Dt 4: 6 your understanding in the **s** of the nations, 5869
4:25 shall do evil in the **s** of the LORD thy 5869
4:37 brought thee out in his **s** with his mighty 6440
6:18 *is* right and good in the **s** of the LORD: 5869
9:18 in doing wickedly in the **s** of the LORD, 5869
12:25 *that which is* right in the **s** of the LORD. 5869
12:28 and right in the **s** of the LORD thy God. 5869
17: 2 that hath wrought wickedness in the **s** of 5869
21: 9 *that which is* right in the **s** of the LORD. 5869
28:34 So that thou shalt be mad for the **s** of thine 4758
28:67 for the **s** of thine eyes which thou shalt see. 4758
31: 7 said unto him in the **s** of all Israel, 5869
31:29 ye will do evil in the **s** of the LORD, 5869
34:12 which Moses shewed in the **s** of all Israel. 5869
Jos 3: 7 I begin to magnify thee in the **s** of all Israel, 5869
4:14 magnified Joshua in the **s** of all Israel; 5869
10:12 he said in the **s** of Israel, Sun, stand thou 5869
23: 5 and drive them from out of your **s**; 6440+3807.1
24:17 which did those great signs in our **s**, and 5869
Jdg 2:11 the children of Israel did evil in the **s** of 5869
3: 7 the children of Israel did evil in the **s** of 5869
3:12 the children of Israel did evil again in the **s** 5869
3:12 they had done evil in the **s** of the LORD. 5869
4: 1 the children of Israel again did evil in the **s** 5869
6: 1 the children of Israel did evil in the **s** of 5869
6:17 If now I have found grace in thy **s**, then 5869
6:21 angel of the LORD departed out of his **s**. 5869
10: 6 the children of Israel did evil again in the **s** 5869
13: 1 the children of Israel did evil again in the **s** 5869
Ru 2: 2 glean ears of corn after *him* in whose **s** I 5869
2:13 Let me find favour in thy **s**, my lord; 5869
1Sa 1:18 Let thine handmaid find grace in thy **s**. 5869
12:17 which ye have done in the **s** of the LORD, 5869
15:17 When thou *wast* little in thine own **s**, 5869
15:19 and didst evil in the **s** of the LORD? 5869
16:22 for he hath found favour in my **s**. 5869
18: 5 he was accepted in the **s** of all the people, 5869
18: 5 and also in the **s** of Saul's servants. 5869
29: 6 in with me in the host *is* good in my **s**: 5869
29: 9 to David, I know that thou *art* good in my **s**, 5869
2Sa 6:22 than thus, and will be base in mine own **s**: 5869
7: 9 have cut off all thine enemies out of thy **s**, 6440
7:19 this was yet a small thing in thy **s**, O Lord 5869
12: 9 of the LORD, to do evil in his **s**? 5869
12:11 he shall lie with thy wives in the **s** of this 5869
13: 5 give me meat, and dress the meat in my **s**, 5869
13: 6 make *me* a couple of cakes in my **s**, that I 5869
13: 8 kneaded *it*, and made cakes in his **s**, and 5869
14:22 knoweth that I have found grace in thy **s**, 5869
16: 4 beseech thee *that* I may find grace in thy **s**, 5869
16:22 his father's concubines in the **s** of all Israel. 5869
22:25 according to my cleanness in his **eye s**. 5869
1Ki 8:25 There shall not fail thee a man in my **s** to sit 6440
9: 7 for my name, will I cast out of my **s**; 6440
11: 6 Solomon did evil in the **s** of the LORD, 5869
11:19 Hadad found great favour in the **s** of 5869
11:38 do that *is* right in my **s**, to keep my statutes 5869
14:22 Judah did evil in the **s** of the LORD, and 5869
15:26 he did evil in the **s** of the LORD, and 5869
15:34 he did evil in the **s** of the LORD, and 5869
16: 7 even for all the evil that he did in the **s** of 5869
16:19 sinned in doing evil in the **s** of the LORD, 5869
16:30 Ahab the son of Omri did evil in the **s** of 5869
21:20 thou hast sold thyself to work evil in the **s** 5869
21:25 to work wickedness in the **s** of the LORD, 5869
22:52 he did evil in the **s** of the LORD, and 5869
2Ki 1:13 fifty thy servants, be precious in thy **s**. 5869
1:14 let my life now be precious in thy **s**. 5869
3: 2 he wrought evil in the **s** of the LORD; 5869
3:18 *but* a light thing in the **s** of the LORD: 5869
8:18 and he did evil in the **s** of the LORD. 5869
8:27 did evil in the **s** of the LORD, as *did* 5869
12: 2 Jehoash did *that* which *was* right in the **s** of 5869
13: 2 he did *that* which *was* evil in the **s** of 5869
13:11 he did *that* which *was* evil in the **s** of 5869
14: 3 he did *that* which *was* right in the **s** of 5869
14:24 he did *that* which *was* evil in the **s** of 5869
15: 3 he did *that* which *was* right in the **s** of 5869
15: 9 he did *that* which *was* evil in the **s** of 5869
15:18 he did *that* which *was* evil in the **s** of 5869

2Ki 15:24 he did that which was evil in the s of 5869
15:28 he did that which was evil in the s of 5869
15:34 he did that which was right in the s of 5869
16: 2 did not that which was right in the s of 5869
17: 2 he did that which was evil in the s of 5869
17:17 sold themselves to do evil in the s of 5869
17:18 with Israel, and removed them out of his s: 6440
17:20 until he had cast them out of his s. 6440
17:23 the LORD removed Israel out of his s, 6440
18: 3 he did that which was right in the s of 5869
20: 3 and have done that which is good in thy s. 5869
21: 2 he did that which was evil in the s of 5869
21: 6 he wrought much wickedness in the s of 5869
21:15 they have done that which was evil in my s, 5869
21:16 in doing that which was evil in the s of 5869
21:20 he did that which was evil in the s of 5869
22: 2 he did that which was right in the s of 5869
23:27 I will remove Judah also out of my s, 6440
23:32 he did that which was evil in the s of 5869
23:37 he did that which was evil in the s of 5869
24: 3 to remove them out of his s, for the sins of 6440
24: 9 he did that which was evil in the s of 5869
24:19 he did that which was evil in the s of 5869
1Ch 2: 3 of Judah, was evil in the s of the LORD; 5869
19:13 the LORD do that which is good in his s. 5869
22: 8 shed much blood upon the earth in my s. 6440
28: 8 in the s of all Israel the congregation of 5869
29:25 Solomon exceedingly in the s of all Israel, 5869
2Ch 6:16 s to sit upon the throne of Israel; 6440+3807.1
7:20 will I cast out of my s, and will make it to 6440
20:32 doing that which was right in the s of 5869
22: 4 Wherefore he did evil in the s of 5869
24: 2 Joash did that which was right in the s of 5869
25: 2 he did that which was right in the s of 5869
26: 4 he did that which was right in the s of 5869
27: 2 he did that which was right in the s of 5869
28: 1 he did not that which was right in the s of 5869
29: 2 he did that which was right in the s of 5869
32:23 that he was magnified in the s of all nations 5869
33: 2 did that which was evil in the s of 5869
33: 6 he wrought much evil in the s of 5869
33:22 he did that which was evil in the s of 5869
34: 2 he did that which was right in the s of 5869
36: 5 he did that which was evil in the s of 5869
36: 9 he did that which was evil in the s of 5869
36:12 he did that which was evil in the s of 5869
Ezr 9: 9 hath extended mercy unto us in the s of 6440
Ne 1:11 him mercy in the s of this man. 6440+3807.1
2: 5 if thy servant have found favour in thy s, 6440
8: 5 Ezra opened the book in the s of all 5869
Est 2:15 Esther obtained favour in the s of all them 5869
2:17 favour in his s more than all the virgins; 6440
5: 2 the court, that she obtained favour in his s: 5869
5: 8 If I have found favour in the s of the king, 5869
7: 3 and said, If I have found favour in thy s, 5869
8: 5 if I have found favour in his s, and the thing 6440
Job 15:15 yea, the heavens are not clean in his s. 5869
18: 3 as beasts, and reputed vile in your s? 5869
19:15 me for a stranger: I am an alien in their s. 5869
21: 8 Their seed is established in their s 6440+3807.1
25: 5 yea, the stars are not pure in his s. 5869
34:26 them as wicked men in the open s of others; 7200
41: 9 shall not one be cast down even at the s of 4758
Ps 5: 5 The foolish shall not stand in thy s: 5869
9:19 let the heathen be judged in thy s. 6440
10: 5 thy judgments are far above out of his s: 5048
19:14 be acceptable in thy s, O LORD, 6440
51: 4 have I sinned, and done this evil in thy s: 5869
72:14 and precious shall their blood be in his s. 5869
76: 7 who may stand in thy s when once thou art 6440
78:12 Marvellous things did he in the s of their 5048
79:10 s by the revenging of the blood of thy 5869
90: 4 For a thousand years in thy s are but 5869
98: 2 he openly shewed in the s of the heathen. 5869
101: 7 he that telleth lies shall not tarry in my s. 5869
116:15 Precious in the s of the LORD is the death 5869
143: 2 for in thy s shall no man living be justified. 6440
Pr 1:17 Surely in vain the net is spread in the s of 5869
3: 4 and good understanding in the s of God and 5869
4: 3 and only beloved in the s of my mother. 6440
Ecc 2:26 to a man that is good in his s wisdom, 6440
6: 9 Better is the s of the eyes than 4758
8: 3 Be not hasty to go out of his s: stand not in 6440
11: 9 of thine heart, and in the s of thine eyes: 4758

Isa 5:21 their own eyes, and prudent in their own s! 6440
11: 3 he shall not judge after the s of his eyes, 4758
26:17 so have we been in thy s, O LORD. 6440
38: 3 and have done that which is good in thy s. 5869
43: 4 Since thou wast precious in my s, thou hast 5869
Jer 4: 1 put away thine abominations out of my s, 6440
7:15 I will cast you out of my s, as I have cast 6440
7:30 children of Judah have done evil in my s, 5869
15: 1 cast them out of my s, and let them go 6440
18:10 If it do evil in my s, that it obey not my 5869
18:23 neither blot out their sin from thy s, 6440+3807.1
19:10 shalt thou break the bottle in the s of 5869
32:12 in the s of Hanameel mine uncle's son, and 5869
34:15 now turned, and had done right in my s, 5869
43: 9 in Tahpanhes, in the s of the men of Judah; 5869
51:24 evil that they have done in Zion in your s, 5869
Eze 4:12 dung that cometh out of man, in their s. 5869
5: 8 in the midst of thee in the s of the nations. 5869
5:14 about thee, in the s of all that pass by. 5869
10: 2 them over the city. And he went in in my s. 5869
10:19 and mounted up from the earth in my s: 5869
12: 3 for removing, and remove by day in their s; 5869
12: 3 from thy place to another place in their s: 5869
12: 4 thou bring forth thy stuff by day in their s, 5869
12: 4 thou shalt go forth at even in their s, as they 5869
12: 5 Dig thou through the wall in their s, and 5869
12: 6 In their s shalt thou bear it upon thy 5869
12: 7 and I bare it upon my shoulder in their s. 5869
16:41 execute judgments upon thee in the s of 5869
20: 9 among whom they were, in whose s I made 5869
20:14 the heathen, in whose s I brought them out. 5869
20:22 that it should not be polluted in the s of 5869
20:22 in whose s I brought them forth. 5869
20:43 ye shall lothe yourselves in your own s for 6440
21:23 be unto them as a false divination in their s, 5869
22:16 in thyself in the s of the heathen, 5869
28:18 earth in the s of all them that behold thee. 5869
28:25 shall be sanctified in them in the s of 5869
36:31 shall lothe yourselves in your own s for 6440
36:34 whereas it lay desolate in the s of all that 5869
39:27 am sanctified in them in the s of many 5869
43:11 write it in their s, that they may keep 5869
Da 4:11 the s thereof to the end of all the earth: 2379
4:20 and the s thereof to all the earth; 2379
Hos 2: 2 put away her whoredoms out of her s, 6440
2:10 now will I discover her lewdness in the s of 5869
6: 2 will raise us up, and we shall live in his s. 6440
Am 9: 3 though they be hid from my s in the bottom 5869
Jnh 2: 4 I said, I am cast out of thy s; yet I will look 5869
Mal 2:17 Every one that doeth evil is good in the s of 5869
Mt 11: 5 The blind receive their s, and the lame walk, 308
11:26 Father: for so it seemed good in thy s. 1715
20:34 and immediately their eyes received s, and 308
Mk 10:51 unto him, Lord, that I might receive my s. 308
10:52 And immediately he received his s, and 308
Lk 1:15 For he shall be great in the s of the Lord, 1799
4:18 and recovering of s to the blind, 309
7:21 and unto many that were blind he gave s. 991
10:21 Father; for so it seemed good in thy s. 1715
15:21 and in thy s, and am no more worthy to be 1799
16:15 men is abomination in the s of God. 1799
18:41 And he said, Lord, that I may receive my s. 308
18:42 And Jesus said unto him, Receive thy s: 308
18:43 And immediately he received his s, and 308
23:48 all the people that came together to that s, 2335
24:31 and he vanished out of their s. 855+1096
Jn 9:11 and I went and washed, and I received s. 308
9:15 also asked him how he had received his s. 308
9:18 that he had been blind, and received his s, 308
9:18 the parents of him that had received his s. 308
Ac 1: 9 and a cloud received him out of their s. 3788
4:19 Whether it be right in the s of God to 1799
7:10 wisdom in the s of Pharaoh king of Egypt; 1726
7:31 When Moses saw it, he wondered at the s: 3705
8:21 for thy heart is not right in the s of God. 1799
9: 9 And he was three days without s, and 991
9:12 his hand on him, that he might receive his s. 308
9:17 that thou mightest receive thy s, and 308
9:18 and he received s forthwith, and arose, and 308
10:31 thine alms are had in remembrance in the s 1799
22:13 said unto me, Brother Saul, receive thy s. 308
Ro 3:20 law there shall no flesh be justified in his s: 1799
12:17 Provide things honest in the s of all men. 1799
2Co 2:17 of God, in the s of God speak we in Christ. 2714

S

2Co 4: 2 to every man's conscience **in the s** of God. *1799*
5: 7 (For we walk by faith, not by s:) *1491*
7:12 that our care for you **in the s** of God might *1799*
8:21 honest *things,* not only **in the s** of the Lord, *1799*
8:21 sight of the Lord, but also **in the s** of men. *1799*
Gal 3:11 *man* is justified by the law **in the s** of God, *3844*
Col 1:22 unblameable and unreproveable in his s: *2714*
1Th 1: 3 **in the s** of God and our Father; *1715*
1Ti 2: 3 and acceptable **in the s** of God our Saviour; *1799*
6:13 I give thee charge **in the s** of God, *1799*
Heb 4:13 any creature *that is* not manifest **in** his s: *1799*
12:21 And so terrible was the s, *that* Moses said, *5324*
13:21 in you *that which is* well pleasing **in** his s, *1799*
Jas 4:10 Humble yourselves **in the s** of the Lord, *1799*
1Pe 3: 4 which is **in the s** of God of great price. *1799*
1Jn 3:22 do those *things* that are pleasing **in** his s. *1799*
Rev 4: 3 about the throne, **in s** like unto an emerald. *3706*
13:13 from heaven on the earth **in the s** of men, *1799*
13:14 he had power to do **in the s** of the beast; *1799*

SIGHTS (1) [SEE]
Lk 21:11 and **fearful s** and great signs shall there be *5400*

SIGN (76) [SIGNED, SIGNS]
Ex 4: 8 neither hearken to the voice of the first s, 226
4: 8 that they will believe the voice of the latter s. 226
8:23 and thy people: to morrow shall this s be. 226
13: 9 it shall be for a s unto thee upon thine hand, 226
31:13 for it *is* a s between me and you throughout 226
31:17 It *is* a s between me and the children of 226
Nu 16:38 they shall be a s unto the children of Israel. 226
26:10 and fifty men: and they became a s. 5251
Dt 6: 8 thou shalt bind them for a s upon thine hand, 226
11:18 and bind them for a s upon your hand, 226
13: 1 of dreams, and giveth thee a s or a wonder, 226
13: 2 the s or the wonder come to pass, whereof he 226
28:46 they shall be upon thee for a s and for a 226
Jos 4: 6 That this may be a s among you, *that* when 226
Jdg 6:17 then shew me a s that thou talkest with me. 226
20:38 Now there was an **appointed** s between 4150
1Sa 2:34 this *shall be* a s unto thee, that shall come 226
14:10 into our hand: and this *shall be* a s unto us. 226
1Ki 13: 3 he gave a s the same day, saying, This *is* 4159
13: 3 This *is* the s which the LORD hath 4159
13: 5 according to the s which the man of God 4159
2Ki 19:29 this *shall be* a s unto thee, Ye shall eat *this* 226
20: 8 What *shall be* the s that the LORD will heal 226
20: 9 This s shalt thou have of the LORD, 226
2Ch 32:24 he spake unto him, and he gave him a s. 4159
Isa 7:11 Ask thee a s of the LORD thy God; ask it 226
7:14 the Lord himself shall give you a s; 226
19:20 it shall be for a s and for a witness unto 226
20: 3 barefoot three years *for* a s and wonder upon 226
37:30 this *shall be* a s unto thee, Ye shall eat *this* 226
38: 7 this *shall be* a s unto thee from the LORD, 226
38:22 What *is* the s that I shall go up *to* the house 226
55:13 for an everlasting s *that* shall not be cut off. 226
66:19 I will set a s among them, and I will send 226
Jer 6: 1 and set up a **s of fire** in Beth-haccerem: 4864
44:29 this *shall be* a s unto you, saith the LORD, 226
Eze 4: 3 This *shall be* a s to the house of Israel. 226
12: 6 for I have set thee *for* a s unto the house of 4159
12:11 Say, I *am* your s: like as I have done, so 4159
14: 8 will make him a s and a proverb, and I will 226
20:12 my sabbaths, to be a s between me and them, 226
20:20 they shall be a s between me and you, that *ye* 226
24:24 Thus Ezekiel is unto you a s: according to 4159
24:27 thou shalt be a s unto them; and they shall 4159
39:15 a man's bone, then shall he set up a s by it, 6725
Da 6: 8 establish the decree, and s the writing, 7560
Mt 12:38 saying, Master, we would see a s from thee. *4592*
12:39 and adulterous generation seeketh after a s; *4592*
12:39 and there shall no s be given to it, but *4592*
12:39 given to it, but the s of the prophet Jonas: *4592*
16: 1 that *he* would shew them a s from heaven. *4592*
16: 4 and adulterous generation seeketh after a s; *4592*
16: 4 and there shall no s be given unto it, but *4592*
16: 4 given unto it, but the s of the prophet Jonas. *4592*
24: 3 and what *shall be* the s of thy coming, and *4592*
24:30 shall appear the s of the Son of man in *4592*
26:48 Now he that betrayed him gave them a s, *4592*
Mk 8:11 seeking of him a s from heaven, *4592*
8:12 Why doth this generation seek after a s? *4592*
8:12 There shall no s be given unto this *4592*
13: 4 what *shall be* the s when all these *things* *4592*
Lk 2:12 And this *shall be* a s unto you; Ye shall find *4592*
2:34 and for a s which shall be spoken against; *4592*
11:16 tempting *him,* sought of him a s from *4592*
11:29 they seek a s; and there shall no sign be *4592*
11:29 and there shall no s be given it, but the sign *4592*
11:29 be given it, but the s of Jonas the prophet. *4592*
11:30 For as Jonas was a s unto the Ninevites, so *4592*
21: 7 what s *will there be* when these *things* shall *4592*
Jn 2:18 unto him, What s shewest thou unto us, *4592*
6:30 unto him, What s shewest thou then, *4592*
Ac 28:11 in the isle, *whose* s *was* Castor and Pollux. *3902*
Ro 4:11 And he received the s of circumcision, *4592*
1Co 1:22 For the Jews require a s, and the Greeks *4592*
14:22 Wherefore tongues are for a s, not to them *4592*
Rev 15: 1 And I saw another s in heaven, great and *4592*

SIGNED (4) [SIGN]
Da 6: 9 Wherefore king Darius s the writing and 7560
6:10 when Daniel knew that the writing *was* s, 7560
6:12 Hast thou not s a decree, that every man 7560
6:13 nor the decree that thou hast s, but 7560

SIGNET (11) [SIGNETS]
Ge 38:18 Thy s, and thy bracelets, and thy staff that 2368
38:25 *are* these, the s, and bracelets, and staff. 2858
Ex 28:11 in stone, *like* the engravings of a s, 2368
28:21 to their names, *like* the engravings of a s; 2368
28:36 grave upon it, *like* the engravings of a s, 2368
39:14 *like* the engravings of a s, every one with 2368
39:30 it a writing, *like to* the engravings of a s, 2368
Jer 22:24 of Judah were the s upon my right hand, 2368
Da 6:17 the king sealed it with his own s, and 5824
6:17 his own signet, and with the s of his lords; 5824
Hag 2:23 the LORD, and will make thee as a s: 2368

SIGNETS (1) [SIGNET]
Ex 39: 6 graven *as* s are graven, with the names of 2368

SIGNIFICATION (1) [SIGNIFY]
1Co 14:10 in the world, and none of them *is* **without** s. *880*

SIGNIFIED (2) [SIGNIFY]
Ac 11:28 s by the Spirit that there should be great *4591*
Rev 1: 1 and s *it* by his angel unto his servant John: *4591*

SIGNIFIETH (1) [SIGNIFY]
Heb 12:27 And this *word,* Yet once *more,* s *1213*

SIGNIFY (4) [SIGNIFICATION, SIGNIFIED, SIGNIFIETH, SIGNIFYING]
Ac 21:26 to s the accomplishment of the days of *1229*
23:15 ye with the council s to the chief captain *1718*
25:27 not withal to s the crimes *laid* against him. *4591*
1Pe 1:11 Spirit of Christ which was in them did s, *1213*

SIGNIFYING (4) [SIGNIFY]
Jn 12:33 This he said, s what death he should die. *4591*
18:32 which he spake, s what death he should die. *4591*
21:19 s by what death he should glorify God. *4591*
Heb 9: 8 The Holy Ghost this s, that the way into *1213*

SIGNS (53) [SIGN]
Ge 1:14 let them be for s, and for seasons, and 226
Ex 4: 9 if they will not believe also these two s, 226
4:17 rod in thine hand, wherewith thou shalt do s. 226
4:28 and all the s which he had commanded him. 226
4:30 and did the s in the sight of the people. 226
7: 3 multiply my s and my wonders in the land of 226
10: 1 that I might shew these my s before him: 226
10: 2 and my s which I have done amongst them; 226
Nu 14:11 for all the s which I have shewed among 226
Dt 4:34 by s, and by wonders, and by war, and by a 226
6:22 the LORD shewed s and wonders, great 226
7:19 the s, and the wonders, and the mighty hand, 226
26: 8 and with s, and with wonders: 226
29: 3 have seen, the s, and those great miracles: 226
34:11 In all the s and the wonders, which 226
Jos 24:17 and which did those great s in our sight, and 226
1Sa 10: 7 let it be, when these s are come unto thee, 226
10: 9 and all those s came to pass that day. 226
Ne 9:10 And shewedst s and wonders upon Pharaoh, 226
Ps 74: 4 they set up their ensigns *for* s. 226
74: 9 We see not our s: *there is* no more any 226
78:43 How he had wrought his s in Egypt, and 226

S

Ps 105:27 They shewed his **s** among them, 226
Isa 8:18 whom the LORD hath given me *are* for **s** 226
Jer 10: 2 and be not dismayed at the **s** of heaven; 226
32:20 Which hast set **s** and wonders in the land of 226
32:21 people Israel out of the land of Egypt with **s**, 226
Da 4: 2 I thought it good to shew the **s** and 852
4: 3 How great *are* his **s**! and how mighty *are* his 852
6:27 and he worketh **s** and wonders in heaven and 852
Mt 16: 3 but can ye not *discern* the **s** of the times? *4592*
24:24 and shall shew great **s** and wonders; *4592*
Mk 13:22 and shall shew **s** and wonders, to seduce, *4592*
16:17 And these **s** shall follow them that believe; *4592*
16:20 and confirming the word with **s** following. *4592*
Lk 1:62 And they **made s** to his father, how he *1770*
21:11 and great **s** shall there be from heaven. *4592*
21:25 And there shall be **s** in the sun, and in *4592*
Jn 4:48 Except ye see **s** and wonders, ye will not *4592*
20:30 And many other **s** truly did Jesus in *4592*
Ac 2:19 in heaven above, and **s** in the earth beneath; *4592*
2:22 among you by miracles and wonders and **s**, *4592*
2:43 and **s** were done by the apostles. *4592*
4:30 and that **s** and wonders may be done by *4592*
5:12 by the hands of the apostles were many **s** *4592*
7:36 shewed wonders and **s** in the land of Egypt, *4592*
8:13 *the* miracles and **s** *which were* done. *4592*
14: 3 and granted **s** and wonders to be done by *4592*
Ro 15:19 Through mighty **s** and wonders, by *4592*
2Co 12:12 Truly the **s** of an apostle were wrought *4592*
12:12 in **s**, and wonders, and mighty deeds. *4592*
2Th 2: 9 with all power and **s** and lying wonders, *4592*
Heb 2: 4 both with **s** and wonders, and with divers *4592*

SIHON (37)
Nu 21:21 Israel sent messengers unto **S** king of 5511
21:23 **S** would not suffer Israel to pass through 5511
21:23 **S** gathered all his people together, and 5511
21:26 For Heshbon *was* the city of **S** the king of 5511
21:27 let the city of **S** be built and prepared: 5511
21:28 out of Heshbon, a flame from the city of **S**: 5511
21:29 his daughters into captivity unto **S** king of 5511
21:34 thou shalt do to him as thou didst unto **S** 5511
32:33 the kingdom of **S** king of the Amorites, and 5511
Dt 1: 4 After he had slain **S** the king of 5511
2:24 I have given into thy hand **S** the Amorite, 5511
2:26 **S** king of Heshbon *with* words of peace, 5511
2:30 **S** king of Heshbon would not let us pass by 5511
2:31 I have begun to give **S** and his land before 5511
2:32 **S** came out against us, he and all his 5511
3: 2 thou shalt do unto him as thou didst unto **S** 5511
3: 6 as we did unto **S** king of Heshbon, 5511
4:46 in the land of **S** king of the Amorites, 5511
29: 7 **S** the king of Heshbon, and Og the king of 5511
31: 4 LORD shall do unto them as he did to **S** 5511
Jos 2:10 **S** and Og, whom ye utterly destroyed. 5511
9:10 to **S** king of Heshbon, and to Og king of 5511
12: 2 **S** king of the Amorites, who dwelt in 5511
12: 5 the border of **S** king of Heshbon. 5511
13:10 And all the cities of **S** king of the Amorites, 5511
13:21 all the kingdom of **S** king of the Amorites, 5511
13:21 Hur, and Reba, *which were* dukes of **S**, 5511
13:27 the rest of the kingdom of **S** king of 5511
Jdg 11:19 Israel sent messengers unto **S** king of 5511
11:20 **S** trusted not Israel to pass through his 5511
11:20 **S** gathered all his people together, and 5511
11:21 the LORD God of Israel delivered **S** and 5511
1Ki 4:19 *in* the country of **S** king of the Amorites, 5511
Ne 9:22 so they possessed the land of **S**, and 5511
Ps 135:11 **S** king of the Amorites, and Og king of 5511
136:19 **S** king of the Amorites: for his mercy 5511
Jer 48:45 a flame from the midst of **S**, and 5511

SIHOR (3)
Jos 13: 3 From **S**, which *is* before Egypt, even unto 7883
Isa 23: 3 by great waters the seed of **S**, the harvest of 7883
Jer 2:18 the way of Egypt, to drink the waters of **S**? 7883

SILAS (13) [SILVANUS]
Ac 15:22 and **S**, chief *men* among the brethren: *4609*
15:27 We have sent therefore Judas and **S**, *4609*
15:32 And Judas and **S**, being prophets also *4609*
15:34 Notwithstanding it pleased **S** to abide there *4609*
15:40 And Paul chose **S**, and departed, *4609*
16:19 they caught Paul and **S**, and drew *them* into *4609*
16:25 And at midnight Paul and **S** prayed, and *4609*
16:29 and fell down before Paul and **S**, *4609*
17: 4 and consorted with Paul and **S**; *4609*
17:10 sent away Paul and **S** by night unto Berea: *4609*
17:14 but **S** and Timotheus abode there still. *4609*
17:15 and receiving a commandment unto **S** and *4609*
18: 5 And when **S** and Timotheus were come *4609*

SILENCE (35) [SILENT]
Jdg 3:19 who said, **Keep s**. And all that stood by 2013
Job 4:16 *there was* **s**, and I heard a voice, *saying*, 1827
29:21 and waited, and **kept s** at my counsel. 1826
31:34 that I **kept s**, *and* went not out *of* the door? 1826
Ps 31:18 Let the lying lips be **put to s**; which speak 481
32: 3 When I **kept s**, my bones waxed old 2790
35:22 **keep** not **s**: O Lord, be not far from me. 2790
39: 2 I was dumb *with* **s**, I held my peace, 1747
50: 3 Our God shall come, and shall not **keep s**: 2790
50:21 These *things* hast thou done, and I **kept s**; 2790
83: 1 **Keep** not thou **s**, O God: hold not thy 1824
94:17 my help, my soul had almost dwelt *in* **s**. 1745
115:17 neither any that go down into **s**. 1745
Ecc 3: 7 a time to **keep s**, and a time to speak; 2814
Isa 15: 1 Ar of Moab is laid waste, *and* **brought to s**; 1820
15: 1 of Moab is laid waste, *and* **brought to s**; 1820
41: 1 **Keep s** before me, O islands; and let 2790
62: 6 make mention of the LORD, keep not **s**, 1824
65: 6 I will not keep **s**, but will recompense, 2814
Jer 8:14 for the LORD our God hath **put us to s**, 1826
La 2:10 of Zion sit upon the ground, *and* **keep s**: 1826
3:28 He sitteth alone and **keepeth s**, because 1826
Am 5:13 Therefore the prudent shall **keep s** in that 1826
8: 3 they shall cast *them* forth with **s**. 2013
Hab 2:20 let all the earth **keep s** before him. 2013
Mt 22:34 heard that he had **put** the Sadducees **to s**, *5392*
Ac 15:12 Then all the multitude **kept s**, and *4601*
21:40 And when there was made a great **s**, *4602*
22: 2 tongue to them, they kept the more **s**: *2271*
1Co 14:28 no interpreter, let him **keep s** in the church; *4601*
14:34 Let your women **keep s** in the churches: *4601*
1Ti 2:11 Let the woman learn in **s** with all *2271*
2:12 usurp authority over the man, but to be in **s**. *2271*
1Pe 2:15 that with well doing *ye* may **put to s** *5392*
Rev 8: 1 there was **s** in heaven about the space of *4602*

SILENT (9) [SILENCE]
1Sa 2: 9 and the wicked shall be **s** in darkness; 1826
Ps 22: 2 and in the night season, and am not **s**. 1747
28: 1 I cry, O LORD, my rock; be not **s** to me: 2790
28: 1 lest, *if* thou be **s** to me, I become like them 2814
30:12 glory may sing *praise* to thee, and not be **s**. 1826
31:17 be ashamed, *and* let them be **s** in the grave. 1826
Isa 47: 5 Sit thou **s**, and get thee into darkness, 1748
Jer 8:14 the defenced cities, and let us be **s** there: 1826
Zec 2:13 **Be s**, O all flesh, before the LORD: for he 2013

SILK (4)
Pr 31:22 of tapestry; her clothing *is* **s** and purple. 8336
Eze 16:10 with fine linen, and I covered thee *with* **s**. 4897
16:13 *of* fine linen, and **s**, and broidered work; 4897
Rev 18:12 and **s**, and scarlet, and all thyine wood, and *4596*

SILLA (1)
2Ki 12:20 the house of Millo, which goeth down *to* **S**. 5538

SILLY (3)
Job 5: 2 the foolish man, and envy slayeth the **s one**. 6601
Hos 7:11 Ephraim also is like a **s** dove, without heart: 6601
2Ti 3: 6 and lead captive **s women** laden with sins, *1133*

SILOAH (1) [SILOAM]
Ne 3:15 the wall of the pool of **S** by the king's 7975

SILOAM (3) [SILOAH]
Lk 13: 4 upon whom the tower in **S** fell, and *4611*
Jn 9: 7 said unto him, Go, wash in the pool of **S**, *4611*
9:11 unto me, Go to the pool of **S**, and wash: *4611*

SILVANUS (4) [SILAS]
2Co 1:19 *even* by me and **S** and Timotheus, was not *4610*
1Th 1: 1 Paul, and **S**, and Timotheus, unto *4610*
2Th 1: 1 Paul, and **S**, and Timotheus, unto *4610*
1Pe 5:12 By **S**, a faithful brother unto you, as I *4610*

SILVER (320) [SILVERLINGS, SILVERSMITH]
Ge 13: 2 *was* very rich in cattle, in **s**, and in gold. 3701

S

Ge	20:16	given thy brother a thousand *pieces* of **s**:	3701
	23:15	the land *is worth* four hundred shekels of **s**;	3701
	23:16	Abraham weighed to Ephron the **s**,	3701
	23:16	four hundred shekels of **s**, current *money*	3701
	24:35	**s**, and gold, and menservants, and	3701
	24:53	the servant brought forth jewels of **s**, and	3701
	37:28	to the Ishmeelites for twenty *pieces* of **s**:	3701
	44: 2	put my cup, the **s** cup, in the sack's mouth	3701
	44: 8	should we steal out of thy lord's house **s** or	3701
	45:22	he gave three hundred *pieces* of **s**,	3701
Ex	3:22	jewels of **s**, and jewels of gold, and	3701
	11: 2	jewels of **s**, and jewels of gold.	3701
	12:35	they borrowed of the Egyptians jewels of **s**,	3701
	20:23	Ye shall not make with me gods of **s**,	3701
	21:32	give unto their master thirty shekels *of* **s**,	3701
	25: 3	shall take of them; gold, and **s**, and brass,	3701
	26:19	thou shalt make forty sockets of **s** under	3701
	26:21	their forty sockets *of* **s**; two sockets under	3701
	26:25	and their sockets *of* **s**, sixteen sockets;	3701
	26:32	*shall be of* gold, upon the four sockets of **s**.	3701
	27:10	of the pillars and their fillets *shall be of* **s**.	3701
	27:11	the hooks of the pillars and their fillets *of* **s**.	3701
	27:17	about the court *shall be* filleted *with* **s**;	3701
	27:17	their hooks *shall be of* **s**, and their sockets	3701
	31: 4	to work in gold, and in **s**, and in brass,	3701
	35: 5	of the LORD; gold, and **s**, and brass,	3701
	35:24	Every one that did offer an offering of **s**	3701
	35:32	to work in gold, and in **s**, and in brass,	3701
	36:24	forty sockets of **s** he made under the twenty	3701
	36:26	their forty sockets *of* **s**; two sockets under	3701
	36:30	their sockets *were* sixteen sockets *of* **s**,	3701
	36:36	and he cast for them four sockets of **s**.	3701
	38:10	of the pillars and their fillets *were of* **s**.	3701
	38:11	the hooks of the pillars and their fillets *of* **s**.	3701
	38:12	the hooks of the pillars and their fillets *of* **s**.	3701
	38:17	the hooks of the pillars and their fillets *of* **s**;	3701
	38:17	the overlaying of their chapiters *of* **s**; and	3701
	38:17	the pillars of the court *were* filleted *with* **s**.	3701
	38:19	their hooks *of* **s**, and the overlaying of their	3701
	38:19	of their chapiters and their fillets *of* **s**.	3701
	38:25	the **s** of them that were numbered of	3701
	38:27	of the hundred talents of **s** were cast	3701
Lev	5:15	with thy estimation *by* shekels of **s**,	3701
	27: 3	thy estimation shall be fifty shekels of **s**,	3701
	27: 6	shall be of the male five shekels of **s**,	3701
	27: 6	thy estimation *shall be* three shekels of **s**.	3701
	27:16	seed *shall be valued* at fifty shekels of **s**.	3701
Nu	7:13	his offering *was* one **s** charger, the weight	3701
	7:13	thirty *shekels,* one **s** bowl of seventy	3701
	7:19	He offered *for* his offering one **s** charger,	3701
	7:19	thirty *shekels,* one **s** bowl of seventy	3701
	7:25	His offering *was* one **s** charger, the weight	3701
	7:25	thirty *shekels,* one **s** bowl of seventy	3701
	7:31	His offering *was* one **s** charger of	3701
	7:31	thirty *shekels,* one **s** bowl of seventy	3701
	7:37	His offering *was* one **s** charger, the weight	3701
	7:37	thirty *shekels,* one **s** bowl of seventy	3701
	7:43	His offering *was* one **s** charger of	3701
	7:43	thirty *shekels,* a **s** bowl of seventy shekels,	3701
	7:49	His offering *was* one **s** charger, the weight	3701
	7:49	thirty *shekels,* one **s** bowl of seventy	3701
	7:55	His offering *was* one **s** charger of	3701
	7:55	thirty *shekels,* one **s** bowl of seventy	3701
	7:61	His offering *was* one **s** charger, the weight	3701
	7:61	thirty *shekels,* one **s** bowl of seventy	3701
	7:67	His offering *was* one **s** charger, the weight	3701
	7:67	thirty *shekels,* one **s** bowl of seventy	3701
	7:73	His offering *was* one **s** charger, the weight	3701
	7:73	thirty *shekels,* one **s** bowl of seventy	3701
	7:79	His offering *was* one **s** charger, the weight	3701
	7:79	thirty *shekels,* one **s** bowl of seventy	3701
	7:84	twelve chargers of **s**, twelve silver bowls,	3701
	7:84	twelve **s** bowls, twelve spoons of gold:	3701
	7:85	Each charger of **s** *weighing* an hundred and	3701
	7:85	all the **s** vessels *weighed* two thousand and	3701
	10: 2	Make thee two trumpets of **s**; of a whole	3701
	22:18	If Balak would give me his house full *of* **s**	3701
	24:13	If Balak would give me his house full *of* **s**	3701
	31:22	the **s**, the brass, the iron, the tin, and	3701
Dt	7:25	thou shalt not desire the **s** or gold *that is* on	3701
	8:13	thy **s** and thy gold is multiplied, and all that	3701
	17:17	shall he greatly multiply to himself **s**	3701
	22:19	amerce him in an hundred *shekels* of **s**,	3701
	22:29	unto the damsel's father fifty *shekels* of **s**,	3701
	29:17	their idols, wood and stone, **s** and gold,	3701
Jos	6:19	all the **s**, and gold, and vessels of brass and	3701
	6:24	only the **s**, and the gold, and the vessels of	3701
	7:21	two hundred shekels *of* **s**, and a wedge of	3701
	7:21	in the midst of my tent, and the **s** under it.	3701
	7:22	*it was* hid in his tent, and the **s** under it.	3701
	7:24	the **s**, and the garment, and the wedge of	3701
	22: 8	with **s**, and with gold, and with brass, and	3701
	24:32	of Shechem for an hundred **pieces of s**:	7192
Jdg	9: 4	ten *pieces* of **s** out of the house of	3701
	16: 5	every one *of us* eleven hundred *pieces* of **s**.	3701
	17: 2	The eleven hundred *shekels* of **s** that were	3701
	17: 2	also in mine ears, behold, the **s** *is* with me;	3701
	17: 3	eleven hundred *shekels* of **s** to his mother,	3701
	17: 3	I had wholly dedicated the **s** unto	3701
	17: 4	his mother took two hundred *shekels* of **s**,	3701
	17:10	I will give thee ten *shekels* of **s** by the year,	3701
1Sa	2:36	crouch to him for a piece of **s** and a morsel	3701
	9: 8	here at hand the fourth part of a shekel of **s**:	3701
2Sa	8:10	*Joram* brought with him vessels of **s**, and	3701
	8:11	with the **s** and gold that he had dedicated of	3701
	18:11	I would have given thee ten *shekels of* **s**,	3701
	18:12	a thousand *shekels of* **s** in mine hand,	3701
	21: 4	We will have no **s** nor gold of Saul, nor of	3701
	24:24	and the oxen for fifty shekels of **s**.	3701
1Ki	7:51	*even* the **s**, and the gold, and the vessels,	3701
	10:21	none *were of* **s**: it was nothing accounted of	3701
	10:22	and **s**, ivory, and apes, and peacocks.	3701
	10:25	vessels of **s**, and vessels of gold, and	3701
	10:27	the king made **s** *to be* in Jerusalem as	3701
	10:29	out of Egypt for six hundred *shekels* of **s**,	3701
	15:15	of the LORD, **s**, and gold, and vessels.	3701
	15:18	Asa took all the **s** and the gold that were	3701
	15:19	I have sent unto thee a present of **s** and	3701
	16:24	hill Samaria of Shemer for two talents of **s**,	3701
	20: 3	Thy **s** and thy gold *is* mine; thy wives also	3701
	20: 5	Thou shalt deliver me thy **s**, and thy gold,	3701
	20: 7	my children, and for my **s**, and for my gold;	3701
	20:39	his life, or else thou shalt pay a talent of **s**.	3701
2Ki	5: 5	took with him ten talents of **s**, and	3701
	5:22	a talent of **s**, and two changes of garments.	3701
	5:23	and bound two talents of **s** in two bags,	3701
	6:25	head was *sold* for fourscore *pieces* of **s**,	3701
	6:25	of a kab of dove's dung for five *pieces* of **s**.	3701
	7: 8	carried thence **s**, and gold, and raiment, and	3701
	12:13	*for* the house of the LORD bowls of **s**,	3701
	12:13	any vessels of gold, or vessels of **s**,	3701
	14:14	he took all the gold and **s**, and all	3701
	15:19	Menahem gave Pul a thousand talents of **s**,	3701
	15:20	of each man fifty shekels *of* **s**, to give to	3701
	16: 8	Ahaz took the **s** and gold that was found *in*	3701
	18:14	king of Judah three hundred talents of **s**	3701
	18:15	Hezekiah gave *him* all the **s** that was found	3701
	20:13	the **s**, and the gold, and the spices, and	3701
	22: 4	that he may sum the **s** which is brought *into*	3701
	23:33	land to a tribute of an hundred talents of **s**,	3701
	23:35	Jehoiakim gave the **s** and the gold to	3701
	23:35	he exacted the **s** and the gold of the people	3701
	25:15	as *were of* gold, *in* gold, and *of* **s**, *in* silver,	3701
	25:15	as *were of* gold, *in* gold, and *of* silver, *in* **s**,	3701
1Ch	18:10	*manner of* vessels of gold and **s** and brass.	3701
	18:11	with the **s** and the gold that he brought from	3701
	19: 6	a thousand talents of **s** to hire them chariots	3701
	22:14	and a thousand thousand talents *of* **s**;	3701
	22:16	the gold, the **s**, and the brass, and the iron,	3701
	28:14	**s** *also* for all instruments of silver by	NIH
	28:14	*silver also* for all instruments of **s** by	3701
	28:15	for the candlesticks of **s** by weight, *both* for	3701
	28:16	and *likewise* **s** for the tables of silver:	3701
	28:16	and *likewise* silver for the tables of **s**:	3701
	28:17	*likewise* **s** by weight for every bason of	NIH
	28:17	*silver* by weight for every bason of **s**:	3701
	29: 2	the **s** for *things of* silver, and the brass for	3701
	29: 2	the silver for *things of* **s**, and the brass for	3701
	29: 3	of mine own proper good, *of* gold and **s**,	3701
	29: 4	and seven thousand talents of refined **s**,	3701
	29: 5	the **s** for *things of* silver, and for all *manner*	3701
	29: 5	the silver for *things of* **s**, and for all *manner*	3701
	29: 7	*of* **s** ten thousand talents, and *of* brass	3701
2Ch	1:15	the king made **s** and gold at Jerusalem *as*	3701
	1:17	a chariot for six hundred *shekels* of **s**,	3701
	2: 7	in **s**, and in brass, and in iron, and in purple,	3701
	2:14	in **s**, in brass, in iron, in stone, and	3701
	5: 1	the **s**, and the gold, and all the instruments,	3701

2Ch 9:14 the country brought gold and **s** to Solomon. 3701
9:20 none *were of* **s**; it was *not* any thing 3701
9:21 and **s**, ivory, and apes, and peacocks. 3701
9:24 vessels of **s**, and vessels of gold, and 3701
9:27 the king made **s** in Jerusalem as stones, 3701
15:18 had dedicated, **s**, and gold, and vessels. 3701
16: 2 Asa brought out **s** and gold out of 3701
16: 3 behold, I have sent thee **s** and gold; go, 3701
17:11 brought Jehoshaphat presents, and tribute **s**; 3701
21: 3 their father gave them great gifts of **s**, and 3701
24:14 and spoons, and vessels of gold and **s**. 3701
25: 6 out of Israel for an hundred talents of **s**. 3701
25:24 *he took* all the gold and the **s**, and all 3701
27: 5 him the same year an hundred talents of **s**, 3701
32:27 he made himself treasuries for **s**, and 3701
36: 3 the land in an hundred talents of **s** 3701
Ezr 1: 4 let the men of his place help him with **s**, 3701
1: 6 strengthened their hands with vessels of **s**, 3701
1: 9 a thousand chargers of **s**, nine and 3701
1:10 **s** basons of a second sort four hundred and 3701
1:11 of **s** *were* five thousand and four hundred. 3701
2:69 five thousand pound *of* **s**, and one hundred 3701
5:14 also of gold and **s** of the house of God, 3702
6: 5 and **s** vessels of the house of God, 3702
7:15 to carry the **s** and gold, which the king and 3702
7:16 all the **s** and gold that thou canst find in all 3702
7:18 to do with the rest of the **s** and gold, 3702
7:22 Unto an hundred talents *of* **s**, and to an 3702
8:25 weighed unto them the **s**, and the gold, and 3701
8:26 their hand six hundred and fifty talents *of* **s**, 3701
8:26 **s** vessels an hundred talents, *and of* gold an 3701
8:28 the **s** and the gold *are* a freewill offering 3701
8:30 and the Levites the weight of the **s**, 3701
8:33 Now on the fourth day was the **s** and 3701
Ne 5:15 and wine, beside forty shekels of **s**; 3701
7:71 two thousand and two hundred pound *of* **s**. 3701
7:72 two thousand pound *of* **s**, and threescore 3701
Est 1: 6 and purple to **s** rings and pillars of marble: 3701
1: 6 the beds *were of* gold and **s**, upon a 3701
3: 9 I will pay ten thousand talents of **s** to 3701
3:11 The **s** *is* given to thee, the people also, 3701
Job 3:15 had gold, who filled their houses *with* **s**: 3701
22:25 and thou shalt have plenty of **s**. 3701
27:16 Though he heap up **s** as the dust, and 3701
27:17 *it* on, and the innocent shall divide the **s**. 3701
28: 1 Surely there is a vein for the **s**, and a place 3701
28:15 neither shall **s** be weighed *for* the price 3701
Ps 12: 6 *as* **s** tried in a furnace of earth, 3701
66:10 proved us: thou hast tried us, as **s** is tried. 3701
68:13 *be as* the wings of a dove covered with **s**, 3701
68:30 *every one* submit himself with pieces of **s**: 3701
105:37 He brought them forth also with **s** and gold: 3701
115: 4 Their idols *are* **s** and gold, the work of 3701
119:72 unto me than thousands of gold and **s**. 3701
135:15 The idols of the heathen *are* **s** and gold, 3701
Pr 2: 4 If thou seekest her as **s**, and searchest for 3701
3:14 of it *is* better than the merchandise of **s**, 3701
8:10 Receive my instruction, and not **s**; and 3701
8:19 fine gold; and my revenue than choice **s**. 3701
10:20 The tongue of the just *is as* choice **s**: 3701
16:16 understanding rather to be chosen than **s**! 3701
17: 3 The fining pot *is* for **s**, and the furnace for 3701
22: 1 *and* loving favour rather than **s** and gold. 3701
25: 4 Take away the dross from the **s**, and 3701
25:11 *is like* apples of gold in pictures of **s**. 3701
26:23 *are like* a potsherd covered with **s** dross. 3701
27:21 *As* the fining pot for **s**, and the furnace for 3701
Ecc 2: 8 I gathered me also **s** and gold, and 3701
5:10 He that loveth **s** shall not be satisfied *with* 3701
5:10 loveth silver shall not be satisfied *with* **s**; 3701
12: 6 Or ever the **s** cord be loosed, or the golden 3701
SS 1:11 make thee borders of gold with studs of **s**. 3701
3:10 He made the pillars thereof *of* **s**, the bottom 3701
8: 9 a wall, we will build upon her a palace of **s**: 3701
8:11 thereof was to bring a thousand *pieces* of **s**. 3701
Isa 1:22 Thy **s** is become dross, thy wine mixt with 3701
2: 7 Their land also is full *of* **s** and gold, 3701
2:20 In that day a man shall cast his idols of **s**, 3701
13:17 against them, which shall not regard **s**; 3701
30:22 also the covering of thy graven images of **s**, 3701
31: 7 every man shall cast away his idols of **s**, 3701
39: 2 the **s**, and the gold, and the spices, and 3701
40:19 it over with gold, and casteth **s** chains. 3701
46: 6 weigh **s** in the balance, *and* hire a 3701
48:10 Behold, I have refined thee, but not with **s**; 3701
60: 9 from far, their **s** and their gold with them, 3701
60:17 for iron I will bring **s**, and for wood brass, 3701
Jer 6:30 Reprobate **s** shall *men* call them, because 3701
10: 4 They deck it with **s** and with gold; 3701
10: 9 **S** spread into plates is brought from 3701
32: 9 the money, *even* seventeen shekels of **s**. 3701
52:19 *in* gold, and *that* which *was of* **s** *in* silver, 3701
52:19 *in* gold, and *that* which *was of* silver *in* **s**, 3701
Eze 7:19 They shall cast their **s** in the streets, and 3701
7:19 their **s** and their gold shall not be able to 3701
16:13 Thus wast thou decked *with* gold and **s**; and 3701
16:17 thy fair jewels of my gold and of my **s**, 3701
22:18 of the furnace; they are *even the* dross *of* **s**. 3701
22:20 *As they* gather **s**, and brass, and iron, and 3701
22:22 As **s** is melted in the midst of the furnace, 3701
27:12 with **s**, iron, tin, and lead, they traded in thy 3701
28: 4 hast gotten gold and **s** into thy treasures: 3701
38:13 to carry away **s** and gold, to take *away* 3701
Da 2:32 his breast and his arms of **s**, his belly and 3702
2:35 the clay, the brass, the **s**, and the gold, 3702
2:45 the brass, the clay, the **s**, and the gold; 3702
5: 2 **s** vessels which his father Nebuchadnezzar 3702
5: 4 of **s**, of brass, of iron, of wood, and 3702
5:23 thou hast praised the gods of **s**, and gold, 3702
11: 8 *and* with their precious vessels *of* **s** and 3701
11:38 **s**, and with precious stones, and pleasant 3701
11:43 power over the treasures of gold and of **s**, 3701
Hos 2: 8 and oil, and multiplied her **s** and gold, 3701
3: 2 I bought her to me for fifteen *pieces* of **s**, 3701
8: 4 *of* their **s** and their gold have they made 3701
9: 6 the pleasant *places* for their **s**, nettles shall 3701
13: 2 have made them molten images of their **s**, 3701
Joel 3: 5 Because ye have taken my **s** and my gold, 3701
Am 2: 6 because they sold the righteous for **s**, and 3701
8: 6 That *we* may buy the poor for **s**, and 3701
Na 2: 9 Take ye the spoil of **s**, take the spoil of 3701
Hab 2:19 it *is* laid over *with* gold and **s**, and *there is* 3701
Zep 1:11 cut down; all they that bear **s** are cut off. 3701
1:18 Neither their **s** nor their gold shall be able 3701
Hag 2: 8 The **s** *is* mine, and the gold *is* mine, 3701
Zec 6:11 take **s** and gold, and make crowns, and 3701
9: 3 heaped up **s** as the dust, and fine gold as 3701
11:12 weighed *for* my price thirty *pieces* of **s**. 3701
11:13 I took the thirty *pieces* of **s**, and cast them 3701
13: 9 will refine them as **s** is refined, and will try 3701
14:14 gold, and **s**, and apparel, in great 3701
Mal 3: 3 he shall sit *as* a refiner and purifier of **s**: 3701
3: 3 sons of Levi, and purge them as gold and **s**, 3701
Mt 10: 9 Provide neither gold, nor **s**, nor brass in your *696*
26:15 covenanted with him for thirty pieces of **s**. *694*
27: 3 brought again the thirty pieces of **s** to *694*
27: 5 And he cast down the pieces of **s** in *694*
27: 6 And the chief priests took the **s** pieces, and *694*
27: 9 saying, And they took the thirty pieces of **s**, *694*
Lk 15: 8 Either what woman having ten pieces of **s**, *1406*
Ac 3: 6 Then Peter said, **S** and gold have I none; but *694*
17:29 or **s**, or stone, graven by art and *696*
19:19 and found *it* fifty thousand *pieces* of **s**. *694*
19:24 which made **s** shrines for Diana, *693*
20:33 I have coveted no *man's* **s**, or gold, or *694*
1Co 3:12 **s**, precious stones, wood, hay, stubble; *696*
2Ti 2:20 there are not only vessels of gold and **of s**, *693*
Jas 5: 3 Your gold and **s** is cankered; and the rust of *696*
1Pe 1:18 not redeemed with corruptible *things, as* **s** *694*
Rev 9:20 idols of gold, and **s**, and brass, and stone, *693*
18:12 and **s**, and precious stones, and of pearls, and *696*

SILVERLINGS (1) [SILVER]
Isa 7:23 there were a thousand vines at a thousand **s**, 3701

SILVERSMITH (1) [SILVER, SMITH]
Ac 19:24 For a certain *man* named Demetrius, a **s**, *695*

SIMEON (50) [SIMEONITES]
Ge 29:33 me this *son* also: and she called his name **S**. 8095
34:25 **S** and Levi, Dinah's brethren, took each 8095
34:30 Jacob said to **S** and Levi, Ye have troubled 8095
35:23 **S**, and Levi, and Judah, and Issachar, and 8095
42:24 took from them **S**, and bound him before 8095
42:36 **S** *is* not, and ye will take Benjamin *away*: 8095
43:23 And he brought **S** out unto them. 8095
46:10 the sons of **S**; Jemuel, and Jamin, and 8095
48: 5 as Reuben and **S**, they shall be mine. 8095

Ge 49: 5 S and Levi *are* brethren; instruments of 8095
Ex 1: 2 Reuben, S, Levi, and Judah, 8095
6:15 the sons of S; Jemuel, and Jamin, and 8095
6:15 these *are* the families of S. 8095
Nu 1: 6 Of S; Shelumiel the son of Zurishaddai. 8095
1:22 Of the children of S, *by* their generations, 8095
1:23 *even* of the tribe of S, *were* fifty and 8095
2:12 which pitch by him *shall be* the tribe of S: 8095
2:12 the captain of the children of S *shall be* 8095
7:36 prince of the children of S, *did offer:* 8095
10:19 of S *was* Shelumiel the son of Zurishaddai. 8095
13: 5 Of the tribe of S, Shaphat the son of Hori. 8095
26:12 The sons of S after their families: 8095
34:20 of the tribe of the children of S, 8095
Dt 27:12 S, and Levi, and Judah, and Issachar, and 8095
Jos 19: 1 the second lot came forth to S, *even* for 8095
19: 1 *even* for the tribe of the children of S 8095
19: 8 children of S according to their families. 8095
19: 9 *was* the inheritance of the children of S: 8095
19: 9 the children of S had their inheritance 8095
21: 4 out of the tribe of S, and out of the tribe of 8099
21: 9 out of the tribe of the children of S, these 8095
Jdg 1: 3 Judah said unto S his brother, Come up 8095
1: 3 with thee into thy lot. So S went with him. 8095
1:17 Judah went with S his brother, and 8095
1Ch 2: 1 Reuben, S, Levi, and Judah, Issachar, and 8095
4:24 The sons of S *were,* Nemuel, and Jamin, 8095
4:42 *even* of the sons of S, five hundred men, 8095
6:65 and out of the tribe of the children of S, and 8095
12:25 Of the children of S, mighty *men* of valour 8095
2Ch 15: 9 of Ephraim and Manasseh, and out of S: 8095
34: 6 and Ephraim, and S, even unto Naphtali, 8095
Eze 48:24 unto the west side, S *shall have* a *portion.* 8095
48:25 by the border of S, from the east side unto 8095
48:33 one gate of S, one gate of Issachar, one gate 8095
Lk 2:25 a man in Jerusalem, whose name *was* S; *4826*
2:34 And S blessed them, and said unto Mary *4826*
3:30 Which was *the son* of S, which was *the son* *4826*
Ac 13: 1 and S that was called Niger, and Lucius of *4826*
15:14 S hath declared how God at the first did *4826*
Rev 7: 7 Of the tribe of S *were* sealed twelve *4826*

SIMEONITES (3) [SIMEON]
Nu 25:14 a prince of a chief house among the S. 8099
26:14 These *are* the families of the S, twenty and 8099
1Ch 27:16 of the S, Shephatiah the son of Maachah: 8099

SIMILITUDE (11) [SIMILITUDES]
Nu 12: 8 and the s of the LORD shall he behold: 8544
Dt 4:12 heard the voice of the words, but saw no s; 8544
4:15 for ye saw no *manner of* s on the day *that* 8544
4:16 the s of any figure, the likeness of male or 8544
2Ch 4: 3 under it *was* the s of oxen, which did 1823
Ps 106:20 Thus they changed their glory into the s of 8403
144:12 polished *after* the s of a palace: 8403
Da 10:16 *one* like the s of the sons of men touched 1823
Ro 5:14 sinned after the s of Adam's transgression, *3667*
Heb 7:15 for that after the s of Melchisedec there *3665*
Jas 3: 9 we men, which are made after the s of God. *3669*

SIMILITUDES (1) [SIMILITUDE]
Hos 12:10 and **used** s by the ministry of the prophets. 1819

SIMON (69) [PETER, SIMON'S]
Mt 4:18 S called Peter, and Andrew his brother, *4613*
10: 2 The first, S, who is called Peter, and *4613*
10: 4 S the Canaanite, and Judas Iscariot, *4613*
13:55 James, and Joses, and S, and Judas? *4613*
16:16 And S Peter answered and said, Thou art *4613*
16:17 said unto him, Blessed art thou, S Bar-jona: *4613*
17:25 saying, What thinkest thou, S? *4613*
26: 6 was in Bethany, in the house of S the leper, *4613*
27:32 they found a man of Cyrene, S by name: *4613*
Mk 1:16 he saw S and Andrew his brother casting a *4613*
1:29 they entered into the house of S and *4613*
1:36 And S and they that were with him *4613*
3:16 And S he surnamed Peter; *4613*
3:18 and Thaddeus, and S the Canaanite, *4613*
6: 3 of James, and Joses, and of Juda, and S? *4613*
14: 3 And being in Bethany in the house of S *4613*
14:37 and saith unto Peter, S, sleepest thou? *4613*
15:21 And they compel one S a Cyrenian, *4613*
Lk 5: 4 he said unto S, Launch out into the deep, *4613*
5: 5 And S answering said unto him, Master, *4613*
5: 8 When S Peter saw *it,* he fell down at Jesus' *4613*
5:10 of Zebedee, which were partners with S. *4613*
5:10 And Jesus said unto S, Fear not; *4613*
6:14 S, (whom he also named Peter,) and *4613*
6:15 the *son* of Alpheus, and S called Zelotes, *4613*
7:40 S, I have somewhat to say unto thee. *4613*
7:43 S answered and said, I suppose that *he,* to *4613*
7:44 and said unto S, Seest thou this woman? *4613*
22:31 And the Lord said, S, Simon, behold, Satan *4613*
22:31 And the Lord said, Simon, S, behold, Satan *4613*
23:26 they laid hold upon one S, a Cyrenian, *4613*
24:34 is risen indeed, and hath appeared to S. *4613*
Jn 1:40 was Andrew, S Peter's brother. *4613*
1:41 He first findeth his own brother S, and *4613*
1:42 he said, Thou art S the son of Jona: *4613*
6: 8 Andrew, S Peter's brother, saith unto him, *4613*
6:68 Then S Peter answered him, Lord, to whom *4613*
6:71 He spake of Judas Iscariot *the son* of S: *4613*
13: 6 Then cometh he to S Peter: and *Peter* saith *4613*
13: 9 S Peter saith unto him, Lord, not my feet *4613*
13:24 S Peter therefore beckoned to him, that *he* *4613*
13:26 he gave *it* to Judas Iscariot, *the son* of S. *4613*
13:36 S Peter said unto him, Lord, whither goest *4613*
18:10 Then S Peter having a sword drew it, and *4613*
18:15 And S Peter followed Jesus, and *so* *4613*
18:25 And S Peter stood and warmed himself. *4613*
20: 2 and cometh to S Peter, and to the other *4613*
20: 6 Then cometh S Peter following him, and *4613*
21: 2 There were together S Peter, and *4613*
21: 3 S Peter saith unto them, I go a fishing. *4613*
21: 7 Now when S Peter heard that it was *4613*
21:11 S Peter went up, and drew the net to land *4613*
21:15 Jesus saith to S Peter, Simon, *son* of Jonas, *4613*
21:15 Jesus saith to Simon Peter, S, *son* of Jonas, *4613*
21:16 S, *son* of Jonas, lovest thou me? *4613*
21:17 third time, S, *son* of Jonas, lovest thou me? *4613*
Ac 1:13 and S Zelotes, and Judas *the brother* of *4613*
8: 9 But there was a certain man, called S, *4613*
8:13 Then S himself believed also: and when he *4613*
8:18 And when S saw that through laying on of *4613*
8:24 Then answered S, and said, Pray ye to *4613*
9:43 many days in Joppa with one S a tanner. *4613*
10: 5 and call for *one* S, whose surname is Peter: *4613*
10: 6 He lodgeth with one S a tanner, *4613*
10:18 And called, and asked whether S, *4613*
10:32 Send therefore to Joppa, and call hither S, *4613*
10:32 he is lodged in the house of *one* S a tanner *4613*
11:13 Send men to Joppa, and call for S, *4613*
2Pe 1: 1 S Peter, a servant and an apostle of Jesus *4826*

SIMON'S (7) [SIMON]
Mk 1:30 But S wife's mother lay sick of a fever, and *4613*
Lk 4:38 of the synagogue, and entered into S house. *4613*
4:38 And S wife's mother was taken with a great *4613*
5: 3 which was S, and prayed him that *he* would *4613*
Jn 12: 4 S *son,* which should betray him, *4613*
13: 2 of Judas Iscariot, S *son,* to betray him; *4613*
Ac 10:17 Cornelius had made inquiry for S house, *4613*

SIMPLE (20) [SIMPLICITY]
Ps 19: 7 of the LORD *is* sure, making wise the s. 6612
116: 6 The LORD preserveth the s: I was brought 6612
119:130 it giveth understanding unto the s. 6612
Pr 1: 4 To give subtilty to the s, to the young man 6612
1:22 How long, ye s **ones,** will ye love 6612
1:32 For the turning away of the s shall slay 6612
7: 7 beheld among the s **ones,** I discerned 6612
8: 5 O ye s, understand wisdom: and, ye fools, 6612
9: 4 Whoso *is* s, let him turn in hither: *as for* 6612
9:13 *she is* s, and knoweth nothing. 6615
9:16 Whoso *is* s, let him turn in hither: and 6612
14:15 The s believeth every word: but the prudent 6612
14:18 The s inherit folly: but the prudent are 6612
19:25 Smite a scorner, and the s will beware: and 6612
21:11 the scorner is punished, the s is made wise: 6612
22: 3 but the s pass on, and are punished. 6612
27:12 *but* the s pass on, *and* are punished. 6612
Eze 45:20 every one that erreth, and for *him that is* s: 6612
Ro 16:18 and fair speeches deceive the hearts of the s. *172*
16:19 *that which is* good, and s concerning evil. *185*

SIMPLICITY (5) [SIMPLE]
2Sa 15:11 they went in their s, and they knew not any 8537
Pr 1:22 How long, ye simple ones, will ye love s? 6612

Ro 12: 8 he that giveth, *let him do it* with **s**; he that 572
2Co 1:12 that in **s** and godly sincerity, not with fleshly 572
11: 3 your minds should be corrupted from the **s** 572

SIMRI (1)
1Ch 26:10 **S** the chief, (for *though* he was not 8113

SIN (448) [SINFUL, SINNED, SINNER, SINNERS, SINNEST, SINNETH, SINNING, SINS]
Ge 4: 7 if thou doest not well, **s** lieth at the door. 2403
18:20 and because their **s** is very grievous; 2403
20: 9 on me and on my kingdom a great **s**? 2401
31:36 what *is* my **s**, that thou hast *so* 2403
39: 9 this great wickedness, and **s** against God? 2398
42:22 saying, Do not **s** against the child; 2398
50:17 the trespass of thy brethren, and their **s**; 2403
Ex 10:17 my **s** only *this* once, and intreat the LORD 2403
16: 1 of Israel came unto the wilderness of **S**, 5512
17: 1 Israel journeyed from the wilderness of **S**, 5512
20:20 fear may be before your faces, that ye **s** not. 2398
23:33 thy land, lest they **make** thee **s** against me: 2398
29:14 fire without the camp: it *is* a **s offering**. 2403
29:36 a bullock *for* a **s offering** for atonement: 2403
30:10 the blood of the **s offering** of atonements: 2403
32:21 thou hast brought *so* great a **s** upon them? 2401
32:30 unto the people, Ye have sinned a great **s**: 2401
32:30 I shall make an atonement for your **s**. 2403
32:31 this people have sinned a great **s**, and 2401
32:32 Yet now, if thou wilt forgive their **s**; and 2403
32:34 when I visit, I will visit their **s** upon them. 2403
34: 7 forgiving iniquity and transgression and **s**, 2403
34: 9 pardon our iniquity and our **s**, and take us 2403
Lev 4: 2 If a soul shall **s** through ignorance against 2398
4: 3 If the priest that is anointed do **s** according 2398
4: 3 do sin according to the **s** of the people; 819
4: 3 let him bring for his **s**, which he hath 2403
4: 3 blemish unto the LORD for a **s offering**. 2403
4: 8 all the fat of the bullock *for* the **s offering**; 2403
4:13 of Israel **s through ignorance**, 7686
4:14 When the **s**, which they have sinned against 2403
4:14 shall offer a young bullock for the **s**, 2403
4:20 as he did with the bullock for a **s offering**, 2403
4:21 it *is* a **s offering** for the congregation. 2403
4:23 Or if his **s**, wherein he hath sinned, come to 2403
4:24 before the LORD: it *is* a **s offering**. 2403
4:25 the blood of the **s offering** with his finger, 2403
4:26 an atonement for him as concerning his **s**, 2403
4:27 if any one of the common people **s** through 2398
4:28 Or if his **s**, which he hath sinned, come to 2403
4:28 for his **s** which he hath sinned. 2403
4:29 his hand upon the head of the **s offering**, 2403
4:29 slay the **s offering** in the place of the burnt 2403
4:32 if he bring a lamb for a **s** offering, he shall 2403
4:33 his hand upon the head of the **s offering**, 2403
4:33 slay it for a **s offering** in the place where 2403
4:34 the blood of the **s offering** with his finger, 2403
4:35 the priest shall make an atonement for his **s** 2403
5: 1 if a soul **s**, and hear the voice of swearing, 2398
5: 6 the LORD for his **s** which he hath sinned, 2403
5: 6 or a kid of the goats, for a **s offering**; 2403
5: 6 an atonement for him concerning his **s**. 2403
5: 7 one for a **s offering**, and the other for a 2403
5: 8 offer *that* which *is* for the **s offering** first, 2403
5: 9 of the **s offering** upon the side of the altar; 2403
5: 9 at the bottom of the altar: it *is* a **s offering**. 2403
5:10 for him for his **s** which he had sinned, 2403
5:11 of an ephah of fine flour for a **s offering**; 2403
5:11 frankincense thereon: for it *is* a **s offering**. 2403
5:12 by fire unto the LORD: it *is* a **s offering**. 2403
5:13 his **s** that he hath sinned in one of these, 2403
5:15 commit a trespass, and **s** through ignorance, 2398
5:17 if a soul **s**, and commit any *of these things* 2398
6: 2 If a soul **s**, and commit a trespass against 2398
6:17 as *is* the **s offering**, and as the trespass 2403
6:25 This *is* the law of the **s offering**: 2403
6:25 the **s offering** be killed before the LORD: 2403
6:26 The priest that **offereth** it **for s** shall eat it: 2398
6:30 no **s offering**, whereof *any* of the blood is 2403
7: 7 As the **s offering** *is*, so *is* the trespass 2403
7:37 of the **s offering**, and of the trespass 2403
8: 2 a bullock *for* the **s offering**, and two rams, 2403
8:14 he brought the bullock *for* the **s offering**: 2403
8:14 the head of the bullock *for* the **s offering**. 2403
9: 2 Take thee a young calf for a **s offering**, and 2403
9: 3 Take ye a kid of the goats for a **s offering**; 2403
9: 7 offer thy **s offering**, and thy burnt offering, 2403
9: 8 the altar, and slew the calf of the **s offering**, 2403
9:10 the caul above the liver of the **s offering**, 2403
9:15 which *was* the **s offering** for the people, 2403
9:15 and slew it, and **offered** it **for s**, as the first. 2398
9:22 came down from offering of the **s offering**, 2403
10:16 diligently sought the goat of the **s offering**, 2403
10:17 Wherefore have ye not eaten the **s offering** 2403
10:19 *this* day have they offered their **s offering** 2403
10:19 *if* I had eaten the **s offering** to day, should 2403
12: 6 or a turtledove, for a **s offering**, 2403
12: 8 and the other for a **s offering**: 2403
14:13 the place where he shall kill the **s offering** 2403
14:13 for as the **s offering** *is* the priest's, *so is* 2403
14:19 the priest shall offer the **s offering**, and 2403
14:22 the one shall be a **s offering**, and the other 2403
14:31 the one *for* a **s offering**, and the other *for* a 2403
15:15 the one *for* a **s offering**, and the other *for* a 2403
15:30 priest shall offer the one *for* a **s offering**, 2403
16: 3 with a young bullock for a **s offering**, 2403
16: 5 Israel two kids of the goats for a **s offering**, 2403
16: 6 shall offer *his* bullock of the **s offering**, 2403
16: 9 lot fell, and offer him *for* a **s offering**. 2403
16:11 shall bring the bullock of the **s offering**, 2403
16:11 shall kill the bullock of the **s offering** 2403
16:15 Then shall he kill the goat of the **s offering**, 2403
16:25 the fat of the **s offering** shall he burn upon 2403
16:27 the bullock for the **s offering**, and the goat 2403
16:27 sin offering, and the goat for the **s offering**, 2403
19:17 thy neighbour, and not suffer **s** upon him. 2399
19:22 the LORD for his **s** which he hath done: 2403
19:22 the **s** which he hath done shall be forgiven 2403
20:20 they shall bear their **s**; they shall die 2399
22: 9 lest they bear **s** for it, and die therefore, if 2399
23:19 one kid of the goats for a **s offering**, 2403
24:15 Whosoever curseth his God shall bear his **s**. 2399
Nu 5: 6 woman shall commit any **s** that men 2403
5: 7 they shall confess their **s** which they have 2403
6:11 priest shall offer the one for a **s offering**, 2403
6:14 first year without blemish for a **s offering**, 2403
6:16 shall offer his **s offering**, and his burnt 2403
7:16 One kid of the goats for a **s offering**: 2403
7:22 One kid of the goats for a **s offering**: 2403
7:28 One kid of the goats for a **s offering**: 2403
7:34 One kid of the goats for a **s offering**: 2403
7:40 One kid of the goats for a **s offering**: 2403
7:46 One kid of the goats for a **s offering**: 2403
7:52 One kid of the goats for a **s offering**: 2403
7:58 One kid of the goats for a **s offering**: 2403
7:64 One kid of the goats for a **s offering**: 2403
7:70 One kid of the goats for a **s offering**: 2403
7:76 One kid of the goats for a **s offering**: 2403
7:82 One kid of the goats for a **s offering**: 2403
7:87 the kids of the goats for **s offering** twelve. 2403
8: 8 bullock shalt thou take for a **s offering**. 2403
8:12 thou shalt offer the one *for* a **s offering**, 2403
9:13 appointed season, that man shall bear his **s**. 2399
12:11 I beseech thee, lay not the **s** upon us, 2403
15:24 and one kid of the goats for a **s offering**. 2403
15:25 their **s offering** before the LORD, 2403
15:27 if any soul **s** through ignorance, then 2398
15:27 a she goat of the first year for a **s offering**. 2403
16:22 shall one man **s**, and wilt thou be wroth 2398
18: 9 every **s offering** of theirs, and every 2403
18:22 the congregation, lest they bear **s**, and die. 2399
18:32 ye shall bear no **s** by reason of it, when ye 2399
19: 9 of separation: it *is* a **purification for s**. 2403
19:17 of the burnt *heifer* of **purification for s**, 2403
27: 3 but died in his own **s**, and had no sons. 2399
28:15 one kid of the goats for a **s offering** unto 2403
28:22 one goat for a **s offering**, to make an 2403
29: 5 one kid of the goats for a **s offering**, 2403
29:11 One kid of the goats *for* a **s offering**; beside 2403
29:11 beside the **s offering** of atonement, and 2403
29:16 one kid of the goats *for* a **s offering**; beside 2403
29:19 one kid of the goats *for* a **s offering**; beside 2403
29:22 one goat for a **s offering**; beside 2403
29:25 one kid of the goats *for* a **s offering**; beside 2403
29:28 one goat for a **s offering**; beside 2403
29:31 one goat for a **s offering**; beside 2403
29:34 one goat for a **s offering**; beside 2403
29:38 one goat for a **s offering**; beside 2403
32:23 and be sure your **s** will find you out. 2403

S

Nu	33:11	and encamped in the wilderness of **S**.	5512
	33:12	their journey out of the wilderness of **S**,	5512
Dt	9:21	I took your **s**, the calf which ye had made,	2403
	9:27	nor to their wickedness, nor to their **s**:	2403
	15: 9	LORD against thee, and it be **s** unto thee.	2399
	19:15	or for any **s**, in any sin that he sinneth:	2403
	19:15	or for any sin, in any **s** that he sinneth:	2399
	20:18	should ye **s** against the LORD your God.	2398
	21:22	if a man have **committed a s** worthy of	2399
	22:26	*there is* in the damsel no **s** *worthy* of death:	2399
	23:21	require it of thee; and it would be **s** in thee.	2399
	23:22	shalt forbear to vow, it shall be no **s** in thee.	2399
	24: 4	thou shalt not **cause** the land **to s**,	2398
	24:15	thee unto the LORD, and it be **s** unto thee.	2399
	24:16	man shall be put to death for his own **s**.	2399
1Sa	2:17	Wherefore the **s** of the young men was very	2403
	2:25	If one man **s** against another, the judge	2398
	2:25	if a man **s** against the LORD, who shall	2398
	12:23	God forbid that I should **s** against	2398
	14:33	Behold, the people **s** against the LORD,	2398
	14:34	**s** not against the LORD in eating with	2398
	14:38	and see wherein this **s** hath been *this* day.	2403
	15:23	For rebellion *is as* the **s** of witchcraft, and	2403
	15:25	pardon my **s**, and turn again with me,	2403
	19: 4	Let not the king **s** against his servant,	2398
	19: 5	then wilt thou **s** against innocent blood,	2398
	20: 1	what *is* my **s** before thy father, that he	2403
2Sa	12:13	The LORD also hath put away thy **s**;	2403
1Ki	8:34	forgive the **s** of thy people Israel, and	2403
	8:35	confess thy name, and turn from their **s**,	2403
	8:36	forgive the **s** of thy servants, and of thy	2403
	8:46	If they **s** against thee, (for *there is* no man	2398
	12:30	this thing became a **s**: for the people went	2403
	13:34	this thing became **s** unto the house of	2403
	14:16	who did **s**, and who made Israel to sin.	2398
	14:16	who did sin, and who **made** Israel **to s**.	2398
	15:26	in his **s** wherewith he made Israel to sin.	2403
	15:26	in his sin wherewith he **made** Israel **to s**.	2398
	15:30	he sinned, and which he **made** Israel **s**,	2398
	15:34	in his **s** wherewith he made Israel to sin.	2403
	15:34	in his sin wherewith he **made** Israel **to s**.	2398
	16: 2	hast **made** my people Israel **to s**,	2398
	16:13	and *by* which they **made** Israel **to s**,	2398
	16:19	in his **s** which he did, to make Israel sin.	2403
	16:19	in his sin which he did, to **make** Israel **s**.	2398
	16:26	in his **s** wherewith he made Israel to sin,	2403
	16:26	in his sin wherewith he **made** Israel **to s**,	2398
	17:18	art thou come unto me to call my **s** to	5771
	21:22	*me* to anger, and **made** Israel **to s**.	2398
	22:52	the son of Nebat, who **made** Israel **to s**:	2398
2Ki	3: 3	the son of Nebat, which **made** Israel **to s**;	2398
	10:29	who **made** Israel **to s**, Jehu departed not	2398
	10:31	sins of Jeroboam, which **made** Israel **to s**.	2398
	12:16	**s** money was not brought *into* the house of	2403
	13: 2	the son of Nebat, which **made** Israel **to s**;	2398
	13: 6	who **made** Israel **s**, *but* walked therein:	2398
	13:11	the son of Nebat, who **made** Israel **s**:	2398
	14: 6	man shall be put to death for his own **s**.	2399
	14:24	the son of Nebat, who **made** Israel **to s**.	2398
	15: 9	the son of Nebat, who **made** Israel **to s**.	2398
	15:18	the son of Nebat, who **made** Israel **to s**.	2398
	15:24	the son of Nebat, who **made** Israel **to s**.	2398
	15:28	the son of Nebat, who **made** Israel **to s**.	2398
	17:21	the LORD, and **made** them **s** a great sin.	2398
	17:21	the LORD, and made them sin a great **s**.	2401
	21:11	hath **made** Judah also **to s** with his idols:	2398
	21:16	beside his **s** where*with* he made Judah to	2403
	21:16	his sin where*with* he **made** Judah **to s**,	2398
	21:17	and all that he did, and his **s** that he sinned,	2403
	23:15	who **made** Israel **to s**, had made, both that	2398
2Ch	6:22	If a man **s** against his neighbour, and	2398
	6:25	forgive the **s** of thy people Israel, and	2403
	6:26	confess thy name, *and* turn from their **s**,	2403
	6:27	forgive the **s** of thy servants, and of thy	2403
	6:36	If they **s** against thee, (for *there is* no man	2398
	7:14	will forgive their **s**, and will heal their land.	2403
2Ch	25: 4	but every man shall die for his own **s**.	2399
	29:21	for a **s offering** for the kingdom, and	2403
	29:23	he goats for the **s offering** before the king	2403
	29:24	the **s offering** *should be made* for all Israel.	2403
	33:19	all his **s**, and his trespass, and the places	2403
Ezr	6:17	for a **s offering** for all Israel, twelve he	2409
	8:35	twelve he goats *for* a **s offering**:	2403
Ne	4: 5	let not their **s** be blotted out from before	2403
	6:13	**s**, and *that* they might have *matter* for an	2398
	10:33	for the **s offerings** to make an atonement	2403
	13:26	Did not Solomon king of Israel **s** by these	2398
	13:26	even him did outlandish women **cause to s**.	2398
Job	2:10	In all this did not Job **s** with his lips.	2398
	5:24	shalt visit thy habitation, and shalt not **s**.	2398
	10: 6	mine iniquity, and searchest after my **s**?	2403
	10:14	If I **s**, then thou markest me, and thou wilt	2398
	13:23	me to know my transgression and my **s**.	2403
	14:16	my steps: dost thou not watch over my **s**?	2403
	20:11	His bones are full *of the* **s** *of* his youth,	NIH
	31:30	(Neither have I suffered my mouth to **s** by	2398
	34:37	For he addeth rebellion unto his **s**,	2403
	35: 3	shall I have, *if I be cleansed* from my **s**?	2403
Ps	4: 4	Stand in awe, and **s** not: commune with	2398
	32: 1	*is* forgiven, whose **s** *is* covered.	2401
	32: 5	I acknowledged my **s** unto thee, and	2403
	32: 5	and thou forgavest the iniquity of my **s**.	2403
	38: 3	*there any* rest in my bones because of my **s**.	2403
	38:18	mine iniquity; I will be sorry for my **s**.	2403
	39: 1	to my ways, that *I* **s** not with my tongue:	2398
	40: 6	and **s offering** hast thou not required.	2401
	51: 2	mine iniquity, and cleanse me from my **s**.	2403
	51: 3	and my **s** *is* ever before me.	2403
	51: 5	and in **s** did my mother conceive me.	2399
	59: 3	my transgression, nor *for* my **s**, O LORD.	2403
	59:12	*For* the **s** of their mouth *and* the words of	2403
	85: 2	of thy people, thou hast covered all their **s**.	2403
	109: 7	be condemned: and let his prayer become **s**.	2401
	109:14	let not the **s** of his mother be blotted out.	2403
	119:11	mine heart, that I might not **s** against thee.	2398
Pr	10:16	*tendeth* to life: the fruit of the wicked to **s**.	2403
	10:19	the multitude of words there wanteth not **s**:	6588
	14: 9	Fools make a mock at **s**: but among	817
	14:34	a nation: but **s** *is* a reproach to any people.	2403
	20: 9	made my heart clean, I am pure from my **s**?	2403
	21: 4	*and* the plowing of the wicked, *is* **s**.	2403
	24: 9	The thought of foolishness *is* **s**: and	2403
Ecc	5: 6	not thy mouth to **cause** thy flesh **to s**;	2398
Isa	3: 9	they declare their **s** as Sodom, they hide *it*	2403
	5:18	of vanity, and **s** as it were with a cart rope:	2403
	6: 7	iniquity is taken away, and thy **s** purged.	2403
	27: 9	and this *is* all the fruit to take away his **s**;	2403
	30: 1	not of my Spirit, that *they* may add **s** to sin:	2403
	30: 1	not of my Spirit, that *they* may add sin to **s**:	2403
	31: 7	own hands have made unto you *for* a **s**.	2399
	53:10	thou shalt make his soul an **offering for s**,	817
	53:12	he bare the **s** of many, and	2399
Jer	16:10	**s** that we have **committed** against	2398+2403
	16:18	their iniquity and their **s** double;	2403
	17: 1	The **s** of Judah *is* written with a pen of iron,	2403
	17: 3	*and* thy high places for **s**, throughout all thy	2403
	18:23	neither blot out their **s** from thy sight, but	2403
	31:34	and I will remember their **s** no more.	2403
	32:35	do this abomination, to **cause** Judah **to s**.	2398
	36: 3	that I may forgive their iniquity and their **s**.	2403
	51: 5	though their land was filled *with* **s** against	817
La	4: 6	than the **punishment of** the **s** of Sodom,	2403
Eze	3:20	he shall die in his **s**, and his righteousness	2403
	3:21	the righteous *man,* that the righteous **s** not,	2398
	3:21	he doth not **s**, he shall surely live, because	2398
	18:24	in his **s** that he hath sinned, in them shall he	2403
	30:15	I will pour my fury upon **S**, the strength of	5512
	30:16	**S** shall have great pain, and No shall be	5512
	33:14	if he turn from his **s**, and do that which is	2403
	40:39	and the **s offering** and the trespass offering.	2403
	42:13	the **s offering**, and the trespass offering;	2403
	43:19	a young bullock for a **s offering**.	2403
	43:21	shalt take the bullock also of the **s offering**,	2403
	43:22	the goats without blemish for a **s offering**;	2403
	43:25	prepare every day a goat *for* a **s offering**:	2403
	44:27	he shall offer his **s offering**, saith the Lord	2403
	44:29	the **s offering**, and the trespass offering;	2403
	45:17	he shall prepare the **s offering**, and	2403
	45:19	shall take of the blood of the **s offering**,	2403
	45:22	of the land a bullock *for* a **s offering**.	2403
	45:23	and a kid of the goats daily *for* a **s offering**.	2403
	45:25	according to the **s offering**, according to	2403
	46:20	the trespass offering and the **s offering**,	2403
Da	9:20	confessing my **s** and the sin of my people	2403
	9:20	my sin and the **s** of my people Israel,	2403
Hos	4: 8	They eat *up* the **s** of my people, and	2403
	8:11	Ephraim hath made many altars to **s**,	2398
	8:11	altars to sin, altars shall be unto him to **s**.	2398

Hos 10: 8 of Aven, the **s** of Israel, shall be destroyed: 2403
12: 8 shall find none iniquity in me that *were* **s**. 2399
13: 2 now they **s** more and more, and have made 2398
13:12 of Ephraim *is* bound up; his **s** *is* hid. 2403
Am 8:14 They that swear by the **s** of Samaria, and 819
Mic 1:13 she *is* the beginning of the **s** to the daughter 2403
3: 8 Jacob his transgression, and to Israel his **s**. 2403
6: 7 the fruit of my body *for* the **s** of my soul? 2403
Zec 13: 1 to the inhabitants of Jerusalem for **s** and 2403
Mt 12:31 All *manner of* **s** and blasphemy shall be *266*
18:21 how oft shall my brother **s** against me, and I *264*
Jn 1:29 which taketh away the **s** of the world. *266*
5:14 **s** no more, lest a worse *thing* come unto thee. *264*
8: 7 unto them, He that is **without s** among you, *361*
8:11 do I condemn thee: go, and **s** no more. *264*
8:34 Whosoever committeth **s** is the servant of *266*
8:34 committeth sin is the servant of **s**. *266*
8:46 Which of you convinceth me of **s**? And if I *266*
9: 2 saying, Master, who did **s**, this *man*, or *264*
9:41 If ye were blind, ye should have no **s**: *266*
9:41 ye say, We see; therefore your **s** remaineth. *266*
15:22 and spoken unto them, they had not had **s**: *266*
15:22 but now they have no cloke for their **s**. *266*
15:24 none other *man* did, they had not had **s**: *266*
16: 8 he will reprove the world of **s**, and *266*
16: 9 Of **s**, because they believe not on me; *266*
19:11 delivered me unto thee hath the greater **s**. *266*
Ac 7:60 Lord, lay not this **s** to their charge. *266*
Ro 3: 9 and Gentiles, that *they* are all under **s**; *266*
3:20 for by the law *is* the knowledge of **s**. *266*
4: 8 the man to whom the Lord will not impute **s**. *266*
5:12 as by one man **s** entered into the world, and *266*
5:12 sin entered into the world, and death by **s**; *266*
5:13 For until the law **s** was in the world: but *266*
5:13 but **s** is not imputed when there is no law. *266*
5:20 But where **s** abounded, grace did much more *266*
5:21 That as **s** hath reigned unto death, even so *266*
6: 1 Shall we continue in **s**, that grace may *266*
6: 2 How shall we, that are dead to **s**, live any *266*
6: 6 *him*, that the body of **s** might be destroyed, *266*
6: 6 that henceforth we should not serve **s**. *266*
6: 7 For he that is dead is freed from **s**. *266*
6:10 For in that he died, he died unto **s** once: but *266*
6:11 ye also yourselves to be dead indeed unto **s**, *266*
6:12 Let not **s** therefore reign in your mortal *266*
6:13 *as* instruments of unrighteousness unto **s**: *266*
6:14 For **s** shall not have dominion over you: *266*
6:15 shall we **s**, because we are not under the law, *264*
6:16 whether of **s** unto death, or of obedience *266*
6:17 that ye were the servants of **s**, but ye have *266*
6:18 Being then made free from **s**, ye became *266*
6:20 For when ye were the servants of **s**, ye were *266*
6:22 But now being made free from **s**, and *266*
6:23 For the wages of **s** *is* death; but the gift of *266*
7: 7 *Is* the law **s**? God forbid. Nay, I had not *266*
7: 7 Nay, I had not known **s**, but by the law: for I *266*
7: 8 But **s**, taking occasion by the commandment, *266*
7: 8 For without the law **s** *was* dead. *266*
7: 9 commandment came, **s** revived, and I died. *266*
7:11 For **s**, taking occasion by the commandment, *266*
7:13 But **s**, that it might appear sin, working death *266*
7:13 But sin, that it might appear **s**, working death *266*
7:13 that **s** by the commandment might become *266*
7:14 law is spiritual: but I am carnal, sold under **s**. *266*
7:17 more I that do it, but **s** that dwelleth in me. *266*
7:20 more I that do it, but **s** that dwelleth in me. *266*
7:23 bringing me into captivity to the law of **s** *266*
7:25 law of God; but with the flesh the law of **s**. *266*
8: 2 Jesus hath made me free from the law of **s** *266*
8: 3 and for **s**, condemned sin in the flesh: *266*
8: 3 and for sin, condemned **s** in the flesh: *266*
8:10 *be* in you, the body *is* dead because of **s**; *266*
14:23 of faith: for whatsoever *is* not of faith is **s**. *266*
1Co 6:18 Every **s** that a man doeth is without *265*
8:12 But when ye **s** so against the brethren, and *264*
8:12 their weak conscience, ye **s** against Christ. *264*
15:34 Awake to righteousness, and **s** not: for some *264*
15:56 The sting of death *is* **s**; *266*
15:56 death *is* sin; and the strength of **s** *is* the law. *266*
2Co 5:21 For he hath made him *to be* **s** for us, *266*
5:21 made him *to be* sin for us, who knew no **s**; *266*
Gal 2:17 *is* therefore Christ the minister of **s**? *266*
3:22 But the scripture hath concluded all under **s**, *266*
Eph 4:26 Be ye angry, and **s** not: let not the sun go *264*
2Th 2: 3 and *that* man of **s** be revealed, the son of *266*
1Ti 5:20 Them that **s** rebuke before all, that others *264*
Heb 3:13 be hardened through the deceitfulness of **s**. *266*
4:15 *points* tempted like as *we are, yet* without **s**. *266*
9:26 to put away **s** by the sacrifice of himself. *266*
9:28 the second time without **s** unto salvation. *266*
10: 6 *sacrifices* for **s** thou hast had no pleasure. *266*
10: 8 and *offering* for **s** thou wouldest not, *266*
10:18 of these *is, there is* no more offering for **s**. *266*
10:26 For if we **s** wilfully after that *we* have *264*
11:25 than to enjoy the pleasures of **s** for a season; *266*
12: 1 and the **s** which doth so easily beset *us*, and *266*
12: 4 yet resisted unto blood, striving against **s**. *266*
13:11 into the sanctuary by the high priest for **s**, *266*
Jas 1:15 when lust hath conceived, it bringeth forth **s**: *266*
1:15 and **s**, when it is finished, bringeth forth *266*
2: 9 ye commit **s**, and are convinced of the law as *266*
4:17 to do good, and doeth *it* not, to him it is **s**. *266*
1Pe 2:22 Who did no **s**, neither was guile found in his *266*
4: 1 hath suffered in the flesh hath ceased from **s**; *266*
2Pe 2:14 full of adultery and that cannot cease from **s**; *266*
1Jn 1: 7 Jesus Christ his Son cleanseth us from all **s**. *266*
1: 8 If we say that we have no **s**, we deceive *266*
2: 1 these *things* write I unto you, that ye **s** not. *264*
2: 1 And if any *man* **s**, we have an advocate with *264*
3: 4 Whosoever committeth **s** transgresseth also *266*
3: 4 the law: for **s** is the transgression of the law. *266*
3: 5 to take away our sins; and in him is no **s**. *266*
3: 8 He that committeth **s** is of the devil; for *266*
3: 9 is born of God doth not commit **s**; *266*
3: 9 and he cannot **s**, because he is born of God. *264*
5:16 If any *man* see his brother **s** a sin *which is* *264*
5:16 If any *man* see his brother sin a **s** *which is* *266*
5:16 he shall give him life for them that **s** not unto *264*
5:16 There is a **s** unto death: I do not say that he *266*
5:17 All unrighteousness is **s**: and there is a sin *266*
5:17 is sin: and there is a **s** not unto death. *266*

SINA (2) [SINAI]
Ac 7:30 **S** an angel of the Lord in a flame of fire in *4614*
7:38 angel which spake to him in the mount **S**, *4614*

SINAI (37) [HOREB, SINA]
Ex 16: 1 of Sin, which *is* between Elim and **S**, 5514
19: 1 day came they *into* the wilderness of **S**. 5514
19: 2 were come *to* the desert of **S**, and 5514
19:11 in the sight of all the people upon mount **S**. 5514
19:18 mount **S** was altogether on a smoke, 5514
19:20 the LORD came down upon mount **S**, 5514
19:23 The people cannot come up to mount **S**: 5514
24:16 glory of the LORD abode upon mount **S**, 5514
31:18 end of communing with him upon mount **S**, 5514
34: 2 come up in the morning unto mount **S**, and 5514
34: 4 in the morning, and went up unto mount **S**, 5514
34:29 when Moses came down from mount **S** 5514
34:32 LORD had spoken with him in mount **S**. 5514
Lev 7:38 the LORD commanded Moses in mount **S**, 5514
7:38 unto the LORD, in the wilderness of **S**. 5514
25: 1 the LORD spake unto Moses in mount **S**, 5514
26:46 the children of Israel in mount **S** by 5514
27:34 Moses for the children of Israel in mount **S**. 5514
Nu 1: 1 spake unto Moses in the wilderness of **S**, 5514
1:19 he numbered them in the wilderness of **S**. 5514
3: 1 the LORD spake with Moses in mount **S**. 5514
3: 4 in the wilderness of **S**, and they had no 5514
3:14 spake unto Moses in the wilderness of **S**, 5514
9: 1 spake unto Moses in the wilderness of **S**, 5514
9: 5 first month at even in the wilderness of **S**: 5514
10:12 their journeys out of the wilderness of **S**; 5514
26:64 the children of Israel in the wilderness of **S**. 5514
28: 6 which was ordained in mount **S** for a sweet 5514
33:15 and pitched in the wilderness of **S**. 5514
33:16 And they removed from the desert of **S**, and 5514
Dt 33: 2 The LORD came from **S**, and rose up 5514
Jdg 5: 5 *even* that **S** from before the LORD God of 5514
Ne 9:13 Thou camest down also upon mount **S**, and 5514
Ps 68: 8 *even* **S** itself *was moved* at the presence of 5514
68:17 *is* among them, *as in* **S**, in the holy *place*. 5514
Gal 4:24 the one from the mount **S**, which gendereth *4614*
4:25 For *this* Agar is mount **S** in Arabia, and *4614*

SINCE (68) [SITH]
Ge 30:30 LORD hath blessed thee **s** my coming: 3807.1
44:28 is torn in pieces; and I saw him not **s**: 2008+5704

Ge 46:30 **s** I have seen thy face, because thou *art* yet 310
Ex 4:10 **s** thou hast spoken unto thy servant: 227+4480
5:23 For **s** I came to Pharaoh to speak in 227+4480
9:18 **s** the foundation 3117+4480+1886.1+3807.1
9:24 the land of Egypt **s** it became a nation. 227+4480
10: 6 **s** the day that they were upon the earth unto 4480
Nu 22:30 upon which thou hast ridden **ever s** *I* 4480+5750
Dt 4:32 **s** the day that God created man upon 4480
34:10 there arose not a prophet **s** in Israel like 5750
Jos 2:12 the LORD, **s** I have shewed you kindness, 3588
14:10 *even* **s** the LORD spake this word 227+4480
Ru 2:11 mother in law **s** the death of thine husband: 310
1Sa 8: 8 **s** the day that I brought them up out of 4480
9:24 time *hath it* been kept for thee **s** *I* said, 3807.1
21: 5 **s** I came out, and the vessels of the young 871.1
29: 3 I have found no *fault* in him **s** he fell 3117+4480
29: 6 for I have not found evil in thee **s** the day of 4480
2Sa 7: 6 **s** the time that I brought up 4480+3807.1
7:11 *as* **s** the time that I commanded judges *to be* 4480
1Ki 8:16 **S** the day that I brought forth my people 4480
2Ki 8: 6 all the fruits of the field **s** the day that she 4480
21:15 **s** the day their fathers came forth out of 4480
1Ch 17: 5 For I have not dwelt in a house **s** the day 4480
17:10 **s** the time that I commanded judges *to be* 4480
2Ch 6: 5 **S** the day that I brought forth my people out 4480
30:26 for **s** the time of Solomon the son of David 4480
31:10 **S** *the people* began to bring the offerings 4480
Ezr 4: 2 we do sacrifice unto him **s** the days of 4480
5:16 **s** that time even until now *hath it been* in 4481
9: 7 **S** the days of our fathers *have* we *been* in a 4480
Ne 8:17 for **s** the days of Jeshua the son of Nun unto 4480
9:32 **s** the time of the kings of Assyria unto this 4480
Job 20: 4 this of old, **s** man was placed upon earth, 4480
38:12 Hast thou commanded the morning **s** thy 4480
Isa 14: 8 the cedars of Lebanon, *saying,* **S** thou 227+4480
16:13 hath spoken concerning Moab **s** that time. 4480
43: 4 **S** thou wast precious in my sight, 834+4480
44: 7 for me, **s** I appointed the ancient people? 4480
64: 4 For **s the beginning of the world** 4480+5769
Jer 7:25 **S** the day that your fathers came forth out 4480
20: 8 For **s** I spake, I cried out, I cried 1767+4480
31:20 for **s** I spake against him, I do 1767+4480
44:18 **s** we left off to burn incense to 227+4480
48:27 for **s** thou spakest of him, 1767+4480
Da 12: 1 such as never was **s** there was a nation *even* 4480
Hag 2:16 **S** those *days* were, when *one* came to 1961+4480
Mt 24:21 such as was not **s** the beginning of the world *575*
Mk 9:21 How long is it ago **s** this came unto him? *5613*
Lk 1:70 which have been **s** the world **began**:) *575*
7:45 this *woman* **s the time** I came in hath *575+3739*
16:16 **s** that time the kingdom of God is preached, *575*
24:21 to day is the third day **s** these *things* *575+3739*
Jn 9:32 **S** the world **began** was it not heard that any *1537*
Ac 3:21 of all his holy prophets **s** the world **began**. *575*
19: 2 Have ye received the Holy Ghost **s** ye *1487*
24:11 twelve days **s** I went up to Jerusalem *575+3739*
Ro 16:25 was kept secret **s** the **world began,** *166+5550*
1Co 15:21 For **s** by man *came* death, by man *came* *1894*
2Co 13: 3 **S** ye seek a proof of Christ speaking in me, *1893*
Col 1: 4 **S** we heard of your faith in Christ Jesus, and NIG
1: 6 **s** the day ye heard of *it,* and knew the grace *575*
1: 9 **s** the day we heard *it,* do not cease to pray *575*
Heb 7:28 which was **s** the law, *maketh* the Son, *3326*
9:26 must he often have suffered **s** the foundation *575*
2Pe 3: 4 for **s** the fathers fell asleep, all *things* *575+3739*
Rev 16:18 such as was not **s** men were upon *575+3739*

SINCERE (2) [SINCERELY, SINCERITY]
Php 1:10 that ye may be **s** and without offence till *1506*
1Pe 2: 2 newborn babes, desire the **s** milk of the word, *97*

SINCERELY (3) [SINCERE]
Jdg 9:16 if ye have done truly and **s,** 8549+871.1
9:19 dealt truly and **s** with Jerubbaal and 8549+871.1
Php 1:16 The one preach Christ of contention, not **s,** *55*

SINCERITY (7) [SINCERE]
Jos 24:14 and serve him in **s** and in truth: 8549
1Co 5: 8 but with the unleavened bread of **s** and *1505*
2Co 1:12 that in simplicity and godly **s,** not with *1505*
2:17 but as of **s,** but as of God, in the sight of *1505*
8: 8 of others, and to prove the **s** of your love. *1103*
Eph 6:24 all them that love our Lord Jesus Christ in **s.** *861*
Tit 2: 7 doctrine *shewing* uncorruptness, gravity, **s,** *861*

SINEW (3) [SINEWS]
Ge 32:32 of Israel eat not *of* the **s** which shrank, 1517
32:32 hollow of Jacob's thigh in the **s** that shrank. 1517
Isa 48: 4 thy neck *is* an iron **s,** and thy brow brass: 1517

SINEWS (5) [SINEW]
Job 10:11 flesh, and hast fenced me with bones and **s.** 1517
30:17 in the night season: and my **s** take no rest. 6207
40:17 the **s** of his stones are wrapt together. 1517
Eze 37: 6 I will lay **s** upon you, and will bring up 1517
37: 8 lo, the **s** and the flesh came up upon them, 1517

SINFUL (8) [SIN]
Nu 32:14 in your fathers' stead, an increase of **s** men, 2400
Isa 1: 4 Ah **s** nation, a people laden with iniquity, 2398
Am 9: 8 the eyes of the Lord GOD *are* upon the **s** 2403
Mk 8:38 words in this adulterous and **s** generation; *268*
Lk 5: 8 Depart from me; for I am a **s** man, O Lord. *268*
24: 7 must be delivered into the hands of **s** men, *268*
Ro 7:13 commandment might become exceeding **s.** *268*
8: 3 God sending his own Son in the likeness of **s** *266*

SINFUL NATURE See CARNAL; FLESH

SING (119) [SANG, SINGER, SINGERS, SINGETH, SINGING, SONG, SONGS, SUNG]
Ex 15: 1 and spake, saying, I will **s** unto the LORD, 7891
15:21 answered them, **S** ye to the LORD, 7891
32:18 *but* the noise of *them that* **s** do I hear. 6031
Nu 21:17 this song, Spring up, O well; **s** ye unto it: 6030
Jdg 5: 3 I, *even* I, will **s** unto the LORD; 7891
5: 3 I will **s** *praise* to the LORD God of Israel. 2167
1Sa 21:11 did they not **s** one to another of him in 6030
2Sa 22:50 and I will **s praises** unto thy name. 2167
1Ch 16: 9 **S** unto him, sing psalms unto him, talk you 7891
16: 9 Sing unto him, **s psalms** unto him, talk you 2167
16:23 **S** unto the LORD, all the earth; shew forth 7891
16:33 shall the trees of the wood **s out** at 7442
2Ch 20:22 when they began to **s** and to praise, 7440
23:13 of musick, and such as taught to *s* praise. NIH
29:30 the princes commanded the Levites to *s* NIH
Job 29:13 I **caused** the widow's heart **to s for joy.** 7442
Ps 7:17 will **s** *praise* to the name of the LORD 2167
9: 2 I will **s** *praise* to thy name, O thou most 2167
9:11 **S** *praises* to the LORD, which dwelleth in 2167
13: 6 I will **s** unto the LORD, because he hath 7891
18:49 the heathen, and **s** *praises* unto thy name. 2167
21:13 *so* will we **s** and praise thy power. 7891
27: 6 I will **s,** yea, I will sing *praises* unto 7891
27: 6 yea, I will **s** *praises* unto the LORD. 2167
30: 4 **S** unto the LORD, O ye saints of his, and 2167
30:12 To the end that *my* glory may **s** *praise* to 2167
33: 2 **s** unto him with the psaltery *and* 2167
33: 3 **S** unto him a new song; play skilfully with 7891
47: 6 **S** *praises* to God, sing *praises:* sing *praises* 2167
47: 6 **s** *praises:* sing *praises* unto our King, 2167
47: 6 sing *praises:* **s** *praises* unto our King, 2167
47: 6 sing *praises* unto our King, **s** *praises.* 2167
47: 7 the earth: **s** ye *praises* with understanding. 2167
51:14 my tongue shall **s aloud** of thy 7442
57: 7 my heart is fixed: I will **s** and give praise. 7891
57: 9 I will **s** unto thee among the nations. 2167
59:16 I will **s** of thy power; yea, I will sing aloud 7891
59:16 I will **s aloud** of thy mercy in the morning: 7442
59:17 Unto thee, O my strength, will I **s:** for God 2167
61: 8 So will I **s** *praise* unto thy name for ever, 2167
65:13 with corn; they shout for joy, they also **s.** 7891
66: 2 **S forth** the honour of his name: make his 2167
66: 4 shall worship thee, and shall **s** unto thee; 2167
66: 4 sing unto thee; they shall **s** *to* thy name. 2167
67: 4 O let the nations be glad and **s for joy**: 7442
68: 4 **S** unto God, sing *praises to* his name: 7891
68: 4 Sing unto God, **s** *praises to* his name: 2167
68:32 **S** unto God, ye kingdoms of the earth; 7891
68:32 the earth; O **s** *praises unto* the Lord; Selah. 2167
71:22 unto thee will I **s** with the harp, O thou 2167
71:23 My lips shall greatly rejoice when I **s** unto 2167
75: 9 I will **s** *praises* to the God of Jacob. 2167
81: 1 **S aloud** unto God our strength: make a 7442
89: 1 I will **s** of the mercies of the LORD for 7891
92: 1 to **s** *praises* unto thy name, O most High: 2167
95: 1 O come, let us **s** unto the LORD: let us 7442
96: 1 O **s** unto the LORD a new song: sing unto 7891
96: 1 new song: **s** unto the LORD, all the earth. 7891

Ps 96: 2 **S** unto the LORD, bless his name; 7891
98: 1 O **s** unto the LORD a new song; for he 7891
98: 4 a loud noise, and rejoice, and **s** *praise.* 2167
98: 5 **S** unto the LORD with the harp; with 2167
101: 1 I will **s** of mercy and judgment: unto thee, 7891
101: 1 judgment: unto thee, O LORD, will I **s**. 2167
104:12 *which* **s** among the branches. 5414+6963
104:33 I will **s** unto the LORD as long as I live: 7891
104:33 I will **s** *praise* to my God while I have my 2167
105: 2 **S** unto him, sing psalms unto him: talk ye 7891
105: 2 Sing unto him, **s psalms** unto him: talk ye 2167
108: 1 I will **s** and give praise, even *with* my 7891
108: 3 I will **s** *praises* unto thee among the nations. 2167
135: 3 **s** *praises* unto his name; for *it is* pleasant. 2167
137: 3 *saying,* **S** us *one* of the songs of Zion. 7891
137: 4 How shall we **s** the LORD'S song in a 7891
138: 1 before the gods will I **s** *praise* unto thee. 2167
138: 5 they shall **s** in the ways of the LORD: 7891
144: 9 I will **s** a new song unto thee, O God: 7891
144: 9 an instrument of ten strings will I **s** *praises* 2167
145: 7 and shall **s** of thy righteousness. 7442
146: 2 I will **s** *praises* unto my God while I have 2167
147: 1 for *it is* good to **s** *praises* unto our God; 2167
147: 7 **S** unto the LORD with thanksgiving; 6030
147: 7 **s** *praise* upon the harp unto our God: 2167
149: 1 **S** unto the LORD a new song, *and* 7891
149: 3 let them **s** *praises* unto him with the timbrel 2167
149: 5 in glory: let them **s aloud** upon their beds. 7442
Pr 29: 6 but the righteous doth **s** and rejoice. 7442
Isa 5: 1 Now will I **s** to my wellbeloved a song of 7891
12: 5 **S** unto the LORD; for he hath done 2167
23:15 after the end of seventy years shall Tyre **s** 7892
23:16 make sweet melody, **s** many songs, that NIH
24:14 They shall lift up their voice, they shall **s**, 7442
26:19 Awake and **s**, ye that dwell in dust: for thy 7442
27: 2 In that day **s** ye unto her, A vineyard of red 6030
35: 6 as a hart, and the tongue of the dumb **s**: 7442
38:20 **s** my songs *to* **the stringed instruments** all 5059
42:10 **S** unto the LORD a new song, *and* 7891
42:11 let the inhabitants of the rock **s**, let them 7442
44:23 **S**, O ye heavens; for the LORD hath done 7442
49:13 **S**, O heavens; and be joyful, O earth; and 7442
52: 8 *with* the voice together shall they **s**: 7442
52: 9 Break forth **into joy**, **s** together, ye waste 7442
54: 1 **S**, O barren, thou *that* didst not bear; 7442
65:14 my servants shall **s** for joy of heart, but 7442
Jer 20:13 **S** unto the LORD, praise ye the LORD: 7891
31: 7 **S** with gladness for Jacob, and shout among 7442
31:12 they shall come and **s** in the height of Zion, 7442
51:48 and all that *is* therein, shall **s** for Babylon: 7442
Eze 27:25 The ships of Tarshish did **s** of thee *in* thy 7788
Hos 2:15 she shall **s** there, as *in* the days of her 6030
Zep 2:14 *their* voice shall **s** in the windows; 7891
3:14 **S**, O daughter of Zion; shout, O Israel; 7442
Zec 2:10 **S** and rejoice, O daughter of Zion: for lo, 7442
Ro 15: 9 among the Gentiles, and **s** unto thy name. *5567*
1Co 14:15 I will **s** with the spirit, and I will sing with *5567*
14:15 and I will **s** with the understanding also. *5567*
Heb 2:12 in the midst of the church will I **s praise** *5214*
Jas 5:13 him pray. Is any merry? let him **s psalms**. *5567*
Rev 15: 3 And they **s** the song of Moses the servant of *103*

SINGED (1)

Da 3:27 nor was a hair of their head **s**, neither were 2761

SINGER (2) [SING]

1Ch 6:33 Heman a **s**, the son of Joel, the son of 7891
Hab 3:19 To the **chief** **s** on my stringed instruments. 5329

SINGERS (38) [SING]

1Ki 10:12 harps also and psalteries for **s**: 7891
1Ch 9:33 these *are* the **s**, chief of the fathers of 7891
15:16 *to be* the **s** with instruments of musick, 7891
15:19 So the **s**, Heman, Asaph, and Ethan, 7891
15:27 the **s**, and Chenaniah the master of the song 7891
15:27 the master of the song *with* the **s**: 7891
2Ch 5:12 Also the Levites *which were* the **s**, all of 7891
5:13 as the trumpeters and **s** *were* as one, 7891
9:11 and harps and psalteries for **s**: 7891
20:21 he appointed **s** unto the LORD, and 7891
23:13 also the **s** with instruments of musick, and 7891
29:28 and the **s** sang, and the trumpeters sounded: 7892
35:15 the **s** the sons of Asaph *were* in their place, 7891
Ezr 2:41 The **s**: the children of Asaph, an hundred 7891
2:70 the **s**, and the porters, and the Nethinims, 7891
7: 7 the **s**, and the porters, and the Nethinims, 7891
7:24 any of the priests and Levites, **s**, porters, 2171
10:24 Of the **s** also; Eliashib: and of the porters; 7891
Ne 7: 1 the porters and the **s** and the Levites were 7891
7:44 The **s**: the children of Asaph, an hundred 7891
7:73 the **s**, and *some* of the people, and 7891
10:28 the priests, the Levites, the porters, the **s**, 7891
10:39 that minister, and the porters, and the **s**: 7891
11:22 the **s** *were* over the business of the house of 7891
11:23 that a certain portion *should be* for the **s**, 7891
12:28 the sons of the **s** gathered themselves 7891
12:29 for the **s** had builded them villages round 7891
12:42 the **s** sang loud, with Jezrahiah *their* 7891
12:45 both the **s** and the porters kept the ward of 7891
12:46 and Asaph of old *there were* chief of the **s**, 7891
12:47 gave the portions of the **s** and the porters, 7891
13: 5 to the Levites, and the **s**, and the porters; 7891
13:10 been given *them:* for the Levites and the **s**, 7891
Ps 68:25 The **s** went before, the players on 7891
87: 7 As well the **s** as the players on instruments 7891
Ecc 2: 8 I gat me *men* **s** and *women* singers, and 7891
2: 8 I gat me *men* singers and *women* **s**, and 7891
Eze 40:44 the chambers of the **s** in the inner court, 7891

SINGETH (1) [SING]

Pr 25:20 so *is* he that **s** songs to a heavy heart. 7891

SINGING (29) [SING]

1Sa 18: 6 **s** and dancing, to meet king Saul, 7891
2Sa 19:35 can I hear any more the voice of **s** *men* and 7891
19:35 singing *men* and **s** *women?* wherefore then 7891
1Ch 6:32 the tabernacle of the congregation with **s**, 7892
13: 8 with **s**, and with harps, and with psalteries, 7892
2Ch 23:18 with rejoicing and with **s**, as it was 7892
30:21 *s* with loud instruments unto the LORD. NIH
35:25 all the **s** *men* and the singing *women* spake 7891
35:25 the **s** *women* spake of Josiah in their 7891
Ezr 2:65 *there were* among them two hundred **s** *men* 7891
2:65 two hundred singing *men* and **s** *women.* 7891
Ne 7:67 and five **s** *men* and singing *women.* 7891
7:67 and five singing *men* and **s** *women.* 7891
12:27 with **s**, *with* cymbals, psalteries, and 7892
Ps 100: 2 come before his presence with **s**. 7445
126: 2 filled *with* laughter, and our tongue *with* **s**: 7440
SS 2:12 the time of the **s** *of birds* is come, and 2158
Isa 14: 7 at rest, *and* is quiet: they break forth *into* **s**. 7440
16:10 in the vineyards there shall be no **s**, 7442
35: 2 and rejoice even *with* joy and **s**: 7444
44:23 break forth *into* **s**, ye mountains, O forest, 7440
48:20 with a voice of **s** declare ye, tell this, 7440
49:13 and break forth *into* **s**, O mountains: 7440
51:11 shall return, and come with **s** *unto* Zion; 7440
54: 1 break forth *into* **s**, and cry aloud, thou *that* 7440
55:12 the hills shall break forth before you *into* **s**, 7440
Zep 3:17 rest in his love, he will joy over thee with **s**. 7440
Eph 5:19 **s** and making melody in your heart to *103*
Col 3:16 **s** with grace in your hearts to the Lord. *103*

SINGLE (2) [SINGLENESS, SINGULAR]

Mt 6:22 if therefore thine eye be **s**, thy whole body *573*
Lk 11:34 therefore when thine eye is **s**, thy whole *573*

SINGLENESS (3) [SINGLE]

Ac 2:46 eat *their* meat with gladness and **s** of heart, *858*
Eph 6: 5 with fear and trembling, in **s** of your heart, *572*
Col 3:22 but in **s** of heart, fearing God: *572*

SINGULAR (1) [SINGLE]

Lev 27: 2 When a man shall **make a s vow**, 5088+6381

SINIM (1)

Isa 49:12 from the west; and these from the land of **S**. 5515

SINITE (2)

Ge 10:17 And the Hivite, and the Arkite, and the **S**, 5513
1Ch 1:15 And the Hivite, and the Arkite, and the **S**, 5513

SINK (6) [SANK, SUNK]

Ps 69: 2 I **s** in deep mire, where *there is* no standing: 2883
69:14 me out of the mire, and let me not **s**: 2883
Jer 51:64 Thus shall Babylon **s**, and shall not rise 8257
Mt 14:30 and beginning to **s**, he cried, saying, Lord, *2670*
Lk 5: 7 filled both the ships, so that they began to **s**. *1036*
9:44 Let these sayings **s down** into your ears: *5087*

SINNED (119) [SIN]

Ex	9:27	and said unto them, I have **s** *this* time:	2398
	9:34	he **s** yet more, and hardened his heart, he	2398
	10:16	I have **s** against the LORD your God, and	2398
	32:30	said unto the people, Ye have **s** a great sin:	2398
	32:31	this people have **s** a great sin, and	2398
	32:33	Whosoever hath **s** against me, him will I	2398
Lev	4: 3	let him bring for his sin, which he hath **s**,	2398
	4:14	which they have **s** against it, is known, then	2398
	4:22	When a ruler hath **s**, and done somewhat	2398
	4:23	Or if his sin, wherein he hath **s**, come to his	2398
	4:28	Or if his sin, which he hath **s**, come to his	2398
	4:28	for his sin which he hath **s**.	2398
	5: 5	he shall confess that he hath **s** in that *thing:*	2398
	5: 6	the LORD for his sin which he hath **s**,	2398
	5:10	for him for his sin which he had **s**,	2398
	5:11	he that **s** shall bring for his offering	2398
	5:13	his sin that he hath **s** in one of these,	2398
	6: 4	it shall be, because he hath **s**, and is guilty,	2398
Nu	6:11	for that he **s** by the dead, and shall hallow	2398
	12:11	done foolishly, and wherein we have **s**.	2398
	14:40	the LORD hath promised: for we have **s**.	2398
	21: 7	came to Moses, and said, We have **s**,	2398
	22:34	said unto the angel of the LORD, I have **s**;	2398
	32:23	behold, ye have **s** against the LORD:	2398
Dt	1:41	unto me, We have **s** against the LORD,	2398
	9:16	ye had **s** against the LORD your God, *and*	2398
	9:18	because of all your sins which ye **s**,	2398
Jos	7:11	Israel hath **s**, and they have also	2398
	7:20	Indeed I have **s** against the LORD God of	2398
Jdg	10:10	We have **s** against thee, both because	2398
	10:15	of Israel said unto the LORD, We have **s**:	2398
	11:27	Wherefore I have not **s** against thee, but	2398
1Sa	7: 6	said there, We have **s** against the LORD.	2398
	12:10	said, We have **s**, because we have forsaken	2398
	15:24	Saul said unto Samuel, I have **s**: for I have	2398
	15:30	he said, I have **s**: *yet* honour me now, I pray	2398
	19: 4	because he hath not **s** against thee, and	2398
	24:11	in mine hand, and I have not **s** against thee;	2398
	26:21	said Saul, I have **s**: return, my son David:	2398
2Sa	12:13	unto Nathan, I have **s** against the LORD.	2398
	19:20	For thy servant doth know that I have **s**:	2398
	24:10	I have **s** greatly *in* that I have done:	2398
	24:17	Lo, I have **s**, and I have done wickedly:	2398
1Ki	8:33	because they have **s** against thee, and	2398
	8:35	is no rain, because they have **s** against thee;	2398
	8:47	We have **s**, and have done perversely,	2398
	8:50	forgive thy people that have **s** against thee,	2398
	15:30	of the sins of Jeroboam which he **s**,	2398
	16:13	*by* which they **s**, and *by* which they made	2398
	16:19	For his sins which he **s** in doing evil in	2398
	18: 9	he said, What have I **s**, that thou wouldest	2398
2Ki	17: 7	that the children of Israel had **s** against	2398
	21:17	and all that he did, and his sin that he **s**,	2398
1Ch	21: 8	I have **s** greatly, because I have done this	2398
	21:17	even I *it is* that have **s** and done evil indeed;	2398
2Ch	6:24	because they have **s** against thee;	2398
	6:26	is no rain, because they have **s** against thee;	2398
	6:37	saying, We have **s**, we have done amiss,	2398
	6:39	forgive thy people which have **s** against	2398
Ne	1: 6	of Israel, which we have **s** against thee:	2398
	1: 6	both I and my father's house have **s**.	2398
	9:29	**s** against thy judgments, (which if a man	2398
Job	1: 5	It may be that my sons have **s**, and	2398
	1:22	In all this Job **s** not, nor charged God	2398
	7:20	I have **s**; what shall I do unto thee, O thou	2398
	8: 4	If thy children have **s** against him, and	2398
	24:19	*so doth* the grave *those which* have **s**.	2398
	33:27	I have **s**, and perverted *that which was*	2398
Ps	41: 4	heal my soul; for I have **s** against thee.	2398
	51: 4	have I **s**, and done *this* evil in thy sight:	2398
	78:17	they **s** yet more against him by provoking	2398
	78:32	For all this they **s** still, and believed not for	2398
	106: 6	We have **s** with our fathers, we have	2398
Isa	42:24	the LORD, he against whom we have **s**?	2398
	43:27	Thy first father hath **s**, and thy teachers	2398
	64: 5	behold, thou art wroth; for we have **s**:	2398
Jer	2:35	with thee, because thou sayest, I have not **s**.	2398
	3:25	for we have **s** against the LORD our God,	2398
	8:14	because we have **s** against the LORD.	2398
	14: 7	are many; we have **s** against thee.	2398
	14:20	of our fathers: for we have **s** against thee.	2398
	33: 8	whereby they have **s** against me, and I will	2398
	33: 8	whereby they have **s**, and whereby they	2398
	40: 3	because ye have **s** against the LORD, and	2398
	44:23	because ye have **s** against the LORD, and	2398
	50: 7	because they have **s** against the LORD,	2398
	50:14	for she hath **s** against the LORD.	2398
La	1: 8	Jerusalem hath **grievously s**;	2398+2399
	5: 7	Our fathers have **s**, *and are* not; *and*	2398
	5:16	*from* our head: woe unto us, that we have **s**!	2398
Eze	18:24	in his sin that he hath **s**, in them shall he	2398
	28:16	of thee *with* violence, and thou hast **s**:	2398
	37:23	wherein they have **s**, and will cleanse them:	2398
Da	9: 5	We have **s**, and have committed iniquity,	2398
	9: 8	our fathers, because we have **s** against thee.	2398
	9:11	of God, because we have **s** against him.	2398
	9:15	we have **s**, we have done wickedly.	2398
Hos	4: 7	they were increased, so they **s** against me:	2398
	10: 9	thou hast **s** from the days of Gibeah:	2398
Mic	7: 9	because I have **s** against him, until he plead	2398
Hab	2:10	many people, and *hast* **s** *against* thy soul.	2398
Zep	1:17	because they have **s** against the LORD:	2398
Mt	27: 4	I have **s** in that I have betrayed *the* innocent	*264*
Lk	15:18	I have **s** against heaven, and before thee,	*264*
	15:21	I have **s** against heaven, and in thy sight, and	*264*
Jn	9: 3	Neither hath this *man* **s**, nor his parents:	*264*
Ro	2:12	For as many as have **s** without law shall also	*264*
	2:12	as many as have **s** in the law shall be judged	*264*
	3:23	For all have **s**, and come short of the glory of	*264*
	5:12	passed upon all men, for that all have **s**:	*264*
	5:14	even over them that had not **s** after	*264*
	5:16	And not as *it was* by one that **s**, *so is* the gift:	*264*
1Co	7:28	But and if thou marry, thou hast not **s**; and	*264*
	7:28	and if a virgin marry, she hath not **s**.	*264*
2Co	12:21	I shall bewail many which have **s already**,	*4258*
	13: 2	I write to them which **heretofore** have **s**,	*4258*
Heb	3:17	*was it* not with them that had **s**,	*264*
2Pe	2: 4	For if God spared not the angels that **s**, but	*264*
1Jn	1:10	If we say that we have not **s**, we make him a	*264*

SINNER (21) [SIN]

Pr	11:31	the earth: much more the wicked and the **s**.	2398
	13: 6	but wickedness overthroweth the **s**.	2403
	13:22	the wealth of the **s** *is* laid up for the just.	2398
Ecc	2:26	to the **s** he giveth travail, to gather and	2398
	7:26	from her; but the **s** shall be taken by her.	2398
	8:12	Though a **s** do evil an hundred *times,* and	2398
	9: 2	as *is* the good, so *is* the **s**; *and* he that	2398
	9:18	of war: but one **s** destroyeth much good.	2398
Isa	65:20	the **s** *being* an hundred years old shall be	2398
Lk	7:37	a woman in the city, which was a **s**,	*268*
	7:39	*this is* that toucheth him: for she is a **s**.	*268*
	15: 7	shall be in heaven over one **s** that repenteth,	*268*
	15:10	the angels of God over one **s** that repenteth.	*268*
	18:13	his breast, saying, God be merciful to me a **s**.	*268*
	19: 7	was gone to be guest with a man *that is* a **s**.	*268*
Jn	9:16	How can a man *that is* a **s** do such miracles?	*268*
	9:24	God the praise: we know that this man is a **s**.	*268*
	9:25	said, Whether he be a **s** *or no,* I know not:	*268*
Ro	3: 7	his glory; why yet am I also judged as a **s**?	*268*
Jas	5:20	that he which converteth the **s** from the error	*268*
1Pe	4:18	where shall the ungodly and the **s** appear?	*268*

SINNERS (48) [SIN]

Ge	13:13	and **s** before the LORD exceedingly.	2400
Nu	16:38	The censers of these **s** against their own	2400
1Sa	15:18	and utterly destroy the **s** the Amalekites,	2400
Ps	1: 1	nor standeth in the way of **s**, nor sitteth in	2400
	1: 5	nor **s** in the congregation of the righteous.	2400
	25: 8	will he teach **s** in the way.	2400
	26: 9	Gather not my soul with **s**, nor my life with	2400
	51:13	and **s** shall be converted unto thee.	2400
	104:35	Let the **s** be consumed out of the earth, and	2400
Pr	1:10	My son, if **s** entice thee, consent thou not.	2400
	13:21	Evil pursueth **s**: but to the righteous good	2400
	23:17	Let not thine heart envy **s**: but *be thou* in	2400
Isa	1:28	and of the **s** *shall be* together,	2400
	13: 9	and he shall destroy the **s** thereof out of it.	2400
	33:14	The **s** in Zion are afraid; fearfulness hath	2400
Am	9:10	All the **s** of my people shall die by	2400
Mt	9:10	many publicans and **s** came and sat down	*268*
	9:11	eateth your Master with publicans and **s**?	*268*
	9:13	to call *the* righteous, but **s** to repentance.	*268*
	11:19	a winebibber, a friend of publicans and **s**.	*268*
	26:45	Son of man is betrayed into the hands of **s**.	*268*
Mk	2:15	and **s** sat also together with Jesus and	*268*

Mk 2:16 Pharisees saw him eat with publicans and s, 268
2:16 he eateth and drinketh with publicans and s? 268
2:17 not to call the righteous, but s to repentance. 268
14:41 Son of man is betrayed into the hands of s. 268
Lk 5:30 do ye eat and drink with publicans and s? 268
5:32 not to call the righteous, but s to repentance. 268
6:32 have ye? for s also love those that love them. 268
6:33 thank have ye? for s also do even the same. 268
6:34 for s also lend to sinners, to receive as much 268
6:34 for sinners also lend to s, to receive as much 268
7:34 a winebibber, a friend of publicans and s. 268
13: 2 Suppose ye that these Galileans were s 268
13: 4 think ye that they were s above all men that 3781
15: 1 him all the publicans and s for to hear him. 268
15: 2 This man receiveth s, and eateth with them. 268
Jn 9:31 Now we know that God heareth not s: but 268
Ro 5: 8 in that, while we were yet s, Christ died for 268
5:19 one man's disobedience many were made s, 268
Gal 2:15 are Jews by nature, and not s of the Gentiles, 268
2:17 we ourselves also are found s, is therefore 268
1Ti 1: 9 for the ungodly and for s, for unholy and 268
1:15 Christ Jesus came into the world to save s; 268
Heb 7:26 separate from s, and made higher than 268
12: 3 such contradiction of s against himself, 268
Jas 4: 8 Cleanse your hands, ye s; and purify your 268
Jude 1:15 of all their hard speeches which ungodly s 268

SINNEST (1) [SIN]
Job 35: 6 If thou s, what doest thou against him? or 2398

SINNETH (22) [SIN]
Nu 15:28 an atonement for the soul that s ignorantly, 7683
15:28 when he s by ignorance before the LORD, 2398
15:29 that s through ignorance, 6213+7684+871.1
Dt 19:15 or for any sin, in any sin that he s: 2398
1Ki 8:46 (for there is no man that s not,) 2398
2Ch 6:36 (for there is no man which s not,) 2398
Pr 8:36 he that s against me wrongeth his own soul: 2398
14:21 He that despiseth his neighbour s: but 2398
19: 2 and he that hasteth with his feet, s. 2398
20: 2 whoso provoketh him to anger s against his 2398
Ecc 7:20 man upon earth, that doeth good, and s not. 2398
Eze 14:13 when the land s against me by trespassing 2398
18: 4 the son is mine: the soul that s, it shall die. 2398
18:20 The soul that s, it shall die. The son shall 2398
33:12 for his righteousness in the day that he s. 2398
1Co 6:18 he that committeth fornication s against his 264
7:36 so require, let him do what he will, he s not: 264
Tit 3:11 and s, being condemned of himself. 264
1Jn 3: 6 Whosoever abideth in him s not: 264
3: 6 whosoever s hath not seen him, 264
3: 8 the devil; for the devil s from the beginning. 264
5:18 We know that whosoever is born of God s 264

SINNING (2) [SIN]
Ge 20: 6 for I also withheld thee from s against me: 2398
Lev 6: 3 any of all these that a man doeth, s therein: 2398

SINS (172) [SIN]
Lev 16:16 because of their transgressions in all their s: 2403
16:21 all their transgressions in all their s, putting 2403
16:30 that ye may be clean from all your s before 2403
16:34 children of Israel for all their s once a year. 2403
26:18 punish you seven times more for your s. 2403
26:21 moe plagues upon you according to your s. 2403
26:24 will punish you yet seven times for your s. 2403
26:28 will chastise you seven times for your s. 2403
Nu 16:26 of theirs, lest ye be consumed in all their s. 2403
Dt 9:18 because of all your s which ye sinned, 2403
Jos 24:19 not forgive your transgressions nor your s. 2403
1Sa 12:19 for we have added unto all our s this evil, 2403
1Ki 14:16 give Israel up because of the s of Jeroboam, 2403
14:22 they provoked him to jealousy with their s 2403
15: 3 he walked in all the s of his father, 2403
15:30 Because of the s of Jeroboam which he 2403
16: 2 to sin, to provoke me to anger with their s; 2403
16:13 For all the s of Baasha, and the sins of Elah 2403
16:13 the s of Elah his son, by which they sinned, 2403
16:19 For his s which he sinned in doing evil in 2403
16:31 walk in the s of Jeroboam the son of Nebat, 2403
2Ki 3: 3 Nevertheless he cleaved unto the s of 2403
10:29 Howbeit from the s of Jeroboam the son of 2399
10:31 for he departed not from the s of Jeroboam, 2403
13: 2 followed the s of Jeroboam the son of 2403
13: 6 Nevertheless they departed not from the s 2403
13:11 he departed not from all the s of Jeroboam 2403
14:24 he departed not from all the s of Jeroboam 2403
15: 9 he departed not from the s of Jeroboam 2403
15:18 he departed not all his days from the s of 2403
15:24 he departed not from the s of Jeroboam 2403
15:28 he departed not from the s of Jeroboam 2403
17:22 For the children of Israel walked in all the s 2403
24: 3 for the s of Manasseh, according to all that 2403
2Ch 28:10 with you, s against the LORD your God? 819
28:13 already, ye intend to add more to our s 2403
Ne 1: 6 confess the s of the children of Israel, 2403
9: 2 stood and confessed their s, and 2403
9:37 thou hast set over us because of our s: 2403
Job 13:23 How many are mine iniquities and s? 2403
Ps 19:13 s; let them not have dominion over me: NIH
25: 7 Remember not the s of my youth, nor my 2403
25:18 and my pain; and forgive all my s. 2403
51: 9 Hide thy face from my s, and blot out all 2399
69: 5 and my s are not hid from thee. 819
79: 9 deliver us, and purge away our s, for thy 2403
90: 8 our secret s in the light of thy countenance. NIH
103:10 He hath not dealt with us after our s; 2399
Pr 5:22 he shall be holden with the cords of his s. 2403
10:12 stirreth up strifes: but love covereth all s. 6588
28:13 He that covereth his s shall not prosper: but 6588
Isa 1:18 though your s be as scarlet, they shall be as 2399
38:17 for thou hast cast all my s behind thy back. 2399
40: 2 of the LORD's hand double for all her s. 2403
43:24 thou hast made me to serve with thy s, 2403
43:25 own sake, and will not remember thy s. 2403
44:22 thy transgressions, and, as a cloud, thy s: 2403
58: 1 and the house of Jacob their s. 2403
59: 2 and your s have hid his face from you, 2403
59:12 before thee, and our s testify against us: 2403
Jer 5:25 your s have withholden good things from 2403
14:10 remember their iniquity, and visit their s. 2403
15:13 that for all thy s, even in all thy borders. 2403
30:14 because thy s were increased. 2403
30:15 because thy s were increased, I have done 2403
50:20 the s of Judah, and they shall not be found: 2403
La 3:39 a man for the punishment of his s? 2399
4:13 For the s of her prophets, and the iniquities 2403
4:22 O daughter of Edom; he will discover thy s. 2403
Eze 16:51 hath Samaria committed half of thy s; 2403
16:52 s that thou hast committed more 2403
18:14 that seeth all his father's s which he hath 2403
18:21 if the wicked will turn from all his s that he 2403
21:24 so that in all your doings your s do appear; 2403
23:49 and ye shall bear the s of your idols: 2399
33:10 If our transgressions and our s be upon us, 2403
33:16 None of his s that he hath committed shall 2403
Da 4:27 break off thy s by righteousness, and 2408
9:16 because for our s, and for the iniquities of 2399
9:24 to make an end of s, and to make 2403
Hos 8:13 remember their iniquity, and visit their s: 2403
9: 9 their iniquity, he will visit their s. 2403
Am 5:12 manifold transgressions and your mighty s: 2403
Mic 1: 5 all this, and for the s of the house of Israel. 2403
6:13 in making thee desolate because of thy s. 2403
7:19 thou wilt cast all their s into the depths of 2403
Mt 1:21 for he shall save his people from their s. 266
3: 6 baptized of him in Jordan, confessing their s. 266
9: 2 be of good cheer; thy s be forgiven thee. 266
9: 5 is easier, to say, Thy s be forgiven thee; 266
9: 6 Son of man hath power on earth to forgive s, 266
26:28 is shed for many for the remission of s. 266
Mk 1: 4 baptism of repentance for the remission of s. 266
1: 5 him in the river of Jordan, confessing their s. 266
2: 5 sick of the palsy, Son, thy s be forgiven thee. 266
2: 7 who can forgive s but God only? 266
2: 9 the sick of the palsy, Thy s be forgiven thee; 266
2:10 Son of man hath power on earth to forgive s, 266
3:28 All s shall be forgiven unto the sons of men, 265
4:12 and their s should be forgiven them. 265
Lk 1:77 unto his people by the remission of their s, 266
3: 3 baptism of repentance for the remission of s; 266
5:20 said unto him, Man, thy s are forgiven thee. 266
5:21 Who can forgive s, but God alone? 266
5:23 is easier, to say, Thy s be forgiven thee; 266
5:24 of man hath power upon earth to forgive s, 266
7:47 Her s, which are many, are forgiven; 266
7:48 And he said unto her, Thy s are forgiven. 266
7:49 Who is this that forgiveth s also? 266

S

Lk 11: 4 And forgive us our **s**; for we also forgive 266
24:47 remission of **s** should be preached in his 266
Jn 8:21 and ye shall seek me, and shall die in your **s**: 266
8:24 unto you, that ye shall die in your **s**: 266
8:24 not that I am *he,* ye shall die in your **s**. 266
9:34 Thou wast altogether born in **s**, and dost thou 266
20:23 Whose soever **s** ye remit, they are remitted 266
20:23 *and* whose soever *s* ye retain, they are NIG
Ac 2:38 name of Jesus Christ for the remission of **s**, 266
3:19 be converted, that your **s** may be blotted out, 266
5:31 repentance to Israel, and forgiveness of **s**. 266
10:43 believeth in him shall receive remission of **s**. 266
13:38 is preached unto you the forgiveness of **s**: 266
22:16 arise, and be baptized, and wash away thy **s**, 266
26:18 that they may receive forgiveness of **s**, and 266
Ro 3:25 for the remission of **s** that are past, 265
4: 7 are forgiven, and whose **s** are covered. 266
7: 5 the motions of **s**, which were by the law, 266
11:27 unto them, when I shall take away their **s**. 266
1Co 15: 3 how that Christ died for our **s** according to 266
15:17 your faith *is* vain; ye are yet in your **s**. 266
Gal 1: 4 Who gave himself for our **s**, that he might 266
Eph 1: 7 the forgiveness of **s**, according to the riches 3900
2: 1 who were dead in trespasses and **s**; 266
2: 5 Even when we were dead in **s**, 3900
Col 1:14 through his blood, *even* the forgiveness of **s**: 266
2:11 in putting off the body of the **s** of the flesh, 266
2:13 being dead in *your* **s** and 3900
1Th 2:16 they might be saved, to fill up their **s** alway: 266
1Ti 5:22 no *man,* neither be partaker of other *men's* **s**: 266
5:24 Some men's **s** are open beforehand, 266
2Ti 3: 6 and lead captive silly women laden with **s**, 266
Heb 1: 3 when he had by himself purged our **s**, 266
2:17 to make reconciliation for the **s** of 266
5: 1 he may offer both gifts and sacrifices for **s**: 266
5: 3 the people, so also for himself, to offer for **s**. 266
7:27 first for his own **s**, *and* then for the people's: 266
8:12 and their **s** and their iniquities will I 266
9:28 So Christ was once offered to bear the **s** of 266
10: 2 should have had no more conscience of **s**. 266
10: 3 a remembrance *again made* of **s** every year. 266
10: 4 of bulls and of goats should take away **s**. 266
10:11 which can never take away **s**: 266
10:12 he had offered one sacrifice for **s** for ever, 266
10:17 And their **s** and iniquities will I remember no 266
10:26 there remaineth no more sacrifice for **s**, 266
Jas 5:15 and if he have committed **s**, they shall be 266
5:20 from death, and shall hide a multitude of **s**. 266
1Pe 2:24 Who his own self bare our **s** in his own body 266
2:24 that we, being dead to **s**, should live unto 266
3:18 For Christ also hath once suffered for **s**, 266
4: 8 for charity shall cover the multitude of **s**. 266
2Pe 1: 9 forgotten that *he* was purged from his old **s**. 266
1Jn 1: 9 If we confess our **s**, he is faithful and just to 266
1: 9 he is faithful and just to forgive us *our* **s**, and 266
2: 2 And he is the propitiation for our **s**: and 266
2: 2 but also for *the* **s** *of* the whole world. NIG
2:12 *your* **s** are forgiven you for his name's sake. 266
3: 5 that he was manifested to take away our **s**; 266
4:10 sent his Son *to be* the propitiation for our **s**. 266
Rev 1: 5 and washed us from our **s** in his own blood, 266
18: 4 that ye be not partakers of her **s**, and that ye 266
18: 5 For her **s** have reached unto heaven, and God 266

SION (8) [ZION]
Dt 4:48 even unto mount **S**, which *is* Hermon, 7865
Mt 21: 5 Tell ye the daughter of **S**, Behold, thy King 4622
Jn 12:15 Fear not, daughter of **S**: behold, thy King 4622
Ro 9:33 I lay in **S** a stumblingstone and rock of 4622
11:26 There shall come out of **S** the Deliverer, 4622
Heb 12:22 But ye are come unto mount **S**, and 4622
1Pe 2: 6 I lay in **S** a chief corner stone, elect, 4622
Rev 14: 1 and lo, a Lamb stood on the mount **S**, and 4622

SIPHMOTH (1)
1Sa 30:28 to *them* which *were* in **S**, and to *them* 8224

SIPPAI (1)
1Ch 20: 4 time Sibbechai the Hushathite slew **S**, 5598

SIR (12) [SIRS]
Ge 43:20 said, O **s**, we came indeed down at the first 113
Mt 13:27 the householder came and said unto him, **S**, 2962
21:30 And he answered and said, I *go,* **s**: and 2962
27:63 Saying, **S**, we remember that that deceiver 2962
Jn 4:11 The woman saith unto him, **S**, thou hast 2962
4:15 **S**, give me this water, that I thirst not, 2962
4:19 The woman saith unto him, **S**, I perceive 2962
4:49 unto him, **S**, come down ere my child die. 2962
5: 7 **S**, I have no man, when the water is 2962
12:21 and desired him, saying, **S**, we would see 2962
20:15 him to be the gardener, saith unto him, **S**, 2962
Rev 7:14 And I said unto him, **S**, thou knowest. 2962

SIRAH (1)
2Sa 3:26 brought him again from the well of **S**: 5626

SIRION (2)
Dt 3: 9 (*Which* Hermon the Sidonians call **S**; and 8303
Ps 29: 6 a calf; Lebanon and **S** like a young unicorn. 8303

SIRS (7) [SIR]
Ac 7:26 them at one *again,* saying, **S**, ye are brethren; 435
14:15 And saying, **S**, why do ye these *things?* We 435
16:30 And brought them out, and said, **S**, 2962
19:25 and said, **S**, ye know that by this craft we 435
27:10 And said unto them, **S**, I perceive that *this* 435
27:21 and said, **S**, *ye* should have hearkened unto 435
27:25 Wherefore, **s**, be of good cheer: for I believe 435

SISAMAI (2)
1Ch 2:40 Eleasah begat **S**, and Sisamai begat 5581
2:40 begat Sisamai, and **S** begat Shallum, 5581

SISERA (21)
Jdg 4: 2 the captain of whose host *was* **S**, which 5516
4: 7 I will draw unto thee to the river Kishon **S**, 5516
4: 9 for the LORD shall sell **S** into the hand of 5516
4:12 they shewed **S** that Barak the son of 5516
4:13 **S** gathered together all his chariots, 5516
4:14 LORD hath delivered **S** into thine hand: 5516
4:15 the LORD discomfited **S**, and all *his* 5516
4:15 so that **S** lighted down off *his* chariot, and 5516
4:16 all the host of **S** fell upon the edge of 5516
4:17 Howbeit **S** fled away on his feet to the tent 5516
4:18 Jael went out to meet **S**, and said unto him, 5516
4:22 behold, as Barak pursued **S**, Jael came out 5516
4:22 **S** lay dead, and the nail *was* in his temples. 5516
5:20 the stars in their courses fought against **S**. 5516
5:26 with the hammer she smote **S**, she smote 5516
5:28 The mother of **S** looked out at a window, 5516
5:30 to **S** a prey of divers colours, a prey of 5516
1Sa 12: 9 he sold them into the hand of **S**, captain of 5516
Ezr 2:53 The children of Barkos, the children of **S**, 5516
Ne 7:55 the children of **S**, the children of Tamah, 5516
Ps 83: 9 as *to* **S**, as *to* Jabin, at the brook of Kison: 5516

SISMAI See SISAMAI

SISTER (109) [SISTER'S, SISTERS]
Ge 4:22 iron: and the **s** of Tubal-cain *was* Naamah. 269
12:13 Say, I pray thee, thou *art* my **s**: that it may be 269
12:19 Why saidst thou, She *is* my **s**? so I might 269
20: 2 Abraham said of Sarah his wife, She *is* my **s**: 269
20: 5 Said he not unto me, She *is* my **s**? and she, 269
20:12 yet indeed *she is* my **s**; she *is* the daughter of 269
24:30 when he heard the words of Rebekah his **s**, 269
24:59 they sent away Rebekah their **s**, and her 269
24:60 and said unto her, Thou *art* our **s**, 269
25:20 of Padan-aram, the **s** to Laban the Syrian. 269
26: 7 *him* of his wife; and he said, She *is* my **s**: 269
26: 9 how saidst thou, She *is* my **s**? And Isaac said 269
28: 9 the **s** of Nebajoth, to be his wife. 269
30: 1 bare Jacob no *children,* Rachel envied her **s**; 269
30: 8 great wrestlings have I wrestled with my **s**, 269
34:13 said, because he had defiled Dinah their **s**: 269
34:14 to give our **s** to one that is uncircumcised; 269
34:27 the city, because they had defiled their **s**. 269
34:31 Should he deal with our **s** as with a harlot? 269
36: 3 Ishmael's daughter, **s** of Nebajoth. 269
36:22 and Hemam; and Lotan's **s** *was* Timna. 269
46:17 and Ishui, and Beriah, and Serah their **s**: 269
Ex 2: 4 his **s** stood afar off, to wit what would be 269
2: 7 said his **s** to Pharaoh's daughter, Shall I go 269
6:20 Amram took him Jochebed his **father's s** to 1733
6:23 of Amminadab, **s** of Naashon, to wife; 269
15:20 the **s** of Aaron, took a timbrel in her hand; 269
Lev 18: 9 The nakedness of thy **s**, the daughter of thy 269
18:11 begotten of thy father, she *is* thy **s**, thou shalt 269

Lev 18:12 not uncover the nakedness of thy father's s: 269
18:13 not uncover the nakedness of thy mother's s: 269
18:18 Neither shalt thou take a wife to her s, to vex 269
20:17 if a man shall take his s, his father's 269
20:19 not uncover the nakedness of thy mother's s, 269
20:19 of thy mother's sister, nor of thy father's s: 269
21: 3 And for his s a virgin, that is nigh unto him, 269
Nu 6: 7 for his brother, or for his s, when they die: 269
25:18 the daughter of a prince of Midian, their s, 269
26:59 and Moses, and Miriam their s. 269
Dt 27:22 Cursed *be* he that lieth with his s, 269
Jdg 15: 2 *is* not her younger s fairer than she? take her, 269
Ru 1:15 thy **s in law** is gone back unto her people, 2994
1:15 her gods: return thou after thy **s in law**. 2994
2Sa 13: 1 that Absalom the son of David had a fair s, 269
13: 2 *so* vexed, that he fell sick for his s Tamar; 269
13: 4 I love Tamar, my brother Absalom's s. 269
13: 5 let my s Tamar come, and give me meat, and 269
13: 6 let Tamar my s come, and make *me* a couple 269
13:11 and said unto her, Come lie with me, my s. 269
13:20 hold now thy peace, my s: he *is* thy brother; 269
13:22 because he had forced his s Tamar. 269
13:32 from the day that he forced his s Tamar. 269
17:25 of Nahash, s to Zeruiah Joab's mother. 269
1Ki 11:19 that he gave him *to* wife the s of his own 269
11:19 his own wife, the s of Tahpenes the queen. 269
11:20 the s of Tahpenes bare him Genubath his 269
2Ki 11: 2 the daughter of king Joram, s of Ahaziah, 269
1Ch 1:39 Hori, and Homam: and Timna *was* Lotan's s. 269
3: 9 sons of the concubines, and Tamar their s. 269
3:19 and Hananiah, and Shelomith their s: 269
4: 3 and the name of their s *was* Hazelelponi: 269
4:19 the sons of *his* wife Hodiah the s of Naham, 269
7:15 Machir took to wife *the* s of Huppim and NIH
7:18 his s Hammoleketh bare Ishod, and Abiezer, 269
7:30 and Ishuai, and Beriah, and Serah their s. 269
7:32 and Shomer, and Hotham, and Shua their s. 269
2Ch 22:11 the priest, (for she was the s of Ahaziah,) 269
Job 17:14 to the worm, *Thou art* my mother, and my s. 269
Pr 7: 4 Say unto wisdom, Thou *art* my s; and 269
SS 4: 9 hast ravished my heart, my s, *my* spouse; 269
4:10 How fair is thy love, my s, *my* spouse! 269
4:12 A garden inclosed *is* my s, *my* spouse; 269
5: 1 I am come into my garden, my s, *my* spouse: 269
5: 2 my s, my love, my dove, my undefiled: 269
8: 8 We have a little s, and she hath no breasts: 269
8: 8 what shall we do for our s in the day when 269
Jer 3: 7 And her treacherous s Judah saw *it*. 269
3: 8 yet her treacherous s Judah feared not, but 269
3:10 yet for all this her treacherous s Judah hath 269
22:18 or, Ah s! they shall not lament for him, 269
Eze 16:45 thou *art* the s of thy sisters, which lothed 269
16:46 thine elder s *is* Samaria, she and 269
16:46 thy younger s, that dwelleth at thy right 269
16:48 the Lord GOD, Sodom thy s hath not done, 269
16:49 this was the iniquity of thy s Sodom, pride, 269
16:56 For thy s Sodom was not mentioned by thy 269
22:11 another in thee hath humbled his s, 269
23: 4 *were* Aholah the elder, and Aholibah her s: 269
23:11 when her s Aholibah saw *this*, she was more 269
23:11 in her whoredoms more than her s in *her* 269
23:18 like as my mind was alienated from her s. 269
23:31 Thou hast walked in the way of thy s; 269
23:33 desolation, *with* the cup of thy s Samaria. 269
44:25 or for s that hath had no husband, 269
Mt 12:50 the same is my brother, and s, and mother. *79*
Mk 3:35 the same is my brother, and my s, and mother. *79*
Lk 10:39 And she had a s called Mary, which also sat at *79*
10:40 dost thou not care that my s hath left me to *79*
Jn 11: 1 the town of Mary and her s Martha. *79*
11: 5 Jesus loved Martha, and her s, and Lazarus. *79*
11:28 and called Mary her s secretly, saying, *79*
11:39 Martha, the s of him that was dead, saith unto *79*
19:25 and his mother's s, Mary the *wife* of *79*
Ro 16: 1 I commend unto you Phebe our s, which is a *79*
16:15 and his s, and Olympas, and all the saints *79*
1Co 7:15 or a s is not under bondage in such *cases:* but *79*
9: 5 Have we not power to lead about a s, a wife, *79*
Jas 2:15 If a brother or s be naked, and destitute of *79*
2Jn 1:13 The children of thy elect s greet thee. Amen. *79*

SISTER'S (7) [SISTER]

Ge 24:30 the earring and bracelets upon his s hands, 269
29:13 when Laban heard the tidings of Jacob his s 269
Lev 20:17 he hath uncovered his s nakedness; he shall 269
1Ch 7:15 and Shuppim, whose s name *was* Maachah;) 269
Eze 23:32 Thou shalt drink *of* thy s cup deep and large: 269
Ac 23:16 And when Paul's s son heard of *their* lying in *79*
Col 4:10 saluteth you, and Marcus, **s son** to Barnabas, *431*

SISTERS (19) [SISTER]

Jos 2:13 my s, and all that they have, and deliver our 269
1Ch 2:16 Whose s *were* Zeruiah, and Abigail. And 269
Job 1: 4 sent and called for their three s to eat and 269
42:11 all his s, and all *they that had been of* his 269
Eze 16:45 thou *art* the sister of thy s, which lothed their 269
16:51 hast justified thy s in all thine abominations 269
16:52 Thou also, which hast judged thy s, 269
16:52 thy shame, in that thou hast justified thy s. 269
16:55 When thy s, Sodom and her daughters, 269
16:61 when thou shalt receive thy s, thine elder and 269
Hos 2: 1 Ammi; and to your s, Ruhamah. 269
Mt 13:56 And his s, are they not all with us? Whence *79*
19:29 or s, or father, or mother, or wife, or children, *79*
Mk 6: 3 and are not his s here with us? And they were *79*
10:29 or s, or father, or mother, or wife, or children, *79*
10:30 and s, and mothers, and children, and lands, *79*
Lk 14:26 and children, and brethren, and s, yea, *79*
Jn 11: 3 Therefore *his* s sent unto him, saying, Lord, *79*
1Ti 5: 2 as mothers; the younger as s, with all purity. *79*

SIT (113) [DOWNSITTING, SAT, SATEST, SEAT, SEATED, SEATS, SEATWARD, SITTEST, SITTETH, SITTING]

Ge 27:19 arise, I pray thee, s and eat of my venison, 3427
Nu 32: 6 brethren go to war, and shall ye s here? 3427
Jdg 5:10 ye that s in judgment, and walk by the way. 3427
Ru 3:18 said she, **S still**, my daughter, until thou 3427
4: 1 *Ho*, such a one, turn aside, s **down** here. 3427
4: 2 elders of the city, and said, S ye **down** here. 3427
1Sa 9:22 **made** them s in the chiefest place among 5414
16:11 for we will not s **down** till he come hither. 5437
20: 5 I should **not fail to** s with the king at meat: 3427
2Sa 19: 8 Behold, the king doth s in the gate. 3427
1Ki 1:13 after me, and he shall s upon my throne? 3427
1:17 after me, and he shall s upon my throne. 3427
1:20 that *thou* shouldest tell them who shall s on 3427
1:24 after me, and he shall s upon my throne? 3427
1:27 who should s on the throne of my lord 3427
1:30 and he shall s upon my throne in my stead; 3427
1:35 that he may come and s upon my throne; 3427
1:48 which hath given *one* to s on my throne *this* 3427
3: 6 that thou hast given him a son to s on his 3427
8:20 s on the throne of Israel, as the LORD 3427
8:25 man in my sight to s on the throne of Israel; 3427
2Ki 7: 3 to another, Why s we here until we die? 3427
7: 4 if we s still here, we die also. Now therefore NIH
10:30 thy children of the fourth *generation* shall s 3427
15:12 Thy sons shall s on the throne of Israel unto 3427
18:27 *hath he* not *sent me* to the men which s on 3427
1Ch 28: 5 he hath chosen Solomon my son to s upon 3427
2Ch 6:16 in my sight to s upon the throne of Israel; 3427
Ps 26: 5 of evildoers; and will not s with the wicked. 3427
69:12 They that s in the gate speak against me; 3427
107:10 Such as s in darkness and in the shadow of 3427
110: 1 said unto my Lord, S thou at my right hand, 3427
119:23 Princes also did s *and* speak against me: *but* 3427
127: 2 to **s up** late, to eat the bread of sorrows: 3427
132:12 their children also shall s upon thy throne 3427
Ecc 10: 6 in great dignity, and the rich s in low place. 3427
Isa 3:26 she *being* desolate shall s upon the ground. 3427
14:13 I will s also upon the mount of 3427
16: 5 he shall s upon it in truth in the tabernacle 3427
30: 7 concerning this, Their strength *is* to **s still**. 7674
36:12 *hath he* not *sent me* to the men that s upon 3427
42: 7 them that **s in** darkness out of the prison 3427
47: 1 Come down, and s in the dust, O virgin 3427
47: 1 daughter of Babylon, s on the ground: 3427
47: 5 S thou silent, and get thee into darkness, 3427
47: 8 I shall not s *as* a widow, neither shall I 3427
47:14 *be* a coal to warm at, *nor* fire to s before it. 3427
52: 2 the dust; arise, *and* **s down**, O Jerusalem: 3427
Jer 8:14 Why do we **s still**? assemble yourselves, 3427
13:13 even the kings that s upon David's throne, 3427
13:18 to the queen, Humble yourselves, **s down**: 3427
16: 8 to s with them to eat and to drink. 3427
33:17 David shall never want a man to s upon 3427
36:15 **S down** now, and read it in our ears. 3427
36:30 He shall have none to s upon the throne of 3427

Jer 48:18 come down from *thy* glory, and **s** in thirst; 3427
La 1: 1 How doth the city **s** solitary, *that was* full 3427
2:10 The elders of the daughter of Zion **s** upon 3427
Eze 26:16 they shall **s** upon the ground, and 3427
28: 2 hast said, I *am* a God, I **s** *in* the seat of God, 3427
33:31 they **s** before thee *as* my people, and 3427
44: 3 he shall **s** in it to eat bread before 3427
Da 7: 9 cast *down,* and the Ancient of days did **s**, 3488
7:26 the judgment shall **s**, and they shall take 3488
Joel 3:12 for there will I **s** to judge all the heathen 3427
Mic 4: 4 they shall **s** every man under his vine and 3427
7: 8 when I **s** in darkness, the LORD *shall be* a 3427
Zec 3: 8 thou, and thy fellows that **s** before thee: 3427
6:13 and shall **s** and rule upon his throne: 3427
Mal 3: 3 he shall **s** *as* a refiner and purifier of silver: 3427
Mt 8:11 and shall **s down** with Abraham, and Isaac, *347*
14:19 And he commanded the multitude to **s down** *347*
15:35 And he commanded the multitude to **s down** *377*
19:28 when the Son of man shall **s** in the throne *2523*
19:28 ye also shall **s** upon twelve thrones, *2523*
20:21 Grant that these my two sons may **s**, *2523*
20:23 baptized *with:* but to **s** on my right hand, *2523*
22:44 unto my Lord, **S** thou on my right hand, *2521*
23: 2 and the Pharisees **s** in Moses' seat: *2523*
25:31 then shall he **s** upon the throne of his glory: *2523*
26:36 **S** ye here, while I go and pray yonder. *2523*
Mk 6:39 **make** all **s down** by companies upon *347*
8: 6 And he commanded the people to **s down** on *377*
10:37 said unto him, Grant unto us that we may **s**, *2523*
10:40 But to **s** on my right hand and on my left *2523*
12:36 said to my Lord, **S** thou on my right hand, *2521*
14:32 his disciples, **S** ye here, while I shall pray. *2523*
Lk 1:79 To give light to them that **s** in darkness and *2521*
9:14 **Make** them **s down** by fifties in a *2625*
9:15 And they did so, and **made** *them* all **s down**. *347*
12:37 and **make** them to **s down to meat**, and *347*
13:29 and shall **s down** in the kingdom of God. *347*
14: 8 a wedding, **s** not **down** in the highest room; *2625*
14:10 go and **s down** in the lowest room; *377*
14:10 presence of them that **s at meat with** thee. *4873*
16: 6 and **s down** quickly, and write fifty. *2523*
17: 7 from the field, Go and **s down to meat**? *377*
20:42 said to my Lord, **S** thou on my right hand, *2521*
22:30 **s** on thrones judging the twelve tribes of *2523*
22:69 Hereafter shall the Son of man **s** on *2521*
Jn 6:10 And Jesus said, Make the men **s down**. *377*
Ac 2:30 *he* would raise up Christ to **s** on his throne; *2523*
2:34 unto my Lord, **S** thou on my right hand, *2521*
8:31 that *he* would come up and **s** with him. *2523*
1Co 8:10 knowledge **s at meat** in the idol's temple, *2621*
Eph 2: 6 **made** *us* **s together** in heavenly *places* in *4776*
Heb 1:13 **S** on my right hand, until I make thine *2521*
Jas 2: 3 say unto him, **S** thou here in a good place; *2521*
2: 3 thou there, or **s** here under my footstool: *2521*
Rev 3:21 To him that overcometh will I grant to **s** *2523*
17: 3 I saw a woman **s** upon a scarlet coloured *2521*
18: 7 I **s** a queen, and am no widow, and shall see *2521*
19:18 and of them that **s** on them, and the flesh of *2521*

SITH (3) [SINCE]

Jer 15: 7 *s* they return not from their ways. NIH
23:38 **s** ye say, The burden of the LORD; 518
Eze 35: 6 **s** thou hast not hated blood, even blood shall 518

SITHRI See ZITHRI

SITNAH (1)

Ge 26:21 for that also: and he called the name of it **S**. 7856

SITTEST (7) [SITH]

Ex 18:14 why **s** thou thyself alone, and all the people 3427
Dt 6: 7 shalt talk of them when thou **s** in thine 3427
11:19 speaking of them when thou **s** in thine 3427
Ps 50:20 Thou **s** *and* speakest against thy brother; 3427
Pr 23: 1 When thou **s** to eat with a ruler, 3427
Jer 22: 2 that **s** upon the throne of David, thou, and 3427
Ac 23: 3 for **s** thou to judge me after the law, and *2521*

SITTETH (42) [SITH]

Ex 11: 5 from the firstborn of Pharaoh that **s** upon 3427
Lev 15: 4 every thing, whereon he **s**, shall be unclean. 3427
15: 6 he that **s** on *any* thing whereon he sat that 3427
15:20 every *thing* also that she **s** upon shall be 3427
15:23 or on *any* thing whereon she **s**, when he 3427
15:26 whatsoever she **s** upon shall be unclean, 3427
Dt 17:18 when he **s** upon the throne of his kingdom, 3427
1Ki 1:46 also Solomon **s** on the throne of 3427
Est 6:10 Mordecai the Jew, that **s** at the king's gate: 3427
Ps 1: 1 of sinners, nor **s** in the seat of the scornful. 3427
2: 4 He that **s** in the heavens shall laugh: 3427
10: 8 He **s** in the lurking places of the villages: 3427
29:10 The LORD **s** upon the flood; yea, 3427
29:10 the flood; yea, the LORD **s** King for ever. 3427
47: 8 God **s** upon the throne of his holiness. 3427
99: 1 he **s** *between* the cherubims; let the earth be 3427
Pr 9:14 For she **s** at the door of her house, on a seat 3427
20: 8 A king that **s** in the throne of judgment 3427
31:23 when he **s** among the elders of the land. 3427
SS 1:12 While the king *s* at his table, my spikenard NIH
Isa 28: 6 for a spirit of judgment to him that **s** in 3427
40:22 *It is* he that **s** upon the circle of the earth, 3427
Jer 17:11 *As* the partridge **s** *on eggs,* and 1716
29:16 of the king that **s** upon the throne of David, 3427
La 3:28 He **s** alone and keepeth silence, because 3427
Zec 1:11 behold, all the earth **s still**, and is at rest. 3427
5: 7 this *is* a woman that **s** in the midst of 3427
Mt 23:22 throne of God, and by him that **s** thereon. *2521*
Lk 14:28 **s** not **down** first, and counteth the cost, *2523*
14:31 **s** not **down** first, and consulteth whether he *2523*
22:27 he that **s at meat**, or he that serveth? *345*
22:27 *is* not he that **s at meat**? but I am among you *345*
1Co 14:30 If *any thing* be revealed to another that **s** *2521*
Col 3: 1 where Christ **s** on the right hand of God. *2521*
2Th 2: 4 so that he as God **s** in the temple of God, *2523*
Rev 5:13 *be* unto him that **s** upon the throne, and *2521*
6:16 hide us from the face of him that **s** on *2521*
7:10 Salvation to our God which **s** upon *2521*
7:15 he that **s** on the throne shall dwell among *2521*
17: 1 of the great whore that **s** upon many waters: *2521*
17: 9 seven mountains, on which the woman **s**. *2521*
17:15 where the whore **s**, are peoples, and *2521*

SITTING (43) [SITH]

Dt 22: 6 the dam **s** upon the young, or upon 7257
Jdg 3:20 he was **s** in a summer parlour, which he had 3427
1Ki 10: 5 the **s** of his servants, and the attendance of 4186
13:14 man of God, and found him **s** under an oak: 3427
22:19 I saw the LORD **s** on his throne, and 3427
2Ki 4:38 the sons of the prophets *were* **s** before him: 3427
9: 5 the captains of the host *were* **s**; 3427
2Ch 9: 4 the **s** of his servants, and the attendance of 4186
9:18 stays on each side of the **s** place, and 3427
18:18 I saw the LORD **s** upon his throne, and 3427
Ne 2: 6 said unto me, (the queen also **s** by him,) 3427
Est 5:13 long as I see Mordecai the Jew **s** at 3427
Isa 6: 1 died I saw also the Lord **s** upon a throne, 3427
Jer 17:25 and princes **s** upon the throne of David, 3427
22: 4 house kings **s** upon the throne of David, 3427
22:30 **s** upon the throne of David, and ruling any 3427
38: 7 the king then **s** in the gate of Benjamin; 3427
La 3:63 Behold their **s down**, and their rising up; 3427
Mt 9: 9 named Matthew, **s** at the receipt of custom: *2521*
11:16 It is like unto children **s** in the markets, and *2521*
20:30 two blind men **s** by the way side, *2521*
21: 5 and **s** upon an ass, and a colt the foal of an *1910*
26:64 Hereafter shall ye see the Son of man **s** on *2521*
27:36 And **s down** they watched him there; *2521*
27:61 other Mary, **s** over against the sepulchre. *2521*
Mk 2: 6 But there were certain of the scribes **s** there, *2521*
2:14 he saw Levi the *son* of Alpheus **s** at *2521*
5:15 **s**, and clothed, and in his right mind: *2521*
14:62 ye shall see the Son of man **s** on the right *2521*
16: 5 they saw a young man **s** on the right side, *2521*
Lk 2:46 **s** in the midst of the doctors, both hearing *2516*
5:17 doctors of the law **s** *by,* which were come *2521*
5:27 named Levi, **s** at the receipt of custom: *2521*
7:32 They are like unto children **s** in *2521*
8:35 **s** at the feet of Jesus, clothed, and in his *2521*
10:13 ago repented, **s** in sackcloth and ashes. *2521*
Jn 2:14 and doves, and the changers of money **s**: *2521*
12:15 behold, thy King cometh, **s** on an ass's colt. *2521*
20:12 And seeth two angels in white **s**, the one at *2516*
Ac 2: 2 it filled all the house where they were **s**. *2521*
8:28 and **s** in his chariot read Esaias the prophet. *2521*
25: 6 and the next day **s** in the judgment seat, *2523*
Rev 4: 4 the seats I saw four and twenty elders **s**, *2521*

SITUATE (3) [SITUATION]

1Sa 14: 5 The forefront of the one *was* **s** northward 4690

Eze 27: 3 O thou that art s at the entry of the sea, 3427
Na 3: 8 populous No, that was s among the rivers, 3427

SITUATION (2) [SITUATE]

2Ki 2:19 I pray thee, the s of *this* city *is* pleasant, 4186
Ps 48: 2 Beautiful for s, the joy of the whole earth, 5131

SIVAN (1)

Est 8: 9 that *is,* the month S, on the three and 5510

SIX (202) [SIXSCORE, SIXTH]

Ge 7: 6 Noah *was* s hundred years old when 8337
7:11 In the s hundredth year of Noah's life, 8337
8:13 it came to pass in the s hundredth and 8337
16:16 Abram *was* fourscore and s years old, 8337
30:20 with me, because I have born him s sons: 8337
31:41 two daughters, and s years for thy cattle: 8337
46:26 all the souls *were* threescore and s; 8337
Ex 12:37 about s hundred thousand on foot *that were* 8337
14: 7 And he took s hundred chosen chariots, and 8337
16:26 S days ye shall gather it; but on the seventh 8337
20: 9 S days shalt thou labour, and do all thy 8337
20:11 For *in* s days the LORD made heaven and 8337
21: 2 a Hebrew servant, s years he shall serve: 8337
23:10 s years thou shalt sow thy land, and 8337
23:12 S days thou shalt do thy work, and on 8337
24:16 and the cloud covered it s days: 8337
25:32 s branches shall come out of the sides of it; 8337
25:33 in the s branches that come out of 8337
25:35 according to the s branches that proceed out 8337
26: 9 s curtains by themselves, and shalt double 8337
26:22 westward thou shalt make s boards. 8337
28:10 S of their names on one stone, and the *other* 8337
28:10 the *other* s names of the rest on the other 8337
31:15 S days may work be done; but in 8337
31:17 for *in* s days the LORD made heaven and 8337
34:21 S days thou shalt work, but on the seventh 8337
35: 2 S days shall work be done, but on 8337
36:16 and s curtains by themselves. 8337
36:27 the tabernacle westward he made s boards. 8337
37:18 s branches going out of the sides thereof; 8337
37:19 throughout the s branches going out of 8337
37:21 according to the s branches going out of it. 8337
38:26 for s hundred thousand and three thousand 8337
Lev 12: 5 of her purifying threescore and s days. 8337
23: 3 S days shall work be done: but the seventh 8337
24: 6 thou shalt set them *in* two rows, s on a row, 8337
25: 3 S years thou shalt sow thy field, and 8337
25: 3 s years thou shalt prune thy vineyard, and 8337
Nu 1:21 *were* forty and s thousand and 8337
1:25 and five thousand s hundred and fifty. 8337
1:27 and fourteen thousand and s hundred. 8337
1:46 Even all they that were numbered were s 8337
2: 4 and fourteen thousand and s hundred. 8337
2: 9 and s thousand and four hundred, 8337
2:11 *were* forty and s thousand and 8337
2:15 and five thousand and s hundred and fifty. 8337
2:31 fifty and seven thousand and s hundred. 8337
2:32 their hosts *were* s hundred thousand 8337
3:28 *were* eight thousand and s hundred, 8337
3:34 upward, *were* s thousand and two hundred. 8337
4:40 two thousand and s hundred and thirty. 8337
7: 3 s covered wagons, and twelve oxen; 8337
11:21 amongst whom I *am, are* s hundred 8337
26:41 and five thousand and s hundred. 8337
26:51 s hundred thousand and a thousand seven 8337
31:32 was s hundred thousand and 8337
31:37 the LORD'S tribute of the sheep was s 8337
31:38 the beeves *were* thirty and s thousand; of 8337
31:44 And thirty and s thousand beeves, 8337
35: 6 the Levites *there shall be* s cities for refuge, 8337
35:13 *of these* cities which ye shall give s cities 8337
35:15 These s cities shall be a refuge, *both* for 8337
Dt 5:13 S days thou shalt labour, and do all thy 8337
15:12 be sold unto thee, and serve thee s years; 8337
15:18 servant *to thee,* in serving thee s years: 8337
16: 8 S days thou shalt eat unleavened bread: and 8337
Jos 6: 3 the city once. Thus shalt thou do s days. 8337
6:14 returned *into* the camp: so they did s days. 8337
7: 5 of Ai smote of them about thirty and s men: 8337
15:59 and Eltekon; s cities with their villages. 8337
15:62 and En-gedi; s cities with their villages. 8337
Jdg 3:31 which slew *of* the Philistines s hundred 8337
12: 7 Jephthah judged Israel s years. Then died 8337
18:11 s hundred men appointed *with* weapons of 8337
18:16 the s hundred men appointed *with* their 8337
18:17 s hundred men that were appointed *with* 8337
20:15 and s thousand men that drew sword, 8337
20:47 s hundred men turned and fled to 8337
Ru 3:15 he measured s *measures* of barley, and 8337
3:17 These s *measures* of barley gave he me; 8337
1Sa 13: 5 s thousand horsemen, and people as 8337
13:15 present with him, about s hundred men. 8337
14: 2 the people that *were* with him *were* about s 8337
17: 4 whose height *was* s cubits and a span. 8337
17: 7 his spear's head *weighed* s hundred shekels 8337
23:13 *which were* about s hundred, arose and 8337
27: 2 he passed over with the s hundred men that 8337
30: 9 and the s hundred men that *were* with him, 8337
2Sa 2:11 of Judah was seven years and s months. 8337
5: 5 over Judah seven years and s months: 8337
6:13 the ark of the LORD had gone s paces, 8337
15:18 s hundred men which came after him from 8337
21:20 that had on every hand s fingers, and 8337
21:20 on every foot s toes, four and twenty *in* 8337
1Ki 6: 6 the middle *was* s cubits broad, and the third 8337
10:14 in one year was s hundred threescore 8337
10:14 hundred threescore and s talents of gold, 8337
10:16 s hundred *shekels* of gold went to one 8337
10:19 The throne had s steps, and the top of 8337
10:20 one side and on the other upon the s steps: 8337
10:29 went out of Egypt for s hundred *shekels* of 8337
11:16 (For s months did Joab remain there with 8337
16:23 twelve years: s years reigned he in Tirzah. 8337
2Ki 5: 5 s thousand *pieces* of gold, and ten changes 8337
11: 3 her hid *in* the house of the LORD s years. 8337
13:19 shouldest have smitten five or s times; 8337
15: 8 reign over Israel in Samaria s months. 8337
1Ch 3: 4 *These* s were born unto him in Hebron; and 8337
3: 4 there he reigned seven years and s months: 8337
3:22 and Bariah, and Neariah, and Shaphat, s. 8337
4:27 Shimei had sixteen sons and s daughters; 8337
7: 2 and twenty thousand and s hundred. 8337
7: 4 s and thirty thousand *men:* for they had 8337
7:40 to battle *was* twenty and s thousand men. 8337
8:38 Azel had s sons, whose names *are* these, 8337
9: 6 and their brethren, s hundred and ninety. 8337
9: 9 nine hundred and fifty and s. 8337
9:44 Azel had s sons, whose names *are* these, 8337
12:24 spear *were* s thousand and eight hundred, 8337
12:26 of Levi four thousand and s hundred. 8337
12:35 and eight thousand and s hundred. 8337
20: 6 s *on each hand,* and six *on each foot:* and 8337
20: 6 six *on each hand,* and s *on each foot:* and 8337
21:25 So David gave to Ornan for the place s 8337
23: 4 and s thousand *were* officers and judges: 8337
25: 3 and Jeshaiah, Hashabiah, and Mattithiah, s, 8337
26:17 Eastward *were* s Levites, northward four a 8337
2Ch 1:17 brought forth out of Egypt a chariot for s 8337
2: 2 and s hundred to oversee them. 8337
2:17 and three thousand and s hundred. 8337
2:18 s hundred overseers to set the people a 8337
3: 8 fine gold, *amounting* to s hundred talents. 8337
9:13 to Solomon in one year was s hundred 8337
9:13 and threescore and s talents of gold; 8337
9:15 s hundred *shekels* of beaten gold went to 8337
9:18 *there were* s steps to the throne, with a 8337
9:19 one side and on the other upon the s steps. 8337
16: 1 In the s and thirtieth year of the reign of 8337
22:12 he was with them hid in the house of God s 8337
26:12 of valour *were* two thousand and s hundred. 8337
29:33 the consecrated *things were* s hundred oxen 8337
35: 8 s hundred *small cattle,* and three hundred 8337
Ezr 2:10 children of Bani, s hundred forty and two. 8337
2:11 of Bebai, s hundred twenty and three. 8337
2:13 of Adonikam, s hundred sixty and six. 8337
2:13 of Adonikam, six hundred sixty and s. 8337
2:14 of Bigvai, two thousand fifty and s. 8337
2:22 The men of Netophah, fifty and s. 8337
2:26 and Gaba, s hundred twenty and one. 8337
2:30 of Magbish, an hundred fifty and s. 8337
2:35 three thousand and s hundred and thirty. 8337
2:60 of Nekoda, s hundred fifty and two. 8337
2:66 horses *were* seven hundred thirty and s; 8337
2:67 s thousand seven hundred and twenty. 8337
8:26 I even weighed unto their hand s hundred 8337
8:35 ninety and s rams, seventy and 8337
Ne 5:18 *me* daily *was* one ox *and* s choice sheep; 8337

S

Ne 7:10 children of Arah, **s** hundred fifty and two. 8337
7:15 of Binnui, **s** hundred forty and eight. 8337
7:16 of Bebai, **s** hundred twenty and eight. 8337
7:18 **s** hundred threescore and seven. 8337
7:20 children of Adin, **s** hundred fifty and five. 8337
7:30 and Geba, **s** hundred twenty and one. 8337
7:62 of Nekoda, **s** hundred forty and two. 8337
7:68 Their horses, seven hundred thirty and **s**: 8337
7:69 **s** thousand seven hundred and twenty asses. 8337
Est 2:12 *to wit,* **s** months with oil of myrrh, and 8337
2:12 **s** months with sweet odours, and with *other* 8337
Job 5:19 He shall deliver thee in **s** troubles: yea, 8337
42:12 **s** thousand camels, and a thousand yoke of 8337
Pr 6:16 These **s** *things* doth the LORD hate: yea, 8337
Isa 6: 2 each one had **s** wings; with twain he 8337
Jer 34:14 when he hath served thee **s** years, thou shalt 8337
52:23 were ninety and **s** pomegranates on a side; 8337
52:30 persons *were* four thousand and **s** hundred. 8337
Eze 9: 2 **s** men came from the way of the higher 8337
40: 5 in the man's hand a measuring reed of **s** 8337
40:12 the little chambers *were* **s** cubits on this 8337
40:12 cubits on this side, and **s** cubits on that side. 8337
41: 1 **s** cubits broad on the one side, and 8337
41: 1 and **s** cubits broad on the other side, 8337
41: 3 the door, **s** cubits; and the breadth of 8337
41: 5 he measured the wall of the house, **s** cubits; 8337
41: 8 chambers *were* a full reed of **s** great cubits. 8337
46: 1 the east shall be shut the **s** working days; 8337
46: 4 day *shall be* **s** lambs without blemish, 8337
46: 6 without blemish, and **s** lambs, and a ram: 8337
Da 3: 1 *and* the breadth thereof **s** cubits: 8353
Mt 17: 1 And after **s** days Jesus taketh Peter, James, *1803*
Mk 9: 2 And after **s** days Jesus taketh with *him* *1803*
Lk 4:25 was shut up three years and **s** months, *1803*
13:14 There are **s** days in which *men* ought to *1803*
Jn 2: 6 And there were set there **s** waterpots of *1803*
2:20 and **s** years was this temple in building, *1803*
12: 1 Then Jesus **s** days before the passover came *1803*
Ac 11:12 Moreover these **s** brethren accompanied *1803*
18:11 he continued *there* a year and **s** months, *1803*
Jas 5:17 *by the space of* three years and **s** months. *1803*
Rev 4: 8 And the four beasts had each of them **s** *1803*
13:18 number *is* **S hundred threescore** *and* **six**. *5516*
13:18 number *is* **Six hundred threescore** *and* **s**. *5516*
14:20 of a thousand *and* **s hundred** furlongs. *1812*

SIXSCORE (2) [SIX]
1Ki 9:14 Hiram sent to the king **s** 3967+6242+2050.1
Jnh 4:11 wherein are more than **s** thousand 6240+8147

SIXTEEN (23) [SIXTEENTH]
Ge 46:18 she bare unto Jacob, *even* **s** souls. 6240+8337
Ex 26:25 and their sockets *of* silver, **s** sockets; 6240+8337
36:30 their sockets *were* **s** sockets *of* silver, 6240+8337
Nu 26:22 **threescore and s** thousand 7657+8337+2050.1
31:40 the persons *were* **s** thousand; of 6240+8337
31:46 And **s** thousand persons;) 6240+8337
31:52 was **s** thousand seven hundred and 6240+8337
Jos 15:41 **s** cities with their villages. 6240+8337
19:22 *at* Jordan: **s** cities with their villages. 6240+8337
2Ki 13:10 in Samaria, *and reigned* **s** years. 6240+8337
14:21 which *was* **s** years old, and made him 6240+8337
15: 2 **S** years old was he when he *began* to 6240+8337
15:33 and he reigned **s** years in Jerusalem. 6240+8337
16: 2 reigned **s** years in Jerusalem, and 6240+8337
1Ch 4:27 Shimei had **s** sons and six daughters; 6240+8337
24: 4 **s** chief *men* of the house of *their* 6240+8337
2Ch 13:21 and two sons, and **s** daughters. 6240+8337
26: 1 who *was* **s** years old, and made him 6240+8337
26: 3 **S** years old *was* Uzziah when he 6240+8337
27: 1 and he reigned **s** years in Jerusalem. 6240+8337
27: 8 and reigned **s** years in Jerusalem. 6240+8337
28: 1 and he reigned **s** years in Jerusalem: 6240+8337
Ac 27:37 ship two hundred **threescore** *and* **s** *1440+1803*

SIXTEENTH (3) [SIXTEEN]
1Ch 24:14 fifteenth to Bilgah, the **s** to Immer, 6240+8337
25:23 The **s** to Hananiah, *he,* his sons, and 6240+8337
2Ch 29:17 in the **s** day of the first month they 6240+8337

SIXTH (47) [SIX]
Ge 1:31 and the morning were the **s** day. 8345
30:19 conceived again, and bare Jacob the **s** son. 8345
Ex 16: 5 that on the **s** day they shall prepare *that* 8345
16:22 *that* on the **s** day they gathered twice as 8345
16:29 he giveth you on the **s** day the bread of two 8345
26: 9 shalt double the **s** curtain in the forefront of 8345
Lev 25:21 my blessing upon you in the **s** year, 8345
Nu 7:42 On the **s** day Eliasaph the son of Deuel, 8345
29:29 on the **s** day eight bullocks, two rams, *and* 8345
Jos 19:32 The **s** lot came out to the children of 8345
2Sa 3: 5 the **s**, Ithream, by Eglah David's wife. 8345
1Ki 16: 8 **s** year of Asa king of Judah *began* Elah 8337
2Ki 18:10 *even* in the **s** year of Hezekiah, that *is* 8337
1Ch 2:15 Ozem the **s**, David the seventh: 8345
3: 3 of Abital: the **s**, Ithream by Eglah his wife. 8345
12:11 Attai the **s**, Eliel the seventh, 8345
24: 9 The fifth to Malchijah, the **s** to Mijamin, 8345
25:13 The **s** *to* Bukkiah, *he,* his sons, and 8345
26: 3 Elam the fifth, Jehohanan the **s**, 8345
26: 5 Ammiel the **s**, Issachar the seventh, 8345
27: 9 The **s** *captain* for the sixth month *was* Ira 8345
27: 9 The sixth *captain* for the **s** month *was* Ira 8345
Ezr 6:15 which *was in* the **s** year of the reign of 8353
Ne 3:30 Hanun the **s** son of Zalaph, another piece. 8345
Eze 4:11 also water by measure, the **s** *part* of a hin: 8345
8: 1 it came to pass in the **s** year, in the sixth 8345
8: 1 in the **s** *month,* in the fifth *day* of 8345
39: 2 **leave** but **the s part** of thee, and will cause 8338
45:13 the **s** *part* of an ephah of a homer of wheat, 8345
45:13 ye shall **give the s part** of an ephah of a 8341
46:14 the **s** *part* of an ephah, and the third *part* of 8345
Hag 1: 1 in the **s** month, in the first day of 8345
1:15 the four and twentieth day of the **s** month, 8345
Mt 20: 5 Again he went out about the **s** and *1623*
27:45 Now from the **s** hour there was darkness *1623*
Mk 15:33 And when the **s** hour was come, there was *1623*
Lk 1:26 And in the **s** month the angel Gabriel was *1623*
1:36 and this is the **s** month with her, who was *1623*
23:44 And it was about the **s** hour, and there was *1623*
Jn 4: 6 on the well: *and* it was about the **s** hour. *1623*
19:14 of the passover, and about the **s** hour: *1623*
Ac 10: 9 up upon the house to pray about the **s** hour: *1623*
Rev 6:12 And I beheld when he had opened the **s** *1623*
9:13 And the **s** angel sounded, and I heard a *1623*
9:14 Saying to the **s** angel which had *1623*
16:12 And the **s** angel poured out his vial upon *1623*
21:20 The fifth, sardonyx; the **s**, sardius; *1623*

SIXTY (15) [SIXTYFOLD, THREESCORE]
Ge 5:15 Mahalaleel lived **s** and five years, and 8346
5:18 Jared lived an hundred **s** and two years, 8346
5:20 all the days of Jared were nine hundred **s** 8346
5:21 Enoch lived **s** and five years, and 8346
5:23 all the days of Enoch were three hundred **s** 8346
5:27 days of Methuselah were nine hundred **s** 8346
Lev 27: 3 twenty years old even unto **s** years old, 8346
27: 7 if *it be* from **s** years old and above; if *it be* a 8346
Nu 7:88 *were* twenty and four bullocks, the rams **s**, 8346
7:88 four bullocks, the rams sixty, the he goats **s**, 8346
7:88 he goats sixty, the lambs of the first year **s**. 8346
Ezr 2:13 of Adonikam, six hundred **s** and six. 8346
Mt 13:23 some an hundred*fold,* some **s**, some thirty. *1835*
Mk 4: 8 and some **s**, and some an hundred. *1835*
4:20 some thirty*fold,* some **s**, and some an *1835*

SIXTYFOLD (1) [SIXTY]
Mt 13: 8 some an hundred*fold,* some **s**, some *1835*

SIZE (5)
Ex 36: 9 four cubits: the curtains *were* all of one **s**. 4060
36:15 the eleven curtains *were* of one **s**. 4060
1Ki 6:25 cherubims *were* of one measure and one **s**. 7095
7:37 had one casting, one measure, *and* one **s**. 7095
1Ch 23:29 and for all *manner of* measure and **s**; 4060

SKIES (5) [SKY]
2Sa 22:12 dark waters, *and* thick clouds of the **s**. 7834
Ps 18:11 *were* dark waters *and* thick clouds of the **s**. 7834
77:17 the **s** sent out a sound: thine arrows also 7834
Isa 45: 8 and let the **s** pour down righteousness: 7834
Jer 51: 9 unto heaven, and is lifted up *even* to the **s**. 7834

SKILFUL (7) [SKILL]
1Ch 5:18 **s** in war, *were* four and forty thousand 3925
15:22 instructed about the song, because he *was* **s**. 995
28:21 willing **s** *man,* for any *manner of* service: 2451
2Ch 2:14 **s** to work in gold, and in silver, in brass, 3045

Eze 21:31 the hand of brutish men, *and* **s** to destroy. 2796
Da 1: 4 **s** in all wisdom, and cunning in knowledge, 7919
Am 5:16 and such as are **s** of lamentation to wailing. 3045

SKILFULLY (1) [SKILL]
Ps 33: 3 him a new song; play **s** with a loud noise. 3190

SKILFULNESS (1) [SKILL]
Ps 78:72 and guided them by the **s** of his hands. 8394

SKILL (7) [SKILFUL, SKILFULLY, SKILFULNESS, UNSKILFUL]
1Ki 5: 6 **can s** to hew timber like unto 3045
2Ch 2: 7 that can **s** to grave with the cunning *men* 3045
2: 8 for I know that thy servants can **s** to cut 3045
34:12 all that could **s** of instruments of musick. 995
Ecc 9:11 nor yet favour to men of **s**; 3045
Da 1:17 and **s** in all learning and wisdom: 7919
9:22 I am now come forth to **give** thee **s** and 7919

SKIN (77) [FORESKIN, FORESKINS, GOATSKINS, SHEEPSKINS, SKINS]
Ex 22:27 his covering only, it *is* his raiment for his **s**: 5785
29:14 of the bullock, and his **s**, and his dung, 5785
34:29 that Moses wist not that the **s** of his face 5785
34:30 saw Moses, behold, the **s** of his face shone; 5785
34:35 of Moses, that the **s** of Moses' face shone: 5785
Lev 4:11 the **s** of the bullock, and all his flesh, 5785
7: 8 *even* the priest shall have to himself the **s** of 5785
11:32 vessel of wood, or raiment, or **s**, or sack, 5785
13: 2 When a man shall have in the **s** of his flesh 5785
13: 2 it be in the **s** of his flesh like the plague of 5785
13: 3 the priest shall look on the plague in the **s** 5785
13: 3 the plague in sight *be* deeper than the **s** of 5785
13: 4 If the bright spot *be* white in the **s** of his 5785
13: 4 in sight *be* not deeper than the **s**, and 5785
13: 5 at a stay, *and* the plague spread not in the **s**; 5785
13: 6 and the plague spread not in the **s**, 5785
13: 7 But if the scab spread much abroad in the **s**, 5785
13: 8 the scab spreadeth in the **s**, then the priest 5785
13:10 *if* the rising *be* white in the **s**, and it have 5785
13:11 It *is* an old leprosy in the **s** of his flesh, and 5785
13:12 if a leprosy break out abroad in the **s**, and 5785
13:12 the leprosy cover all the **s** of *him that hath* 5785
13:18 in which, *even* in the **s** thereof, was a boil, 5785
13:20 it *be* in sight lower than the **s**, and the hair 5785
13:21 *if* it *be* not lower than the **s**, but *be* 5785
13:22 if it spread much abroad in the **s**, then 5785
13:24 in the **s** whereof *there is* a hot burning, and 5785
13:25 and it *be* in sight deeper than the **s**; 5785
13:26 it *be* no lower than the *other* **s**, but *be* 5785
13:27 *and* if it be spread much abroad in the **s**, 5785
13:28 *and* spread not in the **s**, but it *be* somewhat 5785
13:30 behold, *if* it *be* in sight deeper than the **s**; 5785
13:31 it *be* not in sight deeper than the **s**, and 5785
13:32 the scall *be* not in sight deeper than the **s**; 5785
13:34 behold, *if* the scall be not spread in the **s**, 5785
13:34 the skin, nor *be* in sight deeper than the **s**; 5785
13:35 if the scall spread much in the **s** after his 5785
13:36 behold, *if* the scall be spread in the **s**, 5785
13:38 a woman have in the **s** of their flesh bright 5785
13:39 *if* the bright spots in the **s** of their flesh *be* 5785
13:39 it *is* a freckled spot *that* groweth in the **s**: 5785
13:43 as the leprosy appeareth in the **s** of 5785
13:48 whether in a **s**, or in any thing made of 5785
13:48 in a skin, or in any thing made of **s**; 5785
13:49 or in the **s**, either in the warp, or in 5785
13:49 or in the woof, or in any thing of **s**; 5785
13:51 or in a **s**, *or* in any work that is made of 5785
13:51 in a skin, *or* in any work that is made of **s**; 5785
13:52 in woollen or in linen, or any thing of **s**, 5785
13:53 or in the woof, or in any thing of **s**; 5785
13:56 or out of the **s**, or out of the warp, or out of 5785
13:57 or in the woof, or in any thing of **s**; 5785
13:58 whatsoever thing of **s** *it be*, which thou 5785
15:17 every garment, and every **s**, whereon is 5785
Nu 19: 5 her **s**, and her flesh, and her blood, with her 5785
Job 2: 4 the LORD, and said, **S** for skin, yea, 5785
2: 4 the LORD, and said, Skin for **s**, yea, 5785
7: 5 my **s** is broken, and become loathsome. 5785
10:11 Thou hast clothed me with **s** and flesh, and 5785
16:15 I have sewed sackcloth upon my **s**, and 1539
18:13 It shall devour the strength of his **s**: 5785
19:20 My bone cleaveth to my **s** and to my flesh, 5785
19:20 and I am escaped with the **s** of my teeth. 5785
19:26 *though* after my **s** *worms* destroy this *body*, 5785
30:30 My **s** is black upon me, and my bones are 5785
41: 7 Canst thou fill his **s** with barbed irons? or 5785
Ps 102: 5 of my groaning my bones cleave to my **s**. 1320
Jer 13:23 Can the Ethiopian change his **s**, or 5785
La 3: 4 My flesh and my **s** hath he made old; 5785
4: 8 their **s** cleaveth to their bones; it is 5785
5:10 Our **s** was black like an oven because of 5785
Eze 16:10 shod thee *with* badgers' **s**, and I girded thee NIH
37: 6 and cover you with **s**, and put breath in you, 5785
37: 8 upon them, and the **s** covered them above: 5785
Mic 3: 2 who pluck off their **s** from off them, and 5785
3: 3 my people, and flay their **s** from off them; 5785
Mk 1: 6 and with a girdle of a **s** about his loins; *1193*

SKINK See SNAIL

SKINS (24) [SKIN]
Ge 3:21 wife did the LORD God make coats of **s**, 5785
27:16 she put the **s** of the kids of the goats upon 5785
Ex 25: 5 rams' **s** dyed red, and badgers' skins, and 5785
25: 5 dyed red, and badgers' **s**, and shittim wood, 5785
26:14 a covering for the tent *of* rams' **s** dyed red, 5785
26:14 and a covering above of badgers' **s**. 5785
35: 7 rams' **s** dyed red, and badgers' skins, and 5785
35: 7 dyed red, and badgers' **s**, and shittim wood, 5785
35:23 goats' *hair*, and red **s** of rams, and 5785
35:23 of rams, and badgers' **s**, brought *them*. 5785
36:19 he made a covering for the tent *of* rams' **s** 5785
36:19 and a covering of badgers' **s** above *that*. 5785
39:34 the covering of rams' **s** dyed red, and 5785
39:34 the covering of badgers' **s**, and the vail of 5785
Lev 13:59 *in* the warp, or woof, or any thing of **s**, 5785
16:27 they shall burn in the fire their **s**, and their 5785
Nu 4: 6 shall put thereon the covering of badgers' **s**, 5785
4: 8 the same with a covering of badgers' **s**, 5785
4:10 thereof within a covering of badgers' **s**, 5785
4:11 cover it with a covering of badgers' **s**, and 5785
4:12 cover them with a covering of badgers' **s**, 5785
4:14 spread upon it a covering of badgers' **s**, 5785
4:25 the covering of the **badgers' s** that *is* above 8476
31:20 all that is made of **s**, and all work of goats' 5785

SKIP (1) [SKIPPED, SKIPPEDST, SKIPPING]
Ps 29: 6 He **maketh** them also **to s** like a calf; 7540

SKIPPED (2) [SKIP]
Ps 114: 4 The mountains **s** like rams, *and* the little 7540
114: 6 Ye mountains, *that* ye **s** like rams; *and* 7540

SKIPPEDST (1) [SKIP]
Jer 48:27 since thou spakest of him, thou **s for joy**. 5110

SKIPPING (1) [SKIP]
SS 2: 8 upon the mountains, **s** upon the hills. 7092

SKIRT (12) [SKIRTS]
Dt 22:30 his father's wife, nor discover his father's **s**. 3671
27:20 because he uncovereth his father's **s**. 3671
Ru 3: 9 spread therefore thy **s** over thine handmaid; 3671
1Sa 15:27 he laid hold upon the **s** of his mantle, and 3671
24: 4 and cut off the **s** of Saul's robe privily. 3671
24: 5 smote him, because he had cut off Saul's **s**. 3671
24:11 see, yea see the **s** of thy robe in my hand: 3671
24:11 for in that I cut off the **s** of thy robe, and 3671
Eze 16: 8 I spread my **s** over thee, and covered thy 3671
Hag 2:12 If one bear holy flesh in the **s** of his 3671
2:12 and with his **s** do touch bread, or pottage, or 3671
Zec 8:23 even shall take hold of the **s** of him that is a 3671

SKIRTS (7) [SKIRT]
Ps 133: 2 that went down to the **s** of his garments; 6310
Jer 2:34 Also in thy **s** is found the blood of the souls 3671
13:22 For the greatness of thine iniquity are thy **s** 7757
13:26 Therefore will I discover thy **s** upon thy 7757
La 1: 9 Her filthiness *is* in her **s**; she remembereth 7757
Eze 5: 3 a few in number, and bind them in thy **s**. 3671
Na 3: 5 I will discover thy **s** upon thy face, and 7757

SKULL (5)
Jdg 9:53 Abimelech's head, and all to brake his **s**. 1538
2Ki 9:35 they found no more of her than the **s**, and 1538
Mt 27:33 that is to say, a place of a **s**, *2898*
Mk 15:22 being interpreted, The place of a **s**. *2898*
Jn 19:17 forth into a place called *the place* of a **s**, *2898*

S

SKY (7) [SKIES]
Dt 33:26 in thy help, and in his excellency *on* the **s**. 7834
Job 37:18 Hast thou with him spread out the **s**, 7834
Mt 16: 2 *It will be* fair weather: for the **s** is red. *3772*
16: 3 for the **s** is red and lowring. O *ye* *3772*
16: 3 ye can discern the face of the **s**; *3772*
Lk 12:56 ye can discern the face of the **s** and of *3772*
Heb 11:12 *so many* as the stars of the **s** in multitude, *3772*

SLACK (8) [SLACKED, SLACKNESS]
Dt 7:10 he will not be **s** to him that hateth him, 309
23:21 LORD thy God, thou shalt not **s** to pay it: 309
Jos 10: 6 **S** not thy hand from thy servants; 7503
18: 3 How long *are* you **s** to go to possess 7503
2Ki 4:24 and go *forward;* **s** not *thy* riding for me, 6113
Pr 10: 4 *He becometh* poor that dealeth *with* a **s** 7423
Zep 3:16 *and to* Zion, Let not thine hands be **s**. 7503
2Pe 3: 9 The Lord is not **s** concerning *his* promise, *1019*

SLACKED (1) [SLACK]
Hab 1: 4 Therefore the law is **s**, and judgment doth 6313

SLACKNESS (1) [SLACK]
2Pe 3: 9 *his* promise, as some *men* count **s**; *1022*

SLAIN (183) [SLAY]
Ge 4:23 for I have **s** a man to my wounding, and 2026
34:27 The sons of Jacob came upon the **s**, and 2491
Lev 14:51 dip them in the blood of the **s** bird, and 7819
26:17 and ye shall be **s** before your enemies; 5062
Nu 11:22 Shall the flocks and the herds be **s** for them, 7819
14:16 therefore he hath **s** them in the wilderness. 7819
19:16 whosoever toucheth one **that is s** with a 2491
19:18 a bone, or one **s**, or one dead, or a grave: 2491
22:33 surely now also I had **s** thee, and saved her 2026
23:24 eat *of* the prey, and drink the blood of the **s**. 2491
25:14 Now the name of the Israelite that was **s**, 5221
25:14 *even* that was **s** with the Midianitish 5221
25:15 Midianitish woman that was **s** *was* Cozbi, 5221
25:18 which was **s** in the day of the plague for 5221
31: 8 beside *the rest of* them **that were s**; 2491
31:19 whosoever hath touched *any* **s**, purify *both* 2491
Dt 1: 4 After he had **s** Sihon the king of 5221
21: 1 If *one* be found **s** in the land which 2491
21: 1 *and* it be not known who hath **s** him: 5221
21: 2 cities which *are* round about him that is **s**: 2491
21: 3 *that* the city *which is* next unto the **s** *man*, 2491
21: 6 *that are* next unto the **s** *man*, shall wash 2491
28:31 Thine ox *shall be* **s** before thine eyes, and 2873
32:42 *and that* with the blood of the **s** and of 2491
Jos 11: 6 will I deliver them up all **s** before Israel: 2491
13:22 the sword among them that were **s** by them. 2491
Jdg 9:18 have **s** his sons, threescore and ten persons, 2026
15:16 with the jaw of an ass have I **s** a thousand 5221
20: 4 the husband of the woman that was **s**, 7523
20: 5 me by night, *and* thought to have **s** me: 2026
1Sa 4:11 sons of Eli, Hophni and Phinehas, were **s**. 4191
18: 7 Saul hath **s** his thousands, and David his ten 5221
19: 6 *As* the LORD liveth, he shall not be **s**. 4191
19:11 thy life to night, to morrow thou *shalt be* **s**. 4191
20:32 and said unto him, Wherefore shall he be **s**? 4191
21:11 Saul hath **s** his thousands, and David his ten 5221
22:21 Abiathar shewed David that Saul had **s** 2026
31: 1 and fell down **s** in mount Gilboa. 2491
31: 8 when the Philistines came to strip the **s**, 2491
2Sa 1:16 I have **s** the LORD's anointed. 4191
1:19 The beauty of Israel *is* **s** upon thy high 2491
1:22 From the blood of the **s**, from the fat of 2491
1:25 *thou wast* **s** in thine high places. 2491
3:30 he had **s** their brother Asahel at Gibeon in 4191
4:11 when wicked men have **s** a righteous 2026
12: 9 hast **s** him with the sword of the children of 2026
13:30 Absalom hath **s** all the king's sons, and 5221
13:32 Let not my lord suppose *that* they have **s** all 4191
18: 7 Where the people of Israel were **s** before 5062
21:12 when the Philistines had **s** Saul in Gilboa: 5221
21:16 *with* a new *sword*, thought to have **s** David. 5221
1Ki 1:19 he hath **s** oxen and fat cattle and sheep in 2076
1:25 hath **s** oxen and fat cattle and sheep in 2076
9:16 **s** the Canaanites that dwelt in the city, and 2026
11:15 of the host was gone up to bury the **s**, 2491
13:26 which hath torn him, and **s** him, 4191
16:16 hath conspired, and hath also **s** the king: 5221
19: 1 withal how he had **s** all the prophets with 2026
19:10 and **s** thy prophets with the sword; 2026
19:14 and **s** thy prophets with the sword; 2026
2Ki 3:23 the kings are **surely s**, and they have 2717+2717
11: 2 from among the king's sons which were **s**; 4191
11: 2 from Athaliah, so that he was not **s**. 4191
11: 8 that cometh within the ranges, let him be **s**: 4191
11:15 Let her not be **s** *in* the house of the LORD. 4191
11:16 *into* the king's house: and there was she **s**. 4191
14: 5 that he slew his servants which had **s** 5221
1Ch 5:22 For there fell down many **s**, because 2491
10: 1 and fell down **s** in mount Gilboa. 2491
10: 8 when the Philistines came to strip the **s**, 2491
11:11 he lift up his spear against three hundred **s** 2491
2Ch 13:17 there fell down **s** of Israel five hundred 2491
21:13 also hast **s** thy brethren of thy father's 2026
22: 1 Arabians to the camp had **s** all the eldest. 2026
22: 9 when they had **s** him, they buried him: 4191
22:11 from among the king's sons that were **s**, 4191
23:14 followeth her, let him be **s** with the sword. 4191
23:21 after that they had **s** Athaliah with 4191
28: 9 ye have **s** them in a rage *that* reacheth up 2026
Est 7: 4 to be destroyed, to be **s**, and to perish. 2026
9:11 On that day the number of those that were **s** 2026
9:12 The Jews have **s** and destroyed five 2026
Job 1:15 they have **s** the servants with the edge of 5221
1:17 **s** the servants with the edge of the sword; 5221
39:30 up blood: and where the **s** *are*, there *is* she. 2491
Ps 62: 3 ye shall be **s** all of you: as a bowing wall 7523
88: 5 the dead, like the **s** that lie in the grave, 2491
89:10 broken Rahab in pieces, as one that is **s**; 2491
Pr 7:26 yea, many strong *men have been* **s** by her. 2026
22:13 *is* a lion without, I shall be **s** in the streets. 7523
24:11 unto death, and *those that are* ready to be **s**; 2027
Isa 10: 4 and they shall fall under the **s**. 2026
14:19 *and as* the raiment of those that are **s**, 2026
14:20 hast destroyed thy land, *and* **s** thy people: 2026
22: 2 thy **s** *men are* not slain with the sword, nor 2491
22: 2 thy slain *men are* not **s** with the sword, nor 2491
26:21 her blood, and shall no more cover her **s**. 2026
27: 7 is he **s** according to the slaughter of them 2026
27: 7 to the slaughter of them that are **s** by him? 2026
34: 3 Their **s** also shall be cast out, and their stink 2491
66:16 and the **s** of the LORD shall be many. 2491
Jer 9: 1 night for the **s** of the daughter of my 2491
14:18 the field, then behold the **s** with the sword: 2491
18:21 *let* their young men *be* **s** by the sword in 5221
25:33 the **s** of the LORD shall be at that day 2491
33: 5 whom I have **s** in mine anger and in my 5221
41: 4 came to pass the second day after *he* had **s** 4191
41: 9 whom he had **s** because of Gedaliah, 5221
41: 9 of Nethaniah filled it *with them that were* **s**. 2491
41:16 after *that* he had **s** Gedaliah the son of 5221
41:18 Ishmael the son of Nethaniah had **s** 5221
51: 4 Thus the **s** shall fall in the land of 2491
51:47 and all her **s** shall fall in the midst of her. 2491
51:49 As Babylon *hath caused* the **s** of Israel to 2491
51:49 at Babylon shall fall the **s** of all the earth. 2491
La 2:20 the prophet be **s** in the sanctuary of 2026
2:21 thou hast **s** *them* in the day of thine anger; 2026
3:43 thou hast **s**, thou hast not pitied. 2026
4: 9 *They that be* **s** with the sword are better 2491
4: 9 are better than *they that be* **s** with hunger: 2491
Eze 6: 4 I will cast down your **s** *men* before your 2491
6: 7 the **s** shall fall in the midst of you, and 2491
6:13 when their **s** *men* shall be among their idols 2491
9: 7 the house, and fill the courts *with* the **s**: 2491
11: 6 Ye have multiplied your **s** in this city, 2491
11: 6 ye have filled the streets thereof *with* the **s**. 2491
11: 7 Your **s** whom ye have laid in the midst of 2491
16:21 That thou hast **s** my children, and 7819
21:14 doubled the third time, the sword of the **s**: 2491
21:14 it *is* the sword of the great *men that are* **s**, 2491
21:29 the necks of *them that are* **s** of the wicked, 2491
23:39 For when they had **s** their children to their 7819
26: 6 *are* in the field shall be **s** by the sword; 2026
28: 8 thou shalt die the deaths of *them that are* **s** 2491
30: 4 when the **s** shall fall in Egypt, and 2491
30:11 against Egypt, and fill the land *with* the **s**. 2491
31:17 him unto *them that be* **s** with the sword; 2491
31:18 with *them that be* **s** with the sword. 2491
32:20 the midst of *them that are* **s** by the sword: 2491
32:21 they lie uncircumcised, **s** by the sword. 2491
32:22 all of them **s**, fallen by the sword: 2491
32:23 all of them **s**, fallen by the sword, 2491

Eze 32:24 all of them **s**, fallen by the sword, 2491
32:25 in the midst of the **s** with all her multitude: 2491
32:25 all of them uncircumcised, **s** by the sword: 2491
32:25 he is put in the midst of *them that be* **s**. 2491
32:26 all of them uncircumcised, **s** by the sword, 2490
32:28 shalt lie with *them that are* **s** with 2491
32:29 are laid by *them that were* **s** by the sword: 2491
32:30 which are gone down with the **s**; 2491
32:30 they lie uncircumcised with *them that be* **s** 2491
32:31 and all his army **s** by the sword, 2491
32:32 with *them that are* **s** with the sword, 2491
35: 8 I will fill his mountains *with* his **s** *men:* in 2491
35: 8 shall they fall *that are* **s** with the sword. 2491
37: 9 O breath, and breathe upon these **s**, that 2026
Da 2:13 went forth that the wise *men* should be **s**; 6992
2:13 they sought Daniel and his fellows to be **s**. 6992
5:30 *was* Belshazzar the king of the Chaldeans **s**. 6992
7:11 I beheld *even* till the beast *was* **s**, and 6992
11:26 shall overflow: and many shall fall down **s**. 2491
Hos 6: 5 I have **s** them by the words of my mouth: 2026
Am 4:10 your young men have I **s** with the sword, 2026
Na 3: 3 *there is* a multitude of **s**, and a great 2491
Zep 2:12 Ethiopians also, ye *shall be* **s** by my sword. 2491
Lk 9:22 scribes, and be **s**, and be raised the third day. *615*
Ac 2:23 and by wicked hands have crucified and **s**: *337*
5:36 who was **s**; and all, as many as obeyed him, *337*
7:42 have ye offered to me **s beasts** and *4968*
7:52 they have **s** them which shewed before of *615*
13:28 *yet* desired they Pilate that he should be **s**. *337*
23:14 that *we* will eat nothing until we have **s** Paul. *615*
Eph 2:16 by the cross, having **s** the enmity thereby: *615*
Heb 11:37 were tempted, were **s** with the sword: *599+5408*
Rev 2:13 who was **s** among you, where Satan *615*
5: 6 stood a Lamb as *it had been* **s**, having seven *4969*
5: 9 for thou wast **s**, and hast redeemed us to *4969*
5:12 Worthy is the Lamb that was **s** to receive *4969*
6: 9 of them that were **s** for the word of God, *4969*
11:13 in the earthquake were **s** of men seven *615*
13: 8 Lamb **s** from the foundation of the world. *4969*
18:24 and of all that were **s** upon the earth. *4969*
19:21 And the remnant were **s** with the sword of *615*

SLANDER (3) [SLANDERED, SLANDERERS, SLANDEREST, SLANDERETH, SLANDEROUSLY, SLANDERS]
Nu 14:36 by bringing up a **s** upon the land, 1681
Ps 31:13 For I have heard the **s** of many: fear *was* on 1681
Pr 10:18 lying lips, and he that uttereth a **s**, *is* a fool. 1681

SLANDERED (1) [SLANDER]
2Sa 19:27 he hath **s** thy servant unto my lord the king; 7270

SLANDERERS (1) [SLANDER]
1Ti 3:11 *be* grave, not **s**, sober, faithful in all *things.* *1228*

SLANDEREST (1) [SLANDER]
Ps 50:20 thou **s** thine own mother's son. 1848+5414

SLANDERETH (1) [SLANDER]
Ps 101: 5 Whoso privily **s** his neighbour, him will I 3960

SLANDEROUSLY (1) [SLANDER]
Ro 3: 8 And not *rather,* (as we be **s reported**, and *987*

SLANDERS (2) [SLANDER]
Jer 6:28 *are* all grievous revolters, walking with **s**: 7400
9: 4 every neighbour will walk *with* **s**. 7400

SLANG (1)
1Sa 17:49 **s** *it,* and smote the Philistine in his 7049

SLAUGHTER (56)
Ge 14:17 after his return from the **s** of Chedorlaomer, 5221
Jos 10:10 and slew them *with* a great **s** at Gibeon, and 4347
10:20 an end of slaying them *with* a very great **s**, 4347
Jdg 11:33 plain of the vineyards, *with* a very great **s**. 4347
15: 8 he smote them hip and thigh *with* a great **s**: 4347
1Sa 4:10 there was a very great **s**; for there fell of 4347
4:17 there hath been also a great **s** among 4046
6:19 smitten *many* of the people *with* a great **s**. 4347
14:14 **s**, which Jonathan and his armourbearer **made**, 4347+5221
14:30 for had there not been now a much greater **s** 4347
17:57 as David returned from the **s** of 5221
18: 6 when David was returned from the **s** of 5221
19: 8 and slew them *with* a great **s**; 4347
23: 5 their cattle, and smote them *with* a great **s**. 4347
2Sa 1: 1 when David was returned from the **s** of 5221
17: 9 There is a **s** among the people that follow 4046
18: 7 there was there a great **s** that day *of* twenty 4046
1Ki 20:21 and slew the Syrians with a great **s**. 4347
2Ch 13:17 and his people slew them *with* a great **s**: 4347
25:14 after that Amaziah was come from the **s** of 5221
28: 5 of Israel, who smote him *with* a great **s**. 4347
Est 9: 5 **s**, and destruction, and did what they would 2027
Ps 44:22 day long; we are counted as sheep for the **s**. 2878
Pr 7:22 as an ox goeth to the **s**, or as a fool to 2874
Isa 10:26 to the **s** of Midian at the rock Oreb: 4347
14:21 Prepare **s** for his children for the iniquity of 4293
27: 7 is he slain according to the **s** of them that 2027
30:25 streams of waters in the day of the great **s**, 2027
34: 2 he hath delivered them to the **s**. 2874
34: 6 and a great **s** in the land of Idumea. 2874
53: 7 he is brought as a lamb to the **s**, and as a 2874
65:12 and ye shall all bow down to the **s**: 2874
Jer 7:32 of the son of Hinnom, but the valley of **s**: 2028
11:19 like a lamb *or* an ox *that* is brought to the **s**; 2873
12: 3 pull them out like sheep for the **s**, and 2878
12: 3 and prepare them for the day of **s**. 2028
19: 6 of the son of Hinnom, but The valley of **s**. 2028
25:34 for the days of your **s** and of your 2873
48:15 chosen young men are gone down to the **s**, 2874
50:27 all her bullocks; let them go down to the **s**: 2874
51:40 I will bring them down like lambs to the **s**, 2873
Eze 9: 2 and every man a **s** weapon in his hand; 4660
21:10 It is sharpened to make a **sore s**; *it is* 2873+2874
21:15 ah, *it is* made bright, *it is* wrapt up for the **s**. 2874
21:22 to open the mouth in the **s**, 7524
21:28 for the **s** *it is* furbished, to consume because 2874
26:15 the **s** is **made** in the midst of thee? 2026+2027
Hos 5: 2 the revolters are profound to make **s**, 7819
Ob 1: 9 of the mount of Esau may be cut off by **s**. 6993
Zec 11: 4 LORD my God; Feed the flock of the **s**; 2028
11: 7 I will feed the flock of **s**, *even* you, O poor 2028
Ac 8:32 was this, He was led as a sheep to the **s**; *4967*
9: 1 and **s** against the disciples of the Lord, *5408*
Ro 8:36 we are accounted as sheep for the **s**. *4967*
Heb 7: 1 who met Abraham returning from the **s** of *2871*
Jas 5: 5 have nourished your hearts, as in a day of **s**. *4967*

SLAVE (1) [SLAVES]
Jer 2:14 *is* he a homeborn *s*? why is he spoiled? NIH

SLAVE DRIVERS See TASKMASTERS

SLAVE MASTERS See TASKMASTERS

SLAVE TRADERS See MENSTEALERS

SLAVES (1) [SLAVE]
Rev 18:13 and chariots, and **s**, and souls of men. *4983*

SLAY (117) [MANSLAYER, MANSLAYERS, SLAIN, SLAYER, SLAYETH, SLAYING, SLEW, SLEWEST]
Ge 4:14 *that* every one that findeth me shall **s** me. 2026
18:25 to **s** the righteous with the wicked: 4191
20: 4 Lord, wilt thou **s** also a righteous nation? 2026
20:11 and they will **s** me for my wife's sake. 2026
22:10 his hand, and took the knife to **s** his son. 7819
27:41 are at hand; then will I **s** my brother Jacob. 2026
34:30 themselves together against me, and **s** me; 5221
37:18 they conspired against him to **s** him. 4191
37:20 and let us **s** him, and cast him into some pit, 2026
37:26 What profit *is it* if we **s** our brother, and 2026
42:37 saying, **S** my two sons, if I bring him not to 4191
43:16 *these* men home, and **s**, and make ready; 2873
Ex 2:15 heard this thing, he sought to **s** Moses. 2026
4:23 behold, I will **s** thy son, *even* thy firstborn. 2026
5:21 to put a sword in their hand to **s** us. 2026
21:14 upon his neighbour, to **s** him with guile; 2026
23: 7 and the innocent and righteous **s** thou not: 2026
29:16 thou shalt **s** the ram, and thou shalt take his 7819
32:12 to **s** them in the mountains, and to consume 2026
32:27 **s** every man his brother, and every man his 2026
Lev 4:29 **s** the sin offering in the place of the burnt 7819
4:33 **s** it for a sin offering in the place where 7819
14:13 he shall **s** the lamb in the place where he 7819
20:15 be put to death: and ye shall **s** the beast. 2026
Nu 19: 3 and *one* shall **s** her before his face: 7819
25: 5 **S** ye every one his men that were joined 2026
35:19 The revenger of blood himself shall **s** 4191

Nu 35:19 when he meeteth him, he shall **s** him. 4191
35:21 the revenger of blood shall **s** the murderer, 4191
Dt 9:28 he hath brought them out to **s** them in 4191
19: 6 because the way is long, and **s** him; 5221+5315
27:25 Cursed *be* he that taketh reward to **s** 5221+5315
Jos 13:22 did the children of Israel **s** with the sword 2026
Jdg 8:19 ye had saved them alive, I would not **s** you. 2026
8:20 unto Jether his firstborn, Up, *and* **s** them. 2026
9:54 said unto him, Draw thy sword, and **s** me, 4191
1Sa 2:25 because the LORD would **s** them. 4191
5:10 God of Israel to us, to **s** us and our people. 4191
5:11 own place, that it **s** us not, and our people: 4191
14:34 man his sheep, and **s** *them* here, and eat; 7819
15: 3 **s** both man and woman, infant and 4191
19: 5 innocent blood, to **s** David without a cause? 4191
19:11 to watch him, and to **s** him in the morning: 4191
19:15 him up to me in the bed, that I may **s** him. 4191
20: 8 if there be in me iniquity, **s** me thyself; 4191
20:33 it was determined of his father to **s** David. 4191
22:17 Turn, and **s** the priests of the LORD; 4191
2Sa 1: 9 Stand, I pray thee, upon me, and **s** me: 4191
3:37 not of the king to **s** Abner the son of Ner. 4191
21: 2 Saul sought to **s** them in his zeal to 5221
1Ki 1:51 he will not **s** his servant with the sword. 4191
3:26 the living child, and **in no wise s** it. 4191+4191
3:27 the living child, and **in no wise s** it: 4191+4191
15:28 of Asa king of Judah did Baasha **s** him, 4191
17:18 my sin to remembrance, and to **s** my son? 4191
18: 9 thy servant into the hand of Ahab, to **s** me? 4191
18:12 and he cannot find thee, he shall **s** me: 2026
18:14 Behold, Elijah *is here:* and he shall **s** me. 2026
19:17 escapeth the sword of Hazael shall Jehu **s**: 4191
19:17 from the sword of Jehu shall Elisha **s**. 4191
20:36 art departed from me, a lion shall **s** thee. 5221
2Ki 8:12 their young *men* wilt thou **s** with the sword, 2026
10:25 and to the captains, Go in, *and* **s** them; 5221
17:26 behold, they **s** them, because they know not 4191
2Ch 20:23 **utterly to s** and destroy *them:* and 2763
23:14 **S** her not *in* the house of the LORD. 4191
Ne 4:11 and **s** them, and cause the work to cease. 2026
6:10 for they will come to **s** thee; yea, in 2026
6:10 yea, in the night will they come to **s** thee. 2026
Est 8:11 to destroy, to **s**, and to cause to perish, 2026
Job 9:23 If the scourge **s** suddenly, he will laugh at 4191
13:15 Though he **s** me, *yet* will I trust in him: but 6991
20:16 of asps: the viper's tongue shall **s** him. 2026
Ps 34:21 Evil shall **s** the wicked: and they that hate 4191
37:14 *and* to **s** such as be of upright conversation. 2873
37:32 the righteous, and seeketh to **s** him. 4191
59:11 **S** them not, lest my people forget: 2026
94: 6 They **s** the widow and the stranger, and 2026
109:16 that *he* might even **s** the broken in heart. 4191
139:19 Surely thou wilt **s** the wicked, O God: 6991
Pr 1:32 For the turning away of the simple shall **s** 2026
Isa 11: 4 with the breath of his lips shall he **s** 4191
14:30 with famine, and he shall **s** thy remnant. 2026
27: 1 and he shall **s** the dragon that *is* in the sea. 2026
65:15 for the Lord GOD shall **s** thee, and call his 4191
Jer 5: 6 Wherefore a lion out of the forest shall **s** 5221
15: 3 the sword to **s**, and the dogs to tear, and 2026
18:23 me to **s** *me:* forgive not their iniquity, 4194
20: 4 and shall **s** them with the sword. 5221
29:21 and he shall **s** them before your eyes; 5221
40:14 the son of Nethaniah to **s** thee? 5221+5315
40:15 I will **s** Ishmael the son of Nethaniah, and 5221
40:15 know *it:* wherefore should he **s** thee, 5221+5315
41: 8 them that said unto Ishmael, **S** us not: 4191
50:27 **S** all her bullocks; let them go down to 2717
Eze 9: 6 **S** utterly old *and* young, both maids, and 2026
13:19 to **s** the souls that should not die, and 4191
23:47 they shall **s** their sons and their daughters, 2026
26: 8 He shall **s** with the sword thy daughters in 2026
26:11 he shall **s** thy people by the sword, and 2026
40:39 to **s** thereon the burnt offering and the sin 7819
44:11 they shall **s** the burnt offering and 7819
Da 2:14 which was gone forth to **s** the wise *men* of 6992
Hos 2: 3 set her like a dry land, and **s** her with thirst. 4191
9:16 yet will I **s** *even* the beloved *fruit* of their 4191
Am 2: 3 will **s** all the princes thereof with him, 2026
9: 1 and I will **s** the last of them with the sword: 2026
9: 4 I command the sword, and it shall **s** them: 2026
Hab 1:17 and not spare continually to **s** the nations? 2026
Zec 11: 5 Whose possessors **s** them, and 2026
Lk 11:49 and *some* of them they shall **s** and persecute: *615*
19:27 bring hither, and **s** *them* before me. *2695*
Jn 5:16 and sought to **s** him, because he had done *615*
Ac 5:33 cut *to the heart,* and took counsel to **s** them. *337*
9:29 the Grecians: but they went about to **s** him. *337*
11: 7 saying unto me, Arise, Peter; **s** and eat. *2380*
Rev 9:15 and a year, for to **s** the third *part* of men. *615*

SLAYER (19) [SLAY]

Nu 35:11 that the **s** may flee thither, which killeth 7523
35:24 the congregation shall judge between the **s** 5221
35:25 the congregation shall deliver the **s** out of 7523
35:26 if the **s** shall at any time come *without* 7523
35:27 and the revenger of blood kill the **s**; 7523
35:28 after the death of the high priest the **s** shall 7523
Dt 4:42 That the **s** might flee thither, which should 7523
19: 3 three parts, that every **s** may flee thither. 7523
19: 4 this *is* the case of the **s**, which shall flee 7523
19: 6 Lest the avenger of the blood pursue the **s**, 7523
Jos 20: 3 That the **s** that killeth *any* person unawares 7523
20: 5 they shall not deliver the **s** up into his hand; 7523
20: 6 shall the **s** return, and come unto his own 7523
21:13 her suburbs, *to be* a city of refuge for the **s**; 7523
21:21 *to be* a city of refuge for the **s**; 7523
21:27 her suburbs, *to be* a city of refuge for the **s**; 7523
21:32 her suburbs, *to be* a city of refuge for the **s**; 7523
21:38 her suburbs, *to be* a city of refuge for the **s**; 7523
Eze 21:11 to give it into the hand of the **s**. 2026

SLAYETH (5) [SLAY]

Ge 4:15 said unto him, Therefore whosoever **s** Cain, 2026
Dt 22:26 and **s** him, even so *is* this matter: 7523
Job 5: 2 the foolish man, and envy **s** the silly one. 4191
Eze 28: 9 Wilt thou yet say before him that **s** thee, 2026
28: 9 and no God, in the hand of him that **s** thee. 2490

SLAYING (7) [SLAY]

Jos 8:24 when Israel had made an end of **s** all 2026
10:20 the children of Israel had made an end of **s** 5221
Jdg 9:56 unto his father, in **s** his seventy brethren: 2026
1Ki 17:20 widow with whom I sojourn, by **s** her son? 4191
Isa 22:13 and gladness, **s** oxen, and killing sheep, 2026
57: 5 **s** the children in the valleys under the clifts 7819
Eze 9: 8 while they were **s** them, and I *was* left, 5221

SLEEP (82) [ASLEEP, SLEEPER, SLEEPEST, SLEEPETH, SLEEPING, SLEPT]

Ge 2:21 the LORD God caused a **deep s** to fall 8639
15:12 was going down, a **deep s** fell upon Abram; 8639
28:11 his pillows, and **lay down** in that place **to s**. 7901
28:16 Jacob awaked out of his **s**, and he said, 8142
31:40 and my **s** departed from mine eyes. 8142
Ex 22:27 wherein shall he **s**? and it shall come to 7901
Dt 24:12 *be* poor, thou shalt not **s** with his pledge: 7901
24:13 that he may **s** in his own raiment, and 7901
31:16 Behold, thou shalt **s** with thy fathers; 7901
Jdg 16:14 he awaked out of his **s**, and went away with 8142
16:19 she **made** him **s** upon her knees; and 3462
16:20 he awoke out of his **s**, and said, I will go 8142
1Sa 3: 3 God *was,* and Samuel was laid down *to s;* NIH
26:12 a **deep s** from the LORD was fallen upon 8639
2Sa 7:12 thou shalt **s** with thy fathers, I will set up 7901
1Ki 1:21 when my lord the king shall **s** with his 7901
Est 6: 1 On that night could not the king **s**, and 8142
Job 4:13 of the night, when **deep s** falleth on men. 8639
7:21 for now shall I **s** in the dust; and thou shalt 7901
14:12 shall not awake, nor be raised out of their **s**. 8142
33:15 of the night, when **deep s** falleth upon men, 8639
Ps 4: 8 I will both lay me down in peace, and **s**: 3462
13: 3 mine eyes, lest I **s** the *sleep of* death; 3462
13: 3 lighten mine eyes, lest I sleep the *s of* death; NIH
76: 5 are spoiled, they have slept their **s**: 8142
76: 6 and horse *are* **cast into a dead s**. 7290
78:65 the Lord awaked as one out of **s**, *and* like a 3463
90: 5 them away as with a flood; they are *as* a **s**: 8142
121: 4 keepeth Israel shall neither slumber nor **s**. 3462
127: 2 of sorrows: *for* so he giveth his beloved **s**. 8142
132: 4 I will not give **s** to mine eyes, *or* slumber to 8153
Pr 3:24 shalt lie down, and thy **s** shall be sweet. 8142
4:16 For they **s** not, except they have done 3462
4:16 their **s** is taken away, unless they cause 8142
6: 4 Give not **s** to thine eyes, nor slumber to 8142
6: 9 How long wilt thou **s**, O sluggard? 7901
6: 9 when wilt thou arise out of thy **s**? 8142
6:10 *Yet* a little **s**, a little slumber, a little folding 8142

Pr 6:10 a little folding of the hands to **s**: 7901
19:15 Slothfulness casteth into a **deep s**; and 8639
20:13 Love not **s**, lest thou come to poverty; 8142
24:33 *Yet* a little **s**, a little slumber, a little folding 8142
24:33 a little folding of the hands to **s**: 7901
Ecc 5:12 The **s** of a labouring *man is* sweet, 8142
5:12 of the rich will not suffer him to **s**. 3462
8:16 neither day nor night seeth **s** with his eyes:) 8142
SS 5: 2 I **s**, but my heart waketh: *it is* the voice of 3463
Isa 5:27 none shall slumber nor **s**; neither shall 3462
29:10 poured out upon you the spirit of **deep s**, 8639
Jer 31:26 and beheld; and my **s** was sweet unto me. 8142
51:39 **s** a perpetual sleep, and not wake, saith 3462
51:39 sleep a perpetual **s**, and not wake, saith 8142
51:57 and they shall **s** a perpetual sleep, 3462
51:57 and they shall sleep a perpetual **s**, 8142
Eze 34:25 in the wilderness, and **s** in the woods. 3462
Da 2: 1 was troubled, and his **s** brake from him. 8142
6:18 before him: and his **s** went from him. 8139
8:18 I was **in a deep s** on my face toward 7290
10: 9 was I **in a deep s** on my face, and my face 7290
12: 2 many of them that **s** in the dust of the earth 3463
Zec 4: 1 as a man that is wakened out of his **s**, 8142
Mt 1:24 Then Joseph being raised from **s** did as *5258*
26:45 unto them, **S** on now, and take your rest: *2518*
Mk 4:27 And should **s**, and rise night and day, and *2518*
14:41 unto them, **S** on now, and take your rest: *2518*
Lk 9:32 they that were with him were heavy with **s**: *5258*
22:46 And said unto them, Why **s** ye? rise and *2518*
Jn 11:11 but I go, that I may **awake** him **out of s**. *1852*
11:12 his disciples, Lord, if he **s**, he shall do well. *2837*
11:13 that he had spoken of taking of rest in **s**. *5258*
Ac 13:36 **fell on s**, and was laid unto his fathers, and *2837*
16:27 of the prison **awaking out of** his **s**, *1096+1853*
20: 9 named Eutychus, being fallen into a deep **s**: *5258*
20: 9 he sunk down with **s**, and fell down from *5258*
Ro 13:11 that now *it is* high time to awake out of **s**: *5258*
1Co 11:30 and sickly among you, and many **s**. *2837*
15:51 We shall not all **s**, but we shall all be *2837*
1Th 4:14 them also which **s** in Jesus will God bring *2837*
5: 6 Therefore let us not **s**, as *do* others; but *2518*
5: 7 For they that **s** sleep in the night; and *2518*
5: 7 For they that sleep **s** in the night; and *2518*
5:10 died for us, that, whether we wake or **s**, *2518*

SLEEPER (1) [SLEEP]
Jnh 1: 6 said unto him, What meanest thou, O **s**? 7290

SLEEPEST (4) [SLEEP]
Ps 44:23 Awake, why **s** thou, O Lord? arise, cast *us* 3462
Pr 6:22 when thou **s**, it shall keep thee; and 7901
Mk 14:37 and saith unto Peter, Simon, **s** thou? *2518*
Eph 5:14 Awake thou that **s**, and arise from the dead, *2518*

SLEEPETH (7) [SLEEP]
1Ki 18:27 *or* peradventure he **s**, and must be awaked. 3463
Pr 10: 5 he that **s** in harvest *is* a son that causeth 7290
Hos 7: 6 their baker **s** all the night; *in* the morning it 3463
Mt 9:24 for the maid is not dead, but **s**. And they *2518*
Mk 5:39 and weep? the damsel is not dead, but **s**. *2518*
Lk 8:52 he said, Weep not; she is not dead, but **s**. *2518*
Jn 11:11 he saith unto them, Our friend Lazarus **s**; *2837*

SLEEPING (6) [SLEEP]
1Sa 26: 7 Saul lay **s** within the trench, and his spear 3463
Isa 56:10 **s**, lying down, loving to slumber. 1957
Mk 13:36 Lest coming suddenly he find you **s**. *2518*
14:37 and findeth them **s**, and saith unto Peter, *2518*
Lk 22:45 to his disciples, he found them **s** for sorrow, *2837*
Ac 12: 6 the same night Peter was **s** between two *2837*

SLEIGHT (1)
Eph 4:14 every wind of doctrine, by the **s** of men, *2940*

SLEPT (49) [SLEEP]
Ge 2:21 a deep sleep to fall upon Adam, and he **s**: 3462
41: 5 he **s** and dreamed the second time: and 3462
2Sa 11: 9 Uriah **s** *at* the door of the king's house with 7901
1Ki 2:10 So David **s** with his fathers, and was buried 7901
3:20 while thine handmaid **s**, and laid it in her 3463
11:21 when Hadad heard in Egypt that David **s** 7901
11:43 Solomon **s** with his fathers, and was buried 7901
14:20 he **s** with his fathers, and Nadab his son 7901
14:31 Rehoboam **s** with his fathers, and 7901
15: 8 Abijam **s** with his fathers; and they buried 7901
15:24 Asa **s** with his fathers, and was buried with 7901
16: 6 So Baasha **s** with his fathers, and 7901
16:28 So Omri **s** with his fathers, and was buried 7901
19: 5 as he lay and **s** under a juniper tree, 3462
22:40 So Ahab **s** with his fathers; and Ahaziah his 7901
22:50 Jehoshaphat **s** with his fathers, and 7901
2Ki 8:24 Joram **s** with his fathers, and was buried 7901
10:35 Jehu **s** with his fathers: and they buried him 7901
13: 9 Jehoahaz **s** with his fathers; and they buried 7901
13:13 Joash **s** with his fathers; and Jeroboam sat 7901
14:16 Jehoash **s** with his fathers, and was buried 7901
14:22 after that the king **s** with his fathers. 7901
14:29 Jeroboam **s** with his fathers, *even* with 7901
15: 7 So Azariah **s** with his fathers; and 7901
15:22 Menahem **s** with his fathers; and 7901
15:38 Jotham **s** with his fathers, and was buried 7901
16:20 Ahaz **s** with his fathers, and was buried 7901
20:21 Hezekiah **s** with his fathers: and 7901
21:18 Manasseh **s** with his fathers, and 7901
24: 6 So Jehoiakim **s** with his fathers: and 7901
2Ch 9:31 Solomon **s** with his fathers, and he was 7901
12:16 Rehoboam **s** with his fathers, and 7901
14: 1 So Abijah **s** with his fathers, and 7901
16:13 Asa **s** with his fathers, and died in the one 7901
21: 1 Now Jehoshaphat **s** with his fathers, and 7901
26: 2 after that the king **s** with his fathers. 7901
26:23 So Uzziah **s** with his fathers, and 7901
27: 9 Jotham **s** with his fathers, and they buried 7901
28:27 Ahaz **s** with his fathers, and they buried 7901
32:33 Hezekiah **s** with his fathers, and they buried 7901
33:20 So Manasseh **s** with his fathers, and 7901
Job 3:13 lien *still* and been quiet, I should have **s**: 3462
Ps 3: 5 I laid me down and **s**; I awaked; for 3462
76: 5 are spoiled, they have **s** their sleep: 5123
Mt 13:25 But while men **s**, his enemy came and *2518*
25: 5 they all slumbered and **s**. *2518*
27:52 and many bodies of saints which **s** arose, *2837*
28:13 by night, and stole him *away* while we **s**. *2837*
1Co 15:20 *and* become the firstfruits of them that **s**. *2837*

SLEW (196) [SLAY]
Ge 4: 8 rose up against Abel his brother, and **s** him. 2026
4:25 another seed instead of Abel, whom Cain **s**. 2026
34:25 upon the city boldly, and **s** all the males. 2026
34:26 they **s** Hamor and Shechem his son with 2026
38: 7 sight of the LORD; and the LORD **s** him. 4191
38:10 the LORD: wherefore he **s** him also. 4191
49: 6 for in their anger they **s** a man, and in their 2026
Ex 2:12 he **s** the Egyptian, and hid him in the sand. 5221
13:15 that the LORD **s** all the firstborn in 2026
Lev 8:15 he **s** *it;* and Moses took the blood, and put *it* 7819
8:23 he **s** *it;* and Moses took of the blood of it, 7819
9: 8 the altar, and **s** the calf of the sin offering, 7819
9:12 he **s** the burnt offering; and Aaron's sons 7819
9:15 and **s** it, and offered it for sin, as the first. 7819
9:18 He **s** also the bullock and the ram *for* a 7819
Nu 31: 7 and they **s** all the males. 2026
31: 8 they **s** the kings of Midian, beside *the rest* 2026
31: 8 Balaam also the son of Beor they **s** with 2026
Jos 8:21 then they turned again, and **s** the men of Ai. 5221
9:26 the children of Israel, that they **s** them not. 2026
10:10 **s** them *with* a great slaughter at Gibeon, 5221
10:11 the children of Israel **s** with the sword. 2026
10:26 and **s** them, and hanged them on five trees: 4191
11:17 kings he took, and smote them, and **s** them. 4191
Jdg 1: 4 they **s** *of* them in Bezek ten thousand men. 5221
1: 5 they **s** the Canaanites and the Perizzites. 5221
1:10 they **s** Sheshai, and Ahiman, and Talmai. 5221
1:17 they **s** the Canaanites that inhabited 5221
3:29 they **s** *of* Moab at that time about ten 5221
3:31 which **s** *of* the Philistines six hundred men 5221
7:25 they **s** Oreb upon the rock Oreb, and Zeeb 2026
7:25 Zeeb they **s** at the winepress of Zeeb, and 2026
8:17 tower of Penuel, and **s** the men of the city. 2026
8:18 What manner of men *were they* whom ye **s** 2026
8:21 **s** Zebah and Zalmunna, and took away 2026
9: 5 **s** his brethren the sons of Jerubbaal, 2026
9:24 Abimelech their brother, which **s** them; 2026
9:44 *people* that *were* in the fields, and **s** them. 5221
9:45 **s** the people that *was* therein, and 2026
9:54 that *men* say not of me, A woman **s** him. 2026
12: 6 and **s** him at the passages of Jordan: 7819
14:19 **s** thirty men of them, and took their spoil, 5221
15:15 took it, and **s** a thousand men therewith. 5221

Jdg 16:24 of our country, which **s** many of us. 2491
16:30 So the dead which he **s** at his death were 4191
16:30 were moe than *they* which he **s** in his life. 4191
20:45 and **s** two thousand men of them. 5221
1Sa 1:25 they **s** a bullock, and brought the child to 7819
4: 2 they **s** of the army in the field about four 5221
11:11 **s** the Ammonites until the heat of the day: 5221
14:13 and his armourbearer **s** after him. 4191
14:32 oxen, and calves, and **s** *them* on the ground: 7819
14:34 ox with him *that* night, and **s** *them* there. 7819
17:35 by his beard, and smote him, and **s** him. 4191
17:36 Thy servant **s** both the lion and the bear: 5221
17:50 a stone, and smote the Philistine, and **s** him; 4191
17:51 and **s** him, and cut off his head therewith. 4191
18:27 and **s** of the Philistines two hundred men; 5221
19: 5 **s** the Philistine, and the LORD wrought a 5221
19: 8 and **s** them *with* a great slaughter; 5221
22:18 **s** on that day fourscore and five persons 4191
29: 5 Saul **s** his thousands, and David his ten 5221
30: 2 they **s** not any, either great or small, but 4191
31: 2 the Philistines **s** Jonathan, and Abinadab, 5221
2Sa 1:10 **s** him, because I was sure that he could not 4191
3:30 So Joab and Abishai his brother **s** Abner, 2026
4: 7 **s** him, and beheaded him, and took his 4191
4:10 I took hold of him, and **s** him in Ziklag, 2026
4:12 and they **s** them, and cut off their hands and 2026
8: 5 David **s** of the Syrians two and 5221
10:18 David **s** *the men of* seven hundred chariots 2026
14: 6 but the one smote the other, and **s** him. 4191
14: 7 for the life of his brother whom he **s**; 2026
18:15 and smote Absalom, and **s** him. 4191
21: 1 bloody house, because he **s** the Gibeonites. 4191
21:18 Sibbechai the Hushathite **s** Saph, 5221
21:19 **s** *the brother of* Goliath the Gittite, 5221
21:21 son of Shimea the brother of David **s** him. 5221
23: 8 eight hundred, whom he **s** at one time. 2491
23:12 and defended it, and **s** the Philistines: 5221
23:18 and **s** them, and had the name among three. 2491
23:20 many acts, he **s** two lionlike men of Moab: 5221
23:20 **s** a lion in the midst of a pit in time of 5221
23:21 he **s** an Egyptian, a goodly man: and 5221
23:21 and **s** him with his own spear. 2026
1Ki 1: 9 Adonijah **s** sheep and oxen and fat cattle by 2076
2: 5 whom he **s**, and shed the blood of war in 2026
2:32 better than he, and **s** them with the sword, 2026
2:34 went up, and fell upon him, and **s** him: 4191
11:24 when David **s** them *of Zobah:* and 2026
13:24 a lion met him by the way, and **s** him: 4191
16:11 *that* he **s** all the house of Baasha: 5221
18:13 when Jezebel **s** the prophets of the LORD, 2026
18:40 to the brook Kishon, and **s** them there. 7819
19:21 **s** them, and boiled their flesh with 2076
20:20 they **s** every one his man: and the Syrians 5221
20:21 and **s** the Syrians with a great slaughter. 5221
20:29 the children of Israel **s** *of* the Syrians an 5221
20:36 from him, a lion found him, and **s** him. 5221
2Ki 9:31 *Had* Zimri peace, who **s** his master? 2026
10: 7 **s** seventy persons, and put their heads in 7819
10: 9 I conspired against my master, and **s** him: 2026
10: 9 and slew him: but who **s** all these? 5221
10:11 So Jehu **s** all that remained of the house of 5221
10:14 **s** them at the pit of the shearing house, 7819
10:17 he **s** all that remained unto Ahab in 5221
11:18 **s** Mattan the priest of Baal before the altars. 2026
11:20 they **s** Athaliah with the sword *beside* 4191
12:20 **s** Joash *in* the house of Millo, 5221
14: 5 that he **s** his servants which had slain 5221
14: 6 the children of the murderers he **s** not: 4191
14: 7 He **s** *of* Edom in the valley of salt ten 5221
14:19 sent after him to Lachish, and **s** him there. 4191
15:10 and **s** him, and reigned in his stead. 4191
15:14 and **s** him, and reigned in his stead. 4191
15:30 and **s** him, and reigned in his stead, 4191
16: 9 *the people of* it captive to Kir, and **s** Rezin. 4191
17:25 lions among them, which **s** *some* of them. 2026
21:23 and **s** the king in his own house. 4191
21:24 the people of the land **s** all them that had 5221
23:20 he **s** all the priests of the high places that 2076
23:29 he **s** him at Megiddo, when he had seen 4191
25: 7 they **s** the sons of Zedekiah before his eyes, 7819
25:21 and **s** them at Riblah in the land of Hamath. 4191
1Ch 2: 3 in the sight of the LORD; and he **s** him. 4191
7:21 men of Gath that were born in *that* land **s**, 2026
10: 2 the Philistines **s** Jonathan, and Abinadab, 5221
10:14 therefore he **s** him, and turned the kingdom 4191
11:14 and delivered it, and **s** the Philistines; 5221
11:20 he **s** *them,* and had a name among the three. 2491
11:22 many acts; he **s** two lionlike men of Moab: 5221
11:22 and **s** a lion in a pit in a snowy day. 5221
11:23 he **s** an Egyptian, a man of *great* stature, 5221
11:23 and **s** him with his own spear. 2026
18: 5 David **s** of the Syrians two and 5221
18:12 Moreover Abishai the son of Zeruiah **s** of 5221
19:18 David **s** of the Syrians seven thousand *men* 2026
20: 4 at which time Sibbechai the Hushathite **s** 5221
20: 5 Elhanan the son of Jair **s** Lahmi the brother 5221
20: 7 the son of Shimea David's brother **s** him. 5221
2Ch 13:17 his people **s** them *with* a great slaughter: 5221
21: 4 **s** all his brethren with the sword, and 2026
22: 8 that ministered to Ahaziah, he **s** them. 2026
22:11 him from Athaliah, so that she **s** him not. 4191
23:15 gate *by* the king's house, they **s** her there. 4191
23:17 **s** Mattan the priest of Baal before the altars. 2026
24:22 his father had done to him, but **s** his son. 2026
24:25 and **s** him on his bed, and he died: 2026
25: 3 that he **s** his servants that had killed 2026
25: 4 he **s** not their children, but *did* as it is 4191
25:27 sent to Lachish after him, and **s** him there. 4191
28: 6 For Pekah the son of Remaliah **s** in Judah 2026
28: 7 **s** Maaseiah the king's son, and Azrikam 2026
32:21 they that came forth of his own bowels **s** 5307
33:24 against him, and **s** him in his own house. 4191
33:25 the people of the land **s** all them that had 5221
36:17 who **s** their young men with the sword in 2026
Ne 9:26 **s** thy prophets which testified against them 2026
Est 9: 6 in Shushan the palace the Jews **s** and 2026
9:10 the enemy of the Jews, **s** they; 2026
9:15 and **s** three hundred men at Shushan; 2026
9:16 **s** of their foes seventy and five thousand, 2026
Ps 78:31 **s** the fattest of them, and smote down 2026
78:34 When he **s** them, then they sought him: and 2026
105:29 their waters into blood, and **s** their fish. 4191
135:10 smote great nations, and **s** mighty kings; 2026
136:18 **s** famous kings: for his mercy *endureth* for 2026
Isa 66: 3 He that killeth an ox *is as if* he **s** a man; 5221
Jer 20:17 Because he **s** me not from the womb; or 4191
26:23 who **s** him with the sword, and cast his 5221
39: 6 the king of Babylon **s** the sons of Zedekiah 7819
39: 6 also the king of Babylon **s** all the nobles of 7819
41: 2 **s** him, whom the king of Babylon had made 4191
41: 3 Ishmael also **s** all the Jews that were with 5221
41: 7 that Ishmael the son of Nethaniah **s** them, 7819
41: 8 and **s** them not among their brethren. 4191
52:10 the king of Babylon **s** the sons of Zedekiah 7819
52:10 he **s** also all the princes of Judah in Riblah. 7819
La 2: 4 **s** all *that were* pleasant to the eye, in 2026
Eze 9: 7 And they went forth, and **s** in the city. 5221
23:10 her daughters, and **s** her with the sword: 2026
40:41 whereupon they **s** *their sacrifices.* 7819
40:42 wherewith they **s** the burnt offering 7819
Da 3:22 the flame of the fire **s** those men that took 6992
5:19 whom he would he **s**; and whom he would 6992
Mt 2:16 **s** all the children that were in Bethlehem, *337*
21:39 and cast *him* out of the vineyard, and **s** *him.* *615*
22: 6 and entreated *them* spitefully, and **s** *them.* *615*
23:35 whom ye **s** between the temple and *5407*
Lk 13: 4 whom the tower in Siloam fell, and **s** them, *615*
Ac 5:30 up Jesus, whom ye **s** and hanged on a tree. *1315*
10:39 whom they **s** and hanged on a tree: *337*
22:20 and kept the raiment of them that **s** him. *337*
Ro 7:11 deceived me, and by it **s** *me.* *615*
1Jn 3:12 was of *that* wicked one, and **s** his brother. *4969*
3:12 And wherefore **s** he him? Because his own *4969*

SLEWEST (1) [SLAY]
1Sa 21: 9 whom thou **s** in the valley of Elah, behold, 5221

SLIDDEN (1) [SLIDE]
Jer 8: 5 is this people of Jerusalem **s back** *by* a 7725

SLIDE (3) [BACKSLIDER, BACKSLIDING, BACKSLIDINGS, SLIDDEN, SLIDETH]
Dt 32:35 recompence; their foot shall **s** in *due* time: 4131
Ps 26: 1 also in the LORD; *therefore* I shall not **s**. 4571
37:31 God *is* in his heart; none of his steps shall **s**. 4571

SLIDETH (1) [SLIDE]
Hos 4:16 For Israel **s back** as a backsliding heifer: 5637

SLIGHTLY (2)
Jer 6:14 hurt of *the daughter of* my people s, 5921+7043
8:11 hurt of the daughter of my people s, 5921+7043

SLIME (2) [SLIMEPITS]
Ge 11: 3 brick for stone, and s had they for morter. 2564
Ex 2: 3 daubed it with s and with pitch, and put 2564

SLIMEPITS (1) [PIT, SLIME]
Ge 14:10 the vale of Siddim *was* full of s; 875+875+2564

SLING (8) [SLINGERS, SLINGS, SLINGSTONES]
Jdg 20:16 every one could s stones at a hair *breadth,* 7049
1Sa 17:40 even in a scrip; and his s *was* in his hand: 7050
17:50 David prevailed over the Philistine with a s 7050
25:29 them shall he s out *as out* of the middle of a 7049
25:29 he sling out *as out* of the middle of a s. 7050
Pr 26: 8 As *he that* bindeth a stone in a s, so *is* he 4773
Jer 10:18 I will s out the inhabitants of the land at 7049
Zec 9:15 shall devour, and subdue *with* s stones; 7050

SLINGERS (1) [SLING]
2Ki 3:25 howbeit the s went about *it,* and smote it. 7051

SLINGS (1) [SLING]
2Ch 26:14 habergeons, and bows, and s to cast stones. 7050

SLINGSTONES (1) [SLING, STONE]
Job 41:28 s are turned with him into stubble. 68+7050

SLIP (5) [SLIPPERY, SLIPPETH, SLIPS, SLIPT]
2Sa 22:37 steps under me; so that my feet did not s. 4571
Job 12: 5 He that is ready to s with *his* feet *is as* a 4571
Ps 17: 5 goings in thy paths, *that* my footsteps s not. 4131
18:36 my steps under me, that my feet did not s. 4571
Heb 2: 1 lest at any time we should let *them* s. *3901*

SLIPPERY (3) [SLIP]
Ps 35: 6 Let their way be dark and s: and let 2519
73:18 Surely thou didst set them in s *places:* thou 2513
Jer 23:12 be unto them as s *ways* in the darkness: 2519

SLIPPETH (3) [SLIP]
Dt 19: 5 the head s from the helve, and lighteth upon 5394
Ps 38:16 when my foot s, they magnify *themselves* 4131
94:18 When I said, My foot s; thy mercy, 4131

SLIPS (1) [SLIP]
Isa 17:10 and shalt set it *with* strange s: 2156

SLIPT (2) [SLIP]
1Sa 19:10 he s away out of Saul's presence, and 6362
Ps 73: 2 almost gone; my steps had well nigh s. 8210

SLOTHFUL (15) [SLOTHFULNESS]
Jdg 18: 9 be not s to go, *and* to enter to possess 6101
Pr 12:24 bear rule: but the s shall be under tribute. 7423
12:27 The s *man* roasteth not that which he took 7423
15:19 The way of the s *man is* as a hedge of 6102
18: 9 He also that is s in his work is brother to 7503
19:24 A s *man* hideth his hand in *his* bosom, and 6102
21:25 The desire of the s killeth him; for his 6102
22:13 The s *man* saith, *There is* a lion without, 6102
24:30 I went by the field of the s, and by 376+6102
26:13 The s *man* saith, *There is* a lion in the way; 6102
26:14 upon his hinges, so *doth* the s upon his bed. 6102
26:15 The s hideth his hand in *his* bosom; 6102
Mt 25:26 said unto him, *Thou* wicked and s servant, *3636*
Ro 12:11 Not s in business; fervent in spirit; *3636*
Heb 6:12 That ye be not s, but followers of them who *3576*

SLOTHFULNESS (2) [SLOTHFUL]
Pr 19:15 S casteth into a deep sleep; and an idle soul 6103
Ecc 10:18 By much s the building decayeth; and 6103

SLOW (15) [SLOWLY]
Ex 4:10 but I *am* s of speech, and of a slow tongue. 3515
4:10 but I *am* slow of speech, and of a s tongue. 3515
Ne 9:17 s to anger, and of great kindness, and 750
Ps 103: 8 gracious, s to anger, and plenteous in mercy. 750
145: 8 s to anger, and of great mercy. 750
Pr 14:29 *He that is* s to wrath *is* of great 750
15:18 but *he that is* s to anger appeaseth strife. 750
16:32 *He that is* s to anger *is* better than 750
Joel 2:13 s to anger, and of great kindness, and 750
Jnh 4: 2 s to anger, and of great kindness, and 750
Na 1: 3 The LORD *is* s to anger, and great in 750
Lk 24:25 s of heart to believe all that the prophets *1021*
Tit 1:12 *are* alway liars, evil beasts, s bellies. *692*
Jas 1:19 be swift to hear, s to speak, slow to wrath: *1021*
1:19 be swift to hear, slow to speak, s to wrath: *1021*

SLOWLY (1) [SLOW]
Ac 27: 7 And when we had sailed s many days, and *1020*

SLUCES (1)
Isa 19:10 all that make s *and* ponds for fish. 7938

SLUG See SNAIL

SLUGGARD (6)
Pr 6: 6 Go to the ant, thou s; consider her ways, 6102
6: 9 How long wilt thou sleep, O s? when wilt 6102
10:26 the eyes, so *is* the s to them that send him. 6102
13: 4 The soul of the s desireth, and *hath* nothing: 6102
20: 4 The s will not plow by reason of the cold; 6102
26:16 The s *is* wiser in his own conceit than seven 6102

SLUMBER (10) [SLUMBERED, SLUMBERETH, SLUMBERINGS]
Ps 121: 3 be moved: he that keepeth thee will not s. 5123
121: 4 he that keepeth Israel shall neither s nor 5123
132: 4 sleep to mine eyes, *or* s to mine eyelids, 8572
Pr 6: 4 sleep to thine eyes, nor s to thine eyelids. 8572
6:10 *Yet* a little sleep, a little s, a little folding of 8572
24:33 *Yet* a little sleep, a little s, a little folding of 8572
Isa 5:27 none shall s nor sleep; neither shall 5123
56:10 sleeping, lying down, loving to s. 5123
Na 3:18 Thy shepherds s, O king of Assyria: 5123
Ro 11: 8 God hath given them the spirit of s, *2659*

SLUMBERED (1) [SLUMBER]
Mt 25: 5 the bridegroom tarried, they all s and slept. *3573*

SLUMBERETH (1) [SLUMBER]
2Pe 2: 3 lingereth not, and their damnation s not. *3573*

SLUMBERINGS (1) [SLUMBER]
Job 33:15 sleep falleth upon men, in s upon the bed; 8572

SLY See BACKBITING; BACKBITINGS

SMALL (97) [SMALLEST]
Ge 19:11 the house with blindness, both s and great; 6996
30:15 *Is it* a s matter that thou hast taken my 4592
Ex 9: 9 it shall become s dust in all the land of Egypt, 80
16:14 upon the face of the wilderness *there lay* a s 1851
16:14 *as* s as the hoar frost on the ground. 1851
18:22 but every s matter they shall judge: 6996
18:26 but every s matter they judged themselves. 6996
30:36 thou shalt beat *some* of it very s, and put of 1854
Lev 16:12 his hands full of sweet incense beaten s, 1851
Nu 16: 9 *Seemeth it but* a s thing unto you, that 4592
16:13 *Is it* a s thing that thou hast brought us up 4592
32:41 and took the s towns thereof, 2333
Dt 1:17 you shall hear the s as well as the great; 6996
9:21 and stamped it, *and* ground *it* very s, 2912
9:21 *it* very small, *even* until *it was as* s as dust: 1854
25:13 in thy bag divers weights, a great and a s. 6996
25:14 house divers measures, a great and a s. 6996
32: 2 as the s rain upon the tender herb, and 8164
1Sa 5: 9 both s and great, and they had emerods in 6996
20: 2 my father will do nothing *either* great or s, 6996
30: 2 either great or s, but carried *them* away, 6996
30:19 neither s nor great, neither sons nor 6996
2Sa 7:19 this was yet a s thing in thy sight, O Lord 6994
17:13 until there be not one s stone found there. 6872
22:43 did I beat them *as* s as the dust of the earth, 7833
1Ki 2:20 she said, I desire one s petition of thee; 6996
19:12 in the fire: and after the fire a still s voice. 1851
22:31 saying, Fight neither with s nor great, 6996
2Ki 19:26 Therefore their inhabitants *were* of s power, 7116
23: 2 and all the people, both s and great: 6996
23: 6 stampt *it* s to powder, and cast the powder 1854
23:15 *and* stampt *it* s to powder, and burnt 1854
25:26 both s and great, and the captains of 6996
1Ch 17:17 *yet* this was a s thing in thine eyes, O God; 6994
25: 8 ward against *ward,* as well the s as 6996
26:13 they cast lots, as well the s as the great, 6996
2Ch 15:13 whether s or great, whether man or woman. 6996
18:30 saying, Fight ye not with s or great, 6996
24:24 For the army of the Syrians came with a s 4705

S

2Ch 31:15 by courses, as well *to* the great as *to* the **s**: 6996
34:30 the Levites, and all the people, great and **s**: 6996
35: 8 six hundred *s cattle,* and three hundred NIH
35: 9 for passover *offerings* five thousand *s cattle,* NIH
36:18 great and **s**, and the treasures of the house 6996
Est 1: 5 both unto great and **s**, seven days, in 6996
1:20 their husbands honour, both to great and **s**. 6996
Job 3:19 The **s** and great *are* there; and the servant *is* 6996
8: 7 Though thy beginning was **s**, yet thy latter 4705
15:11 *Are* the consolations of God **s** with thee? 4592
36:27 For he **maketh s** the drops of water: 1639
37: 6 likewise *to* the **s** rain, and *to* the great rain 4306
Ps 18:42 did I **beat** them **s** as the dust before 7833
104:25 both **s** and great beasts. 6996
115:13 that fear the LORD, *both* **s** and great. 6996
119:141 I *am* **s** and despised: *yet* do not I forget thy 6810
Pr 24:10 in the day of adversity, thy strength *is* **s**. 6862
Ecc 2: 7 **s**s cattle above all that were in Jerusalem 6629
Isa 1: 9 had left unto us a **very s** remnant, 4592+3509.1
7:13 *Is it* a **s thing** for you to weary men, but 4592
16:14 the remnant *shall be* very **s** *and* feeble. 4213
22:24 and the issue, all vessels of **s quantity**, 6996
29: 5 of thy strangers shall be like **s** dust, 1851
37:27 Therefore their inhabitants *were* of **s** power, 7116
40:15 are counted as the **s dust** of the balance: 7834
41:15 **beat** *them* **s**, and shalt make the hills as 1854
43:23 Thou hast not brought me the **s cattle** of 7716
54: 7 For a **s** moment have I forsaken thee; but 6996
60:22 a thousand, and a **s one** a strong nation: 6810
Jer 16: 6 the great and the **s** shall die in this land: 6996
30:19 also glorify them, and they shall not be **s**. 6819
44:28 Yet a **s** number that escape the sword shall 4962
49:15 I will make thee **s** among the heathen, *and* 6996
Eze 16:20 *Is this* of thy whoredoms a **s matter**, 4592
34:18 *Seemeth it* a **s thing** unto you to have eaten 4592
Da 11:23 and shall become strong with a **s** people. 4592
Am 7: 2 *by* whom shall Jacob arise? for he *is* **s**. 6996
7: 5 *by* whom shall Jacob arise? for he *is* **s**. 6996
8: 5 **making** the ephah **s**, and the shekel great, 6994
Ob 1: 2 I have made thee **s** among the heathen: 6996
Zec 4:10 For who hath despised the day of **s** *things?* 6996
Mk 3: 9 that a **s ship** should wait on him because *4142*
8: 7 And they had a few **s fishes**: and *2485*
Jn 2:15 when he had made a scourge of **s cords**, *4979*
6: 9 hath five barley loaves, and two **s fishes**: *3795*
Ac 12:18 there was no **s** stir among the soldiers, *3641*
15: 2 and Barnabas had no **s** dissension and *3641*
19:23 And the same time there arose no **s** stir *3641*
19:24 brought no **s** gain unto the craftsmen; *3641*
26:22 this day, witnessing both to **s** and great, *3398*
27:20 no **s** tempest lay on *us,* all hope that we *3641*
1Co 4: 3 But with me it is a **very s** *thing* that I *1646*
Jas 3: 4 *yet* are they turned about with a **very s** *1646*
Rev 11:18 and them that fear thy name, **s** and great; *3398*
13:16 *both* **s** and great, rich and poor, free and *3398*
19: 5 and ye that fear him, both **s** and great. *3398*
19:18 *men,* both free and bond, both **s** and great. *3398*
20:12 the dead, **s** and great, stand before God; *3398*

SMALL COPPER COINS See MITES

SMALLEST (2) [SMALL]
1Sa 9:21 a Benjamite, of the **s** of the tribes of Israel? 6996
1Co 6: 2 are ye unworthy to judge the **s matters**? *1646*

SMALLEST LETTER See JOT

SMALLEST STROKE See TITTLE

SMART (1)
Pr 11:15 He that is surety for a stranger shall **s** 7321+7451

SMELL (20) [SMELLED, SMELLETH, SMELLING, SWEETSMELLING]
Ge 27:27 he smelled the **s** of his raiment, and 7381
27:27 the **s** of my son *is* as the smell of a field 7381
27:27 the smell of my son *is* as the **s** of a field 7381
Ex 30:38 to **s** thereto, shall even be cut off from his 7306
Lev 26:31 I will not **s** the savour of your sweet 7306
Dt 4:28 which neither see, nor hear, nor eat, nor **s**. 7306
Ps 45: 8 All thy garments *s of* myrrh, and aloes, *and* NIH
115: 6 hear not: noses have they, but they **s** not: 7306
SS 1:12 my spikenard sendeth forth the **s** thereof. 7381
2:13 vines *with* the tender grape give a *good* **s**. 7381
4:10 and the **s** of thine ointments than all spices! 7381
4:11 the **s** of thy garments *is* like the smell of 7381
4:11 the smell of thy garments *is* like the **s** of 7381
7: 8 the vine, and the **s** of thy nose like apples; 7381
7:13 The mandrakes give a **s**, and at our gates 7381
Isa 3:24 *that* instead of **sweet s** there shall be stink; 1314
Da 3:27 nor the **s** of fire had passed on them. 7382
Hos 14: 6 be as the olive tree, and his **s** as Lebanon. 7381
Am 5:21 and I will not **s** in your solemn assemblies. 7306
Php 4:18 an odour of a **sweet s**, a sacrifice *2175*

SMELLED (2) [SMELL]
Ge 8:21 the LORD **s** a sweet savour; and 7306
27:27 he **s** the smell of his raiment, and 7306

SMELLETH (1) [SMELL]
Job 39:25 he **s** the battle afar off, the thunder of 7306

SMELLING (3) [SMELL]
SS 5: 5 my fingers *with* **sweet s** myrrh, upon 5674
5:13 his lips *like* lilies, dropping **sweet s** myrrh. 5674
1Co 12:17 the whole *were* hearing, where *were* the **s**? *3750*

SMITE (125) [SMITERS, SMITEST, SMITETH, SMITING, SMITTEN, SMOTE, SMOTEST]
Ge 8:21 neither will I again **s** any more every *thing* 5221
32: 8 **s** it, then the *other* company which is left 5221
32:11 lest he will come and **s** me, *and* the mother 5221
Ex 3:20 **s** Egypt with all my wonders which I will 5221
7:17 I will **s** with the rod that *is* in mine hand 5221
8: 2 behold, I will **s** all thy borders with frogs: 5062
8:16 out thy rod, and **s** the dust of the land, 5221
9:15 that I may **s** thee and thy people with 5221
12:12 will **s** all the firstborn in the land of Egypt, 5221
12:13 to destroy *you,* when I **s** the land of Egypt. 5221
12:23 For the LORD will pass through to **s** 5062
12:23 to come in unto your houses to **s** *you.* 5062
17: 6 thou shalt **s** the rock, and there shall come 5221
21:18 one **s** another with a stone, or with *his* fist, 5221
21:20 if a man **s** his servant, or his maid, with a 5221
21:26 if a man **s** the eye of his servant, or the eye 5221
21:27 if he **s out** his manservant's tooth, or 5307
Nu 14:12 I will **s** them with the pestilence, and 5221
22: 6 *that* we may **s** them, and *that* I may drive 5221
24:17 shall **s** the corners of Moab, and destroy all 4272
25:17 Vex the Midianites, and **s** them: 5221
35:16 if he **s** him with an instrument of iron, so 5221
35:17 if he **s** him with throwing a stone, 5221
35:18 Or *if* he **s** him with a hand weapon of 5221
35:21 Or in enmity **s** him with his hand, that he 5221
Dt 7: 2 thou shalt **s** them, *and* utterly destroy them; 5221
13:15 Thou shalt **surely s** the inhabitants of 5221+5221
19:11 **s** him mortally that he die, and fleeth into 5221
20:13 thou shalt **s** every male thereof with 5221
28:22 The LORD shall **s** thee with a 5221
28:27 The LORD will **s** thee with the botch of 5221
28:28 The LORD shall **s** thee with madness, and 5221
28:35 The LORD shall **s** thee in the knees, and 5221
33:11 **s** through the loins of them that rise against 4272
Jos 7: 3 or three thousand men go up and **s** Ai; 5221
10: 4 and help me, that we may **s** Gibeon: 5221
10:19 your enemies, and **s the hindmost** of them; 2179
12: 6 of the LORD and the children of Israel **s**: 5221
13:12 for these did Moses **s**, and cast them out. 5221
Jdg 6:16 and thou shalt **s** the Midianites as one man. 5221
20:31 they began to **s** of the people, *and* kill, as at 5221
20:39 Benjamin began to **s** *and* kill of the men of 5221
21:10 **s** the inhabitants of Jabesh-gilead with 5221
1Sa 15: 3 Now go and **s** Amalek, and utterly destroy 5221
17:46 I will **s** thee, and take thine head from thee; 5221
18:11 I will **s** David even to the wall *with it.* And 5221
19:10 Saul sought to **s** David even to the wall 5221
20:33 Saul cast a javelin at him to **s** him: 5221
23: 2 Shall I go and **s** these Philistines? 5221
23: 2 Go, and **s** the Philistines, and save Keilah. 5221
26: 8 now therefore let me **s** him, I pray thee, 5221
26: 8 and I will not **s** him the second time. NIH
26:10 the LORD liveth, the LORD shall **s** him; 5062
2Sa 2:22 wherefore should I **s** thee to the ground? 5221
5:24 before thee, to **s** the host of the Philistines. 5221
13:28 and when I say unto you, **S** Amnon; 5221
15:14 and **s** the city with the edge of the sword. 5221
17: 2 him shall flee; and I will **s** the king only: 5221
18:11 why didst thou not **s** him there to 5221
1Ki 14:15 For the LORD shall **s** Israel, as a reed is 5221

1Ki	20:35	the word of the LORD, S me, I pray thee.	5221
	20:35	I pray thee. And the man refused to s him.	5221
	20:37	another man, and said, S me, I pray thee.	5221
2Ki	3:19	ye shall s every fenced city, and	5221
	6:18	said, S this people, I pray thee,	5221
	6:21	shall I s *them?* shall I smite *them?*	5221
	6:21	shall I smite *them?* shall I s *them?*	5221
	6:22	Thou shalt not s *them:* wouldest thou smite	5221
	6:22	Thou shalt not smite *them:* wouldest thou s	5221
	9:7	thou shalt s the house of Ahab thy master,	5221
	9:27	and said, S him also in the chariot.	5221
	13:17	for thou shalt s the Syrians in Aphek,	5221
	13:18	unto the king of Israel, S upon the ground.	5221
	13:19	*it:* whereas now thou shalt s Syria	5221
1Ch	14:15	for God is gone forth before thee to s	5221
2Ch	21:14	*with* a great plague will the LORD s thy	5062
Ps	121:6	The sun shall not s thee by day, nor	5221
	141:5	Let the righteous s me; *it shall be* a	1986
Pr	19:25	S a scorner, and the simple will beware:	5221
Isa	3:17	Therefore the Lord will s **with a scab**	5596
	10:24	he shall s thee with a rod, and shall lift up	5221
	11:4	he shall s the earth with the rod of his	5221
	11:15	shall s it in *the* seven streams, and	5221
	19:22	the LORD shall s Egypt: *he* shall smite	5062
	19:22	*he* shall s and heal *it:* and they shall return	5062
	49:10	neither shall the heat nor sun s them:	5221
	58:4	debate, and to s with the fist of wickedness:	5221
Jer	18:18	let us s him with the tongue, and let us not	5221
	21:6	I will s the inhabitants of this city, both	5221
	21:7	he shall s them with the edge of the sword;	5221
	43:11	he shall s the land of Egypt, *and*	5221
	46:13	should come and s the land of Egypt.	5221
	49:28	Nebuchadrezzar king of Babylon shall s,	5221
Eze	5:2	take a third *part, and* s about it with a knife:	5221
	6:11	S with thine hand, and stamp with thy foot,	5221
	9:5	Go ye after him through the city, and s:	5221
	21:12	upon my people: s therefore upon *thy* thigh.	5606
	21:14	s *thine* hands together, and let the sword be	5221
	21:17	I will also s mine hands together, and I will	5221
	32:15	when I shall s all them that dwell therein,	5221
	39:3	I will s thy bow out of thy left hand, and	5221
Am	3:15	I will s the winter house with the summer	5221
	6:11	he will s the great house *with* breaches, and	5221
	9:1	he said, S the lintel of the door, that	5221
Mic	5:1	they shall s the judge of Israel with a rod	5221
Na	2:10	the knees s **together**, and much pain *is* in	6375
Zec	9:4	her out, and he will s her power in the sea;	5221
	10:11	shall s the waves in the sea, and all	5221
	11:6	they shall s the land, and out of their hand	3807
	12:4	I will s every horse with astonishment, and	5221
	12:4	will s every horse of the people with	5221
	13:7	s the shepherd, and the sheep shall be	5221
	14:12	s all the people that have fought against	5062
	14:18	where*with* the LORD will s the heathen	5062
Mal	4:6	lest I come and s the earth *with* a curse.	5221
Mt	5:39	whosoever shall s thee on thy right cheek,	*4474*
	24:49	And shall begin to s *his* fellowservants, and	*5180*
	26:31	I will s the shepherd, and the sheep of	*3960*
Mk	14:27	I will s the shepherd, and the sheep shall be	*3960*
Lk	22:49	unto him, Lord, shall we s with the sword?	*3960*
Ac	23:2	that stood by him to s him on the mouth.	*5180*
	23:3	God shall s thee, *thou* whited wall:	*5180*
2Co	11:20	exalt himself, if a man s you on the face.	*1194*
Rev	11:6	and to s the earth with all plagues, as often	*3960*
	19:15	that with it he should s the nations:	*3960*

SMITERS (1) [SMITE]

Isa	50:6	I gave my back to the s, and my cheeks to	5221

SMITEST (2) [SMITE]

Ex	2:13	the wrong, Wherefore s thou thy fellow?	5221
Jn	18:23	of the evil: but if well, why s thou me?	*1194*

SMITETH (13) [SMITE]

Ex	21:12	He that s a man, so that he die, shall be	5221
	21:15	he that s his father, or his mother, shall be	5221
Dt	25:11	husband out of the hand of him that s him,	5221
	27:24	Cursed *be* he that s his neighbour secretly.	5221
Jos	15:16	He that s Kirjath-sepher, and taketh it,	5221
Jdg	1:12	He that s Kirjath-sepher, and taketh it,	5221
2Sa	5:8	s the Jebusites, and the lame and the blind,	5221
1Ch	11:6	Whosoever s the Jebusites first shall be	5221
Job	26:12	by his understanding he s **through**	4272
Isa	9:13	For the people turneth not unto him that s	5221
La	3:30	He giveth *his* cheek to him that s him: he is	5221
Eze	7:9	ye shall know that I *am* the LORD that s.	5221
Lk	6:29	*And* unto him that s thee on the *one* cheek	*5180*

SMITH (3) [COPPERSMITH, GOLDSMITH, GOLDSMITH'S, GOLDSMITHS, SILVERSMITH, SMITHS]

1Sa	13:19	Now there was no s found throughout all	2796
Isa	44:12	The s *with* the tongs both worketh in	1270+2796
	54:16	I have created the s that bloweth the coals	2796

SMITHS (4) [SMITH]

2Ki	24:14	and all the craftsmen and s:	4525
	24:16	craftsmen and s a thousand, all *that were*	4525
Jer	24:1	with the carpenters and s, from Jerusalem,	4525
	29:2	Jerusalem, and the carpenters, and the s,	4525

SMITING (5) [SMITE]

Ex	2:11	he spied an Egyptian s a Hebrew, *one* of his	5221
2Sa	8:13	from s of the Syrians in the valley of salt,	5221
1Ki	20:37	smote him, so that in s he wounded *him.*	5221
2Ki	3:24	they went forward s the Moabites, even in	5221
Mic	6:13	Therefore also will I make *thee* sick in s	5221

SMITTEN (63) [SMITE]

Ex	7:25	after *that* the LORD had s the river.	5221
	9:31	the flax and the barley was s: for the barley	5221
	9:32	the wheat and the rye were not s: for they	5221
	22:2	be found breaking up, and be s that he die,	5221
Nu	14:42	that ye be not s before your enemies.	5062
	22:28	that thou hast s me these three times?	5221
	22:32	Wherefore hast thou s thine ass these three	5221
	33:4	which the LORD had s among them:	5221
Dt	1:42	lest ye be s before your enemies.	5062
	28:7	rise up against thee *to be* s before thy face:	5062
	28:25	The LORD shall cause thee *to be* s before	5062
Jdg	1:8	s it with the edge of the sword, and set	5221
	20:32	They *are* s **down** before us, as at the first.	5062
	20:36	children of Benjamin saw that they were s:	5062
	20:39	Surely they are s **down** before us,	5062+5062
1Sa	4:2	Israel was s before the Philistines:	5062
	4:3	Wherefore hath the LORD s us to day	5062
	4:10	Israel was s, and they fled every man into	5062
	5:12	the men that died not were s with	5221
	6:19	the LORD had s *many* of the people *with*	5221
	7:10	and they were s before Israel.	5062
	13:4	all Israel heard say *that* Saul had s a	5221
	30:1	and s Ziklag, and burnt it with fire;	5221
2Sa	2:31	the servants of David had s of Benjamin,	5221
	8:9	that David had s all the host of Hadadezer,	5221
	8:10	had fought against Hadadezer, and s him:	5221
	10:15	when the Syrians saw that they were s	5062
	10:19	saw that they were s before Israel,	5062
	11:15	ye from him, that he may be s, and die.	5221
1Ki	8:33	When thy people Israel be s **down** before	5062
	11:15	after he had s every male in Edom;	5221
2Ki	2:14	when he also had s the waters, they parted	5221
	3:23	surely slain, and they have s one another:	5221
	13:19	*Thou* shouldest have s five or six times;	5221
	13:19	hadst thou s Syria till *thou* hadst consumed	5221
	14:10	Thou hast **indeed** s Edom, and	5221+5221
1Ch	18:9	s all the host of Hadarezer king of Zobah;	5221
	18:10	had fought against Hadarezer, and s him;	5221
2Ch	20:22	were come against Judah; and they were s.	5062
	25:16	forbear; why shouldest thou be s? Then	5221
	25:19	Thou sayest, Lo, thou hast s the Edomites;	5221
	26:20	to go out, because the LORD had s him.	5060
	28:17	again the Edomites had come and s Judah,	5221
Job	16:10	they have s me upon the cheek	5221
Ps	3:7	for thou hast s all mine enemies *upon*	5221
	69:26	For they persecute *him* whom thou hast s;	5221
	102:4	My heart is s, and withered like grass; so	5221
	143:3	he hath s my life **down** to the ground;	1792
Isa	5:25	his hand against them, and hath s them:	5221
	24:12	and the gate is s *with* destruction.	3807
	27:7	Hath he s him, as he smote those that smote	5221
	53:4	him stricken, s of God, and afflicted.	5221
Jer	2:30	In vain have I s your children;	5221
	14:19	why hast thou s us, and *there is* no healing	5221
	37:10	For though ye had s the whole army of	5221
Eze	22:13	I have s mine hand at thy dishonest gain	5221
	33:21	came unto me, saying, The city is s.	5221
	40:1	the fourteenth year after that the city was s,	5221
Hos	6:1	heal us; he hath s, and he will bind us up.	5221
	9:16	Ephraim is s, their root is dried up,	5221

Am 4: 9 I have s you with blasting and mildew: 5221
Ac 23: 3 commandest me to be s contrary to *5180*
Rev 8:12 and the third *part* of the sun was s, and *4141*

SMOKE (45) [SMOKING]
Ge 19:28 the s of the country went up as the smoke 7008
19:28 the smoke of the country went up as the s 7008
Ex 19:18 mount Sinai was altogether on a s, because 6225
19:18 the s thereof ascended as the smoke of a 6227
19:18 the smoke thereof ascended as the s of a 6227
Dt 29:20 and his jealousy shall s against that man, 6225
Jos 8:20 the s of the city ascended up to heaven, and 6227
8:21 that the s of the city ascended, then 6227
Jdg 20:38 that they should make a great flame with s 6227
20:40 to arise up out of the city *with* a pillar of s, 6227
2Sa 22: 9 There went up a s out of his nostrils, and 6227
Job 41:20 Out of his nostrils goeth s, as *out of* a 6227
Ps 18: 8 There went up a s out of his nostrils, and 6227
37:20 into s shall they consume *away*. 6227
68: 2 As s is driven away, *so* drive *them* away: 6227
74: 1 *why* doth thine anger s against the sheep of 6225
102: 3 For my days are consumed like s, and 6227
104:32 he toucheth the hills, and they s. 6225
119:83 For I am become like a bottle in the s; 7008
144: 5 touch the mountains, and they shall s. 6225
Pr 10:26 as s to the eyes, so *is* the sluggard to them 6227
SS 3: 6 out of the wilderness like pillars of s, 6227
Isa 4: 5 a cloud and s by day, and the shining of a 6227
6: 4 that cried, and the house was filled *with* s. 6227
9:18 they shall mount up *like* the lifting up of s. 6227
14:31 for there shall come from the north a s, and 6227
34:10 nor day; the s thereof shall go up for ever: 6227
51: 6 for the heavens shall vanish away like s, 6227
65: 5 These *are* a s in my nose, a fire that burneth 6227
Hos 13: 3 the floor, and as the s out of the chimney. 6227
Joel 2:30 in the earth, blood, and fire, and pillars of s. 6227
Na 2:13 I will burn her chariots in the s, and 6227
Ac 2:19 blood, and fire, and vapour of s: *2586*
Rev 8: 4 And the s of the incense, *which came* with *2586*
9: 2 and there arose a s out of the pit, as *2586*
9: 2 out of the pit, as the s of a great furnace; *2586*
9: 2 the air were darkened by reason of the s of *2586*
9: 3 And there came out of the s locusts upon *2586*
9:17 mouths issued fire and s and brimstone. *2586*
9:18 the fire, and by the s, and by the brimstone, *2586*
14:11 And the s of their torment ascendeth up for *2586*
15: 8 And the temple was filled with s from *2586*
18: 9 when they shall see the s of her burning, *2586*
18:18 And cried when they saw the s of her *2586*
19: 3 And her s rose up for ever and ever. *2586*

SMOKING (5) [SMOKE]
Ge 15:17 behold a s furnace, and a burning lamp that 6227
Ex 20:18 noise of the trumpet, and the mountain s: 6226
Isa 7: 4 for the two tails of these s firebrands, 6226
42: 3 and the s flax shall he not quench: 3544
Mt 12:20 he not break, and s flax shall he not quench, *5188*

SMOOTH (6) [SMOOTHER, SMOOTHETH]
Ge 27:11 brother *is* a hairy man, and I *am* a s man: 2509
27:16 upon his hands, and upon the s of his neck: 2513
1Sa 17:40 chose him five s stones out of the brook, 2512
Isa 30:10 speak unto us s *things*, prophesy deceits: 2513
57: 6 Among the s *stones* of the stream *is* thy 2511
Lk 3: 5 and the rough ways *shall be* made s; *3006*

SMOOTHER (2) [SMOOTH]
Ps 55:21 *The words of* his mouth were s than butter, 2505
Pr 5: 3 a honeycomb, and her mouth *is* s than oil: 2509

SMOOTHETH (1) [SMOOTH]
Isa 41: 7 he that s *with* the hammer him that smote 2505

SMOTE (230) [SMITE]
Ge 14: 5 s the Rephaims in Ashteroth Karnaim, and 5221
14: 7 s all the country of the Amalekites, and 5221
14:15 and s them, and pursued them unto Hobah, 5221
19:11 they s the men that *were at* the door of 5221
36:35 who s Midian in the field of Moab, 5221
Ex 7:20 and s the waters that *were* in the river, 5221
8:17 s the dust of the earth, and it became lice in 5221
9:25 the hail s throughout all the land of Egypt 5221
9:25 the hail s every herb of the field, and brake 5221
12:27 when he s the Egyptians, and delivered our 5062
12:29 that at midnight the LORD s all 5221
21:19 his staff, then shall he that s *him* be quit: 5221
Nu 3:13 *for* on the day that I s all the firstborn in 5221
8:17 on the day that I s every firstborn in 5221
11:33 the LORD s the people *with* a very great 5221
14:45 s them, and discomfited them, *even* unto 5221
20:11 and with his rod he s the rock twice: 5221
21:24 Israel s him with the edge of the sword, 5221
21:35 So they s him, and his sons, and all his 5221
22:23 Balaam s the ass, to turn her *into* the way. 5221
22:25 foot against the wall: and he s her again. 5221
22:27 was kindled, and he s the ass with a staff. 5221
24:10 and he s his hands **together**: 5606
32: 4 *Even* the country which the LORD s 5221
35:21 he that s *him* shall surely be put to death; 5221
Dt 2:33 we s him, and his sons, and all his people. 5221
3: 3 we s him until none was left to him 5221
4:46 whom Moses and the children of Israel s, 5221
25:18 by the way, and **s the hindmost** of thee, 2179
29: 7 out against us unto battle, and we s them: 5221
Jos 7: 5 the men of Ai s of them about thirty and 5221
7: 5 and s them in the going down: 5221
8:22 they s them, so that *they* let none of them 5221
8:24 *unto* Ai, and s it with the edge of the sword. 5221
9:18 the children of Israel s them not, because 5221
10:10 and s them to Azekah, and unto Makkedah. 5221
10:26 afterward Joshua s them, and slew them, 5221
10:28 s it with the edge of the sword, and the king 5221
10:30 he s it with the edge of the sword, and all 5221
10:32 s it with the edge of the sword, and all 5221
10:33 Joshua s him and his people, until *he* had 5221
10:35 s it with the edge of the sword, and all 5221
10:37 s it with the edge of the sword, and the king 5221
10:39 they s them with the edge of the sword, and 5221
10:40 So Joshua s all the country of the hills, and 5221
10:41 Joshua s them from Kadesh-barnea even 5221
11: 8 who s them, and chased them unto great 5221
11: 8 they s them, until *they* left them none 5221
11:10 and s the king thereof with the sword: 5221
11:11 they s all the souls that *were* therein with 5221
11:12 s them with the edge of the sword, *and* 5221
11:14 every man they s with the edge of 5221
11:17 kings he took, and s them, and slew them. 5221
12: 1 which the children of Israel s, and 5221
12: 7 the children of Israel s on *this* side Jordan 5221
13:21 whom Moses s with the princes of Midian, 5221
19:47 s it with the edge of the sword, and 5221
20: 5 because he s his neighbour unwittingly, and 5221
Jdg 1:25 they s the city with the edge of the sword; 5221
3:13 went and s Israel, and possessed the city of 5221
4:21 s the nail into his temples, and fastened *it* 8628
5:26 with the hammer she s Sisera, she smote off 1986
5:26 she **s off** his head, when she had pierced 4277
7:13 a tent, and s it that it fell, and overturned it, 5221
8:11 east of Nobah and Jogbehah, and s the host: 5221
9:43 and he rose up against them, and s them. 5221
11:21 into the hand of Israel, and they s them: 5221
11:33 he s them from Aroer, even till thou come 5221
12: 4 the men of Gilead s Ephraim, because 5221
15: 8 he s them hip and thigh *with* a great 5221
18:27 they s them with the edge of the sword, and 5221
20:35 the LORD s Benjamin before Israel: and 5062
20:37 s all the city with the edge of the sword. 5221
20:48 s them with the edge of the sword, as well 5221
1Sa 4: 8 these *are* the Gods that s the Egyptians with 5221
5: 6 s them with emerods, *even* Ashdod and 5221
5: 9 he s the men of the city, both small and 5221
6: 9 we shall know that *it is* not his hand *that* s 5060
6:19 he s the men of Beth-shemesh, because 5221
6:19 even he s of the people fifty thousand 5221
7:11 pursued the Philistines, and s them, 5221
13: 3 Jonathan s the garrison of the Philistines 5221
14:31 they s the Philistines that day from 5221
14:48 s the Amalekites, and delivered Israel out 5221
15: 7 Saul s the Amalekites from Havilah *until* 5221
17:35 s him, and delivered *it* out of his mouth: 5221
17:35 *him* by his beard, and s him, and slew him. 5221
17:49 slang *it,* and s the Philistine in his forehead, 5221
17:50 a stone, and s the Philistine, and slew him; 5221
19:10 and he s the javelin into the wall: 5221
22:19 s he with the edge of the sword, both men 5221
23: 5 and s them *with* a great slaughter. 5221
24: 5 that David's heart s him, because he had 5221
25:38 ten days *after,* that the LORD s Nabal, 5062
27: 9 David s the land, and left neither man nor 5221

1Sa	30:17	David s them from the twilight even unto	5221
2Sa	1:15	fall upon him. And he s him that he died.	5221
	2:23	s him under the fifth *rib*, that the spear	5221
	3:27	s him there *under* the fifth *rib*, that he died,	5221
	4: 6	they s him under the fifth *rib:* and Rechab	5221
	4: 7	they s him, and slew him, and	5221
	5:20	and David s them there, and said,	5221
	5:25	s the Philistines from Geba until thou come	5221
	6: 7	God s him there for *his* error; and there he	5221
	8: 1	that David s the Philistines, and	5221
	8: 2	he s Moab, and measured them with a line,	5221
	8: 3	David s also Hadadezer, the son of Rehob,	5221
	10:18	s Shobach the captain of their host,	5221
	11:21	Who s Abimelech the son of Jerubbesheth?	5221
	14: 6	but the one s the other, and slew him.	5221
	14: 7	they said, Deliver him that s his brother,	5221
	18:15	armour compassed about and s Absalom,	5221
	20:10	so he s him therewith in the fifth *rib*, and	5221
	21:17	and s the Philistine, and killed him.	5221
	23:10	s the Philistines until his hand was weary,	5221
	24:10	David's heart s him after that he had	5221
	24:17	when he saw the angel that s the people,	5221
1Ki	15:20	s Ijon, and Dan, and Abel-beth-maachah,	5221
	15:27	Baasha s him at Gibbethon,	5221
	15:29	*that* he s all the house of Jeroboam;	5221
	16:10	Zimri went in and s him, and killed him,	5221
	20:21	s the horses and chariots, and slew	5221
	20:37	the man s him, so that in smiting he	5221
	22:24	and s Micaiah on the cheek, and said,	5221
	22:34	s the king of Israel between the joints of	5221
2Ki	2: 8	s the waters, and they were divided hither	5221
	2:14	s the waters, and said, Where *is* the LORD	5221
	3:24	the Israelites rose up and s the Moabites, so	5221
	3:25	howbeit the slingers went about *it*, and s it.	5221
	6:18	he s them with blindness according to	5221
	8:21	s the Edomites which compassed him	5221
	9:24	s Jehoram between his arms, and the arrow	5221
	10:25	they s them with the edge of the sword;	5221
	10:32	Hazael s them in all the coasts of Israel;	5221
	12:21	of Shomer, his servants, s him, and he died;	5221
	13:18	the ground. And he s thrice, and stayed.	5221
	15: 5	the LORD s the king, so that he was a	5060
	15:10	s him before the people, and slew him, and	5221
	15:14	and s Shallum the son of Jabesh in Samaria,	5221
	15:16	Menahem s Tiphsah, and all that *were*	5221
	15:16	opened not *to him*, therefore he s *it; and*	5221
	15:25	against him, and s him in Samaria,	5221
	15:30	s him, and slew him, and reigned in his	5221
	18: 8	He s the Philistines, *even* unto Gaza, and	5221
	19:35	s in the camp of the Assyrians an hundred	5221
	19:37	and Sharezer *his sons* s him with the sword:	5221
	25:21	the king of Babylon s them, and slew them	5221
	25:25	s Gedaliah, that he died, and the Jews and	5221
1Ch	1:46	which s Midian in the field of Moab,	5221
	4:41	s their tents, and the habitations that were	5221
	4:43	they s the rest of the Amalekites that were	5221
	13:10	he s him, because he put his hand to	5221
	14:11	to Baal-perazim; and David s them there.	5221
	14:16	they s the host of the Philistines from	5221
	18: 1	that David s the Philistines, and	5221
	18: 2	he s Moab; and the Moabites became	5221
	18: 3	David s Hadarezer king of Zobah unto	5221
	20: 1	And Joab s Rabbah, and destroyed it.	5221
	21: 7	with this thing; therefore he s Israel.	5221
2Ch	13:15	that God s Jeroboam and all Israel before	5062
	14:12	So the LORD s the Ethiopians before Asa,	5062
	14:14	they s all the cities round about Gerar;	5221
	14:15	They s also the tents of cattle, and	5221
	16: 4	they s Ijon, and Dan, and Abel-maim, and	5221
	18:23	and s Micaiah upon the cheek, and said,	5221
	18:33	s the king of Israel between the joints of	5221
	21: 9	s the Edomites which compassed him in,	5221
	21:18	after all this the LORD s him in his	5062
	22: 5	at Ramoth-gilead: and the Syrians s Joram.	5221
	25:11	and s *of* the children of Seir ten thousand.	5221
	25:13	s three thousand of them, and took much	5221
	28: 5	they s him, and carried away a great	5221
	28: 5	of Israel, who s him *with* a great slaughter.	5221
	28:23	unto the gods of Damascus, which s him:	5221
Ne	13:25	s certain of them, and pluckt off their hair,	5221
Est	9: 5	Thus the Jews s all their enemies *with*	5221
Job	1:19	s the four corners of the house, and it fell	5060
	2: 7	s Job with sore boils from the sole of his	5221
Ps	60: T	s of Edom in the valley of salt twelve	5221
	78:20	Behold, he s the rock, that the waters	5221
	78:31	and **s down** the chosen *men* of Israel.	3766
	78:51	s all the firstborn in Egypt; the chief of	5221
	78:66	he s his enemies in the hinder parts: he put	5221
	105:33	He s their vines also and their fig trees; and	5221
	105:36	He s also all the firstborn in their land,	5221
	135: 8	Who s the firstborn of Egypt, both of man	5221
	135:10	Who s great nations, and slew mighty	5221
	136:10	To him that s Egypt in their firstborn:	5221
	136:17	To him which s great kings: for his mercy	5221
SS	5: 7	found me, they s me, they wounded me;	5221
Isa	10:20	shall no more again stay upon him that s	5221
	14: 6	He who s the people in wrath *with* a	5221
	14:29	the rod of him that s thee is broken:	5221
	27: 7	smitten him, as he s those that smote him?	4347
	27: 7	smitten him, as he smote those that s him?	5221
	30:31	be beaten down, *which* s with a rod.	5221
	37:36	s in the camp of the Assyrians an hundred	5221
	37:38	and Sharezer his sons s him with the sword;	5221
	41: 7	*with* the hammer him that s the anvil,	1986
	57:17	of his covetousness was I wroth, and s him:	5221
	60:10	for in my wrath I s thee, but in my favour	5221
Jer	20: 2	Pashur s Jeremiah the prophet, and put him	5221
	31:19	that I was instructed, I s upon *my* thigh:	5606
	37:15	s him, and put him *in* prison *in* the house of	5221
	41: 2	s Gedaliah the son of Ahikam the son of	5221
	46: 2	which Nebuchadrezzar king of Babylon s	5221
	47: 1	the Philistines, before that Pharaoh s Gaza.	5221
	52:27	the king of Babylon s them, and put them	5221
Da	2:34	which s the image upon his feet *that were*	4223
	2:35	the stone that s the image became a great	4223
	5: 6	and his knees s one against another.	5368
	8: 7	and s the ram, and brake his two horns:	5221
Jnh	4: 7	and it s the gourd, that it withered.	5221
Hag	2:17	I s you with blasting and with mildew and	5221
Mt	26:51	servant of the high priest's, and **s off** his ear.	*851*
	26:67	s *him* **with the palms of** their **hands**,	*4474*
	26:68	unto us, *thou* Christ, Who is he that s thee?	*3817*
	27:30	and took the reed, and s him on the head.	*5180*
Mk	14:47	and s a servant of the high priest, and	*3817*
	15:19	And they s him on the head with a reed,	*5180*
Lk	18:13	unto heaven, but s upon his breast, saying,	*5180*
	22:50	And one of them s the servant of the high	*3960*
	22:63	that held Jesus mocked him, and s *him*.	*1194*
	22:64	saying, Prophesy, who is it that s thee?	*3817*
	23:48	were done, s their breasts, and returned.	*5180*
Jn	18:10	and s the high priest's servant, and cut off	*3817*
	19: 3	and they s him **with** their **hands**.	*1325+4475*
Ac	7:24	him that was oppressed, and s the Egyptian:	*3960*
	12: 7	and he s Peter on the side, and raised him	*3960*
	12:23	And immediately *the* angel of the Lord s	*3960*

SMOTEST (1) [SMITE]

Ex	17: 5	thy rod, wherewith thou s the river, take in	5221

SMYRNA (2)

Rev	1:11	and unto S, and unto Pergamos, and	*4667*
	2: 8	And unto the angel of the church in S write;	*4668*

SNAIL (2)

Lev	11:30	and the lizard, and the s, and the mole.	2546
Ps	58: 8	As a s *which* melteth, let *every one of them*	7642

SNARE (47) [ENSNARED, SNARED, SNARES]

Ex	10: 7	How long shall this *man* be a s unto us?	4170
	23:33	their gods, it will surely be a s unto thee.	4170
	34:12	lest it be for a s in the midst of thee:	4170
Dt	7:16	their gods; for that *will be* a s unto thee.	4170
Jdg	2: 3	and their gods shall be a s unto you.	4170
	8:27	which *thing* became a s unto Gideon, and	4170
1Sa	18:21	that she may be a s to him, and that	4170
	28: 9	wherefore then **layest** thou **a s** for my life,	5367
Job	18: 8	by his own feet, and he walketh upon a s.	7639
	18:10	The s *is* laid for him in the ground, and	2256
Ps	69:22	Let their table become a s before them: and	6341
	91: 3	Surely he shall deliver thee from the s of	6341
	106:36	their idols: which were a s unto them.	4170
	119:110	The wicked have laid a s for me: yet I erred	6341
	124: 7	Our soul is escaped as a bird out of the s of	6341
	124: 7	the s is broken, and we are escaped.	6341
	140: 5	The proud have hid a s for me, and cords;	6341
	141: 9	Keep me from the s *which* they have laid	6341
	142: 3	I walked have they privily laid a s for me.	6341
Pr	7:23	as a bird hasteth to the s, and knoweth not	6341

S

Pr 18: 7 and his lips *are* the **s** of his soul. 4170
20:25 *It is* a **s** to the man *who* devoureth *that* 4170
22:25 thou learn his ways, and get a **s** to thy soul. 4170
29: 6 the transgression of an evil man *there is* a **s**: 4170
29: 8 Scornful men **bring** a city **into a s**: but 6315
29:25 The fear of man bringeth a **s**: but 4170
Ecc 9:12 and as the birds that are caught in the **s**; 6341
Isa 8:14 and for a **s** to the inhabitants of Jerusalem. 4170
24:17 Fear, and the pit, and the **s**, *are* upon thee, 6341
24:18 the midst of the pit shall be taken in the **s**: 6341
29:21 **lay a s** for him that reproveth in the gate, 6983
Jer 48:43 Fear, and the pit, and the **s**, *shall be* upon 6341
48:44 up out of the pit shall be taken in the **s**: 6341
50:24 I have **laid a s** for thee, and thou art also 3369
La 3:47 Fear and a **s** is come upon us, desolation 6354
Eze 12:13 upon him, and he shall be taken in my **s**: 4686
17:20 he shall be taken in my **s**, and I will bring 4686
Hos 5: 1 because ye have been a **s** on Mizpah, and 6341
9: 8 the prophet *is* a **s** of a fowler in all his 6341
Am 3: 5 Can a bird fall in a **s** upon the earth, 6341
3: 5 shall *one* take up a **s** from the earth, and 6341
Lk 21:35 For as a **s** shall it come on all them that *3803*
Ro 11: 9 Let their table be made a **s**, and a trap, and *3803*
1Co 7:35 not that I may cast a **s** upon you, but *1029*
1Ti 3: 7 he fall into reproach and the **s** of the devil. *3803*
6: 9 that will be rich fall into temptation and a **s**, *3803*
2Ti 2:26 recover themselves out of the **s** of the devil, *3803*

SNARED (9) [SNARE]
Dt 7:25 nor take *it* unto thee, lest thou be **s** therein: 3369
12:30 Take heed to thyself that thou be not **s** by 5367
Ps 9:16 the wicked is **s** in the work of his own 5367
Pr 6: 2 Thou art **s** with the words of thy mouth, 3369
12:13 The wicked is **s** by the transgression of *his* 4170
Ecc 9:12 so *are* the sons of men **s** in an evil time, 3369
Isa 8:15 fall, and be broken, and be **s**, and be taken. 3369
28:13 and be broken, and **s**, and taken. 3369
42:22 *they are* all of them **s** in holes, and they are 6351

SNARES (14) [SNARE]
Jos 23:13 they shall be **s** and traps unto you, and 6341
2Sa 22: 6 me about; the **s** of death prevented me: 4170
Job 22:10 Therefore **s** *are* round about thee, and 6341
40:24 it with his eyes: *his* nose pierceth through **s**. 4170
Ps 11: 6 Upon the wicked he shall rain **s**, fire and 6341
18: 5 me about: the **s** of death prevented me. 4170
38:12 They also that seek after my life **lay s** *for* 5367
64: 5 they commune of laying **s** privily; they say, 4170
Pr 13:14 of life, to depart from the **s** of death. 4170
14:27 of life, to depart from the **s** of death. 4170
22: 5 Thorns *and* **s** *are* in the way of the froward: 6341
Ecc 7:26 whose heart *is* **s** and nets, *and* her hands *as* 4685
Jer 5:26 *men:* they lay wait, as he that setteth **s**; 3353
18:22 a pit to take me, and hid **s** for my feet. 6341

SNATCH (1)
Isa 9:20 he shall **s** on the right hand, and be hungry; 1504

SNEERED See DERIDED

SNORTING (1)
Jer 8:16 The **s** of his horses was heard from Dan: 5170

SNOUT (1)
Pr 11:22 *As* a jewel of gold in a swine's **s**, *so is* a fair 639

SNOW (24) [SNOWY]
Ex 4: 6 it out, behold, his hand *was* leprous as **s**. 7950
Nu 12:10 behold, Miriam *became* leprous, *white* as **s**: 7950
2Sa 23:20 slew a lion in the midst of a pit in time of **s**: 7950
2Ki 5:27 out from his presence a leper *as white* as **s**. 7950
Job 6:16 reason of the ice, *and* wherein the **s** is hid: 7950
9:30 If I wash myself with **s** water, and make my 7950
24:19 Drought and heat consume the **s** waters: *so* 7950
37: 6 For he saith to the **s**, Be thou *on* the earth; 7950
38:22 thou entered into the treasures of the **s**? 7950
Ps 51: 7 wash me, and I shall be whiter than **s**. 7950
68:14 kings in it, it was *white as* **s** in Salmon. 7949
147:16 He giveth **s** like wool: he scattereth 7950
148: 8 Fire, and hail; **s**, and vapour; stormy wind 7950
Pr 25:13 As the cold of **s** in the time of harvest, *so* 7950
26: 1 As **s** in summer, and as rain in harvest, so 7950
31:21 She is not afraid of the **s** for her household: 7950
Isa 1:18 be as scarlet, they shall be as white as **s**; 7950
55:10 the **s** from heaven, and returneth not thither, 7950
Jer 18:14 Will *a man* leave the **s** of Lebanon *which* 7950
La 4: 7 Her Nazarites were purer than **s**, they were 7950
Da 7: 9 whose garment *was* white as **s**, and the hair 8517
Mt 28: 3 like lightning, and his raiment white as **s**: *5510*
Mk 9: 3 became shining, exceeding white as **s**; *5510*
Rev 1:14 hairs *were* white like wool, *as* white as **s**; *5510*

SNOWY (1) [SNOW]
1Ch 11:22 and slew a lion in a pit in a **s** day. 7950

SNUFFDISHES (3) [DISH, SNUFFETH]
Ex 25:38 and the **s** thereof, *shall be of* pure gold. 4289
37:23 and his snuffers, and his **s**, *of* pure gold. 4289
Nu 4: 9 and his **s**, and all the oil vessels thereof, 4289

SNUFFED (2) [SNUFFETH]
Jer 14: 6 they **s up** the wind like dragons; 7602
Mal 1:13 what a weariness *is it!* and ye have **s** at it, 5301

SNUFFERS (6) [SNUFFETH]
Ex 37:23 and his **s**, and his snuffdishes, *of* pure gold. 4457
1Ki 7:50 the **s**, and the basons, and the spoons, and 4212
2Ki 12:13 **s**, basons, trumpets, any vessels of gold, or 4212
25:14 the **s**, and the spoons, and all the vessels of 4212
2Ch 4:22 the **s**, and the basons, and the spoons, and 4212
Jer 52:18 the **s**, and the bowls, and the spoons, and 4212

SNUFFETH (1) [SNUFFDISHES, SNUFFED, SNUFFERS]
Jer 2:24 *that* **s up** the wind at her pleasure; 7602

SO (1689) [FORSOMUCH, HOWSOEVER, INSOMUCH, SOEVER, WHATSOEVER, WHENSOEVER, WHEREINSOEVER, WHERESOEVER, WHITHERSOEVER, WHOMSOEVER, WHOSO, WHOSOEVER] See Index

SOAKED (1)
Isa 34: 7 their land shall be **s** with blood, and 7301

SOAP See FULLER; SOPE

SOBER (12) [SOBRIETY]
2Co 5:13 or whether we be **s**, *it is* for your cause. *4993*
1Th 5: 6 as *do* others; but let us watch and be **s**. *3525*
5: 8 But let us, who are of the day, be **s**, *3525*
1Ti 3: 2 vigilant, **s**, of good behaviour, given to *4998*
3:11 not slanderers, **s**, faithful in all *things*. *3524*
Tit 1: 8 a lover of good *men*, **s**, just, holy, *4998*
2: 2 That the aged men be **s**, grave, temperate, *3524*
2: 4 they may **teach** the young *women* **to be s**, *4994*
2: 6 *men* likewise exhort to be **s minded**. *4993*
1Pe 1:13 be **s**, and hope to the end for the grace that *3525*
4: 7 be ye therefore **s**, and watch unto prayer. *4993*
5: 8 Be **s**, be vigilant; because your adversary *3525*

SOBERLY (2) [SOBRIETY]
Ro 12: 3 but to think **s**, according as God hath dealt *4993*
Tit 2:12 and worldly lusts we should live **s**, *4996*

SOBERNESS (1) [SOBRIETY]
Ac 26:25 but speak forth *the* words of truth and **s**. *4997*

SOBRIETY (2) [SOBER, SOBERLY, SOBERNESS]
1Ti 2: 9 modest apparel, with shamefastness and **s**; *4997*
2:15 in faith and charity and holiness with **s**. *4997*

SOCHO (1)
1Ch 4:18 Heber the father of **S**, and Jekuthiel 7755

SOCHOH (1)
1Ki 4:10 to him *pertained* **S**, and all the land of 7755

SOCKET (1) [SOCKETS]
Ex 38:27 of the hundred talents, a talent for a **s**. 134

SOCKETS (54) [SOCKET]
Ex 26:19 thou shalt make forty **s** of silver under 134
26:19 two **s** under one board for his two tenons, 134
26:19 two **s** under another board for his two 134
26:21 their forty **s** *of* silver; two sockets under one 134
26:21 two **s** under one board, and two sockets 134
26:21 one board, and two **s** under another board. 134
26:25 and their **s** *of* silver, sixteen sockets; 134
26:25 and their sockets *of* silver, sixteen **s**; 134
26:25 two **s** under one board, and two sockets 134
26:25 one board, and two **s** under another board. 134
26:32 *shall be of* gold, upon the four **s** of silver. 134

Ex 26:37 and thou shalt cast five **s** of brass for them. 134
27:10 and their twenty **s** *shall be of* brass; 134
27:11 his twenty pillars and their twenty **s** *of* brass; 134
27:12 fifty cubits: their pillars ten, and their **s** ten. 134
27:14 their pillars three, and their **s** three. 134
27:15 *cubits:* their pillars three, and their **s** three. 134
27:16 their pillars *shall be* four, and their **s** four. 134
27:17 hooks *shall be of* silver, and their **s** *of* brass. 134
27:18 *of* fine twined linen, and their **s** *of* brass. 134
35:11 and his boards, his bars, his pillars, and his **s**, 134
35:17 their **s**, and the hanging for the door of 134
36:24 forty **s** of silver he made under the twenty 134
36:24 two **s** under one board for his two tenons, 134
36:24 two **s** under another board for his two 134
36:26 their forty **s** *of* silver; two sockets under one 134
36:26 two **s** under one board, and two sockets 134
36:26 one board, and two **s** under another board. 134
36:30 their **s** *were* sixteen sockets *of* silver, 134
36:30 their sockets *were* sixteen **s** *of* silver, 134
36:30 sockets *of* silver, under every board two **s**. 134
36:36 *of* gold; and he cast for them four **s** of silver. 134
36:38 with gold: but their five **s** *were of* brass. 134
38:10 *were* twenty, and their brasen **s** twenty; 134
38:11 *were* twenty, and their **s** *of* brass twenty; 134
38:12 fifty cubits, their pillars ten, and their **s** ten; 134
38:14 their pillars three, and their **s** three. 134
38:15 their pillars three, and their **s** three. 134
38:17 the **s** for the pillars *were of* brass; the hooks 134
38:19 pillars *were* four, and their **s** *of* brass four; 134
38:27 of silver were cast the **s** of the sanctuary, 134
38:27 of the sanctuary, and the **s** of the vail; 134
38:27 an hundred **s** of the hundred talents, a talent 134
38:30 therewith he made the **s** to the door of 134
38:31 the **s** of the court round about, and 134
38:31 the **s** of the court gate, and all the pins of 134
39:33 his boards, his bars, and his pillars, and his **s**, 134
39:40 and his **s**, and the hanging for the court gate, 134
40:18 fastened his **s**, and set up the boards thereof, 134
Nu 3:36 and the **s** thereof, and all the vessels thereof, 134
3:37 and their **s**, and their pins, and their cords. 134
4:31 and the pillars thereof, and **s** thereof, 134
4:32 their **s**, and their pins, and their cords, 134
SS 5:15 *as* pillars of marble, set upon **s** of fine gold: 134

SOCO See SHOCHO; SHOCO; SOCHO

SOCOH (2)
Jos 15:35 Jarmuth, and Adullam, **S**, and Azekah, 7755
15:48 in the mountains, Shamir, and Jattir, and **S**, 7755

SOD (2) [SODDEN]
Ge 25:29 Jacob **s** pottage: and Esau came from 2102
2Ch 35:13 the *other* holy *offerings* **s** they in pots, and 1310

SODA See NITRE

SODDEN (6) [SOD]
Ex 12: 9 **s at all** with water, but roast with 1310+1311
Lev 6:28 the earthen vessel wherein it is **s** shall be 1310
6:28 if it be **s** in a brasen pot, it shall be both 1310
Nu 6:19 the priest shall take the **s** shoulder of 1311
1Sa 2:15 for he will not have **s** flesh of thee, but raw. 1310
La 4:10 The hands of the pitiful women have **s** their 1310

SODERING (1)
Isa 41: 7 smote the anvil, saying, It *is* ready for the **s**: 1694

SODI (1)
Nu 13:10 the tribe of Zebulun, Gaddiel the son of **S**. 5476

SODOM (48) [SODOMA, SODOMITE, SODOMITES]
Ge 10:19 as thou goest unto **S**, and Gomorrah, and 5467
13:10 before the LORD destroyed **S** and 5467
13:12 of the plain, and pitched his tent toward **S**. 5467
13:13 the men of **S** *were* wicked and 5467
14: 2 *That these* made war with Bera king of **S**, 5467
14: 8 there went out the king of **S**, and the king 5467
14:10 the kings of **S** and Gomorrah fled, and 5467
14:11 they took all the goods of **S** and Gomorrah, 5467
14:12 who dwelt in **S**, and his goods, and 5467
14:17 the king of **S** went out to meet him after his 5467
14:21 the king of **S** said unto Abram, Give me 5467
14:22 Abram said to the king of **S**, I have lift up 5467
18:16 rose up from thence, and looked toward **S**: 5467
18:20 Because the cry of **S** and Gomorrah is 5467
18:22 their faces from thence, and went toward **S**: 5467
18:26 If I find in **S** fifty righteous within the city, 5467
19: 1 there came two angels to **S** at even; and 5467
19: 1 Sodom at even; and Lot sat in the gate of **S**: 5467
19: 4 the men of the city, *even* the men of **S**, 5467
19:24 the LORD rained upon **S** and 5467
19:28 he looked toward **S** and Gomorrah, and 5467
Dt 29:23 like the overthrow of **S**, and Gomorrah, 5467
32:32 For their vine *is* of the vine of **S**, and of 5467
Isa 1: 9 we should have been as **S**, *and* we should 5467
1:10 the word of the LORD, ye rulers of **S**; 5467
3: 9 they declare their sin as **S**, they hide *it* not. 5467
13:19 shall be as when God overthrew **S** and 5467
Jer 23:14 they are all of them unto me as **S**, and 5467
49:18 As *in* the overthrow of **S** and Gomorrah 5467
50:40 As God overthrew **S** and Gomorrah and 5467
La 4: 6 greater than the punishment of the sin of **S**, 5467
Eze 16:46 at thy right hand, *is* **S** and her daughters. 5467
16:48 the Lord GOD, **S** thy sister hath not done, 5467
16:49 this was the iniquity of thy sister **S**, pride, 5467
16:53 the captivity of **S** and her daughters, and 5467
16:55 When thy sisters, **S** and her daughters, 5467
16:56 For thy sister **S** was not mentioned by thy 5467
Am 4:11 as God overthrew **S** and Gomorrah, and 5467
Zep 2: 9 Surely Moab shall be as **S**, and the children 5467
Mt 10:15 It shall be more tolerable for the land of **S** *4670*
11:23 have been done in thee, had been done in **S**, *4670*
11:24 for the land of **S** in the day of judgment, *4670*
Mk 6:11 It shall be more tolerable for **S** and *4670*
Lk 10:12 it shall be more tolerable in that day for **S**, *4670*
17:29 But the *same* day that Lot went out of **S** it *4670*
2Pe 2: 6 And turning the cities of **S** and *4670*
Jude 1: 7 *Even* as **S** and Gomorrha, and the cities *4670*
Rev 11: 8 which spiritually is called **S** and Egypt, *4670*

SODOMA (1) [SODOM]
Ro 9:29 we had been as **S**, and been made like unto *4670*

SODOMITE (1) [SODOM]
Dt 23:17 of Israel, nor a **s** of the sons of Israel. 6945

SODOMITES (4) [SODOM]
1Ki 14:24 there were also **s** in the land: *and* they did 6945
15:12 he took away the **s** out of the land, and 6945
22:46 the remnant of the **s**, which remained in 6945
2Ki 23: 7 he brake down the houses of the **s**, 6945

SOEVER (16) [EVER, SO]
Lev 15: 9 **what** saddle **s** he rideth upon that hath 834+3605
17: 3 **What man s** *there be* of the house of 376+376
22: 4 **What man s** of the seed of Aaron *is* a 376+376
Dt 12:32 **What** thing **s** I command you, 834+3605
2Sa 15:35 *that* **what** thing **s** thou shalt hear out 834+3605
24: 3 how many **s** they be, an hundredfold, 3509.1
1Ki 8:38 and supplication **s** be *made* by any man, 3605
2Ch 6:29 what supplication **s** shall be *made* of any 834
19:10 **what** cause **s** shall come to you of 834+3605
Mk 3:28 blasphemies **wherewith s** they shall *302+3745*
6:10 **In what place s** ye enter into a *1437+3699*
11:24 What *things* **s** ye desire, when ye pray, *302*
Jn 5:19 for what *things* **s** he doeth, these also *302+3739*
20:23 Whose **s** sins ye remit, they are remitted unto *302*
20:23 *and* whose **s** *sins* ye retain, they are retained. *302*
Ro 3:19 Now we know that **what** *things* **s** the law *3745*

SOFT (8) [SOFTER, SOFTLY]
Job 23:16 For God **maketh** my heart **s**, and 7401
41: 3 unto thee? will he speak **s** *words* unto thee? 7390
Ps 65:10 thou **makest** it **s** with showers: 4127
Pr 15: 1 A **s** answer turneth away wrath: but 7390
25:15 and a **s** tongue breaketh the bone. 7390
Mt 11: 8 A man clothed in **s** raiment? behold, *3120*
11: 8 they that wear **s** *clothing* are in kings' *3120*
Lk 7:25 A man clothed in **s** raiment? Behold, *3120*

SOFTER (1) [SOFT]
Ps 55:21 his words were **s** than oil, yet *were* they 7401

SOFTLY (7) [SOFT]
Ge 33:14 I will lead on **s**, according as 328+3807.1
Jdg 4:21 went **s** unto him, and 3814+871.1+1886.1
Ru 3: 7 *of corn:* and she came **s**, 3909+871.1+1886.1
1Ki 21:27 and fasted, and lay in sackcloth, and went **s**. 328
Isa 8: 6 the waters of Shiloah that go **s**, 328+3807.1
38:15 himself hath done *it:* I shall **go s** all my 1718

Ac 27:13 And when the south wind **blew s**, *5285*

SOIL (1)
Eze 17: 8 It *was* planted in a good s by great waters, 7704

SOJOURN (33) [SOJOURNED, SOJOURNER, SOJOURNERS, SOJOURNETH, SOJOURNING]
Ge 12:10 Abram went down into Egypt to s there; 1481
19: 9 said *again, This* one *fellow* came in to s, 1481
26: 3 S in this land, and I will be with thee, and 1481
47: 4 For to s in the land are we come; 1481
Ex 12:48 when a stranger shall s with thee, and 1481
Lev 17: 8 or of the strangers which s among you, 1481
17:10 or of the strangers that s among you, 1481
17:13 or of the strangers that s among you, 1481
19:33 if a stranger s with thee in your land, 1481
20: 2 or of the strangers that s in Israel, 1481
25:45 of the strangers that do s among you, 1481
Nu 9:14 if a stranger shall s among you, and 1481
15:14 if a stranger s with you, or whosoever *be* 1481
Jdg 17: 8 to s where he could find *a place:* 1481
17: 9 I go to s where I may find *a place.* 1481
Ru 1: 1 went to s in the country of Moab, 1481
1Ki 17:20 evil upon the widow with whom I s, 1481
2Ki 8: 1 and s wheresoever thou canst sojourn: 1481
8: 1 and sojourn wheresoever thou canst s: 1481
Ps 120: 5 Woe is me, that I s *in* Mesech, *that* I dwell 1481
Isa 23: 7 her own feet shall carry her afar off to s. 1481
52: 4 went down aforetime *into* Egypt to s there; 1481
Jer 42:15 faces to enter *into* Egypt, and go to s there; 1481
42:17 set their faces to go *into* Egypt to s there; 1481
42:22 the place whither ye desire to go *and* to s. 1481
43: 2 thee to say, Go not *into* Egypt to s there: 1481
44:12 faces to go *into* the land of Egypt to s there, 1481
44:14 which are gone into the land of Egypt to s 1481
44:28 that are gone into the land of Egypt to s 1481
La 4:15 the heathen, They shall no more s *there.* 1481
Eze 20:38 them forth out of the country where they s, 4033
47:22 to the strangers that s among you, 1481
Ac 7: 6 his seed should s in a strange land; *1510+3941*

SOJOURNED (12) [SOJOURN]
Ge 20: 1 between Kadesh and Shur, and s in Gerar. 1481
21:23 and to the land wherein thou hast s. 1481
21:34 Abraham s in the Philistines' land many 1481
32: 4 I have s with Laban, and stayed *there* until 1481
35:27 *is* Hebron, where Abraham and Isaac s. 1481
Dt 18: 6 where he s, and come with all the desire of 1481
26: 5 s there with a few, and became there a 1481
Jdg 17: 7 of Judah, who *was* a Levite, and he s there. 1481
19:16 also of mount Ephraim; and he s in Gibeah: 1481
2Ki 8: 2 s in the land of the Philistines seven years. 1481
Ps 105:23 *into* Egypt; and Jacob s in the land of Ham. 1481
Heb 11: 9 By faith he s in the land of promise, as *in* a *3939*

SOJOURNER (8) [SOJOURN]
Ge 23: 4 I *am* a stranger and a s with you: give me a 8453
Lev 22:10 eat *of* the holy *thing:* a s of the priest's, 8453
25:35 *yea, though he be* a stranger, or a s; that he 8453
25:40 *and* as a s, he shall be with thee, *and* 8453
25:47 if a s or stranger wax rich by thee, and 1616
25:47 sell himself unto the stranger *or* s by thee, 8453
Nu 35:15 for the stranger, and for the s among them: 8453
Ps 39:12 with thee, *and* a s, as all my fathers *were.* 8453

SOJOURNERS (3) [SOJOURN]
Lev 25:23 for ye *were* strangers and s with me. 8453
2Sa 4: 3 to Gittaim, and were s there until this day.) 1481
1Ch 29:15 before thee, and s, as *were* all our fathers: 8453

SOJOURNETH (15) [SOJOURN]
Ex 3:22 of her that s in her house, jewels of silver, 1481
12:49 and unto the stranger that s among you. 1481
Lev 16:29 or a stranger that s among you: 1481
17:12 neither shall any stranger that s among you 1481
18:26 nor any stranger that s among you: 1481
25: 6 and for thy stranger that s with thee, 1481
Nu 15:15 also for the stranger that s *with you,* an 1481
15:16 and for the stranger that s with you. 1481
15:26 and the stranger that s among them; 1481
15:29 and for the stranger that s among them. 1481
19:10 unto the stranger that s among them, for a 1481
Jos 20: 9 and for the stranger that s among them, 1481
Ezr 1: 4 remaineth in any place where he s, 1481

S

Eze 14: 7 or of the stranger that s in Israel, 1481
47:23 to pass, *that* in what tribe the stranger s, 1481

SOJOURNING (3) [SOJOURN]
Ex 12:40 Now the s of the children of Israel, 4186
Jdg 19: 1 that there was a certain Levite s on the side 1481
1Pe 1:17 pass the time of your s *here* in fear: *3940*

SOLACE (1)
Pr 7:18 the morning: let us s ourselves with loves. 5965

SOLD (82) [SELL]
Ge 25:33 to him: and he s his birthright unto Jacob. 4376
31:15 for he hath s us, and hath quite devoured 4376
37:28 s Joseph to the Ishmeelites for twenty 4376
37:36 the Medanites s him into Egypt unto 4376
41:56 the storehouses, and s unto the Egyptians; 7666
42: 6 he *it was* that s to all the people of the land: 7666
45: 4 Joseph your brother, whom ye s into Egypt. 4376
45: 5 angry with yourselves, that ye s me hither: 4376
47:20 for the Egyptians s every man his field, 4376
47:22 gave them: wherefore they s not their lands. 4376
Ex 22: 3 then he shall be s for his theft. 4376
Lev 25:23 The land shall not be s for ever: for the land 4376
25:25 hath s away *some* of his possession, and 4376
25:25 shall he redeem **that which** his brother s. 4465
25:27 the overplus unto the man to whom he s it; 4376
25:28 **that which is** s shall remain in the hand of 4465
25:29 redeem it within a whole year after it is s; 4465
25:33 the house **that was** s, and the city of his 4465
25:34 of the suburbs of their cities may not be s; 4376
25:39 by thee be waxen poor, and be s unto thee; 4376
25:42 they shall not be s as bondmen. 4376+4466
25:48 After *that* he is s he may be redeemed 4376
25:50 that he was s to him unto the year of jubile: 4376
27:20 or if he have s the field to another man, 4376
27:27 it shall be s according to thy estimation. 4376
27:28 of his possession, shall be s or redeemed: 4376
Dt 15:12 be s unto thee, and serve thee six years; 4376
28:68 there ye shall be s unto your enemies for 4376
32:30 except their Rock had s them, and 4376
Jdg 2:14 he s them into the hands of their enemies 4376
3: 8 he s them into the hand of 4376
4: 2 the LORD s them into the hand of Jabin 4376
10: 7 he s them into the hands of the Philistines, 4376
1Sa 12: 9 he s them into the hand of Sisera, captain of 4376
1Ki 21:20 thou hast s thyself to work evil in the sight 4376
2Ki 6:25 until an ass's head was s for fourscore NIH
7: 1 a measure of fine flour *be* s for a shekel, NIH
7:16 So a measure of fine flour was s for a NIH
17:17 s themselves to do evil in the sight of 4376
Ne 5: 8 the Jews, which were s unto the heathen; 4376
5: 8 or shall they be s unto us? Then held they 4376
13:15 *them* in the day wherein they s victuals. 4376
13:16 s on the sabbath unto the children of Judah, 4376
Est 7: 4 For we are s, I and my people, to be 4376
7: 4 if we had been s for bondmen and 4376
Ps 105:17 *even* Joseph, *who* was s for a servant: 4376
Isa 50: 1 of my creditors *is it* to whom I have s 4376
50: 1 for your iniquities have you s yourselves, 4376
52: 3 Ye have s yourselves for nought; 4376
Jer 34:14 a Hebrew, which hath been s unto thee; 4376
La 5: 4 for money; our wood is s *unto us.* 4242+871.1
Eze 7:13 the seller shall not return to that which is s, 4465
Joel 3: 3 and s a girl for wine, that they might drink. 4376
3: 6 the children of Jerusalem have ye s unto 4376
3: 7 out of the place whither ye have s them, 4376
Am 2: 6 because they s the righteous for silver, and 4376
Mt 10:29 Are not two sparrows s for a farthing? and *4453*
13:46 went and s all that he had, and bought it. *4097*
18:25 his lord commanded him to be s, and *4097*
21:12 and cast out all them that s and bought in *4453*
21:12 and the seats of them that s doves, *4453*
26: 9 For this ointment might have been s for *4097*
Mk 11:15 and began to cast out them that s and *4453*
11:15 and the seats of them that s doves; *4453*
14: 5 For it might have been s for more than *4097*
Lk 12: 6 Are not five sparrows s for two farthings, *4453*
17:28 did eat, they drank, they bought, they s, *4453*
19:45 and began to cast out them that s therein, *4453*
Jn 2:14 And found in the temple those that s oxen *4453*
2:16 And said unto them that s doves, *4453*
12: 5 Why was not this ointment s for three *4097*
Ac 2:45 And s their possessions and goods, and *4097*

Ac 4:34 were possessors of lands or houses **s** them, *4453*
4:34 brought the prices of the *things* that were **s**, *4097*
4:37 **s** *it*, and brought the money, and laid *it* at *4453*
5: 1 with Sapphira his wife, **s** a possession, *4453*
5: 4 and after it was **s**, was it not in thine own *4097*
5: 8 Tell me whether ye **s** the land for so much? *591*
7: 9 moved with envy, **s** Joseph into Egypt: *591*
Ro 7:14 law is spiritual: but I am carnal, **s** under sin. *4097*
1Co 10:25 Whatsoever is **s** in the shambles, *that* eat, *4453*
Heb 12:16 who for one morsel of meat **s** his birthright. *591*

SOLDIER (5) [FELLOWSOLDIER, SOLDIERS, SOLDIERS']
Jn 19:23 and made four parts, to every **s** a part; *4757*
Ac 10: 7 a devout **s** of them that waited on him *4757*
28:16 to dwell by himself with a **s** that kept him. *4757*
2Ti 2: 3 as a good **s** of Jesus Christ. *4757*
2: 4 please him who hath **chosen** *him* **to be a s**. *4758*

SOLDIERS (29) [SOLDIER]
1Ch 7: 4 *were* bands of **s** for war, six and 6635
7:11 two hundred *s*, *fit to* go out *for* war NIH
2Ch 25:13 the **s** of the army which Amaziah sent back, 1121
Ezr 8:22 ashamed to require of the king a band *of s* NIH
Isa 15: 4 the **armed s** of Moab shall cry out; 2502
Mt 8: 9 a man under authority, having **s** under me: *4757*
27:27 Then the **s** of the governor took Jesus into *4757*
27:27 and gathered unto him the whole band *of s*. NIG
28:12 they gave large money unto the **s**, *4757*
Mk 15:16 And the **s** led him away into the hall, *4757*
Lk 3:14 And *the* **s** likewise demanded of him, *4754*
7: 8 having under me **s**, and I say unto one, Go, *4757*
23:36 And the **s** also mocked him, coming to *him*, *4757*
Jn 19: 2 And the **s** platted a crown of thorns, and *4757*
19:23 Then the **s**, when they had crucified Jesus, *4757*
19:24 cast lots. These *things* therefore the **s** did. *4757*
19:32 Then came the **s**, and brake the legs of *4757*
19:34 But one of the **s** with a spear pierced his *4757*
Ac 12: 4 delivered *him* to four quaternions of **s** to *4757*
12: 6 night Peter was sleeping between two **s**, *4757*
12:18 there was no small stir among the **s**, *4757*
21:32 Who immediately took **s** and centurions, *4757*
21:32 when they saw the chief captain and the **s**, *4757*
21:35 that he was borne of the **s** for the violence *4757*
23:10 commanded the **s** to go down, and to take *4753*
23:23 Make ready two hundred **s** to go to *4757*
23:31 Then the **s**, as it was commanded them, *4757*
27:31 Paul said to the centurion and to the **s**, *4757*
27:32 Then the **s** cut off the ropes of the boat, and *4757*

SOLDIERS' (1) [SOLDIER]
Ac 27:42 And the **s** counsel was to kill the prisoners, *4757*

SOLE (12) [SOLES]
Ge 8: 9 the dove found no rest for the **s** of her foot, 3709
Dt 28:35 from the **s** of thy foot unto the top of thy 3709
28:56 which would not adventure to set the **s** of 3709
28:65 neither shall the **s** of thy foot have rest: 3709
Jos 1: 3 Every place that the **s** of your foot shall 3709
2Sa 14:25 from the **s** of his foot even to the crown of 3709
2Ki 19:24 with the **s** of my feet have I dried up all 3709
Job 2: 7 smote Job with sore boils from the **s** of his 3709
Isa 1: 6 From the **s** of the foot even unto the head 3709
37:25 with the **s** of my feet have I dried up all 3709
Eze 1: 7 the **s** of their feet *was* like the sole of a 3709
1: 7 the sole of their feet *was* like the **s** of a 3709

SOLEMN (29) [SOLEMNITIES, SOLEMNITY, SOLEMNLY]
Lev 23:36 it *is* a **s assembly**; *and* ye shall do no 6116
Nu 10:10 in your **s days**, and in the beginnings of 4150
15: 3 or in a freewill offering, or in your **s feasts**, 4150
29:35 the eighth day ye shall have a **s assembly**; 6116
Dt 16: 8 on the seventh day *shall be* a **s assembly** to 6116
16:15 Seven days shalt thou **keep a s feast** unto 2287
2Ki 10:20 Jehu said, Proclaim a **s assembly** for Baal. 6116
2Ch 2: 4 and on the **s feasts** of the LORD our God. 4150
7: 9 in the eighth day they made a **s assembly**: 6116
8:13 and on the new moons, and on the **s feasts**, 4150
Ne 8:18 on the eighth day *was* a **s assembly**, 6116
Ps 81: 3 in the time appointed, on our **s feast** day. 2282
92: 3 the psaltery; upon the harp with a **s sound**. 1902
Isa 1:13 *it is* iniquity, even the **s meeting**. 6116
La 1: 4 because none come to the **s feasts**: 4150
2: 6 the LORD hath caused the **s feasts** and 4150
2: 7 of the LORD, as *in* the day of a **s feast**. 4150
2:22 Thou hast called as *in* a **s** day my terrors 4150
Eze 36:38 as the flock of Jerusalem in her **s feasts**; 4150
46: 9 come before the LORD in the **s feasts**, 4150
Hos 2:11 and her sabbaths, and all her **s feasts**. 4150
9: 5 What will ye do in the **s** day, and in the day 4150
12: 9 in tabernacles, as *in* the days of the **s feast**. 4150
Joel 1:14 call a **s assembly**, gather the elders *and* 6116
2:15 in Zion, sanctify a fast, call a **s assembly**: 6116
Am 5:21 and I will not smell in your **s assemblies**. 6116
Na 1:15 O Judah, keep thy **s feasts**, perform thy 2282
Zep 3:18 *them that are* sorrowful for the **s assembly**, 4150
Mal 2: 3 your faces, *even* the dung of your **s feasts**; 2282

SOLEMNITIES (3) [SOLEMN]
Isa 33:20 Look upon Zion, the city of our **s**: 4150
Eze 45:17 in the sabbaths in all **s** of the house of 4150
46:11 in the **s** the meat offering shall be an ephah 4150

SOLEMNITY (2) [SOLEMN]
Dt 31:10 in the **s** of the year of release, in the feast of 4150
Isa 30:29 as *in* the night when a holy **s** is kept; 2282

SOLEMNLY (2) [SOLEMN]
Ge 43: 3 man did **s protest** unto us, saying, 5749+5749
1Sa 8: 9 howbeit yet **protest s** unto them, and 5749+5749

SOLES (7) [SOLE]
Dt 11:24 Every place whereon the **s** of your feet 3709
Jos 3:13 as soon as the **s** of the feet of the priests 3709
4:18 the **s** of the priests' feet were lift up unto 3709
1Ki 5: 3 until the LORD put them under the **s** of 3709
Isa 60:14 bow themselves down at the **s** of thy feet; 3709
Eze 43: 7 and the place of the **s** of my feet, 3709
Mal 4: 3 for they shall be ashes under the **s** of your 3709

SOLITARILY (1) [SOLITARY]
Mic 7:14 which dwell **s** *in* the wood, in 910+3807.1

SOLITARY (7) [SOLITARILY]
Job 3: 7 Lo, let that night be **s**, let no joyful voice 1565
30: 3 For want and famine *they were* **s**; flying 1565
Ps 68: 6 God setteth the **s** in families: he bringeth 3173
107: 4 They wandered in the wilderness in a **s** 3452
Isa 35: 1 and the **s place** shall be glad *for* them; 6723
La 1: 1 How doth the city sit **s**, *that was* full of 910
Mk 1:35 and departed into a **s** place, and *2048*

SOLOMON (281) [JEDIDIAH, SOLOMON'S]
2Sa 5:14 Shammua, and Shobab, and Nathan, and **S**, 8010
12:24 she bare a son, and he called his name **S**: 8010
1Ki 1:10 and the mighty *men*, and **S** his brother, 8010
1:11 spake unto Bath-sheba the mother of **S**, 8010
1:12 thine own life, and the life of thy son **S**. 8010
1:13 Assuredly **S** thy son shall reign after me, 8010
1:17 *saying*, Assuredly **S** thy son shall reign 8010
1:19 but **S** thy servant hath he not called. 8010
1:21 and my son **S** shall be *counted* offenders. 8010
1:26 and thy servant **S**, hath he not called. 8010
1:30 Assuredly **S** thy son shall reign after me, 8010
1:33 cause **S** my son to ride upon mine own 8010
1:34 with the trumpet, and say, God save king **S**. 8010
1:37 even so be he with **S**, and make his throne 8010
1:38 caused **S** to ride upon king David's mule, 8010
1:39 of oil out of the tabernacle, and anointed **S**. 8010
1:39 and all the people said, God save king **S**. 8010
1:43 Verily our lord king David hath made **S** 8010
1:46 also **S** sitteth on the throne of the kingdom. 8010
1:47 God make the name of **S** better than thy 8010
1:50 Adonijah feared because of **S**, and arose, 8010
1:51 it was told **S**, saying, Behold, 8010
1:51 Behold, Adonijah feareth king **S**: 8010
1:51 Let king **S** swear unto me to day that he 8010
1:52 **S** said, If he will shew himself a worthy 8010
1:53 So king **S** sent, and they brought him down 8010
1:53 he came and bowed himself to king **S**: and 8010
1:53 and **S** said unto him, Go to thine house. 8010
2: 1 and he charged **S** his son, saying, 8010
2:12 sat **S** upon the throne of David his father; 8010
2:13 came to Bath-sheba the mother of **S**. 8010
2:17 he said, Speak, I pray thee, unto **S** the king, 8010
2:19 Bath-sheba therefore went unto king **S**, 8010
2:22 king **S** answered and said unto his mother, 8010
2:23 king **S** sware by the LORD, saying, God 8010
2:25 king **S** sent by the hand of Benaiah the son 8010
2:27 So **S** thrust out Abiathar from being priest 8010

S

1Ki	2:29	it was told king **S** that Joab was fled unto	8010
	2:29	**S** sent Benaiah the son of Jehoiada, saying,	8010
	2:41	it was told **S** that Shimei had gone from	8010
	2:45	king **S** *shall be* blessed, and the throne of	8010
	2:46	kingdom was established in the hand of **S**.	8010
	3: 1	**S** made affinity with Pharaoh king of	8010
	3: 3	**S** loved the LORD, walking in the statutes	8010
	3: 4	a thousand burnt offerings did **S** offer up on	8010
	3: 5	In Gibeon the LORD appeared to **S** in a	8010
	3: 6	**S** said, Thou hast shewed unto thy servant	8010
	3:10	the Lord, that **S** had asked this thing.	8010
	3:15	**S** awoke; and behold, *it was* a dream.	8010
	4: 1	So king **S** was king over all Israel.	8010
	4: 7	**S** had twelve officers over all Israel, which	8010
	4:11	which had Taphath the daughter of **S** to	8010
	4:15	he also took Basmath the daughter of **S** to	8010
	4:21	**S** reigned over all kingdoms from the river	8010
	4:21	and served **S** all the days of his life.	8010
	4:25	Dan even to Beer-sheba, all the days of **S**.	8010
	4:26	**S** had forty thousand stalls of horses for his	8010
	4:27	those officers provided victual for king **S**,	8010
	4:29	God gave **S** wisdom and	8010
	4:34	came of all people to hear the wisdom of **S**,	8010
	5: 1	king of Tyre sent his servants unto **S**;	8010
	5: 2	And **S** sent to Hiram, saying,	8010
	5: 7	to pass, when Hiram heard the words of **S**,	8010
	5: 8	Hiram sent to **S**, saying, I have considered	8010
	5:10	So Hiram gave **S** cedar trees and fir trees	8010
	5:11	**S** gave Hiram twenty thousand measures of	8010
	5:11	pure oil: thus gave **S** to Hiram year by year.	8010
	5:12	the LORD gave **S** wisdom, as he promised	8010
	5:12	there was peace between Hiram and **S**; and	8010
	5:13	king **S** raised a levy out of all Israel; and	8010
	5:15	**S** had threescore and ten thousand that bare	8010
	6: 2	the house which king **S** built for	8010
	6:11	the word of the LORD came to **S**, saying,	8010
	6:14	So **S** built the house, and finished it.	8010
	6:21	So **S** overlaid the house within with pure	8010
	7: 1	**S** was building his own house thirteen	8010
	7: 8	**S** made also a house for Pharaoh's	8010
	7:13	And king **S** sent and fet Hiram out of Tyre.	8010
	7:14	he came to king **S**, and wrought all his	8010
	7:40	made king **S** *for* the house of the LORD:	8010
	7:45	which Hiram made to king **S** *for* the house	8010
	7:47	**S** left all the vessels *unweighed,* because	8010
	7:48	**S** made all the vessels that *pertained unto*	8010
	7:51	So was ended all the work that king **S** made	8010
	7:51	**S** brought in the *things* which David his	8010
	8: 1	**S** assembled the elders of Israel, and all	8010
	8: 1	children of Israel, unto king **S** *in* Jerusalem,	8010
	8: 2	king **S** at the feast in the month Ethanim,	8010
	8: 5	king **S**, and all the congregation of Israel,	8010
	8:12	spake **S**, The LORD said that *he* would	8010
	8:22	**S** stood before the altar of the LORD in	8010
	8:54	*that* when **S** had made an end of praying all	8010
	8:63	**S** offered a sacrifice of peace offerings,	8010
	8:65	at that time **S** held a feast, and all Israel	8010
	9: 1	when **S** had finished the building of	8010
	9: 2	That the LORD appeared to **S** the second	8010
	9:10	when **S** had built the two houses, the house	8010
	9:11	of Tyre had furnished **S** with cedar trees	8010
	9:11	king **S** gave Hiram twenty cities in the land	8010
	9:12	to see the cities which **S** had given him;	8010
	9:15	this *is* the reason of the levy which king **S**	8010
	9:17	**S** built Gezer, and Beth-horon the nether,	8010
	9:19	all the cities of store that **S** had, and cities	8010
	9:19	that which **S** desired to build in Jerusalem,	8010
	9:21	upon those did **S** levy a tribute of	8010
	9:22	of the children of Israel did **S** make no	8010
	9:24	unto her house which **S** had built for her:	NIH
	9:25	three times in a year did **S** offer burnt	8010
	9:26	king **S** made a navy *of ships* in	8010
	9:27	of the sea, with the servants of **S**.	8010
	9:28	and twenty talents, and brought *it* to king **S**.	8010
	10: 1	of **S** concerning the name of the LORD,	8010
	10: 2	when she was come to **S**, she communed	8010
	10: 3	**S** told her all her questions: there was not	8010
	10:10	which the queen of Sheba gave to king **S**.	8010
	10:13	king **S** gave unto the queen of Sheba all her	8010
	10:13	besides *that* which **S** gave her of his royal	8010
	10:14	Now the weight of gold that came to **S** in	8010
	10:16	king **S** made two hundred targets *of* beaten	8010
	10:21	was nothing accounted of in the days of **S**.	8010
	10:23	So king **S** exceeded all the kings of	8010
	10:24	all the earth sought to **S**, to hear his	8010
	10:26	**S** gathered together chariots and horsemen:	8010
	10:28	And **S** had horses brought out of Egypt, and	8010
	11: 1	king **S** loved many strange women,	8010
	11: 2	after their gods: **S** clave unto these in love.	8010
	11: 4	For it came to pass, when **S** was old,	8010
	11: 5	For **S** went after Ashtoreth the goddess of	8010
	11: 6	**S** did evil in the sight of the LORD, and	8010
	11: 7	did **S** build a high place for Chemosh,	8010
	11: 9	And the LORD was angry with **S**, because	8010
	11:11	Wherefore the LORD said unto **S**,	8010
	11:14	the LORD stirred up an adversary unto **S**,	8010
	11:25	was an adversary to Israel all the days of **S**,	8010
	11:27	**S** built Millo, *and* repaired the breaches of	8010
	11:28	**S** seeing the young man that he was	8010
	11:31	will rent the kingdom out of the hand of **S**,	8010
	11:40	**S** sought therefore to kill Jeroboam.	8010
	11:40	and was in Egypt until the death of **S**.	8010
	11:41	the rest of the acts of **S**, and all that he did,	8010
	11:41	not written in the book of the acts of **S**?	8010
	11:42	the time that **S** reigned in Jerusalem over	8010
	11:43	**S** slept with his fathers, and was buried in	8010
	12: 2	he was fled from the presence of king **S**,	8010
	12: 6	that stood before **S** his father while he *yet*	8010
	12:21	kingdom again to Rehoboam the son of **S**.	8010
	12:23	the son of **S**, king of Judah, and unto all	8010
	14:21	Rehoboam the son of **S** reigned in Judah.	8010
	14:26	all the shields of gold which **S** had made.	8010
2Ki	21: 7	to **S** his son, In this house, and	8010
	23:13	which **S** the king of Israel had builded for	8010
	24:13	cut in pieces all the vessels of gold which **S**	8010
	25:16	the bases which **S** had made for the house	8010
1Ch	3: 5	and Shobab, and Nathan, and **S**, four,	8010
	6:10	in the temple that **S** built in Jerusalem:)	8010
	6:32	until **S** had built the house of the LORD in	8010
	14: 4	Shammua, and Shobab, Nathan, and **S**,	8010
	18: 8	wherewith **S** made the brasen sea, and	8010
	22: 5	**S** my son *is* young and tender, and	8010
	22: 6	he called for **S** his son, and charged him to	8010
	22: 7	David said to **S**, My son, *as for* me, it was	8010
	22: 9	for his name shall be **S**, and I will give	8010
	22:17	all the princes of Israel to help **S** his son,	8010
	23: 1	*of* days, he made **S** his son king over Israel.	8010
	28: 5	he hath chosen **S** my son to sit upon	8010
	28: 6	he said unto me, **S** thy son, he shall build	8010
	28: 9	thou, **S** my son, know thou the God of thy	8010
	28:11	David gave to **S** his son the pattern of	8010
	28:20	David said to **S** his son, Be strong and	8010
	29: 1	**S** my son, whom alone God hath chosen, *is*	8010
	29:19	give unto **S** my son a perfect heart, to keep	8010
	29:22	they made **S** the son of David king	8010
	29:23	**S** sat on the throne of the LORD as king	8010
	29:24	submitted themselves unto **S** the king.	8010
	29:25	the LORD magnified **S** exceedingly in	8010
	29:28	honour: and **S** his son reigned in his stead.	8010
2Ch	1: 1	**S** the son of David was strengthened in his	8010
	1: 2	**S** spake unto all Israel, to the captains of	8010
	1: 3	So **S**, and all the congregation with him,	8010
	1: 5	and **S** and the congregation sought *unto* it.	8010
	1: 6	**S** went up thither to the brasen altar before	8010
	1: 7	In that night did God appear unto **S**, and	8010
	1: 8	**S** said unto God, Thou hast shewed great	8010
	1:11	God said to **S**, Because this was in thine	8010
	1:13	**S** came *from his journey* to the high place	8010
	1:14	**S** gathered chariots and horsemen: and	8010
	1:16	And **S** had horses brought out of Egypt, and	8010
	2: 1	**S** determined to build a house for the name	8010
	2: 2	**S** told out threescore and ten thousand men	8010
	2: 3	**S** sent to Huram the king of Tyre, saying,	8010
	2:11	which he sent to **S**, Because the LORD	8010
	2:17	**S** numbered all the strangers that *were* in	8010
	3: 1	**S** began to build the house of the LORD at	8010
	3: 3	Now these *are the things wherein* **S** was	8010
	4:11	to make for king **S** for the house of God;	8010
	4:16	did Huram his father make to king **S** for	8010
	4:18	Thus **S** made all these vessels in great	8010
	4:19	**S** made all the vessels that *were for*	8010
	5: 1	Thus all the work that **S** made for the house	8010
	5: 1	**S** brought in *all the things* that David his	8010
	5: 2	**S** assembled the elders of Israel, and all	8010
	5: 6	Also king **S**, and all the congregation of	8010
	6: 1	said **S**, The LORD hath said that *he* would	8010
	6:13	For **S** had made a brasen scaffold, of five	8010
	7: 1	Now when **S** had made an end of praying,	8010

2Ch 7: 5 king **S** offered a sacrifice of twenty and 8010
7: 7 Moreover **S** hallowed the middle of 8010
7: 7 the brasen altar which **S** had made was not 8010
7: 8 Also at the same time **S** kept the feast seven 8010
7:10 and to **S**, and to Israel his people. 8010
7:11 Thus **S** finished the house of the LORD, 8010
7:12 the LORD appeared to **S** by night, and 8010
8: 1 wherein **S** had built the house of 8010
8: 2 the cities which Huram had restored to **S**, 8010
8: 2 **S** built them, and caused the children of 8010
8: 3 **S** went *to* Hamath-zobah, and 8010
8: 4 all the store cities that **S** had, and all 8010
8: 6 all that **S** desired to build in Jerusalem, and 8010
8: 8 them did **S** make to pay tribute until this 8010
8: 9 of the children of Israel did **S** make no 8010
8:11 **S** brought up the daughter of Pharaoh out 8010
8:12 **S** offered burnt offerings unto the LORD 8010
8:16 Now all the work of **S** was prepared unto 8010
8:17 went **S** to Ezion-geber, and to Eloth, at 8010
8:18 they went with the servants of **S** to Ophir, 8010
8:18 talents of gold, and brought *them* to king **S**. 8010
9: 1 the queen of Sheba heard of the fame of **S**, 8010
9: 1 she came to prove **S** with hard questions at 8010
9: 1 when she was come to **S**, she communed 8010
9: 2 **S** told her all her questions: and there was 8010
9: 2 there was nothing hid from **S** which he told 8010
9: 3 queen of Sheba had seen the wisdom of **S**, 8010
9: 9 spice as the queen of Sheba gave king **S**. 8010
9:10 the servants of **S**, which brought gold from 8010
9:12 king **S** gave to the queen of Sheba all her 8010
9:13 Now the weight of gold that came to **S** in 8010
9:14 of the country brought gold and silver to **S**. 8010
9:15 king **S** made two hundred targets *of* beaten 8010
9:20 all the drinking vessels of king **S** *were of* 8010
9:20 *not* any thing accounted of in the days of **S**. 8010
9:22 king **S** passed all the kings of the earth in 8010
9:23 kings of the earth sought the presence of **S**, 8010
9:25 **S** had four thousand stalls for horses and 8010
9:28 they brought unto **S** horses out of Egypt, 8010
9:29 Now the rest of the acts of **S**, first and last, 8010
9:30 **S** reigned in Jerusalem over all Israel forty 8010
9:31 **S** slept with his fathers, and he was buried 8010
10: 2 whither he had fled from the presence of **S** 8010
10: 6 stood before **S** his father while he *yet* lived, 8010
11: 3 Speak unto Rehoboam the son of **S**, king of 8010
11:17 made Rehoboam the son of **S** strong, 8010
11:17 they walked in the way of David and **S**. 8010
12: 9 also the shields of gold which **S** had made. 8010
13: 6 the servant of **S** the son of David, is risen 8010
13: 7 themselves against Rehoboam the son of **S**, 8010
30:26 for since the time of **S** the son of David 8010
33: 7 God had said to David and to **S** his son, 8010
35: 3 Put the holy ark in the house which **S** 8010
35: 4 and according to the writing of **S** his son. 8010
Ne 12:45 commandment of David, *and* of **S** his son. 8010
13:26 Did not **S** king of Israel sin by these *things?* 8010
Ps 72: T *A Psalm* for **S**. 8010
127: T A Song of degrees for **S**. 8010
Pr 1: 1 The proverbs of **S** the son of David, king of 8010
10: 1 The proverbs of **S**. A wise son maketh a 8010
25: 1 These *are* also proverbs of **S**, which 8010
SS 1: 5 as the tents of Kedar, as the curtains of **S**. 8010
3: 9 King **S** made himself a chariot of the wood 8010
3:11 behold king **S** with the crown where*with* 8010
8:11 **S** had a vineyard at Baal-hamon; he let out 8010
8:12 thou, O **S**, *must have* a thousand, and 8010
Jer 52:20 which king **S** had made in the house of 8010
Mt 1: 6 David the king begat **S** of *her that had been* *4672*
1: 7 And **S** begat Roboam; and Roboam begat *4672*
6:29 That even **S** in all his glory was not arrayed *4672*
12:42 parts of the earth to hear the wisdom of **S**; *4672*
12:42 and behold, a greater than **S** *is* here. *4672*
Lk 11:31 parts of the earth to hear the wisdom of **S**; *4672*
11:31 and behold, a greater than **S** *is* here. *4672*
12:27 *that* **S** in all his glory was not arrayed like *4672*
Ac 7:47 But **S** built him a house. *4672*

SOLOMON'S (25) [SOLOMON]
1Ki 4:22 **S** provision for one day was thirty measures 8010
4:27 for all that came unto king **S** table, 8010
4:30 **S** wisdom excelled the wisdom of all 8010
5:16 Besides the chief of **S** officers which *were* 8010
5:18 **S** builders and Hiram's builders did hew 8010
6: 1 in the fourth year of **S** reign over Israel, 8010
9: 1 all **S** desire which he was pleased to do, 8010
9:16 it *for* a present unto his daughter, **S** wife. 8010
9:23 chief of the officers that *were* over **S** work, 8010
10: 4 when the queen of Sheba had seen all **S** 8010
10:21 all king **S** drinking vessels *were of* gold, 8010
11:26 an Ephrathite of Zereda, **S** servant, 8010+3807.1
1Ch 3:10 **S** son *was* Rehoboam, Abia his son, Asa his 8010
2Ch 7:11 all that came into **S** heart to make in 8010
8:10 these *were* the chief of king **S** 8010+3807.1
Ezr 2:55 The children of **S** servants: the children of 8010
2:58 and the children of **S** servants, 8010
Ne 7:57 The children of **S** servants: the children of 8010
7:60 and the children of **S** servants, 8010
11: 3 and the children of **S** servants. 8010
SS 1: 1 The song of songs, which *is* **S**. 8010+3807.1
3: 7 Behold his bed, which *is* **S**; 8010+3807.1
Jn 10:23 And Jesus walked in the temple in **S** porch. *4672*
Ac 3:11 unto them in the porch that is called **S**, *4672*
5:12 they were all with one accord in **S** porch. *4672*

SOME (231) [SOMEBODY, SOMETHING, SOMETIME, SOMETIMES, SOMEWHAT] See Index

SOMEBODY (2) [SOME] See Index

SOMETHING (8) [SOME, THING] See Index

SOMETIME (3) [SOME, TIME] See Index

SOMETIMES (3) [SOME, TIME] See Index

SOMEWHAT (25) [SOME, WHAT] See Index

SON (2374) [SON'S, SONS, SONS']
Ge 4:17 of the city, after the name of his **s**, Enoch. 1121
4:25 she bare a **s**, and called his name Seth: 1121
4:26 to Seth, *to* him also there was born a **s**; and 1121
5: 3 and begat *a* **s** in his own likeness, NIH
5:28 and two years, and begat a **s**: 1121
9:24 knew what his younger **s** had done unto 1121
11:31 Terah took Abram his **s**, and Lot the son of 1121
11:31 Lot the **s** of Haran his son's son, and Sarai 1121
11:31 Lot the son of Haran his son's **s**, and Sarai 1121
11:31 his daughter in law, his **s** Abram's wife; 1121
12: 5 Lot his brother's **s**, and all their substance 1121
14:12 they took Lot, Abram's brother's **s**, 1121
16:11 shalt bear a **s**, and shalt call his name 1121
16:15 Hagar bare Abram a **s**: and Abram called 1121
17:16 will bless her, and give thee a **s** also of her: 1121
17:19 Sarah thy wife shall bear thee a **s** indeed; 1121
17:23 Abraham took Ishmael his **s**, and all that 1121
17:25 Ishmael his **s** *was* thirteen years old, 1121
17:26 Abraham circumcised, and Ishmael his **s**. 1121
18:10 and lo, Sarah thy wife shall have a **s**. 1121
18:14 to the time of life, and Sarah shall have a **s**. 1121
19:12 **s in law**, and thy sons, and thy daughters, 2860
19:37 the firstborn bare a **s**, and called his name 1121
19:38 she also bare a **s**, and called his name 1121
21: 2 and bare Abraham a **s** in his old age, 1121
21: 3 Abraham called the name of his **s** that was 1121
21: 4 Abraham circumcised his **s** Isaac being 1121
21: 5 when his **s** Isaac was born unto him. 1121
21: 7 for I have born *him* a **s** in his old age. 1121
21: 9 And Sarah saw the **s** of Hagar the Egyptian, 1121
21:10 Cast out this bondwoman and her **s**: 1121
21:10 for the **s** of this bondwoman shall not be 1121
21:10 bondwoman shall not be heir with my **s**, 1121
21:11 in Abraham's sight because of his **s**. 1121
21:13 also of the **s** of the bondwoman will I make 1121
21:23 nor with my **s**, nor with my son's son: 5209
21:23 nor with my son, nor with my **son's s**: 5220
22: 2 he said, Take now thy **s**, thine only *son* 1121
22: 2 Take now thy son, thine only **s** Isaac, NIH
22: 3 Isaac his **s**, and clave the wood for 1121
22: 6 burnt offering, and laid *it* upon Isaac his **s**; 1121
22: 7 he said, Here *am* I, my **s**. And he said, 1121
22: 8 Abraham said, My **s**, God will provide 1121
22: 9 bound Isaac his **s**, and laid him on the altar 1121
22:10 his hand, and took the knife to slay his **s**. 1121
22:12 seeing thou hast not withheld thy **s**, thine 1121
22:12 not withheld thy son, thine only **s** from me. NIH
22:13 up for a burnt offering in the stead of his **s**. 1121
22:16 hast not withheld thy **s**, thine only *son:* 1121
22:16 hast not withheld thy son, thine only **s**: NIH
23: 8 and intreat for me to Ephron the **s** of Zohar, 1121
24: 3 that thou shalt not take a wife unto my **s** of 1121

S

Ge 24: 4 and take a wife unto my **s** Isaac. 1121
24: 5 must I needs bring thy **s** again unto the land 1121
24: 6 Beware thou that thou bring not my **s** 1121
24: 7 thou shalt take a wife unto my **s** from 1121
24: 8 my oath: only bring not my **s** thither again. 1121
24:15 **s** of Milcah, the wife of Nahor, 1121
24:24 I *am* the daughter of Bethuel the **s** of 1121
24:36 Sarah my master's wife bare a **s** to my 1121
24:37 Thou shalt not take a wife to my **s** of 1121
24:38 to my kindred, and take a wife unto my **s**. 1121
24:40 thou shalt take a wife for my **s** of my 1121
24:44 hath appointed out for my master's **s**. 1121
24:47 The daughter of Bethuel, Nahor's **s**, 1121
24:48 my master's brother's daughter unto his **s**. 1121
25: 6 sent them away from Isaac his **s**, while he 1121
25: 9 in the field of Ephron the **s** of Zohar 1121
25:11 of Abraham, that God blessed his **s** Isaac; 1121
25:12 Abraham's **s**, whom Hagar the Egyptian, 1121
25:19 *are* the generations of Isaac, Abraham's **s**: 1121
27: 1 he called Esau his eldest **s**, and said unto 1121
27: 1 his eldest son, and said unto him, My **s**: 1121
27: 5 heard when Isaac spake to Esau his **s**. 1121
27: 6 Rebekah spake unto Jacob her **s**, saying, 1121
27: 8 Now therefore, my **s**, obey my voice 1121
27:13 said unto him, Upon me *be* thy curse, my **s**: 1121
27:15 took goodly raiment of her eldest **s** Esau, 1121
27:15 and put them upon Jacob her younger **s**: 1121
27:17 had prepared, into the hand of her **s** Jacob. 1121
27:18 and he said, Here *am* I; who *art* thou, my **s**? 1121
27:20 Isaac said unto his **s**, How *is it that* thou 1121
27:20 it *that* thou hast found *it so* quickly, my **s**? 1121
27:21 I pray thee, that I may feel thee, my **s**, 1121
27:21 whether thou *be* my very **s** Esau or not. 1121
27:24 he said, *Art* thou my very **s** Esau? And he 1121
27:26 Come near now, and kiss me, my **s**. 1121
27:27 the smell of my **s** *is* as the smell of a field 1121
27:32 And he said, I *am* thy **s**, thy firstborn Esau. 1121
27:37 and what shall I do now unto thee, my **s**? 1121
27:42 these words of Esau her elder **s** were told to 1121
27:42 she sent and called Jacob her younger **s**, 1121
27:43 Now therefore, my **s**, obey my voice; and 1121
28: 5 **s** of Bethuel the Syrian, the brother of 1121
28: 9 the daughter of Ishmael Abraham's **s**, 1121
29: 5 unto them, Know ye Laban the **s** of Nahor? 1121
29:12 and that he *was* Rebekah's **s**: 1121
29:13 heard the tidings of Jacob his sister's **s**, 1121
29:32 bare a **s**, and she called his name Reuben: 1121
29:33 she conceived again, and bare a **s**; and said, 1121
29:33 he hath therefore given me this *s* also: NIH
29:34 she conceived again, and bare a **s**; and said, 1121
29:35 she conceived again, and bare a **s**: and 1121
30: 5 And Bilhah conceived, and bare Jacob a **s**. 1121
30: 6 also heard my voice, and hath given me a **s**: 1121
30: 7 conceived again, and bare Jacob a second **s**. 1121
30:10 And Zilpah Leah's maid bare Jacob a **s**. 1121
30:12 And Zilpah Leah's maid bare Jacob a second **s**. 1121
30:17 she conceived, and bare Jacob the fifth **s**. 1121
30:19 conceived again, and bare Jacob the sixth **s**. 1121
30:23 she conceived, and bare a **s**; and said, 1121
30:24 The LORD shall add to me another **s**. 1121
34: 2 when Shechem the **s** of Hamor the Hivite, 1121
34: 8 The soul of my **s** Shechem longeth for your 1121
34:18 pleased Hamor, and Shechem Hamor's **s**. 1121
34:20 Shechem his **s** came unto the gate of their 1121
34:24 unto Shechem his **s** hearkened all that went 1121
34:26 Shechem his **s** with the edge of the sword, 1121
35:17 Fear not; thou shalt have this **s** also. 1121
36:10 Eliphaz the **s** of Adah the wife of Esau, 1121
36:10 Reuel the **s** of Bashemath the wife of Esau. 1121
36:12 Timna was concubine to Eliphaz Esau's **s**; 1121
36:15 the sons of Eliphaz the firstborn *s* of Esau; NIH
36:17 these *are* the sons of Reuel Esau's **s**; 1121
36:32 Bela the **s** of Beor reigned in Edom: and 1121
36:33 Jobab the **s** of Zerah of Bozrah reigned in 1121
36:35 Husham died, and Hadad the **s** of Bedad, 1121
36:38 Baal-hanan the **s** of Achbor reigned in his 1121
36:39 Baal-hanan the **s** of Achbor died, and 1121
37: 3 because he *was* the **s** of his old age: 1121
37:34 his loins, and mourned for his **s** many days. 1121
37:35 For I will go down into the grave unto my **s** 1121
38: 3 she conceived, and bare a **s**; and he called 1121
38: 4 she conceived again, and bare a **s**; and 1121
38: 5 she yet again conceived, and bare a **s**; and 1121
38:11 father's house, till Shelah my **s** be grown: 1121
38:26 because that I gave her not to Shelah my **s**. 1121
42:38 he said, My **s** shall not go down with you; 1121
43:29 brother Benjamin, his mother's **s**, and said, 1121
43:29 he said, God be gracious unto thee, my **s**. 1121
45: 9 and say unto him, Thus saith thy **s** Joseph, 1121
45:28 *It is* enough; Joseph my **s** *is* yet alive: 1121
46:10 and Shaul the **s** of a Canaanitish woman. 1121
47:29 he called his **s** Joseph, and said unto him, 1121
48: 2 Behold, thy **s** Joseph cometh unto thee: 1121
48:19 his father refused, and said, I know *it*, my **s**, 1121
49: 9 from the prey, my **s**, thou art gone up: 1121
50:23 **s** of Manasseh were brought up upon 1121
Ex 1:16 the stools; if it *be* a **s**, then ye shall kill him: 1121
1:22 Every **s** that is born ye shall cast into 1121
2: 2 the woman conceived, and bare a **s**: and 1121
2:10 Pharaoh's daughter, and he became her **s**. 1121
2:22 she bare *him* a **s**, and he called his name 1121
4:22 Israel *is* my **s**, *even* my firstborn: 1121
4:23 I say unto thee, Let my **s** go, that he may 1121
4:23 behold, I will slay thy **s**, *even* thy firstborn. 1121
4:25 cut off the foreskin of her **s**, and cast *it* at 1121
6:15 and Shaul the **s** of a Canaanitish woman: 1121
6:25 Eleazar Aaron's **s** took him *one* of 1121
10: 2 that thou mayest tell in the ears of thy **s**, 1121
10: 2 of thy son's **s**, what things I have wrought 1121
13: 8 thou shalt shew thy **s** in that day, saying, 1121
13:14 it shall be when thy **s** asketh thee in time to 1121
20:10 thou, nor thy **s**, nor thy daughter, 1121
21: 9 if he have betrothed her unto his **s**, he shall 1121
21:31 Whether he have gored a **s**, or have gored a 1121
23:12 and the **s** of thy handmaid, and the stranger, 1121
29:30 *And* that **s** that is priest in his stead shall 1121
31: 2 I have called by name Bezaleel the **s** of Uri, 1121
31: 2 of Uri, the **s** of Hur, of the tribe of Judah: 1121
31: 6 the **s** of Ahisamach, of the tribe of Dan: 1121
32:29 even every man upon his **s**, and upon his 1121
33:11 servant Joshua, the **s** of Nun, a young man, 1121
35:30 hath called by name Bezaleel the **s** of Uri, 1121
35:30 of Uri, the **s** of Hur, of the tribe of Judah; 1121
35:34 *both* he, and Aholiab, the **s** of Ahisamach, 1121
38:21 the hand of Ithamar, **s** to Aaron the priest. 1121
38:22 Bezaleel the **s** of Uri, the son of Hur, of 1121
38:22 of Uri, the **s** of Hur, of the tribe of Judah, 1121
38:23 **s** of Ahisamach, of the tribe of Dan, 1121
Lev 12: 6 are fulfilled, for a **s**, or for a daughter, 1121
21: 2 for his **s**, and for his daughter, and for his 1121
24:10 the **s** of an Israelitish woman, whose father 1121
24:10 *this* **s** of the Israelitish *woman* and a man of 1121
24:11 the Israelitish woman's **s** blasphemed 1121
25:49 Either his uncle, or his uncle's **s**, 1121
Nu 1: 5 *tribe of* Reuben; Elizur the **s** of Shedeur. 1121
1: 6 Of Simeon; Shelumiel the **s** of Zurishaddai. 1121
1: 7 Of Judah; Nahshon the **s** of Amminadab. 1121
1: 8 Of Issachar; Nethaneel the **s** of Zuar. 1121
1: 9 Of Zebulun; Eliab the **s** of Helon. 1121
1:10 of Ephraim; Elishama the **s** of Ammihud: 1121
1:10 of Manasseh; Gamaliel the **s** of Pedahzur. 1121
1:11 Of Benjamin; Abidan the **s** of Gideoni. 1121
1:12 Of Dan; Ahiezer the **s** of Ammishaddai. 1121
1:13 Of Asher; Pagiel the **s** of Ocran. 1121
1:14 Of Gad; Eliasaph the **s** of Deuel. 1121
1:15 Of Naphtali; Ahira the **s** of Enan. 1121
1:20 Israel's **eldest s**, *by* their generations, 1060
2: 3 Nahshon the **s** of Amminadab *shall be* 1121
2: 5 Nethaneel the **s** of Zuar *shall be* captain of 1121
2: 7 Eliab the **s** of Helon *shall be* captain of 1121
2:10 of Reuben *shall be* Elizur the **s** of Shedeur. 1121
2:12 *shall be* Shelumiel the **s** of Zurishaddai. 1121
2:14 of Gad *shall be* Eliasaph the **s** of Reuel. 1121
2:18 *shall be* Elishama the **s** of Ammihud. 1121
2:20 *shall be* Gamaliel the **s** of Pedahzur. 1121
2:22 Benjamin *shall be* Abidan the **s** of Gideoni. 1121
2:25 *shall be* Ahiezer the **s** of Ammishaddai. 1121
2:27 of Asher *shall be* Pagiel the **s** of Ocran. 1121
2:29 of Naphtali *shall be* Ahira the **s** of Enan. 1121
3:24 Gershonites *shall be* Eliasaph the **s** of Lael. 1121
3:30 *shall be* Elizaphan the **s** of Uzziel. 1121
3:32 Eleazar the **s** of Aaron the priest *shall be* 1121
3:35 of Merari *was* Zuriel the **s** of Abihail: 1121
4:16 *to* the office of Eleazar the **s** of Aaron 1121
4:28 hand of Ithamar the **s** of Aaron the priest. 1121
4:33 under the hand of Ithamar the **s** of Aaron 1121
7: 8 under the hand of Ithamar the **s** of Aaron 1121
7:12 first day was Nahshon the **s** of Amminadab, 1121

Nu	7:17	this *was* the offering of Nahshon the **s** of	1121
	7:18	On the second day Nethaneel the **s** of Zuar,	1121
	7:23	this *was* the offering of Nethaneel the **s** of	1121
	7:24	On the third day Eliab the **s** of Helon,	1121
	7:29	this *was* the offering of Eliab the **s** of	1121
	7:30	On the fourth day Elizur the **s** of Shedeur,	1121
	7:35	this *was* the offering of Elizur the **s** of	1121
	7:36	On the fifth day Shelumiel the **s** of	1121
	7:41	this *was* the offering of Shelumiel the **s** of	1121
	7:42	On the sixth day Eliasaph the **s** of Deuel,	1121
	7:47	this *was* the offering of Eliasaph the **s** of	1121
	7:48	On the seventh day Elishama the **s** of	1121
	7:53	this *was* the offering of Elishama the **s** of	1121
	7:54	On the eighth day *offered* Gamaliel the **s** of	1121
	7:59	this *was* the offering of Gamaliel the **s** of	1121
	7:60	On the ninth day Abidan the **s** of Gideoni,	1121
	7:65	this *was* the offering of Abidan the **s** of	1121
	7:66	On the tenth day Ahiezer the **s** of	1121
	7:71	this *was* the offering of Ahiezer the **s** of	1121
	7:72	On the eleventh day Pagiel the **s** of Ocran,	1121
	7:77	this *was* the offering of Pagiel the **s** of	1121
	7:78	On the twelfth day Ahira the **s** of Enan,	1121
	7:83	this *was* the offering of Ahira the **s** of Enan.	1121
	10:14	over his host *was* Nahshon the **s** of	1121
	10:15	of Issachar *was* Nethaneel the **s** of Zuar.	1121
	10:16	of Zebulun *was* Eliab the **s** of Helon.	1121
	10:18	over his host *was* Elizur the **s** of Shedeur.	1121
	10:19	*was* Shelumiel the **s** of Zurishaddai.	1121
	10:20	of Gad *was* Eliasaph the **s** of Deuel.	1121
	10:22	over his host *was* Elishama the **s** of	1121
	10:23	Manasseh *was* Gamaliel the **s** of Pedahzur.	1121
	10:24	of Benjamin *was* Abidan the **s** of Gideoni.	1121
	10:25	over his host *was* Ahiezer the **s** of	1121
	10:26	of Asher *was* Pagiel the **s** of Ocran.	1121
	10:27	of Naphtali *was* Ahira the **s** of Enan.	1121
	10:29	the **s** of Raguel the Midianite,	1121
	11:28	Joshua the **s** of Nun, the servant of Moses,	1121
	13: 4	tribe of Reuben, Shammua the **s** of Zaccur.	1121
	13: 5	the tribe of Simeon, Shaphat the **s** of Hori.	1121
	13: 6	tribe of Judah, Caleb the **s** of Jephunneh.	1121
	13: 7	the tribe of Issachar, Igal the **s** of Joseph.	1121
	13: 8	the tribe of Ephraim, Oshea the **s** of Nun.	1121
	13: 9	the tribe of Benjamin, Palti the **s** of Raphu.	1121
	13:10	the tribe of Zebulun, Gaddiel the **s** of Sodi.	1121
	13:11	the tribe of Manasseh, Gaddi the **s** of Susi.	1121
	13:12	the tribe of Dan, Ammiel the **s** of Gemalli.	1121
	13:13	the tribe of Asher, Sethur the **s** of Michael.	1121
	13:14	tribe of Naphtali, Nahbi the **s** of Vophsi.	1121
	13:15	Of the tribe of Gad, Geuel the **s** of Machi.	1121
	13:16	Moses called Oshea the **s** of Nun, Jehoshua.	1121
	14: 6	Joshua the **s** of Nun, and Caleb the son of	1121
	14: 6	son of Nun, and Caleb the **s** of Jephunneh,	1121
	14:30	save Caleb the **s** of Jephunneh, and	1121
	14:30	son of Jephunneh, and Joshua the **s** of Nun.	1121
	14:38	Joshua the **s** of Nun, and Caleb the son of	1121
	14:38	son of Nun, and Caleb the **s** of Jephunneh,	1121
	16: 1	Now Korah, the **s** of Izhar, the son of	1121
	16: 1	the **s** of Kohath, the son of Levi, and	1121
	16: 1	the **s** of Levi, and Dathan and Abiram,	1121
	16: 1	On, the **s** of Peleth, sons of Reuben,	1121
	16:37	Speak unto Eleazar the **s** of Aaron	1121
	20:25	Take Aaron and Eleazar his **s**, and	1121
	20:26	and put them upon Eleazar his **s**:	1121
	20:28	and put them upon Eleazar his **s**;	1121
	22: 2	Balak the **s** of Zippor saw all that Israel had	1121
	22: 4	Balak the **s** of Zippor *was* king of	1121
	22: 5	unto Balaam the **s** of Beor to Pethor,	1121
	22:10	Balak the **s** of Zippor, king of Moab,	1121
	22:16	to him, Thus saith Balak the **s** of Zippor,	1121
	23:18	hear; hearken unto me, thou **s** of Zippor:	1121
	23:19	neither the **s** of man, that he should repent:	1121
	24: 3	Balaam the **s** of Beor hath said, and	1121
	24:15	Balaam the **s** of Beor hath said, and	1121
	25: 7	when Phinehas, the **s** of Eleazar, the son of	1121
	25: 7	the son of Eleazar, the **s** of Aaron the priest,	1121
	25:11	Phinehas, the **s** of Eleazar, the son of Aaron	1121
	25:11	the son of Eleazar, the **s** of Aaron the priest,	1121
	25:14	*was* Zimri, the **s** of Salu, a prince of a chief	1121
	26: 1	and unto Eleazar the **s** of Aaron the priest,	1121
	26: 5	Reuben, the **eldest s** of Israel: the children	1060
	26:33	Zelophehad the **s** of Hepher had no sons,	1121
	26:65	save Caleb the **s** of Jephunneh, and	1121
	26:65	son of Jephunneh, and Joshua the **s** of Nun.	1121
	27: 1	the **s** of Hepher, the son of Gilead, the son	1121
	27: 1	the **s** of Gilead, the son of Machir,	1121
	27: 1	the son of Gilead, the **s** of Machir,	1121
	27: 1	the son of Machir, the **s** of Manasseh,	1121
	27: 1	of the families of Manasseh the **s** of Joseph:	1121
	27: 4	among his family, because he hath no **s**?	1121
	27: 8	have no **s**, then ye shall cause his	1121
	27:18	Take thee Joshua the **s** of Nun, a man in	1121
	31: 6	and Phinehas the **s** of Eleazar the priest,	1121
	31: 8	Balaam also the **s** of Beor they slew with	1121
	32:12	Save Caleb the **s** of Jephunneh	1121
	32:12	the Kenezite, and Joshua the **s** of Nun:	1121
	32:28	Joshua the **s** of Nun, and the chief fathers	1121
	32:33	unto half the tribe of Manasseh the **s** of	1121
	32:39	the children of Machir the **s** of Manasseh	1121
	32:40	Moses gave Gilead unto Machir the **s** of	1121
	32:41	Jair the **s** of Manasseh went and took	1121
	34:17	Eleazar the priest, and Joshua the **s** of Nun.	1121
	34:19	tribe of Judah, Caleb the **s** of Jephunneh.	1121
	34:20	of Simeon, Shemuel the **s** of Ammihud.	1121
	34:21	tribe of Benjamin, Elidad the **s** of Chislon.	1121
	34:22	of the children of Dan, Bukki the **s** of Jogli.	1121
	34:23	of Manasseh, Hanniel the **s** of Ephod.	1121
	34:24	of Ephraim, Kemuel the **s** of Shiphtan.	1121
	34:25	of Zebulun, Elizaphan the **s** of Parnach.	1121
	34:26	children of Issachar, Paltiel the **s** of Azzan.	1121
	34:27	children of Asher, Ahihud the **s** of Shelomi.	1121
	34:28	of Naphtali, Pedahel the **s** of Ammihud.	1121
	36: 1	the **s** of Machir, the son of Manasseh, of	1121
	36: 1	the son of Machir, the **s** of Manasseh, of	1121
	36:12	of the sons of Manasseh the **s** of Joseph,	1121
Dt	1:31	as a man doth bear his **s**, in all the way that	1121
	1:36	Save Caleb the **s** of Jephunneh, he shall see	1121
	1:38	*But* Joshua the **s** of Nun, which standeth	1121
	3:14	Jair the **s** of Manasseh took all the country	1121
	5:14	thou, nor thy **s**, nor thy daughter, nor thy	1121
	6: 2	thou, and thy **s**, and thy son's son, all	1121
	6: 2	thou, and thy son, and thy son's **s**, all	1121
	6:20	*And* when thy **s** asketh thee in time to	1121
	6:21	thou shalt say unto thy **s**, We were	1121
	7: 3	thy daughter thou shalt not give unto his **s**,	1121
	7: 3	nor his daughter shalt thou take unto thy **s**.	1121
	7: 4	For they will turn away thy **s** from	1121
	8: 5	as a man chasteneth his **s**, *so* the LORD	1121
	10: 6	Eleazar his **s** ministered in the priest's	1121
	11: 6	the sons of Eliab, the **s** of Reuben:	1121
	12:18	thy **s**, and thy daughter, and	1121
	13: 6	the **s** of thy mother, or thy son, or	1121
	13: 6	or thy **s**, or thy daughter, or the wife of thy	1121
	16:11	thy **s**, and thy daughter, and	1121
	16:14	thy **s**, and thy daughter, and	1121
	18:10	found among you *any one* that maketh his **s**	1121
	21:15	and *if* the firstborn **s** be hers that was hated:	1121
	21:16	*that* he may not make the **s** of the beloved	1121
	21:16	beloved firstborn before the **s** of the hated,	1121
	21:17	he shall acknowledge the **s** of the hated *for*	1121
	21:18	If a man have a stubborn and rebellious **s**,	1121
	21:20	This our **s** *is* stubborn and rebellious,	1121
	23: 4	they hired against thee Balaam the **s** of	1121
	28:56	towards her **s**, and towards her daughter,	1121
	31:23	he gave Joshua the **s** of Nun a charge,	1121
	32:44	of the people, he and Hoshea the **s** of Nun.	1121
	34: 9	Joshua the **s** of Nun was full *of* the spirit of	1121
Jos	1: 1	that the LORD spake unto Joshua the **s** of	1121
	2: 1	Joshua the **s** of Nun sent out of Shittim two	1121
	2:23	came to Joshua the **s** of Nun, and told him	1121
	6: 6	Joshua the **s** of Nun called the priests, and	1121
	6:26	in his youngest **s** shall he set up the gates of	NIH
	7: 1	for Achan, the **s** of Carmi, the son of Zabdi,	1121
	7: 1	of Carmi, the **s** of Zabdi, the son of Zerah,	1121
	7: 1	of Carmi, the son of Zabdi, the **s** of Zerah,	1121
	7:18	Achan, the **s** of Carmi, the son of Zabdi,	1121
	7:18	of Carmi, the **s** of Zabdi, the son of Zerah,	1121
	7:18	of Carmi, the son of Zabdi, the **s** of Zerah,	1121
	7:19	said unto Achan, My **s**, give, I pray thee,	1121
	7:24	took Achan the **s** of Zerah, and the silver,	1121
	13:22	Balaam also the **s** of Beor, the soothsayer,	1121
	13:31	the children of Machir the **s** of Manasseh,	1121
	14: 1	Joshua the **s** of Nun, and the heads of	1121
	14: 6	Caleb the **s** of Jephunneh the Kenezite said	1121
	14:13	gave unto Caleb the **s** of Jephunneh Hebron	1121
	14:14	became the inheritance of Caleb the **s** of	1121
	15: 6	up *to* the stone of Bohan the **s** of Reuben:	1121
	15: 8	the border went up *by* the valley of the **s** of	1121
	15:13	unto Caleb the **s** of Jephunneh he gave a	1121

Jos 15:17 Othniel the **s** of Kenaz, the brother of 1121
17: 2 Manasseh the **s** of Joseph by their families. 1121
17: 3 Zelophehad, the **s** of Hepher, the son of 1121
17: 3 the **s** of Gilead, the son of Machir, 1121
17: 3 the son of Gilead, the **s** of Machir, 1121
17: 3 the **s** of Manasseh, had no sons, but 1121
17: 4 before Joshua the **s** of Nun, and before 1121
18:16 *lieth* before the valley of the **s** of Hinnom, 1121
18:17 descended *to* the stone of Bohan the **s** of 1121
19:49 to Joshua the **s** of Nun among them: 1121
19:51 Joshua the **s** of Nun, and the heads of 1121
21: 1 unto Joshua the **s** of Nun, and unto 1121
21:12 gave they to Caleb the **s** of Jephunneh for 1121
22:13 Phinehas the **s** of Eleazar the priest, 1121
22:20 Did not Achan the **s** of Zerah commit a 1121
22:31 Phinehas the **s** of Eleazar the priest said 1121
22:32 Phinehas the **s** of Eleazar the priest, and 1121
24: 9 Balak the **s** of Zippor, king of Moab, arose 1121
24: 9 called Balaam the **s** of Beor to curse you: 1121
24:29 that Joshua the **s** of Nun, the servant of 1121
24:33 Eleazar the **s** of Aaron died; and 1121
24:33 in a hill that pertained to Phinehas his **s**, 1121
Jdg 1:13 Othniel the **s** of Kenaz, Caleb's younger 1121
2: 8 Joshua the **s** of Nun, the servant of 1121
3: 9 *even* Othniel the **s** of Kenaz, 1121
3:11 And Othniel the **s** of Kenaz died. 1121
3:15 Ehud the **s** of Gera, a Benjamite, a man 1121
3:31 after him was Shamgar the **s** of Anath, 1121
4: 6 called Barak the **s** of Abinoam out of 1121
4:12 they shewed Sisera that Barak the **s** of 1121
5: 1 and Barak the **s** of Abinoam on that day, 1121
5: 6 In the days of Shamgar the **s** of Anath, 1121
5:12 thy captivity captive, thou **s** of Abinoam. 1121
6:11 his **s** Gideon threshed wheat by 1121
6:29 Gideon the **s** of Joash hath done this thing. 1121
6:30 Bring out thy **s**, that he may die: 1121
7:14 save the sword of Gideon the **s** of Joash, 1121
8:13 Gideon the **s** of Joash returned from battle 1121
8:22 both thou, and thy **s**, and thy son's son also: 1121
8:22 both thou, and thy son, and thy son's **s** also: 1121
8:23 over you, neither shall my **s** rule over you: 1121
8:29 Jerubbaal the **s** of Joash went and dwelt in 1121
8:31 she also bare him a **s**, whose name he 1121
8:32 Gideon the **s** of Joash died in a good old 1121
9: 1 Abimelech the **s** of Jerubbaal went to 1121
9: 5 notwithstanding yet Jotham the youngest **s** 1121
9:18 made Abimelech, the **s** of his maidservant, 1121
9:26 Gaal the **s** of Ebed came with his brethren, 1121
9:28 Gaal the **s** of Ebed said, Who *is* Abimelech, 1121
9:28 *is* not *he* the **s** of Jerubbaal? and Zebul his 1121
9:30 city heard the words of Gaal the **s** of Ebed, 1121
9:31 Gaal the **s** of Ebed and his brethren be 1121
9:35 Gaal the **s** of Ebed went out, and stood *in* 1121
9:57 upon them came the curse of Jotham the **s** 1121
10: 1 arose to defend Israel Tola the **s** of Puah, 1121
10: 1 of Puah, the **s** of Dodo, a man of Issachar; 1121
11: 1 *man* of valour, and he *was* the **s** of a harlot: 1121
11: 2 for thou *art* the **s** of a strange woman. 1121
11:25 any thing better than Balak the **s** of Zippor, 1121
11:34 beside her he had neither **s** nor daughter. 1121
12:13 after him Abdon the **s** of Hillel, 1121
12:15 Abdon the **s** of Hillel the Pirathonite died, 1121
13: 3 but thou shalt conceive, and bear a **s**. 1121
13: 5 For lo, thou *shalt* conceive, and bear a **s**; 1121
13: 7 Behold, thou *shalt* conceive, and bear a **s**; 1121
13:24 the woman bare a **s**, and called his name 1121
15: 6 the **s in law** of the Timnite, because he had 2860
17: 2 Blessed *be thou* of the LORD, my **s**. 1121
17: 3 unto the LORD from my hand for my **s**, 1121
18:30 Jonathan, the **s** of Gershom, the son of 1121
18:30 the **s** of Manasseh, he and his sons were 1121
19: 5 the damsel's father said unto his **s in law**, 2860
20:28 Phinehas, the **s** of Eleazar, the son of 1121
20:28 the son of Eleazar, the **s** of Aaron, 1121
Ru 4:13 gave her conception, and she bare a **s**. 1121
4:17 a name, saying, There is a **s** born to Naomi; 1121
1Sa 1: 1 the **s** of Jeroham, the son of Elihu, the son 1121
1: 1 the **s** of Elihu, the son of Tohu, the son of 1121
1: 1 the **s** of Tohu, the son of Zuph, 1121
1: 1 son of Tohu, the **s** of Zuph, an Ephrathite: 1121
1:20 that she bare a **s**, and called his name 1121
1:23 and gave her **s** suck until she weaned him. 1121
3: 6 he answered, I called not, my **s**; lie down 1121
3:16 Eli called Samuel, and said, Samuel, my **s**. 1121
4:16 And he said, What is there done, my **s**? 1121
4:20 *unto her,* Fear not; for thou hast born a **s**. 1121
7: 1 sanctified Eleazar his **s** to keep the ark of 1121
9: 1 the **s** of Abiel, the son of Zeror, the son of 1121
9: 1 the son of Abiel, the **s** of Zeror, the son of 1121
9: 1 the son of Zeror, the **s** of Bechorath, 1121
9: 1 of Bechorath, the **s** of Aphiah, a Benjamite, 1121
9: 2 he had a **s**, whose name *was* Saul, a choice 1121
9: 3 Kish said to Saul his **s**, Take now one of 1121
10: 2 for you, saying, What shall I do for my **s**? 1121
10:11 What *is* this *that* is come unto the **s** of 1121
10:21 and Saul the **s** of Kish was taken: 1121
13:16 Jonathan his **s**, and the people that were 1121
13:22 and with Jonathan his **s** was there found. 1121
14: 1 that Jonathan the **s** of Saul said unto 1121
14: 3 Ahiah, the **s** of Ahitub, Ichabod's brother, 1121
14: 3 the **s** of Phinehas, the son of Eli, 1121
14: 3 the son of Phinehas, the **s** of Eli, 1121
14:39 though it be in Jonathan my **s**, he shall 1121
14:40 and Jonathan my **s** will be on the other side. 1121
14:42 Cast *lots* between me and Jonathan my **s**. 1121
14:50 host *was* Abner, the **s** of Ner, Saul's uncle. 1121
14:51 Ner the father of Abner *was* the **s** of Abiel. 1121
16:18 I have seen a **s** of Jesse the Beth-lehemite, 1121
16:19 said, Send me David thy **s**, which *is* with 1121
16:20 sent *them* by David his **s** unto Saul. 1121
17:12 Now David *was* the **s** of that Ephrathite of 1121
17:17 Jesse said unto David his **s**, Take now for 1121
17:55 of the host, Abner, whose **s** *is* this youth? 1121
17:56 Inquire thou whose **s** the stripling *is.* 1121
17:58 to him, Whose **s** *art* thou, *thou* young man? 1121
17:58 *I am* the **s** of thy servant Jesse 1121
18:18 that I should be **s in law** to the king? 2860
18:21 Thou shalt *this* day be my **s in law** in 2859
18:22 now therefore be the king's **s in law**. 2859
18:23 to you a light *thing* to be a king's **s in law**, 2859
18:26 David well to be the king's **s in law**: 2859
18:27 that he might be the king's **s in law**. 2859
19: 1 Saul spake to Jonathan his **s**, and to all his 1121
19: 2 Jonathan Saul's **s** delighted much in David: 1121
20:27 Saul said unto Jonathan his **s**, 1121
20:27 Wherefore cometh not the **s** of Jesse to 1121
20:30 Thou **s** of the perverse rebellious *woman,* 1121
20:30 the **s** of Jesse to thine own confusion, 1121
20:31 For as long as the **s** of Jesse liveth upon 1121
22: 7 will the **s** of Jesse give every one of you 1121
22: 8 *there is* none that sheweth me that my **s** 1121
22: 8 son hath made *a league* with the **s** of Jesse, 1121
22: 8 sheweth unto me that my **s** hath stirred up 1121
22: 9 said, I saw the **s** of Jesse coming to Nob, 1121
22: 9 to Nob, to Ahimelech the **s** of Ahitub: 1121
22:11 the **s** of Ahitub, and all his father's house, 1121
22:12 Saul said, Hear now, thou **s** of Ahitub. 1121
22:13 thou and the **s** of Jesse, in that thou hast 1121
22:14 which *is* the king's **s in law**, and goeth at 2860
22:20 one of the sons of Ahimelech the **s** of 1121
23: 6 when Abiathar the **s** of Ahimelech fled to 1121
23:16 Jonathan Saul's **s** arose, and went to David 1121
24:16 Saul said, *Is* this thy voice, my **s** David? 1121
25: 8 hand unto thy servants, and to thy **s** David. 1121
25:10 who *is* the **s** of Jesse? there be many 1121
25:17 for he *is such* a **s** of Belial, that *a man* 1121
25:44 David's wife, to Phalti the **s** of Laish, 1121
26: 5 Abner the **s** of Ner, the captain of his host: 1121
26: 6 to Abishai the **s** of Zeruiah, brother to Joab, 1121
26:14 to Abner the **s** of Ner, saying, Answerest 1121
26:17 and said, *Is* this thy voice, my **s** David? 1121
26:21 return, my **s** David: for I will no more do 1121
26:25 said to David, Blessed *be* thou, my **s** David: 1121
27: 2 unto Achish, the **s** of Maoch, king of Gath. 1121
30: 7 Ahimelech's **s**, I pray thee, bring me hither 1121
2Sa 1: 4 and Saul and Jonathan his **s** are dead also. 1121
1: 5 thou that Saul and Jonathan his **s** be dead? 1121
1:12 for Jonathan his **s**, and for the people of 1121
1:13 *I am* the **s** of a stranger, an Amalekite. 1121
1:17 over Saul and over Jonathan his **s**: 1121
2: 8 Abner the **s** of Ner, captain of Saul's host, 1121
2: 8 took Ish-bosheth the **s** of Saul, and 1121
2:10 Ish-bosheth Saul's **s** *was* forty years old 1121
2:12 Abner the **s** of Ner, and the servants of 1121
2:12 the servants of Ish-bosheth the **s** of Saul, 1121
2:13 Joab the **s** of Zeruiah, and the servants of 1121
2:15 which *pertained* to Ish-bosheth the **s** of 1121
3: 3 Absalom the **s** of Maacah the daughter of 1121

2Sa 3: 4 the fourth, Adonijah the **s** of Haggith; and 1121
3: 4 and the fifth, Shephatiah the **s** of Abital; 1121
3:14 sent messengers to Ish-bosheth Saul's **s**, 1121
3:15 *even* from Phaltiel the **s** of Laish. 1121
3:23 Abner the **s** of Ner came to the king, and 1121
3:25 Thou knowest Abner the **s** of Ner, that he 1121
3:28 ever from the blood of Abner the **s** of Ner: 1121
3:37 not of the king to slay Abner the **s** of Ner. 1121
4: 1 when Saul's **s** heard that Abner was dead in 1121
4: 2 Saul's **s** had two men *that were* captains of 1121
4: 4 Jonathan, Saul's **s**, had a son *that was* lame 1121
4: 4 had a **s** *that was* lame of *his* feet, *and* 1121
4: 8 Behold the head of Ish-bosheth the **s** of 1121
7:14 I will be his father, and he shall be my **s**. If 1121
8: 3 the **s** of Rehob, king of Zobah, 1121
8:10 Toi sent Joram his **s** unto king David, 1121
8:12 of Hadadezer, **s** of Rehob, king of Zobah. 1121
8:16 Joab the **s** of Zeruiah *was* over the host; 1121
8:16 Jehoshaphat the **s** of Ahilud *was* recorder; 1121
8:17 Zadok the **s** of Ahitub, and Ahimelech 1121
8:17 Ahimelech the **s** of Abiathar, *were* 1121
8:18 Benaiah the **s** of Jehoiada *was over* both 1121
9: 3 Jonathan hath yet a **s**, *which is* lame on *his* 1121
9: 4 of Machir, the **s** of Ammiel, in Lo-debar. 1121
9: 5 of Machir, the **s** of Ammiel, from Lo-debar. 1121
9: 6 the **s** of Jonathan, the son of Saul, 1121
9: 6 the son of Jonathan, the **s** of Saul, 1121
9: 9 I have given unto thy master's **s** all that 1121
9:10 that thy master's **s** may have food to eat: 1121
9:10 Mephibosheth thy master's **s** shall eat bread 1121
9:12 Mephibosheth had a young **s**, whose name 1121
10: 1 and Hanun his **s** reigned in his stead. 1121
10: 2 I will shew kindness unto Hanun the **s** of 1121
11:21 Who smote Abimelech the **s** of 1121
11:27 and she became his wife, and bare him a **s**. 1121
12:24 she bare a **s**, and he called his name 1121
13: 1 that Absalom the **s** of David had a fair 1121
13: 1 and Amnon the **s** of David loved her. 1121
13: 3 the **s** of Shimeah David's brother: 1121
13: 4 Why *art* thou, *being* the king's **s**, lean from 1121
13:25 Nay, my **s**, let us not all now go, 1121
13:32 the **s** of Shimeah David's brother, answered 1121
13:37 the **s** of Ammihud, king of Geshur. 1121
13:37 And *David* mourned for his **s** every day. 1121
14: 1 Now Joab the **s** of Zeruiah perceived that 1121
14:11 to destroy any more, lest they destroy my **s**. 1121
14:11 there shall not one hair of thy **s** fall to 1121
14:16 my **s** together out of the inheritance of God. 1121
15:27 Ahimaaz thy **s**, and Jonathan the son of 1121
15:27 thy son, and Jonathan the **s** of Abiathar. 1121
15:36 Ahimaaz Zadok's **s**, and NIH
15:36 Zadok's *son*, and Jonathan Abiathar's *s*; and NIH
16: 3 the king said, And where *is* thy master's **s**? 1121
16: 5 whose name *was* Shimei, the **s** of Gera: 1121
16: 8 kingdom into the hand of Absalom thy **s**: 1121
16: 9 said Abishai the **s** of Zeruiah unto the king, 1121
16:11 and to all his servants, Behold, my **s**, 1121
16:19 *should* I not *serve* in the presence of his **s**? 1121
17:25 which Amasa *was* a man's **s**, whose name 1121
17:27 that Shobi the **s** of Nahash of Rabbah of 1121
17:27 Machir the **s** of Ammiel of Lo-debar, and 1121
18: 2 a third part under the hand of Abishai the **s** 1121
18:12 put forth mine hand against the king's **s**: 1121
18:18 I have no **s** to keep my name in 1121
18:19 said Ahimaaz the **s** of Zadok, Let me now 1121
18:20 no tidings, because the king's **s** is dead. 1121
18:22 said Ahimaaz the **s** of Zadok yet again to 1121
18:22 Joab said, Wherefore wilt thou run, my **s**, 1121
18:27 like the running of Ahimaaz the **s** of Zadok. 1121
18:33 thus he said, O my **s** Absalom, my son, 1121
18:33 my son Absalom, my **s**, my son Absalom: 1121
18:33 my son Absalom, my son, my **s** Absalom: 1121
18:33 died for thee, O Absalom, my **s**, my son. 1121
18:33 died for thee, O Absalom, my son, my **s**. 1121
19: 2 that day *how* the king was grieved for his **s**. 1121
19: 4 O my **s** Absalom, O Absalom, my son, 1121
19: 4 son Absalom, O Absalom, my **s**, my son. 1121
19: 4 son Absalom, O Absalom, my son, my **s**. 1121
19:16 Shimei the **s** of Gera, a Benjamite, 1121
19:18 Shimei the **s** of Gera fell down before 1121
19:21 Abishai the **s** of Zeruiah answered and said, 1121
19:24 Mephibosheth the **s** of Saul came down to 1121
20: 1 *was* Sheba, the **s** of Bichri, a Benjamite: 1121
20: 1 neither have we inheritance in the **s** of 1121
20: 2 *and* followed Sheba the **s** of Bichri: 1121
20: 6 Now shall Sheba the **s** of Bichri do us more 1121
20: 7 to pursue after Sheba the **s** of Bichri. 1121
20:10 brother pursued after Sheba the **s** of Bichri. 1121
20:13 to pursue after Sheba the **s** of Bichri. 1121
20:21 Sheba the **s** of Bichri by name, 1121
20:22 they cut off the head of Sheba the **s** of 1121
20:23 Benaiah the **s** of Jehoiada *was* over 1121
20:24 Jehoshaphat the **s** of Ahilud *was* recorder: 1121
21: 7 the **s** of Jonathan the son of Saul, because 1121
21: 7 the son of Jonathan the **s** of Saul, because 1121
21: 7 between David and Jonathan the **s** of Saul. 1121
21: 8 whom she brought up for Adriel the **s** of 1121
21:12 the bones of Jonathan his **s** from the men of 1121
21:13 of Saul and the bones of Jonathan his **s**; 1121
21:14 Jonathan his **s** buried they in the country of 1121
21:17 Abishai the **s** of Zeruiah succoured him, 1121
21:19 where Elhanan the **s** of Jaare-oregim, 1121
21:21 Jonathan the **s** of Shimea the brother of 1121
23: 1 David the **s** of Jesse said, and the man *who* 1121
23: 9 after him *was* Eleazar the **s** of Dodo 1121
23:11 after him *was* Shammah the **s** of Agee 1121
23:18 the brother of Joab, the **s** of Zeruiah, 1121
23:20 Benaiah the **s** of Jehoiada, the son of a 1121
23:20 the **s** of a valiant man, of Kabzeel, who had 1121
23:22 These *things* did Benaiah the **s** of Jehoiada, 1121
23:24 Elhanan the **s** of Dodo *of* Beth-lehem, 1121
23:26 the Paltite, Ira the **s** of Ikkesh the Tekoite, 1121
23:29 Heleb the **s** of Baanah, a Netophathite, 1121
23:29 Ittai the **s** of Ribai out of Gibeah of 1121
23:33 Ahiam the **s** of Sharar the Hararite, 1121
23:34 Eliphelet the **s** of Ahasbai, the son of 1121
23:34 son of Ahasbai, the **s** of the Maachathite, 1121
23:34 Eliam the **s** of Ahithophel the Gilonite, 1121
23:36 Igal the **s** of Nathan of Zobah, Bani 1121
23:37 armourbearer to Joab the **s** of Zeruiah, 1121
1Ki 1: 5 Adonijah the **s** of Haggith exalted himself, 1121
1: 7 he conferred with Joab the **s** of Zeruiah, 1121
1: 8 Benaiah the **s** of Jehoiada, and Nathan 1121
1:11 Hast thou not heard that Adonijah the **s** of 1121
1:12 own life, and the life of thy **s** Solomon. 1121
1:13 Assuredly Solomon thy **s** shall reign after 1121
1:17 *saying,* Assuredly Solomon thy **s** shall 1121
1:21 my **s** Solomon shall be *counted* offenders. 1121
1:26 Benaiah the **s** of Jehoiada, and thy servant 1121
1:30 Assuredly Solomon thy **s** shall reign after 1121
1:32 the prophet, and Benaiah the **s** of Jehoiada. 1121
1:33 cause Solomon my **s** to ride upon mine own 1121
1:36 Benaiah the **s** of Jehoiada answered 1121
1:38 Benaiah the **s** of Jehoiada, and 1121
1:42 Jonathan the **s** of Abiathar the priest came: 1121
1:44 Benaiah the **s** of Jehoiada, and 1121
2: 1 and he charged Solomon his **s**, saying, 1121
2: 5 also what Joab the **s** of Zeruiah did to me, 1121
2: 5 unto Abner the **s** of Ner, and unto Amasa 1121
2: 5 unto Amasa the **s** of Jether, whom he slew, 1121
2: 8 *thou hast* with thee Shimei the **s** of Gera, 1121
2:13 Adonijah the **s** of Haggith came to 1121
2:22 the priest, and for Joab the **s** of Zeruiah. 1121
2:25 by the hand of Benaiah the **s** of Jehoiada; 1121
2:29 Solomon sent Benaiah the **s** of Jehoiada, 1121
2:32 knowing *thereof, to wit,* Abner the **s** of Ner, 1121
2:32 host of Israel, and Amasa the **s** of Jether, 1121
2:34 So Benaiah the **s** of Jehoiada went up, and 1121
2:35 the king put Benaiah the **s** of Jehoiada in 1121
2:39 unto Achish **s** of Maachah king of Gath. 1121
2:46 So the king commanded Benaiah the **s** of 1121
3: 6 that thou hast given him a **s** to sit on his 1121
3:20 at midnight, and took my **s** from beside me, 1121
3:21 it was not my **s**, which I did bear. 1121
3:22 the living *is* my **s**, and the dead *is* thy son. 1121
3:22 the living *is* my son, and the dead *is* thy **s**. 1121
3:22 the dead *is* thy **s**, and the living *is* my son. 1121
3:22 the dead *is* thy son, and the living *is* my **s**. 1121
3:23 This *is* my **s** that liveth, and thy son *is* 1121
3:23 *is* my son that liveth, and thy **s** *is* the dead: 1121
3:23 thy **s** *is* the dead, and my son *is* the living. 1121
3:23 thy son *is* the dead, and my **s** *is* the living. 1121
3:26 for her bowels yerned upon her **s**, and 1121
4: 2 he had; Azariah the **s** of Zadok the priest, 1121
4: 3 Jehoshaphat the **s** of Ahilud, the recorder. 1121
4: 4 Benaiah the **s** of Jehoiada *was* over 1121
4: 5 Azariah the **s** of Nathan *was* over 1121
4: 5 Zabud the **s** of Nathan *was* principal 1121

1Ki 4: 6 Adoniram the **s** of Abda *was* over 1121
4: 8 The **s** of Hur, in mount Ephraim: 1121
4: 9 The **s** of Dekar, in Makaz, and in Shaalbim, 1121
4:10 The **s** of Hesed, in Aruboth; to him 1121
4:11 The **s** of Abinadab, *in* all the region of Dor; 1121
4:12 Baana the **s** of Ahilud; *to him pertained* 1121
4:13 The **s** of Geber, in Ramoth-gilead; to him 1121
4:13 to him *pertained* the towns of Jair the **s** of 1121
4:14 Ahinadab the **s** of Iddo *had* Mahanaim: 1121
4:16 Baanah the **s** of Hushai *was* in Asher and 1121
4:17 Jehoshaphat the **s** of Paruah, in Issachar: 1121
4:18 Shimei the **s** of Elah, in Benjamin: 1121
4:19 Geber the **s** of Uri *was* in the country of 1121
5: 5 spake unto David my father, saying, Thy **s**, 1121
5: 7 which hath given unto David a wise **s** over 1121
7:14 He *was* a widow's **s** of the tribe of 1121
8:19 thy **s** that shall come forth out of thy loins, 1121
11:12 *but* I will rend it out of the hand of thy **s**. 1121
11:13 will give one tribe to thy **s** for David my 1121
11:20 sister of Tahpenes bare him Genubath his **s**, 1121
11:23 *another* adversary, Rezon the **s** of Eliadah, 1121
11:26 Jeroboam the **s** of Nebat, an Ephrathite of 1121
11:36 unto his **s** will I give one tribe, that David 1121
11:43 and Rehoboam his **s** reigned in his stead. 1121
12: 2 to pass, when Jeroboam the **s** of Nebat, 1121
12:15 the Shilonite unto Jeroboam the **s** of Nebat. 1121
12:16 neither *have we* inheritance in the **s** of 1121
12:21 again to Rehoboam the **s** of Solomon. 1121
12:23 the **s** of Solomon, king of Judah, and 1121
13:11 his **s** came and told him all the works that 1121
14: 1 At that time Abijah the **s** of Jeroboam fell 1121
14: 5 cometh to ask a thing of thee for her **s**; 1121
14:20 and Nadab his **s** reigned in his stead. 1121
14:21 Rehoboam the **s** of Solomon reigned in 1121
14:31 And Abijam his **s** reigned in his stead. 1121
15: 1 the **s** of Nebat reigned Abijam over Judah. 1121
15: 4 to set up his **s** after him, and to establish 1121
15: 8 and Asa his **s** reigned in his stead. 1121
15:18 the **s** of Tabrimon, the son of Hezion, 1121
15:18 of Tabrimon, the **s** of Hezion, king of Syria, 1121
15:24 and Jehoshaphat his **s** reigned in his stead. 1121
15:25 Nadab the **s** of Jeroboam *began* to reign 1121
15:27 Baasha the **s** of Ahijah, of the house of 1121
15:33 **s** of Ahijah to reign over all Israel in 1121
16: 1 the word of the LORD came to Jehu the **s** 1121
16: 3 like the house of Jeroboam the **s** of Nebat. 1121
16: 6 and Elah his **s** reigned in his stead. 1121
16: 7 also by the hand of the prophet Jehu the **s** 1121
16: 8 **s** of Baasha to reign over Israel in Tirzah, 1121
16:13 the sins of Elah his **s**, *by* which they sinned, 1121
16:21 half of the people followed Tibni the **s** of 1121
16:22 people that followed Tibni the **s** of Ginath: 1121
16:26 in all the way of Jeroboam the **s** of Nebat, 1121
16:28 and Ahab his **s** reigned in his stead. 1121
16:29 Ahab the **s** of Omri to reign over Israel: 1121
16:29 Ahab the **s** of Omri reigned over Israel in 1121
16:30 Ahab the **s** of Omri did evil in the sight of 1121
16:31 walk in the sins of Jeroboam the **s** of Nebat, 1121
16:34 set up the gates thereof in his youngest *s* NIH
16:34 which he spake by Joshua the **s** of Nun. 1121
17:12 I may go in and dress it for me and my **s**, 1121
17:13 and after make for thee and for thy **s**. 1121
17:17 *that* the **s** of the woman, the mistress of 1121
17:18 my sin to remembrance, and to slay my **s**? 1121
17:19 he said unto her, Give me thy **s**. And he 1121
17:20 with whom I sojourn, by slaying her **s**? 1121
17:23 and Elijah said, See, thy **s** liveth. 1121
19:16 Jehu the **s** of Nimshi shalt thou anoint to be 1121
19:16 Elisha the **s** of Shaphat of Abel-meholah 1121
19:19 and found Elisha the **s** of Shaphat, 1121
21:22 like the house of Jeroboam the **s** of Nebat, 1121
21:22 like the house of Baasha the **s** of Ahijah, 1121
22: 8 *is* yet one man, Micaiah the **s** of Imlah, 1121
22: 9 said, Hasten *hither* Micaiah the **s** of Imlah. 1121
22:11 Zedekiah the **s** of Chenaanah made him 1121
22:24 Zedekiah the **s** of Chenaanah went near, 1121
22:26 of the city, and to Joash the king's **s**; 1121
22:40 and Ahaziah his **s** reigned in his stead. 1121
22:41 Jehoshaphat the **s** of Asa *began* to reign 1121
22:49 said Ahaziah the **s** of Ahab unto 1121
22:50 and Jehoram his **s** reigned in his stead. 1121
22:51 Ahaziah the **s** of Ahab *began* to reign over 1121
22:52 in the way of Jeroboam the **s** of Nebat, 1121
2Ki 1:17 the **s** of Jehoshaphat king of Judah; 1121
1:17 king of Judah; because he had no **s**. 1121
3: 1 Now Jehoram the **s** of Ahab *began* to reign 1121
3: 3 unto the sins of Jeroboam the **s** of Nebat, 1121
3:11 and said, Here *is* Elisha the **s** of Shaphat, 1121
3:27 he took his eldest **s** that should have 1121
4: 6 that she said unto her **s**, Bring me yet a 1121
4:16 to the time of life, thou shalt embrace a **s**. 1121
4:17 bare a **s** at that season that Elisha had said 1121
4:28 she said, Did I desire a **s** of my lord? did I 1121
4:36 come in unto him, he said, Take up thy **s**. 1121
4:37 and took up her **s**, and went out. 1121
6:28 This woman said unto me, Give thy **s**, 1121
6:28 to day, and we will eat my **s** to morrow. 1121
6:29 So we boiled my **s**, and did eat him: and 1121
6:29 next day, Give thy **s**, that we may eat him: 1121
6:29 that we may eat him: and she hath hid her **s**. 1121
6:31 if the head of Elisha the **s** of Shaphat shall 1121
6:32 See ye how this **s** of a murderer hath sent to 1121
8: 1 whose **s** he had restored to life, saying, 1121
8: 5 the woman, whose **s** he had restored to life, 1121
8: 5 O king, this *is* the woman, and this *is* her **s**, 1121
8: 9 Thy **s** Ben-hadad king of Syria hath sent 1121
8:16 in the fifth year of Joram the **s** of Ahab 1121
8:16 Jehoram the **s** of Jehoshaphat king of Judah 1121
8:24 and Ahaziah his **s** reigned in his stead. 1121
8:25 In the twelfth year of Joram the **s** of Ahab 1121
8:25 **s** of Jehoram king of Judah *begin* to reign. 1121
8:27 for he *was* the **s in law** of the house of 2860
8:28 he went with Joram the **s** of Ahab to 1121
8:29 Ahaziah the **s** of Jehoram king of Judah 1121
8:29 down to see Joram the **s** of Ahab in Jezreel, 1121
9: 2 look out there Jehu the **s** of Jehoshaphat 1121
9: 2 the son of Jehoshaphat the **s** of Nimshi, 1121
9: 9 like the house of Jeroboam the **s** of Nebat, 1121
9: 9 like the house of Baasha the **s** of Ahijah: 1121
9:14 So Jehu the **s** of Jehoshaphat the son of 1121
9:14 So Jehu the son of Jehoshaphat the **s** of 1121
9:20 the driving *is* like the driving of Jehu the **s** 1121
9:29 in the eleventh year of Joram the **s** of Ahab 1121
10:15 he lighted on Jehonadab the **s** of Rechab 1121
10:23 Jehu went, and Jehonadab the **s** of Rechab, 1121
10:29 Howbeit *from* the sins of Jeroboam the **s** of 1121
10:35 And Jehoahaz his **s** reigned in his stead. 1121
11: 1 mother of Ahaziah saw that her **s** was dead, 1121
11: 2 took Joash the **s** of Ahaziah, and stale him 1121
11: 4 the LORD, and shewed them the king's **s**. 1121
11:12 he brought forth the king's **s**, and put 1121
12:21 For Jozachar the **s** of Shimeath, and 1121
12:21 Jehozabad the **s** of Shomer, his servants, 1121
12:21 and Amaziah his **s** reigned in his stead. 1121
13: 1 twentieth year of Joash the **s** of Ahaziah 1121
13: 1 **s** of Jehu *began* to reign over Israel in 1121
13: 2 followed the sins of Jeroboam the **s** of 1121
13: 3 into the hand of Ben-hadad the **s** of Hazael, 1121
13: 9 and Joash his **s** reigned in his stead. 1121
13:10 **s** of Jehoahaz to reign over Israel in 1121
13:11 all the sins of Jeroboam the **s** of Nebat, 1121
13:24 and Ben-hadad his **s** reigned in his stead. 1121
13:25 Jehoash the **s** of Jehoahaz took again out of 1121
13:25 of Ben-hadad the **s** of Hazael the cities, 1121
14: 1 In the second year of Joash **s** of Jehoahaz 1121
14: 1 Amaziah the **s** of Joash king of Judah. 1121
14: 8 the **s** of Jehoahaz son of Jehu, king of 1121
14: 8 the son of Jehoahaz **s** of Jehu, king of 1121
14: 9 Give thy daughter to my **s** to wife: 1121
14:13 the **s** of Jehoash the son of Ahaziah, 1121
14:13 the son of Jehoash the **s** of Ahaziah, 1121
14:16 and Jeroboam his **s** reigned in his stead. 1121
14:17 Amaziah the **s** of Joash king of Judah lived 1121
14:17 **s** of Jehoahaz king of Israel fifteen years. 1121
14:23 In the fifteenth year of Amaziah the **s** of 1121
14:23 **s** of Joash king of Israel *began* to reign in 1121
14:24 all the sins of Jeroboam the **s** of Nebat, 1121
14:25 the **s** of Amittai, the prophet, which *was* of 1121
14:27 by the hand of Jeroboam the **s** of Joash. 1121
14:29 and Zachariah his **s** reigned in his stead. 1121
15: 1 **s** of Amaziah king of Judah to reign. 1121
15: 5 Jotham the king's **s** *was* over the house, 1121
15: 7 and Jotham his **s** reigned in his stead. 1121
15: 8 **s** of Jeroboam reign over Israel in Samaria 1121
15: 9 from the sins of Jeroboam the **s** of Nebat, 1121
15:10 Shallum the **s** of Jabesh conspired against 1121
15:13 Shallum the **s** of Jabesh *began* to reign in 1121
15:14 For Menahem the **s** of Gadi went up from 1121

S

2Ki 15:14 smote Shallum the **s** of Jabesh in Samaria, 1121
15:17 Menahem the **s** of Gadi to reign over Israel, 1121
15:18 from the sins of Jeroboam the **s** of Nebat, 1121
15:22 and Pekahiah his **s** reigned in his stead. 1121
15:23 **s** of Menahem *began* to reign over Israel in 1121
15:24 from the sins of Jeroboam the **s** of Nebat, 1121
15:25 Pekah the **s** of Remaliah, a captain of his, 1121
15:27 **s** of Remaliah *began* to reign over Israel in 1121
15:28 from the sins of Jeroboam the **s** of Nebat, 1121
15:30 Hoshea the **s** of Elah made a conspiracy 1121
15:30 against Pekah the **s** of Remaliah, 1121
15:30 in the twentieth year of Jotham the **s** of 1121
15:32 In the second year of Pekah the **s** of 1121
15:32 the **s** of Uzziah king of Judah to reign. 1121
15:37 king of Syria, and Pekah the **s** of Remaliah. 1121
15:38 and Ahaz his **s** reigned in his stead. 1121
16: 1 In the seventeenth year of Pekah the **s** of 1121
16: 1 **s** of Jotham king of Judah *began* to reign. 1121
16: 3 yea, and made his **s** to pass through the fire, 1121
16: 5 Pekah **s** of Remaliah king of Israel came up 1121
16: 7 saying, I *am* thy servant and thy **s**: 1121
16:20 and Hezekiah his **s** reigned in his stead. 1121
17: 1 **s** of Elah to reign in Samaria over Israel 1121
17:21 they made Jeroboam the **s** of Nebat king: 1121
18: 1 year of Hoshea **s** of Elah king of Israel, 1121
18: 1 *that* Hezekiah the **s** of Ahaz king of Judah 1121
18: 9 which *was* the seventh year of Hoshea **s** of 1121
18:18 there came out to them Eliakim the **s** of 1121
18:18 and Joah the **s** of Asaph the recorder. 1121
18:26 said Eliakim the **s** of Hilkiah, and Shebna, 1121
18:37 came Eliakim the **s** of Hilkiah, which *was* 1121
18:37 and Joah the **s** of Asaph the recorder, 1121
19: 2 to Esai the prophet the **s** of Amoz. 1121
19:20 Isaiah the **s** of Amoz sent to Hezekiah, 1121
19:37 And Esarhaddon his **s** reigned in his stead. 1121
20: 1 the prophet Isaiah the **s** of Amoz came to 1121
20:12 the **s** of Baladan, king of Babylon, 1121
20:21 and Manasseh his **s** reigned in his stead. 1121
21: 6 he made his **s** pass through the fire, and 1121
21: 7 to Solomon his **s**, In this house, and 1121
21:18 and Amon his **s** reigned in his stead. 1121
21:24 the people of the land made Josiah his **s** 1121
21:26 and Josiah his **s** reigned in his stead. 1121
22: 3 *that* the king sent Shaphan the **s** of Azaliah, 1121
22: 3 the **s** of Meshullam, the scribe, *to* the house 1121
22:12 Ahikam the **s** of Shaphan, and Achbor 1121
22:12 Achbor the **s** of Michaiah, and Shaphan 1121
22:14 the wife of Shallum the **s** of Tikvah, the son 1121
22:14 the **s** of Harhas, keeper of the wardrobe; 1121
23:10 that no man might make his **s** or his 1121
23:15 the high place which Jeroboam the **s** of 1121
23:30 the people of the land took Jehoahaz the **s** 1121
23:34 Pharaoh-nechoh made Eliakim the **s** of 1121
24: 6 and Jehoiachin his **s** reigned in his stead. 1121
25:22 even over them he made Gedaliah the **s** of 1121
25:22 the son of Ahikam, the **s** of Shaphan, ruler. 1121
25:23 even Ishmael the **s** of Nethaniah, and 1121
25:23 Johanan the **s** of Careah, and Seraiah 1121
25:23 Seraiah the **s** of Tanhumeth 1121
25:23 Jaazaniah the **s** of a Maachathite, they and 1121
25:25 *that* Ishmael the **s** of Nethaniah, the son of 1121
25:25 the **s** of Elishama, of the seed royal, came, 1121
1Ch 1:43 the children of Israel; Bela the **s** of Beor: 1121
1:44 Jobab the **s** of Zerah of Bozrah reigned in 1121
1:46 Husham was dead, Hadad the **s** of Bedad, 1121
1:49 Baal-hanan the **s** of Achbor reigned in his 1121
2:18 Caleb the **s** of Hezron begat *children* of 1121
2:45 the **s** of Shammai *was* Maon: and 1121
2:50 These were the sons of Caleb the **s** of Hur, 1121
3: 2 Absalom the **s** of Maachah the daughter of 1121
3: 2 the fourth, Adonijah the **s** of Haggith: 1121
3:10 Solomon's **s** *was* Rehoboam, Abia his son, 1121
3:10 Abia his **s**, Asa his son, Jehoshaphat his 1121
3:10 Abia his son, Asa his **s**, Jehoshaphat his 1121
3:10 his son, Asa his son, Jehoshaphat his **s**, 1121
3:11 Joram his **s**, Ahaziah his son, Joash his son, 1121
3:11 Joram his son, Ahaziah his **s**, Joash his son, 1121
3:11 Joram his son, Ahaziah his son, Joash his **s**, 1121
3:12 Amaziah his **s**, Azariah his son, Jotham his 1121
3:12 his son, Azariah his **s**, Jotham his son, 1121
3:12 his son, Azariah his son, Jotham his **s**, 1121
3:13 Ahaz his **s**, Hezekiah his son, Manasseh his 1121
3:13 Ahaz his son, Hezekiah his **s**, Manasseh his 1121
3:13 his son, Hezekiah his son, Manasseh his **s**, 1121
3:14 Amon his **s**, Josiah his son. 1121
3:14 Amon his son, Josiah his **s**. 1121
3:16 Jeconiah his **s**, Zedekiah his son. 1121
3:16 Jeconiah his son, Zedekiah his **s**. 1121
3:17 the sons of Jeconiah; Assir, Salathiel his **s**, 1121
3:19 the **s** of Zerubbabel; Meshullam, and 1121
4: 2 Reaiah the **s** of Shobal begat Jahath; and 1121
4: 8 and the families of Aharhel the **s** of Harum. 1121
4:15 the sons of Caleb the **s** of Jephunneh; Iru, 1121
4:21 The sons of Shelah the **s** of Judah *were*, Er 1121
4:25 Shallum his **s**, Mibsam his son, Mishma his 1121
4:25 his son, Mibsam his **s**, Mishma his son. 1121
4:25 his son, Mibsam his son, Mishma his **s**. 1121
4:26 Hamuel his **s**, Zacchur his son, Shimei his 1121
4:26 his son, Zacchur his **s**, Shimei his son. 1121
4:26 his son, Zacchur his son, Shimei his **s**. 1121
4:34 and Jamlech, and Joshah the **s** of Amaziah, 1121
4:35 Joel, and Jehu the **s** of Josibiah, the son of 1121
4:35 the **s** of Seraiah, the son of Asiel, 1121
4:35 the son of Seraiah, the **s** of Asiel, 1121
4:37 Ziza the **s** of Shiphi, the son of Allon, 1121
4:37 the **s** of Allon, the son of Jedaiah, the son 1121
4:37 the son of Allon, the **s** of Jedaiah, the son 1121
4:37 the son of Jedaiah, the **s** of Shimri, 1121
4:37 the son of Shimri, the **s** of Shemaiah; 1121
5: 1 unto the sons of Joseph the **s** of Israel: 1121
5: 4 Shemaiah his **s**, Gog his son, Shimei his 1121
5: 4 his son, Gog his **s**, Shimei his son, 1121
5: 4 his son, Gog his son, Shimei his **s**, 1121
5: 5 Micah his **s**, Reaia his son, Baal his son, 1121
5: 5 Micah his son, Reaia his **s**, Baal his son, 1121
5: 5 Micah his son, Reaia his son, Baal his **s**, 1121
5: 6 Beerah his **s**, whom Tilgath-pilneser king 1121
5: 8 Bela the **s** of Azaz, the son of Shema, 1121
5: 8 the **s** of Shema, the son of Joel, who dwelt 1121
5: 8 the son of Shema, the **s** of Joel, who dwelt 1121
5:14 These *are* the children of Abihail the **s** of 1121
5:14 the **s** of Jaroah, the son of Gilead, the son 1121
5:14 the son of Jaroah, the **s** of Gilead, the son 1121
5:14 the son of Gilead, the **s** of Michael, 1121
5:14 the **s** of Jeshishai, the son of Jahdo, the son 1121
5:14 of Jeshishai, the **s** of Jahdo, the son of Buz; 1121
5:14 of Jeshishai, the son of Jahdo, the **s** of Buz; 1121
5:15 Ahi the **s** of Abdiel, the son of Guni, 1121
5:15 Ahi the son of Abdiel, the **s** of Guni, 1121
6:20 Libni his **s**, Jahath his son, Zimmah his son, 1121
6:20 Libni his son, Jahath his **s**, Zimmah his son, 1121
6:20 Libni his son, Jahath his son, Zimmah his **s**, 1121
6:21 Joah his **s**, Iddo his son, Zerah his son, 1121
6:21 Joah his son, Iddo his **s**, Zerah his son, 1121
6:21 Joah his son, Iddo his son, Zerah his **s**, 1121
6:21 Iddo his son, Zerah his son, Jeaterai his **s**. 1121
6:22 Amminadab his **s**, Korah his son, Assir his 1121
6:22 his son, Korah his **s**, Assir his son, 1121
6:22 his son, Korah his son, Assir his **s**, 1121
6:23 Elkanah his **s**, and Ebiasaph his son, and 1121
6:23 and Ebiasaph his **s**, and Assir his son, 1121
6:23 and Ebiasaph his son, and Assir his **s**, 1121
6:24 Tahath his **s**, Uriel his son, Uzziah his son, 1121
6:24 Tahath his son, Uriel his **s**, Uzziah his son, 1121
6:24 his son, Uzziah his **s**, and Shaul his son. 1121
6:24 his son, Uzziah his son, and Shaul his **s**. 1121
6:26 Zophai his **s**, and Nahath his son, 1121
6:26 Zophai his son, and Nahath his **s**, 1121
6:27 Eliab his **s**, Jeroham his son, Elkanah his 1121
6:27 Eliab his son, Jeroham his **s**, Elkanah his 1121
6:27 his son, Jeroham his son, Elkanah his **s**. 1121
6:29 Mahli, Libni his **s**, Shimei his son, Uzza his 1121
6:29 Libni his son, Shimei his **s**, Uzza his son, 1121
6:29 Libni his son, Shimei his son, Uzza his **s**, 1121
6:30 Shimea his **s**, Haggiah his son, Asaiah his 1121
6:30 his son, Haggiah his **s**, Asaiah his son. 1121
6:30 his son, Haggiah his son, Asaiah his **s**. 1121
6:33 Heman a singer, the **s** of Joel, the son of 1121
6:33 a singer, the son of Joel, the **s** of Shemuel, 1121
6:34 The **s** of Elkanah, the son of Jeroham, 1121
6:34 the **s** of Jeroham, the son of Eliel, the son 1121
6:34 of Jeroham, the **s** of Eliel, the son of Toah, 1121
6:34 of Jeroham, the son of Eliel, the **s** of Toah, 1121
6:35 The **s** of Zuph, the son of Elkanah, the son 1121
6:35 The son of Zuph, the **s** of Elkanah, the son 1121
6:35 the **s** of Mahath, the son of Amasai, 1121
6:35 the son of Mahath, the **s** of Amasai, 1121
6:36 The **s** of Elkanah, the son of Joel, the son of 1121

1Ch 6:36 the **s** of Joel, the son of Azariah, 1121
6:36 the son of Joel, the **s** of Azariah, 1121
6:36 the son of Azariah, the **s** of Zephaniah, 1121
6:37 The **s** of Tahath, the son of Assir, the son of 1121
6:37 The son of Tahath, the **s** of Assir, the son of 1121
6:37 the son of Assir, the **s** of Ebiasaph, the son 1121
6:37 the son of Ebiasaph, the **s** of Korah, 1121
6:38 The **s** of Izhar, the son of Kohath, the son 1121
6:38 the **s** of Kohath, the son of Levi, the son of 1121
6:38 of Kohath, the **s** of Levi, the son of Israel. 1121
6:38 of Kohath, the son of Levi, the **s** of Israel. 1121
6:39 *even* Asaph the **s** of Berachiah, the son of 1121
6:39 the son of Berachiah, the **s** of Shimea, 1121
6:40 The **s** of Michael, the son of Baaseiah, 1121
6:40 The son of Michael, the **s** of Baaseiah, 1121
6:40 the son of Baaseiah, the **s** of Malchiah, 1121
6:41 The **s** of Ethni, the son of Zerah, the son of 1121
6:41 The son of Ethni, the **s** of Zerah, the son of 1121
6:41 of Ethni, the son of Zerah, the **s** of Adaiah, 1121
6:42 The **s** of Ethan, the son of Zimmah, the son 1121
6:42 The son of Ethan, the **s** of Zimmah, the son 1121
6:42 the son of Zimmah, the **s** of Shimei, 1121
6:43 The **s** of Jahath, the son of Gershom, 1121
6:43 the **s** of Gershom, the son of Levi. 1121
6:43 the son of Gershom, the **s** of Levi. 1121
6:44 Ethan the **s** of Kishi, the son of Abdi, 1121
6:44 of Kishi, the **s** of Abdi, the son of Malluch, 1121
6:44 of Kishi, the son of Abdi, the **s** of Malluch, 1121
6:45 The **s** of Hashabiah, the son of Amaziah, 1121
6:45 the **s** of Amaziah, the son of Hilkiah, 1121
6:45 the son of Amaziah, the **s** of Hilkiah, 1121
6:46 The **s** of Amzi, the son of Bani, the son of 1121
6:46 The son of Amzi, the **s** of Bani, the son of 1121
6:46 of Amzi, the son of Bani, the **s** of Shamer, 1121
6:47 The **s** of Mahli, the son of Mushi, the son 1121
6:47 the **s** of Mushi, the son of Merari, the son 1121
6:47 of Mushi, the **s** of Merari, the son of Levi. 1121
6:47 of Mushi, the son of Merari, the **s** of Levi. 1121
6:50 Eleazar his **s**, Phinehas his son, Abishua his 1121
6:50 Eleazar his son, Phinehas his **s**, Abishua his 1121
6:50 his son, Phinehas his son, Abishua his **s**, 1121
6:51 Bukki his **s**, Uzzi his son, Zerahiah his son, 1121
6:51 Bukki his son, Uzzi his **s**, Zerahiah his son, 1121
6:51 Bukki his son, Uzzi his son, Zerahiah his **s**, 1121
6:52 Meraioth his **s**, Amariah his son, Ahitub his 1121
6:52 his son, Amariah his **s**, Ahitub his son, 1121
6:52 his son, Amariah his son, Ahitub his **s**, 1121
6:53 Zadok his **s**, Ahimaaz his son. 1121
6:53 Zadok his son, Ahimaaz his **s**. 1121
6:56 they gave to Caleb the **s** of Jephunneh. 1121
7:16 Maachah the wife of Machir bare a **s**, and 1121
7:17 the **s** of Machir, the son of Manasseh. 1121
7:17 the son of Machir, the **s** of Manasseh. 1121
7:20 Bered his **s**, and Tahath his son, and 1121
7:20 Tahath his **s**, and Eladah his son, and 1121
7:20 and Eladah his **s**, and Tahath his son, 1121
7:20 and Eladah his son, and Tahath his **s**, 1121
7:21 Zabad his **s**, and Shuthelah his son, and 1121
7:21 and Shuthelah his **s**, and Ezer, and Elead, 1121
7:23 and bare a **s**, and he called his name Beriah, 1121
7:25 Rephah *was* his **s**, also Resheph, and 1121
7:25 and Telah his **s**, and Tahan his son, 1121
7:25 and Telah his son, and Tahan his **s**, 1121
7:26 Laadan his **s**, Ammihud his son, 1121
7:26 Laadan his son, Ammihud his **s**, 1121
7:26 his son, Ammihud his son, Elishama his **s**, 1121
7:27 Non his **s**, Jehoshua his son. 1121
7:27 Non his son, Jehoshua his **s**. 1121
7:29 In these dwelt the children of Joseph the **s** 1121
7:35 the **s** of his brother Helem; Zophah, and 1121
8:30 his firstborn **s** Abdon, and Zur, and Kish, 1121
8:34 the **s** of Jonathan *was* Merib-baal; and 1121
8:37 Rapha *was* his **s**, Eleasah his son, Azel his 1121
8:37 *was* his son, Eleasah his **s**, Azel his son: 1121
8:37 *was* his son, Eleasah his son, Azel his **s**: 1121
9: 4 Uthai the **s** of Ammihud, the son of Omri, 1121
9: 4 the **s** of Omri, the son of Imri, the son of 1121
9: 4 son of Omri, the **s** of Imri, the son of Bani, 1121
9: 4 son of Omri, the son of Imri, the **s** of Bani, 1121
9: 4 of the children of Pharez the **s** of Judah. 1121
9: 7 Sallu the **s** of Meshullam, the son of 1121
9: 7 the **s** of Hodaviah, the son of Hasenuah, 1121
9: 7 the son of Hodaviah, the **s** of Hasenuah, 1121
9: 8 Ibneiah the **s** of Jeroham, and Elah the son 1121
9: 8 Elah the **s** of Uzzi, the son of Michri, and 1121
9: 8 the **s** of Michri, and Meshullam the son of 1121
9: 8 Meshullam the **s** of Shephathiah, the son of 1121
9: 8 the **s** of Reuel, the son of Ibnijah; 1121
9: 8 the son of Reuel, the **s** of Ibnijah; 1121
9:11 Azariah the **s** of Hilkiah, the son of 1121
9:11 the **s** of Meshullam, the son of Zadok, 1121
9:11 the **s** of Zadok, the son of Meraioth, the son 1121
9:11 the son of Zadok, the **s** of Meraioth, the son 1121
9:11 the son of Meraioth, the **s** of Ahitub, 1121
9:12 Adaiah the **s** of Jeroham, the son of Pashur, 1121
9:12 the **s** of Pashur, the son of Malchijah, and 1121
9:12 the **s** of Malchijah, and Maasiai the son of 1121
9:12 Maasiai the **s** of Adiel, the son of Jahzerah, 1121
9:12 the **s** of Jahzerah, the son of Meshullam, 1121
9:12 the son of Jahzerah, the **s** of Meshullam, 1121
9:12 the **s** of Meshillemith, the son of Immer; 1121
9:12 the son of Meshillemith, the **s** of Immer; 1121
9:14 Shemaiah the **s** of Hasshub, the son of 1121
9:14 the **s** of Azrikam, the son of Hashabiah, 1121
9:14 the son of Azrikam, the **s** of Hashabiah, 1121
9:15 and Galal, and Mattaniah the **s** of Micah, 1121
9:15 of Micah, the **s** of Zichri, the son of Asaph; 1121
9:15 of Micah, the son of Zichri, the **s** of Asaph; 1121
9:16 Obadiah the **s** of Shemaiah, the son of 1121
9:16 the **s** of Galal, the son of Jeduthun, and 1121
9:16 the **s** of Jeduthun, and Berechiah the son of 1121
9:16 Berechiah the **s** of Asa, the son of Elkanah, 1121
9:16 Berechiah the son of Asa, the **s** of Elkanah, 1121
9:19 Shallum the **s** of Kore, the son of Ebiasaph, 1121
9:19 the **s** of Ebiasaph, the son of Korah, and 1121
9:19 the **s** of Korah, and his brethren, 1121
9:20 Phinehas the **s** of Eleazar was the ruler over 1121
9:21 *And* Zechariah the **s** of Meshelemiah *was* 1121
9:36 his firstborn **s** Abdon, then Zur, and Kish, 1121
9:40 the **s** of Jonathan *was* Merib-baal: and 1121
9:43 Rephaiah his **s**, Eleasah his son, Azel his 1121
9:43 his son, Eleasah his **s**, Azel his son. 1121
9:43 his son, Eleasah his son, Azel his **s**. 1121
10:14 turned the kingdom unto David the **s** of 1121
11: 6 So Joab the **s** of Zeruiah went first up, and 1121
11:12 after him *was* Eleazar the **s** of Dodo, 1121
11:22 Benaiah the **s** of Jehoiada, the son of a 1121
11:22 the **s** of a valiant man of Kabzeel, who had 1121
11:24 These *things* did Benaiah the **s** of Jehoiada, 1121
11:26 Elhanan the **s** of Dodo of Beth-lehem, 1121
11:28 Ira the **s** of Ikkesh the Tekoite, Abi-ezer 1121
11:30 Heled the **s** of Baanah the Netophathite, 1121
11:31 Ithai the **s** of Ribai of Gibeah, 1121
11:34 Jonathan the **s** of Shage the Hararite, 1121
11:35 Ahiam the **s** of Sacar the Hararite, 1121
11:35 of Sacar the Hararite, Eliphal the **s** of Ur, 1121
11:37 Hezro the Carmelite, Naarai the **s** of Ezbai, 1121
11:38 brother of Nathan, Mibhar the **s** of Haggeri, 1121
11:39 the armourbearer of Joab the **s** of Zeruiah, 1121
11:41 Uriah the Hittite, Zabad the **s** of Ahlai, 1121
11:42 Adina the **s** of Shiza the Reubenite, 1121
11:43 Hanan the **s** of Maachah, and Joshaphat 1121
11:45 Jediael the **s** of Shimri, and Joha his 1121
12: 1 himself close because of Saul the **s** of Kish: 1121
12:18 *we,* David, and on thy side, thou **s** of Jesse: 1121
15:17 So the Levites appointed Heman the **s** of 1121
15:17 of his brethren, Asaph the **s** of Berechiah; 1121
15:17 their brethren, Ethan the **s** of Kushaiah; 1121
16:38 Obed-edom also the **s** of Jeduthun and 1121
17:13 I will be his father, and he shall be my **s**: 1121
18:10 He sent Hadoram his **s** to king David, 1121
18:12 Moreover Abishai the **s** of Zeruiah slew of 1121
18:15 Joab the **s** of Zeruiah *was* over the host; 1121
18:15 and Jehoshaphat the **s** of Ahilud, recorder. 1121
18:16 Zadok the **s** of Ahitub, and Abimelech 1121
18:16 Abimelech the **s** of Abiathar, *were* 1121
18:17 Benaiah the **s** of Jehoiada *was* over 1121
19: 1 Ammon died, and his **s** reigned in his stead. 1121
19: 2 I will shew kindness unto Hanun the **s** of 1121
20: 5 Elhanan the **s** of Jair slew Lahmi 1121
20: 6 and he also was the **s** of the giant. 3205
20: 7 Jonathan the **s** of Shimea David's brother 1121
22: 5 Solomon my **s** *is* young and tender, and 1121
22: 6 he called for Solomon his **s**, and 1121
22: 7 David said to Solomon, My **s**, *as for* me, 1121
22: 9 Behold, a **s** *shall be* born to thee, who shall 1121
22:10 he shall be my **s**, and I *will be* his father; 1121
22:11 Now, my **s**, the LORD be with thee; and 1121

1Ch	22:17	the princes of Israel to help Solomon his **s**,	1121
	23: 1	he made Solomon his **s** king over Israel.	1121
	24: 6	Shemaiah the **s** of Nethaneel the scribe,	1121
	24: 6	Ahimelech the **s** of Abiathar, and *before*	1121
	24:29	the **s** of Kish *was* Jerahmeel.	1121
	26: 1	Of the Korhites *was* Meshelemiah the **s** of	1121
	26: 6	Also unto Shemaiah his **s** were sons born,	1121
	26:14	*for* Zechariah his **s**, a wise counseller,	1121
	26:24	Shebuel the **s** of Gershom, the son of	1121
	26:24	the **s** of Moses, *was* ruler of the treasures.	1121
	26:25	Rehabiah his **s**, and Jeshaiah his son, and	1121
	26:25	Jeshaiah his **s**, and Joram his son, and	1121
	26:25	Joram his **s**, and Zichri his son, and	1121
	26:25	and Zichri his **s**, and Shelomith his son.	1121
	26:25	and Zichri his son, and Shelomith his **s**.	1121
	26:28	Saul the **s** of Kish, and Abner the son of	1121
	26:28	Abner the **s** of Ner, and Joab the son of	1121
	26:28	and Joab the **s** of Zeruiah, had dedicated;	1121
	27: 2	month *was* Jashobeam the **s** of Zabdiel:	1121
	27: 5	third month *was* Benaiah the **s** of Jehoiada,	1121
	27: 6	and *in* his course *was* Ammizabad his **s**.	1121
	27: 7	of Joab, and Zebadiah his **s** after him:	1121
	27: 9	month *was* Ira the **s** of Ikkesh the Tekoite:	1121
	27:16	the Reubenites *was* Eliezer the **s** of Zichri:	1121
	27:16	Shephatiah the **s** of Maachah:	1121
	27:17	Of the Levites, Hashabiah the **s** of Kemuel:	1121
	27:18	of Issachar, Omri the **s** of Michael:	1121
	27:19	Of Zebulun, Ishmaiah the **s** of Obadiah:	1121
	27:19	of Naphtali, Jerimoth the **s** of Azriel:	1121
	27:20	of Ephraim, Hoshea the **s** of Azaziah:	1121
	27:20	tribe of Manasseh, Joel the **s** of Pedaiah:	1121
	27:21	in Gilead, Iddo the **s** of Zechariah:	1121
	27:21	of Benjamin, Jaasiel the **s** of Abner:	1121
	27:22	Of Dan, Azareel the **s** of Jeroham.	1121
	27:24	Joab the **s** of Zeruiah began to number, but	1121
	27:25	treasures *was* Azmaveth the **s** of Adiel:	1121
	27:25	the castles, *was* Jehonathan the **s** of Uzziah:	1121
	27:26	of the ground *was* Ezri the **s** of Chelub:	1121
	27:29	in the valleys *was* Shaphat the **s** of Adlai:	1121
	27:32	Jehiel the **s** of Hachmoni *was* with	1121
	27:34	after Ahithophel *was* Jehoiada the **s** of	1121
	28: 5	he hath chosen Solomon my **s** to sit upon	1121
	28: 6	he said unto me, Solomon thy **s**, he shall	1121
	28: 6	for I have chosen him to be my **s**, and I will	1121
	28: 9	thou, Solomon my **s**, know thou the God of	1121
	28:11	David gave to Solomon his **s** the pattern of	1121
	28:20	And David said to Solomon his **s**, Be strong	1121
	29: 1	Solomon my **s**, whom alone God hath	1121
	29:19	give unto Solomon my **s** a perfect heart,	1121
	29:22	they made Solomon the **s** of David king	1121
	29:26	Thus David the **s** of Jesse reigned over all	1121
	29:28	and Solomon his **s** reigned in his stead.	1121
2Ch	1: 1	Solomon the **s** of David was strengthened	1121
	1: 5	that Bezaleel the **s** of Uri, the son of Hur,	1121
	1: 5	the son of Uri, the **s** of Hur, had made,	1121
	2:12	who hath given to David the king a wise **s**,	1121
	2:14	The **s** of a woman of the daughters of Dan,	1121
	6: 9	thy **s** which shall come forth out of thy	1121
	9:29	the seer against Jeroboam the **s** of Nebat?	1121
	9:31	and Rehoboam his **s** reigned in his stead.	1121
	10: 2	when Jeroboam the **s** of Nebat, who *was* in	1121
	10:15	the Shilonite to Jeroboam the **s** of Nebat.	1121
	10:16	*we have* none inheritance in the **s** of Jesse:	1121
	11: 3	Speak unto Rehoboam the **s** of Solomon,	1121
	11:17	made Rehoboam the **s** of Solomon strong,	1121
	11:18	daughter of Jerimoth the **s** of David *to* wife,	1121
	11:18	Abihail the daughter of Eliab the **s** of Jesse;	1121
	11:22	Rehoboam made Abijah the **s** of Maachah	1121
	12:16	and Abijah his **s** reigned in his stead.	1121
	13: 6	Yet Jeroboam the **s** of Nebat, the servant of	1121
	13: 6	the servant of Solomon the **s** of David,	1121
	13: 7	against Rehoboam the **s** of Solomon,	1121
	14: 1	Asa his **s** reigned in his stead. In his days	1121
	15: 1	the spirit of God came upon Azariah the **s**	1121
	17: 1	Jehoshaphat his **s** reigned in his stead, and	1121
	17:16	next him *was* Amasiah the **s** of Zichri,	1121
	18: 7	the same *is* Micaiah the **s** of Imla.	1121
	18: 8	said, Fetch quickly Micaiah the **s** of Imla.	1121
	18:10	Zedekiah the **s** of Chenaanah had made him	1121
	18:23	Zedekiah the **s** of Chenaanah came near,	1121
	18:25	of the city, and to Joash the king's **s**;	1121
	19: 2	Jehu the **s** of Hanani the seer went out to	1121
	19:11	Zebadiah the **s** of Ishmael, the ruler of	1121
	20:14	upon Jahaziel the **s** of Zechariah, the son of	1121
	20:14	the **s** of Benaiah, the son of Jeiel, the son of	1121
	20:14	the son of Benaiah, the **s** of Jeiel, the son of	1121
	20:14	the son of Jeiel, the **s** of Mattaniah,	1121
	20:34	written in the book of Jehu the **s** of Hanani,	1121
	20:37	Eliezer the **s** of Dodavah of Mareshah	1121
	21: 1	And Jehoram his **s** reigned in his stead.	1121
	21:17	so that there was never a **s** left him,	1121
	22: 1	Ahaziah his youngest **s** king in his stead:	1121
	22: 1	So Ahaziah the **s** of Jehoram king of Judah	1121
	22: 5	went with Jehoram the **s** of Ahab king of	1121
	22: 6	Azariah the **s** of Jehoram king of Judah	1121
	22: 6	to see Jehoram the **s** of Ahab at Jezreel,	1121
	22: 7	with Jehoram against Jehu the **s** of Nimshi,	1121
	22: 9	said they, he *is* the **s** of Jehoshaphat,	1121
	22:10	mother of Ahaziah saw that her **s** was dead,	1121
	22:11	took Joash the **s** of Ahaziah, and stole him	1121
	23: 1	Azariah the **s** of Jeroham, and Ishmael	1121
	23: 1	Ishmael the **s** of Jehohanan, and Azariah	1121
	23: 1	Azariah the **s** of Obed, and Maaseiah	1121
	23: 1	Maaseiah the **s** of Adaiah, and Elishaphat	1121
	23: 1	Elishaphat the **s** of Zichri, into covenant	1121
	23: 3	unto them, Behold, the king's **s** shall reign,	1121
	23:11	they brought out the king's **s**, and put upon	1121
	24:20	the spirit of God came upon Zechariah the **s**	1121
	24:22	his father had done to him, but slew his **s**.	1121
	24:26	Zabad the **s** of Shimeath an Ammonitess,	1121
	24:26	Jehozabad the **s** of Shimrith a Moabitess.	1121
	24:27	And Amaziah his **s** reigned in his stead.	1121
	25:17	sent to Joash, the **s** of Jehoahaz, the son of	1121
	25:17	the **s** of Jehu, king of Israel, saying, Come,	1121
	25:18	Give thy daughter to my **s** to wife:	1121
	25:23	the **s** of Joash, the son of Jehoahaz,	1121
	25:23	the son of Joash, the **s** of Jehoahaz,	1121
	25:25	Amaziah the **s** of Joash king of Judah lived	1121
	25:25	**s** of Jehoahaz king of Israel fifteen years.	1121
	26:21	and Jotham his **s** *was* over the king's house,	1121
	26:22	Isaiah the prophet, the **s** of Amoz, write.	1121
	26:23	and Jotham his **s** reigned in his stead.	1121
	27: 9	and Ahaz his **s** reigned in his stead.	1121
	28: 3	incense in the valley of the **s** of Hinnom,	1121
	28: 6	For Pekah the **s** of Remaliah slew in Judah	1121
	28: 7	slew Maaseiah the king's **s**, and Azrikam	1121
	28:12	Azariah the **s** of Johanan, Berechiah the son	1121
	28:12	Berechiah the **s** of Meshillemoth, and	1121
	28:12	Jehizkiah the **s** of Shallum, and Amasa	1121
	28:12	son of Shallum, and Amasa the **s** of Hadlai,	1121
	28:27	and Hezekiah his **s** reigned in his stead.	1121
	29:12	Mahath the **s** of Amasai, and Joel the son of	1121
	29:12	son of Amasai, and Joel the **s** of Azariah,	1121
	29:12	Kish the **s** of Abdi, and Azariah the son of	1121
	29:12	son of Abdi, and Azariah the **s** of Jehalelel:	1121
	29:12	Joah the **s** of Zimmah, and Eden the son of	1121
	29:12	the son of Zimmah, and Eden the **s** of Joah:	1121
	30:26	for since the time of Solomon the **s** of	1121
	31:14	Kore the **s** of Imnah the Levite, the porter	1121
	32:20	the prophet Isaiah the **s** of Amoz, prayed	1121
	32:32	the **s** of Amoz, *and* in the book of the kings	1121
	32:33	And Manasseh his **s** reigned in his stead.	1121
	33: 6	the fire in the valley of the **s** of Hinnom:	1121
	33: 7	had said to David and to Solomon his **s**,	1121
	33:20	and Amon his **s** reigned in his stead.	1121
	33:25	the people of the land made Josiah his **s**	1121
	34: 8	he sent Shaphan the **s** of Azaliah, and	1121
	34: 8	and Joah the **s** of Joahaz the recorder,	1121
	34:20	Ahikam the **s** of Shaphan, and Abdon	1121
	34:20	Abdon the **s** of Micah, and Shaphan	1121
	34:22	the wife of Shallum the **s** of Tikvath,	1121
	34:22	the **s** of Hasrah, keeper of the wardrobe;	1121
	35: 3	the **s** of David king of Israel did build;	1121
	35: 4	according to the writing of Solomon his **s**.	1121
	36: 1	the people of the land took Jehoahaz the **s**	1121
	36: 8	and Jehoiachin his **s** reigned in his stead.	1121
Ezr	3: 2	stood up Jeshua the **s** of Jozadak, and	1121
	3: 2	Zerubbabel the **s** of Shealtiel, and	1121
	3: 8	began Zerubbabel the **s** of Shealtiel, and	1121
	3: 8	Jeshua the **s** of Jozadak, and the remnant of	1121
	5: 1	the prophet, and Zechariah the **s** of Iddo,	1247
	5: 2	rose up Zerubbabel the **s** of Shealtiel, and	1247
	5: 2	Jeshua the **s** of Jozadak, and began to build	1247
	6:14	the prophet and Zechariah the **s** of Iddo.	1247
	7: 1	Ezra the **s** of Seraiah, the son of Azariah,	1121
	7: 1	the **s** of Azariah, the son of Hilkiah,	1121
	7: 1	the son of Azariah, the **s** of Hilkiah,	1121
	7: 2	The **s** of Shallum, the son of Zadok, the son	1121

Ezr 7: 2 the s of Zadok, the son of Ahitub, 1121
7: 2 the son of Zadok, the s of Ahitub, 1121
7: 3 The s of Amariah, the son of Azariah, 1121
7: 3 the s of Azariah, the son of Meraioth, 1121
7: 3 the son of Azariah, the s of Meraioth, 1121
7: 4 The s of Zerahiah, the son of Uzzi, the son 1121
7: 4 the s of Uzzi, the son of Bukki, 1121
7: 4 the son of Uzzi, the s of Bukki, 1121
7: 5 The s of Abishua, the son of Phinehas, 1121
7: 5 the s of Phinehas, the son of Eleazar, 1121
7: 5 the son of Phinehas, the s of Eleazar, 1121
7: 5 of Eleazar, the s of Aaron the chief priest: 1121
8: 4 Elihoenai the s of Zerahiah, and with him 1121
8: 5 the s of Jahaziel, and with him three 1121
8: 6 Ebed the s of Jonathan, and with him fifty 1121
8: 7 Jeshaiah the s of Athaliah, and with him 1121
8: 8 Zebadiah the s of Michael, and with him 1121
8: 9 Obadiah the s of Jehiel, and with him two 1121
8:10 the s of Josiphiah, and with him an hundred 1121
8:11 Zechariah the s of Bebai, and with him 1121
8:12 Johanan the s of Hakkatan, and with him an 1121
8:18 of Mahli, the s of Levi, the son of Israel; 1121
8:18 of Mahli, the son of Levi, the s of Israel; 1121
8:33 hand of Meremoth the s of Uriah the priest; 1121
8:33 with him *was* Eleazar the s of Phinehas; 1121
8:33 with them *was* Jozabad the s of Jeshua, and 1121
8:33 and Noadiah the s of Binnui, Levites; 1121
10: 2 Shechaniah the s of Jehiel, *one* of the sons 1121
10: 6 went into the chamber of Johanan the s of 1121
10:15 Only Jonathan the s of Asahel and 1121
10:15 Jahaziah the s of Tikvah were employed 1121
10:18 *namely,* of the sons of Jeshua the s of 1121
Ne 1: 1 The words of Nehemiah the s of Hachaliah. 1121
3: 2 next to them builded Zaccur the s of Imri. 1121
3: 4 next unto them repaired Meremoth the s of 1121
3: 4 Meremoth the son of Urijah, the s of Koz. 1121
3: 4 next unto them repaired Meshullam the s of 1121
3: 4 the son of Berechiah, the s of Meshezabeel. 1121
3: 4 next unto them repaired Zadok the s of 1121
3: 6 old gate repaired Jehoiada the s of Paseah, 1121
3: 6 and Meshullam the s of Besodeiah; 1121
3: 8 Next unto him repaired Uzziel the s of 1121
3: 8 Next unto him also repaired Hananiah the s 1121
3: 9 next unto them repaired Rephaiah the s of 1121
3:10 next unto them repaired Jedaiah the s of 1121
3:10 next unto him repaired Hattush the s of 1121
3:11 Malchijah the s of Harim, and Hashub 1121
3:11 Hashub the s of Pahath-moab, repaired 1121
3:12 next unto him repaired Shallum the s of 1121
3:14 the dung gate repaired Malchiah the s of 1121
3:15 repaired Shallun the s of Col-hozeh, 1121
3:16 After him repaired Nehemiah the s of 1121
3:17 repaired the Levites, Rehum the s of Bani. 1121
3:18 their brethren, Bavai the s of Henadad, 1121
3:19 next to him repaired Ezer the s of Jeshua, 1121
3:20 After him Baruch the s of Zabbai earnestly 1121
3:21 After him repaired Meremoth the s of 1121
3:21 son of Urijah the s of Koz another piece, 1121
3:23 After him repaired Azariah the s of 1121
3:23 of Maaseiah the s of Ananiah by his house. 1121
3:24 After him repaired Binnui the s of Henadad 1121
3:25 Palal the s of Uzai, over against the turning 1121
3:25 After him Pedaiah the s of Parosh. 1121
3:29 After them repaired Zadok the s of Immer 1121
3:29 After him repaired also Shemaiah the s of 1121
3:30 After him repaired Hananiah the s of 1121
3:30 Hanun the sixth s of Zalaph, another piece. 1121
3:30 After him repaired Meshullam the s of 1121
3:31 s unto the place of the Nethinims, 1121
6:10 the s of Delaiah the son of Mehetabeel, 1121
6:10 the son of Delaiah the s of Mehetabeel, 1121
6:18 he *was* the s in law of Shechaniah the son 2860
6:18 he *was* the son in law of Shechaniah the s 1121
6:18 his s Johanan had taken the daughter of 1121
6:18 daughter of Meshullam the s of Berechiah. 1121
8:17 for since the days of Jeshua the s of Nun 1121
10: 1 the s of Hachaliah, and Zidkijah, 1121
10: 9 both Jeshua the s of Azaniah, Binnui of 1121
10:38 the priest the s of Aaron shall be with 1121
11: 4 Athaiah the s of Uzziah, the son of 1121
11: 4 the s of Zechariah, the son of Amariah, 1121
11: 4 the son of Zechariah, the s of Amariah, 1121
11: 4 the son of Amariah, the s of Shephatiah, 1121
11: 4 the son of Shephatiah, the s of Mahalaleel, 1121
11: 5 Maaseiah the s of Baruch, the son of 1121
11: 5 the s of Col-hozeh, the son of Hazaiah, 1121
11: 5 the s of Hazaiah, the son of Adaiah, the son 1121
11: 5 the s of Adaiah, the son of Joiarib, 1121
11: 5 the son of Adaiah, the s of Joiarib, 1121
11: 5 the son of Joiarib, the s of Zechariah, 1121
11: 5 the son of Zechariah, the s of Shiloni. 1121
11: 7 Sallu the s of Meshullam, the son of Joed, 1121
11: 7 the s of Joed, the son of Pedaiah, the son of 1121
11: 7 the son of Joed, the s of Pedaiah, the son of 1121
11: 7 the son of Pedaiah, the s of Kolaiah, 1121
11: 7 the s of Maaseiah, the son of Ithiel, the son 1121
11: 7 the s of Ithiel, the son of Jesaiah. 1121
11: 7 the son of Ithiel, the s of Jesaiah. 1121
11: 9 Joel the s of Zichri *was* their overseer: 1121
11: 9 Judah the s of Senuah *was* second over 1121
11:10 the priests: Jedaiah the s of Joiarib, Jachin, 1121
11:11 Seraiah the s of Hilkiah, the son of 1121
11:11 the s of Meshullam, the son of Zadok, 1121
11:11 the s of Zadok, the son of Meraioth, the son 1121
11:11 the son of Zadok, the s of Meraioth, the son 1121
11:11 the son of Meraioth, the s of Ahitub, 1121
11:12 Adaiah the s of Jeroham, the son of 1121
11:12 the s of Pelaliah, the son of Amzi, the son 1121
11:12 the son of Pelaliah, the s of Amzi, the son 1121
11:12 the son of Amzi, the s of Zechariah, the son 1121
11:12 the s of Pashur, the son of Malchiah, 1121
11:12 the son of Pashur, the s of Malchiah, 1121
11:13 Amashai the s of Azareel, the son of 1121
11:13 the s of Ahasai, the son of Meshillemoth, 1121
11:13 the s of Meshillemoth, the son of Immer, 1121
11:13 the son of Meshillemoth, the s of Immer, 1121
11:14 *was* Zabdiel, the s of *one of* the great *men.* 1121
11:15 Shemaiah the s of Hashub, the son of 1121
11:15 the s of Azrikam, the son of Hashabiah, 1121
11:15 the s of Hashabiah, the son of Bunni; 1121
11:15 the son of Hashabiah, the s of Bunni; 1121
11:17 Mattaniah the s of Micha, the son of Zabdi, 1121
11:17 of Micha, the s of Zabdi, the son of Asaph, 1121
11:17 of Micha, the son of Zabdi, the s of Asaph, 1121
11:17 Abda the s of Shammua, the son of Galal, 1121
11:17 the s of Galal, the son of Jeduthun. 1121
11:17 the son of Galal, the s of Jeduthun. 1121
11:22 at Jerusalem *was* Uzzi the s of Bani, 1121
11:22 the s of Hashabiah, the son of Mattaniah, 1121
11:22 the s of Mattaniah, the son of Micha. 1121
11:22 the son of Mattaniah, the s of Micha. 1121
11:24 Pethahiah the s of Meshezabeel, of 1121
11:24 of the children of Zerah the s of Judah, 1121
12: 1 went up with Zerubbabel the s of Shealtiel, 1121
12:23 even until the days of Johanan the s of 1121
12:24 Sherebiah, and Jeshua the s of Kadmiel, 1121
12:26 These *were* in the days of Joiakim the s of 1121
12:26 the s of Jozadak, and in the days of 1121
12:35 *namely,* Zechariah the s of Jonathan, 1121
12:35 the s of Shemaiah, the son of Mattaniah, 1121
12:35 the s of Mattaniah, the son of Michaiah, 1121
12:35 the s of Michaiah, the son of Zaccur, 1121
12:35 the s of Zaccur, the son of Asaph: 1121
12:35 the son of Zaccur, the s of Asaph: 1121
12:45 of David, *and* of Solomon his s. 1121
13:13 next to them *was* Hanan the s of Zaccur, 1121
13:13 the son of Zaccur, the s of Mattaniah: 1121
13:28 of Joiada, the s of Eliashib the high priest, 1121
13:28 *was* s in law to Sanballat the Horonite: 2860
Est 2: 5 the s of Jair, the son of Shimei, the son of 1121
2: 5 the son of Jair, the s of Shimei, the son of 1121
2: 5 son of Shimei, the s of Kish, a Benjamite; 1121
3: 1 Haman the s of Hammedatha the Agagite, 1121
3:10 gave it unto Haman the s of Hammedatha 1121
8: 5 Haman the s of Hammedatha the Agagite, 1121
9:10 The ten sons of Haman the s of 1121
9:24 Because Haman the s of Hammedatha, 1121
Job 18:19 He shall neither have s nor nephew among 5209
25: 6 and the s of man, *which is* a worm? 1121
32: 2 was kindled the wrath of Elihu the s of 1121
32: 6 Elihu the s of Barachel the Buzite answered 1121
35: 8 thy righteousness *may profit* the s of man. 1121
Ps 2: 7 LORD hath said unto me, Thou *art* my S; 1121
2:12 Kiss the S, lest he be angry, and ye perish 1248
3: T of David, when he fled from Absalom his s. 1121
8: 4 and the s of man, that thou visitest him? 1121
50:20 thou slanderest thine own mother's s. 1121
72: 1 and thy righteousness unto the king's s. 1121

Ps	72:20	The prayers of David the **s** of Jesse are	1121
	80:17	upon the **s** of man *whom* thou madest	1121
	86:16	and save the **s** of thine handmaid.	1121
	89:22	nor the **s** of wickedness afflict him.	1121
	116:16	*am* thy servant, *and* the **s** of thy handmaid:	1121
	144: 3	*or* the **s** of man, that thou makest account of	1121
	146: 3	*nor* in the **s** of man, in whom *there is* no	1121
Pr	1: 1	The proverbs of Solomon the **s** of David,	1121
	1: 8	My **s**, hear the instruction of thy father, and	1121
	1:10	My **s**, if sinners entice thee, consent thou	1121
	1:15	My **s**, walk not thou in the way with them;	1121
	2: 1	My **s**, if thou wilt receive my words, and	1121
	3: 1	My **s**, forget not my law; but let thine heart	1121
	3:11	My **s**, despise not the chastening of	1121
	3:12	even as a father the **s** *in whom* he	1121
	3:21	My **s**, let not them depart from thine eyes:	1121
	4: 3	For I was my father's **s**, tender and	1121
	4:10	Hear, O my **s**, and receive my sayings; and	1121
	4:20	My **s**, attend to my words; incline thine ear	1121
	5: 1	My **s**, attend unto my wisdom, *and*	1121
	5:20	why wilt thou, my **s**, be ravisht with a	1121
	6: 1	My **s**, if thou be surety for thy friend,	1121
	6: 3	Do this now, my **s**, and deliver thyself,	1121
	6:20	My **s**, keep thy father's commandment, and	1121
	7: 1	My **s**, keep my words, and lay up my	1121
	10: 1	A wise **s** maketh a glad father: but a foolish	1121
	10: 1	a foolish **s** *is* the heaviness of his mother.	1121
	10: 5	He that gathereth in summer *is* a wise **s**: *but*	1121
	10: 5	he that sleepeth in harvest *is* a **s** that	1121
	13: 1	A wise **s** *heareth his* father's instruction:	1121
	13:24	He that spareth his rod hateth his **s**: but	1121
	15:20	A wise **s** maketh a glad father: but a foolish	1121
	17: 2	A wise servant shall have rule over a **s** that	1121
	17:25	A foolish **s** *is* a grief to his father, and	1121
	19:13	A foolish **s** *is* the calamity of his father: and	1121
	19:18	Chasten thy **s** while there is hope, and	1121
	19:26	*is* a **s** that causeth shame, and	1121
	19:27	Cease, my **s**, to hear the instruction *that*	1121
	23:15	My **s**, if thine heart be wise, my heart shall	1121
	23:19	my **s**, and be wise, and guide thine heart in	1121
	23:26	My **s**, give me thine heart, and let thine	1121
	24:13	My **s**, eat thou honey, because *it is* good;	1121
	24:21	My **s**, fear thou the LORD and the king:	1121
	27:11	My **s**, be wise, and make my heart glad,	1121
	28: 7	Whoso keepeth the law *is* a wise **s**: but	1121
	29:17	Correct thy **s**, and he shall give thee rest;	1121
	29:21	shall have him become *his* **s** at the length.	4497
	30: 1	The words of Agur the **s** of Jakeh, *even*	1121
	31: 2	What, my **s**? and what, the son of my	1248
	31: 2	what, the **s** of my womb? and what, the son	1248
	31: 2	of my womb? and what, the **s** of my vows?	1248
Ecc	1: 1	the **s** of David, king in Jerusalem.	1121
	5:14	he begetteth a **s**, and *there is* nothing in his	1121
	10:17	when thy king *is* the **s** of nobles, and	1121
	12:12	further, by these, my **s**, be admonished:	1121
Isa	1: 1	The vision of Isaiah the **s** of Amoz,	1121
	2: 1	The word that Isaiah the **s** of Amoz saw	1121
	7: 1	it came to pass in the days of Ahaz the **s** of	1121
	7: 1	the **s** of Uzziah king of Judah, *that* Rezin	1121
	7: 1	and Pekah the **s** of Remaliah, king of Israel,	1121
	7: 3	to meet Ahaz, thou, and Shear-jashub thy **s**,	1121
	7: 4	Rezin with Syria, and of the **s** of Remaliah.	1121
	7: 5	Ephraim, and the **s** of Remaliah,	1121
	7: 6	king in the midst of it, *even* the **s** of Tabeal:	1121
	7: 9	and the head of Samaria *is* Remaliah's **s**.	1121
	7:14	bear a **S**, and shall call his name Immanuel.	1121
	8: 2	and Zechariah the **s** of Jeberechiah.	1121
	8: 3	and she conceived, and bare a **s**.	1121
	8: 6	and rejoice in Rezin and Remaliah's **s**;	1121
	9: 6	unto us a child is born, unto us a **S** is given:	1121
	13: 1	which Isaiah the **s** of Amoz did see.	1121
	14:12	from heaven, O Lucifer, **s** of the morning!	1121
	14:22	remnant, and **s**, and nephew, saith	5209
	19:11	I *am* the **s** of the wise, the son of ancient	1121
	19:11	the son of the wise, the **s** of ancient kings?	1121
	20: 2	spake the LORD by Isaiah the **s** of Amoz,	1121
	22:20	that I will call my servant Eliakim the **s** of	1121
	36: 3	Hilkiah's **s**, which *was* over the house, and	1121
	36: 3	and Joah, Asaph's **s**, the recorder.	1121
	36:22	came Eliakim, the **s** of Hilkiah, that *was*	1121
	36:22	and Joah, the **s** of Asaph, the recorder,	1121
	37: 2	unto Isaiah the prophet the **s** of Amoz.	1121
	37:21	Isaiah the **s** of Amoz sent unto Hezekiah,	1121
	37:38	and Esar-haddon his **s** reigned in his stead.	1121
	38: 1	Isaiah the prophet the **s** of Amoz came unto	1121
	39: 1	the **s** of Baladan, king of Babylon,	1121
	49:15	not have compassion on the **s** of her womb?	1121
	51:12	of the **s** of man *which* shall be made *as*	1121
	56: 2	and the **s** of man *that* layeth hold on it;	1121
	56: 3	Neither let the **s** of the stranger, that hath	1121
Jer	1: 1	The words of Jeremiah the **s** of Hilkiah,	1121
	1: 2	days of Josiah the **s** of Amon king of Judah,	1121
	1: 3	It came also in the days of Jehoiakim the **s**	1121
	1: 3	of Zedekiah the **s** of Josiah king of Judah,	1121
	6:26	*as* for an only *s*, most bitter lamentation:	NIH
	7:31	which *is* in the valley of the **s** of Hinnom,	1121
	7:32	nor the valley of the **s** of Hinnom, but	1121
	15: 4	of Manasseh the **s** of Hezekiah king of	1121
	19: 2	go forth unto the valley of the **s** of Hinnom,	1121
	19: 6	nor The valley of the **s** of Hinnom, but The	1121
	20: 1	Now Pashur the **s** of Immer the priest,	1121
	21: 1	sent unto him Pashur the **s** of Melchiah,	1121
	21: 1	Zephaniah the **s** of Maaseiah the priest,	1121
	22:11	Shallum the **s** of Josiah king of Judah,	1121
	22:18	Jehoiakim the **s** of Josiah king of Judah;	1121
	22:24	though Coniah the **s** of Jehoiakim king of	1121
	24: 1	Jeconiah the **s** of Jehoiakim king of Judah,	1121
	25: 1	of Jehoiakim the **s** of Josiah king of Judah,	1121
	25: 3	From the thirteenth year of Josiah the **s** of	1121
	26: 1	**s** of Josiah king of Judah came this word	1121
	26:20	Urijah the **s** of Shemaiah of Kirjath-jearim,	1121
	26:22	*namely,* Elnathan the **s** of Achbor, and	1121
	26:24	Nevertheless the hand of Ahikam the **s** of	1121
	27: 1	**s** of Josiah king of Judah came this word	1121
	27: 7	serve him, and his **s**, and his son's son,	1121
	27: 7	serve him, and his son, and his son's **s**,	1121
	27:20	**s** of Jehoiakim king of Judah from	1121
	28: 1	*that* Hananiah the **s** of Azur the prophet,	1121
	28: 4	Jeconiah the **s** of Jehoiakim king of Judah,	1121
	29: 3	By the hand of Elasah the **s** of Shaphan,	1121
	29: 3	of Shaphan, and Gemariah the **s** of Hilkiah,	1121
	29:21	of Ahab the **s** of Kolaiah, and of Zedekiah,	1121
	29:21	and of Zedekiah, the **s** of Maaseiah,	1121
	29:25	to Zephaniah the **s** of Maaseiah the priest,	1121
	31:20	*Is* Ephraim my dear **s**? *is he* a pleasant	1121
	32: 7	Hanameel the **s** of Shallum thine uncle	1121
	32: 8	So Hanameel mine uncle's **s** came to me in	1121
	32: 9	bought the field of Hanameel my uncle's **s**,	1121
	32:12	the purchase unto Baruch the **s** of Neriah,	1121
	32:12	the **s** of Maaseiah, in the sight of Hanameel	1121
	32:12	in the sight of Hanameel mine uncle's *s*, and	NIH
	32:16	the purchase unto Baruch the **s** of Neriah,	1121
	32:35	which *are* in the valley of the **s** of Hinnom,	1121
	33:21	that he should not have a **s** to reign upon	1121
	35: 1	of Jehoiakim the **s** of Josiah king of Judah,	1121
	35: 3	I took Jaazaniah the **s** of Jeremiah, the son	1121
	35: 3	the **s** of Habaziniah, and his brethren, and	1121
	35: 4	of Hanan, the **s** of Igdaliah, a man of God,	1121
	35: 4	the chamber of Maaseiah the **s** of Shallum,	1121
	35: 6	for Jonadab the **s** of Rechab our father	1121
	35: 8	**s** of Rechab our father in all that he hath	1121
	35:14	The words of Jonadab the **s** of Rechab,	1121
	35:16	Because the sons of Jonadab the **s** of	1121
	35:19	Jonadab the **s** of Rechab shall not want a	1121
	36: 1	of Jehoiakim the **s** of Josiah king of Judah,	1121
	36: 4	Jeremiah called Baruch the **s** of Neriah:	1121
	36: 8	Baruch the **s** of Neriah did according to all	1121
	36: 9	of Jehoiakim the **s** of Josiah king of Judah,	1121
	36:10	in the chamber of Gemariah the **s** of	1121
	36:11	When Michaiah the **s** of Gemariah, the son	1121
	36:11	the son of Gemariah, the **s** of Shaphan,	1121
	36:12	Delaiah the **s** of Shemaiah, and	1121
	36:12	Elnathan the **s** of Achbor, and	1121
	36:12	Gemariah the **s** of Shaphan, and	1121
	36:12	Zedekiah the **s** of Hananiah, and all	1121
	36:14	Therefore all the princes sent Jehudi the **s**	1121
	36:14	the **s** of Shelemiah, the son of Cushi,	1121
	36:14	the **s** of Cushi, unto Baruch, saying,	1121
	36:14	So Baruch the **s** of Neriah took the roll in	1121
	36:26	the king commanded Jerahmeel the **s** of	1121
	36:26	Seraiah the **s** of Azriel, and Shelemiah	1121
	36:26	Shelemiah the **s** of Abdeel, to take Baruch	1121
	36:32	it to Baruch the scribe, the **s** of Neriah;	1121
	37: 1	king Zedekiah the **s** of Josiah reigned	1121
	37: 1	instead of Coniah the **s** of Jehoiakim,	1121
	37: 3	Zedekiah the king sent Jehucal the **s** of	1121
	37: 3	Zephaniah the **s** of Maaseiah the priest to	1121
	37:13	the **s** of Shelemiah, the son of Hananiah;	1121

Jer	37:13	the son of Shelemiah, the **s** of Hananiah;	1121
	38: 1	Shephatiah the **s** of Mattan, and	1121
	38: 1	Gedaliah the **s** of Pashur, and Jucal the son	1121
	38: 1	Jucal the **s** of Shelemiah, and Pashur	1121
	38: 1	and Pashur the **s** of Malchiah,	1121
	38: 6	cast him into the dungeon of Malchiah the **s**	1121
	39:14	committed him unto Gedaliah the **s** of	1121
	39:14	the son of Ahikam the **s** of Shaphan,	1121
	40: 5	*he said,* Go back also to Gedaliah the **s** of	1121
	40: 5	the son of Ahikam the **s** of Shaphan,	1121
	40: 6	went Jeremiah unto Gedaliah the **s** of	1121
	40: 7	the **s** of Ahikam governor in the land,	1121
	40: 8	even Ishmael the **s** of Nethaniah, and	1121
	40: 8	Seraiah the **s** of Tanhumeth, and the sons of	1121
	40: 8	Jezaniah the **s** of a Maachathite, they and	1121
	40: 9	Gedaliah the **s** of Ahikam the son of	1121
	40: 9	Gedaliah the son of Ahikam the **s** of	1121
	40:11	that he had set over them Gedaliah the **s** of	1121
	40:11	the son of Ahikam the **s** of Shaphan;	1121
	40:13	Moreover Johanan the **s** of Kareah, and	1121
	40:14	Ishmael the **s** of Nethaniah to slay thee?	1121
	40:14	Gedaliah the **s** of Ahikam believed them	1121
	40:15	Johanan the **s** of Kareah spake to Gedaliah	1121
	40:15	I will slay Ishmael the **s** of Nethaniah, and	1121
	40:16	Gedaliah the **s** of Ahikam said unto	1121
	40:16	Ahikam said unto Johanan the **s** of Kareah,	1121
	41: 1	*that* Ishmael the **s** of Nethaniah the son of	1121
	41: 1	*that* Ishmael the son of Nethaniah the **s** of	1121
	41: 1	came unto Gedaliah the **s** of Ahikam to	1121
	41: 2	arose Ishmael the **s** of Nethaniah, and	1121
	41: 2	smote Gedaliah the **s** of Ahikam the son of	1121
	41: 2	smote Gedaliah the son of Ahikam the **s** of	1121
	41: 6	Ishmael the **s** of Nethaniah went forth from	1121
	41: 6	Come to Gedaliah the **s** of Ahikam.	1121
	41: 7	that Ishmael the **s** of Nethaniah slew them,	1121
	41: 9	Ishmael the **s** of Nethaniah filled it *with*	1121
	41:10	committed to Gedaliah the **s** of Ahikam:	1121
	41:10	Ishmael the **s** of Nethaniah carried them	1121
	41:11	when Johanan the **s** of Kareah, and all	1121
	41:11	heard of all the evil that Ishmael the **s** of	1121
	41:12	went to fight with Ishmael the **s** of	1121
	41:13	with Ishmael saw Johanan the **s** of Kareah,	1121
	41:14	and went unto Johanan the **s** of Kareah.	1121
	41:15	Ishmael the **s** of Nethaniah escaped from	1121
	41:16	took Johanan the **s** of Kareah, and all	1121
	41:16	recovered from Ishmael the **s** of Nethaniah,	1121
	41:16	after *that* he had slain Gedaliah the **s** of	1121
	41:18	Ishmael the **s** of Nethaniah had slain	1121
	41:18	had slain Gedaliah the **s** of Ahikam,	1121
	42: 1	Johanan the **s** of Kareah, and Jezaniah	1121
	42: 1	Jezaniah the **s** of Hoshaiah, and all	1121
	42: 8	called he Johanan the **s** of Kareah, and	1121
	43: 2	spake Azariah the **s** of Hoshaiah, and	1121
	43: 2	Johanan the **s** of Kareah, and all the proud	1121
	43: 3	Baruch the **s** of Neriah setteth thee on	1121
	43: 4	So Johanan the **s** of Kareah, and all	1121
	43: 5	Johanan the **s** of Kareah, and all	1121
	43: 6	the **s** of Ahikam the son of Shaphan,	1121
	43: 6	the son of Ahikam the **s** of Shaphan,	1121
	43: 6	the prophet, and Baruch the **s** of Neriah.	1121
	45: 1	prophet spake unto Baruch the **s** of Neriah,	1121
	45: 1	in the fourth year of Jehoiakim the **s** of	1121
	46: 2	of Jehoiakim the **s** of Josiah king of Judah.	1121
	49:18	neither shall a **s** of man dwell in it.	1121
	49:33	abide there, nor *any* **s** of man dwell in it.	1121
	50:40	neither shall any **s** of man dwell therein.	1121
	51:43	neither doth *any* **s** of man pass thereby.	1121
	51:59	commanded Seraiah the **s** of Neriah,	1121
	51:59	the son of Neriah, the **s** of Maaseiah,	1121
Eze	1: 3	the **s** of Buzi, in the land of the Chaldeans	1121
	2: 1	**S** of man, stand upon thy feet, and I will	1121
	2: 3	he said unto me, **S** of man, I send thee to	1121
	2: 6	thou, **s** of man, be not afraid of them,	1121
	2: 8	thou, **s** of man, hear what I say unto thee;	1121
	3: 1	unto me, **S** of man, eat that thou findest;	1121
	3: 3	he said unto me, **S** of man, cause thy belly	1121
	3: 4	he said unto me, **S** of man, go, get thee unto	1121
	3:10	Moreover he said unto me, **S** of man, all	1121
	3:17	**S** of man, I have made thee a watchman	1121
	3:25	thou, O **s** of man, behold, they shall put	1121
	4: 1	Thou also, **s** of man, take thee a tile, and	1121
	4:16	he said unto me, **S** of man, behold,	1121
	5: 1	thou, **s** of man, take thee a sharp knife,	1121
	6: 2	**S** of man, set thy face towards	1121
	7: 2	Also, thou **s** of man, thus saith the Lord	1121
	8: 5	said he unto me, **S** of man, lift up thine	1121
	8: 6	**S** of man, seest thou what they do?	1121
	8: 8	he unto me, **S** of man, dig now in the wall:	1121
	8:11	in the midst of them stood Jaazaniah the **s**	1121
	8:12	said he unto me, **S** of man, hast thou seen	1121
	8:15	unto me, Hast thou seen *this,* O **s** of man?	1121
	8:17	unto me, Hast thou seen *this,* O **s** of man?	1121
	11: 1	among whom I saw Jaazaniah the **s** of	1121
	11: 1	Pelatiah the **s** of Benaiah, princes of	1121
	11: 2	said he unto me, **S** of man, these *are*	1121
	11: 4	against them, prophesy, O **s** of man.	1121
	11:13	that Pelatiah the **s** of Benaiah died.	1121
	11:15	**S** of man, thy brethren, *even* thy brethren,	1121
	12: 2	**S** of man, thou dwellest in the midst of a	1121
	12: 3	Therefore thou **s** of man, prepare thee stuff	1121
	12: 9	**S** of man, hath not the house of Israel,	1121
	12:18	**S** of man, eat thy bread with quaking, and	1121
	12:22	**S** of man, what *is* that proverb *that* ye have	1121
	12:27	**S** of man, behold, *they of* the house of	1121
	13: 2	**S** of man, prophesy against the prophets of	1121
	13:17	Likewise thou **s** of man, set thy face against	1121
	14: 3	**S** of man, these men have set up their idols	1121
	14:13	**S** of man, when the land sinneth against me	1121
	14:20	they shall deliver neither **s** nor daughter;	1121
	15: 2	**S** of man, What is the vine tree more than	1121
	16: 2	**S** of man, cause Jerusalem to know her	1121
	17: 2	**S** of man, put forth a riddle, and speak a	1121
	18: 4	the father, so also the soul of the **s** *is* mine:	1121
	18:10	If he beget a **s** *that is* a robber, a shedder of	1121
	18:14	Now lo, *if* he beget a **s**, that seeth all his	1121
	18:19	doth not the **s** bear the iniquity of	1121
	18:19	When the **s** hath done that which is lawful	1121
	18:20	The **s** shall not bear the iniquity of	1121
	18:20	shall the father bear the iniquity of the **s**:	1121
	20: 3	**S** of man, speak unto the elders of Israel,	1121
	20: 4	Wilt thou judge them, **s** of man, wilt thou	1121
	20:27	Therefore, **s** of man, speak unto the house	1121
	20:46	**S** of man, set thy face toward the south, and	1121
	21: 2	**S** of man, set thy face toward Jerusalem,	1121
	21: 6	Sigh therefore, thou **s** of man, with	1121
	21: 9	**S** of man, prophesy, and say, Thus saith	1121
	21:10	it contemneth the rod of my **s**, *as* every tree.	1121
	21:12	Cry and howl, **s** of man: for it shall be upon	1121
	21:14	**s** of man, prophesy, and smite *thine* hands	1121
	21:19	Also, thou **s** of man, appoint thee two ways,	1121
	21:28	thou, **s** of man, prophesy and say,	1121
	22: 2	Now, thou **s** of man, wilt thou judge, wilt	1121
	22:18	**S** of man, the house of Israel is to me	1121
	22:24	**S** of man, say unto her, Thou *art* the land	1121
	23: 2	**S** of man, there were two women,	1121
	23:36	**S** of man, wilt thou judge Aholah and	1121
	24: 2	**S** of man, write thee the name of the day,	1121
	24:16	**S** of man, behold, I take away from thee	1121
	24:25	Also, thou **s** of man, *shall it* not *be* in	1121
	25: 2	**S** of man, set thy face against	1121
	26: 2	**S** of man, because that Tyrus hath said	1121
	27: 2	Now, thou **s** of man, take up a lamentation	1121
	28: 2	**S** of man, say unto the prince of Tyrus,	1121
	28:12	**S** of man, take up a lamentation upon	1121
	28:21	**S** of man, set thy face against Zidon, and	1121
	29: 2	**S** of man, set thy face against Pharaoh king	1121
	29:18	**S** of man, Nebuchadrezzar king of Babylon	1121
	30: 2	**S** of man, prophesy and say, Thus saith	1121
	30:21	**S** of man, I have broken the arm of Pharaoh	1121
	31: 2	**S** of man, speak unto Pharaoh king of	1121
	32: 2	**S** of man, take up a lamentation for	1121
	32:18	**S** of man, wail for the multitude of Egypt,	1121
	33: 2	**S** of man, speak to the children of thy	1121
	33: 7	So thou, O **s** of man, I have set thee a	1121
	33:10	Therefore, O thou **s** of man, speak unto	1121
	33:12	Therefore, thou **s** of man, say unto	1121
	33:24	**S** of man, they that inhabit those wastes of	1121
	33:30	Also, thou **s** of man, the children of thy	1121
	34: 2	**S** of man, prophesy against the shepherds	1121
	35: 2	**S** of man, set thy face against mount Seir,	1121
	36: 1	Also, thou **s** of man, prophesy unto	1121
	36:17	**S** of man, when the house of Israel dwelt in	1121
	37: 3	unto me, **S** of man, can these bones live?	1121
	37: 9	prophesy, **s** of man, and say to the wind,	1121
	37:11	he said unto me, **S** of man, these bones *are*	1121
	37:16	Moreover, thou **s** of man, take thee one	1121
	38: 2	**S** of man, set thy face against Gog, the land	1121
	38:14	**s** of man, prophesy and say unto Gog,	1121

Eze	39: 1	Therefore thou **s** of man, prophesy against	1121
	39:17	thou **s** of man, thus saith the Lord GOD;	1121
	40: 4	**S** of man, behold with thine eyes, and	1121
	43: 7	he said unto me, **S** of man, the place of my	1121
	43:10	Thou **s** of man, shew the house to the house	1121
	43:18	he said unto me, **S** of man, thus saith	1121
	44: 5	**S** of man, mark well, and behold with thine	1121
	44:25	or for mother, or for **s**, or for daughter,	1121
	47: 6	he said unto me, **S** of man, hast thou seen	1121
Da	3:25	the form of the fourth *is* like the **S** of God.	1247
	5:22	thou his **s**, O Belshazzar, hast not humbled	1247
	7:13	*one* like the **S** of man came with the clouds	1247
	8:17	he said unto me, Understand, O **s** of man:	1121
	9: 1	In the first year of Darius the **s** of	1121
Hos	1: 1	the **s** of Beeri, in the days of Uzziah,	1121
	1: 1	in the days of Jeroboam the **s** of Joash,	1121
	1: 3	which conceived, and bare him a **s**.	1121
	1: 8	she conceived, and bare a **s**.	1121
	11: 1	I loved him, and called my **s** out of Egypt.	1121
	13:13	he *is* an unwise **s**; for he should not stay	1121
Joel	1: 1	LORD that came to Joel the **s** of Pethuel.	1121
Am	1: 1	in the days of Jeroboam the **s** of Joash king	1121
	7:14	*was* no prophet, neither *was* I a prophet's **s**;	1121
	8:10	I will make it as the mourning of an only *s*,	NIH
Jnh	1: 1	LORD came unto Jonah the **s** of Amittai,	1121
Mic	6: 5	what Balaam the **s** of Beor answered him;	1121
	7: 6	For the **s** dishonoureth the father,	1121
Zep	1: 1	which came unto Zephaniah the **s** of Cushi,	1121
	1: 1	the **s** of Gedaliah, the son of Amariah,	1121
	1: 1	the **s** of Amariah, the son of Hizkiah,	1121
	1: 1	the son of Amariah, the **s** of Hizkiah,	1121
	1: 1	in the days of Josiah the **s** of Amon, king of	1121
Hag	1: 1	prophet unto Zerubbabel the **s** of Shealtiel,	1121
	1: 1	to Joshua the **s** of Josedech the high priest,	1121
	1:12	Zerubbabel the **s** of Shealtiel, and	1121
	1:12	Joshua the **s** of Josedech the high priest,	1121
	1:14	the spirit of Zerubbabel the **s** of Shealtiel,	1121
	1:14	the spirit of Joshua the **s** of Josedech	1121
	2: 2	Speak now to Zerubbabel the **s** of Shealtiel,	1121
	2: 2	to Joshua the **s** of Josedech the high priest	1121
	2: 4	be strong, O Joshua, **s** of Josedech, the high	1121
	2:23	my servant, the **s** of Shealtiel,	1121
Zec	1: 1	the **s** of Berechiah, the son of Iddo	1121
	1: 1	the **s** of Iddo the prophet, saying,	1121
	1: 7	the **s** of Berechiah, the son of Iddo	1121
	1: 7	the **s** of Iddo the prophet, saying,	1121
	6:10	go *into* the house of Josiah the **s** of	1121
	6:11	set *them* upon the head of Joshua the **s** of	1121
	6:14	to Jedaiah, and to Hen the **s** of Zephaniah,	1121
	12:10	as one mourneth for *his* only *s*, and shall be	NIH
Mal	1: 6	A **s** honoureth *his* father, and a servant his	1121
	3:17	as a man spareth his own **s** that serveth	1121
Mt	1: 1	the **s** of David, the son of Abraham.	*5207*
	1: 1	the son of David, the **s** of Abraham.	*5207*
	1:20	saying, Joseph, *thou* **s** of David, fear not to	*5207*
	1:21	And she shall bring forth a **s**, and thou shalt	*5207*
	1:23	and shall bring forth a **s**, and they shall call	*5207*
	1:25	till she had brought forth her firstborn **s**:	*5207*
	2:15	saying, Out of Egypt have I called my **s**.	*5207*
	3:17	saying, This is my beloved **S**, in whom I	*5207*
	4: 3	to him, he said, If thou be the **S** of God,	*5207*
	4: 6	If thou be the **S** of God, cast thyself down:	*5207*
	4:21	James the *s* of Zebedee, and John his	NIG
	7: 9	whom if his **s** ask bread, will he give him a	*5207*
	8:20	the **S** of man hath not where to lay *his* head.	*5207*
	8:29	we to do with thee, Jesus, *thou* **S** of God?	*5207*
	9: 2	**S**, be of good cheer; thy sins be forgiven	*5043*
	9: 6	But that ye may know that the **S** of man	*5207*
	9:27	crying, and saying, *Thou* **S** of David,	*5207*
	10: 2	the *s* of Zebedee, and John his brother;	NIG
	10: 3	James the *s* of Alpheus, and Lebbeus,	NIG
	10:23	cities of Israel, till the **S** of man be come.	*5207*
	10:37	and he that loveth **s** or daughter more than	*5207*
	11:19	The **S** of man came eating and drinking,	*5207*
	11:27	and no *man* knoweth the **S**, but the Father;	*5207*
	11:27	save the **S**, and *he* to whomsoever the Son	*5207*
	11:27	*he* to whomsoever the **S** will reveal *him*.	*5207*
	12: 8	For the **S** of man is Lord even of	*5207*
	12:23	and said, Is this the **s** of David?	*5207*
	12:32	speaketh a word against the **S** of man,	*5207*
	12:40	so shall the **S** of man be three days and	*5207*
	13:37	He that soweth the good seed is the **S** of	*5207*
	13:41	The **S** of man shall send forth his angels,	*5207*
	13:55	Is not this the carpenter's **s**? is not his	*5207*
	14:33	saying, Of a truth thou art the **S** of God.	*5207*
	15:22	mercy on me, O Lord, *thou* **S** of David;	*5207*
	16:13	Whom do men say that I the **S** of man am?	*5207*
	16:16	Thou art the Christ, the **S** of the living God.	*5207*
	16:27	For the **S** of man shall come in the glory of	*5207*
	16:28	till they see the **S** of man coming in his	*5207*
	17: 5	which said, This is my beloved **S**, in whom	*5207*
	17: 9	Tell the vision to no *man*, until the **S** of	*5207*
	17:12	Likewise shall also the **S** of man suffer of	*5207*
	17:15	Lord, have mercy on my **s**: for he is	*5207*
	17:22	The **S** of man shall be betrayed into	*5207*
	18:11	For the **S** of man is come to save that which	*5207*
	19:28	when the **S** of man shall sit in the throne of	*5207*
	20:18	the **S** of man shall be betrayed unto	*5207*
	20:28	Even as the **S** of man came not to be	*5207*
	20:30	mercy on us, O Lord, *thou* **S** of David.	*5207*
	20:31	mercy on us, O Lord, *thou* **S** of David.	*5207*
	21: 9	cried, saying, Hosanna to the **S** of David:	*5207*
	21:15	and saying, Hosanna to the **S** of David;	*5207*
	21:28	and he came to the first, and said, **S**,	*5043*
	21:37	But last *of all* he sent unto them his **s**,	*5207*
	21:37	his son, saying, They will reverence my **s**.	*5207*
	21:38	But when the husbandmen saw the **s**,	*5207*
	22: 2	which made a marriage for his **s**,	*5207*
	22:42	whose **s** is he? They say unto him, *The Son*	*5207*
	22:42	is he? They say unto him, *The* **S** of David.	NIG
	22:45	then call him Lord, how is he his **s**?	*5207*
	23:35	unto the blood of Zacharias **s** of Barachias,	*5207*
	24:27	so shall also the coming of the **S** of man be.	*5207*
	24:30	shall appear the sign of the **S** of man in	*5207*
	24:30	they shall see the **S** of man coming in	*5207*
	24:37	so shall also the coming of the **S** of man be.	*5207*
	24:39	so shall also the coming of the **S** of man be.	*5207*
	24:44	for in such an hour as you think not the **S** of	*5207*
	25:13	nor the hour wherein the **S** of man cometh.	*5207*
	25:31	When the **S** of man shall come in his glory,	*5207*
	26: 2	the **S** of man is betrayed to be crucified.	*5207*
	26:24	The **S** of man goeth as it is written of him:	*5207*
	26:24	woe unto that man by whom the **S** of man	*5207*
	26:45	the **S** of man is betrayed into the hands of	*5207*
	26:63	us whether thou be the Christ, the **S** of God.	*5207*
	26:64	Hereafter shall ye see the **S** of man sitting	*5207*
	27:40	If thou be the **S** of God, come down from	*5207*
	27:43	have him: for he said, I am the **S** of God.	*5207*
	27:54	saying, Truly this was the **S** of God.	*5207*
	28:19	and of the **S**, and of the Holy Ghost:	*5207*
Mk	1: 1	of the gospel of Jesus Christ, the **S** of God;	*5207*
	1:11	*saying*, Thou art my beloved **S**, in whom I	*5207*
	1:19	he saw James the **s** of Zebedee, and John his	NIG
	2: 5	of the palsy, **S**, thy sins be forgiven thee.	*5043*
	2:10	But that ye may know that the **S** of man	*5207*
	2:14	he saw Levi the *s* of Alpheus sitting at	NIG
	2:28	Therefore the **S** of man is Lord also of	*5207*
	3:11	and cried, saying, Thou art the **S** of God.	*5207*
	3:17	And James the *s* of Zebedee, and John	NIG
	3:18	and James the *s* of Alpheus, and Thaddeus,	NIG
	5: 7	Jesus, *thou* **S** of the most high God?	*5207*
	6: 3	the **s** of Mary, the brother of James, and	*5207*
	8:31	that the **S** of man must suffer many *things*,	*5207*
	8:38	of him also shall the **S** of man be ashamed,	*5207*
	9: 7	of the cloud, saying, This is my beloved **S**:	*5207*
	9: 9	till the **S** of man were risen from the dead.	*5207*
	9:12	and how it is written of the **S** of man,	*5207*
	9:17	said, Master, I have brought unto thee my **s**,	*5207*
	9:31	The **S** of man is delivered into the hands of	*5207*
	10:33	the **S** of man shall be delivered unto	*5207*
	10:45	For even the **S** of man came not to be	*5207*
	10:46	blind Bartimeus, the **s** of Timeus,	*5207*
	10:47	and say, Jesus, *thou* **S** of David,	*5207*
	10:48	*Thou* **S** of David, have mercy on me.	*5207*
	12: 6	Having yet therefore one **s**,	*5207*
	12: 6	saying, They will reverence my **s**.	*5207*
	12:35	How say the scribes that Christ is the **S** of	*5207*
	12:37	him Lord; and whence is he *then* his **s**?	*5207*
	13:12	the brother to death, and the father the **s**;	*5043*
	13:26	shall they see the **S** of man coming in	*5207*
	13:32	are in heaven, neither the **S**, but the Father.	*5207*
	13:34	*For the* **S** *of man is* as a man taking a far	NIG
	14:21	The **S** of man indeed goeth, as it is written	*5207*
	14:21	woe to that man by whom the **S** of man is	*5207*
	14:41	the **S** of man is betrayed into the hands of	*5207*
	14:61	Art thou the Christ, the **S** of the Blessed?	*5207*
	14:62	ye shall see the **S** of man sitting on the right	*5207*
	15:39	he said, Truly this man was the **S** of God.	*5207*

Lk 1:13 and thy wife Elisabeth shall bear thee a **s**, *5207*
1:31 and bring forth a **s**, and shalt call his name *5207*
1:32 and shall be called the **S** of the Highest: *5207*
1:35 be born of thee shall be called the **S** of God. *5207*
1:36 she hath also conceived a **s** in her old age: *5207*
1:57 be delivered; and she brought forth a **s**. *5207*
2: 7 And she brought forth her firstborn **s**, and *5207*
2:48 and his mother said unto him, **S**, why hast *5043*
3: 2 the word of God came unto John the **s** of *5207*
3:22 which said, Thou art my beloved **S**; *5207*
3:23 the **s** of Joseph, which was *the son* of Heli, *5207*
3:23 the son of Joseph, which was *the* **s** of Heli, NIG
3:24 Which was *the* **s** of Matthat, which was NIG
3:24 which was *the* **s** of Levi, which was *the son* NIG
3:24 *the son* of Levi, which was *the* **s** of Melchi, NIG
3:24 which was *the* **s** of Janna, which was NIG
3:24 *the son* of Janna, which was *the* **s** of Joseph, NIG
3:25 Which was *the* **s** of Mattathias, which was NIG
3:25 which was *the* **s** of Amos, which was NIG
3:25 which was *the* **s** of Naum, which was NIG
3:25 *the son* of Naum, which was *the* **s** of Esli, NIG
3:25 *the son* of Esli, which was *the* **s** of Nagge, NIG
3:26 Which was *the* **s** of Maath, which was NIG
3:26 which was *the* **s** of Mattathias, which was NIG
3:26 which was *the* **s** of Semei, which was NIG
3:26 which was *the* **s** of Joseph, which was NIG
3:26 *the son* of Joseph, which was *the* **s** of Juda, NIG
3:27 Which was *the* **s** of Joanna, which was NIG
3:27 *son* of Joanna, which was *the* **s** of Rhesa, NIG
3:27 *son* of Rhesa, which was *the* **s** of Zorobabel, NIG
3:27 which was *the* **s** of Salathiel, which was NIG
3:27 *son* of Salathiel, which was *the* **s** of Neri, NIG
3:28 Which was *the* **s** of Melchi, which was NIG
3:28 which was *the* **s** of Addi, which was *the son* NIG
3:28 *the son* of Addi, which was *the* **s** of Cosam, NIG
3:28 which was *the* **s** of Elmodam, which was NIG
3:28 *the son* of Elmodam, which was *the* **s** of Er, NIG
3:29 Which was *the* **s** of Jose, which was *the son* NIG
3:29 *the son* of Jose, which was *the* **s** of Eliezer, NIG
3:29 *the son* of Eliezer, which was *the* **s** of Jorim, NIG
3:29 which was *the* **s** of Matthat, which was NIG
3:29 *the son* of Matthat, which was *the* **s** of Levi, NIG
3:30 Which was *the* **s** of Simeon, which was NIG
3:30 which was *the* **s** of Juda, which was *the son* NIG
3:30 *the son* of Juda, which was *the* **s** of Joseph, NIG
3:30 *the son* of Joseph, which was *the* **s** of Jonan, NIG
3:30 *son* of Jonan, which was *the* **s** of Eliakim, NIG
3:31 Which was *the* **s** of Melea, which was NIG
3:31 *son* of Melea, which was *the* **s** of Menan, NIG
3:31 *son* of Menan, which was *the* **s** of Mattatha, NIG
3:31 which was *the* **s** of Nathan, which was NIG
3:31 *son* of Nathan, which was *the* **s** of David, NIG
3:32 Which was *the* **s** of Jesse, which was NIG
3:32 which was *the* **s** of Obed, which was *the son* NIG
3:32 *the son* of Obed, which was *the* **s** of Booz, NIG
3:32 *the son* of Booz, which was *the* **s** of Salmon, NIG
3:32 *son* of Salmon, which was *the* **s** of Naasson, NIG
3:33 Which was *the* **s** of Aminadab, which was NIG
3:33 which was *the* **s** of Aram, which was NIG
3:33 *the son* of Aram, which was *the* **s** of Esrom, NIG
3:33 which was *the* **s** of Phares, which was NIG
3:33 *the son* of Phares, which was *the* **s** of Juda, NIG
3:34 Which was *the* **s** of Jacob, which was NIG
3:34 *the son* of Jacob, which was *the* **s** of Isaac, NIG
3:34 *son* of Isaac, which was *the* **s** of Abraham, NIG
3:34 which was *the* **s** of Thara, which was NIG
3:34 *son* of Thara, which was *the* **s** of Nachor, NIG
3:35 Which was *the* **s** of Saruch, which was NIG
3:35 which was *the* **s** of Ragau, which was NIG
3:35 which was *the* **s** of Phalec, which was NIG
3:35 which was *the* **s** of Heber, which was NIG
3:35 *the son* of Heber, which was *the* **s** of Sala, NIG
3:36 Which was *the* **s** of Cainan, which was NIG
3:36 which was *the* **s** of Arphaxad, which was NIG
3:36 which was *the* **s** of Sem, which was *the son* NIG
3:36 *the son* of Sem, which was *the* **s** of Noe, NIG
3:36 *the son* of Noe, which was *the* **s** of Lamech, NIG
3:37 Which was *the* **s** of Mathusala, which was NIG
3:37 which was *the* **s** of Enoch, which was NIG
3:37 *the son* of Enoch, which was *the* **s** of Jared, NIG
3:37 *son* of Jared, which was *the* **s** of Maleleel, NIG
3:37 *son* of Maleleel, which was *the* **s** of Cainan, NIG
3:38 Which was *the* **s** of Enos, which was *the son* NIG
3:38 *the son* of Enos, which was *the* **s** of Seth, NIG
3:38 which was *the* **s** of Adam, which was NIG
3:38 *the son* of Adam, which was *the* **s** of God. NIG
4: 3 said unto him, If thou be the **S** of God, *5207*
4: 9 and said unto him, If thou be the **S** of God, *5207*
4:22 And they said, Is not this Joseph's **s**? *5207*
4:41 and saying, Thou art Christ the **S** of God. *5207*
5:24 But that ye may know that the **S** of man *5207*
6: 5 That the **S** of man is Lord also of *5207*
6:15 James the **s** of Alpheus, and Simon called NIG
6:22 your name as evil, for the **S** of man's sake. *5207*
7:12 the only **s** of his mother, and she was a *5207*
7:34 The **S** of man is come eating and drinking; *5207*
8:28 with thee, Jesus, *thou* **S** of God most high? *5207*
9:22 The **S** of man must suffer many *things,* and *5207*
9:26 of him shall the **S** of man be ashamed, *5207*
9:35 of the cloud, saying, This is my beloved **S**: *5207*
9:38 Master, I beseech thee, look upon my **s**: *5207*
9:41 and suffer you? Bring thy **s** hither. *5207*
9:44 for the **S** of man shall be delivered into *5207*
9:56 For the **S** of man is not come to destroy *5207*
9:58 the **S** of man hath not where to lay *his* head. *5207*
10: 6 And if the **s** of peace be there, your peace *5207*
10:22 and no *man* knoweth who the **S** is, but *5207*
10:22 but the **S**, and *he* to whom the Son will *5207*
10:22 and *he* to whom the **S** will reveal *him.* *5207*
11:11 *If* a **s** shall ask bread of any of you that is a *5207*
11:30 shall also the **S** of man be to this *5207*
12: 8 him shall the **S** of man also confess before *5207*
12:10 shall speak a word against the **S** of man, *5207*
12:40 for the **S** of man cometh at an hour when ye *5207*
12:53 The father shall be divided against the **s**, *5207*
12:53 against the son, and the **s** against the father; *5207*
15:13 And not many days after the younger **s** *5207*
15:19 And am no more worthy to be called thy **s**: *5207*
15:21 And the **s** said unto him, Father, I have *5207*
15:21 and am no more worthy to be called thy **s**. *5207*
15:24 For this my **s** was dead, and is alive again; *5207*
15:25 Now his elder **s** was in the field: and as he *5207*
15:30 But as soon as this thy **s** was come, *5207*
15:31 **S**, thou art ever with me, and all that I have *5043*
16:25 But Abraham said, **S**, remember that thou *5043*
17:22 to see one of the days of the **S** of man, *5207*
17:24 so shall also the **S** of man be in his day. *5207*
17:26 shall it be also in the days of the **S** of man. *5207*
17:30 Even thus shall it be in the day when the **S** *5207*
18: 8 Nevertheless when the **S** of man cometh, *5207*
18:31 the **S** of man shall be accomplished. *5207*
18:38 he cried, saying, Jesus, *thou* **S** of David, *5207*
18:39 *so* much the more, *Thou* **S** of David, *5207*
19: 9 forsomuch as he also is a **s** of Abraham. *5207*
19:10 For the **S** of man is come to seek and *5207*
20:13 I will send my beloved **s**: it may be they *5207*
20:41 How say they that Christ is David's **s**? *5207*
20:44 calleth him Lord, how is he then his **s**? *5207*
21:27 shall they see the **S** of man coming in a *5207*
21:36 to pass, and to stand before the **S** of man. *5207*
22:22 And truly the **S** of man goeth, as it was *5207*
22:48 betrayest thou the **S** of man with a kiss? *5207*
22:69 Hereafter shall the **S** of man sit on the right *5207*
22:70 said they all, Art thou then the **S** of God? *5207*
24: 7 The **S** of man must be delivered into *5207*
Jn 1:18 the only begotten **S**, which is in the bosom *5207*
1:34 and bare record that this is the **S** of God. *5207*
1:42 he said, Thou art Simon the **s** of Jona: *5207*
1:45 Jesus of Nazareth, the **s** of Joseph. *5207*
1:49 unto him, Rabbi, thou art the **S** of God; *5207*
1:51 and descending upon the **S** of man. *5207*
3:13 *even* the **S** of man which is in heaven. *5207*
3:14 *even* so must the **S** of man be lifted up: *5207*
3:16 the world, that he gave his only begotten **S**, *5207*
3:17 For God sent not his **S** into the world to *5207*
3:18 in the name of the only begotten **S** of God. *5207*
3:35 The Father loveth the **S**, and hath given all *5207*
3:36 He that believeth on the **S** hath everlasting *5207*
3:36 he that believeth not the **S** shall not see life; *5207*
4: 5 of ground that Jacob gave to his **s** Joseph. *5207*
4:46 whose **s** was sick at Capernaum. *5207*
4:47 that he would come down, and heal his **s**: *5207*
4:50 saith unto him, Go *thy way;* thy **s** liveth. *5207*
4:51 met him, and told *him,* saying, Thy **s** liveth. *3816*
4:53 the which Jesus said unto him, Thy **s** liveth: *5207*
5:19 The **S** can do nothing of himself, but *5207*
5:19 he doeth, these also doeth the **S** likewise. *5207*
5:20 For the Father loveth the **S**, and *5207*

Jn 5:21 so the **S** quickeneth whom he will. 5207
5:22 hath committed all judgment unto the **S**: 5207
5:23 That all *men* should honour the **S**, even as 5207
5:23 He that honoureth not the **S** honoureth not 5207
5:25 when the dead shall hear the voice of the **S** 5207
5:26 hath he given to the **S** to have life in 5207
5:27 judgment also, because he is the **S** of man. 5207
6:27 which the **S** of man shall give unto you: 5207
6:40 that every one which seeth the **S**, and 5207
6:42 the **s** of Joseph, whose father and mother 5207
6:53 Except ye eat the flesh of the **S** of man, and 5207
6:62 if ye shall see the **S** of man ascend up 5207
6:69 thou art *that* Christ, the **S** of the living God. 5207
6:71 He spake of Judas Iscariot *the s* of Simon: NIG
8:28 When ye have lift up the **S** of man, then 5207
8:35 in the house for ever: *but* the **s** abideth ever. 5207
8:36 If the **S** therefore shall make you free, 5207
9:19 And they asked them, saying, Is this your **s**, 5207
9:20 We know that this is our **s**, and that he was 5207
9:35 Dost thou believe on the **S** of God? 5207
10:36 because I said, I am the **S** of God? 5207
11: 4 that the **S** of God might be glorified 5207
11:27 that thou art the Christ, the **S** of God, 5207
12: 4 Simon's *s*, which should betray him, NIG
12:23 that the **S** of man should be glorified. 5207
12:34 sayest thou, The **S** of man must be lift up? 5207
12:34 man must be lift up? who is this **S** of man? 5207
13: 2 of Judas Iscariot, Simon's *s*, to betray him; NIG
13:26 he gave *it* to Judas Iscariot, *the s* of Simon. NIG
13:31 Now is the **S** of man glorified, and God is 5207
14:13 that the Father may be glorified in the **S**. 5207
17: 1 glorify thy **S**, that thy Son also may glorify 5207
17: 1 thy Son, that thy **S** also may glorify thee: 5207
17:12 none of them is lost, but the **s** of perdition; 5207
19: 7 because he made himself the **S** of God. 5207
19:26 unto his mother, Woman, behold thy **s**. 5207
20:31 that Jesus is the Christ, the **S** of God; 5207
21:15 saith to Simon Peter, Simon, *s* of Jonas, NIG
21:16 Simon, *s* of Jonas, lovest thou me? NIG
21:17 Simon, *s* of Jonas, lovest thou me? NIG
Ac 1:13 James *the s* of Alpheus, and Simon Zelotes, NIG
3:13 of our fathers, hath glorified his **S** Jesus; 3816
3:26 you first God, having raised up his **S** Jesus, 3816
4:36 being interpreted, The **s** of consolation,) 5207
7:21 him up, and nourished him for her own **s**. 5207
7:56 the **S** of man standing on the right hand of 5207
8:37 I believe that Jesus Christ is the **S** of God. 5207
9:20 in the synagogues, that he is the **S** of God. 5207
13:21 and God gave unto them Saul the **s** of Cis, 5207
13:22 and said, I have found David the **s** of Jesse, NIG
13:33 Thou art my **S**, this day have I begotten 5207
16: 1 the **s** of a certain woman, 5207
23: 6 I am a Pharisee, the **s** of a Pharisee: 5207
23:16 And when Paul's sister's **s** heard of *their* 5207
Ro 1: 3 Concerning his **S** Jesus Christ our Lord, 5207
1: 4 *And* declared *to be* the **S** of God with 5207
1: 9 I serve with my spirit in the gospel of his **S**, 5207
5:10 reconciled to God by the death of his **S**, 5207
8: 3 God sending his own **S** in the likeness of 5207
8:29 *to be* conformed to the image of his **S**, 5207
8:32 He that spared not his own **S**, but 5207
9: 9 time will I come, and Sara shall have a **s**. 5207
1Co 1: 9 fellowship of his **S** Jesus Christ our Lord. 5207
4:17 who is my beloved **s**, and faithful in 5043
15:28 shall the **S** also himself be subject unto him 5207
2Co 1:19 For the **S** of God, Jesus Christ, who was 5207
Gal 1:16 To reveal his **S** in me, that I might preach 5207
2:20 the flesh I live by the faith of the **S** of God, 5207
4: 4 God sent forth his **S**, made of a woman, 5207
4: 6 God hath sent forth the Spirit of his **S** into 5207
4: 7 thou art no more a servant, but a **s**; 5207
4: 7 and if a **s**, then an heir of God through 5207
4:30 Cast out the bondwoman and her **s**: for 5207
4:30 for the **s** of the bondwoman shall not be 5207
4:30 not be heir with the **s** of the freewoman. 5207
Eph 4:13 and of the knowledge of the **S** of God, 5207
Php 2:22 the proof of him, that, as a **s** *with the* father, 5043
Col 1:13 *us* into the kingdom of his dear **S**: 5207
4:10 and Marcus, **sister's s** to Barnabas, 431
1Th 1:10 And to wait for his **S** from heaven, 5207
2Th 2: 3 man of sin be revealed, the **s** of perdition; 5207
1Ti 1: 2 Unto Timothy, *my* own **s** in the faith: 5043
1:18 This charge I commit unto thee, **s** Timothy, 5043
2Ti 1: 2 To Timothy, *my* dearly beloved **s**: Grace, 5043
2: 1 Thou therefore, my **s**, be strong in the grace 5043
Tit 1: 4 *mine* own **s** after the common faith: 5043
Phm 1:10 I beseech thee for my **s** Onesimus, whom I 5043
Heb 1: 2 in these last days spoken unto us by *his* **S**, 5207
1: 5 Thou art my **S**, this day have I begotten 5207
1: 5 to him a Father, and he shall be to me a **S**? 5207
1: 8 But unto the **S** *he saith,* Thy throne, O God, 5207
2: 6 or the **s** of man, that thou visitest him? 5207
3: 6 But Christ as a **S** over his own house; 5207
4:14 Jesus the **S** of God, let us hold fast *our* 5207
5: 5 but he that said unto him, Thou art my **S**, 5207
5: 8 Though he were a **S**, *yet* learned he 5207
6: 6 seeing they crucify to themselves the **S** of 5207
7: 3 of life; but made like unto the **S** of God; 5207
7:28 which was since the law, *maketh* the **S**, 5207
10:29 who hath trodden under foot the **S** of God, 5207
11:17 the promises offered up *his* only begotten *s*, NIG
11:24 refused to be called the **s** of Pharaoh's 5207
12: 5 My **s**, despise not thou the chastening of 5207
12: 6 and scourgeth every **s** whom he receiveth. 5207
12: 7 for what **s** is *he* whom the father chasteneth 5207
Jas 2:21 when he had offered Isaac his **s** upon 5207
1Pe 5:13 saluteth you; and *so doth* Marcus my **s**. 5207
2Pe 1:17 This is my beloved **S**, in whom I am well 5207
2:15 following the way of Balaam *the s* of Bosor, NIG
1Jn 1: 3 with the Father, and with his **S** Jesus Christ. 5207
1: 7 the blood of Jesus Christ his **S** cleanseth us 5207
2:22 that denieth the Father and the **S**. 5207
2:23 Whosoever denieth the **S**, the same hath not 5207
2:23 *he that acknowledgeth the* **S** *hath the Father* NIG
2:24 ye also shall continue in the **S**, and in 5207
3: 8 For this purpose the **S** of God was 5207
3:23 believe on the name of his **S** Jesus Christ, 5207
4: 9 that God sent his only begotten **S** into 5207
4:10 sent his **S** *to be* the propitiation for our sins. 5207
4:14 do testify that the Father sent the **S** *to be* 5207
4:15 Whosoever shall confess that Jesus is the **S** 5207
5: 5 he that believeth that Jesus is the **S** of God? 5207
5: 9 of God which he hath testified of his **S**. 5207
5:10 He that believeth on the **S** of God hath 5207
5:10 not the record that God gave of his **S**. 5207
5:11 to us eternal life, and this life is in his **S**. 5207
5:12 He that hath the **S** hath life; *and* he that 5207
5:12 he that hath not the **S** of God hath not life. 5207
5:13 that believe on the name of the **S** of God; 5207
5:13 that ye may believe on the name of the **S** of 5207
5:20 And we know that the **S** of God is come, 5207
5:20 him *that is* true, *even* in his **S** Jesus Christ. 5207
2Jn 1: 3 the **S** of the Father, in truth and love. 5207
1: 9 of Christ, he hath both the Father and the **S**. 5207
Rev 1:13 candlesticks one like unto the **S** of man, 5207
2:18 These *things* saith the **S** of God, who hath 5207
14:14 upon the cloud one sat like unto the **S** of 5207
21: 7 and I will be his God, and he shall be my **s**. 5207

SON'S (22) [SON]

Ge 11:31 Lot the son of Haran his **s** son, and Sarai 1121
16:15 Abram called his **s** name, which Hagar 1121
21:23 nor with my son, nor with my **s son**: 5220
24:51 and go, and let her be thy master's **s** wife, 1121
27:25 near to me, and I will eat of my **s** venison, 1121
27:31 my father arise, and eat of his **s** venison, 1121
30:14 Give me, I pray thee, of thy **s** mandrakes. 1121
30:15 wouldest thou take away my **s** mandrakes 1121
30:15 lie with thee to night for thy **s** mandrakes. 1121
30:16 for surely I have hired thee with my **s** 1121
37:32 know now whether it *be* thy **s** coat or no. 1121
37:33 he knew it, and said, *It is* my **s** coat; an evil 1121
Ex 10: 2 of thy **s** son, what things I have wrought in 1121
Lev 18:10 The nakedness of thy **s** daughter, or of thy 1121
18:15 she *is* thy **s** wife; thou shalt not uncover her 1121
18:17 neither shalt thou take her **s** daughter, or 1121
Dt 6: 2 thou, and thy son, and thy **s** son, all 1121
Jdg 8:22 both thou, and thy son, and thy **s** son also: 1121
1Ki 11:35 I will take the kingdom out of his **s** hand, 1121
21:29 in his **s** days will I bring the evil upon his 1121
Pr 30: 4 and what *is* his **s** name, if thou canst tell? 1121
Jer 27: 7 shall serve him, and his son, and his **s** son, 1121

SONG (78) [SING]

Ex 15: 1 the children of Israel this **s** unto 7892
15: 2 The LORD *is* my strength and **s**, and he is 2176
Nu 21:17 Israel sang this **s**, Spring up, O well; 7892
Dt 31:19 Now therefore write ye this **s** for you, 7892

Dt	31:19	that this **s** may be a witness for me against	7892
	31:21	that this **s** shall testify against them as a	7892
	31:22	Moses therefore wrote this **s** the same day,	7892
	31:30	congregation of Israel the words of this **s**,	7892
	32:44	spake all the words of this **s** in the ears of	7892
Jdg	5:12	awake, awake, utter a **s**: arise, Barak, and	7892
2Sa	22: 1	**s** in the day *that* the LORD had delivered	7892
1Ch	6:31	the service of **s** *in* the house of the LORD,	7892
	15:22	chief of the Levites, *was* for **s**:	4853
	15:22	he instructed about the **s**, because he *was*	4853
	15:27	Chenaniah the master of the **s** *with*	4853
	25: 6	father for **s** *in* the house of the LORD,	7892
2Ch	29:27	the **s** of the LORD began *also* with	7892
Job	30: 9	now am I their **s**, yea, I am their byword.	5058
Ps	18: T	**s** in the day *that* the LORD delivered him	7892
	28: 7	and with my **s** will I praise him.	7892
	30: T	**S** *at* the dedication of the house of David.	7892
	33: 3	Sing unto him a new **s**; play skilfully with a	7892
	40: 3	he hath put a new **s** in my mouth,	7892
	42: 8	in the night his **s** *shall be* with me, *and*	7892
	45: T	the sons of Korah, Maschil, A **S** of loves.	7892
	46: T	for the sons of Korah, A **S** upon Alamoth.	7892
	48: T	A **S** *and* Psalm for the sons of Korah.	7892
	65: T	chief Musician, A Psalm *and* **S** of David.	7892
	66: T	To the chief Musician, A **S** *or* Psalm.	7892
	67: T	chief Musician on Neginoth, A Psalm *or* **S**.	7892
	68: T	the chief Musician, A Psalm *or* **S** of David.	7892
	69:12	and *I was* the **s** of the drunkards.	5058
	69:30	I will praise the name of God with a **s**; and	7892
	75: T	Al-taschith, A Psalm *or* **S** of Asaph.	7892
	76: T	on Neginoth, A Psalm *or* **S** of Asaph.	7892
	77: 6	I call to remembrance my **s** in the night:	5058
	83: T	A **S** *or* Psalm of Asaph.	7892
	87: T	A Psalm *or* **S** for the sons of Korah.	7892
	88: T	A **S** *or* Psalm for the sons of Korah. To	7892
	92: T	A Psalm *or* **S** for the sabbath day.	7892
	96: 1	O sing unto the LORD a new **s**: sing unto	7892
	98: 1	O sing unto the LORD a new **s**; for he	7892
	108: T	A **S** *or* Psalm of David.	7892
	118:14	The LORD *is* my strength and **s**, and	2176
	120: T	A **S** of degrees.	7892
	121: T	A **S** of degrees.	7892
	122: T	A **S** of degrees of David.	7892
	123: T	A **S** of degrees.	7892
	124: T	A **S** of degrees of David.	7892
	125: T	A **S** of degrees.	7892
	126: T	A **S** of degrees.	7892
	127: T	A **S** of degrees for Solomon.	7892
	128: T	A **S** of degrees.	7892
	129: T	A **S** of degrees.	7892
	130: T	A **S** of degrees.	7892
	131: T	A **S** of degrees of David.	7892
	132: T	A **S** of degrees.	7892
	133: T	A **S** of degrees of David.	7892
	134: T	A **S** of degrees.	7892
	137: 3	us away captive required of us a **s**;	1697+7892
	137: 4	How shall we sing the LORD'S **s** in a	7892
	144: 9	I will sing a new **s** unto thee, O God:	7892
	149: 1	Sing unto the LORD a new **s**, *and*	7892
Ecc	7: 5	than for a man to hear the **s** of fools.	7892
SS	1: 1	The **s** of songs, which *is* Solomon's.	7892
Isa	5: 1	Now will I sing to my wellbeloved a **s** of	7892
	12: 2	JEHOVAH *is* my strength and *my* **s**;	2176
	24: 9	They shall not drink wine with a **s**;	7892
	26: 1	In that day shall this **s** be sung in the land	7892
	30:29	Ye shall have a **s**, as *in* the night when a	7892
	42:10	Sing unto the LORD a new **s**, *and*	7892
La	3:14	to all my people; *and* their **s** all the day.	5058
Eze	33:32	thou *art* unto them as a very lovely **s** *of* one	7892
Rev	5: 9	And they sung a new **s**, saying, Thou art	*5603*
	14: 3	And they sung as *it were* a new **s** before	*5603*
	14: 3	and no *man* could learn *that* **s** but	*5603*
	15: 3	And they sing the **s** of Moses the servant of	*5603*
	15: 3	and the **s** of the Lamb, saying, Great and	*5603*

SONGS (20) [SING]

Ge	31:27	and with **s**, with tabret, and with harp?	7892
1Ki	4:32	and his **s** were a thousand and five.	7892
1Ch	25: 7	*that were* instructed in the **s** of the LORD,	7892
Ne	12:46	and **s** of praise and thanksgiving unto God.	7892
Job	35:10	God my Maker, who giveth **s** in the night;	2158
Ps	32: 7	thou shalt compass me about *with* **s** of	7438
	119:54	Thy statutes have been my **s** in the house of	2158
	137: 3	*saying,* Sing us *one* of the **s** of Zion.	7892
Pr	25:20	so *is* he that singeth **s** to a heavy heart.	7892
SS	1: 1	The song of **s**, which *is* Solomon's.	7892
Isa	23:16	make sweet melody, sing many **s**, that thou	7892
	24:16	uttermost part of the earth have we heard **s**,	2158
	35:10	come to Zion with **s** and everlasting joy	7440
	38:20	we will sing my **s** *to* the stringed	5058
Eze	26:13	I will cause the noise of thy **s** to cease; and	7892
Am	5:23	Take thou away from me the noise of thy **s**;	7892
	8: 3	the **s** of the temple shall be howlings in that	7892
	8:10	and all your **s** into lamentation;	7892
Eph	5:19	in psalms and hymns and spiritual **s**,	*5603*
Col	3:16	in psalms and hymns and spiritual **s**,	*5603*

SONS (1076) [SON]

Ge	5: 4	and he begat **s** and daughters:	1121
	5: 7	seven years, and begat **s** and daughters:	1121
	5:10	fifteen years, and begat **s** and daughters:	1121
	5:13	forty years, and begat **s** and daughters:	1121
	5:16	thirty years, and begat **s** and daughters:	1121
	5:19	hundred years, and begat **s** and daughters:	1121
	5:22	hundred years, and begat **s** and daughters:	1121
	5:26	and two years, and begat **s** and daughters:	1121
	5:30	and five years, and begat **s** and daughters:	1121
	6: 2	That the **s** of God saw the daughters of men	1121
	6: 4	when the **s** of God came in unto	1121
	6:10	Noah begat three **s**, Shem, Ham, and	1121
	6:18	thy **s**, and thy wife, and thy sons' wives	1121
	7: 7	his **s**, and his wife, and his sons' wives with	1121
	7:13	the **s** of Noah, and Noah's wife, and	1121
	7:13	the three wives of his **s** with them, into	1121
	8:16	and thy **s**, and thy sons' wives with thee.	1121
	8:18	his **s**, and his wife, and his sons' wives with	1121
	9: 1	God blessed Noah and his **s**, and said unto	1121
	9: 8	unto Noah, and to his **s** with him, saying,	1121
	9:18	the **s** of Noah, that went forth of the ark,	1121
	9:19	These *are* the three **s** of Noah: and of them	1121
	10: 1	Now these *are* the generations of the **s** of	1121
	10: 1	and unto them were **s** born after the flood.	1121
	10: 2	The **s** of Japheth; Gomer, and Magog, and	1121
	10: 3	the **s** of Gomer; Ashkenaz, and Riphath,	1121
	10: 4	the **s** of Javan; Elishah, and Tarshish,	1121
	10: 6	the **s** of Ham; Cush, and Mizraim, and	1121
	10: 7	the **s** of Cush; Seba, and Havilah, and	1121
	10: 7	and the **s** of Raamah; Sheba, and Dedan.	1121
	10:20	These *are* the **s** of Ham, after their families,	1121
	10:25	unto Eber were born two **s**: the name of one	1121
	10:29	and Jobab: all these *were* the **s** of Joktan.	1121
	10:31	These *are* the **s** of Shem, after their	1121
	10:32	These *are* the families of the **s** of Noah,	1121
	11:11	hundred years, and begat **s** and daughters.	1121
	11:13	three years, and begat **s** and daughters.	1121
	11:15	three years, and begat **s** and daughters.	1121
	11:17	thirty years, and begat **s** and daughters.	1121
	11:19	nine years, and begat **s** and daughters.	1121
	11:21	seven years, and begat **s** and daughters.	1121
	11:23	hundred years, and begat **s** and daughters.	1121
	11:25	nineteen years, and begat **s** and daughters.	1121
	19:12	thy **s**, and thy daughters, and	1121
	19:14	Lot went out, and spake unto his **s in law**,	2860
	19:14	one that mocked unto his **s in law**.	2860
	23: 3	and spake unto the **s** of Heth, saying,	1121
	23:11	in the presence of the **s** of my people give I	1121
	23:16	had named in the audience of the **s** of Heth,	1121
	23:20	of a buryingplace by the **s** of Heth.	1121
	25: 3	the **s** of Dedan were Asshurim, and	1121
	25: 4	the **s** of Midian; Ephah, and Epher, and	1121
	25: 6	unto the **s** of the concubines,	1121
	25: 9	his **s** Isaac and Ishmael buried him in	1121
	25:10	which Abraham purchased of the **s** of Heth:	1121
	25:13	these *are* the names of the **s** of Ishmael,	1121
	25:16	These *are* the **s** of Ishmael, and these *are*	1121
	27:29	and let thy mother's **s** bow down to thee:	1121
	29:34	unto me, because I have born him three **s**:	1121
	30:20	with me, because I have born him six **s**:	1121
	30:35	and gave *them* into the hand of his **s**.	1121
	31: 1	he heard the words of Laban's **s**, saying,	1121
	31:17	and set his **s** and his wives upon camels;	1121
	31:28	hast not suffered me to kiss my **s** and my	1121
	31:55	kissed his **s** and his daughters, and	1121
	32:22	his eleven **s**, and passed over the ford	3206
	34: 5	now his **s** were with his cattle in the field:	1121
	34: 7	the **s** of Jacob came out of the field when	1121

Ge	34:13	the **s** of Jacob answered Shechem and	1121
	34:25	that two of the **s** of Jacob, Simeon and	1121
	34:27	The **s** of Jacob came upon the slain, and	1121
	35: 5	and they did not pursue after the **s** of Jacob.	1121
	35:22	Israel heard *it.* Now the **s** of Jacob were	1121
	35:23	The **s** of Leah; Reuben, Jacob's firstborn,	1121
	35:24	The **s** of Rachel; Joseph, and Benjamin:	1121
	35:25	the **s** of Bilhah, Rachel's handmaid; Dan,	1121
	35:26	the **s** of Zilpah, Leah's handmaid; Gad,	1121
	35:26	these *are* the **s** of Jacob, which were born to	1121
	35:29	and his **s** Esau and Jacob buried him.	1121
	36: 5	these *are* the **s** of Esau, which were born	1121
	36: 6	his **s**, and his daughters, and all the persons	1121
	36:10	These *are* the names of Esau's **s**;	1121
	36:11	the **s** of Eliphaz were Teman, Omar, Zepho,	1121
	36:12	these *were* the **s** of Adah Esau's wife.	1121
	36:13	these *are* the **s** of Reuel; Nahath, and Zerah,	1121
	36:13	these were the **s** of Bashemath Esau's wife.	1121
	36:14	these were the **s** of Aholibamah,	1121
	36:15	These *were* dukes of the **s** of Esau: the sons	1121
	36:15	the **s** of Eliphaz the firstborn *son* of Esau;	1121
	36:16	the land of Edom; these *were* the **s** of Adah.	1121
	36:17	these *are* the **s** of Reuel Esau's son;	1121
	36:17	these *are* the **s** of Bashemath Esau's wife.	1121
	36:18	these *are* the **s** of Aholibamah Esau's wife;	1121
	36:19	These *are* the **s** of Esau, who *is* Edom, and	1121
	36:20	These *are* the **s** of Seir the Horite,	1121
	37: 2	the lad *was* with the **s** of Bilhah, and	1121
	37: 2	and with the **s** of Zilpah, his father's wives:	1121
	37:35	all his **s** and all his daughters rose up to	1121
	41:50	unto Joseph were born two **s** before	1121
	42: 1	Jacob said unto his **s**, Why do ye look one	1121
	42: 5	the **s** of Israel came to buy *corn* among	1121
	42:11	We *are* all one man's **s**; we *are* true *men,*	1121
	42:13	the **s** of one man in the land of Canaan;	1121
	42:32	We *be* twelve brethren, **s** of our father; one	1121
	42:37	saying, Slay my two **s**, if I bring him not to	1121
	44:27	Ye know that my wife bare me two **s**:	NIH
	46: 5	and the **s** of Israel carried Jacob their father,	1121
	46: 7	His **s**, and his sons' sons with him,	1121
	46: 7	His sons, and his sons' **s** with him,	1121
	46: 8	which came into Egypt, Jacob and his **s**:	1121
	46: 9	the **s** of Reuben; Hanoch, and Phallu, and	1121
	46:10	the **s** of Simeon; Jemuel, and Jamin, and	1121
	46:11	the **s** of Levi; Gershon, Kohath, and Merari.	1121
	46:12	the **s** of Judah; Er, and Onan, and Shelah,	1121
	46:12	the **s** of Pharez were Hezron and Hamul.	1121
	46:13	the **s** of Issachar; Tola, and Phuvah, and	1121
	46:14	the **s** of Zebulun; Sered, and Elon, and	1121
	46:15	These *be* the **s** of Leah, which she bare unto	1121
	46:15	all the souls of his **s** and his daughters *were*	1121
	46:16	the **s** of Gad; Ziphion, and Haggi, Shuni,	1121
	46:17	the **s** of Asher; Jimnah, and Ishuah, and	1121
	46:17	and the **s** of Beriah; Heber, and Malchiel.	1121
	46:18	These *are* the **s** of Zilpah, whom Laban	1121
	46:19	The **s** of Rachel Jacob's wife; Joseph, and	1121
	46:21	the **s** of Benjamin *were* Belah, and Becher,	1121
	46:22	These *are* the **s** of Rachel, which were born	1121
	46:23	And the **s** of Dan; Hushim.	1121
	46:24	the **s** of Naphtali; Jahzeel, and Guni, and	1121
	46:25	These *are* the **s** of Bilhah, which Laban	1121
	46:27	the **s** of Joseph, which were born him in	1121
	48: 1	he took with him his two **s**, Manasseh and	1121
	48: 5	now thy two **s**, Ephraim and Manasseh,	1121
	48: 8	Israel beheld Joseph's **s**, and said, Who *are*	1121
	48: 9	Joseph said unto his father, They *are* my **s**,	1121
	49: 1	Jacob called unto his **s**, and said,	1121
	49: 2	and hear, ye **s** of Jacob;	1121
	49:33	had made an end of commanding his **s**,	1121
	50:12	his **s** did unto him according as he	1121
	50:13	For his **s** carried him into the land of	1121
Ex	3:22	ye shall put *them* upon your **s**, and	1121
	4:20	Moses took his wife and his **s**, and set them	1121
	6:14	The **s** of Reuben the firstborn of Israel;	1121
	6:15	the **s** of Simeon; Jemuel, and Jamin, and	1121
	6:16	these *are* the names of the **s** of Levi	1121
	6:17	The **s** of Gershon; Libni, and Shimi,	1121
	6:18	the **s** of Kohath; Amram, and Izhar, and	1121
	6:19	the **s** of Merari; Mahali and Mushi:	1121
	6:21	the **s** of Izhar; Korah, and Nepheg, and	1121
	6:22	the **s** of Uzziel; Mishael, and Elzaphan,	1121
	6:24	the **s** of Korah; Assir, and Elkanah, and	1121
	10: 9	our old, with our **s** and with our daughters,	1121
	12:24	an ordinance to thee and to thy **s** for ever.	1121
	18: 3	her two **s**; of which the name of the one	1121
	18: 5	came with his **s** and his wife unto Moses	1121
	18: 6	and thy wife, and her two **s** with her.	1121
	21: 4	and she have born him **s** or daughters;	1121
	22:29	the firstborn of thy **s** shalt thou give unto	1121
	27:21	his **s** shall order it from evening to morning	1121
	28: 1	his **s** with him, from among the children of	1121
	28: 1	and Abihu, Eleazar and Ithamar, Aaron's **s**.	1121
	28: 4	his **s**, that he may minister unto me in	1121
	28:40	for Aaron's **s** thou shalt make coats, and	1121
	28:41	upon Aaron thy brother, and his **s** with him;	1121
	28:43	they shall be upon Aaron, and upon his **s**,	1121
	29: 4	his **s** thou shalt bring unto the door of	1121
	29: 8	thou shalt bring his **s**, and put coats upon	1121
	29: 9	Aaron and his **s**, and put the bonnets on	1121
	29: 9	and thou shalt consecrate Aaron and his **s**.	1121
	29:10	his **s** shall put their hands upon the head of	1121
	29:15	his **s** shall put their hands upon the head of	1121
	29:19	his **s** shall put their hands upon the head of	1121
	29:20	upon the tip of the right ear of his **s**, and	1121
	29:21	upon his **s**, and upon the garments of his	1121
	29:21	and upon the garments of his **s** with him:	1121
	29:21	and his **s**, and his sons' garments with him.	1121
	29:24	hands of Aaron, and in the hands of his **s**;	1121
	29:27	*is* for Aaron, and of *that* which *is* for his **s**:	1121
	29:32	and his **s** shall eat the flesh of the ram,	1121
	29:35	thus shalt thou do unto Aaron, and to his **s**,	1121
	29:44	I will sanctify also both Aaron and his **s**,	1121
	30:19	and his **s** shall wash their hands and	1121
	30:30	thou shalt anoint Aaron and his **s**, and	1121
	31:10	the garments of his **s**, to minister in	1121
	32: 2	of your **s**, and of your daughters, and	1121
	32:26	all the **s** of Levi gathered themselves	1121
	34:16	thou take of their daughters unto thy **s**, and	1121
	34:16	make thy **s** go a whoring after their gods.	1121
	34:20	All the firstborn of thy **s** thou shalt redeem:	1121
	35:19	the garments of his **s**, to minister in	1121
	39:27	*of* woven work for Aaron, and for his **s**,	1121
	40:12	his **s** unto the door of the tabernacle of	1121
	40:14	thou shalt bring his **s**, and clothe them with	1121
	40:31	and Aaron and his **s** washed their hands and	1121
Lev	1: 5	the priests, Aaron's **s**, shall bring the blood,	1121
	1: 7	the **s** of Aaron the priest shall put fire upon	1121
	1: 8	the priests, Aaron's **s**, shall lay the parts,	1121
	1:11	the priests, Aaron's **s**, shall sprinkle his	1121
	2: 2	he shall bring it to Aaron's **s** the priests:	1121
	3: 2	Aaron's **s** the priests shall sprinkle	1121
	3: 5	Aaron's **s** shall burn it on the altar upon	1121
	3: 8	Aaron's **s** shall sprinkle the blood thereof	1121
	3:13	the **s** of Aaron shall sprinkle the blood	1121
	6: 9	Command Aaron and his **s**, saying, This *is*	1121
	6:14	the **s** of Aaron shall offer it before	1121
	6:16	remainder thereof shall Aaron and his **s** eat:	1121
	6:20	This *is* the offering of Aaron and of his **s**,	1121
	6:22	the priest of his **s** that is anointed in his	1121
	6:25	Speak unto Aaron and to his **s**, saying,	1121
	7:10	and dry, shall all the **s** of Aaron have,	1121
	7:33	He among the **s** of Aaron, that offereth	1121
	7:34	unto his **s** by a statute for ever from among	1121
	7:35	of Aaron, and of the anointing of his **s**,	1121
	8: 2	Take Aaron and his **s** with him, and	1121
	8: 6	Moses brought Aaron and his **s**, and	1121
	8:13	Moses brought Aaron's **s**, and put coats	1121
	8:14	his **s** laid their hands upon the head of	1121
	8:18	his **s** laid their hands upon the head of	1121
	8:22	his **s** laid their hands upon the head of	1121
	8:24	he brought Aaron's **s**, and Moses put of	1121
	8:30	upon his **s**, and upon his sons' garments	1121
	8:30	and his **s**, and his sons' garments with him.	1121
	8:31	Moses said unto Aaron and to his **s**,	1121
	8:31	Aaron and his **s** shall eat it.	1121
	8:36	his **s** did all things which the LORD	1121
	9: 1	*that* Moses called Aaron and his **s**, and	1121
	9: 9	the **s** of Aaron brought the blood unto him:	1121
	9:12	Aaron's **s** presented unto him the blood,	1121
	9:18	Aaron's **s** presented unto him the blood,	1121
	10: 1	Nadab and Abihu, the **s** of Aaron,	1121
	10: 4	the **s** of Uzziel the uncle of Aaron,	1121
	10: 6	unto Eleazar and unto Ithamar his **s**,	1121
	10: 9	nor strong drink, thou, nor thy **s** with thee,	1121
	10:12	and unto Ithamar his **s** that were left,	1121
	10:14	and thy **s**, and thy daughters with thee:	1121
	10:16	Ithamar the **s** of Aaron which were left	1121
	13: 2	the priest, or unto one of his **s** the priests:	1121

Lev 16: 1 after the death of the two **s** of Aaron, 1121
17: 2 unto his **s**, and unto all the children of 1121
21: 1 Speak unto the priests the **s** of Aaron, and 1121
21:24 to his **s**, and unto all the children of Israel. 1121
22: 2 Speak unto Aaron and to his **s**, that they 1121
22:18 to his **s**, and unto all the children of Israel, 1121
26:29 ye shall eat the flesh of your **s**, and the flesh 1121
Nu 2:14 the captain of the **s** of Gad *shall be* Eliasaph 1121
2:18 the captain of the **s** of Ephraim *shall be* 1121
2:22 the captain of the **s** of Benjamin *shall be* 1121
3: 2 these *are* the names of the **s** of Aaron; 1121
3: 3 These *are* the names of the **s** of Aaron, 1121
3: 9 give the Levites unto Aaron and to his **s**: 1121
3:10 And thou shalt appoint Aaron and his **s**, and 1121
3:17 these were the **s** of Levi by their names; 1121
3:18 these *are* the names of the **s** of Gershon by 1121
3:19 the **s** of Kohath by their families; Amram, 1121
3:20 the **s** of Merari by their families; Mahli, 1121
3:25 the charge of the **s** of Gershon in 1121
3:29 The families of the **s** of Kohath shall pitch 1121
3:36 charge of the **s** of Merari *shall be* 1121
3:38 *shall be* Moses, and Aaron and his **s**, 1121
3:48 is *to be* redeemed, unto Aaron and to his **s**. 1121
3:51 were redeemed unto Aaron and to his **s**, 1121
4: 2 Take the sum of the **s** of Kohath from 1121
4: 2 sons of Kohath from among the **s** of Levi, 1121
4: 4 This *shall be* the service of the **s** of Kohath 1121
4: 5 his **s**, and they shall take down the covering 1121
4:15 his **s** have made an end of covering 1121
4:15 the **s** of Kohath shall come to bear *it*: but 1121
4:15 These *things are* the burden of the **s** of 1121
4:19 holy *things*: Aaron and his **s** shall go in, 1121
4:22 Take also the sum of the **s** of Gershon, 1121
4:27 his **s** shall be all the service of the sons of 1121
4:27 his sons shall be all the service of the **s** of 1121
4:28 This *is* the service of the families of the **s** of 1121
4:29 *As for* the **s** of Merari, thou shalt number 1121
4:33 This *is* the service of the families of the **s** of 1121
4:34 the **s** of the Kohathites after their families, 1121
4:38 those that were numbered of the **s** of 1121
4:41 of the families of the **s** of Gershon, 1121
4:42 numbered of the families of the **s** of Merari, 1121
4:45 numbered of the families of the **s** of Merari, 1121
6:23 Speak unto Aaron and unto his **s**, saying, 1121
7: 7 four oxen he gave unto the **s** of Gershon, 1121
7: 8 eight oxen he gave unto the **s** of Merari, 1121
7: 9 unto the **s** of Kohath he gave none: because 1121
8:13 before his **s**, and offer them *for* an offering 1121
8:19 to his **s** from among the children of Israel, 1121
8:22 before Aaron, and before his **s**: 1121
10: 8 the **s** of Aaron, the priests, shall blow with 1121
10:17 the **s** of Gershon and the sons of Merari set 1121
10:17 of Gershon and the **s** of Merari set forward, 1121
13:33 the **s** of Anak, *which come* of the giants: 1121
16: 1 Dathan and Abiram, the **s** of Eliab, and On, 1121
16: 1 the son of Peleth, **s** of Reuben, took *men*: 1121
16: 7 *ye take* too much upon you, ye **s** of Levi. 1121
16: 8 unto Korah, Hear, I pray you, ye **s** of Levi: 1121
16:10 and all thy brethren the **s** of Levi with thee: 1121
16:12 to call Dathan and Abiram, the **s** of Eliab: 1121
16:27 and their **s**, and their little children. 1121
18: 1 Thou and thy **s** and thy father's house with 1121
18: 1 thy **s** with thee shall bear the iniquity of 1121
18: 2 thy **s** with thee *shall minister* before 1121
18: 7 thy **s** with thee shall keep your priest's 1121
18: 8 and to thy **s**, by an ordinance for ever. 1121
18: 9 *shall be* most holy for thee and for thy **s**. 1121
18:11 to thy **s** and to thy daughters with thee, by a 1121
18:19 and thy **s** and thy daughters with thee, 1121
21:29 he hath given his **s** that escaped, and 1121
21:35 smote him, and his **s**, and all his people, 1121
26: 8 And the **s** of Pallu; Eliab. 1121
26: 9 the **s** of Eliab; Nemuel, and Dathan, and 1121
26:12 The **s** of Simeon after their families: 1121
26:19 The **s** of Judah *were* Er and Onan: and Er 1121
26:20 And the **s** of Judah after their families were, 1121
26:21 the **s** of Pharez were; of Hezron, the family 1121
26:23 *Of* the **s** of Issachar after their families: 1121
26:26 *Of* the **s** of Zebulun after their families: 1121
26:28 The **s** of Joseph after their families *were* 1121
26:29 *Of* the **s** of Manasseh: of Machir, the family 1121
26:30 These *are* the **s** of Gilead: *of* Jeezer, 1121
26:33 Zelophehad the son of Hepher had no **s**, 1121
26:35 These *are* the **s** of Ephraim after their 1121
26:36 these *are* the **s** of Shuthelah: of Eran, 1121
26:37 These *are* the families of the **s** of Ephraim 1121
26:37 These *are* the **s** of Joseph after their 1121
26:38 The **s** of Benjamin after their families: 1121
26:40 the **s** of Bela were Ard and Naaman: 1121
26:41 These *are* the **s** of Benjamin after their 1121
26:42 These *are* the **s** of Dan after their families: 1121
26:45 Of the **s** of Beriah: of Heber, the family of 1121
26:47 These *are* the families of the **s** of Asher 1121
26:48 *Of* the **s** of Naphtali after their families: 1121
27: 3 but died in his own sin, and had no **s**. 1121
36: 1 of the families of the **s** of Joseph, 1121
36: 3 *if* they be married to any of the **s** of 1121
36: 5 The tribe of the **s** of Joseph hath said well. 1121
36:11 were married unto their father's brothers' **s**: 1121
36:12 of the **s** of Manasseh the son of Joseph, 1121
Dt 1:28 moreover we have seen the **s** of 1121
2:33 we smote him, and his **s**, and all his people. 1121
4: 9 but teach them thy **s**, and thy sons' sons; 1121
4: 9 but teach them thy sons, and thy sons' **s**; 1121
11: 6 did unto Dathan and Abiram, the **s** of Eliab, 1121
12:12 ye, and your **s**, and your daughters, and 1121
12:31 for even their **s** and their daughters they 1121
18: 5 of the LORD, him and his **s** for ever. 1121
21: 5 the priests the **s** of Levi shall come near; 1121
21:16 when he maketh his **s** to inherit *that* which 1121
23:17 of Israel, nor a sodomite of the **s** of Israel. 1121
28:32 Thy **s** and thy daughters *shall be* given unto 1121
28:41 Thou shalt beget **s** and daughters, but 1121
28:53 the flesh of thy **s** and of thy daughters, 1121
31: 9 delivered it unto the priests the **s** of Levi, 1121
32: 8 when he separated the **s** of Adam, 1121
32:19 because of the provoking of his **s**, 1121
Jos 7:24 his **s**, and his daughters, and his oxen, and 1121
15:14 Caleb drove thence the three **s** of Anak, 1121
17: 3 son of Manasseh, had no **s**, but daughters: 1121
17: 6 Manasseh had an inheritance among his **s**: 1121
17: 6 the rest of Manasseh's **s** had the land of 1121
24:32 **s** of Hamor the father of Shechem for an 1121
Jdg 1:20 and he expelled thence the three **s** of Anak. 1121
3: 6 gave their daughters to their **s**, and 1121
8:19 *were* my brethren, *even* the **s** of my mother: 1121
8:30 and ten **s** of his body begotten: 1121
9: 2 either that all the **s** of Jerubbaal, *which are* 1121
9: 5 slew his brethren the **s** of Jerubbaal, 1121
9:18 have slain his **s**, threescore and ten persons, 1121
9:24 and ten **s** of Jerubbaal might come, 1121
10: 4 he had thirty **s** that rode on thirty ass colts, 1121
11: 2 Gilead's wife bare him **s**; and *his* wife's 1121
11: 2 *his* wife's **s** grew up, and they thrust out 1121
12: 9 he had thirty **s**, and thirty daughters, 1121
12: 9 in thirty daughters from abroad for his **s**. 1121
12:14 he had forty **s** and thirty nephews, that rode 1121
17: 5 and teraphim, and consecrated one of his **s**, 1121
17:11 young man was unto him as one of his **s**. 1121
18:30 his **s** were priests to the tribe of Dan until 1121
19:22 the men of the city, certain **s** of Belial, 1121
Ru 1: 1 of Moab, he, and his wife, and his two **s**. 1121
1: 2 the name of his two **s** Mahlon and Chilion, 1121
1: 3 and she was left, and her two **s**. 1121
1: 5 the woman was left of her two **s** and 3206
1:11 *are there* yet *any moe* **s** in my womb, 1121
1:12 also to night, and should also bear **s**; 1121
4:15 which *is* better to thee than seven **s**, 1121
1Sa 1: 3 the two **s** of Eli, Hophni and Phinehas, 1121
1: 4 and to all her **s** and her daughters, portions: 1121
1: 8 *am* not I better to thee than ten **s**? 1121
2:12 Now the **s** of Eli *were* sons of Belial; 1121
2:12 Now the sons of Eli *were* **s** of Belial; 1121
2:21 and bare three **s** and two daughters. 1121
2:22 and heard all that his **s** did unto all Israel; 1121
2:24 Nay, my **s**; for *it is* no good report that I 1121
2:29 honourest thy **s** above me, to make 1121
2:34 that shall come upon thy two **s**, on Hophni 1121
3:13 because his **s** made themselves vile, and 1121
4: 4 the two **s** of Eli, Hophni and Phinehas, 1121
4:11 the two **s** of Eli, Hophni and Phinehas, 1121
4:17 thy two **s** also, Hophni and Phinehas, 1121
8: 1 that he made his **s** judges over Israel. 1121
8: 3 his **s** walked not in his ways, but 1121
8: 5 thou art old, and thy **s** walk not in thy ways: 1121
8:11 He will take your **s**, and appoint *them* for 1121
12: 2 grayheaded; and behold, my **s** *are* with you: 1121
14:49 Now the **s** of Saul were Jonathan, and 1121

1Sa	16: 1	for I have provided me a king among his **s**.	1121
	16: 5	he sanctified Jesse and his **s**, and	1121
	16:10	Jesse made seven of his **s** to pass before	1121
	17:12	whose name *was* Jesse; and he had eight **s**:	1121
	17:13	the three eldest **s** of Jesse went *and*	1121
	17:13	the names of his three **s** that went to	1121
	22:20	one of the **s** of Ahimelech the son of	1121
	28:19	to morrow *shalt* thou and thy **s** *be* with me:	1121
	30: 3	their wives, and their **s**, and their daughters,	1121
	30: 6	every man for his **s** and for his daughters:	1121
	30:19	neither **s** nor daughters, neither spoil,	1121
	31: 2	followed hard upon Saul and upon his **s**;	1121
	31: 2	and Abinadab, and Malchishua, Saul's **s**.	1121
	31: 6	his three **s**, and his armourbearer, and	1121
	31: 7	that Saul and his **s** were dead, they forsook	1121
	31: 8	and his three **s** fallen in mount Gilboa.	1121
	31:12	the bodies of his **s** from the wall of	1121
2Sa	2:18	there were three **s** of Zeruiah there, Joab,	1121
	3: 2	unto David were **s** born in Hebron: and	1121
	3:39	these men the **s** of Zeruiah *be* too hard for	1121
	4: 2	the **s** of Rimmon a Beerothite, of	1121
	4: 5	the **s** of Rimmon the Beerothite, Rechab	1121
	4: 9	the **s** of Rimmon the Beerothite, and	1121
	5:13	there were yet **s** and daughters born to	1121
	6: 3	Uzzah and Ahio, the **s** of Abinadab,	1121
	8:18	and David's **s** were chief rulers.	1121
	9:10	Thou therefore, and thy **s**, and thy servants,	1121
	9:10	Now Ziba had fifteen **s** and	1121
	9:11	shall eat at my table, as one of the king's **s**.	1121
	13:23	and Absalom invited all the king's **s**.	1121
	13:27	let Amnon and all the king's **s** go with him.	1121
	13:29	all the king's **s** arose, and every man gat	1121
	13:30	Absalom hath slain all the king's **s**, and	1121
	13:32	have slain all the young men the king's **s**;	1121
	13:33	to think *that* all the king's **s** are dead:	1121
	13:35	unto the king, Behold, the king's **s** come:	1121
	13:36	the king's **s** came, and lift up their voice	1121
	14: 6	thy handmaid had two **s**, and they two	1121
	14:27	unto Absalom there were born three **s**, and	1121
	15:27	your two **s** with you, Ahimaaz thy son, and	1121
	15:36	*they have* there with them their two **s**,	1121
	16:10	have I to do with you, ye **s** of Zeruiah?	1121
	19: 5	the lives of thy **s** and of thy daughters, and	1121
	19:17	his fifteen **s** and his twenty servants with	1121
	19:22	have I to do with you, ye **s** of Zeruiah,	1121
	21: 6	Let seven men of his **s** be delivered unto us,	1121
	21: 8	the king took the two **s** of Rizpah	1121
	21: 8	the five **s** of Michal the daughter of Saul,	1121
	21:16	which *was* of the **s** of the giant,	3211
	21:18	slew Saph, which *was* of the **s** of the giant.	3211
	23: 6	*the **s** of* Belial *shall be* all of them as thorns	NIH
	23:32	*of* the **s** of Jashen, Jonathan,	1121
1Ki	1: 9	called all his brethren the king's **s**, and all	1121
	1:19	hath called all the **s** of the king, and	1121
	1:25	hath called all the king's **s**, and the captains	1121
	2: 7	shew kindness unto the **s** of Barzillai	1121
	4: 3	Elihoreph and Ahiah, the **s** of Shisha,	1121
	4:31	and Chalcol, and Darda, the **s** of Mahol:	1121
	11:20	household among the **s** of Pharaoh.	1121
	12:31	the people, which were not of the **s** of Levi.	1121
	13:12	For his **s** had seen what way the man of	1121
	13:13	he said unto his **s**, Saddle me the ass.	1121
	13:27	he spake to his **s**, saying, Saddle me the ass.	1121
	13:31	that he spake to his **s**, saying, When I am	1121
	18:31	the number of the tribes of the **s** of Jacob,	1121
	20:35	a certain man of the **s** of the prophets said	1121
	21:10	set two men, **s** of Belial, before him, to bear	1121
2Ki	2: 3	the **s** of the prophets that *were at* Beth-el	1121
	2: 5	the **s** of the prophets that *were* at Jericho	1121
	2: 7	And fifty men of the **s** of the prophets went,	1121
	2:15	when the **s** of the prophets which *were* to	1121
	4: 1	wives of the **s** of the prophets unto Elisha,	1121
	4: 1	to take unto him my two **s** to be bondmen.	3206
	4: 4	shut the door upon thee and upon thy **s**,	1121
	4: 5	and shut the door upon her and upon her **s**,	1121
	4:38	the **s** of the prophets *were* sitting before	1121
	4:38	and seethe pottage for the **s** of the prophets.	1121
	5:22	two young men of the **s** of the prophets:	1121
	6: 1	the **s** of the prophets said unto Elisha,	1121
	9:26	and the blood of his **s**, saith the LORD;	1121
	10: 1	Ahab had seventy **s** in Samaria. And Jehu	1121
	10: 2	seeing your master's **s** *are* with you, and	1121
	10: 3	out the best and meetest of your master's **s**,	1121
	10: 6	ye the heads of the men your master's **s**,	1121

	10: 6	Now the king's **s**, *being* seventy persons,	1121
	10: 7	that they took the king's **s**, and	1121
	10: 8	have brought the heads of the king's **s**.	1121
	11: 2	stale him from among the king's **s** which	1121
	15:12	Thy **s** shall sit on the throne of Israel unto	1121
	17:17	they caused their **s** and their daughters to	1121
	19:37	Sharezer *his* **s** smote him with the sword:	NIH
	20:18	of thy **s** that shall issue from thee,	1121
	25: 7	they slew the **s** of Zedekiah before his eyes,	1121
1Ch	1: 5	The **s** of Japheth; Gomer, and Magog, and	1121
	1: 6	the **s** of Gomer; Ashchenaz, and Riphath,	1121
	1: 7	the **s** of Javan; Elishah, and Tarshish,	1121
	1: 8	The **s** of Ham; Cush, and Mizraim, Put, and	1121
	1: 9	the **s** of Cush; Seba, and Havilah, and	1121
	1: 9	And the **s** of Raamah; Sheba, and Dedan.	1121
	1:17	The **s** of Shem; Elam, and Asshur, and	1121
	1:19	unto Eber were born two **s**: the name of	1121
	1:23	and Jobab. All these *were* the **s** of Joktan.	1121
	1:28	The **s** of Abraham; Isaac, and Ishmael.	1121
	1:31	and Kedemah. These *are* the **s** of Ishmael.	1121
	1:32	Now the **s** of Keturah,	1121
	1:32	And the **s** of Jokshan; Sheba, and Dedan.	1121
	1:33	the **s** of Midian; Ephah, and Epher, and	1121
	1:33	and Eldaah. All these *are* the **s** of Keturah.	1121
	1:34	begat Isaac. The **s** of Isaac; Esau and Israel.	1121
	1:35	The **s** of Esau; Eliphaz, Reuel, and Jeush,	1121
	1:36	The **s** of Eliphaz; Teman, and Omar, Zephi,	1121
	1:37	The **s** of Reuel; Nahath, Zerah, Shammah,	1121
	1:38	the **s** of Seir; Lotan, and Shobal, and	1121
	1:39	the **s** of Lotan; Hori, and Homam: and	1121
	1:40	The **s** of Shobal; Alian, and Manahath, and	1121
	1:40	And the **s** of Zibeon; Aiah, and Anah.	1121
	1:41	The **s** of Anah; Dishon. And the sons of	1121
	1:41	the **s** of Dishon; Amram, and Eshban, and	1121
	1:42	The **s** of Ezer; Bilhan, and Zavan, *and*	1121
	1:42	*and* Jakan. The **s** of Dishan; Uz, and Aran.	1121
	2: 1	These *are* the **s** of Israel; Reuben, Simeon,	1121
	2: 3	The **s** of Judah; Er, and Onan, and Shelah:	1121
	2: 4	and Zerah. All the **s** of Judah *were* five.	1121
	2: 5	The **s** of Pharez; Hezron, and Hamul.	1121
	2: 6	the **s** of Zerah; Zimri, and Ethan, and	1121
	2: 7	the **s** of Carmi; Achar, the troubler of	1121
	2: 8	And the **s** of Ethan; Azariah.	1121
	2: 9	The **s** also of Hezron, that were born unto	1121
	2:16	the **s** of Zeruiah; Abishai, and Joab, and	1121
	2:18	her **s** *are* these; Jesher, and Shobab, and	1121
	2:23	All these *belonged to* the **s** of Machir	1121
	2:25	the **s** of Jerahmeel the firstborn of Hezron	1121
	2:27	the **s** of Ram the firstborn of Jerahmeel	1121
	2:28	the **s** of Onam were, Shammai, and Jada.	1121
	2:28	the **s** of Shammai; Nadab, and Abishur.	1121
	2:30	the **s** of Nadab; Seled, and Appaim: but	1121
	2:31	the **s** of Appaim; Ishi. And the sons of Ishi;	1121
	2:31	the **s** of Ishi; Sheshan. And the children of	1121
	2:32	the **s** of Jada the brother of Shammai;	1121
	2:33	the **s** of Jonathan; Peleth, and Zaza.	1121
	2:33	and Zaza. These were the **s** of Jerahmeel.	1121
	2:34	Now Sheshan had no **s**, but daughters.	1121
	2:42	Now the **s** of Caleb the brother of	1121
	2:42	and the **s** of Mareshah the father of Hebron.	1121
	2:43	the **s** of Hebron; Korah, and Tappuah, and	1121
	2:47	the **s** of Jahdai; Regem, and Jotham, and	1121
	2:50	These were the **s** of Caleb the son of Hur,	1121
	2:52	Shobal the father of Kirjath-jearim had **s**;	1121
	2:54	The **s** of Salma; Beth-lehem, and	1121
	3: 1	Now these were the **s** of David, which were	1121
	3: 9	*These were* all the **s** of David, beside	1121
	3: 9	beside the **s** of the concubines, and	1121
	3:15	the **s** of Josiah *were*, the firstborn Johanan,	1121
	3:16	the **s** of Jehoiakim: Jeconiah his son,	1121
	3:17	the **s** of Jeconiah; Assir, Salathiel his son,	1121
	3:19	And the **s** of Pedaiah *were*, Zerubbabel, and	1121
	3:21	the **s** of Hananiah; Pelatiah, and Jesaiah:	1121
	3:21	the **s** of Rephaiah, the sons of Arnan,	1121
	3:21	the **s** of Arnan, the sons of Obadiah,	1121
	3:21	the sons of Arnan, the **s** of Obadiah,	1121
	3:21	the sons of Obadiah, the **s** of Shechaniah.	1121
	3:22	the **s** of Shechaniah; Shemaiah: and	1121
	3:22	the **s** of Shemaiah; Hattush, and Igeal, and	1121
	3:23	the **s** of Neariah; Elioenai, and Hezekiah,	1121
	3:24	the **s** of Elioenai *were*, Hodaiah, and	1121
	4: 1	The **s** of Judah; Pharez, Hezron, and Carmi,	1121
	4: 4	These *are* the **s** of Hur, the firstborn of	1121
	4: 6	These *were* the **s** of Naarah.	1121

1Ch 4: 7	the s of Helah *were,* Zereth, and Jezoar,	1121
4:13	the s of Kenaz; Othniel, and Seraiah: and	1121
4:13	and Seraiah: and the s of Othniel; Hathath.	1121
4:15	the s of Caleb the son of Jephunneh; Iru,	1121
4:15	and Naam: and the s of Elah, even Kenaz.	1121
4:16	the s of Jehaleleel; Ziph, and Ziphah, Tiria,	1121
4:17	the s of Ezra *were,* Jether, and Mered, and	1121
4:18	these *are* the s of Bithiah the daughter of	1121
4:19	the s of *his* wife Hodiah the sister of	1121
4:20	the s of Shimon *were,* Amnon, and Rinnah,	1121
4:20	the s of Ishi *were,* Zoheth, and Ben-zoheth.	1121
4:21	The s of Shelah the son of Judah *were,* Er	1121
4:24	The s of Simeon *were,* Nemuel, and Jamin,	1121
4:26	the s of Mishma; Hamuel his son,	1121
4:27	Shimei had sixteen s and six daughters;	1121
4:42	*even* of the s of Simeon, five hundred men,	1121
4:42	and Rephaiah, and Uzziel, the s of Ishi.	1121
5: 1	Now the s of Reuben the firstborn of Israel,	1121
5: 1	his birthright was given unto the s of	1121
5: 3	The s, *I say,* of Reuben the firstborn of	1121
5: 4	The s of Joel; Shemaiah his son, Gog his	1121
5:18	The s of Reuben, and the Gadites, and	1121
6: 1	The s of Levi; Gershon, Kohath, and	1121
6: 2	the s of Kohath; Amram, Izhar, and	1121
6: 3	The s also of Aaron; Nadab, and Abihu,	1121
6:16	The s of Levi; Gershom, Kohath, and	1121
6:17	these *be* the names of the s of Gershom;	1121
6:18	the s of Kohath *were,* Amram, and Izhar,	1121
6:19	The s of Merari; Mahli, and Mushi.	1121
6:22	The s of Kohath; Amminadab his son,	1121
6:25	the s of Elkanah; Amasai, and Ahimoth.	1121
6:26	the s of Elkanah; Zophai his son, and	1121
6:28	the s of Samuel; the firstborn Vashni, and	1121
6:29	The s of Merari; Mahli, Libni his son,	1121
6:33	Of the s of the Kohathites: Heman a singer,	1121
6:44	their brethren the s of Merari *stood* on	1121
6:49	his s offered upon the altar of the burnt	1121
6:50	these *are* the s of Aaron; Eleazar his son,	1121
6:54	of the s of Aaron, of the families of	1121
6:57	to the s of Aaron they gave the cities of	1121
6:61	unto the s of Kohath, which were left of	1121
6:62	to the s of Gershom throughout their	1121
6:63	Unto the s of Merari *were given* by lot,	1121
6:66	*the residue* of the families of the s of	1121
6:70	for the family of the remnant of the s of	1121
6:71	Unto the s of Gershom *were given* out of	1121
7: 1	Now the s of Issachar *were,* Tola, and	1121
7: 2	the s of Tola; Uzzi, and Rephaiah, and	1121
7: 3	the s of Uzzi; Izrahiah: and the sons of	1121
7: 3	the s of Izrahiah; Michael, and Obadiah,	1121
7: 4	*men:* for they had many wives and s.	1121
7: 6	*The s of* Benjamin; Bela, and Becher, and	NIH
7: 7	the s of Bela; Ezbon, and Uzzi, and Uzziel,	1121
7: 8	the s of Becher; Zemira, and Joash, and	1121
7: 8	and Alameth. All these *are* the s of Becher.	1121
7:10	The s also of Jediael; Bilhan: and the sons	1121
7:10	the s of Bilhan; Jeush, and Benjamin, and	1121
7:11	All these the s of Jediael, by the heads of	1121
7:12	children of Ir, *and* Hushim, the s of Aher.	1121
7:13	The s of Naphtali; Jahziel, and Guni, and	1121
7:13	and Jezer, and Shallum, the s of Bilhah.	1121
7:14	The s of Manasseh; Ashriel, whom she	1121
7:16	and his s *were* Ulam and Rakem.	1121
7:17	the s of Ulam; Bedan. These *were* the sons	1121
7:17	These *were* the s of Gilead, the son of	1121
7:19	the s of Shemida were, Ahian, and	1121
7:20	the s of Ephraim; Shuthelah, and Bered his	1121
7:30	The s of Asher; Imnah, and Isuah, and	1121
7:31	the s of Beriah; Heber, and Malchiel,	1121
7:33	the s of Japhlet; Pasach, and Bimhal, and	1121
7:34	the s of Shamer; Ahi, and Rohgah,	1121
7:36	The s of Zophah; Suah, and Harnepher, and	1121
7:38	the s of Jether; Jephunneh, and Pispah, and	1121
7:39	the s of Ulla; Arah, and Haniel, and Rezia.	1121
8: 3	the s of Bela were, Addar, and Gera, and	1121
8: 6	these *are* the s of Ehud: these *are* the heads	1121
8:10	These *were* his s, heads of the fathers.	1121
8:12	The s of Elpaal; Eber, and Misham, and	1121
8:16	and Ispah, and Joha, the s of Beriah;	1121
8:18	and Jezliah, and Jobab, the s of Elpaal;	1121
8:21	and Beraiah, and Shimrath, the s of Shimhi;	1121
8:25	and Penuel, the s of Shashak;	1121
8:27	and Eliah, and Zichri, the s of Jeroham.	1121
8:35	the s of Micah *were,* Pithon, and Melech,	1121
8:38	And Azel had six s, whose names *are* these,	1121
8:38	and Hanan. All these *were* the s of Azel.	1121
8:39	the s of Eshek his brother *were,* Ulam his	1121
8:40	the s of Ulam were mighty men of valour,	1121
8:40	archers, and had many s, and sons' sons,	1121
8:40	and sons' s, an hundred and fifty.	1121
8:40	fifty. All these *are* of the s of Benjamin.	1121
9: 5	Asaiah the firstborn, and his s.	1121
9: 6	of the s of Zerah; Jeuel, and their brethren,	1121
9: 7	of the s of Benjamin; Sallu the son of	1121
9:14	the son of Hashabiah, of the s of Merari;	1121
9:30	*some* of the s of the priests made	1121
9:32	of the s of the Kohathites, *were* over	1121
9:41	the s of Micah *were,* Pithon, and Melech,	1121
9:44	And Azel had six s, whose names *are* these,	1121
9:44	and Hanan: these *were* the s of Azel.	1121
10: 2	followed hard after Saul, and after his s;	1121
10: 2	and Malchishua, the s of Saul.	1121
10: 6	his three s, and all his house died together.	1121
10: 7	that Saul and his s were dead, then	1121
10: 8	and his s fallen in mount Gilboa.	1121
10:12	the bodies of his s, and brought them to	1121
11:34	The s of Hashem the Gizonite, Jonathan	1121
11:44	and Jehiel the s of Hothan the Aroerite,	1121
11:46	the s of Elnaam, and Ithmah the Moabite,	1121
12: 3	Joash, the s of Shemaah the Gibeathite;	1121
12: 3	Jeziel, and Pelet, the s of Azmaveth; and	1121
12: 7	and Zebadiah, the s of Jeroham of Gedor.	1121
12:14	These *were* of the s of Gad, captains of	1121
14: 3	and David begat moe s and daughters.	1121
15: 5	Of the s of Kohath; Uriel the chief, and	1121
15: 6	Of the s of Merari; Asaiah the chief, and	1121
15: 7	Of the s of Gershom; Joel the chief, and	1121
15: 8	Of the s of Elizaphan; Shemaiah the chief,	1121
15: 9	Of the s of Hebron; Eliel the chief, and	1121
15:10	Of the s of Uzziel; Amminadab the chief,	1121
15:17	of the s of Merari their brethren, Ethan	1121
16:42	of God. And the s of Jeduthun *were* porters.	1121
17:11	thy seed after thee, which shall be of thy s;	1121
18:17	the s of David *were* chief about the king.	1121
21:20	and his four s with him hid themselves.	1121
23: 6	them *into* courses among the s of Levi,	1121
23: 8	The s of Laadan; the chief *was* Jehiel, and	1121
23: 9	The s of Shimei; Shelomith, and Haziel,	1121
23:10	And the s of Shimei *were,* Jahath, Zina, and	1121
23:10	Beriah. These four *were* the s of Shimei.	1121
23:11	Jeush and Beriah had not many s; therefore	1121
23:12	The s of Kohath; Amram, Izhar, Hebron,	1121
23:13	The s of Amram; Aaron and Moses: and	1121
23:13	the most holy *things,* he and his s for ever,	1121
23:14	his s were named of the tribe of Levi.	1121
23:15	The s of Moses *were,* Gershom, and	1121
23:16	*Of* the s of Gershom, Shebuel *was*	1121
23:17	the s of Eliezer *were,* Rehabiah the chief.	1121
23:17	Eliezer had none other s; but the sons of	1121
23:17	but the s of Rehabiah were very many.	1121
23:18	*Of* the s of Izhar; Shelomith the chief.	1121
23:19	*Of* the s of Hebron; Jeriah the first,	1121
23:20	*Of* the s of Uzziel; Michah the first, and	1121
23:21	The s of Merari; Mahli, and Mushi.	1121
23:21	Mushi. The s of Mahli; Eleazar, and Kish.	1121
23:22	Eleazar died, and had no s, but daughters:	1121
23:22	and their brethren the s of Kish took them.	1121
23:23	The s of Mushi; Mahli, and Eder, and	1121
23:24	These *were* the s of Levi after the house of	1121
23:28	Because their office *was* to wait on the s of	1121
23:32	the charge of the s of Aaron their brethren,	1121
24: 1	Now *these are* the divisions of the s of	1121
24: 1	The s of Aaron; Nadab, and Abihu,	1121
24: 3	both Zadok of the s of Eleazar, and	1121
24: 3	and Ahimelech of the s of Ithamar,	1121
24: 4	there were moe chief men found of the s of	1121
24: 4	the sons of Eleazar than of the s of Ithamar;	1121
24: 4	Among the s of Eleazar *there were* sixteen	1121
24: 4	eight among the s of Ithamar according to	1121
24: 5	were of the s of Eleazar, and of the sons of	1121
24: 5	the sons of Eleazar, and of the s of Ithamar.	1121
24:20	the rest of the s of Levi *were these:* Of	1121
24:20	of Levi *were these:* Of the s of Amram;	1121
24:20	Shubael: of the s of Shubael; Jehdeiah.	1121
24:21	of the s of Rehabiah, the first *was* Isshiah.	1121
24:22	Shelomoth: of the s of Shelomoth; Jahath.	1121
24:23	the s *of Hebron;* Jeriah *the first,* Amariah	1121
24:24	*Of* the s of Uzziel; Michah: of the sons of	1121

1Ch	24:24	Michah: of the **s** of Michah; Shamir.	1121
	24:25	*was* Isshiah: of the **s** of Isshiah; Zechariah.	1121
	24:26	The **s** of Merari *were* Mahli and Mushi:	1121
	24:26	and Mushi: the **s** of Jaaziah; Beno.	1121
	24:27	The **s** of Merari by Jaaziah; Beno, and	1121
	24:28	Of Mahli *came* Eleazar, who had no **s**.	1121
	24:30	The **s** also of Mushi; Mahli, and Eder, and	1121
	24:30	These *were* the **s** of the Levites after	1121
	24:31	**s** of Aaron in the presence of David	1121
	25: 1	separated to the service of the **s** of Asaph,	1121
	25: 2	Of the **s** of Asaph; Zaccur, and Joseph, and	1121
	25: 2	the **s** of Asaph under the hands of Asaph,	1121
	25: 3	the **s** of Jeduthun; Gedaliah, and Zeri, and	1121
	25: 4	the **s** of Heman; Bukkiah, Mattaniah,	1121
	25: 5	All these *were* the **s** of Heman the king's	1121
	25: 5	God gave to Heman fourteen **s** and	1121
	25: 9	who with his brethren and **s** *were* twelve:	1121
	25:10	*he*, his **s**, and his brethren, *were* twelve:	1121
	25:11	*he*, his **s**, and his brethren, *were* twelve:	1121
	25:12	*he*, his **s**, and his brethren, *were* twelve:	1121
	25:13	*he*, his **s**, and his brethren, *were* twelve:	1121
	25:14	*he*, his **s**, and his brethren, *were* twelve:	1121
	25:15	*he*, his **s**, and his brethren, *were* twelve:	1121
	25:16	*he*, his **s**, and his brethren, *were* twelve:	1121
	25:17	*he*, his **s**, and his brethren, *were* twelve:	1121
	25:18	*he*, his **s**, and his brethren, *were* twelve:	1121
	25:19	*he*, his **s**, and his brethren, *were* twelve:	1121
	25:20	*he*, his **s**, and his brethren, *were* twelve:	1121
	25:21	*he*, his **s**, and his brethren, *were* twelve:	1121
	25:22	*he*, his **s**, and his brethren, *were* twelve:	1121
	25:23	*he*, his **s**, and his brethren, *were* twelve:	1121
	25:24	*he*, his **s**, and his brethren, *were* twelve:	1121
	25:25	*he*, his **s**, and his brethren, *were* twelve:	1121
	25:26	*he*, his **s**, and his brethren, *were* twelve:	1121
	25:27	*he*, his **s**, and his brethren, *were* twelve:	1121
	25:28	*he*, his **s**, and his brethren, *were* twelve:	1121
	25:29	*he*, his **s**, and his brethren, *were* twelve:	1121
	25:30	*he*, his **s**, and his brethren, *were* twelve:	1121
	25:31	*he*, his **s**, and his brethren, *were* twelve.	1121
	26: 1	the son of Kore, of the **s** of Asaph.	1121
	26: 2	the **s** of Meshelemiah *were*, Zechariah	1121
	26: 4	Moreover the **s** of Obed-edom *were*,	1121
	26: 6	Also unto Shemaiah his son were **s** born,	1121
	26: 7	The **s** of Shemaiah; Othni, and Rephael,	1121
	26: 8	All these of the **s** of Obed-edom: they and	1121
	26: 8	they and their **s** and their brethren,	1121
	26: 9	Meshelemiah had **s** and brethren,	1121
	26:10	of the children of Merari, had **s**;	1121
	26:11	all the **s** and brethren of Hosah *were*	1121
	26:15	to his **s** the house of Asuppim.	1121
	26:19	of the porters among the **s** of Kore,	1121
	26:19	sons of Kore, and among the **s** of Merari.	1121
	26:21	*As concerning* the **s** of Laadan; the sons of	1121
	26:21	the **s** of the Gershonite Laadan,	1121
	26:22	The **s** of Jehieli; Zetham, and Joel his	1121
	26:29	his **s** *were* for the outward business over	1121
	27:32	the son of Hachmoni *was* with the king's **s**:	1121
	28: 1	of his **s**, with the officers, and *with*	1121
	28: 4	among the **s** of my father he liked me to	1121
	28: 5	of all my **s**, (for the LORD hath given me	1121
	28: 5	(for the LORD hath given me many **s**,)	1121
	29:24	and all the **s** likewise of king David,	1121
2Ch	5:12	of Jeduthun, with their **s** and their brethren,	1121
	11:14	his **s** had cast them off from executing	1121
	11:21	begat twenty and eight **s**, and	1121
	13: 5	to him and to his **s** *by* a covenant of salt?	1121
	13: 8	the LORD in the hand of the **s** of David;	1121
	13: 9	the **s** of Aaron, and the Levites, and	1121
	13:10	*are* the **s** of Aaron, and the Levites *wait*	1121
	13:21	begat twenty and two **s**, and	1121
	20:14	of Mattaniah, a Levite of the **s** of Asaph,	1121
	21: 2	he had brethren the **s** of Jehoshaphat,	1121
	21: 2	all these *were* the **s** of Jehoshaphat king of	1121
	21: 7	to give a light to him and to his **s** for ever.	1121
	21:17	king's house, and his **s** also, and his wives;	1121
	21:17	save Jehoahaz, the youngest of his **s**.	1121
	22: 8	the **s** of the brethren of Ahaziah,	1121
	22:11	stole him from among the king's **s** that	1121
	23: 3	as the LORD hath said of the **s** of David.	1121
	23:11	Jehoiada and his **s** anointed him, and said,	1121
	24: 3	two wives; and he begat **s** and daughters.	1121
	24: 7	For the **s** of Athaliah, *that* wicked woman,	1121
	24:25	for the blood of the **s** of Jehoiada the priest,	1121
	24:27	Now *concerning* his **s**, and the greatness of	1121
	26:18	but to the priests the **s** of Aaron,	1121
	28: 8	**s**, and daughters, and took also away much	1121
	29: 9	our **s** and our daughters and our wives *are*	1121
	29:11	My **s**, be not now negligent: for the LORD	1121
	29:12	son of Azariah, of the **s** of the Kohathites:	1121
	29:12	of the **s** of Merari, Kish the son of Abdi,	1121
	29:13	of the **s** of Elizaphan; Shimri, and Jeiel:	1121
	29:13	of the **s** of Asaph; Zechariah, and	1121
	29:14	of the **s** of Heman; Jehiel, and Shimei: and	1121
	29:14	of the **s** of Jeduthun; Shemaiah, and Uzziel.	1121
	29:21	he commanded the priests the **s** of Aaron to	1121
	31:18	their wives, and their **s**, and their daughters,	1121
	31:19	Also of the **s** of Aaron the priests,	1121
	32:33	chiefest of the sepulchres of the **s** of David:	1121
	34:12	Obadiah, the Levites, of the **s** of Merari;	1121
	34:12	and Meshullam, of the **s** of the Kohathites,	1121
	35:14	the priests the **s** of Aaron *were busied* in	1121
	35:14	and for the priests the **s** of Aaron.	1121
	35:15	the singers the **s** of Asaph *were* in their	1121
	36:20	his **s** until the reign of the kingdom of	1121
Ezr	3: 9	stood Jeshua *with* his **s** and his brethren,	1121
	3: 9	and his brethren, Kadmiel and his **s**,	1121
	3: 9	Kadmiel and his sons, the **s** of Judah,	1121
	3: 9	the **s** of Henadad, *with* their sons and	1121
	3: 9	*with* their **s** and their brethren the Levites.	1121
	3:10	the Levites the **s** of Asaph with cymbals,	1121
	6:10	pray for the life of the king, and of his **s**.	1123
	7:23	against the realm of the king and his **s**?	1123
	8: 2	Of the **s** of Phinehas; Gershom: of the sons	1121
	8: 2	of the **s** of Ithamar; Daniel: of the sons of	1121
	8: 2	Daniel: of the **s** of David; Hattush.	1121
	8: 3	Of the **s** of Shechaniah, of the sons of	1121
	8: 3	the sons of Shechaniah, of the **s** of Pharosh;	1121
	8: 4	Of the **s** of Pahath-moab; Elihoenai the son	1121
	8: 5	Of the **s** of Shechaniah; the son of Jahaziel,	1121
	8: 6	Of the **s** also of Adin; Ebed the son of	1121
	8: 7	of the **s** of Elam; Jeshaiah the son of	1121
	8: 8	of the **s** of Shephatiah; Zebadiah the son of	1121
	8: 9	Of the **s** of Joab; Obadiah the son of Jehiel,	1121
	8:10	of the **s** of Shelomith; the son of Josiphiah,	1121
	8:11	of the **s** of Bebai; Zechariah the son of	1121
	8:12	of the **s** of Azgad; Johanan the son of	1121
	8:13	of the last **s** of Adonikam, whose names *are*	1121
	8:14	Of the **s** also of Bigvai; Uthai, and Zabbud,	1121
	8:15	and found there none of the **s** of Levi.	1121
	8:18	of the **s** of Mahli, the son of Levi, the son	1121
	8:18	with his **s** and his brethren, eighteen;	1121
	8:19	with him Jeshaiah of the **s** of Merari,	1121
	8:19	of Merari, his brethren and their **s**, twenty;	1121
	9: 2	daughters for themselves, and for their **s**:	1121
	9:12	give not your daughters unto their **s**,	1121
	9:12	neither take their daughters unto your **s**,	1121
	10: 2	*one* of the **s** of Elam, answered and	1121
	10:18	among the **s** of the priests there were found	1121
	10:18	*namely*, of the **s** of Jeshua the son of	1121
	10:20	of the **s** of Immer; Hanani, and Zebadiah.	1121
	10:21	of the **s** of Harim; Maaseiah, and Elijah,	1121
	10:22	of the **s** of Pashur; Elioenai, Maaseiah,	1121
	10:25	of the **s** of Parosh; Ramiah, and Jeziah, and	1121
	10:26	of the **s** of Elam; Mattaniah, Zechariah,	1121
	10:27	of the **s** of Zattu; Elioenai, Eliashib,	1121
	10:28	Of the **s** also of Bebai; Jehohanan,	1121
	10:29	of the **s** of Bani; Meshullam, Malluch, and	1121
	10:30	of the **s** of Pahath-moab; Adna, and Chelal,	1121
	10:31	*of* the **s** of Harim; Eliezer, Ishijah,	1121
	10:33	Of the **s** of Hashum; Mattenai, Mattathah,	1121
	10:34	Of the **s** of Bani; Maadai, Amram, and Uel,	1121
	10:43	Of the **s** of Nebo; Jeiel, Mattithiah, Zabad,	1121
Ne	3: 3	the fish gate did the **s** of Hassenaah build,	1121
	4:14	your **s**, and your daughters, your wives, and	1121
	5: 2	We, our **s**, and our daughters, *are* many:	1121
	5: 5	we bring into bondage our **s** and our	1121
	10: 9	Binnui of the **s** of Henadad, Kadmiel;	1121
	10:28	their wives, their **s**, and their daughters,	1121
	10:30	the land, nor take their daughters for our **s**:	1121
	10:36	Also the firstborn of our **s**, and of our	1121
	11: 6	All the **s** of Perez that dwelt at Jerusalem	1121
	11: 7	these *are* the **s** of Benjamin; Sallu the son	1121
	11:22	Of the **s** of Asaph, the singers *were* over	1121
	12:23	The **s** of Levi, the chief of the fathers,	1121
	12:28	the **s** of the singers gathered themselves	1121
	12:35	*certain* of the priests' **s** with trumpets;	1121
	13:25	shall not give your daughters unto their **s**,	1121
	13:25	nor take their daughters unto your **s**, or	1121

Ne 13:28 *one* of the **s** of Joiada, the son of Eliashib 1121
Est 9:10 The ten **s** of Haman the son of 1121
9:12 the palace, and the ten **s** of Haman; 1121
9:13 let Haman's ten **s** be hanged upon 1121
9:14 and they hanged Haman's ten **s**. 1121
9:25 and his **s** should be hanged on the gallows. 1121
Job 1: 2 there were born unto him seven **s** and 1121
1: 4 his **s** went and feasted *in their* houses, 1121
1: 5 It may be that my **s** have sinned, and 1121
1: 6 Now there was a day when the **s** of God 1121
1:13 there was a day when his **s** and 1121
1:18 Thy **s** and thy daughters *were* eating and 1121
2: 1 Again there was a day when the **s** of God 1121
14:21 His **s** come to honour, and he knoweth *it* 1121
38: 7 and all the **s** of God shouted for joy? 1121
38:32 or canst thou guide Arcturus with his **s**? 1121
42:13 He had also seven **s** and three daughters. 1121
42:16 and saw his **s**, and his sons' sons, 1121
42:16 and saw his sons, and his sons' **s**, 1121
Ps 4: 2 O ye **s** of men, how long *will ye turn* my 1121
31:19 them that trust in thee before the **s** of men! 1121
33:13 from heaven; he beholdeth all the **s** of men. 1121
42: T chief Musician, Maschil, for the **s** of Korah. 1121
44: T To the chief Musician for the **s** of Korah, 1121
45: T for the **s** of Korah, Maschil, A Song of 1121
46: T To the chief Musician for the **s** of Korah, 1121
47: T chief Musician, A Psalm for the **s** of Korah. 1121
48: T A Song *and* Psalm for the **s** of Korah. 1121
49: T chief Musician, A Psalm for the **s** of Korah. 1121
57: 4 *even* the **s** of men, whose teeth *are* spears 1121
58: 1 do ye judge uprightly, O ye **s** of men? 1121
77:15 thy people, the **s** of Jacob and Joseph. 1121
84: T upon Gittith, A Psalm for the **s** of Korah. 1121
85: T chief Musician, A Psalm for the **s** of Korah. 1121
87: T A Psalm *or* Song for the **s** of Korah. 1121
88: T A Song *or* Psalm for the **s** of Korah. To 1121
89: 6 *who* among the **s** of the mighty can be 1121
106:37 they sacrificed their **s** and their daughters 1121
106:38 *even* the blood of their **s** and of their 1121
144:12 That our **s** *may be* as plants grown up in 1121
145:12 To make known to the **s** of men his mighty 1121
Pr 8: 4 I call; and my voice *is* to the **s** of man. 1121
8:31 and my delights *were* with the **s** of men. 1121
Ecc 1:13 this sore travail hath God given to the **s** of 1121
2: 3 till I might see what *was* that good for the **s** 1121
2: 8 and the delights of the **s** of men, 1121
3:10 which God hath given to the **s** of men to be 1121
3:18 heart concerning the estate of the **s** of men, 1121
3:19 For that which befalleth the **s** of men 1121
8:11 the heart of the **s** of men is fully set in them 1121
9: 3 also the heart of the **s** of men is full *of* evil, 1121
9:12 so *are* the **s** of men snared in an evil time, 1121
SS 2: 3 of the wood, so *is* my beloved among the **s**. 1121
Isa 37:38 Sharezer his **s** smote him with the sword; 1121
39: 7 of thy **s** that shall issue from thee, 1121
43: 6 bring my **s** from far, and my daughters 1121
45:11 Ask me of *things* to come concerning my **s**, 1121
49:22 they shall bring thy **s** in *their* arms, and 1121
51:18 *There is* none to guide her among all the **s** 1121
51:18 hand of all the **s** *that* she hath brought up. 1121
51:20 Thy **s** have fainted, they lie at the head of 1121
52:14 and his form more than the **s** of men: 1121
56: 5 a name better than *of* **s** and *of* daughters: 1121
56: 6 Also the **s** of the stranger, that join 1121
57: 3 draw near hither, ye **s** of the sorceress, 1121
60: 4 thy **s** shall come from far, and 1121
60: 9 to bring thy **s** from far, their silver and 1121
60:10 the **s** of strangers shall build up thy walls, 1121
60:14 The **s** also of them that afflicted thee shall 1121
61: 5 the **s** of the alien *shall be* your plowmen 1121
62: 5 marrieth a virgin, *so* shall thy **s** marry thee: 1121
62: 8 the **s** of the stranger shall not drink thy 1121
Jer 3:24 and their herds, their **s** and their daughters. 1121
5:17 *which* thy **s** and thy daughters should eat: 1121
6:21 and the **s** together shall fall upon them; 1121
7:31 to burn their **s** and their daughters in 1121
11:22 their **s** and their daughters shall die by 1121
13:14 even the fathers and the **s** together, saith 1121
14:16 them, their wives, nor their **s**, nor their 1121
16: 2 neither shalt thou have **s** nor daughters in 1121
16: 3 For thus saith the LORD concerning the **s** 1121
19: 5 to burn their **s** with fire *for* burnt offerings 1121
19: 9 I will cause them to eat the flesh of their **s** 1121
29: 6 Take ye wives, and beget **s** and daughters; 1121
29: 6 take wives for your **s**, and give your 1121
29: 6 that they may bear **s** and daughters; 1121
32:19 *are* open upon all the ways of the **s** of men: 1121
32:35 to cause their **s** and their daughters to pass 1121
35: 3 all his **s**, and the whole house of 1121
35: 4 into the chamber of the **s** of Hanan, the son 1121
35: 5 I set before the **s** of the house of 1121
35: 6 no wine, *neither* ye, nor your **s** for ever: 1121
35: 8 we, our wives, our **s**, nor our daughters; 1121
35:14 that he commanded his **s** not to drink wine, 1121
35:16 Because the **s** of Jonadab the son of Rechab 1121
39: 6 the king of Babylon slew the **s** of Zedekiah 1121
40: 8 Johanan and Jonathan the **s** of Kareah, and 1121
40: 8 the **s** of Ephai the Netophathite, and 1121
48:46 for thy **s** are taken captives, and 1121
49: 1 thus saith the LORD; Hath Israel no **s**? 1121
52:10 the king of Babylon slew the **s** of Zedekiah 1121
La 4: 2 The precious **s** of Zion, comparable to fine 1121
Eze 5:10 Therefore the fathers shall eat the **s** in 1121
5:10 of thee, and the **s** shall eat their fathers; 1121
14:16 they shall deliver neither **s** nor daughters; 1121
14:18 they shall deliver neither **s** nor daughters, 1121
14:22 be brought forth, *both* **s** and daughters: 1121
16:20 Moreover thou hast taken thy **s** and thy 1121
20:31 when *ye* make your **s** to pass through 1121
23: 4 were mine, and they bare **s** and daughters. 1121
23:10 they took her **s** and her daughters, and slew 1121
23:25 they shall take thy **s** and thy daughters; and 1121
23:37 have also caused their **s**, whom they bare 1121
23:47 they shall slay their **s** and their daughters, 1121
24:21 your **s** and your daughters whom ye have 1121
24:25 set their minds, their **s** and their daughters, 1121
40:46 these *are* the **s** of Zadok among the sons of 1121
40:46 these *are* the sons of Zadok among the **s** of 1121
44:15 the priests the Levites, the **s** of Zadok, 1121
46:16 If the prince give a gift unto any of his **s**, 1121
46:18 he shall give his **s** inheritance out of his 1121
48:11 priests that are sanctified of the **s** of Zadok; 1121
Da 5:21 he *was* driven from the **s** of men; and 1123
10:16 *one* like the similitude of the **s** of men 1121
11:10 his **s** shall be stirred up, and shall assemble 1121
Hos 1:10 unto them, *Ye are* the **s** of the living God. 1121
Joel 1:12 joy is withered away from the **s** of men. 1121
2:28 your **s** and your daughters shall prophesy, 1121
3: 8 I will sell your **s** and your daughters into 1121
Am 2:11 I raised up of your **s** for prophets, and 1121
7:17 thy **s** and thy daughters shall fall by 1121
Mic 5: 7 not for man, nor waiteth for the **s** of men. 1121
Zec 9:13 raised up thy **s**, O Zion, against thy sons, 1121
9:13 O Zion, against thy **s**, O Greece, and 1121
Mal 3: 3 he shall purify the **s** of Levi, and 1121
3: 6 therefore ye **s** of Jacob are not consumed. 1121
Mt 20:20 mother of Zebedee's children with her **s**, *5207*
20:21 Grant that these my two **s** may sit, *5207*
21:28 A *certain* man had two **s**; and he came to *5043*
26:37 with *him* Peter and the two **s** of Zebedee, *5207*
Mk 3:17 which is, The **s** of thunder:) *5207*
3:28 All sins shall be forgiven unto the **s** of men, *5207*
10:35 And James and John, the **s** of Zebedee, *5207*
Lk 5:10 *was* also James, and John, *the* **s** of Zebedee, *5207*
11:19 by whom do your **s** cast *them* out? *5207*
15:11 And he said, A certain man had two **s**: *5207*
Jn 1:12 to them gave he power to become the **s** of *5043*
21: 2 and the *s* of Zebedee, and two other of his NIG
Ac 2:17 and your **s** and your daughters shall *5207*
7:16 of the **s** of Emmor the *father* of Sychem. *5207*
7:29 the land of Madian, where he begat two **s**. *5207*
19:14 And there were seven **s** of *one* Sceva, *5207*
Ro 8:14 by the Spirit of God, they are the **s** of God. *5207*
8:19 for the manifestation of the **s** of God. *5207*
1Co 4:14 but as my beloved **s** I warn *you*. *5043*
2Co 6:18 and ye shall be my **s** and daughters, *5207*
Gal 4: 5 that we might receive the **adoption of s**. *5206*
4: 6 And because ye are **s**, God hath sent forth *5207*
4:22 For it is written, that Abraham had two **s**, *5207*
Eph 3: 5 was not made known unto the **s** of men, *5207*
Php 2:15 and harmless, the **s** of God without rebuke, *5043*
Heb 2:10 by whom *are* all *things*, in bringing many **s** *5207*
7: 5 And verily they that are of the **s** of Levi *5207*
11:21 was a dying, blessed both the **s** of Joseph; *5207*
12: 7 God dealeth with you as with **s**; *5207*
12: 8 then are ye bastards, and not **s**. *5207*
1Jn 3: 1 that we should be called the **s** of God: *5043*
3: 2 now are we the **s** of God, and it doth not yet *5043*

S

SONS' (26) [SON]
Ge 6:18 and thy wife, and thy **s** wives with thee. 1121
7: 7 and his wife, and his **s** wives with him, 1121
8:16 and thy sons, and thy **s** wives with thee. 1121
8:18 and his wife, and his **s** wives with him: 1121
46: 7 His sons, and his **s** sons with him, 1121
46: 7 his **s** daughters, and all his seed brought he 1121
46:26 out of his loins, besides Jacob's **s** wives, 1121
Ex 29:21 and his sons, and his **s** garments with him. 1121
29:28 his **s** by a statute for ever from 1121+3807.1
29:29 the holy garments of Aaron shall be his **s** 1121
39:41 his **s** garments, to minister in the priest's 1121
Lev 2: 3 offering *shall be* Aaron's and his **s**: 1121+3807.1
2:10 offering *shall be* Aaron's and his **s**: 1121+3807.1
7:31 but the breast shall be Aaron's and his **s**. 1121
8:27 upon his **s** hands, and waved them *for* a 1121
8:30 his sons, and upon his **s** garments with him; 1121
8:30 and his sons, and his **s** garments with him. 1121
10:13 because it *is* thy due, and thy **s** due, 1121
10:14 for *they be* thy due, and thy **s** due, 1121
10:15 it shall be thine, and thy **s** with thee, by a 1121
24: 9 it shall be Aaron's and his **s**; and 1121+3807.1
Dt 4: 9 but teach them thy sons, and thy **s** sons; 1121
1Ch 8:40 and **s** sons, an hundred and fifty. 1121
Job 42:16 and saw his sons, and his **s** sons, 1121
Eze 46:16 inheritance thereof shall be his **s**; 1121+3807.1
46:17 but his inheritance shall be his **s** for them. 1121

SOON (65) [SOONER] See Index

SOONER (2) [SOON] See Index

SOOTHED See MOLLIFIED

SOOTHSAYER (1) [SOOTHSAYERS, SOOTHSAYING]
Jos 13:22 Balaam also the son of Beor, the **s**, did 7080

SOOTHSAYER'S See MEONENIM

SOOTHSAYERS (6) [SOOTHSAYER]
Isa 2: 6 *are* **s** like the Philistines, and they please 6049
Da 2:27 the magicians, the **s**, shew unto the king; 1505
4: 7 the astrologers, the Chaldeans, and the **s**: 1505
5: 7 in the astrologers, the Chaldeans, and the **s**. 1505
5:11 astrologers, Chaldeans, *and* **s**; 1505
Mic 5:12 thine hand; and thou shalt have no *more* **s**: 6049

SOOTHSAYING (1) [SOOTHSAYER]
Ac 16:16 which brought her masters much gain by **s**: *3132*

SOP (4)
Jn 13:26 He it is, to whom I shall give a **s**, *5596*
13:26 dipped *it*. And when he had dipped the **s**, *5596*
13:27 And after the **s** Satan entered into him. *5596*
13:30 having received the **s** went immediately *5596*

SOPATER (1)
Ac 20: 4 And there accompanied him into Asia **S** of *4986*

SOPE (2)
Jer 2:22 wash thee with nitre, and take thee much **s**, 1287
Mal 3: 2 he *is* like a refiner's fire, and like fullers' **s**: 1287

SOPHERETH (2)
Ezr 2:55 the children of Sotai, the children of **S**, 5618
Ne 7:57 the children of Sotai, the children of **S**, 5618

SORCERER (2) [SORCERY]
Ac 13: 6 they found a certain **s**, a false prophet, *3097*
13: 8 But Elymas the **s** (for so is his name by *3097*

SORCERERS (6) [SORCERY]
Ex 7:11 Pharaoh also called the wise men and the **s**: 3784
Jer 27: 9 nor to your **s**, which speak unto you, 3786
Da 2: 2 and the **s**, and the Chaldeans, 3784
Mal 3: 5 I will be a swift witness against the **s**, and 3784
Rev 21: 8 and whoremongers, and **s**, and idolaters, *5332*
22:15 and **s**, and whoremongers, and murderers, *5333*

SORCERESS (1) [SORCERY]
Isa 57: 3 draw near hither, ye sons of the **s**, the seed 6049

SORCERIES (5) [SORCERY]
Isa 47: 9 their perfection for the multitude of thy **s**, 3785
47:12 and with the multitude of thy **s**, 3785
Ac 8:11 of long time *he* had bewitched them with **s**. *3095*
Rev 9:21 nor of their **s**, nor of their fornication, *5331*
18:23 for by thy **s** were all nations deceived. *5331*

SORCERY (1) [SORCERER, SORCERERS, SORCERESS, SORCERIES]
Ac 8: 9 which beforetime in the *same* city **used s**, *3096*

SORE (98) [SORELY, SORER, SORES]
Ge 19: 9 And they pressed **s** upon the man, *even* Lot, 3966
20: 8 in their ears: and the men were **s** afraid. 3966
31:30 **s longedst** after thy father's house, 3700+3700
34:25 when they were **s**, that two of the sons of 3510
41:56 the famine **waxed s** in the land of Egypt. 2388
41:57 that the famine was *so* **s** in all lands. 2388
43: 1 And the famine *was* **s** in the land. 3515
47: 4 for the famine *is* **s** in the land of Canaan: 3515
47:13 for the famine *was* very **s**, so that the land 3515
50:10 with a great and very **s** lamentation: 3515
Ex 14:10 marched after them; and they were **s** afraid: 3966
Lev 13:42 or bald forehead, a white reddish **s**; 5061
13:43 *if* the rising of the **s** *be* white reddish in his 5061
Nu 22: 3 Moab was **s** afraid of the people, because 3966
Dt 6:22 shewed signs and wonders, great and **s**, 7451
28:35 with a **s** botch that cannot be healed, 7451
28:59 and **s** sicknesses, and of long continuance. 7451
Jos 9:24 we were **s** afraid of our lives because of 3966
Jdg 10: 9 of Ephraim; so that Israel was **s** distressed. 3966
14:17 he told her, because she **lay s upon** him: 6693
15:18 he was **s** athirst, and called on the LORD, 3966
20:34 men out of all Israel, and the battle was **s**: 3513
21: 2 up their voices, and **wept s**; 1058+1065+1419
1Sa 1: 6 her adversary also **provoked** her **s**, 3707+3708
1:10 prayed unto the LORD, and **wept s**. 1058+1058
5: 7 for his hand is **s** upon us, and upon Dagon 7185
14:52 there was **s** war against the Philistines all 2389
17:24 the man, fled from him, and were **s** afraid. 3966
21:12 was **s** afraid of Achish the king of Gath. 3966
28:15 Saul answered, I am **s** distressed; for 3966
28:20 was **s** afraid, because of the words of 3966
28:21 saw that he was **s** troubled, and said unto 3966
31: 3 the battle **went s** against Saul, and 3513
31: 3 and he was **s** wounded of the archers. 3966
31: 4 would not; for he was **s** afraid: 3966
2Sa 2:17 there was a very **s** battle that day; 7186
13:36 and all his servants **wept** very **s**. 1058+1065
1Ki 17:17 his sickness was so **s**, that there was no 2389
18: 2 And *there was* a **s** famine in Samaria. 2389
2Ki 3:26 Moab saw that the battle was too **s** for him, 2388
6:11 king of Syria was **s troubled** for this thing; 5590
20: 3 And Hezekiah **wept s**. 1058+1065+1419
1Ch 10: 3 the battle **went s** against Saul, and 3513
10: 4 would not; for he was **s** afraid. 3966
2Ch 6:28 whatsoever **s** or whatsoever sickness *there* 5061
6:29 when every one shall know his own **s** and 5061
21:19 so he died of **s** diseases. And his people 7451
28:19 **transgressed s** against the LORD. 4603+4604
35:23 Have me away; for I am **s** wounded. 3966
Ezr 10: 1 children: for the people **wept** very **s**. 1058+1059
Ne 2: 2 sorrow of heart. Then I was very **s** afraid, 7235
13: 8 it grieved me **s**: therefore I cast forth all 3966
Job 2: 7 smote Job with **s** boils from the sole of his 7451
5:18 For he **maketh s**, and bindeth up: 3510
Ps 2: 5 and vex them in his **s displeasure**. 2740
6: 3 My soul is also **s** vexed: but thou, 3966
6:10 all mine enemies be ashamed and **s** vexed: 3966
38: 2 in me, and thy hand **presseth** me **s**. 5181+5921
38: 8 I am feeble and **s** broken: I have 3966+5704
38:11 and my friends stand aloof from my **s**; 5061
44:19 Though thou hast **s broken** us in the place 1794
55: 4 My heart is **s pained** within me: and 2342
71:20 which hast shewed me great and **s** troubles, 7451
77: 2 my **s** ran in the night, and ceased not: 3027
118:13 Thou hast **thrust s** at me that *I* might 1760+1760
118:18 The LORD hath **chastened** me **s**: 3256+3256
Ecc 1:13 this **s** travail hath God given to the sons of 7451
4: 8 This *is* also vanity, yea, it *is* a **s** travail. 7451
5:13 There is a **s** evil *which* I have seen under 2470
5:16 this also *is* a **s** evil, *that* in all points as he 2470
Isa 27: 1 In that day the LORD with his **s** and great 7186
38: 3 And Hezekiah **wept s**. 1058+1065+1419
59:11 like bears, and **mourn s** like doves: 1897+1897
64: 9 Be not wroth **very s**, O LORD, 3966+5704
64:12 hold thy peace, and afflict us **very s**? 3966+5704
Jer 13:17 mine eye shall **weep s**, and run down 1830+1830

S

Jer 22:10 *but* **weep s** for him that goeth away: 1058+1058
50:12 Your mother shall be **s** confounded; 3966
52: 6 the famine was **s** in the city, so that there 2388
La 1: 2 She **weepeth s** in the night, and 1058+1058
3:52 Mine enemies **chased** me **s**, like a 6679+6679
Eze 14:21 How much more when I send my four **s** 7451
21:10 is sharpened to make a **s slaughter**; 2873+2874
27:35 their kings shall be **s afraid**, they 8175+8178
Da 6:14 was **s** displeased with himself, and set *his* 7690
Mic 2:10 it shall destroy *you,* even *with* a **s** 4834
Zec 1: 2 The LORD hath been **s displeased** 7107+7110
1:15 I am very **s displeased** with 7107+7110
Mt 17: 6 *it,* they fell on their face, and were **s** afraid. *4970*
17:15 for he is lunatick, and **s** vexed: for ofttimes *2560*
21:15 to the Son of David; they were **s displeased**, *23*
Mk 6:51 they were **s** amazed in themselves beyond *3029*
9: 6 not what to say; for they were **s afraid**. *1630*
9:26 and rent him **s**, and came out of *him:* and *4183*
14:33 and began to be **s amazed**, and to be very *1568*
Lk 2: 9 round about them: and they were **s** afraid. *3173*
Ac 20:37 And *they* all wept **s**, and fell on Paul's *2425*
Rev 16: 2 grievous **s** upon the men which had *1668*

SOREK (1)
Jdg 16: 4 that he loved a woman in the valley of **S**, 7796

SORELY (2) [SORE]
Ge 49:23 The archers have **s grieved** him, and shot *at* 4843
Isa 23: 5 shall they be **s pained** *at* the report of Tyre. 2342

SORER (1) [SORE]
Heb 10:29 Of how much **s** punishment, suppose ye, *5501*

SORES (4) [SORE]
Isa 1: 6 *but* wounds, and bruises, and putrifying **s**: 4347
Lk 16:20 which was laid at his gate, **full of s**, *1669*
16:21 moreover the dogs came and licked his **s**. *1668*
Rev 16:11 of heaven because of their pains and their **s**, *1668*

SORROW (70) [SORROWED, SORROWETH, SORROWFUL, SORROWING, SORROWS, SORRY]
Ge 3:16 I will greatly multiply thy **s** and 6093
3:16 in **s** thou shalt bring forth children; and 6089
3:17 in **s** shalt thou eat *of* it all the days of thy 6093
42:38 shall ye bring down my gray hairs with **s** to 3015
44:29 ye shall bring down my gray hairs with **s** to 7451
44:31 of thy servant our father with **s** to the grave. 3015
Ex 15:14 **s** shall take hold on the inhabitants of 2427
Lev 26:16 consume the eyes, and **cause s** of heart: 1727
Dt 28:65 and failing of eyes, and **s** of mind: 1671
1Ch 4: 9 saying, Because I bare *him* with **s**. 6090
Ne 2: 2 this *is* nothing *else* but **s** of heart. Then I 7455
Est 9:22 which was turned unto them from **s** to joy, 3015
Job 3:10 *mother's* womb, nor hid **s** from mine eyes. 5999
6:10 yea, I would harden myself in **s**; let him not 2427
17: 7 Mine eye also is dim by reason of **s**, and 3708
41:22 and **s** is turned into joy before him. 1670
Ps 13: 2 in my soul, *having* **s** in my heart daily? 3015
38:17 to halt, and my **s** *is* continually before me. 4341
39: 2 *even* from good; and my **s** was stirred. 3511
55:10 mischief also and **s** *are* in the midst of it. 5999
90:10 yet *is* their strength labour and **s**; 205
107:39 low through oppression, affliction, and **s**. 3015
116: 3 gat hold upon me: I found trouble and **s**. 3015
Pr 10:10 He that winketh *with* the eye causeth **s**: but 6094
10:22 it maketh rich, and he addeth no **s** with it. 6089
15:13 but by **s** of the heart the spirit *is* broken. 6094
17:21 He that begetteth a fool *doeth it* to his **s**: 8424
23:29 who hath **s**? who hath contentions? who hath 17
Ecc 1:18 he that increaseth knowledge increaseth **s**. 4341
5:17 *he hath* much **s** and wrath with his sickness. 3707
7: 3 **S** *is* better than laughter: for by the sadness 3708
11:10 Therefore remove **s** from thy heart, and 3708
Isa 5:30 behold darkness *and* **s**, and the light is 6862
14: 3 the LORD shall give thee rest from thy **s**, 6090
17:11 heap in the day of grief and of desperate **s**. 3511
29: 2 and there shall be heaviness and **s**: 592
35:10 gladness, and **s** and sighing shall flee away. 3015
50:11 have of mine hand; ye shall lie down in **s**. 4620
51:11 joy; *and* **s** and mourning shall flee away. 3015
65:14 ye shall cry for **s** of heart, and shall howl 3511
Jer 8:18 *When* I would comfort myself against **s**, 3015
20:18 I forth out of the womb to see labour and **s**, 3015
30:15 thy **s** *is* incurable for the multitude of thine 4341
31:12 and they shall not **s** any more at all. 1669
31:13 and make them rejoice from their **s**. 3015
45: 3 for the LORD hath added grief to my **s**; 4341
49:23 *there is* **s** on the sea; it cannot be quiet. 1674
51:29 the land shall tremble and **s**: for every 2342
La 1:12 see if there be any **s** like unto my sorrow, 4341
1:12 see if there be any sorrow like unto my **s**, 4341
1:18 I pray you, all people, and behold my **s**: 4341
3:65 Give them **s** of heart, thy curse unto them. 4044
Eze 23:33 shalt be filled *with* drunkenness and **s**, 3015
Hos 8:10 they shall **s** a little for the burden of 2490
Lk 22:45 his disciples, he found them sleeping for **s**, *3077*
Jn 16: 6 *things* unto you, **s** hath filled your heart. *3077*
16:20 but your **s** shall be turned into joy. *3077*
16:21 A woman when she is in travail hath **s**, *3077*
16:22 And ye now therefore have **s**: but I will see *3077*
Ro 9: 2 great heaviness and continual **s** in my heart. *3601*
2Co 2: 3 I should have **s** from *them of* whom I ought *3077*
2: 7 should be swallowed up with overmuch **s**. *3077*
7:10 For godly **s** worketh repentance to salvation *3077*
7:10 but the **s** of the world worketh death. *3077*
Php 2:27 me also, lest I should have **s** upon sorrow. *3077*
2:27 me also, lest I should have sorrow upon **s**. *3077*
1Th 4:13 them which are asleep, that ye **s** not, *3076*
Rev 18: 7 so much torment and **s** give her: *3997*
18: 7 and am no widow, and shall see no **s**. *3997*
21: 4 be no more death, neither **s**, nor crying, *3997*

SORROWED (2) [SORROW]
2Co 7: 9 made sorry, but that ye **s** to repentance: *3076*
7:11 For behold this selfsame *thing,* that ye **s** *3076*

SORROWETH (1) [SORROW]
1Sa 10: 2 **s** for you, saying, What shall I do for my 1672

SORROWFUL (18) [SORROW]
1Sa 1:15 No, my lord, I *am* a woman of a **s** spirit: 7186
Job 6: 7 my soul refused to touch *are* as my **s** meat. 1741
Ps 69:29 I *am* poor and **s**: let thy salvation, O God, 3510
Pr 14:13 Even in laughter the heart is **s**; and the end 3510
Jer 31:25 and I have replenished every **s** soul. 1669
Zep 3:18 I will gather *them that are* **s** for the solemn 3013
Zec 9: 5 Gaza also *shall see it,* and be very **s**, and 2342
Mt 19:22 man heard *that* saying, he went away **s**: *3076*
26:22 And they were exceeding **s**, and *3076*
26:37 and began to be **s** and very heavy. *3076*
26:38 My soul is **exceeding s**, *even* unto death: *4036*
Mk 14:19 And they began to be **s**, and to say unto him *3076*
14:34 My soul is **exceeding s** unto death: *4036*
Lk 18:23 And when he heard this, he was **very s**: *4036*
18:24 And when Jesus saw that he was **very s**, *4036*
Jn 16:20 and ye shall be **s**, but your sorrow shall be *3076*
2Co 6:10 As **s**, yet alway rejoicing; as poor, *3076*
Php 2:28 ye may rejoice, and *that* I may be the **less s**. *253*

SORROWING (2) [SORROW]
Lk 2:48 behold, thy father and I have sought thee **s**. *3600*
Ac 20:38 **S** most *of all* for the words which he spake, *3600*

SORROWS (22) [SORROW]
Ex 3: 7 of their taskmasters; for I know their **s**; 4341
2Sa 22: 6 The **s** of hell compassed me about; 2256
Job 9:28 I am afraid of all my **s**, I know that thou 6094
21:17 upon them! *God* distributeth **s** in his anger. 2256
39: 3 forth their young ones, they cast out their **s**. 2256
Ps 16: 4 Their **s** shall be multiplied *that* hasten *after* 6094
18: 4 The **s** of death compassed me, and 2256
18: 5 The **s** of hell compassed me about: 2256
32:10 Many **s** *shall be* to the wicked: but he that 4341
116: 3 The **s** of death compassed me, and the pains 2256
127: 2 up early, to sit up late, to eat the bread of **s**: 6089
Ecc 2:23 For all his days *are* **s**, and his travail grief; 4341
Isa 13: 8 **s** shall take hold of *them;* they shall be in 2256
53: 3 a man of **s**, and acquainted with grief: 4341
53: 4 he hath borne our griefs, and carried our **s**: 4341
Jer 13:21 shall not **s** take thee, as a woman in travail? 2256
49:24 and **s** have taken her as a woman in travail. 2256
Da 10:16 by the vision my **s** are turned upon me, and 6735
Hos 13:13 The **s** of a travailing *woman* shall come 2256
Mt 24: 8 All these *are* the beginning of **s**. *5604*
Mk 13: 8 and troubles: these *are* the beginnings of **s**. *5604*
1Ti 6:10 pierced themselves through with many **s**. *3601*

SORRY (14) [SORROW]
1Sa 22: 8 *there is* none of you that is **s** for me, or 2470

S

Ne 8:10 neither be ye s; for the joy of the LORD *is* 6087
Ps 38:18 mine iniquity; I will be s for my sin. 1672
Isa 51:19 are come unto thee; who shall be s for thee? 5110
Mt 14: 9 And the king was s: nevertheless for *3076*
17:23 be raised *again.* And they were exceeding s. *3076*
18:31 they were very s, and came and told unto *3076*
Mk 6:26 And the king was **exceeding s**; *yet* for his *4036*
2Co 2: 2 For if I **make** you s, who is he then *3076*
2: 2 but *the same* which is **made** s by me? *3076*
7: 8 For though I **made** you s with a letter, I do *3076*
7: 8 that the same epistle hath **made** you s, *3076*
7: 9 not that ye were **made** s, but that ye *3076*
7: 9 for ye were **made** s after a godly manner, *3076*

SORT (21) [SORTS]
Ge 6:19 two of every *s* shalt thou bring into the ark, NIH
6:20 two of every *s* shall come unto thee, to keep NIH
7:14 fowl after his kind, every bird of every s. 3671
2Ki 24:14 save the **poorest** s of the people of the land. 1803
1Ch 24: 5 they divided by lot, one *s* with another; NIH
29:14 willingly after this *s*? for all *things come* of NIH
2Ch 30: 5 *it* of a long *time in such s* as it was written. NIH
Ezr 1:10 silver basons of a **second** s four hundred 4932
4: 8 Jerusalem to Artaxerxes the king **in this** s: 3660
Ne 6: 4 they sent unto me four times after this s; 1697
Eze 23:42 with the men of the common s *were* brought 120
39: 4 thee unto the ravenous birds of every s, 3671
44:30 of every *s* of your oblations, shall be NIH
Da 1:10 than the children which *are* of your s? 1524
3:29 no other God that can deliver **after** this s. 3509.4
Ac 17: 5 unto *them* certain lewd fellows of the **baser** s, *60*
Ro 15:15 written the more boldly unto you in some s, *3313*
1Co 3:13 shall try every man's work **of what** s it is. *3697*
2Co 7:11 *thing,* that ye sorrowed **after a** godly s, *2596*
2Ti 3: 6 For of this s are they which creep into NIG
3Jn 1: 6 forward on their journey **after a** godly s, *516*

SORTS (7) [SORT]
Dt 22:11 Thou shalt not wear a **garment of divers** s, 8162
Ne 5:18 and once in ten days store of all *s of* wine: NIH
Ps 78:45 He sent **divers** s *of flies* among them, 6157
105:31 there came **divers** s *of flies, and* lice in all 6157
Ecc 2: 8 **musical instruments**, and that **of all s.** 7705+7705
Eze 27:24 *were* thy merchants in **all s of things,** 4360
38: 4 all of them clothed with **all** s *of armour,* 4358

SOSIPATER (1)
Ro 16:21 and Lucius, and Jason, and **S**, my kinsmen, *4989*

SOSTHENES (2)
Ac 18:17 Then all the Greeks took **S**, the *chief* ruler *4988*
1Co 1: 1 through the will of God, and **S** *our* brother, *4988*

SOTAI (2)
Ezr 2:55 the children of **S**, the children of Sophereth, 5479
Ne 7:57 the children of **S**, the children of Sophereth, 5479

SOTTISH (1)
Jer 4:22 they *are* s children, and they have none 5530

SOUGHT (126) [SEEK]
Ge 43:30 he s *where* to weep; and he entered into *his* 1245
Ex 2:15 heard this thing, he s to slay Moses. 1245
4:19 for all the men are dead which s thy life. 1245
4:24 that the LORD met him, and s to kill him. 1245
33: 7 *that* every one which s the LORD went 1245
Lev 10:16 Moses **diligently** s the goat of the sin 1875+1875
Nu 35:23 and *was* not his enemy, neither s his harm: 1245
Dt 13:10 he hath s to thrust thee away from 1245
Jos 2:22 the pursuers s *them* throughout all the way, 1245
Jdg 14: 4 that he s an occasion against the Philistines: 1245
18: 1 in those days the tribe of the Danites s them 1245
1Sa 10:21 when they s him, he could not be found. 1245
13:14 the LORD hath s him a man after his own 1245
14: 4 *by* which Jonathan s to go over unto 1245
19:10 Saul s to smite David even to the wall with 1245
23:14 Saul s him every day, but God delivered 1245
27: 4 *to* Gath: and he s no more again for him. 1245
2Sa 3:17 Ye s **for** David in times past to be king 1245
4: 8 son of Saul thine enemy, which s thy life; 1245
17:20 when they had s and could not find *them,* 1245
21: 2 Saul s to slay them in his zeal to 1245
1Ki 1: 2 Let there be s for my lord the king a young 1245
1: 3 So they s **for** a fair damsel throughout all 1245
10:24 all the earth s to Solomon, to hear his 1245
11:40 Solomon s therefore to kill Jeroboam. 1245
2Ki 2:17 and they s three days, but found him not. 1245
1Ch 15:13 for that we s him not after the due order. 1875
26:31 year of the reign of David they were **s for,** 1875
2Ch 1: 5 Solomon and the congregation s *unto* it. 1875
9:23 all the kings of the earth s the presence of 1245
14: 7 because we have s the LORD our God, 1875
14: 7 we have s *him,* and he hath given us rest on 1875
15: 4 of Israel, and s him, he was found of them. 1245
15:15 and s him with their whole desire; 1245
16:12 yet in his disease he s not *to* the LORD, 1875
17: 3 of his father David, and s not unto Baalim; 1875
17: 4 s to the *LORD* God of his father, and 1875
22: 9 he s Ahaziah: and they caught him, (for he 1245
22: 9 who s the LORD with all his heart. 1875
25:15 Why hast thou s **after** the gods of 1875
25:20 because they s **after** the gods of Edom. 1875
26: 5 he s God in the days of Zechariah, who had 1875
26: 5 as long as he s the LORD, God made him 1875
Ezr 2:62 These s their register *among* those that 1245
Ne 7:64 These s their register *among* those that 1245
12:27 they s the Levites out of all their places, 1245
Est 2: 2 Let there be fair young virgins s for 1245
2:21 and s to lay hand on the king Ahasuerus. 1245
3: 6 wherefore Haman s to destroy all the Jews 1245
6: 2 who s to lay hand on the king Ahasuerus. 1245
9: 2 to lay hand on such as s their hurt: 1245
Ps 34: 4 I s the LORD, and he heard me, and 1875
37:36 yea, I s him, but he could not be found. 1245
77: 2 In the day of my trouble I s the Lord: 1875
78:34 When he slew them, then they s him: and 1875
86:14 the assemblies of violent *men* have **s after** 1245
111: 2 **s out** of all them that have pleasure therein. 1875
119:10 With my whole heart have I s thee: O let 1875
119:94 save me; for I have s thy precepts. 1875
Ecc 2: 3 I s in mine heart to give myself unto wine, 8446
7:29 but they have s **out** many inventions. 1245
12: 9 and **s out,** *and* set in order many proverbs. 2713
12:10 The Preacher s to find out acceptable 1245
SS 3: 1 By night on my bed I s *him* whom my soul 1245
3: 1 soul loveth: I s him, but I found him not. 1245
3: 2 soul loveth: I s him, but I found him not. 1245
5: 6 I s him, but I could not find him; I called 1245
Isa 62:12 shalt be called, **S out**, A city not forsaken. 1875
65: 1 I am s of *them that* asked not *for me:* I am 1875
65: 1 *for me:* I am found of *them that* s me not: 1245
65:10 lie down in, for my people that have s me. 1875
Jer 8: 2 whom they have s, and whom they have 1875
10:21 and have not s the LORD: 1875
26:21 his words, the king s to put him to death: 1245
44:30 of Babylon, his enemy, and that s his life. 1245
50:20 the iniquity of Israel shall be **s for**, and 1245
La 1:19 while they s their meat, to relieve their 1245
Eze 22:30 I s **for** a man among them, that *should* 1245
26:21 *shalt be* no *more:* though thou be **s for,** 1245
34: 4 neither have ye s that which was lost; 1245
Da 2:13 they s Daniel and his fellows to be slain. 1156
4:36 my counsellers and my lords s unto me; 1156
6: 4 princes s to find occasion against Daniel 1156
8:15 and s **for** the meaning, then behold, 1245
Ob 1: 6 searched out! *how* are his hid things **s up**! 1158
Zep 1: 6 *those* that have not s the LORD, nor 1245
Zec 6: 7 s to go that *they* might walk to and 1245
Mt 2:20 for they are dead which s the young child's *2212*
21:46 But when they s to lay hands on him, *2212*
26:16 And from that time he s opportunity to *2212*
26:59 the council, s false witness against Jesus, *2212*
Mk 11:18 heard *it,* and s how they might destroy him: *2212*
12:12 And they s to lay hold on him, but *2212*
14: 1 the scribes s how they might take him by *2212*
14:11 And he s how he might conveniently betray *2212*
14:55 all the council s **for** witness against Jesus to *2212*
Lk 2:44 and they s him among *their* kinsfolk and *327*
2:48 thy father and I have s thee sorrowing. *2212*
2:49 he said unto them, How *is it* that ye s me? *2212*
4:42 and the people s him, and came unto him, *2212*
5:18 and they s *means* to bring him in, and to lay *2212*
6:19 And the whole multitude s to touch him: *2212*
11:16 tempting *him,* s of him a sign from heaven. *2212*
13: 6 and he came and s fruit thereon, *2212*
19: 3 And he s to see Jesus who he was; and *2212*
19:47 and the chief of the people s to destroy him, *2212*
20:19 the scribes the same hour s to lay hands on *2212*

S

Lk 22: 2 and scribes s how they might kill him; *2212*
22: 6 s opportunity to betray him unto them in *2212*
Jn 5:16 and s to slay him, because he had done *2212*
5:18 Therefore the Jews s the more to kill him, *2212*
7: 1 in Jewry, because the Jews s to kill him. *2212*
7:11 Then the Jews s him at the feast, and said, *2212*
7:30 Then they s to take him: but no *man* laid *2212*
10:39 Therefore they s again to take him: but *2212*
11: 8 Master, the Jews of late s to stone thee; *2212*
11:56 Then s they **for** Jesus, and spake among *2212*
19:12 *And* from thenceforth Pilate s to release *2212*
Ac 12:19 And when Herod had s **for** him, and *1934*
17: 5 and s to bring them out to the people. *2212*
Ro 9:32 Because *they* s *it* not by faith, but as *it were* NIG
10:20 saith, I was found of them that s me not; *2212*
1Th 2: 6 Nor of men s we glory, neither of you, *2212*
2Ti 1:17 was in Rome, he s me **out** very diligently, *2212*
Heb 8: 7 should no place have been s **for** the second. *2212*
12:17 though he s it **carefully** with tears. *1567*

SOUL (458) [SOUL'S, SOULS]

Ge 2: 7 breath of life; and man became a living s. 5315
12:13 and my s shall live because of thee. 5315
17:14 that s shall be cut off from his people; 5315
19:20 (*is* it not a little one?) and my s shall live. 5315
27: 4 that my s may bless thee before I die. 5315
27:19 eat of my venison, that thy s may bless me. 5315
27:25 my son's venison, that my s may bless thee. 5315
27:31 his son's venison, that thy s may bless me. 5315
34: 3 his s clave unto Dinah the daughter of 5315
34: 8 The s of my son Shechem longeth for your 5315
35:18 as her s was in departing (for she died) 5315
42:21 in that we saw the anguish of his s, when he 5315
49: 6 O my s, come not thou into their secret; 5315
Ex 12:15 that s shall be cut off from Israel. 5315
12:19 even that s shall be cut off from 5315
30:12 man a ransom for his s unto the LORD, 5315
31:14 that s shall be cut off from amongst his 5315
Lev 4: 2 If a s shall sin through ignorance against 5315
5: 1 if a s sin, and hear the voice of swearing, 5315
5: 2 Or if a s touch any unclean thing, 5315
5: 4 Or if a s swear, pronouncing with *his* lips to 5315
5:15 If a s commit a trespass, and sin through 5315
5:17 if a s sin, and commit any *of these things* 5315
6: 2 If a s sin, and commit a trespass against 5315
7:18 the s that eateth of it shall bear his iniquity. 5315
7:20 the s that eateth *of* the flesh of the sacrifice 5315
7:20 even that s shall be cut off from his people. 5315
7:21 Moreover the s that shall touch any unclean 5315
7:21 even that s shall be cut off from his people. 5315
7:25 even the s that eateth *it* shall be cut off 5315
7:27 Whatsoever s *it be* that eateth any *manner* 5315
7:27 even that s shall be cut off from his people. 5315
17:10 I will even set my face against *that* s that 5315
17:11 blood *that* maketh an atonement for the s. 5315
17:12 of Israel, No s of you shall eat blood, 5315
17:15 every s that eateth that which died of itself, 5315
19: 8 that s shall be cut off from among his 5315
20: 6 the s that turneth after such as have familiar 5315
20: 6 I will even set my face against that s, and 5315
22: 3 that s shall be cut off from my presence: 5315
22: 6 The s which hath touched *any* such shall be 5315
22:11 if the priest buy *any* s with his money, 5315
23:29 For whatsoever s *it be* that shall not be 5315
23:30 whatsoever s *it be* that doeth any work in 5315
23:30 the same s will I destroy from among his 5315
26:11 amongst you: and my s shall not abhor you. 5315
26:15 or if your s abhor my judgments, so that *ye* 5315
26:30 of your idols, and my s shall abhor you. 5315
26:43 and because their s abhorred my statutes. 5315
Nu 9:13 even the same s shall be cut off from 5315
11: 6 now our s *is* dried away: *there is* nothing at 5315
15:27 if any s sin through ignorance, then he shall 5315
15:28 the priest shall make an atonement for the s 5315
15:30 the s that doeth *ought* presumptuously, 5315
15:30 that s shall be cut off from among his 5315
15:31 that s shall utterly be cut off; 5315
19:13 and that s shall be cut off from Israel: 5315
19:20 that s shall be cut off from among 5315
19:22 the s that toucheth *it* shall be unclean until 5315
21: 4 the s of the people was much discouraged 5315
21: 5 and our s loatheth *this* light bread. 5315
30: 2 or swear an oath to bind his s with a bond; 5315
30: 4 her bond wherewith she hath bound her s, 5315
30: 4 every bond wherewith she hath bound her s 5315
30: 5 her bonds wherewith she hath bound her s, 5315
30: 6 out of her lips, wherewith she bound her s; 5315
30: 7 her bonds wherewith she bound her s shall 5315
30: 8 wherewith she bound her s, of none effect: 5315
30:10 or bound her s by a bond with an oath; 5315
30:11 every bond wherewith she bound her s shall 5315
30:12 or concerning the bond of her s, shall not 5315
30:13 and every binding oath to afflict the s, 5315
31:28 one s of five hundred, *both* of the persons, 5315
Dt 4: 9 heed to thyself, and keep thy s diligently, 5315
4:29 him with all thy heart and with all thy s. 5315
6: 5 and with all thy s, and with all thy might. 5315
10:12 God with all thy heart and with all thy s, 5315
11:13 him with all your heart and with all your s, 5315
11:18 these my words in your heart and in your s, 5315
12:15 all thy gates, whatsoever thy s lusteth after, 5315
12:20 eat flesh, because thy s longeth to eat flesh; 5315
12:20 eat flesh, whatsoever thy s lusteth after. 5315
12:21 thou shalt eat in thy gates whatsoever thy s 5315
13: 3 God with all your heart and with all your s. 5315
13: 6 or thy friend, which *is* as thine own s, 5315
14:26 money for whatsoever thy s lusteth after, 5315
14:26 or for whatsoever thy s desireth: 5315
26:16 them with all thine heart, and with all thy s. 5315
30: 2 with all thine heart and with all thy s; 5315
30: 6 and with all thy s, that thou mayest live. 5315
30:10 God with all thine heart, and with all thy s. 5315
Jos 22: 5 him with all your heart and with all your s. 5315
Jdg 5:21 O my s, thou hast trodden down strength. 5315
10:16 his s was grieved for the misery of Israel. 5315
16:16 *so* that his s was vexed unto death; 5315
1Sa 1:10 she *was* in bitterness of s, and prayed unto 5315
1:15 have poured out my s before the LORD. 5315
1:26 O my lord, *as* thy s liveth, my lord, 5315
2:16 *then* take *as much* as thy s desireth; 5315
17:55 *As* thy s liveth, O king, I cannot tell. 5315
18: 1 that the s of Jonathan was knit with the soul 5315
18: 1 that the soul of Jonathan was knit with the s 5315
18: 1 and Jonathan loved him as his own s. 5315
18: 3 because he loved him as his own s. 5315
20: 3 *as* thy s liveth, *there is* but a step between 5315
20: 4 Whatsoever thy s desireth, I will even do *it* 5315
20:17 for he loved him as he loved his own s. 5315
23:20 to all the desire of thy s to come down; 5315
24:11 yet thou huntest my s to take it. 5315
25:26 *as* the LORD liveth, and *as* thy s liveth, 5315
25:29 is risen to pursue thee, and to seek thy s: 5315
25:29 the s of my lord shall be bound in 5315
26:21 my s was precious in thine eyes this day: 5315
30: 6 because the s of all the people was grieved, 5315
2Sa 4: 9 who hath redeemed my s out of all 5315
5: 8 and the blind, *that are* hated of David's s, 5315
11:11 *as* thou livest, and *as* thy s liveth, I will not 5315
13:39 *the s of* king David longed to go forth unto NIH
14:19 woman answered and said, *As* thy s liveth, 5315
1Ki 1:29 that hath redeemed my s out of all distress, 5315
2: 4 truth with all their heart and with all their s, 5315
8:48 with all their s, in the land of their enemies, 5315
11:37 thou shalt reign according to all that thy s 5315
17:21 let this child's s come into him again. 5315
17:22 the s of the child came into him again, and 5315
2Ki 2: 2 and *as* thy s liveth, I will not leave thee. 5315
2: 4 and *as* thy s liveth, I will not leave thee. 5315
2: 6 and *as* thy s liveth, I will not leave thee. 5315
4:27 Let her alone; for her s *is* vexed within her: 5315
4:30 and *as* thy s liveth, I will not leave thee. 5315
23: 3 statutes with all *their* heart and all *their* s, 5315
23:25 with all his s, and with all his might, 5315
1Ch 22:19 and your s to seek the LORD your God; 5315
2Ch 6:38 with all their s in the land of their captivity, 5315
15:12 with all their heart and with all their s; 5315
34:31 with all his heart, and with all his s, 5315
Job 3:20 is in misery, and life unto the bitter in s; 5315
6: 7 The things *that* my s refused to touch *are* as 5315
7:11 I will complain in the bitterness of my s. 5315
7:15 So that my s chooseth strangling, *and* 5315
9:21 I *were* perfect, *yet* would I not know my s: 5315
10: 1 My s is weary of my life; I will leave my 5315
10: 1 I will speak in the bitterness of my s. 5315
12:10 In whose hand *is* the s of every living *thing*, 5315
14:22 and his s within him shall mourn. 5315
16: 4 I also could speak as ye *do*: if your s were 5315
19: 2 How long will ye vex my s, and break me 5315

Job 21:25 another dieth in the bitterness of his **s**, and 5315
23:13 and *what* his **s** desireth, even *that* he doeth. 5315
24:12 and the **s** of the wounded crieth out: 5315
27: 2 and the Almighty, *who* hath vexed my **s**; 5315
27: 8 hath gained, when God taketh away his **s**? 5315
30:15 they pursue my **s** as the wind: and 5082
30:16 now my **s** is poured out upon me; the days 5315
30:25 was *not* my **s** grieved for the poor? 5315
31:30 mouth to sin by wishing a curse to his **s**.) 5315
33:18 He keepeth back his **s** from the pit, and 5315
33:20 life abhorreth bread, and his **s** dainty meat. 5315
33:22 his **s** draweth near unto the grave, and 5315
33:28 He will deliver his **s** from going into 5315
33:30 To bring back his **s** from the pit, to be 5315
Ps 3: 2 Many *there be* which say of my **s**, *There is* 5315
6: 3 My **s** is also sore vexed: but thou, 5315
6: 4 Return, O LORD, deliver my **s**: O save 5315
7: 2 Lest he tear my **s** like a lion, rending *it* in 5315
7: 5 Let the enemy persecute my **s**, and take *it;* 5315
11: 1 how say ye to my **s**, Flee *as* a bird *to* your 5315
11: 5 and him that loveth violence his **s** hateth. 5315
13: 2 How long shall I take counsel in my **s**, 5315
16: 2 *O my s*, thou hast said unto the LORD, NIH
16:10 For thou wilt not leave my **s** in hell; 5315
17:13 deliver my **s** from the wicked, *which is* thy 5315
19: 7 of the LORD *is* perfect, converting the **s**: 5315
22:20 Deliver my **s** from the sword; my darling 5315
22:29 and none can keep alive his own **s**. 5315
23: 3 He restoreth my **s**: he leadeth me in 5315
24: 4 who hath not lift up his **s** unto vanity, 5315
25: 1 Unto thee, O LORD, do I lift up my **s**. 5315
25:13 His **s** shall dwell at ease; and his seed shall 5315
25:20 O keep my **s**, and deliver me: let me not be 5315
26: 9 Gather not my **s** with sinners, nor my life 5315
30: 3 thou hast brought up my **s** from the grave: 5315
31: 7 thou hast known my **s** in adversities; 5315
31: 9 with grief, *yea,* my **s** and my belly. 5315
33:19 To deliver their **s** from death, and to keep 5315
33:20 Our **s** waiteth for the LORD: he *is* our 5315
34: 2 My **s** shall make her boast in the LORD: 5315
34:22 The LORD redeemeth the **s** of his 5315
35: 3 say unto my **s**, I *am* thy salvation. 5315
35: 4 and put to shame that seek after my **s**: 5315
35: 7 without cause they have digged for my **s**. 5315
35: 9 my **s** shall be joyful in the LORD: it shall 5315
35:12 me evil for good *to* the spoiling of my **s**. 5315
35:13 I humbled my **s** with fasting; and my prayer 5315
35:17 rescue my **s** from their destructions, 5315
40:14 confounded together that seek after my **s** to 5315
41: 4 heal my **s**; for I have sinned against thee. 5315
42: 1 so panteth my **s** after thee, O God. 5315
42: 2 My **s** thirsteth for God, for the living God: 5315
42: 4 these *things,* I pour out my **s** in me: 5315
42: 5 Why art thou cast down, O my **s**? and 5315
42: 6 O my God, my **s** is cast down within me: 5315
42:11 Why art thou cast down, O my **s**? and 5315
43: 5 Why art thou cast down, O my **s**? and 5315
44:25 For our **s** is bowed down to the dust: 5315
49: 8 (For the redemption of their **s** is precious, 5315
49:15 God will redeem my **s** from the power of 5315
49:18 Though whiles he lived he blessed his **s**: 5315
54: 3 against me, and oppressors seek after my **s**: 5315
54: 4 the Lord *is* with them that uphold my **s**. 5315
55:18 He hath delivered my **s** in peace from 5315
56: 6 mark my steps, when they wait for my **s**. 5315
56:13 For thou hast delivered my **s** from death: 5315
57: 1 for my **s** trusteth in thee: yea, in the shadow 5315
57: 4 My **s** *is* among lions: *and* I lie *even among* 5315
57: 6 a net for my steps; my **s** is bowed down: 5315
59: 3 For lo, they lie in wait for my **s**: the mighty 5315
62: 1 Truly my **s** waiteth upon God: from him 5315
62: 5 My **s**, wait thou only upon God; for my 5315
63: 1 my **s** thirsteth for thee, my flesh longeth for 5315
63: 5 My **s** shall be satisfied as *with* marrow and 5315
63: 8 My **s** followeth hard after thee: thy right 5315
63: 9 those *that* seek my **s**, to destroy *it,* shall go 5315
66: 9 Which holdeth our **s** in life, and 5315
66:16 I will declare what he hath done for my **s**. 5315
69: 1 for the waters are come in unto *my* **s**. 5315
69:10 I wept, *and chastened* my **s** with fasting, 5315
69:18 Draw nigh unto my **s**, *and* redeem it: 5315
70: 2 and confounded that seek after my **s**: 5315
71:10 they that lay wait for my **s** take counsel 5315
71:13 *and* consumed that are adversaries to my **s**; 5315
71:23 and my **s**, which thou hast redeemed. 5315
72:14 He shall redeem their **s** from deceit and 5315
74:19 O deliver not the **s** of thy turtledove unto 5315
77: 2 ceased not: my **s** refused to be comforted. 5315
78:50 he spared not their **s** from death, but 5315
84: 2 My **s** longeth, yea, even fainteth for 5315
86: 2 Preserve my **s**; for I *am* holy: O thou my 5315
86: 4 Rejoice the **s** of thy servant: for unto thee, 5315
86: 4 for unto thee, O Lord, do I lift up my **s**. 5315
86:13 thou hast delivered my **s** from the lowest 5315
86:14 of violent *men* have sought after my **s**; 5315
88: 3 For my **s** is full of troubles: and my life 5315
88:14 LORD, why castest thou off my **s**? 5315
89:48 shall he deliver his **s** from the hand of 5315
94:17 my help, my **s** had almost dwelt *in* silence. 5315
94:19 within me thy comforts delight my **s**. 5315
94:21 together against the **s** of the righteous, 5315
103: 1 Bless the LORD, O my **s**: and all that is 5315
103: 2 O my **s**, and forget not all his benefits: 5315
103:22 of his dominion: bless the LORD, O my **s**. 5315
104: 1 Bless the LORD, O my **s**. O LORD my 5315
104:35 Bless thou the LORD, O my **s**. Praise ye 5315
106:15 their request; but sent leanness into their **s**. 5315
107: 5 Hungry and thirsty, their **s** fainted in them. 5315
107: 9 For he satisfieth the longing **s**, and 5315
107: 9 and filleth the hungry **s** *with* goodness. 5315
107:18 Their **s** abhorreth all *manner of* meat; and 5315
107:26 their **s** is melted because of trouble. 5315
109:20 and of them that speak evil against my **s**. 5315
109:31 to save *him* from those that condemn his **s**. 5315
116: 4 O LORD, I beseech thee, deliver my **s**. 5315
116: 7 Return unto thy rest, O my **s**; for 5315
116: 8 For thou hast delivered my **s** from death, 5315
119:20 My **s** breaketh for the longing *that it hath* 5315
119:25 My **s** cleaveth unto the dust: quicken thou 5315
119:28 My **s** melteth for heaviness: strengthen thou 5315
119:81 My **s** fainteth for thy salvation: *but* I hope 5315
119:109 My **s** *is* continually in my hand: yet do I not 5315
119:129 therefore doth my **s** keep them. 5315
119:167 My **s** hath kept thy testimonies; and *I* love 5315
119:175 Let my **s** live, and it shall praise thee; and 5315
120: 2 Deliver my **s**, O LORD, from lying lips, 5315
120: 6 My **s** hath long dwelt with him that hateth 5315
121: 7 thee from all evil: he shall preserve thy **s**. 5315
123: 4 Our **s** is exceedingly filled *with* 5315
124: 4 the stream had gone over our **s**: 5315
124: 5 Then the proud waters had gone over our **s**. 5315
124: 7 Our **s** is escaped as a bird out of the snare 5315
130: 5 my **s** doth wait, and in his word do I hope. 5315
130: 6 My **s** *waiteth* for the Lord more than they 5315
131: 2 his mother: my **s** *is even* as a weaned child. 5315
138: 3 strengthenedst me *with* strength in my **s**. 5315
139:14 and *that* my **s** knoweth right well. 5315
141: 8 in thee is my trust; leave not my **s** destitute. 5315
142: 4 refuge failed me; no man cared for my **s**. 5315
142: 7 Bring my **s** out of prison, that *I* may praise 5315
143: 3 For the enemy hath persecuted my **s**; 5315
143: 6 my **s** *thirsteth* after thee, as a thirsty land. 5315
143: 8 I should walk; for I lift up my **s** unto thee. 5315
143:11 for thy righteousness' sake bring my **s** out 5315
143:12 and destroy all them that afflict my **s**: 5315
146: 1 ye the LORD. Praise the LORD, O my **s**. 5315
Pr 2:10 and knowledge is pleasant unto thy **s**; 5315
3:22 So shall they be life unto thy **s**, and grace to 5315
6:30 if he steal to satisfy his **s** when he is 5315
6:32 he *that* doeth it destroyeth his own **s**. 5315
8:36 that sinneth *against* me wrongeth his own **s**: 5315
10: 3 The LORD will not suffer the **s** of 5315
11:17 The merciful man doeth good to his own **s**: 5315
11:25 The liberal **s** shall be made fat: and he that 5315
13: 2 the **s** of the transgressors *shall eat* violence. 5315
13: 4 The **s** of the sluggard desireth, and 5315
13: 4 but the **s** of the diligent shall be made fat. 5315
13:19 The desire accomplished is sweet to the **s**: 5315
13:25 righteous eateth to the satisfying of his **s**: 5315
15:32 refuseth instruction despiseth his own **s**: 5315
16:17 he that keepeth his way preserveth his **s**. 5315
16:24 sweet to the **s**, and health to the bones. 5315
18: 7 and his lips *are* the snare of his **s**. 5315
19: 2 Also, *that* the **s** *be* without knowledge, *it is* 5315
19: 8 He that getteth wisdom loveth his own **s**: 5315
19:15 and an idle **s** shall suffer hunger. 5315
19:16 the commandment keepeth his own **s**; 5315
19:18 and let not thy **s** spare for his crying. 5315

S

Pr	20: 2	him to anger sinneth against his own s.	5315
	21:10	The s of the wicked desireth evil:	5315
	21:23	and his tongue keepeth his s from troubles.	5315
	22: 5	he that doth keep his s shall be far from	5315
	22:23	and spoil the s of those that spoiled them.	5315
	22:25	learn his ways, and get a snare to thy s.	5315
	23:14	the rod, and shalt deliver his s from hell.	5315
	24:12	heart consider it? and he that keepeth thy s,	5315
	24:14	the knowledge of wisdom be unto thy s:	5315
	25:13	for he refresheth the s of his masters.	5315
	25:25	As cold waters to a thirsty s, so is good	5315
	27: 7	The full s loatheth a honeycomb; but to	5315
	27: 7	to the hungry s every bitter thing is sweet.	5315
	29:10	hate the upright: but the just seek his s.	5315
	29:17	yea, he shall give delight unto thy s.	5315
	29:24	is partner with a thief hateth his own s:	5315
Ecc	2:24	that he should make his s enjoy good in his	5315
	4: 8	do I labour, and bereave my s of good?	5315
	6: 2	that he wanteth nothing for his s of all that	5315
	6: 3	his s be not filled with good, and also that	5315
	7:28	Which yet my s seeketh, but I find not:	5315
SS	1: 7	Tell me, O thou whom my s loveth,	5315
	3: 1	on my bed I sought him whom my s loveth:	5315
	3: 2	I will seek him whom my s loveth:	5315
	3: 3	to whom I said, Saw ye him whom my s	5315
	3: 4	but I found him whom my s loveth:	5315
	5: 6	my s failed when he spake: I sought him,	5315
	6:12	my s made me like the chariots of	5315
Isa	1:14	and your appointed feasts my s hateth:	5315
	3: 9	Woe unto their s! for they have rewarded	5315
	10:18	and of his fruitful field, both s and body:	5315
	26: 8	the desire of our s is to thy name, and to	5315
	26: 9	With my s have I desired thee in the night;	5315
	29: 8	but he awaketh, and his s is empty:	5315
	29: 8	behold, he is faint, and his s hath appetite:	5315
	32: 6	to make empty the s of the hungry, and	5315
	38:15	softly all my years in the bitterness of my s.	5315
	38:17	thou hast in love to my s delivered it from	5315
	42: 1	mine elect, in whom my s delighteth;	5315
	44:20	that he cannot deliver his s, nor say, Is there	5315
	51:23	which have said to thy s, Bow down,	5315
	53:10	when thou shalt make his s an offering for	5315
	53:11	He shall see of the travail of his s, and	5315
	53:12	he hath poured out his s unto death:	5315
	55: 2	and let your s delight itself in fatness.	5315
	55: 3	hear, and your s shall live; and I will make	5315
	58: 3	wherefore have we afflicted our s, and	5315
	58: 5	a day for a man to afflict his s? is it to bow	5315
	58:10	if thou draw out thy s to the hungry, and	5315
	58:10	to the hungry, and satisfy the afflicted s;	5315
	58:11	satisfy thy s in drought, and make fat thy	5315
	61:10	my s shall be joyful in my God;	5315
	66: 3	and their s delighteth in their abominations.	5315
Jer	4:10	whereas the sword reacheth unto the s).	5315
	4:19	my peace, because thou hast heard, O my s,	5315
	4:31	for my s is wearied because of murderers.	5315
	5: 9	shall not my s be avenged on such a nation	5315
	5:29	shall not my s be avenged on such a nation	5315
	6: 8	O Jerusalem, lest my s depart from thee;	5315
	9: 9	shall not my s be avenged on such a nation	5315
	12: 7	I have given the dearly beloved of my s	5315
	13:17	my s shall weep in secret places for your	5315
	14:19	hath thy s lothed Zion? why hast thou	5315
	18:20	for they have digged a pit for my s.	5315
	20:13	for he hath delivered the s of the poor from	5315
	31:12	their s shall be as a watered garden; and	5315
	31:14	I will satiate the s of the priests with	5315
	31:25	For I have satiated the weary s, and I have	5315
	31:25	and I have replenished every sorrowful s.	5315
	32:41	with my whole heart and with my whole s.	5315
	38:16	As the LORD liveth, that made us this s,	5315
	38:17	thy s shall live, and this city shall not be	5315
	38:20	shall be well unto thee, and thy s shall live.	5315
	50:19	his s shall be satisfied upon mount Ephraim	5315
	51: 6	of Babylon, and deliver every man his s:	5315
	51:45	deliver ye every man his s from the fierce	5315
La	1:11	pleasant things for meat to relieve the s:	5315
	1:16	the comforter that should relieve my s is far	5315
	2:12	when their s was poured out into their	5315
	3:17	thou hast removed my s far off from peace:	5315
	3:20	My s hath them still in remembrance, and	5315
	3:24	The LORD is my portion, saith my s;	5315
	3:25	that wait for him, to the s that seeketh him.	5315
	3:58	thou hast pleaded the causes of my s;	5315
Eze	3:19	his iniquity; but thou hast delivered thy s.	5315
	3:21	he is warned; also thou hast delivered thy s.	5315
	4:14	behold, my s hath not been polluted:	5315
	18: 4	as the s of the father, so also the soul of	5315
	18: 4	the father, so also the s of the son is mine:	5315
	18: 4	son is mine: the s that sinneth, it shall die.	5315
	18:20	The s that sinneth, it shall die. The son shall	5315
	18:27	is lawful and right, he shall save his s alive.	5315
	24:21	of your eyes, and that which your s pitieth;	5315
	33: 5	he that taketh warning shall deliver his s.	5315
	33: 9	his iniquity; but thou hast delivered thy s.	5315
Hos	9: 4	for their bread for their s shall not come	5315
Jnh	2: 5	waters compassed me about, even to the s:	5315
	2: 7	When my s fainted within me I	5315
Mic	6: 7	the fruit of my body for the sin of my s?	5315
	7: 1	to eat: my s desired the firstripe fruit.	5315
Hab	2: 4	his s which is lifted up is not upright in	5315
	2:10	many people, and hast sinned against thy s.	5315
Zec	11: 8	my s lothed them, and their soul also	5315
	11: 8	lothed them, and their s also abhorred me.	5315
Mt	10:28	kill the body, but are not able to kill the s:	5590
	10:28	fear him which is able to destroy both s	5590
	12:18	my beloved, in whom my s is well pleased:	5590
	16:26	gain the whole world, and lose his own s?	5590
	16:26	shall a man give in exchange for his s?	5590
	22:37	and with all thy s, and with all thy mind.	5590
	26:38	My s is exceeding sorrowful, even unto	5590
Mk	8:36	gain the whole world, and lose his own s?	5590
	8:37	shall a man give in exchange for his s?	5590
	12:30	and with all thy s, and with all thy mind,	5590
	12:33	and with all the s, and with all the strength,	5590
	14:34	My s is exceeding sorrowful unto death:	5590
Lk	1:46	Mary said, My s doth magnify the Lord,	5590
	2:35	a sword shall pierce through thy own s	5590
	10:27	and with all thy s, and with all thy strength,	5590
	12:19	And I will say to my s, Soul, thou hast	5590
	12:19	And I will say to my soul, S, thou hast	5590
	12:20	this night thy s shall be required of thee:	5590
Jn	12:27	Now is my s troubled; and what shall I say?	5590
Ac	2:27	Because thou wilt not leave my s in hell,	5590
	2:31	of Christ, that his s was not left in hell,	5590
	2:43	And fear came upon every s: and	5590
	3:23	And it shall come to pass, that every s,	5590
	4:32	believed were of one heart and of one s:	5590
Ro	2: 9	upon every s of man that doeth evil,	5590
	13: 1	Let every s be subject unto the higher	5590
1Co	15:45	The first man Adam was made a living s;	5590
2Co	1:23	I call God for a record upon my s,	5590
1Th	5:23	and I pray God your whole spirit and s and	5590
Heb	4:12	piercing even to the dividing asunder of s	5590
	6:19	Which hope we have as an anchor of the s,	5590
	10:38	my s shall have no pleasure in him.	5590
	10:39	of them that believe to the saving of the s.	5590
Jas	5:20	error of his way shall save a s from death,	5590
1Pe	2:11	from fleshly lusts, which war against the s;	5590
2Pe	2: 8	vexed his righteous s from day to day with	5590
3Jn	1: 2	and be in health, even as thy s prospereth.	5590
Rev	16: 3	and every living s died in the sea.	5590
	18:14	And the fruits that thy s lusted after are	5590

SOUL'S (1) [SOUL]

Job	16: 4	as ye do: if your soul were in my s stead,	5315

SOULS (78) [SOUL]

Ge	12: 5	and the s that they had gotten in Haran;	5315
	46:15	all the s of his sons and his daughters were	5315
	46:18	these she bare unto Jacob, even sixteen s.	5315
	46:22	were born to Jacob: all the s were fourteen.	5315
	46:25	bare these unto Jacob: all the s were seven.	5315
	46:26	All the s that came with Jacob into Egypt,	5315
	46:26	all the s were threescore and six;	5315
	46:27	which were born him in Egypt, were two s:	5315
	46:27	all the s of the house of Jacob, which came	5315
Ex	1: 5	all the s that came out of the loins of Jacob	5315
	1: 5	out of the loins of Jacob were seventy s:	5315
	12: 4	take it according to the number of the s;	5315
	30:15	to make an atonement for your s.	5315
	30:16	to make an atonement for your s.	5315
Lev	16:29	ye shall afflict your s, and do no work at	5315
	16:31	ye shall afflict your s, by a statute for ever.	5315
	17:11	the altar to make an atonement for your s:	5315
	18:29	even the s that commit them shall be cut off	5315
	20:25	ye shall not make your s abominable by	5315
	23:27	ye shall afflict your s, and offer an offering	5315

Lev 23:32 a sabbath of rest, and ye shall afflict your **s**: 5315
Nu 16:38 censers of these sinners against their own **s**, 5315
29: 7 and ye shall afflict your **s**: 5315
30: 9 wherewith they have bound their **s**, 5315
31:50 to make an atonement for our **s** before 5315
Jos 10:28 them, and all the **s** that *were* therein; 5315
10:30 of the sword, and all the **s** that *were* therein; 5315
10:32 of the sword, and all the **s** that *were* therein, 5315
10:35 all the **s** that *were* therein he utterly 5315
10:37 and all the **s** that *were* therein; 5315
10:37 it utterly, and all the **s** that *were* therein. 5315
10:39 utterly destroyed all the **s** that *were* therein; 5315
11:11 they smote all the **s** that *were* therein with 5315
23:14 ye know in all your hearts and in all your **s**, 5315
1Sa 25:29 the **s** of thine enemies, them shall he sling 5315
Ps 72:13 needy, and shall save the **s** of the needy. 5315
97:10 he preserveth the **s** of his saints; 5315
Pr 11:30 a tree of life; and he that winneth **s** *is* wise. 5315
14:25 A true witness delivereth **s**: but a deceitful 5315
Isa 57:16 before me, and the **s** *which* I have made. 5397
Jer 2:34 Also in thy skirts is found the blood of the **s** 5315
6:16 and ye shall find rest for your **s**. 5315
26:19 *might* we procure great evil against our **s**. 5315
44: 7 commit ye *this* great evil against your **s**, 5315
La 1:19 they sought their meat, to relieve their **s**. 5315
Eze 7:19 they shall not satisfy their **s**, neither fill 5315
13:18 upon the head of every stature to hunt **s**! 5315
13:18 Will ye hunt the **s** of my people, and will ye 5315
13:18 will ye save the **s** alive *that come* unto you? 5315
13:19 to slay the **s** that should not die, and to save 5315
13:19 and to save the **s** alive that should not live, 5315
13:20 where*with* ye there hunt the **s** to make *them* 5315
13:20 them from your arms, and will let the **s** go, 5315
13:20 *even* the **s** that ye hunt to make *them* fly. 5315
14:14 *but* their own **s** by their righteousness, 5315
14:20 deliver their own **s** by their righteousness. 5315
18: 4 Behold, all **s** *are* mine; as the soul of 5315
22:25 they have devoured **s**; they have taken 5315
22:27 to shed blood, *and* to destroy **s**, to get 5315
Mt 11:29 in heart: and ye shall find rest unto your **s**. *5590*
Lk 21:19 In your patience possess ye your **s**. *5590*
Ac 2:41 added *unto them* about three thousand **s**. *5590*
7:14 and all his kindred, threescore and fifteen **s**. *5590*
14:22 Confirming the **s** of the disciples, *and* *5590*
15:24 subverting your **s**, saying, *Ye must* be *5590*
27:37 ship two hundred threescore *and* sixteen **s**. *5590*
1Th 2: 8 but also our own **s**, because ye were dear *5590*
Heb 13:17 for they watch for your **s**, as they that must *5590*
Jas 1:21 which is able to save your **s**. *5590*
1Pe 1: 9 of your faith, *even* the salvation of *your* **s**. *5590*
1:22 Seeing ye have purified your **s** in obeying *5590*
2:25 unto the Shepherd and Bishop of your **s**. *5590*
3:20 that is, eight **s** were saved by water. *5590*
4:19 the keeping of their **s** *to him* in well doing, *5590*
2Pe 2:14 cannot cease from sin; beguiling unstable **s**: *5590*
Rev 6: 9 I saw under the altar the **s** of them that were *5590*
18:13 and chariots, and slaves, and **s** of men. *5590*
20: 4 *I saw* the **s** of them that were beheaded for *5590*

SOUND (89) [SOUNDED, SOUNDETH, SOUNDING, SOUNDNESS, SOUNDS]

Ex 28:35 his **s** shall be heard when he goeth in unto 6963
Lev 25: 9 thou **cause** the trumpet of the jubile **to s** 5674
25: 9 **make** the trumpet **s** throughout all your 5674
26:36 the **s** of a shaken leaf shall chase them; and 6963
Nu 10: 7 shall blow, but you shall not **s an alarm**. 7321
Jos 6: 5 *and* when ye hear the **s** of the trumpet, 6963
6:20 when the people heard the **s** of the trumpet, 6963
2Sa 5:24 when thou hearest the **s** of a going in 6963
6:15 and with the **s** of the trumpet. 6963
15:10 As soon as ye hear the **s** of the trumpet, 6963
1Ki 1:40 so that the earth rent with the **s** of them. 6963
1:41 when Joab heard the **s** of the trumpet, he 6963
14: 6 *so,* when Ahijah heard the **s** of her feet, 6963
18:41 drink; for *there is* a **s** of abundance of rain. 6963
2Ki 6:32 *is* not the **s** of his master's feet behind him? 6963
1Ch 14:15 when thou shalt hear a **s** of going in 6963
15:19 *were appointed* to **s** with cymbals of brass; 8085
15:28 with **s** of the cornet, and with trumpets, and 6963
16: 5 but Asaph **made a s** with cymbals; 8085
16:42 cymbals for those that should **make a s**, 8085
2Ch 5:13 to make one **s** to be heard in praising and 6963
Ne 4:20 *therefore* ye hear the **s** of the trumpet, 6963
Job 15:21 A dreadful **s** *is* in his ears: in prosperity 6963
21:12 and harp, and rejoice at the **s** of the organ. 6963
37: 2 and the **s** *that* goeth out of his mouth. 1899
39:24 neither believeth he that *it is* the **s** of 6963
Ps 47: 5 a shout, the LORD with the **s** of a trumpet. 6963
77:17 the skies sent out a **s**: thine arrows also 6963
89:15 *is* the people that know the **joyful s**: 8643
92: 3 the psaltery; upon the harp with a **solemn s**. 1902
98: 6 **s** of cornet make a joyful noise before 6963
119:80 Let my heart be **s** in thy statutes; that I be 8549
150: 3 Praise him with the **s** of the trumpet: 8629
Pr 2: 7 He layeth up **s wisdom** for the righteous: 8454
3:21 thine eyes: keep **s wisdom** and discretion: 8454
8:14 Counsel *is* mine, and **s wisdom**: I *am* 8454
14:30 A **s** heart *is* the life of the flesh: but 4832
Ecc 12: 4 when the **s** of the grinding is low, and 6963
Isa 16:11 Wherefore my bowels shall **s** like a harp for 1993
Jer 4:19 hast heard, O my soul, the **s** of the trumpet, 6963
4:21 the standard, *and* hear the **s** of the trumpet? 6963
6:17 *saying,* Hearken to the **s** of the trumpet. 6963
8:16 the whole land trembled at the **s** of 6963
25:10 the **s** of the millstones, and the light of 6963
42:14 nor hear the **s** of the trumpet, nor have 6963
48:36 Therefore mine heart shall **s** for Moab like 1993
48:36 mine heart shall **s** like pipes for the men of 1993
50:22 A **s** of battle *is* in the land, and of great 6963
51:54 A **s** of a cry *cometh* from Babylon, and 6963
Eze 10: 5 the **s** of the cherubims' wings was heard 6963
26:13 the **s** of thy harps shall be no more heard. 6963
26:15 Shall not the isles shake at the **s** of thy fall, 6963
27:28 The suburbs shall shake at the **s** of the cry 6963
31:16 I made the nations to shake at the **s** of his 6963
33: 4 whosoever heareth the **s** of the trumpet, 6963
33: 5 He heard the **s** of the trumpet, and took not 6963
Da 3: 5 *That* at what time ye hear the **s** of 7032
3: 7 when all the people heard the **s** of 7032
3:10 that every man that shall hear the **s** of 7032
3:15 that at what time ye hear the **s** of the cornet, 7032
Joel 2: 1 and **s an alarm** in my holy mountain: 7321
Am 2: 2 *and* with the **s** of the trumpet: 6963
6: 5 That chant to the **s** of the viol, *and* invent to 6310
Mt 6: 2 *thine* alms, do not **s a trumpet** before thee, *4537*
24:31 And he shall send his angels with a great **s** *5456*
Lk 15:27 because he hath received him *safe and* **s**. *5198*
Jn 3: 8 and thou hearest the **s** thereof, but canst not *5456*
Ac 2: 2 And suddenly there came a **s** from heaven *2279*
Ro 10:18 their **s** went into all the earth, and *5353*
1Co 14: 7 *And* even *things* without life giving **s**, *5456*
14: 8 For if the trumpet give an uncertain **s**, *5456*
15:52 for the **trumpet** shall **s**, and the dead shall *4537*
1Ti 1:10 other *thing that* is contrary to **s** doctrine; *5198*
2Ti 1: 7 but of power, and of love, and of a **s mind**. *4995*
1:13 Hold fast the form of **s** words, which thou *5198*
4: 3 come when they will not endure **s** doctrine; *5198*
Tit 1: 9 that he may be able by **s** doctrine both to *5198*
1:13 that they may be **s** in the faith; *5198*
2: 1 But speak thou *the things* which become **s** *5198*
2: 2 grave, temperate, **s** in faith, in charity, *5198*
2: 8 **S** speech that cannot be condemned; that he *5199*
Heb 12:19 And the **s** of a trumpet, and the voice of *2279*
Rev 1:15 and his voice as the **s** of many waters. *5456*
8: 6 seven trumpets prepared themselves to **s**. *4537*
8:13 of the three angels, which are yet to **s**. *4537*
9: 9 the **s** of their wings *was* as the sound of *5456*
9: 9 the sound of their wings *was* as the **s** of *5456*
10: 7 when he shall begin to **s**, the mystery of *4537*
18:22 the **s** of a millstone shall be heard no more *5456*

SOUNDED (18) [SOUND]

Ex 19:19 when the voice of the trumpet **s long**, and 1980
1Sa 20:12 when I have **s** my father about to morrow 2713
2Ch 7: 6 and the priests **s trumpets** before them, and 2690
13:14 and the priests **s** with the trumpets. 2690
23:13 of the land rejoiced, and **s** with trumpets, 8628
29:28 and the singers sang, and the trumpeters **s**: 2690
Ne 4:18 And he that **s** the trumpet *was* by me. 8628
Lk 1:44 as soon as the voice of thy salutation **s** in *1096*
Ac 27:28 And **s**, and found *it* twenty fathoms: and *1001*
27:28 they **s** again, and found *it* fifteen fathoms. *1001*
1Th 1: 8 For from you **s out** the word of the Lord *1837*
Rev 8: 7 The first angel **s**, and there followed hail *4537*
8: 8 And the second angel **s**, and as *it were* a *4537*
8:10 And the third angel **s**, and there fell a great *4537*
8:12 And the fourth angel **s**, and the third *part* of *4537*
9: 1 And the fifth angel **s**, and I saw a star fall *4537*

S

Rev 9:13 And the sixth angel **s**, and I heard a voice *4537*
11:15 And the seventh angel **s**; and there were *4537*

SOUNDETH (1) [SOUND]
Ex 19:13 when the trumpet **s long**, they shall come 4900

SOUNDING (7) [SOUND]
1Ch 15:16 psalteries and harps and cymbals, **s**, 8085
2Ch 5:12 and twenty priests **s** with trumpets:) 2690
13:12 his priests with **s** trumpets to cry alarm 8643
Ps 150: 5 praise him upon the **high s** cymbals. 8643
Isa 63:15 the **s** of thy bowels and of thy mercies 1995
Eze 7: 7 and not the **s again** of the mountains. 1906
1Co 13: 1 I am become *as* **s** brass, or a tinkling *2278*

SOUNDNESS (4) [SOUND]
Ps 38: 3 *There is* no **s** in my flesh because of thine 4974
38: 7 and *there is* no **s** in my flesh. 4974
Isa 1: 6 foot even unto the head *there is* no **s** in it; 4974
Ac 3:16 this **perfect s** in the presence of you all. *3647*

SOUNDS (1) [SOUND]
1Co 14: 7 harp, except they give a distinction in the **s**, *5353*

SOUR (5)
Isa 18: 5 and the **s grape** is ripening in the flower, 1155
Jer 31:29 The fathers have eaten a **s grape**, and 1155
31:30 every man that eateth the **s grape**, his teeth 1155
Eze 18: 2 The fathers have eaten **s grapes**, and 1155
Hos 4:18 Their drink is **s**; they have committed 5493

SOUTH (143) [SOUTHWARD]
Ge 12: 9 going on still toward the **s**. 5045
13: 1 all that he had, and Lot with him, into the **s**. 5045
13: 3 he went on his journeys from the **s** even to 5045
20: 1 from thence toward the **s** country, 5045
24:62 for he dwelt in the **s** country. 5045
28:14 to the east, and to the north, and to the **s**: 5045
Ex 26:18 boards on the **s** side southward. 5045+1886.5
26:35 on the side of the tabernacle toward the **s**: 8486
27: 9 for the **s** side southward *there shall be* 5045
36:23 twenty boards for the **s** side southward: 5045
38: 9 on the **s** side southward the hangings of 5045
Nu 2:10 On the **s side** *shall be* the standard of 8486
10: 6 the camps that lie on the **s side** shall take 8486
13:22 they ascended by the **s**, and came unto 5045
13:29 The Amalekites dwell in the land of the **s**: 5045
21: 1 Arad the Canaanite, which dwelt *in* the **s**, 5045
33:40 which dwelt in the **s** in the land of Canaan, 5045
34: 3 your **s** quarter shall be from the wilderness 5045
34: 3 your **s** border shall be the outmost coast of 5045
34: 4 your border shall turn from the **s** to 5045
34: 4 the going forth thereof shall be from the **s** 5045
35: 5 *on* the **s** side two thousand cubits, and 5045
Dt 1: 7 in the vale, and in the **s**, and by the sea side, 5045
33:23 possess thou the west and the **s**. 1864
34: 3 the **s**, and the plain of the valley of Jericho, 5045
Jos 10:40 of the **s**, and of the vale, and of the springs, 5045
11: 2 of the plains **s** of Cinneroth, and in 5045
11:16 all the **s** *country*, and all the land of 5045
12: 3 and from the **s**, under Ashdoth-pisgah: 8486
12: 8 in the **s** *country;* the Hittites, the Amorites, 5045
13: 4 From the **s**, all the land of the Canaanites, 8486
15: 1 *was* the uttermost part of the **s** *coast.* 8486
15: 2 their **s** border was from the shore of the salt 5045
15: 3 it went out to the **s side** to 5045
15: 3 ascended up on the **s side** unto 5045
15: 4 were at the sea: this shall be your **s** coast. 5045
15: 7 which *is* on the **s side** of the river: 5045
15: 8 unto the **s** side of the Jebusite; 4480+5045
15:19 a blessing; for thou hast given me a **s** land; 5045
18: 5 Judah shall abide in their coast on the **s**, 5045
18:13 near the hill that *lieth* on the **s side** of 5045
18:15 the **s** quarter *was* from the end of 5045+1886.5
18:16 to the side of Jebusi on the **s**, and 5045
18:19 bay of the salt sea at the **s** end of Jordan: 5045
18:19 south end of Jordan: this *was* the **s** coast. 5045
19: 8 cities to Baalath-beer, Ramath of the **s**. 5045
19:34 reacheth to Zebulun on the **s side**, and 5045
Jdg 1: 9 and in the **s**, and in the valley. 5045
1:15 for thou hast given me a **s** land; give me 5045
1:16 of Judah, which *lieth* in the **s** of Arad; 5045
21:19 to Shechem, and on the **s** of Lebonah. 5045
1Sa 20:41 David arose out of *a place* toward the **s**, and 5045
23:19 of Hachilah, which *is* on the **s** of Jeshimon? 3225
23:24 of Maon, in the plain on the **s** of Jeshimon. 3225
27:10 Against the **s** of Judah, and against 5045
27:10 against the **s** of the Jerahmeelites, and 5045
27:10 and against the **s** of the Kenites. 5045
30: 1 that the Amalekites had invaded the **s**, and 5045
30:14 We made an invasion *upon* the **s** of 5045
30:14 to Judah, and upon the **s** of Caleb; 5045
30:27 to *them* which *were* in **s** Ramoth, and 5045
2Sa 24: 7 they went out to the **s** of Judah, *even to* 5045
1Ki 7:25 three looking toward the **s**, and 5045
7:39 of the house eastward over against the **s**. 5045
1Ch 9:24 toward the east, west, north, and **s**. 5045
2Ch 4: 4 three looking toward the **s**, and 5045
4:10 of the east end, over against the **s**. 5045+1886.5
28:18 of the **s** of Judah, and had taken 5045
Job 9: 9 and Pleiades, and the chambers of the **s**. 8486
37: 9 Out of the **s** cometh the whirlwind: and 2315
37:17 when he quieteth the earth by the **s** *wind?* 1864
39:26 *and* stretch her wings toward the **s**? 8486
Ps 75: 6 the east, nor from the west, nor from the **s**. 4057
78:26 and by his power he brought in the **s wind**. 8486
89:12 The north and the **s** thou hast created them: 3225
107: 3 the west, from the north, and from the **s**. 3220
126: 4 O LORD, as the streams in the **s**. 5045
Ecc 1: 6 The wind goeth toward the **s**, and 1864
11: 3 if the tree fall toward the **s**, or toward 1864
SS 4:16 Awake, O north wind; and come thou **s**; 8486
Isa 21: 1 As whirlwinds in the **s** pass through; *so* 5045
30: 6 The burden of the beasts of the **s**: into 5045
43: 6 Give *up;* and to the **s**, Keep not back: 8486
Jer 13:19 The cities of the **s** shall be shut up, and 5045
17:26 and from the mountains, and from the **s**, 5045
32:44 of the valley, and in the cities of the **s**: 5045
33:13 in the cities of the **s**, and in the land of 5045
Eze 20:46 set thy face toward the **s**, and 8486+1886.5
20:46 drop *thy word* toward the **s**, and 1864
20:46 prophesy against the forest of the **s** field; 5045
20:47 say to the forest of the **s**, Hear the word of 5045
20:47 all faces from the **s** to the north shall be 5045
21: 4 against all flesh from the **s** *to* the north: 5045
40: 2 which *was* as the frame of a city on the **s**. 5045
40:24 After that he brought me toward the **s**, and 1864
40:24 the south, and behold a gate toward the **s**: 1864
40:27 *was* a gate in the inner court toward the **s**: 1864
40:27 he measured from gate to gate toward the **s** 1864
40:28 he brought me to the inner court by the **s** 1864
40:28 he measured the **s** gate according to these 1864
40:44 and their prospect *was* toward the **s**: 1864
40:45 whose prospect *is* toward the **s**, 1864
41:11 the north, and another door toward the **s**: 1864
42:12 the **s** *was* a door in the head of the way, 1864
42:13 The north chambers *and* the **s** chambers, 1864
42:18 He measured the **s** side, five hundred reeds, 1864
46: 9 shall go out *by* the way of the **s** gate; 5045
46: 9 he that entereth *by* the way of the **s** gate 5045
47: 1 side of the house, at the **s** *side* of the altar. 5045
47:19 the **s** side southward, from Tamar *even* to 5045
47:19 *is* the **s** side southward. 8486+1886.5+1886.5
48:10 toward the **s** five and twenty thousand *in* 5045
48:16 the **s** side four thousand and five hundred, 5045
48:17 toward the **s** two hundred and fifty, and 5045
48:28 the border of Gad, at the **s** side southward, 5045
48:33 *at* the **s** side four thousand and five hundred 5045
Da 8: 9 toward the **s**, and toward the east, and 5045
11: 5 the king of the **s** shall be strong, and *one* of 5045
11: 6 for the king's daughter of the **s** shall come 5045
11: 9 So the king of the **s** shall come into *his* 5045
11:11 the king of the **s** shall be moved with 5045
11:14 many stand up against the king of the **s**: 5045
11:15 the arms of the **s** shall not withstand, 5045
11:25 his courage against the king of the **s** with a 5045
11:25 the king of the **s** shall be stirred up to battle 5045
11:29 he shall return, and come toward the **s**; 5045
11:40 at the time of the end shall the king of the **s** 5045
Ob 1:19 *they of* the **s** shall possess the mount of 5045
1:20 shall possess the cities of the **s**. 5045
Zec 6: 6 the grisled go forth toward the **s** country. 8486
7: 7 when *men* inhabited the **s** and the plain? 5045
9:14 and shall go with whirlwinds of the **s**. 8486
14: 4 the north, and half of it toward the **s**. 5045
14:10 plain from Geba to Rimmon **s** of Jerusalem: 5045
Mt 12:42 *The* queen of the **s** shall rise up in *3558*
Lk 11:31 *The* queen of the **s** shall rise up in *3558*
12:55 And when *ye see* the **s wind** blow, ye say, *3558*

Lk 13:29 and *from* the s, and shall sit down in 3558
Ac 8:26 go toward the s unto the way that goeth 3314
27:12 and lieth toward the s **west** and north west. 3047
27:13 And when the s **wind** blew softly, 3558
28:13 and after one day the s **wind** blew, and 3558
Rev 21:13 on the s three gates; and on the west three 3558

SOUTHWARD (24) [SOUTH]
Ge 13:14 s, and eastward, and westward: 5045+1886.5
Ex 26:18 twenty boards on the south side s. 8486+1886.5
27: 9 for the south side s *there shall be* 8486+1886.5
36:23 twenty boards for the south side s: 8486+1886.5
38: 9 on the south side s the hangings of 8486+1886.5
40:24 on the side of the tabernacle s. 5045+1886.5
Nu 3:29 on the side of the tabernacle s. 8486+1886.5
13:17 Get you up this *way* s, and 5045+871.1+1886.1
Dt 3:27 s, and eastward, and behold *it* with 8486+1886.5
Jos 15: 1 the wilderness of Zin s *was* 5045+1886.5
15: 2 from the bay that looketh s: 5045+1886.5
15:21 the coast of Edom s were Kabzeel, 5045+1886.5
17: 9 *unto* the river Kanah, s of the river: 5045+1886.5
17:10 S *it was* Ephraim's, and 5045+1886.5
18:13 the side of Luz, which *is* Beth-el, s; 5045+1886.5
18:14 compassed the corner of the sea s, 5045+1886.5
18:14 hill that *lieth* before Beth-horon s; 5045+1886.5
1Sa 14: 5 and the other s over against Gibeah. 4480+5045
1Ch 26:15 To Obed-edom s; and to his sons 5045+1886.5
26:17 s four a day, and toward Asuppim 5045+1886.5
Eze 47:19 the south side s, from Tamar *even* 8486+1886.5
47:19 to the great sea. And *this is* the south side s. 5045
48:28 border of Gad, at the south side s, 8486+1886.5
Da 8: 4 and northward, and s; 5045+1886.5

SOW (37) [SEW, SOWED, SOWEDST, SOWER, SOWEST, SOWETH, SOWING, SOWN]
Ge 47:23 *here is* seed for you, and ye shall s the land. 2232
Ex 23:10 six years thou shalt s thy land, and 2232
Lev 19:19 shalt not s thy field **with** mingled **seed**: 2232
25: 3 Six years thou shalt s thy field, and 2232
25: 4 thou shalt neither s thy field, nor prune thy 2232
25:11 ye shall not s, neither reap that which 2232
25:20 behold, we shall not s, nor gather in our 2232
25:22 ye shall s the eighth year, and eat *yet* of old 2232
26:16 ye shall s your seed in vain, for your 2232
Dt 22: 9 shalt not s thy vineyard with divers **seeds**: 2232
2Ki 19:29 in the third year s ye, and reap, and 2232
Job 4: 8 and s wickedness, reap the same. 2232
31: 8 *Then* let me s, and let another eat; yea, 2232
Ps 107:37 s the fields, and plant vineyards, which may 2232
126: 5 They that s in tears shall reap in joy. 2232
Ecc 11: 4 He that observeth the wind shall not s; and 2232
11: 6 In the morning s thy seed, and in 2232
Isa 28:24 Doth the plowman plow all day to s? 2232
30:23 that thou shalt s the ground withal; 2232
32:20 Blessed *are* ye that s beside all waters, 2232
37:30 in the third year s ye, and reap, and 2232
Jer 4: 3 fallow ground, and s not among thorns. 2232
31:27 that I will s the house of Israel and 2232
35: 7 nor s seed, nor plant vineyard, nor have 2232
Hos 2:23 I will s her unto me in the earth; and I will 2232
10:12 S to yourselves in righteousness, reap in 2232
Mic 6:15 Thou shalt s, but thou shalt not reap; 2232
Zec 10: 9 I will s them among the people: and they 2232
Mt 6:26 for they s not, neither do they reap, *4687*
13: 3 saying, Behold, a sower went forth to s; *4687*
13:27 Sir, didst not thou s good seed in thy field? *4687*
Mk 4: 3 Behold, there went out a sower to s: *4687*
Lk 8: 5 A sower went out to s his seed: and as he *4687*
12:24 for they neither s nor reap; which neither *4687*
19:21 not down, and reapest that thou didst not s. *4687*
19:22 I laid not down, and reaping that I did not s: *4687*
2Pe 2:22 The s that was washed to *her* wallowing in *5300*

SOWED (10) [SOW]
Ge 26:12 Isaac s in that land, and received in 2232
Jdg 9:45 beat down the city, and s it *with* salt. 2232
Mt 13: 4 And when he s, some *seeds* fell by the way *4687*
13:24 unto a man which s good seed in his field: *4687*
13:25 enemy came and s tares among the wheat, *4687*
13:31 which a man took, and s in his field: *4687*
13:39 The enemy that s them is the devil; *4687*
25:26 thou knewest that I reap where I s not, and *4687*
Mk 4: 4 And it came to pass, as *he* s, some fell by *4687*
Lk 8: 5 and as he s, some fell by the way side; and *4687*

SOWEDST (1) [SOW]
Dt 11:10 where thou s thy seed, and wateredst *it* with 2232

SOWER (8) [SOW]
Isa 55:10 that it may give seed to the s, and bread to 2232
Jer 50:16 Cut off the s from Babylon, and him that 2232
Mt 13: 3 saying, Behold, a s went forth to sow; *4687*
13:18 Hear ye therefore the parable of the s. *4687*
Mk 4: 3 Hearken; Behold, there went out a s to sow: *4687*
4:14 The s soweth the word. *4687*
Lk 8: 5 A s went out to sow his seed: and as he *4687*
2Co 9:10 Now he that ministereth seed to the s both *4687*

SOWEST (3) [SOW]
1Co 15:36 *that* which thou s is not quickened, *4687*
15:37 And *that* which thou s, thou sowest not that *4687*
15:37 thou s not that body that shall be, but *4687*

SOWETH (15) [SOW]
Pr 6:14 deviseth mischief continually; he s discord. 7971
6:19 and he that s discord among brethren. 7971
11:18 *to* him that s righteousness *shall be* a sure 2232
16:28 A froward man s strife: and a whisperer 7971
22: 8 He that s iniquity shall reap vanity: and 2232
Am 9:13 and the treader of grapes him that s seed; 4900
Mt 13:37 He that s the good seed is the Son of man; *4687*
Mk 4:14 The sower s the word. *4687*
Jn 4:36 that both he that s and he that reapeth may *4687*
4:37 And herein is *that* saying true, One s, *4687*
2Co 9: 6 But this *I say,* He which s sparingly shall *4687*
9: 6 he which s bountifully shall reap also *4687*
Gal 6: 7 for whatsoever a man s, that shall he also *4687*
6: 8 For he that s to his flesh shall of the flesh *4687*
6: 8 he that s to the Spirit shall of the Spirit reap *4687*

SOWING (2) [SOW]
Lev 11:37 if *any part* of their carcase fall upon any s 2221
26: 5 and the vintage shall reach unto the s **time**: 2233

SOWN (32) [SOW]
Ex 23:16 thy labours, which thou hast s in the field: 2232
Lev 11:37 fall upon any sowing seed which is to be s, 2232
Dt 21: 4 which is neither eared nor s, and shall strike 2232
22: 9 lest the fruit of *thy* seed which thou hast s, 2232
29:23 salt, *and* burning, *that* it is not s, 2232
Jdg 6: 3 *so* it was, when Israel had s, that 2232
Ps 97:11 Light is s for the righteous, and 2232
Isa 19: 7 every thing s by the brooks, shall wither, 4218
40:24 not be planted; yea, they shall not be s: 2232
61:11 as the garden causeth the **things that are** s 2221
Jer 2: 2 in the wilderness, in a land *that was* not s. 2232
12:13 They have s wheat, but shall reap thorns: 2232
Eze 36: 9 turn unto you, and ye shall be tilled and s: 2232
Hos 8: 7 For they have s the wind, and they shall 2232
Na 1:14 *that* no more of thy name be s: 2232
Hag 1: 6 Ye have s much, and bring in little; *ye* eat, 2232
Mt 13:19 catcheth away that which was s in his heart. *4687*
25:24 reaping where thou hast not s, and *4687*
Mk 4:15 they by the way side, where the word is s; *4687*
4:15 taketh away the word that was s in their *4687*
4:16 And these are they likewise which are s on *4687*
4:18 And these are they which are s among *4687*
4:20 And these are they which are s on good *4687*
4:31 which, when it is s in the earth, *4687*
4:32 But when it is s, it groweth up, and *4687*
1Co 9:11 If we have s unto you spiritual *things, is it* *4687*
15:42 It is s in corruption; it is raised in *4687*
15:43 It is s in dishonour; it is raised in glory: it is *4687*
15:43 it is s in weakness; it is raised in power: *4687*
15:44 It is s a natural body; it is raised a spiritual *4687*
2Co 9:10 and multiply your **seed** s, and increase *4703*
Jas 3:18 And the fruit of righteousness is s in peace *4687*

SPACE (27)
Ge 29:14 And he abode with him the s of a month. 3117
32:16 and put a s betwixt drove and drove. 7305
Lev 25: 8 the s of the seven sabbaths of years shall be 3117
25:30 if it be not redeemed within the s of a full 4390
Dt 2:14 the s in which we came from 3117
Jos 3: 4 Yet there shall be a s between you and it, 7350
1Sa 26:13 hill afar off; a great s *being* between them: 4725
Ezr 9: 8 now for a little s grace hath been *shewed* 7281
Jer 28:11 **within the s of** two full years. 5750+871.1
Eze 40:12 The s also before the little chambers *was* 1366

S

Eze 40:12 and the **s** *was* one cubit on that side: 1366
Lk 22:59 And about the **s** of one hour **after** another *1339*
Ac 5: 7 And it was about the **s** of three hours **after**, *1292*
5:34 to put the apostles forth a **little s**; *1024*
7:42 sacrifices *by the s of* forty years in NIG
13:20 *them* judges about *the s of* four hundred NIG
13:21 tribe of Benjamin, *by the s of* forty years. NIG
15:33 And after they had **tarried** *there* **a s**, *4160+5550*
19: 8 and spake boldly **for the s of** three months, *1909*
19:10 And this continued **by the s of** two years; *1909*
19:34 all with one voice about **the s of** two hours *1909*
20:31 that *by the s of* three years I ceased not to NIG
Jas 5:17 it rained not on the earth *by the s of* three NIG
Rev 2:21 And I gave her **s** to repent of her *5550*
8: 1 there was silence in heaven about the **s** of NIG
14:20 by the **s of** a thousand *and* six hundred *575*
17:10 he cometh, he must continue a short *s*. NIG

SPAIN (2)
Ro 15:24 Whensoever I take my journey into **S**, I will *4681*
15:28 them this fruit, I will come by you into **S**. *4681*

SPAKE (588) [SPEAK] See Index

SPAKEST (10) [SPEAK] See Index

SPAN (8) [SPANNED]
Ex 28:16 a **s** *shall be* the length thereof, and a span 2239
28:16 and a **s** *shall be* the breadth thereof. 2239
39: 9 a **s** *was* the length thereof, and a span 2239
39: 9 and a **s** the breadth thereof, *being* doubled. 2239
1Sa 17: 4 whose height *was* six cubits and a **s**. 2239
Isa 40:12 meted out heaven with the **s**, and 2239
La 2:20 eat their fruit, *and* children of a **s long**? 2949
Eze 43:13 the edge thereof round about *shall be* a **s**: 2239

SPANNED (1) [SPAN]
Isa 48:13 and my right hand hath **s** the heavens: 2946

SPARE (40) [SPARED, SPARETH, SPARING, SPARINGLY]
Ge 18:24 not **s** the place for the fifty righteous that 5375
18:26 then I will **s** all the place for their sakes. 5375
Dt 13: 8 neither shalt thou **s**, neither shalt thou 2550
29:20 The LORD will not **s** him, but then 5545
1Sa 15: 3 destroy all that they have, and **s** them not; 2550
Ne 13:22 **s** me according to the greatness of 2347+5921
Job 6:10 harden myself in sorrow; let him not **s**: 2550
16:13 cleaveth my reins asunder, and doth not **s**; 2550
20:13 *Though* he **s** it, and forsake it not; but 2550
27:22 For *God* shall cast upon him, and not **s**: 2550
30:10 far from me, and **s** not to spit in my face. 2820
Ps 39:13 O **s** me, that I may recover strength, before 8159
72:13 He shall **s** the poor and needy, and 2347+5921
Pr 6:34 he will not **s** in the day of vengeance. 2550
19:18 is hope, and let not thy soul **s** for his crying. 5375
Isa 9:19 fuel of the fire: no man shall **s** his brother. 2550
13:18 of the womb; their eye shall not **s** children. 2347
30:14 that is broken in pieces; he shall not **s**: 2550
54: 2 **s** not, lengthen thy cords, and 2820
58: 1 Cry aloud, **s** not, lift up thy voice like a 2820
Jer 13:14 I will not pity, nor **s**, nor have mercy, but 2347
21: 7 he shall not **s** them, neither have pity, 2347
50:14 bend the bow, shoot at her, **s** no arrows: 2550
51: 3 **s** ye not her young men; destroy ye utterly 2550
Eze 5:11 also diminish *thee;* neither shall mine eye **s**, 2347
7: 4 mine eye shall not **s** thee, neither will I 2347
7: 9 mine eye shall not **s**, neither will I have 2347
8:18 mine eye shall not **s**, neither will I have 2347
9: 5 let not your eye **s**, neither have ye pity: 2347
9:10 *as for* me also, mine eye shall not **s**, 2347
24:14 neither will I **s**, neither will I repent; 2347
Joel 2:17 **S** thy people, O LORD, and give not thine 2347
Jnh 4:11 should not I **s** Nineveh, *that* great city, 2347
Hab 1:17 and not **s** continually to slay the nations? 2550
Mal 3:17 I will **s** them, as a man spareth his own son 2550
Lk 15:17 of my father's **have** bread **enough and to s**, *4052*
Ro 11:21 *take heed* lest he also **s** not thee. *5339*
1Co 7:28 shall have trouble in the flesh: but I **s** you. *5339*
2Co 1:23 that to **s** you I came not as yet unto Corinth. *5339*
13: 2 all other, that, if I come again, I will not **s**: *5339*

SPARED (12) [SPARE]
1Sa 15: 9 Saul and the people **s** Agag, and the best of 2550
15:15 for the people **s** the best of the sheep and 2550
24:10 *mine eye* **s** thee; and I said, I will not put 2347
2Sa 12: 4 he **s** to take of his own flock and of his own 2550
21: 7 the king **s** Mephibosheth, the son of 2550
2Ki 5:20 my master hath **s** Naaman this Syrian, 2820
Ps 78:50 he **s** not their soul from death, but 2820
Eze 20:17 Nevertheless mine eye **s** them from 2347
Ro 8:32 He that **s** not his own Son, but *5339*
11:21 For if God **s** not the natural branches, *5339*
2Pe 2: 4 For if God **s** not the angels that sinned, but *5339*
2: 5 And **s** not the old world, but saved Noah *5339*

SPARETH (4) [SPARE]
Pr 13:24 He that **s** his rod hateth his son: but he that 2820
17:27 He that hath knowledge **s** his words: *and* 2820
21:26 day long: but the righteous giveth and **s** not. 2820
Mal 3:17 as a man **s** his own son that serveth him. 2550

SPARING (1) [SPARE]
Ac 20:29 wolves enter in among you, not **s** the flock. *5339*

SPARINGLY (2) [SPARE]
2Co 9: 6 But this *I say,* He which soweth **s** shall reap *5340*
9: 6 which soweth sparingly shall reap also **s**; *5340*

SPARK (2) [SPARKS]
Job 18: 5 put out, and the **s** of his fire shall not shine. 7632
Isa 1:31 the maker of it as a **s**, and they shall both 5213

SPARKLED (1)
Eze 1: 7 they **s** like the colour of burnished brass. 5340

SPARKS (4) [SPARK]
Job 5: 7 unto trouble, as the **s** fly upward. 1121+7565
41:19 go burning lamps, *and* **s** of fire leap out. 3590
Isa 50:11 that compass *yourselves* about with **s**: 2131
50:11 your fire, and in the **s** *that* ye have kindled. 2131

SPARROW (2) [SPARROWS]
Ps 84: 3 the **s** hath found a house, and the swallow a 6833
102: 7 and am as a **s** alone upon the housetop. 6833

SPARROWS (4) [SPARROW]
Mt 10:29 Are not two **s** sold for a farthing? and *4765*
10:31 ye are of more value than many **s**. *4765*
Lk 12: 6 Are not five **s** sold for two farthings, and *4765*
12: 7 ye are of more value than many **s**. *4765*

SPAT (1) [SPIT]
Jn 9: 6 he **s** on the ground, and made clay of *4429*

SPEAK (513) [SPAKE, SPAKEST, SPEAKER, SPEAKEST, SPEAKETH, SPEAKING, SPEAKINGS, SPEECH, SPEECHES, SPEECHLESS, SPOKEN, SPOKESMAN, UNSPEAKABLE] See Index

SPEAKER (2) [SPEAK] See Index

SPEAKEST (17) [SPEAK] See Index

SPEAKETH (74) [SPEAK] See Index

SPEAKING (62) [SPEAK] See Index

SPEAKINGS (1) [SPEAK] See Index

SPEAR (45) [SPEAR'S, SPEARMEN, SPEARS]
Jos 8:18 Stretch out the **s** that *is* in thy hand toward 3591
8:18 Joshua stretched out the **s** that *he had* in his 3591
8:26 wherewith he stretched out the **s**, 3591
Jdg 5: 8 or **s** seen among forty thousand in Israel? 7420
1Sa 13:22 that there was neither sword nor **s** found in 2595
17: 7 the staff of his **s** *was* like a weaver's beam; 2595
17:45 a sword, and with a **s**, and with a shield: 2595
17:47 the LORD saveth not with sword and **s**: 2595
21: 8 is there not here under thine hand **s** or 2595
22: 6 having his **s** in his hand, and all his servants 2595
26: 7 and his **s** stuck in the ground *at* his bolster: 2595
26: 8 with the **s** even to the earth at once, and 2595
26:11 take thou now the **s** that *is at* his bolster, 2595
26:12 So David took the **s** and the cruse of water 2595
26:16 now see where the king's **s** *is,* and the cruse 2595
26:22 and said, Behold, the king's **s**; 2595
2Sa 1: 6 behold, Saul leaned upon his **s**; 2595
2:23 **s** smote him under the fifth *rib,* that 2595
2:23 fifth *rib,* that the **s** came out behind him; 2595
21:16 the weight of whose **s** *weighed* three 7013
21:19 the staff of whose **s** *was* like a weaver's 2595
23: 7 be fenced *with* iron and the staff of a **s**; 2595

2Sa 23: 8 *he lift up his* **s** against eight hundred, NIH
23:18 he lift up his **s** against three hundred, and 2595
23:21 the Egyptian had a **s** in his hand; but 2595
23:21 plucked the **s** out of the Egyptian's hand, 2595
23:21 and slew him with his own **s**. 2595
1Ch 11:11 he lift up his **s** against three hundred slain 2595
11:20 for lifting up his **s** against three hundred, 2595
11:23 in the Egyptian's hand *was* a **s** like a 2595
11:23 pluckt the **s** out of the Egyptian's hand, and 2595
11:23 and slew him with his own **s**. 2595
12:24 and **s** *were* six thousand and eight hundred, 7420
12:34 with shield and **s** thirty and seven thousand. 7420
20: 5 whose **s** staff *was* like a weaver's beam. 2595
2Ch 25: 5 forth *to* war, that could handle **s** and shield. 7420
Job 39:23 against him, the glittering **s** and the shield. 2595
41:26 the **s**, the dart, nor the habergeon. 2595
41:29 he laugheth at the shaking of a **s**. 3591
Ps 35: 3 Draw out also the **s**, and stop *the way* 2595
46: 9 the bow, and cutteth the **s** in sunder; 2595
Jer 6:23 They shall lay hold on bow and **s**; they *are* 3591
Na 3: 3 both the bright sword and the glittering **s**: 2595
Hab 3:11 *and* at the shining of thy glittering **s**. 2595
Jn 19:34 But one of the soldiers with a **s** pierced his *3057*

SPEAR'S (1) [SPEAR]

1Sa 17: 7 his **s** head *weighed* six hundred shekels *of* 2595

SPEARMEN (2) [MAN, SPEAR]

Ps 68:30 Rebuke the company of **s**, the multitude of 7070
Ac 23:23 *and* ten, and **s** two hundred, *1187*

SPEARS (16) [SPEAR]

1Sa 13:19 Lest the Hebrews make *them* swords or **s**: 2595
2Ki 11:10 hundreds did the priest give king David's **s** 2595
2Ch 11:12 in every several city *he put* shields and **s**, 7420
14: 8 had an army *of men* that bare targets and **s**, 7420
23: 9 delivered to the captains of hundreds **s**, 2595
26:14 **s**, and helmets, and habergeons, and bows, 7420
Ne 4:13 with their swords, their **s**, and their bows. 7420
4:16 the *other* half of them held both the **s**, 7420
4:21 half of them held the **s** from the rising of 7420
Job 41: 7 with barbed irons? or his head with fish **s**? 6767
Ps 57: 4 whose teeth *are* **s** and arrows, and 2595
Isa 2: 4 and their **s** into pruninghooks: 2595
Jer 46: 4 furbish the **s**, *and* put on the brigandines. 7420
Eze 39: 9 the **s**, and they shall burn them with fire 7420
Joel 3:10 into swords, and your pruninghooks into **s**: 7420
Mic 4: 3 and their **s** into pruninghooks: 2595

SPECIAL (2) [ESPECIALLY, SPECIALLY]

Dt 7: 6 chosen thee to be a **s** people unto himself, 5459
Ac 19:11 And God wrought **s** miracles *3588+3756+5177*

SPECIALLY (6) [SPECIAL]

Dt 4:10 **S** the day that thou stoodest before NIH
Ac 25:26 and **s** before thee, O king Agrippa, that, *3122*
1Ti 4:10 Saviour of all men, **s** of those that believe. *3122*
5: 8 and **s** for those of his own house, he hath *3122*
Tit 1:10 and deceivers, **s** they of the circumcision: *3122*
Phm 1:16 **s** to me, but how much more unto thee, *3122*

SPECK OF SAWDUST See MOTE

SPECKLED (11)

Ge 30:32 removing from thence all the **s** and 5348
30:32 and the spotted and **s** among the goats: 5348
30:33 every one that *is* not **s** and spotted amongst 5348
30:35 all the she goats that were **s** and spotted, 5348
30:39 forth cattle ringstraked, **s**, and spotted. 5348
31: 8 If he said thus, The **s** shall be thy wages; 5348
31: 8 be thy wages; then all the cattle bare **s**: 5348
31:10 the cattle *were* ringstraked, **s**, and grisled. 5348
31:12 the cattle *are* ringstraked, **s**, and grisled: 5348
Jer 12: 9 Mine heritage *is* unto me *as* a **s** bird, 6641
Zec 1: 8 him *were there* red horses, **s**, and white. 8320

SPECTACLE (1)

1Co 4: 9 for we are made a **s** unto the world, and *2302*

SPED (1) [SPEED]

Jdg 5:30 Have they not **s**? have they *not* divided 4672

SPEECH (49) [SPEAK]

Ge 4:23 ye wives of Lamech, hearken unto my **s**: 565
11: 1 earth was *of* one language, and *of* one **s**. 1697
11: 7 they may not understand one another's **s**. 8193
Ex 4:10 but I *am* slow of **s**, and of a slow tongue. 6310
Dt 22:14 give occasions of **s** against her, and 1697
22:17 he hath given occasions of **s** *against her,* 1697
32: 2 drop as the rain, my **s** shall distil as the dew, 565
2Sa 14:20 To fetch about *this* form of **s** hath thy 1697
19:11 seeing the **s** of all Israel is come to the king, 1697
1Ki 3:10 the **s** pleased the Lord, that Solomon had 1697
2Ch 32:18 they cried with a loud voice **in the Jews' s** 3066
Ne 13:24 their children spake half **in the s of Ashdod**, 797
Job 12:20 He removeth away the **s** of the trusty, and 8193
13:17 Hear diligently my **s**, and my declaration 4405
21: 2 Hear diligently my **s**, and let this be your 4405
24:25 me a liar, and make my **s** nothing worth? 4405
29:22 not again; and my **s** dropped upon them. 4405
37:19 *for* we cannot order *our* **s** by reason of NIH
Ps 17: 6 incline thine ear unto me, *and* hear my **s**. 565
19: 2 Day unto day uttereth **s**, and night unto night 562
19: 3 *There is* no **s** nor language, *where* their voice 562
Pr 7:21 With her much **fair s** she caused him to 3948
17: 7 Excellent **s** becometh not a fool: much less 8193
SS 4: 3 like a thread of scarlet, and thy **s** *is* comely: 4057
Isa 28:23 and hear my voice; hearken, and hear my **s**. 565
29: 4 thy **s** shall be low out of the dust, and 565
29: 4 and thy **s** shall whisper out of the dust. 565
32: 9 ye careless daughters, give ear unto my **s**. 565
33:19 a people of a deeper **s** than *thou* canst 8193
Jer 31:23 As yet they shall use this **s** in the land of 1697
Eze 1:24 the voice of **s**, as the noise of a host: 1999
3: 5 thou *art* not sent to a people of a strange **s** 8193
3: 6 Not to many people of a strange **s** and of a 8193
Hab 3: 2 I have heard thy **s**, *and* was afraid: 8088
Mt 26:73 art *one* of them; for thy **s** bewrayeth thee. *2981*
Mk 7:32 *was* deaf, and had an **impediment in** his **s**; *3424*
14:70 art a Galilean, and thy **s** agreeth *thereto.* *2981*
Jn 8:43 Why do ye not understand my **s**? *even* *2981*
Ac 14:11 their voices, saying **in the s of Lycaonia**, *3072*
20: 7 and continued *his* **s** until midnight. *3056*
1Co 2: 1 came not with excellency of **s** or *3056*
2: 4 And my **s** and my preaching *was* not with *3056*
4:19 not the **s** of them which are puffed up, but *3056*
2Co 3:12 such hope, we use great **plainness of s**: *3954*
7: 4 Great *is* my **boldness of s** toward you, *3954*
10:10 presence *is* weak, and *his* **s** contemptible. *3056*
11: 6 But though *I be* rude in **s**, yet not in *3056*
Col 4: 6 Let your **s** *be* alway with grace, *3056*
Tit 2: 8 Sound **s** that cannot be condemned; that he *3056*

SPEECHES (7) [SPEAK]

Nu 12: 8 even apparently, and not in **dark s**; 2420
Job 6:26 the **s** of one that is desperate, *which are* as 561
15: 3 or *with* **s** wherewith he can do no good? 4405
32:14 neither will I answer him with your **s**. 561
33: 1 hear my **s**, and hearken to all my words. 4405
Ro 16:18 and **fair s** deceive the hearts of the simple. *2129*
Jude 1:15 of all *their* hard **s** which ungodly sinners NIG

SPEECHLESS (3) [SPEAK]

Mt 22:12 having a wedding garment? And he was **s**. *5392*
Lk 1:22 for he beckoned unto them, and remained **s**. *2974*
Ac 9: 7 the men which journeyed with him stood **s**, *1769*

SPEED (11) [SPED, SPEEDILY, SPEEDY]

Ge 24:12 **send** me **good s** *this* day, and 6440+7136+3807.1
1Sa 20:38 cried after the lad, **Make s**, haste, stay not. 4120
2Sa 15:14 **make s** to depart, lest he overtake us 4116
1Ki 12:18 Therefore king Rehoboam **made s** to get *him* 553
2Ch 10:18 king Rehoboam **made s** to get *him* up to *his* 553
Ezr 6:12 have made a decree; let it be done **with s**. 629
Isa 5:19 Let him **make s**, *and* hasten his work, 4116
5:26 and behold, they shall come with **s** swiftly: 4120
Ac 17:15 for to come to him **with all s**, *5030+5613*
2Jn 1:10 not into *your* house, neither bid him **God s**: *5463*
1:11 For he that biddeth him **God s** is partaker *5463*

SPEEDILY (19) [SPEED]

Ge 44:11 they **s** took down every man his sack to 4116
1Sa 27: 1 **s escape** into the land of 4422+4422
2Sa 17:16 of the wilderness, but **s pass over**; 5674+5674
2Ch 35:13 and **divided** *them* **s** among all the people. 7323
Ezr 6:13 Darius the king had sent, so they did **s**. 629
7:17 That thou mayest buy **s** with this money 629
7:21 of heaven, shall require of you, *it* be done **s**, 629
7:26 let judgment be executed **s** upon him, 629

S

Est 2: 9 and he s gave her her things for purification, 926
Ps 31: 2 Bow down thine ear to me; deliver me s: 4120
69:17 thy servant; for I am in trouble: hear me s. 4118
79: 8 let thy tender mercies s prevent us: for we 4118
102: 2 in the day *when* I call answer me s. 4118
143: 7 Hear me s, O LORD: my spirit faileth: 4118
Ecc 8:11 *against* an evil work is not executed s, 4120
Isa 58: 8 and thine health shall spring forth s: 4120
Joel 3: 4 s will I return your recompence upon your 4120
Zec 8:21 Let us **go** s to pray before 1980+1980
Lk 18: 8 I tell you that he will avenge them s. *1722+5034*

SPEEDY (1) [SPEED]
Zep 1:18 for he shall make even a s riddance of all 926

SPELT See RIE

SPEND (7) [SPENDEST, SPENDETH, SPENT]
Dt 32:23 upon them; I will s mine arrows upon them. 3615
Job 21:13 They s their days in wealth, and in a 3615
36:11 serve *him,* they shall s their days in 3615
Ps 90: 9 we s our years as a tale *that is told.* 3615
Isa 55: 2 Wherefore do ye s money for *that which is* 8254
Ac 20:16 because he would not s the **time** in Asia: *5551*
2Co 12:15 And I will very gladly s and be spent for *1159*

SPENDEST (1) [SPEND]
Lk 10:35 and whatsoever thou **s more,** when I come *4325*

SPENDETH (3) [SPEND]
Pr 21:20 of the wise; but a foolish man **s** it **up.** 1104
29: 3 he that keepeth company with harlots s *his* 6
Ecc 6:12 all the days of his vain life which he s as a 6213

SPENT (19) [SPEND]
Ge 21:15 the water was s in the bottle, and she cast 3615
47:18 *it* from my lord, how that our money is s; 8552
Lev 26:20 your strength shall be s in vain: for your 8552
Jdg 19:11 when they *were* by Jebus, the day was far s; 7286
1Sa 9: 7 for the bread is s in our vessels, and *there is* 235
Job 7: 6 a weaver's shuttle, and are s without hope. 3615
Ps 31:10 For my life is s with grief, and my years 3615
Isa 49: 4 I have s my strength for nought, and 3615
Jer 37:21 until all the bread in the city were s. 8552
Mk 5:26 many physicians, and had s all that she had, *1159*
6:35 And when the day was now far s, *1096*
Lk 8:43 which had s all *her* living upon physicians, *4321*
15:14 And when he had s all, there arose a mighty *1159*
24:29 and the day is **far** s. *2235+2827*
Ac 17:21 strangers which were there s their **time** in *2119*
18:23 And after he had s some time *there,* he *4160*
27: 9 Now when much time was s, and *1230*
Ro 13:12 The night is **far** s, the day is at hand: let us *4298*
2Co 12:15 I will very gladly spend and be s for you; *1550*

SPEW See BELCH; SPUE

SPICE (5) [SPICED, SPICERY, SPICES]
Ex 35:28 s, and oil for the light, and for the anointing 1314
1Ki 10:15 *of* the traffick of the *s* merchants, and *of* all NIH
2Ch 9: 9 neither was there any such s as the queen of 1314
SS 5: 1 I have gathered my myrrh with my s; I have 1313
Eze 24:10 and s it well, and let the bones be burnt. 7543

SPICED (1) [SPICE]
SS 8: 2 I would cause thee to drink of s wine, of 7544

SPICERY (1) [SPICE]
Ge 37:25 from Gilead with their camels bearing s 5219

SPICES (31) [SPICE]
Ge 43:11 s, and myrrh, nuts, and almonds: 5219
Ex 25: 6 s for anointing oil, and for sweet incense, 1314
30:23 Take thou also unto thee principal s, 1314
30:34 Take unto thee **sweet** s, stacte, and onycha, 5561
30:34 *these* **sweet** s with pure frankincense: 5561
35: 8 s for anointing oil, and for the sweet 1314
37:29 and the pure incense of **sweet** s, 5561
1Ki 10: 2 *with* camels that bare s, and very much 1314
10:10 of s very great store, and precious stones: 1314
10:10 there came no more such abundance of s as 1314
10:25 and armour, and s, horses, and mules, 1314
2Ki 20:13 the s, and the precious ointment, and all 1314
1Ch 9:29 and the oil, and the frankincense, and the s. 1314
9:30 of the priests made the ointment of the s. 1314
2Ch 9: 1 camels that bare s, and gold in abundance, 1314
9: 9 of s great abundance, and precious stones: 1314
9:24 raiment, harness, and s, horses, and mules, 1314
16:14 divers kinds *of s* prepared by NIH
32:27 for s, and for shields, and for all *manner of* 1314
SS 4:10 and the smell of thine ointments than all s! 1314
4:14 myrrh and aloes, with all the chief s: 1314
4:16 my garden, *that* the s thereof may flow out. 1314
5:13 His cheeks *are* as a bed of s, *as* sweet 1314
6: 2 to the beds of s, to feed in the gardens, and 1314
8:14 or to a young hart upon the mountains of s. 1314
Isa 39: 2 the s, and the precious ointment, and all 1314
Eze 27:22 occupied in thy fairs with chief of all s, 1314
Mk 16: 1 and Salome, had bought *sweet* s, that they *759*
Lk 23:56 they returned, and prepared s and ointments; *759*
24: 1 bringing the s which they had prepared, and *759*
Jn 19:40 and wound it in linen clothes with the s, *759*

SPIDER (1) [SPIDER'S]
Pr 30:28 The s taketh hold with her hands, and *is* in 8079

SPIDER'S (2) [SPIDER]
Job 8:14 be cut off, and whose trust *shall be* a s web. 5908
Isa 59: 5 cockatrice' eggs, and weave the s web: 5908

SPIED (6) [SPY]
Ex 2:11 he s an Egyptian smiting a Hebrew, *one* of 7200
Jos 6:22 the two men that had **s out** the country, 7270
2Ki 9:17 he s the company of Jehu as he came, and 7200
13:21 they s a band *of men;* and they cast the man 7200
23:16 he s the sepulchres that *were* there in 7200
23:24 all the abominations that were s in the land 7200

SPIES (14) [SPY]
Ge 42: 9 of them, and said unto them, Ye *are* s; 7270
42:11 we *are* true *men,* thy servants are no s. 7270
42:14 *is it* that I spake unto you, saying, Ye *are* s: 7270
42:16 else by the life of Pharaoh surely ye *are* s. 7270
42:30 to us, and took us for s of the country. 7270
42:31 unto him, We *are* true *men;* we are no s: 7270
42:34 shall I know that ye *are* no s, but *that* ye *are* 7270
Nu 21: 1 *tell* that Israel came *by* the way of the s; 871
Jos 6:23 the young men that were s went in, and 7270
Jdg 1:24 the s saw a man come forth out of the city, 8104
1Sa 26: 4 David therefore sent out s, and 7270
2Sa 15:10 Absalom sent s throughout all the tribes of 7270
Lk 20:20 And they watched *him,* and sent forth s, *1455*
Heb 11:31 when she had received the s with peace. *2685*

SPIKENARD (5)
SS 1:12 my s sendeth forth the smell thereof. 5373
4:13 with pleasant fruits; camphire, with s, 5373
4:14 S and saffron; calamus and cinnamon, 5373
Mk 14: 3 box of ointment of s very precious; *3487+4101*
Jn 12: 3 took Mary a pound of ointment of s, *3487+4101*

SPILLED (3) [SPILT]
Ge 38: 9 brother's wife, that he s *it* on the ground, 7843
Mk 2:22 and the wine is s, and the bottles will be *1632*
Lk 5:37 and be s, and the bottles shall perish. *1632*

SPILT (1) [SPILLED]
2Sa 14:14 needs die, and *are* as water s on the ground, 5064

SPIN (3) [SPUN]
Ex 35:25 all the women that were wise hearted did s 2901
Mt 6:28 they grow; they toil not, neither do they s: *3514*
Lk 12:27 they toil not, they s not; and yet I say unto *3514*

SPINDLE (1)
Pr 31:19 She layeth her hands to the s, and her hands 3601

SPIRIT (505) [SPIRITS, SPIRITUAL, SPIRITUALLY]
Ge 1: 2 the S of God moved upon the face of 7307
6: 3 My s shall not always strive with man, 7307
41: 8 it came to pass in the morning that his s 7307
41:38 as this *is,* a man in whom the s of God *is?* 7307
45:27 the s of Jacob their father revived: 7307
Ex 6: 9 hearkened not unto Moses for anguish of s, 7307
28: 3 whom I have filled with the s of wisdom, 7307
31: 3 I have filled him *with* the s of God, 7307
35:21 every one whom his s made willing, *and* 7307
35:31 he hath filled him *with* the s of God, 7307
Lev 20:27 A man also or woman that hath a **familiar** s, 178
Nu 5:14 the s of jealousy come upon him, and he be 7307
5:14 or if the s of jealousy come upon him, and 7307

S

Nu	5:30	Or when the **s** of jealousy cometh upon	7307
	11:17	I will take of the **s** which *is* upon thee, and	7307
	11:25	took of the **s** that *was* upon him, and gave *it*	7307
	11:25	to pass, that when the **s** rested upon them,	7307
	11:26	the **s** rested upon them; and they *were* of	7307
	11:29	that the LORD would put his **s** upon	7307
	14:24	because he had another **s** with him, and	7307
	24: 2	and the **s** of God came upon him.	7307
	27:18	a man in whom *is* the **s**, and lay thine hand	7307
Dt	2:30	for the LORD thy God hardened his **s**, and	7307
	34: 9	Joshua the son of Nun was full *of* the **s** of	7307
Jos	5: 1	neither was there **s** in them any more,	7307
Jdg	3:10	the **s** of the LORD came upon him, and	7307
	6:34	the **s** of the LORD came upon Gideon,	7307
	9:23	God sent an evil **s** between Abimelech	7307
	11:29	the **s** of the LORD came upon Jephthah,	7307
	13:25	the **s** of the LORD began to move him at	7307
	14: 6	the **s** of the LORD came mightily upon	7307
	14:19	the **s** of the LORD came upon him, and	7307
	15:14	the **s** of the LORD came mightily upon	7307
	15:19	his **s** came again, and he revived:	7307
1Sa	1:15	my lord, I *am* a woman of a sorrowful **s**:	7307
	10: 6	the **s** of the LORD will come upon thee,	7307
	10:10	the **s** of God came upon him, and	7307
	11: 6	the **s** of God came upon Saul when he	7307
	16:13	the **s** of the LORD came upon David from	7307
	16:14	the **s** of the LORD departed from Saul,	7307
	16:14	an evil **s** from the LORD troubled him.	7307
	16:15	an evil **s** from God troubleth thee.	7307
	16:16	when the evil **s** from God is upon thee,	7307
	16:23	when the *evil* **s** from God was upon Saul,	7307
	16:23	was well, and the evil **s** departed from him.	7307
	18:10	that the evil **s** from God came upon Saul,	7307
	19: 9	the evil **s** from the LORD was upon Saul,	7307
	19:20	the **s** of God was upon the messengers of	7307
	19:23	the **s** of God was upon him also, and	7307
	28: 7	Seek me a woman that hath a **familiar s**,	178
	28: 7	*there is* a woman that hath a **familiar s** at	178
	28: 8	divine unto me by the **familiar s**, and	178
	30:12	he had eaten, his **s** came again to him:	7307
2Sa	23: 2	The **S** of the LORD spake by me, and	7307
1Ki	10: 5	of the LORD; there was no more **s** in her.	7307
	18:12	that the **s** of the LORD shall carry thee	7307
	21: 5	said unto him, Why is thy **s** so sad,	7307
	22:21	there came forth a **s**, and stood before	7307
	22:22	I will be a lying **s** in the mouth of all his	7307
	22:23	the LORD hath put a lying **s** in the mouth	7307
	22:24	Which way went the **s** of the LORD from	7307
2Ki	2: 9	let a double portion of thy **s** be upon me.	7307
	2:15	The **s** of Elijah doth rest on Elisha.	7307
	2:16	lest peradventure the **s** of the LORD hath	7307
1Ch	5:26	the God of Israel stirred up the **s** of Pul	7307
	5:26	the **s** of Tilgath-pilneser king of Assyria,	7307
	10:13	asking *counsel* of *one that had* a **familiar s**,	178
	12:18	the **s** came upon Amasai, *who was* chief of	7307
	28:12	the pattern of all that he had by the **s**, of	7307
2Ch	9: 4	of the LORD; there was no more **s** in her.	7307
	15: 1	the **s** of God came upon Azariah the son of	7307
	18:20	there came out a **s**, and stood before	7307
	18:21	be a lying **s** in the mouth of all his prophets.	7307
	18:22	the LORD hath put a lying **s** in the mouth	7307
	18:23	Which way went the **s** of the LORD from	7307
	20:14	came the **s** of the LORD in the midst of	7307
	21:16	up against Jehoram the **s** of the Philistines,	7307
	24:20	the **s** of God came upon Zechariah the son	7307
	33: 6	dealt with a **familiar s**, and with wizards:	178
	36:22	the LORD stirred up the **s** of Cyrus king	7307
Ezr	1: 1	the LORD stirred up the **s** of Cyrus king	7307
	1: 5	with all *them* whose **s** God had raised,	7307
Ne	9:20	Thou gavest also thy good **s** to instruct	7307
	9:30	testifiedst against them by thy **s** in thy	7307
Job	4:15	a **s** passed before my face; the hair of my	7307
	6: 4	the poison whereof drinketh up my **s**:	7307
	7:11	I will speak in the anguish of my **s**;	7307
	10:12	and thy visitation hath preserved my **s**.	7307
	15:13	That thou turnest thy **s** against God, and	7307
	20: 3	the **s** of my understanding causeth me to	7307
	21: 4	*so,* why should not my **s** be troubled?	7307
	26: 4	and whose **s** came from thee?	5397
	26:13	By his **s** he hath garnished the heavens;	7307
	27: 3	*is* in me, and the **s** of God *is* in my nostrils;	7307
	32: 8	*there is* a **s** in man: and the inspiration of	7307
	32:18	*of* matter, the **s** within me constraineth me.	7307
	33: 4	The **S** of God hath made me, and the breath	7307
	34:14	upon *man, if* he gather unto himself his **s**	7307
Ps	31: 5	Into thine hand I commit my **s**: thou hast	7307
	32: 2	and in whose **s** *there is* no guile.	7307
	34:18	and saveth such as be of a contrite **s**.	7307
	51:10	O God; and renew a right **s** within me.	7307
	51:11	and take not thy holy **S** from me.	7307
	51:12	and uphold me *with thy* free **s**.	7307
	51:17	The sacrifices of God *are* a broken **s**:	7307
	76:12	He shall cut off the **s** of princes: *he is*	7307
	77: 3	I complained, and my **s** was overwhelmed.	7307
	77: 6	own heart: and my **s** made diligent search.	7307
	78: 8	and whose **s** was not stedfast with God.	7307
	104:30	Thou sendest forth thy **s**, they are created:	7307
	106:33	Because they provoked his **s**, so that he	7307
	139: 7	Whither shall I go from thy **s**? or	7307
	142: 3	When my **s** was overwhelmed within me,	7307
	143: 4	Therefore is my **s** overwhelmed within me;	7307
	143: 7	my **s** faileth: hide not thy face from me,	7307
	143:10	thy **s** *is* good; lead me into the land of	7307
Pr	1:23	behold, I will pour out my **s** unto you, I will	7307
	11:13	he that is of a faithful **s** concealeth	7307
	14:29	but *he that is* hasty of **s** exalteth folly.	7307
	15: 4	but perverseness therein *is* a breach in the **s**.	7307
	15:13	but by sorrow of the heart the **s** *is* broken.	7307
	16:18	and a haughty **s** before a fall.	7307
	16:19	Better *it is to be* of an humble **s** with	7307
	16:32	he that ruleth his **s** than he that taketh a	7307
	17:22	a medicine: but a broken **s** drieth the bones.	7307
	17:27	a man of understanding is of an excellent **s**.	7307
	18:14	The **s** of a man will sustain his infirmity;	7307
	18:14	but a wounded **s** who can bear?	7307
	20:27	The **s** of man *is* the candle of the LORD,	5397
	25:28	He that *hath* no rule over his own **s** *is like* a	7307
	29:23	but honour shall uphold the humble in **s**.	7307
Ecc	1:14	and behold, all *is* vanity and vexation of **s**.	7307
	1:17	I perceived that this also *is* vexation of **s**.	7307
	2:11	all *was* vanity and vexation of **s**, and	7307
	2:17	unto me: for all *is* vanity and vexation of **s**.	7307
	2:26	This also *is* vanity and vexation of **s**.	7307
	3:21	Who knoweth the **s** of man that goeth	7307
	3:21	the **s** of the beast that goeth downward to	7307
	4: 4	This *is* also vanity and vexation of **s**.	7307
	4: 6	hands full *with* travail and vexation of **s**.	7307
	4:16	Surely this also *is* vanity and vexation of **s**.	7307
	6: 9	this *is* also vanity and vexation of **s**.	7307
	7: 8	the patient in **s** *is* better than the proud in	7307
	7: 8	patient in spirit *is* better than the proud in **s**.	7307
	7: 9	Be not hasty in thy **s** to be angry: for anger	7307
	8: 8	*There is* no man that hath power over the **s**	7307
	8: 8	hath power over the spirit to retain the **s**;	7307
	10: 4	If the **s** of the ruler rise up against thee,	7307
	11: 5	thou knowest not what *is* the way of the **s**,	7307
	12: 7	and the **s** shall return unto God who gave it.	7307
Isa	4: 4	the midst thereof by the **s** of judgment,	7307
	4: 4	spirit of judgment, and by the **s** of burning.	7307
	11: 2	the **S** of the LORD shall rest upon him,	7307
	11: 2	the **s** of wisdom and understanding,	7307
	11: 2	understanding, the **s** of counsel and might,	7307
	11: 2	the **s** of knowledge and of the fear of	7307
	19: 3	the **s** of Egypt shall fail in the midst	7307
	19:14	The LORD hath mingled a perverse **s** in	7307
	26: 9	*with* my **s** within me will I seek thee early:	7307
	28: 6	for a **s** of judgment to him that sitteth in	7307
	29: 4	as of one that hath a **familiar s**, out of	178
	29:10	poured out upon you the **s** of deep sleep,	7307
	29:24	They also that erred in **s** shall come to	7307
	30: 1	that cover *with* a covering, but not of my **S**,	7307
	31: 3	not God; and their horses flesh, and not **s**.	7307
	32:15	Until the **s** be poured upon us from on high,	7307
	34:16	and his **s** it hath gathered them.	7307
	38:16	and in all these *things is* the life of my **s**:	7307
	40: 7	the **s** of the LORD bloweth upon it:	7307
	40:13	Who hath directed the **s** of the LORD, or	7307
	42: 1	soul delighteth; I have put my **s** upon him:	7307
	42: 5	upon it, and **s** to them that walk therein:	7307
	44: 3	dry *ground:* I will pour my **s** upon thy seed,	7307
	48:16	the Lord GOD, and his **S**, hath sent me.	7307
	54: 6	thee as a woman forsaken and grieved in **s**,	7307
	57:15	him also *that is* of a contrite and humble **s**,	7307
	57:15	to revive the **s** of the humble, and to revive	7307
	57:16	for the **s** should fail before me, and	7307
	59:19	the **s** of the LORD shall lift up a standard	7307
	59:21	My **s** that *is* upon thee, and my words	7307
	61: 1	The **S** of the Lord GOD *is* upon me;	7307

Isa	61: 3	the garment of praise for the **s** of heaviness;	7307
	63:10	they rebelled, and vexed his holy **S**:	7307
	63:11	where *is* he that put his holy **S** within him?	7307
	63:14	the **S** of the LORD caused him to rest:	7307
	65:14	of heart, and shall howl for vexation of **s**.	7307
	66: 2	*even* to *him that is* poor and of a contrite **s**,	7307
Jer	51:11	the LORD hath raised up the **s** of	7307
Eze	1:12	whither the **s** was to go, they went; *and*	7307
	1:20	Whithersoever the **s** was to go, they went,	7307
	1:20	to go, they went, thither *was their* **s** to go;	7307
	1:20	for the **s** of the living creature *was* in	7307
	1:21	for the **s** of the living creature *was* in	7307
	2: 2	the **s** entered into me when he spake unto	7307
	3:12	the **s** took me up, and I heard behind me a	7307
	3:14	So the **s** lifted me up, and took me away,	7307
	3:14	and I went in bitterness, in the heat of my **s**;	7307
	3:24	the **s** entered into me, and set me upon my	7307
	8: 3	the **s** lift me up between the earth and	7307
	10:17	*these* lift up themselves *also:* for the **s** of	7307
	11: 1	Moreover the **s** lift me up, and brought me	7307
	11: 5	the **S** of the LORD fell upon me, and	7307
	11:19	and I will put a new **s** within you;	7307
	11:24	Afterwards the **s** took me up, and	7307
	11:24	brought me in vision by the **S** of God into	7307
	13: 3	that follow their own **s**, and have seen	7307
	18:31	and make you a new heart and a new **s**:	7307
	21: 7	every **s** shall faint, and all knees shall be	7307
	36:26	give you, and a new **s** will I put within you:	7307
	36:27	I will put my **s** within you, and cause you to	7307
	37: 1	carried me out in the **s** of the LORD, and	7307
	37:14	shall put my **s** in you, and ye shall live,	7307
	39:29	for I have poured out my **s** upon the house	7307
	43: 5	So the **s** took me up, and brought me into	7307
Da	2: 1	wherewith his **s** was troubled, and his sleep	7307
	2: 3	and my **s** was troubled to know the dream.	7307
	4: 8	and in whom *is* the **s** of the holy gods:	7308
	4: 9	I know that the **s** of the holy gods *is* in thee,	7308
	4:18	for the **s** of the holy gods *is* in thee.	7308
	5:11	in whom *is* the **s** of the holy gods;	7308
	5:12	Forasmuch as an excellent **s**, and	7308
	5:14	that the **s** of the gods *is* in thee, and	7308
	6: 3	princes, because an excellent **s** *was* in him;	7308
	7:15	I Daniel was grieved in my **s** in the midst of	7308
Hos	4:12	for the **s** of whoredoms hath caused *them* to	7307
	5: 4	for the **s** of whoredoms *is* in the midst of	7307
Joel	2:28	that I will pour out my **s** upon all flesh;	7307
	2:29	in those days will I pour out my **s**.	7307
Mic	2: 7	of Jacob, is the **s** of the LORD straitened?	7307
	2:11	If a man walking *in* the **s** and falsehood do	7307
	3: 8	truly I am full *of* power by the **s** of	7307
Hag	1:14	the LORD stirred up the **s** of Zerubbabel	7307
	1:14	the **s** of Joshua the son of Josedech the high	7307
	1:14	and the **s** of all the remnant of the people;	7307
	2: 5	of Egypt, so my **s** remaineth among you:	7307
Zec	4: 6	Not by might, nor by power, but by my **s**,	7307
	6: 8	have quieted my **s** in the north country.	7307
	7:12	hath sent in his **s** by the former prophets:	7307
	12: 1	and formeth the **s** of man within him.	7307
	12:10	the **s** of grace and of supplications:	7307
	13: 2	and the unclean **s** to pass out of the land.	7307
Mal	2:15	Yet had he the residue of the **s**. And	7307
	2:15	Therefore take heed to your **s**, and let none	7307
	2:16	therefore take heed to your **s**, that ye deal	7307
Mt	3:16	he saw the **S** of God descending like a	*4151*
	4: 1	Then was Jesus led up of the **S** into	*4151*
	5: 3	Blessed *are* the poor in **s**: for theirs is	*4151*
	10:20	the **S** of your Father which speaketh in you.	*4151*
	12:18	I will put my **s** upon him, and he shall shew	*4151*
	12:28	But if I cast out devils by the **S** of God,	*4151*
	12:43	When the unclean **s** is gone out of a man,	*4151*
	14:26	the sea, they were troubled, saying, It is a **s**;	*5326*
	22:43	How then doth David in **s** call him Lord,	*4151*
	26:41	the **s** indeed *is* willing, but the flesh *is*	*4151*
Mk	1:10	and the **S** like a dove descending upon him:	*4151*
	1:12	And immediately the **S** driveth him into	*4151*
	1:23	in their synagogue a man with an unclean **s**;	*4151*
	1:26	And when the unclean **s** had torn him, and	*4151*
	2: 8	when Jesus perceived in his **s** that they so	*4151*
	3:30	Because they said, He hath an unclean **s**.	*4151*
	5: 2	out of the tombs a man with an unclean **s**,	*4151*
	5: 8	Come out of the man, *thou* unclean **s**.	*4151*
	6:49	they supposed *it* had been a **s**, and	*5326*
	7:25	whose young daughter had an unclean **s**,	*4151*
	8:12	And he sighed deeply in his **s**, and saith,	*4151*
	9:17	unto thee my son, which hath a dumb **s**:	*4151*
	9:20	he saw him, straightway the **s** tare him;	*4151*
	9:25	he rebuked the foul **s**, saying unto him,	*4151*
	9:25	*Thou* dumb and deaf **s**, I charge thee,	*4151*
	9:26	And *the* **s** cried, and rent him sore, and	NIG
	14:38	The **s** truly *is* ready, but the flesh *is* weak.	*4151*
Lk	1:17	And he shall go before him in the **s** and	*4151*
	1:47	And my **s** hath rejoiced in God my Saviour.	*4151*
	1:80	and waxed strong in **s**, and was in	*4151*
	2:27	And he came by the **S** into the temple: and	*4151*
	2:40	and waxed strong in **s**, filled with wisdom:	*4151*
	4: 1	and was led by the **S** into the wilderness,	*4151*
	4:14	And Jesus returned in the power of the **S**	*4151*
	4:18	The **S** of the Lord *is* upon me,	*4151*
	4:33	which had a **s** of an unclean devil, and	*4151*
	8:29	(For he had commanded the unclean **s** to	*4151*
	8:55	And her **s** came again, and she arose	*4151*
	9:39	a **s** taketh him, and he suddenly crieth out;	*4151*
	9:42	tare *him.* And Jesus rebuked the unclean **s**,	*4151*
	9:55	Ye know not what manner of **s** ye are of.	*4151*
	10:21	In that hour Jesus rejoiced in **s**, and said,	*4151*
	11:13	give the Holy **S** to them that ask him?	*4151*
	11:24	When the unclean **s** is gone out of a man,	*4151*
	13:11	there was a woman which had a **s** of	*4151*
	23:46	Father, into thy hands I commend my **s**:	*4151*
	24:37	and supposed that *they* had seen a **s**.	*4151*
	24:39	for a **s** hath not flesh and bones, as ye see	*4151*
Jn	1:32	I saw the **S** descending from heaven like a	*4151*
	1:33	Upon whom thou shalt see the **S**	*4151*
	3: 5	Except a man be born of water and *of* the **S**,	*4151*
	3: 6	and that which is born of the **S** is spirit.	*4151*
	3: 6	and that which is born of the Spirit is **s**.	*4151*
	3: 8	so is every one that is born of the **S**.	*4151*
	3:34	for God giveth not the **S** by measure *unto*	*4151*
	4:23	worshippers shall worship the Father in **s**	*4151*
	4:24	God *is* a **S**: and they that worship him must	*4151*
	4:24	that worship him must worship *him* in **s**	*4151*
	6:63	It is the **s** that quickeneth; the flesh	*4151*
	6:63	unto you, *they* are **s**, and *they* are life.	*4151*
	7:39	(But this spake he of the **S**, which they that	*4151*
	11:33	he groaned in the **s**, and was troubled,	*4151*
	13:21	he was troubled in **s**, and testified, and said,	*4151*
	14:17	*Even* the **S** of truth; whom the world cannot	*4151*
	15:26	*even* the **S** of truth, which proceedeth from	*4151*
	16:13	Howbeit when he, the **S** of truth, is come,	*4151*
Ac	2: 4	other tongues, as the **S** gave them utterance.	*4151*
	2:17	I will pour out of my **S** upon all flesh:	*4151*
	2:18	I will pour out in those days of my **S**;	*4151*
	5: 9	agreed together to tempt the **S** of the Lord?	*4151*
	6:10	the wisdom and the **s** by which he spake.	*4151*
	7:59	and saying, Lord Jesus, receive my **s**.	*4151*
	8:29	Then the **S** said unto Philip, Go near, and	*4151*
	8:39	the **S** of the Lord caught away Philip,	*4151*
	10:19	the **S** said unto him, Behold, three men	*4151*
	11:12	And the **S** bade me go with them,	*4151*
	11:28	signified by the **S** that there should be great	*4151*
	16: 7	into Bithynia: but the **S** suffered them not.	*4151*
	16:16	a certain damsel possessed with a **s** of	*4151*
	16:18	being grieved, turned and said to the **s**,	*4151*
	17:16	for them at Athens, his **s** was stirred in him,	*4151*
	18: 5	Paul was pressed in **s**, and testified to	*4151*
	18:25	and being fervent in the **s**, he spake and	*4151*
	19:15	And the evil **s** answered and said, Jesus I	*4151*
	19:16	And the man in whom the evil **s** was leapt	*4151*
	19:21	*things* were ended, Paul purposed in the **s**,	*4151*
	20:22	I go bound in the **s** unto Jerusalem,	*4151*
	21: 4	who said to Paul through the **S**, that *he*	*4151*
	23: 8	there is no resurrection, neither angel nor **s**:	*4151*
	23: 9	but if a **s** or an angel hath spoken to him,	*4151*
Ro	1: 4	according to the **S** of holiness, by	*4151*
	1: 9	whom I serve with my **s** in the gospel of his	*4151*
	2:29	of the heart, in the **s**, *and* not *in* the letter;	*4151*
	7: 6	that we should serve in newness of **s**, and	*4151*
	8: 1	who walk not after the flesh, but after the **S**.	*4151*
	8: 2	For the law of the **S** of life in Christ Jesus	*4151*
	8: 4	who walk not after the flesh, but after the **S**.	*4151*
	8: 5	they *that are* after the **S** the *things* of	*4151*
	8: 5	*that are* after the Spirit the *things* of the **S**.	*4151*
	8: 9	but in the **S**, if so be that the Spirit of God	*4151*
	8: 9	if so be that the **S** of God dwell in you.	*4151*
	8: 9	Now if any *man* have not the **S** of Christ,	*4151*
	8:10	but the **S** *is* life because of righteousness.	*4151*
	8:11	But if the **S** of him that raised up Jesus	*4151*
	8:11	mortal bodies by his **S** that dwelleth in you.	*4151*

Ro 8:13 if ye through the **S** do mortify the deeds of 4151
8:14 For as many as are led by the **S** of God, 4151
8:15 For ye have not received the **s** of bondage 4151
8:15 but ye have received the **S** of adoption, 4151
8:16 The **S** itself beareth witness with our spirit, 4151
8:16 The Spirit itself beareth witness with our **s**, 4151
8:23 which have the firstfruits of the **S**, 4151
8:26 Likewise the **S** also helpeth our infirmities: 4151
8:26 the **S** itself maketh intercession for us with 4151
8:27 hearts knoweth what *is* the mind of the **S**, 4151
11: 8 God hath given them the **s** of slumber, 4151
12:11 in business; fervent in **s**; serving the Lord; 4151
15:19 and wonders, by the power of the **S** of God; 4151
15:30 Christ's sake, and for the love of the **S**, 4151
1Co 2: 4 but in demonstration of the **S** and of power: 4151
2:10 God hath revealed *them* unto us by his **S**: 4151
2:10 for the **S** searcheth all *things*, yea, the deep 4151
2:11 a man, save the **s** of man which is in him? 4151
2:11 of God knoweth no *man*, but the **S** of God. 4151
2:12 not the **s** of the world, but the Spirit which 4151
2:12 of the world, but the **S** which is of God; 4151
2:14 receiveth not the *things* of the **S** of God: 4151
3:16 and *that* the **S** of God dwelleth in you? 4151
4:21 a rod, or in love, and *in* the **s** of meekness? 4151
5: 3 I verily, as absent in body, but present in **s**, 4151
5: 4 when ye are gathered together, and my **s**, 4151
5: 5 that the **s** may be saved in the day of 4151
6:11 of the Lord Jesus, and by the **S** of our God. 4151
6:17 But he that is joined unto the Lord is one **s**. 4151
6:20 your body, and in your **s**, which are God's. 4151
7:34 that she may be holy both in body and in **s**: 4151
7:40 and I think also that *I* have the **S** of God. 4151
12: 3 that no *man* speaking by the **S** of God 4151
12: 4 there are diversities of gifts, but the same **S**. 4151
12: 7 But the manifestation of the **S** is given to 4151
12: 8 For to one is given by the **S** the word of 4151
12: 8 the word of knowledge by the same **S**; 4151
12: 9 To another faith by the same **S**; to another 4151
12: 9 another the gifts of healing by the same **S**; 4151
12:11 these worketh *that* one and the selfsame **S**, 4151
12:13 For by one **S** are we all baptized into one 4151
12:13 and have been all made to drink into one **S**. 4151
14: 2 howbeit in the **s** he speaketh mysteries. 4151
14:14 my **s** prayeth, but my understanding is 4151
14:15 I will pray with the **s**, and will pray with 4151
14:15 I will sing with the **s**, and I will sing with 4151
14:16 Else when thou shalt bless with the **s**, 4151
15:45 the last Adam *was made* a quickening **s**. 4151
16:18 For they have refreshed my **s** and yours: 4151
2Co 1:22 and given the earnest of the **S** in our hearts. 4151
2:13 I had no rest in my **s**, because I found not 4151
3: 3 with ink, but with the **S** of the living God; 4151
3: 6 not of the letter, but of the **s**: 4151
3: 6 for the letter killeth, but the **s** giveth life. 4151
3: 8 How shall not the ministration of the **s** be 4151
3:17 Now the Lord is *that* **S**: and where 4151
3:17 where the **S** of the Lord *is*, there *is* liberty. 4151
3:18 glory to glory, even as by the **S** of the Lord. 4151
4:13 We having the same **s** of faith, according as 4151
5: 5 also hath given unto us the earnest of the **S**. 4151
7: 1 from all filthiness of the flesh and **s**, 4151
7:13 because his **s** was refreshed by you all. 4151
11: 4 or *if* ye receive another **s**, which ye have 4151
12:18 walked we not in the same **s**? *walked we* 4151
Gal 3: 2 Received ye the **S** by the works of the law, 4151
3: 3 having begun in the **S**, are ye now made 4151
3: 5 He therefore that ministereth to you the **S**, 4151
3:14 that we might receive the promise of the **S** 4151
4: 6 God hath sent forth the **S** of his Son into 4151
4:29 persecuted him that was *born* after the **S**, 4151
5: 5 For we through the **S** wait for the hope of 4151
5:16 Walk in the **S**, and ye shall not fulfil 4151
5:17 For the flesh lusteth against the **S**, and 4151
5:17 the Spirit, and the **S** against the flesh: 4151
5:18 But if ye be led of the **S**, ye are not under 4151
5:22 But the fruit of the **S** is love, joy, peace, 4151
5:25 If we live in the **S**, let us also walk in 4151
5:25 live in the Spirit, let us also walk in the **S**. 4151
6: 1 restore such a one in the **s** of meekness; 4151
6: 8 he that soweth to the **S** shall of the Spirit 4151
6: 8 he that soweth to the Spirit shall of the **S** 4151
6:18 of our Lord Jesus Christ *be* with your **s**. 4151
Eph 1:13 ye were sealed with *that* holy **S** of promise, 4151
1:17 may give unto you the **s** of wisdom and 4151
2: 2 the **s** that now worketh in the children of 4151
2:18 both have access by one **S** unto the Father. 4151
2:22 for a habitation of God through the **S**. 4151
3: 5 his holy apostles and prophets by the **S**; 4151
3:16 to be strengthened with might by his **S** in 4151
4: 3 Endeavouring to keep the unity of the **S** in 4151
4: 4 *There is* one body, and one **S**, even as ye 4151
4:23 And be renewed in the **s** of your mind; 4151
4:30 And grieve not the holy **S** of God, 4151
5: 9 (For the fruit of the **S** *is* in all goodness and 4151
5:18 wherein is excess; but be filled with the **S**; 4151
6:17 and the sword of the **S**, which is the word 4151
6:18 with all prayer and supplication in the **S**, 4151
Php 1:19 and the supply of the **S** of Jesus Christ, 4151
1:27 of your affairs, that ye stand fast in one **s**, 4151
2: 1 if any fellowship of the **S**, if any bowels 4151
3: 3 which worship God in the **s**, and rejoice in 4151
Col 1: 8 also declared unto us your love in the **S**. 4151
2: 5 yet am I with you in the **s**, joying and 4151
1Th 4: 8 who hath also given unto us his holy **S**. 4151
5:19 Quench not the **S**. 4151
5:23 and *I pray God* your whole **s** and soul and 4151
2Th 2: 2 or be troubled, neither by **s**, nor by word, 4151
2: 8 whom the Lord shall consume with the **s** of 4151
2:13 to salvation through sanctification of the **S** 4151
1Ti 3:16 justified in the **S**, seen of angels, 4151
4: 1 Now the **S** speaketh expressly, that in 4151
4:12 in charity, in **s**, in faith, in purity. 4151
2Ti 1: 7 For God hath not given us the **s** of fear; but 4151
4:22 The Lord Jesus Christ *be* with thy **s**. Grace 4151
Phm 1:25 of our Lord Jesus Christ *be* with your **s**. 4151
Heb 4:12 even to the dividing asunder of soul and **s**, 4151
9:14 who through the eternal **S** offered himself 4151
10:29 and hath done despite unto the **S** of grace? 4151
Jas 2:26 For as the body without the **s** is dead, so 4151
4: 5 the **s** that dwelleth in us lusteth to envy? 4151
1Pe 1: 2 through sanctification of the **S**, 4151
1:11 what manner of time the **S** of Christ which 4151
1:22 the **S** unto unfeigned love of the brethren, 4151
3: 4 *even the ornament* of a meek and quiet **s**, 4151
3:18 death in the flesh, but quickened by the **S**: 4151
4: 6 the flesh, but live according to God in the **s**. 4151
4:14 happy *are ye;* for the **s** of glory and of God 4151
1Jn 3:24 in us, by the **S** which he hath given us. 4151
4: 1 believe not every **s**, but try the spirits 4151
4: 2 Hereby know ye the **S** of God: Every spirit 4151
4: 2 Every **s** that confesseth that Jesus Christ is 4151
4: 3 And every **s** that confesseth not that Jesus 4151
4: 3 and this is *that* **s** of antichrist, whereof you NIG
4: 6 Hereby know we the **s** of truth, and 4151
4: 6 we the spirit of truth, and the **s** of error. 4151
4:13 he in us, because he hath given us of his **S**. 4151
5: 6 And it is the **S** that beareth witness, because 4151
5: 6 that beareth witness, because the **S** is truth. 4151
5: 8 the **S**, and the water, and the blood: 4151
Jude 1:19 sensual, having not the **S**. 4151
Rev 1:10 I was in the **s** on the Lord's day, and 4151
2: 7 let him hear what the **S** saith unto 4151
2:11 let him hear what the **S** saith unto 4151
2:17 let him hear what the **S** saith unto 4151
2:29 let him hear what the **S** saith unto 4151
3: 6 let him hear what the **S** saith unto 4151
3:13 let him hear what the **S** saith unto 4151
3:22 let him hear what the **S** saith unto 4151
4: 2 And immediately I was in the **s**: and 4151
11:11 a half the **s** of life from God entered into 4151
14:13 Yea, saith the **S**, that they may rest from 4151
17: 3 So he carried me away in the **s** into 4151
18: 2 and the hold of every foul **s**, and a cage of 4151
19:10 for the testimony of Jesus is the **s** of 4151
21:10 And he carried me away in the **s** to a great 4151
22:17 And the **S** and the bride say, Come. And let 4151

[HOLY] SPIRIT See [HOLY] GHOST

SPIRITIST See WIZARD

SPIRITS (46) [SPIRIT]

Lev 19:31 Regard not them that have **familiar s**, 178
20: 6 that turneth after such as have **familiar s**, 178
Nu 16:22 said, O God, the God of the **s** of all flesh, 7307
27:16 the LORD, the God of the **s** of all flesh, 7307
Dt 18:11 or a consulter with **familiar s**, or a wizard, 178
1Sa 28: 3 Saul had put away those that had **familiar s**, 178

1Sa 28: 9 he hath cut off those that have **familiar** s, 178
2Ki 21: 6 and dealt with **familiar** s and wizards: 178
23:24 Moreover the *workers with* **familiar** s, and 178
Ps 104: 4 Who maketh his angels s; his ministers a 7307
Pr 16: 2 own eyes; but the LORD weigheth the s. 7307
Isa 8:19 Seek unto them that have **familiar** s, and 178
19: 3 to them that have **familiar** s, and to 178
Zec 6: 5 These *are* the four s of the heavens, 7307
Mt 8:16 and he cast out the s with *his* word, and *4151*
10: 1 he gave them power against unclean s, *4151*
12:45 taketh with himself seven other s more *4151*
Mk 1:27 commandeth he even the unclean s, *4151*
3:11 And unclean s, when they saw him, *4151*
5:13 And the unclean s went out, and *4151*
6: 7 two; and gave them power over unclean s; *4151*
Lk 4:36 and power he commandeth the unclean s, *4151*
6:18 And they that were vexed with unclean s: *4151*
7:21 *their* infirmities and plagues, and of evil s; *4151*
8: 2 which had been healed of evil s and *4151*
10:20 rejoice not, that the s are subject unto you; *4151*
11:26 taketh to *him* seven other s more wicked *4151*
Ac 5:16 and *them which were* vexed with unclean s: *4151*
8: 7 For unclean s, crying with loud voice, *4151*
19:12 from them, and the evil s went out of them. *4151*
19:13 had evil s the name of the Lord Jesus, *4151*
1Co 12:10 to another discerning of s; *4151*
14:32 And the s of the prophets are subject to *4151*
1Ti 4: 1 giving heed to seducing s, and doctrines of *4151*
Heb 1: 7 Who maketh his angels s, and his ministers *4151*
1:14 Are they not all ministering s, sent forth to *4151*
12: 9 rather be in subjection unto the Father of s, *4151*
12:23 and to the s of just *men* made perfect, *4151*
1Pe 3:19 he went and preached unto the s in prison; *4151*
1Jn 4: 1 but try the s whether they are of God: *4151*
Rev 1: 4 from the seven s which are before his *4151*
3: 1 These *things* saith he that hath the seven s *4151*
4: 5 the throne, which are the seven s of God. *4151*
5: 6 which are the seven s of God sent forth into *4151*
16:13 And I saw three unclean s like frogs *come* *4151*
16:14 For they are the s of devils, working *4151*

SPIRITUAL (28) [SPIRIT]
Hos 9: 7 the s man *is* mad, for the multitude of thine 7307
Ro 1:11 that I may impart unto you some s gift, *4152*
7:14 For we know that the law is s: but I am *4152*
15:27 s *things,* their duty is also to minister unto *4152*
1Co 2:13 comparing s *things* with spiritual. *4152*
2:13 comparing spiritual *things* with s. *4152*
2:15 But he that is s judgeth all *things,* yet he *4152*
3: 1 could not speak unto you as unto s, but *4152*
9:11 If we have sown unto you s *things, is it* a *4152*
10: 3 And did all eat the same s meat; *4152*
10: 4 And did all drink the same s drink: for they *4152*
10: 4 for they drank of *that* s Rock that followed *4152*
12: 1 Now concerning s *gifts,* brethren, I would *4152*
14: 1 and desire s *gifts,* but rather that ye may *4152*
14:12 forasmuch as ye are zealous of s *gifts,* seek *4151*
14:37 any *man* think himself to be a prophet, or s, *4152*
15:44 is sown a natural body; it is raised a s body. *4152*
15:44 is a natural body, and there is a s body. *4152*
15:46 Howbeit *that was* not first *which is* s, but *4152*
15:46 *is* natural; *and* afterward *that which is* s. *4152*
Gal 6: 1 man be overtaken in a fault, ye which are s, *4152*
Eph 1: 3 who hath blessed us with all s blessings in *4152*
5:19 in psalms and hymns and s songs, *4152*
6:12 against s wickedness in high *places.* *4152*
Col 1: 9 his will in all wisdom and s understanding; *4152*
3:16 another in psalms and hymns and s songs, *4152*
1Pe 2: 5 as lively stones, are built *up* a s house, *4152*
2: 5 a holy priesthood, to offer up s sacrifices, *4152*

SPIRITUALLY (3) [SPIRIT]
Ro 8: 6 but to be s minded *is* life and peace. *4151*
1Co 2:14 know *them,* because they are s discerned. *4153*
Rev 11: 8 which s is called Sodom and Egypt, *4153*

SPIT (11) [SPAT, SPITTED, SPITTING, SPITTLE]
Lev 15: 8 if he that hath the issue s upon him that is 7556
Nu 12:14 If her father had **but** s in her face, 3417+3417
Dt 25: 9 and s in his face, and shall answer and say, 3417
Job 30:10 far from me, and spare not to s in my face. 7536
Mt 26:67 Then did they s in his face, and *1716*
27:30 And they s upon him, and took the reed, *1716*
Mk 7:33 his ears, and he s, and touched his tongue; *4429*
8:23 and when he had s on his eyes, and put *his* *4429*
10:34 and shall s **upon** him, and shall kill him: *1716*
14:65 And some began to s **on** him, and to cover *1716*
15:19 and did s **upon** him, and bowing *their* *1716*

SPITE (1) [SPITEFULLY]
Ps 10:14 seen *it;* for thou beholdest mischief and s, 3708

SPITEFULLY (2) [SPITE]
Mt 22: 6 and **entreated** *them* s, and slew *them.* *5195*
Lk 18:32 and s **entreated,** and spitted on: *5195*

SPITTED (1) [SPIT]
Lk 18:32 and spitefully entreated, and s on: *1716*

SPITTING (1) [SPIT]
Isa 50: 6 I hid not my face from shame and s. 7536

SPITTLE (3) [SPIT]
1Sa 21:13 and let his s fall down upon his beard. 7388
Job 7:19 nor let me alone till I swallow down my s? 7536
Jn 9: 6 and made clay of the s, and he anointed *4427*

SPLENDID See GOODLIER; GOODLIEST; GOODLY

SPLINT See ROLLER

SPLIT See CLAVE

SPOIL (118) [SPOILED, SPOILER, SPOILERS, SPOILEST, SPOILETH, SPOILING, SPOILS]
Ge 49:27 the prey, and at night he shall divide the s. 7998
Ex 3:22 and ye shall s the Egyptians. 5337
15: 9 I will overtake, I will divide the s; 7998
Nu 31: 9 **took** the s of all their cattle, and all their 962
31:11 they took all the s, and all the prey, *both* of 7998
31:12 the prey, and the s, unto Moses, and 7998
31:53 (*For* the men of war had **taken** s, every man 962
Dt 2:35 and the s of the cities which we took. 7998
3: 7 all the cattle, and the s of the cities, we took 7998
13:16 thou shalt gather all the s of it into 7998
13:16 all the s thereof every whit, for the LORD 7998
20:14 all that is in the city, *even* all the s thereof, 7998
20:14 thou shalt eat the s of thine enemies, 7998
Jos 8: 2 only the s thereof, and the cattle thereof, 7998
8:27 the s of that city Israel took for a prey unto 7998
11:14 all the s of these cities, and the cattle, 7998
22: 8 divide the s of your enemies with your 7998
Jdg 5:30 *meet* for the necks of *them that take* the s? 7998
14:19 took their s, and gave change *of garments* 2488
1Sa 14:30 of the s of their enemies which they found? 7998
14:32 the people flew upon the s, and took sheep, 7998
14:36 s them until the morning light, and let us not 962
15:19 didst fly upon the s, and didst evil in 7998
15:21 the people took of the s, sheep and oxen, 7998
30:16 of all the great s that they had taken out of 7998
30:19 neither sons nor daughters, neither s, 7998
30:20 *other* cattle, and said, This *is* David's s. 7998
30:22 we will not give them *ought* of the s that 7998
30:26 he sent of the s unto the elders of Judah, 7998
30:26 Behold a present for you of the s of 7998
2Sa 3:22 a troop, and brought in a great s with them: 7998
8:12 of Amalek, and of the s of Hadadezer, 7998
12:30 he brought forth the s of the city in great 7998
23:10 the people returned after him only to s. 6584
2Ki 3:23 one another: now therefore, Moab, to the s. 7998
21:14 become a prey and a s to all their enemies; 4933
1Ch 20: 2 he brought also exceeding much s *out* of 7998
2Ch 14:13 and they carried away very much s. 7998
14:14 for there was *exceeding* much s in them. 961
15:11 of the s *which* they had brought, 7998
20:25 his people came to take away the s of them, 7998
20:25 they were three days in gathering of the s, 7998
24:23 sent all the s of them unto the king of 7998
25:13 three thousand of them, and took much s. 961
28: 8 took also away much s from them, and 7998
28: 8 from them, and brought the s to Samaria. 7998
28:14 the s before the princes and all 961
28:15 with the s clothed all *that were* naked 7998
Ezr 9: 7 and to a s, and to confusion of face, 961
Est 3:13 and *to take* the s of them for a prey. 7998
8:11 and *to take* the s of them for a prey, 7998
9:10 but on the s laid they not their hand. 961
Job 29:17 and pluckt the s out of his teeth. 2964
Ps 44:10 and they which hate us s for themselves. 8154

Ps 68:12 she that tarried at home divided the **s**. 7998
89:41 All that pass by the way **s** him: he is a 8155
109:11 he hath; and let the strangers **s** his labour. 962
119:162 at thy word, as one that findeth great **s**. 7998
Pr 1:13 we shall fill our houses *with* **s**: 7998
16:19 than to divide the **s** with the proud. 7998
22:23 and **s** the soul of those that spoiled them. 6906
24:15 of the righteous; **s** not his resting place: 7703
31:11 in her, so that he shall have no need of **s**. 7998
SS 2:15 the foxes, the little foxes, that **s** the vines: 2254
Isa 3:14 the **s** of the poor *is* in your houses. 1500
8: 4 the **s** of Samaria shall be taken away before 7998
9: 3 *and* as *men* rejoice when they divide the **s**. 7998
10: 6 to take the **s**, and to take the prey, and 7998
11:14 they shall **s** them of the east together: 962
17:14 This *is* the portion of them that **s** us, and 8154
33: 1 when thou shalt cease to **s**, thou shalt be 7703
33: 4 your **s** shall be gathered *like* the gathering 7998
33:23 is the prey of a great **s** divided; the lame 7998
42:22 *for* a **s**, and none saith, Restore. 4933
42:24 Who gave Jacob for a **s**, and Israel to 4933
53:12 and he shall divide the **s** with the strong; 7998
Jer 5: 6 *and* a wolf of the evenings shall **s** them, 7703
6: 7 violence and **s** is heard in her; before me 7701
15:13 thy treasures will I give to the **s** without 957
17: 3 thy substance *and* all thy treasures to the **s**, 957
20: 5 which shall **s** them, and take them, and 962
20: 8 I spake, I cried out, I cried violence and **s**; 7701
30:16 they that **s** thee shall be a spoil, and all that 7601
30:16 they that spoil thee shall be a **s**, and all that 4933
47: 4 Because of the day that cometh to **s** all 7703
47: 4 for the LORD *will* **s** the Philistines, 7703
49:28 go up to Kedar, and **s** the men of the east. 7703
49:32 and the multitude of their cattle a **s**: 7998
50:10 Chaldea shall be a **s**: all that spoil her shall 7998
50:10 all that **s** her shall be satisfied, saith 7997
Eze 7:21 and to the wicked of the earth for a **s**; 7998
14:15 they **s** it, so that it be desolate, that no man 7921
25: 7 and will deliver thee for a **s** to the heathen; 957
26: 5 and it shall become a **s** to the nations. 957
26:12 they shall **make a s** of thy riches, and 7997
29:19 and **take** her **s**, and take her prey; 7997+7998
32:12 they shall **s** the pomp of Egypt, and all 7703
38:12 To **take a s**, and to take a prey; to 7997+7998
38:13 unto thee, Art thou come to **take a s**? 7997+7998
38:13 *away* cattle and goods, to take a great **s**? 7998
39:10 they shall **s** those that spoiled them, and 7997
45: 9 remove violence and **s**, and 7701
Da 11:24 among them the prey, and **s**, and riches: 7998
11:33 by flame, by captivity, and by **s**, *many* days. 961
Hos 10: 2 down their altars, he shall **s** their images. 7703
13:15 he shall **s** the treasure of all pleasant 8154
Na 2: 9 **Take** ye **the s** of silver, take the spoil of 962
2: 9 ye the spoil of silver, **take the s** of gold: 962
Hab 2: 8 all the remnant of the people shall **s** thee; 7997
2:17 the **s** of beasts, *which* made them afraid, 7701
Zep 2: 9 the residue of my people shall **s** them, and 962
Zec 2: 9 and they shall be a **s** to their servants: 7998
14: 1 thy **s** shall be divided in the midst of thee. 7998
Mt 12:29 and **s** his goods, except he first bind *1283*
12:29 strong *man?* and then he will **s** his house. *1283*
Mk 3:27 and **s** his goods, except he will first bind *1283*
3:27 strong *man;* and then he will **s** his house. *1283*
Col 2: 8 Beware lest any *man* **s** you through *4812*

SPOILED (55) [SPOIL]
Ge 34:27 **s** the city, because they had defiled their 962
34:29 and **s** even all that *was* in the house. 962
Ex 12:36 *as they required.* And they **s** the Egyptians. 5337
Dt 28:29 shalt be only oppressed and **s** evermore, 1497
Jdg 2:14 them into the hands of spoilers that **s** them, 8155
2:16 them out of the hand of those that **s** them. 8154
1Sa 14:48 Israel out of the hands of them that **s** them. 8154
17:53 after the Philistines, and they **s** their tents. 8155
2Ki 7:16 went out, and **s** the tents of the Syrians. 962
2Ch 14:14 they **s** all the cities; for there was *exceeding* 962
Job 12:17 He leadeth counsellers away **s**, and 7758
12:19 He leadeth princes away **s**, and 7758
Ps 76: 5 The stouthearted are **s**, they have slept their 7997
Pr 22:23 and spoil the soul of those that **s** them. 6906
Isa 13:16 their houses shall be **s**, and their wives 8155
18: 2 trodden down, whose land the rivers have **s**. 958
18: 7 under foot, whose land the rivers have **s**, 958
24: 3 shall be utterly emptied, and **utterly s**: 962+962
33: 1 to thee that spoilest, and thou *wast* not **s**; 7703
33: 1 thou shalt cease to spoil, thou shalt be **s**; 7703
42:22 this *is* a people robbed and **s**; *they are* all of 8154
Jer 2:14 *is* he a homeborn *slave?* why is he **s**? 957
4:13 than eagles. Woe unto us! for we are **s**. 7703
4:20 destruction is cried; for the whole land is **s**: 7703
4:20 suddenly are my tents **s**, *and* my curtains in 7703
4:30 when thou art **s**, what wilt thou do? 7703
9:19 wailing is heard out of Zion, How are we **s**! 7703
10:20 My tabernacle is **s**, and all my cords are 7703
21:12 deliver *him that is* **s** out of the hand of 1497
22: 3 deliver the **s** out of the hand of 1497
25:36 *shall be heard:* for the LORD *hath* **s** their 7703
48: 1 for it is **s**: Kiriathaim is confounded *and* 7703
48:15 Moab is **s**, and gone up *out of* her cities, 7703
48:20 and cry; tell ye *it* in Arnon, that Moab is **s**, 7703
49: 3 Howl, O Heshbon, for Ai is **s**: cry, 7703
49:10 his seed is **s**, and his brethren, and 7703
51:55 Because the LORD *hath* **s** Babylon, and 7703
Eze 18: 7 hath **s** none by violence, hath given his 1497
18:12 the poor and needy, hath **s** by violence, 1497
18:16 neither hath **s** by violence, *but* hath given 1497
18:18 **s** *his* brother by violence, and did *that* 1497
23:46 and *will* give them to be removed and **s**. 957
39:10 they shall spoil those that **s** them, and 7997
Hos 10:14 thy people, and all thy fortresses shall be **s**, 7703
10:14 as Shalman **s** Beth-arbel in the day of 7701
Am 3:11 from thee, and thy palaces shall be **s**. 962
5: 9 That strengtheneth the **s** against the strong, 7701
5: 9 so that the **s** shall come against the fortress. 7701
Mic 2: 4 *and* say, We be **utterly s**: 7703+7703
Hab 2: 8 Because thou hast **s** many nations, all 7997
Zec 2: 8 he sent me unto the nations which **s** you: 7997
11: 2 cedar is fallen; because the mighty are **s**: 7703
11: 3 of the shepherds; for their glory is **s**: 7703
11: 3 of young lions; for the pride of Jordan is **s**. 7703
Col 2:15 *And* having **s** principalities and powers, *554*

SPOILER (9) [SPOIL]
Isa 16: 4 thou a covert to them from the face of the **s**: 7703
16: 4 the extortioner is at an end, the **s** ceaseth, 7701
21: 2 dealeth treacherously, and the **s** spoileth. 7703
Jer 6:26 for the **s** shall suddenly come upon us. 7703
15: 8 mother of the young men a **s** at noonday: 7703
48: 8 the **s** shall come upon every city, and 7703
48:18 for the **s** of Moab shall come upon thee, 7703
48:32 the **s** is fallen upon thy summer fruits and 7703
51:56 Because the **s** is come upon her, *even* upon 7703

SPOILERS (7) [SPOIL]
Jdg 2:14 he delivered them into the hands of **s** that 8154
1Sa 13:17 the **s** came out of the camp of 7843
14:15 the garrison, and the **s**, they also trembled, 7843
2Ki 17:20 and delivered them into the hand of **s**, 8154
Jer 12:12 The **s** are come upon all high places 7703
51:48 for the **s** shall come unto her from 7703
51:53 *yet* from me shall **s** come unto her, saith 7703

SPOILEST (1) [SPOIL]
Isa 33: 1 Woe to thee that **s**, and thou *wast* not 7703

SPOILETH (4) [SPOIL]
Ps 35:10 and the needy from him that **s** him? 1497
Isa 21: 2 dealeth treacherously, and the spoiler **s**. 7703
Hos 7: 1 *and* the troop *of robbers* **s** without. 6584
Na 3:16 the cankerworm **s**, and flieth away. 6584

SPOILING (5) [SPOIL]
Ps 35:12 They rewarded me evil for good *to* the **s** of 7908
Isa 22: 4 of the **s** of the daughter of my people. 7701
Jer 48: 3 *be* from Horonaim, **s** and great destruction. 7701
Hab 1: 3 for **s** and violence *are* before me: and 7701
Heb 10:34 and took joyfully the **s** of your goods, *724*

SPOILS (5) [SPOIL]
Jos 7:21 When I saw among the **s** a goodly 7998
1Ch 26:27 Out of the **s won** in battles did they 7998
Isa 25:11 their pride together with the **s** of their hands. 698
Lk 11:22 wherein he trusted, and divideth his **s**. *4661*
Heb 7: 4 patriarch Abraham gave the tenth of the **s**. *205*

SPOKEN (287) [SPEAK] See Index

SPOKES (1)
1Ki 7:33 their naves, and their felloes, and their **s**, 2840

SPOKESMAN (1) [MAN, SPEAK]
Ex 4:16 he shall be thy **s** unto the people: and 1696

SPONGE See SPUNGE

SPOON (12) [SPOONS]
Nu 7:14 One **s** of ten *shekels* of gold, full *of* 3709
7:20 One **s** of gold of ten *shekels,* full *of* 3709
7:26 One golden **s** of ten *shekels,* full *of* incense: 3709
7:32 One golden **s** *of* ten *shekels,* full *of* incense: 3709
7:38 One golden **s** of ten *shekels,* full *of* incense: 3709
7:44 One golden **s** of ten *shekels,* full *of* incense: 3709
7:50 One golden **s** of ten *shekels,* full *of* incense: 3709
7:56 One golden **s** of ten *shekels,* full *of* incense: 3709
7:62 One golden **s** of ten *shekels,* full *of* incense: 3709
7:68 One golden **s** of ten *shekels,* full *of* incense: 3709
7:74 One golden **s** of ten *shekels,* full *of* incense: 3709
7:80 One golden **s** of ten *shekels,* full *of* incense: 3709

SPOONS (12) [SPOON]
Ex 25:29 **s** thereof, and covers thereof, and 3709
37:16 his **s**, and his bowls, and *his* covers to cover 3709
Nu 4:7 the **s**, and the bowls, and covers to cover 3709
7:84 twelve silver bowls, twelve **s** of gold: 3709
7:86 The golden **s** *were* twelve, full *of* incense, 3709
7:86 all the gold of the **s** *was* an hundred and 3709
1Ki 7:50 and the **s**, and the censers *of* pure gold; 3709
2Ki 25:14 the **s**, and all the vessels of brass wherewith 3709
2Ch 4:22 the basons, and the **s**, and the censers, 3709
24:14 to offer *withal,* and **s**, and vessels of gold 3709
Jer 52:18 the **s**, and all the vessels of brass wherewith 3709
52:19 the candlesticks, and the **s**, and the cups; 3709

SPORT (6) [SPORTING]
Jdg 16:25 Call for Samson, that he may **make us s**. 7832
16:25 of the prison house; and he **made** them **s**: 6711
16:27 women, that beheld while Samson **made s**. 7832
Pr 10:23 *It is* as **s** to a fool to do mischief: but a man 7814
26:19 his neighbour, and saith, Am not I **in s**? 7832
Isa 57:4 Against whom do ye **s** yourselves? 6026

SPORTING (2) [SPORT]
Ge 26:8 behold, Isaac *was* **s with** Rebekah his wife. 6711
2Pe 2:13 **s** themselves with their own deceivings *1792*

SPOT (25) [SPOTS, SPOTTED, UNSPOTTED]
Lev 13:2 or **bright s**, and it be in the skin of his flesh 934
13:4 If the **bright s** *be* white in the skin of his 934
13:19 or a **bright s**, white, *and* somewhat reddish, 934
13:23 if the **bright s** stay in his place, *and* 934
13:24 *flesh* that burneth have a white **bright s**, 934
13:25 *if* the hair in the **bright s** be turned white, 934
13:26 *there be* no white hair in the **bright s**, and 934
13:28 if the **bright s** stay in his place, *and* 934
13:39 it *is* a **freckled s** *that* groweth in the skin: 933
14:56 a rising, and for a scab, and for a **bright s**: 934
Nu 19:2 that they bring thee a red heifer **without s**, 8549
28:3 two lambs of the first year **without s** day 8549
28:9 day two lambs of the first year **without s**, 8549
28:11 seven lambs of the first year **without s**; 8549
29:17 fourteen lambs of the first year **without s**: 8549
29:26 fourteen lambs of the first year **without s**: 8549
Dt 32:5 their **s** *is* not *the spot* of his children: 3971
32:5 their spot *is* not *the* **s** of his children: NIH
Job 11:15 then shalt thou lift up thy face without **s**; 3971
SS 4:7 *art* all fair, my love; *there is* no **s** in thee. 3971
Eph 5:27 not having **s**, or wrinkle, or any such *thing;* *4696*
1Ti 6:14 thou keep *this* commandment **without s**, *784*
Heb 9:14 Spirit offered himself **without s** to God, *299*
1Pe 1:19 as of a lamb without blemish and **without s**: *784*
2Pe 3:14 of him in peace, **without s**, and blameless. *784*

SPOTS (6) [SPOT]
Lev 13:38 have in the skin of their flesh **bright s**, 934
13:38 their flesh bright spots, *even* white **bright s**; 934
13:39 *if* the **bright s** in the skin of their flesh *be* 934
Jer 13:23 change his skin, or the leopard his **s**? 2272
2Pe 2:13 **S** *they are* and blemishes, *4696*
Jude 1:12 These are **s** in your feasts of charity when *4694*

SPOTTED (7) [SPOT]
Ge 30:32 from thence all the speckled and **s** cattle, 2921
30:32 and the **s** and speckled among the goats: 2921
30:33 *is* not speckled and **s** amongst the goats, 2921
30:35 the he goats that were ringstraked and **s**, 2921
30:35 all the she goats that were speckled and **s**, 2921
30:39 forth cattle ringstraked, speckled, and **s**. 2921
Jude 1:23 hating even the garment **s** by the flesh. *4695*

SPOUSE (6) [SPOUSES]
SS 4:8 *my* **s**, with me from Lebanon: 3618
4:9 hast ravished my heart, my sister, *my* **s**; 3618
4:10 How fair is thy love, my sister, *my* **s**! 3618
4:11 Thy lips, O *my* **s**, drop *as* the honeycomb: 3618
4:12 A garden inclosed *is* my sister, *my* **s**; 3618
5:1 I am come into my garden, my sister, *my* **s**: 3618

SPOUSES (2) [SPOUSE]
Hos 4:13 and your **s** shall commit adultery. 3618
4:14 nor your **s** when they commit adultery: 3618

SPRANG (8) [SPRING]
Ge 41:6 blasted with the east wind **s up** after them. 6779
Mk 4:5 and immediately it **s up**, because *it* had no *1816*
4:8 and did yield fruit that **s up** and increased; *305*
Lk 8:7 and the thorns **s up with** *it,* and choked it. *4855*
8:8 and **s up**, and bare fruit an hundredfold. *5453*
Ac 16:29 and **s in**, and came trembling, and *1530*
Heb 7:14 For *it is* evident that our Lord **s** out of Juda; *393*
11:12 Therefore **s** there even of one, and him as *1080*

SPREAD (109) [OVERSPREAD, SPREADEST, SPREADETH, SPREADING, SPREADINGS]
Ge 10:18 the families of the Canaanites **s abroad**. 6327
28:14 thou shalt **s abroad** to the west, and to 6555
33:19 a parcel of a field, where he had **s** his tent, 5186
35:21 and **s** his tent beyond the tower of Edar. 5186
Ex 9:29 I will **s abroad** my hands unto the LORD; 6566
9:33 **s abroad** his hands unto the LORD: 6566
37:9 the cherubims **s out** *their* wings on high, 6566
40:19 he **s abroad** the tent over the tabernacle, 6566
Lev 13:5 at a stay, *and* the plague **s** not in the skin; 6581
13:6 and the plague **s** not in the skin, 6581
13:7 if the scab **s much abroad** in 6581+6581
13:22 if it **s much abroad** in the skin, then 6581+6581
13:23 in his place, *and* **s** not, it *is* a burning boil; 6581
13:27 *and* if it be **s much abroad** in 6581+6581
13:28 *and* **s** not in the skin, but it *be* somewhat 6581
13:32 *if* the scall **s** not, and there be in it no 6581
13:34 behold, *if* the scall be not **s** in the skin, 6581
13:35 if the scall **s much** in the skin after 6581+6581
13:36 behold, *if* the scall be **s** in the skin, 6581
13:51 if the plague be **s** in the garment, either in 6581
13:53 behold, the plague be not **s** in the garment, 6581
13:55 changed his colour, and the plague be not **s**; 6581
14:39 *if* the plague be **s** in the walls of the house; 6581
14:44 and behold, *if* the plague be **s** in the house, 6581
14:48 behold, the plague hath not **s** in the house, 6581
Nu 4:6 shall **s** over *it* a cloth wholly of blue, and 6566
4:7 upon the table of shewbread they shall **s** a 6566
4:8 they shall **s** upon them a cloth of scarlet, 6566
4:11 upon the golden altar they shall **s** a cloth of 6566
4:13 from the altar, and **s** a purple cloth thereon: 6566
4:14 they shall **s** upon it a covering of badgers' 6566
11:32 they **s** *them* **all abroad** for 7849+7849
24:6 As the valleys are they **s forth**, as gardens 5186
Dt 22:17 they shall **s** the cloth before the elders of 6566
Jdg 8:25 We will willingly give *them.* And they **s** a 6566
15:9 pitched in Judah, and **s** themselves in Lehi. 5203
Ru 3:9 **s** therefore thy skirt over thine handmaid; 6566
1Sa 30:16 behold *they were* **s abroad** upon all 5203
2Sa 5:18 and **s** themselves in the valley of Rephaim. 5203
5:22 and **s** themselves in the valley of Rephaim. 5203
16:22 So they **s** Absalom a tent upon the top of 5186
17:19 and **s** a covering over the well's mouth, 6566
17:19 well's mouth, and **s** ground corn thereon; 7849
21:10 and **s** it for her upon the rock, 5186
22:43 mire of the street, *and* did **s** them **abroad**. 7554
1Ki 6:32 **s** gold upon the cherubims, and upon 7286
8:7 For the cherubims **s forth** *their* two wings 6566
8:22 and **s forth** his hands *toward* heaven: 6566
8:38 and **s forth** his hands towards this house: 6566
8:54 from kneeling on his knees with his hands **s** 6566
2Ki 8:15 and **s** *it* on his face, so that he died: 6566
19:14 of the LORD, and **s** it before the LORD. 6566
1Ch 14:9 and **s** themselves in the valley of Rephaim. 6584
14:13 again **s** themselves **abroad** in the valley. 6584
28:18 that **s out** *their wings,* and covered the ark 6566
2Ch 3:13 **s** themselves **forth** twenty cubits: 6566

2Ch 5: 8 For the cherubims **s forth** *their* wings over 6566
6:12 of Israel, and **s forth** his hands: 6566
6:13 and **s forth** his hands towards heaven, 6566
6:29 and shall **s forth** his hands in this house: 6566
26: 8 his name **s abroad** even to the entering in 1980
26:15 his name **s** far abroad; for he was 3318
Ezr 9: 5 **s out** my hands unto the LORD my God, 6566
Job 29:19 My root *was* **s out** by the waters, and 6605
37:18 Hast thou with him **s out** the sky, *which is* 7554
Ps 105:39 He **s** a cloud for a covering; and fire to give 6566
140: 5 cords; they have **s** a net by the way side; 6566
Pr 1:17 Surely in vain the net *is* **s** in the sight of any 2219
Isa 1:15 when ye **s forth** your hands, I will hide 6566
14:11 the worm is **s** under thee, and the worms 3331
19: 8 they that **s** nets upon the waters shall 6566
25: 7 and the vail that is **s** over all nations. 5259
25:11 he shall **s forth** his hands in the midst of 6566
33:23 their mast, they could not **s** the sail: 6566
37:14 of the LORD, and **s** it before the LORD. 6566
42: 5 he that **s forth** the earth, and that which 7554
58: 5 to **s** sackcloth and ashes *under him?* wilt 3331
65: 2 I have **s out** mine hands all the day unto a 6566
Jer 8: 2 they shall **s** them before the sun, and 7849
10: 9 Silver **s into plates** is brought from 7554
43:10 and he shall **s** his royal pavilion over them. 5186
48:40 an eagle, and shall **s** his wings over Moab. 6566
49:22 as the eagle, and **s** his wings over Bozrah: 6566
La 1:10 The adversary hath **s out** his hand upon all 6566
1:13 he hath **s** a net for my feet, he hath turned 6566
Eze 2:10 he **s** it before me; and it *was* written within 6566
12:13 My net also will I **s** upon him, and he shall 6566
16: 8 I **s** my skirt over thee, and covered thy 6566
17:20 I will **s** my net upon him, and he shall be 6566
19: 8 the provinces, and **s** their net over him: 6566
26:14 thou shalt be *a place* to **s** nets **upon**; 4894
32: 3 **s out** my net over thee with a company of 6566
47:10 they shall be a **place to s forth** nets; 4894
Hos 5: 1 a snare on Mizpah, and a net **s** upon Tabor. 6566
7:12 they shall go, I will **s** my net upon them; 6566
14: 6 His branches shall **s**, and his beauty shall be 1980
Joel 2: 2 as the morning **s** upon the mountains: 6566
Hab 1: 8 their horsemen shall **s** themselves, and 6335
Zec 1:17 through prosperity shall yet be **s abroad**; 6327
2: 6 for I have **s** you **abroad** as the four winds 6566
Mal 2: 3 your seed, and **s** dung upon your faces, 2219
Mt 9:31 **s abroad** his **fame** in all that country. *1310*
21: 8 And a very great multitude **s** their garments *4766*
Mk 1:28 And immediately his fame **s abroad** *1831*
6:14 heard *of him;* (for his name was **s abroad**:) *5318*
11: 8 And many **s** their garments in the way: and *4766*
Lk 19:36 as he went, they **s** their clothes in the way. *5291*
Ac 4:17 But that it **s** no further among the people, *1268*
1Th 1: 8 place your faith to God-ward is **s abroad**; *1831*

SPREADEST (1) [SPREAD]
Eze 27: 7 was that **which** thou **s forth** to be thy sail; 4666

SPREADETH (14) [SPREAD]
Lev 13: 8 the scab **s** in the skin, then the priest shall 6581
Dt 32:11 **s abroad** her wings, taketh them, 6566
Job 9: 8 Which alone **s out** the heavens, and 5186
26: 9 face of *his* throne, *and* **s** his cloud upon it. 6576
36:30 he **s** his light upon it, and covereth 6566
41:30 he **s** sharp pointed *things* upon the mire. 7502
Pr 29: 5 A man that flattereth his neighbour **s** a net 6566
Isa 25:11 as he that swimmeth **s forth** *his hands* to 6566
40:19 the goldsmith **s** it **over** with gold, and 7554
40:22 and **s** them **out** as a tent to dwell in: 4969
44:24 that **s abroad** the earth by myself; 7554
Jer 4:31 *that* bewaileth herself, *that* **s** her hands, 6566
17: 8 *that* **s out** her roots by the river, and 7971
La 1:17 Zion **s forth** her hands, *and there is* none to 6566

SPREADING (4) [SPREAD]
Lev 13:57 it *is* a **s** *plague:* thou shalt burn that wherein 6524
Ps 37:35 and **s** himself like a green bay tree. 6168
Eze 17: 6 it grew, and became a **s** vine of low stature, 5628
26: 5 It shall be *a place for* the **s** of nets in 4894

SPREADINGS (1) [SPREAD]
Job 36:29 Also can *any* understand the **s** of 4666

SPRIGS (2)
Isa 18: 5 he shall both cut off the **s** with pruning 2150
Eze 17: 6 brought forth branches, and shot forth **s**. 6288

SPRING (23) [DAYSPRING, SPRANG, SPRINGETH, SPRINGING, SPRINGS, SPRUNG, WATERSPRINGS, WELLSPRING]
Nu 21:17 Israel sang this song, **S up**, O well; sing ye 5927
Dt 8: 7 depths that **s out** of the valleys and hills; 3318
Jdg 19:25 when the day began to **s**, they let her go. 5927
1Sa 9:26 it came to pass about the **s** of the day, 5927
2Ki 2:21 he went forth unto the **s** of the waters, and 4161
Job 5: 6 neither doth trouble **s** out of the ground; 6779
38:27 **cause** the bud of the tender herb **to s forth**? 6779
Ps 85:11 Truth shall **s out** of the earth; and 6779
92: 7 When the wicked **s** as the grass, and 6524
Pr 25:26 *is as* a troubled fountain, and a corrupt **s**. 4726
SS 4:12 *my* spouse; a **s** shut up, a fountain sealed. 1530
Isa 42: 9 before they **s forth** I tell you of them. 6779
43:19 I will do a new *thing;* now it shall **s forth**; 6779
44: 4 they shall **s up** *as* among the grass, 6779
45: 8 and let righteousness **s up** together; 6779
58: 8 and thine health shall **s forth** speedily: 6779
58:11 and like a **s** of water, whose waters fail not. 4161
61:11 **causeth** the things that are sown in it **to s forth**; 6779
61:11 **cause** righteousness and praise **to s forth** 6779
Eze 17: 9 it shall wither *in* all the leaves of her **s**, 6780
Hos 13:15 his **s** shall become dry, and his fountain 4726
Joel 2:22 for the pastures of the wilderness do **s**, 1876
Mk 4:27 and day, and the seed should **s** and grow up, *985*

SPRINGETH (4) [SPRING]
1Ki 4:33 even unto the hyssop that **s out** of the wall: 3318
2Ki 19:29 the second year **that which s of the same**; 7823
Isa 37:30 the second year **that which s of the same**: 7823
Hos 10: 4 thus judgment **s up** as hemlock in 6524

SPRINGING (5) [SPRING]
Ge 26:19 and found there a well of **s** water. 2416
2Sa 23: 4 *as* the tender grass *s* out of the earth by clear NIH
Ps 65:10 with showers: thou blessest the **s** thereof. 6780
Jn 4:14 him a well of water **s up** into everlasting life. *242*
Heb 12:15 lest any root of bitterness **s** up trouble *you,* *5453*

SPRINGS (16) [SPRING]
Dt 4:49 the sea of the plain, under the **s** of Pisgah. 794
Jos 10:40 of the vale, and of the **s**, and all their kings: 794
12: 8 in the **s**, and in the wilderness, and in 794
15:19 me a south land; give me also **s** of water. 1543
15:19 he gave her the upper **s**, and the nether 1543
15:19 her the upper springs, and the nether **s**. 1543
Jdg 1:15 me a south land; give me also **s** of water. 1543
1:15 Caleb gave her the upper **s** and the nether 1543
1:15 gave her the upper springs and the nether **s**. 1543
Job 38:16 Hast thou entered into the **s** of the sea? or 5033
Ps 87: 7 *shall be there:* all my **s** *are* in thee. 4599
104:10 He sendeth the **s** into the valleys, *which* run 4599
Isa 35: 7 a pool, and the thirsty land **s** of water: 4002
41:18 a pool of water, and the dry land **s** of water. 4161
49:10 even by the **s** of water shall he guide them. 4002
Jer 51:36 I will dry up her sea, and make her **s** dry. 4726

SPRINKLE (31) [SPRINKLED, SPRINKLETH, SPRINKLING]
Ex 9: 8 let Moses **s** it towards the heaven in 2236
29:16 and **s** *it* round about upon the altar. 2236
29:20 and **s** the blood upon the altar round about. 2236
29:21 **s** *it* upon Aaron, and upon his garments, 5137
Lev 1: 5 **s** the blood round about upon the altar that 2236
1:11 shall **s** his blood round about upon the altar. 2236
3: 2 Aaron's sons the priests shall **s** the blood 2236
3: 8 Aaron's sons shall **s** the blood thereof 2236
3:13 the sons of Aaron shall **s** the blood thereof 2236
4: 6 **s** of the blood seven times before 5137
4:17 **s** *it* seven times before the LORD, 5137
5: 9 he shall **s** of the blood of the sin offering 5137
7: 2 the blood thereof shall he **s** round about 2236
14: 7 he shall **s** upon him that is to be cleansed 5137
14:16 shall **s** of the oil with his finger seven times 5137
14:27 the priest shall **s** with his right finger *some* 5137
14:51 running water, and **s** the house seven times: 5137
16:14 **s** *it* with his finger upon the mercy seat 5137
16:14 before the mercy seat shall he **s** of 5137
16:15 **s** it upon the mercy seat, and before 5137
16:19 he shall **s** of the blood upon it with his 5137
17: 6 the priest shall **s** the blood upon the altar of 2236

S

Nu 8: 7 **S** water of purifying upon them, and 5137
18:17 thou shalt **s** their blood upon the altar, and 2236
19: 4 **s** of her blood directly before the tabernacle 5137
19:18 **s** *it* upon the tent, and upon all the vessels, 5137
19:19 the clean *person* shall **s** upon the unclean 5137
2Ki 16:15 **s** upon it all the blood of the burnt offering, 2236
Isa 52:15 So shall he **s** many nations; the kings shall 5137
Eze 36:25 will I **s** clean water upon you, and ye shall 2236
43:18 offerings thereon, and to **s** blood thereon. 2236

SPRINKLED (25) [SPRINKLE]
Ex 9:10 Moses **s** it *up* toward heaven; and it became 2236
24: 6 and half of the blood he **s** on the altar. 2236
24: 8 the blood, and **s** *it* on the people, and said, 2236
Lev 6:27 when there is **s** of the blood thereof upon 5137
6:27 thou shalt wash that whereon it was **s** in 5137
8:11 And he **s** thereof upon the altar seven times, 5137
8:19 Moses **s** the blood upon the altar round 2236
8:24 Moses **s** the blood upon the altar round 2236
8:30 **s** *it* upon Aaron, *and* upon his garments, 5137
9:12 which he **s** round about upon the altar. 2236
9:18 which he **s** upon the altar round about, 2236
Nu 19:13 the water of separation was not **s** upon him, 2236
19:20 the water of separation hath not been **s** 2236
2Ki 9:33 *some* of her blood was **s** on the wall, and 5137
16:13 **s** the blood of his peace offerings, upon 2236
2Ch 29:22 received the blood, and **s** *it* on the altar: 2236
29:22 the rams, they **s** the blood upon the altar: 2236
29:22 and they **s** the blood upon the altar. 2236
30:16 the priests **s** the blood, *which they received* 2236
35:11 and the priests **s** *the blood* from their hands, 2236
Job 2:12 and **s** dust upon their heads toward heaven. 2236
Isa 63: 3 their blood shall be **s** upon my garments, 5137
Heb 9:19 and **s** both the book, and all the people, *4472*
9:21 Moreover he **s** with blood both *4472*
10:22 having *our* hearts **s** from an evil *4472*

SPRINKLETH (2) [SPRINKLE]
Lev 7:14 it shall be the priest's that **s** the blood of 2236
Nu 19:21 that he that **s** the water of separation shall 5137

SPRINKLING (4) [SPRINKLE]
Heb 9:13 and the ashes of a heifer **s** the unclean, *4472*
11:28 he kept the passover, and the **s** of blood, *4378*
12:24 and to the blood of **s**, that speaketh better *4473*
1Pe 1: 2 and **s** of the blood of Jesus Christ: *4473*

SPROUT (1)
Job 14: 7 that it will **s** again, and that the tender 2498

SPRUNG (7) [SPRING]
Ge 41:23 blasted with the east wind, **s up** after them: 6779
Lev 13:42 it *is* a leprosy **s up** in his bald head, or his 6524
Mt 4:16 the region and shadow of death light is **s up**. *393*
13: 5 and forthwith they **s up**, because *they* had *1816*
13: 7 and the thorns **s up**, and choked them: *305*
13:26 But when the blade was **s up**, and *985*
Lk 8: 6 and as soon as it was **s up**, it withered *5453*

SPUE (4) [SPUED, SPUING]
Lev 18:28 That the land **s** not you **out** also, when ye 6958
20:22 I bring you to dwell therein, **s** you not **out**. 6958
Jer 25:27 **s**, and fall, and rise no more, because of 7006
Rev 3:16 cold nor hot, I will **s** thee out of my mouth. *1692*

SPUED (1) [SPUE]
Lev 18:28 as it **s out** the nations that *were* before you. 6958

SPUING (1) [SPUE]
Hab 2:16 and **shameful s** *shall be* on thy glory. 7022

SPUN (2) [SPIN]
Ex 35:25 brought that which they had **s**, *both* of blue, 4299
35:26 stirred them up in wisdom **s** goats' *hair*. 2901

SPUNGE (3)
Mt 27:48 and took a **s**, and filled *it* with vinegar, and *4699*
Mk 15:36 And one ran and filled a **s** *full* of vinegar, *4699*
Jn 19:29 and they filled a **s** with vinegar, and put *it* *4699*

SPY (12) [ESPIED, ESPY, SPIED, SPIES]
Nu 13:16 men which Moses sent to **s out** the land. 8446
13:17 Moses sent them to **s out** the land of 8446
21:32 Moses sent to **s out** Jaazer, and they took 7270
Jos 2: 1 sent out of Shittim two men to **s** secretly, 7270
6:25 which Joshua sent to **s out** Jericho. 7270
Jdg 18: 2 to **s out** the land, and to search it; 7270
18:14 answered the five men that went to **s out** 7270
18:17 the five men that went to **s out** the land 7270
2Sa 10: 3 and to **s** it **out**, and to overthrow it? 7270
2Ki 6:13 Go and **s** where he *is*, that I may send and 7200
1Ch 19: 3 and to overthrow, and to **s out** the land? 7270
Gal 2: 4 who came in privily to **s out** our liberty *2684*

SQUADS OF FOUR SOLDIERS See QUATERNIONS

SQUARE (3) [FOURSQUARE, SQUARED, SQUARES, STONESQUARERS]
1Ki 7: 5 all the doors and posts *were* **s**, *with* 7251
Eze 43:16 twelve broad, **s** in the four squares thereof. 7251
45: 2 five hundred *in breadth*, **s** round about; 7251

SQUARED (1) [SQUARE]
Eze 41:21 The posts of the temple *were* **s**, *and* the face 7251

SQUARES (2) [SQUARE]
Eze 43:16 twelve broad, square in the four **s** thereof. 7253
43:17 and fourteen broad in the four **s** thereof; 7253

STABILITY (1) [STABLE]
Isa 33: 6 and knowledge shall be the **s** of thy times, 530

STABLE (2) [STABILITY, UNSTABLE]
1Ch 16:30 the world also shall be **s**, that it be not 3559
Eze 25: 5 And I will make Rabbah a **s** for camels, and 5116

STABLISH (15) [STABLISHED, STABLISHETH]
2Sa 7:13 I will **s** the throne of his kingdom for ever. 3559
1Ch 17:11 be of thy sons; and I will **s** his kingdom. 3559
17:12 me a house, and I will **s** his throne for ever. 3559
18: 3 as he went to **s** his dominion by the river 5324
2Ch 7:18 will I **s** the throne of thy kingdom, 6965
Est 9:21 To **s** *this* among them, that they should 6965
Ps 89: 4 Thy seed will I **s** for ever, and build up thy 3559
119:38 **S** thy word unto thy servant, who *is* 6965
Isa 9: 7 to **s** it with judgment and with justice from 5582
Ro 16:25 Now to him that is of power to **s** you *4741*
1Th 3:13 To the end *he* may **s** your hearts *4741*
2Th 2:17 and **s** you in every good word and work. *4741*
3: 3 who shall **s** you, and keep *you* from evil. *4741*
Jas 5: 8 Be ye also patient; **s** your hearts: for *4741*
1Pe 5:10 make you perfect, **s**, strengthen, settle *you*. *4741*

STABLISHED (10) [STABLISH]
Lev 25:30 house that *is* in the walled city shall be **s** 6965
Dt 19:15 of three witnesses, shall the matter be **s**. 6965
1Sa 20:31 thou shalt not be **s**, nor thy kingdom. 3559
2Sa 7:16 thy kingdom shall be **s** for ever before thee: 539
7:16 before thee: thy throne shall be **s** for ever. 3559
2Ch 17: 5 Therefore the LORD **s** the kingdom in his 3559
Ps 93: 1 the world also is **s**, *that* it cannot be moved. 3559
148: 6 He hath also **s** them for ever and ever: 5975
Col 2: 7 and built up in him, and **s** in the faith, *950*
2Pe 1:12 ye know *them*, and be **s** in the present truth. *4741*

STABLISHETH (3) [STABLISH]
Pr 29: 4 The king by judgment **s** the land: but 5975
Hab 2:12 a town with blood, and **s** a city by iniquity! 3559
2Co 1:21 Now he which **s** us with you in Christ, and *950*

STACHYS (1)
Ro 16: 9 our helper in Christ, and **S** my beloved. *4720*

STACKS (1)
Ex 22: 6 so that the **s of corn**, or the standing corn, 1430

STACTE (1)
Ex 30:34 sweet spices, **s**, and onycha, and galbanum; 5198

STADIA See FURLONGS

STAFF (43) [HANDSTAVES, STAVES]
Ge 32:10 for with my **s** I passed over this Jordan; 4731
38:18 thy bracelets, and thy **s** that *is* in thine hand. 4294
38:25 *are* these, the signet, and bracelets, and **s**. 4294
Ex 12:11 shoes on your feet, and your **s** in your hand; 4731
21:19 walk abroad upon his **s**, then shall he that 4938
Lev 26:26 *And* when I have broken the **s** of your 4294
Nu 13:23 and they bare it between two upon a **s**; 4132
22:27 was kindled, and he smote the ass with a **s**. 4731
Jdg 6:21 forth the end of the **s** that *was* in his hand, 4938

1Sa 17: 7 the **s** of his spear *was* like a weaver's beam; 6086
17:40 he took his **s** in his hand, and chose him 4731
2Sa 3:29 or that leaneth on a **s**, or that falleth on 6418
21:19 the **s** of whose spear *was* like a weaver's 6086
23: 7 be fenced *with* iron and the **s** of a spear; 6086
23:21 he went down to him with a **s**, and 7626
2Ki 4:29 take my **s** in thine hand, and go *thy way:* if 4938
4:29 and lay my **s** upon the face of the child. 4938
4:31 and laid the **s** upon the face of the child; 4938
18:21 thou trustest upon the **s** of this bruised reed, 4938
1Ch 11:23 he went down to him with a **s**, and 7626
20: 5 whose spear **s** *was* like a weaver's beam. 6086
Ps 23: 4 thy rod and thy **s** they comfort me. 4938
105:16 the land: he brake the whole **s** of bread. 4294
Isa 3: 1 and from Judah the stay and the **s**, 4938
9: 4 the **s** of his shoulder, the rod of his 4294
10: 5 and the **s** in their hand *is* mine indignation. 4294
10:15 as if the **s** should lift up *itself, as if it were* 4294
10:24 shall lift up his **s** against thee, after 4294
14: 5 The LORD hath broken the **s** of 4294
28:27 the fitches are beaten out with a **s**, and 4294
30:32 *in* every *place* where the grounded **s** shall 4294
36: 6 thou trustest in the **s** of this broken reed, 4938
Jer 48:17 How is the strong **s** broken, *and* 4294
Eze 4:16 I will break the **s** of bread in Jerusalem: 4294
5:16 upon you, and will break your **s** of bread: 4294
14:13 will break the **s** of the bread thereof, and 4294
29: 6 they have been a **s** of reed to the house of 4938
Hos 4:12 and their **s** declareth unto them: 4731
Zec 8: 4 every man with his **s** in his hand for very 4938
11:10 I took my **s**, *even* Beauty, and cut it 4731
11:14 I cut asunder mine other **s**, *even* Bands, 4731
Mk 6: 8 nothing for *their* journey, save a **s** only; *4464*
Heb 11:21 worshipped, *leaning* upon the top of his **s**. *4464*

STAFFS See STAVES

STAG See HART

STAGGER (3) [STAGGERED, STAGGERETH]
Job 12:25 he **maketh** them **to s** like a drunken *man.* 8582
Ps 107:27 **s** like a drunken *man,* and are at their wit's 5128
Isa 29: 9 *with* wine; they **s**, but not *with* strong drink. 5128

STAGGERED (1) [STAGGER]
Ro 4:20 He **s** not at the promise of God through *1252*

STAGGERETH (1) [STAGGER]
Isa 19:14 as a drunken *man* **s** in his vomit. 8582

STAIN (3)
Job 3: 5 Let darkness and the shadow of death **s** it; 1350
Isa 23: 9 to **s** the pride of all glory, *and* to bring into 2490
63: 3 my garments, and I will **s** all my raiment. 1351

STAIRS (10)
1Ki 6: 8 they went up with **winding s** into 3883
2Ki 9:13 and put *it* under him on the top of the **s**, and 4609
Ne 3:15 unto the **s** that go down from the city of 4609
9: 4 stood up upon the **s** of the Levites, Jeshua, 4608
12:37 they went up by the **s** of the city of David, 4609
SS 2:14 in the secret places of the **s**, let me see thy 4095
Eze 40: 6 went up the **s** thereof, and measured 4609
43:17 and his **s** *shall* look toward the east. 4609
Ac 21:35 And when he came upon the **s**, so it was, *304*
21:40 Paul stood on the **s**, and beckoned with *304*

STAKES (2)
Isa 33:20 not one of the **s** thereof shall ever be 3489
54: 2 lengthen thy cords, and strengthen thy **s**; 3489

STALE (2) [STEAL]
Ge 31:20 Jacob **s away unawares** to Laban 1589+3820
2Ki 11: 2 **s** him from among the king's sons which 1589

STALK (3) [STALKS]
Ge 41: 5 seven ears of corn came up upon one **s**, 7070
41:22 seven ears came up in one **s**, full and good: 7070
Hos 8: 7 it hath no **s**: the bud shall yield no meal: if 7054

STALKS (1) [STALK]
Jos 2: 6 hid them with the **s** of flax, which she had 6086

STALL (3) [STALLED, STALLS]
Am 6: 4 and the calves out of the midst of the **s**; 4770
Mal 4: 2 go forth, and grow up as calves of the **s**. 4770
Lk 13:15 sabbath loose his ox or *his* ass from the **s**, *5336*

STALLED (1) [STALL]
Pr 15:17 love is, than a **s** ox and hatred therewith. 75

STALLS (4) [STALL]
1Ki 4:26 Solomon had forty thousand **s** of horses for 723
2Ch 9:25 And Solomon had four thousand **s** for horses 723
32:28 **s** for all *manner of* beasts, and cotes for 723
Hab 3:17 the fold, and *there shall be* no herd in the **s**: 7517

STAMMERERS (1) [STAMMERING]
Isa 32: 4 the tongue of the **s** shall be ready to speak 5926

STAMMERING (2) [STAMMERERS]
Isa 28:11 For with **s** lips and another tongue will he 3934
33:19 of a **s** tongue, *that thou canst* not 3932

STAMP (2) [STAMPED, STAMPING, STAMPT]
2Sa 22:43 I did **s** them as the mire of the street, *and* 1854
Eze 6:11 thine hand, and **s** with thy foot, and say, 7554

STAMPED (7) [STAMP]
Dt 9:21 with fire, and **s** it, *and* ground *it* very small, 3807
2Ch 15:16 and **s** *it,* and burnt *it* at the brook Kidron. 1854
Eze 25: 6 **s** with the feet, and rejoiced in heart with 7554
Da 7: 7 and **s** the residue with the feet of it: 7512
7:19 in pieces, and **s** the residue with his feet; 7512
8: 7 him down to the ground, and **s upon** him: 7429
8:10 of the stars to the ground, and **s** upon them. 7429

STAMPING (1) [STAMP]
Jer 47: 3 At the noise of the **s** of the hoofs of his 8161

STAMPT (2) [STAMP]
2Ki 23: 6 **s** *it* **small** to powder, and cast the powder 1854
23:15 *and* **s** *it* **small** to powder, and burnt 1854

STANCHED (1)
Lk 8:44 and immediately her issue of blood **s**. *2476*

STAND (274) [STANDEST, STANDETH, STANDING, STOOD, STOODEST]
Ge 19: 9 they said, **S** back. And they said *again, This* 5066
24:13 Behold, I **s** *here* by the well of water; and 5324
24:43 Behold, I **s** by the well of water; and it shall 5324
Ex 7:15 thou shalt **s** by the river's brink against he 5324
8:20 early in the morning, and **s** before Pharaoh; 3320
9:11 the magicians could not **s** before Moses 5975
9:13 and **s** before Pharaoh, and say unto him, 3320
14:13 **s still**, and see the salvation of the LORD, 3320
17: 6 I will **s** before thee there upon the rock in 5975
17: 9 to morrow I will **s** on the top of the hill 5324
18:14 all the people **s** by thee from morning unto 5324
33:10 all the people saw the cloudy pillar **s** *at* 5975
33:21 a place by me, and thou shalt **s** upon a rock: 5324
Lev 18:23 neither shall any woman **s** before a beast to 5975
19:16 neither shalt thou **s** against the blood of thy 5975
26:37 ye shall have no **power to s** before your 8617
27:14 as the priest shall estimate it, so shall it **s**. 6965
27:17 according to thy estimation it shall **s**. 6965
Nu 1: 5 these *are* the names of the men that shall **s** 5975
9: 8 **S still**, and I will hear what the LORD 5975
11:16 that they may **s** there with thee. 3320
16: 9 to **s** before the congregation to minister 5975
23: 3 **S** by thy burnt offering, and I will go: 3320
23:15 unto Balak, **S** here by thy burnt offering, 3320
27:21 he shall **s** before Eleazar the priest, 5975
30: 4 all her vows shall **s**, and every bond 6965
30: 4 wherewith she hath bound her soul shall **s**. 6965
30: 5 wherewith she hath bound her soul, shall **s**: 6965
30: 7 day that he heard *it:* then her vows shall **s**, 6965
30: 7 wherewith she bound her soul shall **s**. 6965
30: 9 have bound their souls, shall **s** against her. 6965
30:11 all her vows shall **s**, and every bond 6965
30:11 bond wherewith she bound her soul shall **s**. 6965
30:12 concerning the bond of her soul, shall not **s**: 6965
35:12 until he **s** before the congregation in 5975
Dt 5:31 **s** thou here by me, and I will speak unto 5975
7:24 there shall no man *be able to* **s** before thee, 3320
9: 2 *of whom* thou hast heard *say,* Who can **s** 3320
10: 8 to **s** before the LORD to minister unto 5975
11:25 There shall no man *be able to* **s** before you: 3320
18: 5 to **s** to minister in the name of the LORD, 5975
18: 7 as all his brethren the Levites *do,* which **s** 5975

S

Dt 19:17 between whom the controversy *is,* shall **s** 5975
24:11 Thou shalt **s** abroad, and the man to whom 5975
25: 8 *if* he **s** *to it,* and say, I like not to take her; 5975
27:12 These shall **s** upon mount Gerizzim to bless 5975
27:13 these shall **s** upon mount Ebal to curse; 5975
29:10 Ye **s** *this* day all of you before the LORD 5324
Jos 1: 5 There shall not any man *be able to* **s** before 3320
3: 8 water of Jordan, ye shall **s still** in Jordan. 5975
3:13 from above; and they shall **s** *upon* a heap. 5975
7:12 Therefore the children of Israel could not **s** 6965
7:13 thou canst not **s** before thine enemies, 6965
10: 8 there shall not a man of them **s** before thee. 5975
10:12 of Israel, Sun, **s** thou **still** upon Gibeon; 1826
20: 4 shall **s** *at* the entering of the gate of the city, 5975
20: 6 until he **s** before the congregation for 5975
23: 9 no man hath *been able to* **s** before you unto 5975
Jdg 2:14 that they could not any longer **s** before their 5975
4:20 **S** *in* the door of the tent, and it shall be, 5975
1Sa 6:20 Who is able to **s** before this holy LORD 5975
9:27 **s** thou **still** a while, that I may shew thee 5975
12: 7 Now therefore **s still**, that I may reason 3320
12:16 Now therefore **s** and see this great thing, 3320
14: 9 we will **s still** in our place, and will not go 5975
16:22 Let David, I pray thee, **s** before me; 5975
19: 3 **s** beside my father in the field where thou 5975
2Sa 1: 9 **S**, I pray thee, upon me, and slay me: 5975
18:30 king said *unto him,* Turn aside, *and* **s** here. 3320
1Ki 1: 2 let her **s** before the king, and let her cherish 5975
8:11 So that the priests could not **s** to minister 5975
10: 8 which **s** continually before thee, *and* 5975
17: 1 God of Israel liveth, before whom I **s**, 5975
18:15 LORD of hosts liveth, before whom I **s**, 5975
19:11 and **s** upon the mount before the LORD. 5975
2Ki 3:14 of hosts liveth, before whom I **s**, surely, 5975
5:11 **s**, and call on the name of the LORD his 5975
5:16 before whom I **s**, I will receive none. 5975
6:31 the son of Shaphat shall **s** on him *this* day. 5975
10: 4 stood not before him: how then shall we **s**? 5975
1Ch 21:16 saw the angel of the LORD **s** between 5975
23:30 to **s** every morning to thank and praise 5975
2Ch 5:14 So that the priests could not **s** to minister by 5975
9: 7 which **s** continually before thee, and 5975
20: 9 we **s** before this house, and in thy presence, 5975
20:17 **s** ye *still,* and see the salvation of 5975
29:11 for the LORD hath chosen you to **s** before 5975
34:32 **caused** all that were present in Jerusalem and Benjamin **to s** 5975
35: 5 **s** in the holy *place* according to 5975
Ezr 9:15 for *we* cannot **s** before thee because of this. 5975
10:13 much rain, and *we are* not able to **s** without, 5975
10:14 Let now our rulers of all the congregation **s**, 5975
Ne 7: 3 while they **s by**, let them shut the doors, 5975
9: 5 **S up** *and* bless the LORD your God for 6965
Est 3: 4 to see whether Mordecai's matters would **s**: 5975
8:11 to **s** for their life, to destroy, to slay, and 5975
Job 8:15 shall lean upon his house, but it shall not **s**: 5975
19:25 *that* he shall **s** *at* the latter *day* upon 6965
30:20 hear me: I **s** *up,* and thou regardest me *not.* 5975
33: 5 set *thy words* in order before me, **s up**. 3320
37:14 **s still**, and consider the wondrous works of 5975
38:14 as clay *to* the seal; and they **s** as a garment. 3320
41:10 him up: who then is able to **s** before me? 3320
Ps 1: 5 Therefore the ungodly shall not **s** in 6965
4: 4 **S in awe**, and sin not: commune with your 7264
5: 5 The foolish shall not **s** in thy sight: 3320
20: 8 and fallen: but we are risen, and **s upright**. 5749
24: 3 and who shall **s** in his holy place? 6965
30: 7 thou hast **made** my mountain **to s** strong: 5975
33: 8 let all the inhabitants of the world **s in awe** 1481
35: 2 and buckler, and **s up** for mine help. 6965
38:11 and my friends **s** aloof from my sore; 5975
38:11 from my sore; and my kinsmen **s** afar off. 5975
45: 9 right hand did **s** the queen in gold of Ophir. 5324
73: 7 Their eyes **s out** with fatness: they have 3318
76: 7 who may **s** in thy sight when once thou art 5975
78:13 and he **made** the waters **to s** as a heap. 5324
89:28 and my covenant *shall* **s fast** with him. 539
89:43 and hast not **made** him **to s** in the battle. 6965
94:16 who will **s up** for me against the workers of 3320
109: 6 over him: and let Satan **s** at his right hand. 5975
109:31 For he shall **s** at the right hand of the poor, 5975
111: 8 They **s fast** for ever and ever, *and are* done 5564
122: 2 Our feet shall **s** within thy gates, 5975
130: 3 mark iniquities, O Lord, who shall **s**? 5975
134: 1 which by night **s** in the house of 5975
135: 2 Ye that **s** in the house of the LORD, in 5975
147:17 ice like morsels: who can **s** before his cold? 5975
Pr 12: 7 but the house of the righteous shall **s**. 5975
19:21 the counsel of the LORD, that shall **s**. 6965
22:29 he shall **s** before kings; he shall not stand 3320
22:29 he shall not **s** before mean *men.* 3320
25: 6 and **s** not in the place of great *men:* 5975
27: 4 but who is **able to s** before envy? 5975
Ecc 4:15 with the second child that shall **s** *up* in his 5975
8: 3 **s** not in an evil thing; for he doeth 5975
Isa 7: 7 Thus saith the Lord GOD, It shall not **s**, 6965
8:10 speak the word, and it shall not **s**: 6965
11:10 which shall **s** for an ensign of the people; 5975
14:24 and as I have purposed, *so* shall it **s**: 6965
21: 8 I **s** continually upon the watchtower in 5975
27: 9 the groves and images shall not **s up**. 6965
28:18 and your agreement with hell shall not **s**; 6965
32: 8 and by liberal *things* shall he **s**. 6965
40: 8 but the word of our God shall **s** for ever. 6965
44:11 let them **s** *up; yet* they shall fear, *and* 5975
46:10 My counsel shall **s**, and I will do all my 6965
47:12 **S** now with thine enchantments, and 5975
47:13 **s** *up,* and save thee from *these things* that 5975
48:13 *when* I call unto them, they **s** *up* together. 5975
50: 8 let us **s** together: who *is* mine adversary? let 5975
51:17 Awake, awake, **s up**, O Jerusalem, 6965
61: 5 strangers shall **s** and feed your flocks, and 5975
65: 5 Which say, **S** by thyself, come not near to 7126
Jer 6:16 **S** ye in the ways, and see, and ask for 5975
7: 2 **S** in the gate of the LORD's house, and 5975
7:10 come and **s** before me in this house, which 5975
14: 6 the wild asses did **s** in the high places, 5975
15:19 thee again, *and* thou shalt **s** before me: 5975
17:19 **s** in the gate of the children of the people, 5975
26: 2 **S** in the court of the LORD's house, and 5975
35:19 not want a man to **s** before me for ever. 5975
44:28 shall know whose words shall **s**, mine, or 6965
44:29 shall **surely s** against you for evil: 6965+6965
46: 4 and **s forth** with *your* helmets; 3320
46:14 say ye, **S fast**, and prepare thee; for 3320
46:21 they did not **s**, because the day of their 5975
48:19 inhabitant of Aroer, **s** by the way and espy; 5975
49:19 who *is* that shepherd that will **s** before me? 5975
50:44 who *is* that shepherd that will **s** before me? 5975
51:50 escaped the sword, go *away,* **s** not **still**: 5975
Eze 2: 1 **s** upon thy feet, and I will speak unto thee. 5975
13: 5 to **s** in the battle in the day of the LORD. 5975
17:14 that by keeping of his covenant it might **s**. 5975
22:30 **s** in the gap before me for the land, that *I* 5975
27:29 from their ships, they shall **s** upon the land; 5975
29: 7 and **madest** all their loins **to be at a s**. 5976
31:14 neither their trees **s up** in their height, 5975
33:26 Ye **s** upon your sword, ye work 5975
44:11 they shall **s** before them to minister unto 5975
44:15 they shall **s** before me to offer unto me 5975
44:24 in controversy they shall **s** in judgment; 5975
46: 2 shall **s** by the post of the gate, and 5975
47:10 *that* the fishers shall **s** upon it from En-gedi 5975
Da 1: 4 such as *had* ability in them to **s** in 5975
1: 5 that at the end thereof they might **s** before 5975
2:44 all these kingdoms, and it shall **s** for ever. 6966
7: 4 **made s** upon the feet as a man, and a man's 6966
8: 4 so that no beasts might **s** before him, 5975
8: 7 there was no power in the ram to **s** before 5975
8:22 four kingdoms shall **s up** out of the nation, 5975
8:23 understanding dark sentences, shall **s up**. 5975
8:25 he shall also **s up** against the Prince of 5975
10:11 words that I speak unto thee, and **s** upright: 5975
11: 2 there *shall* **s up** yet three kings in Persia; 5975
11: 3 a mighty king shall **s up**, that shall rule 5975
11: 4 when he shall **s up**, his kingdom shall be 5975
11: 6 of the arm; neither shall he **s**, nor his arm: 5975
11: 7 out of a branch of her roots shall *one* **s up** 5975
11:14 in those times there shall many **s up** against 5975
11:16 his own will, and none shall **s** before him: 5975
11:16 he shall **s** in the glorious land, which by his 5975
11:17 she shall not **s** *on his side,* neither be for 5975
11:20 shall **s up** in his estate a raiser of taxes *in* 5975
11:21 in his estate shall **s up** a vile person, to 5975
11:25 and mighty army; but he shall not **s**: 5975
11:31 arms shall **s** on his part, and they shall 5975
12: 1 at that time shall Michael **s up**, the great 5975
12:13 and **s** in thy lot at the end of the days. 5975

Am 2:15 Neither shall he s that handleth the bow; 5975
Mic 5: 4 he shall s and feed in the strength of 5975
Na 1: 6 Who can s before his indignation? and 5975
2: 8 S, stand, shall they cry; but none shall look 5975
2: 8 Stand, s, shall they cry; but none shall look 5975
Hab 2: 1 I will s upon my watch, and set me upon 5975
Zec 3: 7 thee places to walk among these that s by. 5975
4:14 that s by the Lord of the whole earth. 5975
14: 4 his feet shall s in that day upon the mount 5975
14:12 consume away while they s upon their feet, 5975
Mal 3: 2 who shall s when he appeareth? for he is 5975
Mt 12:25 or house divided against itself shall not s: 2476
12:26 how shall then his kingdom s? 2476
12:47 thy mother and thy brethren s without, 2476
20: 6 unto them, Why s ye here all the day idle? 2476
24:15 s in the holy place, (whoso readeth, let him 2476
Mk 3: 3 man which had the withered hand, S forth. 1453
3:24 against itself, that kingdom cannot s. 2476
3:25 divided against itself, that house cannot s. 2476
3:26 be divided, he cannot s, but hath an end. 2476
9: 1 That there be some of them that s here, 2476
11:25 And when ye s praying, forgive, if ye have 4739
Lk 1:19 I am Gabriel, that s in the presence of God; 3936
6: 8 Rise up, and s forth in the midst. 2476
8:20 Thy mother and thy brethren s without, 2476
11:18 against himself, how shall his kingdom s? 2476
13:25 and ye begin to s without, and to knock at 2476
21:36 to pass, and to s before the Son of man. 2476
Jn 11:42 of the people which s by I said it, that they 4026
Ac 1:11 of Galilee, why s ye gazing up into heaven? 2476
4:10 even by him doth this man s here before 3936
5:20 s and speak in the temple to the people all 2476
8:38 And he commanded the chariot to s still: 2476
10:26 But Peter took him up, saying, S up; 450
14:10 Said with a loud voice, S upright on thy feet. 450
25:10 said Paul, I s at Cesar's judgment seat, 2476
26: 6 And now I s and am judged for the hope of 2476
26:16 But rise, and s upon thy feet: for I have 2476
Ro 5: 2 access by faith into this grace wherein we s, 2476
9:11 of God according to election might s, 3306
14: 4 holden up: for God is able to make him s. 2476
14:10 for we shall all s before the judgment seat 3936
1Co 2: 5 That your faith should not s in the wisdom 1510
15: 1 also you have received, and wherein ye s; 2476
15:30 And why s we in jeopardy every hour? 2793
16:13 Watch ye, s fast in the faith, quit you like 4739
2Co 1:24 are helpers of your joy: for by faith ye s. 2476
Gal 4:20 to change my voice; for I s in doubt of you. 639
5: 1 S fast therefore in the liberty wherewith 4739
Eph 6:11 that ye may be able to s against the wiles of 2476
6:13 in the evil day, and having done all, to s. 2476
6:14 S therefore, having your loins girt about 2476
Php 1:27 of your affairs, that ye s fast in one spirit, 4739
4: 1 my joy and crown, so s fast in the Lord, 4739
Col 4:12 that ye may s perfect and complete in all 2476
1Th 3: 8 For now we live, if ye s fast in the Lord. 4739
2Th 2:15 s fast, and hold the traditions which ye 4739
Jas 2: 3 S thou there, or sit here under my footstool: 2476
1Pe 5:12 this is the true grace of God wherein ye s. 2476
Rev 3:20 Behold, I s at the door, and knock: if any 2476
6:17 wrath is come; and who shall be able to s? 2476
10: 5 And the angel which I saw s upon the sea 2476
15: 2 s on the sea of glass, having the harps of 2476
18:15 shall s afar off for the fear of her torment, 2476
20:12 the dead, small and great, s before God; 2476

STANDARD (18) [STANDARD-BEARER, STANDARDS]

Nu 1:52 every man by his own s, throughout their 1714
2: 2 children of Israel shall pitch by his own s, 1714
2: 3 s of the camp of Judah pitch throughout 1714
2:10 On the south side shall be the s of the camp 1714
2:18 On the west side shall be the s of the camp 1714
2:25 The s of the camp of Dan shall be on 1714
10:14 In the first place went the s of the camp of 1714
10:18 the s of the camp of Reuben set forward 1714
10:22 the s of the camp of the children of 1714
10:25 the s of the camp of the children of Dan set 1714
Isa 49:22 the Gentiles, and set up my s to the people: 5251
59:19 the spirit of the LORD shall lift up a s 5127
62:10 out the stones; lift up a s for the people. 5251
Jer 4: 6 Set up the s toward Zion: retire, stay not: 5251
4:21 How long shall I see the s, and hear 5251
50: 2 the nations, and publish, and set up a s; 5251
51:12 Set up the s upon the walls of Babylon, 5251
51:27 Set ye up a s in the land, blow the trumpet 5251

STANDARD-BEARER (1) [BEAR, STANDARD]

Isa 10:18 and they shall be as when a s fainteth. 5263

STANDARDS (3) [STANDARD]

Nu 2:17 every man in his place by their s. 1714
2:31 They shall go hindmost with their s. 1714
2:34 so they pitched by their s, and so they set 1714

STANDEST (6) [STAND]

Ge 24:31 of the LORD; wherefore s thou without? 5975
Ex 3: 5 for the place whereon thou s is holy 5975
Jos 5:15 for the place whereon thou s is holy. 5975
Ps 10: 1 Why s thou afar off, O LORD? why hidest 5975
Ac 7:33 for the place where thou s is holy ground. 2476
Ro 11:20 they were broken off, and thou s by faith. 2476

STANDETH (30) [STAND]

Nu 14:14 that thy cloud s over them, and that thou 5975
Dt 1:38 s before thee, he shall go in thither: 5975+3807.1
17:12 will not hearken unto the priest that s to 5975
29:15 with him that s here with us this day before 5975
Jdg 16:26 may feel the pillars whereupon the house s, 3559
Est 6: 5 unto him, Behold, Haman s in the court. 5975
7: 9 good for the king, s in the house of Haman. 5975
Ps 1: 1 nor s in the way of sinners, nor sitteth in 5975
26:12 My foot s in an even place: in 5975
33:11 The counsel of the LORD s for ever, 5975
82: 1 God s in the congregation of the mighty; 5324
119:161 a cause: but my heart s in awe of thy word. 6342
Pr 8: 2 She s in the top of high places by the way, 5324
SS 2: 9 behold, he s behind our wall, he looketh 5975
Isa 3:13 The LORD s up to plead, and standeth to 5324
3:13 up to plead, and s to judge the people. 5975
46: 7 and set him in his place, and he s; 5975
59:14 away backward, and justice s afar off: 5975
Da 12: 1 the great prince which s for the children of 5975
Zec 11:16 that that is broken, nor feed that that s still: 5324
Jn 1:26 but there s one among you, whom ye know 2476
3:29 which s and heareth him, rejoiceth greatly 2476
Ro 14: 4 to his own master he s or falleth. Yea, 4739
1Co 7:37 Nevertheless he that s stedfast in his heart, 2476
8:13 I will eat no flesh while the world s, lest I 1519
10:12 Wherefore let him that thinketh he s take 2476
2Ti 2:19 Nevertheless the foundation of God s sure, 2476
Heb 10:11 And every priest s daily ministering and 2476
Jas 5: 9 the judge s before the door. 2476
Rev 10: 8 the hand of the angel which s upon the sea 2476

STANDING (55) [STAND]

Ex 22: 6 stacks of corn, or the s corn, or the field, 7054
26:15 for the tabernacle of shittim wood s up. 5975
36:20 for the tabernacle of shittim wood, s up. 5975
Lev 26: 1 neither rear you up a s image, 4676
Nu 22:23 the ass saw the angel of the LORD s in 5324
22:31 he saw the angel of the LORD s in 5324
Dt 23:25 When thou comest into the s corn of thy 7054
23:25 move a sickle unto thy neighbour's s corn. 7054
Jdg 15: 5 he let them go into the s corn of 7054
15: 5 also the s corn, with the vineyards and 7054
1Sa 19:20 Samuel s as appointed over them, the spirit 5975
22: 6 and all his servants were s about him;) 5324
1Ki 13:25 in the way, and the lion s by the carcase: 5975
13:28 and the ass and the lion s by the carcase: 5975
22:19 all the host of heaven s by him on his right 5975
2Ch 9:18 sitting place, and two lions s by the stays: 5975
18:18 all the host of heaven s on his right hand 5975
Est 5: 2 when the king saw Esther the queen s in 5975
Ps 69: 2 I sink in deep mire, where there is no s: 4613
107:35 He turneth the wilderness into a s water, and 98
114: 8 Which turned the rock into a s water, the flint 98
Da 8: 6 which I had seen s before the river, and 5975
Am 9: 1 I saw the Lord s upon the altar: and he said, 5324
Mic 1:11 of Beth-ezel; he shall receive of you his s. 5979
5:13 and thy s images out of the midst of thee; 4676
Zec 3: 1 he shewed me Joshua the high priest s 5975
3: 1 and Satan s at his right hand to resist him. 5975
6: 5 which go forth from s before the Lord of all 3320
Mt 6: 5 for they love to pray s in the synagogues 2476
16:28 I say unto you, There be some s here, 2476
20: 3 and saw others s idle in the marketplace, 2476
20: 6 and found others s idle, and saith unto 2476
Mk 3:31 his brethren and his mother, and, s without, 2476

Mk 13:14 by Daniel the prophet, **s** where it ought not, *2476*
Lk 1:11 **s** on the right side of the altar of incense. *2476*
5: 2 And saw two ships **s** by the lake: but *2476*
9:27 I tell you of a truth, there be some **s** here, *2476*
18:13 **s** afar off, would not lift up so much as *his* *2476*
Jn 8: 9 left alone, and the woman **s** in the midst. *2476*
19:26 saw *his* mother, and the disciple **s by**, *3936*
20:14 and saw Jesus **s**, and knew not that it was *2476*
Ac 2:14 But Peter, **s up** with the eleven, lift up his *2476*
4:14 And beholding the man which was healed **s** *2476*
5:23 and the keepers **s** without before the doors: *2476*
5:25 the men whom ye put in prison are **s** in *2476*
7:55 and Jesus **s** on the right hand of God, *2476*
7:56 the Son of man **s** on the right hand of God. *2476*
22:20 I also was **s by**, and consenting unto his *2186*
24:21 this one voice, that I cried **s** among them, *2476*
Heb 9: 8 while as the first tabernacle was yet **s**: *4714*
2Pe 3: 5 and the earth **s** out of the water and in *4921*
Rev 7: 1 And after these *things* I saw four angels **s** *2476*
11: 4 the two candlesticks **s** before the God of *2476*
18:10 **S** afar off for the fear of her torment, *2476*
19:17 And I saw an angel **s** in the sun; and *2476*

STANK (3) [STINK]
Ex 8:14 them together upon heaps: and the land **s**. 887
16:20 until the morning, and it bred worms, and **s**: 887
2Sa 10: 6 when the children of Ammon saw that they **s** 887

STAR (15) [STARE, STARS]
Nu 24:17 there shall come a **S** out of Jacob, and 3556
Am 5:26 and Chiun your images, the **s** of your god, 3556
Mt 2: 2 for we have seen his **s** in the east, and *792*
2: 7 inquired of them diligently what time the **s** *792*
2: 9 and lo, the **s**, which they saw in the east, *792*
2:10 When they saw the **s**, they rejoiced *with* *792*
Ac 7:43 of Moloch, and the **s** of your god Remphan, *798*
1Co 15:41 for *one* **s** differeth from *another* star in glory. *792*
15:41 for *one* star differeth from *another* **s** in glory. *792*
2Pe 1:19 and the **day s** arise in your hearts: *5459*
Rev 2:28 And I will give him the morning **s**. *792*
8:10 and there fell a great **s** from heaven, *792*
8:11 And the name of the **s** is called Wormwood: *792*
9: 1 and I saw a **s** fall from heaven unto the earth: *792*
22:16 of David, *and* the bright and morning **s**. *792*

STARE (1)
Ps 22:17 tell all my bones: they look *and* **s** upon me. 7200

STARGAZERS (1) [GAZE, STAR]
Isa 47:13 the astrologers, the **s**, 2374+3556+871.1+1886.1

STARS (51) [STAR]
Ge 1:16 light to rule the night: *he made* the **s** also. 3556
15: 5 Look now towards heaven, and tell the **s**, 3556
22:17 multiply thy seed as the **s** of the heaven, 3556
26: 4 I will make thy seed to multiply as the **s** of 3556
37: 9 and the eleven **s** made obeisance to me. 3556
Ex 32:13 I will multiply your seed as the **s** of heaven, 3556
Dt 1:10 you *are this* day as the **s** of heaven for 3556
4:19 thou seest the sun, and the moon, and the **s**, 3556
10:22 made thee as the **s** of heaven for multitude. 3556
28:62 whereas ye were as the **s** of heaven for 3556
Jdg 5:20 the **s** in their courses fought against Sisera. 3556
1Ch 27:23 increase Israel like to the **s** of the heavens. 3556
Ne 4:21 the rising of the morning till the **s** appeared. 3556
9:23 children also multipliedst thou as the **s** 3556
Job 3: 9 Let the **s** of the twilight thereof be dark; 3556
9: 7 and it riseth not; and sealeth up the **s**. 3556
22:12 behold the height of the **s**, how high they 3556
25: 5 yea, the **s** are not pure in his sight. 3556
38: 7 When the morning **s** sang together, and 3556
Ps 8: 3 the work of thy fingers, the moon and the **s**, 3556
136: 9 The moon and **s** to rule by night: for his 3556
147: 4 He telleth the number of the **s**; he calleth 3556
148: 3 sun and moon: praise him, all ye **s** of light. 3556
Ecc 12: 2 the sun, or the light, or the moon, or the **s**, 3556
Isa 13:10 For the **s** of heaven and the constellations 3556
14:13 I will exalt my throne above the **s** of God: 3556
Jer 31:35 the moon and of the **s** for a light by night, 3556
Eze 32: 7 the heaven, and make the **s** thereof dark; 3556
Da 8:10 *some* of the host and of the **s** to the ground, 3556
12: 3 turn many to righteousness as the **s** for ever 3556
Joel 2:10 and the **s** shall withdraw their shining: 3556
3:15 and the **s** shall withdraw their shining. 3556
Am 5: 8 *Seek him* that maketh the **seven s** and 3598
Ob 1: 4 though *thou* set thy nest among the **s**, 3556
Na 3:16 thy merchants above the **s** of heaven: 3556
Mt 24:29 and the **s** shall fall from heaven, and *792*
Mk 13:25 And the **s** of heaven shall fall, *792*
Lk 21:25 in the sun, and in the moon, and in the **s**; *798*
Ac 27:20 And when neither sun nor **s** in many days *798*
1Co 15:41 of the moon, and another glory of the **s**: *792*
Heb 11:12 *so many* as the **s** of the sky in multitude, and *798*
Jude 1:13 wandering **s**, to whom is reserved *792*
Rev 1:16 And he had in his right hand seven **s**: and *792*
1:20 The mystery of the seven **s** which thou *792*
1:20 The seven **s** are the angels of the seven *792*
2: 1 These *things* saith he that holdeth the seven **s** *792*
3: 1 the seven spirits of God, and the seven **s**; *792*
6:13 And the **s** of heaven fell unto the earth, *792*
8:12 *part* of the moon, and the third *part* of the **s**; *792*
12: 1 and upon her head a crown of twelve **s**: *792*
12: 4 And his tail drew the third *part* of the **s** of *792*

STATE (14)
Ge 43: 7 The man asked us straitly of our **s**, and NIH
2Ch 24:13 they set the house of God in his **s**, and 4971
Est 1: 7 according to the **s** of the king. 3027
2:18 gave gifts, according to the **s** of the king. 3027
Ps 39: 5 verily every man **at** his **best s** *is* altogether 5324
Pr 27:23 Be thou diligent to know the **s** of thy 6440
28: 2 knowledge the **s** *thereof* shall be prolonged. 3651
Isa 22:19 and from thy **s** shall he pull thee down. 4612
Mt 12:45 the last *s* of that man is worse than the first. NIG
Lk 11:26 the last *s* of that man is worse than the first. NIG
Php 2:19 of good comfort, when I know your **s**. *3588+4012*
2:20 who will naturally care for your **s**. *3588+4012*
4:11 for I have learned, in whatsoever *s* I am, NIG
Col 4: 7 All my **s** shall Tychicus declare unto you, *2596*

STATELY (1)
Eze 23:41 satest upon a **s** bed, and a table prepared 3520

STATION (1)
Isa 22:19 I will drive thee from thy **s**, and from thy 4673

STATURE (17)
Nu 13:32 that we saw in it *are* men of a **great s**. 4060
1Sa 16: 7 his countenance, or on the height of his **s**; 6967
2Sa 21:20 where was a man of *great* **s**, that had on 4067
1Ch 11:23 a man of *great* **s**, five cubits *high;* and in 4060
20: 6 where was a man of *great* **s**, whose fingers 4060
SS 7: 7 This thy **s** is like to a palm tree, and 6967
Isa 10:33 the high ones of **s** *shall be* hewn down, and 6967
45:14 of Ethiopia and of the Sabeans, men of **s**, 4060
Eze 13:18 make kerchiefs upon the head of every **s** to 6967
17: 6 and became a spreading vine of low **s**, 6967
19:11 her **s** was exalted among the thick 6967
31: 3 with a shadowing shrowd, and of a high **s**; 6967
Mt 6:27 thought can add one cubit unto his **s**? *2244*
Lk 2:52 And Jesus increased in wisdom and **s**, and *2244*
12:25 taking thought can add to his **s** one cubit? *2244*
19: 3 not for the press, because he was little of **s**. *2244*
Eph 4:13 unto the measure of the **s** of the fulness of *2244*

STATUTE (35) [STATUTES]
Ex 15:25 there he made for them a **s** and 2706
27:21 *it shall be* a **s** for ever unto their generations 2708
28:43 *it shall be* a **s** for ever unto him and his seed 2708
29: 9 office shall be theirs for a perpetual **s**: 2708
29:28 his sons' by a **s** for ever from the children 2706
30:21 it shall be a **s** for ever to them, *even* to him 2706
Lev 3:17 *It shall be* a perpetual **s** for your 2708
6:18 *It shall be* a **s** for ever in your generations 2706
6:22 *it is* a **s** for ever unto the LORD; it shall be 2706
7:34 unto his sons by a **s** for ever from among 2706
7:36 *by* a **s** for ever throughout their generations. 2708
10: 9 *it shall be* a **s** for ever throughout your 2708
10:15 and thy sons' with thee, by a **s** for ever; 2706
16:29 *this* shall be a **s** for ever unto you: *that* in 2708
16:31 ye shall afflict your souls, *by* a **s** for ever. 2708
16:34 this shall be an everlasting **s** unto you, 2708
17: 7 This shall be a **s** for ever unto them 2708
23:14 *it shall be* a **s** for ever throughout your 2708
23:21 **s** for ever in all your dwellings throughout 2708
23:31 *it shall be* a **s** for ever throughout your 2708
23:41 *It shall be* a **s** for ever in your generations: 2708
24: 3 *it shall be* a **s** for ever in your generations. 2708

Lev 24: 9 the LORD made by fire, *by* a perpetual **s**. 2706
Nu 18:11 to thy daughters with thee, by a **s** for ever: 2706
18:19 and thy daughters with thee, by a **s** for ever: 2706
18:23 *it shall be* a **s** for ever throughout your 2708
19:10 sojourneth among them, for a **s** for ever. 2708
19:21 it shall be a perpetual **s** unto them, that he 2708
27:11 it shall be unto the children of Israel a **s** of 2708
35:29 So these *things* shall be for a **s** of judgment 2708
Jos 24:25 set them a **s** and an ordinance in Shechem. 2706
1Sa 30:25 that he made it a **s** and an ordinance for 2706
Ps 81: 4 For this *was* a **s** for Israel, *and* a law of 2706
Da 6: 7 consulted together to establish a royal **s**, 7010
6:15 Persians *is,* That no decree nor **s** which 7010

STATUTES (132) [STATUTE]

Ge 26: 5 my commandments, my **s**, and my laws. 2708
Ex 15:26 to his commandments, and keep all his **s**, 2706
18:16 and I do make *them* know the **s** of God, and 2706
Lev 10:11 **s** which the LORD hath spoken unto them 2706
18: 5 Ye shall therefore keep my **s**, and my 2708
18:26 Ye shall therefore keep my **s** and my 2708
19:19 Ye shall keep my **s**. Thou shalt not let thy 2708
19:37 Therefore shall ye observe all my **s**, and all 2708
20: 8 ye shall keep my **s**, and do them: I *am* 2708
20:22 Ye shall therefore keep all my **s**, and all my 2708
25:18 Wherefore ye shall do my **s**, and keep my 2708
26: 3 If ye walk in my **s**, and keep my 2708
26:15 if ye shall despise my **s**, or if your soul 2708
26:43 and because their soul abhorred my **s**. 2708
26:46 These *are* the **s** and judgments and laws, 2706
Nu 30:16 These *are* the **s**, which the LORD 2706
Dt 4: 1 O Israel, unto the **s** and unto the judgments, 2706
4: 5 Behold, I have taught you **s** and judgments, 2706
4: 6 which shall hear all these **s**, and say, 2706
4: 8 that hath **s** and judgments *so* righteous as 2706
4:14 commanded me at that time to teach you **s** 2706
4:40 Thou shalt keep therefore his **s**, and his 2706
4:45 and the **s**, and the judgments, 2706
5: 1 the **s** and judgments which I speak in your 2706
5:31 the **s**, and the judgments, which thou shalt 2706
6: 1 the **s**, and the judgments, 2706
6: 2 to keep all his **s** and his commandments, 2708
6:17 his testimonies, and his **s**, which he hath 2706
6:20 and the **s**, and the judgments, 2706
6:24 LORD commanded us to do all these **s**, 2706
7:11 and the **s**, and the judgments, 2706
8:11 his judgments, and his **s**, which I command 2708
10:13 commandments of the LORD, and his **s**, 2708
11: 1 his **s**, and his judgments, and 2708
11:32 ye shall observe to do all the **s** and 2706
12: 1 These *are* the **s** and judgments, which ye 2706
16:12 and thou shalt observe and do these **s**. 2706
17:19 keep all the words of this law and these **s**, 2706
26:16 thy God hath commanded thee to do these **s** 2706
26:17 to keep his **s**, and his commandments, and 2706
27:10 do his commandments and his **s**, which I 2706
28:15 and his **s** which I command thee *this* day; 2708
28:45 and his **s** which he commanded thee: 2708
30:10 his **s** which are written in this book of 2708
30:16 and his **s** and his judgments, 2708
2Sa 22:23 and *as for* his **s**, I did not depart from them. 2708
1Ki 2: 3 to keep his **s**, *and* his commandments, and 2708
3: 3 walking in the **s** of David his father: 2708
3:14 to keep my **s** and my commandments, 2706
6:12 if thou wilt walk in my **s**, and execute my 2708
8:58 and his **s**, and his judgments, 2706
8:61 to walk in his **s**, and to keep his 2706
9: 4 *and* wilt keep my **s** and my judgments: 2706
9: 6 *and* my **s** which I have set before you, 2708
11:11 thou hast not kept my covenant and my **s**, 2708
11:33 *to keep* my **s** and my judgments, as *did* 2708
11:34 he kept my commandments and my **s**: 2708
11:38 to keep my **s** and my commandments, 2708
2Ki 17: 8 walked in the **s** of the heathen, whom 2708
17:13 and keep my commandments *and* my **s**, 2708
17:15 they rejected his **s**, and his covenant that he 2706
17:19 walked in the **s** of Israel which they made. 2708
17:34 neither do they after their **s**, or after their 2708
17:37 the **s**, and the ordinances, and the law, and 2706
23: 3 his **s** with all *their* heart and all *their* soul, 2708
1Ch 22:13 if thou takest heed to fulfil the **s** and 2706
29:19 thy **s**, and to do all *these things,* and 2706
2Ch 7:17 and shalt observe my **s** and my judgments; 2706
7:19 and forsake my **s** and my commandments, 2708
19:10 and commandment, **s** and judgments, 2706
33: 8 according to the whole law and the **s** and 2706
34:31 his testimonies, and his **s**, with all his heart, 2706
Ezr 7:10 to do *it,* and to teach in Israel **s** and 2706
7:11 of the LORD, and of his **s** to Israel. 2706
Ne 1: 7 nor the **s**, nor the judgments, 2706
9:13 and true laws, good **s** and commandments: 2706
9:14 commandedst them precepts, **s**, and laws, 2706
10:29 our Lord, and his judgments and his **s**; 2706
Ps 18:22 and I did not put away his **s** from me. 2708
19: 8 The **s** of the LORD *are* right, rejoicing 6490
50:16 What hast thou to do to declare my **s**, or 2706
89:31 If they break my **s**, and keep not my 2708
105:45 That they might observe his **s**, and keep his 2706
119: 5 that my ways were directed to keep thy **s**! 2706
119: 8 I will keep thy **s**: O forsake me not utterly. 2706
119:12 *art* thou, O LORD: teach me thy **s**. 2706
119:16 I will delight myself in thy **s**: I will not 2708
119:23 *but* thy servant did meditate in thy **s**. 2706
119:26 and thou heardest me: teach me thy **s**. 2706
119:33 Teach me, O LORD, the way of thy **s**; and 2706
119:48 I have loved; and I will meditate in thy **s**. 2706
119:54 Thy **s** have been my songs in the house of 2706
119:64 is full *of* thy mercy: teach me thy **s**. 2706
119:68 *art* good, and doest good; teach me thy **s**. 2706
119:71 have been afflicted; that I might learn thy **s**. 2706
119:80 Let my heart be sound in thy **s**; that I be not 2706
119:83 in the smoke; *yet* do I not forget thy **s**. 2706
119:112 I have inclined mine heart to perform thy **s** 2706
119:117 I will have respect unto thy **s** continually. 2706
119:118 trodden down all them that err from thy **s**: 2706
119:124 unto thy mercy, and teach me thy **s**. 2706
119:135 shine upon thy servant; and teach me thy **s**. 2706
119:145 hear me, O LORD: I will keep thy **s**. 2706
119:155 far from the wicked: for they seek not thy **s**. 2706
119:171 when thou hast taught me thy **s**. 2706
147:19 his **s** and his judgments unto Israel. 2706
Jer 44:10 nor in my **s**, that I set before you and before 2708
44:23 nor walked in his law, nor in his **s**, nor in 2708
Eze 5: 6 my **s** more than the countries that *are* round 2708
5: 6 and my **s**, they have not walked in them. 2708
5: 7 *and* have not walked in my **s**, neither have 2708
11:12 for ye have not walked in my **s**, 2706
11:20 That they may walk in my **s**, and keep mine 2708
18: 9 Hath walked in my **s**, and hath kept my 2708
18:17 my judgments, hath walked in my **s**; 2708
18:19 *and* hath kept all my **s**, and hath done them, 2708
18:21 keep all my **s**, and do that which is lawful 2708
20:11 I gave them my **s**, and shewed them my 2708
20:13 they walked not in my **s**, and they despised 2708
20:16 walked not in my **s**, but polluted my 2708
20:18 Walk ye not in the **s** of your fathers, 2706
20:19 walk in my **s**, and keep my judgments, and 2708
20:21 they walked not in my **s**, neither kept my 2708
20:24 had despised my **s**, and had polluted my 2708
20:25 Wherefore I gave them also **s** *that were* not 2706
33:15 walk in the **s** of life, without committing 2708
36:27 cause you to walk in my **s**, and ye shall 2706
37:24 and observe my **s**, and do them. 2708
44:24 my laws and my **s** in all mine assemblies; 2708
Mic 6:16 For the **s** of Omri are kept, and all 2708
Zec 1: 6 my words and my **s**, which I commanded 2706
Mal 4: 4 for all Israel, *with* the **s** and judgments. 2706

STAVES (49) [STAFF]

Ex 25:13 thou shalt make **s** of shittim wood, and 905
25:14 thou shalt put the **s** into the rings by the sides 905
25:15 The **s** shall be in the rings of the ark: 905
25:27 rings be for places of the **s** to bear the table. 905
25:28 thou shalt make the **s** *of* shittim wood, and 905
27: 6 thou shalt make **s** for the altar, staves of 905
27: 6 **s** of shittim wood, and overlay them with 905
27: 7 the **s** shall be put into the rings, and 905
27: 7 the **s** shall be upon the two sides of the altar, 905
30: 4 they shall be for places for the **s** to bear it 905
30: 5 thou shalt make the **s** *of* shittim wood, and 905
35:12 The ark, and the **s** thereof, *with* the mercy 905
35:13 his **s**, and all his vessels, and the shewbread, 905
35:15 the incense altar and his **s**, and the anointing 905
35:16 his **s**, and all his vessels, the laver and his 905
37: 4 he made **s** of shittim wood, and 905
37: 5 he put the **s** into the rings by the sides of 905
37:14 the places for the **s** to bear the table. 905
37:15 he made the **s** *of* shittim wood, and 905

Ex 37:27 to be places for the **s** to bear it withal. 905
37:28 he made the **s** *of* shittim wood, and 905
38: 5 of the grate of brass, *to be* places for the **s**. 905
38: 6 he made the **s** *of* shittim wood, and 905
38: 7 he put the **s** into the rings on the sides of 905
39:35 and the **s** thereof, and the mercy seat, 905
39:39 his **s**, and all his vessels, the laver and his 905
40:20 set the **s** on the ark, and put the mercy seat 905
Nu 4: 6 wholly of blue, and shall put in the **s** thereof. 905
4: 8 badgers' skins, and shall put in the **s** thereof. 905
4:11 badgers' skins, and shall put to the **s** thereof: 905
4:14 of badgers' skins, and put to the **s** of it. 905
21:18 the direction of the lawgiver, with their **s**. 4938
1Sa 17:43 *Am* I a dog, that thou comest to me with **s**? 4731
1Ki 8: 7 covered the ark and the **s** thereof above. 905
8: 8 they drew out the **s**, that the ends of 905
8: 8 that the ends of the **s** were seen out in 905
1Ch 15:15 upon their shoulders with the **s** thereon, 4133
2Ch 5: 8 covered the ark and the **s** thereof above. 905
5: 9 they drew out the **s** *of the ark,* that the ends 905
5: 9 **s** were seen from the ark before the oracle; 905
Hab 3:14 Thou didst strike through with his **s** 4294
Zec 11: 7 I took unto me two **s**; the one I called 4731
Mt 10:10 neither two coats, neither shoes, nor yet **s**: *4464*
26:47 him a great multitude with swords and **s**, *3586*
26:55 a thief with swords and **s** for to take me? *3586*
Mk 14:43 him a great multitude with swords and **s**, *3586*
14:48 a thief, with swords and *with* **s** to take me? *3586*
Lk 9: 3 neither **s**, nor scrip, neither bread, *4464*
22:52 as against a thief, with swords and **s**? *3586*

STAY (33) [STAYED, STAYETH, STAYS]
Ge 19:17 behind thee, neither **s** thou in all the plain; 5975
Ex 9:28 I will let you go, and ye shall **s** no longer. 5975
Lev 13: 5 *if* the plague in his sight be **at a s**, *and* 5975
13:23 if the bright spot **s** in his place, *and* 5975
13:28 if the bright spot **s** in his place, *and* 5975
13:37 if the scall be in his sight **at a s**, and 5975
Jos 10:19 **s** you not, *but* pursue after your enemies, 5975
Ru 1:13 would ye **s** for them from having husbands? 5702
1Sa 15:16 **S**, and I will tell thee what the LORD hath 7503
20:38 cried after the lad, Make speed, haste, **s** not. 5975
2Sa 22:19 of my calamity: but the LORD was my **s**. 4937
24:16 **s** now thine hand. And the angel of 7503
1Ch 21:15 *It is* enough, **s** now thine hand. 7503
Job 37: 4 he will not **s** them when his voice is heard. 6117
38:37 or who can **s** the bottles of heaven, 7901
Ps 18:18 of my calamity: but the LORD was my **s**. 4937
Pr 28:17 shall flee to the pit; let no man **s** him. 8551
SS 2: 5 **S** me with flagons, comfort me with apples: 5564
Isa 3: 1 and from Judah the **s** and the staff, 4937
3: 1 the whole **s** of bread, and the whole stay of 4937
3: 1 stay of bread, and the whole **s** of water, 4937
10:20 shall no more again **s** upon him that smote 8172
10:20 shall **s** upon the LORD, the Holy One of 8172
19:13 *even they that are* the **s** of the tribes thereof. 6438
29: 9 **S** yourselves, and wonder; cry ye out, and 4102
30:12 and perverseness, and **s** thereon: 8172
31: 1 **s** on horses, and trust in chariots, because 8172
48: 2 and **s** themselves upon the God of Israel; 5564
50:10 name of the LORD, and **s** upon his God. 8172
Jer 4: 6 retire, **s** not: for I will bring evil from 5975
20: 9 weary with forbearing, and I could not **s**. NIH
Da 4:35 none can **s** his hand, or say unto him, 4223
Hos 13:13 for he should not **s** long in *the place of* 5975

STAYED (31) [STAY]
Ge 8:10 he **s** yet other seven days; and again he sent 2342
8:12 he **s** yet other seven days; and sent forth 3176
32: 4 sojourned with Laban, and **s** *there* until now: 309
Ex 10:24 only let your flocks and your herds be **s**: 3322
17:12 Aaron and Hur **s up** his hands, the one on 8551
Nu 16:48 and the living; and the plague was **s**. 6113
16:50 of the congregation: and the plague was **s**. 6113
25: 8 So the plague was **s** from the children of 6113
Dt 10:10 I **s** in the mount, according to the first time, 5975
Jos 10:13 the sun stood still, and the moon **s**, until 5975
1Sa 20:19 *when* thou hast **s three days**, *then* 8027
24: 7 So David **s** his servants with *these* words, 8156
30: 9 where those that were left behind **s**. 5975
2Sa 17:17 Now Jonathan and Ahimaaz **s** by En-rogel; 5975
24:21 that the plague may be **s** from the people. 6113
24:25 the land, and the plague was **s** from Israel. 6113
1Ki 22:35 the king was **s up** in *his* chariot against 5975
2Ki 4: 6 *There is* not a vessel more. And the oil **s**. 5975
13:18 the ground. And he smote thrice, and **s**. 5975
15:20 turned back, and **s** not there in the land. 5975
1Ch 21:22 that the plague may be **s** from the people. 6113
2Ch 18:34 howbeit the king of Israel **s** *himself* **up** in 5975
Job 38:11 and here shall thy proud waves be **s**? 7896
Ps 106:30 and *so* the plague was **s**. 6113
Isa 26: 3 *whose* mind *is* **s** *on thee:* because 5564
La 4: 6 as in a moment, and no hands **s** on her. 2342
Eze 31:15 floods thereof, and the great waters were **s**: 3607
Hag 1:10 Therefore the heaven over you is **s** from 3607
1:10 from dew, and the earth is **s** *from* her fruit. 3607
Lk 4:42 sought him, and came unto him, and **s** him, *2722*
Ac 19:22 but he himself **s** in Asia for a season. *1907*

STAYETH (1) [STAY]
Isa 27: 8 he **s** his rough wind in the day of the east 1898

STAYS (4) [STAY]
1Ki 10:19 *there were* **s** on either side on the place of 3027
10:19 of the seat, and two lions stood beside the **s**. 3027
2Ch 9:18 **s** on each side of the sitting place, and 3027
9:18 and two lions standing by the **s**: 3027

STEAD (94) [STEADS] See Index

STEADFAST (1) [STEDFAST]
Job 11:15 yea, thou shalt be **s**, and shalt not fear. 3332

STEADS (1) [STEAD]
1Ch 5:22 And they dwelt **in** their **s** until the captivity. 8478

STEADY (1)
Ex 17:12 his hands were **s** until the going down of 530

STEAL (22) [MENSTEALERS, STALE, STEALETH, STEALING, STEALTH, STOLE, STOLEN]
Ge 31:27 flee away secretly, and **s away from** me; 1589
44: 8 should we **s** out of thy lord's house silver or 1589
Ex 20:15 Thou shalt not **s**. 1589
22: 1 If a man shall **s** an ox, or a sheep, and 1589
Lev 19:11 Ye shall not **s**, neither deal falsely, 1589
Dt 5:19 Neither shalt thou **s**. 1589
2Sa 19: 3 as people being ashamed **s away** when they 1589
Pr 6:30 if he **s** to satisfy his soul when he is hungry; 1589
30: 9 **s**, and take the name of my God *in vain.* 1589
Jer 7: 9 *Will ye* **s**, murder, and commit adultery, 1589
23:30 that **s** my words every one from his 1589
Mt 6:19 and where thieves break through and **s**: *2813*
6:20 where thieves do not break through nor **s**: *2813*
19:18 shalt not commit adultery, Thou shalt not **s**, *2813*
27:64 and **s** him *away,* and say unto the people, *2813*
Mk 10:19 not commit adultery, Do not kill, Do not **s**, *2813*
Lk 18:20 not commit adultery, Do not kill, Do not **s**, *2813*
Jn 10:10 but for to **s**, and to kill, and to destroy: *2813*
Ro 2:21 thou that preachest *a man* should not **s**, *2813*
2:21 *a man* should not steal, dost thou **s**? *2813*
13: 9 Thou shalt not kill, Thou shalt not **s**, *2813*
Eph 4:28 Let him that stole **s** no more: but rather let *2813*

STEALETH (3) [STEAL]
Ex 21:16 he that **s** a man, and selleth him, or if he be 1589
Job 27:20 a tempest **s** him **away** in the night. 1589
Zec 5: 3 for every one that **s** shall be cut off *as* on 1589

STEALING (2) [STEAL]
Dt 24: 7 If a man be found **s** any of his brethren of 1589
Hos 4: 2 and killing, and **s**, and committing adultery, 1589

STEALTH (1) [STEAL]
2Sa 19: 3 the people gat them by **s** that day *into* 1589

STEDFAST (10) [STEADFAST, STEDFASTLY, STEDFASTNESS]
Ps 78: 8 and whose spirit was not **s** with God. 539
78:37 neither were they **s** in his covenant. 539
Da 6:26 **s** for ever, and his kingdom *that* which shall 7011
1Co 7:37 Nevertheless he that standeth **s** in *his* heart, *1476*
15:58 my beloved brethren, be ye **s**, unmoveable, *1476*
2Co 1: 7 And our hope of you *is* **s**, knowing, that as *949*
Heb 2: 2 For if the word spoken by angels was **s**, and *949*
3:14 if we hold the beginning of *our* confidence **s** *949*
6:19 both sure and **s**, and which entereth into that *949*
1Pe 5: 9 Whom resist **s** in the faith, knowing that *4731*

STEDFASTLY (10) [STEDFAST]
Ru 1:18 When she saw that she *was* **s minded** to go 553

S

2Ki 8:11 he settled his countenance **s**, until *he* was 7760
Lk 9:51 he **s set** his face to go to Jerusalem, *4741*
Ac 1:10 And while they **looked s** toward heaven as *816*
2:42 And they **continued s** in the apostles' *4342*
6:15 all that sat in the council, **looking s** on him, *816*
7:55 **looked** up **s** into heaven, and saw the glory *816*
14: 9 who **s beholding** him, and perceiving that he *816*
2Co 3: 7 that the children of Israel could not **s behold** *816*
3:13 that the children of Israel could not **s look** to *816*

STEDFASTNESS (2) [STEDFAST]
Col 2: 5 your order, and the **s** of your faith in Christ. *4733*
2Pe 3:17 error of the wicked, fall from your own **s**. *4740*

STEEL (4)
2Sa 22:35 so that a bow of **s** is broken *by* mine arms. 5154
Job 20:24 *and* the bow of **s** shall strike him through. 5154
Ps 18:34 so that a bow of **s** is broken *by* mine arms. 5154
Jer 15:12 iron break the northern iron and the **s**? 5178

STEEP (5)
Eze 38:20 the **s places** shall fall, and every wall shall 4095
Mic 1: 4 the waters *that are* poured down a **s place**. 4174
Mt 8:32 ran violently down a **s place** into the sea, *2911*
Mk 5:13 the herd ran violently down a **s place** into *2911*
Lk 8:33 the herd ran violently down a **s place** into *2911*

STEM (1)
Isa 11: 1 there shall come forth a rod out of the **s** of 1503

STEP (2) [FOOTSTEPS, STEPPED, STEPPETH, STEPS]
1Sa 20: 3 *there is* but a **s** between me and death. 6587
Job 31: 7 If my **s** hath turned out of the way, and 838

STEPHANAS (4)
1Co 1:16 And I baptized also the household of **S**: *4734*
16:15 brethren, (ye know the house of **S**, *4734*
16:17 I am glad of the coming of **S** and *4734*
16: S Corinthians was written from Philippi by **S**, *4734*

STEPHEN (7)
Ac 6: 5 and they chose **S**, a man full of faith and *4736*
6: 8 And **S**, full of faith and power, did great *4736*
6: 9 of Cilicia and of Asia, disputing with **S**. *4736*
7:59 And they stoned **S**, calling upon *God,* and *4736*
8: 2 And devout men carried **S** *to his burial,* and *4736*
11:19 arose about **S** travelled as far as Phenice, *4736*
22:20 And when the blood of thy martyr **S** was *4736*

STEPPED (1) [STEP]
Jn 5: 4 first after the troubling of the water **s in**, *1684*

STEPPETH (1) [STEP]
Jn 5: 7 I am coming, another **s down** before me. *2597*

STEPS (38) [STEP]
Ex 20:26 Neither shalt thou go up by **s** unto mine 4609
2Sa 22:37 Thou hast enlarged my **s** under me; so 6806
1Ki 10:19 The throne had six **s**, and the top of 4609
10:20 the one side and on the other upon the six **s**: 4609
2Ch 9:18 *there were* six **s** to the throne, with a 4609
9:19 the one side and on the other upon the six **s**. 4609
Job 14:16 For now thou numberest my **s**: dost thou 6806
18: 7 The **s** of his strength shall be straitened, and 6806
23:11 My foot hath held his **s**, his way have I kept, 838
29: 6 When *I* washed my **s** with butter, and 1978
31: 4 not he see my ways, and count all my **s**? 6806
31:37 declare unto him the number of my **s**; 6806
Ps 17:11 They have now compassed us *in* our **s**: 838
18:36 Thou hast enlarged my **s** under me, that my 6806
37:23 The **s** of a *good* man are ordered by 4703
37:31 God *is* in his heart; none of his **s** shall slide. 838
44:18 neither have our **s** declined from thy way; 838
56: 6 they hide themselves, they mark my **s**, 6119
57: 6 They have prepared a net for my **s**; my soul 6471
73: 2 were almost gone; my **s** had well nigh slipt. 838
85:13 and shall set *us* in the way of his **s**. 6471
119:133 Order my **s** in thy word: and let not any 6471
Pr 4:12 When thou goest thy **s** shall not be 6806
5: 5 go down *to* death; her **s** take hold on hell. 6806
16: 9 his way: but the LORD directeth his **s**. 6806
Isa 26: 6 the feet of the poor, *and* the **s** of the needy. 6471
Jer 10:23 *it is* not in man that walketh to direct his **s**. 6806
La 4:18 They hunt our **s**, that *we* cannot go in our 6806
Eze 40:22 they went up unto it by seven **s**; and 4609
40:26 *there were* seven **s** to go up to it, and 4609
40:31 and the going up to it *had* eight **s**. 4609
40:34 that side: and the going up to it *had* eight **s**. 4609
40:37 that side: and the going up to it *had* eight **s**. 4609
40:49 *he brought me* by the **s** whereby they went 4609
Da 11:43 and the Ethiopians *shall be* at his **s**. 4703
Ro 4:12 who also walk in the **s** of *that* faith of our *2487*
2Co 12:18 same spirit? *walked we* not in the same **s**? *2487*
1Pe 2:21 us an example, that ye should follow his **s**: *2487*

STERN (1)
Ac 27:29 they cast four anchors out of the **s**, and *4403*

STEW See POTTAGE

STEWARD (13) [STEWARDS, STEWARDSHIP]
Ge 15: 2 the **s** of my house *is* this Eliezer of 1121+4943
43:19 they came near to the **s** of 376+834+5921
44: 1 he commanded the **s** of his house, 834+5921
44: 4 Joseph said unto his **s**, Up, 834+1004+5921
1Ki 16: 9 of Arza **s** of *his* house in Tirzah. 834+5921
Mt 20: 8 the lord of the vineyard saith unto his **s**, *2012*
Lk 8: 3 And Joanna the wife of Chuza Herod's **s**, *2012*
12:42 Who then is *that* faithful and wise **s**, *3623*
16: 1 was a certain rich man, which had a **s**; *3623*
16: 2 for thou mayest be no longer **s**. *3621*
16: 3 Then the **s** said within himself, What shall I *3623*
16: 8 And the lord commended the unjust **s**, *3623*
Tit 1: 7 bishop must be blameless, as the **s** of God; *3623*

STEWARDS (4) [STEWARD]
1Ch 28: 1 the **s** over all the substance and 8269
1Co 4: 1 of Christ, and **s** of the mysteries of God. *3623*
4: 2 Moreover it is required in **s**, that a man be *3623*
1Pe 4:10 as good **s** of the manifold grace of God. *3623*

STEWARDSHIP (3) [STEWARD]
Lk 16: 2 give an account of thy **s**; for thou mayest be *3622*
16: 3 for my lord taketh away from me the **s**: *3622*
16: 4 what to do, that, when I am put out of the **s**, *3622*

STICK (14) [CANDLESTICK, CANDLESTICKS, STICKETH, STICKS, STUCK]
2Ki 6: 6 he cut down a **s**, and cast *it* in thither; 6086
Job 33:21 and his bones *that* were not seen **s out**. 8192
41:17 they **s together**, that they cannot be 3920
Ps 38: 2 For thine arrows **s fast** in me, and thy hand 5181
La 4: 8 it is withered, it is become like a **s**. 6086
Eze 29: 4 I will **cause** the fish of thy rivers **to s** unto 1692
29: 4 all the fish of thy rivers shall **s** unto thy 1692
37:16 take thee one **s**, and write upon it, 6086
37:16 take another **s**, and write upon it, 6086
37:16 the **s** of Ephraim, and *for* all the house of 6086
37:17 join them one to another into one **s**; and 6086
37:19 Behold, I *will* take the **s** of Joseph, which *is* 6086
37:19 *even* with the **s** of Judah, and make them 6086
37:19 make them one **s**, and they shall be one in 6086

STICKETH (1) [STICK]
Pr 18:24 there is a friend *that* **s closer** than a brother. 1695

STICKS (6) [STICK]
Nu 15:32 they found a man that gathered **s** upon 6086
15:33 they that found him gathering **s** brought 6086
1Ki 17:10 the widow woman *was* there gathering of **s**: 6086
17:12 behold, I *am* gathering two **s**, that I may go 6086
Eze 37:20 the **s** whereon thou writest shall be in thine 6086
Ac 28: 3 And when Paul had gathered a bundle of **s**, *5434*

STIFF (4) [STIFFENED, STIFFNECKED]
Dt 31:27 For I know thy rebellion, and thy **s** neck: 7186
Ps 75: 5 your horn on high: speak *not* with a **s** neck. 6277
Jer 17:23 **made** their neck **s**, that *they* might not hear, 7185
Eze 2: 4 *they are* impudent children and **s** hearted. 2389

STIFFENED (1) [STIFF]
2Ch 36:13 he **s** his neck, and hardened his heart from 7185

STIFFNECKED (9) [NECK, STIFF]
Ex 32: 9 and behold, it *is* a **s** people: 6203+7186
33: 3 midst of thee; for thou *art* a **s** people: 6203+7186
33: 5 children of Israel, Ye *are* a **s** people: 6203+7186
34: 9 for it *is* a **s** people; and pardon our 6203+7186
Dt 9: 6 for thou *art* a **s** people. 6203+7186
9:13 and behold, it *is* a **s** people: 6203+7186

Dt 10:16 foreskin of your heart, and be no more **s**. 6203
2Ch 30: 8 Now be ye not **s**, as your fathers 6203+7185
Ac 7:51 Ye **s** and uncircumcised in heart and ears, *4644*

STILL (101) [STILLED, STILLEST, STILLETH]

Ge 12: 9 going on **s** toward the south. 5265+2050.1
41:21 they *were* **s** ill favoured, as at the beginning. NIH
Ex 9: 2 refuse to let *them* go, and wilt hold them **s**, 5750
14:13 **stand s**, and see the salvation of 3320
15:16 of thine arm they shall be *as* **s** as a stone; 1826
23:11 seventh *year* thou shalt let it rest and **lie s**; 5203
Lev 13:57 if it appear **s** in the garment, either in 5750
Nu 9: 8 **Stand s**, and I will hear what the LORD 5975
14:38 men that went to search the land, lived **s**. NIH
Jos 3: 8 water of Jordan, ye shall **stand s** in Jordan. 5975
10:12 of Israel, Sun, **stand** thou **s** upon Gibeon; 1826
10:13 the sun **stood s**, and the moon stayed, 1826
10:13 So the sun **stood s** in the midst of heaven, 5975
11:13 *as for* the cities that **stood s** in their 5975
24:10 therefore he **blessed** you **s**: 1288+1288
Jdg 18: 9 *are* ye **s**? be not slothful to go, *and* to enter 2814
Ru 3:18 said she, **Sit s**, my daughter, until thou 3427
1Sa 9:27 **stand** thou **s** a while, that I may shew thee 5975
12: 7 Now therefore **stand s**, that I may reason 3320
12:25 if ye shall **s do wickedly**, ye shall be 7489+7489
14: 9 we will **stand s** in our place, and will not 5975
26:25 great things, and also shalt **s prevail**. 3201+3201
2Sa 2:23 where Asahel fell down and died **stood s**. 5975
2:28 all the people **stood s**, and pursued after 5975
11: 1 But David tarried **s** at Jerusalem. NIH
14:32 *had been* good for me *to have been* there **s**: 5750
16: 5 he came forth, and cursed **s** as he came. NIH
18:30 And he turned aside, and **stood s**. 5975
20:12 the man saw that all the people **stood s**, 5975
20:12 that every one that came by him **stood s**. 5975
1Ki 19:12 in the fire: and after the fire a **s** small voice. 1827
22: 3 we *be* **s**, and take it not out of the hand of 2814
2Ki 2:11 **s went on**, and talked, that behold, 1980+1980
7: 4 if we sit **s** here, we die also. Now therefore 3427
12: 3 the people **s** sacrificed and burnt incense in 5750
15: 4 and burnt incense **s** on the high places. 5750
15:35 and burnt incense **s** in the high places. 5750
2Ch 20:17 stand ye **s**, and see the salvation of NIH
22: 9 had no power to **keep s** the kingdom. 6113
33:17 Nevertheless the people did sacrifice **s** in 5750
Ne 12:39 and they **stood s** in the prison gate. 5975
Job 2: 3 **s** he holdeth fast his integrity, 5750
2: 9 unto him, Dost thou **s** retain thine integrity? 5750
3:13 For now should I have lien **s** and been quiet, NIH
4:16 It **stood s**, but I could not discern the form 5975
20:13 it not; but **keep** it **s** within his mouth: 4513
32:16 but **stood s**, *and* answered no more:) 5975
37:14 **stand s**, and consider the wondrous works 5975
Ps 4: 4 your own heart upon your bed, and be **s**. 1826
8: 2 that *thou* mightest **s** the enemy and 7673
23: 2 he leadeth me beside the **s** waters. 4496
46:10 Be **s**, and know that I *am* God: I will be 7503
49: 9 That he should **s** live for ever, *and* not see 5750
68:21 the hairy scalp of such a one as **goeth on s** 1980
76: 8 from heaven; the earth feared, and was **s**, 8252
78:32 For all this they sinned **s**, and believed not 5750
83: 1 hold not thy peace, and be not **s**, O God. 8252
84: 4 they will be **s** praising thee. Selah. 5750
92:14 They shall **s** bring forth fruit in old age; 5750
107:29 a calm, so that the waves thereof are **s**. 2814
139:18 the sand: when I awake, I am **s** with thee. 5750
Ecc 12: 9 he **s** taught the people knowledge; 5750
Isa 5:25 turned away, but his hand *is* stretched out **s**. 5750
9:12 turned away, but his hand *is* stretched out **s**. 5750
9:17 turned away, but his hand *is* stretched out **s**. 5750
9:21 turned away, but his hand *is* stretched out **s**. 5750
10: 4 turned away, but his hand *is* stretched out **s**. 5750
23: 2 Be **s**, ye inhabitants of the isle; thou whom 1826
30: 7 concerning this, Their strength *is* to **sit s**. 7674
42:14 I have been **s**, *and* refrained myself: 2790
Jer 8:14 Why do we **sit s**? assemble yourselves, and 3427
23:17 They **say s** unto them that despise me, 559+559
27:11 those will I let **remain s** in their own land, 3240
31:20 I do earnestly remember him **s**: 5750
42:10 If ye will **s** abide in this land, then will I 7725
47: 6 up thyself into thy scabbard, rest, and be **s**. 1826
51:50 escaped the sword, go *away*, **stand** not **s**: 5975
La 3:20 soul hath *them* **s in remembrance**, 2142+2142
Eze 33:30 the children of thy people **s** are talking NIH

41: 7 a winding about **s** upward 4605+1886.5+3807.1
41: 7 **s** upward round about 4605+1886.5+3807.1
41: 7 the breadth of the house *was* **s** upward, NIH
Hab 3:11 *and* moon **stood s** in *their* habitation: 5975
Zec 1:11 behold, all the earth **sitteth s**, and is at rest. 3427
11:16 that is broken, nor feed that that **standeth s**. 5324
Mt 20:32 And Jesus **stood s**, and called them, and *2476*
Mk 4:39 the wind, and said unto the sea, Peace, be **s**. *5392*
10:49 And Jesus **stood s**, and commanded him to *2476*
Lk 7:14 and they that bare *him* **stood s**. And he *2476*
Jn 7: 9 *words* unto them, he abode **s** in Galilee. NIG
11: 6 he abode two days **s** in the *same* place NIG
11:20 and met him: but Mary sat **s** in the house. NIG
Ac 8:38 And he commanded the chariot to **stand s**: *2476*
15:34 it pleased Silas to abide there **s**. NIG
17:14 but Silas and Timotheus **abode** there **s**. *5278*
Ro 11:23 they also, if they **bide** not **s in** unbelief, *1961*
1Ti 1: 3 As I besought thee to abide **s** at Ephesus, NIG
Rev 22:11 He that is unjust, let him be unjust **s**: and *2089*
22:11 and he which is filthy, let him be filthy **s**: *2089*
22:11 *he that is* righteous, let him be righteous **s**: *2089*
22:11 and *he that is* holy, let him be holy **s**: *2089*

STILLBORN See UNTIMELY

STILLED (2) [STILL]

Nu 13:30 Caleb **s** the people before Moses, and said, 2013
Ne 8:11 So the Levites **s** all the people, saying, 2814

STILLEST (1) [STILL]

Ps 89: 9 when the waves thereof arise, thou **s** them. 7623

STILLETH (1) [STILL]

Ps 65: 7 Which **s** the noise of the seas, the noise of 7623

STING (2) [STINGETH, STINGS]

1Co 15:55 O death, where *is* thy **s**? O grave, where *is* *2759*
15:56 The **s** of death *is* sin; *2759*

STINGETH (1) [STING]

Pr 23:32 it biteth like a serpent, and **s** like an adder. 6567

STINGS (1) [STING]

Rev 9:10 and there were **s** in their tails: *2759*

STINK (8) [STANK, STINKETH, STINKING, STUNK]

Ge 34:30 Ye have troubled me to **make me to s** 887
Ex 7:18 *is* in the river shall die, and the river shall **s**; 887
16:24 it did not **s**, neither was there any worm 887
Ps 38: 5 My wounds **s** *and* are corrupt because of my 887
Isa 3:24 *that* instead of sweet smell there shall be **s**; 4716
34: 3 their **s** shall come up *out of* their carcases, 889
Joel 2:20 his **s** shall come up, and his ill savour shall 889
Am 4:10 I have made the **s** of your camps to come up 889

STINKETH (2) [STINK]

Isa 50: 2 their fish **s**, because *there is* no water, and 887
Jn 11:39 saith unto him, Lord, by this time he **s**: *3605*

STINKING (1) [STINK]

Ecc 10: 1 of the apothecary to send forth a **s savour**: 887

STIR (20) [STIRRED, STIRRETH, STIRS]

Nu 24: 9 who shall **s** him **up**? Blessed *is* he that 6965
Job 17: 8 the innocent shall **s up** himself against 5782
41:10 None *is so* fierce that **dare s** him **up**: who 5782
Ps 35:23 **S up** thyself, and awake to my judgment, 5782
78:38 anger away, and did not **s up** all his wrath. 5782
80: 2 Benjamin and Manasseh **s up** thy strength, 5782
Pr 15: 1 away wrath: but grievous words **s up** anger. 5927
SS 2: 7 that ye **s** not **up**, nor awake *my* love, till he 5782
3: 5 that ye **s** not **up**, nor awake *my* love, till he 5782
8: 4 that ye **s** not **up**, nor awake *my* love, 5782
Isa 10:26 the LORD of hosts shall **s up** a scourge 5782
13:17 Behold, I will **s up** the Medes against them, 5782
42:13 he shall **s up** jealousy like a man of war: 5782
Da 11: 2 shall **s up** all against the realm of Grecia. 5782
11:25 he shall **s up** his power and his courage 5782
Ac 12:18 there was no small **s** among the soldiers, *5017*
19:23 And the same time there arose no small **s** *5017*
2Ti 1: 6 remembrance that *thou* **s up** the gift of God, *329*
2Pe 1:13 to **s** you **up** by putting *you* in *1326*
3: 1 in both which I **s up** your pure minds by *1326*

STIRRED (23) [STIR]

Ex 35:21 every one whose heart **s** him **up**, and 5375

Ex 35:26 all the women whose heart **s** them **up** in 5375
36: 2 *even* every one whose heart **s** him **up** to 5375
1Sa 22: 8 sheweth unto me that my son hath **s up** my 6965
26:19 If the LORD have **s** thee **up** against me, 5496
1Ki 11:14 the LORD **s up** an adversary unto 6965
11:23 God **s** him **up** *another* adversary, Rezon 6965
21:25 the LORD, whom Jezebel his wife **s up**. 5496
1Ch 5:26 the God of Israel **s up** the spirit of Pul king 5782
2Ch 21:16 Moreover the LORD **s up** against 5782
36:22 the LORD **s up** the spirit of Cyrus king of 5782
Ezr 1: 1 the LORD **s up** the spirit of Cyrus king of 5782
Ps 39: 2 *even* from good; and my sorrow was **s**. 5916
Da 11:10 his sons shall be **s up**, and shall assemble a 1624
11:10 shall he return, and be **s up**, *even* to his 1624
11:25 the king of the south shall be **s up** to battle 1624
Hag 1:14 the LORD **s up** the spirit of Zerubbabel 5782
Ac 6:12 And they **s up** the people, and the elders, *4787*
13:50 But the Jews **s up** the devout and *3951*
14: 2 But the unbelieving Jews **s up** the Gentiles, *1892*
17:13 they came thither also, and **s up** the people. *4531*
17:16 for them at Athens, his spirit was **s** in him, *3947*
21:27 **s up** all the people, and laid hands on him, *4797*

STIRRETH (8) [STIR]

Dt 32:11 As an eagle **s up** her nest, fluttereth over 5782
Pr 10:12 Hatred **s up** strifes: but love covereth all 5782
15:18 A wrathful man **s up** strife: but *he that is* 1624
28:25 He that is of a proud heart **s up** strife: but 1624
29:22 An angry man **s up** strife, and a furious 1624
Isa 14: 9 it **s up** the dead for thee, *even* all the chief 5782
64: 7 that **s up** himself to take hold of thee: 5782
Lk 23: 5 saying, He **s up** the people, *383*

STIRS (1) [STIR]

Isa 22: 2 Thou *that art* full *of* **s**, a tumultuous city, 8663

STOCK (8) [STOCKS]

Lev 25:47 by thee, or to the **s** of the stranger's family: 6133
Job 14: 8 and the **s** thereof die in the ground; 1503
Isa 40:24 yea, their **s** shall not take root in the earth: 1503
44:19 shall I fall down to the **s** of a tree? 944
Jer 2:27 Saying to a **s**, Thou *art* my father; and to a 6086
10: 8 and foolish: the **s** *is* a doctrine of vanities. 6086
Ac 13:26 children of the **s** of Abraham, and *1085*
Php 3: 5 of the **s** of Israel, of the tribe of Benjamin, *1085*

STOCKS (9) [STOCK]

Job 13:27 Thou puttest my feet also in the **s**, and 5465
33:11 He putteth my feet in the **s**, he marketh all 5465
Pr 7:22 or as a fool to the correction of the **s**; 5914
Jer 3: 9 committed adultery with stones and with **s**. 6086
20: 2 put him in the **s** that *were* in the high gate 4115
20: 3 Pashur brought forth Jeremiah out of the **s**. 4115
29:26 shouldest put him in prison, and in the **s**. 6729
Hos 4:12 My people ask *counsel* at their **s**, and 6086
Ac 16:24 and made their feet fast in the **s**. *3586*

STOICKS (1)

Ac 17:18 and of the **S**, encountered him. *4770*

STOLE (4) [STEAL]

2Sa 15: 6 Absalom **s** the hearts of the men of Israel. 1589
2Ch 22:11 **s** him from among the king's sons that were 1589
Mt 28:13 by night, and **s** him *away* while we slept. *2813*
Eph 4:28 Let him that **s** steal no more: but rather let *2813*

STOLEN (15) [STEAL]

Ge 30:33 the sheep, that *shall be counted* **s** with me. 1589
31:19 Rachel had **s** the images that *were* her 1589
31:26 that thou hast **s away unawares** to 1589+3824
31:30 *yet* wherefore hast thou **s** my gods? 1589
31:32 For Jacob knew not that Rachel had **s** them. 1589
31:39 *whether* **s** by day, or stolen by night. 1589
31:39 *whether* stolen by day, or **s** by night. 1589
40:15 For **indeed** I was **s away** out of 1589+1589
Ex 22: 7 to keep, and it be **s** out of the man's house; 1589
22:12 if it be **s** from him, he shall make 1589+1589
Jos 7:11 have also **s**, and dissembled also, and 1589
2Sa 19:41 our brethren the men of Judah **s** thee **away**, 1589
21:12 which had **s** them from the street of 1589
Pr 9:17 **S** waters are sweet, and bread *eaten* in 1589
Ob 1: 5 would they not have **s** till they had enough? 1589

STOMACH'S (1) [STOMACHER]

1Ti 5:23 but use a little wine for thy **s** sake and *4751*

STOMACHER (1) [STOMACH'S]

Isa 3:24 instead of a **s** a girding of sackcloth; *and* 6614

STONE (192) [BRIMSTONE, CHALKSTONES, HAILSTONES, HAIL-STONES, HEADSTONE, SLINGSTONES, STONE'S, STONED, STONES, STONESQUARERS, STONEST, STONING, STONY, STUMBLINGSTONE]

Ge 2:12 land *is* good: there *is* bdellium and the onyx **s**. 68
11: 3 they had brick for **s**, and slime had they for 68
28:18 and took the **s** that he had put *for* his pillows, 68
28:22 this **s**, which I have set *for* a pillar, shall be 68
29: 2 and a great **s** *was* upon the well's mouth. 68
29: 3 and they rolled the **s** from the well's mouth, 68
29: 3 put the **s** again upon the well's mouth in his 68
29: 8 and *till* they roll the **s** from the well's mouth; 68
29:10 rolled the **s** from the well's mouth, and 68
31:45 And Jacob took a **s**, and set it up *for* a pillar. 68
35:14 where he talked with him, *even* a pillar of **s**: 68
49:24 (from thence *is* the shepherd, the **s** of Israel:) 68
Ex 4:25 Zipporah took a **sharp s**, and cut off 6864
7:19 both in *vessels of* wood, and in *vessels of* **s**. 68
8:26 before their eyes, and will they not **s** us? 5619
15: 5 they sank into the bottom as a **s**. 68
15:16 of thine arm they shall be *as* still as a **s**; 68
17: 4 this people? they be almost ready to **s** me. 5619
17:12 they took a **s**, and put *it* under him, and he sat 68
20:25 if thou wilt make me an altar of **s**, thou shalt 68
20:25 of stone, thou shalt not build it *of* **hewn s**: 1496
21:18 one smite another with a **s**, or with *his* fist, 68
24:10 as it were a paved work of a **sapphire s**, 5601
24:12 and I will give thee tables of **s**, and a law, and 68
28:10 Six of their names on one **s**, and the *other* six 68
28:10 the *other* six names of the rest on the other **s**, 68
28:11 *With* the work of an engraver in **s**, *like* 68
31:18 two tables of Testimony, tables of **s**, 68
34: 1 Hew thee two tables of **s** like unto the first: 68
34: 4 he hewed two tables of **s** like unto the first; 68
34: 4 and took in his hand the two tables of **s**. 68
Lev 20: 2 the people of the land shall **s** him with 7275
20:27 they shall **s** them with stones: their blood 7275
24:14 his head, and let all the congregation **s** him. 7275
24:16 congregation shall **certainly s** him: 7275+7275
24:23 out of the camp, and **s** him with stones. 7275
26: 1 neither shall ye set up *any* image of **s** in your 68
Nu 14:10 all the congregation bade **s** them with 7275
15:35 all the congregation shall **s** him with stones 7275
35:17 if he smite him with throwing a **s**, 68
35:23 Or with any **s**, wherewith *a man* may die, 68
Dt 4:13 and he wrote them upon two tables of **s**. 68
4:28 wood and **s**, which neither see, nor hear, 68
5:22 he wrote them in two tables of **s**, and 68
9: 9 up into the mount to receive the tables of **s**, 68
9:10 the LORD delivered unto me two tables of **s** 68
9:11 *that* the LORD gave me the two tables of **s**, 68
10: 1 Hew thee two tables of **s** like unto the first, 68
10: 3 and hewed two tables of **s** like unto the first, 68
13:10 thou shalt **s** him with stones, that he die; 5619
17: 5 and shalt **s** them with stones, till they die. 5619
21:21 all the men of his city shall **s** him with 7275
22:21 the men of her city shall **s** her with stones 5619
22:24 ye shall **s** them with stones that they die; 5619
28:36 there shalt thou serve other gods, wood and **s**. 68
28:64 nor thy fathers have known, *even* wood and **s**. 68
29:17 their idols, wood and **s**, silver and gold, 68
Jos 4: 5 take ye up every man of you a **s** upon his 68
15: 6 the border went up *to* the **s** of Bohan the son 68
18:17 descended *to* the **s** of Bohan the son of 68
24:26 took a great **s**, and set it up there under an 68
24:27 Behold, this **s** shall be a witness unto us; 68
Jdg 9: 5 *being* threescore and ten persons, upon one **s**: 68
9:18 upon one **s**, and have made Abimelech, 68
1Sa 6:14 stood there, where *there was* a great **s**: 68
6:15 of gold *were,* and put *them* on the great **s**: 68
6:18 even unto the great **s** *of* Abel, NIH
6:18 *which* **s** *remaineth* unto this day in the field NIH
7:12 Samuel took a **s**, and set *it* between Mizpeh 68
14:33 roll a great **s** unto me *this* day. 68
17:49 took thence a **s**, and slang *it*, and smote 68
17:49 his forehead, that the **s** sunk into his forehead; 68
17:50 over the Philistine with a sling and with a **s**, 68
20:19 was *in hand,* and shalt remain by the **s** Ezel. 68
25:37 heart died within him, and he became *as* a **s**. 68
2Sa 17:13 until there be not one **small s** found there. 6872

S

2Sa 20: 8 When they *were* at the great **s** which *is* in 68
1Ki 1: 9 and oxen and fat cattle by the **s** of Zoheleth, 68
6: 7 was built *of* **s** made ready *before it was* 68
6:18 all *was* cedar; there was no **s** seen. 68
6:36 the inner court *with* three rows of **hewed s**, 1496
8: 9 nothing in the ark save the two tables of **s**, 68
21:10 *then* carry him out, and **s** him, that he may 5619
2Ki 3:25 every good piece of land cast every man his **s**, 68
12:12 hewers of **s**, and to buy timber and 68
12:12 hewed **s** to repair the breaches of the house of 68
19:18 but the work of men's hands, wood and **s**: 68
22: 6 to buy timber and hewn **s** to repair the house. 68
1Ch 22:14 timber also and **s** have I prepared; and 68
22:15 hewers and workers of **s** and timber, and 68
2Ch 2:14 in silver, in brass, in iron, in **s**, and in timber, 68
34:11 and builders gave they *it*, to buy hewn **s**, 68
Ne 4: 3 go up, he shall even break down their **s** wall. 68
9:11 into the deeps, as a **s** into the mighty waters. 68
Job 28: 2 of the earth, and brass *is* molten *out of* the **s**. 68
38: 6 or who laid the corner **s** thereof; 68
38:30 The waters are hid as *with* a **s**, and the face of 68
41:24 His heart is as firm as a **s**; yea, as hard as a 68
Ps 91:12 *their* hands, lest thou dash thy foot against a **s**. 68
118:22 The **s** *which* the builders refused is become 68
118:22 refused is become the head *s* of the corner. NIH
Pr 17: 8 A gift *is as* a precious **s** in the eyes of him that 68
24:31 and the **s** wall thereof was broken down. 68
26: 8 As *he that* bindeth a **s** in a sling, so *is* he that 68
26:27 and he that rolleth a **s**, it will return upon him. 68
27: 3 A **s** *is* heavy, and the sand weighty; but 68
Isa 8:14 for a **s** of stumbling and for a rock of offence 68
28:16 Behold, I lay in Zion for a foundation a **s**, 68
28:16 lay in Zion for a foundation a stone, a tried **s**, 68
28:16 a precious corner *s*, a sure foundation: NIH
37:19 but the work of men's hands, wood and **s**: 68
Jer 2:27 and to a **s**, Thou hast brought me forth: 68
51:26 they shall not take of thee a **s** for a corner, 68
51:26 a stone for a corner, nor a **s** for foundations; 68
51:63 *that* thou shalt bind a **s** to it, and cast it into 68
La 3: 9 He hath inclosed my ways with **hewn s**, 1496
3:53 my life in the dungeon, and cast a **s** upon me. 68
Eze 1:26 of a throne, as the appearance of a sapphire **s**: 68
10: 1 appeared over them as it were a sapphire **s**, 68
10: 9 of the wheels *was* as the colour of a beryl **s**. 68
16:40 they shall **s** thee with stones, and thrust thee 7275
20:32 families of the countries, to serve wood and **s**. 68
23:47 the company shall **s** them with stones, and 7275
28:13 every precious **s** *was* thy covering, 68
40:42 the four tables *were* of hewn **s** for the burnt 68
Da 2:34 Thou sawest till that a **s** was cut out without 69
2:35 the **s** that smote the image became a great 69
2:45 Forasmuch as thou sawest that the **s** was cut 69
5: 4 of silver, of brass, of iron, of wood, and of **s**. 69
5:23 gold, of brass, iron, wood, and **s**, which see 69
6:17 a **s** was brought, and laid upon the mouth of 69
Am 5:11 ye have built houses of **hewn s**, but ye shall 1496
Hab 2:11 For the **s** shall cry out of the wall, and 68
2:19 Awake; to the dumb **s**, Arise, it shall teach! 68
Hag 2:15 from before a **s** was laid upon a stone in 68
2:15 from before a stone was laid upon a **s** in 68
Zec 3: 9 For behold the **s** that I have laid before 68
3: 9 before Joshua; upon one **s** *shall be* seven eyes: 68
7:12 they made their hearts *as* an **adamant s**, 8068
12: 3 Jerusalem a burdensome **s** for all people: 68
Mt 4: 6 at any time thou dash thy foot against a **s**. *3037*
7: 9 if his son ask bread, will he give him a **s**? *3037*
21:42 The **s** which the builders rejected, *3037*
21:44 And whosoever shall fall on this **s** shall be *3037*
24: 2 There shall not be left here one **s** upon *3037*
27:60 he rolled a great **s** to the door of *3037*
27:66 sealing the **s**, and setting a watch. *3037*
28: 2 came and rolled back the **s** from the door, *3037*
Mk 12:10 The **s** which the builders rejected is become *3037*
13: 2 there shall not be left one **s** upon another, *3037*
15:46 rolled a **s** unto the door of the sepulchre. *3037*
16: 3 Who shall roll us away the **s** from the door *3037*
16: 4 they saw that the **s** was rolled away: *3037*
Lk 4: 3 command this **s** that it be made bread. *3037*
4:11 at any time thou dash thy foot against a **s**. *3037*
11:11 of you that is a father, will he give him a **s**? *3037*
19:44 they shall not leave in thee one **s** upon *3037*
20: 6 if we say, Of men; all the people will **s** us: *2642*
20:17 The **s** which the builders rejected, *3037*
20:18 Whosoever shall fall upon that **s** shall be *3037*
21: 6 in the which there shall not be left one **s** *3037*
23:53 laid it in a sepulchre *that was* **hewn in s**, *2991*
24: 2 And they found the **s** rolled away from *3037*
Jn 1:42 which is by interpretation, A **s**. *4074*
2: 6 And there were set there six waterpots of **s**, *3035*
8: 7 sin among you, let him first cast a **s** at her. *3037*
10:31 Then the Jews took up stones again to **s** *3034*
10:32 for which of those works do ye **s** me? *3034*
10:33 saying, For a good work we **s** thee not; *3034*
11: 8 Master, the Jews of late sought to **s** thee; *3034*
11:38 the grave. It was a cave, and a **s** lay upon it. *3037*
11:39 Jesus said, Take ye away the **s**. Martha, *3037*
11:41 Then they took away the **s** *from the place* *3037*
20: 1 seeth the **s** taken away from the sepulchre. *3037*
Ac 4:11 This is the **s** which was set at nought of you *3037*
14: 5 to use *them* despitefully, and to **s** them, *3036*
17:29 or silver, or **s**, graven by art and *3037*
2Co 3: 3 not in tables **of s**, but in fleshy tables of *3035*
Eph 2:20 Christ himself being the chief corner *s*; NIG
1Pe 2: 4 To whom coming, *as unto* a living **s**, *3037*
2: 6 Behold, I lay in Sion a chief corner **s**, elect, *3037*
2: 7 the **s** which the builders disallowed, *3037*
2: 8 And a **s** of stumbling, and a rock of *3037*
Rev 2:17 and will give him a white **s**, and in *5586*
2:17 and in the **s** a new name written, *5586*
4: 3 to look upon like a jasper and a sardine **s**: *3037*
9:20 idols of gold, and silver, and brass, and **s**, *3035*
16:21 *every s* about the weight of a talent: NIG
17: 4 with gold and precious **s** and pearls, *3037*
18:21 And a mighty angel took up a **s** like a great *3037*
21:11 her light *was* like unto a **s** most precious, *3037*
21:11 *even* like a jasper **s**, clear as crystal; *3037*

STONE'S (1) [STONE]

Lk 22:41 And he was withdrawn from them about a **s** *3037*

STONED (22) [STONE]

Ex 19:13 he shall **surely** be **s**, or shot through; 5619+5619
21:28 the ox shall be **surely s**, and his flesh 5619+5619
21:29 the ox shall be **s**, and his owner also shall 5619
21:32 shekels *of* silver, and the ox shall be **s**. 5619
Nu 15:36 and **s** him with stones, and he died; 7275
Jos 7:25 all Israel **s** him *with* stones, and 7275
7:25 with fire, after they had **s** them with stones. 5619
1Ki 12:18 all Israel **s** him with stones, that he died. 7275
21:13 the city, and **s** him with stones, that he died. 5619
21:14 to Jezebel, saying, Naboth is **s**, and is dead. 5619
21:15 when Jezebel heard that Naboth was **s**, and 5619
2Ch 10:18 the children of Israel **s** him with stones, 7275
24:21 **s** him *with* stones at the commandment of 7275
Mt 21:35 beat one, and killed another, and **s** another. *3036*
Jn 8: 5 law commanded us, that such should be **s**: *3036*
Ac 5:26 the people, lest they should have been **s**. *3034*
7:58 and **s** *him*: and the witnesses laid down *3036*
7:59 And they **s** Stephen, calling upon *God*, and *3036*
14:19 and, having **s** Paul, drew *him* out of *3034*
2Co 11:25 once was I **s**, thrice I suffered shipwrack, *3034*
Heb 11:37 They were **s**, they were sawn asunder, *3034*
12:20 it shall be **s**, or thrust through with a dart: *3036*

STONES (175) [STONE]

Ge 28:11 he took of the **s** of *that* place, and put *them for* 68
31:46 Jacob said unto his brethren, Gather **s**; and 68
31:46 and they took **s**, and made a heap: 68
Ex 25: 7 Onyx **s**, and stones to be set in the ephod, and 68
25: 7 **s** to be set in the ephod, and in the breastplate. 68
28: 9 thou shalt take two onyx **s**, and grave on them 68
28:11 shalt thou engrave the two **s** with the names of 68
28:12 thou shalt put the two **s** upon the shoulders of 68
28:12 *for* **s** of memorial unto the children of Israel: 68
28:17 thou shalt set in it settings of **s**, *even* four 68
28:17 set in it settings of stones, *even* four rows of **s**: 68
28:21 the **s** shall be with the names of the children 68
31: 5 in cutting of **s**, to set *them*, and in carving of 68
35: 9 onyx **s**, and stones to be set for the ephod, 68
35: 9 **s** to be set for the ephod, and for 68
35:27 the rulers brought onyx **s**, and stones to be set, 68
35:27 **s** to be set, for the ephod, and for 68
35:33 in the cutting of **s**, to set *them*, and in carving 68
39: 6 they wrought onyx **s** inclosed *in* ouches *of* 68
39: 7 *that they should be* **s** for a memorial to 68
39:10 they set in it four rows of **s**: *the first* row *was* 68
39:14 the **s** *were* according to the names of 68
Lev 14:40 they take away the **s** in which the plague *is*, 68

Lev 14:42 they shall take other **s**, and put *them* in 68
14:42 and put *them* in the place of *those* **s**; 68
14:43 after *that* he hath taken away the **s**, and 68
14:45 the **s** of it, and the timber thereof, and all 68
20: 2 the people of the land shall stone him with **s**. 68
20:27 they shall stone them with **s**: their blood *shall* 68
21:20 be scurvy, or scabbed, or hath his **s** broken; 810
24:23 cursed out of the camp, and stone him with **s**. 68
Nu 14:10 all the congregation bade stone them with **s**. 68
15:35 all the congregation shall stone him with **s** 68
15:36 the camp, and stoned him with **s**, and he died; 68
Dt 8: 9 a land whose **s** *are* iron, and out of whose hills 68
13:10 And thou shalt stone him with **s**, that he die; 68
17: 5 and shalt stone them with **s**, till they die. 68
21:21 all the men of his city shall stone him with **s**, 68
22:21 the men of her city shall stone her with **s** that 68
22:24 and ye shall stone them with **s** that they die; 68
23: 1 He that is wounded in the **s**, or hath *his* 1795
27: 2 that thou shalt set thee up great **s**, and 68
27: 4 *that* ye shall set up these **s**, which I command 68
27: 5 altar unto the LORD thy God, an altar of **s**: 68
27: 6 the altar of the LORD thy God *of* whole **s**: 68
27: 8 thou shalt write upon the **s** all the words of 68
Jos 4: 3 twelve **s**, and ye shall carry them over with 68
4: 6 to come, saying, What mean you by these **s**? 68
4: 7 these **s** shall be for a memorial unto 68
4: 8 took up twelve **s** out of the midst of Jordan, 68
4: 9 Joshua set up twelve **s** in the midst of Jordan, 68
4:20 those twelve **s**, which they took out of Jordan, 68
4:21 in time to come, saying, What *mean* these **s**? 68
7:25 all Israel stoned him *with* **s**, and burned them 68
7:25 with fire, after they had stoned them with **s**. 68
7:26 they raised over him a great heap of **s** unto 68
8:29 raise thereon a great heap of **s**, *that remaineth* 68
8:31 an altar of whole **s**, over which no *man* hath 68
8:32 he wrote there upon the **s** a copy of the law of 68
10:11 that the LORD cast down great **s** from 68
10:18 Roll great **s** upon the mouth of the cave, and 68
10:27 laid great **s** in the cave's mouth, *which remain* 68
Jdg 20:16 every one could sling **s** at a hair *breadth*, and 68
1Sa 17:40 and chose him five smooth **s** out of the brook, 68
2Sa 12:30 *was* a talent of gold with the precious **s**: 68
16: 6 he cast **s** at David, and at all the servants of 68
16:13 as he went, and threw **s** at him, and cast dust. 68
18:17 and laid a very great heap of **s** upon him: 68
1Ki 5:17 they brought great **s**, costly stones, *and* 68
5:17 great stones, costly **s**, *and* hewed stones, 68
5:17 great stones, costly stones, *and* hewed **s**, 68
5:18 they prepared timber and **s** to build the house. 68
7: 9 All these *were of* costly **s**, according to 68
7: 9 according to the measures of **hewed s**, 1496
7:10 the foundation *was of* costly **s**, *even* great 68
7:10 *even* great **s**, stones of ten cubits, and 68
7:10 **s** of ten cubits, and stones of eight cubits. 68
7:10 stones of ten cubits, and **s** of eight cubits. 68
7:11 above *were* costly **s**, after the measures of 68
7:11 after the measures of **hewed s**, and cedars. 1496
7:12 about *was with* three rows *of* **hewed s**, 1496
10: 2 and very much gold, and precious **s**: 68
10:10 and of spices very great store, and precious **s**: 68
10:11 great plenty of almug trees, and precious **s**. 68
10:27 the king made silver *to be* in Jerusalem as **s**, 68
12:18 and all Israel stoned him with **s**, that he died. 68
15:22 they took away the **s** of Ramah, and 68
18:31 Elijah took twelve **s**, according to the number 68
18:32 *with* the **s** he built an altar in the name of 68
18:38 the **s**, and the dust, and licked up the water 68
21:13 the city, and stoned him with **s**, that he died. 68
2Ki 3:19 and mar every good piece of land with **s**. 68
3:25 only in Kir-haraseth left *they* the **s** thereof; 68
16:17 under it, and put it upon a pavement of **s**. 68
1Ch 12: 2 the right hand and the left in *hurling* **s** and 68
20: 2 talent of gold, and *there were* precious **s** in it; 68
22: 2 he set masons to hew wrought **s** to build 68
29: 2 onyx **s**, and *stones* to be set, glistering stones, 68
29: 2 onyx stones, and *s* to be set, NIH
29: 2 glistering **s**, and of divers colours, and 68
29: 2 all *manner of* precious **s**, and marble stones in 68
29: 2 precious stones, and marble **s** in abundance. 68
29: 8 they with whom *precious* **s** were found gave 68
2Ch 1:15 and gold at Jerusalem *as plenteous* as **s**, 68
3: 6 he garnished the house with precious **s** for 68
9: 1 and gold in abundance, and precious **s**: 68
9: 9 and of spices great abundance, and precious **s**: 68
9:10 brought algum trees and precious **s**. 68
9:27 the king made silver in Jerusalem as **s**, and 68
10:18 and the children of Israel stoned him with **s**, 68
16: 6 they carried away the **s** of Ramah, and 68
24:21 stoned him *with* **s** at the commandment of 68
26:14 habergeons, and bows, and slings to cast **s**. 68
26:15 to shoot arrows and great **s** withal. 68
32:27 for precious **s**, and for spices, and for shields, 68
Ezr 5: 8 which *is* builded *with* great **s**, and timber *is* 69
6: 4 *With* three rows of great **s**, and a row of new 69
Ne 4: 2 will they revive the **s** out of the heaps of 68
Job 5:23 For thou shalt be in league with the **s** of 68
6:12 *Is* my strength the strength of **s**? or *is* my flesh 68
8:17 about the heap, *and* seeth the place of **s**. 68
14:19 The waters wear the **s**: thou washest away 68
22:24 and *the gold of* Ophir as the **s** of the brooks. 6697
28: 3 the **s** of darkness, and the shadow of death. 68
28: 6 The **s** of it *are* the place of sapphires: and 68
40:17 the sinews of his **s** are wrapt together. 6344
41:30 Sharp **s** *are* under him: he spreadeth sharp 2789
Ps 102:14 For thy servants take pleasure in her **s**, and 68
137: 9 and dasheth thy little ones against the **s**. 5553
144:12 *that* our daughters *may be* as **corner s**, 2106
Ecc 3: 5 A time to cast away **s**, and a time to gather 68
3: 5 away stones, and a time to gather **s** together; 68
10: 9 Whoso removeth **s** shall be hurt therewith; 68
Isa 5: 2 **gathered out** the **s** thereof, and planted it 5619
9:10 fallen down, but we will build *with* **hewn s**: 1496
14:19 with a sword, that go down to the **s** of the pit; 68
27: 9 when he maketh all the **s** of the altar as 68
34:11 the line of confusion, and the **s** of emptiness. 68
54:11 I will lay thy **s** with fair colours, and lay thy 68
54:12 and all thy borders of pleasant **s**. 68
57: 6 Among the smooth *s* of the stream *is* thy NIH
60:17 and for wood brass, and for **s** iron: 68
62:10 cast up, cast up the highway; gather out the **s**; 68
Jer 3: 9 committed adultery with **s** and with stocks. 68
43: 9 Take great **s** in thine hand, and hide them in 68
43:10 will set his throne upon these **s** that I have 68
La 3:16 He hath also broken my teeth with **gravel s**, 2687
4: 1 the **s** of the sanctuary are poured out in the top 68
Eze 16:40 they shall stone thee with **s**, and thrust thee 68
23:47 And the company shall stone them with **s**, and 68
26:12 they shall lay thy **s** and thy timber and 68
27:22 of all spices, and with all precious **s**, and gold. 68
28:14 and down in the midst of the **s** of fire. 68
28:16 from the midst of the **s** of fire. 68
Da 11:38 and with precious **s**, and pleasant things. 68
Mic 1: 6 I will pour down the **s** thereof into the valley, 68
Zec 5: 4 it with the timber thereof and the **s** thereof. 68
9:15 they shall devour, and subdue *with* sling **s**; 68
9:16 for *they shall be as* the **s** of a crown, lifted up 68
Mt 3: 9 that God is able of these **s** to raise up *3037*
4: 3 command that these **s** be made bread. *3037*
Mk 5: 5 crying, and cutting himself with **s**. *3037*
12: 4 and at him they **cast s**, and wounded *him* in *3036*
13: 1 see what manner of **s** and what buildings *3037*
Lk 3: 8 That God is able of these **s** to raise up *3037*
19:40 the **s** would immediately cry out. *3037*
21: 5 how it was adorned with goodly **s** and gifts, *3037*
Jn 8:59 Then took they up **s** to cast at him: but *3037*
10:31 Then the Jews took up **s** again to stone him. *3037*
1Co 3:12 silver, precious **s**, wood, hay, stubble; *3037*
2Co 3: 7 written *and* engraven in **s**, was glorious, *3037*
1Pe 2: 5 Ye also, as lively **s**, are built *up* a spiritual *3037*
Rev 18:12 and precious **s**, and of pearls, and *3037*
18:16 with gold, and precious **s**, and pearls: *3037*
21:19 garnished with all *manner of* precious **s**. *3037*

STONESQUARERS (1) [SQUARE, STONE]

1Ki 5:18 Hiram's builders did hew *them*, and the **s**: 1382

STONEST (2) [STONE]

Mt 23:37 and **s** them which are sent unto thee, *3036*
Lk 13:34 and **s** them that are sent unto thee; *3036*

STONING (1) [STONE]

1Sa 30: 6 for the people spake of **s** him, because 5619

STONY (7) [STONE]

Ps 141: 6 When their judges are overthrown in **s** 5553
Eze 11:19 I will take the **s** heart out of their flesh, and 68
36:26 I will take away the **s** heart out of your flesh, 68
Mt 13: 5 Some fell upon **s** *places*, where they had *4075*

Mt	13:20	But he that received the seed into **s** *places,*	4075
Mk	4: 5	And some fell on **s ground**, where it had	4075
	4:16	they likewise which are sown on **s ground**;	4075

STOOD (339) [STAND]

Ge	18: 2	and looked, and lo, three men **s** by him:	5324
	18: 8	he **s** by them under the tree, and they did	5975
	18:22	but Abraham **s** yet before the LORD.	5975
	19:27	to the place where he **s** before the LORD:	5975
	23: 3	Abraham **s up** from before his dead, and	6965
	23: 7	Abraham **s up**, and bowed himself to	6965
	24:30	and behold, he **s** by the camels at the well.	5975
	28:13	the LORD **s** above it, and said,	5324
	37: 7	and lo, my sheaf arose, and also **s upright**;	5324
	37: 7	your sheaves **s round about**, and	5437
	41: 1	and behold, he **s** by the river.	5975
	41: 3	**s** by the *other* kine upon the brink of	5975
	41:17	behold, I **s** upon the bank of the river:	5975
	41:46	Joseph *was* thirty years old when he **s**	5975
	43:15	went down *to* Egypt, and **s** before Joseph.	5975
	45: 1	himself before all them that **s** by him;	5324
	45: 1	there **s** no man with him, while Joseph	5975
Ex	2: 4	his sister **s** afar off, to wit what would be	3320
	2:17	Moses **s up** and helped them, and	6965
	5:20	met Moses and Aaron, who **s** in the way,	5324
	9:10	ashes of the furnace, and **s** before Pharaoh;	5975
	14:19	from before their face, and **s** behind them:	5975
	15: 8	the floods **s upright** as a heap, *and*	5324
	18:13	the people **s** by Moses from the morning	5975
	19:17	and they **s** at the nether part of the mount.	3320
	20:18	people saw *it,* they removed, and **s** afar off.	5975
	20:21	the people **s** afar off, and Moses drew near	5975
	32:26	Moses **s** in the gate of the camp, and said,	5975
	33: 8	**s** every man *at* his tent door, and	5324
	33: 9	**s** *at* the door of the tabernacle, and	5975
	34: 5	**s** with him there, and proclaimed the name	3320
Lev	9: 5	drew near and **s** before the LORD.	5975
Nu	11:32	the people **s up** all that day, and all *that*	6965
	12: 5	**s** *in* the door of the tabernacle, and	5975
	16:18	**s** *in* the door of the tabernacle of	5975
	16:27	**s** *in* the door of their tents, and their wives,	5324
	16:48	he **s** between the dead and the living; and	5975
	22:22	the angel of the LORD **s** in the way for an	3320
	22:24	the angel of the LORD **s** in a path of	5975
	22:26	went further, and **s** in a narrow place,	5975
	23: 6	lo, *he* **s** by his burnt sacrifice, he, and	5324
	23:17	he **s** by his burnt offering, and the princes	5324
	27: 2	they **s** before Moses, and before Eleazar	5975
Dt	4:11	ye came near and **s** under the mountain;	5975
	5: 5	(I **s** between the LORD and you at that	5975
	31:15	the pillar of the cloud **s** over the door of	5975
Jos	3:16	the waters which came down from above **s**	5975
	3:17	**s** firm on dry *ground* in the midst of Jordan,	5975
	4: 3	out of the place where the priests' feet **s**	4673
	4: 9	which bare the ark of the covenant **s**:	4673
	4:10	For the priests which bare the ark **s** in	5975
	5:13	there **s** a man over against him with his	5975
	8:33	**s** on this side the ark and on that side before	5975
	10:13	the sun **s still**, and the moon stayed,	1826
	10:13	So the sun **s still** in the midst of heaven,	5975
	11:13	*as for* the cities that **s still** in their strength,	5975
	20: 9	of blood, until he **s** before the congregation.	5975
	21:44	there **s** not a man of all their enemies before	5975
Jdg	3:19	And all that **s** by him went out from him.	5975
	6:31	Joash said unto all that **s** against him, Will	5975
	7:21	they **s** every man in his place round about	5975
	9: 7	he went and **s** in the top of mount Gerizim,	5975
	9:35	and **s** *in* the entering of the gate of the city:	5975
	9:44	and **s** *in* the entering of the gate of the city:	5975
	16:29	two middle pillars upon which the house **s**,	3559
	18:16	of Dan, **s** *by* the entering of the gate.	5324
	18:17	the priest **s** *in* the entering of the gate with	5324
	20:28	the son of Aaron, **s** before it in those days,)	5975
1Sa	1:26	I *am* the woman that **s** by thee here,	5324
	3:10	**s**, and called as at other times, Samuel,	3320
	4:20	the time of her death the *women* that **s**	5324
	6:14	a Beth-shemite, and **s** there, where *there*	5975
	10:23	when he **s** among the people, he was higher	3320
	16:21	David came to Saul, and **s** before him: and	5975
	17: 3	the Philistines **s** on a mountain on the one	5975
	17: 3	Israel **s** on a mountain on the other side:	5975
	17: 8	he **s** and cried unto the armies of Israel,	5975
	17:26	David spake to the men that **s** by him,	5975
	17:51	**s** upon the Philistine, and took his sword,	5975
	22: 7	Saul said unto his servants that **s** about him,	5324
	22:17	the king said unto the footmen that **s** about	5324
	26:13	and **s** on the top of a hill afar off;	5975
2Sa	1:10	So I **s** upon him, and slew him, because	5975
	2:23	where Asahel fell down and died **s still**.	5975
	2:25	became one troop, and **s** on the top of a hill.	5975
	2:28	all the people **s still**, and pursued after	5975
	13:31	all his servants **s** *by* with their clothes rent.	5324
	15: 2	up early, and **s** beside the way of the gate:	5975
	18: 4	the king **s** by the gate side, and all	5975
	18:30	stand here. And he turned aside, and **s still**.	5975
	20:11	one of Joab's men **s** by him, and said,	5975
	20:12	when the man saw that all the people **s still**,	5975
	20:12	saw that every one that came by him **s still**.	5975
	20:15	bank against the city, and it **s** in the trench:	5975
	23:12	he **s** in the midst of the ground, and	3320
1Ki	1:28	the king's presence, and **s** before the king.	5975
	3:15	**s** before the ark of the covenant of	5975
	3:16	unto the king, and **s** before him.	5975
	7:25	It **s** upon twelve oxen, three looking toward	5975
	8:14	(and all the congregation of Israel **s**;)	5975
	8:22	Solomon **s** before the altar of the LORD	5975
	8:55	he **s**, and blessed all the congregation of	5975
	10:19	of the seat, and two lions **s** beside the stays.	5975
	10:20	twelve lions **s** there on the one side and	5975
	12: 6	that **s** before Solomon his father while he	5975
	12: 8	up with him, *and* which **s** before him:	5975
	13: 1	and Jeroboam **s** by the altar to burn incense.	5975
	13:24	was cast in the way, and the ass **s** by it,	5975
	13:24	stood by it, the lion also **s** by the carcase.	5975
	19:13	and **s** *in* the entering in of the cave.	5975
	22:21	**s** before the LORD, and said, I will	5975
2Ki	2: 7	of the prophets went, and **s** to view afar off:	5975
	2: 7	to view afar off: and they two **s** by Jordan.	5975
	2:13	and went back, and **s** by the bank of Jordan;	5975
	3:21	on armour, and upward, and **s** in the border.	5975
	4:12	when he had called her, she **s** before him.	5975
	4:15	when he had called her, she **s** in the door.	5975
	5: 9	and **s** *at* the door of the house of Elisha.	5975
	5:15	his company, and came, and **s** before him:	5975
	5:25	he went in, and **s** before his master.	5975
	8: 9	and came and **s** before him, and said,	5975
	9:17	there **s** a watchman on the tower in Jezreel,	5975
	10: 4	said, Behold, two kings **s** not before him:	5975
	10: 9	**s**, and said to all the people, Ye *be*	5975
	11:11	the guard **s**, every man with his weapons in	5975
	11:14	behold, the king **s** by a pillar, as the manner	5975
	13:21	of Elisha, he revived, and **s up** on his feet.	6965
	18:17	and **s** by the conduit of the upper pool,	5975
	18:28	Rab-shakeh **s** and cried with a loud voice in	5975
	23: 3	the king **s** by a pillar, and made a covenant	5975
	23: 3	And all the people **s** to the covenant.	5975
1Ch	6:39	his brother Asaph, who **s** on his right hand,	5975
	6:44	their brethren the sons of Merari *s* on	NIH
	21: 1	Satan **s** *up* against Israel, and	5975
	21:15	the angel of the LORD **s** by	5975
	28: 2	David the king **s up** upon his feet, and	6965
2Ch	3:13	they **s** on their feet, and their faces *were*	5975
	4: 4	It **s** upon twelve oxen, three looking toward	5975
	5:12	**s** *at* the east *end* of the altar, and with them	5975
	6: 3	and all the congregation of Israel **s**.	5975
	6:12	he **s** before the altar of the LORD in	5975
	6:13	upon it he **s**, and kneeled *down* upon his	5975
	7: 6	trumpets before them, and all Israel **s**.	5975
	9:19	twelve lions **s** there on the one side and	5975
	10: 6	**s** before Solomon his father while he *yet*	5975
	10: 8	brought up with him, that **s** before him.	5975
	13: 4	Abijah **s up** upon mount Zemaraim,	6965
	18:20	**s** before the LORD, and said, I will entice	5975
	20: 5	Jehoshaphat **s** in the congregation of Judah	5975
	20:13	all Judah **s** before the LORD, with their	5975
	20:19	**s up** to praise the LORD God of Israel	6965
	20:20	Jehoshaphat **s** and said, Hear me, O Judah,	5975
	20:23	Moab **s up** against the inhabitants of mount	5975
	23:13	the king **s** at his pillar at the entering in, and	5975
	24:20	which **s** above the people, and said unto	5975
	28:12	**s up** against them that came from the war,	6965
	29:26	the Levites **s** with the instruments of David,	5975
	30:16	they **s** in their place after their manner,	5975
	34:31	the king **s** in his place, and made a	5975
	35:10	the priests **s** in their place, and the Levites	5975
Ezr	2:63	holy *things* till there **s** *up* a priest with Urim	5975
	3: 2	**s up** Jeshua the son of Jozadak, and	6965
	3: 9	**s** Jeshua *with* his sons and his brethren,	5975

Ezr 10:10 Ezra the priest s up, and said unto them, 6965
Ne 7:65 things, till there s up a priest with Urim 5975
8: 4 Ezra the scribe s upon a pulpit of wood, 5975
8: 4 beside him s Mattithiah, and Shema, and 5975
8: 5 and when he opened it, all the people s up: 5975
8: 7 the law: and the people s in their place. NIH
9: 2 s and confessed their sins, and the iniquities 5975
9: 3 they s up in their place, and read in 6965
9: 4 s up upon the stairs of the Levites, Jeshua, 6965
12:39 and they s still in the prison gate. 5975
12:40 So s the two companies of them that gave 5975
Est 5: 1 and s in the inner court of the king's house, 5975
5: 9 that he s not up, nor moved for him, he was 6965
7: 7 Haman s up to make request for his life to 5975
8: 4 So Esther arose, and s before the king, 5975
9:16 s for their lives, and had rest from their 5975
Job 4:15 before my face; the hair of my flesh s up: 5568
4:16 It s still, but I could not discern the form 5975
29: 8 and the aged arose, and s up. 5975
30:28 I s up, and I cried in the congregation. 6965
32:16 but s still, and answered no more:) 5975
Ps 33: 9 it was done; he commanded, and it s fast. 5975
104: 6 the waters s above the mountains. 5975
106:23 had not Moses his chosen s before him in 5975
106:30 s up Phinehas, and executed judgment: 5975
Isa 6: 2 Above it s the seraphims: each one had six 5975
36: 2 he s by the conduit of the upper pool in 5975
36:13 Rabshakeh s, and cried with a loud voice in 5975
Jer 15: 1 Though Moses and Samuel s before me, 5975
18:20 Remember that I s before thee to speak 5975
19:14 he s in the court of the LORD's house; 5975
23:18 For who hath s in the counsel of 5975
23:22 if they had s in my counsel, and had caused 5975
28: 5 in the presence of all the people that s in 5975
36:21 in the ears of all the princes which s beside 5975
44:15 all the women that s by, a great multitude, 5975
46:15 they s not, because the LORD did drive 5975
48:45 They that fled s under the shadow of 5975
La 2: 4 he s with his right hand as an adversary, 5324
Eze 1:21 when those s, these stood; and when those 5975
1:21 when those stood, these s; and when those 5975
1:24 when they s, they let down their wings. 5975
1:25 when they s, and had let down their wings. 5975
3:23 behold, the glory of the LORD s there, 5975
8:11 there s before them seventy men of 5975
8:11 in the midst of them s Jaazaniah the son of 5975
9: 2 they went in, and s beside the brasen altar. 5975
10: 3 Now the cherubims s on the right side of 5975
10: 4 and s over the threshold of the house; NIH
10: 6 then he went in, and s beside the wheels. 5975
10:17 When they s, these stood; and when they 5975
10:17 When they stood, these s; and when they 5975
10:18 of the house, and s over the cherubims. 5975
10:19 every one s at the door of the east gate of 5975
11:23 s upon the mountain which is on the east 5975
21:21 For the king of Babylon s at the parting of 5975
37:10 they lived, and s up upon their feet, 5975
40: 3 and a measuring reed; and he s in the gate. 5975
43: 6 me out of the house; and the man s by me. 5975
47: 1 for the forefront of the house s toward NIH
Da 1:19 Azariah: therefore s they before the king. 5975
2: 2 So they came and s before the king. 5975
2:31 brightness was excellent, s before thee; 6966
3: 3 they s before the image that 6966
7:10 ten thousand times ten thousand s before 6966
7:16 I came near unto one of them that s by, 6966
8: 3 there s before the river a ram which had 5975
8:15 there s before me as the appearance of a 5975
8:17 So he came near where I s: and when he 5977
8:22 that being broken, whereas four s up for it, 5975
10:11 spoken this word unto me, I s trembling. 5975
10:16 spake, and said unto him that s before me, 5975
11: 1 even I, s to confirm and to strengthen him. 5977
12: 5 and behold, there s other two, 5975
Hos 10: 9 there they s: the battle in Gibeah against 5975
Am 7: 7 the Lord s upon a wall made by a 5324
Ob 1:14 Neither shouldest thou have s in 5975
Hab 3: 6 He s, and measured the earth: he beheld, 5975
3:11 The sun and moon s still in their habitation: 5975
Zec 1: 8 he s among the myrtle trees that were in 5975
1:10 the man that s among the myrtle trees 5975
1:11 the LORD that s among the myrtle trees, 5975
3: 3 filthy garments, and s before the angel. 5975
3: 4 and spake unto those that s before him, 5975
3: 5 And the angel of the LORD s by. 5975
Mt 2: 9 and s over where the young child was. 2476
12:46 his mother and his brethren s without, 2476
13: 2 sat; and the whole multitude s on the shore. 2476
20:32 And Jesus s still, and called them, and said, 2476
26:73 And after a while came unto him they that s 2476
27:11 And Jesus s before the governor: and 2476
27:47 Some of them that s there, when they heard 2476
Mk 10:49 And Jesus s still, and commanded him to 2476
11: 5 And certain of them that s there said unto 2476
14:47 And one of them that s by drew a sword, 3936
14:60 And the high priest s up in the midst, and 450
14:69 and began to say to them that s by, This is 3936
14:70 they that s by said again to Peter, 3936
15:35 And some of them that s by, when they 3936
15:39 which s over against him, saw that he so 3936
Lk 4:16 on the sabbath day, and s up for to read. 450
4:39 And he s over her, and rebuked the fever; 2186
5: 1 of God, he s by the lake of Gennesaret, 2476
6: 8 in the midst. And he arose and s forth. 2476
6:17 and s in the plain, and the company of his 2476
7:14 and they that bare him s still. And he said, 2476
7:38 And s at his feet behind him weeping, and 2476
9:32 his glory, and the two men that s with him. 4921
10:25 a certain lawyer s up, and tempted him, 450
17:12 ten men that were lepers, which s afar off: 2476
18:11 The Pharisee s and prayed thus with 2476
18:40 And Jesus s, and commanded him to be 2476
19: 8 And Zaccheus s, and said unto the Lord; 2476
19:24 And he said unto them that s by, Take from 3936
23:10 And the chief priests and scribes s and 2476
23:35 And the people s beholding. And the rulers 2476
23:49 s afar off, beholding these things. 2476
24: 4 two men s by them in shining garments: 2186
24:36 Jesus himself s in the midst of them, and 2476
Jn 1:35 Again the next day after John s, and two of 2476
6:22 when the people which s on the other side 2476
7:37 Jesus s and cried, saying, If any man thirst, 2476
11:56 as they s in the temple, What think ye, 2476
12:29 that s by, and heard it, said that it 2476
18: 5 which betrayed him, s with them. 2476
18:16 But Peter s at the door without. Then went 2476
18:18 officers s there, who had made a fire of 2476
18:18 and Peter s with them, and warmed himself. 2476
18:22 one of the officers which s by stroke Jesus 3936
18:25 And Simon Peter s and warmed himself. 2476
19:25 Now there s by the cross of Jesus his 2476
20:11 But Mary s without at the sepulchre 2476
20:19 came Jesus and s in the midst, and 2476
20:26 and s in the midst, and said, Peace be unto 2476
21: 4 was now come, Jesus s on the shore: 2476
Ac 1:10 two men s by them in white apparel; 3936
1:15 And in those days Peter s up in the midst of 450
3: 8 And he leaping up s, and walked, and 2476
4:26 The kings of the earth s up, and the rulers 3936
5:34 Then s there up one in the council, 450
9: 7 And the men which journeyed with him s 2476
9:39 and all the widows s by him weeping, and 3936
10:17 and s before the gate, 2186
10:30 a man s before me in bright clothing, 2476
11:13 which s and said unto him, Send men to 2476
11:28 And there s up one of them named Agabus, 450
12:14 ran in, and told how Peter s before the gate. 2476
13:16 Then Paul s up, and beckoning with his hand 450
14:20 as the disciples s round about him, 2944
16: 9 There s a man of Macedonia, and 2476
17:22 Then Paul s in the midst of Mars' hill, and 2476
21:40 Paul s on the stairs, and beckoned with 2476
22:13 and s, and said unto me, Brother Saul, 2186
22:25 Paul said unto the centurion that s by, Is it 2476
23: 2 that s by him to smite him on the mouth. 3936
23: 4 And they that s by said, Revilest thou 3936
23:11 And the night following the Lord s by him, 2186
24:20 doing in me, while I s before the council, 2476
25: 7 came down from Jerusalem s round about, 4026
25:18 Against whom when the accusers s up, they 2476
27:21 But after long abstinence Paul s forth in 2476
27:23 For there s by me this night the angel of 3936
2Ti 4:16 At my first answer no man s with me, but 4836
4:17 Notwithstanding the Lord s with me, and 3936
Heb 9:10 Which s only in meats and drinks, and NIG
Rev 5: 6 s a Lamb as it had been slain, having seven 2476
7: 9 s before the throne, and before the Lamb, 2476
7:11 And all the angels s round about the throne, 2476

Rev 8: 2 And I saw the seven angels which **s** before *2476*
8: 3 And another angel came and **s** at the altar, *2476*
11: 1 and the angel **s**, saying, Rise, and *2476*
11:11 into them, and they **s** upon their feet; *2476*
12: 4 the dragon **s** before the woman which was *2476*
13: 1 And I **s** upon the sand of the sea, and saw a *2476*
14: 1 and lo, a Lamb **s** on the mount Sion, and *2476*
18:17 and as many as trade by sea, **s** afar off, *2476*

STOODEST (3) [STAND]
Nu 22:34 for I knew not that thou **s** in the way 5324
Dt 4:10 *Specially* the day that thou **s** before 5975
Ob 1:11 In the day that thou **s** on the other side, 5975

STOOL (1) [FOOTSTOOL, STOOLS]
2Ki 4:10 and a table, and a **s**, and a candlestick: 3678

STOOLS (1) [STOOL]
Ex 1:16 the Hebrew women, and see *them* upon the **s**; 70

STOOP (4) [STOOPED, STOOPETH, STOOPING]
Job 9:13 his anger, the proud helpers do **s** under him. 7817
Pr 12:25 Heaviness in the heart of man **maketh** it **s**: 7812
Isa 46: 2 They **s**, they bow down together; 7164
Mk 1: 7 of whose shoes I am not worthy to **s down** *2955*

STOOPED (7) [STOOP]
Ge 49: 9 he **s down**, he couched as a lion, and as an 3766
1Sa 24: 8 David **s** *with his* face to the earth, and 6915
28:14 he **s** *with his* face to the ground, and 6915
2Ch 36:17 or maiden, old man, or **him that s for age**: 3486
Jn 8: 6 But Jesus **s** down, and with *his* finger wrote *2955*
8: 8 And again he **s** down, and wrote on *2955*
20:11 she **s down**, **and looked** into the sepulchre, *3879*

STOOPETH (1) [STOOP]
Isa 46: 1 Bel boweth down, Nebo **s**, their idols were 7164

STOOPING (2) [STOOP]
Lk 24:12 and **s down**, he beheld the linen clothes laid *3879*
Jn 20: 5 And he **s down**, **and looking** in, saw *3879*

STOP (7) [STOPPED, STOPPETH, STOPT, UNSTOPPED]
1Ki 18:44 and get thee down, that the rain **s** thee not. 6113
2Ki 3:19 **s** all wells of water, and mar every good 5640
2Ch 32: 3 his mighty *men* to **s** the waters of 5640
Ps 35: 3 **s** *the way* against them that persecute me: 5462
107:42 rejoice: and all iniquity shall **s** her mouth. 7092
Eze 39:11 it *shall* **s** the *noses of the* passengers: and 2629
2Co 11:10 no *man* shall **s** me of this boasting in *5420*

STOPPED (14) [STOP]
Ge 8: 2 and the windows of heaven were **s**, 5534
26:15 the Philistims had **s** them, and filled them 5640
26:18 for the Philistims had **s** them after the death 5640
Lev 15: 3 or his flesh be **s** from his issue, it *is* his 2856
2Ki 3:25 they **s** all the wells of water, and felled all 5640
2Ch 32:30 This same Hezekiah also **s** the upper 5640
Ne 4: 7 *and* that the breaches began to be **s**, then 5640
Ps 63:11 the mouth of them that speak lies shall be **s**. 5534
Jer 51:32 *that* the passages are **s**, and the reeds they 8610
Zec 7:11 and **s** their ears, that *they* should not hear. 3513
Ac 7:57 and **s** their ears, and ran upon him with one *4912*
Ro 3:19 that every mouth may be **s**, and all *5420*
Tit 1:11 Whose **mouths** must be **s**, who subvert *1993*
Heb 11:33 obtained promises, **s** the mouths of lions, *5420*

STOPPETH (4) [STOP]
Job 5:16 poor hath hope, and iniquity **s** her mouth. 7092
Ps 58: 4 *they are* like the deaf adder *that* **s** her ear; 331
Pr 21:13 Whoso **s** his ears at the cry of the poor, 331
Isa 33:15 that **s** his ears from hearing of blood, and 331

STOPT (1) [STOP]
2Ch 32: 4 who **s** all the fountains, and the brook that 5640

STORE (25) [STOREHOUSE, STOREHOUSES]
Ge 26:14 of herds, and **great s** of servants: 7227
41:36 *that* food shall be for **s** to the land against 6487
Lev 25:22 her fruits come in ye shall eat *of* the old **s**. NIH
26:10 ye shall eat **old s**, and bring forth 3462+3465
Dt 28: 5 Blessed *shall be* thy basket and thy **s**. 4863
28:17 Cursed *shall be* thy basket and thy **s**. 4863
32:34 *Is* not this **laid up in s** with me, *and* 3647
1Ki 9:19 all the cities of **s** that Solomon had, 4543
10:10 of spices very **great s**, and precious stones: 7235
2Ki 20:17 *that* which thy fathers have **laid up in s** unto 686
1Ch 29:16 all this **s** that we have prepared to build 1995
2Ch 8: 4 all the **s** cities, which he built in Hamath. 4543
8: 6 all the **s** cities that Solomon had, and all 4543
11:11 and **s** of victual, and *of* oil and wine. 214
16: 4 and all the **s** cities of Naphtali. 4543
17:12 and he built in Judah castles, and cities of **s**. 4543
31:10 and that which is left *is* this **great s**. 1995
Ne 5:18 and once in ten days **s** of all *sorts of* wine: 7235
Ps 144:13 **all manner of s**: 413+2177+2177+4480
Isa 39: 6 *that* which thy fathers have **laid up in s** until 686
Am 3:10 who **s up** violence and robbery in their 686
Na 2: 9 for *there is* none end of the **s and** glory out 8498
1Co 16: 2 week let every one of you lay by him **in s**, *2343*
1Ti 6:19 **Laying up in s** for themselves a good *597*
2Pe 3: 7 are now, by the same word are **kept in s**, *2343*

STOREHOUSE (2) [HOUSE, STORE]
Mal 3:10 Bring ye all the tithes into the **s**, that 214+1004
Lk 12:24 which neither have **s** nor barn; and God *5009*

STOREHOUSES (6) [HOUSE, STORE]
Ge 41:56 Joseph opened all **the s**, 834+871.1+1992.1
Dt 28: 8 command the blessing upon thee in thy **s**, 618
1Ch 27:25 and over the **s** in the fields, in the cities, and 214
2Ch 32:28 **S** also for the increase of corn, and wine, 4543
Ps 33: 7 as a heap: he layeth up the depth in **s**. 214
Jer 50:26 her from the utmost border, open her **s**: 3965

STORIES (5) [STORY]
Ge 6:16 second, and third **s** shalt thou make it. NIH
Eze 41:16 the galleries round about on their three **s**, NIH
42: 3 *was* gallery against gallery in three **s**. NIH
42: 6 For they *were* in three **s**, but had not pillars NIH
Am 9: 6 *It is* he that buildeth his **s** in the heaven, and 4609

STORK (5)
Lev 11:19 the **s**, the heron after her kind, and 2624
Dt 14:18 the **s**, and the heron after her kind, and 2624
Ps 104:17 *as for* the **s**, the fir trees *are* her house. 2624
Jer 8: 7 the **s** in the heaven knoweth her appointed 2624
Zec 5: 9 for they had wings like the wings of a **s**: 2624

STORM (14) [STORMY]
Job 21:18 and as chaff that the **s** carrieth away. 5492
27:21 and **as a s hurleth** him out of his place. 8175
Ps 55: 8 I would hasten my escape from the windy **s** 5584
83:15 and make them afraid with thy **s**. 5492
107:29 He maketh the **s** a calm, so that the waves 5591
Isa 4: 6 and for a covert from **s** and from rain. 2230
25: 4 a refuge from the **s**, a shadow from 2230
25: 4 when the blast of the terrible ones *is* as a **s** 2230
28: 2 as a tempest of hail *and* a destroying **s**, 8178
29: 6 *with* **s** and tempest, and the flame of 5492
Eze 38: 9 Thou shalt ascend and come like a **s**, 7722
Na 1: 3 *hath* his way in the whirlwind and in the **s**, 8183
Mk 4:37 And there arose a great **s** of wind, and *2978*
Lk 8:23 there came down a **s** of wind on the lake; *2978*

STORMY (4) [STORM]
Ps 107:25 For he commandeth, and raiseth the **s** wind, 5591
148: 8 and vapour; **s** wind fulfilling his word: 5591
Eze 13:11 shall fall; and a **s** wind shall rent *it*. 5591
13:13 I will even rent *it with* a **s** wind in my fury; 5591

STORY (2) [STORIES]
2Ch 13:22 *are* written in the **s** of the prophet Iddo. 4097
24:27 behold they *are* written in the **s** of the book 4097

STOUT (4) [STOUTHEARTED, STOUTNESS]
Job 4:11 the **s lion's** whelps are scattered abroad. 3833
Isa 10:12 I will punish the fruit of the **s** heart of 1433
Da 7:20 whose look *was* more **s** than his fellows. 7260
Mal 3:13 Your words have been **s** against me, 2388

STOUTHEARTED (2) [HEART, STOUT]
Ps 76: 5 The **s** are spoiled, they have slept their 47+3820
Isa 46:12 Hearken unto me, ye **s**, that *are* far from 47+3820

STOUTNESS (1) [STOUT]
Isa 9: 9 that say in the pride and **s** of heart, 1433

STRAIGHT (28) [STRAIGHTWAY]
Jos 6: 5 shall ascend up every man **s before** him. 5048

Jos 6:20 every man s **before** him, and they took 5048
1Sa 6:12 the kine **took** the s way to the way of 3474
2Ch 32:30 **brought** it s down to the west *side* of 3474
Ps 5: 8 **make** thy way s before my face. 3474
Pr 4:25 and let thine eyelids **look** s before thee. 3474
Ecc 1:15 *That which is* crooked cannot be **made** s: 8626
7:13 for who can **make** *that* s, which he hath 8626
Isa 40: 3 **make** s in the desert a highway for our 3474
40: 4 the crooked shall be **made** s, and the rough 4334
42:16 light before them, and crooked things s. 4334
45: 2 and **make** the crooked places s: 3474
Jer 31: 9 to walk by the rivers of waters in a s way, 3477
Eze 1: 7 their feet *were* s feet; and the sole of their 3477
1: 9 they went every one s **forward**. 413+5676+6440
1:12 they went every one s **forward**: 413+5676+6440
1:23 under the firmament *were* their wings s, 3477
10:22 they went every one s **forward**. 413+5676+6440
Mt 3: 3 ye the way of the Lord, make his paths s. *2117*
Mk 1: 3 ye the way of the Lord, make his paths s. *2117*
Lk 3: 4 ye the way of the Lord, make his paths s. *2117*
3: 5 and the crooked shall be made s, and *2117*
13:13 and immediately she was **made** s, and *461*
Jn 1:23 **Make** s the way of the Lord, as said *2116*
Ac 9:11 and go into the street which is called S, and *2117*
16:11 we **came with a** s **course** to Samothracia, *2113*
21: 1 we came with a s **course** unto Cos, and *2113*
Heb 12:13 And make s paths for your feet, lest *that* *3717*

STRAIGHTWAY (42) [STRAIGHT]
1Sa 9:13 be come *into* the city, ye shall s find him, 3651
28:20 Saul fell s all along on the earth, and 4116
Pr 7:22 He goeth after her s, as an ox goeth to 6597
Da 10:17 for me, s there remained no strength in me, 6258
Mt 3:16 he was baptized, went up s out of the water: *2112*
4:20 And they s left *their* nets, and *2112*
14:22 And s Jesus constrained his disciples to get *2112*
14:27 But s Jesus spake unto them, saying, Be of *2112*
21: 2 and s ye shall find an ass tied, and a colt *2112*
21: 3 hath need of them; and s he will send them. *2112*
25:15 his several ability; and s took his journey. *2112*
27:48 And s one of them ran, and took a spunge, *2112*
Mk 1:10 And s coming up out of the water, he saw *2112*
1:18 And s they forsook their nets, and *2112*
1:20 And s he called them: and they left their *2112*
1:21 s on the sabbath day he entered into *2112*
2: 2 And s many were gathered together, *2112*
3: 6 s took counsel with the Herodians against *2112*
5:29 And s the fountain of her blood was dried *2112*
5:42 And s the damsel arose, and walked; *2112*
6:25 And she came in s with haste unto the king, *2112*
6:45 And s he constrained his disciples to get *2112*
6:54 come out of the ship, s they knew him, *2112*
7:35 And s his ears were opened, *2112*
8:10 And s he entered into a ship with his *2112*
9:15 And s all the people, when they beheld *2112*
9:20 and when he saw him, s the spirit tare him; *2112*
9:24 And s the father of the child cried out, and *2112*
11: 3 need of him; and s he will send him hither. *2112*
14:45 he goeth s to him, and saith, Master, *2112*
15: 1 And s in the morning the chief priests held *2112*
Lk 5:39 No *man* also having drunk old *wine* s *2112*
8:55 And her spirit came again, and she arose s: *3916*
12:54 the west, s ye say, There cometh a shower; *2112*
14: 5 will not s pull him out on the sabbath day? *2112*
Jn 13:32 him in himself, and shall s glorify him. *2112*
Ac 5:10 Then fell she down s at his feet, and *3916*
9:20 And s he preached Christ in *2112*
16:33 and was baptized, he and all his, s. *3916*
22:29 Then s they departed from him which *2112*
23:30 I sent s to thee, and gave commandment to *1824*
Jas 1:24 s forgetteth what manner of *man* he was. *2112*

STRAIN (1)
Mt 23:24 which **s out** a gnat, and swallow a camel. *1368*

STRAIT (10) [STRAITEN, STRAITENED, STRAITENETH, STRAITEST, STRAITLY, STRAITNESS, STRAITS]
1Sa 13: 6 the men of Israel saw that they were **in a** s, 6887
2Sa 24:14 David said unto Gad, I am in a great s: 6887
2Ki 6: 1 the place where we dwell with thee is too s 6862
1Ch 21:13 And David said unto Gad, I am **in a** great s: 6887
Job 36:16 would he have removed thee out of the s 6862
Isa 49:20 in thine ears, The place *is* too s for me: 6862
Mt 7:13 Enter ye in at the s gate: for wide *is* *4728*
7:14 Because s *is* the gate, and narrow *is* *4728*
Lk 13:24 Strive to enter in at the s gate: for many, *4728*
Php 1:23 For I am **in a** s betwixt two, having a desire *4912*

STRAITEN (1) [STRAIT]
Jer 19: 9 and they that seek their lives, shall s them. 6693

STRAITENED (8) [STRAIT]
Job 18: 7 The steps of his strength shall be s, and 3334
37:10 is given: and the breadth of the waters is s. 4164
Pr 4:12 When thou goest thy steps shall not be s; 3334
Eze 42: 6 *the building* was s more than the lowest and 680
Mic 2: 7 of Jacob, is the spirit of the LORD s? 7114
Lk 12:50 and how am I s till it be accomplished! *4912*
2Co 6:12 Ye are not s in us, *4729*
6:12 in us, but ye are s in your own bowels. *4729*

STRAITENETH (1) [STRAIT]
Job 12:23 he enlargeth the nations, and s them *again*. 5148

STRAITEST (1) [STRAIT]
Ac 26: 5 that after the **most** s sect of our religion I *196*

STRAITLY (11) [STRAIT]
Ge 43: 7 The man **asked** us s of our state, and 7592+7592
Ex 13:19 for he had s **sworn** the children of 7650+7650
Jos 6: 1 Now Jericho was **s shut up** 5462+5462+2050.1
1Sa 14:28 **s charged** the people **with an oath**, 7650+7650
Mt 9:30 and Jesus s **charged** them, saying, See *that* *1690*
Mk 1:43 And he s **charged** him, and forthwith sent *1690*
3:12 And he s charged them that they should not *4183*
5:43 And he charged them s that no *man* should *4183*
Lk 9:21 And he s **charged** them, and *2008*
Ac 4:17 among the people, let us s **threaten** them, *546*
5:28 Did not we s **command** you that *you* *3852+3853*

STRAITNESS (5) [STRAIT]
Dt 28:53 hath given thee, in the siege, and in the s, 4689
28:55 nothing left him in the siege, and in the s, 4689
28:57 of all *things* secretly in the siege and s, 4689
Job 36:16 *into* a broad place, where *there is* no s; 4164
Jer 19: 9 the flesh of his friend in the siege and s, 4689

STRAITS (2) [STRAIT]
Job 20:22 fulness of his sufficiency he shall be **in** s: 3334
La 1: 3 her persecutors overtook her between the s. 4712

STRAKE (3) [STRIKE]
2Sa 12:15 the LORD s the child that Uriah's wife 5062
20:10 bowels to the ground, and s him not again; NIH
Ac 27:17 the quicksands, s sail, and so were driven. *5465*

STRAKES (2)
Ge 30:37 pilled white s in them, and made the white 6479
Lev 14:37 *be* in the walls of the house with **hollow** s, 8258

STRANDS See WIRES

STRANGE (76) [STRANGELY, STRANGER, STRANGER'S, STRANGERS, STRANGERS']
Ge 35: 2 Put away the s gods that *are* among you, 5236
35: 4 they gave unto Jacob all the s gods which 5236
42: 7 **made** himself s unto them, and 5234
Ex 2:22 he said, I have been a stranger in a s land. 5237
18: 3 for he said, I have been an alien in a s land: 5237
21: 8 to sell her unto a s nation he shall have no 5237
30: 9 Ye shall offer no s incense thereon, nor 2114
Lev 10: 1 offered s fire before the LORD, 2114
Nu 3: 4 when they offered s fire before the LORD, 2114
26:61 when they offered s fire before the LORD. 2114
Dt 32:12 lead him, and *there was* no s god with him. 5236
32:16 They provoked him to jealousy with s *gods*, 2114
Jos 24:20 serve s gods, then he will turn and do you 5236
24:23 *said he*, the s gods which *are* among you, 5236
Jdg 10:16 they put away the s gods from among them, 5236
11: 2 for thou *art* the son of a s woman. 312
1Sa 7: 3 *then* put away the s gods and Ashtaroth 5236
1Ki 11: 1 king Solomon loved many s women, 5237
11: 8 likewise did he for all his s wives, 5237
2Ki 19:24 I have digged and drunk s waters, and 2114
2Ch 14: 3 For he took away the altars of the s *gods*, 5236
33:15 he took away the s gods, and the idol out of 5236
Ezr 10: 2 have taken s wives of the people of 5237
10:10 have transgressed, and have taken s wives, 5237
10:11 people of the land, and from the s wives. 5237

S

Ezr 10:14 let all *them* which have taken s wives in our 5237
10:17 s wives by the first day of the first month. 5237
10:18 there were found that had taken s wives: 5237
10:44 All these had taken s wives: and *some* of 5237
Ne 13:27 to transgress against our God in marrying s 5237
Job 19: 3 ashamed *that* you **make** yourselves s to me. 1970
19:17 My breath is s to my wife, though I 2114
31: 3 a s **punishment** to the workers of iniquity? 5235
Ps 44:20 or stretched out our hands to a s god; 2114
81: 9 There shall no s god be in thee; 2114
81: 9 neither shall thou worship *any* s god. 5236
114: 1 of Jacob from a people of s **language**; 3937
137: 4 we sing the LORD'S song in a s land? 5236
144: 7 of great waters, from the hand of s children; 5236
144:11 and deliver me from the hand of s children, 5236
Pr 2:16 To deliver thee from the s woman, 2114
5: 3 For the lips of a s *woman* drop *as* a 2114
5:20 be ravisht with a s *woman,* and embrace 2114
6:24 from the flattery of the tongue of a s 5237
7: 5 That *they* may keep thee from the s woman, 2114
20:16 and take a pledge of him for a s *woman.* 5237
21: 8 The way of man *is* froward and s: but *as for* 2054
22:14 The mouth of s *women is* a deep pit: he that 2114
23:27 a deep ditch; and a s *woman is* a narrow pit. 5237
23:33 Thine eyes shall behold s *women,* and 2114
27:13 and take a pledge of him for a s *woman.* 5237
Isa 17:10 pleasant plants, and shalt set it *with* s slips: 2114
28:21 that *he* may do his work, his s work; 2114
28:21 and bring to pass his act, his s act. 5237
43:12 when *there was* no s *god* among you: 2114
Jer 2:21 the degenerate plant of a s vine unto me? 5237
5:19 served s gods in your land, so shall ye serve 5236
8:19 their graven images, *and* with s vanities? 5236
Eze 3: 5 For thou *art* not sent to a people of a s 6012
3: 6 Not to many people of a s speech and of a 6012
Da 11:39 he do in the most strong holds with a s god, 5236
Hos 5: 7 for they have begotten s children: now shall 2114
8:12 my law, *but* they were counted as a s *thing.* 2114
Zep 1: 8 and all such as are clothed with s apparel. 5237
Mal 2:11 and hath married the daughter of a s god. 5236
Lk 5:26 saying, We have seen s *things* to day. *3861*
Ac 7: 6 That his seed should sojourn in a s land; *245*
17:18 He seemeth to be a setter forth of s gods: *3581*
17:20 For thou bringest certain s *things* to our *3579*
26:11 I persecuted *them* even unto s cities. *1854*
Heb 11: 9 as *in* a s *country,* dwelling in tabernacles *245*
13: 9 carried about with divers and s doctrines. *3581*
1Pe 4: 4 Wherein they **think it** s that you run not *3579*
4:12 **think it** not s concerning the fiery trial *3579*
4:12 as though *some* s *thing* happened unto you: *3581*
Jude 1: 7 and going after s flesh, are set forth for an *2087*

STRANGELY (1) [STRANGE]

Dt 32:27 adversaries should **behave** themselves s, 5234

STRANGER (129) [STRANGE]

Ge 15:13 Know of a surety that thy seed shall be a s 1616
17: 8 after thee, the land wherein thou art a s, 4033
17:12 or bought with money of any s, 1121+5236
17:27 and bought with money of the s, 1121+5236
23: 4 I *am* a s and a sojourner with you: give me 1616
28: 4 mayest inherit the land wherein thou art a s, 4033
37: 1 dwelt in the land wherein his father was a s, 4033
Ex 2:22 he said, I have been a s in a strange land. 1616
12:19 whether he be a s, or born in the land. 1616
12:43 There shall no s eat thereof: 1121+5236
12:48 when a s shall sojourn with thee, and 1616
12:49 and unto the s that sojourneth among you. 1616
20:10 thy cattle, nor thy s that *is* within thy gates: 1616
22:21 Thou shalt neither vex a s, nor oppress him: 1616
23: 9 Also thou shalt not oppress a s: for ye know 1616
23: 9 for ye know the heart of a s, seeing ye were 1616
23:12 thy handmaid, and the s, may be refreshed. 1616
29:33 a s shall not eat *thereof,* because they *are* 2114
30:33 or whosoever putteth *any* of it upon a s, 2114
Lev 16:29 or a s that sojourneth among you: 1616
17:12 neither shall any s that sojourneth among 1616
17:15 or a s, he shall both wash his clothes, and 1616
18:26 nor any s that sojourneth among you: 1616
19:10 thou shalt leave them for the poor and s: 1616
19:33 if a s sojourn with thee in your land, 1616
19:34 *But* the s that dwelleth with you shall be 1616
22:10 There shall no s eat *of* the holy *thing:* a 2114
22:12 daughter also be *married* unto a s, 376+2114
22:13 but there shall no s eat thereof. 2114
23:22 shalt leave them unto the poor, and to the s: 1616
24:16 as well the s, as he that is born in the land, 1616
24:22 as well for the s, as for one of your own 1616
25: 6 and for thy s that sojourneth with thee, 8453
25:35 *yea, though he be* a s, or a sojourner; 1616
25:47 if a sojourner or s wax rich by thee, and 8453
25:47 sell himself unto the s *or* sojourner by thee, 1616
Nu 1:51 the s that cometh nigh shall be put to death. 2114
3:10 the s that cometh nigh shall be put to death. 2114
3:38 the s that cometh nigh shall be put to death. 2114
9:14 if a s shall sojourn among you, and 1616
9:14 both for the s, and for him that was born in 1616
15:14 if a s sojourn with you, or whosoever *be* 1616
15:15 also for the s that sojourneth *with you,* an 1616
15:15 ye *are,* so shall the s be before the LORD. 1616
15:16 and for the s that sojourneth with you. 1616
15:26 and the s that sojourneth among them; 1616
15:29 and for the s that sojourneth among them. 1616
15:30 *whether he be* born in the land, or a s, 1616
16:40 s, which *is* not of the seed of Aaron, 376+2214
18: 4 and a s shall not come nigh unto you. 2114
18: 7 the s that cometh nigh shall be put to death. 2114
19:10 unto the s that sojourneth among them, 1616
35:15 for the s, and for the sojourner among 1616
Dt 1:16 and his brother, and the s *that is* with him. 1616
5:14 thy cattle, nor thy s that *is* within thy gates; 1616
10:18 the fatherless and widow, and loveth the s, 1616
10:19 Love ye therefore the s: for ye were 1616
14:21 thou shalt give it unto the s that *is* in thy 1616
14:29 the s, and the fatherless, and the widow, 1616
16:11 the s, and the fatherless, and the widow, 1616
16:14 the s, and the fatherless, and the widow, 1616
17:15 thou mayest not set a s over thee, 376+5237
23: 7 because thou wast a s in his land. 1616
23:20 Unto a s thou mayest lend upon usury; but 5237
24:17 shalt not pervert the judgment of the s, 1616
24:19 it shall be for the s, for the fatherless, and 1616
24:20 it shall be for the s, for the fatherless, and 1616
24:21 it shall be for the s, for the fatherless, and 1616
25: 5 dead shall not marry without unto a s: 376+2214
26:11 and the Levite, and the s that *is* among you. 1616
26:12 the s, the fatherless, and the widow, 1616
26:13 unto the s, to the fatherless, and to 1616
27:19 *be* he that perverteth the judgment of the s, 1616
28:43 The s that *is* within thee shall get up above 1616
29:11 your wives, and thy s that *is* in thy camp, 1616
29:22 the s that shall come from a far land, 5237
31:12 and thy s that *is* within thy gates, 1616
Jos 8:33 as well the s, as he that was born among 1616
20: 9 and for the s that sojourneth among them, 1616
Jdg 19:12 will not turn aside hither into the city of a s, 5237
Ru 2:10 take knowledge of me, seeing I *am* a s? 5237
2Sa 1:13 I *am* the son of a s, an Amalekite. 376+1616
15:19 the king: for thou *art* a s, and also an exile. 5237
1Ki 3:18 *there was* no s with us in the house, 2114
8:41 Moreover concerning a s, that *is* not of thy 5237
8:43 do according to all that the s calleth to thee 5237
2Ch 6:32 Moreover concerning the s, which *is* not of 5237
6:33 do according to all that the s calleth to thee 5237
Job 15:19 was given, and no s passed among them. 2114
19:15 and my maidens, count me for a s: 2114
31:32 The s did not lodge in the street: *but* 1616
Ps 39:12 for I *am* a s with thee, *and* a sojourner, 1616
69: 8 I am become a s unto my brethren, and 2114
94: 6 They slay the widow and the s, and 1616
119:19 I *am* a s in the earth: hide not thy 1616
Pr 2:16 *even* from the s *which* flattereth with her 5237
5:10 and thy labours *be* in the house of a s; 5237
5:20 and embrace the bosom of a s? 5237
6: 1 *if* thou hast stricken thy hand with a s, 2114
7: 5 from the s *which* flattereth with her words. 5237
11:15 He that is surety for a s shall smart *for it:* 2114
14:10 and a s doth not intermeddle with his joy. 2114
20:16 Take his garment that is surety *for* a s: and 2114
27: 2 own mouth; a s, and not thine own lips. 5237
27:13 Take his garment that is surety *for* a s, and 2114
Ecc 6: 2 power to eat thereof, but a s eateth it: 376+5237
Isa 56: 3 Neither let the son of the s, that hath joined 5236
56: 6 Also the sons of the s, that join themselves 5236
62: 8 the sons of the s shall not drink thy wine, 5236
Jer 7: 6 *If* ye oppress not the s, the fatherless, and 1616
14: 8 why shouldest thou be as a s in the land, 1616
22: 3 to the s, the fatherless, nor the widow, 1616

S

Eze 14: 7 or of the **s** that sojourneth in Israel, 1616
22: 7 have they dealt by oppression with the **s**: 1616
22:29 they have oppressed the **s** wrongfully. 1616
44: 9 No **s**, uncircumcised in heart, 1121+5236
44: 9 of any **s** that *is* among the children of 1121+5236
47:23 to pass, *that* in what tribe the **s** sojourneth, 1616
Ob 1:12 of thy brother in the day that he became a **s**; 5235
Zec 7:10 nor the fatherless, the **s**, nor the poor; 1616
Mal 3: 5 that turn aside the **s** *from his right,* and 1616
Mt 25:35 me drink: I was a **s**, and ye took me in: *3581*
25:38 When saw we thee a **s**, and took *thee* in? or *3581*
25:43 I was a **s**, and ye took me not in: naked, and *3581*
25:44 or a **s**, or naked, or sick, or in prison, and *3581*
Lk 17:18 returned to give glory to God, save this **s**. *241*
24:18 Art thou only a **s** in Jerusalem, and hast not *3939*
Jn 10: 5 And a **s** will they not follow, but will flee *245*
Ac 7:29 and was a **s** in the land of Madian, where he *3941*

STRANGER'S (2) [STRANGE]
Lev 22:25 Neither from a **s** hand shall ye offer 1121+5236
25:47 by thee, or to the stock of the **s** family: 1616

STRANGERS (79) [STRANGE]
Ge 31:15 Are we not counted of him **s**? for he hath 5237
36: 7 the land wherein they were **s** could not bear 4033
Ex 6: 4 of their pilgrimage, wherein they were **s**. 1481
22:21 for ye were **s** in the land of Egypt. 1616
23: 9 seeing ye were **s** in the land of Egypt. 1616
Lev 17: 8 or of the **s** which sojourn among you, 1616
17:10 or of the **s** that sojourn among you, 1616
17:13 or of the **s** that sojourn among you, 1616
19:34 for ye were **s** in the land of Egypt: 1616
20: 2 or of the **s** that sojourn in Israel, that giveth 1616
22:18 of the house of Israel, or of the **s** in Israel, 1616
25:23 for ye *were* **s** and sojourners with me. 1616
25:45 Moreover of the children of the **s** that do 8453
Dt 10:19 for ye were **s** in the land of Egypt. 1616
24:14 of thy **s** that *are* in thy land within thy 1616
31:16 go a whoring after the gods of the **s** of 5236
Jos 8:35 and the **s** that were conversant among them. 1616
2Sa 22:45 **S** shall submit themselves unto me: 1121+5236
22:46 **S** shall fade away, and they shall be 1121+5236
1Ch 16:19 ye were *but* few, even a few, and **s** in it. 1481
22: 2 David commanded to gather together the **s** 1616
29:15 For we *are* **s** before thee, and sojourners, 1616
2Ch 2:17 Solomon numbered all the **s** that *were* 376+1616
15: 9 the **s** with them out of Ephraim and 1481
30:25 and the **s** that came out of the land of Israel, 1616
Ne 9: 2 separated themselves from all **s**, 1121+5236
13:30 Thus cleansed I them from all **s**, and 5236
Ps 18:44 **s** shall submit themselves unto me. 1121+5236
18:45 The **s** shall fade away, and be afraid 1121+5236
54: 3 For **s** are risen up against me, and 2114
105:12 men in number; yea, *very* few, and **s** in it. 1481
109:11 that he hath; and let the **s** spoil his labour. 2114
146: 9 The LORD preserveth the **s**; he relieveth 1616
Pr 5:10 Lest **s** be filled *with* thy wealth; and 2114
Isa 1: 7 **s** devour it in your presence, and *it is* 2114
1: 7 and *it is* desolate, as overthrown by **s**. 2114
2: 6 they please themselves in the children of **s**. 5237
5:17 the waste places of the fat ones shall **s** eat. 1481
14: 1 the **s** shall be joined with them, and 1616
25: 2 a palace of **s** to be no city; it shall never be 2114
25: 5 Thou shalt bring down the noise of **s**, as 2114
29: 5 Moreover the multitude of thy **s** shall be 2114
60:10 the sons of **s** shall build up thy walls, and 5236
61: 5 **s** shall stand and feed your flocks, and 2114
Jer 2:25 for I have loved **s**, and after them will I go. 2114
3:13 hast scattered thy ways to the **s** under every 2114
5:19 shall ye serve **s** in a land *that is* not yours. 2114
30: 8 **s** shall no more serve themselves of him: 2114
35: 7 live many days in the land where ye *be* **s**. 1481
51:51 for **s** are come into the sanctuaries of 2114
La 5: 2 Our inheritance is turned to **s**, our houses to 2114
Eze 7:21 I will give it into the hands of the **s** for a 2114
11: 9 deliver you into the hands of **s**, and 2114
16:32 *which* taketh **s** instead of her husband. 2114
28: 7 Behold therefore, I *will* bring **s** upon thee, 2114
28:10 of the uncircumcised by the hand of **s**: 2114
30:12 and all that is therein, by the hand of **s**: 2114
31:12 **s**, the terrible of the nations, have cut him 2114
44: 7 ye have brought *into my sanctuary* **s**, 1121+5236
47:22 to the **s** that sojourn among you, 1616
Hos 7: 9 **S** have devoured his strength, and 2114
8: 7 if so be it yield, *the* **s** shall swallow it up. 2114
Joel 3:17 there shall no **s** pass through her any more. 2214
Ob 1:11 in the day that the **s** carried away captive 2114
Mt 17:25 or tribute? of their own children, or of **s**? *245*
17:26 Peter saith unto him, Of **s**. Jesus saith unto *245*
27: 7 with them the potter's field, to bury **s** in. *3581*
Jn 10: 5 from him: for they know not the voice of **s**. *245*
Ac 2:10 and **s** of Rome, Jews and proselytes, *1927*
13:17 exalted the people when *they* **dwelt as s** in *3940*
17:21 **s** which were there spent their time in *3581*
Eph 2:12 and **s** from the covenants of promise, *3581*
2:19 Now therefore ye are no more **s** and *3581*
1Ti 5:10 brought up children, if she have **lodged s**, *3580*
Heb 11:13 and confessed that they were **s** and *3581*
13: 2 Be not forgetful to **entertain s**: for thereby *5381*
1Pe 1: 1 to the **s** scattered throughout Pontus, *3927*
2:11 I beseech *you* as **s** and pilgrims, *3941*
3Jn 1: 5 thou doest to the brethren, and to **s**; *3581*

STRANGERS' (1) [STRANGE]
Pr 5:17 be only thine own, and not **s** with thee. 2114

STRANGLED (4) [STRANGLING]
Na 2:12 **s** for his lionesses, and filled his holes *with* 2614
Ac 15:20 and *from* things **s**, and *from* blood. *4156*
15:29 and from **things s**, and from fornication: *4156*
21:25 and from **s**, and from fornication. *4156*

STRANGLING (1) [STRANGLED]
Job 7:15 So that my soul chooseth **s**, *and* 4267

STRAW (16)
Ge 24:25 We have both **s** and provender enough, and 8401
24:32 gave **s** and provender for the camels, and 8401
Ex 5: 7 Ye shall no more give the people **s** to make 8401
5: 7 let them go and gather **s** for themselves. 8401
5:10 Thus saith Pharaoh, I will not give you **s**. 8401
5:11 get you **s** where you can find *it:* yet not 8401
5:12 land of Egypt to gather stubble instead of **s**. 8401
5:13 *your* daily tasks, as when there was **s**. 8401
5:16 *There is* no **s** given unto thy servants, and 8401
5:18 for there shall no **s** be given you, yet shall 8401
Jdg 19:19 Yet there is both **s** and provender for our 8401
1Ki 4:28 Barley also and **s** for the horses and 8401
Job 41:27 He esteemeth iron as **s**, *and* brass as rotten 8401
Isa 11: 7 and the lion shall eat **s** like the ox. 8401
25:10 *even* as **s** is trodden down for the dunghill. 4963
65:25 and the lion shall eat **s** like the bullock: 8401

STRAWED (5) [STROWED]
Ex 32:20 **s** *it* upon the water, and made the children 2219
Mt 21: 8 from the trees, and **s** *them* in the way. *4766*
25:24 and gathering where thou hast not **s**: *1287*
25:26 I sowed not, and gather where I have not **s**: *1287*
Mk 11: 8 off the trees, and **s** *them* in the way. *4766*

STREAKED See RINGSTRAKED

STREAM (12) [STREAMS]
Nu 21:15 *at* the **s** of the brooks that goeth down to 793
Job 6:15 *and* as the **s** of brooks they pass away; 650
Ps 124: 4 the **s** had gone over our soul: 5158
Isa 27:12 the channel of the river unto the **s** of Egypt, 5158
30:28 his breath, as an overflowing **s**, shall reach 5158
30:33 like a **s** of brimstone, doth kindle it. 5158
57: 6 Among the smooth *stones* of the **s** *is* thy 5158
66:12 the glory of the Gentiles like a flowing **s**: 5158
Da 7:10 A fiery **s** issued and came forth from before 5103
Am 5:24 as waters, and righteousness as a mighty **s**. 5158
Lk 6:48 the **s** beat vehemently upon that house, and *4215*
6:49 against which the **s** did beat vehemently, *4215*

STREAMS (12) [STREAM]
Ex 7:19 upon their **s**, upon their rivers, and 5104
8: 5 forth thine hand with thy rod over the **s**, 5104
Ps 46: 4 the **s** whereof shall make glad the city of 6388
78:16 He brought **s** also out of the rock, and 5140
78:20 waters gushed out, and the **s** overflowed; 5158
126: 4 O LORD, as the **s** in the south. 650
SS 4:15 well of living waters, and **s** from Lebanon. 5140
Isa 11:15 shall smite it in *the* seven **s**, and make *men* 5158
30:25 **s** of waters in the day of the great slaughter, 2988
33:21 *be* unto us a place of broad rivers *and* **s**; 2975
34: 9 the **s** thereof shall be turned into pitch, and 5158
35: 6 shall waters break out, and **s** in the desert. 5158

STREET (36) [STREETS]

Ge 19: 2 Nay; but we will abide in the **s** all night. 7339
Dt 13:16 the spoil of it into the midst of the **s** thereof, 7339
Jos 2:19 go out of the doors of thy house into the **s**, 2351
Jdg 19:15 went in, he sat him down in a **s** of the city: 7339
19:17 he saw a wayfaring man in the **s** of the city: 7339
19:20 wants *lie* upon me; only lodge not in the **s**. 7339
2Sa 21:12 which had stolen them from the **s** of 7339
22:43 I did stamp them as the mire of the **s**, *and* 2351
2Ch 29: 4 and gathered them together into the east **s**, 7339
32: 6 gathered them together to him in the **s** of 7339
Ezr 10: 9 all the people sat in the **s** of the house of 7339
Ne 8: 1 into the **s** that *was* before the water gate; 7339
8: 3 he read therein before the **s** that *was* before 7339
8:16 in the **s** of the water gate, and in the street 7339
8:16 and in the **s** of the gate of Ephraim. 7339
Est 4: 6 forth to Mordecai unto the **s** of the city, 7339
6: 9 bring him on horseback through the **s** of 7339
6:11 brought him on horseback through the **s** of 7339
Job 18:17 and he shall have no name in the **s**. 2351
29: 7 the city, *when* I prepared my seat in the **s**; 7339
31:32 The stranger did not lodge in the **s**: *but* 2351
Pr 7: 8 Passing through the **s** near her corner; and 7784
Isa 42: 2 nor cause his voice to be heard in the **s**. 2351
51:23 and as the **s**, to them that went over. 2351
59:14 for truth is fallen in the **s**, and equity cannot 7339
Jer 37:21 daily a piece of bread out of the bakers' **s**, 2351
La 2:19 that faint for hunger in the top of every **s**. 2351
4: 1 are poured out in the top of every **s**. 2351
Eze 16:24 and hast made thee a high place in every **s**. 7339
16:31 and makest thine high place in every **s**; 7339
Da 9:25 the **s** shall be built again, and the wall, 7339
Ac 9:11 and go into the **s** which is called Straight, *4505*
12:10 they went out, and passed on through one **s**; *4505*
Rev 11: 8 And their dead bodies *shall lie* in the **s** of *4113*
21:21 and the **s** of the city *was* pure gold, as *it* *4113*
22: 2 In the midst of the **s** of it, and of either side *4113*

STREETS (65) [STREET]

2Sa 1:20 in Gath, publish *it* not in the **s** of Askelon; 2351
1Ki 20:34 thou shalt make **s** for thee in Damascus, 2351
Ps 18:42 I did cast them out as the dirt in the **s**. 2351
55:11 and guile depart not from her **s**. 7339
144:13 forth thousands and ten thousands in our **s**: 2351
144:14 that *there be* no complaining in our **s**. 7339
Pr 1:20 she uttereth her voice in the **s**: 7339
5:16 *and* rivers of waters in the **s**. 7339
7:12 now in the **s**, and lieth in wait at every 7339
22:13 *is* a lion without, I shall be slain in the **s**. 7339
26:13 *There is* a lion in the way; a lion *is* in the **s**. 7339
Ecc 12: 4 the doors shall be shut in the **s**, when 7784
12: 5 and the mourners go about the **s**: 7784
SS 3: 2 go about the city in the **s** and in the broad 7784
Isa 5:25 carcases were torn in the midst of the **s**. 2351
10: 6 to tread them down like the mire of the **s**. 2351
15: 3 In their **s** they shall gird themselves with 2351
15: 3 in their **s**, every one shall howl, weeping 7339
24:11 *There is* a crying for wine in the **s**; all joy is 2351
51:20 they lie at the head of all the **s**, as a wild 2351
Jer 5: 1 ye to and fro through the **s** of Jerusalem, 2351
7:17 cities of Judah and in the **s** of Jerusalem? 2351
7:34 from the **s** of Jerusalem, the voice of mirth, 2351
9:21 *and* the young men from the **s**. 7339
11: 6 in the **s** of Jerusalem, saying, Hear ye 2351
11:13 *according to* the number of the **s** of 2351
14:16 shall be cast out in the **s** of Jerusalem 2351
33:10 in the **s** of Jerusalem, that are desolate, 2351
44: 6 cities of Judah and in the **s** of Jerusalem; 2351
44: 9 land of Judah, and in the **s** of Jerusalem? 2351
44:17 cities of Judah, and in the **s** of Jerusalem: 2351
44:21 in the **s** of Jerusalem, ye, and your fathers, 2351
48:38 the housetops of Moab, and in the **s** thereof: 7339
49:26 Therefore her young men shall fall in her **s**, 7339
50:30 Therefore shall her young men fall in the **s**, 7339
51: 4 and *they that are* thrust through in her **s**. 2351
La 2:11 and the sucklings swoon in the **s** of the city. 7339
2:12 when they swooned as the wounded in the **s** 7339
2:21 and the old lie on the ground in the **s**: 2351
4: 5 that did feed delicately are desolate in the **s**: 2351
4: 8 than a coal; they are not known in the **s**: 2351
4:14 They have wandered *as* blind *men* in the **s**, 2351
4:18 hunt our steps, that *we* cannot go in our **s**: 7339
Eze 7:19 They shall cast their silver in the **s**, and 2351
11: 6 ye have filled the **s** thereof *with* the slain. 2351
26:11 of his horses shall he tread down all thy **s**: 2351
28:23 into her pestilence, and blood into her **s**; 2351
Am 5:16 Wailing *shall be* in all **s**; and they shall say 7339
Mic 7:10 she be trodden down as the mire of the **s**. 2351
Na 2: 4 The chariots shall rage in the **s**, they shall 2351
3:10 were dashed in pieces at the top of all the **s**: 2351
Zep 3: 6 I made their **s** waste, that none passeth by: 2351
Zec 8: 4 and old women dwell in the **s** of Jerusalem, 7339
8: 5 the **s** of the city shall be full *of* boys and 7339
8: 5 *of* boys and girls playing in the **s** thereof. 7339
9: 3 the dust, and fine gold as the mire of the **s**. 2351
10: 5 *enemies* in the mire of the **s** in the battle: 2351
Mt 6: 2 do in the synagogues and in the **s**, *4505*
6: 5 the synagogues and in the corners of the **s**, *4113*
12:19 shall any *man* hear his voice in the **s**. *4113*
Mk 6:56 they laid the sick in the **s**, and besought him *58*
Lk 10:10 go *your ways* out into the **s** of the same, *4113*
13:26 thy presence, and thou hast taught in our **s**. *4113*
14:21 Go out quickly into the **s** and lanes of *4113*
Ac 5:15 that *they* brought forth the sick into the **s**, *4113*

STRENGTH (242) [STRENGTHEN, STRENGTHENED, STRENGTHENEDST, STRENGTHENETH, STRENGTHENING, STRONG, STRONGER, STRONGEST, STRONGLY]

Ge 4:12 it shall not henceforth yield unto thee her **s**; 3581
49: 3 my might, and the beginning of my **s**, 202
49:24 his bow abode in **s**, and the arms of his 386
Ex 13: 3 for by **s** of hand the LORD brought you 2392
13:14 By **s** of hand the LORD brought us out 2392
13:16 for by **s** of hand the LORD brought us 2392
14:27 the sea returned to his **s** when the morning 386
15: 2 The LORD *is* my **s** and song, and he is 5797
15:13 thou hast guided *them* in thy **s** unto thy 5797
Lev 26:20 your **s** shall be spent in vain: for your land 3581
Nu 23:22 he hath as it were the **s** of an unicorn. 8443
24: 8 he hath as it were the **s** of an unicorn: 8443
Dt 21:17 for he *is* the beginning of his **s**; the right of 202
33:25 brass; and as thy days, *so shall* thy **s** *be*. 1679
Jos 11:13 *as for* the cities that stood still in their **s**, 8510
14:11 as my **s** *was* then, even so *is* my strength 3581
14:11 even so *is* my **s** now, for war, both to go 3581
Jdg 5:21 O my soul, thou hast trodden down **s**. 5797
8:21 for as the man *is, so is* his **s**. And Gideon 1369
16: 5 see wherein his great **s** *lieth*, and by what 3581
16: 6 wherein thy great **s** *lieth*, and 3581
16: 9 it toucheth the fire. So his **s** was not known. 3581
16:15 hast not told me wherein thy great **s** *lieth*. 3581
16:17 my **s** will go from me, and I shall become 3581
16:19 to afflict him, and his **s** went from him. 3581
1Sa 2: 4 and they that stumbled are girt with **s**. 2428
2: 9 in darkness; for by **s** shall no man prevail. 3581
2:10 he shall give **s** unto his king, and exalt 5797
15:29 also the **S** of Israel will not lie nor repent: 5331
28:20 there was no **s** in him; for he had eaten no 3581
28:22 eat, that thou mayest have **s**, when thou 3581
2Sa 22:33 God *is* my **s** *and* power: and he maketh my 4581
22:40 For thou hast girded me with **s** to battle: 2428
1Ki 19: 8 went in the **s** of that meat forty days and 3581
2Ki 9:24 **drew** a bow **with** his **full s**, 3027+4390+871.1
18:20 *I have* counsel and **s** for the war. 1369
19: 3 to the birth, and *there is* not **s** to bring forth. 3581
1Ch 16:11 Seek the LORD and his **s**, seek his face 5797
16:27 **s** and gladness *are* in his place. 5797
16:28 give unto the LORD glory and **s**. 5797
26: 8 able men for **s** for the service, 3581
29:12 *it is* to make great, and to **give s** unto all. 2388
2Ch 6:41 thy resting place, thou, and the ark of thy **s**: 5797
13:20 Neither did Jeroboam recover **s** again in 3581
Ne 4:10 The **s** of the bearers of burdens is decayed, 3581
8:10 for the joy of the LORD *is* your **s**. 4581
Job 6:11 What *is* my **s**, that I should hope? and 3581
6:12 *Is* my **s** the strength of stones? or *is* my 3581
6:12 *Is* my strength the **s** of stones? or *is* my 3581
9: 4 *He is* wise in heart, and mighty in **s**: 3581
9:19 If *I speak* of **s**, lo, *he is* strong: and if of 3581
12:13 With him *is* wisdom and **s**, he hath counsel 1369
12:16 With him *is* **s** and wisdom: the deceived 5797
12:21 and weakeneth the **s** of the mighty. 4206
18: 7 The steps of his **s** shall be straitened, and 202
18:12 His **s** shall be hunger-bitten, and 202
18:13 It shall devour the **s** of his skin: *even* 905
18:13 *even* the firstborn of death shall devour his **s**. 905
21:23 One dieth in his full **s**, *being* wholly at ease 6106

Job	23: 6	great power? No; but he would put *s* in me.	NIH
	26: 2	*how* savest thou the arm *that hath* no **s**?	5797
	30: 2	whereto *might* the **s** of their hands profit	3581
	36: 5	and despiseth not *any: he is* mighty **in s** *and*	3581
	36:19	*no,* not gold, nor all the forces of **s**.	3581
	37: 6	the small rain, and *to* the great rain of his **s**.	5797
	39:11	Wilt thou trust him, because his **s** *is* great?	3581
	39:19	Hast thou given the horse **s**? hast thou	1369
	39:21	paweth in the valley, and rejoiceth in *his* **s**.	3581
	40:16	his **s** *is* in his loins, and his force *is* in	3581
	41:22	In his neck remaineth **s**, and sorrow is	5797
Ps	8: 2	sucklings hast thou ordained **s** because	5797
	18: 1	I will love thee, O LORD, my **s**.	2391
	18: 2	my God, my **s**, in whom I will trust;	6697
	18:32	*It is* God that girdeth me *with* **s**, and	2428
	18:39	For thou hast girded me *with* **s** unto	2428
	19:14	O LORD, my **s**, and my redeemer.	6697
	20: 6	heaven with the saving **s** of his right hand.	1369
	21: 1	The king shall joy in thy **s**, O LORD; and	5797
	21:13	Be thou exalted, LORD, in thine own **s**: *so*	5797
	22:15	My **s** is dried up like a potsherd; and	3581
	22:19	O LORD: O my **s**, haste thee to help me.	360
	27: 1	the LORD *is* the **s** of my life; of whom	4581
	28: 7	The LORD *is* my **s** and my shield;	5797
	28: 8	The LORD *is* their **s**, and he *is* the saving	5797
	28: 8	and he *is* the saving **s** of his anointed.	4581
	29: 1	give unto the LORD glory and **s**.	5797
	29:11	The LORD will give **s** unto his people;	5797
	31: 4	have laid privily for me: for thou *art* my **s**.	4581
	31:10	my **s** faileth because of mine iniquity, and	3581
	33:16	a mighty *man* is not delivered by much **s**.	3581
	33:17	neither shall he deliver *any* by his great **s**.	2428
	37:39	*he is* their **s** in the time of trouble.	4581
	38:10	My heart panteth, my **s** faileth me: as for	3581
	39:13	O spare me, that I may **recover s**, before I	1082
	43: 2	For thou *art* the God of my **s**: why dost	4581
	46: 1	God *is* our refuge and **s**, a very present help	5797
	52: 7	Lo, *this is* the man *that* made not God his **s**;	4581
	54: 1	by thy name, and judge me by thy **s**.	1369
	59: 9	*Because of* his **s** will I wait upon thee:	5797
	59:17	Unto thee, O my **s**, will I sing: for God *is*	5797
	60: 7	*is* mine; Ephraim also *is* the **s** of mine head;	4581
	62: 7	the rock of my **s**, *and* my refuge, *is* in God.	5797
	65: 6	Which by his **s** setteth fast the mountains;	3581
	68:28	Thy God hath commanded thy **s**:	5797
	68:34	Ascribe ye **s** unto God: his excellency *is*	5797
	68:34	*is* over Israel, and his **s** *is* in the clouds.	5797
	68:35	the God of Israel *is* he that giveth **s** and	5797
	71: 9	old age; forsake me not when my **s** faileth.	3581
	71:16	I will go in the **s** of the Lord GOD: I will	1369
	71:18	until I have shewed thy **s** unto *this*	2220
	73: 4	no bands in their death: but their **s** *is* firm.	193
	73:26	*but* God *is* the **s** of my heart, and	6697
	74:13	Thou didst divide the sea by thy **s**:	5797
	77:14	thou hast declared thy **s** among the people.	5797
	78: 4	his **s**, and his wonderful works that he hath	5807
	78:51	the chief of *their* **s** in the tabernacles of Ham:	202
	78:61	delivered his **s** into captivity, and his glory	5797
	80: 2	and Benjamin and Manasseh stir up thy **s**,	1369
	81: 1	Sing aloud unto God our **s**: make a joyful	5797
	84: 5	Blessed *is* the man whose **s** *is* in thee;	5797
	84: 7	They go from **s** to strength, *every one of*	2428
	84: 7	They go from strength to **s**, *every one of*	2428
	86:16	give thy **s** unto thy servant, and save	5797
	88: 4	into the pit: I am as a man *that hath* no **s**:	353
	89:17	For thou *art* the glory of their **s**: and in thy	5797
	90:10	if by reason of **s** *they be* fourscore years,	1369
	90:10	yet *is* their **s** labour and sorrow;	7296
	93: 1	the LORD is clothed with **s**, *wherewith* he	5797
	95: 4	of the earth: the **s** of the hills *is* his also.	8443
	96: 6	**s** and beauty *are* in his sanctuary.	5797
	96: 7	give unto the LORD glory and **s**.	5797
	99: 4	The king's **s** also loveth judgment;	5797
	102:23	He weakened my **s** in the way;	3581
	103:20	the LORD, ye his angels, that excel in **s**,	3581
	105: 4	Seek the LORD, and his **s**: seek his face	5797
	105:36	firstborn in their land, the chief of all their **s**.	202
	108: 8	*is* mine; Ephraim also *is* the **s** of mine head;	4581
	110: 2	The LORD shall send the rod of thy **s** out	5797
	118:14	The LORD *is* my **s** and song, and	5797
	132: 8	into thy rest; thou, and the ark of thy **s**.	5797
	138: 3	*and* strengthenedst me *with* **s** in my soul.	5797
	140: 7	O GOD the Lord, the **s** of my salvation,	5797
	144: 1	Blessed *be* the LORD my **s**,	6697
	147:10	He delighteth not in the **s** of the horse:	1369
Pr	8:14	I *am* understanding; I have **s**.	1369
	10:29	The way of the LORD *is* **s** to the upright:	4581
	14: 4	but much increase *is* by the **s** of the ox.	3581
	20:29	The glory of young men *is* their **s**: and	3581
	21:22	casteth down the **s** of the confidence	5797
	24: 5	yea, a man of knowledge increaseth **s**.	3581
	24:10	faint in the day of adversity, thy **s** *is* small.	3581
	31: 3	Give not thy **s** unto women, nor thy ways to	2428
	31:17	She girdeth her loins with **s**, and	5797
	31:25	**S** and honour *are* her clothing; and she shall	5797
Ecc	9:16	said I, Wisdom *is* better than **s**:	1369
	10:10	whet the edge, then must he put to more **s**:	2428
	10:17	due season, for **s**, and not for drunkenness.	1369
Isa	5:22	and men of **s** to mingle strong drink:	2428
	10:13	By the **s** of my hand I have done *it,* and	3581
	12: 2	for the LORD JEHOVAH *is* my **s** and	5797
	17:10	hast not been mindful of the rock of thy **s**,	4581
	23: 4	*even* the **s** of the sea, saying, I travail not,	4581
	23:10	O daughter of Tarshish: *there is* no more **s**.	4206
	23:14	ships of Tarshish: for your **s** is laid waste.	4581
	25: 4	For thou hast been a **s** to the poor,	4581
	25: 4	a **s** to the needy in his distress, a refuge	4581
	26: 4	in the LORD JEHOVAH *is* everlasting **s**:	6697
	27: 5	Or let him take hold of my **s**, *that* he may	4581
	28: 6	for **s** to them that turn the battle to the gate.	1369
	30: 2	to strengthen themselves in the **s** of	4581
	30: 3	Therefore shall the **s** of Pharaoh be your	4581
	30: 7	I cried concerning this, Their **s** *is* to sit still.	7293
	30:15	and in confidence shall be your **s**:	1369
	33: 6	the stability of thy times, *and* **s** of salvation:	2633
	36: 5	vain words) *I have* counsel and **s** for war:	1369
	37: 3	to the birth, and *there is* not **s** to bring forth.	3581
	40: 9	good tidings, lift up thy voice with **s**;	3581
	40:29	to *them that have* no might he increaseth **s**.	6109
	40:31	wait upon the LORD shall renew *their* **s**;	3581
	41: 1	O islands; and let the people renew *their* **s**:	3581
	42:25	the fury of his anger, and the **s** of battle:	5807
	44:12	and worketh it with the **s** of his arms:	3581
	44:12	yea, he is hungry, and his **s** faileth:	3581
	45:24	in the LORD have I righteousness and **s**:	5797
	49: 4	I have spent my **s** for nought, and in vain:	3581
	49: 5	of the LORD, and my God shall be my **s**.	5797
	51: 9	Awake, awake, put on **s**, O arm of	5797
	52: 1	Awake, awake; put on thy **s**, O Zion; put on	5797
	62: 8	by his right hand, and by the arm of his **s**,	5797
	63: 1	travelling in the greatness of his **s**?	3581
	63: 6	and I will bring down their **s** to the earth.	5332
	63:15	where *is* thy zeal and thy **s**, the sounding of	1369
Jer	16:19	my **s**, and my fortress, and my refuge in	5797
	20: 5	Moreover I will deliver all the **s** of this city,	2633
	51:53	she should fortify the height of her **s**,	5797
La	1: 6	they are gone without **s** before the pursuer.	3581
	1:14	he hath made my **s** to fall, the Lord hath	3581
	3:18	My **s** and my hope is perished from	5331
Eze	24:21	the excellency of your **s**, the desire of your	5797
	24:25	*be* in the day when I take from them their **s**,	4581
	30:15	will pour my fury upon Sin, the **s** of Egypt;	4581
	30:18	the pomp of her **s** shall cease in her: *as for*	5797
	33:28	and the pomp of her **s** shall cease;	5797
Da	2:37	thee a kingdom, power, and **s**, and glory.	8632
	2:41	there shall be in it of the **s** of the iron,	5326
	10: 8	great vision, and there remained no **s** in me:	3581
	10: 8	in me into corruption, and I retained no **s**.	3581
	10:16	turned upon me, and I have retained no **s**.	3581
	10:17	straightway there remained no **s** in me,	3581
	11: 2	by his **s** through his riches he shall stir up	2393
	11:15	neither *shall there be any* **s** to withstand.	3581
	11:17	He shall also set his face to enter with the **s**	8633
	11:31	they shall pollute the sanctuary *of* **s**, and	4581
Hos	7: 9	Strangers have devoured his **s**, and	3581
	12: 3	and by his **s** he had power with God:	202
Joel	2:22	the fig tree and the vine do yield their **s**.	2428
	3:16	and the **s** of the children of Israel.	4581
Am	3:11	he shall bring down thy **s** from thee, and	5797
	6:13	we not taken to us horns by our own **s**?	2392
Mic	5: 4	shall stand and feed in the **s** of the LORD,	5797
Na	3: 9	Ethiopia and Egypt *were* her **s**, and *it was*	6109
	3:11	thou also shalt seek **s** because of the enemy.	4581
Hab	3:19	The Lord GOD *is* my **s**, and he will make	2428
Hag	2:22	I will destroy the **s** of the kingdoms of	2392
Zec	12: 5	The inhabitants of Jerusalem *shall be* my **s** in	556
Mk	12:30	and with all thy mind, and with all thy **s**:	*2479*
	12:33	and with all the **s**, and to love *his* neighbour	*2479*

Lk 1:51 He hath shewed **s** with his arm; he hath 2904
10:27 and with all thy **s**, and with all thy mind; 2479
Ac 3: 7 his feet and ankle bones **received s**, 4732
9:22 But Saul **increased** the more **in s**, and 1743
Ro 5: 6 For when we were yet **without s**, in due time 772
1Co 15:56 of death *is* sin; and the **s** of sin *is* the law. 1411
2Co 1: 8 we were pressed out of measure, above **s**, 1411
12: 9 for my **s** is made perfect in weakness. 1411
Heb 9:17 otherwise it is of no **s** at all whilst 2480
11:11 Through faith also Sara herself received **s** 1411
Rev 1:16 countenance *was* as the sun shineth in his **s**. 1411
3: 8 for thou hast a little **s**, and hast kept my 1411
5:12 and **s**, and honour, and glory, and blessing. 2479
12:10 and **s**, and the kingdom of our God, and 1411
17:13 shall give their power and **s** unto the beast. 1849

STRENGTHEN (32) [STRENGTH]

Dt 3:28 and encourage him, and **s** him: 553
Jdg 16:28 I pray thee, and **s** me, I pray thee, 2388
1Ki 20:22 **s** thyself, and mark, and see what thou 2388
Ezr 6:22 to **s** their hands in the work of the house of 2388
Ne 6: 9 Now therefore, *O God*, **s** my hands. 2388
Job 16: 5 *But* I would **s** you with my mouth, and 553
Ps 20: 2 from the sanctuary, and **s** thee out of Zion; 5582
27:14 of good courage, and he shall **s** thine heart: 553
31:24 of good courage, and he shall **s** your heart, 553
41: 3 The LORD will **s** him upon the bed of 5582
68:28 **s**, O God, that which thou hast wrought for 5810
89:21 be established: mine arm also shall **s** him. 553
119:28 **s** thou me according unto thy word. 6965
Isa 22:21 **s** him *with* thy girdle, and I will commit thy 2388
30: 2 to **s** themselves in the strength of Pharaoh, 5810
33:23 they could not well **s** their mast, they could 2388
35: 3 **S** ye the weak hands, and confirm 2388
41:10 I will **s** thee; yea, I will help thee; yea, I will 553
54: 2 lengthen thy cords, and **s** thy stakes; 2388
Jer 23:14 they **s** also the hands of evildoers, that none 2388
Eze 7:13 neither shall any **s** himself in the iniquity of 2388
16:49 neither did she **s** the hand of the poor and 2388
30:24 I will **s** the arms of the king of Babylon, 2388
30:25 I will **s** the arms of the king of Babylon, 2388
34:16 was broken, and will **s** that which was sick: 2388
Da 11: 1 *even* I, stood to confirm and to **s** him. 4581
Am 2:14 the strong shall not **s** his force, neither shall 553
Zec 10: 6 I will **s** the house of Judah, and I will save 1396
10:12 I will **s** them in the LORD; and they shall 1396
Lk 22:32 when thou art converted, **s** thy brethren. 4741
1Pe 5:10 make you perfect, stablish, **s**, settle *you*. 4599
Rev 3: 2 Be watchful, and **s** the *things* which remain, 4741

STRENGTHENED (39) [STRENGTH]

Ge 48: 2 and Israel **s** himself, and sat upon the bed. 2388
Jdg 3:12 the LORD **s** Eglon the king of Moab 2388
7:11 afterward shall thine hands be **s** to go down 2388
1Sa 23:16 *into* the wood, and **s** his hand in God. 2388
2Sa 2: 7 Therefore now let your hands be **s**, and 2388
1Ch 11:10 who **s** themselves with him in his kingdom, 2388
2Ch 1: 1 Solomon the son of David was **s** in his 2388
11:17 So they **s** the kingdom of Judah, and 2388
12: 1 had **s** himself, he forsook the law of 2393
12:13 So king Rehoboam **s** himself in Jerusalem, 2388
13: 7 have **s** themselves against Rehoboam the son 553
17: 1 in his stead, and **s** himself against Israel. 2388
21: 4 he **s** himself, and slew all his brethren with 2388
23: 1 in the seventh year Jehoiada **s** himself, and 2388
24:13 set the house of God in his state, and **s** it. 553
25:11 Amaziah **s** himself, and led forth his 2388
26: 8 in of Egypt: for he **s** *himself* exceedingly. 2388
28:20 unto him, and distressed him, but **s** him not. 2388
32: 5 Also he **s** himself, and built up all the wall 2388
Ezr 1: 6 all *they that were* about them **s** their hands 2388
7:28 I was **s** as the hand of the LORD my God 2388
Ne 2:18 So they **s** their hands for *this* good *work*. 2388
Job 4: 3 and thou hast **s** the weak hands. 2388
4: 4 was falling, and thou hast **s** the feeble knees. 553
Ps 52: 7 his riches, *and* **s** himself in his wickedness. 5810
147:13 For he hath **s** the bars of thy gates; he hath 2388
Pr 8:28 when *he* **s** the fountains of the deep: 5810
Eze 13:22 **s** the hands of the wicked, that *he* should 2388
34: 4 The diseased have ye not **s**, neither have ye 2388
Da 10:18 like the appearance of a man, and he **s** me, 2388
10:19 I was **s**, and said, Let my lord speak; 2388
10:19 said, Let my lord speak; for thou hast **s** me. 2388
11: 6 begat her, and he that **s** her in *these* times. 2388
11:12 ten thousands: but he shall not be **s** *by it*. 5810
Hos 7:15 Though I have bound *and* **s** their arms, 2388
Ac 9:19 And when he had received meat, he was **s**. 1765
Eph 3:16 to be **s** with might by his Spirit in the inner 2901
Col 1:11 **S** with all might, according to his glorious 1412
2Ti 4:17 the Lord stood with me, and **s** me; 1743

STRENGTHENEDST (1) [STRENGTH]

Ps 138: 3 *and* **s** me *with* strength in my soul. 7292

STRENGTHENETH (7) [STRENGTH]

Job 15:25 and **s** himself against the Almighty. 1396
Ps 104:15 to shine, and bread *which* **s** man's heart. 5582
Pr 31:17 her loins with strength, and **s** her arms. 553
Ecc 7:19 Wisdom **s** the wise more than ten mighty 5810
Isa 44:14 which he **s** for himself among the trees of 553
Am 5: 9 That **s** the spoiled against the strong, so 1082
Php 4:13 I can do all *things* through Christ which **s** 1743

STRENGTHENING (2) [STRENGTH]

Lk 22:43 an angel unto him from heaven, **s** him. 1765
Ac 18:23 and Phrygia in order, **s** all the disciples. 1991

STRETCH (50) [OUTSTRETCHED, STRETCHED, STRETCHEDST, STRETCHEST, STRETCHETH, STRETCHING]

Ex 3:20 I will **s out** my hand, and smite Egypt with 7971
7: 5 when I **s forth** mine hand upon Egypt, and 5186
7:19 **s out** thine hand upon the waters of Egypt, 5186
8: 5 **S forth** thine hand with thy rod over 5186
8:16 **S out** thy rod, and smite the dust of 5186
9:15 For now I will **s out** my hand, that I may 7971
9:22 **S forth** thine hand toward heaven, 5186
10:12 **S out** thine hand over the land of Egypt for 5186
10:21 **S out** thine hand toward heaven, 5186
14:16 **s out** thine hand over the sea, and divide it: 5186
14:26 unto Moses, **S out** thine hand over the sea, 5186
25:20 the cherubims shall **s forth** *their* wings on 6566
Jos 8:18 **S out** the spear that *is* in thy hand toward 5186
1Sa 24: 6 to **s forth** mine hand against him, 7971
26: 9 for who can **s forth** his hand against 7971
26:11 The LORD forbid that *I* should **s forth** 7971
26:23 I would not **s forth** mine hand against 7971
2Sa 1:14 How wast thou not afraid to **s forth** thine 7971
2Ki 21:13 I will **s** over Jerusalem the line of Samaria, 5186
Job 11:13 and **s out** thine hands toward him; 6566
30:24 Howbeit *he* will not **s out** *his* hand to 7971
39:26 *and* **s** her wings toward the south? 6566
Ps 68:31 Ethiopia shall soon **s out** her hands unto 7323
138: 7 thou shalt **s forth** thine hand against 7971
143: 6 I **s forth** my hands unto thee: my soul 6566
Isa 28:20 For the bed is shorter than that *a man* can **s** 8311
31: 3 When the LORD shall **s out** his hand, 5186
34:11 he shall **s out** upon it the line of confusion, 5186
54: 2 let them **s forth** the curtains of thine 5186
Jer 6:12 for I will **s out** my hand upon 5186
10:20 *there is* none to **s forth** my tent any more, 5186
15: 6 therefore will I **s out** my hand against thee, 5186
51:25 I will **s out** mine hand upon thee, and 5186
Eze 6:14 So will I **s out** mine hand upon them, and 5186
14: 9 I will **s out** my hand upon him, and 5186
14:13 will I **s out** mine hand upon it, and 5186
25: 7 I will **s out** mine hand upon thee, and 5186
25:13 I will also **s out** mine hand upon Edom, and 5186
25:16 I *will* **s out** mine hand upon the Philistines, 5186
30:25 and he shall **s** it **out** upon the land of Egypt. 5186
35: 3 and I will **s out** mine hand against thee, and 5186
Da 11:42 He shall **s forth** his hand also upon 7971
Am 6: 4 **s** themselves upon their couches, and 5628
Zep 1: 4 I will also **s out** mine hand upon Judah, and 5186
2:13 he will **s out** his hand against the north, 5186
Mt 12:13 saith he to the man, **S forth** thine hand. 1614
Mk 3: 5 he saith unto the man, **S forth** thine hand. 1614
Lk 6:10 he said unto the man, **S forth** thy hand. 1614
Jn 21:18 thou shalt **s forth** thy hands, and 1614
2Co 10:14 For we **s** not ourselves **beyond** *our* 5239

STRETCHED (71) [STRETCH]

Ge 22:10 Abraham **s forth** his hand, and took 7971
48:14 Israel **s out** his right hand, and laid *it* upon 7971
Ex 6: 6 and I will redeem you with a **s out** arm, and 5186
8: 6 Aaron **s out** his hand over the waters of 5186
8:17 for Aaron **s out** his hand with his rod, and 5186
9:23 Moses **s forth** his rod toward heaven: and 5186
10:13 Moses **s forth** his rod over the land of 5186

Ex 10:22 Moses **s forth** his hand toward heaven; 5186
14:21 Moses **s out** his hand over the sea; and 5186
14:27 Moses **s forth** his hand over the sea, and 5186
Dt 4:34 and by a **s out** arm, and by great terrors, 5186
5:15 through a mighty hand and by a **s out** arm: 5186
7:19 and the mighty hand, and the **s out** arm, 5186
9:29 by thy mighty power and by thy **s out** arm. 5186
11: 2 his mighty hand, and his **s out** arm, 5186
Jos 8:18 Joshua **s out** the spear that *he had* in his 5186
8:19 they ran as soon as *he* had **s out** his hand: 5186
8:26 hand back, wherewith he **s out** the spear, 5186
2Sa 24:16 when the angel **s out** his hand *upon* 7971
1Ki 6:27 they **s forth** the wings of the cherubims, 6566
8:42 of thy strong hand, and of thy **s out** arm;) 5186
17:21 he **s** himself upon the child three times, 4058
2Ki 4:34 he **s** himself upon the child; and the flesh of 1457
4:35 fro; and went up, and **s** himself upon him: 1457
17:36 of Egypt with great power and a **s out** arm, 5186
1Ch 21:16 having a drawn sword in his hand **s out** 5186
2Ch 6:32 and thy mighty hand, and thy **s out** arm; 5186
Job 38: 5 or who hath **s** the line upon it? 5186
Ps 44:20 or **s out** our hands to a strange god; 6566
88: 9 upon thee, I have **s out** my hands unto thee. 7849
136: 6 To him that **s out** the earth above 7554
136:12 With a strong hand, and with a **s out** arm: 5186
Pr 1:24 I have **s out** my hand, and no man 5186
Isa 3:16 walk with **s forth** necks and wanton eyes, 5186
5:25 he hath **s forth** his hand against them, and 5186
5:25 not turned away, but his hand *is* **s out** still. 5186
9:12 not turned away, but his hand *is* **s out** still. 5186
9:17 not turned away, but his hand *is* **s out** still. 5186
9:21 not turned away, but his hand *is* **s out** still. 5186
10: 4 not turned away, but his hand *is* **s out** still. 5186
14:26 this *is* the hand that is **s out** upon all 5186
14:27 who shall disannul *it?* and his hand *is* **s out**, 5186
16: 8 her branches are **s out**, they are gone over 5203
23:11 He **s out** his hand over the sea, he shook 5186
42: 5 he that created the heavens, and **s** them **out**; 5186
45:12 have **s out** the heavens, and all their host 5186
51:13 that hath **s forth** the heavens, and laid 5186
Jer 6: 4 for the shadows of the evening are **s out**. 5186
10:12 hath **s out** the heavens by his discretion. 5186
32:17 the earth by thy great power and **s out** arm, 5186
32:21 and with a **s out** arm, and with great terror; 5186
51:15 hath **s out** the heaven by his understanding. 5186
La 2: 8 he hath **s out** a line, he hath not withdrawn 5186
Eze 1:11 their wings *were* **s** upward; two *wings* of 6504
1:22 **s forth** over their heads above. 5186
10: 7 *one* cherub **s forth** his hand from between 7971
16:27 I have **s out** my hand over thee, and 5186
20:33 with a **s out** arm, and with fury poured out, 5186
20:34 with a **s out** arm, and with fury poured out. 5186
Hos 7: 5 of wine; he **s out** his hand with scorners. 4900
Am 6: 7 the banquet of them that **s** themselves shall 5628
Zec 1:16 and a line shall be **s forth** upon Jerusalem. 5186
Mt 12:13 And he **s** *it* **forth**; and it was restored *1614*
12:49 And he **s forth** his hand toward his *1614*
14:31 And immediately Jesus **s forth** *his* hand, *1614*
26:51 one of them which were with Jesus **s out** *1614*
Mk 3: 5 And he **s** *it* **out**: and his hand was restored *1614*
Lk 22:53 the temple, ye **s forth** no hands against me: *1614*
Ac 12: 1 Now about that time Herod the king **s forth** *1911*
26: 1 Then Paul **s forth** the hand, and *1614*
Ro 10:21 All day long have I **s forth** my hands unto *1600*

STRETCHEDST (1) [STRETCH]
Ex 15:12 Thou **s out** thy right hand, the earth 5186

STRETCHEST (1) [STRETCH]
Ps 104: 2 who **s out** the heavens like a curtain: 5186

STRETCHETH (7) [STRETCH]
Job 15:25 For he **s out** his hand against God, and 5186
26: 7 He **s out** the north over the empty place, 5186
Pr 31:20 She **s out** her hand to the poor; yea, 6566
Isa 40:22 that **s out** the heavens as a curtain, and 5186
44:13 The carpenter **s out** *his* rule; he marketh it 5186
44:24 all *things;* that **s forth** the heavens alone; 5186
Zec 12: 1 which **s forth** the heavens, and layeth 5186

STRETCHING (2) [STRETCH]
Isa 8: 8 the **s out** of his wings shall fill the breadth 4298
Ac 4:30 By **s forth** thine hand to heal; and *1614*

STRICKEN (18) [STRIKE]
Ge 18:11 and Sarah *were* old *and* **well s** in age; 935
24: 1 Abraham was old, *and* **well s** in age: and 935
Jos 13: 1 Now Joshua was old *and* **s** in years; and 935
13: 1 Thou art old *and* **s** in years, and 935
23: 1 that Joshua waxed old *and* **s** in age. 935
23: 2 and said unto them, I am old *and* **s** in age: 935
Jdg 5:26 she had pierced and **s through** his temples. 2498
1Ki 1: 1 Now king David was old *and* **s** in years; and 935
Pr 6: 1 *if* thou hast **s** thy hand with a stranger, 8628
23:35 They have **s** me, *shalt thou say, and* I was 5221
Isa 1: 5 Why should ye be **s** any more? ye will 5221
16: 7 shall ye mourn; surely *they are* **s**. 5218
53: 4 yet we did esteem him **s**, smitten of God, 5060
53: 8 for the transgression of my people was he **s**. 5061
Jer 5: 3 thou hast **s** them, but they have not grieved; 5221
La 4: 9 **s through** for *want of* the fruits of the field. 1856
Lk 1: 7 and they both were *now* **well s** in years. *4260*
1:18 an old man, and my wife **well s** in years. *4260*

STRIFE (39) [STRIVE]
Ge 13: 7 there was a **s** between the herdmen of 7379
13: 8 Let there be no **s**, I pray thee, between me 4808
Nu 27:14 in the **s** of the congregation, to sanctify me 4808
Dt 1:12 and your burden, and your **s**? 7379
Jdg 12: 2 my people were at great **s** with the children 7379
2Sa 19: 9 all the people were **at s** throughout all 1777
Ps 31:20 secretly in a pavilion from the **s** of tongues. 7379
55: 9 for I have seen violence and **s** in the city. 7379
80: 6 Thou makest us a **s** unto our neighbours: 4066
106:32 They angered *him* also at the waters of **s**, so 4808
Pr 15:18 A wrathful man stirreth up **s**: but *he that is* 4066
15:18 but *he that is* slow to anger appeaseth **s**. 7379
16:28 A froward man soweth **s**: and a whisperer 4066
17: 1 than a house full *of* sacrifices with **s**. 7379
17:14 The beginning of **s** *is as* when one letteth 4066
17:19 He loveth transgression that loveth **s**: *and* 4683
20: 3 *It is* an honour for a man to cease from **s**: 7379
22:10 go out; yea, **s** and reproach shall cease. 1779
26:17 *and* meddleth with **s** *belonging* not to him, 7379
26:20 where *there is* no talebearer, the **s** ceaseth. 4066
26:21 to fire; so *is* a contentious man to kindle **s**. 7379
28:25 He that is of a proud heart stirreth up **s**: but 4066
29:22 An angry man stirreth up **s**, and a furious 4066
30:33 so the forcing of wrath bringeth forth **s**. 7379
Isa 58: 4 ye fast for **s** and debate, and to smite with 7379
Jer 15:10 that thou hast borne me a man of **s** and 7379
Eze 47:19 from Tamar *even* to the waters of **s** *in* 4808
48:28 from Tamar *unto* the waters of **s** *in* Kadesh, 4808
Hab 1: 3 and there are *that* raise up **s** and contention. 7379
Lk 22:24 And there was also a **s** among them, which *5379*
Ro 13:13 and wantonness, not in **s** and envying. *2054*
1Co 3: 3 and **s**, and divisions, are ye not carnal, and *2054*
Gal 5:20 emulations, wrath, **s**, seditions, heresies, *2052*
Php 1:15 indeed preach Christ even of envy and **s**; *2054*
2: 3 *Let* nothing *be done* through **s** or vainglory; *2052*
1Ti 6: 4 cometh envy, **s**, railings, evil surmisings, *2054*
Heb 6:16 for confirmation *is* to them an end of all **s**. *485*
Jas 3:14 ye have bitter envying and **s** in your hearts, *2052*
3:16 and **s** *is,* there *is* confusion and every evil *2052*

STRIFES (4) [STRIVE]
Pr 10:12 Hatred stirreth up **s**: but love covereth all 4066
2Co 12:20 envyings, wraths, **s**, backbitings, *2052*
1Ti 6: 4 but doting about questions and **s of words**, *3055*
2Ti 2:23 knowing that they do gender **s**. *3163*

STRIKE (12) [STRAKE, STRICKEN, STRIKER, STRIKETH, STROKE, STROKES, STROOKE, STRUCK]
Ex 12: 7 **s** *it* on the two side posts and on the upper 5414
12:22 **s** the lintel and the two side posts with 5060
Dt 21: 4 shall **s off** the heifer's **neck** there in 6202
2Ki 5:11 **s** his hand over the place, and recover 5130
Job 17: 3 who *is* he *that* will **s** hands with me? 8628
20:24 *and* the bow of steel shall **s** him **through**. 2498
Ps 110: 5 The Lord at thy right hand shall **s through** 4272
Pr 7:23 Till a dart **s through** his liver; as a bird 6398
17:26 just *is* not good, *nor* to **s** princes for equity. 5221
22:26 Be not thou *one* of them that **s** hands, *or* 8628
Hab 3:14 Thou didst **s through** with his staves 5344
Mk 14:65 **s** him **with the palms of** their **hands**. *906+4475*

STRIKER (2) [STRIKE]
1Ti 3: 3 Not given to wine, no **s**, not greedy of filthy *4131*

S

Tit 1: 7 not soon angry, not given to wine, no **s**, *4131*

STRIKETH (3) [STRIKE]
Job 34:26 He **s** them as wicked *men* in the open sight 5606
Pr 17:18 A man void of understanding **s** hands, *and* 8628
Rev 9: 5 the torment of a scorpion, when he **s** a man. *3817*

STRING (2) [STRINGED, STRINGS]
Ps 11: 2 they make ready their arrow upon the **s**, 3499
Mk 7:35 and the **s** of his tongue was loosed, and *1199*

STRINGED (3) [STRING]
Ps 150: 4 praise him with **s instruments** and organs. 4482
Isa 38:20 **sing** my songs *to* **the s instruments** all 5059
Hab 3:19 To the chief singer on my **s instruments**. 5058

STRINGS (4) [STRING]
Ps 21:12 *arrows* upon thy **s** against the face of them. 4340
33: 2 the psaltery *and* an **instrument of ten s**. 6218
92: 3 Upon an **instrument of ten s**, and upon 6218
144: 9 an **instrument of ten s** will I sing *praises* 6218

STRIP (7) [STRIPPED, STRIPT]
Nu 20:26 **s** Aaron of his garments, and put them upon 6584
1Sa 31: 8 when the Philistines came to **s** the slain, 6584
1Ch 10: 8 when the Philistines came to **s** the slain, 6584
Isa 32:11 **s** ye, and make ye bare, and gird *sackcloth* 6584
Eze 16:39 they shall **s** thee also of thy clothes, and 6584
23:26 They shall also **s** thee **out of** thy clothes, 6584
Hos 2: 3 Lest I **s** her naked, and set her as *in* the day 6584

STRIPE (2) [STRIPES]
Ex 21:25 for burning, wound for wound, **s** for stripe. 2250
21:25 for burning, wound for wound, stripe for **s**. 2250

STRIPES (17) [STRIPE]
Dt 25: 3 Forty **s** he may **give** him, *and* not exceed: 5221
25: 3 beat him above these *with* many **s**, then 4347
2Sa 7:14 and with the **s** of the children of men: 5061
Ps 89:32 with the rod, and their iniquity with **s**. 5061
Pr 17:10 a wise *man* than an hundred **s** into a fool. 5221
19:29 for scorners, and **s** for the back of fools. 4112
20:30 so *do* **s** the inward parts of the belly. 4347
Isa 53: 5 upon him; and with his **s** we are healed. 2250
Lk 12:47 to his will, shall be beaten with many *s*. NIG
12:48 and did commit *things* worthy of **s**, *4127*
12:48 shall be beaten with few *s*. For unto NIG
Ac 16:23 And when they had laid many **s** upon them, *4127*
16:33 same hour of the night, and washed *their* **s**; *4127*
2Co 6: 5 In **s**, in imprisonments, in tumults, *4127*
11:23 in **s** above measure, in prisons more *4127*
11:24 Of the Jews five times received I forty *s* NIG
1Pe 2:24 by whose **s** ye were healed. *3468*

STRIPLING (1)
1Sa 17:56 king said, Inquire thou whose son the **s** *is*. 5958

STRIPPED (6) [STRIP]
Nu 20:28 Moses **s** Aaron of his garments, and 6584
1Sa 31: 9 **s off** his armour, and sent into the land of 6584
1Ch 10: 9 when they had **s** him, they took his head, 6584
Job 22: 6 and **s** the naked of their clothing. 6584
Mt 27:28 And they **s** him, and put on him a scarlet *1562*
Lk 10:30 which **s him of his raiment**, and *1562*

STRIPT (7) [STRIP]
Ge 37:23 that they **s** Joseph **out of** his coat, 6584
Ex 33: 6 the children of Israel **s** themselves of their 5337
1Sa 18: 4 Jonathan **s** himself of the robe that *was* 6584
19:24 he **s off** his clothes also, and 6584
2Ch 20:25 which they **s off** for themselves, 5337
Job 19: 9 He hath **s** me of my glory, and taken 6584
Mic 1: 8 I will wail and howl, I will go **s** and naked: 7758

STRIVE (22) [STRIFE, STRIFES, STRIVED, STRIVEN, STRIVETH, STRIVING, STRIVINGS, STROVE]
Ge 6: 3 My spirit shall not always **s** with man, 1777
26:20 the herdmen of Gerar did **s** with Isaac's 7378
Ex 21:18 if men **s together**, and one smite another 7378
21:22 If men **s**, and hurt a woman with child, so 5327
Dt 25:11 When men **s** together one with another, 5327
33: 8 *with* whom thou didst **s** at the waters of 7378
Jdg 11:25 did he **ever s** against Israel, or did he 7378+7378
Job 33:13 Why dost thou **s** against him? for he giveth 7378
Ps 35: 1 O LORD, with them that **s with** me: 3401
Pr 3:30 **S** not with a man without cause, if he have 7378
25: 8 Go not forth hastily to **s**, lest *thou know not* 7378
Isa 41:11 and they that **s with** thee shall perish. 7379
45: 9 *Let* the potsherd *s* with the potsherds of NIH
Hos 4: 4 Yet let no man **s**, nor reprove another: 7378
4: 4 for thy people *are* as they that **s** with 7378
Mt 12:19 He shall not **s**, nor cry; neither shall any *2051*
Lk 13:24 **S** to enter in at the strait gate: for many, I say *75*
Ro 15:30 that *ye* **s together with** me in *your* prayers *4865*
2Ti 2: 5 And if a man also **s for masteries**, *yet* is he *118*
2: 5 *yet* is he not crowned, except he **s** lawfully. *118*
2:14 that *they* **s** not **about words** to no profit, *3054*
2:24 And the servant of the Lord must not **s**; but *3164*

STRIVED (1) [STRIVE]
Ro 15:20 Yea, so have I **s** to preach the gospel, *5389*

STRIVEN (1) [STRIVE]
Jer 50:24 because thou hast **s** against the LORD. 1624

STRIVETH (2) [STRIVE]
Isa 45: 9 Woe unto him that **s** with his maker! 7378
1Co 9:25 And every *man* that **s for the mastery** is *75*

STRIVING (3) [STRIVE]
Php 1:27 with one mind **s together** for the faith of *4866*
Col 1:29 I also labour, **s** according to his working, *75*
Heb 12: 4 not yet resisted unto blood, **s** against sin. *464*

STRIVINGS (3) [STRIVE]
2Sa 22:44 Thou also hast delivered me from the **s** of 7379
Ps 18:43 Thou hast delivered me from the **s** of 7379
Tit 3: 9 and contentions, and **s** about the law; *3163*

STROKE (14) [STRIKE]
Dt 17: 8 and plea, and between **s** and stroke, 5061
17: 8 and plea, and between stroke and **s**, 5061
19: 5 his hand **fetcheth a s** with the axe to cut 5080
21: 5 every controversy and every **s** be *tried:* 5061
Est 9: 5 all their enemies *with* the **s** of the sword, 4347
Job 23: 2 my **s** is heavier than my groaning. 3027
36:18 *beware* lest he take thee away with *his* **s**: 5607
Ps 39:10 Remove thy **s** away from me: I am 5061
Isa 14: 6 the people in wrath *with* a continual **s**, 4347
30:26 and healeth the **s** of their wound. 4273
Eze 24:16 from thee the desire of thine eyes with a **s**: 4046
Mt 26:51 and **s** a servant of the high priest's, and *3960*
Lk 22:64 they **s** him on the face, and asked him, *5180*
Jn 18:22 **s** Jesus **with the palm of** his **hand**, *1325+4475*

STROKES (1) [STRIKE]
Pr 18: 6 into contention, and his mouth calleth for **s**. 4112

STRONG (255) [STRENGTH]
Ge 49:14 Issachar *is* a **s** ass couching down between 1634
49:24 the arms of his hands were **made s** by 6339
Ex 6: 1 for with a **s** hand shall he let them go, and 2389
6: 1 with a **s** hand shall he drive them out of his 2389
10:19 the LORD turned a mighty **s** west wind, 2389
13: 9 for with a **s** hand hath the LORD brought 2389
14:21 LORD caused the sea to go *back* by a **s** 5794
Lev 10: 9 Do not drink wine nor **s drink**, thou, 7941
Nu 6: 3 separate *himself* from wine and **s drink**, 7941
6: 3 no vinegar of wine, or vinegar of **s drink**, 7941
13:18 whether they *be* **s** or weak, few or many; 2389
13:19 dwell in, whether in tents, or in **s holds**; 4013
13:28 Nevertheless the people *be* **s** that dwell in 5794
20:20 him with much people, and with a **s** hand. 2389
21:24 the border of the children of Ammon *was* **s**. 5794
24:21 **S** *is* thy dwelling place, and thou puttest thy 386
28: 7 **s wine** to be poured unto the LORD *for* a 7941
Dt 2:36 there was not one city too **s** for us: 7682
11: 8 that ye may be **s**, and go in and possess 2388
14:26 or for **s drink**, or for whatsoever thy soul 7941
29: 6 neither have you drunk wine or **s drink**: 7941
31: 6 Be **s** and of a good courage, fear not, nor be 2388
31: 7 of all Israel, Be **s** and of a good courage: 2388
31:23 said, Be **s** and of a good courage: 2388
Jos 1: 6 Be **s** and of a good courage: for unto this 2388
1: 7 Only be thou **s** and very courageous, 2388
1: 9 Be **s** and of a good courage; be not afraid, 2388
1:18 to death: only be **s** and of a good courage. 2388
10:25 nor be dismayed, be **s** and of good courage: 2388
14:11 As yet I *am as* **s** *this* day as *I was* in the day 2389
17:13 when the children of Israel were **waxen s**, 2388

Jos 17:18 have iron chariots, *and* though they *be* **s**. 2389
19:29 turneth *to* Ramah, and to the **s** city Tyre; 4013
23: 9 out from before you great nations and **s**: 6099
Jdg 1:28 it came to pass, when Israel was **s**, that they 2388
6: 2 in the mountains, and caves, and **s holds**. 4679
9:51 there was a **s** tower within the city, and 5797
13: 4 drink not wine nor **s drink**, and eat not any 7941
13: 7 now drink no wine nor **s drink**, neither eat 7941
13:14 neither let her drink wine or **s drink**, 7941
14:14 and out of the **s** came forth sweetness. 5794
18:26 when Micah saw that they *were* too **s** for 2389
1Sa 1:15 I have drunk neither wine nor **s drink**, but 7941
4: 9 Be **s**, and quit yourselves like men, O ye 2388
14:52 when Saul saw any **s** man, or any valiant 1368
23:14 David abode in the wilderness in **s holds**, 4679
23:19 hide himself with us in **s holds** in the wood, 4679
23:29 and dwelt in **s holds** at En-gedi. 4679
2Sa 3: 6 that Abner **made** himself **s** for the house of 2388
5: 7 Nevertheless David took the **s hold** of 4686
10:11 If the Syrians be too **s** for me, then 2388
10:11 if the children of Ammon be too **s** for thee, 2388
11:25 **make** thy battle *more* **s** against the city, and 2388
15:12 the conspiracy was **s**; for the people 533
16:21 shall the hands of all that *are* with thee be **s**. 2388
22:18 He delivered me from my **s** enemy, *and* 5794
22:18 that hated me: for they were too **s** for me. 553
24: 7 came *to* the **s hold** of Tyre, and *to* all 4013
1Ki 2: 2 be thou **s** therefore, and shew thyself a 2388
8:42 of thy **s** hand, and of thy stretched out arm;) 2389
19:11 a great and **s** wind rent the mountains, and 2389
2Ki 2:16 be with thy servants fifty **s** men; 1121+2428
8:12 their **s holds** wilt thou set on fire, and 4013
24:16 a thousand, all *that were* **s** *and* apt for war, 1368
1Ch 19:12 If the Syrians be too **s** for me, then thou 2388
19:12 if the children of Ammon be too **s** for thee, 2388
22:13 be **s**, and of good courage; dread not, nor be 2388
26: 7 whose brethren *were* **s** men, Elihu, and 2428
26: 9 Meshelemiah had sons and brethren, **s** men, 2428
28:10 a house for the sanctuary: be **s**, and do *it*. 2388
28:20 Be **s** and of good courage, and do *it*: fear 2388
2Ch 11:11 he fortified the **s holds**, and put captains in 4694
11:12 and spears, and **made** them exceeding **s**, 2388
11:17 and **made** Rehoboam the son of Solomon **s**, 553
15: 7 Be ye **s** therefore, and let not your hands be 2388
16: 9 to **shew** himself **s** in the behalf of *them* 2388
25: 8 if thou *wilt* go, do *it*, be **s** for the battle: 2388
26:15 he was marvellously helped, till he was **s**. 2388
26:16 when he was **s**, his heart was lifted up to *his* 2393
32: 7 Be **s** and courageous, be not afraid nor 2388
Ezr 9:12 that ye may be **s**, and eat the good of 2388
Ne 1:10 by thy great power, and by thy **s** hand. 2389
9:25 they took **s** cities, and a fat land, and 1219
Job 8: 2 the words of thy mouth *be like* a **s** wind? 3524
9:19 If *I speak* of strength, lo, *he is* **s**: and if of 533
30:21 with thy **s** hand thou opposest thyself 6108
33:19 and the multitude of his bones *with* **s** *pain*: 386
37:18 *which is* **s**, *and* as a molten looking glass? 2389
39:28 upon the crag of the rock, and the **s place**. 4686
40:18 His bones *are as* **s pieces** of brass; his bones 650
Ps 10:10 that the poor may fall by his **s** *ones*. 6099
18:17 He delivered me from my **s** enemy, and 5794
18:17 which hated me: for they were too **s** for me. 553
19: 5 *and* rejoiceth as a **s** *man* to run a race. 1368
22:12 **s** *bulls* of Bashan have beset me round. 47
24: 8 the LORD **s** and mighty, the LORD 5808
30: 7 thou hast made my mountain to stand **s**: 5797
31: 2 be thou my **s** rock, for a house of defence to 4581
31:21 me his marvellous kindness in a **s** city. 4692
35:10 the poor from him that is too **s** for him, 2389
38:19 But mine enemies *are* lively, *and* they are **s**: 6105
60: 9 Who will bring me *into* the **s** city? who will 4692
61: 3 for me, *and* a **s** tower from the enemy. 5797
71: 3 Be thou my **s** habitation, whereunto *I* may 6697
71: 7 unto many; but thou *art* my **s** refuge. 5797
80:15 the branch *that* thou **madest s** for thyself. 553
80:17 upon the son of man *whom* thou **madest s** 553
89: 8 of hosts, who *is* a **s** LORD like unto thee? 2626
89:10 thou hast scattered thine enemies with thy **s** 5797
89:13 **s** is thy hand, *and* high is thy right hand. 5810
89:40 thou hast brought his **s holds** to ruin. 4013
108:10 Who will bring me *into* the **s** city? who will 4013
136:12 With a **s** hand, and with a stretched out 2389
144:14 *That* our oxen *may be* **s to labour**; 5445
Pr 7:26 yea, many **s** *men have been* slain by her. 6099
10:15 The rich *man's* wealth *is* his **s** city: 5797
11:16 retaineth honour: and **s** *men* retain riches. 6184
14:26 In the fear of the LORD *is* **s** confidence: 5797
18:10 The name of the LORD *is* a **s** tower: 5797
18:11 The rich *man's* wealth *is* his **s** city, and as a 5797
18:19 offended *is harder to be won* than a **s** city: 5797
20: 1 Wine *is* a mocker, **s drink** *is* raging: and 7941
21:14 and a reward in the bosom **s** wrath. 5794
24: 5 A wise man *is* **s**; yea, a man of knowledge 5797
30:25 The ants *are* a people not **s**, yet they 5794
31: 4 to drink wine; nor for princes **s drink**: 7941
31: 6 Give **s drink** unto him that is ready to 7941
Ecc 9:11 nor the battle to the **s**, neither yet bread to 1368
12: 3 the **s** men shall bow themselves, and 2428
SS 8: 6 for love *is* **s** as death; jealousy *is* cruel as 5794
Isa 1:31 the **s** shall be as tow, and the maker of it as 2634
5:11 the morning, *that* they may follow **s drink**; 7941
5:22 and men of strength to mingle **s drink**: 7941
8: 7 **s** and many, *even* the king of Assyria, and 6099
8:11 For the LORD spake thus to me with a **s** 2393
17: 9 In that day shall his **s** cities be as a forsaken 4581
23:11 *city*, to destroy the **s holds** thereof. 4581
24: 9 **s drink** shall be bitter to them that drink it. 7941
25: 3 Therefore shall the **s** people glorify thee, 5794
26: 1 We have a **s** city; salvation will *God* 5797
27: 1 **s** sword shall punish leviathan the piercing 2389
28: 2 the LORD hath a mighty and **s** one, 533
28: 7 and through **s drink** are out of the way; 7941
28: 7 and the prophet have erred through **s drink**, 7941
28: 7 they are out of the way through **s drink**; 7941
28:22 ye not mockers, lest your bands be **made s**: 2388
29: 9 they stagger, but not *with* **s drink**. 7941
31: 1 in horsemen, because they are very **s**; but 6105
31: 9 he shall pass over *to* his **s hold** for fear, 5553
35: 4 that are of a fearful heart, Be **s**, fear not: 2388
40:10 the Lord GOD will come with **s** *hand*, and 2389
40:26 of *his* might, for that *he is* **s** in power; 533
41:21 bring forth your **s** *reasons*, saith the King of 6110
53:12 and he shall divide the spoil with the **s**; 6099
56:12 and we will fill ourselves with **s drink**; 7941
60:22 a thousand, and a small one a **s** nation: 6099
Jer 8:16 at the sound of the neighing of his **s ones**; 47
21: 5 with an outstretched hand and with a **s** arm, 2389
32:21 with a **s** hand, and with a stretched out arm, 2389
47: 3 of his **s** *horses*, at the rushing of his chariots, 47
48:14 We *are* mighty and **s** men for the war? 2428
48:17 How is the **s** staff broken, *and* the beautiful 5797
48:18 upon thee, *and* he shall destroy thy **s holds**. 4013
48:41 the **s holds** are surprised, and the mighty 4679
49:19 of Jordan against the habitation of the **s**: 386
50:34 Their redeemer *is* **s**; the LORD of hosts *is* 2389
50:44 of Jordan unto the habitation of the **s**: 386
51:12 **make** the watch **s**, set up the watchmen, 2388
La 2: 2 wrath the **s holds** of the daughter of Judah; 4013
2: 5 he hath destroyed his **s holds**, and 4013
Eze 3: 8 I have made thy face **s** against their faces, 2389
3: 8 and thy forehead **s** against their foreheads. 2389
3:14 but the hand of the LORD was **s** upon me. 2388
7:24 I will also make the pomp of the **s** to cease; 5794
19:11 she had **s** rods for the sceptres of them that 5797
19:12 her **s** rods were broken and withered; 5797
19:14 that she hath no **s** rod *to be* a sceptre to 5797
22:14 thine heart endure, or can thine hands be **s**, 2388
26:11 thy **s** garrisons shall go down to the ground. 5797
26:17 which wast **s** in the sea, she and 2389
30:21 to bind it, to **make** it **s** to hold the sword. 2388
30:22 his arms, the **s**, and that which was broken; 2389
32:21 The **s** among the mighty shall speak to him 410
34:16 I will destroy the fat and the **s**; I will feed 2389
Da 2:40 the fourth kingdom shall be **s** as iron: 8624
2:42 *so* the kingdom shall be partly **s**, and 8624
4:11 was **s**, and the height thereof reached unto 8631
4:20 that thou sawest, which grew, and was **s**, 8631
4:22 O king, that art grown and become **s**: 8631
7: 7 dreadful and terrible, and **s** exceedingly; 8624
8: 8 when he was **s**, the great horn was broken; 6105
10:19 peace *be* unto thee, be **s**, yea, be strong. 2388
10:19 peace *be* unto thee, be strong, yea, be **s**. 2388
11: 5 the king of the south shall be **s**, and *one* of 2388
11: 5 he shall be **s** above him, and 2388
11:23 and shall become **s** with a small people. 6105
11:24 forecast his devices against the **s holds**, 4013
11:32 people that do know their God shall be **s**, 2388
11:39 Thus shall he do in the **most s** holds with a 4581

Joel 1: 6 **s**, and without number, whose teeth *are* 6099
2: 2 a great people and a **s**; there hath not been 6099
2: 5 the stubble, as a **s** people set in battle array. 6099
2:11 for *he is* **s** that executeth his word: for 6099
3:10 into spears: let the weak say, I *am* **s**. 1368
Am 2: 9 of the cedars, and he *was* **s** as the oaks; 2634
2:14 the **s** shall not strengthen his force, 2389
5: 9 That strengtheneth the spoiled against the **s**, 5794
Mic 2:11 prophesy unto thee of wine and of **s drink**; 7941
4: 3 many people, and rebuke **s** nations afar off; 6099
4: 7 and her that was cast far off a **s** nation: 6099
4: 8 the **s hold** of the daughter of Zion, 6077
5:11 of thy land, and throw down all thy **s holds**: 4013
6: 2 and ye **s** foundations of the earth: 386
Na 1: 7 *is* good, a **s hold** in the day of trouble; 4581
2: 1 watch the way, **make** *thy* loins **s**, 2388
3:12 All thy **s holds** *shall be like* fig trees with 4013
3:14 waters for the siege, fortify thy **s holds**: 4013
3:14 and tread the morter, **make s** the brickkiln. 2388
Hab 1:10 they shall deride every **s hold**; for they 4013
Hag 2: 4 Yet now be **s**, O Zerubbabel, saith 2388
2: 4 be **s**, O Joshua, son of Josedech, the high 2388
2: 4 be **s**, all ye people of the land, saith 2388
Zec 8: 9 Let your hands be **s**, ye that hear in these 2388
8:13 a blessing: fear not, *but* let your hands be **s**. 2388
8:22 **s** nations shall come to seek the LORD of 6099
9: 3 Tyrus did build herself a **s hold**, and 4692
9:12 Turn ye to the **s hold**, ye prisoners of hope: 1225
Mt 12:29 Or else how can one enter into a **s** *man's* *2478*
12:29 except he first bind the **s** *man?* and then *2478*
Mk 3:27 No *man* can enter into a **s** *man's* house, and *2478*
3:27 except he will first bind the **s** *man;* and then *2478*
Lk 1:15 and shall drink neither wine nor **s drink**; *4608*
1:80 and **waxed s** in spirit, and was in *2901*
2:40 and **waxed s** in spirit, filled with wisdom: *2901*
11:21 When a **s** *man* armed keepeth his palace, *2478*
Ac 3:16 faith in his name hath **made** this *man* **s**, *4732*
Ro 4:20 but was **s** in faith, giving glory to God; *1743*
15: 1 that are **s** ought to bear the infirmities of *1415*
1Co 4:10 we *are* weak, but ye *are* **s**; ye *are* *2478*
16:13 fast in the faith, quit you like men, be **s**. *2901*
2Co 10: 4 God to the pulling down of **s holds**;) *3794*
12:10 for when I am weak, then am I **s**. *1415*
13: 9 are glad, when we are weak, and ye are **s**: *1415*
Eph 6:10 be **s** in the Lord, and in the power of his *1743*
2Th 2:11 And for this cause God shall send them **s** *1753*
2Ti 2: 1 be **s** in the grace that is in Christ Jesus. *1743*
Heb 5: 7 and supplications with **s** crying and *2478*
5:12 as have need of milk, and not of **s** meat. *4731*
5:14 But **s** meat belongeth to *them that are* of *4731*
6:18 God to lie, we might have a **s** consolation, *2478*
11:34 out of weakness were **made s**, waxed *1743*
1Jn 2:14 because ye are **s**, and the word of God *2478*
Rev 5: 2 And I saw a **s** angel proclaiming with a *2478*
18: 2 And he cried mightily with a **s** voice, *3173*
18: 8 for **s** *is* the Lord God who judgeth her. *2478*

STRONGER (21) [STRENGTH]
Ge 25:23 *the one* people shall be **s** than *the other* 553
30:41 whensoever the **s** cattle did conceive, 7194
30:42 the feebler were Laban's, and the **s** Jacob's. 7194
Nu 13:31 against the people; for they *are* **s** than we. 2389
Jdg 14:18 what *is* **s** than a lion? And he said unto 5794
2Sa 1:23 swifter than eagles, they were **s** than lions. 1396
3: 1 David **waxed s** and stronger, and the house 1980
3: 1 David waxed stronger and **s**, and the house 2390
13:14 but, being **s** than she, forced her, and 2388
1Ki 20:23 therefore they were **s** than we; but let us 2388
20:23 and surely we shall be **s** than they. 2388
20:25 *and* surely we shall be **s** than they. 2388
Job 17: 9 clean hands shall be **s and stronger**. 555+3254
17: 9 clean hands shall be **stronger and s**. 555+3254
Ps 105:24 and **made** them **s** than their enemies. 6105
142: 6 from my persecutors; for they are **s** than I. 553
Jer 20: 7 thou art **s than** I, and hast prevailed: I am 2388
31:11 from the hand of *him that was* **s** than he. 2389
Lk 11:22 But when a **s than** he shall come upon *him,* *2478*
1Co 1:25 and the weakness of God is **s than** men. *2478*
10:22 the Lord to jealousy? are we **s than** he? *2478*

STRONGEST (1) [STRENGTH]
Pr 30:30 A lion *which is* **s** among beasts, and 1368

STRONGLY (1) [STRENGTH]
Ezr 6: 3 and *let* the foundations thereof *be* **s laid**; 5446

STROOKE (1) [STRIKE]
1Sa 2:14 he **s** *it* into the pan, or kettle, or caldron, 5221

STROVE (14) [STRIVE]
Ge 26:20 of the well Esek; because they **s** with him. 6229
26:21 digged another well, and **s** for that also: 7378
26:22 digged another well; and for that they **s** not: 7378
Ex 2:13 two men of the Hebrews **s together**: 5327
Lev 24:10 and a man of Israel **s together** in the camp; 5327
Nu 20:13 the children of Israel **s** with the LORD, 7378
26: 9 who **s** against Moses and against Aaron in 5327
26: 9 of Korah, when they **s** against the LORD: 5327
2Sa 14: 6 they two **s together** in the field, and 5327
Ps 60: T when he **s** with Aram-naharaim and 5327
Da 7: 2 the four winds of the heaven **s** upon 1519
Jn 6:52 The Jews therefore **s** amongst themselves, *3164*
Ac 7:26 day he shewed himself unto them as they **s**, *3164*
23: 9 and **s**, saying, We find no evil in this man: *1264*

STROWED (1) [STRAWED]
2Ch 34: 4 **s** *it* upon the graves of them that had 2236

STRUCK (1) [STRIKE]
2Ch 13:20 and the LORD **s** him, and he died. 5062

STRUGGLED (1)
Ge 25:22 the children **s together** within her; and 7533

STUBBLE (18)
Ex 5:12 of Egypt to **gather s** instead of straw. 7179+7197
15: 7 forth thy wrath, *which* consumed them as **s**. 7179
Job 13:25 and fro? and wilt thou pursue the dry **s**? 7179
21:18 They are as **s** before the wind, and as chaff 8401
41:28 slingstones are turned with him into **s**. 7179
41:29 Darts are counted as **s**: he laugheth at 7179
Ps 83:13 them like a wheel; as the **s** before the wind. 7179
Isa 5:24 Therefore as the fire devoureth the **s**, and 7179
33:11 shall conceive chaff, ye shall bring forth **s**: 7179
40:24 the whirlwind shall take them away as **s**. 7179
41: 2 *to* his sword, *and* as driven **s** *to* his bow. 7179
47:14 Behold, they shall be as **s**; the fire shall 7179
Jer 13:24 Therefore will I scatter them as the **s** that 7179
Joel 2: 5 noise of a flame of fire that devoureth the **s**, 7179
Ob 1:18 the house of Esau for **s**, and they shall 7179
Na 1:10 they shall be devoured as **s** fully dry. 7179
Mal 4: 1 yea, and all that do wickedly, shall be **s**: 7179
1Co 3:12 silver, precious stones, wood, hay, **s**; *2562*

STUBBORN (5) [STUBBORNNESS]
Dt 21:18 If a man have a **s** and rebellious son, 5637
21:20 This our son *is* **s** and rebellious, he will not 5637
Jdg 2:19 their own doings, nor from their **s** way. 7186
Ps 78: 8 their fathers, a **s** and rebellious generation; 5637
Pr 7:11 (She *is* loud and **s**; her feet abide not in her 5637

STUBBORNNESS (2) [STUBBORN]
Dt 9:27 look not unto the **s** of this people, nor to 7190
1Sa 15:23 and **s** *is as* iniquity and idolatry. 6484

STUCK (3) [STICK]
1Sa 26: 7 and his spear **s** in the ground *at* his bolster: 4600
Ps 119:31 I have **s** unto thy testimonies: O LORD, 1692
Ac 27:41 and the forepart **s fast**, and *2043*

STUDIETH (2) [STUDY]
Pr 15:28 The heart of the righteous **s** to answer: but 1897
24: 2 For their heart **s** destruction, and their lips 1897

STUDS (1)
SS 1:11 We will make thee borders of gold with **s** 5351

STUDY (3) [STUDIETH]
Ecc 12:12 and much **s** *is* a weariness of the flesh. 3854
1Th 4:11 And that *ye* **s** to be quiet, and to do your *5389*
2Ti 2:15 **S** to shew thyself approved unto God, *4704*

STUFF (16)
Ge 31:37 Whereas thou hast searched all my **s**, 3627
31:37 hast thou found of all thy household **s**? 3627
45:20 Also regard not your **s**; for the good of all 3627
Ex 22: 7 unto his neighbour money or **s** to keep, 3627
36: 7 For the **s** *they had* was sufficient for all 4399

Jos 7:11 they have put *it* even amongst their own **s**. 3627
1Sa 10:22 Behold, he hath hid himself among the **s**. 3627
25:13 and two hundred abode by the **s**. 3627
30:24 so *shall* his part *be* that tarrieth by the **s**: 3627
Ne 13: 8 I cast forth all the household **s** of Tobiah 3627
Eze 12: 3 prepare thee **s** for removing, and remove by 3627
12: 4 shalt thou bring forth thy **s** by day in their 3627
12: 4 by day in their sight, as **s** for removing: 3627
12: 7 I brought forth my **s** by day, as stuff for 3627
12: 7 as **s** for captivity, and in the even I digged 3627
Lk 17:31 upon the housetop, and his **s** in the house, *4632*

STUMBLE (19) [STUMBLED, STUMBLETH, STUMBLING, STUMBLINGBLOCK, STUMBLINGBLOCKS, STUMBLINGSTONE]
Pr 3:23 *in* thy way safely, and thy foot shall not **s**. 5062
4:12 and when thou runnest, thou shalt not **s**. 3782
4:19 as darkness: they know not at what they **s**. 3782
Isa 5:27 None *shall be* weary nor **s** amongst them; 3782
8:15 many among them shall **s**, and fall, and 3782
28: 7 they err in vision, they **s** *in* judgment. 6328
59:10 we **s** at noonday as *in* the night; *we are* in 3782
63:13 in the wilderness, *that* they should not **s**? 3782
Jer 13:16 before your feet **s** upon the dark mountains, 5062
18:15 they have **caused** them **to s** in their ways 3782
20:11 therefore my persecutors shall **s**, and 3782
31: 9 in a straight way, wherein they shall not **s**: 3782
46: 6 they shall **s**, and fall toward the north by 3782
50:32 the most proud shall **s** and fall, and 3782
Da 11:19 but he shall **s** and fall, and not be found. 3782
Na 2: 5 they shall **s** in their walk; they shall make 3782
3: 3 of *their* corpses; they **s** upon their corpses: 3782
Mal 2: 8 ye have **caused** many **to s** at the law; 3782
1Pe 2: 8 *even to them* which **s** at the word, *4350*

STUMBLED (6) [STUMBLE]
1Sa 2: 4 and they that **s** are girt with strength. 3782
1Ch 13: 9 his hand to hold the ark; for the oxen **s**. 8058
Ps 27: 2 upon me to eat up my flesh, they **s** and fell. 3782
Jer 46:12 for the mighty *man* hath **s** against 3782
Ro 9:32 the law. For they **s** at *that* stumblingstone; *4350*
11:11 say then, Have they **s** that they should fall? *4417*

STUMBLETH (4) [STUMBLE]
Pr 24:17 and let not thine heart be glad when he **s**: 3782
Jn 11: 9 he **s** not, because he seeth the light of this *4350*
11:10 he **s**, because there is no light in him. *4350*
Ro 14:21 nor *any thing* whereby thy brother **s**, or *4350*

STUMBLING (3) [STUMBLE]
Isa 8:14 for a stone of **s** and for a rock of offence to 5063
1Pe 2: 8 And a stone of **s**, and a rock of offence, *4348*
1Jn 2:10 and there is none **occasion of s** in him. *4625*

STUMBLINGBLOCK (12) [STUMBLE]
Lev 19:14 nor put a **s** before the blind, but shalt fear 4383
Isa 57:14 take up the **s** out of the way of my people. 4383
Eze 3:20 and I lay a **s** before him, he shall die: 4383
7:19 because it is the **s** of their iniquity. 4383
14: 3 put the **s** of their iniquity before their face: 4383
14: 4 putteth the **s** of his iniquity before his face, 4383
14: 7 putteth the **s** of his iniquity before his face, 4383
Ro 11: 9 and a **s**, and a recompence unto them: *4625*
14:13 that no *man* put a **s** or an occasion to fall in *4348*
1Co 1:23 unto the Jews a **s**, and unto the Greeks *4625*
8: 9 of yours become a **s** to them that are weak. *4348*
Rev 2:14 who taught Balac to cast a **s** before *4625*

STUMBLINGBLOCKS (2) [STUMBLE]
Jer 6:21 I will lay **s** before this people, and 4383
Zep 1: 3 fishes of the sea, and the **s** with the wicked; 4384

STUMBLINGSTONE (2) [STONE, STUMBLE]
Ro 9:32 the law. For they stumbled at *that* **s**; *3037+4348*
9:33 I lay in Sion a **s** and rock of offence: *3037+4348*

STUMP (4)
1Sa 5: 4 only *the* **s** *of* Dagon was left to him. NIH
Da 4:15 Nevertheless leave the **s** of his roots in 6136
4:23 yet leave the **s** of the roots thereof in 6136
4:26 whereas they commanded to leave the **s** of 6136

STUNK (1) [STINK]
Ex 7:21 the river **s**, and the Egyptians could not drink 887

STUPID See UNLEARNED

SUAH (1)
1Ch 7:36 **S**, and Harnepher, and Shual, and Beri, and 5477

SUBDUE (8) [SUBDUED, SUBDUEDST, SUBDUETH]
Ge 1:28 multiply, and replenish the earth, and **s** it: 3533
1Ch 17:10 Moreover I will **s** all thine enemies. 3665
Ps 47: 3 He shall **s** the people under us, and 1696
Isa 45: 1 hand I have holden, to **s** nations before him; 7286
Da 7:24 from the first, and he shall **s** three kings. 8214
Mic 7:19 he will **s** our iniquities; and thou wilt cast 3533
Zec 9:15 they shall devour, and **s** *with* sling stones; 3533
Php 3:21 he is able even to **s** all *things* unto himself. *5293*

SUBDUED (19) [SUBDUE]
Nu 32:22 the land be **s** before the LORD: then 3533
32:29 and the land shall be **s** before you; 3533
Dt 20:20 city that maketh war with thee, until it be **s**. 3381
Jos 18: 1 And the land was **s** before them. 3533
Jdg 3:30 So Moab was **s** that day under the hand of 3665
4:23 So God **s** on that day Jabin the king of 3665
8:28 Thus was Midian **s** before the children of 3665
11:33 Thus the children of Ammon were **s** before 3665
1Sa 7:13 So the Philistines were **s**, and they came no 3665
2Sa 8: 1 David smote the Philistines, and **s** them: 3665
8:11 he had dedicated of all nations which he **s**; 3533
22:40 them that rose up against me hast thou **s** 3766
1Ch 18: 1 **s** them, and took Gath and her towns out of 3665
20: 4 the children of the giant: and they were **s**. 3665
22:18 the land is **s** before the LORD, and before 3533
Ps 18:39 thou hast **s** under me those that rose up 3766
81:14 I should soon have **s** their enemies, and 3665
1Co 15:28 And when all *things* shall be **s** unto him, *5293*
Heb 11:33 Who through faith **s** kingdoms, *2610*

SUBDUEDST (1) [SUBDUE]
Ne 9:24 thou **s** before them the inhabitants of 3665

SUBDUETH (3) [SUBDUE]
Ps 18:47 avengeth me, and **s** the people under me. 1696
144: 2 whom I trust; who **s** my people under me. 7286
Da 2:40 **s** all *things:* and as iron that breaketh all 2827

SUBJECT (17) [SUBJECTED, SUBJECTION]
Lk 2:51 came to Nazareth, and was **s** unto them: *5293*
10:17 even the devils are **s** unto us through thy *5293*
10:20 rejoice not, that the spirits are **s** unto you; *5293*
Ro 8: 7 for it is not **s** to the law of God, *5293*
8:20 For the creature was **made s** to vanity, *5293*
13: 1 Let every soul be **s** unto the higher powers. *5293*
13: 5 Wherefore *ye* must needs be **s**, not only for *5293*
1Co 14:32 And the spirits of the prophets are **s to** *5293*
15:28 shall the Son also himself be **s** unto him *5293*
Eph 5:24 Therefore as the church is **s** unto Christ, so *5293*
Col 2:20 living in the world, are ye **s to ordinances,** *1379*
Tit 3: 1 Put them in mind to be **s** to principalities *5293*
Heb 2:15 death were all their lifetime **s** to bondage. *1777*
Jas 5:17 Elias was a man **s to like passions** as we *3663*
1Pe 2:18 Servants, *be* **s to** *your* masters with all fear; *5293*
3:22 and powers being **made s** unto him. *5293*
5: 5 all *of you* be **s** one to another, and *5293*

SUBJECTED (1) [SUBJECT]
Ro 8:20 by reason of him who hath **s** *the same,* in *5293*

SUBJECTION (14) [SUBJECT]
Ps 106:42 they were **brought into s** under their hand. 3665
Jer 34:11 **brought** them **into s** for servants and 3533
34:16 to return, and **brought** them **into s**, to be 3533
1Co 9:27 I keep under my body, and **bring** *it* **into s**: *1396*
2Co 9:13 your professed **s** unto the gospel of Christ, *5292*
Gal 2: 5 To whom we gave place by **s**, no, not for an *5292*
1Ti 2:11 Let the woman learn in silence with all **s**. *5292*
3: 4 having *his* children in **s** with all gravity; *5292*
Heb 2: 5 For unto *the* angels hath he not **put in s** *5293*
2: 8 Thou hast **put** all *things* **in s** under his feet. *5293*
2: 8 For in that *he* **put** all **in s under** him, *5293*
12: 9 shall we not much rather be in **s** unto *5293*
1Pe 3: 1 ye wives, *be* in **s** to your own husbands; *5293*
3: 5 being **in s** unto their own husbands: *5293*

SUBMISSIVE See SUBJECTION

SUBMIT (12) [SUBMITTED, SUBMITTING]
Ge 16: 9 thy mistress, and **s** thyself under her hands. 6031
2Sa 22:45 Strangers shall **s** themselves unto me: 3584
Ps 18:44 the strangers shall **s** themselves unto me. 3584
66: 3 shall thine enemies **s** themselves unto thee. 3584
68:30 *till every one* **s** himself with pieces of 7511
1Co 16:16 That ye **s** yourselves unto such, and *5293*
Eph 5:22 **s** yourselves unto your own husbands, *5293*
Col 3:18 **s** yourselves unto your own husbands, *5293*
Heb 13:17 have the rule over you, and **s** yourselves: *5226*
Jas 4: 7 **S** yourselves therefore to God. Resist *5293*
1Pe 2:13 **S** yourselves to every ordinance of man for *5293*
5: 5 *ye* younger, **s** yourselves unto the elder. *5293*

SUBMITTED (3) [SUBMIT]
1Ch 29:24 **s** themselves unto Solomon the king. 5414
Ps 81:15 The haters of the LORD should have **s** 3584
Ro 10: 3 have not **s** themselves unto *5293*

SUBMITTING (1) [SUBMIT]
Eph 5:21 **S** yourselves one to another in the fear of *5293*

SUBORNED (1)
Ac 6:11 Then they **s** men, which said, We have *5260*

SUBSCRIBE (2) [SUBSCRIBED]
Isa 44: 5 another shall **s** *with* his hand unto 3789
Jer 32:44 **s** evidences, and seal *them,* and 3789

SUBSCRIBED (2) [SUBSCRIBE]
Jer 32:10 I **s** the evidence, and sealed *it,* and 3789
32:12 in the presence of the witnesses that **s** 3789

SUBSTANCE (50)
Ge 7: 4 every **living s** that I have made will I 3351
7:23 every **living s** was destroyed which *was* 3351
12: 5 all their **s** that they had gathered, and 7399
13: 6 for their **s** was great, so that they could not 7399
15:14 afterward shall they come out with great **s**. 7399
34:23 *Shall* not their cattle and their **s** and 7075
36: 6 his cattle, and all his beasts, and all his **s**, 7075
Dt 11: 6 and all the **s** that *was* in their possession, 3351
33:11 his **s**, and accept the work of his hands: 2428
Jos 14: 4 their suburbs for their cattle and for their **s**. 7075
1Ch 27:31 All these *were* the rulers of the **s** which *was* 7399
28: 1 the stewards over all the **s** and 7399
2Ch 21:17 carried away all the **s** that was found in 7399
31: 3 portion of his **s** for the burnt offerings, 7399
32:29 for God had given him **s** very much. 7399
35: 7 these *were* of the king's **s**. 7399
Ezr 8:21 and for our little ones, and for all our **s**. 7399
10: 8 all his **s** should be forfeited, and 7399
Job 1: 3 His **s** also was seven thousand sheep, and 4735
1:10 his hands, and his **s** is increased in the land. 4735
5: 5 and the robber swalloweth up their **s**. 2428
6:22 or, Give a reward for me of your **s**? 3581
15:29 not be rich, neither shall his **s** continue, 2428
20:18 according to *his* **s** *shall* the restitution *be,* 2428
22:20 Whereas our **s** is not cut down, but 7009
30:22 me to ride *upon it,* and dissolvest my **s**. 8454
Ps 17:14 and leave the rest of their **s** to their babes. NIH
105:21 him lord of his house, and ruler of all his **s**: 7075
139:15 My **s** was not hid from thee, when I was 6108
139:16 eyes did see my **s**, **yet being unperfect**; 1564
Pr 1:13 We shall find all precious **s**, we shall fill 1952
3: 9 Honour the LORD with thy **s**, and 1952
6:31 he shall give all the **s** of his house. 1952
8:21 *I* may cause those that love me to inherit **s**; 3426
10: 3 but he casteth away the **s** of the wicked. 1942
12:27 but the **s** of a diligent man *is* precious. 1952
28: 8 by usury and unjust gain increaseth his **s**, 1952
29: 3 company with harlots spendeth *his* **s**. 1952
SS 8: 7 if a man would give all the **s** of his house 1952
Isa 6:13 teil tree, and as an oak, whose **s** *is* in them, 4678
6:13 *so* the holy seed *shall be* the **s** thereof. 4678
Jer 15:13 Thy **s** and thy treasures will I give to 2428
17: 3 I will give thy **s** *and* all thy treasures to 2428
Hos 12: 8 I am become rich, I have found me out **s**: 202
Ob 1:13 nor have laid *hands* on their **s** in the day of 2428
Mic 4:13 their **s** unto the Lord of the whole earth. 2428
Lk 8: 3 which ministered unto him of their **s**. *5225*
15:13 and there wasted his **s** with riotous living. *3776*
Heb 10:34 have in heaven a better and an enduring **s**. *5223*
11: 1 Now faith is the **s** of *things* hoped for, *5287*

SUBTIL (3) [SUBTILTY]
Ge 3: 1 Now the serpent was more **s** than any beast 6175
2Sa 13: 3 and Jonadab *was* a very **s** man. 2450
Pr 7:10 *with* the attire of a harlot, and **s** of heart. 5341

SUBTILLY (3) [SUBTILTY]
1Sa 23:22 it is told me *that* he **dealeth very s**. 6191+6191
Ps 105:25 hate his people, to **deal s** with his servants. 5230
Ac 7:19 The same **dealt s with** our kindred, and *2686*

SUBTILTY (6) [SUBTIL, SUBTILLY]
Ge 27:35 Thy brother came with **s**, and hath taken 4820
2Ki 10:19 Jehu did *it* in **s**, to the intent that *he* might 6122
Pr 1: 4 To give **s** to the simple, to the young man 6195
Mt 26: 4 consulted that they might take Jesus by **s**, *1388*
Ac 13:10 And said, O full of all **s** and all mischief, *1388*
2Co 11: 3 as the serpent beguiled Eve through his **s**, *3834*

SUBURBS (115)
Lev 25:34 the field of the **s** of their cities may not be 4054
Nu 35: 2 ye shall give *also* unto the Levites **s** for 4054
35: 3 the **s** of them shall be for their cattle, and 4054
35: 4 the **s** of the cities, which ye shall give unto 4054
35: 5 this shall be to them the **s** of the cities. 4054
35: 7 eight cities: them *shall ye give* with their **s**. 4054
Jos 14: 4 save cities to dwell *in,* with their **s** for their 4054
21: 2 to dwell in, with the **s** thereof for our cattle. 4054
21: 3 of the LORD, these cities and their **s**. 4054
21: 8 lot unto the Levites these cities with their **s**, 4054
21:11 of Judah, with the **s** thereof round about it. 4054
21:13 of Aaron the priest Hebron with her **s**, 4054
21:13 refuge for the slayer; and Libnah with her **s**, 4054
21:14 Jattir with her **s**, and Eshtemoa with her 4054
21:14 with her suburbs, and Eshtemoa with her **s**, 4054
21:15 Holon with her **s**, and Debir with her 4054
21:15 with her suburbs, and Debir with her **s**, 4054
21:16 Ain with her **s**, and Juttah with her suburbs, 4054
21:16 Juttah with her **s**, *and* Beth-shemesh with 4054
21:16 her suburbs, *and* Beth-shemesh with her **s**; 4054
21:17 Gibeon with her **s**, Geba with her suburbs, 4054
21:17 Gibeon with her suburbs, Geba with her **s**, 4054
21:18 Anathoth with her **s**, and Almon with her 4054
21:18 with her suburbs, and Almon with her **s**; 4054
21:19 the priests, *were* thirteen cities with their **s**. 4054
21:21 For they gave them Shechem with her **s** in 4054
21:21 refuge for the slayer; and Gezer with her **s**, 4054
21:22 Kibzaim with her **s**, and Beth-horon with 4054
21:22 her suburbs, and Beth-horon with her **s**; 4054
21:23 out of the tribe of Dan, Eltekeh with her **s**, 4054
21:23 with her suburbs, Gibbethon with her **s**, 4054
21:24 Aijalon with her **s**, Gath-rimmon with her 4054
21:24 with her suburbs, Gath-rimmon with her **s**; 4054
21:25 Tanach with her **s**, and Gath-rimmon with 4054
21:25 her suburbs, and Gath-rimmon with her **s**; 4054
21:26 All the cities *were* ten with their **s** for 4054
21:27 *they gave* Golan in Bashan with her **s**, 4054
21:27 and Beeshterah with her **s**; two cities. 4054
21:28 Kishon with her **s**, Dabareh with her 4054
21:28 with her suburbs, Dabareh with her **s**, 4054
21:29 Jarmuth with her **s**, En-gannim with her 4054
21:29 with her suburbs, En-gannim with her **s**; 4054
21:30 Mishal with her **s**, Abdon with her suburbs, 4054
21:30 Mishal with her suburbs, Abdon with her **s**, 4054
21:31 Helkath with her **s**, and Rehob with her 4054
21:31 with her suburbs, and Rehob with her **s**; 4054
21:32 of Naphtali, Kedesh in Galilee with her **s**, 4054
21:32 Hammoth-dor with her **s**, and Kartan with 4054
21:32 with her suburbs, and Kartan with her **s**; 4054
21:33 families *were* thirteen cities with their **s**. 4054
21:34 Jokneam with her **s**, and Kartah with her 4054
21:34 with her suburbs, and Kartah with her **s**, 4054
21:35 Dimnah with her **s**, Nahalal with her 4054
21:35 with her suburbs, Nahalal with her **s**; 4054
21:36 Bezer with her **s**, and Jahazah with her 4054
21:36 with her suburbs, and Jahazah with her **s**, 4054
21:37 Kedemoth with her **s**, and Mephaath with 4054
21:37 with her suburbs, and Mephaath with her **s**; 4054
21:38 tribe of Gad, Ramoth in Gilead with her **s**, 4054
21:38 for the slayer; and Mahanaim with her **s**, 4054
21:39 Heshbon with her **s**, Jazer with her suburbs; 4054
21:39 Heshbon with her suburbs, Jazer with her **s**; 4054
21:41 *were* forty and eight cities with their **s**. 4054
21:42 These cities were every one with their **s** 4054
2Ki 23:11 which *was* in the **s**, and burnt the chariots 6503

1Ch 5:16 in her towns, and in all the s of Sharon, 4054
6:55 of Judah, and the s thereof round about it. 4054
6:57 Libnah with her s, and Jattir, and 4054
6:57 and Jattir, and Eshtemoa, with their s, 4054
6:58 Hilen with her s, Debir with her suburbs, 4054
6:58 Hilen with her suburbs, Debir with her s, 4054
6:59 Ashan with her s, and Beth-shemesh with 4054
6:59 her suburbs, and Beth-shemesh with her s: 4054
6:60 Geba with her s, and Alemeth with her 4054
6:60 Alemeth with her s, and Anathoth with her 4054
6:60 with her suburbs, and Anathoth with her s. 4054
6:64 gave to the Levites *these* cities with their s. 4054
6:67 Shechem in mount Ephraim with her s; 4054
6:67 *they gave* also Gezer with her s, 4054
6:68 Jokmeam with her s, and Beth-horon with 4054
6:68 her suburbs, and Beth-horon with her s, 4054
6:69 Aijalon with her s, and Gath-rimmon with 4054
6:69 her suburbs, and Gath-rimmon with her s: 4054
6:70 Aner with her s, and Bileam with her 4054
6:70 with her suburbs, and Bileam with her s, 4054
6:71 Golan in Bashan with her s, and Ashtaroth 4054
6:71 with her suburbs, and Ashtaroth with her s: 4054
6:72 Kedesh with her s, Daberath with her 4054
6:72 with her suburbs, Daberath with her s, 4054
6:73 Ramoth with her s, and Anem with her 4054
6:73 with her suburbs, and Anem with her s: 4054
6:74 Mashal with her s, and Abdon with her 4054
6:74 with her suburbs, and Abdon with her s, 4054
6:75 Hukok with her s, and Rehob with her 4054
6:75 with her suburbs, and Rehob with her s: 4054
6:76 Kedesh in Galilee with her s, and Hammon 4054
6:76 Hammon with her s, and Kirjathaim with 4054
6:76 her suburbs, and Kirjathaim with her s. 4054
6:77 Rimmon with her s, Tabor with her 4054
6:77 with her suburbs, Tabor with her s: 4054
6:78 Bezer in the wilderness with her s, and 4054
6:78 with her suburbs, and Jahzah with her s, 4054
6:79 Kedemoth also with her s, and Mephaath 4054
6:79 with her suburbs, and Mephaath with her s: 4054
6:80 Ramoth in Gilead with her s, and 4054
6:80 with her suburbs, and Mahanaim with her s, 4054
6:81 Heshbon with her s, and Jazer with her 4054
6:81 with her suburbs, and Jazer with her s. 4054
13: 2 and Levites *which are* in their cities *and* s, 4054
2Ch 11:14 For the Levites left their s and 4054
31:19 *which were* in the fields of the s of their 4054
Eze 27:28 The s shall shake at the sound of the cry of 4054
45: 2 fifty cubits round about *for* the s thereof. 4054
48:15 *place* for the city, for dwelling, and for s: 4054
48:17 the s of the city shall be toward the north 4054

SUBVERT (2) [SUBVERTED, SUBVERTING]
La 3:36 To s a man in his cause, the Lord approveth 5791
Tit 1:11 must be stopped, who s whole houses, *396*

SUBVERTED (1) [SUBVERT]
Tit 3:11 Knowing that *he that is* such is s, and *1612*

SUBVERTING (2) [SUBVERT]
Ac 15:24 s your souls, saying, *Ye must* be *384*
2Ti 2:14 to no profit, *but* to the s of the hearers. *2692*

SUCATHITES See SUCHATHITES

SUCCEED (1) [SUCCEEDED, SUCCEEDEST, SUCCESS]
Dt 25: 6 *that* the firstborn which she beareth shall s 6965

SUCCEEDED (3) [SUCCEED]
Dt 2:12 the children of Esau s them, when they had 3423
2:21 and they s them, and dwelt in their stead: 3423
2:22 they s them, and dwelt in their stead *even* 3423

SUCCEEDEST (2) [SUCCEED]
Dt 12:29 and thou s them, and dwellest in their land; 3423
19: 1 thou s them, and dwellest in their cities, 3423

SUCCESS (1) [SUCCEED]
Jos 1: 8 and then thou shalt have good s. 7919

SUCCOTH (18)
Ge 33:17 Jacob journeyed to S, and built him a 5523
33:17 the name of the place is called S. 5523
Ex 12:37 of Israel journeyed from Rameses to S, 5523
13:20 they took their journey from S, and 5523
Nu 33: 5 removed from Rameses, and pitched in S. 5523
33: 6 they departed from S, and pitched in 5523
Jos 13:27 and Beth-nimrah, and S, and Zaphon, 5523
Jdg 8: 5 he said unto the men of S, Give, I pray you, 5523
8: 6 the princes of S said, *Are* the hands of 5523
8: 8 him as the men of S had answered *him.* 5523
8:14 caught a young man of the men of S, and 5523
8:14 he described unto him the princes of S, and 5523
8:15 he came unto the men of S, and said, 5523
8:16 and with them he taught the men of S. 5523
1Ki 7:46 in the clay ground between S and Zarthan. 5523
2Ch 4:17 in the clay ground between S and 5523
Ps 60: 6 and mete out the valley of S. 5523
108: 7 and mete out the valley of S. 5523

SUCCOTH-BENOTH (1)
2Ki 17:30 the men of Babylon made S, and the men 5524

SUCCOUR (3) [SUCCOURED, SUCCOURER]
2Sa 8: 5 when the Syrians of Damascus came to s 5826
18: 3 now *it is* better that thou s us out of 5826
Heb 2:18 he is able to s them that are tempted. *997*

SUCCOURED (2) [SUCCOUR]
2Sa 21:17 Abishai the son of Zeruiah s him, and 5826
2Co 6: 2 and in the day of salvation have I s thee: *997*

SUCCOURER (1) [SUCCOUR]
Ro 16: 2 for she hath been a s of many, and *4368*

SUCH (249) See Index

SUCHATHITES (1)
1Ch 2:55 the Tirathites, the Shimeathites, *and* S. 7756

SUCK (19) [SUCKED, SUCKING, SUCKLING, SUCKLINGS]
Ge 21: 7 that Sarah should have given children s? 3243
Dt 32:13 he made him to s honey out of the rock, 3243
33:19 for they shall s *of* the abundance of 3243
1Sa 1:23 and gave her son s until she weaned him. 3243
1Ki 3:21 I rose in the morning to give my child s, 3243
Job 3:12 or why the breasts that I should s? 3243
20:16 He shall s the poison of asps: the viper's 3243
39:30 Her young ones also s up blood: and where 5966
Isa 60:16 Thou shalt also s the milk of the Gentiles, 3243
60:16 the Gentiles, and shalt s the breast of kings: 3243
66:11 That ye may s, and be satisfied with 3243
66:12 shall ye s, ye shall be borne upon *her* sides, 3243
La 4: 3 the breast, they give s to their young ones: 3243
Eze 23:34 Thou shalt even drink it and s *it* out, and 4680
Joel 2:16 the children, and those that s the breasts: 3243
Mt 24:19 and to them that give s in those days. *2337*
Mk 13:17 and to them that give s in those days. *2337*
Lk 21:23 and to them that give s, in those days, *2337*
23:29 and the paps which never gave s. *2337*

SUCKED (2) [SUCK]
SS 8: 1 my brother, that s the breasts of my mother! 3243
Lk 11:27 bare thee, and the paps which thou hast s. *2337*

SUCKING (5) [SUCK]
Nu 11:12 as a nursing father beareth the s child, 3243
1Sa 7: 9 Samuel took a s lamb, and offered it *for* a 2461
Isa 11: 8 the s child shall play on the hole of the asp, 3243
49:15 Can a woman forget her s child, that *she* 5764
La 4: 4 The tongue of the s child cleaveth to 3243

SUCKLING (3) [SUCK]
Dt 32:25 the s *also* with the man of gray hairs. 3243
1Sa 15: 3 infant and s, ox and sheep, camel and ass. 3243
Jer 44: 7 off from you man and woman, child and s, 3243

SUCKLINGS (4) [SUCK]
1Sa 22:19 children and s, and oxen, and asses, and 3243
Ps 8: 2 s hast thou ordained strength because 3243
La 2:11 and the s swoon in the streets of the city. 3243
Mt 21:16 of babes and s thou hast perfected praise? *2337*

SUDDEN (3) [SUDDENLY]
Job 22:10 round about thee, and s fear troubleth thee; 6597
Pr 3:25 Be not afraid of s fear, neither of 6597
1Th 5: 3 then s destruction cometh upon them, *160*

SUDDENLY (41) [SUDDEN]
Nu 6: 9 if any man die very s by him, 6597+6621+871.1
12: 4 the LORD spake s unto Moses, and 6597
35:22 if he thrust him s without enmity, or 6621+871.1

Dt	7: 4	be kindled against you, and destroy thee s.	4118
Jos	10: 9	Joshua therefore came unto them s, *and*	6597
	11: 7	against them by the waters of Merom s;	6597
2Sa	15:14	lest he overtake us s, and bring evil upon	4116
2Ch	29:36	the people: for the thing was *done* s.	6597+871.1
Job	5: 3	taking root: but s I cursed his habitation.	6597
	9:23	If the scourge slay s, he will laugh at	6597
Ps	6:10	let them return *and* be ashamed s.	7281
	64: 4	s do they shoot at him, and fear not.	6597
	64: 7	*with* an arrow; s shall they be wounded.	6597
Pr	6:15	Therefore shall his calamity come s;	6597
	6:15	s shall he be broken without remedy.	6621
	24:22	For their calamity shall rise s; and	6597
	29: 1	shall s be destroyed, and that without	6621
Ecc	9:12	in an evil time, when it falleth s upon them.	6597
Isa	29: 5	passeth away: yea, it shall be at an instant s.	6597
	30:13	whose breaking cometh s at an instant.	6597
	47:11	desolation shall come upon thee s,	6597
	48: 3	I did *them* s, and they came to pass.	6597
Jer	4:20	s are my tents spoiled, *and* my curtains in a	6597
	6:26	for the spoiler shall s come upon us.	6597
	15: 8	I have caused *him* to fall upon it s, and	6597
	18:22	when thou shalt bring a troop s upon them:	6597
	49:19	I will s make him run away from her: and	7280
	50:44	I will make them s run away from her: and	7280
	51: 8	Babylon is s fallen and destroyed: howl for	6597
Hab	2: 7	Shall they not rise up s that *shall* bite thee,	6621
Mal	3: 1	whom ye seek, shall s come to his temple,	6597
Mk	9: 8	And s, when they had looked round about,	*1819*
	13:36	Lest coming s he find you sleeping.	*1810*
Lk	2:13	And s there was with the angel a multitude	*1810*
	9:39	a spirit taketh him, and he s crieth out;	*1810*
Ac	2: 2	And s there came a sound from heaven as of	*869*
	9: 3	s there shined round about him a light from	*1810*
	16:26	And s there was a great earthquake, so	*869*
	22: 6	s there shone from heaven a great light	*1810*
	28: 6	should have swollen, or fallen down dead s:	*869*
1Ti	5:22	Lay hands s on no *man,* neither be partaker	*5030*

SUE (1)

Mt	5:40	And if any man will s thee **at the law**, and	*2919*

SUFFER (96) [LONGSUFFERING, SUFFERED, SUFFEREST, SUFFERETH, SUFFERING, SUFFERINGS]

Ex	12:23	will not s the destroyer to come in unto	5414
	22:18	Thou shalt not s a witch **to live**.	2421
Lev	2:13	s the salt of the covenant of thy God **to be lacking**	7673
	19:17	thy neighbour, and not s sin upon him.	5375
	22:16	Or s them **to bear** the iniquity of trespass,	5375
Nu	21:23	Sihon would not s Israel to pass through his	5414
Jos	10:19	of them; s them not to enter into their cities:	5414
Jdg	1:34	for they would not s them to come down to	5414
	15: 1	But her father would not s him to go in.	5414
	16:26	S me that I may feel the pillars whereupon	3240
2Sa	14:11	that thou wouldest **not** s the revengers of	4480
1Ki	15:17	that *he* might not s *any* to go out or come in	5414
Est	3: 8	it *is* not for the king's profit to s them.	3240
Job	9:18	He will not s me to take my breath, but	5414
	21: 3	S me that I may speak; and after that I have	5375
	24:11	*and* tread *their* winepresses, and s **thirst**.	6770
	36: 2	S me a little, and I will shew thee that *I*	3803
Ps	9:13	consider my trouble *which I* s of them that	NIH
	16:10	neither wilt thou s thine Holy One to see	5414
	34:10	The young lions do lack, and s **hunger**:	7456
	55:22	he shall never s the righteous to be moved.	5414
	88:15	ready to die from *my* youth *up: while* I s	5375
	89:33	take from him, nor s my faithfulness **to fail**.	8266
	101: 5	a high look and a proud heart will not I s.	3201
	121: 3	He will not s thy foot to be moved: he that	5414
Pr	10: 3	not s the soul of the righteous **to famish**:	7456
	19:15	deep sleep; and an idle soul shall s **hunger**.	7456
	19:19	*A man* of great wrath *shall* s punishment:	5375
Ecc	5: 6	S not thy mouth to cause thy flesh to sin;	5414
	5:12	the abundance of the rich will not s him to	3240
Eze	44:20	their heads, nor s *their* locks **to grow long**;	7971
Mt	3:15	answering said unto him, S *it to be so* now:	*863*
	8:21	Lord, s me first to go and bury my father.	*2010*
	8:31	s us to go away into the herd of swine.	*2010*
	16:21	and s many *things* of the elders and	*3958*
	17:12	Likewise shall also the Son of man s of	*3958*
	17:17	how long shall I s you? bring him hither to	*430*
	19:14	S little children, and forbid them not,	*863*
	23:13	neither s ye them that are entering to go in.	*863*
Mk	7:12	And ye s him no more to do ought for his	*863*
	8:31	that the Son of man must s many *things,*	*3958*
	9:12	that he must s many *things,* and be set at	*3958*
	9:19	how long shall I s you? bring him unto me.	*430*
	10:14	S the little children to come unto me, and	*863*
	11:16	And would not s that any *man* should carry	*863*
Lk	8:32	they besought him that he would s them to	*2010*
	9:22	The Son of man must s many *things,* and	*3958*
	9:41	how long shall I be with you, and s you?	*430*
	9:59	Lord, s me first to go and bury my father.	*2010*
	17:25	But first must he s many *things,* and	*3958*
	18:16	S little children to come unto me, and	*863*
	22:15	to eat this passover with you before I s:	*3958*
	22:51	And Jesus answered and said, S ye thus far.	*1439*
	24:46	and thus it behoved Christ to s, and to rise	*3958*
Ac	2:27	neither wilt thou s thine Holy One to see	*1325*
	3:18	that Christ should s, he hath so fulfilled.	*3958*
	5:41	counted worthy to s **shame** for his name.	*818*
	7:24	And seeing one *of them* s **wrong**, he defended	*91*
	9:16	great *things* he must s for my name's sake.	*3958*
	13:35	not s thine Holy One to see corruption.	*1325*
	21:39	s me to speak unto the people.	*2010*
	26:23	That Christ should s, *and* that he *should be*	*3805*
Ro	8:17	be that we s **with** *him,* that we may be also	*4841*
1Co	3:15	*man's* work shall be burnt, he shall s **loss**:	*2210*
	4:12	we bless; being persecuted, we s *it:*	*430*
	6: 7	why do ye not rather s *yourselves to* be	NIG
	9:12	s all *things,* lest we should hinder	*4722*
	10:13	who will not s you to be tempted above that	*1439*
	12:26	And whether one member s, all	*3958*
	12:26	all the members s **with** *it;* or one member	*4841*
2Co	1: 6	of the same sufferings which we also s:	*3958*
	11:19	For ye s fools gladly, seeing ye *yourselves*	*430*
	11:20	For ye s, if a man bring you into bondage,	*430*
Gal	5:11	why do I yet s **persecution**?	*1377*
	6:12	only lest they should s **persecution** for	*1377*
Php	1:29	to believe on him, but also to s for his sake;	*3958*
	4:12	to be hungry, both to abound and to s **need**.	*5302*
1Th	3: 4	you before that we should s **tribulation**;	*2346*
2Th	1: 5	of the kingdom of God, for which ye also s:	*3958*
1Ti	2:12	But I s not a woman to teach, nor to usurp	*2010*
	4:10	therefore we both labour and s **reproach**,	*3679*
2Ti	1:12	For the which cause I also s these *things:*	*3958*
	2: 9	Wherein I s **trouble**, as an evil doer,	*2553*
	2:12	If we s, we shall also reign with *him:* if we	*5278*
	3:12	godly in Christ Jesus shall s **persecution**.	*1377*
Heb	11:25	Choosing rather to s **affliction with**	*4778*
	13: 3	with *them; and* them which s **adversity**,	*2558*
	13:22	brethren, s the word of exhortation:	*430*
1Pe	2:20	ye do well, and s *for it,* ye take it patiently,	*3958*
	3:14	But and if ye s for righteousness' sake,	*3958*
	3:17	that *ye* s for well doing, than for evil doing.	*3958*
	4:15	But let none of you s as a murderer, or *as* a	*3958*
	4:16	Yet if *any man* s as a Christian, let him not	NIG
	4:19	Wherefore let them that s according to	*3958*
Rev	2:10	none *of those things* which thou shalt s:	*3958*
	11: 9	shall not s their dead bodies to be put in	*863*

SUFFERED (50) [SUFFER]

Ge	20: 6	therefore s I thee not to touch her.	5414
	31: 7	ten times; but God s him not to hurt me.	5414
	31:28	hast not s me to kiss my sons and my	5203
Dt	8: 3	s thee **to hunger**, and fed thee with manna,	7456
	18:14	the LORD thy God hath not s thee so	5414
Jdg	3:28	toward Moab, and s not a man to pass over.	5414
1Sa	24: 7	and s them not to rise against Saul.	5414
2Sa	21:10	s neither the birds of the air to rest on them	5414
1Ch	16:21	He s no man to do them wrong: yea,	3240
Job	31:30	(Neither have I s my mouth to sin by	5414
Ps	105:14	He s no man to do them wrong: yea,	3240
Jer	15:15	know that for thy sake I have s rebuke.	5375
Mt	3:15	us to fulfil all righteousness. Then he s him.	*863*
	19: 8	of the hardness of your hearts s you to put	*2010*
	24:43	would not have s his house to be broken up.	*1439*
	27:19	for I have s many *things* this day in a dream	*3958*
Mk	1:34	and s not the devils to speak, because	*863*
	5:19	Howbeit Jesus s him not, but saith unto him,	*863*
	5:26	And had s many *things* of many physicians,	*3958*
	5:37	And he s no *man* to follow him, save Peter,	*863*
	10: 4	Moses s to write a bill of divorcement, and	*2010*
Lk	4:41	And he rebuking *them* s them not to speak:	*1439*
	8:32	them to enter into them. And he s them.	*2010*
	8:51	the house, he s no *man* to go in, save Peter,	*863*
	12:39	not have s his house to be broken through.	*863*

Lk 13: 2 the Galileans, because they **s** such *things?* *3958*
24:26 Ought not Christ to have **s** these *things,* and *3958*
Ac 13:18 years **s** he their **manners** in the wilderness. *5159*
14:16 Who in times past **s** all nations to walk in *1439*
16: 7 go into Bithynia: but the Spirit **s** them not. *1439*
17: 3 that Christ must needs have **s**, and *3958*
19:30 in unto the people, the disciples **s** him not. *1439*
28:16 Paul was **s** to dwell by himself with a *2010*
2Co 7:12 nor for his cause that **s wrong**, but that our *91*
11:25 thrice I **s shipwrack**, a night and a day I *3489*
Gal 3: 4 Have ye **s** so many *things* in vain? if *it be* *3958*
Php 3: 8 for whom I have **s** the **loss** of all *things,* and *2210*
1Th 2: 2 But even after that we had **s before**, and *4310*
2:14 for ye also have **s** like *things* of your own *3958*
Heb 2:18 For in that he himself hath **s** being tempted, *3958*
5: 8 he obedience by *the things* which he **s**; *3958*
7:23 *they* were **not s** to continue by reason of *2967*
9:26 must he often have **s** since the foundation *3958*
13:12 with his own blood, **s** without the gate. *3958*
1Pe 2:21 because Christ also **s** for us, leaving us an *3958*
2:23 when he **s**, he threatened not; but *3958*
3:18 For Christ also hath once **s** for sins, the just *3958*
4: 1 then as Christ hath **s** for us in the flesh, *3958*
4: 1 for he that hath **s** in the flesh hath ceased *3958*
5:10 after that ye have **s** a while, make you *3958*

SUFFEREST (1) [SUFFER]
Rev 2:20 because thou **s** *that* woman Jezebel, *1439*

SUFFERETH (5) [SUFFER]
Ps 66: 9 soul in life, and **s** not our feet to be moved. 5414
107:38 and **s** not their cattle **to decrease**. 4591
Mt 11:12 until now the kingdom of heaven **s violence**, *971*
Ac 28: 4 the sea, yet Vengeance **s** not to live. *1439*
1Co 13: 4 Charity **s long**, *and* is kind; charity envieth *3114*

SUFFERING (5) [SUFFER]
Ac 27: 7 the wind not **s** us, we sailed under Crete, *4330*
Heb 2: 9 for the **s** of death, crowned with glory and *3804*
Jas 5:10 for an example of **s affliction**, and *2552*
1Pe 2:19 toward God endure grief, **s** wrongfully. *3958*
Jude 1: 7 an example, **s** the vengeance of eternal fire. *5254*

SUFFERINGS (10) [SUFFER]
Ro 8:18 For I reckon that the **s** of *this* present time *3804*
2Co 1: 5 For as the **s** of Christ abound in us, so *3804*
1: 6 of the same **s** which we also suffer: *3804*
1: 7 that as you are partakers of the **s**, so *3804*
Php 3:10 his resurrection, and the fellowship of his **s**, *3804*
Col 1:24 Who now rejoice in my **s** for you, and *3804*
Heb 2:10 captain of their salvation perfect through **s**. *3804*
1Pe 1:11 when it testified beforehand the **s** of Christ, *3804*
4:13 inasmuch as ye are partakers of Christ's **s**; *3804*
5: 1 and a witness of the **s** of Christ, and also a *3804*

SUFFICE (7) [SUFFICED, SUFFICETH, SUFFICIENCY, SUFFICIENT, SUFFICIENTLY]
Nu 11:22 and the herds be slain for them, to **s** them? 4672
11:22 be gathered together for them, to **s** them? 4672
Dt 3:26 the LORD said unto me, Let it **s** thee; 7227
1Ki 20:10 if the dust of Samaria shall **s** for handfuls 5606
Eze 44: 6 let it **s** you of all your abominations, 7227
45: 9 Let it **s** you, O princes of Israel: 7227
1Pe 4: 3 For the time past of *our* life may **s** us to have *713*

SUFFICED (3) [SUFFICE]
Jdg 21:14 and yet so they **s** them not. 4672
Ru 2:14 and she did eat, and was **s**, and left. 7646
2:18 to her that she had reserved after she was **s**. 7648

SUFFICETH (1) [SUFFICE]
Jn 14: 8 Lord, shew us the Father, and it **s** us. *714*

SUFFICIENCY (3) [SUFFICE]
Job 20:22 In the fulness of his **s** he shall be in straits: 5607
2Co 3: 5 *thing* as of ourselves; but our **s** *is* of God; *2426*
9: 8 always having all **s** in all *things,* may abound *841*

SUFFICIENT (13) [SUFFICE]
Ex 36: 7 For the stuff *they had* was **s** for all the work 1767
Dt 15: 8 shalt surely lend him **s for** his need, *in that* 1767
33: 7 let his hands *be* **s** for him; and be thou a 7227
Pr 25:16 eat **so much as is s** for thee, lest thou be 1767
Isa 40:16 Lebanon *is* not **s** to burn, nor the beasts 1767
40:16 nor the beasts thereof **s** *for* a burnt offering. 1767
Mt 6:34 of itself. **S** unto the day *is* the evil thereof. *713*
Lk 14:28 the cost, whether he have **s** to finish it? *3588*
Jn 6: 7 Two hundred pennyworth of bread is not **s** *714*
2Co 2: 6 **S** to such *a man is* this punishment, *2425*
2:16 unto life. And who *is* **s** for these *things?* *2425*
3: 5 Not that we are **s** of ourselves to think any *2425*
12: 9 And he said unto me, My grace is **s** for thee: *714*

SUFFICIENTLY (2) [SUFFICE]
2Ch 30: 3 had not sanctified themselves **s**, 4078+3807.1
Isa 23:18 to eat **s**, and for durable clothing. 7654+3807.1

SUIT (3) [SUITS]
Jdg 17:10 and a **s** of apparel, and thy victuals. 6187
2Sa 15: 4 that every man which hath *any* **s** or 7379
Job 11:19 yea, many shall **make s** unto thee. 2470

SUITS (1) [SUIT]
Isa 3:22 The **changeable s of apparel**, and 4254

SUKKIIMS (1)
2Ch 12: 3 the Lubims, the **S**, and the Ethiopians. 5525

SUKKITES See SUKKIIMS

SULPHUR See BRIMSTONE

SUM (21)
Ex 21:30 If there be laid on him a **s of money**, then 3724
30:12 When thou takest the **s** of the children of 7218
38:21 This is the **s** of the tabernacle, *even* of 6485
Nu 1: 2 Take ye the **s** of all the congregation of 7218
1:49 neither take the **s** of them among 7218
4: 2 Take the **s** of the sons of Kohath from 7218
4:22 Take also the **s** of the sons of Gershon, 7218
26: 2 Take the **s** of all the congregation of 7218
26: 4 *Take the s of the people,* from twenty years NIH
31:26 Take the **s** of the prey that was taken, *both* 7218
31:49 Thy servants have taken the **s** of the men of 7218
2Sa 24: 9 Joab gave *up* the **s** of the number of 4557
2Ki 22: 4 that he may **s** the silver which is brought 8552
1Ch 21: 5 Joab gave the **s** of the number of the people 4557
Est 4: 7 of the **s** of the money that Haman had 6575
Ps 139:17 O God: how great is the **s** of them! 7218
Eze 28:12 Thou sealest up the **s**, full *of* wisdom, and 8508
Da 7: 1 the dream, *and* told the **s** of the matters. 7217
Ac 7:16 **s** of money of the sons of Emmor the *father* *5092*
22:28 With a great **s** obtained I this freedom. *2774*
Heb 8: 1 *things* which we have spoken *this is* the **s**: *2774*

SUMMER (27)
Ge 8:22 **s** and winter, and day and night shall not 7019
Jdg 3:20 he was sitting in a **s** parlour, which he had 4747
3:24 Surely he covereth his feet in *his* **s** 4747
2Sa 16: 1 an hundred of **s fruits**, and a bottle of wine. 7019
16: 2 and **s fruit** for the young men to eat; 7019
Ps 32: 4 my moisture is turned into the drought of **s**. 7019
74:17 of the earth: thou hast made **s** and winter. 7019
Pr 6: 8 Provideth her meat in the **s**, *and* 7019
10: 5 He that gathereth in **s** *is* a wise son: *but* 7019
26: 1 As snow in **s**, and as rain in harvest, so 7019
30:25 yet they prepare their meat in the **s**; 7019
Isa 16: 9 for the shouting for thy **s fruits** and for thy 7019
18: 6 the fowls shall **s** upon them, and all 6972
28: 4 *and* as the hasty fruit before the **s**; 7019
Jer 8:20 is past, the **s** is ended, and we are not saved. 7019
40:10 **s fruits**, and oil, and put *them* in your 7019
40:12 and gathered wine and **s fruits** very much. 7019
48:32 the spoiler is fallen upon thy **s fruits** and 7019
Da 2:35 became like the chaff of the **s** 7007
Am 3:15 I will smite the winter house with the **s** 7019
8: 1 unto me: and behold, a basket of **s fruit**. 7019
8: 2 I said, A basket of **s fruit**. Then said 7019
Mic 7: 1 am as when they have gathered the **s fruits**, 7019
Zec 14: 8 the hinder sea: in **s** and in winter shall it be. 7019
Mt 24:32 putteth forth leaves, ye know that **s** *is* nigh: *2330*
Mk 13:28 putteth forth leaves, ye know that **s** is near: *2330*
Lk 21:30 know of your own selves that **s** is now nigh *2330*

SUMPTUOUSLY (1)
Lk 16:19 and fine linen, and fared **s** every day: *2988*

SUN (160) [SUNRISING]
Ge 15:12 when the **s** was going down, a deep sleep 8121
15:17 when the **s** went down, and it was dark, 8121
19:23 The **s** was risen upon the earth when Lot 8121

S

Ge	28:11	there all night, because the **s** was set;	8121
	32:31	as he passed over Penuel the **s** rose upon	8121
	37: 9	the **s** and the moon and the eleven stars	8121
Ex	16:21	and when the **s** waxed hot, it melted.	8121
	17:12	were steady until the going down of the **s**.	8121
	22: 3	If the **s** be risen upon him, *there shall be*	8121
	22:26	thou shalt deliver it unto him by that the **s**	8121
Lev	22: 7	when the **s** is down, he shall be clean, and	8121
Nu	2: 3	on the east side toward the **rising of the s**	4217
	25: 4	them up before the LORD against the **s**,	8121
Dt	4:19	when thou seest the **s**, and the moon, and	8121
	11:30	by the way where the **s** goeth down, in	8121
	16: 6	at the going down of the **s**, *at* the season	8121
	17: 3	either the **s**, or moon, or any of the host of	8121
	23:11	when the **s** is down, he shall come into	8121
	24:13	the pledge again when the **s** goeth down,	8121
	24:15	his hire, neither shall the **s** go down upon it;	8121
	33:14	the precious fruits brought forth by the **s**,	8121
Jos	1: 4	great sea *toward* the going down of the **s**,	8121
	8:29	as soon as the **s** was down,	8121
	10:12	he said in the sight of Israel, **S**, stand thou	8121
	10:13	the **s** stood still, and the moon stayed,	8121
	10:13	So the **s** stood still in the midst of heaven,	8121
	10:27	pass at the time of the going down of the **s**,	8121
	12: 1	*other* side Jordan toward the rising of the **s**,	8121
Jdg	5:31	*let* them that love him *be* as the **s** when he	8121
	8:13	returned from battle before the **s** was up,	2775
	9:33	*that* in the morning, as soon as the **s** is up,	8121
	14:18	on the seventh day before the **s** went down,	2775
	19:14	the **s** went down upon them *when they*	8121
1Sa	11: 9	To morrow, by *that time* the **s** be hot,	8121
2Sa	2:24	the **s** went down when they were come to	8121
	3:35	or ought else, till the **s** be down.	8121
	12:11	lie with thy wives in the sight of this **s**.	8121
	12:12	this thing before all Israel, and before the **s**.	8121
	23: 4	*when* the **s** riseth, *even* a morning without	8121
1Ki	22:36	the host about the going down of the **s**,	8121
2Ki	3:22	the **s** shone upon the water, and	8121
	23: 5	to the **s**, and to the moon, and to	8121
	23:11	that the kings of Judah had given to the **s**,	8121
	23:11	and burnt the chariots of the **s** with fire.	8121
2Ch	18:34	about the time of the **s** going down he died.	8121
Ne	7: 3	of Jerusalem be opened until the **s** be hot;	8121
Job	8:16	He *is* green before the **s**, and his branch	8121
	9: 7	Which commandeth the **s**, and it riseth not;	2775
	30:28	I went mourning without the **s**: I stood up,	2535
	31:26	If I beheld the **s** when it shined, or the moon	216
Ps	19: 4	In them hath he set a tabernacle for the **s**,	8121
	50: 1	called the earth from the rising of the **s** unto	8121
	58: 8	of a woman, *that* they may not see the **s**.	8121
	72: 5	They shall fear thee as long as the **s** and	8121
	72:17	name shall be continued as long as the **s**:	8121
	74:16	thou hast prepared the light and the **s**.	8121
	84:11	For the LORD God *is* a **s** and shield:	8121
	89:36	for ever, and his throne as the **s** before me.	8121
	104:19	for seasons: the **s** knoweth his going down.	8121
	104:22	The **s** ariseth, they gather themselves	8121
	113: 3	From the rising of the **s** unto the going	8121
	121: 6	The **s** shall not smite thee by day, nor	8121
	136: 8	The **s** to rule by day: for his mercy *endureth*	8121
	148: 3	Praise ye him, **s** and moon: praise him,	8121
Ecc	1: 3	all his labour which he taketh under the **s**?	8121
	1: 5	The **s** also ariseth, and the sun goeth down,	8121
	1: 5	the **s** goeth down, and hasteth to his place	8121
	1: 9	and *there is* no new *thing* under the **s**.	8121
	1:14	seen all the works that are done under the **s**;	8121
	2:11	and *there was* no profit under the **s**.	8121
	2:17	the work that is wrought under the **s** *is*	8121
	2:18	my labour which I *had* taken under the **s**:	8121
	2:19	I have shewed myself wise under the **s**.	8121
	2:20	of all the labour which I took under the **s**.	8121
	2:22	wherein he *hath* laboured under the **s**?	8121
	3:16	moreover I saw under the **s** the place of	8121
	4: 1	the oppressions that *are* done under the **s**:	8121
	4: 3	seen the evil work that is done under the **s**.	8121
	4: 7	I returned, and I saw vanity under the **s**.	8121
	4:15	all the living which walk under the **s**,	8121
	5:13	is a sore evil *which* I have seen under the **s**,	8121
	5:18	he taketh under the **s** all the days of his life,	8121
	6: 1	is an evil which I have seen under the **s**,	8121
	6: 5	Moreover he hath not seen the **s**, nor known	8121
	6:12	a man what shall be after him under the **s**?	8121
	7:11	*by it there is* profit to them that see the **s**.	8121
	8: 9	unto every work that is done under the **s**:	8121
	8:15	a man hath no better *thing* under the **s**,	8121
	8:15	his life, which God giveth him under the **s**.	8121
	8:17	find out the work that is done under the **s**:	8121
	9: 3	among all *things* that are done under the **s**,	8121
	9: 6	ever in any *thing* that is done under the **s**.	8121
	9: 9	which he hath given thee under the **s**,	8121
	9: 9	in thy labour which thou takest under the **s**.	8121
	9:11	I returned, and saw under the **s**, that	8121
	9:13	This wisdom have I seen also under the **s**,	8121
	10: 5	is an evil *which* I have seen under the **s**,	8121
	11: 7	*thing it is* for the eyes to behold the **s**:	8121
	12: 2	While the **s**, or the light, or the moon, or	8121
SS	1: 6	because the **s** hath looked upon me:	8121
	6:10	clear as the **s**, *and* terrible as *an army* with	2535
Isa	13:10	the **s** shall be darkened in his going forth,	8121
	24:23	shall be confounded, and the **s** ashamed,	2535
	30:26	of the moon shall be as the light of the **s**,	2535
	30:26	the light of the **s** shall be sevenfold, as	2535
	38: 8	which is gone down in the **s** dial of Ahaz,	8121
	38: 8	So the **s** returned ten degrees, by which	8121
	41:25	from the rising of the **s** shall he call upon	8121
	45: 6	they may know from the rising of the **s**,	8121
	49:10	neither shall the heat nor **s** smite them:	8121
	59:19	and his glory from the rising of the **s**.	8121
	60:19	The **s** shall be no more thy light by day;	8121
	60:20	Thy **s** shall no more go down; neither shall	8121
Jer	8: 2	they shall spread them before the **s**, and	8121
	15: 9	her **s** is gone down while *it was* yet day:	8121
	31:35	which giveth the **s** for a light by day, *and*	8121
Eze	8:16	and they worshipped the **s** towards the east.	8121
	32: 7	I will cover the **s** with a cloud, and	8121
Da	6:14	he laboured till the going down of the **s** to	8122
Joel	2:10	the **s** and the moon shall be dark, and	8121
	2:31	The **s** shall be turned into darkness, and	8121
	3:15	The **s** and the moon shall be darkened, and	8121
Am	8: 9	that I will cause the **s** to go down at noon,	8121
Jnh	4: 8	it came to pass, when the **s** did arise,	8121
	4: 8	the **s** beat upon the head of Jonah, that he	8121
Mic	3: 6	the **s** shall go down over the prophets, and	8121
Na	3:17	*but* when the **s** ariseth they flee away, and	8121
Hab	3:11	The **s** *and* moon stood still in *their*	8121
Mal	1:11	For from the rising of the **s** even unto	8121
	4: 2	unto you that fear my name shall the **S** of	8121
Mt	5:45	for he maketh his **s** to rise on the evil and	*2246*
	13: 6	And when the **s** was up, they were	*2246*
	13:43	Then shall the righteous shine forth as the **s**	*2246*
	17: 2	and his face did shine as the **s**, and	*2246*
	24:29	of those days shall the **s** be darkened,	*2246*
Mk	1:32	And at even, when the **s** did set,	*2246*
	4: 6	But when the **s** was up, it was scorched;	*2246*
	13:24	the **s** shall be darkened, and the moon shall	*2246*
	16: 2	unto the sepulchre at the rising of the **s**.	*2246*
Lk	4:40	Now when the **s** was setting, all they that	*2246*
	21:25	And there shall be signs in the **s**, and in	*2246*
	23:45	And the **s** was darkened, and the vail of	*2246*
Ac	2:20	The **s** shall be turned into darkness, and	*2246*
	13:11	shalt be blind, not seeing the **s** for a season.	*2246*
	26:13	above the brightness of the **s**, shining round	*2246*
	27:20	And when neither **s** nor stars in many days	*2246*
1Co	15:41	*There is* one glory of the **s**, and	*2246*
Eph	4:26	let not the **s** go down upon your wrath:	*2246*
Jas	1:11	For the **s** is no sooner risen with a burning	*2246*
Rev	1:16	his countenance *was* as the **s** shineth in his	*2246*
	6:12	and the **s** became black as sackcloth of hair,	*2246*
	7:16	neither shall the **s** light on them, nor any	*2246*
	8:12	and the third *part* of the **s** was smitten, and	*2246*
	9: 2	and the **s** and the air were darkened by	*2246*
	10: 1	and his face *was* as *it were* the **s**, and	*2246*
	12: 1	a woman clothed with the **s**, and the moon	*2246*
	16: 8	fourth angel poured out his vial upon the **s**;	*2246*
	19:17	And I saw an angel standing in the **s**; and	*2246*
	21:23	And the city had no need of the **s**, neither of	*2246*
	22: 5	they need no candle, neither light of the **s**;	*2246*

SUNDER (7) [SUNDERED]

Ps	46: 9	the bow, and **cutteth** the spear **in s**;	7112
	107:14	of death, and **brake** their bands **in s**.	5423
	107:16	gates of brass, and **cut** the bars of iron **in s**.	1438
Isa	27: 9	the altar as chalkstones that are **beaten in s**,	5310
	45: 2	gates of brass, and **cut in s** the bars of iron:	1438
Na	1:13	off thee, and will **burst** thy bonds **in s**.	5423
Lk	12:46	and will **cut** him **in s**, and will appoint *him*	*1371*

SUNDERED (1) [SUNDER]
Job 41:17 they stick together, that they cannot be **s**. 6504

SUNDRY (1)
Heb 1: 1 God, who **at s** times and in divers manners *3588*

SUNG (6) [SING]
Ezr 3:11 they **s** together by course in praising and 6030
Isa 26: 1 In that day shall this song be **s** in the land 7891
Mt 26:30 And when they had **s a hymn**, they went *5214*
Mk 14:26 And when they had **s a hymn**, they went *5214*
Rev 5: 9 And they **s** a new song, saying, Thou art *103*
14: 3 And they **s** as *it were* a new song before *103*

SUNK (7) [SINK]
1Sa 17:49 that the stone **s** into his forehead; 2883
2Ki 9:24 at his heart, and he **s down** in his chariot. 3766
Ps 9:15 The heathen are **s down** in the pit *that* they 2883
Jer 38: 6 but mire: so Jeremiah **s** in the mire. 2883
38:22 thy feet are **s** in the mire, *and* they are 2883
La 2: 9 Her gates are **s** into the ground; he hath 2883
Ac 20: 9 he **s down** with sleep, and fell down from *2702*

SUNRISING (10) [RISE, SUN]
Nu 21:11 which *is* before Moab, toward the **s**. 4217+8121
34:15 Jordan *near* Jericho eastward, toward the **s**. 4217
Dt 4:41 on *this* side Jordan toward the **s**; 4217+8121
4:47 on *this* side Jordan *toward* the **s**; 4217+8121
Jos 1:15 you on *this* side Jordan *toward* the **s**. 4217+8121
13: 5 all Lebanon, *toward* the **s**, 4217+8121+1886.1
19:12 **s** unto the border of Chisloth-tabor, 4217+8121
19:27 turneth *toward* **the s** *to* 4217+8121+1886.1
19:34 upon Jordan *toward* **the s**. 4217+8121+1886.1
Jdg 20:43 over against Gibeah toward the **s**. 4217+8121

SUP (3) [SUPPED, SUPPER]
Hab 1: 9 their faces shall **s up** *as* the east wind, and 4041
Lk 17: 8 Make ready wherewith I may **s**, and *1172*
Rev 3:20 and will **s** with him, and he with me. *1172*

SUPERFLUITY (1) [SUPERFLUOUS]
Jas 1:21 lay apart all filthiness and **s** of naughtiness, *4050*

SUPERFLUOUS (3) [SUPERFLUITY]
Lev 21:18 or he that hath a flat nose, or any thing **s**, 8311
22:23 or a lamb that **hath any thing s** or 8311
2Co 9: 1 to the saints, it is **s** for me to write to you: *4053*

SUPERSCRIPTION (5)
Mt 22:20 saith unto them, Whose *is* this image and **s**? *1923*
Mk 12:16 saith unto them, Whose *is* this image and **s**? *1923*
15:26 And the **s** of his accusation was written *1923*
Lk 20:24 Whose image and **s** hath it? They answered *1923*
23:38 And a **s** also was written over him in letters *1923*

SUPERSTITION (1) [SUPERSTITIOUS]
Ac 25:19 questions against him of their own **s**, *1175*

SUPERSTITIOUS (1) [SUPERSTITION]
Ac 17:22 I perceive that in all *things* ye are **too s**. *1174*

SUPERVISION See SCHOOLMASTER

SUPPED (1) [SUP]
1Co 11:25 when *he* had **s**, saying, This cup is the new *1172*

SUPPER (14) [SUP]
Mk 6:21 that Herod on his birthday made a **s** to his *1173*
Lk 14:12 When thou makest a dinner or a **s**, call not *1173*
14:16 A certain man made a great **s**, and *1173*
14:17 And sent his servant at **s** time to say to *1173*
14:24 men which were bidden shall taste of my **s**. *1173*
22:20 Likewise also the cup after **s**, saying, *1172*
Jn 12: 2 There they made him a **s**; and Martha *1173*
13: 2 And **s** being ended, the devil having now *1173*
13: 4 He riseth from **s**, and laid aside *his* *1173*
21:20 which also leaned on his breast at **s**, and *1173*
1Co 11:20 one place, *this* is not to eat the Lord's **s**. *1173*
11:21 every one taketh before *other* his own **s**: *1173*
Rev 19: 9 are called unto the marriage **s** of the Lamb. *1173*
19:17 gather yourselves together unto the **s** of *1173*

SUPPLANT (1) [SUPPLANTED]
Jer 9: 4 for every brother will **utterly s**, 6117+6117

SUPPLANTED (1) [SUPPLANT]
Ge 27:36 for he hath **s** me these two times: he took 6117

SUPPLE (1)
Eze 16: 4 neither wast thou washed in water to **s** *thee;* 4935

SUPPLIANTS (1)
Zep 3:10 From beyond the rivers of Ethiopia my **s**, 6282

SUPPLICATION (39) [SUPPLICATIONS]
1Sa 13:12 and I have not **made s** unto the LORD: 2470
1Ki 8:28 to his **s**, O LORD my God, to hearken 8467
8:30 hearken thou to the **s** of thy servant, and 8467
8:33 pray, and **make s** unto thee in this house: 2603
8:38 and **s** soever be *made* by any man, 8467
8:45 hear thou *in* heaven their prayer and their **s**, 8467
8:47 **make s** unto thee in the land of them *that* 2603
8:49 and their **s** *in* heaven thy dwelling place, 8467
8:52 That thine eyes may be open unto the **s** of 8467
8:52 unto the **s** of thy people Israel, to hearken 8467
8:54 all this prayer and **s** unto the LORD, 8467
8:59 wherewith I have **made s** before 2603
9: 3 and thy **s**, that thou hast **made** before me: 8467
2Ch 6:19 to his **s**, O LORD my God, to hearken 8467
6:24 pray and **make s** before thee in this house; 2603
6:29 *or* what **s** soever shall be *made* of any man, 8467
6:35 from the heavens their prayer and their **s**, 8467
33:13 heard his **s**, and brought him again *to* 8467
Est 4: 8 to **make s** unto him, and to make request 2603
Job 8: 5 and **make** thy **s** to the Almighty; 2603
9:15 *but* I would **make s** to my judge. 2603
Ps 6: 9 The LORD hath heard my **s**; the LORD 8467
30: 8 O LORD; and unto the LORD I **made s**. 2603
55: 1 O God; and hide not thyself from my **s**. 8467
119:170 Let my **s** come before thee: deliver me 8467
142: 1 voice unto the LORD did I **make** my **s**. 2603
Isa 45:14 they shall **make s** unto thee, *saying,* Surely 6419
Jer 36: 7 It may be they will present their **s** before 8467
37:20 let my **s**, I pray thee, be accepted before 8467
38:26 I presented my **s** before the king, 8467
42: 2 our **s** be accepted before thee, and pray for 8467
42: 9 unto whom ye sent me to present your **s** 8467
Da 6:11 and **making s** before his God. 2604
9:20 presenting my **s** before the LORD my God 8467
Hos 12: 4 he wept, and **made s** unto him: he found 2603
Ac 1:14 continued with one accord in prayer and **s**, *1162*
Eph 6:18 always with all prayer and **s** in the Spirit, *1162*
6:18 with all perseverance and **s** for all saints; *1162*
Php 4: 6 **s** with thanksgiving let your requests be *1162*

SUPPLICATIONS (21) [SUPPLICATION]
2Ch 6:21 Hearken therefore unto the **s** of thy servant, 8469
6:39 their prayer and their **s**, and maintain their 8467
Job 41: 3 Will he make many **s** unto thee? will he 8469
Ps 28: 2 Hear the voice of my **s**, when I cry unto 8469
28: 6 because he hath heard the voice of my **s**. 8469
31:22 the voice of my **s** when I cried unto thee. 8469
86: 6 my prayer; and attend to the voice of my **s**. 8469
116: 1 he hath heard my voice *and* my **s**. 8469
130: 2 thine ears be attentive to the voice of my **s**. 8469
140: 6 my God: hear the voice of my **s**, O LORD. 8469
143: 1 my prayer, O LORD, give ear to my **s**: 8469
Jer 3:21 weeping *and* **s** of the children of Israel: 8469
31: 9 with weeping, and with **s** will I lead them: 8469
Da 9: 3 to seek *by* prayer and **s**, with fasting, and 8469
9:17 his **s**, and cause thy face to shine upon thy 8469
9:18 for we do not present our **s** before thee for 8469
9:23 At the beginning of thy **s** 8469
Zec 12:10 of Jerusalem, the spirit of grace and of **s**: 8469
1Ti 2: 1 therefore that, first of all, **s**, prayers, *1162*
5: 5 and continueth in **s** and prayers night and *1162*
Heb 5: 7 up prayers and **s** with strong crying and *2428*

SUPPLIED (2) [SUPPLY]
1Co 16:17 which was lacking on your part they have **s**. *378*
2Co 11: 9 brethren which came from Macedonia **s**: *4322*

SUPPLIES See CELLARS; STUFF

SUPPLIETH (2) [SUPPLY]
2Co 9:12 service not only **s** the want of the saints, *4322*
Eph 4:16 and compacted by that which every joint **s**, *2024*

SUPPLY (5) [SUPPLIED, SUPPLIETH]
2Co 8:14 your abundance *may be a* **s** for their want, NIG

2Co 8:14 that their abundance also may be *a s* for NIG
Php 1:19 and the **s** of the Spirit of Jesus Christ, *2024*
2:30 *his* life, to **s** your lack of service toward me. *378*
4:19 But my God shall **s** all your need according *4137*

SUPPORT (2)
Ac 20:35 so labouring *ye* ought to **s** the weak, *482*
1Th 5:14 comfort the feebleminded, **s** the weak, *472*

SUPPORTS See UNDERSETTERS

SUPPOSE (10) [SUPPOSED, SUPPOSING]
2Sa 13:32 Let not my lord **s** *that* they have slain all 559
Lk 7:43 said, I **s** that *he,* to whom he forgave most. *5274*
12:51 **S** ye that I am come to give peace on earth? *1380*
13: 2 **S** ye that these Galileans were sinners *1380*
Jn 21:25 I **s** that even the world itself could not *3633*
Ac 2:15 as ye **s**, seeing it is *but* the third hour of *5274*
1Co 7:26 I **s** therefore that this is good for the present *3543*
2Co 11: 5 For I **s** *I* was not a whit behind the very *3049*
Heb 10:29 **s** ye, shall he be thought worthy, *1380*
1Pe 5:12 as I **s**, I have written briefly, exhorting, and *3049*

SUPPOSED (8) [SUPPOSE]
Mt 20:10 they **s** that they should have received more; *3543*
Mk 6:49 they **s** *it* had been a spirit, and cried out: *1380*
Lk 3:23 about thirty years of age, being (as was **s**) *3543*
24:37 affrighted, and **s** that *they* had seen a spirit. *1380*
Ac 7:25 For he **s** his brethren would have *3543*
21:29 whom they **s** that Paul had brought into *3543*
25:18 none accusation of *such things* as I **s**: *5282*
Php 2:25 Yet I **s** it necessary to send to you *2233*

SUPPOSING (7) [SUPPOSE]
Lk 2:44 **s** him to have been in the company, *3543*
Jn 20:15 She, **s** him to be the gardener, saith unto *1380*
Ac 14:19 *him* out of the city, **s** he had been dead. *3543*
16:27 **s** that the prisoners had been fled. *3543*
27:13 **s** that *they* had obtained *their* purpose, *1380*
Php 1:16 **s** to add affliction to my bonds: *3633*
1Ti 6: 5 of the truth, **s** that gain is godliness: *3543*

SUPREME (1)
1Pe 2:13 Lord's sake: whether *it be* to the king, as **s**; *5242*

SUPREME COMMANDER See TARTAN

SUR (1)
2Ki 11: 6 a third *part shall be* at the gate of **S**; and 5495

SURE (41) [SURELY, SURETIES, SURETISHIP, SURETY]
Ge 23:17 all the borders round about, were **made s** 6965
23:20 were **made s** unto Abraham for a 6965
Ex 3:19 I am **s** that the king of Egypt will not let 3045
Nu 32:23 and be **s** your sin will find you out. 3045
Dt 12:23 Only be **s** that thou eat not the blood: 2388
1Sa 2:35 I will build him a **s** house; and he shall walk 539
20: 7 be **s** that evil is determined by him. 3045
25:28 will certainly make my lord a **s** house; 539
2Sa 1:10 I was **s** that he could not live after *that* he 3045
23: 5 ordered in all *things,* and **s**: 8104
1Ki 11:38 and build thee a **s** house, as I built for David, 539
Ne 9:38 because of all this we make a **s** covenant, 548
Job 24:22 he riseth up, and no *man* is **s** of life. 539
Ps 19: 7 the testimony of the LORD *is* **s**, 539
93: 5 Thy testimonies are very **s**: 539
111: 7 and judgment; all his commandments *are* **s**. 539
Pr 6: 3 go, humble thyself, and **make s** thy friend. 7292
11:15 smart *for it:* and he that hateth suretiship *is* **s**. 982
11:18 *to* him that soweth righteousness *shall be* a **s** 571
Isa 22:23 I will fasten him *as* a nail in a **s** place; and 539
22:25 shall the nail that is fastened in the **s** place be 539
28:16 corner *stone,* a **s foundation**: 3245+4143
32:18 in **s** dwellings, and in quiet resting places; 4009
33:16 *shall be* given him; his waters *shall be* **s**. 539
55: 3 with you, *even* the **s** mercies of David. 539
Da 2:45 *is* certain, and the interpretation thereof **s**. 540
4:26 thy kingdom *shall be* **s** unto thee, after that 7011
Mt 27:64 that the sepulchre be **made s** until the third *805*
27:65 go your way, **make** *it* as **s** as you can. *805*
27:66 So they went, and **made** the sepulchre **s**, *805*
Lk 10:11 notwithstanding be ye **s** of this, that *1097*
Jn 6:69 and are **s** that thou art *that* Christ, *1097*
16:30 Now are we **s** that thou knowest all *things,* *1492*
Ac 13:34 I will give you the **s** mercies of David. *4103*
Ro 2: 2 But we are **s** that the judgment of God is *1492*
4:16 to the end the promise might be **s** to all *949*
15:29 And I am **s** that, when I come unto you, *1492*
2Ti 2:19 the foundation of God standeth **s**, *4731*
Heb 6:19 both **s** and stedfast, and which entereth into *804*
2Pe 1:10 to make your calling and election **s**: *949*
1:19 We have also a **more s** word of prophecy; *949*

SURELY (284) [SURE] See Index

SURETIES (1) [SURE]
Pr 22:26 strike hands, *or* of them that are **s** for debts. 6148

SURETISHIP (1) [SURE]
Pr 11:15 smart *for it:* and he that hateth **s** *is* sure. 8628

SURETY (14) [SURE]
Ge 15:13 **Know of a s** that thy seed shall be a 3045+3045
18:13 **I of a s** bear *a child,* which am old? 552+637
26: 9 and said, Behold, **of a s** she *is* thy wife: 389
43: 9 I will be **s for** him; of my hand shalt thou 6148
44:32 For thy servant **became s** for the lad unto 6148
Job 17: 3 Lay down now, **put** me **in a s** with thee; 6148
Ps119:122 Be **s for** thy servant for good: let not 6148
Pr 6: 1 My son, if thou be **s** for thy friend, *if* thou 6148
11:15 He that is **s** for a stranger shall smart *for it:* 6148
17:18 **becometh s** in the presence of his 6148+6161
20:16 Take his garment that is **s** *for* a stranger: 6148
27:13 Take his garment that is **s** *for* a stranger, 6148
Ac 12:11 he said, Now I know **of a s**, that the Lord *230*
Heb 7:22 much was Jesus made a **s** of a better *1450*

SURFEITING (1)
Lk 21:34 any time your hearts be overcharged with **s**, *2897*

SURMISINGS (1)
1Ti 6: 4 cometh envy, strife, railings, evil **s**, *5283*

SURNAME (8) [SURNAMED]
Isa 44: 5 and **s** *himself* by the name of Israel. 3655
Mt 10: 3 and Lebbeus, whose **s** was Thaddeus; *1941*
Ac 10: 5 and call for *one* Simon, whose **s** is Peter: *1941*
10:32 and call hither Simon, whose **s** is Peter; *1941*
11:13 and call for Simon, whose **s** is Peter; *1941*
12:12 the mother of John, whose **s** was Mark; *1941*
12:25 took with *them* John, whose **s** was Mark. *1941*
15:37 to take with *them* John, whose **s** was Mark. *2564*

SURNAMED (8) [SURNAME]
Isa 45: 4 I have **s** thee, though thou hast not known 3655
Mk 3:16 And Simon he **s** Peter; *2007*
3:17 (and he **s** them Boanerges, which is, *2007+3686*
Lk 22: 3 Then entered Satan into Judas **s** Iscariot, *1941*
Ac 1:23 who was **s** Justus, and Matthias. *1941*
4:36 who by the apostles was **s** Barnabas, *1941*
10:18 which was **s** Peter, were lodged there. *1941*
15:22 *namely,* Judas **s** Barsabas, and Silas, *1941*

SURPRISED (3)
Isa 33:14 are afraid; fearfulness hath **s** the hypocrites. 270
Jer 48:41 the strong holds are **s**, and the mighty 8610
51:41 *how* is the praise of the whole earth **s**! 8610

SURVIVE See ABIDE; ABIDETH; ABIDING

SURVIVORS See RESIDUE

SUSA See SHUSHAN; SUSANCHITES

SUSANCHITES (1)
Ezr 4: 9 the **S**, the Dehavites, *and* the Elamites, 7801

SUSANNA (1)
Lk 8: 3 and **S**, and many others, which ministered *4677*

SUSI (1)
Nu 13:11 the tribe of Manasseh, Gaddi the son of **S**. 5485

SUSPENSE See TARRIED; TARRIEST; TARRIETH; TARRY; TARRYING

SUSPICIONS See SURMISINGS

SUSTAIN (4) [SUSTAINED, SUSTENANCE]
1Ki 17: 9 a widow woman there to **s** thee. 3557
Ne 9:21 forty years didst thou **s** them in 3557
Ps 55:22 upon the LORD, and he shall **s** thee: 3557

Pr 18:14 The spirit of a man will **s** his infirmity; but 3557

SUSTAINED (3) [SUSTAIN]

Ge 27:37 and with corn and wine have I **s** him: 5564
Ps 3: 5 and slept; I awaked; for the LORD **s** me. 5564
Isa 59:16 unto him; and his righteousness, it **s** him. 5564

SUSTENANCE (3) [SUSTAIN]

Jdg 6: 4 left no **s** for Israel, neither sheep, nor ox, 4241
2Sa 19:32 he had **provided** the king **of s** while he lay 3557
Ac 7:11 great affliction: and our fathers found no **s**. *5527*

SWADDLED (2) [SWADDLING]

La 2:22 those that I have **s** and brought up hath 2946
Eze 16: 4 wast not salted at all, nor **s at all**. 2853+2853

SWADDLING (3) [SWADDLED]

Job 38: 9 and thick darkness a **s band** for it, 2854
Lk 2: 7 and **wrapped** him **in s clothes**, and *4683*
2:12 shall find *the* babe **wrapped in s clothes**, *4683*

SWALLOW (23) [SWALLOWED, SWALLOWETH]

Nu 16:30 the earth open her mouth, and **s** them **up**, 1104
16:34 for they said, Lest the earth **s** us **up** *also*. 1104
2Sa 20:19 why wilt thou **s up** the inheritance of 1104
20:20 be it from me, that I should **s up** or destroy. 1104
Job 7:19 nor let me alone till I **s down** my spittle? 1104
20:18 for shall he restore, and shall not **s** *it* **down**: 1104
Ps 21: 9 the LORD shall **s** them **up** in his wrath, 1104
56: 1 for man would **s** me **up**; he fighting daily 7602
56: 2 Mine enemies would daily **s** *me* **up**: 7602
57: 3 the reproach of him that would **s** me **up**. 7602
69:15 neither let the deep **s** me **up**, and let not 1104
84: 3 the **s** a nest for herself, where she may lay 1866
Pr 1:12 Let us **s** them **up** alive as the grave; and 1104
26: 2 as the **s** by flying, so the curse causeless 1866
Ecc 10:12 but the lips of a fool will **s up** himself. 1104
Isa 25: 8 He will **s up** death in victory; and the Lord 1104
38:14 Like a crane *or* a **s**, so did I chatter: I did 5693
Jer 8: 7 and the **s** observe the time of their coming; 5693
Hos 8: 7 if so be it yield, *the* strangers shall **s** it **up**. 1104
Am 8: 4 Hear this, O ye that **s up** the needy, even to 7602
Ob 1:16 they shall **s down**, and they shall be as 3886
Jnh 1:17 had prepared a great fish to **s up** Jonah. 1104
Mt 23:24 which strain out a gnat, and **s** a camel. *2666*

SWALLOWED (26) [SWALLOW]

Ex 7:12 but Aaron's rod **s up** their rods. 1104
15:12 out thy right hand, the earth **s** them. 1104
Nu 16:32 **s** them **up**, and their houses, and all 1104
26:10 **s** them **up** together with Korah, when that 1104
Dt 11: 6 **s** them **up**, and their households, and 1104
2Sa 17:16 lest the king be **s up**, and all the people that 1104
Job 6: 3 of the sea: therefore my words are **s up**. 3886
20:15 He hath **s down** riches, and he shall vomit 1104
37:20 if a man speak, surely he shall be **s up**. 1104
Ps 35:25 let them not say, We have **s** him **up**. 1104
106:17 The earth opened and **s up** Dathan, and 1104
124: 3 they had **s** us **up** quick, when their wrath 1104
Isa 28: 7 through strong drink, they are **s up** of wine, 1104
49:19 and they that **s** thee **up** shall be far away. 1104
Jer 51:34 he hath **s** me **up** like a dragon, 1104
51:44 out of his mouth that which he hath **s up**: 1105
La 2: 2 The Lord hath **s up** all the habitations of 1104
2: 5 he hath **s up** Israel, he hath swallowed up 1104
2: 5 up Israel, he hath **s up** all her palaces: 1104
La 2:16 they say, We have **s** *her* **up**: certainly this *is* 1104
Eze 36: 3 *you* desolate, and **s** you **up** on every side, 7602
Hos 8: 8 Israel is **s up**: now shall they be among 1104
1Co 15:54 that is written, Death is **s up** in victory. *2666*
2Co 2: 7 one should be **s up** with overmuch sorrow. *2666*
5: 4 that mortality might be **s up** of life. *2666*
Rev 12:16 **s up** the flood which the dragon cast out of *2666*

SWALLOWETH (2) [SWALLOW]

Job 5: 5 and the robber **s up** their substance. 7602
39:24 He **s** the ground with fierceness and rage: 1572

SWAN (2)

Lev 11:18 the **s**, and the pelican, and the gier eagle, 8580
Dt 14:16 The little owl, and the great owl, and the **s**, 8580

SWARE (78) [SWEAR]

Ge 21:31 because there they **s** both of them. 7650
24: 7 spake unto me, and that **s** unto me, saying, 7650
24: 9 and **s** to him concerning that matter. 7650
25:33 Swear to me *this* day; and he **s** to him: 7650
26: 3 I will perform the oath which I **s** unto 7650
26:31 in the morning, and **s** one to another: 7650
31:53 And Jacob **s** by the fear of his father Isaac. 7650
47:31 he **s** unto him. And Israel bowed himself 7650
50:24 land unto the land which he **s** to Abraham, 7650
Ex 13: 5 which he **s** unto thy fathers to give thee, 7650
13:11 as he **s** unto thee and to thy fathers, and 7650
33: 1 unto the land which I **s** unto Abraham, 7650
Nu 14:16 people into the land which he **s** unto them, 7650
14:23 Surely they shall not see the land which I **s** 7650
14:30 *concerning* which I **s** to make you 3027+5375
32:10 kindled the same time, and he **s**, saying, 7650
32:11 shall see the land which I **s** unto Abraham, 7650
Dt 1: 8 possess the land which the LORD **s** unto 7650
1:34 your words, and was wroth, and **s**, saying, 7650
1:35 which I **s** to give unto your fathers, 7650
2:14 among the host, as the LORD **s** unto them. 7650
4:21 **s** that I should not go over Jordan, and 7650
4:31 of thy fathers which he **s** unto them. 7650
6:10 into the land which he **s** unto thy fathers, 7650
6:18 possess the good land which the LORD **s** 7650
6:23 to give us the land which he **s** unto our 7650
7:12 and the mercy which he **s** unto thy fathers: 7650
7:13 in the land which he **s** unto thy fathers to 7650
8: 1 possess the land which the LORD **s** unto 7650
8:18 his covenant which he **s** unto thy fathers, 7650
9: 5 word which the LORD **s** unto thy fathers, 7650
10:11 which I **s** unto their fathers to give unto 7650
11: 9 which the LORD **s** unto your fathers to 7650
11:21 in the land which the LORD **s** unto your 7650
26: 3 LORD **s** unto our fathers for to give us. 7650
28:11 in the land which the LORD **s** unto thy 7650
30:20 land which the LORD **s** unto thy fathers, 7650
31:20 into the land which I **s** unto their fathers, 7650
31:21 I have brought them into the land which I **s**. 7650
31:23 of Israel into the land which I **s** unto them: 7650
34: 4 This *is* the land which I **s** unto Abraham, 7650
Jos 1: 6 which I **s** unto their fathers to give them. 7650
5: 6 unto whom the LORD **s** that *he* would not 7650
5: 6 which the LORD **s** unto their fathers that 7650
6:22 and all that she hath, as ye **s** unto her. 7650
9:15 the princes of the congregation **s** unto them. 7650
9:20 because of the oath which we **s** unto them. 7650
14: 9 Moses **s** on that day, saying, Surely 7650
21:43 land which he **s** to give unto their fathers; 7650
21:44 according to all that he **s** unto their fathers: 7650
Jdg 2: 1 have brought you unto the land which I **s** 7650
1Sa 19: 6 Saul **s**, *As* the LORD liveth, he shall not 7650
20: 3 David **s** moreover, and said, Thy father 7650
24:22 David **s** unto Saul. And Saul went home; 7650
28:10 Saul **s** to her by the LORD, saying, *As* 7650
2Sa 3:35 David **s**, saying, So do God to me, and 7650
19:23 shalt not die. And the king **s** unto him. 7650
21:17 the men of David **s** unto him, saying, 7650
1Ki 1:29 the king **s**, and said, *As* the LORD liveth, 7650
1:30 Even as I **s** unto thee by the LORD God of 7650
2: 8 and I **s** to him by the LORD, saying, 7650
2:23 king Solomon **s** by the LORD, saying, 7650
2Ki 25:24 Gedaliah **s** to them, and to their men, and 7650
2Ch 15:14 they **s** unto the LORD with a loud voice, 7650
Ezr 10: 5 do according to this word. And they **s**. 7650
Ps 95:11 *Unto* whom I **s** in my wrath that they 7650
132: 2 How he **s** unto the LORD, *and* 7650
Jer 38:16 So Zedekiah the king **s** secretly unto 7650
40: 9 of Ahikam the son of Shaphan **s** unto them 7650
Eze 16: 8 I **s** unto thee, and entered into a covenant 7650
Da 12: 7 **s** by him that liveth for ever that *it shall be* 7650
Mk 6:23 And he **s** unto her, Whatsoever thou shalt *3660*
Lk 1:73 The oath which he **s** to our father Abraham, *3660*
Heb 3:11 So I **s** in my wrath, They shall not enter *3660*
3:18 And to whom **s** he that *they* should not *3660*
6:13 could swear by no greater, he **s** by himself, *3660*
7:21 unto him, The Lord **s** and will not repent, *3660*
Rev 10: 6 And **s** by him that liveth for ever and ever, *3660*

SWAREST (5) [SWEAR]

Ex 32:13 to whom thou **s** by thine own self, and 7650
Nu 11:12 unto the land which thou **s** unto their 7650
Dt 26:15 as thou **s** unto our fathers, a land that 7650
1Ki 1:17 thou **s** by the LORD thy God unto thine 7650
Ps 89:49 *which* thou **s** unto David in thy truth? 7650

S

SWARM (3) [SWARMS]
Ex 8:24 there came a grievous **s** *of flies* into 6157
8:24 the land was corrupted by reason of the **s** 6157
Jdg 14: 8 *there was* a **s** of bees and honey in 5712

SWARMS (5) [SWARM]
Ex 8:21 I will send **s** *of flies* upon thee, and 6157
8:21 of the Egyptians shall be full of **s** *of flies,* 6157
8:22 that no **s** *of flies* shall be there; 6157
8:29 I will intreat the LORD that the **s** *of flies* 6157
8:31 and he removed the **s** *of flies* from Pharaoh, 6157

SWEAR (60) [FORSWEAR, SWARE, SWAREST, SWEARERS, SWEARETH, SWEARING, SWORN]
Ge 21:23 **s** unto me here by God that thou wilt not 7650
21:24 And Abraham said, I will **s**. 7650
24: 3 I will **make** thee **s** by the LORD, the God 7650
24:37 my master **made** me **s**, saying, Thou shalt 7650
25:33 Jacob said, **S** to me *this* day; and he sware 7650
47:31 he said, **S** unto me. And he sware unto him. 7650
50: 5 My father **made** me **s**, saying, Lo, I die: 7650
50: 6 thy father, according as he **made** thee **s**. 7650
Ex 6: 8 *concerning* the which I did **s** to give 3027+5375
Lev 5: 4 Or if a soul **s**, pronouncing with *his* lips to 7650
19:12 ye shall not **s** by my name falsely, 7650
Nu 30: 2 or **s** an oath to bind his soul with a bond; 7650
Dt 6:13 and serve him, and shalt **s** by his name. 7650
10:20 to him shalt thou cleave, and **s** by his name. 7650
Jos 2:12 I pray you, **s** unto me by the LORD, 7650
2:17 this thine oath which thou hast **made** us **s**. 7650
2:20 of thine oath which thou hast **made** us **to s**. 7650
23: 7 nor **cause to s** *by them,* neither serve them, 7650
Jdg 15:12 Samson said unto them, **S** unto me, that ye 7650
1Sa 20:17 Jonathan caused David to **s** again, because 7650
24:21 **S** now therefore unto me by the LORD, 7650
30:15 he said, **S** unto me by God, that thou wilt 7650
2Sa 19: 7 for I **s** by the LORD, if thou go not forth, 7650
1Ki 1:13 lord O king, **s** unto thine handmaid, saying, 7650
1:51 Let king Solomon **s** unto me to day that he 7650
2:42 Did I not **make** thee **to s** by the LORD, 7650
8:31 an oath be laid upon him to **cause** him **to s**, 422
2Ch 6:22 and an oath be laid upon him to **make** him **s**, 422
36:13 who had **made** him **s** by God: 7650
Ezr 10: 5 **made** the chief priests, the Levites, and all Israel, **to s** 7650
Ne 13:25 off their hair, and **made** them **s** by God, 7650
Isa 3: 7 In that day shall he **s**, saying, I will not be a 5375
19:18 of Canaan, and **s** to the LORD of hosts: 7650
45:23 every knee shall bow, every tongue shall **s**. 7650
48: 1 which **s** by the name of the LORD, and 7650
65:16 he that sweareth in the earth shall **s** by 7650
Jer 4: 2 thou shalt **s**, The LORD liveth, in truth, 7650
5: 2 The LORD liveth; surely they **s** falsely. 7650
7: 9 **s** falsely, and burn incense unto Baal, and 7650
12:16 to **s** by my name, The LORD liveth; 7650
12:16 as they taught my people to **s** by Baal; then 7650
22: 5 I **s** by myself, saith the LORD, 7650
32:22 which thou didst **s** to their fathers to give 7650
Hos 4:15 up *to* Beth-aven, nor **s**, The LORD liveth. 7650
Am 8:14 They that **s** by the sin of Samaria, and say, 7650
Zep 1: 5 that worship *and* that **s** by the LORD, 7650
1: 5 by the LORD, and that **s** by Malcham; 7650
Mt 5:34 But I say unto you, **S** not at all; neither by *3660*
5:36 Neither shalt thou **s** by thy head, because *3660*
23:16 Whosoever shall **s** by the temple, *3660*
23:16 whosoever shall **s** by the gold of *3660*
23:18 And, Whosoever shall **s** by the altar, it is *3660*
23:20 Whoso therefore shall **s** by the altar, *3660*
23:21 And whoso shall **s** by the temple, *3660*
23:22 And he that shall **s** by heaven, sweareth by *3660*
26:74 Then began he to curse and to **s**, *saying,* I *3660*
Mk 14:71 But he began to curse and to **s**, *saying,* I *3660*
Heb 6:13 because he could **s** by no greater, he sware *3660*
6:16 For men verily **s** by the greater: and an oath *3660*
Jas 5:12 **s** not, neither by heaven, neither by *3660*

SWEARERS (1) [SWEAR]
Mal 3: 5 against false **s**, and against those that 7650

SWEARETH (11) [SWEAR]
Lev 6: 3 and lieth concerning it, and **s** falsely; 7650
Ps 15: 4 *He that* **s** to *his own* hurt, and changeth not. 7650
63:11 in God; every one that **s** by him shall glory: 7650
Ecc 9: 2 *and* he that **s**, as he that feareth an oath. 7650
Isa 65:16 he that **s** in the earth shall swear by the God 7650
Zec 5: 3 every one that **s** shall be cut off *as* on that 7650
5: 4 into the house of him that **s** falsely by my 7650
Mt 23:18 but whosoever **s** by the gift that is upon it, *3660*
23:20 the altar, **s** by it, and by all *things* thereon. *3660*
23:21 **s** by it, and by him that dwelleth therein. *3660*
23:22 **s** by the throne of God, and by him that *3660*

SWEARING (4) [SWEAR]
Lev 5: 1 and hear the voice of **s**, and *is* a witness, 423
Jer 23:10 for because of **s** the land mourneth; 423
Hos 4: 2 By **s**, and lying, and killing, and stealing, 422
10: 4 **s** falsely in making a covenant: 422

SWEAT (3)
Ge 3:19 In the **s** of thy face shalt thou eat bread, 2188
Eze 44:18 *themselves* with any thing that causeth **s**. 3154
Lk 22:44 his **s** was as it were great drops of blood *2402*

SWEEP (3) [SWEEPING, SWEPT]
Isa 14:23 I will **s** it with the besom of destruction, 2894
28:17 the hail shall **s away** the refuge of lies, and 3261
Lk 15: 8 and **s** the house, and seek diligently till she *4563*

SWEEPING (1) [SWEEP]
Pr 28: 3 poor *is like* a **s** rain which leaveth no food. 5502

SWEET (108) [SWEETER, SWEETLY, SWEETNESS, SWEETSMELLING]
Ge 8:21 the LORD smelled a **s** savour; and 5207
Ex 15:25 into the waters, the waters were **made s**: 4985
25: 6 spices for anointing oil, and for **s** incense, 5561
29:18 it *is* a **s** savour, an offering made by fire 5207
29:25 for a **s** savour before the LORD: 5207
29:41 to the drink offering thereof, for a **s** savour, 5207
30: 7 Aaron shall burn thereon **s** incense every 5561
30:23 and of **s** cinnamon half so much, 1314
30:23 and of **s** calamus two hundred and 1314
30:34 Take unto thee **s spices**, stacte, and onycha, 5561
30:34 *these* **s spices** with pure frankincense: 5561
31:11 **s** incense for the holy *place:* according to 5561
35: 8 for anointing oil, and for the **s** incense, 5561
35:15 the **s** incense, and the hanging for the door 5561
35:28 for the anointing oil, and for the **s** incense. 5561
37:29 and the pure incense of **s spices**, 5561
39:38 the **s** incense, and the hanging for 5561
40:27 he burnt **s** incense thereon; as the LORD 5561
Lev 1: 9 by fire, of a **s** savour unto the LORD. 5207
1:13 by fire, of a **s** savour unto the LORD. 5207
1:17 by fire, of a **s** savour unto the LORD. 5207
2: 2 by fire, of a **s** savour unto the LORD: 5207
2: 9 by fire, of a **s** savour unto the LORD. 5207
2:12 they shall not be burnt on the altar for a **s** 5207
3: 5 by fire, of a **s** savour unto the LORD. 5207
3:16 of the offering made by fire for a **s** savour: 5207
4: 7 of the altar of **s** incense before the LORD, 5561
4:31 the priest shall burn *it* upon the altar for a **s** 5207
6:15 shall burn *it upon* the altar *for* a **s** savour, 5207
6:21 thou offer *for* a **s** savour unto the LORD. 5207
8:21 it *was* a burnt sacrifice for a **s** savour, *and* 5207
8:28 they *were* consecrations for a **s** savour: it *is* 5207
16:12 and his hands full of **s** incense beaten small, 5561
17: 6 burn the fat for a **s** savour unto the LORD. 5207
23:13 by fire unto the LORD *for* a **s** savour: 5207
23:18 made by fire, of **s** savour unto the LORD. 5207
26:31 will not smell the savour of your **s odours**. 5207
Nu 4:16 the **s** incense, and the daily meat offering, 5561
15: 3 to make a **s** savour unto the LORD, of 5207
15: 7 *of* wine, *for* a **s** savour unto the LORD. 5207
15:10 by fire, of a **s** savour unto the LORD. 5207
15:13 by fire, of a **s** savour unto the LORD. 5207
15:14 by fire, of a **s** savour unto the LORD; 5207
15:24 for a **s** savour unto the LORD, with his 5207
18:17 by fire, for a **s** savour unto the LORD. 5207
28: 2 made by fire, *for* a **s** savour unto me, 5207
28: 6 which was ordained in mount Sinai for a **s** 5207
28: 8 by fire, *of* a **s** savour unto the LORD. 5207
28:13 *for* a burnt offering *of* a **s** savour, 5207
28:24 by fire, *of* a **s** savour unto the LORD: 5207
28:27 ye shall offer the burnt offering for a **s** 5207
29: 2 ye shall offer a burnt offering for a **s** savour 5207
29: 6 according unto their manner, for a **s** savour, 5207
29: 8 offering unto the LORD *for* a **s** savour; 5207
29:13 by fire, *of* a **s** savour unto the LORD; 5207

Nu 29:36 by fire, *of* a **s** savour unto the LORD: 5207
2Sa 23: 1 of Jacob, and the **s** psalmist of Israel, said, 5273
2Ch 2: 4 *and* to burn before him **s** incense, and 5561
13:11 evening burnt sacrifices and **s** incense: 5561
16:14 in the bed which was filled *with* **s odours** 1314
Ezr 6:10 That they may offer sacrifices of **s savours** 5208
Ne 8:10 drink the **s**, and send portions unto *them* for 4477
Est 2:12 six months with **s odours**, and with *other* 1314
Job 20:12 Though wickedness be **s** in his mouth, 4985
21:33 The clods of the valley shall be **s** unto him, 4985
38:31 Canst thou bind the **s influences** of 4575
Ps 55:14 We **took s** counsel together, *and* 4985
104:34 My meditation of him shall be **s**: I will be 6149
119:103 How **s** are thy words unto my taste! 4452
141: 6 they shall hear my words; for they are **s**. 5276
Pr 3:24 shalt lie down, and thy sleep shall be **s**. 6149
9:17 Stolen waters are **s**, and bread *eaten* in 4985
13:19 The desire accomplished is **s** to the soul: 6149
16:24 **s** to the soul, and health to the bones. 4966
20:17 Bread of deceit *is* **s** to a man; but 6156
23: 8 shalt thou vomit up, and lose thy **s** words. 5273
24:13 and the honeycomb, *which is* **s** to thy taste: 4966
27: 7 *to* the hungry soul every bitter *thing is* **s**. 4966
Ecc 5:12 The sleep of a labouring *man is* **s**, 4966
11: 7 Truly the light *is* **s**, and a pleasant *thing it is* 4966
SS 2: 3 and his fruit *was* **s** to my taste. 4966
2:14 for **s** *is* thy voice, and thy countenance *is* 6156
5: 5 my fingers *with* **s smelling** myrrh, upon 5674
5:13 cheeks *are* as a bed of spices, *as* **s** flowers: 4840
5:13 lips *like* lilies, dropping **s smelling** myrrh. 5674
5:16 His mouth *is* **most s**: yea, he *is* altogether 4477
Isa 3:24 *that* instead of **s smell** there shall be stink; 1314
5:20 that put bitter for **s**, and sweet for bitter! 4966
5:20 that put bitter for sweet, and **s** for bitter! 4966
23:16 **make s** melody, sing many songs, that thou 3190
43:24 Thou hast bought me no **s cane** with 7070
49:26 with their own blood, as with **s wine**: 6071
Jer 6:20 and the **s** cane from a far country? 2896
6:20 nor your sacrifices **s** unto me. 6149
31:26 and beheld; and my sleep was **s** unto me. 6149
Eze 6:13 the place where they did offer **s** savour to 5207
16:19 thou hast even set it before them for a **s** 5207
20:28 there also they made their **s** savour, and 5207
20:41 I will accept you with *your* **s** savour, 5207
Da 2:46 offer an oblation and **s odours** unto him. 5208
Am 9:13 the mountains shall drop **s wine**, and all 6071
Mic 6:15 and **s wine**, but shalt not drink wine. 8492
Mk 16: 1 and Salome, had bought *s* spices, that they NIG
2Co 2:15 For we are unto God a **s savour** of Christ, *2175*
Php 4:18 an odour of a **s smell**, a sacrifice *2175*
Jas 3:11 send forth at the same place **s** *water* *1099*
Rev 10: 9 but it shall be in thy mouth **s** as honey. *1099*
10:10 it up; and it was in my mouth **s** as honey: *1099*

SWEETER (3) [SWEET]
Jdg 14:18 the sun went down, What *is* **s** than honey? 4966
Ps 19:10 **s** also than honey and the honeycomb. 4966
119:103 my taste! *yea, s* than honey to my mouth! NIH

SWEETLY (2) [SWEET]
Job 24:20 forget him; the worm shall **feed s on** him; 4988
SS 7: 9 for my beloved, that goeth *down* **s**, 4339+3807.1

SWEETNESS (5) [SWEET]
Jdg 9:11 Should I forsake my **s**, and my good fruit, 4987
14:14 and out of the strong came forth **s**. 4966
Pr 16:21 and the **s** of the lips increaseth learning. 4986
27: 9 *doth* the **s** of a man's friend by hearty 4986
Eze 3: 3 and it was in my mouth as honey for **s**. 4966

SWEETSMELLING (1) [SMELL, SWEET]
Eph 5: 2 and a sacrifice to God for a **s** savour. *2175*

SWELL (4) [SWELLED, SWELLING, SWELLINGS, SWOLLEN]
Nu 5:21 make thy thigh to rot, and thy belly to **s**; 6639
5:22 to **make** *thy* belly **to s**, and *thy* thigh to rot: 6638
5:27 and her belly shall **s**, and her thigh shall rot: 6638
Dt 8: 4 neither did thy foot **s**, these forty years. 1216

SWELLED (1) [SWELL]
Ne 9:21 clothes waxed not old, and their feet **s** not. 1216

SWELLING (7) [SWELL]
Ps 46: 3 *though* the mountains shake with the **s** 1346
Isa 30:13 **s out** in a high wall, whose breaking 1158
Jer 12: 5 then how wilt thou do in the **s** of Jordan? 1347
49:19 he shall come up like a lion from the **s** of 1347
50:44 he shall come up like a lion from the **s** of 1347
2Pe 2:18 For when they speak **great s** *words* of *5246*
Jude 1:16 their mouth speaketh **great s** *words*, *5246*

SWELLINGS (1) [SWELL]
2Co 12:20 strifes, backbitings, whisperings, **s**, tumults: *5450*

SWEPT (4) [SWEEP]
Jdg 5:21 The river of Kishon **s** them **away**, 1640
Jer 46:15 Why are thy valiant *men* **s away**? 5502
Mt 12:44 he findeth *it* empty, **s**, and garnished. *4563*
Lk 11:25 he cometh, he findeth *it* **s** and garnished. *4563*

SWERVED (1)
1Ti 1: 6 From which some having **s** have turned aside *795*

SWIFT (20) [SWIFTER, SWIFTLY]
Dt 28:49 the end of the earth, *as* **s** as the eagle flieth; NIH
1Ch 12: 8 *were* as **s** as the roes upon the mountains: 4116
Job 9:26 They are passed away as the **s** ships: as 16
24:18 He *is* **s** as the waters; their portion is cursed 7031
Pr 6:18 feet that be **s** in running to mischief, 4116
Ecc 9:11 under the sun, that the race *is* not to the **s**, 7031
Isa 18: 2 *saying,* Go, ye **s** messengers, to a nation 7031
19: 1 the LORD rideth upon a **s** cloud, and 7031
30:16 and, We will ride upon the **s**; therefore shall 7031
30:16 therefore shall they that pursue you be **s**. 7043
66:20 and upon mules, and upon **s beasts**, 3753
Jer 2:23 *thou art* a **s** dromedary traversing her ways; 7031
46: 6 Let not the **s** flee away, nor the mighty *man* 7031
Am 2:14 Therefore the flight shall perish from the **s**, 7031
2:15 *he that is* **s** of foot shall not deliver *himself*: 7031
Mic 1:13 of Lachish, bind the chariot to the **s beast**: 7409
Mal 3: 5 I will be a **s** witness against the sorcerers, 4116
Ro 3:15 Their feet *are* **s** to shed blood: *3691*
Jas 1:19 let every man be **s** to hear, slow to speak, *5036*
2Pe 2: 1 and bring upon themselves **s** destruction. *5031*

SWIFTER (6) [SWIFT]
2Sa 1:23 they were **s** than eagles, they were stronger 7043
Job 7: 6 My days are **s** than a weaver's shuttle, and 7043
9:25 Now my days are **s** than a post: they flee 7043
Jer 4:13 his horses are **s** than eagles. Woe unto us! 7043
La 4:19 Our persecutors are **s** than the eagles of 7031
Hab 1: 8 Their horses also are **s** than the leopards, 7043

SWIFTLY (4) [SWIFT]
Ps 147:15 *upon* earth: his word runneth **very s**. 4120+5704
Isa 5:26 and behold, they shall come with speed **s**: 7031
Da 9:21 the beginning, being caused to fly **s**, 3288+871.1
Joel 3: 4 **s** *and* speedily will I return your 7031

SWIM (6) [SWIMMEST, SWIMMETH]
2Ki 6: 6 and cast *it* in thither; and the iron did **s**. 6687
Ps 6: 6 all the night **make** I my bed **to s**; 7811
Isa 25:11 swimmeth spreadeth forth *his hands* to **s**: 7811
Eze 47: 5 for the waters were risen, waters to **s** in, 7813
Ac 27:42 lest any *of them* should **s out**, and escape. *1579*
27:43 commanded that they which could **s** should *2860*

SWIMMEST (1) [SWIM]
Eze 32: 6 with thy blood the land wherein thou **s**, 6824

SWIMMETH (1) [SWIM]
Isa 25:11 as he that **s** spreadeth forth *his hands* to 7811

SWINE (16) [SWINE'S]
Lev 11: 7 the **s**, though he divide the hoof, and 2386
Dt 14: 8 the **s**, because it divideth the hoof, 2386
Mt 7: 6 neither cast ye your pearls before **s**, *5519*
8:30 off from them a herd of many **s** feeding. *5519*
8:31 suffer us to go away into the herd of **s**. *5519*
8:32 come out, they went into the herd of **s**: *5519*
8:32 the whole herd of **s** ran violently down a *5519*
Mk 5:11 the mountains a great herd of **s** feeding. *5519*
5:12 saying, Send us into the **s**, that we may *5519*
5:13 spirits went out, and entered into the **s**: *5519*
5:14 And they that fed the **s** fled, and told *it* in *5519*
5:16 with the devil, and *also* concerning the **s**. *5519*
Lk 8:32 And there was there a herd of many **s** *5519*
8:33 out of the man, and entered into the **s**: *5519*
15:15 and he sent him into his fields to feed **s**. *5519*
15:16 his belly with the husks that the **s** did eat: *5519*

SWINE'S (4) [SWINE]
Pr 11:22 *As* a jewel of gold in a s snout, *so is* a fair 2386
Isa 65: 4 which eat s flesh, and broth of abominable 2386
66: 3 an oblation, *as if he offered* s blood; 2386
66:17 eating s flesh, and the abomination, and 2386

SWOLLEN (1) [SWELL]
Ac 28: 6 they looked when he should have s, *4092*

SWOON (1) [SWOONED]
La 2:11 and the sucklings s in the streets of the city. 5848

SWOONED (1) [SWOON]
La 2:12 when they s as the wounded in the streets 5848

SWORD (424) [SWORDS]
Ge 3:24 a flaming s which turned every way, 2719
27:40 by thy s shalt thou live, and shalt serve thy 2719
31:26 my daughters, as captives taken with the s? 2719
34:25 took each man his s, and came upon 2719
34:26 and Shechem his son with the edge of the s, 2719
48:22 out of the hand of the Amorite with my s 2719
Ex 5: 3 fall upon us with pestilence, or with the s. 2719
5:21 to put a s in their hand to slay us. 2719
15: 9 I will draw my s, my hand shall destroy 2719
17:13 and his people with the edge of the s. 2719
18: 4 and delivered me from the s of Pharaoh: 2719
22:24 shall wax hot, and I will kill you with the s; 2719
32:27 Put every man his s by his side, *and* go in 2719
Lev 26: 6 neither shall the s go through your land. 2719
26: 7 and they shall fall before you by the s. 2719
26: 8 your enemies shall fall before you by the s. 2719
26:25 I will bring a s upon you, that shall avenge 2719
26:33 the heathen, and will draw out a s after you: 2719
26:36 they shall flee, as fleeing from a s; and 2719
26:37 as it were before a s, when none pursueth: 2719
Nu 14: 3 to fall by the s, *that* our wives and 2719
14:43 there before you, and ye shall fall by the s: 2719
19:16 one that is slain with a s in the open fields, 2719
20:18 lest I come out against thee with the s. 2719
21:24 Israel smote him with the edge of the s, 2719
22:23 in the way, and his s drawn in his hand: 2719
22:29 I would there were a s in mine hand, 2719
22:31 in the way, and his s drawn in his hand: 2719
31: 8 also the son of Beor they slew with the s. 2719
Dt 13:15 of that city with the edge of the s, 2719
13:15 the cattle thereof, with the edge of the s. 2719
20:13 every male thereof with the edge of the s: 2719
28:22 with the s, and with blasting, and 2719
32:25 The s without, and terror within, 2719
32:41 If I whet my glittering s, and mine hand 2719
32:42 with blood, and my s shall devour flesh; 2719
33:29 and who *is* the s of thy excellency! 2719
Jos 5:13 against him with his s drawn in his hand: 2719
6:21 and sheep, and ass, with the edge of the s. 2719
8:24 they were all fallen on the edge of the s, 2719
8:24 *unto* Ai, and smote it with the edge of the s. 2719
10:11 whom the children of Israel slew with the s. 2719
10:28 smote it with the edge of the s, and the king 2719
10:30 he smote it with the edge of the s, and all 2719
10:32 smote it with the edge of the s, and all 2719
10:35 smote it with the edge of the s, and all 2719
10:37 smote it with the edge of the s, and the king 2719
10:39 they smote them with the edge of the s, and 2719
11:10 and smote the king thereof with the s: 2719
11:11 that *were* therein with the edge of the s, 2719
11:12 smote them with the edge of the s, *and* 2719
11:14 man they smote with the edge of the s, 2719
13:22 did the children of Israel slay with the s 2719
19:47 smote it with the edge of the s, and 2719
24:12 *but* not with thy s, nor with thy bow. 2719
Jdg 1: 8 smitten it with the edge of the s, and set 2719
1:25 they smote the city with the edge of the s; 2719
4:15 with the edge of the s before Barak; 2719
4:16 host of Sisera fell upon the edge of the s; 2719
7:14 This *is* nothing else save the s of Gideon 2719
7:18 say, *The* s of the LORD, and of Gideon. NIH
7:20 The s of the LORD, and of Gideon. 2719
7:22 the LORD set every man's s against his 2719
8:10 and twenty thousand men that drew s. 2719
8:20 the youth drew not his s: for he feared, 2719
9:54 and said unto him, Draw thy s, and slay me, 2719
18:27 they smote them with the edge of the s, and 2719
20: 2 four hundred thousand footmen that drew s. 2719
20:15 and six thousand men that drew s, 2719
20:17 four hundred thousand men that drew s: 2719
20:25 thousand men; all these drew the s. 2719
20:35 and an hundred men: all these drew the s. 2719
20:37 smote all the city with the edge of the s. 2719
20:46 and five thousand men that drew the s; 2719
20:48 smote them with the edge of the s, as well 2719
21:10 of Jabesh-gilead with the edge of the s, 2719
1Sa 13:22 that there was neither s nor spear found in 2719
14:20 every man's s was against his fellow, *and* 2719
15: 8 all the people with the edge of the s. 2719
15:33 As thy s hath made women childless, so 2719
17:39 David girded his s upon his armour, and 2719
17:45 Thou comest to me with a s, and with a 2719
17:47 know that the LORD saveth not with s 2719
17:50 but *there was* no s in the hand of David. 2719
17:51 took his s, and drew it out of the sheath 2719
18: 4 even to his s, and to his bow, and to his 2719
21: 8 there not here under thine hand spear or s? 2719
21: 8 for I have neither brought my s nor my 2719
21: 9 priest said, The s of Goliath the Philistine, 2719
22:10 and gave him the s of Goliath the Philistine. 2719
22:13 in that thou hast given him bread and a s, 2719
22:19 smote he with the edge of the s, both men 2719
22:19 and asses, and sheep, with the edge of the s. 2719
25:13 unto his men, Gird you on every man his s. 2719
25:13 they girded on every man his s; and 2719
25:13 his sword; and David also girded on his s: 2719
31: 4 Draw thy s, and thrust me through 2719
31: 4 therefore Saul took a s, and fell upon it. 2719
31: 5 he fell likewise upon his s, and died with 2719
2Sa 1:12 of Israel; because they were fallen by the s. 2719
1:22 and the s of Saul returned not empty. 2719
2:16 and *thrust* his s in his fellow's side; 2719
2:26 and said, Shall the s devour for ever? 2719
3:29 or that falleth on the s, or that lacketh 2719
11:25 for the s devoureth one as well as another: 2719
12: 9 thou hast killed Uriah the Hittite with the s, 2719
12: 9 hast slain him with the s of the children of 2719
12:10 the s shall never depart from thine house, 2719
15:14 and smite the city with the edge of the s. 2719
18: 8 more people that day than the s devoured. 2719
20: 8 upon it a girdle with a s fastened upon his 2719
20:10 Amasa took no heed to the s that *was* in 2719
21:16 he being girded *with* a new s, thought to NIH
23:10 was weary, and his hand clave unto the s: 2719
24: 9 thousand valiant men that drew the s; 2719
1Ki 1:51 that he will not slay his servant with the s. 2719
2: 8 I will not put thee to death with the s. 2719
2:32 better than he, and slew them with the s, 2719
3:24 the king said, Bring me a s. And they 2719
3:24 And they brought a s before the king. 2719
19: 1 how he had slain all the prophets with the s. 2719
19:10 and slain thy prophets with the s; 2719
19:14 and slain thy prophets with the s; 2719
19:17 *that* him that escapeth the s of Hazael shall 2719
19:17 him that escapeth from the s of Jehu shall 2719
2Ki 6:22 whom thou hast taken captive with thy s 2719
8:12 their young *men* wilt thou slay with the s, 2719
10:25 they smote them with the edge of the s; 2719
11:15 him that followeth her kill with the s. 2719
11:20 they slew Athaliah with the s *beside* 2719
19: 7 I will cause him to fall by the s in his own 2719
19:37 and Sharezer *his sons* smote him with the s: 2719
1Ch 5:18 men *able to* bear buckler and s, and 2719
10: 4 Draw thy s, and thrust me through 2719
10: 4 So Saul took a s, and fell upon it. 2719
10: 5 he fell likewise on the s, and died. 2719
21: 5 and an hundred thousand men that drew s: 2719
21: 5 and ten thousand men that drew s. 2719
21:12 while that the s of thine enemies overtaketh 2719
21:12 or else three days the s of the LORD, 2719
21:16 having a drawn s in his hand stretched out 2719
21:27 he put up his s again into the sheath 2719
21:30 of the s of the angel of the LORD. 2719
2Ch 20: 9 *as* the s, judgment, or pestilence, or famine, 2719
21: 4 slew all his brethren with the s, and 2719
23:14 followeth her, let him be slain with the s. 2719
23:21 after that they had slain Athaliah with the s. 2719
29: 9 our fathers have fallen by the s, and 2719
32:21 his own bowels slew him there with the s. 2719
36:17 who slew their young men with the s in 2719
36:20 them that had escaped from the s carried he 2719
Ezr 9: 7 to the s, to captivity, and to a spoil, and 2719

Ne 4:18 every one had his **s** girded by his side, and 2719
Est 9: 5 all their enemies *with* the stroke of the **s**, 2719
Job 1:15 slain the servants with the edge of the **s**; 2719
1:17 slain the servants with the edge of the **s**; 2719
5:15 he saveth the poor from the **s**, from their 2719
5:20 and in war from the power of the **s**. 2719
15:22 of darkness, and he *is* waited for of the **s**. 2719
19:29 Be ye afraid of the **s**: for wrath *bringeth* 2719
19:29 for wrath *bringeth* the punishments of the **s**, 2719
20:25 yea, the **glistering s** cometh out of his gall: 1300
27:14 If his children be multiplied, *it is* for the **s**: 2719
33:18 the pit, and his life from perishing by the **s**. 7973
36:12 they shall perish by the **s**, and they shall die 7973
39:22 neither turneth he back from the **s**. 2719
40:19 he that made him can make his **s** to 2719
41:26 The **s** of him that layeth at him cannot hold: 2719
Ps 7:12 If he turn not, he will whet his **s**; he hath 2719
17:13 my soul from the wicked, *which is* thy **s**: 2719
22:20 Deliver my soul from the **s**; my darling 2719
37:14 The wicked have drawn out the **s**, and 2719
37:15 Their **s** shall enter into their own heart, and 2719
42:10 *As* with a **s** in my bones, mine enemies 7524
44: 3 not the land in possession by their own **s**, 2719
44: 6 in my bow, neither shall my **s** save me. 2719
45: 3 Gird thy **s** upon *thy* thigh, O *most* mighty, 2719
57: 4 and arrows, and their tongue a sharp **s**. 2719
63:10 They shall fall by the **s**: they shall be a 2719
64: 3 Who whet their tongue like a **s**, *and* 2719
76: 3 the shield, and the **s**, and the battle. 2719
78:62 He gave his people over also unto the **s**; 2719
78:64 Their priests fell by the **s**; and their widows 2719
89:43 Thou hast also turned the edge of his **s**, and 2719
144:10 David his servant from the hurtful **s**. 2719
149: 6 and a twoedged **s** in their hand; 2719
Pr 5: 4 bitter as wormwood, sharp as a twoedged **s**. 2719
12:18 is that speaketh like the piercings of a **s**: 2719
25:18 *is* a maul, and a **s**, and a sharp arrow. 2719
SS 3: 8 every man *hath* his **s** upon his thigh 2719
Isa 1:20 and rebel, ye shall be devoured *with* the **s**: 2719
2: 4 nation shall not lift up **s** against nation, 2719
3:25 Thy men shall fall by the **s**, and thy mighty 2719
13:15 that is joined *unto them* shall fall by the **s**. 2719
14:19 thrust through with a **s**, that go down to 2719
21:15 from the drawn **s**, and from the bent bow, 2719
22: 2 thy slain *men are* not slain with the **s**, nor 2719
27: 1 strong **s** shall punish leviathan the piercing 2719
31: 8 shall the Assyrian fall with the **s**, not of a 2719
31: 8 the **s**, not of a mean man, shall devour him: 2719
31: 8 he shall flee from the **s**, and his young men 2719
34: 5 For my **s** shall be bathed in heaven: behold, 2719
34: 6 The **s** of the LORD is filled *with* blood, 2719
37: 7 I will cause him to fall by the **s** in his own 2719
37:38 and Sharezer his sons smote him with the **s**; 2719
41: 2 he gave *them* as the dust *to* his **s**, *and* 2719
49: 2 he hath made my mouth like a sharp **s**; 2719
51:19 and destruction, and the famine, and the **s**: 2719
65:12 Therefore will I number you to the **s**, and 2719
66:16 by his **s** will the LORD plead with all 2719
Jer 2:30 your own **s** hath devoured your prophets, 2719
4:10 whereas the **s** reacheth unto the soul). 2719
5:12 upon us; neither shall we see **s** nor famine: 2719
5:17 wherein thou trustedst, with the **s**. 2719
6:25 for the **s** of the enemy *and* fear *is* on every 2719
9:16 I will send a **s** after them, till I have 2719
11:22 the young men shall die by the **s**; their sons 2719
12:12 for the **s** of the LORD *shall* devour from 2719
14:12 I will consume them by the **s**, and by 2719
14:13 say unto them, Ye shall not see the **s**, 2719
14:15 **S** and famine shall not be in this land; 2719
14:15 By **s** and famine shall those prophets be 2719
14:16 because of the famine and the **s**; 2719
14:18 the field, then behold the slain with the **s**: 2719
15: 2 such as *are* for the **s**, to the sword; and 2719
15: 2 such as *are* for the sword, to the **s**; and 2719
15: 3 the **s** to slay, and the dogs to tear, and 2719
15: 9 the residue of them will I deliver to the **s** 2719
16: 4 they shall be consumed by the **s**, and 2719
18:21 pour out their *blood* by the force of the **s**; 2719
18:21 *let* their young men *be* slain by the **s** in 2719
19: 7 I will cause them to fall by the **s** before 2719
20: 4 they shall fall by the **s** of their enemies, and 2719
20: 4 and shall slay them with the **s**. 2719
21: 7 from the **s**, and from the famine, 2719
21: 7 he shall smite them with the edge of the **s**; 2719
21: 9 that abideth in this city shall die by the **s**, 2719
24:10 I will send the **s**, the famine, and 2719
25:16 of the **s** that I will send among them. 2719
25:27 of the **s** which I will send among you. 2719
25:29 for I *will* call for a **s** upon all 2719
25:31 he will give them *that are* wicked to the **s**, 2719
26:23 who slew him with the **s**, and cast his dead 2719
27: 8 with the **s**, and with the famine, and 2719
27:13 thou and thy people, by the **s**, by 2719
29:17 Behold, I will send upon them the **s**, 2719
29:18 I will persecute them with the **s**, with 2719
31: 2 The people which were left of the **s** found 2719
32:24 because of the **s**, and *of* the famine, and 2719
32:36 the hand of the king of Babylon by the **s**, 2719
33: 4 thrown down by the mounts, and by the **s**; 2719
34: 4 of thee, Thou shalt not die by the **s**: 2719
34:17 to the **s**, to the pestilence, and to 2719
38: 2 that remaineth in this city shall die by the **s**, 2719
39:18 thou shalt not fall by the **s**, but thy life shall 2719
41: 2 of Ahikam the son of Shaphan with the **s**, 2719
42:16 come to pass, *that* the **s**, which ye feared, 2719
42:17 they shall die by the **s**, by the famine, and 2719
42:22 know certainly that ye shall die by the **s**, 2719
43:11 and such *as are* for the **s** to the sword. 2719
43:11 and such *as are* for the sword to the **s**. 2719
44:12 they shall *even* be consumed by the **s**, *and* 2719
44:12 the greatest, by the **s** and by the famine: 2719
44:13 by the **s**, by the famine, and by 2719
44:18 have been consumed by the **s** and by 2719
44:27 land of Egypt shall be consumed by the **s** 2719
44:28 Yet a small number that escape the **s** shall 2719
46:10 the **s** shall devour, and it shall be satiate 2719
46:14 for the **s** shall devour round about thee. 2719
46:16 land of our nativity, from the oppressing **s**. 2719
47: 6 O thou **s** of the LORD, how long *will it be* 2719
48: 2 O Madmen; the **s** shall pursue thee. 2719
48:10 cursed *be* he that keepeth back his **s** from 2719
49:37 I will send the **s** after them, till I have 2719
50:16 for fear of the oppressing **s** they shall turn 2719
50:35 A **s** *is* upon the Chaldeans, saith 2719
50:36 A **s** *is* upon the liars; and they shall dote: 2719
50:36 a **s** *is* upon her mighty *men;* and they shall 2719
50:37 A **s** *is* upon their horses, and upon their 2719
50:37 a **s** *is* upon her treasures; and they shall be 2719
51:50 Ye that have escaped the **s**, go *away,* stand 2719
La 1:20 abroad the **s** bereaveth, at home *there is* as 2719
2:21 and my young men are fallen by the **s**; 2719
4: 9 *They that be* slain with the **s** are better than 2719
5: 9 our lives because of the **s** of the wilderness. 2719
Eze 5: 2 the wind; and I will draw out a **s** after them. 2719
5:12 a third *part* shall fall by the **s** round about 2719
5:12 and I will draw out a **s** after them. 2719
5:17 and I will bring the **s** upon thee. 2719
6: 3 *will* bring a **s** upon you, and I will destroy 2719
6: 8 that shall escape the **s** among the nations, 2719
6:11 for they shall fall by the **s**, by the famine, 2719
6:12 *he* that *is* near shall fall by the **s**; and he that 2719
7:15 The **s** *is* without, and the pestilence and 2719
7:15 he that *is* in the field shall die with the **s**; 2719
11: 8 Ye have feared the **s**; and I will bring a 2719
11: 8 I will bring a **s** upon you, saith the Lord 2719
11:10 Ye shall fall by the **s**; I will judge you in 2719
12:14 and I will draw out the **s** after them. 2719
12:16 I will leave a few men of them from the **s**, 2719
14:17 Or *if* I bring a **s** upon that land, and say, 2719
14:17 that land, and say, **S**, go through the land; 2719
14:21 the **s**, and the famine, and the noisome 2719
17:21 with all his bands shall fall by the **s**, 2719
21: 3 will draw forth my **s** out of his sheath, and 2719
21: 4 shall my **s** go forth out of his sheath against 2719
21: 5 have drawn forth my **s** out of his sheath: 2719
21: 9 Say, A **s**, a sword is sharpened, and 2719
21: 9 a **s** is sharpened, and also furbished: 2719
21:11 this **s** is sharpened, and it *is* furbished, 2719
21:12 terrors by reason of the **s** shall be upon my 2719
21:13 and what if *the* **s** contemn even the rod? NIH
21:14 let the **s** be doubled the third time, 2719
21:14 be doubled the third time, the **s** of the slain: 2719
21:14 it *is* the **s** of the great *men that are* slain, 2719
21:15 I have set the point of the **s** against all their 2719
21:19 that the **s** of the king of Babylon may come: 2719
21:20 that the **s** may come to Rabbath of 2719
21:28 even say thou, The **s**, the sword *is* drawn: 2719
21:28 even say thou, The sword, the **s** *is* drawn: 2719

Eze 23:10 and her daughters, and slew her with the s: 2719
23:25 and thy remnant shall fall by the s: 2719
24:21 whom ye have left shall fall by the s. 2719
25:13 and they of Dedan shall fall by the s. 2719
26: 6 *are* in the field shall be slain by the s; 2719
26: 8 He shall slay with the s thy daughters in 2719
26:11 he shall slay thy people by the s, and 2719
28:23 of her by the s upon her on every side; 2719
29: 8 I *will* bring a s upon thee, and cut off man 2719
30: 4 the s shall come upon Egypt, and great pain 2719
30: 5 is in league, shall fall with them by the s. 2719
30: 6 tower of Syene shall they fall in it by the s, 2719
30:17 and of Phi-beseth shall fall by the s: 2719
30:21 to bind it, to make it strong to hold the s. 2719
30:22 and I will cause the s to fall out of his hand. 2719
30:24 king of Babylon, and put my s in his hand: 2719
30:25 when I shall put my s into the hand of 2719
31:17 with him unto *them that be* slain with the s; 2719
31:18 with *them that be* slain with the s. 2719
32:10 when I shall brandish my s before them; 2719
32:11 The s of the king of Babylon shall come 2719
32:20 in the midst of *them that are* slain by the s: 2719
32:20 she is delivered *to* the s: draw her and 2719
32:21 they lie uncircumcised, slain by the s. 2719
32:22 about him: all of them slain, fallen by the s: 2719
32:23 all of them slain, fallen by the s, 2719
32:24 her grave, all of them slain, fallen by the s, 2719
32:25 all of them uncircumcised, slain by the s: 2719
32:26 all of them uncircumcised, slain by the s, 2719
32:28 shalt lie with *them that are* slain with the s. 2719
32:29 are laid by *them that were* slain by the s: 2719
32:30 with *them that be* slain by the s, 2719
32:31 and all his army slain by the s, 2719
32:32 with *them that are* slain with the s, 2719
33: 2 unto them, When I bring the s upon a land, 2719
33: 3 *If* when he seeth the s come upon the land, 2719
33: 4 if the s come, and take him away, his blood 2719
33: 6 if the watchman see the s come, and 2719
33: 6 if the s come, and take *any* person from 2719
33:26 Ye stand upon your s, ye work 2719
33:27 that *are* in the wastes shall fall by the s, 2719
35: 5 force of the s in the time of their calamity, 2719
35: 8 shall they fall *that are* slain with the s. 2719
38: 8 the land *that is* brought back from the s, 2719
38:21 I will call *for* a s against him throughout all 2719
38:21 every man's s shall be against his brother. 2719
39:23 of their enemies: so fell they all by the s. 2719
Da 11:33 yet they shall fall by the s, and by flame, 2719
Hos 1: 7 nor by s, nor by battle, by horses, nor by 2719
2:18 I will break the bow and the s and the battle 2719
7:16 their princes shall fall by the s for the rage 2719
11: 6 the s shall abide on his cities, and 2719
13:16 they shall fall by the s: their infants shall be 2719
Joel 2: 8 *when* they fall upon the s, they shall not be 7973
Am 1:11 he did pursue his brother with the s, 2719
4:10 your young men have I slain with the s, and 2719
7: 9 against the house of Jeroboam with the s. 2719
7:11 Jeroboam shall die by the s, and Israel shall 2719
7:17 and thy daughters shall fall by the s, 2719
9: 1 and I will slay the last of them with the s: 2719
9: 4 thence will I command the s, and it shall 2719
9:10 the sinners of my people shall die by the s, 2719
Mic 4: 3 nation shall not lift up a s against nation, 2719
5: 6 shall waste the land of Assyria with the s, 2719
6:14 thou deliverest will I give up to the s. 2719
Na 2:13 and the s shall devour thy young lions: 2719
3: 3 The horseman lifteth up both the bright s 2719
3:15 the s shall cut thee off, it shall eat thee up 2719
Zep 2:12 Ethiopians also, ye *shall be* slain by my s. 2719
Hag 2:22 every one by the s of his brother. 2719
Zec 9:13 and made thee as the s of a mighty *man.* 2719
11:17 the s *shall be* upon his arm, and upon his 2719
13: 7 Awake, O s, against my shepherd, and 2719
Mt 10:34 on earth: I came not to send peace, but a s. *3162*
26:51 and drew his s, and stroke a servant of *3162*
26:52 unto him, Put up again thy s into his place: *3162*
26:52 for all they that take the s shall perish with *3162*
26:52 that take the sword shall perish with the s. *3162*
Mk 14:47 And one of them that stood by drew a s, *3162*
Lk 2:35 a s shall pierce through thy own soul also,) *4501*
21:24 And they shall fall by the edge of the s, and *3162*
22:36 and he that hath no s, let him sell his *3162*
22:49 unto him, Lord, shall we smite with the s? *3162*
Jn 18:10 Then Simon Peter having a s drew it, and *3162*
18:11 unto Peter, Put up thy s into the sheath: *3162*
Ac 12: 2 killed James the brother of John with the s. *3162*
16:27 he drew out his s, and would have killed *3162*
Ro 8:35 or famine, or nakedness, or peril, or s? *3162*
13: 4 be afraid; for he beareth not the s in vain: *3162*
Eph 6:17 and the s of the Spirit, which is the word of *3162*
Heb 4:12 powerful, and sharper than any twoedged s, *3162*
11:34 violence of fire, escaped the edge of the s, *3162*
11:37 were tempted, were slain with the s: *3162*
Rev 1:16 out of his mouth went a sharp twoedged s: *4501*
2:12 *things* saith he which hath the sharp s *4501*
2:16 will fight against them with the s of my *4501*
6: 4 and there was given unto him a great s. *3162*
6: 8 to kill with s, and with hunger, and *4501*
13:10 he that killeth with the s must be killed with *3162*
13:10 with the sword must be killed with the s. *3162*
13:14 which had the wound by a s, and did live. *3162*
19:15 And out of his mouth goeth a sharp s, *4501*
19:21 And the remnant were slain with the s of *4501*
19:21 which *s* proceeded out of his mouth: NIG

SWORDS (24) [SWORD]

1Sa 13:19 Lest the Hebrews make *them* s or spears: 2719
2Ki 3:26 with him seven hundred men that drew s, 2719
Ne 4:13 the people after *their* families with their s, 2719
Ps 55:21 were softer than oil, yet *were* they **drawn** s. 6609
59: 7 s *are* in their lips: for who, *say they,* doth 2719
Pr 30:14 whose teeth *are as* s, and their jaw teeth *as* 2719
SS 3: 8 They all hold s, *being* expert in war: 2719
Isa 2: 4 they shall beat their s into plowshares, and 2719
21:15 For they fled from the s, from the drawn 2719
Eze 16:40 and thrust thee through with their s. 2719
23:47 with stones, and dispatch them with their s; 2719
28: 7 they shall draw their s against the beauty of 2719
30:11 they shall draw their s against Egypt, and 2719
32:12 By the s of the mighty will I cause thy 2719
32:27 they have laid their s under their heads, but 2719
38: 4 and shields, all of them handling s: 2719
Joel 3:10 Beat your plowshares into s, and 2719
Mic 4: 3 they shall beat their s into plowshares, and 2719
Mt 26:47 and with him a great multitude with s and *3162*
26:55 Are ye come out as against a thief with s *3162*
Mk 14:43 and with him a great multitude with s and *3162*
14:48 a thief, with s and *with* staves to take me? *3162*
Lk 22:38 And they said, Lord, behold, here *are* two s. *3162*
22:52 as against a thief, with s and staves? *3162*

SWORN (48) [SWEAR]

Ge 22:16 said, By myself have I s, saith the Lord, 7650
Ex 13:19 for he had **straitly** s the children of 7650+7650
17:16 Because the Lord hath s 3027+3678+5921
Lev 6: 5 Or all *that* about which he hath s falsely; 7650
Dt 7: 8 he would keep the oath which he had s unto 7650
13:17 multiply thee, as he hath s unto thy fathers; 7650
19: 8 as he hath s unto thy fathers, and give thee 7650
28: 9 people unto himself, as he hath s unto thee, 7650
29:13 as he hath s unto thy fathers, to Abraham, 7650
31: 7 hath s unto their fathers to give them; 7650
Jos 9:18 the princes of the congregation had s unto 7650
9:19 We have s unto them by the Lord God 7650
Jdg 2:15 and as the Lord had s unto them: 7650
21: 1 Now the men of Israel had s in Mizpeh, 7650
21: 7 seeing we have s by the Lord that *we* 7650
21:18 for the children of Israel have s, saying, 7650
1Sa 3:14 I have s unto the house of Eli, 7650
20:42 forasmuch as we have s both of us in 7650
2Sa 3: 9 as the Lord hath s to David, even so I do 7650
21: 2 and the children of Israel had s unto them: 7650
2Ch 15:15 for they had s with all their heart, and 7650
Ne 6:18 For *there were* many in Judah s unto 1167+7621
9:15 the land which thou hadst s to give them. 3027
Ps 24: 4 up his soul unto vanity, nor s deceitfully. 7650
89: 3 my chosen, I have s unto David my servant, 7650
89:35 Once have I s by my holiness that I will not 7650
102: 8 they that are mad against me are s against 7650
110: 4 The Lord hath s, and will not repent, 7650
119:106 I have s, and I will perform *it,* that *I* will 7650
132:11 The Lord hath s *in* truth unto David; 7650
Isa 14:24 The Lord of hosts hath s, saying, 7650
45:23 I have s by myself, the word is gone out of 7650
54: 9 for *as* I have s that the waters of Noah 7650
54: 9 have I s that *I* would not be wroth with 7650
62: 8 The Lord hath s by his right hand, and 7650
Jer 5: 7 and s by *them that are* no gods: 7650

S

Jer 11: 5 That *I* may perform the oath which I have **s** 7650
44:26 Behold, I have **s** by my great name, 7650
49:13 For I have **s** by myself, saith the LORD, 7650
51:14 The LORD of hosts hath **s** by himself, 7650
Eze 21:23 in their sight, to them that have **s** oaths: 7650
Am 4: 2 The Lord GOD hath **s** by his holiness, 7650
6: 8 The Lord GOD hath **s** by himself, saith 7650
8: 7 The LORD hath **s** by the excellency of 7650
Mic 7:20 which thou hast **s** unto our fathers from 7650
Ac 2:30 knowing that God had **s** with an oath to *3660*
7:17 which God had **s** to Abraham, the people *3660*
Heb 4: 3 as *he* said, As I have **s** in my wrath, if they *3660*

SYCAMINE (1)
Lk 17: 6 ye might say unto this **s tree**, Be thou *4807*

SYCAMORE-FIG See SYCOMORE

SYCHAR (1)
Jn 4: 5 he to a city of Samaria, which is called **S**, *4965*

SYCHEM (2) [SHECHEM]
Ac 7:16 And were carried over into **S**, and laid in *4966*
7:16 of the sons of Emmor the *father* of **S**. *4966*

SYCOMORE (7) [SYCOMORES]
1Ki 10:27 cedars made he *to be* as the **s trees** that *are* 8256
1Ch 27:28 the **s trees** that *were* in the low plains *was* 8256
2Ch 1:15 cedar trees made he as the **s trees** that *are* 8256
9:27 cedar trees made he as the **s trees** that *are* 8256
Ps 78:47 vines with hail, and their **s trees** with frost. 8256
Am 7:14 I *was* a herdman, and a gatherer of **s fruit**: 8256
Lk 19: 4 and climbed up into a **s tree** to see him: *4809*

SYCOMORES (1) [SYCOMORE]
Isa 9:10 the **s** are cut down, but we will change 8256

SYENE (2)
Eze 29:10 from the tower of **S** even unto the border of 5482
30: 6 from the tower of **S** shall they fall in it by 5482

SYNAGOGUE (43) [SYNAGOGUE'S, SYNAGOGUES]
Mt 12: 9 was departed thence, he went into their **s**: *4864*
13:54 he taught them in their **s**, insomuch that *4864*
Mk 1:21 on the sabbath day he entered into the **s**, *4864*
1:23 And there was in their **s** a man with an *4864*
1:29 when they were come out of the **s**, *4864*
3: 1 And he entered again into the **s**; and *4864*
5:22 there cometh one of the **rulers of the s**, *752*
5:36 he saith unto the **ruler of the s**, Be not *752*
5:38 he cometh to the house of the **ruler of the s**, *752*
6: 2 day was come, he began to teach in the **s**: *4864*
Lk 4:16 he went into the **s** on the sabbath day, *4864*
4:20 And the eyes of all *them that were* in the **s** *4864*
4:28 And all *they* in the **s**, when they heard these *4864*
4:33 And in the **s** there was a man, which had a *4864*
4:38 And he arose out of the **s**, and entered into *4864*
6: 6 that he entered into the **s** and taught: *4864*
7: 5 loveth our nation, and he hath built us a **s**. *4864*
8:41 named Jairus, and he was a ruler of the **s**: *4864*
13:14 And the **ruler of the s** answered with *752*
Jn 6:59 These *things* said he in the **s**, as he taught in *4864*
9:22 he *was* Christ, he should be **put out of the s**. *656*
12:42 *him,* lest they should be **put out of the s**: *656*
18:20 I ever taught in the **s**, and in the temple, *4864*
Ac 6: 9 Then there arose certain of the **s**, which is *4864*
6: 9 which is called *the s* of the Libertines, and NIG
13:14 and went into the **s** on the sabbath day, and *4864*
13:15 the prophets the **rulers of the s** sent unto *752*
13:42 And when the Jews were gone out of the **s**, *4864*
14: 1 that they went *both* together into the **s** of *4864*
17: 1 to Thessalonica, where was a **s** of the Jews: *4864*
17:10 who coming *thither* went into the **s** of *4864*
17:17 Therefore disputed he in the **s** with *4864*
18: 4 And he reasoned in the **s** every sabbath, and *4864*
18: 7 whose house joined hard to the **s**. *4864*
18: 8 And Crispus, the *chief* **ruler of the s**, *752*
18:17 the *chief* **ruler of the s**, and beat *him* before *752*
18:19 but he himself entered into the **s**, and *4864*
18:26 And he began to speak boldly in the **s**: *4864*
19: 8 And he went into the **s**, and spake boldly *4864*
22:19 beat in every **s** them that believed on thee: *4864*
26:11 And I punished them oft in every **s**, and *4864*
Rev 2: 9 are Jews, and are not, but *are* the **s** of Satan. *4864*
3: 9 Behold, I *will* make *them* of the **s** of Satan, *4864*

SYNAGOGUE'S (2) [SYNAGOGUE]
Mk 5:35 there came from the **ruler of the s** *house* *752*
Lk 8:49 there cometh one from the **ruler of the s** *752*

SYNAGOGUES (24) [SYNAGOGUE]
Ps 74: 8 they have burnt up all the **s** of God in 4150
Mt 4:23 teaching in their **s** and preaching the gospel *4864*
6: 2 as the hypocrites do in the **s** and in *4864*
6: 5 *are:* for they love to pray standing in the **s** *4864*
9:35 teaching in their **s**, and preaching *4864*
10:17 and they will scourge you in their **s**; *4864*
23: 6 rooms at feasts, and the chief seats in the **s**, *4864*
23:34 *some* of them shall ye scourge in your **s**, *4864*
Mk 1:39 And he preached in their **s** throughout all *4864*
12:39 And the chief seats in the **s**, and *4864*
13: 9 to councils; and in the **s** ye shall be beaten: *4864*
Lk 4:15 And he taught in their **s**, being glorified of *4864*
4:44 And he preached in the **s** of Galilee. *4864*
11:43 for ye love the uppermost seats in the **s**, and *4864*
12:11 And when they bring you unto the **s**, and *4864*
13:10 And he was teaching in one of the **s** on *4864*
20:46 and the highest seats in the **s**, and the chief *4864*
21:12 persecute *you,* delivering *you* up to *the* **s**, *4864*
Jn 16: 2 They shall put you **out of the s**: yea, the time *656*
Ac 9: 2 desired of him letters to Damascus to the **s**, *4864*
9:20 straightway he preached Christ in the **s**, *4864*
13: 5 they preached the word of God in the **s** of *4864*
15:21 being read in the **s** every sabbath day. *4864*
24:12 the people, neither in the **s**, nor in the city: *4864*

SYNTYCHE (1)
Php 4: 2 I beseech Euodias, and beseech **S**, that *they* *4941*

SYRACUSE (1)
Ac 28:12 And landing at **S**, we tarried *there* three *4946*

SYRIA (75) [SYRIA-DAMASCUS, SYRIA-MAACHAH, SYRIACK, SYRIAN, SYRIANS, SYROPHENICIAN]
Jdg 10: 6 the gods of **S**, and the gods of Zidon, and 758
2Sa 8: 6 Then David put garrisons in **S** of Damascus: 758
8:12 Of **S**, and of Moab, and of the children of 758
15: 8 vowed a vow while I abode at Geshur in **S**, 758
1Ki 10:29 kings of the Hittites, and for the kings of **S**, 758
11:25 and he abhorred Israel, and reigned over **S**. 758
15:18 of Tabrimon, the son of Hezion, king of **S**, 758
19:15 anoint Hazael to be king over **S**: 758
20: 1 Ben-hadad the king of **S** gathered all his host 758
20:20 Ben-hadad the king of **S** escaped on a horse 758
20:22 for at the return of the year the king of **S** will 758
20:23 the servants of the king of **S** said unto him, 758
22: 1 continued three years without war between **S** 758
22: 3 take it not out of the hand of the king of **S**? 758
22:31 But the king of **S** commanded his thirty and 758
2Ki 5: 1 captain of the host of the king of **S**, 758
5: 1 the LORD had given deliverance unto **S**: 758
5: 5 the king of **S** said, Go to, go, and I will send 758
6: 8 Then the king of **S** warred against Israel, and 758
6:11 Therefore the heart of the king of **S** was sore 758
6:23 So the bands of **S** came no more into 758
6:24 that Ben-hadad king of **S** gathered all his 758
7: 5 come to the uttermost part of the camp of **S**, 758
8: 7 Ben-hadad the king of **S** was sick; and it was 758
8: 9 Thy son Ben-hadad king of **S** hath sent me to 758
8:13 shewed me *that* thou *shalt be* king over **S**. 758
8:28 against Hazael king of **S** in Ramoth-gilead; 758
8:29 when he fought against Hazael king of **S**. 758
9:14 and all Israel, because of Hazael king of **S**. 758
9:15 when he fought with Hazael king of **S**.) 758
12:17 Hazael king of **S** went up, and fought against 758
12:18 king's house, and sent *it* to Hazael king of **S**: 758
13: 3 them into the hand of Hazael king of **S**, 758
13: 4 because the king of **S** oppressed them. 758
13: 7 for the king of **S** had destroyed them, and 758
13:17 and the arrow of deliverance from **S**: 758
13:19 hadst thou smitten **S** till *thou* hadst 758
13:19 consumed *it:* whereas now thou shalt smite **S** 758
13:22 Hazael king of **S** oppressed Israel all 758
13:24 So Hazael king of **S** died; and Ben-hadad his 758
15:37 to send against Judah Rezin the king of **S**, 758
16: 5 Rezin king of **S** and Pekah son of Remaliah 758
16: 6 At that time Rezin king of **S** recovered Elath 758
16: 6 Rezin king of Syria recovered Elath to **S**, 758
16: 7 and save me out of the hand of the king of **S**, 758
2Ch 1:17 and *for* the kings of **S**, by their means. 758

2Ch 16: 2 and sent to Ben-hadad king of **S**, 758
16: 7 Because thou hast relied on the king of **S**, 758
16: 7 is the host of the king of **S** escaped out of 758
18:10 With these thou shalt push **S** until they be 758
18:30 Now the king of **S** had commanded 758
20: 2 thee from beyond the sea on this side **S**; 758
22: 5 against Hazael king of **S** at Ramoth-gilead: 758
22: 6 when he fought with Hazael king of **S**. 758
24:23 *that* the host of **S** came up against him: 758
28: 5 delivered him into the hand of the king of **S**; 758
28:23 Because the gods of the kings of **S** help 758
Isa 7: 1 *that* Rezin the king of **S**, and Pekah the son 758
7: 2 **S** is confederate with Ephraim. 758
7: 4 for the fierce anger of Rezin with **S**, and 758
7: 5 Because **S**, Ephraim, and the son of 758
7: 8 For the head of **S** *is* Damascus, and the head 758
17: 3 from Damascus, and the remnant of **S**: 758
Eze 16:57 time of *thy* reproach of the daughters of **S**, 758
27:16 **S** *was* thy merchant by reason of 758
Hos 12:12 Jacob fled *into* the country of **S**, and 758
Am 1: 5 the people of **S** shall go into captivity unto 758
Mt 4:24 And his fame went throughout all **S**: and *4947*
Lk 2: 2 made when Cyrenius was governor of **S**.) *4947*
Ac 15:23 the Gentiles in Antioch and **S** and Cilicia: *4947*
15:41 And he went through **S** and Cilicia, *4947*
18:18 and sailed thence into **S**, and with him *4947*
20: 3 wait for him, as he was about to sail into **S**, *4947*
21: 3 and sailed into **S**, and landed at Tyre: *4947*
Gal 1:21 Afterwards I came into the regions of **S** and *4947*

SYRIACK (1) [SYRIA]
Da 2: 4 spake the Chaldeans to the king **in S**, O king, 762

SYRIA-DAMASCUS (1) [DAMASCUS, SYRIA]
1Ch 18: 6 David put *garrisons* in **S**; and 758+1834

SYRIA-MAACHAH (1) [SYRIA]
1Ch 19: 6 and out of **S**, and out of Zobah. 758

SYRIAN (12) [SYRIA]
Ge 25:20 the daughter of Bethuel the **S** of Padan-aram, 761
25:20 of Padan-aram, the sister to Laban the **S**. 761
28: 5 son of Bethuel the **S**, the brother of Rebekah, 761
31:20 Jacob stale away unawares to Laban the **S**, 761
31:24 God came to Laban the **S** in a dream by 761
Dt 26: 5 A **S** ready to perish *was* my father, and 761
2Ki 5:20 my master hath spared Naaman this **S**, 761
18:26 pray thee, to thy servants **in the S language**; 762
Ezr 4: 7 of the letter *was* written **in the S tongue**, 762
4: 7 and interpreted **in the S tongue**. 762
Isa 36:11 unto thy servants **in the S language**; 762
Lk 4:27 them was cleansed, saving Naaman the **S**. *4948*

SYRIAN PHOENICIA See SYROPHENICIAN

SYRIANS (61) [SYRIA]
2Sa 8: 5 when the **S** of Damascus came to succour 758
8: 5 David slew of the **S** two and 758
8: 6 the **S** became servants to David, and 758
8:13 from smiting of the **S** in the valley of salt, 758
10: 6 Ammon sent and hired the **S** of Beth-rehob, 758
10: 6 and the **S** of Zoba, twenty thousand footmen, 758
10: 8 the **S** of Zoba, and of Rehob, and Ish-tob, 758
10: 9 of Israel, and put *them* in array against the **S**: 758
10:11 If the **S** be too strong for me, then thou shalt 758
10:13 *were* with him, unto the battle against the **S**: 758
10:14 when the children of Ammon saw that the **S** 758
10:15 when the **S** saw that they were smitten 758
10:16 brought out the **S** that *were* beyond the river: 758
10:17 the **S** set *themselves* in array against David, 758
10:18 the **S** fled before Israel; and David slew 758
10:18 *the men of* seven hundred chariots of the **S**, 758
10:19 So the **S** feared to help the children of 758
1Ki 20:20 and the **S** fled; and Israel pursued them: and 758
20:21 and slew the **S** with a great slaughter. 758
20:26 that Ben-hadad numbered the **S**, and went up 758
20:27 flocks of kids; but the **S** filled the country. 758
20:28 saith the LORD, Because the **S** have said, 758
20:29 the children of Israel slew *of* the **S** an 758
22:11 With these shalt thou push the **S**, 758
22:35 was stayed up in *his* chariot against the **S**, 758
2Ki 5: 2 the **S** had gone out *by* companies, and 758
6: 9 a place; for thither the **S** are come down. 758
7: 4 come, and let us fall unto the host of the **S**: 758
7: 5 in the twilight, to go unto the camp of the **S**: 758
7: 6 For the Lord had made the host of the **S** to 758
7:10 We came to the camp of the **S**, and behold, 758
7:12 I will now shew you what the **S** have done to 758
7:14 the king sent after the host of the **S**, saying, 758
7:15 which the **S** had cast away in their haste. 758
7:16 went out, and spoiled the tents of the **S**. 758
8:28 in Ramoth-gilead; and the **S** wounded Joram. 761
8:29 which the **S** had given him at Ramah, 761
9:15 of the wounds which the **S** had given him, 761
13: 5 they went out from under the hand of the **S**: 758
13:17 for thou shalt smite the **S** in Aphek, till *thou* 758
16: 6 the **S** came *to* Elath, and dwelt there unto 726
24: 2 bands of the **S**, and bands of the Moabites, 758
1Ch 18: 5 when the **S** of Damascus came to help 758
18: 5 David slew of the **S** two and 758
18: 6 the **S** became David's servants, and 758
19:10 of Israel, and put *them* in array against the **S**. 758
19:12 If the **S** be too strong for me, then thou shalt 758
19:14 him drew nigh before the **S** unto the battle; 758
19:15 when the children of Ammon saw that the **S** 758
19:16 when the **S** saw that they were put to 758
19:16 drew forth the **S** that *were* beyond the river: 758
19:17 had put the battle in array against the **S**, 758
19:18 the **S** fled before Israel; and David slew of 758
19:18 David slew of the **S** seven thousand *men* 758
19:19 neither would the **S** help the children of 758
2Ch 18:34 up in *his* chariot against the **S** until the even: 758
22: 5 at Ramoth-gilead: and the **S** smote Joram. 7421
24:24 For the army of the **S** came with a small 758
Isa 9:12 The **S** before, and the Philistines behind; and 758
Jer 35:11 and for fear of the army of the **S**: 758
Am 9: 7 from Caphtor, and the **S** from Kir? 758

SYROPHENICIAN (1) [PHENICIA, SYRIA]
Mk 7:26 The woman was a Greek, a **S** by nation; *4949*

T

TAANACH (6)
Jos 12:21 The king of **T**, one; the king of Megiddo, 8590
17:11 the inhabitants of **T** and her towns, and 8590
Jdg 1:27 and her towns, nor **T** and her towns, 8590
5:19 fought the kings of Canaan in **T** by 8590
1Ki 4:12 *to him pertained* **T** and Megiddo, and 8590
1Ch 7:29 **T** and her towns, Megiddo and her towns, 8590

TAANATH-SHILOH (1) [SHILOH]
Jos 16: 6 the border went about eastward *unto* **T**, and 8387

TABALIAH See TEBALIAH

TABBAOTH (2)
Ezr 2:43 the children of Hasupha, the children of **T**, 2884
Ne 7:46 the children of Hashupha, the children of **T**, 2884

TABBATH (1)
Jdg 7:22 *and* to the border of Abel-meholah, unto **T**. 2888

TABEAL (1)
Isa 7: 6 a king in the midst of it, *even* the son of **T**: 2870

TABEEL (1)
Ezr 4: 7 **T**, and the rest of their companions, 2870

TABERAH (2)
Nu 11: 3 he called the name of the place **T**: because 8404
Dt 9:22 at **T**, and at Massah, and 8404

TABERNACLE (328) [TABERNACLES]
Ex 25: 9 *after* the pattern of the **t**, and the pattern of 4908
26: 1 Moreover thou shalt make the **t** *with* ten 4908
26: 6 with the taches: and it shall be one **t**. 4908
26: 7 *of* goats' *hair* to be a covering upon the **t**: 4908
26: 9 the sixth curtain in the forefront of the **t**. 168
26:12 shall hang over the backside of the **t**. 4908
26:13 it shall hang over the sides of the **t** on this 4908
26:15 thou shalt make boards for the **t** *of* shittim 4908
26:17 shalt thou make for all the boards of the **t**. 4908

Ex	26:18	thou shalt make the boards for the **t**,	4908
	26:20	for the second side of the **t** on the north	4908
	26:22	for the sides of the **t** westward thou shalt	4908
	26:23	for the corners of the **t** in the two sides.	4908
	26:26	five for the boards of the one side of the **t**,	4908
	26:27	bars for the boards of the other side of the **t**,	4908
	26:27	five bars for the boards of the side of the **t**,	4908
	26:30	thou shalt rear up the **t** according to	4908
	26:35	table on the side of the **t** toward the south:	4908
	27: 9	thou shalt make the court of the **t**: for	4908
	27:19	All the vessels of the **t** in all the service	4908
	27:21	In the **t** of the congregation without the vail,	168
	28:43	when they come in unto the **t** of	168
	29: 4	unto the door of the **t** of the congregation,	168
	29:10	be brought before the **t** of the congregation:	168
	29:11	*by* the door of the **t** of the congregation.	168
	29:30	when he cometh into the **t** of	168
	29:32	*by* the door of the **t** of the congregation.	168
	29:42	the **t** of the congregation before the LORD:	168
	29:43	and *the t* shall be sanctified by my glory.	NIH
	29:44	And I will sanctify the **t** of the congregation,	168
	30:16	shalt appoint it for the service of the **t** of	168
	30:18	thou shalt put it between the **t** of	168
	30:20	When they go into the **t** of the congregation,	168
	30:26	thou shalt anoint the **t** of the congregation	168
	30:36	put of it before the Testimony in the **t** of	168
	31: 7	The **t** of the congregation, and the ark of	168
	31: 7	*is* thereupon, and all the furniture of the **t**,	168
	33: 7	Moses took the **t**, and pitched it without	168
	33: 7	and called it the **T** of the Congregation.	168
	33: 7	went out unto the **T** of the Congregation,	168
	33: 8	to pass, when Moses went out unto the **t**,	168
	33: 8	after Moses, until he was gone into the **t**.	168
	33: 9	it came to pass, as Moses entered into the **t**,	168
	33: 9	stood *at* the door of the **t**, and *the* LORD	168
	33:10	saw the cloudy pillar stand *at* the **t** door:	168
	33:11	a young man, departed not out of the **t**.	168
	35:11	The **t**, his tent, and his covering, his taches,	4908
	35:15	for the door at the entering in of the **t**,	4908
	35:18	The pins of the **t**, and the pins of the court,	4908
	35:21	to the work of the **t** of the congregation,	168
	36: 8	the **t** made ten curtains *of* fine twined linen,	4908
	36:13	another with the taches: so it became one **t**.	4908
	36:14	*of* goats' *hair* for the tent over the **t**:	4908
	36:20	he made boards for the **t** *of* shittim wood,	4908
	36:22	thus did he make for all the boards of the **t**.	4908
	36:23	he made boards for the **t**; twenty boards for	4908
	36:25	for the other side of the **t**, *which is* toward	4908
	36:27	for the sides of the **t** westward he made six	4908
	36:28	two boards made he for the corners of the **t**	4908
	36:31	five for the boards of the one side of the **t**,	4908
	36:32	bars for the boards of the other side of the **t**,	4908
	36:32	five bars for the boards of the **t** for the sides	4908
	36:37	he made a hanging for the **t** door *of* blue,	168
	38: 8	which assembled *at* the door of the **t** of	168
	38:20	all the pins of the **t**, and of the court round	4908
	38:21	This is the sum of the **t**, *even* of	4908
	38:21	*even* of the **t** of Testimony, as it was	4908
	38:30	to the door of the **t** of the congregation,	168
	38:31	all the pins of the **t**, and all the pins of	4908
	39:32	Thus was all the work of the **t** of the tent of	4908
	39:33	they brought the **t** unto Moses, the tent,	4908
	39:38	and the hanging for the **t** door,	168
	39:40	and all the vessels of the service of the **t**,	4908
	40: 2	set up the **t** of the tent of the congregation.	4908
	40: 5	and put the hanging of the door to the **t**.	4908
	40: 6	door of the **t** of the tent of the congregation.	4908
	40: 9	anoint the **t**, and all that *is* therein, and	4908
	40:12	his sons unto the door of the **t** of	168
	40:17	*day* of the month, *that* the **t** was reared up.	4908
	40:18	Moses reared up the **t**, and fastened his	4908
	40:19	he spread abroad the tent over the **t**, and	4908
	40:21	he brought the ark into the **t**, and set up	4908
	40:22	upon the side of the **t** northward, without	4908
	40:24	the table, on the side of the **t** southward.	4908
	40:28	he set up the hanging at the door of the **t**.	4908
	40:29	door of the **t** of the tent of the congregation,	4908
	40:33	he reared up the court round about the **t**	4908
	40:34	and the glory of the LORD filled the **t**.	4908
	40:35	the glory of the LORD filled the **t**.	4908
	40:36	the cloud was taken up from over the **t**,	4908
	40:38	For the cloud of the LORD *was* upon the **t**	4908
Lev	1: 1	spake unto him out of the **t** of	168
	1: 3	the **t** of the congregation before the LORD.	168
	1: 5	*is by* the door of the **t** of the congregation.	168
	3: 2	kill it *at* the door of the **t** of	168
	3: 8	and kill it before the **t** of the congregation:	168
	3:13	and kill it before the **t** of the congregation:	168
	4: 4	the **t** of the congregation before the LORD;	168
	4: 5	and bring it to the **t** of the congregation:	168
	4: 7	which *is* in the **t** of the congregation;	168
	4: 7	which *is at* the door of the **t** of	168
	4:14	bring him before the **t** of the congregation.	168
	4:16	bullock's blood to the **t** of the congregation:	168
	4:18	that *is* in the **t** of the congregation, and shall	168
	4:18	which *is at* the door of the **t** of	168
	6:16	in the court of the **t** of the congregation they	168
	6:26	in the court of the **t** of the congregation.	168
	6:30	**t** of the congregation to reconcile *withal* in	168
	8: 3	unto the door of the **t** of the congregation.	168
	8: 4	unto the door of the **t** of the congregation.	168
	8:10	anointed the **t** and all that *was* therein,	4908
	8:31	Boil the flesh *at* the door of the **t** of	168
	8:33	ye shall not go out of the door of the **t** of	168
	8:35	Therefore shall ye abide *at* the door of the **t**	168
	9: 5	commanded before the **t** of the congregation:	168
	9:23	Aaron went into the **t** of the congregation,	168
	10: 7	ye shall not go out from the door of the **t** of	168
	10: 9	when ye go into the **t** of the congregation,	168
	12: 6	unto the door of the **t** of the congregation,	168
	14:11	*at* the door of the **t** of the congregation:	168
	14:23	unto the door of the **t** of the congregation,	168
	15:14	unto the door of the **t** of the congregation,	168
	15:29	to the door of the **t** of the congregation.	168
	15:31	when they defile my **t** that *is* among them.	4908
	16: 7	*at* the door of the **t** of the congregation.	168
	16:16	so shall he do for the **t** of the congregation,	168
	16:17	there shall be no man in the **t** of	168
	16:20	the holy *place*, and the **t** of the congregation,	168
	16:23	Aaron shall come into the **t** of	168
	16:33	he shall make an atonement for the **t** of	168
	17: 4	bringeth it not unto the door of the **t** of	168
	17: 4	the LORD before the **t** of the LORD;	4908
	17: 5	unto the door of the **t** of the congregation,	168
	17: 6	*at* the door of the **t** of the congregation,	168
	17: 9	bringeth it not unto the door of the **t** of	168
	19:21	unto the door of the **t** of the congregation,	168
	24: 3	the Testimony, in the **t** of the congregation,	168
	26:11	I will set my **t** amongst you: and my soul	4908
Nu	1: 1	in the **t** of the congregation, on the first *day*	168
	1:50	thou shalt appoint the Levites over the **t** of	4908
	1:50	they shall bear the **t**, and all the vessels	4908
	1:50	unto it, and shall encamp round about the **t**.	4908
	1:51	when the **t** setteth forward, the Levites shall	4908
	1:51	when the **t** is to be pitched, the Levites	4908
	1:53	the Levites shall pitch round about the **t** of	4908
	1:53	the Levites shall keep the charge of the **t** of	4908
	2: 2	far off about the **t** of the congregation shall	168
	2:17	the **t** of the congregation shall set forward	168
	3: 7	before the **t** of the congregation,	168
	3: 7	the congregation, to do the service of the **t**.	4908
	3: 8	they shall keep all the instruments of the **t** of	168
	3: 8	children of Israel, to do the service of the **t**.	4908
	3:23	shall pitch behind the **t** westward.	4908
	3:25	the charge of the sons of Gershon in the **t** of	168
	3:25	of the congregation *shall be* the **t**,	4908
	3:25	the hanging for the door of the **t** of	168
	3:26	which *is* by the **t**, and by the altar round	4908
	3:29	shall pitch on the side of the **t** southward.	4908
	3:35	*these* shall pitch on the side of the **t**	4908
	3:36	sons of Merari *shall be* the boards of the **t**,	4908
	3:38	those that encamp before the **t** toward	4908
	3:38	*even* before the **t** of the congregation	168
	4: 3	to do the work in the **t** of the congregation.	168
	4: 4	sons of Kohath in the **t** of the congregation,	168
	4:15	sons of Kohath in the **t** of the congregation.	168
	4:16	*and* the oversight of all the **t**, and of all that	4908
	4:23	to do the work in the **t** of the congregation.	168
	4:25	they shall bear the curtains of the **t**, and	4908
	4:25	the **t** of the congregation, his covering, and	168
	4:25	the hanging for the door of the **t** of	168
	4:26	which *is* by the **t** and by the altar round	4908
	4:28	sons of Gershon in the **t** of the congregation:	168
	4:30	to do the work of the **t** of the congregation.	168
	4:31	according to all their service in the **t** of	168
	4:31	the boards of the **t**, and the bars thereof,	4908
	4:33	all their service, in the **t** of the congregation,	168
	4:35	for the work in the **t** of the congregation:	168

Nu 4:37 all that *might* do service in the t of 168
4:39 for the work in the t of the congregation, 168
4:41 of all that *might* do service in the t of 168
4:43 for the work in the t of the congregation, 168
4:47 the service of the burden in the t of 168
5:17 of the dust that is in the floor of the t 4908
6:10 to the door of the t of the congregation: 168
6:13 he shall be brought unto the door of the t of 168
6:18 *at* the door of the t of the congregation, 168
7: 1 on the day that Moses had fully set up the t, 4908
7: 3 an ox: and they brought them before the t. 4908
7: 5 that they may be to do the service of the t of 168
7:89 when Moses was gone into the t of 168
8: 9 thou shalt bring the Levites before the t of 168
8:15 to do the service of the t of the congregation: 168
8:19 of Israel in the t of the congregation, 168
8:22 in the t of the congregation before Aaron, 168
8:24 upon the service of the t of the congregation: 168
8:26 shall minister with their brethren in the t of 168
9:15 on the day that the t was reared up, 4908
9:15 the cloud covered the t, *namely,* the tent of 4908
9:15 at even there was upon the t as it were 4908
9:17 And when the cloud was taken up from the t, 168
9:18 as long as the cloud abode upon the t they 4908
9:19 when the cloud tarried long upon the t 4908
9:20 when the cloud was a few days upon the t; 4908
9:22 or a year, that the cloud tarried upon the t, 4908
10: 3 thee at the door of the t of the congregation. 168
10:11 *that* the cloud was taken up from off the t 4908
10:17 the t was taken down; and the sons of 4908
10:17 sons of Merari set forward, bearing the t. 4908
10:21 *the other* did set up the t against they came. 4908
11:16 bring them unto the t of the congregation, 168
11:24 the people, and set them round about the t. 168
11:26 were written, but went not out unto the t: 168
12: 4 Come out ye three unto the t of 168
12: 5 stood *in* the door of the t, and called Aaron 168
12:10 the cloud departed from off the t; and 168
14:10 the glory of the LORD appeared in the t of 168
16: 9 to do the service of the t of the LORD, 4908
16:18 stood *in* the door of the t of the congregation 168
16:19 unto the door of the t of the congregation: 168
16:24 Get you up from about the t of Korah, 4908
16:27 So they gat up from the t of Korah, Dathan, 4908
16:42 that they looked toward the t of 168
16:43 Aaron came before the t of the congregation. 168
16:50 unto the door of the t of the congregation: 168
17: 4 thou shalt lay them up in the t of 168
17: 7 rods before the LORD in the t of Witness. 168
17: 8 that on the morrow Moses went into the t of 168
17:13 near unto the t of the LORD shall die: 4908
18: 2 thy sons with thee *shall minister* before the t 168
18: 3 keep thy charge, and the charge of all the t: 168
18: 4 keep the charge of the t of the congregation, 168
18: 4 the congregation, for all the service of the t: 168
18: 6 to do the service of the t of the congregation. 168
18:21 *even* the service of the t of the congregation. 168
18:22 come nigh the t of the congregation, 168
18:23 the Levites shall do the service of the t of 168
18:31 for it *is* your reward for your service in the t 168
19: 4 sprinkle of her blood directly before the t of 168
19:13 not himself, defileth the t of the LORD; 4908
20: 6 unto the door of the t of the congregation, 168
25: 6 who *were* weeping *before* the door of the t 168
27: 2 *by* the door of the t of the congregation, 168
31:30 which keep the charge of the t of 4908
31:47 which kept the charge of the t of 4908
31:54 and brought it into the t of the congregation, 168
Dt 31:14 present yourselves in the t of 168
31:14 presented themselves in the t of 168
31:15 the LORD appeared in the t in a pillar of a 168
31:15 of the cloud stood over the door of the t. 168
Jos 18: 1 and set up the t of the congregation there. 168
19:51 *at* the door of the t of the congregation. 168
22:19 wherein the LORD'S t dwelleth, and 4908
22:29 of the LORD our God that *is* before his t. 4908
1Sa 2:22 *at* the door of the t of the congregation. 168
2Sa 6:17 in the midst of the t that David had pitched 168
7: 6 but have walked in a tent and in a t. 4908
1Ki 1:39 the priest took a horn of oil out of the t, 168
2:28 And Joab fled unto the t of the LORD, and 168
2:29 that Joab was fled unto the t of the LORD; 168
2:30 Benaiah came to the t of the LORD, and 168
8: 4 the t of the congregation, and all the holy 168
8: 4 all the holy vessels that *were* in the t, 168
1Ch 6:32 of the t of the congregation with singing, 168
6:48 *of* service of the t of the house of God. 4908
9:19 of the service, keepers of the gates of the t: 168
9:21 of the door of the t of the congregation. 168
9:23 *namely,* the house of the t, by wards. 168
16:39 before the t of the LORD in the high place 4908
17: 5 tent to tent, and from *one* t *to another.* 4908
21:29 For the t of the LORD, which Moses 4908
23:26 *they* shall no *more* carry the t, nor any 4908
23:32 that they should keep the charge of the t of 168
2Ch 1: 3 for there was the t of the congregation of 168
1: 5 he put before the t of the LORD: 4908
1: 6 which *was* at the t of the congregation, and 168
1:13 from before the t of the congregation, and 168
5: 5 the t of the congregation, and all the holy 168
5: 5 all the holy vessels that *were* in the t, these 168
24: 6 congregation of Israel, for the t of Witness? 168
Job 5:24 thou shalt know that thy t *shall be in* peace; 168
18: 6 The light shall be dark in his t, and 168
18:14 His confidence shall be rooted out of his t, 168
18:15 It shall dwell in his t, because *it is* none of 168
19:12 against me, and encamp round about my t. 168
20:26 it shall go ill with him that is left in his t. 168
29: 4 when the secret of God *was* upon my t; 168
31:31 If the men of my t said not, O that we had of 168
36:29 of the clouds, *or* the noise of his t? 5521
Ps 15: 1 LORD, who shall abide in thy t? who shall 168
19: 4 the world. In them hath he set a t for the sun, 168
27: 5 in the secret of his t shall he hide me; 168
27: 6 will I offer in his t sacrifices of joy; 168
61: 4 I will abide in thy t for ever: I will trust in 168
76: 2 In Salem also is his t, and his dwelling 5520
78:60 So that he forsook the t of Shiloh, the tent 4908
78:67 Moreover he refused the t of Joseph, and 168
132: 3 Surely I will not come into the t of my 168
Pr 14:11 but the t of the upright shall flourish. 168
Isa 4: 6 there shall be a t for a shadow in 5521
16: 5 he shall sit upon it in truth in the t of David, 168
33:20 a t *that* shall not be taken down; 168
Jer 10:20 My t is spoiled, and all my cords are broken: 168
La 2: 4 to the eye, in the t of the daughter of Zion: 168
2: 6 he hath violently taken away his t, as *if it* 7900
Eze 37:27 My t also shall be with them: yea, I will be 4908
41: 1 other side, *which was* the breadth of the t. 168
Am 5:26 But ye have borne the t of your Moloch and 5522
9:11 In that day will I raise up the t of David 5521
Ac 7:43 ye took up the t of Moloch, and the star of *4633*
7:44 Our fathers had the t of Witness in *4633*
7:46 and desired to find a t for the God of Jacob. *4638*
15:16 and will build again the t of David, *4633*
2Co 5: 1 our earthly house of *this* t were dissolved, *4636*
5: 4 For we that are in *this* t do groan, *4636*
Heb 8: 2 and of the true t, which the Lord pitched, *4633*
8: 5 of God when he was about to make the t: *4633*
9: 2 For there was a t made; the first, wherein *4633*
9: 3 the t which is called the holiest of all; *4633*
9: 6 the priests went always into the first t, *4633*
9: 8 while as the first t was yet standing: *4633*
9:11 by a greater and more perfect t, not made *4633*
9:21 he sprinkled with blood both the t, *4633*
13:10 they have no right to eat which serve the t. *4633*
2Pe 1:13 I think it meet, as long as I am in this t, *4638*
1:14 that shortly *I* must put off *this* my t, *4638*
Rev 13: 6 and his t, and them that dwell in heaven. *4633*
15: 5 the temple of the t of the testimony in *4633*
21: 3 the t of God *is* with men, and he will dwell *4633*

TABERNACLES (30) [TABERNACLE]

Lev 23:34 feast of t *for* seven days unto the LORD. 5521
Nu 24: 5 are thy tents, O Jacob, *and* thy t, O Israel! 4908
Dt 16:13 Thou shalt observe the feast of t seven 5521
16:16 in the feast of weeks, and in the feast of t: 5521
31:10 of the year of release, in the feast of t, 5521
2Ch 8:13 in the feast of weeks, and in the feast of t. 5521
Ezr 3: 4 They kept also the feast of t, as it is written, 5521
Job 11:14 and let not wickedness dwell in thy t. 168
12: 6 The t of robbers prosper, and they that 168
15:34 and fire shall consume the t of bribery. 168
22:23 thou shalt put away iniquity far from thy t. 168
Ps 43: 3 bring me unto thy holy hill, and to thy t. 4908
46: 4 the holy *place* of the t of the most High. 4908
78:51 the chief of *their* strength in the t of Ham: 168
83: 6 The t of Edom, and the Ishmaelites; 168

Ps 84: 1 How amiable *are* thy **t**, O LORD of hosts! 4908
118:15 and salvation *is* in the **t** of the righteous: 168
132: 7 We will go into his **t**: we will worship at 4908
Da 11:45 he shall plant the **t** of his palace between 168
Hos 9: 6 shall possess them: thorns *shall be* in their **t**. 168
12: 9 of Egypt will yet make thee to dwell in **t**, 168
Zec 14:16 LORD of hosts, and to keep the feast of **t**. 5521
14:18 that come not up to keep the feast of **t**. 5521
14:19 that come not up to keep the feast of **t**. 5521
Mal 2:12 out of the **t** of Jacob, and him that offereth 168
Mt 17: 4 if thou wilt, let us make here three **t**: *4633*
Mk 9: 5 and let us make three **t**; one for thee, and *4633*
Lk 9:33 and let us make three **t**; one for thee, and *4633*
Jn 7: 2 Now the Jews' feast of **t** was at hand. *4634*
Heb 11: 9 as *in* a strange *country,* dwelling in **t** with *4633*

TABITHA (2)

Ac 9:36 was at Joppa a certain disciple named **T**, *5000*
9:40 and turning *him* to the body said, **T**, arise. *5000*

TABLE (73) [TABLES]

Ex 25:23 Thou shalt also make a **t** *of* shittim wood: 7979
25:27 be for places of the staves to bear the **t**. 7979
25:28 that the **t** may be borne with them. 7979
25:30 thou shalt set upon the **t** shewbread before 7979
26:35 thou shalt set the **t** without the vail, and 7979
26:35 the candlestick over against the **t** on 7979
26:35 and thou shalt put the **t** on the north side. 7979
30:27 the **t** and all his vessels, and the candlestick 7979
31: 8 the **t** and his furniture, and the pure 7979
35:13 The **t**, and his staves, and all his vessels, 7979
37:10 he made the **t** *of* shittim wood: two cubits 7979
37:14 the places for the staves to bear the **t**. 7979
37:15 and overlaid them with gold, to bear the **t**. 7979
37:16 he made the vessels which *were* upon the **t**, 7979
39:36 The **t**, *and* all the vessels thereof, and 7979
40: 4 thou shalt bring in the **t**, and set in order 7979
40:22 he put the **t** in the tent of the congregation, 7979
40:24 over against the **t**, on the side of 7979
Lev 24: 6 a row, upon the pure **t** before the LORD. 7979
Nu 3:31 the **t**, and the candlestick, and the altars, 7979
4: 7 upon the **t** of shewbread they shall spread a 7979
Jdg 1: 7 cut off, gathered *their meat* under my **t**: 7979
1Sa 20:29 Therefore he cometh not unto the king's **t**. 7979
20:34 So Jonathan arose from the **t** in fierce 7979
2Sa 9: 7 and thou shalt eat bread at my **t** continually. 7979
9:10 master's son shall eat bread alway at my **t**. 7979
9:11 *said the king,* he shall eat at my **t**, 7979
9:13 for he did eat continually at the king's **t**; 7979
19:28 among them that did eat at thine own **t**. 7979
1Ki 2: 7 and let them be of *those* that eat at thy **t**: 7979
4:27 for all that came unto king Solomon's **t**, 7979
7:48 the altar of gold, and the **t** *of* gold, 7979
10: 5 the meat of his **t**, and the sitting of his 7979
13:20 it came to pass, as they sat at the **t**, that 7979
18:19 four hundred, which eat *at* Jezebel's **t**. 7979
2Ki 4:10 and a **t**, and a stool, and a candlestick: 7979
1Ch 28:16 of shewbread, for **every t**; 7979+7979+2050.1
2Ch 9: 4 the meat of his **t**, and the sitting of his 7979
13:11 also *set they* in order upon the pure **t**; 7979
29:18 the shewbread **t**, with all the vessels 7979
Ne 5:17 Moreover *there were* at my **t** an hundred 7979
Job 36:16 that which should be set on thy **t** *should be* 7979
Ps 23: 5 Thou preparest a **t** before me in 7979
69:22 Let their **t** become a snare before them: and 7979
78:19 Can God furnish a **t** in the wilderness? 7979
128: 3 children like olive plants round about thy **t**. 7979
Pr 3: 3 write them upon the **t** of thine heart: 3871
7: 3 write them upon the **t** of thine heart. 3871
9: 2 her wine; she hath also furnished her **t**. 7979
SS 1:12 While the king *sitteth* at his **t**, my spikenard 4524
Isa 21: 5 Prepare the **t**, watch *in* the watchtower, eat, 7979
30: 8 write it before them in a **t**, and note it in a 3871
65:11 that prepare a **t** for *that* troop, and 7979
Jer 17: 1 *it is* graven upon the **t** of their heart, and 3871
Eze 23:41 a stately bed, and a **t** prepared before it, 7979
39:20 Thus ye shall be filled at my **t** *with* horses 7979
41:22 This *is* the **t** that *is* before the LORD. 7979
44:16 they shall come near to my **t**, to minister 7979
Da 11:27 and they shall speak lies at one **t**; 7979
Mal 1: 7 The **t** of the LORD *is* contemptible. 7979
1:12 ye say, The **t** of the LORD *is* polluted; 7979
Mt 15:27 the crumbs which fall from their masters' **t**. *5132*
Mk 7:28 yet the dogs under the **t** eat of *5132*
Lk 1:63 And he asked for a **writing t**, and wrote, *4093*
16:21 crumbs which fell from the rich *man's* **t**: *5132*
22:21 him that betrayeth me *is* with me on the **t**. *5132*
22:30 may eat and drink at my **t** in my kingdom, *5132*
Jn 12: 2 of them that **sat at the t with** him. *4873*
13:28 Now no *man* at the **t** knew for what intent he *345*
Ro 11: 9 Let their **t** be made a snare, and a trap, and *5132*
1Co 10:21 ye cannot be partakers of the Lord's **t**, and *5132*
10:21 of the Lord's table, and of the **t** of devils. *5132*
Heb 9: 2 and the **t**, and the shewbread; *5132*

TABLES (56) [TABLE, TABLETS]

Ex 24:12 I will give thee **t** of stone, and a law, and 3871
31:18 two **t** of Testimony, tables of stone, 3871
31:18 two tables of Testimony, **t** of stone, 3871
32:15 the two **t** of the Testimony *were* in his 3871
32:15 the **t** *were* written on both their sides; 3871
32:16 the **t** *were* the work of God, and the writing 3871
32:16 *was* the writing of God, graven upon the **t**. 3871
32:19 he cast the **t** out of his hands, and 3871
34: 1 Hew thee two **t** of stone like unto the first: 3871
34: 1 I will write upon *these* **t** the words that 3871
34: 1 tables the words that were in the first **t**, 3871
34: 4 he hewed two **t** of stone like unto the first; 3871
34: 4 and took in his hand the two **t** of stone. 3871
34:28 he wrote upon the **t** the words of 3871
34:29 the two **t** of Testimony in Moses' hand, 3871
Dt 4:13 and he wrote them upon two **t** of stone. 3871
5:22 he wrote them in two **t** of stone, and 3871
9: 9 up into the mount to receive the **t** of stone, 3871
9: 9 *even* the **t** of the covenant which 3871
9:10 the LORD delivered unto me two **t** of 3871
9:11 *that* the LORD gave me the two **t** of stone, 3871
9:11 tables of stone, *even* the **t** of the covenant. 3871
9:15 the two **t** of the covenant *were* in my two 3871
9:17 I took the two **t**, and cast them out of my 3871
10: 1 Hew thee two **t** of stone like unto the first, 3871
10: 2 I will write on the **t** the words that were in 3871
10: 2 that were in the first **t** which thou brakest, 3871
10: 3 hewed two **t** of stone like unto the first, and 3871
10: 3 the mount, having the two **t** in mine hand. 3871
10: 4 he wrote on the **t**, according to the first 3871
10: 5 and put the **t** in the ark which I had made; 3871
1Ki 8: 9 *There was* nothing in the ark save the two **t** 3871
1Ch 28:16 *by* weight *he gave* gold for the **t** of 7979
28:16 and *likewise* silver for the **t** of silver: 7979
2Ch 4: 8 He made also ten **t**, and placed *them* in 7979
4:19 the **t** whereon the shewbread *was set;* 7979
5:10 *There was* nothing in the ark save the two **t** 3871
Isa 28: 8 For all **t** are full *of* vomit *and* filthiness, *so* 7979
Eze 40:39 in the porch of the gate *were* two **t** on this 7979
40:39 two **t** on that side, to slay thereon the burnt 7979
40:40 to the entry of the north gate, *were* two **t**; 7979
40:40 *was* at the porch of the gate, *were* two **t**. 7979
40:41 Four **t** *were* on this side, and four tables on 7979
40:41 four **t** on that side, by the side of the gate; 7979
40:41 eight **t**, whereupon they slew *their* 7979
40:42 the four **t** *were* of hewn stone for the burnt 7979
40:43 and upon the **t** *was* the flesh of the offering. 7979
Hab 2: 2 Write the vision, and make *it* plain upon **t**, 3871
Mt 21:12 and overthrew the **t** of the moneychangers, *5132*
Mk 7: 4 of cups, and pots, brasen vessels, and of **t**. *2825*
11:15 and overthrew the **t** of the money-changers, *5132*
Jn 2:15 the changers' money, and overthrew the **t**; *5132*
Ac 6: 2 should leave the word of God, and serve **t**. *5132*
2Co 3: 3 not in **t** of stone, but in fleshy tables of *4109*
3: 3 tables of stone, but in fleshy **t** of the heart. *4109*
Heb 9: 4 rod that budded, and the **t** of the covenant; *4109*

TABLETS (3) [TABLES]

Ex 35:22 and earrings, and rings, and **t**, 3558
Nu 31:50 chains, and bracelets, rings, earrings, and **t**, 3558
Isa 3:20 and the **t**, and the earrings, 1004+5315

TABOR (10) [AZNOTH-TABOR, CHISLOTH-TABOR]

Jos 19:22 the coast reacheth to **T**, and Shahazimah, 8396
Jdg 4: 6 *saying,* Go and draw toward mount **T**, and 8396
4:12 son of Abinoam was gone up *to* mount **T**. 8396
4:14 So Barak went down from mount **T**, and 8396
8:18 of men *were they* whom ye slew at **T**? 8396
1Sa 10: 3 thou shalt come to the plain of **T**, and 8396
1Ch 6:77 with her suburbs, **T** with her suburbs: 8396
Ps 89:12 **T** and Hermon shall rejoice in thy name. 8396
Jer 46:18 Surely as **T** *is* among the mountains, and 8396

Hos 5: 1 snare on Mizpah, and a net spread upon **T**. 8396

TABRET (4) [TABRETS]
Ge 31:27 and with songs, with **t**, and with harp? 8596
1Sa 10: 5 and a **t**, and a pipe, and a harp, before them; 8596
Job 17: 6 of the people; and aforetime I was *as* a **t**. 8611
Isa 5:12 and the viol, the **t**, and pipe, and wine, 8596

TABRETS (5) [TABRET]
1Sa 18: 6 with **t**, with joy, and with instruments of 8596
Isa 24: 8 The mirth of **t** ceaseth, the noise of them 8596
30:32 lay upon him, *it* shall be with **t** and harps: 8596
Jer 31: 4 thou shalt again be adorned *with* thy **t**, and 8596
Eze 28:13 the workmanship of thy **t** and of thy pipes 8596

TABRIMMON See TABRIMON

TABRIMON (1)
1Ki 15:18 the son of **T**, the son of Hezion, king of 2886

TABRING (1)
Na 2: 7 the voice of doves, **t** upon their breasts. 8608

TACHES (10)
Ex 26: 6 thou shalt make fifty **t** of gold, and 7165
26: 6 and couple the curtains together with the **t**: 7165
26:11 thou shalt make fifty **t** of brass, and put 7165
26:11 put the **t** into the loops, and couple the tent 7165
26:33 thou shalt hang up the vail under the **t**, 7165
35:11 his **t**, and his boards, his bars, his pillars, 7165
36:13 he made fifty **t** of gold, and coupled 7165
36:13 the curtains one unto another with the **t**: 7165
36:18 he made fifty **t** of brass to couple the tent 7165
39:33 his **t**, his boards, his bars, and his pillars, 7165

TACHMONITE (1)
2Sa 23: 8 The **T** that sat in the seat, chief among 8461

TACKLING (1) [TACKLINGS]
Ac 27:19 *out* with our own hands the **t** of the ship. *4631*

TACKLINGS (1) [TACKLING]
Isa 33:23 Thy **t** are loosed; they could not well 2256

TADMOR (2)
1Ki 9:18 and **T** in the wilderness, in the land, 8412
2Ch 8: 4 he built **T** in the wilderness, and all 8412

TAHAN (2) [TAHANITES]
Nu 26:35 of **T**, the family of the Tahanites. 8465
1Ch 7:25 and Telah his son, and **T** his son, 8465

TAHANITES (1) [TAHAN]
Nu 26:35 of Tahan, the family of the **T**. 8470

TAHAPANES (1) [TAHPANHES]
Jer 2:16 and **T** have broken the crown of thy head. 8471

TAHASH See THAHASH

TAHATH (6)
Nu 33:26 from Makheloth, and encamped at **T**. 8480
33:27 they departed from **T**, and pitched at Tarah. 8480
1Ch 6:24 **T** his son, Uriel his son, Uzziah his son, 8480
6:37 The son of **T**, the son of Assir, the son of 8480
7:20 **T** his son, and Eladah his son, and 8480
7:20 his son, and Eladah his son, and **T** his son, 8480

TAHKEMONITE See TACHMONITE

TAHPANHES (5) [TAHAPANES, TEHAPHNEHES]
Jer 43: 7 of the LORD: thus came they *even* to **T**. 8471
43: 8 word of the LORD unto Jeremiah in **T**, 8471
43: 9 *is* at the entry of Pharaoh's house in **T**, 8471
44: 1 at **T**, and at Noph, and in the country of 8471
46:14 in Migdol, and publish in Noph and in **T**: 8471

TAHPENES (3)
1Ki 11:19 of his own wife, the sister of **T** the queen. 8472
11:20 the sister of **T** bare him Genubath his son, 8472
11:20 whom **T** weaned in Pharaoh's house: 8472

TAHREA (1)
1Ch 9:41 and Melech, and **T**, *and Ahaz*. 8475

TAHTIM-HODSHI (1)
2Sa 24: 6 they came to Gilead, and to the land of **T**; 8483

TAIL (10) [TAILS]
Ex 4: 4 Put forth thine hand, and take it by the **t**. 2180
Dt 28:13 shall make thee the head, and not the **t**; 2180
28:44 he shall be the head, and thou shalt be the **t**. 2180
Jdg 15: 4 turned **t** to tail, and put a firebrand in 2180
15: 4 turned tail to **t**, and put a firebrand in 2180
Job 40:17 He moveth his **t** like a cedar: the sinews of 2180
Isa 9:14 LORD will cut off from Israel head and **t**, 2180
9:15 the prophet that teacheth lies, he *is* the **t**. 2180
19:15 which the head or **t**, branch or rush, 2180
Rev 12: 4 And his **t** drew the third *part* of the stars of *3769*

TAILS (6) [TAIL]
Jdg 15: 4 put a firebrand in the midst between two **t**. 2180
Isa 7: 4 neither be fainthearted for the two **t** of 2180
Rev 9:10 And they had **t** like unto scorpions, and *3769*
9:10 and there were stings in their **t**: *3769*
9:19 their power is in their mouth, and in their **t**: *3769*
9:19 for their **t** *were* like unto serpents, and *3769*

TAKE (874) [OVERTAKE, TAKEN, TAKER, TAKEST, TAKETH, TAKING, TOOK, TOOKEST, UNTAKEN] See Index

TAKEN (338) [TAKE] See Index

TAKER (1) [TAKE] See Index

TAKEST (9) [TAKE] See Index

TAKETH (74) [TAKE] See Index

TAKING (20) [TAKE] See Index

TALE (5) [TALEBEARER, TALES]
Ex 5: 8 the **t** of the bricks, which they did make 4971
5:18 yet shall ye deliver the **t** of bricks. 8506
1Sa 18:27 and they **gave** them **in full t** to the king, 4390
1Ch 9:28 that they should bring them in and out by **t**. 4557
Ps 90: 9 we spend our years as a **t** *that is told*. 1899

TALEBEARER (6) [BEAR, TALE]
Lev 19:16 go up and down *as* a **t** among thy people: 7400
Pr 11:13 A **t** revealeth secrets: but he that is of 1980+7400
18: 8 The words of a **t** *are* as wounds, and 5372
20:19 He that goeth about *as* a **t** revealeth secrets: 7400
26:20 so where *there is* no **t**, the strife ceaseth. 5372
26:22 The words of a **t** *are* as wounds, and 5372

TALENT (14) [TALENTS]
Ex 25:39 *Of* a **t** of pure gold shall he make it, with all 3603
37:24 *Of* a **t** *of* pure gold made he it, and all 3603
38:27 of the hundred talents, a **t** for a socket. 3603
2Sa 12:30 the weight whereof *was* a **t** of gold with 3603
1Ki 20:39 his life, or else thou shalt pay a **t** of silver. 3603
2Ki 5:22 a **t** of silver, and two changes of garments. 3603
23:33 an hundred talents of silver, and a **t** of gold. 3603
1Ch 20: 2 found it to weigh a **t** of gold, and 3603
2Ch 36: 3 an hundred talents of silver and a **t** of gold. 3603
Zec 5: 7 behold, there *was* lift up a **t** of lead: and 3603
Mt 25:24 Then he which had received the one **t** came *5007*
25:25 and went and hid thy **t** in the earth: *5007*
25:28 Take therefore the **t** from him, and give *it* *5007*
Rev 16:21 *every stone* about the **weight of a t**: *5006*

TALENTS (51) [TALENT]
Ex 38:24 was twenty and nine **t**, and seven hundred 3603
38:25 of the congregation *was* an hundred **t**, 3603
38:27 of the hundred **t** of silver were cast 3603
38:27 an hundred sockets of the hundred **t**, 3603
38:29 the brass of the offering *was* seventy **t**, and 3603
1Ki 9:14 Hiram sent to the king sixscore **t** of gold. 3603
9:28 four hundred and twenty **t**, and brought *it* to 3603
10:10 the king an hundred and twenty **t** of gold, 3603
10:14 six hundred threescore and six **t** of gold, 3603
16:24 hill Samaria of Shemer for **two t** of silver, 3603
2Ki 5: 5 took with him ten **t** of silver, and 3603
5:23 Naaman said, Be content, take **two t**. 3603
5:23 and bound **two t** of silver in two bags, 3603
15:19 Menahem gave Pul a thousand **t** of silver, 3603
18:14 king of Judah three hundred **t** of silver 3603
18:14 talents of silver and thirty **t** of gold. 3603
23:33 put the land to a tribute of an hundred **t** of 3603
1Ch 19: 6 the children of Ammon sent a thousand **t** of 3603
22:14 the LORD an hundred thousand **t** *of* gold, 3603
22:14 and a thousand thousand **t** *of* silver; 3603
29: 4 *Even* three thousand **t** of gold, of the gold 3603

1Ch 29: 4 and seven thousand **t** of refined silver, 3603
29: 7 of the house of God *of* gold five thousand **t** 3603
29: 7 *of* silver ten thousand **t**, and *of* brass 3603
29: 7 *of* brass eighteen thousand **t**, and 3603
29: 7 and one hundred thousand **t** *of* iron. 3603
2Ch 3: 8 with fine gold, *amounting* to six hundred **t**. 3603
8:18 thence four hundred and fifty **t** of gold, 3603
9: 9 the king an hundred and twenty **t** of gold, 3603
9:13 and threescore and six **t** of gold; 3603
25: 6 out of Israel for an hundred **t** of silver. 3603
25: 9 what *shall we* do for the hundred **t** which I 3603
27: 5 him the same year an hundred **t** of silver, 3603
36: 3 condemned the land in an hundred **t** of 3603
Ezr 7:22 Unto an hundred **t** *of* silver, and to an 3604
8:26 their hand six hundred and fifty **t** *of* silver, 3603
8:26 silver vessels an hundred **t**, *and of* gold an 3603
8:26 hundred talents, *and of* gold an hundred **t**; 3603
Est 3: 9 I will pay ten thousand **t** of silver to 3603
Mt 18:24 unto him, which ought him ten thousand **t**. *5007*
25:15 And unto one he gave five **t**, to another *5007*
25:16 Then he that had received the five **t** went *5007*
25:16 with the same, and made *them* other five **t**. *5007*
25:20 And *so* he that had received five **t** came and *5007*
25:20 five talents came and brought other five **t**, *5007*
25:20 Lord, thou deliveredst unto me five **t**: *5007*
25:20 I have gained besides them five **t** moe. *5007*
25:22 He also that had received two **t** came and *5007*
25:22 said, Lord, thou deliveredst unto me two **t**: *5007*
25:22 I have gained two other **t** besides them. *5007*
25:28 and give *it* unto him which hath ten **t**. *5007*

TALES (2) [TALE]
Eze 22: 9 In thee are men that **carry t** to shed blood: 7400
Lk 24:11 And their words seemed to them as **idle t**, *3026*

TALITHA (1)
Mk 5:41 by the hand, and said unto her, **T** CUMI; *5008*

TALK (24) [TALKED, TALKERS, TALKEST, TALKETH, TALKING] See Index

TALKED (42) [TALK] See Index

TALKERS (2) [TALK] See Index

TALKEST (3) [TALK] See Index

TALKETH (2) [TALK] See Index

TALKING (9) [TALK] See Index

TALL (5) [TALLER]
Dt 2:10 a people great, and many, and **t**, as 7311
2:21 A people great, and many, and **t**, as 7311
9: 2 A people great and **t**, the children of 7311
2Ki 19:23 will cut down the **t** cedar trees thereof, *and* 6967
Isa 37:24 I will cut down the **t** cedars thereof, *and* 6967

TALLER (1) [TALL]
Dt 1:28 The people *is* greater and **t** than we; 7311

TALMAI (6)
Nu 13:22 where Ahiman, Sheshai, and **T**, 8526
Jos 15:14 Sheshai, and Ahiman, and **T**, the children 8526
Jdg 1:10 and they slew Sheshai, and Ahiman, and **T**. 8526
2Sa 3: 3 Maacah the daughter of **T** king of Geshur; 8526
13:37 Absalom fled, and went to **T**, the son of 8526
1Ch 3: 2 Maachah the daughter of **T** king of Geshur: 8526

TALMON (5)
1Ch 9:17 and **T**, and Ahiman, and their brethren: 2929
Ezr 2:42 the children of Ater, the children of **T**, 2929
Ne 7:45 the children of Ater, the children of **T**, 2929
11:19 **T**, and their brethren that kept the gates, 2929
12:25 Obadiah, Meshullam, **T**, Akkub, 2929

TAMAH (1)
Ne 7:55 the children of Sisera, the children of **T**, 8547

TAMAR (24) [BAAL-TAMAR, HAZAZON-TAMAR, HAZEZON-TAMAR]
Ge 38: 6 for Er his firstborn, whose name *was* **T**. 8559
38:11 said Judah to **T** his daughter in law, 8559
38:11 as his brethren *did.* And **T** went and 8559
38:13 it was told **T**, saying, Behold thy father in 8559
38:24 **T** thy daughter in law hath played 8559
Ru 4:12 house of Pharez, whom **T** bare unto Judah, 8559
2Sa 13: 1 David had a fair sister, whose name *was* **T**; 8559
13: 2 *so* vexed, that he fell sick for his sister **T**; 8559
13: 4 Amnon said unto him, I love **T**, my brother 8559
13: 5 let my sister **T** come, and give me meat, 8559
13: 6 let **T** my sister come, and make *me* a 8559
13: 7 David sent home to **T**, saying, Go now *to* 8559
13: 8 So **T** went *to* her brother Amnon's house; 8559
13:10 Amnon said unto **T**, Bring the meat *into* 8559
13:10 **T** took the cakes which she had made, and 8559
13:19 **T** put ashes on her head, and rent her 8559
13:20 So **T** remained desolate *in* her brother 8559
13:22 because he had forced his sister **T**. 8559
13:32 from the day that he forced his sister **T**. 8559
14:27 and one daughter, whose name *was* **T**: 8559
1Ch 2: 4 **T** his daughter in law bare him Pharez and 8559
3: 9 sons of the concubines, and **T** their sister. 8559
Eze 47:19 from **T** *even* to the waters of strife *in* 8559
48:28 the border shall be even from **T** *unto* 8559

TAMBOURINE; TAMBOURINES See TABRET; TABRETS; TIMBREL

TAME (2) [TAMED]
Mk 5: 4 in pieces: neither could any *man* **t** him. *1150*
Jas 3: 8 But the tongue can no man **t**; *it is* an unruly *1150*

TAMED (2) [TAME]
Jas 3: 7 is **t**, and hath been tamed of mankind: *1150*
3: 7 is tamed, and hath been **t** of mankind: *1150*

TAMMUZ (1)
Eze 8:14 behold, there sat women weeping for **T**. 8542

TANACH (1)
Jos 21:25 **T** with her suburbs, and Gath-rimmon with 8590

TANHUMETH (2)
2Ki 25:23 Seraiah the son of **T** the Netophathite, and 8576
Jer 40: 8 Seraiah the son of **T**, and the sons of Ephai 8576

TANNER (3)
Ac 9:43 many days in Joppa with one Simon a **t**. *1038*
10: 6 He lodgeth with one Simon a **t**, *1038*
10:32 he is lodged in the house of *one* Simon a **t** *1038*

TAPESTRY (2)
Pr 7:16 I have deckt my bed *with* **coverings of t**, 4765
31:22 She maketh herself **coverings of t**; 4765

TAPHATH (1)
1Ki 4:11 which had **T** the daughter of Solomon to 2955

TAPPUAH (6) [BETH-TAPPUAH]
Jos 12:17 The king of **T**, one; the king of Hepher, 8599
15:34 And Zanoah, and En-gannim, **T**, and Enam, 8599
16: 8 The border went *out* from **T** westward *unto* 8599
17: 8 *Now* Manasseh had the land of **T**: but 8599
17: 8 **T** on the border of Manasseh *belonged* to 8599
1Ch 2:43 Korah, and **T**, and Rekem, and Shema. 8599

TAR PITS See SLIMEPITS

TARAH (2)
Nu 33:27 departed from Tahath, and pitched at **T**. 8646
33:28 they removed from **T**, and pitched in 8646

TARALAH (1)
Jos 18:27 And Rekem, and Irpeel, and **T**, 8634

TARE (4) [TEAR]
2Sa 13:31 and **t** his garments, and lay on the earth; 7167
2Ki 2:24 and **t** forty and two children of them. 1234
Mk 9:20 he saw him, straightway the spirit **t** him; *4682*
Lk 9:42 **t** *him.* And Jesus rebuked the unclean spirit, *4952*

TAREA (1)
1Ch 8:35 and Melech, and **T**, and Ahaz. 8390

TARES (8)
Mt 13:25 enemy came and sowed **t** among the wheat, *2215*
13:26 brought forth fruit, then appeared the **t** also. *2215*
13:27 in thy field? from whence then hath it **t**? *2215*
13:29 lest while ye gather up the **t**, ye root up also *2215*
13:30 Gather ye together first the **t**, and bind them *2215*
13:36 Declare unto us the parable of the **t** of *2215*
13:38 but the **t** are the children of the wicked one; *2215*

Mt 13:40 As therefore the **t** are gathered and burnt in *2215*

TARGET (3) [TARGETS]
1Sa 17: 6 and a **t** of brass between his shoulders. 3591
1Ki 10:16 six hundred *shekels* of gold went to one **t**. 6793
2Ch 9:15 *shekels* of beaten gold went to one **t**. 6793

TARGETS (3) [TARGET]
1Ki 10:16 king Solomon made two hundred **t** *of* 6793
2Ch 9:15 king Solomon made two hundred **t** *of* 6793
14: 8 Asa had an army *of men* that bare **t** and 6793

TARPELITES (1)
Ezr 4: 9 the **T**, the Apharsites, the Archevites, 2967

TARRIED (32) [TARRY]
Ge 24:54 the men that *were* with him, and **t all night**; 3885
28:11 **t** there **all night**, because the sun was set; 3885
31:54 did eat bread, and **t all night** in the mount. 3885
Nu 9:19 when the cloud **t long** upon the tabernacle 748
9:22 a year, that the cloud **t** upon the tabernacle, 748
Jdg 3:25 they **t** till *they* were ashamed: and behold, 2342
3:26 Ehud escaped while they **t**, and passed 4102
19: 8 they **t** until afternoon, and they did eat both 4102
Ru 2: 7 until now, that she **t** a little in the house. 3427
1Sa 13: 8 he **t** seven days, according to the set time 3176
14: 2 Saul **t** in the uttermost part of Gibeah under 3427
2Sa 11: 1 But David **t** *still* at Jerusalem. 3427
15:17 after him, and **t** *in* a place that *was* far off. 5975
15:29 of God again *to* Jerusalem: and they **t** there. 3427
20: 5 he **t longer** than the set time which he had 309
2Ki 2:18 came again to him, (for he **t** at Jericho,) 3427
1Ch 20: 1 David **t** at Jerusalem. And Joab smote 3427
Ps 68:12 she that **t** at home divided the spoil. 5116
Mt 25: 5 While the bridegroom **t**, they all slumbered *5549*
Lk 1:21 marvelled that he **t** *so* **long** in the temple. *5549*
2:43 the child Jesus **t behind** in Jerusalem; *5278*
Jn 3:22 and there he **t** with them, and baptized. *1304*
Ac 9:43 that he **t** many days in Joppa with one *3306*
15:33 And after they had **t** *there* **a space**, *4160+5550*
18:18 And Paul *after this* **t** *there* yet a good while, *4357*
20: 5 These going before **t for** us at Troas. *3306*
20:15 we arrived at Samos, and **t** at Trogyllium; *3306*
21: 4 finding disciples, we **t** there seven days: *1961*
21:10 And as we **t** *there* many days, there came *1961*
25: 6 And when he had **t** among them more than *1304*
27:33 This day is the fourteenth day that ye have **t** *4328*
28:12 landing at Syracuse, we **t** *there* three days. *1961*

TARRIEST (1) [TARRY]
Ac 22:16 And now why **t** thou? arise, and *3195*

TARRIETH (2) [TARRY]
1Sa 30:24 so *shall* his part *be* that **t** by the stuff: 3427
Mic 5: 7 showers upon the grass, that **t** not for man, 6960

TARRY (51) [TARRIED, TARRIEST, TARRIETH, TARRYING]
Ge 19: 2 **t all night**, and wash your feet, and ye shall 3885
27:44 **t** with him a few days, until thy brother's 3427
30:27 **t**: *for* I have learned by experience that NIH
45: 9 of all Egypt: come down unto me, **t** not: 5975
Ex 12:39 were thrust out of Egypt, and could not **t**, 4102
24:14 he said unto the elders, **T** ye here for us, 3427
Lev 14: 8 shall **t abroad** out of his tent seven days. 3427
Nu 22:19 I pray you, **t** ye also here *this* night, 3427
Jdg 5:28 in coming? why **t** the wheels of his chariots? 309
6:18 And he said, I will **t** until thou come again. 3427
19: 6 and **t all night**, and let thine heart be merry. 3885
19: 9 towards evening, I pray you **t all night**: 3885
19:10 the man would not **t** *that* **night**, but he rose 3885
Ru 1:13 Would ye **t** for them till they were grown? 7663
3:13 **T** this night, and it shall be in the morning, 3885
1Sa 1:23 thee good; **t** until thou have weaned him; 3427
10: 8 seven days shalt thou **t**, till I come to thee, 3176
14: 9 say thus unto us, **T** until we come to you; 1826
2Sa 10: 5 **T** at Jericho until your beards be grown, 3427
11:12 **T** here to day also, and to morrow I will let 3427
15:28 See, I will **t** in the plain of the wilderness, 4102
18:14 said Joab, I may not **t** thus with thee. 3176
19: 7 there will not **t** one with thee *this* night: 3885
2Ki 2: 2 Elijah said unto Elisha, **T** here, I pray thee; 3427
2: 4 said unto him, Elisha, **T** here, I pray thee; 3427
2: 6 Elijah said unto him, **T**, I pray thee, here; 3427
7: 9 if we **t** till the morning light, *some* mischief 2442
9: 3 Then open the door, and flee, and **t** not. 2442
14:10 glory *of this*, and **t** at home: for why 3427
1Ch 19: 5 **T** at Jericho until your beards be grown, 3427
Ps 101: 7 he that telleth lies shall not **t** in my sight. 3559
Pr 23:30 They that **t long** at the wine; they that go to 309
Isa 46:13 not be far off, and my salvation shall not **t**: 309
Jer 14: 8 man *that* turneth aside to **t for a night**? 3885
Hab 2: 3 though it **t**, wait for it; because it will 4102
2: 3 because it will surely come, it will not **t**. 309
Mt 26:38 unto death: **t** ye here, and watch with me. *3306*
Mk 14:34 sorrowful unto death: **t** ye here, and watch. *3306*
Lk 24:29 is far spent. And he went in to **t** with them. *3306*
24:49 but **t** ye in the city of Jerusalem, until ye be *2523*
Jn 4:40 they besought him that *he* would **t** with *3306*
21:22 If I will that he **t** till I come, what *is that* to *3306*
21:23 but, If I will that he **t** till I come, what *is* *3306*
Ac 10:48 Then prayed they him to **t** certain days. *1961*
18:20 When they desired *him* to **t** longer time *3306*
28:14 and were desired to **t** with them seven days: *1961*
1Co 11:33 ye come together to eat, **t** one **for** another. *1551*
16: 7 but I trust to **t** a while with you, if the Lord *1961*
16: 8 But I will **t** at Ephesus until Pentecost. *1961*
1Ti 3:15 But if I **t long**, that thou mayest know how *1019*
Heb 10:37 he that shall come will come, and will not **t**. *5549*

TARRYING (2) [TARRY]
Ps 40:17 and my deliverer; **make** no **t**, O my God. 309
70: 5 and my deliverer; O LORD, **make** no **t**. 309

TARSHISH (24) [THARSHISH]
Ge 10: 4 Elishah, and **T**, Kittim, and Dodanim. 8659
1Ch 1: 7 Elishah, and **T**, Kittim, and Dodanim. 8659
2Ch 9:21 For the king's ships went *to* **T** with 8659
9:21 every three years once came the ships of **T** 8659
20:36 himself with him to make ships to go *to* **T**: 8659
20:37 that they were not able to go to **T**. 8659
Est 1:14 **T**, Meres, Marsena, *and* Memucan, 8659
Ps 48: 7 Thou breakest the ships of **T** with an east 8659
72:10 The kings of **T** and *of* the isles shall bring 8659
Isa 2:16 upon all the ships of **T**, and upon all 8659
23: 1 Howl, ye ships of **T**; for it is laid waste, so 8659
23: 6 Pass ye over to **T**; howl, ye inhabitants of 8659
23:10 thy land as a river, O daughter of **T**: 8659
23:14 Howl, ye ships of **T**: for your strength is 8659
60: 9 the ships of **T** first, to bring thy sons from 8659
66:19 *to* **T**, Pul, and Lud, that draw the bow, 8659
Jer 10: 9 Silver spread into plates is brought from **T**, 8659
Eze 27:12 **T** *was* thy merchant by reason of 8659
27:25 The ships of **T** did sing of thee *in* thy 8659
38:13 Sheba, and Dedan, and the merchants of **T**, 8659
Jnh 1: 3 Jonah rose up to flee unto **T** from 8659
1: 3 *to* Joppa; and he found a ship going *to* **T**: 8659
1: 3 to go with them unto **T** from the presence 8659
4: 2 Therefore I fled before unto **T**: for I knew 8659

TARSUS (5)
Ac 9:11 house of Judas for *one* called Saul, of **T**: *5018*
9:30 down to Cesarea, and sent him forth to **T**. *5019*
11:25 Then departed Barnabas to **T**, for to seek *5019*
21:39 Paul said, I am a man *which am* a Jew of **T**, *5018*
22: 3 *which am* a Jew, born in **T**, *a city* in Cilicia, *5019*

TARTAK (1)
2Ki 17:31 the Avites made Nibhaz and **T**, and 8662

TARTAN (2)
2Ki 18:17 the king of Assyria sent **T** and Rabsaris 8661
Isa 20: 1 In the year that **T** came unto Ashdod, 8661

TASK (2) [TASKMASTERS, TASKS]
Ex 5:14 Wherefore have ye not fulfilled your **t** in 2706
5:19 *ought* from your bricks of *your* daily **t**. 1697

TASKMASTERS (6) [MASTER, TASK]
Ex 1:11 Therefore they did set over them **t** to 4522+8269
3: 7 have heard their cry by reason of their **t**; 5065
5: 6 Pharaoh commanded the same day the **t** of 5065
5:10 the **t** of the people went out, and 5065
5:13 the **t** hasted *them*, saying, Fulfil your 5065
5:14 which Pharaoh's **t** had set over them, 5065

TASKS (1) [TASK]
Ex 5:13 Fulfil your works, *your* daily **t**, as when 1697

TASTE (22) [TASTED, TASTETH]
Ex 16:31 the **t** of it *was* like wafers *made* with honey. 2940

Nu 11: 8 and the **t** of it was as the taste of fresh oil. 2940
11: 8 and the taste of it was as the **t** of fresh oil. 2940
1Sa 14:43 I **did but t** a little honey with the end 2938+2938
2Sa 3:35 and more also, if I **t** bread, or ought else, 2938
19:35 can thy servant **t** what I eat or what I drink? 2938
Job 6: 6 or is there *any* **t** in the white of an egg? 2940
6:30 cannot my **t** discern perverse things? 2441
12:11 ear try words? and the mouth **t** his meat? 2938
Ps 34: 8 O **t** and see that the LORD *is* good: 2938
119:103 How sweet are thy words unto my **t**! 2441
Pr 24:13 the honeycomb, *which is* sweet to thy **t**: 2441
SS 2: 3 and his fruit *was* sweet to my **t**. 2441
Jer 48:11 therefore his **t** remained in him, and 2940
Jnh 3: 7 man nor beast, herd nor flock, **t** any thing: 2938
Mt 16:28 standing here, which shall not **t** of death, *1089*
Mk 9: 1 that stand here, which shall not **t** of death, *1089*
Lk 9:27 standing here, which shall not **t** of death, *1089*
14:24 which were bidden shall **t** of my supper. *1089*
Jn 8:52 keep my saying, he shall never **t** of death. *1089*
Col 2:21 (Touch not; **t** not; handle not; *1089*
Heb 2: 9 that he by the grace of God should **t** death *1089*

TASTED (8) [TASTE]
1Sa 14:24 So none of the people **t** *any* food. 2938
14:29 because I **t** a little of this honey. 2938
Da 5: 2 Belshazzar, whiles *he* **t** the wine, 2942
Mt 27:34 when he had **t** *thereof,* he would not drink. *1089*
Jn 2: 9 When the ruler of the feast had **t** the water *1089*
Heb 6: 4 and have **t** of the heavenly gift, and *1089*
6: 5 And have **t** the good word of God, and *1089*
1Pe 2: 3 If so be ye have **t** that the Lord *is* gracious. *1089*

TASTELESS See UNSAVOURY

TASTETH (1) [TASTE]
Job 34: 3 the ear trieth words, as the mouth **t** meat. 2938

TASTY See SAVOURY

TATNAI (4)
Ezr 5: 3 At the same time came to them **T**, 8674
5: 6 The copy of the letter that **T**, governor on 8674
6: 6 Now *therefore,* **T**, governor beyond 8674
6:13 **T**, governor on *this* side the river, 8674

TATTENAI See TATNAI

TATTLERS (1)
1Ti 5:13 not only idle, but **t** also and busybodies, *5397*

TAUGHT (81) [TEACH]
Dt 4: 5 I have **t** you statutes and judgments, 3925
31:22 the same day, and **t** it the children of Israel. 3925
Jdg 8:16 and with them he **t** the men of Succoth. 3045
2Ki 17:28 **t** them how they should fear the LORD. 3384
2Ch 6:27 when thou hast **t** them the good way, 3384
17: 9 they **t** in Judah, and *had* the book of the law 3925
17: 9 all the cities of Judah, and **t** the people. 3925
23:13 of musick, and such as **t** to *sing* praise. 3045
30:22 **t** the good **knowledge** of 7919+7922
35: 3 said unto the Levites that **t** all Israel, 995
Ne 8: 9 the Levites that **t** the people, said unto all 995
Ps 71:17 O God, thou hast **t** me from my youth: and 3925
119:102 from thy judgments: for thou hast **t** me. 3384
119:171 when thou hast **t** me thy statutes. 3925
Pr 4: 4 He **t** me also, and said unto me, Let thine 3384
4:11 I have **t** thee in the way of wisdom; I have 3384
31: 1 the prophecy that his mother **t** him. 3256
Ecc 12: 9 was wise, he still **t** the people knowledge; 3925
Isa 29:13 their fear towards me is **t** *by* the precept of 3925
40:13 or *being* his counseller hath **t** him? 3045
40:14 **t** him in the path of judgment, and 3925
40:14 **t** him knowledge, and shewed to him 3925
54:13 all thy children *shall be* **t** of the LORD; 3928
Jer 2:33 hast thou also **t** the wicked ones thy ways. 3925
9: 5 they have **t** their tongue to speak lies, *and* 3925
9:14 after Baalim, which their fathers **t** them: 3925
12:16 as they **t** my people to swear by Baal; then 3925
13:21 for thou hast **t** them *to be* captains, *and* 3925
28:16 thou hast **t** rebellion against the LORD. 1696
29:32 he hath **t** rebellion against the LORD. 1696
32:33 though *I* **t** them, rising up early and 3925
Eze 23:48 that all women may be **t** not to do after 3256
Hos 10:11 Ephraim *is as* a heifer *that is* **t**, *and* 3925
11: 3 I **t** Ephraim also **to go**, taking them by their 7270
Zec 13: 5 for man **t** me *to keep cattle* from my youth. 7069
Mt 5: 2 he opened his mouth, and **t** them, saying, *1321*
7:29 For he **t** them as *one* having authority, and *1321*
13:54 he **t** them in their synagogue, insomuch that *1321*
28:15 took the money, and did as they were **t**: *1321*
Mk 1:21 day he entered into the synagogue, and **t**. *1321*
1:22 for he **t** them as *one* that had authority, and *1321*
2:13 multitude resorted unto him, and he **t** them. *1321*
4: 2 And he **t** them many *things* by parables, *1321*
6:30 what they had done, and what they had **t**. *1321*
9:31 For he **t** his disciples, and said unto them, *1321*
10: 1 and, as he was wont, he **t** them again. *1321*
11:17 And he **t**, saying unto them, Is it not *1321*
12:35 and said, while he **t** in the temple, *1321*
Lk 4:15 And he **t** in their synagogues, *1321*
4:31 of Galilee, and **t** them on the sabbath days. *1321*
5: 3 sat down, and **t** the people out of the ship. *1321*
6: 6 that he entered into the synagogue and **t**: *1321*
11: 1 us to pray, as John also **t** his disciples. *1321*
13:26 thy presence, and thou hast **t** in our streets. *1321*
19:47 And he **t** daily in the temple. But the chief *1321*
20: 1 as he **t** the people in the temple, and *1321*
Jn 6:45 the prophets, And they shall be all **t** of God. *1318*
6:59 he in the synagogue, as he **t** in Capernaum. *1321*
7:14 feast Jesus went up into the temple, and **t**. *1321*
7:28 Then cried Jesus in the temple as he **t**, *1321*
8: 2 unto him; and he sat down, and **t** them. *1321*
8:20 Jesus in the treasury, as he **t** in the temple: *1321*
8:28 but as my Father hath **t** me, I speak these *1321*
18:20 I ever **t** in the synagogue, and in the temple, *1321*
Ac 4: 2 Being grieved that they **t** the people, and *1321*
5:21 into the temple early in the morning, and **t**. *1321*
11:26 and **t** much people, and the disciples were *1321*
14:21 and had **t** many, they returned *again* to *3100*
15: 1 came down from Judea **t** the brethren, *1321*
18:25 and **t** diligently the *things* of the Lord, *1321*
20:20 and have **t** you publickly, and from house *1321*
22: 3 **t** according to the perfect manner of the law *3811*
Gal 1:12 neither was I **t** *it,* but by the revelation of *1321*
6: 6 Let him that is **t** in the word communicate *2727*
Eph 4:21 and have been **t** by him, as the truth is in *1321*
Col 2: 7 stablished in the faith, as ye have been **t**, *1321*
1Th 4: 9 for ye yourselves are **t of God** to love one *2312*
2Th 2:15 hold the traditions which ye have been **t**, *1321*
Tit 1: 9 fast the faithful word as *he* hath been **t**, *1322*
1Jn 2:27 and is no lie, and even as it hath **t** you, *1321*
Rev 2:14 who **t** Balac to cast a stumblingblock *1321*

TAUNT (2) [TAUNTING]
Jer 24: 9 a reproach and a proverb, a **t** and a curse, 8148
Eze 5:15 So it shall be a reproach and a **t**, 1422

TAUNTING (1) [TAUNT]
Hab 2: 6 and a **t** proverb against him, and say, 4426

TAVERNS (1)
Ac 28:15 us as far as Appii forum, and The three **t**: *4999*

TAX BOOTH See RECEIPT OF CUSTOM

TAX COLLECTOR See PUBLICAN

TAXATION (1) [TAXED, TAXES, TAXING]
2Ki 23:35 of every one according to his **t**, to give *it* 6187

TAXED (4) [TAXATION]
2Ki 23:35 he **t** the land to give the money according 6186
Lk 2: 1 that all the world should be **t**. *583*
2: 3 And all went to be **t**, every one into his own *583*
2: 5 To be **t** with Mary his espoused wife, *583*

TAXES (1) [TAXATION]
Da 11:20 shall stand up in his estate a raiser of **t** *in* 5065

TAXING (2) [TAXATION]
Lk 2: 2 (*And* this **t** was first made when Cyrenius *582*
Ac 5:37 rose up Judas of Galilee in the days of the **t**, *582*

TEACH (109) [TAUGHT, TEACHER, TEACHERS, TEACHEST, TEACHETH, TEACHING]
Ex 4:12 thy mouth, and **t** thee what thou shalt say. 3384
4:15 his mouth, and will **t** you what ye shall do. 3384
18:20 thou shalt **t** them ordinances and laws, and 2094
24:12 I have written; that thou mayest **t** them. 3384
35:34 he hath put in his heart that *he* may **t**, 3384

T

Lev 10:11 that *ye* may **t** the children of Israel all 3384
14:57 To **t** when *it is* unclean, and when *it is* 3384
Dt 4: 1 and unto the judgments, which I **t** you, 3925
4: 9 but **t** them thy sons, and thy sons' sons; 3045
4:10 the earth, and *that* they may **t** their children. 3925
4:14 LORD commanded me at that time to **t** 3925
5:31 and the judgments, which thou shalt **t** them, 3925
6: 1 the LORD your God commanded to **t** you, 3925
6: 7 thou shalt **t** them **diligently** unto thy 8150
11:19 ye shall **t** them your children, speaking of 3925
17:11 sentence of the law which they shall **t** thee, 3384
20:18 That they **t** you not to do after all their 3925
24: 8 to all that the priests the Levites shall **t** you: 3384
31:19 song for you, and **t** it the children of Israel: 3925
33:10 They shall **t** Jacob thy judgments, and 3384
Jdg 3: 2 to **t** them war, at the least such as before 3925
13: 8 **t** us what we shall do unto the child that 3384
1Sa 12:23 but I will **t** you the good and the right way: 3384
2Sa 1:18 (Also he bade *them* **t** the children of Judah 3925
1Ki 8:36 that thou **t** them the good way wherein they 3384
2Ki 17:27 let him **t** them the manner of the God of 3384
2Ch 17: 7 and to Michaiah, to **t** in the cities of Judah. 3925
Ezr 7:10 to do *it*, and to **t** in Israel statutes and 3925
7:25 thy God; and **t** ye them that know *them* not. 3046
Job 6:24 **T** me, and I will hold my tongue: and 3384
8:10 Shall not they **t** thee, *and* tell thee, and 3384
12: 7 ask now the beasts, and they shall **t** thee; 3384
12: 8 Or speak to the earth, and it shall **t** thee: 3384
21:22 Shall *any* **t** God knowledge? seeing he 3925
27:11 I will **t** you by the hand of God: *that* which 3384
32: 7 and multitude of years should **t** wisdom. 3045
33:33 hold thy peace, and I shall **t** thee wisdom. 502
34:32 *That which* I see not **t** thou me: if I have 3384
37:19 **T** us what we shall say unto him; *for* we 3045
Ps 25: 4 me thy ways, O LORD; **t** me thy paths. 3925
25: 5 Lead me in thy truth, and **t** me: for thou *art* 3925
25: 8 will he **t** sinners in the way. 3384
25: 9 and the meek will he **t** his way. 3925
25:12 him shall he **t** in the way *that* he shall 3384
27:11 **T** me thy way, O LORD, and lead me in a 3384
32: 8 and **t** thee in the way which thou shalt go: 3384
34:11 I will **t** you the fear of the LORD. 3925
45: 4 thy right hand shall **t** thee terrible *things*. 3384
51:13 *Then* will I **t** transgressors thy ways; and 3925
60: T Michtam of David, to **t**; 3925
86:11 **T** me thy way, O LORD; I will walk in 3384
90:12 So **t** *us* to number our days, that we may 3045
105:22 at his pleasure; and **t** his senators **wisdom**. 2449
119:12 *art* thou, O LORD: **t** me thy statutes. 3925
119:26 and thou heardest me: **t** me thy statutes. 3925
119:33 **T** me, O LORD, the way of thy statutes; 3384
119:64 is full *of* thy mercy: **t** me thy statutes. 3925
119:66 **T** me good judgment and knowledge: for I 3925
119:68 *art* good, and doest good; **t** me thy statutes. 3925
119:108 O LORD, and **t** me thy judgments. 3925
119:124 unto thy mercy, and **t** me thy statutes. 3925
119:135 upon thy servant; and **t** me thy statutes. 3925
132:12 and my testimony that I shall **t** them, 3925
143:10 **T** me to do thy will; for thou *art* my God: 3925
Pr 9: 9 **t** a just *man*, and he will increase in 3045
Isa 2: 3 he will **t** us of his ways, and we will walk 3384
28: 9 Whom shall he **t** knowledge? and whom 3384
28:26 instruct him to discretion, *and* doth **t** him. 3384
Jer 9:20 **t** your daughters wailing, and every one her 3925
31:34 they shall **t** no more every man his 3925
Eze 44:23 they shall **t** my people *the difference* 3384
Da 1: 4 whom *they* might **t** the learning and 3925
Mic 3:11 the priests thereof **t** for hire, and 3384
4: 2 he will **t** us of his ways, and we will walk 3384
Hab 2:19 Awake; to the dumb stone, Arise, it shall **t**! 3384
Mt 5:19 least commandments, and shall **t** men so, *1321*
5:19 **t** *them*, the same shall be called great in *1321*
11: 1 he departed thence to **t** and to preach in *1321*
28:19 Go ye therefore, and **t** all nations, *3100*
Mk 4: 1 And he began again to **t** by the sea side: *1321*
6: 2 was come, he began to **t** in the synagogue: *1321*
6:34 and he began to **t** them many *things*. *1321*
8:31 And he began to **t** them, that the Son of *1321*
Lk 11: 1 Lord, **t** us to pray, as John also taught his *1321*
12:12 For the Holy Ghost shall **t** you in the same *1321*
Jn 7:35 among the Gentiles, and **t** the Gentiles? *1321*
9:34 altogether born in sins, and dost thou **t** us? *1321*
14:26 he shall **t** you all *things*, and bring all *1321*
Ac 1: 1 of all that Jesus began both to do and **t**, *1321*
4:18 commanded them not to speak at all nor **t** *1321*
5:28 you that *you* should not **t** in this name? *1321*
5:42 they ceased not to **t** and preach Jesus *1321*
16:21 And **t** customs, which are not lawful for us *2605*
1Co 4:17 as I **t** every where in every church. *1321*
11:14 Doth not even nature itself **t** you, that, if a *1321*
14:19 that *by my voice* I might **t** others also, *2727*
1Ti 1: 3 charge some that *they* **t** no **other doctrine**, *2085*
2:12 But I suffer not a woman to **t**, nor to usurp *1321*
3: 2 given to hospitality, **apt to t**; *1317*
4:11 These *things* command and **t**. *1321*
6: 2 of the benefit. These *things* **t** and exhort. *1321*
6: 3 If any *man* **t otherwise**, and consent not to *2085*
2Ti 2: 2 who shall be able to **t** others also. *1321*
2:24 but be gentle unto all *men*, **apt to t**, patient, *1317*
Tit 2: 4 they may **t** the young *women* **to be sober**, *4994*
Heb 5:12 ye have need that *one* **t** you again which *be* *1321*
8:11 And they shall not **t** every man his *1321*
1Jn 2:27 in you, and ye need not that any *man* **t** you: *1321*
Rev 2:20 to **t** and to seduce my servants to commit *1321*

TEACHER (6) [TEACH]

1Ch 25: 8 the small as the great, the **t** as the scholar. 995
Hab 2:18 the molten image, and a **t** of lies, that 3384
Jn 3: 2 we know that thou art a **t** come from God: *1320*
Ro 2:20 An instructor of the foolish, a **t** of babes, *1320*
1Ti 2: 7 a **t** of the Gentiles in faith and verity. *1320*
2Ti 1:11 and an apostle, and a **t** of the Gentiles. *1320*

TEACHERS (14) [TEACH]

Ps 119:99 I have more understanding than all my **t**: 3925
Pr 5:13 have not obeyed the voice of my **t**, 3384
Isa 30:20 yet shall not thy **t** be removed into a corner 3384
30:20 any more, but thine eyes shall see thy **t**: 3384
43:27 and thy **t** have transgressed against me. 3887
Ac 13: 1 that was at Antioch certain prophets and **t**; *1320*
1Co 12:28 thirdly **t**, after that miracles, then gifts of *1320*
12:29 *are* all **t**? *are* all workers of miracles? *1320*
Eph 4:11 some, evangelists; and some, pastors and **t**; *1320*
1Ti 1: 7 Desiring to be **t of the law**; *3547*
2Ti 4: 3 own lusts shall they heap to themselves **t**, *1320*
Tit 2: 3 not given to much wine, **t of good things**; *2567*
Heb 5:12 For when for the time ye ought to be **t**, *1320*
2Pe 2: 1 even as there shall be **false t** among you, *5572*

TEACHEST (8) [TEACH]

Ps 94:12 O LORD, and **t** him out of thy law; 3925
Mt 22:16 thou art true, and **t** the way of God in truth, *1321*
Mk 12:14 of men, but **t** the way of God in truth: *1321*
Lk 20:21 we know that thou sayest and **t** rightly, *1321*
20:21 person *of any*, but **t** the way of God truly: *1321*
Ac 21:21 that thou **t** all the Jews which are among *1321*
Ro 2:21 Thou therefore which **t** another, *1321*
2:21 which teachest another, **t** thou not thyself? *1321*

TEACHETH (16) [TEACH]

2Sa 22:35 He **t** my hands to war; so that a bow of 3925
Job 35:11 Who **t** us more than the beasts of the earth, 502
36:22 God exalteth by his power: who **t** like him? 3384
Ps 18:34 He **t** my hands to war, so that a bow of 3925
94:10 he that **t** man knowledge, *shall not he* 3925
144: 1 which **t** my hands to war, *and* my fingers to 3925
Pr 6:13 speaketh with his feet, he **t** with his fingers; 3384
16:23 The heart of the wise **t** his mouth, and 7919
Isa 9:15 and the prophet that **t** lies, he *is* the tail. 3384
48:17 I *am* the LORD thy God which **t** thee to 3925
Ac 21:28 that **t** all *men* every where against *1321*
Ro 12: 7 *our* ministering: or he that **t**, on teaching; *1321*
1Co 2:13 not in the words which man's wisdom **t**, *1318*
2:13 but which the Holy Ghost **t**; *1318*
Gal 6: 6 unto him that **t** in all good *things*. *2727*
1Jn 2:27 as the same anointing **t** you of all *things*, *1321*

TEACHING (25) [TEACH]

2Ch 15: 3 and without a **t** priest, and without law. 3384
Jer 32:33 **t** *them*, yet they have not hearkened to 3925
Mt 4:23 **t** in their synagogues and preaching *1321*
9:35 **t** in their synagogues, and preaching *1321*
15: 9 **t** for doctrines the commandments of men. *1321*
21:23 of the people came unto him as he was **t**, *1321*
26:55 I sat daily with you **t** in the temple, and *1321*
28:20 **T** them to observe all *things* whatsoever I *1321*
Mk 6: 6 And he went round about the villages, **t**. *1321*
7: 7 **t** for doctrines the commandments of men. *1321*

T

Mk 14:49 I was daily with you in the temple **t**, and *1321*
Lk 5:17 as he was **t**, that there were Pharisees and *1321*
13:10 And he was **t** in one of the synagogues on *1321*
13:22 **t**, and journeying towards Jerusalem. *1321*
21:37 And in the day time he was **t** in the temple; *1321*
23: 5 up the people, **t** throughout all Jewry, *1321*
Ac 5:25 are standing in the temple, and **t** the people. *1321*
15:35 **t** and preaching the word of the Lord, *1321*
18:11 six months, **t** the word of God among them. *1321*
28:31 **t** those *things* which concern the Lord Jesus *1321*
Ro 12: 7 *our* ministering: or he that teacheth, on **t**; *1319*
Col 1:28 every man, and **t** every man in all wisdom; *1321*
3:16 **t** and admonishing one another in psalms *1321*
Tit 1:11 **t** *things* which *they* ought not, for filthy *1321*
2:12 **T** us that denying ungodliness and worldly *3811*

TEAR (13) [TARE, TEARETH, TEARS, TORN]
Jdg 8: 7 I will **t** your flesh with the thorns of 1758
Ps 7: 2 Lest he **t** my soul like a lion, rending *it* in 2963
35:15 I knew *it* not; they did **t** *me,* and ceased not: 7167
50:22 lest I **t** *you* **in pieces**, and *there be* none to 2963
Jer 15: 3 the dogs to **t**, and the fowls of the heaven, 5498
16: 7 Neither shall *men* **t** *themselves* for them in 6536
Eze 13:20 I will **t** them from your arms, and will let 7167
13:21 Your kerchiefs also will I **t**, and deliver my 7167
Hos 5:14 I, *even* I, will **t** and go away; I will take 2963
13: 8 them like a lion: the wild beast shall **t** them. 1234
Am 1:11 his anger did **t** perpetually, and he kept his 2963
Na 2:12 The lion did **t in pieces** enough for his 2963
Zec 11:16 flesh of the fat, and **t** their claws **in pieces**. 6561

TEARETH (6) [TEAR]
Dt 33:20 and **t** the arm with the crown of the head. 2963
Job 16: 9 He **t** *me in* his wrath, who hateth me: 2963
18: 4 He **t** himself in his anger: shall the earth be 2963
Mic 5: 8 and **t in pieces**, and none can deliver. 2963
Mk 9:18 And wheresoever he taketh him, he **t** him: *4486*
Lk 9:39 and it **t** him that he foameth again, and *4682*

TEARS (36) [TEAR]
2Ki 20: 5 I have heard thy prayer, I have seen thy **t**: 1832
Est 8: 3 besought him with **t** to put away 1058
Job 16:20 *but* mine eye poureth out *t* unto God. NIH
Ps 6: 6 bed to swim; I water my couch with my **t**. 1832
39:12 ear unto my cry; hold not thy peace at my **t**: 1832
42: 3 My **t** have been my meat day and night, 1832
56: 8 put thou my **t** into thy bottle: *are they* not in 1832
80: 5 Thou feedest them with the bread of **t**; and 1832
80: 5 and givest them **t** to drink *in great* measure. 1832
116: 8 mine eyes from **t**, *and* my feet from falling. 1832
126: 5 They that sow in **t** shall reap in joy. 1832
Ecc 4: 1 the **t** of such as were oppressed, and 1832
Isa 16: 9 I will water thee *with* my **t**, O Heshbon, 1832
25: 8 the Lord GOD will wipe away **t** from off 1832
38: 5 I have heard thy prayer, I have seen thy **t**: 1832
Jer 9: 1 mine eyes a fountain of **t**, that I might weep 1832
9:18 that our eyes may run down *with* **t**, and 1832
13:17 run down *with* **t**, because the LORD'S 1832
14:17 Let mine eyes run down *with* **t** night and 1832
31:16 voice from weeping, and thine eyes from **t**: 1832
La 1: 2 in the night, and her **t** *are* on her cheeks: 1832
2:11 Mine eyes do fail with **t**, my bowels are 1832
2:18 let **t** run down like a river day and night: 1832
Eze 24:16 nor weep, neither shall thy **t** run down. 1832
Mal 2:13 covering the altar of the LORD *with* **t**, 1832
Mk 9:24 cried out, and said with **t**, Lord, I believe; *1144*
Lk 7:38 and began to wash his feet with **t**, and *1144*
7:44 but she hath washed my feet with **t**, and *1144*
Ac 20:19 of mind, and *with* many **t**, and temptations, *1144*
20:31 not to warn every one night and day with **t**. *1144*
2Co 2: 4 of heart I wrote unto you with many **t**; *1144*
2Ti 1: 4 desiring to see thee, being mindful of thy **t**, *1144*
Heb 5: 7 **t** unto him that was able to save him from *1144*
12:17 though he sought it carefully with **t**. *1144*
Rev 7:17 God shall wipe away all **t** from their eyes. *1144*
21: 4 And God shall wipe away all **t** from their *1144*

TEATS (3)
Isa 32:12 They *shall* lament for the **t**, for the pleasant 7699
Eze 23: 3 there they bruised the **t** of their virginity. 1717
23:21 in bruising thy **t** by the Egyptians for 1717

TEBAH (1)
Ge 22:24 she bare also **T**, and Gaham, and Thahash, 2875

TEBALIAH (1)
1Ch 26:11 Hilkiah the second, **T** the third, 2882

TEBETH (1)
Est 2:16 which *is* the month **T**, in the seventh year 2887

TEDIOUS (1)
Ac 24: 4 that I be not further **t** unto thee, *1465*

TEETH (49) [TOOTH]
Ge 49:12 *be* red with wine, and *his* **t** white with milk. 8127
Nu 11:33 while the flesh *was* yet between their **t**, 8127
Dt 32:24 I will also send the **t** of beasts upon them, 8127
1Sa 2:13 with a fleshhook of three **t** in his hand; 8127
Job 4:10 and the **t** of the young lions, are broken. 8127
13:14 Wherefore do I take my flesh in my **t**, and 8127
16: 9 he gnasheth upon me with his **t**; 8127
19:20 and I am escaped with the skin of my **t**. 8127
29:17 the wicked, and pluckt the spoil out of his **t**. 8127
41:14 of his face? his **t** *are* terrible round about. 8127
Ps 3: 7 thou hast broken the **t** of the ungodly. 8127
35:16 *they* gnashed upon me *with* their **t**. 8127
37:12 the just, and gnasheth upon him *with* his **t**. 8127
57: 4 whose **t** *are* spears and arrows, and 8127
58: 6 Break their **t**, O God, in their mouth: 8127
58: 6 break out the **great t** of the young lions, 4459
112:10 he shall gnash *with* his **t**, and melt away: 8127
124: 6 who hath not given us *as* a prey to their **t**. 8127
Pr 10:26 As vinegar to the **t**, and as smoke to 8127
30:14 whose **t** *are as* swords, and their jaw teeth 8127
30:14 *are as* swords, and their **jaw t** *as* knives, 4973
SS 4: 2 Thy **t** *are* like a flock of *sheep that are* even 8127
6: 6 Thy **t** *are* as a flock of sheep which go up 8127
Isa 41:15 a new sharp threshing instrument having **t**: 6374
Jer 31:29 and the children's **t** are set on edge. 8127
31:30 the sour grape, his **t** shall be set on edge. 8127
La 2:16 they hiss and gnash the **t**: they say, 8127
3:16 He hath also broken my **t** with gravel 8127
Eze 18: 2 and the children's **t** are set on edge? 8127
Da 7: 5 ribs in the mouth of it between the **t** of it: 8128
7: 7 strong exceedingly; and it had great iron **t**: 8128
7:19 whose **t** *were of* iron, and his nails *of* brass; 8128
Joel 1: 6 whose **t** *are* the teeth of a lion, and he hath 8127
1: 6 whose teeth *are* the **t** of a lion, and he hath 8127
Am 4: 6 I also have given you cleanness of **t** in all 8127
Mic 3: 5 that bite with their **t**, and cry, Peace; 8127
Zec 9: 7 and his abominations from between his **t**: 8127
Mt 8:12 there shall be weeping and gnashing of **t**. *3599*
13:42 there shall be wailing and gnashing of **t**. *3599*
13:50 there shall be wailing and gnashing of **t**. *3599*
22:13 there shall be weeping and gnashing of **t**. *3599*
24:51 there shall be weeping and gnashing of **t**. *3599*
25:30 there shall be weeping and gnashing of **t**. *3599*
27:44 crucified with him, **cast** the same **in** his **t**. *3679*
Mk 9:18 and gnasheth with his **t**, and pineth away: *3599*
Lk 13:28 There shall be weeping and gnashing of **t**, *3599*
Ac 7:54 and they gnashed on him *with their* **t**. *3599*
Rev 9: 8 and their **t** were as *the teeth* of lions. *3599*
9: 8 and their teeth were as *the* **t** of lions. NIG

TEHAPHNEHES (1) [TAHPANHES]
Eze 30:18 At **T** also the day shall be darkened, when I 8471

TEHINNAH (1)
1Ch 4:12 and Paseah, and **T** the father of Irnahash. 8468

TEIL (1)
Isa 6:13 as a **t tree**, and as an oak, whose substance *is* 424

TEKEL (2)
Da 5:25 MENE, MENE, **T**, UPHARSIN. 8625
5:27 **T**; Thou art weighed in the balances, and 8625

TEKOA (6) [TEKOAH, TEKOITE, TEKOITES]
1Ch 2:24 wife bare him Ashur the father of **T**. 8620
4: 5 Ashur the father of **T** had two wives, Helah 8620
2Ch 11: 6 built even Beth-lehem, and Etam, and **T**, 8620
20:20 and went forth into the wilderness of **T**: 8620
Jer 6: 1 blow the trumpet in **T**, and set up a sign of 8620
Am 1: 1 who was among the herdmen of **T**, 8620

TEKOAH (3) [TEKOA]
2Sa 14: 2 Joab sent to **T**, and fetcht thence a wise 8620
14: 4 when the woman of **T** spake to the king, 8621
14: 9 the woman of **T** said unto the king, 8621

TEKOITE (3) [TEKOA]
2Sa 23:26 the Paltite, Ira the son of Ikkesh the T, 8621
1Ch 11:28 Ira the son of Ikkesh the T, Abi-ezer 8621
27: 9 month *was* Ira the son of Ikkesh the T: 8621

TEKOITES (2) [TEKOA]
Ne 3: 5 next unto them the T repaired; but 8621
3:27 After them the T repaired another piece, 8621

TEL-ABIB (1)
Eze 3:15 I came to them of the captivity *at* T, 8512

TELAH (1)
1Ch 7:25 and T his son, and Tahan his son, 8520

TELAIM (1)
1Sa 15: 4 numbered them in T, two hundred thousand 2923

TELASSAR (1) [THELASAR]
Isa 37:12 and the children of Eden which *were* in T? 8515

TELEM (2)
Jos 15:24 Ziph, and T, and Bealoth, 2928
Ezr 10:24 and of the porters; Shallum, and T, and Uri. 2928

TEL-HARESHA (1) [TEL-HARSA]
Ne 7:61 T, Cherub, Addon, and Immer: 8521

TEL-HARSA (1) [TEL-HARESHA]
Ezr 2:59 T, Cherub, Addan, *and* Immer: 8521

TELL (217) [FORETELL, FORETOLD, TELLEST, TELLETH, TELLING, TOLD] See Index

TELLEST (1) [TELL] See Index

TELLETH (7) [TELL] See Index

TELLING (3) [TELL] See Index

TEL-MELAH (2)
Ezr 2:59 these *were* they which went up from T, 8528
Ne 7:61 these *were* they which went up *also* from T, 8528

TEMA (5)
Ge 25:15 Hadar, and T, Jetur, Naphish, and 8485
1Ch 1:30 and Dumah, Massa, Hadad, and T, 8485
Job 6:19 The troops of T looked, the companies of 8485
Isa 21:14 The inhabitants of the land of T brought 8485
Jer 25:23 T, and Buz, and all *that are* in the utmost 8485

TEMAH See TAMAH; THAMAH

TEMAN (11) [TEMANI, TEMANITE, TEMANITES]
Ge 36:11 the sons of Eliphaz were T, Omar, Zepho, 8487
36:15 duke T, duke Omar, duke Zepho, 8487
36:42 Duke Kenaz, duke T, duke Mibzar, 8487
1Ch 1:36 T, and Omar, Zephi, and Gatam, Kenaz, 8487
1:53 Duke Kenaz, duke T, duke Mibzar, 8487
Jer 49: 7 LORD of hosts; *Is* wisdom no more in T? 8487
49:20 hath purposed against the inhabitants of T: 8487
Eze 25:13 I will make it desolate from T; and they of 8487
Am 1:12 I will send a fire upon the T, which shall 8487
Ob 1: 9 thy mighty *men,* O T, shall be dismayed, 8487
Hab 3: 3 God came from T, and the Holy One from 8487

TEMANI (1) [TEMAN]
Ge 36:34 Husham of the land of T reigned in his 8489

TEMANITE (6) [TEMAN]
Job 2:11 Eliphaz the T, and Bildad the Shuhite, and 8489
4: 1 Then Eliphaz the T answered and said, 8489
15: 1 Then answered Eliphaz the T, and said, 8489
22: 1 Then Eliphaz the T answered and said, 8489
42: 7 the LORD said to Eliphaz the T, 8489
42: 9 So Eliphaz the T and Bildad the Shuhite 8489

TEMANITES (1) [TEMAN]
1Ch 1:45 Husham of the land of the T reigned in his 8489

TEMENI (1)
1Ch 4: 6 and Hepher, and T, and Haahashtari. 8488

TEMPER (1) [TEMPERANCE, TEMPERATE, TEMPERED, UNTEMPERED]
Eze 46:14 *part* of a hin of oil, to t with the fine flour; 7450

TEMPERANCE (4) [TEMPER]
Ac 24:25 t, and judgment to come, Felix trembled, *1466*
Gal 5:23 Meekness, t: against such there is no law. *1466*
2Pe 1: 6 And to knowledge t; and to temperance *1466*
1: 6 and to t patience; and to patience godliness; *1466*

TEMPERATE (3) [TEMPER]
1Co 9:25 t in all *things.* Now they *do it* to obtain a *1467*
Tit 1: 8 a lover of good *men,* sober, just, holy, t; *1468*
2: 2 grave, t, sound in faith, in charity, *4998*

TEMPERED (3) [TEMPER]
Ex 29: 2 cakes unleavened t with oil, and 1101
30:35 the apothecary, t **together**, pure *and* holy: 4414
1Co 12:24 but God hath t the body **together**, *4786*

TEMPEST (18) [TEMPESTUOUS]
Job 9:17 For he breaketh me with a t, and 8183
27:20 a t stealeth him away in the night. 5492
Ps 11: 6 fire and brimstone, and a horrible t: 7307
55: 8 my escape from the windy storm *and* t. 5591
83:15 So persecute them with thy t, and 5591
Isa 28: 2 *which* as a t of hail *and* a destroying storm, 2230
29: 6 *with* storm and t, and the flame of 5591
30:30 *with* scattering, and t, and hailstones. 2230
32: 2 from the wind, and a covert from the t; 2230
54:11 **tossed with** t, *and* not comforted, behold, 5590
Am 1:14 with a t in the day of the whirlwind: 5591
Jnh 1: 4 there was a mighty t in the sea, so that 5591
1:12 for I know that for my sake this great t *is* 5591
Mt 8:24 And behold, there arose a great t in the sea, *4578*
Ac 27:18 And we being exceedingly **tossed with a t**, *5492*
27:20 no small t lay on *us,* all hope that we *5494*
Heb 12:18 nor unto blackness, and darkness, and t, *2366*
2Pe 2:17 clouds that are carried with a t; *2978*

TEMPESTUOUS (4) [TEMPEST]
Ps 50: 3 and it shall be very t round about him. 8175
Jnh 1:11 unto us? for the sea wrought, and was t. 5590
1:13 the sea wrought, and was t against them. 5590
Ac 27:14 But not long after there arose against it a t *5189*

TEMPLE (204) [TEMPLES]
1Sa 1: 9 a seat by a post of the t of the LORD. 1964
3: 3 ere the lamp of God went out in the t of 1964
2Sa 22: 7 he did hear my voice out of his t, and 1964
1Ki 6: 3 the porch before the t of the house, 1964
6: 5 round about, *both* of the t and of the oracle: 1964
6:17 the house, that *is,* the t before it, was forty 1964
6:33 So also made he for the door of the t posts 1964
7:21 he set up the pillars in the porch of the t: 1964
7:50 for the doors of the house, *to wit,* of the t. 1964
2Ki 11:10 that *were* in the t of the LORD. 1004
11:11 from the right corner of the t to the left 1004
11:11 of the temple to the left corner of the t, 1004
11:11 of the temple, *along* by the altar and the t. 1004
11:13 she came to the people *into* the t of 1004
18:16 *gold from* the doors of the t of the LORD, 1964
23: 4 to bring forth out of the t of the LORD all 1964
24:13 of Israel had made in the t of the LORD, 1964
1Ch 6:10 in the t that Solomon built in Jerusalem:) 1004
10:10 and fastened his head *in* the t of Dagon. 1004
2Ch 3:17 he reared up the pillars before the t, one on 1964
4: 7 and set *them* in the t, five on the right hand, 1964
4: 8 placed *them* in the t, five on the right side, 1964
4:22 and the doors of the house of the t, 1964
23:10 from the right side of the t to the left side of 1004
23:10 side of the temple to the left side of the t, 1004
23:10 *along* by the altar and the t, by the king 1004
26:16 went into the t of the LORD to burn 1964
27: 2 howbeit he entered not into the t of 1964
29:16 t of the LORD into the court of the house 1964
35:20 all this, when Josiah had prepared the t, 1004
36: 7 and put them in his t at Babylon. 1964
Ezr 3: 6 the foundation of the t of the LORD was 1964
3:10 laid the foundation of the t of the LORD, 1964
4: 1 the t unto the LORD God of Israel; 1964
5:14 which Nebuchadnezzar took out of the t 1965
5:14 brought them into the t of Babylon, 1965
5:14 those did Cyrus the king take out of the t of 1965
5:15 carry them into the t that *is* in Jerusalem, 1965
6: 5 forth out of the t which *is* at Jerusalem, 1965
6: 5 brought *again* unto the t which *is* at 1965
Ne 6:10 within the t, and let us shut the doors of 1964

Ne 6:10 and let us shut the doors of the **t**: 1964
6:11 *being* as I *am*, would go into the **t** to save 1964
Ps 5: 7 in thy fear will I worship toward thy holy **t**. 1964
11: 4 The LORD *is* in his holy **t**, the LORD'S 1964
18: 6 he heard my voice out of his **t**, and my cry 1964
27: 4 of the LORD, and to inquire in his **t**. 1964
29: 9 in his **t** doth every one speak of *his* glory. 1964
48: 9 O God, in the midst of thy **t**. 1964
65: 4 goodness of thy house, *even* of thy holy **t**. 1964
68:29 Because of thy **t** at Jerusalem shall kings 1964
79: 1 thy holy **t** have they defiled; they have laid 1964
138: 2 I will worship toward thy holy **t**, and 1964
Isa 6: 1 high and lifted up, and his train filled the **t**. 1964
44:28 and *to* the **t**, Thy foundation shall be laid. 1964
66: 6 of noise from the city, a voice from the **t**, 1964
Jer 7: 4 saying, The **t** of the LORD, The temple of 1964
7: 4 The **t** of the LORD, The temple of 1964
7: 4 The **t** of the LORD, *are* these. 1964
24: 1 two baskets of figs *were* set before the **t** of 1964
50:28 LORD our God, the vengeance of his **t**. 1964
51:11 of the LORD, the vengeance of his **t**. 1964
Eze 8:16 behold, *at* the door of the **t** of the LORD, 1964
8:16 *with* their backs toward the **t** of 1964
41: 1 Afterward he brought me to the **t**, and 1964
41: 4 and the breadth, twenty cubits, before the **t**: 1964
41:15 with the inner **t**, and the porches of 1964
41:20 palm trees made, and *on* the wall of the **t**. 1964
41:21 The posts of the **t** *were* squared, *and* 1964
41:23 And the **t** and the sanctuary had two doors. 1964
41:25 on the doors of the **t**, cherubims and 1964
42: 8 and lo, before the **t** *were* an hundred cubits. 1964
Da 5: 2 taken out of the **t** which *was* in Jerusalem; 1965
5: 3 **t** of the house of God which *was* at 1965
Am 8: 3 the songs of the **t** shall be howlings in that 1964
Jnh 2: 4 yet I will look again toward thy holy **t**. 1964
2: 7 prayer came in unto thee, into thine holy **t**. 1964
Mic 1: 2 against you, the Lord from his holy **t**. 1964
Hab 2:20 the LORD *is* in his holy **t**: let all the earth 1964
Hag 2:15 laid upon a stone in the **t** of the LORD: 1964
2:18 the foundation of the LORD'S **t** was laid, 1964
Zec 6:12 and he shall build the **t** of the LORD: 1964
6:13 Even he shall build the **t** of the LORD; 1964
6:14 for a memorial in the **t** of the LORD. 1964
6:15 and build in the **t** of the LORD, 1964
8: 9 of hosts was laid, that the **t** might be built. 1964
Mal 3: 1 ye seek, shall suddenly come to his **t**, 1964
Mt 4: 5 and setteth him on a pinnacle of the **t**, *2411*
12: 5 days the priests in the **t** profane the sabbath, *2411*
12: 6 That in this place is *one* greater than the **t**. *2411*
21:12 And Jesus went into the **t** of God, and *2411*
21:12 out all them that sold and bought in the **t**, *2411*
21:14 *the* blind and *the* lame came to him in the **t**; *2411*
21:15 and the children crying in the **t**, and saying, *2411*
21:23 And when he was come into the **t**, the chief *2411*
23:16 which say, Whosoever shall swear by the **t**, *3485*
23:16 whosoever shall swear by the gold of the **t**, *3485*
23:17 the gold, or the **t** that sanctifieth the gold? *3485*
23:21 And whoso shall swear by the **t**, *3485*
23:35 whom ye slew between the **t** and the altar. *3485*
24: 1 Jesus went out, and departed from the **t**: *2411*
24: 1 *him* for to shew him the buildings of the **t**. *2411*
26:55 I sat daily with you teaching in the **t**, and *2411*
26:61 I am able to destroy the **t** of God, and *3485*
27: 5 he cast down the pieces of silver in the **t**, *3485*
27:40 *Thou* that destroyest the **t**, and buildest *it* in *3485*
27:51 the vail of the **t** was rent in twain from *3485*
Mk 11:11 Jesus entered into Jerusalem, and into the **t**: *2411*
11:15 and Jesus went into the **t**, and began to cast *2411*
11:15 cast out them that sold and bought in the **t**, *2411*
11:16 *man* should carry *any* vessel through the **t**. *2411*
11:27 and as he was walking in the **t**, there come *2411*
12:35 and said, while he taught in the **t**, *2411*
13: 1 And as he went out of the **t**, one of his *2411*
13: 3 the mount of Olives over against the **t**, *2411*
14:49 I was daily with you in the **t** teaching, and *2411*
14:58 I will destroy this **t** that is made with hands, *3485*
15:29 *thou* that destroyest the **t**, and buildest *it* in *3485*
15:38 And the vail of the **t** was rent in twain from *3485*
Lk 1: 9 when he went into the **t** of the Lord. *3485*
1:21 marvelled that he tarried *so* long in the **t**. *3485*
1:22 perceived that he had seen a vision in the **t**: *3485*
2:27 And he came by the Spirit into the **t**: and *2411*
2:37 which departed not from the **t**, but *2411*
2:46 after three days they found him in the **t**, *2411*
4: 9 and set him on a pinnacle of the **t**, and *2411*
11:51 which perished between the altar and the **t**: *3624*
18:10 Two men went up into the **t** to pray; *2411*
19:45 And he went into the **t**, and began to cast *2411*
19:47 And he taught daily in the **t**. But the chief *2411*
20: 1 as he taught the people in the **t**, and *2411*
21: 5 And as some spake of the **t**, how it was *2411*
21:37 in the day time he was teaching in the **t**; *2411*
21:38 came early in the morning to him in the **t**, *2411*
22:52 and captains of the **t**, and the elders, *2411*
22:53 When I was daily with you in the **t**, *2411*
23:45 and the vail of the **t** was rent in the midst. *3485*
24:53 And were continually in the **t**, praising and *2411*
Jn 2:14 And found in the **t** those that sold oxen and *2411*
2:15 he drove *them* all out of the **t**, and the sheep *2411*
2:19 Destroy this **t**, and in three days I will raise *3485*
2:20 Forty and six years was this **t** in building, *3485*
2:21 But he spake of the **t** of his body. *3485*
5:14 Afterward Jesus findeth him in the **t**, and *2411*
7:14 midst of the feast Jesus went up into the **t**, *2411*
7:28 Then cried Jesus in the **t** as he taught, *2411*
8: 2 in the morning he came again into the **t**, *2411*
8:20 Jesus in the treasury, as he taught in the **t**: *2411*
8:59 but Jesus hid himself, and went out of the **t**, *2411*
10:23 And Jesus walked in the **t** in Solomon's *2411*
11:56 as they stood in the **t**, What think ye, *2411*
18:20 I ever taught in the synagogue, and in the **t**, *2411*
Ac 2:46 continuing daily with one accord in the **t**, *2411*
3: 1 John went up together into the **t** at the hour *2411*
3: 2 whom they laid daily at the gate of the **t** *2411*
3: 2 to ask alms of them that entered into the **t**; *2411*
3: 3 seeing Peter and John about to go into the **t**, *2411*
3: 8 walked, and entered with them into the **t**, *2411*
3:10 sat for alms at the Beautiful gate of the **t**: *2411*
4: 1 and the captain of the **t**, and the Sadducees, *2411*
5:20 speak in the **t** to the people all the words of *2411*
5:21 they entered into the **t** early in the morning, *2411*
5:24 the *high* priest and the captain of the **t** and *2411*
5:25 whom ye put in prison are standing in the **t**, *2411*
5:42 And daily in the **t**, and in every house, they *2411*
19:27 also that the **t** of the great goddess Diana *2411*
21:26 himself with them entered into the **t**, *2411*
21:27 when they saw him in the **t**, stirred up all *2411*
21:28 and further brought Greeks also into the **t**, *2411*
21:29 supposed that Paul had brought into the **t**.) *2411*
21:30 they took Paul, and drew him out of the **t**: *2411*
22:17 even while I prayed in the **t**, I was in a *2411*
24: 6 Who also hath gone about to profane the **t**: *2411*
24:12 And they neither found me in the **t** *2411*
24:18 Jews from Asia found me purified in the **t**, *2411*
25: 8 neither against the **t**, nor *yet* against Cesar, *2411*
26:21 these causes the Jews caught me in the **t**, *2411*
1Co 3:16 Know ye not that ye are the **t** of God, and *3485*
3:17 If any *man* defile the **t** of God, him shall *3485*
3:17 for the **t** of God is holy, which *temple* ye *3485*
3:17 the temple of God is holy, which *t* ye are. NIG
6:19 know ye not that your body is the **t** of *3485*
8:10 hast knowledge sit at meat in the **idol's t**, *1493*
9:13 about holy *things* live of *the things of* the **t**? *2411*
2Co 6:16 And what agreement hath the **t** of God with *3485*
6:16 for ye are the **t** of the living God; as God *3485*
Eph 2:21 together groweth unto a holy **t** in the Lord: *3485*
2Th 2: 4 so that he as God sitteth in the **t** of God, *3485*
Rev 3:12 will I make a pillar in the **t** of my God, *3485*
7:15 and serve him day and night in his **t**: *3485*
11: 1 and measure the **t** of God, and the altar, and *3485*
11: 2 But the court which is without the **t** leave *3485*
11:19 And the **t** of God was opened in heaven, *3485*
11:19 there was seen in his **t** the ark of his *3485*
14:15 And another angel came out of the **t**, *3485*
14:17 And another angel came out of the **t** which *3485*
15: 5 the **t** of the tabernacle of the testimony in *3485*
15: 6 And the seven angels came out of the **t**, *3485*
15: 8 And the **t** was filled with smoke from *3485*
15: 8 and no *man* was able to enter into the **t**, *3485*
16: 1 And I heard a great voice out of the **t** *3485*
16:17 there came a great voice out of the **t** of *3485*
21:22 And I saw no **t** therein: for the Lord God *3485*
21:22 God Almighty and the Lamb are the **t** of it. *3485*

TEMPLE SERVANTS See NETHINIMS

TEMPLES (9) [TEMPLE]

Jdg 4:21 smote the nail into his **t**, and fastened *it* into 7541

T

Jdg	4:22	Sisera lay dead, and the nail *was* in his t.	7541
	5:26	she had pierced and stricken through his t.	7541
SS	4:3	thy t *are* like a piece of a pomegranate	7541
	6:7	As a piece of a pomegranate *are* thy t	7541
Hos	8:14	hath forgotten his Maker, and buildeth t;	1964
Joel	3:5	have carried into your t my goodly pleasant	1964
Ac	7:48	Howbeit the most High dwelleth not in t	*3485*
	17:24	earth, dwelleth not in t made with hands;	*3485*

TEMPORAL (1)

2Co	4:18	for the *things* which are seen *are* t; but	*4340*

TEMPORARY See TEMPORAL

TEMPORARY RESIDENT See SOJOURN; SOJOURNED; SOJOURNER; SOJOURNERS; SOJOURNETH; SOJOURNING

TEMPT (14) [TEMPTATION, TEMPTATIONS, TEMPTED, TEMPTER, TEMPTETH, TEMPTING]

Ge	22:1	that God did t Abraham, and said unto him,	5254
Ex	17:2	with me? wherefore do ye t the LORD?	5254
Dt	6:16	Ye shall not t the LORD your God, as ye	5254
Isa	7:12	I will not ask, neither will I t the LORD.	5254
Mal	3:15	yea, *they that* t God are even delivered.	974
Mt	4:7	Thou shalt not t the Lord thy God.	*1598*
	22:18	and said, Why t ye me, *ye* hypocrites?	*3985*
Mk	12:15	said unto them, Why t ye me?	*3985*
Lk	4:12	is said, Thou shalt not t the Lord thy God.	*1598*
	20:23	and said unto them, Why t ye me?	*3985*
Ac	5:9	How *is it* that ye have agreed together to t	*3985*
	15:10	Now therefore why t ye God, to put a yoke	*3985*
1Co	7:5	that Satan t you not for your incontinency.	*3985*
	10:9	Neither let us t Christ, as some of them also	*1598*

TEMPTATION (16) [TEMPT]

Ps	95:8	*and* as *in* the day of t in the wilderness:	4531
Mt	6:13	And lead us not into t, but deliver us from	*3986*
	26:41	Watch and pray, that ye enter not into t:	*3986*
Mk	14:38	Watch ye and pray, lest ye enter into t.	*3986*
Lk	4:13	And when the devil had ended all the t,	*3986*
	8:13	a while believe, and in time of t fall away.	*3986*
	11:4	And lead us not into t; but deliver us from	*3986*
	22:40	said unto them, Pray that *ye* enter not into t.	*3986*
	22:46	sleep ye? rise and pray, lest ye enter into t.	*3986*
1Co	10:13	There hath no t taken you but such as is	*3986*
	10:13	will with the t also make a way to escape,	*3986*
Gal	4:14	And my t which was in my flesh ye	*3986*
1Ti	6:9	But they that will be rich fall into t and	*3986*
Heb	3:8	in the day of t in the wilderness:	*3986*
Jas	1:12	Blessed *is* the man that endureth t:	*3986*
Rev	3:10	I also will keep thee from the hour of t,	*3986*

TEMPTATIONS (8) [TEMPT]

Dt	4:34	by t, by signs, and by wonders, and by war,	4531
	7:19	The great t which thine eyes saw, and	4531
	29:3	The great t which thine eyes have seen,	4531
Lk	22:28	which have continued with me in my t.	*3986*
Ac	20:19	of mind, and *with* many tears, and t,	*3986*
Jas	1:2	count *it* all joy when ye fall into divers t;	*3986*
1Pe	1:6	ye are in heaviness through manifold t:	*3986*
2Pe	2:9	knoweth *how* to deliver the godly out of t,	*3986*

TEMPTED (25) [TEMPT]

Ex	17:7	because they t the LORD, saying, Is	5254
Nu	14:22	have t me *now* these ten times, and	5254
Dt	6:16	LORD your God, as ye t *him* in Massah.	5254
Ps	78:18	they t God in their heart by asking meat for	5254
	78:41	they turned *back* and t God, and limited	5254
	78:56	Yet they t and provoked the most high	5254
	95:9	When your fathers t me, proved me, and	5254
	106:14	in the wilderness, and t God in the desert.	5254
Mt	4:1	into the wilderness to be t of the devil.	*3985*
Mk	1:13	in the wilderness forty days, t of Satan;	*3985*
Lk	4:2	Being forty days t of the devil. And in	*3985*
	10:25	lawyer stood up, and t him, saying, Master,	*1598*
1Co	10:9	as some of them also t, and were destroyed	*3985*
	10:13	who will not suffer you to be t above that	*3985*
Gal	6:1	considering thyself, lest thou also be t.	*3985*
1Th	3:5	lest by some means the tempter have t you,	*3985*
Heb	2:18	For in that he himself hath suffered being t,	*3985*
	2:18	he is able to succour them that are t.	*3985*
	3:9	When your fathers t me, proved me, and	*3985*
	4:15	was in all *points* t like as *we are, yet*	*3985*
	11:37	they were sawn asunder, were t,	*3985*
Jas	1:13	Let no *man* say when he is t, I am tempted	*3985*
	1:13	*man* say when he is tempted, I am t of God:	*3985*
	1:13	for God **cannot be t** with evil,	*551+1510*
	1:14	But every man is t, when he is drawn away	*3985*

TEMPTER (2) [TEMPT]

Mt	4:3	And when the t came to him, he said,	*3985*
1Th	3:5	lest by some means the t have tempted you,	*3985*

TEMPTETH (1) [TEMPT]

Jas	1:13	be tempted with evil, neither t he any *man:*	*3985*

TEMPTING (7) [TEMPT]

Mt	16:1	t desired him that *he* would shew them a	*3985*
	19:3	came unto him, t him, and saying unto him,	*3985*
	22:35	asked *him a question,* t him, and saying,	*3985*
Mk	8:11	seeking of him a sign from heaven, t him.	*3985*
	10:2	for a man to put away *his* wife? t him.	*3985*
Lk	11:16	t *him,* sought of him a sign from heaven.	*3985*
Jn	8:6	This they said, t him, that they might have	*3985*

TEN (248) [TEN'S, TENS, TENTH]

Ge	5:14	of Cainan were nine hundred and t years:	6235
	16:3	after Abram had dwelt t years in the land of	6235
	18:32	Peradventure t shall be found there. And he	6235
	24:10	the servant took t camels of the camels of	6235
	24:22	two bracelets for her hands of t *shekels*	6235
	24:55	abide with us *a few* days, at the least t;	6218
	31:7	and changed my wages t times;	6235
	31:41	and thou hast changed my wages t times.	6235
	32:15	forty kine, and t bulls, twenty she asses,	6235
	32:15	and ten bulls, twenty she asses, and t foals.	6235
	42:3	Joseph's t brethren went down to buy corn	6235
	45:23	t asses laden with the good things of Egypt,	6235
	45:23	t she asses laden with corn and bread and	6235
	46:27	came into Egypt, *were* **threescore and t**.	7657
	50:3	mourned for him **threescore and t**	7657
	50:22	and Joseph lived an hundred and t years.	6235
	50:26	*being* an hundred and t years old:	6235
Ex	15:27	of water, and **threescore and t** palm trees:	7657
	26:1	*with* t curtains *of* fine twined linen,	6235
	26:16	T cubits *shall be* the length of a board, and	6235
	27:12	their pillars t, and their sockets ten.	6235
	27:12	their pillars ten, and their sockets t.	6235
	34:28	of the covenant, the t commandments.	6235
	36:8	made t curtains *of* fine twined linen,	6235
	36:21	The length of a board *was* t cubits, and	6235
	38:12	their pillars t, and their sockets ten;	6235
	38:12	their pillars ten, and their sockets t;	6235
Lev	26:8	an hundred of you shall put **t thousand** to	7233
	26:26	t women shall bake your bread in one oven,	6235
	27:5	and for the female t shekels.	6235
	27:7	and for the female t shekels.	6235
Nu	7:14	One spoon of t *shekels* of gold, full *of*	6235
	7:20	One spoon of gold of t *shekels,* full *of*	6235
	7:26	One golden spoon of t *shekels,* full *of*	6235
	7:32	One golden spoon *of* t *shekels,* full *of*	6235
	7:38	One golden spoon of t *shekels,* full *of*	6235
	7:44	One golden spoon of t *shekels,* full *of*	6235
	7:50	One golden spoon of t *shekels,* full *of*	6235
	7:56	One golden spoon of t *shekels,* full *of*	6235
	7:62	One golden spoon of t *shekels,* full *of*	6235
	7:68	One golden spoon of t *shekels,* full *of*	6235
	7:74	One golden spoon of t *shekels,* full *of*	6235
	7:80	One golden spoon of t *shekels,* full *of*	6235
	7:86	full *of* incense, *weighing* t *shekels* apiece,	6235
	11:19	nor two days, nor five days, neither t days,	6235
	11:32	he that gathered least gathered t homers:	6235
	14:22	have tempted me *now* these t times, and	6235
	29:23	And on the fourth day t bullocks, two rams,	6235
	33:9	of water, and **threescore and t** palm trees;	7657
Dt	4:13	you to perform, *even* t commandments;	6235
	10:4	to the first writing, the t commandments,	6235
	10:22	down into Egypt with **threescore and t**	7657
	32:30	two put **t thousand** to flight, except their	7233
	33:2	and he came with **t thousands** of saints:	7233
	33:17	they *are* the **t thousands** of Ephraim, and	7233
Jos	15:57	and Timnah; t cities with their villages.	6235
	17:5	there fell t portions to Manasseh, beside	6235
	21:5	out of the half tribe of Manasseh, t cities.	6235
	21:26	All the cities *were* t with their suburbs for	6235
	22:14	with him t princes, of each chief house a	6235
	24:29	died, *being* an hundred and t years old.	6235
Jdg	1:4	they slew *of* them in Bezek t thousand men.	6235
	1:7	**Threescore and t** kings, having their	7657

Jdg	2: 8	died, *being* an hundred and t years old.	6235
	3:29	they slew *of* Moab at that time about t	6235
	4: 6	take with thee t thousand men of	6235
	4:10	he went up with t thousand men at his feet:	6235
	4:14	and t thousand men after him.	6235
	6:27	Gideon took t men of his servants, and	6235
	7: 3	and there remained t thousand.	6235
	8:30	Gideon had **threescore and** t sons of his	7657
	9: 2	*which are* **threescore and** t persons,	7657
	9: 4	they gave him **threescore and** t *pieces* of	7657
	9: 5	*being* **threescore and** t persons, upon one	7657
	9:18	**threescore and** t persons, upon one stone,	7657
	9:24	the cruelty *done* to the **threescore and** t	7657
	12:11	judged Israel; and he judged Israel t years.	6235
	12:14	that rode on **threescore and** t ass colts:	7651
	17:10	I will give thee t *shekels* of silver by	6235
	20:10	we will take t men of an hundred	6235
	20:10	and a thousand out of t **thousand**,	7233
	20:34	there came against Gibeah t thousand	6235
Ru	1: 4	and they dwelled there about t years.	6235
	4: 2	he took t men of the elders of the city, and	6235
1Sa	1: 8	*am* not I better to thee than t sons?	6235
	6:19	fifty thousand and **threescore and** t men:	7657
	15: 4	and t thousand men of Judah.	6235
	17:17	of this parched *corn*, and these t loaves,	6235
	17:18	carry these t cheeses unto the captain of	6235
	18: 7	his thousands, and David his t **thousands**.	7233
	18: 8	have ascribed unto David t **thousands**,	7233
	21:11	his thousands, and David his t **thousands**?	7233
	25: 5	David sent out t young men, and	6235
	25:38	it came to pass about t days *after*, that	6235
	29: 5	his thousands, and David his t **thousands**?	7233
2Sa	15:16	the king left t women, *which were*	6235
	18: 3	now *thou art* worth t thousand of us:	6235
	18:11	I would have given thee t *shekels of* silver,	6235
	18:15	t young men that bare Joab's armour	6235
	19:43	We have t parts in the king, and we have	6235
	20: 3	the king took the t women *his* concubines,	6235
1Ki	4:23	**T** fat oxen, and twenty oxen out of	6235
	5:14	to Lebanon, t thousand a month *by* courses:	6235
	5:15	Solomon had **threescore and** t thousand	7657
	6: 3	t cubits *was* the breadth thereof before	6235
	6:23	cherubims *of* olive tree, each t cubits high.	6235
	6:24	the uttermost part of the other *were* t cubits.	6235
	6:25	the other cherub *was* t cubits: both	6235
	6:26	The height of the one cherub *was* t cubits,	6235
	7:10	stones of t cubits, and stones of eight	6235
	7:23	t cubits from the one brim to the other:	6235
	7:24	t in a cubit, compassing the sea round	6235
	7:27	he made t bases of brass; four cubits *was*	6235
	7:37	After this *manner* he made the t bases:	6235
	7:38	made he t lavers of brass: one laver	6235
	7:38	upon every one of the t bases one laver.	6235
	7:43	the t bases, and ten lavers on the bases;	6235
	7:43	the ten bases, and t lavers on the bases;	6235
	11:31	he said to Jeroboam, Take thee t pieces:	6235
	11:31	of Solomon, and will give t tribes to thee:	6235
	11:35	and will give it unto thee, *even* t tribes.	6235
	14: 3	take with thee t loaves, and cracknels, and	6235
2Ki	5: 5	took with him t talents of silver, and	6235
	5: 5	*pieces* of gold, and t changes of raiment.	6235
	13: 7	and t chariots, and ten thousand footmen;	6235
	13: 7	and ten chariots, and t thousand footmen;	6235
	14: 7	He slew *of* Edom in the valley of salt t	6235
	15:17	over Israel, *and reigned* t years in Samaria.	6235
	20: 9	shall the shadow go forward t degrees, or	6235
	20: 9	forward ten degrees, or go back t degrees?	6235
	20:10	thing for the shadow to go down t degrees:	6235
	20:10	let the shadow return backward t degrees.	6235
	20:11	he brought the shadow t degrees backward,	6235
	24:14	*even* t thousand captives, and all	6240
	25:25	and t men with him, and smote Gedaliah,	6235
1Ch	6:61	the half *tribe* of Manasseh, by lot, t cities.	6235
	21: 5	Judah *was* four hundred **threescore and** t	7657
	29: 7	thousand talents and t **thousand** drams,	7239
	29: 7	*of* silver t thousand talents, and *of* brass	6235
2Ch	2: 2	Solomon told out **threescore and** t	7657
	2:18	he set **threescore and** t thousand of them	7657
	4: 1	and t cubits the height thereof.	6235
	4: 2	Also he made a molten sea of t cubits from	6235
	4: 3	t in a cubit, compassing the sea round	6235
	4: 6	He made also t lavers, and put five on	6235
	4: 7	he made t candlesticks of gold according to	6235
	4: 8	He made also t tables, and placed *them* in	6235
	14: 1	In his days the land was quiet t years.	6235
	25:11	smote *of* the children of Seir t thousand.	6235
	25:12	*other* t thousand *left* alive did the children	6235
	27: 5	t thousand measures of wheat, and	6235
	27: 5	of wheat, and t thousand of barley.	6235
	29:32	was **threescore and** t bullocks, an hundred	7657
	30:24	a thousand bullocks and t thousand sheep:	6235
	36: 9	three months and t days in Jerusalem:	6235
	36:21	to fulfil **threescore and** t years.	7657
Ezr	1:10	basons of a second sort four hundred and t,	6235
	8:12	and with him an hundred and t males.	6235
	8:24	and t of their brethren with them,	6235
Ne	4:12	by them came, they said unto us t times,	6235
	5:18	and once in t days store of all *sorts of* wine:	6235
	11: 1	to bring one of t to dwell in Jerusalem	6235
Est	3: 9	I will pay t thousand talents of silver to	6235
	9:10	The t sons of Haman the son of	6235
	9:12	the palace, and the t sons of Haman;	6235
	9:13	let Haman's t sons be hanged upon	6235
	9:14	and they hanged Haman's t sons.	6235
Job	19: 3	These t times have ye reproached me:	6235
Ps	3: 6	I will not be afraid of t **thousands** of	7233
	33: 2	the psaltery *and* an **instrument of t strings**.	6218
	90:10	of our years *are* **threescore** years **and** t;	7657
	91: 7	thy side, and t **thousand** at thy right hand;	7233
	92: 3	Upon an **instrument of t strings**, and	6218
	144: 9	an **instrument of t strings** will I sing	6218
	144:13	and t **thousands** in our streets:	7231
Ecc	7:19	Wisdom strengtheneth the wise more than t	6235
SS	5:10	and ruddy, the chiefest among t **thousand**.	7233
Isa	5:10	t acres of vineyard shall yield one bath, and	6235
	38: 8	the sun dial of Ahaz, t degrees backward.	6235
	38: 8	So the sun returned t degrees, by which	6235
Jer	41: 1	princes of the king, even t men with him,	6235
	41: 2	the t men that were with him, and	6235
	41: 8	t men were found among them that said	6235
	42: 7	it came to pass after t days, that the word of	6235
Eze	40:11	the breadth of the entry of the gate, t cubits;	6235
	41: 2	the breadth of the door *was* t cubits; and	6235
	42: 4	before the chambers *was* a walk of t cubits	6235
	45: 1	and the breadth *shall be* t thousand.	6235
	45: 3	and the breadth of t thousand:	6235
	45: 5	*the* t thousand of breadth, shall also	6235
	45:14	out of the cor, *which is* a homer of t baths;	6235
	45:14	homer of ten baths; for t baths *are* a homer:	6235
	48: 9	*in* length, and *of* t thousand *in* breadth.	6235
	48:10	and toward the west t thousand *in* breadth,	6235
	48:10	toward the east t thousand *in* breadth, and	6235
	48:13	*in* length, and t thousand *in* breadth:	6235
	48:13	and the breadth t thousand.	6235
	48:18	holy *portion shall be* t thousand eastward,	6235
	48:18	and t thousand westward:	6235
Da	1:12	Prove thy servants, I beseech thee, t days;	6235
	1:14	in this matter, and proved them t days.	6235
	1:15	at the end of t days their countenances	6235
	1:20	he found them t times better than all	6235
	7: 7	that *were* before it; and it had t horns.	6236
	7:10	t **thousand** times ten thousand stood before	7240
	7:10	ten thousand times t **thousand** stood before	7240
	7:20	of the t horns that *were* in his head, and	6236
	7:24	the t horns out of this kingdom *are* ten	6236
	7:24	the ten horns out of this kingdom *are* t	6236
	11:12	and he shall cast down *many* t **thousands**:	7239
Am	5: 3	went forth *by* an hundred shall leave t,	6235
	6: 9	if there remain t men in one house,	6235
Mic	6: 7	*or* with t **thousands** of rivers of oil?	7233
Hag	2:16	heap of twenty *measures*, there were *but* t:	6235
Zec	1:12	hast had indignation these **threescore and** t	7657
	5: 2	and the breadth thereof t cubits.	6235
	8:23	In those days *it shall come to pass*, that t	6235
Mt	18:24	which ought him t **thousand** talents.	*3463*
	20:24	And when the t heard *it*, they were moved	*1176*
	25: 1	of heaven be likened unto t virgins,	*1176*
	25:28	and give *it* unto him which hath t talents.	*1176*
Mk	10:41	And when the t heard *it*, they began to be	*1176*
Lk	14:31	consulteth whether he be able with t	*1176*
	15: 8	Either what woman having t pieces of	*1176*
	17:12	there met him t men *that were* lepers,	*1176*
	17:17	answering said, Were there not t cleansed?	*1176*
	19:13	And he called his t servants, and	*1176*
	19:13	and delivered them t pounds, and said unto	*1176*
	19:16	Lord, thy pound hath gained t pounds.	*1176*
	19:17	very little, have thou authority over t cities.	*1176*
	19:24	and give *it* to him that hath t pounds.	*1176*

Lk 19:25 they said unto him, Lord, he hath **t** pounds.) *1176*
Ac 23:23 and horsemen **threescore** *and* **t**, and *1440*
25: 6 had tarried among them more than **t** days, *1176*
1Co 4:15 For though you have **t thousand** instructors *3463*
14:19 than **t thousand** words in an *unknown* *3463*
Jude 1:14 the Lord cometh with **t thousands** of his *3461*
Rev 2:10 and ye shall have tribulation **t** days: *1176*
5:11 the number of them was **t thousand** times *3461*
5:11 them was ten thousand times **t thousand**, *3461*
12: 3 having seven heads and **t** horns, and *1176*
13: 1 having seven heads and **t** horns, and *1176*
13: 1 and upon his horns **t** crowns, and upon his *1176*
17: 3 having seven heads and **t** horns. *1176*
17: 7 which hath the seven heads and **t** horns. *1176*
17:12 And the **t** horns which thou sawest are ten *1176*
17:12 And the ten horns which thou sawest are **t** *1176*
17:16 And the **t** horns which thou sawest upon *1176*

TEN'S (1) [TEN]
Ge 18:32 And he said, I will not destroy *it* for **t** sake. 6235

TEND (1) [TENDETH]
Pr 21: 5 The thoughts of the diligent *t* only to NIH

TENDER (40) [TENDERHEARTED, TENDERNESS]
Ge 18: 7 fetcht a calf **t** and good, and gave *it* unto a 7390
29:17 Leah was **t** eyed; but Rachel was beautiful 7390
33:13 My lord knoweth that the children *are* **t**, 7390
Dt 28:54 *So that* the man *that is* **t** among you, and 7390
28:56 The **t** and delicate *woman* among you, 7390
32: 2 as the small rain upon the **t herb**, and as 1877
2Sa 23: 4 *as* the **t grass** *springing* out of the earth by 1877
2Ki 22:19 Because thine heart was **t**, and thou hast 7401
1Ch 22: 5 Solomon my son *is* young and **t**, and 7390
29: 1 *is yet* young and **t**, and the work *is* great: 7390
2Ch 13: 7 when Rehoboam was young and **t** hearted, 7390
34:27 Because thine heart was **t**, and thou didst 7401
Job 14: 7 that the **t branch** thereof will not cease. 3127
38:27 to cause the bud of the **t herb** to spring 1877
Ps 25: 6 thy **t mercies** and thy lovingkindnesses; 7356
40:11 Withhold not thou thy **t mercies** from me, 7356
51: 1 of thy **t mercies** blot out my transgressions. 7356
69:16 according to the multitude of thy **t mercies**. 7356
77: 9 hath he in anger shut up his **t mercies**? 7356
79: 8 let thy **t mercies** speedily prevent us: 7356
103: 4 thee *with* lovingkindness and **t mercies**; 7356
119:77 Let thy **t mercies** come *unto* me, that I may 7356
119:156 Great *are* thy **t mercies**, O LORD: 7356
145: 9 and his **t mercies** *are* over all his works. 7356
Pr 4: 3 **t** and only *beloved* in the sight of my 7390
12:10 but the **t mercies** of the wicked *are* cruel. 7356
27:25 the **t grass** sheweth itself, and herbs of 1877
SS 2:13 the vines *with* the **t grape** give a *good* 5563
2:15 spoil the vines: for our vines *have* **t grapes**. 5563
7:12 *whether* the **t grape** appear, *and* 5563
Isa 47: 1 for thou shalt no more be called **t** and 7390
53: 2 he shall grow up before him as a **t plant**, 3126
Eze 17:22 off from the top of his young twigs a **t one**, 7390
Da 1: 9 and **t love** with the prince of the eunuchs. 7356
4:15 of iron and brass, in the **t grass** of the field; 1883
4:23 of iron and brass, in the **t grass** of the field; 1883
Mt 24:32 When his branch is yet **t**, and putteth forth *527*
Mk 13:28 When her branch is yet **t**, and putteth forth *527*
Lk 1:78 Through the **t mercy** of our God; *1656+4698*
Jas 5:11 that the Lord is very pitiful, and of **t mercy**. *3629*

TENDERHEARTED (1) [HEART, TENDER]
Eph 4:32 one to another, **t**, forgiving one another, *2155*

TENDERNESS (1) [TENDER]
Dt 28:56 foot upon the ground for delicateness and **t**, 7391

TENDETH (5) [TEND]
Pr 10:16 The labour of the righteous *t* to life: the fruit NIH
11:19 As righteousness *t* to life: so he that NIH
11:24 more than is meet, but *it t* to poverty. NIH
14:23 but the talk of the lips *t* only to penury. NIH
19:23 The fear of the LORD *t* to life: and *he that* NIH

TENONS (6)
Ex 26:17 Two **t** *shall there be* in one board, set in 3027
26:19 two sockets under one board for his two **t**, 3027
26:19 sockets under another board for his two **t**. 3027
36:22 One board had two **t**, equally distant one 3027
36:24 two sockets under one board for his two **t**, 3027
36:24 sockets under another board for his two **t**. 3027

TENOR (2)
Ge 43: 7 we told him according to the **t** of these 6310
Ex 34:27 for after the **t** of these words I have made a 6310

TENS (3) [TENS]
Ex 18:21 rulers of fifties, and rulers of **t**: 6235
18:25 of hundreds, rulers of fifties, and rulers of **t**. 6235
Dt 1:15 captains over **t**, and officers among your 6235

TENT (98) [TENTMAKERS, TENTS]
Ge 9:21 and he was uncovered within his **t**. 168
12: 8 pitched his **t**, *having* Beth-el on the west, 168
13: 3 unto the place where his **t** had been at 168
13:12 the plain, and **pitched** his **t** toward Sodom. 167
13:18 Abram **removed** his **t**, and came and 167
18: 1 he sat *in* the **t** door in the heat of the day; 168
18: 2 *them,* he ran to meet them from the **t** door, 168
18: 6 Abraham hastened into the **t** unto Sarah, 168
18: 9 thy wife? And he said, Behold, in the **t**. 168
18:10 Sarah heard *it in* the **t** door, which *was* 168
24:67 Isaac brought her into his mother Sarah's **t**, 168
26:17 **pitched** his **t** in the valley of Gerar, and 2583
26:25 name of the LORD, and pitched his **t** there: 168
31:25 Now Jacob had pitched his **t** in the mount: 168
31:33 Laban went into Jacob's **t**, and into Leah's 168
31:33 into Leah's **t**, and into the two maidservants' 168
31:33 went he out of Leah's **t**, and entered into 168
31:33 of Leah's tent, and entered into Rachel's **t**. 168
31:34 Laban searched all the **t**, but found *them* not. 168
33:18 and **pitched** his **t** before the city. 2583
33:19 a parcel of a field, where he had spread his **t**, 168
35:21 and spread his **t** beyond the tower of Edar. 168
Ex 18: 7 of *their* welfare; and they came into the **t**. 168
26:11 and couple the **t** together, that it may be one. 168
26:12 that remaineth of the curtains of the **t**, 168
26:13 in the length of the curtains of the **t**, 168
26:14 thou shalt make a covering for the **t** *of* rams' 168
26:36 shalt make a hanging for the door of the **t**, 168
33: 8 stood every man *at* his **t** door, and 168
33:10 and worshipped, every man *in* his **t** door. 168
35:11 his **t**, and his covering, his taches, and 168
36:14 he made curtains *of* goats' *hair* for the **t** over 168
36:18 he made fifty taches of brass to couple the **t** 168
36:19 he made a covering for the **t** *of* rams' skins 168
39:32 of the **t** of the congregation finished: 168
39:33 the **t**, and all his furniture, his taches, 168
39:40 the tabernacle, for the **t** of the congregation, 168
40: 2 the tabernacle of the **t** of the congregation. 168
40: 6 of the tabernacle of the **t** of the congregation. 168
40: 7 thou shalt set the laver between the **t** of 168
40:19 he spread abroad the **t** over the tabernacle, 168
40:19 and put the covering of the **t** above upon it; 168
40:22 he put the table in the **t** of the congregation, 168
40:24 he put the candlestick in the **t** of 168
40:26 he put the golden altar in the **t** of 168
40:29 of the tabernacle of the **t** of the congregation, 168
40:30 he set the laver between the **t** of 168
40:32 When they went into the **t** of 168
40:34 a cloud covered the **t** of the congregation, 168
40:35 Moses was not able to enter into the **t** of 168
Lev 14: 8 shall tarry abroad out of his **t** seven days. 168
Nu 3:25 the **t**, the covering thereof, and the hanging 168
9:15 *namely,* the **t** of the Testimony: 168
11:10 their families, every man in the door of his **t**: 168
19:14 This *is* the law, when a man dieth in a **t**: 168
19:14 all that come into the **t**, and all that *is* in 168
19:14 come into the tent, and all that *is* in the **t**, 168
19:18 sprinkle *it* upon the **t**, and upon all 168
25: 8 he went after the man of Israel into the **t**, 6898
Jos 7:21 they *are* hid in the earth in the midst of my **t**, 168
7:22 sent messengers, and they ran unto the **t**; 168
7:22 *it was* hid in his **t**, and the silver under it. 168
7:23 And they took them out of the midst of the **t**, 168
7:24 and his sheep, and his **t**, and all that he had: 168
Jdg 4:11 pitched his **t** unto the plain of Zaanaim, 168
4:17 Howbeit Sisera fled away on his feet to the **t** 168
4:18 when he had turned in unto her into the **t**, 168
4:20 Stand *in* the door of the **t**, and it shall be, 168
4:21 Jael Heber's wife took a nail of the **t**, and 168
4:22 when he came into her *t*, behold, Sisera lay NIH
5:24 blessed shall she be above women in the **t**. 168
7: 8 all *the rest of* Israel every man unto his **t**, 168

Jdg	7:13	came unto a **t**, and smote it that it fell, and	168
	7:13	it fell, and overturned it, that the **t** lay along.	168
	20:8	We will not any *of us* go to his **t**,	168
1Sa	4:10	and they fled every man into his **t**:	168
	13:2	rest of the people he sent every man to his **t**.	168
	17:54	*to* Jerusalem; but he put his armour in his **t**.	168
2Sa	7:6	but have walked in a **t** and in a tabernacle.	168
	16:22	So they spread Absalom a **t** upon the top of	168
	18:17	and all Israel fled every one to his **t**.	168
	19:8	for Israel had fled every man to his **t**.	168
	20:22	they retired from the city, every man to his **t**.	168
2Ki	7:8	they went into one **t**, and did eat and drink,	168
	7:8	entered into another **t**, and carried thence	168
1Ch	15:1	for the ark of God, and pitched for it a **t**.	168
	16:1	set it in the midst of the **t** that David had	168
	17:5	have gone from **t** to tent, and from *one*	168
	17:5	have gone from tent to **t**, and from *one*	168
2Ch	1:4	for he had pitched a **t** for it at Jerusalem.	168
	25:22	and they fled every man to his **t**.	168
Ps	78:60	of Shiloh, the **t** *which* he placed among men;	168
Isa	13:20	neither shall the Arabian **pitch t** there;	167
	38:12	and is removed from me as a shepherd's **t**:	168
	40:22	and spreadeth them out as a **t** to dwell in:	168
	54:2	Enlarge the place of thy **t**, and let them	168
Jer	10:20	*there is* none to stretch forth my **t** any more,	168
	37:10	*yet* should they rise up every man in his **t**,	168

TENTH (81) [TENS]

Ge	8:5	the waters decreased continually until the **t**	6224
	8:5	in the **t** *month*, on the first *day* of	6224
	28:22	me I will **surely give the t** unto thee.	6237+6237
Ex	12:3	In the **t** *day* of this month they shall take to	6218
	16:36	Now an omer *is* the **t** *part* of an ephah.	6224
	29:40	with the one lamb a **t deal** of flour mingled	6241
Lev	5:11	**t** *part* of an ephah of fine flour for a sin	6224
	6:20	the **t** *part* of an ephah of fine flour *for* a	6224
	14:10	**three t deals** of fine flour *for* a meat	6241+7969
	14:21	**one t deal** of fine flour mingled with	259+6241
	16:29	on the **t** *day* of the month, ye shall afflict	6218
	23:13	two **t deals** *of* fine flour mingled with oil,	6241
	23:17	habitations two wave loaves of two **t deals**:	6241
	23:27	Also on the **t** *day* of this seventh month	6218
	24:5	two **t deals** shall be *in* one cake.	6241
	25:9	to sound on the **t** *day* of the seventh month,	6218
	27:32	the **t** shall be holy unto the LORD.	6224
Nu	5:15	the **t** *part* of an ephah of barley meal;	6224
	7:66	On the **t** day Ahiezer the son of	6224
	15:4	**t deal** *of* flour mingled with the fourth *part*	6241
	15:6	**t deals** *of* flour mingled with the third *part*	6241
	15:9	**t deals** *of* flour mingled with half a hin of	6241
	18:21	I have given the children of Levi all the **t** in	4643
	18:26	it for the LORD, *even* a **t** *part* of the tithe.	4643
	28:5	a **t** *part* of an ephah *of* flour for a meat	6224
	28:9	and two **t deals** *of* flour *for* a meat offering,	6241
	28:12	three **t deals** *of* flour *for* a meat offering,	6241
	28:12	and two **t deals** *of* flour *for* a meat offering,	6241
	28:13	a **several t deal** of flour mingled	6241+6241
	28:20	three **t deals** shall ye offer for a bullock,	6241
	28:20	for a bullock, and two **t deals** for a ram;	6241
	28:21	A **several t deal** shalt thou offer for	6241+6241
	28:28	three **t deals** unto one bullock, two tenth	6241
	28:28	unto one bullock, two **t deals** unto one ram,	6241
	28:29	A **several t deal** unto one lamb,	6241+6241
	29:3	three **t deals** for a bullock, *and* two tenth	6241
	29:3	for a bullock, *and* two **t deals** for a ram,	6241
	29:4	one **t deal** for one lamb, throughout	6241
	29:7	ye shall have on the **t** *day* of this seventh	6218
	29:9	three **t deals** to a bullock, *and* two tenth	6241
	29:9	to a bullock, *and* two **t deals** to one ram,	6241
	29:10	A **several t deal** for one lamb,	6241+6241
	29:14	three **t deals** unto every bullock of	6241
	29:14	two **t deals** to each ram of the two rams,	6241
	29:15	a **several t deal** to each lamb of	6241+6241
Dt	23:2	even *to* his **t** generation shall he not enter	6224
	23:3	even *to* their **t** generation shall they not	6224
Jos	4:19	the people came up out of Jordan on the **t**	6218
1Sa	8:15	he will **take the t** of your seed, and of your	6237
	8:17	He will **take the t** of your sheep: and	6237
2Ki	25:1	in the **t** month, in the tenth *day* of	6224
	25:1	the tenth month, in the **t** *day* of the month,	6218
1Ch	12:13	Jeremiah the **t**, Machbanai the eleventh.	6224
	24:11	The ninth to Jeshua, the **t** to Shecaniah,	6224
	25:17	The **t** *to* Shimei, *he*, his sons, and	6224
	27:13	The **t** *captain* for the tenth month *was*	6224
	27:13	The tenth *captain* for the **t** month *was*	6224
Ezr	10:16	sat down in the first day of the **t** month to	6224
Est	2:16	into his house royal in the **t** month,	6224
Isa	6:13	yet in it *shall be* a **t**, and *it* shall return, and	6224
Jer	32:1	in the **t** year of Zedekiah king of Judah,	6224
	39:1	in the **t** month, came Nebuchadrezzar king	6224
	52:4	in the **t** month, in the tenth *day* of	6224
	52:4	the tenth month, in the **t** *day* of the month,	6218
	52:12	the fifth month, in the **t** *day* of the month,	6218
Eze	20:1	in the fifth *month,* the **t** *day* of the month,	6218
	24:1	Again in the ninth year, in the **t** month,	6224
	24:1	the tenth month, in the **t** *day* of the month,	6218
	29:1	In the **t** year, in the tenth *month,* in	6224
	29:1	in the **t** *month,* in the twelfth *day* of	6224
	33:21	in the **t** *month,* in the fifth *day* of	6224
	40:1	of the year, in the **t** *day* of the month,	6218
	45:11	that the bath may contain the **t part** of a	4643
	45:11	and the ephah the **t** *part* of a homer:	6224
	45:14	*ye shall offer* the **t part** of a bath out of	4643
Zec	8:19	the fast of the seventh, and the fast of the **t**,	6224
Jn	1:39	him that day: for it was about the **t** hour.	*1182*
Heb	7:2	To whom also Abraham gave a **t** *part* of all;	*1181*
	7:4	patriarch Abraham gave the **t** of the spoils.	*1181*
Rev	11:13	and the **t** *part* of the city fell, and in	*1182*
	21:20	the ninth, a topaz; the **t**, a chrysoprasus;	*1182*

TENTMAKERS (1) [MAKE, TENT]

Ac	18:3	for *by* their occupation they were **t**.	*4635*

TENTS (66) [TENT]

Ge	4:20	he was the father of such as dwell in **t**, and	168
	9:27	and he shall dwell in the **t** of Shem;	168
	13:5	with Abram, had flocks, and herds, and **t**.	168
	25:27	and Jacob *was* a plain man, dwelling in **t**.	168
	31:33	and into the two maidservants' **t**;	168
Ex	16:16	ye every man for *them* which *are* in his **t**.	168
Nu	1:52	the children of Israel shall **pitch** their **t**,	2583
	9:17	there the children of Israel **pitched** their **t**.	2583
	9:18	upon the tabernacle they **rested in** the **t**.	2583
	9:20	of the LORD they **abode in** their **t**,	2583
	9:22	the children of Israel **abode in** their **t**, and	2583
	9:23	of the LORD they **rested in** the **t**,	2583
	13:19	dwell in, whether in **t**, or in strong holds;	4264
	16:26	from the **t** of these wicked men, and	168
	16:27	stood *in* the door of their **t**, and their wives,	168
	24:2	he saw Israel abiding *in his t* according to	NIH
	24:5	How goodly are thy **t**, O Jacob, *and*	168
Dt	1:27	ye murmured in your **t**, and said,	168
	1:33	to search you out a place to **pitch** your **t** *in,*	2583
	5:30	Go say to them, Get you into your **t** again.	168
	11:6	their **t**, and all the substance that *was* in their	168
	16:7	shalt turn in the morning, and go unto thy **t**.	168
	33:18	in thy going out; and, Issachar, in thy **t**.	168
Jos	3:14	when the people removed from their **t**,	168
	22:4	get ye unto your **t**, *and* unto the land of your	168
	22:6	sent them away: and they went unto their **t**.	168
	22:7	Joshua sent them away also unto their **t**,	168
	22:8	Return with much riches unto your **t**, and	168
Jdg	6:5	they came up with their cattle and their **t**,	168
	8:11	of them that dwelt in **t** on the east of Nobah	168
1Sa	17:53	the Philistines, and they spoiled their **t**.	4264
2Sa	11:11	The ark, and Israel, and Judah, abide in **t**;	5521
	20:1	the son of Jesse: every man to his **t**, O Israel.	168
1Ki	8:66	went unto their **t** joyful and glad of heart for	168
	12:16	to your **t**, O Israel: now see to thine own	168
	12:16	David. So Israel departed unto their **t**.	168
2Ki	7:7	left their **t**, and their horses, and their asses,	168
	7:10	and asses tied, and the **t** as they *were*.	168
	7:16	went out, and spoiled the **t** of the Syrians.	4264
	8:21	the chariots: and the people fled into their **t**.	168
	13:5	the children of Israel dwelt in their **t**,	168
	14:12	and they fled every man to their **t**.	168
1Ch	4:41	smote their **t**, and the habitations that were	168
	5:10	they dwelt in their **t** throughout all the east	168
2Ch	7:10	month he sent the people away into their **t**,	168
	10:16	every man to your **t**, O Israel: *and* now,	168
	10:16	thine own house. So all Israel went to their **t**.	168
	14:15	They smote also the **t** of cattle, and	168
	31:2	to praise in the gates of the **t** of	4264
Ezr	8:15	and there **abode** we **in t** three days:	2583
Ps	69:25	be desolate; *and* let none dwell in their **t**.	168
	78:55	made the tribes of Israel to dwell in their **t**.	168
	84:10	than to dwell in the **t** of wickedness.	168
	106:25	murmured in their **t**, *and* hearkened not unto	168

Ps 120: 5 *in* Mesech, *that* I dwell in the **t** of Kedar! 168
SS 1: 5 as the **t** of Kedar, as the curtains of Solomon. 168
1: 8 and feed thy kids beside the shepherds' **t**. 4908
Jer 4:20 suddenly are my **t** spoiled, *and* my curtains 168
6: 3 they shall pitch *their* **t** against her round 168
30:18 I *will* bring again the captivity of Jacob's **t**, 168
35: 7 but all your days ye shall dwell in **t**; 168
35:10 we have dwelt in **t**, and have obeyed, and 168
49:29 Their **t** and their flocks shall they take *away:* 168
Hab 3: 7 I saw the **t** of Cushan in affliction: *and* 168
Zec 12: 7 The LORD also shall save the **t** of Judah 168
14:15 and of all the beasts that shall be in these **t**, 4264

TERAH (11) [THARA]
Ge 11:24 lived nine and twenty years, and begat **T**: 8646
11:25 Nahor lived after he begat **T** an hundred 8646
11:26 **T** lived seventy years, and begat Abram, 8646
11:27 Now these *are* the generations of **T**: 8646
11:27 **T** begat Abram, Nahor, and Haran; and 8646
11:28 Haran died before his father **T** in the land 8646
11:31 **T** took Abram his son, and Lot the son of 8646
11:32 the days of **T** were two hundred and 8646
11:32 five years: and **T** died in Haran. 8646
Jos 24: 2 *even* **T**, the father of Abraham, and 8646
1Ch 1:26 Serug, Nahor, **T**, 8646

TERAPHIM (6)
Jdg 17: 5 and **t**, and consecrated one of his sons, 8655
18:14 **t**, and a graven image, and a molten image? 8655
18:17 the ephod, and the **t**, and the molten image: 8655
18:18 the ephod, and the **t**, and the molten image. 8655
18:20 the **t**, and the graven image, and went in 8655
Hos 3: 4 and without an ephod, and *without* **t**: 8655

TEREBINTH See TEIL

TERESH (2)
Est 2:21 Bigthan and **T**, of those which kept 8657
6: 2 that Mordecai had told of Bigthana and **T**, 8657

TERMED (2)
Isa 62: 4 Thou shalt no more be **t** Forsaken; 559
62: 4 neither shall thy land any more be **t** 559

TERRACES (1)
2Ch 9:11 the king made *of* the algum trees **t** to 4546

TERRESTRIAL (2)
1Co 15:40 *are* also celestial bodies, and bodies **t**: *1919*
15:40 *is* one, and the *glory* of the **t** *is* another. *1919*

TERRIBLE (52) [TERRIFY]
Ex 34:10 for it *is* a **t** thing that I will do with thee. 3372
Dt 1:19 *through* all that great and **t** wilderness, 3372
7:21 thy God *is* among you, a mighty God and **t**. 3372
8:15 led thee through *that* great and **t** wilderness, 3372
10:17 of lords, a great God, a mighty, and a **t**, 3372
10:21 and **t** *things,* which thine eyes have seen. 3372
Jdg 13: 6 the countenance of an angel of God, very **t**: 3372
2Sa 7:23 to do for you great things and **t**, for thy 3372
Ne 1: 5 the great and **t** God, that keepeth covenant 3372
4:14 *which is* great and **t**, and fight for your 3372
9:32 the great, the mighty, and the **t** God, 3372
Job 37:22 out of the north: with God *is* **t** majesty. 3372
39:20 a grasshopper? the glory of his nostrils *is* **t**. 367
41:14 doors of his face? his teeth *are* **t** round about. 367
Ps 45: 4 and thy right hand shall teach thee **t** *things.* 3372
47: 2 For the LORD most High *is* **t**; *he is* a 3372
65: 5 *By* **t** *things* in righteousness wilt thou 3372
66: 3 Say unto God, How **t** *art thou in* thy works! 3372
66: 5 *he is* **t** *in his* doing toward the children of 3372
68:35 O God, *thou art* **t** out of thy holy places: 3372
76:12 of princes: *he is* **t** to the kings of the earth. 3372
99: 3 Let them praise thy great and **t** name; *for* it 3372
106:22 land of Ham, *and* **t** *things* by the Red sea. 3372
145: 6 *men* shall speak of the might of thy **t acts**: 3372
SS 6: 4 as Jerusalem, **t** as *an army* with banners. 366
6:10 as the sun, *and* **t** as *an army* with banners? 366
Isa 13:11 and will lay low the haughtiness of the **t**. 6184
18: 2 to a people **t** from their beginning hitherto; 3372
18: 7 from a people **t** from their beginning 3372
21: 1 *so* it cometh from the desert, from a **t** land. 3372
25: 3 the city of the **t** nations shall fear thee. 6184
25: 4 when the blast of the **t ones** *is* as a storm 6184
25: 5 the branch of the **t ones** shall be brought 6184
29: 5 the multitude of the **t ones** *shall be* as chaff 6184
29:20 For the **t one** is brought **to nought**, and 6184
49:25 and the prey of the **t** shall be delivered: 6184
64: 3 When thou didst **t things** *which* we looked 3372
Jer 15:21 I will redeem thee out of the hand of the **t**. 6184
20:11 the LORD *is* with me as a mighty **t one**: 6184
La 5:10 black like an oven because of the **t** famine. 2152
Eze 1:22 creature *was* as the colour of the **t** crystal, 3372
28: 7 strangers upon thee, the **t** of the nations: 6184
30:11 his people with him, the **t** of the nations, 6184
31:12 strangers, the **t** of the nations, have cut him 6184
32:12 to fall, the **t** of the nations, all of them: 6184
Da 2:31 before thee; and the form thereof *was* **t**. 1763
7: 7 dreadful and **t**, and strong exceedingly; 574
Joel 2:11 the day of the LORD *is* great and very **t**; 3372
2:31 and the **t** day of the LORD come. 3372
Hab 1: 7 They *are* **t** and dreadful: their judgment and 366
Zep 2:11 The LORD *will be* **t** unto them: for he will 3372
Heb 12:21 And so **t** was the sight, *that* Moses said, *5398*

TERRIBLENESS (3) [TERRIFY]
Dt 26: 8 with great **t**, and with signs, and 4172
1Ch 17:21 to make thee a name of greatness and **t**, 3372
Jer 49:16 Thy **t** hath deceived thee, *and* the pride of 8606

TERRIBLY (3) [TERRIFY]
Isa 2:19 when he ariseth to **shake t** the earth. 6206
2:21 when he ariseth to **shake t** the earth. 6206
Na 2: 3 and the fir trees shall be **t shaken.** 7477

TERRIFIED (4) [TERRIFY]
Dt 20: 3 neither be ye **t** because of them; 6206
Lk 21: 9 hear of wars and commotions, be not **t**: *4422*
24:37 But they were **t** and affrighted, and *4422*
Php 1:28 And in nothing **t** by *your* adversaries: *4426*

TERRIFIEST (1) [TERRIFY]
Job 7:14 me with dreams, and **t** me through visions: 1204

TERRIFY (4) [TERRIBLE, TERRIBLENESS, TERRIBLY, TERRIFIED, TERRIFIEST, TERROR, TERRORS]
Job 3: 5 upon it; let the blackness of the day **t** it. 1204
9:34 away from me, and let not his fear **t** me: 1204
31:34 or did the contempt of families **t** me, that I 2865
2Co 10: 9 That I may not seem as if *I* would **t** you by *1629*

TERROR (29) [TERRIFY]
Ge 35: 5 the **t** of God was upon the cities that *were* 2847
Lev 26:16 I will even appoint over you **t**, consumption, 928
Dt 32:25 The sword without, and **t** within, 367
34:12 in all the great **t** which Moses shewed in 4172
Jos 2: 9 that your **t** is fallen upon us, and that all 367
Job 31:23 For destruction from God *was* a **t** to me, 6343
33: 7 Behold, my **t** shall not make thee afraid, 367
Ps 91: 5 Thou shalt not be afraid for the **t** by night; 6343
Isa 10:33 of hosts, shall lop the bough with **t**: 4637
19:17 the land of Judah shall be a **t** unto Egypt, 2283
33:18 Thine heart shall meditate **t**. Where *is* 367
54:14 and from **t**; for it shall not come near thee. 4288
Jer 17:17 Be not a **t** unto me: thou *art* my hope in 4288
20: 4 I will make thee a **t** to thyself, and to all thy 4032
32:21 with a stretched out arm, and with great **t**; 4172
Eze 26:17 which cause their **t** *to be* on all that haunt it. 2851
26:21 I will make thee a **t**, and thou *shalt be* no 1091
27:36 thou shalt be a **t**, and never *shalt be* any 1091
28:19 thou shalt be a **t**, and never *shalt* thou *be* 1091
32:23 which caused **t** in the land of the living. 2851
32:24 which caused their **t** in the land of 2851
32:25 though their **t** was caused in the land of 2851
32:26 though they caused their **t** in the land of 2851
32:27 though *they were* the **t** of the mighty in 2851
32:30 with their **t** *they are* ashamed of their 2851
32:32 For I have caused my **t** in the land of 2851
Ro 13: 3 For rulers are not a **t** to good works, but *5401*
2Co 5:11 Knowing therefore the **t** of the Lord, *5401*
1Pe 3:14 happy *are ye:* and be not afraid of their **t**, *5401*

TERRORS (15) [TERRIFY]
Dt 4:34 and by a stretched out arm, and by great **t**, 4172
Job 6: 4 the **t** of God do set *themselves* in array 1161
18:11 **T** shall make him afraid on every side, and 1091
18:14 and it shall bring him to the king of **t**. 1091
20:25 sword cometh out of his gall: **t** *are* upon him. 367
24:17 if *one* know *them, they are in* the **t** of 1091
27:20 **T** take hold on him as waters, a tempest 1091

Job 30:15 T are turned upon me: they pursue my soul 1091
Ps 55: 4 and the t of death are fallen upon me. 367
73:19 they are utterly consumed with t. 1091
88:15 youth *up: while* I suffer thy t I am distracted. 367
88:16 wrath goeth over me; thy t have cut me off. 1161
Jer 15: 8 to fall upon it suddenly, and t *upon* the city. 928
La 2:22 Thou hast called as *in* a solemn day my t 4032
Eze 21:12 t by reason of the sword shall be upon my 4048

TERTIUS (1)
Ro 16:22 I T, who wrote *this* epistle, salute you in *5060*

TERTULLUS (2)
Ac 24: 1 and *with* a certain orator *named* T, *5061*
24: 2 And when he was called *forth,* T began to *5061*

TESTAMENT (14) [TESTIFY]
Mt 26:28 For this is my blood of the new t, which is *1242*
Mk 14:24 unto them, This is my blood of the new t, *1242*
Lk 22:20 saying, This cup *is* the new t in my blood, *1242*
1Co 11:25 saying, This cup is the new t in my blood: *1242*
2Co 3: 6 hath made us able ministers of the new t; *1242*
3:14 untaken away in the reading of the old t; *1242*
Heb 7:22 much was Jesus made a surety of a better t. *1242*
9:15 this cause he is the mediator of the new t, *1242*
9:15 transgressions that were under the first t, *1242*
9:16 For where a t *is,* there must also of *1242*
9:17 For a t *is* of force after *men* are dead: *1242*
9:18 Whereupon neither the first *t* was dedicated NIG
9:20 This *is* the blood of the t which God hath *1242*
Rev 11:19 was seen in his temple the ark of his t: *1242*

TESTATOR (2) [TESTIFY]
Heb 9:16 must also of necessity be the death of the t. *1303*
9:17 it is of no strength at all whilst the t liveth. *1303*

TESTIFIED (24) [TESTIFY]
Ex 21:29 it hath been t to his owner, and he hath not 5749
Dt 19:18 *and* hath t falsely against his brother; 6030
Ru 1:21 seeing the LORD hath t against me, and 6030
2Sa 1:16 for thy mouth hath t against thee, saying, 6030
2Ki 17:13 Yet the LORD t against Israel, and 5749
17:15 his testimonies which he t against them; 5749
2Ch 24:19 unto the LORD; and they t against them: 5749
Ne 9:26 slew thy prophets which t against them to 5749
13:15 I t *against them* in the day wherein they 5749
13:21 I t against them, and said unto them, 5749
Jn 4:39 which t, He told me all that ever I did. *3140*
4:44 For Jesus himself t, that a prophet hath no *3140*
13:21 and t, and said, Verily, verily, I say unto *3140*
Ac 8:25 when they had t and preached the word of *1263*
18: 5 and t to the Jews *that* Jesus *was* Christ. *1263*
23:11 for as thou hast t of me in Jerusalem, so *1263*
28:23 he expounded and t the kingdom of God, *1263*
1Co 15:15 we have t of God that he raised up Christ: *3140*
1Th 4: 6 as we also have forewarned you and t. *1263*
1Ti 2: 6 a ransom for all, to be t in due time. *3142*
Heb 2: 6 But one in a certain place t, saying, What is *1263*
1Pe 1:11 when it t **beforehand** the sufferings of *4303*
1Jn 5: 9 witness of God which he hath t of his Son. *3140*
3Jn 1: 3 and t of the truth *that is* in thee, *3140*

TESTIFIEDST (2) [TESTIFY]
Ne 9:29 t against them, that *thou* mightest bring 5749
9:30 t against them by thy spirit in thy prophets: 5749

TESTIFIETH (5) [TESTIFY]
Hos 7:10 the pride of Israel t to his face: and they do 6030
Jn 3:32 And what he hath seen and heard, that he t; *3140*
21:24 This is the disciple which t of these *things,* *3140*
Heb 7:17 For *he* t, Thou *art* a priest for ever after *3140*
Rev 22:20 He which t these *things* saith, Surely I *3140*

TESTIFY (29) [TESTAMENT, TESTATOR, TESTIFIED, TESTIFIEDST, TESTIFIETH, TESTIFYING, TESTIMONIES, TESTIMONY]
Nu 35:30 one witness shall not t against *any* person 6030
Dt 8:19 I t against you *this* day that ye shall surely 5749
19:16 man to t against him *that which is* wrong; 6030
31:21 that this song shall t against them as a 6030
32:46 Set your hearts unto all the words which I t 5749
Ne 9:34 where*with* thou didst t against them. 5749
Job 15: 6 and not I; yea, thine own lips t against thee. 6030
Ps 50: 7 O Israel, and I will t against thee: 5749
81: 8 Hear, O my people, and I will t unto thee: 5749
Isa 59:12 before thee, and our sins t against us: 6030
Jer 14: 7 though our iniquities t against us, 6030
Hos 5: 5 the pride of Israel doth t to his face: 6030
Am 3:13 Hear ye, and t in the house of Jacob, 5749
Mic 6: 3 wherein have I wearied thee? t against me. 6030
Lk 16:28 that he may t unto them, lest they also *1263*
Jn 2:25 And needed not that any should t of man: *3140*
3:11 that we do know, and t that we have seen; *3140*
5:39 and they are they which t of me. *3140*
7: 7 but me it hateth, because I t of it, that *3140*
15:26 from the Father, he shall t of me: *3140*
Ac 2:40 And with many other words did he t and *1263*
10:42 to t that it is he which was ordained of God *1263*
20:24 to t the gospel of the grace of God. *1263*
26: 5 me from the beginning, if they would t, *3140*
Gal 5: 3 For I t again to every man that is *3143*
Eph 4:17 This I say therefore, and t in the Lord, *3143*
1Jn 4:14 do t that the Father sent the Son *to be* *3140*
Rev 22:16 I Jesus have sent mine angel to t unto you *3140*
22:18 For I t unto every *man* that heareth *4828*

TESTIFYING (3) [TESTIFY]
Ac 20:21 T both to the Jews, and *also* to the Greeks, *1263*
Heb 11: 4 that he was righteous, God t of his gifts: *3140*
1Pe 5:12 t that this is the true grace of God wherein *1957*

TESTIMONIES (36) [TESTIFY]
Dt 4:45 These *are* the t, and the statutes, and 5713
6:17 his t, and his statutes, which he hath 5713
6:20 What *mean* the t, and the statutes, and 5713
1Ki 2: 3 and his judgments, and his t, 5715
2Ki 17:15 and his t which he testified against them; 5715
23: 3 to keep his commandments and his t and 5715
1Ch 29:19 thy t, and thy statutes, and to do all *these* 5715
2Ch 34:31 and his t, and his statutes, with all his heart, 5715
Ne 9:34 unto thy commandments and thy t, 5715
Ps 25:10 unto such as keep his covenant and his t. 5713
78:56 the most high God, and kept not his t: 5713
93: 5 Thy t are very sure: holiness becometh 5713
99: 7 they kept his t, and the ordinance *that* he 5713
119: 2 Blessed *are* they that keep his t, *and* 5713
119:14 I have rejoiced in the way of thy t, as *much* 5715
119:22 and contempt; for I have kept thy t. 5713
119:24 Thy t also *are* my delight *and* 5713
119:31 I have stuck unto thy t: O LORD, put me 5715
119:36 Incline my heart unto thy t, and not to 5715
119:46 I will speak of thy t also before kings, and 5713
119:59 on my ways, and turned my feet unto thy t. 5713
119:79 unto me, and those that have known thy t. 5713
119:95 me to destroy me: *but* I will consider thy t. 5713
119:99 my teachers: for thy t *are* my meditation. 5715
119:111 Thy t have I taken as an heritage for ever: 5715
119:119 the earth *like* dross: therefore I love thy t. 5713
119:125 me understanding, that I may know thy t. 5713
119:129 Thy t *are* wonderful: therefore doth my 5715
119:138 Thy t *that* thou hast commanded *are* 5713
119:144 The righteousness of thy t *is* everlasting: 5715
119:146 unto thee; save me, and I shall keep thy t. 5713
119:152 Concerning thy t, I have known of old that 5713
119:157 *yet* do I not decline from thy t. 5715
119:167 My soul hath kept thy t; and *I* love them 5713
119:168 I have kept thy precepts and thy t: for all 5713
Jer 44:23 in his law, nor in his statutes, nor in his t; 5715

TESTIMONY (76) [TESTIFY]
Ex 16:34 so Aaron laid it up before the T, to be kept. 5715
25:16 thou shalt put into the ark the T which I 5715
25:21 in the ark thou shalt put the T that I shall 5715
25:22 cherubims which *are* upon the ark of the T, 5715
26:33 in thither within the vail the ark of the T: 5715
26:34 the ark of the T in the most holy *place.* 5715
27:21 which *is* before the T, Aaron and his sons 5715
30: 6 it before the vail that *is* by the ark of the T, 5715
30: 6 before the mercy seat that *is* over the T, 5715
30:26 and the ark of the T, 5715
30:36 put of it before the T in the tabernacle of 5715
31: 7 the ark of the T, and the mercy seat that *is* 5715
31:18 two tables of T, tables of stone, 5715
32:15 the two tables of the T *were* in his hand: 5715
34:29 with the two tables of T in Moses' hand, 5715
38:21 *even* of the tabernacle of T, as it was 5715
39:35 The ark of the T, and the staves thereof, 5715
40: 3 thou shalt put therein the ark of the T, and 5715
40: 5 gold for the incense before the ark of the T, 5715

T

Ex 40:20 he took and put the **T** into the ark, and 5715
40:21 the covering, and covered the ark of the **T**; 5715
Lev 16:13 cover the mercy seat that *is* upon the **T**, 5715
24: 3 Without the vail of the **T**, in the tabernacle 5715
Nu 1:50 the Levites over the tabernacle of **T**, 5715
1:53 shall pitch round about the tabernacle of **T**, 5715
1:53 shall keep the charge of the tabernacle of **T**. 5715
4: 5 and cover the ark of **T** with it: 5715
7:89 the mercy seat that *was* upon the ark of **T**, 5715
9:15 the tabernacle, *namely,* the tent of the **T**: 5715
10:11 taken up from off the tabernacle of the **T**. 5715
17: 4 tabernacle of the congregation before the **T**, 5715
17:10 Bring Aaron's rod again before the **T**, 5715
Jos 4:16 the priests that bear the ark of the **T**, 5715
Ru 4: 7 to his neighbour: and this *was* a **t** in Israel. 8584
2Ki 11:12 the crown upon him, and *gave him* the **T**; 5715
2Ch 23:11 and *gave him* the **T**, and made him king. 5715
Ps 19: 7 the **t** of the LORD *is* sure, making wise 5715
78: 5 For he established a **t** in Jacob, and 5715
81: 5 This he ordained in Joseph *for* a **t**, when he 5715
119:88 so shall I keep the **t** of thy mouth. 5715
122: 4 tribes of the LORD, *unto* the **t** of Israel, 5715
132:12 and my **t** that I shall teach them, 5713
Isa 8:16 Bind up the **t**, seal the law among my 8584
8:20 To the law and to the **t**: if they speak not 8584
Mt 8: 4 offer the gift that Moses commanded for a **t** *3142*
10:18 for a **t** against them and the Gentiles. *3142*
Mk 1:44 Moses commanded, for a **t** unto them. *3142*
6:11 shake off the dust under your feet for a **t** *3142*
13: 9 and kings for my sake, for a **t** against them. *3142*
Lk 5:14 as Moses commanded, for a **t** unto them. *3142*
9: 5 dust from your feet for a **t** against them. *3142*
21:13 And it shall turn to you for a **t**. *3142*
Jn 3:32 he testifieth; and no *man* receiveth his **t**. *3141*
3:33 He that hath received his **t** hath set to *his* *3141*
5:34 But I receive not **t** from man: *3141*
8:17 in your law, that the **t** of two men is true. *3141*
21:24 these *things:* and we know that his **t** is true. *3141*
Ac 13:22 to whom also he **gave t**, and said, I have *3140*
14: 3 which **gave t** unto the word of his grace, *3140*
22:18 for they will not receive thy **t** concerning *3141*
1Co 1: 6 Even as the **t** of Christ was confirmed in *3142*
2: 1 declaring unto you the **t** of God. *3142*
2Co 1:12 the **t** of our conscience, that in simplicity *3142*
2Th 1:10 (because our **t** among you was believed) *3142*
2Ti 1: 8 therefore ashamed of the **t** of our Lord, *3142*
Heb 3: 5 for a **t** of those *things* which were to be *3142*
11: 5 for before his translation he had this **t**, *3140*
Rev 1: 2 and of the **t** of Jesus Christ, and of all *3141*
1: 9 word of God, and for the **t** of Jesus Christ. *3141*
6: 9 word of God, and for the **t** which they held: *3141*
11: 7 And when they shall have finished their **t**, *3141*
12:11 of the Lamb, and by the word of their **t**; *3141*
12:17 of God, and have the **t** of Jesus Christ. *3141*
15: 5 the temple of the tabernacle of the **t** in *3142*
19:10 and of thy brethren that have the **t** of Jesus: *3141*
19:10 for the **t** of Jesus is the spirit of prophecy. *3141*

TETRARCH (7)

Mt 14: 1 At that time Herod the **t** heard of the fame *5076*
Lk 3: 1 and Herod being **t** of Galilee, and *5075*
3: 1 and his brother Philip **t** of Iturea and of *5075*
3: 1 and Lysanias the **t** of Abilene, *5075*
3:19 But Herod the **t**, being reproved by him for *5076*
9: 7 Now Herod the **t** heard of all that was done *5076*
Ac 13: 1 had been brought up with Herod the **t**, *5076*

THADDEUS (2)

Mt 10: 3 and Lebbeus, whose surname was **T**; *2280*
Mk 3:18 and **T**, and Simon the Canaanite, *2280*

THAHASH (1)

Ge 22:24 and Gaham, and **T**, and Maachah. 8477

THAMAH (1)

Ezr 2:53 the children of Sisera, the children of **T**, 8547

THAMAR (1)

Mt 1: 3 And Judas begat Phares and Zara of **T**; and *2283*

THAN (483) See Index

THANK (27) [THANKED, THANKFUL, THANKFULNESS, THANKING, THANKS, THANKSGIVING, THANKSGIVINGS, THANKWORTHY, UNTHANKFUL]

1Ch 16: 4 to **t** and praise the LORD God of Israel: 3034
16: 7 to **t** the LORD into the hand of Asaph 3034
23:30 to stand every morning to **t** and praise 3034
29:13 we **t** thee, and praise thy glorious name. 3034
2Ch 29:31 **t offerings** into the house of the LORD. 8426
29:31 brought in sacrifices and **t offerings**; 8426
33:16 thereon peace offerings and **t offerings**, 8426
Da 2:23 I **t** thee, and praise thee, O thou God of my 3029
Mt 11:25 that time Jesus answered and said, I **t** thee, *1843*
Lk 6:32 love them which love you, what **t** have ye? *5485*
6:33 which do good to you, what **t** have ye? *5485*
6:34 whom ye hope to receive, what **t** have ye? *5485*
10:21 and said, I **t** thee, O Father, Lord of heaven *1843*
17: 9 Doth he **t** that servant because he did *2192+5485*
18:11 and prayed thus with himself, God, I **t** thee, *2168*
Jn 11:41 Father, I **t** thee that thou hast heard me. *2168*
Ro 1: 8 I **t** my God through Jesus Christ for you all, *2168*
7:25 I **t** God through Jesus Christ our Lord. So *2168*
1Co 1: 4 I **t** my God always on your behalf, for *2168*
1:14 I **t** God that I baptized none of you, but *2168*
14:18 I **t** my God, I speak with tongues more than *2168*
Php 1: 3 I **t** my God upon every remembrance of *2168*
1Th 2:13 For this cause also **t** we God without *2168*
2Th 1: 3 We are bound to **t** God always for you, *2168*
1Ti 1:12 And I **t** Christ Jesus our Lord, *2192+5485*
2Ti 1: 3 I **t** God, whom I serve from *my* *2192+5485*
Phm 1: 4 I **t** my God, making mention of thee always *2168*

THANKED (3) [THANK]

2Sa 14:22 his face, and bowed himself, and **t** the king: 1288
Ac 28:15 Paul saw, he **t** God, and took courage. *2168*
Ro 6:17 But God be **t**, that ye were the servants of *5485*

THANKFUL (3) [THANK]

Ps 100: 4 be **t** unto him, *and* bless his name. 3034
Ro 1:21 glorified *him* not as God, neither were **t**; *2168*
Col 3:15 also ye are called in one body; and be ye **t**. *2170*

THANKFULNESS (1) [THANK]

Ac 24: 3 in all places, most noble Felix, with all **t**. *2169*

THANKING (1) [THANK]

2Ch 5:13 to be heard in praising and **t** the LORD; 3034

THANKS (73) [THANK]

2Sa 22:50 Therefore I will **give t** unto thee, 3034
1Ch 16: 8 **Give t** unto the LORD, call upon his 3034
16:34 O **give t** unto the LORD; for *he is* good; 3034
16:35 that *we* may **give t** to thy holy name, 3034
16:41 to **give t** to the LORD, because his mercy 3034
25: 3 a harp, to **give t** and to praise the LORD. 3034
2Ch 31: 2 to **give t**, and to praise in the gates of 3034
Ezr 3:11 in praising and **giving t** unto the LORD; 3034
Ne 12:24 over against them, to praise *and* to **give t**, 3034
12:31 two great *companies of them that gave* **t**, 8426
12:38 the other *company of them that gave* **t** went 8426
12:40 *of them that gave* **t** in the house of God, 8426
Ps 6: 5 of thee: in the grave who shall **give** thee **t**? 3034
18:49 Therefore will I **give t** unto thee, 3034
30: 4 **give t** at the remembrance of his holiness. 3034
30:12 my God, I will **give t** unto thee for ever. 3034
35:18 I will **give** thee **t** in the great congregation: 3034
75: 1 Unto thee, O God, do we **give t**, *unto thee* 3034
75: 1 do we give thanks, *unto thee* do we **give t**: 3034
79:13 sheep of thy pasture will **give** thee **t** for 3034
92: 1 *It is a* good *thing* to **give t** unto the LORD, 3034
97:12 **give t** at the remembrance of his holiness. 3034
105: 1 O **give t** unto the LORD; call upon his 3034
106: 1 O **give t** unto the LORD; for *he is* good: 3034
106:47 to **give t** unto thy holy name, *and* 3034
107: 1 O **give t** unto the LORD, for *he is* good: 3034
118: 1 O **give t** unto the LORD; for *he is* good: 3034
118:29 O **give t** unto the LORD; for *he is* good: 3034
119:62 At midnight I will rise to **give t** unto thee 3034
122: 4 to **give t** unto the name of the LORD. 3034
136: 1 O **give t** unto the LORD; for *he is* good: 3034
136: 2 O **give t** unto the God of gods: for his 3034
136: 3 O **give t** to the Lord of lords: for his mercy 3034
136:26 O **give t** unto the God of heaven: for his 3034
140:13 Surely the righteous shall **give t** unto thy 3034
Da 6:10 prayed, and **gave t** before his God, as he 3029

Mt 15:36 and **gave t**, and brake *them*, and gave to his *2168*
26:27 and **gave t**, and gave *it* to them, saying, *2168*
Mk 8: 6 and **gave t**, and brake, and gave to his *2168*
14:23 and when he had **given t**, he gave *it* to *2168*
Lk 2:38 in that instant **gave t** *likewise* **unto** the Lord, *437*
17:16 down on *his* face at his feet, **giving** him **t**: *2168*
22:17 and **gave t**, and said, Take this, and *2168*
22:19 and **gave t**, and brake *it*, and gave unto *2168*
Jn 6:11 and when he had **given t**, he distributed to *2168*
6:23 eat bread, after that the Lord had **given t**:) *2168*
Ac 27:35 and **gave t** to God in presence of *them* all: *2168*
Ro 14: 6 eateth to the Lord, for he **giveth** God **t**; *2168*
14: 6 to the Lord he eateth not, and **giveth** God **t**. *2168*
16: 4 unto whom not only I **give t**, but also all *2168*
1Co 10:30 I evil spoken of for *that for* which I **give t**? *2168*
11:24 And when he had **given t**, he brake *it*, and *2168*
14:16 the unlearned say Amen at thy **giving of t**, *2169*
14:17 For thou verily **givest t** well, but the other *2168*
15:57 But **t** *be* to God, which giveth us *5485*
2Co 1:11 **t** may be **given** by many on our behalf. *2168*
2:14 Now **t** *be* unto God, which always causeth *5485*
8:16 But **t** *be* to God, which put the same earnest *5485*
9:15 **T** *be* unto God for his unspeakable gift. *5485*
Eph 1:16 Cease not to **give t** for you, *2168*
5: 4 are not convenient: but rather **giving of t**. *2169*
5:20 **Giving t** always for all *things* unto God and *2168*
Col 1: 3 We **give t** to God and the Father of our *2168*
1:12 **Giving t** unto the Father, which hath made *2168*
3:17 **giving t** to God and the Father by him. *2168*
1Th 1: 2 We **give t** to God always for you all, *2168*
3: 9 For what **t** can we render to God again for *2169*
5:18 In every *thing* **give t**: for this *is* the will of *2168*
2Th 2:13 But we are bound to **give t** alway to God *2168*
1Ti 2: 1 prayers, intercessions, *and* **giving of t**, *2169*
Heb 13:15 the fruit of *our* lips **giving t** to his name. *3670*
Rev 4: 9 honour and **t** to him that sat on the throne, *2169*
11:17 Saying, We **give** thee **t**, O Lord God *2168*

THANKSGIVING (28) [GIVE, THANK]
Lev 7:12 If he offer it for a **t**, then he shall offer with 8426
7:12 he shall offer with the sacrifice of **t** 8426
7:13 the sacrifice of **t** of his peace offerings. 8426
7:15 **t** shall be eaten the same day that it is 8426
22:29 when ye will offer a sacrifice of **t** unto 8426
Ne 11:17 *was* the principal to begin the **t** in prayer: 3034
12: 8 *which was* over the **t**, he and his brethren. 1960
12:46 and songs of praise and **t** unto God. 3034
Ps 26: 7 That *I* may publish with the voice of **t**, and 8426
50:14 Offer unto God **t**; and pay thy vows unto 8426
69:30 with a song; and will magnify him with **t**. 8426
95: 2 Let us come before his presence with **t**, *and* 8426
100: 4 Enter *into* his gates with **t**, *and* into his 8426
107:22 let them sacrifice the sacrifices of **t**, and 8426
116:17 I will offer to thee the sacrifice of **t**, and 8426
147: 7 Sing unto the LORD with **t**; sing *praise* 8426
Isa 51: 3 found therein, **t**, and the voice of melody. 8426
Jer 30:19 out of them shall proceed **t** and the voice of 8426
Am 4: 5 offer a **sacrifice of t** with leaven, and 8426
Jnh 2: 9 I will sacrifice unto thee with the voice of **t**; 8426
2Co 4:15 that the abundant grace might through the **t** *2169*
9:11 which causeth through us **t** to God. *2169*
Php 4: 6 supplication with **t** let your requests be *2169*
Col 2: 7 have been taught, abounding therein with **t**. *2169*
4: 2 in prayer, and watch in the same with **t**; *2169*
1Ti 4: 3 to be received with **t** of them which believe *2169*
4: 4 to be refused, if it be received with **t**: *2169*
Rev 7:12 and **t**, and honour, and power, and might, *2169*

THANKSGIVINGS (2) [GIVE, THANK]
Ne 12:27 both with **t**, and with singing, 8426
2Co 9:12 but is abundant also by many **t** unto God; *2169*

THANKWORTHY (1) [THANK, WORTH]
1Pe 2:19 For this *is* **t**, if a man for conscience toward *5485*

THARA (1) [TERAH]
Lk 3:34 which was *the son* of **T**, which was *the son* *2291*

THARSHISH (4) [TARSHISH]
1Ki 10:22 For the king had at sea a navy of **T** with 8659
10:22 once in three years came the navy of **T**, 8659
22:48 Jehoshaphat made ships of **T** to go to Ophir 8659
1Ch 7:10 and Zethan, and **T**, and Ahishahar. 8659

THAT (12914) [THOSE] See Index

THE (64039) See Index

THEATRE (2)
Ac 19:29 they rushed with one accord into the **t**. *2302*
19:31 *he* would not adventure himself into the **t**. *2302*

THEBEZ (3)
Jdg 9:50 went Abimelech to **T**, and 8405
9:50 and encamped against **T**, and took it. 8405
2Sa 11:21 upon him from the wall, that he died in **T**? 8405

THEE (3826) [THOU] See Index

THEE-WARD (1) [THOU]
1Sa 19: 4 his works *have been* to **t** very good: 3509.2

THEFT (2) [THEFTS, THIEF, THIEVES]
Ex 22: 3 have nothing, then he shall be sold for his **t**. 1591
22: 4 If the **t** be certainly found in his hand alive, 1591

THEFTS (3) [THEFT]
Mt 15:19 murders, adulteries, fornications, **t**, *2829*
Mk 7:22 **T**, covetousness, wickedness, deceit, *2829*
Rev 9:21 nor of their fornication, nor of their **t**. *2809*

THEIR (3931) [THEY] See Index

THEIRS (21) [THEY] See Index

THELASAR (1) [TELASSAR]
2Ki 19:12 and the children of Eden which *were* in **T**? 8515

THEM (6429) [THEY] See Index

THEMSELVES (409) [SELF, THEY] See Index

THEN (2168) See Index

THENCE (145) [THENCEFORTH] See Index

THENCEFORTH (4) [THENCE] See Index

THEOPHILUS (2)
Lk 1: 3 write unto thee in order, most excellent **T**, *2321*
Ac 1: 1 The former treatise have I made, O **T**, of all *2321*

THERE (2299) See Index

THEREABOUT (1) [ABOUT] See Index

THEREAT (3) [AT]
Ex 30:19 wash their hands and their feet **t**: 4480+5105.2
40:31 washed their hands and their feet **t**: 4480+5105.2
Mt 7:13 and many there be which go in **t**: *846+1223*

THEREBY (21) [BY] See Index

THEREFORE (1237) See Index

THEREFROM (3) [FROM] See Index

THEREIN (230) [IN] See Index

THEREINTO (1) [INTO] See Index

THEREOF (908) [OF] See Index

THEREON (66) [ON] See Index

THEREOUT (2) [OUT] See Index

THERETO (20) [TO] See Index

THEREUNTO (9) [UNTO] See Index

THEREUPON (5) [UPON] See Index

THEREWITH (36) [WITH] See Index

THESE (1225) [THIS] See Index

THESSALONIANS (5) [THESSALONICA]
Ac 20: 4 and of the **T**, Aristarchus and Secundus; *2331*
1Th 1: 1 unto the church of the **T** *which is* in God *2331*
5: S The first *epistle* unto the **T** was written *2331*
2Th 1: 1 unto the church of the **T** in God our Father *2331*
3: S The second *epistle* to the **T** was written *2331*

THESSALONICA (6) [THESSALONIANS]
Ac 17: 1 and Apollonia, they came to **T**, *2332*
17:11 These were more noble than those in **T**, *2332*
17:13 But when the Jews of **T** had knowledge *2332*
27: 2 a Macedonian of **T**, being with us. *2331*

Php 4:16 For even in **T** ye sent once and again unto *2332*
2Ti 4:10 *this* present world, and is departed unto **T**; *2332*

THEUDAS (1)
Ac 5:36 For before these days rose up **T**, *2333*

THEY (7376) [THEIR, THEIRS, THEM, THEMSELVES] See Index

THICK (39) [THICKER, THICKNESS]
Ex 10:22 there was a **t** darkness in all the land of 653
19: 9 Lo, I come unto thee in a **t** cloud, 5645
19:16 a **t** cloud upon the mount, and the voice of 3515
20:21 Moses drew near unto the **t darkness** 6205
Lev 23:40 the boughs of **t** trees, and willows of 5687
Dt 4:11 *with* darkness, clouds, and **t darkness**. 6205
5:22 of the cloud, and of the **t darkness**, *with* a 6205
32:15 thou art waxed fat, thou art **grown t**, 5666
2Sa 18: 9 the mule went under the **t boughs** of a great 7730
22:12 dark waters, *and* **t clouds** of the skies. 5645
1Ki 7: 6 and the **t beam** *were* before them. 5646
7:26 it *was* a handbreadth **t**, and the brim thereof 5672
8:12 said that *he* would dwell in the **t darkness**. 6205
2Ki 8:15 that he took a **t cloth**, and dipt *it* in water, 4346
2Ch 6: 1 said that *he* would dwell in the **t darkness**. 6205
Ne 8:15 palm branches, and branches of **t** trees, 5687
Job 15:26 *his* neck, upon the **t** bosses of his bucklers: 5672
22:14 **T clouds** *are* a covering to him, that he 5645
26: 8 He bindeth up the waters in his **t clouds**; 5645
37:11 Also by watering he wearieth the **t cloud**: 5645
38: 9 and **t darkness** a swaddling band for it, 6205
Ps 18:11 *were* dark waters *and* **t clouds** of the skies. 5645
18:12 *that was* before him his **t clouds** passed, 5645
74: 5 as he had lifted up axes upon the **t** trees. 5442
Isa 44:22 I have blotted out, as a **t cloud**, 5645
Eze 6:13 every green tree, and under every **t** oak, 5687
8:11 his hand; and a **t** cloud of incense went up. 6282
19:11 stature was exalted among the **t branches**, 5688
20:28 all the **t** trees, and they offered there their 5687
31: 3 and his top was among the **t boughs**. 5688
31:10 hath shot up his top among the **t boughs**, 5688
31:14 shoot up their top among the **t boughs**, 5688
41:12 the wall of the building *was* five cubits **t** 7341
41:25 *there were* **t** planks upon the face of 5646
41:26 side chambers of the house, and **t planks**. 5646
Joel 2: 2 a day of clouds and of **t darkness**, 6205
Hab 2: 6 and to him that ladeth himself with **t clay**! 5671
Zep 1:15 a day of clouds and **t darkness**, 6205
Lk 11:29 when the people were **gathered t together**, *1865*

THICKER (2) [THICK]
1Ki 12:10 My little *finger* shall be **t** than my father's 5666
2Ch 10:10 My little *finger* shall be **t** than my father's 5666

THICKET (2) [THICKETS]
Ge 22:13 behold behind *him* a ram caught in a **t** by 5442
Jer 4: 7 The lion is come up from his **t**, and 5441

THICKETS (4) [THICKET]
1Sa 13: 6 in **t**, and in rocks, and in high places, and 2337
Isa 9:18 shall kindle in the **t** of the forest, and 5442
10:34 he shall cut down the **t** of the forest with 5442
Jer 4:29 they shall go into **t**, and climb up upon 5645

THICKNESS (4) [THICK]
2Ch 4: 5 the **t** of it *was* a handbreadth, and the brim 5672
Jer 52:21 and the **t** thereof *was* four fingers: 5672
Eze 41: 9 The **t** of the wall, which *was* for the side 7341
42:10 The chambers *were* in the **t** of the wall of 7341

THIEF (28) [THEFT]
Ex 22: 2 If a **t** be found breaking up, and be smitten 1590
22: 7 if the **t** be found, let him pay double. 1590
22: 8 If the **t** be not found, then the master of 1590
Dt 24: 7 that **t** shall die; and thou shalt put evil away 1590
Job 24:14 and needy, and in the night is as a **t**. 1590
30: 5 (they cried after them as *after* a **t**;) 1590
Ps 50:18 When thou sawest a **t**, then 1590
Pr 6:30 *Men* do not despise a **t**, if he steal to satisfy 1590
29:24 Whoso is partner with a **t** hateth his own 1590
Jer 2:26 As the **t** is ashamed when he is found, so 1590
Hos 7: 1 the **t** cometh in, *and* the troop *of robbers* 1590
Joel 2: 9 they shall enter in at the windows like a **t**. 1590
Zec 5: 4 and it shall enter into the house of the **t**, and 1590
Mt 24:43 known in what watch the **t** would come, *2812*
26:55 Are ye come out as against a **t** with swords *3027*
Mk 14:48 as against a **t**, with swords and *with* staves *3027*
Lk 12:33 where no **t** approacheth, neither moth *2812*
12:39 had known what hour the **t** would come, *2812*
22:52 as against a **t**, with swords and staves? *3027*
Jn 10: 1 other way, the same is a **t** and a robber. *2812*
10:10 The **t** cometh not, but for to steal, and *2812*
12: 6 but because he was a **t**, and had the bag, *2812*
1Th 5: 2 of the Lord so cometh as a **t** in the night. *2812*
5: 4 that *that* day should overtake you as a **t**. *2812*
1Pe 4:15 or *as* a **t**, or *as* an evildoer, or as a busybody *2812*
2Pe 3:10 But the day of the Lord will come as a **t** in *2812*
Rev 3: 3 I will come on thee as a **t**, and thou shalt *2812*
16:15 Behold, I come as a **t**. Blessed *is* he that *2812*

THIEVES (16) [THEFT]
Isa 1:23 princes *are* rebellious, and companions of **t**: 1590
Jer 48:27 was he found among **t**? for since thou 1590
49: 9 if **t** by night, they will destroy till they have 1590
Ob 1: 5 If **t** came to thee, if robbers by night, 1590
Mt 6:19 and where **t** break through and steal: *2812*
6:20 and where **t** do not break through nor steal: *2812*
21:13 of prayer; but ye have made it a den of **t**. *3027*
27:38 Then were there two **t** crucified with him, *3027*
27:44 The **t** also, which were crucified with him, *3027*
Mk 11:17 of prayer? but ye have made it a den of **t**. *3027*
15:27 And with him they crucify two **t**; the one *3027*
Lk 10:30 and fell among **t**, which stripped him of his *3027*
10:36 neighbour unto him that fell among the **t**? *3027*
19:46 of prayer: but ye have made it a den of **t**. *3027*
Jn 10: 8 All that ever came before me are **t** and *2812*
1Co 6:10 Nor **t**, nor covetous, nor drunkards, *2812*

THIGH (21) [THIGHS]
Ge 24: 2 Put, I pray thee, thy hand under my **t**: 3409
24: 9 the servant put his hand under the **t** of 3409
32:25 against him, he touched the hollow of his **t**; 3409
32:25 the hollow of Jacob's **t** was out of joint, 3409
32:31 rose upon him, and he halted upon his **t**. 3409
32:32 which *is* upon the hollow of the **t**, unto this 3409
32:32 he touched the hollow of Jacob's **t** in 3409
47:29 thy hand under my **t**, and deal kindly and 3409
Nu 5:21 when the LORD doth make thy **t** to rot, 3409
5:22 to make *thy* belly to swell, and *thy* **t** to rot: 3409
5:27 and her belly shall swell, and her **t** shall rot: 3409
Jdg 3:16 gird it under his raiment upon his right **t**. 3409
3:21 took the dagger from his right **t**, and 3409
15: 8 them hip and **t** *with* a great slaughter: 3409
Ps 45: 3 Gird thy sword upon *thy* **t**, O *most* mighty, 3409
SS 3: 8 every man *hath* his sword upon his **t** 3409
Isa 47: 2 thy locks, make bare the leg, uncover the **t**, 7785
Jer 31:19 that I was instructed, I smote upon *my* **t**: 3409
Eze 21:12 my people: smite therefore upon *thy* **t**. 3409
24: 4 every good piece, the **t**, and the shoulder; 3409
Rev 19:16 on *his* vesture and on his **t** a name written, *3382*

THIGHS (3) [THIGH]
Ex 28:42 from the loins even unto the **t** they shall 3409
SS 7: 1 the joints of thy **t** *are* like jewels, the work 3409
Da 2:32 arms of silver, his belly and his **t** of brass, 3410

THIMNATHAH (1)
Jos 19:43 And Elon, and **T**, and Ekron, 8553

THIN (9)
Ge 41: 6 seven **t** ears and blasted with the east wind 1851
41: 7 the seven **t** ears devoured the seven rank 1851
41:23 withered, **t**, *and* blasted with the east wind, 1851
41:24 the **t** ears devoured the seven good ears: 1851
41:27 the seven **t** and ill favoured kine that came 7534
Ex 39: 3 they did beat the gold into **t plates**, and 6341
Lev 13:30 *there be* in it a yellow **t** hair; then the priest 1851
1Ki 7:29 oxen *were certain* additions **made** of **t** 4174
Isa 17: 4 *that* the glory of Jacob shall be **made t**, and 1809

THINE (933) [THOU] See Index

THING (548) [ANYTHING, NOTHING, SOMETHING, THINGS, THINGS'] See Index

THINGS (1161) [THING] See Index

THINGS' (1) [THING] See Index

THINK (65) [BETHINK, THINKEST, THINKETH, THINKING, THOUGHT, THOUGHTEST, THOUGHTS]
Ge 40:14 But **t on** me when it shall be well with thee, 2142

Nu 36: 6 marry to whom they t **best**; 2896+5869+871.1
2Sa 13:33 to t *that* all the king's sons are dead: 559
2Ch 13: 8 now ye t to withstand the kingdom of 559
Ne 5:19 T upon me, my God, for good, *according to* 2142
6: 6 saith *it, that* thou and the Jews t to rebel: 2803
6:14 t thou upon Tobiah and Sanballat according 2142
Est 4:13 T not with thyself that *thou* shalt escape *in* 1819
Job 31: 1 mine eyes; why then should I t upon a maid? 995
41:32 after him; *one* would t the deep to be hoary. 2803
Ecc 8:17 though a wise *man* t to know *it,* yet shall he 559
Isa 10: 7 meaneth not so, neither doth his heart t so; 2803
Jer 23:27 Which t to cause my people to forget my 2803
29:11 For I know the thoughts that I t towards 2803
Eze 38:10 thy mind, and thou shalt t an evil thought: 2803
Da 7:25 most High, and t to change times and laws: 5452
Jnh 1: 6 if so be that God will t upon us, that we 6245
Zec 11:12 If ye t good, give *me* my price; 5869+871.1
Mt 3: 9 And t not to say within yourselves, *1380*
5:17 T not that I am come to destroy the law, or *3543*
6: 7 as the heathen *do:* for they t that they shall *1380*
9: 4 Wherefore t ye evil in your hearts? *1760*
10:34 T not that I am come to send peace on *3543*
18:12 How t ye? if a man have an hundred sheep, *1380*
21:28 But what t you? A *certain* man had two *1380*
22:42 Saying, What t ye of Christ? whose son is *1380*
24:44 for in such an hour as you t not the Son of *1380*
26:66 What t ye? They answered and said, He is *1380*
Mk 14:64 what t ye? And they all condemned him to *5316*
Lk 12:40 of man cometh at an hour when ye t not. *1380*
13: 4 t ye that they were sinners above all men *1380*
Jn 5:39 for in them ye t ye have eternal life: *1380*
5:45 Do not t that I will accuse you to *1380*
11:56 as they stood in the temple, What t ye, *1380*
16: 2 that whosoever killeth you will t that he *1380*
Ac 13:25 *his* course, he said, Whom t ye that I am? *5282*
17:29 we ought not to t that the Godhead is like *3543*
26: 2 I t myself happy, king Agrippa, because *2233*
Ro 12: 3 not to t *of himself* more **highly** than he *5252*
12: 3 *of himself* more highly than he ought to t; *5426*
12: 3 but to t soberly, according as God hath *5426*
1Co 4: 6 that ye might learn in us not to t *of men* *5426*
4: 9 For I t that God hath set forth us *1380*
7:36 But if any *man* t that *he* behaveth himself *3543*
7:40 and I t also that *I* have the Spirit of God. *1380*
8: 2 And if any *man* t that *he* knoweth any *1380*
12:23 the body, which we t to be less honourable, *1380*
14:37 If any *man* t himself to be a prophet, or *1380*
2Co 3: 5 Not that we are sufficient of ourselves to t *3049*
10: 2 wherewith I t to be bold against some, *3049*
10: 2 which t of us as if we walked according to *3049*
10: 7 let him of himself t this again, that, as he *is* *3049*
10:11 Let such a one t this, that, such as we are in *3049*
11:16 I say again, Let no *man* t me a fool; *1380*
12: 6 lest any *man* should t of me above *that* *3049*
12:19 t you that we excuse ourselves unto you? *1380*
Gal 6: 3 For if a man t himself to be something, *1380*
Eph 3:20 abundantly above all that we ask or t, *3539*
Php 1: 7 Even as it is meet for me to t this of you all, *5426*
4: 8 if *there be* any praise, t on these *things.* *3049*
Jas 1: 7 For let not that man t that he shall receive *3633*
4: 5 Do ye t that the scripture saith in vain, *1380*
1Pe 4: 4 Wherein they t **it strange** that you run not *3579*
4:12 t **it** not **strange** concerning the fiery trial *3579*
2Pe 1:13 Yea, I t it meet, as long as I am in this *2233*

THINKEST (9) [THINK]

2Sa 10: 3 said unto Hanun their lord, T 5869+871.1
1Ch 19: 3 T thou that David doth honour thy 5869+871.1
Job 35: 2 T thou this to be right, *that* thou saidst, 2803
Mt 17:25 saying, What t thou, Simon? *1380*
22:17 Tell us therefore, What t thou? Is it lawful *1380*
26:53 T thou that I cannot now pray to my Father, *1380*
Lk 10:36 Which now of these three, t thou, *1380*
Ac 28:22 But we desire to hear of thee what thou t: *5426*
Ro 2: 3 And t thou this, O man, that judgest them *3049*

THINKETH (6) [THINK]

2Sa 18:27 Me t the running of the foremost *is* like 7200
Ps 40:17 and needy; *yet* the Lord t upon me: 2803
Pr 23: 7 For as he t in his heart, so *is* he: Eat and 8176
1Co 10:12 Wherefore let him that t he standeth take *1380*
13: 5 her own, is not easily provoked, t no evil; *3049*
Php 3: 4 If any other *man* t that *he hath whereof he* *1380*

THINKING (2) [THINK]

2Sa 4:10 t to have brought good tidings, 5869+871.1
5: 6 in hither: t, David cannot come in hither. 559

THIRD (182) [THREE]

Ge 1:13 and the morning were the t day. 7992
2:14 the name of the t river *is* Hiddekel: that *is it* 7992
6:16 second, and t *stories* shalt thou make it. 7992
22: 4 on the t day Abraham lift up his eyes, and 7992
31:22 it was told Laban on the t day that Jacob 7992
32:19 the t, and all that followed the droves, 7992
34:25 it came to pass on the t day, when they 7992
40:20 it came to pass the t day, *which was* 7992
42:18 Joseph said unto them the t day, This do, 7992
50:23 Joseph saw Ephraim's children of the t 8029
Ex 19: 1 In the t month, when the children of Israel 7992
19:11 be ready against the t day: for the third day 7992
19:11 for the t day the LORD will come down in 7992
19:15 unto the people, Be ready against the t day: 7969
19:16 it came to pass on the t day in the morning, 7992
20: 5 of the fathers upon the children unto the t 8029
28:19 the t row a ligure, an agate, and 7992
34: 7 unto the t and to the fourth *generation.* 8029
39:12 the t row, a ligure, an agate, and 7992
Lev 7:17 on the t day shall be burnt with fire. 7992
7:18 peace offerings be eaten at all on the t day, 7992
19: 6 if ought remain until the t day, it shall be 7992
19: 7 if it be eaten at all on the t day, it *is* 7992
Nu 2:24 And they shall go forward in the t **rank**. 7992
7:24 On the t day Eliab the son of Helon, 7992
14:18 of the fathers upon the children unto the t 8029
15: 6 flour mingled with the t *part* of a hin of oil. 7992
15: 7 for a drink offering thou shalt offer the t 7992
19:12 He shall purify himself with it on the t day, 7992
19:12 if he purify not himself the t day, then 7992
19:19 sprinkle upon the unclean on the t day, 7992
28:14 the t *part* of a hin unto a ram, and a fourth 7992
29:20 on the t day eleven bullocks, two rams, 7992
31:19 and your captives on the t day, 7992
Dt 5: 9 of the fathers upon the children unto the t 8029
23: 8 of the LORD *in* their t generation. 7992
26:12 all the tithes of thine increase the t year, 7992
Jos 9:17 and came unto their cities on the t day. 7992
19:10 the t lot came up for the children of 7992
Jdg 20:30 the children of Benjamin on the t day, 7992
1Sa 3: 8 the LORD called Samuel again the t **time**. 7992
17:13 unto him Abinadab, and the t Shammah. 7992
19:21 Saul sent messengers again the t **time**, and 7992
20: 5 myself in the fields unto the t *day* at even. 7992
20:12 *or* the t *day,* and behold, *if there be* good 7992
30: 1 his men were come *to* Ziklag on the t day, 7992
2Sa 1: 2 It came even to pass on the t day, that 7992
3: 3 the t, Absalom the son of Maacah 7992
18: 2 David sent forth a t **part** of the people 7992
18: 2 a t **part** under the hand of Abishai the son 7992
18: 2 a t **part** under the hand of Ittai the Gittite. 7992
1Ki 3:18 it came to pass the t day after that I was 7992
6: 6 and the t *was* seven cubits broad: 7992
6: 8 and out of the middle into the t. 7992
12:12 all the people came to Rehoboam the t day, 7992
12:12 saying, Come to me again the t day. 7992
15:28 Even in the t year of Asa king of Judah did 7969
15:33 In the t year of Asa king of Judah *began* 7969
18: 1 of the LORD came to Elijah in the t year, 7992
18:34 he said, **Do** *it* **the t time**. And they did *it* 8027
18:34 *it* the third time. And they **did** *it* **the t time**. 8027
22: 2 it came to pass on the t year, that 7992
2Ki 1:13 he sent again a captain of the t fifty with 7992
1:13 the t captain of fifty went up, and came 7992
11: 5 A t *part* of you that enter in on the sabbath 7992
11: 6 a t *part shall be* at the gate of Sur; and 7992
11: 6 and a t *part* at the gate behind the guard: 7992
18: 1 Now it came to pass in the t year of Hoshea 7969
19:29 in the t year sow ye, and reap, and 7992
20: 5 on the t day thou shalt go up *unto* the house 7992
20: 8 up *into* the house of the LORD the t day? 7992
1Ch 2:13 Abinadab the second, and Shimma the t, 7992
3: 2 The t, Absalom the son of Maachah 7992
3:15 the t Zedekiah, the fourth Shallum. 7992
8: 1 Ashbel the second, and Aharah the t, 7992
8:39 Jehush the second, and Eliphelet the t. 7992
12: 9 the first, Obadiah the second, Eliab the t, 7992
23:19 Jahaziel the t, and Jekameam the fourth. 7992

1Ch 24: 8 The t to Harim, the fourth to Seorim, 7992
24:23 Jahaziel the t, Jekameam the fourth. 7992
25:10 The t *to* Zaccur, *he,* his sons, and 7992
26: 2 Jediael the second, Zebadiah the t, 7992
26: 4 Joah the t, and Sacar the fourth, and 7992
26:11 Hilkiah the second, Tebaliah the t, 7992
27: 5 The t captain of the host for the third month 7992
27: 5 The third captain of the host for the t month 7992
2Ch 10:12 all the people came to Rehoboam on the t 7992
10:12 saying, Come again to me on the t day. 7992
15:10 together *at* Jerusalem in the t month, 7992
17: 7 Also in the t year of his reign he sent to his 7969
23: 4 A t *part* of you entering on the sabbath, 7992
23: 5 a t *part shall be* at the king's house; and 7992
23: 5 and a t *part* at the gate of the foundation: 7992
27: 5 unto him, both the second year, and the t. 7992
31: 7 In the t month they began to lay 7992
Ezr 6:15 this house was finished on the t day of 8532
Ne 10:32 to charge ourselves yearly with the t *part* of 7992
Est 1: 3 In the t year of his reign, he made a feast 7969
5: 1 Now it came to pass on the t day, 7992
8: 9 scribes called at that time in the t month, 7992
Job 42:14 and the name of the t, Keren-happuch. 7992
Isa 19:24 In that day shall Israel be the t with Egypt 7992
37:30 in the t year sow ye, and reap, and 7992
Jer 38:14 t entry that *is* in the house of the LORD: 7992
Eze 5: 2 Thou shalt burn with fire a t *part* in 7992
5: 2 thou shalt take a t *part, and* smite about it 7992
5: 2 a t *part* thou shalt scatter in the wind; and 7992
5:12 A t *part* of thee shall die with 7992
5:12 a t *part* shall fall by the sword round about 7992
5:12 I will scatter a t *part* into all the winds, and 7992
10:14 the t the face of a lion, and the fourth 7992
21:14 let the sword be doubled the t **time,** 7992
31: 1 in the t *month,* in the first *day* of the month, 7992
46:14 of an ephah, and the t *part* of a hin of oil, 7992
Da 1: 1 In the t year of the reign of Jehoiakim king 7969
2:39 another t kingdom of brass, which shall 8523
5: 7 and shall be the t ruler in the kingdom. 8523
5:16 and shalt be the t ruler in the kingdom. 8531
5:29 that *he* should be the t ruler in the kingdom. 8531
8: 1 In the t year of the reign of king Belshazzar 7969
10: 1 In the t year of Cyrus king of Persia a thing 7969
Hos 6: 2 in the t day he will raise us up, and we shall 7992
Zec 6: 3 in the t chariot white horses; and in 7992
13: 8 *and* die; but the t shall be left therein. 7992
13: 9 I will bring the t *part* through the fire, and 7992
Mt 16:21 and be killed, and be raised *again* the t day. *5154*
17:23 the t day he shall be raised *again.* And they *5154*
20: 3 And he went out about the t hour, and *5154*
20:19 and the t day he shall rise again. *5154*
22:26 the second also, and the t, unto the seventh. *5154*
26:44 away again, and prayed the t **time,** *1537+5154*
27:64 that the sepulchre be made sure until the t *5154*
Mk 9:31 after that he is killed, he shall rise the t day. *5154*
10:34 kill him: and the t day he shall rise again. *5154*
12:21 neither left he *any* seed: and the t likewise. *5154*
14:41 And he cometh the t **time,** and saith unto *5154*
15:25 And it was the t hour, and they crucified *5154*
Lk 9:22 and be slain, and be raised the t day. *5154*
12:38 or come in the t watch, and find *them* so, *5154*
13:32 and the t *day* I shall be perfected. *5154*
18:33 to death: and the t day he shall rise again. *5154*
20:12 And again he sent a t: and they wounded *5154*
20:31 And the t took her; and in like manner *5154*
23:22 And he said unto them the t **time,** Why, *5154*
24: 7 and be crucified, and the t day rise again. *5154*
24:21 to day is the t day since these *things* were *5154*
24:46 and to rise from the dead the t day: *5154*
Jn 2: 1 And the t day there was a marriage in Cana *5154*
21:14 This *is* now the t **time** *that* Jesus shewed *5154*
21:17 He saith unto him the t **time,** Simon, *son* of *5154*
21:17 because he said unto him the t **time,** *5154*
Ac 2:15 seeing it is *but* the t hour of the day. *5154*
10:40 Him God raised up the t day, and *5154*
20: 9 and fell down from the t **loft,** and *5152*
23:23 two hundred, at the t hour of the night; *5154*
27:19 And the t *day* we cast *out* with our own *5154*
1Co 15: 4 that he rose *again* the t day according to *5154*
2Co 12: 2 such a one caught up to the t heaven. *5154*
12:14 the t *time* I am ready to come to you; *5154*
13: 1 This *is* the t *time* I am coming to you. *5154*
Rev 4: 7 and the t beast had a face as a man, and *5154*
6: 5 And when he had opened the t seal, I heard *5154*
6: 5 I heard the t beast say, Come and see. *5154*
8: 7 and the t *part* of trees was burnt up, and all *5154*
8: 8 and the t *part* of the sea became blood; *5154*
8: 9 And the t *part* of the creatures which were *5154*
8: 9 and the t *part* of the ships were destroyed. *5154*
8:10 And the t angel sounded, and there fell a *5154*
8:10 and it fell upon the t *part* of the rivers, and *5154*
8:11 the t *part* of the waters became wormwood; *5154*
8:12 and the t *part* of the sun was smitten, and *5154*
8:12 and the t *part* of the moon, and the third *5154*
8:12 *part* of the moon, and the t *part* of the stars; *5154*
8:12 so as the t *part* of them was darkened and *5154*
8:12 and the day shone not for a t *part* of it, *5154*
9:15 and a year, for to slay the t *part* of men. *5154*
9:18 By these three was the t *part* of men killed, *5154*
11:14 *and* behold, the t woe cometh quickly. *5154*
12: 4 And his tail drew the t *part* of the stars of *5154*
14: 9 And *the* t angel followed them, saying with *5154*
16: 4 And the t angel poured out his vial upon *5154*
21:19 the second, sapphire; the t, a chalcedony; *5154*

THIRDLY (1) [THREE]

1Co 12:28 t teachers, after that miracles, then gifts of *5154*

THIRST (31) [ATHIRST, BLOODTHIRSTY, THIRSTED, THIRSTETH, THIRSTY]

Ex 17: 3 and our children and our cattle with t? 6772
Dt 28:48 in t, and in nakedness, and in want of all 6772
29:19 of mine heart, to add drunkenness *to* t: 6771
Jdg 15:18 now shall I die for t, and fall into the hand 6772
2Ch 32:11 over yourselves to die by famine and by t, 6772
Ne 9:15 water for them out of the rock for their t, 6772
9:20 and gavest them water for their t. 6772
Job 24:11 *and* tread *their* winepresses, and **suffer** t. 6770
Ps 69:21 and in my t they gave me vinegar to drink. 6772
104:11 of the field: the wild asses quench their t. 6772
Isa 5:13 and their multitude dried up with t. 6772
41:17 *there is* none, *and* their tongue faileth for t, 6772
49:10 They shall not hunger nor t; neither shall 6770
50: 2 because *there is* no water, and dieth for t. 6772
Jer 2:25 from being unshod, and thy throat from t: 6773
48:18 come down from *thy* glory, and sit in t; 6772
La 4: 4 child cleaveth to the roof of his mouth for t: 6772
Hos 2: 3 set her like a dry land, and slay her with t. 6772
Am 8:11 nor a t for water, but of hearing the words 6772
8:13 the fair virgins and young men faint for t. 6772
Mt 5: 6 which do hunger and t after righteousness: *1372*
Jn 4:13 Whosoever drinketh of this water shall t *1372*
4:14 the water that I shall give him shall never t; *1372*
4:15 Sir, give me this water, that I t not, *1372*
6:35 and he that believeth on me shall never t. *1372*
7:37 Jesus stood and cried, saying, If any *man* t, *1372*
19:28 the scripture might be fulfilled, saith, I t. *1372*
Ro 12:20 feed him; if he t, give him drink: *1372*
1Co 4:11 and t, and are naked, and are buffeted, and *1372*
2Co 11:27 in hunger and t, in fastings often, in cold *1373*
Rev 7:16 shall hunger no more, neither t any more; *1372*

THIRSTED (2) [THIRST]

Ex 17: 3 the people t there for water; and the people 6770
Isa 48:21 they t not *when* he led them through 6770

THIRSTETH (4) [THIRST]

Ps 42: 2 My soul t for God, for the living God: 6770
63: 1 my soul t for thee, my flesh longeth for 6770
143: 6 my soul *t* after thee, as a thirsty land. Selah. NIH
Isa 55: 1 Ho, every one that t, come ye to the waters, 6771

THIRSTY (17) [THIRST]

Jdg 4:19 pray thee, a little water to drink; for I am t. 6770
2Sa 17:29 and weary, and t, in the wilderness. 6771
Ps 63: 1 in a dry and t land, where no water is; 5889
107: 5 Hungry and t, their soul fainted in them. 6771
143: 6 my soul *thirsteth* after thee, as a t land. 5889
Pr 25:21 and if he *be* t, give him water to drink: 6771
25:25 *As* cold waters to a t soul, so *is* good news 5889
Isa 21:14 of Tema brought water to him that was t, 6771
29: 8 or as when a t *man* dreameth, and behold, 6771
32: 6 and he will cause the drink of the t to fail. 6771
35: 7 a pool, and the t **land** springs of water: 6774
44: 3 For I will pour water upon *him that is* t, and 6771
65:13 my servants shall drink, but ye shall be t: 6770
Eze 19:13 in the wilderness, in a dry and t ground. 6772
Mt 25:35 I was t, and ye gave me drink: I was a *1372*

Mt 25:37 and fed *thee?* or t, and gave *thee* drink? *1372*
25:42 no meat: I was t, and ye gave me no drink: *1372*

THIRTEEN (15) [THIRTEENTH]
Ge 17:25 Ishmael his son *was* t years old, 6240+7969
Nu 3:43 and **threescore and t.** 7657+7969+2050.1
3:46 **threescore and t** of 7657+7969+1886.1+2050.1
29:13 t young bullocks, two rams, *and* 6240+7969
29:14 unto every bullock of the t bullocks, 6240+7969
Jos 19: 6 Sharuhen; t cities and their villages: 6240+7969
21: 4 out of the tribe of Benjamin, t cities. 6240+7969
21: 6 tribe of Manasseh in Bashan, t cities. 6240+7969
21:19 *were* t cities with their suburbs. 6240+7969
21:33 *were* t cities with their suburbs. 6240+7969
1Ki 7: 1 was building his own house t years, 6240+7969
1Ch 6:60 their families *were* t cities. 6240+7969
6:62 tribe of Manasseh in Bashan, t cities. 6240+7969
26:11 and brethren of Hosah *were* t. 6240+7969
Eze 40:11 *and* the length of the gate, t cubits. 6240+7969

THIRTEENTH (11) [THIRTEEN]
Ge 14: 4 and *in* the t year they rebelled. 6240+7969
1Ch 24:13 The t to Huppah, the fourteenth to 6240+7969
25:20 The t *to* Shubael, *he,* his sons, and 6240+7969
Est 3:12 called on the t day of the first month, 6240+7969
3:13 upon the t *day* of the twelfth month, 6240+7969
8:12 *namely,* upon the t *day* of the twelfth 6240+7969
9: 1 on the t day of the same, 6240+7969
9:17 On the t day of the month Adar; and 6240+7969
9:18 together on the t *day* thereof, 6240+7969
Jer 1: 2 of Judah, in the t year of his reign. 6240+7969
25: 3 From the t year of Josiah the son of 6240+7969

THIRTIETH (9) [THIRTY]
2Ki 15:13 the nine and t year of Uzziah king of Judah; 7970
15:17 t year of Azariah king of Judah *began* 7970
25:27 t year of the captivity of Jehoiachin king of 7970
2Ch 15:19 unto the five and t year of the reign of Asa. 7970
16: 1 t year of the reign of Asa Baasha king of 7970
Ne 5:14 the two and t year of Artaxerxes the king, 7970
13: 6 t year of Artaxerxes king of Babylon came 7970
Jer 52:31 t year of the captivity of Jehoiachin king of 7970
Eze 1: 1 Now it came to pass in the t year, in 7970

THIRTY (174) [THIRTIETH, THIRTYFOLD]
Ge 5: 3 Adam lived an hundred and t years, and 7970
5: 5 Adam lived were nine hundred and t years: 7970
5:16 he begat Jared eight hundred and t years, 7970
6:15 it fifty cubits, and the height of it t cubits. 7970
11:12 Arphaxad lived five and t years, and 7970
11:14 And Salah lived t years, and begat Eber: 7970
11:16 Eber lived four and t years, and 7970
11:17 he begat Peleg four hundred and t years, 7970
11:18 And Peleg lived t years, and begat Reu: 7970
11:20 Reu lived two and t years, and begat Serug: 7970
11:22 And Serug lived t years, and begat Nahor: 7970
18:30 Peradventure there shall t be found there. 7970
18:30 he said, I will not do *it,* if I find t there. 7970
25:17 an hundred and t and seven years: 7970
32:15 T milch camels with their colts, forty kine, 7970
41:46 Joseph *was* t years old when he stood 7970
46:15 his sons and his daughters *were* t and three. 7970
47: 9 my pilgrimage *are* an hundred and t years: 7970
Ex 6:16 years of the life of Levi *were* an hundred t 7970
6:18 of the life of Kohath *were* an hundred t 7970
6:20 *were* an hundred and t and seven years. 7970
12:40 in Egypt, *was* four hundred and t years. 7970
12:41 at the end of the four hundred and t years, 7970
21:32 he shall give unto their master t shekels *of* 7970
26: 8 The length of one curtain *shall be* t cubits, 7970
36:15 The length of one curtain *was* t cubits, and 7970
38:24 and seven hundred and t shekels, 7970
Lev 12: 4 the blood of her purifying three and t days; 7970
27: 4 then thy estimation shall be t shekels. 7970
Nu 1:35 *were* t and two thousand and two hundred. 7970
1:37 *were* t and five thousand and four hundred. 7970
2:21 *were* t and two thousand and two hundred. 7970
2:23 *were* t and five thousand and four hundred. 7970
4: 3 From t years old and upward even until 7970
4:23 From t years old and upward until fifty 7970
4:30 From t years old and upward even unto 7970
4:35 From t years old and upward even unto 7970
4:39 From t years old and upward even unto 7970
4:40 were two thousand and six hundred and t. 7970
4:43 From t years old and upward even unto 7970
4:47 From t years old and upward even unto 7970
7:13 t *shekels,* one silver bowl of seventy 7970
7:19 t *shekels,* one silver bowl of seventy 7970
7:25 t *shekels,* one silver bowl of seventy 7970
7:31 t *shekels,* one silver bowl of seventy 7970
7:37 t *shekels,* one silver bowl of seventy 7970
7:43 t *shekels,* a silver bowl of seventy shekels, 7970
7:49 t *shekels,* one silver bowl of seventy 7970
7:55 t *shekels,* one silver bowl of seventy 7970
7:61 t *shekels,* one silver bowl of seventy 7970
7:67 t *shekels,* one silver bowl of seventy 7970
7:73 t *shekels,* one silver bowl of seventy 7970
7:79 t *shekels,* one silver bowl of seventy 7970
7:85 and t *shekels,* each bowl seventy: 7970
20:29 they mourned for Aaron t days, *even* all 7970
26: 7 three thousand and seven hundred and t. 7970
26:37 t and two thousand and five hundred. 7970
26:51 and a thousand seven hundred and t. 7970
31:35 t and two thousand persons in all, 7970
31:36 seven and t thousand and five hundred 7970
31:38 the beeves *were* t and six thousand; of 7970
31:39 the asses *were* t thousand and five hundred; 7970
31:40 of which the LORD's tribute *was* t and 7970
31:43 t thousand *and* seven thousand and 7970
31:44 And t and six thousand beeves, 7970
31:45 And t thousand asses and five hundred, 7970
Dt 2:14 the brook Zered, *was* t and eight years; 7970
34: 8 for Moses in the plains of Moab t days: 7970
Jos 7: 5 the men of Ai smote of them about t and 7970
8: 3 Joshua chose out t thousand mighty *men* of 7970
12:24 king of Tirzah, one: all the kings t and one. 7970
Jdg 10: 4 he had t sons that rode on thirty ass colts, 7970
10: 4 he had thirty sons that rode on t ass colts, 7970
10: 4 they had t cities, which are called 7970
12: 9 he had t sons, and thirty daughters, 7970
12: 9 t daughters, *whom* he sent abroad, and 7970
12: 9 took in t daughters from abroad for his 7970
12:14 he had forty sons and t nephews, that rode 7970
14:11 that they brought t companions to be with 7970
14:12 I will give you t sheets and thirty change of 7970
14:12 you thirty sheets and t change of garments: 7970
14:13 shall ye give me t sheets and thirty change 7970
14:13 me thirty sheets and t change of garments. 7970
14:19 slew t men of them, and took their spoil, 7970
20:31 to Gibeah in the field, about t men of Israel. 7970
20:39 kill of the men of Israel about t persons: 7970
1Sa 4:10 for there fell of Israel t thousand footmen. 7970
9:22 were bidden, which *were* about t persons. 7970
11: 8 and the men of Judah t thousand. 7970
13: 5 t thousand chariots, and six thousand 7970
2Sa 5: 4 David *was* t years old when he *began* to 7970
5: 5 in Jerusalem he reigned t and three years 7970
6: 1 all the chosen *men* of Israel, t thousand. 7970
23:13 three of the t chief went down, and came to 7970
23:23 He was more honourable than the t, but 7970
23:24 Asahel the brother of Joab *was* one of the t; 7970
23:39 Uriah the Hittite: t and seven *in* all. 7970
1Ki 2:11 t and three years reigned he in Jerusalem. 7970
4:22 Solomon's provision for one day was t 7970
5:13 all Israel; and the levy was t thousand men. 7970
6: 2 and the height thereof t cubits. 7970
7: 2 fifty cubits, and the height thereof t cubits, 7970
7: 6 and the breadth thereof t cubits: 7970
7:23 a line of t cubits did compass it round 7970
16:23 In the t and first year of Asa king of Judah 7970
16:29 in the t and eighth year of Asa king of 7970
20: 1 *there were* t and two kings with him, and 7970
20:15 and they were two hundred and t two: 7970
20:16 the t and two kings that helped him. 7970
22:31 the king of Syria commanded his t and 7970
22:42 Jehoshaphat *was* t and five years old when 7970
2Ki 8:17 T and two years old was he when he *began* 7970
13:10 In the t and seventh year of Joash king of 7970
15: 8 In the t and eighth year of Azariah king of 7970
18:14 talents of silver and t talents of gold. 7970
22: 1 he reigned t and one years in Jerusalem. 7970
1Ch 3: 4 in Jerusalem he reigned t and three years. 7970
7: 4 t thousand *men:* for they had many wives 7970
7: 7 and two thousand and t and four. 7970
11:15 Now three of the t captains went down to 7970
11:25 he was honourable among the t, but 7970
11:42 a captain of the Reubenites, and t with him, 7970
12: 4 a mighty *man* among the t, and over 7970

1Ch 12: 4 *man* among the thirty, and over the **t**; 7970
12:34 with shield and spear **t** and seven thousand. 7970
15: 7 and his brethren an hundred and **t**: 7970
19: 7 So they hired **t** and two thousand chariots, 7970
23: 3 were numbered from the age of **t** years 7970
23: 3 man by man, was **t** and eight thousand. 7970
27: 6 *who was* mighty among the **t**, and 7970
27: 6 mighty among the thirty, and above the **t**: 7970
29:27 **t** and three *years* reigned he in Jerusalem. 7970
2Ch 3:15 he made before the house two pillars of **t** 7970
4: 2 a line of **t** cubits did compass it round 7970
16:12 Asa in the **t** and ninth year of his reign was 7970
20:31 *he was* **t** and five years old when he *began* 7970
21: 5 Jehoram *was* **t** and two years old when he 7970
21:20 **T** and two *years* old was he when he *began* 7970
24:15 and **t** years old *was he* when he died. 7970
34: 1 he reigned in Jerusalem one and **t** years. 7970
35: 7 to the number of **t** thousand, and 7970
Ezr 1: 9 **t** chargers of gold, a thousand chargers of 7970
1:10 **T** basons of gold, silver basons of a second 7970
2:35 three thousand and six hundred and **t**. 7970
2:42 of Shobai, *in* all an hundred **t** and nine. 7970
2:65 *there were* seven thousand three hundred **t** 7970
2:66 Their horses *were* seven hundred **t** and six; 7970
Ezr 2:67 Their camels, four hundred **t** and five; 7970
Ne 7:38 three thousand nine hundred and **t**. 7970
7:45 children of Shobai, an hundred **t** and eight. 7970
7:67 *there were* seven thousand three hundred **t** 7970
7:68 Their horses, seven hundred **t** and six: 7970
7:69 *Their* camels, four hundred **t** and five: 7970
7:70 five hundred and **t** priests' garments. 7970
Est 4:11 to come in unto the king these **t** days. 7970
Jer 38:10 Take from hence **t** men with thee, and 7970
52:29 captive from Jerusalem eight hundred **t** 7970
Eze 40:17 **t** chambers *were* upon the pavement. 7970
41: 6 one over another, and **t** *in* order; 7970
46:22 joined *of* forty *cubits* long and **t** broad: 7970
Da 6: 7 ask a petition of any God or man for **t** days, 8533
6:12 *a petition* of any God or man within **t** days, 8533
12:12 thousand three hundred *and* five and **t** days. 7970
Zec 11:12 So they weighed *for* my price **t** *pieces* of 7970
11:13 I took the **t** *pieces* of silver, and cast them 7970
Mt 13:23 some an hundred*fold,* some sixty, some **t**. *5144*
26:15 And they covenanted with him for **t** pieces *5144*
27: 3 brought again the **t** pieces of silver to *5144*
27: 9 saying, And they took the **t** pieces of silver, *5144*
Mk 4: 8 some **t**, and some sixty, and some an *5144*
Lk 3:23 And Jesus himself began *to be* about **t** *5144*
Jn 5: 5 which had an infirmity **t** *and* eight years. *5144*
6:19 rowed about five and twenty or **t** furlongs, *5144*
Gal 3:17 which was four hundred and **t** years after, *5144*

THIRTYFOLD (2) [THIRTY]
Mt 13: 8 hundred*fold,* some sixty*fold,* some **t**. *5144*
Mk 4:20 some **t**, some sixty, and some an *5144*

THIS (2786) [THESE] See Index

THISTLE (5) [THISTLES]
2Ki 14: 9 The **t** that *was* in Lebanon sent to the cedar 2336
14: 9 that *was* in Lebanon, and trode down the **t**. 2336
2Ch 25:18 The **t** that *was* in Lebanon sent to the cedar 2336
25:18 that *was* in Lebanon, and trode down the **t**. 2336
Hos 10: 8 and the **t** shall come up on their altars; 1863

THISTLES (3) [THISTLE]
Ge 3:18 and **t** shall it bring forth to thee; 1863
Job 31:40 Let **t** grow instead of wheat, and 2336
Mt 7:16 *men* gather grapes of thorns, or figs of **t**? *5146*

THITHER (95) [THITHERWARD] See Index

THITHERWARD (3) [THITHER] See Index

THOMAS (12)
Mt 10: 3 **T**, and Matthew the publican; *2381*
Mk 3:18 and **T**, and James the *son* of Alpheus, and *2381*
Lk 6:15 Matthew and **T**, James the *son* of Alpheus, *2381*
Jn 11:16 Then said **T**, which is called Didymus, *2381*
14: 5 **T** saith unto him, Lord, we know not *2381*
20:24 But **T**, one of the twelve, called Didymus, *2381*
20:26 his disciples were within, and **T** with them: *2381*
20:27 Then saith he to **T**, Reach hither thy finger, *2381*
20:28 And **T** answered and said unto him, *2381*
20:29 **T**, because thou hast seen me, thou hast *2381*
21: 2 and **T** called Didymus, and Nathanael of *2381*
Ac 1:13 and John, and Andrew, Philip, and **T**, *2381*

THONG; THONGS See LATCHET; SHOELATCHET; WITHS

THONGS (1)
Ac 22:25 And as they bound him with **t**, Paul said *2438*

THORN (7) [THORNS]
Job 41: 2 his nose? or bore his jaw through with a **t**? 2336
Pr 26: 9 *As* a **t** goeth up into the hand of a drunkard, 2336
Isa 55:13 Instead of the **t** shall come up the fir tree, 5285
Eze 28:24 nor *any* grieving **t** of all *that are* round 6975
Hos 10: 8 the **t** and the thistle shall come up on their 6975
Mic 7: 4 the *most* upright *is sharper* than a **t hedge**: 4534
2Co 12: 7 there was given to me a **t** in the flesh, *4647*

THORNBUSH See BRAMBLE

THORNS (50) [THORN]
Ge 3:18 **T** also and thistles shall it bring forth to 6975
Ex 22: 6 catch in **t**, so that the stacks of corn, or 6975
Nu 33:55 **t** in your sides, and shall vex you in 6796
Jos 23:13 scourges in your sides, and **t** in your eyes, 6796
Jdg 2: 3 they shall be *as* **t** in your sides, and NIH
8: 7 I will tear your flesh with the **t** of 6975
8:16 **t** of the wilderness and briers, and 6975
2Sa 23: 6 *the sons of* Belial *shall be* all of them as **t** 6975
2Ch 33:11 which took Manasseh among the **t**, and 2336
Job 5: 5 taketh it *even* out of the **t**, and the robber 6791
Ps 58: 9 Before your pots can feel the **t**, he shall take 329
118:12 like bees; they are quenched as the fire of **t**: 6975
Pr 15:19 way of the slothful *man is* as a hedge of **t**: 2312
22: 5 **T** *and* snares *are* in the way of the froward: 6791
24:31 it was all grown over *with* **t**, *and* nettles had 7063
Ecc 7: 6 For as the crackling of **t** under a pot, so 5518
SS 2: 2 As the lily among **t**, so *is* my love among 2336
Isa 5: 6 but there shall come up briers and **t**: 7898
7:19 and upon all **t**, and upon all bushes. 5285
7:23 it shall *even* be for briers and **t**. 7898
7:24 all the land shall become briers and **t**. 7898
7:25 not come thither the fear of briers and **t**: 7898
9:18 it shall devour the briers and **t**, and 7898
10:17 it shall burn and devour his **t** and his briers 7898
27: 4 set the briers *and* **t** against me in battle? 7898
32:13 Upon the land of my people shall come up **t** 6975
33:12 *as* **t** cut up shall they be burnt in the fire. 6975
34:13 **t** shall come up *in* her palaces, nettles and 5518
Jer 4: 3 your fallow ground, and sow not among **t**. 6975
12:13 They have sown wheat, but shall reap **t**: 6975
Eze 2: 6 though briers and **t** *be* with thee, and 5544
Hos 2: 6 I will hedge up thy way with **t**, and make a 5518
9: 6 possess them: **t** *shall be* in their tabernacles. 2336
Na 1:10 For while *they be* folden together *as* **t**, and 5518
Mt 7:16 Do *men* gather grapes of **t**, or figs of *173*
13: 7 And some fell among **t**; and the thorns *173*
13: 7 and the **t** sprung up, and choked them: *173*
13:22 He also that received seed among the **t** is he *173*
27:29 And when they had platted a crown of **t**, *173*
Mk 4: 7 And some fell among **t**, and the thorns grew *173*
4: 7 and the **t** grew up, and choked it, and *173*
4:18 And these are they which are sown among **t**; *173*
15:17 and platted a crown **of t**, and put *it* about his *174*
Lk 6:44 For of **t** *men* do not gather figs, nor of a *173*
8: 7 And some fell among **t**; and the thorns *173*
8: 7 and the **t** sprang up with *it*, and choked it. *173*
8:14 And that which fell among **t** are they, which, *173*
Jn 19: 2 And the soldiers platted a crown of **t**, and *173*
19: 5 wearing the crown **of t**, and the purple robe. *174*
Heb 6: 8 But that which beareth **t** and briers *is* *173*

THOROUGHLY (2) [THROUGHLY]
Ge 11: 3 and **burn** *them* **t**. 8313+8316+3807.1
Ex 21:19 and shall **cause** *him* **to be t healed.** 7495+7495

THOSE (465) [THAT] See Index

THOU (5474) [THEE, THEE-WARD, THINE, THY, THYSELF, YOU] See Index

THOUGH (233) [ALTHOUGH] See Index

THOUGHT (81) [THINK]
Ge 20:11 Abraham said, Because I **t**, Surely the fear of 559
38:15 Judah saw her, he **t** her to be a harlot; 2803
48:11 said unto Joseph, I had not **t** to see thy face: 6419

Ge 50:20 as for you, ye t evil against me; *but* 2803
Ex 32:14 the LORD repented of the evil which he t 1696
Nu 24:11 I t to promote thee unto great honour; but lo, 559
33:56 I shall do unto you, as I t to do unto them. 1819
Dt 15: 9 Beware that there be not a t in thy wicked 1697
19:19 as he had t to have done unto his brother: 2161
Jdg 15: 2 **verily** t that thou hadst utterly hated 559+559
20: 5 upon me by night, *and* t to have slain me: 1819
Ru 4: 4 I t to advertise thee, saying, Buy *it* before 559
1Sa 1:13 therefore Eli t she had been drunken. 2803
9: 5 leave *caring* for the asses, and **take** t for us. 1672
18:25 Saul t to make David fall by the hand of 2803
20:26 for he t, Something hath befallen him, he *is* 559
2Sa 4:10 who *t* that I would have given him a reward NIH
13: 2 Amnon t it hard for him to do any 5869+871.1
14:13 hast thou t such a thing against the people 2803
19:18 and to do what he t good. 5869+871.1
21:16 he being girded *with* a new *sword,* t to have 559
2Ki 5:11 and went away, and said, Behold, I t, 559
2Ch 11:22 his brethren: for *he t* to make him king. NIH
32: 1 fenced cities, and t to win them for himself. 559
Ne 6: 2 plain of Ono. But they t to do me mischief. 2803
Est 3: 6 he t scorn to lay hands on Mordecai 5869+871.1
6: 6 Now Haman t in his heart, To whom would 559
Job 12: 5 lamp despised in the t of him that is at ease. 6248
42: 2 and *that* no t can be withholden from thee. 4209
Ps 48: 9 We have t of thy lovingkindness, O God, 1819
49:11 Their inward *t is, that* their houses *shall* NIH
64: 6 both the inward *t* of every one *of them,* and NIH
73:16 When I t to know this, it *was* too painful 2803
119:59 I t **on** my ways, and turned my feet unto 2803
139: 2 thou understandest my t afar off. 7454
Pr 24: 9 The t of foolishness *is* sin: and the scorner 2154
30:32 or if thou hast t **evil**, *lay thine* hand upon 2161
Ecc 10:20 Curse not the king, no not in thy t; and 4093
Isa 14:24 Surely as I have t, so shall it come to pass; 1819
Jer 18: 8 I will repent of the evil that I t to do unto 2803
Eze 38:10 thy mind, and thou shalt think an evil t: 4284
Da 4: 2 I t it good to shew the signs and 6925
6: 3 the king t to set him over the whole realm. 6246
Am 4:13 and declareth unto man what *is* his t, 7808
Zec 1: 6 Like as the LORD of hosts t to do unto us, 2161
8:14 As I t to punish you, when your fathers 2161
8:15 So again have I t in these days to do well 2161
Mal 3:16 the LORD, and that t upon his name. 2803
Mt 1:20 But while he t **on** these *things,* behold, *1760*
6:25 **Take** no t for your life, what ye shall eat, *3309*
6:27 Which of you by **taking** t can add one cubit *3309*
6:28 And why **take** ye t for raiment? *3309*
6:31 Therefore **take** no t, saying, What shall we *3309*
6:34 **Take** therefore no t for the morrow: for *3309*
6:34 for the morrow shall **take** t for the *things* of *3309*
10:19 **take** no t how or what ye shall speak: *3309*
Mk 13:11 **take** no t **beforehand** what ye shall speak, *4305*
14:72 me thrice. And when he t **thereon**, he wept. *1911*
Lk 7: 7 Wherefore neither t I myself **worthy** to *515*
9:47 And Jesus, perceiving the t of their heart, *1261*
12:11 **take** ye no t how or what *thing* ye shall *3309*
12:17 And he t within himself, saying, What shall *1260*
12:22 **Take** no t for your life, what ye shall eat; *3309*
12:25 And which of you with **taking** t can add to *3309*
12:26 *which is* least, why **take** ye t for the rest? *3309*
19:11 they t that the kingdom of God should *1380*
Jn 11:13 they t that he had spoken of taking of rest *1380*
13:29 For some *of them* t, because Judas had *1380*
Ac 8:20 thou hast t that the gift of God may be *3543*
8:22 if perhaps the t of thine heart may be *1963*
10:19 While Peter t on the vision, the Spirit said *1760*
12: 9 done by the angel; but t he saw a vision. *1380*
15:38 But Paul t not **good** to take him with *them,* *515*
26: 8 Why should it be t *a thing* incredible with *2919*
26: 9 I verily t with myself, that *I* ought to do *1380*
1Co 13:11 I understood as a child, I t as a child: *3049*
2Co 9: 5 Therefore I t it necessary to exhort *2233*
10: 5 bringing into captivity every t to *3540*
Php 2: 6 t it not robbery to be equal with God: *2233*
1Th 3: 1 we t it **good** to be left at Athens alone; *2106*
Heb 10:29 suppose ye, shall he be t **worthy**, *515*

THOUGHTEST (1) [THINK]
Ps 50:21 thou t that I was altogether *such a one* as 1819

THOUGHTS (57) [THINK]
Ge 6: 5 *that* every imagination of the t of his heart 4284
Jdg 5:15 of Reuben *there were* great t of heart. 2711
1Ch 28: 9 understandeth all the imaginations of the t: 4284
29:18 of the t of the heart of thy people, 4284
Job 4:13 In t from the visions of the night, 5587
17:11 are broken off, *even* the t of my heart. 4180
20: 2 Therefore do my t cause me to answer, and 5587
21:27 I know your t, and the devices *which* ye 4284
Ps 10: 4 not seek *after God:* God *is* not *in* all his t. 4209
33:11 for ever, the t of his heart to all generations. 4284
40: 5 hast done, and thy t *which are* to us-ward: 4284
56: 5 all their t *are* against me for evil. 4284
92: 5 are thy works! *and* thy t are very deep. 4284
94:11 The LORD knoweth the t of man, 4284
94:19 In the multitude of my t within me thy 8312
119:113 I hate *vain* t: but thy law do I love. 5588
139:17 How precious also are thy t unto me, 7454
139:23 know my heart: try me, and know my t: 8312
146: 4 to his earth; in that *very* day his t perish. 6250
Pr 12: 5 The t of the righteous *are* right: *but* 4284
15:26 The t of the wicked *are* an abomination to 4284
16: 3 the LORD, and thy t shall be established. 4284
21: 5 The t of the diligent *tend* only to 4284
Isa 55: 7 his way, and the unrighteous man his t: 4284
55: 8 For my t *are* not your thoughts, neither *are* 4284
55: 8 For my thoughts *are* not your t, neither *are* 4284
55: 9 your ways, and my t than your thoughts. 4284
55: 9 your ways, and my thoughts than your t. 4284
59: 7 their t *are* thoughts of iniquity; wasting and 4284
59: 7 their thoughts *are* t of iniquity; wasting and 4284
65: 2 a way *that was* not good, after their own t; 4284
66:18 For I *know* their works and their t: it shall 4284
Jer 4:14 How long shall thy vain t lodge within 4284
6:19 *even* the fruit of their t, because they have 4284
23:20 till he have performed the t of his heart: 4209
29:11 For I know the t that I think towards you, 4284
29:11 the LORD, t of peace, and not of evil, 4284
Da 2:29 thy t came *into thy mind* upon thy bed, 7476
2:30 *that* thou mightest know the t of thy heart. 7476
4: 5 the t upon my bed and the visions of my 2031
4:19 for one hour, and his t troubled him. 7476
5: 6 his t troubled him, so that the joints of his 7476
5:10 let not thy t trouble thee, nor let thy 7476
Mic 4:12 they know not the t of the LORD, 4284
Mt 9: 4 And Jesus knowing their t said, *1761*
12:25 And Jesus knew their t, and said unto them, *1761*
15:19 For out of the heart proceed evil t, murders, *1261*
Mk 7:21 proceed evil t, adulteries, fornications, *1261*
Lk 2:35 that the t of many hearts may be revealed. *1261*
5:22 But when Jesus perceived their t, *1261*
6: 8 But he knew their t, and said to the man *1261*
11:17 But he, knowing their t, said unto them, *1270*
24:38 and why do t arise in your hearts? *1261*
Ro 2:15 and *their* t the mean while accusing or *3053*
1Co 3:20 The Lord knoweth the t of the wise, *1261*
Heb 4:12 and *is* a discerner of the t and intents of *1761*
Jas 2: 4 and are become judges of evil t? *1261*

THOUSAND (521) [THOUSANDS]
Ge 20:16 I have given thy brother a t *pieces* of silver: 505
Ex 12:37 about six hundred t on foot *that were* men, 505
32:28 there fell of the people that day about three t 505
38:25 a t seven hundred and threescore and 505
38:26 for six hundred t and three thousand and 505
38:26 and three t and five hundred and fifty *men.* 505
38:28 of the t seven hundred seventy and 505
38:29 and **two** t and four hundred shekels. 505
Lev 26: 8 an hundred of you shall put **ten** t to flight: 7233
Nu 1:21 *were* forty and six t and five hundred. 505
1:23 *were* fifty and nine t and three hundred. 505
1:25 *were* forty and five t six hundred and fifty. 505
1:27 and fourteen t and six hundred. 505
1:29 *were* fifty and four t and four hundred. 505
1:31 *were* fifty and seven t and four hundred. 505
1:33 of Ephraim, *were* forty t and five hundred. 505
1:35 *were* thirty and two t and two hundred. 505
1:37 *were* thirty and five t and four hundred. 505
1:39 and two t and seven hundred. 505
1:41 *were* forty and one t and five hundred. 505
1:43 *were* fifty and three t and four hundred. 505
1:46 they that were numbered were six hundred t 505
1:46 and three t and five hundred and fifty. 505
2: 4 and fourteen t and six hundred. 505
2: 6 *were* fifty and four t and four hundred. 505
2: 8 *were* fifty and seven t and four hundred. 505

Nu 2: 9 in the camp of Judah *were* an hundred t 505
2: 9 fourscore t and six thousand and 505
2: 9 and six t and four hundred, 505
2:11 *were* forty and six t and five hundred. 505
2:13 *were* fifty and nine t and three hundred. 505
2:15 *were* forty and five t and six hundred and 505
2:16 in the camp of Reuben *were* an hundred t 505
2:16 fifty and one t and four hundred and fifty, 505
2:19 of them, *were* forty t and five hundred. 505
2:21 *were* thirty and two t and two hundred. 505
2:23 *were* thirty and five t and four hundred, 505
2:24 of the camp of Ephraim *were* an hundred t 505
2:24 and eight t and an hundred, 505
2:26 and two t and seven hundred. 505
2:28 *were* forty and one t and five hundred. 505
2:30 *were* fifty and three t and four hundred. 505
2:31 in the camp of Dan *were* an hundred t 505
2:31 and fifty and seven t and six hundred. 505
2:32 throughout their hosts *were* six hundred t 505
2:32 and three t and five hundred and fifty. 505
3:22 that were numbered of them *were* seven t 505
3:28 and upward, *were* eight t and six hundred, 505
3:34 and upward, *were* six t and two hundred. 505
3:39 and upward, *were* twenty and two t. 505
3:43 two t two hundred and threescore and 505
3:50 a t three hundred and threescore and 505
4:36 by their families were **two** t seven hundred 505
4:40 were **two** t and six hundred and thirty. 505
4:44 their families, were three t and two hundred. 505
4:48 were eight t and five hundred and fourscore. 505
7:85 all the silver vessels *weighed* **two** t and 505
11:21 amongst whom I *am, are* six hundred t 505
16:49 they that died in the plague were fourteen t 505
25: 9 died in the plague were twenty and four t. 505
26: 7 and three t and seven hundred and thirty. 505
26:14 twenty and two t and two hundred. 505
26:18 numbered of them, forty t and five hundred. 505
26:22 threescore and sixteen t and five hundred. 505
26:25 threescore and four t and three hundred. 505
26:27 of them, threescore t and five hundred. 505
26:34 of them, fifty and two t and seven hundred. 505
26:37 of them, thirty and two t and five hundred. 505
26:41 them *were* forty and five t and six hundred. 505
26:43 *were* threescore and four t and four hundred. 505
26:47 *who were* fifty and three t and four hundred. 505
26:50 them *were* forty and five t and four hundred. 505
26:51 six hundred t and a thousand seven hundred 505
26:51 and a t seven hundred and thirty. 505
26:62 numbered of them were twenty and three t, 505
31: 4 Of every tribe a t, throughout all the tribes of 505
31: 5 a t of *every* tribe, twelve thousand armed for 505
31: 5 of *every* tribe, twelve t armed for war. 505
31: 6 a t of *every* tribe, them and Phinehas the son 505
31:32 was six hundred t and seventy thousand and 505
31:32 and seventy t and five thousand sheep, 505
31:32 and seventy thousand and five t sheep, 505
31:33 And threescore and twelve t beeves, 505
31:34 And threescore and one t asses, 505
31:35 thirty and two t persons in all, of women that 505
31:36 was *in* number three hundred t and seven 505
31:36 seven and thirty t and five hundred sheep: 505
31:38 the beeves *were* thirty and six t; of which 505
31:39 And the asses *were* thirty t and five hundred; 505
31:40 the persons *were* sixteen t; of which 505
31:43 unto the congregation was three hundred t 505
31:43 thirty t *and* seven thousand and five hundred 505
31:43 thirty thousand *and* seven t and five hundred 505
31:44 And thirty and six t beeves, 505
31:45 And thirty t asses and five hundred, 505
31:46 And sixteen t persons;) 505
31:52 was sixteen t seven hundred and 505
35: 4 the city and outward a t cubits round about. 505
35: 5 without the city *on* the east side **two** t cubits, 505
35: 5 *on* the south side **two** t cubits, and *on* 505
35: 5 *on* the west side **two** t cubits, and *on* 505
35: 5 and *on* the north side **two** t cubits; 505
Dt 1:11 God of your fathers make you a t times 505
7: 9 keep his commandments to a t generations; 505
32:30 How should one chase a t, and two put ten 505
32:30 two put **ten** t to flight, except their Rock 7233
Jos 3: 4 and it, about **two** t cubits by measure: 505
4:13 About forty t prepared for war passed over 505
7: 3 *but* let about **two** or three t men go up 505
7: 4 up thither of the people about three t men: 505
8: 3 Joshua chose out thirty t mighty *men* of 505
8:12 he took about five t men, and set them to lie 505
8:25 both of men and women, *were* twelve t, 505
23:10 One man of you shall chase a t: for 505
Jdg 1: 4 and they slew *of* them in Bezek ten t men. 505
3:29 they slew *of* Moab at that time about ten t 505
4: 6 take with thee ten t men of the children of 505
4:10 and he went up with ten t men at his feet: 505
4:14 from mount Tabor, and ten t men after him. 505
5: 8 or spear seen among forty t in Israel? 505
7: 3 returned of the people twenty and two t; 505
7: 3 and two thousand; and there remained ten t. 505
8:10 about fifteen t *men,* all that were left of all 505
8:10 and twenty t men that drew sword. 505
8:26 the golden earrings that he requested was a t 505
9:49 died also, about a t men and women. 505
12: 6 that time of the Ephraimites forty and two t. 505
15:11 three t men of Judah went to the top of 505
15:15 and took it, and slew a t men therewith. 505
15:16 with the jaw of an ass have I slain a t men. 505
16:27 *there were* upon the roof about three t men 505
20: 2 four hundred t footmen that drew sword. 505
20:10 an hundred of a t, and a thousand out of ten 505
20:10 of a thousand, and a t out of ten thousand, 505
20:10 of a thousand, and a thousand out of **ten t,** 7233
20:15 cities twenty and six t men that drew sword, 505
20:17 were numbered four hundred t men that 505
20:21 the Israelites that day twenty and two t men. 505
20:25 the children of Israel again eighteen t men; 505
20:34 there came against Gibeah ten t chosen men 505
20:35 day twenty and five t and an hundred men: 505
20:44 there fell of Benjamin eighteen t men; all 505
20:45 they gleaned of them in the highways five t 505
20:45 unto Gidom, and slew **two** t men of them. 505
20:46 and five t men that drew the sword; 505
21:10 the congregation sent thither twelve t men of 505
1Sa 4: 2 of the army in the field about four t men. 505
4:10 for there fell of Israel thirty t footmen. 505
6:19 even he smote of the people fifty t 505
11: 8 the children of Israel were three hundred t, 505
11: 8 and the men of Judah thirty t. 505
13: 2 Saul chose him three t *men* of Israel; 505
13: 2 *whereof* **two** t were with Saul in Michmash 505
13: 2 a t were with Jonathan in Gibeah of 505
13: 5 thirty t chariots, and six thousand horsemen, 505
13: 5 six t horsemen, and people as the sand which 505
15: 4 two hundred t footmen, and ten thousand 505
15: 4 thousand footmen, and ten t men of Judah. 505
17: 5 the weight of the coat *was* five t shekels *of* 505
17:18 these ten cheeses unto the captain of *their* t, 505
18:13 from him, and made him his captain over a t; 505
24: 2 Saul took three t chosen men out of all 505
25: 2 he had three t sheep, and a thousand goats: 505
25: 2 he had three thousand sheep, and a t goats: 505
26: 2 having three t chosen men of Israel with 505
2Sa 6: 1 together all the chosen *men* of Israel, thirty t. 505
8: 4 David took from him a t *chariots,* and 505
8: 4 hundred horsemen, and twenty t footmen: 505
8: 5 slew of the Syrians two and twenty t men. 505
8:13 in the valley of salt, *being* eighteen t *men.* 505
10: 6 twenty t footmen, and of king Maacah a 505
10: 6 of king Maacah a t men, and of Ish-tob 505
10: 6 thousand men, and of Ish-tob twelve t men. 505
10:18 forty t horsemen, and smote Shobach 505
17: 1 Let me now choose out twelve t men, and 505
18: 3 but now *thou art* worth ten t of us: therefore 505
18: 7 a great slaughter that day *of* twenty t *men.* 505
18:12 Though I should receive a t *shekels of* silver 505
19:17 *there were* a t men of Benjamin with him, 505
24: 9 there were in Israel eight hundred t valiant 505
24: 9 the men of Judah *were* five hundred t men. 505
24:15 from Dan even to Beer-sheba seventy t men. 505
1Ki 3: 4 a t burnt offerings did Solomon offer up on 505
4:26 Solomon had forty t stalls of horses for his 505
4:26 for his chariots, and twelve t horsemen. 505
4:32 he spake three t proverbs: and his songs 505
4:32 and his songs were a t and five. 505
5:11 Solomon gave Hiram twenty t measures of 505
5:13 of all Israel; and the levy was thirty t men. 505
5:14 them to Lebanon, ten t a month *by* courses: 505
5:15 had threescore and ten t that bare burdens, 505
5:15 and fourscore t hewers in the mountains; 505
5:16 three t and three hundred, which ruled over 505
7:26 flowers of lilies: it contained **two** t baths. 505

1Ki	8:63	two and twenty **t** oxen, and an hundred and	505
	8:63	and an hundred and twenty **t** sheep.	505
	10:26	he had a **t** and four hundred chariots, and	505
	10:26	hundred chariots, and twelve **t** horsemen,	505
	12:21	fourscore **t** chosen *men,* which were	505
	19:18	Yet I have left *me* seven **t** in Israel, all	505
	20:15	*even* all the children of Israel, *being* seven **t**.	505
	20:29	the Syrians an hundred **t** footmen in one day.	505
	20:30	and seven **t** of the men that were left.	505
2Ki	3: 4	rendered unto the king of Israel an hundred **t**	505
	3: 4	and an hundred **t** rams, *with* the wool.	505
	5: 5	six **t** *pieces* of gold, and ten changes of	505
	13: 7	and ten chariots, and ten **t** footmen;	505
	14: 7	He slew *of* Edom in the valley of salt ten **t**,	505
	15:19	Menahem gave Pul a **t** talents of silver,	505
	18:23	and I will deliver thee **two t** horses,	505
	19:35	Assyrians an hundred fourscore and five **t**:	505
	24:14	*even* ten **t** captives, and all the craftsmen and	505
	24:16	*even* seven **t**, and craftsmen and smiths a	505
	24:16	craftsmen and smiths a **t**, all *that were* strong	505
1Ch	5:18	*were* four and forty **t** seven hundred and	505
	5:21	*of* their camels fifty **t**, and *of* sheep two	505
	5:21	*of* sheep two hundred and fifty **t**, and	505
	5:21	*of* asses **two t**, and *of* men an hundred	505
	5:21	two thousand, and *of* men an hundred **t**.	505
	7: 2	of David two and twenty **t** and six hundred.	505
	7: 4	thirty **t** *men:* for they had many wives and	505
	7: 5	by their genealogies fourscore and seven **t**.	505
	7: 7	and two **t** and thirty and four.	505
	7: 9	of valour, *was* twenty **t** and two hundred.	505
	7:11	*were* seventeen **t** and two hundred *soldiers,*	505
	7:40	*and* to battle *was* twenty and six **t** men.	505
	9:13	a **t** and seven hundred and threescore;	505
	12:14	over an hundred, and the greatest over a **t**.	505
	12:24	and spear *were* six **t** and eight hundred,	505
	12:25	valour for the war, seven **t** and one hundred.	505
	12:26	Of the children of Levi four **t** and	505
	12:27	with him *were* three **t** and seven hundred;	505
	12:29	of Benjamin, the kindred of Saul, three **t**:	505
	12:30	And of the children of Ephraim twenty **t** and	505
	12:31	And of the half tribe of Manasseh eighteen **t**,	505
	12:33	of war, fifty **t**, which could keep rank:	505
	12:34	of Naphtali a **t** captains, and with them with	505
	12:34	with shield and spear thirty and seven **t**.	505
	12:35	in war twenty and eight **t** and six hundred.	505
	12:36	as went forth to battle, expert in war, forty **t**.	505
	12:37	war for the battle, an hundred and twenty **t**.	505
	16:15	the word *which* he commanded to a **t**	505
	18: 4	David took from him a **t** chariots, and	505
	18: 4	seven **t** horsemen, and twenty thousand	505
	18: 4	thousand horsemen, and twenty **t** footmen:	505
	18: 5	slew of the Syrians two and twenty **t** men.	505
	18:12	the Edomites in the valley of salt eighteen **t**.	505
	19: 6	the children of Ammon sent a **t** talents of	505
	19: 7	So they hired thirty and two **t** chariots, and	505
	19:18	David slew of the Syrians seven **t** *men*	505
	19:18	forty **t** footmen, and killed Shophach	505
	21: 5	And all *they of* Israel were a **t** thousand and	505
	21: 5	And all *they of* Israel were a thousand **t** and	505
	21: 5	and an hundred **t** men that drew sword:	505
	21: 5	and ten **t** men that drew sword.	505
	21:14	and there fell of Israel seventy **t** men.	505
	22:14	of the LORD an hundred **t** talents *of* gold,	505
	22:14	*of* gold, and a **t** thousand talents *of* silver;	505
	22:14	*of* gold, and a thousand **t** talents *of* silver;	505
	23: 3	man by man, was thirty and eight **t**.	505
	23: 4	four **t** *were* to set forward the work of	505
	23: 4	and six **t** *were* officers and judges:	505
	23: 5	Moreover four **t** *were* porters; and	505
	23: 5	four **t** praised the LORD with	505
	26:30	men of valour, a **t** and seven hundred,	505
	26:32	*were* **two t** and seven hundred chief fathers,	505
	27: 1	*of* every course *were* twenty and four **t**.	505
	27: 2	and in his course *were* twenty and four **t**.	505
	27: 4	his course likewise *were* twenty and four **t**.	505
	27: 5	and in his course *were* twenty and four **t**.	505
	27: 7	and in his course *were* twenty and four **t**.	505
	27: 8	and in his course *were* twenty and four **t**.	505
	27: 9	and in his course *were* twenty and four **t**.	505
	27:10	and in his course *were* twenty and four **t**.	505
	27:11	and in his course *were* twenty and four **t**.	505
	27:12	and in his course *were* twenty and four **t**.	505
	27:13	and in his course *were* twenty and four **t**.	505
	27:14	and in his course *were* twenty and four **t**.	505
	27:15	and in his course *were* twenty and four **t**.	505
	29: 4	*Even* three **t** talents of gold, of the gold of	505
	29: 4	and seven **t** talents of refined silver,	505
	29: 7	of the house of God *of* gold five **t** talents	505
	29: 7	gold five thousand talents and **ten t** drams,	7239
	29: 7	*of* silver ten **t** talents, and *of* brass eighteen	505
	29: 7	*of* brass **eighteen t**	505+7239+8083+2050.1
	29: 7	and one hundred **t** talents *of* iron.	505
	29:21	*even* a **t** bullocks, a thousand rams, *and*	505
	29:21	a **t** rams, *and* a thousand lambs, with their	505
	29:21	a thousand rams, *and* a **t** lambs, with their	505
2Ch	1: 6	and offered a **t** burnt offerings upon it.	505
	1:14	he had a **t** and four hundred chariots, and	505
	1:14	hundred chariots, and twelve **t** horsemen,	505
	2: 2	out threescore and ten **t** men to bear burdens,	505
	2: 2	fourscore **t** to hew in the mountain, and	505
	2: 2	and three **t** and six hundred to oversee them.	505
	2:10	twenty **t** measures of beaten wheat, and	505
	2:10	twenty **t** measures of barley, and	505
	2:10	twenty **t** baths of wine, and twenty thousand	505
	2:10	baths of wine, and twenty **t** baths of oil.	505
	2:17	fifty **t** and three thousand and six hundred.	505
	2:17	fifty thousand and three **t** and six hundred.	505
	2:18	and ten **t** of them *to be* bearers of burdens,	505
	2:18	fourscore **t** *to be* hewers in the mountain,	505
	2:18	three **t** and six hundred overseers to set	505
	4: 5	*and* it received and held three **t** baths.	505
	7: 5	offered a sacrifice of twenty and two **t** oxen,	505
	7: 5	and an hundred and twenty **t** sheep:	505
	9:25	And Solomon had four **t** stalls for horses and	505
	9:25	and chariots, and twelve **t** horsemen;	505
	11: 1	fourscore **t** chosen *men,* which were	505
	12: 3	hundred chariots, and threescore **t** horsemen:	505
	13: 3	of war, *even* four hundred **t** chosen men:	505
	13: 3	him with eight hundred **t** chosen men,	505
	13:17	there fell down slain of Israel five hundred **t**	505
	14: 8	and spears, out of Judah three hundred **t**;	505
	14: 8	drew bows, two hundred and fourscore **t**:	505
	14: 9	the Ethiopian with a host of a **t** thousand,	505
	14: 9	the Ethiopian with a host of a thousand **t**,	505
	15:11	seven hundred oxen and seven **t** sheep.	505
	17:11	seven **t** and seven hundred rams, and	505
	17:11	and seven **t** and seven hundred he goats.	505
	17:14	him mighty *men* of valour three hundred **t**.	505
	17:15	and with him two hundred and fourscore **t**.	505
	17:16	with him two hundred **t** mighty *men* of	505
	17:17	*men* with bow and shield two hundred **t**.	505
	17:18	and fourscore **t** ready prepared for the war.	505
	25: 5	found them three hundred **t** choice *men, able*	505
	25: 6	He hired also an hundred **t** mighty *men* of	505
	25:11	and smote *of* the children of Seir ten **t**.	505
	25:12	*other* ten **t** *left* alive did the children of Judah	505
	25:13	smote three **t** of them, and took much spoil.	505
	26:12	of the mighty *men* of valour *were* **two t**	505
	26:13	three hundred **t** and seven thousand and	505
	26:13	and seven **t** and five hundred,	505
	27: 5	ten **t** measures of wheat, and ten thousand of	505
	27: 5	measures of wheat, and ten **t** of barley.	505
	28: 6	in Judah an hundred and twenty **t** in one day,	505
	28: 8	captive of their brethren two hundred **t**,	505
	29:33	*were* six hundred oxen and three **t** sheep.	505
	30:24	did give to the congregation a **t** bullocks	505
	30:24	a thousand bullocks and seven **t** sheep;	505
	30:24	the princes gave to the congregation a **t**	505
	30:24	a thousand bullocks and ten **t** sheep:	505
	35: 7	to the number of thirty **t**, and three thousand	505
	35: 7	of thirty thousand, and three **t** bullocks:	505
	35: 8	the priests for the passover *offerings* **two t**	505
	35: 9	for passover *offerings* five **t** *small cattle,*	505
Ezr	1: 9	a **t** chargers of silver, nine and	505
	1:10	four hundred and ten, *and* other vessels a **t**.	505
	1:11	and of silver *were* five **t** and four hundred.	505
	2: 3	**two t** an hundred seventy and two.	505
	2: 6	*and* Joab, **two t** eight hundred and twelve.	505
	2: 7	of Elam, a **t** two hundred fifty and four.	505
	2:12	of Azgad, a **t** two hundred twenty and two.	505
	2:14	The children of Bigvai, **two t** fifty and six.	505
	2:31	other Elam, a **t** two hundred fifty and four.	505
	2:35	of Senaah, three **t** and six hundred and thirty.	505
	2:37	The children of Immer, a **t** fifty and two.	505
	2:38	of Pashur, a **t** two hundred forty and seven.	505
	2:39	The children of Harim, a **t** and seventeen.	505
	2:64	together *was* **forty** *and* **two t**	505+702+7239
	2:65	of whom *there were* seven **t** three hundred	505

Ezr	2:67	*their* asses, six **t** seven hundred and twenty.	505
	2:69	**threescore and one t**	505+7239+8337+2050.1
	2:69	five **t** pound *of* silver, and one hundred	505
	8:27	Also twenty basons of gold, of a **t** drams;	505
Ne	3:13	and a **t** cubits on the wall unto the dung gate.	505
	7: 8	**two t** an hundred seventy and two.	505
	7:11	Joab, **two t** and eight hundred *and* eighteen.	505
	7:12	of Elam, a **t** two hundred fifty and four.	505
	7:17	**two t** three hundred twenty and two.	505
	7:19	of Bigvai, **two t** threescore and seven.	505
	7:34	other Elam, a **t** two hundred fifty and four.	505
	7:38	of Senaah, three **t** nine hundred and thirty.	505
	7:40	The children of Immer, a **t** fifty and two.	505
	7:41	of Pashur, a **t** two hundred forty and seven.	505
	7:42	The children of Harim, a **t** *and* seventeen.	505
	7:66	together *was* **forty** *and* **two t**	505+702+7239
	7:67	of whom *there were* seven **t** three hundred	505
	7:69	five: six **t** seven hundred and twenty asses.	505
	7:70	The Tirshatha gave to the treasure a **t** drams	505
	7:71	of the work twenty **t** drams *of* gold,	7239
	7:71	and **two t** and two hundred pound *of* silver.	505
	7:72	people gave *was* twenty **t** drams *of* gold,	7239
	7:72	**two t** pound *of* silver, and threescore and	505
Est	3: 9	I will pay ten **t** talents of silver to the hands	505
	9:16	and slew of their foes seventy and five **t**, but	505
Job	1: 3	His substance also was seven **t** sheep, and	505
	1: 3	three **t** camels, and five hundred yoke of	505
	9: 3	with him, he cannot answer him one of a **t**.	505
	33:23	with him, an interpreter, one among a **t**,	505
	42:12	for he had fourteen **t** sheep, and six thousand	505
	42:12	six **t** camels, and a thousand yoke of oxen,	505
	42:12	a **t** yoke of oxen, and a thousand she asses.	505
	42:12	a thousand yoke of oxen, and a **t** she asses.	505
Ps	50:10	forest *is* mine, *and* the cattle upon a **t** hills.	505
	60: T	smote of Edom in the valley of salt twelve **t**.	505
	68:17	The chariots of God *are* **twenty t**,	7239
	84:10	For a day in thy courts *is* better than a **t**.	505
	90: 4	For a **t** years in thy sight *are but* as yesterday	505
	91: 7	A **t** shall fall at thy side, and ten thousand at	505
	91: 7	fall at thy side, and **ten t** at thy right hand;	7233
	105: 8	the word *which* he commanded to a **t**	505
Ecc	6: 6	though he live a **t** years twice *told,* yet hath	505
	7:28	one man among a **t** have I found; but	505
SS	4: 4	whereon there hang a **t** bucklers, all shields	505
	5:10	and ruddy, the chiefest among **ten t**.	7233
	8:11	fruit thereof was to bring a **t** *pieces* of silver.	505
	8:12	*must have* a **t**, and those that keep the fruit	505
Isa	7:23	where there were a **t** vines at a thousand	505
	7:23	where there were a thousand vines at a **t**	505
	30:17	One **t** *shall flee* at the rebuke of one; at	505
	36: 8	of Assyria, and I will give thee **two t** horses,	505
	37:36	an hundred and fourscore and five **t**:	505
	60:22	A little one shall become a **t**, and a small one	505
Jer	52:28	in the seventh year three **t** Jews and three	505
	52:30	all the persons *were* four **t** and six hundred.	505
Eze	45: 1	twenty **t** *reeds,* and the breadth *shall be* ten	505
	45: 1	and the breadth *shall be* ten **t**.	505
	45: 3	thou measure the length of five and twenty **t**,	505
	45: 3	twenty thousand, and the breadth of ten **t**:	505
	45: 5	*the* five and twenty **t** of length, and *the* ten	505
	45: 5	*the* ten **t** of breadth, shall also the Levites,	505
	45: 6	the possession of the city five **t** broad,	505
	45: 6	thousand broad, and five and twenty **t** long,	505
	47: 3	went forth east*ward,* he measured a **t** cubits,	505
	47: 4	Again he measured a **t**, and brought me	505
	47: 4	Again he measured a **t**, and brought me	505
	47: 5	Afterward he measured a **t**; *and it was* a river	505
	48: 8	offer *of* five and twenty **t** *reeds in* breadth,	505
	48: 9	*shall be of* five and twenty **t** *in* length,	505
	48: 9	thousand *in* length, and *of* ten **t** *in* breadth.	505
	48:10	the north five and twenty **t** *in length,* and	505
	48:10	and toward the west ten **t** *in* breadth,	505
	48:10	toward the east ten **t** *in* breadth, and	505
	48:10	toward the south five and twenty **t** *in* length:	505
	48:13	*shall have* five and twenty **t** *in* length,	505
	48:13	thousand *in* length, and ten **t** *in* breadth:	505
	48:13	all the length *shall be* five and twenty **t**, and	505
	48:13	and twenty thousand, and the breadth ten **t**.	505
	48:15	the five **t**, that are left in the breadth over	505
	48:15	breadth over against the five and twenty **t**,	505
	48:16	the north side four **t** and five hundred, and	505
	48:16	the south side four **t** and five hundred, and	702
	48:16	and on the east side four **t** and five hundred,	505
	48:16	and the west side four **t** and five hundred.	505
	48:18	of the holy *portion shall be* ten **t** eastward,	505
	48:18	ten thousand eastward, and ten **t** westward:	505
	48:20	and twenty **t** by five and twenty thousand:	505
	48:20	and twenty thousand by five and twenty **t**:	505
	48:21	twenty **t** of the oblation toward the east	505
	48:21	the five and twenty **t** toward the west border,	505
	48:30	north side, four **t** and five hundred measures.	505
	48:32	And at the east side four **t** and five hundred:	505
	48:33	*at* the south side four **t** and five hundred	505
	48:34	*At* the west side four **t** and five hundred,	505
	48:35	*It was* round about eighteen **t** *measures:* and	505
Da	5: 1	Belshazzar the king made a great feast to a **t**	506
	5: 1	of his lords, and drank wine before the **t**.	506
	7:10	**t** thousands ministered unto him, and	506
	7:10	**ten t** times ten thousand stood before him:	7240
	7:10	ten thousand times **ten t** stood before him:	7240
	8:14	unto me, Unto **two t** and three hundred days;	505
	12:11	*there shall be* a **t** two hundred and	505
	12:12	cometh to the **t** three hundred *and* five and	505
Am	5: 3	The city that went out *by* a **t** shall leave an	505
Jnh	4:11	wherein are more than sixscore **t** persons	7239
Mt	14:21	And they that had eaten were about **five t**	*4000*
	15:38	And they that did eat were **four t** men,	*5070*
	16: 9	remember the five loaves of the **five t**,	*4000*
	16:10	Neither the seven loaves of the **four t**, and	*5070*
	18:24	unto him, which ought him **ten t** talents.	*3463*
Mk	5:13	place into the sea, (they were about **two t**,)	*1367*
	6:44	did eat *of* the loaves were about **five t** men.	*4000*
	8: 9	And they that had eaten were about **four t**:	*5070*
	8:19	When I brake the five loaves among **five t**,	*4000*
	8:20	And when the seven among **four t**,	*5070*
Lk	9:14	For they were about **five t** men. And he	*4000*
	14:31	consulteth whether he be able with ten **t** to	*5505*
	14:31	him that cometh against him with twenty **t**?	*5505*
Jn	6:10	the men sat down, *in* number about **five t**.	*4000*
Ac	2:41	were added *unto them* about **three t** souls.	*5153*
	4: 4	the number of the men was about five **t**.	*5505*
	19:19	and found *it* **fifty t** *pieces* of silver.	*3461+4002*
	21:38	leddest out into the wilderness **four t** men	*5070*
Ro	11: 4	I have reserved to myself **seven t** men,	*2035*
1Co	4:15	For though you have **ten t** instructors in	*3463*
	10: 8	and fell in one day three and twenty **t**.	*5505*
	14:19	than **ten t** words in an *unknown* tongue.	*3463*
2Pe	3: 8	that one day *is* with the Lord as a **t** years,	*5507*
	3: 8	a thousand years, and a **t** years as one day.	*5507*
Rev	5:11	the number of them was **ten t** times ten	*3461*
	5:11	of them was ten thousand times **ten t**,	*3461*
	7: 4	four **t** of all the tribes of the children of	*5505*
	7: 5	Of the tribe of Juda *were* sealed twelve **t**.	*5505*
	7: 5	the tribe of Reuben *were* sealed twelve **t**.	*5505*
	7: 5	Of the tribe of Gad *were* sealed twelve **t**.	*5505*
	7: 6	Of the tribe of Aser *were* sealed twelve **t**.	*5505*
	7: 6	tribe of Nephthalim *were* sealed twelve **t**.	*5505*
	7: 6	the tribe of Manasses *were* sealed twelve **t**.	*5505*
	7: 7	the tribe of Simeon *were* sealed twelve **t**.	*5505*
	7: 7	Of the tribe of Levi *were* sealed twelve **t**.	*5505*
	7: 7	Of the tribe of Isachar *were* sealed twelve **t**.	*5505*
	7: 8	the tribe of Zabulon *were* sealed twelve **t**.	*5505*
	7: 8	Of the tribe of Joseph *were* sealed twelve **t**.	*5505*
	7: 8	the tribe of Benjamin *were* sealed twelve **t**.	*5505*
	9:16	*were* **two hundred t thousand**:	*1417+3461*
	9:16	*were* **two hundred thousand t**:	*1417+3461*
	11: 3	they shall prophesy a **t** two hundred *and*	*5507*
	11:13	the earthquake were slain of men seven **t**:	*5505*
	12: 6	that they should feed her there a **t** two	*5507*
	14: 1	and with him an hundred forty *and* four **t**,	*5505*
	14: 3	but the hundred *and* forty *and* four **t**,	*5505*
	14:20	by the space of a **t** *and* six hundred	*5507*
	20: 2	and Satan, and bound him a **t** years,	*5507*
	20: 3	no more, till the **t** years should be fulfilled:	*5507*
	20: 4	they lived and reigned with Christ a **t** years.	*5507*
	20: 5	not again until the **t** years were finished.	*5507*
	20: 6	and shall reign with him a **t** years.	*5507*
	20: 7	And when the **t** years are expired, Satan	*5507*
	21:16	the city with the reed, twelve **t** furlongs.	*5505*

THOUSANDS (62) [THOUSAND]

Ge	24:60	be thou *the mother* of **t** of millions, and	505
Ex	18:21	*to be* rulers of **t**, *and* rulers of hundreds,	505
	18:25	rulers of **t**, rulers of hundreds, rulers of	505
	20: 6	shewing mercy unto **t** of them that love me,	505
	34: 7	Keeping mercy for **t**, forgiving iniquity and	505
Nu	1:16	the tribes of their fathers, heads of **t** in Israel.	505
	10: 4	*which are* heads of the **t** of Israel,	505

T

Nu 10:36 Return, O LORD, *unto* the many t of Israel. 505
31: 5 So there were delivered out of the t of Israel, 505
31:14 *with* the captains over t, and captains over 505
31:48 the officers which *were* over t of the host, 505
31:48 the captains of t, and captains of hundreds, 505
31:52 of the captains of t, and of the captains of 505
31:54 the priest took the gold of the captains of t 505
Dt 1:15 captains over t, and captains over hundreds, 505
5:10 shewing mercy unto t of them that love me 505
33: 2 and he came with **ten** t of saints: 7233
33:17 they *are* the **ten** t of Ephraim, and they *are* 7233
33:17 of Ephraim, and they *are* the t of Manasseh. 505
Jos 22:14 house of their fathers among the t of Israel. 505
22:21 and said unto the heads of the t of Israel, 505
22:30 heads of the t of Israel which *were* with him, 505
1Sa 8:12 And he will appoint him captains over t, and 505
10:19 the LORD by your tribes, and by your t. 505
18: 7 Saul hath slain his t, and David his ten 505
18: 7 slain his thousands, and David his **ten** t. 7233
18: 8 They have ascribed unto David **ten** t, and 7233
18: 8 and to me they have ascribed *but* t: 505
21:11 Saul hath slain his t, and David his ten 505
21:11 slain his thousands, and David his **ten** t? 7233
22: 7 *and* make you all captains of t, and 505
23:23 that I will search him out throughout all the t 505
29: 2 Philistines passed on by hundreds, and by t: 505
29: 5 Saul slew his t, and David his ten thousands? 505
29: 5 slew his thousands, and David his **ten** t? 7233
2Sa 18: 1 set captains of t and captains of hundreds 505
18: 4 the people came out by hundreds and by t. 505
1Ch 12:20 captains of the t that *were* of Manasseh. 505
13: 1 David consulted with the captains of t and 505
15:25 the elders of Israel, and the captains over t, 505
26:26 the captains over t and hundreds, and 505
27: 1 chief fathers and captains of t and hundreds, 505
28: 1 the captains over the t, and captains over 505
29: 6 and the captains of t and of hundreds, 505
2Ch 1: 2 to the captains of t and of hundreds, and 505
17:14 Of Judah, the captains of t; Adnah the chief, 505
25: 5 made them captains over t, and captains over 505
Ps 3: 6 I will not be afraid of **ten** t of people, 7233
68:17 God *are* twenty thousand, *even* t of angels: 505
119:72 of thy mouth *is* better unto me than t of gold 505
144:13 *that* our sheep may **bring forth** t and 503
144:13 forth thousands and **ten** t in our streets: 7231
Jer 32:18 Thou shewest lovingkindness unto t, and 505
Da 7:10 thousand t ministered unto him, and 506
11:12 and he shall cast down *many* **ten** t: 7239
Mic 5: 2 *though thou* be little among the t of Judah, 505
6: 7 Will the LORD be pleased with t of rams, 505
6: 7 of rams, *or* with **ten** t of rivers of oil? 7233
Ac 21:20 how many t of Jews there are which *3461*
Jude 1:14 the Lord cometh with **ten** t of his saints, *3461*
Rev 5:11 times ten thousand, and t of thousands; *5505*
5:11 times ten thousand, and thousands of t; *5505*

THREAD (7)

Ge 14:23 That I will not *take* from a t even to a 2339
38:28 and bound upon his hand a **scarlet** t, 8144
38:30 that had the **scarlet** t upon his hand: 8144
Jos 2:18 thou shalt bind this line of scarlet t in 2339
Jdg 16: 9 as a t of tow is broken when it toucheth 6616
16:12 he brake them from off his arms like a t. 2339
SS 4: 3 Thy lips *are* like a t of scarlet, and 2339

THREATEN (1) [THREATENED, THREATENING, THREATENINGS]

Ac 4:17 among the people, let us **straitly** t them, *546*

THREATENED (2) [THREATEN]

Ac 4:21 So when they had **further** t *them,* they let *4324*
1Pe 2:23 when he suffered, he t not; but *546*

THREATENING (1) [THREATEN]

Eph 6: 9 do the same *things* unto them, forbearing t: *547*

THREATENINGS (2) [THREATEN]

Ac 4:29 And now, Lord, behold their t: and *547*
9: 1 yet breathing out t and slaughter against *547*

THREE (485) [THIRD, THIRDLY, THREEFOLD, THRICE]

Ge 5:22 after he begat Methuselah t hundred years, 7969
5:23 all the days of Enoch were t hundred sixty 7969
6:10 Noah begat t sons, Shem, Ham, and 7969
6:15 length of the ark *shall be* t hundred cubits, 7969
7:13 the t wives of his sons with them, into 7969
9:19 These *are* the t sons of Noah: and of them 7969
9:28 Noah lived after the flood t hundred and 7969
11:13 he begat Salah four hundred and t years, 7969
11:15 he begat Eber four hundred and t years, 7969
14:14 t hundred and eighteen, and pursued *them* 7969
15: 9 Take me a heifer of **t years old**, and a she 8027
15: 9 a she goat of **t years old**, and a ram of three 8027
15: 9 a ram of **t years old**, and a turtle-dove, and 8027
18: 2 and looked, and lo, t men stood by him: 7969
18: 6 Make ready quickly t measures of fine 7969
29: 2 lo, there *were* t flocks of sheep lying by it; 7969
29:34 unto me, because I have born him t sons: 7969
30:36 he set t days' journey betwixt himself and 7969
38:24 it came to pass about t months after, that it 7969
40:10 in the vine *were* t branches: and it *was* as 7969
40:12 of it: The t branches *are* three days: 7969
40:12 of it: The three branches *are* t days: 7969
40:13 Yet within t days shall Pharaoh lift up thine 7969
40:16 behold, *I had* t white baskets on my head: 7969
40:18 The t baskets *are* three days: 7969
40:18 The three baskets *are* t days: 7969
40:19 Yet within t days shall Pharaoh lift up thy 7969
42:17 he put them all together into ward t days. 7969
45:22 to Benjamin he gave t hundred *pieces* of 7969
46:15 his sons and his daughters *were* thirty and t. 7969
Ex 2: 2 *was a* goodly *child,* she hid him t months. 7969
3:18 t days' journey into the wilderness, 7969
5: 3 t days' journey into the desert, and 7969
6:18 Kohath *were* an hundred thirty and t years. 7969
7: 7 Aaron fourscore and t years old, when they 7969
8:27 We will go t days' journey into 7969
10:22 darkness in all the land of Egypt t days: 7969
10:23 neither rose any from his place for t days: 7969
15:22 they went t days in the wilderness, and 7969
21:11 if he do not these t unto her, then shall she 7969
23:14 T times thou shalt keep a feast unto me in 7969
23:17 T times in the year all thy males shall 7969
25:32 t branches of the candlestick out of the one 7969
25:32 t branches of the candlestick out of 7969
25:33 T bowls made like unto almonds, *with* a 7969
25:33 t bowls made like almonds in the other 7969
27: 1 and the height thereof *shall be* t cubits. 7969
27:14 their pillars t, and their sockets three. 7969
27:14 their pillars three, and their sockets t. 7969
27:15 fifteen *cubits:* their pillars t, and 7969
27:15 their pillars three, and their sockets t. 7969
32:28 there fell of the people that day about t 7969
37:18 t branches of the candlestick out of the one 7969
37:18 t branches of the candlestick out of 7969
37:19 T bowls made after the fashion of almonds 7969
37:19 t bowls made like almonds in another 7969
38: 1 and t cubits the height thereof. 7969
38:14 their pillars t, and their sockets three. 7969
38:14 their pillars three, and their sockets t. 7969
38:15 their pillars t, and their sockets three. 7969
38:15 their pillars three, and their sockets t. 7969
38:26 t thousand and five hundred and fifty *men.* 7969
Lev 12: 4 continue in the blood of her purifying t and 7969
14:10 t **tenth deals** of fine flour *for* a meat 6241+7969
19:23 t years shall it be as uncircumcised unto 7969
25:21 it shall bring forth fruit for t years. 7969
27: 6 for the female thy estimation *shall be* t 7969
Nu 1:23 *were* fifty and nine thousand and t hundred. 7969
1:43 *were* fifty and t thousand and four hundred. 7969
1:46 and t thousand and five hundred and fifty. 7969
2:13 *were* fifty and nine thousand and t hundred. 7969
2:30 *were* fifty and t thousand and four hundred. 7969
2:32 and t thousand and five hundred and fifty. 7969
3:50 a thousand t hundred and threescore and 7969
4:44 were t thousand and two hundred. 7969
10:33 the mount of the LORD t days' journey: 7969
10:33 went before them *in* the t days' journey, 7969
12: 4 Come out ye t unto the tabernacle of 7969
12: 4 of the congregation. And they t came out. 7969
15: 9 t tenth deals *of* flour mingled with half a 7969
22:28 that thou hast smitten me these t times? 7969
22:32 hast thou smitten thine ass these t times? 7969
22:33 saw me, and turned from me these t times: 7969
24:10 thou hast altogether blessed *them* these t 7969
26: 7 t thousand and seven hundred and thirty. 7969
26:25 and four thousand and t hundred. 7969
26:47 *were* fifty and t thousand and four hundred. 7969

T

Nu 26:62 of them were twenty and t thousand, 7969
28:12 t tenth deals *of* flour *for* a meat offering, 7969
28:20 t tenth deals shall ye offer for a bullock, 7969
28:28 t tenth deals unto one bullock, two tenth 7969
29: 3 t tenth deals for a bullock, *and* two tenth 7969
29: 9 t tenth deals to a bullock, *and* two tenth 7969
29:14 t tenth deals unto every bullock of 7969
31:36 was *in* number t hundred thousand and 7969
31:43 the congregation was t hundred thousand 7969
33: 8 went t days' journey in the wilderness of 7969
33:39 and t years old when he died in mount Hor. 7969
35:14 Ye shall give t cities on *this* side Jordan, 7969
35:14 t cities shall ye give in the land of Canaan, 7969
Dt 4:41 Moses severed t cities on *this* side Jordan 7969
14:28 At the end of t years thou shalt bring forth 7969
16:16 T times in a year shall all thy males appear 7969
17: 6 the mouth of two witnesses, or t witnesses, 7969
19: 2 Thou shalt separate t cities for thee in 7969
19: 3 **divide** the coasts of thy land, which the LORD thy God giveth thee to inherit, **into t parts,** 8027
19: 7 Thou shalt separate t cities for thee. 7969
19: 9 shalt thou add t cities moe for thee, 7969
19: 9 add three cities moe for thee, beside these t: 7969
19:15 or at the mouth of t witnesses, shall 7969
Jos 1:11 for within t days ye shall pass over this 7969
2:16 hide yourselves there t days, until 7969
2:22 unto the mountain, and abode there t days, 7969
3: 2 it came to pass after t days, that the officers 7969
7: 3 or t thousand men go up and smite Ai; 7969
7: 4 thither of the people about t thousand men: 7969
9:16 it came to pass at the end of t days after 7969
15:14 And Caleb drove thence the t sons of Anak, 7969
17:11 and her towns, *even* t countries. 7969
18: 4 Give out from among you t men for *each* 7969
21:32 and Kartan with her suburbs; t cities. 7969
Jdg 1:20 and he expelled thence the t sons of Anak. 7969
7: 6 hand to their mouth, were t hundred men: 7969
7: 7 By the t hundred men that lapped will I 7969
7: 8 his tent, and retained *those* t hundred men: 7969
7:16 he divided the t hundred men *into* three 7969
7:16 he divided the three hundred men *into* t 7969
7:20 the t companies blew the trumpets, and 7969
7:22 the t hundred blew the trumpets, and 7969
8: 4 and the t hundred men that *were* with him, 7969
9:22 When Abimelech had reigned t years over 7969
9:43 divided them into t companies, and 7969
10: 2 he judged Israel twenty and t years, and 7969
11:26 by the coasts of Arnon, t hundred years? 7969
14:14 they could not *in* t days expound the riddle. 7969
15: 4 Samson went and caught t hundred foxes, 7969
15:11 t thousand men of Judah went to the top of 7969
16:15 thou hast mocked me these t times, and 7969
16:27 *there were* upon the roof about t thousand 7969
19: 4 and he abode with him t days: 7969
1Sa 1:24 with t bullocks, and one ephah of flour, and 7969
2:13 with a fleshhook of t teeth in his hand; 7969
2:21 and bare t sons and two daughters. 7969
9:20 as for thine asses that were lost t days ago, 7969
10: 3 there shall meet thee t men going up to God 7969
10: 3 one carrying t kids, and another carrying 7969
10: 3 another carrying t loaves of bread, and 7969
11: 8 the children of Israel were t hundred 7969
11:11 that Saul put the people *in* t companies; 7969
13: 2 Saul chose him t thousand *men* of Israel; 7969
13:17 the camp of the Philistines *in* t companies: 7969
17:13 the t eldest sons of Jesse went *and* 7969
17:13 the names of his t sons that went to 7969
17:14 and the t eldest followed Saul. 7969
20:19 *when* thou hast **stayed t days,** *then* 8027
20:20 I will shoot t arrows on the side *thereof,* as 7969
20:41 to the ground, and bowed himself t times: 7969
21: 5 kept from us about **these t days,** 8032+8543
24: 2 Saul took t thousand chosen men out of all 7969
25: 2 he had t thousand sheep, and a thousand 7969
26: 2 having t thousand chosen men of Israel 7969
30:12 drunk *any* water, t days and three nights. 7969
30:12 drunk *any* water, three days and t nights. 7969
30:13 left me, because t days agone I fell sick. 7969
31: 6 his t sons, and his armourbearer, and all his 7969
31: 8 and his t sons fallen in mount Gilboa. 7969
2Sa 2:18 there were t sons of Zeruiah there, Joab, 7969
2:31 *so that* t hundred and threescore men died. 7969
5: 5 and t years over all Israel and Judah. 7969
6:11 house of Obed-edom the Gittite t months: 7969
13:38 and went to Geshur, and was there t years. 7969
14:27 unto Absalom there were born t sons, and 7969
18:14 he took t darts in his hand, and thrust them 7969
20: 4 Assemble me the men of Judah *within* t 7969
21: 1 there was a famine in the days of David t 7969
21:16 the weight of whose spear *weighed* t 7969
23: 9 *one* of the t mighty *men* with David, 7969
23:13 t of the thirty chief went down, and came to 7969
23:16 the t mighty *men* brake through the host of 7969
23:17 These *things* did *these* t mighty *men.* 7969
23:18 the son of Zeruiah, *was* chief among t. 7969
23:18 he lift up his spear against t hundred, and 7969
23:18 and slew them, and had the name among t. 7969
23:19 Was he not most honourable of t? therefore 7969
23:19 howbeit he attained not unto the *first* t. 7969
23:22 and had the name among t mighty *men.* 7969
23:23 the thirty, but he attained not to the *first* t. 7969
24:12 I offer thee t *things;* choose thee one of 7969
24:13 wilt thou flee t months before thine 7969
24:13 that there be t days' pestilence in thy land? 7969
1Ki 2:11 thirty and t years reigned he in Jerusalem. 7969
2:39 it came to pass at the end of t years, 7969
4:32 he spake t thousand proverbs: and his songs 7969
5:16 t thousand and three hundred, which ruled 7969
5:16 three thousand and t hundred, which ruled 7969
6:36 he built the inner court *with* t rows of 7969
7: 4 *there were* windows *in* t rows, and 7969
7: 4 and light *was* against light *in* t ranks. 7969
7: 5 and light *was* against light *in* t ranks. 7969
7:12 the great court round about *was with* t rows 7969
7:25 t looking toward the north, and 7969
7:25 t looking toward the west, and 7969
7:25 t looking toward the south, and 7969
7:25 the south, and t looking toward the east: 7969
7:27 and t cubits the height of it. 7969
9:25 t times in a year did Solomon offer burnt 7969
10:17 *he made* t hundred shields *of* beaten gold; 7969
10:17 t pound *of* gold went to one shield: 7969
10:22 once in t years came the navy of Tharshish, 7969
11: 3 princesses, and t hundred concubines: 7969
12: 5 Depart yet *for* t days, then come again to 7969
15: 2 T years reigned he in Jerusalem. And his 7969
17:21 he stretched himself upon the child t times, 7969
22: 1 they continued t years without war between 7969
2Ki 2:17 and they sought t days, but found him not. 7969
3:10 that the LORD hath called these t kings 7969
3:13 for the LORD hath called these t kings 7969
9:32 there looked out to him two *or* t eunuchs. 7969
12: 6 it was *so, that* in the t and twentieth year of 7969
13: 1 In the t and twentieth year of Joash the son 7969
13:25 T times did Joash beat him, and 7969
17: 5 went up *to* Samaria, and besieged it t years. 7969
18:10 at the end of t years they took it: *even* in 7969
18:14 king of Judah t hundred talents of silver 7969
23:31 and t years old when he *began* to reign; 7969
23:31 and he reigned t months in Jerusalem. 7969
24: 1 and Jehoiakim became his servant t years: 7969
24: 8 and he reigned in Jerusalem t months. 7969
25:17 the height of the chapiter t cubits; and 7969
25:18 second priest, and the t keepers of the door: 7969
1Ch 2: 3 *which* t were born unto him of the daughter 7969
2:16 Abishai, and Joab, and Asahel, t. 7969
2:22 who had t and twenty cities in the land of 7969
3: 4 in Jerusalem he reigned thirty and t years. 7969
3:23 Elioenai, and Hezekiah, and Azrikam, t. 7969
7: 6 Bela, and Becher, and Jediael, t. 7969
10: 6 his t sons, and all his house died together. 7969
11:11 he lift up his spear against t hundred slain 7969
11:12 the Ahohite, who *was one* of the t mighties. 7969
11:15 Now t of the thirty captains went down to 7969
11:18 the t brake through the host of 7969
11:19 drink it. These *things* did *these* t mightiest. 7969
11:20 the brother of Joab, he was chief of the t: 7969
11:20 for lifting up his spear against t hundred, 7969
11:20 he slew *them,* and had a name among the t. 7969
11:21 Of the t, he was more honourable than 7969
11:21 howbeit he attained not to the *first* t. 7969
11:24 and had the name among the t mighties. 7969
11:25 the thirty, but attained not to the *first* t: 7969
12:27 with him *were* t thousand and 7969
12:29 the kindred of Saul, t thousand: 7969
12:39 there they were with David t days, eating 7969
13:14 of Obed-edom in his house t months. 7969
21:10 I offer thee t *things:* choose thee one of 7969

1Ch 21:12 Either t years' famine; or three months to 7969
21:12 or t months to be destroyed before thy foes, 7969
21:12 or else t days the sword of the LORD, 7969
23: 8 chief *was* Jehiel, and Zetham, and Joel, t. 7969
23: 9 Shelomith, and Haziel, and Haran, t. 7969
23:23 of Mushi; Mahli, and Eder, and Jeremoth, t. 7969
24:18 The t and twentieth to Delaiah, the four and 7969
25: 5 to Heman fourteen sons and t daughters. 7969
25:30 The t and twentieth to Mahazioth, *he,* his 7969
29: 4 *Even* t thousand talents of gold, of the gold 7969
29:27 thirty and t *years* reigned he in Jerusalem. 7969
2Ch 2: 2 t thousand and six hundred to oversee 7969
2:17 and t thousand and six hundred. 7969
2:18 t thousand and six hundred overseers to set 7969
4: 4 t looking toward the north, and 7969
4: 4 t looking toward the west, and 7969
4: 4 t looking toward the south, and 7969
4: 4 the south, and t looking toward the east: 7969
4: 5 *and* it received and held t thousand baths. 7969
6:13 t cubits high, and had set it in the midst of 7969
7:10 on the t and twentieth day of the seventh 7969
8:13 on the solemn feasts, t times in the year, 7969
9:16 t hundred shields *made he of* beaten gold: 7969
9:16 t hundred *shekels* of gold went to one 7969
9:21 every t years once came the ships of 7969
10: 5 Come again unto me after t days. 7969
11:17 the son of Solomon strong, t years: 7969
11:17 for t years they walked in the way of David 7969
13: 2 He reigned t years in Jerusalem. 7969
14: 8 spears, out of Judah t hundred thousand; 7969
14: 9 thousand thousand, and t hundred chariots; 7969
17:14 with him mighty *men* of valour t hundred 7969
20:25 they were t days in gathering of the spoil, 7969
25: 5 found them t hundred thousand choice 7969
25:13 smote t thousand of them, and took much 7969
26:13 t hundred thousand and seven thousand and 7969
29:33 six hundred oxen and t thousand sheep. 7969
31:16 of males, from t years old and upward, 7969
35: 7 of thirty thousand, and t thousand bullocks: 7969
35: 8 hundred *small cattle,* and t hundred oxen. 7969
36: 2 and t years old when he *began* to reign, 7969
36: 2 and he reigned t months in Jerusalem. 7969
36: 9 he reigned t months and ten days in 7969
Ezr 2: 4 of Shephatiah, t hundred seventy and two. 7969
2:11 of Bebai, six hundred twenty and t. 7969
2:17 of Bezai, t hundred twenty and three. 7969
2:17 of Bezai, three hundred twenty and t. 7969
2:19 of Hashum, two hundred twenty and t. 7969
2:21 of Beth-lehem, an hundred twenty and t. 7969
2:25 and Beeroth, seven hundred and forty and t. 7969
2:28 and Ai, two hundred twenty and t. 7969
2:32 children of Harim, t hundred and twenty. 7969
2:34 of Jericho, t hundred forty and five. 7969
2:35 t thousand and six hundred and thirty. 7969
2:36 of Jeshua, nine hundred seventy and t. 7969
2:58 *were* t hundred ninety and two. 7969
2:64 *and* two thousand t hundred *and* threescore, 7969
2:65 of whom *there were* seven thousand t 7969
6: 4 *With* t rows of great stones, and a row of 8532
8: 5 of Jahaziel, and with him t hundred males. 7969
8:15 and there abode we in tents t days: 7969
8:32 came *to* Jerusalem, and abode there t days. 7969
10: 8 *that* whosoever would not come within t 7969
10: 9 together *unto* Jerusalem within t days. 7969
Ne 2:11 I came to Jerusalem, and was there t days. 7969
7: 9 of Shephatiah, t hundred seventy and two. 7969
7:17 two thousand t hundred twenty and two. 7969
7:22 of Hashum, t hundred twenty and eight. 7969
7:23 of Bezai, t hundred twenty and four. 7969
7:29 and Beeroth, seven hundred forty and t. 7969
7:32 of Beth-el and Ai, an hundred twenty and t. 7969
7:35 children of Harim, t hundred and twenty. 7969
7:36 of Jericho, t hundred forty and five. 7969
7:38 t thousand nine hundred and thirty. 7969
7:39 of Jeshua, nine hundred seventy and t. 7969
7:60 *were* t hundred ninety and two. 7969
7:66 two thousand t hundred and threescore, 7969
7:67 of whom *there were* seven thousand t 7969
Est 4:16 neither eat nor drink t days, night or day; 7969
8: 9 on the t and twentieth *day* thereof; 7969
9:15 and slew t hundred men at Shushan; 7969
Job 1: 2 born unto him seven sons and t daughters. 7969
1: 3 t thousand camels, and five hundred yoke 7969
1: 4 sent and called for their t sisters to eat and 7969
1:17 The Chaldeans made out t bands, and 7969
2:11 Now when Job's t friends heard of all this 7969
32: 1 So these t men ceased to answer Job, 7969
32: 3 Also against his t friends was his wrath 7969
32: 5 *was* no answer in the mouth of *these* t men, 7969
42:13 He had also seven sons and t daughters. 7969
Pr 30:15 There are t *things that* are never satisfied, 7969
30:18 There be t *things which* are too wonderful 7969
30:21 For t *things* the earth is disquieted, and 7969
30:29 There be t *things* which go well, yea, 7969
Isa 15: 5 *shall flee* unto Zoar, a heifer of **t years old**: 7992
16:14 saying, Within t years, as the years of a 7969
17: 6 t berries in the top of the uppermost bough, 7969
20: 3 barefoot t years *for* a sign and wonder upon 7969
Jer 25: 3 this day, that *is* the t and twentieth year, 7969
36:23 *that* when Jehudi had read t or four leaves, 7969
48:34 unto Horonaim, *as* a heifer of **t years old**: 7992
52:24 second priest, and the t keepers of the door: 7969
52:28 in the seventh year t thousand Jews and 7969
52:28 year three thousand Jews and t and twenty: 7969
52:30 In the t and twentieth year of 7969
Eze 4: 5 of the days, t hundred and ninety days: 7969
4: 9 t hundred and ninety days shalt thou eat 7969
14:14 Though these t men, Noah, Daniel, and 7969
14:16 *Though* these t men *were* in it, *as* I live, 7969
14:18 Though these t men *were* in it, *as* I live, 7969
40:10 of the gate eastward *were* t on this side, 7969
40:10 *were* three on this side, and t on that side; 7969
40:10 on that side; they t *were* of one measure: 7969
40:21 the little chambers thereof *were* t on this 7969
40:21 *were* three on this side and t on that side; 7969
40:48 the breadth of the gate *was* t cubits on this 7969
40:48 cubits on this side, and t cubits on that side. 7969
41: 6 the side chambers *were* t, one over another, 7969
41:16 the galleries round about on their t *stories,* 7969
41:22 The altar *of* wood *was* t cubits high, and 7969
42: 3 *was* gallery against gallery in t *stories.* 7992
42: 6 For they *were* in t *stories,* but had not 8027
48:31 t gates northward; one gate of Reuben, 7969
48:32 t gates; and one gate of Joseph, one gate of 7969
48:33 t gates; one gate of Simeon, one gate of 7969
48:34 and five hundred, *with* their t gates; 7969
Da 1: 5 so nourishing them t years, that at the end 7969
3:23 these t men, Shadrach, Meshach, and 8532
3:24 Did not we cast t men bound into the midst 8532
6: 2 over these t presidents; of whom Daniel 8532
6:10 he kneeled upon his knees t times a day, 8532
6:13 but maketh his petition t times a day. 8532
7: 5 *it had* t ribs in the mouth of it between 8532
7: 8 before whom there were t of the first horns 8532
7:20 which came up, and before whom t fell; 8532
7:24 from the first, and he shall subdue t kings. 8532
8:14 Unto two thousand and t hundred days; 7969
10: 2 In those days I Daniel was mourning t full 7969
10: 3 at all, till t whole weeks were fulfilled. 7969
11: 2 there *shall* stand up yet t kings in Persia; 7969
12:12 cometh to the thousand t hundred *and* five 7969
Am 1: 3 For t transgressions of Damascus, and 7969
1: 6 For t transgressions of Gaza, and for four, 7969
1: 9 For t transgressions of Tyrus, and for four, 7969
1:11 For t transgressions of Edom, and for four, 7969
1:13 For t transgressions of the children of 7969
2: 1 For t transgressions of Moab, and for four, 7969
2: 4 For t transgressions of Judah, and for four, 7969
2: 6 For t transgressions of Israel, and for four, 7969
4: 4 *and* your tithes after t years: 7969
4: 7 when *there were* yet t months to 7969
4: 8 So two *or* t cities wandered unto one city, 7969
Jnh 1:17 Jonah was in the belly of the fish t days 7969
1:17 the belly of the fish three days and t nights. 7969
3: 3 an exceeding great city of t days' journey. 7969
Zec 11: 8 T shepherds also I cut off in one month; 7969
Mt 12:40 For as Jonas was t days and three nights in *5140*
12:40 three days and t nights in the whale's belly; *5140*
12:40 so shall the Son of man be t days and *5140*
12:40 and t nights in the heart of the earth. *5140*
13:33 woman took, and hid in t measures of meal, *5140*
15:32 because they continue with me now t days, *5140*
17: 4 if thou wilt, let us make here t tabernacles: *5140*
18:16 t witnesses every word may be established. *5140*
18:20 or t are gathered together in my name, *5140*
26:61 the temple of God, and to build it in t days. *5140*
27:40 and buildest *it* in t days, save thyself. *5140*
27:63 was yet alive, After t days I will rise *again.* *5140*

Mk 8: 2 they have now been with me t days, *5140*
8:31 and be killed, and after t days rise again. *5140*
9: 5 and let us make t tabernacles; one for thee, *5140*
14: 5 been sold for more than **t hundred** pence, *5145*
14:58 within t days I will build another made *5140*
15:29 the temple, and buildest *it* in t days, *5140*
Lk 1:56 And Mary abode with her about t months, *5140*
2:46 *that* after t days they found him in *5140*
4:25 when the heaven was shut up t years and *5140*
9:33 and let us make t tabernacles; one for thee, *5140*
10:36 Which now of these t, thinkest thou, *5140*
11: 5 and say unto him, Friend, lend me t loaves; *5140*
12:52 t against two, and two against three. *5140*
12:52 three against two, and two against **t**. *5140*
13: 7 *these* t years I come seeking fruit on this fig *5140*
13:21 woman took and hid in t measures of meal, *5140*
Jn 2: 6 the Jews, containing two or t firkins apiece. *5140*
2:19 this temple, and in t days I will raise it up. *5140*
2:20 and wilt thou rear it up in t days? *5140*
12: 5 not this ointment sold for **t hundred** pence, *5145*
21:11 of great fishes, an hundred and fifty *and* t: *5140*
Ac 2:41 added *unto them* about **t thousand** souls. *5153*
5: 7 And it was about the space of t hours after, *5140*
7:20 nourished up in his father's house t months: *5140*
9: 9 And he was t days without sight, and *5140*
10:19 said unto him, Behold, t men seek thee: *5140*
11:10 And this was done **t times**: and *1909+5151*
11:11 immediately there were t men already *5140*
17: 2 t sabbath days reasoned with them out of *5140*
19: 8 and spake boldly for the space of t months, *5140*
20: 3 And *there* abode t months: and when *5140*
20:31 that *by the space of* **t years** I ceased not to *5148*
25: 1 after t days he ascended from Cesarea to *5140*
28: 7 and lodged *us* t days courteously. *5140*
28:11 And after t months we departed in a ship of *5140*
28:12 landing at Syracuse, we tarried *there* t days. *5140*
28:15 us as far as Appii forum, and The t taverns: *5140*
28:17 that after t days Paul called the chief of *5140*
1Co 10: 8 and fell in one day t and twenty thousand. *5140*
13:13 now abideth faith, hope, charity, these t; *5140*
14:27 or at the most *by* t, and *that* by course; *5140*
14:29 Let the prophets speak two or t, and let *5140*
2Co 13: 1 t witnesses shall every word be established. *5140*
Gal 1:18 Then after t years I went up to Jerusalem to *5140*
1Ti 5:19 but before two or t witnesses. *5140*
Heb 10:28 without mercy under two or t witnesses: *5140*
11:23 was hid **t months** of his parents, because *5150*
Jas 5:17 it rained not on the earth *by the space of* t *5140*
1Jn 5: 7 For there are t that bear record in heaven, *5140*
5: 7 and the Holy Ghost: and these t are one. *5140*
5: 8 And there are t that bear witness in earth, *5140*
5: 8 and the blood: and *these* t agree in one. *5140*
Rev 6: 6 and t measures of barley for a penny; *5140*
8:13 other voices of the trumpet of the t angels, *5140*
9:18 By these t was the third *part* of men killed, *5140*
11: 9 nations shall see their dead bodies t days *5140*
11:11 And after t days and a half the spirit of life *5140*
16:13 And I saw t unclean spirits like frogs *come* *5140*
16:19 And the great city was *divided* into t parts, *5140*
21:13 On the east t gates; on the north three gates; *5140*
21:13 On the east three gates; on the north t gates; *5140*
21:13 on the south t gates; and on the west three *5140*
21:13 south three gates; and on the west t gates. *5140*

THREEFOLD (1) [THREE]
Ecc 4:12 and a t cord is not quickly broken. 8027

THREESCORE (93) [SIXTY]
Ge 25: 7 hundred **t and fifteen** years. 2568+7657+2050.1
25:26 Isaac *was* t years old when she bare them. 8346
46:26 sons' wives, all the souls *were* t and six; 8346
46:27 which came into Egypt, *were* **t and ten**. 7657
50: 3 the Egyptians mourned for him **t and ten** 7657
Ex 15:27 wells of water, and **t and ten** palm trees: 7657
38:25 **t and fifteen** 2568+7657+2050.1+2050.1
Lev 12: 5 continue in the blood of her purifying t 8346
Nu 1:27 *were* **t and fourteen** thousand 702+7657+2050.1
1:39 *were* t and two thousand and 8346
2: 4 *were* **t and fourteen** thousand 702+7657+2050.1
2:26 *were* t and two thousand and 8346
3:43 and **t and thirteen**. 7657+7969+2050.1
3:46 **t and thirteen** of 7657+7969+1886.1+2050.1
3:50 a thousand three hundred and t and 8346
26:22 **t and sixteen** thousand and 7657+8337+2050.1
26:25 t and four thousand and three hundred. 8346
26:27 of them, t thousand and five hundred. 8346
26:43 *were* t and four thousand and four hundred. 8346
31:33 **t and twelve** thousand 7657+8147+2050.1
31:34 And t and one thousand asses, 8346
31:37 *and* **t and fifteen**. 2568+7657+2050.1
31:38 tribute *was* **t and twelve**. 7657+8147+2050.1
31:39 tribute *was* **t and one**. 259+8346+2050.1
33: 9 of water, and **t and ten** palm trees; 7657
Dt 3: 4 t cities, all the region of Argob, 8346
10:22 went down into Egypt with **t and ten** 7657
Jos 13:30 towns of Jair, which *are* in Bashan, t cities: 8346
Jdg 1: 7 **T and ten** kings, having their thumbs 7657
8:14 *even* **t and seventeen** men. 7651+7657+2050.1
8:30 Gideon had **t and ten** sons of his body 7657
9: 2 *which are* **t and ten** persons, reign over 7657
9: 4 they gave him **t and ten** *pieces* of silver out 7657
9: 5 *being* **t and ten** persons, upon one stone: 7657
9:18 **t and ten** persons, upon one stone, and 7657
9:24 That the cruelty *done* to the **t and ten** sons 7657
12:14 that rode on **t and ten** ass colts: 7651
1Sa 6:19 people fifty thousand and **t and ten** men: 7657
2Sa 2:31 *so that* three hundred and t men died. 8346
1Ki 4:13 t great cities *with* walls and brasen bars: 8346
4:22 of fine flour, and t measures of meal, 8346
5:15 Solomon had **t and ten** thousand that bare 7657
6: 2 the length thereof *was* t cubits, and 8346
10:14 to Solomon in one year was six hundred t 8346
2Ki 25:19 t men of the people of the land that were 8346
1Ch 2:21 whom he married when he *was* t years old; 8346
2:23 and the towns thereof, *even* t cities. 8346
5:18 and forty thousand seven hundred and t, 8346
9:13 a thousand and seven hundred and t; 8346
16:38 Obed-edom with their brethren, t and eight; 8346
21: 5 Judah *was* four hundred **t and ten** thousand 7657
26: 8 the service, *were* t and two of Obed-edom. 8346
2Ch 2: 2 Solomon told out **t and ten** thousand men 7657
2:18 he set **t and ten** thousand of them *to be* 7657
3: 3 cubits after the first measure *was* t cubits, 8346
9:13 six hundred and t and six talents of gold; 8346
11:21 he took eighteen wives, and t concubines; 8346
11:21 and eight sons, and t daughters.) 8346
12: 3 hundred chariots, and t thousand horsemen: 8346
29:32 was **t and ten** bullocks, an hundred rams, 7657
36:21 she kept sabbath, to fulfil **t and ten** years. 7657
Ezr 2: 9 children of Zaccai, seven hundred and t. 8346
2:64 *and* two thousand three hundred *and* t, 8346
2:69 **t and one thousand** 505+7239+8337+2050.1
6: 3 the height thereof t cubits, *and* the breadth 8361
6: 3 *and* the breadth thereof t cubits; 8361
8:10 and with him an hundred and t males. 8346
8:13 and Shemaiah, and with them t males. 8346
Ne 7:14 children of Zaccai, seven hundred and t. 8346
7:18 of Adonikam, six hundred t and seven. 8346
7:19 of Bigvai, two thousand t and seven. 8346
7:66 *and* two thousand three hundred and t, 8346
7:72 *of* silver, and t and seven priests' garments. 8346
11: 6 that dwelt at Jerusalem *were* four hundred t 8346
Ps 90:10 The days of our years *are* t years **and ten**; 7657
SS 3: 7 t valiant *men are* about it, of the valiant of 8346
6: 8 There *are* t queens, and 8346
Isa 7: 8 within t and five years shall Ephraim be 8346
Jer 52:25 t men of the people of the land, that were 8346
Eze 40:14 He made also posts *of* t cubits, even unto 8346
Da 3: 1 whose height *was* t cubits, *and* the breadth 8361
5:31 *being* about t and two year old. 8361
9:25 *shall be* seven weeks, and t and two weeks: 8346
9:26 after t and two weeks shall Messiah be cut 8346
Zec 1:12 thou hast had indignation these **t and ten** 7657
Lk 24:13 which was from Jerusalem *about* t furlongs. *1835*
Ac 7:14 all his kindred, **t and fifteen** souls. *1440+4002*
23:23 and horsemen t *and* **ten**, and spearmen two *1440*
27:37 in the ship two hundred t *and* **sixteen** *1440+1803*
1Ti 5: 9 be taken into the number under t years old, *1835*
Rev 11: 3 a thousand two hundred *and* t days, *1835*
12: 6 there a thousand two hundred *and* t days. *1835*
13:18 and his number *is* **Six hundred** t *and* six. *5516*

THRESH (4) [THRESHED, THRESHETH, THRESHING, THRESHINGFLOOR, THRESHINGFLOORS, THRESHINGPLACE]
Isa 41:15 thou shalt t the mountains, and beat *them* 1758
Jer 51:33 *is* like a threshingfloor, *it is* time to t her: 1869
Mic 4:13 Arise and t, O daughter of Zion: for I will 1758

Hab 3:12 thou didst **t** the heathen in anger. 1758

THRESHED (3) [THRESH]
Jdg 6:11 his son Gideon **t** wheat by the winepress, 2251
Isa 28:27 For the fitches are not **t** with a threshing 1758
Am 1: 3 they have **t** Gilead with threshing 1758

THRESHETH (1) [THRESH]
1Co 9:10 that he that **t** in hope should be partaker of *248*

THRESHING (10) [THRESH]
Lev 26: 5 And your **t** shall reach unto the vintage, and 1786
2Sa 24:22 **t instruments** and *other* instruments of 4173
2Ki 13: 7 and had made them like the dust by **t**. 1758
1Ch 21:20 hid themselves. Now Ornan was **t** wheat. 1758
21:23 the **t instruments** for wood, and the wheat 4173
Isa 21:10 O my **t**, and the corn of my floor: 4098
28:27 For the fitches are not threshed with a **t** 2742
28:28 because he will not ever be **t** it, 156+156
41:15 I will make thee a new sharp **t instrument** 4173
Am 1: 3 they have threshed Gilead with **t** 2742

THRESHINGFLOOR (17) [FLOOR, THRESH]
Ge 50:10 they came to the **t** of Atad, which *is* beyond 1637
Nu 15:20 as *ye do* the heave offering of the **t**, so 1637
18:27 as though it were the corn of the **t**, and 1637
18:30 unto the Levites as the increase of the **t**, 1637
Ru 3: 2 he winnoweth barley to night in the **t**. 1637
2Sa 6: 6 when they came to Nachon's **t**, Uzzah put 1637
24:18 rear an altar unto the LORD in the **t** of 1637
24:21 David said, To buy the **t** of thee, to build an 1637
24:24 So David bought the **t** and the oxen for fifty 1637
1Ch 13: 9 when they came unto the **t** of Chidon, Uzza 1637
21:15 the angel of the LORD stood by the **t** of 1637
21:18 set up an altar unto the LORD in the **t** of 1637
21:21 went out of the **t**, and bowed himself to 1637
21:22 said to Ornan, Grant me the place of *this* **t**, 1637
21:28 him in the **t** of Ornan the Jebusite, 1637
2Ch 3: 1 in the place that David had prepared in the **t** 1637
Jer 51:33 The daughter of Babylon *is* like a **t**, *it is* 1637

THRESHINGFLOORS (2) [FLOOR, THRESH]
1Sa 23: 1 fight against Keilah, and they rob the **t**. 1637
Da 2:35 and became like the chaff of the summer **t**; 147

THRESHINGPLACE (1) [PLACE, THRESH]
2Sa 24:16 the angel of the LORD was by the **t** of 1637

THRESHOLD (14) [THRESHOLDS]
Jdg 19:27 the house, and her hands *were* upon the **t**. 5592
1Sa 5: 4 palms of his hands *were* cut off upon the **t**; 4670
5: 5 tread on the **t** of Dagon in Ashdod unto this 4670
1Ki 14:17 *and* when she came to the **t** of the door, 5592
Eze 9: 3 whereupon he was, to the **t** of the house. 4670
10: 4 *and stood* over the **t** of the house; 4670
10:18 departed from off the **t** of the house, 4670
40: 6 and measured the **t** of the gate, 5592
40: 6 the other **t** *of the gate, which was* one reed 5592
40: 7 the **t** of the gate by the porch of the gate 5592
43: 8 In their setting of their **t** by my thresholds, 5592
46: 2 and he shall worship at the **t** of the gate: 5592
47: 1 waters issued out from under the **t** of 4670
Zep 1: 9 will I punish all those that leap on the **t**, 4670

THRESHOLDS (3) [THRESHOLD]
Ne 12:25 *were* porters keeping the ward at the **t** of 624
Eze 43: 8 In their setting of their threshold by my **t**, 5592
Zep 2:14 in the windows; desolation *shall be* in the **t**: 5592

THREW (6) [THROW]
2Sa 16:13 he went, and **t** stones at him, and cast dust. 5619
2Ki 9:33 So they **t** her **down**: and *some* of her blood 8058
2Ch 31: 1 **t down** the high places and the altars out of 5422
Mk 12:42 and she **t** in two mites, which make a *906*
Lk 9:42 the devil **t** him **down**, and tare *him*. And *4486*
Ac 22:23 cast *off their* clothes, and **t** dust into the air, *906*

THREWEST (1) [THROW]
Ne 9:11 and their persecutors thou **t** into the deeps, 7993

THRICE (15) [THREE]
Ex 34:23 **T** in the year shall all your men 6471+7969
34:24 the LORD thy God **t** in the year. 6471+7969
2Ki 13:18 And he smote **t**, and stayed. 6471+7969
13:19 now thou shalt smite Syria *but* **t**. 6471+7969
Mt 26:34 before *the* cock crow, thou shalt deny me **t**. *5151*
26:75 Before *the* cock crow, thou shalt deny me **t**. *5151*
Mk 14:30 *the* cock crow twice, thou shalt deny me **t**. *5151*
14:72 *the* cock crow twice, thou shalt deny me **t**. *5151*
Lk 22:34 before that thou shalt **t** deny that *thou* *5151*
22:61 Before *the* cock crow, thou shalt deny me **t**. *5151*
Jn 13:38 shall not crow, till thou hast denied me **t**. *5151*
Ac 10:16 This was done **t**: and the vessel was *1909+5151*
2Co 11:25 **T** was I beaten with rods, once was I *5151*
11:25 **t** I suffered shipwrack, a night and a day I *5151*
12: 8 For this *thing* I besought the Lord **t**, that it *5151*

THROAT (7)
Ps 5: 9 their **t** *is* an open sepulchre; they flatter 1627
69: 3 my **t** is dried: mine eyes fail while *I* wait 1627
115: 7 walk not: neither speak they through their **t**. 1627
Pr 23: 2 put a knife to thy **t**, if thou *be* a man given 3930
Jer 2:25 from being unshod, and thy **t** from thirst: 1627
Mt 18:28 on him, and **took** *him* **by the t**, saying, *4155*
Ro 3:13 Their **t** *is* an open sepulchre; with their *2995*

THRONE (176) [THRONES]
Ge 41:40 only *in* the **t** will I be greater than thou. 3678
Ex 11: 5 firstborn of Pharaoh that sitteth upon his **t**, 3678
12:29 **t** unto the firstborn of the captive that *was* 3678
Dt 17:18 when he sitteth upon the **t** of his kingdom, 3678
1Sa 2: 8 and to make them inherit the **t** of glory: 3678
2Sa 3:10 to set up the **t** of David over Israel and 3678
7:13 I will stablish the **t** of his kingdom for ever. 3678
7:16 thy **t** shall be stablished for ever. 3678
14: 9 and the king and his **t** *be* guiltless. 3678
1Ki 1:13 reign after me, and he shall sit upon my **t**? 3678
1:17 reign after me, and he shall sit upon my **t**. 3678
1:20 sit on the **t** of my lord the king after him. 3678
1:24 reign after me, and he shall sit upon my **t**? 3678
1:27 who should sit on the **t** of my lord the king 3678
1:30 and he shall sit upon my **t** in my stead; 3678
1:35 that he may come and sit upon my **t**; 3678
1:37 make his **t** greater than the throne of my 3678
1:37 make his throne greater than the **t** of my 3678
1:46 also Solomon sitteth on the **t** of 3678
1:47 and make his **t** greater than thy throne. 3678
1:47 and make his throne greater than thy **t**. 3678
1:48 which hath given *one* to sit on my **t** *this* 3678
2: 4 fail thee (said he) a man on the **t** of Israel. 3678
2:12 sat Solomon upon the **t** of David his father; 3678
2:19 sat down on his **t**, and caused a seat to be 3678
2:24 set me on the **t** of David my father, and 3678
2:33 and upon his house, and upon his **t**, 3678
2:45 the **t** of David shall be established before 3678
3: 6 thou hast given him a son to sit on his **t**, 3678
5: 5 whom I will set upon thy **t** in thy room, 3678
7: 7 he made a porch for the **t** where he might 3678
8:20 sit on the **t** of Israel, as the LORD 3678
8:25 a man in my sight to sit on the **t** of Israel; 3678
9: 5 I will establish the **t** of thy kingdom upon 3678
9: 5 There shall not fail thee a man upon the **t** of 3678
10: 9 in thee, to set thee on the **t** of Israel: 3678
10:18 Moreover the king made a great **t** of ivory, 3678
10:19 The **t** had six steps, and the top of 3678
10:19 and the top of the **t** *was* round behind: 3678
16:11 he *began* to reign, as soon as he sat on his **t**, 3678
22:10 the king of Judah sat each on his **t**, 3678
22:19 I saw the LORD sitting on his **t**, and 3678
2Ki 10: 3 set *him* on his father's **t**, and fight for your 3678
10:30 fourth *generation* shall sit on the **t** of Israel. 3678
11:19 And he sat on the **t** of the kings. 3678
13:13 his fathers; and Jeroboam sat upon his **t**: 3678
15:12 Thy sons shall sit on the **t** of Israel unto 3678
25:28 set his **t** above the throne of the kings that 3678
25:28 set his throne above the **t** of the kings that 3678
1Ch 17:12 a house, and I will stablish his **t** for ever. 3678
17:14 and his **t** shall be established for evermore. 3678
22:10 I will establish the **t** of his kingdom over 3678
28: 5 **t** of the kingdom of the LORD over Israel. 3678
29:23 Solomon sat on the **t** of the LORD as king 3678
2Ch 6:10 am set on the **t** of Israel, as the LORD 3678
6:16 a man in my sight to sit upon the **t** of Israel; 3678
7:18 will I stablish the **t** of thy kingdom, 3678
9: 8 which delighted in thee to set thee on his **t**, 3678
9:17 Moreover the king made a great **t** of ivory, 3678
9:18 *there were* six steps to the **t**, with a 3678
9:18 *which were* fastened to the **t**, and stays on 3678
18: 9 king of Judah sat either of them on his **t**, 3678

2Ch 18:18 I saw the LORD sitting upon his **t**, and 3678
23:20 and set the king upon the **t** of the kingdom. 3678
Ne 3: 7 unto the **t** of the governor on *this* side 3678
Est 1: 2 when the king Ahasuerus sat on the **t** of his 3678
5: 1 the king sat upon his royal **t** in the royal 3678
Job 26: 9 He holdeth back the face of *his* **t**, *and* 3678
36: 7 with kings *are they* on the **t**; yea, he doth 3678
Ps 9: 4 my cause; thou satest in the **t** judging right. 3678
9: 7 he hath prepared his **t** for judgment. 3678
11: 4 holy temple, the LORD'S **t** *is* in heaven: 3678
45: 6 Thy **t**, O God, *is* for ever and ever: 3678
47: 8 God sitteth upon the **t** of his holiness. 3678
89: 4 and build up thy **t** to all generations. 3678
89:14 and judgment *are* the habitation of thy **t**: 3678
89:29 for ever, and his **t** as the days of heaven. 3678
89:36 for ever, and his **t** as the sun before me. 3678
89:44 to cease, and cast his **t** down to the ground. 3678
93: 2 Thy **t** is established of old: thou *art* from 3678
94:20 Shall the **t** of iniquity have fellowship *with* 3678
97: 2 and judgment *are* the habitation of his **t**. 3678
103:19 The LORD hath prepared his **t** in 3678
132:11 the fruit of thy body will I set upon thy **t**. 3678
132:12 their children also shall sit upon thy **t** for 3678
Pr 16:12 for the **t** is established by righteousness. 3678
20: 8 A king that sitteth in the **t** of judgment 3678
20:28 the king: and his **t** is upholden by mercy. 3678
25: 5 his **t** shall be established in righteousness. 3678
29:14 the poor, his **t** shall be established for ever. 3678
Isa 6: 1 died I saw also the Lord sitting upon a **t**, 3678
9: 7 upon the **t** of David, and upon his kingdom, 3678
14:13 I will exalt my **t** above the stars of God: 3678
16: 5 And in mercy shall the **t** be established: and 3678
22:23 he shall be for a glorious **t** to his father's 3678
47: 1 *there is* no **t**, O daughter of the Chaldeans; 3678
66: 1 The heaven *is* my **t**, and the earth *is* my 3678
Jer 1:15 they shall set every one his **t** *at* the entering 3678
3:17 At that time they shall call Jerusalem the **t** 3678
13:13 even the kings that sit upon David's **t**, 3678
14:21 do not disgrace the **t** of thy glory: 3678
17:12 A glorious high **t** from the beginning *is* 3678
17:25 and princes sitting upon the **t** of David, 3678
22: 2 that sittest upon the **t** of David, thou, and 3678
22: 4 this house kings sitting upon the **t** of David, 3678
22:30 sitting upon the **t** of David, and ruling any 3678
29:16 of the king that sitteth upon the **t** of David, 3678
33:17 man to sit upon the **t** of the house of Israel; 3678
33:21 should not have a son to reign upon his **t**; 3678
36:30 He shall have none to sit upon the **t** of 3678
43:10 will set his **t** upon these stones that I have 3678
49:38 I will set my **t** in Elam, and will destroy 3678
52:32 set his **t** above the throne of the kings that 3678
52:32 set his throne above the **t** of the kings that 3678
La 5:19 thy **t** from generation to generation. 3678
Eze 1:26 *was* over their heads *was* the likeness of a **t**, 3678
1:26 upon the likeness of the **t** *was* the likeness 3678
10: 1 as the appearance of the likeness of a **t**. 3678
43: 7 the place of my **t**, and the place of the soles 3678
Da 5:20 he was deposed from his kingly **t**, and 3764
7: 9 his **t** *was like* the fiery flame, *and* 3764
Jnh 3: 6 he arose from his **t**, and he laid his robe 3678
Hag 2:22 I will overthrow the **t** of kingdoms, and 3678
Zec 6:13 the glory, and shall sit and rule upon his **t**: 3678
6:13 he shall be a priest upon his **t**: and 3678
Mt 5:34 at all; neither by heaven; for it is God's **t**: 2362
19:28 when the Son of man shall sit in the **t** of his 2362
23:22 sweareth by the **t** of God, and by him that 2362
25:31 then shall he sit upon the **t** of his glory: 2362
Lk 1:32 the Lord God shall give unto him the **t** of 2362
Ac 2:30 *he* would raise up Christ to sit on his **t**; 2362
7:49 Heaven *is* my **t**, and earth *is* my footstool: 2362
12:21 sat upon his **t**, and made an oration unto 968
Heb 1: 8 But unto the Son *he saith,* Thy **t**, O God, 2362
4:16 therefore come boldly unto the **t** of grace, 2362
8: 1 who is set on the right hand of the **t** of 2362
12: 2 is set down at the right hand of the **t** of 2362
Rev 1: 4 the seven spirits which are before his **t**; 2362
3:21 will I grant to sit with me in my **t**, 2362
3:21 and am set down with my Father in his **t**. 2362
4: 2 a **t** was set in heaven, and one sat on 2362
4: 2 was set in heaven, and one sat on the **t**. 2362
4: 3 and *there was* a rainbow round about the **t**, 2362
4: 4 And round about the **t** *were* four and 2362
4: 5 And out of the **t** proceeded lightnings and 2362
4: 5 seven lamps of fire burning before the **t**, 2362
4: 6 And before the **t** *there was* a sea of glass 2362
4: 6 and in the midst of the **t**, and round about 2362
4: 6 midst of the throne, and round about the **t**, 2362
4: 9 honour and thanks to him that sat on the **t**, 2362
4:10 fall down before him that sat on the **t**, 2362
4:10 and ever, and cast their crowns before the **t**, 2362
5: 1 him that sat on the **t** a book written within 2362
5: 6 in the midst of the **t** and of the four beasts, 2362
5: 7 of the right hand of him that sat upon the **t**. 2362
5:11 the voice of many angels round about the **t** 2362
5:13 *be* unto him that sitteth upon the **t**, and 2362
6:16 us from the face of him that sitteth on the **t**, 2362
7: 9 stood before the **t**, and before the Lamb, 2362
7:10 to our God which sitteth upon the **t**, 2362
7:11 And all the angels stood round about the **t**, 2362
7:11 and fell before the **t** on their faces, and 2362
7:15 Therefore are they before the **t** of God, and 2362
7:15 he that sitteth on the **t** shall dwell among 2362
7:17 For the Lamb which is in the midst of the **t** 2362
8: 3 the golden altar which was before the **t**. 2362
12: 5 child was caught up unto God, and *to* his **t**. 2362
14: 3 sung as *it were* a new song before the **t**, 2362
14: 5 for they are without fault before the **t** of 2362
16:17 of heaven, from the **t**, saying, It is done. 2362
19: 4 and worshipped God that sat on the **t**, 2362
19: 5 And a voice came out of the **t**, saying, 2362
20:11 And I saw a great white **t**, and him that sat 2362
21: 5 And he that sat upon the **t** said, Behold, 2362
22: 1 proceeding out of the **t** of God and of 2362
22: 3 but the **t** of God and of the Lamb shall be in 2362

THRONES (9) [THRONE]
Ps 122: 5 For there are set **t** of judgment, the thrones 3678
122: 5 of judgment, the **t** of the house of David. 3678
Isa 14: 9 it hath raised up from their **t** all the kings of 3678
Eze 26:16 of the sea shall come down from their **t**, 3678
Da 7: 9 I beheld till the **t** were cast *down,* and 3764
Mt 19:28 ye also shall sit upon twelve **t**, judging 2362
Lk 22:30 sit on **t** judging the twelve tribes of Israel. 2362
Col 1:16 whether *they be* **t**, or dominions, or 2362
Rev 20: 4 And I saw **t**, and they sat upon them, and 2362

THRONG (2) [THRONGED, THRONGING]
Mk 3: 9 of the multitude, lest they should **t** him. 2346
Lk 8:45 the multitude **t** thee and press *thee,* and 4912

THRONGED (2) [THRONG]
Mk 5:24 and much people followed him, and **t** him. 4918
Lk 8:42 a dying. (But as he went the people **t** him. 4846

THRONGING (1) [THRONG]
Mk 5:31 Thou seest the multitude **t** thee, and 4918

THROUGH (463) [THROUGHOUT] See Index

THROUGHLY (12) [THOROUGHLY]
2Ki 11:18 and his images brake they in pieces **t**, 3190
Job 6: 2 Oh that my grief were **t weighed**, 8254+8254
Ps 51: 2 Wash me **t** from mine iniquity, and 7235
Jer 6: 9 They shall **t glean** the remnant of 5953+5953
7: 5 For if you **t amend** your ways and 3190+3190
7: 5 if you **t execute** judgment between a 6213+6213
50:34 he shall **t plead** their cause, that he 7378+7378
Eze 16: 9 I **t washed away** thy blood from thee, and 7857
Mt 3:12 and he will **t purge** his floor, and gather his 1245
Lk 3:17 and he will **t purge** his floor, and 1245
2Co 11: 6 we *have been* **t** made manifest 1722+3956
2Ti 3:17 **t furnished** unto all good works. 1822

THROUGHOUT (162) [THROUGH] See Index

THROW (9) [OVERTHROW, THREWEST, THROWING, THROWN]
Jdg 2: 2 of this land; you shall **t down** their altars: 5422
6:25 **t down** the altar of Baal that thy father 2040
2Sa 20:15 with Joab battered the wall, to **t** *it* **down**. 5307
2Ki 9:33 he said, **T** her **down**. So they threw her 8058
Jer 1:10 and to **t down**, to build, and to plant. 2040
31:28 to **t down**, and to destroy, and to afflict; 2040
Eze 16:39 they shall **t down** thine eminent place, and 2040
Mic 5:11 thy land, and **t down** all thy strong holds: 2040
Mal 1: 4 They shall build, but I will **t down**; 2040

THROWING (1) [THROW]
Nu 35:17 if he smite him with **t** a stone, 3027

THROWN (19) [THROW]
Ex 15: 1 and his rider hath he **t** into the sea. 7411
15:21 and his rider hath he **t** into the sea. 7411
Jdg 6:32 because he hath **t down** his altar. 5422
2Sa 20:21 his head *shall be* **t** to thee over the wall. 7993
1Ki 19:10 **t down** thine altars, and slain thy prophets 2040
19:14 **t down** thine altars, and slain thy prophets 2040
Jer 31:40 plucked up, nor **t down** any more for ever. 2040
33: 4 which are **t down** by the mounts, and 5422
50:15 are fallen, her walls are **t down**: 2040
La 2: 2 he hath **t down** in his wrath the strong 2040
2:17 he hath **t down**, and hath not pitied: and 2040
Eze 29: 5 I will leave thee *t* into the wilderness, thee NIH
38:20 the mountains shall be **t down**, and 2040
Na 1: 6 like fire, and the rocks are **t down** by him. 5422
Mt 24: 2 upon another, that shall not be **t down**. *2647*
Mk 13: 2 upon another, that shall not be **t down**. *2647*
Lk 4:35 And when the devil had **t** him in the midst, *4496*
21: 6 upon another, that shall not be **t down**. *2647*
Rev 18:21 shall *that* great city Babylon be **t** down, *906*

THRUST (50) [THRUSTETH]
Ex 11: 1 **surely t** you **out** hence altogether. 1644+1644
12:39 because they were **t out** of Egypt, and 1644
Nu 22:25 she **t** herself unto the wall, and 3905
25: 8 **t** both of them **through**, the man of Israel, 1856
35:20 if he **t** him of hatred, or hurl at him by 1920
35:22 if he **t** him suddenly without enmity, or 1920
Dt 13: 5 to **t** thee out of the way which the LORD 5080
13:10 he hath sought to **t** thee **away** from 5080
15:17 **t** *it* through his ear unto the door, and 5414
33:27 he shall **t out** the enemy from before thee; 1644
Jdg 3:21 from his right thigh, and **t** it into his belly: 8628
6:38 **t** the fleece **together**, and wringed the dew 2115
9:41 Zebul **t out** Gaal and his brethren, that *they* 1644
9:54 his young man **t** him **through**, and he died. 1856
11: 2 and they **t out** Jephthah, and said unto him, 1644
1Sa 11: 2 that *I* may **t out** all your right eyes, and 5365
31: 4 thy sword, and **t** me **through** therewith; 1856
31: 4 uncircumcised come and **t** me **through**, 1856
2Sa 2:16 and *t* his sword in his fellow's side; NIH
18:14 and **t** them through the heart of Absalom, 8628
23: 6 Belial *shall be* all of them as thorns **t away**, 5074
1Ki 2:27 So Solomon **t out** Abiathar from being 1644
2Ki 4:27 Gehazi came near to **t** her **away**. And 1920
1Ch 10: 4 thy sword, and **t** me **through** therewith; 1856
2Ch 26:20 and they **t** him **out** from thence; 926
Ps 118:13 Thou hast **t sore** at me that *I* might 1760+1760
Isa 13:15 Every one that is found shall be **t through**; 1856
14:19 **t through** with a sword, that go down to 2944
Jer 51: 4 and *they that are* **t through** in her streets. 1856
Eze 16:40 and **t** thee **through** with their swords. 1333
34:21 Because ye have **t** with side and 1920
46:18 by oppression to **t** them out of their NIH
Joel 2: 8 Neither shall one **t** another; they shall walk 1766
Zec 13: 3 shall **t** him **through** when he prophesieth. 1856
Lk 4:29 and **t** him **out** of the city, and led him unto *1544*
5: 3 prayed him that *he* would **t out** a little from *1877*
10:15 exalted to heaven, shalt be **t down** to hell. *2601*
13:28 kingdom of God, and you yourselves **t out**. *1544*
Jn 20:25 and **t** my hand into his side, I will not *906*
20:27 reach *hither* thy hand, and **t** *it* into my side: *906*
Ac 7:27 he that did his neighbour wrong **t** him **away**, *683*
7:39 but **t** *him* **from** *them,* and in their hearts *683*
16:24 **t** them into the inner prison, and made their *906*
16:37 and now do they **t** us **out** privily? *1544*
27:39 if it were possible, to **t in** the ship. *1856*
Heb 12:20 it shall be stoned, or **t through** with a dart: *2700*
Rev 14:15 sat on the cloud, **T in** thy sickle, and reap: *3992*
14:16 And he that sat on the cloud **t in** his sickle *906*
14:18 **T in** thy sharp sickle, and gather *3992*
14:19 And the angel **t in** his sickle into the earth, *906*

THRUSTETH (1) [THRUST]
Job 32:13 out wisdom: God **t** him **down**, not man. 5086

THUMB (6) [THUMBS]
Ex 29:20 upon the **t** of their right hand, and upon 931
Lev 8:23 upon the **t** of his right hand, and upon 931
14:14 upon the **t** of his right hand, and upon 931
14:17 upon the **t** of his right hand, and upon 931
14:25 upon the **t** of his right hand, and upon 931
14:28 upon the **t** of his right hand, and upon 931

THUMBS (3) [THUMB]
Lev 8:24 upon the **t** of their right hands, and upon 931
Jdg 1: 6 and cut off his **t** and his great toes. 931+3027
1: 7 their **t** and their great toes cut off, 931+3027

THUMMIM (5)
Ex 28:30 of judgment the Urim and the **T**; 8550
Lev 8: 8 put in the breastplate the Urim and the **T**. 8550
Dt 33: 8 *Let* thy **T** and thy Urim *be* with thy holy 8550
Ezr 2:63 stood *up* a priest with Urim and with **T**. 8550
Ne 7:65 till there stood *up* a priest with Urim and **T**. 8550

THUNDER (19) [THUNDERBOLTS, THUNDERED, THUNDERETH, THUNDERINGS, THUNDERS]
Ex 9:23 the LORD sent **t** and hail, and the fire ran 6963
9:29 *and* the **t** shall cease, neither shall there be 6963
1Sa 2:10 out of heaven shall he **t** upon them: 7481
7:10 the LORD thundered with a great **t** on that 6963
12:17 the LORD, and he shall send **t** and rain; 6963
12:18 and the LORD sent **t** and rain that day: 6963
Job 26:14 but the **t** of his power who can understand? 7482
28:26 and a way for the lightning of the **t**: 6963
38:25 of waters, or a way for the lightning of **t**; 6963
39:19 hast thou clothed his neck with **t**? 7483
39:25 the **t** of the captains, and the shouting. 7482
40: 9 or, canst thou **t** with a voice like him? 7481
Ps 77:18 The voice of thy **t** *was* in the heaven: 7482
81: 7 I answered thee in the secret place of **t**: 7482
104: 7 at the voice of thy **t** they hasted away. 7482
Isa 29: 6 be visited of the LORD of hosts with **t**, 7482
Mk 3:17 them Boanerges, which is, The sons of **t**:) *1027*
Rev 6: 1 and I heard, as *it were* the noise of **t**, one of *1027*
14: 2 many waters, and as the voice of a great **t**: *1027*

THUNDERBOLTS (1) [THUNDER]
Ps 78:48 also to the hail, and their flocks to **hot t**. 7565

THUNDERED (4) [THUNDER]
1Sa 7:10 the LORD **t** with a great thunder on that 7481
2Sa 22:14 The LORD **t** from heaven, and the most 7481
Ps 18:13 The LORD also **t** in the heavens, and 7481
Jn 12:29 stood *by,* and heard *it,* said that it **t**: *1027+1096*

THUNDERETH (3) [THUNDER]
Job 37: 4 he **t** with the voice of his excellency; and 7481
37: 5 God **t** marvellously with his voice; 7481
Ps 29: 3 the God of glory **t**: the LORD *is* upon 7481

THUNDERINGS (6) [THUNDER]
Ex 9:28 that there be no *more* mighty **t** and hail; and 6963
20:18 all the people saw the **t**, and the lightnings, 6963
Rev 4: 5 proceeded lightnings and **t** and voices: *1027*
8: 5 and **t**, and lightnings, and an earthquake. *1027*
11:19 and **t**, and an earthquake, and great hail. *1027*
19: 6 and as the voice of mighty **t**, saying, *1027*

THUNDERS (7) [THUNDER]
Ex 9:33 the **t** and hail ceased, and the rain was not 6963
9:34 the rain and the hail and the **t** were ceased, 6963
19:16 that there were **t** and lightnings, and a thick 6963
Rev 10: 3 he had cried, seven **t** uttered their voices. *1027*
10: 4 And when the seven **t** had uttered their *1027*
10: 4 Seal *up those things* which the seven **t** *1027*
16:18 there were voices, and **t**, and lightnings; *1027*

THUS (737) See Index

THWART See DISANNUL; DISANNULLED

THWARTED See NOUGHT

THY (4607) [THOU] See Index

THYATIRA (4)
Ac 16:14 a seller of purple, of the city of **T**, *2363*
Rev 1:11 and unto **T**, and unto Sardis, and *2363*
2:18 And unto the angel of the church in **T** *2363*
2:24 But unto you I say, and unto the rest in **T**, *2363*

THYINE (1)
Rev 18:12 and all **t** wood, and all *manner* vessels of *2367*

THYSELF (215) [SELF, THOU] See Index

TIBERIAS (3)
Jn 6: 1 the sea of Galilee, *which is* the *sea* of **T**. *5085*
6:23 (Howbeit there came other boats from **T** *5085*

T

Jn 21: 1 again to the disciples at the sea of **T**; *5085*

TIBERIUS (1)
Lk 3: 1 Now in the fifteenth year of the reign of **T** *5086*

TIBHATH (1)
1Ch 18: 8 Likewise from **T**, and from Chun, cities of 2880

TIBNI (3)
1Ki 16:21 half of the people followed **T** the son of 8402
16:22 people that followed **T** the son of Ginath: 8402
16:22 son of Ginath: so **T** died, and Omri reigned. 8402

TIDAL (2)
Ge 14: 1 king of Elam, and **T** king of nations; 8413
14: 9 *with* **T** king of nations, and Amraphel king 8413

TIDINGS (46)
Ge 29:13 when Laban heard the **t** of Jacob his sister's 8088
Ex 33: 4 when the people heard these evil **t**, they 1697
1Sa 4:19 when she heard the **t** that the ark of God 8052
11: 4 and told the **t** in the ears of the people: 1697
11: 5 they told him the **t** of the men of Jabesh. 1697
11: 6 came upon Saul when he heard those **t**, 1697
27:11 to bring *t to* Gath, saying, Lest they should NIH
2Sa 4: 4 was five years old when the **t** came of Saul 8052
4:10 is dead, thinking to have **brought good t**, 1319
4:10 I would have given him a **reward for** *his* **t**: 1309
13:30 in the way, that **t** came to David, saying, 8052
18:19 Let me now run, and **bear** the king **t**, 1319
18:20 Thou *shalt* not bear **t** this day, but 1309
18:20 this day, but thou shalt **bear t** another day: 1319
18:20 this day thou shalt **bear** no **t**, because 1319
18:22 my son, seeing that thou hast no **t** ready? 1309
18:25 If he *be* alone, *there is* **t** in his mouth. 1309
18:26 And the king said, He also **bringeth t**. 1319
18:27 He *is* a good man, and cometh with good **t**. 1309
18:31 and Cushi said, **T**, my lord the king: 1319
1Ki 1:42 thou *art* a valiant man, and **bringest** good **t**. 1319
2:28 **t** came to Joab: for Joab had turned after 8052
14: 6 for I *am* sent to thee *with* heavy *t*. NIH
2Ki 7: 9 this day *is* a day of **good t**, and we hold our 1309
1Ch 10: 9 to **carry t** unto their idols, and to 1319
Ps 112: 7 He shall not be afraid of evil **t**: his heart is 8052
Isa 40: 9 O Zion, that **bringest good t**, get thee up 1319
40: 9 O Jerusalem, that **bringest good t**, lift up 1319
41:27 give to Jerusalem one that **bringeth good t**. 1319
52: 7 are the feet of him that **bringeth good t**, 1319
52: 7 that **bringeth good t** of good, 1319
61: 1 me to **preach good t unto** the meek; 1319
Jer 20:15 Cursed *be* the man who **brought t** to my 1319
37: 5 that besieged Jerusalem heard **t** of them, 8088
49:23 for they have heard evil **t**: they are 8052
Eze 21: 7 that thou shalt answer, For the **t**; because 8052
Da 11:44 **t** out of the east and out of the north shall 8052
Na 1:15 the feet of him that **bringeth good t**, 1319
Lk 1:19 unto thee, and to **shew** thee these **glad t**. *2097*
2:10 for behold, I **bring** you **good t** of great joy, *2097*
8: 1 **shewing the glad t** of the kingdom of God: *2097*
Ac 11:22 Then **t** of these *things* came unto the ears of *3056*
13:32 And we **declare** unto you **glad t**, how that *2097*
21:31 **t** came unto the chief captain of the band, *5334*
Ro 10:15 of peace, and **bring glad t** of good *things!* *2097*
1Th 3: 6 and **brought** us **good t** of your faith and *2097*

TIE (2) [TIED]
1Sa 6: 7 **t** the kine to the cart, and bring their calves 631
Pr 6:21 thine heart, *and* **t** them about thy neck. 6029

TIED (8) [TIE]
Ex 39:31 they **t** unto it a lace of blue, to fasten *it* on 5414
1Sa 6:10 **t** them to the cart, and shut up their calves at 631
2Ki 7:10 horses **t**, and asses tied, and the tents as they 631
7:10 and asses **t**, and the tents as they *were*. 631
Mt 21: 2 and straightway ye shall find an ass **t**, and *1210*
Mk 11: 2 ye shall find a colt **t**, whereon never man *1210*
11: 4 found the colt **t** by the door without in a *1210*
Lk 19:30 which at your entering ye shall find a colt **t**, *1210*

TIGLATH-PILESER (3) [PUL, TILGATH-PILNESER]
2Ki 15:29 In the days of Pekah king of Israel came **T** 8407
16: 7 So Ahaz sent messengers to **T** king of 8407
16:10 king Ahaz went *to* Damascus to meet **T** 8407

TIGRIS See HIDDEKEL

TIKVAH (2) [TIKVATH]
2Ki 22:14 the wife of Shallum the son of **T**, the son of 8616
Ezr 10:15 Jahaziah the son of **T** were employed about 8616

TIKVATH (1) [TIKVAH]
2Ch 34:22 the wife of Shallum the son of **T**, the son of 8616

TILE (1) [TILING]
Eze 4: 1 take thee a **t**, and lay it before thee, and 3843

TILGATH-PILNESER (3) [TIGLATH-PILESER]
1Ch 5: 6 whom **T** king of Assyria carried away 8407
5:26 the spirit of **T** king of Assyria, and 8407
2Ch 28:20 **T** king of Assyria came unto him, and 8407

TILING (1) [TILE]
Lk 5:19 let him down through the **t** with *his* couch *2766*

TILL (169) [TILLAGE, TILLED, TILLER, TILLEST, TILLETH] See Index

TILLAGE (3) [TILL]
1Ch 27:26 **t** of the ground *was* Ezri the son of Chelub: 5656
Ne 10:37 have the tithes in all the cities of our **t**. 5656
Pr 13:23 Much food *is in* the **t** of the poor: but 5215

TILLED (2) [TILL]
Eze 36: 9 turn unto you, and ye shall be **t** and sown: 5647
36:34 the desolate land shall be **t**, whereas it lay 5647

TILLER (1) [TILL]
Ge 4: 2 of sheep, but Cain was a **t** of the ground. 5647

TILLEST (1) [TILL]
Ge 4:12 When thou **t** the ground, it shall not 5647

TILLETH (2) [TILL]
Pr 12:11 He that **t** his land shall be satisfied *with* 5647
28:19 He that **t** his land shall have plenty *of* 5647

TILON (1)
1Ch 4:20 and Rinnah, Ben-hanan, and **T**. 8436

TIMBER (26)
Ex 31: 5 of stones, to set *them*, and in carving of **t**, 6086
Lev 14:45 the **t** thereof, and all the morter of 6086
1Ki 5: 6 can skill to hew **t** like unto the Sidonians. 6086
5: 8 I will do all thy desire concerning **t** of 6086
5: 8 timber of cedar, and concerning **t** of fir. 6086
5:18 so they prepared **t** and stones to build 6086
6:10 they rested on the house with **t** of cedar. 6086
15:22 the **t** thereof, where*with* Baasha had 6086
2Ki 12:12 to buy **t** and hewed stone to repair 6086
22: 6 to buy **t** and hewn stone to repair the house. 6086
1Ch 14: 1 **t** of cedars, with masons and carpenters, 6086
22:14 **t** also and stone have I prepared; and 6086
22:15 hewers and workers of stone and **t**, and 6086
2Ch 2: 8 thy servants can skill to cut **t** in Lebanon; 6086
2: 9 Even to prepare me **t** in abundance: for 6086
2:10 give to thy servants, the hewers that cut **t**, 6086
2:14 in silver, in brass, in iron, in stone, and in **t**, 6086
16: 6 the **t** thereof, where*with* Baasha was a 6086
34:11 **t** for couplings, and to floor the houses 6086
Ezr 5: 8 **t** *is* laid in the walls, and this work goeth fast 636
6: 4 rows of great stones, and a row of new **t**: 636
6:11 let **t** be pulled down from his house, and 636
Ne 2: 8 that he may give me **t** to make beams for 6086
Eze 26:12 they shall lay thy stones and thy **t** and 6086
Hab 2:11 and the beam out of the **t** shall answer it. 6086
Zec 5: 4 shall consume it with the **t** thereof and 6086

TIMBREL (5) [TIMBRELS]
Ex 15:20 the sister of Aaron, took a **t** in her hand; 8596
Job 21:12 They take the **t** and harp, and rejoice at 8596
Ps 81: 2 Take a psalm, and bring hither the **t**, 8596
149: 3 let them sing *praises* unto him with the **t** 8596
150: 4 Praise him with the **t** and dance: praise him 8596

TIMBRELS (5) [TIMBREL]
Ex 15:20 all the women went out after her with **t** and 8596
Jdg 11:34 his daughter came out to meet him with **t** 8596
2Sa 6: 5 and on **t**, and on cornets, and on cymbals. 8596
1Ch 13: 8 with **t**, and with cymbals, and 8596
Ps 68:25 *them were* the damsels **playing** with **t**. 8608

TIME (619) [BEFORETIME, BETIMES, DAYTIME, LIFETIME, MEALTIME, OFTENTIMES, OFTTIMES, SEEDTIME, SOMETIME, SOMETIMES, TIMES, UNTIMELY]

Ge 4: 3 in process of **t** it came to pass, that Cain 3117
17:21 bear unto thee at this **set t** in the next year. 4150
18:10 return unto thee according to the **t** of life; 6256
18:14 At the **t appointed** I will return unto thee, 4150
18:14 according to the **t** of life, and Sarah shall 6256
21: 2 at the **set t** of which God had spoken to 4150
21:22 it came to pass at that **t**, that Abimelech 6256
22:15 unto Abraham out of heaven the **second t**, 8145
24:11 by a well of water at the **t** of the evening, 6256
24:11 *even* the **t** that *women* go out to draw 6256
26: 8 to pass, when he had been there a long **t**, 3117
29: 7 neither *is it* **t** that the cattle should be 6256
29:34 Now *this* **t** will my husband be joined unto 6471
30:33 righteousness answer for me in **t** to come, 3117
31:10 it came to pass at the **t** that the cattle 6256
38: 1 it came to pass at that **t**, that Judah went 6256
38:12 **in process of t** the daughter 3117+7235+1886.1
38:27 it came to pass in the **t** of her travail, that, 6256
39: 5 it came to pass from the **t** *that* he had made 227
39:11 it came to pass about this **t**, that *Joseph* 3117
41: 5 he slept and dreamed the **second t**: and 8145
43:10 surely now we had returned this **second t**. 6471
43:18 in our sacks at the **first t** *are* we brought in; 8462
43:20 we came indeed down at the **first t** to buy 8462
47:29 the **t** drew nigh that Israel must die: and 3117
Ex 2:23 pass in **process of t**, 3117+7227+1886.1+1886.1
8:32 Pharaoh hardened his heart at this **t** also, 6471
9: 5 the LORD appointed a **set t**, saying, 4150
9:14 For I will at this **t** send all my plagues upon 6471
9:18 to morrow about *this* **t** I will cause it to rain 6256
9:27 and said unto them, I have sinned *this* **t**: 6471
13:14 be when thy son asketh thee **in t to come**, 4279
21:19 only he shall pay *for* the **loss of** his **t**, and 7674
21:29 to push with his horn **in t past**, 4480+8032+8543
21:36 ox *hath* used to push **in t past**, 4480+8032+8543
23:15 in the **t appointed** of the month Abib; 4150
34:18 in the **t** of the month Abib: 4150
34:21 in **earing t** and in harvest thou shalt rest. 2758
Lev 13:58 it shall be washed the **second t**, and 8145
15:25 many days out of the **t** of her separation, 6256
15:25 or if it run beyond the **t** of her separation; NIH
18:18 besides the other in her life *t*. NIH
25:32 may the Levites redeem at **any t**. 5769
25:50 according to the **t** of a hired servant shall it 3117
26: 5 the vintage shall reach unto the **sowing t**: 2233
Nu 10: 6 When you blow an alarm the **second t**, then 8145
13:20 Now the **t** *was* the time of the first ripe 3117
13:20 Now the time *was* the **t** of the first ripe 3117
14:14 **by day t** in a pillar of a cloud, and in a 3119
20:15 and we have dwelt in Egypt a long **t**; 3117
22: 4 Zippor *was* king of the Moabites at that **t**. 6256
23:23 according to *this* **t** it shall be said of Jacob 6256
26:10 **what t** the fire devoured two hundred and 871.1
32:10 LORD'S anger was kindled the same **t**, 3117
35:26 if the slayer shall **at any t come** 3318+3318
Dt 1: 9 I spake unto you at that **t**, saying, I am not 6256
1:16 I charged your judges at that **t**, saying, 6256
1:18 I commanded you at that **t** all the things 6256
2:20 giants dwelt therein **in old t**; and 6440+3807.1
2:34 we took all his cities at that **t**, and 6256
3: 4 we took all his cities at that **t**, there was not 6256
3: 8 we took at that **t** out of the hand of the two 6256
3:12 *which* we possessed at that **t**, from Aroer, 6256
3:18 I commanded you at that **t**, saying, 6256
3:21 I commanded Joshua at that **t**, saying, 6256
3:23 I besought the LORD at that **t**, saying, 6256
4:14 the LORD commanded me at that **t** to 6256
5: 5 between the LORD and you at that **t**, 6256
6:20 *And* when thy son asketh thee **in t to come**, 4279
9:19 the LORD hearkened unto me at that **t** 6471
9:20 and I prayed for Aaron also the same **t**. 6256
10: 1 At that **t** the LORD said unto me, 6256
10: 8 At that **t** the LORD separated the tribe of 6256
10:10 according to the first **t**, forty days and 3117
10:10 the LORD hearkened unto me at that **t** 6471
16: 9 *t as thou* beginnest *to put* the sickle to NIH
19: 4 whom he hated not **in t past**; 4480+8032+8543
19: 6 as he hated him not **in t past**. 4480+8032+8543
19:14 which they of **old t** have set in thine 7223
20:19 When thou shalt besiege a city a long **t**, 3117
32:35 recompence; their foot shall slide in *due* **t**: 6256
Jos 2: 5 it came to pass *about the* **t** of shutting of NIH
3:15 all his banks all the **t** of harvest,) 3117
4: 6 your children ask *their fathers* **in t to come**, 4279
4:21 children shall ask their fathers **in t to come**, 4279
5: 2 At that **t** the LORD said unto Joshua, 6256
5: 2 again the children of Israel the **second t**. 8145
6:16 it came to pass at the seventh **t**, when 6471
6:26 Joshua adjured *them* at that **t**, saying, 6256
8:14 he and all his people, at a **t appointed**, 4150
10:27 it came to pass at the **t** of the going down of 6256
10:42 and their land did Joshua take *at* one **t**, 6471
11: 6 for to morrow about this **t** will I deliver 6256
11:10 Joshua at that **t** turned back, and 6256
11:18 Joshua made war a long **t** with all those 3117
11:21 at that **t** came Joshua, and cut off 6256
22:24 **In t to come** your children might speak 4279
22:27 may not say to our children **in t to come**, 4279
22:28 say to us or to our generations **in t to come**, 4279
23: 1 it came to pass a long **t** after that 3117
24: 2 dwelt on the *other* side of the flood in **old t**, 5769
Jdg 3:29 they slew *of* Moab at that **t** about ten 6256
4: 4 wife of Lapidoth, she judged Israel at that **t**. 6256
9: 8 The trees **went forth on a t** to anoint 1980+1980
10:14 let them deliver you in the **t** of your 6256
11: 4 it came to pass **in process of t**, 3117+4480
11:26 did ye not recover *them* within that **t**? 6256
12: 6 there fell at that **t** of the Ephraimites forty 6256
13:23 as *at this* **t** have told us *such things* as these. 6256
14: 4 for at that **t** the Philistines had dominion 6256
14: 8 after a **t** he returned to take her, and 3117
15: 1 in the **t** of wheat harvest, that Samson 3117
18:31 all the **t** that the house of God was in 3117
20:15 numbered at that **t** out of the cities twenty 3117
21:14 Benjamin came again at that **t**; and 6256
21:22 for ye did not give unto them at *this* **t**, 6256
21:24 children of Israel departed thence at that **t**, 6256
Ru 4: 7 **in former t** in Israel concerning 6440+3807.1
1Sa 1: 4 when the **t** was that Elkanah offered, he 3117
1:20 when the **t** was come about after Hannah 3117
3: 2 it came to pass at that **t**, when Eli *was* laid 3117
3: 8 LORD called Samuel again the **third t**. 7992
4:20 about the **t** of her death the *women* that 6256
7: 2 abode in Kirjath-jearim, that the **t** was long: 3117
9:13 you up; for about *this* **t** ye shall find him. 3117
9:16 To morrow about *this* **t** I will send thee a 6256
9:24 for unto *this* **t** *hath it* been kept for thee 4150
11: 9 To morrow, by *that* **t** the sun be hot, ye shall NIH
13: 8 according to the **set t** that Samuel *had* 4150
14:18 For the ark of God was at that **t** with 3117
14:21 the Philistines **before that t**, 865+8032+3509.1
18:19 it came to pass at the **t** when Merab Saul's 6256
19:21 Saul sent messengers again the **third t**. 7992
20:12 sounded my father about to morrow *any* **t**, 6256
20:35 the field at the **t appointed** with David, 4150
26: 8 and I will not *smite* him the **second t**. 8138
27: 7 the **t** that David dwelt in the country 3117+4557
2Sa 2:11 the **t** that David was king in Hebron 3117+4557
5: 2 Also **in t past**, when Saul was 865+1571+8032
7: 6 **t** that I brought up the children of Israel out 3117
7:11 *as* since the **t** that I commanded judges *to* 3117
11: 1 at the **t** when kings go forth *to battle*, that 6256
14: 2 be as a woman *that had* a long **t** mourned 3117
14:29 when he sent again the **second t**, he would 8145
17: 7 Ahithophel hath given *is* not good at this **t**. 6471
20: 5 he tarried longer than the **set t** which he 4150
20:18 They were wont to speak in **old t**, saying, 7223
23: 8 eight hundred, whom he slew at one **t**. 6471
23:13 came to David in the **harvest t** unto 7105
23:20 slew a lion in the midst of a pit in **t** of 3117
24:15 from the morning even to the **t** appointed: 6256
1Ki 1: 6 his father had not displeased him at **any t** in 3117
2:26 I will not at this **t** put thee to death, because 3117
8:65 at that **t** Solomon held a feast, and all Israel 6256
9: 2 LORD appeared to Solomon the **second t**, 8145
11:29 it came to pass at that **t** when Jeroboam 6256
11:42 the **t** that Solomon reigned in Jerusalem 3117
14: 1 At that **t** Abijah the son of Jeroboam fell 6256
15:23 Nevertheless in the **t** of his old age he was 6256
18:29 they prophesied until *the* **t** of the offering of NIH
18:34 he said, **Do** *it* **the second t**. And they did *it* 8138
18:34 they **did** *it* **the second t**. And he said, Do *it* 8138
18:34 he said, **Do** *it* **the third t**. And they did *it* 8027
18:34 the third time. And they **did** *it* **the third t**. 8027

1Ki 18:36 it came to pass at *the* **t** *of* the offering of NIH
18:44 it came to pass at the seventh **t**, that he said, NIH
19: 2 of one of them *by* to morrow about *this* **t**. 6256
19: 7 of the LORD came again the **second t**, 8145
20: 6 servants unto thee to morrow about *this* **t**, 6256
2Ki 3: 6 Jehoram went out of Samaria the same **t**, 3117
4:16 About this season, according to the **t** of life, 6256
4:17 had said unto her, according to the **t** of life. 6256
5:26 *Is it* a **t** to receive money, and to receive 6256
7: 1 To morrow about *this* **t** *shall* a measure of 6256
7:18 shall be to morrow about *this* **t** in the gate 6256
8:22 Then Libnah revolted at the same **t**. 6256
10: 6 Then he wrote a letter the **second t** to them, 8145
10: 6 come to me to Jezreel by to morrow *this* **t**. 6256
10:36 the **t** that Jehu reigned over Israel in 3117
16: 6 At that **t** Rezin king of Syria recovered 6256
18:16 At that **t** did Hezekiah cut off *the gold from* 6256
20:12 At that **t** Berodach-baladan, the son of 6256
24:10 At that **t** the servants of Nebuchadnezzar 6256
1Ch 9:20 was the ruler over them **in t past**, 6440+3807.1
9:25 *were* to come after seven days from **t** to 6256
9:25 after seven days from time to **t** with them. 6256
11: 2 *And* moreover **in t past**, even when 8032+8543
11:11 against three hundred slain *by him* at one **t**. 6471
12:22 For at *that* **t** day by day there came to 6256
17:10 since the **t** that I commanded judges *to be* 3117
20: 1 at the **t** that kings go out *to battle,* Joab led 6256
20: 4 **at which t** Sibbechai the Hushathite slew 227
21:28 At that **t** when David saw that the LORD 6256
29:22 the son of David king the **second t**, 8145
29:27 the **t** that he reigned over Israel *was* forty 3117
2Ch 7: 8 Also at the same **t** Solomon kept the feast 6256
13:18 of Israel were brought under at that **t**, 6256
15:11 they offered unto the LORD the same **t**, 3117
16: 7 at that **t** Hanani the seer came to Asa king 6256
16:10 oppressed *some* of the people the same **t**. 6256
18:34 about the **t** of the sun going down he died. 6256
21:10 The same **t** also did Libnah revolt from 6256
21:19 that **in process of t**, 3117+3117+4480+3807.1
24:11 that at *what* **t** the chest was brought unto 6256
25:27 Now after the **t** that Amaziah did turn away 6256
28:16 At that **t** did king Ahaz send unto the kings 6256
28:22 in the **t** of his distress did he trespass yet 6256
30: 3 For they could not keep it at that **t**, because 6256
30: 5 for they had not done *it* of a long *t in such* NIH
30:26 for since the **t** of Solomon the son of David 3117
35:17 that were present kept the passover at that **t**, 6256
Ezr 4:10 *are on this* side the river, and at **such a t**. 3706
4:11 men *on this* side the river, and **at such a t**. 3706
4:15 moved sedition within the same of old **t**: 3118
4:17 beyond the river: Peace, and **at such a t**. 3706
4:19 it is found that this city of old **t** *hath* made 3118
5: 3 At the same **t** came to them Tatnai, 2166
5:16 since **that t** even until now *hath it been* in 116
7:12 of heaven, perfect *peace,* and **at such a t**. 3706
8:34 and all the weight was written at that **t**. 6256
10:13 *it is* a **t** of much rain, and *we are* not able to 6256
Ne 2: 6 the king to send me; and I set him a **t**. 2165
4:16 it came to pass from that **t** forth, *that* 3117
4:22 Likewise at the same **t** said I unto 6256
5:14 Moreover from the **t** that I was appointed to 3117
6: 1 (though at that **t** I had not set up the doors 6256
6: 5 the fifth **t** with an open letter in his hand; 6471
9:27 in the **t** of their trouble, when they cried 6256
9:32 since the **t** of the kings of Assyria unto this 3117
12:44 at that **t** were some appointed over 3117
13: 6 in all this *t* was not I at Jerusalem: for in NIH
13:21 From that **t** forth came they no *more* on 6256
Est 2:19 were gathered together the **second t**, 8145
4:14 if thou altogether holdest thy peace at this **t**, 6256
4:14 come to the kingdom for *such* a **t** as this? 6256
8: 9 were the king's scribes called at that **t** in 6256
9:27 according to their *appointed* **t** every year; 2165
Job 6:17 What **t** they wax warm, they vanish: 6256
7: 1 *Is there* not an **appointed t** to man upon 6635
9:19 of judgment, who shall **set me a t** *to plead?* 3259
14:13 that thou wouldest appoint me a **set t**, and 2706
14:14 all the days of my **appointed t** will I wait, 6635
15:32 It shall be accomplished before his **t**, and 3117
22:16 Which were cut down out of **t**, 6256
30: 3 flying *into* the wilderness **in former t** 570
38:23 Which I have reserved against the **t** of 6256
39: 1 Knowest thou the **t** when the wild goats of 6256
39: 2 knowest thou the **t** when they bring forth? 6256
39:18 What **t** she lifteth up herself on high, 6256
Ps 4: 7 more than *in* the **t** *that* their corn and 6256
21: 9 them as a fiery oven in the **t** of thine anger: 6256
27: 5 For in the **t** of trouble he shall hide me in 3117
32: 6 unto thee in a **t** when thou mayest be found: 6256
37:19 They shall not be ashamed in the evil **t**: and 6256
37:39 *he is* their strength in the **t** of trouble. 6256
41: 1 the LORD will deliver him in **t** of trouble. 3117
56: 3 *What* **t** I am afraid, I will trust in thee. 3117
69:13 *is* unto thee, O LORD, *in* an acceptable **t**: 6256
71: 9 Cast me not off in the **t** of old age; 6256
78:38 **many a t** turned he his anger away, and 7235
81: 3 in the **t appointed**, on our solemn feast 3677
81:15 but their **t** should have endured for ever. 6256
89:47 Remember how **short** my **t** is: 2465
102:13 for the **t** to favour her, yea, the set time, 6256
102:13 time to favour her, yea, the **set t**, is come. 4150
105:19 Until the **t** that his word came: the word of 6256
113: 2 the name of the LORD from **this t forth** 6258
115:18 we will bless the LORD from **this t forth** 6258
119:126 *It is* **t** for *thee,* LORD, to work: *for* they 6256
121: 8 and thy coming in from **this t forth**, 6258
129: 1 **Many a t** have they afflicted me from my 7227
129: 2 **Many a t** have they afflicted me from my 7227
Pr 25:13 As the cold of snow in the **t** of harvest, *so* 3117
25:19 Confidence in an unfaithful *man* in **t** of 3117
31:25 and she shall rejoice in **t** to come. 3117
Ecc 1:10 it hath been already **of old t**, 5769+3807.1
3: 1 and a **t** to every purpose under the heaven: 6256
3: 2 A **t** to be born, and a time to die; a time to 6256
3: 2 A time to be born, and a **t** to die; a time to 6256
3: 2 a **t** to plant, and a time to pluck up *that* 6256
3: 2 and a **t** to pluck up *that which is* planted; 6256
3: 3 A **t** to kill, and a time to heal; a time to 6256
3: 3 A time to kill, and a **t** to heal; a time to 6256
3: 3 a **t** to break down, and a time to build *up;* 6256
3: 3 a time to break down, and a **t** to build *up;* 6256
3: 4 A **t** to weep, and a time to laugh; a time to 6256
3: 4 A time to weep, and a **t** to laugh; a time to 6256
3: 4 to laugh; a **t** to mourn, and a time to dance; 6256
3: 4 to laugh; a time to mourn, and a **t** to dance; 6256
3: 5 A **t** to cast away stones, and a time to 6256
3: 5 and a **t** to gather stones together; 6256
3: 5 a **t** to embrace, and a time to refrain from 6256
3: 5 and a **t** to refrain from embracing; 6256
3: 6 A **t** to get, and a time to lose; a time to 6256
3: 6 A time to get, and a **t** to lose; a time to 6256
3: 6 to lose; a **t** to keep, and a time to cast away; 6256
3: 6 to lose; a time to keep, and a **t** to cast away; 6256
3: 7 A **t** to rent, and a time to sew; a time to 6256
3: 7 A time to rent, and a **t** to sew; a time to 6256
3: 7 a **t** to keep silence, and a time to speak; 6256
3: 7 a time to keep silence, and a **t** to speak; 6256
3: 8 A **t** to love, and a time to hate; a time of 6256
3: 8 A time to love, and a **t** to hate; a time of 6256
3: 8 to hate; a **t** of war, and a time of peace. 6256
3: 8 to hate; a time of war, and a **t** of peace. 6256
3:11 He hath made every *thing* beautiful in his **t**: 6256
3:17 for *there is* a **t** there for every purpose and 6256
7:17 why shouldest thou die before thy **t**? 6256
8: 5 a wise *man's* heart discerneth *both* **t** and 6256
8: 6 Because to every purpose there is **t** and 6256
8: 9 *there is* a **t** wherein one man ruleth over 6256
9:11 but **t** and chance happeneth to them all. 6256
9:12 For man also knoweth not his **t**: as 6256
9:12 so *are* the sons of men snared in an evil **t**, 6256
SS 2:12 the **t** of the singing *of birds* is come, and 6256
Isa 11:11 **second t** to recover the remnant of his 8145
13:22 her **t** *is* near to come, and her days shall not 6256
16:13 hath spoken concerning Moab since that **t**. 227
18: 7 In that **t** shall the present be brought unto 6256
20: 2 At the same **t** spake the LORD by Isaiah 6256
26:17 *that* **draweth near the t** of her delivery, 7126
28:19 From the **t** that it goeth forth it shall take 1767
30: 8 that it may be for the **t** to come for ever and 3117
33: 2 our salvation also in the **t** of trouble. 6256
39: 1 At that **t** Merodach-baladan, the son of 6256
42:14 I have **long t** holden my peace; I have been 5769
42:23 *who* will hearken and hear for the **t to come**? 268
44: 8 have not I told thee from **that t**, and 227
45:21 who hath declared this from **ancient t**? 6924
45:21 *who* hath told it from **that t**? *have* not I 227
48: 6 I have shewed thee new *things* from **this t**, 6258
48: 8 from **that t** *that* thine ear was not opened: 227

Isa 48:16 from the **t** that it was, there *am* I: 6256
49: 8 In an acceptable **t** have I heard thee, and 6256
60:22 I the LORD will hasten it in his **t**. 6256
Jer 1:13 of the LORD came unto me the **second t**, 8145
2:20 For **of old t** I have broken thy yoke, 4480+5769
2:27 in the **t** of their trouble they will say, Arise, 6256
2:28 if they can save thee in the **t** of thy trouble: 6256
3: 4 Wilt thou not from **this t** cry unto me, 6258
3:17 At that **t** they shall call Jerusalem 6256
4:11 At that **t** shall it be said to this people and 6256
6:15 at the **t** *that* I visit them they shall be cast 6256
8: 1 At that **t**, saith the LORD, they shall bring 6256
8: 7 the swallow observe the **t** of their coming; 6256
8:12 in the **t** of their visitation they shall be cast 6256
8:15 but no good *came; and* for a **t** of health, and 6256
10:15 in the **t** of their visitation they shall perish. 6256
11:12 they shall not save them at all in the **t** of 6256
11:14 for I will not hear *them* in the **t** that they 6256
13: 3 of the LORD came unto me the **second t**, 8145
14: 8 of Israel, the saviour thereof in **t** of trouble, 6256
14:19 and for the **t** of healing, and behold trouble. 6256
15:11 enemy to entreat thee *well* in the **t** of evil, 6256
15:11 in the time of evil, and in the **t** of affliction. 6256
18:23 deal *thus* with them in the **t** of thine anger. 6256
27: 7 son's son, until the very **t** of his land come: 6256
30: 7 it *is* even the **t** of Jacob's trouble; but 6256
31: 1 At the same **t**, saith the LORD, will I be 6256
33: 1 LORD came unto Jeremiah the **second t**, 8145
33:15 In those days, and at that **t**, will I cause 6256
39:10 them vineyards and fields at the same **t**. 3117
46:17 *but* a noise; he hath passed the **t appointed**. 4150
46:21 upon them, *and* the **t** of their visitation. 6256
49: 8 of Esau upon him, the **t** *that* I will visit him. 6256
49:19 who will **appoint** me **the t**? and who *is* that 3259
50: 4 In those days, and in that **t**, saith 6256
50:16 him that handleth the sickle in the **t** of 6256
50:20 In those days, and in that **t**, saith 6256
50:27 their day is come, the **t** of their visitation. 6256
50:31 thy day is come, the **t** *that* I will visit thee. 6256
50:44 who will **appoint** me **the t**? and who *is* that 3259
51: 6 for this *is* the **t** of the LORD's vengeance; 6256
51:18 in the **t** of their visitation they shall perish. 6256
51:33 *is* like a threshingfloor, *it is* **t** to thresh her: 6256
51:33 and the **t** of her harvest shall come. 6256
La 5:20 forget us for ever, *and* forsake us so long **t**? 3117
Eze 4:10 a day: from **t** to time shalt thou eat it. 6256
4:10 a day: from time to **t** shalt thou eat it. 6256
4:11 of a hin: from **t** to time shalt thou drink. 6256
4:11 of a hin: from time to **t** shalt thou drink. 6256
7: 7 the **t** is come, the day of trouble *is* near, and 6256
7:12 The **t** is come, the day draweth near: let not 6256
16: 8 behold, thy **t** *was* the time of love; 6256
16: 8 behold, thy time *was* the **t** of love; 6256
16:57 as *at* the **t** of *thy* reproach of the daughters 6256
21:14 let the sword be doubled the **third t**, 7992
22: 3 that her **t** may come, and maketh idols 6256
26:20 with the people of **old t**, and shall set thee 5769
27:34 *In* the **t** when *thou shalt be* broken by 6256
30: 3 cloudy day; it shall be the **t** of the heathen. 6256
35: 5 force of the sword in the **t** of their calamity, 6256
35: 5 in the **t** *that their* iniquity *had* an end: 6256
38:10 *that* at the same **t** shall things come into thy 3117
38:17 *Art* thou he of whom I have spoken in old **t** 3117
38:18 it shall come to pass at the same **t** when 3117
Da 2: 8 know of certainty that ye would gain the **t**, 5732
2: 9 to speak before me, till the **t** be changed: 5732
2:16 of the king that he would give him **t**, 2166
3: 5 *That* **at what t** ye hear 0.2+1768+5732+871.2
3: 7 Therefore at that **t**, when all the people 2166
3: 8 Wherefore at that **t** certain Chaldeans came 2166
3:15 Now if ye be ready that at what **t** ye hear 5732
4:36 At the same **t** my reason returned unto me; 2166
7:12 lives were prolonged for a season and **t**. 5732
7:22 the **t** came that the saints possessed 2166
7:25 they shall be given into his hand until a **t** 5732
7:25 until a time and times and the dividing of **t**. 5732
8:17 for at the **t** of the end *shall be* the vision. 6256
8:19 for at the **t appointed** the end *shall be*. 4150
8:23 in the **latter t** of their kingdom, when 319
9:21 touched me about the **t** of the evening 6256
10: 1 *was* true, but the **t appointed** *was* long: 6635
11:24 against the strong holds, even for a **t**. 6256
11:27 for yet the end *shall be* at the **t appointed**. 4150
11:29 At the **t appointed** he shall return, and 4150
11:35 make *them* white, *even* to the **t** of the end: 6256
11:35 the end: because *it is* yet for a **t appointed**. 4150
11:40 at the **t** of the end shall the king of 6256
12: 1 at that **t** shall Michael stand up, the great 6256
12: 1 there shall be a **t** of trouble, such as never 6256
12: 1 there was a nation *even* to that same **t**: 6256
12: 1 at that **t** thy people shall be delivered, 6256
12: 4 and seal the book, *even* to the **t** of the end: 6256
12: 7 that liveth for ever that *it shall be* for a **t**, 4150
12: 9 closed up and sealed till the **t** of the end. 6256
12:11 from the **t** *that* the daily *sacrifice* shall be 6256
Hos 2: 9 take *away* my corn in the **t** thereof, and 6256
9:10 as the firstripe in the fig tree at her **first t**: 7225
10:12 for *it is* **t** to seek the LORD, till he come 6256
Joel 3: 1 For behold, in those days, and in that **t**, 6256
Am 5:13 the prudent shall keep silence in that **t**; 6256
5:13 keep silence in that time; for it *is* an evil **t**. 6256
Jnh 3: 1 the LORD came unto Jonah the **second t**, 8145
Mic 2: 3 shall ye go haughtily: for this **t** *is* evil. 6256
3: 4 will even hide his face from them at that **t**, 6256
5: 3 until the **t** *that* she which travaileth hath 6256
Na 1: 9 affliction shall not rise up the **second t**. 6471
Hab 2: 3 For the vision *is* yet for an **appointed t**, but 4150
Zep 1:12 it shall come to pass at that **t**, *that* I will 6256
3:19 at that **t** I *will* undo all that afflict thee: 6256
3:20 At that **t** will I bring you *again,* even in 6256
3:20 you *again,* even in the **t** that I gather you: 6256
Hag 1: 2 This people say, The **t** is not come, 6256
1: 2 the **t** that the LORD's house should be 6256
1: 4 *Is it* **t** for you, O ye, to dwell in your cieled 6256
Zec 10: 1 Ask ye of the LORD rain in the **t** of 6256
14: 7 to pass, *that* at evening **t** it shall be light. 6256
Mal 3:11 vine **cast** her **fruit before the t** in the field, 7921
Mt 1:11 **about the t** they were carried away to *1909*
2: 7 inquired of them diligently what **t** the star *5550*
2:16 according to the **t** which he had diligently *5550*
4: 6 **lest at any t** thou dash thy foot against a *3379*
4:17 From **that t** Jesus began to preach, and *5119*
5:21 have heard that it was said by them **of old t**, *744*
5:25 **lest at any t** the adversary deliver thee to *3379*
5:27 have heard that it was said by them **of old t**, *744*
5:33 heard that it hath been said by them **of old t**, *744*
8:29 come hither to torment us before the **t**? *2540*
11:25 At that **t** Jesus answered and said, I thank *2540*
12: 1 At that **t** Jesus went on the sabbath day *2540*
13:15 **lest at any t** they should see with *their* *3379*
13:30 in the **t** of harvest I will say to the reapers, *2540*
14: 1 At that **t** Herod the tetrarch heard of *2540*
14:15 *This* is a desert place, and the **t** is now past; *5610*
16:21 From **that t forth** began Jesus to shew unto *5119*
18: 1 At the same **t** came the disciples unto Jesus, *5610*
21:34 And when the **t** of the fruit drew near, *2540*
24:21 the beginning of the world to **this t**, *3568+3588*
25:19 After a long **t** the lord of those servants *5550*
26:16 And from that **t** he sought opportunity to *5119*
26:18 The Master saith, My **t** is at hand; *2540*
26:42 He went away again the **second t**, *1208+1537*
26:44 away again, and prayed the **third t**, *1537+5154*
Mk 1:15 And saying, The **t** is fulfilled, *2540*
4:12 **lest at any t** they should be converted, and *3379*
4:17 in themselves, and so endure but **for a t**; *4340*
6:35 a desert place, and now the **t** *is* far passed: *5610*
10:30 shall receive an hundredfold now in this **t**, *2540*
11:13 but leaves; for the **t** of figs was not *yet.* *2540*
13:19 which God created unto **this t**, *3568+3588*
13:33 and pray: for ye know not when the **t** is. *2540*
14:41 And he cometh the **third t**, and saith unto *5154*
14:72 And the **second t** *the* cock crew. *1208+1537*
Lk 1:10 were praying without at the **t** of incense. *5610*
1:57 Now Elisabeth's full **t** came that she should *5550*
4: 5 kingdoms of the world in a moment of **t**. *5550*
4:11 **lest at any t** thou dash thy foot against a *3379*
4:27 And many lepers were in Israel **in the t of** *1909*
7:45 this *woman* **since the t** I came in hath *575+3739*
8:13 and in **t** of temptation fall away. *2540*
8:27 which had devils long **t**, and ware no *5550*
9:51 when the **t** was come that he should be *2250*
12: 1 **In the mean t**, when there were *1722+3739*
12:56 but how *is it that* ye do not discern this **t**? *2540*
13:35 see me, until *the* **t** come when ye shall say, NIG
14:17 And sent his servant at supper **t** to say to *5610*
15:29 **neither** transgressed I **at any t** thy *2532+3763*
16:16 since **that t** the kingdom of God is *5119*
18:30 not receive manifold more in this *present* **t**, *2540*

T

Lk 19:44 thou knewest not the **t** of thy visitation. *2540*
20: 9 and went into a far country for a long **t**. *5550*
21: 8 saying, I am *Christ;* and the **t** draweth near: *2540*
21:34 **lest at any t** your hearts be overcharged *3379*
21:37 And in the **day** **t** he was teaching in *2250*
23: 7 who himself also was at Jerusalem at that **t**. *2250*
23:22 And he said unto them the **third** **t**, Why, *5154*
Jn 1:18 No *man* hath seen God **at any t**; the only *4455*
3: 4 can he enter the **second** **t** into his mother's *1208*
5: 6 knew that he had been now a long **t** *in that* *5550*
5:37 Ye have neither heard his voice **at any t**, *4455*
6:66 From that *t* many of his disciples went back, NIG
7: 6 Jesus said unto them, My **t** is not yet come: *2540*
7: 6 is not yet come: but your **t** is alway ready. *2540*
7: 8 this feast; for my **t** is not yet full come. *2540*
11:39 saith unto him, Lord, **by this** **t** he stinketh: *2235*
14: 9 Have I been so long **t** with you, and *5550*
16: 2 yea, the **t** cometh, that whosoever killeth *5610*
16: 4 have I told you, that when the **t** shall come, *5610*
16:25 but the **t** cometh, when I shall no more *5610*
21:14 This *is* now the **third** **t** *that* Jesus shewed *5154*
21:16 He saith to him again the **second** **t**, Simon, *1208*
21:17 He saith unto him the **third** **t**, Simon, *5154*
21:17 because he said unto him the **third** **t**, *5154*
Ac 1: 6 wilt thou at this **t** restore again the kingdom *5550*
1:21 with us all the **t** that the Lord Jesus went in *5550*
7:13 And at the second **t** Joseph was made NIG
7:17 But when the **t** of the promise drew nigh, *5550*
7:20 In which **t** Moses was born, and *2540*
8: 1 And at that **t** there was a great persecution *2250*
8:11 that of long **t** *he* had bewitched them with *5550*
10:15 *spake* unto him again the **second** **t**, *1208+1537*
11: 8 **nothing** common or unclean hath
at any t *3763+3956*
12: 1 Now about that **t** Herod the king stretched *2540*
13:18 And about the **t** of forty years suffered he *5550*
14: 3 Long **t** therefore abode they speaking *5550*
14:28 And there they abode long **t** with *5550*
15:21 For Moses of old **t** hath in every city them *1074*
17:21 strangers which were there **spent** their **t** in *2119*
18:20 When they desired *him* to tarry longer **t** *5550*
18:23 And after he had spent some **t** *there,* he *5550*
19:23 And the same **t** there arose no small stir *2540*
20:16 because he would not **spend** the **t** in Asia: *5551*
24:25 and answered, Go *thy way* for *this* **t**; *3568*
27: 9 Now when much **t** was spent, and *5550*
Ro 3:26 To declare, *I say,* at this **t** his righteousness: *2540*
5: 6 in due **t** Christ died for the ungodly. *2540*
8:18 **t** *are* not worthy to be compared with *2540*
9: 9 At this **t** will I come, and Sara shall have a *2540*
11: 5 at *this* present **t** also there is a remnant *2540*
13:11 And that, knowing the **t**, that now *it is* high *2540*
13:11 **now** *it is* **high** **t** to awake out of *2235+5610*
1Co 4: 5 Therefore judge nothing before the **t**, *2540*
7: 5 the other, except *it be* with consent for a **t**, *2540*
7:29 But this I say, brethren, the **t** *is* short: *2540*
9: 7 Who goeth a warfare **any** **t** at his own *4218*
15: 8 of me also, as of one **born out of due** **t**. *1626*
16:12 but *his* will was not at all to come **at this** **t**; *3568*
16:12 come when he shall **have convenient** **t**. *2119*
2Co 6: 2 I have heard thee in a **t** accepted, and in *2540*
6: 2 behold, now *is* the accepted **t**; behold, *2540*
8:14 *that* now at *this* **t** your abundance *may be a* *2540*
12:14 the third *t* I am ready to come to you; NIG
13: 1 This *is* the third *t* I am coming to you. In NIG
13: 2 *you,* as if I were present the second *t*; NIG
Gal 1:13 conversation **in t past** in the Jews' religion, *4218*
4: 2 governors until the **t** **appointed** of *4287*
4: 4 But when the fulness of the **t** was come, *5550*
5:21 as I have also **told** *you* **in t past**, *4302*
Eph 2: 2 Wherein **in t past** ye walked according to *4218*
2:11 that ye *being* **in t passed** Gentiles in *4218*
2:12 That at that **t** ye were without Christ, *2540*
5:16 Redeeming the **t**, because the days are evil. *2540*
Col 4: 5 them that are without, redeeming the **t**. *2540*
1Th 2: 5 For neither **at any t** used we flattering *4218*
2:17 being taken from you for a short **t** in *2540*
2Th 2: 6 that he might be revealed in his **t**. *2540*
1Ti 2: 6 a ransom for all, to be testified in due **t**. *2540*
6:19 a good foundation against the **t** **to come**, *3195*
2Ti 4: 3 For the **t** will come when they will not *2540*
4: 6 and the **t** of my departure is at hand. *2540*
4: S Paul was brought before Nero the second **t**. NIG
Phm 1:11 Which **in t past** was to thee unprofitable, *4218*

Heb 1: 1 **in t** past unto the fathers by **the** prophets, *3588*
1: 5 unto which of the angels said he **at any t**, *4218*
1:13 But to which of the angels said he **at any t**, *4218*
2: 1 **lest at any t** we should let *them* slip. *3379*
4: 7 saying in David, To day, after so long a **t**; *5550*
4:16 and find grace to help **in t of need**. *2121*
5:12 For when for the **t** ye ought to be teachers, *5550*
9: 9 Which *was* a figure for the **t** *then* present, *2540*
9:10 imposed *on them* until the **t** of reformation. *2540*
9:28 **second** **t** without sin unto salvation. *1208+1537*
11:32 for the **t** would fail me to tell of Gedeon, *5550*
Jas 4:14 that appeareth for a little *t*, and then NIG
1Pe 1: 5 salvation ready to be revealed in the last **t**. *2540*
1:11 what manner of **t** the Spirit of Christ which *2540*
1:17 pass the **t** of your sojourning *here* in fear: *5550*
2:10 Which **in t past** *were* not a people, but *4218*
3: 5 For after this manner **in the old t** the holy *4218*
4: 2 rest of *his* **t** in the flesh to the lusts of men, *5550*
4: 3 For the **t** past of *our* life may suffice us to *5550*
4:17 For the **t** *is come* that judgment must begin *2540*
5: 6 of God, that he may exalt you in **due** **t**: *2540*
2Pe 1:21 For the prophecy came not **in old t** by *4218*
2: 3 whose judgment now **of a long** **t** lingereth *1597*
2:13 that count it pleasure to riot in the day **t**. NIG
1Jn 2:18 Little children, it is the last **t**: and as ye *5610*
2:18 whereby we know that it is the last **t**. *5610*
4:12 No *man* hath seen God **at any t**. If we love *4455*
Jude 1:18 you there should be mockers in the last **t**, *5550*
Rev 1: 3 are written therein: for the **t** *is* at hand. *2540*
10: 6 are therein, that there should be **t** no longer: *5550*
11:18 thy wrath is come, and the **t** of the dead, *2540*
12:12 he knoweth that he hath *but* a short **t**. *2540*
12:14 where she is nourished for a **t**, and times, *2540*
12:14 and times, and half a **t**, from the face of *2540*
14:15 for the **t** is come for thee to reap; for *5610*
22:10 prophecy of this book: for the **t** is at hand. *2540*

TIMES (146) [TIME]

Ge 27:36 for he hath supplanted me these **two** **t**: he 6471
31: 7 deceived me, and changed my wages ten **t**; 4489
31:41 and thou hast changed my wages ten **t**. 4489
33: 3 and bowed himself to the ground seven **t**, 6471
43:34 Benjamin's mess was five **t** so much as any 3027
Ex 23:14 Three **t** thou shalt keep a feast unto me in 7272
23:17 Three **t** in the year all thy males shall 6471
Lev 4: 6 sprinkle of the blood seven **t** before 6471
4:17 sprinkle *it* seven **t** before the LORD, 6471
8:11 he sprinkled thereof upon the altar seven **t**, 6471
14: 7 is to be cleansed from the leprosy seven **t**, 6471
14:16 with his finger seven **t** before the LORD: 6471
14:27 in his left hand seven **t** before the LORD: 6471
14:51 and sprinkle the house seven **t**: 6471
16: 2 that he come not at all **t** into the holy *place* 6256
16:14 of the blood with his finger seven **t**. 6471
16:19 of the blood upon it with his finger seven **t**, 6471
19:26 shall ye use enchantment, nor **observe** **t**. 6049
25: 8 of years unto thee, seven **t** seven years; 6471
26:18 I will punish you seven *t* more for your sins. NIH
26:21 I will bring seven *t* moe plagues upon you NIH
26:24 will punish you yet seven *t* for your sins. NIH
26:28 will chastise you seven *t* for your sins. NIH
Nu 14:22 have tempted me *now* these ten **t**, and 6471
19: 4 the tabernacle of the congregation seven **t**: 6471
22:28 that thou hast smitten me these three **t**? 7272
22:32 hast thou smitten thine ass these three **t**? 7272
22:33 saw me, and turned from me these three **t**: 7272
24: 1 he went not, as **at other** **t**, to 6471+6471+871.1
24:10 hast altogether blessed *them* these three **t**. 6471
Dt 1:11 God of your fathers make you a thousand **t** 6471
2:10 Emims dwelt therein **in t past**, 6440+3807.1
4:42 hated him not **in t past**; 4480+8032+8543
16:16 Three **t** in a year shall all thy males appear 6471
18:10 *or* an **observer of** **t**, or an enchanter, or 6049
18:14 hearkened unto **observers of** **t**, and 6049
Jos 6: 4 day ye shall compass the city seven **t**, 6471
6:15 the city after the same manner seven **t**: 6471
6:15 that day they compassed the city seven **t**. 6471
Jdg 13:25 began to **move** him **at** **t** in the camp of Dan, 6470
16:15 thou hast mocked me these three **t**, and 6471
16:20 I will go out as **at other** **t** 6471+6471+871.1
20:30 against Gibeah, as **at other** **t**. 6471+6471+871.1
20:31 as **at other** **t**, in the highways, 6471+6471+871.1
1Sa 3:10 and called as **at other** **t**, 6471+6471+871.1
18:10 with his hand, as **at other** **t**: 3117+3117+871.1

1Sa 19: 7 he was in his presence, as in t past. 865+8032
20:25 at other t, even upon a seat 6471+6471+871.1
20:41 to the ground, and bowed himself three t: 6471
2Sa 3:17 in t past to be king over 1571+1571+8032+8543
1Ki 8:59 of his people Israel at all t, 3117+3117+871.1
9:25 three t in a year did Solomon offer burnt 6471
17:21 he stretched himself upon the child three t, 6471
18:43 is nothing. And he said, Go again seven t. 6471
22:16 How many t shall I adjure thee that thou 6471
2Ki 4:35 the child neesed seven t, and the child 6471
5:10 Go and wash in Jordan seven t, and 6471
5:14 and dipped himself seven t in Jordan, 6471
13:19 Thou shouldest have smitten five or six t; 6471
13:25 Three t did Joash beat him, and 6471
19:25 and of ancient t that I have formed it? 3117
21: 6 observed t, and used enchantments, and 6049
1Ch 12:32 were men that had understanding of the t, 6256
21: 3 The LORD make his people an hundred t 6471
29:30 the t that went over him, and over Israel, 6256
2Ch 8:13 on the solemn feasts, three t in the year, 6471
15: 5 in those t there was no peace to him that 6256
18:15 How many t shall I adjure thee that thou 6471
33: 6 also he observed t, and used enchantments, 6049
Ezr 10:14 wives in our cities come at appointed t, 6256
Ne 4:12 by them came, they said unto us ten t, 6471
6: 4 Yet they sent unto me four t after this sort; 6471
9:28 many t didst thou deliver them according to 6256
10:34 of our fathers, at t appointed year by year, 6256
13:31 at t appointed, and for the firstfruits. 6256
Est 1:13 said to the wise men, which knew the t, 6256
9:31 To confirm these days of Purim in their t 2165
Job 19: 3 These ten t have ye reproached me: you are 6471
24: 1 seeing t are not hidden from the Almighty, 6256
Ps 9: 9 for the oppressed, a refuge in t of trouble. 6256
10: 1 why hidest thou thyself in t of trouble? 6256
12: 6 tried in a furnace of earth, purified seven t. 7659
31:15 My t are in thy hand: deliver me from 6256
34: 1 I will bless the LORD at all t: his praise 6256
44: 1 thou didst in their days, in the t of old. 3117
62: 8 Trust in him at all t; ye people, pour out 6256
77: 5 the days of old, the years of ancient t. 5769
106: 3 and he that doeth righteousness at all t. 6256
106:43 Many t did he deliver them; but 6471
119:20 that it hath unto thy judgments at all t. 6256
119:164 Seven t a day do I praise thee because NIH
Pr 5:19 let her breasts satisfy thee at all t; and 6256
17:17 A friend loveth at all t, and a brother is 6256
24:16 For a just man falleth seven t, and riseth up NIH
Ecc 8:12 Though a sinner do evil an hundred t, and NIH
Isa 14:31 and none shall be alone in his appointed t. 4151
33: 6 knowledge shall be the stability of thy t, 6256
37:26 and of ancient t, that I have formed it? 3117
46:10 from ancient t the things that are not yet 6924
Jer 8: 7 in the heaven knoweth her appointed t; 4150
Eze 12:27 and he prophesieth of the t that are far off. 6256
Da 1:20 he found them ten t better than all 3027
2:21 he changeth the t and the seasons: 5732
3:19 seven t more than it was wont to be heat. NIH
4:16 unto him; and let seven t pass over him. 5732
4:23 of the field, till seven t pass over him; 5732
4:25 of heaven, and seven t shall pass over thee, 5732
4:32 as oxen, and seven t shall pass over thee, 5732
6:10 he kneeled upon his knees three t a day, 2166
6:13 but maketh his petition three t a day. 2166
7:10 ten thousand t ten thousand stood before NIH
7:25 most High, and think to change t and laws: 2166
7:25 until a time and t and the dividing of time. 5732
9:25 and the wall, even in troublous t. 6256
11: 6 and he that strengthened her in these t. 6256
11:14 in those t there shall many stand up against 6256
12: 7 ever that it shall be for a time, t, and a half; 4150
Mt 16: 3 but can ye not discern the signs of the t? 2540
18:21 against me, and I forgive him? till seven t? 2034
18:22 unto him, I say not unto thee, Until seven t: 2034
18:22 seven times: but, Until seventy t seven. 1441
Lk 17: 4 And if he trespass against thee seven t in a 2034
17: 4 and seven t in a day turn again to thee, 2034
21:24 until the t of the Gentiles be fulfilled. 2540
Ac 1: 7 It is not for you to know the t or 5550
3:19 when the t of refreshing shall come from 2540
3:21 Whom the heaven must receive until the t 5550
11:10 And this was done three t: and 1909+5151
14:16 Who in t past suffered all nations to walk in 1074
17:26 and hath determined the t before appointed, 2540
17:30 And the t of this ignorance God winked at; 5550
Ro 11:30 For as ye in t past have not believed God, 4218
2Co 11:24 Of the Jews five t received I forty stripes 3999
Gal 1:23 That he which persecuted us in t past now 4218
4:10 observe days, and months, and t, and years. 2540
Eph 1:10 That in the dispensation of the fulness of t 2540
2: 3 in t past in the lusts of our flesh, 4218
1Th 5: 1 But of the t and the seasons, brethren, 5550
1Ti 4: 1 that in the latter t some shall depart from 2540
6:15 Which in his t he shall shew, who is 2540
2Ti 3: 1 that in the last days perilous t shall come. 2540
Tit 1: 3 But hath in due t manifested his word 2540
Heb 1: 1 who at sundry t and in divers manners 4181
1Pe 1:20 but was manifest in these last t for you, 5550
Rev 5:11 the number of them was ten thousand t ten NIG
12:14 and t, and half a time, from the face of 2540

TIMEUS (1)
Mk 10:46 of people, blind Bartimeus, the son of T, 5090

TIMNA (4)
Ge 36:12 T was concubine to Eliphaz Esau's son; 8555
36:22 and Hemam; and Lotan's sister was T. 8555
1Ch 1:36 and Gatam, Kenaz, and T, and Amalek. 8555
1:39 and Homam: and T was Lotan's sister. 8555

TIMNAH (5)
Ge 36:40 duke T, duke Alvah, duke Jetheth, 8555
Jos 15:10 down to Beth-shemesh, and passed on to T: 8553
15:57 Cain, Gibeah, and T; ten cities with their 8553
1Ch 1:51 duke T, duke Aliah, duke Jetheth, 8555
2Ch 28:18 T with the villages thereof, Gimzo also and 8553

TIMNATH (8)
Ge 38:12 and went up unto his sheepshearers to T, he 8553
38:13 Behold thy father in law goeth up to T to 8553
38:14 in an open place, which is by the way to T; 8553
Jdg 14: 1 Samson went down to T, and saw a woman 8553
14: 1 saw a woman in T of the daughters of 8553
14: 2 I have seen a woman in T of the daughters 8553
14: 5 to T, and came to the vineyards of 8553
14: 5 and came to the vineyards of T: 8553

TIMNATH-HERES (1) [TIMNATH-SERAH]
Jdg 2: 9 him in the border of his inheritance in T, 8556

TIMNATH-SERAH (2) [TIMNATH-HERES]
Jos 19:50 which he asked, even T in mount Ephraim: 8556
24:30 him in the border of his inheritance in T, 8556

TIMNITE (1)
Jdg 15: 6 the son in law of the T, because he had 8554

TIMON (1)
Ac 6: 5 and T, and Parmenas, and Nicolas a 5096

TIMOTHEUS (19) [TIMOTHY]
Ac 16: 1 named T, the son of a certain woman, 5095
17:14 to the sea: but Silas and T abode there still. 5095
17:15 and T for to come to him with all speed, 5095
18: 5 and T were come from Macedonia, 5095
19:22 that ministered unto him, T and Erastus; 5095
20: 4 and Gaius of Derbe, and T; and of Asia, 5095
Ro 16:21 T my workfellow, and Lucius, and Jason, 5095
1Co 4:17 For this cause have I sent unto you T, 5095
16:10 Now if T come, see that he may be with 5095
16: S and Fortunatus, and Achaicus, and T. 5095
2Co 1:19 even by me and Silvanus and T, was not 5095
Php 1: 1 Paul and T, the servants of Jesus Christ, 5095
2:19 But I trust in the Lord Jesus to send T 5095
Col 1: 1 by the will of God, and T our brother, 5095
1Th 1: 1 Paul, and Silvanus, and T, unto the church 5095
3: 2 And sent T, our brother, and minister of 5095
3: 6 But now when T came from you unto us, 5095
2Th 1: 1 Paul, and Silvanus, and T, unto the church 5095
2Ti 4: S The second epistle unto T, ordained 5095

TIMOTHY (9) [TIMOTHEUS]
2Co 1: 1 and T our brother, unto the church of God 5095
1Ti 1: 2 Unto T, my own son in the faith: Grace, 5095
1:18 This charge I commit unto thee, son T, 5095
6:20 O T, keep that which is committed to thy 5095
6: S The first to T was written from Laodicea, 5095
2Ti 1: 2 To T, my dearly beloved son: Grace, 5095
Phm 1: 1 prisoner of Jesus Christ, and T our brother, 5095

Heb 13:23 Know ye that *our* brother **T** is set at liberty; *5095*
13: S Written to the Hebrews from Italy by **T**. *5095*

TIN (5)
Nu 31:22 the brass, the iron, the **t**, and the lead, 913
Isa 1:25 away thy dross, and take away all thy **t**: 913
Eze 22:18 all they *are* brass, and **t**, and iron, and lead, 913
22:20 and brass, and iron, and lead, and **t**, 913
27:12 with silver, iron, **t**, and lead, they traded in 913

TINDER See TOW

TINGLE (3)
1Sa 3:11 the ears of every one that heareth it shall **t**. 6750
2Ki 21:12 heareth of it, both his ears shall **t**. 6750
Jer 19: 3 which whosoever heareth, his ears shall **t**. 6750

TINKLING (3)
Isa 3:16 *as* they go, and **making a t** with their feet: 5913
3:18 of *their* **t ornaments** *about their feet,* 5914
1Co 13: 1 am become *as* sounding brass, or a **t** cymbal. *214*

TIP (9)
Ex 29:20 put *it* upon the **t** of the *right* ear of Aaron, 8571
29:20 upon the **t** of the right ear of his sons, and 8571
Lev 8:23 put *it* upon the **t** of Aaron's right ear, and 8571
8:24 Moses put of the blood upon the **t** of their 8571
14:14 the priest shall put *it* upon the **t** of the right 8571
14:17 **t** of the right ear of him that is to be 8571
14:25 put *it* upon the **t** of the right ear of him that 8571
14:28 **t** of the right ear of him that is to be 8571
Lk 16:24 that he may dip the **t** of his finger in water, *206*

TIPHSAH (2)
1Ki 4:24 from **T** even to Azzah, over all the kings on 8607
2Ki 15:16 Menahem smote **T**, and all that *were* 8607

TIRAS (2)
Ge 10: 2 and Javan, and Tubal, and Meshech, and **T**. 8494
1Ch 1: 5 and Javan, and Tubal, and Meshech, and **T**. 8494

TIRATHITES (1)
1Ch 2:55 the **T**, the Shimeathites, *and* Suchathites. 8654

TIRE (1) [TIRED, TIRES]
Eze 24:17 bind the **t of** thine **head** upon thee, and 6287

TIRED (1) [TIRE]
2Ki 9:30 and **t** her head, and looked out at a window. 3190

TIRES (2) [TIRE]
Isa 3:18 and *their* **round t like the moon**, 7720
Eze 24:23 your **t** *shall be* upon your heads, and 6287

TIRHAKAH (2)
2Ki 19: 9 when he heard say of **T** king of Ethiopia, 8640
Isa 37: 9 he heard say concerning **T** king of 8640

TIRHANAH (1)
1Ch 2:48 Caleb's concubine, bare Sheber, and **T**. 8647

TIRIA (1)
1Ch 4:16 Ziph, and Ziphah, **T**, and Asareel. 8493

TIRSHATHA (5)
Ezr 2:63 the **T** said unto them, that they should not 8660
Ne 7:65 the **T** said unto them, that they should not 8660
7:70 The **T** gave to the treasure a thousand 8660
8: 9 which *is* the **T**, and Ezra the priest 8660
10: 1 the **T**, the son of Hachaliah, and Zidkijah, 8660

TIRZAH (18)
Nu 26:33 and Noah, Hoglah, Milcah, and **T**. 8656
27: 1 Noah, and Hoglah, and Milcah, and **T**. 8656
36:11 **T**, and Hoglah, and Milcah, and Noah, 8656
Jos 12:24 The king of **T**, one: all the kings thirty and 8656
17: 3 Mahlah, and Noah, Hoglah, Milcah, and **T**. 8656
1Ki 14:17 wife arose, and departed, and came to **T**: 8656
15:21 left off building of Ramah, and dwelt in **T**. 8656
15:33 son of Ahijah to reign over all Israel in **T**, 8656
16: 6 slept with his fathers, and was buried in **T**: 8656
16: 8 the son of Baasha to reign over Israel in **T**, 8656
16: 9 conspired against him, as he *was* in **T**, 8656
16: 9 house of Arza steward of *his* house in **T**. 8656
16:15 of Judah did Zimri reign seven days in **T**. 8656
16:17 all Israel with him, and they besieged **T**. 8656
16:23 twelve years: six years reigned he in **T**. 8656
2Ki 15:14 Menahem the son of Gadi went up from **T**, 8656
15:16 *were* therein, and the coasts thereof from **T**: 8656
SS 6: 4 Thou *art* beautiful, O my love, as **T**, 8656

TISHBITE (6)
1Ki 17: 1 Elijah the **T**, *who was* of the inhabitants of 8664
21:17 word of the LORD came to Elijah the **T**, 8664
21:28 word of the LORD came to Elijah the **T**, 8664
2Ki 1: 3 angel of the LORD said to Elijah the **T**, 8664
1: 8 his loins. And he said, It *is* Elijah the **T**. 8664
9:36 which he spake by his servant Elijah the **T**, 8664

TITHE (14) [TITHES, TITHING]
Lev 27:30 all the **t** of the land, *whether* of the seed of 4643
27:32 *concerning* the **t** of the herd, or of the flock, 4643
Nu 18:26 it for the LORD, *even* a tenth *part* of the **t**. 4643
Dt 12:17 Thou mayest not eat within thy gates the **t** 4643
14:22 Thou shalt **truly t** all the increase of 6237+6237
14:23 the **t** of thy corn, of thy wine, and of thine 4643
14:28 all the **t** of thine increase the same year, 4643
2Ch 31: 5 the **t** of all *things* brought they in 4643
31: 6 they also brought in the **t** of oxen and 4643
31: 6 the **t** of holy *things* which were consecrated 4643
Ne 10:38 the Levites shall bring up the **t** of the tithes 4643
13:12 Then brought all Judah the **t** of the corn and 4643
Mt 23:23 for ye **pay t of** mint and anise and cummin, *586*
Lk 11:42 for ye **t** mint and rue and all *manner of* *586*

TITHES (24) [TITHE]
Ge 14:20 into thy hand. And he gave him **t** of all. 4643
Lev 27:31 if a man will at all redeem *ought* of his **t**, 4643
Nu 18:24 the **t** of the children of Israel, which they 4643
18:26 When ye take of the children of Israel the **t** 4643
18:28 offering unto the LORD of all your **t**, 4643
Dt 12: 6 your **t**, and heave offerings of your hand, 4643
12:11 your **t**, and the heave offering of your hand, 4643
26:12 all the **t** of thine increase the third year, 4643
2Ch 31:12 brought in the offerings and the **t** and 4643
Ne 10:37 the **t** of our ground unto the Levites, 4643
10:37 that the same Levites *might* have the **t** in all 6237
10:38 with the Levites, when the Levites **take t**: 6237
10:38 the Levites shall bring up the tithe of the **t** 4643
12:44 for the firstfruits, and for the **t**, 4643
13: 5 the vessels, and the **t** of the corn, the new 4643
Am 4: 4 *every* morning, *and* your **t** after three years: 4643
Mal 3: 8 have we robbed thee? *In* **t** and offerings. 4643
3:10 Bring ye all the **t** into the storehouse, that 4643
Lk 18:12 in the week, I **give t** of all that I possess. *586*
Heb 7: 5 to **take t** of the people according to the law, *586*
7: 6 counted from them **received t** of Abraham, *1183*
7: 8 And here men that die receive **t**; but *1181*
7: 9 as *I* may so say, Levi also, who receiveth **t**, *1181*
7: 9 who receiveth tithes, **payed t** in Abraham. *1183*

TITHING (2) [TITHE]
Dt 26:12 When thou hast made an end of **t** all 6237
26:12 *which is* the year of **t**, and hast given *it* unto 4643

TITLE (3) [TITLES]
2Ki 23:17 he said, What **t** *is* that that I see? And 6725
Jn 19:19 And Pilate wrote a **t**, and put *it* on *5102*
19:20 This **t** then read many of the Jews: for *5102*

TITLES (2) [TITLE]
Job 32:21 neither let me **give flattering t** unto man. 3655
32:22 For I know not to **give flattering t**; *in so* 3655

TITTLE (2)
Mt 5:18 or one **t** shall in no wise pass from the law, *2762*
Lk 16:17 earth to pass, than one **t** of the law to fail. *2762*

TITUS (15)
2Co 2:13 because I found not **T** my brother: *5103*
7: 6 comforted us by the coming of **T**; *5103*
7:13 the more joyed we for the joy of **T**, *5103*
7:14 so our boasting, which *I made* before **T**, *5103*
8: 6 Insomuch that we desired **T**, that as he had *5103*
8:16 earnest care into the heart of **T** for you. *5103*
8:23 Whether *any do inquire* of **T**, *he is* my *5103*
12:18 I desired **T**, and with *him* I sent a brother. *5103*
12:18 Did **T** make a gain of you? walked we not *5103*
13: S *a city* of Macedonia, by **T** and Lucas. *5103*
Gal 2: 1 with Barnabas, and took **T** with *me* also. *5103*
2: 3 But neither **T**, who was with me, being a *5103*

2Ti 4:10 Crescens to Galatia, **T** unto Dalmatia. *5103*
Tit 1: 4 To **T**, *mine* own son after the common *5103*
3: S It was written to **T**, ordained the first *5103*

TIZITE (1)
1Ch 11:45 son of Shimri, and Joha his brother, the **T**, 8491

TO (13641) [HERETOFORE, HITHERTO, INTO, THERETO, WHERETO] See Index

TOAH (1)
1Ch 6:34 of Jeroham, the son of Eliel, the son of **T**, 8430

TOB (2)
Jdg 11: 3 his brethren, and dwelt in the land of **T**: 2897
11: 5 went to fetch Jephthah out of the land of **T**: 2897

TOB-ADONIJAH (1)
2Ch 17: 8 and Adonijah, and Tobijah, and **T**, Levites; 2899

TOBIAH (15)
Ezr 2:60 the children of **T**, the children of Nekoda, 2900
Ne 2:10 and **T** the servant, the Ammonite, 2900
2:19 **T** the servant, the Ammonite, and 2900
4: 3 Now **T** the Ammonite *was* by him, and 2900
4: 7 **T**, and the Arabians, and the Ammonites, 2900
6: 1 **T**, and Geshem the Arabian, and the rest of 2900
6:12 for **T** and Sanballat had hired him. 2900
6:14 think thou upon **T** and Sanballat according 2900
6:17 nobles of Judah sent many letters unto **T**, 2900
6:17 and *the letters* of **T** came unto them. 2900
6:19 to him. *And* **T** sent letters to put me in fear. 2900
7:62 the children of **T**, the children of Nekoda, 2900
13: 4 of the house of our God, *was* allied unto **T**: 2900
13: 7 of the evil that Eliashib did for **T**, 2900
13: 8 I cast forth all the household stuff of **T** out 2900

TOBIJAH (3)
2Ch 17: 8 and **T**, and Tob-adonijah, Levites; 2900
Zec 6:10 *even* of Heldai, of **T**, and of Jedaiah, 2900
6:14 to **T**, and to Jedaiah, and to Hen the son of 2900

TOCHEN (1)
1Ch 4:32 Ain, Rimmon, and **T**, and Ashan, 8507

TODAY See TO DAY

TOE (6) [TOES]
Ex 29:20 upon the **great t** of their right foot, and 931
Lev 8:23 and upon the **great t** of his right foot. 931
14:14 and upon the **great t** of his right foot: 931
14:17 and upon the **great t** of his right foot, 931
14:25 and upon the **great t** of his right foot: 931
14:28 and upon the **great t** of his right foot, 931

TOES (7) [TOE]
Lev 8:24 and upon the **great t** of their right feet: 931
Jdg 1: 6 and cut off his thumbs and his **great t**. 7272
1: 7 their thumbs and their **great t** cut off, 7272
2Sa 21:20 on every foot six **t**, four and twenty *in* 676
1Ch 20: 6 whose **fingers and t** *were* four and twenty, 676
Da 2:41 whereas thou sawest the feet and **t**, part of 677
2:42 And *as* the **t** of the feet *were* part of iron, and 677

TOGARMAH (4)
Ge 10: 3 of Gomer; Ashkenaz, and Riphath, and **T**. 8425
1Ch 1: 6 of Gomer; Ashchenaz, and Riphath, and **T**. 8425
Eze 27:14 They of the house of **T** traded in thy fairs 8425
38: 6 the house of **T** *of* the north quarters, and all 8425

TOGETHER (484) [ALTOGETHER] See Index

TOHU (1)
1Sa 1: 1 the son of **T**, the son of Zuph, 8459

TOI (3) [TOU]
2Sa 8: 9 When **T** king of Hamath heard that David 8583
8:10 Then **T** sent Joram his son unto king David, 8583
8:10 for Hadadezer had wars with **T**. And *Joram* 8583

TOIL (4) [TOILED, TOILING]
Ge 5:29 us concerning our work and **t** of our hands, 6093
41:51 *said he*, hath made me forget all my **t**, and 5999
Mt 6:28 they grow; they **t** not, neither do they spin: *2872*
Lk 12:27 they **t** not, they spin not; and yet I say unto *2872*

TOILED (1) [TOIL]
Lk 5: 5 we have **t** all the night, and have taken *2872*

TOILING (1) [TOIL]
Mk 6:48 And he saw them **t** in rowing; for the wind *928*

TOKEN (14) [TOKENS]
Ge 9:12 This *is* the **t** of the covenant which I make 226
9:13 it shall be for a **t** of a covenant between me 226
9:17 said unto Noah, This *is* the **t** of the covenant, 226
17:11 it shall be a **t** of the covenant betwixt me and 226
Ex 3:12 this *shall be* a **t** unto thee, that I have sent 226
12:13 the blood shall be to you for a **t** upon 226
13:16 it shall be for a **t** upon thine hand, and 226
Nu 17:10 to be kept for a **t** against the rebels; 226
Jos 2:12 unto my father's house, and give me a true **t**: 226
Ps 86:17 Shew me a **t** for good; that they which hate 226
Mk 14:44 he that betrayed him had given them a **t**, *4953*
Php 1:28 which is to them an **evident t** of perdition, *1732*
2Th 1: 5 *Which is* a **manifest t** of the righteous *1730*
3:17 own hand, which is the **t** in every epistle: *4592*

TOKENS (7) [TOKEN]
Dt 22:15 bring forth *the* **t** *of* the damsel's virginity NIH
22:17 *yet these are the* **t** *of* my daughter's NIH
22:20 *the* **t** *of* virginity be not found for NIH
Job 21:29 go by the way? and do ye not know their **t**, 226
Ps 65: 8 in the uttermost parts are afraid at thy **t**: 226
135: 9 *Who* sent **t** and wonders into the midst of 226
Isa 44:25 That frustrateth the **t** of the liars, and 226

TOKHATH See TIKVATH

TOLA (6) [TOLAITES]
Ge 46:13 **T**, and Phuvah, and Job, and Shimron. 8439
Nu 26:23 *of* **T**, the family of the Tolaites: of Pua, 8439
Jdg 10: 1 arose to defend Israel **T** the son of Puah, 8439
1Ch 7: 1 Now the sons of Issachar *were*, **T**, and 8439
7: 2 And the sons of **T**; Uzzi, and Rephaiah, and 8439
7: 2 heads of their fathers' house, *to wit*, of **T**: 8439

TOLAD (1)
1Ch 4:29 And at Bilhah, and at Ezem, and at **T**, 8434

TOLAITES (1) [TOLA]
Nu 26:23 *of* Tola, the family of the **T**: of Pua, 8440

TOLD (283) [TELL] See Index

TOLERABLE (6)
Mt 10:15 It shall be **more t** for the land of Sodom and *414*
11:22 It shall be **more t** for Tyre and Sidon at *414*
11:24 that it shall be **more t** for the land of Sodom *414*
Mk 6:11 It shall be **more t** for Sodom and *414*
Lk 10:12 that it shall be **more t** in that day for Sodom, *414*
10:14 But it shall be **more t** for Tyre and Sidon at *414*

TOLL (3)
Ezr 4:13 walls set up *again, then* will they not pay **t**, 4061
4:20 **t**, tribute, and custom, *was* paid unto them. 4061
7:24 it *shall* not *be* lawful to impose **t**, tribute, or 4061

TOMB (3) [TOMBS]
Job 21:32 to the grave, and shall remain in the **t**. 1430
Mt 27:60 And laid it in his own new **t**, which he had *3419*
Mk 6:29 and took up his corpse, and laid it in a **t**. *3419*

TOMBS (6) [TOMB]
Mt 8:28 coming out of the **t**, exceeding fierce, so *3419*
23:29 because ye build the **t** of the prophets, and *5028*
Mk 5: 2 immediately there met him out of the **t** a *3419*
5: 3 Who had *his* dwelling among the **t**; *3419*
5: 5 and in the **t**, crying, and cutting himself *3418*
Lk 8:27 neither abode in *any* house, but in the **t**. *3418*

TOMORROW See TO MORROW

TONGS (6)
Ex 25:38 the **t** thereof, and the snuffdishes thereof, 4457
Nu 4: 9 his **t**, and his snuffdishes, and all the oil 4457
1Ki 7:49 and the lamps, and the **t** *of* gold, 4457
2Ch 4:21 the flowers, and the lamps, and the **t**, 4457
Isa 6: 6 *which* he had taken with the **t** from off 4457
44:12 The smith *with* the **t** both worketh in 4621

TONGUE (129) [DOUBLETONGUED, TONGUES]

Ge	10: 5	every one after his **t**, after their families,	3956
Ex	4:10	but I *am* slow of speech, and of a slow **t**.	3956
	11: 7	of Israel shall not a dog move his **t**,	3956
Dt	28:49	a nation whose **t** thou shalt not understand;	3956
Jos	10:21	none moved his **t** against any of	3956
Jdg	7: 5	one that lappeth of the water with his **t**,	3956
2Sa	23: 2	spake by me, and his word *was* in my **t**.	3956
Ezr	4: 7	of the letter *was* written **in the Syrian t**,	762
	4: 7	and interpreted **in the** Syrian **t**.	762
Est	7: 4	and bondwomen, I had **held** my **t**,	2790
Job	5:21	Thou shalt be hid from the scourge of the **t**:	3956
	6:24	Teach me, and I will **hold** my **t**: and	2790
	6:30	Is there iniquity in my **t**? cannot my taste	3956
	13:19	for now, if I **hold** my **t**, I shall give up	2790
	15: 5	and thou choosest the **t** of the crafty.	3956
	20:12	in his mouth, *though* he hide it under his **t**;	3956
	20:16	poison of asps: the viper's **t** shall slay him.	3956
	27: 4	not speak wickedness, nor my **t** utter deceit.	3956
	29:10	their **t** cleaved to the roof of their mouth.	3956
	33: 2	my mouth, my **t** hath spoken in my mouth.	3956
	41: 1	his **t** with a cord *which* thou lettest down?	3956
Ps	5: 9	an open sepulchre; they flatter with their **t**.	3956
	10: 7	fraud: under his **t** *is* mischief and vanity.	3956
	12: 3	*and* the **t** that speaketh proud *things:*	3956
	12: 4	Who have said, With our **t** will we prevail;	3956
	15: 3	*He that* backbiteth not with his **t**, nor doeth	3956
	22:15	my **t** cleaveth *to* my jaws; and thou hast	3956
	34:13	Keep thy **t** from evil, and thy lips from	3956
	35:28	my **t** shall speak of thy righteousness *and*	3956
	37:30	and his **t** talketh of judgment.	3956
	39: 1	heed to my ways, that *I* sin not with my **t**:	3956
	39: 3	the fire burned: *then* spake I with my **t**,	3956
	45: 1	*the* king: my **t** *is* the pen of a ready writer.	3956
	50:19	thy mouth to evil, and thy **t** frameth deceit.	3956
	51:14	my **t** shall sing aloud of thy righteousness.	3956
	52: 2	Thy **t** deviseth mischiefs; like a sharp rasor,	3956
	52: 4	all devouring words, O thou deceitful **t**.	3956
	57: 4	and arrows, and their **t** a sharp sword.	3956
	64: 3	Who whet their **t** like a sword, *and*	3956
	64: 8	So they shall make their own **t** to fall upon	3956
	66:17	my mouth, and *he was* extolled with my **t**.	3956
	68:23	*and* the **t** of thy dogs in the same.	3956
	71:24	My **t** also shall talk of thy righteousness all	3956
	73: 9	and their **t** walketh through the earth.	3956
	109: 2	they have spoken against me *with* a lying **t**.	3956
	119:172	My **t** shall speak of thy word: for all thy	3956
	120: 2	from lying lips, *and* from a deceitful **t**.	3956
	120: 3	what shall be done unto thee, thou false **t**?	3956
	126: 2	filled *with* laughter, and our **t** *with* singing:	3956
	137: 6	let my **t** cleave to the roof of my mouth;	3956
	139: 4	For *there is* not a word in my **t**, *but* lo,	3956
Pr	6:17	a lying **t**, and hands that shed innocent	3956
	6:24	from the flattery of the **t** of a strange	3956
	10:20	The **t** of the just *is as* choice silver:	3956
	10:31	but the froward **t** shall be cut out.	3956
	12:18	of a sword: but the **t** of the wise *is* health.	3956
	12:19	for ever: but a lying **t** *is* but for a moment.	3956
	15: 2	The **t** of the wise useth knowledge aright:	3956
	15: 4	A wholesome **t** *is* a tree of life: but	3956
	16: 1	the answer of the **t**, *is* from the LORD.	3956
	17: 4	*and* a liar giveth ear to a naughty **t**.	3956
	17:20	he that hath a perverse **t** falleth into	3956
	18:21	Death and life *are* in the power of the **t**: and	3956
	21: 6	The getting of treasures by a lying **t** *is* a	3956
	21:23	and his **t** keepeth his soul from troubles.	3956
	25:15	and a soft **t** breaketh the bone.	3956
	25:23	*doth* an angry countenance a backbiting **t**.	3956
	26:28	A lying **t** hateth *those that are* afflicted by	3956
	28:23	favour than he that flattereth with the **t**.	3956
	31:26	and in her **t** *is* the law of kindness.	3956
SS	4:11	honey and milk *are* under thy **t**; and	3956
Isa	3: 8	because their **t** and their doings *are* against	3956
	11:15	the LORD shall utterly destroy the **t** of	3956
	28:11	and another **t** will he speak to this people.	3956
	30:27	*of* indignation, and his **t** as a devouring fire:	3956
	32: 4	the **t** of the stammerers shall be ready to	3956
	33:19	of a stammering **t**, *that thou canst* not	3956
	35: 6	leap as a hart, and the **t** of the dumb sing:	3956
	41:17	*there is* none, *and* their **t** faileth for thirst,	3956
	45:23	every knee shall bow, every **t** shall swear.	3956
	50: 4	The Lord GOD hath given me the **t** of	3956
	54:17	every **t** *that* shall rise against thee in	3956
	57: 4	make ye a wide mouth, *and* draw out the **t**?	3956
	59: 3	your **t** hath muttered perverseness.	3956
Jer	9: 5	they have taught their **t** to speak lies, *and*	3956
	9: 8	Their **t** *is as* an arrow shot out; it speaketh	3956
	18:18	let us smite him with the **t**, and let us not	3956
La	4: 4	The **t** of the sucking child cleaveth to	3956
Eze	3:26	I will make thy **t** cleave to the roof of thy	3956
Da	1: 4	the learning and the **t** of the Chaldeans.	3956
Hos	7:16	fall by the sword for the rage of their **t**:	3956
Am	6:10	shall he say, **Hold** thy **t**: for *we may* not	2013
Mic	6:12	and their **t** *is* deceitful in their mouth.	3956
Hab	1:13	**holdest** thy **t** when the wicked devoureth	2790
Zep	3:13	neither shall a deceitful **t** be found in their	3956
Zec	14:12	their **t** shall consume away in their mouth.	3956
Mk	7:33	into his ears, and he spit, and touched his **t**;	*1100*
	7:35	and the string of his **t** was loosed, and	*1100*
Lk	1:64	and his **t** *loosed,* and he spake, and	*1100*
	16:24	the tip of his finger in water, and cool my **t**;	*1100*
Jn	5: 2	which is called **in the Hebrew t** Bethesda,	*1447*
Ac	1:19	as that field is called in their proper **t**,	*1258*
	2: 8	And how hear we every man in our own **t**,	*1258*
	2:26	did my heart rejoice, and my **t** was glad;	*1100*
	21:40	he spake unto *them* in the Hebrew **t**,	*1258*
	22: 2	that he spake in the Hebrew **t** to them,	*1258*
	26:14	and saying in the Hebrew **t**, Saul, Saul,	*1258*
Ro	14:11	to me, and every **t** shall confess to God.	*1100*
1Co	14: 2	For he that speaketh in an *unknown* **t**	*1100*
	14: 4	He that speaketh in an *unknown* **t** edifieth	*1100*
	14: 9	except ye utter by the **t** words easy to be	*1100*
	14:13	in an *unknown* **t** pray that he may interpret.	*1100*
	14:14	For if I pray in an *unknown* **t**, my spirit	*1100*
	14:19	than ten thousand words in an *unknown* **t**.	*1100*
	14:26	hath a doctrine, hath a **t**, hath a revelation,	*1100*
	14:27	If any *man* speak in an *unknown* **t**, *let it be*	*1100*
Php	2:11	And *that* every **t** should confess that Jesus	*1100*
Jas	1:26	and bridleth not his **t**, but deceiveth his own	*1100*
	3: 5	Even so the **t** is a little member, and	*1100*
	3: 6	And the **t** *is* a fire, a world of iniquity: so	*1100*
	3: 6	so is the **t** amongst our members, that it	*1100*
	3: 8	But the **t** can no man tame; *it is* an unruly	*1100*
1Pe	3:10	let him refrain his **t** from evil, and his lips	*1100*
1Jn	3:18	let us not love in word, neither in **t**;	*1100*
Rev	5: 9	and **t**, and people, and nation;	*1100*
	9:11	whose name **in the Hebrew t** *is* Abaddon,	*1447*
	9:11	but in the Greek *t* hath *his* name Apollyon.	NIG
	14: 6	and kindred, and **t**, and people,	*1100*
	16:16	place called **in the Hebrew t** Armageddon.	*1447*

TONGUES (36) [TONGUE]

Ge	10:20	after their **t**, in their countries, *and* in their	3956
	10:31	after their **t**, in their lands, after their	3956
Ps	31:20	secretly in a pavilion from the strife of **t**.	3956
	55: 9	Destroy, O Lord, *and* divide their **t**: for I	3956
	78:36	and they lied unto him with their **t**.	3956
	140: 3	They have sharpened their **t** like a serpent;	3956
Isa	66:18	that *I* will gather all nations and **t**;	3956
Jer	9: 3	they bend their **t** *like* their bow *for* lies:	3956
	23:31	that use their **t**, and say, He saith.	3956
Mk	16:17	cast out devils; they shall speak with new **t**;	*1100*
Ac	2: 3	And there appeared unto them cloven **t** like	*1100*
	2: 4	and began to speak with other **t**, as	*1100*
	2:11	we do hear them speak in our **t**	*1100*
	10:46	For they heard them speak with **t**, and	*1100*
	19: 6	and they spake with **t**, and prophesied.	*1100*
Ro	3:13	with their **t** they have used deceit;	*1100*
1Co	12:10	of spirits; to another *divers* kinds of **t**;	*1100*
	12:10	to another the interpretation of **t**:	*1100*
	12:28	helps, governments, diversities of **t**.	*1100*
	12:30	do all speak with **t**? do all interpret?	*1100*
	13: 1	Though I speak with the **t** of men and	*1100*
	13: 8	whether *there be* **t**, they shall cease;	*1100*
	14: 5	I would that ye all spake with **t**, but rather	*1100*
	14: 5	prophesieth than he that speaketh with **t**,	*1100*
	14: 6	if I come unto you speaking with **t**,	*1100*
	14:18	my God, I speak with **t** more than you all:	*1100*
	14:21	With *men* of **other t** and other lips will I	*2084*
	14:22	Wherefore **t** are for a sign, not to them that	*1100*
	14:23	and all speak with **t**, and there come in	*1100*
	14:39	to prophesy, and forbid not to speak with **t**.	*1100*
Rev	7: 9	all nations, and kindreds, and people, and **t**,	*1100*
	10:11	and nations, and **t**, and kings.	*1100*
	11: 9	*they* of the people and kindreds and **t** and	*1100*
	13: 7	him over all kindreds, and **t**, and nations.	*1100*
	16:10	and they gnawed their **t** for pain,	*1100*

Rev 17:15 and multitudes, and nations, and **t**. *1100*

TOO (51) See Index

TOOK (752) [TAKE] See Index

TOOKEST (2) [TAKE] See Index

TOOL (4)

Ex 20:25 for if thou lift up thy **t** upon it, thou hast 2719
32: 4 fashioned it with a **graving t**, after he had 2747
Dt 27: 5 thou shalt not lift up *any* iron *t* upon them. NIH
1Ki 6: 7 nor axe *nor* any **t** of iron heard in the house, 3627

TOOTH (11) [CHEEK-TEETH, TEETH, TOOTH'S]

Ex 21:24 Eye for eye, **t** for tooth, hand for hand, 8127
21:24 Eye for eye, tooth for **t**, hand for hand, 8127
21:27 if he smite out his manservant's **t**, or 8127
21:27 manservant's tooth, or his maidservant's **t**; 8127
Lev 24:20 Breach for breach, eye for eye, **t** for tooth: 8127
24:20 Breach for breach, eye for eye, tooth for **t**: 8127
Dt 19:21 eye for eye, **t** for tooth, hand for hand, 8127
19:21 eye for eye, tooth for **t**, hand for hand, 8127
Pr 25:19 *man* in time of trouble *is like* a broken **t**, 8127
Mt 5:38 An eye for an eye, and a **t** for a tooth: *3599*
5:38 An eye for an eye, and a tooth for a **t**: *3599*

TOOTH'S (1) [TOOTH]

Ex 21:27 he shall let him go free for his **t** sake. 8127

TOP (90) [HOUSETOP, HOUSETOPS, TOPS]

Ge 11: 4 a tower, whose **t** *may reach* unto heaven; 7218
28:12 the earth, and the **t** of it reached to heaven: 7218
28:18 *for* a pillar, and poured oil upon the **t** of it. 7218
Ex 17: 9 to morrow I will stand on the **t** of the hill 7218
17:10 Aaron, and Hur went up *to* the **t** of the hill. 7218
19:20 upon mount Sinai, on the **t** of the mount: 7218
19:20 the LORD called Moses *up* to the **t** of 7218
24:17 **t** of the mount in the eyes of the children of 7218
28:32 there shall be a hole in the **t** of it, in 7218
30: 3 the **t** thereof, and the sides thereof round 1406
34: 2 present thyself there to me in the **t** of 7218
37:26 *both* the **t** of it, and the sides thereof round 1406
Nu 14:40 gat them up into the **t** of the mountain, 7218
14:44 they presumed to go up unto the hill **t**: 7218
20:28 and Aaron died there in the **t** of the mount: 7218
21:20 in the country of Moab, *to* the **t** of Pisgah, 7218
23: 9 For from the **t** of the rocks I see him, and 7218
23:14 to the **t** of Pisgah, and built seven altars, 7218
23:28 Balak brought Balaam *unto* the **t** of Peor, 7218
Dt 3:27 Get thee up *into* the **t** of Pisgah, and lift up 7218
28:35 the sole of thy foot unto the **t of** thy **head**. 6936
33:16 upon the **t of the head** of him *that was* 6936
34: 1 *to* the **t** of Pisgah, that *is* over against 7218
Jos 15: 8 the border went up to the **t** of the mountain 7218
15: 9 the border was drawn from the **t** of the hill 7218
Jdg 6:26 the LORD thy God upon the **t** of this rock, 7218
9: 7 and stood in the **t** of mount Gerizim, 7218
9:25 in wait for him in the **t** of the mountains, 7218
9:36 there come people down from the **t** of 7218
9:51 and gat them up to the **t** of the tower. 1406
15: 8 and dwelt in the **t** of the rock Etam. 5585
15:11 three thousand men of Judah went to the **t** 5585
16: 3 carried them up to the **t** of a hill that *is* 7218
1Sa 9:25 with Saul upon the **t of the house**. 1406
9:26 Samuel called Saul to the **t of the house**, 1406
26:13 and stood on the **t** of a hill afar off; 7218
2Sa 2:25 one troop, and stood on the **t** of a hill. 7218
15:32 that *when* David was come to the **t** *of* 7218
16: 1 when David was a little past the **t** *of* 7218
16:22 Absalom a tent upon the **t of the house**; 1406
1Ki 7:17 for the chapiters which *were* upon the **t** of 7218
7:18 to cover the chapiters that *were* upon the **t**, 7218
7:19 (And the chapiters that *were* upon the **t** of 7218
7:22 upon the **t** of the pillars *was* lily work: so 7218
7:35 in the **t** of the base *was there* a round 7218
7:35 on the **t** of the base the ledges thereof and 7218
7:41 that *were* on the **t** of the *two* pillars; 7218
7:41 which *were* upon the **t** of the pillars; 7218
10:19 and the **t** of the throne *was* round behind: 7218
18:42 Elijah went up to the **t** of Carmel; and 7218
2Ki 1: 9 behold, he sat on the **t** of a hill. And he 7218
9:13 put *it* under him on the **t** of the stairs, and 1634
23:12 the altars that *were* on the **t** of the upper 1406
2Ch 3:15 the chapiter that *was* on the **t** *of each* of 7218
4:12 the chapiters *which were* on the **t** of the two 7218
4:12 chapiters which *were* on the **t** of the pillars; 7218
25:12 brought them unto the **t** of the rock, and 7218
25:12 cast them down from the **t** of the rock, 7218
Est 5: 2 drew near, and touched the **t** of the sceptre. 7218
Ps 72:16 in the earth upon the **t** of the mountains; 7218
Pr 8: 2 She standeth in the **t** of high places by 7218
23:34 or as he that lieth upon the **t** of a mast. 7218
SS 4: 8 look from the **t** of Amana, from the top of 7218
4: 8 from the **t** of Shenir and Hermon, from 7218
Isa 2: 2 be established in the **t** of the mountains, 7218
17: 6 three berries in the **t** of the uppermost 7218
30:17 till ye be left as a beacon upon the **t** of a 7218
42:11 let them shout from the **t** of the mountains. 7218
La 2:19 that faint for hunger in the **t** of every street. 7218
4: 1 are poured out in the **t** of every street. 7218
Eze 17: 4 He cropt off the **t** of his young twigs, and 7218
17:22 will set *it;* I will crop off from the **t** of his 7218
24: 7 she set it upon the **t** of a rock; she poured it 6706
24: 8 I have set her blood upon the **t** of a rock, 6706
26: 4 from her, and make her like the **t** of a rock. 6706
26:14 I will make thee like the **t** of a rock: 6706
31: 3 and his **t** was among the thick boughs. 6788
31:10 he hath shot up his **t** among the thick 6788
31:14 neither shoot up their **t** among the thick 6788
43:12 Upon the **t** of the mountain the whole limit 7218
Am 1: 2 and the **t** of Carmel shall wither. 7218
9: 3 though they hide themselves in the **t** of 7218
Mic 4: 1 be established in the **t** of the mountains, 7218
Na 3:10 dashed in pieces at the **t** of all the streets: 7218
Zec 4: 2 with a bowl upon the **t** of it, and his seven 7218
4: 2 which *were* upon the **t** thereof: 7218
Mt 27:51 was rent in twain from the **t** to the bottom; *509*
Mk 15:38 was rent in twain from the **t** to the bottom. *509*
Jn 19:23 without seam, woven from the **t** throughout. *509*
Heb 11:21 worshipped, *leaning* upon the **t** of his staff. *206*

TOPAZ (5)

Ex 28:17 row *shall be* a sardius, a **t**, and a carbuncle: 6357
39:10 *first* row *was* a sardius, a **t**, and a carbuncle: 6357
Job 28:19 The **t** of Ethiopia shall not equal it, 6357
Eze 28:13 **t**, and the diamond, the beryl, the onyx, and 6357
Rev 21:20 the eighth, beryl; the ninth, a **t**; the tenth, *5116*

TOPHEL (1)

Dt 1: 1 **T**, and Laban, and Hazeroth, and Dizahab. 8603

TOPHET (9) [TOPHETH]

Isa 30:33 For **T** *is* ordained of old; yea, for the king it 8613
Jer 7:31 they have built the high places of **T**, 8612
7:32 that it shall no more be called **T**, 8612
7:32 for they shall bury in **T**, till there be no 8612
19: 6 that this place shall no more be called **T**, 8612
19:11 they shall bury *them* in **T**, till *there be* no 8612
19:12 and *even* make this city as **T**: 8612
19:13 shall be defiled as the place of **T**, because 8612
19:14 came Jeremiah from **T**, whither the LORD 8612

TOPHETH (1) [TOPHET]

2Ki 23:10 he defiled **T**, which *is* in the valley of 8612

TOPMOST See OUTMOST; UPPERMOST

TOPS (10) [TOP]

Ge 8: 5 were the **t** of the mountains seen. 7218
2Sa 5:24 of a going in the **t** of the mulberry trees, 7218
1Ki 7:16 to set upon the **t** of the pillars: 7218
1Ch 14:15 of going in the **t** of the mulberry trees, 7218
Job 24:24 and cut off as the **t** of the ears of corn. 7218
Isa 2:21 into the **t** of the ragged rocks, for fear of 5585
15: 3 on the **t of** their **houses**, and in their streets, 1406
Eze 6:13 in all the **t** of the mountains, and 7218
Hos 4:13 They sacrifice upon the **t** of the mountains, 7218
Joel 2: 5 Like the noise of chariots on the **t** of 7218

TORCH (1) [TORCHES]

Zec 12: 6 the wood, and like a **t** of fire in a sheaf; 3940

TORCHES (3) [TORCH]

Na 2: 3 the chariots *shall be* with flaming **t** in 6393
2: 4 they shall seem like **t**, they shall run like 3940
Jn 18: 3 thither with lanterns and **t** and weapons. *2985*

TORMENT (11) [TORMENTED, TORMENTORS, TORMENTS]

Mt 8:29 art thou come hither to **t** us before the time? *928*

T

Mk 5: 7 I adjure thee by God, that thou **t** me not. *928*
Lk 8:28 of God most high? I beseech thee, **t** me not. *928*
16:28 lest they also come into this place of **t**. *931*
1Jn 4:18 because fear hath **t**. He that feareth is not *2851*
Rev 9: 5 and their **t** *was* as the torment of a scorpion, *929*
9: 5 and their torment *was* as the **t** of a scorpion, *929*
14:11 And the smoke of their **t** ascendeth up for *929*
18: 7 so much **t** and sorrow give her: *929*
18:10 Standing afar off for the fear of her **t**, saying, *929*
18:15 shall stand afar off for the fear of her **t**, *929*

TORMENTED (8) [TORMENT]
Mt 8: 6 lieth at home sick of the palsy, grievously **t**. *928*
Lk 16:24 cool my tongue; for I am **t** in this flame. *3600*
16:25 but now he is comforted, and thou art **t**. *3600*
Heb 11:37 and goatskins; being destitute, afflicted, **t**; *2558*
Rev 9: 5 but that they should be **t** five months: *928*
11:10 these two prophets **t** them that dwelt on *928*
14:10 and he shall be **t** with fire and brimstone in *928*
20:10 and shall be **t** day and night for ever and *928*

TORMENTORS (1) [TORMENT]
Mt 18:34 lord was wroth, and delivered him to the **t**, *930*

TORMENTS (2) [TORMENT]
Mt 4:24 that were taken with divers diseases and **t**, *931*
Lk 16:23 being in **t**, and seeth Abraham afar off, and *931*

TORN (17) [TEAR]
Ge 31:39 **That which was t** ***of beasts*** I brought not 2966
44:28 and I said, Surely he is **t in pieces**; 2963+2963
Ex 22:13 If it be **t in pieces**, *then* let him bring 2963+2963
22:13 he shall not make good that which was **t**. 2966
22:31 neither shall ye eat *any* flesh *that is* **t** *of* 2966
Lev 7:24 the fat of **that which is t** *with beasts*, may 2966
17:15 **that which was t** *with beasts, whether it be* 2966
22: 8 is **t** *with beasts*, he shall not eat to defile 2966
1Ki 13:26 which hath **t** him, and slain him, 7665
13:28 lion had not eaten the carcase, nor **t** the ass. 7665
Isa 5:25 their carcases were **t** in the midst of 5478
Jer 5: 6 that goeth out thence shall be **t in pieces**: 2963
Eze 4:14 that which dieth of itself, or is **t in pieces**; 2966
44:31 of itself, or **t**, whether it be fowl or beast. 2966
Hos 6: 1 for he hath **t**, and he will heal us; he hath 2963
Mal 1:13 ye brought *that which was* **t**, and the lame, 1497
Mk 1:26 And when the unclean spirit had **t** him, and *4682*

TORTOISE (1)
Lev 11:29 and the mouse, and the **t** after his kind, 6632

TORTURED (1)
Heb 11:35 and others were **t**, not accepting *5178*

TOSS (2) [TOSSED, TOSSINGS]
Isa 22:18 **surely violently turn and t** 6801+6801+6802
Jer 5:22 though the waves thereof **t** themselves, 1607

TOSSED (7) [TOSS]
Ps 109:23 I am **t up and down** as the locust. 5287
Pr 21: 6 by a lying tongue *is* a vanity **t to and fro** 5086
Isa 54:11 **t with tempest**, *and* not comforted, behold, 5590
Mt 14:24 now in the midst of the sea, **t** with waves: *928*
Ac 27:18 we being exceedingly **t with a tempest**, *5492*
Eph 4:14 **t to and fro**, and carried about with every *2831*
Jas 1: 6 wave of the sea driven with the wind and **t**. *4494*

TOSSINGS (1) [TOSS]
Job 7: 4 I am full ***of* t to and fro** unto the dawning 5076

TOTTERING (1)
Ps 62: 3 a bowing wall *shall ye be, and as* a **t** fence. 1760

TOU (2) [TOI]
1Ch 18: 9 Now when **T** king of Hamath heard how 8583
18:10 (for Hadarezer had war with **T**;) and 8583

TOUCH (48) [TOUCHED, TOUCHETH, TOUCHING]
Ge 3: 3 not eat of it, neither shall ye **t** it, lest ye die. 5060
20: 6 therefore suffered I thee not to **t** her. 5060
Ex 19:12 *not* up into the mount, or **t** the border of it: 5060
19:13 There shall not a hand **t** it, but he shall 5060
Lev 5: 2 Or if a soul **t** any unclean thing, whether *it* 5060
5: 3 Or if he **t** the uncleanness of man, 5060
6:27 Whatsoever shall **t** the flesh thereof shall be 5060
7:21 Moreover the soul that shall **t** any unclean 5060
11: 8 ye not eat, and their carcase shall ye not **t**; 5060
11:31 whosoever doth **t** them, when they be dead, 5060
12: 4 she shall **t** no hallowed *thing*, nor come into 5060
Nu 4:15 they shall not **t** *any* holy *thing*, lest they die. 5060
16:26 these wicked men, and **t** nothing of theirs, 5060
Dt 14: 8 eat of their flesh, nor **t** their dead carcase. 5060
Jos 9:19 of Israel: now therefore we may not **t** them. 5060
Ru 2: 9 the young men that *they* shall not **t** thee? 5060
2Sa 14:10 to me, and he shall not **t** thee any more. 5060
18:12 Beware *that* none *t* the young man NIH
23: 7 the man *that* shall **t** them must be fenced 5060
1Ch 16:22 *Saying*, **T** not mine anointed, and do my 5060
Job 1:11 **t** all that he hath, and he will curse thee to 5060
2: 5 **t** his bone and his flesh, and he will curse 5060
5:19 yea, in seven there shall no evil **t** thee. 5060
6: 7 The things *that* my soul refused to **t** *are* as 5060
Ps 105:15 *Saying*, **T** not mine anointed, and do my 5060
144: 5 **t** the mountains, and they shall smoke. 5060
Isa 52:11 **t** no unclean *thing*; go ye out of the midst 5060
Jer 12:14 that **t** the inheritance which I have caused 5060
La 4:14 so that *men* could not **t** their garments. 5060
4:15 depart, depart, **t** not, when they fled away 5060
Hag 2:12 with his skirt do **t** bread, or pottage, or 5060
2:13 If *one that is* unclean *by* a dead body **t** any 5060
Mt 9:21 If I may but **t** his garment, I shall be whole. *681*
14:36 And besought him that they might only **t** *681*
Mk 3:10 insomuch that *they* pressed upon him for to **t** *681*
5:28 For she said, If I may **t** but his clothes, *681*
6:56 besought him that they might **t** if it were but *681*
8:22 man unto him, and besought him to **t** him. *681*
10:13 young children to him, that he should **t** them: *681*
Lk 6:19 And the whole multitude sought to **t** him: *681*
11:46 ye yourselves **t** not the burdens with one of *4379*
18:15 unto him also infants, that he would **t** them: *681*
Jn 20:17 Jesus saith unto her, **T** me not; for I am not *681*
1Co 7: 1 *It is* good for a man not to **t** a woman. *681*
2Co 6:17 and **t** not the unclean *thing*; and I will *681*
Col 2:21 (**T** not; taste not; handle not; *681*
Heb 11:28 lest he that destroyed the firstborn should **t** *2345*
12:20 And if *so much as* a beast **t** the mountain, *2345*

TOUCHED (49) [TOUCH]
Ge 26:29 as we have not **t** thee, and as we have done 5060
32:25 against him, he **t** the hollow of his thigh; 5060
32:32 he **t** the hollow of Jacob's thigh in 5060
Lev 22: 6 The soul which hath **t** *any* such shall be 5060
Nu 19:18 upon him that **t** a bone, or one slain, or one 5060
31:19 whosoever hath **t** *any* slain, purify *both* 5060
Jdg 6:21 **t** the flesh and the unleavened *cakes*; and 5060
1Sa 10:26 a band of men, whose hearts God had **t**. 5060
1Ki 6:27 so that the wing of the one **t** the *one* wall, 5060
6:27 the wing of the other cherub **t** the other 5060
6:27 their wings **t** one another in the midst of 5060
19: 5 an angel **t** him, and said unto him, Arise 5060
19: 7 and **t** him, and said, Arise *and* eat; 5060
2Ki 13:21 **t** the bones of Elisha, he revived, and 5060
Est 5: 2 drew near, and **t** the top of the sceptre. 5060
Job 19:21 my friends; for the hand of God hath **t** me. 5060
Isa 6: 7 my mouth, and said, Lo, this hath **t** thy lips; 5060
Jer 1: 9 put forth his hand, and **t** my mouth. 5060
Eze 3:13 of the living creatures that **t** one another, 5401
Da 8: 5 of the whole earth, and **t** not the ground: 5060
8:18 the ground: but he **t** me, and set me upright. 5060
9:21 **t** me about the time of the evening oblation. 5060
10:10 behold, a hand **t** me, which set me upon my 5060
10:16 *one* like the similitude of the sons of men **t** 5060
10:18 and **t** me *one* like the appearance of a man, 5060
Mt 8: 3 put forth *his* hand, and **t** him, saying, I will; *681*
8:15 And he **t** her hand, and the fever left her: and *681*
9:20 behind *him*, and **t** the hem of his garment: *681*
9:29 Then **t** he their eyes, saying, According to *681*
14:36 and as many as **t** were made perfectly whole. *681*
17: 7 And Jesus came and **t** them, and said, Arise, *681*
20:34 had compassion *on them*, and **t** their eyes: *681*
Mk 1:41 and **t** him, and saith unto him, I will; *681*
5:27 came in the press behind, and **t** his garment. *681*
5:30 in the press, and said, Who **t** my clothes? *681*
5:31 thronging thee, and sayest thou, Who **t** me? *681*
6:56 and as many as **t** him were made whole. *681*
7:33 into his ears, and he spit, and **t** his tongue; *681*
Lk 5:13 put forth *his* hand, and **t** him, saying, I will: *681*
7:14 And he came and **t** the bier: and they that *681*
8:44 behind *him*, and **t** the border of his garment: *681*
8:45 And Jesus said, Who **t** me? When all denied, *681*

T

Lk 8:45 and press *thee,* and sayest thou, Who t me? *681*
8:46 And Jesus said, Somebody hath t me: for I *681*
8:47 all the people for what cause she had t him, *681*
22:51 ye thus far. And he t his ear, and healed him. *681*
Ac 27: 3 And the next *day* we t at Sidon. And Julius *2609*
Heb 4:15 be **t with the feeling** of our infirmities; *4834*
12:18 not come unto the mount that might be t, *5584*

TOUCHETH (40) [TOUCH]
Ge 26:11 He that t this man or his wife shall surely 5060
Ex 19:12 whosoever t the mount shall be surely put 5060
29:37 whatsoever t the altar shall be holy. 5060
30:29 most holy: whatsoever t them shall be holy. 5060
Lev 6:18 by fire: every one that t them shall be holy. 5060
7:19 the flesh that t any unclean *thing* shall not 5060
11:24 whosoever t the carcase of them shall be 5060
11:26 every one that t them shall be unclean. 5060
11:27 whoso t their carcase shall be unclean until 5060
11:36 that which t their carcase shall be unclean. 5060
11:39 he that t the carcase thereof shall be 5060
15: 5 whosoever t his bed shall wash his clothes, 5060
15: 7 he that t the flesh of him that hath the issue 5060
15:10 whosoever t any *thing* that was under him 5060
15:11 whomsoever he t that hath the issue, and 5060
15:12 that he t which hath the issue, shall be 5060
15:19 whosoever t her shall be unclean until 5060
15:21 whosoever t her bed shall wash his clothes, 5060
15:22 whosoever t any thing that she sat upon 5060
15:23 *any* thing whereon she sitteth, when he t it, 5060
15:27 whosoever t those *things* shall be unclean, 5060
22: 4 whoso t any *thing that is* unclean *by* 5060
22: 5 Or whosoever t any creeping thing, 5060
Nu 19:11 He that t the dead *body* of any man shall be 5060
19:13 Whosoever t the dead *body* of *any* man that 5060
19:16 whosoever t one that is slain with a sword 5060
19:21 he that t the water of separation shall be 5060
19:22 whatsoever the unclean *person* t shall be 5060
19:22 the soul that t *it* shall be unclean until even. 5060
Jdg 16: 9 as a thread of tow is broken when it t 7306
Job 4: 5 it t thee, and thou art troubled. 5060
Ps 104:32 it trembleth: he t the hills, and they smoke. 5060
Pr 6:29 whosoever t her shall not be innocent. 5060
Eze 17:10 not utterly wither, when the east wind t it? 5060
Hos 4: 2 they break out, and blood t blood. 5060
Am 9: 5 the Lord God of hosts *is* he that t 5060
Zec 2: 8 for he that t you toucheth the apple of his 5060
2: 8 for he that toucheth you t the apple of his 5060
Lk 7:39 what manner of woman *this is* that t him: *681*
1Jn 5:18 and *that* wicked one t him not. *681*

TOUCHING (30) [TOUCH]
Ge 27:42 Behold, thy brother Esau, **as** t thee, 3807.1
Lev 5:13 **as** t his sin that he hath sinned in one of 5921
Nu 8:26 Thus shalt thou do unto the Levites t their 871.1
1Sa 20:23 *as* t the matter which thou and I have NIH
2Ki 22:18 *As* t the words which thou hast heard; NIH
Ezr 7:24 that t any of the priests and Levites, singers, NIH
Job 37:23 T the Almighty, we cannot find him out: NIH
Ps 45: 1 I speak of the things which I have made t 3807.1
Isa 5: 1 a song of my beloved t his vineyard. 3807.1
Jer 1:16 I will utter my judgments against them t all 5921
21:11 t the house of the king of Judah, 3807.1
22:11 For thus saith the Lord t Shallum the son 413
Eze 7:13 for the vision *is* t the whole multitude 413
Mt 18:19 That if two of you shall agree on earth **as** t *4012*
22:31 But **as** t the resurrection of the dead, *4012*
Mk 12:26 And **as** t the dead, that they rise: have ye *4012*
Lk 23:14 have found no fault in this man *t those* NIG
Ac 5:35 what ye intend to do **as** t these men. *1909*
21:25 **As** t the Gentiles which believe, we have *4012*
24:21 T the resurrection of the dead I am called in *4012*
26: 2 t all *the things* whereof I am accused of *4012*
Ro 11:28 but **as** t the election, *they are* beloved for *2596*
1Co 8: 1 Now **as** t things offered unto idols, *4012*
16:12 **As** t *our* brother Apollos, I greatly desired *4012*
2Co 9: 1 For **as** t the ministering to the saints, it is *4012*
Php 3: 5 of the Hebrews; **as** t the law, a Pharisee; *2596*
3: 6 t the righteousness which is in the law, *2596*
Col 4:10 (t whom ye received commandments: *4012*
1Th 4: 9 But as t brotherly love ye need not that *I* *4012*
2Th 3: 4 And we have confidence in the Lord t you, *1909*

TOW (3)
Jdg 16: 9 as a thread of t is broken when it toucheth 5296
Isa 1:31 the strong shall be as t, and the maker of it 5296
43:17 they are extinct, they are quenched as t. 6594

TOWARD (265) [TOWARDS] See Index

TOWARDS (81) [TOWARD] See Index

TOWEL (2)
Jn 13: 4 and took a t, and girded himself. *3012*
13: 5 to wipe *them* with the t wherewith he was *3012*

TOWER (48) [TOWERS, WATCHTOWER]
Ge 11: 4 Go to, let us **build** us a city and a t, 4026
11: 5 came down to see the city and the t, 4026
35:21 and spread his tent beyond the t of Edar. 4026
Jdg 8: 9 again in peace, I will break down this t. 4026
8:17 he beat down the t of Penuel, and slew 4026
9:46 when all the men of the t of Shechem heard 4026
9:47 that all the men of the t of Shechem were 4026
9:49 that all the men of the t of Shechem died 4026
9:51 But there was a strong t within the city, and 4026
9:51 to them, and gat them up to the top of the t. 4026
9:52 Abimelech came unto the t, and 4026
9:52 went hard unto the door of the t to burn it 4026
2Sa 22: 3 my **high** t, and my refuge, my saviour; 4869
22:51 *He is* the t of salvation for his king: and 4024
2Ki 5:24 when he came to the t, he took *them* from 6076
9:17 there stood a watchman on the t in Jezreel, 4026
17: 9 from the t of the watchmen to the fenced 4026
18: 8 from the t of the watchmen to the fenced 4026
2Ch 20:24 when Judah came toward the **watch** t in 4707
Ne 3: 1 even unto the t of Meah they sanctified it, 4026
3: 1 they sanctified it, unto the t of Hananeel. 4026
3:11 the other piece, and the t of the furnaces. 4026
3:25 the t which lieth out from the king's high 4026
3:26 gate toward the east, and the t that lieth out. 4026
3:27 over against the great t that lieth out, 4026
12:38 from beyond the t of the furnaces even unto 4026
12:39 the t of Hananeel, and the tower of Meah, 4026
12:39 the tower of Hananeel, and the t of Meah, 4026
Ps 18: 2 the horn of my salvation, *and* my **high** t. 4869
61: 3 for me, *and* a strong t from the enemy. 4026
144: 2 my **high** t, and my deliverer; my shield, 4869
Pr 18:10 The name of the Lord *is* a strong t: 4026
SS 4: 4 Thy neck *is* like the t of David builded for 4026
7: 4 Thy neck *is* as a t of ivory; thine eyes *like* 4026
7: 4 thy nose *is* as the t of Lebanon which 4026
Isa 2:15 upon every high t, and upon every fenced 4026
5: 2 built a t in the midst of it, and also made a 4026
Jer 6:27 I have set thee *for* a t *and* a fortress among 969
31:38 t of Hananeel unto the gate of the corner. 4026
Eze 29:10 from the t of Syene even unto the border of 4024
30: 6 from the t of Syene shall they fall in it by 4024
Mic 4: 8 thou, O t of the flock, the strong hold of 4026
Hab 2: 1 set me upon the t, and will watch to see 4692
Zec 14:10 *from* the t of Hananeel unto the king's 4026
Mt 21:33 and built a t, and let it out to husbandmen, *4444*
Mk 12: 1 and built a t, and let it out to husbandmen, *4444*
Lk 13: 4 upon whom the t in Siloam fell, and *4444*
14:28 For which of you, intending to build a t, *4444*

TOWERS (17) [TOWER]
2Ch 14: 7 about *them* walls, and t, gates, and bars, 4026
26: 9 Moreover Uzziah built t in Jerusalem at 4026
26:10 Also he built t in the desert, and 4026
26:15 invented by cunning *men,* to be on the t 4026
27: 4 and in the forests he built castles and t. 4026
32: 5 raised *it* up to the t, and another wall 4026
Ps 48:12 and go round about her: tell the t thereof. 4026
SS 8:10 I *am* a wall, and my breasts like t: then 4026
Isa 23:13 they set up the t thereof, they raised up 971
30:25 day of the great slaughter, when the t fall. 4026
32:14 the forts and t shall be for dens for ever, 975
33:18 where *is* he that counted the t? 4026
Eze 26: 4 the walls of Tyrus, and break down her t: 4026
26: 9 and with his axes he shall break down thy t. 4026
27:11 and the Gammadims were in thy t: 4026
Zep 1:16 the fenced cities, and against the high t. 6438
3: 6 their t are desolate; I made their streets 6438

TOWN (13) [TOWNCLERK, TOWNS]
Jos 2:15 for her house *was* upon the t wall, and 7023
1Sa 16: 4 the elders of the t trembled at his coming, 5892
23: 7 by entering into a t that hath gates and bars. 5892
27: 5 let them give me a place in some t in 5892

Hab	2:12	Woe to him that buildeth a **t** with blood,	5892
Mt	10:11	And into whatsoever city or **t** ye shall enter,	*2968*
Mk	8:23	man by the hand, and led him out of the **t**;	*2968*
	8:26	saying, Neither go into the **t**, nor tell *it* to	*2968*
	8:26	go into the town, nor tell *it* to any in the **t**.	*2968*
Lk	5:17	which were come out of every **t** of Galilee,	*2968*
Jn	7:42	and out of the **t** of Bethlehem, where David	*2968*
	11: 1	the **t** of Mary and her sister Martha.	*2968*
	11:30	Now Jesus was not yet come into the **t**, but	*2968*

TOWNCLERK (1) [TOWN]

Ac	19:35	And when the **t** had appeased the people,	*1122*

TOWNS (45) [TOWN]

Ge	25:16	their names, by their **t**, and by their castles;	2691
Nu	32:41	and took the **small t** thereof,	2333
Dt	3: 5	and bars; beside unwalled **t** a great many.	5892
Jos	13:30	all the **t** of Jair, which *are* in Bashan,	2333
	15:45	Ekron, with her **t** and her villages:	1323
	15:47	Ashdod *with* her **t** and her villages,	1323
	15:47	Gaza *with* her **t** and her villages,	1323
	17:11	and in Asher Beth-shean and her **t**,	1323
	17:11	Ibleam and her **t**, and the inhabitants of Dor	1323
	17:11	the inhabitants of Dor and her **t**, and	1323
	17:11	the inhabitants of Endor and her **t**, and	1323
	17:11	the inhabitants of Taanach and her **t**, and	1323
	17:11	and the inhabitants of Megiddo and her **t**,	1323
	17:16	*both they* who *are* of Beth-shean and her **t**,	1323
Jdg	1:27	out *the inhabitants of* Beth-shean and her **t**,	1323
	1:27	and her towns, nor Taanach and her **t**,	1323
	1:27	nor the inhabitants of Dor and her **t**,	1323
	1:27	nor the inhabitants of Ibleam and her **t**,	1323
	1:27	nor the inhabitants of Megiddo and her **t**:	1323
	11:26	While Israel dwelt in Heshbon and her **t**,	1323
	11:26	in Aroer and her **t**, and in all the cities that	1323
1Ki	4:13	to him *pertained* the **t** of Jair the son of	2333
1Ch	2:23	Aram, with the **t** of Jair, from them,	2333
	2:23	from them, with Kenath, and the **t** thereof,	1323
	5:16	in her **t**, and in all the suburbs of Sharon,	1323
	7:28	habitations *were,* Beth-el and the **t** thereof,	1323
	7:28	and westward Gezer, with the **t** thereof;	1323
	7:28	Shechem also and the **t** thereof, unto Gaza	1323
	7:28	towns thereof, unto Gaza and the **t** thereof:	1323
	7:29	Beth-shean and her **t**, Taanach and	1323
	7:29	Taanach and her **t**, Megiddo and her towns,	1323
	7:29	Megiddo and her **t**, Dor and her towns.	1323
	7:29	Megiddo and her towns, Dor and her **t**.	1323
	8:12	who built Ono, and Lod, with the **t** thereof:	1323
	18: 1	and her **t** out of the hand of the Philistines.	1323
2Ch	13:19	Beth-el with the **t** thereof, and Jeshanah	1323
	13:19	Jeshanah with the **t** thereof, and Ephrain	1323
	13:19	and Ephrain with the **t** thereof.	1323
Est	9:19	of the villages, that dwelt in the unwalled **t**,	5892
Jer	19:15	upon all her **t** all the evil that I have	5892
Zec	2: 4	*as* **t without walls** for the multitude of men	6519
Mk	1:38	he said unto them, Let us go into the next **t**,	*2969*
	8:27	his disciples, into the **t** of Cesarea Philippi:	*2968*
Lk	9: 6	And they departed, and went through the **t**,	*2968*
	9:12	that they may go into the **t** and	*2968*

TRACHONITIS (1)

Lk	3: 1	tetrarch of Iturea and of the region of **T**,	*5139*

TRACONITIS See TRACHONITIS

TRADE (5) [TRADED, TRADING]

Ge	34:10	dwell and **t** you therein, and get you	5503
	34:21	let them dwell in the land, and **t** therein;	5503
	46:32	for their **t** hath been **to feed cattle**;	376+4735
	46:34	Thy servants' **t** hath been **about cattle**	376+4735
Rev	18:17	and sailers, and as many as **t** by sea,	*2038*

TRADED (5) [TRADE]

Eze	27:12	iron, tin, and lead, they **t** in thy fairs.	5414
	27:13	they **t** the persons of men and vessels of	5414
	27:14	They of the house of Togarmah **t** in thy	5414
	27:17	they **t** in thy market wheat of Minnith, and	5414
Mt	25:16	the five talents went and **t** with the same,	*2038*

TRADERS See TRAFFICK; TRAFFICKERS

TRADING (1) [TRADE]

Lk	19:15	how much every *man* had **gained by t**.	*1281*

TRADITION (11) [TRADITIONS]

Mt	15: 2	Why do thy disciples transgress the **t** of	*3862*
	15: 3	the commandment of God by your **t**?	*3862*
	15: 6	of God of none effect by your **t**.	*3862*
Mk	7: 3	eat not, holding the **t** of the elders.	*3862*
	7: 5	disciples according to the **t** of the elders,	*3862*
	7: 8	ye hold the **t** of men, *as* the washing of pots	*3862*
	7: 9	of God, that ye may keep your own **t**.	*3862*
	7:13	word of God of none effect through your **t**,	*3862*
Col	2: 8	and vain deceit, after the **t** of men,	*3862*
2Th	3: 6	and not after the **t** which he received of us.	*3862*
1Pe	1:18	**received by t from** your **fathers**;	*3970*

TRADITIONS (2) [TRADITION]

Gal	1:14	being more exceedingly zealous of the **t** of	*3862*
2Th	2:15	and hold the **t** which ye have been taught,	*3862*

TRAFFICK (5) [TRAFFICKERS]

Ge	42:34	you your brother, and ye shall **t** in the land.	5503
1Ki	10:15	*of* the **t** of the *spice* merchants, and *of* all	4536
Eze	17: 4	young twigs, and carried it into a land of **t**;	3667
	28: 5	*and* by thy **t** hast thou increased thy riches,	7404
	28:18	of thine iniquities, by the iniquity of thy **t**;	7404

TRAFFICKERS (1) [TRAFFICK]

Isa	23: 8	whose **t** *are* the honourable of the earth?	3667

TRAIN (3) [TRAINED]

1Ki	10: 2	she came to Jerusalem with a very great **t**,	2428
Pr	22: 6	**T up** a child in the way he should go: and	2596
Isa	6: 1	and lifted up, and his **t** filled the temple.	7757

TRAINED (1) [TRAIN]

Ge	14:14	he armed his **t** *servants,* born in his own	2593

TRAITOR (1) [TRAITORS, TREASON]

Lk	6:16	and Judas Iscariot, which also was the **t**.	*4273*

TRAITORS (1) [TRAITOR]

2Ti	3: 4	**T**, heady, highminded, lovers of pleasures	*4273*

TRAMPLE (3)

Ps	91:13	and the dragon shalt thou **t under feet**.	7429
Isa	63: 3	them in mine anger, and **t** them in my fury;	7429
Mt	7: 6	lest they **t** them under their feet, and	*2662*

TRANCE (5)

Nu	24: 4	falling *into a* **t**, but having his eyes open:	NIH
	24:16	falling *into a* **t**, but having his eyes open:	NIH
Ac	10:10	but while they made ready, he fell into a **t**,	*1611*
	11: 5	and in a **t** I saw a vision, A certain vessel	*1611*
	22:17	while I prayed in the temple, I was in a **t**;	*1611*

TRANQUILLITY (1)

Da	4:27	the poor; if it may be a lengthening of thy **t**.	7963

TRANSFER See TRANSLATE

TRANSFERRED (1)

1Co	4: 6	I have **in a figure t** to myself and	*3345*

TRANSFIGURED (2)

Mt	17: 2	And was **t** before them: and his face did	*3339*
Mk	9: 2	by themselves: and he was **t** before them.	*3339*

TRANSFORMED (3) [TRANSFORMING]

Ro	12: 2	but be ye **t** by the renewing of your mind,	*3339*
2Co	11:14	for Satan himself is **t** into an angel of light.	*3345*
	11:15	also be **t** as the ministers of righteousness;	*3345*

TRANSFORMING (1) [TRANSFORMED]

2Co	11:13	**t** themselves into the apostles of Christ.	*3345*

TRANSGRESS (14) [TRANSGRESSED, TRANSGRESSEST, TRANSGRESSETH, TRANSGRESSING, TRANSGRESSION, TRANSGRESSIONS, TRANSGRESSOR, TRANSGRESSORS]

Nu	14:41	Wherefore now do ye **t** the commandment	5674
1Sa	2:24	I hear: *ye* **make** the LORD'S people **to t**.	5674
2Ch	24:20	Why **t** ye the commandments of	5674
Ne	1: 8	saying, *If* ye **t**, I will scatter you abroad	4603
	13:27	to **t** against our God in marrying strange	4603
Ps	17: 3	I am purposed *that* my mouth shall not **t**.	5674
	25: 3	let them be ashamed which **t** without cause.	898
Pr	28:21	for for a piece of bread *that* man will **t**.	6586
Jer	2:20	thy bands; and thou saidst, I will not **t**;	5674
Eze	20:38	you the rebels, and them that **t** against me:	6586

T

Am 4: 4 Come *to* Beth-el, and t; *at* Gilgal multiply 6586
Mt 15: 2 Why do thy disciples t the tradition of 3845
15: 3 Why do you also t the commandment of 3845
Ro 2:27 the letter and circumcision dost t the law? 3848

TRANSGRESSED (34) [TRANSGRESS]
Dt 26:13 I have not t thy commandments, 5674
Jos 7:11 they have also t my covenant which I 5674
7:15 he hath t the covenant of the LORD, 5674
23:16 When ye have t the covenant of 5674
Jdg 2:20 Because that this people hath t my 5674
1Sa 14:33 he said, Ye have t: roll a great stone unto me 898
15:24 for I have t the commandment of 5674
1Ki 8:50 all their transgressions wherein they have t 6586
2Ki 18:12 t his covenant, *and* all that Moses 5674
1Ch 2: 7 of Israel, who t in the thing accursed. 4603
5:25 they t against the God of their fathers, and 4603
2Ch 12: 2 because they had t against the LORD, 4603
26:16 for he t against the LORD his God, and 4603
28:19 and t **sore** against the LORD. 4603+4604
36:14 t very **much** after all 4603+4604
Ezr 10:10 Ye have t, and have taken strange wives, 4603
10:13 for we are many that have t in this thing. 6586
Isa 24: 5 because they have t the laws, changed 5674
43:27 and thy teachers have t against me. 6586
66:24 carcases of the men that have t against me: 6586
Jer 2: 8 the pastors also t against me, and 6586
2:29 ye all have t against me, saith the LORD. 6586
3:13 that thou hast t against the LORD thy 6586
33: 8 whereby they have t against me. 6586
34:18 I will give the men that have t my 5674
La 3:42 We have t and have rebelled: thou hast not 6586
Eze 2: 3 they and their fathers have t against me, 6586
18:31 all your transgressions, whereby ye have t; 6586
Da 9:11 Yea, all Israel have t thy law, even by 5674
Hos 6: 7 they like men have t the covenant: 5674
7:13 because they have t against me: though I 6586
8: 1 because they have t my covenant, and 5674
Zep 3:11 thy doings, wherein thou hast t against me: 6586
Lk 15:29 neither t I at any time thy commandment: 3928

TRANSGRESSEST (1) [TRANSGRESS]
Est 3: 3 Why t thou the king's commandment? 5674

TRANSGRESSETH (4) [TRANSGRESS]
Pr 16:10 of the king: his mouth t not in judgment. 4603
Hab 2: 5 Yea also, because he t *by* wine, *he is* a proud 898
1Jn 3: 4 committeth sin t also the **law**: 458+4160
2Jn 1: 9 Whosoever t, 3845

TRANSGRESSING (2) [TRANSGRESS]
Dt 17: 2 of the LORD thy God, in t his covenant, 5674
Isa 59:13 In t and lying against the LORD, and 6586

TRANSGRESSION (51) [TRANSGRESS]
Ex 34: 7 forgiving iniquity and t and sin, and 6588
Nu 14:18 forgiving iniquity and t, and by no means 6588
Jos 22:22 in rebellion, or if in t against the LORD, 4604
1Sa 24:11 see that *there is* neither evil nor t in mine 6588
1Ch 9: 1 were carried away to Babylon for their t. 4604
10:13 t which he **committed** against 4603+4604
2Ch 29:19 Ahaz in his reign did cast away in his t, 4604
Ezr 9: 4 of the t of those that had been carried away; 4604
10: 6 of the t of them that had been carried away. 4604
Job 7:21 why dost thou not pardon my t, and 6588
8: 4 and he have cast them away for their t; 6588
13:23 sins? make me to know my t and my sin. 6588
14:17 My t *is* sealed up in a bag, and thou sewest 6588
33: 9 I am clean without t, I *am* innocent; 6588
34: 6 my right? my wound *is* incurable without t. 6588
Ps 19:13 and I shall be innocent from *the* great t. 6588
32: 1 Blessed *is he whose* t *is* forgiven, 6588
36: 1 The t of the wicked saith within my heart, 6588
59: 3 not *for* my t, nor *for* my sin, O LORD. 6588
89:32 will I visit their t with the rod, and 6588
107:17 Fools because of their t, and because 1870+6588
Pr 12:13 The wicked is snared by the t of *his* lips: 6588
17: 9 He that covereth a t seeketh love; but 6588
17:19 He loveth t that loveth strife: *and* he that 6588
19:11 and *it is* his glory to pass over a t. 6588
28: 2 For the t of a land many *are* the princes 6588
28:24 his father or his mother, and saith, *It is* no t; 6588
29: 6 In the t of an evil man *there is* a snare: but 6588
29:16 the wicked are multiplied, t increaseth: 6588
29:22 up strife, and a furious man aboundeth in t. 6588
Isa 24:20 and the t thereof shall be heavy upon it; and 6588
53: 8 for the t of my people was he stricken. 6588
57: 4 *are* ye not children of t, a seed of falsehood, 6588
58: 1 shew my people their t, and the house of 6588
59:20 unto them that turn from t in Jacob, 6588
Eze 33:12 shall not deliver him in the day of his t: 6588
Da 8:12 against the daily *sacrifice* by reason of t, 6588
8:13 the daily *sacrifice,* and the t of desolation, 6588
9:24 to finish the t, and to make an end of sins, 6588
Am 4: 4 *at* Gilgal multiply t; and bring your 6586
Mic 1: 5 For the t of Jacob *is* all this, and for the sins 6588
1: 5 What *is* the t of Jacob? *is it* not Samaria? 6588
3: 8 to declare unto Jacob his t, and to Israel his 6588
6: 7 shall I give my firstborn *for* my t, the fruit 6588
7:18 passeth by the t of the remnant of his 6588
Ac 1:25 and apostleship, from which Judas **by** t **fell**, 3845
Ro 4:15 for where no law is, *there is* no t. 3847
5:14 not sinned after the similitude of Adam's t, 3847
1Ti 2:14 but the woman being deceived was in the t. 3847
Heb 2: 2 and every t and disobedience received a 3847
1Jn 3: 4 also the law: for sin is the t **of the law**. 458

TRANSGRESSIONS (48) [TRANSGRESS]
Ex 23:21 him not; for he will not pardon your t: 6588
Lev 16:16 and because of their t in all their sins: 6588
16:21 all their t in all their sins, putting them 6588
Jos 24:19 he will not forgive your t nor your sins. 6588
1Ki 8:50 all their t wherein they have transgressed 6588
Job 31:33 If I covered my t as Adam, by hiding mine 6588
35: 6 or *if* thy t be multiplied, what doest thou 6588
36: 9 and their t that they have exceeded. 6588
Ps 5:10 cast them out in the multitude of their t; 6588
25: 7 not the sins of my youth, nor my t: 6588
32: 5 I said, I will confess my t unto the LORD; 6588
39: 8 Deliver me from all my t: make me not 6588
51: 1 of thy tender mercies blot out my t. 6588
51: 3 For I acknowledge my t: and my sin *is* ever 6588
65: 3 *as for* our t, thou shalt purge them away. 6588
103:12 *so* far hath he removed our t from us. 6588
Isa 43:25 *am* he that blotteth out thy t for mine own 6588
44:22 thick cloud, thy t, and, as a cloud, thy sins: 6588
50: 1 and for your t *is* your mother put away. 6588
53: 5 he *was* wounded for our t, *he was* bruised 6588
59:12 For our t are multiplied before thee, and 6588
59:12 for our t *are* with us; and *as for* our 6588
Jer 5: 6 because their t are many, *and* 6588
La 1: 5 hath afflicted her for the multitude of her t: 6588
1:14 The yoke of my t is bound by his hand: 6588
1:22 as thou hast done unto me for all my t: 6588
Eze 14:11 be polluted any more with all their t; 6588
18:22 All his t that he hath committed, they shall 6588
18:28 turneth away from all his t that he hath 6588
18:30 Repent, and turn *yourselves* from all your t; 6588
18:31 Cast away from you all your t, whereby ye 6588
21:24 in that your t are discovered, so that in all 6588
33:10 If our t and our sins *be* upon us, and 6588
37:23 detestable things, nor with any of their t: 6588
39:24 according to their t have I done unto them, 6588
Am 1: 3 For three t of Damascus, and for four, I will 6588
1: 6 For three t of Gaza, and for four, I will not 6588
1: 9 For three t of Tyrus, and for four, I will not 6588
1:11 For three t of Edom, and for four, I will not 6588
1:13 For three t of the children of Ammon, and 6588
2: 1 For three t of Moab, and for four, I will not 6588
2: 4 For three t of Judah, and for four, I will not 6588
2: 6 For three t of Israel, and for four, I will not 6588
3:14 That in the day that I shall visit the t of 6588
5:12 For I know your manifold t and 6588
Mic 1:13 for the t of Israel were found in thee. 6588
Gal 3:19 It was added because of t, till the seed 3847
Heb 9:15 for the redemption of the t that were under 3847

TRANSGRESSOR (5) [TRANSGRESS]
Pr 21:18 for the righteous, and the t for the upright. 898
22:12 and he overthroweth the words of the t. 898
Isa 48: 8 wast called a t from the womb. 6586
Gal 2:18 which I destroyed, I make myself a t. 3848
Jas 2:11 *if* thou kill, thou art become a t of the law. 3848

TRANSGRESSORS (20) [TRANSGRESS]
Ps 37:38 the t shall be destroyed together: the end of 6586
51:13 *Then* will I teach t thy ways; and 6586
59: 5 be not merciful to any wicked t. Selah. 898

Ps119:158 I beheld the t, and was grieved; because 898
Pr 2:22 the earth, and the t shall be rooted out of it. 898
11: 3 but the perverseness of t shall destroy them. 898
11: 6 but t shall be taken in their own naughtiness. 898
13: 2 but the soul of the t *shall eat* violence. 898
13:15 giveth favour: but the way of t *is* hard. 898
23:28 *for* a prey, and increaseth the t among men. 898
26:10 both rewardeth the fool, and rewardeth t. 5674
Isa 1:28 the destruction of the t and of the sinners 6586
46: 8 bring *it* again to mind, O ye t. 6586
53:12 he was numbered with the t; and he bare 6586
53:12 of many, and made intercession for the t. 6586
Da 8:23 when the t are come to the full, a king of 6586
Hos 14: 9 walk in them: but the t shall fall therein. 6586
Mk 15:28 And he was numbered with the t. *459*
Lk 22:37 in me, And he was reckoned among the t: *459*
Jas 2: 9 and are convinced of the law as t. *3848*

TRANSLATE (1) [TRANSLATED, TRANSLATION]
2Sa 3:10 To t the kingdom from the house of Saul, 5674

TRANSLATED (3) [TRANSLATE]
Col 1:13 hath t *us* into the kingdom of his dear Son: *3179*
Heb 11: 5 By faith Enoch was t that *he* should not see *3346*
11: 5 and was not found, because God had t him: *3346*

TRANSLATION (1) [TRANSLATE]
Heb 11: 5 for before his t he had this testimony, *3331*

TRANSPARENT (1)
Rev 21:21 of the city *was* pure gold, as *it were* t glass. *1307*

TRAP (4) [TRAPS]
Job 18:10 in the ground, and a t for him in the way. 4434
Ps 69:22 *been* for *their* welfare, *let it become* a t. 4170
Jer 5:26 setteth snares; they set a t, they catch men. 4889
Ro 11: 9 and a t, and a stumblingblock, and a *2339*

TRAPS (1) [TRAP]
Jos 23:13 they shall be snares and t unto you, and 4170

TRAVAIL (31) [TRAVAILED, TRAVAILEST, TRAVAILETH, TRAVAILING]
Ge 38:27 it came to pass in the time of her t, that, 3205
Ex 18: 8 all the t that had come upon them by 8513
Nu 20:14 Thou knowest all the t that hath befallen 8513
Ps 48: 6 them there, *and* pain, as of a woman **in** t. 3205
Ecc 1:13 this sore t hath God given to the sons of 6045
2:23 For all his days *are* sorrows, and his t grief; 6045
2:26 to the sinner he giveth t, to gather and 6045
3:10 I have seen the t, which God hath given to 6045
4: 4 I considered all t, and every right work, 5999
4: 6 than both the hands full *with* t and 5999
4: 8 This *is* also vanity, yea, it *is* a sore t. 6045
5:14 those riches perish by evil t: and 6045
Isa 23: 4 saying, I t not, nor bring forth children, 2342
53:11 He shall see of the t of his soul, *and* 5999
54: 1 cry aloud, thou *that* didst not t **with child**: 2342
Jer 4:31 I have heard a voice as of a woman **in** t, 2470
6:24 hold of us, *and* pain, as of a woman **in** t. 3205
13:21 not sorrows take thee, as a woman **in** t? 3205
22:23 upon thee, the pain as of a woman **in** t. 3205
30: 6 and see whether a man doth t **with child**? 3205
30: 6 as a woman **in** t, and all faces are turned 3205
49:24 sorrows have taken her as a woman **in** t. 3205
50:43 hold of him, *and* pangs as of a woman **in** t. 3205
La 3: 5 and compassed *me* with gall and t. 8513
Mic 4: 9 for pangs have taken thee as a woman **in** t. 3205
4:10 O daughter of Zion, like a woman **in** t: 3205
Jn 16:21 A woman when she is **in** t hath sorrow, *5088*
Gal 4:19 of whom I t **in birth** again until Christ be *5605*
1Th 2: 9 ye remember, brethren, our labour and t: *3449*
5: 3 upon them, as t upon a *woman* with child; *5604*
2Th 3: 8 wrought with labour and t night and day, *3449*

TRAVAILED (5) [TRAVAIL]
Ge 35:16 and Rachel t, and she had hard labour. 3205
38:28 it came to pass, when she t, that *the one* put 3205
1Sa 4:19 were dead, she bowed herself and t; 3205
Isa 66: 7 Before she t, she brought forth; before her 2342
66: 8 for as soon as Zion t, she brought forth her 2342

TRAVAILEST (1) [TRAVAIL]
Gal 4:27 break forth and cry, thou that t not: *5605*

TRAVAILETH (7) [TRAVAIL]
Job 15:20 The wicked *man* t **with pain** all his days, 2342
Ps 7:14 he t with iniquity, and hath conceived 2254
Isa 13: 8 they shall be in pain as a woman that t: 3205
21: 3 upon me, as the pangs of a woman that t: 3205
Jer 31: 8 and her that t **with child** together: 3205
Mic 5: 3 until the time *that* she which t hath brought 3205
Ro 8:22 and t **in pain together** until now. *4944*

TRAVAILING (3) [TRAVAIL]
Isa 42:14 *now* will I cry like a t **woman**; I will 3205
Hos 13:13 The sorrows of a t *woman* shall come upon 3205
Rev 12: 2 t **in birth**, and pained to be delivered. *5605*

TRAVEL (2) [TRAVELLED, TRAVELLER, TRAVELLERS, TRAVELLETH, TRAVELLING]
Ac 19:29 of Macedonia, Paul's **companions in** t, *4898*
2Co 8:19 of the churches to t **with** us with this grace, *4898*

TRAVELLED (1) [TRAVEL]
Ac 11:19 that arose about Stephen t as far as Phenice, *1330*

TRAVELLER (2) [TRAVEL]
2Sa 12: 4 there came a t unto the rich man, and 1982
Job 31:32 in the street: *but* I opened my doors to the t. 734

TRAVELLERS (1) [TRAVEL]
Jdg 5: 6 and the t walked *through* byways. 1980+5410

TRAVELLETH (2) [TRAVEL]
Pr 6:11 So shall thy poverty come as one that t, and 1980
24:34 So shall thy poverty come *as* one that t; and 1980

TRAVELLING (3) [TRAVEL]
Isa 21:13 ye lodge, O ye t **companies** of Dedanim. 736
63: 1 t in the greatness of his strength? 6808
Mt 25:14 *of heaven is* as a man **t into a far country,** *589*

TRAVERSING (1)
Jer 2:23 *thou art* a swift dromedary t her ways; 8308

TRAYS See SNUFFDISHES

TREACHEROUS (9) [TREACHERY]
Isa 21: 2 the t **dealer** dealeth treacherously, and 898
24:16 the t **dealers** have dealt treacherously; yea, 898
24:16 the t **dealers** have dealt very treacherously. 898
Jer 3: 7 returned not. And her t sister Judah saw *it.* 901
3: 8 yet her t sister Judah feared not, but went 898
3:10 yet for all this her t sister Judah hath not 901
3:11 hath justified herself more than t Judah. 898
9: 2 they *be* all adulterers, an assembly of t *men.* 898
Zep 3: 4 Her prophets *are* light *and* t persons: 900

TREACHEROUSLY (23) [TREACHERY]
Jdg 9:23 the men of Shechem **dealt** t with Abimelech: 898
Isa 21: 2 the treacherous dealer **dealeth** t, and 898
24:16 the treacherous dealers have **dealt** t; yea, 898
24:16 treacherous dealers have **dealt very** t. 898+899
33: 1 **dealest** t, and they dealt not treacherously 898
33: 1 and they **dealt** not t with thee! 898
33: 1 *and* when thou shalt make an end to **deal** t, 898
33: 1 they shall **deal** t with thee. 898
48: 8 I knew *that* thou wouldest **deal very** t, 898+898
Jer 3:20 Surely *as* a wife t departeth from her 898
3:20 so have you **dealt** t with me, O house of 898
5:11 the house of Judah have **dealt very** t 898+898
12: 1 are all they happy that **deal very** t? 898+899
12: 6 thy father, even they have **dealt** t with thee; 898
La 1: 2 *her:* all her friends have **dealt** t with her, 898
Hos 5: 7 They have **dealt** t against the LORD: 898
6: 7 there have they **dealt** t against me. 898
Hab 1:13 lookest thou upon them that **deal** t, 898
Mal 2:10 why do we **deal** t every man against his 898
2:11 Judah hath **dealt** t, and an abomination is 898
2:14 of thy youth, against whom thou hast **dealt** t: 898
2:15 let none **deal** t against the wife of his youth. 898
2:16 take heed to your spirit, that ye **deal** not t. 898

TREACHERY (1) [TREACHEROUS, TREACHEROUSLY]
2Ki 9:23 and said to Ahaziah, *There is* t, O Ahaziah. 4820

TREAD (33) [TREADER, TREADERS, TREADETH, TREADING, TRODDEN, TRODE]
Dt 11:24 the soles of your feet shall t shall be yours: 1869

T

Dt 11:25 you upon all the land that ye shall **t** upon, 1869
33:29 and thou shalt **t** upon their high places. 1869
Jos 1: 3 that the sole of your foot shall **t upon,** 1869
1Sa 5: 5 **t** on the threshold of Dagon in Ashdod unto 1869
Job 24:11 *and* **t** *their* winepresses, and suffer thirst. 1869
40:12 and **t down** the wicked in their place. 1915
Ps 7: 5 let him **t down** my life upon the earth, and 7429
44: 5 through thy name will we **t** them **under** that 947
60:12 for he *it is that* shall **t down** our enemies. 947
91:13 Thou shalt **t** upon the lion and adder: 1869
108:13 for he *it is that* shall **t down** our enemies. 947
Isa 1:12 required this at your hand, to **t** my courts? 7429
10: 6 **t** them **down** like the mire of 4823+7760
14:25 and upon my mountains **t** him **under foot:** 947
16:10 the treaders shall **t out** no wine in *their* 1869
26: 6 The foot shall **t** it **down,** *even* the feet of 7429
63: 3 for I will **t** them in mine anger, and 1869
63: 6 And I will **t down** the people in mine anger, 947
Jer 25:30 as they that **t** *the grapes,* against all 1869
48:33 none shall **t** *with* shouting; *their* shouting 1869
Eze 26:11 the hoofs of his horses shall he **t down** 7429
34:18 ye must **t down** with your feet the residue 7429
Da 7:23 and shall **t** it **down,** and break it in pieces. 1759
Hos 10:11 *and* loveth to **t out** *the corn;* but I passed 1758
Mic 1: 3 and **t** upon the high places of the earth. 1869
5: 5 when he shall **t** in our palaces, then 1869
6:15 thou shalt **t** the olives, but thou shalt not 1869
Na 3:14 go into clay, and **t** the morter, make strong 7429
Zec 10: 5 they shall be as mighty *men,* which **t down** 947
Mal 4: 3 ye shall **t down** the wicked; for they shall 6072
Lk 10:19 I give unto you power to **t** on serpents and *3961*
Rev 11: 2 the holy city shall they **t under foot** forty *3961*

TREADER (1) [TREAD]
Am 9:13 and the **t** of grapes him that soweth seed; 1869

TREADERS (1) [TREAD]
Isa 16:10 the **t** shall tread out no wine in *their* 1869

TREADETH (10) [TREAD]
Dt 25: 4 not muzzle the ox when he **t out** *the corn.* 1758
Job 9: 8 and **t** upon the waves of the sea. 1869
Isa 41:25 as *upon* morter, and as the potter **t** clay. 7429
63: 2 thy garments like him that **t** in the winefat? 1869
Am 4:13 **t** upon the high places of the earth, 1869
Mic 5: 6 our land, and when he **t** within our borders. 1869
5: 8 both **t down,** and teareth in pieces, and 7429
1Co 9: 9 the mouth of the ox that **t out the corn.** *248*
1Ti 5:18 shalt not muzzle the ox that **t out the corn.** *248*
Rev 19:15 and he **t** the winepress of the fierceness and *3961*

TREADING (4) [TREAD]
Ne 13:15 In those days saw I in Judah *some* **t** wine 1869
Isa 7:25 forth of oxen, and for the **t** of lesser cattle. 4823
22: 5 of **t down,** and of perplexity by the Lord 4001
Am 5:11 as your **t** *is* upon the poor, 1318

TREASON (5) [TRAITOR]
1Ki 16:20 the acts of Zimri, and his **t** that he wrought, 7195
2Ki 11:14 rent her clothes, and cried, **T,** Treason. 7195
11:14 rent her clothes, and cried, Treason, **T.** 7195
2Ch 23:13 rent her clothes, and said, **T,** Treason. 7195
23:13 rent her clothes, and said, Treason, **T.** 7195

TREASURE (37) [TREASURED, TREASURER, TREASURERS, TREASURES, TREASUREST, TREASURIES, TREASURY]
Ge 43:23 your father, hath given you **t** in your sacks: 4301
Ex 1:11 they built for Pharaoh **t** cities, Pithom and 4543
19: 5 ye shall be a **peculiar t** unto me above all 5459
Dt 28:12 The LORD shall open unto thee his good **t,** 214
1Ch 29: 8 *them* to the **t** of the house of the LORD, 214
Ezr 2:69 They gave after their ability unto the **t** of 214
5:17 let there be search made in the king's **t** 1596
7:20 bestow *it* out of the king's **t** house. 1596
Ne 7:70 The Tirshatha gave to the **t** a thousand drams 214
7:71 *some* of the chief of the fathers gave to the **t** 214
10:38 our God, to the chambers, into the **t** house. 214
Ps 17:14 whose belly thou fillest *with* thy hid *t:* they NIH
135: 4 unto himself, *and* Israel for his **peculiar t.** 5459
Pr 15: 6 *In* the house of the righteous *is* much **t:** but 2633
15:16 little with the fear of the LORD than great **t** 214
21:20 *There is* **t** to be desired and oil in 214
Ecc 2: 8 the **peculiar t** of kings and of 5459
Isa 33: 6 of salvation: the fear of the LORD *is* his **t.** 214
Eze 22:25 they have taken the **t** and precious things; 2633
Da 1: 2 he brought the vessels *into* the **t** house of his 214
Hos 13:15 he shall spoil the **t** of all pleasant vessels. 214
Mt 6:21 For where your **t** is, there will your heart be *2344*
12:35 A good man out of the good **t** of the heart *2344*
12:35 an evil man out of the evil **t** bringeth forth *2344*
13:44 the kingdom of heaven is like unto **t** hid in *2344*
13:52 which bringeth forth out of his **t** *things* *2344*
19:21 to the poor, and thou shalt have **t** in heaven: *2344*
Mk 10:21 to the poor, and thou shalt have **t** in heaven: *2344*
Lk 6:45 A good man out of the good **t** of his heart *2344*
6:45 an evil man out of the evil **t** of his heart *2344*
12:21 So *is* he that **layeth up t** for himself, and *2343*
12:33 a **t** in the heavens that faileth not, where no *2344*
12:34 For where your **t** is, there will your heart be *2344*
18:22 the poor, and thou shalt have **t** in heaven: *2344*
Ac 8:27 who had the charge of all her **t,** and had *1047*
2Co 4: 7 But we have this **t** in earthen vessels, *2344*
Jas 5: 3 ye have **heaped t together** for the last *2343*

TREASURED (1) [TREASURE]
Isa 23:18 it shall not be **t** nor laid up; for her 686

TREASURER (2) [TREASURE]
Ezr 1: 8 bring forth by the hand of Mithredath the **t,** 1489
Isa 22:15 Go, get thee unto this **t,** *even* unto Shebna, 5532

TREASURERS (4) [TREASURE]
Ezr 7:21 do make a decree to all the **t** which *are* 1490
Ne 13:13 I **made t** over the treasuries, Shelemiah 686
Da 3: 2 and the captains, the judges, the **t,** 1411
3: 3 and captains, the judges, the **t,** 1411

TREASURES (62) [TREASURE]
Dt 32:34 in store with me, *and* sealed up among my **t**? 214
33:19 of the seas, and *of* **t** hid in the sand. 8226
1Ki 7:51 did he put among the **t** of the house of 214
14:26 he took away the **t** of the house of 214
14:26 of the LORD, and the **t** of the king's house; 214
15:18 the gold that were left in the **t** of the house of 214
15:18 the **t** of the king's house, and delivered them 214
2Ki 12:18 all the gold that was found in the **t** of 214
14:14 in the **t** of the king's house, and hostages, 214
16: 8 in the **t** of the king's house, and sent *it for* a 214
18:15 the LORD, and in the **t** of the king's house. 214
20:13 of his armour, and all that was found in his **t:** 214
20:15 there is nothing among my **t** that I have not 214
24:13 he carried out thence all the **t** of the house of 214
24:13 the **t** of the king's house, and cut in pieces 214
1Ch 26:20 Ahijah *was* over the **t** of the house of God, 214
26:20 and over the **t** of the dedicate *things.* 214
26:22 *which were* over the **t** of the house of 214
26:24 the son of Moses, *was* ruler of the **t.** 214
26:26 his brethren *were* over all the **t** of 214
27:25 over the king's **t** *was* Azmaveth the son of 214
2Ch 5: 1 put he among the **t** of the house of God. 214
8:15 concerning any matter, or concerning the **t.** 214
12: 9 took away the **t** of the house of the LORD, 214
12: 9 of the LORD, and the **t** of the king's house; 214
16: 2 gold out of the **t** of the house of the LORD 214
25:24 the **t** of the king's house, the hostages also, 214
36:18 the **t** of the house of the LORD, and 214
36:18 and the **t** of the king, and of his princes; 214
Ezr 6: 1 where the **t** were laid up in Babylon. 1596
Ne 12:44 some appointed over the chambers for the **t,** 214
Job 3:21 and dig for it more than for **hid t;** 4301
38:22 Hast thou entered into the **t** of the snow? or 214
38:22 the snow? or hast thou seen the **t** of the hail, 214
Pr 2: 4 as silver, and searchest for her as *for* **hid t;** 4301
8:21 me to inherit substance; and I will fill their **t.** 214
10: 2 **T** of wickedness profit nothing: but 214
21: 6 The getting of **t** by a lying tongue *is* a vanity 214
Isa 2: 7 and gold, neither *is there any* end of their **t;** 214
10:13 have robbed their **t,** and I have put down 6259
30: 6 their **t** upon the bunches of camels, to a 214
39: 2 of his armour, and all that was found in his **t:** 214
39: 4 there is nothing among my **t** that I have not 214
45: 3 I will give thee the **t** of darkness, and 214
Jer 10:13 and bringeth forth the wind out of his **t.** 214
15:13 thy **t** will I give to the spoil without price, 214
17: 3 give thy substance *and* all thy **t** to the spoil, 214
20: 5 all the **t** of the kings of Judah will I give into 214
41: 8 for we have **t** in the field, *of* wheat, and 4301
48: 7 thou hast trusted in thy works and in thy **t,** 214

Jer 49: 4 that trusted in her t, *saying,* Who shall come 214
50:37 a sword *is* upon her t; and they shall be 214
51:13 abundant in t, thine end is come, *and* 214
51:16 and bringeth forth the wind out of his t. 214
Eze 28: 4 and hast gotten gold and silver into thy t: 214
Da 11:43 he shall have power over the t of gold and 4362
Mic 6:10 Are there yet the t of wickedness *in* 214
Mt 2:11 and when they had opened their t, *2344*
6:19 Lay not up for yourselves t upon earth, *2344*
6:20 But lay up for yourselves t in heaven, *2344*
Col 2: 3 In whom are hid all the t of wisdom and *2344*
Heb 11:26 of Christ greater riches than the t in Egypt: *2344*

TREASUREST (1) [TREASURE]
Ro 2: 5 impenitent heart t up unto thyself wrath *2343*

TREASURIES (10) [TREASURE]
1Ch 9:26 over the chambers and t of the house of God. 214
28:11 of the t thereof, and of the upper chambers 1597
28:12 of the t of the house of God, and of 214
28:12 of God, and of the t of the dedicate *things:* 214
2Ch 32:27 he made himself t for silver, and for gold, 214
Ne 13:12 and the new wine and the oil unto the t. 214
13:13 I made treasurers over the t, Shelemiah 214
Est 3: 9 of the business, to bring *it* into the king's t. 1595
4: 7 to pay to the king's t for the Jews, 1595
Ps 135: 7 for the rain; he bringeth the wind out of his t. 214

TREASURY (9) [TREASURE]
Jos 6:19 they shall come *into* the t of the LORD. 214
6:24 they put *into* the t of the house of 214
Jer 38:11 went *into* the house of the king under the t, 214
Mt 27: 6 It is not lawful for to put them into the t, *2878*
Mk 12:41 And Jesus sat over against the t, and *1049*
12:41 how the people cast money into the t: *1049*
12:43 than all they which have cast into the t: *1049*
Lk 21: 1 the rich *men* casting their gifts into the t. *1049*
Jn 8:20 These words spake Jesus in the t, as he *1049*

TREATISE (1)
Ac 1: 1 The former t have I made, O Theophilus, *3056*

TREATY See LEAGUE

TREE (201) [TREES]
Ge 1:11 *and* the fruit t yielding fruit after his kind, 6086
1:12 the t yielding fruit, whose seed *was* in 6086
1:29 upon the face of all the earth, and every t, 6086
1:29 in the which *is* the fruit of a t yielding seed; 6086
2: 9 to grow every t that is pleasant to the sight, 6086
2: 9 the t of life also in the midst of the garden, 6086
2: 9 and the t of knowledge of good and evil. 6086
2:16 Of every t of the garden thou mayest freely 6086
2:17 of the t of the knowledge of good and evil, 6086
3: 1 Ye shall not eat of every t of the garden? 6086
3: 3 of the fruit of the t which *is* in the midst of 6086
3: 6 when the woman saw that the t *was* good 6086
3: 6 a t to be desired to make *one* wise, she took 6086
3:11 Hast thou eaten of the t, whereof I 6086
3:12 with me, she gave me of the t, and I did eat. 6086
3:17 hast eaten of the t, of which I commanded 6086
3:22 take also of the t of life, and eat, and 6086
3:24 every way, to keep the way of the t of life. 6086
18: 4 your feet, and rest yourselves under the t: 6086
18: 8 he stood by them under the t, and they did 6086
30:37 and of the hazel and **chesnut** t; 6196
40:19 from off thee, and shall hang thee on a t; 6086
Ex 9:25 of the field, and brake every t of the field. 6086
10: 5 shall eat every t which groweth for you out 6086
15:25 the LORD shewed him a t, *which* when he 6086
Lev 27:30 *or* of the fruit of the t, *is* the LORD's: 6086
Nu 6: 4 he eat nothing that is made of the vine t, 1612
Dt 12: 2 and upon the hills, and under every green t: 6086
19: 5 a stroke with the axe to cut down the t, 6086
20:19 thou shalt not cut them down (for the t of 6086
21:22 *be* put to death, and thou hang him on a t: 6086
21:23 body shall not remain all night upon the t, 6086
22: 6 to be before thee in the way in any t, 6086
24:20 When thou beatest thine **olive** t, thou shalt 2132
Jos 8:29 the king of Ai he hanged on a t until 6086
8:29 should take his carcase down from the t, 6086
Jdg 4: 5 she dwelt under the **palm** t of Deborah 8560
9: 8 they said unto the **olive** t, Reign thou over 2132
9: 9 the **olive** t said unto them, Should I leave 2132
9:10 the trees said to the **fig** t, Come thou, *and* 8384
9:11 the **fig** t said unto them, Should I forsake 8384
1Sa 14: 2 under a **pomegranate** t which *is* in Migron: 7416
22: 6 (now Saul abode in Gibeah under a t in 815
31:13 buried *them* under a t at Jabesh, and 815
1Ki 4:25 man under his vine and under his **fig** t, 8384
4:33 from the **cedar** t that *is* in Lebanon even 730
6:23 oracle he made two cherubims *of* olive t, 6086
6:31 of the oracle he made doors of olive t: 6086
6:32 The two doors also *were* of olive t; and 6086
6:33 for the door of the temple posts of olive t, 6086
6:34 the two doors *were* of fir t: the two leaves 6086
14:23 on every high hill, and under every green t. 6086
19: 4 and came and sat down under a **juniper** t: 7574
19: 5 as he lay and slept under a **juniper** t, 7574
2Ki 3:19 shall fell every good t, and stop all wells of 6086
16: 4 and on the hills, and under every green t. 6086
17:10 in every high hill, and under every green t: 6086
18:31 every one of his **fig** t, and drink ye every 8384
2Ch 3: 5 the greater house he cieled with fir t, 6086
28: 4 and on the hills, and under every green t. 6086
Est 2:23 therefore they were both hanged on a t: 6086
Job 14: 7 For there is hope of a t, if it be cut down, 6086
19:10 and mine hope hath he removed like a t. 6086
24:20 and wickedness shall be broken as a t. 6086
Ps 1: 3 he shall be like a t planted by the rivers of 6086
37:35 and spreading himself like a green **bay** t. 249
52: 8 I *am* like a green **olive** t in the house of 2132
92:12 The righteous shall flourish like the **palm** t: 8558
Pr 3:18 She *is* a t of life to them that lay hold upon 6086
11:30 The fruit of the righteous *is* a t of life; and 6086
13:12 but *when* the desire cometh, *it is* a t of life. 6086
15: 4 A wholesome tongue *is* a t of life: but 6086
27:18 Whoso keepeth the **fig** t shall eat the fruit 8384
Ecc 11: 3 if the t fall toward the south, or toward 6086
11: 3 *in* the place where the t falleth, there it 6086
12: 5 the **almond** t shall flourish, and 8247
SS 2: 3 As the **apple** t among the trees of 8598
2:13 The **fig** t putteth forth her green figs, and 8384
7: 7 This thy stature is like to a **palm** t, and 8558
7: 8 I said, I will go up to the **palm** t, I will take 8558
8: 5 I raised thee up under the **apple** t: there thy 8598
Isa 6:13 as a **teil** t, and as an oak, whose substance *is* 424
17: 6 as the shaking of an **olive** t, two *or* 2132
24:13 *there shall be* as the shaking of an **olive** t, 2132
34: 4 the vine, and as a falling *fig* from the **fig** t. 8384
36:16 every one *of* his **fig** t, and drink ye every 8384
40:20 no oblation chooseth a t *that* will not rot; 6086
41:19 the **shittah** t, and the myrtle, and the oil 7848
41:19 shittah tree, and the myrtle, and the oil t; 6086
41:19 I will set in the desert the **fir** t, *and* 1265
41:19 *and* the pine, and the **box** t together: 8391
44:19 shall I fall down to the stock of a t? 6086
44:23 ye mountains, O forest, and every t therein: 6086
55:13 Instead of the thorn shall come up the **fir** t, 1265
55:13 of the brier shall come up the **myrtle** t: 1918
56: 3 let the eunuch say, Behold, I *am* a dry t. 6086
57: 5 yourselves with idols under every green t, 6086
60:13 the **fir** t, the pine tree, and the box together, 1265
60:13 the fir tree, the **pine** t, and the box together, 8410
65:22 for as the days of a t *are* the days of my 6086
66:17 in the gardens behind one *t* in the midst, NIH
Jer 1:11 And I said, I see a rod of an **almond** t. 8247
2:20 and under every green t thou wanderest, 6086
3: 6 high mountain and under every green t, 6086
3:13 ways to the strangers under every green t, 6086
8:13 nor figs on the **fig** t, and the leaf shall fade; 8384
10: 3 for *one* cutteth a t out of the forest, 6086
10: 5 They *are* upright as the **palm** t, but 8560
11:16 A green **olive** t, fair, *and* of goodly fruit: 2132
11:19 *saying,* Let us destroy the t with the fruit 6086
17: 8 For he shall be as a t planted by the waters, 6086
Eze 6:13 under every green t, and under every thick 6086
15: 2 What is the vine t more than any tree, *or* 6086
15: 2 What is the vine tree more than any t, *or* 6086
15: 6 As the vine t among the trees of the forest, 6086
17: 5 *it* by great waters, *and* set it *as* a **willow** t. 6851
17:24 I the LORD have brought down the high t, 6086
17:24 have exalted the low t, have dried up 6086
17:24 have dried up the green t, and have made 6086
17:24 and have made the dry t to flourish: 6086
20:47 it shall devour every green t in thee, and 6086
20:47 every green tree in thee, and every dry t: 6086
21:10 it contemneth the rod of my son, *as* every t. 6086
31: 8 nor any t in the garden of God was like 6086

Eze 34:27 the **t** of the field shall yield her fruit, and 6086
36:30 I will multiply the fruit of the **t**, and 6086
41:18 so that a **palm t** *was* between a cherub and 8561
41:19 man *was* toward the **palm t** on the one side, 8561
41:19 the face of a young lion toward the **palm t** 8561
Da 4:10 a **t** in the midst of the earth, and the height 363
4:11 The **t** grew, and was strong, and the height 363
4:14 Hew down the **t**, and cut off his branches, 363
4:20 The **t** that thou sawest, which grew, and 363
4:23 saying, Hew the **t** down, and destroy it; 363
4:26 to leave the stump of the **t** roots; 363
Hos 9:10 as the firstripe in the **fig t** at her first time: 8384
14: 6 his beauty shall be as the **olive t**, and his 2132
14: 8 I *am* like a green **fir t**. From me is thy fruit 1265
Joel 1: 7 laid my vine waste, and barked my **fig t**: 8384
1:12 vine is dried up, and the **fig t** languisheth; 8384
1:12 the **pomegranate t**, the palm tree also, and 7416
1:12 the **palm t** also, and the apple tree, 8558
1:12 the palm tree also, and the **apple t**, 8598
2:22 for the **t** beareth her fruit, the fig tree and 6086
2:22 the **fig t** and the vine do yield their 8384
Mic 4: 4 man under his vine and under his **fig t**; 8384
Hab 3:17 Although the **fig t** shall not blossom, 8384
Hag 2:19 the **fig t**, and the pomegranate, and 8384
2:19 and the pomegranate, and the olive **t**, 6086
Zec 3:10 under the vine and under the **fig t**. 8384
11: 2 Howl, **fir t**; for the cedar is fallen; because 1265
Mt 3:10 every **t** which bringeth not forth good fruit *1186*
7:17 so every good **t** bringeth forth good fruit; *1186*
7:17 but a corrupt **t** bringeth forth evil fruit. *1186*
7:18 A good **t** cannot bring forth evil fruit, *1186*
7:18 neither *can* a corrupt **t** bring forth good *1186*
7:19 Every **t** that bringeth not forth good fruit is *1186*
12:33 Either make the **t** good, and his fruit good; *1186*
12:33 or else make the **t** corrupt, and his fruit *1186*
12:33 fruit corrupt: for the **t** is known by *his* fruit. *1186*
13:32 and becometh a **t**, so that the birds of the air *1186*
21:19 And when he saw a **fig t** in the way, *4808*
21:19 And presently the **fig t** withered away. *4808*
21:20 How soon is the **fig t** withered away! *4808*
21:21 not only do this which is done to the **fig t**, *4808*
24:32 Now learn a parable of the **fig t**; When his *4808*
Mk 11:13 And seeing a **fig t** afar off having leaves, *4808*
11:20 they saw the **fig t** dried up from the roots. *4808*
11:21 the **fig t** which thou cursedst is withered *4808*
13:28 Now learn a parable of the **fig t**; When her *4808*
Lk 3: 9 every **t** therefore which bringeth not forth *1186*
6:43 For a good **t** bringeth not forth corrupt *1186*
6:43 neither doth a corrupt **t** bring forth good *1186*
6:44 For every **t** is known by his own fruit. *1186*
13: 6 A certain *man* had a **fig t** planted in his *4808*
13: 7 years I come seeking fruit on this **fig t**, *4808*
13:19 and it grew, and waxed a great **t**; and *1186*
17: 6 ye might say unto this **sycamine t**, Be thou *4807*
19: 4 climbed up into a **sycomore t** to see him: *4809*
21:29 a parable; Behold the **fig t**, and all the trees; *4808*
23:31 For if they do these *things* in a green **t**, *3586*
Jn 1:48 when thou wast under the **fig t**, I saw thee. *4808*
1:50 I saw thee under the **fig t**, believest thou? *4808*
Ac 5:30 up Jesus, whom ye slew and hanged on a **t**. *3586*
10:39 whom they slew and hanged on a **t**: *3586*
13:29 they took *him* down from the **t**, and *3586*
Ro 11:17 and thou, being a **wild olive t**, wert graffed in *65*
11:17 of the root and fatness of the **olive t**; *1636*
11:24 cut out of the **olive t which is wild** by nature, *65*
11:24 contrary to nature into a **good olive t**: *2565*
11:24 *branches,* be graffed into their own **olive t**? *1636*
Gal 3:13 Cursed *is* every one that hangeth on a **t**: *3586*
Jas 3:12 Can the **fig t**, my brethren, bear olive *4808*
1Pe 2:24 self bare our sins in his own body on the **t**, *3586*
Rev 2: 7 overcometh will I give to eat of the **t** of life, *3586*
6:13 *even* as a **fig t** casteth her untimely figs, *4808*
7: 1 on the earth, nor on the sea, nor on any **t**. *1186*
9: 4 neither any green *thing,* neither any **t**; *1186*
22: 2 side of the river, *was there* the **t** of life, *3586*
22: 2 the leaves of the **t** *were* for the healing of *3586*
22:14 that they may have right to the **t** of life, and *3586*

TREES (157) [TREE]

Ge 3: 2 We may eat of the fruit of the **t** of 6086
3: 8 LORD God amongst the **t** of the garden. 6086
23:17 and all the **t** that *were* in the field, 6086
Ex 10:15 all the fruit of the **t** which the hail had left: 6086
10:15 there remained not any green thing in the **t**, 6086
15:27 of water, and threescore and ten **palm t**: 8558
Lev 19:23 shall have planted all *manner of* **t** for food, 6086
23:40 you on the first day the boughs of goodly **t**, 6086
23:40 branches of **palm t**, and the boughs of thick 8558
23:40 the boughs of thick **t**, and willows of 6086
26: 4 and the **t** of the field shall yield their fruit. 6086
26:20 neither shall the **t** of the land yield their 6086
Nu 24: 6 as the **t of lign aloes** *which* the LORD hath 174
24: 6 *and* as **cedar t** beside the waters. 730
33: 9 of water, and threescore and ten **palm t**; 8558
Dt 6:11 thou diggedst not, vineyards and **olive t**, 2132
8: 8 and vines, and **fig t**, and pomegranates; 8384
16:21 Thou shalt not plant thee a grove *of* any **t** 6086
20:19 thou shalt not destroy the **t** thereof by 6086
20:20 Only the **t** which thou knowest that they *be* 6086
20:20 thou knowest that they *be* not **t** for meat, 6086
28:40 Thou shalt have **olive t** throughout all thy 2132
28:42 All thy **t** and fruit of thy land shall 6086
34: 3 of Jericho, the city of **palm t**, unto Zoar. 8558
Jos 10:26 and slew them, and hanged them on five **t**: 6086
10:26 they were hanging upon the **t** until 6086
10:27 they took them down off the **t**, and 6086
Jdg 1:16 went up out of the city of **palm t** with 8558
3:13 and possessed the city of **palm t**. 8558
9: 8 The **t** went forth on a time to anoint a king 6086
9: 9 and man, and go to be promoted over the **t**? 6086
9:10 the **t** said to the fig tree, Come thou, *and* 6086
9:11 and go to be promoted over the **t**? 6086
9:12 said the **t** unto the vine, Come thou, *and* 6086
9:13 and man, and go to be promoted over the **t**? 6086
9:14 said all the **t** unto the bramble, Come thou, 6086
9:15 the bramble said unto the **t**, If in truth ye 6086
9:48 cut down a bough from the **t**, and took it, 6086
2Sa 5:11 and cedar **t**, and carpenters, and masons: 6086
5:23 upon them over against the **mulberry t**. 1057
5:24 of a going in the tops of the **mulberry t**, 1057
1Ki 4:33 he spake of **t**, from the cedar tree that *is* in 6086
5: 6 command thou that they hew me **cedar t** out 730
5:10 So Hiram gave Solomon cedar **t** and 6086
5:10 and fir **t** *according to* all his desire. 6086
6:29 of cherubims and **palm t** and open flowers, 8561
6:32 of cherubims and **palm t** and open flowers, 8561
6:32 upon the cherubims, and upon the **palm t**. 8561
6:35 and **palm t** and open flowers: 8561
7:36 he graved cherubims, lions, and **palm t**, 8561
9:11 of Tyre had furnished Solomon with cedar **t** 6086
9:11 Solomon with cedar trees and fir **t**, 6086
10:11 in from Ophir great plenty of almug **t**, 6086
10:12 the king made *of* the almug **t** pillars for 6086
10:12 there came no such almug **t**, nor were seen 6086
10:27 cedars made he *to be* as the **sycomore t** that 8256
2Ki 3:25 the wells of water, and felled all the good **t**: 6086
19:23 will cut down the tall **cedar t** thereof, *and* 730
19:23 trees thereof, *and* the choice **fir t** thereof: 1265
1Ch 14:14 upon them over against the **mulberry t**. 1057
14:15 of going in the tops of the **mulberry t**, 1057
16:33 shall the **t** of the wood sing out at 6086
22: 4 Also cedar **t** in abundance: for 6086
27:28 over the **olive t** and the sycomore trees that 2132
27:28 the **sycomore t** that *were* in the low plains 8256
2Ch 1:15 **cedar t** made he as the sycomore trees that 730
1:15 cedar trees made he as the **sycomore t** that 8256
2: 8 Send me also cedar **t**, fir trees, and 6086
2: 8 **fir t**, and algum trees, out of Lebanon: 1265
2: 8 fir trees, and **algum t**, out of Lebanon: 418
3: 5 and set thereon **palm t** and chains. 8561
9:10 brought algum **t** and precious stones. 6086
9:11 the king made *of* the algum **t** terraces to 6086
9:27 **cedar t** made he as the sycomore trees that 730
9:27 cedar trees made he as the **sycomore t** that 8256
28:15 the city of **palm t**, to their brethren: 8558
Ezr 3: 7 to bring cedar **t** from Lebanon to the sea of 6086
Ne 8:15 palm branches, and branches of thick **t**, 6086
9:25 and oliveyards, and fruit **t** in abundance: 6086
10:35 the firstfruits of all fruit of all **t**, year by 6086
10:37 the fruit of all *manner of* **t**, of wine and 6086
Job 40:21 He lieth under the **shady t**, in the covert of 6628
40:22 The **shady t** cover him *with* their shadow; 6628
Ps 74: 5 as he had lifted up axes upon the thick **t**. 6086
78:47 with hail, and their **sycomore t** with frost. 8256
96:12 shall all the **t** of the wood rejoice 6086
104:16 The **t** of the LORD are full *of sap;* 6086
104:17 *as for* the stork, the **fir t** *are* her house. 1265
105:33 He smote their vines also and their **fig t**; 8384

Ps 105:33 fig trees; and brake the **t** of their coasts. 6086
148: 9 all hills; fruitful **t**, and all cedars: 6086
Ecc 2: 5 and I planted **t** in them of all *kind of* fruits: 6086
2: 6 therewith the wood that bringeth forth **t**: 6086
SS 2: 3 As the apple tree among the **t** of the wood, 6086
4:14 and cinnamon, with all **t** of frankincense; 6086
Isa 7: 2 as the **t** of the wood are moved with 6086
10:19 the rest of the **t** of his forest shall be few, 6086
14: 8 the **fir t** rejoice at thee, *and* the cedars of 1265
37:24 cedars thereof, *and* the choice **fir t** thereof: 1265
44:14 for himself among the **t** of the forest: 6086
55:12 all the **t** of the field shall clap *their* hands. 6086
61: 3 that they might be called **t** of righteousness, 352
Jer 5:17 they shall eat up thy vines and thy **fig t**: 8384
6: 6 Hew ye down **t**, and cast a mount against 6097
7:20 upon the **t** of the field, and upon the fruit of 6086
17: 2 their groves by the green **t** upon the high 6086
Eze 15: 2 *than* a branch which is among the **t** of 6086
15: 6 As the vine tree among the **t** of the forest, 6086
17:24 all the **t** of the field shall know that I 6086
20:28 all the thick **t**, and they offered there their 6086
27: 5 They have made all thy *ship* boards of **fir t** 1265
31: 4 sent out her little rivers unto all the **t** of 6086
31: 5 was exalted above all the **t** of the field, 6086
31: 8 the **fir t** were not like his boughs, and 1265
31: 8 the **chesnut t** were not like his branches; 6196
31: 9 so that all the **t** of Eden, that *were* in 6086
31:14 To the end that none of all the **t** by 6086
31:14 neither their **t** stand up in their height, 352
31:15 and all the **t** of the field fainted for him. 6086
31:16 all the **t** of Eden, the choice and best of 6086
31:18 and in greatness among the **t** of Eden? 6086
31:18 yet shalt thou be brought down with the **t** of 6086
40:16 and upon *each* post *were* **palm t**. 8561
40:22 and their arches, and their **palm t**, 8561
40:26 it had **palm t**, one on this side, and 8561
40:31 and **palm t** *were* upon the posts thereof: 8561
40:34 **palm t** *were* upon the posts thereof, on this 8561
40:37 **palm t** *were* upon the posts thereof, on this 8561
41:18 *it was* made *with* cherubims and **palm t**, 8561
41:20 the door *were* cherubims and **palm t** made, 8561
41:25 doors of the temple, cherubims and **palm t**, 8561
41:26 **palm t** on the one side and on the other 8561
47: 7 at the bank of the river *were* very many **t** 6086
47:12 and on that side, shall grow all **t** for meat, 6086
Hos 2:12 I will destroy her vines and her **fig t**, 8384
Joel 1:12 *even* all the **t** of the field, are withered: 6086
1:19 the flame hath burnt all the **t** of the field. 6086
Am 4: 9 and your vineyards and your **fig t** and 8384
4: 9 your fig trees and your **olive t** increased, 2132
Na 2: 3 and the **fir t** shall be terribly shaken. 1265
3:12 All thy strong holds *shall be like* **fig t** with 8384
Zec 1: 8 he stood among the **myrtle t** that *were* in 1918
1:10 the man that stood among the **myrtle t** 1918
1:11 the LORD that stood among the **myrtle t**, 1918
4: 3 two **olive t** by it, one upon the right *side* of 2132
4:11 What *are* these two **olive t** upon the right 2132
Mt 3:10 also the axe is laid unto the root of the **t**: *1186*
21: 8 others cut down branches from the **t**, and *1186*
Mk 8:24 and said, I see men as **t**, walking. *1186*
11: 8 and others cut down branches off the **t**, *1186*
Lk 3: 9 also the axe is laid unto the root of the **t**: *1186*
21:29 a parable; Behold the fig tree, and all the **t**; *1186*
Jn 12:13 Took branches of **palm t**, and went forth to *5404*
Jude 1:12 **t** whose fruit withereth, without fruit, *1186*
Rev 7: 3 Hurt not the earth, neither the sea, nor the **t**, *1186*
8: 7 and the third *part* of **t** was burnt up, and all *1186*
11: 4 These are the two **olive t**, and the two *1636*

TREMBLE (29) [TREMBLED, TREMBLETH, TREMBLING]

Dt 2:25 shall **t**, and be in anguish because of thee. 7264
20: 3 fear not, and do not **t**, neither be ye terrified 2648
Ezr 10: 3 of those that **t** at the commandment of our 2730
Job 9: 6 out of her place, and the pillars thereof **t**. 6426
26:11 The pillars of heaven **t** and are astonished 7322
Ps 60: 2 Thou hast **made** the earth **to t**; thou hast 7493
99: 1 The LORD reigneth; let the people **t**: 7264
114: 7 **T**, thou earth, at the presence of the Lord, 2342
Ecc 12: 3 day when the keepers of the house shall **t**, 2111
Isa 5:25 the hills did **t**, and their carcases were torn 7264
14:16 *Is* this the man that **made** the earth **to t**, 7264
32:11 **T**, ye *women* that are at ease; be troubled, 2729
64: 2 *that* the nations may **t** at thy presence. 7264
66: 5 word of the LORD, ye that **t** at his word; 2730
Jer 5:22 will ye not **t** at my presence, which have 2342
10:10 at his wrath the earth shall **t**, and 7493
33: 9 shall fear and **t** for all the goodness and 7264
51:29 the land shall **t** and sorrow: for every 7493
Eze 26:16 shall **t** at every moment, and be astonished 2729
26:18 Now shall the isles **t** *in* the day of thy fall; 2729
32:10 they shall **t** at every moment, every man for 2729
Da 6:26 in every dominion of my kingdom *men* **t** 2112
Hos 11:10 then the children shall **t** from the west. 2729
11:11 They shall **t** as a bird out of Egypt, and as a 2729
Joel 2: 1 let all the inhabitants of the land **t**: for 7264
2:10 quake before them; the heavens shall **t**: 7493
Am 8: 8 Shall not the land **t** for this, and every one 7264
Hab 3: 7 *and* the curtains of the land of Midian did **t**. 7264
Jas 2:19 doest well: the devils also believe, and **t**. *5425*

TREMBLED (21) [TREMBLE]

Ge 27:33 Isaac **t** very exceedingly, and said, 2729+2731
Ex 19:16 so that all the people that *was* in the camp **t**. 2729
Jdg 5: 4 the earth **t**, and the heavens dropped, 7493
1Sa 4:13 for his heart **t** for the ark of God. 1961+2730
14:15 they also **t**, and the earth quaked: 2729
16: 4 the elders of the town **t** at his coming, and 2729
28: 5 he was afraid, and his heart greatly **t**. 2729
2Sa 22: 8 the earth shook and **t**; the foundations of 7493
Ezr 9: 4 were assembled unto me every one that **t** at 2730
Ps 18: 7 the earth shook and **t**; the foundations also 7493
77:18 lightened the world: the earth **t** and shook. 7264
97: 4 enlightened the world: the earth saw, and **t**. 2342
Jer 4:24 lo, they **t**, and all the hills moved lightly. 7493
8:16 the whole land **t** at the sound of 7493
Da 5:19 languages, **t** and feared before him: 2112
Hab 3:10 The mountains saw thee, *and* they **t**: 2342
3:16 When I heard, my belly **t**; my lips quivered 7264
3:16 entered into my bones, and I **t** in myself, 7264
Mk 16: 8 for they **t** and were amazed: *2192+5156*
Ac 7:32 and the God of Jacob. Then Moses **t**, *1096+1790*
24:25 and judgment to come, Felix **t**, *1096+1719*

TREMBLETH (4) [TREMBLE]

Job 37: 1 At this also my heart **t**, and is moved out of 2729
Ps 104:32 He looketh on the earth, and it **t**: 7460
119:120 My flesh **t** for fear of thee; and I am afraid 5568
Isa 66: 2 and of a contrite spirit, and **t** at my word. 2730

TREMBLING (26) [TREMBLE]

Ex 15:15 men of Moab, **t** shall take hold upon them; 7461
Dt 28:65 the LORD shall give thee there a **t** heart, 7268
1Sa 13: 7 in Gilgal, and all the people followed him **t**. 2729
14:15 And there was **t** in the host, in the field, and 2731
14:15 the earth quaked: so it was a very great **t**. 2731
Ezr 10: 9 **t** because of *this* matter, and for the great 7460
Job 4:14 Fear came upon me, and **t**, which made all 7461
21: 6 I am afraid, and **t** taketh hold on my flesh. 6427
Ps 2:11 the LORD with fear, and rejoice with **t**. 7461
55: 5 Fearfulness and **t** are come upon me, and 7461
Isa 51:17 thou hast drunken the dregs of the cup of **t**, 8653
51:22 I have taken out of thine hand the cup of **t**, 8653
Jer 30: 5 We have heard a voice of **t**, of fear, and 2731
Eze 12:18 drink thy water with **t** and with carefulness; 7269
26:16 they shall clothe themselves with **t**; 2731
Da 10:11 he had spoken this word unto me, I stood **t**. 7460
Hos 13: 1 When Ephraim spake **t**, he exalted *himself* 7578
Zec 12: 2 I *will* make Jerusalem a cup of **t** unto all 7478
Mk 5:33 But the woman fearing and **t**, *5141*
Lk 8:47 she came **t**, and falling down before him, *5141*
Ac 9: 6 And he **t** and astonished said, Lord, *5141*
16:29 and came **t**, and fell down before Paul and *1790*
1Co 2: 3 in weakness, and in fear, and in much **t**. *5156*
2Co 7:15 how with fear and **t** you received him. *5156*
Eph 6: 5 with fear and **t**, in singleness of your heart, *5156*
Php 2:12 out your own salvation with fear and **t**. *5156*

TRENCH (8)

1Sa 17:20 he came to the **t**, as the host was going 4570
26: 5 Saul lay in the **t**, and the people pitched 4570
26: 7 Saul lay sleeping within the **t**, and his spear 4570
2Sa 20:15 a bank against the city, and it stood in the **t**: 2426
1Ki 18:32 he made a **t** about the altar, as great as 8585
18:35 the altar; and he filled the **t** also *with* water. 8585
18:38 and licked up the water that *was* in the **t**. 8585
Lk 19:43 that thine enemies shall cast a **t** about thee, *5482*

TRESPASS (82) [TRESPASSED, TRESPASSES, TRESPASSING]

Ge	31:36	and said to Laban, What *is* my t?	6588
	50:17	the t of thy brethren, and their sin;	6588
	50:17	forgive the t of the servants of the God of	6588
Ex	22: 9	For all manner of t, *whether it be* for ox,	6588
Lev	5: 6	he shall bring his **t offering** unto the LORD	817
	5: 7	he shall bring for his t, which he hath	817
	5:15	If a soul **commit a** t, and sin through	4603+4604
	5:15	he shall bring for his t unto the LORD a	817
	5:15	the shekel of the sanctuary, for a **t offering**:	817
	5:16	for him with the ram of the **t offering**,	817
	5:18	for a **t offering**, unto the priest:	817
	5:19	It *is* a **t offering**: he hath certainly trespassed	817
	6: 2	**commit a** t against the LORD, and	4603+4604
	6: 5	it appertaineth, in the day of his **t offering**.	819
	6: 6	he shall bring his **t offering** unto	817
	6: 6	for a **t offering**, unto the priest:	817
	6:17	as *is* the sin offering, and as the **t offering**.	817
	7: 1	Likewise this *is* the law of the **t offering**:	817
	7: 2	burnt offering shall they kill the **t offering**:	817
	7: 5	by fire unto the LORD: it *is* a **t offering**.	817
	7: 7	As the sin offering *is*, so *is* the **t offering**:	817
	7:37	of the **t offering**, and of the consecrations,	817
	14:12	offer him for a **t offering**, and the log of oil,	817
	14:13	offering *is* the priest's, *so is* the **t offering**:	817
	14:14	take *some* of the blood of the **t offering**,	817
	14:17	right foot, upon the blood of the **t offering**:	817
	14:21	he shall take one lamb *for* a **t offering** to be	817
	14:24	priest shall take the lamb of the **t offering**,	817
	14:25	he shall kill the lamb of the **t offering**, and	817
	14:25	take *some* of the blood of the **t offering**,	817
	14:28	upon the place of the blood of the **t offering**:	817
	19:21	he shall bring his **t offering** unto	817
	19:21	*even* a ram for a **t offering**.	817
	19:22	**t offering** before the LORD for his sin	817
	22:16	Or suffer them to bear the iniquity of t,	819
	26:40	with their t which they trespassed against	4604
Nu	5: 6	to **do a** t against the LORD, and	4603+4604
	5: 7	he shall recompense his t with the principal	817
	5: 8	have no kinsman to recompense the t unto,	817
	5: 8	*let* the t *be* recompensed unto the LORD,	817
	5:12	and **commit a** t against him,	4603+4604
	5:27	and have **done** t against her husband,	4603+4604
	6:12	bring a lamb of the first year for a **t offering**:	817
	18: 9	of theirs, and every **t offering** of theirs,	817
	31:16	to commit t against the LORD in	4604
Jos	7: 1	the children of Israel **committed a** t	4603+4604
	22:16	What t *is* this that ye have committed	4604
	22:20	**commit a** t in the accursed thing,	4603+4604
	22:31	ye have not **committed** this t against	4603+4604
1Sa	6: 3	but in any wise return him a **t offering**:	817
	6: 4	What *shall be* the **t offering** which we shall	817
	6: 8	of gold, which ye return him *for* a **t offering**,	817
	6:17	returned *for* a **t offering** unto the LORD;	817
	25:28	I pray thee, forgive the t of thine handmaid:	6588
1Ki	8:31	If any man t against his neighbour, and	2398
2Ki	12:16	The t money and sin money was not brought	817
1Ch	21: 3	*thing?* why will he be a **cause of** t to Israel?	819
2Ch	19:10	ye shall even warn them that they t not	816
	19:10	your brethren: this do, and ye shall not **t**.	816
	24:18	upon Judah and Jerusalem for this their **t**.	819
	28:13	intend to add *more* to our sins and to our **t**:	819
	28:13	for our t is great, and *there is* fierce wrath	819
	28:22	in the time of his distress did he t yet more	4603
	33:19	his t, and the places wherein he built high	4604
Ezr	9: 2	and rulers hath been chief in this **t**.	4604
	9: 6	and our t is grown up unto the heavens.	819
	9: 7	*have* we *been* in a great t unto this day;	819
	9:13	us for our evil deeds, and for our great t,	819
	10:10	strange wives, to increase the t of Israel.	819
	10:19	*they offered* a ram of the flock for their **t**.	819
Eze	15: 8	because they have **committed a t**,	4603+4604
	17:20	will plead with him there *for* his t that he	4604
	18:24	in his t that he hath trespassed, and in his	4604
	20:27	in that they have **committed a t**	4603+4604
	40:39	and the sin offering and the **t offering**.	817
	42:13	and the sin offering, and the **t offering**;	817
	44:29	and the sin offering, and the **t offering**;	817
	46:20	where the priests shall boil the **t offering**	817
Da	9: 7	of their t that they have trespassed against	4604
Mt	18:15	Moreover if thy brother shall t against thee,	*264*
Lk	17: 3	If thy brother t against thee, rebuke him; and	*264*
	17: 4	And if he t against thee seven times in a day,	*264*

TRESPASSED (15) [TRESPASS]

Lev	5:19	he hath **certainly** t against the LORD.	816+816
	26:40	with their trespass which they t against me,	4603
Nu	5: 7	give *it* unto *him* against whom he **hath** t.	816
Dt	32:51	Because ye t against me among	4603
2Ch	26:18	go out of the sanctuary; for thou hast t;	4603
	29: 6	For our fathers have t, and done *that* which	4603
	30: 7	which t against the LORD God of their	4603
	33:23	but Amon t more and more.	819
Ezr	10: 2	We have t against our God, and have taken	4603
Eze	17:20	*for* his trespass that he hath t against me.	4603
	18:24	in his trespass that he hath t, and in his sin	4603
	39:23	because they t against me, therefore hid I	4603
	39:26	all their trespasses whereby they have t	4603
Da	9: 7	of their trespass that they have t against	4603
Hos	8: 1	my covenant, and t against my law.	6586

TRESPASSES (12) [TRESPASS]

Ezr	9:15	behold, we *are* before thee in our t: for *we*	819
Ps	68:21	scalp of such a one as goeth on still in his t.	817
Eze	39:26	all their t whereby they have trespassed	4604
Mt	6:14	For if ye forgive men their t, your heavenly	*3900*
	6:15	But if ye forgive not men their t,	*3900*
	6:15	neither will your Father forgive your t.	*3900*
	18:35	forgive not every one his brother their t.	*3900*
Mk	11:25	which is in heaven may forgive you your t.	*3900*
	11:26	Father which is in heaven forgive your t.	*3900*
2Co	5:19	not imputing their t unto them;	*3900*
Eph	2: 1	you *hath he quickened,* who were dead in t	*3900*
Col	2:13	with him, having forgiven you all t;	*3900*

TRESPASSING (2) [TRESPASS]

Lev	6: 7	any *thing* of all that he hath done in t therein.	819
Eze	14:13	sinneth against me by t **grievously**,	4603+4604

TRIAL (6) [TRY]

Job	9:23	he will laugh at the t of the innocent.	4531
Eze	21:13	Because *it is* a t, and what if *the sword*	974
2Co	8: 2	How that in a great t of affliction	*1382*
Heb	11:36	And others had t of *cruel* mockings and	*3984*
1Pe	1: 7	That the t of your faith, *being* much more	*1383*
	4:12	think it not strange concerning the **fiery t**	*4451*

TRIBE (242) [TRIBES]

Ex	31: 2	of Uri, the son of Hur, of the t of Judah:	4294
	31: 6	the son of Ahisamach, of the t of Dan:	4294
	35:30	of Uri, the son of Hur, of the t of Judah;	4294
	35:34	the son of Ahisamach, of the t of Dan.	4294
	38:22	of Uri, the son of Hur, of the t of Judah,	4294
	38:23	of the t of Dan, an engraver, and a cunning	4294
Lev	24:11	the daughter of Dibri, of the t of Dan:)	4294
Nu	1: 4	with you there shall be a man of every t;	4294
	1: 5	of *the* t *of* Reuben; Elizur the son of	NIH
	1:21	*even* of the t of Reuben, *were* forty and	4294
	1:23	*even* of the t of Simeon, *were* fifty and	4294
	1:25	*even* of the t of Gad, *were* forty and	4294
	1:27	*even* of the t of Judah, *were* threescore and	4294
	1:29	*even* of the t of Issachar, *were* fifty and	4294
	1:31	*even* of the t of Zebulun, *were* fifty and	4294
	1:33	*even* of the t of Ephraim, *were* forty	4294
	1:35	*even* of the t of Manasseh, *were* thirty and	4294
	1:37	*even* of the t of Benjamin, *were* thirty and	4294
	1:39	*even* of the t of Dan, *were* threescore and	4294
	1:41	*even* of the t of Asher, *were* forty and	4294
	1:43	*even* of the t of Naphtali, *were* fifty and	4294
	1:47	the Levites after the t of their fathers were	4294
	1:49	Only thou shalt not number the t of Levi,	4294
	2: 5	next unto him *shall be* the t of Issachar:	4294
	2: 7	*Then* the t of Zebulun: and Eliab the son of	4294
	2:12	those which pitch by him *shall be* the t of	4294
	2:14	the t of Gad: and the captain of the sons of	4294
	2:20	by him *shall be* the t of Manasseh: and	4294
	2:22	the t of Benjamin: and the captain of	4294
	2:27	those that encamp by him *shall be* the t of	4294
	2:29	the t of Naphtali: and the captain of	4294
	3: 6	Bring the t of Levi near, and present them	4294
	4:18	Cut ye not off the t of the families of	7626
	7:12	the son of Amminadab, of the t of Judah:	4294
	10:15	over the host of the t of the children of	4294
	10:16	over the host of the t of the children of	4294
	10:19	over the host of the t of the children of	4294
	10:20	over the host of the t of the children of Gad	4294
	10:23	over the host of the t of the children of	4294
	10:24	over the host of the t of the children of	4294

T

Nu	10:26	over the host of the **t** of the children of	4294
	10:27	over the host of the **t** of the children of	4294
	13: 2	of every **t** of their fathers shall ye send a	4294
	13: 4	of the **t** of Reuben, Shammua the son of	4294
	13: 5	Of the **t** of Simeon, Shaphat the son of	4294
	13: 6	Of the **t** of Judah, Caleb the son of	4294
	13: 7	Of the **t** of Issachar, Igal the son of Joseph.	4294
	13: 8	Of the **t** of Ephraim, Oshea the son of Nun.	4294
	13: 9	Of the **t** of Benjamin, Palti the son of	4294
	13:10	Of the **t** of Zebulun, Gaddiel the son of	4294
	13:11	Of the **t** of Joseph, *namely,* of the tribe of	4294
	13:11	*namely,* of the **t** of Manasseh, Gaddi	4294
	13:12	Of the **t** of Dan, Ammiel the son of	4294
	13:13	Of the **t** of Asher, Sethur the son of	4294
	13:14	Of the **t** of Naphtali, Nahbi the son of	4294
	13:15	Of the **t** of Gad, Geuel the son of Machi.	4294
	18: 2	thy brethren also *of* the **t** of Levi, the tribe	4294
	18: 2	the **t** of thy father, bring thou with thee,	7626
	31: 4	Of every **t** a thousand, throughout all	4294
	31: 5	a thousand of *every* **t**, twelve thousand	4294
	31: 6	a thousand of *every* **t**, them and Phinehas	4294
	32:33	unto half the **t** of Manasseh the son of	7626
	34:13	give unto the nine tribes, and *to* the half **t**:	4294
	34:14	For the **t** of the children of Reuben	4294
	34:14	the **t** of the children of Gad according to	4294
	34:14	half the **t** of Manasseh have received their	4294
	34:15	the half **t** have received their inheritance on	4294
	34:18	ye shall take one prince of every **t**,	4294
	34:19	Of the **t** of Judah, Caleb the son of	4294
	34:20	of the **t** of the children of Simeon,	4294
	34:21	Of the **t** of Benjamin, Elidad the son of	4294
	34:22	the prince of the **t** of the children of Dan,	4294
	34:23	for the **t** of the children of Manasseh,	4294
	34:24	the prince of the **t** of the children of	4294
	34:25	the prince of the **t** of the children of	4294
	34:26	the prince of the **t** of the children of	4294
	34:27	the prince of the **t** of the children of Asher,	4294
	34:28	the prince of the **t** of the children of	4294
	36: 3	shall be put to the inheritance of the **t**	4294
	36: 4	of the **t** whereunto they are received:	4294
	36: 4	from the inheritance of the **t** of our fathers.	4294
	36: 5	The **t** of the sons of Joseph hath said well.	4294
	36: 6	only to the family of the **t** of their father	4294
	36: 7	children of Israel remove from **t** to tribe:	4294
	36: 7	children of Israel remove from tribe to **t**:	4294
	36: 7	to the inheritance of the **t** of his fathers.	4294
	36: 8	that possesseth an inheritance in any **t** of	4294
	36: 8	shall be wife unto one of the family of the **t**	4294
	36: 9	remove from *one* **t** to another tribe;	4294
	36: 9	remove from *one* tribe to another **t**;	4294
	36:12	their inheritance remained in the **t** of	4294
Dt	1:23	I took twelve men of you, one of a **t**:	7626
	3:13	of Og, gave I unto the half **t** of Manasseh;	7626
	10: 8	At that time the LORD separated the **t** of	7626
	18: 1	priests the Levites, *and* all the **t** of Levi,	7626
	29: 8	the Gadites, and to the half **t** of Manasseh.	7626
	29:18	among you man, or woman, or family, or **t**,	7626
Jos	1:12	to half the **t** of Manasseh, spake Joshua,	7626
	3:12	of the tribes of Israel, out of every **t** a man.	7626
	4: 2	men out of the people, out of every **t** a man,	7626
	4: 4	the children of Israel, out of every **t** a man:	7626
	4:12	of Gad, and half the **t** of Manasseh,	7626
	7: 1	the son of Zerah, of the **t** of Judah,	4294
	7:14	*that* the **t** which the LORD taketh shall	7626
	7:16	their tribes; and the **t** of Judah was taken:	7626
	7:18	son of Zerah, of the **t** of Judah, was taken.	4294
	12: 6	the Gadites, and the half **t** of Manasseh.	7626
	13: 7	the nine tribes, and the half **t** of Manasseh,	7626
	13:14	Only unto the **t** of Levi he gave none	7626
	13:15	Moses gave unto the **t** of the children of	4294
	13:24	Moses gave *inheritance* unto the **t** of Gad,	4294
	13:29	Moses gave *inheritance* unto the half **t** of	7626
	13:29	*this* was *the possession* of the half **t** of	4294
	13:33	unto the **t** of Levi Moses gave not *any*	7626
	14: 2	for the nine tribes, and *for* the half **t**.	4294
	14: 3	and a half **t** on the *other* side Jordan:	4294
	15: 1	was the lot of the **t** of the children of Judah	4294
	15:20	This *is* the inheritance of the **t** of	4294
	15:21	the uttermost cities of the **t** of the children	4294
	16: 8	This *is* the inheritance of the **t** of	4294
	17: 1	There was also a lot for the **t** of Manasseh;	4294
	18: 4	out from among you three men for *each* **t**:	7626
	18: 7	and Reuben, and half the **t** of Manasseh,	7626
	18:11	the lot of the **t** of the children of Benjamin	4294
	18:21	Now the cities of the **t** of the children of	4294
	19: 1	*even* for the **t** of the children of Simeon	4294
	19: 8	This *is* the inheritance of the **t** of	4294
	19:23	This *is* the inheritance of the **t** of	4294
	19:24	the fifth lot came out for the **t** of	4294
	19:31	This *is* the inheritance of the **t** of	4294
	19:39	This *is* the inheritance of the **t** of	4294
	19:40	*And* the seventh lot came out for the **t** of	4294
	19:48	This *is* the inheritance of the **t** of	4294
	20: 8	upon the plain out of the **t** of Reuben,	4294
	20: 8	Ramoth in Gilead out of the **t** of Gad, and	4294
	20: 8	Golan in Bashan out of the **t** of Manasseh.	4294
	21: 4	had by lot out of the **t** of Judah, and out of	4294
	21: 4	out of the **t** of Simeon, and out of the tribe	4294
	21: 4	and out of the **t** of Benjamin, thirteen cities.	4294
	21: 5	lot out of the families of the **t** of Ephraim,	4294
	21: 5	out of the **t** of Dan, and out of the half tribe	4294
	21: 5	and out of the half **t** of Manasseh, ten cities.	4294
	21: 6	lot out of the families of the **t** of Issachar,	4294
	21: 6	out of the **t** of Asher, and out of the tribe of	4294
	21: 6	out of the **t** of Naphtali, and out of the half	4294
	21: 6	out of the half **t** of Manasseh in Bashan,	4294
	21: 7	by their families *had* out of the **t** of Reuben,	4294
	21: 7	out of the **t** of Gad, and out of the tribe of	4294
	21: 7	and out of the **t** of Zebulun, twelve cities.	4294
	21: 9	they gave out of the **t** of the children of	4294
	21: 9	out of the **t** of the children of Simeon, these	4294
	21:17	out of the **t** of Benjamin, Gibeon with her	4294
	21:20	cities of their lot out of the **t** of Ephraim.	4294
	21:23	out of the **t** of Dan, Eltekeh with her	4294
	21:25	out of the half **t** of Manasseh, Tanach with	4294
	21:27	out of the *other* half **t** of Manasseh *they*	4294
	21:28	out of the **t** of Issachar, Kishon with her	4294
	21:30	out of the **t** of Asher, Mishal with her	4294
	21:32	out of the **t** of Naphtali, Kedesh in Galilee	4294
	21:34	rest of the Levites, out of the **t** of Zebulun,	4294
	21:36	out of the **t** of Reuben, Bezer with her	4294
	21:38	out of the **t** of Gad, Ramoth in Gilead with	4294
	22: 1	the Gadites, and the half **t** of Manasseh,	4294
	22: 7	Now to the *one* half of the **t** of Manasseh	7626
	22: 9	of Gad and the half **t** of Manasseh returned,	7626
	22:10	the half **t** of Manasseh built there an altar	7626
	22:11	the half **t** of Manasseh have built an altar	7626
	22:13	of Gad, and to the half **t** of Manasseh,	7626
	22:15	of Gad, and to the half **t** of Manasseh,	7626
	22:21	and the half **t** of Manasseh answered,	7626
Jdg	18: 1	in those days the **t** of the Danites sought	7626
	18:19	or that thou be a priest unto a **t** and a family	7626
	18:30	his sons were priests to the **t** of Dan until	7626
	20:12	sent men through all the **t** of Benjamin,	7626
	21: 3	that there should be to day one **t** lacking in	7626
	21: 6	There is one **t** cut off from Israel *this* day.	7626
	21:17	that a **t** be not destroyed out of Israel.	7626
	21:24	every man to his **t** and to his family, and	7626
1Sa	9:21	of all the families of the **t** of Benjamin?	7626
	10:20	to come near, the **t** of Benjamin was taken.	7626
	10:21	When he had caused the **t** of Benjamin to	7626
1Ki	7:14	He *was* a widow's son of the **t** of Naphtali,	4294
	11:13	will give one **t** to thy son for David my	7626
	11:32	(But he shall have one **t** for my servant	7626
	11:36	unto his son will I give one **t**, that David	7626
	12:20	the house of David, but the **t** of Judah only.	7626
	12:21	with the **t** of Benjamin, an hundred and	7626
2Ki	17:18	there was none left but the **t** of Judah only.	7626
1Ch	5:18	the Gadites, and half the **t** of Manasseh,	7626
	5:23	the children of the half **t** of Manasseh dwelt	7626
	5:26	the half **t** of Manasseh, and brought them	7626
	6:60	out of the **t** of Benjamin; Geba with her	4294
	6:61	which were left of the family of *that* **t**,	4294
	6:61	*were cities given* out of the half **t**,	4294
	6:61	*namely, out of* the half *t* of Manasseh,	NIH
	6:62	their families out of the **t** of Issachar,	4294
	6:62	out of the **t** of Asher, and out of the tribe of	4294
	6:62	out of the **t** of Naphtali, and out of the tribe	4294
	6:62	out of the **t** of Manasseh in Bashan,	4294
	6:63	out of the **t** of Reuben, and out of the tribe	4294
	6:63	out of the **t** of Gad, and out of the tribe of	4294
	6:63	and out of the **t** of Zebulun, twelve cities.	4294
	6:65	they gave by lot out of the **t** of the children	4294
	6:65	out of the **t** of the children of Simeon, and	4294
	6:65	out of the **t** of the children of Benjamin,	4294
	6:66	of their coasts out of the **t** of Ephraim.	4294
	6:70	out of the half **t** of Manasseh; Aner with	4294
	6:71	out of the family of the half **t** of Manasseh,	4294

1Ch 6:72 out of the t of Issachar; Kedesh with her 4294
6:74 out of the t of Asher; Mashal with her 4294
6:76 out of the t of Naphtali; Kedesh in Galilee 4294
6:77 Merari *were given* out of the t of Zebulun, 4294
6:78 *were given them* out of the t of Reuben, 4294
6:80 out of the t of Gad; Ramoth in Gilead with 4294
12:31 of the half t of Manasseh eighteen 4294
12:37 the Gadites, and of the half t of Manasseh, 7626
23:14 his sons were named of the t of Levi. 7626
26:32 the Gadites, and the half t of Manasseh, 7626
27:20 of the half t of Manasseh, Joel the son of 7626
27:21 Of the half *t* of Manasseh in Gilead, NIH
Ps 78:67 of Joseph, and chose not the t of Ephraim: 7626
78:68 chose the t of Judah, the mount Zion which 7626
Eze 47:23 *that* in what t the stranger sojourneth, 7626
Lk 2:36 the daughter of Phanuel, of the t of Aser: 5443
Ac 13:21 a man of the t of Benjamin, *by the space of* 5443
Ro 11: 1 the seed of Abraham, *of* the t of Benjamin. 5443
Php 3: 5 of the stock of Israel, of the t of Benjamin, 5443
Heb 7:13 *things* are spoken pertaineth to another t, 5443
7:14 of which t Moses spake nothing concerning 5443
Rev 5: 5 behold, the Lion of the t of Juda, the root of 5443
7: 5 Of the t of Juda *were* sealed twelve 5443
7: 5 Of the t of Reuben *were* sealed twelve 5443
7: 5 Of the t of Gad *were* sealed twelve 5443
7: 6 Of the t of Aser *were* sealed twelve 5443
7: 6 Of the t of Nephthalim *were* sealed twelve 5443
7: 6 Of the t of Manasses *were* sealed twelve 5443
7: 7 Of the t of Simeon *were* sealed twelve 5443
7: 7 Of the t of Levi *were* sealed twelve 5443
7: 7 Of the t of Isachar *were* sealed twelve 5443
7: 8 Of the t of Zabulon *were* sealed twelve 5443
7: 8 Of the t of Joseph *were* sealed twelve 5443
7: 8 Of the t of Benjamin *were* sealed twelve 5443

TRIBES (112) [TRIBE]

Ge 49:16 judge his people, as one of the t of Israel. 7626
49:28 All these *are* the twelve t of Israel: and 7626
Ex 24: 4 according to the twelve t of Israel. 7626
28:21 shall they be according to the twelve t. 7626
39:14 with his name, according to the twelve t. 7626
Nu 1:16 princes of the t of their fathers, heads of 4294
7: 2 who *were* the princes of the t, and were 4294
24: 2 abiding *in his tents* according to their t; 7626
26:55 according to the names of the t of their 4294
30: 1 Moses spake unto the heads of the t 4294
31: 4 throughout all the t of Israel, shall ye send 4294
32:28 the chief fathers of the t of the children of 4294
33:54 according to the t of your fathers ye shall 4294
34:13 commanded to give unto the nine t, 4294
34:15 The two t and the half tribe have received 4294
36: 3 sons of the *other* t of the children of Israel, 7626
36: 9 every one of the t of the children of Israel 4294
Dt 1:13 known among your t, and I will make them 7626
1:15 So I took the chief of your t, wise men, and 7626
1:15 over tens, and officers among your t. 7626
5:23 *even* all the heads of your t, and 7626
12: 5 out of all your t to put his name there, 7626
12:14 the LORD shall choose in one of thy t, 7626
16:18 thy God giveth thee, throughout thy t: 7626
18: 5 thy God hath chosen him out of all thy t, 7626
29:10 your captains of your t, your elders, and 7626
29:21 him unto evil out of all the t of Israel, 7626
31:28 Gather unto me all the elders of your t, and 7626
33: 5 *and* the t of Israel were gathered together. 7626
Jos 3:12 take ye twelve men out of the t of Israel, 7626
4: 5 according unto the number of the t of 7626
4: 8 according to the number of the t of 7626
7:14 ye shall be brought according to your t: 7626
7:16 the morning, and brought Israel by their t; 7626
11:23 Israel according to their divisions by their t. 7626
12: 7 which Joshua gave unto the t of Israel *for* a 7626
13: 7 this land for an inheritance unto the nine t, 7626
14: 1 the heads of the fathers of the t of 4294
14: 2 for the nine t, and *for* the half tribe. 4294
14: 3 Moses had given the inheritance of two t 4294
14: 4 For the children of Joseph were two t, 4294
18: 2 among the children of Israel seven t, 7626
19:51 the heads of the fathers of the t of 4294
21: 1 unto the heads of the fathers of the t of 4294
21:16 her suburbs; nine cities out of those two t. 7626
22:14 house a prince throughout all the t of Israel; 4294
23: 4 to be an inheritance for your t, from Jordan, 7626
24: 1 Joshua gathered all the t of Israel to 7626
Jdg 18: 1 not fallen unto them among the t of Israel. 7626
20: 2 of all the people, *even* of all the t of Israel, 7626
20:10 of an hundred throughout all the t of Israel, 7626
20:12 the t of Israel sent men through all the tribe 7626
21: 5 Who *is there* among all the t of Israel that 7626
21: 8 What one *is there* of the t of Israel that 7626
21:15 that the LORD had made a breach in the t 7626
1Sa 2:28 did I choose him out of all the t of Israel to 7626
9:21 of the smallest of the t of Israel? 7626
10:19 yourselves before the LORD by your t, 7626
10:20 when Samuel had caused all the t of Israel 7626
15:17 *wast* thou not *made* the head of the t of 7626
2Sa 5: 1 came all the t of Israel to David unto 7626
7: 7 spake I a word with any of the t of Israel, 7626
15: 2 Thy servant *is* of one of the t of Israel. 7626
15:10 Absalom sent spies throughout all the t of 7626
19: 9 were at strife throughout all the t of Israel, 7626
20:14 he went through all the t of Israel unto 7626
24: 2 Go now through all the t of Israel, 7626
1Ki 8: 1 elders of Israel, and all the heads of the t, 4294
8:16 I chose no city out of all the t of Israel to 7626
11:31 of Solomon, and will give ten t to thee: 7626
11:32 the city which I have chosen out of all the t 7626
11:35 and will give it unto thee, *even* ten t. 7626
14:21 LORD did choose out of all the t of Israel, 7626
18:31 according to the number of the t of the sons 7626
2Ki 21: 7 which I have chosen out of all t of Israel, 7626
1Ch 27:16 Furthermore over the t of Israel: the ruler 7626
27:22 These *were* the princes of the t of Israel. 7626
28: 1 the princes of the t, and the captains of 7626
29: 6 of the fathers and princes of the t of Israel, 7626
2Ch 5: 2 elders of Israel, and all the heads of the t, 4294
6: 5 t of Israel to build a house *in,* that my name 7626
11:16 after them out of all the t of Israel such as 7626
12:13 had chosen out of all the t of Israel, 7626
33: 7 which I have chosen before all the t of 7626
Ezr 6:17 according to the number of the t of Israel. 7625
Ps 78:55 made the t of Israel to dwell in their tents. 7626
105:37 *was* not *one* feeble *person* among their t. 7626
122: 4 Whither the t go up, the tribes of 7626
122: 4 the tribes go up, the t of the LORD, 7626
Isa 19:13 *even they that are* the stay of the t thereof. 7626
49: 6 be my servant to raise up the t of Jacob, 7626
63:17 servants' sake, the t of thine inheritance. 7626
Eze 37:19 the t of Israel his fellows, and will put them 7626
45: 8 to the house of Israel according to their t. 7626
47:13 the land according to the twelve t of Israel: 7626
47:21 land unto you according to the t of Israel. 7626
47:22 inheritance with you among the t of Israel. 7626
48: 1 Now these *are* the names of the t. From 7626
48:19 city shall serve it out of all the t of Israel. 7626
48:23 As for the rest of the t, from the east side 7626
48:29 *by lot* unto the t of Israel for inheritance, 7626
48:31 *shall be* after the names of the t of Israel: 7626
Hos 5: 9 among the t of Israel have I made known 7626
Hab 3: 9 *according to* the oaths of the t, *even thy* 4294
Zec 9: 1 the eyes of man, as of all the t of Israel, 7626
Mt 19:28 judging the twelve t of Israel. 5443
24:30 and then shall all the t of the earth mourn, 5443
Lk 22:30 sit on thrones judging the twelve t of Israel. 5443
Ac 26: 7 Unto which *promise* our **twelve t**, 1429
Jas 1: 1 to the twelve t which are scattered abroad, 5443
Rev 7: 4 four thousand of all the t of the children of 5443
21:12 which are *the names* of the twelve t of 5443

TRIBULATION (22) [TRIBULATIONS]

Dt 4:30 When thou art in t, and all these things are 6862
Jdg 10:14 let them deliver you in the time of your t. 6869
1Sa 26:24 and let him deliver me out of all t. 6869
Mt 13:21 for when t or persecution ariseth because 2347
24:21 For then shall be great t, such as was not 2347
24:29 Immediately after the t of those days shall 2347
Mk 13:24 But in those days, after that t, the sun shall 2347
Jn 16:33 In the world ye shall have t: but be of good 2347
Ac 14:22 that we must through much t enter into 2347
Ro 2: 9 T and anguish, upon every soul of man that 2347
5: 3 knowing that t worketh patience; 2347
8:35 *shall* t, or distress, or persecution, or 2347
12:12 Rejoicing in hope; patient in t; 2347
2Co 1: 4 Who comforteth us in all our t, that we may 2347
7: 4 I am exceeding joyful in all our t. 2347
1Th 3: 4 we told you before that we should **suffer t**; 2346
2Th 1: 6 to recompense t to them that trouble you; 2347
Rev 1: 9 and companion in t, and in the kingdom 2347

T

Rev 2: 9 and t, and poverty, (but thou art rich) 2347
2:10 may be tried; and ye shall have t ten days: 2347
2:22 that commit adultery with her into great t, 2347
7:14 These are they which came out of great t, 2347

TRIBULATIONS (4) [TRIBULATION]
1Sa 10:19 you out of all your adversities and your t; 6869
Ro 5: 3 And not only *so*, but we glory in t also: 2347
Eph 3:13 Wherefore I desire that *ye* faint not at my t 2347
2Th 1: 4 all your persecutions and t that ye endure: 2347

TRIBUTARIES (4) [TRIBUTE]
Dt 20:11 that is found therein shall be t unto thee, 4522
Jdg 1:30 dwelt among them, and became t. 4522
1:33 and of Beth-anath became t unto them. 4522
1:35 of Joseph prevailed, so that they became t. 4522

TRIBUTARY (1) [TRIBUTE]
La 1: 1 among the provinces, *how* is she become t! 4522

TRIBUTE (37) [TRIBUTARIES, TRIBUTARY]
Ge 49:15 to bear, and became a servant unto t. 4522
Nu 31:28 levy a t unto the LORD of the men of war 4371
31:37 the LORD'S t of the sheep was six 4371
31:38 of which the LORD'S t *was* threescore 4371
31:39 of which the LORD'S t *was* threescore 4371
31:40 of which the LORD'S t *was* thirty and 4371
31:41 Moses gave the t, *which was* the LORD'S 4371
Dt 16:10 *with* a t of a freewill offering of thine hand, 4530
Jos 16:10 unto this day, and serve under t. 4522
17:13 that they put the Canaanites to t; 4522
Jdg 1:28 that they put the Canaanites to t, and 4522
2Sa 20:24 Adoram *was* over the t: and 4522
1Ki 4: 6 Adoniram the son of Abda *was* over the t. 4522
9:21 upon those did Solomon levy a t of 4522
12:18 sent Adoram, who *was* over the t; 4522
2Ki 23:33 put the land to a t of an hundred talents of 6066
2Ch 8: 8 them did Solomon make to pay t until this 4522
10:18 sent Hadoram that *was* over the t; 4522
17:11 brought Jehoshaphat presents, and t silver; 4853
Ezr 4:13 t, and custom, and *so* thou shalt endamage 1093
4:20 and toll, t, and custom, *was* paid unto them. 1093
6: 8 *even* of the t beyond the river, 4061
7:24 to impose toll, t, or custom, upon them. 1093
Ne 5: 4 We have borrowed money for the king's t, 4060
Est 10: 1 the king Ahasuerus laid a t upon the land, 4522
Pr 12:24 bear rule: but the slothful shall be under t. 4522
Mt 17:24 they that received t **money** came to Peter, 1323
17:24 and said, Doth not your master pay t? 1323
17:25 do the kings of the earth take custom or t? 2778
22:17 Is it lawful to give t unto Cesar, or not? 2778
22:19 Shew me the t money. And they brought 2778
Mk 12:14 Is it lawful to give t to Cesar, or not? 2778
Lk 20:22 Is it lawful for us to give t unto Cesar, or 5411
23: 2 and forbidding to give t to Cesar, saying 5411
Ro 13: 6 For for this cause pay you t also: for they 5411
13: 7 t to whom tribute *is due;* custom to whom 5411
13: 7 tribute to whom t *is due;* custom to whom 5411

TRICKERY See GUILE

TRICKLETH (1)
La 3:49 Mine eye t **down**, and ceaseth not, without 5064

TRIED (20) [TRY]
Dt 21: 5 every controversy and every stroke be *t*: NIH
2Sa 22:31 way *is* perfect; the word of the LORD *is* t: 6884
Job 23:10 *when* he hath t me, I shall come forth as 974
34:36 My desire *is that* Job may be t unto the end 974
Ps 12: 6 *as* silver t in a furnace of earth, 6884
17: 3 thou hast t me, *and* shalt find nothing; 6884
18:30 the word of the LORD is t: he *is* a buckler 6884
66:10 proved us: thou hast t us, as silver is tried. 6884
66:10 proved us: thou hast tried us, as silver is t. 6884
105:19 word came: the word of the LORD t him. 6884
Isa 28:16 in Zion for a foundation a stone, a t stone, 976
Jer 12: 3 hast seen me, and t mine heart towards thee: 974
Da 12:10 shall be purified, and made white, and t; 6884
Zec 13: 9 is refined, and will try them as gold is t: 974
Heb 11:17 when he was t, offered up Isaac: 3985
Jas 1:12 for when he is t, he shall receive the crown 1384
1Pe 1: 7 though it be t with fire, might be found 1381
Rev 2: 2 thou hast t them which say *they* are 3985
2:10 *some* of you into prison, that ye may be t; 3985
3:18 I counsel thee to buy of me gold t in 4448

TRIEST (3) [TRY]
1Ch 29:17 that thou t the heart, and hast pleasure in 974
Jer 11:20 that t the reins and the heart, 974
20:12 that t the righteous, *and* seest the reins and 974

TRIETH (5) [TRY]
Job 34: 3 For the ear t words, as the mouth tasteth 974
Ps 7: 9 for the righteous God t the hearts and reins. 974
11: 5 The LORD t the righteous: but the wicked 974
Pr 17: 3 for gold: but the LORD t the hearts. 974
1Th 2: 4 pleasing men, but God, which t our hearts. 1381

TRIMMED (2) [TRIMMEST]
2Sa 19:24 nor t his beard, nor washed his clothes, 6213
Mt 25: 7 all those virgins arose, and t their lamps. 2885

TRIMMEST (1) [TRIMMED]
Jer 2:33 Why t thou thy way to seek love? therefore 3190

TRIPOLIS See TARPELITES

TRIUMPH (10) [TRIUMPHED, TRIUMPHING]
2Sa 1:20 lest the daughters of the uncircumcised t. 5937
Ps 25: 2 let not mine enemies t over me. 5970
41:11 because mine enemy doth not t over me. 7321
47: 1 shout unto God with the voice of t. 7440
60: 8 my shoe: Philistia, t thou because of me. 7321
92: 4 thy work: I will t in the works of thy hands. 7442
94: 3 the wicked, how long shall the wicked t? 5937
106:47 unto thy holy name, *and* to t in thy praise. 7623
108: 9 I cast out my shoe; over Philistia will I t. 7321
2Co 2:14 which always **causeth** us **to** t in Christ, and 2358

TRIUMPHED (2) [TRIUMPH]
Ex 15: 1 the LORD, for he hath t **gloriously**: 1342+1342
15:21 the LORD, for he hath t **gloriously**; 1342+1342

TRIUMPHING (2) [TRIUMPH]
Job 20: 5 That the t of the wicked *is* short, and 7445
Col 2:15 a shew of *them* openly, t **over** them in it. 2358

TROAS (6)
Ac 16: 8 they passing by Mysia came down to T. 5174
16:11 Therefore loosing from T, we came with a 5174
20: 5 These going before tarried for us at T. 5174
20: 6 and came unto them to T in five days; 5174
2Co 2:12 when I came to T to *preach* Christ's gospel, 5174
2Ti 4:13 The cloke that I left at T with Carpus, 5174

TRODDEN (27) [TREAD]
Dt 1:36 to him will I give the land that he hath t 1869
Jos 14: 9 Surely the land whereon thy feet have t 1869
Jdg 5:21 O my soul, thou hast t **down** strength. 1869
Job 22:15 the old way which wicked men have t? 1869
28: 8 The lion's whelps have not t it, nor 1869
Ps119:118 Thou hast t **down** all them that err from thy 5541
Isa 5: 5 the wall thereof, and it shall be t **down**: 4823
14:19 stones of the pit; as a carcase t **under feet**. 947
18: 2 a nation meted out and t **down**, whose land 4001
18: 7 a nation meted out and t **under foot**, 4001
25:10 Moab shall be t **down** under him, *even* as 1758
25:10 *even* as straw is t **down** for the dunghill. 1758
28: 3 drunkards of Ephraim, shall be t under feet: 7429
28:18 pass through, then ye shall be t **down** by it. 4823
63: 3 I have t the winepress alone; and of 1869
63:18 our adversaries have t **down** thy sanctuary. 947
Jer 12:10 they have t my portion **under foot**, 947
La 1:15 The Lord hath t **under foot** all my mighty 5541
1:15 the Lord hath t the virgin, the daughter of 1869
Eze 34:19 they eat **that which** ye have t with your 4823
Da 8:13 and the host to be t **under foot**? 4823
Mic 7:10 now shall she be t **down** as the mire of 4823
Mt 5:13 be cast out, and to be t **under foot** of men. 2662
Lk 8: 5 and it was t **down**, and the fowls of the air 2662
21:24 Jerusalem shall be t **down** of the Gentiles, 3961
Heb 10:29 who hath t **under foot** the Son of God, and 2662
Rev 14:20 And the winepress was t without the city, 3961

TRODE (8) [TREAD]
Jdg 9:27 t *the grapes*, and made merry, and 1869
20:43 t them **down** with ease over against Gibeah 1869
2Ki 7:17 the people t **upon** him in the gate, and 7429
7:20 for the people t **upon** him in the gate, and 7429
9:33 and on the horses: and he t her **under foot**. 7429
14: 9 *was* in Lebanon, and t **down** the thistle. 7429

2Ch 25:18 *was* in Lebanon, and **t down** the thistle. 7429
Lk 12: 1 insomuch that *they* t one **upon** another, *2662*

TROGYLLIUM (1)
Ac 20:15 *day* we arrived at Samos, and tarried at T; *5175*

TROOP (13) [TROOPS]
Ge 30:11 Leah said, A t cometh: and she called his 1409
49:19 Gad, a t shall overcome him: but he shall 1416
1Sa 30: 8 saying, Shall I pursue after this t? 1416
2Sa 2:25 became one t, and stood on the top of a hill. 92
3:22 of David and Joab came from *pursuing* a t, 1416
22:30 For by thee I have run *through* a t: by my 1416
23:11 Philistines were gathered together into a t, 2416
23:13 the t of the Philistines pitched in the valley 2416
Ps 18:29 For by thee I have run *through* a t; and 1416
Isa 65:11 that prepare a table for *that* t, and 1409
Jer 18:22 when thou shalt bring a t suddenly upon 1416
Hos 7: 1 *and* the t *of robbers* spoileth without. 1416
Am 9: 6 and hath founded his t in the earth; 92

TROOPS (7) [TROOP]
Job 6:19 The t of Tema looked, the companies of 734
19:12 His t come together, and raise up their way 1416
Jer 5: 7 **assembled** themselves **by** t *in* the harlots' 1413
Hos 6: 9 as t *of robbers* wait for a man, *so* 1416
Mic 5: 1 Now **gather** thyself **in** t, O daughter of 1413
5: 1 gather thyself in troops, O daughter of t: 1416
Hab 3:16 the people, he will **invade** them **with** his t. 1464

TROPHIMUS (3)
Ac 20: 4 Timotheus; and of Asia, Tychicus and T. *5161*
21:29 before with him in the city T an Ephesian, *5161*
2Ti 4:20 but **T** have I left at Miletum sick. *5161*

TROUBLE (110) [TROUBLED, TROUBLEDST, TROUBLER, TROUBLES, TROUBLEST, TROUBLETH, TROUBLING, TROUBLOUS]
Jos 6:18 make the camp of Israel a curse, and t it. 5916
7:25 the LORD shall t thee this day. And all 5916
Jdg 11:35 and thou art one of them that t me: 5916
2Ki 19: 3 This day *is* a day of t, and of rebuke, and 6869
1Ch 22:14 in my t I have prepared for the house of 6040
2Ch 15: 4 when they in their t did turn unto 6862
29: 8 Jerusalem, and he hath delivered them to t, 2189
32:18 on the wall, to affright them, and to t them; 926
Ne 9:27 in the time of their t, when they cried unto 6869
9:32 let not all the t seem little before thee, 8513
Job 3:26 had I rest, neither was I quiet; yet t came. 7267
5: 6 neither doth t spring out of the ground; 5999
5: 7 Yet man is born unto t, as the sparks fly 5999
14: 1 of a woman *is* of few days, and full of t. 7267
15:24 T and anguish shall make him afraid; 6862
27: 9 Will God hear his cry when t cometh upon 6869
30:25 Did not I weep for him that was **in** t? 3117+7186
34:29 he giveth quietness, who then can **make** t? 7561
38:23 Which I have reserved against the time of t, 6862
Ps 3: 1 LORD, how are they increased that t me! 6862
9: 9 for the oppressed, a refuge in times of t. 6869
9:13 consider my t *which I suffer* of them that 6040
10: 1 *why* hidest thou *thyself* in times of t? 6869
13: 4 those that t me rejoice when I am moved. 6862
20: 1 The LORD hear thee in the day of t; 6869
22:11 Be not far from me; for t *is* near; for *there* 6869
27: 5 For in the time of t he shall hide me in his 7451
31: 7 for thou hast considered my t; thou hast 6040
31: 9 mercy upon me, O LORD, for I am in t: 6887
32: 7 hiding place; thou shalt preserve me from t; 6862
37:39 *he is* their strength in the time of t. 6869
41: 1 the LORD will deliver him in time of t. 7451
46: 1 and strength, a very present help in t. 6869
50:15 call upon me in the day of t: I will deliver 6869
54: 7 For he hath delivered me out of all t: and 6869
59:16 my defence and refuge in the day of my t. 6862
60:11 Give us help from t: for vain *is* the help of 6862
66:14 my mouth hath spoken, when I was in t. 6862
69:17 not thy face from thy servant; for I am **in** t: 6887
73: 5 They *are* not in t *as other* men; neither are 5999
77: 2 In the day of my t I sought the Lord: 6869
78:33 he consume in vanity, and their years in t. 928
78:49 wrath, and indignation, and t, *by* sending 6869
81: 7 Thou calledst in t, and I delivered thee; 6869
86: 7 In the day of my t I will call upon thee: 6869
91:15 I *will be* with him in t; I will deliver him, 6869
102: 2 thy face from me in the day *when* I am in t; 6862
107: 6 they cried unto the LORD in their t, *and* 6862
107:13 they cried unto the LORD in their t, *and* 6862
107:19 they cry unto the LORD in their t, 6862
107:26 the depths: their soul is melted because of t. 7451
107:28 they cry unto the LORD in their t, and 6862
108:12 Give us help from t: for vain *is* the help of 6862
116: 3 gat hold upon me: I found t and sorrow. 6869
119:143 T and anguish have taken hold on me: 6862
138: 7 Though I walk in the midst of t, thou wilt 6869
142: 2 before him; I shewed before him my t. 6869
143:11 righteousness' sake bring my soul out of t. 6869
Pr 11: 8 The righteous is delivered out of t, and 6869
12:13 of *his* lips: but the just shall come out of t. 6869
15: 6 but in the revenues of the wicked *is* t. 5916
15:16 LORD than great treasure and t therewith. 4103
25:19 *man* in time of t *is like* a broken tooth, 6869
Isa 1:14 they are a t unto me; I am weary to bear 2960
8:22 behold t and darkness, dimness of anguish; 6869
17:14 behold at eveningtide t; *and* before 1091
22: 5 For *it is* a day of t, and of treading down, 4103
26:16 LORD, in t have they visited thee, 6862
30: 6 into the land of t and anguish, from whence 6869
33: 2 our salvation also in the time of t. 6869
37: 3 This day *is* a day of t, and of rebuke, and 6869
46: 7 he not answer, nor save him out of his t. 6869
65:23 shall not labour in vain, nor bring forth for t; 928
Jer 2:27 in the time of their t they will say, Arise, 7451
2:28 if they can save thee in the time of thy t: 7451
8:15 *and* for a time of health, and behold t. 1205
11:12 not save them at all in the time of their t. 7451
11:14 in the time that they cry unto me for their t. 7451
14: 8 of Israel, the saviour thereof in time of t, 6869
14:19 and for the time of healing, and behold t. 1205
30: 7 it *is* even the time of Jacob's t; but he shall 6869
51: 2 for in the day of t they shall be against her 7451
La 1:21 all mine enemies have heard of my t; 7451
Eze 7: 7 the day of t *is* near, and not the sounding 4103
32:13 neither shall the foot of man t them any 1804
32:13 any more, nor the hoofs of beasts t them. 1804
Da 4:19 or the interpretation thereof, t thee. 927
5:10 let not thy thoughts t thee, nor let thy 927
11:44 of the east and out of the north shall t him: 926
12: 1 there shall be a time of t, such as never was 6869
Na 1: 7 *is* good, a strong hold in the day of t; 6869
Hab 3:16 in myself, that I might rest in the day of t: 6869
Zep 1:15 a day of t and distress, a day of wasteness 6869
Mt 26:10 unto them, Why t ye the woman? *2873+3930*
Mk 14: 6 Let her alone; why t you her? *2873+3930*
Lk 7: 6 to him, saying unto him, Lord, t not thyself: *4660*
8:49 Thy daughter is dead; t not the Master. *4660*
11: 7 shall answer and say, T me not: *2873+3930*
Ac 15:19 my sentence is, that *we* t not them, *3926*
16:20 being Jews, do **exceedingly** t our city, *1613*
20:10 and embracing *him* said, T not yourselves; *2350*
1Co 7:28 Nevertheless such shall have t in the flesh: *2347*
2Co 1: 4 be able to comfort them which are in any t, *2347*
1: 8 have you ignorant of our t which came to *2347*
Gal 1: 7 but there be some that t you, and *5015*
5:12 I would they were even cut off which t you. *387*
6:17 From henceforth let no *man* t me: *2873+3930*
2Th 1: 6 recompense tribulation to them that t you; *2346*
2Ti 2: 9 Wherein I **suffer** t, as an evil doer, *2553*
Heb 12:15 lest any root of bitterness springing up t *1776*

TROUBLED (68) [TROUBLE]
Ge 34:30 Ye have t me to make me to stink among 5916
41: 8 to pass in the morning that his spirit was t; 6470
45: 3 answer him; for they were t at his presence. 926
Ex 14:24 the cloud, and t the host of the Egyptians, 2000
Jos 7:25 Joshua said, Why hast thou t us? 5916
1Sa 14:29 said Jonathan, My father hath t the land: 5916
16:14 and an evil spirit from the LORD t him. 1204
28:21 saw that he was sore t, and said unto him, 926
2Sa 4: 1 were feeble, and all the Israelites were t. 926
1Ki 18:18 he answered, I have not t Israel; but thou, 5916
2Ki 6:11 the king of Syria was **sore** t for this thing; 5590
Ezr 4: 4 the people of Judah, and t them in building, 926
Job 4: 5 thou faintest; it toucheth thee, and thou art t. 926
21: 4 if *it were so,* why should not my spirit be t? 7114
23:15 Therefore am I t at his presence: when I 926
34:20 the people shall be t at midnight, and 1607
Ps 30: 7 thou didst hide thy face, *and* I was t. 926
38: 6 I am t; I am bowed down greatly; I go 5753

T

Ps 46: 3 *Though* the waters thereof roar *and* be **t**, 2560
48: 5 they were **t**, *and* hasted away. 926
77: 3 I remembered God, and was **t**: 1993
77: 4 eyes waking: I am *so* **t** that I cannot speak. 6470
77:16 they were afraid: the depths also were **t**. 7264
83:17 Let them be confounded and **t** for ever; yea, 926
90: 7 by thine anger, and by thy wrath are we **t**. 926
104:29 Thou hidest thy face, they are **t**: thou takest 926
Pr 25:26 down before the wicked *is as* a **t** fountain, 7515
Isa 32:10 Many days and years shall ye be **t**, 7264
32:11 that are at ease; be **t**, ye careless ones: 7264
57:20 the wicked *are* like the **t** sea, when it cannot 1644
Jer 31:20 therefore my bowels are **t** for him; I will 1993
La 1:20 my bowels are **t**; mine heart is turned 2560
2:11 eyes do fail with tears, my bowels are **t**, 2560
Eze 7:27 the hands of the people of the land shall be **t**: 926
26:18 the isles that *are* in the sea shall be **t** at thy 926
27:35 they shall be **t** *in their* countenance. 7481
Da 2: 1 wherewith his spirit was **t**, and his sleep 6470
2: 3 and my spirit was **t** to know the dream. 6470
4: 5 my bed and the visions of my head **t** me. 927
4:19 for one hour, and his thoughts **t** him. 927
5: 6 his thoughts **t** him, so that the joints of his 927
5: 9 *was* king Belshazzar greatly **t**, and 927
7:15 *my* body, and the visions of my head **t** me. 927
7:28 my cogitations much **t** me, and 927
Zec 10: 2 they were **t**, because *there was* no shepherd. 6031
Mt 2: 3 the king had heard *these things*, he was **t**, *5015*
14:26 on the sea, they were **t**, saying, It is a spirit; *5015*
24: 6 see that ye be not **t**: for all *these things* *2360*
Mk 6:50 For they all saw him, and were **t**. *5015*
13: 7 of wars and rumours of wars, be ye not **t**: *2360*
Lk 1:12 And when Zacharias saw *him*, he was **t**, *5015*
1:29 And when she saw *him*, she was **t** at his *1298*
10:41 thou art careful and **t** about many *things*: *5182*
24:38 And he said unto them, Why are ye **t**? and *5015*
Jn 5: 4 season into the pool, and **t** the water: *5015*
5: 7 Sir, I have no man, when the water is **t**, *5015*
11:33 he groaned in the spirit, and was **t**, *5015*
12:27 Now is my soul **t**; and what shall I say? *5015*
13:21 he was **t** in spirit, and testified, and said, *5015*
14: 1 Let not your heart be **t**: ye believe in God, *5015*
14:27 Let not your heart be **t**, neither let it be *5015*
Ac 15:24 that certain which went out from us have **t** *5015*
17: 8 And they **t** the people and the rulers of *5015*
2Co 4: 8 *We are* **t** on every *side*, yet not distressed; *2346*
7: 5 *we were* **t** on every *side*; without *were* *2346*
2Th 1: 7 And to you who are **t** rest with us, when *2346*
2: 2 or be **t**, neither by spirit, nor by word, *2360*
1Pe 3:14 be not afraid of their terror, neither be **t**; *5015*

TROUBLEDST (1) [TROUBLE]
Eze 32: 2 **t** the waters with thy feet, and fouledst their 1804

TROUBLEMAKER See PESTILENT

TROUBLER (1) [TROUBLE]
1Ch 2: 7 Achar, the **t** of Israel, who transgressed in 5916

TROUBLES (12) [TROUBLE]
Dt 31:17 and many evils and **t** shall befall them; 6869
31:21 when many evils and **t** are befallen them, 6869
Job 5:19 He shall deliver thee in six **t**: yea, in seven 6869
Ps 25:17 The **t** of my heart are enlarged: O bring 6869
25:22 Redeem Israel, O God, out of all his **t**. 6869
34: 6 heard *him*, and saved him out of all his **t**. 6869
34:17 and delivereth them out of all their **t**. 6869
71:20 which hast shewed me great and sore **t**, 6869
88: 3 For my soul is full of **t**: and my life 7451
Pr 21:23 and his tongue keepeth his soul from **t**. 6869
Isa 65:16 because the former **t** are forgotten, and 6869
Mk 13: 8 and there shall be famines and **t**: *5016*

TROUBLEST (1) [TROUBLE]
Mk 5:35 is dead: why **t** thou the Master any further? *4660*

TROUBLETH (10) [TROUBLE]
1Sa 16:15 Behold now, an evil spirit from God **t** thee. 1204
1Ki 18:17 said unto him, *Art* thou he that **t** Israel? 5916
Job 22:10 *are* round about thee, and sudden fear **t** thee; 926
23:16 my heart soft, and the Almighty **t** me: 926
Pr 11:17 but *he that is* cruel **t** his own flesh. 5916
11:29 He that **t** his own house shall inherit 5916
15:27 He that is greedy of gain **t** his own house; 5916
Da 4: 9 the holy gods *is* in thee, and no secret **t** thee, 598

Lk 18: 5 Yet because this widow **t** me, I will *2873+3930*
Gal 5:10 but he that **t** you shall bear *his* judgment, *5015*

TROUBLING (2) [TROUBLE]
Job 3:17 There the wicked cease *from* **t**; and 7267
Jn 5: 4 then first after the **t** of the water stepped in, *5016*

TROUBLOUS (1) [TROUBLE]
Da 9:25 be built again, and the wall, even in **t** times. 6695

TROUGH (1) [KNEADINGTROUGHS, TROUGHS]
Ge 24:20 emptied her pitcher into the **t**, and ran again 8268

TROUGHS (2) [TROUGH]
Ge 30:38 watering **t** when the flocks came to drink, 8268
Ex 2:16 and filled the **t** to water their father's flock. 7298

TROUSERS See HOSEN

TROW (1)
Lk 17: 9 *things* that were commanded him? I **t** not. *1380*

TRUCEBREAKERS (1) [BREAK]
2Ti 3: 3 **t**, false accusers, incontinent, fierce, *786*

TRUE (81) [TRUTH]
Ge 42:11 we *are* **t** *men*, thy servants are no spies. 3651
42:19 If ye *be* **t** *men*, let one of your brethren be 3651
42:31 unto him, We *are* **t** *men*; we are no spies: 3651
42:33 Hereby shall I know that ye *are* **t** *men*; 3651
42:34 *that* ye *are* **t** *men*: *so* will I deliver you your 3651
Dt 17: 4 and behold, *it is* **t**, *and* the thing certain, 571
22:20 if this thing be **t**, *and the tokens of* virginity 571
Jos 2:12 my father's house, and give me a **t** token: 571
Ru 3:12 now it is **t** that I *am thy* near kinsman: 551
2Sa 7:28 thy words be **t**, and thou hast promised this 571
1Ki 10: 6 It was a **t** report that I heard in mine own 571
22:16 *that which is* **t** in the name of the LORD? 571
2Ch 9: 5 *It was* a **t** report which I heard in mine own 571
15: 3 season Israel *hath been* without the **t** God, 571
Ne 9:13 **t** laws, good statutes and commandments: 571
Ps 19: 9 the judgments of the LORD *are* **t** *and* 571
119:160 Thy word *is* **t** *from* the beginning: and 571
Pr 14:25 A **t** witness delivereth souls: but a deceitful 571
Jer 10:10 the LORD *is* the **t** God, he *is* the living 571
42: 5 The LORD be a **t** and faithful witness 571
Eze 18: 8 hath executed **t** judgment between man and 571
Da 3:14 *Is it* **t**, O Shadrach, Meshach, and 6656
3:24 and said unto the king, **T**, O king. 3330
6:12 The king answered and said, The thing *is* **t**, 3330
8:26 and the morning which was told *is* **t**: 571
10: 1 the thing *was* **t**, but the time appointed *was* 571
Zec 7: 9 Execute **t** judgment, and shew mercy and 571
Mt 22:16 we know that thou art **t**, and teachest *227*
Mk 12:14 we know that thou art **t**, and carest for no *227*
Lk 16:11 who will commit to your trust the **t** *riches*? *228*
Jn 1: 9 *That* was the **t** Light, which lighteth every *228*
3:33 testimony hath set to *his* seal that God is **t**. *227*
4:23 when the **t** worshippers shall worship *228*
4:37 And herein is *that* saying **t**, One soweth, *228*
5:31 I bear witness of myself, my witness is not **t**. *227*
5:32 the witness which he witnesseth of me is **t**. *227*
6:32 my Father giveth you the **t** bread from *228*
7:18 the same is **t**, and no unrighteousness is in *227*
7:28 but he that sent me is **t**, whom ye know not. *228*
8:13 bearest record of thyself; thy record is not **t**. *227*
8:14 I bear record of myself, *yet* my record is **t**: *227*
8:16 And yet if I judge, my judgment is **t**: for I *227*
8:17 your law, that the testimony of two men is **t**. *227*
8:26 but he that sent me is **t**; and I speak to *227*
10:41 all *things* that John spake of this *man* were **t**. *227*
15: 1 I am the **t** vine, and my Father is *228*
17: 3 that they might know thee the only **t** God, *228*
19:35 he that saw *it* bare record, and his record is **t**: *228*
19:35 and he knoweth that he saith **t**, that ye might *227*
21:24 and we know that his testimony is **t**. *227*
Ac 12: 9 wist not that it was **t** which was done by *227*
Ro 3: 4 yea, let God be **t**, but every man a liar; as it *227*
2Co 1:18 But *as* God *is* **t**, our word toward you was *4103*
6: 8 and good report: as deceivers, and *yet* **t**; *227*
Eph 4:24 is created in righteousness and **t** holiness. *225*
Php 4: 3 And I intreat thee also, **t** yokefellow, *1103*
4: 8 Finally, brethren, whatsoever *things* are **t**, *227*
1Th 1: 9 God from idols to serve the living and **t** God, *228*
1Ti 3: 1 *This is* a **t** saying, If a man desire the office *4103*

Tit 1:13 This witness is t. Wherefore rebuke them 227
Heb 8: 2 and of the t tabernacle, which the Lord 228
9:24 with hands, *which are* the figures of the t; 228
10:22 Let us draw near with a t heart in full 228
1Pe 5:12 testifying that this is the t grace of God 227
2Pe 2:22 unto them according to the t proverb, 227
1Jn 2: 8 unto you, which *thing* is t in him and in you: 227
2: 8 darkness is past, and the t light now shineth. 228
5:20 that we may know him *that is* t, and we are 228
5:20 and we are in him *that is* t, *even* in his Son 228
5:20 This is the t God, and eternal life. 228
3Jn 1:12 bear record; and ye know that our record is t. 227
Rev 3: 7 he *that is* t, he that hath the key of David, 228
3:14 saith the Amen, the faithful and t witness, 228
6:10 saying, How long, O Lord, holy and t, 228
15: 3 just and t *are* thy ways, thou King of saints. 228
16: 7 t and righteous *are* thy judgments. 228
19: 2 For t and righteous *are* his judgments: for he 228
19: 9 unto me, These are the t sayings of God. 228
19:11 that sat upon him *was* called Faithful and T, 228
21: 5 Write: for these words are t and faithful. 228
22: 6 unto me, These sayings *are* faithful and t: 228

TRULY (42) [TRUTH]

Ge 4:24 t Lamech seventy and sevenfold. 2050.1
24:49 if ye will deal kindly and t with my master, 571
47:29 my thigh, and deal kindly and t with me; 571
48:19 t his younger brother shall be greater than 199
Nu 14:21 *as* t *as* I live, all the earth shall be filled *with* 199
14:28 Say unto them, *As* t *as* I live, saith NIH
Dt 14:22 Thou shalt t **tithe** all the increase of 6237+6237
Jos 2:14 that we will deal kindly and t with thee. 571
2:24 T the LORD hath delivered into our hands 3588
Jdg 9:16 if ye have done t and sincerely, 571+871.1
9:19 If ye then have dealt t and sincerely 571+871.1
1Sa 20: 3 t *as* the LORD liveth, and *as* thy soul 199
Job 36: 4 For t my words *shall* not *be* false: *he that is* 551
Ps 62: 1 T my soul waiteth upon God: from him 389
73: 1 T God *is* good to Israel, *even* to such as are 389
116:16 Oh LORD, t I *am* thy servant; I *am* thy 3588
Pr 12:22 but they that deal t *are* his delight. 530
Ecc 11: 7 T the light *is* sweet, and a pleasant *thing* 2050.1
Jer 3:23 T in vain *is salvation hoped for* from 403
3:23 t in the LORD our God *is* the salvation of 403
10:19 but I said, T this *is* a grief, and I must bear it. 389
28: 9 that the LORD hath t sent him. 571+871.1
Eze 18: 9 and hath kept my judgments, to deal t; 571
Mic 3: 8 t I am full *of* power by the spirit of 199
Mt 9:37 The harvest t is plenteous, but the labourers 3303
17:11 Elias t shall first come, and restore all 3303
27:54 saying, T this was the Son of God. 230
Mk 14:38 The spirit t *is* ready, but the flesh *is* weak. 3303
15:39 he said, T this man was the Son of God. 230
Lk 10: 2 The harvest t *is* great, but the labourers *are* 3303
11:48 T ye bear witness that ye allow the deeds of 686
20:21 *of any,* but teachest the way of God t: 225+1909
22:22 And t the Son of man goeth, as it was 3303
Jn 4:18 hast is not thy husband: *in* that saidst thou t. 227
20:30 And many other signs t did Jesus in 3303
Ac 1: 5 For John t baptized with water; but ye shall 3303
3:22 For Moses t said unto the fathers, 3303
5:23 The prison t found we shut with all safety, 3303
2Co 12:12 T the signs of an apostle were wrought 3303
Heb 7:23 And they t were many priests, because 3303
11:15 And t, if they had been mindful of that 3303
1Jn 1: 3 and t our fellowship *is* with the Father, and NIG

TRUMP (2) [TRUMPET]

1Co 15:52 in the twinkling of an eye, at the last t: 4536
1Th 4:16 of the archangel, and with the t of God: 4536

TRUMPET (61) [TRUMP, TRUMPETERS, TRUMPETS]

Ex 19:13 when the t soundeth long, they shall come 3104
19:16 and the voice of the t exceeding loud; 7782
19:19 when the voice of the t sounded long, and 7782
20:18 the noise of the t, and the mountain 7782
Lev 25: 9 shalt thou cause the t of the jubile to sound 7782
25: 9 in the day of atonement shall ye make the t 7782
Nu 10: 4 if they blow *but* with one *t*, then the princes, NIH
Jos 6: 5 *and* when ye hear the sound of the t, all 7782
6:20 when the people heard the sound of the t, 7782
Jdg 3:27 that he blew a t in the mountain of 7782
6:34 came upon Gideon, and he blew a t; 7782
7:16 he put a t in every man's hand, with empty 7782
7:18 When I blow with a t, I and all that *are* with 7782
1Sa 13: 3 And Saul blew the t throughout all the land, 7782
2Sa 2:28 So Joab blew a t, and all the people stood 7782
6:15 with shouting, and with the sound of the t. 7782
15:10 As soon as ye hear the sound of the t, then 7782
18:16 Joab blew the t, and the people returned 7782
20: 1 he blew a t, and said, We have no part in 7782
20:22 he blew a t, and they retired from the city, 7782
1Ki 1:34 blow ye with the t, and say, God save king 7782
1:39 they blew the t; and all the people said, 7782
1:41 when Joab heard the sound of the t, he said, 7782
Ne 4:18 And he that sounded the t *was* by me. 7782
4:20 *therefore* ye hear the sound of the t, 7782
Job 39:24 believeth he that *it is* the sound of the t. 7782
Ps 47: 5 a shout, the LORD with the sound of a t. 7782
81: 3 Blow up the t in the new moon, in the time 7782
150: 3 Praise him with the sound of the t: 7782
Isa 18: 3 and when *he* bloweth a t, hear ye. 7782
27:13 *that* the great t shall be blown, and 7782
58: 1 lift up thy voice like a t, and shew my 7782
Jer 4: 5 and say, Blow ye the t in the land: 7782
4:19 hast heard, O my soul, the sound of the t, 7782
4:21 the standard, *and* hear the sound of the t? 7782
6: 1 blow the t in Tekoa, and set up a sign of 7782
6:17 *saying,* Hearken to the sound of the t. 7782
42:14 nor hear the sound of the t, nor have hunger 7782
51:27 blow the t among the nations, prepare 7782
Eze 7:14 They have blown the t, even to make all 8619
33: 3 he blow the t, and warn the people; 7782
33: 4 whosoever heareth the sound of the t, and 7782
33: 5 He heard the sound of the t, and took not 7782
33: 6 blow not the t, and the people be not 7782
Hos 5: 8 the cornet in Gibeah, *and* the t in Ramah: 2689
8: 1 *Set* the t to thy mouth. *He shall come* as an 7782
Joel 2: 1 Blow ye the t in Zion, and sound an alarm 7782
2:15 Blow the t in Zion, sanctify a fast, call a 7782
Am 2: 2 with shouting, *and* with the sound of the t: 7782
3: 6 Shall a t be blown in the city, and 7782
Zep 1:16 A day of the t and alarm against the fenced 7782
Zec 9:14 the Lord GOD shall blow the t, and 7782
Mt 6: 2 *thine* alms, do not **sound a t** before thee, 4537
24:31 send his angels with a great sound of a t, 4536
1Co 14: 8 For if the t give an uncertain sound, 4536
15:52 for the t shall **sound**, and the dead shall be 4537
Heb 12:19 And the sound of a t, and the voice of 4536
Rev 1:10 heard behind me a great voice, as of a t, 4536
4: 1 heard *was* as *it were* of a t talking with me; 4536
8:13 the other voices of the t of the three angels, 4536
9:14 Saying to the sixth angel which had the t, 4536

TRUMPETERS (4) [TRUMPET]

2Ki 11:14 and the princes and the t by the king, 2689
2Ch 5:13 to pass, as the t and singers *were* as one, 2690
29:28 and the singers sang, and the t sounded: 2689
Rev 18:22 and musicians, and of pipers, and t, 4538

TRUMPETS (51) [TRUMPET]

Lev 23:24 a memorial of **blowing of t**, a holy 8643
Nu 10: 2 Make thee two t of silver; of a whole piece 2689
10: 8 of Aaron, the priests, shall blow with the t; 2689
10: 9 then ye shall blow an alarm with the t; 2689
10:10 ye shall blow with the t over your burnt 2689
29: 1 it is a day of **blowing** the t unto you. 8643
31: 6 and the t to blow in his hand. 2689
Jos 6: 4 bear before the ark seven t of rams' horns: 7782
6: 4 and the priests shall blow with the t. 7782
6: 6 let seven priests bear seven t of rams' horns 7782
6: 8 that the seven priests bearing the seven t of 7782
6: 8 on before the LORD, and blew with the t: 7782
6: 9 went before the priests that blew *with* the t, 7782
6: 9 *priests* going on, and blowing with the t. 7782
6:13 seven priests bearing seven t of rams' horns 7782
6:13 went on continually, and blew with the t: 7782
6:13 *priests* going on, and blowing with the t. 7782
6:16 when the priests blew with the t, Joshua 7782
6:20 shouted when *the priests* blew with the t: 7782
Jdg 7: 8 took victuals in their hand, and their t: 7782
7:18 blow ye the t also on every side of all 7782
7:19 they blew the t, and brake the pitchers that 7782
7:20 the three companies blew the t, and 7782
7:20 the t in their right hands to blow *withal:* 7782
7:22 the three hundred blew the t, and 7782
2Ki 9:13 and blew with t, saying, Jehu is king. 7782
11:14 of the land rejoiced, and blew with t: 2689

T

2Ki	12:13	snuffers, basons, **t**, any vessels of gold, or	2689
1Ch	13: 8	and with cymbals, and with **t**.	2689
	15:24	did blow with the **t** before the ark of God:	2689
	15:28	of the cornet, and with **t**, and with cymbals,	2689
	16: 6	Jahaziel the priests with **t** continually	2689
	16:42	with them Heman and Jeduthun *with* **t** and	2689
2Ch	5:12	and twenty priests sounding with **t**:)	2689
	5:13	when *they* lift up *their* voice with the **t** and	2689
	7: 6	the priests **sounded** **t** before them, and	2690
	13:12	his priests with sounding **t** to cry alarm	2689
	13:14	and the priests sounded with the **t**.	2689
	15:14	with shouting, and with **t**, and with cornets.	2689
	20:28	and **t** unto the house of the LORD.	2689
	23:13	and the princes and the **t** by the king:	2689
	23:13	of the land rejoiced, and sounded with **t**,	2689
	29:26	of David, and the priests with the **t**.	2689
	29:27	song of the LORD began *also* with the **t**,	2689
Ezr	3:10	they set the priests in their apparel with **t**,	2689
Ne	12:35	*certain* of the priests' sons with **t**;	2689
	12:41	Elioenai, Zechariah, *and* Hananiah, with **t**;	2689
Job	39:25	He saith among the **t**, Ha, ha; and	7782
Ps	98: 6	With **t** and sound of cornet make a joyful	2689
Rev	8: 2	and to them were given seven **t**.	*4536*
	8: 6	And the seven angels which had the seven **t**	*4536*

TRUST (134) [TRUSTED, TRUSTEDST, TRUSTEST, TRUSTETH, TRUSTING, TRUSTY]

Jdg	9:15	*then* come *and* **put** your **t** in my shadow:	2620
Ru	2:12	under whose wings thou art come to **t**.	2620
2Sa	22: 3	The God of my rock; in him will I **t**: *he is*	2620
	22:31	he *is* a buckler to all them that **t** in him.	2620
2Ki	18:20	Now on whom dost thou **t**, that thou	982
	18:21	*is* Pharaoh king of Egypt unto all that **t** on	982
	18:22	say unto me, We **t** in the LORD our God:	982
	18:24	**put** thy **t** on Egypt for chariots and	982
	18:30	Neither let Hezekiah **make** you **t** in	982
1Ch	5:20	of them; because they **put** their **t** in him.	982
2Ch	32:10	Whereon do ye **t**, that ye abide in the siege	982
Job	4:18	Behold, he **put** no **t** in his servants; and his	539
	8:14	cut off, and whose **t** *shall be* a spider's web.	4009
	13:15	Though he slay me, *yet* will I **t** in him: but	3176
	15:15	Behold, he **putteth** no **t** in his saints; yea,	539
	15:31	Let not him that is deceived **t** in vanity:	539
	35:14	*is* before him; therefore **t** thou in him.	2342
	39:11	Wilt thou **t** him, because his strength *is*	982
Ps	2:12	blessed *are* all they that **put** their **t** in him.	2620
	4: 5	and **put** your **t** in the LORD.	982
	5:11	let all those that **put** their **t** in thee rejoice:	2620
	7: 1	O LORD my God, in thee do I **put** my **t**:	2620
	9:10	they that know thy name will **put** their **t** in	982
	11: 1	In the LORD **put** I my **t**: how say ye to	2620
	16: 1	O God: for in thee do I **put** my **t**.	2620
	17: 7	**put** their **t** *in thee* from those that rise up	2620
	18: 2	my God, my strength, in whom I will **t**;	2620
	18:30	he *is* a buckler to all those that **t** in him.	2620
	20: 7	Some *t* in chariots, and some in horses: but	NIH
	25: 2	O my God, I **t** in thee: let me not be	982
	25:20	me not be ashamed; for I **put** my **t** in thee.	2620
	31: 1	In thee, O LORD, do I **put** my **t**; let me	2620
	31: 6	regard lying vanities: but I **t** in the LORD.	982
	31:19	*which* thou hast wrought for them that **t** in	2620
	34:22	none of them that **t** in him shall be desolate.	2620
	36: 7	the children of men **put** their **t** under	2620
	37: 3	**T** in the LORD, and do good; *so* shalt thou	982
	37: 5	**t** also in him; and he shall bring *it* to pass.	982
	37:40	and save them, because they **t** in him.	2620
	40: 3	see *it,* and fear, and shall **t** in the LORD.	982
	40: 4	*is that* man that maketh the LORD his **t**,	4009
	44: 6	For I will not **t** in my bow, neither shall my	982
	49: 6	They that **t** in their wealth, and	982
	52: 8	I **t** in the mercy of God for ever and ever.	982
	55:23	live out half their days; but I will **t** in thee.	982
	56: 3	*What* time I am afraid, I will **t** in thee.	982
	56: 4	will praise his word, in God I have **put** my **t**;	982
	56:11	In God have I **put** my **t**: I will not be afraid	982
	61: 4	I will **t** in the covert of thy wings. Selah.	2620
	62: 8	**T** in him at all times; ye people, pour out	982
	62:10	**T** not in oppression, and become not vain in	982
	64:10	be glad in the LORD, and shall **t** in him;	2620
	71: 1	In thee, O LORD, do I **put** my **t**: let me	2620
	71: 5	Lord GOD: *thou art* my **t** from my youth.	4009
	73:28	I have put my **t** in the Lord GOD, that *I*	4268
	91: 2	and my fortress: my God; in him will I **t**.	982
	91: 4	and under his wings shalt thou **t**:	2620
	115: 9	O Israel, **t** thou in the LORD: he *is* their	982
	115:10	O house of Aaron, **t** in the LORD: he *is*	982
	115:11	Ye that fear the LORD, **t** in the LORD:	982
	118: 8	*It is* better to **t** in the LORD than to put	2620
	118: 9	*It is* better to **t** in the LORD than to put	2620
	119:42	him that reproacheth me: for I **t** in thy word.	982
	125: 1	They that **t** in the LORD *shall be* as mount	982
	141: 8	in thee is my **t**; leave not my soul destitute.	2620
	143: 8	in the morning; for in thee do I **t**:	982
	144: 2	my shield, and *he* in whom I **t**;	2620
	146: 3	**Put** not your **t** in princes, *nor* in the son of	982
Pr	3: 5	**T** in the LORD with all thine heart; and	982
	22:19	That thy **t** may be in the LORD, I have	4009
	28:25	he that **putteth** his **t** in the LORD shall be	982
	29:25	whoso **putteth** his **t** in the LORD shall be	982
	30: 5	he *is* a shield unto them that **put** their **t** in	2620
	31:11	The heart of her husband doth *safely* **t** in her,	982
Isa	12: 2	*is* my salvation; I will **t**, and not be afraid:	982
	14:32	and the poor of his people shall **t** in it.	2620
	26: 4	**T** ye in the LORD for ever: for in	982
	30: 2	and to **t** in the shadow of Egypt.	2620
	30: 3	the **t** in the shadow of Egypt *your*	2622
	30:12	**t** in oppression and perverseness, and	982
	31: 1	and **t** in chariots, because *they are* many;	982
	36: 5	now on whom dost thou **t**, that thou rebellest	982
	36: 6	*is* Pharaoh king of Egypt to all that **t** in him.	982
	36: 7	say to me, We **t** in the LORD our God:	982
	36: 9	**put** thy **t** on Egypt for chariots and	982
	36:15	Neither let Hezekiah **make** you **t** in	982
	42:17	that **t** in graven images, that say to	982
	50:10	let him **t** in the name of the LORD, and	982
	51: 5	upon me, and on mine arm shall they **t**.	3176
	57:13	he that **putteth** his **t** in me shall possess	2620
	59: 4	*they* **t** in vanity, and speak lies;	982
Jer	7: 4	**T** ye not in lying words, saying, The temple	982
	7: 8	Behold, ye **t** in lying words, *that* cannot	982
	7:14	wherein ye **t**, and unto the place which I	982
	9: 4	of his neighbour, and **t** ye not in any brother:	982
	28:15	but thou **makest** this people **to** **t** in a lie.	982
	29:31	sent him not, and he **caused** you **to** **t** in a lie:	982
	39:18	because thou hast **put** thy **t** in me, saith	982
	46:25	even Pharaoh, and *all* them that **t** in him:	982
	49:11	*them* alive; and let thy widows **t** in me.	982
Eze	16:15	thou didst **t** in thine own beauty, and	982
	33:13	if he **t** to his own righteousness, and	982
Hos	10:13	because thou didst **t** in thy way, in	982
Am	6: 1	in Zion, and **t** in the mountain of Samaria,	982
Mic	7: 5	**T** ye not in a friend, put ye not confidence in	539
Na	1: 7	and he knoweth them that **t** in him.	2620
Zep	3:12	and they shall **t** in the name of the LORD.	2620
Mt	12:21	And in his name shall the Gentiles **t**.	*1679*
Mk	10:24	how hard is it for them that **t** in riches to	*3982*
Lk	16:11	who will **commit to** your **t** the true *riches?*	*4100*
Jn	5:45	accuseth you, *even* Moses, in whom ye **t**.	*1679*
Ro	15:12	the Gentiles; in him shall the Gentiles **t**.	*1679*
	15:24	for I **t** to see you in my journey, and to be	*1679*
1Co	16: 7	but I **t** to tarry a while with you, if the Lord	*1679*
2Co	1: 9	that we should not **t** in ourselves, but	*3982*
	1:10	in whom we **t** that he will yet deliver *us;*	*1679*
	1:13	I **t** you shall acknowledge even to the end;	*1679*
	3: 4	And such **t** have we through Christ to	*4006*
	5:11	I **t** also are made manifest in your	*1679*
	10: 7	If any *man* **t** to himself that *he* is Christ's,	*3982*
	13: 6	But I **t** that ye shall know that we are not	*1679*
Php	2:19	But I **t** in the Lord Jesus to send Timotheus	*1679*
	2:24	But I **t** in the Lord that I also myself shall	*3982*
	3: 4	that *he hath whereof he* might **t** in the flesh,	*3982*
1Th	2: 4	of God to be **put in** **t** with the gospel,	*4100*
1Ti	1:11	which was **committed to** my **t**.	*4100*
	4:10	because we **t** in the living God,	*1679*
	6:17	nor **t** in uncertain riches, but in the living	*1679*
	6:20	keep that which is **committed to** *thy* **t**,	*3872*
Phm	1:22	for I **t** that through your prayers I shall be	*1679*
Heb	2:13	And again, I will **put** my **t** in him.	*3982*
	13:18	for we **t** we have a good conscience, in all	*3982*
2Jn	1:12	but I **t** to come unto you, and speak face to	*1679*
3Jn	1:14	But I **t** *I* shall shortly see thee, and we shall	*1679*

TRUSTED (29) [TRUST]

Dt	32:37	*are* their gods, *their* rock in whom they **t**,	2620
Jdg	11:20	Sihon **t** not Israel to pass through his coast:	539
	20:36	they **t** unto the liers in wait which they had	982
2Ki	18: 5	He **t** in the LORD God of Israel; so	982
Ps	13: 5	I have **t** in thy mercy; my heart shall rejoice	982

T

Ps 22: 4 Our fathers t in thee: they trusted, and 982
22: 4 in thee: they t, and thou didst deliver them. 982
22: 5 they t in thee, and were not confounded. 982
22: 8 He t on the LORD *that* he would deliver 1556
26: 1 I have t also in the LORD; *therefore* I shall 982
28: 7 my heart t in him, and I am helped: 982
31:14 I t in thee, O LORD: I said, Thou *art* my 982
33:21 in him, because we have t in his holy name. 982
41: 9 Yea, mine own familiar friend, in whom I t, 982
52: 7 t in the abundance of his riches, *and* 982
78:22 not in God, and t not in his salvation: 982
Isa 47:10 For thou hast t in thy wickedness: thou hast 982
Jer 13:25 thou hast forgotten me, and t in falsehood. 982
48: 7 For because thou hast t in thy works and 982
49: 4 that t in her treasures, *saying,* Who shall 982
Da 3:28 delivered his servants that t in him, and 7365
Zep 3: 2 not correction; she t not in the LORD; 982
Mt 27:43 He t in God; let him deliver him now, if he *3982*
Lk 11:22 *from him* all his armour wherein he t, *3982*
18: 9 t in themselves that they were righteous, *3982*
24:21 But we t that it had been he which should *1679*
Eph 1:12 the praise of his glory, who **first** t in Christ: *4276*
1:13 In whom ye also *t,* after that ye heard NIG
1Pe 3: 5 who t in God, adorned themselves, being in *1679*

TRUSTEDST (3) [TRUST]
Dt 28:52 wherein thou t, throughout all thy land: 982
Jer 5:17 fenced cities, wherein thou t, with the sword. 982
12: 5 *wherein* thou t, *they wearied thee,* then 982

TRUSTEST (6) [TRUST]
2Ki 18:19 What confidence *is* this where*in* thou t? 982
18:21 thou t upon the staff of this bruised reed, 982
19:10 Let not thy God in whom thou t deceive 982
Isa 36: 4 What confidence *is* this where*in* thou t? 982
36: 6 Lo, thou t in the staff of this broken reed, on 982
37:10 in whom thou t, deceive thee, saying, 982

TRUSTETH (17) [TRUST]
Job 40:23 he t that he can draw up Jordan into his 982
Ps 21: 7 For the king t in the LORD, and 982
32:10 he that t in the LORD, mercy shall compass 982
34: 8 *is* good: blessed *is* the man *that* t in him. 2620
57: 1 for my soul t in thee: yea, in the shadow of 2620
84:12 of hosts, blessed *is* the man that t in thee. 982
86: 2 thou my God, save thy servant that t in thee. 982
115: 8 unto them; *so is* every one that t in them. 982
135:18 unto them: *so is* every one that t in them. 982
Pr 11:28 He that t in his riches shall fall: but 982
16:20 and whoso t in the LORD, happy *is* he. 982
28:26 He that t in his own heart *is* a fool: but 982
Isa 26: 3 mind *is* stayed *on thee:* because he t in thee. 982
Jer 17: 5 Cursed *be* the man that t in man, and 982
17: 7 Blessed *is* the man that t in the LORD, and 982
Hab 2:18 of lies, that the maker of his work t therein, 982
1Ti 5: 5 t in God, and continueth in supplications *1679*

TRUSTING (1) [TRUST]
Ps 112: 7 his heart is fixed, t in the LORD. 982

TRUSTY (1) [TRUST]
Job 12:20 He removeth away the speech of the t, and 539

TRUTH (235) [TRUE, TRULY, TRUTH'S]
Ge 24:27 destitute my master of his mercy and his t: 571
32:10 of all the t, which thou hast shewed unto thy 571
42:16 be proved, whether *there be any* t in you: 571
Ex 18:21 such as fear God, men of t, 571
34: 6 abundant in goodness and t, 571
Dt 13:14 behold, *if it be* t, *and* the thing certain, *that* 571
32: 4 a God of t and without iniquity, just and 530
Jos 24:14 and serve him in sincerity and in t: 571
Jdg 9:15 If in t ye anoint me king over you, *then* 571
1Sa 12:24 and serve him in t with all your heart: 571
21: 5 **Of a** t women *have been* kept from us 518+3588
2Sa 2: 6 the LORD shew kindness and t unto you: 571
15:20 back thy brethren: mercy and t *be* with thee. 571
1Ki 2: 4 to walk before me in t with all their heart 571
3: 6 according as he walked before thee in t, and 571
17:24 the word of the LORD in thy mouth *is* t. 571
2Ki 19:17 **Of a** t, LORD, the kings of Assyria have 551
20: 3 now how I have walked before thee in t 571
20:19 *Is it* not *good,* if peace and t be in my days? 571
2Ch 18:15 but the t to me in the name of the LORD? 571
31:20 and right and t before the LORD his God. 571
Est 9:30 of Ahasuerus, *with* words of peace and t, 571
Job 9: 2 I know *it is* so **of a** t: but how should man be 551
Ps 15: 2 and speaketh the t in his heart. 571
25: 5 Lead me in thy t, and teach me: for thou *art* 571
25:10 t unto such as keep his covenant and 571
26: 3 before mine eyes: and I have walked in thy t. 571
30: 9 the dust praise thee? shall it declare thy t? 571
31: 5 thou hast redeemed me, O LORD God of t. 571
33: 4 *is* right; and all his works *are done* in t. 530
40:10 and thy t from the great congregation. 571
40:11 and thy t continually preserve me. 571
43: 3 O send out thy light and thy t: let them lead 571
45: 4 because of t and meekness *and* 571
51: 6 Behold, thou desirest t in the inward parts: 571
54: 5 unto mine enemies: cut them off in thy t. 571
57: 3 God shall send forth his mercy and his t. 571
57:10 unto the heavens, and thy t unto the clouds. 571
60: 4 that *it* may be displayed because of the t. 7189
61: 7 O prepare mercy and t, *which* may preserve 571
69:13 thy mercy hear me, in the t of thy salvation. 571
71:22 thee with the psaltery, *even* thy t, O my God: 571
85:10 Mercy and t are met together; righteousness 571
85:11 T shall spring out of the earth; and 571
86:11 me thy way, O LORD; I will walk in thy t: 571
86:15 longsuffering, and plenteous in mercy and t. 571
89:14 mercy and t shall go before thy face. 571
89:49 *which* thou swarest unto David in thy t? 530
91: 4 his t *shall be thy* shield and buckler. 571
96:13 with righteousness, and the people with his t. 530
98: 3 and his t toward the house of Israel: 530
100: 5 his t *endureth* to all generations. 530
108: 4 and thy t *reacheth* unto the clouds. 571
111: 8 and ever, *and are* done in t and uprightness. 571
117: 2 the t of the LORD *endureth* for ever. 571
119:30 I have chosen the way of t: thy judgments 530
119:43 take not the word of t utterly out of my 571
119:142 and thy law *is* the t. 571
119:151 O LORD; and all thy commandments *are* t. 571
132:11 The LORD hath sworn *in* t unto David; 571
138: 2 name for thy lovingkindness and for thy t: 571
145:18 call upon him, to all that call upon him in t. 571
146: 6 all that therein is: which keepeth t for ever: 571
Pr 3: 3 Let not mercy and t forsake thee: bind them 571
8: 7 For my mouth shall speak t; and 571
12:17 *He that* speaketh t sheweth forth 530
12:19 The lip of t shall be established for ever: but 571
14:22 and t *shall be to* them that devise good. 571
16: 6 By mercy and t iniquity is purged: and 571
20:28 Mercy and t preserve the king: and 571
22:21 thee know the certainty of the words of t; 571
22:21 that *thou* mightest answer the words *of* t to 571
23:23 Buy the t, and sell *it* not; *also* wisdom, and 571
Ecc 12:10 *was* written *was* upright, *even* words of t. 571
Isa 5: 9 **Of a** t many houses shall be desolate, 518+3808
10:20 the LORD, the Holy One of Israel, in t. 571
16: 5 he shall sit upon it in t in the tabernacle of 571
25: 1 *thy* counsels of old *are* faithfulness *and* t. 544
26: 2 that the righteous nation which keepeth the t 529
37:18 **Of a** t, LORD, the kings of Assyria have 551
38: 3 how I have walked before thee in t and 571
38:18 go down into the pit cannot hope for thy t. 571
38:19 to the children shall make known thy t. 571
39: 8 For there shall be peace and t in my days. 571
42: 3 he shall bring forth judgment unto t. 571
43: 9 be justified: or let them hear, and say, *It is* t. 571
48: 1 of Israel, *but* not in t, nor in righteousness. 571
59: 4 calleth for justice, nor any pleadeth for t: 530
59:14 for t is fallen in the street, and equity cannot 571
59:15 Yea, t faileth; and he *that* departeth from evil 571
61: 8 I will direct their work in t, and I will make 571
65:16 the earth shall bless himself in the God of t; 543
65:16 in the earth shall swear by the God of t; 543
Jer 4: 2 in t, in judgment, and in righteousness; 571
5: 1 that executeth judgment, that seeketh the t; 530
5: 3 O LORD, *are* not thine eyes upon the t? 530
7:28 t is perished, and is cut off from their mouth. 530
9: 3 they are not valiant for the t upon the earth; 530
9: 5 one his neighbour, and will not speak the t: 571
26:15 for of a t the LORD hath sent me unto you 571
33: 6 unto them the abundance of peace and t. 571
Da 2:47 **Of a** t *it is,* that your God *is* a God of 4481+7187
4:37 all whose works *are* t, and his ways 7187
7:16 stood *by,* and asked him the t of all this. 3330
7:19 I would **know the** t of the fourth beast, 3321

Da 8:12 and it cast down the t to the ground; 571
9:13 from our iniquities, and understand thy t. 571
10:21 thee that which is noted in the scripture of t: 571
11: 2 now will I shew thee the t. Behold, 571
Hos 4: 1 because *there is* no t, nor mercy, 571
Mic 7:20 Thou wilt perform the t to Jacob, *and* 571
Zec 8: 3 and Jerusalem shall be called a city of t; and 571
8: 8 I will be their God, in t and in righteousness. 571
8:16 Speak ye every man the t to his neighbour; 571
8:16 execute the judgment of t and peace in your 571
8:19 therefore love the t and peace. 571
Mal 2: 6 The law of t was in his mouth, and 571
Mt 14:33 saying, Of a t thou art the Son of God. *230*
15:27 And she said, T, Lord: yet the dogs eat of *3483*
22:16 art true, and teachest the way of God in t, *225*
Mk 5:33 fell down before him, and told him all the t. *225*
12:14 of men, but teachest the way of God in t: *225*
12:32 unto him, Well, Master, thou hast said the t: *225*
Lk 4:25 But I tell you of a t, many widows were in *225*
9:27 But I tell you of a t, there be some standing *230*
12:44 Of a t I say unto you, that he will make him *230*
21: 3 And he said, Of a t I say unto you, that this *230*
22:59 Of a t this *fellow* also was with him: *225+1909*
Jn 1:14 begotten of the Father,) full of grace and t. *225*
1:17 *but* grace and t came by Jesus Christ. *225*
3:21 But he that doeth t cometh to the light, *225*
4:23 shall worship the Father in spirit and *in* t: *225*
4:24 him must worship *him* in spirit and *in* t. *225*
5:33 unto John, and he bare witness unto the t. *225*
6:14 This is of a t *that* prophet that should come *230*
7:40 *this* saying, said, Of a t this is the Prophet. *230*
8:32 And ye shall know the t, and the truth shall *225*
8:32 the truth, and the t shall make you free. *225*
8:40 a man that hath told you the t, which I have *225*
8:44 and abode not in the t, because there is no *225*
8:44 not in the truth, because there is no t in him. *225*
8:45 And because I tell *you* the t, ye believe me *225*
8:46 And if I say the t, why do ye not believe me? *225*
14: 6 unto him, I am the way, the t, and the life: *225*
14:17 *Even* the Spirit of t; whom the world cannot *225*
15:26 *even* the Spirit of t, which proceedeth from *225*
16: 7 Nevertheless I tell you the t; It is expedient *225*
16:13 Howbeit when he, the Spirit of t, is come, *225*
16:13 of truth, is come, he will guide you into all t: *225*
17:17 Sanctify them through thy t: thy word is *225*
17:17 them through thy truth: thy word is t. *225*
17:19 they also might be sanctified through the t. *225*
18:37 that I should bear witness unto the t. *225*
18:37 Every one that is of the t heareth my voice. *225*
18:38 Pilate saith unto him, What is t? And when *225*
Ac 4:27 For of a t against thy holy child Jesus, *225+1909*
10:34 Of a t I perceive that God is no *225+1909*
26:25 but speak forth *the* words of t and *225*
Ro 1:18 of men, who hold the t in unrighteousness; *225*
1:25 Who changed the t of God into a lie, and *225*
2: 2 to t against them which commit such *things*. *225*
2: 8 and do not obey the t, but *225*
2:20 form of knowledge and of the t in the law. *225*
3: 7 For if the t of God hath *more* abounded *225*
9: 1 I say the t in Christ, I lie not, my conscience *225*
15: 8 minister of the circumcision for the t of God, *225*
1Co 5: 8 with the unleavened bread of sincerity and t. *225*
13: 6 not in iniquity, but rejoiceth in the t; *225*
14:25 and report that God is in you of a t. *3689*
2Co 4: 2 by manifestation of the t commending *225*
6: 7 By the word of t, by the power of God, *225*
7:14 but as we spake all *things* to you in t, even *225*
7:14 which *I made* before Titus, is found a t. *225*
11:10 *As* the t of Christ is in me, no *man* shall stop *225*
12: 6 I shall not be a fool; for I will say the t: *225*
13: 8 For we can do nothing against the t, but *225*
13: 8 do nothing against the truth, but for the t. *225*
Gal 2: 5 that the t of the gospel might continue with *225*
2:14 uprightly according to the t of the gospel, *225*
3: 1 that *you* should not obey the t, *225*
4:16 your enemy, because I tell you the t? *226*
5: 7 did hinder you that *ye* should not obey the t? *225*
Eph 1:13 also *trusted,* after that ye heard the word of t, *225*
4:15 But speaking the t in love, may grow *up* *226*
4:21 have been taught by him, as the t is in Jesus: *225*
4:25 speak every man t with his neighbour: *225*
5: 9 *is* in all goodness and righteousness and t;) *225*
6:14 having your loins girt about with t, and *225*
Php 1:18 in pretence, or in t, Christ is preached; *225*
Col 1: 5 whereof ye heard before in the word of the t *225*
1: 6 heard of *it,* and knew the grace of God in t: *225*
1Th 2:13 of men, but as it is in t, the word of God, *230*
2Th 2:10 because they received not the love of the t, *225*
2:12 all might be damned who believed not the t, *225*
2:13 sanctification of the Spirit and belief of the t: *225*
1Ti 2: 4 and to come unto the knowledge of the t. *225*
2: 7 (I speak the t in Christ, *and* lie not;) *225*
3:15 the living God, the pillar and ground of the t. *225*
4: 3 of them which believe and know the t. *225*
6: 5 and destitute of the t, supposing that gain is *225*
2Ti 2:15 be ashamed, rightly dividing the word of t. *225*
2:18 Who concerning the t have erred, saying that *225*
2:25 repentance to the acknowledging of the t; *225*
3: 7 able to come to the knowledge of the t. *225*
3: 8 so do these also resist the t: *225*
4: 4 they shall turn away *their* ears from the t, *225*
Tit 1: 1 the acknowledging of the t which is after *225*
1:14 commandments of men, that turn from the t. *225*
Heb 10:26 *we* have received the knowledge of the t, *225*
Jas 1:18 his own will begat he us with the word of t, *225*
3:14 glory not, and lie *not* against the t. *225*
5:19 if any of you do err from the t, and *225*
1Pe 1:22 t through the Spirit unto unfeigned love of *225*
2Pe 1:12 and be stablished in the present t. *225*
2: 2 by reason of whom the way of t shall be evil *225*
1Jn 1: 6 walk in darkness, we lie, and do not the t: *225*
1: 8 we deceive ourselves, and the t is not in us. *225*
2: 4 is a liar, and the t is not in him. *225*
2:21 written unto you because ye know not the t, *225*
2:21 ye know it, and that no lie is of the t. *225*
2:27 anointing teacheth you of all *things,* and is t, *227*
3:18 neither in tongue; but in deed and in t. *225*
3:19 And hereby we know that we are of the t, *225*
4: 6 Hereby know we the spirit of t, and the spirit *225*
5: 6 that beareth witness, because the Spirit is t. *225*
2Jn 1: 1 and her children, whom I love in the t; *225*
1: 1 but also all they that have known the t; *225*
1: 3 the Son of the Father, in t and love. *225*
1: 4 that I found of thy children walking in t, *225*
3Jn 1: 1 the wellbeloved Gaius, whom I love in the t. *225*
1: 3 and testified of the t *that is* in thee, *225*
1: 3 *that is* in thee, even as thou walkest in the t. *225*
1: 4 joy than to hear that my children walk in t. *225*
1: 8 that we might be fellowhelpers to the t. *225*
1:12 good report of all *men,* and of the t itself: *225*

TRUTH'S (2) [TRUTH]
Ps 115: 1 give glory, for thy mercy, *and* for thy t sake. 571
2Jn 1: 2 For the t sake, which dwelleth in us, and *225*

TRY (17) [TRIAL, TRIED, TRIEST, TRIETH, TRYING]
Jdg 7: 4 the water, and I will t them for thee there: 6884
2Ch 32:31 God left him, to t him, that *he* might know 5254
Job 7:18 every morning, *and* t him every moment? 974
12:11 Doth not the ear t words? and the mouth 974
Ps 11: 4 his eyes behold, his eyelids t, the children of 974
26: 2 and prove me; t my reins and my heart. 6884
139:23 my heart: t me, and know my thoughts: 974
Jer 6:27 that thou mayest know and t their way. 974
9: 7 Behold, I will melt them, and t them; 974
17:10 I the LORD search the heart, *I* t the reins, 974
La 3:40 Let us search and t our ways, and 2713
Da 11:35 to t them, and to purge, and to make *them* 6884
Zec 13: 9 is refined, and will t them as gold is tried: 974
1Co 3:13 the fire shall t every man's work of what *1381*
1Pe 4:12 concerning the fiery trial which is to t you, *3986*
1Jn 4: 1 but t the spirits whether they are of God: *1381*
Rev 3:10 to t them that dwell upon the earth. *3985*

TRYING (1) [TRY]
Jas 1: 3 Knowing *this,* that the t of your faith *1383*

TRYPHENA (1)
Ro 16:12 Salute T and Tryphosa, who labour in *5170*

TRYPHOSA (1)
Ro 16:12 Salute Tryphena and T, who labour in *5173*

TUBAL (8)
Ge 10: 2 and Javan, and T, and Meshech, and Tiras. 8422
1Ch 1: 5 and Javan, and T, and Meshech, and Tiras. 8422
Isa 66:19 Lud, that draw the bow, *to* T, and Javan, 8422
Eze 27:13 Javan, T, and Meshech, they *were* thy 8422
32:26 There *is* Meshech, T, and all her multitude: 8422

Eze 38: 2 the chief prince of Meshech and **T**, and 8422
38: 3 O Gog, the chief prince of Meshech and **T**: 8422
39: 1 O Gog, the chief prince of Meshech and **T**: 8422

TUBAL-CAIN (2)

Ge 4:22 Zillah, she also bare **T**, an instructor of 8423
4:22 and iron: and the sister of **T** *was* Naamah. 8423

TUCKED INTO BELT See GIRDED

TUMBLED (1)

Jdg 7:13 a cake of barley bread **t** into the host of 2015

TUMORS See EMERODS

TUMULT (16) [TUMULTS, TUMULTUOUS]

1Sa 4:14 he said, What *meaneth* the noise of this **t**? 1995
2Sa 18:29 I saw a great **t**, but I knew not what *it was.* 1995
2Ki 19:28 and thy **t** is come up into mine ears, 7600
Ps 65: 7 of their waves, and the **t** of the people. 1995
74:23 the **t** of those that rise up against thee 7588
83: 2 For lo, thine enemies **make a t**: and 1993
Isa 33: 3 At the noise of the **t** the people fled; at 1995
37:29 thy **t**, is come up into mine ears, therefore 7600
Jer 11:16 with the noise of a great **t** he hath kindled 1999
Hos 10:14 Therefore shall a **t** arise among thy people, 7588
Am 2: 2 Moab shall die with **t**, with shouting, *and* 7588
Zec 14:13 *that* a great **t** from the LORD shall be 4103
Mt 27:24 but *that* rather a **t** was made, he took water, *2351*
Mk 5:38 and seeth *the* **t**, and them that wept and *2351*
Ac 21:34 he could not know the certainty for the **t**, *2351*
24:18 neither with multitude, nor with **t**. *2351*

TUMULTS (3) [TUMULT]

Am 3: 9 behold the great **t** in the midst thereof, and 4103
2Co 6: 5 in **t**, in labours, in watchings, in fastings; *181*
12:20 backbitings, whisperings, swellings, **t**: *181*

TUMULTUOUS (3) [TUMULT]

Isa 13: 4 a **t** noise of the kingdoms of nations 7588
22: 2 *that art* full *of* stirs, a **t** city, a joyous city: 1993
Jer 48:45 and the crown of the head of the **t** ones. 7588

TUNNEL See CONDUIT

TURBAN See MITRE

TURBANS See BONNETS; TIRES

TURN (283) [OVERTURN, TURNED, TURNEST, TURNETH, TURNING]

Ge 19: 2 Behold now, my lords, **t in**, I pray you, 5493
24:49 that I may **t** to the right hand, or to the left. 6437
27:44 a few days, until thy brother's fury **t away**; 7725
27:45 Until thy brother's anger **t away** from thee, 7725
Ex 3: 3 I will now **t aside**, and see this great sight, 5493
14: 2 that they **t** and encamp before Pi-hahiroth, 7725
23:27 I will make all thine enemies **t** their **backs** 6203
32:12 **T** from thy fierce wrath, and repent of *this* 7725
Lev 13:16 Or if the raw flesh **t again**, and be changed 7725
19: 4 **T** ye not unto idols, nor make to yourselves 6437
Nu 14:25 To morrow **t** you, and get you *into* 6437
20:17 we will not **t** *to* the right hand nor *to* 5186
21:22 we will not **t** into the fields, or into 5186
22:23 Balaam smote the ass, to **t** her *into* the way. 5186
22:26 where *was* no way to **t** *either to* the right 5186
32:15 For if ye **t away** from after him, he will yet 7725
34: 4 your border shall **t** from the south to 5437
Dt 1: 7 **T** you, and take your journey, and go *to* 6437
1:40 **t** ye, and take your journey into 6437
2: 3 mountain long enough: **t** you northward. 6437
2:27 I will neither **t** *unto* the right hand nor *to* 5493
4:30 if thou **t** to the LORD thy God, and 7725
5:32 ye shall not **t aside** *to* the right hand or 5493
7: 4 For they will **t away** thy son from 5493
11:16 ye **t aside**, and serve other gods, and 5493
11:28 **t aside** out of the way which I command 5493
13: 5 he hath spoken to **t** *you* **away** from 5627
13:17 that the LORD may **t** from the fierceness 7725
14:25 shalt thou **t** *it* into money, and bind up 5414
16: 7 thou shalt **t** in the morning, and go unto thy 6437
17:17 wives to himself, that his heart **t** not **away**: 5493
17:20 that *he* **t** not **aside** from the commandment, 5493
23:13 shalt **t back** and cover that which cometh 7725
23:14 thing in thee, and **t** away from thee. 7725
30: 3 the LORD thy God will **t** thy captivity, 7725
30:10 if thou **t** unto the LORD thy God with all 7725
30:17 if thine heart **t away**, so that thou wilt not 6437
31:20 will they **t** unto other gods, and serve them, 6437
31:29 **t aside** from the way which I have 5493
Jos 1: 7 **t** not from it *to* the right hand or *to* the left, 5493
22:16 to **t away** *this* day from following 7725
22:18 that ye must **t away** *this* day from 7725
22:23 That we have built us an altar to **t** from 7725
22:29 **t** *this* day from following the LORD, 7725
23: 6 that *ye* **t** not **aside** therefrom *to* the right 5493
24:20 he will **t** and do you hurt, and 7725
Jdg 4:18 said unto him, **T in**, my lord, turn in to me; 5493
4:18 said unto him, Turn in, my lord, **t in** to me; 5493
11: 8 Therefore we **t again** to thee now, that thou 7725
19:11 let us **t in** into this city of the Jebusites, and 5493
19:12 We will not **t aside** hither into the city of a 5493
20: 8 neither will we any *of us* **t** into his house. 5493
Ru 1:11 Naomi said, **T again**, my daughters: why 7725
1:12 **T again**, my daughters, go *your way;* for I 7725
4: 1 *Ho,* such a one, **t aside**, sit down here. 5493
1Sa 12:20 yet **t** not **aside** from following the LORD, 5493
12:21 **t** ye not **aside**: for *then should ye go* after 5493
14: 7 **t** thee; behold, I *am* with thee according to 5186
15:25 pardon my sin, and **t again** with me, 7725
15:30 and before Israel, and **t again** with me, 7725
22:17 **T**, and slay the priests of the LORD; 5437
22:18 to Doeg, **T** thou, and fall upon the priests. 5437
2Sa 2:21 **T** thee **aside** to thy right hand or to thy left, 5186
2:21 Asahel would not **t aside** from following of 5493
2:22 to Asahel, **T** thee **aside** from following me: 5493
2:23 Howbeit he refused to **t aside**: 5493
14:19 none can **t to the right hand** or to the left 3231
14:24 Let him **t** to his own house, and let him not 5437
15:31 **t** the counsel of Ahithophel **into foolishness**. 5528
18:30 the king said *unto him,* **T aside**, *and* 5437
19:37 Let thy servant, I pray thee, **t back again**, 7725
1Ki 8:33 shall **t again** to thee, and confess thy name, 7725
8:35 confess thy name, and **t** from their sin, 7725
9: 6 *But* if you shall **at all t** from following me, 7725
11: 2 *for* surely they will **t away** your heart after 5186
12:27 shall the heart of this people **t again** unto 7725
13: 9 nor **t again** by the *same* way that thou 7725
13:17 nor **t again** to go by the way that thou 7725
17: 3 **t** thee eastward, and hide thyself by 6437
22:34 **T** thine hand, and carry me out of the host; 2015
2Ki 1: 6 **t again** unto the king that sent you, and 7725
4:10 he cometh to us, *that* he shall **t** *in* thither. 5493
9:18 **t** thee behind me. And the watchman told, 5437
9:19 thou to do with peace? **t** thee behind me. 5437
17:13 **T** ye from your evil ways, and keep my 7725
18:24 wilt thou **t away** the face of one captain of 7725
19:28 I will **t** thee **back** by the way by which thou 7725
20: 5 **T again**, and tell Hezekiah the captain of 7725
1Ch 12:23 to Hebron, to **t** the kingdom of Saul to him, 5437
14:14 **t away** from them, and come upon them 5437
2Ch 6:26 confess thy name, *and* **t** from their sin, 7725
6:37 **t** and pray unto thee in the land of their 7725
6:42 **t** not **away** the face of thine anointed: 7725
7:14 my face, and **t** from their wicked ways; 7725
7:19 if ye **t away**, and forsake my statutes and 7725
15: 4 when they in their trouble did **t** unto 7725
18:33 he said to *his* chariot man, **T** thine hand, 2015
25:27 after the time that Amaziah did **t away** 5493
29:10 that his fierce wrath may **t away** from us. 7725
30: 6 **t again** unto the LORD God of Abraham, 7725
30: 8 that the fierceness of his wrath may **t away** 7725
30: 9 For if ye **t again** unto the LORD, 7725
30: 9 and will not **t away** *his* face from you, 5493
35:22 Nevertheless Josiah would not **t** his face 5437
Ne 1: 9 *if* ye **t** unto me, and keep my 7725
4: 4 **t** their reproach upon their own head, and 7725
9:26 testified against them to **t** them to thee, 7725
Est 2:12 Now when every maid's **t** was come to go 8447
2:15 Now when the **t** of Esther, the daughter of 8447
Job 5: 1 and to which of the saints wilt thou **t**? 6437
14: 6 **T** from him, that he may rest, till he shall 8159
23:13 he *is* in one *mind,* and who can **t** him? and 7725
24: 4 They **t** the needy out of the way: the poor 5186
34:15 and man shall **t again** unto dust. 7725
Ps 4: 2 how long *will ye* **t** my glory into shame? NIH
7:12 If he **t** not, he will whet his sword; he hath 7725
18:37 neither did I **t again** till they were 7725
21:12 Therefore shalt thou **make** them **t** their 7896
22:27 shall remember and **t** unto the LORD: 7725

Ps	25:16	T thee unto me, and have mercy upon me;	6437
	40: 4	not the proud, nor such as t aside to lies.	7750
	44:10	Thou makest us to t back from the enemy:	7725
	56: 9	unto thee, then shall mine enemies t back:	7725
	60: 1	been displeased; O t thyself to us again.	7725
	69:16	t unto me according to the multitude of thy	6437
	80: 3	T us again, O God, and cause thy face to	7725
	80: 7	T us again, O God of hosts, and cause thy	7725
	80:19	T us again, O LORD God of hosts,	7725
	85: 4	T us, O God of our salvation, and	7725
	85: 8	his saints: but let them not t again to folly.	7725
	86:16	O t unto me, and have mercy upon me;	6437
	101: 3	I hate the work of them that t aside; it shall	7750
	104: 9	that they t not again to cover the earth.	7725
	106:23	to t away his wrath, lest he should destroy	7725
	119:37	T away mine eyes from beholding vanity;	5674
	119:39	T away my reproach which I fear: for thy	5674
	119:79	Let those that fear thee t unto me, and	7725
	125: 5	As for such as t aside unto their crooked	5186
	126: 4	T again our captivity, O LORD, as	7725
	132:10	For thy servant David's sake t not away	7725
	132:11	in truth unto David; he will not t from it;	7725
Pr	1:23	T you at my reproof: behold, I will pour	7725
	4:15	pass not by it, t from it, and pass away.	7847
	4:27	T not to the right hand nor to the left:	5186
	9: 4	Whoso is simple, let him t in hither: as for	5493
	9:16	Whoso is simple, let him t in hither: and	5493
	24:18	and he t away his wrath from him.	7725
	25:10	to shame, and thine infamy t not away.	7725
	29: 8	into a snare: but wise men t away wrath.	7725
Ecc	3:20	all are of the dust, and all t to dust again.	7725
SS	2:17	t, my beloved, and be thou like a roe or a	5437
	6: 5	T away thine eyes from me, for they have	5437
Isa	1:25	I will t my hand upon thee, and purely	7725
	10: 2	To t aside the needy from judgment, and	5186
	13:14	they shall every man t to his own people,	6437
	14:27	is stretched out, and who shall t it back?	7725
	19: 6	they shall t the rivers far away; and	2186
	22:18	surely violently t and toss	6801+6801+6802
	23:17	she shall t to her hire, and shall commit	7725
	28: 6	for strength to them that t the battle to	7725
	29:21	and t aside the just for a thing of nought.	5186
	30:11	ye out of the way, t aside out of the path,	5186
	30:21	when ye t to the right hand, and when ye	541
	30:21	to the right hand, and when ye t to the left.	8041
	31: 6	T ye unto him from whom the children of	7725
	36: 9	wilt thou t away the face of one captain of	7725
	37:29	I will t thee back by the way by which thou	7725
	58:13	If thou t away thy foot from the sabbath,	7725
	59:20	unto them that t from transgression in	7725
Jer	2:24	in her occasion who can t her away?	7725
	2:35	surely his anger shall t from me.	7725
	3: 7	I said after she had done all these things, T	7725
	3:14	T, O backsliding children, saith	7725
	3:19	My father; and shalt not t away from me.	7725
	4:28	not repent, neither will I t back from it.	7725
	6: 9	t back thine hand as a grapegatherer into	7725
	8: 4	not arise? shall he t away, and not return?	7725
	13:16	he t it into the shadow of death, and make it	7760
	18: 8	whom I have pronounced, t from their evil,	7725
	18:20	and to t away thy wrath from them.	7725
	21: 4	I will t back the weapons of war that are in	5437
	25: 5	T ye again now every one from his evil	7725
	26: 3	and t every man from his evil way,	7725
	29:14	I will t away your captivity, and I will	7725
	31:13	for I will t their mourning into joy, and	2015
	31:18	as a bullock unaccustomed to the yoke; t	7725
	31:21	t again, O virgin of Israel, turn again to	7725
	31:21	virgin of Israel, t again to these thy cities,	7725
	32:40	that I will not t away from them, to do	7725
	44: 5	nor inclined their ear to t from their	7725
	49: 8	Flee ye, t back, dwell deep, O inhabitants	6437
	50:16	for fear of the oppressing sword they shall t	6437
La	2:14	thine iniquity, to t away thy captivity;	7725
	3:35	To t aside the right of a man before	5186
	3:40	try our ways, and t again to the LORD.	7725
	5:21	T thou us unto thee, O LORD, and	7725
Eze	3:19	he t not from his wickedness, nor from his	7725
	3:20	When a righteous man doth t from his	7725
	4: 8	thou shalt not t thee from one side to	2015
	7:22	My face will I t also from them, and	5437
	8: 6	t thee yet again, and thou shalt see greater	7725
	8:13	T thee yet again, and thou shalt see greater	7725
	8:15	t thee yet again, and thou shalt see greater	7725
	14: 6	Repent, and t yourselves from your idols;	7725
	14: 6	t away your faces from all your	7725
	18:21	if the wicked will t from all his sins that he	7725
	18:30	t yourselves from all your transgressions;	7725
	18:32	wherefore t yourselves, and live ye.	7725
	33: 9	if thou warn the wicked of his way to t	7725
	33: 9	if he do not t from his way, he shall die in	7725
	33:11	but that the wicked t from his way and live:	7725
	33:11	t ye, turn ye from your evil ways; for why	7725
	33:11	turn ye, t ye from your evil ways; for why	7725
	33:14	if he t from his sin, and do that which is	7725
	33:19	if the wicked t from his wickedness, and	7725
	36: 9	I will t unto you, and ye shall be tilled and	6437
	38: 4	I will t thee back, and put hooks into thy	7725
	38:12	to t thine hand upon the desolate places that	7725
	39: 2	I will t thee back, and leave but the sixth	7725
Da	9:13	that we might t from our iniquities, and	7725
	11:18	After this shall he t his face unto the isles,	7725
	11:18	reproach he shall cause it to t upon him.	7725
	11:19	he shall t his face towards the fort of his	7725
	12: 3	they that t many to righteousness as	6663
Hos	5: 4	They will not frame their doings to t unto	7725
	12: 6	Therefore t thou to thy God: keep mercy	7725
	14: 2	Take with you words, and t to the LORD:	7725
Joel	2:12	t ye even to me with all your heart, and	7725
	2:13	and t unto the LORD your God:	7725
Am	1: 3	I will not t away the punishment thereof;	7725
	1: 6	I will not t away the punishment thereof;	7725
	1: 8	and I will t mine hand against Ekron:	7725
	1: 9	I will not t away the punishment thereof;	7725
	1:11	I will not t away the punishment thereof;	7725
	1:13	I will not t away the punishment thereof;	7725
	2: 1	I will not t away the punishment thereof;	7725
	2: 4	I will not t away the punishment thereof;	7725
	2: 6	I will not t away the punishment thereof;	7725
	2: 7	the poor, and t aside the way of the meek:	5186
	5: 7	Ye who t judgment to wormwood, and	2015
	5:12	they t aside the poor in the gate from their	5186
	8:10	I will t your feasts into mourning, and	2015
Jnh	3: 8	let them t every one from his evil way, and	7725
	3: 9	Who can tell if God will t and repent, and	7725
	3: 9	repent, and t away from his fierce anger,	7725
Mic	7:19	He will t again, he will have compassion	7725
Zep	2: 7	shall visit them, and t away their captivity.	7725
	3: 9	then will I t to the people a pure language,	2015
	3:20	when I t back your captivity before your	7725
Zec	1: 3	T ye unto me, saith the LORD of hosts,	7725
	1: 3	I will t unto you, saith the LORD of hosts.	7725
	1: 4	T ye now from your evil ways, and	7725
	9:12	T ye to the strong hold, ye prisoners of	7725
	10: 9	shall live with their children, and t again.	7725
	13: 7	and I will t mine hand upon the little ones.	7725
Mal	2: 6	and did t many away from iniquity.	7725
	3: 5	that t aside the stranger from his right, and	5186
	4: 6	he shall t the heart of the fathers to	7725
Mt	5:39	on thy right cheek, t to him the other also.	4762
	5:42	that would borrow of thee t not thou away.	654
	7: 6	under their feet, and t again and rent you.	4762
Mk	13:16	And let him that is in the field not t back	1994
Lk	1:16	shall he t to the Lord their God.	1994
	1:17	to t the hearts of the fathers to	1994
	10: 6	rest upon it: if not, it shall t to you again.	344
	17: 4	and seven times in a day t again to thee,	1994
	21:13	And it shall t to you for a testimony.	576
Ac	13: 8	seeking to t away the deputy from the faith.	1294
	13:46	of everlasting life, lo, we t to the Gentiles.	4762
	14:15	t from these vanities unto the living	1994
	26:18	and to t them from darkness to light, and	1994
	26:20	that they should repent and t to God,	1994
Ro	11:26	and shall t away ungodliness from Jacob:	654
2Co	3:16	Nevertheless when it shall t to the Lord,	1994
Gal	4: 9	how t ye again to the weak and	1994
Php	1:19	For I know that this shall t to my salvation	576
2Ti	3: 5	the power thereof: from such t away.	665
	4: 4	And they shall t away their ears from	654
Tit	1:14	of men, that t from the truth.	654
Heb	12:25	t away from him that speaketh from heaven:	654
Jas	3: 3	obey us; and we t about their whole body.	3329
2Pe	2:21	after they have known it, to t from the holy	1994
Rev	11: 6	have power over waters to t them to blood,	4762

TURNED (287) [TURN]

Ge	3:24	a flaming sword which t every way,	2015
	18:22	the men t their faces from thence, and	6437

Ge 19: 3 they **t in** unto him, and entered into his 5493
38: 1 **t in** to a certain Adullamite, whose name 5186
38:16 he **t** unto her by the way, and said, Go to, 5186
42:24 he **t** himself **about** from them, and wept; 5437
Ex 3: 4 when the LORD saw that he **t aside** to 5493
4: 7 behold, it was **t again** as his *other* flesh. 7725
7:15 the rod which was **t** to a serpent shalt thou 2015
7:17 *are* in the river, and they shall be **t** to blood. 2015
7:20 all the waters that *were* in the river were **t** 2015
7:23 Pharaoh **t** and went into his house, 6437
10: 6 he **t** himself, and went out from Pharaoh. 6437
10:19 the LORD **t** a mighty strong west wind, 2015
14: 5 and of his servants was **t** against the people, 2015
32: 8 They have **t aside** quickly out of the way 5493
32:15 Moses **t**, and went down from the mount, 6437
33:11 he **t again** into the camp: but his servant 7725
Lev 13: 3 *when* the hair in the plague is **t** white, and 2015
13: 4 the skin, and the hair thereof be not **t** white; 2015
13:10 it have **t** the hair white, and *there be* quick 2015
13:13 *hath* the plague: it is all **t** white: he *is* clean. 2015
13:17 behold, *if* the plague be **t** into white; then 2015
13:20 the skin, and the hair thereof be **t** white; 2015
13:25 *if* the hair in the bright spot be **t** white, and 2015
Nu 14:43 because ye are **t away** from the LORD, 7725
20:21 wherefore Israel **t** away from him. 5186
21:33 they **t** and went up *by* the way of Bashan: 6437
22:23 the ass **t aside** out of the way, and 5186
22:33 saw me, and **t** from me these three times: 5186
22:33 unless she had **t** from me, surely now also I 5186
25: 4 of the LORD may be **t away** from Israel. 7725
25:11 hath **t** my wrath **away** from the children of 7725
33: 7 **t again** unto Pi-hahiroth, which *is* before 7725
Dt 1:24 they **t** and went up into the mountain, and 6437
2: 1 we **t**, and took our journey into 6437
2: 8 we **t** and passed *by* the way of 6437
3: 1 we **t**, and went up the way to Bashan: and 6437
9:12 **t aside** out of the way which I commanded 5493
9:15 So I **t** and came down from the mount, and 6437
9:16 ye had **t aside** quickly out of the way which 5493
10: 5 I **t** myself and came down from the mount, 6437
23: 5 the LORD thy God **t** the curse into a 2015
31:18 in that they are **t** unto other gods. 6437
Jos 7:12 *but* **t** *their* backs before their enemies, 6437
7:26 So the LORD **t** from the fierceness of his 7725
8:20 *to* the wilderness **t back** upon the pursuers. 2015
8:21 then they **t again**, and slew the men of Ai. 7725
11:10 Joshua at that time **t back**, and took Hazor, 7725
19:12 **t** from Sarid eastward *toward* the sunrising 7725
Jdg 2:17 they **t** quickly out of the way which their 5493
3:19 he himself **t again** from the quarries that 7725
4:18 And when he had **t in** unto her into the tent, 5493
8:33 that the children of Israel **t again**, and 7725
14: 8 and he **t aside** to see the carcase of the lion: 5493
15: 4 **t** tail to tail, and put a firebrand in the midst 6437
18: 3 they **t in** thither, and said unto him, 5493
18:15 they **t** thitherward, and came to the house 5493
18:21 So they **t** and departed, and put the little 6437
18:23 And they **t** their faces, and said unto Micah, 5437
18:26 for him, he **t** and went back unto his house. 6437
19:15 they **t aside** thither, to go in *and* to lodge in 5493
20:41 when the men of Israel **t** *again,* the men of 2015
20:42 Therefore they **t** *their backs* before the men 6437
20:45 they **t** and fled toward the wilderness unto 6437
20:47 six hundred men **t** and fled to 6437
20:48 the men of Israel **t again** upon the children 7725
Ru 3: 8 that the man was afraid, and **t** himself: 3943
4: 1 down here. And he **t aside**, and sat down. 5493
1Sa 6:12 **t** not **aside** *to* the right hand or *to* the left; 5493
8: 3 **t aside** after lucre, and took bribes, and 5186
10: 6 with them, and shalt be **t** into another man. 2015
10: 9 that when he had **t** his back to go from 6437
13:17 one company **t** unto the way that leadeth to 6437
13:18 another company **t** the way to Beth-horon: 6437
13:18 another company **t** *to* the way of the border 6437
14:21 even they also *t* to be with the Israelites that NIH
14:47 whithersoever he **t** himself, he vexed *them.* 6437
15:11 for he is **t back** from following me, and 7725
15:27 as Samuel **t about** to go away, he laid hold 5437
15:31 So Samuel **t again** after Saul; and 7725
17:30 he **t** from him towards another, and 5437
22:18 Doeg the Edomite **t**, and he fell upon 5437
25:12 So David's young men **t** their way, and 2015
2Sa 1:22 the bow of Jonathan **t** not back, and 7734
2:19 in going he **t** not to the right hand nor to 5186

18:30 stand here. And he **t aside**, and stood still. 5437
19: 2 the victory that day was *t* into mourning NIH
22:38 and **t** not **again** until I had consumed them. 7725
1Ki 2:15 howbeit the kingdom is **t about**, and 5437
2:28 for Joab had **t** after Adonijah, though he 5186
2:28 though he **t** not after Absalom. 5186
8:14 the king **t** his face **about**, and blessed all 5437
10:13 So she **t** and went to her own country, she 6437
11: 3 and his wives **t away** his heart. 5186
11: 4 *that* his wives **t away** his heart after other 5186
11: 9 his heart was **t** from the LORD God of 5186
15: 5 **t** not **aside** from any *thing* that he 5493
18:37 and *that* thou hast **t** their heart **back** again. 5437
20:39 a man **t aside**, and brought a man unto me, 5493
21: 4 **t away** his face, and would eat no bread. 5437
22:32 they **t aside** to fight against him: and 5493
22:33 that they **t back** from pursuing him. 7725
22:43 he **t** not **aside** from it, doing *that* which *was* 5493
2Ki 1: 5 when the messengers **t back** unto him, 7725
1: 5 he said unto them, Why are ye now **t back**? 7725
2:24 he **t** back, and looked on them, and 6437
4: 8 as he passed by, he **t in** thither to eat bread. 5493
4:11 he **t** into the chamber, and lay there. 5493
5:12 be clean? So he **t** and went away in a rage. 6437
5:26 man **t** *again* from his chariot to meet thee? 2015
9:23 Joram **t** his hands, and fled, and said to 2015
15:20 So the king of Assyria **t back**, and 7725
16:18 **t** he *from* the house of the LORD for 5437
20: 2 he **t** his face to the wall, and prayed unto 5437
22: 2 **t** not **aside** *to* the right hand or *to* the left. 5493
23:16 as Josiah **t** himself, he spied the sepulchres 6437
23:25 that **t** to the LORD with all his heart, and 7725
23:26 Notwithstanding the LORD **t** not from 7725
23:34 **t** his name *to* Jehoiakim, and took Jehoahaz 5437
24: 1 then he **t** and rebelled against him. 7725
1Ch 10:14 **t** the kingdom unto David the son of Jesse. 5437
21:20 Ornan **t back**, and saw the angel; and 7725
2Ch 6: 3 the king **t** his face, and blessed the whole 5437
9:12 So she **t**, and went away to her own land, 2015
12:12 the wrath of the LORD **t** from him, 7725
18:32 they **t back** *again* from pursuing him. 7725
20:10 they **t** from them, and destroyed them not; 5493
29: 6 have **t away** their faces from the habitation 5437
29: 6 habitation of the LORD, and **t** *their* backs. 5414
36: 4 Jerusalem, and **t** his name *to* Jehoiakim. 5437
Ezr 6:22 **t** the heart of the king of Assyria unto them, 5437
10:14 of our God for this matter be **t** from us. 7725
Ne 2:15 **t back**, and entered by the gate of 7725
9:35 neither **t** they from their wicked works. 7725
13: 2 howbeit our God **t** the curse into a blessing. 2015
Est 9: 1 (though it was **t** *to the contrary,* that 2015
9:22 the month which was **t** unto them from 2015
Job 6:18 The paths of their way are **t aside**; they go 3943
16:11 and **t** me **over** into the hands of the wicked. 3399
19:19 and they whom I loved are **t** against me. 2015
20:14 *Yet* his meat in his bowels is **t**, *it is* the gall 2015
28: 5 and under it is **t up** as it were fire. 2015
30:15 Terrors are **t** upon me: they pursue my soul 2015
30:31 My harp also is *t* to mourning, and NIH
31: 7 If my step hath **t** out of the way, and 5186
34:27 Because they **t back** from him, and 5493
37:12 it is **t** round about by his counsels: that they 2015
38:14 It is **t** as clay *to* the seal; and they stand as a 2015
41:22 and sorrow is **t into joy** before him. 1750
41:28 slingstones are **t** with him **into** stubble. 2015
42:10 the LORD **t** the captivity of Job, when he 7725
Ps 9: 3 When mine enemies are **t** back, they shall 7725
9:17 The wicked shall be **t** into hell, *and* all 7725
30:11 Thou hast **t** for me my mourning into 2015
32: 4 my moisture is **t** into the drought of 2015
35: 4 let them be **t** back and brought to confusion 5472
44:18 Our heart is not **t** back, neither have our 5472
66: 6 He **t** the sea into dry *land:* they went 2015
66:20 *be* God, which hath not **t away** my prayer, 5493
70: 2 let them be **t** backward, and put to 5472
70: 3 Let them be **t back** for a reward of their 7725
78: 9 carrying bows, **t** *back* in the day of battle. 2015
78:38 many a time **t** he his anger **away**, and 7725
78:41 they **t** *back* and tempted God, and 7725
78:44 had **t** their rivers into blood; and 2015
78:57 **t** *back,* and dealt unfaithfully like their 5472
78:57 they were **t aside** like a deceitful bow. 2015
81:14 and **t** my hand against their adversaries. 7725
85: 3 thou hast **t** *thyself* from the fierceness of 7725

Ps 89:43 Thou hast also **t** the edge of his sword, and 7725
105:25 He **t** their heart to hate his people, to deal 2015
105:29 He **t** their waters into blood, and slew their 2015
114: 8 Which **t** the rock *into* a standing water, 2015
119:59 and **t** my feet unto thy testimonies. 7725
126: 1 When the LORD **t again** the captivity of 7725
129: 5 be confounded and **t** back that hate Zion. 5472
Ecc 2:12 I **t** myself to behold wisdom, and madness, 6437
SS 6: 1 whither is thy beloved **t aside**? that we may 6437
Isa 5:25 For all this his anger is not **t away**, but 7725
9:12 For all this his anger is not **t away**, but 7725
9:17 For all this his anger is not **t away**, but 7725
9:21 For all this his anger is not **t away**, but 7725
10: 4 For all this his anger is not **t away**, but 7725
12: 1 thine anger is **t away**, and thou comfortedst 7725
21: 4 the night of my pleasure hath he **t** into fear 7760
28:27 is a cart wheel **t about** upon the cummin; 5437
29:17 Lebanon shall be **t** into a fruitful field, and 7725
34: 9 the streams thereof shall be **t** into pitch, 2015
38: 2 Hezekiah **t** his face toward the wall, and 5437
42:17 They shall be **t** back, they shall be greatly 5472
44:20 a deceived heart hath **t** him **aside**, that he 5186
50: 5 I was not rebellious, neither **t away** back. 5472
53: 6 we have **t** every one to his own way; and 6437
59:14 judgment is **t away** backward, and 5253
63:10 therefore he was **t** to be their enemy, *and* 2015
Jer 2:21 art thou **t** *into* the degenerate plant of a 2015
2:27 for they have **t** *their* back unto me, and 6437
3:10 hath not **t** unto me with her whole heart, 7725
4: 8 anger of the LORD is not **t back** from us. 7725
5:25 Your iniquities have **t away** these *things,* 5186
6:12 their houses shall be **t** unto others, 5437
8: 6 every one **t** to his course, as the horse 7725
11:10 They are **t back** to the iniquities of their 7725
23:22 they should have **t** them from their evil 7725
30: 6 in travail, and all faces are **t** into paleness? 2015
31:18 *to the yoke;* turn thou me, and I shall be **t**; 7725
31:19 Surely after that I was **t**, I repented; and 7725
32:33 they have **t** unto me the back, and not 6437
34:11 afterwards they **t**, and caused the servants 7725
34:15 ye were now **t**, and had done right in my 7725
34:16 ye **t** and polluted my name, and 7725
38:22 sunk in the mire, *and* they are **t away** back. 5472
46: 5 I seen them dismayed *and* **t away** back? 5472
46:21 for they also are **t back**, *and* are fled away 6437
48:39 how hath Moab **t** the back with shame! so 6437
50: 6 they have **t** them **away** *on* the mountains: 7725
La 1:13 spread a net for my feet, he hath **t** me back; 7725
1:20 are troubled; mine heart is **t** within me; 2015
3: 3 Surely against me is he **t**; he turneth his 7725
3:11 He hath **t aside** my ways, and pulled me in 5493
5: 2 Our inheritance is **t** to strangers, our houses 2015
5:15 is ceased; our dance is **t** into mourning. 2015
5:21 us unto thee, O LORD, and we shall be **t**; 7725
Eze 1: 9 they **t** not when they went; they went every 5437
1:12 they went; *and* they **t** not when they went. 5437
1:17 four sides: *and* they **t** not when they went. 5437
10:11 they **t** not as they went, but *to* the place 5437
10:11 they followed it; they **t** not as they went. 5437
10:16 the same wheels also **t** not from beside 5437
17: 6 whose branches **t** toward him, and the roots 6437
26: 2 she is **t** unto me: I shall be replenished, 5437
42:19 He **t about** to the west side, *and* 5437
Da 9:16 thy fury be **t away** from thy city Jerusalem, 7725
10: 8 for my comeliness was **t** in me into 2015
10:16 by the vision my sorrows are **t** upon me, 2015
Hos 7: 8 among the people; Ephraim is a cake not **t**. 2015
11: 8 mine heart is **t** within me, my repentings 2015
14: 4 for mine anger is **t away** from him. 7725
Joel 2:31 The sun shall be **t** into darkness, and 2015
Am 6:12 for ye have **t** judgment into gall, and 2015
Jnh 3:10 their works, that they **t** from their evil way; 7725
Na 2: 2 For the LORD hath **t** *away* the excellency 7725
Hab 2:16 LORD'S right hand shall be **t** unto thee, 5437
Zep 1: 6 And them that are **t back** from the LORD; 5472
Hag 2:17 yet ye *t* not to me, saith the LORD. NIH
Zec 5: 1 I **t**, and lift up mine eyes, and looked, and 7725
6: 1 I **t**, and lift up mine eyes, and looked, and 7725
14:10 All the land shall be **t** as a plain from Geba 5437
Mt 2:22 a dream, he **t aside** into the parts of Galilee: 402
9:22 But Jesus **t** him **about**, and when he saw 1994
16:23 But he **t**, and said unto Peter, Get thee 4762
Mk 5:30 **t** him **about** in the press, and said, 1994
8:33 But when he had **t about** and looked on his 1994
Lk 2:45 they **t back again** to Jerusalem, 5290
7: 9 and **t** him *about,* and said unto the people 4762
7:44 And he **t** to the woman, and said unto 4762
9:55 But he **t**, and rebuked them, and said, 4762
10:23 And he **t** him unto *his* disciples, and 4762
14:25 with him: and he **t**, and said unto them, 4762
17:15 **t back**, and with a loud voice glorified 5290
22:61 And the Lord **t**, and looked upon Peter. 4762
Jn 1:38 Then Jesus **t**, 4762
16:20 but your sorrow shall be **t** into joy. 1096
20:14 when she had thus said, she **t** herself back, 4762
20:16 She **t** herself, and saith unto him, Rabboni; 4762
Ac 2:20 The sun shall be **t** into darkness, and 3344
7:39 and in their hearts **t** *back again* into Egypt, 4762
7:42 Then God **t**, and gave them up to worship 4762
9:35 Saron saw him, and **t to** the Lord. 1994
11:21 and **t unto** the Lord. 1994
15:19 among the Gentiles are **t to** God: 1994
16:18 being grieved, **t** and said to the spirit, 1994
17: 6 These that have **t** the world **upside down** are 387
19:26 hath persuaded and **t away** much people, 3179
1Th 1: 9 how ye **t** to God from idols to serve 1994
1Ti 1: 6 swerved have **t aside** unto vain jangling; 1624
5:15 For some are already **t aside** after Satan. 1624
2Ti 1:15 they which are in Asia be **t away from** me; 654
4: 4 from the truth, and shall be **t** unto fables. 1624
Heb 11:34 in fight, **t to flight** the armies of the aliens. 2827
12:13 lest *that which is* lame be **t out of the way**; 1624
Jas 3: 4 *yet* are they **t about** with a very small 3329
4: 9 let your laughter be **t** to mourning, and 3344
2Pe 2:22 The dog *is* **t** to his own vomit **again**; 1994
Rev 1:12 And I **t** to see the voice that spake with me. 1994
1:12 And being **t**, I saw seven golden 1994

TURNEST (3) [TURN]

1Ki 2: 3 and whithersoever thou **t** thyself: 6437
Job 15:13 That thou **t** thy spirit against God, and 7725
Ps 90: 3 Thou **t** man to destruction; and sayest, 7725

TURNETH (33) [TURN]

Lev 20: 6 the soul that **t** after such as have familiar 6437
Dt 29:18 whose heart **t away** *this* day from 6437
Jos 7: 8 when Israel **t** *their* backs before their 2015
19:27 **t** *toward* the sunrising *to* Beth-dagon, and 7725
19:29 *then* the coast **t** *to* Ramah, and to the strong 7725
19:29 the coast **t** *to* Hosah; and the outgoings 7725
19:34 *then* the coast **t** westward *to* Aznoth-tabor, 7725
Job 39:22 neither **t** he **back** from the sword. 7725
Ps 107:33 He **t** rivers into a wilderness, and 7760
107:35 He **t** the wilderness into a standing water, 7760
146: 9 the way of the wicked he **t upside down**. 5791
Pr 15: 1 A soft answer **t away** wrath: but 7725
17: 8 hath it: whithersoever it **t**, it prospereth. 6437
21: 1 of water: he **t** it whithersoever he will. 5186
26:14 *As* the door **t** upon his hinges, so *doth* 5437
28: 9 He that **t away** his ear from hearing 5493
30:30 among beasts, and **t** not **away** for any; 7725
Ecc 1: 6 the south, and **t about** unto the north; 5437
SS 1: 7 for why should I be as one that **t aside** by 5844
Isa 9:13 For the people **t** not unto him that smiteth 7725
24: 1 **t** it upside down, and scattereth abroad 5753
44:25 that **t** wise *men* backward, and maketh their 7725
Jer 14: 8 as a wayfaring man *that* **t aside** to tarry for 5186
49:24 *and* **t** herself to flee, and fear hath seized on 6437
La 1: 8 yea, she sigheth, and **t** backward. 7725
3: 3 he **t** his hand *against me* all the day. 2015
Eze 18:24 when the righteous **t away** from his 7725
18:26 When a righteous *man* **t away** from his 7725
18:27 when the wicked *man* **t away** from his 7725
18:28 **t away** from all his transgressions that he 7725
33:12 he shall not fall thereby in the day that he **t** 7725
33:18 When the righteous **t** from his 7725
Am 5: 8 **t** the shadow of death into the morning, and 2015

TURNING (18) [TURN]

2Ki 21:13 a dish, wiping *it,* and **t** *it* upside down. 2015
2Ch 26: 9 and at the **t** *of the wall,* and fortified them. 4740
36:13 hardened his heart from **t** unto the LORD 7725
Ne 3:19 up to the armoury *at* the **t** *of the wall.* 4740
3:20 from the **t** *of the wall* unto the door of 4740
3:24 from the house of Azariah unto the **t** *of* 4740
3:25 over against the **t** *of the wall,* and the tower 4740
Pr 1:32 For the **t away** of the simple shall slay 4878
Isa 29:16 Surely your **t** *of things* **upside down** shall 2017

Eze 41:24 the doors had two leaves *apiece,* two t 5437
Mic 2: 4 from me! t away he hath divided our fields. 7725
Lk 23:28 But Jesus t unto them, said, Daughters of *4762*
Jn 21:20 Then Peter, t about, seeth the disciple *1994*
Ac 3:26 in t away every one of you from *his* *654*
9:40 and t *him* to the body said, Tabitha, arise. *1994*
Jas 1:17 is no variableness, neither shadow of t. *5157*
2Pe 2: 6 t the cities of Sodom and Gomorrha into ashes *5077*
Jude 1: 4 ungodly *men,* t the grace of our God into *3346*

TURTLE (2) [TURTLEDOVE, TURTLE-DOVE, TURTLEDOVES, TURTLES]
SS 2:12 and the voice of the t is heard in our land; 8449
Jer 8: 7 the t and the crane and the swallow observe 8449

TURTLEDOVE, TURTLE-DOVE (3) [TURTLE]
Ge 15: 9 years old, and a t, and a young pigeon. 8449
Lev 12: 6 a young pigeon, or a t, for a sin offering, 8449
Ps 74:19 O deliver not the soul of thy t unto 8449

TURTLEDOVES (7) [TURTLE]
Lev 1:14 he shall bring his offering of t, or of young 8449
5: 7 two t, or two young pigeons, unto 8449
5:11 if he be not able to bring two t, or two 8449
14:22 two t, or two young pigeons, such as he is 8449
14:30 he shall offer the one of the t, or of 8449
15:14 on the eighth day he shall take to him two t, 8449
Lk 2:24 the Lord, A pair of t, or two young pigeons. *5167*

TURTLES (3) [TURTLE]
Lev 12: 8 she shall bring two t, or two young 8449
15:29 the eighth day she shall take unto her two t, 8449
Nu 6:10 on the eighth day he shall bring two t, or 8449

TUTORS (1)
Gal 4: 2 But is under t and governors until the time *2012*

TWAIN (17) [TWO]
1Sa 18:21 day be my son in law in *the one of* the t. 8147
2Ki 4:33 shut the door upon them t, and prayed unto 8147
Isa 6: 2 with t he covered his face, and with twain 8147
6: 2 with t he covered his feet, and with twain 8147
6: 2 he covered his feet, and with t he did fly. 8147
Jer 34:18 when they cut the calf in t, and 8147
Eze 21:19 both t shall come forth out of one land: and 8147
Mt 5:41 compel thee to go a mile, go with him t. *1417*
19: 5 to his wife: and they t shall be one flesh? *1417*
19: 6 Wherefore they are no more t, but *1417*
21:31 Whether of *them* t did the will of *his* *1417*
27:21 Whether of the t will ye *that* I release unto *1417*
27:51 the vail of the temple was rent in t from *1417*
Mk 10: 8 And they t shall be one flesh: so then *1417*
10: 8 so then they are no more t, but one flesh. *1417*
15:38 And the vail of the temple was rent in t *1417*
Eph 2:15 for to make in himself of t one new man, *so* *1417*

TWELFTH (23) [TWELVE]
Nu 7:78 On the t day Ahira the son of Enan, 6240+8147
1Ki 19:19 *oxen* before him, and he with the t: 6240+8147
2Ki 8:25 In the t year of Joram the son of 6240+8147
17: 1 In the t year of Ahaz king of Judah 6240+8147
25:27 in the t month, on the seven and 6240+8147
1Ch 24:12 eleventh to Eliashib, the t to Jakim, 6240+8147
25:19 The t to Hashabiah, *he,* his sons, and 6240+8147
27:15 The t *captain* for the twelfth month 6240+8147
27:15 The twelfth *captain* for the t month 6240+8147
2Ch 34: 3 t year he began to purge Judah and 6240+8147
Ezr 8:31 on the t *day* of the first month, 6240+8147
Est 3: 7 in the t year of king Ahasuerus, 6240+8147
3: 7 the t *month,* that *is,* the month Adar. 6240+8147
3:13 *even* upon the thirteenth *day* of the t 6240+8147
8:12 the thirteenth *day* of the t month, 6240+8147
9: 1 Now in the t month, that *is,* 6240+8147
Jer 52:31 in the t month, in the five and 6240+8147
Eze 29: 1 in the tenth *month,* in the t *day* of 6240+8147
32: 1 it came to pass in the t year, in 6240+8147
32: 1 in the t month, in the first *day* of 6240+8147
32:17 It came to pass also in the t year, 6240+8147
33:21 it came to pass in the t year of our 6240+8147
Rev 21:20 the eleventh, a jacinth; the t, an amethyst. *1428*

TWELVE (189) [TWELFTH]
Ge 5: 8 Seth were nine hundred and t years: 6240+8147
14: 4 T years they served Chedorlaomer, 6240+8147
17:20 t princes shall he beget, and I will 6240+8147
25:16 t princes according to their nations. 6240+8147
35:22 *it.* Now the sons of Jacob were t: 6240+8147
42:13 they said, Thy servants *are* t 6240+8147
42:32 We *be* t brethren, sons of our father; 6240+8147
49:28 All these *are* the t tribes of Israel: 6240+8147
Ex 15:27 where *were* t wells of water, and 6240+8147
24: 4 an altar under the hill, and t pillars, 6240+8147
24: 4 according to the t tribes of Israel. 6240+8147
28:21 t, according to their names, *like* 6240+8147
28:21 they be according to the t tribes. 6240+8147
39:14 t, according to their names, *like* 6240+8147
39:14 his name, according to the t tribes. 6240+8147
Lev 24: 5 fine flour, and bake t cakes thereof: 6240+8147
Nu 1:44 the princes of Israel, *being* t men: 6240+8147
7: 3 six covered wagons, and t oxen; 6240+8147
7:84 t chargers of silver, twelve silver 6240+8147
7:84 t silver bowls, twelve spoons of 6240+8147
7:84 silver bowls, t spoons of gold: 6240+8147
7:86 The golden spoons *were* t, full *of* 6240+8147
7:87 the burnt offering *were* t bullocks, 6240+8147
7:87 the rams t, the lambs of the first year 6240+8147
7:87 the lambs of the first year t, 6240+8147
7:87 kids of the goats for sin offering t. 6240+8147
17: 2 to the house of their fathers t rods: 6240+8147
17: 6 to their fathers' houses, *even* t rods: 6240+8147
29:17 on the second day *ye shall offer* t 6240+8147
31: 5 t thousand armed for war. 6240+8147
31:33 threescore and t thousand 7657+8147+2050.1
31:38 *was* threescore and t. 7657+8147+2050.1
33: 9 in Elim *were* t fountains of water, 6240+8147
Dt 1:23 I took t men of you, one of a tribe: 6240+8147
Jos 3:12 ye t men out of the tribes of Israel, 6240+8147
4: 2 Take you t men out of the people, 6240+8147
4: 3 t stones, and ye shall carry them over 6240+8147
4: 4 Joshua called the t men, whom he 6240+8147
4: 8 t stones out of the midst of Jordan, 6240+8147
4: 9 Joshua set up t stones in the midst of 6240+8147
4:20 those t stones, which they took out of 6240+8147
8:25 both of men and women, *were* t 6240+8147
18:24 and Gaba; t cities with their villages. 6240+8147
19:15 t cities with their villages. 6240+8147
21: 7 out of the tribe of Zebulun, t cities. 6240+8147
21:40 the Levites, were *by* their lot t cities. 6240+8147
Jdg 19:29 into t pieces, and sent her into all 6240+8147
21:10 the congregation sent thither t 6240+8147
2Sa 2:15 went over by number t of Benjamin, 6240+8147
2:15 and t of the servants of David. 6240+8147
10: 6 and of Ish-tob t thousand men. 6240+8147
17: 1 Let me now choose out t thousand 6240+8147
1Ki 4: 7 Solomon had t officers over all 6240+8147
4:26 and t thousand horsemen. 6240+8147
7:15 a line of t cubits did compass either 6240+8147
7:25 It stood upon t oxen, three looking 6240+8147
7:44 one sea, and t oxen under the sea; 6240+8147
10:20 t lions stood there on the one side 6240+8147
10:26 and t thousand horsemen, 6240+8147
11:30 *was* on him, and rent it *in* t pieces: 6240+8147
16:23 Omri to reign over Israel, t years: 6240+8147
18:31 Elijah took t stones, according to 6240+8147
19:19 who *was* plowing *with* t yoke *of* 6240+8147
2Ki 3: 1 king of Judah, and reigned t years. 6240+8147
21: 1 Manasseh *was* t years old when he 6240+8147
1Ch 6:63 out of the tribe of Zebulun, t cities. 6240+8147
9:22 in the gates *were* two hundred and t. 6240+8147
15:10 and his brethren an hundred and t. 6240+8147
25: 9 with his brethren and sons *were* t: 6240+8147
25:10 *he,* his sons, and his brethren, *were* t: 6240+8147
25:11 *he,* his sons, and his brethren, *were* t: 6240+8147
25:12 *he,* his sons, and his brethren, *were* t: 6240+8147
25:13 *he,* his sons, and his brethren, *were* t: 6240+8147
25:14 *he,* his sons, and his brethren, *were* t: 6240+8147
25:15 *he,* his sons, and his brethren, *were* t: 6240+8147
25:16 *he,* his sons, and his brethren, *were* t: 6240+8147
25:17 *he,* his sons, and his brethren, *were* t: 6240+8147
25:18 *he,* his sons, and his brethren, *were* t: 6240+8147
25:19 *he,* his sons, and his brethren, *were* t: 6240+8147
25:20 *he,* his sons, and his brethren, *were* t: 6240+8147
25:21 *he,* his sons, and his brethren, *were* t: 6240+8147
25:22 *he,* his sons, and his brethren, *were* t: 6240+8147
25:23 *he,* his sons, and his brethren, *were* t: 6240+8147
25:24 *he,* his sons, and his brethren, *were* t: 6240+8147
25:25 *he,* his sons, and his brethren, *were* t: 6240+8147
25:26 *he,* his sons, and his brethren, *were* t: 6240+8147

1Ch 25:27 *he,* his sons, and his brethren, *were* t: 6240+8147
25:28 *he,* his sons, and his brethren, *were* t: 6240+8147
25:29 *he,* his sons, and his brethren, *were* t: 6240+8147
25:30 *he,* his sons, and his brethren, *were* t: 6240+8147
25:31 *he,* his sons, and his brethren, *were* t. 6240+8147
2Ch 1:14 and t thousand horsemen, 6240+8147
4: 4 It stood upon t oxen, three looking 6240+8147
4:15 One sea, and t oxen under it. 6240+8147
9:19 t lions stood there on the one side 6240+8147
9:25 chariots, and t thousand horsemen; 6240+8147
12: 3 With t **hundred** chariots, and 505+3967+2050.1
33: 1 Manasseh *was* t years old when he 6240+8147
Ezr 2: 6 two thousand eight hundred and t. 6240+8147
2:18 children of Jorah, an hundred and t. 6240+8147
6:17 sin offering for all Israel, t he goats, 6236+8648
8:24 I separated t of the chief of 6240+8147
8:35 t bullocks for all Israel, ninety and 6240+8147
8:35 t he goats *for* a sin offering: 6240+8147
Ne 5:14 *that is,* t years, I and my brethren 6240+8147
7:24 children of Hariph, an hundred *and* t. 6240+8147
Est 2:12 after that she had been t months, 6240+8147
Ps 60: T smote of Edom in the valley of salt t 6240+8147
Jer 52:20 t brasen bulls that *were* under 6240+8147
52:21 a fillet of t cubits did compass it; and 6240+8147
Eze 43:16 the altar *shall be* t *cubits* long, twelve 6240+8147
43:16 t broad, square in the four squares 6240+8147
47:13 according to the t tribes of Israel: 6240+8147
Da 4:29 At the end of t months he walked in 6236+8648
Mt 9:20 which was diseased with an issue of blood t *1427*
10: 1 And when he had called unto *him* his t *1427*
10: 2 Now the names of the t apostles are these; *1427*
10: 5 These t Jesus sent forth, and *1427*
11: 1 an end of commanding his t disciples, *1427*
14:20 the fragments that remained t baskets full. *1427*
19:28 ye also shall sit upon t thrones, judging *1427*
19:28 judging the t tribes of Israel. *1427*
20:17 And Jesus going up to Jerusalem took the t *1427*
26:14 Then one of the t, called Judas Iscariot, *1427*
26:20 the even was come, he sat down with the t. *1427*
26:47 one of the t, came, and with him a great *1427*
26:53 he shall presently give me more than t *1427*
Mk 3:14 And he ordained t, that they should be with *1427*
4:10 they that were about him with the t asked *1427*
5:25 which had an issue of blood t years, *1427*
5:42 walked; for she was *of the age* of t years. *1427*
6: 7 And he calleth unto *him* the t, and began to *1427*
6:43 And they took up t baskets full of *1427*
8:19 took ye up? They say unto him, T. *1427*
9:35 and called the t, and saith unto them, *1427*
10:32 And he took again the t, and began to tell *1427*
11:11 he went out unto Bethany with the t. *1427*
14:10 And Judas Iscariot, one of the t, went unto *1427*
14:17 And in the evening he cometh with the t. *1427*
14:20 and said unto them, *It is* one of the t, *1427*
14:43 one of the t, and with him a great multitude *1427*
Lk 2:42 And when he was t years old, they went up *1427*
6:13 and of them he chose t, whom also he *1427*
8: 1 kingdom of God: and the t *were* with him, *1427*
8:42 about t years of age, and she lay a dying. *1427*
8:43 And a woman having an issue of blood t *1427*
9: 1 Then he called his t disciples together, and *1427*
9:12 then came the t, and said unto him, *1427*
9:17 fragments that remained to them t baskets. *1427*
18:31 Then he took unto *him* the t, and said unto *1427*
22: 3 being of the number of the t. *1427*
22:14 he sat down, and the t apostles with him. *1427*
22:30 sit on thrones judging the t tribes of Israel. *1427*
22:47 one of the t, went before them, and *1427*
Jn 6:13 filled t baskets with the fragments of *1427*
6:67 Then said Jesus unto the t, Will ye also go *1427*
6:70 Have not I chosen you t, and one of you is *1427*
6:71 *that* should betray him, being one of the t. *1427*
11: 9 Are there not t hours in the day? *1427*
20:24 But Thomas, one of the t, called Didymus, *1427*
Ac 6: 2 Then the t called the multitude of *1427*
7: 8 and Jacob *begat* the t patriarchs. *1427*
19: 7 And all the men were about t. *1177*
24:11 t days since I went up to Jerusalem for to *1177*
26: 7 Unto which *promise* our t **tribes**, *1429*
1Co 15: 5 that he was seen of Cephas, then of the t: *1427*
Jas 1: 1 to the t tribes which are scattered abroad, *1427*
Rev 7: 5 Of the tribe of Juda *were* sealed t thousand. *1427*
7: 5 Of the tribe of Reuben *were* sealed t *1427*
7: 5 Of the tribe of Gad *were* sealed t thousand. *1427*
7: 6 Of the tribe of Aser *were* sealed t thousand. *1427*
7: 6 Of the tribe of Nephthalim *were* sealed t *1427*
7: 6 Of the tribe of Manasses *were* sealed t *1427*
7: 7 Of the tribe of Simeon *were* sealed t *1427*
7: 7 Of the tribe of Levi *were* sealed t thousand. *1427*
7: 7 Of the tribe of Isachar *were* sealed t *1427*
7: 8 Of the tribe of Zabulon *were* sealed t *1427*
7: 8 Of the tribe of Joseph *were* sealed t *1427*
7: 8 Of the tribe of Benjamin *were* sealed t *1427*
12: 1 and upon her head a crown of t stars: *1427*
21:12 and had t gates, and at the gates twelve *1427*
21:12 and at the gates t angels, and names written *1427*
21:12 which are *the names* of the t tribes of *1427*
21:14 And the wall of the city had t foundations, *1427*
21:14 in them the names of the t apostles of *1427*
21:16 the city with the reed, t thousand furlongs. *1427*
21:21 And the t gates *were* twelve pearls; *1427*
21:21 And the twelve gates *were* t pearls; *1427*
22: 2 which bare t *manner of* fruits, *and* *1427*

TWENTIETH (36) [TWENTY]

Ge 8:14 on the seven and t day of the month, 6242
Ex 12:18 the one and t day of the month at even. 6242
Nu 10:11 it came to pass on the t *day* of the second 6242
1Ki 15: 9 in the t year of Jeroboam king of Israel 6242
2Ki 12: 6 t year of king Jehoash the priests had not 6242
13: 1 t year of Joash the son of Ahaziah king of 6242
15:30 in the t year of Jotham the son of Uzziah. 6242
25:27 on the seven and t *day* of the month, 6242
1Ch 24:16 nineteenth to Pethahiah, the t to Jehezekel, 6242
24:17 The one and t to Jachin, the two and 6242
24:17 twentieth to Jachin, the two and t to Gamul, 6242
24:18 The three and t to Delaiah, the four and 6242
24:18 to Delaiah, the four and t to Maaziah. 6242
25:27 The t to Eliathah, *he,* his sons, and 6242
25:28 The one and t to Hothir, *he,* his sons, and 6242
25:29 The two and t to Giddalti, *he,* his sons, and 6242
25:30 The three and t to Mahazioth, *he,* his sons, 6242
25:31 The four and t to Romamti-ezer, *he,* his 6242
2Ch 7:10 t day of the seventh month he sent 6242
Ezr 10: 9 the ninth month, on the t *day* of the month; 6242
Ne 1: 1 *in* the t year, as I was in Shushan 6242
2: 1 *in* the t year of Artaxerxes the king, 6242
5:14 from the t year even unto the two 6242
Est 8: 9 on the three and t *day* thereof; 6242
Jer 25: 3 unto this day, that *is* the three and t year, 6242
52:30 t year of Nebuchadrezzar Nebuzar-adan 6242
52:31 in the five and t *day* of the month, 6242
Eze 29:17 it came to pass in the seven and t year, 6242
40: 1 In the five and t year of our captivity, in 6242
Da 10: 4 And in the four and t day of the first month, 6242
Hag 1:15 In the four and t day of the sixth month, 6242
2: 1 *month,* in the one and t *day* of the month, 6242
2:10 t *day* of the ninth *month,* in the second year 6242
2:18 t day of the ninth *month, even* from the day 6242
2:20 Haggai in the four and t *day* of the month, 6242
Zec 1: 7 the four and t day of the eleventh month, 6242

TWENTY (293) [TWENTIETH, TWENTY'S]

Ge 6: 3 his days shall be an hundred and t years. 6242
11:24 Nahor lived nine and t years, and 6242
18:31 Peradventure there shall be t found there. 6242
23: 1 was an hundred and seven and t years old: 6242
31:38 This t years *have* I *been* with thee; thy ewes 6242
31:41 Thus have I been t years in thy house; 6242
32:14 t he goats, two hundred ewes, and 6242
32:14 he goats, two hundred ewes, and t rams, 6242
32:15 and ten bulls, t she asses, and ten foals. 6242
37:28 sold Joseph to the Ishmeelites for t *pieces* 6242
Ex 26: 2 of one curtain *shall be* eight and t cubits, 6242
26:18 t boards on the south side southward. 6242
26:19 forty sockets of silver under the t boards; 6242
26:20 on the north side *there shall be* t boards: 6242
27:10 the t pillars thereof and their twenty sockets 6242
27:10 and their t sockets *shall be of* brass; 6242
27:11 his t pillars and their twenty sockets *of* 6242
27:11 twenty pillars and their t sockets *of* brass; 6242
27:16 of the court *shall be* a hanging of t cubits, 6242
30:13 (a shekel *is* t gerahs:) a half shekel *shall be* 6242
30:14 from t years old and above, shall give an 6242
36: 9 The length of one curtain *was* t and 6242
36:23 t boards for the south side southward: 6242
36:24 forty sockets of silver he made under the t 6242
36:25 toward the north corner, he made t boards, 6242

Ex 38:10 Their pillars *were* t, and their brasen 6242
38:10 *were* twenty, and their brasen sockets t; 6242
38:11 their pillars *were* t, and their sockets *of* 6242
38:11 *were* twenty, and their sockets *of* brass t; 6242
38:18 t cubits *was* the length, and the height in 6242
38:24 was t and nine talents, and seven hundred 6242
38:26 from t years old and upward, for six 6242
Lev 27: 3 of the male from t years old even unto sixty 6242
27: 5 if *it be* from five years old even unto t 6242
27: 5 thy estimation shall be of the male t 6242
27:25 the sanctuary: t gerahs shall be the shekel. 6242
Nu 1: 3 From t years old and upward, all that *are* 6242
1:18 from t years old and upward, by their polls. 6242
1:20 every male from t years old and upward, 6242
1:22 every male from t years old and upward, 6242
1:24 from t years old and upward, all that *were* 6242
1:26 from t years old and upward, all that *were* 6242
1:28 from t years old and upward, all that *were* 6242
1:30 from t years old and upward, all that *were* 6242
1:32 from t years old and upward, all that *were* 6242
1:34 from t years old and upward, all that *were* 6242
1:36 from t years old and upward, all that *were* 6242
1:38 from t years old and upward, all that *were* 6242
1:40 from t years old and upward, all that *were* 6242
1:42 from t years old and upward, all that *were* 6242
1:45 their fathers, from t years old and upward, 6242
3:39 and upward, *were* t and two thousand. 6242
3:43 were t and two thousand two hundred and 6242
3:47 thou take *them:* (the shekel *is* t gerahs:) 6242
7:86 the spoons *was* an hundred and t *shekels.* 6242
7:88 the sacrifice of the peace offerings *were* t 6242
8:24 from t and five years old and upward they 6242
11:19 nor five days, neither ten days, nor t days; 6242
14:29 from t years old and upward, 6242
18:16 shekel of the sanctuary, which *is* t gerahs. 6242
25: 9 those that died in the plague were t and 6242
26: 2 from t years old and upward, throughout 6242
26: 4 *Take the sum of the people,* from t years 6242
26:14 t and two thousand and two hundred. 6242
26:62 those that were numbered of them were t 6242
32:11 from t years old and upward, shall see 6242
33:39 Aaron *was* an hundred and t and 6242
Dt 31: 2 I *am* an hundred and t years old *this* day; 6242
34: 7 an hundred and t years old when he died: 6242
Jos 15:32 all the cities *are* t and nine, with their 6242
19:30 Rehob: t and two cities with their villages. 6242
Jdg 4: 3 t years he mightily oppressed the children 6242
7: 3 there returned of the people t and 6242
8:10 and t thousand men that drew sword. 6242
10: 2 he judged Israel t and three years, and died, 6242
10: 3 and judged Israel t and two years. 6242
11:33 *even* t cities, and unto the plain of 6242
15:20 Israel in the days of the Philistines t years. 6242
16:31 his father. And he judged Israel t years. 6242
20:15 numbered at that time out of the cities t 6242
20:21 to the ground of the Israelites that day t 6242
20:35 destroyed of the Benjamites that day t 6242
20:46 all which fell that day of Benjamin were t 6242
1Sa 7: 2 for it was t years: and all the house of Israel 6242
14:14 his armourbearer made, was about t men, 6242
2Sa 3:20 to David *to* Hebron, and t men with him. 6242
8: 4 and t thousand footmen: 6242
8: 5 of the Syrians two and t thousand men. 6242
9:10 Now Ziba had fifteen sons and t servants. 6242
10: 6 t thousand footmen, and of king Maacah a 6242
18: 7 great slaughter that day *of* t thousand *men.* 6242
19:17 his fifteen sons and his t servants with him; 6242
21:20 every foot six toes, four and t *in* number; 6242
24: 8 at the end of nine months and t days. 6242
1Ki 4:23 t oxen out of the pastures, and an hundred 6242
5:11 Solomon gave Hiram t thousand measures 6242
5:11 his household, and t measures of pure oil: 6242
6: 2 the breadth thereof t *cubits,* and the height 6242
6: 3 t cubits *was* the length thereof, according to 6242
6:16 he built t cubits on the sides of the house, 6242
6:20 the oracle in the forepart *was* t cubits in 6242
6:20 t cubits in breadth, and twenty cubits in 6242
6:20 and t cubits in the height thereof: 6242
8:63 two and t thousand oxen, and an hundred 6242
8:63 and an hundred and t thousand sheep. 6242
9:10 it came to pass at the end of t years, 6242
9:11 king Solomon gave Hiram t cities in 6242
9:28 four hundred and t talents, and brought *it* to 6242
10:10 the king an hundred and t talents of gold, 6242
14:20 Jeroboam reigned *were* two and t years: 6242
15:33 over all Israel in Tirzah, t and four years. 6242
16: 8 In the t and sixth year of Asa king of Judah 6242
16:10 in the t and seventh year of Asa king of 6242
16:15 In the t and seventh year of Asa king of 6242
16:29 of Omri reigned over Israel in Samaria t 6242
20:30 *there* a wall fell upon t and seven thousand 6242
22:42 he reigned t and five years in Jerusalem. 6242
2Ki 4:42 t loaves of barley, and full ears of corn in 6242
8:26 t years old *was* Ahaziah when he *began* to 6242
10:36 Jehu reigned over Israel in Samaria *was* t 6242
14: 2 He was t and five years old when he *began* 6242
14: 2 and reigned t and nine years in Jerusalem. 6242
15: 1 In the t and seventh year of Jeroboam king 6242
15:27 over Israel in Samaria, *and reigned* t years. 6242
15:33 t years old was he when he *began* to reign, 6242
16: 2 T years old *was* Ahaz when he *began* to 6242
18: 2 T and five years old was he when he *began* 6242
18: 2 he reigned t and nine years in Jerusalem. 6242
21:19 Amon *was* t and two years old when he 6242
23:31 Jehoahaz *was* t and three years old when he 6242
23:36 Jehoiakim *was* t and five year old when he 6242
24:18 Zedekiah *was* t and one years old when he 6242
1Ch 2:22 had three and t cities in the land of Gilead. 6242
7: 2 David two and t thousand and six hundred. 6242
7: 7 were reckoned by their genealogies t and 6242
7: 9 of valour, *was* t thousand and two hundred. 6242
7:40 *and* to battle *was* t and six thousand men. 6242
12:28 *of* his father's house t and two captains. 6242
12:30 of the children of Ephraim t thousand and 6242
12:35 of the Danites expert in war t and 6242
12:37 for the battle, an hundred and t thousand. 6242
15: 5 and his brethren an hundred and t: 6242
15: 6 and his brethren two hundred and t: 6242
18: 4 and t thousand footmen: 6242
18: 5 of the Syrians two and t thousand men. 6242
20: 6 whose fingers and toes *were* four and t, 6242
23: 4 t and four thousand *were* to set forward 6242
23:24 from the age of t years and upward. 6242
23:27 the Levites *were* numbered from t years old 6242
27: 1 *of* every course *were* t and four thousand. 6242
27: 2 and in his course *were* t and four thousand. 6242
27: 4 in his course likewise *were* t and 6242
27: 5 and in his course *were* t and four thousand. 6242
27: 7 and in his course *were* t and four thousand. 6242
27: 8 and in his course *were* t and four thousand. 6242
27: 9 and in his course *were* t and four thousand. 6242
27:10 and in his course *were* t and four thousand. 6242
27:11 and in his course *were* t and four thousand. 6242
27:12 and in his course *were* t and four thousand. 6242
27:13 and in his course *were* t and four thousand. 6242
27:14 and in his course *were* t and four thousand. 6242
27:15 and in his course *were* t and four thousand. 6242
27:23 David took not the number of them from t 6242
2Ch 2:10 t thousand measures of beaten wheat, and 6242
2:10 t thousand measures of barley, and 6242
2:10 t thousand baths of wine, and 6242
2:10 baths of wine, and t thousand baths of oil. 6242
3: 3 threescore cubits, and the breadth t cubits. 6242
3: 4 t cubits, and the height *was* an hundred and 6242
3: 4 and the height *was* an hundred and t: 6242
3: 8 t cubits, and the breadth thereof twenty 6242
3: 8 and the breadth thereof t cubits: 6242
3:11 the wings of the cherubims *were* t cubits 6242
3:13 cherubims spread themselves forth t cubits: 6242
4: 1 t cubits the length thereof, and 6242
4: 1 t cubits the breadth thereof, and ten cubits 6242
5:12 and t priests sounding with trumpets:) 6242
7: 5 king Solomon offered a sacrifice of t and 6242
7: 5 and an hundred and t thousand sheep: 6242
8: 1 it came to pass at the end of t years, 6242
9: 9 the king an hundred and t talents of gold, 6242
11:21 begat t and eight sons, and 6242
13:21 begat t and two sons, and 6242
20:31 he reigned t and five years in Jerusalem. 6242
25: 1 Amaziah *was* t and five years old *when* he 6242
25: 1 he reigned t and nine years in Jerusalem. 6242
25: 5 and he numbered them from t years old and 6242
27: 1 Jotham *was* t and five years old when he 6242
27: 8 and t years old when he *began* to reign, 6242
28: 1 Ahaz *was* t years old when he *began* to 6242
28: 6 an hundred and t thousand in one day, 6242
29: 1 to reign *when he was* five and t years old, 6242
29: 1 he reigned nine and t years in Jerusalem. 6242

2Ch 31:17 the Levites from t years old and upward, 6242
33:21 and t years old when he *began* to reign, 6242
36: 2 Jehoahaz *was* t and three years old when he 6242
36: 5 Jehoiakim *was* t and five years old when he 6242
36:11 and t years old when he *began* to reign, 6242
Ezr 1: 9 chargers of silver, nine and t knives, 6242
2:11 children of Bebai, six hundred t and three. 6242
2:12 a thousand two hundred t and two. 6242
2:17 of Bezai, three hundred t and three. 6242
2:19 of Hashum, two hundred t and three. 6242
2:21 of Beth-lehem, an hundred t and three. 6242
2:23 men of Anathoth, an hundred t and eight. 6242
2:26 of Ramah and Gaba, six hundred t and one. 6242
2:27 men of Michmas, an hundred t and two. 6242
2:28 of Beth-el and Ai, two hundred t and three. 6242
2:32 The children of Harim, three hundred and t. 6242
2:33 Hadid, and Ono, seven hundred t and five. 6242
2:41 children of Asaph, an hundred t and eight. 6242
2:67 six thousand seven hundred and t. 6242
3: 8 appointed the Levites from t years old and 6242
8:11 of Bebai, and with him t and eight males. 6242
8:19 of Merari, his brethren and their sons, t; 6242
8:20 the Levites, two hundred and t Nethinims: 6242
8:27 Also t basons of gold, of a thousand drams; 6242
Ne 6:15 So the wall was finished in the t and 6242
7:16 children of Bebai, six hundred t and eight. 6242
7:17 two thousand three hundred t and two. 6242
7:22 of Hashum, three hundred t and eight. 6242
7:23 children of Bezai, three hundred t and four. 6242
7:27 men of Anathoth, an hundred t and eight. 6242
7:30 of Ramah and Geba, six hundred t and one. 6242
7:31 of Michmas, an hundred and t and two. 6242
7:32 of Beth-el and Ai, an hundred t and three. 6242
7:35 The children of Harim, three hundred and t. 6242
7:37 Hadid, and Ono, seven hundred t and one. 6242
7:69 six thousand seven hundred and t asses. 6242
7:71 of the work t thousand drams *of* gold, 8147
7:72 *that* which the rest of the people gave *was* t 8147
9: 1 Now in the t and fourth day of this month 6242
11: 8 Sallai, nine hundred t and eight. 6242
11:12 the work of the house *were* eight hundred t 6242
11:14 *men* of valour, an hundred t and eight: 6242
Est 1: 1 an hundred and seven and t provinces:) 6242
8: 9 an hundred t and seven provinces, 6242
9:30 to the hundred t and seven provinces of 6242
Ps 68:17 The chariots of God *are* **t thousand,** 7239
Jer 52: 1 and t year old when he *began* to reign, 6242
52:28 year three thousand Jews and three and t: 6242
Eze 4:10 shalt eat *shall be* by weight, t shekels a day: 6242
8:16 and the altar, *were* about five and t men, 6242
11: 1 at the door of the gate five and t men; 6242
40:13 the breadth *was* five and t cubits, 6242
40:21 and the breadth five and t cubits. 6242
40:25 and the breadth five and t cubits. 6242
40:29 cubits long, and five and t cubits broad. 6242
40:30 round about *were* five and t cubits long, 6242
40:33 cubits long, and five and t cubits broad. 6242
40:36 and the breadth five and t cubits. 6242
40:49 The length of the porch *was* t cubits, and 6242
41: 2 forty cubits: and the breadth, t cubits. 6242
41: 4 So he measured the length thereof, t cubits; 6242
41: 4 and the breadth, t cubits, before the temple: 6242
41:10 the chambers *was* the wideness of t 6242
42: 3 Over against the t *cubits* which *were* for 6242
45: 1 t thousand *reeds,* and the breadth *shall be* 6242
45: 3 measure the length of five and t thousand, 6242
45: 5 *the* five and t thousand of length, and 6242
45: 5 for a possession *for* t chambers. 6242
45: 6 and five and t thousand long, 6242
45:12 the shekel *shall be* t gerahs: twenty shekels, 6242
45:12 t shekels, five and twenty shekels, 6242
45:12 five and t shekels, fifteen shekels, 6242
48: 8 *of* five and t thousand *reeds in* breadth, 6242
48: 9 *shall be of* five and t thousand *in* length, 6242
48:10 the north five and t thousand *in length,* and 6242
48:10 the south five and t thousand *in* length: 6242
48:13 *shall have* five and t thousand *in* length, 6242
48:13 all the length *shall be* five and t thousand, 6242
48:15 over against the five and t thousand, 6242
48:20 t thousand by five and twenty thousand: 6242
48:20 twenty thousand by five and t thousand: 6242
48:21 t thousand of the oblation toward the east 6242
48:21 and t thousand toward the west border, 6242
Da 6: 1 over the kingdom an hundred and t princes, 6243
10:13 of Persia withstood me one and t days: 6242
Hag 2:16 when *one* came to a heap of t *measures,* 6242
2:16 *vessels out of* the press, there were *but* t. 6242
Zec 5: 2 the length thereof *is* t cubits, and 6242
Lk 14:31 that cometh against him with t thousand? *1501*
Jn 6:19 rowed about five and t or thirty furlongs, *1501*
Ac 1:15 together were about an hundred *and* t,) *1501*
27:28 And sounded, and found *it* t fathoms: and *1501*
1Co 10: 8 and fell in one day three and t thousand. *1501*
Rev 4: 4 about the throne *were* four and t seats: *1501*
4: 4 the seats I saw four and t elders sitting, *1501*
4:10 t elders fall down before him that sat on *1501*
5: 8 *and* t elders fell down before the Lamb, *1501*
5:14 And the four *and* t elders fell down and *1501*
11:16 And the four and t elders, which sat before *1501*
19: 4 And the four and t elders and the four *1501*

TWENTY'S (1) [TWENTY]
Ge 18:31 And he said, I will not destroy *it* for t sake. 6242

TWICE (17) [TWO]
Ge 41:32 that the dream was doubled unto Pharaoh t; 6471
Ex 16: 5 it shall be t as much as they gather daily. 4932
16:22 sixth day they gathered t **as much** bread, 4932
Nu 20:11 and with his rod he smote the rock t: 6471
1Sa 18:11 *it.* And David avoided out of his presence t. 6471
1Ki 11: 9 of Israel, which had appeared unto him t, 6471
2Ki 6:10 and saved himself there, not once nor t. 8147
Ne 13:20 ware lodged without Jerusalem once or t. 8147
Job 33:14 For God speaketh once, yea t, 8147+871.1
40: 5 yea, t; but I will proceed no further. 8147
42:10 also the LORD gave Job t as much as he 4932
Ps 62:11 God hath spoken once; t have I heard this; 8147
Ecc 6: 6 though he live a thousand years t *told,* yet 6471
Mk 14:30 *even* in this night, before *the* cock crow t, *1364*
14:72 Before *the* cock crow t, thou shalt deny me *1364*
Lk 18:12 I fast t in the week, I give tithes of all that I *1364*
Jude 1:12 without fruit, t dead, plucked up by *1364*

TWIGS (2)
Eze 17: 4 He cropt off the top of his **young** t, and 3242
17:22 from the top of his **young** t a tender one, 3127

TWILIGHT (9)
1Sa 30:17 David smote them from the t even unto 5399
2Ki 7: 5 they rose up in the t, to go unto the camp of 5399
7: 7 Wherefore they arose and fled in the t, and 5399
Job 3: 9 Let the stars of the t thereof be dark; let it 5399
24:15 eye also of the adulterer waiteth for the t, 5399
Pr 7: 9 In the t, in the evening, in the black and 5399
Eze 12: 6 *thy* shoulders, *and* carry *it* forth in the t: 5939
12: 7 I brought *it* forth in the t, *and* I bare *it* upon 5939
12:12 them shall bear upon *his* shoulder in the t, 5939

TWINED (21)
Ex 26: 1 tabernacle *with* ten curtains *of* fine t linen, 7806
26:31 scarlet, and fine t linen *of* cunning work: 7806
26:36 and purple, and scarlet, and fine t linen, 7806
27: 9 t linen of an hundred cubits long for one 7806
27:16 and purple, and scarlet, and fine t linen, 7806
27:18 the height five cubits *of* fine t linen, and 7806
28: 6 and *of* purple, *of* scarlet, and fine t linen, 7806
28: 8 and purple, and scarlet, and fine t linen. 7806
28:15 *of* purple, and *of* scarlet, and *of* fine t linen, 7806
36: 8 tabernacle made ten curtains *of* fine t linen, 7806
36:35 and purple, and scarlet, and fine t linen: 7806
36:37 purple, and scarlet, and fine t linen, 7806
38: 9 hangings of the court *were of* fine t linen, 7806
38:16 the court round about *were of* fine t linen. 7806
38:18 and purple, and scarlet, and fine t linen: 7806
39: 2 and purple, and scarlet, and fine t linen. 7806
39: 5 and purple, and scarlet, and fine t linen; 7806
39: 8 and purple, and scarlet, and fine t linen. 7806
39:24 and purple, and scarlet, *and* t *linen.* 7806
39:28 and linen breeches *of* fine t linen, 7806
39:29 a girdle *of* fine t linen, and blue, and 7806

TWINKLING (1)
1Co 15:52 In a moment, in the t of an eye, at the last *4493*

TWINS (6)
Ge 25:24 behold, *there were* t in her womb. 8380
38:27 that, behold, t *were* in her womb. 8380
SS 4: 2 whereof every one **beareth** t, and none *is* 8382
4: 5 breasts *are* like two young roes *that are* t, 8380

SS 6: 6 whereof every one **beareth t**, and *there is* 8382
7: 3 breasts *are* like two young roes *that are* **t**. 8380

TWIST See WREST

TWISTED See PLATTED; TWINED

TWO (835) [SECOND, TWAIN, TWICE, TWOEDGED, TWOFOLD]

Ge 1:16 God made **t** great lights; the greater light to 8147
4:19 Lamech took unto him **t** wives: the name of 8147
5:18 Jared lived an hundred sixty and **t** years, 8147
5:20 Jared were nine hundred sixty and **t** years: 8147
5:26 Lamech seven hundred eighty and **t** years, 8147
5:28 lived an hundred eighty and **t** years, 8147
6:19 **t** of every *sort* shalt thou bring into the ark, 8147
6:20 **t** of every *sort* shall come unto thee, to keep 8147
7: 2 of beasts that *are* not clean by **t**, the male 8147
7: 9 There went in **t** and two unto Noah into 8147
7: 9 went in two and **t** unto Noah into the ark, 8147
7:15 **t** and two of all flesh, wherein *is* the breath 8147
7:15 two and **t** of all flesh, wherein *is* the breath 8147
9:22 his father, and told his **t** brethren without. 8147
10:25 unto Eber were born **t** sons: the name of 8147
11:10 and begat Arphaxad **t years** after the flood: 8141
11:19 Peleg lived after he begat Reu **t hundred** 3967
11:20 Reu lived **t** and thirty years, and 8147
11:21 Reu lived after he begat Serug **t hundred** 3967
11:23 Serug lived after he begat Nahor **t hundred** 3967
11:32 the days of Terah were **t hundred** and 3967
19: 1 there came **t** angels to Sodom at even; and 8147
19: 8 I have **t** daughters which have not known 8147
19:15 Arise, take thy wife, and thy **t** daughters, 8147
19:16 and upon the hand of his **t** daughters; 8147
19:30 the mountain, and his **t** daughters with him; 8147
19:30 he dwelt in a cave, he and his **t** daughters. 8147
22: 3 took **t** of his young men with him, and 8147
24:22 **t** bracelets for her hands of ten *shekels* 8147
25:23 **T** nations *are* in thy womb, and two manner 8147
25:23 **t** manner of people shall be separated from 8147
27: 9 fetch me from thence **t** good kids of 8147
27:36 for he hath supplanted me these **t times**: he 6471
29:16 Laban had **t** daughters: the name of 8147
31:33 and into the **t** maidservants' tents; 8147
31:41 I served thee fourteen years for thy **t** 8147
32: 7 and herds, and the camels, into **t** bands; 8147
32:10 this Jordan; and now I am become **t** bands. 8147
32:14 **T hundred** she goats, and twenty he goats, 3967
32:14 **t hundred** ewes, and twenty rams, 3967
32:22 took his **t** wives, and his two 8147
32:22 his **t** womenservants, and his eleven sons, 8147
33: 1 and unto Rachel, and unto the **t** handmaids. 8147
34:25 that **t** of the sons of Jacob, Simeon and 8147
40: 2 Pharaoh was wroth against **t** *of* his officers, 8147
41: 1 to pass at the end of **t full years**, 3117+8141
41:50 unto Joseph were born **t** sons before 8147
42:37 saying, Slay my **t** sons, if I bring him not to 8147
44:27 Ye know that my wife bare me **t** *sons:* 8147
45: 6 For these **t years** *hath* the famine *been* in 8141
46:27 were born him in Egypt, *were* **t** souls: 8147
48: 1 he took with him his **t** sons, Manasseh and 8147
48: 5 now thy **t** sons, Ephraim and Manasseh, 8147
49:14 ass couching down between **t burdens**: 4942
Ex 2:13 **t** men of the Hebrews strove together: 8147
4: 9 if they will not believe also these **t** signs, 8147
12: 7 strike *it* on the **t** side posts and on the upper 8147
12:22 the **t** side posts with the blood that *is* in 8147
12:23 on the **t** side posts, the LORD will pass 8147
16:22 **t** omers for one *man:* and all the rulers of 8147
16:29 you on the sixth day the bread of **t days**; 3117
18: 3 her **t** sons; of which the name of the one 8147
18: 6 and thy wife, and her **t** sons with her. 8147
21:21 Notwithstanding, if he continue a day or **t**, 3117
25:10 **t cubits** and a half *shall be* the length 520
25:12 and **t** rings *shall be* in the one side of it, and 8147
25:12 side of it, and **t** rings in the other side of it. 8147
25:17 **t cubits** and a half *shall be* the length 520
25:18 thou shalt make **t** cherubims *of* gold, 8147
25:18 make them, in the **t** ends of the mercy seat. 8147
25:19 make the cherubims on the **t** ends thereof. 8147
25:22 from between the **t** cherubims which *are* 8147
25:23 **t cubits** *shall be* the length thereof, and 520
25:35 *there shall be* a knop under **t** branches of 8147
25:35 a knop under **t** branches of the same, and 8147
25:35 and a knop under **t** branches of the same, 8147
26:17 **T** tenons *shall there be* in one board, set in 8147
26:19 **t** sockets under one board for his two 8147
26:19 two sockets under one board for his **t** 8147
26:19 **t** sockets under another board for his two 8147
26:19 two sockets under another board for his **t** 8147
26:21 **t** sockets under one board, and two sockets 8147
26:21 and **t** sockets under another board. 8147
26:23 **t** boards shalt thou make for the corners of 8147
26:23 the corners of the tabernacle in the **t sides**. 3411
26:24 them both; they shall be for the **t** corners. 8147
26:25 **t** sockets under one board, and two sockets 8147
26:25 and **t** sockets under another board. 8147
26:27 of the tabernacle, for the **t sides** westward. 3411
27: 7 the staves shall be upon the **t** sides of 8147
28: 7 It shall have the **t** shoulderpieces *thereof* 8147
28: 7 *thereof* joined at the **t** edges thereof; 8147
28: 9 thou shalt take **t** onyx stones, and grave on 8147
28:11 shalt thou engrave the **t** stones with 8147
28:12 thou shalt put the **t** stones upon 8147
28:12 upon his **t** shoulders for a memorial. 8147
28:14 **t** chains *of* pure gold at the ends; 8147
28:23 thou shalt make upon the breastplate **t** rings 8147
28:23 shalt put the **t** rings on the two ends of 8147
28:23 shalt put the two rings on the **t** ends of 8147
28:24 thou shalt put the **t** wreathen *chains of* gold 8147
28:24 **t** rings *which are* on the ends of 8147
28:25 *the other* **t** ends of the two wreathen *chains* 8147
28:25 *the other* two ends of the **t** wreathen *chains* 8147
28:25 *chains* thou shalt fasten in the **t** ouches, 8147
28:26 thou shalt make **t** rings of gold, and 8147
28:26 thou shalt put them upon the **t** ends of 8147
28:27 **t** *other* rings of gold thou shalt make, and 8147
28:27 shalt put them on the **t** sides of the ephod 8147
29: 1 young bullock, and **t** rams without blemish, 8147
29: 3 the basket, with the bullock and the **t** rams. 8147
29:13 the **t** kidneys, and the fat that *is* upon them, 8147
29:22 the **t** kidneys, and the fat that *is* upon them, 8147
29:38 **t** lambs of the first year day by day 8147
30: 2 **t cubits** *shall be* the height thereof: the horns 520
30: 4 **t** golden rings shalt thou make to it under 8147
30: 4 by the **t** corners thereof, upon the two sides 8147
30: 4 upon the **t** sides of it shalt thou make *it;* and 8147
30:23 *even* **t hundred** and fifty *shekels,* and 3967
30:23 and of sweet calamus **t hundred** and 3967
31:18 **t** tables of Testimony, tables of stone, 8147
32:15 the **t** tables of the Testimony *were* in his 8147
34: 1 Hew thee **t** tables of stone like unto 8147
34: 4 he hewed **t** tables of stone like unto 8147
34: 4 and took in his hand the **t** tables of stone. 8147
34:29 the **t** tables of Testimony in Moses' hand, 8147
36:22 One board had **t** tenons, equally distant one 8147
36:24 **t** sockets under one board for his two 8147
36:24 two sockets under one board for his **t** 8147
36:24 **t** sockets under another board for his two 8147
36:24 two sockets under another board for his **t** 8147
36:26 **t** sockets under one board, and two sockets 8147
36:26 and **t** sockets under another board. 8147
36:28 **t** boards made he for the corners of 8147
36:28 the corners of the tabernacle in the **t sides**. 3411
36:30 *of* silver, under every board **t** sockets. 8147
37: 1 **t cubits** and a half *was* the length of it, and 520
37: 3 even **t** rings upon the one side of it, and 8147
37: 3 of it, and **t** rings upon the other side of it. 8147
37: 6 **t cubits** and a half *was* the length thereof, 520
37: 7 he made **t** cherubims *of* gold, beaten out of 8147
37: 7 he them, on the **t** ends of the mercy seat; 8147
37: 8 he the cherubims on the **t** ends thereof. 8147
37:10 **t cubits** *was* the length thereof, and a cubit 520
37:21 a knop under **t** branches of the same, and 8147
37:21 a knop under **t** branches of the same, and 8147
37:21 and a knop under **t** branches of the same, 8147
37:25 and **t cubits** *was* the height of it; 520
37:27 he made **t** rings of gold for it under 8147
37:27 by the **t** corners of it, upon the two sides 8147
37:27 two corners of it, upon the **t** sides thereof, 8147
38:29 and **t thousand** and four hundred shekels. 505
39: 4 by the **t** edges was it coupled together. 8147
39:16 they made **t** ouches *of* gold, and two gold 8147
39:16 made two ouches *of* gold, and **t** gold rings; 8147
39:16 put the **t** rings in the two ends of 8147
39:16 put the two rings in the **t** ends of 8147
39:17 they put the **t** wreathen *chains of* gold in 8147
39:17 in the **t** rings on the ends of the breastplate. 8147

T

Ex 39:18 the t ends of the two wreathen *chains* they 8147
39:18 the two ends of the t wreathen *chains* they 8147
39:18 *chains* they fastened in the t ouches, 8147
39:19 they made t rings of gold, and put *them* on 8147
39:19 put *them* on the t ends of the breastplate, 8147
39:20 they made t *other* golden rings, and 8147
39:20 put them on the t sides of the ephod 8147
Lev 3: 4 the t kidneys, and the fat that *is* on them, 8147
3:10 the t kidneys, and the fat that *is* upon them, 8147
3:15 the t kidneys, and the fat that *is* upon them, 8147
4: 9 the t kidneys, and the fat that *is* upon them, 8147
5: 7 t turtledoves, or two young pigeons, 8147
5: 7 two turtledoves, or t young pigeons, 8147
5:11 if he be not able to bring t turtledoves, or 8147
5:11 or t young pigeons, then he that sinned 8147
7: 4 the t kidneys, and the fat that *is* on them, 8147
8: 2 t rams, and a basket of unleavened bread; 8147
8:16 the t kidneys, and their fat, and 8147
8:25 the t kidneys, and their fat, and the right 8147
12: 5 she shall be unclean t **weeks**, as *in* her 7620
12: 8 she shall bring t turtles, or two young 8147
12: 8 shall bring two turtles, or t young pigeons; 8147
14: 4 for him that is to be cleansed t birds alive 8147
14:10 on the eighth day he shall take t he lambs 8147
14:22 t turtledoves, or two young pigeons, 8147
14:22 two turtledoves, or t young pigeons, 8147
14:49 he shall take to cleanse the house t birds, 8147
15:14 on the eighth day he shall take to him t 8147
15:14 or t young pigeons, and come before 8147
15:29 on the eighth day she shall take unto her t 8147
15:29 or t young pigeons, and bring them unto 8147
16: 1 after the death of the t sons of Aaron, 8147
16: 5 Israel t kids of the goats for a sin offering, 8147
16: 7 he shall take the t goats, and present them 8147
16: 8 Aaron shall cast lots upon the t goats; 8147
23:13 the meat offering thereof *shall be* t tenth 8147
23:17 Ye shall bring out of your habitations t 8147
23:17 two wave loaves of t tenth deals: 8147
23:18 and one young bullock, and t rams: 8147
23:19 t lambs of the first year for a sacrifice of 8147
23:20 before the LORD, with the t lambs: 8147
24: 5 t tenth deals shall be *in* one cake. 8147
24: 6 thou shalt set them *in* t rows, six on a row, 8147
Nu 1:35 *were* thirty and t thousand and 8147
1:35 and two thousand and t **hundred**. 3967
1:39 and t thousand and seven hundred. 8147
2:21 *were* thirty and t thousand and 8147
2:21 and two thousand and t **hundred**. 3967
2:26 and t thousand and seven hundred. 8147
3:34 upward, *were* six thousand and t **hundred**. 3967
3:39 and upward, *were* twenty and t thousand. 8147
3:43 t thousand two hundred and threescore and 8147
3:43 two thousand t **hundred** and threescore 3967
3:46 that are *to be* redeemed of the t **hundred** 3967
4:36 families were t **thousand** seven hundred 505
4:40 were t **thousand** and six hundred and thirty. 505
4:44 were three thousand and t **hundred**. 3967
6:10 on the eighth day he shall bring t turtles, 8147
6:10 or t young pigeons, to the priest, 8147
7: 3 a wagon for t of the princes, and for *each* 8147
7: 7 T wagons and four oxen he gave unto 8147
7:17 t oxen, five rams, five he goats, five lambs 8147
7:23 t oxen, five rams, five he goats, five lambs 8147
7:29 t oxen, five rams, five he goats, five lambs 8147
7:35 t oxen, five rams, five he goats, five lambs 8147
7:41 t oxen, five rams, five he goats, five lambs 8147
7:47 t oxen, five rams, five he goats, five lambs 8147
7:53 t oxen, five rams, five he goats, five lambs 8147
7:59 t oxen, five rams, five he goats, five lambs 8147
7:65 t oxen, five rams, five he goats, five lambs 8147
7:71 t oxen, five rams, five he goats, five lambs 8147
7:77 t oxen, five rams, five he goats, five lambs 8147
7:83 t oxen, five rams, five he goats, five lambs 8147
7:85 all the silver vessels *weighed* t **thousand** 505
7:89 from between the t cherubims: 8147
9:22 Or *whether it were* t **days**, or a month, or 3117
10: 2 Make thee t trumpets of silver; of a whole 8147
11:19 nor t **days**, nor five days, neither ten days, 3117
11:26 there remained t *of the* men in the camp, 8147
11:31 as it were t **cubits** *high* upon the face of 520
13:23 and they bare it between t upon a staff; 8147
15: 6 thou shalt prepare *for* a meat offering t 8147
16: 2 t **hundred** and fifty princes of 3967
16:17 his censer, t **hundred** and fifty censers; 3967
16:35 consumed the t **hundred** and fifty men that 3967
22:22 his ass, and his t servants *were* with him. 8147
26:10 what time the fire devoured t **hundred** and 3967
26:14 twenty and t thousand and two hundred. 8147
26:14 twenty and two thousand and t **hundred**. 3967
26:34 fifty and t thousand and seven hundred. 8147
26:37 thirty and t thousand and five hundred. 8147
28: 3 t lambs of the first year without spot day by 8147
28: 9 on the sabbath day t lambs of the first year 8147
28: 9 t tenth deals *of* flour *for* a meat offering, 8147
28:11 t young bullocks, and one ram, seven lambs 8147
28:12 t tenth deals *of* flour *for* a meat offering, 8147
28:19 t young bullocks, and one ram, and 8147
28:20 for a bullock, and t tenth deals for a ram; 8147
28:27 t young bullocks, one ram, seven lambs of 8147
28:28 one bullock, t tenth deals unto one ram, 8147
29: 3 for a bullock, *and* t tenth deals for a ram, 8147
29: 9 to a bullock, *and* t tenth deals to one ram, 8147
29:13 t rams, *and* fourteen lambs of the first year; 8147
29:14 t tenth deals to each ram of the two rams, 8147
29:14 two tenth deals to each ram of the t rams, 8147
29:17 t rams, fourteen lambs of the first year 8147
29:20 on the third day eleven bullocks, t rams, 8147
29:23 t rams, *and* fourteen lambs of the first year 8147
29:26 t rams, *and* fourteen lambs of the first year 8147
29:29 t rams, *and* fourteen lambs of the first year 8147
29:32 t rams, *and* fourteen lambs of the first year 8147
31:27 **divide** the prey **into t parts**; between them 2673
31:35 thirty and t thousand persons in all, 8147
31:40 LORD'S tribute *was* thirty and t persons. 8147
34:15 The t tribes and the half tribe have received 8147
35: 5 the city *on* the east side t **thousand** cubits, 505
35: 5 and *on* the south side t **thousand** cubits, and 505
35: 5 *on* the west side t **thousand** cubits, and 505
35: 5 and *on* the north side t **thousand** cubits; 505
35: 6 to them ye shall add forty and t cities. 8147
Dt 3: 8 we took at that time out of the hand of the t 8147
3:21 your God hath done unto these t kings: 8147
4:13 and he wrote them upon t tables of stone. 8147
4:47 Og king of Bashan, t kings of the Amorites, 8147
5:22 he wrote them in t tables of stone, and 8147
9:10 the LORD delivered unto me t tables of 8147
9:11 *that* the LORD gave me the t tables of 8147
9:15 the t tables of the covenant *were* in my two 8147
9:15 the two tables of the covenant *were* in my t 8147
9:17 I took the t tables, and cast them out of my 8147
9:17 cast them out of my t hands, and 8147
10: 1 Hew thee t tables of stone like unto 8147
10: 3 hewed t tables of stone like unto the first, 8147
10: 3 having the t tables in mine hand. 8147
14: 6 cleaveth the cleft *into* t claws, *and* 8147
17: 6 At the mouth of t witnesses, or 8147
18: 3 and the t **cheeks**, and the maw. 3895
19:15 at the mouth of t witnesses, or at the mouth 8147
21:15 If a man have t wives, one beloved, and 8147
32:30 t put ten thousand to flight, except their 8147
Jos 2: 1 Joshua the son of Nun sent out of Shittim t 8147
2: 4 the woman took the t men, and hid them, 8147
2:10 what you did unto the t kings of 8147
2:23 So the t men returned, and descended from 8147
3: 4 and it, about t **thousand** cubits by measure: 505
6:22 Joshua had said unto the t men that had 8147
7: 3 *but* let about t or three **thousand** men go up 505
7:21 t **hundred** shekels *of* silver, and a wedge of 3967
9:10 all that he did to the t kings of 8147
14: 3 For Moses had given the inheritance of t 8147
14: 4 For the children of Joseph were t tribes, 8147
15:60 and Rabbah; t cities with their villages. 8147
19:30 twenty and t cities with their villages. 8147
21:16 her suburbs; nine cities out of those t tribes. 8147
21:25 and Gath-rimmon with her suburbs; t cities. 8147
21:27 and Beeshterah with her suburbs; t cities. 8147
24:12 *even* the t kings of the Amorites; 8147
Jdg 3:16 Ehud made him a dagger which had t 8147
5:30 the prey; to every man a damsel *or* ts; 7361
7: 3 of the people twenty and t thousand; 8147
7:25 they took t princes of the Midianites, Oreb 8147
8:12 took the t kings of Midian, Zebah and 8147
9:44 the t *other* companies ran upon all 8147
10: 3 and judged Israel twenty and t years. 8147
11:37 let me alone t months, that I may go up and 8147
11:38 he sent her away *for* t months: and 8147
11:39 it came to pass at the end of t months, 8147
12: 6 of the Ephraimites forty and t thousand. 8147

T

Jdg 15: 4 put a firebrand in the midst between t tails. 8147
15:13 they bound him with t new cords, and 8147
16: 3 the t posts, and went away with them, bar 8147
16:28 avenged of the Philistines for my t eyes. 8147
16:29 Samson took hold of the t middle pillars 8147
17: 4 his mother took t **hundred** *shekels* of 3967
19:10 *there were* with him t asses saddled, 6776
20:21 that day twenty and t thousand men. 8147
20:45 and slew t **thousand** men of them. 505
Ru 1: 1 of Moab, he, and his wife, and his t sons. 8147
1: 2 the name of his t sons Mahlon and Chilion, 8147
1: 3 and she was left, and her t sons. 8147
1: 5 the woman was left of her t sons and 8147
1: 7 and her t daughters in law with her; 8147
1: 8 Naomi said unto her t daughters in law, 8147
1:19 So they t went until they came *to* 8147
4:11 which t did build the house of Israel: 8147
1Sa 1: 2 he had t wives; the name of the one *was* 8147
1: 3 the t sons of Eli, Hophni and Phinehas, 8147
2:21 and bare three sons and t daughters. 8147
2:34 that shall come upon thy t sons, on Hophni 8147
4: 4 the t sons of Eli, Hophni and Phinehas, 8147
4:11 the t sons of Eli, Hophni and Phinehas, 8147
4:17 thy t sons also, Hophni and Phinehas, 8147
6: 7 make a new cart, and take t milch kine, 8147
6:10 took t milch kine, and tied them to the cart, 8147
10: 2 thou shalt find t men by Rachel's sepulchre 8147
10: 4 salute thee, and give thee t *loaves* of bread; 8147
11:11 so that t of them were not left together. 8147
13: 1 when he had reigned t years over Israel, 8147
13: 2 *whereof* t **thousand** were with Saul in 505
14:49 the names of his t daughters *were these;* 8147
15: 4 t **hundred** thousand footmen, and 3967
18:27 and slew of the Philistines t **hundred** men; 3967
23:18 they t made a covenant before the LORD: 8147
25:13 and t **hundred** abode by the stuff. 3967
25:18 took t **hundred** loaves, and two bottles of 3967
25:18 t bottles of wine, and five sheep ready 8147
25:18 t **hundred** cakes *of figs,* and laid *them* on 3967
27: 3 *even* David with his t wives, Ahinoam 8147
28: 8 t men with him, and they came to 8147
30: 5 David's t wives were taken captives, 8147
30:10 for t **hundred** abode *behind,* which were so 3967
30:12 of a cake *of figs,* and t clusters of raisins: 8147
30:18 and David rescued his t wives. 8147
30:21 David came to the t **hundred** men, 3967
2Sa 1: 1 and David had abode t days in Ziklag; 8147
2: 2 his t wives also, Ahinoam the Jezreelitess, 8147
2:10 to reign over Israel, and reigned t years. 8147
4: 2 Saul's son had t men *that were* captains of 8147
8: 2 even *with* t lines measured he to put to 8147
8: 5 David slew of the Syrians t and 8147
12: 1 unto him, There were t men in one city; 8147
13:23 it came to pass after t **full years,** 3117+8141
14: 6 thy handmaid had t sons, and they two 8147
14: 6 they t strove together in the field, and 8147
14:26 t **hundred** shekels after the king's weight. 3967
14:28 So Absalom dwelt t **full years** in 3117+8141
15:11 with Absalom went t **hundred** men out of 3967
15:27 your t sons with you, Ahimaaz thy son, and 8147
15:36 *they have* there with them their t sons, 8147
16: 1 upon them t **hundred** *loaves of* bread, and 3967
18:24 David sat between the t gates: and 8147
21: 8 the king took the t sons of Rizpah 8147
23:20 he slew t lionlike men of Moab: 8147
1Ki 2: 5 what he did to the t captains of the hosts of 8147
2:32 who fell upon t men more righteous and 8147
2:39 that t of the servants of Shimei ran away 8147
3:16 came there t women, *that were* harlots, 8147
3:18 us in the house, save we t in the house. 8147
3:25 Divide the living child in t, and give half to 8147
5:12 and they t made a league *together.* 8147
5:14 were in Lebanon, *and* t months at home: 8147
6:23 within the oracle he made t cherubims *of* 8147
6:32 The t doors also *were of* olive tree; and 8147
6:34 the t doors *were* of fir tree: the two leaves 8147
6:34 the t leaves of the one door *were* folding, 8147
6:34 the t leaves of the other door *were* folding. 8147
7:15 For he cast t pillars *of* brass, of eighteen 8147
7:16 he made t chapiters *of* molten brass, to set 8147
7:18 t rows round about upon the one network, 8147
7:20 the chapiters upon the t pillars *had* 8147
7:20 the pomegranates *were* t **hundred** *in* rows 3967
7:24 the knops *were* cast *in* t rows, when it was 8147
7:26 of lilies: it contained t **thousand** baths. 505
7:41 The t pillars, and the two bowls of 8147
7:41 the t bowls of the chapiters that *were* on 8147
7:41 that *were* on the top of the t pillars; NIH
7:41 the t networks, to cover the two bowls of 8147
7:41 to cover the t bowls of the chapiters which 8147
7:42 four hundred pomegranates for the t 8147
7:42 *even* t rows *of* pomegranates for one 8147
7:42 to cover the t bowls of the chapiters that 8147
8: 7 forth *their* t **wings** over the place of the ark, 3671
8: 9 *There was* nothing in the ark save the t 8147
8:63 t and twenty thousand oxen, and 8147
9:10 when Solomon had built the t houses, 8147
10:16 king Solomon made t **hundred** targets *of* 3967
10:19 the seat, and t lions stood beside the stays. 8147
11:29 and they t *were* alone in the field: 8147
12:28 made t calves of gold, and said unto them, 8147
14:20 the days which Jeroboam reigned *were* t 8147
15:25 of Judah, and reigned over Israel t **years.** 8141
16: 8 to reign over Israel in Tirzah, t **years.** 8141
16:21 the people of Israel divided into t **parts:** 2677
16:24 Samaria of Shemer for t **talents** of silver, 3603
16:29 over Israel in Samaria twenty and t years. 8147
17:12 behold, I *am* gathering t sticks, that I may 8147
18:21 said, How long halt ye between t opinions? 8147
18:23 Let them therefore give us t bullocks; and 8147
18:32 as great as would contain t **measures** of 5429
20: 1 *there were* thirty and t kings with him, and 8147
20:15 and they were t **hundred** and thirty two: 3967
20:15 and they were two hundred and thirty t: 8147
20:16 the thirty and t kings that helped him. 8147
20:27 before them like t little flocks of kids; 8147
21:10 set t men, sons of Belial, before him, to 8147
21:13 there came in t men, children of Belial, 8147
22:31 t captains that had rule over *his* chariots, 8147
22:51 of Judah, and reigned t **years** over Israel. 8141
2Ki 1:14 burnt up the t captains of the former fifties 8147
2: 6 I will not leave thee. And they t went on. 8147
2: 7 to view afar off: and they t stood by Jordan. 8147
2: 8 so that they t went over on dry *ground.* 8147
2:12 his own clothes, and rent them in t pieces. 8147
2:24 there came forth t she bears out of 8147
2:24 and tare forty and t children of them. 8147
4: 1 the creditor is come to take unto him my t 8147
5:17 be given to thy servant t mules' burden of 6776
5:22 t young men of the sons of the prophets: 8147
5:22 talent of silver, and t changes of garments. 8147
5:23 Naaman said, Be content, take t **talents.** 3603
5:23 and bound t **talents** of silver in two bags, 3603
5:23 and bound two talents of silver in t bags, 8147
5:23 with t changes of garments, and laid *them* 8147
5:23 and laid *them* upon t of his servants; 8147
7: 1 t **measures** of barley for a shekel, in 5429
7:14 They took therefore t chariot horses; and 8147
7:16 t **measures** of barley for a shekel, 5429
7:18 **T measures** of barley for a shekel, and 5429
8:17 t years old was he when he *began* to reign; 8147
8:26 **T** and twenty years old *was* Ahaziah when 8147
9:32 there looked out to him t *or* three eunuchs. 8147
10: 4 said, Behold, t kings stood not before him: 8147
10: 8 Lay ye them *in* t heaps *at* the entering in of 8147
10:14 the shearing house, *even* t and forty men; 8147
11: 7 t parts of all you that go forth on 8147
15: 2 he reigned t and fifty years in Jerusalem. 8147
15:23 over Israel in Samaria, *and reigned* t **years.** 8141
15:27 In the t and fiftieth year of Azariah king of 8147
17:16 *even* t calves, and made a grove, and 8147
18:23 and I will deliver thee t **thousand** horses, 505
21: 5 in the t courts of the house of the LORD. 8147
21:19 and t years old when he *began* to reign, 8147
21:19 and he reigned t years in Jerusalem. 8147
23:12 in the t courts of the house of the LORD, 8147
25: 4 *by* the way of the gate between t **walls,** 2346
25:16 The t pillars, one sea, and the bases which 8147
1Ch 1:19 unto Eber were born t sons: the name of 8147
4: 5 Ashur the father of Tekoa had t wives, 8147
5:21 *of* sheep t **hundred** and fifty thousand, and 3967
5:21 *of* asses t **thousand**, and *of* men an hundred 505
7: 2 whose number *was* in the days of David t 8147
7: 7 and t thousand and thirty and four. 8147
7: 9 *was* twenty thousand and t **hundred.** 3967
7:11 t **hundred** *soldiers, fit to* go out *for* war 3967
9:22 to be porters in the gates *were* t **hundred** 3967
11:21 he was more honourable than the t; 8147

T

1Ch 11:22 many acts; he slew t lionlike men of Moab: 8147
12:28 *of* his father's house twenty and t captains. 8147
12:32 the heads of them *were* **t hundred**; and 3967
15: 6 and his brethren **t hundred** and twenty: 3967
15: 8 the chief, and his brethren **t hundred**: 3967
18: 5 David slew of the Syrians t and 8147
19: 7 So they hired thirty and t thousand chariots, 8147
24:17 to Jachin, the t and twentieth to Gamul, 8147
25: 7 was **t hundred** fourscore and eight. 3967
25:29 The t and twentieth to Giddalti, *he,* his 8147
26: 8 *were* threescore and t of Obed-edom. 8147
26:17 four a day, and toward Asuppim t *and* two. 8147
26:17 four a day, and toward Asuppim two *and* t. 8147
26:18 four at the causeway, *and* t at Parbar. 8147
26:32 *were* **t thousand** and seven hundred chief 505
2Ch 3:10 in the most holy house he made t 8147
3:15 Also he made before the house t pillars of 8147
4: 3 T rows *of* oxen *were* cast, when it was cast. 8147
4:12 *To wit,* the t pillars, and the pommels, and 8147
4:12 the chapiters *which were* on the top of the t 8147
4:12 the t wreaths to cover the two pommels of 8147
4:12 the two wreaths to cover the t pommels of 8147
4:13 four hundred pomegranates on the t 8147
4:13 t rows *of* pomegranates on each wreath, to 8147
4:13 to cover the t pommels of the chapiters 8147
5:10 *There was* nothing in the ark save the t 8147
7: 5 a sacrifice of twenty and t thousand oxen, 8147
8:10 *even* **t hundred** and fifty, that bare rule 3967
9:15 king Solomon made **t hundred** targets *of* 3967
9:18 and t lions standing by the stays: 8147
13:21 begat twenty and t sons, and 8147
14: 8 **t hundred** and fourscore thousand: 3967
17:15 with him **t hundred** and 3967
17:16 with him **t hundred** thousand mighty *men* 3967
17:17 with bow and shield **t hundred** thousand. 3967
21: 5 and t years old when he *began* to reign, 8147
21:19 in process of time, after the end of t years, 8147
21:20 t *years* old was he when he *began* to reign, 8147
22: 2 t years old *was* Ahaziah when he *began* to 8147
24: 3 Jehoiada took for him t wives; and he begat 8147
26: 3 he reigned fifty and t years in Jerusalem. 8147
26:12 the mighty *men* of valour *were* **t thousand** 505
28: 8 of their brethren **t hundred** thousand, 3967
29:32 an hundred rams, *and* **t hundred** lambs: 3967
33: 5 in the t courts of the house of the LORD. 8147
33:21 Amon *was* t and twenty years old when he 8147
33:21 to reign, and reigned t years in Jerusalem. 8147
35: 8 priests for the passover *offerings* **t thousand** 505
Ezr 2: 3 **t thousand** an hundred seventy and two. 505
2: 3 two thousand an hundred seventy and **t**. 8147
2: 4 of Shephatiah, three hundred seventy and **t**. 8147
2: 6 Joab, **t thousand** eight hundred and twelve. 505
2: 7 a thousand **t hundred** fifty and four. 3967
2:10 children of Bani, six hundred forty and **t**. 8147
2:12 a thousand **t hundred** twenty and two. 3967
2:12 a thousand two hundred twenty and **t**. 8147
2:14 children of Bigvai, **t thousand** fifty and six. 505
2:19 of Hashum, **t hundred** twenty and three. 3967
2:24 The children of Azmaveth, forty and **t**. 8147
2:27 men of Michmas, an hundred twenty and **t**. 8147
2:28 and Ai, **t hundred** twenty and three. 3967
2:29 The children of Nebo, fifty and **t**. 8147
2:31 a thousand **t hundred** fifty and four. 3967
2:37 children of Immer, a thousand fifty and **t**. 8147
2:38 a thousand **t hundred** forty and seven. 3967
2:58 *were* three hundred ninety and **t**. 8147
2:60 children of Nekoda, six hundred fifty and **t**. 8147
2:64 *was* **forty** *and* **t thousand** 505+702+7239
2:65 *there were* among them **t hundred** singing 3967
2:66 six; their mules, **t hundred** forty and five; 3967
6:17 **t hundred** rams, four hundred lambs; 3969
8: 4 and with him **t hundred** males. 3967
8: 9 with him **t hundred** and eighteen males. 3967
8:20 **t hundred** and twenty Nethinims: 3967
8:27 t vessels of fine copper, precious as gold. 8147
10:13 neither *is this* a work of one day or t: 8147
Ne 5:14 from the twentieth year even unto the t 8147
6:15 *day* of *the month* Elul, in fifty and t days. 8147
7: 8 **t thousand** an hundred seventy and two. 505
7: 8 two thousand an hundred seventy and **t**. 8147
7: 9 of Shephatiah, three hundred seventy and **t**. 8147
7:10 children of Arah, six hundred fifty and **t**. 8147
7:11 **t thousand** and eight hundred *and* eighteen. 505
7:12 a thousand **t hundred** fifty and four. 3967
7:17 **t thousand** three hundred twenty and two. 505
7:17 two thousand three hundred twenty and **t**. 8147
7:19 of Bigvai, **t thousand** threescore and seven. 505
7:28 The men of Beth-azmaveth, forty and **t**. 8147
7:31 of Michmas, an hundred and twenty and **t**. 8147
7:33 The men of the other Nebo, fifty and **t**. 8147
7:34 a thousand **t hundred** fifty and four. 3967
7:40 children of Immer, a thousand fifty and **t**. 8147
7:41 a thousand **t hundred** forty and seven. 3967
7:60 *were* three hundred ninety and **t**. 8147
7:62 of Nekoda, six hundred forty and **t**. 8147
7:66 *was* **forty** *and* **t thousand** 505+702+7239
7:67 they had **t hundred** forty and five singing 3967
7:68 six: their mules, **t hundred** forty and five: 3967
7:71 **t thousand** and two hundred pound *of* silver. 505
7:71 and **t hundred** pound *of* silver. 3967
7:72 **t thousand** pound *of* silver, and threescore 505
11:12 the house *were* eight hundred twenty and **t**: 8147
11:13 of the fathers, **t hundred** forty and two: 3967
11:13 of the fathers, two hundred forty and **t**: 8147
11:18 in the holy city *were* **t hundred** fourscore 3967
11:19 the gates, *were* an hundred seventy and **t**. 8147
12:31 appointed t great *companies of them that* 8147
12:40 So stood the t *companies of them that gave* 8147
13: 6 for in the t and thirtieth year of Artaxerxes 8147
Est 2:21 t of the king's chamberlains, Bigthan and 8147
6: 2 and Teresh, t of the king's chamberlains, 8147
9:27 that they would keep these t days according 8147
Job 13:20 Only do not t *things* unto me: then will I 8147
42: 7 against thee, and against thy t friends: 8147
Pr 30: 7 T *things* have I required of thee; deny me 8147
30:15 The horseleach hath t daughters, 8147
Ecc 4: 9 T *are* better than one; because they have a 8147
4:11 Again, if t lie together, then they have heat: 8147
4:12 prevail against him, t shall withstand him; 8147
SS 4: 5 Thy t breasts *are* like two young roes *that* 8147
4: 5 Thy two breasts *are* like t young roes *that* 8147
6:13 As it were the company of **t armies**. 4264
7: 3 Thy t breasts *are* like two young roes *that* 8147
7: 3 Thy two breasts *are* like t young roes *that* 8147
8:12 those that keep the fruit thereof **t hundred**. 3967
Isa 7: 4 neither be fainthearted for the t tails of 8147
7:21 shall nourish a young cow, and t sheep; 8147
17: 6 t *or* three berries in the top of 8147
22:11 Ye made also a ditch between the **t walls** 2346
36: 8 and I will give thee **t thousand** horses, 505
45: 1 to open before him the **t leaved gates**; 1817
47: 9 these t *things* shall come to thee *in* a 8147
51:19 These t *things* are come unto thee; 8147
Jer 2:13 For my people have committed t evils; 8147
3:14 t of a family, and I will bring you *to* Zion: 8147
24: 1 t baskets of figs *were* set before the temple 8147
28: 3 Within **t full years** *will* I bring again 3117+8141
28:11 within the space of **t full years**. 3117+8141
33:24 The t families which the LORD hath 8147
39: 4 by the gate betwixt the **t walls**: 2346
52: 7 *by* the way of the gate between the **t walls**, 2346
52:20 The t pillars, one sea, and twelve brasen 8147
52:29 eight hundred thirty and t persons: 8147
Eze 1:11 t *wings* of every one *were* joined one to 8147
1:11 one to another, and t covered their bodies. 8147
1:23 every one had t, which covered on this 8147
1:23 covered on this *side,* and every one had t, 8147
21:19 Also, thou son of man, appoint thee t ways, 8147
21:21 at the head of the t ways, to use divination: 8147
23: 2 Son of man, there were t women, 8147
35:10 These t nations and these two countries 8147
35:10 and these t countries shall be mine, 8147
37:22 they shall be no more t nations, 8147
37:22 neither shall they be divided into t 8147
40: 9 the posts thereof, t cubits; and the porch of 8147
40:39 in the porch of the gate *were* t tables on this 8147
40:39 t tables on that side, to slay thereon 8147
40:40 to the entry of the north gate, *were* t tables; 8147
40:40 *was* at the porch of the gate, *were* t tables. 8147
41: 3 measured the post of the door, t cubits; 8147
41:18 and a cherub; and *every* cherub had t faces; 8147
41:22 cubits high, and the length thereof t cubits; 8147
41:23 the temple and the sanctuary had t doors. 8147
41:24 the doors had t leaves *apiece,* two turning 8147
41:24 the doors had two leaves *apiece,* t turning 8147
41:24 t *leaves* for the one door, and two leaves 8147
41:24 one door, and t leaves for the other *door.* 8147
43:14 *even* to the lower settle *shall be* t cubits, 8147

Eze 45:15 lamb out of the flock, out of **t hundred**, 3967
46:19 there *was* a place on the **t sides** westward. 3411
47:13 tribes of Israel: Joseph *shall have* **t** portions. NIH
48:17 city shall be toward the north **t hundred** 3967
48:17 toward the south **t hundred** and fifty, and 3967
48:17 toward the east **t hundred** and fifty, and 3967
48:17 and toward the west **t hundred** and fifty. 3967
Da 5:31 *being* about threescore and **t** year old. 8648
8: 3 before the river a ram which had **t horns**: 7161
8: 3 the **t horns** *were* high; but one *was* higher 7161
8: 6 he came to the ram that had **t horns**, 7161
8: 7 and smote the ram, and brake his **t** horns: 8147
8:14 Unto **t thousand** and three hundred days; 505
8:20 The ram which thou sawest having **t horns** 7161
9:25 seven weeks, and threescore and **t** weeks: 8147
9:26 and **t** weeks shall Messiah be cut off, 8147
12: 5 and behold, there stood other **t**, 8147
12:11 *there shall be* a thousand **t hundred** and 3967
Hos 6: 2 After **t days** will he revive us: in the third 3117
10:10 when *they* shall bind themselves in their **t** 8147
Am 1: 1 king of Israel, **t year** before the earthquake. 8141
3: 3 Can **t** walk together, except they be agreed? 8147
3:12 taketh out of the mouth of the lion **t** legs, 8147
4: 8 So **t** *or* three cities wandered unto one city, 8147
Zec 4: 3 **t** olive trees by it, one upon the right *side* of 8147
4:11 What *are* these **t** olive trees upon the right 8147
4:12 What *be these* **t** olive branches which 8147
4:12 **t** golden pipes empty the golden *oil* out of 8147
4:14 Then said he, These *are* the **t** anointed ones, 8147
5: 9 there came out **t** women, and the wind *was* 8147
6: 1 there came four chariots out from between **t** 8147
11: 7 I took unto me **t** staves; the one I called 8147
13: 8 **t** parts therein shall be cut off *and* die; 8147
Mt 2:16 coasts thereof, from **t years old** and under, *1332*
4:18 saw **t** brethren, Simon called Peter, and *1417*
4:21 he saw other **t** brethren, James the *son* of *1417*
6:24 No *man* can serve **t** masters: for either he *1417*
8:28 there met him **t** possessed with devils, *1417*
9:27 **t** blind men followed him, crying, and *1417*
10:10 neither **t** coats, neither shoes, nor yet *1417*
10:29 Are not **t** sparrows sold for a farthing? and *1417*
11: 2 works of Christ, he sent **t** of his disciples, *1417*
14:17 We have here but five loaves, and **t** fishes. *1417*
14:19 and the **t** fishes, and looking up to heaven, *1417*
18: 8 rather than having **t** hands or two feet to be *1417*
18: 8 or **t** feet to be cast into everlasting fire. *1417*
18: 9 rather than having **t** eyes to be cast into hell *1417*
18:16 *then* take with thee one or **t** more, *1417*
18:16 that in the mouth of **t** or three witnesses *1417*
18:19 That if **t** of you shall agree on earth as *1417*
18:20 For where **t** or three are gathered together *1417*
20:21 Grant that these my **t** sons may sit, *1417*
20:24 with indignation against the **t** brethren. *1417*
20:30 **t** blind men sitting by the way side, *1417*
21: 1 mount of Olives, then sent Jesus **t** disciples, *1417*
21:28 A *certain* man had **t** sons; and he came to *1417*
22:40 On these **t** commandments hang all the law *1417*
24:40 Then shall **t** be in the field; the one shall be *1417*
24:41 **T** *women shall be* grinding at the mill; *1417*
25:15 to another **t**, and to another one; *1417*
25:17 And likewise he that *had received* **t**, he also *1417*
25:17 *had received* two, he also gained other **t**. *1417*
25:22 He also that had received **t** talents came *1417*
25:22 Lord, thou deliveredst unto me **t** talents: *1417*
25:22 I have gained **t** other talents besides them. *1417*
26: 2 Ye know that after **t** days is *the feast of* *1417*
26:37 with *him* Peter and the **t** sons of Zebedee, *1417*
26:60 At the last came **t** false witnesses, *1417*
27:38 Then were there **t** thieves crucified with *1417*
Mk 5:13 into the sea, (they were about **t thousand**,) *1367*
6: 7 and began to send them forth by **t** and two; *1417*
6: 7 and began to send them forth by two and **t**; *1417*
6: 9 shod with sandals; and not put on **t** coats. *1417*
6:37 and buy **t hundred** pennyworth of bread, *1250*
6:38 they knew, they say, Five, and **t** fishes. *1417*
6:41 had taken the five loaves and the **t** fishes, *1417*
6:41 and the **t** fishes divided he among *them* all. *1417*
9:43 than having **t** hands to go into hell, into *1417*
9:45 than having **t** feet to be cast into hell, *1417*
9:47 than having **t** eyes to be cast into hell fire: *1417*
11: 1 he sendeth forth **t** of his disciples, *1417*
11: 4 door without in a place where **t** ways met; NIG
12:42 and she threw in **t** mites, which make a *1417*
14: 1 After **t** days was *the feast of* the passover, *1417*
14:13 And he sendeth forth **t** of his disciples, and *1417*
15:27 And with him they crucify **t** thieves; *1417*
16:12 he appeared in another form unto **t** of them, *1417*
Lk 2:24 A pair of turtledoves, or **t** young pigeons. *1417*
3:11 and saith unto them, He that hath **t** coats, *1417*
5: 2 And saw **t** ships standing by the lake: but *1417*
7:19 And John calling unto *him* **t** of his disciples *1417*
7:41 There was a certain creditor which had **t** *1417*
9: 3 neither money; neither have **t** coats apiece. *1417*
9:13 have no more but five loaves and **t** fishes; *1417*
9:16 he took the five loaves and the **t** fishes, *1417*
9:30 And behold, there talked with him **t** men, *1417*
9:32 and the **t** men that stood with him. *1417*
10: 1 and sent them **t** and two before his face into *1417*
10: 1 and **t** before his face into every city and *1417*
10:35 he took out **t** pence, and gave *them* to *1417*
12: 6 Are not five sparrows sold for **t** farthings, *1417*
12:52 three against **t**, and two against three. *1417*
12:52 three against two, and **t** against three. *1417*
15:11 And he said, A certain man had **t** sons: *1417*
16:13 No servant can serve **t** masters: for either *1417*
17:34 in that night there shall be **t** *men* in one *1417*
17:35 **T** *women* shall be grinding together; *1417*
17:36 **T** *men* shall be in the field; the one shall be *1417*
18:10 **T** men went up into the temple to pray; *1417*
19:29 *mount* of Olives, he sent **t** of his disciples, *1417*
21: 2 poor widow casting in thither **t** mites. *1417*
22:38 they said, Lord, behold, here *are* **t** swords. *1417*
23:32 And there were also **t** other, malefactors, *1417*
24: 4 **t** men stood by them in shining garments: *1417*
24:13 **t** of them went *that* same day to a village *1417*
Jn 1:35 day *after* John stood, and **t** of his disciples; *1417*
1:37 And the **t** disciples heard him speak, and *1417*
1:40 One of the **t** which heard John speak, and *1417*
2: 6 containing **t** or three firkins apiece. *1417*
4:40 tarry with them: and he abode there **t** days. *1417*
4:43 Now after **t** days he departed thence, and *1417*
6: 7 **T hundred** pennyworth of bread is not *1250*
6: 9 hath five barley loaves, and **t** small fishes: *1417*
8:17 that the testimony of **t** men is true. *1417*
11: 6 he abode **t** days *still* in the *same* place *1417*
19:18 and **t** other with him, on either side one, *1417*
20:12 And seeth **t** angels in white sitting, the one *1417*
21: 2 of Zebedee, and **t** other of his disciples. *1417*
21: 8 from land, but as it were **t hundred** cubits,) *1250*
Ac 1:10 **t** men stood by them in white apparel; *1417*
1:23 And they appointed **t**, Joseph called *1417*
1:24 shew whether of these **t** thou hast chosen, *1417*
7:29 the land of Madian, where he begat **t** sons. *1417*
9:38 Peter was there, they sent unto him **t** men, *1417*
10: 7 he called **t** of his household servants, and *1417*
12: 6 night Peter was sleeping between **t** soldiers, *1417*
12: 6 between two soldiers, bound with **t** chains: *1417*
19:10 And this continued by the space of **t** years; *1417*
19:22 So he sent into Macedonia **t** of them that *1417*
19:34 all with one voice about the space of **t** *1417*
21:33 commanded *him* to be bound with **t** chains; *1417*
23:23 And he called unto *him* **t** centurions, *1417*
23:23 Make ready **t hundred** soldiers to go to *1250*
23:23 *and* ten, and spearmen **t hundred**, *1250*
24:27 But after **t years** Porcius Festus came into *1333*
27:37 And we were in all in the ship **t hundred** *1250*
27:41 And falling into a place **where t seas met**, *1337*
28:30 And Paul dwelt **t** whole **years** in his own *1333*
1Co 6:16 one body? for **t**, saith *he,* shall be one flesh. *1417*
14:27 *let it be* by **t**, or at the most *by* three, and *1417*
14:29 Let the prophets speak **t** or three, and *1417*
2Co 13: 1 In the mouth of **t** or three witnesses shall *1417*
Gal 4:22 For it is written, that Abraham had **t** sons, *1417*
4:24 for these are the **t** covenants; the one from *1417*
Eph 5:31 unto his wife, and they **t** shall be one flesh. *1417*
Php 1:23 For I am in a strait betwixt **t**, having a *1417*
1Ti 5:19 but before **t** or three witnesses. *1417*
Heb 6:18 That by **t** immutable things, in which *it was* *1417*
10:28 Moses' law died without mercy under **t** *1417*
Rev 2:12 which hath the sharp sword **with t edges**; *1366*
9:12 behold, there come **t** woes more hereafter. *1417*
9:16 **t hundred thousand thousand**: *1417+3461*
11: 2 they tread under foot forty *and* **t** months. *1417*
11: 3 And I will give *power* unto my **t** witnesses, *1417*
11: 3 they shall prophesy a thousand **t hundred** *1250*
11: 4 These are the **t** olive trees, and the two *1417*
11: 4 the **t** candlesticks standing before the God *1417*
11:10 these **t** prophets tormented them that dwelt *1417*

Rev 12: 6 should feed her there a thousand **t** **hundred** *1250*
12:14 And to the woman were given **t** wings of a *1417*
13: 5 unto him to continue forty *and* **t** months. *1417*
13:11 and he had **t** horns like a lamb, and *1417*

TWOEDGED (4) [EDGE, TWO]
Ps 149: 6 in their mouth, and a **t** sword in their hand; 6374
Pr 5: 4 is bitter as wormwood, sharp as a **t** sword. 6310
Heb 4:12 powerful, and sharper than any **t** sword, *1366*
Rev 1:16 and out of his mouth went a sharp **t** sword: *1366*

TWOFOLD (1) [TWO]
Mt 23:15 ye make him **t** **more** *the* child of hell **than** *1362*

TYCHICUS (7)
Ac 20: 4 Timotheus; and of Asia, **T** and Trophimus. *5190*
Eph 6:21 *and* how I do, **T**, a beloved brother and *5190*
6: S from Rome unto the Ephesians by **T**. *5190*
Col 4: 7 All my state shall **T** declare unto you, *5190*
4: S Written from Rome to the Colossians by **T** *5190*
2Ti 4:12 And **T** have I sent to Ephesus. *5190*
Tit 3:12 When I shall send Artemas unto thee, or **T**, *5190*

TYRANNUS (1)
Ac 19: 9 disputing daily in the school of one **T**. *5181*

TYRE (37) [TYRUS]
Jos 19:29 turneth *to* Ramah, and to the strong city **T**; 6865
2Sa 5:11 Hiram king of **T** sent messengers to David, 6865
24: 7 came *to* the strong hold of **T**, and *to* all 6865
1Ki 5: 1 Hiram king of **T** sent his servants unto 6865
7:13 king Solomon sent and fet Hiram out of **T**. 6865
7:14 his father *was* a man **of** **T**, a worker in 6876
9:11 (*Now* Hiram the king of **T** had furnished 6865
9:12 Hiram came out from **T** to see the cities 6865
1Ch 14: 1 Now Hiram king of **T** sent messengers to 6865
22: 4 they **of** **T** brought much cedar wood to 6876
2Ch 2: 3 Solomon sent to Huram the king of **T**, 6865
2:11 Huram the king of **T** answered in writing, 6865
2:14 his father *was* a man of **T**, skilful to work 6876
Ezr 3: 7 oil, unto them of Zidon, and to them of **T**, 6876
Ne 13:16 There dwelt **men** **of** **T** also therein, which 6876
Ps 45:12 the daughter of **T** *shall be there* with a gift; 6865
83: 7 the Philistines with the inhabitants of **T**; 6865
87: 4 behold Philistia, and **T**, with Ethiopia; 6865
Isa 23: 1 The burden of **T**. Howl, ye ships of 6865
23: 5 they be sorely pained *at* the report of **T**. 6865
23: 8 Who hath taken this counsel against **T**, 6865
23:15 that **T** shall be forgotten seventy years, 6865
23:15 after the end of seventy years shall **T** sing 6865
23:17 *that* the LORD will visit **T**, and she shall 6865
Joel 3: 4 O **T**, and Zidon, and all the coasts of 6865
Mt 11:21 had been done in **T** and Sidon they would *5184*
11:22 It shall be more tolerable for **T** and Sidon at *5184*
15:21 and departed into the coasts of **T** and *5184*
Mk 3: 8 and they about **T** and Sidon, a great *5184*
7:24 and went into the borders of **T** and Sidon, *5184*
7:31 departing from the coasts of **T** and Sidon, *5184*
Lk 6:17 and *from* the sea coast of **T** and Sidon, *5184*
10:13 for if the mighty works had been done in **T** *5184*
10:14 But it shall be more tolerable for **T** and *5184*
Ac 12:20 was highly displeased with them **of** **T** *5183*
21: 3 and sailed into Syria, and landed at **T**: *5184*
21: 7 when we had finished *our* course from **T**, *5184*

TYRUS (22) [TYRE]
Jer 25:22 all the kings of **T**, and all the kings of 6865
27: 3 to the king of **T**, and to the king of Zidon, 6865
47: 4 *and* to cut off from **T** and Zidon every 6865
Eze 26: 2 because that **T** hath said against Jerusalem, 6865
26: 3 O **T**, and will cause many nations to come 6865
26: 4 they shall destroy the walls of **T**, and 6865
26: 7 I *will* bring upon **T** Nebuchadrezzar king of 6865
26:15 Thus saith the Lord GOD to **T**; Shall not 6865
27: 2 son of man, take up a lamentation for **T**; 6865
27: 3 say unto **T**, O thou that art situate at 6865
27: 3 O **T**, thou hast said, I *am* of perfect beauty. 6865
27: 8 thy wise *men*, O **T**, *that* were in thee, 6865
27:32 over thee, *saying,* What *city is* like **T**, 6865
28: 2 Son of man, say unto the prince of **T**, 6865
28:12 take up a lamentation upon the king of **T**, 6865
29:18 his army to serve a great service against **T**: 6865
29:18 yet had he no wages, nor his army, for **T**, 6865
Hos 9:13 Ephraim, as I saw **T**, *is* planted in a 6865
Am 1: 9 For three transgressions of **T**, and for four, 6865
1:10 I will send a fire on the wall of **T**, 6865
Zec 9: 2 **T**, and Zidon, though it be very wise. 6865
9: 3 **T** did build herself a strong hold, and 6865

U

UCAL (1)
Pr 30: 1 spake unto Ithiel, even unto Ithiel and **U**. 401

UEL (1)
Ezr 10:34 Of the sons of Bani; Maadai, Amram, and **U**, 177

UGLY See NOISOME

ULAI (2)
Da 8: 2 I saw in a vision, and I was by the river of **U**. 195
8:16 heard a man's voice between *the banks of* **U**, 195

ULAM (4)
1Ch 7:16 and his sons *were* **U** and Rakem. 198
7:17 the sons of **U**; Bedan. These *were* the sons of 198
8:39 the sons of Eshek his brother *were*, **U** his 198
8:40 the sons of **U** were mighty men of valour, 198

ULLA (1)
1Ch 7:39 the sons of **U**; Arah, and Haniel, and Rezia. 5925

UMMAH (1)
Jos 19:30 **U** also, and Aphek, and Rehob: twenty and 5981

UNACCUSTOMED (1) [ACCUSTOMED]
Jer 31:18 as a bullock **u** *to the yoke;* turn thou 3808+3925

UNADVISEDLY (1) [ADVISE]
Ps 106:33 his spirit, so that he **spake** **u** with his lips. 981

UNAWARES (12) [AWARE]
Ge 31:20 Jacob **stale** **away** **u** to Laban 1589+3820
31:26 that thou hast **stolen** **away** **u** to me, 1589+3824
Nu 35:11 flee thither, which killeth *any* person at **u**. 7684
35:15 *any* person **u** may flee thither. 7684+871.1
Dt 4:42 should kill his neighbour **u**, 1097+1847+871.1
Jos 20: 3 the slayer that killeth *any* person **u** 7684+871.1
20: 9 that whosoever killeth *any* person at **u** 7684
Ps 35: 8 Let destruction come upon him at **u**; 3045+3808
Lk 21:34 *this* life, and *so* that day come upon you **u**. *160*
Gal 2: 4 because of false brethren **u** **brought** **in**, *3920*
Heb 13: 2 for thereby some have entertained angels **u**. *2990*
Jude 1: 4 For there are certain men **crept** **in** **u**, *3921*

UNBELIEF (16) [BELIEVE, UNBELIEVERS, UNBELIEVING]
Mt 13:58 mighty works there, because of their **u**. *570*
17:20 Jesus said unto them, Because of your **u**: *570*
Mk 6: 6 And he marvelled because of their **u**. And he *570*
9:24 with tears, Lord, I believe; help thou mine **u**. *570*
16:14 and upbraided them with their **u** and *570*
Ro 3: 3 shall their **u** make the faith of God without *570*
4:20 not at the promise of God through **u**; *570*
11:20 because of **u** they were broken off, and *570*
11:23 And they also, if they bide not still in **u**, *570*
11:30 have now obtained mercy through their **u**: *543*
11:32 For God hath concluded *them* all in **u**, *543*
1Ti 1:13 because I did *it* ignorantly in **u**. *570*
Heb 3:12 lest there be in any of you an evil heart of **u**, *570*
3:19 see that they could not enter in because of **u**. *570*
4: 6 first preached entered not in because of **u**, *543*
4:11 any *man* fall after the same example of **u**. *543*

UNBELIEVER See INFIDEL

UNBELIEVERS (4) [UNBELIEF]
Lk 12:46 and will appoint *him* his portion with the **u**. *571*
1Co 6: 6 to law with brother, and that before the **u**. *571*
14:23 or **u**, will they not say that ye are mad? *571*
2Co 6:14 Be ye not unequally yoked together with **u**: *571*

UNBELIEVING (6) [UNBELIEF]
Ac 14: 2 But the **u** Jews stirred up the Gentiles, and *544*
1Co 7:14 For the **u** husband is sanctified by the wife, *571*

1Co 7:14 and the **u** wife is sanctified by the husband: *571*
7:15 But if the **u** depart, let him depart. A brother *571*
Tit 1:15 them that are defiled and **u** *is* nothing pure; *571*
Rev 21: 8 and **u**, and the abominable, and murderers, *571*

UNBLAMEABLE (2) [BLAME, UNBLAMEABLY]
Col 1:22 to present you holy and **u** and *299*
1Th 3:13 To the end *he* may stablish your hearts **u** in *273*

UNBLAMEABLY (1) [UNBLAMEABLE]
1Th 2:10 **u** we behaved ourselves among you that *274*

UNCERTAIN (2) [CERTAIN, UNCERTAINLY]
1Co 14: 8 For if the trumpet give an **u** sound, who shall *82*
1Ti 6:17 nor trust in **u** riches, but in the living God, *83*

UNCERTAINLY (1) [UNCERTAIN]
1Co 9:26 I therefore so run, not as **u**; so fight I, not as *84*

UNCHANGEABLE (1) [CHANGE]
Heb 7:24 he continueth ever, hath an **u** priesthood. *531*

UNCIRCUMCISED (43) [CIRCUMCISE, UNCIRCUMCISION]
Ge 17:14 the **u** man *child* whose flesh of his foreskin 6189
34:14 this thing, to give our sister to one that is **u**; 6190
Ex 6:12 shall Pharaoh hear me, who *am* of **u** lips? 6189
6:30 I *am* of **u** lips, and how shall Pharaoh 6189
12:48 the land: for no **u person** shall eat thereof. 6189
Lev 19:23 ye shall **count** the fruit thereof **as u**: 6188+6190
19:23 three years shall it be as **u** unto you: it shall 6189
26:41 if then their **u** hearts be humbled, and they 6189
Jos 5: 7 for they were **u**, because they had not 6189
Jdg 14: 3 that thou goest to take a wife of the **u** 6189
15:18 for thirst, and fall into the hand of the **u**? 6189
1Sa 14: 6 let us go over unto the garrison of these **u**: 6189
17:26 for who *is* this **u** Philistine, that he should 6189
17:36 this **u** Philistine shall be as one of them, 6189
31: 4 lest these **u** come and thrust me through, 6189
2Sa 1:20 lest the daughters of the **u** triumph. 6189
1Ch 10: 4 lest these **u** come and abuse me. 6189
Isa 52: 1 there shall no more come into thee the **u** 6189
Jer 6:10 their ear *is* **u**, and they cannot hearken: 6189
9:25 all *them which are* circumcised with the **u**; 6190
9:26 for all *these* nations *are* **u**, and all the house 6189
9:26 and all the house of Israel *are* **u** in the heart. 6189
Eze 28:10 Thou shalt die the deaths of the **u** by 6189
31:18 thou shalt lie in the midst of the **u** with 6189
32:19 go down, and be thou laid with the **u**. 6189
32:21 gone down, they lie **u**, slain by the sword. 6189
32:24 which are gone down **u** into the nether 6189
32:25 all of them **u**, slain by the sword: 6189
32:26 all of them **u**, slain by the sword, 6189
32:27 lie with the mighty *that are* fallen of the **u**, 6189
32:28 thou shalt be broken in the midst of the **u**, 6189
32:29 they shall lie with the **u**, and with them that 6189
32:30 they lie **u** with *them that be* slain by 6189
32:32 he shall be laid in the midst of the **u** with 6189
44: 7 **u** in heart, and uncircumcised in flesh, to be 6189
44: 7 **u** in flesh, to be in my sanctuary, to pollute 6189
44: 9 No stranger, **u** in heart, nor uncircumcised 6189
44: 9 uncircumcised in heart, nor **u** in flesh, 6189
Ac 7:51 Ye stiffnecked and **u** in heart and ears, ye do *564*
11: 3 Saying, Thou wentest in to men **u**, *203+2192*
Ro 4:11 of the faith which he had *yet* being **u**: *203*
4:12 which he had being *yet* **u**. *203+1722*
1Co 7:18 let him not **become u**. Is any called in *1986*

UNCIRCUMCISION (16) [UNCIRCUMCISED]
Ro 2:25 of the law, thy circumcision is made **u**. *203*
2:26 Therefore if the **u** keep the righteousness of *203*
2:26 shall not his **u** be counted for circumcision? *203*
2:27 And shall not **u** which is by nature, if it fulfil *203*
3:30 circumcision by faith, and **u** through faith. *203*
4: 9 the circumcision *only,* or upon the **u** also? *203*
4:10 when he was in circumcision, or in **u**? Not in *203*
4:10 Not in circumcision, but in **u**. *203*
1Co 7:18 Is any called in **u**? let him not be *203*
7:19 and **u** is nothing, but the keeping of *203*
Gal 2: 7 when they saw that the gospel of the **u** was *203*
5: 6 circumcision availeth any *thing,* nor **u**; *203*
6:15 circumcision availeth any *thing,* nor **u**, *203*
Eph 2:11 who are called **U** by that which is called *203*
Col 2:13 dead in *your* sins and the **u** of your flesh, *203*
3:11 circumcision nor **u**, barbarian, Scythian, *203*

UNCLE (10) [UNCLE'S]
Lev 10: 4 the sons of Uzziel the **u** of Aaron, and 1730
25:49 Either his **u**, or his uncle's son, 1730
1Sa 10:14 Saul's **u** said unto him and to his servant, 1730
10:15 Saul's **u** said, Tell me, I pray thee, 1730
10:16 Saul said unto his **u**, He told us plainly that 1730
14:50 host *was* Abner, the son of Ner, Saul's **u**. 1730
1Ch 27:32 Also Jonathan David's **u** *was* a counseller, 1730
Est 2:15 the daughter of Abihail the **u** of Mordecai, 1730
Jer 32: 7 Hanameel the son of Shallum thine **u** *shall* 1730
Am 6:10 a man's **u** shall take him up, and he that 1730

UNCLE'S (7) [UNCLE]
Lev 20:20 if a man shall lie with his **u wife**, he hath 1733
20:20 he hath uncovered his **u** nakedness: 1730
25:49 Either his uncle, or his **u** son, may redeem 1730
Est 2: 7 up Hadassah, that *is,* Esther, his **u** daughter: 1730
Jer 32: 8 So Hanameel mine **u** son came to me in 1730
32: 9 I bought the field of Hanameel my **u** son, 1730
32:12 in the sight of Hanameel mine **u** *son,* and 1730

UNCLEAN (194) [CLEAN, UNCLEANNESS, UNCLEANNESSES]
Lev 5: 2 Or if a soul touch any **u** thing, whether *it be* 2931
5: 2 whether *it be* a carcase of an **u** beast, or a 2931
5: 2 or a carcase of **u** cattle, or the carcase of 2931
5: 2 or the carcase of **u** creeping things, and *if* it 2931
5: 2 from him; he also shall be **u**, and guilty. 2931
7:19 the flesh that toucheth any **u** *thing* shall not 2931
7:21 Moreover the soul that shall touch any **u** 2931
7:21 or *any* **u** beast, or any abominable unclean 2931
7:21 or any abominable **u** *thing,* and eat of 2931
10:10 and unholy, and between **u** and clean; 2931
11: 4 but divideth not the hoof; he *is* **u** unto you. 2931
11: 5 but divideth not the hoof; he *is* **u** unto you. 2931
11: 6 but divideth not the hoof; he *is* **u** unto you. 2931
11: 7 yet he cheweth not the cud; he *is* **u** to you. 2931
11: 8 shall ye not touch; they *are* **u** to you. 2931
11:24 for these ye shall be **u**: whosoever toucheth 2930
11:24 carcase of them shall be **u** until the even. 2930
11:25 wash his clothes, and be **u** until the even. 2930
11:26 nor cheweth the cud, *are* **u** unto you: 2931
11:26 every one that toucheth them shall be **u**. 2930
11:27 that go on *all* four, those *are* **u** unto you: 2931
11:27 whoso toucheth their carcase shall be **u** 2930
11:28 wash his clothes, and be **u** until the even: 2930
11:28 unclean until the even: they *are* **u** unto you. 2931
11:29 These also *shall be* **u** unto you among 2931
11:31 These *are* **u** to you among all that creep: 2931
11:31 they be dead, shall be **u** until the even. 2930
11:32 when they are dead, doth fall, it shall be **u**; 2930
11:32 into water, and it shall be **u** until the even; 2930
11:33 them falleth, whatsoever *is* in it shall be **u**; 2930
11:34 on which *such* water cometh shall be **u**: 2930
11:34 be drunk in every *such* vessel shall be **u**. 2930
11:35 *any part* of their carcase falleth shall be **u**; 2930
11:35 *for* they *are* **u**, and shall be unclean unto 2931
11:35 they *are* unclean, and shall be **u** unto you. 2931
11:36 that which toucheth their carcase shall be **u**. 2930
11:38 carcase fall thereon, it *shall be* **u** unto you. 2931
11:39 the carcase thereof shall be **u** until the even. 2930
11:40 wash his clothes, and be **u** until the even: 2930
11:40 wash his clothes, and be **u** until the even. 2930
11:43 neither shall ye **make** yourselves **u** with 2933
11:47 To make a difference between the **u** and 2931
12: 2 she shall be **u** seven days; according to 2930
12: 2 separation for her infirmity shall she be **u**. 2930
12: 5 she shall be **u** two weeks, as *in* her 2930
13: 3 shall look on him, and **pronounce** him **u**. 2930
13: 8 then the priest shall **pronounce** him **u**: 2930
13:11 the priest shall **pronounce** him **u**, *and* 2930
13:11 *and* shall not shut him up: for he *is* **u**. 2931
13:14 raw flesh appeareth in him, he shall be **u**. 2930
13:15 the raw flesh, and **pronounce** him to be **u**: 2930
13:15 *for* the raw flesh *is* **u**: it *is* a leprosy. 2931
13:20 the priest shall **pronounce** him **u**: 2930
13:22 then the priest shall **pronounce** him **u**: 2930
13:25 the priest shall **pronounce** him **u**: 2930
13:27 then the priest shall **pronounce** him **u**: 2930
13:30 then the priest shall **pronounce** him **u**: 2930
13:36 priest shall not seek for yellow hair: he *is* **u**. 2931
13:44 He *is* a leprous man, he *is* **u**: the priest shall 2931
13:44 shall **pronounce** him **utterly u**, 2930+2930
13:45 *his* upper lip, and shall cry, **U**, unclean. 2931
13:45 *his* upper lip, and shall cry, Unclean, **u**. 2931

Lev 13:46 *shall be* in him he shall be defiled; he *is* **u**: 2931
13:51 the plague *is* a fretting leprosy; it *is* **u**. 2931
13:55 and the plague be not spread; it *is* **u**; 2931
13:59 to pronounce it clean, or to **pronounce** it **u**. 2930
14:36 that all that *is* in the house be not *made* **u**: 2930
14:40 they shall cast them into an **u** place without 2931
14:41 scrape off without the city into an **u** place: 2931
14:44 it *is* a fretting leprosy in the house: it *is* **u**. 2931
14:45 *them* forth out of the city into an **u** place. 2931
14:46 that it is shut up shall be **u** until the even. 2930
14:57 To teach when *it is* **u**, and when *it is* clean: 2931
15: 2 out of his flesh, *because of* his issue he *is* **u**. 2931
15: 4 whereon he lieth that hath the issue, is **u**: 2930
15: 4 every thing, whereon he sitteth, shall be **u**. 2930
15: 5 *himself* in water, and be **u** until the even. 2930
15: 6 *himself* in water, and be **u** until the even. 2930
15: 7 *himself* in water, and be **u** until the even. 2930
15: 8 *himself* in water, and be **u** until the even. 2930
15: 9 rideth upon that hath the issue shall be **u**. 2930
15:10 was under him shall be **u** until the even: 2930
15:10 *himself* in water, and be **u** until the even. 2930
15:11 *himself* in water, and be **u** until the even. 2930
15:16 his flesh in water, and be **u** until the even. 2930
15:17 washed with water, and be **u** until the even. 2930
15:18 in water, and be **u** until the even. 2930
15:19 whosoever toucheth her shall be **u** until 2930
15:20 she lieth upon in her separation shall be **u**: 2930
15:20 *thing* also that she sitteth upon shall be **u**. 2930
15:21 *himself* in water, and be **u** until the even. 2930
15:22 *himself* in water, and be **u** until the even. 2930
15:23 he toucheth it, he shall be **u** until the even. 2930
15:24 be upon him, he shall be **u** seven days; 2930
15:24 and all the bed whereon he lieth shall be **u**. 2930
15:25 the days of her separation: she *shall be* **u**. 2931
15:26 whatsoever she sitteth upon shall be **u**, 2931
15:27 whosoever toucheth those *things* shall be **u**, 2930
15:27 *himself* in water, and be **u** until the even. 2930
15:33 and of him that lieth with her which is **u**. 2931
17:15 *himself* in water, and be **u** until the even: 2930
20:21 take his brother's wife, it *is* an **u thing**: 5079
20:25 put difference between clean beasts and **u**, 2931
20:25 and between **u** fowls and clean: 2931
20:25 which I have separated from you as **u**. 2930
22: 4 whoso toucheth any *thing that is* **u** *by* 2931
22: 5 whereby he may be **made u**, or a man of 2930
22: 6 hath touched *any* such shall be **u** until even, 2930
27:11 if *it be* any **u** beast, of which they do not 2931
27:27 if *it be* of an **u** beast, then he shall redeem *it* 2931
Nu 6: 7 He shall not **make** himself **u** for his father, 2930
9:10 of your posterity shall be **u** by reason of a 2931
18:15 the firstling of **u** beasts shalt thou redeem. 2931
19: 7 and the priest shall be **u** until the even. 2930
19: 8 flesh in water, and shall be **u** until the even. 2930
19:10 wash his clothes, and be **u** until the even: 2930
19:11 *body* of any man shall be **u** seven days. 2930
19:13 was not sprinkled upon him, he shall be **u**; 2931
19:14 all that *is* in the tent, shall be **u** seven days. 2930
19:15 which hath no covering bound upon it, *is* **u**. 2931
19:16 of a man, or a grave, shall be **u** seven days. 2930
19:17 for an **u** *person* they shall take of the ashes 2931
19:19 the clean *person* shall sprinkle upon the **u** 2931
19:20 the man that shall be **u**, and shall not purify 2930
19:20 hath not been sprinkled upon him; he *is* **u**. 2931
19:21 water of separation shall be **u** until even. 2930
19:22 whatsoever the **u** *person* toucheth shall be 2931
19:22 the unclean *person* toucheth shall be **u**; 2930
19:22 the soul that toucheth *it* shall be **u** until 2930
Dt 12:15 the **u** and the clean may eat thereof, as of 2931
12:22 the **u** and the clean shall eat of them alike. 2931
14: 7 not the hoof; *therefore* they *are* **u** unto you. 2931
14: 8 yet *cheweth* not the cud, it *is* **u** unto you: 2931
14:10 and scales ye may not eat; it *is* **u** unto you. 2931
14:19 every creeping thing that flieth *is* **u** unto 2931
15:22 the **u** and the clean *person shall eat it* alike, 2931
23:14 that he see no **u** thing in thee, and 6172
26:14 **u** *use,* nor given *ought* thereof for the dead: 2931
Jos 22:19 if the land of your possession *be* **u**, *then* 2931
Jdg 13: 4 nor strong drink, and eat not any **u** *thing:* 2931
13: 7 neither eat any **u** *thing:* for the child shall 2932
13:14 nor eat any **u** *thing:* all that I commanded 2932
2Ch 23:19 that none *which was* **u** in any thing should 2931
Ezr 9:11 *is* an **u** land with the filthiness of the people 5079
Job 14: 4 Who can bring a clean *thing* out of an **u**? 2931
36:14 die in youth, and their life *is* among the **u**. 6945

Ecc 9: 2 to the good and to the clean, and to the **u**; 2931
Isa 6: 5 because I *am* a man of **u** lips, and I dwell in 2931
6: 5 I dwell in the midst of a people of **u** lips: 2931
35: 8 the **u** shall not pass over it; but it *shall be* 2931
52: 1 into thee the uncircumcised and the **u**. 2931
52:11 touch no **u** *thing;* go ye out of the midst of 2931
64: 6 we are all as an **u** *thing,* and all our 2931
La 4:15 *it is* **u**; depart, depart, touch not, when they 2931
Eze 22:26 have they shewed *difference* between the **u** 2931
44:23 cause them to discern between the **u** and 2931
Hos 9: 3 and they shall eat **u** *things* in Assyria. 2931
Hag 2:13 If *one that is* **u** *by* a dead body touch any of 2931
2:13 dead body touch any of these, shall it be **u**? 2930
2:13 the priests answered and said, It shall be **u**. 2930
2:14 and *that* which they offer there *is* **u**. 2931
Zec 13: 2 and the **u** spirit to pass out of the land. 2932
Mt 10: 1 he gave them power against **u** spirits, to cast *169*
12:43 When the **u** spirit is gone out of a man, *169*
Mk 1:23 in their synagogue a man with an **u** spirit; *169*
1:26 And when the **u** spirit had torn him, and *169*
1:27 for with authority commandeth he even the **u** *169*
3:11 And **u** spirits, when they saw him, fell down *169*
3:30 Because they said, He hath an **u** spirit. *169*
5: 2 him out of the tombs a man with an **u** spirit, *169*
5: 8 Come out of the man, *thou* **u** spirit. *169*
5:13 And the **u** spirits went out, and entered into *169*
6: 7 two; and gave them power over **u** spirits; *169*
7:25 whose young daughter had an **u** spirit, *169*
Lk 4:33 which had a spirit of an **u** devil, and *169*
4:36 and power he commandeth the **u** spirits, *169*
6:18 And they that were vexed with **u** spirits: and *169*
8:29 (For he had commanded the **u** spirit to come *169*
9:42 and tare *him.* And Jesus rebuked the **u** spirit, *169*
11:24 When the **u** spirit is gone out of a man, *169*
Ac 5:16 and *them which were* vexed with **u** spirits: *169*
8: 7 For **u** spirits, crying with loud voice, *169*
10:14 never eaten any *thing that is* common or **u**. *169*
10:28 that *I* should not call any man common or **u**. *169*
11: 8 or **u** hath at any time entered into my mouth. *169*
Ro 14:14 Lord Jesus, that *there is* nothing **u** of itself: *2839*
14:14 but to him that esteemeth any *thing* to be **u**, *2839*
14:14 any *thing* to be unclean, to him *it is* **u**. *2839*
1Co 7:14 else were your children **u**; but now are they *169*
2Co 6:17 and touch not the **u** *thing;* and I will receive *169*
Eph 5: 5 nor **u** *person,* nor covetous man who is an *169*
Heb 9:13 and the ashes of a heifer sprinkling the **u**, *2840*
Rev 16:13 And I saw three **u** spirits like frogs *come* out *169*
18: 2 and a cage of every **u** and hateful bird. *169*

UNCLEANNESS (40) [UNCLEAN]

Lev 5: 3 Or if he touch the **u** of man, 2932
5: 3 whatsoever **u** *it be* that a man shall be 2932
7:20 unto the LORD, having his **u** upon him, 2932
7:21 touch any unclean *thing, as* the **u** of man, 2932
14:19 for him that is to be cleansed from his **u**; 2932
15: 3 this shall be his **u** in his issue: *whether* his 2932
15: 3 flesh be stopped from his issue, it *is* his **u**. 2932
15:25 all the days of the issue of her **u** shall be as 2932
15:26 shall be unclean, as the **u** of her separation. 2932
15:30 before the LORD for the issue of her **u**. 2932
15:31 separate the children of Israel from their **u**; 2932
15:31 that they die not in their **u**, when they defile 2932
16:16 because of the **u** of the children of Israel, 2932
16:16 among them in the midst of their **u**. 2932
16:19 hallow it from the **u** of the children of 2932
18:19 as long as she is put apart for her **u**. 2932
22: 3 having his **u** upon him, that soul shall be 2932
22: 5 or a man of whom he may **take u**, 2930
22: 5 take uncleanness, whatsoever **u** he hath; 2932
Nu 5:19 if thou hast not gone aside *to* **u** *with* 2932
19:13 he shall be unclean; his **u** *is* yet upon him. 2932
Dt 23:10 that is not clean by reason of **u** that NIH
24: 1 because he hath found some **u** in her: 6172
2Sa 11: 4 with her; for she was purified from her **u**: 2932
2Ch 29:16 brought out all the **u** that they found in 2932
Ezr 9:11 it from one end to another with their **u**. 2932
Eze 36:17 their way was before me as the **u** of a 2932
39:24 According to their **u** and according to their 2932
Zec 13: 1 inhabitants of Jerusalem for sin and for **u**. 5079
Mt 23:27 within full of dead *men's* bones, and of all **u**. *167*
Ro 1:24 Wherefore God also gave them up to **u** *167*
6:19 ye have yielded your members servants to **u** *167*
2Co 12:21 and have not repented of the **u** and *167*
Gal 5:19 fornication, **u**, lasciviousness, *167*

Eph 4:19 to work all **u** with greediness. *167*
5: 3 But fornication, and all **u**, or covetousness, *167*
Col 3: 5 fornication, **u**, inordinate affection, *167*
1Th 2: 3 *was* not of deceit, nor of **u**, nor in guile: *167*
4: 7 For God hath not called us unto **u**, but *167*
2Pe 2:10 that walk after the flesh in the lust of **u**, *3394*

UNCLEANNESSES (1) [UNCLEAN]
Eze 36:29 I will also save you from all your **u**: and 2932

UNCLOTHED (1) [CLOTHE]
2Co 5: 4 not for that we would be **u**, but *1562*

UNCOMELY (2) [COMELINESS]
1Co 7:36 *he* **behaveth** himself **u** toward his virgin, *807*
12:23 our **u** *parts* have more abundant comeliness. *809*

UNCONDEMNED (2) [CONDEMN]
Ac 16:37 They have beaten us openly **u**, *178*
22:25 to scourge a man *that is* a Roman, and **u**? *178*

UNCORRUPTIBLE (1) [CORRUPT, UNCORRUPTNESS]
Ro 1:23 And changed the glory of the **u** God into an *862*

UNCORRUPTNESS (1) [UNCORRUPTIBLE]
Tit 2: 7 in doctrine *shewing* **u**, gravity, sincerity, *90*

UNCOVER (26) [COVER, UNCOVERED, UNCOVERETH]
Lev 10: 6 unto Ithamar his sons, **U** not your heads, 6544
18: 6 is near of kin to him, to **u** *their* nakedness: 1540
18: 7 nakedness of thy mother, shalt thou not **u**: 1540
18: 7 thy mother; thou shalt not **u** her nakedness. 1540
18: 8 of thy father's wife shalt thou not **u**: 1540
18: 9 *even* their nakedness thou shalt not **u**. 1540
18:10 *even* their nakedness thou shalt not **u**: 1540
18:11 *is* thy sister, thou shalt not **u** her nakedness. 1540
18:12 Thou shalt not **u** the nakedness of thy 1540
18:13 Thou shalt not **u** the nakedness of thy 1540
18:14 Thou shalt not **u** the nakedness of thy 1540
18:15 Thou shalt not **u** the nakedness of thy 1540
18:15 son's wife; thou shalt not **u** her nakedness. 1540
18:16 Thou shalt not **u** the nakedness of thy 1540
18:17 Thou shalt not **u** the nakedness of a woman 1540
18:17 daughter's daughter, to **u** her nakedness; 1540
18:18 to vex *her*, to **u** her nakedness, besides 1540
18:19 approach unto a woman to **u** her nakedness, 1540
20:18 her sickness, and shall **u** her nakedness; 1540
20:19 thou shalt not **u** the nakedness of thy 1540
21:10 shall not **u** his head, nor rend his clothes; 6544
Nu 5:18 **u** the woman's head, and put the offering of 6544
Ru 3: 4 go in, and **u** his feet, and lay thee down; 1540
Isa 47: 2 **u** thy locks, make bare the leg, uncover 1540
47: 2 thy locks, make bare the leg, **u** the thigh, 1540
Zep 2:14 for he shall **u** the cedar work. 6168

UNCOVERED (17) [UNCOVER]
Ge 9:21 was drunken; and he was **u** within his tent. 1540
Lev 20:11 father's wife hath **u** his father's nakedness: 1540
20:17 he hath **u** his sister's nakedness; he shall 1540
20:18 and she hath **u** the fountain of her blood: 1540
20:20 he hath **u** his uncle's nakedness: 1540
20:21 he hath **u** his brother's nakedness; 1540
Ru 3: 7 and **u** his feet, and laid her down. 1540
2Sa 6:20 who **u** himself to day in the eyes of 1540
Isa 20: 4 and barefoot, even with *their* buttocks **u**, 2834
22: 6 of men *and* horsemen, and Kir **u** the shield. 6168
47: 3 Thy nakedness shall be **u**, yea, thy shame 1540
Jer 49:10 I have **u** his secret places, and he shall not 1540
Eze 4: 7 thine arm *shall be* **u**, and thou shalt 2834
Hab 2:16 drink thou also, and let thy **foreskin** be **u**: 6188
Mk 2: 4 for the press, they **u** the roof where he was: *648*
1Co 11: 5 prophesieth with *her* head **u** dishonoureth *177*
11:13 is it comely that a woman pray unto God **u**? *177*

UNCOVERETH (3) [UNCOVER]
Lev 20:19 for he **u** his near kin: they shall bear their 6168
Dt 27:20 because he **u** his father's skirt. 1540
2Sa 6:20 as one of the vain *fellows* **shamelessly u** 1540

UNCTION (1)
1Jn 2:20 But ye have an **u** from the Holy One, and *5545*

UNDEFILED (7) [DEFILE]
Ps 119: 1 Blessed *are* the **u** in the way, who walk in 8549
SS 5: 2 to me, my sister, my love, my dove, my **u**: 8535
6: 9 My dove, my **u** *is but* one; she *is* the *only* 8535
Heb 7:26 *who is* holy, harmless, **u**, separate from *283*
13: 4 Marriage *is* honourable in all, and the bed **u**: *283*
Jas 1:27 Pure religion and **u** before God and *283*
1Pe 1: 4 and **u**, and that fadeth not away, reserved in *283*

UNDER (392) See Index

UNDERGARMENT See BREECHES

UNDERGIRDING (1) [GIRD]
Ac 27:17 had taken up, they used helps, **u** the ship; *5269*

UNDERNEATH (3) See Index

UNDERSETTERS (4)
1Ki 7:30 the four corners thereof had **u**: under 3802
7:30 under the laver *were* **u** molten, at the side 3802
7:34 *there were* four **u** to the four corners of one 3802
7:34 *and* the **u** *were* of the *very* base itself. 3802

UNDERSTAND (91) [UNDERSTANDEST, UNDERSTANDETH, UNDERSTANDING, UNDERSTOOD]
Ge 11: 7 that they may not **u** one another's speech. 8085
41:15 *that* thou canst **u** a dream to interpret it. 8085
Nu 16:30 ye shall **u** that these men have provoked 3045
Dt 9: 3 **U** therefore *this* day, that the LORD thy 3045
9: 6 **U** therefore, that the LORD thy God 3045
28:49 a nation whose tongue thou shalt not **u**; 8085
2Ki 18:26 for we **u** *it*: and talk not with us in 8085
1Ch 28:19 **made** me **u** in writing by *his* hand upon 7919
Ne 8: 3 and the women, and those that could **u**; 995
8: 7 the Levites, **caused** the people **to u** the law: 995
8: 8 the sense, and **caused** *them* **to u** the reading. 995
8:13 the scribe, even to **u** the words of the law. 7919
Job 6:24 and **cause** me **to u** wherein I have erred. 995
23: 5 and **u** what he would say unto me. 995
26:14 but the thunder of his power who can **u**? 995
32: 9 neither do the aged **u** judgment. 995
36:29 Also can *any* **u** the spreadings of the clouds, 995
Ps 14: 2 to see if there were *any* that did **u**, *and* 7919
19:12 Who can **u** *his* errors? cleanse thou me from 995
53: 2 to see if there were *any* that did **u**, that did 7919
82: 5 They know not, neither will they **u**; 995
92: 6 man knoweth not; neither doth a fool **u** this. 995
94: 8 **U**, ye brutish among the people: and 995
107:43 will observe these *things*, even they shall **u** 995
119:27 **Make** me **to u** the way of thy precepts: so 995
119:100 I **u** more than the ancients, because I keep 995
Pr 1: 6 To **u** a proverb, and the interpretation; 995
2: 5 shalt thou **u** the fear of the LORD, and 995
2: 9 shalt thou **u** righteousness, and judgment, 995
8: 5 O ye simple, **u** wisdom: and, ye fools, be ye 995
14: 8 The wisdom of the prudent *is* to **u** his way: 995
19:25 *and* he will **u** knowledge. 995
20:24 how can a man then **u** his own way? 995
28: 5 Evil men **u** not judgment: but they that seek 995
28: 5 but they that seek the LORD **u** all *things*. 995
29:19 for though he **u** he will not answer. 995
Isa 6: 9 tell this people, Hear ye indeed, but **u** not; 995
6:10 **u** *with* their heart, and convert, and 995
28: 9 whom shall he **make to u** doctrine? 995
28:19 it shall be a vexation only *to* **u** the report. 995
32: 4 The heart also of the rash shall **u** knowledge, 995
33:19 a stammering tongue, *that thou canst* not **u**. 998
36:11 for we **u** *it*: and speak not to us in the Jews' 8085
41:20 and know, and consider, and **u** together, 7919
43:10 and believe me, and **u** that I *am* he: 995
44:18 *and* their hearts, that *they* cannot **u**. 7919
56:11 and they *are* shepherds *that* cannot **u**: 995+3045
Jer 9:12 Who *is* the wise man, that may **u** this? and 995
Eze 3: 6 whose words thou canst not **u**. 8085
Da 8:16 said, Gabriel, **make** this *man* **to u** the vision. 995
8:17 he said unto me, **U**, O son of man: for at 995
9:13 turn from our iniquities, and **u** thy truth. 7919
9:23 therefore **u** the matter, and consider 995
9:25 Know therefore and **u**, *that* from the going 7919
10:11 **u** the words that I speak unto thee, and 995
10:12 first day that thou didst set thine heart to **u**, 995
10:14 Now I am come to **make** thee **u** what shall 995
11:33 they that **u** among the people shall instruct 7919
12:10 none of the wicked shall **u**; but the wise shall 995
12:10 shall understand; but the wise shall **u**. 995
Hos 4:14 therefore the people *that* doth not **u** shall fall. 995
14: 9 he shall **u** these *things*? prudent, and he shall 995

Mic 4:12 of the LORD, neither **u** they his counsel: 995
Mt 13:13 hearing they hear not, neither do they **u**. *4920*
13:14 By hearing ye shall hear, and shall not **u**; *4920*
13:15 and should **u** with *their* heart, and *4920*
15:10 and said unto them, Hear, and **u**: *4920*
15:17 Do not ye yet **u**, that whatsoever entereth in *3539*
16: 9 Do ye not yet **u**, neither remember the five *3539*
16:11 How *is it that* ye do not **u** that I spake *it* not *3539*
24:15 the holy place, (whoso readeth, let him **u**:) *3539*
Mk 4:12 and hearing they may hear, and not **u**; *4920*
7:14 Hearken unto me every one of you, and **u**: *4920*
8:17 perceive ye not yet, neither **u**? have ye your *4920*
8:21 said unto them, How *is it that* ye do not **u**? *4920*
13:14 where it ought not, (let him that readeth **u**,) *3539*
14:68 I know not, neither **u** I what thou sayest. *1987*
Lk 8:10 not see, and hearing they might not **u**. *4920*
24:45 that *they* might **u** the scriptures, *4920*
Jn 8:43 Why do ye not **u** my speech? *even* because *1097*
12:40 nor **u** with *their* heart, and be converted, *3539*
Ac 24:11 Because that thou mayest **u**, that there are *1097*
28:26 say, Hearing ye shall hear, and shall not **u**; *4920*
28:27 and **u** with *their* heart, and should be *4920*
Ro 15:21 and they that have not heard shall **u**. *4920*
1Co 12: 3 Wherefore I **give** you **to u**, that no *man* *1107*
13: 2 and **u** all mysteries, and all knowledge; *1492*
Eph 3: 4 ye may **u** my knowledge in the mystery of *3539*
Php 1:12 But I would ye should **u**, brethren, that *1097*
Heb 11: 3 Through faith we **u** that the worlds were *3539*
2Pe 2:12 speak evil of *the things* that they **u not**; *50*

UNDERSTANDEST (4) [UNDERSTAND]
Job 15: 9 know not? *what* **u** thou, which *is* not in us? 995
Ps 139: 2 mine uprising, thou **u** my thought afar off. 995
Jer 5:15 thou knowest not, neither **u** what they say. 8085
Ac 8:30 and said, **U** thou what thou readest? *1097*

UNDERSTANDETH (11) [UNDERSTAND]
1Ch 28: 9 and **u** all the imaginations of the thoughts: 995
Job 28:23 God **u** the way thereof, and he knoweth 995
Ps 49:20 Man *that is* in honour, and **u** not, is like 995
Pr 8: 9 They *are* all plain to him that **u**, and right to 995
14: 6 but knowledge *is* easy unto him that **u**. 995
Jer 9:24 glory in this, that *he* **u** and knoweth me, 7919
Mt 13:19 and **u** *it* not, then cometh the wicked one, *4920*
13:23 and **u** *it;* which also beareth fruit, and *4920*
Ro 3:11 There is none that **u**, there is none that *4920*
1Co 14: 2 for no *man* **u** *him;* howbeit in the spirit he *191*
14:16 seeing he **u** not what thou sayest? *1492*

UNDERSTANDING (160) [UNDERSTAND]
Ex 31: 3 in **u**, and in knowledge, and in all *manner* 8394
35:31 in **u**, and in knowledge, and in all *manner* 8394
36: 1 **u** to know how to work all *manner of* work 8394
Dt 1:13 **u**, and known among your tribes, and I will 995
4: 6 and your **u** in the sight of the nations, 998
4: 6 this great nation *is* a wise and **u** people. 995
32:28 of counsel, neither *is there any* **u** in them. 8394
1Sa 25: 3 *she was* a woman of good **u**, and of a 7922
1Ki 3: 9 thy servant an **u** heart to judge thy people, 8085
3:11 hast asked for thyself **u** to discern judgment; 995
3:12 lo, I have given thee a wise and an **u** heart; 995
4:29 Solomon wisdom and **u** exceeding much, 8394
7:14 **u**, and cunning to work all works in brass. 8394
1Ch 12:32 *were men* that **had u** of the times, 998+3045
22:12 Only the LORD give thee wisdom and **u**, 998
2Ch 2:12 endued with prudence and **u**, that might 998
2:13 endued with **u**, of Huram my father's, 998
26: 5 who **had u** in the visions of God: 995
Ezr 8:16 also for Joiarib, and for Elnathan, *men* of **u**. 995
8:18 God upon us they brought us a man of **u**, 7922
Ne 8: 2 and women, and all that could hear with **u**, 995
10:28 every one having knowledge, *and* **having u**; 995
Job 12: 3 I have **u** as well as you; I *am* not inferior to 3824
12:12 ancient *is* wisdom; and *in* length of days **u**. 8394
12:13 and strength, he hath counsel and **u**. 8394
12:20 and taketh *away* the **u** of the aged. 2940
17: 4 For thou hast hid their heart from **u**: 7922
20: 3 and the spirit of my **u** causeth me to answer. 998
26:12 and by his **u** he smiteth through the proud. 8394
28:12 be found? and where *is* the place of **u**? 998
28:20 and where *is* the place of **u**? 998
28:28 that *is* wisdom; and to depart from evil *is* **u**. 998
32: 8 inspiration of the Almighty **giveth** them **u**. 995
34:10 Therefore hearken unto me, ye men of **u**: 3824
34:16 If now *thou hast* **u**, hear this: hearken to 998
34:34 Let men of **u** tell me, and let a wise man 3824
38: 4 of the earth? declare, if thou hast **u**. 998
38:36 or who hath given **u** to the heart? 998
39:17 neither hath he imparted to her **u**. 998
Ps 32: 9 the horse, *or* as the mule, *which have* no **u**: 995
47: 7 King of all the earth: sing ye *praises* with **u**. 7919
49: 3 the meditation of my heart *shall be of* **u**. 8394
111:10 a good **u** have all they that do *his* 7922
119:34 **Give** me **u**, and I shall keep thy law; yea, 995
119:73 **give** me **u**, that I may learn thy 995
119:99 I **have** more **u** than all my teachers: for thy 7919
119:104 Through thy precepts I get **u**: therefore I hate 995
119:125 **give** me **u**, that I may know thy testimonies. 995
119:130 giveth light; it **giveth u** unto the simple. 995
119:144 *is* everlasting: **give** me **u**, and I shall live. 995
119:169 O LORD: **give** me **u** according to thy word. 995
147: 5 and of great power: his **u** *is* infinite. 8394
Pr 1: 2 and instruction; to perceive the words of **u**; 998
1: 5 a man of **u** shall attain unto wise counsels: 995
2: 2 unto wisdom, *and* apply thine heart to **u**; 8394
2: 3 *and* liftest up thy voice for **u**; 8394
2: 6 out of his mouth *cometh* knowledge and **u**. 8394
2:11 shall preserve thee, **u** shall keep thee: 8394
3: 4 and good **u** in the sight of God and man. 7922
3: 5 thine heart; and lean not unto thine own **u**. 998
3:13 findeth wisdom, and the man *that* getteth **u**. 8394
3:19 by **u** hath he established the heavens. 8394
4: 1 instruction of a father, and attend to know **u**. 998
4: 5 Get wisdom, get **u**: forget *it* not; 998
4: 7 get wisdom: and with all thy getting get **u**. 998
5: 1 my wisdom, *and* bow thine ear to my **u**: 8394
6:32 adultery with a woman lacketh **u**: 3820
7: 4 *art* my sister; and call **u** *thy* kinswoman: 998
7: 7 among the youths, a young man void of **u**, 3820
8: 1 not wisdom cry? and **u** put forth her voice? 8394
8: 5 and, ye fools, be ye of an **u** heart. 995
8:14 and sound wisdom: I *am* **u**; I have strength. 998
9: 4 *as for* him that wanteth **u**, she saith to him, 3820
9: 6 the foolish, and live; and go in the way of **u**. 998
9:10 and the knowledge of the holy *is* **u**. 998
9:16 *as for* him that wanteth **u**, she saith to him, 3820
10:13 In the lips of him that **hath u** wisdom is 995
10:13 rod *is* for the back of him that is void of **u**. 3820
10:23 do mischief: but a man of **u** hath wisdom. 8394
11:12 but a man of **u** holdeth his peace. 8394
12:11 he that followeth vain *persons is* void of **u**. 3820
13:15 Good **u** giveth favour: but the way of 7922
14:29 *He that is* slow to wrath *is* of great **u**: but 8394
14:33 resteth in the heart of him that **hath u**: 995
15:14 The heart of him that **hath u** seeketh 995
15:21 but a man of **u** walketh uprightly. 8394
15:32 but he that heareth reproof getteth **u**. 3820
16:16 and to get **u** rather to be chosen than silver! 998
16:22 **U** *is* a wellspring of life unto him that hath 7922
17:18 A man void of **u** striketh hands, *and* 3820
17:24 Wisdom *is* before him that **hath u**; but 995
17:27 *and* a man of **u** is of an excellent spirit. 8394
17:28 that shutteth his lips *is esteemed a man* of **u**. 995
18: 2 A fool hath no delight in **u**, but that his 8394
19: 8 own soul: he that keepeth **u** shall find good. 8394
19:25 reprove one that **hath u**, *and* he will 995
20: 5 deep water; but a man of **u** will draw it out. 8394
21:16 The man that wandereth out of the way of **u** 7919
21:30 *There is* no wisdom nor **u** nor counsel 8394
23:23 *it* not; *also* wisdom, and instruction, and **u**. 998
24: 3 a house builded; and by **u** it is established: 8394
24:30 by the vineyard of the man void of **u**; 3820
28: 2 by a man of **u** *and* knowledge the state 995
28:11 but the poor that hath **u** searcheth him out. 995
28:16 The prince that wanteth **u** *is* also a great 8394
30: 2 than *any* man, and have not the **u** of a man. 998
Ecc 9:11 bread to the wise, nor yet riches to men of **u**, 995
Isa 11: 2 the spirit of wisdom and **u**, the spirit of 998
11: 3 shall **make** him **of quick u** in the fear of 7306
27:11 for it *is* a people of no **u**: therefore he that 998
29:14 and the **u** of their prudent *men* shall be hid. 998
29:16 say of him that framed it, He had no **u**? 995
29:24 that erred in spirit shall **come to u**, 998+3045
40:14 and shewed to him the way of **u**? 8394
40:28 is weary? *there is* no searching of his **u**. 8394
44:19 neither *is there* knowledge nor **u** to say, 8394
Jer 3:15 shall feed you with knowledge and **u**. 7919
4:22 *are* sottish children, and they **have** none **u**: 995

Jer 5:21 now this, O foolish people, and without **u**; 3820
51:15 and hath stretched out the heaven by his **u**. 8394
Eze 28: 4 with thine **u** thou hast gotten thee riches, 8394
Da 1: 4 **u** science, and such as *had* ability in them to 995
1:17 and Daniel had **u** in all visions and dreams. 995
1:20 *in* all matters of wisdom *and* **u**, that the king 998
2:21 and knowledge to them that know **u**: 999
4:34 mine **u** returned unto me, and I blessed 4486
5:11 days of thy father light and **u** and wisdom, 7924
5:12 knowledge, and **u**, interpreting of dreams, 7924
5:14 *that* light and **u** and excellent wisdom is 7924
8:23 and **u** dark sentences, shall stand up. 995
9:22 I am now come forth to give thee skill and **u**. 998
10: 1 the thing, and had **u** of the vision. 998
11:35 *some* of them of **u** shall fall, to try them, 7919
Hos 13: 2 *and* idols according to their own **u**, all of it 8394
Ob 1: 7 a wound under thee: *there is* none **u** in him. 8394
1: 8 of Edom, and **u** out of the mount of Esau? 8394
Mt 15:16 And Jesus said, Are ye also yet **without u**? *801*
Mk 7:18 saith unto them, Are ye so **without u** also? *801*
12:33 and with all the **u**, and with all the soul, and *4907*
Lk 1: 3 having had perfect **u** of all *things* from *3877*
2:47 all that heard him were astonished at his **u** *4907*
24:45 Then opened he their **u**, that *they* might *3563*
Ro 1:31 **Without u**, covenant-breakers, *801*
1Co 1:19 will bring to nothing the **u** of the prudent. *4907*
14:14 my spirit prayeth, but my **u** is unfruitful. *3563*
14:15 the spirit, and will pray with the **u** also: *3563*
14:15 the spirit, and I will sing with the **u** also. *3563*
14:19 I had rather speak five words with my **u**, *3563*
14:20 Brethren, be not children in **u**: howbeit in *5424*
14:20 in malice be ye children, but in **u** be men. *5424*
Eph 1:18 The eyes of your **u** being enlightened; *1271*
4:18 Having the **u** darkened, being alienated *1271*
5:17 but **u** what the will of the Lord *is*. *4920*
Php 4: 7 which passeth all **u**, shall keep your hearts *3563*
Col 1: 9 of his will in all wisdom and spiritual **u**; *4907*
2: 2 unto all riches of the full assurance of **u**, *4907*
1Ti 1: 7 **u** neither what they say, nor whereof they *3539*
2Ti 2: 7 and the Lord give thee **u** in all *things*. *4907*
1Jn 5:20 and hath given us an **u**, that we may know *1271*
Rev 13:18 Let him that hath **u** count the number of *3563*

UNDERSTOOD (37) [UNDERSTAND]
Ge 42:23 they knew not that Joseph **u** *them;* for he 8085
Dt 32:29 O that they were wise, *that* they **u** this, 7919
1Sa 4: 6 they **u** that the ark of the LORD was come 3045
26: 4 and **u** that Saul was come in very deed. 3045
2Sa 3:37 all Israel **u** that day that it was not of 3045
Ne 8:12 they had **u** the words that were declared unto 995
13: 7 **u** of the evil that Eliashib did for Tobiah, 995
Job 13: 1 seen all *this,* mine ear hath heard and **u** it. 995
42: 3 therefore have I uttered that I **u** not; 995
Ps 73:17 into the sanctuary of God; *then* **u** I their end. 995
81: 5 *where* I heard a language *that* I **u** not. 3045
106: 7 Our fathers **u** not thy wonders in Egypt; 7919
Isa 40:21 have ye not **u** *from* the foundations of 995
44:18 They have not known nor **u**: for he hath shut 995
Da 8:27 I was astonished at the vision, but none **u** *it*. 995
9: 2 In the first year of his reign I Daniel **u** by 995
10: 1 he **u** the thing, and had understanding of 995
12: 8 I heard, but I **u** not: then said I, O my lord, 995
Mt 13:51 Have ye **u** all these *things?* They say unto *4920*
16:12 Then **u** they how that he bade *them* not *4920*
17:13 Then the disciples **u** that he spake unto *4920*
26:10 When Jesus **u** *it,* he said unto them, *1097*
Mk 9:32 But they **u not** *that* saying, and were afraid to *50*
Lk 2:50 And they **u** not the saying which he spake *4920*
9:45 But they **u not** this saying, and it was hid *50*
18:34 And they **u** none of these *things:* and *4920*
Jn 8:27 They **u** not that he spake to them of *1097*
10: 6 they **u** not what *things* they were which he *1097*
12:16 These *things* **u** not his disciples at the first: *1097*
Ac 7:25 For he supposed his brethren would have **u** *4920*
7:25 hand would deliver them: but they **u** not. *4920*
23:27 having **u** that he was a Roman. *3129*
23:34 and when he **u** that *he was* of Cilicia; *4441*
Ro 1:20 being **u** by the things that are made, *3539*
1Co 13:11 I spake as a child, I **u** as a child, I thought *5426*
14: 9 ye utter by the tongue words **easy to be u**, *2154*
2Pe 3:16 in which are some *things* **hard to be u**, *1425*

UNDERTAKE (1) [UNDERTOOK]
Isa 38:14 O LORD, I am oppressed; **u** for me. 6148

UNDERTOOK (1) [UNDERTAKE]
Est 9:23 the Jews **u** to do as they had begun, and 6901

UNDO (2) [DO, UNDONE]
Isa 58: 6 to **u** the heavy burdens, and to let 5425
Zep 3:19 that time I *will* **u** all that afflict thee: 854+6213

UNDONE (5) [UNDO]
Nu 21:29 thou art **u**, O people of Chemosh: he hath given 6
Jos 11:15 he **left** nothing **u** of all that the LORD 5493
Isa 6: 5 for I am **u**; because I *am* a man of unclean 1820
Mt 23:23 *ye* to have done, and not to **leave** the other **u**. *863*
Lk 11:42 *ye* to have done, and not to **leave** the other **u**. *863*

UNDRESSED (2) [DRESS]
Lev 25: 5 neither gather the grapes of thy **vine u**: 5139
25:11 nor gather *the grapes* in it of thy **vine u**. 5139

UNEQUAL (2) [EQUAL, UNEQUALLY]
Eze 18:25 my way equal? are not your ways **u**? 3808+8505
18:29 ways equal? are not your ways **u**? 3808+8505

UNEQUALLY (1) [UNEQUAL]
2Co 6:14 Be ye not **u yoked together** with *2086*

UNFAILING LOVE See LOVINGKINDNESS

UNFAITHFUL (1) [FAITH, UNFAITHFULLY]
Pr 25:19 Confidence in an **u** *man* in time of trouble *is* 898

UNFAITHFULLY (1) [UNFAITHFUL]
Ps 78:57 turned *back,* and **dealt u** like their fathers: 898

UNFAITHFULNESS See WHOREDOM

UNFEIGNED (4) [FEIGN]
2Co 6: 6 by kindness, by the Holy Ghost, by love **u**, *505*
1Ti 1: 5 and *of* a good conscience, and *of* faith **u**: *505*
2Ti 1: 5 When I call to remembrance the **u** faith that *505*
1Pe 1:22 the Spirit unto **u** love of the brethren, *505*

UNFIT See REPROBATE; REPROBATES

UNFORGIVING See TRUCEBREAKERS

UNFORMED See UNPERFECT

UNFRUITFUL (6) [FRUIT]
Mt 13:22 choke the word, and he becometh **u**. *175*
Mk 4:19 choke the word, and it becometh **u**. *175*
1Co 14:14 my spirit prayeth, but my understanding is **u**. *175*
Eph 5:11 And have no fellowship with the **u** works of *175*
Tit 3:14 works for necessary uses, that they be not **u**. *175*
2Pe 1: 8 **u** in the knowledge of our Lord Jesus Christ. *175*

UNGIRDED (1) [GIRD]
Ge 24:32 he **u** *his* camels, and gave straw and 6605

UNGODLINESS (4) [GOD, UNGODLY]
Ro 1:18 of God is revealed from heaven against all **u** *763*
11:26 and shall turn away **u** from Jacob: *763*
2Ti 2:16 for they will increase unto more **u**. *763*
Tit 2:12 Teaching us that denying **u** and worldly lusts *763*

UNGODLY (27) [UNGODLINESS]
2Sa 22: 5 the floods of **u men** made me afraid; 1100
2Ch 19: 2 Shouldest thou help the **u**, and love them 7563
Job 16:11 God hath delivered me to the **u**, and 5760
34:18 *Thou art* wicked? *and* to princes, *Ye are* **u**? 7563
Ps 1: 1 that walketh not in the counsel of the **u**, 7563
1: 4 The **u** *are* not so: but *are* like the chaff 7563
1: 5 Therefore the **u** shall not stand in 7563
1: 6 but the way of the **u** shall perish. 7563
3: 7 thou hast broken the teeth of the **u**. 7563
18: 4 and the floods of **u men** made me afraid. 1100
43: 1 plead my cause against an **u** nation: 2623+3808
73:12 Behold, these *are* the **u**, who prosper in 7563
Pr 16:27 An **u** man diggeth up evil: and in his lips 1100
19:28 An **u** witness scorneth judgment: and 1100
Ro 4: 5 but believeth on him that justifieth the **u**, *765*
5: 6 in due time Christ died for the **u**. *765*
1Ti 1: 9 for the **u** and for sinners, for unholy and *765*
1Pe 4:18 where shall the **u** and the sinner appear? *765*
2Pe 2: 5 in the flood upon the world of the **u**; *765*
2: 6 ensample unto **those that** after should **live u**; *764*
3: 7 the day of judgment and perdition of **u** men. *765*
Jude 1: 4 **u** *men,* turning the grace of our God into *765*

U

Jude 1:15 to convince all *that are* **u** among them of all *765*
1:15 **u** deeds which they have ungodly *763*
1:15 deeds which they have **u committed,** *764*
1:15 of all *their* hard *speeches* which **u** sinners *765*
1:18 who should walk after their own **u** lusts. *763*

UNGRATEFUL See UNTHANKFUL

UNHOLY (4) [HOLY]
Lev 10:10 *ye* may put difference between holy and **u,** 2455
1Ti 1: 9 and for sinners, for **u** and profane, *462*
2Ti 3: 2 disobedient to parents, unthankful, **u,** *462*
Heb 10:29 an **u** *thing,* and hath done despite unto *2839*

UNICORN (6) [UNICORNS]
Nu 23:22 he hath as it were the strength of an **u.** 7214
24: 8 he hath as it were the strength of an **u:** 7214
Job 39: 9 Will the **u** be willing to serve thee, or 7214
39:10 Canst thou bind the **u** *with* his band in 7214
Ps 29: 6 a calf; Lebanon and Sirion like a young **u.** 7214
92:10 horn shalt thou exalt like *the horn of* an **u:** 7214

UNICORNS (3) [UNICORN]
Dt 33:17 and his horns *are like* the horns of **u:** 7214
Ps 22:21 thou hast heard me from the horns of the **u.** 7214
Isa 34: 7 the **u** shall come down with them, and 7214

UNINTENTIONALLY See UNAWARES

UNITE (1) [UNITED, UNITY]
Ps 86:11 in thy truth: **u** my heart to fear thy name. 3161

UNITED (1) [UNITE]
Ge 49: 6 their assembly, mine honour, be not thou **u:** 3161

UNITY (3) [UNITE]
Ps 133: 1 *it is* for brethren to dwell **together in u.** 3162
Eph 4: 3 Endeavouring to keep the **u** of the Spirit in *1775*
4:13 Till we all come in the **u** of the faith, and *1775*

UNJUST (17) [JUST, UNJUSTLY]
Ps 43: 1 O deliver me from the deceitful and **u** man. 5766
Pr 11: 7 and the hope of **u** *men* perisheth. 205
28: 8 and **u gain** increaseth his substance, 8636
29:27 An **u** man is an abomination to the just: and 5766
Zep 3: 5 he faileth not; but the **u** knoweth no shame. 5767
Mt 5:45 and sendeth rain on the just and *on* the **u.** *94*
Lk 16: 8 And the lord commended the **u** steward, *93*
16:10 he that is **u** in the least is unjust also in much. *94*
16:10 he that is unjust in the least is **u** also in much. *94*
18: 6 the Lord said, Hear what the **u** judge saith. *93*
18:11 **u,** adulterers, or even as this publican. *94*
Ac 24:15 of the dead, both of the just and **u.** *94*
1Co 6: 1 go to law before the **u,** and not before *94*
1Pe 3:18 the just for the **u,** that he might bring us to *94*
2Pe 2: 9 to reserve the **u** unto the day of judgment *to* *94*
Rev 22:11 He that is **u,** let him be unjust still: and *91*
22:11 He that is unjust, let him be **u** still: and *91*

UNJUSTLY (2) [UNJUST]
Ps 82: 2 How long will ye judge **u,** and accept 5766
Isa 26:10 in the land of uprightness will he **deal u,** 5765

UNKNOWN (9) [KNOW]
Ac 17:23 altar with this inscription, TO *THE* **U** GOD. *57*
1Co 14: 2 For he that speaketh in an **u** tongue NIG
14: 4 He that speaketh in an *u* tongue edifieth NIG
14:13 Wherefore let him that speaketh in an *u* NIG
14:14 For if I pray in an *u* tongue, my spirit NIG
14:19 than ten thousand words in an *u* tongue. NIG
14:27 If any *man* speak in an *u* tongue, *let it be* by NIG
2Co 6: 9 As **u,** and *yet* well known; as dying, and *50*
Gal 1:22 And was **u** by face unto the churches of Judea *50*

UNLADE (1) [LADE]
Ac 21: 3 for there the ship was to **u** *her* burden. *670*

UNLAWFUL (2) [LAW]
Ac 10:28 Ye know how that it is an **u** *thing* for a man *111*
2Pe 2: 8 soul from day to day with *their* **u** deeds;) *459*

UNLEARNED (6) [LEARN]
Ac 4:13 and perceived that they were **u** and *62*
1Co 14:16 of the **u** say Amen at thy giving of thanks, *2399*
14:23 and there come in *those that are* **u,** or *2399*
14:24 or *one* **u,** he is convinced of all, he is *2399*
2Ti 2:23 But foolish and **u** questions avoid, *521*
2Pe 3:16 which *they that are* **u** and unstable wrest, *261*

UNLEAVENED (61) [LEAVEN]
Ge 19: 3 and did bake **u bread,** and they did eat. 4682
Ex 12: 8 in that night, roast with fire, and **u bread;** 4682
12:15 Seven days shall ye eat **u bread;** even 4682
12:17 ye shall observe the *feast of* **u bread;** for in 4682
12:18 ye shall eat **u bread,** until the one and 4682
12:20 in all your habitations shall ye eat **u bread.** 4682
12:39 they baked **u** cakes of the dough which 4682
13: 6 Seven days thou shalt eat **u bread,** and 4682
13: 7 **U bread** shall be eaten seven days; and 4682
23:15 Thou shalt keep the feast of **u bread:** 4682
23:15 thou shalt eat **u bread** seven days, as I 4682
29: 2 **u** bread, and cakes unleavened tempered 4682
29: 2 cakes **u** tempered with oil, and 4682
29: 2 with oil, and wafers **u** anointed with oil: 4682
29:23 one wafer out of the basket of the **u bread** 4682
34:18 The feast of **u bread** shalt thou keep: 4682
34:18 seven days thou shalt eat **u bread,** as I 4682
Lev 2: 4 *it shall be* **u** cakes of fine flour mingled 4682
2: 4 with oil, or **u** wafers anointed with oil. 4682
2: 5 it shall be *of* fine flour **u,** mingled with oil. 4682
6:16 *with* **u bread** shall it be eaten in the holy 4682
7:12 of thanksgiving **u** cakes mingled with oil, 4682
7:12 **u** wafers anointed with oil, and 4682
8: 2 and two rams, and a basket of **u bread;** 4682
8:26 out of the basket of **u bread,** that *was* 4682
8:26 he took one **u** cake, and a cake of oiled 4682
23: 6 *is* the feast of **u bread** unto the LORD: 4682
23: 6 seven days ye must eat **u bread.** 4682
Nu 6:15 a basket of **u bread,** cakes *of* fine flour 4682
6:15 wafers of **u bread** anointed with oil, and 4682
6:17 the LORD, with the basket of **u bread:** 4682
6:19 one **u** cake out of the basket, and 4682
6:19 one **u** wafer, and shall put *them* upon 4682
9:11 *and* eat it with **u bread** and bitter *herbs.* 4682
28:17 seven days shall **u bread** be eaten. 4682
Dt 16: 3 seven days shalt thou eat **u bread** 4682
16: 8 Six days thou shalt eat **u bread:** and on 4682
16:16 in the feast of **u bread,** and in the feast of 4682
Jos 5:11 **u** *cakes,* and parched *corn* in the selfsame 4682
Jdg 6:19 a kid, and **u** *cakes of* an ephah of flour: 4682
6:20 Take the flesh and the **u** *cakes,* and 4682
6:21 touched the flesh and the **u** *cakes;* and 4682
6:21 the **u** *cakes.* Then the angel of the LORD 4682
1Sa 28:24 kneaded *it,* and did bake **u bread** thereof: 4682
2Ki 23: 9 they did eat of the **u bread** among their 4682
1Ch 23:29 for the **u** cakes, and for *that which is baked* 4682
2Ch 8:13 *even* in the feast of **u bread,** and in 4682
30:13 the feast of **u bread** in the second month, 4682
30:21 of **u bread** seven days with great gladness: 4682
35:17 and the feast of **u bread** seven days. 4682
Ezr 6:22 kept the feast of **u bread** seven days with 4682
Eze 45:21 feast of seven days; **u bread** shall be eaten. 4682
Mt 26:17 Now the first *day* of the *feast of* **u bread** *106*
Mk 14: 1 *the feast of* the passover, and *of* **u bread:** *106*
14:12 And the first day of **u bread,** when they *106*
Lk 22: 1 Now the feast of **u bread** drew nigh, *106*
22: 7 Then came the day of **u bread,** when *106*
Ac 12: 3 Peter also. (Then were the days of **u bread.**) *106*
20: 6 from Philippi after the days of **u bread,** *106*
1Co 5: 7 that ye may be a new lump, as ye are **u.** *106*
5: 8 but with the **u bread** of sincerity and truth. *106*

UNLESS (8)
Lev 22: 6 shall not eat of the holy *things,* **u** he 518+3588
Nu 22:33 **u** she had turned from me, surely now also I 194
2Sa 2:27 **u** thou hadst spoken, surely then 3588+3884
Ps 27:13 *I had fainted,* **u** I had believed to see 3884
94:17 **U** the LORD *had been* my help, my soul 3884
119:92 **U** thy law *had been* my delights, I should 3884
Pr 4:16 taken away, **u** they cause *some* to fall. 518+3808
1Co 15: 2 **u** ye have believed in vain. *1487+1622+3361*

UNLOAD See UNLADE

UNLOADED See UNGIRDED

UNLOOSE (3) [LOOSE]
Mk 1: 7 shoes I am not worthy to stoop down and **u.** *3089*
Lk 3:16 of whose shoes I am not worthy to **u:** *3089*
Jn 1:27 whose shoe's latchet I am not worthy to **u.** *3089*

UNMARRIED (4) [MARRY]
1Co 7: 8 I say therefore to the **u** and widows, It is good *22*
7:11 let her remain **u**, or be reconciled to *her* *22*
7:32 He *that is* **u** careth for the *things* that belong *22*
7:34 The **u** *woman* careth for the *things* of *22*

UNMERCIFUL (1) [MERCY]
Ro 1:31 without natural affection, implacable, **u**: *415*

UNMINDFUL (1) [MIND]
Dt 32:18 Of the Rock *that* begat thee thou art **u**, and 7876

UNMOVEABLE (2) [MOVE]
Ac 27:41 and remained **u**, but the hinder part was *761*
1Co 15:58 my beloved brethren, be ye stedfast, **u**, *277*

UNNI (3)
1Ch 15:18 **U**, Eliab, and Benaiah, and Maaseiah, and 6042
15:20 **U**, and Eliab, and Maaseiah, and Benaiah, 6042
Ne 12: 9 Also Bakbukiah and **U**, their brethren, *were* 6042

UNOCCUPIED (1) [OCCUPY]
Jdg 5: 6 the highways were **u**, and the travellers 2308

UNPERFECT (1) [PERFECT]
Ps 139:16 eyes did see my **substance, yet being u**; 1564

UNPLOWED See FALLOW

UNPOSSIBLE (4) [IMPOSSIBLE, POSSIBLE]
Mt 17:20 and nothing shall be **u** unto you. *101*
19:26 and said unto them, With men this is **u**; *102*
Lk 1:37 For with God nothing shall be **u**. *101*
18:27 The *things which are* **u** with men are *102*

UNPREPARED (1) [PREPARE]
2Co 9: 4 and find you **u**, we (that we say not, you) *532*

UNPRESENTABLE See UNCOMELY

UNPROFITABLE (7) [PROFIT, UNPROFITABLENESS]
Job 15: 3 Should he reason *with* **u** talk? or 3808
Mt 25:30 And cast ye the **u** servant into outer *888*
Lk 17:10 are commanded you, say, We are **u** servants: *888*
Ro 3:12 out of the way, they are together become **u**; *889*
Tit 3: 9 about the law; for they are **u** and vain. *512*
Phm 1:11 Which in time past was to thee **u**, but *890*
Heb 13:17 and not with grief: for that *is* **u** for you. *255*

UNPROFITABLENESS (1) [UNPROFITABLE]
Heb 7:18 going before for the weakness and **u** thereof. *512*

UNPUNISHED (11) [PUNISH]
Pr 11:21 *join* in hand, the wicked shall not be **u**: 5352
16: 5 *though* hand *join* in hand, he shall not be **u**. 5352
17: 5 he that is glad at calamities shall not be **u**. 5352
19: 5 A false witness shall not be **u**, and *he that* 5352
19: 9 A false witness shall not be **u**, and *he that* 5352
Jer 25:29 and should ye be **utterly u**? 5352+5352
25:29 Ye shall not be **u**: for I *will* call for a sword 5352
30:11 and will not **leave** thee **altogether u**. 5352+5352
46:28 yet will I not **leave** thee **wholly u**. 5352+5352
49:12 thou he *that* shall **altogether go u**? 5352+5352
49:12 thou shalt not **go u**, but thou shalt surely 5352

UNQUENCHABLE (2) [QUENCH]
Mt 3:12 but will burn up the chaff with **u** fire. *762*
Lk 3:17 but the chaff he will burn with fire **u**. *762*

UNREASONABLE (2) [REASON]
Ac 25:27 For it seemeth to me **u** to send a prisoner, *249*
2Th 3: 2 And that we may be delivered from **u** and *824*

UNREBUKEABLE (1) [REBUKE]
1Ti 6:14 **u**, until the appearing of our Lord Jesus *423*

UNREPENTANT See IMPENITENT

UNREPROVEABLE (1) [REPROVE]
Col 1:22 you holy and unblameable and **u** in his sight: *410*

UNRIGHTEOUS (9) [RIGHT, UNRIGHTEOUSLY, UNRIGHTEOUSNESS]
Ex 23: 1 hand with the wicked to be an **u** witness. 2555
Job 27: 7 and he that riseth up against me as the **u**. 5767
Ps 71: 4 out of the hand of the **u** and cruel *man*. 5765
Isa 10: 1 Woe unto them that decree **u** decrees, and 205
55: 7 forsake his way, and the **u** man his thoughts: 205
Lk 16:11 ye have not been faithful in the **u** mammon, *94*
Ro 3: 5 *Is* God **u** who taketh vengeance? (I speak as a *94*
1Co 6: 9 Know ye not that the **u** shall not inherit *94*
Heb 6:10 For God *is* not **u** to forget your work and *94*

UNRIGHTEOUSLY (1) [UNRIGHTEOUS]
Dt 25:16 all that do such *things, and* all that do **u**, 5766

UNRIGHTEOUSNESS (21) [UNRIGHTEOUS]
Lev 19:15 Ye shall do no **u** in judgment: thou shalt 5766
19:35 Ye shall do no **u** in judgment, in meteyard, 5766
Ps 92:15 *he is* my rock, and *there is* no **u** in him. 5766
Jer 22:13 him that buildeth his house by **u**, 3808+6664
Lk 16: 9 to yourselves friends of the mammon of **u**; *93*
Jn 7:18 sent him, the same is true, and no **u** is in him. *93*
Ro 1:18 heaven against all ungodliness and **u** of men, *93*
1:18 of men, who hold the truth in **u**; *93*
1:29 Being filled with all **u**, fornication, *93*
2: 8 the truth, but obey **u**, indignation and wrath, *93*
3: 5 But if our **u** commend the righteousness of *93*
6:13 ye your members *as* instruments of **u** unto sin: *93*
9:14 we say then? *Is there* **u** with God? God forbid. *93*
2Co 6:14 what fellowship hath righteousness with **u**? *458*
2Th 2:10 And with all deceivableness of **u** in them that *93*
2:12 believed not the truth, but had pleasure in **u**. *93*
Heb 8:12 For I will be merciful to their **u**, and their sins *93*
2Pe 2:13 And shall receive the reward of **u**, *as* they that *93*
2:15 *the son* of Bosor, who loved the wages of **u**; *93*
1Jn 1: 9 us *our* sins, and to cleanse us from all **u**. *93*
5:17 All **u** is sin: and there is a sin not unto death. *93*

UNRIPE (1) [RIPE]
Job 15:33 He shall shake off his **u grape** as the vine, 1154

UNRULY (4)
1Th 5:14 exhort you, brethren, warn *them that are* **u**, *813*
Tit 1: 6 faithful children not accused of riot or **u**. *506*
1:10 For there are many **u** and vain talkers and *506*
Jas 3: 8 *it is* an **u** evil, full of deadly poison. *183*

UNSANDALED See SHOE; SHOE'S; SHOES

UNSATIABLE (1) [SATIATE]
Eze 16:28 the Assyrians, because thou wast **u**; 1115+7654

UNSAVOURY (2) [SAVOUR]
2Sa 22:27 with the froward thou wilt **shew** thyself **u**. 6617
Job 6: 6 Can **that which is u** be eaten without salt? 8602

UNSCHOOLED See UNLEARNED

UNSEARCHABLE (5) [SEARCH]
Job 5: 9 Which doeth great *things* and **u**; 369+2714
Ps 145: 3 to be praised; and his greatness *is* **u**. 369+2714
Pr 25: 3 for depth, and the heart of kings *is* **u**. 369+2714
Ro 11:33 how **u** *are* his judgments, and his ways past *419*
Eph 3: 8 *I* should preach among the Gentiles the **u** *421*

UNSEEMLY (2) [SEEM]
Ro 1:27 men with men working that which is **u**, and *808*
1Co 13: 5 Doth not **behave** itself **u**, seeketh not her *807*

UNSHOD (1) [SHOD]
Jer 2:25 Withhold thy foot from being **u**, and 3182

UNSKILFUL (1) [SKILL]
Heb 5:13 For every one that useth milk *is* **u** in *552*

UNSPEAKABLE (3) [SPEAK]
2Co 9:15 Thanks *be* unto God for his **u** gift. *411*
12: 4 and heard **u** words, which *it is* not lawful for *731*
1Pe 1: 8 ye rejoice with joy **u** and full of glory: *412*

UNSPIRITUAL See CARNAL

UNSPOTTED (1) [SPOT]
Jas 1:27 *and* to keep himself **u** from the world. *784*

UNSTABLE (4) [STABLE]
Ge 49: 4 **U** as water, thou shalt not excel; because 6349
Jas 1: 8 A double minded man *is* **u** in all his ways. *182*
2Pe 2:14 cannot cease from sin; beguiling **u** souls: *793*
3:16 which *they that are* unlearned and **u** wrest, *793*

UNSTOPPED (1) [STOP]
Isa 35: 5 and the ears of the deaf shall be **u**. 6605

UNTAKEN (1) [TAKE]
2Co 3:14 **u away** in the reading of the old 343+3361

UNTEMPERED (5) [TEMPER]
Eze 13:10 and lo, others daubed it *with* **u** *morter:* 8602
13:11 Say unto them which daub *it with* **u** *morter,* 8602
13:14 the wall that ye have daubed *with* **u** *morter,* 8602
13:15 upon them that have daubed it *with* **u** 8602
22:28 her prophets have daubed them *with* **u** 8602

UNTENDED See UNDRESSED

UNTHANKFUL (2) [THANK]
Lk 6:35 for he is kind unto the **u** and *to the* evil. *884*
2Ti 3: 2 disobedient to parents, **u**, unholy, *884*

UNTIL (366) See Index

UNTIMELY (4) [TIME]
Job 3:16 Or as a hidden **u birth** I had not been; 5309
Ps 58: 8 *like* the **u birth** of a woman, *that* they may 5309
Ecc 6: 3 I say, *that* an **u birth** *is* better than he. 5309
Rev 6:13 *even* as a fig tree casteth her **u figs**, when *3653*

UNTO (9005) [HEREUNTO, THEREUNTO, WHEREUNTO]
See Index

UNTOWARD (1)
Ac 2:40 Save yourselves from this **u** generation. *4646*

UNWALLED (3) [WALL]
Dt 3: 5 and bars; beside **u** towns a great many. 6521
Est 9:19 of the villages, that dwelt in the **u** towns, 6519
Eze 38:11 I will go up to the land of **u villages**; 6519

UNWASHEN (3) [WASH]
Mt 15:20 but to eat with **u** hands defileth not a man. *449*
Mk 7: 2 that is to say, with **u**, hands, they found fault. *449*
7: 5 of the elders, but eat bread with **u** hands? *449*

UNWEIGHED (1) [WEIGH]
1Ki 7:47 Solomon left all the vessels **u**, because NIH

UNWISE (4) [WISDOM]
Dt 32: 6 the LORD, O foolish people and **u**? 2450+3808
Hos 13:13 he *is* an **u** son; for he should not stay 2450+3808
Ro 1:14 the barbarians; both to the wise, and to the **u**. *453*
Eph 5:17 Wherefore be ye not **u**, but *878*

UNWITTINGLY (3) [WIT]
Lev 22:14 if a man eat *of* the holy *thing* **u**, then 7684+871.1
Jos 20: 3 *and* **u** may flee thither: 1097+1847+871.1
20: 5 he smote his neighbour **u**, 1097+1847+871.1

UNWORTHILY (2) [UNWORTHY]
1Co 11:27 and drink *this* cup of the Lord **u**, shall be *371*
11:29 For he that eateth and drinketh **u**, eateth and *371*

UNWORTHY (2) [UNWORTHILY, WORTH]
Ac 13:46 judge yourselves **u** of everlasting life, *514+3756*
1Co 6: 2 are ye **u** to judge the smallest matters? *370*

UP (2381) [UPON, UPPER, UPPERMOST, UPSIDE, UPWARD]
See Index

UPBRAID (2) [UPBRAIDED, UPBRAIDETH]
Jdg 8:15 Zalmunna, with whom ye did **u** me, saying, 2778
Mt 11:20 Then began he to **u** the cities wherein most *3679*

UPBRAIDED (1) [UPBRAID]
Mk 16:14 and **u** them with their unbelief and *3679*

UPBRAIDETH (1) [UPBRAID]
Jas 1: 5 that giveth to all *men* liberally, and **u** not; *3679*

UPHARSIN (1)
Da 5:25 MENE, MENE, TEKEL, **U**. 6537+2050.3

UPHAZ (2)
Jer 10: 9 and gold from **U**, the work of the workman, 210
Da 10: 5 whose loins *were* girded with fine gold of **U**: 210

UPHELD (1) [UPHOLD]
Isa 63: 5 salvation unto me; and my fury, it **u** me. 5564

UPHOLD (8) [UPHELD, UPHOLDEN, UPHOLDEST, UPHOLDETH, UPHOLDING]
Ps 51:12 thy salvation; and **u** me *with thy* free spirit. 5564
54: 4 the Lord *is* with them that **u** my soul. 5564
119:116 **U** me according unto thy word, that I may 5564
Pr 29:23 but honour shall **u** the humble in spirit. 8551
Isa 41:10 I will **u** thee with the right hand of my 8551
42: 1 Behold my servant, whom I **u**; mine elect, 8551
63: 5 and I wondered that *there was* none to **u**: 5564
Eze 30: 6 They also that **u** Egypt shall fall; and 5564

UPHOLDEN (2) [UPHOLD]
Job 4: 4 Thy words have **u** him that was falling, and 6965
Pr 20:28 the king: and his throne is **u** by mercy. 5582

UPHOLDEST (1) [UPHOLD]
Ps 41:12 thou **u** me in mine integrity, and settest me 8551

UPHOLDETH (4) [UPHOLD]
Ps 37:17 be broken: but the LORD **u** the righteous. 5564
37:24 for the LORD **u** *him with* his hand. 5564
63: 8 hard after thee: thy right hand **u** me. 8551
145:14 The LORD **u** all that fall, and raiseth up 5564

UPHOLDING (1) [UPHOLD]
Heb 1: 3 and **u** all *things* by the word of his power, *5342*

UPON (2763) [THEREUPON, UP, WHEREUPON] See Index

UPPER (25) [UP]
Ex 12: 7 and on the **u door post** of the houses, 4947
Lev 13:45 he shall put a covering upon *his* **u lip**, and 8222
Dt 24: 6 the nether or the **u millstone** to pledge: 7393
Jos 15:19 he gave her the **u** springs, and the nether 5942
16: 5 was Ataroth-addar, unto Beth-horon the **u**; 5945
Jdg 1:15 Caleb gave her the **u** springs and the nether 5942
2Ki 1: 2 in his **u chamber** that *was* in Samaria, 5944
18:17 and stood by the conduit of the **u** pool, 5945
23:12 *were* on the top of the **u chamber** of Ahaz, 5944
1Ch 7:24 the nether, and the **u**, and Uzzen-sherah.) 5945
28:11 of the **u chambers** thereof, and of the inner 5944
2Ch 3: 9 And he overlaid the **u chambers** with gold. 5944
8: 5 Also he built Beth-horon the **u**, and 5945
32:30 This same Hezekiah also stopped the **u** 5945
Isa 7: 3 at the end of the conduit of the **u** pool in 5945
36: 2 he stood by the conduit of the **u** pool in 5945
Eze 42: 5 Now the **u** chambers *were* shorter: for 5945
Zep 2:14 the bittern shall lodge in the **u lintels** of it; 3730
Mk 14:15 And he will shew you a large **u room** *508*
Lk 22:12 And he shall shew you a large **u room** *508*
Ac 1:13 they went up into an **u room**, where abode *5253*
9:37 had washed, they laid *her* in an **u chamber**. *5253*
9:39 they brought him into the **u chamber**: *5253*
19: 1 Paul having passed through the **u** coasts *510*
20: 8 there were many lights in the **u chamber**, *5253*

UPPERMOST (6) [UP]
Ge 40:17 in the **u** basket *there was* of all *manner of* 5945
Isa 17: 6 *or* three berries in the top of the **u bough**, 534
17: 9 an **u** branch, which they left because of NIH
Mt 23: 6 And love the **u rooms** at feasts, and *4411*
Mk 12:39 the synagogues, and the **u rooms** at feasts: *4411*
Lk 11:43 for ye love the **u seats** in the synagogues, *4410*

UPRIGHT (68) [UPRIGHTNESS]
Ge 37: 7 and lo, my sheaf arose, and also **stood u**; 5324
Ex 15: 8 the floods **stood u** as a heap, *and* the depths 5324
Lev 26:13 the bands of your yoke, and made you go **u**. 6968
1Sa 29: 6 thou *hast been* **u**, and thy going out and 3477
2Sa 22:24 I was also **u** before him, and have kept 8549
22:26 with the **u** man thou wilt shew thyself 8549
22:26 the upright man thou wilt **shew** thyself **u**. 8552
2Ch 29:34 for the Levites *were* more **u** in heart to 3477
Job 1: 1 that man was perfect and **u**, and one that 3477
1: 8 a perfect and an **u** man, one that feareth 3477
2: 3 a perfect and an **u** man, one that feareth 3477
8: 6 If thou *wert* pure and **u**; surely now he 3477
12: 4 the just **u** *man is* laughed to scorn. 8549
17: 8 **U** *men* shall be astonied at this, and 3477
Ps 7:10 *is* of God, which saveth the **u** in heart. 3477
11: 2 that *they* may privily shoot at the **u** in heart. 3477
11: 7 his countenance doth behold the **u**. 3477
18:23 I was also **u** before him, and I kept myself 8549
18:25 with an **u** man thou wilt shew thyself 8549
18:25 an upright man thou wilt **shew** thyself **u**; 8552

Ps 19:13 shall I be **u**, and I shall be innocent from 8552
20: 8 and fallen: but we are risen, and **stand u**. 5749
25: 8 Good and **u** *is* the LORD: therefore 3477
32:11 and shout for joy, all *ye that are* **u** in heart. 3477
33: 1 ye righteous: *for* praise is comely for the **u**. 3477
36:10 and thy righteousness to the **u** in heart. 3477
37:14 *and* to slay such as be of **u** conversation. 3477
37:18 The LORD knoweth the days of the **u**: 8549
37:37 Mark the perfect *man*, and behold the **u**: 3477
49:14 the **u** shall have dominion over them in 3477
64:10 in him; and all the **u** in heart shall glory. 3477
92:15 To shew that the LORD *is* **u**: *he is* my 3477
94:15 and all the **u** in heart shall follow it. 3477
97:11 and gladness for the **u** in heart. 3477
111: 1 in the assembly of the **u**, and *in* 3477
112: 2 the generation of the **u** shall be blessed. 3477
112: 4 Unto the **u** there ariseth light in 3477
119:137 O LORD, and **u** *are* thy judgments. 3477
125: 4 and to *them that are* **u** in their hearts. 3477
140:13 thy name: the **u** shall dwell in thy presence. 3477
Pr 2:21 For the **u** shall dwell *in* the land, and 3477
10:29 The way of the LORD *is* strength to the **u**: 8537
11: 3 The integrity of the **u** shall guide them: but 3477
11: 6 The righteousness of the **u** shall deliver 3477
11:11 By the blessing of the **u** the city is exalted: 3477
11:20 *such as are* **u** in *their* way *are* his delight. 8549
12: 6 but the mouth of the **u** shall deliver them. 3477
13: 6 Righteousness keepeth *him that is* **u** in 8537
14:11 but the tabernacle of the **u** shall flourish. 3477
15: 8 but the prayer of the **u** *is* his delight. 3477
16:17 The highway of the **u** *is* to depart from evil: 3477
21:18 and the transgressor for the **u**. 3477
21:29 but *as for* the **u**, he directeth his way. 3477
28:10 the **u** shall have good *things* in possession. 8549
29:10 The bloodthirsty hate the **u**: but the just 8535
29:27 *he that is* **u** in the way *is* abomination to 3477
Ecc 7:29 have I found, that God hath made man **u**; 3477
12:10 *that which was* written *was* **u**, *even* words 3476
SS 1: 4 thy love more than wine: the **u** love thee. 4339
Isa 26: 7 thou, **most u**, dost weigh the path of 3477
Jer 10: 5 They *are* **u** as the palm tree, but speak not: 4749
Da 8:18 but he touched me, and set me **u**. 5921+5977
10:11 that I speak unto thee, and stand **u**: 5921+5977
11:17 his whole kingdom, and **u ones** with him; 3477
Mic 7: 2 *there is* none **u** among men: they all lie in 3477
7: 4 the *most* **u** *is sharper* than a thorn hedge: 3477
Hab 2: 4 his soul *which* is lifted up is not **u** in him: 3474
Ac 14:10 Said with a loud voice, Stand **u** on thy feet. *3717*

UPRIGHTLY (12) [UPRIGHTNESS]

Ps 15: 2 He that walketh **u**, and 8549
58: 1 do ye judge **u**, O ye sons of men? 4339
75: 2 receive the congregation I will judge **u**. 4339
84:11 he withhold from them that walk **u**. 8549+871.1
Pr 2: 7 *he is* a buckler to them that walk **u**. 8537
10: 9 He that walketh **u** walketh surely: 8537+871.1
15:21 but a man of understanding walketh **u**. 3474
28:18 Whoso walketh **u** shall be saved: but 8549
Isa 33:15 that walketh righteously, and speaketh **u**; 4339
Am 5:10 and they abhor him that speaketh **u**. 8549
Mic 2: 7 my words do good to him that walketh **u**? 3477
Gal 2:14 But when I saw that they **walked** not **u** *3716*

UPRIGHTNESS (19) [UPRIGHT, UPRIGHTLY]

Dt 9: 5 or for the **u** of thine heart, 3476
1Ki 3: 6 and in **u** of heart with thee; 3483
9: 4 in integrity of heart, and in **u**, 3476
1Ch 29:17 thou triest the heart, and hast pleasure in **u**. 4339
29:17 in the **u** of mine heart I have willingly 3476
Job 4: 6 thy hope; and the **u** of thy ways? 8537
33: 3 My words *shall be of* the **u** of my heart: 3476
33:23 among a thousand, to shew unto man his **u**: 3476
Ps 9: 8 shall minister judgment to the people in **u**. 4339
25:21 Let integrity and **u** preserve me; for I wait 3476
111: 8 and ever, *and are* done in truth and **u**. 3477
119: 7 I will praise thee with **u** of heart, when I 3476
143:10 spirit *is* good; lead me into the land of **u**. 4334
Pr 2:13 Who leave the paths of **u**, to walk in 3476
14: 2 He that walketh in his **u** feareth 3476
28: 6 Better *is* the poor that walketh in his **u**, 8537
Isa 26: 7 The way of the just *is* **u**: thou, most upright, 4339
26:10 in the land of **u** will he deal unjustly, and 5229
57: 2 in their beds, *each one* walking *in* his **u**. 5228

UPRISING (1)

Ps 139: 2 Thou knowest my downsitting and mine **u**, 6965

UPROAR (8)

1Ki 1:41 *is this* noise of the city being **in an u**? 1993
Mt 26: 5 Not on the feast *day*, lest there be an **u** *2351*
Mk 14: 2 Not on the feast *day*, lest there be an **u** of *2351*
Ac 17: 5 and **set** all the city **on an u**, and assaulted *2350*
19:40 to be called in question for this day's **u**, *4714*
20: 1 And after the **u** was ceased, Paul called *2351*
21:31 of the band, that all Jerusalem was **in an u**. *4797*
21:38 which before these days **madest an u**, and *387*

UPSIDE (5) [UP]

2Ki 21:13 wiping *it*, and turning *it* **u down**. 5921+6440
Ps 146: 9 the way of the wicked he **turneth u down**. 5791
Isa 24: 1 turneth it **u down**, and scattereth abroad 6440
29:16 Surely your **turning** *of things* **u down** shall 2017
Ac 17: 6 These that have **turned** the world **u down** *387*

UPWARD (61) [UP] See Index

UR (5)

Ge 11:28 the land of his nativity, in **U** of the Chaldees. 218
11:31 they went forth with them from **U** of 218
15: 7 I *am* the LORD that brought thee out of **U** 218
1Ch 11:35 of Sacar the Hararite, Eliphal the son of **U**, 218
Ne 9: 7 broughtest him forth out of **U** of 218

URBAN (1)

Ro 16: 9 Salute **U** our helper in Christ, and *3773*

URBANUS See URBAN

URGE (1) [URGED]

Lk 11:53 the Pharisees began to **u** *him* vehemently, *1758*

URGED (6) [URGE]

Ge 33:11 have enough. And he **u** him, and he took *it*. 6484
Jdg 16:16 **u** him, *so* that his soul was vexed unto death; 509
19: 7 rose up to depart, his father in law **u** him: 6484
2Ki 2:17 when they **u** him till *he* was ashamed, he 6484
5:16 And he **u** him to take *it*; but he refused. 6484
5:23 he **u** him, and bound two talents of silver in 6555

URGENT (2)

Ex 12:33 the Egyptians were **u** upon the people, that 2388
Da 3:22 the king's commandment *was* **u**, 2685

URI (8)

Ex 31: 2 I have called by name Bezaleel the son of **U**, 221
35:30 hath called by name Bezaleel the son of **U**, 221
38:22 Bezaleel the son of **U**, the son of Hur, of 221
1Ki 4:19 Geber the son of **U** *was* in the country of 221
1Ch 2:20 And Hur begat **U**, and Uri begat Bezaleel. 221
2:20 And Hur begat Uri, and **U** begat Bezaleel. 221
2Ch 1: 5 that Bezaleel the son of **U**, the son of Hur, 221
Ezr 10:24 of the porters; Shallum, and Telem, and **U**. 221

URIAH (26) [URIAH'S, URIAS, URIJAH]

2Sa 11: 3 daughter of Eliam, the wife of **U** the Hittite? 223
11: 6 sent to Joab, *saying*, Send me **U** the Hittite. 223
11: 6 Uriah the Hittite. And Joab sent **U** to David. 223
11: 7 when **U** was come unto him, David 223
11: 8 And David said to **U**, Go down to thy house, 223
11: 8 And **U** departed out of the king's house, and 223
11: 9 **U** slept *at* the door of the king's house with 223
11:10 saying, **U** went not down unto his house, 223
11:10 David said unto **U**, Camest thou not from *thy* 223
11:11 And **U** said unto David, The ark, and Israel, 223
11:12 And David said to **U**, Tarry here to day also, 223
11:12 So **U** abode in Jerusalem that day, and 223
11:14 a letter to Joab, and sent *it* by the hand of **U**. 223
11:15 Set ye **U** in the forefront of the hottest battle, 223
11:16 that he assigned **U** unto a place where he 223
11:17 of David; and **U** the Hittite died also. 223
11:21 Thy servant **U** the Hittite is dead also. 223
11:24 and thy servant **U** the Hittite is dead also. 223
11:26 when the wife of **U** heard that Uriah her 223
11:26 when the wife of Uriah heard that **U** her 223
12: 9 thou hast killed **U** the Hittite with the sword, 223
12:10 hast taken the wife of **U** the Hittite to be thy 223
23:39 **U** the Hittite: thirty and seven *in* all. 223
1Ch 11:41 **U** the Hittite, Zabad the son of Ahlai, 223
Ezr 8:33 hand of Meremoth the son of **U** the priest; 223

Isa 8: 2 **U** the priest, and Zechariah the son of 223

URIAH'S (1) [URIAH]
2Sa 12:15 the LORD strake the child that **U** wife bare 223

URIAS (1) [URIAH]
Mt 1: 6 of *her that had been* the *wife* of **U**; *3774*

URIEL (4)
1Ch 6:24 Tahath his son, **U** his son, Uzziah his son, 222
15: 5 **U** the chief, and his brethren an hundred and 222
15:11 for **U**, Asaiah, and Joel, Shemaiah, and Eliel, 222
2Ch 13: 2 *was* Michaiah the daughter of **U** of Gibeah. 222

URIJAH (12) [URIAH]
1Ki 15: 5 save only in the matter of **U** the Hittite. 223
2Ki 16:10 king Ahaz sent to **U** the priest the fashion of 223
16:11 **U** the priest built an altar according to all 223
16:11 **U** the priest made *it* against king Ahaz came 223
16:15 king Ahaz commanded **U** the priest, saying, 223
16:16 Thus did **U** the priest, according to all that 223
Ne 3: 4 unto them repaired Meremoth the son of **U**, 223
3:21 After him repaired Meremoth the son of **U** 223
8: 4 Anaiah, and **U**, and Hilkiah, and Maaseiah, 223
Jer 26:20 **U** the son of Shemaiah of Kirjath-jearim, 223
26:21 but when **U** heard *it,* he was afraid, and fled, 223
26:23 they fet forth **U** out of Egypt, and 223

URIM (7)
Ex 28:30 shalt put in the breastplate of judgment the **U** 224
Lev 8: 8 also he put in the breastplate the **U** and 224
Nu 27:21 after the judgment of **U** before the LORD: 224
Dt 33: 8 and thy **U** *be* with thy holy one, 224
1Sa 28: 6 by dreams, nor by **U**, nor by prophets. 224
Ezr 2:63 holy *things* till there stood *up* a priest with **U** 224
Ne 7:65 *things,* till there stood *up* a priest with **U** 224

URINE See PISS

US (1449) [WE] See Index

USE (35) [USED, USES, USEST, USETH, USING]
Lev 7:24 *with beasts,* may be used in any *other* **u**: 4399
19:26 neither shall ye **u enchantment**, 5172
Nu 10: 2 that thou mayest **u** them for 1961+3807.1
15:39 own eyes, after which ye **u** to go a whoring: NIH
Dt 26:14 **u**, nor given *ought* thereof for the dead: NIH
2Sa 1:18 the children of Judah the *u of the* bow: NIH
1Ch 12: 2 could **u** both **the right hand** and the left in 3231
28:15 according to the **u** of every candlestick. 5656
Jer 23:31 that **u** their tongues, and say, He saith. 3947
31:23 As yet they shall **u**s this speech in the land 559
46:11 in vain shalt thou **u many** medicines; *for* 7235
Eze 12:23 they shall no more **u** it **as a proverb** in 4911
16:44 proverbs shall **u** *this* **proverb** against thee, 4911
18: 2 that ye **u** this **proverb** concerning 4911+4912
18: 3 any more to **u** this **proverb** in Israel. 4911+4912
21:21 of the two ways, to **u divination**: 7080+7081
Mt 5:44 pray for them which **despitefully u** you, *1908*
6: 7 But when ye pray, **u** not **vain repetitions**, *945*
Lk 6:28 pray for them which **despitefully u** you. *1908*
Ac 14: 5 to **u** *them* **despitefully**, and to stone them, *5195*
Ro 1:26 natural **u** into that which is against nature: *5540*
1:27 leaving the natural **u** of the woman, *5540*
1Co 7:21 if thou mayest be made free, **u** *it* rather. *5530*
7:31 And they that **u** this world, as not abusing *5530*
2Co 1:17 was thus minded, did I **u** lightness? *5530*
3:12 such hope, we **u** great plainness of speech: *5530*
13:10 lest being present I should **u** sharpness, *5530*
Gal 5:13 only **u** not liberty for an occasion to NIG
Eph 4:29 but that which *is* good to the **u** of edifying, *5532*
1Ti 1: 8 that the law *is* good, if a man **u** it lawfully; *5530*
3:10 then let them **u the office of** a **deacon**, *1247*
5:23 but **u** a little wine for thy stomach's sake *5530*
2Ti 2:21 and **meet for** the master's **u**, *and* *2173*
Heb 5:14 *even* those who by reason of **u** have their *1838*
1Pe 4: 9 **U** hospitality one to another without NIG

USED (22) [USE]
Ex 21:36 Or *if* it be known that the ox *hath* **u to push** 5056
Lev 7:24 torn *with beasts,* may be **u** in any *other* use: 6213
Jdg 14:10 there a feast; for so **u** the young men **to do**. 6213
14:20 whom he had **u as** his friend. 3807.1
2Ki 17:17 **u divination** and enchantments, and 7080+7081
21: 6 **u enchantments**, and dealt with familiar 5172
2Ch 33: 6 **u enchantments**, and used witchcraft, and 5172
33: 6 **u witchcraft**, and dealt with a familiar 3784
Jer 2:24 A wild ass **u to** the wilderness, 3928
Eze 22:29 of the land have **u oppression**, 6231+6233
35:11 according to thine envy which thou hast **u** 6213
Hos 12:10 **u similitudes** by the ministry of 1819
Mk 2:18 of John and of the Pharisees **u to** fast: *1510*
Ac 8: 9 beforetime in the *same* city **u sorcery**, *3096*
19:19 Many also of them which **u** curious arts *4238*
27:17 they **u** helps, undergirding the ship; *5530*
Ro 3:13 with their tongues they have **u deceit**; *1387*
1Co 9:12 Nevertheless we have not **u** this power; but *5530*
9:15 But I have **u** none of these *things:* neither *5530*
1Th 2: 5 For neither at any time **u** we flattering *1096*
1Ti 3:13 For they that have **u the office of** a **deacon** *1247*
Heb 10:33 became companions of them that were so **u**. *390*

USELESS See NOUGHT

USES (1) [USE]
Tit 3:14 to maintain good works for necessary **u**, *5532*

USEST (1) [USE]
Ps119:132 as thou **u to do** unto those that love thy 4941

USETH (7) [USE]
Dt 18:10 *or* that **u divination**, *or* an observer 7080+7081
Est 6: 8 be brought which the king *u* to wear, NIH
Pr 15: 2 tongue of the wise **u** knowledge **aright**: 3190
18:23 The poor **u intreaties**; but the rich 8469
Jer 22:13 *that* **u** his neighbour's **service** without 5647
Eze 16:44 every one that **u proverbs** shall use *this* 4911
Heb 5:13 For every one that **u** milk *is* unskilful in *3348*

USING (2) [USE]
Col 2:22 Which all are to perish with the **u**;) after *671*
1Pe 2:16 not **u** *your* liberty for a cloke of *2192*

USUAL See WONT

USURER (1) [USURY]
Ex 22:25 thou shalt not be to him as an **u**, 5383

USURP (1)
1Ti 2:12 nor to **u authority over** the man, but to be in *831*

USURY (24) [USURER]
Ex 22:25 neither shalt thou lay upon him **u**. 5392
Lev 25:36 Take thou no **u** of him, or increase: but 5392
25:37 Thou shalt not give him thy money upon **u**, 5392
Dt 23:19 Thou shalt not **lend upon u** to thy brother; 5391
23:19 **u** of money, usury of victuals, usury of any 5392
23:19 usury of money, **u** of victuals, usury of any 5392
23:19 **u** of any thing that is lent upon usury: 5392
23:19 usury of any thing that is **lent upon u**: 5391
23:20 Unto a stranger thou mayest **lend upon u**; 5391
23:20 thy brother thou shalt not **lend upon u**: 5391
Ne 5: 7 the rulers, and said unto them, You exact **u**, 4855
5:10 and corn: I pray you, let us leave off this **u**. 4855
Ps 15: 5 *He that* putteth not out his money to **u**, 5392
Pr 28: 8 He that by **u** and unjust gain increaseth his 5392
Isa 24: 2 as *with* the **taker of u**, so *with* the giver of 5378
24: 2 of usury, so *with* the **giver of u** to him. 5383
Jer 15:10 I have neither **lent on u**, nor *men* have lent 5383
15:10 on usury, nor *men* have **lent** to me **on u**; 5383
Eze 18: 8 He *that* hath not given forth upon **u**, 5392
18:13 Hath given forth upon **u**, and hath taken 5392
18:17 *that* hath not received **u** nor increase, 5392
22:12 thou hast taken **u** and increase, and 5392
Mt 25:27 I should have received mine own with **u**. *5110*
Lk 19:23 I might have required *mine own* with **u**? *5110*

US-WARD (3) [WE]
Ps 40: 5 and thy thoughts *which are* to **u**: 413+5105.1
Eph 1:19 greatness of his power to **u** who believe, *1473*
2Pe 3: 9 but is longsuffering to **u**, not willing that *1473*

UTENSILS See FURNITURE

UTHAI (2)
1Ch 9: 4 **U** the son of Ammihud, the son of Omri, 5793
Ezr 8:14 **U**, and Zabbud, and with them seventy 5793

UTMOST (11) [UTTER]
Ge 49:26 unto the **u bound** of the everlasting hills: 8379
Nu 22:36 border of Arnon, which *is* in the **u** coast. 7097

Nu 22:41 that thence he might see the **u part** of 7097
23:13 thou shalt see but the **u part** of them, and 7097
Dt 34: 2 and all the land of Judah, unto the **u** sea, 314
Jer 9:26 and Moab, and all *that are* **in the u** corners, 7112
25:23 and Buz, and all *that are* **in the u** corners, 7112
49:32 all winds them *that are* **in the u** corners; 7112
50:26 Come against her from the **u border**, 7093
Joel 2:20 his hinder part towards the **u** sea, and 314
Lk 11:31 for she came from the **u parts** of the earth *4009*

UTTER (46) [UTMOST, UTTERANCE, UTTERED, UTTERETH, UTTERING, UTTERLY, UTTERMOST]

Lev 5: 1 or known *of it;* if he do not **u** *it,* then 5046
Jos 2:14 life for yours, if ye **u** not this our business. 5046
2:20 if thou **u** this our business, then we will be 5046
Jdg 5:12 awake, awake, **u** a song: arise, Barak, and 1696
1Ki 20:42 a man whom I **appointed to u destruction**, 2764
Job 8:10 tell thee, and **u** words out of their heart? 3318
15: 2 Should a wise *man* **u** vain knowledge, and 6030
27: 4 speak wickedness, nor my tongue **u** deceit. 1897
33: 3 and my lips shall **u** knowledge clearly. 4448
Ps 78: 2 in a parable: I will **u** dark sayings of old: 5042
94: 4 *How long* shall they **u** *and* speak hard 5042
106: 2 Who can **u** the mighty acts of the LORD? 4448
119:171 My lips shall **u** praise, when thou hast 5042
145: 7 They shall **abundantly u** the memory of 5042
Pr 14: 5 will not lie: but a false witness will **u** lies. 6315
23:33 and thine heart shall **u** perverse things. 1696
Ecc 1: 8 man cannot **u** *it:* the eye is not satisfied 1696
5: 2 let not thine heart be hasty to **u** *any* thing 3318
Isa 32: 6 and to **u** error against the LORD, 1696
48:20 tell this, **u** it *even* to the end of the earth; 3318
Jer 1:16 I will **u** my judgments against them 1696
25:30 and **u** his voice from his holy habitation; 5414
Eze 10: 5 wings was heard *even* to the **u** court, 2435
24: 3 **u** a parable unto the rebellious house, and 4911
40:31 the arches thereof *were* toward the **u** court; 2435
40:37 the posts thereof *were* toward the **u** court; 2435
42: 1 he brought me forth into the **u** court, 2435
42: 3 the pavement which *was* for the **u** court, 2435
42: 7 towards the **u** court on the forepart of 2435
42: 8 that *were* in the **u** court *was* fifty cubits: 2435
42: 9 as one goeth into them from the **u** court. 2435
42:14 go out of the holy *place* into the **u** court, 2435
44:19 when they go forth into the **u** court, 2435
44:19 *even* into the **u** court to the people, 2435
46:20 that *they* bear *them* not out into the **u** court, 2435
46:21 he brought me forth into the **u** court, 2435
47: 2 led me about the way without unto the **u** 2351
Joel 2:11 the LORD shall **u** his voice before his 5414
3:16 of Zion, and **u** his voice from Jerusalem; 5414
Am 1: 2 from Zion, and **u** his voice from Jerusalem; 5414
Na 1: 8 he will make an **u end** of the place thereof, 3617
1: 9 he *will* make an **u end**: affliction shall not 3617
Zec 14:11 and there shall be no more **u destruction**; 2764
Mt 13:35 I will **u** *things which have been* kept secret *2044*
1Co 14: 9 except ye **u** by the tongue words easy to be *1325*
2Co 12: 4 which *it is* not lawful for a man to **u.** *2980*

UTTERANCE (5) [UTTER]

Ac 2: 4 other tongues, as the Spirit gave them **u**. *669*
1Co 1: 5 by him, in all **u**, and *in* all knowledge; *3056*
2Co 8: 7 and **u**, and knowledge, and *in* all diligence, *3056*
Eph 6:19 And for me, that **u** may be given unto me, *3056*
Col 4: 3 that God would open unto us a door of **u**, *3056*

UTTERED (17) [UTTER]

Nu 30: 6 she vowed, or **u ought out** of her lips, 4008
30: 8 **that which** she **u** with her lips, 4008
Jdg 11:11 Jephthah **u** all his words before the LORD 1696
2Sa 22:14 and the most High **u** his voice. 5414
Ne 6:19 deeds before me, and **u** my words to him. 3318
Job 26: 4 To whom hast thou **u** words? and 5046
42: 3 therefore have I **u** that I understood not; 5046
Ps 46: 6 he **u** his voice, the earth melted. 5414
66:14 Which my lips have **u**, and my mouth hath 6475
Jer 48:34 *even* unto Jahaz, have they **u** their voice, 5414
51:55 like great waters, a noise of their voice is **u**: 5414
Hab 3:10 the deep **u** his voice, *and* lift up his hands 5414
Ro 8:26 for us with groanings which **cannot be u**. *215*
Heb 5:11 and hard to be **u**, seeing ye are dull of *3004*
Rev 10: 3 he had cried, seven thunders **u** their voices. *2980*
10: 4 And when the seven thunders had **u** their *2980*
10: 4 *up those things* which the seven thunders **u**, *2980*

UTTERETH (9) [UTTER]

Job 15: 5 For thy mouth **u** thine iniquity, and 502
Ps 19: 2 Day unto day **u** speech, and night unto 5042
Pr 1:20 she **u** her voice in the streets: 5414
1:21 in the city she **u** her words, *saying,* 559
10:18 lying lips, and he that **u** a slander, *is* a fool. 3318
29:11 A fool **u** all his mind: but a wise *man* 3318
Jer 10:13 When he **u** his voice, *there is* a multitude of 5414
51:16 When he **u** *his* voice, *there is* a multitude of 5414
Mic 7: 3 the great *man,* he **u** his mischievous desire: 1696

UTTERING (1) [UTTER]

Isa 59:13 and **u** from the heart words of falsehood. 1897

UTTERLY (101) [UTTER]

Ex 17:14 for I will **u put out** the remembrance 4229+4229
22:17 If her father **u refuse** to give her unto 3985+3985
22:20 the LORD only, he shall be **u destroyed.** 2763
23:24 thou shalt **u overthrow** them, and 2040+2040
Lev 13:44 shall **pronounce** him **u unclean,** 2930+2930
26:44 to **destroy** them **u**, and to break my 3615
Nu 15:31 that soul shall **u** be **cut off;** 3772+3772
21: 2 my hand, then I will **u destroy** their cities. 2763
21: 3 and they **u destroyed** them and their cities: 2763
30:12 **u made** them **void** on the day he 6565+6565
Dt 2:34 **u destroyed** the men, and the women, and 2763
3: 6 we **u destroyed** them, as we did unto Sihon 2763
3: 6 **u destroying** the men, women, and 2763
4:26 that ye shall soon **u perish** from off the land 6+6
4:26 *your* days upon it, but shall **u** be destroyed. NIH
7: 2 thou shalt smite them, *and* **u destroy** 2763+2763
7:26 *but* thou shalt **u detest** it, and 8262+8262
7:26 detest it, and thou shalt **u abhor** it; 8581+8581
12: 2 Ye shall **u destroy** all the places, 6+6
13:15 **destroying** it **u**, and all that *is* therein, 2763
20:17 thou shalt **u destroy** them; 2763+2763
31:29 death ye will **u corrupt** *yourselves,* 7843+7843
Jos 2:10 and Og, whom ye **u destroyed.** 2763
6:21 they **u destroyed** all that *was* in the city, 2763
8:26 until *he* had **u destroyed** all the inhabitants 2763
10: 1 had taken Ai, and had **u destroyed** it; 2763
10:28 the king thereof he **u destroyed**, them, 2763
10:35 that *were* therein he **u destroyed** that day, 2763
10:37 **destroyed** it **u**, and all the souls that *were* 2763
10:39 **u destroyed** all the souls that *were* therein; 2763
10:40 but **u destroyed** all that breathed, 2763
11:11 **u destroying** *them:* there was not any left 2763
11:12 of the sword, *and* he **u destroyed** them, 2763
11:20 that *he* might **destroy** them **u**, *and* that they 2763
11:21 Joshua **destroyed** them **u** with their cities. 2763
17:13 but did not **u drive** them **out.** 3423+3423
Jdg 1:17 that inhabited Zephath, and **u destroyed** it: 2763
1:28 and did not **u drive** them **out.** 3423+3423
15: 2 thought that thou hadst **u hated** her; 8130+8130
21:11 Ye shall **u destroy** every male, and 2763
1Sa 15: 3 **u destroy** all that they have, and 2763
15: 8 **u destroyed** all the people with the edge of 2763
15: 9 *was* good, and would not **u destroy** them: 2763
15: 9 *was* vile and refuse, that they **destroyed u.** 2763
15:15 thy God; and the rest we have **u destroyed.** 2763
15:18 and **u destroy** the sinners the Amalekites, 2763
15:20 and have **u destroyed** the Amalekites. 2763
15:21 **things** which should have been **u destroyed,** 2764
27:12 **made** his people Israel **u to abhor** him; 887+887
2Sa 17:10 *is* as the heart of a lion, shall **u melt:** 4549+4549
23: 7 they shall be **u burnt** with fire in 8313+8313
1Ki 9:21 of Israel also were not able **u** to **destroy,** 2763
2Ki 19:11 done to all lands, by **destroying** them **u**: 2763
1Ch 4:41 **destroyed** them **u** unto this day, and 2763
2Ch 20:23 **u to slay** and destroy *them:* and when they 2763
31: 1 until *they* had **u destroyed** *them all.* Then 3615
32:14 those nations that my fathers **u destroyed,** 2763
Ne 9:31 sake thou didst not **u consume** them, 3617
Ps 37:24 he fall, he shall not be **u cast down**: 2904
73:19 they are **u** consumed with terrors. 8552
89:33 lovingkindness will I not **u take** from him, 6331
119: 8 thy statutes: O forsake me not **u.** 3966+5704
119:43 take not the word of truth **u** out of 3966+5704
SS 8: 7 for love, it would **u** be **contemned.** 936+936
Isa 2:18 And the idols he shall **u** abolish. 3632
6:11 without man, and the land be **u** desolate, 8077
11:15 the LORD shall **u destroy** the tongue of 2763
24: 3 The land shall be **u emptied,** 1238+1238
24: 3 shall be utterly emptied, and **u spoiled**: 962+962

Isa 24:19 The earth is **u broken down**, 7489+7489
34: 2 he hath **u destroyed** them, he hath 2763
37:11 done to all lands by **destroying** them **u**; 2763
40:30 and the young men shall **u fall**: 3782+3782
56: 3 The LORD hath **u separated** me from 914+914
60:12 yea, *those* nations shall be **u wasted**. 2717+2717
Jer 9: 4 for every brother will **u supplant**, 6117+6117
12:17 I will **u pluck up** and destroy that 5428+5428
14:19 Hast thou **u rejected** Judah? hath thy 3988+3988
23:39 will **u forget** you, and I will forsake 5377+5382
25: 9 will **u destroy** them, and make them an 2763
25:29 and should ye be **u unpunished**? 5352+5352
50:21 waste and **u destroy** after them, saith 2763
50:26 cast her up as heaps, and **destroy** her **u**: 2763
51: 3 her young men; **destroy** ye **u** all her host. 2763
51:58 walls of Babylon shall be **u broken**, 6209+6209
La 5:22 thou hast **u rejected** us; thou art very 3988+3988
Eze 9: 6 Slay **u** old *and* young, both maids, 4889+3807.1
17:10 shall it not **u wither**, when the east 3001+3001
27:31 they shall **make** themselves **u bald** 7139+7139
29:10 make the land of Egypt **u waste** *and* 2721+2723
Da 11:44 fury to destroy, and **u** to **make away** many. 2763
Hos 1: 6 but I will **u take them away**. 5375+5375
10:15 shall the king of Israel **u** be **cut off**. 1820+1820
Am 9: 8 saving that I will not **u destroy** 8045+8045
Mic 2: 4 *and* say, We be **u spoiled**: 7703+7703
Na 1:15 no more pass through thee; he is **u** cut off. 3605
Zep 1: 2 I will **u** consume all *things* from off the land, 622
Zec 11:17 his right eye shall be **u darkened**. 3543+3543
1Co 6: 7 therefore there is **u** a fault among you, *3654*
2Pe 2:12 and shall **u perish** in their own corruption; *2704*
Rev 18: 8 famine; and she shall be **u burnt** with fire: *2618*

UTTERMOST (28) [UTTER]
Ex 26: 4 likewise shalt thou make in the **u** edge of 7020
36:11 likewise he made in the **u** side of *another* 7020
36:17 he made fifty loops upon the **u** edge of 7020
Nu 11: 1 consumed *them that were* in the **u parts** of 7097
20:16 *are* in Kadesh, a city in the **u** of thy border: 7097
Dt 11:24 even unto the **u** sea shall your coast be. 314
Jos 15: 1 *was* the **u part** of the south *coast*. 4480+7097
15: 5 the bay of the sea at the **u part** of Jordan: 7097
15:21 the **u** cities of the tribe of 4480+7097
1Sa 14: 2 Saul tarried in the **u part** of Gibeah under a 7097
1Ki 6:24 from the **u part** of the one wing unto 7098
6:24 unto the **u part** of the other *were* ten cubits. 7098
2Ki 7: 5 when they were come to the **u part** of 7097
7: 8 when these lepers came to the **u part** of 7097
Ne 1: 9 you cast out unto the **u part** of the heaven, 7097
Ps 2: 8 the **u parts** of the earth *for* thy possession. 657
65: 8 They also that dwell in the **u parts** are 7099
139: 9 *and* dwell in the **u parts** of the sea; 319
Isa 7:18 that *is* in the **u part** of the rivers of Egypt, 7097
24:16 From the **u part** of the earth have we heard 3671
Mt 5:26 out thence, till thou hast paid the **u** farthing. *2078*
12:42 for she came from the **u parts** of the earth *4009*
Mk 13:27 from the **u part** of the earth to the uttermost *206*
13:27 part of the earth to the **u part** of heaven. *206*
Ac 1: 8 and unto the **u part** of the earth. *2078*
24:22 I will **know the u** of your matter. *1231*
1Th 2:16 for the wrath is come upon them to the **u**. *5056*
Heb 7:25 them to the **u** that come unto God by him, *3838*

UZ (7)
Ge 10:23 **U**, and Hul, and Gether, and Mash. 5780
36:28 children of Dishan *are* these; **U**, and Aran. 5780
1Ch 1:17 and **U**, and Hul, and Gether, and Meshech. 5780
1:42 Jakan. The sons of Dishan; **U**, and Aran. 5780
Job 1: 1 There was a man in the land of **U**, 5780
Jer 25:20 all the kings of the land of **U**, and all 5780
La 4:21 of Edom, that dwellest in the land of **U**; 5780

UZAI (1)
Ne 3:25 Palal the son of **U**, over against the turning 186

UZAL (2)
Ge 10:27 And Hadoram, and **U**, and Diklah, 187
1Ch 1:21 Hadoram also, and **U**, and Diklah, 187

UZZA (10) [UZZAH]
2Ki 21:18 of his own house, in the garden of **U**: 5798
21:26 buried in his sepulchre in the garden of **U**: 5798
1Ch 6:29 Libni his son, Shimei his son, **U** his son, 5798
8: 7 removed them, and begat **U**, and Ahihud. 5798
13: 7 and **U** and Ahio drave the cart. 5798
13: 9 **U** put forth his hand to hold the ark; 5798
13:10 of the LORD was kindled against **U**, 5798
13:11 the LORD had made a breach upon **U**: 5798
Ezr 2:49 The children of **U**, the children of Paseah, 5798
Ne 7:51 the children of **U**, the children of Phaseah, 5798

UZZAH (4) [PEREZ-UZZA, PEREZ-UZZAH, UZZA]
2Sa 6: 3 **U** and Ahio, the sons of Abinadab, 5798
6: 6 **U** put forth *his hand* to the ark of God, and 5798
6: 7 of the LORD was kindled against **U**; 5798
6: 8 the LORD had made a breach upon **U**: 5798

UZZEN SHEERAH See UZZEN-SHERAH

UZZEN-SHERAH (1)
1Ch 7:24 the nether, and the upper, and **U**.) 242

UZZI (11)
1Ch 6: 5 Abishua begat Bukki, and Bukki begat **U**, 5813
6: 6 **U** begat Zerahiah, and Zerahiah begat 5813
6:51 Bukki his son, **U** his son, Zerahiah his son, 5813
7: 2 **U**, and Rephaiah, and Jeriel, and Jahmai, 5813
7: 3 the sons of **U**; Izrahiah: and the sons of 5813
7: 7 **U**, and Uzziel, and Jerimoth, and Iri, five; 5813
9: 8 Elah the son of **U**, the son of Michri, and 5813
Ezr 7: 4 of Zerahiah, the son of **U**, the son of Bukki, 5813
Ne 11:22 Levites at Jerusalem *was* **U** the son of Bani, 5813
12:19 And of Joiarib, Mattenai; of Jedaiah, **U**; 5813
12:42 **U**, and Jehohanan, and Malchijah, and 5813

UZZIA (1)
1Ch 11:44 **U** the Ashterathite, Shama and Jehiel 5814

UZZIAH (27) [AZARIAH]
2Ki 15:13 and thirtieth year of **U** king of Judah; 5818
15:30 the twentieth year of Jotham the son of **U**. 5818
15:32 Jotham the son of **U** king of Judah to reign. 5818
15:34 he did according to all that his father **U** had 5818
1Ch 6:24 Uriel his son, **U** his son, and Shaul his son. 5818
27:25 in the castles, *was* Jehonathan the son of **U**: 5818
2Ch 26: 1 all the people of Judah took **U**, who *was* 5818
26: 3 Sixteen years old *was* **U** when he *began* to 5818
26: 8 the Ammonites gave gifts to **U**: and 5818
26: 9 Moreover **U** built towers in Jerusalem at 5818
26:11 Moreover **U** had a host of fighting *men*, 5818
26:14 **U** prepared for them throughout all the host 5818
26:18 they withstood **U** the king, and said unto 5818
26:18 unto him, *It pertaineth* not unto thee, **U**, 5818
26:19 **U** was wroth, and *had* a censer in his hand 5818
26:21 **U** the king was a leper unto the day of his 5818
26:22 Now the rest of the acts of **U**, first and last, 5818
26:23 So **U** slept with his fathers, and they buried 5818
27: 2 according to all that his father **U** did: 5818
Ezr 10:21 Elijah, and Shemaiah, and Jehiel, and **U**. 5818
Ne 11: 4 Athaiah the son of **U**, the son of Zechariah, 5818
Isa 1: 1 and Jerusalem in the days of **U**, 5818
6: 1 In the year that king **U** died I saw also 5818
7: 1 the son of **U** king of Judah, *that* Rezin 5818
Hos 1: 1 in the days of **U**, Jotham, Ahaz, *and* 5818
Am 1: 1 Israel in the days of **U** king of Judah, 5818
Zec 14: 5 earthquake in the days of **U** king of Judah: 5818

UZZIEL (16) [UZZIELITES]
Ex 6:18 Amram, and Izhar, and Hebron, and **U**: 5816
6:22 the sons of **U**; Mishael, and Elzaphan, and 5816
Lev 10: 4 the sons of **U** the uncle of Aaron, and 5816
Nu 3:19 Amram, and Izehar, Hebron, and **U**. 5816
3:30 Kohathites *shall be* Elizaphan the son of **U**. 5816
1Ch 4:42 Neariah, and Rephaiah, and **U**, the sons of 5816
6: 2 Amram, Izhar, and Hebron, and **U**. 5816
6:18 and Izhar, and Hebron, and **U**. 5816
7: 7 Uzzi, and **U**, and Jerimoth, and Iri, five; 5816
15:10 Of the sons of **U**; Amminadab the chief, 5816
23:12 Amram, Izhar, Hebron, and **U**, four. 5816
23:20 *Of* the sons of **U**; Michah the first, and 5816
24:24 *Of* the sons of **U**; Michah: of the sons of 5816
25: 4 **U**, Shebuel, and Jerimoth, Hananiah, 5816
2Ch 29:14 of the sons of Jeduthun; Shemaiah, and **U**. 5816
Ne 3: 8 Next unto him repaired **U** the son of 5816

UZZIELITES (2) [UZZIEL]
Nu 3:27 of the Hebronites, and the family of the **U**: 5817
1Ch 26:23 the Izharites, the Hebronites, *and* the **U**: 5817

V

VAGABOND (3) [VAGABONDS]
Ge 4:12 a fugitive and a v shalt thou be in the earth. 5110
4:14 and I shall be a fugitive and a v in the earth; 5110
Ac 19:13 Then certain of the v Jews, exorcists, *4022*

VAGABONDS (1) [VAGABOND]
Ps 109:10 Let his children be **continually** v, 5128+5128

VAIL (45) [VAILS]
Ge 24:65 therefore she took a v, and covered herself. 6809
38:14 covered her with a v, and wrapped herself, 6809
38:19 laid by her v from her, and put on 6809
Ex 26:31 thou shalt make a v *of* blue, and purple, 6532
26:33 thou shalt hang up the v under the taches, 6532
26:33 within the v the ark of the Testimony: 6532
26:33 the v shall divide unto you between 6532
26:35 thou shalt set the table without the v, and 6532
27:21 of the congregation without the v, 6532
30:6 thou shalt put it before the v that *is* by 6532
34:33 speaking with them, he put a v on his face. 4533
34:34 he took the v off, until he came out. 4533
34:35 Moses put the v upon his face again, 4533
35:12 the mercy seat, and the v of the covering, 6532
36:35 he made a v *of* blue, and purple, and 6532
38:27 of the sanctuary, and the sockets of the v; 6532
39:34 of badgers' skins, and the v of the covering, 6532
40:3 and cover the ark with the v. 6532
40:21 set up the v of the covering, and 6532
40:22 of the tabernacle northward, without the v. 6532
40:26 in the tent of the congregation before the v: 6532
Lev 4:6 the LORD, before the v of the sanctuary. 6532
4:17 times before the LORD, *even* before the v. 6532
16:2 *place* within the v before the mercy seat, 6532
16:12 beaten small, and bring *it* within the v: 6532
16:15 bring his blood within the v, and do with 6532
21:23 Only he shall not go in unto the v, 6532
24:3 Without the v of the Testimony, in 6532
Nu 4:5 they shall take down the covering v, and 6532
18:7 every thing of the altar, and within the v; 6532
Ru 3:15 Bring the v that *thou hast* upon thee, and 4304
2Ch 3:14 he made the v *of* blue, and purple, and 6532
SS 5:7 the keepers of the walls took away my v 7289
Isa 25:7 and the v that is spread over all nations. 4541
Mt 27:51 the v of the temple was rent in twain from *2665*
Mk 15:38 And the v of the temple was rent in twain *2665*
Lk 23:45 the v of the temple was rent in the midst. *2665*
2Co 3:13 not as Moses, *which* put a v over his face, *2571*
3:14 for until this day remaineth the same v *2571*
3:14 which *v* is done away in Christ. NIG
3:15 Moses is read, the v is upon their heart. *2571*
3:16 turn to the Lord, the v shall be taken away. *2571*
Heb 6:19 and which entereth into that within the v; *2665*
9:3 And after the second v, the tabernacle *2665*
10:20 through the v, that is to say, his flesh; *2665*

VAILS (1) [VAIL]
Isa 3:23 and the fine linen, and the hoods, and the v. 7289

VAIN (112) [VAINGLORY, VAINLY, VANITIES, VANITY]
Ex 5:9 and let them not regard v words. 8267
20:7 take the name of the LORD thy God in v; 7723
20:7 hold him guiltless that taketh his name in v. 7723
Lev 26:16 ye shall sow your seed in v, for your 7385
26:20 your strength shall be spent in v: for your 7385
Dt 5:11 take the name of the LORD thy God in v: 7723
5:11 hold *him* guiltless that taketh his name in v. 7723
32:47 For it *is* not a v thing for you; because it *is* 7386
Jdg 9:4 wherewith Abimelech hired v and 7386
11:3 there were gathered v men to Jephthah, and 7386
1Sa 12:21 *should ye go* after v *things,* which cannot 8414
12:21 cannot profit nor deliver; for they *are* v. 8414
25:21 Surely **in** v have I kept all 8267+1886.1+3807.1
2Sa 6:20 as one of the v *fellows* shamelessly 7386
2Ki 17:15 became v, and *went* after the heathen that 1891
18:20 Thou sayest, (but *they are but* v words,) 8193
2Ch 13:7 there are gathered unto him v men, 7386
Job 9:29 *If* I be wicked, why then labour I **in** v? 1892
11:11 For he knoweth v men: he seeth 7723
11:12 For v man would be wise, though man be 5014
15:2 Should a wise *man* utter v knowledge, and 7307
16:3 Shall v words have an end? or 7307
21:34 How then comfort ye me **in** v, seeing *in* 1892
27:12 seen *it;* why then are ye thus **altogether** v? 1892
35:16 Therefore doth Job open his mouth **in** v; 1892
39:16 not hers: her labour *is* in v without fear; 7385
41:9 Behold, the hope of him is **in** v: shall *not* 3576
Ps 2:1 and the people imagine a v *thing?* 7385
26:4 I have not sat with v persons, neither will I 7723
33:17 A horse *is* a v **thing** for safety: neither shall 8267
39:6 Surely every man walketh **in a** v **shew**: 6754
39:6 surely they are disquieted **in** v: he heapeth 1892
60:11 help from trouble: for v *is* the help of man. 7723
62:10 and become not v in robbery: 1891
73:13 Verily I have cleansed my heart *in* v, and 7385
89:47 wherefore hast thou made all men **in** v? 7723
108:12 help from trouble: for v *is* the help of man. 7723
119:113 I hate *v* thoughts: but thy law do I love. NIH
127:1 the house, they labour **in** v that build it: 7723
127:1 the city, the watchman waketh *but* **in** v. 7723
127:2 *It is* v for you to rise up early, to sit up late, 7723
139:20 *and* thine enemies take *thy name* in v. 7723
Pr 1:17 Surely **in** v the net *is* spread in the sight of 2600
12:11 he that followeth v *persons is* void of 7386
28:19 he that followeth after v *persons* shall have 7386
30:9 steal, and take the name of my God *in* v. NIH
31:30 Favour *is* deceitful, and beauty *is* v: *but* 1892
Ecc 6:12 all the days of his v life which he spendeth 1892
Isa 1:13 Bring no more v oblations; incense *is* an 7723
30:7 For the Egyptians shall help **in** v, and to no 1892
36:5 *sayest thou,* (but *they are but* v words) 8193
45:18 he hath established it, he created it not **in** v, 8414
45:19 unto the seed of Jacob, Seek ye me **in** v: 8414
49:4 I said, I have laboured in v, I have spent my 7385
49:4 spent my strength for nought, and **in** v: 1892
65:23 They shall not labour in v, nor bring forth 7385
Jer 2:5 walked after vanity, and are **become** v? 1891
2:30 **In** v have I smitten your 7723+1886.1+3807.1
3:23 Truly in v *is salvation hoped for* from 8267
4:14 How long shall thy v thoughts lodge within 205
4:30 in v shalt thou make thyself fair; 7723
6:29 the founder melteth **in** v: 7723+1886.1+3807.1
8:8 certainly **in** v made he *it;* the pen of 8267
8:8 made he *it;* the pen of the scribes *is* in v. 8267
10:3 For the customs of the people *are* v: for *one* 1892
23:16 they **make** you v: they speak a vision of 1891
46:11 in v shalt thou use many medicines; *for* 7723
50:9 a mighty expert *man;* none shall return **in** v. 7387
51:58 the people shall labour in v, and the folk in 7385
La 2:14 Thy prophets have seen v and 7723
4:17 for us, our eyes as yet failed for our v help: 1892
Eze 6:10 *that* I have not said in v that *I* would do this 2600
12:24 For there shall be no more any v vision nor 7723
13:7 Have ye not seen a v vision, and have ye 7723
Zec 10:2 have told false dreams; they comfort **in** v: 1892
Mal 3:14 Ye have said, It *is* v to serve God: and 7723
Mt 6:7 But when ye pray, **use not** v **repetitions**, *945*
15:9 But **in** v they do worship me, teaching for *3155*
Mk 7:7 Howbeit **in** v do they worship me, *3155*
Ac 4:25 and the people imagine v *things?* *2756*
Ro 1:21 but became **v** in their imaginations, and *3154*
13:4 be afraid; for he beareth not the sword **in** v: *1500*
1Co 3:20 the thoughts of the wise, that they are v. *3152*
15:2 unto you, unless ye have believed **in** v. *1500*
15:10 which was *bestowed* upon me was not **in** v; *2756*
15:14 then *is* our preaching v, and your faith *is* *2756*
15:14 our preaching vain, and your faith *is* also v. *2756*
15:17 And if Christ be not raised, your faith *is* v; *3152*
15:58 that your labour is not **in** v in the Lord. *2756*
2Co 6:1 that ye receive not the grace of God in v. *2756*
9:3 lest our boasting of you should be **in** v in *2758*
Gal 2:2 by any means I should run, or had run, in v. *2756*
2:21 *come* by the law, then Christ is dead **in** v. *1432*
3:4 Have ye suffered so many *things* **in** v? if *it* *1500*
3:4 so many *things* in vain? if *it be* yet **in** v. *1500*
4:11 lest I have bestowed upon you labour **in** v. *1500*
5:26 Let us not be desirous of **v glory**, *2755*
Eph 5:6 Let no *man* deceive you with v words: for *2756*
Php 2:16 that I have not run in v, neither laboured in *2756*
2:16 have not run in vain, neither laboured in v. *2756*
Col 2:8 spoil you through philosophy and v deceit, *2756*
1Th 2:1 entrance in unto you, that it was not in v: *2756*

1Th 3: 5 have tempted you, and our labour be in v. *2756*
1Ti 1: 6 swerved have turned aside unto v **jangling**; *3150*
6:20 avoiding profane *and* v **babblings**, and *2757*
2Ti 2:16 But shun profane *and* v **babblings**: for they *2757*
Tit 1:10 many unruly and v **talkers** and deceivers, *3151*
3: 9 the law; for they are unprofitable and v. *3152*
Jas 1:26 his own heart, this *man's* religion *is* v. *3152*
2:20 But wilt thou know, O v man, that faith *2756*
4: 5 Do ye think that the scripture saith **in** v, *2761*
1Pe 1:18 from your v conversation received by *3152*

VAINGLORY (1) [GLORY, VAIN]
Php 2: 3 *Let* nothing *be done* through strife or v; but *2754*

VAINLY (1) [VAIN]
Col 2:18 hath not seen, v puft up by his fleshly mind, *1500*

VAIZATHA See VAJEZATHA

VAJEZATHA (1)
Est 9: 9 and Arisai, and Aridai, and V, 2055

VALE (9) [VALLEY]
Ge 14: 3 All these were joined together in the v of 6010
14: 8 they joined battle with them in the v of 6010
14:10 the v of Siddim *was* full of slimepits; 6010
37:14 So he sent him out of the v of Hebron, and 6010
Dt 1: 7 in the v, and in the south, and by the sea 8219
Jos 10:40 of the v, and of the springs, and all their 8219
1Ki 10:27 *to be* as the sycomore trees that *are* in the v, 8219
2Ch 1:15 trees that *are* in the v for abundance. 8219
Jer 33:13 in the cities of the v, and in the cities of 8219

VALIANT (31) [VALOUR]
1Sa 14:52 or any v man, he took him unto him. 2428
16:18 a mighty v *man,* and a man of war, and 2428
18:17 only be thou v for me, and fight 1121+2428
26:15 David said to Abner, *Art* not thou a v man? NIH
31:12 All the v men arose, and went all night, and 2428
2Sa 2: 7 hands be strengthened, and be ye v: 1121+2428
11:16 a place where he knew that v men *were.* 2428
13:28 be courageous, and be v. 1121+2428
17:10 he also *that is* v, whose heart *is* as 1121+2428
17:10 and *they* which *be* with him *are* v men. 2428
23:20 the son of a v man, of Kabzeel, who had 2428
24: 9 thousand v men that drew the sword; 2428
1Ki 1:42 for thou *art* a v man, and bringest good 2428
1Ch 5:18 of v men, men *able to* bear buckler and 2428
7: 2 *they were* v *men* of might in their 1368
10:12 all the v men, and took away the body of 2428
11:22 the son of a v man of Kabzeel, who had 2428
11:26 Also the v *men* of the armies *were,* Asahel 1368
28: 1 the mighty *men,* and with all the v men, 2428
2Ch 13: 3 in array with an army of v *men* of war, 1368
26:17 priests of the LORD, *that were* v men: 2428
28: 6 thousand in one day, *which were* all v men; 2428
Ne 11: 6 four hundred threescore and eight v men. 2428
SS 3: 7 threescore v *men are* about it, of the valiant 1368
3: 7 valiant *men are* about it, of the v of Israel. 1368
Isa 10:13 I have put down the inhabitants like a v *man:* 47
33: 7 Behold, their v **ones** shall cry without: 691
Jer 9: 3 they are not v for the truth upon the earth; 1396
46:15 Why are thy v *men* swept away? they stood 47
Na 2: 3 *men is* made red, the v men *are* in scarlet: 2428
Heb 11:34 were made strong, waxed v in fight, *2478*

VALIANTEST (1) [VALOUR]
Jdg 21:10 thither twelve thousand men of the v, 1121+2428

VALIANTLY (6) [VALOUR]
Nu 24:18 for his enemies; and Israel shall do v. 2428
1Ch 19:13 let us **behave** ourselves v for our people, 2388
Ps 60:12 Through God we shall do v: for he *it is that* 2428
108:13 Through God we shall do v: for he *it is that* 2428
118:15 the right hand of the LORD doeth v. 2428
118:16 the right hand of the LORD doeth v. 2428

VALLEY (140) [VALE, VALLEYS]
Ge 14:17 at the v of Shaveh, which *is* the king's dale. 6010
26:17 pitched his tent in the v of Gerar, and 5158
26:19 Isaac's servants digged in the v, and 5158
Nu 14:25 and the Canaanites dwelt in the v.) 6010
21:12 and pitched in the v of Zared. 5158
21:20 from Bamoth *in* the v, that *is* in the country 1516
32: 9 For when they went up unto the v of 5158
Dt 1:24 came unto the v of Eshcol, and searched it 5158
3:16 half the v, and the border, even unto 5158
3:29 So we abode in the v over against 1516
4:46 in the v over against Beth-peor, 1516
21: 4 shall bring down the heifer unto a rough v, 5158
21: 4 strike off the heifer's neck there in the v: 5158
21: 6 over the heifer that is beheaded in the v: 5158
34: 3 the south, and the plain of the v of Jericho, 1237
34: 6 he buried him in a v in the land of Moab, 1516
Jos 7:24 and they brought them *unto* the v of Achor. 6010
7:26 was called, The v of Achor, unto this day. 6010
8:11 now *there was* a v between them and Ai. 1516
8:13 went that night into the midst of the v. 6010
10:12 and thou, Moon, in the v of Ajalon. 6010
11: 2 in the v, and in the borders of Dor on 8219
11: 8 and unto the v of Mizpeh eastward; 1237
11:16 the v, and the plain, and the mountain of 8219
11:16 mountain of Israel, and the v of the same; 8219
11:17 even unto Baal-gad in the v of Lebanon 1237
12: 7 from Baal-gad in the v of Lebanon even 1237
13:19 and Zareth-shahar in the mount of the v, 6010
13:27 in the v, Beth-aram, and Beth-nimrah, and 6010
15: 7 the border went up toward Debir from the v 6010
15: 8 the border went up *by* the v of the son of 1516
15: 8 that *lieth* before the v of Hinnom westward, 1516
15: 8 which *is* at the end of the v of the giants 6010
15:33 *And* in the v, Eshtaol, and Zoreah, and 8219
17:16 in the land of the v have chariots of iron, 6010
17:16 and *they* who *are* of the v of Jezreel. 6010
18:16 *lieth* before the v of the son of Hinnom, 1516
18:16 which *is* in the v of the giants on the north, 6010
18:16 descended *to* the v of Hinnom, to the side 1516
18:21 and Beth-hoglah, and the v of Keziz, 6010
19:14 the outgoings thereof are *in* the v of 1516
19:27 to the v of Jiphthah-el toward the north side 1516
Jdg 1: 9 the mountain, and in the south, and in the v. 8219
1:19 could not drive out the inhabitants of the v, 6010
1:34 not suffer them to come down to the v: 6010
5:15 he was sent on foot into the v. For 6010
6:33 went over, and pitched in the v of Jezreel. 6010
7: 1 side of them, by the hill of Moreh, in the v. 6010
7: 8 host of Midian was beneath him in the v. 6010
7:12 all the children of the east lay along in the v 6010
16: 4 that he loved a woman in the v of Sorek, 5158
18:28 and it was in the v that *lieth* by Beth-rehob. 6010
1Sa 6:13 *were* reaping *their* wheat harvest in the v: 6010
13:18 to the v of Zeboim toward the wilderness. 1516
15: 5 to a city of Amalek, and laid wait in the v. 5158
17: 2 pitched by the v of Elah, and set the battle 6010
17: 3 other side: and *there was* a v between them. 1516
17:19 all the men of Israel, *were* in the v of Elah, 6010
17:52 until thou come *to* the v, and to the gates of 1516
21: 9 whom thou slewest in the v of Elah, 6010
31: 7 Israel that *were* on the *other* side of the v, 6010
2Sa 5:18 and spread themselves in the v of Rephaim. 6010
5:22 and spread themselves in the v of Rephaim. 6010
8:13 from smiting of the Syrians in the v of salt, 1516
23:13 the troop of the Philistines pitched in the v 6010
2Ki 2:16 him upon some mountain, or into some v. 1516
3:16 the LORD, Make this v full of ditches. 5158
3:17 yet that v shall be filled *with* water, that ye 5158
14: 7 He slew *of* Edom in the v of salt ten 1516
23:10 which *is* in the v of the children of Hinnom, 1516
1Ch 4:14 the father of the v of Charashim; 1516
4:39 *even* unto the east *side* of the v, to seek 1516
10: 7 Israel that *were* in the v saw that they fled, 6010
11:15 Philistines encamped in the v of Rephaim. 6010
14: 9 and spread themselves in the v of Rephaim. 6010
14:13 again spread themselves abroad in the v. 6010
18:12 Edomites in the v of salt eighteen thousand. 1516
2Ch 14:10 they set the battle in array in the v of 1516
20:26 assembled themselves in the v of Berachah; 6010
20:26 The v of Berachah, unto *this* day. 6010
25:11 went *to* the v of salt, and smote *of* 1516
26: 9 at the v gate, and at the turning *of the wall,* 1516
28: 3 Moreover he burnt incense in the v of 1516
33: 6 the fire in the v of the son of Hinnom: 1516
33:14 on the west *side* of Gihon, in the v, even to 5158
35:22 and came to fight in the v of Megiddo. 1237
Ne 2:13 I went out by night by the gate of the v, 1516
2:15 entered by the gate of the v, and *so* 1516
3:13 The v gate repaired Hanun, and 1516
11:30 they dwelt from Beer-sheba unto the v of 1516
11:35 Lod, and Ono, the v of craftsmen. 1516

Job 21:33 The clods of the v shall be sweet unto him, 5158
39:21 He paweth in the v, and rejoiceth in *his* 6010
Ps 23: 4 though I walk through the v of the shadow 1516
60: T smote of Edom in the v of salt twelve 1516
60: 6 and mete out the v of Succoth. 6010
84: 6 *Who* passing through the v of Baca make it 6010
108: 7 and mete out the v of Succoth. 6010
Pr 30:17 the ravens of the v shall pick it out, and 5158
SS 6:11 the garden of nuts to see the fruits of the v, 5158
Isa 17: 5 it shall be as he that gathereth ears in the v 6010
22: 1 The burden of the v of vision. What aileth 1516
22: 5 the Lord GOD of hosts in the v of vision, 1516
28: 4 which *is* on the head of the fat v, shall be a 1516
28:21 he shall be wroth as *in* the v of Gibeon, 6010
40: 4 Every v shall be exalted, and 1516
63:14 As a beast goeth down into the v, the Spirit 1237
65:10 the v of Achor a place for the herds to lie 6010
Jer 2:23 see thy way in the v, know what thou hast 1516
7:31 which *is* in the v of the son of Hinnom, 1516
7:32 nor the v of the son of Hinnom, but 1516
7:32 the son of Hinnom, but the v of slaughter: 1516
19: 2 go forth unto the v of the son of Hinnom, 1516
19: 6 nor The v of the son of Hinnom, but The 1516
19: 6 the son of Hinnom, but The v of slaughter. 1516
21:13 O inhabitant of the v, *and* rock of the plain, 6010
31:40 the whole v of the dead bodies, and of 6010
32:35 which *are* in the v of the son of Hinnom, 1516
32:44 in the cities of the v, and in the cities of 8219
47: 5 is cut off *with* the remnant of their v: 6010
48: 8 the v also shall perish, and the plain shall 6010
49: 4 thy flowing v, O backsliding daughter? 6010
Eze 37: 1 set me down in the midst of the v which 1237
37: 2 *there were* very many in the open v; 1237
39:11 the v of the passengers *on* the east of 1516
39:11 and they shall call *it* The v of Hamon-gog. 1516
39:15 till the buriers have buried it in the v of 1516
Hos 1: 5 that I will break the bow of Israel in the v 6010
2:15 and the v of Achor for a door of hope: 6010
Joel 3: 2 will bring them down into the v of 6010
3:12 and come up to the v of Jehoshaphat: 6010
3:14 Multitudes, multitudes in the v of decision: 6010
3:14 for the day of the LORD *is* near in the v of 6010
3:18 and shall water the v of Shittim. 5158
Mic 1: 6 pour down the stones thereof into the v, 1516
Zec 12:11 as the mourning of Hadadrimmon in the v 1237
14: 4 the west, *and there shall be* a very great v; 1516
14: 5 ye shall flee *to* the v of the mountains; 1516
14: 5 for the v of the mountains shall reach unto 1516
Lk 3: 5 Every v shall be filled, and every mountain *5327*

VALLEYS (28) [VALLEY]

Nu 24: 6 As the v are they spread forth, as gardens 5158
Dt 8: 7 and depths that spring out of the v and hills; 1237
11:11 *is* a land of hills and v, *and* drinketh water 1237
Jos 9: 1 in the v, and in all the coasts of the great 8219
12: 8 in the v, and in the plains, and in 8219
1Ki 20:28 he *is* not God of the v, therefore will I 6010
1Ch 12:15 they put to flight all *them of* the v, 6010
27:29 over the herds *that were* in the v *was* 6010
Job 30: 6 To dwell in the clifts of the v, *in* caves of 5158
39:10 or will he harrow the v after thee? 6010
Ps 65:13 the v also are covered over with corn; 6010
104: 8 they go down *by* the v unto the place which 1237
104:10 He sendeth the springs into the v, 5158
SS 2: 1 am the rose of Sharon, *and* the lily of the v. 6010
Isa 7:19 shall rest all of them in the desolate v, and 5158
22: 7 *that* thy choicest v shall be full *of* chariots, 6010
28: 1 which *are* on the head of the fat v of them 1516
41:18 and fountains in the midst of the v: 1237
57: 5 slaying the children in the v under the clifts 5158
Jer 49: 4 Wherefore gloriest thou in the v, 6010
Eze 6: 3 and to the hills, to the rivers, and to the v; 1516
7:16 be on the mountains like doves of the v, 1516
31:12 and in all the v his branches are fallen, 1516
32: 5 and fill the v *with* thy height. 1516
35: 8 in thy v, and in all thy rivers, shall they fall 1516
36: 4 to the hills, to the rivers, and to the v, to 1516
36: 6 and to the hills, to the rivers, and to the v, 1516
Mic 1: 4 the v shall be cleft, as wax before the fire, 6010

VALOUR (37) [VALIANT, VALIANTEST, VALIANTLY]

Jos 1:14 all the mighty *men* of v, and help them; 2428
6: 2 the king thereof, *and* the mighty *men* of v. 2428
8: 3 chose out thirty thousand mighty *men* of v, 2428
10: 7 war with him, and all the mighty *men* of v. 2428
Jdg 3:29 thousand men, all lusty, and all men of v; 2428
6:12 LORD *is* with thee, thou mighty *man* of v. 2428
11: 1 the Gileadite was a mighty *man* of v, 2428
18: 2 men of v, from Zorah and from Eshtaol, 2428
20:44 thousand men; all these *were* men of v. 2428
20:46 drew the sword; all these *were* men of v. 2428
1Ki 11:28 the man Jeroboam *was* a mighty *man* of v: 2428
2Ki 5: 1 he was also a mighty *man* in v, *but he was* 2428
24:14 all the princes, and all the mighty *men* of v, 2428
1Ch 5:24 Hodaviah, and Jahdiel, mighty *men* of v, 2428
7: 7 the house of *their* fathers, mighty *men* of v; 2428
7: 9 mighty *men* of v, *was* twenty thousand and 2428
7:11 mighty *men* of v, *were* seventeen thousand 2428
7:40 choice *and* mighty *men* of v, chief of 2428
8:40 the sons of Ulam were mighty men of v, 2428
12:21 *rovers:* for they *were* all mighty *men* of v, 2428
12:25 mighty *men* of v for the war, 2428
12:28 a young man mighty of v, and *of* his 2428
12:30 and eight hundred, mighty *men* of v, 2428
26: 6 their father: for they *were* mighty *men* of v. 2428
26:30 men of v, a thousand and seven hundred, 2428
26:31 them mighty *men* of v at Jazer of Gilead. 2428
26:32 his brethren, men of v, *were* two thousand 2428
2Ch 13: 3 chosen men, *being* mighty *men* of v. 2428
14: 8 all these *were* mighty *men* of v. 2428
17:13 the men of war, mighty *men* of v, *were* in 2428
17:14 with him mighty *men* of v three hundred 2428
17:16 two hundred thousand mighty *men* of v. 2428
17:17 Eliada a mighty *man* of v, and with him 2428
25: 6 v out of Israel for an hundred talents of 2428
26:12 of the mighty *men* of v *were* two thousand 2428
32:21 which cut off all the mighty *men* of v, and 2428
Ne 11:14 mighty *men* of v, an hundred twenty and 2428

VALUE (7) [VALUED, VALUEST]

Lev 27: 8 before the priest, and the priest shall v him; 6186
27: 8 his ability that vowed shall the priest v him. 6186
27:12 the priest shall v it, whether it be good or 6186
Job 13: 4 forgers of lies, ye *are* all physicians **of no** v. 457
Mt 10:31 ye are of **more v than** many sparrows. *1308*
27: 9 whom they of the children of Israel did v; *5091*
Lk 12: 7 ye are of **more v than** many sparrows. *1308*

VALUED (4) [VALUE]

Lev 27:16 a homer of barley seed *shall be* v at fifty NIH
Job 28:16 It cannot be v with the gold of Ophir, 5541
28:19 equal it, neither shall it be v with pure gold. 5541
Mt 27: 9 pieces of silver, the price of him that was v, *5091*

VALUEST (1) [VALUE]

Lev 27:12 as thou v it, *who art* the priest, so shall it 6187

VANIAH (1)

Ezr 10:36 V, Meremoth, Eliashib, 2057

VANISH (4) [VANISHED, VANISHETH]

Job 6:17 What time they wax warm, they v: when it 6789
Isa 51: 6 for the heavens shall v **away** like smoke, 4414
1Co 13: 8 *there be* knowledge, it shall v **away**. *2673*
Heb 8:13 and waxeth old *is* ready to v **away**. *854*

VANISHED (2) [VANISH]

Jer 49: 7 from the prudent? is their wisdom v? 5628
Lk 24:31 knew him; and he v **out of their sight**. *855+1096*

VANISHETH (2) [VANISH]

Job 7: 9 *As* the cloud is consumed and v **away**: so 1980
Jas 4:14 appeareth for a little *time*, and then v **away**. *853*

VANITIES (13) [VAIN]

Dt 32:21 have provoked me to anger with their v: 1892
1Ki 16:13 LORD God of Israel to anger with their v. 1892
16:26 LORD God of Israel to anger with their v. 1892
Ps 31: 6 I have hated them that regard lying v: but 1892
Ecc 1: 2 Vanity of v, saith the Preacher, vanity of 1892
1: 2 of vanities, saith the Preacher, vanity of v; 1892
5: 7 and many words *there are* also *divers* v: 1892
12: 8 Vanity of v, saith the Preacher; all *is* 1892
Jer 8:19 their graven images, *and* with strange v? 1892
10: 8 and foolish: the stock *is* a doctrine of v. 1892
14:22 Are there *any* among the v of the Gentiles 1892
Jnh 2: 8 They that observe lying v forsake their own 1892
Ac 14:15 turn from these v unto the living God, *3152*

VANITY (86) [VAIN]
2Ki 17:15 they followed v, and became vain, and 1892
Job 7: 3 So am I made to possess months of v, and 7723
7:16 live alway: let me alone; for my days *are* v. 1892
15:31 Let not him that is deceived trust in v: 7723
15:31 in vanity: for v shall be his recompence. 7723
15:35 bring forth v, and their belly prepareth 205
31: 5 If I have walked with v, or *if* my foot hath 7723
35:13 Surely God will not hear v, neither will 7723
Ps 4: 2 *how long* will ye love v, *and* seek after 7385
10: 7 fraud: under his tongue *is* mischief and v. 205
12: 2 They speak v every one with his neighbour: 7723
24: 4 who hath not lift up his soul unto v, 7723
39: 5 every man at his best state *is* altogether v. 1892
39:11 like a moth: surely every man *is* v. Selah. 1892
41: 6 if he come to see *me*, he speaketh v: 7723
62: 9 Surely men of low degree *are* v, *and* men of 1892
62: 9 they *are* altogether *lighter* than v. 1892
78:33 Therefore their days did he consume in v, 1892
94:11 the thoughts of man, that they *are* v. 1892
119:37 Turn away mine eyes from beholding v; 7723
144: 4 Man is like to v: his days *are* as a shadow 1892
144: 8 Whose mouth speaketh v, and their right 7723
144:11 whose mouth speaketh v, and their right 7723
Pr 13:11 Wealth *gotten* by v shall be diminished: but 1892
21: 6 treasures by a lying tongue *is* a v tossed to 1892
22: 8 He that soweth iniquity shall reap v: and 205
30: 8 Remove far from me v and lies: give me 7723
Ecc 1: 2 V of vanities, saith the Preacher, vanity of 1892
1: 2 of vanities, saith the Preacher, v of vanities; 1892
1: 2 the Preacher, vanity of vanities; all *is* v. 1892
1:14 and behold, all *is* v and vexation of spirit. 1892
2: 1 enjoy pleasure: and behold, this also *is* v. 1892
2:11 all *was* v and vexation of spirit, and 1892
2:15 Then I said in my heart, that this also *is* v. 1892
2:17 unto me: for all *is* v and vexation of spirit. 1892
2:19 myself wise under the sun. This *is* also v. 1892
2:21 his portion. This also *is* v and a great evil. 1892
2:23 taketh not rest in the night. This *is* also v. 1892
2:26 This also *is* v and vexation of spirit. 1892
3:19 no preeminence above a beast: for all *is* v. 1892
4: 4 This *is* also v and vexation of spirit. 1892
4: 7 Then I returned, and I saw v under the sun. 1892
4: 8 This *is* also v, yea, it *is* a sore travail. 1892
4:16 Surely this also *is* v and vexation of spirit. 1892
5:10 abundance *with* increase: this *is* also v. 1892
6: 2 eateth it: this *is* v, and it *is* an evil disease. 1892
6: 4 For he cometh in with v, and departeth in 1892
6: 9 this *is* also v and vexation of spirit. 1892
6:11 there be many things that increase v, 1892
7: 6 so *is* the laughter of the fool: this also *is* v. 1892
7:15 All *things* have I seen in the days of my v: 1892
8:10 city where they had so done: this *is* also v. 1892
8:14 There is a v which is done upon the earth; 1892
8:14 of the righteous: I said that this also *is* v. 1892
9: 9 thou lovest all the days of the life of thy v, 1892
9: 9 thee under the sun, all the days of thy v: 1892
11: 8 for they shall be many. All that cometh *is* v. 1892
11:10 thy flesh: for childhood and youth *are* v. 1892
12: 8 V of vanities, saith the Preacher; all *is* 1892
12: 8 of vanities, saith the Preacher; all *is* v. 1892
Isa 5:18 them that draw iniquity with cords of v, 7723
30:28 to sift the nations with the sieve of v: 7723
40:17 are counted to him less than nothing, and v. 8414
40:23 he maketh the judges of the earth as v. 8414
41:29 Behold, they *are* all v; their works *are* 205
44: 9 that make a graven image *are* all of them v; 8414
57:13 v shall take *them*: but he that putteth his 1892
58: 9 putting forth of the finger, and speaking v; 205
59: 4 *they* trust in v, and speak lies; 8414
Jer 2: 5 have walked after v, and are become vain? 1892
10:15 They *are* v, *and* the work of errors: in 1892
16:19 v, and *things* wherein *there is* no profit. 1892
18:15 they have burnt incense to v, and they have 7723
51:18 They *are* v, the work of errors: in the time 1892
Eze 13: 6 They have seen v and lying divination, 7723
13: 8 Because ye have spoken v, and seen lies, 7723
13: 9 hand shall be upon the prophets that see v, 7723
13:23 Therefore ye shall see no more v, 7723
21:29 Whiles *they* see v unto thee, whiles *they* 7723
22:28 them *with* untempered *morter*, seeing v, 7723
Hos 12:11 surely they are v: they sacrifice bullocks in 7723
Hab 2:13 people shall weary themselves for very v? 7385
Zec 10: 2 For the idols have spoken v, and the diviners 205
Ro 8:20 For the creature was made subject to v, *3153*
Eph 4:17 other Gentiles walk, in the v of their mind, *3153*
2Pe 2:18 when they speak great swelling *words* of v, *3153*

VAPOUR (5) [VAPOURS]
Job 36:27 they pour down rain according to the v 108
36:33 the cattle also concerning the v. 5927
Ps 148: 8 Fire, and hail; snow, and v; stormy wind 7008
Ac 2:19 blood, and fire, and v of smoke: *822*
Jas 4:14 It is even a v, that appeareth for a little *time*, *822*

VAPOURS (3) [VAPOUR]
Ps 135: 7 He causeth the v to ascend from the ends of 5387
Jer 10:13 he causeth the v to ascend from the ends of 5387
51:16 he causeth the v to ascend from the ends of 5387

VARIABLENESS (1) [VARIANCE]
Jas 1:17 with whom is no v, neither shadow of *3883*

VARIANCE (2) [VARIABLENESS]
Mt 10:35 For I am come to **set** a man **at** v against his *1369*
Gal 5:20 Idolatry, witchcraft, hatred, v, emulations, *2054*

VARIED See DIVERS; DIVERSE

VASHNI (1)
1Ch 6:28 sons of Samuel; the firstborn V, and Abiah. 2059

VASHTI (10)
Est 1: 9 Also V the queen made a feast for 2060
1:11 To bring V the queen before the king with 2060
1:12 the queen V refused to come at the king's 2060
1:15 What shall *we* do unto the queen V 2060
1:16 V the queen hath not done wrong to 2060
1:17 The king Ahasuerus commanded V 2060
1:19 That V come no *more* before king 2060
2: 1 he remembered V, and what she had done, 2060
2: 4 pleaseth the king be queen instead of V. 2060
2:17 her head, and made her queen instead of V. 2060

VAT; VATS See CELLARS; FATS; LIQUORS; PRESSES

VAUNT (1) [VAUNTETH]
Jdg 7: 2 lest Israel v themselves against me, saying, 6286

VAUNTETH (1) [VAUNT]
1Co 13: 4 charity v not itself, is not puffed up, *4068*

VEGETABLES See PULSE

VEHEMENT (3) [VEHEMENTLY]
SS 8: 6 coals of fire, *which hath* a **most v flame**. 7957
Jnh 4: 8 did arise, that God prepared a v east wind; 2759
2Co 7:11 yea, *what* fear, yea, *what* v **desire**, *1972*

VEHEMENTLY (5) [VEHEMENT]
Mk 14:31 But he spake the more v, If I should *1537+4053*
Lk 6:48 the stream **beat** v **upon** that house, and *4366*
6:49 **against** which the stream did **beat** v, and *4366*
11:53 and the Pharisees began to urge *him* v, *1171*
23:10 and scribes stood and v accused him. *2159*

VEIL, VEILS See KERCHIEFS; LOCKS; MUFFLERS; VAIL; VAILS

VEIN (1)
Job 28: 1 Surely there is a v for the silver, and 4161

VENGEANCE (45) [AVENGE, AVENGED, AVENGER, AVENGETH, AVENGING, REVENGE, REVENGED, REVENGER, REVENGERS, REVENGES, REVENGETH, REVENGING]
Ge 4:15 v shall be **taken** on him sevenfold. 5358
Dt 32:35 To me *belongeth* v, and recompence; 5359
32:41 I will render v to mine enemies, and 5359
32:43 will render v to his adversaries, and will be 5359
Jdg 11:36 forasmuch as the LORD hath taken v for 5360
Ps 58:10 righteous shall rejoice when he seeth the v: 5359
94: 1 O LORD God, to whom v belongeth; 5360
94: 1 O God, to whom v belongeth, shew thyself. 5360
99: 8 though thou **tookest** v of their inventions. 5358
149: 7 To execute v upon the heathen, *and* 5360
Pr 6:34 therefore he will not spare in the day of v. 5359
Isa 34: 8 For *it is* the day of the LORD'S v, *and* 5359
35: 4 behold, your God will come *with* v, 5359
47: 3 I will take v, and I will not meet *thee as* a 5359
59:17 he put on the garments of v *for* clothing, 5359

V

Isa 61: 2 the LORD, and the day of v of our God; 5359
63: 4 For the day of v *is* in mine heart, and 5359
Jer 11:20 and the heart, let me see thy v on them: 5360
20:12 and the heart, let me see thy v on them: 5360
46:10 a day of v, that *he* may avenge him of his 5360
50:15 for it *is* the v of the LORD: 5360
50:15 **take** v upon her; as she hath done, do unto 5358
50:28 to declare in Zion the v of the LORD our 5360
50:28 of the LORD our God, the v of his temple. 5360
51: 6 for this *is* the time of the LORD'S v; 5360
51:11 because it *is* the v of the LORD, 5360
51:11 of the LORD, the v of his temple. 5360
51:36 plead thy cause, and **take** v for thee; 5358+5360
La 3:60 Thou hast seen all their v *and* all their 5360
Eze 24: 8 cause fury to come up to **take** v; 5358+5359
25:12 the house of Judah by **taking** v, 5358+5359
25:14 I will lay my v upon Edom by the hand of 5360
25:14 they shall know my v, saith the Lord 5360
25:15 have **taken** v with a despiteful heart, 5358+5359
25:17 I will execute great v upon them with 5360
25:17 when I shall lay my v upon them. 5360
Mic 5:15 I will execute v in anger and fury upon 5359
Na 1: 2 the LORD will **take** v on his adversaries, 5358
Lk 21:22 For these be *the* days of v, that all *things* *1557*
Ac 28: 4 escaped the sea, yet V suffereth not to live. *1349*
Ro 3: 5 *Is* God unrighteous who taketh v? (I speak *3709*
12:19 for it is written, V *is* mine; I will repay, *1557*
2Th 1: 8 taking v on them that know not God, and *1557*
Heb 10:30 V *belongeth* unto me, I will recompense, *1557*
Jude 1: 7 an example, suffering the v of eternal fire. *1349*

VENISON (8)
Ge 25:28 loved Esau, because he did eat of *his* v: 6718
27: 3 and go out to the field, and take me *some* v; 6718
27: 5 Esau went to the field to hunt for v, *and* 6718
27: 7 Bring me v, and make me savoury meat, 6718
27:19 arise, I pray thee, sit and eat of my v, that 6718
27:25 *it* near to me, and I will eat of my son's v, 6718
27:31 Let my father arise, and eat of his son's v, 6718
27:33 where *is* he that hath taken v, and brought *it* 6718

VENOM (1) [VENOMOUS]
Dt 32:33 poison of dragons, and the cruel v of asps. 7219

VENOMOUS (1) [VENOM]
Ac 28: 4 And when the barbarians saw the *v* beast NIG

VENT (1)
Job 32:19 my belly *is* as wine *which* hath no v; 6605

VENTURE (2)
1Ki 22:34 a *certain* man drew a bow at a v, and 8537
2Ch 18:33 a *certain* man drew a bow at a v, and 8537

VERIFIED (3) [VERITY]
Ge 42:20 so shall your words be v, and ye shall not 539
1Ki 8:26 God of Israel, let thy word, I pray thee, be v, 539
2Ch 6:17 O LORD God of Israel, let thy word be v, 539

VERILY (140) [VERITY] See Index

VERITY (2) [VERIFIED, VERILY]
Ps 111: 7 The works of his hands *are* v and judgment; 571
1Ti 2: 7 a teacher of the Gentiles in faith and v. *225*

VERMILION (2)
Jer 22:14 *it is* cieled with cedar, and painted with v. 8350
Eze 23:14 images of the Chaldeans pourtrayed with v, 8350

VERY (257) See Index

VESSEL (46) [VESSELS]
Lev 6:28 the earthen v wherein it is sodden shall be 3627
11:32 whether *it be* any v of wood, or raiment, or 3627
11:32 whatsoever v *it be,* wherein *any* work is 3627
11:33 every earthen v, whereinto *any* of them 3627
11:34 all drink that may be drunk in every *such* v 3627
14: 5 killed in an earthen v over running water: 3627
14:50 birds in an earthen v over running water: 3627
15:12 the v of earth, that he toucheth which hath 3627
15:12 every v of wood shall be rinsed in water. 3627
Nu 5:17 priest shall take holy water in an earthen v; 3627
19:15 every open v, which hath no covering 3627
19:17 running water shall be put thereto in a v: 3627
Dt 23:24 but thou shalt not put *any* in thy v. 3627
1Sa 21: 5 though it were sanctified *this* day in the v. 3627
1Ki 17:10 Fetch me, I pray thee, a little water in a v, 3627
2Ki 4: 6 that she said unto her son, Bring me yet a v. 3627
4: 6 he said unto her, *There is* not a v more. 3627
Ps 2: 9 shalt dash them in pieces like a potter's v. 3627
31:12 dead man out of mind: I am like a broken v. 3627
Pr 25: 4 and there shall come forth a v for the finer. 3627
Isa 30:14 of the potters' v that is broken in pieces; 5035
66:20 in a clean v *into* the house of the LORD. 3627
Jer 18: 4 the v that he made of clay was marred in 3627
18: 4 so he made it again another v, as seemed 3627
19:11 this city, as *one* breaketh a potter's v, 3627
22:28 *is he* a v wherein *is* no pleasure? 3627
25:34 And ye shall fall like a pleasant v. 3627
32:14 put them in an earthen v, that they may 3627
48:11 and hath not been emptied from v to vessel, 3627
48:11 and hath not been emptied from vessel to v, 3627
48:38 for I have broken Moab like a v wherein *is* 3627
51:34 crushed me, he hath made me an empty v, 3627
Eze 4: 9 put them in one v, and make thee bread 3627
15: 3 will *men* take a pin of it to hang any v 3627
Hos 8: 8 now shall they be among the Gentiles as a v 3627
Mk 11:16 *man* should carry *any* v through the temple. *4632*
Lk 8:16 covereth it with a v, or putteth *it* under a *4632*
Jn 19:29 Now there was set a v full of vinegar: and *4632*
Ac 9:15 Go *thy way:* for he is a chosen v unto me, *4632*
10:11 and a certain v descending unto him, *4632*
10:16 the v was received up again into heaven. *4632*
11: 5 a trance I saw a vision, A certain v descend, *4632*
Ro 9:21 of the same lump to make one v unto *4632*
1Th 4: 4 know how to possess his v in sanctification *4632*
2Ti 2:21 he shall be a v unto honour, sanctified, and *4632*
1Pe 3: 7 as unto the weaker v, and as *being* heirs *4632*

VESSELS (154) [VESSEL]
Ge 43:11 take of the best fruits in the land in your v, 3627
Ex 7:19 both in *v of* wood, and in *vessels of* stone. NIH
7:19 both in *vessels of* wood, and in *v of* stone. NIH
25:39 pure gold shall he make it, with all these v. 3627
27: 3 all the v thereof thou shalt make *of* brass. 3627
27:19 All the v of the tabernacle in all the service 3627
30:27 the table and all his v, and the candlestick 3627
30:27 the candlestick and his v, and the altar of 3627
30:28 the altar of burnt offering with all his v, 3627
35:13 his staves, and all his v, and the shewbread, 3627
35:16 and all his v, the laver and his foot, 3627
37:16 he made the v which *were* upon the table, 3627
37:24 pure gold made he it, and all the v thereof. 3627
38: 3 he made all the v of the altar, the pots, and 3627
38: 3 all the v thereof made he *of* brass. 3627
38:30 brasen grate for it, and all the v of the altar, 3627
39:36 all the v thereof, and the shewbread, 3627
39:37 and all the v thereof, and the oil for light, 3627
39:39 and all his v, the laver and his foot, 3627
39:40 all the v of the service of the tabernacle, 3627
40: 9 shalt hallow it, and all the v thereof: 3627
40:10 and all his v, and sanctify the altar: 3627
Lev 8:11 anointed the altar and all his v, both 3627
Nu 1:50 over all the v thereof, and over all *things* 3627
1:50 bear the tabernacle, and all the v thereof; 3627
3:31 the v of the sanctuary wherewith they 3627
3:36 all the v thereof, and all that serveth 3627
4: 9 his snuffdishes, and all the oil v thereof, 3627
4:10 all the v thereof within a covering of 3627
4:14 they shall put upon it all the v thereof, 3627
4:14 and the basons, all the v of the altar; 3627
4:15 all the v of the sanctuary, as the camp is to 3627
4:16 *is,* in the sanctuary, and in the v thereof. 3627
7: 1 both the altar and all the v thereof, and 3627
7:85 all the silver v *weighed* two thousand and 3627
18: 3 only they shall not come nigh the v of 3627
19:18 upon all the v, and upon the persons that 3627
Jos 6:19 the silver, and gold, and v of brass and iron, 3627
6:24 and the gold, and the v of brass and of iron, 3627
Ru 2: 9 go unto the v, and drink of *that* which 3627
1Sa 9: 7 for the bread is spent in our v, and *there is* 3627
21: 5 the v of the young men are holy, and 3627
2Sa 8:10 *Joram* brought with him v of silver, and 3627
8:10 and v of gold, and vessels of brass: 3627
8:10 and vessels of gold, and v of brass: 3627
17:28 earthen v, and wheat, and barley, and flour, 3627
1Ki 7:45 all these v, which Hiram made to king 3627
7:47 Solomon left all the v *unweighed,* because 3627
7:48 Solomon made all the v that *pertained unto* 3627
7:51 *even* the silver, and the gold, and the v, 3627

1Ki 8: 4 all the holy v that *were* in the tabernacle, 3627
10:21 all king Solomon's drinking v *were of* gold, 3627
10:21 all the v of the house of the forest of 3627
10:25 v of silver, and vessels of gold, and 3627
10:25 v of gold, and garments, and armour, and 3627
15:15 of the LORD, silver, and gold, and v. 3627
2Ki 4: 3 borrow thee v abroad of all thy neighbours, 3627
4: 3 abroad of all thy neighbours, *even* empty v; 3627
4: 4 shalt pour out into all those v, and 3627
4: 5 upon her sons, who brought *the* v to her; NIH
4: 6 it came to pass, when the v were full, 3627
7:15 lo, all the way *was* full *of* garments and v, 3627
12:13 trumpets, any v of gold, or vessels of silver, 3627
12:13 trumpets, any vessels of gold, or v of silver, 3627
14:14 all the v that were found *in* the house of 3627
23: 4 LORD all the v that were made for Baal, 3627
24:13 cut in pieces all the v of gold which 3627
25:14 all the v of brass wherewith they 3627
25:16 the brass of all these v was without weight. 3627
1Ch 9:28 of them had the charge of the ministering v, 3627
9:29 them also *were* appointed to oversee the v, 3627
18: 8 and the pillars, and the v of brass. 3627
18:10 *with him* all *manner of* v of gold and silver 3627
22:19 of the LORD, and the holy v of God, 3627
23:26 nor any v of it for the service thereof. 3627
28:13 for all the v of service in the house of 3627
2Ch 4:18 Thus Solomon made all these v in great 3627
4:19 Solomon made all the v that *were for* 3627
5: 5 all the holy v that *were* in the tabernacle, 3627
9:20 all the drinking v of king Solomon *were of* 3627
9:20 all the v of the house of the forest of 3627
9:24 v of silver, and vessels of gold, and 3627
9:24 v of gold, and raiment, harness, and spices, 3627
15:18 had dedicated, silver, and gold, and v. 3627
24:14 whereof were made v for the house of 3627
24:14 *even* v to minister, and to offer *withal,* and 3627
24:14 and spoons, and v of gold and silver. 3627
25:24 all the v that were found in the house of 3627
28:24 Ahaz gathered together the v of the house 3627
28:24 cut in pieces the v of the house of God, and 3627
29:18 with all the v thereof, and the shewbread 3627
29:18 the shewbread table, with all the v thereof. 3627
29:19 Moreover all the v, which king Ahaz in his 3627
36: 7 Nebuchadnezzar also carried of the v of 3627
36:10 with the goodly v of the house of 3627
36:18 And all the v of the house of God, great and 3627
36:19 and destroyed all the goodly v thereof. 3627
Ezr 1: 6 strengthened their hands with v of silver, 3627
1: 7 Also Cyrus the king brought forth the v of 3627
1:10 and ten, *and* other v a thousand. 3627
1:11 All the v of gold and of silver *were* five 3627
5:14 the v also of gold and silver of the house of 3984
5:15 said unto him, Take these v, go, carry them 3984
6: 5 the golden and silver v of the house of God, 3984
7:19 The v also that *are* given thee for 3984
8:25 them the silver, and the gold, and the v, 3627
8:26 silver v an hundred talents, *and of* gold an 3627
8:27 and two v of fine copper, precious as gold. 3627
8:28 the v *are* holy also; and the silver and 3627
8:30 of the silver, and the gold, and the v, 3627
8:33 the v weighed in the house of our God by 3627
Ne 10:39 where *are* the v of the sanctuary, and 3627
13: 5 the v, and the tithes of the corn, the new 3627
13: 9 thither brought I again the v of the house of 3627
Est 1: 7 *they* gave *them* drink in v of gold, 3627
1: 7 (the v being diverse one from another,) 3627
Isa 18: 2 even in v of bulrushes upon the waters, 3627
22:24 and the issue, all v of small quantity, 3627
22:24 of small quantity, from the v of cups, 3627
22:24 vessels of cups, even to all the v of flagons. 3627
52:11 be ye clean, that bear the v of the LORD. 3627
65: 4 and broth of abominable *things is in* their v; 3627
Jer 14: 3 no water; they returned *with* their v empty; 3627
27:16 the v of the LORD's house *shall* now 3627
27:18 that the v which are left in the house of 3627
27:19 concerning the residue of the v that remain 3627
27:21 concerning the v that remain *in* the house 3627
28: 3 this place all the v of the LORD's house, 3627
28: 6 to bring again the v of the LORD's house, 3627
40:10 oil, and put *them* in your v, and dwell in 3627
48:12 shall empty his v, and break their bottles. 3627
49:29 and all their v, and their camels; 3627
52:18 all the v of brass wherewith they 3627
52:20 the brass of all these v was without weight. 3627

V

Eze 27:13 of men and v of brass in thy market. 3627
Da 1: 2 with part of the v of the house of God: 3627
1: 2 he brought the v *into* the treasure house of 3627
5: 2 silver v which his father Nebuchadnezzar 3984
5: 3 they brought the golden v that were taken 3984
5:23 they have brought the v of his house before 3984
11: 8 *and* with their precious v *of* silver and 3627
Hos 13:15 he shall spoil the treasure of all pleasant v. 3627
Hag 2:16 for to draw out fifty v *out of* the press, NIH
Mt 13:48 and gathered the good into v, but cast the bad *30*
25: 4 But the wise took oil in their v with their *30*
Mk 7: 4 of cups, and pots, **brasen** v, and of tables. *5473*
Ro 9:22 endured with much longsuffering *the* v of *4632*
9:23 the riches of his glory on the v of mercy, *4632*
2Co 4: 7 But we have this treasure in earthen v, *4632*
2Ti 2:20 But in a great house there are not only v of *4632*
Heb 9:21 the tabernacle, and all the v of the ministry. *4632*
Rev 2:27 as the v of a potter *shall* they be broken to *4632*
18:12 and all *manner* v of ivory, and all *manner* *4632*
18:12 and all *manner* v of most precious wood, *4632*

VESTMENTS (2) [VESTURE]
2Ki 10:22 Bring forth v for all the worshippers of 3830
10:22 of Baal. And he brought them forth v. 4403

VESTRY (1) [VESTURE]
2Ki 10:22 he said unto *him* that *was* over the v, 4458

VESTURE (8) [VESTMENTS, VESTRY, VESTURES]
Dt 22:12 thee fringes upon the four quarters of thy v, 3682
Ps 22:18 among them, and cast lots upon my v. 3830
102:26 as a v shalt thou change them, and 3830
Mt 27:35 and upon my v did they cast lots. *2441*
Jn 19:24 and for my v they did cast lots. *2441*
Heb 1:12 And as a v shalt thou fold them up, and *4018*
Rev 19:13 And he *was* clothed with a v dipt in blood: *2440*
19:16 And he hath on *his* v and on his thigh a *2440*

VESTURES (1) [VESTURE]
Ge 41:42 arrayed him in v of fine linen, and put a gold 899

VEX (15) [VEXATION, VEXATIONS, VEXED]
Ex 22:21 Thou shalt neither v a stranger, nor oppress 3238
Lev 18:18 to v *her,* to uncover her nakedness, 6887
19:33 with thee in your land, ye shall not v him. 3238
Nu 25:17 V the Midianites, and smite them: 6887
25:18 For they v you with their wiles, 6887
33:55 shall v you in the land wherein ye dwell. 6887
2Sa 12:18 how will he then v himself, if we tell 6213+7451
2Ch 15: 6 for God did v them with all adversity. 2000
Job 19: 2 How long will ye v my soul, and break me 3013
Ps 2: 5 his wrath, and v them in his sore displeasure. 926
Isa 7: 6 v it, and let us make a breach therein for us, 6973
11:13 envy Judah, and Judah shall not v Ephraim. 6887
Eze 32: 9 I will also v the hearts of many people, 3707
Hab 2: 7 awake that *shall* v thee, and thou shalt be 2111
Ac 12: 1 forth *his* hands to v certain of the church. *2559*

VEXATION (14) [VEX]
Dt 28:20 shall send upon thee cursing, v, and rebuke, 4103
Ecc 1:14 and behold, all *is* vanity and v of spirit. 7469
1:17 folly: I perceived that this also *is* v of spirit. 7475
2:11 all *was* vanity and v of spirit, and *there was* 7469
2:17 unto me: for all *is* vanity and v of spirit. 7469
2:22 of all his labour, and of the v of his heart, 7475
2:26 This also *is* vanity and v of spirit. 7469
4: 4 This *is* also vanity and v of spirit. 7469
4: 6 the hands full *with* travail and v of spirit. 7469
4:16 Surely this also *is* vanity and v of spirit. 7475
6: 9 the desire: this *is* also vanity and v of spirit. 7469
Isa 9: 1 dimness *shall* not *be* such as *was* in her v, 4164
28:19 it shall be a v only *to* understand the report. 2113
65:14 of heart, and shall howl for v of spirit. 7667

VEXATIONS (1) [VEX]
2Ch 15: 5 great v *were* upon all the inhabitants of 4103

VEXED (22) [VEX]
Nu 20:15 and the Egyptians v us, and our fathers: 7489
Jdg 2:18 of them that oppressed them and v them. 1766
10: 8 that year they v and oppressed the children 7492
16:16 *so* that his soul was v unto death; 7114
1Sa 14:47 he turned himself, he v *them.* 7561
2Sa 13: 2 Amnon was *so* v, that he fell sick for his 3334
2Ki 4:27 Let her alone; for her soul *is* v within her: 4843

Ne 9:27 into the hand of their enemies, who v them: 6887
Job 27: 2 and the Almighty, *who* hath v my soul; 4843
Ps 6: 2 O LORD, heal me; for my bones are v. 926
6: 3 My soul is also sore v: but thou, O LORD, 926
6:10 Let all mine enemies be ashamed and sore v: 926
Isa 63:10 they rebelled, and v his holy Spirit: 6087
Eze 22: 5 mock thee, *which art* infamous *and* much v. 4103
22: 7 in thee have they v the fatherless and 3238
22:29 and have v the poor and needy: 3238
Mt 15:22 my daughter is grievously v **with a devil**. *1139*
17:15 for he is lunatick, and sore v: for ofttimes *3958*
Lk 6:18 And they that were v with unclean spirits: *3791*
Ac 5:16 *them which were* v with unclean spirits: *3791*
2Pe 2: 7 v with the filthy conversation of *2669*
2: 8 v *his* righteous soul from day to day with *928*

VIAL (8) [VIALS]
1Sa 10: 1 Samuel took a v of oil, and poured *it* upon 6378
Rev 16: 2 and poured out his v upon the earth; *5357*
16: 3 And the second angel poured out his v *5357*
16: 4 And the third angel poured out his v upon *5357*
16: 8 And the fourth angel poured out his v upon *5357*
16:10 And the fifth angel poured out his v upon *5357*
16:12 And the sixth angel poured out his v upon *5357*
16:17 And the seventh angel poured out his v into *5357*

VIALS (5) [VIAL]
Rev 5: 8 and golden v full of odours, which are *5357*
15: 7 seven golden v full of the wrath of God, *5357*
16: 1 pour out the v of the wrath of God upon *5357*
17: 1 of the seven angels which had the seven v, *5357*
21: 9 the seven v full of the seven last plagues, *5357*

VICTORY (12)
2Sa 19: 2 the v that day was *turned* into mourning 8668
23:10 the LORD wrought a great v that day; 8668
23:12 and the LORD wrought a great v. 8668
1Ch 29:11 and the glory, and the v, and the majesty: 5331
Ps 98: 1 and his holy arm, hath **gotten** him the v. 3467
Isa 25: 8 He will swallow up death in v; and 5331
Mt 12:20 till he send forth judgment unto v. *3534*
1Co 15:54 that is written, Death is swallowed up in v. *3534*
15:55 where *is* thy sting? O grave, where *is* thy v? *3534*
15:57 which giveth us the v through our Lord *3534*
1Jn 5: 4 and this is the v that overcometh the world, *3529*
Rev 15: 2 them that had **gotten the** v over the beast, *3528*

VICTUAL (5) [VICTUALS]
Ex 12:39 had they prepared for themselves *any* v. 6720
Jdg 20:10 to fetch v for the people, that *they* may do, 6720
1Ki 4:27 those officers **provided** v for king 3557
2Ch 11:11 in them, and store of v, and *of* oil and wine. 3978
11:23 he gave them v in abundance. And he 4202

VICTUALS (17) [VICTUAL]
Ge 14:11 and all their v, and went their way. 400
Lev 25:37 upon usury, nor lend him thy v for increase. 400
Dt 23:19 usury of money, usury of v, usury of any 400
Jos 1:11 the people, saying, Prepare you v; 6720
9:11 Take v with you for the journey, and go to 6720
9:14 the men took of their v, and asked not 6718
Jdg 7: 8 So the people took v in their hand, and their 6720
17:10 by the year, and a suit of apparel, and thy v. 4241
1Sa 22:10 gave him v, and gave him the sword of 6720
1Ki 4: 7 which **provided** v for the king and his 3557
11:18 and appointed him v, and gave him land. 3899
Ne 10:31 or any v on the sabbath day to sell, 7668
13:15 *them* in the day wherein they sold v. 6718
Jer 40: 5 So the captain of the guard gave him v and 737
44:17 for *then* had we plenty of v, and were well, 3899
Mt 14:15 go into the villages, and buy themselves v. *1033*
Lk 9:12 country round about, and lodge, and get v: *1979*

VIEW (4) [VIEWED]
Jos 2: 1 Go v the land, even Jericho. 7200
7: 2 unto them, saying, Go up and v the country. 7270
2Ki 2: 7 and stood to v afar off: 4480+5048
2:15 which *were* to v at Jericho saw him, 4480+5048

VIEWED (4) [VIEW]
Jos 7: 2 the country. And the men went up and v Ai. 7270
Ezr 8:15 I v the people, and the priests, and 995
Ne 2:13 the dung port, and v the walls of Jerusalem, 7663
2:15 v the wall, and turned back, and entered by 7663

VIGILANT (2)
1Ti 3: 2 v, sober, of good behaviour, given to *3524*
1Pe 5: 8 Be sober, be v; because your adversary *1127*

VIGOROUS See LIVELY

VIGOROUSLY See THROUGHLY

VILE (19) [VILELY, VILER, VILEST]
Dt 25: 3 then thy brother should seem v unto thee. 7034
Jdg 19:24 but unto this man do not so v a thing. 5039
1Sa 3:13 because his sons **made** themselves v, 7043
15: 9 every thing *that was* v and refuse, that they 5240
2Sa 6:22 I will yet be more v than thus, and will be 7043
Job 18: 3 as beasts, *and* **reputed** v in your sight? 2933
40: 4 Behold, I am v; what shall I answer thee? 7043
Ps 15: 4 In whose eyes a v *person* is contemned; but 3988
Isa 32: 5 The v **person** shall be no more called 5036
32: 6 For the v **person** will speak villany, and 5036
Jer 15:19 if thou take forth the precious from the v, 2151
29:17 and will make them like v figs, 8182
La 1:11 and consider; for I am become v. 2151
Da 11:21 in his estate shall stand up a v **person**, to 959
Na 1:14 I will make thy grave; for thou art v. 7043
3: 6 **make** thee v, and will set thee as a 5034
Ro 1:26 For this cause God gave them up unto v *819*
Php 3:21 Who shall change our v body, that it may *5014*
Jas 2: 2 there come in also a poor *man* in v raiment; *4508*

VILELY (1) [VILE]
2Sa 1:21 the shield of the mighty is v **cast away**, 1602

VILER (1) [VILE]
Job 30: 8 of base men: they were v than the earth. 5217

VILEST (1) [VILE]
Ps 12: 8 on every side, when the v men are exalted. 2149

VILLAGE (10) [VILLAGES]
Mt 21: 2 Go into the v over against you, and *2968*
Mk 11: 2 Go your way into the v over against you: *2968*
Lk 8: 1 that he went throughout every city and v, *2968*
9:52 and entered into a v of the Samaritans, *2968*
9:56 to save *them*. And they went to another v. *2968*
10:38 they went, that he entered into a certain v: *2968*
17:12 And as he entered into a certain v, *2968*
19:30 Go ye into the v over against *you;* in *2968*
24:13 two of them went *that* same day to a v *2968*
24:28 And they drew nigh unto the v, *2968*

VILLAGES (75) [VILLAGE]
Ex 8:13 out of the v, and out of the fields. 2691
Lev 25:31 the houses of the v which have no wall 2691
Nu 21:25 in Heshbon, and in all the v thereof. 1323
21:32 they took the v thereof, and drove out 1323
32:42 and the v thereof, and called it Nobah, 1323
Jos 13:23 after their families, the cities and v thereof. 2691
13:28 after their families, the cities, and their v. 2691
15:32 the cities *are* twenty and nine, with their v. 2691
15:36 Gederothaim; fourteen cities with their v. 2691
15:41 and Makkedah; sixteen cities with their v. 2691
15:44 and Mareshah; nine cities with their v. 2691
15:45 Ekron, with her towns and her v: 2691
15:46 all that *lay* near Ashdod, with their v: 2691
15:47 Ashdod *with* her towns and her v, 2691
15:47 Gaza *with* her towns and her v, 2691
15:51 Holon, and Giloh; eleven cities with their v. 2691
15:54 *is* Hebron, and Zior; nine cities with their v. 2691
15:57 Gibeah, and Timnah; ten cities with their v. 2691
15:59 and Eltekon; six cities with their v. 2691
15:60 and Rabbah; two cities with their v. 2691
15:62 of salt, and En-gedi; six cities with their v. 2691
16: 9 of Manasseh, all the cities with their v. 2691
18:24 and Gaba; twelve cities with their v. 2691
18:28 *and* Kirjath; fourteen cities with their v. 2691
19: 6 and Sharuhen; thirteen cities and their v: 2691
19: 7 Ether, and Ashan; four cities and their v: 2691
19: 8 all the v that *were* round about these cities 2691
19:15 and Beth-lehem: twelve cities with their v. 2691
19:16 to their families, these cities with their v. 2691
19:22 were *at* Jordan: sixteen cities with their v. 2691
19:23 to their families, the cities and their v. 2691
19:30 Rehob: twenty and two cities with their v. 2691
19:31 to their families, these cities with their v. 2691
19:38 Beth-shemesh; nineteen cities with their v. 2691

Jos 19:39 to their families, the cities and their v. 2691
19:48 to their families, these cities with their v. 2691
21:12 the fields of the city, and the v thereof, 2691
Jdg 5: 7 *The inhabitants of* the v ceased, they ceased 6520
5:11 *towards the inhabitants* of his v in Israel: 6520
1Sa 6:18 *both* of fenced cities, and of country v, 3724
1Ch 4:32 their v *were,* Etam, and Ain, Rimmon, and 2691
4:33 all their v that *were* round about the same 2691
6:56 the fields of the city, and the v thereof, 2691
9:16 that dwelt in the v of the Netophathites. 2691
9:22 reckoned by their genealogy in their v, 2691
9:25 their brethren, *which were* in their v, 2691
27:25 in the cities, and in the v, and in the castles, 3723
2Ch 28:18 Shocho with the v thereof, and Timnah 1323
28:18 Timnah with the v thereof, Gimzo also and 1323
28:18 Gimzo also and the v thereof: 1323
Ne 6: 2 let us meet together in *some one of* the v in 3715
11:25 for the v, with their fields, *some* of 2691
11:25 *in* the v thereof, and at Dibon, and *in* 1323
11:25 *in* the v thereof, and at Jekabzeel, and *in* 1323
11:25 and at Jekabzeel, and *in* the v thereof, 2691
11:27 and at Beer-sheba, and *in* the v thereof, 1323
11:28 and at Mekonah, and in the v thereof, 1323
11:30 Zanoah, Adullam, and *in* their v, 2691
11:30 *at* Azekah, and *in* the v thereof. 1323
11:31 and Aija, and Beth-el, and *in* their v, 1323
12:28 and from the v of Netophathi; 2691
12:29 for the singers had builded them v round 2691
Est 9:19 Therefore the Jews of the v, that dwelt in 6521
Ps 10: 8 He sitteth in the lurking places of the v: 2691
SS 7:11 go forth *into* the field; let us lodge in the v. 3723
Isa 42:11 the cities thereof lift up *their voice,* the v 2691
Eze 38:11 I will go up to the land of **unwalled** v; 6519
Hab 3:14 through with his staves the head of his v: 6518
Mt 9:35 And Jesus went about all the cities and v, *2968*
14:15 that they may go into the v, and *2968*
Mk 6: 6 And he went round about the v, teaching. *2968*
6:36 and *into* the v, and buy themselves bread: *2968*
6:56 he entered, into v, or cities, or country, *2968*
Lk 13:22 And he went through the cities and v, *2968*
Ac 8:25 preached the gospel in many v of *2968*

VILLANY (2)
Isa 32: 6 For the vile person will speak v, and 5039
Jer 29:23 Because they have committed v in Israel, 5039

VINE (61) [VINEDRESSERS, VINES, VINEYARD, VINEYARDS, VINTAGE]
Ge 40: 9 In my dream, behold, a v *was* before me; 1612
40:10 in the v *were* three branches: and it *was* as 1612
49:11 Binding his foal unto the v, and his ass's 1612
49:11 and his ass's colt unto the **choice** v; 8322
Lev 25: 5 gather the grapes of thy v **undressed**: 5139
25:11 gather *the grapes* in it of thy v **undressed**. 5139
Nu 6: 4 he eat nothing that is made of the v tree, 3196
Dt 32:32 For their v *is* of the vine of Sodom, and 1612
32:32 For their vine *is* of the v of Sodom, and 1612
Jdg 9:12 said the trees unto the v, Come thou, *and* 1612
9:13 the v said unto them, Should I leave my 1612
13:14 eat of any *thing* that cometh of the v, 1612+3196
1Ki 4:25 every man under his v and under his fig 1612
2Ki 4:39 found a wild v, and gathered thereof wild 1612
18:31 *then* eat ye every man of his own v, and 1612
Job 15:33 He shall shake off his unripe grape as the v, 1612
Ps 80: 8 Thou hast brought a v out of Egypt: 1612
80:14 from heaven, and behold, and visit this v; 1612
128: 3 Thy wife *shall be* as a fruitful v by the sides 1612
SS 6:11 *and* to see whether the v flourished, *and* 1612
7: 8 also thy breasts shall be as clusters of the v, 1612
7:12 let us see if the v flourish, *whether* 1612
Isa 5: 2 planted it *with* the **choicest** v, and built a 8321
16: 8 of Heshbon languish, *and* the v of Sibmah: 1612
16: 9 with the weeping of Jazer the v of Sibmah: 1612
24: 7 The new wine mourneth, the v languisheth, 1612
32:12 for the pleasant fields, for the fruitful v. 1612
34: 4 as the leaf falleth off from the v, and as a 1612
36:16 eat ye every one *of* his v, and every one *of* 1612
Jer 2:21 Yet I had planted thee a **noble** v, wholly a 8321
2:21 degenerate **plant of** a strange v unto me? 1612
6: 9 glean the remnant of Israel as a v: 1612
8:13 *there shall be* no grapes on the v, nor figs 1612
48:32 O v of Sibmah, I will weep for thee with 1612
Eze 15: 2 What is the v tree more than any tree, *or* 1612
15: 6 As the v tree among the trees of the forest, 1612
17: 6 and became a spreading v of low stature, 1612
17: 6 so it became a v, and brought forth 1612
17: 7 this v did bend her roots toward him, and 1612
17: 8 might bear fruit, that *it* might be a goodly v. 1612
19:10 Thy mother *is* like a v in thy blood, 1612
Hos 10: 1 Israel *is* an empty v, he bringeth forth fruit 1612
14: 7 shall revive *as* the corn, and grow as the v: 1612
Joel 1: 7 He hath laid my v waste, and barked my fig 1612
1:12 The v is dried up, and the fig tree 1612
2:22 the fig tree and the v do yield their strength. 1612
Mic 4: 4 But they shall sit every man under his v and 1612
Na 2: 2 them out, and marred their v **branches**. 2156
Hag 2:19 as yet the v, and the fig tree, and 1612
Zec 3:10 under the v and under the fig tree. 1612
8:12 the v shall give her fruit, and the ground 1612
Mal 3:11 neither shall your v cast her fruit before 1612
Mt 26:29 not drink henceforth of this fruit of the v, *288*
Mk 14:25 I will drink no more of the fruit of the v, *288*
Lk 22:18 I will not drink of the fruit of the v, *288*
Jn 15: 1 I am the true v, and my Father is *288*
15: 4 bear fruit of itself, except it abide in the v; *288*
15: 5 I am the v, ye *are* the branches: He that *288*
Jas 3:12 either a v, figs? so *can* no fountain *both* yield *288*
Rev 14:18 and gather the clusters of the v of the earth; *288*
14:19 and gathered the v of the earth, and cast *it* *288*

VINE GROWERS See VINEDRESSERS

VINEDRESSERS (5) [VINE]
2Ki 25:12 the guard left of the poor of the land to be v 3755
2Ch 26:10 husbandmen *also,* and v in the mountains, 3755
Isa 61: 5 the alien *shall be* your plowmen and your v. 3755
Jer 52:16 left *certain* of the poor of the land for v 3755
Joel 1:11 howl, O ye v, for the wheat and for 3755

VINEGAR (13)
Nu 6: 3 *and* shall drink no v of wine, or vinegar of 2558
6: 3 no vinegar of wine, or v of strong drink, 2558
Ru 2:14 of the bread, and dip thy morsel in the v. 2558
Ps 69:21 and in my thirst they gave me v to drink. 2558
Pr 10:26 As v to the teeth, and as smoke to the eyes, 2558
25:20 *and as* v upon nitre, so *is* he that singeth 2558
Mt 27:34 They gave him v to drink mingled with *3690*
27:48 and filled *it* with v, and put *it* on a reed, and *3690*
Mk 15:36 And one ran and filled a spunge *full* of v, *3690*
Lk 23:36 coming to *him,* and offering him v, *3690*
Jn 19:29 Now there was set a vessel full of v: and *3690*
19:29 and they filled a spunge with v, and put *it* *3690*
19:30 When Jesus therefore had received the v, *3690*

VINES (12) [VINE]
Nu 20: 5 or of figs, or v, or of pomegranates; 1612
Dt 8: 8 and v, and fig trees, and pomegranates; 1612
Ps 78:47 He destroyed their v with hail, and 1612
105:33 He smote their v also and their fig trees; 1612
SS 2:13 the v *with* the tender grape give a *good* 1612
2:15 the foxes, the little foxes, that spoil the v: 3754
2:15 the vines: for our v *have* tender grapes. 3754
Isa 7:23 where there were a thousand v at a 1612
Jer 5:17 they shall eat up thy v and thy fig trees: 1612
31: 5 Thou shalt yet plant v upon the mountains 3754
Hos 2:12 I will destroy her v and her fig trees, 1612
Hab 3:17 not blossom, neither *shall* fruit *be* in the v; 1612

VINEYARD (69) [VINE]
Ge 9:20 *to be* a husbandman, and he planted a v: 3754
Ex 22: 5 If a man shall cause a field or v to be eaten, 3754
22: 5 of the best of his own v, shall he make 3754
23:11 In like manner thou shalt deal with thy v, 3754
Lev 19:10 thou shalt not glean thy v, neither shalt thou 3754
19:10 shalt thou gather *every* grape of thy v; 3754
25: 3 six years thou shalt prune thy v, and 3754
25: 4 shalt neither sow thy field, nor prune thy v. 3754
Dt 20: 6 what man *is he* that hath planted a v, and 3754
22: 9 Thou shalt not sow thy v with divers seeds: 3754
22: 9 hast sown, and the fruit of thy v, be defiled. 3754
23:24 When thou comest into thy neighbour's v, 3754
24:21 When thou gatherest the grapes of thy v, 3754
28:30 thou shalt plant a v, and shalt not gather 3754
1Ki 21: 1 *that* Naboth the Jezreelite had a v, 3754
21: 2 spake unto Naboth, saying, Give me thy v, 3754
21: 2 I will give thee for it a better v than it; *or,* 3754
21: 6 said unto him, Give me thy v for money; 3754
21: 6 please thee, I will give thee *another* v for it: 3754
21: 6 and he answered, I will not give thee my v. 3754

1Ki 21: 7 I will give thee the v of Naboth 3754
21:15 take possession of the v of Naboth 3754
21:16 that Ahab rose up to go down to the v of 3754
21:18 behold, *he is* in the v of Naboth, whither he 3754
Ps 80:15 the v which thy right hand hath planted, 3657
Pr 24:30 by the v of the man void of understanding; 3754
31:16 with the fruit of her hands she planteth a v. 3754
SS 1: 6 *but* mine own v have I not kept. 3754
8:11 Solomon had a v at Baal-hamon; he let out 3754
8:11 he let out the v unto keepers; 3754
8:12 My v, which *is* mine, *is* before me: thou, 3754
Isa 1: 8 daughter of Zion is left as a cottage in a v, 3754
3:14 for ye have eaten up the v; the spoil of 3754
5: 1 a song of my beloved touching his v. 3754
5: 1 My wellbeloved hath a v in a very fruitful 3754
5: 3 judge, I pray you, betwixt me and my v. 3754
5: 4 What could have been done more to my v, 3754
5: 5 go to, I will tell you what I *will* do to my v: 3754
5: 7 For the v of the LORD of hosts *is* 3754
5:10 ten acres of v shall yield one bath, and 3754
27: 2 that day sing ye unto her, A v of red wine. 3754
Jer 12:10 Many pastors have destroyed my v, 3754
35: 7 nor plant v, nor have *any:* but all your days 3754
35: 9 neither have we v, nor field, nor seed: 3754
Mic 1: 6 a heap of the field, *and* as plantings of a v: 3754
Mt 20: 1 in the morning to hire labourers into his v. *290*
20: 2 for a penny a day, he sent them into his v. *290*
20: 4 Go ye also into the v, and whatsoever is *290*
20: 7 He saith unto them, Go ye also into the v; *290*
20: 8 the lord of the v saith unto his steward, *290*
21:28 and said, Son, go work to day in my v. *290*
21:33 which planted a v, and hedged it round *290*
21:39 and cast *him* out of the v, and slew *him.* *290*
21:40 When the lord therefore of the v cometh, *290*
21:41 and will let out *his* v unto other husbandmen, *290*
Mk 12: 1 A *certain* man planted a v, and set a hedge *290*
12: 2 from the husbandmen of the fruit of the v. *290*
12: 8 and killed *him,* and cast *him* out of the v. *290*
12: 9 What shall therefore the lord of the v do? *290*
12: 9 and will give the v unto others. *290*
Lk 13: 6 A certain *man* had a fig tree planted in his v; *290*
13: 7 Then said he unto the **dresser of** his v, *289*
20: 9 A certain man planted a v, and let it forth to *290*
20:10 they should give him of the fruit of the v: *290*
20:13 Then said the lord of the v, What shall I do? *290*
20:15 So they cast him out of the v, and killed *him.* *290*
20:15 shall the lord of the v do unto them? *290*
20:16 and shall give the v to others. *290*
1Co 9: 7 who planteth a v, and eateth not of the fruit *290*

VINEYARDS (45) [VINE]

Nu 16:14 or given us inheritance of fields and v: 3754
20:17 pass through the fields, or through the v, 3754
21:22 will not turn into the fields, or into the v; 3754
22:24 of the LORD stood in a path of the v, 3754
Dt 6:11 which thou diggedst not, v and olive trees, 3754
28:39 Thou shalt plant v, and dress *them,* but 3754
Jos 24:13 of the v and oliveyards which ye planted 3754
Jdg 9:27 gathered their v, and trode *the grapes,* and 3754
11:33 twenty cities, and unto the plain of the v, 3754
14: 5 *to* Timnath, and came to the v of Timnath: 3754
15: 5 the standing corn, with the v *and* olives. 3754
21:20 Go and lie in wait in the v; 3754
21:21 come ye out of the v, and catch you every 3754
1Sa 8:14 your v, and your oliveyards, *even* the best 3754
8:15 of your v, and give to his officers, and 3754
22: 7 of Jesse give every one of you fields and v, 3754
2Ki 5:26 v, and sheep, and oxen, and menservants, 3754
18:32 of corn and wine, a land of bread and v, 3754
19:29 reap, and plant v, and eat the fruits thereof. 3754
1Ch 27:27 over the v *was* Shimei the Ramathite: over 3754
27:27 over the increase of the v for the wine 3754
Ne 5: 3 v, and houses, that we might buy corn, 3754
5: 4 *and that upon* our lands and v. 3754
5: 5 *them;* for other men have our lands and v. 3754
5:11 to them, even *this* day, their lands, their v, 3754
9:25 v, and oliveyards, and fruit trees in 3754
Job 24:18 he beholdeth not the way of the v. 3754
Ps 107:37 sow the fields, and plant v, which may 3754
Ecc 2: 4 I builded me houses; I planted me v: 3754
SS 1: 6 they made me the keeper of the v; *but* 3754
1:14 *as* a cluster of camphire in the v of En-gedi. 3754
7:12 Let us get up early to the v; let us see if 3754
Isa 16:10 in the v there shall be no singing, 3754
36:17 of corn and wine, a land of bread and v. 3754
37:30 reap, and plant v, and eat the fruit thereof. 3754
65:21 inhabit *them;* and they shall plant v, and 3754
Jer 32:15 and v shall be possessed again in this land. 3754
39:10 gave them v and fields at the same time. 3754
Eze 28:26 and shall build houses, and plant v; 3754
Hos 2:15 I will give her her v from thence, and 3754
Am 4: 9 and your v and your fig trees and 3754
5:11 ye have planted pleasant v, but ye shall not 3754
5:17 in all v *shall be* wailing: for I will pass 3754
9:14 inhabit *them;* and they shall plant v, and 3754
Zep 1:13 not inhabit *them;* and they shall plant v, but 3754

VINTAGE (10) [VINE]

Lev 26: 5 your threshing shall reach unto the v, and 1210
26: 5 and the v shall reach unto the sowing time: 1210
Jdg 8: 2 of Ephraim better than the v of Abi-ezer? 1210
Job 24: 6 and they gather the v of the wicked. 3754
Isa 16:10 I have made *their* v shouting to cease. NIH
24:13 as the gleaning grapes when the v is done. 1210
32:10 ye careless *women:* for the v shall fail, 1210
Jer 48:32 upon thy summer fruits and upon thy v. 1210
Mic 7: 1 as the grapegleanings of the v: 1210
Zec 11: 2 for the forest of the v is come down. 1210

VIOL (2) [VIOLS]

Isa 5:12 and the v, the tabret, and pipe, and wine, 5035
Am 6: 5 That chant to the sound of the v, *and* 5035

VIOLATED (1)

Eze 22:26 Her priests have v my law, and 2554

VIOLENCE (57) [VIOLENT, VIOLENTLY]

Ge 6:11 before God, and the earth was filled *with* v. 2555
6:13 for the earth is filled *with* v through them; 2555
Lev 6: 2 or in a **thing taken away by** v, or 1498
2Sa 22: 3 my saviour; thou savest me from v. 2555
Ps 11: 5 and him that loveth v his soul hateth. 2555
55: 9 for I have seen v and strife in the city. 2555
58: 2 you weigh the v of your hands in the earth. 2555
72:14 shall redeem their soul from deceit and v: 2555
73: 6 as a chain; v covereth them *as* a garment. 2555
Pr 4:17 of wickedness, and drink the wine of v. 2555
10: 6 but v covereth the mouth of the wicked. 2555
10:11 but v covereth the mouth of the wicked. 2555
13: 2 but the soul of the transgressors *shall eat* v. 2555
28:17 A man that **doeth** v to the blood of *any* 6231
Isa 53: 9 because he had done no v, neither *was any* 2555
59: 6 and the act of v *is* in their hands. 2555
60:18 V shall no more be heard in thy land, 2555
Jer 6: 7 v and spoil is heard in her; before me 2555
20: 8 I spake, I cried out, I cried v and spoil; 2555
22: 3 do no wrong, **do** no v, to the stranger, 2554
22:17 and for oppression, and for v, to do *it.* 4835
51:35 The v done to me and *to* my flesh *be* upon 2555
51:46 and v in the land, ruler against ruler. 2555
Eze 7:11 V is risen up into a rod of wickedness: 2555
7:23 *of* bloody crimes, and the city is full *of* v. 2555
8:17 for they have filled the land *with* v, and 2555
12:19 of the v of all them that dwell therein. 2555
18: 7 hath spoiled none by v, hath given his 1500
18:12 the poor and needy, hath spoiled by v, 1500
18:16 neither hath spoiled by v, *but* hath given his 1500
18:18 spoiled *his* brother by v, and did *that* which 1499
28:16 they have filled the midst of thee *with* v, 2555
45: 9 remove v and spoil, and execute judgment 2555
Joel 3:19 for the v against the children of Judah, 2555
Am 3:10 who store up v and robbery in their palaces. 2555
6: 3 and cause the seat of v to come near; 2555
Ob 1:10 For *thy* v against thy brother Jacob shame 2555
Jnh 3: 8 and from the v that *is* in their hands. 2555
Mic 2: 2 they covet fields, and **take** *them* **by** v; and 1497
6:12 For the rich *men* thereof are full *of* v, and 2555
Hab 1: 2 *even* cry out unto thee *of* v, and thou wilt 2555
1: 3 for spoiling and v *are* before me: and 2555
1: 9 They shall come all for v: their faces shall 2555
2: 8 *for* the v of the land, *of* the city, and *of* all 2555
2:17 For the v of Lebanon shall cover thee, and 2555
2:17 *for* the v of the land, *of* the city, and *of* all 2555
Zep 1: 9 which fill their masters' houses *with* v and 2555
3: 4 the sanctuary, they have **done** v to the law. 2554
Mal 2:16 for *one* covereth v with his garment, 2555
Mt 11:12 now the kingdom of heaven **suffereth** v, *971*
Lk 3:14 And he said unto them, Do v to no man, *1286*

Ac 5:26 the officers, and brought them without v: *970*
21:35 that he was borne of the soldiers for the v of *970*
24: 7 with great v took *him* away out of our hands, *970*
27:41 the hinder part was broken with the v of *970*
Heb 11:34 Quenched the v of fire, escaped the edge of *1411*
Rev 18:21 Thus with v shall *that* great city Babylon be *3731*

VIOLENT (10) [VIOLENCE]
2Sa 22:49 thou hast delivered me from the v man. 2555
Ps 7:16 his v **dealing** shall come down upon his 2555
18:48 thou hast delivered me from the v man. 2555
86:14 the assemblies of v *men* have sought after 6184
140: 1 the evil man: preserve me from the v man; 2555
140: 4 of the wicked; preserve me from the v man; 2555
140:11 evil shall hunt the v man to overthrow *him.* 2555
Pr 16:29 A v man enticeth his neighbour, and 2555
Ecc 5: 8 **v perverting** of judgment and justice in a 1499
Mt 11:12 suffereth violence, and the v take it by force. *973*

VIOLENTLY (10) [VIOLENCE]
Ge 21:25 Abimelech's servants had v **taken away.** 1497
Lev 6: 4 restore that which he **took** v **away,** 1497+1500
Dt 28:31 thine ass *shall be* v **taken away** from 1497
Job 20:19 he hath v **taken away** a house which he 1497
24: 2 they v **take away** flocks, and feed *thereof.* 1497
Isa 22:18 He will **surely** v **turn and toss** 6801+6801+6802
La 2: 6 he hath v **taken away** his tabernacle, as *if it* 2554
Mt 8:32 the whole herd of swine **ran** v down a steep *3729*
Mk 5:13 the herd **ran** v down a steep place into *3729*
Lk 8:33 the herd **ran** v down a steep place into *3729*

VIOLS (2) [VIOL]
Isa 14:11 down *to* the grave, *and* the noise of thy v: 5035
Am 5:23 for I will not hear the melody of thy v. 5035

VIPER (3) [VIPER'S, VIPERS]
Isa 30: 6 and old lion, the v and fiery flying serpent, 660
59: 5 that which is crushed breaketh out *into* a v. 660
Ac 28: 3 there came a v out of the heat, and *2191*

VIPER'S (1) [VIPER]
Job 20:16 poison of asps: the v tongue shall slay him. 660

VIPERS (4) [VIPER]
Mt 3: 7 he said unto them, O generation of v, *2191*
12:34 O generation of v, how can ye, being evil, *2191*
23:33 *Ye* serpents, *ye* generation of v, how can ye *2191*
Lk 3: 7 O generation of v, who hath warned you to *2191*

VIRGIN (33) [VIRGIN'S, VIRGINITY, VIRGINS]
Ge 24:16 a v, neither had any man known her: 1330
24:43 *that when* the v cometh forth to draw *water,* 5959
Lev 21: 3 for his sister a v, that is nigh unto him, 1330
21:14 he shall take a v of his own people to wife. 1330
Dt 22:19 he hath brought up an evil name upon a v 1330
22:23 If a damsel *that is* a v be betrothed unto a 1330
22:28 If a man find a damsel *that is* a v, which is 1330
32:25 shall destroy both the young man and the v, 1330
2Sa 13: 2 for she *was* a v; and Amnon thought it hard 1330
1Ki 1: 2 be sought for my lord the king a young v: 1330
2Ki 19:21 The v the daughter of Zion hath despised 1330
Isa 7:14 a V shall conceive, and bear a Son, and 5959
23:12 O thou oppressed v, daughter of Zidon: 1330
37:22 The v, the daughter of Zion, hath despised 1330
47: 1 sit in the dust, O v daughter of Babylon, 1330
62: 5 For *as* a young man marrieth a v, *so* 1330
Jer 14:17 for the v daughter of my people is broken 1330
18:13 who hath heard such *things:* the v of Israel 1330
31: 4 and thou shalt be built, O v of Israel: 1330
31:13 shall the v rejoice in the dance, both young 1330
31:21 turn again, O v of Israel, turn again to these 1330
46:11 Go up *into* Gilead, and take balm, O v, 1330
La 1:15 the Lord hath trodden the v, the daughter of 1330
2:13 I may comfort thee, O v daughter of Zion? 1330
Joel 1: 8 Lament like a v girded with sackcloth for 1330
Am 5: 2 The v of Israel is fallen; she shall no more 1330
Mt 1:23 a v shall be with child, and shall bring forth *3933*
Lk 1:27 To a v espoused to a man whose name was *3933*
1Co 7:28 and if a v marry, she hath not sinned. *3933*
7:34 is difference *also* between a wife and a v. *3933*
7:36 behaveth himself uncomely toward his v, *3933*
7:37 decreed in his heart that *he* will keep his v, *3933*
2Co 11: 2 that *I* may present *you as* a chaste v to *3933*

VIRGIN'S (1) [VIRGIN]
Lk 1:27 house of David; and the v name *was* Mary. *3933*

VIRGINITY (9) [VIRGIN]
Lev 21:13 And he shall take a wife in her v. 1331
Dt 22:15 bring forth *the tokens of* the damsel's v 1331
22:17 *yet* these *are the tokens of* my daughter's v. 1331
22:20 *the tokens of* v be not found for the damsel: 1331
Jdg 11:37 and bewail my v, I and my fellows. 1331
11:38 and bewailed her v upon the mountains. 1331
Eze 23: 3 and there they bruised the teats of their v. 1331
23: 8 they bruised the breasts of her v, and 1331
Lk 2:36 with a husband seven years from her v; *3932*

VIRGINS (22) [VIRGIN]
Ex 22:17 pay money according to the dowry of v. 1330
Jdg 21:12 of Jabesh-gilead four hundred young v, 1330
2Sa 13:18 the king's daughters *that were* v apparelled. 1330
Est 2: 2 Let there be fair young v sought for 1330
2: 3 the fair young v unto Shushan the palace, 1330
2:17 and favour in his sight more than all the v; 1330
2:19 when the v were gathered together 1330
Ps 45:14 the v her companions that follow her *shall* 1330
SS 1: 3 poured forth, therefore do the v love thee. 5959
6: 8 and v without number. 5959
Isa 23: 4 do I nourish up young men, *nor* bring up v. 1330
La 1: 4 her v *are* afflicted, and she *is* in bitterness. 1330
1:18 my v and my young men are gone into 1330
2:10 the v of Jerusalem hang down their heads 1330
2:21 my v and my young men are fallen by 1330
Am 8:13 In that day shall the fair v and young men 1330
Mt 25: 1 kingdom of heaven be likened unto ten v, *3933*
25: 7 Then all those v arose, and trimmed their *3933*
25:11 Afterward came also the other v, saying, *3933*
Ac 21: 9 had four daughters, v, which did prophesy. *3933*
1Co 7:25 Now concerning v I have no commandment *3933*
Rev 14: 4 not defiled with women; for they are v. *3933*

VIRTUE (7) [VIRTUOUS, VIRTUOUSLY]
Mk 5:30 in himself that v had gone out of him, *1411*
Lk 6:19 for there went v out of him, and *1411*
8:46 for I perceive that v is gone out of me. *1411*
Php 4: 8 if *there be* any v, and if *there be* any praise, *703*
2Pe 1: 3 of him that hath called us to glory and v: *703*
1: 5 giving all diligence, add to your faith v; *703*
1: 5 add to your faith virtue; and to v knowledge; *703*

VIRTUOUS (3) [VIRTUE]
Ru 3:11 people doth know that thou *art* a v woman. 2428
Pr 12: 4 A v woman *is* a crown to her husband: but 2428
31:10 Who can find a v woman? for her price *is* 2428

VIRTUOUSLY (1) [VIRTUE]
Pr 31:29 Many daughters have done v, but 2428

VISAGE (3) [VISION]
Isa 52:14 his v *was* so marred more than *any* man, 4758
La 4: 8 Their v is blacker than a coal; they are not 8389
Da 3:19 the form of his v was changed against 600

VISIBLE (1) [VISION]
Col 1:16 and that are in earth, v and invisible, *3707*

VISION (79) [VISAGE, VISIBLE, VISIONS]
Ge 15: 1 of the LORD came unto Abram in a v, 4236
Nu 12: 6 will make myself known unto him in a v, 4759
24: 4 which saw the v of the Almighty, 4236
24:16 *which* saw the v of the Almighty, 4236
1Sa 3: 1 in those days; *there was* no open v. 2377
3:15 And Samuel feared to shew Eli the v. 4759
2Sa 7:17 according to all this v, so did Nathan speak 2384
1Ch 17:15 according to all this v, so did Nathan speak 2377
2Ch 32:32 they *are* written in the v of Isaiah 2377
Job 20: 8 he shall be chased away as a v of the night. 2384
33:15 In a dream, *in* a v of the night, when deep 2384
Ps 89:19 thou spakest in v to thy holy one, and 2377
Pr 29:18 Where *there is* no v, the people perish: but 2377
Isa 1: 1 The v of Isaiah the son of Amoz, which he 2377
21: 2 A grievous v is declared unto me; 2380
22: 1 The burden of the valley of v. What aileth 2384
22: 5 the Lord GOD of hosts in the valley of v, 2384
28: 7 they err in v, they stumble *in* judgment. 7203
29: 7 shall be as a dream of a night v. 2377
29:11 the v of all is become unto you as 2380
Jer 14:14 they prophesy unto you a false v and 2377

Jer 23:16 they speak a v of their own heart, *and* 2377
La 2: 9 prophets also find no v from the LORD. 2377
Eze 7:13 for the v *is* touching the whole multitude 2377
7:26 shall they seek a v of the prophet; but 2377
8: 4 according to the v that I saw in the plain. 4758
11:24 brought me in v by the Spirit of God into 4758
11:24 So the v that I had seen went up from me. 4758
12:22 days are prolonged, and every v faileth? 2377
12:23 days are at hand, and the effect of every v. 2377
12:24 For there shall be no more any vain v nor 2377
12:27 The v that he seeth *is* for many days *to* 2377
13: 7 Have ye not seen a vain v, and have ye not 4236
43: 3 *it was* according to the appearance of the v 4758
43: 3 *even* according to the v that I saw when I 4758
43: 3 the visions *were* like the v that I saw by 4758
Da 2:19 the secret revealed unto Daniel in a night v. 2376
7: 2 said, I saw in my v by night, and behold, 2376
8: 1 of king Belshazzar a v appeared unto me, 2377
8: 2 I saw in a v; and it came to pass, when I 2377
8: 2 I saw in a v, and I was by the river of Ulai. 2377
8:13 How long *shall be* the v *concerning* 2377
8:15 had seen the v, and sought for the meaning, 2377
8:16 Gabriel, make this *man* to understand the v. 4758
8:17 for at the time of the end *shall be* the v. 2377
8:26 the v of the evening and the morning which 4758
8:26 wherefore shut thou up the v; for *it shall be* 2377
8:27 I was astonished at the v, but 4758
9:21 whom I had seen in the v at the beginning, 2377
9:23 understand the matter, and consider the v. 4758
9:24 to seal up the v and prophecy, and to anoint 2377
10: 1 the thing, and had understanding of the v. 4758
10: 7 I Daniel alone saw the v: for the men that 4759
10: 7 the men that were with me saw not the v; 4759
10: 8 saw this great v, and there remained no 4759
10:14 latter days: for yet the v *is* for *many* days. 2377
10:16 by the v my sorrows are turned upon me, 4759
11:14 shall exalt themselves to establish the v; 2377
Ob 1: 1 The v of Obadiah. Thus saith the Lord 2377
Mic 3: 6 *shall be* unto you, that *ye* shall not have a v; 2377
Na 1: 1 The book of the v of Nahum the Elkoshite. 2377
Hab 2: 2 Write the v, and make *it* plain upon tables, 2377
2: 3 For the v *is* yet for an appointed time, but 2377
Zec 13: 4 shall be ashamed every one of his v, 2384
Mt 17: 9 Tell the v to no *man,* until the Son of man *3705*
Lk 1:22 they perceived that he had seen a v in *3701*
24:23 that *they* had also seen a v of angels, *3701*
Ac 9:10 and to him said the Lord in a v, Ananias. *3705*
9:12 And hath seen in a v a man named Ananias *3705*
10: 3 He saw in a v evidently, about the ninth *3705*
10:17 what *this* v which he had seen should mean, *3705*
10:19 While Peter thought on the v, the Spirit said *3705*
11: 5 and in a trance I saw a v, A certain vessel *3705*
12: 9 done by the angel; but thought he saw a v. *3705*
16: 9 And a v appeared to Paul in the night; *3705*
16:10 And after he had seen the v, *3705*
18: 9 spake the Lord to Paul in the night by a v, *3705*
26:19 I was not disobedient unto the heavenly v: *3701*
Rev 9:17 And thus I saw the horses in the v, and *3706*

VISIONS (24) [VISION]

Ge 46: 2 God spake unto Israel in the v of the night, 4759
2Ch 9:29 in the v of Iddo the seer against Jeroboam 2378
26: 5 who had understanding in the v of God: 7200
Job 4:13 In thoughts from the v of the night, 2384
7:14 with dreams, and terrifiest me through v: 2384
Eze 1: 1 heavens were opened, and I saw v of God. 4759
8: 3 brought me in the v of God to Jerusalem, 4759
13:16 which see v of peace for her, and *there is* 2377
40: 2 In the v of God brought he me into the land 4759
43: 3 the v *were* like the vision that I saw by 4759
Da 1:17 Daniel had understanding in all v and 2377
2:28 the v of thy head upon thy bed, *are* these; 2376
4: 5 my bed and the v of my head troubled me. 2376
4: 9 tell *me* the v of my dream that I have seen, 2376
4:10 Thus *were* the v of mine head in my bed; 2376
4:13 I saw in the v of my head upon my bed, and 2376
7: 1 a dream and v of his head upon his bed: 2376
7: 7 After this I saw in the night v, and behold, 2376
7:13 I saw in the night v, and behold, *one* like 2376
7:15 and the v of my head troubled me. 2376
Hos 12:10 I have multiplied v, and used similitudes by 2377
Joel 2:28 dream dreams, your young men shall see v: 2384
Ac 2:17 and your young men shall see v, and *3706*
2Co 12: 1 I will come to v and revelations of *3701*

VISIT (38) [VISITATION, VISITED, VISITEST, VISITETH, VISITING]

Ge 50:24 God will **surely** v you, and bring you 6485+6485
50:25 God will **surely** v you, and ye shall 6485+6485
Ex 13:19 saying, God will **surely** v you; 6485+6485
32:34 nevertheless in the day when I v, I will visit 6485
32:34 when I visit, I will v their sin upon them. 6485
Lev 18:25 therefore I do v the iniquity thereof upon it, 6485
Job 5:24 thou shalt v thy habitation, and shalt not 6485
7:18 *that* thou shouldest v him every morning, 6485
Ps 59: 5 God of Israel, awake to v all the heathen: 6485
80:14 from heaven, and behold, and v this vine; 6485
89:32 will I v their transgression with the rod, 6485
106: 4 unto thy people: O v me with thy salvation; 6485
Isa 23:17 *that* the LORD will v Tyre, and she shall 6485
Jer 3:16 neither shall they v *it;* neither shall *that* be 6485
5: 9 Shall I not v for these *things?* saith 6485
5:29 Shall I not v for these *things?* saith 6485
6:15 at the time *that* I v them they shall be cast 6485
9: 9 Shall I not v them for these *things?* saith 6485
14:10 remember their iniquity, and v their sins. 6485
15:15 v me, and revenge me of my persecutors; 6485
23: 2 I will v upon you the evil of your doings, 6485
27:22 there shall they be until the day that I v 6485
29:10 be accomplished at Babylon I will v you, 6485
32: 5 there shall he be until I v him, saith 6485
49: 8 Esau upon him, the time *that* I will v him. 6485
50:31 thy day is come, the time *that* I will v thee. 6485
La 4:22 he will v thine iniquity, O daughter of 6485
Hos 2:13 I will v upon her the days of Baalim, 6485
8:13 he remember their iniquity, and v their sins: 6485
9: 9 their iniquity, he will v their sins. 6485
Am 3:14 That in the day that I shall v 6485
3:14 upon him I will also v the altars of Beth-el: 6485
Zep 2: 7 for the LORD their God shall v them, and 6485
Zec 11:16 *which* shall not v those that be cut off, 6485
Ac 7:23 it came into his heart to v his brethren *1980*
15:14 how God at the first did v the Gentiles, *1980*
15:36 v our brethren in every city where we have *1980*
Jas 1:27 To v the fatherless and widows in their *1980*

VISITATION (15) [VISIT]

Nu 16:29 or if they be visited after the v of all men; 6486
Job 10:12 favour, and thy v hath preserved my spirit. 6486
Isa 10: 3 what will ye do in the day of v, and in 6486
Jer 8:12 in the time of their v they shall be cast 6486
10:15 in the time of their v they shall perish. 6486
11:23 men of Anathoth, *even* the year of their v. 6486
23:12 *even* the year of their v, saith the LORD. 6486
46:21 come upon them, *and* the time of their v. 6486
48:44 *even* upon Moab, the year of their v, 6486
50:27 for their day is come, the time of their v. 6486
51:18 in the time of their v they shall perish. 6486
Hos 9: 7 The days of v are come, the days of 6486
Mic 7: 4 the day of thy watchmen *and* thy v cometh; 6486
Lk 19:44 because thou knewest not the time of thy v. *1984*
1Pe 2:12 shall behold, glorify God in the day of v. *1984*

VISITED (23) [VISIT]

Ge 21: 1 the LORD v Sarah as he had said, and 6485
Ex 3:16 I have **surely** v you, and *seen* that 6485+6485
4:31 when they heard that the LORD had v 6485
Nu 16:29 if they be v after the visitation of all men; 6485
Jdg 15: 1 that Samson v his wife with a kid; 6485
Ru 1: 6 had v his people in giving them bread. 6485
1Sa 2:21 the LORD v Hannah, so that she 6485
Job 35:15 because *it is* not so, he hath v *in* his anger; 6485
Ps 17: 3 thou hast v *me* in the night; thou hast tried 6485
Pr 19:23 abide satisfied; he shall not be v *with* evil. 6485
Isa 24:22 and after many days shall they be v. 6485
26:14 therefore hast thou v and destroyed them, 6485
26:16 LORD, in trouble have they v thee, 6485
29: 6 Thou shalt be v of the LORD of hosts 6485
Jer 6: 6 this is the city to be v; she *is* wholly 6485
23: 2 driven them away, and have not v them: 6485
Eze 38: 8 After many days thou shalt be v: in 6485
Zec 10: 3 for the LORD of hosts hath v his flock 6485
Mt 25:36 I was sick, and ye v me: I was in prison, *1980*
25:43 sick, and in prison, and ye v me not. *1980*
Lk 1:68 for he hath v and redeemed his people, *1980*
1:78 whereby the dayspring from on high hath v *1980*
7:16 among us; and, That God hath v his people. *1980*

VISITEST (3) [VISIT]
Ps 8: 4 and the son of man, that thou v him? 6485
65: 9 Thou v the earth, and waterest it: 6485
Heb 2: 6 of him? or the son of man, that thou v him? *1980*

VISITETH (1) [VISIT]
Job 31:14 and when he v, what shall I answer him? 6485

VISITING (4) [VISIT]
Ex 20: 5 v the iniquity of the fathers upon 6485
34: 7 *that* will by no means clear *the guilty;* v 6485
Nu 14:18 by no means clearing *the guilty,* v 6485
Dt 5: 9 v the iniquity of the fathers upon 6485

VOCATION (1)
Eph 4: 1 beseech you that *ye* walk worthy of the v *2821*

VOICE (505) [VOICES]
Ge 3: 8 they heard the v of the LORD God 6963
3:10 I heard thy v in the garden, and I was 6963
3:17 Because thou hast hearkened unto the v of 6963
4:10 the v of thy brother's blood crieth unto me 6963
4:23 his wives, Adah and Zillah, Hear my v; 6963
16: 2 And Abram hearkened to the v of Sarai. 6963
21:12 hath said unto thee, hearken unto her v; 6963
21:16 she sat over against *him,* and lift up her v, 6963
21:17 God heard the v of the lad; and the angel of 6963
21:17 for God hath heard the v of the lad where 6963
22:18 be blessed; because thou hast obeyed my v. 6963
26: 5 Because that Abraham obeyed my v, and 6963
27: 8 obey my v according to *that* which I 6963
27:13 only obey my v, and go fetch me *them.* 6963
27:22 The v *is* Jacob's voice, but the hands *are* 6963
27:22 The voice *is* Jacob's v, but the hands *are* 6963
27:38 my father. And Esau lift up his v, and wept. 6963
27:43 Now therefore, my son, obey my v; and 6963
29:11 and lifted up his v, and wept. 6963
30: 6 hath also heard my v, and hath given me a 6963
39:14 me to lie with me, and I cried with a loud v: 6963
39:15 when he heard that I lifted up my v and 6963
39:18 it came to pass, as I lift up my v and cried, 6963
Ex 3:18 they shall hearken to thy v: and thou shalt 6963
4: 1 will not believe me, nor hearken unto my v: 6963
4: 8 neither hearken to the v of the first sign, 6963
4: 8 that they will believe the v of the latter 6963
4: 9 these two signs, neither hearken unto thy v, 6963
5: 2 that I should obey his v to let Israel go? 6963
15:26 If thou wilt diligently hearken to the v of 6963
18:19 Hearken now unto my v, I will give thee 6963
18:24 So Moses hearkened to the v of his father 6963
19: 5 if ye will obey my v indeed, and keep my 6963
19:16 and the v of the trumpet exceeding loud; 6963
19:19 when the v of the trumpet sounded long, 6963
19:19 and God answered him by a v. 6963
23:21 Beware of him, and obey his v, 6963
23:22 if thou shalt indeed obey his v, and do all 6963
24: 3 and all the people answered *with* one v, and 6963
32:18 *It is* not the v of *them that* shout for 6963
32:18 neither *is it* the v of *them that* cry for being 6963
Lev 5: 1 hear the v of swearing, and *is* a witness, 6963
Nu 7:89 he heard the v of one speaking unto him 6963
14: 1 all the congregation lifted up their v, and 6963
14:22 ten times, and have not hearkened to my v; 6963
20:16 he heard our v, and sent an angel, and 6963
21: 3 the LORD hearkened to the v of Israel, 6963
Dt 1:34 the LORD heard the v of your words, and 6963
1:45 the LORD would not hearken to your v, 6963
4:12 ye heard the v of the words, but saw no 6963
4:12 but saw no similitude; only *ye heard* a v. 6963
4:30 thy God, and shalt be obedient unto his v; 6963
4:33 Did *ever* people hear the v of God speaking 6963
4:36 Out of heaven he made thee to hear his v, 6963
5:22 and of the thick darkness, *with* a great v: 6963
5:23 when ye heard the v out of the midst of 6963
5:24 we have heard his v out of the midst of 6963
5:25 if we hear the v of the LORD our God any 6963
5:26 that hath heard the v of the living God 6963
5:28 the LORD heard the v of your words, 6963
5:28 I have heard the v of the words of this 6963
8:20 ye would not be obedient unto the v of 6963
9:23 ye believed him not, nor hearkened to his v. 6963
13: 4 obey his v, and you shall serve him, and 6963
13:18 When thou shalt hearken to the v of 6963
15: 5 Only if thou carefully hearken unto the v of 6963
18:16 Let me not hear again the v of the LORD 6963
21:18 which will not obey the v of his father, or 6963
21:18 or the v of his mother, and *that,* when they 6963
21:20 and rebellious, he will not obey our v; 6963
26: 7 the LORD heard our v, and looked on our 6963
26:14 I have hearkened to the v of the LORD 6963
26:17 his judgments, and to hearken unto his v: 6963
27:10 obey the v of the LORD thy God, 6963
27:14 say unto all the men of Israel *with* a loud v, 6963
28: 1 if thou shalt hearken diligently unto the v 6963
28: 2 if thou shalt hearken unto the v of 6963
28:15 if thou wilt not hearken unto the v of 6963
28:45 thou hearkenedst not unto the v of 6963
28:62 thou wouldest not obey the v of 6963
30: 2 shalt obey his v according to all that I 6963
30: 8 shalt return and obey the v of the LORD, 6963
30:10 If thou shalt hearken unto the v of 6963
30:20 *and* that thou mayest obey his v, and 6963
33: 7 the v of Judah, and bring him unto his 6963
Jos 5: 6 they obeyed not the v of the LORD: 6963
6:10 not shout, nor make any noise with your v, 6963
10:14 that the LORD hearkened unto the v of a 6963
22: 2 have obeyed my v in all that I commanded 6963
24:24 God will we serve, and his v will we obey. 6963
Jdg 2: 2 ye have not obeyed my v: why have ye 6963
2: 4 that the people lift up their v, and wept. 6963
2:20 and have not hearkened unto my v; 6963
6:10 ye dwell: but ye have not obeyed my v. 6963
9: 7 lift up his v, and cried, and said unto them, 6963
13: 9 God hearkened to the v of Manoah; and 6963
18: 3 they knew the v of the young man 6963
18:25 Let not thy v be heard among us, lest angry 6963
20:13 the v of their brethren the children of Israel: 6963
Ru 1: 9 and they lift up their v, and wept. 6963
1:14 they lift up their v, and wept again: and 6963
1Sa 1:13 her lips moved, but her v was not heard: 6963
2:25 hearkened not unto the v of their father, 6963
8: 7 Hearken unto the v of the people in all that 6963
8: 9 Now therefore hearken unto their v: 6963
8:19 the people refused to obey the v of Samuel; 6963
8:22 Hearken unto their v, and make them a 6963
12: 1 I have hearkened unto your v in all that ye 6963
12:14 obey his v, and not rebel against 6963
12:15 But if ye will not obey the v of the LORD, 6963
15: 1 hearken thou unto the v of the words of 6963
15:19 didst thou not obey the v of the LORD, 6963
15:20 I have obeyed the v of the LORD, and 6963
15:22 as in obeying the v of the LORD? 6963
15:24 I feared the people, and obeyed their v. 6963
19: 6 And Saul hearkened unto the v of Jonathan: 6963
24:16 that Saul said, *Is* this thy v, my son David? 6963
24:16 And Saul lift up his v, and wept. 6963
25:35 I have hearkened to thy v, and 6963
26:17 Saul knew David's v, and said, *Is* this thy 6963
26:17 and said, *Is* this thy v, my son David? 6963
26:17 David said, *It is* my v, my lord, O king. 6963
28:12 saw Samuel, she cried with a loud v: 6963
28:18 Because thou obeyedst not the v of 6963
28:21 thine handmaid hath obeyed thy v, and 6963
28:22 hearken thou also unto the v of thine 6963
28:23 and he hearkened unto their v. 6963
30: 4 the people that *were* with him lift up their v 6963
2Sa 3:32 the king lift up his v, and wept at the grave 6963
12:18 and he would not hearken unto our v: 6963
13:14 Howbeit he would not hearken unto her v: 6963
13:36 sons came, and lift up their v and wept: 6963
15:23 all the country wept *with* a loud v, and 6963
19: 4 the king cried *with* a loud v, O my son 6963
19:35 can I hear any more the v of singing *men* 6963
22: 7 he did hear my v out of his temple, and 6963
22:14 and the most High uttered his v. 6963
1Ki 8:55 all the congregation of Israel *with* a loud v, 6963
17:22 the LORD heard the v of Elijah; and 6963
18:26 *there was* no v, nor any that answered. 6963
18:29 that *there was* neither v, nor any to answer, 6963
19:12 in the fire: and after the fire a still small v. 6963
19:13 *there came* a v unto him, and said, 6963
20:25 And he hearkened unto their v, and did so. 6963
20:36 Because thou hast not obeyed the v of 6963
2Ki 4:31 but *there was* neither v, nor hearing. 6963
7:10 neither v of man, but horses tied, and asses 6963
10: 6 *be* mine, and *if* ye will hearken unto my v, 6963
18:12 Because they obeyed not the v of 6963
18:28 cried with a loud v in the Jews' language, 6963

V

2Ki 19:22 against whom hast thou exalted *thy* v, and 6963
1Ch 15:16 sounding, by lifting up the v with joy. 6963
2Ch 5:13 when *they* lift up *their* v with the trumpets 6963
15:14 they sware unto the LORD with a loud v, 6963
20:19 God of Israel with a loud v on high. 6963
30:27 their v was heard, and their prayer came *up* 6963
32:18 they cried with a loud v in the Jews' speech 6963
Ezr 3:12 laid before their eyes, wept with a loud v; 6963
10:12 and said *with* a loud v, 6963
Ne 9: 4 cried with a loud v unto the LORD their 6963
Job 2:12 him not, they lifted up their v, and wept; 6963
3: 7 be solitary, let no **joyful** v come therein. 7445
3:18 they hear not the v of the oppressor. 6963
4:10 the v of the fierce lion, and the teeth of 6963
4:16 *there was* silence, and I heard a v, *saying,* 6963
9:16 believe that he had hearkened unto my v. 6963
30:31 and my organ into the v of them that weep. 6963
33: 8 I have heard the v of *thy* words, 6963
34:16 hear this: hearken to the v of my words. 6963
37: 2 Hear attentively the noise of his v, and 6963
37: 4 After it a v roareth: he thundereth with 6963
37: 4 he thundereth with the v of his excellency; 6963
37: 4 he will not stay them when his v is heard. 6963
37: 5 God thundereth marvellously with his v; 6963
38:34 Canst thou lift up thy v to the clouds, 6963
40: 9 or, canst thou thunder with a v like him? 6963
Ps 3: 4 I cried unto the LORD *with* my v, and 6963
5: 2 Hearken unto the v of my cry, my King, 6963
5: 3 My v shalt thou hear *in* the morning, 6963
6: 8 for the LORD hath heard the v of my 6963
18: 6 he heard my v out of his temple, and 6963
18:13 in the heavens, and the Highest gave his v; 6963
19: 3 nor language, *where* their v is not heard. 6963
26: 7 That *I* may publish with the v of 6963
27: 7 Hear, O LORD, *when* I cry *with* my v: 6963
28: 2 Hear the v of my supplications, when I cry 6963
28: 6 he hath heard the v of my supplications. 6963
29: 3 The v of the LORD *is* upon the waters: 6963
29: 4 The v of the LORD *is* powerful; the voice 6963
29: 4 the v of the LORD *is* full of majesty. 6963
29: 5 The v of the LORD breaketh the cedars; 6963
29: 7 The v of the LORD divideth the flames of 6963
29: 8 The v of the LORD shaketh 6963
29: 9 The v of the LORD maketh the hinds to 6963
31:22 nevertheless thou heardest the v of my 6963
42: 4 with the v of joy and praise, *with* a 6963
44:16 For the v of him that reproacheth and 6963
46: 6 he uttered his v, the earth melted. 6963
47: 1 shout unto God with the v of triumph. 6963
55: 3 Because of the v of the enemy, because 6963
55:17 and cry aloud: and he shall hear my v. 6963
58: 5 Which will not hearken to the v of 6963
64: 1 Hear my v, O God, in my prayer: 6963
66: 8 and make the v of his praise to be heard: 6963
66:19 *me;* he hath attended to the v of my prayer. 6963
68:33 lo, he doth send out his v, *and that* a mighty 6963
68:33 send out his voice, *and that* a mighty v. 6963
74:23 Forget not the v of thine enemies: 6963
77: 1 I cried unto God *with* my v, *even* unto God 6963
77: 1 *with* my voice, *even* unto God *with* my v; 6963
77:18 The v of thy thunder *was* in the heaven: 6963
81:11 my people would not hearken to my v; and 6963
86: 6 and attend to the v of my supplications. 6963
93: 3 O LORD, the floods have lifted up their v; 6963
95: 7 of his hand. To day if ye will hear his v, 6963
98: 5 with the harp, and the v of a psalm. 6963
102: 5 By reason of the v of my groaning my 6963
103:20 hearkening unto the v of his word. 6963
104: 7 at the v of thy thunder they hasted away. 6963
106:25 hearkened not unto the v of the LORD. 6963
116: 1 because he hath heard my v *and* 6963
118:15 The v of rejoicing and salvation *is* in 6963
119:149 Hear my v according unto thy 6963
130: 2 Lord, hear my v: let thine ears be attentive 6963
130: 2 let thine ears be attentive to the v of my 6963
140: 6 hear the v of my supplications, O LORD. 6963
141: 1 give ear unto my v, when I cry unto thee. 6963
142: 1 I cried unto the LORD *with* my v; 6963
142: 1 *with* my v unto the LORD did I make my 6963
Pr 1:20 she uttereth her v in the streets: 6963
2: 3 *and* liftest up thy v for understanding; 6963
5:13 have not obeyed the v of my teachers, 6963
8: 1 and understanding put forth her v? 6963
8: 4 I call; and my v *is* to the sons of man. 6963
27:14 He that blesseth his friend with a loud v, 6963
Ecc 5: 3 a fool's v *is known* by multitude of words. 6963
5: 6 wherefore should God be angry at thy v, 6963
10:20 for a bird of the air shall carry the v, and 6963
12: 4 he shall rise up at the v of the bird, and 6963
SS 2: 8 The v of my beloved! behold, he cometh 6963
2:12 and the v of the turtle is heard in our land; 6963
2:14 me see thy countenance, let me hear thy v; 6963
2:14 for sweet *is* thy v, and thy countenance *is* 6963
5: 2 *it is* the v of my beloved that knocketh 6963
8:13 the companions hearken to thy v: 6963
Isa 6: 4 the posts of the door moved at the v of him 6963
6: 8 Also I heard the v of the Lord, saying, 6963
10:30 Lift up thy v, O daughter of Gallim: 6963
13: 2 exalt the v unto them, shake the hand, 6963
15: 4 their v shall be heard *even* unto Jahaz: 6963
24:14 They shall lift up their v, they shall sing, 6963
28:23 Give ye ear, and hear my v; hearken, and 6963
29: 4 thy v shall be, as of one that hath a familiar 6963
30:19 he will be very gracious unto thee at the v 6963
30:30 the LORD shall cause his glorious v to be 6963
30:31 For through the v of the LORD shall 6963
31: 4 he will not be afraid of their v, nor abase 6963
32: 9 ye women that are at ease, hear my v; 6963
36:13 cried with a loud v in the Jews' language, 6963
37:23 against whom hast thou exalted *thy* v, and 6963
40: 3 The v of him that crieth in the wilderness, 6963
40: 6 The v said, Cry. And he said, What shall I 6963
40: 9 good tidings, lift up thy v with strength; 6963
42: 2 nor cause his v to be heard in the street. 6963
42:11 the cities thereof lift up *their v,* the villages NIH
48:20 with a v of singing declare ye, tell this, 6963
50:10 that obeyeth the v of his servant, 6963
51: 3 thanksgiving, and the v of melody. 6963
52: 8 Thy watchmen shall lift up the v; *with* 6963
52: 8 *with* the v together shall they sing: 6963
58: 1 lift up thy v like a trumpet, and shew my 6963
58: 4 to make your v to be heard on high. 6963
65:19 the v of weeping shall be no more heard in 6963
65:19 no more heard in her, nor the v of crying. 6963
66: 6 A v of noise from the city, a voice from 6963
66: 6 of noise from the city, a v from the temple, 6963
66: 6 a v of the LORD that rendereth 6963
Jer 3:13 ye have not obeyed my v, saith 6963
3:21 A v was heard upon the high places, 6963
3:25 have not obeyed the v of the LORD our 6963
4:15 For a v declareth from Dan, and 6963
4:16 give out their v against the cities of Judah. 6963
4:31 For I have heard a v as of a woman in 6963
4:31 the v of the daughter of Zion, 6963
6:23 their v roareth like the sea; and they ride 6963
7:23 Obey my v, and I will be your God, and 6963
7:28 This *is* a nation that obeyeth not the v of 6963
7:34 the v of mirth, and the voice of gladness, 6963
7:34 the voice of mirth, and the v of gladness, 6963
7:34 the v of the bridegroom, and the voice of 6963
7:34 of the bridegroom, and the v of the bride: 6963
8:19 Behold the v of the cry of the daughter of 6963
9:10 neither can *men* hear the v of the cattle; 6963
9:13 have not obeyed my v, neither walked 6963
9:19 For a v of wailing is heard out of Zion, 6963
10:13 When he uttereth his v, *there is* a multitude 6963
11: 4 saying, Obey my v, and do them, 6963
11: 7 and protesting, saying, Obey my v. 6963
16: 9 the v of mirth, and the voice of gladness, 6963
16: 9 the voice of mirth, and the v of gladness, 6963
16: 9 the v of the bridegroom, and the voice of 6963
16: 9 of the bridegroom, and the v of the bride. 6963
18:10 that *it* obey not my v, then I will repent of 6963
18:19 hearken to the v of them that contend with 6963
22:20 lift up thy v in Bashan, and cry from 6963
22:21 thy youth, that thou obeyedst not my v. 6963
25:10 Moreover I will take from them the v of 6963
25:10 the v of gladness, the voice of 6963
25:10 the v of the bridegroom, and the voice of 6963
25:10 the v of the bride, the sound of 6963
25:30 and utter his v from his holy habitation; 6963
25:36 A v of the cry of the shepherds, and 6963
26:13 and obey the v of the LORD your God; 6963
30: 5 We have heard a v of trembling, of fear, 6963
30:19 and the v of them that make merry: 6963
31:15 A v was heard in Ramah, lamentation, *and* 6963
31:16 Refrain thy v from weeping, and thine eyes 6963
32:23 they obeyed not thy v, neither walked in 6963

Jer	33:11	The v of joy, and the voice of gladness,	6963
	33:11	The voice of joy, and the v of gladness,	6963
	33:11	the v of the bridegroom, and the voice of	6963
	33:11	of the bridegroom, and the v of the bride,	6963
	33:11	of the bride, the v of them that shall say,	6963
	35: 8	Thus have we obeyed the v of Jonadab	6963
	38:20	I beseech thee, the v of the LORD, which	6963
	40: 3	have not obeyed his v, therefore this thing	6963
	42: 6	we will obey the v of the LORD our God,	6963
	42: 6	when we obey the v of the LORD our	6963
	42:13	neither obey the v of the LORD your God,	6963
	42:21	ye have not obeyed the v of the LORD	6963
	43: 4	the people, obeyed not the v of the LORD,	6963
	43: 7	for they obeyed not the v of the LORD:	6963
	44:23	have not obeyed the v of the LORD,	6963
	46:22	The v thereof shall go like a serpent;	6963
	48: 3	A v of crying *shall be* from Horonaim,	6963
	48:34	*even* unto Jahaz, have they uttered their v,	6963
	50:28	The v of them that flee and escape out of	6963
	50:42	their v shall roar like the sea, and they shall	6963
	51:16	When he uttereth *his* v, *there is* a multitude	6963
	51:55	and destroyed out of her the great v;	6963
	51:55	great waters, a noise of their v is uttered:	6963
La	3:56	Thou hast heard my v: hide not thine ear at	6963
Eze	1:24	as the v of the Almighty, the voice of	6963
	1:24	the v of speech, as the noise of a host:	6963
	1:25	there was a v from the firmament that *was*	6963
	1:28	my face, and I heard a v of one that spake.	6963
	3:12	I heard behind me a v of a great rushing,	6963
	8:18	though they cry in mine ears *with* a loud v,	6963
	9: 1	He cried also in mine ears *with* a loud v,	6963
	10: 5	as the v of the Almighty God when he	6963
	11:13	cried *with* a loud v, and said, Ah Lord	6963
	19: 9	that his v should no more be heard upon	6963
	21:22	the slaughter, to lift up the v with shouting,	6963
	23:42	a v of a multitude being at ease *was* with	6963
	27:30	shall cause their v to be heard against thee,	6963
	33:32	lovely song *of* one that hath a pleasant v,	6963
	43: 2	his v *was* like a noise of many waters: and	6963
Da	4:31	there fell a v from heaven, *saying,* O king	7032
	6:20	he cried with a lamentable v unto Daniel:	7032
	7:11	of the v of the great words which the horn	7032
	8:16	I heard a man's v between *the banks of*	6963
	9:10	Neither have we obeyed the v of	6963
	9:11	that *they* might not obey thy v;	6963
	9:14	which he doeth: for we obeyed not his v.	6963
	10: 6	the v of his words like the voice of a	6963
	10: 6	the voice of his words like the v of a	6963
	10: 9	Yet heard I the v of his words: and when I	6963
	10: 9	when I heard the v of his words, then was I	6963
Joel	2:11	the LORD shall utter his v before his	6963
	3:16	out of Zion, and utter his v from Jerusalem;	6963
Am	1: 2	from Zion, and utter his v from Jerusalem;	6963
Jnh	2: 2	of hell cried I, *and* thou heardest my v.	6963
	2: 9	I will sacrifice unto thee with the v of	6963
Mic	6: 1	the mountains, and let the hills hear thy v.	6963
	6: 9	The LORD's v crieth unto the city, and	6963
Na	2: 7	her maids *shall* lead *her* as *with* the v of	6963
	2:13	the v of thy messengers shall no more be	6963
Hab	3:10	the deep uttered his v, *and* lift up his hands	6963
	3:16	belly trembled; my lips quivered at the v:	6963
Zep	1:14	*even* the v of the day of the LORD:	6963
	2:14	*their* v shall sing in the windows;	6963
	3: 2	She obeyed not the v; she received not	6963
Hag	1:12	obeyed the v of the LORD their God, and	6963
Zec	6:15	if ye will diligently obey the v of	6963
	11: 3	*There is* a v of the howling of	6963
	11: 3	a v of the roaring of young lions; for	6963
Mt	2:18	In Rama was there a v heard, lamentation,	*5456*
	3: 3	The v of one crying in the wilderness,	*5456*
	3:17	And lo a v from heaven, saying, This is my	*5456*
	12:19	neither shall any *man* hear his v in	*5456*
	17: 5	and behold a v out of the cloud, which said,	*5456*
	27:46	the ninth hour Jesus cried with a loud v,	*5456*
	27:50	when he had cried again with a loud v,	*5456*
Mk	1: 3	The v of one crying in the wilderness,	*5456*
	1:11	And there came a v from heaven,	*5456*
	1:26	and cried with a loud v, he came out of	*5456*
	5: 7	And cried with a loud v, and said,	*5456*
	9: 7	and a v came out of the cloud, saying,	*5456*
	15:34	at the ninth hour Jesus cried with a loud v,	*5456*
	15:37	And Jesus cried with a loud v, and gave up	*5456*
Lk	1:42	And she spake out with a loud v,	*5456*
	1:44	as soon as the v of thy salutation sounded	*5456*
	3: 4	The v of one crying in the wilderness,	*5456*
	3:22	and a v came from heaven, which said,	*5456*
	4:33	unclean devil, and cried out with a loud v,	*5456*
	8:28	down before him, and with a loud v said,	*5456*
	9:35	And there came a v out of the cloud,	*5456*
	9:36	And when the v was past, Jesus was found	*5456*
	11:27	certain woman of the company lift up her v,	*5456*
	17:15	and with a loud v glorified God,	*5456*
	19:37	praise God with a loud v for all the mighty	*5456*
	23:46	And when Jesus had cried with a loud v,	*5456*
Jn	1:23	I *am* the v of one crying in the wilderness,	*5456*
	3:29	because of the bridegroom's v:	*5456*
	5:25	when the dead shall hear the v of the Son of	*5456*
	5:28	all that are in the graves shall hear his v,	*5456*
	5:37	Ye have neither heard his v at any time,	*5456*
	10: 3	porter openeth; and the sheep hear his v:	*5456*
	10: 4	the sheep follow him: for they know his v.	*5456*
	10: 5	for they know not the v of strangers.	*5456*
	10:16	also I must bring, and they shall hear my v;	*5456*
	10:27	My sheep hear my v, and I know them, and	*5456*
	11:43	he cried with a loud v, Lazarus, come forth.	*5456*
	12:28	Then came there a v from heaven, *saying,* I	*5456*
	12:30	This v came not because of me, but	*5456*
	18:37	Every one that is of the truth heareth my v.	*5456*
Ac	2:14	lift up his v, and said unto them, Ye men of	*5456*
	4:24	they lift up their v to God with one accord,	*5456*
	7:31	as he drew near to behold *it,* the v of	*5456*
	7:57	Then they cried out with a loud v, and	*5456*
	7:60	and cried with a loud v, Lord,	*5456*
	8: 7	For unclean spirits, crying with loud v,	*5456*
	9: 4	and heard a v saying unto him, Saul, Saul,	*5456*
	9: 7	hearing a v, but seeing no *man.*	*5456*
	10:13	And there came a v to him, Rise, Peter; kill,	*5456*
	10:15	And *the* v *spake* unto him again the second	*5456*
	11: 7	And I heard a v saying unto me, Arise,	*5456*
	11: 9	But *the* v answered me again from heaven,	*5456*
	12:14	And when she knew Peter's v, she opened	*5456*
	12:22	*saying, It is* the v of a god, and not of a	*5456*
	14:10	Said with a loud v, Stand upright on thy	*5456*
	16:28	But Paul cried with a loud v, saying,	*5456*
	19:34	all with one v about the space of two hours	*5456*
	22: 7	and heard a v saying unto me, Saul, Saul,	*5456*
	22: 9	they heard not the v of him that spake to	*5456*
	22:14	and shouldest hear the v of his mouth.	*5456*
	24:21	Except *it be* for this one v, that I cried	*5456*
	26:10	put to death, I gave my v **against** *them.*	*5586*
	26:14	I heard a v speaking unto me, and saying in	*5456*
	26:24	Festus said with a loud v, Paul, thou art	*5456*
1Co	14:11	if I know not the meaning of the v,	*5456*
	14:19	that *by my* v I might teach others also,	NIG
Gal	4:20	present with you now, and to change my v;	*5456*
1Th	4:16	with the v of the archangel, and with	*5456*
Heb	3: 7	Ghost saith, To day if ye will hear his v,	*5456*
	3:15	it is said, To day if ye will hear his v,	*5456*
	4: 7	as it is said, To day if ye will hear his v,	*5456*
	12:19	the sound of a trumpet, and the v of words;	*5456*
	12:19	which *v* they that heard intreated that	NIG
	12:26	Whose v then shook the earth: but now he	*5456*
2Pe	1:17	when there came such a v to him from	*5456*
	1:18	And this v which came from heaven we	*5456*
	2:16	the dumb ass speaking with man's v forbad	*5456*
Rev	1:10	and heard behind me a great v, as of a	*5456*
	1:12	And I turned to see the v that spake with	*5456*
	1:15	and his v as the sound of many waters.	*5456*
	3:20	if any *man* hear my v, and open the door, I	*5456*
	4: 1	the first v which I heard *was* as *it were* of a	*5456*
	5: 2	a strong angel proclaiming with a loud v,	*5456*
	5:11	I heard the v of many angels round about	*5456*
	5:12	Saying with a loud v, Worthy is the Lamb	*5456*
	6: 6	And I heard a v in the midst of the four	*5456*
	6: 7	I heard the v of the fourth beast say, Come	*5456*
	6:10	And they cried with a loud v, saying,	*5456*
	7: 2	he cried with a loud v to the four angels,	*5456*
	7:10	And cried with a loud v, saying, Salvation	*5456*
	8:13	saying with a loud v, Woe, woe, woe,	*5456*
	9:13	I heard a v from the four horns of	*5456*
	10: 3	And cried with a loud v, as *when* a lion	*5456*
	10: 4	I heard a v from heaven saying unto me,	*5456*
	10: 7	But in the days of the v of the seventh	*5456*
	10: 8	And the v which I heard from heaven spake	*5456*
	11:12	And they heard a great v from heaven	*5456*
	12:10	And I heard a loud v saying in heaven,	*5456*
	14: 2	And I heard a v from heaven, as the voice	*5456*
	14: 2	as the v of many waters, and as the voice of	*5456*

Rev 14: 2 and as the v of a great thunder: *5456*
14: 2 I heard the v of harpers harping with their *5456*
14: 7 Saying with a loud v, Fear God, and *5456*
14: 9 saying with a loud v, If any *man* worship *5456*
14:13 And I heard a v from heaven saying unto *5456*
14:15 crying with a loud v to him that sat on *5456*
16: 1 And I heard a great v out of the temple *5456*
16:17 there came a great v out of the temple of *5456*
18: 2 And he cried mightily with a strong v, *5456*
18: 4 And I heard another v from heaven, saying, *5456*
18:22 And the v of harpers, and musicians, and *5456*
18:23 and the v of the bridegroom and of *5456*
19: 1 And after these *things* I heard a great v of *5456*
19: 5 And a v came out of the throne, saying, *5456*
19: 6 And I heard as *it were* the v of a great *5456*
19: 6 and as the v of many waters, and as *5456*
19: 6 and as the v of mighty thunderings, saying, *5456*
19:17 and he cried with a loud v, saying to all *5456*
21: 3 And I heard a great v out of heaven saying, *5456*

VOICES (17) [VOICE]
Jdg 21: 2 and lift up their v, and wept sore; 6963
1Sa 11: 4 and all the people lift up their v, and wept. 6963
Lk 17:13 And they lifted up *their* v, and said, Jesus, *5456*
23:23 And they were instant with loud v, *5456*
23:23 And the v of them and of the chief priests *5456*
Ac 13:27 nor *yet* the v of the prophets which are read *5456*
14:11 they lift up their v, saying in the speech of *5456*
22:22 and *then* lift up their v, and said, *5456*
1Co 14:10 so many kinds of v in the world, and *5456*
Rev 4: 5 and thunderings and v: *5456*
8: 5 and there were v, and thunderings, and *5456*
8:13 other v of the trumpet of the three angels, *5456*
10: 3 he had cried, seven thunders uttered their v. *5456*
10: 4 the seven thunders had uttered their v, *5456*
11:15 and there were great v in heaven, saying, *5456*
11:19 and v, and thunderings, and an earthquake, *5456*
16:18 And there were v, and thunders, and *5456*

VOID (24)
Ge 1: 2 the earth was without form, and v; and 922
Nu 30:12 **utterly made** them v on the day he 6565+6565
30:12 her husband hath **made** them v; and 6565
30:13 establish it, or her husband may **make** it v. 6565
30:15 if he shall **any ways make** them v 6565+6565
Dt 32:28 For they *are* a nation v of counsel, neither *is* 6
1Ki 22:10 in a v **place** *in* the entrance of the gate of 1637
2Ch 18: 9 they sat in a v **place** *at* the entering in of 1637
Ps 89:39 Thou hast **made** v the covenant of thy 5010
119:126 to work: *for* they have **made** v thy law. 6565
Pr 7: 7 a young man v of understanding, 2638
10:13 a rod *is* for the back of him that is v of 2638
11:12 He that is v of wisdom despiseth his 2638
12:11 he that followeth vain *persons is* v of 2638
17:18 A man v of understanding striketh hands, 2638
24:30 by the vineyard of the man v of 2638
Isa 55:11 it shall not return unto me v, but it shall 7387
Jer 4:23 the earth, and lo, *it was* without form, and v; 922
19: 7 And I will **make** v the counsel of Judah and 1238
Na 2:10 She *is* empty, and v, and waste: and 4003
Ac 24:16 to have always a conscience v **of offence** *677*
Ro 3:31 Do we then **make** v the law through faith? *2673*
4:14 faith is **made** v, and the promise made of *2758*
1Co 9:15 that any *man* should **make** my glorying v. *2758*

VOLUME (2)
Ps 40: 7 in the v of the book *it is* written of me, 4039
Heb 10: 7 I come (in the v of the book it is written of *2777*

VOLUNTARILY (1) [VOLUNTARY]
Eze 46:12 or peace offerings v unto the LORD, 5071

VOLUNTARY (4) [VOLUNTARILY]
Lev 1: 3 he shall offer it of his own v **will** at 7522
7:16 of his offering *be* a vow, or a v **offering**, 5071
Eze 46:12 Now when the prince shall prepare a v 5071
Col 2:18 beguile you of your reward in a v humility *2309*

VOMIT (8) [VOMITED, VOMITETH]
Job 20:15 down riches, and he shall v them **up** again: 6958
Pr 23: 8 *which* thou hast eaten shalt thou v **up**, 6958
25:16 lest thou be filled there*with*, and v it. 6958
26:11 As a dog returneth to his v, *so* a fool 6892
Isa 19:14 as a drunken *man* staggereth in his v. 6892
28: 8 For all tables are full *of* v *and* filthiness, *so* 6892
Jer 48:26 Moab also shall wallow in his v, and 6892
2Pe 2:22 The dog *is* turned to his own v again; *1829*

VOMITED (1) [VOMIT]
Jnh 2:10 and it v **out** Jonah upon the dry *land*. 6958

VOMITETH (1) [VOMIT]
Lev 18:25 and the land *itself* v **out** her inhabitants. 6958

VOPHSI (1)
Nu 13:14 the tribe of Naphtali, Nahbi the son of V. 2058

VOW (41) [VOWED, VOWEDST, VOWEST, VOWETH, VOWS]
Ge 28:20 Jacob vowed a v, saying, If God will be 5088
31:13 *and* where thou vowedst a v unto me: 5088
Lev 7:16 if the sacrifice of his offering *be* a v, or 5088
22:21 unto the LORD to accomplish *his* v, 5088
22:23 but for a v it shall not be accepted. 5088
27: 2 a man shall **make a singular** v, 5088+6381
Nu 6: 2 woman shall separate *themselves* to v a 5087
6: 2 *themselves* to vow a v of a Nazarite, 5088
6: 5 All the days of the v of his separation there 5088
6:21 according to the v which he vowed, so 5088
15: 3 or a sacrifice in performing a v, or in a 5088
15: 8 or *for* a sacrifice in performing a v, or 5088
21: 2 Israel vowed a v unto the LORD, and 5088
30: 2 If a man v a vow unto the LORD, or 5087
30: 2 If a man vow a v unto the LORD, or 5088
30: 3 If a woman also v a vow unto the LORD, 5087
30: 3 If a woman also vow a v unto the LORD, 5088
30: 4 her father hear her v, and her bond 5088
30: 8 then he shall make her v which she vowed, 5088
30: 9 every v of a widow, and of her that is 5088
30:13 Every v, and every binding oath to afflict 5088
Dt 12:11 all your choice vows which ye v unto 5087
23:18 the house of the LORD thy God for any v: 5088
23:21 When thou shalt v a vow unto the LORD 5087
23:21 When thou shalt vow a v unto the LORD 5088
23:22 if thou shalt forbear to v, it shall be no sin 5087
Jdg 11:30 Jephthah vowed a v unto the LORD, and 5088
11:39 who did with her *according to* his v which 5088
1Sa 1:11 she vowed a v, and said, O LORD of 5088
1:21 the LORD the yearly sacrifice, and his v. 5088
2Sa 15: 7 I pray thee, let me go and pay my v, 5088
15: 8 For thy servant vowed a v while I abode at 5088
Ps 65: 1 and unto thee shall the v be performed. 5088
76:11 V, and pay unto the LORD your God: 5087
Ecc 5: 4 When thou vowest a v unto God, defer not 5088
5: 5 Better *is it* that thou shouldest not v, 5087
5: 5 than that thou shouldest v and not pay. 5087
Isa 19:21 they shall v a vow unto the LORD, and 5087
19:21 they shall vow a v unto the LORD, and 5088
Ac 18:18 shorn *his* head in Cenchrea: for he had a v. *2171*
21:23 We have four men which have a v on them; *2171*

VOWED (18) [VOW]
Ge 28:20 Jacob v a vow, saying, If God will be with 5087
Lev 27: 8 according to his ability that v shall 5087
Nu 6:21 This *is* the law of the Nazarite who hath v, 5087
6:21 according to the vow which he v, so 5087
21: 2 Israel v a vow unto the LORD, and said, 5087
30: 6 when she v, or uttered ought out of her lips, 5088
30: 8 then he shall make her vow which she v^s, 5921
30:10 if she v *in* her husband's house, or 5087
Dt 23:23 according as thou hast v unto the LORD 5087
Jdg 11:30 Jephthah v a vow unto the LORD, and 5087
11:39 her *according to* his vow which he had v: 5087
1Sa 1:11 she v a vow, and said, O LORD of hosts, 5087
2Sa 15: 7 which I have v unto the LORD, 5087
15: 8 For thy servant v a vow while I abode at 5087
Ps 132: 2 *and* v unto the mighty *God* of Jacob; 5087
Ecc 5: 4 in fools: pay that which thou hast v. 5087
Jer 44:25 surely perform our vows that we have v, 5087
Jnh 2: 9 I will pay *that* that I have v. 5087

VOWEDST (1) [VOW]
Ge 31:13 the pillar, *and* where thou v a vow unto me: 5087

VOWEST (2) [VOW]
Dt 12:17 nor any of thy vows which thou v, 5087
Ecc 5: 4 When thou v a vow unto God, defer not to 5087

VOWETH (1) [VOW]
Mal 1:14 v, and sacrificeth unto the Lord a corrupt 5087

VOWS (30) [VOW]
Lev 22:18 that will offer his oblation for all his **v**, and 5088
23:38 beside all your **v**, and beside all your 5088
Nu 29:39 besides your **v**, and your freewill offerings, 5088
30: 4 all her **v** shall stand, and every bond 5088
30: 5 not any of her **v**, or of her bonds wherewith 5088
30: 7 day that he heard *it:* then her **v** shall stand, 5088
30:11 all her **v** shall stand, and every bond 5088
30:12 proceeded out of her lips concerning her **v**, 5088
30:14 he establisheth all her **v**, or all her bonds, 5088
Dt 12: 6 your **v**, and your freewill offerings, and 5088
12:11 all your choice **v** which ye vow unto 5088
12:17 nor any of thy **v** which thou vowest, 5088
12:26 thy **v**, thou shalt take, and go unto the place 5088
Job 22:27 he shall hear thee, and thou shalt pay thy **v**. 5088
Ps 22:25 I will pay my **v** before them that fear him. 5088
50:14 and pay thy **v** unto the most High: 5088
56:12 Thy **v** *are* upon me, O God: I will render 5088
61: 5 For thou, O God, hast heard my **v**: 5088
61: 8 for ever, that I may daily perform my **v**. 5088
66:13 with burnt offerings: I will pay thee my **v**, 5088
116:14 I will pay my **v** unto the LORD now in 5088
116:18 I will pay my **v** unto the LORD now in 5088
Pr 7:14 with me; *this* day have I payed my **v**. 5088
20:25 *which is* holy, and after **v** to make inquiry. 5088
31: 2 of my womb? and what, the son of my **v**? 5088
Jer 44:25 We will surely perform our **v** that we have 5088
44:25 ye will surely accomplish your **v**, and 5088
44:25 your vows, and surely perform your **v**. 5088
Jnh 1:16 a sacrifice unto the LORD, and made **v**. 5088
Na 1:15 keep thy solemn feasts, perform thy **v**: 5088

VOYAGE (1)
Ac 27:10 I perceive that *this* **v** will be with hurt and *4144*

VULTURE (2) [VULTURE'S, VULTURES]
Lev 11:14 And the **v**, and the kite after his kind; 1676
Dt 14:13 And the kite, and the **v** after his kind, 1772

VULTURE'S (1) [VULTURE]
Job 28: 7 and which the **v** eye hath not seen: 344

VULTURES (1) [VULTURE]
Isa 34:15 there shall the **v** also be gathered, every one 1772

W

WADI See BROOKS

WAFER (3) [WAFERS]
Ex 29:23 one **w** out of the basket of the unleavened 7550
Lev 8:26 one **w**, and put *them* on the fat, and 7550
Nu 6:19 one unleavened **w**, and shall put *them* upon 7550

WAFERS (5) [WAFER]
Ex 16:31 the taste of it *was* like **w** *made* with honey. 6838
29: 2 and **w** unleavened anointed with oil: 7550
Lev 2: 4 with oil, or unleavened **w** anointed with oil. 7550
7:12 unleavened **w** anointed with oil, and 7550
Nu 6:15 **w** of unleavened bread anointed with oil, 7550

WAG (3) [WAGGING]
Jer 18:16 thereby shall be astonished, and **w** his head. 5110
La 2:15 **w** their head at the daughter of Jerusalem, 5128
Zep 2:15 passeth by her shall hiss, *and* **w** his hand. 5128

WAGES (18)
Ge 29:15 for nought? tell me, what *shall* thy **w** *be?* 4909
30:28 Appoint me thy **w**, and I will give *it.* 7939
31: 7 deceived me, and changed my **w** ten times; 4909
31: 8 If he said thus, The speckled shall be thy **w**; 7939
31:41 and thou hast changed my **w** ten times. 4909
Ex 2: 9 nurse it for me, and I will give *thee* thy **w**. 7939
Lev 19:13 neither rob *him:* the **w** of him that is hired 6468
Jer 22:13 useth his neighbour's service **without w**, 2600
Eze 29:18 yet had he no **w**, nor his army, for Tyrus, 7939
29:19 her prey; and it shall be the **w** for his army. 7939
Hag 1: 6 he that **earneth w** earneth wages *to put it* 7936
1: 6 he that earneth wages **earneth w** *to put it* 7936
Mal 3: 5 those that oppress the hireling in *his* **w**, 7939
Lk 3:14 *any* falsely; and be content with your **w**. *3800*
Jn 4:36 And he that reapeth receiveth **w**, and *3408*
Ro 6:23 For the **w** of sin *is* death; but the gift of *3800*
2Co 11: 8 taking **w** *of them,* to do you service. *3800*
2Pe 2:15 who loved the **w** of unrighteousness; *3408*

WAGGING (2) [WAG]
Mt 27:39 that passed by, reviled him, **w** their heads, *2795*
Mk 15:29 **w** their heads, and saying, Ah, *thou* that *2795*

WAGON (1) [WAGONS]
Nu 7: 3 a **w** for two of the princes, and for *each* one 5699

WAGONS (9) [WAGON]
Ge 45:19 take you **w** out of the land of Egypt for 5699
45:21 Joseph gave them **w**, according to 5699
45:27 when he saw the **w** which Joseph had sent 5699
46: 5 in the **w** which Pharaoh had sent to carry 5699
Nu 7: 3 six covered **w**, and twelve oxen; 5699
7: 6 Moses took the **w** and the oxen, and 5699
7: 7 Two **w** and four oxen he gave unto the sons 5699
7: 8 four **w** and eight oxen he gave unto 5699
Eze 23:24 **w**, and wheels, and with an assembly of 7393

WAIL (3) [WAILED, WAILING]
Eze 32:18 **w** for the multitude of Egypt, and cast them 5091
Mic 1: 8 Therefore I will **w** and howl, I will go stript 5594
Rev 1: 7 and all kindreds of the earth shall **w** *2875*

WAILED (1) [WAIL]
Mk 5:38 and them that wept and **w** greatly. *214*

WAILING (16) [WAIL]
Est 4: 3 the Jews, and fasting, and weeping, and **w**; 4553
Jer 9:10 mountains will I take up a weeping and **w**, 5092
9:18 let them make haste, and take up a **w** for us, 5092
9:19 For a voice of **w** is heard out of Zion, 5092
9:20 teach your daughters **w**, and every one her 5092
Eze 7:11 of theirs: neither *shall there be* **w** for them. 5089
27:31 thee with bitterness of heart *and* bitter **w**. 4553
27:32 in their **w** they shall take up a lamentation 5204
Am 5:16 **W** *shall be* in all streets; and they shall say 4553
5:16 and such as are skilful of lamentation to **w**. 4553
5:17 in all vineyards *shall be* **w**: for I will pass 4553
Mic 1: 8 I will make a **w** like the dragons, and 4553
Mt 13:42 there shall be **w** and gnashing of teeth. *2805*
13:50 there shall be **w** and gnashing of teeth. *2805*
Rev 18:15 for the fear of her torment, weeping and **w**, *3996*
18:19 and cried, weeping and **w**, saying, Alas, *3996*

WAIT (106) [AWAIT, WAITED, WAITETH, WAITING]
Ex 21:13 if a man **lie** not **in w**, but God deliver *him* 6658
Nu 3:10 and they shall **w on** their priest's office: 8104
8:24 upward they shall go in to **w** upon 6633+6635
35:20 or hurl at him by **laying of w**, that he die; 6660
35:22 upon him any thing without **laying of w**, 6660
Dt 19:11 and **lie in w** for him, and rise up against him, 693
Jos 8: 4 Behold, ye shall **lie in w against** the city, 693
8:13 and their **liers in w** on the west of the city, 6119
Jdg 9:25 the men of Shechem set **liers in w** for him in 693
9:32 that *is* with thee, *and* **lie in w** in the field: 693
9:34 they **laid w** against Shechem *in* four 693
9:35 people that *were* with him, from **lying in w**. 3993
9:43 **laid w** in the field, and looked, and behold, 693
16: 2 **laid w** for him all night in the gate of 693
16: 9 Now *there were* men **lying in w**, 693
16:12 *there were* **liers in w** abiding in the chamber. 693
20:29 Israel set **liers in w** round about Gibeah. 693
20:33 the **liers in w** of Israel came forth out of 693
20:36 they trusted unto the **liers in w** which they 693
20:37 the **liers in w** hasted, and rushed upon 693
20:37 the **liers in w** drew *themselves* along, and 693
20:38 between the men of Israel and the **liers in w**, 693
21:20 Go and **lie in w** in the vineyards; 693
1Sa 15: 2 how he laid *w* for him in the way, when he NIH
15: 5 a city of Amalek, and **laid w** in the valley. 7378
22: 8 against me, to **lie in w**, as at this day? 693
22:13 rise against me, to **lie in w**, as at this day? 693
2Ki 6:33 what should I **w** for the LORD any 3176
1Ch 23:28 Because their office *was* to **w on** the sons 3027
2Ch 5:11 *and* did not *then* **w** by course: 8104
13:10 and the Levites **w** upon *their* business: NIH
Ezr 8:31 and of such as **lay in w** by the way. 693

Job 14:14 all the days of my appointed time will I w, 3176
17:13 If I w, the grave is mine house: I have made 6960
31: 9 or if I have laid w at my neighbour's door; 693
38:40 and abide in the covert to lie in w? 695
Ps 10: 9 He lieth in w secretly as a lion in his den: 693
10: 9 he lieth in w to catch the poor: he doth catch 693
25: 3 Yea, let none that w on thee be ashamed: 6960
25: 5 of my salvation; on thee do I w all the day. 6960
25:21 uprightness preserve me; for I w on thee. 6960
27:14 W on the LORD: be of good courage, and 6960
27:14 thine heart: w, I say, on the LORD. 6960
37: 7 in the LORD, and w patiently for him: 2342
37: 9 those that w upon the LORD, they shall 6960
37:34 W on the LORD, and keep his way, and 6960
39: 7 now, Lord, what w I for? my hope is in 6960
52: 9 thou hast done it: and I will w on thy name; 6960
56: 6 mark my steps, when they w for my soul. 6960
59: 3 For lo, they lie in w for my soul: the mighty 693
59: 9 Because of his strength will I w upon thee: 8104
62: 5 My soul, w thou only upon God; for my 1826
69: 3 mine eyes fail while I w for my God. 3176
69: 6 Let not them that w on thee, O Lord GOD 6960
71:10 they that lay w for my soul take counsel 8104
104:27 These w all upon thee; that thou mayest 7663
123: 2 so our eyes w upon the LORD our God, NIH
130: 5 I w for the LORD, my soul doth wait, and 6960
130: 5 my soul doth w, and in his word do I hope. 6960
145:15 The eyes of all w upon thee; and 7663
Pr 1:11 Come with us, let us lay w for blood, 693
1:18 they lay w for their own blood; they lurk 693
7:12 in the streets, and lieth in w at every corner.) 693
12: 6 The words of the wicked are to lie in w for 693
20:22 but w on the LORD, and he shall save 6960
23:28 She also lieth in w as for a prey, and 693
24:15 Lay not w, O wicked man, against 693
Isa 8:17 I will w upon the LORD, that hideth his 2442
30:18 therefore will the LORD w, that he may 2442
30:18 blessed are all they that w for him. 2442
40:31 they that w upon the LORD shall renew 6960
42: 4 the earth: and the isles shall w for his law. 3176
49:23 for they shall not be ashamed that w for 6960
51: 5 the isles shall w upon me, and on mine arm 6960
59: 9 we w for light, but behold obscurity; 6960
60: 9 Surely the isles shall w for me, and 6960
Jer 5:26 people are found wicked men: they lay w, 7789
9: 8 with his mouth, but in heart he layeth his w. 696
14:22 therefore we will w upon thee: for thou 6960
La 3:10 He was unto me as a bear lying in w, and 693
3:25 The LORD is good unto them that w for 6960
3:26 quietly w for the salvation of the LORD. 1748
4:19 they laid w for us in the wilderness. 693
Hos 6: 9 as troops of robbers w for a man, so 2442
7: 6 their heart like an oven, whiles they lie in w: 693
12: 6 judgment, and w on thy God continually. 6960
Mic 7: 2 they all lie in w for blood; they hunt every 693
7: 7 I will w for the God of my salvation: 3176
Hab 2: 3 though it tarry, w for it; because it will 2442
Zep 3: 8 Therefore w ye upon me, saith the LORD, 2442
Mk 3: 9 that a small ship should w on him because 4342
Lk 11:54 Laying w for him, and seeking to catch 1748
12:36 And ye yourselves like unto men that w for 4327
Ac 1: 4 but w for the promise of the Father, which, 4037
20: 3 and when the Jews laid w for him, 1096+1917
20:19 which befell me by the lying in w of 1917
23:16 Paul's sister's son heard of their lying in w, 1747
23:21 for there lie in w for him of them moe than 1748
23:30 me how that the Jews laid w for the man, 1917
25: 3 laying w in the way to kill him. 1747+4160
Ro 8:25 see not, then do we with patience w for it. 553
12: 7 Or ministry, let us w on our ministering: or NIG
1Co 9:13 they which w at the altar are partakers with 4332
Gal 5: 5 For we through the Spirit w for the hope of 553
Eph 4:14 whereby they lie in w to deceive; 3180
1Th 1:10 And to w for his Son from heaven, whom he 362

WAITED (35) [WAIT]

Ge 49:18 I have w for thy salvation, O LORD. 6960
1Ki 20:38 w for the king by the way, and 5975
2Ki 5: 2 she w on Naaman's wife. 1961+6440+3807.1
1Ch 6:32 they w on their office according to their 5975
6:33 these are they that w with their children. 5975
9:18 Who hitherto w in the king's gate eastward: NIH
2Ch 7: 6 the priests w on their offices: the Levites 5975
17:19 These w on the king, besides those whom 8334
35:15 king's seer; and the porters w at every gate; NIH
Ne 12:44 for the priests and for the Levites that w. 5975
Job 6:19 the companies of Sheba w for them. 6960
15:22 of darkness, and he is w for of the sword. 6822
29:21 and w, and kept silence at my counsel. 3176
29:23 they w for me as for the rain; and 3176
30:26 evil came unto me: and when I w for light, 3176
32: 4 Now Elihu had w till Job had spoken, 2442
32:11 Behold, I w for your words; I gave ear to 3176
32:16 When I had w, (for they spake not, but 3176
Ps 40: 1 I w patiently for the LORD; and 6960+6960
106:13 his works; they w not for his counsel: 2442
119:95 The wicked have w for me to destroy me: 6960
Isa 25: 9 we have w for him, and he will save us: 6960
25: 9 we have w for him, we will be glad and 6960
26: 8 O LORD, have we w for thee; 6960
33: 2 be gracious unto us; we have w for thee: 6960
Eze 19: 5 Now when she saw that she had w, and 3176
Mic 1:12 For the inhabitant of Maroth w carefully 2342
Zec 11:11 the poor of the flock that w upon me knew 8104
Mk 15:43 which also w for the kingdom of God, 4327
Lk 1:21 And the people w for Zacharias, and 4328
23:51 who also himself w for the kingdom of 4327
Ac 10: 7 soldier of them that w on him continually; 4342
10:24 And Cornelius w for them, and had called 4328
17:16 Now while Paul w for them at Athens, his 1551
1Pe 3:20 when once the longsuffering of God w in 1551

WAITETH (11) [WAIT]

Job 24:15 The eye also of the adulterer w for 8104
Ps 33:20 Our soul w for the LORD: he is our help 2442
62: 1 Truly my soul w upon God: from him 1747
65: 1 Praise w for thee, O God, in Zion: and 1747
130: 6 My soul w for the Lord more than they that NIH
Pr 27:18 he that w on his master shall be honoured. 8104
Isa 64: 4 what he hath prepared for him that w for 2442
Da 12:12 Blessed is he that w, and cometh to 2442
Mic 5: 7 not for man, nor w for the sons of men. 3176
Ro 8:19 w for the manifestation of the sons of God. 553
Jas 5: 7 the husbandman w for the precious fruit of 1551

WAITING (8) [WAIT]

Nu 8:25 they shall cease w upon the service thereof, 6635
Pr 8:34 at my gates, w at the posts of my doors. 8104
Lk 2:25 and devout, w for the consolation of Israel: 4327
8:40 received him: for they were all w for him. 4328
Jn 5: 3 withered, w for the moving of the water. 1551
Ro 8:23 w for the adoption, to wit, the redemption of 553
1Co 1: 7 w for the coming of our Lord Jesus Christ: 553
2Th 3: 5 of God, and into the patient w for Christ. 5281

WAKE (4) [AWAKE, AWAKED, AWAKEST, AWAKETH, AWAKING, AWOKE, WAKED, WAKENED, WAKENETH, WAKETH, WAKING]

Jer 51:39 and not w, saith the LORD. 6974
51:57 a perpetual sleep, and not w, saith the King, 6974
Joel 3: 9 w up the mighty men, let all the men of 5782
1Th 5:10 died for us, that, whether we w or sleep, 1127

WAKED (1) [WAKE]

Zec 4: 1 w me, as a man that is wakened out of his 5782

WAKENED (2) [WAKE]

Joel 3:12 Let the heathen be w, and come up to 5782
Zec 4: 1 as a man that is w out of his sleep, 5782

WAKENETH (2) [WAKE]

Isa 50: 4 he w morning by morning, he wakeneth 5782
50: 4 he w mine ear to hear as the learned. 5782

WAKETH (2) [WAKE]

Ps 127: 1 keep the city, the watchman w but in vain. 8245
SS 5: 2 I sleep, but my heart w: it is the voice of 5782

WAKING (1) [WAKE]

Ps 77: 4 Thou holdest mine eyes w: I am so 8109

WALK (212) [WALKED, WALKEDST, WALKEST, WALKETH, WALKING]

Ge 13:17 w through the land in the length of it and 1980
17: 1 w before me, and be thou perfect. 1980
24:40 unto me, The LORD, before whom I w, 1980
48:15 my fathers Abraham and Isaac did w, 1980
Ex 16: 4 whether they will w in my law, or no. 1980
18:20 shew them the way wherein they must w, 1980

Ex	21:19	w abroad upon his staff, then shall he that	1980
Lev	18: 3	neither shall ye w in their ordinances.	1980
	18: 4	and keep mine ordinances, to w therein:	1980
	20:23	ye shall not w in the manners of the nation,	1980
	26: 3	If ye w in my statutes, and keep my	1980
	26:12	I will w among you, and will be your God,	1980
	26:21	if ye w contrary unto me, and will not	1980
	26:23	these *things,* but will w contrary unto me;	1980
	26:24	will I also w contrary unto you, and	1980
	26:27	hearken unto me, but w contrary unto me;	1980
	26:28	I will w contrary unto you also in fury;	1980
Dt	5:33	You shall w in all the ways which	1980
	8: 6	thy God, to w in his ways, and to fear him.	1980
	8:19	w after other gods, and serve them, and	1980
	10:12	to w in all his ways, and to love him, and	1980
	11:22	to w in all his ways, and to cleave unto	1980
	13: 4	Ye shall w after the LORD your God, and	1980
	13: 5	LORD thy God commanded thee to w in.	1980
	19: 9	thy God, and to w ever in his ways;	1980
	26:17	to w in his ways, and to keep his statutes,	1980
	28: 9	of the LORD thy God, and w in his ways.	1980
	29:19	though I w in the imagination of mine	1980
	30:16	to w in his ways, and to keep his	1980
Jos	18: 8	Go and w through the land, and describe it,	1980
	22: 5	to w in all his ways, and to keep his	1980
Jdg	2:22	keep the way of the LORD to w therein,	1980
	5:10	ye that sit in judgment, and w by the way.	1980
1Sa	2:30	of thy father, should w before me for ever:	1980
	2:35	he shall w before mine anointed for ever.	1980
	8: 5	art old, and thy sons w not in thy ways:	1980
1Ki	2: 3	to w in his ways, to keep his statutes, *and*	1980
	2: 4	to w before me in truth with all their heart	1980
	3:14	if thou wilt w in my ways, to keep my	1980
	3:14	as thy father David did w, then I will	1980
	6:12	if thou wilt w in my statutes, and execute	1980
	6:12	keep all my commandments to w in them;	1980
	8:23	mercy with thy servants that w before thee	1980
	8:25	that they w before me as thou hast walked	1980
	8:36	them the good way wherein they should w,	1980
	8:58	to w in all his ways, and to keep his	1980
	8:61	to w in his statutes, and to keep his	1980
	9: 4	if thou wilt w before me, as David thy	1980
	11:38	wilt w in my ways, and do that *is* right in	1980
	16:31	as if it had been a light thing for him to w	1980
2Ki	10:31	Jehu took no heed to w in the law of	1980
	23: 3	to w after the LORD, and to keep his	1980
2Ch	6:14	that w before thee with all their hearts:	1980
	6:16	take heed to their way to w in my law,	1980
	6:27	them the good way, wherein they should w;	1980
	6:31	to w in thy ways, so long as they live in	1980
	7:17	*as for* thee, if thou wilt w before me,	1980
	34:31	to w after the LORD, and to keep his	1980
Ne	5: 9	ought ye not to w in the fear of our God	1980
	10:29	and into an oath, to w in God's law,	1980
Ps	12: 8	The wicked w on every side, when	1980
	23: 4	though I w through the valley of	1980
	26:11	*as for* me, I will w in mine integrity:	1980
	48:12	**W about** Zion, and go round about her:	5437
	56:13	that *I* may w before God in the light of	1980
	78:10	of God, and refused to w in his law;	1980
	82: 5	they understand; they **w on** in darkness:	1980
	84:11	he withhold from them that w uprightly.	1980
	86:11	thy way, O LORD; I will w in thy truth:	1980
	89:15	they shall w, O LORD, in the light of thy	1980
	89:30	my law, and w not in my judgments;	1980
	101: 2	I will w within my house with a perfect	1980
	115: 7	feet *have* they, but they w not:	1980
	116: 9	I will w before the LORD in the land of	1980
	119: 1	the way, who w in the law of the LORD.	1980
	119: 3	also do no iniquity: they w in his ways.	1980
	119:45	I will w at liberty: for I seek thy precepts.	1980
	138: 7	Though I w in the midst of trouble,	1980
	143: 8	me to know the way wherein I should w;	1980
Pr	1:15	My son, w not thou in the way with them;	1980
	2: 7	*he is* a buckler to them that w uprightly.	1980
	2:13	to w in the ways of darkness;	1980
	2:20	That thou mayest w in the way of good	1980
	3:23	shalt thou w *in* thy way safely, and thy foot	1980
Ecc	4:15	I considered all the living which w under	1980
	6: 8	that knoweth to w before the living?	1980
	11: 9	w in the ways of thine heart, and in	1980
Isa	2: 3	us of his ways, and we will w in his paths:	1980
	2: 5	and let us w in the light of the LORD.	1980
	3:16	w with stretched forth necks and	1980
	8:11	instructed me that *I* should not w in the way	1980
	30: 2	That w to go down *into* Egypt, and	1980
	30:21	saying, This *is* the way, w ye in it, when ye	1980
	35: 9	but the redeemed shall w *there:*	1980
	40:31	be weary; *and* they shall w, and not faint.	1980
	42: 5	upon it, and spirit to them that w therein:	1980
	42:24	for they would not w in his ways,	1980
	50:11	w in the light of your fire, and in the sparks	1980
	59: 9	for brightness, *but* we w in darkness.	1980
Jer	3:17	neither shall they w any more after	1980
	3:18	In those days the house of Judah shall w	1980
	6:16	w therein, and ye shall find rest for your	1980
	6:16	But they said, We will not w *therein.*	1980
	6:25	not forth *into* the field, nor w by the way;	1980
	7: 6	neither w after other gods to your hurt:	1980
	7: 9	and w after other gods whom ye know not;	1980
	7:23	w ye in all the ways that I have commanded	1980
	9: 4	every neighbour will w *with* slanders.	1980
	13:10	which w in the imagination of their heart,	1980
	13:10	w after other gods, to serve them, and	1980
	16:12	ye w every one after the imagination of his	1980
	18:12	we will w after our own devices, and	1980
	18:15	to w *in* paths, *in* a way not cast up;	1980
	23:14	*they* commit adultery, and w in lies:	1980
	26: 4	to w in my law, which I have set before	1980
	31: 9	I will **cause** them **to** w by the rivers of	1980
	42: 3	may shew us the way wherein we may w,	1980
La	5:18	which is desolate, the foxes w upon it.	1980
Eze	11:20	That they may w in my statutes, and keep	1980
	20:18	W ye not in the statutes of your fathers,	1980
	20:19	w in my statutes, and keep my judgments,	1980
	33:15	w in the statutes of life, without committing	1980
	36:12	Yea, I will **cause** men **to** w upon you,	1980
	36:27	cause you to w in my statutes, and ye shall	1980
	37:24	they shall also w in my judgments, and	1980
	42: 4	before the chambers *was* a w of ten cubits	4109
Da	4:37	those that w in pride he *is* able to abase.	1981
	9:10	to w in his laws, which he set before us by	1980
Hos	11:10	They shall w after the LORD: he shall	1980
	14: 9	*are* right, and the just shall w in them:	1980
Joel	2: 8	they shall w every one in his path:	1980
Am	3: 3	Can two w together, except they be agreed?	1980
Mic	4: 2	us of his ways, and we will w in his paths:	1980
	4: 5	For all people will w every one in the name	1980
	4: 5	we will w in the name of the LORD our	1980
	6: 8	and to w humbly with thy God?	1980
	6:16	house of Ahab, and ye w in their counsels;	1980
Na	2: 5	they shall stumble in their w; they shall	1979
Hab	3:15	Thou didst w through the sea *with* thine	1869
	3:19	he will **make** me **to** w upon mine high	1869
Zep	1:17	that they shall w like blind *men,* because	1980
Zec	1:10	the LORD hath sent to **w to and fro**	1980
	3: 7	If thou wilt w in my ways, and if thou wilt	1980
	3: 7	I will give thee **places to** w among these	4108
	6: 7	sought to go that *they* might **w to and fro**	1980
	6: 7	Get ye *hence,* **w to and fro** through	1980
	10:12	they shall **w up and down** in his name,	1980
Mt	9: 5	be forgiven thee; or to say, Arise, and w?	4043
	11: 5	and the lame w, the lepers are cleansed, and	4043
	15:31	the lame to w, and the blind to see:	4043
Mk	2: 9	to say, Arise, and take up thy bed, and w?	4043
	7: 5	Why w not thy disciples according to	4043
Lk	5:23	be forgiven thee; or to say, Rise up and w?	4043
	7:22	how that the blind see, the lame w,	4043
	11:44	the men that w over *them* are not aware *of*	4043
	13:33	Nevertheless I must w to day, and	4198
	20:46	which desire to w in long robes, and	4043
	24:17	have one to another, as ye w, and are sad?	4043
Jn	5: 8	unto him, Rise, take up thy bed, and w.	4043
	5:11	same said unto me, Take up thy bed, and w.	4043
	5:12	said unto thee, Take up thy bed, and w?	4043
	7: 1	for he would not w in Jewry, because	4043
	8:12	he that followeth me shall not w in	4043
	11: 9	If any *man* w in the day, he stumbleth not,	4043
	11:10	But if a man w in the night, he stumbleth,	4043
	12:35	W while ye have the light, lest darkness	4043
Ac	3: 6	of Jesus Christ of Nazareth rise up and w.	4043
	3:12	or holiness we had made this *man* to w?	4043
	14:16	Who in times past suffered all nations to w	4198
	21:21	neither to w after the customs.	4043
Ro	4:12	who also w in the steps of *that* faith of our	4748
	6: 4	so we also should w in newness of life.	4043
	8: 1	in Christ Jesus who w not after the flesh,	4043
	8: 4	who w not after the flesh, but after	4043

Ro	13:13	Let us **w** honestly, as in the day; not in	*4043*
1Co	3: 3	divisions, are ye not carnal, and **w** as men?	*4043*
	7:17	Lord hath called every one, so let him **w**.	*4043*
2Co	5: 7	(For we **w** by faith, not by sight:)	*4043*
	6:16	and **w in** *them;* and I will be their God, and	*1704*
	10: 3	For though we **w** in the flesh, we do not	*4043*
Gal	5:16	**W** in the Spirit, and ye shall not fulfil	*4043*
	5:25	live in the Spirit, let us also **w** in the Spirit.	*4748*
	6:16	And as many as **w** according to this rule,	*4748*
Eph	2:10	before ordained that we should **w** in them.	*4043*
	4: 1	beseech you that *ye* **w** worthy of	*4043*
	4:17	that ye henceforth **w** not as other Gentiles	*4043*
	4:17	ye henceforth walk not as other Gentiles **w**,	*4043*
	5: 2	And **w** in love, as Christ also hath loved us,	*4043*
	5: 8	*ye* light in the Lord: **w** as children of light:	*4043*
	5:15	See then that ye **w** circumspectly, not as	*4043*
Php	3:16	*let us* **w** by the same rule, *let us* mind	*4748*
	3:17	and mark them which **w** so as ye have us	*4043*
	3:18	(For many **w**, of whom I have told you	*4043*
Col	1:10	That ye might **w** worthy of the Lord unto	*4043*
	2: 6	Christ Jesus the Lord, *so* **w** ye in him:	*4043*
	4: 5	**W** in wisdom toward them that are without,	*4043*
1Th	2:12	That ye would **w** worthy of God, who hath	*4043*
	4: 1	ye have received of us how ye ought to **w**	*4043*
	4:12	That ye may **w** honestly toward them that	*4043*
2Th	3:11	For we hear that *there are* some which **w**	*4043*
2Pe	2:10	But chiefly them that **w** after the flesh in	*4198*
1Jn	1: 6	and **w** in darkness, we lie, and do not	*4043*
	1: 7	But if we **w** in the light, as he is in the light,	*4043*
	2: 6	abideth in him ought himself also so to **w**,	*4043*
2Jn	1: 6	is love, that we **w** after his commandments.	*4043*
	1: 6	heard from the beginning, ye should **w** in it.	*4043*
3Jn	1: 4	joy than to hear that my children **w** in truth.	*4043*
Jude	1:18	who should **w** after their own ungodly	*4198*
Rev	3: 4	and they shall **w** with me in white:	*4043*
	9:20	which neither can see, nor hear, nor **w**:	*4043*
	16:15	lest he **w** naked, and they see his shame.	*4043*
	21:24	which are saved shall **w** in the light of it:	*4043*

WALKED (122) [WALK]

Ge	5:22	Enoch **w** with God after he begat	1980
	5:24	Enoch **w** with God: and he *was* not;	1980
	6: 9	in his generations, *and* Noah **w** with God.	1980
Ex	2: 5	her maidens **w** along by the river's side;	1980
	14:29	the children of Israel **w** upon dry *land* in	1980
Lev	26:40	and that also they have **w** contrary unto me;	1980
	26:41	*And that* I also have **w** contrary unto them,	1980
Jos	5: 6	For the children of Israel **w** forty years in	1980
Jdg	2:17	out of the way which their fathers **w** in,	1980
	5: 6	and the travellers **w** *through* byways.	1980
	11:16	**w** through the wilderness unto the Red sea,	1980
1Sa	8: 3	his sons **w** not in his ways, but turned aside	1980
	12: 2	I have **w** before you from my childhood	1980
2Sa	2:29	his men **w** all that night through the plain,	1980
	7: 6	but have **w** in a tent and in a tabernacle.	1980
	7: 7	In all *the places* wherein I have **w** with all	1980
	11: 2	and **w** upon the roof of the king's house:	1980
1Ki	3: 6	according as he **w** before thee in truth, and	1980
	8:25	that they walk before me as thou hast **w**	1980
	9: 4	as David thy father **w**, in integrity of heart,	1980
	11:33	have not **w** in my ways, to do *that* which *is*	1980
	15: 3	he **w** in all the sins of his father, which he	1980
	15:26	**w** in the way of his father, and in his sin	1980
	15:34	**w** in the way of Jeroboam and in his sin	1980
	16: 2	thou hast **w** in the way of Jeroboam, and	1980
	16:26	For he **w** in all the way of Jeroboam the son	1980
	22:43	he **w** in all the ways of Asa his father;	1980
	22:52	**w** in the way of his father, and in the way	1980
2Ki	4:35	he returned, and **w** in the house to and fro;	1980
	8:18	he **w** in the way of the kings of Israel,	1980
	8:27	he **w** in the way of the house of Ahab, and	1980
	13: 6	who made Israel sin, *but* **w** therein:	1980
	13:11	who made Israel sin: *but* he **w** therein.	1980
	16: 3	he **w** in the way of the kings of Israel, yea,	1980
	17: 8	**w** in the statutes of the heathen, whom	1980
	17:19	**w** in the statutes of Israel which they made.	1980
	17:22	For the children of Israel **w** in all the sins of	1980
	20: 3	remember now how I have **w** before thee in	1980
	21:21	he **w** in all the way that his father walked	1980
	21:21	he walked in all the way that his father **w**	1980
	21:22	and **w** not in the way of the LORD.	1980
	22: 2	**w** in all the way of David his father, and	1980
1Ch	17: 6	Wheresoever I have **w** with all Israel, spake	1980
	17: 8	been with thee whithersoever thou hast **w**,	1980
2Ch	6:16	walk in my law, as thou hast **w** before me.	1980
	7:17	as David thy father **w**, and do according to	1980
	11:17	for three years they **w** in the way of David	1980
	17: 3	he **w** in the first ways of his father David,	1980
	17: 4	**w** in his commandments, and not after	1980
	20:32	he **w** in the way of Asa his father, and	1980
	21: 6	he **w** in the way of the kings of Israel,	1980
	21:12	Because thou hast not **w** in the ways of	1980
	21:13	hast **w** in the way of the kings of Israel, and	1980
	22: 3	He also **w** in the ways of the house of	1980
	22: 5	He **w** also after their counsel, and	1980
	28: 2	For he **w** in the ways of the kings of Israel,	1980
	34: 2	**w** in the ways of David his father, and	1980
Est	2:11	Mordecai **w** every day before the court of	1980
Job	29: 3	*and when* by his light I **w** *through* darkness;	1980
	31: 5	If I have **w** with vanity, or *if* my foot hath	1980
	31: 7	mine heart **w** after mine eyes, and *if any*	1980
	38:16	or hast thou **w** in the search of the depth?	1980
Ps	26: 1	O LORD; for I have **w** in mine integrity:	1980
	26: 3	before mine eyes: and I have **w** in thy truth.	1980
	55:14	*and* **w** unto the house of God in company.	1980
	81:12	*and* they **w** in their own counsels.	1980
	81:13	unto me, *and* Israel had **w** in my ways!	1980
	142: 3	In the way wherein I **w** have they privily	1980
Isa	9: 2	The people that **w** in darkness have seen a	1980
	20: 3	Like as my servant Isaiah hath **w** naked and	1980
	38: 3	how I have **w** before thee in truth and	1980
Jer	2: 5	have **w** after vanity, and are become vain?	1980
	2: 8	and **w** after *things that* do not profit.	1980
	7:24	**w** in the counsels *and* in the imagination of	1980
	8: 2	after whom they have **w**, and whom they	1980
	9:13	not obeyed my voice, neither **w** therein;	1980
	9:14	have **w** after the imagination of their own	1980
	11: 8	**w** every one in the imagination of their evil	1980
	16:11	have **w** after other gods, and have served	1980
	32:23	obeyed not thy voice, neither **w** in thy law;	1980
	44:10	nor **w** in my law, nor in my statutes, that I	1980
	44:23	nor **w** in his law, nor in his statutes, nor in	1980
Eze	5: 6	and my statutes, they have not **w** in them.	1980
	5: 7	*and* have not **w** in my statutes, neither have	1980
	11:12	for ye have not **w** in my statutes,	1980
	16:47	Yet hast thou not **w** after their ways,	1980
	18: 9	Hath **w** in my statutes, and hath kept my	1980
	18:17	my judgments, hath **w** in my statutes;	1980
	20:13	they **w** not in my statutes, and they	1980
	20:16	**w** not in my statutes, but polluted my	1980
	20:21	they **w** not in my statutes, neither kept my	1980
	23:31	Thou hast **w** in the way of thy sister;	1980
	28:14	thou hast **w up and down** in the midst of	1980
Da	4:29	At the end of twelve months he **w** in	1981
Hos	5:11	he willingly **w** after the commandment.	1980
Am	2: 4	to err, after the which their fathers have **w**:	1980
Na	2:11	**w**, *and* the lion's whelp, and none made	1980
Zec	1:11	We have **w to and fro** through the earth,	1980
	6: 7	So they **w to and fro** through the earth.	1980
Mal	2: 6	he **w** with me in peace and equity, and	1980
	3:14	that we have **w** mournfully before	1980
Mt	14:29	the ship, he **w** on the water, to go to Jesus.	*4043*
Mk	1:16	Now as he **w** by the sea of Galilee, he saw	*4043*
	5:42	And straightway the damsel arose, and **w**;	*4043*
	16:12	as they **w**, and went into the country.	*4043*
Jn	1:36	And looking upon Jesus as he **w**, he saith,	*4043*
	5: 9	made whole, and took up his bed, and **w**:	*4043*
	6:66	went back, and **w** no more with him.	*4043*
	7: 1	After these *things* Jesus **w** in Galilee: for he	*4043*
	10:23	And Jesus **w** in the temple in Solomon's	*4043*
	11:54	**w** no more openly among the Jews;	*4043*
Ac	3: 8	and **w**, and entered with them into	*4043*
	14: 8	from his mother's womb, who never had **w**:	*4043*
	14:10	upright on thy feet. And he leaped and **w**.	*4043*
2Co	10: 2	which think of us as if we **w** according to	*4043*
	12:18	**w** we not in the same spirit? *walked we* not	*4043*
	12:18	the same spirit? *w we* not in the same steps?	NIG
Gal	2:14	But when I saw that they **w** not **uprightly**	*3716*
Eph	2: 2	Wherein in time past ye **w** according to	*4043*
Col	3: 7	In the which ye also **w** sometime, when ye	*4043*
1Pe	4: 3	when we **w** in lasciviousness, lusts,	*4198*
1Jn	2: 6	himself also so to walk, even as he **w**.	*4043*

WALKEDST (1) [WALK]

Jn	21:18	and **w** whither thou wouldest:	*4043*

WALKEST (7) [WALK]

Dt	6: 7	when thou **w** by the way, and when thou	1980

W

Dt 11:19 when thou w by the way, when thou liest 1980
1Ki 2:42 w *abroad* any whither, that thou shalt surely 1980
Isa 43: 2 when thou w through the fire, thou shalt not 1980
Ac 21:24 but *that* thou thyself also **w orderly**, and *4748*
Ro 14:15 with *thy* meat, now w thou not charitably. *4043*
3Jn 1: 3 *that is* in thee, even as thou w in the truth. *4043*

WALKETH (41) [WALK]

Ge 24:65 What man *is* this that w in the field to meet 1980
Dt 23:14 For the LORD thy God w in the midst of 1980
1Sa 12: 2 now behold, the king w before you: and 1980
Job 18: 8 net by his own feet, and he w upon a snare. 1980
22:14 seeth not; and he w *in* the circuit of heaven. 1980
34: 8 of iniquity, and w with wicked men. 1980
Ps 1: 1 Blessed *is* the man that w not in the counsel 1980
15: 2 He that w uprightly, and 1980
39: 6 Surely every man w in a vain shew: 1980
73: 9 and their tongue w through the earth. 1980
91: 6 *Nor* for the pestilence *that* w in darkness; 1980
101: 6 he that w in a perfect way, he shall serve 1980
104: 3 who w upon the wings of the wind: 1980
128: 1 that feareth the LORD; that w in his ways. 1980
Pr 6:12 a wicked man, w *with* a froward mouth. 1980
10: 9 He that w uprightly walketh surely: but 1980
10: 9 He that walketh uprightly w surely: but 1980
13:20 He that w with wise *men* shall be wise: but 1980
14: 2 He that w in his uprightness feareth 1980
15:21 but a man of understanding w uprightly. 1980
19: 1 Better *is* the poor that w in his integrity, 1980
20: 7 The just *man* w in his integrity: his children 1980
28: 6 Better *is* the poor that w in his uprightness, 1980
28:18 Whoso w uprightly shall be saved: but 1980
28:26 but whoso w wisely, he shall be delivered. 1980
Ecc 2:14 *are* in his head; but the fool w in darkness: 1980
10: 3 when he that is a fool w by the way, 1980
Isa 33:15 He that w righteously, and 1980
50:10 that w *in* darkness, and hath no light? 1980
65: 2 which w *in* a way *that was* not good, 1980
Jer 10:23 *it is* not in man that w to direct his steps. 1980
23:17 they say *unto* every one that w after 1980
Eze 11:21 *as for them* whose heart w after the heart of 1980
Mic 2: 7 do not my words do good to him that w 1980
Mt 12:43 he **w through** dry places, *1330*
Lk 11:24 **w through** dry places, seeking rest; *1330*
Jn 12:35 for he that w in darkness knoweth not *4043*
2Th 3: 6 from every brother that w disorderly, *4043*
1Pe 5: 8 the devil, as a roaring lion, **w about**, *4043*
1Jn 2:11 and w in darkness, and knoweth not *4043*
Rev 2: 1 who w in the midst of the seven golden *4043*

WALKING (30) [WALK]

Ge 3: 8 they heard the voice of the LORD God w 1980
Dt 2: 7 he knoweth thy w *through* this great 1980
1Ki 3: 3 w in the statutes of David his father: 1980
16:19 in w in the way of Jeroboam, and in his sin 1980
Job 1: 7 in the earth, and from w **up and down** in it. 1980
2: 2 in the earth, and from w **up and down** in it. 1980
31:26 it shined, or the moon w *in* brightness; 1980
Ecc 10: 7 and princes w as servants upon the earth. 1980
Isa 3:16 w and mincing *as* they go, and making a 1980
20: 2 And he did so, w naked and barefoot. 1980
57: 2 in their beds, *each one* w *in* his uprightness. 1980
Jer 6:28 *are* all grievous revolters, w with slanders: 1980
Da 3:25 w in the midst of the fire, and they have no 1981
Mic 2:11 If a man w *in* the spirit and falsehood do 1980
Mt 4:18 And Jesus, w by the sea of Galilee, saw two *4043*
14:25 night Jesus went unto them, w on the sea. *4043*
14:26 And when the disciples saw him w on *4043*
Mk 6:48 w upon the sea, and would have passed by *4043*
6:49 But when they saw him w upon the sea, *4043*
8:24 looked up, and said, I see men as trees, w. *4043*
11:27 and as he was w in the temple, there come *4043*
Lk 1: 6 w in all the commandments and *4198*
Jn 6:19 they see Jesus w on the sea, and drawing *4043*
Ac 3: 8 w, and leaping, and praising God. *4043*
3: 9 And all the people saw him w and *4043*
9:31 and w in the fear of the Lord, and in *4198*
2Co 4: 2 not w in craftiness, nor handling the word *4043*
2Pe 3: 3 last days scoffers, w after their own lusts, *4198*
2Jn 1: 4 that I found of thy children w in truth, *4043*
Jude 1:16 complainers, w after their own lusts; *4198*

WALL (179) [UNWALLED, WALLED, WALLS]

Ge 49: 6 and in their selfwill they digged down a w. 7794
49:22 by a well; *whose* branches run over the w. 7791
Ex 14:22 the waters *were* a w unto them on their 2346
14:29 the waters *were* a w unto them on their 2346
Lev 14:37 which in sight *are* lower than the w; 7023
25:31 the houses of the villages which have no w 2346
Nu 22:24 a w *being* on this side, and a wall on that 1447
22:24 *being* on this side, and a w on that side. 1447
22:25 she thrust herself unto the w, and 7023
22:25 and crusht Balaam's foot against the w: 7023
35: 4 *shall reach* from the w of the city and 7023
Jos 2:15 for her house *was* upon the town w, and 2346
2:15 the town wall, and she dwelt upon the w. 2346
6: 5 the w of the city shall fall down flat, 2346
6:20 that the w fell down flat, so that the people 2346
1Sa 18:11 I will smite David even to the w *with it.* 7023
19:10 Saul sought to smite David even to the w 7023
19:10 and he smote the javelin into the w: 7023
20:25 at other times, *even* upon a seat by the w: 7023
25:16 They were a w unto us both by night and 2346
25:22 light *any that* pisseth against the w. 7023
25:34 light *any that* pisseth against the w. 7023
31:10 they fastened his body to the w of 2346
31:12 the bodies of his sons from the w of 2346
2Sa 11:20 ye not that they would shoot from the w? 2346
11:21 a piece of a millstone upon him from the w, 2346
11:21 why went ye nigh the w? then say thou, 2346
11:24 the shooters shot from off the w upon thy 2346
18:24 *up* to the roof over the gate unto the w, 2346
20:15 people that *were* with Joab battered the w, 2346
20:21 his head *shall be* thrown to thee over the w. 2346
22:30 a troop: by my God have I leaped over a w. 7791
1Ki 3: 1 and the w of Jerusalem round about. 2346
4:33 unto the hyssop that springeth out of the w: 7023
6: 5 against the w of the house he built 7023
6: 6 for without *in the* w of the house he made NIH
6:27 that the wing of the one touched the *one* w, 7023
6:27 of the other cherub touched the other w; 7023
6:31 *and* side posts *were* a fifth *part of the* w. NIH
6:33 posts of olive tree, a fourth *part of the* w. NIH
9:15 the w of Jerusalem, and Hazor, and 2346
14:10 Jeroboam *him that* pisseth against the w, 7023
16:11 he left him not *one that* pisseth against a w, 7023
20:30 *there* a w fell upon twenty and 2346
21:21 from Ahab *him that* pisseth against the w, 7023
21:23 The dogs shall eat Jezebel by the w of 2426
2Ki 3:27 offered him *for* a burnt offering upon the w. 2346
4:10 a little chamber, I pray thee, on the w; 7023
6:26 king of Israel was passing by upon the w, 2346
6:30 he passed by upon the w, and the people 2346
9: 8 from Ahab *him that* pisseth against the w, 7023
9:33 *some* of her blood was sprinkled on the w, 7023
14:13 brake down the w of Jerusalem from 2346
18:26 in the ears of the people that *are* on the w. 2346
18:27 not *sent me* to the men which sit on the w, 2346
20: 2 he turned his face to the w, and prayed unto 7023
2Ch 3:11 five cubits, reaching to the w of the house: 7023
3:12 five cubits, reaching to the w of the house: 7023
25:23 brake down the w of Jerusalem from 2346
26: 6 brake down the w of Gath, and the wall of 2346
26: 6 the w of Jabneh, and the wall of Ashdod, 2346
26: 6 the w of Ashdod, and built cities about 2346
26: 9 at the turning *of the* w, and fortified them. NIH
27: 3 and on the w of Ophel he built much. 2346
32: 5 built up all the w that was broken, and 2346
32: 5 another w without, and repaired Millo *in* 2346
32:18 the people of Jerusalem that *were* on the w, 2346
33:14 Now after this he built a w without the city 2346
36:19 brake down the w of Jerusalem, and 2346
Ezr 5: 3 to build this house, and to make up this w? 846
9: 9 to give us a w in Judah and in Jerusalem. 1447
Ne 1: 3 the w of Jerusalem also *is* broken down, 2346
2: 8 for the w of the city, and for the house that 2346
2:15 viewed the w, and turned back, and 2346
2:17 and let us build *up* the w of Jerusalem, 2346
3: 8 they fortified Jerusalem unto the broad w. 2346
3:13 a thousand cubits on the w unto the dung 2346
3:15 the w of the pool of Siloah by the king's 2346
3:19 up to the armoury *at* the turning *of the* w. NIH
3:20 from the turning *of the* w unto the door of NIH
3:24 the turning *of the* w, even unto the corner. NIH
3:25 over against the turning *of the* w, and NIH
3:27 that lieth out, even unto the w of Ophel. 2346
4: 1 Sanballat heard that we builded the w, 2346
4: 3 he shall even break down their stone w. 2346

Ne 4: 6 So built we the **w**; and all the wall was 2346
4: 6 all the **w** was joined together unto the half 2346
4:10 so that we are not able to build the **w**. 2346
4:13 set I in the lower places behind the **w**, 2346
4:15 that we returned all of us to the **w**, 2346
4:17 They which builded on the **w**, and they that 2346
4:19 and large, and we *are* separated upon the **w**, 2346
5:16 Yea also I continued in the work of this **w**, 2346
6: 1 heard that I had builded the **w**, and 2346
6: 6 for which cause thou buildest the **w**, 2346
6:15 So the **w** was finished in the twenty and 2346
7: 1 when the **w** was built, and I had set up 2346
12:27 at the dedication of the **w** of Jerusalem they 2346
12:30 the people, and the gates, and the **w**. 2346
12:31 brought up the princes of Judah upon the **w**, 2346
12:31 hand upon the **w** toward the dung gate: 2346
12:37 at the going up of the **w**, above the house of 2346
12:38 and the half of the people upon the **w**, 2346
12:38 of the furnaces even unto the broad **w**; 2346
13:21 said unto them, Why lodge ye about the **w**? 2346
Ps 18:29 and by my God have I leaped over a **w**. 7791
62: 3 as a bowing **w** *shall ye be, and as a* 7023
Pr 18:11 and as a high **w** in his own conceit. 2346
24:31 and the stone **w** thereof was broken down. 1444
SS 2: 9 behold, he standeth behind our **w**, 3796
8: 9 If she *be* a **w**, we will build upon her a 2346
8:10 I *am* a **w**, and my breasts like towers: then 2346
Isa 2:15 every high tower, and upon every fenced **w**, 2346
5: 5 *and* break down the **w** thereof, and it shall 1447
22:10 have ye broken down to fortify the **w**. 2346
25: 4 the terrible ones *is* as a storm *against* the **w**. 7023
30:13 swelling out in a high **w**, whose breaking 2346
36:11 in the ears of the people that *are* on the **w**. 2346
36:12 not *sent me* to the men that sit upon the **w**, 2346
38: 2 Hezekiah turned his face toward the **w**, 7023
59:10 We grope for the **w** like the blind, and 7023
Jer 15:20 thee unto this people a fenced brasen **w**: 2346
49:27 I will kindle a fire in the **w** of Damascus, 2346
51:44 unto him: yea, the **w** of Babylon shall fall. 2346
La 2: 8 The LORD hath purposed to destroy the **w** 2346
2: 8 he made the rampart and the **w** to lament; 2346
2:18 unto the Lord, O **w** of the daughter of Zion, 2346
Eze 4: 3 set it *for* a **w** of iron between thee and 7023
8: 7 and when I looked, behold a hole in the **w**. 7023
8: 8 he unto me, Son of man, dig now in the **w**: 7023
8: 8 when I had digged in the **w**, behold a door. 7023
8:10 pourtrayed upon the **w** round about. 7023
12: 5 Dig thou through the **w** in their sight, and 7023
12: 7 in the even I digged through the **w** with 7023
12:12 they shall dig through the **w** to carry out 7023
13:10 one built up a **w**, and lo, others daubed it 2434
13:12 Lo, when the **w** is fallen, shall it not be said 7023
13:14 So will I break down the **w** that ye have 7023
13:15 will I accomplish my wrath upon the **w**, 7023
13:15 The **w** *is* no *more,* neither they that daubed 7023
23:14 when she saw men pourtrayed upon the **w**, 7023
38:20 and every **w** shall fall to the ground. 2346
40: 5 behold a **w** on the outside of the house 2346
41: 5 After he measured the **w** of the house, 7023
41: 6 they entered into the **w** which *was* of 7023
41: 6 but they had not hold in the **w** of the house. 7023
41: 9 The thickness of the **w**, which *was* for 7023
41:12 the **w** of the building *was* five cubits thick 7023
41:17 by all the **w** round about within 7023
41:20 trees made, and *on* the **w** of the temple. 7023
42: 7 the **w** that *was* without over against 1447
42:10 of the **w** of the court toward the east, 1444
42:12 *even* the way directly before the **w** toward 1448
42:20 it had a **w** round about, five hundred *reeds* 2346
43: 8 my posts, and the **w** between me and them, 7023
Da 5: 5 the plaister of the **w** of the king's palace: 3797
9:25 and the **w**, even in troublous times. 2742
Hos 2: 6 **make a w**, that she shall not find her 1443+1447
Joel 2: 7 they shall climb the **w** like men of war; 2346
2: 9 they shall run upon the **w**, they shall climb 2346
Am 1: 7 I will send a fire on the **w** of Gaza, 2346
1:10 I will send a fire on the **w** of Tyrus, 2346
1:14 I will kindle a fire in the **w** of Rabbah, and 2346
5:19 leaned his hand on the **w**, and a serpent bit 7023
7: 7 the Lord stood upon a **w** made by a 2346
Na 2: 5 they shall make haste *to* the **w** thereof, and 2346
3: 8 *was* the sea, *and* her **w** *was* from the sea? 2346
Hab 2:11 For the stone shall cry out of the **w**, and 7023
Zec 2: 5 will be unto her a **w** of fire round about, 2346
Ac 9:25 and let *him* down by the **w** in a basket. *5038*
23: 3 God shall smite thee, *thou* whited **w**: *5109*
2Co 11:33 in a basket was I let down by the **w**, *5038*
Eph 2:14 hath broken down the **middle w** of *3320*
Rev 21:12 And had a **w** great and high, and *5038*
21:14 And the **w** of the city had twelve *5038*
21:15 and the gates thereof, and the **w** thereof. *5038*
21:17 And he measured the **w** thereof, an hundred *5038*
21:18 And the building of the **w** of it was *of* *5038*
21:19 And the foundations of the **w** of the city *5038*

WALLED (4) [WALL]

Lev 25:29 if a man sell a dwelling house in a **w** city, 2346
25:30 the house that *is* in the **w** city shall be 2346
Nu 13:28 and the cities *are* **w**, *and* very great: 1219
Dt 1:28 the cities *are* great and **w up** to heaven; and 1219

WALLOW (4) [WALLOWED, WALLOWING]

Jer 6:26 *thee* with sackcloth, and **w** thyself in ashes: 6428
25:34 **w** yourselves *in the ashes,* ye principal of 6428
48:26 Moab also shall **w** in his vomit, and he also 5606
Eze 27:30 they shall **w** themselves in the ashes: 6428

WALLOWED (2) [WALLOW]

2Sa 20:12 Amasa **w** in blood in the midst of 1556
Mk 9:20 and he fell on the ground, and **w** foaming. *2947*

WALLOWING (1) [WALLOW]

2Pe 2:22 The sow that was washed to *her* **w** in *2946*

WALLS (66) [WALL]

Lev 14:37 *if* the plague *be* in the **w** of the house with 7023
14:39 *if* the plague be spread in the **w** of 7023
Dt 3: 5 All these cities *were* fenced *with* high **w**, 2346
28:52 until thy high and fenced **w** come down, 2346
1Ki 4:13 threescore great cities *with* **w** and 2346
6: 5 *against* the **w** of the house round about, 7023
6: 6 not be fastened in the **w** of the house. 7023
6:15 he built the **w** of the house within with 7023
6:15 floor of the house, and the **w** of the cieling: 7023
6:16 the floor and the **w** with boards of cedar: 7023
6:29 he carved all the **w** of the house round 7023
2Ki 25: 4 *by* the way of the gate between **two w**, 2346
25:10 brake down the **w** of Jerusalem round 2346
1Ch 29: 4 to overlay the **w** of the houses *withal:* 7023
2Ch 3: 7 and the **w** thereof, and the doors thereof, 7023
3: 7 with gold; and graved cherubims on the **w**. 7023
8: 5 fenced cities, *with* **w**, gates, and bars; 2346
14: 7 make about *them* **w**, and towers, gates, and 2346
Ezr 4:12 have set up the **w** *thereof,* and joined 7792
4:13 the **w** set up *again, then* will they not pay 7792
4:16 be builded *again,* and the **w** thereof set up, 7792
5: 8 timber *is* laid in the **w**, and this work goeth 3797
5: 9 to build this house, and to make up these **w**? 846
Ne 2:13 dung port, and viewed the **w** of Jerusalem, 2346
4: 7 heard that the **w** of Jerusalem were made 2346
Job 24:11 *Which* make oil within their **w**, *and* 7791
Ps 51:18 unto Zion: build thou the **w** of Jerusalem. 2346
55:10 night they go about it upon the **w** thereof: 2346
122: 7 Peace be within thy **w**, *and* 2426
Pr 25:28 a city *that is* broken down, *and* without **w**. 2346
SS 5: 7 the keepers of the **w** took away my vail 2346
Isa 22: 5 breaking down the **w**, and of crying to 7023
22:11 Ye made also a ditch between the **two w** 2346
25:12 the fortress of the high fort of thy **w** shall 2346
26: 1 salvation will *God* appoint *for* **w** and 2346
49:16 *my* hands; thy **w** *are* continually before me. 2346
56: 5 within my **w** a place and a name better than 2346
60:10 the sons of strangers shall build up thy **w**, 2346
60:18 thou shalt call thy **w** Salvation, and 2346
62: 6 I have set watchmen upon thy **w**, 2346
Jer 1:15 against all the **w** thereof round about, and 2346
1:18 and brasen **w** against the whole land, 2346
5:10 Go ye up upon her **w**, and destroy; but 8284
21: 4 which besiege you without the **w**, and I will 2346
39: 4 by the gate betwixt the **two w**: 2346
39: 8 and brake down the **w** of Jerusalem. 2346
50:15 are fallen, her **w** are thrown down: 2346
51:12 Set up the standard upon the **w** of Babylon, 2346
51:58 The broad **w** of Babylon shall be utterly 2346
52: 7 *by* the way of the gate between the **two w**, 2346
52:14 brake down all the **w** of Jerusalem round 2346
La 2: 7 the hand of the enemy the **w** of her palaces; 2346
Eze 26: 4 they shall destroy the **w** of Tyrus, and 2346

W

Eze 26: 9 he shall set engines of war against thy **w**, 2346
26:10 thy **w** shall shake at the noise of 2346
26:12 they shall break down thy **w**, and 2346
27:11 thine army *were* upon thy **w** round about, 2346
27:11 they hanged their shields upon thy **w** round 2346
33:30 still are talking against thee by the **w** 7023
38:11 all of them dwelling without **w**, and 2346
41:13 and the building, with the **w** thereof, 7023
41:22 and the **w** thereof, *were of* wood: 7023
41:25 palm trees, like as *were* made upon the **w**; 7023
Mic 7:11 *In* the day that thy **w** are *to be* built, *in* that 1447
Zec 2: 4 **towns without w** for the multitude of men 6519
Heb 11:30 By faith the **w** of Jericho fell down, *5038*

WANDER (14) [WANDERED, WANDERERS, WANDEREST, WANDERETH, WANDERING, WANDERINGS]

Ge 20:13 when God **caused** me **to w** from my 8582
Nu 14:33 your children shall **w** in the wilderness 7462
32:13 he **made** them **w** in the wilderness forty 5128
Dt 27:18 Cursed *be* he that **maketh** the blind **to w** 7686
Job 12:24 **causeth** them **to w** in a wilderness *where* 8582
38:41 ones cry unto God, they **w** for lack of meat. 8582
Ps 55: 7 Lo, *then* would I **w** far off, *and* remain in 5074
59:15 Let them **w up and down** for meat, and 5128
107:40 **causeth** them **to w** in the wilderness, 8582
119:10 O let me not **w** from thy commandments. 7686
Isa 47:15 they shall **w** every one to his quarter; 8582
Jer 14:10 Thus have they loved to **w**, they have not 5128
48:12 that shall **cause** him **to w**, and shall empty 6808
Am 8:12 they shall **w** from sea to sea, and from 5128

WANDERED (10) [WANDER]

Ge 21:14 and **w** in the wilderness of Beer-sheba. 8582
Jos 14:10 while *the children of* Israel **w** in 1980
Ps 107: 4 They **w** in the wilderness in a solitary way; 8582
Isa 16: 8 unto Jazer, they **w** *through* the wilderness: 8582
La 4:14 They have **w** *as* blind *men* in the streets, 5128
4:15 touch not, when they fled away and **w**: 5128
Eze 34: 6 My sheep **w** through all the mountains, and 7686
Am 4: 8 So two *or* three cities **w** unto one city, 5128
Heb 11:37 they **w about** in sheepskins and goatskins; *4022*
11:38 they **w** in deserts, and *in* mountains, and *4105*

WANDERERS (2) [WANDER]

Jer 48:12 the LORD, that I will send unto him **w**, 6808
Hos 9:17 and they shall be **w** among the nations. 5074

WANDEREST (1) [WANDER]

Jer 2:20 high hill and under every green tree thou **w**, 6808

WANDERETH (6) [WANDER]

Job 15:23 He **w abroad** for bread, *saying,* Where *is* 5074
Pr 21:16 The man that **w** out of the way of 8582
27: 8 As a bird that **w** from her nest, so *is* a man 5074
27: 8 her nest, so *is* a man that **w** from his place. 5074
Isa 16: 3 hide the outcasts; bewray not him that **w**. 5074
Jer 49: 5 and none shall gather up him that **w**. 5074

WANDERING (6) [WANDER]

Ge 37:15 and behold, *he was* **w** in the field: 8582
Pr 26: 2 As the bird by **w**, as the swallow by flying, 5110
Ecc 6: 9 Better *is* the sight of the eyes than the **w** of 1980
Isa 16: 2 *that,* as a **w** bird cast out of the nest, *so* 5074
1Ti 5:13 *to be* idle, **w about** from house to house; *4022*
Jude 1:13 **w** stars, to whom is reserved the blackness *4107*

WANDERINGS (1) [WANDER]

Ps 56: 8 Thou tellest my **w**: put thou my tears into 5112

WANT (31) [WANTED, WANTETH, WANTING, WANTS]

Dt 28:48 in **w** of all *things:* and he shall put a yoke of 2640
28:57 for she shall eat them for **w** of all *things* 2640
Jdg 18:10 a place where *there is* no **w** of any thing 4270
19:19 thy servants: *there is* no **w** of any thing. 4270
Job 24: 8 embrace the rock **for w of** a shelter. 1097+4480
30: 3 For **w** and famine *they were* solitary; flying 2639
31:19 If I have seen *any* perish for **w** of clothing, 1097
Ps 23: 1 The LORD *is* my shepherd; I shall not **w**. 2637
34: 9 for *there is* no **w** to them that fear him. 4270
34:10 they that seek the LORD shall not **w** any 2637
Pr 6:11 that travelleth, and thy **w** as an armed man. 4270
10:21 feed many: but fools die for **w** of wisdom. 2638
13:23 there is *that is* destroyed for **w of** judgment. 3808
13:25 but the belly of the wicked shall **w**. 2637
14:28 in the **w** of people *is* the destruction of 657
21: 5 but *of* every one that is hasty only to **w**. 4270
22:16 giveth to the rich, *shall* surely *come* to **w**. 4270
24:34 that travelleth; and thy **w** as an armed man. 4270
Isa 34:16 of these shall fail, none shall **w** her mate: 6485
Jer 33:17 David shall never **w** a man to sit upon 3772
33:18 Neither shall the priests the Levites **w** a 3772
35:19 Jonadab the son of Rechab shall not **w** a 3772
La 4: 9 stricken through for *w of* the fruits of NIH
Eze 4:17 That they may **w** bread and water, and 2637
Am 4: 6 and **w** of bread in all your places: 2640
Mk 12:44 but she of her **w** did cast in all that she had, *5304*
Lk 15:14 in that land; and he began to be **in w**. *5302*
2Co 8:14 abundance *may be a supply* for their **w**, *5303*
8:14 also may be *a supply* for your **w**: *5303*
9:12 not only supplieth the **w** of the saints, *5303*
Php 4:11 Not that I speak in respect of **w**: for I have *5304*

WANTED (3) [WANT]

Jer 44:18 we have **w** all *things,* and have been 2637
Jn 2: 3 And when they **w** wine, the mother of Jesus *5302*
2Co 11: 9 And when I was present with you, and **w**, *5302*

WANTETH (7) [WANT]

Dt 15: 8 sufficient for his need, *in that* which he **w**. 2637
Pr 9: 4 *as for* him that **w** understanding, she saith 2638
9:16 *as for* him that **w** understanding, she saith 2638
10:19 In the multitude of words there **w** not sin: 2308
28:16 The prince that **w** understanding *is* also a 2638
Ecc 6: 2 that he **w** nothing for his soul of all that he 2638
SS 7: 2 *is like* a round goblet, *which* **w** not liquor: 2637

WANTING (8) [WANT]

2Ki 10:19 and all his priests; let none be **w**: 6485
10:19 whosoever shall be **w**, he shall not live. 6485
Pr 19: 7 *them with* words, *yet* they *are* **w** *to him.* 3808
Ecc 1:15 and **that which is w** cannot be numbered. 2642
Da 5:27 weighed in the balances, and art found **w**. 2627
Tit 1: 5 shouldest set in order the *things* that are **w**, *3007*
3:13 that nothing be **w** unto them. *3007*
Jas 1: 4 ye may be perfect and entire, **w** nothing. *3007*

WANTON (3) [WANTONNESS]

Isa 3:16 walk with stretched forth necks and **w** eyes, 8265
1Ti 5:11 when they have *begun to* **wax w against** *2691*
Jas 5: 5 lived in pleasure on the earth, and been **w**; *4684*

WANTONNESS (2) [WANTON]

Ro 13:13 not in chambering and **w**, not in strife and *766*
2Pe 2:18 the lusts of the flesh, through much **w**, *766*

WANTS (2) [WANT]

Jdg 19:20 howsoever *let* all thy **w** *lie* upon me; 4270
Php 2:25 and he that ministered to my **w**. *5532*

WAR (225) [WARFARE, WARRED, WARRETH, WARRING, WARRIOR, WARRIORS, WARS]

Ge 14: 2 *That these* made **w** with Bera king of 4421
Ex 1:10 to pass, that, when there falleth out any **w**, 4421
13:17 the people repent when they see **w**, 4421
15: 3 The LORD *is* a man of **w**: the LORD *is* 4421
17:16 **w** with Amalek from generation *to* 4421
32:17 *There is* a noise of **w** in the camp. 4421
Nu 1: 3 all that *are able to* go forth *to* **w** in Israel: 6635
1:20 upward, all that *were able to* go forth *to* **w**; 6635
1:22 upward, all that *were able to* go forth *to* **w**; 6635
1:24 upward, all that *were able to* go forth *to* **w**; 6635
1:26 upward, all that *were able to* go forth *to* **w**; 6635
1:28 upward, all that *were able to* go forth *to* **w**; 6635
1:30 upward, all that *were able to* go forth *to* **w**; 6635
1:32 upward, all that *were able to* go forth *to* **w**; 6635
1:34 upward, all that *were able to* go forth *to* **w**; 6635
1:36 upward, all that *were able to* go forth *to* **w**; 6635
1:38 upward, all that *were able to* go forth *to* **w**; 6635
1:40 upward, all that *were able to* go forth *to* **w**; 6635
1:42 upward, all that *were able to* go forth *to* **w**; 6635
1:45 all that *were able to* go forth *to* **w** in Israel; 6635
10: 9 if ye go *to* **w** in your land against 4421
26: 2 all that *are able to* go *to* **w** in Israel. 6635
31: 3 Arm some of yourselves unto the **w**, and 6635
31: 4 the tribes of Israel, shall ye send to the **w**. 6635
31: 5 *every* tribe, twelve thousand armed for **w**. 6635
31: 6 Moses sent them to the **w**, a thousand of 6635
31: 6 to the **w**, with the holy instruments, and 6635
31:21 Eleazar the priest said unto the men of **w** 6635
31:27 between them that took the **w** upon them, 4421

Nu 31:28 of the men of **w** which went out to battle: 4421
31:32 of the prey which the men of **w** had caught, 6635
31:36 *was* the portion of them that went out to **w**, 6635
31:49 the men of **w** which *are* under our charge, 4421
31:53 (*For* the men of **w** had taken spoil, 6635
32: 6 Shall your brethren go to **w**, and shall ye sit 4421
32:20 ye will go armed before the LORD to **w**, 4421
32:27 every man armed for **w**, before the LORD 6635
Dt 1:41 had girded on every man his weapons of **w**, 4421
2:14 until all the generation of the men of **w** 4421
2:16 when all the men of **w** were consumed and 4421
3:18 of Israel, all *that are* **meet for the w.** 1121+2428
4:34 by **w**, and by a mighty hand, and by a 4421
20:12 will make **w** against thee, then thou shalt 4421
20:19 long time, in **making w** against it to take it, 3898
20:20 against the city that maketh **w** with thee, 4421
21:10 When thou goest forth to **w** against thine 4421
24: 5 taken a new wife, he shall not go out to **w**, 6635
Jos 4:13 About forty thousand prepared for **w** 6635
5: 4 *that were* males, *even* all the men of **w**, 4421
5: 6 till all the people *that were* men of **w**, 4421
6: 3 all *ye* men of **w**, *and* go round about 4421
8: 1 take all the people of **w** with thee, 4421
8: 3 So Joshua arose, and all the people of **w**, 4421
8:11 *even the people* of **w** that *were* with him, 4421
10: 5 before Gibeon, and **made w** against it. 3898
10: 7 he, and all the people of **w** with him, and 4421
10:24 said unto the captains of the men of **w** 4421
11: 7 and all the people of **w** with him, 4421
11:18 Joshua made **w** a long time with all those 4421
11:23 by their tribes. And the land rested from **w**. 4421
14:11 for **w**, both to go out, and to come in. 4421
14:15 the Anakims. And the land had rest from **w**. 4421
17: 1 because he was a man of **w**, therefore 4421
22:12 *at* Shiloh, to go up to **w** against them. 6635
Jdg 3: 2 to teach them **w**, at the least such as before 4421
3:10 and he judged Israel, and went out to **w**: 4421
5: 8 chose new gods; then *was* **w** in the gates: 3901
11: 4 that the children of Ammon **made w** 3898
11: 5 that when the children of Ammon **made w** 3898
11:27 but thou doest me wrong to **w** against me: 3898
18:11 hundred men appointed *with* weapons of **w**. 4421
18:16 men appointed *with* their weapons of **w**, 4421
18:17 that were appointed *with* weapons of **w**. 4421
20:17 that drew sword: all these *were* men of **w**. 4421
21:22 reserved not to each man his wife in the **w**: 4421
1Sa 8:12 to make his instruments of **w**, and 4421
14:52 there was sore **w** against the Philistines all 4421
16:18 a mighty valiant *man*, and a man of **w**, and 4421
17:33 a youth, and he a man of **w** from his youth. 4421
18: 5 Saul set him over the men of **w**, and he was 4421
19: 8 there was **w** again: and David went out, 4421
23: 8 Saul called all the people together to **w**, 4421
28:15 for the Philistines **make w** against me, and 3898
2Sa 1:27 and the weapons of **w** perished! 4421
3: 1 Now there was long **w** between the house 4421
3: 6 while there was **w** between the house of 4421
11: 7 the people did, and how the **w** prospered. 4421
11:18 told David all the things concerning the **w**; 4421
11:19 telling the matters of the **w** unto the king, 4421
17: 8 thy father *is* a man of **w**, and will not lodge 4421
21:15 Moreover the Philistines had yet **w** again 4421
22:35 He teacheth my hands to **w**; so that a bow 4421
1Ki 2: 5 shed the blood of **w** in peace, and put 4421
2: 5 put the blood of **w** upon his girdle that *was* 4421
9:22 they *were* men of **w**, and his servants, and 4421
14:30 there was **w** between Rehoboam and 4421
15: 6 there was **w** between Rehoboam and 4421
15: 7 there was **w** between Abijam and 4421
15:16 there was **w** between Asa and Baasha king 4421
15:32 there was **w** between Asa and Baasha king 4421
20:18 or whether they be come out for **w**, 4421
22: 1 they continued three years without **w** 4421
2Ki 8:28 **w** against Hazael king of Syria in 4421
13:25 out of the hand of Jehoahaz his father by **w**. 4421
14: 7 took Selah by **w**, and called the name of it 4421
16: 5 king of Israel came up *to* Jerusalem to **w**: 4421
18:20 *I have* counsel and strength for the **w**. 4421
24:16 all *that were* strong *and* apt for **w**, 4421
25: 4 all the men of **w** *fled* by night *by* the way of 4421
25:19 an officer that was set over the men of **w**, 4421
1Ch 5:10 in the days of Saul they made **w** with 4421
5:18 skilful in **w**, *were* four and forty thousand 4421
5:18 and threescore, that went out *to* the **w**. 6635
5:19 they made **w** with the Hagarites, with Jetur, 4421
5:22 many slain, because the **w** *was* of God. 4421
7: 4 *were* bands of soldiers for **w**, six and 4421
7:11 two hundred *soldiers, fit to* go out *for* **w** 6635
7:40 genealogy of them *that were apt* to the **w** 6635
12: 1 among the mighty *men*, helpers of the **w**. 4421
12: 8 *and* men of **w** *fit* for the battle, that could 6635
12:23 the bands that were ready armed to the **w**, 6635
12:24 and eight hundred, ready armed to the **w**. 6635
12:25 mighty *men* of valour for the **w**, 6635
12:33 expert in **w**, with all instruments of war, 4421
12:33 expert in war, with all instruments of **w**, 4421
12:35 of the Danites expert in **w** twenty and 4421
12:36 forth to battle, expert in **w**, forty thousand. 4421
12:37 with all *manner of* instruments of **w** for 6635
12:38 All these men of **w**, that could keep rank, 4421
18:10 (for Hadarezer **had w with** 376+1961+4421
20: 4 that there arose **w** at Gezer with 4421
20: 5 there was **w** again with the Philistines; and 4421
20: 6 yet again there was **w** at Gath, where was a 4421
28: 3 because thou *hast been* a man of **w**, and 4421
2Ch 6:34 If thy people go out to **w** against their 4421
8: 9 they *were* men of **w**, and chief of his 4421
13: 2 there was **w** between Abijah and Jeroboam. 4421
13: 3 in array with an army of valiant *men* of **w**, 4421
14: 6 had rest, and he had no **w** in those years; 4421
15:19 there was no *more* **w** unto the five and 4421
17:10 that they **made** no **w** against Jehoshaphat. 3898
17:13 the men of **w**, mighty *men* of valour, 4421
17:18 thousand ready prepared for the **w**. 6635
18: 3 and *we will be* with thee in the **w**. 4421
22: 5 **w** against Hazael king of Syria at 4421
25: 5 thousand choice *men, able to* go forth *to* **w**, 6635
26:11 fighting *men*, that went out to **w** by bands, 6635
26:13 that made **w** with mighty power, 4421
28:12 up against them that came from the **w**, 6635
32: 6 he set captains of **w** over the people, and 4421
33:14 put captains of **w** in all the fenced cities of 2428
35:21 but against the house wherewith I have **w**: 4421
Job 5:20 and in **w** from the power of the sword. 4421
10:17 upon me; changes and **w** *are* against me. 6635
38:23 of trouble, against the day of battle and **w**? 4421
Ps 18:34 He teacheth my hands to **w**, so that a bow 4421
27: 3 though **w** should rise against me, in this 4421
55:21 than butter, but **w** *was* in his heart: 7128
68:30 scatter thou the people *that* delight in **w**. 7128
120: 7 *for* peace: but when I speak, they *are* for **w**. 4421
140: 2 are they gathered together *for* **w**. 4421
144: 1 which teacheth my hands to **w**, *and* 7128
Pr 20:18 by counsel: and with good advice make **w**. 4421
24: 6 For by wise counsel thou shalt make thy **w**: 4421
Ecc 3: 8 to hate; a time of **w**, and a time of peace. 4421
8: 8 *there is* no discharge in *that* **w**; neither shall 4421
9:18 Wisdom *is* better than weapons of **w**: but 7128
SS 3: 8 They all hold swords, *being* expert in **w**: 4421
Isa 2: 4 neither shall they learn **w** any more. 4421
3: 2 The mighty *man*, and the man of **w**, 4421
3:25 fall by the sword, and thy mighty in the **w**. 4421
7: 1 went up *towards* Jerusalem to **w** against it, 4421
21:15 bent bow, and from the grievousness of **w**. 4421
36: 5 *I have* counsel and strength for **w**: 4421
37: 9 He is come forth to **make w** with thee. 3898
41:12 they that **w** against thee shall be as nothing, 4421
42:13 he shall stir up jealousy like a man of **w**: 4421
Jer 4:19 the sound of the trumpet, the alarm of **w**. 4421
6: 4 Prepare ye **w** against her; arise, and let us 4421
6:23 set in array as men for **w** against thee, 4421
21: 2 king of Babylon **maketh w** against us; 3898
21: 4 I *will* turn back the weapons of **w** that *are* 4421
28: 8 of **w**, and of evil, and of pestilence. 4421
38: 4 of the men of **w** that remain in this city, 4421
39: 4 all the men of **w**, then they fled, and 4421
41: 3 that were found there, *and* the men of **w**. 4421
41:16 *even* mighty men of **w**, and the women, and 4421
42:14 the land of Egypt, where we shall see no **w**, 4421
48:14 We *are* mighty and strong men for the **w**? 4421
49: 2 that I will cause an alarm of **w** to be heard 4421
49:26 all the men of **w** shall be cut off in that day, 4421
50:30 all her men of **w** shall be cut off in that day, 4421
51:20 Thou *art* my battle axe *and* weapons of **w**: 4421
51:32 with fire, and the men of **w** are affrighted. 4421
52: 7 all the men of **w** fled, and went forth out of 4421
52:25 which had the charge of the men of **w**; 4421
Eze 17:17 and great company make for him in the **w**, 4421

Eze 26: 9 he shall set engines of **w** against thy walls, 6904
27:10 of Phut were in thine army, thy men of **w**: 4421
27:27 all thy men of **w**, that *are* in thee, and in all 4421
32:27 gone down *to* hell with their weapons of **w**: 4421
39:20 with mighty *men,* and *with* all men of **w**, 4421
Da 7:21 the same horn made **w** with the saints, and 7129
9:26 unto the end of the **w** desolations *are* 4421
Joel 2: 7 they shall climb the wall like men of **w**; 4421
3: 9 Prepare **w**, wake up the mighty *men,* let all 4421
3: 9 mighty *men,* let all the men of **w** draw near; 4421
Mic 2: 8 that pass by securely *as men* averse from **w**. 4421
3: 5 they even prepare **w** against him. 4421
4: 3 neither shall they learn **w** any more. 4421
Lk 14:31 **make w against** another king, *1519+4171+4820*
23:11 And Herod with his **men of w** set him at *4753*
2Co 10: 3 in the flesh, we do not **w** after the flesh: *4754*
1Ti 1:18 that thou by them mightest **w** a good *4754*
Jas 4: 1 *even* of your lusts that **w** in your members? *4754*
4: 2 ye fight and **w**, yet ye have not, because ye *4170*
1Pe 2:11 fleshly lusts, which **w** against the soul; *4754*
Rev 11: 7 bottomless *pit* shall make **w** against them, *4171*
12: 7 And there was **w** in heaven: Michael and *4171*
12:17 went to make **w** with the remnant of her *4171*
13: 4 who is able to **make w** with him? *4170*
13: 7 And it was given unto him to make **w** with *4171*
17:14 These shall **make w** with the Lamb, and *4170*
19:11 righteousness he doth judge and **make w**. *4170*
19:19 gathered together to make **w** against him *4171*

WARD (22) [WARDS]

Ge 40: 3 he put them in **w** *in* the house of the captain 4929
40: 4 and they continued a season in **w**. 4929
40: 7 *were* with him in the **w** of his lord's house, 4929
41:10 put me in **w** *in* the captain of the guard's 4929
42:17 he put them all together into **w** three days. 4929
Lev 24:12 they put him in **w**, that the mind of 4929
Nu 15:34 they put him in **w**, because it was not 4929
2Sa 20: 3 put them *in* **w**, and fed them, but 1004+4931
1Ch 12:29 them had kept the **w** of the house of Saul. 4931
25: 8 **w** against *ward,* as well the small as 4931
25: 8 ward against *w*, as well the small as NIH
26:16 causeway of the going up, **w** against ward. 4929
26:16 causeway of the going up, ward against **w**. 4929
Ne 12:24 the man of God, **w** over against ward, 4929
12:24 the man of God, ward over against **w**, 4929
12:25 *were* porters keeping the **w** at 4929
12:45 and the porters kept the **w** of their God, 4931
12:45 of their God, and the **w** of the purification, 4931
Isa 21: 8 and I *am* set in my **w** whole nights: 4931
Jer 37:13 a captain of the **w** *was* there, whose name 6488
Eze 19: 9 they put him in **w** in chains, and 5474
Ac 12:10 they were past the first and the second **w**, *5438*

WARDROBE (2)

2Ki 22:14 the son of Harhas, keeper of the **w**; 899
2Ch 34:22 the son of Hasrah, keeper of the **w**; 899

WARDS (3) [WARD]

1Ch 9:23 *namely,* the house of the tabernacle, by **w**. 4931
26:12 chief men, *having* **w** one against another, 4931
Ne 13:30 appointed the **w** of the priests and 4931

WARE (8) [AWARE, WARES, WEAR]

Ne 10:31 *if* the people of the land bring **w** or 4728
13:16 all *manner of* **w**, and sold on the sabbath 4377
13:20 sellers of all *kind of* **w** lodged without 4465
Mt 24:50 for *him,* and in an hour that he is not **w of**, *1097*
Lk 8:27 and **w** no clothes, neither abode in *any* *1737*
12:46 for *him,* and at an hour when he is not **w**, *1097*
Ac 14: 6 They were **w** of *it,* and fled unto Lystra and *4894*
2Ti 4:15 Of whom **be** thou **w** also; for he hath *5442*

WARES (5) [WARE]

Jer 10:17 Gather up thy **w** out of the land, 3666
Eze 27:16 of the multitude of the **w of** thy **making**: 4639
27:18 in the multitude of the **w of** thy **making**, 4639
27:33 When thy **w** went forth out of the seas, 5801
Jnh 1: 5 cast forth the **w** that *were* in the ship into 3627

WARFARE (5) [WAR]

1Sa 28: 1 gathered their armies together for **w**, 6635
Isa 40: 2 cry unto her, that her **w** is accomplished, 6635
1Co 9: 7 Who **goeth a w** any time at his own *4754*
2Co 10: 4 (For the weapons of our **w** *are* not carnal, *4752*
1Ti 1:18 that thou by them mightest war a good **w**; *4752*

WARM (8) [LUKEWARM]

2Ki 4:34 and the flesh of the child **waxed w**. 2552
Job 6:17 What time they **wax w**, they vanish: 2215
37:17 How thy garments *are* **w**, when he quieteth 2525
Ecc 4:11 have heat: but how can one be **w** *alone?* 3179
Isa 44:15 for he will take thereof, and **w** himself; yea, 2552
44:16 and saith, Aha, I am **w**, I have seen the fire: 2552
47:14 *there shall* not *be* a coal to **w** at, *nor* fire to 2552
Hag 1: 6 *ye* clothe you, but there is none **w**; and he 2527

WARMED (6) [WARMETH, WARMING]

Job 31:20 *if* he were *not* **w** with the fleece of my 2552
Mk 14:54 with the servants, and **w** himself at the fire. *2328*
Jn 18:18 and they **w** themselves: and Peter stood *2328*
18:18 and Peter stood with them, and **w** himself. *2328*
18:25 And Simon Peter stood and **w** himself. *2328*
Jas 2:16 Depart in peace, be you **w** and filled; *2328*

WARMETH (2) [WARMED]

Job 39:14 her eggs in the earth, and **w** them in dust, 2552
Isa 44:16 yea, he **w** himself, and saith, Aha, I am 2552

WARMING (1) [WARMED]

Mk 14:67 And when she saw Peter **w** himself, *2328*

WARN (11) [FOREWARN, FOREWARNED, WARNED, WARNING]

2Ch 19:10 ye shall even **w** them that they trespass not 2094
Eze 3:18 nor speakest to **w** the wicked from his 2094
3:19 Yet if thou **w** the wicked, and he turn not 2094
3:21 Nevertheless if thou **w** the righteous *man,* 2094
33: 3 he blow the trumpet, and **w** the people; 2094
33: 7 word at my mouth, and **w** them from me. 2094
33: 8 if thou dost not speak to **w** the wicked from 2094
33: 9 if thou **w** the wicked of his way to turn 2094
Ac 20:31 years I ceased not to **w** every one night *3560*
1Co 4:14 but as my beloved sons I **w** *you.* *3560*
1Th 5:14 brethren, **w** *them that are* unruly, *3560*

WARNED (10) [WARN]

2Ki 6:10 the man of God told him and **w** him of, 2094
Ps 19:11 Moreover by them *is* thy servant **w**: *and* 2094
Eze 3:21 he shall surely live, because he is **w**; 2094
33: 6 not the trumpet, and the people be not **w**; 2094
Mt 2:12 And being **w of God** in a dream that *they* *5537*
2:22 being **w of God** in a dream, *5537*
3: 7 who hath **w** you to flee from the wrath to *5263*
Lk 3: 7 who hath **w** you to flee from the wrath to *5263*
Ac 10:22 was **w from God** by a holy angel to send *5537*
Heb 11: 7 being **w of God** of *things* not seen as yet, *5537*

WARNING (8) [WARN]

Jer 6:10 I speak, and **give w**, that they may hear? 5749
Eze 3:17 at my mouth, and **give** them **w** from me. 2094
3:18 and thou **givest** him not **w**, 2094
3:20 because thou hast not **given** him **w**, he shall 2094
33: 4 the sound of the trumpet, and **taketh** not **w**; 2094
33: 5 the sound of the trumpet, and **took** not **w**; 2094
33: 5 But he that **taketh w** shall deliver his soul. 2094
Col 1:28 **w** every man, and teaching every man in all *3560*

WARP (9)

Lev 13:48 Whether *it be* in the **w**, or woof; of linen, or 8359
13:49 either in the **w**, or in the woof, or in any 8359
13:51 either in the **w**, or in the woof, or in a skin, 8359
13:52 whether **w** or woof, in woollen or in linen, 8359
13:53 either in the **w**, or in the woof, or in any 8359
13:56 the skin, or out of the **w**, or out of the woof: 8359
13:57 either in the **w**, or in the woof, or in any 8359
13:58 either **w**, or woof, or whatsoever thing of 8359
13:59 either *in* the **w**, or woof, or any thing of 8359

WARRED (9) [WAR]

Nu 31: 7 they **w** against the Midianites, as 6633
31:42 which Moses divided from the men that **w**, 6633
Jos 24: 9 arose and **w** against Israel, and sent and 3898
1Ki 14:19 how he **w**, and how he reigned, 3898
20: 1 and besieged Samaria, and **w** against it. 3898
22:45 his might that he shewed, and how he **w**, 3898
2Ki 6: 8 the king of Syria **w** against Israel, and 3898
14:28 how he **w**, and how he recovered 3898
2Ch 26: 6 he went forth and **w** against the Philistines, 3898

WARRETH (1) [WAR]

2Ti 2: 4 No *man* that **w** entangleth himself with *4754*

WARRING (3) [WAR]
2Ki 19: 8 found the king of Assyria **w** against 3898
Isa 37: 8 found the king of Assyria **w** against 3898
Ro 7:23 **w against** the law of my mind, and *497*

WARRIOR (1) [WAR]
Isa 9: 5 For every battle of the **w** *is* with confused 5431

WARRIORS (2) [WAR]
1Ki 12:21 thousand chosen *men,* which were **w**, 4421+6213
2Ch 11: 1 thousand chosen *men,* which were **w**, 4421+6213

WARS (15) [WAR]
Nu 21:14 Wherefore it is said in the book of the **w** of 4421
Jdg 3: 1 as had not known all the **w** of Canaan; 4421
2Sa 8:10 for Hadadezer **had w with** Toi. 376+1961+4421
1Ki 5: 3 the **w** which were about him on every side, 4421
1Ch 22: 8 blood abundantly, and hast made great **w**: 4421
2Ch 12:15 *there were* **w** between Rehoboam and 4421
16: 9 from henceforth thou shalt have **w**. 4421
27: 7 acts of Jotham, and all his **w**, and his ways, 4421
Ps 46: 9 He maketh **w** to cease unto the end of 4421
Mt 24: 6 And ye shall hear of **w** and rumours of *4171*
24: 6 ye shall hear of wars and rumours of **w**: *4171*
Mk 13: 7 And when ye shall hear of **w** and *4171*
13: 7 ye shall hear of wars and rumours of **w**, *4171*
Lk 21: 9 But when ye shall hear of **w** and *4171*
Jas 4: 1 From whence *come* **w** and fightings among *4171*

WART See WEN

WAS (4531) [BE] See Index

WASH (89) [UNWASHEN, WASHED, WASHEST, WASHING, WASHINGS, WASHPOT]
Ge 18: 4 **w** your feet, and rest yourselves under 7364
19: 2 **w** your feet, and ye shall rise up early, and 7364
24:32 water to **w** his feet, and the men's feet that 7364
Ex 2: 5 the daughter of Pharaoh came down to **w** 7364
19:10 to morrow, and let them **w** their clothes, 3526
29: 4 and shalt **w** them with water. 7364
29:17 **w** the inwards of him, and his legs, and 7364
30:18 to **w** *withal:* and thou shalt put it between 7364
30:19 and his sons shall **w** their hands and 7364
30:20 they shall **w** *with* water, that they die not; 7364
30:21 So they shall **w** their hands and their feet, 7364
40:12 the congregation, and **w** them with water. 7364
40:30 the altar, and put water there, to **w** *withal.* 7364
Lev 1: 9 and his legs shall he **w** in water: 7364
1:13 he shall **w** the inwards and the legs with 7364
6:27 thou shalt **w** that whereon it was sprinkled 3526
9:14 he did **w** the inwards and the legs, and 7364
11:25 of the carcase of them shall **w** his clothes, 3526
11:28 he that beareth the carcase of them shall **w** 3526
11:40 he that eateth of the carcase of it shall **w** his 3526
11:40 he also that beareth the carcase of it shall **w** 3526
13: 6 and he shall **w** his clothes, and be clean. 3526
13:34 and he shall **w** his clothes, and be clean. 3526
13:54 the priest shall command that they **w** 3526
13:58 thing of skin *it be,* which thou shalt **w**, 3526
14: 8 he that is to be cleansed shall **w** his clothes, 3526
14: 8 off all his hair, and **w** *himself* in water, 7364
14: 9 he shall **w** his clothes, also he shall wash 3526
14: 9 also he shall **w** his flesh in water, and 7364
14:47 he that lieth in the house shall **w** his 3526
14:47 he that eateth in the house shall **w** his 3526
15: 5 whosoever toucheth his bed shall **w** his 3526
15: 6 sat that hath the issue shall **w** his clothes, 3526
15: 7 him that hath the issue shall **w** his clothes, 3526
15: 8 he shall **w** his clothes, and bathe *himself* in 3526
15:10 he that beareth *any of* those *things* shall **w** 3526
15:11 he shall **w** his clothes, and bathe *himself* in 3526
15:13 **w** his clothes, and bathe his flesh in running 3526
15:16 he shall **w** all his flesh in water, and 7364
15:21 whosoever toucheth her bed shall **w** his 3526
15:22 thing that she sat upon shall **w** his clothes, 3526
15:27 shall **w** his clothes, and bathe *himself* in 3526
16: 4 therefore shall he **w** his flesh in water, and 7364
16:24 he shall **w** his flesh with water in the holy 7364
16:26 goat for the scapegoat shall **w** his clothes, 3526
16:28 he that burneth them shall **w** his clothes, 3526
17:15 he shall both **w** his clothes, and 3526
17:16 if he **w** *them* not, nor bathe his flesh; then 3526
22: 6 shall not eat of the holy *things,* unless he **w** 7364
Nu 8: 7 let them **w** their clothes, and *so* 3526
19: 7 the priest shall **w** his clothes, and he shall 3526
19: 8 he that burneth her shall **w** his clothes in 3526
19:10 the ashes of the heifer shall **w** his clothes, 3526
19:19 he shall purify him*self,* and **w** his clothes, 3526
19:21 the water of separation shall **w** his clothes; 3526
31:24 ye shall **w** your clothes on the seventh day, 3526
Dt 21: 6 *that are* next unto the slain *man,* shall **w** 7364
23:11 cometh on, he shall **w** *himself* with water: 7364
Ru 3: 3 **W** *thyself* therefore, and anoint thee, and 7364
1Sa 25:41 *let* thine handmaid *be* a servant to **w** 7364
2Sa 11: 8 Go down to thy house, and **w** thy feet. 7364
2Ki 5:10 Go and **w** in Jordan seven times, and 7364
5:12 may I not **w** in them, and be clean? So he 7364
5:13 when he saith to thee, **W**, and be clean? 7364
2Ch 4: 6 and five on the left, to **w** in them: 7364
4: 6 but the sea *was* for the priests to **w** in. 7364
Job 9:30 If I **w** myself with snow water, and 7364
Ps 26: 6 I will **w** mine hands in innocency: so will I 7364
51: 2 **W** me throughly from mine iniquity, and 3526
51: 7 **w** me, and I shall be whiter than snow. 3526
58:10 he shall **w** his feet in the blood of 7364
Isa 1:16 **W** ye, make you clean; put away the evil of 7364
Jer 2:22 For though thou **w** thee with nitre, and 3526
4:14 **w** thine heart from wickedness, 3526
Eze 23:40 for whom thou didst **w** *thyself,* paintedst 7364
Mt 6:17 anoint thine head, and **w** thy face; *3538*
15: 2 for they **w** not their hands when they eat *3538*
Mk 7: 3 except they **w** *their* hands oft, eat not, *3538*
7: 4 from the market, except they **w**, they eat not. *907*
Lk 7:38 and began to **w** his feet with tears, and *1026*
Jn 9: 7 said unto him, Go, **w** in the pool of Siloam, *3538*
9:11 unto me, Go to the pool of Siloam, and **w**: *3538*
13: 5 and began to **w** the disciples' feet, and *3538*
13: 6 saith unto him, Lord, dost thou **w** my feet? *3538*
13: 8 saith unto him, Thou shalt never **w** my feet. *3538*
13: 8 Jesus answered him, If I **w** thee not, *3538*
13:10 He that is washed needeth not save to **w** *his* *3538*
13:14 ye also ought to **w** one another's feet. *3538*
Ac 22:16 arise, and be baptized, and **w away** thy sins, *628*

WASHBASIN See WASHPOT

WASHED (45) [WASH]
Ge 43:24 and gave *them* water, and they **w** their feet; 7364
43:31 he **w** his face, and went out, and 7364
49:11 he **w** his garments in wine, and his clothes 3526
Ex 19:14 the people; and they **w** their clothes. 3526
40:31 and Aaron and his sons **w** their hands and 7364
40:32 when they came near unto the altar, they **w**; 7364
Lev 8: 6 and his sons, and **w** them with water. 7364
8:21 And he **w** the inwards and the legs in water; 7364
13:55 shall look on the plague, after *that* it is **w**: 3526
13:58 it shall be **w** the second time, and shall be 3526
15:17 shall be **w** with water, and be unclean until 3526
Nu 8:21 were purified, and they **w** their clothes; 3526
Jdg 19:21 and they **w** their feet, and did eat and drink. 7364
2Sa 12:20 **w**, and anointed *himself,* and changed his 7364
19:24 nor trimmed his beard, nor **w** his clothes, 3526
1Ki 22:38 *one* **w** the chariot in the pool of Samaria; 7857
22:38 licked up his blood; and they **w** his armour; 7364
2Ch 4: 6 for the burnt offering they **w** in them; 1740
Job 29: 6 When *I* **w** my steps with butter, and 7364
Ps 73:13 *in* vain, and **w** my hands in innocency. 7364
Pr 30:12 and *yet* is not **w** from their filthiness. 7364
SS 5: 3 I have **w** my feet; how shall I defile them? 7364
5:12 rivers of waters, **w** with milk, *and* fitly set. 7364
Isa 4: 4 When the Lord shall have **w away** the filth 7364
Eze 16: 4 neither wast thou **w** in water to supple *thee;* 7364
16: 9 **w** I thee with water; yea, I throughly 7364
16: 9 I **throughly w away** thy blood from thee, 7857
40:38 the gates, where they **w** the burnt offering. 1740
Mt 27:24 and **w** *his* hands before the multitude, *633*
Lk 7:44 but she hath **w** my feet with tears, and *1026*
11:38 that he had not first **w** before dinner. *907*
Jn 9: 7 his way therefore, and **w**, and came seeing. *3538*
9:11 and I went and **w**, and I received sight. *3538*
9:15 He put clay upon mine eyes, and I **w**, *3538*
13:10 He that is **w** needeth not save to wash *his* *3068*
13:12 So after he had **w** their feet, and had taken *3538*
13:14 *your* Lord and Master, have **w** your feet; *3538*
Ac 9:37 whom when they had **w**, they laid *her* in an *3068*
16:33 same hour of the night, and **w** *their* stripes; *3068*
1Co 6:11 but ye are **w**, but ye are sanctified, but ye are *628*
1Ti 5:10 if she have **w** the saints' feet, *3538*

Heb 10:22 and *our* bodies **w** with pure water. *3068*
2Pe 2:22 The sow that was **w** to *her* wallowing in *3068*
Rev 1: 5 and **w** us from our sins in his own blood, *3068*
7:14 and have **w** their robes, and made them *4150*

WASHERMAN'S See FULLER'S

WASHEST (1) [WASH]
Job 14:19 thou **w away** the things which grow out of 7857

WASHING (10) [WASH]
Lev 13:56 the plague *be* somewhat dark after the **w** of 3526
2Sa 11: 2 from the roof he saw a woman **w** *herself;* 7364
Ne 4:23 *saving that* every one put them off *for* **w**. 4325
SS 4: 2 *are* even shorn, which came up from the **w**; 7367
6: 6 as a flock of sheep which go up from the **w**, 7367
Mk 7: 4 *as* the **w** of cups, and pots, brasen vessels, *909*
7: 8 tradition of men, *as* the **w** of pots and cups: *909*
Lk 5: 2 gone out of them, and were **w** *their* nets. *637*
Eph 5:26 cleanse *it* with the **w** of water by the word, *3067*
Tit 3: 5 by the **w** of regeneration, and renewing of *3067*

WASHINGS (1) [WASH]
Heb 9:10 drinks, and divers **w**, and carnal ordinances, *909*

WASHPOT (2) [POT, WASH]
Ps 60: 8 Moab *is* my **w**; over Edom will I cast 5518+7366
108: 9 Moab *is* my **w**; over Edom will I cast 5518+7366

WAST (66) [BE] See Index

WASTE (64) [WASTED, WASTENESS, WASTER, WASTES, WASTETH, WASTING]
Lev 26:31 I will make your cities **w**, and bring your 2723
26:33 land shall be desolate, and your cities **w**. 2723
Nu 21:30 we have **laid** *them* **w** even unto Nophah, 8074
Dt 32:10 and in the **w** howling wilderness; 8414
1Ki 17:14 The barrel of meal shall not **w**, neither shall 3615
2Ki 19:25 that thou shouldest be to **lay w** fenced cities 7582
1Ch 17: 9 neither shall the children of wickedness **w** 1086
Ne 2: 3 *lieth* **w**, and the gates thereof are consumed 2720
2:17 how Jerusalem *lieth* **w**, and the gates 2720
Job 30: 3 wilderness in former time desolate and **w**. 4875
38:27 To satisfy the desolate and **w** *ground;* and 4875
Ps 79: 7 and **laid w** his dwelling place. 8074
80:13 The boar out of the wood doth **w** it, and 3765
Isa 5: 6 I will lay it **w**: it shall not be pruned, nor 1326
5:17 the **w places** of the fat ones shall strangers 2723
15: 1 Because in the night Ar of Moab is **laid w**, 7703
15: 1 because in the night Kir of Moab is **laid w**, 7703
23: 1 for it is **laid w**, so that *there is* no house, 7703
23:14 of Tarshish: for your strength is **laid w**. 7703
24: 1 **maketh** it **w**, and turneth it upside down, 1110
33: 8 The highways **lie w**, the wayfaring man 8074
34:10 from generation to generation it shall **lie w**; 2717
37:18 the kings of Assyria have **laid w** all 2717
37:26 that thou shouldest be to **lay w** defenced 7582
42:15 I will **make w** mountains and hills, and 2717
49:17 they that **made** thee **w** shall go forth of 2717
49:19 For thy **w** and thy desolate places, and 2723
51: 3 he will comfort all her **w places**; and 2723
52: 9 sing together, ye **w places** of Jerusalem: 2723
58:12 *be* of thee shall build the old **w places**: 2723
61: 4 they shall repair the **w** cities, 2721
64:11 and all our pleasant things are **laid w**. 2723
Jer 2:15 *and* yelled, and they made his land **w**: 8047
4: 7 *and* thy cities shall be **laid w**, without an 5327
27:17 live: wherefore should this city be **laid w**? 2723
46:19 for Noph shall be **w** and desolate without 8047
49:13 a desolation, a reproach, a **w**, and a curse; 2721
50:21 **w** and utterly destroy after them, saith 2717
Eze 5:14 Moreover I will make thee **w**, and 2723
6: 6 dwelling places the cities shall be **laid w**, 2717
6: 6 that your altars may be **laid w** and 2717
12:20 the cities that are inhabited shall be **laid w**, 2717
19: 7 desolate palaces, and he **laid w** their cities; 2717
26: 2 I shall be replenished, *now* she is **laid w**: 2717
29: 9 the land of Egypt shall be desolate and **w**; 2723
29:10 make the land of Egypt **utterly w** 2721+2723
29:12 her cities among the cities *that are* **laid w** 2717
30:12 I will **make** the land **w**, and all that is 8074
35: 4 I will lay thy cities **w**, and thou shalt be 2723
36:35 the **w** and desolate and ruined cities *are* 2720
36:38 shall the **w** cities be filled *with* flocks of 2720
38: 8 of Israel, which have been always **w**: 2723

Joel 1: 7 He hath laid my vine **w**, and barked my fig 8047
Am 7: 9 the sanctuaries of Israel shall be **laid w**; 2717
9:14 they shall build the **w** cities, and 8074
Mic 5: 6 they shall **w** the land of Assyria with 7462
Na 2:10 She *is* empty, and void, and **w**: and 1110
3: 7 flee from thee, and say, Nineveh is **laid w**: 7703
Zep 3: 6 I **made** their streets **w**, that none passeth 2717
Hag 1: 4 in your cieled houses, and this house *lie* **w**? 2720
1: 9 Because of mine house that *is* **w**, and 2720
Mal 1: 3 his heritage **w** for the dragons of 8077
Mt 26: 8 saying, To what purpose *is* this **w**? *684*
Mk 14: 4 said, Why was this **w** of the ointment made? *684*

WASTED (16) [WASTE]
Nu 14:33 until your carcases be **w** in the wilderness. 8552
24:22 Nevertheless the Kenite shall be **w**, 1197
Dt 2:14 of war were **w** out from among the host, 8552
1Ki 17:16 *And* the barrel of meal **w** not, neither did 3615
1Ch 20: 1 **w** the country of the children of Ammon, 7843
Ps 137: 3 they that **w** us *required of us* mirth, 8437
Isa 6:11 Until the cities be **w** without inhabitant, and 7582
19: 5 and the river shall be **w** and dried up. 2717
60:12 yea, *those* nations shall be **utterly w**. 2717+2717
Jer 44: 6 and they are **w** *and* desolate, as *at* this day. 2723
Eze 30: 7 shall be in the midst of the cities *that are* **w**. 2717
Joel 1:10 The field is **w**, the land mourneth; for 7703
1:10 for the corn is **w**, the new wine is dried up, 7703
Lk 15:13 there **w** his substance with riotous living. *1287*
16: 1 accused unto him that he had **w** his goods. *1287*
Gal 1:13 I persecuted the church of God, and **w** it: *4199*

WASTENESS (1) [WASTE]
Zep 1:15 and distress, a day of **w** and desolation, 7722

WASTER (2) [WASTE]
Pr 18: 9 his work *is* brother to him that is a great **w**. 7843
Isa 54:16 and I have created the **w** to destroy. 7843

WASTES (7) [WASTE]
Isa 61: 4 they shall build the old **w**, they shall raise 2723
Jer 49:13 all the cities thereof shall be perpetual **w**. 2723
Eze 33:24 they that inhabit those **w** of the land of 2723
33:27 surely *they* that *are* in the **w** shall fall by 2723
36: 4 to the desolate **w**, and to the cities that are 2723
36:10 be inhabited, and the **w** shall be builded: 2723
36:33 in the cities, and the **w** shall be builded. 2723

WASTETH (3) [WASTE]
Job 14:10 man dieth, and **w away**: yea, man giveth up 2522
Ps 91: 6 *nor* for the destruction *that* **w** at noonday. 7736
Pr 19:26 He that **w** *his* father, *and* chaseth away *his* 7703

WASTING (2) [WASTE]
Isa 59: 7 **w** and destruction are in their paths. 7701
60:18 **w** nor destruction within thy borders; 7701

WATCH (61) [WATCHED, WATCHER, WATCHERS, WATCHES, WATCHETH, WATCHFUL, WATCHING, WATCHINGS, WATCHMAN, WATCHMAN'S, WATCHMEN, WATCHT, WATCHTOWER]
Ge 31:49 The LORD **w** between me and thee, 6822
Ex 14:24 that in the morning **w** the LORD looked 821
Jdg 7:19 the camp *in* the beginning of the middle **w**; 821
7:19 *and* they had but newly set the **w**: 8104
1Sa 11:11 into the midst of the host in the morning **w**, 821
19:11 to **w** him, and to slay him in the morning: 8104
2Sa 13:34 the young man that **kept** the **w** lift up his 6822
2Ki 11: 5 be keepers of the **w** of the king's house; 4931
11: 6 so shall ye keep the **w** of the house, that it 4931
11: 7 even they shall keep the **w** of the house of 4931
2Ch 20:24 when Judah came toward the **w tower** in 4707
23: 6 all the people shall keep the **w** of 4931
Ezr 8:29 **W** ye, and keep *them,* until ye weigh *them* 8245
Ne 4: 9 set a **w** against them day and night, because 4929
7: 3 every one in his **w**, and every one *to be* 4929
Job 7:12 or a whale, that thou settest a **w** over me? 4929
14:16 my steps: dost thou not **w** over my sin? 8104
Ps 90: 4 when it is past, and *as* a **w** in the night. 821
102: 7 I **w**, and am as a sparrow alone upon 8245
130: 6 more than they that **w** for the morning: 8104
130: 6 *I say, more than* they that **w** for 8104
141: 3 Set a **w**, O LORD, before my mouth; 8108
Isa 21: 5 the table, **w** *in* the watchtower, eat, drink: 6822
29:20 and all that **w** for iniquity are cut off: 8245

Jer 5: 6 a leopard shall w over their cities: 8245
31:28 so will I w over them, to build, and to plant, 8245
44:27 I *will* w over them for evil, and not for 8245
51:12 make the w strong, set up the watchmen, 4929
Na 2: 1 keep the munition, w the way, make *thy* 6822
Hab 2: 1 I will stand upon my w, and set me upon 4931
2: 1 will w to see what he will say unto me, and 6822
Mt 14:25 And in the fourth w of the night Jesus went *5438*
24:42 W therefore: for ye know not what hour *1127*
24:43 had known in what w the thief would come, *5438*
25:13 W therefore, for ye know neither the day *1127*
26:38 unto death: tarry ye here, and w with me. *1127*
26:40 What, could ye not w with me one hour? *1127*
26:41 W and pray, that ye enter not into *1127*
27:65 Pilate said unto them, Ye have a w: go your *2892*
27:66 sealing the stone, and setting a w. *2892*
28:11 some of the w came into the city, and *2892*
Mk 6:48 about the fourth w of the night he cometh *5438*
13:33 Take ye heed, w and pray: for ye know not *69*
13:34 his work, and commanded the porter to w. *1127*
13:35 W ye therefore: for ye know not when *1127*
13:37 And what I say unto you I say unto all, W. *1127*
14:34 sorrowful unto death: tarry ye here, and w. *1127*
14:37 couldest not thou w one hour? *1127*
14:38 W ye and pray, lest ye enter into *1127*
Lk 2: 8 **keeping** w over their flock by night. *5438+5442*
12:38 And if he shall come in the second w, or *5438*
12:38 or come in the third w, and find *them* so, *5438*
21:36 W ye therefore, and pray always, that ye may *69*
Ac 20:31 Therefore w, and remember, that *by* *1127*
1Co 16:13 W ye, stand fast in the faith, quit you like *1127*
Col 4: 2 and w in the same with thanksgiving; *1127*
1Th 5: 6 as *do* others; but let us w and be sober. *1127*
2Ti 4: 5 But w thou in all *things,* endure afflictions, *3525*
Heb 13:17 for they w for your souls, as they that must *69*
1Pe 4: 7 be ye therefore sober, and w unto prayer. *3525*
Rev 3: 3 If therefore thou shalt not w, I will come on *1127*

WATCHED (12) [WATCH]

Jer 20:10 All my familiars w for my halting, 8104
31:28 *that* like as I have w over them, to pluck up, 8245
La 4:17 in our watching we have w for a nation 6822
Da 9:14 Therefore hath the LORD w upon the evil, 8245
Mt 24:43 he would have w, and would not have *1127*
27:36 And sitting down they w him there; *5083*
Mk 3: 2 And they w him, whether he would heal *3906*
Lk 6: 7 And the scribes and Pharisees w him, *3906*
12:39 he would have w, and not have suffered his *1127*
14: 1 bread on the sabbath day, that they w him. *3906*
20:20 And they w *him,* and sent forth spies, *3906*
Ac 9:24 And they w the gates day and night to kill *3906*

WATCHER (2) [WATCH]

Da 4:13 a w and a holy one came down from 5894
4:23 whereas the king saw a w and a holy one 5894

WATCHERS (2) [WATCH]

Jer 4:16 *that* w come from a far country, and 5341
Da 4:17 *This* matter *is* by the decree of the w, and 5894

WATCHES (5) [WATCH]

Ne 7: 3 appoint w of the inhabitants of Jerusalem, 4931
12: 9 *were* over against them in the w. 4931
Ps 63: 6 my bed, *and* meditate on thee in the *night* w. 821
119:148 Mine eyes prevent the *night* w, that *I* might 821
La 2:19 in the beginning of the w, pour out thine 821

WATCHETH (3) [WATCH]

Ps 37:32 The wicked w the righteous, and seeketh to 6822
Eze 7: 6 is come: it w for thee; behold, it is come. 6974
Rev 16:15 Blessed *is* he that w, and keepeth his *1127*

WATCHFUL (1) [WATCH]

Rev 3: 2 Be w, and strengthen the *things* which *1127*

WATCHING (6) [WATCH]

1Sa 4:13 Eli sat upon a seat *by* the wayside w: 6822
Pr 8:34 w daily at my gates, waiting at the posts of 8245
La 4:17 in our w we have watched for a nation *that* 6836
Mt 27:54 w Jesus, saw the earthquake, and *5083*
Lk 12:37 the lord when he cometh shall find w: *1127*
Eph 6:18 and w thereunto with all perseverance and *69*

WATCHINGS (2) [WATCH]

2Co 6: 5 in tumults, in labours, in w, in fastings; *70*
11:27 painfulness, in w often, in hunger and thirst, *70*

WATCHMAN (18) [WATCH]

2Sa 18:24 the w went *up* to the roof over the gate unto 6822
18:25 the w cried, and told the king. And the king 6822
18:26 the w saw another man running: and 6822
18:26 the w called unto the porter, and said, 6822
18:27 the w said, Me thinketh the running of 6822
2Ki 9:17 there stood a w on the tower in Jezreel, 6822
9:18 the w told, saying, The messenger came to 6822
9:20 the w told, saying, He came even unto 6822
Ps 127: 1 keep the city, the w waketh *but* in vain. 8104
Isa 21: 6 Go, set a w, let him declare what he seeth. 6822
21:11 to me out of Seir, W, what of the night? 8104
21:11 what of the night? W, what of the night? 8104
21:12 The w said, The morning cometh, and 8104
Eze 3:17 I have made thee a w unto the house of 6822
33: 2 man of their coasts, and set him for their w: 6822
33: 6 if the w see the sword come, and blow not 6822
33: 7 I have set thee a w unto the house of Israel; 6822
Hos 9: 8 The w of Ephraim *was* with my God: *but* 6822

WATCHMAN'S (1) [WATCH]

Eze 33: 6 but his blood will I require at the w hand. 6822

WATCHMEN (12) [WATCH]

1Sa 14:16 the w of Saul in Gibeah of Benjamin 6822
2Ki 17: 9 from the tower of the w to the fenced city. 5341
18: 8 from the tower of the w to the fenced city. 5341
SS 3: 3 The w that go about the city found me: 8104
5: 7 The w that went about the city found me, 8104
Isa 52: 8 Thy w shall lift up the voice; *with* the voice 6822
56:10 His w *are* blind: they are all ignorant, they 6822
62: 6 I have set w upon thy walls, O Jerusalem, 8104
Jer 6:17 Also I set w over you, *saying,* Hearken to 6822
31: 6 *that* the w upon the mount Ephraim shall 5341
51:12 set up the w, prepare the ambushes: 8104
Mic 7: 4 the day of thy w *and* thy visitation cometh; 6822

WATCHT (1) [WATCH]

Ps 59: T Saul sent, and they w the house to kill him. 8104

WATCHTOWER (2) [TOWER, WATCH]

Isa 21: 5 the table, watch *in* the w, eat, drink: 6844
21: 8 I stand continually upon the w in 4707

WATER (396) [WATERCOURSE, WATERED, WATEREDST, WATEREST, WATERETH, WATERFLOOD, WATERING, WATERPOT, WATERPOTS, WATERS, WATERSPOUTS, WATERSPRINGS]

Ge 2:10 a river went out of Eden to w the garden; 8248
16: 7 her by a fountain of w in the wilderness, 4325
18: 4 Let a little w, I pray you, be fetched, and 4325
21:14 and a bottle of w, and gave *it* unto Hagar, 4325
21:15 the w was spent in the bottle, and she cast 4325
21:19 opened her eyes, and she saw a well of w; 4325
21:19 filled the bottle *with* w, and gave the lad 4325
21:25 because of a well of w, 4325
24:11 by a well of w at the time of the evening, 4325
24:11 the time that *women* go out to draw *w*. NIH
24:13 Behold, I stand *here* by the well of w; and 4325
24:13 of the men of the city come out to draw w: 4325
24:17 I pray thee, drink a little w of thy pitcher. 4325
24:19 she said, I will draw *w* for thy camels also, NIH
24:20 ran again unto the well to draw *w*, and NIH
24:32 w to wash his feet, and the men's feet that 4325
24:43 Behold, I stand by the well of w; and 4325
24:43 *when* the virgin cometh forth to draw *w*, NIH
24:43 I pray thee, a little w of thy pitcher to drink; 4325
24:45 drew *w*: and I said unto her, Let me drink, NIH
26:18 Isaac digged again the wells of w, 4325
26:19 and found there a well of springing w. 4325
26:20 Isaac's herdmen, saying, The w *is* ours: 4325
26:32 and said unto him, We have found w. 4325
29: 7 w ye the sheep, and go *and* feed *them.* 8248
29: 8 the well's mouth; then we w the sheep. 8248
37:24 and the pit *was* empty, *there was* no w in it. 4325
43:24 gave *them* w, and they washed their feet; 4325
49: 4 Unstable as w, thou shalt not excel; 4325
Ex 2:10 she said, Because I drew him out of the w. 4325
2:16 they came and **drew** w, and filled 1802
2:16 filled the troughs to w their father's flock. 8248
2:19 also **drew** w **enough** for us, and 1802+1802
4: 9 that thou shalt take of the w of the river, 4325

Ex	4: 9	the w which thou takest out of the river	4325
	7:15	lo, he goeth out unto the w; and thou shalt	4325
	7:18	the Egyptians shall lothe to drink of the w	4325
	7:19	their ponds, and upon all their pools of w,	4325
	7:21	the Egyptians could not drink of the w of	4325
	7:24	digged round about the river *for* w to drink;	4325
	7:24	for they could not drink of the w of	4325
	8:20	lo, he cometh forth to the w; and say unto	4325
	12: 9	nor sodden at all with w, but roast with fire;	4325
	15:22	days in the wilderness, and found no w.	4325
	15:27	where *were* twelve wells of w, and	4325
	17: 1	and *there was* no w for the people to drink.	4325
	17: 2	and said, Give us w that we may drink.	4325
	17: 3	the people thirsted there for w; and	4325
	17: 6	the rock, and there shall come w out of it,	4325
	20: 4	or that *is* in the w under the earth:	4325
	23:25	and he shall bless thy bread, and thy w;	4325
	29: 4	and shalt wash them with w.	4325
	30:18	and the altar, and thou shalt put w therein.	4325
	30:20	they shall wash *with* w, that they die not;	4325
	32:20	strawed *it* upon the w, and made	4325
	34:28	he did neither eat bread, nor drink w.	4325
	40: 7	and the altar, and shalt put w therein.	4325
	40:12	of the congregation, and wash them with w.	4325
	40:30	and the altar, and put w there,	4325
Lev	1: 9	his inwards and his legs shall he wash in w:	4325
	1:13	shall wash the inwards and the legs with w:	4325
	6:28	it shall be both scoured, and rinsed in w.	4325
	8: 6	and his sons, and washed them with w.	4325
	8:21	he washed the inwards and the legs in w;	4325
	11:32	it must be put into w, and it shall be	4325
	11:34	*that* on which *such* w cometh shall be	4325
	11:36	or pit, *wherein there is* plenty of w,	4325
	11:38	if *any* w be put upon the seed, and *any part*	4325
	14: 5	killed in an earthen vessel over running w:	4325
	14: 6	the bird *that was* killed over the running w:	4325
	14: 8	off all his hair, and wash *himself* in w,	4325
	14: 9	also he shall wash his flesh in w, and	4325
	14:50	birds in an earthen vessel over running w:	4325
	14:51	in the running w, and sprinkle the house	4325
	14:52	with the running w, and with the living	4325
	15: 5	bathe *himself* in w, and be unclean until	4325
	15: 6	bathe *himself* in w, and be unclean until	4325
	15: 7	bathe *himself* in w, and be unclean until	4325
	15: 8	bathe *himself* in w, and be unclean until	4325
	15:10	bathe *himself* in w, and be unclean until	4325
	15:11	hath not rinsed his hands in w, he shall	4325
	15:11	bathe *himself* in w, and be unclean until	4325
	15:12	every vessel of wood shall be rinsed in w.	4325
	15:13	bathe his flesh in running w, and shall be	4325
	15:16	he shall wash all his flesh in w, and	4325
	15:17	shall be washed with w, and be unclean	4325
	15:18	they shall *both* bathe *themselves* in w, and	4325
	15:21	bathe *himself* in w, and be unclean until	4325
	15:22	bathe *himself* in w, and be unclean until	4325
	15:27	bathe *himself* in w, and be unclean until	4325
	16: 4	therefore shall he wash his flesh in w, and	4325
	16:24	he shall wash his flesh with w in the holy	4325
	16:26	bathe his flesh in w, and afterward come	4325
	16:28	bathe his flesh in w, and afterward he shall	4325
	17:15	bathe *himself* in w, and be unclean until	4325
	22: 6	*things,* unless he wash his flesh with w.	4325
Nu	5:17	the priest shall take holy w in an earthen	4325
	5:17	the priest shall take, and put *it* into the w:	4325
	5:18	the priest shall have in his hand the bitter w	4325
	5:19	be thou free from this bitter w that causeth	4325
	5:22	this w that causeth the curse shall go into	4325
	5:23	and he shall blot *them* out with the bitter w:	4325
	5:24	to drink the bitter w that causeth the curse:	4325
	5:24	the w that causeth the curse shall enter into	4325
	5:26	shall cause the woman to drink the w.	4325
	5:27	when he hath made her to drink the w, then	4325
	5:27	that the w that causeth the curse shall enter	4325
	8: 7	Sprinkle w of purifying upon them, and	4325
	19: 7	he shall bathe his flesh in w, and	4325
	19: 8	that burneth her shall wash his clothes in w,	4325
	19: 8	bathe his flesh in w, and shall be unclean	4325
	19: 9	the children of Israel for a w of separation:	4325
	19:13	the w of separation was not sprinkled upon	4325
	19:17	running w shall be put thereto in a vessel:	4325
	19:18	dip *it* in the w, and sprinkle *it* upon the tent,	4325
	19:19	bathe *himself* in w, and shall be clean at	4325
	19:20	the w of separation hath not been sprinkled	4325
	19:21	that he that sprinkleth the w of separation	4325
	19:21	he that toucheth the w of separation shall	4325
	20: 2	there was no w for the congregation: and	4325
	20: 5	neither *is there any* w to drink.	4325
	20: 8	it shall give forth his w, and thou shalt	4325
	20: 8	thou shalt bring forth to them w out of	4325
	20:10	must we fetch you w out of this rock?	4325
	20:11	the w came out abundantly, and	4325
	20:13	This *is* the w of Meribah; because	4325
	20:17	neither will we drink *of* the w of the wells:	4325
	20:19	if I and my cattle drink *of* thy w, then I will	4325
	20:24	ye rebelled against my word at the w of	4325
	21: 5	for *there is* no bread, neither *is there any* w;	4325
	21:16	the people together, and I will give them w.	4325
	24: 7	He shall pour the w out of his buckets, and	4325
	27:14	to sanctify me at the w before their eyes:	4325
	27:14	that *is* the w of Meribah in Kadesh *in*	4325
	31:23	nevertheless it shall be purified with the w	4325
	31:23	not the fire ye shall make go through the w.	4325
	33: 9	in Elim *were* twelve fountains of w, and	4325
	33:14	where was no w for the people to drink.	4325
Dt	2: 6	ye shall also buy w of them for money,	4325
	2:28	and give me w for money, that I may drink:	4325
	8: 7	a land of brooks of w, of fountains and	4325
	8:15	and drought, where *there was* no w;	4325
	8:15	who brought thee forth w out of the rock of	4325
	9: 9	I neither did eat bread nor drink w:	4325
	9:18	nor drink w, because of all your sins which	4325
	11: 4	how he made the w of the Red sea to	4325
	11:11	*and* drinketh w of the rain of heaven:	4325
	12:16	ye shall pour it upon the earth as w.	4325
	12:24	eat it; thou shalt pour it upon the earth as w.	4325
	15:23	thou shalt pour it upon the ground as w.	4325
	23: 4	you not with bread and with w in the way,	4325
	23:11	cometh on, he shall wash *himself* with w:	4325
	29:11	of thy wood unto the drawer of thy w:	4325
Jos	2:10	dried up the w of the Red sea for you,	4325
	3: 8	When ye are come to the brink of the w of	4325
	3:15	the ark were dipped in the brim of the w,	4325
	7: 5	of the people melted, and became as w.	4325
	9:21	and drawers of w unto all the congregation;	4325
	9:23	and drawers of w for the house of my God.	4325
	9:27	and drawers of w for the congregation,	4325
	15: 9	hill unto the fountain of the w of Nephtoah,	4325
	15:19	me a south land; give me also springs of w.	4325
	16: 1	unto the w of Jericho on the east,	4325
Jdg	1:15	me a south land; give me also springs of w.	4325
	4:19	Give me, I pray thee, a little w to drink;	4325
	5: 4	the clouds also dropped w.	4325
	5:11	w, there shall they rehearse the righteous	NIH
	5:25	He asked w, *and* she gave *him* milk;	4325
	6:38	the dew out of the fleece, a bowl full *of* w.	4325
	7: 4	bring them down unto the w, and I will try	4325
	7: 5	So he brought down the people unto the w:	4325
	7: 5	Every one that lappeth of the w with his	4325
	7: 6	bowed down upon their knees to drink w.	4325
	15:19	*was* in the jaw, and there came w thereout;	4325
1Sa	7: 6	drew w, and poured *it* out before	4325
	9:11	found young maidens going out to draw w,	4325
	25:11	my w, and my flesh that I have killed for	4325
	26:11	and the cruse of w, and let us go.	4325
	26:12	and the cruse of w from Saul's bolster;	4325
	26:16	and the cruse of w that *was at* his bolster.	4325
	30:11	and he did eat; and they made him drink w;	4325
	30:12	nor drunk *any* w, three days and	4325
2Sa	14:14	needs die, and *are* as w spilt on the ground,	4325
	17:20	They be gone over the brook of w.	4325
	17:21	Arise, and pass quickly over the w:	4325
	21:10	from the beginning of harvest until w	4325
	23:15	Oh that one would give me drink *of* the w	4325
	23:16	drew w out of the well of Beth-lehem,	4325
1Ki	13: 8	neither will I eat bread nor drink w in this	4325
	13: 9	saying, Eat no bread, nor drink w,	4325
	13:16	neither will I eat bread nor drink w with	4325
	13:17	Thou shalt eat no bread nor drink w there,	4325
	13:18	that he may eat bread and drink w.	4325
	13:19	and did eat bread in his house, and drank w.	4325
	13:22	hast eaten bread and drunk w in the place,	4325
	13:22	say to thee, Eat no bread, and drink no w;	4325
	14:15	as a reed is shaken in the w, and he shall	4325
	17:10	Fetch me, I pray thee, a little w in a vessel,	4325
	18: 4	in a cave, and fed them *with* bread and w.)	4325
	18: 5	unto all fountains of w, and unto all brooks:	4325
	18:13	in a cave, and fed them *with* bread and w?	4325
	18:33	Fill four barrels *with* w, and pour *it* on	4325

1Ki 18:35 the **w** ran round about the altar; and 4325
18:35 and he filled the trench also *with* **w**. 4325
18:38 and licked up the **w** that *was* in the trench. 4325
19: 6 on the coals, and a cruse of **w** *at* his head. 4325
22:27 bread of affliction and with **w** of affliction, 4325
2Ki 2:19 but the **w** *is* naught, and the ground barren. 4325
3: 9 there was no **w** for the host, and for 4325
3:11 which poured **w** on the hands of Elijah. 4325
3:17 yet that valley shall be filled *with* **w**, that ye 4325
3:19 stop all wells of **w**, and mar every good 4325
3:20 there came **w** by the way of Edom, and 4325
3:20 and the country was filled with **w**. 4325
3:22 the sun shone upon the **w**, and the Moabites 4325
3:22 the Moabites saw the **w** on the other side *as* 4325
3:25 they stopped all the wells of **w**, and 4325
6: 5 felling a beam, the axe head fell into the **w**: 4325
6:22 set bread and **w** before them, that they may 4325
8:15 dipt *it* in **w**, and spread *it* on his face, so 4325
20:20 and a conduit, and brought **w** into the city, 4325
1Ch 11:17 Oh that one would give me drink *of* the **w** 4325
11:18 drew **w** out of the well of Beth-lehem, 4325
2Ch 18:26 bread of affliction and with **w** of affliction, 4325
32: 4 kings of Assyria come, and find much **w**? 4325
Ezr 10: 6 he did eat no bread, nor drink **w**: 4325
Ne 3:26 unto *the place* over against the **w** gate 4325
8: 1 into the street that *was* before the **w** gate; 4325
8: 3 the **w** gate from the morning until midday, 4325
8:16 in the street of the **w** gate, and in the street 4325
9:15 broughtest forth **w** for them out of the rock 4325
9:20 and gavest them **w** for their thirst. 4325
12:37 of David, even unto the **w** gate east*ward*. 4325
13: 2 children of Israel with bread and with **w**, 4325
Job 8:11 without mire? can the flag grow without **w**? 4325
9:30 If I wash myself with snow **w**, and 4325
14: 9 *Yet* through the sent of **w** it will bud, and 4325
15:16 *is* man, which drinketh iniquity like **w**? 4325
22: 7 Thou hast not given **w** to the weary to 4325
34: 7 like Job, *who* drinketh up scorning like **w**? 4325
36:27 For he maketh small the drops of **w**: 4325
Ps 1: 3 be like a tree planted by the rivers of **w**, 4325
6: 6 bed to swim; I **w** my couch with my tears. 4529
22:14 I am poured out like **w**, and all my bones 4325
42: 1 As the hart panteth after the **w** brooks, so 4325
63: 1 in a dry and thirsty land, where no **w** is; 4325
65: 9 it *with* the river of God, *which* is full *of* **w**: 4325
66:12 we went through fire and through **w**: 4325
72: 6 mown grass: as showers that **w** the earth. 2222
77:17 The clouds poured out **w**: the skies sent out 4325
79: 3 Their blood have they shed like **w** round 4325
88:17 They came round about me daily like **w**; 4325
107:35 turneth the wilderness into a standing **w**, 4325
109:18 so let it come into his bowels like **w**, and 4325
114: 8 Which turned the rock *into* a standing **w**, 4325
Pr 8:24 *there were* no fountains abounding with **w**. 4325
17:14 of strife *is as* when one letteth out **w**: 4325
20: 5 Counsel in the heart of man *is like* deep **w**; 4325
21: 1 the hand of the LORD, *as* the rivers of **w**: 4325
25:21 and if he *be* thirsty, give him **w** to drink: 4325
27:19 As *in* **w** face *answereth* to face, so the heart 4325
30:16 the earth *that* is not filled *with* **w**; and 4325
Ecc 2: 6 I made me pools of **w**, to water therewith 4325
2: 6 to **w** therewith the wood that bringeth forth 8248
Isa 1:22 is become dross, thy wine mixt with **w**: 4325
1:30 leaf fadeth, and as a garden that hath no **w**. 4325
3: 1 stay of bread, and the whole stay of **w**, 4325
12: 3 Therefore with joy shall ye draw **w** out of 4325
14:23 a possession for the bittern, and pools of **w**: 4325
16: 9 I will **w** thee *with* my tears, O Heshbon, 7301
21:14 of Tema brought **w** to him that was thirsty, 4325
22:11 the two walls for the **w** of the old pool: 4325
27: 3 do keep it; I will **w** it every moment: 8248
30:14 or to take **w** *withal* out of the pit. 4325
30:20 bread of adversity, and the **w** of affliction, 4325
32: 2 as rivers of **w** in a dry place, as the shadow 4325
35: 7 a pool, and the thirsty land springs of **w**: 4325
37:25 I have digged, and drunk **w**; and with 4325
41:17 *When* the poor and needy seek **w**, and 4325
41:18 I will make the wilderness a pool of **w**, and 4325
41:18 of water, and the dry land springs of **w**. 4325
44: 3 For I will pour **w** upon *him that is* thirsty, 4325
44: 4 the grass, as willows by the **w** courses. 4325
44:12 he drinketh no **w**, and is faint. 4325
49:10 even by the springs of **w** shall he guide 4325
50: 2 because *there is* no **w**, and dieth for thirst. 4325
58:11 like a spring of **w**, whose waters fail not. 4325
63:12 dividing the **w** before them, to make 4325
Jer 2:13 broken cisterns, that can hold no **w**. 4325
8:14 given us **w** of gall to drink, because 4325
9:15 and give them **w** of gall to drink. 4325
13: 1 put it upon thy loins, and put it not in **w**. 4325
14: 3 they came to the pits, *and* found no **w**; 4325
23:15 and make them drink the **w** of gall: 4325
38: 6 in the dungeon *there was* no **w**, but mire: 4325
La 1:16 mine eye runneth down *with* **w**, because 4325
2:19 pour out thine heart like **w** before the face 4325
3:48 Mine eye runneth down *with* rivers of **w** for 4325
5: 4 We have drunken our **w** for money; 4325
Eze 4:11 Thou shalt drink also **w** by measure, 4325
4:16 they shall drink **w** by measure, and 4325
4:17 That they may want bread and **w**, and 4325
7:17 be feeble, and all knees shall be weak *as* **w**. 4325
12:18 drink thy **w** with trembling and 4325
12:19 and drink their **w** with astonishment, 4325
16: 4 neither wast thou washed in **w** to supple 4325
16: 9 washed I thee with **w**; yea, I throughly 4325
17: 7 that *he* might **w** it by the furrows of her 8248
21: 7 and all knees shall be weak *as* **w**: 4325
24: 3 on a pot, set *it* on, and also pour **w** into it: 4325
26:12 and thy dust in the midst of the **w**. 4325
31:14 stand up in their height, all that drink **w**: 4325
31:16 and best of Lebanon, all that drink **w**, 4325
32: 6 I will also **w** with thy blood the land 8248
36:25 will I sprinkle clean **w** upon you, and 4325
Da 1:12 them give us pulse to eat, and **w** to drink. 4325
Hos 2: 5 that give *me* my bread and my **w**, my wool 4325
5:10 I will pour out my wrath upon them like **w**. 4325
10: 7 her king is cut off as the foam upon the **w**. 4325
Joel 3:18 and shall **w** the valley of Shittim. 8248
Am 4: 8 cities wandered unto one city, to drink **w**; 4325
8:11 nor a thirst for **w**, but of hearing the words 4325
Jnh 3: 7 any thing: let them not feed, nor drink **w**: 4325
Na 2: 8 Nineveh *is* of old like a pool of **w**: yet they 4325
Hab 3:10 the overflowing of the **w** passed by: 4325
Zec 9:11 thy prisoners out of the pit wherein *is* no **w**. 4325
Mt 3:11 I indeed baptize you with **w** unto *5204*
3:16 went up straightway out of the **w**: *5204*
10:42 cup of cold *w* only in the name of a disciple, NIG
14:28 it be thou, bid me come unto thee on the **w**. *5204*
14:29 the ship, he walked on the **w**, to go to Jesus. *5204*
17:15 he falleth into the fire, and oft into the **w**. *5204*
27:24 he took **w**, and washed *his* hands before *5204*
Mk 1: 8 I indeed have baptized you with **w**: but *5204*
1:10 And straightway coming up out of the **w**, *5204*
9:41 For whosoever shall give you a cup of **w** to *5204*
14:13 meet you a man bearing a pitcher of **w**: *5204*
Lk 3:16 unto *them* all, I indeed baptize you with **w**; *5204*
7:44 thou gavest me no **w** for my feet: *5204*
8:23 and they were filled *with* **w**, and were in NIG
8:24 rebuked the wind and the raging of the **w**: *5204*
8:25 for he commandeth even the winds and **w**, *5204*
16:24 that he may dip the tip of his finger in **w**, *5204*
22:10 a man meet you, bearing a pitcher of **w**; *5204*
Jn 1:26 answered them, saying, I baptize with **w**: *5204*
1:31 therefore am I come baptizing with **w**. *5204*
1:33 but he that sent me to baptize with **w**, *5204*
2: 7 saith unto them, Fill the waterpots with **w**. *5204*
2: 9 When the ruler of the feast had tasted the **w** *5204*
2: 9 (but the servants which drew the **w** knew;) *5204*
3: 5 Except a man be born of **w** and *of* *5204*
3:23 to Salim, because there was much **w** there: *5204*
4: 7 cometh a woman of Samaria to draw **w**: *5204*
4:10 and he would have given thee living **w**. *5204*
4:11 from whence then hast thou *that* living **w**? *5204*
4:13 Whosoever drinketh of this **w** shall thirst *5204*
4:14 But whosoever drinketh of the **w** that I *5204*
4:14 the **w** that I shall give him shall be in him a *5204*
4:14 well of **w** springing up into everlasting life. *5204*
4:15 Sir, give me this **w**, that I thirst not, *5204*
4:46 of Galilee, where he made the **w** wine. *5204*
5: 3 withered, waiting for the moving of the **w**. *5204*
5: 4 season into the pool, and troubled the **w**: *5204*
5: 4 first after the troubling of the **w** stepped in, *5204*
5: 7 Sir, I have no man, when the **w** is troubled, *5204*
7:38 of his belly shall flow rivers of living **w**. *5204*
13: 5 he poureth **w** into a bason, and began to *5204*
19:34 and forthwith came there out blood and **w**. *5204*
Ac 1: 5 For John truly baptized with **w**; but ye shall *5204*
8:36 on *their* way, they came unto a certain **w**: *5204*

Ac 8:36 and the eunuch said, See, *here is* w; 5204
8:38 and they went down both into the w, 5204
8:39 And when they were come up out of the w, 5204
10:47 Can any *man* forbid w, that these should 5204
11:16 that he said, John indeed baptized with w; 5204
Eph 5:26 cleanse *it* with the washing of w by 5204
1Ti 5:23 **Drink** no longer w, but use a little wine for 5202
Heb 9:19 with w, and scarlet wool, and hyssop, and 5204
10:22 and *our* bodies washed with pure w. 5204
Jas 3:11 send forth at the same place sweet *w* NIG
3:12 so *can* no fountain *both* yield salt w and 5204
1Pe 3:20 that is, eight souls were saved by w. 5204
2Pe 2:17 These are wells **without** w, clouds that are 504
3: 5 and the earth standing out of the w and 5204
3: 5 standing out of the water and in the w: 5204
3: 6 then was, being overflowed with w, 5204
1Jn 5: 6 This is he that came by w and blood, 5204
5: 6 not by w only, but by water and blood. 5204
5: 6 not by water only, but by w and blood. 5204
5: 8 the Spirit, and the w, and the blood: 5204
Jude 1:12 clouds *they are* **without** w, carried about of 504
Rev 12:15 And the serpent cast out of his mouth w as 5204
16:12 and the w thereof was dried up, that 5204
21: 6 of the fountain of the w of life freely. 5204
22: 1 And he shewed me a pure river of w of life, 5204
22:17 let him take the w of life freely. 5204

WATERCOURSE (2) [WATER]

2Ch 32:30 also stopped the upper w of Gihon, 4161+4325
Job 38:25 Who hath divided a w for the overflowing 8585

WATERED (11) [WATER]

Ge 2: 6 and w the whole face of the ground. 8248
13:10 of Jordan, that it *was* **well** w every where, 4945
29: 2 by it; for out of that well they w the flocks: 8248
29: 3 w the sheep, and put the stone again upon 8248
29:10 w the flock of Laban his mother's brother. 8248
Ex 2:17 and helped them, and w their flock. 8248
2:19 drew water enough for us, and w the flock. 8248
Pr 11:25 he that watereth shall be w also himself. 3384
Isa 58:11 thou shalt be like a w garden, and like a 7302
Jer 31:12 their soul shall be as a w garden; and 7302
1Co 3: 6 I have planted, Apollos w; but God gave 4222

WATEREDST (1) [WATER]

Dt 11:10 and w *it* with thy foot, as a garden of herbs: 8248

WATEREST (2) [WATER]

Ps 65: 9 Thou visitest the earth, and w it: 7783
65:10 *Thou* w the ridges thereof **abundantly**: 7301

WATERETH (5) [WATER]

Ps 104:13 He w the hills from his chambers: the earth 8248
Pr 11:25 and he that w shall be watered also himself. 7301
Isa 55:10 w the earth, and maketh it bring forth and 7301
1Co 3: 7 that planteth any *thing,* neither he that w; 4222
3: 8 Now he that planteth and he that w are one: 4222

WATERFALLS See WATERSPOUTS

WATERFLOOD (1) [FLOOD, WATER]

Ps 69:15 Let not the w overflow me, 4325+7641

WATERING (3) [WATER]

Ge 30:38 w troughs when the flocks came to drink, 4325
Job 37:11 Also by w he wearieth the thick cloud: 7377
Lk 13:15 ass from the stall, and lead *him* away to w? 4222

WATERPOT (1) [POT, WATER]

Jn 4:28 The woman then left her w, and went her 5201

WATERPOTS (2) [POT, WATER]

Jn 2: 6 And there were set there six w of stone, 5201
2: 7 saith unto them, Fill the w with water. 5201

WATERS (287) [WATER]

Ge 1: 2 of God moved upon the face of the w. 4325
1: 6 there be a firmament in the midst of the w, 4325
1: 6 let it divide the w from the waters. 4325
1: 6 let it divide the waters from the w. 4325
1: 7 divided the w which *were* under 4325
1: 7 the w which *were* above the firmament: 4325
1: 9 Let the w under the heaven be gathered 4325
1:10 the gathering together of the w called he 4325
1:20 Let the w bring forth abundantly 4325
1:21 which the w brought forth abundantly, 4325
1:22 fill the w in the seas, and let fowl multiply 4325
6:17 do bring a flood of w upon the earth, 4325
7: 6 when the flood of w was upon the earth. 4325
7: 7 into the ark, because of the w of the flood. 4325
7:10 that the w of the flood were upon the earth. 4325
7:17 the w increased, and bare up the ark, and 4325
7:18 the w prevailed, and were increased greatly 4325
7:18 and the ark went upon the face of the w. 4325
7:19 the w prevailed exceedingly upon the earth; 4325
7:20 Fifteen cubits upward did the w prevail; 4325
7:24 the w prevailed upon the earth an hundred 4325
8: 1 to pass over the earth, and the w asswaged; 4325
8: 3 the w returned from off the earth 4325
8: 3 and fifty days the w were abated. 4325
8: 5 the w decreased continually until the tenth 4325
8: 7 until the w were dried up from off 4325
8: 8 to see if the w were abated from off 4325
8: 9 for the w *were* on the face of the whole 4325
8:11 Noah knew that the w were abated from off 4325
8:13 the w were dried up from off the earth: 4325
9:11 be cut off any more by the w of a flood; 4325
9:15 the w shall no more become a flood to 4325
Ex 7:17 hand upon the w which *are* in the river, 4325
7:19 stretch out thine hand upon the w of Egypt, 4325
7:20 and smote the w that *were* in the river, 4325
7:20 all the w that *were* in the river were turned 4325
8: 6 Aaron stretched out his hand over the w of 4325
14:21 the sea dry *land,* and the w were divided. 4325
14:22 the w *were* a wall unto them on their right 4325
14:26 that the w may come again upon 4325
14:28 the w returned, and covered the chariots, 4325
14:29 the w *were* a wall unto them on their right 4325
15: 8 with the blast of thy nostrils the w were 4325
15:10 they sank as lead in the mighty w. 4325
15:19 the LORD brought again the w of the sea 4325
15:23 they could not drink of the w of Marah, 4325
15:25 *which* when he had cast into the w, 4325
15:25 into the waters, the w were made sweet: 4325
15:27 and they encamped there by the w. 4325
Lev 11: 9 These shall ye eat of all that *are* in the w: 4325
11: 9 whatsoever hath fins and scales in the w, 4325
11:10 of all that move in the w, and of any living 4325
11:10 and of any living thing which *is* in the w, 4325
11:12 hath no fins nor scales in the w, 4325
11:46 every living creature that moveth in the w, 4325
Nu 21:22 we will not drink *of* the w of the well: 4325
24: 6 *and* as cedar trees beside the w. 4325
24: 7 his seed *shall be* in many w, and his king 4325
Dt 4:18 the likeness of any fish that *is* in the w 4325
5: 8 or that *is* in the w beneath the earth: 4325
10: 7 Gudgodah to Jotbath, a land of rivers of w. 4325
14: 9 These ye shall eat of all that *are* in the w: 4325
32:51 of Israel at the w of Meribah-Kadesh, 4325
33: 8 *with* whom thou didst strive at the w of 4325
Jos 3:13 all the earth, shall rest in the w of Jordan, 4325
3:13 *that* the w of Jordan shall be cut off *from* 4325
3:13 off *from* the w that come down from above; 4325
3:16 That the w which came down from above 4325
4: 7 That the w of Jordan were cut off before 4325
4: 7 over Jordan, the w of Jordan were cut off: 4325
4:18 the w of Jordan returned unto their place, 4325
4:23 For the LORD your God dried up the w of 4325
5: 1 heard that the LORD had dried up the w 4325
11: 5 and pitched together at the w of Merom, 4325
11: 7 against them by the w of Merom suddenly; 4325
15: 7 the border passed towards the w of 4325
18:15 and went out to the well of w of Nephtoah: 4325
Jdg 5:19 Canaan in Taanach by the w of Megiddo; 4325
7:24 take before them the w unto Beth-barah and 4325
7:24 and took the w unto Beth-barah and Jordan. 4325
2Sa 5:20 enemies before me, as the breach of w. 4325
12:27 and have taken the city of w. 4325
22:12 dark w, *and* thick clouds of the skies. 4325
22:17 he took me; he drew me out of many w; 4325
2Ki 2: 8 smote the w, and they were divided hither 4325
2:14 smote the w, and said, Where *is* 4325
2:14 when he also had smitten the w, they parted 4325
2:21 he went forth unto the spring of the w, and 4325
2:21 saith the LORD, I have healed these w; 4325
2:22 So the w were healed unto this day, 4325
5:12 better than all the w of Israel? 4325
18:31 and drink ye every one the w of his cistern: 4325
19:24 I have digged and drunk strange w, and 4325
1Ch 14:11 by mine hand like the breaking forth of w: 4325

2Ch	32: 3	his mighty *men* to stop the **w** of	4325
Ne	9:11	into the deeps, as a stone into the mighty **w**.	4325
Job	3:24	and my roarings are poured out like the **w**.	4325
	5:10	the earth, and sendeth **w** upon the fields:	4325
	11:16	*and* remember *it* as **w** *that* pass away:	4325
	12:15	he withholdeth the **w**, and they dry up:	4325
	14:11	*As* the **w** fail from the sea, and the flood	4325
	14:19	The **w** wear the stones: thou washest away	4325
	22:11	not see; and abundance of **w** cover thee.	4325
	24:18	He *is* swift as the **w**; their portion is cursed	4325
	24:19	Drought and heat consume the snow **w**: *so*	4325
	26: 5	Dead *things* are formed from under the **w**,	4325
	26: 8	He bindeth up the **w** in his thick clouds;	4325
	26:10	He hath compassed the **w** with bounds,	4325
	27:20	Terrors take hold on him as **w**, a tempest	4325
	28: 4	*even the* **w** forgotten of the foot:	NIH
	28:25	and he weigheth the **w** by measure.	4325
	29:19	My root *was* spread out by the **w**, and	4325
	30:14	**w**: in the desolation they rolled themselves	NIH
	37:10	and the breadth of the **w** is straitened.	4325
	38:25	a watercourse for the **overflowing of w**,	7858
	38:30	The **w** are hid as *with* a stone, and the face	4325
	38:34	that abundance of **w** may cover thee?	4325
Ps	18:11	his pavilion round about him *were* dark **w**	4325
	18:15	the channels of **w** were seen, and	4325
	18:16	he took me, he drew me out of many **w**.	4325
	23: 2	he leadeth me beside the still **w**.	4325
	29: 3	The voice of the LORD *is* upon the **w**:	4325
	29: 3	the LORD *is* upon many **w**.	4325
	32: 6	surely in the floods of great **w** they shall	4325
	33: 7	He gathereth the **w** of the sea together as a	4325
	46: 3	*Though* the **w** thereof roar *and* be troubled,	4325
	58: 7	Let them melt away as **w** *which* run	4325
	69: 1	O God; for the **w** are come in unto *my* soul.	4325
	69: 2	I am come into deep **w**, where the floods	4325
	69:14	them that hate me, and out of the deep **w**.	4325
	73:10	and **w** of a full *cup* are wrung out to them.	4325
	74:13	brakest the heads of the dragons in the **w**.	4325
	77:16	The **w** saw thee, O God, the waters saw	4325
	77:16	waters saw thee, O God, the **w** saw thee;	4325
	77:19	thy path in the great **w**, and thy footsteps	4325
	78:13	and he made the **w** to stand as a heap.	4325
	78:16	and caused **w** to run down like rivers.	4325
	78:20	that the **w** gushed out, and the streams	4325
	81: 7	I proved thee at the **w** of Meribah. Selah.	4325
	93: 4	high *is* mightier than the noise of many **w**,	4325
	104: 3	layeth the beams of his chambers in the **w**:	4325
	104: 6	the **w** stood above the mountains.	4325
	105:29	He turned their **w** into blood, and slew their	4325
	105:41	He opened the rock, and the **w** gushed out;	4325
	106:11	the **w** covered their enemies: there was not	4325
	106:32	They angered *him* also at the **w** of strife, so	4325
	107:23	the sea in ships, that do business in great **w**;	4325
	114: 8	the flint into a fountain of **w**.	4325
	119:136	Rivers of **w** run down mine eyes, because	4325
	124: 4	the **w** had overwhelmed us, the stream had	4325
	124: 5	Then the proud **w** had gone over our soul.	4325
	136: 6	that stretched out the earth above the **w**:	4325
	144: 7	rid me, and deliver me out of great **w**,	4325
	147:18	causeth his wind to blow, *and* the **w** flow.	4325
	148: 4	and ye **w** that *be* above the heavens.	4325
Pr	5:15	Drink **w** out of thine own cistern, and	4325
	5:15	and **running w** out of thine own well.	5140
	5:16	*and* rivers of **w** in the streets.	4325
	8:29	that the **w** should not pass his	4325
	9:17	Stolen **w** are sweet, and bread *eaten* in	4325
	18: 4	The words of a man's mouth *are as* deep **w**,	4325
	25:25	*As* cold **w** to a thirsty soul, so *is* good news	4325
	30: 4	who hath bound the **w** in a garment?	4325
Ecc	11: 1	Cast thy bread upon the **w**: for thou shalt	4325
SS	4:15	a well of living **w**, and streams from	4325
	5:12	*are* as *the eyes of* doves by the rivers of **w**,	4325
	8: 7	Many **w** cannot quench love, neither can	4325
Isa	8: 6	Forsomuch as this people refuseth the **w** of	4325
	8: 7	the Lord bringeth up upon them the **w** of	4325
	11: 9	of the LORD, as the **w** cover the sea.	4325
	15: 6	For the **w** of Nimrim shall be desolate:	4325
	15: 9	For the **w** of Dimon shall be full *of* blood:	4325
	17:12	a rushing like the rushing of mighty **w**.	4325
	17:13	shall rush like the rushing of many **w**:	4325
	18: 2	even in vessels of bulrushes upon the **w**,	4325
	19: 5	the **w** shall fail from the sea, and the river	4325
	19: 8	they that spread nets upon the **w** shall	4325
	22: 9	ye gathered together the **w** of the lower	4325
	23: 3	by great **w** the seed of Sihor, the harvest of	4325
	28: 2	as a flood of mighty **w** overflowing,	4325
	28:17	and the **w** shall overflow the hiding place.	4325
	30:25	streams of **w** in the day of the great	4325
	32:20	Blessed *are* ye that sow beside all **w**,	4325
	33:16	*shall be* given him; his **w** *shall be* sure.	4325
	35: 6	for in the wilderness shall **w** break out, and	4325
	36:16	drink ye every one the **w** of his own cistern;	4325
	40:12	Who hath measured the **w** in the hollow of	4325
	43: 2	When thou passest through the **w**, I *will be*	4325
	43:16	way in the sea, and a path in the mighty **w**;	4325
	43:20	because I give **w** in the wilderness, *and*	4325
	48: 1	and are come forth out of the **w** of Judah,	4325
	48:21	he caused the **w** to flow out of the rock for	4325
	48:21	clave the rock also, and the **w** gushed out.	4325
	51:10	hath dried the sea, the **w** of the great deep;	4325
	54: 9	For this *is as* the **w** of Noah unto me: for *as*	4325
	54: 9	for *as* I have sworn that the **w** of Noah	4325
	55: 1	come ye to the **w**, and he that hath no	4325
	57:20	cannot rest, whose **w** cast up mire and dirt.	4325
	58:11	and like a spring of water, whose **w** fail not.	4325
	64: 2	fire burneth, the fire causeth the **w** to boil,	4325
Jer	2:13	have forsaken me the fountain of living **w**,	4325
	2:18	the way of Egypt, to drink the **w** of Sihor?	4325
	2:18	way of Assyria, to drink the **w** of the river?	4325
	6: 7	As a fountain casteth out her **w**, so	4325
	9: 1	O that my head were **w**, and mine eyes a	4325
	9:18	*with* tears, and our eyelids gush out with **w**.	4325
	10:13	*there is* a multitude of **w** in the heavens,	4325
	14: 3	nobles have sent their little ones to the **w**:	4325
	15:18	unto me as a liar, *and as* **w** *that* fail?	4325
	17: 8	For he shall be as a tree planted by the **w**,	4325
	17:13	the LORD, the fountain of living **w**.	4325
	18:14	shall the cold flowing **w** that come from	4325
	31: 9	I will cause them to walk by the rivers of **w**	4325
	41:12	found him by the great **w** that *are* in	4325
	46: 7	a flood, whose **w** are moved as the rivers?	4325
	46: 8	and *his* **w** are moved like the rivers;	4325
	47: 2	**w** rise up out of the north, and shall be an	4325
	48:34	for the **w** also of Nimrim shall be desolate.	4325
	50:38	A drought *is* upon her **w**; and they shall be	4325
	51:13	O thou that dwellest upon many **w**,	4325
	51:16	*there is* a multitude of **w** in the heavens;	4325
	51:55	when her waves do roar like great **w**,	4325
La	3:54	**W** flowed over mine head; *then* I said, I am	4325
Eze	1:24	like the noise of great **w**, as the voice of	4325
	17: 5	he placed *it* by great **w**, *and* set it *as* a	4325
	17: 8	It *was* planted in a good soil by great **w**,	4325
	19:10	*is* like a vine in thy blood, planted by the **w**:	4325
	19:10	and full of branches by reason of many **w**.	4325
	26:19	upon thee, and great **w** shall cover thee;	4325
	27:26	Thy rowers have brought thee into great **w**:	4325
	27:34	broken by the seas in the depths of the **w**,	4325
	31: 4	The **w** made him great, the deep set him up	4325
	31: 5	became long because of the multitude of **w**,	4325
	31: 7	of his branches: for his root was by great **w**.	4325
	31:14	by the **w** exalt themselves for their height,	4325
	31:15	floods thereof, and the great **w** were stayed:	4325
	32: 2	troubledst the **w** with thy feet, and	4325
	32:13	the beasts thereof from besides the great **w**;	4325
	32:14	will I make their **w** deep, and cause their	4325
	34:18	to have drunk of the deep **w**, but ye must	4325
	43: 2	his voice *was* like a noise of many **w**: and	4325
	47: 1	**w** issued out from under the threshold of	4325
	47: 1	the **w** came down from under from the right	4325
	47: 2	behold, there ran out **w** on the right side.	4325
	47: 3	and he brought me through the **w**;	4325
	47: 3	the waters; the **w** *were* to the ankles.	4325
	47: 4	a thousand, and brought me through the **w**;	4325
	47: 4	the waters; the **w** *were to* the knees.	4325
	47: 4	me through; the **w** *were* to the loins.	4325
	47: 5	for the **w** were risen, waters to swim in,	4325
	47: 5	for the waters were risen, **w** to swim in,	4325
	47: 8	These **w** issue out toward the east country,	4325
	47: 8	forth into the sea, the **w** shall be healed.	4325
	47: 9	of fish, because these **w** shall come thither:	4325
	47:12	their **w** they issued out of the sanctuary:	4325
	47:19	from Tamar *even* to the **w** of strife *in*	4325
	48:28	from Tamar *unto* the **w** of strife *in* Kadesh,	4325
Da	12: 6	in linen, which *was* upon the **w** of the river,	4325
	12: 7	which *was* upon the **w** of the river, when he	4325
Joel	1:20	for the rivers of **w** are dried up, and the fire	4325
	3:18	all the rivers of Judah shall flow *with* **w**,	4325
Am	5: 8	that calleth for the **w** of the sea, and	4325

Am 5:24 let judgment run down as **w**, and 4325
9: 6 he that calleth for the **w** of the sea, and 4325
Jnh 2: 5 The **w** compassed me about, *even* to 4325
Mic 1: 4 as the **w** *that are* poured down a steep 4325
Na 3: 8 *that had* the **w** round about it, 4325
3:14 Draw thee **w** for the siege, fortify thy 4325
Hab 2:14 of the LORD, as the **w** cover the sea. 4325
3:15 thine horses, *through* the heap of great **w**. 4325
Zec 14: 8 *that* living **w** shall go out from Jerusalem: 4325
Mt 8:32 place into the sea, and perished in the **w**. *5204*
Mk 9:22 into the fire, and into the **w**, to destroy him: *5204*
2Co 11:26 *in* perils of **w**, *in* perils of robbers, *4215*
Rev 1:15 and his voice as the sound of many **w**. *5204*
7:17 shall lead them unto living fountains of **w**: *5204*
8:10 of the rivers, and upon the fountains of **w**; *5204*
8:11 the third *part* of the **w** became wormwood; *5204*
8:11 and many men died of the **w**, because *5204*
11: 6 have power over **w** to turn them to blood, *5204*
14: 2 as the voice of many **w**, and as the voice of *5204*
14: 7 and the sea, and the fountains of **w**. *5204*
16: 4 his vial upon the rivers and fountains of **w**; *5204*
16: 5 And I heard the angel of the **w** say, *5204*
17: 1 the great whore that sitteth upon many **w**: *5204*
17:15 he saith unto me, The **w** which thou sawest, *5204*
19: 6 and as the voice of many **w**, and as *5204*

WATERSPOUTS (1) [WATER]

Ps 42: 7 calleth unto deep at the noise of thy **w**: 6794

WATERSPRINGS (2) [SPRING, WATER]

Ps 107:33 and the **w** into dry ground; 4161+4325
107:35 and dry ground into **w**; 4161+4325

WAVE (32) [WAVED, WAVES]

Ex 29:24 shalt **w** them *for* a wave offering before 5130
29:24 shalt wave them *for* a **w offering** before 8573
29:26 **w** it *for* a wave offering before the LORD: 5130
29:26 wave it *for* a **w offering** before 8573
29:27 shalt sanctify the breast of the **w offering**, 8573
Lev 7:30 waved *for* a **w offering** before the LORD. 8573
7:34 For the **w** breast and the heave shoulder 8573
8:27 waved them *for* a **w offering** before 8573
8:29 waved it *for* a **w offering** before 8573
9:21 waved *for* a **w offering** before the LORD; 8573
10:14 the **w** breast and heave shoulder shall ye eat 8573
10:15 the **w** breast shall they bring with 8573
10:15 to **w** *it for* a wave offering before 5130
10:15 to wave *it for* a **w offering** before 8573
14:12 **w** them *for* a wave offering before 5130
14:12 wave them *for* a **w offering** before 8573
14:24 the priest shall **w** them *for* a wave offering 5130
14:24 the priest shall wave them *for* a **w offering** 8573
23:11 he shall **w** the sheaf before the LORD, 5130
23:11 after the sabbath the priest shall **w** it. 5130
23:12 ye shall offer that day when ye **w** the sheaf 5130
23:15 that ye brought the sheaf of the **w offering**; 8573
23:17 habitations two **w** loaves of two tenth deals: 8573
23:20 the priest shall **w** them with the bread of 5130
23:20 *for* a **w offering** before the LORD, 8573
Nu 5:25 and shall **w** the offering before the LORD, 5130
6:20 the priest shall **w** them *for* a wave offering 5130
6:20 the priest shall wave them *for* a **w offering** 8573
6:20 with the **w** breast and heave shoulder: 8573
18:11 with all the **w offerings** of the children of 8573
18:18 as the **w** breast and as the right shoulder are 8573
Jas 1: 6 for he that wavereth is like a **w** of the sea *2830*

WAVED (6) [WAVE]

Ex 29:27 which is **w**, and which is heaved up, of 5130
Lev 7:30 that the breast may be **w** *for* a wave 5130
8:27 **w** them *for* a wave offering before 5130
8:29 **w** it *for* a wave offering before the LORD: 5130
9:21 the right shoulder Aaron **w** *for* a wave 5130
14:21 one lamb *for* a trespass offering to be **w**, 8573

WAVERETH (1) [WAVERING]

Jas 1: 6 for he that **w** is like a wave of the sea *1252*

WAVERING (2) [WAVERETH]

Heb 10:23 fast the profession of *our* hope **without w**; *186*
Jas 1: 6 But let him ask in faith, nothing **w**: for he *1252*

WAVES (26) [WAVE]

2Sa 22: 5 When the **w** of death compassed me, 4867
Job 9: 8 and treadeth upon the **w** of the sea. 1116
38:11 and here shall thy proud **w** be stayed? 1530
Ps 42: 7 all thy **w** and thy billows are gone over me. 4867
65: 7 the noise of their **w**, and the tumult of 1530
88: 7 and thou hast afflicted *me with* all thy **w**. 4867
89: 9 when the **w** thereof arise, thou stillest them. 1530
93: 3 up their voice; the floods lift up their **w**. 1796
93: 4 *yea, than* the mighty **w** of the sea. 4867
107:25 which lifteth up the **w** thereof. 1530
107:29 storm a calm, so that the **w** thereof are still. 1530
Isa 48:18 and thy righteousness as the **w** of the sea: 1530
51:15 that divided the sea, whose **w** roared: 1530
Jer 5:22 though the **w** thereof toss themselves, 1530
31:35 which divideth the sea when the **w** thereof 1530
51:42 she is covered with the multitude of the **w** 1530
51:55 when her **w** do roar like great waters, 1530
Eze 26: 3 as the sea causeth his **w** to come up. 1530
Jnh 2: 3 all thy billows and thy **w** passed over me. 1530
Zec 10:11 shall smite the **w** in the sea, and all 1530
Mt 8:24 that the ship was covered with the **w**: *2949*
14:24 now in the midst of the sea, tossed with **w**: *2949*
Mk 4:37 and the **w** beat into the ship, so that it was *2949*
Lk 21:25 with perplexity; the sea and the **w** roaring; *4535*
Ac 27:41 part was broken with the violence of the **w**. *2949*
Jude 1:13 Raging **w** of the sea, foaming out their own *2949*

WAVY See BUSHY

WAX (24) [WAXED, WAXEN, WAXETH, WAXING]

Ex 22:24 my wrath shall **w hot**, and I will kill you 2734
32:10 that my wrath may **w hot** against them, and 2734
32:11 why doth thy wrath **w hot** against thy 2734
32:22 Let not the anger of my lord **w hot**: 2734
Lev 25:47 or stranger **w rich** by thee, 3027+5381
25:47 thy brother *that dwelleth* by him **w poor**, 4134
1Sa 3: 2 his eyes began *to* **w** dim, *that* he could not NIH
Job 6:17 What time they **w warm**, they vanish: 2215
14: 8 Though the root thereof **w old** in the earth, 2204
Ps 22:14 my heart is like **w**; it is melted in the midst 1749
68: 2 as **w** melteth before the fire, *so* let 1749
97: 5 The hills melted like **w** at the presence of 1749
102:26 yea, all of them shall **w old** like a garment; 1086
Isa 17: 4 and the fatness of his flesh shall **w lean**. 7329
29:22 neither shall his face now **w pale**. 2357
50: 9 lo, they all shall **w old** as a garment; 1086
51: 6 the earth shall **w old** like a garment, and 1086
Jer 6:24 our hands **w feeble**: anguish hath taken 7503
Mic 1: 4 as **w** before the fire, *and* as the waters *that* 1749
Mt 24:12 the love of many shall **w cold**. *5594*
Lk 12:33 provide yourselves bags which **w** not **old**, *3822*
1Ti 5:11 have *begun to* **w wanton against** Christ, *2691*
2Ti 3:13 and seducers shall **w** worse and worse, *4298*
Heb 1:11 and they all shall **w old** as *doth* a garment; *3822*

WAXED (38) [WAX]

Ge 18:12 After I am **w old** shall I have pleasure, 1086
26:13 the man **w great**, and went forward, 1431
41:56 and the famine **w sore** in the land of Egypt. 2388
Ex 1: 7 and multiplied, and **w** exceeding **mighty**; 6105
1:20 the people multiplied, and **w** very **mighty**. 6105
16:21 and when the sun **w hot**, it melted. 2552
19:19 **w louder and louder**, Moses spake, 2390+3966
32:19 Moses' anger **w hot**, and he cast the tables 2734
Nu 11:23 Is the LORD'S hand **w short**? 7114
Dt 8: 4 Thy raiment **w** not **old** upon thee, 1086
32:15 Jeshurun **w fat**, and kicked: thou art waxed 8080
32:15 thou art **w fat**, thou art grown thick, 8080
Jos 23: 1 that Joshua **w old** *and* stricken in age. 2204
1Sa 2: 5 and she that hath many children is **w feeble**. 535
2Sa 3: 1 David **w stronger** and stronger, and 1980
3: 1 the house of Saul **w weaker** and weaker. 1980
21:15 against the Philistines: and David **w faint**. 5774
2Ki 4:34 and the flesh of the child **w warm**. 2552
1Ch 11: 9 So David **w greater** and greater: 1980+1980
2Ch 13:21 Abijah **w mighty**, and married fourteen 2388
17:12 Jehoshaphat **w** great exceedingly; and 1980
24:15 Jehoiada **w old**, and was full *of* days when 2204
Ne 9:21 their clothes **w** not **old**, and their feet 1086
Est 9: 4 for *this* man Mordecai **w greater** and 1980
Ps 32: 3 my bones **w old** through my roaring all 1086
Jer 49:24 Damascus is **w feeble**, *and* turneth herself 7503
50:43 the report of them, and his hands **w feeble**: 7503
Da 8: 8 Therefore the he goat **w** very **great**: and 1431
8: 9 which **w** exceeding great, toward the south, 4480
8:10 it **w great**, *even* to the host of heaven; and 1431

Mt 13:15 For this people's heart is **w gross**, and *their* *3975*
Lk 1:80 and **w strong** in spirit, and was in *2901*
2:40 and **w strong** in spirit, filled with wisdom: *2901*
13:19 and it grew, and **w** a great tree; and *1096+1519*
Ac 13:46 Then Paul and Barnabas **w bold**, and said, *3955*
28:27 For the heart of this people is **w gross**, and *3975*
Heb 11:34 were made strong, **w** valiant in fight, *1096*
Rev 18: 3 the merchants of the earth are **w rich** *4147*

WAXEN (11) [WAX]
Ge 19:13 the cry of them is **w great** before the face 1431
Lev 25:25 If thy brother be **w poor**, and hath sold 4134
25:35 if thy brother be **w poor**, and fallen in 4134
25:39 brother *that dwelleth* by thee be **w poor**, 4134
Dt 29: 5 your clothes are not **w old** upon you, and 1086
29: 5 and thy shoe is not **w old** upon thy foot. 1086
31:20 and filled *themselves,* and **w fat**; 1878
Jos 17:13 when the children of Israel were **w strong**, 2388
Jer 5:27 they are become great, and **w rich**. 6238
5:28 They are **w fat**, they shine: yea, 8080
Eze 16: 7 thou hast increased and **w great**, and 1431

WAXETH (2) [WAX]
Ps 6: 7 it **w old** because of all mine enemies. 6275
Heb 8:13 and **w old** *is* ready to vanish away. *1095*

WAXING (1) [WAX]
Php 1:14 in the Lord, **w confident** by my bonds, *3982*

WAY (665) [BYWAYS, HIGHWAY, HIGHWAYS, WAYFARING, WAYMARKS, WAYS, WAYSIDE]
Ge 3:24 a flaming sword which **turned every** w, 2015
3:24 every way, to keep the **w** of the tree of life. 1870
6:12 for all flesh had corrupted his **w** upon 1870
12:19 behold thy wife, take *her,* and go thy **w**. NIH
14:11 and all their victuals, and went their **w**. NIH
16: 7 by the fountain in the **w** to Shur. 1870
18:16 went with them to **bring** them **on** the **w**. 7971
18:19 they shall keep the **w** of the LORD, to do 1870
18:33 the LORD went his **w**, as soon as he had NIH
21:16 her down over against *him* a **good w off**, 7368
24:27 I *being* in the **w**, the LORD led me to 1870
24:40 send his angel with thee, and prosper thy **w**; 1870
24:42 if now thou do prosper my **w** which I go: 1870
24:48 which had led me in the right **w** to take my 1870
24:56 seeing the LORD hath prospered my **w**; 1870
24:61 the servant took Rebekah, and went his **w**. NIH
24:62 Isaac came from the **w** of the well Lahai-roi; 935
25:34 and drink, and rose up, and went his **w**: NIH
28:20 will keep me in this **w** that I go, and 1870
32: 1 Jacob went on his **w**, and the angels of God 1870
33:16 So Esau returned that day on his **w** unto 1870
35: 3 and was with me in the **w** which I went. 1870
35:16 a **little w** to come to Ephrath: 776+3530+1886.1
35:19 and was buried in the **w** to Ephrath, 1870
38:14 open place, which *is* by the **w** to Timnath; 1870
38:16 he turned unto her by the **w**, and said, 1870
38:21 *is* the harlot, that *was* openly by the **w side**? 1870
42:25 and to give them provision for the **w**: 1870
42:38 if mischief befall him by the **w** in the which 1870
45:21 and gave them provision for the **w**. 1870
45:23 and bread and meat for his father by the **w**. 1870
45:24 unto them, See that ye fall not out by the **w**. 1870
48: 7 died by me in the land of Canaan in the **w**, 1870
48: 7 but a little **w** to come unto Ephrath: 776
48: 7 I buried her there in the **w** of Ephrath; 1870
49:17 Dan shall be a serpent by the **w**, an adder in 1870
Ex 2:12 he looked **this w** and that way, and 3541
2:12 he looked this way and **that w**, and 3541
4:24 it came to pass by the **w** in the inn, that 1870
5:20 and Aaron, who stood **in the w**, 7125+3807.1
13:17 that God led them not *through* the **w** of 1870
13:18 *through* the **w** of the wilderness of the Red 1870
13:21 in a pillar of a cloud, to lead them the **w**; 1870
18: 8 travail that had come upon them by the **w**, 1870
18:20 shalt shew them the **w** *wherein* they must 1870
18:27 and he **went** his **w** into his own land. 1980
23:20 to keep thee in the **w**, and to bring thee into 1870
32: 8 out of the **w** which I commanded them: 1870
33: 3 lest I consume thee in the **w**. 1870
33:13 shew me now thy **w**, that I may know thee, 1870
Nu 13:17 Get you up this *w* southward, and go up into NIH
14:25 get you *into* the wilderness *by* the **w** of 1870
20:17 we will go *by* the king's *high* **w**, we will 1870
20:19 said unto him, We will go by the **high w**: 4546
21: 1 heard *tell* that Israel came *by* the **w** of 1870
21: 4 they journeyed from mount Hor *by* the **w** of 1870
21: 4 was much discouraged because of the **w**. 1870
21:22 *but* we will go along by the king's *high* **w**, 1870
21:33 and went up *by* the **w** of Bashan: 1870
22:22 the angel of the LORD stood in the **w** for 1870
22:23 the angel of the LORD standing in the **w**, 1870
22:23 the ass turned aside out of the **w**, and 1870
22:23 smote the ass, to turn her *into* the **w**. 1870
22:26 where *was* no **w** to turn *either to* the right 1870
22:31 the angel of the LORD standing in the **w**, 1870
22:32 because *thy* **w** is perverse before me: 1870
22:34 for I knew not that thou stoodest in the **w** 1870
24:25 to his place: and Balak also went his **w**. 1870
Dt 1: 2 the **w** of mount Seir unto Kadesh-barnea.) 1870
1:19 which you saw *by* the **w** of the mountain of 1870
1:22 bring us word again by what **w** we must go 1870
1:31 doth bear his son, in all the **w** that ye went, 1870
1:33 Who went in the **w** before you, to search 1870
1:33 to shew you by what **w** ye should go, and 1870
1:40 into the wilderness *by* the **w** of the Red sea. 1870
2: 1 into the wilderness *by* the **w** of the Red sea, 1870
2: 8 through the **w** of the plain from Elath, and 1870
2: 8 passed *by* the **w** of the wilderness of Moab. 1870
2:27 I will go along by the **high** w, I will neither 1870
3: 1 we turned, and went up the **w** to Bashan: 1870
6: 7 when thou walkest by the **w**, and when thou 1870
8: 2 thou shalt remember all the **w** which 1870
9:12 out of the **w** which I commanded them; 1870
9:16 ye had turned aside quickly out of the **w** 1870
11:19 when thou walkest by the **w**, when thou 1870
11:28 turn aside out of the **w** which I command 1870
11:30 by the **w** where the sun goeth down, in 1870
13: 5 to thrust thee out of the **w** which 1870
14:24 if the **w** be too long for thee, so that thou 1870
17:16 Ye shall henceforth return no more that **w**. 1870
19: 3 Thou shalt prepare thee a **w**, and divide 1870
19: 6 because the **w** is long, and slay him; 1870
22: 4 brother's ass or his ox fall down by the **w**, 1870
22: 6 to be before thee in the **w** in any tree, 1870
23: 4 you not with bread and with water in the **w**, 1870
24: 9 LORD thy God did unto Miriam by the **w**, 1870
25:17 what Amalek did unto thee by the **w**, 1870
25:18 How he met thee by the **w**, and smote 1870
27:18 maketh the blind to wander out of the **w**. 1870
28: 7 they shall come out against thee one **w**, and 1870
28:25 thou shalt go out one **w** against them, and 1870
28:68 by the **w** where*of* I spake unto thee, 1870
31:29 turn aside from the **w** which I have 1870
Jos 1: 8 for then thou shalt make thy **w** prosperous, 1870
2: 7 the men pursued after them the **w** to Jordan 1870
2:16 and afterward may ye go your **w**. 1870
2:22 pursuers sought *them* throughout all the **w**, 1870
3: 4 that ye may know the **w** by which ye must 1870
3: 4 for ye have not passed *this* **w** heretofore. 1870
5: 4 of war, died in the wilderness by the **w**, 1870
5: 5 by the **w** as they came forth out of Egypt, 1870
5: 7 they had not circumcised them by the **w**. 1870
8:15 and fled *by* the **w** of the wilderness. 1870
8:20 they had no power to flee **this w** or 2008
8:20 had no power to flee this way or **that w**: 2008
10:10 chased them *along* the **w** that goeth up to 1870
12: 3 sea on the east, the **w** to Beth-jeshimoth; 1870
23:14 *this* day I am going the **w** of all the earth: 1870
24:17 preserved us in all the **w** wherein we went, 1870
Jdg 2:17 they turned quickly out of the **w** which 1870
2:19 own doings, nor from their stubborn **w**. 1870
2:22 whether they will keep the **w** of 1870
5:10 ye that sit in judgment, and walk by the **w**. 1870
8:11 Gideon went up *by* the **w** of them that 1870
9:25 they robbed all that came along *that* **w** by 1870
18: 5 that we may know whether our **w** which we 1870
18: 6 before the LORD *is* your **w** wherein ye 1870
18:22 *And* when they were a **good w** from 7368
18:26 the children of Dan went their **w**: and 1870
19: 5 a morsel of bread, and afterward go your **w**. NIH
19: 9 to morrow get you early on your **w**, that 1870
19:14 they passed on and went *their w*; and NIH
19:27 of the house, and went out to go his **w**: 1870
20:42 men of Israel unto the **w** of the wilderness; 1870
Ru 1: 7 they went on the **w** to return unto the land 1870
1:12 go *your w*; for I am too old to have a NIH
1Sa 1:18 So the woman went her **w**, and did eat, and 1870

W

1Sa 6: 9 if it goeth up *by* the w of his own coast *to* 1870
6:12 the kine took the straight w to the way of 1870
6:12 the kine took the straight way to the w of 1870
9: 6 peradventure he can shew us our w that we 1870
9: 8 I give to the man of God, to tell us our w. 1870
12:23 I will teach you the good and the right w: 1870
13:17 one company turned unto the w that leadeth 1870
13:18 another company turned the w to 1870
13:18 another company turned *to* the w of 1870
15: 2 how he laid *wait* for him in the w, when he 1870
15:20 have gone the w which the LORD sent 1870
17:52 Philistines fell down by the w to Shaaraim, 1870
20:22 go *thy w*: for the LORD hath sent thee NIH
24: 3 he came to the sheepcotes by the w, where 1870
24: 7 rose up out of the cave, and went on *his* w. 1870
25:12 So David's young men turned their w, and 1870
26: 3 which *is* before Jeshimon, by the w. 1870
26:25 So David went on his w, and Saul returned 1870
28:22 have strength, when thou goest on *thy* w. 1870
30: 2 carried *them* away, and went on their w. 1870
2Sa 2:24 that *lieth* before Giah *by* the w of 1870
13:30 it came to pass, while they *were* in the w, 1870
13:34 there came much people by the w of the hill 1870
15: 2 and stood beside the w of the gate: 1870
15:23 toward the w of the wilderness. 1870
16:13 as David and his men went by the w, 1870
18:23 Ahimaaz ran *by* the w of the plain, and 1870
19:36 Thy servant will go a little *w* over Jordan NIH
22:31 *As for* God, his w *is* perfect; the word of 1870
22:33 *and* power: and he maketh my w perfect. 1870
1Ki 1:49 and rose up, and went every man his w. 1870
2: 2 I go the w of all the earth: be thou strong 1870
2: 4 saying, If thy children take heed to their w, 1870
8:25 so that thy children take heed to their w, 1870
8:32 the wicked, to bring his w upon his head; 1870
8:36 that thou teach them the good w wherein 1870
11:29 Ahijah the Shilonite found him in the w; 1870
13: 9 nor turn again by the *same* w that thou 1870
13:10 So he went another w, and returned not by 1870
13:10 returned not by the w that he came to 1870
13:12 father said unto them, What w went he? 1870
13:12 For his sons had seen what w the man of 1870
13:17 nor turn again to go by the w that thou 1870
13:24 a lion met him by the w, and slew him: 1870
13:24 his carcase was cast in the w, and the ass 1870
13:25 saw the carcase cast in the w, and the lion 1870
13:26 him back from the w heard *thereof,* he said, 1870
13:28 he went and found his carcase cast in the w, 1870
13:33 Jeroboam returned not from his evil w, 1870
15:26 walked in the w of his father, and in his sin 1870
15:34 walked in the w of Jeroboam and in his sin 1870
16: 2 thou hast walked in the w of Jeroboam, and 1870
16:19 in walking in the w of Jeroboam, and in his 1870
16:26 For he walked in all the w of Jeroboam 1870
18: 6 Ahab went one w by himself, and 1870
18: 6 Obadiah went another w by himself. 1870
18: 7 as Obadiah was in the w, behold Elijah met 1870
19:15 return on thy w to the wilderness of 1870
20:38 waited for the king by the w, and 1870
22:24 **Which** w went the spirit of 335+2088
22:52 walked in the w of his father, and in 1870
22:52 in the w of his mother, and in the way of 1870
22:52 in the w of Jeroboam the son of Nebat, 1870
2Ki 2:23 as he was going up by the w, there came 1870
3: 8 he said, Which w shall we go up? And he 1870
3: 8 The w through the wilderness of Edom. 1870
3:20 there came water by the w of Edom, and 1870
4:29 go *thy w*: if thou meet any man, salute him NIH
5:19 in peace. So he departed from him a little w. 776
6:19 This *is* not the w, neither *is* this the city: 1870
7:15 all the w *was* full *of* garments and vessels, 1870
8:18 he walked in the w of the kings of Israel, 1870
8:27 he walked in the w of the house of Ahab, 1870
9:27 *this,* he fled *by* the w of the garden house. 1870
10:12 as he *was at* the shearing house in the w, 1870
11:16 she went *by* the w by the which the horses 1870
11:19 came *by* the w of the gate of the guard *to* 1870
16: 3 he walked in the w of the kings of Israel, 1870
19:28 I will turn thee back by the w by which 1870
19:33 By the w that he came, *by the same* shall he 1870
21:21 he walked in all the w that his father 1870
21:22 and walked not in the w of the LORD. 1870
22: 2 walked in all the w of David his father, and 1870
25: 4 all the men of war *fled* by night *by* the w of 1870
25: 4 and *the king* went the w toward the plain. 1870
2Ch 6:16 that thy children take heed to their w to 1870
6:23 by recompensing his w upon his own head; 1870
6:27 when thou hast taught them the good w, 1870
6:34 enemies by the w that thou shalt send them, 1870
11:17 for three years they walked in the w of 1870
18:23 Which w went the spirit of the LORD 1870
20:32 he walked in the w of Asa his father, and 1870
21: 6 he walked in the w of the kings of Israel, 1870
21:13 hast walked in the w of the kings of Israel, 1870
Ezr 8:21 to seek of him a right w for us, and for our 1870
8:22 to help us against the enemy in the w: 1870
8:31 and of such as lay in wait by the w. 1870
Ne 8:10 Go *your w*, eat the fat, and drink the sweet, NIH
8:12 all the people went *their w* to eat, and NIH
9:12 to give them light in the w wherein they 1870
9:19 from them by day, to lead them in the w; 1870
9:19 and the w wherein they should go. 1870
Est 4:17 So Mordecai went his w, and did according NIH
Job 3:23 *Why is light given* to a man whose w is hid, 1870
6:18 The paths of their w are turned aside; 1870
8:19 this *is* the joy of his w, and out of the earth 1870
12:24 wander in a wilderness *where there is* no w. 1870
16:22 I shall go the w *whence* I shall not return. 734
17: 9 The righteous also shall hold on his w, and 1870
18:10 in the ground, and a trap for him in the w. 5410
19: 8 He hath fenced up my w that I cannot pass, 734
19:12 raise up their w against me, and 1870
21:29 Have ye not asked them that go by the w? 1870
21:31 Who shall declare his w to his face? and 1870
22:15 Hast thou marked the old w which wicked 734
23:10 he knoweth the w that I take: *when* he hath 1870
23:11 his w have I kept, and not declined. 1870
24: 4 They turn the needy out of the w: the poor 1870
24:18 he beholdeth not the w of the vineyards. 1870
24:24 they are **taken out of the** w as all *other,* 7092
28:23 God understandeth the w thereof, and 1870
28:26 and a w for the lightning of the thunder: 1870
29:25 I chose out their w, and sat chief, and 1870
31: 7 If my step hath turned out of the w, and 1870
36:23 Who hath enjoined him his w? or who can 1870
38:19 Where *is* the w *where* light dwelleth? and 1870
38:24 By what w is the light parted, 1870
38:25 or a w for the lightning of thunder; 1870
Ps 1: 1 nor standeth in the w of sinners, nor sitteth 1870
1: 6 For the LORD knoweth the w of 1870
1: 6 but the w of the ungodly shall perish. 1870
2:12 lest he be angry, and ye perish *from* the w, 1870
5: 8 make thy w straight before my face. 1870
18:30 *As for* God, his w *is* perfect: the word of 1870
18:32 *with* strength, and maketh my w perfect. 1870
25: 8 will he teach sinners in the w. 1870
25: 9 and the meek will he teach his w. 1870
25:12 him shall he teach in the w *that* he shall 1870
27:11 Teach me thy w, O LORD, and lead me in 1870
32: 8 and teach thee in the w which thou shalt go: 1870
35: 3 stop *the* w against them that persecute me: NIH
35: 6 Let their w be dark and slippery: and let 1870
36: 4 he setteth himself in a w *that is* not good; 1870
37: 5 Commit thy w unto the LORD; trust also 1870
37: 7 because of him who prospereth *in* his w, 1870
37:23 by the LORD: and he delighteth in his w. 1870
37:34 keep his w, and he shall exalt thee to inherit 1870
44:18 neither have our steps declined from thy w; 734
49:13 This their w *is* their folly: yet their posterity 1870
67: 2 That thy w may be known upon earth, 1870
77:13 Thy w, O God, *is* in the sanctuary: who *is* 1870
77:19 Thy w *is* in the sea, and thy path in 1870
78:50 He made a w to his anger; he spared not 5410
80:12 that all they which pass by the w do pluck 1870
85:13 and shall set *us* in the w of his steps. 1870
86:11 Teach me thy w, O LORD; I will walk in 1870
89:41 All that pass by the w spoil him: he is a 1870
101: 2 I will behave myself wisely in a perfect w. 1870
101: 6 he that walketh in a perfect w, he shall 1870
102:23 He weakened my strength in the w; 1870
107: 4 wandered in the wilderness in a solitary w; 1870
107: 7 he led them forth by the right w, that *they* 1870
107:40 in the wilderness, *where there is* no w. 1870
110: 7 He shall drink of the brook in the w: 1870
119: 1 Blessed *are* the undefiled in the w, 1870
119: 9 shall a young man cleanse his w? 734
119:14 I have rejoiced in the w of thy testimonies, 1870
119:27 Make me to understand the w of thy 1870

Ps	119:29	Remove from me the w of lying: and	1870
	119:30	I have chosen the w of truth:	1870
	119:32	I will run the w of thy commandments,	1870
	119:33	Teach me, O LORD, the w of thy statutes;	1870
	119:37	and quicken thou me in thy w.	1870
	119:101	I have refrained my feet from every evil w,	734
	119:104	I hate every false w.	734
	119:128	things to be right; and I hate every false w.	734
	139:24	see if there be any wicked w in me, and	1870
	139:24	in me, and lead me in the w everlasting.	1870
	140: 5	they have spread a net by the w side;	3027+4570
	142: 3	In the w wherein I walked have they privily	734
	143: 8	cause me to know the w wherein I should	1870
	146: 9	the w of the wicked he turneth upside	1870
Pr	1:15	My son, walk not thou in the w with them;	1870
	1:31	shall they eat of the fruit of their own w,	1870
	2: 8	and preserveth the w of his saints.	1870
	2:12	To deliver thee from the w of the evil man,	1870
	2:20	That thou mayest walk in the w of good	1870
	3:23	shalt thou walk in thy w safely, and	1870
	4:11	I have taught thee in the w of wisdom;	1870
	4:14	and go not in the w of evil men.	1870
	4:19	The w of the wicked is as darkness:	1870
	5: 8	Remove thy w far from her, and come not	1870
	6:23	and reproofs of instruction are the w of life:	1870
	7: 8	her corner; and he went the w to her house,	1870
	7:27	Her house is the w to hell, going down to	1870
	8: 2	standeth in the top of high places by the w,	1870
	8:13	the evil w, and the froward mouth, do I	1870
	8:20	I lead in the w of righteousness, in the midst	734
	8:22	possessed me in the beginning of his w,	1870
	9: 6	and live; and go in the w of understanding.	1870
	10:17	He is in the w of life that keepeth	734
	10:29	The w of the LORD is strength to	1870
	11: 5	of the perfect shall direct his w:	1870
	11:20	such as are upright in their w are his	1870
	12:15	The w of a fool is right in his own eyes: but	1870
	12:26	but the w of the wicked seduceth them.	1870
	12:28	In the w of righteousness is life; and in	734
	13: 6	keepeth him that is upright in the w:	1870
	13:15	but the w of transgressors is hard.	1870
	14: 8	of the prudent is to understand his w:	1870
	14:12	There is a w which seemeth right unto a	1870
	15: 9	The w of the wicked is an abomination	1870
	15:10	is grievous unto him that forsaketh the w:	734
	15:19	The w of the slothful man is as a hedge of	1870
	15:19	but the w of the righteous is made plain.	734
	15:24	The w of life is above to the wise, that he	734
	16: 9	A man's heart deviseth his w: but	1870
	16:17	he that keepeth his w preserveth his soul.	1870
	16:25	There is a w that seemeth right unto a man,	1870
	16:29	and leadeth him into the w that is not good.	1870
	16:31	if it be found in the w of righteousness.	1870
	19: 3	The foolishness of man perverteth his w:	1870
	20:14	but when he is gone his w, then he boasteth.	235
	20:24	how can a man then understand his own w?	1870
	21: 2	Every w of a man is right in his own eyes:	1870
	21: 8	The w of man is froward and strange: but	1870
	21:16	The man that wandereth out of the w of	1870
	21:29	but as for the upright, he directeth his w.	1870
	22: 5	and snares are in the w of the froward:	1870
	22: 6	a child in the w he should go:	1870+5921+6310
	23:19	and be wise, and guide thine heart in the w.	1870
	26:13	slothful man saith, There is a lion in the w;	1870
	28:10	the righteous to go astray in an evil w,	1870
	29:27	he that is upright in the w is abomination to	1870
	30:19	The w of an eagle in the air; the way of a	1870
	30:19	in the air; the w of a serpent upon a rock;	1870
	30:19	the w of a ship in the midst of the sea; and	1870
	30:19	of the sea; and the w of a man with a maid.	1870
	30:20	Such is the w of an adulterous woman;	1870
Ecc	9: 7	Go thy w, eat thy bread with joy, and	NIH
	10: 3	when he that is a fool walketh by the w,	1870
	11: 5	As thou knowest not what is the w of	1870
	12: 5	fears shall be in the w, and the almond tree	1870
SS	1: 8	go thy w forth by the footsteps of	3318
Isa	3:12	thee to err, and destroy the w of thy paths.	1870
	8:11	I should not walk in the w of this people,	1870
	9: 1	grievously afflict her by the w of the sea,	1870
	15: 5	for in the w of Horonaim they shall raise up	1870
	26: 7	The w of the just is uprightness: thou,	734
	26: 8	Yea, in the w of thy judgments, O LORD,	734
	28: 7	and through strong drink are out of the w;	8582
	28: 7	they are out of the w through strong drink;	8582
	30:11	Get ye out of the w, turn aside out of	1870
	30:21	saying, This is the w, walk ye in it, when ye	1870
	35: 8	a w, and it shall be called The way of	1870
	35: 8	and it shall be called The w of holiness;	1870
	37:29	I will turn thee back by the w by which	1870
	37:34	By the w that he came, by the same shall he	1870
	40: 3	Prepare ye the w of the LORD,	1870
	40:14	and shewed to him the w of understanding?	1870
	40:27	My w is hid from the LORD, and	1870
	41: 3	even by the w that he had not gone with his	734
	42:16	I will bring the blind by a w that they knew	1870
	43:16	which maketh a w in the sea, and a path in	1870
	43:19	I will even make a w in the wilderness, and	1870
	48:15	and he shall make his w prosperous.	1870
	48:17	which leadeth thee by the w that thou	1870
	49:11	I will make all my mountains a w, and	1870
	51:10	that hath made the depths of the sea a w for	1870
	53: 6	we have turned every one to his own w;	1870
	55: 7	Let the wicked forsake his w, and	1870
	56:11	they all look to their own w, every one for	1870
	57:10	Thou art wearied in the greatness of thy w;	1870
	57:14	Cast ye up, cast ye up, prepare the w,	1870
	57:14	take up the stumblingblock out of the w of	1870
	57:17	he went on frowardly in the w of his heart.	1870
	59: 8	The w of peace they know not; and there is	1870
	62:10	prepare you the w of the people; cast up,	1870
	65: 2	which walketh in a w that was not good,	1870
Jer	2:17	thy God, when he led thee by the w?	1870
	2:18	now what hast thou to do in the w of Egypt,	1870
	2:18	or what hast thou to do in the w of Assyria,	1870
	2:23	see thy w in the valley, know what thou	1870
	2:33	Why trimmest thou thy w to seek love?	1870
	2:36	thou about so much to change thy w?	1870
	3:21	for they have perverted their w, and	1870
	4: 7	the destroyer of the Gentiles is on his w;	5265
	4:18	Thy w and thy doings have procured these	1870
	5: 4	for they know not the w of the LORD,	1870
	5: 5	for they have known the w of the LORD,	1870
	6:16	where is the good w, and walk therein,	1870
	6:25	not forth into the field, nor walk by the w;	1870
	6:27	that thou mayest know and try their w.	1870
	10: 2	Learn not the w of the heathen, and be not	1870
	10:23	I know that the w of man is not in himself:	1870
	12: 1	Wherefore doth the w of the wicked	1870
	18:11	return ye now every one from his evil w,	1870
	18:15	to walk in paths, in a w not cast up;	1870
	21: 8	I set before you the w of life, and the way	1870
	21: 8	you the way of life, and the w of death.	1870
	23:12	Wherefore their w shall be unto them as	1870
	23:22	should have turned them from their evil w,	1870
	25: 5	ye again now every one from his evil w,	1870
	25:35	the shepherds shall have no w to flee,	4498
	26: 3	and turn every man from his evil w,	1870
	28:11	And the prophet Jeremiah went his w.	1870
	31: 9	walk by the rivers of waters in a straight w,	1870
	31:21	even the w which thou wentest:	1870
	32:39	one w, that they may fear me for ever, for	1870
	35:15	Return ye now every man from his evil w,	1870
	36: 3	they may return every man from his evil w;	1870
	36: 7	and will return every one from his evil w:	1870
	39: 4	by the w of the king's garden, by the gate	1870
	39: 4	and he went out the w of the plain.	1870
	42: 3	may shew us the w wherein we may walk,	1870
	48:19	of Aroer, stand by the w and espy;	1870
	50: 5	They shall ask the w to Zion with their	1870
	52: 7	went forth out of the city by night by the w	1870
	52: 7	and they went by the w of the plain.	1870
Eze	3:18	to warn the wicked from his wicked w,	1870
	3:19	nor from his wicked w, he shall die in his	1870
	7:27	I will do unto them after their w, and	1870
	8: 5	lift up thine eyes now the w towards	1870
	8: 5	So I lift up mine eyes the w toward	1870
	9: 2	six men came from the w of the higher	1870
	9:10	I will recompense their w upon their head.	1870
	11:21	I will recompense their w upon their own	1870
	13:22	he should not return from his wicked w,	1870
	14:22	and ye shall see their w and their doings:	1870
	16:25	built thy high place at every head of the w,	1870
	16:27	which are ashamed of thy lewd w.	1870
	16:31	thine eminent place in the head of every w,	1870
	16:43	I also will recompense thy w upon thine	1870
	18:25	Yet ye say, The w of the Lord is not equal.	1870
	18:25	O house of Israel; Is not my w equal?	1870
	18:29	of Israel, The w of the Lord is not equal.	1870

Eze 21:16 **Go thee one w or other**, *either* on the right 258
21:19 choose *it,* at the head of the **w** to the city. 1870
21:20 Appoint a **w**, that the sword may come to 1870
21:21 of Babylon stood at the parting of the **w**, 1870
22:31 their own **w** have I recompensed upon their 1870
23:13 she was defiled, *that* they took both one **w**, 1870
23:31 Thou hast walked in the **w** of thy sister; 1870
33: 8 not speak to warn the wicked from his **w**, 1870
33: 9 if thou warn the wicked of his **w** to turn 1870
33: 9 if he do not turn from his **w**, he shall die in 1870
33:11 that the wicked turn from his **w** and live: 1870
33:17 people say, The **w** of the Lord is not equal: 1870
33:17 but *as for* them, their **w** is not equal. 1870
33:20 Yet ye say, The **w** of the Lord is not equal. 1870
36:17 they defiled it by their own **w** and by their 1870
36:17 their **w** was before me as the uncleanness 1870
36:19 according to their **w** and according to their 1870
42: 1 into the utter court, the **w** toward the north: 1870
42: 4 ten cubits breadth inward, a **w** of one cubit; 1870
42:11 the **w** before them *was* like the appearance 1870
42:12 the south *was* a door in the head of the **w**, 1870
42:12 *even* the **w** directly before the wall toward 1870
43: 2 God of Israel came from the **w** of the east: 1870
43: 4 **w** of the gate whose prospect *is* toward 1870
44: 1 he brought me back the **w** of the gate of 1870
44: 3 he shall enter by the **w** of the porch of *that* 1870
44: 3 and shall go out by the **w** of the same. 1870
44: 4 brought he me the **w** of the north gate 1870
46: 2 the prince shall enter by the **w** of the porch 1870
46: 8 he shall go in *by* the **w** of the porch of *that* 1870
46: 8 and he shall go forth by the **w** thereof. 1870
46: 9 he that entereth in *by* the **w** of the north 1870
46: 9 shall go out *by* the **w** of the south gate; 1870
46: 9 he that entereth *by* the **w** of the south gate 1870
46: 9 shall go forth *by* the **w** of the north gate: 1870
46: 9 he shall not return *by* the **w** of the gate 1870
47: 2 brought he me out *of* the **w** of the gate 1870
47: 2 led me about the **w** without unto the utter 1870
47: 2 utter gate *by* the **w** that looketh east*ward;* 1870
47:15 from the great sea, the **w** of Hethlon, as 1870
48: 1 From the north end to the coast of the **w** of 1870
Da 12: 9 he said, Go thy **w**, Daniel: for the words *are* NIH
12:13 go thou thy **w** till the end *be:* for thou shalt NIH
Hos 2: 6 I will hedge up thy **w** with thorns, and 1870
6: 9 the company of priests murder *in* the **w** by 1870
10:13 because thou didst trust in thy **w**, in 1870
13: 7 as a leopard by the **w** will I observe *them:* 1870
Am 2: 7 the poor, and turn aside the **w** of the meek: 1870
Jnh 3: 8 let them turn every one from his evil **w**, and 1870
3:10 that they turned from their evil **w**; 1870
Na 1: 3 the LORD *hath* his **w** in the whirlwind 1870
2: 1 keep the munition, watch the **w**, make *thy* 1870
Zec 10: 2 therefore they went their **w** as a flock, NIH
Mal 2: 8 ye are departed out of the **w**; ye have 1870
3: 1 and he shall prepare the **w** before me: 1870
Mt 2:12 departed into their own country another **w**. 3598
3: 3 Prepare ye the **w** of the Lord, make his *3598*
4:15 *by* the **w** of the sea, beyond Jordan, *3598*
5:24 there thy gift before the altar, and go thy **w**; NIG
5:25 whiles thou art in the **w** with him; *3598*
7:13 for wide *is* the gate, and broad *is* the **w**, *3598*
7:14 and narrow *is* the **w**, which leadeth unto *3598*
8: 4 See thou tell no *man;* but go thy **w**, NIG
8:13 Jesus said unto the centurion, Go thy **w**; NIG
8:28 so that no *man* might pass by that **w**. *3598*
8:30 And there was a **good w off** from them a *3112*
10: 5 Go not into the **w** of the Gentiles, and *3598*
11:10 which shall prepare thy **w** before thee. *3598*
13: 4 some *seeds* fell by the **w** side, and the fowls *3598*
13:19 This is he which received seed by the **w** *3598*
13:25 tares among the wheat, and went his **w**. NIG
15:32 them away fasting, lest they faint in the **w**. *3598*
20: 4 right I will give you. And they **went** their **w**. *565*
20:14 Take *that* thine *is,* and go thy **w**: I will give NIG
20:17 took the twelve disciples apart in the **w**, *3598*
20:30 two blind men sitting by the **w** side, *3598*
21: 8 multitude spread their garments in the **w**; *3598*
21: 8 from the trees, and strawed *them* in the **w**. *3598*
21:19 And when he saw a fig tree in the **w**, *3598*
21:32 For John came unto you in the **w** of *3598*
22:16 art true, and teachest the **w** of God in truth, *3598*
22:22 and left him, and went their **w**. NIG
27:65 go your **w**, make *it* as sure as you can. NIG
Mk 1: 2 which shall prepare thy **w** before thee. *3598*
1: 3 Prepare ye the **w** of the Lord, make his *3598*
1:44 thou say nothing to any *man:* but go thy **w**, NIG
2:11 up thy bed, and go thy **w** into thine house. NIG
4: 4 some fell by the **w side**, and the fowls of *3598*
4:15 And these are they by the **w side**, where *3598*
7:29 he said unto her, For this saying go thy **w**; NIG
8: 3 their own houses, they will faint by the **w**: *3598*
8:27 and by the **w** he asked his disciples, *3598*
9:33 ye disputed among yourselves by the **w**? *3598*
9:34 for by the **w** they had disputed among *3598*
10:17 And when he was gone forth into the **w**, *3598*
10:21 go thy **w**, sell whatsoever thou hast, and NIG
10:32 And they were in the **w** going up to *3598*
10:52 And Jesus said unto him, Go thy **w**; NIG
10:52 his sight, and followed Jesus in the **w**. *3598*
11: 2 Go your **w** into the village over against you: NIG
11: 4 And they went their **w**, and found the colt NIG
11: 8 And many spread their garments in the **w**: *3598*
11: 8 off the trees, and strawed *them* in the **w**. *3598*
12:12 and they left him, and went their **w**. NIG
12:14 of men, but teachest the **w** of God in truth: *3598*
16: 7 But go your **w**, tell his disciples and Peter NIG
Lk 1:79 to guide our feet into the **w** of peace. *3598*
3: 4 Prepare ye the **w** of the Lord, make his *3598*
4:30 through the midst of them went *his* **w**, NIG
5:19 And when they could not find by what *w* NIG
7:22 Go *your* **w**, and tell John what *things* ye NIG
7:27 which shall prepare thy **w** before thee. *3598*
8: 5 and as he sowed, some fell by the **w side**; *3598*
8:12 Those by the **w side** are they that hear; then *3598*
8:39 And he went his **w**, and NIG
9:57 it came to pass *that,* as they went in the **w**, *3598*
10: 4 nor shoes: and salute no *man* by the **w**. *3598*
10:31 there came down a certain priest that **w**: *3598*
12:58 *as thou art* in the **w**, give diligence that *thou* *3598*
14:32 Or else, while the other is yet a **great w off**, *4206*
15:20 But when he was yet a **great w** off, *3112*
17:19 go *thy* **w**: thy faith hath made thee whole. NIG
18:35 a certain blind man sat by the **w side** *3598*
19: 4 tree to see him: for he was to pass that **w**. NIG
19:32 And they that were sent went their **w**, and NIG
19:36 he went, they spread their clothes in the **w**. *3598*
20:21 *of any,* but teachest the **w** of God truly: *3598*
22: 4 And he went his **w**, and communed with NIG
24:32 while he talked with us by the **w**, and *3598*
24:35 they told what *things were done* in the **w**, *3598*
Jn 1:23 Make straight the **w** of the Lord, as said *3598*
4:28 and went her **w** into the city, and saith to NIG
4:50 saith unto him, Go *thy* **w**; thy son liveth. NIG
4:50 had spoken unto him, and he went *his* **w**. NIG
8:21 I go my **w**, and ye shall seek me, and NIG
9: 7 He went his **w** therefore, and washed, and NIG
10: 1 but climbeth up **some other w**, the same is a *237*
11:28 she went her **w**, and called Mary her sister NIG
14: 4 whither I go ye know, and the **w** ye know. *3598*
14: 5 thou goest; and how can we know the **w**? *3598*
14: 6 unto him, I am the **w**, the truth, and the life: *3598*
16: 5 But now I go my **w** to him that sent me; and NIG
18: 8 therefore ye seek me, let these go their **w**: NIG
Ac 8:26 go toward the south unto the **w** that goeth *3598*
8:36 And as they went on *their* **w**, they came *3598*
8:39 no more: and he went *on* his **w** rejoicing. *3598*
9: 2 that if he found any of *this* **w**, whether they *3598*
9:15 Go *thy* **w**: for he is a chosen vessel unto me, NIG
9:17 And Ananias went his **w**, and entered into NIG
9:17 that appeared unto thee in the **w** as thou *3598*
9:27 them how he had seen the Lord in the **w**, *3598*
15: 3 And being **brought on** their **w** by *4311*
16:17 which shew unto us the **w** of salvation. *3598*
18:25 This *man* was instructed in the **w** of *3598*
18:26 expounded unto him the **w** of God more *3598*
19: 9 spake evil of *that* **w** before the multitude, *3598*
19:23 time there arose no small stir about *that* **w**. *3598*
21: 5 we departed and went *our* **w**; and *they* all NIG
21: 5 *our way;* and *they* all brought us on our **w**, NIG
22: 4 And I persecuted this **w** unto the death, *3598*
24:14 that after the **w** which they call heresy, so *3598*
24:22 having more perfect knowledge of *that* **w**, *3598*
24:25 and answered, Go *thy* **w** for *this* time; NIG
25: 3 laying wait in the **w** to kill him. *3598*
26:13 O king, I saw in the **w** a light from heaven, *3598*
Ro 3: 2 Much every **w**: chiefly, because that unto *5158*
3:12 They are all **gone out of the w**, they are *1578*
3:17 And the **w** of peace have they not known: *3598*

Ro 14:13 **put** a stumblingblock or an occasion to fall **in** *his* brother's **w**. *5087*
15:24 to be **brought on** my **w** thitherward by you, *4311*
1Co 10:13 the temptation also make a **w to escape**, *1545*
12:31 yet shew I unto you a more excellent **w**. *3598*
16: 7 For I will not see you now by the **w**; but I *3938*
2Co 1:16 of you to be **brought on** *my* **w** toward *4311*
Php 1:18 notwithstanding, every **w**, whether in *5158*
Col 2:14 and took it out of the **w**, nailing it to *his* *3319*
1Th 3:11 Lord Jesus Christ, direct our **w** unto you. *3598*
2Th 2: 7 *will let,* until he be taken out of the **w**. *3319*
Heb 5: 2 and on them that are **out of the w**; *4105*
9: 8 that the **w** into the holiest *of all* was not yet *3598*
10:20 *By* a new and living **w**, which he hath *3598*
12:13 *that which is* lame be **turned out of the w**; *1624*
Jas 1:24 and **goeth** his **w**, and straightway forgetteth *565*
2:25 and had sent *them* out another **w**? *3598*
5:20 error of his **w** shall save a soul from death, *3598*
2Pe 2: 2 by reason of whom the **w** of truth shall be *3598*
2:15 Which have forsaken the right **w**, and *3598*
2:15 following the **w** of Balaam *the son* of *3598*
2:21 not to have known the **w** of righteousness, *3598*
3: 1 up your pure minds **by w of** remembrance: *1722*
Jude 1:11 for they have gone in the **w** of Cain, and *3598*
Rev 16:12 that the **w** of the kings of the east might be *3598*

WAYFARING (6) [FARE, WAY]
Jdg 19:17 he saw a **w** man in the street of the city: 732
2Sa 12: 4 to dress for the **w man** that was come unto 732
Isa 33: 8 lie waste, the **w man** ceaseth: 734+5674
35: 8 the **w men**, though fools, shall not 1870+1980
Jer 9: 2 in the wilderness a lodging place of **w men**; 732
14: 8 as a **w man** *that* turneth aside to tarry for a 732

WAYMARKS (1) [MARK, WAY]
Jer 31:21 Set thee up **w**, make thee high heaps: 6725

WAYS (205) [WAY]
Ge 19: 2 ye shall rise up early, and go on your **w**. 1870
Lev 20: 4 **any w hide** their eyes from the man, 5956+5956
26:22 and your *high* **w** shall be desolate. 1870
Nu 30:15 if he shall **any w make** them **void** 6565+6565
Dt 5:33 You shall walk in all the **w** which 1870
8: 6 thy God, to walk in his **w**, and to fear him. 1870
10:12 to walk in all his **w**, and to love him, and 1870
11:22 to walk in all his **w**, and to cleave unto him; 1870
19: 9 LORD thy God, and to walk ever in his **w**; 1870
26:17 to walk in his **w**, and to keep his statutes, 1870
28: 7 thee one way, and flee before thee seven **w**. 1870
28: 9 of the LORD thy God, and walk in his **w**. 1870
28:25 and flee seven **w** before them: 1870
28:29 and thou shalt not prosper in thy **w**: 1870
30:16 to walk in his **w**, and to keep his 1870
32: 4 for all his **w** *are* judgment: a God of truth 1870
Jos 22: 5 to walk in all his **w**, and to keep his 1870
1Sa 8: 3 his sons walked not in his **w**, but 1870
8: 5 art old, and thy sons walk not in thy **w**: 1870
18:14 David behaved himself wisely in all his **w**; 1870
2Sa 22:22 For I have kept the **w** of the LORD, and 1870
1Ki 2: 3 to walk in his **w**, to keep his statutes, *and* 1870
3:14 if thou wilt walk in my **w**, to keep my 1870
8:39 and give to every man according to his **w**, 1870
8:58 to walk in all his **w**, and to keep his 1870
11:33 have not walked in my **w**, to do *that* which 1870
11:38 wilt walk in my **w**, and do that *is* right in 1870
22:43 walked in all the **w** of Asa his father; 1870
2Ki 17:13 Turn ye from your evil **w**, and keep my 1870
2Ch 6:30 unto every man according unto all his **w**, 1870
6:31 to walk in thy **w**, so long as they live in 1870
7:14 my face, and turn from their wicked **w**; 1870
13:22 acts of Abijah, and his **w**, and his sayings, 1870
17: 3 he walked in the first **w** of his father David, 1870
17: 6 his heart was lift up in the **w** of 1870
21:12 Because thou hast not walked in the **w** of 1870
21:12 nor in the **w** of Asa king of Judah, 1870
22: 3 He also walked in the **w** of the house of 1870
27: 6 he prepared his **w** before the LORD his 1870
27: 7 acts of Jotham, and all his wars, and his **w**, 1870
28: 2 For he walked in the **w** of the kings of 1870
28:26 Now the rest of his acts and of all his **w**, 1870
32:13 **any w able** to deliver their lands out 3201+3201
34: 2 walked in the **w** of David his father, and 1870
Job 4: 6 thy hope; and the uprightness of thy **w**? 1870
13:15 but I will maintain mine own **w** before him. 1870
21:14 for we desire not the knowledge of thy **w**. 1870
22: 3 *is it* gain *to him,* that thou makest thy **w** 1870
22:28 and the light shall shine upon thy **w**. 1870
24:13 they know not the **w** thereof, nor abide in 1870
24:23 he resteth; yet his eyes *are* upon their **w**. 1870
26:14 Lo, these *are* parts of his **w**: but how little a 1870
30:12 they raise up against me the **w** of their 734
31: 4 Doth not he see my **w**, and count all my 1870
34:11 cause every man to find according to *his* **w**. 734
34:21 For his eyes *are* upon the **w** of man, and 1870
34:27 and would not consider any of his **w**: 1870
40:19 He *is* the chief of the **w** of God: he that 1870
Ps 10: 5 His **w** are always grievous; thy judgments 1870
18:21 For I have kept the **w** of the LORD, and 1870
25: 4 Shew me thy **w**, O LORD; teach me thy 1870
39: 1 I said, I will take heed to my **w**, that *I* sin 1870
51:13 *Then* will I teach transgressors thy **w**; and 1870
81:13 unto me, *and* Israel had walked in my **w**! 1870
84: 5 in thee; in whose heart *are* the **w** *of them.* 4546
91:11 charge over thee, to keep thee in all thy **w**. 1870
95:10 *their* heart, and they have not known my **w**: 1870
103: 7 He made known his **w** unto Moses, his acts 1870
119: 3 also do no iniquity: they walk in his **w**. 1870
119: 5 O that my **w** were directed to keep thy 1870
119:15 in thy precepts, and have respect unto thy **w**. 734
119:26 I have declared my **w**, and thou heardest 1870
119:59 I thought on my **w**, and turned my feet unto 1870
119:168 for all my **w** *are* before thee. 1870
125: 5 for such as turn aside *unto* their **crooked w**, 6128
128: 1 feareth the LORD; that walketh in his **w**. 1870
138: 5 they shall sing in the **w** of the LORD: 1870
139: 3 and art acquainted *with* all my **w**. 1870
145:17 The LORD *is* righteous in all his **w**, and 1870
Pr 1:19 So *are* the **w** of every one that is greedy of 734
2:13 to walk in the **w** of darkness; 1870
2:15 Whose **w** *are* crooked, and *they* froward in 734
3: 6 In all thy **w** acknowledge him, and he shall 1870
3:17 Her **w** *are* ways of pleasantness, and all her 1870
3:17 Her ways *are* **w** of pleasantness, and all her 1870
3:31 the oppressor, and choose none of his **w**. 1870
4:26 of thy feet, and let all thy **w** be established. 1870
5: 6 her **w** are moveable, *that* thou canst not 4570
5:21 For the **w** of man *are* before the eyes of 1870
6: 6 thou sluggard; consider her **w**, and be wise: 1870
7:25 Let not thine heart decline to her **w**, go not 1870
8:32 for blessed *are they that* keep my **w**. 1870
9:15 To call passengers who go right *on* their **w**: 734
10: 9 but he that perverteth his **w** shall be known. 1870
14: 2 he that is perverse in his **w** despiseth him. 1870
14:12 but the end thereof *are* the **w** of death. 1870
14:14 in heart shall be filled with his own **w**: 1870
16: 2 All the **w** of a man *are* clean in his own 1870
16: 7 When a man's **w** please the LORD, 1870
16:25 but the end thereof *are* the **w** of death. 1870
17:23 of the bosom to pervert the **w** of judgment. 734
19:16 *but* he that despiseth his **w** shall die. 1870
22:25 Lest thou learn his **w**, and get a snare to thy 734
23:26 and let thine eyes observe my **w**. 1870
28: 6 than *he that is* perverse in *his* **w**, though he 1870
28:18 *he that is* perverse in *his* **w** shall fall at 1870
31: 3 nor thy **w** to *that which* destroyeth kings. 1870
31:27 She looketh well to the **w** of her household, 1979
Ecc 11: 9 walk in the **w** of thine heart, and in 1870
SS 3: 2 the city in the streets and in the **broad w**, 7339
Isa 2: 3 he will teach us of his **w**, and we will walk 1870
42:24 for they would not walk in his **w**, 1870
45:13 in righteousness, and I will direct all his **w**: 1870
49: 9 They shall feed in the **w**, and their pastures 1870
55: 8 neither *are* your **w** my ways, saith 1870
55: 8 neither *are* your ways my **w**, saith 1870
55: 9 so are my **w** higher than your ways, and 1870
55: 9 so are my ways higher than your **w**, and 1870
57:18 I have seen his **w**, and will heal him: I will 1870
58: 2 seek me daily, and delight to know my **w**, 1870
58:13 shalt honour him, not doing thine own **w**, 1870
63:17 why hast thou made us to err from thy **w**, 1870
64: 5 *those that* remember thee in thy **w**: 1870
66: 3 they have chosen their own **w**, and 1870
Jer 2:23 *art* a swift dromedary traversing her **w**; 1870
2:33 thou also taught the wicked ones thy **w**. 1870
3: 2 In the **w** hast thou sat for them, as 1870
3:13 hast scattered thy **w** to the strangers under 1870
6:16 Stand ye in the **w**, and see, and ask for 1870
7: 3 Amend your **w** and your doings, and I will 1870

Jer 7: 5 For if you throughly amend your w and 1870
7:23 walk ye in all the w that I have commanded 1870
12:16 if they will diligently learn the w of my 1870
15: 7 *sith* they return not from their w. 1870
16:17 For mine eyes *are* upon all their w: they are 1870
17:10 even to give every man according to his w, 1870
18:11 and make your w and your doings good. 1870
18:15 stumble in their w *from* the ancient paths, 1870
23:12 be unto them as slippery *w* in the darkness: NIH
26:13 Therefore now amend your w and 1870
32:19 for thine eyes *are* open upon all the w of 1870
32:19 to give every one according to his w, and 1870
La 1: 4 The w of Zion do mourn, because 1870
3: 9 He hath inclosed my w with hewn stone, 1870
3:11 He hath turned aside my w, and pulled me 1870
3:40 Let us search and try our w, and turn again 1870
Eze 7: 3 will judge thee according to thy w, and 1870
7: 4 I will recompense thy w upon thee, and 1870
7: 8 I will judge thee according to thy w, and 1870
7: 9 I will recompense thee according to thy w 1870
14:23 when ye see their w and their doings: 1870
16:47 Yet hast thou not walked after their w, 1870
16:47 wast corrupted more than they in all thy w. 1870
16:61 thou shalt remember thy w, and 1870
18:23 *and* not that he should return from his w, 1870
18:25 not my way equal? are not your w unequal? 1870
18:29 O house of Israel, are not my w equal? 1870
18:29 my ways equal? are not your w unequal? 1870
18:30 of Israel, every one according to his w, 1870
20:43 there shall ye remember your w, and all 1870
20:44 not according to your wicked w, 1870
21:19 Also, thou son of man, appoint thee two w, 1870
21:21 at the head of the two w, to use divination: 1870
24:14 according to thy w, and according to thy 1870
28:15 Thou *wast* perfect in thy w from the day 1870
33:11 turn ye, turn ye from your evil w; for why 1870
33:20 I will judge you every one after his w. 1870
36:31 shall ye remember your own evil w, and 1870
36:32 and confounded for your own w, 1870
Da 4:37 whose works *are* truth, and his w judgment: 735
5:23 hand thy breath *is*, and whose *are* all thy w, 735
Hos 4: 9 I will punish them for their w, and 1870
9: 8 prophet *is* a snare of a fowler in all his w, 1870
12: 2 and *will* punish Jacob according to his w; 1870
14: 9 for the w of the LORD *are* right, and 1870
Joel 2: 7 they shall march every one on his w, and 1870
Mic 4: 2 he will teach us of his w, and we will walk 1870
Na 2: 4 justle one against another in the **broad** w: 7339
Hab 3: 6 hills did bow: his w *are* everlasting. 1979
Hag 1: 5 the LORD of hosts; Consider your w. 1870
1: 7 the LORD of hosts; Consider your w. 1870
Zec 1: 4 Turn ye now from your evil w, and 1870
1: 6 according to our w, and according to our 1870
3: 7 If thou wilt walk in my w, and if thou wilt 1870
Mal 2: 9 according as ye have not kept my w, but 1870
Mt 8:33 and went their w into the city, and NIG
22: 5 But they made light of *it*, and went their w, NIG
Mk 11: 4 door without in a place where two w met; NIG
Lk 1:76 the face of the Lord to prepare his w; *3598*
3: 5 and the rough w *shall be* made smooth; *3598*
10: 3 Go your w: behold, I send you forth as NIG
10:10 go *your* w out into the streets of the same, NIG
Jn 11:46 But some of them went their w to NIG
Ac 2:28 Thou hast made known to me the w of life; *3598*
13:10 wilt thou not cease to pervert the right w of *3598*
14:16 suffered all nations to walk in their own w. *3598*
Ro 3:16 Destruction and misery *are* in their w: *3598*
11:33 his judgments, and his w past finding out! *3598*
1Co 4:17 remembrance of my w which be in Christ, *3598*
Heb 3:10 *their* heart; and they have not known my w. *3598*
Jas 1: 8 double minded man *is* unstable in all his w. *3598*
1:11 also shall the rich *man* fade away in his w. *4197*
2Pe 2: 2 And many shall follow their **pernicious** w; *684*
Rev 15: 3 just and true *are* thy w, thou King of saints. *3598*
16: 1 Go your w, and pour out the vials of NIG

W

WAYSIDE (1) [SIDE, WAY]
1Sa 4:13 sat upon a seat *by* the w watching: 1870+3027

WAYWARDNESS See BACKSLIDERS; BACKSLIDING

WE (1844) [OUR, OURS, OURSELVES, US, US-WARD] See Index

WEAK (46) [WEAKEN, WEAKENED, WEAKENETH, WEAKER, WEAKNESS]
Nu 13:18 whether they *be* strong or w, few or many; 7504
Jdg 16: 7 then shall I be w, and be as another man. 2470
16:11 shall I be w, and be as another man. 2470
16:17 I shall become w, and be like any *other* 2470
2Sa 3:39 I *am this* day w, though anointed king; and 7390
17: 2 upon him while he *is* weary and w handed, 7504
2Ch 15: 7 and let not your hands be w: 7503
Job 4: 3 and thou hast strengthened the w hands. 7504
Ps 6: 2 mercy upon me, O LORD; for I *am* w: 536
109:24 My knees are w through fasting; and 3782
Isa 14:10 unto thee, Art thou also **become** w as we? 2470
35: 3 Strengthen ye the w hands, and confirm 7504
Eze 7:17 be feeble, and all knees shall be w *as* water. 1980
16:30 How w is thine heart, saith the Lord GOD, 535
21: 7 and all knees shall be w *as* water: 1980
Joel 3:10 into spears: let the w say, I *am* strong. 2523
Mt 26:41 the spirit indeed *is* willing, but the flesh *is* w. *772*
Mk 14:38 The spirit truly *is* ready, but the flesh *is* w. *772*
Ac 20:35 so labouring *ye* ought to support the w, *770*
Ro 4:19 And being not w in faith, he considered not *770*
8: 3 not do, in that it was w through the flesh, *770*
14: 1 Him that is w in the faith receive you, *but* *770*
14: 2 all *things*: another, who is w, eateth herbs. *770*
14:21 or is offended, or is *made* w. *770*
15: 1 strong ought to bear the infirmities of the w, *102*
1Co 1:27 God hath chosen the w *things* of the world to *772*
4:10 we *are* w, but ye *are* strong; ye *are* *772*
8: 7 and their conscience being w is defiled. *772*
8: 9 become a stumblingblock to them that are w. *770*
8:10 shall not the conscience of him which is w *772*
8:11 And through thy knowledge shall the w *770*
8:12 the brethren, and wound their w conscience, *770*
9:22 To the w became I as weak, that I might gain *772*
9:22 To the weak became I as w, that I might gain *772*
9:22 became I as weak, that I might gain the w: *772*
11:30 For this cause many *are* w and sickly among *772*
2Co 10:10 but *his* bodily presence *is* w, and *his* speech *772*
11:21 as though we had been w. *770*
11:29 Who is w, and I am not weak? who is *770*
11:29 Who is weak, and I am not w? who is *770*
12:10 for when I am w, then am I strong. *770*
13: 3 which to you-ward is not w, but is mighty in *770*
13: 4 For we also are w in him, but we shall live *770*
13: 9 are glad, when we are w, and ye are strong: *770*
Gal 4: 9 how turn ye again to the w and *772*
1Th 5:14 comfort the feebleminded, support the w, *772*

WEAK-WILLED See SILLY

WEAKEN (1) [WEAK]
Isa 14:12 to the ground, which didst w the nations! 2522

WEAKENED (3) [WEAK]
Ezr 4: 4 the people of the land w the hands of 7503
Ne 6: 9 Their hands shall be w from the work, 7503
Ps 102:23 He w my strength in the way; he shortened 6031

WEAKENETH (2) [WEAK]
Job 12:21 and w the strength of the mighty. 7503
Jer 38: 4 for thus he w the hands of the men of war 7503

WEAKER (3) [WEAK]
2Sa 3: 1 the house of Saul **waxed** w and weaker. 1980
3: 1 and the house of Saul waxed weaker and w. 1800
1Pe 3: 7 as unto the w vessel, and as *being* heirs *772*

WEAKNESS (7) [WEAK]
1Co 1:25 and the w of God is stronger than men. *772*
2: 3 And I was with you in w, and in fear, and *769*
15:43 it is sown in w; it is raised in power: *769*
2Co 12: 9 for my strength is made perfect in w. *769*
13: 4 For though he was crucified through w, *769*
Heb 7:18 of the commandment going before for the w *772*
11:34 out of w were made strong, waxed valiant in *769*

WEALTH (27) [WEALTHY]
Ge 34:29 all their w, and all their little ones, and their 2428
Dt 8:17 might of mine hand hath gotten me this w. 2428
8:18 for *it is* he that giveth thee power to get w, 2428
Ru 2: 1 a mighty man of w, of the family of 2428
1Sa 2:32 in all *the* w which *God* shall give Israel: NIH
2Ki 15:20 *even* of all the mighty *men* of w, of each 2428

2Ch 1:11 thou hast not asked riches, w, or honour, 5233
1:12 I will give thee riches, and w, and honour, 5233
Ezr 9:12 nor seek their peace or their w for ever: 2896
Est 10: 3 seeking the w of his people, and 2896
Job 21:13 They spend their days in w, and in a 2896
31:25 If I rejoiced because my w *was* great, and 2428
Ps 44:12 and dost not increase *thy* w by their price. NIH
49: 6 They that trust in their w, and 2428
49:10 person perish, and leave their w to others. 2428
112: 3 **W** and riches *shall be* in his house: and 1952
Pr 5:10 Lest strangers be filled *with* thy w; and 3581
10:15 The rich *man's* w *is* his strong city: 1952
13:11 **W** *gotten* by vanity shall be diminished: but 1952
13:22 the w of the sinner *is* laid up for the just. 2428
18:11 The rich *man's* w *is* his strong city, and as a 1952
19: 4 **W** maketh many friends; but the poor is 1952
Ecc 5:19 also to whom God hath given riches and w, 5233
6: 2 w, and honour, so that he wanteth nothing 5233
Zec 14:14 the w of all the heathen round about shall 2428
Ac 19:25 ye know that by this craft we have our w. *2142*
1Co 10:24 seek his own, but every man another's *w*. NIG

WEALTHY (2) [WEALTH]
Ps 66:12 but thou broughtest us out into a w *place*. 7310
Jer 49:31 Arise, get you up unto the w nation, 7961

WEANED (12)
Ge 21: 8 the child grew, and was w: and 1580
21: 8 a great feast the *same* day that Isaac was w. 1580
1Sa 1:22 *I will not go up* until the child be w, and 1580
1:23 thee good; tarry until thou have w him; 1580
1:23 and gave her son suck until she w him. 1580
1:24 when she had w him, she took him up with 1580
1Ki 11:20 whom Tahpenes w in Pharaoh's house: 1580
Ps 131: 2 as a **child** that is w of his mother: 1580
131: 2 of his mother: my soul *is even* as a w **child**. 1580
Isa 11: 8 the w **child** shall put his hand on 1580
28: 9 them that are w from the milk, *and* 1580
Hos 1: 8 Now when she had w Lo-ruhamah, 1580

WEAPON (8) [WEAPONS]
Nu 35:18 Or *if* he smite him with a hand w of wood, 3627
Dt 23:13 thou shalt have a paddle upon thy w; and 240
2Ch 23:10 every man having his w in his hand, 7973
Ne 4:17 the work, and with the other *hand* held a w. 7973
Job 20:24 He shall flee from the iron w, *and* the bow 5402
Isa 54:17 No w *that* is formed against thee shall 3627
Eze 9: 1 even every man *with* his destroying w in 3627
9: 2 and every man a slaughter w in his hand; 3627

WEAPONS (21) [WEAPON]
Ge 27: 3 thy w, thy quiver and thy bow, and go out 3627
Dt 1:41 when ye had girded on every man his w of 3627
Jdg 18:11 six hundred men appointed *with* w of war. 3627
18:16 the six hundred men appointed *with* their w 3627
18:17 men that were appointed *with* w of war. 3627
1Sa 21: 8 brought my sword nor my w with me, 3627
2Sa 1:27 mighty fallen, and the w of war perished! 3627
2Ki 11: 8 every man with his w in his hand: 3627
11:11 every man with his w in his hand, 3627
2Ch 23: 7 every man with his w in his hand; 3627
Ecc 9:18 Wisdom *is* better than w of war: but 3627
Isa 13: 5 the LORD, and the w of his indignation, 3627
Jer 21: 4 I *will* turn back the w of war that *are* in 3627
22: 7 against thee, every one with his w: 3627
50:25 hath brought forth the w of his indignation: 3627
51:20 Thou *art* my battle axe *and* w of war: 3627
Eze 32:27 which are gone down *to* hell with their w of 3627
39: 9 shall set on fire and burn the w, both 5402
39:10 for they shall burn the w with fire: 5402
Jn 18: 3 thither with lanterns and torches and w. *3696*
2Co 10: 4 (For the w of our warfare *are* not carnal, *3696*

WEAR (12) [WARE, WEARETH, WEARING]
Ex 18:18 Thou wilt **surely** w **away**, both thou, 5034+5034
Dt 22: 5 The woman shall not w that which 1961+5921
22:11 Thou shalt not w a garment of divers sorts, 3847
1Sa 2:28 to burn incense, to w an ephod before me? 5375
22:18 and five persons that did w a linen ephod. 5375
Est 6: 8 be brought which the king *useth* to w, 3847
Job 14:19 The waters w the stones: thou washest 7833
Isa 4: 1 eat our own bread, and w our own apparel: 3847
Da 7:25 shall w **out** the saints of the most High, and 1080
Zec 13: 4 neither shall they w a rough garment to 3847
Mt 11: 8 they that w soft *clothing* are in kings' *5409*
Lk 9:12 And *when* the day began to w **away**, then *2827*

WEARETH (1) [WEAR]
Jas 2: 3 And ye have respect to him that w the gay *5409*

WEARIED (14) [WEARY]
Ge 19:11 so that they w themselves to find the door. 3811
Isa 43:23 with an offering, nor w thee with incense. 3021
43:24 thou hast w me with thine iniquities. 3021
47:13 Thou art w in the multitude of thy counsels. 3811
57:10 Thou art w in the greatness of thy way; 3021
Jer 4:31 for my soul is w because of murderers. 5888
12: 5 they have w thee, then how canst thou 3811
12: 5 *they w thee,* then how wilt thou do in NIH
Eze 24:12 She hath w *herself with* lies, and her great 3811
Mic 6: 3 wherein have I w thee? testify against me. 3811
Mal 2:17 Ye have w the LORD with your words. 3021
2:17 Wherein have we w *him?* When ye say, 3021
Jn 4: 6 Jesus therefore, being w with *his* journey, *2872*
Heb 12: 3 lest ye be w and faint in your minds. *2577*

WEARIETH (2) [WEARY]
Job 37:11 Also by watering he w the thick cloud: 2959
Ecc 10:15 The labour of the foolish w every one of 3021

WEARINESS (3) [WEARY]
Ecc 12:12 no end; and much study *is* a w of the flesh. 3024
Mal 1:13 what a w *is it!* and ye have snuffed at it, 4972
2Co 11:27 In w and painfulness, in watchings often, *2873*

WEARING (3) [WEAR]
1Sa 14: 3 the LORD'S priest in Shiloh, w an ephod. 5375
Jn 19: 5 w the crown of thorns, and the purple robe. *5409*
1Pe 3: 3 and of w of gold, or of putting on of *4025*

WEARISOME (1) [WEARY]
Job 7: 3 and w nights are appointed to me. 5999

WEARY (42) [WEARIED, WEARIETH, WEARINESS, WEARISOME]
Ge 27:46 I am w of my life because of the daughters 6973
Dt 25:18 behind thee, when thou *wast* faint and w; 3023
Jdg 4:21 for he was fast asleep and w. So he died. 5774
8:15 should give bread unto thy men *that are* w? 3287
2Sa 16:14 came w, and refreshed themselves there. 5889
17: 2 I will come upon him while he *is* w and 3023
17:29 and w, and thirsty, in the wilderness. 5889
23:10 smote the Philistines until his hand was w, 3021
Job 3:17 and there the w be at rest. 3019+3581
10: 1 My soul is w of my life; I will leave my 5354
16: 7 now he hath **made** me w: thou hast made 3811
22: 7 Thou hast not given water to the w to drink, 5889
Ps 6: 6 I am w with my groaning; all the night 3021
68: 9 confirm thine inheritance, when it was w. 3811
69: 3 I am w of my crying: my throat is dried: 3021
Pr 3:11 the LORD; neither be w of his correction: 6973
25:17 lest he be w *of* thee, and *so* hate thee. 7646
Isa 1:14 are a trouble unto me; I am w to bear *them.* 3811
5:27 None *shall be* w nor stumble amongst 5889
7:13 *Is it* a small thing for you to w men, but 3811
7:13 to weary men, but will ye w my God also? 3811
16:12 when it is seen that Moab is w on the high 3811
28:12 rest *wherewith* ye may cause the w to rest; 5889
32: 2 as the shadow of a great rock in a w land. 5889
40:28 ends of the earth, fainteth not, neither is w? 3021
40:30 Even the youths shall faint and be w, and 3021
40:31 they shall run, and not be w; *and* they shall 3021
43:22 but thou hast been w of me, O Israel. 3021
46: 1 *they are* a burden to the w *beast.* 5889
50: 4 to speak a word in season to *him that is* w: 3287
Jer 2:24 all they that seek her will not w themselves; 3286
6:11 of the LORD; I am w with holding in: 3811
9: 5 *and* w themselves to commit iniquity. 3811
15: 6 and destroy thee; I am w with repenting. 3811
20: 9 I was w with forbearing, and I could not 3811
31:25 For I have satiated the w soul, and I have 5889
51:58 and the folk in the fire, and they shall be w. 3286
51:64 they shall be w. Thus far *are* the words of 3286
Hab 2:13 the people shall w themselves for very 3286
Lk 18: 5 lest by her continual coming she w me. *5299*
Gal 6: 9 And let us not be w in well doing: for in *1573*
2Th 3:13 But ye, brethren, be not w in well doing. *1573*

WEASEL (1)
Lev 11:29 the w, and the mouse, and the tortoise after 2467

WEATHER (4)
Job 37:22 **Fair** w cometh out of the north: with God 2091
Pr 25:20 *As* he that taketh away a garment in cold w, 3117
Mt 16: 2 it is evening, ye say, *It will be* **fair** w: *2105*
16: 3 in the morning, *It will be* **foul** w to day: *5494*

WEAVE (2) [WEAVER, WEAVER'S, WEAVEST, WOVE, WOVEN]
Isa 19: 9 they that w networks, shall be confounded. 707
59: 5 cockatrice' eggs, and w the spider's web: 707

WEAVER (2) [WEAVE]
Ex 35:35 in scarlet, and in fine linen, and of the w, 707
Isa 38:12 I have cut off like a w my life: he will cut 707

WEAVER'S (5) [WEAVE]
1Sa 17: 7 And the staff of his spear *was* like a w beam; 707
2Sa 21:19 the staff of whose spear *was* like a w beam. 707
1Ch 11:23 in the Egyptian's hand *was* a spear like a w 707
20: 5 whose spear staff *was* like a w beam. 707
Job 7: 6 My days are swifter than a w **shuttle**, and 708

WEAVEST (1) [WEAVE]
Jdg 16:13 If thou w the seven locks of my head with 707

WEB (4) [WEBS]
Jdg 16:13 the seven locks of my head with the w. 4545
16:14 with the pin of the beam, and with the w. 4545
Job 8:14 and whose trust *shall be* a spider's w. 1004
Isa 59: 5 cockatrice' eggs, and weave the spider's w: 6980

WEBS (1) [WEB]
Isa 59: 6 Their w shall not become garments, 6980

WEDDING (7) [WEDLOCK]
Mt 22: 3 to call them that were bidden to the w: *1062*
22: 8 The w is ready, but they which were bidden *1062*
22:10 good: and the w was furnished with guests. *1062*
22:11 he saw there a man which had not on a w *1062*
22:12 how camest thou in hither not having a w *1062*
Lk 12:36 their lord, when he will return from the w; *1062*
14: 8 When thou art bidden of any *man* to a w, *1062*

WEDGE (3)
Jos 7:21 a w of gold of fifty shekels weight, then 3956
7:24 the w of gold, and his sons, and his 3956
Isa 13:12 even a man than the **golden** w of Ophir. 3800

WEDLOCK (1) [WEDDING]
Eze 16:38 as *women* that **break** w and shed blood are 5003

WEED See COCKLE

WEEDS (1)
Jnh 2: 5 the w *were* wrapt about my head. 5488

WEEK (13) [WEEKS]
Ge 29:27 Fulfil her w, and we will give thee this also 7620
29:28 Jacob did so, and fulfilled her w: and 7620
Da 9:27 confirm the covenant with many *for* one w: 7620
9:27 *in* the midst of the w he shall cause 7620
Mt 28: 1 to dawn towards the first *day* of the w, *4521*
Mk 16: 2 early in the morning the first *day* of the w, *4521*
16: 9 *Jesus* was risen early the first *day* of the w, *4521*
Lk 18:12 I fast twice in the w, I give tithes of all that *4521*
24: 1 Now upon the first *day* of the w, very early *4521*
Jn 20: 1 The first *day* of the w cometh Mary *4521*
20:19 day at evening, being the first *day* of the w, *4521*
Ac 20: 7 And upon the first *day* of the w, when *4521*
1Co 16: 2 Upon the first *day* of the w let every one of *4521*

WEEKS (15) [WEEK]
Ex 34:22 thou shalt observe the feast of w, of 7620
Lev 12: 5 she shall be unclean **two** w, as *in* her 7620
Nu 28:26 after your w *be out,* ye shall have a holy 7620
Dt 16: 9 Seven w shalt thou number unto thee: 7620
16: 9 begin to number the seven w from *such* 7620
16:10 thou shalt keep the feast of w unto 7620
16:16 in the feast of w, and in the feast of 7620
2Ch 8:13 in the feast of w, and in the feast of 7620
Jer 5:24 he reserveth unto us the appointed w of 7620
Da 9:24 Seventy w are determined upon thy people 7620
9:25 the Messiah the Prince *shall be* seven w, 7620
9:25 *be* seven weeks, and threescore and two w: 7620
9:26 and two w shall Messiah be cut off, 7620
10: 2 I Daniel was mourning three **full** w. 3117+7620
10: 3 till three **whole** w were fulfilled. 3117+7620

WEEP (49) [WEEPEST, WEEPETH, WEEPING, WEPT]
Ge 23: 2 came to mourn for Sarah, and to w for her. 1058
43:30 he sought *where* to w; and he entered into 1058
Nu 11:10 Moses heard the people w throughout their 1058
11:13 for they w unto me, saying, Give us flesh, 1058
1Sa 11: 5 What aileth the people that they w? 1058
30: 4 wept, until they had no more power to w. 1058
2Sa 1:24 Ye daughters of Israel, w over Saul, 1058
12:21 thou didst fast and w for the child, *while it* 1058
2Ch 34:27 didst rend thy clothes, and w before me; 1058
Ne 8: 9 the LORD your God; mourn not, nor w. 1058
Job 27:15 in death: and his widows shall not w. 1058
30:25 Did not I w for him that was in trouble? 1058
30:31 and my organ into the voice of them that w. 1058
Ecc 3: 4 A time to w, and a time to laugh; a time to 1058
Isa 15: 2 and *to* Dibon, the high places, to w: 1065
22: 4 I will w bitterly, labour not to comfort me, 1065
30:19 thou shalt w no **more**: he will be 1058+1058
33: 7 the ambassadors of peace shall w bitterly. 1058
Jer 9: 1 that I might w day and night for the slain of 1058
13:17 my soul shall w in secret places for *your* 1058
13:17 mine eye shall w **sore**, and run down 1830+1830
22:10 W ye not for the dead, neither bemoan him: 1058
22:10 *but* w **sore** for him that goeth away: 1058+1058
48:32 I will w for thee with the weeping of Jazer: 1058
La 1:16 For these *things* I w; mine eye, mine eye 1058
Eze 24:16 yet neither shalt thou mourn nor w, 1058
24:23 ye shall not mourn nor w; but ye shall pine 1058
27:31 they shall w for thee with bitterness of 1058
Joel 1: 5 Awake, ye drunkards, and w; and howl, 1058
2:17 w between the porch and the altar, and 1058
Mic 1:10 ye *it* not at Gath, w ye not **at all**: 1058+1058
Zec 7: 3 Should I w in the fifth month, 1058
Mk 5:39 unto them, Why make ye *this* ado, and w? *2799*
Lk 6:21 Blessed *are ye* that w now: for ye shall *2799*
6:25 that laugh now: for ye shall mourn and w. *2799*
7:13 on her, and said unto her, W not. *2799*
8:52 but he said, W not; she is not dead, but *2799*
23:28 w not for me, but weep for yourselves, and *2799*
23:28 but w for yourselves, and for your children. *2799*
Jn 11:31 saying, She goeth unto the grave to w there. *2799*
16:20 That ye shall w and lament, but the world *2799*
Ac 21:13 What mean ye to w and to break *2799+4160*
Ro 12:15 that do rejoice, and w with them that weep. *2799*
12:15 that do rejoice, and weep with them that w. *2799*
1Co 7:30 And they that w, as though they wept not; *2799*
Jas 4: 9 Be afflicted, and mourn, and w: let your *2799*
5: 1 ye rich *men,* w and howl for your miseries *2799*
Rev 5: 5 And one of the elders saith unto me, W not: *2799*
18:11 And the merchants of the earth *shall* w and *2799*

WEEPEST (3) [WEEP]
1Sa 1: 8 her husband to her, Hannah, why w thou? 1058
Jn 20:13 they say unto her, Woman, why w thou? *2799*
20:15 Jesus saith unto her, Woman, why w thou? *2799*

WEEPETH (4) [WEEP]
2Sa 19: 1 the king w and mourneth for Absalom. 1058
2Ki 8:12 Hazael said, Why w my lord? And he 1058
Ps 126: 6 He that goeth forth and w, bearing precious 1058
La 1: 2 She w **sore** in the night, and her tears 1058+1058

WEEPING (44) [WEEP]
Nu 25: 6 who *were* w *before* the door of 1058
Dt 34: 8 so the days of w *and* mourning for Moses 1065
2Sa 3:16 her husband went with her along w behind 1058
15:30 and they went up, w as they went up. 1058
Ezr 3:13 joy from the noise of the w of the people: 1065
10: 1 w and casting himself down before 1058
Est 4: 3 the Jews, and fasting, and w, and wailing; 1065
Job 16:16 My face is foul with w, and on mine 1065
Ps 6: 8 the LORD hath heard the voice of my w. 1065
30: 5 w may endure for a night, but joy *cometh* 1065
102: 9 like bread, and mingled my drink with w, 1065
Isa 15: 3 every one shall howl, w abundantly. 1065
15: 5 for *by* the mounting up of Luhith with w 1065
16: 9 Therefore I will bewail with the w of Jazer 1065
22:12 day did the Lord GOD of hosts call to w, 1065
65:19 the voice of w shall be no more heard in 1065
Jer 3:21 w *and* supplications of the children of 1065

W

Jer 9:10 For the mountains will I take up a w and 1065
31: 9 They shall come with w, and 1065
31:15 heard in Ramah, lamentation, *and* bitter w; 1065
31:15 Rahel w for her children refused to be 1058
31:16 Refrain thy voice from w, and thine eyes 1065
41: 6 to meet them, w all along as he went: 1058
48: 5 of Luhith **continual** w shall go up; 1065+1065
48:32 I will weep for thee with the w of Jazer: 1065
50: 4 children of Judah together, going and w: 1058
Eze 8:14 behold, there sat women w for Tammuz. 1058
Joel 2:12 and with w, and with mourning: 1065
Mal 2:13 *with* tears, *with* w, and *with* crying out, 1065
Mt 2:18 lamentation, and w, and great mourning, *2805*
2:18 Rachel w for her children, and would not *2799*
8:12 there shall be w and gnashing of teeth. *2805*
22:13 there shall be w and gnashing of teeth. *2805*
24:51 there shall be w and gnashing of teeth. *2805*
25:30 there shall be w and gnashing of teeth. *2805*
Lk 7:38 And stood at his feet behind *him* w, and *2799*
13:28 There shall be w and gnashing of teeth, *2805*
Jn 11:33 When Jesus therefore saw her w, and *2799*
11:33 and the Jews also w which came with her, *2799*
20:11 But Mary stood without at the sepulchre w: *2799*
Ac 9:39 and all the widows stood by him w, and *2799*
Php 3:18 told you often, and now tell *you* even w, *2799*
Rev 18:15 for the fear of her torment, w and wailing, *2799*
18:19 and cried, w and wailing, saying, Alas, *2799*

WEIGH (6) [UNWEIGHED, WEIGHED, WEIGHETH, WEIGHING, WEIGHT, WEIGHTIER, WEIGHTS, WEIGHTY]
1Ch 20: 2 found it to w a talent of gold, and 4948
Ezr 8:29 keep *them,* until ye w *them* before the chief 8254
Ps 58: 2 you w the violence of your hands in 6424
Isa 26: 7 most upright, dost w the path of the just. 6424
46: 6 w silver in the balance, *and* hire a 8254
Eze 5: 1 take thee balances to w, and divide 4948

WEIGHED (17) [WEIGH]
Ge 23:16 Abraham w to Ephron the silver, which he 8254
Nu 7:85 all the silver vessels *w* two thousand and NIH
1Sa 2: 3 of knowledge, and by him actions are w. 8505
17: 7 his spear's head *w* six hundred shekels *of* NIH
2Sa 14:26 he w the hair of his head *at* two hundred 8254
21:16 the weight of whose spear *w* three hundred NIH
Ezr 8:25 w unto them the silver, and the gold, and 8254
8:26 I even w unto their hand six hundred and 8254
8:33 the vessels w in the house of our God by 8254
Job 6: 2 Oh that my grief were **throughly** w, 8254+8254
28:15 neither shall silver be w *for* the price 8254
31: 6 Let me be w in an even balance, that God 8254
Isa 40:12 w the mountains in scales, and the hills in a 8254
Jer 32: 9 *was* in Anathoth, and w him the money, 8254
32:10 w *him* the money in the balances. 8254
Da 5:27 Thou art w in the balances, and art found 8625
Zec 11:12 So they w *for* my price thirty *pieces* of 8254

WEIGHETH (2) [WEIGH]
Job 28:25 the winds; and he w the waters by measure. 8505
Pr 16: 2 his own eyes; but the LORD w the spirits. 8505

WEIGHING (2) [WEIGH]
Nu 7:85 Each charger of silver *w* an hundred and NIH
7:86 full *of* incense, *w* ten *shekels* apiece, NIH

WEIGHT (58) [WEIGH]
Ge 24:22 took a golden earring of half a shekel w, 4948
24:22 two bracelets for her hands of ten *shekels* w 4948
43:21 the mouth of his sack, our money in **full** w: 4948
Ex 30:34 of each shall there be a like *w*: NIH
Lev 19:35 in meteyard, in w, or in measure. 4948
26:26 shall deliver *you* your bread again by w: 4948
Nu 7:13 the w thereof *was* an hundred and 4948
7:19 the w whereof *was* an hundred and 4948
7:25 the w whereof *was* an hundred and 4948
7:31 one silver charger of the w of an hundred 4948
7:37 the w whereof *was* an hundred and 4948
7:43 one silver charger of the w of an hundred 4948
7:49 the w whereof *was* an hundred and 4948
7:55 one silver charger of the w of an hundred 4948
7:61 the w whereof *was* an hundred and 4948
7:67 the w whereof *was* an hundred and 4948
7:73 the w whereof *was* an hundred and 4948
7:79 the w whereof *was* an hundred and 4948
Dt 25:15 *But* thou shalt have a perfect and just w, 68
Jos 7:21 and a wedge of gold of fifty shekels w, then 4948
Jdg 8:26 the w of the golden earrings that he 4948
1Sa 17: 5 the w of the coat *was* five thousand shekels 4948
2Sa 12:30 the w whereof *was* a talent of gold with 4948
14:26 *at* two hundred shekels after the king's w. 68
21:16 the w of whose spear *weighed* three 4948
21:16 three hundred *shekels* of brass *in* w, 4948
1Ki 7:47 neither was the w of the brass found out. 4948
10:14 Now the w of gold that came to Solomon in 4948
2Ki 25:16 the brass of all these vessels was without w. 4948
1Ch 21:25 the place six hundred shekels of gold *by* w. 4948
22: 3 and brass in abundance without w; 4948
22:14 of brass and iron without w; for it is in 4948
28:14 *He gave* of gold by w for *things of* gold, 4948
28:14 *also* for all instruments of silver by w, 4948
28:15 Even the w for the candlesticks of gold, and 4948
28:15 by w for every candlestick, and *for* 4948
28:15 for the candlesticks of silver by w, *both* for 4948
28:16 *by* w *he gave* gold for the tables of 4948
28:17 for the golden basons *he gave gold* by w for 4948
28:17 *likewise silver* by w for every bason of 4948
28:18 for the altar of incense refined gold by w; 4948
2Ch 3: 9 the w of the nails *was* fifty shekels of gold. 4948
4:18 for the w of the brass could not be found 4948
9:13 Now the w of gold that came to Solomon in 4948
Ezr 8:30 and the Levites the w of the silver, 4948
8:34 By number *and* by w of every one: and 4948
8:34 and all the w was written at that time. 4948
Job 28:25 To make the w for the winds; and 4948
Pr 11: 1 to the LORD: but a just w *is* his delight. 68
16:11 A just w and balance *are* the LORD'S: 6425
Jer 52:20 the brass of all these vessels was without w. 4948
Eze 4:10 thy meat which thou shalt eat *shall be* by w, 4946
4:16 they shall eat bread by w, and with care; 4948
Zec 5: 8 he cast the w of lead upon the mouth thereof. 68
Jn 19:39 and aloes, about an hundred pound *w*. NIG
2Co 4:17 a far more exceeding *and* eternal w of glory; *922*
Heb 12: 1 let us lay aside every w, and the sin which *3591*
Rev 16:21 *every stone* about the w **of a talent**: *5006*

WEIGHTIER (1) [WEIGH]
Mt 23:23 and have omitted the w *matters* of the law, *926*

WEIGHTS (6) [WEIGH]
Lev 19:36 just w, a just ephah, and a just hin, shall ye 68
Dt 25:13 not have in thy bag **divers** w, 68+68+2050.1
Pr 16:11 all the w of the bag *are* his work. 68
20:10 **Divers** w, *and* divers measures, 68+68+2050.1
20:23 **Divers** w *are* an abomination unto 68+68+2050.1
Mic 6:11 and with the bag of deceitful w? 68

WEIGHTY (2) [WEIGH]
Pr 27: 3 A stone *is* heavy, and the sand w; but 5192
2Co 10:10 For *his* letters, say they, *are* w and powerful; *926*

WELDING See SODERING

WELFARE (7) [WELL]
Ge 43:27 he asked them of *their* w, and said, *Is* your 7965
Ex 18: 7 they asked each other of *their* w; and 7965
1Ch 18:10 to inquire of his w, and to congratulate him, 7965
Ne 2:10 man to seek the w of the children of Israel. 2896
Job 30:15 and my w passeth away as a cloud. 3444
Ps 69:22 *that which should have been* for *their* w, 7965
Jer 38: 4 for this man seeketh not the w of this 7965

WELL (258) [BEER-LAHAI-ROI, WELFARE, WELL'S, WELLBELOVED, WELL-BELOVED, WELLFAVOURED, WELLS, WELLSPRING]
Ge 4: 7 If thou doest w, *shalt thou* not be accepted? 3190
4: 7 if thou doest not w, sin lieth at the door. 3190
12:13 that it may be w with me for thy sake; and 3190
12:16 he **entreated** Abram w for her sake: and 3190
13:10 that it *was* w **watered** every where, 4945
16:14 Wherefore the w was called Beer-lahai-roi; 875
18:11 and Sarah *were* old *and* w **stricken** in age; 935
21:19 opened her eyes, and she saw a w of water; 875
21:25 because of a w of water, 875
21:30 a witness unto me, that I have digged this w. 875
24: 1 Abraham was old, *and* w **stricken** in age: 935
24:11 by a w of water at the time of the evening, 875
24:13 Behold, I stand *here* by the w of water; and 5869
24:16 she went down to the w, and filled her 5869
24:20 and ran again unto the w to draw *water,* and 875
24:29 Laban ran out unto the man, unto the w. 5869

Ge 24:30 behold, he stood by the camels at the **w**. 5869
24:42 I came this day unto the **w**, and said, 5869
24:43 Behold, I stand by the **w** of water; and 5869
24:45 she went down unto the **w**, and drew *water:* 5869
24:62 came from the way of the **w Lahai-roi**; 883
25:11 and Isaac dwelt by the **w Lahai-roi**. 883
26:19 and found there a **w** of springing water. 875
26:20 he called the name of the **w** Esek; because 875
26:21 they digged another **w**, and strove for that 875
26:22 removed from thence, and digged another **w**; 875
26:25 and there Isaac's servants digged a **w**. 875
26:32 told him concerning the **w** which they had 875
29: 2 and behold a **w** in the field, and lo, 875
29: 2 for out of that **w** they watered the flocks: 875
29: 6 he said unto them, *Is* he **w**? And they said, 7965
29: 6 they said, *He is* **w**: and behold, Rachel his 7965
29:17 but Rachel was beautiful and **w** favoured. 3303
32: 9 to thy kindred, and I will **deal w** with thee: 3190
37:14 see whether it be **w** with thy brethren, and 7965
37:14 with thy brethren, and **w** with the flocks; 7965
39: 6 was *a* goodly *person,* and **w** favoured. 3303
40:14 think on me when it shall be **w** with thee, 3190
41: 2 there came up out of the river seven **w** 3303
41: 4 leanfleshed kine did eat up the seven **w** 3303
41:18 river seven kine, fatfleshed and **w** favoured; 3303
43:27 said, *Is* your father **w**, the old man of whom 7965
45:16 **pleased** Pharaoh **w**, and his 3190+5869+871.1
49:22 *even* a fruitful bough by a **w**; 5869
Ex 1:20 Therefore God **dealt w** with the midwives: 3190
2:15 the land of Midian: and he sat down by a **w**. 875
4:14 I know that he can **speak w**. And 1696+1696
10:29 Moses said, Thou hast spoken **w**, I will see 3651
Lev 24:16 **as w** the stranger, as he that is born in 3509.1
24:22 **as w for** the stranger, as for one of your 3509.1
Nu 11:18 for *it was* **w** with us in Egypt: therefore 2895
13:30 for we are **w able to overcome** it. 3201+3201
21:16 that *is* the **w** whereof the LORD spake unto 875
21:17 Israel sang this song, Spring up, O **w**; 875
21:18 The princes digged the **w**, the nobles of 875
21:22 we will not drink *of* the waters of the **w**: 875
36: 5 The tribe of the sons of Joseph hath said **w**. 3651
Dt 1:17 you shall hear the small **as w as** the great; 3509.1
1:23 the saying **pleased** me **w**: 3190+5869+871.1
3:20 **as w as** *unto* you, and *until* they also 3509.1
4:40 that it may **go w** with thee, and with thy 3190
5:14 and thy maidservant may rest **as w as** thou. 3644
5:16 and that it may **go w** with thee, 3190
5:28 they have **w** *said* all that they have spoken. 3190
5:29 that it might be **w** with them, and with their 3190
5:33 *that it may be* **w** with you, and *that* ye may 2895
6: 3 observe to do *it;* that it may be **w** with thee, 3190
6:18 that it may be **w** with thee, and *that* thou 3190
7:18 shalt **w remember** what the LORD 2142+2142
12:25 that it may **go w** with thee, and with thy 3190
12:28 that it may **go w** with thee, and with thy 3190
15:16 and thine house, because he is **w** with thee; 2895
18:17 They have **w** *spoken that* which they have 3190
19:13 from Israel, that *it may go* **w** with thee. 2895
20: 8 lest his brethren's heart faint **as w as** his 3509.1
22: 7 that it may be **w** with thee, and *that* thou 3190
Jos 8:33 **as w** the stranger, as he that was born 3509.1
18:15 went out to the **w** of waters of Nephtoah: 4599
Jdg 7: 1 and pitched beside the **w** of Harod: 5869
9:16 if ye have dealt **w** with Jerubbaal and his 2896
14: 3 her for me; for she **pleaseth** me **w**. 3474+5869
14: 7 and she **pleased** Samson **w**. 3474+5869+871.1
20:48 **as w** the men of *every* city, as the beast, 4480
Ru 3: 1 rest for thee, that it may be **w** with thee? 3190
3:13 perform unto thee the part of a kinsman, **w**; 2896
1Sa 9:10 said Saul to his servant, **W** said; come, 2896
16:16 play with his hand, and thou shalt be **w**. 2895
16:17 Provide me now a man that can play **w**, and 3190
16:23 was **w**, and the evil spirit departed from 2895
18:26 it **pleased** David **w** to be 3474+5869+871.1
19:22 and came to a great **w** that *is* in Sechu: 953
20: 7 If he say thus, *It is* **w**; thy servant shall have 2896
24:18 day how that thou hast dealt **w** with me: 2896
24:19 find his enemy, will he let him go **w** away? 2896
24:20 I **know w** that thou shalt surely be king, 3045
25:31 when the LORD shall have **dealt w** with 3190
2Sa 3:13 he said, **W**; I will make a league with thee: 2896
3:26 which brought him again from the **w** of 953
6:19 **as w** to the women as men, 4480+3807.1
11:25 for the sword devoureth one **as w** as 3509.1
17: 4 saying **pleased** Absalom **w**, 3474+5869+871.1
17:18 in Bahurim, which had a **w** in his court; 875
17:21 that they came up out of the **w**, and went and 875
18:28 and said unto the king, **All is w**. 7965
19: 6 then it had **pleased** thee **w**. 3477+5869+871.1
23:15 drink *of* the water of the **w** of Beth-lehem, 953
23:16 drew water out of the **w** of Beth-lehem, 953
1Ki 2:18 Bath-sheba said, **W**; I will speak for thee 2896
8:18 thou **didst w** that it was in thine heart. 2895
18:24 people answered and said, It is **w** spoken. 2896
2Ki 4:23 nor sabbath. And she said, *It shall be* **w**. 7965
4:26 and say unto her, *Is it* **w** with thee? 7965
4:26 *is it* **w** with thy husband? *is it* well with 7965
4:26 *is it* **w** with the child? And she answered, 7965
4:26 with the child? And she answered, *It is* **w**. 7965
5:21 the chariot to meet him, and said, *Is all* **w**? 7965
5:22 he said, *All is* **w**. My master hath sent me, 7965
7: 9 they said one to another, We do not **w**: 3651
9:11 *one* said unto him, *Is all* **w**? 7965
10:30 Because thou hast **done w** in executing *that* 2895
25:24 of Babylon; and it shall be **w** with you. 3190
1Ch 11:17 drink *of* the water of the **w** of Beth-lehem, 953
11:18 drew water out of the **w** of Beth-lehem, 953
25: 8 ward against *ward,* **as w** the small as 3509.1
26:13 they cast lots, **as w** the small as the great, 3509.1
2Ch 6: 8 thou **didst w** *in* that it was in thine heart: 2895
12:12 and also in Judah things went **w**. 2896
31:15 **as w** *to* the great as *to* the small: 3509.1
Ne 2:13 even before the dragon **w**, and to the dung 5869
Job 12: 3 I have understanding **as w as** you; I *am* not 3644
33:31 **Mark w**, O Job, hearken unto me: hold thy 7181
Ps 48:13 Mark ye **w** her bulwarks, consider her 3820
49:18 praise thee, when thou **doest w** to thyself. 3190
73: 2 my steps had **w nigh** slipt. 369+3509.1
78:29 So they did eat, and were **w** filled: for he 3966
84: 6 through the valley of Baca make it a **w**; 4599
87: 7 **As w** the singers as the players on 2050.1
119:65 Thou hast dealt **w** with thy servant, 2896
128: 2 *shalt* thou *be,* and *it shall be* **w** with thee. 2896
139:14 and *that* my soul knoweth **right w**. 3966
Pr 5:15 and running waters out of thine own **w**. 875
10:11 The mouth of a righteous *man is* a **w** of 4726
11:10 When it **goeth w** with the righteous, 2898
13:10 but with the **w advised** *is* wisdom. 3289
14:15 but the prudent *man* **looketh w** to his going. 995
24:32 I saw, *and* considered *it* **w**: I looked upon *it,* NIH
27:23 state of thy flocks, *and* look **w** to thy herds. 3820
30:29 There be three *things* which go **w**, yea, 2895
31:27 She **looketh w** to the ways of her 6822
Ecc 8:12 yet surely I know that it shall be **w** with 2896
8:13 it shall not be **w** with the wicked, 2896
SS 4:15 a **w** of living waters, and streams from 875
Isa 1:17 Learn to **do w**; seek judgment, relieve 3190
3:10 that *it shall be* **w** *with him:* for they shall 2896
3:24 instead of **w set hair** baldness; and 4639+4748
25: 6 of marrow, of wines on the lees **w refined**. 2212
33:23 they could not **w** strengthen their mast, 3653
42:21 The LORD is **w pleased** for his 2654
Jer 1:12 the LORD unto me, Thou hast **w** seen: 3190
7:23 that it may be **w** unto you. 3190
15:11 Verily it shall be **w** with thy remnant; 2896
15:11 enemy to entreat thee *w* in the time of evil, NIH
22:15 and justice, *and* then *it was* **w** with him? 2896
22:16 *it was* **w** *with him: was* not this to know 2896
38:20 so it shall be **w** unto thee, and thy soul shall 3190
39:12 **look w** to him, and do him no harm; 5869+7760
40: 4 come; and I will **look w** unto thee: 5869+7760
40: 9 king of Babylon, and it shall be **w** with you. 3190
42: 6 that it may be **w** with us, when we obey 3190
44:17 of victuals, and were **w**, and saw no evil. 2896
Eze 24: 5 *and* **make** it **boil w**, and let them 7570+7571
24:10 and spice it **w**, and let the bones be burnt. 4841
33:32 and can play **w** on an instrument: 2895
44: 5 **mark w**, and behold with thine eyes, 3820+7760
44: 5 **mark w** the entering in of the house, 3820+7760
47:14 ye shall inherit it, one **as w as** another: 3509.1
Da 1: 4 **w** favoured, and skilful in all wisdom, and 2896
3:15 *w*: but if ye worship not, ye shall be cast NIH
Jnh 4: 4 said the LORD, Doest thou **w** to be angry? 3190
4: 9 Doest thou **w** to be angry for the gourd? 3190
4: 9 he said, I **do w** to be angry, *even* unto 3190
Zec 8:15 in these days to **do w** unto Jerusalem 3190
Mt 3:17 my beloved Son, in whom I am **w pleased**. *2106*
12:12 Wherefore it is lawful to do **w** on *2573*

Mt 12:18 in whom my soul is w **pleased**: *2106*
15: 7 **w** did Esaias prophesy of you, saying, *2573*
17: 5 my beloved Son, in whom I am w **pleased**; *2106*
25:21 **W** *done, thou* good and faithful servant: *2095*
25:23 **W** *done,* good and faithful servant; *2095*
Mk 1:11 my beloved Son, in whom I am w **pleased**. *2106*
7: 6 **W** hath Esaias prophesied of you *2573*
7: 9 **Full w** ye reject the commandment of God, *2573*
7:37 saying, He hath done all *things* w: *2573*
12:28 perceiving that he had answered them w, *2573*
12:32 W, Master, thou hast said the truth: *2573*
Lk 1: 7 they both were *now* w **stricken** in years. *4260*
1:18 old man, and my wife **w stricken** in years. *4260*
3:22 my beloved Son; in thee I am w **pleased**. *2106*
6:26 when all men shall speak w of you: *2573*
13: 9 *w*: and if not, *then* after that thou shalt cut it NIG
19:17 he said unto him, W, *thou* good servant: *2095*
20:39 answering said, Master, thou hast w said. *2573*
Jn 2:10 and when *men* have w **drunk**, then *3182*
4: 6 Now Jacob's w was there. Jesus therefore, *4077*
4: 6 wearied with *his* journey, sat thus on the w: *4077*
4:11 nothing to draw with, and the w is deep: *5421*
4:12 which gave us the w, and drank thereof *5421*
4:14 w of water springing up into everlasting *4077*
4:17 Thou hast w said, I have no husband: *2573*
8:48 Say we not w that thou art a Samaritan, and *2573*
11:12 Lord, if he sleep, he shall **do** w. *4982*
13:13 and Lord: and ye say w; for *so* I am. *2573*
18:23 of the evil: but if w, why smitest thou me? *2573*
Ac 10:33 and thou hast w done that thou art come. *2573*
10:47 have received the Holy Ghost **as w as** *2531*
15:29 which if ye keep yourselves, ye shall do w. *2095*
15:29 ye shall do well. **Fare** ye w. *4517*
16: 2 Which was w **reported of** by the brethren *3140*
25:10 I done no wrong, as thou **very** w knowest. *2573*
28:25 W spake the Holy Ghost by Esaias *2573*
Ro 2: 7 To them who by patient continuance in w *18*
11:20 W; because of unbelief they were broken *2573*
1Co 7:37 heart that *he* will keep his virgin, doeth w. *2573*
7:38 then he that giveth *her* in marriage doeth w; *2573*
9: 5 **as** w as other apostles, and *as* the brethren *2532*
10: 5 with many of them God was not w **pleased**: *2106*
14:17 For thou verily givest thanks w, but *2573*
2Co 6: 9 As unknown, and *yet* w **known**; as dying, *1921*
11: 4 not accepted, ye might w bear with *him*. *2573*
Gal 4:17 They zealously affect you, *but* not w; yea, *2573*
5: 7 Ye did run w; who did hinder you that *ye* *2573*
6: 9 And let us not be weary in w doing: for in *2570*
Eph 6: 3 That it may be w with thee, and *2095*
Php 4:14 Notwithstanding ye have w done, that ye *2573*
4:18 a sacrifice acceptable, w **pleasing** to God. *2101*
Col 3:20 *things:* for this is w **pleasing** unto the Lord. *2101*
2Th 3:13 But ye, brethren, be not weary in w **doing**. *2569*
1Ti 3: 4 One that ruleth w his own house, having *his* *2573*
3:12 *their* children and their own houses w. *2573*
3:13 w purchase to themselves a good degree, *2573*
5:10 W **reported** of for good works; if she have *3140*
5:17 Let the elders that rule w be counted *2573*
2Ti 1:18 *unto me* at Ephesus, thou knowest **very** w. *957*
Tit 2: 9 to **please** *them* w in all *things;* not *1510+2101*
Heb 4: 2 the gospel preached, **as** w as unto them: *2509*
13:16 for with such sacrifices God is w **pleased**. *2100*
13:21 working in you *that which is* w **pleasing** in *2101*
Jas 2: 8 love thy neighbour as thyself, ye do w: *2573*
2:19 that there is one God; thou doest w: *2573*
1Pe 2:14 and *for* the praise of them that **do** w. *17*
2:15 that with w **doing** *ye* may put to silence *15*
2:20 but if, when ye **do** w, and suffer *for it,* ye take *15*
3: 6 as long as ye **do** w, and are not afraid *with* *15*
3:17 that *ye* suffer for w **doing**, than for evil doing. *15*
4:19 the keeping of their souls *to him* in w **doing**, *16*
2Pe 1:17 my beloved Son, in whom I am w **pleased**. *2106*
1:19 whereunto ye do w that ye take heed, *2573*
3Jn 1: 6 journey after a godly sort, thou shalt do w: *2573*

WELL'S (6) [WELL]
Ge 29: 2 and a great stone *was* upon the w mouth. 875
29: 3 and they rolled the stone from the w mouth, 875
29: 3 put the stone again upon the w mouth in his 875
29: 8 and *till* they roll the stone from the w mouth; 875
29:10 rolled the stone from the w mouth, and 875
2Sa 17:19 and spread a covering over the w mouth, 875

WELL-BUILT See GOODLIER; GOODLIEST; GOODLY

WELLBELOVED, WELL-BELOVED (6) [LOVE, WELL]
SS 1:13 A bundle of myrrh *is* my w unto me; 1730
Isa 5: 1 Now will I sing to my w a song of my 3039
5: 1 My w hath a vineyard in a very fruitful hill: 3039
Mk 12: 6 Having yet therefore one son, his w, he sent *27*
Ro 16: 5 Salute my w Epenetus, who is the firstfruits of *27*
3Jn 1: 1 The elder unto the w Gaius, whom I love in *27*

WELLFAVOURED (1) [FAVOUR, WELL]
Na 3: 4 of the whoredoms of the w harlot, 2580+2896

WELLS (11) [WELL]
Ge 26:15 For all the w which his father's servants had 875
26:18 Isaac digged again the w of water, 875
Ex 15:27 where *were* twelve w of water, and 5869
Nu 20:17 neither will we drink *of* the water of the w: 875
Dt 6:11 w digged, which thou diggedst not, 953
2Ki 3:19 stop all w of water, and mar every good 4599
3:25 they stopped all the w of water, and 4599
2Ch 26:10 towers in the desert, and digged many w: 953
Ne 9:25 w digged, vineyards, and oliveyards, and 953
Isa 12: 3 ye draw water out of the w of salvation. 4599
2Pe 2:17 These are w without water, clouds that are *4077*

WELLSPRING (2) [SPRING, WELL]
Pr 16:22 Understanding *is* a w of life unto him that 4726
18: 4 *and* the w of wisdom *as* a flowing brook. 4726

WEN (1)
Lev 22:22 or **having a** w, or scurvy, or scabbed, 2990

WENCH (1)
2Sa 17:17 a w went and told them; and they went and 8198

WENT (1400) [GO] See Index

WENTEST (14) [GO] See Index

WEPT (71) [WEEP]
Ge 21:16 against *him,* and lift up her voice, and w. 1058
27:38 And Esau lift up his voice, and w. 1058
29:11 and lifted up his voice, and w. 1058
33: 4 on his neck, and kissed him: and they w. 1058
37:35 son mourning. Thus his father w for him. 1058
42:24 he turned himself about from them, and w; 1058
43:30 he entered into *his* chamber, and w there. 1058
45: 2 he w **aloud**: and 1065+5414+6963+871.1
45:14 upon his brother Benjamin's neck, and w; 1058
45:14 and wept; and Benjamin w upon his neck. 1058
45:15 kissed all his brethren, and w upon them: 1058
46:29 his neck, and w on his neck a good while. 1058
50: 1 and w upon him, and kissed him. 1058
50:17 And Joseph w when they spake unto him. 1058
Ex 2: 6 behold, the babe w. And she had 1058
Nu 11: 4 the children of Israel also w again, and 1058
11:18 for you have w in the ears of the LORD, 1058
11:20 have w before him, saying, Why came we 1058
14: 1 and cried; and the people w that night. 1058
Dt 1:45 ye returned and w before the LORD; but 1058
34: 8 the children of Israel w for Moses in 1058
Jdg 2: 4 that the people lift up their voice, and w. 1058
14:16 And Samson's wife w before him, and said, 1058
14:17 she w before him the seven days, 1058
20:23 and w before the LORD until even, 1058
20:26 w, and sat there before the LORD, and 1058
21: 2 up their voices, and w **sore**; 1058+1065+1419
Ru 1: 9 and they lift up their voice, and w. 1058
1:14 they lift up their voice, and w again: and 1058
1Sa 1: 7 therefore she w, and did not eat. 1058
1:10 prayed unto the LORD, and w **sore**. 1058+1058
11: 4 all the people lift up their voices, and w. 1058
20:41 w one with another, until David exceeded. 1058
24:16 And Saul lift up his voice, and w. 1058
30: 4 *were* with him lift up their voice and w, 1058
2Sa 1:12 w, and fasted until even, for Saul, and 1058
3:32 up his voice, and w at the grave of Abner; 1058
3:32 at the grave of Abner; and all the people w. 1058
3:34 And all the people w again over him. 1058
12:22 the child *was* yet alive, I fasted and w: 1058
13:36 sons came, and lift up their voice and w: 1058
13:36 and all his servants w very **sore**. 1058+1065
15:23 all the country w *with* a loud voice, and 1058
15:30 w as he went up, and had his head covered, 1058
18:33 up to the chamber over the gate, and w: 1058
2Ki 8:11 *he* was ashamed: and the man of God w. 1058

W

2Ki 13:14 w over his face, and said, O my father, 1058
20: 3 And Hezekiah **w sore.** 1058+1065+1419
22:19 and hast rent thy clothes, and w before me; 1058
Ezr 3:12 laid before their eyes, w with a loud voice; 1058
10: 1 children: for the people w very **sore.** 1058+1059
Ne 1: 4 *that* I sat down and w, and mourned *certain* 1058
8: 9 For all the people w, when they heard 1058
Job 2:12 him not, they lifted up their voice, and w; 1058
Ps 69:10 When I w, *and chastened* my soul with 1058
137: 1 of Babylon, there we sat down, yea, we w, 1058
Isa 38: 3 And Hezekiah **w sore.** 1058+1065+1419
Hos 12: 4 he w, and made supplication unto him: 1058
Mt 26:75 me thrice. And he went out, and w bitterly. *2799*
Mk 5:38 and them that w and wailed greatly. *2799*
14:72 And when he thought thereon, he w. *2799*
16:10 had been with him, as they mourned and w. *2799*
Lk 7:32 have mourned to you, and ye have not w. *2799*
8:52 And all w, and bewailed her: but he said, *2799*
19:41 he beheld the city, and w over it, *2799*
22:62 And Peter went out, and w bitterly. *2799*
Jn 11:35 Jesus w. *1145*
20:11 and as she w, she stooped down, and *2799*
Ac 20:37 And *they* all w sore, and fell on *1096+2805*
1Co 7:30 And they that weep, as though they w not; *2799*
Rev 5: 4 And I w much, because no *man* was found *2799*

WERE (2776) [BE] See Index

WERT (6) [BE] See Index

WEST (69) [WESTERN, WESTWARD]

Ge 12: 8 *having* Beth-el on the w, and Hai on 3220
28:14 thou shalt spread abroad to the w, and 3220
Ex 10:19 the LORD turned a mighty strong w wind, 3220
27:12 *for* the breadth of the court on the w side 3220
38:12 for the w side *were* hangings of fifty cubits, 3220
Nu 2:18 On the **w side** *shall be* the standard of 3220
34: 6 for a border: this shall be your w border. 3220
35: 5 *on* the w side two thousand cubits, and 3220
Dt 33:23 possess thou the w and the south. 3220
Jos 8: 9 and Ai, on the **w side** of Ai: 3220
8:12 and Ai, on the **w side** of the city. 3220
8:13 and their liers in wait on the w of the city, 3220
11: 2 and in the borders of Dor on the w, 3220
11: 3 *to* the Canaanite on the east and on the w, 3220
12: 7 Israel smote on *this* side Jordan on the w, 3220
15:12 the w border *was* to the great sea, and 3220
18:14 children of Judah: this *was* the w quarter. 3220
18:15 the border went out on the w, and went out 3220
19:34 reacheth to Asher on the w side, and 3220
1Ki 7:25 three looking toward the w, and 3220
1Ch 9:24 toward the east, w, north, and south. 3220
12:15 *both* toward the east, and toward the w. 4628
2Ch 4: 4 three looking toward the w, and 3220
32:30 brought it straight down to the w *side* of 4628
33:14 on the w *side* of Gihon, in the valley, 4628
Ps 75: 6 nor from the w, nor from the south. 4628
103:12 As far as the east is from the w, *so* far hath 4628
107: 3 from the east, and from the w, from 4628
Isa 11:14 shoulders of the Philistines toward the w; 3220
43: 5 from the east, and gather thee from the w; 4628
45: 6 from the w, that *there is* none besides me. 4628
49:12 lo, these from the north and from the w; 3220
59:19 fear the name of the LORD from the w, 4628
Eze 41:12 end toward the **w** *was* seventy cubits broad; 3220
42:19 He turned about to the w side, *and* 3220
45: 7 from the w side westward, and from 3220
45: 7 from the w border unto the east border. 3220
47:20 The w side also *shall be* the great sea from 3220
47:20 over against Hamath. This *is* the w side. 3220
48: 1 for these are his sides east *and* w; a *portion* 3220
48: 2 from the east side unto the w side, 3220+1886.5
48: 3 from the east side even unto the w 3220+1886.5
48: 4 from the east side unto the w side, 3220+1886.5
48: 5 from the east side unto the w side, 3220+1886.5
48: 6 from the east side even unto the w 3220+1886.5
48: 7 from the east side unto the w side, 3220+1886.5
48: 8 from the east side unto the w side, 3220+1886.5
48: 8 from the east side unto the w side: 3220+1886.5
48:10 and toward the w ten thousand *in* breadth, 3220
48:16 the w side four thousand and 3220+1886.5
48:17 and toward the w two hundred and fifty. 3220
48:21 thousand toward the w border, 3220+1886.5
48:23 from the east side unto the w side, 3220+1886.5
48:24 from the east side unto the w side, 3220+1886.5
48:25 from the east side unto the w side, 3220+1886.5
48:26 from the east side unto the w side, 3220+1886.5
48:27 from the east side unto the w side, 3220+1886.5
48:34 *At* the w side four thousand and 3220
Da 8: 5 a he goat came from the w on the face of 4628
Hos 11:10 then the children shall tremble from the w. 3220
Zec 8: 7 and from **the w** country; 3996+8121+1886.1
14: 4 thereof toward the east and toward the w, 3220
Mt 8:11 That many shall come from the east and w, *1424*
24:27 of the east, and shineth *even* unto the w; *1424*
Lk 12:54 When ye see a cloud rise out of the w, *1424*
13:29 and *from* the w, and from the north, and *1424*
Ac 27:12 and lieth toward the **south** w and *3047*
27:12 lieth toward the south west and **north** w. *5566*
Rev 21:13 south three gates; and on the w three gates. *1424*

WESTERN (1) [WEST]

Nu 34: 6 *as for* the w border, you shall even have 3220

WESTWARD (26) [WEST]

Ge 13:14 southward, and eastward, and w: 3220+1886.5
Ex 26:22 for the sides of the tabernacle w 3220+1886.5
26:27 the tabernacle, for the two sides w. 3220+1886.5
36:27 for the sides of the tabernacle w he 3220+1886.5
36:32 of the tabernacle for the sides w. 3220+1886.5
Nu 3:23 shall pitch behind the tabernacle w. 3220+1886.5
Dt 3:27 lift up thine eyes w, and northward, 3220+1886.5
Jos 5: 1 *were* on the side of Jordan w, 3220+1886.5
15: 8 before the valley of Hinnom w, 3220+1886.5
15:10 from Baalah w unto mount Seir, 3220+1886.5
16: 3 goeth down w to the coast of 3220+1886.5
16: 8 Tappuah w *unto* the river Kanah; 3220+1886.5
18:12 went up through the mountains w; 3220+1886.5
19:26 reacheth to Carmel w, and 3220+1886.5
19:34 coast turneth w *to* Aznoth-tabor, 3220+1886.5
22: 7 brethren on *this* side Jordan w. 3220+1886.5
23: 4 even *unto* the great sea w. 3996+8121+1886.1
1Ch 7:28 and w Gezer, 4628+1886.1+3807.1
26:16 and Hosah *the lot came forth* w, 4628
26:18 At Parbar w, four at the causeway, *and* 4628
26:30 w in all the business of 4628+1886.5
Eze 45: 7 from the west side w, and from 3220+1886.5
46:19 *was* a place on the two sides w. 3220+1886.5
48:18 and ten thousand w: 3220+1886.5
48:21 w over against the five and 3220+1886.5
Da 8: 4 I saw the ram pushing w, 3220+1886.5

WET (6)

Job 24: 8 They are w with the showers of 7372
Da 4:15 let it be w with the dew of heaven, and 6647
4:23 let it be w with the dew of heaven, and 6647
4:25 they *shall* w thee with the dew of heaven, 6647
4:33 his body was w with the dew of heaven, 6647
5:21 his body was w with the dew of heaven; 6647

WHALE (2) [WHALE'S, WHALES]

Job 7:12 *Am* I a sea, or a w, that thou settest a watch 8577
Eze 32: 2 the nations, and thou *art* as a w in the seas: 8577

WHALE'S (1) [WHALE]

Mt 12:40 three days and three nights in the w belly; *2785*

WHALES (1) [WHALE]

Ge 1:21 God created great w, and every living 8577

WHAT (984) [SOMEWHAT, WHATSOEVER] See Index

WHATSOEVER (152) [EVER, SO, WHAT] See Index

WHEAT (51) [WHEATEN]

Ge 30:14 Reuben went in the days of w harvest, and 2406
Ex 9:32 the w and the rye were not smitten: for they 2406
34:22 of the firstfruits of w harvest, and the feast 2406
Nu 18:12 and all the best of the wine, and of the w, 1715
Dt 8: 8 A land of w, and barley, and vines, and 2406
32:14 and goats, with the fat of kidneys of w; 2406
Jdg 6:11 his son Gideon threshed w by 2406
15: 1 in the time of w harvest, that Samson 2406
Ru 2:23 the end of barley harvest and of w harvest; 2406
1Sa 6:13 *they of* Beth-shemesh *were* reaping *their* w 2406
12:17 *Is it* not w harvest to day? I will call unto 2406
2Sa 4: 6 *as though* they would have fetched w; 2406
17:28 w, and barley, and flour, and parched *corn,* 2406
1Ki 5:11 measures of w *for* food to his household, 2406

1Ch 21:20 Now Ornan was threshing w. 2406
21:23 for wood, and the w for the meat offering; 2406
2Ch 2:10 twenty thousand measures of beaten w, and 2406
2:15 Now therefore the w, and the barley, 2406
27: 5 ten thousand measures of w, and 2406
Ezr 6: 9 of the God of heaven, w, salt, wine, and oil, 2591
7:22 to an hundred measures *of* w, and to an 2591
Job 31:40 Let thistles grow instead of w, and 2406
Ps 81:16 have fed them also with the finest of the w: 2406
147:14 *and* filleth thee *with* the finest of the w. 2406
Pr 27:22 a fool in a mortar among w with a pestle, 7383
SS 7: 2 thy belly *is like* a heap of w set about with 2406
Isa 28:25 cast in the principal w and the appointed 2406
Jer 12:13 They have sown w, but shall reap thorns: 2406
23:28 What *is* the chaff to the w? saith 1250
31:12 for w, and for wine, and for oil, and for 1715
41: 8 *of* w, and *of* barley, and *of* oil, and 2406
Eze 4: 9 Take thou also unto thee w, and barley, and 2406
27:17 they traded in thy market w of Minnith, and 2406
45:13 the sixth *part* of an ephah of a homer of w, 2406
Joel 1:11 for the w and for the barley; 2406
2:24 the floors shall be full *of* w, and the fats 1250
Am 5:11 and ye take from him burdens of w: 1250
8: 5 the sabbath, that we may set forth w, 1250
8: 6 of shoes; *yea,* and sell the refuse of the w? 1250
Mt 3:12 his floor, and gather his w into the garner; *4621*
13:25 enemy came and sowed tares among the w, *4621*
13:29 the tares, ye root up also the w with them. *4621*
13:30 burn them: but gather the w into my barn. *4621*
Lk 3:17 and will gather the w into his garner; *4621*
16: 7 And he said, An hundred measures of w. *4621*
22:31 *to have* you, that *he* may sift *you* as w: *4621*
Jn 12:24 Except a corn of w fall into the ground and *4621*
Ac 27:38 the ship, and cast out the w into the sea. *4621*
1Co 15:37 it may chance of w, or of some other *grain:* *4621*
Rev 6: 6 A measure of w for a penny, and *4621*
18:13 and w, and beasts, and sheep, and horses, *4621*

WHEATEN (1) [WHEAT]
Ex 29: 2 with oil: *of* w flour shalt thou make them. 2406

WHEEL (15) [WHEELS]
1Ki 7:32 the height of a w *was* a cubit and half a 212
7:33 the wheels *was* like the work of a chariot w: 212
Ps 83:13 O my God, make them like a w; as 1534
Pr 20:26 the wicked, and bringeth the w over them. 212
Ecc 12: 6 the fountain, or the w broken at the cistern. 1534
Isa 28:27 is a cart w turned about upon the cummin; 212
28:28 nor break *it with* the w of his cart, 1536
Eze 1:15 behold one w upon the earth by the living 212
1:16 their work *was* as it were a w in the middle 212
1:16 *was* as it were a wheel in the middle of a w. 212
10: 9 one w by one cherub, and another wheel by 212
10: 9 and another w by another cherub: 212
10:10 as if a w had been in the midst of a wheel. 212
10:10 as if a wheel had been in the midst of a w. 212
10:13 it was cried unto them in my hearing, O w. 1534

WHEELS (33) [WHEEL]
Ex 14:25 took off their chariot w, that they drave them 212
Jdg 5:28 in coming? why tarry the w of his chariots? 6471
1Ki 7:30 every base had four brasen w, and plates of 212
7:32 under the borders *were* four w; and 212
7:32 the axletrees of the w *were* joined to 212
7:33 the work of the w *was* like the work of a 212
Isa 5:28 like flint, and their w like a whirlwind: 1534
Jer 18: 3 and behold, he wrought a work on the w. 70
47: 3 *and at* the rumbling of his w, the fathers 1534
Eze 1:16 The appearance of the w and their work *was* 212
1:19 living creatures went, the w went by them: 212
1:19 lift up from the earth, the w were lift up. 212
1:20 and the w were lifted up over against them: 212
1:20 the spirit of the living creature *was* in the w. 212
1:21 the w were lifted up over against them: 212
1:21 the spirit of the living creature *was* in the w. 212
3:13 the noise of the w over against them, and 212
10: 2 said, Go in between the w, *even* under 1534
10: 6 saying, Take fire from between the w, 1534
10: 6 then he went in, and stood beside the w. 212
10: 9 behold the four w by the cherubims, 212
10: 9 the appearance of the w *was* as the colour of 212
10:12 and their hands, and their wings, and the w, 212
10:12 round about, *even* the w that they four had. 212
10:13 As for the w, it was cried unto them in my 212
10:16 the cherubims went, the w went by them: 212
10:16 the same w also turned not from beside 212
10:19 the w also *were* besides them, and *every one* 212
11:22 lift up their wings, and the w besides them; 212
23:24 and w, and with an assembly of people, 1534
26:10 of the w, and of the chariots, when he shall 1534
Da 7: 9 the fiery flame, *and* his w *as* burning fire. 1535
Na 3: 2 the noise of the rattling of the w, and of 212

WHELP (3) [WHELPS]
Ge 49: 9 Judah *is* a lion's w: from the prey, my son, 1482
Dt 33:22 of Dan he said, Dan *is* a lion's w: he shall 1482
Na 2:11 *and* the lion's w, and none made *them* 1482

WHELPS (10) [WHELP]
2Sa 17: 8 as a bear **robbed of** her w in the field: 7909
Job 4:11 and the stout lion's w are scattered abroad. 1121
28: 8 The lion's w have not trodden it, nor 1121
Pr 17:12 *Let* a bear robbed of her w meet a man, NIH
Jer 51:38 like lions: they shall yell as lions' w, 1484
Eze 19: 2 she nourished her w among young lions. 1482
19: 3 she brought up one of her w: it became a 1482
19: 5 she took another of her w, *and* made him a 1482
Hos 13: 8 them as a bear *that is* **bereaved of** her w, 7909
Na 2:12 lion did tear in pieces enough for his w, 1484

WHEN (2848) [WHENSOEVER] See Index

WHENCE (72) See Index

WHENSOEVER (3) [EVER, SO, WHEN] See Index

WHERE (401) See Index

WHEREABOUT (1) [ABOUT] See Index

WHEREAS (33) [AS] See Index

WHEREBY (39) [BY] See Index

WHEREFORE (348) See Index

WHEREIN (167) [IN] See Index

WHEREINSOEVER (1) [EVER, IN, SO] See Index

WHEREINTO (4) [INTO] See Index

WHEREOF (71) [OF] See Index

WHEREON (27) [ON] See Index

WHERESOEVER (12) [EVER, SO] See Index

WHERETO (3) [TO] See Index

WHEREUNTO (26) [UNTO] See Index

WHEREUPON (17) [UPON] See Index

WHEREWITH (110) [WITH] See Index

WHEREWITHAL (2) [WITHAL]
Ps 119: 9 W shall a young man cleanse his 4100+871.1
Mt 6:31 shall we drink? or, W shall we be clothed? *5101*

WHET (4)
Dt 32:41 If I w my glittering sword, and mine hand 8150
Ps 7:12 If he turn not, he will w his sword; he hath 3913
64: 3 Who w their tongue like a sword, *and* 8150
Ecc 10:10 he do not w the edge, then must he put to 7043

WHETHER (171) See Index

WHICH (4419) See Index

WHILE (210) [WHILES, WHILST] See Index

WHILES (12) [WHILE] See Index

WHILST (12) [WHILE] See Index

WHIP (2) [WHIPS]
Pr 26: 3 A w for the horse, a bridle for the ass, and 7752
Na 3: 2 The noise of a w, and the noise of 7752

WHIPS (4) [WHIP]
1Ki 12:11 my father hath chastised you with w, but 7752
12:14 my father *also* chastised you with w, but 7752
2Ch 10:11 my father chastised you with w, but I *will* 7752
10:14 my father chastised you with w, but I *will* 7752

WHIRLETH (1) [WHIRLWIND, WHIRLWINDS]
Ecc 1: 6 it w **about continually**, and 1980+5437+5437

WHIRLWIND (27) [WHIRLETH, WIND]
2Ki 2: 1 would take up Elijah *into* heaven by a w, 5591
2:11 and Elijah went up by a w *into* heaven. 5591
Job 37: 9 Out of the south cometh the w: and cold out 5492
38: 1 the LORD answered Job out of the w, 5591
40: 6 the LORD unto Job out of the w, 5591
Ps 58: 9 he shall **take** them **away as with a** w, 8175
Pr 1:27 and your destruction cometh as a w; 5492
10:25 As the w passeth, so *is* the wicked no *more:* 5492
Isa 5:28 counted like flint, and their wheels like a w: 5492
17:13 and like a rolling thing before the w. 5492
40:24 and the w shall take them away as stubble. 5591
41:16 them away, and the w shall scatter them: 5591
66:15 with his chariots like a w, to render his 5492
Jer 4:13 as clouds, and his chariots *shall be* as a w: 5492
23:19 a w of the LORD is gone forth *in* fury, 5591
23:19 is gone forth *in* fury, even a grievous w: 5591
25:32 a great w shall be raised up from the coasts 5591
30:23 the w of the LORD goeth forth *with* fury, 5591
30:23 goeth forth *with* fury, a continuing w: 5591
Eze 1: 4 behold, a w came out of the north, 5591+7307
Da 11:40 the north shall **come** against him **like a** w, 8175
Hos 8: 7 sown the wind, and they shall reap the w: 5492
13: 3 as the chaff *that* is **driven with a** w out of 5590
Am 1:14 with a tempest in the day of the w: 5492
Na 1: 3 *wicked:* the LORD *hath* his way in the w 5492
Hab 3:14 they **came out as a** w to scatter me: 5590
Zec 7:14 I **scattered** them **with a** w among all 5590

WHIRLWINDS (2) [WHIRLETH, WIND]
Isa 21: 1 As w in the south pass through; *so* 5492
Zec 9:14 and shall go with w of the south. 5591

WHISPER (2) [WHISPERED, WHISPERER, WHISPERERS, WHISPERINGS]
Ps 41: 7 All that hate me w together against me: 3907
Isa 29: 4 and thy speech shall w out of the dust. 6850

WHISPERED (1) [WHISPER]
2Sa 12:19 when David saw that his servants w, David 3907

WHISPERER (1) [WHISPER]
Pr 16:28 and a w separateth chief friends. 5372

WHISPERERS (1) [WHISPER]
Ro 1:29 murder, debate, deceit, malignity; w, *5588*

WHISPERINGS (1) [WHISPER]
2Co 12:20 strifes, backbitings, w, swellings, tumults: *5587*

WHIT (5)
Dt 13:16 all the spoil thereof **every** w, for 3632
1Sa 3:18 Samuel told him every w, and hid nothing 1697
Jn 7:23 I have made a man **every** w whole on *3650*
13:10 save to wash *his* feet, but is clean **every** w: *3650*
2Co 11: 5 For I suppose *I* was **not a** w behind *3367*

WHITE (75) [WHITED, WHITER]
Ge 30:35 *and* every one that had *some* w in it, and 3836
30:37 pilled w strakes in them, and made 3836
30:37 made the w appear which *was* in the rods. 3836
40:16 behold, *I had* three w baskets on my head: 2751
49:12 *be* red with wine, and *his* teeth w with milk. 3836
Ex 16:31 it *was* like coriander seed, w; and the taste 3836
Lev 13: 3 and *when* the hair in the plague is turned w, 3836
13: 4 If the bright spot *be* w in the skin of his 3836
13: 4 and the hair thereof be not turned w; 3836
13:10 *if* the rising *be* w in the skin, and it have 3836
13:10 it have turned the hair w, and *there be* 3836
13:13 the plague: it is all turned w: he *is* clean. 3836
13:16 be changed unto w, he shall come unto 3836
13:17 behold, *if* the plague be turned into w; then 3836
13:19 in the place of the boil there be a w rising, 3836
13:19 w, *and* somewhat reddish, and it be shewed 3836
13:20 the skin, and the hair thereof be turned w; 3836
13:21 *there be* no w hairs therein, and *if* it *be* not 3836
13:24 the quick *flesh* that burneth have a w bright 3836
13:24 white bright spot, somewhat reddish, or w; 3836
13:25 *if* the hair in the bright spot be turned w, 3836
13:26 *there be* no w hair in the bright spot, and 3836
13:38 their flesh bright spots, *even* w bright spots; 3836
13:39 spots in the skin of their flesh *be* darkish w; 3836
13:42 or bald forehead, a w reddish sore; 3836
13:43 *if* the rising of the sore *be* w reddish in his 3836
Nu 12:10 behold, Miriam *became* leprous, *w* as snow: NIH
Jdg 5:10 Speak, ye that ride on w asses, ye that sit in 6715
2Ki 5:27 he went out from his presence a leper *as w* NIH
2Ch 5:12 and their brethren, *being* arrayed in **w linen**, 948
Est 1: 6 *Where were* w, green, and blue *hangings,* 2353
1: 6 of red, and blue, and w, and black marble. 1858
8:15 of the king in royal apparel *of* blue and w, 2353
Job 6: 6 or is there *any* taste in the w of an egg? 7388
Ps 68:14 kings in it, it was *w as* snow in Salmon. NIH
Ecc 9: 8 Let thy garments be always w; and let thy 3836
SS 5:10 My beloved *is* w and ruddy, the chiefest 6703
Isa 1:18 be as scarlet, they shall be as w as snow; 3835
Eze 27:18 in the wine of Helbon, and w wool. 6713
Da 7: 9 whose garment *was* w as snow, and the hair 2358
11:35 and to purge, and to **make** *them* w, 3835
12:10 shall be purified, and **made** w, and tried; 3835
Joel 1: 7 *it* away; the branches thereof are **made** w. 3835
Zec 1: 8 him *were there* red horses, speckled, and w. 3836
6: 3 in the third chariot w horses; and in 3836
6: 6 the w go forth after them; and the grisled 3836
Mt 5:36 thou canst not make one hair w or black. *3022*
17: 2 the sun, and his raiment was w as the light. *3022*
28: 3 like lightning, and his raiment w as snow: *3022*
Mk 9: 3 became shining, exceeding w as snow; *3022*
9: 3 so as no fuller on earth can w *them.* *3021*
16: 5 the right side, clothed in a long w garment; *3022*
Lk 9:29 and his raiment *was* w *and* glistering. *3022*
Jn 4:35 the fields; for they are w already to harvest. *3022*
20:12 And seeth two angels in w sitting, the one *3022*
Ac 1:10 two men stood by them in w apparel; *3022*
Rev 1:14 His head and *his* hairs *were* w like wool, *3022*
1:14 hairs *were* white like wool, *as* w as snow; *3022*
2:17 and will give him a w stone, and in *3022*
3: 4 and they shall walk with me in w: *3022*
3: 5 the same shall be clothed in w raiment; *3022*
3:18 and w raiment, that thou mayest be clothed, *3022*
4: 4 twenty elders sitting, clothed in w raiment; *3022*
6: 2 And I saw, and behold a w horse: and *3022*
6:11 And w robes were given unto every one of *3022*
7: 9 clothed with w robes, and palms in their *3022*
7:13 What are these which are arrayed in w *3022*
7:14 **made** them w in the blood of the Lamb. *3021*
14:14 and behold a w cloud, and upon the cloud *3022*
15: 6 clothed in pure and w linen, and *2986*
19: 8 be arrayed in fine linen, clean and w: *2986*
19:11 saw heaven opened, and behold a w horse; *3022*
19:14 in heaven followed him upon w horses, *3022*
19:14 clothed in fine linen, w and clean. *3022*
20:11 And I saw a great w throne, and him that *3022*

WHITED (2) [WHITE]
Mt 23:27 for ye are like unto w sepulchres, *2867*
Ac 23: 3 God shall smite thee, *thou* w wall: *2867*

WHITER (2) [WHITE]
Ps 51: 7 wash me, and I shall be w than snow. 3835
La 4: 7 purer than snow, they were w than milk, 6705

WHITEWASH See MORTER

WHITHER (124) [WHITHERSOEVER] See Index

WHITHERSOEVER (29) [EVER, SO, WHITHER] See Index

WHO (969) [WHOM, WHOMSOEVER, WHOSE, WHOSO, WHOSOEVER] See Index

WHOLE (250) [WHOLESOME, WHOLLY]
Ge 2: 6 and watered the w face of the ground. 3605
2:11 that *is it* which compasseth the w land of 3605
2:13 the same *is it* that compasseth the w land of 3605
7:19 that *were* under the w heaven, 3605
8: 9 for the waters *were* on the face of the w 3605
9:19 and of them was the w earth overspread. 3605
11: 1 the w earth was *of* one language, and 3605
11: 4 abroad upon the face of the w earth. 3605
13: 9 *Is* not the w land before thee? 3605
47:28 so the w **age** of Jacob was an 2416+3117+8141
Ex 10:15 For they covered the face of the w earth, so 3605
12: 6 the w assembly of the congregation of 3605
16: 2 the w congregation of the children of Israel 3605
16: 3 to kill this w assembly with hunger. 3605
16:10 as Aaron spake unto the w congregation of 3605

Ex 19:18 a furnace, and the w mount quaked greatly. 3605
29:18 thou shalt burn the w ram upon the altar: 3605
Lev 3: 9 the fat thereof, *and* the w rump, it shall he 8549
4:12 Even the w bullock shall he carry forth 3605
4:13 if the w congregation of Israel sin through 3605
7:14 of it he shall offer one out of the w oblation 3605
8:21 and Moses burnt the w ram upon the altar: 3605
10: 6 let your brethren, the w house of Israel, 3605
25:29 he may redeem it within a w year after it is 8552
Nu 3: 7 the charge of the w congregation before 3605
8: 9 thou shalt gather the w assembly of 3605
10: 2 of a **w piece** thou shalt make them: 4749
11:20 *But* even a w month, until it come out at 3117
11:21 them flesh, that they may eat a w month. 3117
14: 2 the w congregation said unto them, 3605
14:29 according to your w number, from twenty 3605
20: 1 children of Israel, *even* the w congregation, 3605
20:22 *even* the w congregation, journeyed from 3605
Dt 2:25 the nations *that are* under the w heaven, 3605
4:19 unto all nations under the w heaven. 3605
27: 6 altar of the LORD thy God *of* w stones: 8003
29:23 *And that* the w land thereof *is* brimstone, 3605
33:10 and w *burnt sacrifice* upon thine altar. 3632
Jos 5: 8 in their places in the camp, till they were w. 2421
8:31 an altar of w stones, over which no *man* 8003
10:13 and hasted not to go down about a w day. 8549
11:23 So Joshua took the w land, according to all 3605
18: 1 the w congregation of the children of Israel 3605
22:12 w congregation of the children of Israel 3605
22:16 Thus saith the w congregation of 3605
22:18 that to morrow he will be wroth with the w 3605
Jdg 19: 2 was there four w months. 3117
21:13 the w congregation sent *some* to speak to 3605
2Sa 1: 9 upon me, because my life *is* yet w in me. 3605
3:19 that seemed *good* to the w house of 3605
6:19 *even* among the w multitude of Israel, 3605
14: 7 the w family is risen against thine 3605
1Ki 6:22 the w house he overlaid with gold, until *he* 3605
6:22 also the w altar that *was* by the oracle he 3605
11:34 Howbeit I will not take the w kingdom out 3605
2Ki 9: 8 For the w house of Ahab shall perish: and 3605
2Ch 6: 3 and blessed the w congregation of Israel: 3605
15:15 and sought him with their w desire; 3605
16: 9 run to and fro throughout the w earth, 3605
26:12 The w number of the chief of the fathers of 3605
30:23 the w assembly took counsel to keep other 3605
33: 8 according to the w law and the statutes and 3605
Ezr 2:64 The w congregation together *was* forty *and* 3605
Ne 7:66 The w congregation together *was* forty 3605
Est 3: 6 throughout the w kingdom of Ahasuerus, 3605
Job 5:18 he woundeth, and his hands **make w**. 7495
28:24 of the earth, *and* seeth under the w heaven; 3605
34:13 or who hath disposed the w world? 3605
37: 3 He directeth it under the w heaven, and 3605
41:11 *whatsoever is* under the w heaven *is* mine. 3605
Ps 9: 1 praise *thee*, O LORD, with my w heart; 3605
48: 2 the joy of the w earth, *is* mount Zion, 3605
51:19 burnt offering and w *burnt offering:* then 3632
72:19 let the w earth be filled *with* his glory; 3605
97: 5 at the presence of the Lord of the w earth. 3605
105:16 the land: he brake the w staff of bread. 3605
111: 1 I will praise the LORD with *my* w heart, 3605
119: 2 *and that* seek him with the w heart. 3605
119:10 With my w heart have I sought thee: O let 3605
119:34 yea, I shall observe it with *my* w heart. 3605
119:58 I intreated thy favour with *my* w heart: 3605
119:69 I will keep thy precepts with *my* w heart. 3605
119:145 I cried with *my* w heart; hear me, 3605
138: 1 I will praise thee with my w heart: 3605
Pr 1:12 and w, as those that go down into the pit: 8549
16:33 the w disposing thereof *is* of the LORD. 3605
26:26 shall be shewed before the *w* congregation. NIH
Ecc 12:13 Let us hear the conclusion of the w matter: 3605
12:13 for this *is* the w *duty of* man. 3605
Isa 1: 5 the w head *is* sick, and the whole heart 3605
1: 5 whole head *is* sick, and the w heart faint. 3605
3: 1 the w stay of bread, and the whole stay of 3605
3: 1 stay of bread, and the w stay of water, 3605
6: 3 of hosts: the w earth *is* full of his glory. 3605
10:12 *that* when the Lord hath performed his w 3605
13: 5 of his indignation, to destroy the w land. 3605
14: 7 The w earth is at rest, *and* is quiet: 3605
14:26 purpose that is purposed upon the w earth: 3605
14:29 w Palestina, because the rod of him that 3605
14:31 cry, O city; thou, w Palestina, *art* dissolved: 3605
21: 8 and I *am* set in my ward w nights: 3605
28:22 even determined upon the w earth. 3605
54: 5 The God of the w earth shall he be called. 3605
Jer 1:18 and brasen walls against the w land, 3605
3:10 hath not turned unto me with her w heart, 3605
4:20 is cried; for the w land is spoiled: 3605
4:27 LORD said, The w land shall be desolate; 3605
4:29 The w city shall flee for the noise of 3605
7:15 your brethren, *even* the w seed of Ephraim. 3605
8:16 the w land trembled at the sound of 3605
12:11 the w land is made desolate, because 3605
13:11 have I caused to cleave unto me the w 3605
13:11 house of Israel and the w house of Judah, 3605
Jer 15:10 and a man of contention to the w earth! 3605
19:11 that cannot be **made w** again: 7495
24: 7 for they shall return unto me with their w 3605
25:11 this w land shall be a desolation, *and* 3605
31:40 the w valley of the dead bodies, and of 3605
32:41 them in this land assuredly with my w heart 3605
32:41 with my whole heart and with my w soul. 3605
35: 3 and the w house of the Rechabites; 3605
37:10 For though ye had smitten the w army of 3605
45: 4 planted I *will* pluck up, even this w land. 3605
50:23 How is the hammer of the w earth cut 3605
51:41 *how* is the praise of the w earth surprised! 3605
51:47 her w land shall be confounded, and all her 3605
La 2:15 of beauty, The joy of the w earth? 3605
Eze 5:10 the w remnant of thee will I scatter into all 3605
7:13 for the vision *is* touching the w multitude 3605
10:12 their w body, and their backs, and 3605
15: 5 Behold, when it was w, it was meet for no 8549
32: 4 I will fill the beasts of the w earth with 3605
35:14 When the w earth rejoiceth, I will make 3605
37:11 these bones *are* the w house of Israel: 3605
39:25 have mercy upon the w house of Israel, and 3605
43:11 that they may keep the w form thereof, and 3605
43:12 Upon the top of the mountain the w limit 3605
45: 6 *portion:* it shall be for the w house of Israel. 3605
Da 2:35 a great mountain, and filled the w earth. 3606
2:48 made him ruler over the w province of 3606
6: 1 which should be over the w kingdom; 3606
6: 3 the king thought to set him over the w 3606
7:23 shall devour the w earth, and shall tread it 3606
7:27 the greatness of the kingdom under the w 3606
8: 5 from the west on the face of the w earth, 3605
9:12 for under the w heaven hath not been done 3605
10: 3 till three **w weeks** were fulfilled. 3117+7620
11:17 to enter with the strength of his w kingdom, 3605
Am 1: 6 they carried away captive the w captivity, 8003
1: 9 they delivered up the w captivity to Edom, 8003
3: 1 against the w family which I brought up 3605
Mic 4:13 their substance unto the Lord of the w 3605
Zep 1:18 the w land shall be devoured by the fire of 3605
Zec 4:10 which run to and fro through the w earth. 3605
4:14 that stand by the Lord of the w earth. 3605
5: 3 goeth forth over the face of the w earth: 3605
Mal 3: 9 for ye *have* robbed me, *even* this w nation. 3605
Mt 5:29 not *that* thy w body should be cast into hell. *3650*
5:30 not *that* thy w body should be cast into hell. *3650*
6:22 be single, thy w body shall be full of light. *3650*
6:23 thy w body shall be full of darkness. *3650*
8:32 the w herd of swine ran violently down a *3956*
8:34 the w city came out to meet Jesus: *3956*
9:12 They that be w need not a physician, but *2480*
9:21 If I may but touch his garment, I shall be w. *4982*
9:22 good comfort; thy faith hath **made** thee w. *4982*
9:22 And the woman was **made** w from that *4982*
12:13 and it was restored w, *like* as the other. *5199*
13: 2 sat; and the w multitude stood on the shore. *3956*
13:33 measures of meal, till the w was leavened. *3650*
14:36 many as touched were **made perfectly** w. *1295*
15:28 And her daughter was **made** w from that *2390*
15:31 the maimed *to be* w, the lame to walk, and *5199*
16:26 if he shall gain the w world, and lose his *3650*
26:13 gospel shall be preached in the w world, *3650*
27:27 gathered unto him the w band *of soldiers*. *3650*
Mk 2:17 They that are w have no need of *2480*
3: 5 and his hand was restored w as the other. *5199*
4: 1 the w multitude was by the sea on the land. *3956*
5:28 If I may touch but his clothes, I shall be w. *4982*
5:34 Daughter, thy faith hath **made** thee w; *4982*
5:34 go in peace, and be w of thy plague. *5199*
6:55 And ran through that w region round about, *3650*

W

Mk 6:56 and as many as touched him were **made w**. *4982*
8:36 if he shall gain the w world, and lose his *3650*
10:52 Go thy way; thy faith hath **made** thee **w**. *4982*
12:33 is more than all **w burnt offerings** and *3646*
14: 9 shall be preached throughout the w world, *3650*
15: 1 the elders and scribes and the w council, *3650*
15:16 and they call together the w band. *3650*
15:33 there was darkness over the w land until *3650*
Lk 1:10 And the **w** multitude of the people were *3956*
5:31 They that are **w** need not a physician; *5198*
6:10 and his hand was restored **w** as the other. *5199*
6:19 And the **w** multitude sought to touch him: *3956*
7:10 found the servant **w** that had been sick. *5198*
8:37 Then the **w** multitude of the country of *537*
8:39 published throughout the w city how great *3650*
8:48 thy faith hath **made** thee **w**; go in peace.) *4982*
8:50 believe only, and she shall be **made w**. *4982*
9:25 if he gain the w world, and lose himself, or *3650*
11:34 is single, thy **w** body also is full of light; *3650*
11:36 If thy **w** body therefore *be* full of light, *3650*
11:36 no part dark, the **w** shall be full of light, *3650*
13:21 measures of meal, till the w was leavened. *3650*
17:19 go *thy way:* thy faith hath **made** thee **w**. *4982*
19:37 the **w** multitude of the disciples began to *537*
21:35 them that dwell on the face of the **w** earth. *3956*
23: 1 And the **w** multitude of them arose, and *537*
Jn 4:53 and himself believed, and his **w** house. *3650*
5: 4 was made **w** of whatsoever disease he had. *5199*
5: 6 he saith unto him, Wilt thou be made **w**? *5199*
5: 9 And immediately the man was made **w**, and *5199*
5:11 He answered them, He that made me **w**, *5199*
5:14 said unto him, Behold, thou art made **w**: *5199*
5:15 that it was Jesus, which had made him **w**. *5199*
7:23 I have made a man every whit **w** on *5199*
11:50 the people, and *that* the **w** nation perish not. *3650*
Ac 4: 9 by what *means* he is **made w**; *4982*
4:10 him doth this *man* stand here before you **w**. *5199*
6: 5 And the saying pleased the **w** multitude: *3956*
9:34 Aeneas, Jesus Christ **maketh** thee **w**: *2390*
11:26 that a **w** year they assembled themselves *3650*
13:44 the **w** city together to hear the word of God. *3956*
15:22 the apostles and elders, with the **w** church, *3650*
19:29 And the **w** city was filled with confusion: *3650*
28:30 And Paul dwelt two **w** years in his own *3650*
Ro 1: 8 faith is spoken of throughout the **w** world. *3650*
Ro 8:22 For we know that the **w** creation groaneth *3956*
16:23 and of the **w** church, saluteth you. *3650*
1Co 5: 6 that a little leaven leaveneth the **w** lump? *3650*
12:17 If the **w** body *were* an eye, where *were* *3650*
12:17 If the **w** *were* hearing, where *were* *3650*
14:23 the **w** church be come together into one *3650*
Gal 5: 3 that he is a debtor to do the **w** law. *3650*
5: 9 A little leaven leaveneth the **w** lump. *3650*
Eph 3:15 Of whom the **w** family in heaven and earth *3956*
4:16 From whom the **w** body fitly joined *3956*
6:11 Put on the **w armour** of God, that ye may *3833*
6:13 Wherefore take unto *you* the **w armour** of *3833*
1Th 5:23 and *I pray God* your **w** spirit and soul and *3648*
Tit 1:11 must be stopped, who subvert **w** houses, *3650*
Jas 2:10 For whosoever shall keep the **w** law, and *3650*
3: 2 *and* able also to bridle the **w** body. *3650*
3: 3 obey us; and we turn about their **w** body. *3650*
3: 6 that it defileth the **w** body, and setteth on *3650*
1Jn 2: 2 but also for *the sins of* the **w** world. *3650*
5:19 and the **w** world lieth in wickedness. *3650*
Rev 12: 9 and Satan, which deceiveth the **w** world: *3650*
16:14 the kings of the earth and of the **w** world, *3650*

WHOLESOME (2) [WHOLE]

Pr 15: 4 A **w** tongue *is* a tree of life: but 4832
1Ti 6: 3 and consent not to **w** words, *5198*

WHOLLY (29) [WHOLE]

Lev 6:22 ever unto the LORD; it shall be **w** burnt. 3632
6:23 priest shall be **w** *burnt:* it shall not be eaten. 3632
19: 9 thou shalt not **w reap** the corners 3615+3807.1
Nu 3: 9 they *are* **w given** unto him out of 5414+5414
4: 6 shall spread over *it* a cloth **w** of blue, and 3632
8:16 For they *are* **w given** unto me from 5414+5414
32:11 because they have not **w** followed me: 4390
32:12 for they have **w** followed the LORD. 4390
Dt 1:36 because he hath **w** followed the LORD. 4390
Jos 14: 8 I **w** followed the LORD my God. 4390
14: 9 thou hast **w** followed the LORD my God. 4390
14:14 that he **w** followed the LORD God of 4390
Jdg 17: 3 I had **w dedicated** the silver unto 6942+6942
1Sa 7: 9 offered it *for* a burnt offering **w** unto 3632
1Ch 28:21 all the people *will be* **w** at thy 3605
Job 21:23 his full strength, *being* **w** at ease and quiet. 3605
Isa 22: 1 that thou art **w** gone up to the housetops? 3605
Jer 2:21 planted thee a noble vine, **w** a right seed: 3605
6: 6 she *is* **w** oppression in the midst of her. 3605
13:19 all of it, it shall be **w** carried away captive. 7965
42:15 If ye **w set** your faces to enter *into* 7760+7760
46:28 will I not **leave** thee **w unpunished**. 5352+5352
50:13 not be inhabited, but it shall be **w** desolate: 3605
Eze 11:15 thy kindred, and all the house of Israel **w**, 3605
Am 8: 8 it shall rise up **w** as a flood; and it shall be 3605
9: 5 it shall rise up **w** like a flood; and shall be 3605
Ac 17:16 he saw the city **w given to idolatry**. *1510+2712*
1Th 5:23 And the very God of peace sanctify you **w**; *3651*
1Ti 4:15 upon these *things;* give thyself **w to** them; *1722*

WHOM (763) [WHO] See Index

WHOMSOEVER (20) [EVER, SO, WHO] See Index

WHORE (14) [WHORE'S, WHOREDOM, WHOREDOMS, WHOREMONGER, WHOREMONGERS, WHORES, WHORING, WHORISH]

Lev 19:29 thy daughter, to **cause** her **to be a w**; 2181
21: 7 They shall not take a wife *that is* a **w**, or 2181
21: 9 if she profane herself by **playing the w**, she 2181
Dt 22:21 to **play the w** *in* her father's house: 2181
23:17 There shall be no **w** of the daughters of 6948
23:18 Thou shalt not bring the hire of a **w**, or 2181
Jdg 19: 2 his concubine **played the w** against him, 2181
Pr 23:27 For a **w** *is* a deep ditch; and a strange 2181
Isa 57: 3 the seed of the adulterer and the **w**. 2181
Eze 16:28 Thou hast **played the w** also with 2181
Rev 17: 1 the great **w** that sitteth upon many waters: *4204*
17:15 where the **w** sitteth, are peoples, and *4204*
17:16 these shall hate the **w**, and shall make her *4204*
19: 2 for he hath judged the great **w**, which did *4204*

WHORE'S (1) [WHORE]

Jer 3: 3 thou hadst a **w** forehead, 802+2181

WHOREDOM (22) [WHORE]

Ge 38:24 and also, behold, she *is* with child by **w**. 2183
Lev 19:29 lest the land **fall to w**, and the land become 2181
20: 5 to commit **w** with Molech, from among 2181
Nu 25: 1 the people begun to **commit w** with 2181
Jer 3: 9 came to pass through the lightness of her **w**, 2184
13:27 the lewdness of thy **w**, *and* 2184
Eze 16:17 of men, and didst **commit w** with them, 2181
16:33 come unto thee on every side for thy **w**. 8457
20:30 and **commit** ye **w** after their abominations? 2181
23: 8 her virginity, and poured their **w** upon her. 8457
23:17 they defiled her with their **w**, and she was 8457
23:27 and thy **w** *brought* from the land of Egypt: 2184
43: 7 *neither* they, nor their kings, by their **w**, 2184
43: 9 Now let them put away their **w**, and 2184
Hos 1: 2 the land hath **committed great w**, 2181+2181
4:10 they shall **commit w**, and shall not 2181
4:11 **W** and wine and new wine take *away* 2184
4:13 therefore your daughters shall **commit w**, 2181
4:14 your daughters when they **commit w**, 2181
4:18 they have **committed w continually**: 2181+2181
5: 3 thou **committest w**, *and* Israel is defiled. 2181
6:10 there *is* the **w** of Ephraim, Israel is defiled. 2184

WHOREDOMS (32) [WHORE]

Nu 14:33 bear your **w**, until your carcases be wasted 2184
2Ki 9:22 so long as the **w** of thy mother Jezebel and 2183
2Ch 21:13 like to the **w** of the house of Ahab, and 2181
Jer 3: 2 thou hast polluted the land with thy **w** and 2184
Eze 16:20 be devoured. *Is this* of thy **w** a small matter, 8457
16:22 thy **w** thou hast not remembered the days of 8457
16:25 one that passed by, and multiplied thy **w**. 8457
16:26 hast increased thy **w**, to provoke me to 8457
16:34 is in thee from *other* women in thy **w**, 8457
16:34 whereas none followeth thee to **commit w**: 2181
16:36 thy nakedness discovered through thy **w** 8457
23: 3 they **committed w** in Egypt; 2181
23: 3 in Egypt; they **committed w** in their youth: 2181
23: 7 Thus she committed her **w** with them, 8457
23: 8 Neither left she her **w** *brought* from Egypt: 8457
23:11 in her **w** more than her sister in *her* 8457

Eze 23:11 whoredoms more than her sister in *her* w. 2183
23:14 *that* she increased her w: for when she saw 8457
23:18 So she discovered her w, and 8457
23:19 Yet she multiplied her w, in calling to 8457
23:29 the nakedness of thy w shall be discovered, 2183
23:29 both thy lewdness and thy w. 8457
23:35 bear thou also thy lewdness and thy w. 8457
23:43 Will they now **commit** w with her, 2181+8457
Hos 1: 2 take unto thee a wife of w and children of 2183
1: 2 a wife of whoredoms and children of w: 2183
2: 2 therefore put away her w out of her sight, 2183
2: 4 her children; for they *be the* children of w. 2183
4:12 for the spirit of w hath caused *them* to err, 2183
5: 4 for the spirit of w *is* in the midst of them, 2183
Na 3: 4 Because of the multitude of the w of 2183
3: 4 that selleth nations through her w, and 2183

WHOREMONGER (1) [WHORE]
Eph 5: 5 For this ye know, that no w, nor unclean *4205*

WHOREMONGERS (4) [WHORE]
1Ti 1:10 For w, for them that defile themselves with *4205*
Heb 13: 4 but w and adulterers God will judge. *4205*
Rev 21: 8 and w, and sorcerers, and idolaters, *4205*
22:15 and w, and murderers, and idolaters, and *4205*

WHORES (2) [WHORE]
Eze 16:33 They give gifts to all w: but thou givest thy 2181
Hos 4:14 for themselves are separated with w, and 2181

WHORING (19) [WHORE]
Ex 34:15 they **go a w** after their gods, and 2181
34:16 their daughters **go a w** after their gods, and 2181
34:16 and **make** thy sons **go a w** after their gods. 2181
Lev 17: 7 after whom they have **gone a w**. 2181
20: 5 cut him off, and all that **go a w** after him, 2181
20: 6 after wizards, to **go a w** after them, I will 2181
Nu 15:39 own eyes, after which ye use to **go a w**: 2181
Dt 31:16 **go a w** after the gods of the strangers of 2181
Jdg 2:17 they **went a w** after other gods, and 2181
8:27 all Israel **went** thither **a w** after it: 2181
8:33 **went a w** after Baalim, and 2181
1Ch 5:25 **went a w** after the gods of the people of 2181
2Ch 21:13 **made** Judah and the inhabitants of Jerusalem **to go a w**, 2181
Ps 73:27 thou hast destroyed all them that **go a w** 2181
106:39 and **went a w** with their own inventions. 2181
Eze 6: 9 their eyes, which **go a w** after their idols: 2181
23:30 thou hast **gone a w** after the heathen, 2181
Hos 4:12 they have **gone a w** from under their God. 2181
9: 1 for thou hast **gone a w** from thy God, 2181

WHORISH (3) [WHORE]
Pr 6:26 For by means of a w woman *a man is* 2181
Eze 6: 9 because I am broken with their w heart, 2181
16:30 *things,* the work of an imperious w woman; 2181

WHOSE (314) [WHO] See Index

WHOSO (54) [SO, WHO] See Index

WHOSOEVER (183) [EVER, SO, WHO] See Index

WHY (282) See Index

WICK See TOW

WICK TRIMMERS See SNUFFERS

WICKED (344) [WICKEDLY, WICKEDNESS]
Ge 13:13 the men of Sodom *were* w and 7451
18:23 thou also destroy the righteous with the w? 7563
18:25 to slay the righteous with the w: 7563
18:25 that the righteous should be as the w, 7563
38: 7 was w in the sight of the LORD; 7451
Ex 9:27 *is* righteous, and I and my people *are* w. 7563
23: 1 put not thine hand with the w to be an 7563
23: 7 slay thou not: for I will not justify the w. 7563
Lev 20:17 it *is* a w **thing**; and they shall be cut off in 2617
Nu 16:26 from the tents of these w men, and 7563
Dt 15: 9 Beware that there be not a thought in thy w 1100
17: 5 which have committed that w thing, 7451
23: 9 then keep thee from every w thing. 7451
25: 1 justify the righteous, and condemn the w. 7563
25: 2 if the w *man be* worthy to be beaten, 7563
1Sa 2: 9 and the w shall be silent in darkness; 7563
24:13 Wickedness proceedeth from the w: 7563
30:22 answered all the w men and *men* of Belial, 7451
2Sa 3:34 as *a man* falleth before w men, *so* 5766
4:11 when w men have slain a righteous person 7563
1Ki 8:32 and judge thy servants, condemning the w, 7563
2Ki 17:11 wrought w things to provoke the LORD to 7451
2Ch 6:23 and judge thy servants, by requiting the w, 7563
7:14 seek my face, and turn from their w ways; 7451
24: 7 For the sons of Athaliah, *that* w **woman**, 4849
Ne 9:35 neither turned they from their w works. 7451
Est 7: 6 The adversary and enemy *is* this w Haman. 7451
9:25 he commanded by letters *that* his w device, 7451
Job 3:17 There the w cease *from* troubling; and 7563
8:22 the dwelling place of the w shall come to 7563
9:22 said *it,* He destroyeth the perfect and the w. 7563
9:24 The earth is given into the hand of the w: 7563
9:29 *If* I be w, why then labour I in vain? 7561
10: 3 and shine upon the counsel of the w? 7563
10: 7 Thou knowest that I am not w; and *there is* 7561
10:15 If I be w, woe unto me; and *if* I be 7561
11:20 the eyes of the w shall fail, and they shall 7563
15:20 The w *man* travaileth with pain all his days, 7563
16:11 and turned me over into the hands of the w. 7563
18: 5 the light of the w shall be put out, and 7563
18:21 Surely such *are* the dwellings of the w, and 5767
20: 5 That the triumphing of the w *is* short, and 7563
20:22 every hand of the w shall come *upon* him. 6001
20:29 This *is* the portion of a w man from God, 7563
21: 7 Wherefore do the w live, become old, yea, 7563
21:16 the counsel of the w is far from me. 7563
21:17 How oft is the candle of the w put out! and 7563
21:28 and where *are* the dwelling places of the w? 7563
21:30 That the w is reserved to the day of 7451
22:15 Hast thou marked the old way which w men 205
22:18 but the counsel of the w is far from me. 7563
24: 6 and they gather the vintage of the w. 7563
27: 7 Let mine enemy be as the w, and he that 7563
27:13 This *is* the portion of a w man with God, 7563
29:17 I brake the jaws of the w, and pluckt 5767
31: 3 *Is* not destruction to the w? and a strange 5767
34: 8 of iniquity, and walketh with w men. 7562
34:18 *Is it fit* to say to a king, *Thou art* w? *and* 1100
34:26 He striketh them as w *men* in the open sight 7563
34:36 the end because of *his* answers for w men. 205
36: 6 He preserveth not the life of the w: but 7563
36:17 thou hast fulfilled the judgment of the w: 7563
38:13 that the w might be shaken out of it? 7563
38:15 from the w their light is withholden, and 7563
40:12 and tread down the w in their place. 7563
Ps 7: 9 O let the wickedness of the w come to an 7563
7:11 and God is angry *with the* w every day. NIH
9: 5 the heathen, thou hast destroyed the w, 7563
9:16 the w is snared in the work of his own 7563
9:17 The w shall be turned into hell, *and* all 7563
10: 2 The w in *his* pride doth persecute the poor: 7563
10: 3 For the w boasteth of his heart's desire, and 7563
10: 4 The w, through the pride of his 7563
10:13 Wherefore doth the w contemn God? 7563
10:15 Break thou the arm of the w and the evil 7563
11: 2 For lo, the w bend *their* bow, they make 7563
11: 5 the w and him that loveth violence his soul 7563
11: 6 Upon the w he shall rain snares, fire and 7563
12: 8 The w walk on every side, when the vilest 7563
17: 9 From the w that oppress me, *from* my 7563
17:13 deliver my soul from the w, *which is* thy 7563
22:16 the assembly of the w have inclosed me: 7489
26: 5 of evildoers; and will not sit with the w. 7563
27: 2 When the w, *even* mine enemies and 7489
28: 3 Draw me not away with the w, and with 7563
31:17 let the w be ashamed, *and* let them be silent 7563
32:10 Many sorrows *shall be* to the w: but he that 7563
34:21 Evil shall slay the w: and they that hate 7563
36: 1 The transgression of the w saith within my 7563
36:11 and let not the hand of the w remove me. 7563
37: 7 of the man who bringeth w **devices** to pass. 4209
37:10 a little while, and the w *shall* not *be:* yea, 7563
37:12 The w plotteth against the just, and 7563
37:14 The w have drawn out the sword, and 7563
37:16 hath *is* better than the riches of many w. 7563
37:17 For the arms of the w shall be broken: but 7563
37:20 the w shall perish, and the enemies of 7563
37:21 The w borroweth, and payeth not again: but 7563
37:28 but the seed of the w shall be cut off. 7563
37:32 The w watcheth the righteous, and 7563
37:34 when the w are cut off, thou shalt see *it.* 7563

Ps	37:35	I have seen the **w** in great power, and	7563
	37:38	the end of the **w** shall be cut off.	7563
	37:40	he shall deliver them from the **w**, and	7563
	39: 1	with a bridle, while the **w** *is* before me.	7563
	50:16	unto the **w** God saith, What hast thou to do	7563
	55: 3	because of the oppression of the **w**:	7563
	58: 3	The **w** are estranged from the womb:	7563
	58:10	he shall wash his feet in the blood of the **w**.	7563
	59: 5	be not merciful to any **w** transgressors.	205
	64: 2	Hide me from the secret counsel of the **w**;	7489
	68: 2	*so* let the **w** perish at the presence of God.	7563
	71: 4	O my God, out of the hand of the **w**,	7563
	73: 3	*when* I saw the prosperity of the **w**.	7563
	74:19	**w**: forget not the congregation of thy poor	NIH
	75: 4	and to the **w**, Lift not up the horn:	7563
	75: 8	all the **w** of the earth shall wring *them* out,	7563
	75:10	All the horns of the **w** also will I cut off;	7563
	82: 2	and accept the persons of the **w**?	7563
	82: 4	needy: rid *them* out of the hand of the **w**.	7563
	91: 8	thou behold and see the reward of the **w**.	7563
	92: 7	When the **w** spring as the grass, and	7563
	92:11	mine ears shall hear *my desire* of the **w** that	7489
	94: 3	LORD, how long shall the **w**, how long	7563
	94: 3	the wicked, how long shall the **w** triumph?	7563
	94:13	until the pit be digged for the **w**.	7563
	97:10	he delivereth them out of the hand of the **w**.	7563
	101: 3	I will set no **w** thing before mine eyes:	1100
	101: 4	from me: I will not know a **w** *person*.	7451
	101: 8	I will early destroy all the **w** of the land;	7563
	101: 8	that *I* may cut off all **w** doers from the city of	205
	104:35	out of the earth, and let the **w** be no more.	7563
	106:18	in their company; the flame burnt up the **w**.	7563
	109: 2	For the mouth of the **w** and the mouth of	7563
	109: 6	Set thou a **w** *man* over him: and let Satan	7563
	112:10	The **w** shall see *it*, and be grieved; he shall	7563
	112:10	melt away: the desire of the **w** shall perish.	7563
	119:53	because of the **w** that forsake thy law.	7563
	119:61	The bands of the **w** have robbed me: *but*	7563
	119:95	The **w** have waited for me to destroy me:	7563
	119:110	The **w** have laid a snare for me: yet I erred	7563
	119:119	Thou puttest away all the **w** of the earth	7563
	119:155	Salvation *is* far from the **w**: for they seek	7563
	125: 3	For the rod of the **w** shall not rest upon	7562
	129: 4	he hath cut asunder the cords of the **w**.	7563
	139:19	Surely thou wilt slay the **w**, O God:	7563
	139:24	see if *there be any* **w** way in me, and	6090
	140: 4	O LORD, from the hands of the **w**;	7563
	140: 8	Grant not, O LORD, the desires of the **w**:	7563
	140: 8	further not his **w device**; *lest* they exalt	2162
	141: 4	to practise **w** works with men that work	7562
	141:10	Let the **w** fall into their own nets,	7563
	145:20	that love him: but all the **w** will he destroy.	7563
	146: 9	the way of the **w** he turneth upside down.	7563
	147: 6	he casteth the **w** down to the ground.	7563
Pr	2:14	*and* delight in the frowardness of the **w**;	7451
	2:22	the **w** shall be cut off from the earth, and	7563
	3:25	neither of the desolation of the **w**, when it	7563
	3:33	of the LORD *is* in the house of the **w**:	7563
	4:14	Enter not into the path of the **w**, and go not	7563
	4:19	The way of the **w** *is* as darkness: they know	7563
	5:22	His own iniquities shall take the **w** himself,	7563
	6:12	A naughty person, a **w** man, walketh *with* a	205
	6:18	A heart that deviseth **w** imaginations,	205
	9: 7	he that rebuketh a **w** *man getteth* himself a	7563
	10: 3	but he casteth away the substance of the **w**.	7563
	10: 6	but violence covereth the mouth of the **w**.	7563
	10: 7	*is* blessed: but the name of the **w** shall rot.	7563
	10:11	but violence covereth the mouth of the **w**.	7563
	10:16	*tendeth* to life: the fruit of the **w** to sin.	7563
	10:20	the heart of the **w** *is* little worth.	7563
	10:24	The fear of the **w**, it shall come *upon* him:	7563
	10:25	so *is* the **w** no *more*: but the righteous *is* an	7563
	10:27	but the years of the **w** shall be shortened.	7563
	10:28	but the expectation of the **w** shall perish.	7563
	10:30	but the **w** shall not inhabit the earth.	7563
	10:32	the mouth of the **w** *speaketh* frowardness.	7563
	11: 5	but the **w** shall fall by his own wickedness.	7563
	11: 7	When a **w** man dieth, *his* expectation shall	7563
	11: 8	of trouble, and the **w** cometh in his stead.	7563
	11:10	and when the **w** perish, *there is* shouting.	7563
	11:11	but it is overthrown by the mouth of the **w**.	7563
	11:18	The **w** worketh a deceitful work: but *to* him	7563
	11:21	*join* in hand, the **w** shall not be unpunished:	7451
	11:23	*but* the expectation of the **w** *is* wrath.	7563
	11:31	the earth: much more the **w** and the sinner.	7563
	12: 2	but a man of **w devices** will he condemn.	4209
	12: 5	*but* the counsels of the **w** *are* deceit.	7563
	12: 6	The words of the **w** *are* to lie in wait *for*	7563
	12: 7	The **w** *are* overthrown, and *are* not: but	7563
	12:10	but the tender mercies of the **w** *are* cruel.	7563
	12:12	The **w** desireth the net of evil *men*: but	7563
	12:13	The **w** is snared by the transgression of *his*	7451
	12:21	but the **w** shall be filled *with* mischief.	7563
	12:26	but the way of the **w** seduceth them.	7563
	13: 5	a **w** *man* is loathsome, and cometh to	7563
	13: 9	but the lamp of the **w** shall be put out.	7563
	13:17	A **w** messenger falleth into mischief: but	7563
	13:25	his soul: but the belly of the **w** shall want.	7563
	14:11	The house of the **w** shall be overthrown:	7563
	14:17	and a man of **w devices** is hated.	4209
	14:19	and the **w** at the gates of the righteous.	7563
	14:32	The **w** is driven away in his wickedness:	7563
	15: 6	but in the revenues of the **w** *is* trouble.	7563
	15: 8	The sacrifice of the **w** *is* an abomination to	7563
	15: 9	The way of the **w** *is* an abomination unto	7563
	15:26	The thoughts of the **w** *are* an abomination	7451
	15:28	the mouth of the **w** poureth out evil *things*.	7563
	15:29	The LORD *is* far from the **w**: but	7563
	16: 4	yea, even the **w** for the day of evil.	7563
	17: 4	A **w doer** giveth heed to false lips; *and*	7489
	17:15	He that justifieth the **w**, and he that	7563
	17:23	A **w** *man* taketh a gift out of the bosom to	7563
	18: 3	When the **w** cometh, *then* cometh also	7563
	18: 5	*It is* not good to accept the person of the **w**,	7563
	19:28	and the mouth of the **w** devoureth iniquity.	7563
	20:26	A wise king scattereth the **w**, and	7563
	21: 4	*and* the plowing of the **w**, *is* sin.	7563
	21: 7	The robbery of the **w** shall destroy them;	7563
	21:10	The soul of the **w** desireth evil:	7563
	21:12	*man* wisely considereth the house of the **w**:	7563
	21:12	*God* overthroweth the **w** for *their*	7563
	21:18	The **w** *shall be* a ransom for the righteous,	7563
	21:27	The sacrifice of the **w** *is* abomination:	7563
	21:27	*when* he bringeth it with a **w mind**?	2154
	21:29	A **w** man hardeneth his face: but *as for*	7563
	24:15	O **w** *man*, against the dwelling of	7563
	24:16	up *again*: but the **w** shall fall into mischief.	7563
	24:19	evil *men*, neither be thou envious at the **w**;	7563
	24:20	*man*; the candle of the **w** shall be put out.	7563
	24:24	He that saith unto the **w**, Thou *art*	7563
	25: 5	Take away the **w** *from* before the king, and	7563
	25:26	A righteous *man* falling down before the **w**	7563
	26:23	a **w** heart *are like* a potsherd covered with	7451
	28: 1	The **w** flee when no man pursueth: but	7563
	28: 4	They that forsake the law praise the **w**: but	7563
	28:12	but when the **w** rise, a man is hidden.	7563
	28:15	*so is* a **w** ruler over the poor people.	7563
	28:28	When the **w** rise, men hide themselves: but	7563
	29: 2	when the **w** beareth rule, the people mourn.	7563
	29: 7	*but* the **w** regardeth not to know *it*.	7563
	29:12	ruler hearken to lies, all his servants *are* **w**.	7563
	29:16	When the **w** are multiplied,	7563
	29:27	upright in the way *is* abomination to the **w**.	7563
Ecc	3:17	God shall judge the righteous and the **w**:	7563
	7:15	there is a **w** *man* that prolongeth *his life* in	7563
	7:17	Be not over much **w**, neither be thou	7561
	8:10	so I saw the **w** buried, who had come and	7563
	8:13	it shall not be well with the **w**, neither shall	7563
	8:14	happeneth according to the work of the **w**;	7563
	8:14	there be **w** *men*, to whom it happeneth	7563
	9: 2	*is* one event to the righteous, and to the **w**;	7563
Isa	3:11	Woe unto the **w**! *it shall be* ill *with him*: for	7563
	5:23	Which justify the **w** for reward, and	7563
	11: 4	the breath of his lips shall he slay the **w**.	7563
	13:11	for *their* evil, and the **w** for their iniquity;	7563
	14: 5	The LORD hath broken the staff of the **w**,	7563
	26:10	Let favour be shewed to the **w**, *yet* will he	7563
	32: 7	he deviseth **w devices** to destroy the poor	2154
	48:22	*is* no peace, saith the LORD, unto the **w**.	7563
	53: 9	he made his grave with the **w**, and with	7563
	55: 7	Let the **w** forsake his way, and	7563
	57:20	the **w** *are* like the troubled sea, when it	7563
	57:21	*There is* no peace, saith my God, to the **w**.	7563
Jer	2:33	hast thou also taught the **w ones** thy ways.	7451
	5:26	For among my people are found **w** *men*:	7563
	5:28	yea, they overpass the deeds of the **w**:	7451
	6:29	in vain: for the **w** are not plucked away.	7451
	12: 1	Wherefore doth the way of the **w** prosper?	7563

Jer 15:21 I will deliver thee out of the hand of the w, 7451
17: 9 above all *things,* and **desperately** w: 605
23:19 shall fall grievously upon the head of the w. 7563
25:31 he will give them *that are* w to the sword, 7563
30:23 shall fall with pain upon the head of the w. 7563
Eze 3:18 When I say unto the w, Thou shalt surely 7563
3:18 nor speakest to warn the w from his wicked 7563
3:18 nor speakest to warn the wicked from his w 7563
3:18 the same w *man* shall die in his iniquity; 7563
3:19 Yet if thou warn the w, and he turn not 7563
3:19 nor from his w way, he shall die in his 7563
7:21 a prey, and to the w of the earth for a spoil; 7563
8: 9 behold the w abominations that they do 7451
11: 2 and give w counsel in this city: 7451
13:22 strengthened the hands of the w, that *he* 7451
13:22 that *he* should not return from his w way, 7563
18:20 the wickedness of the w shall be upon him. 7563
18:21 if the w will turn from all his sins that he 7563
18:23 Have I any pleasure at all that the w should 7563
18:24 all the abominations that the w *man* doeth, 7563
18:27 when the w *man* turneth away from his 7563
20:44 not according to your w ways, 7451
21: 3 cut off from thee the righteous and the w. 7563
21: 4 cut off from thee the righteous and the w, 7563
21:25 thou, profane w prince of Israel, whose day 7563
21:29 the necks of *them that are* slain of the w, 7563
30:12 and sell the land into the hand of the w: 7451
33: 8 When I say unto the w, O wicked *man,* 7563
33: 8 the wicked, O w *man,* thou shalt surely die; 7563
33: 8 if thou dost not speak to warn the w from 7563
33: 8 that w *man* shall die in his iniquity; 7563
33: 9 if thou warn the w of his way to turn from 7563
33:11 I have no pleasure in the death of the w; 7563
33:11 but that the w turn from his way and live: 7563
33:12 as for the wickedness of the w, he shall not 7563
33:14 Again, when I say unto the w, Thou shalt 7563
33:15 *If* the w restore the pledge, give again that 7563
33:19 if the w turn from his wickedness, and 7563
Da 12:10 and tried; but the w shall do wickedly: 7563
12:10 none of the w shall understand; but 7563
Mic 6:10 of wickedness *in* the house of the w, 7563
6:11 Shall I count *them* pure with the w 7562
Na 1: 3 will not at all acquit *the w*: the LORD *hath* NIH
1:11 evil against the LORD, a w counseller. 1100
1:15 for the w shall no more pass through thee; 1100
Hab 1: 4 for the w doth compass about the righteous; 7563
1:13 holdest thy tongue when the w devoureth 7563
3:13 the head out of the house of the w, 7563
Zep 1: 3 and the stumblingblocks with the w; 7563
Mal 3:18 discern between the righteous and the w, 7563
4: 3 ye shall tread down the w; for they shall be 7563
Mt 12:45 seven other spirits **more w than** himself, *4191*
12:45 so shall it be also unto this w generation. *4190*
13:19 then cometh the **w one**, and catcheth away *4190*
13:38 but the tares are the children of the **w one**; *4190*
13:49 and sever the w from among the just, *4190*
16: 4 A w and adulterous generation seeketh *4190*
18:32 said unto him, O *thou* w servant, I forgave *4190*
21:41 He will miserably destroy those w *men,* *2556*
25:26 said unto him, *Thou* w and slothful servant, *4190*
Lk 11:26 seven other spirits **more w than** himself; *4191*
19:22 mouth will I judge thee, *thou* w servant. *4190*
Ac 2:23 and by w hands have crucified and slain: *459*
18:14 If it were a matter of wrong or w lewdness, *4190*
1Co 5:13 from among yourselves *that* w *person.* *4190*
Eph 6:16 able to quench all the fiery darts of the w. *4190*
Col 1:21 and enemies in *your* mind by w works, *4190*
2Th 2: 8 And then shall *that* W be revealed, *459*
3: 2 be delivered from unreasonable and w men: *4190*
2Pe 2: 7 vexed with the filthy conversation of the w: *113*
3:17 being led away with the error of the w, *113*
1Jn 2:13 because you have overcome the **w one**. *4190*
2:14 in you, and ye have overcome the **w one**. *4190*
3:12 *who* was of *that* **w one**, and slew his *4190*
5:18 and *that* **w one** toucheth him not. *4190*

WICKEDLY (23) [WICKED]

Ge 19: 7 And said, I pray you, brethren, **do** not *so* **w**. 7489
Dt 9:18 in doing w in the sight of the LORD, 7451
Jdg 19:23 my brethren, *nay,* I pray you, do not *so* w; 7489
1Sa 12:25 if ye shall **still do** w, ye shall be 7489+7489
2Sa 22:22 and have not w **departed** from my God. 7561
24:17 said, Lo, I have sinned, and I have **done** w: 5753
2Ki 21:11 hath **done** w above all that the Amorites 7489
2Ch 6:37 we have done amiss, and have **dealt** w; 7561
20:35 Ahaziah king of Israel, who did **very** w: 7561
22: 3 for his mother was his counseller to **do** w. 7561
Ne 9:33 thou hast done right, but we have **done** w: 7561
Job 13: 7 Will you speak w for God? and 5766
34:12 Yea, surely God will not **do** w, neither will 7561
Ps 18:21 and have not w **departed** from my God. 7561
73: 8 and speak w *concerning* oppression: 7451+871.1
74: 3 *even* all *that* the enemy hath **done** w in 7489
106: 6 have committed iniquity, we have **done** w. 7561
139:20 For they speak against thee w, *and* 4209+3807.1
Da 9: 5 and have **done** w, and have rebelled, 7561
9:15 this day; we have sinned, we have **done** w. 7561
11:32 such as **do** w against the covenant shall he 7561
12:10 and tried; but the wicked shall **do** w: 7561
Mal 4: 1 all the proud, yea, and all that do w, 7564

WICKEDNESS (127) [WICKED]

Ge 6: 5 GOD saw that the w of man *was* great in 7451
39: 9 how then can I do this great w, and 7451
Lev 18:17 *for* they *are* her near kinswomen: it *is* w. 2154
19:29 and the land become full of w. 2154
20:14 if a man take a wife and her mother, it *is* w: 2154
20:14 and they; that there be no w among you. 2154
Dt 9: 4 for the w of these nations the LORD doth 7564
9: 5 for the w of these nations the LORD thy 7564
9:27 this people, nor to their w, nor to their sin: 7562
13:11 shall do no more any such w as this is 7451
17: 2 that hath wrought w in the sight of 7451
28:20 because of the w of thy doings, 7455
Jdg 9:56 Thus God rendered the w of Abimelech, 7451
20: 3 children of Israel, Tell *us,* how was this w? 7451
20:12 What w *is* this that is done among you? 7451
1Sa 12:17 may perceive and see that your w *is* great, 7451
12:20 ye have done all this w: yet turn not aside 7451
24:13 **W** proceedeth from the wicked: 7562
25:39 for the LORD hath returned the w of 7451
2Sa 3:39 reward the doer of evil according to his w. 7451
7:10 neither shall the children of w afflict them 5766
1Ki 1:52 but if w shall be found in him, he shall die. 7451
2:44 Thou knowest all the w which thine heart is 7451
2:44 the LORD shall return thy w upon thine 7451
8:47 done perversely, we have **committed** w; 7561
21:25 which did sell himself to work w in 7451
2Ki 21: 6 he wrought much w in the sight of 7451
1Ch 17: 9 neither shall the children of w waste them 5766
Job 4: 8 plow iniquity, and sow w, reap the same. 5999
11:11 he seeth w also; will he not then consider *it?* 205
11:14 and let not w dwell in thy tabernacles. 5766
20:12 Though w be sweet in his mouth, *though* he 7451
22: 5 *Is* not thy w great? and thine iniquities 7451
24:20 and w shall be broken as a tree. 5766
27: 4 My lips shall not speak w, nor my tongue 5766
34:10 far be it from God, *that he should do* w; and 7562
35: 8 Thy w *may hurt* a man as thou *art;* and thy 7562
Ps 5: 4 thou *art* not a God that hath pleasure in w: 7562
5: 9 their inward *part is* very w; their throat *is* 1942
7: 9 O let the w of the wicked come to an end; 7451
10:15 the evil *man:* seek out his w *till* thou find 7562
28: 4 and according to the w of their endeavours: 7455
45: 7 Thou lovest righteousness, and hatest w: 7562
52: 7 *and* strengthened himself in his w. 1942
55:11 **W** *is* in the midst thereof: deceit and 1942
55:15 for w *is* in their dwellings, *and* 7451
58: 2 Yea, in heart you work w; you weigh 5766
84:10 of my God, than to dwell in the tents of w. 7562
89:22 upon him; nor the son of w afflict him. 5766
94:23 and shall cut them off in their own w; 7451
107:34 for the w of them that dwell therein. 7451
Pr 4:17 For they eat the bread of w, and drink 7562
8: 7 and w *is* an abomination to my lips. 7562
10: 2 Treasures of w profit nothing: but 7562
11: 5 but the wicked shall fall by his own w. 7564
12: 3 A man shall not be established by w: but 7562
13: 6 in the way: but w overthroweth the sinner. 7564
14:32 The wicked is driven away in his w: but 7451
16:12 *It is* an abomination to kings to commit w: 7562
21:12 *God* overthroweth the wicked for *their* w. 7451
26:26 his w shall be shewed before the *whole* 7451
30:20 her mouth, and saith, I have done no w. 205
Ecc 3:16 the place of judgment, *that* w *was* there; 7562
7:15 *man* that prolongeth *his life* in his w. 7451
7:25 *of things,* and to know the w of folly, 7562
8: 8 neither shall w deliver those that are given 7562

Isa 9:18 For w burneth as the fire: it shall devour 7564
47:10 For thou hast trusted in thy w: thou hast 7451
58: 4 and debate, and to smite with the fist of w: 7562
58: 6 to loose the bands of w, to undo the heavy 7562
Jer 1:16 against them touching all their w, 7451
2:19 Thine own w shall correct thee, and 7451
3: 2 land with thy whoredoms and with thy w. 7451
4:14 O Jerusalem, wash thine heart from w, that 7451
4:18 this *is* thy w, because *it is* bitter, because 7451
6: 7 out her waters, so she casteth out her w: 7451
7:12 see what I did to it for the w of my people 7451
8: 6 no man repented him of his w, saying, 7451
12: 4 for the w of them that dwell therein? 7451
14:16 for I will pour their w upon them. 7451
14:20 our w, *and* the iniquity of our fathers: 7562
22:22 be ashamed and confounded for all thy w. 7451
23:11 yea, in my house have I found their w, 7451
23:14 that none doth return from his w: 7451
33: 5 for all whose w I have hid my face from 7451
44: 3 Because of their w which they have 7451
44: 5 nor inclined their ear to turn from their w, 7451
44: 9 Have ye forgotten the w of your fathers, 7451
44: 9 the w of the kings of Judah, and 7451
44: 9 the w of their wives, and your own 7451
44: 9 your own w, and the wickedness of your 7451
44: 9 own wickedness, and the w of your wives, 7451
La 1:22 Let all their w come before thee; and 7451
Eze 3:19 he turn not from his w, nor from his wicked 7562
5: 6 she hath changed my judgments into w 7564
7:11 Violence is risen up into a rod of w: 7562
16:23 it came to pass after all thy w, (woe, 7451
16:57 Before thy w was discovered, as *at* the time 7451
18:20 and the w of the wicked shall be upon him. 7564
18:27 away from his w that he hath committed, 7564
31:11 with him: I have driven him out for his w. 7562
33:12 as for the w of the wicked, he shall not fall 7564
33:12 in the day that he turneth from his w; 7562
33:19 if the wicked turn from his w, and do that 7564
Hos 7: 1 was discovered, and the w of Samaria: 7451
7: 2 in their hearts *that* I remember all their w: 7451
7: 3 They make the king glad with their w, and 7451
9:15 All their w *is* in Gilgal, for there I hated 7451
9:15 for the w of their doings I will drive them 7455
10:13 Ye have plowed w, ye have reaped 7562
10:15 unto you because of your **great** w; 7451+7465
Joel 3:13 the fats overflow; for their w *is* great. 7451
Jnh 1: 2 against it; for their w is come up before me. 7451
Mic 6:10 Are there yet the treasures of w *in* 7562
Na 3:19 for upon whom hath not thy w passed 7451
Zec 5: 8 he said, This *is* w. And he cast it into 7564
Mal 1: 4 they shall call them, The border of w, and, 7564
3:15 yea, they that work w are set up; yea, 7564
Mt 22:18 But Jesus perceived their w, and said, *4189*
Mk 7:22 Thefts, covetousness, w, deceit, *4189*
Lk 11:39 your inward part is full of ravening and w. *4189*
Ac 8:22 Repent therefore of this thy w, and *2549*
25: 5 accuse this man, if there be any *w* in him. NIG
Ro 1:29 fornication, w, covetousness, *4189*
1Co 5: 8 neither with the leaven of malice and w; *4189*
Eph 6:12 against spiritual w in high *places.* *4189*
1Jn 5:19 are of God, and the whole world lieth in w. *4190*

WIDE (15) [WIDENESS]

Dt 15: 8 thou shalt **open** thine hand w unto 6605+6605
15:11 Thou shalt **open** thine hand w unto 6605+6605
1Ch 4:40 the land *was* w, and quiet, and 3027+7342
Job 29:23 they **opened** their mouth w *as* for the latter 6473
30:14 They came *upon me* as a w breaking in *of* 7342
Ps 35:21 they **opened** their mouth w against me, *and* 7337
81:10 **open** thy mouth w, and I will fill it. 7337
104:25 *So is* this great and w sea, 3027+7342
Pr 13: 3 he that **openeth** w his lips shall have 6589
21: 9 than with a brawling woman in a w house. 2267
25:24 with a brawling woman and in a w house. 2267
Isa 57: 4 against whom **make** ye a w mouth, *and* 7337
Jer 22:14 I will build me a w house and 4060
Na 3:13 the gates of thy land shall be **set** w open 6605
Mt 7:13 for w *is* the gate, and broad *is* the way, *4116*

WIDENESS (1) [WIDE]

Eze 41:10 between the chambers *was* the w of twenty 7341

WIDOW (50) [WIDOW'S, WIDOWHOOD, WIDOWS, WIDOWS']

Ge 38:11 Remain a w *at* thy father's house, till Shelah 490
Ex 22:22 Ye shall not afflict any w, or fatherless child. 490
Lev 21:14 A w, or a divorced *woman,* or profane, *or* 490
22:13 if the priest's daughter be a w, or divorced, 490
Nu 30: 9 every vow of a w, and of her that is 490
Dt 10:18 the judgment of the fatherless and w, 490
14:29 the stranger, and the fatherless, and the w, 490
16:11 the stranger, and the fatherless, and the w, 490
16:14 the stranger, and the fatherless, and the w, 490
24:19 the stranger, for the fatherless, and for the w: 490
24:20 the stranger, for the fatherless, and for the w. 490
24:21 the stranger, for the fatherless, and for the w. 490
26:12 the stranger, the fatherless, and the w, 490
26:13 the stranger, to the fatherless, and to the w, 490
27:19 judgment of the stranger, fatherless, and w. 490
2Sa 14: 5 I *am* indeed a w woman, and mine husband 490
1Ki 11:26 mother's name *was* Zeruah, a w woman, 490
17: 9 I have commanded a w woman there to 490
17:10 the w woman *was* there gathering of sticks: 490
17:20 hast thou also brought evil upon the w with 490
Job 24:21 beareth not: and doeth not good to the w. 490
31:16 or have caused the eyes of the w to fail; 490
Ps 94: 6 They slay the w and the stranger, and 490
109: 9 his children be fatherless, and his wife a w. 490
146: 9 he relieveth the fatherless and w: 490
Pr 15:25 but he will establish the border of the w. 490
Isa 1:17 judge the fatherless, plead for the w. 490
1:23 neither doth the cause of the w come unto 490
47: 8 I shall not sit *as* a w, neither shall I know 490
Jer 7: 6 the w, and shed not innocent blood in this 490
22: 3 to the stranger, the fatherless, nor the w, 490
La 1: 1 *how* is she become as a w! she *that was* great 490
Eze 22: 7 have they vexed the fatherless and the w. 490
44:22 Neither shall they take for their wives a w, 490
44:22 of Israel, or a w that had a priest before. 490
Zec 7:10 oppress not the w, nor the fatherless, 490
Mal 3: 5 the w, and the fatherless, and that turn aside 490
Mk 12:42 And there came a certain poor w, and *5503*
12:43 That this poor w hath cast more in, *5503*
Lk 2:37 And she *was* a w of about fourscore and *5503*
4:26 *a city* of Sidon, unto a woman *that was* a w. *5503*
7:12 only son of his mother, and she was a w: *5503*
18: 3 And there was a w in that city; and *5503*
18: 5 Yet because this w troubleth me, I will *5503*
21: 2 And he saw also a certain poor w casting in *5503*
21: 3 that this poor w hath cast in more than *they* *5503*
1Ti 5: 4 But if any w have children or nephews, *5503*
5: 5 Now she that is a w indeed, and desolate, *5503*
5: 9 Let not a w be taken into the number under *5503*
Rev 18: 7 and am no w, and shall see no sorrow. *5503*

WIDOW'S (5) [WIDOW]

Ge 38:14 she put her w garments off from her, and 491
Dt 24:17 nor take a w raiment to pledge: 490
1Ki 7:14 He *was* a w son of the tribe of Naphtali, 490+802
Job 24: 3 they take the w ox for a pledge. 490
29:13 and I caused the w heart to sing for joy. 490

WIDOWHOOD (4) [WIDOW]

Ge 38:19 from her, and put on the garments of her w. 491
2Sa 20: 3 up unto the day of their death, living in w. 491
Isa 47: 9 in one day, the loss of children, and w: 489
54: 4 shalt not remember the reproach of thy w 491

WIDOWS (23) [WIDOW]

Ex 22:24 your wives shall be w, and your children 490
Job 22: 9 Thou hast sent w away empty, and the arms 490
27:15 be buried in death: and his w shall not weep. 490
Ps 68: 5 father of the fatherless, and a judge of the w, 490
78:64 the sword; and their w made no lamentation. 490
Isa 9:17 shall have mercy on their fatherless and w: 490
10: 2 that w may be their prey, and *that* they may 490
Jer 15: 8 Their w are increased to me above the sand 490
18:21 be bereaved of their children, and *be* w; 490
49:11 *them* alive; and let thy w trust in me. 490
La 5: 3 and fatherless, our mothers *are* as w. 490
Eze 22:25 they have made her many w in the midst 490
Lk 4:25 many w were in Israel in the days of Elias, *5503*
Ac 6: 1 their w were neglected in the daily *5503*
9:39 and all the w stood by him weeping, and *5503*
9:41 and when he had called the saints and w, *5503*
1Co 7: 8 I say therefore to the unmarried and w, It is *5503*

W

1Ti	5: 3	Honour **w** that are widows indeed.	5503
	5: 3	Honour widows that are **w** indeed.	5503
	5:11	But the younger **w** refuse: for when they	5503
	5:16	any man or woman that believeth have **w**,	5503
	5:16	that it may relieve them that are **w** indeed.	5503
Jas	1:27	visit the fatherless and **w** in their affliction,	5503

WIDOWS' (3) [WIDOW]

Mt	23:14	for ye devour **w** houses, and for a pretence	5503
Mk	12:40	Which devour **w** houses, and for a pretence	5503
Lk	20:47	Which devour **w** houses, and for a shew	5503

WIFE (396) [WIFE'S, WIVES, WIVES']

Ge	2:24	and his mother, and shall cleave unto his **w**:	802
	2:25	the man and his **w**, and were not ashamed.	802
	3: 8	his **w** hid themselves from the presence of	802
	3:17	thou hast hearkened unto the voice of thy **w**,	802
	3:21	to his **w** did the LORD God make coats of	802
	4: 1	Adam knew Eve his **w**; and she conceived,	802
	4:17	Cain knew his **w**; and she conceived, and	802
	4:25	Adam knew his **w** again; and she bare a son,	802
	6:18	and thy **w**, and thy sons' wives with thee.	802
	7: 7	and his **w**, and his sons' wives with him,	802
	7:13	Noah's **w**, and the three wives of his sons	802
	8:16	thy **w**, and thy sons, and thy sons' wives	802
	8:18	and his **w**, and his sons' wives with him:	802
	11:29	the name of Abram's **w** *was* Sarai; and	802
	11:29	the name of Nahor's **w**, Milcah, the daughter	802
	11:31	his daughter in law, his son Abram's **w**;	802
	12: 5	Abram took Sarai his **w**, and Lot his	802
	12:11	that he said unto Sarai his **w**, Behold now,	802
	12:12	see thee, that they shall say, This *is* his **w**:	802
	12:17	great plagues because of Sarai Abram's **w**.	802
	12:18	didst thou not tell me that she *was* thy **w**?	802
	12:19	so I might have taken her to me to **w**: now	802
	12:19	now therefore behold thy **w**, take *her*, and	802
	12:20	him away, and his **w**, and all that he had.	802
	13: 1	he, and his **w**, and all that he had, and	802
	16: 1	Now Sarai Abram's **w** bare him no *children:*	802
	16: 3	Sarai Abram's **w** took Hagar her maid	802
	16: 3	gave her to her husband Abram to be his **w**.	802
	17:15	God said unto Abraham, *As for* Sarai thy **w**,	802
	17:19	Sarah thy **w** shall bear thee a son indeed;	802
	18: 9	they said unto him, Where *is* Sarah thy **w**?	802
	18:10	of life; and lo, Sarah thy **w** shall have a son.	802
	19:15	Arise, take thy **w**, and thy two daughters,	802
	19:16	upon the hand of his **w**, and upon the hand of	802
	19:26	But his **w** looked back from behind him, and	802
	20: 2	Abraham said of Sarah his **w**, She *is* my	802
	20: 3	which thou hast taken; for she *is* a man's **w**.	1166
	20: 7	Now therefore restore the man *his* **w**; for he	802
	20:12	of my mother; and she became my **w**.	802
	20:14	and restored him Sarah his **w**.	802
	20:17	and his **w**, and his maidservants;	802
	20:18	because of Sarah Abraham's **w**.	802
	21:21	his mother took him a **w** out of the land of	802
	23:19	Abraham buried Sarah his **w** in the cave of	802
	24: 3	that thou shalt not take a **w** unto my son of	802
	24: 4	my kindred, and take a **w** unto my son Isaac.	802
	24: 7	thou shalt take a **w** unto my son from thence.	802
	24:15	son of Milcah, the **w** of Nahor,	802
	24:36	Sarah my master's **w** bare a son to my	802
	24:37	Thou shalt not take a **w** to my son of	802
	24:38	to my kindred, and take a **w** unto my son.	802
	24:40	thou shalt take a **w** for my son of my	802
	24:51	and go, and let her be thy master's son's **w**,	802
	24:67	and took Rebekah, and she became his **w**;	802
	25: 1	again Abraham took a **w**, and her name *was*	802
	25:10	there was Abraham buried, and Sarah his **w**.	802
	25:20	forty years old when he took Rebekah to **w**,	802
	25:21	Isaac intreated the LORD for his **w**,	802
	25:21	of him, and Rebekah his **w** conceived.	802
	26: 7	the men of the place asked *him* of his **w**;	802
	26: 7	for he feared to say, *She is* my **w**; lest,	802
	26: 8	Isaac *was* sporting with Rebekah his **w**.	802
	26: 9	and said, Behold, of a surety she *is* thy **w**:	802
	26:10	people might lightly have lien with thy **w**,	802
	26:11	or his **w** shall surely be put to death.	802
	26:34	Esau was forty years old when he took to **w**	802
	27:46	if Jacob take a **w** of the daughters of Heth,	802
	28: 1	Thou shalt not take a **w** of the daughters of	802
	28: 2	take thee a **w** from thence of the daughters of	802
	28: 6	to Padan-aram, to take him a **w** from thence;	802
	28: 6	Thou shalt not take a **w** of the daughters of	802
	28: 9	the sister of Nebajoth, to be his **w**.	802
	29:21	Give *me* my **w**, for my days are fulfilled,	802
	29:28	he gave him Rachel his daughter to **w** *also.*	802
	30: 4	she gave him Bilhah her handmaid to **w**:	802
	30: 9	Zilpah her maid, and gave her Jacob to **w**.	802
	34: 4	saying, Get me this damsel to **w**.	802
	34: 8	your daughter: I pray you give her him to **w**.	802
	34:12	say unto me: but give me the damsel to **w**.	802
	36:10	Eliphaz the son of Adah the **w** of Esau,	802
	36:10	Reuel the son of Bashemath the **w** of Esau.	802
	36:12	these *were* the sons of Adah Esau's **w**.	802
	36:13	these were the sons of Bashemath Esau's **w**.	802
	36:14	of Anah, daughter of Zibeon, Esau's **w**:	802
	36:17	these *are* the sons of Bashemath Esau's **w**.	802
	36:18	these *are* the sons of Aholibamah Esau's **w**;	802
	36:18	Aholibamah the daughter of Anah, Esau's **w**.	802
	38: 6	Judah took a **w** for Er his firstborn,	802
	38: 8	Go in unto thy brother's **w**, and marry her,	802
	38: 9	when he went in unto his brother's **w**,	802
	38:12	time the daughter of Shuah Judah's **w** died;	802
	38:14	and she was not given unto him to **w**.	802
	39: 7	that his master's **w** cast her eyes upon	802
	39: 8	and said unto his master's **w**, Behold,	802
	39: 9	from me but thee, because thou *art* his **w**:	802
	39:19	when his master heard the words of his **w**,	802
	41:45	he gave him to **w** Asenath the daughter of	802
	44:27	Ye know that my **w** bare me two *sons:*	802
	46:19	The sons of Rachel Jacob's **w**; Joseph, and	802
	49:31	There they buried Abraham and Sarah his **w**;	802
	49:31	there they buried Isaac and Rebekah his **w**;	802
Ex	2: 1	of Levi, and took *to w* a daughter of Levi.	NIH
	4:20	Moses took his **w** and his sons, and set them	802
	6:20	took him Jochebed his father's sister to **w**;	802
	6:23	of Amminadab, sister of Naashon, to **w**;	802
	6:25	took him *one* of the daughters of Putiel to **w**;	802
	18: 2	father in law, took Zipporah, Moses' **w**,	802
	18: 5	and his **w** unto Moses into the wilderness,	802
	18: 6	and thy **w**, and her two sons with her.	802
	20:17	thou shalt not covet thy neighbour's **w**,	802
	21: 3	then his **w** shall go out with him.	802
	21: 4	If his master have given him a **w**, and	802
	21: 4	the **w** and her children shall be her master's,	802
	21: 5	I love my master, my **w**, and my children;	802
	21:10	If he take him another *w*; her food,	NIH
	22:16	he shall surely endow her to be his **w**.	802
Lev	18: 8	The nakedness of thy father's **w** shalt thou	802
	18:14	thou shalt not approach to his **w**:	802
	18:15	she *is* thy son's **w**; thou shalt not uncover her	802
	18:16	uncover the nakedness of thy brother's **w**:	802
	18:18	Neither shalt thou take a **w** to her sister,	802
	18:20	shalt not lie carnally with thy neighbour's **w**,	802
	20:10	committeth adultery with *another* man's **w**,	802
	20:10	committeth adultery with his neighbour's **w**,	802
	20:11	the man that lieth with his father's **w** hath	802
	20:14	if a man take a **w** and her mother, it *is*	802
	20:20	if a man shall lie with his **uncle's w**,	1733
	20:21	if a man shall take his brother's **w**, it *is* an	802
	21: 7	They shall not take a **w** *that is* a whore, or	802
	21:13	And he shall take a **w** in her virginity.	802
	21:14	he shall take a virgin of his own people to **w**.	802
Nu	5:12	If any man's **w** go aside, and commit a	802
	5:14	he be jealous of his **w**, and she be defiled:	802
	5:14	he be jealous of his **w**, and she be not	802
	5:15	shall the man bring his **w** unto the priest,	802
	5:29	when a **w** goeth aside *to another* instead of	802
	5:30	he be jealous over his **w**, and shall set	802
	26:59	And the name of Amram's **w** *was* Jochebed,	802
	30:16	between a man and his **w**, between the father	802
	36: 8	shall be **w** unto one of the family of	802+3807.1
Dt	5:21	Neither shalt thou desire thy neighbour's **w**,	802
	13: 6	or the **w** of thy bosom, or thy friend,	802
	20: 7	what man *is there* that hath betrothed a **w**,	802
	21:11	that thou wouldest have *her* to thy **w**;	802
	21:13	and be her husband, and she shall be thy **w**.	802
	22:13	If any man take a **w**, and go in unto her, and	802
	22:16	I gave my daughter unto this man to **w**, and	802
	22:19	she shall be his **w**; he may not put her away	802
	22:24	because he hath humbled his neighbour's **w**:	802
	22:29	fifty *shekels* of silver, and she shall be his **w**;	802
	22:30	A man shall not take his father's **w**,	802
	24: 1	When a man hath taken a **w**, and	802
	24: 2	she may go and be another man's **w**.	NIH
	24: 3	husband die, which took her *to be* his **w**;	802
	24: 4	may not take her again to be his **w**,	802

Dt 24: 5 When a man hath taken a new **w**, he shall 802
24: 5 shall cheer up his **w** which he hath taken. 802
25: 5 the **w** of the dead shall not marry without 802
25: 5 take her to him to **w**, and perform the duty of 802
25: 7 if the man like not to take his **brother's w**, 2994
25: 7 let his **brother's w** go up to the gate unto 2994
25: 9 shall his **brother's w** come unto him in 2994
25:11 the **w** of the one draweth near for to deliver 802
27:20 Cursed *be* he that lieth with his father's **w**; 802
28:30 Thou shalt betroth a **w**, and another man 802
28:54 toward the **w** of his bosom, and towards 802
Jos 15:16 to him will I give Achsah my daughter to **w**. 802
15:17 and he gave him Achsah his daughter to **w**. 802
Jdg 1:12 to him will I give Achsah my daughter to **w**. 802
1:13 and he gave him Achsah his daughter to **w**. 802
4: 4 a prophetess, the **w** of Lapidoth, 802
4:17 to the tent of Jael the **w** of Heber the Kenite: 802
4:21 Jael Heber's **w** took a nail of the tent, and 802
5:24 Blessed above women shall Jael the **w** of 802
11: 2 Gilead's **w** bare him sons; and *his* wife's 802
13: 2 and his **w** *was* barren, and bare not. 802
13:11 went after his **w**, and came to the man, and 802
13:19 and Manoah and his **w** looked on. 802
13:20 Manoah and his **w** looked on *it,* and fell on 802
13:21 did no more appear to Manoah and to his **w**. 802
13:22 Manoah said unto his **w**, We shall surely die, 802
13:23 his **w** said unto him, If the LORD were 802
14: 2 therefore get her for me to **w**. 802
14: 3 that thou goest to take a **w** of 802
14:15 that they said unto Samson's **w**, Entice thy 802
14:16 And Samson's **w** wept before him, and said, 802
14:20 Samson's **w** was *given* to his companion, 802
15: 1 that Samson visited his **w** with a kid; 802
15: 1 I will go in to my **w** into the chamber. 802
15: 6 because he had taken his **w**, and given her to 802
21: 1 of us give his daughter unto Benjamin to **w**. 802
21:18 Cursed *be* he that giveth a **w** to Benjamin. 802
21:21 catch you every man his **w** of the daughters 802
21:22 we reserved not to each man his **w** in 802
Ru 1: 1 of Moab, he, and his **w**, and his two sons. 802
1: 2 the name of his **w** Naomi, and the name of 802
4: 5 of Ruth the Moabitess, the **w** of the dead, 802
4:10 Ruth the Moabitess, the **w** of Mahlon, 802
4:10 of Mahlon, have I purchased to be my **w**, 802
4:13 So Boaz took Ruth, and she was his **w**: and 802
1Sa 1: 4 he gave to Peninnah his **w**, and to all her 802
1:19 Elkanah knew Hannah his **w**; and 802
2:20 And Eli blessed Elkanah and his **w**, and said, 802
4:19 Phinehas' **w**, was with child, *near* to be 802
14:50 the name of Saul's **w** *was* Ahinoam, 802
18:17 daughter Merab, her will I give thee to **w**: 802
18:19 was given unto Adriel the Meholathite to **w**. 802
18:27 Saul gave him Michal his daughter to **w**. 802
19:11 Michal David's **w** told him, saying, If thou 802
25: 3 *was* Nabal; and the name of his **w** Abigail: 802
25:14 told Abigail, Nabal's **w**, saying, Behold, 802
25:37 his **w** had told him these things, that his 802
25:39 with Abigail, to take her to him to **w**. 802
25:40 sent us unto thee, to take thee to him to **w**. 802
25:42 the messengers of David, and became his **w**. 802
25:44 David's **w**, to Phalti the son of Laish, 802
27: 3 and Abigail the Carmelitess, Nabal's **w**. 802
30: 5 and Abigail the **w** of Nabal the Carmelite. 802
30:22 save *to* every man his **w** and his children, 802
2Sa 2: 2 and Abigail Nabal's **w** the Carmelite. 802
3: 3 of Abigail the **w** of Nabal the Carmelite; 802
3: 5 And the sixth, Ithream, by Eglah David's **w**. 802
3:14 Saul's son, saying, Deliver *me* my **w** Michal, 802
11: 3 of Eliam, the **w** of Uriah the Hittite? 802
11:11 to eat and to drink, and to lie with my **w**? 802
11:26 when the **w** of Uriah heard that Uriah her 802
11:27 and she became his **w**, and bare him a son. 802
12: 9 hast taken his **w** to be thy wife, and hast 802
12: 9 hast taken his wife to be thy **w**, and hast 802
12:10 hast taken the **w** of Uriah the Hittite to be 802
12:10 the wife of Uriah the Hittite to be thy **w**. 802
12:15 the LORD strake the child that Uriah's **w** 802
12:24 And David comforted Bath-sheba his **w**, and 802
1Ki 2:17 he give me Abishag the Shunammite to **w**. 802
2:21 be given to Adonijah thy brother to **w**. 802
4:11 had Taphath the daughter of Solomon to **w**: 802
4:15 took Basmath the daughter of Solomon to **w**: 802
7: 8 whom he had taken *to* **w**, like unto this NIH
9:16 a present unto his daughter, Solomon's **w**. 802
11:19 that he gave him *to* **w** the sister of his own 802
11:19 he gave him *to* wife the sister of his own **w**, 802
14: 2 Jeroboam said to his **w**, Arise, I pray thee, 802
14: 2 that thou be not known to be the **w** of 802
14: 4 Jeroboam's **w** did so, and arose, and went *to* 802
14: 5 the **w** of Jeroboam cometh to ask a thing of 802
14: 6 that he said, Come in, thou **w** of Jeroboam; 802
14:17 Jeroboam's **w** arose, and departed, and 802
16:31 that he took *to* **w** Jezebel the daughter of 802
21: 5 Jezebel his **w** came to him, and said unto 802
21: 7 Jezebel his **w** said unto him, Dost thou now 802
21:25 the LORD, whom Jezebel his **w** stirred up. 802
2Ki 5: 2 a little maid; and she waited on Naaman's **w**. 802
8:18 for the daughter of Ahab was his **w**: and 802
14: 9 Give thy daughter to my son to **w**: 802
22:14 the **w** of Shallum the son of Tikvah, the son 802
1Ch 2:18 of Hezron begat *children* of Azubah *his* **w**, 802
2:24 Abiah Hezron's **w** bare him Ashur the father 802
2:26 Jerahmeel had also another **w**, whose name 802
2:29 the name of the **w** of Abishur *was* Abihail, 802
2:35 gave his daughter to Jarha his servant to **w**; 802
3: 3 of Abital: the sixth, Ithream by Eglah his **w**. 802
4:18 his **w** Jehudijah bare Jered the father of 802
4:19 the sons of *his* **w** Hodiah the sister of 802
7:15 Machir took to **w** *the sister* of Huppim and 802
7:16 Maachah the **w** of Machir bare a son, and 802
7:23 when he went in to his **w**, she conceived, 802
8: 9 he begat of Hodesh his **w**, Jobab, and Zibia, 802
2Ch 8:11 My **w** shall not dwell in the house of David 802
11:18 daughter of Jerimoth the son of David *to* **w**, 802
21: 6 for he had the daughter of Ahab to **w**: and 802
22:11 king Jehoram, the **w** of Jehoiada the priest, 802
25:18 Give thy daughter to my son to **w**: 802
34:22 the **w** of Shallum the son of Tikvath, the son 802
Ezr 2:61 which took a **w** of the daughters of Barzillai 802
Ne 7:63 the daughters of Barzillai the Gileadite *to* **w**, 802
Est 5:10 and called for his friends, and Zeresh his **w**. 802
5:14 said Zeresh his **w** and all his friends unto 802
6:13 Haman told Zeresh his **w** and all his friends 802
6:13 his wise *men* and Zeresh his **w** unto him, 802
Job 2: 9 said his **w** unto him, Dost thou still retain 802
19:17 My breath is strange to my **w**, though I 802
31:10 *Then* let my **w** grind unto another, and 802
Ps 109: 9 children be fatherless, and his **w** a widow. 802
128: 3 Thy **w** *shall be* as a fruitful vine by the sides 802
Pr 5:18 and rejoice with the **w** of thy youth. 802
6:29 So he that goeth in to his neighbour's **w**; 802
18:22 *Whoso* findeth a **w** findeth a good *thing,* and 802
19:13 the contentions of a **w** *are* a continual 802
19:14 and a prudent **w** *is* from the LORD. 802
Ecc 9: 9 Live joyfully with the **w** whom thou lovest 802
Isa 54: 1 than the children of the **married w**, 1166
54: 6 and grieved in spirit, and a **w** of youth, 802
Jer 3: 1 If a man put away his **w**, and she go from 802
3:20 Surely *as* a **w** treacherously departeth from 802
5: 8 every one neighed after his neighbour's **w**. 802
6:11 for even the husband with the **w** shall be 802
16: 2 Thou shalt not take thee a **w**, neither shalt 802
Eze 16:32 *But as* a **w** that committeth adultery, 802
18: 6 neither hath defiled his neighbour's **w**, 802
18:11 and defiled his neighbour's **w**, 802
18:15 of Israel, hath not defiled his neighbour's **w**, 802
22:11 abomination with his neighbour's **w**; 802
24:18 at even my **w** died; and I did in the morning 802
33:26 and ye defile every one his neighbour's **w**: 802
Hos 1: 2 take unto thee a **w** of whoredoms and 802
2: 2 for she *is* not my **w**, neither *am* I her 802
12:12 Israel served for a **w**, and for a wife he kept 802
12:12 served for a wife, and for a **w** he kept *sheep.* 802
Am 7:17 Thy **w** shall be a harlot in the city, and 802
Mal 2:14 witness between thee and the **w** of thy youth, 802
2:14 thy companion, and the **w** of thy covenant. 802
2:15 let none deal treacherously against the **w** of 802
Mt 1: 6 of *her that had been* the **w** of Urias; NIG
1:20 fear not to take unto *thee* Mary thy **w**: *1135*
1:24 had bidden him, and took unto *him* his **w**: *1135*
5:31 been said, Whosoever shall put away his **w**, *1135*
5:32 That whosoever shall put away his **w**, *1135*
14: 3 for Herodias' sake, his brother Philip's **w**. *1135*
18:25 and his **w**, and children, and all that he had, *1135*
19: 3 Is it lawful for a man to put away his **w** for *1135*
19: 5 and mother, and shall cleave to his **w**: *1135*
19: 9 unto you, Whosoever shall put away his **w**, *1135*
19:10 If the case of the man be so with *his* **w**, it is *1135*

Mt 19:29 or mother, or **w**, or children, or lands, *1135*
22:24 his brother shall marry his **w**, and raise up *1135*
22:25 when he had married *a* **w**, deceased, and, NIG
22:25 having no issue, left his **w** unto his brother: *1135*
22:28 Therefore in the resurrection whose **w** shall *1135*
27:19 judgment seat, his **w** sent unto him, saying, *1135*
Mk 6:17 for Herodias' sake, his brother Philip's **w**: *1135*
6:18 not lawful for thee to have thy brother's **w**. *1135*
10: 2 Is it lawful for a man to put away *his* **w**? *1135*
10: 7 his father and mother, and cleave to his **w**; *1135*
10:11 Whosoever shall put away his **w**, and *1135*
10:29 or mother, or **w**, or children, or lands, *1135*
12:19 and leave *his* **w** *behind him,* and leave no *1135*
12:19 that his brother should take his **w**, and *1135*
12:20 and the first took a **w**, and dying left no *1135*
12:23 shall rise, whose **w** shall she be of them? *1135*
12:23 she be of them? for the seven had her to **w**. *1135*
Lk 1: 5 and his **w** *was* of the daughters of Aaron, *1135*
1:13 and thy **w** Elisabeth shall bear thee a son, *1135*
1:18 old man, and my **w** well stricken in years. *1135*
1:24 And after those days his **w** Elisabeth *1135*
2: 5 To be taxed with Mary his espoused **w**, *1135*
3:19 by him for Herodias his brother Philip's **w**, *1135*
8: 3 And Joanna the **w** of Chuza Herod's *1135*
14:20 I have married a **w**, and therefore I cannot *1135*
14:26 and **w**, and children, and brethren, and *1135*
16:18 Whosoever putteth away his **w**, and *1135*
17:32 Remember Lot's **w**. *1135*
18:29 or parents, or brethren, or **w**, or children, *1135*
20:28 having a **w**, and he die without children, *1135*
20:28 that his brother should take *his* **w**, and *1135*
20:29 and the first took a **w**, and died without *1135*
20:30 And the second took her to **w**, and he died *1135*
20:33 Therefore in the resurrection whose **w** of *1135*
20:33 wife of them is she? for seven had her to **w**. *1135*
Jn 19:25 Mary the *w* of Cleophas, and NIG
Ac 5: 1 with Sapphira his **w**, sold a possession, *1135*
5: 2 his **w** also being privy *to it,* and brought a *1135*
5: 7 when his **w**, not knowing what was done, *1135*
18: 2 lately come from Italy, with his **w** Priscilla; *1135*
24:24 when Felix came with his **w** Drusilla, *1135*
1Co 5: 1 that one should have *his* father's **w**. *1135*
7: 2 let every man have his own **w**, and *1135*
7: 3 Let the husband render unto the **w** due *1135*
7: 3 and likewise also the **w** unto the husband. *1135*
7: 4 The **w** hath not power of her own body, but *1135*
7: 4 hath not power of his own body, but the **w**. *1135*
7:10 Let not the **w** depart from *her* husband: *1135*
7:11 and let not the husband put away *his* **w**. *1135*
7:12 If any brother hath a **w** that believeth not, *1135*
7:14 unbelieving husband is sanctified by the **w**, *1135*
7:14 the unbelieving **w** is sanctified by *1135*
7:16 For what knowest thou, O **w**, whether thou *1135*
7:16 O man, whether thou shalt save *thy* **w**? *1135*
7:27 Art thou bound unto a **w**? seek not to be *1135*
7:27 Art thou loosed from a **w**? seek not a wife. *1135*
7:27 Art thou loosed from a wife? seek not a **w**. *1135*
7:33 *are* of the world, how he may please *his* **w**. *1135*
7:34 There is difference *also* between a **w** and a *1135*
7:39 The **w** is bound by the law as long as her *1135*
9: 5 a **w**, as well as other apostles, and *as* *1135*
Eph 5:23 For the husband is the head of the **w**, *1135*
5:28 He that loveth his **w** loveth himself. *1135*
5:31 and shall be joined unto his **w**, and *1135*
5:33 in particular so love his **w** even as himself; *1135*
5:33 the **w** *see* that she reverence *her* husband. *1135*
1Ti 3: 2 the husband of one **w**, vigilant, sober, *1135*
3:12 Let the deacons be the husbands of one **w**, *1135*
5: 9 years old, having been the **w** of one man, *1135*
Tit 1: 6 If any be blameless, the husband of one **w**, *1135*
1Pe 3: 7 giving honour unto the **w**, as unto *1134*
Rev 19: 7 is come, and his **w** hath made herself ready. *1135*
21: 9 I will shew thee the bride, the Lamb's **w**. *1135*

WIFE'S (11) [WIFE]

Ge 3:20 Adam called his **w** name Eve; because 802
20:11 and they will slay me for my **w** sake. 802
36:39 his **w** name *was* Mehetabel, the daughter of 802
Lev 18:11 The nakedness of thy father's **w** daughter, 802
Jdg 11: 2 *his* **w** sons grew up, and they thrust out 802
1Ch 1:50 his **w** name *was* Mehetabel, the daughter of 802
8:29 of Gibeon; whose **w** name *was* Maachah: 802
9:35 Jehiel, whose **w** name *was* Maachah: 802
Mt 8:14 he saw his **w mother** laid, and sick of a *3994*
Mk 1:30 But Simon's **w mother** lay sick of a fever, *3994*
Lk 4:38 And Simon's **w mother** was taken with a *3994*

WILD (44) [WILDERNESS]

Ge 16:12 he will be a **w** man; his hand *will be* against 6501
Lev 26:22 I will also send **w** beasts among you, which 7704
Dt 14: 5 the **w goat**, and the pygarg, and the wild ox, 689
14: 5 the pygarg, and the **w ox**, and the chamois. 8377
1Sa 17:46 of the air, and to the **w beasts** of the earth; 2416
24: 2 and his men upon the rocks of the **w goats**. 3277
2Sa 2:18 *as* light of foot as a **w** roe. 7704+871.1+1886.1
2Ki 4:39 found a **w** vine, and gathered thereof wild 7704
4:39 gathered thereof **w** gourds his lap full, and 7704
14: 9 there passed by a **w** beast that *was* in 7704
2Ch 25:18 there passed by a **w** beast that *was* in 7704
Job 6: 5 Doth the **w ass** bray when he hath grass? or 6501
11:12 though man be born *like* a **w ass's** colt. 6501
24: 5 Behold, *as* **w asses** in the desert, go they 6501
39: 1 Knowest thou the time when the **w goats** of 3277
39: 5 Who hath sent out the **w ass** free? or 6501
39: 5 or who hath loosed the bands of the **w ass**? 6171
39:15 or *that* the **w** beast may break them. 7704
Ps 50:11 and the **w beasts** of the field *are* mine. 2123
80:13 and the **w beast** of the field doth devour it. 2123
104:11 of the field: the **w asses** quench their thirst. 6501
104:18 The high hills *are* a refuge for the **w goats**; 3277
Isa 5: 2 forth grapes, and it brought forth **w grapes**. 891
5: 4 forth grapes, brought it forth **w grapes**? 891
13:21 **w beasts of the desert** shall lie there; and 6728
13:22 the **w beasts of the islands** shall cry in their 338
32:14 a joy of **w asses**, a pasture of flocks; 6501
34:14 The **w beasts of the desert** shall also meet 6728
34:14 also meet with the **w beasts of the island**, 338
51:20 head of all the streets, as a **w bull** *in* a net: 8377
Jer 2:24 A **w ass** used to the wilderness, 6501
14: 6 the **w asses** did stand in the high places, 6501
50:39 Therefore the **w beasts of the desert** with 6728
50:39 the **w beasts of the islands** shall dwell *there,* 338
Da 5:21 and his dwelling *was* with the **w asses**: 6167
Hos 8: 9 up *to* Assyria, a **w ass** alone by himself: 6501
13: 8 like a lion: the **w** beast shall tear them. 7704
Mt 3: 4 and his meat was locusts and **w** honey. *66*
Mk 1: 6 his loins; and he did eat locusts and **w** honey; *66*
1:13 and was with the **w beasts**; and the angels *2342*
Ac 10:12 and **w beasts**, and creeping things, and *2342*
11: 6 and **w beasts**, and creeping things, and *2342*
Ro 11:17 and thou, being a **w olive tree**, wert graffed in *65*
11:24 cut out of the **olive tree which is w** by nature, *65*

WILD GOATS See SATYRS

WILD OX, OXEN See UNICORN; UNICORNS

WILDERNESS (305) [WILD]

Ge 14: 6 unto El-paran, which *is* by the **w**. 4057
16: 7 found her by a fountain of water in the **w**, 4057
21:14 and wandered in the **w** of Beer-sheba. 4057
21:20 and dwelt in the **w**, and became an archer. 4057
21:21 he dwelt in the **w** of Paran: and his mother 4057
36:24 *that* Anah that found the mules in the **w**, 4057
37:22 *but* cast him into this pit that *is* in the **w**, 4057
Ex 3:18 three days' journey into the **w**, 4057
4:27 to Aaron, Go into the **w** to meet Moses. 4057
5: 1 that they may hold a feast unto me in the **w**. 4057
7:16 people go, that they may serve me in the **w**: 4057
8:27 We will go three days' journey into the **w**, 4057
8:28 sacrifice to the LORD your God in the **w**; 4057
13:18 *through* the way of the **w** of the Red sea: 4057
13:20 encamped in Etham, in the edge of the **w**. 4057
14: 3 in the land, the **w** hath shut them in. 4057
14:11 hast thou taken us away to die in the **w**? 4057
14:12 than that we should die in the **w**. 4057
15:22 and they went out into the **w** of Shur; 4057
15:22 they went three days in the **w**, and found no 4057
16: 1 children of Israel came unto the **w** of Sin, 4057
16: 2 against Moses and Aaron in the **w**: 4057
16: 3 for ye have brought us forth into this **w**, to 4057
16:10 that they looked toward the **w**, and behold, 4057
16:14 upon the face of the **w** *there lay* a small 4057
16:32 bread wherewith I have fed you in the **w**, 4057
17: 1 of Israel journeyed from the **w** of Sin, 4057
18: 5 and his wife unto Moses into the **w**, 4057
19: 1 the same day came they *into* the **w** of Sinai. 4057
19: 2 desert of Sinai, and had pitched in the **w**; 4057
Lev 7:38 unto the LORD, in the **w** of Sinai. 4057

Lev	16:10	*and* to let him go for a scapegoat into the **w**.	4057
	16:21	away by the hand of a fit man into the **w**:	4057
	16:22	and he shall let go the goat in the **w**.	4057
Nu	1: 1	the LORD spake unto Moses in the **w** of	4057
	1:19	so he numbered them in the **w** of Sinai.	4057
	3: 4	in the **w** of Sinai, and they had no children:	4057
	3:14	the LORD spake unto Moses in the **w** of	4057
	9: 1	the LORD spake unto Moses in the **w** of	4057
	9: 5	of the first month at even in the **w** of Sinai:	4057
	10:12	took their journeys out of the **w** of Sinai;	4057
	10:12	and the cloud rested in the **w** of Paran.	4057
	10:31	knowest how we are to encamp in the **w**,	4057
	12:16	and pitched in the **w** of Paran.	4057
	13: 3	the LORD sent them from the **w** of Paran:	4057
	13:21	searched the land from the **w** of Zin unto	4057
	13:26	of Israel, unto the **w** of Paran, to Kadesh;	4057
	14: 2	or would God we had died in this **w**!	4057
	14:16	therefore he hath slain them in the **w**.	4057
	14:22	which I did in Egypt and in the **w**, and	4057
	14:25	get you *into* the **w** *by* the way of the Red	4057
	14:29	Your carcases shall fall in this **w**; and	4057
	14:32	your carcases, they shall fall in this **w**.	4057
	14:33	your children shall wander in the **w** forty	4057
	14:33	until your carcases be wasted in the **w**.	4057
	14:35	in this **w** they shall be consumed, and	4057
	15:32	while the children of Israel were in the **w**,	4057
	16:13	with milk and honey, to kill us in the **w**,	4057
	20: 4	the congregation of the LORD into this **w**,	4057
	21: 5	brought us up out of Egypt to die in the **w**?	4057
	21:11	in the **w** which *is* before Moab, toward	4057
	21:13	which *is* in the **w** that cometh out of	4057
	21:18	And from the **w** *they went to* Mattanah:	4057
	21:23	and went out against Israel into the **w**:	4057
	24: 1	but he set his face toward the **w**.	4057
	26:64	the children of Israel in the **w** of Sinai.	4057
	26:65	said of them, They shall surely die in the **w**.	4057
	27: 3	Our father died in the **w**, and he was not in	4057
	27:14	of Meribah in Kadesh *in* the **w** of Zin.	4057
	32:13	he made them wander in the **w** forty years,	4057
	32:15	he will yet again leave them in the **w**;	4057
	33: 6	in Etham, which *is* in the edge of the **w**.	4057
	33: 8	through the midst of the sea into the **w**,	4057
	33: 8	went three days' journey in the **w** of Etham,	4057
	33:11	the Red sea, and encamped in the **w** of Sin.	4057
	33:12	they took their journey out of the **w** of Sin,	4057
	33:15	and pitched in the **w** of Sinai.	4057
	33:36	pitched in the **w** of Zin, which *is* Kadesh.	4057
	34: 3	your south quarter shall be from the **w** of	4057
Dt	1: 1	unto all Israel on *this* side Jordan in the **w**,	4057
	1:19	went *through* all that great and terrible **w**,	4057
	1:31	in the **w**, where thou hast seen how that	4057
	1:40	take your journey into the **w** *by* the way of	4057
	2: 1	took our journey into the **w** *by* the way of	4057
	2: 7	knoweth thy walking *through* this great **w**:	4057
	2: 8	and passed *by* the way of the **w** of Moab.	4057
	2:26	I sent messengers out of the **w** of	4057
	4:43	*Namely,* Bezer in the **w**, in the plain	4057
	8: 2	thy God led thee these forty years in the **w**,	4057
	8:15	led thee through *that* great and terrible **w**,	4057
	8:16	Who fed thee in the **w** with manna,	4057
	9: 7	the LORD thy God to wrath in the **w**:	4057
	9:28	brought them out to slay them in the **w**.	4057
	11: 5	what he did unto you in the **w**, until ye	4057
	11:24	from the **w** and Lebanon, from the river,	4057
	29: 5	I have led you forty years in the **w**:	4057
	32:10	a desert land, and in the waste howling **w**;	3452
	32:51	waters of Meribah-Kadesh, *in* the **w** of Zin;	4057
Jos	1: 4	From the **w** and this Lebanon even unto	4057
	5: 4	the men of war, died in the **w** by the way,	4057
	5: 5	all the people *that were* born in the **w** by	4057
	5: 6	of Israel walked forty years in the **w**,	4057
	8:15	before them, and fled *by* the way of the **w**.	4057
	8:20	the people that fled *to* the **w** turned back	4057
	8:24	in the **w** wherein they chased them, and	4057
	12: 8	in the **w**, and in the south *country;*	4057
	14:10	*the children of* Israel wandered in the **w**:	4057
	15: 1	the **w** of Zin southward *was* the uttermost	4057
	15:61	In the **w**, Beth-arabah, Middin, and	4057
	16: 1	*to* the **w** that goeth up from Jericho	4057
	18:12	the goings out thereof were at the **w** of	4057
	20: 8	they assigned Bezer in the **w** upon the plain	4057
	24: 7	and ye dwelt in the **w** a long season.	4057
Jdg	1:16	the children of Judah *into* the **w** of Judah,	4057
	8: 7	will tear your flesh with the thorns of the **w**	4057
	8:16	thorns of the **w** and briers, and with them	4057
	11:16	and walked through the **w** unto the Red sea,	4057
	11:18	they went along through the **w**, and	4057
	11:22	and from the **w** even unto Jordan.	4057
	20:42	the men of Israel unto the way of the **w**;	4057
	20:45	fled toward the **w** unto the rock of	4057
	20:47	and fled to the **w** unto the rock Rimmon,	4057
1Sa	4: 8	the Egyptians with all the plagues in the **w**.	4057
	13:18	to the valley of Zeboim toward the **w**.	4057
	17:28	hast thou left those few sheep in the **w**?	4057
	23:14	David abode in the **w** in strong holds, and	4057
	23:14	remained in a mountain in the **w** of Ziph.	4057
	23:15	and David *was* in the **w** of Ziph in a wood.	4057
	23:24	David and his men *were* in the **w** of Maon,	4057
	23:25	*into* a rock, and abode in the **w** of Maon.	4057
	23:25	he pursued after David *in* the **w** of Maon.	4057
	24: 1	Behold, David *is* in the **w** of En-gedi.	4057
	25: 1	and went down to the **w** of Paran.	4057
	25: 4	David heard in the **w** that Nabal did shear	4057
	25:14	David sent messengers out of the **w** to	4057
	25:21	I kept all that this *fellow* hath in the **w**,	4057
	26: 2	and went down to the **w** of Ziph,	4057
	26: 2	with him, to seek David in the **w** of Ziph.	4057
	26: 3	David abode in the **w**, and he saw that Saul	4057
	26: 3	he saw that Saul came after him into the **w**.	4057
2Sa	2:24	that *lieth* before Giah *by* the way of the **w**	4057
	15:23	passed over, toward the way of the **w**.	4057
	15:28	See, I will tarry in the plain of the **w**,	4057
	16: 2	that such as be faint in the **w** may drink.	4057
	17:16	Lodge not *this* night in the plains of the **w**,	4057
	17:29	*is* hungry, and weary, and thirsty, in the **w**.	4057
1Ki	2:34	he was buried in his own house in the **w**.	4057
	9:18	and Tadmor in the **w**, in the land,	4057
	19: 4	he himself went a day's journey into the **w**,	4057
	19:15	return on thy way to the **w** of Damascus:	4057
2Ki	3: 8	The way through the **w** of Edom.	4057
1Ch	5: 9	in of the **w** from the river Euphrates:	4057
	6:78	Bezer in the **w** with her suburbs, and	4057
	12: 8	David into the hold to the **w** men of might,	4057
	21:29	which Moses made in the **w**, and the altar	4057
2Ch	1: 3	servant of the LORD had made in the **w**.	4057
	8: 4	he built Tadmor in the **w**, and all the store	4057
	20:16	the end of the brook, before the **w** of Jeruel.	4057
	20:20	and went forth into the **w** of Tekoa:	4057
	20:24	came toward the watch tower in the **w**,	4057
	24: 9	servant of God laid upon Israel in the **w**.	4057
Ne	9:19	mercies forsookest them not in the **w**:	4057
	9:21	forty years didst thou sustain them in the **w**,	4057
Job	1:19	there came a great wind from the **w**, and	4057
	12:24	causeth them to wander in a **w** *where there*	8414
	24: 5	the **w** *yieldeth* food for them *and* for *their*	6160
	30: 3	flying *into* the **w** in former time desolate	6723
	38:26	*where* no man *is; on* the **w**, wherein *there is*	4057
	39: 6	Whose house I have made the **w**, and	6160
Ps	29: 8	The voice of the LORD shaketh the **w**;	4057
	29: 8	the LORD shaketh the **w** of Kadesh.	4057
	55: 7	I wander far off, *and* remain in the **w**.	4057
	63: T	of David, when he was in the **w** of Judah.	4057
	65:12	They drop *upon* the pastures of the **w**: and	4057
	68: 7	when thou didst march through the **w**;	3452
	72: 9	They **that dwell in the w** shall bow before	6728
	74:14	*to be* meat to the people **inhabiting the w**.	6728
	78:15	He clave the rocks in the **w**, and gave *them*	4057
	78:17	him by provoking the most High in the **w**.	6723
	78:19	they said, Can God furnish a table in the **w**?	4057
	78:40	How oft did they provoke him in the **w**, *and*	4057
	78:52	and guided them in the **w** like a flock.	4057
	95: 8	*and* as *in* the day of temptation in the **w**:	4057
	102: 6	I am like a pelican of the **w**: I am like an	4057
	106: 9	them through the depths, as *through* the **w**.	4057
	106:14	lusted exceedingly in the **w**, and	4057
	106:26	against them, to overthrow them in the **w**:	4057
	107: 4	They wandered in the **w** in a solitary way;	4057
	107:33	He turneth rivers into a **w**, and	4057
	107:35	He turneth the **w** into a standing water, and	4057
	107:40	causeth them to wander in the **w**,	8414
	136:16	To him which led his people through the **w**:	4057
Pr	21:19	*It is* better to dwell in the **w**, than with	776+4057
SS	3: 6	Who *is* this that cometh out of the **w** like	4057
	8: 5	Who *is* this that cometh up from the **w**,	4057
Isa	14:17	*That* made the world as a **w**, and	4057
	16: 1	*to* the ruler of the land from Sela to the **w**,	4057
	16: 8	unto Jazer, they wandered *through* the **w**:	4057
	23:13	founded it for **them that dwell in the w**:	6728

Isa 27:10 the habitation forsaken, and left like a **w**: 4057
32:15 the **w** be a fruitful field, and the fruitful 4057
32:16 judgment shall dwell in the **w**, and 4057
33: 9 Sharon is like a **w**; and Bashan and 6160
35: 1 The **w** and the solitary place shall be glad 4057
35: 6 for in the **w** shall waters break out, and 4057
40: 3 The voice of him that crieth in the **w**, 4057
41:18 I will make the **w** a pool of water, and 4057
41:19 I will plant in the **w** the cedar, the shittah 4057
42:11 Let the **w** and the cities thereof lift up *their* 4057
43:19 I will even make a way in the **w**, *and* 4057
43:20 because I give waters in the **w**, *and* rivers in 4057
50: 2 I dry up the sea, I make the rivers a **w**: 4057
51: 3 he will make her **w** like Eden, and 4057
63:13 as a horse in the **w**, *that* they should not 4057
64:10 Thy holy cities are a **w**, Zion is a 4057
64:10 Zion is a **w**, Jerusalem a desolation. 4057
Jer 2: 2 when thou wentest after me in the **w**, 4057
2: 6 that led us through the **w**, through a land of 4057
2:24 A wild ass used to the **w**, *that* snuffeth up 4057
2:31 Have I been a **w** unto Israel? a land of 4057
3: 2 thou sat for them, as the Arabian in the **w**; 4057
4:11 A dry wind of the high places in the **w** 4057
4:26 lo, the fruitful place *was* a **w**, and all 4057
9: 2 O that I had in the **w** a lodging place of 4057
9:10 for the habitations of the **w** a lamentation, 4057
9:12 the land perisheth *and* is burnt up like a **w**, 4057
9:26 in the utmost corners, that dwell in the **w**: 4057
12:10 made my pleasant portion a desolate **w**. 4057
12:12 come upon all high places through the **w**: 4057
13:24 that passeth away by the wind of the **w**. 4057
17: 6 shall inhabit the parched places in the **w**, 4057
22: 6 *yet* surely I will make thee a **w** *and* 4057
23:10 the pleasant places of the **w** are dried up, 4057
31: 2 were left of the sword found grace in the **w**; 4057
48: 6 your lives, and be like the heath in the **w**. 4057
50:12 the hindermost of the nations *shall be* a **w**, 4057
51:43 cities are a desolation, a dry land, and a **w**, 6160
La 4: 3 *is* become cruel, like the ostriches in the **w**. 4057
4:19 they laid wait for us in the **w**. 4057
5: 9 *of* our lives because of the sword of the **w**. 4057
Eze 6:14 more desolate than the **w** toward Diblath, 4057
19:13 now she *is* planted in the **w**, in a dry and 4057
20:10 land of Egypt, and brought them into the **w**. 4057
20:13 of Israel rebelled against me in the **w**: 4057
20:13 pour out my fury upon them in the **w**, 4057
20:15 also I lifted up my hand unto them in the **w**, 4057
20:17 neither did I make an end of them in the **w**. 4057
20:18 I said unto their children in the **w**, Walk ye 4057
20:21 my anger against them in the **w**. 4057
20:23 up mine hand unto them also in the **w**, 4057
20:35 I will bring you into the **w** of the people, 4057
20:36 Like as I pleaded with your fathers in the **w** 4057
23:42 sort *were* brought Sabeans from the **w**, 4057
29: 5 I will leave thee *thrown* into the **w**, thee 4057
34:25 they shall dwell safely in the **w**, and 4057
Hos 2: 3 make her as a **w**, and set her like a dry land, 4057
2:14 bring her *into* the **w**, and speak comfortably 4057
9:10 I found Israel like grapes in the **w**; I saw 4057
13: 5 I did know thee in the **w**, in the land of 4057
13:15 of the LORD *shall* come up from the **w**, 4057
Joel 1:19 the fire hath devoured the pastures of the **w**, 4057
1:20 the fire hath devoured the pastures of the **w**. 4057
2: 3 before them, and behind them a desolate **w**; 4057
2:22 for the pastures of the **w** do spring, for 4057
3:19 and Edom shall be a desolate **w**, 4057
Am 2:10 led you forty years through the **w**, 4057
5:25 and offerings in the **w** forty years, 4057
6:14 in of Hemath unto the river of the **w**. 6160
Zep 2:13 Nineveh a desolation, *and* dry like a **w**. 4057
Mal 1: 3 his heritage waste for the dragons of the **w**. 4057
Mt 3: 1 the Baptist, preaching in the **w** of Judea, *2048*
3: 3 saying, The voice of one crying in the **w**, *2048*
4: 1 Spirit into the **w** to be tempted of the devil. *2048*
11: 7 What went ye out into the **w** to see? *2048*
15:33 should we have so much bread in the **w**, *2047*
Mk 1: 3 The voice of one crying in the **w**, *2048*
1: 4 John did baptize in the **w**, and preach *2048*
1:12 the Spirit driveth him into the **w**. *2048*
1:13 And he was there in the **w** forty days, *2048*
8: 4 satisfy these *men* with bread here in the **w**? *2047*
Lk 3: 2 unto John the son of Zacharias in the **w**. *2048*
3: 4 saying, The voice of one crying in the **w**, *2048*
4: 1 and was led by the Spirit into the **w**, *2048*
5:16 And he withdrew himself into the **w**, and *2048*
7:24 What went ye out into the **w** for to see? *2048*
8:29 and was driven of the devil into the **w**.) *2048*
15: 4 doth not leave the ninety and nine in the **w**, *2048*
Jn 1:23 I *am* the voice of one crying in the **w**, *2048*
3:14 as Moses lifted up the serpent in the **w**, *2048*
6:49 Your fathers did eat manna in the **w**, and *2048*
11:54 went thence unto a country near to the **w**, *2048*
Ac 7:30 there appeared to him in the **w** of mount *2048*
7:36 and in the Red sea, and in the **w** forty years. *2048*
7:38 that was in the church in the **w** with *2048*
7:42 *by the space of* forty years in the **w**? *2048*
7:44 had the tabernacle of Witness in the **w**, *2048*
13:18 years suffered he their manners in the **w**. *2048*
21:38 leddest out into the **w** four thousand men *2048*
1Co 10: 5 for they were overthrown in the **w**. *2048*
2Co 11:26 *in* perils in the **w**, *in* perils in the sea, *2047*
Heb 3: 8 in the day of temptation in the **w**: *2048*
3:17 had sinned, whose carcases fell in the **w**? *2048*
Rev 12: 6 And the woman fled into the **w**, where she *2048*
12:14 that she might fly into the **w**, into her place, *2048*
17: 3 he carried me away in the spirit into the **w**: *2048*

WILES (2) [WILILY]
Nu 25:18 For they vex you with their **w**, 5231
Eph 6:11 that ye may be able to stand against the **w** *3180*

WILFULLY (1) [WILL]
Heb 10:26 For if we sin **w** after that *we* have received *1596*

WILILY (1) [WILES]
Jos 9: 4 They did work **w**, and went and 6195+871.1

WILL (200 of 3837) [FREEWILL, SELFWILL, SELFWILLED, WILFULLY, WILLETH, WILLING, WILLINGLY, WILT, WOULD] See Introduction and Index
Ge 24:49 now if ye **w** deal kindly and truly with my 3426
Lev 1: 3 he shall offer it of his own **voluntary w** at 7522
19: 5 the LORD, ye shall offer it at your own **w**. 7522
22:19 *Ye shall offer* at your own **w** a male 7522
22:29 unto the LORD, offer *it* at your own **w**. 7522
26:21 contrary unto me, and **w** not hearken unto me; 14
Dt 21:14 then thou shalt let her go whither she **w**; 5315
25: 7 he **w** not perform the duty of my husband's 14
29:20 The LORD **w** not spare him, but then 14
33:16 *for* the **good w** of him that dwelt in 7522
Ru 3:13 if he **w** not do the part of a kinsman to thee, 2654
Ezr 7:18 and gold, *that* do after the **w** of your God. 7470
Job 1:11 and he **w** curse thee to thy face. 518+3808
2: 5 and he **w** curse thee to thy face. 518+3808
9: 3 If he **w** contend with him, he cannot answer 2654
Ps 27:12 Deliver me not over unto the **w** of mine 5315
40: 8 I delight to do thy **w**, O my God: yea, 7522
41: 2 thou wilt not deliver him unto the **w** of his 5315
143:10 Teach me to do thy **w**; for thou *art* my God: 7522
Pr 21: 1 of water: he turneth it whithersoever he **w**. 2654
Ecc 4:13 who **w** no more be admonished. 3045
Isa 30: 9 children *that* **w** not hear the law of 14
Eze 3: 7 the house of Israel **w** not hearken unto thee; 14
3: 7 unto thee; for they **w** not hearken unto me: 14
16:27 delivered thee unto the **w** of them that hate 5315
21:27 I **w**s overturn, overturn, overturn it: and 7760
Da 3:18 O king, that we **w** not serve thy gods, 383
4:17 giveth it to whomsoever he **w**, and 6634
4:25 of men, and giveth it to whomsoever he **w**. 6634
4:32 of men, and giveth it to whomsoever he **w**. 6634
4:35 he doeth according to his **w** in the army of 6634
5:21 he appointeth over it whomsoever he **w**. 6634
8: 4 he did according to his **w**, and 7522
11: 3 great dominion, and do according to his **w**. 7522
11:16 him shall do according to his own **w**, 7522
11:36 the king shall do according to his **w**; and 7522
Zec 12: 3 in that day **w** I make Jerusalem a 1961
Mal 2:13 or receiveth *it with* **good w** at your hand. 7522
Mt 2:13 for Herod **w** seek the young child to *3195*
5:40 And if any man **w** sue thee at the law, and *2309*
6:10 Thy **w** be done in earth, as *it is* in heaven. *2307*
7:21 he that doeth the **w** of my Father which is *2307*
8: 3 *his* hand, and touched him, saying, I **w**; *2309*
11:14 And if ye **w** receive *it,* this is Elias, *2309*
11:27 *he* to whomsoever the Son **w** reveal *him.* *1014*
12:50 For whosoever shall do the **w** of my Father *2307*
15:32 and I **w** not send them away fasting, *2309*
16:24 If any *man* **w** come after me, let him deny *2309*

Mt	16:25	For whosoever **w** save his life shall lose it:	*2309*
	18:14	it is not the **w** of your Father which is in	*2307*
	20:14	I **w** give unto this last, even as unto thee.	*2309*
	20:15	Is it not lawful for me to do what I **w** with	*2309*
	20:26	but whosoever **w** be great among you,	*2309*
	20:27	And whosoever **w** be chief among you,	*2309*
	20:32	said, What **w** ye *that* I shall do unto you?	*2309*
	21:29	He answered and said, I **w** not: but	*2309*
	21:31	Whether of *them* twain did the **w** of *his*	*2307*
	23: 4	they *themselves* **w** not move them with	*2309*
	26:15	And said *unto them,* What **w** ye give me,	*2309*
	26:39	nevertheless not as I **w**, but as thou *wilt.*	*2309*
	26:42	from me, except I drink it, thy **w** be done.	*2307*
	27:17	Whom **w** ye *that* I release unto you?	*2309*
	27:21	Whether of the twain **w** ye *that* I release	*2309*
	27:43	let him deliver him now, if he **w** have him:	*2309*
Mk	1:41	and touched him, and saith unto him, I **w**;	*2309*
	3:35	For whosoever shall do the **w** of God,	*2307*
	6:25	I **w** that thou give me by and by in a	*2309*
	8:34	unto them, Whosoever **w** come after me,	*2309*
	8:35	For whosoever **w** save his life shall lose it;	*2309*
	10:43	but whosoever **w** be great among you,	*2309*
	10:44	And whosoever of you **w** be the chiefest,	*2309*
	14: 7	whensoever ye **w** ye may do them good:	*2309*
	14:36	nevertheless not that I **w**, but what thou	*2309*
	15: 9	**W** ye *that* I release unto you the King of	*2309*
	15:12	What **w** ye then *that* I shall do *unto him*	*2309*
Lk	2:14	and on earth peace, **good w** towards men.	*2107*
	4: 6	unto me; and to whomsoever I **w** I give it.	*2309*
	5:13	*his* hand, and touched him, saying, I **w**:	*2309*
	9:23	If any *man* **w** come after me, let him deny	*2309*
	9:24	For whosoever **w** save his life shall lose it:	*2309*
	10:22	and *he* to whom the Son **w** reveal *him.*	*1014*
	11: 2	Thy **w** be done, as in heaven, so in earth.	*2307*
	12:47	which knew his lord's **w**, and prepared not	*2307*
	12:47	not *himself,* neither did according to his **w**,	*2307*
	12:49	and what **w** I, if it be already kindled?	*2309*
	13:31	and depart hence: for Herod **w** kill thee.	*2309*
	18: 8	I tell you that he **w** avenge them speedily.	*4160*
	19:14	We **w** not have this *man* to reign over us.	*2309*
	22:42	nevertheless not my **w**, but thine, be done.	*2307*
	23:25	but he delivered Jesus to their **w**.	*2307*
Jn	1:13	not of blood, nor of the **w** of the flesh,	*2307*
	1:13	the flesh, nor of the **w** of man, but of God.	*2307*
	4:34	My meat is to do the **w** of him that sent me,	*2307*
	5:21	so the Son quickeneth whom he **w**.	*2309*
	5:30	is just; because I seek not mine own **w**,	*2307*
	5:30	but the **w** of the Father which hath sent me.	*2307*
	5:40	And ye **w** not come to me, that ye might	*2309*
	6:38	not to do mine own **w**, but the will of him	*2307*
	6:38	own will, but the **w** of him that sent me.	*2307*
	6:39	And this is the Father's **w** which hath sent	*2307*
	6:40	And this is the **w** of him that sent me,	*2307*
	6:67	Jesus unto the twelve, **W** ye also go away?	*2309*
	7:17	If any *man* **w** do his will, he shall know of	*2309*
	7:17	If any *man* will do his **w**, he shall know of	*2307*
	7:35	Whither **w** he go, that we shall not find	*3195*
	7:35	**w** he go unto the dispersed among	*3195*
	8:44	and the lusts of your father ye **w** do.	*2309*
	9:27	hear *it* again? **w** ye also be his disciples?	*2309*
	9:31	of God, and doeth his **w**, him he heareth.	*2307*
	15: 7	ye shall ask what ye **w**, and it shall be done	*2309*
	17:24	Father, I **w** that they also, whom thou hast	*2309*
	18:39	**w** ye therefore *that* I release unto you	*1014*
	21:22	If I **w** that he tarry till I come, what *is that*	*2309*
	21:23	but, If I **w** that he tarry till I come, what *is*	*2309*
Ac	13:22	mine own heart, which shall fulfil all my **w**.	*2307*
	13:36	served his own generation by the **w** of God,	*1012*
	17:18	And some said, What **w** this babbler say?	*2309*
	17:31	in the which he **w** judge the world in	*3195*
	18:15	look ye *to it;* for I **w** be no judge of such	*1014*
	18:21	but I **w** return again unto you, if God will.	*2309*
	18:21	but I will return again unto you, if God **w**.	*2309*
	21:14	saying, The **w** of the Lord be done.	*2307*
	22:14	that *thou* shouldest know his **w**, and	*2307*
	27:10	I perceive that *this* voyage **w** be with hurt	*3195*
Ro	1:10	journey by the **w** of God to come unto you.	*2307*
	2:18	And knowest *his* **w**, and approvest	*2307*
	7:18	dwelleth no good *thing:* for to **w** is present	*2309*
	9:18	Therefore hath he mercy on whom he **w**	*2309*
	9:18	*have mercy,* and whom he **w** he hardeneth.	*2309*
	9:19	yet find fault? For who hath resisted his **w**?	*1013*
	12: 2	and acceptable, and perfect, **w** of God.	*2307*
	15:32	come unto you with joy by the **w** of God,	*2307*
1Co	1: 1	of Jesus Christ through the **w** of God,	*2307*
	4:19	you shortly, if the Lord **w**, and will know,	*2309*
	4:21	What **w** ye? shall I come unto you with a	*2309*
	7:36	and need so require, let him do what he **w**,	*2309*
	7:37	but hath power over his own **w**, and hath so	*2307*
	7:39	is at liberty to be married to whom she **w**;	*2309*
	9:17	but if **against** my **w**, a dispensation *of*	*210*
	12:11	dividing to every man severally as he **w**.	*1014*
	14:35	And if they **w** learn any *thing,* let them ask	*2309*
	16: 7	For I **w** not see you now by the way; but I	*2309*
	16:12	*his* **w** was not at all to come at this time;	*2307*
2Co	1: 1	an apostle of Jesus Christ by the **w** of God,	*2307*
	8: 5	to the Lord, and unto us by the **w** of God.	*2307*
	8:11	*of it;* that as *there was* a readiness to **w**,	*2309*
Gal	1: 4	according to the **w** of God and our Father:	*2307*
Eph	1: 1	an apostle of Jesus Christ by the **w** of God,	*2307*
	1: 5	according to the good pleasure of his **w**,	*2307*
	1: 9	made known unto us the mystery of his **w**,	*2307*
	1:11	all *things* after the counsel of his own **w**:	*2307*
	5:17	understanding what the **w** of the Lord *is.*	*2307*
	6: 6	doing the **w** of God from the heart;	*2307*
	6: 7	With **good w** doing service, as to the Lord,	*2133*
Php	1:15	and strife; and some also of **good w**:	*2107*
	2:13	it is God which worketh in you both to **w**	*2309*
	2:23	as I shall see **how it w go** with me.	*3588+4012*
Col	1: 1	an apostle of Jesus Christ by the **w** of God,	*2307*
	1: 9	*with* the knowledge of his **w** in all wisdom	*2307*
	2:23	indeed a shew of wisdom in **w worship**,	*1479*
	4:12	and complete in all the **w** of God.	*2307*
1Th	4: 3	For this is the **w** of God, *even* your	*2307*
	5:18	for this *is* the **w** of God in Christ Jesus	*2307*
1Ti	2: 4	Who **w have** all men to be saved, and	*2309*
	2: 8	I **w** therefore that men pray every where,	*1014*
	5:11	wax wanton against Christ, they **w** marry;	*2309*
	5:14	I **w** therefore that the younger *women*	*1014*
	6: 9	But they that **w** be rich fall into temptation	*1014*
2Ti	1: 1	an apostle of Jesus Christ by the **w** of God,	*2307*
	2:26	*who are* taken captive by him at his **w**.	*2307*
	3:12	all that **w** live godly in Christ Jesus shall	*2309*
Tit	3: 8	these *things* I **w** that thou affirm constantly,	*1014*
Heb	2: 4	of the Holy Ghost, according to his own **w**?	*2308*
	2:13	And again, I **w** put my trust in him.	*1510*
	10: 7	it is written of me,) to do thy **w**, O God.	*2307*
	10: 9	said he, Lo, I come to do thy **w**, O God.	*2307*
	10:10	By the which **w** we are sanctified through	*2307*
	10:36	that, after ye have done the **w** of God,	*2307*
	13:21	you perfect in every good work to do his **w**,	*2307*
Jas	1:18	**Of his own w** begat he us with the word of	*1014*
	4: 4	**w** be a friend of the world is the enemy of	*1014*
	4:15	If the Lord **w**, we shall live, and do this, or	*2309*
1Pe	2:15	For so is the **w** of God, that with well doing	*2307*
	3:10	For he that **w** love life, and see good days,	*2309*
	3:17	For *it is* better, if the **w** of God be so,	*2307*
	4: 2	to the lusts of men, but to the **w** of God.	*2307*
	4: 3	us to have wrought the **w** of the Gentiles,	*2307*
	4:19	**w** of God commit the keeping of their souls	*2307*
2Pe	1:12	Wherefore I **w** not be negligent to put you	*3195*
	1:21	came not in old time by the **w** of man:	*2307*
1Jn	2:17	he that doeth the **w** of God abideth for ever.	*2307*
	5:14	that, if we ask any *thing* according to his **w**,	*2307*
3Jn	1:13	but I **w** not with ink and pen write unto	*2309*
Jude	1: 5	I **w** therefore put you in remembrance,	*1014*
Rev	3:16	nor hot, I **w** spue thee out of my mouth.	*3195*
	11: 5	And if any *man* **w** hurt them,	*2309*
	11: 5	and if any *man* **w** hurt them, he must in this	*2309*
	11: 6	earth with all plagues, as often as they **w**.	*2309*
	17:17	God hath put in their hearts to fulfil his **w**,	*1106*
	22:17	And whosoever **w**, let him take the water of	*2309*

WILLETH (1) [WILL]

Ro	9:16	So then *it is* not of him that **w**, nor of him	*2309*

WILLING (32) [WILL]

Ge	24: 5	Peradventure the woman will not be **w** to	14
	24: 8	if the woman will not be **w** to follow thee,	14
Ex	35: 5	whosoever *is* of a **w** heart, let him bring it,	5081
	35:21	and every one whom his spirit **made w**, *and*	5068
	35:22	as many as were **w** hearted, *and*	5081
	35:29	The children of Israel brought a **w offering**	5071
	35:29	whose heart **made** them **w** to bring for all	5068
1Ch	28: 9	him with a perfect heart and with a **w** mind:	2655
	28:21	**w** skilful *man,* for any *manner of* service:	5081
	29: 5	is **w** to consecrate his service *this* day unto	5068
Job	39: 9	Will the unicorn be **w** to serve thee, or	14

W

Ps 110: 3 Thy people *shall be* w in the day of thy 5071
Isa 1:19 If ye be w and obedient, ye shall eat the good 14
Mt 1:19 and not w to make her a publick example, *2309*
26:41 the spirit indeed *is* w, but the flesh *is* weak. *4289*
Mk 15:15 And *so* Pilate, w to content the people, *1014*
Lk 10:29 But he, w to justify himself, said unto *2309*
22:42 Saying, Father, if thou be w, remove this *1014*
23:20 Pilate therefore, w to release Jesus, spake *2309*
Jn 5:35 ye were w for a season to rejoice in his *2309*
Ac 24:27 and Felix, w to shew the Jews a pleasure, *2309*
25: 9 But Festus, w to do the Jews a pleasure, *2309*
27:43 But the centurion, w to save Paul, *1014*
Ro 9:22 w to shew *his* wrath, and to make his power *2309*
2Co 5: 8 and w rather to be absent from the body, *2106*
8: 3 *their* power *they were* **w of themselves**; *830*
8:12 For if there be first a w **mind**, *it is* accepted *4288*
1Th 2: 8 we were w to have imparted unto you, *2106*
1Ti 6:18 ready to distribute, **w to communicate**; *2843*
Heb 6:17 w more abundantly to shew unto the heirs *1014*
13:18 in all *things* w to live honestly. *2309*
2Pe 3: 9 not w that any should perish, but that all *1014*

WILLINGLY (25) [WILL]
Ex 25: 2 of every man that **giveth** it w with his heart 5068
Jdg 5: 2 when the people w **offered** themselves. 5068
5: 9 that **offered** themselves w among 5068
8:25 We will w **give** *them*. And they 5414+5414
1Ch 29: 6 the rulers over the king's work, **offered** w, 5068
29: 9 for that they **offered** w, because 5068
29: 9 with perfect heart they **offered** w to 5068
29:14 that we should be able to **offer** *so* w after 5068
29:17 heart I have w **offered** all these *things:* 5068
29:17 are present here, to **offer** w unto thee. 5068
2Ch 17:16 who w **offered** himself unto the LORD; 5068
35: 8 his princes gave w unto the people, 5071+3807.1
Ezr 1: 6 beside all *that* was w **offered**. 5068
3: 5 of every one that w **offered** a freewill 5068
7:16 **offering** w for the house of their God 5069
Ne 11: 2 that w **offered** themselves to dwell at 5068
Pr 31:13 flax, and worketh w with her hands. 2656+871.1
La 3:33 For he doth not afflict w nor grieve 3820+4480
Hos 5:11 he w walked after the commandment. 2974
Jn 6:21 Then they w received him into the ship: *2309*
Ro 8:20 not w, but by reason of him who hath *1635*
1Co 9:17 For if I do this *thing* w, I have a reward: but *1635*
Phm 1:14 not be as *it were* of necessity, but w. *1595+2596*
1Pe 5: 2 oversight *thereof,* not by constraint, but w; *1596*
2Pe 3: 5 For this they w are ignorant of, that by *2309*

WILLOW (1) [WILLOWS]
Eze 17: 5 *it* by great waters, *and* set it *as* a **w tree**. 6851

WILLOWS (5) [WILLOW]
Lev 23:40 boughs of thick trees, and w of the brook; 6155
Job 40:22 the w of the brook compass him about. 6155
Ps 137: 2 We hanged our harps upon the w in 6155
Isa 15: 7 shall they carry away to the brook of the w. 6155
44: 4 among the grass, as w by the water courses. 6155

WILT (245) [WILL] See Index

WILY See FROWARD

WIMPLES (1)
Isa 3:22 and the w, and the crisping pins, 4304

WIN (2) [WINNETH, WON]
2Ch 32: 1 and thought to w them for himself. 1234
Php 3: 8 count *them but* dung, that I may w Christ, *2770*

WIND (123) [WHIRLWIND, WHIRLWINDS, WINDING, WINDS, WINDY, WOUND]
Ge 8: 1 God made a w to pass over the earth, and 7307
41: 6 blasted with the **east** w sprang up after 6921
41:23 withered, thin, *and* blasted with the **east** w, 6921
41:27 the **east** w shall be seven years of famine. 6921
Ex 10:13 the LORD brought an east w upon 7307
10:13 the east w brought the locusts. 7307
10:19 the LORD turned a mighty strong west w, 7307
14:21 to go *back* by a strong east w all *that* night, 7307
15:10 Thou didst blow with thy w, the sea 7307
Nu 11:31 there went forth a w from the LORD, and 7307
2Sa 22:11 and he was seen upon the wings of the w. 7307
1Ki 18:45 the heaven was black *with* clouds and w, 7307
19:11 a great and strong w rent the mountains, 7307
19:11 *but* the LORD *was* not in the w: 7307
19:11 after the w an earthquake; *but* the LORD 7307
2Ki 3:17 Ye shall not see w, neither shall ye see rain; 7307
Job 1:19 there came a great w from the wilderness, 7307
6:26 of one that is desperate, *which are* as w? 7307
7: 7 O remember that my life *is* w: mine eye 7307
8: 2 the words of thy mouth *be like* a strong w? 7307
15: 2 and fill his belly *with* the **east** w? 6921
21:18 They are as stubble before the w, and 7307
27:21 The **east** w carrieth him away, and 6921
30:15 they pursue my soul as the w: and 7307
30:22 Thou liftest me up to the w; thou causest 7307
37:17 when he quieteth the earth by the south *w?* NIH
37:21 but the w passeth, and cleanseth them. 7307
38:24 *which* scattereth the **east** w upon the earth? 6921
Ps 1: 4 *are* like the chaff which the w driveth away. 7307
18:10 yea, he did fly upon the wings of the w. 7307
18:42 I beat them small as the dust before the w: 7307
35: 5 Let them be as chaff before the w: and 7307
48: 7 the ships of Tarshish with an east w. 7307
78:26 He caused an **east** w to blow in the heaven: 6921
78:26 by his power he brought in the **south** w. 8486
78:39 a w that passeth away, and cometh not 7307
83:13 like a wheel; as the stubble before the w. 7307
103:16 For the w passeth over it, and it is gone; 7307
104: 3 who walketh upon the wings of the w: 7307
107:25 he commandeth, and raiseth the stormy w, 7307
135: 7 he bringeth the w out of his treasuries. 7307
147:18 he causeth his w to blow, *and* the waters 7307
148: 8 and vapour; stormy w fulfilling his word: 7307
Pr 11:29 troubleth his own house shall inherit the w: 7307
25:14 false gift *is like* clouds and w without rain. 7307
25:23 The north w driveth away rain: so *doth* an 7307
27:16 hideth the w, and the ointment of his right 7307
30: 4 who hath gathered the w in his fists? 7307
Ecc 1: 6 The w goeth toward the south, and 7307
1: 6 the w returneth *again* according to his 7307
5:16 profit hath he that hath laboured for the w? 7307
11: 4 He that observeth the w shall not sow; and 7307
SS 4:16 Awake, O **north** w; and come thou south; 6828
Isa 7: 2 the trees of the wood are moved with the w. 7307
11:15 with his mighty w shall he shake his hand 7307
17:13 as the chaff of the mountains before the w, 7307
26:18 in pain, we have as it were brought forth w; 7307
27: 8 he stayeth his rough w in the day of the east 7307
27: 8 his rough wind in the day of the **east** w. 6921
32: 2 a man shall be as a hiding place from the w, 7307
41:16 the w shall carry them away, and 7307
41:29 their molten images *are* w and confusion. 7307
57:13 the w shall carry them all away; 7307
64: 6 our iniquities, like the w, have taken us 7307
Jer 2:24 *that* snuffeth up the w at her pleasure; 7307
4:11 A dry w of the high places in 7307
4:12 *Even* a full w from those *places* shall come 7307
5:13 the prophets shall become w, and the word 7307
10:13 bringeth forth the w out of his treasures. 7307
13:24 passeth away by the w of the wilderness. 7307
14: 6 they snuffed up the w like dragons; 7307
18:17 I will scatter them as *with* an east w before 7307
22:22 The w shall eat up all thy pastors, and 7307
51: 1 that rise up against me, a destroying w; 7307
51:16 bringeth forth the w out of his treasures. 7307
Eze 5: 2 a third *part* thou shalt scatter in the w; and 7307
12:14 I will scatter toward every w all that *are* 7307
13:11 shall fall; and a stormy w shall rent *it.* 7307
13:13 I will even rent *it with* a stormy w in my 7307
17:10 utterly wither, when the east w toucheth it? 7307
19:12 and the east w dried up her fruit: 7307
27:26 the east w hath broken thee in the midst of 7307
37: 9 Prophesy unto the w, prophesy, son of man, 7307
37: 9 prophesy, son of man, and say to the w, 7307
Da 2:35 the w carried them away, that no place was 7308
Hos 4:19 The w hath bound her up in her wings, and 7307
8: 7 For they have sown the w, and they shall 7307
12: 1 Ephraim feedeth on w, and followeth after 7307
12: 1 on wind, and followeth after the **east** w: 6921
13:15 among *his* brethren, an east w shall come, 7307
13:15 the w of the LORD *shall* come up from NIH
Am 4:13 createth the w, and declareth unto man 7307
Jnh 1: 4 the LORD sent out a great w into the sea, 7307
4: 8 that God prepared a vehement east w; 7307
Hab 1: 9 their faces shall sup up *as* the **east** w, and 6921
Zec 5: 9 two women, and the w *was* in their wings; 7307
Mt 11: 7 to see? A reed shaken with the w? *417*

W

Mt 14:24 tossed with **w**aves: for the **w** was contrary. 417
14:30 But when he saw the **w** boysterous, he was 417
14:32 they were come into the ship, the **w** ceased. 417
Mk 4:37 And there arose a great storm of **w**, and 417
4:39 and rebuked the **w**, and said unto the sea, 417
4:39 And the **w** ceased, and there was a great 417
4:41 is this, that even the **w** and the sea obey him? 417
6:48 in rowing; for the **w** was contrary unto them: 417
6:51 up unto them into the ship; and the **w** ceased: 417
Lk 7:24 for to see? A reed shaken with the **w**? 417
8:23 there came down a storm of **w** on the lake; 417
8:24 and rebuked the **w** and the raging of 417
12:55 And when *ye see* the **south w** blow, ye say, 3558
Jn 3: 8 The **w** bloweth where it listeth, and 4151
6:18 And the sea arose by reason of a great **w** that 417
Ac 2: 2 from heaven as of a rushing mighty **w**, 4157
27: 7 the **w** not suffering us, we sailed under 417
27:13 And when the **south w** blew softly, 3558
27:14 after there arose against it a tempestuous **w**, 417
27:15 and could not bear up into the **w**, we let *her* 417
27:40 and hoised up the mainsail to the **w**, and 4154
28:13 and after one day the **south w** blew, and 3558
Eph 4:14 and carried about with every **w** of doctrine, 417
Jas 1: 6 is like a wave of the sea **driven with the w** 416
Rev 6:13 when she is shaken of a mighty **w**. 417
7: 1 that the **w** should not blow on the earth, 417

WINDING (3) [WIND]
1Ki 6: 8 they went up with **w stairs** into the middle 3883
Eze 41: 7 a **w about** still upward to the side 5437
41: 7 for the **w about** of the house *went* still 5437

WINDOW (16) [WINDOWS]
Ge 6:16 A **w** shalt thou make to the ark, and in a 6672
8: 6 that Noah opened the **w** of the ark which he 2474
26: 8 king of the Philistims looked out at a **w**, 2474
Jos 2:15 she let them down by a cord through the **w**: 2474
2:18 in the **w** which thou didst let us down by: 2474
2:21 and she bound the scarlet line in the **w**. 2474
Jdg 5:28 The mother of Sisera looked out at a **w**, and 2474
1Sa 19:12 So Michal let David down through a **w**: and 2474
2Sa 6:16 Michal Saul's daughter looked through a **w**, 2474
2Ki 9:30 and tired her head, and looked out at a **w**. 2474
9:32 he lift up his face to the **w**, and said, Who *is* 2474
13:17 he said, Open the **w** eastward. And he 2474
1Ch 15:29 looking out at a **w** saw king David dancing 2474
Pr 7: 6 For at the **w** of my house I looked through 2474
Ac 20: 9 And there sat in a **w** a certain young man 2376
2Co 11:33 And through a **w** in a basket was I let down 2376

WINDOWS (30) [WINDOW]
Ge 7:11 and the **w** of heaven were opened. 699
8: 2 the deep and the **w** of heaven were stopped, 699
1Ki 6: 4 for the house he made **w** of narrow lights. 2474
7: 4 *there were* **w** *in* three rows, and light *was* 8261
7: 5 and posts *were* square, *with the* **w**: 8260
2Ki 7: 2 *if* the LORD would make **w** in heaven, 699
7:19 *if* the LORD should make **w** in heaven, 699
Ecc 12: 3 and those that look out of the **w** be darkened, 699
SS 2: 9 behind our wall, he looketh forth at the **w**, 2474
Isa 24:18 for the **w** from on high are open, and 699
54:12 I will make thy **w** *of* agates, and thy gates 8121
60: 8 fly as a cloud, and as the doves to their **w**? 699
Jer 9:21 For death is come up into our **w**, *and* 2474
22:14 and large chambers, and cutteth him out **w**; 2474
Eze 40:16 *there were* narrow **w** to the little chambers, 2474
40:16 **w** *were* round about inward: and upon *each* 2474
40:22 their **w**, and their arches, and their palm 2474
40:25 *there were* **w** in it and in the arches thereof 2474
40:25 arches thereof round about, like those **w**: 2474
40:29 *there were* **w** in it and in the arches thereof 2474
40:33 *there were* **w** therein and in the arches 2474
40:36 arches thereof, and the **w** to it round about: 2474
41:16 the narrow **w**, and the galleries round about 2474
41:16 *from* the ground up to the **w**, and 2474
41:16 to the windows, and the **w** *were* covered; 2474
41:26 *there were* narrow **w** and palm trees on 2474
Da 6:10 his **w** being open in his chamber toward 3551
Joel 2: 9 they shall enter in at the **w** like a thief. 2474
Zep 2:14 *their* voice shall sing in the **w**; 2474
Mal 3:10 if I will not open you the **w** of heaven, and 699

WINDS (23) [WINDY]
Job 28:25 To make the weight for the **w**; and 7307
Jer 49:32 I will scatter into all **w** them *that are* in 7307
49:36 upon Elam will I bring the four **w** from 7307
49:36 and will scatter them towards all those **w**; 7307
Eze 5:10 remnant of thee will I scatter into all the **w**. 7307
5:12 I will scatter a third *part* into all the **w**, and 7307
17:21 that remain shall be scattered towards all **w**: 7307
37: 9 Come from the four **w**, O breath, and 7307
Da 7: 2 the four **w** of the heaven strove upon 7308
8: 8 notable ones toward the four **w** of heaven. 7307
11: 4 shall be divided toward the four **w** of 7307
Zec 2: 6 for I have spread you abroad as the four **w** 7307
Mt 7:25 and the **w** blew, and beat upon that house; 417
7:27 and the **w** blew, and beat upon that house; 417
8:26 he arose, and rebuked the **w** and the sea; 417
8:27 is this, that even the **w** and the sea obey him? 417
24:31 gather together his elect from the four **w**, 417
Mk 13:27 gather together his elect from the four **w**, 417
Lk 8:25 for he commandeth even the **w** and water, 417
Ac 27: 4 under Cyprus, because the **w** were contrary. 417
Jas 3: 4 they be so great, and are driven of fierce **w**, 417
Jude 1:12 *they are* without water, carried about of **w**; 417
Rev 7: 1 holding the four **w** of the earth, that the wind 417

WINDY (1) [WINDS]
Ps 55: 8 I would hasten my escape from the **w** storm 7307

WINE (232) [WINEBIBBER, WINEBIBBERS, WINEFAT, WINEPRESS, WINEPRESSES, WINES]
Ge 9:21 he drank of the **w**, and was drunken; and 3196
9:24 Noah awoke from his **w**, and knew what his 3196
14:18 king of Salem brought forth bread and **w**: 3196
19:32 let us make our father drink **w**, and we will 3196
19:33 they made their father drink **w** that night: 3196
19:34 let us make him drink **w** this night also; and 3196
19:35 they made their father drink **w** that night 3196
27:25 and he brought him **w**, and he drank. 3196
27:28 of the earth, and plenty of corn and **w**: 8492
27:37 and with corn and **w** have I sustained him: 8492
49:11 he washed his garments in **w**, and 3196
49:12 *His* eyes *shall be* red with **w**, and *his* teeth 3196
Ex 29:40 the fourth *part* of a hin of **w** *for* a drink 3196
Lev 10: 9 Do not drink **w** nor strong drink, thou, 3196
23:13 the drink offering thereof *shall be of* **w**, 3196
Nu 6: 3 He shall separate *himself* from **w** and 3196
6: 3 *and* shall drink no vinegar of **w**, or 3196
6:20 and after *that* the Nazarite may drink **w**. 3196
15: 5 the fourth *part* of a hin *of* **w** for a drink 3196
15: 7 thou shalt offer the third *part* of a hin *of* **w**, 3196
15:10 bring for a drink offering half a hin *of* **w**, 3196
18:12 and all the best of the **w**, and of the wheat, 8492
28: 7 **strong w** to be poured unto the LORD *for* 7941
28:14 their drink offerings shall be half a hin of **w** 3196
Dt 7:13 thy land, thy corn, and thy **w**, and thine oil, 8492
11:14 gather in thy corn, and thy **w**, and thine oil. 8492
12:17 or of thy **w**, or of thy oil, or the firstlings of 8492
14:23 of thy **w**, and of thine oil, and the firstlings 8492
14:26 or for **w**, or for strong drink, or 3196
16:13 thou hast gathered in thy corn and thy **w**: 3342
18: 4 of thy **w**, and of thy oil, and the first of 8492
28:39 dress *them*, but shalt neither drink *of* the **w**, 3196
28:51 **w**, or oil, *or* the increase of thy kine, or 8492
29: 6 neither have you drunk **w** or strong drink: 3196
32:33 Their **w** *is* the poison of dragons, and 3196
32:38 *and* drank the **w** of their drink offerings? 3196
33:28 Jacob *shall be* upon a land of corn and **w**; 8492
Jos 9: 4 and **w** bottles, old, and rent, and bound up; 3196
9:13 these bottles of **w**, which we filled, 3196
Jdg 9:13 Should I leave my **w**, which cheereth God 8492
13: 4 drink not **w** nor strong drink, and eat not 3196
13: 7 now drink no **w** nor strong drink, 3196
13:14 neither let her drink **w** or strong drink, 3196
19:19 there is bread and **w** also for me, and 3196
1Sa 1:14 be drunken? put away thy **w** from thee. 3196
1:15 I have drunk neither **w** nor strong drink, but 3196
1:24 a bottle of **w**, and brought him *unto* 3196
10: 3 and another carrying a bottle of **w**: 3196
16:20 a bottle of **w**, and a kid, and sent *them* by 3196
25:18 two bottles of **w**, and five sheep ready 3196
25:37 when the **w** was gone out of Nabal, and 3196
2Sa 6:19 a flagon *of* **w**. So all the people departed NIH
13:28 now when Amnon's heart is merry with **w**, 3196
16: 1 of summer fruits, and a bottle of **w**. 3196
16: 2 the **w**, that such as be faint in 3196
2Ki 18:32 a land of corn and **w**, a land of bread and 8492

W

1Ch	9:29	the w, and the oil, and the frankincense,	3196
	12:40	w, and oil, and oxen, and sheep abundantly:	3196
	16: 3	a good piece *of flesh,* and a flagon *of* w.	NIH
	27:27	over the increase of the vineyards for the w	3196
2Ch	2:10	twenty thousand baths of w, and	3196
	2:15	and the barley, the oil, and the w,	3196
	11:11	and store of victual, and *of* oil and w.	3196
	31: 5	w, and oil, and honey, and of all	8492
	32:28	also for the increase of corn, and w, and oil;	8492
Ezr	6: 9	the God of heaven, wheat, salt, w, and oil,	2562
	7:22	to an hundred baths *of* w, and to an	2562
Ne	2: 1	Artaxerxes the king, *that* w *was* before him:	3196
	2: 1	I took up the w, and gave *it* unto the king.	3196
	5:11	*of* the corn, the w, and the oil, that ye exact	8492
	5:15	had taken of them bread and w, beside forty	3196
	5:18	and once in ten days store of all *sorts of* w:	3196
	10:37	*of* trees, of w and of oil, unto the priests,	8492
	10:39	of the **new** w, and the oil, unto	8492
	13: 5	tithes of the corn, the **new** w, and the oil,	8492
	13:12	the **new** w and the oil unto the treasuries.	8492
	13:15	*some* treading w **presses** on the sabbath,	1660
	13:15	as also w, grapes, and figs, and all *manner*	3196
Est	1: 7	royal w in abundance, according to	3196
	1:10	the heart of the king was merry with w,	3196
	5: 6	king said unto Esther at the banquet of w,	3196
	7: 2	on the second day at the banquet of w,	3196
	7: 7	the king arising from the banquet of w in	3196
	7: 8	garden into the place of the banquet of w;	3196
Job	1:13	drinking w in their eldest brother's house:	3196
	1:18	drinking w in their eldest brother's house:	3196
	32:19	my belly *is* as w *which* hath no vent;	3196
Ps	4: 7	time *that* their corn and their w increased.	8492
	60: 3	made us to drink the w *of* astonishment.	3196
	75: 8	the LORD *there is* a cup, and the w is red;	3196
	78:65	a mighty *man* that shouteth by reason of w.	3196
	104:15	w *that* maketh glad the heart of man,	3196
Pr	3:10	and thy presses shall burst out with **new** w.	8492
	4:17	of wickedness, and drink the w of violence.	3196
	9: 2	killed her beasts; she hath mingled her w;	3196
	9: 5	and drink of the w *which* I have mingled.	3196
	20: 1	W *is* a mocker, strong drink *is* raging: and	3196
	21:17	he that loveth w and oil shall not be rich.	3196
	23:30	They that tarry long at the w; they that go	3196
	23:30	at the wine; they that go to seek **mixt** w.	4469
	23:31	Look not thou upon the w when it is red,	3196
	31: 4	O Lemuel, *it is* not for kings to drink w;	3196
	31: 6	and w unto those that be of heavy hearts.	3196
Ecc	2: 3	sought in mine heart to give myself unto w,	3196
	9: 7	and drink thy w with a merry heart;	3196
	10:19	is made for laughter, and w maketh merry:	3196
SS	1: 2	of his mouth: for thy love *is* better than w.	3196
	1: 4	we will remember thy love more than w:	3196
	4:10	how much better is thy love than w! and	3196
	5: 1	I have drunk my w with my milk:	3196
	7: 9	the roof of thy mouth like the best w,	3196
	8: 2	I would cause thee to drink of spiced w,	3196
Isa	1:22	is become dross, thy w mixt with water:	5435
	5:11	continue until night, *till* w inflame them!	3196
	5:12	and the viol, the tabret, and pipe, and w,	3196
	5:22	Woe unto *them that are* mighty to drink w,	3196
	16:10	the treaders shall tread out no w in *their*	3196
	22:13	killing sheep, eating flesh, and drinking w:	3196
	24: 7	The **new** w mourneth, the vine languisheth,	8492
	24: 9	They shall not drink w with a song;	3196
	24:11	*There is* a crying for w in the streets; all joy	3196
	27: 2	day sing ye unto her, A vineyard of **red** w.	2561
	28: 1	valleys of them that are overcome with w.	3196
	28: 7	they also have erred through w, and	3196
	28: 7	strong drink, they are swallowed up of w,	3196
	29: 9	they are drunken, but not *with* w;	3196
	36:17	a land of corn and w, a land of bread and	8492
	49:26	with their own blood, as with **sweet** w:	6071
	51:21	thou afflicted, and drunken, but not with w:	3196
	55: 1	buy w and milk without money and without	3196
	56:12	*say they,* I will fetch w, and we will fill	3196
	62: 8	sons of the stranger shall not drink thy w,	8492
	65: 8	As the **new** w is found in the cluster, and	8492
Jer	13:12	Every bottle shall be filled *with* w:	3196
	13:12	that every bottle shall be filled *with* w?	3196
	23: 9	like a man whom w hath overcome,	3196
	25:15	Take the w cup of this fury at mine hand,	3196
	31:12	for w, and for oil, and for the young of	8492
	35: 2	of the chambers, and give them w to drink.	3196
	35: 5	the house of the Rechabites pots full *of* w,	3196
	35: 5	and cups, and I said unto them, Drink ye w.	3196
	35: 6	they said, We will drink no w: for Jonadab	3196
	35: 6	saying, Ye shall drink no w, *neither* ye,	3196
	35: 8	to drink no w all our days, we, our wives,	3196
	35:14	that he commanded his sons not to drink w,	3196
	40:10	ye, gather ye w, and summer fruits, and oil,	3196
	40:12	gathered w and summer fruits very much.	3196
	48:33	I have caused w to fail from the wine	3196
	48:33	caused wine to fail from the w **presses**:	3342
	51: 7	the nations have drunken of her w;	3196
La	2:12	say to their mothers, Where *is* corn and w?	3196
Eze	27:18	in the w of Helbon, and white wool.	3196
	44:21	Neither shall any priest drink w, when they	3196
Da	1: 5	king's meat, and of the w which he drank:	3196
	1: 8	nor with the w which he drank:	3196
	1:16	and the w that they should drink;	3196
	5: 1	his lords, and drank w before the thousand.	2562
	5: 2	Belshazzar, whiles *he* tasted the w,	2562
	5: 4	They drank w, and praised the gods of	2562
	5:23	and thy concubines, *have* drunk w in them;	2562
	10: 3	neither came flesh nor w in my mouth,	3196
Hos	2: 8	w, and oil, and multiplied her silver and	8492
	2: 9	my w in the season thereof, and	8492
	2:22	shall hear the corn, and the w, and the oil;	8492
	3: 1	look to other gods, and love flagons of w.	6025
	4:11	Whoredom and w and new wine take *away*	3196
	4:11	and wine and **new** w take *away* the heart.	8492
	7: 5	have made *him* sick *with* bottles of w;	3196
	7:14	they assemble themselves for corn and w,	8492
	9: 2	feed them, and the **new** w shall fail in her.	8492
	9: 4	They shall not offer w *offerings* to	3196
	14: 7	the sent thereof *shall be* as the w of	3196
Joel	1: 5	howl, all ye drinkers of w, because of	3196
	1: 5	ye drinkers of wine, because of the **new** w,	6071
	1:10	the **new** w is dried up, the oil languisheth.	8492
	2:19	w, and oil, and ye shall be satisfied	8492
	2:24	and the fats shall overflow *with* w and oil.	8492
	3: 3	and sold a girl for w, that they might drink.	3196
	3:18	*that* the mountains shall drop down **new** w,	6071
Am	2: 8	they drink the w of the condemned *in*	3196
	2:12	ye gave the Nazarites w to drink;	3196
	5:11	but ye shall not drink w of them.	3196
	6: 6	That drink w in bowls, and	3196
	9:13	the mountains shall drop **sweet** w, and	6071
	9:14	plant vineyards, and drink the w thereof;	3196
Mic	2:11	*saying,* I will prophesy unto thee of w and	3196
	6:15	and **sweet** w, but shalt not drink wine.	8492
	6:15	and sweet wine, but shalt not drink w.	3196
Hab	2: 5	Yea also, because he transgresseth *by* w,	3196
Zep	1:13	plant vineyards, but not drink the w thereof.	3196
Hag	1:11	upon the **new** w, and upon the oil, and	8492
	2:12	or pottage, or w, or oil, or any meat, shall it	3196
Zec	9:15	shall drink, *and* make a noise as *through* w;	3196
	9:17	young men cheerful, and **new** w the maids.	8492
	10: 7	and their heart shall rejoice as *through* w:	3196
Mt	9:17	Neither do *men* put new w into old bottles:	*3631*
	9:17	and the w runneth out, and the bottles	*3631*
	9:17	but they put new w into new bottles, and	*3631*
Mk	2:22	And no *man* putteth new w into old bottles:	*3631*
	2:22	else the new w doth burst the bottles, and	*3631*
	2:22	and the w is spilled, and the bottles will be	*3631*
	2:22	but new w must be put into new bottles.	*3631*
	15:23	And they gave him to drink w mingled with	*3631*
Lk	1:15	and shall drink neither w nor strong drink;	*3631*
	5:37	And no *man* putteth new w into old bottles;	*3631*
	5:37	else the new w will burst the bottles, and	*3631*
	5:38	But new w must be put into new bottles;	*3631*
	5:39	No *man* also having drunk old *w*	NIG
	7:33	came neither eating bread nor drinking w;	*3631*
	10:34	pouring in oil and w, and set him on his	*3631*
Jn	2: 3	And when they wanted w, the mother of	*3631*
	2: 3	of Jesus saith unto him, They have no w.	*3631*
	2: 9	feast had tasted the water *that was* made w,	*3631*
	2:10	man at the beginning doth set forth good w;	*3631*
	2:10	*but* thou hast kept the good w until now.	*3631*
	4:46	of Galilee, where he made the water w.	*3631*
Ac	2:13	*These men* are full of **new** w.	*1098*
Ro	14:21	*is* good neither to eat flesh, nor to drink w,	*3631*
Eph	5:18	And be not drunk with w, wherein is	*3631*
1Ti	3: 3	Not **given to** w, no striker, not greedy of	*3943*
	3: 8	not doubletongued, not given to much w,	*3631*
	5:23	but use a little w for thy stomach's sake	*3631*
Tit	1: 7	not soon angry, not **given to** w, no striker,	*3943*
	2: 3	not false accusers, not given to much w,	*3631*

1Pe 4: 3 lusts, **excess of w**, revellings, banquetings, *3632*
Rev 6: 6 and *see* thou hurt not the oil and the **w**. *3631*
14: 8 she made all nations drink of the **w** of *3631*
14:10 The same shall drink of the **w** of the wrath *3631*
16:19 to give unto her the cup of the **w** of *3631*
17: 2 made drunk with the **w** of her fornication. *3631*
18: 3 For all nations have drunk of the **w** of *3631*
18:13 and **w**, and oil, and fine flour, and wheat, *3631*

WINEBIBBER (2) [WINE]
Mt 11:19 and a **w**, a friend of publicans and sinners. *3630*
Lk 7:34 and a **w**, a friend of publicans and sinners. *3630*

WINEBIBBERS (1) [WINE]
Pr 23:20 Be not amongst **w**; amongst riotous eaters 3196

WINEFAT (2) [WINE]
Isa 63: 2 garments like him that treadeth in the **w**? 1660
Mk 12: 1 about *it,* and digged *a place for* the **w**, *5276*

WINEPRESS (15) [PRESS, WINE]
Nu 18:27 and as the fulness of the **w**. 3342
18:30 and as the increase of the **w**. 3342
Dt 15:14 and out of thy floor, and out of thy **w**: 3342
Jdg 6:11 his son Gideon threshed wheat by the **w**, 1660
7:25 Zeeb they slew at the **w** of Zeeb, and 3342
2Ki 6:27 out of the barnfloor, or out of the **w**? 3342
Isa 5: 2 the midst of it, and also made a **w** therein: 3342
63: 3 I have trodden the **w** alone; and of 6333
La 1:15 the virgin, the daughter of Judah, *as in* a **w**. 1660
Hos 9: 2 The floor and the **w** shall not feed them, 3342
Mt 21:33 and digged a **w** in it, and built a tower, and *3025*
Rev 14:19 cast *it* into the great **w** of the wrath of God. *3025*
14:20 And the **w** was trodden without the city, *3025*
14:20 and blood came out of the **w**, *even* unto *3025*
19:15 and he treadeth the **w** of *3025+3631*

WINEPRESSES (2) [PRESS, WINE]
Job 24:11 *and* tread *their* **w**, and suffer thirst. 3342
Zec 14:10 the tower of Hananeel unto the king's **w**. 3342

WINES (2) [WINE]
Isa 25: 6 a feast of **w on the lees**, of fat things full of 8105
25: 6 of marrow, of **w on the lees** well refined. 8105

WING (13) [LONGWINGED, WINGED, WINGS]
1Ki 6:24 five cubits *was* the one **w** of the cherub, 3671
6:24 and five cubits the other **w** of the cherub: 3671
6:24 from the uttermost part of the one **w** unto 3671
6:27 that the **w** of the one touched the *one* wall, 3671
6:27 the **w** of the other cherub touched the other 3671
2Ch 3:11 *one* **w** of the one *cherub was* five cubits, 3671
3:11 the other **w** *was likewise* five cubits, 3671
3:11 reaching to the **w** of the other cherub. 3671
3:12 *one* **w** of the other cherub *was* five cubits, 3671
3:12 the other **w** *was* five cubits *also,* joining to 3671
3:12 *also,* joining to the **w** of the other cherub. 3671
Isa 10:14 there was none that moved the **w**, or 3671
Eze 17:23 and under it shall dwell all fowl of every **w**; 3671

WINGED (2) [WING]
Ge 1:21 their kind, and every **w** fowl after his kind: 3671
Dt 4:17 the likeness of any **w** fowl that flieth in 3671

WINGS (76) [WING]
Ex 19: 4 *how* I bare you on eagles' **w**, and 3671
25:20 the cherubims shall stretch forth *their* **w** on 3671
25:20 covering the mercy seat with their **w**, 3671
37: 9 the cherubims spread out *their* **w** on high, 3671
37: 9 covered with their **w** over the mercy seat, 3671
Lev 1:17 he shall cleave it with the **w** thereof, *but* 3671
Dt 32:11 spreadeth abroad her **w**, taketh them, 3671
32:11 taketh them, beareth them on her **w**: 84
Ru 2:12 under whose **w** thou art come to trust. 3671
2Sa 22:11 and he was seen upon the **w** of the wind. 3671
1Ki 6:27 they stretched forth the **w** of the cherubims, 3671
6:27 their **w** touched one another in the midst of 3671
8: 6 to the most holy *place,* even under the **w** of 3671
8: 7 For the cherubims spread forth *their* **two w** 3671
1Ch 28:18 that spread out *their* **w**, and covered the ark NIH
2Ch 3:11 the **w** of the cherubims *were* twenty cubits 3671
3:13 The **w** of these cherubims spread 3671
5: 7 into the most holy *place,* even under the **w** 3671
5: 8 For the cherubims spread forth *their* **w** over 3671
Job 39:13 *Gavest thou* the goodly **w** unto 3671
39:13 or **w** and feathers *unto* the ostrich? 84
39:26 *and* stretch her **w** toward the south? 3671
Ps 17: 8 hide me under the shadow of thy **w**, 3671
18:10 yea, he did fly upon the **w** of the wind. 3671
36: 7 put their trust under the shadow of thy **w**. 3671
55: 6 O that I had **w** like a dove, *for then* would I 83
57: 1 in the shadow of thy **w** will I make my 3671
61: 4 I will trust in the covert of thy **w**. Selah. 3671
63: 7 in the shadow of thy **w** will I rejoice. 3671
68:13 *yet shall ye be as* the **w** of a dove covered 3671
91: 4 and under his **w** shalt thou trust: 3671
104: 3 who walketh upon the **w** of the wind: 3671
139: 9 *If* I take the **w** of the morning, *and* dwell in 3671
Pr 23: 5 for *riches* certainly make themselves **w**; 3671
Ecc 10:20 and that which hath **w** shall tell the matter. 3671
Isa 6: 2 each one had six **w**; with twain he covered 3671
8: 8 the stretching out of his **w** shall fill 3671
18: 1 Woe to the land shadowing with **w**, 3671
40:31 they shall mount up *with* **w** as eagles; 83
Jer 48: 9 Give **w** unto Moab, that it may flee and 6731
48:40 an eagle, and shall spread his **w** over Moab. 3671
49:22 as the eagle, and spread his **w** over Bozrah: 3671
Eze 1: 6 had four faces, and every one had four **w**. 3671
1: 8 *they had* the hands of a man under their **w** 3671
1: 8 and they four had their faces and their **w**. 3671
1: 9 Their **w** *were* joined one to another; they 3671
1:11 their **w** *were* stretched upward; two *wings* 3671
1:11 two *w* of every one *were* joined one to NIH
1:23 under the firmament *were* their **w** straight, 3671
1:24 they went, I heard the noise of their **w**, 3671
1:24 when they stood, they let down their **w**. 3671
1:25 when they stood, *and* had let down their **w**. 3671
3:13 *I heard* also the noise of the **w** of the living 3671
10: 5 the sound of the cherubims' **w** was heard 3671
10: 8 the form of a man's hand under their **w**. 3671
10:12 their hands, and their **w**, and the wheels, 3671
10:16 when the cherubims lift up their **w** to 3671
10:19 the cherubims lift up their **w**, and 3671
10:21 four faces apiece, and every one four **w**; 3671
10:21 of the hands of a man *was* under their **w**. 3671
11:22 did the cherubims lift up their **w**, and 3671
17: 3 A great eagle with great **w**, longwinged, 3671
17: 7 was also another great eagle with great **w** 3671
Da 7: 4 The first *was* like a lion, and had eagle's **w**: 1611
7: 4 I beheld till the **w** thereof were pluckt, and 1611
7: 6 which had upon the back of it four **w** of a 1611
Hos 4:19 The wind hath bound her up in her **w**, and 3671
Zec 5: 9 two women, and the wind *was* in their **w**; 3671
5: 9 for they had **w** like the wings of a stork: 3671
5: 9 for they had wings like the **w** of a stork: 3671
Mal 4: 2 of righteousness arise with healing in his **w**; 3671
Mt 23:37 a hen gathereth her chickens under *her* **w**, *4420*
Lk 13:34 as a hen *doth gather* her brood under *her* **w**, *4420*
Rev 4: 8 And the four beasts had each of them six **w** *4420*
9: 9 the sound of their **w** *was* as the sound of *4420*
12:14 And to the woman were given two **w** of a *4420*

WINK (2) [WINKED, WINKETH]
Job 15:12 thee away? and what do thine eyes **w** at, 7335
Ps 35:19 *neither* let them **w** *with* the eye that hate me 7169

WINKED (1) [WINK]
Ac 17:30 And the times of *this* ignorance God **w** at; *5237*

WINKETH (2) [WINK]
Pr 6:13 He **w** with his eyes, he speaketh with his 7169
10:10 He that **w** *with* the eye causeth sorrow: but 7169

WINNETH (1) [WIN]
Pr 11:30 *is* a tree of life; and he that **w** souls *is* wise. 3947

WINNOWED (1) [WINNOWETH]
Isa 30:24 which hath been **w** with the shovel and 2219

WINNOWETH (1) [WINNOWED]
Ru 3: 2 he **w** barley to night in the threshingfloor. 2219

WINTER (14) [WINTERED, WINTERHOUSE]
Ge 8:22 summer and **w**, and day and night shall not 2779
Ps 74:17 of the earth: thou hast made summer and **w**. 2779
SS 2:11 For lo, the **w** is past, the rain is over *and* 5638
Isa 18: 6 all the beasts of the earth shall **w** upon 2778
Am 3:15 I will smite the **w** house with the summer 2779
Zec 14: 8 hinder sea: in summer and in **w** shall it be. 2779
Mt 24:20 But pray ye that your flight be not in the **w**, *5494*

Mk 13:18 pray ye that your flight be not in the w. 5494
Jn 10:22 the feast of the dedication, and it was w. 5494
Ac 27:12 the haven was not commodious to w in, 3915
27:12 might attain to Phenice, and there to w; 3914
1Co 16: 6 be that I will abide, yea, and w with you, 3914
2Ti 4:21 Do thy diligence to come before w. 5494
Tit 3:12 for I have determined there to w. 3914

WINTERED (1) [WINTER]
Ac 28:11 which had w in the isle, whose sign was 3914

WINTERHOUSE (1) [HOUSE, WINTER]
Jer 36:22 Now the king sat in the w in 1004+2779

WIPE (8) [WIPED, WIPETH, WIPING]
2Ki 21:13 I will w Jerusalem as a man wipeth a dish, 4229
Ne 13:14 w not out my good deeds that I have done 4229
Isa 25: 8 the Lord God will w away tears from off 4229
Lk 7:38 and did w them with the hairs of her head, 1591
10:11 cleaveth on us, we do w off against you: 631
Jn 13: 5 to w them with the towel wherewith he was 1591
Rev 7:17 God shall w away all tears from their eyes. 1813
21: 4 And God shall w away all tears from their 1813

WIPED (4) [WIPE]
Pr 6:33 and his reproach shall not be w away. 4229
Lk 7:44 and w them with the hairs of her head. 1591
Jn 11: 2 and w his feet with her hair, whose brother 1591
12: 3 feet of Jesus, and w his feet with her hair: 1591

WIPETH (2) [WIPE]
2Ki 21:13 I will wipe Jerusalem as a man w a dish, 4229
Pr 30:20 she eateth, and w her mouth, and saith, 4229

WIPING (1) [WIPE]
2Ki 21:13 a dish, w it, and turning it upside down. 4229

WIRES (1)
Ex 39: 3 cut it into w, to work it in the blue, and 6616

WISDOM (234) [UNWISE]
Ex 28: 3 whom I have filled with the spirit of w, 2451
31: 3 in w, and in understanding, and 2451
31: 6 of all that are wise hearted I have put w, 2451
35:26 heart stirred them up in w spun goats' hair. 2451
35:31 in w, in understanding, and in knowledge, 2451
35:35 Them hath he filled with w of heart, 2451
36: 1 in whom the Lord put w and 2451
36: 2 in whose heart the Lord had put w, 2451
Dt 4: 6 and do them; for this is your w and 2451
34: 9 the son of Nun was full of the spirit of w; 2451
2Sa 14:20 according to the w of an angel of God, 2451
20:22 woman went unto all the people in her w. 2451
1Ki 2: 6 Do therefore according to thy w, and let not 2451
3:28 for they saw that the w of God was in him, 2451
4:29 God gave Solomon w and 2451
4:30 Solomon's w excelled the wisdom of all 2451
4:30 Solomon's wisdom excelled the w of all 2451
4:30 of the east country, and all the w of Egypt. 2451
4:34 there came of all people to hear the w of 2451
4:34 of the earth, which had heard of his w. 2451
5:12 the Lord gave Solomon w, as he 2451
7:14 he was filled with w, and understanding, 2451
10: 4 queen of Sheba had seen all Solomon's w, 2451
10: 6 in mine own land of thy acts and of thy w. 2451
10: 7 thy w and prosperity exceedeth the fame 2451
10: 8 before thee, and that hear thy w. 2451
10:23 the kings of the earth for riches and for w. 2451
10:24 to hear his w, which God had put in his 2451
11:41 of Solomon, and all that he did, and his w, 2451
1Ch 22:12 Only the Lord give thee w and 7922
2Ch 1:10 Give me now w and knowledge, that I may 2451
1:11 hast asked w and knowledge for thyself, 2451
1:12 W and knowledge is granted unto thee; and 2451
9: 3 when the queen of Sheba had seen the w of 2451
9: 5 mine own land of thine acts, and of thy w: 2451
9: 6 the one half of the greatness of thy w was 2451
9: 7 continually before thee, and hear thy w. 2451
9:22 all the kings of the earth in riches and w. 2451
9:23 to hear his w, that God had put in his heart. 2451
Ezr 7:25 thou, Ezra, after the w of thy God, that is in 2452
Job 4:21 in them go away? they die, even without w. 2451
6:13 help in me? and is w driven quite from me? 8454
11: 6 that he would shew thee the secrets of w, 2451
12: 2 ye are the people, and w shall die with you. 2451
12:12 With the ancient is w; and in length of days 2451
12:13 With him is w and strength, he hath counsel 2451
12:16 With him is strength and w: the deceived 8454
13: 5 hold your peace, and it should be your w. 2451
15: 8 of God? and dost thou restrain w to thyself? 2451
26: 3 hast thou counselled him that hath no w? 2451
28:12 where shall w be found? and where is 2451
28:18 of pearls: for the price of w is above rubies. 2451
28:20 Whence then cometh w? and where is 2451
28:28 Behold, the fear of the Lord, that is w; 2451
32: 7 and multitude of years should teach w. 2451
32:13 Lest ye should say, We have found out w: 2451
33:33 hold thy peace, and I shall teach thee w. 2451
34:35 and his words were without w. 7919
36: 5 not any: he is mighty in strength and w. 3820
38:36 Who hath put w in the inward parts? or 2451
38:37 Who can number the clouds in w? or 2451
39:17 Because God hath deprived her of w, 2451
39:26 Doth the hawk fly by thy w, and stretch her 998
Ps 37:30 The mouth of the righteous speaketh w, and 2451
49: 3 My mouth shall speak of w; and 2454
51: 6 hidden part thou shalt make me to know w. 2451
90:12 that we may apply our hearts unto w. 2451
104:24 in w hast thou made them all: the earth is 2451
105:22 at his pleasure; and teach his senators w. 2449
111:10 fear of the Lord is the beginning of w: 2451
136: 5 To him that by w made the heavens: for his 8394
Pr 1: 2 To know w and instruction; to perceive 2451
1: 3 To receive the instruction of w, justice, and 7919
1: 7 but fools despise w and instruction. 2451
1:20 W crieth without; she uttereth her voice in 2454
2: 2 So that thou incline thine ear unto w, and 2451
2: 6 For the Lord giveth w: out of his mouth 2451
2: 7 He layeth up sound w for the righteous: 8454
2:10 When w entereth into thine heart, and 2451
3:13 Happy is the man that findeth w, and 2451
3:19 The Lord by w hath founded the earth; 2451
3:21 thine eyes: keep sound w and discretion: 8454
4: 5 Get w, get understanding: forget it not; 2451
4: 7 W is the principal thing; therefore 2451
4: 7 is the principal thing; therefore get w: 2451
4:11 I have taught thee in the way of w; I have 2451
5: 1 attend unto my w, and bow thine ear to my 2451
7: 4 Say unto w, Thou art my sister; and 2451
8: 1 Doth not w cry? and understanding put 2451
8: 5 O ye simple, understand w: and, ye fools, 6195
8:11 For w is better than rubies; and all 2451
8:12 I w dwell with prudence, and find out 2451
8:14 Counsel is mine, and sound w: I am 8454
9: 1 W hath builded her house, she hath hewn 2454
9:10 fear of the Lord is the beginning of w: 2451
10:13 In the lips of him that hath understanding w 2451
10:21 feed many: but fools die for want of w. 3820
10:23 but a man of understanding hath w. 2451
10:31 The mouth of the just bringeth forth w: but 2451
11: 2 cometh shame: but with the lowly is w. 2451
11:12 He that is void of w despiseth his 3820
12: 8 shall be commended according to his w: 7922
13:10 but with the well advised is w. 2451
14: 6 A scorner seeketh w, and findeth it not: but 2451
14: 8 The w of the prudent is to understand his 2451
14:33 W resteth in the heart of him that hath 2451
15:21 Folly is joy to him that is destitute of w: but 3820
15:33 fear of the Lord is the instruction of w; 2451
16:16 How much better is it to get w than gold! 2451
17:16 there a price in the hand of a fool to get w, 2451
17:24 W is before him that hath understanding; 2451
18: 1 seeketh and intermeddleth with all w. 8454
18: 4 and the wellspring of w as a flowing brook. 2451
19: 8 He that getteth w loveth his own soul: 3820
21:30 There is no w nor understanding nor 2451
23: 4 not to be rich: cease from thine own w. 998
23: 9 for he will despise the w of thy words. 7922
23:23 also w, and instruction, and understanding. 2451
24: 3 Through w is a house builded; and 2451
24: 7 W is too high for a fool: he openeth not his 2454
24:14 So shall the knowledge of w be unto thy 2451
29: 3 Whoso loveth w rejoiceth his father: but 2451
29:15 The rod and reproof give w: but a child left 2451
30: 3 I neither learned w, nor have 2451
31:26 She openeth her mouth with w; and in her 2451
Ecc 1:13 search out by w concerning all 2451+2050.2
1:16 have gotten more w than all they that have 2451
1:16 my heart had great experience of w and 2451

Ecc 1:17 I gave my heart to know **w**, and to know 2451
1:18 For in much **w** *is* much grief: and he that 2451
2: 3 (yet acquainting mine heart with **w**) 2451
2: 9 in Jerusalem: also my **w** remained with me. 2451
2:12 I turned myself to behold **w**, and madness, 2451
2:13 I saw that **w** excelleth folly, as far as light 2451
2:21 For there is a man whose labour *is* in **w**, 2451
2:26 giveth to a man that *is* good in his sight **w**, 2451
7:11 **W** *is* good with an inheritance: and *by it* 2451
7:12 For **w** *is* a defence, *and* money *is* a defence: 2451
7:12 the excellency of knowledge *is, that* **w** 2451
7:19 **W** strengtheneth the wise more than ten 2451
7:23 All this have I proved by **w**: I said, I will be 2451
7:25 to seek out **w**, and the reason *of things,* and 2451
8: 1 a man's **w** maketh his face to shine, and 2451
8:16 When I applied mine heart to know **w**, and 2451
9:10 nor knowledge, nor **w**, in the grave, 2451
9:13 This **w** have I seen also under the sun, and 2451
9:15 and he by his **w** delivered the city; 2451
9:16 said I, **W** *is* better than strength: 2451
9:16 nevertheless the poor *man's* **w** *is* despised, 2451
9:18 **W** *is* better than weapons of war: but 2451
10: 1 a little folly *him that is* in reputation for **w** 2451
10: 3 his **w** faileth *him,* and he saith to every one 3820
10:10 more strength: but **w** *is* profitable to direct. 2451
Isa 10:13 of my hand I have done *it,* and by my **w**; 2451
11: 2 the spirit of **w** and understanding, the spirit 2451
29:14 for the **w** of their wise *men* shall perish, 2451
33: 6 **w** and knowledge shall be the stability of 2451
47:10 Thy **w** and thy knowledge, it hath perverted 2451
Jer 8: 9 of the LORD; and what **w** *is* in them? 2451
9:23 Let not the wise *man* glory in his **w**, 2451
10:12 he hath established the world by his **w**, and 2451
49: 7 LORD of hosts; *Is* **w** no more in Teman? 2451
49: 7 from the prudent? is their **w** vanished? 2451
51:15 he hath established the world by his **w**, and 2451
Eze 28: 4 With thy **w** and with thine understanding 2451
28: 5 By thy great **w** *and* by thy traffick hast thou 2451
28: 7 their swords against the beauty of thy **w**, 2451
28:12 up the sum, full *of* **w**, and perfect in beauty. 2451
28:17 thou hast corrupted thy **w** by reason of thy 2451
Da 1: 4 skilful in all **w**, and cunning in knowledge, 2451
1:17 and skill in all learning and **w**: 2451
1:20 *in* all matters of **w** *and* understanding, 2451
2:14 **w** to Arioch the captain of the king's guard, 2942
2:20 for ever and ever: for **w** and might are his: 2452
2:21 he giveth **w** unto the wise, and 2452
2:23 who hast given me **w** and might, and 2452
2:30 this secret *is* not revealed to me for *any* **w** 2452
5:11 of thy father light and understanding and **w**, 2452
5:11 and wisdom, like the **w** of the gods, 2452
5:14 and excellent **w** is found in thee. 2452
Mic 6: 9 and *the man of* **w** shall see thy name: 8454
Mt 11:19 sinners. But **w** is justified of her children. *4678*
12:42 parts of the earth to hear the **w** of Solomon; *4678*
13:54 Whence hath this *man* this **w**, and *4678*
Mk 6: 2 and what **w** *is this* which is given unto him, *4678*
Lk 1:17 and the disobedient to the **w** of the just; *5428*
2:40 and waxed strong in spirit, filled with **w**: *4678*
2:52 And Jesus increased in **w** and stature, and *4678*
7:35 But **w** is justified of all her children. *4678*
11:31 parts of the earth to hear the **w** of Solomon; *4678*
11:49 Therefore also said the **w** of God, I will *4678*
21:15 For I will give you a mouth and **w**, *4678*
Ac 6: 3 full of the Holy Ghost and **w**, whom we *4678*
6:10 And they were not able to resist the **w** and *4678*
7:10 **w** in the sight of Pharaoh king of Egypt; *4678*
7:22 And Moses was learned in all the **w** of *4678*
Ro 11:33 O the depth of the riches both of the **w** and *4678*
1Co 1:17 not with **w** of words, lest the cross of Christ *4678*
1:19 I will destroy the **w** of the wise, and *4678*
1:20 hath not God made foolish the **w** of this *4678*
1:21 For after that in the **w** of God the world by *4678*
1:21 of God the world by **w** knew not God, *4678*
1:22 require a sign, and the Greeks seek after **w**: *4678*
1:24 Christ the power of God, and the **w** of God. *4678*
1:30 who of God is made unto us **w**, and *4678*
2: 1 not with excellency of speech or of **w**, *4678*
2: 4 *was* not with enticing words of man's **w**, *4678*
2: 5 That your faith should not stand in the **w** of *4678*
2: 6 Howbeit we speak **w** among *them that are* *4678*
2: 6 yet not the **w** of this world, nor of *4678*
2: 7 But we speak the **w** of God in a mystery, *4678*
2: 7 *even* the hidden *w*, which God ordained NIG
2:13 not in the words which man's **w** teacheth, *4678*
3:19 For the **w** of this world is foolishness with *4678*
12: 8 to one is given by the Spirit the word of **w**; *4678*
2Co 1:12 not with fleshly **w**, but by the grace of God, *4678*
Eph 1: 8 he hath abounded toward us in all **w** *4678*
1:17 may give unto you the spirit of **w** and *4678*
3:10 by the church the manifold **w** of God, *4678*
Col 1: 9 *with* the knowledge of his will in all **w** *4678*
1:28 and teaching every man in all **w**; *4678*
2: 3 In whom are hid all the treasures of **w** and *4678*
2:23 Which *things* have indeed a shew of **w** in *4678*
3:16 word of Christ dwell in you richly in all **w**; *4678*
4: 5 Walk in **w** toward them that are without, *4678*
Jas 1: 5 If any of you lack **w**, let him ask of God, *4678*
3:13 his works with meekness of **w**. *4678*
3:15 This **w** descendeth not from above, but *4678*
3:17 But the **w** that is from above is first pure, *4678*
2Pe 3:15 **w** given unto him hath written unto you; *4678*
Rev 5:12 and **w**, and strength, and honour, and glory, *4678*
7:12 and **w**, and thanksgiving, and honour, and *4678*
13:18 Here is **w**. Let him that hath understanding *4678*
17: 9 *And* here *is* the mind which hath **w**. *4678*

WISE (247) [WISELY, WISER]

Ge 3: 6 a tree to be desired to **make** *one* **w**, she 7919
41: 8 of Egypt, and all the **w men** thereof: 2450
41:33 let Pharaoh look out a man discreet and **w**, 2450
41:39 *there is* none so discreet and **w** as thou *art:* 2450
Ex 7:11 Pharaoh also called the **w men** and 2450
22:23 If thou **afflict** them **in any w**, 6031+6031
23: 8 for the gift blindeth the **w**, and 6493
28: 3 thou shalt speak unto all *that are* **w** hearted, 2450
31: 6 in the hearts of all that are **w** hearted I have 2450
35:10 every **w** hearted among you shall come, 2450
35:25 all the women that were **w** hearted did spin 2450
36: 1 and Aholiab, and every **w** hearted man, 2450
36: 2 and Aholiab, and every **w** hearted man, 2450
36: 4 all the **w** *men,* that wrought all the work of 2450
36: 8 every **w** hearted *man* among them that 2450
Lev 7:24 but ye shall **in no w eat** of it. 398+398+3808
19:17 thou shalt **in any w rebuke** thy 3198+3198
27:19 the field will **in any w redeem** it, 1350+1350
Nu 6:23 **On this w** ye shall bless the children of 3541
Dt 1:13 Take ye **w** men, and understanding, and 2450
1:15 **w** men, and known, and made them heads 2450
4: 6 Surely this great nation *is* a **w** and 2450
16:19 for a gift doth blind the eyes of the **w**, and 2450
17:15 Thou shalt **in any w set** *him* king 7760+7760
21:23 shalt **in any w bury** him that day; 6912+6912
22: 7 thou shalt **in any w let** the dam **go**, 7971+7971
32:29 O that they were **w**, *that* they understood 2449
Jos 6:18 **in any w** keep *yourselves* from 7535
23:12 Else if ye do **in any w go back**, 7725+7725
Jdg 5:29 Her **w** ladies answered *her, yea,* 2450
1Sa 6: 3 **in any w return** him a trespass 7725+7725
2Sa 14: 2 fetcht thence a **w** woman, and said unto 2450
14:20 my lord *is* **w**, according to the wisdom of 2450
20:16 cried a **w** woman out of the city, Hear, 2450
1Ki 2: 9 for thou *art* a **w** man, and knowest what 2450
3:12 I have given thee a **w** and an understanding 2450
3:26 the living child, and **in no w slay** it. 4191+4191
3:27 the living child, and **in no w slay** it: 4191+4191
5: 7 which hath given unto David a **w** son over 2450
11:22 howbeit **let** me **go in any w**. 7971+7971
1Ch 26:14 his son, a **w** counseller, they cast lots; 7922
27:32 *was* a counseller, a **w** man, and a scribe: 995
2Ch 2:12 who hath given to David the king a **w** son, 2450
Est 1:13 the king said to the **w** *men,* which knew 2450
6:13 said his **w** *men* and Zeresh his wife unto 2450
Job 5:13 He taketh the **w** in their own craftiness: and 2450
9: 4 *He is* **w** in heart, and mighty in strength: 2450
11:12 For vain man would be **w**, though man be 3823
15: 2 Should a **w** *man* utter vain knowledge, and 2450
15:18 Which **w** *men* have told from their fathers, 2450
17:10 for I cannot find *one* **w** *man* among you. 2450
22: 2 as he that is **w** may be profitable unto 7919
32: 9 Great men are not *always* **w**: neither do 2449
34: 2 O ye **w** *men;* and give ear unto me, 2450
34:34 tell me, and let a **w** man hearken unto me. 2450
37:24 he respecteth not any *that are* **w** of heart. 2450
Ps 2:10 Be **w** now therefore, O ye kings: 7919
19: 7 the LORD *is* sure, **making w** the simple. 2449
36: 3 he hath left off to be **w**, *and* to do good. 7919
37: 8 fret not thyself **in any w** to do evil. 389

Ps	49:10	For he seeth *that* **w** *men* die, likewise	2450
	94: 8	and ye fools, when will ye be **w**?	7919
	107:43	Whoso *is* **w**, and will observe these *things,*	2450
Pr	1: 5	A **w** *man* will hear, and will increase	2450
	1: 5	understanding shall attain unto **w counsels**:	8458
	1: 6	the words of the **w**, and their dark sayings.	2450
	3: 7	Be not **w** in thine own eyes: fear	2450
	3:35	The **w** shall inherit glory: but shame shall	2450
	6: 6	consider her ways, and be **w**:	2449
	8:33	and be **w**, and refuse *it* not.	2449
	9: 8	rebuke a **w** *man,* and he will love thee.	2450
	9: 9	Give *instruction* to a **w** *man,* and he will be	2450
	9:12	If thou be **w**, thou shalt be wise for thyself:	2449
	9:12	If thou be wise, thou shalt be **w** for thyself:	2449
	10: 1	A **w** son maketh a glad father: but a foolish	2450
	10: 5	He that gathereth in summer *is* a **w** son: *but*	7919
	10: 8	The **w** in heart will receive	2450
	10:14	**W** *men* lay up knowledge: but the mouth of	2450
	10:19	not sin: but he that refraineth his lips *is* **w**.	7919
	11:29	the fool *shall be* servant to the **w** of heart.	2450
	11:30	tree of life; and he that winneth souls *is* **w**.	2450
	12:15	but he that hearkeneth unto counsel *is* **w**.	2450
	12:18	a sword: but the tongue of the **w** *is* health.	2450
	13: 1	A **w** son *heareth his* father's instruction: but	2450
	13:14	The law of the **w** *is* a fountain of life,	2450
	13:20	He that walketh with **w** *men* shall be wise:	2450
	13:20	He that walketh with wise *men* shall be **w**:	2449
	14: 1	Every **w** woman buildeth her house: but	2450
	14: 3	but the lips of the **w** shall preserve them.	2450
	14:16	A **w** *man* feareth, and departeth from evil:	2450
	14:24	The crown of the **w** *is* their riches: *but*	2450
	14:35	The king's favour *is* toward a **w** servant:	7919
	15: 2	The tongue of the **w** useth knowledge	2450
	15: 7	The lips of the **w** disperse knowledge: but	2450
	15:12	neither will he go unto the **w**.	2450
	15:20	A **w** son maketh a glad father: but a foolish	2450
	15:24	The way of life *is* above to the **w**, that *he*	7919
	15:31	the reproof of life abideth among the **w**.	2450
	16:14	of death: but a **w** man will pacify it.	2450
	16:21	The **w** in heart shall be called prudent: and	2450
	16:23	The heart of the **w** teacheth his mouth, and	2450
	17: 2	A **w** servant shall have rule over a son that	7919
	17:10	A reproof entereth more into a **w** *man* than	995
	17:28	when he holdeth his peace, is counted **w**:	2450
	18:15	and the ear of the **w** seeketh knowledge.	2450
	19:20	that thou mayest be **w** in thy latter end.	2449
	20: 1	whosoever is deceived thereby is not **w**.	2449
	20:26	A **w** king scattereth the wicked, and	2450
	21:11	scorner is punished, the simple is **made w**:	2449
	21:11	when the **w** is instructed, he receiveth	2450
	21:20	be desired and oil in the dwelling of the **w**;	2450
	21:22	A **w** *man* scaleth the city of the mighty, and	2450
	22:17	hear the words of the **w**, and apply thine	2450
	23:15	My son, if thine heart be **w**, my heart shall	2449
	23:19	and be **w**, and guide thine heart in the way.	2449
	23:24	he that begetteth a **w** *child* shall have joy of	2450
	24: 5	A **w** man *is* strong; yea, a man of	2450
	24: 6	For by **w counsel** thou shalt make thy war:	8458
	24:23	These *things* also *belong* to the **w**. *It is* not	2450
	25:12	*so is* a **w** reprover upon an obedient ear.	2450
	26: 5	to his folly, lest he be **w** in his own conceit.	2450
	26:12	Seest thou a man **w** in his own conceit?	2450
	27:11	My son, be **w**, and make my heart glad,	2449
	28: 7	Whoso keepeth the law *is* a **w** son: but	995
	28:11	The rich man *is* **w** in his own conceit; but	2450
	29: 8	into a snare: but **w** *men* turn away wrath.	2450
	29: 9	If a **w** man contendeth with a foolish man,	2450
	29:11	but a **w** *man* keepeth it in *till* afterwards.	2450
	30:24	the earth, but they *are* **exceeding w**:	2449+2450
Ecc	2:14	The **w** *man's* eyes *are* in his head; but	2450
	2:15	even to me; and why was I then more **w**?	2449
	2:16	For *there is* no remembrance of the **w** more	2450
	2:16	And how dieth the **w** *man?* as the fool.	2450
	2:19	who knoweth whether he shall be a **w** *man*	2450
	2:19	where*in* I have **shewed** myself **w** under	2449
	4:13	and a **w** child than an old and foolish king,	2450
	6: 8	For what hath the **w** more than the fool?	2450
	7: 4	The heart of the **w** *is* in the house of	2450
	7: 5	*It is* better to hear the rebuke of the **w**,	2450
	7: 7	Surely oppression maketh a **w** *man* mad;	2450
	7:16	over much; neither **make** thyself over **w**:	2449
	7:19	Wisdom strengtheneth the **w** more than ten	2450
	7:23	I said, I will be **w**; but it *was* far from me.	2449
	8: 1	Who *is* as the **w** *man?* and who knoweth	2450
	8: 5	a **w** *man's* heart discerneth *both* time and	2450
	8:17	though a **w** *man* think to know *it,* yet shall	2450
	9: 1	the righteous, and the **w**, and their works,	2450
	9:11	to the strong, neither yet bread to the **w**,	2450
	9:15	Now there was found in it a poor **w** man,	2450
	9:17	The words of **w** *men are* heard in quiet,	2450
	10: 2	A **w** *man's* heart *is* at his right hand; but	2450
	10:12	The words of a **w** *man's* mouth *are*	2450
	12: 9	because the Preacher was **w**,	2450
	12:11	The words of the **w** *are* as goads, and	2450
Isa	5:21	Woe unto *them that are* **w** in their own	2450
	19:11	the counsel of the **w** counsellers of Pharaoh	2450
	19:11	I *am* the son of the **w**, the son of ancient	2450
	19:12	where *are* thy **w** *men?* and let them tell thee	2450
	29:14	for the wisdom of their **w** *men* shall perish,	2450
	31: 2	Yet he also *is* **w**, and will bring evil, and	2450
	44:25	that turneth **w** *men* backward, and	2450
Jer	4:22	they *are* **w** to do evil, but to do good they	2450
	8: 8	We *are* **w**, and the law of the LORD *is*	2450
	8: 9	The **w** *men* are ashamed, they are dismayed	2450
	9:12	Who *is* the **w** man, that may understand	2450
	9:23	Let not the **w** *man* glory in his wisdom,	2450
	10: 7	forasmuch as among all the **w** *men* of	2450
	18:18	nor counsel from the **w**, nor the word from	2450
	50:35	and upon her princes, and upon her **w** *men.*	2450
	51:57	her **w** *men,* her captains, and her rulers, and	2450
Eze	27: 8	thy **w** *men,* O Tyrus, *that* were in thee,	2450
	27: 9	the **w** *men* thereof were in thee thy calkers:	2450
Da	2:12	commanded to destroy all the **w** *men* of	2445
	2:13	the decree went forth that the **w** *men* should	2445
	2:14	which was gone forth to slay the **w** *men* of	2445
	2:18	with the rest of the **w** *men* of Babylon.	2445
	2:21	he giveth wisdom unto the **w**, and	2445
	2:24	ordained to destroy the **w** *men* of Babylon:	2445
	2:24	Destroy not the **w** *men* of Babylon:	2445
	2:27	cannot the **w** *men,* the astrologians,	2445
	2:48	chief of the governors over all the **w** *men* of	2445
	4: 6	in all the **w** *men* of Babylon before me,	2445
	4:18	forasmuch as all the **w** *men* of my kingdom	2445
	5: 7	and said to the **w** *men* of Babylon,	2445
	5: 8	came in all the king's **w** *men:* but	2445
	5:15	now the **w** *men,* the astrologers, have been	2445
	12: 3	they that be **w** shall shine as the brightness	7919
	12:10	but the **w** shall understand.	7919
Hos	14: 9	Who *is* **w**, and he shall understand these	2450
Ob	1: 8	even destroy the **w** *men* out of Edom, and	2450
Zec	9: 2	and Zidon, though it be very **w**.	2449
Mt	1:18	the birth of Jesus Christ was **on this w**:	*3779*
	2: 1	there came **w men** from the east to	*3097*
	2: 7	when he had privily called the **w men**,	*3097*
	2:16	he saw that he was mocked of the **w men**,	*3097*
	2:16	he had diligently inquired of the **w men**.	*3097*
	5:18	one tittle shall **in no w** pass from the law,	*3364*
	7:24	doeth them, I will liken him unto a **w** man,	*5429*
	10:16	be ye therefore **w** as serpents, and	*5429*
	10:42	unto you, he shall **in no w** lose his reward.	*3364*
	11:25	thou hast hid these *things* from the **w** and	*4680*
	21:24	**I in like w** will tell you by what authority I	*2504*
	23:34	unto you prophets, and **w** *men,* and scribes:	*4680*
	24:45	Who then is a faithful and **w** servant,	*5429*
	25: 2	And five of them were **w**, and five *were*	*5429*
	25: 4	But the **w** took oil in their vessels with their	*5429*
	25: 8	And the foolish said unto the **w**, Give us of	*5429*
	25: 9	But the **w** answered, saying, *Not so;*	*5429*
Mk	14:31	with thee, I will **not** deny thee **in any w**.	*3364*
Lk	10:21	that thou hast hid these *things* from the **w**	*4680*
	12:42	Who then is *that* faithful and **w** steward,	*5429*
	13:11	**in no w** lift up *herself.*	*1519+3361+3588+3838*
	18:17	as a little child shall **in no w** enter therein.	*3364*
Jn	6:37	him that cometh to me I will **in no w** cast	*3364*
	21: 1	and **on this w** shewed he *himself.*	*3779*
Ac	7: 6	And God spake **on this w**, That his seed	*3779*
	13:34	to return to corruption, he said **on this w**,	*3779*
	13:41	a work which you shall **in no w** believe,	*3364*
Ro	1:14	both to the **w**, and to the unwise.	*4680*
	1:22	Professing *themselves* to be **w**,	*4680*
	3: 9	are we better *than they?* No, **in no w**:	*3843*
	10: 6	which is of faith speaketh **on this w**,	*3779*
	11:25	lest ye should be **w** in your own conceits;	*5429*
	12:16	low estate. Be not **w** in your own conceits.	*5429*
	16:19	*yet* I would have you **w** unto *that which is*	*4680*
	16:27	To God only **w**, *be* glory through Jesus	*4680*
1Co	1:19	I will destroy the wisdom of the **w**, and	*4680*
	1:20	Where *is* the **w**? where *is* the scribe?	*4680*

1Co 1:26 how that not many w *men* after the flesh, *4680*
1:27 *things* of the world to confound the **w**; *4680*
3:10 as a w masterbuilder, I have laid *4680*
3:18 If any *man* among you seemeth to be w in *4680*
3:18 let him become a fool, that he may be **w**. *4680*
3:19 He taketh the w in their own craftiness. *4680*
3:20 The Lord knoweth the thoughts of the w, *4680*
4:10 for Christ's sake, but ye *are* w in Christ; *5429*
6: 5 that there is not a w *man* amongst you? *4680*
10:15 I speak as to w *men;* judge ye what I say. *5429*
2Co 10:12 themselves amongst themselves, are not w. *4920*
11:19 fools gladly, seeing ye *yourselves* are w. *5429*
Eph 5:15 walk circumspectly, not as fools, but as w, *4680*
1Ti 1:17 immortal, invisible, the only w God, *4680*
2Ti 3:15 which are able to **make** thee w unto *4679*
Heb 4: 4 certain place of the seventh *day* **on this** w, *3779*
Jas 3:13 Who *is* a w *man* and endued with *4680*
Jude 1:25 To the only w God our Saviour, *be* glory *4680*
Rev 21:27 And there shall **in no** w enter into it any *3364*

WISELY (14) [WISE]

Ex 1:10 Come on, let us **deal** w with them; lest they 2449
1Sa 18: 5 Saul sent him, *and* **behaved** himself w: 7919
18:14 David **behaved** himself w in all his ways; 7919
18:15 Saul saw that he **behaved** himself very w, 7919
18:30 *that* David **behaved** himself more w than 7919
2Ch 11:23 he **dealt** w, and dispersed of all his children 995
Ps 58: 5 voice of charmers, charming *never so* w. 2449
64: 9 for they shall w **consider** of his doing. 7919
101: 2 I will **behave** myself w in a perfect way. 7919
Pr 16:20 He that **handleth** a matter w shall find 7919
21:12 The righteous *man* w **considereth** 7919
28:26 whoso walketh w, he shall be 2451+871.1
Ecc 7:10 dost not inquire w concerning this. 2451+4480
Lk 16: 8 the unjust steward, because he had done w: *5430*

WISER (8) [WISE]

1Ki 4:31 For he was w than all men; than Ethan 2449
Job 35:11 and **maketh** us w than the fowls of heaven? 2449
Ps 119:98 hast **made** me w than mine enemies: 2449
Pr 9: 9 to a wise *man,* and he will be yet w: 2449
26:16 The sluggard *is* w in his own conceit than 2450
Eze 28: 3 Behold, thou *art* w than Daniel; *there is* no 2450
Lk 16: 8 generation w than the children of light. *5429*
1Co 1:25 Because the foolishness of God is w **than** *4680*

WISH (6) [WISHED, WISHING]

Job 33: 6 I *am* according to thy w in God's stead: 6310
Ps 40:14 and put to shame that w me evil. 2655
73: 7 they have more than heart could w. 4906
Ro 9: 3 For I could w that myself were accursed *2172*
2Co 13: 9 and this also we w, *even* your perfection. *2172*
3Jn 1: 2 I w above all *things* that thou mayest *2172*

WISHED (2) [WISH]

Jnh 4: 8 and w in himself to die, and said, 7592
Ac 27:29 anchors out of the stern, and w **for** the day. *2172*

WISHING (1) [WISH]

Job 31:30 my mouth to sin by w a curse to his soul.) 7592

WIST (13) [WIT]

Ex 16:15 for they w not what it *was.* And Moses said 3045
34:29 that Moses w not that the skin of his face 3045
Lev 5:17 though he w *it* not, yet is he guilty, and 3045
5:18 his ignorance wherein he erred and w *it* not, 3045
Jos 2: 4 unto me, but I w not whence they *were:* 3045
8:14 he w not that *there were* liers in ambush 3045
Jdg 16:20 he w not that the LORD was departed 3045
Mk 9: 6 For he w not what to say; for they were *1492*
14:40 neither w they what to answer him. *1492*
Lk 2:49 w ye not that I must be about my Father's *1492*
Jn 5:13 And he that was healed w not who it was: *1492*
Ac 12: 9 w not that it was true which was done by *1492*
23: 5 Then said Paul, I w not, brethren, that he *1492*

WIT (21) [UNWITTINGLY, WIST, WIT'S, WITTINGLY, WITTY, WOT, WOTTETH]

Ge 24:21 to w whether the LORD had made his 3045
Ex 2: 4 afar off, to w what would be done to him. 3045
Jos 17: 1 *to* w, for Machir the firstborn of Manasseh, NIH
1Ki 2:32 my father David not knowing *thereof, to* w, NIH
7:50 the doors of the house, *to* w, of the temple. NIH
13:23 *to* w, for the prophet whom he had brought NIH
2Ki 10:29 *to* w, the golden calves that *were in* Beth-el, NIH
1Ch 7: 2 heads of their fathers' house, *to* w, of Tola: NIH
27: 1 *to* w, the chief fathers and captains of NIH
2Ch 4:12 *To* w, the two pillars, and the pommels, and NIH
25: 7 *to* w, *with* all the children of Ephraim. NIH
25:10 Amaziah separated them, **to** w, the army 3807.1
31: 3 *to* w, for the morning and evening burnt NIH
Ne 11: 3 *to* w, Israel, the priests, and the Levites, and NIH
Est 2:12 *to* w, six months with oil of myrrh, and NIH
Jer 25:18 *To* w, Jerusalem, and the cities of Judah, NIH
34: 9 himself of them, *to* w, of a Jew his brother. NIH
Eze 13:16 *To* w, the prophets of Israel which prophesy NIH
Ro 8:23 *to* w, the redemption of our body. NIG
2Co 5:19 **To** w, that God was in Christ reconciling *5613*
8: 1 we do you to w of the grace of God *1107*

WIT'S (1) [WIT]

Ps 107:27 and are **at their** w **end**. 1104+2451+3605

WITCH (2) [WITCHCRAFT, WITCHCRAFTS]

Ex 22:18 Thou shalt not suffer a w to live. 3784
Dt 18:10 observer of times, or an enchanter, or a w, 3784

WITCHCRAFT (3) [CRAFT, WITCH]

1Sa 15:23 For rebellion *is as* the sin of w, and 7081
2Ch 33: 6 **used** w, and dealt with a familiar spirit, and 3784
Gal 5:20 Idolatry, w, hatred, variance, emulations, *5331*

WITCHCRAFTS (4) [CRAFT, WITCH]

2Ki 9:22 thy mother Jezebel and her w *are so* many? 3785
Mic 5:12 I will cut off w out of thine hand; and 3785
Na 3: 4 the mistress of w, that selleth nations 3785
3: 4 and families through her w. 3785

WITH (6016) [HEREWITH, THEREWITH, WHEREWITH] See Index

WITHAL (33) [WHEREWITHAL] See Index

WITHDRAW (11) [WITHDRAWEST, WITHDRAWETH, WITHDRAWN, WITHDREW]

1Sa 14:19 and Saul said unto the priest, W thine hand. 622
Job 9:13 *If* God will not w his anger, the proud 7725
13:21 W thine hand **far** from me: and let not thy 7368
33:17 That *he* may w man *from his* purpose, and 5493
Pr 25:17 W thy foot from thy neighbour's house; 3365
Ecc 7:18 yea, also from this w not thine hand: 3240
Isa 60:20 go down; neither shall thy moon w itself: 622
Joel 2:10 be dark, and the stars shall w their shining: 622
3:15 and the stars shall w their shining. 622
2Th 3: 6 that ye w yourselves from every brother *4724*
1Ti 6: 5 that gain is godliness: from such w thyself. *868*

WITHDRAWEST (1) [WITHDRAW]

Ps 74:11 Why w thou thy hand, even thy right hand? 7725

WITHDRAWETH (1) [WITHDRAW]

Job 36: 7 He w not his eyes from the righteous: but 1639

WITHDRAWN (6) [WITHDRAW]

Dt 13:13 have w the inhabitants of their city, saying, 5080
SS 5: 6 my beloved had w himself, *and* was gone: 2559
La 2: 8 he hath not w his hand from destroying: 7725
Eze 18: 8 *that* hath w his hand from iniquity, 7725
Hos 5: 6 they shall not find *him;* he hath w himself 2502
Lk 22:41 And he was w from them about a stone's *645*

WITHDREW (6) [WITHDRAW]

Ne 9:29 w the shoulder, and hardened their 5414+5637
Eze 20:22 Nevertheless I w mine hand, and 7725
Mt 12:15 But when Jesus knew *it,* he w himself from *402*
Mk 3: 7 But Jesus w himself with his disciples to *402*
Lk 5:16 And he w himself into the wilderness, and *5298*
Gal 2:12 were come, he w and separated himself, *5288*

WITHER (11) [WITHERED, WITHERETH]

Ps 1: 3 his leaf also shall not w; and whatsoever he 5034
37: 2 like the grass, and w as the green herb. 5034
Isa 19: 6 and dried up: the reeds and flags shall w. 7060
19: 7 shall w, be driven away, and *be* no *more.* 3001
40:24 they shall w, and the whirlwind shall take 3001
Jer 12: 4 land mourn, and the herbs of every field w, 3001
Eze 17: 9 and cut off the fruit thereof, that it w? 3001
17: 9 it shall w *in* all the leaves of her spring, 3001
17:10 shall it not **utterly** w, when the east 3001+3001
17:10 it shall w in the furrows where it grew. 3001
Am 1: 2 shall mourn, and the top of Carmel shall w. 3001

WITHERED (25) [WITHER]

Ge 41:23 **w**, thin, *and* blasted with the east wind, 6798
Ps 102: 4 My heart is smitten, and **w** like grass; so 3001
102:11 that declineth; and I am **w** like grass. 3001
Isa 15: 6 for the hay is **w away**, the grass faileth, 3001
27:11 When the boughs thereof are **w**, they shall 3001
La 4: 8 their bones; it is **w**, it is become like a stick. 3001
Eze 19:12 her strong rods were broken and **w**; the fire 3001
Joel 1:12 *even* all the trees of the field, are **w**: 3001
1:12 joy is **w away** from the sons of men. 3001
1:17 barns are broken down; for the corn is **w**. 3001
Am 4: 7 and the piece whereupon it rained not **w**. 3001
Jnh 4: 7 next day, and it smote the gourd, that it **w**. 3001
Mt 12:10 there was a man which had *his* hand **w**. *3584*
13: 6 because *they* had not root, they **w away**. *3583*
21:19 for ever. And presently the fig tree **w away**. *3583*
21:20 saying, How soon is the fig tree **w away**! *3583*
Mk 3: 1 there was a man there which had a **w** hand. *3583*
3: 3 And he saith unto the man which had the **w** *3583*
4: 6 and because *it* had no root, it **w away**. *3583*
11:21 the fig tree which thou cursedst is **w away**. *3583*
Lk 6: 6 there was a man whose right hand was **w**. *3584*
6: 8 and said to the man which had the **w** hand, *3584*
8: 6 it **w away**, because *it* lacked moisture. *3583*
Jn 5: 3 halt, **w**, waiting for the moving of *3584*
15: 6 in me, he is cast forth as a branch, and is **w**; *3583*

WITHERETH (8) [WITHER]

Job 8:12 not cut down, it **w** before any *other* herb. 3001
Ps 90: 6 in the evening it is cut down, and **w**. 3001
129: 6 the housetops, which **w** afore it groweth up: 3001
Isa 40: 7 The grass **w**, the flower fadeth: because 3001
40: 8 The grass **w**, the flower fadeth: but 3001
Jas 1:11 but it **w** the grass, and the flower thereof *3583*
1Pe 1:24 The grass **w**, and the flower thereof falleth *3583*
Jude 1:12 trees whose **fruit w**, without fruit, *5352*

WITHHELD (6) [WITHHOLD]

Ge 20: 6 for I also **w** thee from sinning against me: 2820
22:12 seeing thou hast not **w** thy son, thine only 2820
22:16 hast not **w** thy son, thine only *son:* 2820
30: 2 who hath **w** from thee the fruit of 4513
Job 31:16 If I have **w** the poor from *their* desire, or 4513
Ecc 2:10 from them, I **w** not my heart from any joy; 4513

WITHHELDEST (1) [WITHHOLD]

Ne 9:20 **w** not thy manna from their mouth, and 4513

WITHHOLD (9) [WITHHELD, WITHHELDEST, WITHHOLDEN, WITHHOLDETH]

Ge 23: 6 none of us shall **w** from thee his sepulchre, 3607
2Sa 13:13 the king; for he will not **w** me from thee. 4513
Job 4: 2 but who can **w** himself from speaking? 6113
Ps 40:11 **W** not thou thy tender mercies from me, 3607
84:11 no good *thing* will he **w** from them that 4513
Pr 3:27 **W** not good from them to whom it is due, 4513
23:13 **W** not correction from the child: for *if* thou 4513
Ecc 11: 6 and in the evening **w** not thine hand: 3240
Jer 2:25 **W** thy foot from being unshod, and 4513

WITHHOLDEN (10) [WITHHOLD]

1Sa 25:26 seeing the LORD hath **w** thee from 4513
Job 22: 7 and thou hast **w** bread from the hungry. 4513
38:15 from the wicked their light is **w**, and 4513
42: 2 and *that* no thought can be **w** from thee. 1219
Ps 21: 2 and hast not **w** the request of his lips. 4513
Jer 3: 3 Therefore the showers have been **w**, and 4513
5:25 and your sins have **w** good *things* from you. 4513
Eze 18:16 hath not **w the pledge**, 2254+2258
Joel 1:13 the drink offering is **w** from the house of 4513
Am 4: 7 also I have **w** the rain from you, when *there* 4513

WITHHOLDETH (4) [WITHHOLD]

Job 12:15 Behold, he **w** the waters, and they dry up: 6113
Pr 11:24 *there is* that **w** more than is meet, but 2820
11:26 He that **w** corn, the people shall curse him: 4513
2Th 2: 6 And now ye know what **w** that he might be *2722*

WITHIN (186) [IN] See Index

WITHOUT (426) [, OUT] See Index

WITHS (3)

Jdg 16: 7 If they bind me with seven green **w** that 3499
16: 8 seven green **w** which had not been dried, 3499
16: 9 he brake the **w**, as a thread of tow is broken 3499

WITHSTAND (10) [WITHSTOOD]

Nu 22:32 behold, I went out to **w** thee, because 7854
2Ch 13: 7 and could not **w** them. 2388+6440+3807.1
13: 8 now ye think to **w** the 2388+6440+3807.1
20: 6 so that none is **able to w** thee? 3320+5973
Est 9: 2 no man could **w** them; 5975+6440+3807.1
Ecc 4:12 prevail against him, two shall **w** him; 5048+5975
Da 11:15 the arms of the south shall not **w**, 5975
11:15 neither *shall there be any* strength to **w**. 5975
Ac 11:17 what was I, that I could **w** God? *2967*
Eph 6:13 that ye may be able to **w** in the evil day, and *436*

WITHSTOOD (6) [WITHSTAND]

2Ch 26:18 they **w** Uzziah the king, and 5921+5975
Da 10:13 kingdom of Persia **w** me one 5048+5975+3807.1
Ac 13: 8 **w** them, seeking to turn away the deputy *436*
Gal 2:11 I **w** him to the face, because he was *to be* *436*
2Ti 3: 8 Now as Jannes and Jambres **w** Moses, so *436*
4:15 ware also; for he hath greatly **w** our words. *436*

WITNESS (135) [EYEWITNESSES, WITNESSED, WITNESSES, WITNESSETH, WITNESSING]

Ge 21:30 that they may be a **w** unto me, that I have 5713
31:44 and let it be for a **w** between me and thee. 5707
31:48 This heap *is* a **w** between me and thee *this* 5707
31:50 with us; see, God *is* **w** betwixt me and thee. 5707
31:52 This heap *be* **w**, and *this* pillar *be* witness, 5707
31:52 This heap *be* witness, and *this* pillar *be* **w**, 5713
Ex 20:16 Thou shalt not bear false **w** against thy 5707
22:13 *then* let him bring it *for* **w**, *and* he shall not 5707
23: 1 with the wicked to be an unrighteous **w**. 5707
Lev 5: 1 *is* a **w**, whether he hath seen or known *of it;* 5707
Nu 5:13 be defiled, and *there be* no **w** against her, 5707
17: 7 before the LORD in the tabernacle of **W**. 5715
17: 8 Moses went into the tabernacle of **W**; 5715
18: 2 *shall minister* before the tabernacle of **W**. 5715
35:30 one **w** shall not testify against *any* person *to* 5707
Dt 4:26 I **call** heaven and earth **to w** against you 5749
5:20 Neither shalt thou bear false **w** against thy 5707
17: 6 at the mouth of one **w** he shall not be put to 5707
19:15 One **w** shall not rise up against a man for 5707
19:16 If a false **w** rise up against any man to 5707
19:18 *if* the **w** *be* a false witness, *and* 5707
19:18 *if* the witness *be* a false **w**, *and* 5707
31:19 that this song may be a **w** for me against 5707
31:21 this song shall testify against them as a **w**; 5707
31:26 that it may be there for a **w** against thee. 5707
Jos 22:27 But *that* it *may be* a **w** between us, and you, 5707
22:28 but it *is* a **w** between us and you. 5707
22:34 *be* a **w** between us that the LORD *is* God. 5707
24:27 Behold, this stone shall be a **w** unto us; 5713
24:27 it shall be therefore a **w** unto you, lest ye 5713
Jdg 11:10 The LORD be **w** between us, if we do not 8085
1Sa 12: 3 here I *am:* **w** against me before the LORD, 6030
12: 5 The LORD *is* **w** against you, and 5707
12: 5 against you, and his anointed *is* **w** this day, 5707
12: 5 in my hand. And they answered, *He is* **w**. 5707
1Ki 21:10 before him, to **bear w against** him, saying, 5749
2Ch 24: 6 of Israel, for the tabernacle of **W**? 5715
Job 16: 8 *which* is a **w** *against me:* and my leanness 5707
16: 8 my leanness rising up in me **beareth w** to 6030
16:19 behold my **w** *is* in heaven, and my record *is* 5707
29:11 and when the eye saw *me,* it **gave w to** me: 5749
Ps 89:37 as the moon, and *as* a faithful **w** in heaven. 5707
Pr 6:19 A false **w** *that* speaketh lies, and he that 5707
12:17 forth righteousness: but a false **w** deceit. 5707
14: 5 A faithful **w** will not lie: but a false witness 5707
14: 5 will not lie: but a false **w** will utter lies. 5707
14:25 A true **w** delivereth souls: but a deceitful 5707
14:25 but a deceitful *w* speaketh lies. NIH
19: 5 A false **w** shall not be unpunished, and 5707
19: 9 A false **w** shall not be unpunished, and 5707
19:28 An ungodly **w** scorneth judgment: and 5707
21:28 A false **w** shall perish: but the man that 5707
24:28 Be not a **w** against thy neighbour without 5707
25:18 A man that beareth false **w** against his 5707
Isa 3: 9 The shew of their countenance doth **w** 6030
19:20 for a **w** unto the LORD of hosts in 5707
55: 4 I have given him *for* a **w** to the people, 5707
Jer 29:23 even I know, and *am* a **w**, saith 5707
42: 5 be a true and faithful **w** between us, 5707
La 2:13 What *thing* shall I **take to w** for thee? 5749

Mic	1: 2	let the Lord God be **w** against you,	5707
Mal	2:14	Because the Lord hath been **w** between	5749
	3: 5	I will be a swift **w** against the sorcerers,	5707
Mt	15:19	adulteries, fornications, thefts, **false w**,	*5577*
	19:18	shalt not steal, Thou shalt not **bear false w**,	*5576*
	24:14	in all the world for a **w** unto all nations;	*3142*
	26:59	the council, sought **false w** against Jesus,	*5577*
	26:62	what *is it which* these **w against** thee?	*2649*
	27:13	not how many *things* they **w against** thee?	*2649*
Mk	10:19	not steal, Do not **bear false w**, Defraud not,	*5576*
	14:55	all the council sought for **w** against Jesus to	*3141*
	14:56	For many **bare false w** against him, but	*5576*
	14:56	but *their* **w** agreed not together.	*3141*
	14:57	and **bare false w** against him, saying,	*5576*
	14:59	But neither so did their **w** agree together.	*3141*
	14:60	what *is it which* these **w against** thee?	*2649*
	15: 4	behold how many *things* they **w against**	*2649*
Lk	4:22	And all **bare** him **w**, and wondered at	*3140*
	11:48	Truly ye **bear w** that ye allow the deeds of	*3140*
	18:20	not kill, Do not steal, Do not **bear false w**,	*5576*
	22:71	they said, What need we any further **w**?	*3141*
Jn	1: 7	The same came for a **w**, to bear witness of	*3141*
	1: 7	came for a witness, to **bear w** of the Light,	*3140*
	1: 8	but *was sent* to **bear w** of *that* Light.	*3140*
	1:15	John **bare w** of him, and cried, saying,	*3140*
	3:11	we have seen; and ye receive not our **w**.	*3141*
	3:26	to whom thou **barest w**, behold, the same	*3140*
	3:28	Ye yourselves **bear** me **w**, that I said, I am	*3140*
	5:31	If I **bear w** of myself, my witness is not	*3140*
	5:31	I bear witness of myself, my **w** is not true.	*3141*
	5:32	There is another that **beareth w** of me; and	*3140*
	5:32	I know that the **w** which he witnesseth of	*3141*
	5:33	unto John, and he **bare w** unto the truth.	*3140*
	5:36	But I have greater **w** than *that of* John:	*3141*
	5:36	the same works that I do, **bear w** of me,	*3140*
	5:37	which hath sent me, hath **borne w** of me.	*3140*
	8:18	I am *one* that **bear w** of myself, and	*3140*
	8:18	the Father that sent me **beareth w** of me.	*3140*
	10:25	in my Father's name, they **bear w** of me.	*3140*
	15:27	And ye also shall **bear w**, because ye have	*3140*
	18:23	If I have spoken evil, **bear w** of the evil:	*3140*
	18:37	that I should **bear w** unto the truth.	*3140*
Ac	1:22	must one be ordained *to be* a **w** with us of	*3144*
	4:33	And with great power gave the apostles **w**	*3142*
	7:44	Our fathers had the tabernacle of **W** in	*3142*
	10:43	To him **give** all the prophets **w**,	*3140*
	14:17	Nevertheless he left not himself **without w**,	*267*
	15: 8	which knoweth the hearts, **bare** them **w**,	*3140*
	22: 5	As also the high priest doth **bear** me **w**, and	*3140*
	22:15	For thou shalt be his **w** unto all men of	*3144*
	23:11	so must thou **bear w** also at Rome.	*3140*
	26:16	a **w** both of *these things* which thou hast	*3144*
Ro	1: 9	For God is my **w**, whom I serve with my	*3144*
	2:15	their conscience **also bearing w**, and *their*	*4828*
	8:16	The Spirit itself **beareth w with** our spirit,	*4828*
	9: 1	my conscience **also bearing** me **w** in	*4828*
	13: 9	shalt not steal, Thou shalt not **bear false w**,	*5576*
1Th	2: 5	nor a cloke of covetousness; God *is* **w**:	*3144*
Tit	1:13	This **w** is true. Wherefore rebuke them	*3141*
Heb	2: 4	God **also bearing** *them* **w**, both with signs	*4901*
	10:15	*Whereof* the Holy Ghost also is a **w** to us:	*3140*
	11: 4	by which he **obtained w** that he was	*3140*
Jas	5: 3	the rust of them shall be a **w** against you,	*3142*
1Pe	5: 1	and a **w** of the sufferings of Christ, and	*3144*
1Jn	1: 2	and we have seen *it,* and **bear w**, and	*3140*
	5: 6	And it is the Spirit that **beareth w**, because	*3140*
	5: 8	And there are three that **bear w** in earth,	*3140*
	5: 9	If we receive the **w** of men, the witness of	*3141*
	5: 9	the witness of men, the **w** of God is greater:	*3141*
	5: 9	for this is the **w** of God which he hath	*3141*
	5:10	on the Son of God hath the **w** in himself:	*3141*
3Jn	1: 6	Which have **borne w** of thy charity before	*3140*
Rev	1: 5	*who is* the faithful **w**, *and* the first begotten	*3144*
	3:14	saith the Amen, the faithful and true **w**,	*3144*
	20: 4	them that were beheaded for the **w** of Jesus,	*3141*

WITNESSED (4) [WITNESS]

1Ki	21:13	the men of Belial **w against** him,	5749
Ro	3:21	being **w** by the law and the prophets;	*3140*
1Ti	6:13	who before Pontius Pilate **w** a good	*3140*
Heb	7: 8	there he *receiveth them,* of whom it is **w**	*3140*

WITNESSES (49) [WITNESS]

Nu	35:30	shall be put to death by the mouth of **w**:	5707
Dt	17: 6	At the mouth of two **w**, or three witnesses,	5707
	17: 6	At the mouth of two witnesses, or three **w**,	5707
	17: 7	The hands of the **w** shall be first upon him	5707
	19:15	at the mouth of two **w**, or at the mouth of	5707
	19:15	or at the mouth of three **w**, shall the matter	5707
Jos	24:22	Ye *are* **w** against yourselves that ye have	5707
	24:22	to serve him. And they said, *We are* **w**.	5707
Ru	4: 9	and *unto* all the people, Ye *are* **w** *this* day,	5707
	4:10	the gate of his place: ye *are* **w** *this* day.	5707
	4:11	in the gate, and the elders, said, *We are* **w**.	5707
Job	10:17	Thou renewest thy **w** against me, and	5707
Ps	27:12	for false **w** are risen up against me, and	5707
	35:11	False **w** did rise up; they laid to my charge	5707
Isa	8: 2	I took unto me faithful **w** to record, Uriah	5707
	43: 9	former *things?* let them bring forth their **w**,	5707
	43:10	Ye *are* my **w**, saith the Lord, and	5707
	43:12	therefore ye *are* my **w**, saith the Lord,	5707
	44: 8	and have declared *it?* ye *are* even my **w**.	5707
	44: 9	they *are* their own **w**; they see not,	5707
Jer	32:10	sealed *it,* and **took w**, and	5707+5749
	32:12	in the presence of the **w** that subscribed	5707
	32:25	thee the field for money, and **take w**;	5707+5749
	32:44	and **take w** in the land of Benjamin,	5707+5749
Mt	18:16	or three **w** every word may be established.	*3144*
	23:31	Wherefore ye be **w** unto yourselves, that ye	*3140*
	26:60	yea, though many **false w** came, *yet* found	*5575*
	26:60	they none. At the last came two **false w**,	*5575*
	26:65	what further need have we of **w**?	*3144*
Mk	14:63	and saith, What need we any further **w**?	*3144*
Lk	24:48	And ye are **w** of these *things.*	*3144*
Ac	1: 8	ye shall be **w** unto me both in Jerusalem,	*3144*
	2:32	hath God raised up, whereof we all are **w**.	*3144*
	3:15	raised from the dead; whereof we are **w**.	*3144*
	5:32	And we are his **w** of these things; and *so*	*3144*
	6:13	And set up false **w**, which said, This man	*3144*
	7:58	the **w** laid down their clothes at a young	*3144*
	10:39	And we are **w** of all *things* which he did	*3144*
	10:41	but unto **w** chosen before of God, *even* to	*3144*
	13:31	who are his **w** unto the people.	*3144*
1Co	15:15	Yea, and we are found **false w** of God;	*5575*
2Co	13: 1	or three **w** shall every word be established.	*3144*
1Th	2:10	Ye *are* **w**, and God *also,* how holily and	*3144*
1Ti	5:19	an accusation, but before two or three **w**.	*3144*
	6:12	a good profession before many **w**.	*3144*
2Ti	2: 2	that thou hast heard of me among many **w**,	*3144*
Heb	10:28	died without mercy under two or three **w**:	*3144*
	12: 1	about with so great a cloud of **w**,	*3144*
Rev	11: 3	And I will give *power* unto my two **w**, and	*3144*

WITNESSETH (2) [WITNESS]

Jn	5:32	I know that the witness which he **w** of me	*3140*
Ac	20:23	Save that the Holy Ghost **w** in every city,	*1263*

WITNESSING (1) [WITNESS]

Ac	26:22	unto this day, **w** both to small and great,	*3140*

WITTINGLY (1) [WIT]

Ge	48:14	Manasseh's head, **guiding** his hands **w**;	7919

WITTY (1) [WIT]

Pr	8:12	and find out knowledge of **w inventions**.	4209

WIVES (132) [WIFE]

Ge	4:19	Lamech took unto him two **w**: the name of	802
	4:23	Lamech said unto his **w**, Adah and Zillah,	802
	4:23	ye **w** of Lamech, hearken unto my speech:	802
	6: 2	they took them **w** of all which they chose.	802
	6:18	and thy wife, and thy sons' **w** with thee.	802
	7: 7	and his wife, and his sons' **w** with him,	802
	7:13	the three **w** of his sons with them, into	802
	8:16	and thy sons, and thy sons' **w** with thee.	802
	8:18	and his wife, and his sons' **w** with him:	802
	11:29	Abram and Nahor took them **w**: the name of	802
	28: 9	took unto the **w** which he had Mahalath	802
	30:26	Give *me* my **w** and my children, for whom I	802
	31:17	and set his sons and his **w** upon camels;	802
	31:50	if thou shalt take *other* **w** beside my	802
	32:22	took his two **w**, and his two womenservants,	802
	34:21	let us take their daughters to us for **w**, and let	802
	34:29	their **w** took they captive, and spoiled even	802
	36: 2	Esau took his **w** of the daughters of Canaan;	802
	36: 6	Esau took his **w**, and his sons, and his	802
	37: 2	and with the sons of Zilpah, his father's **w**:	802
	45:19	for your **w**, and bring your father, and come.	802

Ge	46: 5	their father, and their little ones, and their w,	802
	46:26	out of his loins, besides Jacob's sons' w,	802
Ex	19:15	against the third day: come not at *your* w.	802
	22:24	your w shall be widows, and your children	802
	32: 2	which *are* in the ears of your w, of your	802
Nu	14: 3	*that* our w and our children should be a	802
	16:27	their w, and their sons, and their little	802
	32:26	our w, our flocks, and all our cattle,	802
Dt	3:19	your w, and your little ones, and your cattle,	802
	17:17	Neither shall he multiply w to himself,	802
	21:15	If a man have two w, one beloved, and	802
	29:11	your w, and thy stranger that *is* in thy camp,	802
Jos	1:14	Your w, your little ones, and your cattle,	802
Jdg	3: 6	they took their daughters to be their w, and	802
	8:30	of his body begotten: for he had many w.	802
	21: 7	How shall we do for w for them that remain,	802
	21: 7	*we* will not give them of our daughters to w?	802
	21:14	they gave them w which they had saved	802
	21:16	How shall we do for w for them that remain,	802
	21:18	Howbeit we may not give them w of our	802
	21:23	and took *them* w, according to their number,	802
Ru	1: 4	they took them w of the women of Moab;	802
1Sa	1: 2	he had two w; the name of the one *was*	802
	25:43	and they were also both of them his w.	802
	27: 3	*even* David with his two w, Ahinoam	802
	30: 3	their w, and their sons, and their daughters,	802
	30: 5	David's two w were taken captives,	802
	30:18	carried away: and David rescued his two w.	802
2Sa	2: 2	his two w also, Ahinoam the Jezreelitess,	802
	5:13	*him* mo concubines and w out of Jerusalem,	802
	12: 8	thy master's w into thy bosom, and	802
	12:11	I will take thy w before thine eyes, and	802
	12:11	he shall lie with thy w in the sight of this	802
	19: 5	the lives of thy w, and the lives of thy	802
1Ki	11: 3	he had seven hundred w, princesses, and	802
	11: 3	and his w turned away his heart.	802
	11: 4	*that* his w turned away his heart after other	802
	11: 8	likewise did he for all his strange w,	802
	20: 3	thy w also and thy children, *even*	802
	20: 5	and thy gold, and thy w, and thy children;	802
	20: 7	for he sent unto me for my w, and for my	802
2Ki	4: 1	Now there cried a certain woman of the w of	802
	24:15	the king's w, and his officers, and	802
1Ch	4: 5	Ashur the father of Tekoa had two w, Helah	802
	7: 4	thirty thousand *men:* for they had many w	802
	8: 8	them away; Hushim and Baara *were* his w.	802
	14: 3	David took moe w at Jerusalem: and	802
2Ch	11:21	the daughter of Absalom above all his w	802
	11:21	(for he took eighteen w, and	802
	11:23	in abundance. And he desired many w.	802
	13:21	married fourteen w, and begat twenty and	802
	20:13	their little ones, their w, and their children.	802
	21:14	thy children, and thy w, and all thy goods:	802
	21:17	king's house, and his sons also, and his w;	802
	24: 3	Jehoiada took for him two w; and he begat	802
	29: 9	and our w *are* in captivity for this.	802
	31:18	their w, and their sons, and their daughters,	802
Ezr	10: 2	have taken strange w of the people of	802
	10: 3	covenant with our God to put away all the w,	802
	10:10	have transgressed, and have taken strange w,	802
	10:11	people of the land, and from the strange w.	802
	10:14	let all *them* which have taken strange w in	802
	10:17	strange w by the first day of the first month.	802
	10:18	there were found that had taken strange w:	802
	10:19	hands that *they* would put away their w;	802
	10:44	All these had taken strange w: and *some* of	802
	10:44	*some* of them had w by *whom* they had	802
Ne	4:14	your daughters, your w, and your houses.	802
	5: 1	of their w against their brethren the Jews.	802
	10:28	their w, their sons, and their daughters,	802
	12:43	the w also and the children rejoiced: so	802
	13:23	saw I Jews *that* had married w of Ashdod,	802
	13:27	against our God in marrying strange w?	802
Est	1:20	all the w shall give to their husbands honour,	802
Isa	13:16	houses shall be spoiled, and their w ravished.	802
Jer	6:12	unto others, *with their* fields and w together:	802
	8:10	Therefore will I give their w unto others, *and*	802
	14:16	them, their w, nor their sons, nor their	802
	18:21	and let their w be bereaved of their children,	802
	29: 6	Take ye w, and beget sons and daughters;	802
	29: 6	take w for your sons, and give your	802
	29:23	adultery with their neighbours' w,	802
	35: 8	we, our w, our sons, nor our daughters;	802
	38:23	So they *shall* bring out all thy w and thy	802
	44: 9	the wickedness of their w, and your own	802
	44: 9	and the wickedness of your w,	802
	44:15	all the men which knew that their w had	802
	44:25	your w have both spoken with your mouths,	802
Eze	44:22	Neither shall they take for their w a widow,	802
Da	5: 2	and his princes, his w, and his concubines,	7695
	5: 3	and his princes, his w, and his concubines,	7695
	5:23	and thy lords, thy w, and thy concubines,	7695
	6:24	of lions, them, their children, and their w;	5389
Zec	12:12	the house of David apart, and their w apart;	802
	12:12	the house of Nathan apart, and their w apart;	802
	12:13	of the house of Levi apart, and their w apart;	802
	12:13	the family of Shimei apart, and their w apart;	802
	12:14	every family apart, and their w apart.	802
Mt	19: 8	hearts suffered you to put away your w:	*1135*
Lk	17:27	they married *w*, they were given in	NIG
Ac	21: 5	with w and children, till *we were* out of	*1135*
1Co	7:29	that both they that have w be as though	*1135*
Eph	5:22	W, submit yourselves unto your own	*1135*
	5:24	*let* the w *be* to their own husbands in every	*1135*
	5:25	Husbands, love your w, even as Christ also	*1135*
	5:28	So ought men to love their w as their own	*1135*
Col	3:18	W, submit yourselves unto your own	*1135*
	3:19	love *your* w, and be not bitter against them.	*1135*
1Ti	3:11	Even so *must their* w *be* grave,	*1135*
1Pe	3: 1	Likewise, ye w, *be* in subjection to your	*1135*
	3: 1	word be won by the conversation of the w;	*1135*

WIVES' (1) [WIFE]

1Ti	4: 7	But refuse profane and **old** w fables, and	*1126*

WIZARD (2) [WIZARDS]

Lev	20:27	or that is a w, shall surely be put to death:	3049
Dt	18:11	familiar spirits, or a w, or a necromancer.	3049

WIZARDS (9) [WIZARD]

Lev	19:31	neither seek after w, to be defiled by them:	3049
	20: 6	after w, to go a whoring after them, I will	3049
1Sa	28: 3	familiar spirits, and the w, out of the land.	3049
	28: 9	familiar spirits, and the w, out of the land:	3049
2Ki	21: 6	and dealt with familiar spirits and w:	3049
	23:24	the w, and the images, and the idols, and	3049
2Ch	33: 6	and dealt with a familiar spirit, and with w:	3049
Isa	8:19	and unto w that peep, and that mutter:	3049
	19: 3	that have familiar spirits, and to the w.	3049

WOE (106) [WOEFUL, WOES]

Nu	21:29	W to thee, Moab! thou art undone, O people	188
1Sa	4: 7	they said, W unto us: for there hath not been	188
	4: 8	W unto us: who shall deliver us out of	188
Job	10:15	If I be wicked, w unto me; and *if* I be	480
Ps	120: 5	W is me, that I sojourn *in* Mesech, *that* I	190
Pr	23:29	Who hath w? who hath sorrow? who hath	188
Ecc	4:10	w to him *that is* alone when he falleth; for *he*	337
	10:16	W to thee, O land, when thy king *is* a child,	337
Isa	3: 9	W unto their soul! for they have rewarded	188
	3:11	W unto the wicked! *it shall be* ill *with him:*	188
	5: 8	W unto them that join house to house,	1945
	5:11	W unto them that rise up early in	1945
	5:18	W unto them that draw iniquity with cords	1945
	5:20	W unto them that call evil good, and good	1945
	5:21	W unto *them that are* wise in their own	1945
	5:22	W unto *them that are* mighty to drink wine,	1945
	6: 5	said I, W *is* me! for I am undone; because	188
	10: 1	W unto them that decree unrighteous	1945
	17:12	W to the multitude of many people,	1945
	18: 1	W to the land shadowing with wings,	1945
	24:16	My leanness, my leanness, w unto me!	188
	28: 1	W to the crown of pride, to the drunkards	1945
	29: 1	W to Ariel, to Ariel, the city *where* David	1945
	29:15	W unto them that seek deep to hide *their*	1945
	30: 1	W to the rebellious children, saith	1945
	31: 1	W to them that go down to Egypt for help;	1945
	33: 1	W to thee that spoilest, and thou *wast* not	1945
	45: 9	W unto him that striveth with his maker!	1945
	45:10	W unto him that saith unto *his* father,	1945
Jer	4:13	than eagles. W unto us! for we are spoiled.	188
	4:31	spreadeth her hands, *saying,* W *is* me now!	188
	6: 4	W unto us! for the day goeth away, for	188
	10:19	W is me for my hurt! my wound *is* grievous:	188
	13:27	W unto thee, O Jerusalem! wilt thou not be	188
	15:10	W is me, my mother, that thou hast borne	188
	22:13	W unto him that buildeth his house by	1945
	23: 1	W be unto *the* pastors that destroy and	1945

Jer 45: 3 Thou didst say, **W** is me now! for 188
48: 1 of hosts, the God of Israel; **W** unto Nebo! 1945
48:46 **W** be unto thee, O Moab! the people of 188
50:27 **w** unto them! for their day is come, 1945
La 5:16 our head: **w** unto us, that we have sinned! 188
Eze 2:10 therein lamentations, and mourning, and **w**. 1958
13: 3 **W** unto the foolish prophets, that follow 1945
13:18 **W** to *the women* that sew pillows to all 1945
16:23 after all thy wickedness, (**w**, woe unto thee! 188
16:23 after all thy wickedness, (woe, **w** unto thee! 188
24: 6 **W** to the bloody city, to the pot whose scum 188
24: 9 saith the Lord GOD; **W** to the bloody city! 188
30: 2 Lord GOD; Howl ye, **W** worth the day! 1929
34: 2 **W** *be* to the shepherds of Israel that do feed 1945
Hos 7:13 **W** unto them! for they have fled from me: 188
9:12 **w** also to them when I depart from them! 188
Am 5:18 **W** unto *you* that desire the day of 1945
6: 1 **W** to them *that are* at ease in Zion, and trust 1945
Mic 2: 1 **W** to them that devise iniquity, and 1945
7: 1 **W** is me! for I am as when they have 480
Na 3: 1 **W** to the bloody city! it *is* all full *of* lies 1945
Hab 2: 6 **W** to him that increaseth *that which is* not 1945
2: 9 **W** to him that coveteth an evil 1945
2:12 **W** to him that buildeth a town with blood, 1945
2:15 **W** unto him that giveth his neighbour 1945
2:19 **W** unto him that saith to the wood, Awake; 1945
Zep 2: 5 **W** unto the inhabitants of the sea coast, 1945
3: 1 **W** to her that is filthy and polluted, to 1945
Zec 11:17 **W** to the idol shepherd that leaveth 1945
Mt 11:21 **W** unto thee, Chorazin, woe unto thee, *3759*
11:21 Chorazin, **w** unto thee, Bethsaida: *3759*
18: 7 **W** unto the world because of offences: *3759*
18: 7 **w** to that man by whom the offence *3759*
23:13 But **w** unto you, scribes and Pharisees, *3759*
23:14 **W** unto you, scribes and Pharisees, *3759*
23:15 **W** unto you, scribes and Pharisees, *3759*
23:16 **W** unto you, *ye* blind guides, which say, *3759*
23:23 **W** unto you, scribes and Pharisees, *3759*
23:25 **W** unto you, scribes and Pharisees, *3759*
23:27 **W** unto you, scribes and Pharisees, *3759*
23:29 **W** unto you, scribes and Pharisees, *3759*
24:19 And **w** unto them that are with child, *3759*
26:24 **w** unto that man by whom the Son of man *3759*
Mk 13:17 But **w** to them that are with child, and *3759*
14:21 **w** to that man by whom the Son of man is *3759*
Lk 6:24 But **w** unto you that are rich: for ye have *3759*
6:25 **W** unto you that are full: for ye shall *3759*
6:25 **W** unto you that laugh now: for ye shall *3759*
6:26 **W** unto you, when all men shall speak well *3759*
10:13 **W** unto thee, Chorazin, woe unto thee, *3759*
10:13 Chorazin, **w** unto thee, Bethsaida: *3759*
11:42 But **w** unto you, Pharisees! for ye tithe mint *3759*
11:43 **W** unto you, Pharisees! for ye love *3759*
11:44 **W** unto you, scribes and Pharisees, *3759*
11:46 And he said, **W** unto you also, *ye* lawyers! *3759*
11:47 **W** unto you! for ye build the sepulchres of *3759*
11:52 **W** unto you, lawyers! for ye have taken *3759*
17: 1 but **w** *unto him,* through whom they come. *3759*
21:23 But **w** unto them that are with child, and *3759*
22:22 **w** unto that man by whom he is betrayed. *3759*
1Co 9:16 yea, **w** is unto me, if I preach not *3759*
Jude 1:11 **W** unto them! for they have gone in *3759*
Rev 8:13 saying with a loud voice, **W**, woe, woe, *3759*
8:13 saying with a loud voice, Woe, **w**, woe, *3759*
8:13 saying with a loud voice, Woe, woe, **w**, *3759*
9:12 One **w** is past; *and* behold, there come two *3759*
11:14 The second **w** is past; *and* behold, the third *3759*
11:14 *and* behold, the third **w** cometh quickly. *3759*
12:12 **W** to the inhabiters of the earth and of *3759*

WOEFUL (1) [WOE]

Jer 17:16 neither have I desired the **w** day; 605

WOES (1) [WOE]

Rev 9:12 behold, there come two **w** more hereafter. *3759*

WOLF (6) [WOLVES]

Ge 49:27 Benjamin shall ravin *as* a **w**: in the morning 2061
Isa 11: 6 The **w** also shall dwell with the lamb, and 2061
65:25 The **w** and the lamb shall feed together, and 2061
Jer 5: 6 *and* a **w** of the evenings shall spoil them, 2061
Jn 10:12 seeth the **w** coming, and leaveth the sheep, *3074*
10:12 and the **w** catcheth them, and scattereth *3074*

WOLVES (7) [WOLF]

Eze 22:27 Her princes in the midst thereof *are* like **w** 2061
Hab 1: 8 and are more fierce than the evening **w**: 2061
Zep 3: 3 *are* roaring lions; her judges *are* evening **w**; 2061
Mt 7:15 but inwardly they are ravening **w**. *3074*
10:16 I send you forth as sheep in the midst of **w**: *3074*
Lk 10: 3 behold, I send you forth as lambs among **w**. *3074*
Ac 20:29 that after my departing shall grievous **w** *3074*

WOMAN (360) [BONDWOMAN, BONDWOMEN, FREEWOMAN, KINSWOMAN, KINSWOMEN, WOMAN'S, WOMANKIND, WOMEN, WOMEN'S, WOMENSERVANTS]

Ge 2:22 made he a **w**, and brought her unto the man. 802
2:23 she shall be called **W**, because she was taken 802
3: 1 And he said unto the **w**, Yea, hath God said, 802
3: 2 the **w** said unto the serpent, We may eat of 802
3: 4 the serpent said unto the **w**, Ye shall not 802
3: 6 when the **w** saw that the tree *was* good for 802
3:12 The **w** whom thou gavest *to be* with me, 802
3:13 the LORD God said unto the **w**, What *is* 802
3:13 the **w** said, The serpent beguiled me, and 802
3:15 I will put enmity between thee and the **w**, 802
3:16 Unto the **w** he said, I will greatly multiply 802
12:11 I know that thou *art* a fair **w** to look upon: 802
12:14 the Egyptians beheld the **w** that she *was* very 802
12:15 and the **w** was taken into Pharaoh's house. 802
20: 3 a dead man, for the **w** which thou hast taken; 802
24: 5 Peradventure the **w** will not be willing to 802
24: 8 if the **w** will not be willing to follow thee, 802
24:39 Peradventure the **w** will not follow me. 802
24:44 *let* the same *be* the **w** whom the LORD hath 802
46:10 and Shaul the son of a Canaanitish **w**. NIH
Ex 2: 2 the **w** conceived, and bare a son: and 802
2: 9 And the **w** took the child, and nursed it. 802
3:22 every **w** shall borrow of her neighbour, and 802
6:15 and Shaul the son of a **Canaanitish w**: 3669
11: 2 every **w** of her neighbour, jewels of silver, 802
21:22 hurt a **w** with child, so that her fruit depart 802
21:28 If an ox gore a man or a **w**, that they die: 802
21:29 him in, but that he hath killed a man or a **w**; 802
35:29 every man and **w**, whose heart made them 802
36: 6 Let neither man nor **w** make any more work 802
Lev 12: 2 If a **w** have conceived seed, and born a man 802
13:29 If a man or **w** hath a plague upon the head or 802
13:38 a **w** have in the skin of their flesh bright 802
15:18 The **w** also with whom man shall lie *with* 802
15:19 if a **w** have an issue, *and* her issue in her 802
15:25 if a **w** have an issue of her blood many days 802
15:33 of the **w**, and of him that lieth with her 5347
18:17 Thou shalt not uncover the nakedness of a **w** 802
18:19 Also thou shalt not approach unto a **w** to 802
18:23 neither shall any **w** stand before a beast to lie 802
19:20 whosoever lieth carnally with a **w** that *is* a 802
20:13 also lie with mankind, as he lieth with a **w**, 802
20:16 if a **w** approach unto any beast, and lie down 802
20:16 thou shalt kill the **w** and the beast: 802
20:18 if a man shall lie with a **w** having her 802
20:27 A man also or **w** that hath a familiar spirit, or 802
21: 7 neither shall they take a **w** put away from her 802
21:14 or a divorced *w*, or profane, *or* a harlot, NIH
24:10 the son of an Israelitish **w**, whose father *was* 802
24:10 *this* son of the Israelitish *w* and a man of NIH
Nu 5: 6 or **w** shall commit any sin that men commit, 802
5:18 the priest shall set the **w** before the LORD, 802
5:19 say unto the **w**, If no man have lain with 802
5:21 the priest shall charge the **w** with an oath of 802
5:21 the priest shall say unto the **w**, The LORD 802
5:22 to rot: And the **w** shall say, Amen, amen. 802
5:24 he shall cause the **w** to drink the bitter water 802
5:26 afterward shall cause the **w** to drink 802
5:27 and the **w** shall be a curse among her people. 802
5:28 if the **w** be not defiled, but *be* clean; then 802
5:30 shall set the **w** before the LORD, and 802
5:31 and this **w** shall bear her iniquity. 802
6: 2 **w** shall separate *themselves* to vow a vow of 802
12: 1 of the Ethiopian **w** whom he had married: 802
12: 1 for he had married an Ethiopian **w**. 802
25: 6 brought unto his brethren a Midianitish *w* in NIH
25: 8 man of Israel, and the **w** through her belly. 802
25:14 *even* that was slain with the **Midianitish w**, 4084
25:15 the name of the Midianitish **w** that was slain 802
30: 3 If a **w** also vow a vow unto the LORD, and 802
31:17 kill every **w** that hath known man by lying 802

Dt	15:12	a Hebrew man, or a **Hebrew** w, be sold	5680
	17: 2	the LORD thy God giveth thee, man or w,	802
	17: 5	shalt thou bring forth that man or that w,	802
	17: 5	*even that* man or *that* w, and shalt stone	802
	21:11	And seest among the captives a beautiful w,	802
	22: 5	The w shall not wear that which pertaineth	802
	22:14	say, I took this w, and when I came to her,	802
	22:22	If a man be found lying with a w married to	802
	22:22	*both* the man that lay with the w, and	802
	22:22	the man that lay with the woman, and the w:	802
	28:56	The tender and delicate *w* among you,	NIH
	29:18	be among you man, or w, or family, or tribe,	802
Jos	2: 4	the w took the two men, and hid them, and	802
	6:21	both man and w, young and old, and ox, and	802
	6:22	bring out thence the w, and all that she hath,	802
Jdg	4: 9	shall sell Sisera into the hand of a w.	802
	9:53	a certain w cast a piece of a millstone upon	802
	9:54	that *men* say not of me, A w slew him.	802
	11: 2	for thou *art* the son of a strange w.	802
	13: 3	angel of the LORD appeared unto the w,	802
	13: 6	the w came and told her husband, saying,	802
	13: 9	the angel of God came again unto the w as	802
	13:10	the w made haste, and ran, and shewed her	802
	13:11	*Art* thou the man that spakest unto the w?	802
	13:13	Of all that I said unto the w let her beware.	802
	13:24	the w bare a son, and called his name	802
	14: 1	saw a w in Timnath of the daughters of	802
	14: 2	I have seen a w in Timnath of the daughters	802
	14: 3	*Is there* never a w among the daughters of	802
	14: 7	he went down, and talked with the w; and	802
	14:10	So his father went down unto the w: and	802
	16: 4	that he loved a w in the valley of Sorek,	802
	19:26	Then came the w in the dawning of the day,	802
	19:27	the w his concubine *was* fallen down *at*	802
	20: 4	the husband of the w that was slain,	802
	21:11	and every w that hath lien by man.	802
Ru	1: 5	the w was left of her two sons and	802
	3: 8	and behold, a w lay *at* his feet.	802
	3:11	people doth know that thou *art* a virtuous w.	802
	3:14	Let it not be known that a w came *into*	802
	4:11	The LORD make the w that is come into	802
	4:12	the LORD shall give thee of this **young** w.	5291
1Sa	1:15	No, my lord, I *am* a w of a sorrowful spirit:	802
	1:18	So the w went her way, and did eat, and her	802
	1:23	So the w abode, and gave her son suck until	802
	1:26	my lord, I *am* the w that stood by thee here,	802
	2:20	The LORD give thee seed of this w for	802
	15: 3	slay both man and w, infant and suckling,	802
	20:30	Thou son of the perverse rebellious *w*, do	NIH
	25: 3	and *she was* a w of good understanding, and	802
	27: 9	left neither man nor w alive, and took away	802
	27:11	David saved neither man nor w alive,	802
	28: 7	Seek me a w that hath a familiar spirit, that I	802
	28: 7	*there is* a w that hath a familiar spirit at	802
	28: 8	with him, and they came to the w by night:	802
	28: 9	the w said unto him, Behold, thou knowest	802
	28:11	said the w, Whom shall I bring up unto thee?	802
	28:12	when the w saw Samuel, she cried with a	802
	28:12	the w spake to Saul, saying, Why hast thou	802
	28:13	the w said unto Saul, I saw gods ascending	802
	28:21	the w came unto Saul, and saw that he was	802
	28:23	together with the w, compelled him;	802
	28:24	the w had a fat calf in the house; and	802
2Sa	3: 8	me to day with a fault concerning *this* w?	802
	11: 2	from the roof he saw a w washing *herself;*	802
	11: 2	and the w *was* very beautiful to look upon.	802
	11: 3	David sent and inquired after the w. And *one*	802
	11: 5	the w conceived, and sent and told David,	802
	11:21	did not a w cast a piece of a millstone upon	802
	13:17	Put now this *w* out from me, and bolt	NIH
	14: 2	fetcht thence a wise w, and said unto her,	802
	14: 2	be as a w *that had* a long time mourned for	802
	14: 4	when the w of Tekoah spake to the king,	802
	14: 5	I *am* indeed a widow w, and mine husband is	802
	14: 8	the king said unto the w, Go to thine house,	802
	14: 9	the w of Tekoah said unto the king, My lord,	802
	14:12	the w said, Let thine handmaid, I pray thee,	802
	14:13	the w said, Wherefore then hast thou thought	802
	14:18	Then the king answered and said unto the w,	802
	14:18	the w said, Let my lord the king now speak.	802
	14:19	the w answered and said, *As* thy soul liveth,	802
	14:27	she was a w of a fair countenance.	802
	17:19	the w took and spread a covering over	802
	17:20	when Absalom's servants came to the w to	802
	17:20	the w said unto them, They be gone over	802
	20:16	cried a wise w out of the city, Hear, hear;	802
	20:17	near unto her, the w said, *Art* thou Joab?	802
	20:21	the w said unto Joab, Behold, his head *shall*	802
	20:22	the w went unto all the people in her	802
1Ki	3:17	the one w said, O my lord, I and this woman	802
	3:17	O my lord, I and this w dwell in one house;	802
	3:18	that this w was delivered also:	802
	3:22	the other w said, Nay; but the living *is* my	802
	3:26	spake the w whose the living child *was* unto	802
	11:26	mother's name *was* Zeruah, a widow w,	802
	14: 5	that she shall feign herself to be another *w*.	NIH
	17: 9	I have commanded a widow w there to	802
	17:10	the widow w *was* there gathering of sticks:	802
	17:17	*that* the son of the w, the mistress of	802
	17:24	the w said to Elijah, Now *by* this I know that	802
2Ki	4: 1	Now there cried a certain w of the wives of	802
	4: 8	passed to Shunem, where *was* a great w;	802
	4:17	the w conceived, and bare a son at that	802
	6:26	there cried a w unto him, saying, Help,	802
	6:28	This w said unto me, Give thy son,	802
	6:30	when the king heard the words of the w,	802
	8: 1	spake Elisha unto the w, whose son he had	802
	8: 2	the w arose, and did after the saying of	802
	8: 3	that the w returned out of the land of	802
	8: 5	that behold, the w, whose son he had	802
	8: 5	O king, this *is* the w, and this *is* her son,	802
	8: 6	when the king asked the w, she told him.	802
	9:34	Go, see now this cursed *w*, and bury her:	NIH
1Ch	16: 3	both man and w, to every one a loaf of	802
2Ch	2:14	The son of a w of the daughters of Dan, and	802
	15:13	whether small or great, whether man or w.	802
	24: 7	For the sons of Athaliah, *that* **wicked** w,	4849
Est	4:11	do know, that whosoever, *whether* man or w,	802
Job	14: 1	Man *that is* born of a w *is* of few days, and	802
	15:14	*he which is* born of a w, that he should be	802
	25: 4	or how can he be clean *that is* born of a w?	802
	31: 9	If mine heart have been deceived by a w, or	802
Ps	48: 6	them there, *and* pain, as of a w in travail.	NIH
	58: 8	*like* the untimely birth of a w, *that* they may	802
	113: 9	He maketh the barren *w* to keep house,	NIH
Pr	2:16	To deliver thee from the strange w,	802
	5: 3	For the lips of a strange *w* drop *as* a	NIH
	5:20	be ravisht with a strange *w*, and embrace	NIH
	6:24	To keep thee from the evil w, from	802
	6:24	the flattery of the tongue of a strange *w*.	NIH
	6:26	For by means of a whorish w *a man is*	802
	6:32	*But* whoso committeth adultery with a w	802
	7: 5	That *they* may keep thee from the strange w,	802
	7:10	there met him a w *with* the attire of a harlot,	802
	9:13	A foolish w *is* clamorous: *she is* simple, and	802
	11:16	A gracious w retaineth honour: and	802
	11:22	*so is* a fair w which is without discretion.	802
	12: 4	A virtuous w *is* a crown to her husband: but	802
	14: 1	Every wise w buildeth her house: but	802
	20:16	and take a pledge of him for a strange *w*.	NIH
	21: 9	than with a brawling w in a wide house.	802
	21:19	than with a contentious and an angry w.	802
	23:27	deep ditch; and a strange *w is* a narrow pit.	NIH
	25:24	than with a brawling w and in a wide house.	802
	27:13	and take a pledge of him for a strange *w*.	NIH
	27:15	very rainy day and a contentious w are alike.	802
	30:20	Such *is* the way of an adulterous w;	802
	30:23	For an odious *w* when she is married; and	NIH
	31:10	Who can find a virtuous w? for her price *is*	802
	31:30	*but* a w that feareth the LORD, she shall be	802
Ecc	7:26	I find more bitter than death the w,	802
	7:28	but a w among all those have I not found.	802
Isa	13: 8	they shall be in pain as a w that travaileth:	NIH
	21: 3	upon me, as the pangs of a w that travaileth:	NIH
	26:17	Like as a w with child, *that* draweth near	NIH
	42:14	*now* will I cry like a **travailing** w; I will	3205
	45:10	or to the w, What hast thou brought forth?	802
	49:15	Can a w forget her sucking child, that *she*	802
	54: 6	For the LORD hath called thee as a w	802
Jer	4:31	For I have heard a voice as of a w in travail,	NIH
	6: 2	of Zion *to* a comely and delicate *w*.	NIH
	6:24	hold of us, *and* pain, as of a w in travail.	NIH
	13:21	shall not sorrows take thee, as a w in travail?	802
	22:23	upon thee, the pain as of a w in travail.	NIH
	30: 6	as a w in travail, and all faces are turned	NIH
	31: 8	the w with child and her that travaileth with	NIH
	31:22	in the earth, A w shall compass a man.	5347
	44: 7	to cut off from you man and w, child and	802

Jer 48:41 day shall be as the heart of a w in her pangs. 802
49:22 of Edom be as the heart of a w in her pangs. 802
49:24 and sorrows have taken her as a w in travail. NIH
50:43 hold of him, *and* pangs as of a w in travail. NIH
51:22 thee also will I break in pieces man and w; 802
La 1:17 Jerusalem is as a menstruous *w* among NIH
Eze 16:30 *things,* the work of an imperious whorish w; 802
18: 6 neither hath come near to a menstruous w, 802
23:44 as *they* go in unto a w that playeth the harlot: 802
36:17 me as the uncleanness of a **removed** w. 5079
Hos 3: 1 Go yet, love a w beloved of *her* friend, 802
13:13 The sorrows of a travailing *w* shall come NIH
Mic 4: 9 for pangs have taken thee as a w in travail. NIH
4:10 O daughter of Zion, like a w in travail: NIH
Zec 5: 7 this *is* a w that sitteth in the midst of 802
Mt 5:28 That whosoever looketh on a w to lust after 1135
9:20 (And behold, a w, which was diseased with 1135
9:22 And the w was made whole from that 1135
13:33 which a w took, and hid in three measures 1135
15:22 a w of Canaan came out of the same coasts, 1135
15:28 Jesus answered and said unto her, O w, 1135
22:27 And last of all the w died also. 1135
26: 7 There came unto him a w having an 1135
26:10 he said unto them, Why trouble ye the w? 1135
26:13 *there* shall also *this,* that this *w* hath done, NIG
Mk 5:25 And a certain w, which had an issue of 1135
5:33 But the w fearing and trembling, 1135
7:25 For a *certain* w, whose young daughter had 1135
7:26 The w was a Greek, a Syrophenician by 1135
10:12 And if a w shall put away her husband, and 1135
12:22 and left no seed: last of all the w died also. 1135
14: 3 there came a w having an alabaster box of 1135
Lk 4:26 *a city* of Sidon, unto a w *that was* a widow. 1135
7:37 And behold, a w in the city, which was a 1135
7:39 what manner of w *this is* that toucheth him: 1135
7:44 And he turned to the w, and said unto 1135
7:44 and said unto Simon, Seest thou this w? 1135
7:45 this *w* since the time I came in hath not NIG
7:46 this *w* hath anointed my feet with ointment. NIG
7:50 And he said to the w, Thy faith hath saved 1135
8:43 And a w having an issue of blood twelve 1135
8:47 And when the w saw that she was not hid, 1135
10:38 a certain w named Martha received him 1135
11:27 as he spake these *things,* a certain w of 1135
13:11 there was a w which had a spirit of 1135
13:12 he called *her* to *him,* and said unto her, W, 1135
13:16 And ought not this *w*, being a daughter of NIG
13:21 which a w took and hid in three measures 1135
15: 8 Either what w having ten pieces of silver, 1135
20:32 Last of all the w died also. 1135
22:57 he denied him, saying, W, I know him not. 1135
Jn 2: 4 Jesus saith unto her, W, what have I to do 1135
4: 7 There cometh a w of Samaria to draw 1135
4: 9 Then saith the w of Samaria unto him, 1135
4: 9 drink of me, which am a w of Samaria? 1135
4:11 The w saith unto him, Sir, thou hast 1135
4:15 The w saith unto him, Sir, give me this 1135
4:17 The w answered and said, I have no 1135
4:19 The w saith unto him, Sir, I perceive that 1135
4:21 unto her, W, believe me, the hour cometh, 1135
4:25 The w saith unto him, I know that Messias 1135
4:27 and marvelled that he talked with *the* w: 1135
4:28 The w then left her waterpot, and went her 1135
4:39 believed on him for the saying of the w, 1135
4:42 And said unto the w, *Now* we believe, not 1135
8: 3 Pharisees brought unto him a w taken in 1135
8: 4 Master, this w was taken in adultery, in 1135
8: 9 left alone, and the w standing in the midst. 1135
8:10 had lift up *himself,* and saw none but the w, 1135
8:10 but the woman, he said unto her, W, 1135
16:21 A w when she is in travail hath sorrow, 1135
19:26 saith unto his mother, W, behold thy son. 1135
20:13 they say unto her, W, why weepest thou? 1135
20:15 Jesus saith unto her, W, why weepest thou? 1135
Ac 9:36 this *w* was full of good works and NIG
16: 1 named Timotheus, the son of a certain w, 1135
16:14 And a certain w named Lydia, a seller of 1135
17:34 and a w named Damaris, and others with 1135
Ro 1:27 the men, leaving the natural use of the w, 2338
7: 2 For the w which hath a husband is bound 1135
1Co 7: 1 *It is* good for a man not to touch a w. 1135
7: 2 and let **every** w have her own husband. 1538
7:13 And the w which hath a husband that 1135
7:34 The unmarried *w* careth for the *things* of NIG
11: 3 and the head of the w *is* the man; and 1135
11: 5 But every w that prayeth or 1135
11: 6 For if the w be not covered, let her also be 1135
11: 6 but *if it* be a shame for a w to be shorn or 1135
11: 7 of God: but the w is the glory of the man. 1135
11: 8 For the man is not of the w; but the woman 1135
11: 8 is not of the woman; but the w of the man. 1135
11: 9 Neither was the man created for the w; but 1135
11: 9 for the woman; but the w for the man. 1135
11:10 For this cause ought the w to have power 1135
11:11 neither *is* the man without the w, 1135
11:11 neither the w without the man, in the Lord. 1135
11:12 For as the w *is* of the man, *even* so *is* 1135
11:12 the man, *even* so *is* the man also by the w; 1135
11:13 is it comely that a w pray unto God 1135
11:15 But if a w have long hair, it is a glory to 1135
Gal 4: 4 his Son, made of a w, made under the law, 1135
1Th 5: 3 upon them, as travail upon a *w* with child; NIG
1Ti 2:11 Let the w learn in silence with all 1135
2:12 But I suffer not a w to teach, nor to usurp 1135
2:14 the w being deceived was in 1135
5:16 any man or w **that believeth** have widows, 4103
Rev 2:20 because thou sufferest *that* w Jezebel, 1135
12: 1 a w clothed with the sun, and the moon 1135
12: 4 the dragon stood before the w which was 1135
12: 6 And the w fled into the wilderness, 1135
12:13 he persecuted the w which brought forth 1135
12:14 And to the w were given two wings of a 1135
12:15 of his mouth water as a flood after the w, 1135
12:16 And the earth helped the w, and the earth 1135
12:17 And the dragon was wroth with the w, and 1135
17: 3 I saw a w sit upon a scarlet coloured beast, 1135
17: 4 And the w was arrayed in purple and 1135
17: 6 And I saw the w drunken with the blood of 1135
17: 7 I will tell thee the mystery of the w, and 1135
17: 9 seven mountains, on which the w sitteth. 1135
17:18 And the w which thou sawest is *that* great 1135

WOMAN'S (7) [WOMAN]

Ge 38:20 to receive *his* pledge from the w hand: 802
Ex 21:22 according as the w husband will lay upon 802
Lev 24:11 the Israelitish w son blasphemed the name *of* 802
Nu 5:18 uncover the w head, and put the offering of 802
5:25 take the jealousy offering out of the w hand, 802
Dt 22: 5 neither shall a man put on a w garment: 802
1Ki 3:19 this w child died in the night; because 802

WOMANKIND (1) [WOMAN]

Lev 18:22 Thou shalt not lie with mankind, as with w: 802

WOMB (71) [WOMBS]

Ge 25:23 Two nations *are* in thy w, and two manner of 990
25:24 behold, *there were* twins in her w. 990
29:31 saw that Leah *was* hated, he opened her w: 7358
30: 2 hath withheld from thee the fruit of the w? 990
30:22 God hearkened to her, and opened her w. 7358
38:27 her travail, that, behold, twins *were* in her w. 990
49:25 blessings of the breasts, and of the w: 7356
Ex 13: 2 whatsoever openeth the w among 7358
Nu 8:16 instead of such as open every w, 7358
12:12 when he cometh out of his mother's w. 7358
Dt 7:13 he will also bless the fruit of thy w, and 990
Jdg 13: 5 shall be a Nazarite unto God from the w: 990
13: 7 to God from the w to the day of his death. 990
16:17 a Nazarite unto God from my mother's w: 990
Ru 1:11 *are there* yet *any moe* sons in my w, 4578
1Sa 1: 5 but the LORD had shut up her w. 7358
1: 6 because the LORD had shut up her w. 7358
Job 1:21 Naked came I out of my mother's w, and 990
3:10 it shut not up the doors of my *mother's* w, 990
3:11 Why died I not from the w? *why* did I *not* 7358
10:18 hast thou brought me forth out of the w? 7358
10:19 I should have been carried from the w to 990
24:20 The w shall forget him; the worm shall feed 7358
31:15 Did not he that made me in the w make him? 990
31:15 and did not one fashion us in the w? 7358
31:18 and I have guided her from my mother's w;) 990
38: 8 brake forth, *as if* it had issued out of the w? 7358
38:29 Out of whose w came the ice? and the hoary 990
Ps 22: 9 thou *art* he that took me out of the w: 990
22:10 I was cast upon thee from the w: thou *art* 7358
58: 3 The wicked are estranged from the w: 7358
71: 6 By thee have I been holden up from the w: 990
110: 3 in the beauties of holiness from the w of 7358

Ps 127: 3 *and* the fruit of the **w** *is his* reward. 990
139:13 thou hast covered me in my mother's **w**. 990
Pr 30:16 The grave; and the barren **w**; the earth *that* 7356
31: 2 what, the son of my **w**? and what, the son of 990
Ecc 5:15 As he came forth of his mother's **w**, 990
11: 5 *nor* how the bones *do grow* in the **w** of her 990
Isa 13:18 they shall have no pity on the fruit of the **w**; 990
44: 2 formed thee from the **w**, *which* will help 990
44:24 and he that formed thee from the **w**, 990
46: 3 the belly, which are carried from the **w**: 7356
48: 8 wast called a transgressor from the **w**. 990
49: 1 The LORD hath called me from the **w**; 990
49: 5 saith the LORD that formed me from the **w** 990
49:15 not have compassion on the son of her **w**? 990
66: 9 bring forth, and shut *the* **w**? saith thy God. NIH
Jer 1: 5 before thou camest forth out of the **w** I 7358
20:17 Because he slew me not from the **w**; or 7358
20:17 and her **w** *to be* always great *with me*. 7358
20:18 Wherefore came I forth out of the **w** to see 7358
Eze 20:26 pass through *the fire* all that openeth the **w**, 7356
Hos 9:11 and from the **w**, and from the conception. 990
9:14 give them a miscarrying **w** and dry breasts. 7358
9:16 will I slay *even* the beloved *fruit* of their **w**. 990
12: 3 He took his brother by the heel in the **w**, and 990
Mt 19:12 which were so born from *their* mother's **w**: *2836*
Lk 1:15 the Holy Ghost, even from his mother's **w**. *2836*
1:31 thou shalt conceive in *thy* **w**, and *1064*
1:41 of Mary, the babe leaped in her **w**; *2836*
1:42 and blessed *is* the fruit of thy **w**. *2836*
1:44 mine ears, the babe leaped in my **w** for joy. *2836*
2:21 the angel before he was conceived in the **w**. *2836*
2:23 Every male that openeth the **w** shall be *3388*
11:27 Blessed *is* the **w** that bare thee, and *2836*
Jn 3: 4 enter the second time into his mother's **w**, *2836*
Ac 3: 2 man lame from his mother's **w** was carried, *2836*
14: 8 being a cripple from his mother's **w**, *2836*
Ro 4:19 neither *yet* the deadness of Sara's **w**: *3388*
Gal 1:15 who separated me from my mother's **w**, *2836*

WOMBS (2) [WOMB]

Ge 20:18 For the LORD had fast closed up all the **w** 7358
Lk 23:29 and the **w** that never bare, and the paps *2836*

WOMEN (178) [WOMAN]

Ge 14:16 his goods, and the **w** also, and the people. 802
18:11 to be with Sarah after the manner of **w**. 802
24:11 *even* the time that *w* go out to draw *water*. NIH
31:35 before thee; for the custom of **w** *is* upon me. 802
33: 5 up his eyes, and saw the **w** and the children; 802
Ex 1:16 the office of a midwife to the **Hebrew w**, 5680
1:19 Because the **Hebrew w** *are* not as 5680
1:19 Hebrew women *are* not as the Egyptian **w**; 802
2: 7 and call to thee a nurse of the Hebrew **w**, 802
15:20 all the **w** went out after her with timbrels and 802
35:22 they came, both men and **w**, as many as were 802
35:25 all the **w** that were wise hearted did spin 802
35:26 all the **w** whose heart stirred them up in 802
38: 8 of the looking-glasses of *the w* assembling, NIH
Lev 26:26 ten **w** shall bake your bread in one oven, and 802
Nu 31: 9 the children of Israel took *all* the **w** of 802
31:15 unto them, Have ye saved all the **w** alive? 5347
31:18 all the **w** children, that have not known a 802
31:35 of **w** that had not known man by lying with 802
Dt 2:34 the **w**, and the little ones, of every city, 802
3: 6 the men, **w**, and children, of every city. 802
20:14 But the **w**, and the little ones, and the cattle, 802
31:12 **w**, and children, and thy stranger that *is* 802
Jos 8:25 both of men and **w**, *were* twelve thousand, 802
8:35 with the **w**, and the little ones, and 802
Jdg 5:24 Blessed above **w** shall Jael the wife of Heber 802
5:24 blessed shall she be above **w** in the tent. 802
9:49 died also, about a thousand men and **w**. 802
9:51 thither fled all the men and **w**, and all they of 802
16:27 Now the house was full *of* men and **w**; and 802
16:27 the roof about three thousand men and **w**, 802
21:10 of the sword, with the **w** and the children. 802
21:14 had saved alive of the **w** of Jabesh-gilead: 802
21:16 seeing the **w** are destroyed out of Benjamin? 802
Ru 1: 4 they took them wives of the **w of Moab**; 4125
4:14 the **w** said unto Naomi, Blessed *be* 802
4:17 the *w her* neighbours gave it a name, NIH
1Sa 2:22 how they lay with the **w** that assembled *at* 802
4:20 about the time of her death the *w* that stood NIH
15:33 As thy sword hath made **w** childless, so 802
15:33 so shall thy mother be childless among **w**. 802
18: 6 that the **w** came out of all cities of Israel, 802
18: 7 the **w** answered *one another* as they played, 802
21: 4 men have kept themselves at least from **w**. 802
21: 5 Of a truth **w** *have been* kept from us about 802
22:19 both men and **w**, children and sucklings, and 802
30: 2 had taken the **w** captives, that *were* therein: 802
2Sa 1:26 to me was wonderful, passing the love of **w**. 802
6:19 as well to the **w** as men, to every one a cake 802
15:16 the king left ten **w**, *which were* concubines, 802
19:35 singing *men* and singing *w*? wherefore then NIH
20: 3 the king took the ten **w** *his* concubines, 802
1Ki 3:16 came there two **w**, *that were* harlots, unto 802
11: 1 king Solomon loved many strange **w**, 802
11: 1 *w of the* Moabites, Ammonites, Edomites, NIH
2Ki 8:12 and rip up their **w with child**. 2030
15:16 all the **w** therein that were **with child** he 2030
23: 7 where the **w** wove hangings for the grove. 802
2Ch 28: 8 **w**, sons, and daughters, and took also away 802
35:25 the singing *w* spake of Josiah in their NIH
Ezr 2:65 two hundred singing *men* and singing *w*. NIH
10: 1 congregation *of* men and **w** and children: 802
Ne 7:67 and five singing *men* and singing *w*. NIH
8: 2 before the congregation both of men and **w**, 802
8: 3 before the men and the **w**, and those that 802
13:26 *nevertheless* even him did outlandish **w** 802
Est 1: 9 Also Vashti the queen made a feast for the **w** 802
1:17 of the queen shall come abroad unto all **w**, 802
2: 3 to the house of the **w**, unto the custody of 802
2: 3 the king's chamberlain, keeper of the **w**; 802
2: 8 to the custody of Hegai, keeper of the **w**. 802
2: 9 unto the best *place* of the house of the **w**. 802
2:12 according to the manner of the **w**, (for so 802
2:12 with *other* things for the purifying of the **w**;) 802
2:13 of the house of the **w** unto the king's house. 802
2:14 she returned into the second house of the **w**, 802
2:15 the keeper of the **w**, appointed. 802
2:17 the king loved Esther above all the **w**, and 802
3:13 both young and old, little children and **w**, 802
8:11 *both* little ones and **w**, and *to take* the spoil 802
Job 2:10 Thou speakest as one of the foolish *w* NIH
42:15 in all the land were no **w** found *so* fair as 802
Ps 45: 9 *w*: upon thy right hand did stand the queen NIH
Pr 22:14 The mouth of strange *w is* a deep pit: NIH
23:33 Thine eyes shall behold strange *w*, and NIH
31: 3 Give not thy strength unto **w**, nor thy ways 802
Ecc 2: 8 I gat me *men* singers and *w* singers, and NIH
SS 1: 8 If thou know not, O thou fairest among **w**, 802
5: 9 *another* beloved, O thou fairest among **w**? 802
6: 1 thy beloved gone, O thou fairest among **w**? 802
Isa 3:12 *are* their oppressors, and **w** rule over them. 802
4: 1 in that day seven **w** shall take hold of one 802
19:16 In that day shall Egypt be like unto **w**: and 802
27:11 the **w** come, *and* set them on fire: for it *is* a 802
32: 9 Rise up, ye **w** that are at ease, hear my voice; 802
32:10 ye careless *w*: for the vintage shall fail, NIH
32:11 Tremble, ye *w* that are at ease; be troubled, NIH
Jer 7:18 kindle the fire, and the **w** knead *their* dough, 802
9:17 call for the mourning *w*, that they may NIH
9:17 send for cunning *w*, that they may come: NIH
9:20 O ye **w**, and let your ear receive the word of 802
38:22 all the **w** that are left in the king of Judah's 802
38:22 those *w shall* say, Thy friends have set thee NIH
40: 7 **w**, and children, and of the poor of the land, 802
41:16 and the **w**, and the children, and the eunuchs, 802
43: 6 **w**, and children, and the king's daughters, 802
44:15 and all the **w** that stood *by*, a great multitude, 802
44:20 to the **w**, and to all the people which had 802
44:24 to all the **w**, Hear the word of the LORD, 802
50:37 the midst of her; and they shall become as **w**: 802
51:30 their might hath failed; they became as **w**: 802
La 2:20 Shall the **w** eat their fruit, *and* children of a 802
4:10 The hands of the pitiful **w** have sodden their 802
5:11 They ravished the **w** in Zion, *and* the maids 802
Eze 8:14 behold, there sat **w** weeping for Tammuz. 802
9: 6 both maids, and little children, and **w**: 802
13:18 Woe to *the w* that sew pillows to all NIH
16:34 the contrary is in thee from *other* **w** in thy 802
16:38 as *w* that break wedlock and shed blood are NIH
16:41 judgments upon thee in the sight of many **w**: 802
23: 2 Son of man, there were two **w**, the daughters 802
23:10 she became famous among **w**; for they had 802
23:44 unto Aholah and unto Aholibah, the lewd **w**. 802
23:45 and after the manner of *w* that shed blood; NIH

Eze 23:48 that all w may be taught not to do after your 802
Da 11:17 he shall give him the daughter of w, 802
11:37 nor the desire of w, nor regard any god: 802
Hos 13:16 and their w with child shall be ript up. 2030
Am 1:13 they have ript up the w with child at 2030
Mic 2: 9 The w of my people have ye cast out from 802
Na 3:13 thy people in the midst of thee *are* w: 802
Zec 5: 9 there came out two w, and the wind *was* in 802
8: 4 and old w dwell in the streets of Jerusalem, 2205
14: 2 and the houses rifled, and the w ravished; 802
Mt 11:11 Among *them that are* born of w there hath 1135
14:21 five thousand men, beside w and children. 1135
15:38 four thousand men, beside w and children. 1135
24:41 Two *w shall be* grinding at the mill; *the* one NIG
27:55 And many w were there beholding afar off, 1135
28: 5 the angel answered and said unto the w, 1135
Mk 15:40 There were also w looking on afar off: 1135
15:41 many other *w* which came up with him unto NIG
Lk 1:28 *is* with thee: blessed *art* thou among w. 1135
1:42 Blessed *art* thou among w, and blessed *is* 1135
7:28 Among *those that are* born of w there is not 1135
8: 2 And certain w, which had been healed of 1135
17:35 Two *w* shall be grinding together; the one NIG
23:27 and of w, which also bewailed and 1135
23:49 and the w that followed him from Galilee, 1135
23:55 And the w also, which came with him from 1135
24:10 of James, and other *w that were* with them, NIG
24:22 certain w *also* of our company made us 1135
24:24 and found *it* even so as the w had said: 1135
Ac 1:14 with the w, and Mary the mother of Jesus, 1135
5:14 to the Lord, multitudes both of men and w.) 1135
8: 3 and w committed *them* to prison. 1135
8:12 they were baptized, both men and w. 1135
9: 2 of *this* way, whether they were men or w, 1135
13:50 stirred up the devout and honourable w, 1135
16:13 spake unto the w which resorted *thither.* 1135
17: 4 and of the chief w not a few. 1135
17:12 also of honourable w which were Greeks, 1135
22: 4 delivering into prisons both men and w. 1135
Ro 1:26 for even their w did change the natural use 2338
1Co 14:34 Let your w keep silence in the churches: 1135
14:35 for it is a shame for w to speak in 1135
Php 4: 3 help those *w* which laboured with me in NIG
1Ti 2: 9 that w adorn themselves in modest apparel, 1135
2:10 But (which becometh w professing 1135
5: 2 The elder *w* as mothers; the younger as NIG
5:14 I will therefore that the younger *w* marry, NIG
2Ti 3: 6 and lead captive silly w laden with sins, 1133
Tit 2: 3 The aged w likewise, *that they be* in 4247
2: 4 That they may teach the young *w* to be NIG
Heb 11:35 W received their dead raised to life again: 1135
1Pe 3: 5 this manner in the old time the holy w also, 1135
Rev 9: 8 And they had hair as the hair of w, and 1135
14: 4 are they which were not defiled with w; 1135

WOMEN'S (1) [WOMAN]
Est 2:11 every day before the court of the w house, 802

WOMENSERVANTS (3) [SERVE, WOMAN]
Ge 20:14 w, and gave *them* unto Abraham, and 8198
32: 5 and asses, flocks, and menservants, and w: 8198
32:22 his two w, and his eleven sons, and 8198

WON (3) [WIN]
1Ch 26:27 Out of the spoils w in battles did they 7998
Pr 18:19 A brother offended *is harder to be* w than a NIH
1Pe 3: 1 they also may without the word be w by 2770

WONDER (15) [WONDERED, WONDERFUL, WONDERFULLY, WONDERING, WONDERS, WONDROUS, WONDROUSLY]
Dt 13: 1 of dreams, and giveth thee a sign or a w, 4159
13: 2 the sign or the w come to pass, whereof he 4159
28:46 shall be upon thee for a sign and for a w, 4159
2Ch 32:31 who sent unto him to inquire of the w that 4159
Ps 71: 7 I am as a w unto many; but thou *art* my 4159
Isa 20: 3 and w upon Egypt and upon Ethiopia; 4159
29: 9 Stay yourselves, and w; cry ye out, and cry: 8539
29:14 *even* a marvellous work and a w: 6382
Jer 4: 9 be astonished, and the prophets shall w. 8539
Hab 1: 5 and regard, and w marvellously: 8539
Ac 3:10 and they were filled with w and 2285
13:41 Behold *ye* despisers, and w, and perish: 2296
Rev 12: 1 And there appeared a great w in heaven; 4592
12: 3 And there appeared another w in heaven; 4592
17: 8 and they that dwell on the earth shall w, 2296

WONDERED (15) [WONDER]
Isa 59:16 and w that *there was* no intercessor: 8074
63: 5 and I w that *there was* none to uphold: 8074
Zec 3: 8 for they *are* men w at: for behold, I *will* 4159
Mt 15:31 Insomuch that the multitude w, when they 2296
Mk 6:51 in themselves beyond measure, and w. 2296
Lk 2:18 And all they that heard *it* w at those *things* 2296
4:22 w at the gracious words which proceeded 2296
8:25 And they being afraid w, saying one to 2296
9:43 But while they w every one at all *things* 2296
11:14 the dumb spake; and the people w. 2296
24:41 and w, he said unto them, Have ye here any 2296
Ac 7:31 When Moses saw *it,* he w at the sight: and 2296
8:13 and w, beholding *the* miracles and 1839
Rev 13: 3 and all the world w after the beast. 2296
17: 6 when I saw her, I w *with* great admiration. 2296

WONDERFUL (21) [WONDER]
Dt 28:59 the LORD will make thy plagues w, and 6381
2Sa 1:26 thy love to me was w, passing the love of 6381
2Ch 2: 9 which I am about to build *shall be* w great. 6381
Job 42: 3 *things* too w for me, which I knew not. 6381
Ps 40: 5 *are* thy w works *which* thou hast done, and 6381
78: 4 and his w works that he hath done. 6381
107: 8 and *for* his w works to the children of men! 6381
107:15 and *for* his w works to the children of men! 6381
107:21 and *for* his w works to the children of men! 6381
107:31 and *for* his w works to the children of men! 6381
111: 4 He hath made his w works to be 6381
119:129 Thy testimonies *are* w: therefore doth my 6382
139: 6 *Such* knowledge *is* too w for me; it is high, 6383
Pr 30:18 There be three *things which* are too w for 6381
Isa 9: 6 and his name shall be called W, Counseller, 6382
25: 1 thy name; for thou hast done w things; 6382
28:29 which is w in counsel, *and* excellent in 6381
Jer 5:30 A w and horrible thing is committed in 8047
Mt 7:22 and in thy name done many w works? 1411
21:15 and scribes saw the w *things* that he did, 2297
Ac 2:11 speak in our tongues the w works of God. 3167

WONDERFULLY (4) [WONDER]
1Sa 6: 6 when he had wrought w among them, did 5953
Ps 139:14 praise thee; for I am fearfully and w made: 6381
La 1: 9 her last end; therefore she came down w: 6382
Da 8:24 he shall destroy w, and shall prosper, and 6381

WONDERING (3) [WONDER]
Ge 24:21 the man w at her held his peace, to wit 7583
Lk 24:12 w in himself at that which was come to 2296
Ac 3:11 porch that is called Solomon's, greatly w. 1569

WONDERS (55) [WONDER]
Ex 3:20 smite Egypt with all my w which I will do 6381
4:21 see that thou do all *those* w before Pharaoh, 4159
7: 3 my signs and my w in the land of Egypt. 4159
11: 9 that my w may be multiplied in the land of 4159
11:10 and Aaron did all these w before Pharaoh: 4159
15:11 in holiness, fearful *in* praises, doing w? 6382
Dt 4:34 by w, and by war, and by a mighty hand, 4159
6:22 the LORD shewed signs and w, great and 4159
7:19 the w, and the mighty hand, and 4159
26: 8 and with signs, and with w: 4159
34:11 In all the signs and the w, which 4159
Jos 3: 5 for to morrow the LORD will do w among 6381
1Ch 16:12 his w, and the judgments of his mouth; 4159
Ne 9:10 shewedst signs and w upon Pharaoh, and 4159
9:17 neither were mindful of thy w that thou 6381
Job 9:10 finding out; yea, and w without number. 6381
Ps 77:11 surely I will remember thy w of old. 6382
77:14 Thou *art* the God that doest w: thou hast 6382
78:11 and his w that he had shewed them. 6381
78:43 in Egypt, and his w in the field of Zoan: 4159
88:10 Wilt thou shew w to the dead? shall 6382
88:12 Shall thy w be known in the dark? and 6382
89: 5 the heavens shall praise thy w, O LORD: 6382
96: 3 among the heathen, his w among all people. 6381
105: 5 his w, and the judgments of his mouth; 4159
105:27 among them, and w in the land of Ham. 4159
106: 7 Our fathers understood not thy w in Egypt; 6381
107:24 of the LORD, and his w in the deep. 6381
135: 9 sent tokens and w into the midst of thee, 4159

W

Ps 136: 4 To him who alone doeth great w: for his 6381
Isa 8:18 for w in Israel from the LORD of hosts, 4159
Jer 32:20 hast set signs and w in the land of Egypt, 4159
32:21 with w, and with a strong hand, and with a 4159
Da 4: 2 w that the high God hath wrought toward 8540
4: 3 how mighty *are* his w! his kingdom *is* an 8540
6:27 worketh signs and w in heaven and in earth, 8540
12: 6 How long *shall it be to* the end of *these* w? 6382
Joel 2:30 I will shew w in the heavens and in 4159
Mt 24:24 and shall shew great signs and w; *5059*
Mk 13:22 and shall shew signs and w, to seduce, if *it* *5059*
Jn 4:48 Except ye see signs and w, ye will not *5059*
Ac 2:19 And I will shew w in heaven above, and *5059*
2:22 among you by miracles and w and signs, *5059*
2:43 and many w and signs were done by *5059*
4:30 w may be done by the name of thy holy *5059*
5:12 and w wrought among the people; *5059*
6: 8 did great w and miracles among the people. *5059*
7:36 after that he had shewed w and signs in *5059*
14: 3 and w to be done by their hands. *5059*
15:12 w God had wrought among the Gentiles by *5059*
Ro 15:19 Through mighty signs and w, by the power *5059*
2Co 12:12 in signs, and w, and mighty deeds. *5059*
2Th 2: 9 Satan with all power and signs and lying w, *5059*
Heb 2: 4 both with signs and w, and with divers *5059*
Rev 13:13 And he doeth great w, so that he maketh *4592*

WONDROUS (15) [WONDER]
1Ch 16: 9 unto him, talk you of all his w **works**. 6381
Job 37:14 and consider the w **works** of God. 6381
37:16 the w **works** of *him which is* perfect in 4652
Ps 26: 7 and tell of all thy w **works**. 6381
71:17 and hitherto have I declared thy w **works**. 6381
72:18 God of Israel, who only doeth w *things*. 6381
75: 1 for *that* thy name *is* near thy w **works** 6381
78:32 and believed not for his w **works**. 6381
86:10 and doest w *things*: thou *art* God alone. 6381
105: 2 unto him: talk ye of all his w **works**. 6381
106:22 W **works** in the land of Ham, *and* 6381
119:18 that I may behold w *things* out of thy law. 6381
119:27 thy precepts: so shall I talk of thy w **works**. 6381
145: 5 honour of thy majesty, and of thy w works. 6381
Jer 21: 2 deal with us according to all his w **works**, 6381

WONDROUSLY (2) [WONDER]
Jdg 13:19 *the angel* did w; and Manoah and his wife 6381
Joel 2:26 that hath dealt w with you: 6381+3807.1

WONT (9)
Ex 21:29 if the ox *were* w **to push with his horn** in 5056
Nu 22:30 was I **ever** w to do so unto thee? 5532+5532
1Sa 30:31 and his men were w **to haunt**. 1980
2Sa 20:18 were w **to speak** in old time, saying, 1696+1696
Da 3:19 seven *times* more than *it was* w to be heat. 2370
Mt 27:15 Now at *that* feast the governor was w to *1486*
Mk 10: 1 and, as he was w, he taught them again. *1486*
Lk 22:39 and went, **as** he was w, *1485+2596+3588*
Ac 16:13 river side, where prayer was w to be made; *3543*

WOOD (140) [WOODS, WORMWOOD]
Ge 6:14 Make thee an ark of gopher w; rooms shalt 6086
22: 3 clave the w for the burnt offering, and 6086
22: 6 Abraham took the w of the burnt offering, 6086
22: 7 he said, Behold the fire and the w: but 6086
22: 9 laid the w in order, and bound Isaac his 6086
22: 9 and laid him on the altar upon the w. 6086
Ex 7:19 both in *vessels of* w, and in *vessels of* 6086
25: 5 and badgers' skins, and shittim w, 6086
25:10 they shall make an ark of shittim w: 6086
25:13 thou shalt make staves of shittim w, and 6086
25:23 Thou shalt also make a table *of* shittim w: 6086
25:28 thou shalt make the staves *of* shittim w, 6086
26:15 for the tabernacle *of* shittim w standing up. 6086
26:26 thou shalt make bars *of* shittim w; five for 6086
26:32 four pillars of shittim *w* overlaid with gold: NIH
26:37 for the hanging five pillars of shittim *w*, NIH
27: 1 thou shalt make an altar *of* shittim w, 6086
27: 6 staves of shittim w, and overlay them with 6086
30: 1 *of* shittim w shalt thou make it. 6086
30: 5 thou shalt make the staves *of* shittim w, 6086
35: 7 and badgers' skins, and shittim w, 6086
35:24 with whom was found shittim w for any 6086
35:33 of stones, to set *them*, and in carving of w, 6086
36:20 boards for the tabernacle *of* shittim w, 6086
36:31 he made bars of shittim w; five for 6086
36:36 he made thereunto four pillars of shittim *w*, NIH
37: 1 Bezaleel made the ark *of* shittim w: 6086
37: 4 he made staves of shittim w, and 6086
37:10 he made the table *of* shittim w: two cubits 6086
37:15 he made the staves *of* shittim w, and 6086
37:25 he made the incense altar *of* shittim w: 6086
37:28 he made the staves *of* shittim w, and 6086
38: 1 the altar of burnt offering *of* shittim w: 6086
38: 6 he made the staves *of* shittim w, and 6086
Lev 1: 7 and lay the w in order upon the fire: 6086
1: 8 in order upon the w that *is* on the fire which 6086
1:12 the priest shall lay them in order on the w 6086
1:17 the altar, upon the w that *is* upon the fire: 6086
3: 5 which *is* upon the w that *is* on the fire: 6086
4:12 and burn him on the w with fire: 6086
6:12 the priest shall burn w on it every morning, 6086
11:32 whether *it be* any vessel of w, or raiment, 6086
14: 4 clean, and cedar w, and scarlet, and hyssop: 6086
14: 6 the cedar w, and the scarlet, and the hyssop, 6086
14:49 and cedar w, and scarlet, and hyssop: 6086
14:51 he shall take the cedar w, and the hyssop, 6086
14:52 with the cedar w, and with the hyssop, and 6086
15:12 every vessel of w shall be rinsed in water. 6086
Nu 13:20 or lean, whether there be w therein, or not. 6086
19: 6 the priest shall take cedar w, and hyssop, 6086
31:20 of goats' *hair*, and all things made of w. 6086
35:18 *if* he smite him with a hand weapon of w, 6086
Dt 4:28 w and stone, which neither see, nor hear, 6086
10: 1 into the mount, and make thee an ark of w. 6086
10: 3 I made an ark of shittim w, and hewed two 6086
19: 5 As when *a man* goeth into the w with his 3293
19: 5 into the wood with his neighbour to hew w, 6086
28:36 shalt thou serve other gods, w and stone. 6086
28:64 thy fathers have known, *even* w and stone. 6086
29:11 from the hewer of thy w unto the drawer of 6086
29:17 their idols, w and stone, silver and gold, 6086
Jos 9:21 let them be hewers of w and drawers of 6086
9:23 hewers of w and drawers of water for 6086
9:27 Joshua made them that day hewers of w 6086
17:15 *then* get thee up to the w *country*, and 3293
17:18 for it *is* a w, and thou shalt cut it down: 3293
Jdg 6:26 offer a burnt sacrifice with the w of 6086
1Sa 6:14 they clave the w of the cart, and offered 6086
14:25 all *they of* the land came to a w; and 3293
14:26 when the people were come into the w, 3293
23:15 David *was* in the wilderness of Ziph in a w. 2793
23:16 went to David *into* the w, and 2793
23:18 David abode in the w, and Jonathan went to 2793
23:19 himself with us in strong holds in the w, 2793
2Sa 6: 5 on all *manner of instruments made of* fir w, 6086
18: 6 and the battle was in the w of Ephraim; 3293
18: 8 the w devoured more people that day than 3293
18:17 cast him into a great pit in the w, and laid a 3293
24:22 and *other* instruments of the oxen for w. 6086
1Ki 6:15 *and* he covered *them* on the inside with w, 6086
18:23 lay *it* on w, and put no fire *under*: and I will 6086
18:23 and lay *it* on w, and put no fire *under*: 6086
18:33 he put the w in order, and cut the bullock in 6086
18:33 in pieces, and laid *him* on the w, and said, 6086
18:33 pour *it* on the burnt sacrifice, and on the w. 6086
18:38 the w, and the stones, and the dust, and 6086
2Ki 2:24 there came forth two she bears out of the w, 3293
6: 4 they came to Jordan, they cut down w. 6086
19:18 but the work of men's hands, w and stone: 6086
1Ch 16:33 shall the trees of the w sing out at 3293
21:23 the threshing instruments for w, and 6086
22: 4 they of Tyre brought much cedar w to 6086
29: 2 *things of* iron, and w for *things of* wood; 6086
29: 2 *things of* iron, and wood for *things of* w; 6086
2Ch 2:16 we will cut w out of Lebanon, as much as 6086
Ne 8: 4 Ezra the scribe stood upon a pulpit of w, 6086
10:34 and the people, for the w offering, 6086
13:31 for the w offering, at times appointed, and 6086
Job 41:27 iron as straw, *and* brass as rotten w. 6086
Ps 80:13 The boar out of the w doth waste it, and 3293
83:14 As the fire burneth a w, and as the flame 3293
96:12 shall all the trees of the w rejoice 3293
132: 6 we found it in the fields of the w. 3293
141: 7 one cutteth and cleaveth *w* upon the earth. NIH
Pr 26:20 Where no w is, *there* the fire goeth out: so 6086
26:21 *As* coals *are* to burning coals, and w to fire; 6086
Ecc 2: 6 to water therewith the w that bringeth forth 3293
10: 9 he that cleaveth w shall be endangered 6086

SS 2: 3 As the apple tree among the trees of the w, 3293
3: 9 himself a chariot of the w of Lebanon. 6086
Isa 7: 2 as the trees of the w are moved with 3293
10:15 staff should lift up *itself, as if it were* no w. 6086
30:33 the pile thereof *is* fire and much w; 6086
37:19 but the work of men's hands, w and stone: 6086
45:20 they have no knowledge that set up the w 6086
60:17 and for w brass, and for stones iron: 6086
Jer 5:14 and this people w, and it shall devour them. 6086
7:18 The children gather w, and the fathers 6086
28:13 Thou hast broken the yokes of w; but 6086
46:22 come against her with axes, as hewers of w. 6086
La 5: 4 our water for money; our w is sold *unto us.* 6086
5:13 to grind, and the children fell under the w. 6086
Eze 15: 3 Shall w be taken thereof to do *any* work? or 6086
20:32 of the countries, to serve w and stone. 6086
24:10 Heap on w, kindle the fire, consume 6086
39:10 So that they shall take no w out of the field, 6086
41:16 cieled with w round about, and *from* 6086
41:22 The altar *of* w *was* three cubits high, and 6086
41:22 and the walls thereof, *were of* w: 6086
Da 5: 4 of silver, of brass, of iron, of w, and of stone. 636
5:23 gold, of brass, iron, w, and stone, which see 636
Mic 7:14 which dwell solitarily *in* the w, in the midst 3293
Hab 2:19 Woe unto him that saith to the w, Awake; 6086
Hag 1: 8 and bring w, and build the house; 6086
Zec 12: 6 of Judah like a hearth of fire among the w, 6086
1Co 3:12 silver, precious stones, w, hay, stubble; *3586*
2Ti 2:20 and of silver, but also **of w** and of earth; *3585*
Rev 9:20 and silver, and brass, and stone, and of w: *3585*
18:12 and all thyine w, and all *manner* vessels of *3586*
18:12 and all *manner* vessels of most precious w, *3586*

WOODCUTTER See HEWER

WOODS (1) [WOOD]
Eze 34:25 safely in the wilderness, and sleep in the w. 3293

WOOF (9)
Lev 13:48 Whether *it be* in the warp, or w; of linen, or 6154
13:49 or in the w, or in any thing of skin; 6154
13:51 or in the w, or in a skin, *or* in any work that 6154
13:52 whether warp or w, in woollen or in linen, 6154
13:53 or in the w, or in any thing of skin; 6154
13:56 the skin, or out of the warp, or out of the w: 6154
13:57 or in the w, or in any thing of skin; 6154
13:58 or w, or whatsoever thing of skin *it be,* 6154
13:59 *in* the warp, or w, or any thing of skins, 6154

WOOL (14) [WOOLLEN]
Jdg 6:37 Behold, I will put a fleece of w in the floor; 6785
2Ki 3: 4 and an hundred thousand rams, *with* the w. 6785
Ps 147:16 He giveth snow like w: he scattereth 6785
Pr 31:13 She seeketh w, and flax, and 6785
Isa 1:18 they be red like crimson, they shall be as w. 6785
51: 8 and the worm shall eat them like w: 6785
Eze 27:18 in the wine of Helbon, and white w. 6785
34: 3 eat the fat, and ye clothe you with the w, 6785
44:17 no w shall come upon them, whiles they 6785
Da 7: 9 and the hair of his head like the pure w: 6015
Hos 2: 5 my w and my flax, mine oil and my drink. 6785
2: 9 will recover my w and my flax *given* to 6785
Heb 9:19 and scarlet w, and hyssop, and *2053*
Rev 1:14 His head and *his* hairs *were* white like w, *2053*

WOOLLEN (6) [WOOL]
Lev 13:47 *whether it be* a w garment, or a linen 6785
13:48 *it be* in the warp, or woof; of linen, or of w; 6785
13:52 in w or in linen, or any thing of skin, 6785
13:59 of the plague of leprosy in a garment of w 6785
19:19 a garment **mingled of linen and w** 3610+8162
Dt 22:11 of divers sorts, *as* of w and linen together. 6785

WORD (698) [BYWORD, WORD'S, WORDS]
Ge 15: 1 After these things the w of the LORD 1697
15: 4 the w of the LORD *came* unto him, 1697
30:34 I would it might be according to thy w. 1697
37:14 well with the flocks; and bring me w again. 1697
41:40 according unto thy w shall all my people be 6310
44: 2 he did according to the w that Joseph had 1697
44:18 speak a w in my lord's ears, and let not 1697
Ex 8:10 he said, *Be it* according to thy w: that thou 1697
8:13 the LORD did according to the w of 1697
8:31 the LORD did according to the w of 1697
9:20 He that feared the w of the LORD 1697
9:21 he that regarded not the w of the LORD 1697
12:35 the children of Israel did according to the w 1697
14:12 *Is* not this the w that we did tell thee in 1697
32:28 the children of Levi did according to the w 1697
Lev 10: 7 And they did according to the w of Moses. 1697
Nu 3:16 Moses numbered them according to the w 6310
3:51 his sons, according to the w of the LORD, 6310
4:45 Aaron numbered according to the w of 6310
11:23 thou shalt see now whether my w shall 1697
13:26 brought back w unto them, and unto all 1697
14:20 I have pardoned according to thy w: 1697
15:31 Because he hath despised the w of 1697
20:24 ye rebelled against my w at the water of 6310
22: 8 *this* night, and I will bring you w again, 1697
22:18 I cannot go beyond the w of the LORD 6310
22:20 yet the w which I shall say unto thee, 1697
22:35 only the w that I shall speak unto thee, 1697
22:38 the w that God putteth in my mouth, that 1697
23: 5 the LORD put a w in Balaam's mouth, 1697
23:16 put a w in his mouth, and said, Go again 1697
27:21 at his w shall they go out, and at his word 6310
27:21 at his w they shall come in, *both* he, and 6310
30: 2 he shall not break his w, he shall do 1697
36: 5 of Israel according to the w of the LORD, 6310
Dt 1:22 bring us w again by what way we must go 1697
1:25 unto us, and brought us w again, and said, 1697
4: 2 Ye shall not add unto the w which I 1697
5: 5 to shew you the w of the LORD: 1697
8: 3 by every *w* that proceedeth out of the mouth NIH
9: 5 that he may perform the w which 1697
18:20 which shall presume to speak a w in my 1697
18:21 How shall we know the w which 1697
21: 5 by their w shall every controversy and 6310
30:14 the w *is* very nigh unto thee, in thy mouth, 1697
33: 9 for they have observed thy w, and kept thy 565
34: 5 according to the w of the LORD. 6310
Jos 1:13 Remember the w which Moses the servant 1697
6:10 neither shall *any* w proceed out of your 1697
8:27 according unto the w of the LORD which 1697
8:35 There was not a w of all that Moses 1697
14: 7 I brought him w again as *it was* in mine 1697
14:10 *even* since the LORD spake this w unto 1697
19:50 According to the w of the LORD they 6310
22: 9 according to the w of the LORD by 6310
22:32 of Israel, and brought them w again. 1697
1Sa 1:23 only the LORD establish his w. 1697
3: 1 the w of the LORD was precious in those 1697
3: 7 neither was the w of the LORD yet 1697
3:21 Samuel in Shiloh by the w of the LORD. 1697
4: 1 the w of Samuel came to all Israel. 1697
9:27 a while, that I may shew thee the w of God. 1697
15:10 came the w of the LORD unto Samuel, 1697
15:23 Because thou hast rejected the w of 1697
15:26 for thou hast rejected the w of the LORD, 1697
2Sa 3:11 he could not answer Abner a w again, 1697
7: 4 that the w of the LORD came unto 1697
7: 7 spake I a w with any of the tribes of Israel, 1697
7:25 the w that thou hast spoken concerning thy 1697
14:12 speak *one* w unto my lord the king. 1697
14:17 The w of my lord the king shall now be 1697
15:28 until there come w from you to certify me. 1697
19:10 why **speak** ye **not a** w of bringing the king 2790
19:14 so that they sent *this* w unto the king, NIH
22:31 way *is* perfect; the w of the LORD *is* tried: 565
23: 2 spake by me, and his w *was* in my tongue. 4405
24: 4 Notwithstanding the king's w prevailed 1697
24:11 the w of the LORD came unto the prophet 1697
1Ki 2: 4 That the LORD may continue his w which 1697
2:23 if Adonijah have not spoken this w against 1697
2:27 that *he* might fulfil the w of the LORD, 1697
2:30 Benaiah brought the king w again, saying, 1697
2:42 unto me, The w *that* I have heard *is* good. 1697
3:12 Behold, I have done according to thy w: lo, 1697
6:11 the w of the LORD came to Solomon, 1697
6:12 will I perform my w with thee, which I 1697
8:20 the LORD hath performed his w that he 1697
8:26 of Israel, let thy w, I pray thee, be verified, 1697
8:56 there hath not failed one w of all his good 1697
12:22 the w of God came unto Shemaiah the man 1697
12:24 therefore to the w of the LORD, 1697
12:24 according to the w of the LORD. 1697
13: 1 Judah by the w of the LORD unto Beth-el: 1697
13: 2 he cried against the altar in the w of 1697
13: 5 of God had given by the w of the LORD. 1697

W

1Ki	13: 9	was it charged me by the w of the LORD,	1697
	13:17	For it was said to me by the w of	1697
	13:18	an angel spake unto me by the w of	1697
	13:20	that the w of the LORD came unto	1697
	13:26	who was disobedient unto the w of	6310
	13:26	according to the w of the LORD,	1697
	13:32	For the saying which he cried by the w of	1697
	14:18	for him, according to the w of the LORD,	1697
	16: 1	the w of the LORD came to Jehu the son	1697
	16: 7	came the w of the LORD against Baasha,	1697
	16:12	according to the w of the LORD,	1697
	16:34	according to the w of the LORD, which he	1697
	17: 1	nor rain these years, but according to my w.	1697
	17: 2	the w of the LORD came unto him,	1697
	17: 5	did according unto the w of the LORD:	1697
	17: 8	the w of the LORD came unto him,	1697
	17:16	according to the w of the LORD, which he	1697
	17:24	*that* the w of the LORD in thy mouth *is*	1697
	18: 1	that the w of the LORD came to Elijah in	1697
	18:21	And the people answered him not a w.	1697
	18:31	unto whom the w of the LORD came,	1697
	18:36	*that* I have done all these things at thy w.	1697
	19: 9	the w of the LORD *came* to him, and	1697
	20: 9	and brought him w again.	1697
	20:35	unto his neighbour in the w of the LORD,	1697
	21: 4	of the w which Naboth the Jezreelite had	1697
	21:17	the w of the LORD came to Elijah	1697
	21:28	the w of the LORD came to Elijah	1697
	22: 5	I pray thee, at the w of the LORD to day.	1697
	22:13	let thy w, I pray thee, be like the word of	1697
	22:13	be like the w of one of them, and speak *that*	1697
	22:19	Hear thou therefore the w of the LORD:	1697
	22:38	according unto the w of the LORD which	1697
2Ki	1:16	*is* no God in Israel to inquire of his w?	1697
	1:17	So he died according to the w of	1697
	3:12	The w of the LORD is with him.	1697
	4:44	left *thereof,* according to the w of	1697
	6:18	with blindness according to the w of Elisha.	1697
	7: 1	Elisha said, Hear ye the w of the LORD;	1697
	7:16	a shekel, according to the w of the LORD.	1697
	9:26	*ground,* according to the w of the LORD.	1697
	9:36	he said, This *is* the w of the LORD,	1697
	10:10	the earth nothing of the w of the LORD,	1697
	14:25	according to the w of the LORD God of	1697
	15:12	This *was* the w of the LORD which he	1697
	18:28	spake, saying, Hear the w of the great king,	1697
	18:36	held their peace, and answered him not a w:	1697
	19:21	This *is* the w that the LORD hath spoken	1697
	20: 4	that the w of the LORD came to him,	1697
	20:16	unto Hezekiah, Hear the w of the LORD.	1697
	20:19	Good *is* the w of the LORD which thou	1697
	22: 9	and brought the king w again, and said,.	1697
	22:20	And they brought the king w again.	1697
	23:16	according to the w of the LORD which	1697
	24: 2	according to the w of the LORD,	1697
1Ch	10:13	*even* against the w of the LORD, which he	1697
	11: 3	according to the w of the LORD by	1697
	11:10	according to the w of the LORD	1697
	12:23	to him, according to the w of the LORD.	6310
	15:15	as Moses commanded according to the w of	1697
	16:15	the w *which* he commanded to a thousand	1697
	17: 3	that the w of God came to Nathan, saying,	1697
	17: 6	spake I a w to any of the judges of Israel,	1697
	21: 4	Nevertheless the king's w prevailed against	1697
	21: 6	for the king's w was abominable to Joab.	1697
	21:12	advise thyself what w I shall bring again to	1697
	22: 8	the w of the LORD came to me, saying,	1697
2Ch	6:10	hath performed his w that he hath spoken:	1697
	6:17	LORD God of Israel, let thy w be verified,	1697
	10:15	that the LORD might perform his w,	1697
	11: 2	the w of the LORD came to Shemaiah	1697
	12: 7	the w of the LORD came to Shemaiah,	1697
	18: 4	I pray thee, at the w of the LORD to day.	1697
	18:12	let thy w therefore, I pray thee, be like one	1697
	18:18	Therefore hear the w of the LORD;	1697
	30:12	and of the princes, by the w of the LORD.	1697
	34:16	brought the king w back again, saying,	1697
	34:21	our fathers have not kept the w of	1697
	34:28	the same. So they brought the king w again.	1697
	35: 6	that *they* may do according to the w of	1697
	36:21	To fulfil the w of the LORD by the mouth	1697
	36:22	that the w of the LORD *spoken* by	1697
Ezr	1: 1	that the w of the LORD by the mouth of	1697
	6:11	a decree, that whosoever shall alter this w,	6600
	10: 5	that *they* should do according to this w.	1697
Ne	1: 8	the w that thou commandedst thy servant	1697
Est	1:21	the king did according to the w of	1697
	7: 8	As the w went out of the king's mouth,	1697
Job	2:13	seven nights, and none spake a w unto him:	1697
Ps	17: 4	by the w of thy lips I have kept *me from*	1697
	18:30	the w of the LORD is tried: he *is* a buckler	565
	33: 4	For the w of the LORD *is* right; and all his	1697
	33: 6	By the w of the LORD were the heavens	1697
	56: 4	In God I will praise his w, in God I have	1697
	56:10	In God will I praise *his* w: in the LORD	1697
	56:10	*his* word: in the LORD will I praise *his* w.	1697
	68:11	The Lord gave the w: great *was*	562
	103:20	hearkening unto the voice of his w.	1697
	105: 8	the w *which* he commanded to a thousand	1697
	105:19	Until the time that his w came: the word of	1697
	105:19	word came: the w of the LORD tried him.	565
	105:28	it dark; and they rebelled not against his w.	1697
	106:24	the pleasant land, they believed not his w:	1697
	107:20	He sent his w, and healed them, and	1697
	119: 9	by taking heed *thereto* according to thy w.	1697
	119:11	Thy w have I hid in mine heart, that I might	565
	119:16	in thy statutes: I will not forget thy w.	1697
	119:17	thy servant, *that* I may live, and keep thy w.	1697
	119:25	quicken thou me according to thy w.	1697
	119:28	strengthen thou me according unto thy w.	1697
	119:38	Stablish thy w unto thy servant, who *is*	565
	119:41	*even* thy salvation, according to thy w.	565
	119:42	that reproacheth me: for I trust in thy w.	1697
	119:43	take not the w of truth utterly out of my	1697
	119:49	Remember the w unto thy servant,	1697
	119:50	my affliction: for thy w hath quickened me.	565
	119:58	be merciful unto me according to thy w.	565
	119:65	O LORD, according unto thy w.	1697
	119:67	I went astray: but now have I kept thy w.	565
	119:74	see me; because I have hoped in thy w.	1697
	119:76	according to thy w unto thy servant.	565
	119:81	for thy salvation: *but* I hope in thy w.	1697
	119:82	Mine eyes fail for thy w, saying, When wilt	565
	119:89	O LORD, thy w *is* settled in heaven.	1697
	119:101	every evil way, that I might keep thy w.	1697
	119:105	Thy w *is* a lamp unto my feet, and a light	1697
	119:107	O LORD, according unto thy w.	1697
	119:114	and my shield: I hope in thy w.	1697
	119:116	Uphold me according unto thy w, that I may	565
	119:123	and for the w of thy righteousness.	565
	119:133	Order my steps in thy w: and let not any	565
	119:140	Thy w *is* very pure: therefore thy servant	565
	119:147	of the morning, and cried: I hoped in thy w.	1697
	119:148	that *I* might meditate in thy w.	565
	119:154	deliver me: quicken me according to thy w.	565
	119:158	was grieved; because they kept not thy w.	565
	119:160	Thy w *is* true *from* the beginning: and	1697
	119:161	but my heart standeth in awe of thy w.	1697
	119:162	I rejoice at thy w, as one that findeth great	565
	119:169	give me understanding according to thy w.	1697
	119:170	before thee: deliver me according to thy w.	565
	119:172	My tongue shall speak of thy w: for all thy	565
	130: 5	my soul doth wait, and in his w do I hope.	1697
	138: 2	for thou hast magnified thy w above all thy	565
	139: 4	For *there is* not a w in my tongue, *but* lo,	4405
	147:15	*upon* earth: his w runneth very swiftly.	1697
	147:18	He sendeth out his w, and melteth them:	1697
	147:19	He sheweth his w unto Jacob, his statutes	1697
	148: 8	and vapour; stormy wind fulfilling his w:	1697
Pr	12:25	it stoop: but a good w maketh it glad.	1697
	13:13	Whoso despiseth the w shall be destroyed:	1697
	14:15	The simple believeth every w: but	1697
	15:23	a w *spoken* in due season, how good *is it!*	1697
	25:11	A w fitly spoken *is like* apples of gold in	1697
	30: 5	Every w of God *is* pure: he *is* a shield unto	565
Ecc	8: 4	Where the w of a king *is, there is* power:	1697
Isa	1:10	Hear the w of the LORD, ye rulers of	1697
	2: 1	The w that Isaiah the son of Amoz saw	1697
	2: 3	and the w of the LORD from Jerusalem.	1697
	5:24	despised the w of the Holy One of Israel.	565
	8:10	speak the w, and it shall not stand:	1697
	8:20	if they speak not according to this w, *it is*	1697
	9: 8	The Lord sent a w into Jacob, and it hath	1697
	16:13	This *is* the w that the LORD hath spoken	1697
	24: 3	for the LORD hath spoken this w.	1697
	28:13	the w of the LORD was unto them precept	1697
	28:14	Wherefore hear the w of the LORD,	1697
	29:21	That make a man an offender for a w, and	1697

Isa	30:12	Because ye despise this **w**, and trust in	1697
	30:21	thine ears shall hear a **w** behind thee,	1697
	36:21	held their peace, and answered him not a **w**:	1697
	37:22	This *is* the **w** which the LORD hath	1697
	38: 4	came the **w** of the LORD to Isaiah,	1697
	39: 5	Hear the **w** of the LORD of hosts:	1697
	39: 8	Good *is* the **w** of the LORD which thou	1697
	40: 8	but the **w** of our God shall stand for ever.	1697
	41:28	when I asked of them, could answer a **w**.	1697
	44:26	That confirmeth the **w** of his servant, and	1697
	45:23	the **w** is gone out of my mouth *in*	1697
	50: 4	that *I* should know how to speak a **w** in	1697
	55:11	So shall my **w** be that goeth forth out of my	1697
	66: 2	of a contrite spirit, and trembleth at my **w**.	1697
	66: 5	Hear the **w** of the LORD, ye that tremble	1697
	66: 5	of the LORD, ye that tremble at his **w**;	1697
Jer	1: 2	To whom the **w** of the LORD came in	1697
	1: 4	the **w** of the LORD came unto me, saying,	1697
	1:11	the **w** of the LORD came unto me, saying,	1697
	1:12	for I will hasten my **w** to perform it.	1697
	1:13	the **w** of the LORD came unto me	1697
	2: 1	Moreover the **w** of the LORD came to me,	1697
	2: 4	Hear ye the **w** of the LORD, O house of	1697
	2:31	O generation, see ye the **w** of the LORD.	1697
	5:13	become wind, and the **w** *is* not in them:	1699'
	5:14	Because ye speak this **w**, behold, I will	1697
	6:10	the **w** of the LORD is unto them a	1697
	7: 1	The **w** that came to Jeremiah from	1697
	7: 2	proclaim there this **w**, and say, Hear	1697
	7: 2	say, Hear the **w** of the LORD, all *ye of*	1697
	8: 9	lo, they have rejected the **w** of the LORD;	1697
	9:20	Yet hear the **w** of the LORD, O ye	1697
	9:20	let your ear receive the **w** of his mouth, and	1697
	10: 1	Hear ye the **w** which the LORD speaketh	1697
	11: 1	The **w** that came to Jeremiah from	1697
	13: 2	according to the **w** of the LORD, and	1697
	13: 3	the **w** of the LORD came unto me	1697
	13: 8	the **w** of the LORD came unto me, saying,	1697
	13:12	thou shalt speak unto them this **w**;	1697
	14: 1	The **w** of the LORD that came to Jeremiah	1697
	14:17	Therefore thou shalt say this **w** unto them;	1697
	15:16	thy **w** was unto me the joy and rejoicing of	1697
	16: 1	The **w** of the LORD came also unto me,	1697
	17:15	unto me, Where *is* the **w** of the LORD?	1697
	17:20	Hear ye the **w** of the LORD, ye kings of	1697
	18: 1	The **w** which came to Jeremiah from	1697
	18: 5	the **w** of the LORD came to me, saying,	1697
	18:18	from the wise, nor the **w** from the prophet.	1697
	19: 3	say, Hear ye the **w** of the LORD, O kings	1697
	20: 8	the **w** of the LORD was made a reproach	1697
	20: 9	*his w* was in mine heart as a burning fire	NIH
	21: 1	The **w** which came unto Jeremiah from	1697
	21:11	*say*, Hear ye the **w** of the LORD.	1697
	22: 1	the king of Judah, and speak there this **w**,	1697
	22: 2	say, Hear the **w** of the LORD, O king of	1697
	22:29	earth, earth, hear the **w** of the LORD.	1697
	23:18	and hath perceived and heard his **w**?	1697
	23:18	who hath marked his **w**, and heard *it*?	1697
	23:28	he that hath my **w**, let him speak my word	1697
	23:28	my word, let him speak my **w** faithfully.	1697
	23:29	*Is* not my **w** like as a fire? saith	1697
	23:36	for every man's **w** shall be his burden;	1697
	23:38	Because you say this **w**, The burden of	1697
	24: 4	Again the **w** of the LORD came unto me,	1697
	25: 1	The **w** that came to Jeremiah concerning all	1697
	25: 3	the **w** of the LORD hath come unto me,	1697
	26: 1	of Judah came this **w** from the LORD,	1697
	26: 2	thee to speak unto them; diminish not a **w**:	1697
	27: 1	this **w** unto Jeremiah from the LORD,	1697
	27:18	and if the **w** of the LORD be with them,	1697
	28: 7	Nevertheless hear thou now this **w** that I	1697
	28: 9	when the **w** of the prophet shall come to	1697
	28:12	the **w** of the LORD came unto Jeremiah	1697
	29:10	perform my good **w** towards you, in	1697
	29:20	Hear ye therefore the **w** of the LORD,	1697
	29:30	came the **w** of the LORD unto Jeremiah,	1697
	30: 1	The **w** that came to Jeremiah from	1697
	31:10	Hear the **w** of the LORD, O ye nations,	1697
	32: 1	The **w** that came to Jeremiah from	1697
	32: 6	The **w** of the LORD came unto me,	1697
	32: 8	prison according to the **w** of the LORD,	1697
	32: 8	I knew that this *was* the **w** of the LORD.	1697
	32:26	came the **w** of the LORD unto Jeremiah,	1697
	33: 1	Moreover the **w** of the LORD came unto	1697
	33:19	the **w** of the LORD came unto Jeremiah,	1697
	33:23	Moreover the **w** of the LORD came to	1697
	34: 1	The **w** which came unto Jeremiah from	1697
	34: 4	Yet hear the **w** of the LORD, O Zedekiah	1697
	34: 5	for I have pronounced the **w**, saith	1697
	34: 8	*This is* the **w** that came unto Jeremiah from	1697
	34:12	Therefore the **w** of the LORD came to	1697
	35: 1	The **w** which came unto Jeremiah from	1697
	35:12	came the **w** of the LORD unto Jeremiah,	1697
	36: 1	*that* this **w** came unto Jeremiah from	1697
	36:27	the **w** of the LORD came to Jeremiah,	1697
	37: 6	came the **w** of the LORD unto the prophet	1697
	37:17	and said, Is there *any* **w** from the LORD?	1697
	38:21	this *is* the **w** that the LORD hath shewed	1697
	39:15	Now the **w** of the LORD came unto	1697
	40: 1	The **w** which came to Jeremiah from	1697
	42: 7	that the **w** of the LORD came unto	1697
	42:15	therefore hear the **w** of the LORD,	1697
	43: 8	came the **w** of the LORD unto Jeremiah in	1697
	44: 1	The **w** that came to Jeremiah concerning all	1697
	44:16	*As for* the **w** that thou hast spoken unto us	1697
	44:24	all the women, Hear the **w** of the LORD,	1697
	44:26	Therefore hear ye the **w** of the LORD,	1697
	45: 1	The **w** that Jeremiah the prophet spake unto	1697
	46: 1	The **w** of the LORD which came to	1697
	46:13	The **w** that the LORD spake to Jeremiah	1697
	47: 1	The **w** of the LORD that came to Jeremiah	1697
	49:34	The **w** of the LORD that came to Jeremiah	1697
	50: 1	The **w** that the LORD spake against	1697
	51:59	The **w** which Jeremiah the prophet	1697
La	2:17	he hath fulfilled his **w** that he had	565
Eze	1: 3	The **w** of the LORD came expressly unto	1697
	3:16	that the **w** of the LORD came unto me,	1697
	3:17	therefore hear the **w** at my mouth, and	1697
	6: 1	the **w** of the LORD came unto me, saying,	1697
	6: 3	of Israel, hear the **w** of the Lord GOD;	1697
	7: 1	Moreover the **w** of the LORD came unto	1697
	11:14	Again the **w** of the LORD came unto me,	1697
	12: 1	The **w** of the LORD also came unto me,	1697
	12: 8	in the morning came the **w** of the LORD	1697
	12:17	Moreover the **w** of the LORD came to me,	1697
	12:21	the **w** of the LORD came unto me, saying,	1697
	12:25	the **w** that I shall speak shall come to pass;	1697
	12:25	will I say the **w**, and will perform it,	1697
	12:26	Again the **w** of the LORD came to me,	1697
	12:28	the **w** which I have spoken shall be done,	1697
	13: 1	the **w** of the LORD came unto me, saying,	1697
	13: 2	own hearts, Hear ye the **w** of the LORD;	1697
	13: 6	to hope that *they* would confirm the **w**.	1697
	14: 2	the **w** of the LORD came unto me, saying,	1697
	14:12	The **w** of the LORD came again to me,	1697
	15: 1	the **w** of the LORD came unto me, saying,	1697
	16: 1	Again the **w** of the LORD came unto me,	1697
	16:35	O harlot, hear the **w** of the LORD:	1697
	17: 1	the **w** of the LORD came unto me, saying,	1697
	17:11	Moreover the **w** of the LORD came unto	1697
	18: 1	the **w** of the LORD came unto me again,	1697
	20: 2	came the **w** of the LORD unto me, saying,	1697
	20:45	Moreover the **w** of the LORD came unto	1697
	20:46	drop *thy w* toward the south, and	NIH
	20:47	of the south, Hear the **w** of the LORD;	1697
	21: 1	the **w** of the LORD came unto me, saying,	1697
	21: 2	drop *thy w* toward the holy places, and	NIH
	21: 8	Again the **w** of the LORD came unto me,	1697
	21:18	The **w** of the LORD came unto me again,	1697
	22: 1	Moreover the **w** of the LORD came unto	1697
	22:17	the **w** of the LORD came unto me, saying,	1697
	22:23	the **w** of the LORD came unto me, saying,	1697
	23: 1	The **w** of the LORD came again unto me,	1697
	24: 1	the **w** of the LORD came unto me, saying,	1697
	24:15	Also the **w** of the LORD came unto me,	1697
	24:20	The **w** of the LORD came unto me,	1697
	25: 1	The **w** of the LORD came again unto me,	1697
	25: 3	Hear the **w** of the Lord GOD;	1697
	26: 1	*that* the **w** of the LORD came unto me,	1697
	27: 1	The **w** of the LORD came again unto me,	1697
	28: 1	The **w** of the LORD came again unto me,	1697
	28:11	Moreover the **w** of the LORD came unto	1697
	28:20	Again the **w** of the LORD came unto me,	1697
	29: 1	the **w** of the LORD came unto me, saying,	1697
	29:17	the **w** of the LORD came unto me, saying,	1697
	30: 1	The **w** of the LORD came again unto me,	1697
	30:20	*that* the **w** of the LORD came unto me,	1697
	31: 1	*that* the **w** of the LORD came unto me,	1697

Eze	32: 1	*that* the **w** of the LORD came unto me,	1697
	32:17	*that* the **w** of the LORD came unto me,	1697
	33: 1	Again the **w** of the LORD came unto me,	1697
	33: 7	thou shalt hear the **w** at my mouth,	1697
	33:23	the **w** of the LORD came unto me, saying,	1697
	33:30	hear what *is* the **w** that cometh forth from	1697
	34: 1	the **w** of the LORD came unto me, saying,	1697
	34: 7	ye shepherds, hear the **w** of the LORD;	1697
	34: 9	O ye shepherds, hear the **w** of the LORD;	1697
	35: 1	Moreover the **w** of the LORD came unto	1697
	36: 1	of Israel, hear the **w** of the LORD:	1697
	36: 4	of Israel, hear the **w** of the Lord GOD;	1697
	36:16	Moreover the **w** of the LORD came unto	1697
	37: 4	O ye dry bones, hear the **w** of the LORD.	1697
	37:15	The **w** of the LORD came again unto me,	1697
	38: 1	the **w** of the LORD came unto me, saying,	1697
Da	3:28	have changed the king's **w**, and	4406
	4:17	and the demand *by* the **w** of the holy ones:	3983
	4:31	While the **w** *was* in the king's mouth,	4406
	9: 2	where*of* the **w** of the LORD came to	1697
	10:11	when he had spoken this **w** unto me, I stood	1697
Hos	1: 1	The **w** of the LORD that came unto	1697
	1: 2	The beginning of the **w** of the LORD by	1699'
	4: 1	Hear the **w** of the LORD, ye children of	1697
Joel	1: 1	The **w** of the LORD that came to Joel	1697
	2:11	for *he is* strong that executeth his **w**: for	1697
Am	3: 1	Hear this **w** that the LORD hath spoken	1697
	4: 1	Hear this **w**, ye kine of Bashan, that *are* in	1697
	5: 1	Hear ye this **w** which I take up against you,	1697
	7:16	therefore hear thou the **w** of the LORD:	1697
	7:16	drop not *thy* **w** against the house of Isaac.	NIH
	8:12	run to and fro to seek the **w** of the LORD,	1697
Jnh	1: 1	Now the **w** of the LORD came unto Jonah	1697
	3: 1	the **w** of the LORD came unto Jonah	1697
	3: 3	according to the **w** of the LORD.	1697
	3: 6	For **w** came unto the king of Nineveh, and	1697
Mic	1: 1	The **w** of the LORD that came to Micah	1697
	4: 2	and the **w** of the LORD from Jerusalem.	1697
Hab	3: 9	*to* the oaths of the tribes, *even thy* **w**.	562
Zep	1: 1	The **w** of the LORD which came unto	1697
	2: 5	the **w** of the LORD *is* against you;	1697
Hag	1: 1	came the **w** of the LORD by Haggai	1697
	1: 3	came the **w** of the LORD by Haggai	1697
	2: 1	came the **w** of the LORD by the prophet	1697
	2: 5	*According to* the **w** that I covenanted with	1697
	2:10	came the **w** of the LORD by Haggai	1697
	2:20	again the **w** of the LORD came unto	1697
Zec	1: 1	came the **w** of the LORD unto Zechariah,	1697
	1: 7	came the **w** of the LORD unto Zechariah,	1697
	4: 6	This *is* the **w** of the LORD unto	1697
	4: 8	Moreover the **w** of the LORD came unto	1697
	6: 9	the **w** of the LORD came unto me, saying,	1697
	7: 1	*that* the **w** of the LORD came unto	1697
	7: 4	came the **w** of the LORD of hosts unto	1697
	7: 8	the **w** of the LORD came unto Zechariah,	1697
	8: 1	Again the **w** of the LORD of hosts came	1697
	8:18	the **w** of the LORD of hosts came unto	1697
	9: 1	The burden of the **w** of the LORD in	1697
	11:11	me knew that it *was* the **w** of the LORD.	1697
	12: 1	The burden of the **w** of the LORD for	1697
Mal	1: 1	The burden of the **w** of the LORD to	1697
Mt	2: 8	when ye have found *him,* **bring** me **w again,**	*518*
	2:13	and be thou there until I **bring** thee **w**:	*3004*
	4: 4	by every **w** that proceedeth out of	*4487*
	8: 8	but speak the **w** only, and my servant shall	*3056*
	8:16	and he cast out the spirits with *his* **w**, and	*3056*
	12:32	And whosoever speaketh a **w** against	*3056*
	12:36	That every idle **w** that men shall speak,	*4487*
	13:19	When any one heareth the **w** of	*3056*
	13:20	*places,* the same is he that heareth the **w**,	*3056*
	13:21	or persecution ariseth because of the **w**,	*3056*
	13:22	among the thorns is he that heareth the **w**;	*3056*
	13:22	choke the **w**, and he becometh unfruitful.	*3056*
	13:23	the good ground is he that heareth the **w**,	*3056*
	15:23	But he answered her not a **w**. And his	*3056*
	18:16	three witnesses every **w** may be	*4487*
	22:46	And no *man* was able to answer him a **w**,	*3056*
	26:75	And Peter remembered the **w** of Jesus,	*4487*
	27:14	And he answered him to never a **w**;	*4487*
	28: 8	and did run to **bring** his disciples **w**.	*518*
Mk	2: 2	the door: and he preached the **w** unto them.	*3056*
	4:14	The sower soweth the **w**.	*3056*
	4:15	they by the way side, where the **w** is sown;	*3056*
	4:15	taketh away the **w** that was sown in their	*3056*
	4:16	who, when they have heard the **w**,	*3056*
	4:18	are sown among thorns; such as hear the **w**,	*3056*
	4:19	choke the **w**, and it becometh unfruitful.	*3056*
	4:20	such as hear the **w**, and receive *it,* and	*3056*
	4:33	such parables spake he the **w** unto them,	*3056*
	5:36	As soon as Jesus heard the **w** *that was*	*3056*
	7:13	Making the **w** of God of none effect	*3056*
	14:72	And Peter called to mind the **w** that Jesus	*4487*
	16:20	and confirming the **w** with signs following.	*3056*
Lk	1: 2	were eyewitnesses, and ministers of the **w**;	*3056*
	1:38	the Lord; be it unto me according to thy **w**.	*4487*
	2:29	servant depart in peace, according to thy **w**:	*4487*
	3: 2	the **w** of God came unto John the son of	*4487*
	4: 4	live by bread alone, but by every **w** of God.	*4487*
	4:32	at his doctrine: for his **w** was with power.	*3056*
	4:36	saying, What a **w** *is* this!	*3056*
	5: 1	pressed upon him to hear the **w** of God,	*3056*
	5: 5	nevertheless at thy **w** I will let down	*4487*
	7: 7	but say in a **w**, and my servant shall be	*3056*
	8:11	parable is this: The seed is the **w** of God.	*3056*
	8:12	and taketh away the **w** out of their hearts,	*3056*
	8:13	when they hear, receive the **w** with joy;	*3056*
	8:15	having heard the **w**, keep *it,* and bring forth	*3056*
	8:21	my brethren are these which hear the **w** of	*3056*
	10:39	also sat at Jesus' feet, and heard his **w**.	*3056*
	11:28	blessed *are* they that hear the **w** of God, and	*3056*
	12:10	And whosoever shall speak a **w** against	*3056*
	22:61	And Peter remembered the **w** of the Lord,	*3056*
	24:19	and **w** before God and all the people:	*3056*
Jn	1: 1	In the beginning was the **W**, and the Word	*3056*
	1: 1	and the **W** was with God, and the Word	*3056*
	1: 1	Word was with God, and the **W** was God.	*3056*
	1:14	And the **W** was made flesh, and	*3056*
	2:22	and the **w** which Jesus had said.	*3056*
	4:41	many moe believed because of his own **w**;	*3056*
	4:50	And the man believed the **w** that Jesus had	*3056*
	5:24	He that heareth my **w**, and believeth on him	*3056*
	5:38	And ye have not his **w** abiding in you:	*3056*
	8:31	If ye continue in my **w**, *then* are ye my	*3056*
	8:37	kill me, because my **w** hath no place in you.	*3056*
	8:43	*even* because ye cannot hear my **w**.	*3056*
	10:35	unto whom the **w** of God came, and	*3056*
	12:48	the **w** that I have spoken, the same shall	*3056*
	14:24	and the **w** which you hear is not mine, but	*3056*
	15: 3	Now ye are clean through the **w** which I	*3056*
	15:20	Remember the **w** that I said unto you,	*3056*
	15:25	But *this cometh to pass,* that the **w** might be	*3056*
	17: 6	gavest them me; and they have kept thy **w**.	*3056*
	17:14	I have given them thy **w**; and the world	*3056*
	17:17	them through thy truth: thy **w** is truth.	*3056*
	17:20	which shall believe on me through their **w**;	*3056*
Ac	2:41	Then they that gladly received his **w** were	*3056*
	4: 4	Howbeit many of them which heard the **w**	*3056*
	4:29	with all boldness *they* may speak thy **w**,	*3056*
	4:31	and they spake the **w** of God with boldness.	*3056*
	6: 2	It is not reason that we should leave the **w**	*3056*
	6: 4	to prayer, and to the ministry of the **w**.	*3056*
	6: 7	And the **w** of God increased; and	*3056*
	8: 4	abroad went every where preaching the **w**.	*3056*
	8:14	that Samaria had received the **w** of God,	*3056*
	8:25	and preached the **w** of the Lord,	*3056*
	10:36	The **w** which *God* sent unto the children of	*3056*
	10:37	*That* **w**, *I say,* you know, which was	*4487*
	10:44	Ghost fell on all them which heard the **w**.	*3056*
	11: 1	Gentiles had also received the **w** of God.	*3056*
	11:16	Then remembered I the **w** of the Lord,	*4487*
	11:19	preaching the **w** to none but unto *the* Jews	*3056*
	12:24	But the **w** of God grew and multiplied.	*3056*
	13: 5	they preached the **w** of God in	*3056*
	13: 7	and Saul, and desired to hear the **w** of God.	*3056*
	13:15	if ye have *any* **w** of exhortation for	*3056*
	13:26	to you is the **w** of this salvation sent.	*3056*
	13:44	whole city together to hear the **w** of God.	*3056*
	13:46	It was necessary that the **w** of God should	*3056*
	13:48	were glad, and glorified the **w** of the Lord:	*3056*
	13:49	And the **w** of the Lord was published	*3056*
	14: 3	which gave testimony unto the **w** of his	*3056*
	14:25	And when they had preached the **w** in	*3056*
	15: 7	my mouth should hear the **w** of the gospel,	*3056*
	15:35	teaching and preaching the **w** of the Lord,	*3056*
	15:36	where we have preached the **w** of the Lord,	*3056*
	16: 6	of the Holy Ghost to preach the **w** in Asia,	*3056*
	16:32	And they spake unto him the **w** of the Lord,	*3056*
	17:11	in that they received the **w** with all	*3056*

Ac 17:13 w of God was preached of Paul at Berea, 3056
18:11 teaching the w of God among them. 3056
19:10 in Asia heard the w of the Lord Jesus, 3056
19:20 So mightily grew the w of God and 3056
20:32 you to God, and to the w of his grace, 3056
22:22 And they gave him audience unto this w, 3056
28:25 after that Paul had spoken one w, 4487
Ro 9: 6 Not as though the w of God hath taken 3056
9: 9 For this *is* the w of promise, At this time 3056
10: 8 The w is nigh thee, *even* in thy mouth, and 4487
10: 8 that is, the w of faith, which we preach; 4487
10:17 by hearing, and hearing by the w of God. 4487
15:18 make the Gentiles obedient, by w and deed, 3056
1Co 4:20 For the kingdom of God *is* not in w, but 3056
12: 8 For to one is given by the Spirit the w of 3056
12: 8 to another the w of knowledge by the same 3056
14:36 came the w of God out from you? or 3056
2Co 1:18 our w toward you was not yea and nay. 3056
2:17 not as many, which corrupt the w of God: 3056
4: 2 nor handling the w of God deceitfully; 3056
5:19 hath committed unto us the w of 3056
6: 7 By the w of truth, by the power of God, 3056
10:11 such as we are in w by letters when we are 3056
13: 1 three witnesses shall every w be 4487
Gal 5:14 For all the law is fulfilled in one w, *even* in 3056
6: 6 Let him that is taught in the w 3056
Eph 1:13 *trusted,* after that ye heard the w of truth, 3056
5:26 *it* with the washing of water by the w, 4487
6:17 sword of the Spirit, which is the w of God: 4487
Php 1:14 are much more bold to speak the w without 3056
2:16 Holding forth the w of life; that I may 3056
Col 1: 5 whereof ye heard before in the w of 3056
1:25 given to me for you, to fulfil the w of God; 3056
3:16 Let the w of Christ dwell in you richly in 3056
3:17 And whatsoever ye do in w or deed, *do* all 3056
1Th 1: 5 For our gospel came not unto you in w 3056
1: 6 having received the w in much affliction, 3056
1: 8 For from you sounded out the w of 3056
2:13 when ye received the w of God which *ye* 3056
2:13 ye received *it* not as the w of men, but as it 3056
2:13 of men, but as it is in truth, the w of God, 3056
4:15 For this we say unto you by the w of 3056
2Th 2: 2 or be troubled, neither by spirit, nor by w, 3056
2:15 whether by w, or by our epistle. 3056
2:17 and stablish you in every good w and work. 3056
3: 1 that the w of the Lord may have *free* 3056
3:14 And if any *man* obey not our w by *this* 3056
1Ti 4: 5 For it is sanctified by the w of God and 3056
4:12 in w, in conversation, in charity, in spirit, 3056
5:17 especially they who labour in the w and 3056
2Ti 2: 9 unto bonds; but the w of God is not bound. 3056
2:15 be ashamed, rightly dividing the w of truth. 3056
2:17 And their w will eat as *doth* a canker: 3056
4: 2 Preach the w; be instant in season, out of 3056
Tit 1: 3 But hath in due times manifested his w 3056
1: 9 Holding fast the faithful w as *he* hath been 3056
2: 5 that the w of God be not blasphemed. 3056
Heb 1: 3 upholding all *things* by the w of his power, 4487
2: 2 For if the w spoken by angels was stedfast, 3056
4: 2 but the w preached did not profit them, 3056
4:12 For the w of God *is* quick, and powerful, 3056
5:13 milk *is* unskilful in the w of righteousness: 3056
6: 5 And have tasted the good w of God, and 4487
7:28 but the w of the oath, which was since 3056
11: 3 the worlds were framed by the w of God, 4487
12:19 w should not be **spoken** to them any more: 3056
12:27 And this *w*, Yet once *more,* signifieth NIG
13: 7 who have spoken unto you the w of God: 3056
13:22 brethren, suffer the w of exhortation: 3056
Jas 1:18 Of his own will begat he us with the w of 3056
1:21 and receive with meekness the engrafted w, 3056
1:22 But be ye doers of the w, and not hearers 3056
1:23 For if any be a hearer of the w, and not a 3056
3: 2 If any *man* offend not in w, the same *is* a 3056
1Pe 1:23 by the w of God, which liveth and 3056
1:25 But the w of the Lord endureth for ever. 4487
1:25 And this is the w which by the gospel is 4487
2: 2 desire the sincere milk of the w, 3050
2: 8 *even to them* which stumble at the w, 3056
3: 1 that, if any obey not the w, they also may 3056
3: 1 they also may without the w be won by 3056
2Pe 1:19 We have also a more sure w of prophecy; 3056
3: 5 that by the w of God the heavens were of 3056
3: 7 are now, by the same w are kept in store, 3056
1Jn 1: 1 our hands have handled, of the W of life; 3056
1:10 we make him a liar, and his w is not in us. 3056
2: 5 But whoso keepeth his w, in him verily is 3056
2: 7 The old commandment is the w which ye 3056
2:14 and the w of God abideth in you, and 3056
3:18 let us not love in w, neither in tongue; 3056
5: 7 the Father, the W, and the Holy Ghost: 3056
Rev 1: 2 Who bare record of the w of God, and 3056
1: 9 for the w of God, and for the testimony of 3056
3: 8 and hast kept my w, and hast not denied my 3056
3:10 Because thou hast kept the w of my 3056
6: 9 of them that were slain for the w of God, 3056
12:11 the Lamb, and by the w of their testimony; 3056
19:13 and his name is called The W of God. 3056
20: 4 and for the w of God, and which had not 3056

WORD'S (2) [WORD]

2Sa 7:21 For thy w sake, and according to thine own 1697
Mk 4:17 or persecution ariseth for the w sake, 3056

WORDS (547) [WORD]

Ge 24:30 when he heard the w of Rebekah his sister, 1697
24:52 when Abraham's servant heard their w, 1697
27:34 when Esau heard the w of his father, he 1697
27:42 these w of Esau her elder son were told to 1697
31: 1 he heard the w of Laban's sons, saying, 1697
34:18 their w pleased Hamor, and Shechem 1697
37: 8 yet the more for his dreams, and for his w. 1697
39:17 she spake unto him according to these w, 1697
39:19 when his master heard the w of his wife, 1697
42:16 kept in prison, that your w may be proved, 1697
42:20 so shall your w be verified, and ye shall not 1697
43: 7 told him according to the tenor of these w: 1697
44: 6 and he spake unto them these *same* w. 1697
44: 7 Wherefore saith my lord these w? 1697
44:10 Now also *let* it *be* according unto your w: 1697
44:24 my father, we told him the w of my lord. 1697
45:27 they told him all the w of Joseph, which he 1697
49:21 *is* a hind let loose: he giveth goodly w. 561
Ex 4:15 speak unto him, and put w in his mouth: 1697
4:28 Moses told Aaron all the w of the LORD 1697
4:30 Aaron spake all the w which the LORD 1697
5: 9 and let them not regard vain w. 1697
19: 6 These *are* the w which thou shalt speak 1697
19: 7 laid before their faces all these w which 1697
19: 8 Moses returned the w of the people unto 1697
19: 9 Moses told the w of the people unto 1697
20: 1 And God spake all these w, saying, 1697
23: 8 and perverteth the w of the righteous. 1697
24: 3 told the people all the w of the LORD, 1697
24: 3 All the w which the LORD hath said will 1697
24: 4 Moses wrote all the w of the LORD, and 1697
24: 8 hath made with you concerning all these w. 1697
34: 1 I will write upon *these* tables the w that 1697
34:27 said unto Moses, Write thou these w: 1697
34:27 for after the tenor of these w I have made a 1697
34:28 he wrote upon the tables the w of 1697
35: 1 These *are* the w which the LORD hath 1697
Nu 11:24 told the people the w of the LORD, and 1697
12: 6 he said, Hear now my w: If there be a 1697
16:31 had made an end of speaking all these w, 1697
22: 7 and spake unto him the w of Balak. 1697
24: 4 He hath said, which heard the w of God, 561
24:16 which heard the w of God, and knew 561
Dt 1: 1 These *be* the w which Moses spake unto all 1697
1:34 the LORD heard the voice of your w, and 1697
2:26 Sihon king of Heshbon *with* w of peace, 1697
4:10 and I will make them hear my w, 1697
4:12 ye heard the voice of the w, but saw no 1697
4:36 thou heardest his w out of the midst of 1697
5:22 These w the LORD spake unto all your 1697
5:28 the LORD heard the voice of your w, 1697
5:28 I have heard the voice of the w of this 1697
6: 6 these w, which I command thee *this* day, 1697
9:10 on them *was written* according to all the w, 1697
10: 2 I will write on the tables the w that were in 1697
11:18 Therefore shall ye lay up these my w in 1697
12:28 and hear all these w which I command thee, 1697
13: 3 Thou shalt not hearken unto the w of that 1697
16:19 the wise, and pervert the w of the righteous. 1697
17:19 to keep all the w of this law and 1697
18:18 unto thee, and will put my w in his mouth; 1697
18:19 *that* whosoever will not hearken unto my w 1697
27: 3 thou shalt write upon them all the w of this 1697

W

Dt 27: 8 thou shalt write upon the stones all the w of 1697
27:26 Cursed *be* he that confirmeth not *all* the w 1697
28:14 thou shalt not go aside from any of the w 1697
28:58 If thou wilt not observe to do all the w of 1697
29: 1 These *are* the w of the covenant, which 1697
29: 9 Keep therefore the w of this covenant, 1697
29:19 when he heareth the w of this curse, 1697
29:29 that *we* may do all the w of this law. 1697
31: 1 and spake these w unto all Israel. 1697
31:12 and observe to do all the w of this law: 1697
31:24 end of writing the w of this law in a book, 1697
31:28 that I may speak these w in their ears, 1697
31:30 congregation of Israel the w of this song, 1697
32: 1 and hear, O earth, the w of my mouth. 561
32:44 spake all the w of this song in the ears of 1697
32:45 Moses made an end of speaking all these w 1697
32:46 Set your hearts unto all the w which I 1697
32:46 to observe to do, all the w of this law. 1697
33: 3 at thy feet; *every one* shall receive of thy w. 1703
Jos 1:18 will not hearken unto thy w in all that thou 1697
2:21 she said, According unto your w, so *be* it. 1697
3: 9 and hear the w of the LORD your God. 1697
8:34 afterward he read all the w of the law, 1697
22:30 heard the w that the children of Reuben and 1697
24:26 Joshua wrote these w in the book of the law 1697
24:27 for it hath heard all the w of the LORD 561
Jdg 2: 4 these w unto all the children of Israel, 1697
9: 3 ears of all the men of Shechem all these w: 1697
9:30 when Zebul the ruler of the city heard the w 1697
11:10 if we do not so according to thy w. 1697
11:11 Jephthah uttered all his w before 1697
11:28 unto the w of Jephthah which he sent him. 1697
13:12 Manoah said, Now let thy w come to pass. 1697
16:16 when she pressed him daily with her w, and 1697
1Sa 3:19 and did let none of his w fall to the ground. 1697
8:10 Samuel told all the w of the LORD unto 1697
8:21 Samuel heard all the w of the people, and 1697
15: 1 hearken thou unto the voice of the w of 1697
15:24 commandment of the LORD, and thy w: 1697
17:11 all Israel heard those w of the Philistine, 1697
17:23 and spake according to the same w: 1697
17:31 when the w were heard which David spake, 1697
18:23 Saul's servants spake those w in the ears of 1697
18:26 when his servants told David these w, 1697
21:12 David laid up these w in his heart, and 1697
24: 7 So David stayed his servants with *these* w, 1697
24: 9 Wherefore hearest thou men's w, saying, 1697
24:16 made an end of speaking these w unto Saul, 1697
25: 9 to all those w in the name of David, 1697
25:24 and hear the w of thine handmaid. 1697
26:19 let my lord the king hear the w of his 1697
28:20 sore afraid, because of the w of Samuel: 1697
28:21 have hearkened unto thy w which thou 1697
2Sa 3: 8 was Abner very wroth for the w of 1697
7:17 According to all these w, and according to 1697
7:28 thy w be true, and thou hast promised this 1697
14: 3 unto him. So Joab put the w in her mouth. 1697
14:19 he put all these w in the mouth of thine 1697
19:43 the w of the men of Judah were fiercer than 1697
19:43 were fiercer than the w of the men of Israel. 1697
20:17 unto him, Hear the w of thine handmaid. 1697
22: 1 David spake unto the LORD the w of this 1697
23: 1 Now these *be* the last w of David. 1697
1Ki 1:14 will come in after thee, and confirm thy w. 1697
5: 7 when Hiram heard the w of Solomon, 1697
8:59 let these my w, wherewith I have made 1697
10: 7 Howbeit I believed not the w, until I came, 1697
12: 7 speak good w to them, then they will be thy 1697
13:11 the w which he had spoken unto the king, 1697
21:27 it came to pass, when Ahab heard those w, 1697
22:13 the w of the prophets *declare* good unto 1697
2Ki 1: 7 came up to meet you, and told you these w? 1697
6:12 telleth the king of Israel the w that thou 1697
6:30 when the king heard the w of the woman, 1697
18:20 Thou sayest, (but *they are but* vain w,) 1697
18:27 thy master, and to thee, to speak these w? 1697
18:37 and told him the w of Rab-shakeh. 1697
19: 4 thy God will hear all the w of Rab-shakeh, 1697
19: 4 will reprove the w which the LORD thy 1697
19: 6 Be not afraid of the w which thou hast 1697
19:16 hear the w of Sennacherib, which hath sent 1697
22:11 when the king had heard the w of the book 1697
22:13 concerning the w of this book that is found: 1697
22:13 our fathers have not hearkened unto the w 1697
22:16 *even* all the w of the book which the king 1697
22:18 *As touching* the w which thou hast heard; 1697
23: 2 he read in their ears all the w of the book of 1697
23: 3 to perform the w of this covenant that were 1697
23:16 God proclaimed, who proclaimed these w. 1697
23:24 that he might perform the w of the law 1697
1Ch 17:15 According to all these w, and according to 1697
23:27 For by the last w of David, the Levites 1697
25: 5 of Heman the king's seer in the w of God, 1697
2Ch 9: 6 Howbeit I believed not their w, until I 1697
10: 7 please them, and speak good w to them, 1697
11: 4 they obeyed the w of the LORD, and 1697
15: 8 when Asa heard these w, and the prophecy 1697
18:12 the w of the prophets *declare* good to 1697
29:15 by the w of the LORD, to cleanse 1697
29:30 unto the LORD with the w of David, 1697
32: 8 the people rested themselves upon the w of 1697
33:18 the w of the seers that spake to him in 1697
34:19 when the king had heard the w of the law, 1697
34:21 concerning the w of the book that is found: 1697
34:26 *concerning* the w which thou hast heard; 1697
34:27 when thou heardest his w against this place, 1697
34:30 he read in their ears all the w of the book of 1697
34:31 to perform the w of the covenant which are 1697
35:22 hearkened not unto the w of Necho from 1697
36:16 despised his w, and misused his prophets, 1697
Ezr 7:11 *even* a scribe of the w of 1697
9: 4 that trembled at the w of the God of Israel, 1697
Ne 1: 1 The w of Nehemiah the son of Hachaliah. 1697
1: 4 when I heard these w, *that* I sat down and 1697
2:18 as also the king's w that he had spoken 1697
5: 6 angry when I heard their cry and these w. 1697
6: 6 mayest be their king, according to these w. 1697
6: 7 reported to the king according to these w. 1697
6:19 deeds before me, and uttered my w to him. 1697
8: 9 when they heard the w of the law. 1697
8:12 they had understood the w that were 1697
8:13 even to understand the w of the law. 1697
9: 8 *say,* to his seed, and hast performed thy w; 1697
Est 4: 9 and told Esther the w of Mordecai. 1697
4:12 And they told to Mordecai Esther's w. 1697
9:26 Therefore for all the w of this letter, and 1697
9:30 of Ahasuerus, *with* w of peace and truth, 1697
Job 4: 4 Thy w have upholden him that was falling, 4405
6: 3 the sea: therefore my w are swallowed up. 1697
6:10 for I have not concealed the w of the Holy 561
6:25 How forcible are right w! but what doth your 561
6:26 Do ye imagine to reprove w, and 4405
8: 2 *how long shall* the w of thy mouth *be like* a 561
8:10 *and* tell thee, and utter w out of their heart? 4405
9:14 *and* choose out my w *to reason* with him? 1697
11: 2 Should not the multitude of w be 1697
12:11 Doth not the ear try w? and the mouth taste 4405
15:13 and lettest *such* w go out of thy mouth? 4405
16: 3 Shall vain w have an end? or 1697
16: 4 I could heap up w against you, and 4405
18: 2 long *will it be ere* you make an end of w? 4405
19: 2 my soul, and break me in pieces with w? 4405
19:23 O that my w were now written! O that they 4405
22:22 his mouth, and lay up his w in thine heart. 561
23: 5 I would know the w *which* he would 4405
23:12 I have esteemed the w of his mouth more 561
26: 4 To whom hast thou uttered w? and 4405
29:22 After my w they spake not again; and 1697
31:40 instead of barley. The w of Job are ended. 1697
32:11 Behold, I waited for your w; I gave ear to 1697
32:12 that convinced Job, *or* that answered his w: 561
32:14 Now he hath not directed *his* w against me: 4405
33: 1 hear my speeches, and hearken to all my w. 1697
33: 3 My w *shall be of* the uprightness of my 561
33: 5 set *thy* w in order before me, stand up. NIH
33: 8 I have heard the voice of *thy* w, 4405
34: 2 Hear my w, O ye wise *men;* and give ear 4405
34: 3 For the ear trieth w, as the mouth tasteth 4405
34:16 hear this: hearken to the voice of my w. 4405
34:35 and his w *were* without wisdom. 1697
34:37 and multiplieth his w against God. 561
35:16 he multiplieth w without knowledge. 4405
36: 4 For truly my w *shall* not *be* false: *he that is* 4405
38: 2 Who *is* this that darkeneth counsel by w 4405
41: 3 unto thee? will he speak soft *w* unto thee? NIH
42: 7 that after the LORD had spoken these w 1697
Ps 5: 1 Give ear to my w, O LORD, consider my 561
7: T concerning the w of Cush the Benjamite. 1697

Ps	12: 6	The w of the LORD *are* pure words:	565
	12: 6	The words of the LORD *are* pure w:	565
	18: T	who spake unto the LORD the w of this	1697
	19: 4	and their w to the end of the world.	4405
	19:14	Let the w of my mouth, and the meditation	561
	22: 1	helping me, *and from* the w of my roaring?	1697
	36: 3	The w of his mouth *are* iniquity and deceit:	1697
	50:17	and castest my w behind thee.	1697
	52: 4	Thou lovest all devouring w, O thou	1697
	54: 2	O God; give ear to the w of my mouth.	561
	55:21	*The w of* his mouth were smoother than	NIH
	55:21	his w were softer than oil, yet *were* they	1697
	56: 5	Every day they wrest my w: all their	1697
	59:12	the w of their lips let them even be taken in	1697
	64: 3	*bows to shoot* their arrows, *even* bitter w:	1697
	78: 1	incline your ears to the w of my mouth.	561
	106:12	believed they his w; they sang his praise.	1697
	107:11	Because they rebelled against the w of God,	561
	109: 3	They compassed me about also *with* w of	1697
	119:57	I have said that *I* would keep thy w.	1697
	119:103	How sweet are thy w unto my taste!	565
	119:130	The entrance of thy w giveth light; it giveth	1697
	119:139	mine enemies have forgotten thy w.	1697
	138: 4	when they hear the w of thy mouth.	561
	141: 6	in stony places, they shall hear my w;	561
Pr	1: 2	to perceive the w of understanding;	561
	1: 6	the w of the wise, and their dark sayings.	1697
	1:21	in the city she uttereth her w, *saying,*	561
	1:23	I will make known my w unto you.	1697
	2: 1	if thou wilt receive my w, and hide my	561
	2:16	the stranger *which* flattereth with her w;	561
	4: 4	said unto me, Let thine heart retain my w:	1697
	4: 5	neither decline from the w of my mouth.	561
	4:20	My son, attend to my w; incline thine ear	1697
	5: 7	and depart not from the w of my mouth.	561
	6: 2	Thou art snared with the w of thy mouth,	561
	6: 2	thou art taken with the w of thy mouth,	561
	7: 1	keep my w, and lay up my commandments	561
	7: 5	the stranger *which* flattereth with her w.	561
	7:24	and attend to the w of my mouth.	561
	8: 8	All the w of my mouth *are* in righteousness;	561
	10:19	In the multitude of w there wanteth not sin:	1697
	12: 6	The w of the wicked *are* to lie in wait *for*	1697
	15: 1	away wrath: but grievous w stir up anger.	1697
	15:26	but *the w of* the pure *are* pleasant words.	NIH
	15:26	but *the words of* the pure *are* pleasant w.	561
	16:24	Pleasant w *are as* a honeycomb, sweet to	561
	17:27	He that hath knowledge spareth his w: *and*	561
	18: 4	The w of a man's mouth *are as* deep	1697
	18: 8	The w of a talebearer *are* as wounds, and	1697
	19: 7	he pursueth *them with* w, *yet* they *are*	561
	19:27	*that causeth* to err from the w of knowledge.	561
	22:12	he overthroweth the w of the transgressor.	1697
	22:17	hear the w of the wise, and apply thine	1697
	22:21	thee know the certainty of the w of truth;	561
	22:21	that *thou* mightest answer the w *of* truth to	561
	23: 8	shalt thou vomit up, and lose thy sweet w.	1697
	23: 9	for he will despise the wisdom of thy w.	4405
	23:12	and thine ears to the w of knowledge.	561
	26:22	The w of a talebearer *are* as wounds, and	1697
	29:19	A servant will not be corrected by w:	1697
	29:20	Seest thou a man that is hasty in his w?	1697
	30: 1	The w of Agur the son of Jakeh, *even*	1697
	30: 6	Add thou not unto his w, lest he reprove	1697
	31: 1	The w of king Lemuel, the prophecy that	1697
Ecc	1: 1	The w of the Preacher, the son of David,	1697
	5: 2	thou upon earth: therefore let thy w be few.	1697
	5: 3	a fool's voice *is known* by multitude of w.	1697
	5: 7	and many w *there are* also *divers* vanities:	1697
	7:21	Also take no heed unto all w that are	1697
	9:16	*is* despised, and his w *are* not heard.	1697
	9:17	The w of wise *men are* heard in quiet,	1697
	10:12	The w of a wise *man's* mouth *are* gracious;	1697
	10:13	The beginning of the w of his mouth *is*	1697
	10:14	A fool also is full of w: a man cannot tell	1697
	12:10	Preacher sought to find out acceptable w:	1697
	12:10	*was* written *was* upright, *even* w of truth.	1697
	12:11	The w of the wise *are* as goads, and as nails	1697
Isa	29:11	unto you as the w of a book that is sealed,	1697
	29:18	in that day shall the deaf hear the w of	1697
	31: 2	will bring evil, and will not call back his w:	1697
	32: 7	devices to destroy the poor with lying w,	561
	36: 5	I say, *sayest thou,* (but *they are but* vain w)	1697
	36:12	to thy master and to thee to speak these w?	1697
	36:13	said, Hear ye the w of the great king,	1697
	36:22	and told him the w of Rabshakeh.	1697
	37: 4	thy God will hear the w of Rabshakeh,	1697
	37: 4	will reprove the w which the LORD thy	1697
	37: 6	Be not afraid of the w that thou hast heard,	1697
	37:17	hear all the w of Sennacherib, which hath	1697
	41:26	yea, *there is* none that heareth your w.	561
	51:16	I have put my w in thy mouth, and	1697
	58:13	own pleasure, nor speaking *thine own* w:	1697
	59:13	and uttering from the heart w of falsehood.	1697
	59:21	and my w which I have put in thy mouth,	1697
Jer	1: 1	The w of Jeremiah the son of Hilkiah,	1697
	1: 9	Behold, I have put my w in thy mouth.	1697
	3:12	Go and proclaim these w toward the north,	1697
	5:14	I will make my w in thy mouth fire, and	1697
	6:19	they have not hearkened unto my w,	1697
	7: 4	Trust ye not in lying w, saying, The temple	1697
	7: 8	Behold, ye trust in lying w, *that* cannot	1697
	7:27	Therefore thou shalt speak all these w unto	1697
	11: 2	Hear ye the w of this covenant, and	1697
	11: 3	Cursed *be* the man that obeyeth not the w	1697
	11: 6	Proclaim all these w in the cities of Judah,	1697
	11: 6	Hear ye the w of this covenant, and	1697
	11: 8	I will bring upon them all the w of this	1697
	11:10	which refused to hear my w;	1697
	12: 6	though they speak fair *w* unto thee.	NIH
	13:10	evil people, which refuse to hear my w,	1697
	15:16	Thy w were found, and I did eat them; and	1697
	16:10	thou shalt shew this people all these w,	1697
	18: 2	and there I will cause thee to hear my w.	1697
	18:18	and let us not give heed to any of his w.	1697
	19: 2	proclaim there the w that I shall tell thee,	1697
	19:15	their necks, that *they* might not hear my w.	1697
	22: 5	if ye will not hear these w, I swear by	1697
	23: 9	and because of the w of his holiness.	1697
	23:16	Hearken not unto the w of the prophets that	1697
	23:22	had caused my people to hear my w, then	1697
	23:30	that steal my w every one from his	1697
	23:36	for ye have perverted the w of the living	1697
	25: 8	of hosts; Because ye have not heard my w,	1697
	25:13	I will bring upon that land all my w which I	1697
	25:30	prophesy thou against them all these w,	1697
	26: 2	all the w that I command thee to speak unto	1697
	26: 5	To hearken to the w of my servants	1697
	26: 7	these w in the house of the LORD.	1697
	26:12	against this city all the w that ye have	1697
	26:15	unto you to speak all these w in your ears.	1697
	26:20	against this land according to all the w of	1697
	26:21	and all the princes, heard his w,	1697
	27:12	king of Judah according to all these w,	1697
	27:14	Therefore hearken not unto the w of	1697
	27:16	Hearken not to the w of your prophets that	1697
	28: 6	the LORD perform thy w which thou hast	1697
	29: 1	Now these *are* the w of the letter that	1697
	29:19	Because they have not hearkened to my w,	1697
	29:23	have spoken lying w in my name, which I	1697
	30: 2	Write thee all the w that I have spoken unto	1697
	30: 4	these *are* the w that the LORD spake	1697
	34: 6	Jeremiah the prophet spake all these w unto	1697
	34:18	which have not performed the w of	1697
	35:13	not receive instruction to hearken to my w?	1697
	35:14	The w of Jonadab the son of Rechab,	1697
	36: 2	write therein all the w that I have spoken	1697
	36: 4	mouth of Jeremiah all the w of the LORD,	1697
	36: 6	the w of the LORD in the ears of	1697
	36: 8	reading in the book the w of the LORD *in*	1697
	36:10	read Baruch in the book the w of Jeremiah	1697
	36:11	had heard out of the book all the w of	1697
	36:13	Michaiah declared unto them all the w that	1697
	36:16	to pass when they had heard all the w,	1697
	36:16	We will surely tell the king of all these w.	1697
	36:17	How didst thou write all these w at his	1697
	36:18	He pronounced all these w unto me with	1697
	36:20	and told all the w in the ears of the king.	1697
	36:24	any of his servants that heard all these w.	1697
	36:27	the w which Baruch wrote at the mouth of	1697
	36:28	write in it all the former w that were in	1697
	36:32	w of the book which Jehoiakim king of	1697
	36:32	were added besides unto them many like w.	1697
	37: 2	did hearken unto the w of the LORD,	1697
	38: 1	heard the w that Jeremiah had spoken unto	1697
	38: 4	the people, in speaking such w unto them:	1697
	38:24	Let no man know of these w, and thou shalt	1697
	38:27	he told them according to all these w that	1697

Jer 39:16 I *will* bring my **w** upon this city for evil, 1697
42: 4 the LORD your God according to your **w**; 1697
43: 1 people all the **w** of the LORD their God, 1697
43: 1 God had sent him to them, *even* all these **w**; 1697
44:28 shall know whose **w** shall stand, mine, or 1697
44:29 that ye may know that my **w** shall surely 1697
45: 1 when he had written these **w** in a book at 1697
51:60 *even* all these **w** that are written against 1697
51:61 and shalt see, and shalt read all these **w**; 1697
51:64 be weary. Thus far *are* the **w** of Jeremiah. 1697
Eze 2: 6 neither be afraid of their **w**, though briers 1697
2: 6 be not afraid of their **w**, nor be dismayed at 1697
2: 7 thou shalt speak my **w** unto them, 1697
3: 4 of Israel, and speak with my **w** unto them. 1697
3: 6 whose **w** thou canst not understand. 1697
3:10 all my **w** that I shall speak unto thee receive 1697
12:28 There shall none of my **w** be prolonged any 1697
33:31 they hear thy **w**, but they will not do them: 1697
33:32 for they hear thy **w**, but they do them not. 1697
35:13 and have multiplied your **w** against me: 1697
Da 2: 9 and corrupt **w** to speak before me, 4406
5:10 by reason of the **w** of the king and his lords, 4406
6:14 the king, when he heard *these* **w**, was sore 4406
7:11 of the voice of the great **w** which the horn 4406
7:25 he shall speak *great* **w** against the most 4406
9:12 he hath confirmed his **w**, which he spake 1697
10: 6 the voice of his **w** like the voice of a 1697
10: 9 Yet heard I the voice of his **w**: and when I 1697
10: 9 when I heard the voice of his **w**, then was I 1697
10:11 understand the **w** that I speak unto thee, and 1697
10:12 thy **w** were heard, and I am come for thy 1697
10:12 were heard, and I am come for thy **w**. 1697
10:15 when he had spoken such **w** unto me, I set 1697
12: 4 O Daniel, shut up the **w**, and seal the book, 1697
12: 9 for the **w** *are* closed up and sealed till 1697
Hos 6: 5 I have slain them by the **w** of my mouth: 561
10: 4 They have spoken **w**, swearing falsely in 1697
14: 2 Take with you **w**, and turn to the LORD: 1697
Am 1: 1 The **w** of Amos, who was among 1697
7:10 the land is not able to bear all his **w**. 1697
8:11 but of hearing the **w** of the LORD: 1697
Mic 2: 7 do not my **w** do good to him that walketh 1697
Hag 1:12 the **w** of Haggai the prophet, as the LORD 1697
Zec 1: 6 my **w** and my statutes, which I commanded 1697
1:13 the angel that talked with me *with* good **w** 1697
1:13 me *with* good words *and* comfortable **w**. 1697
7: 7 *Should ye* not *hear* the **w** which 1697
7:12 the **w** which the LORD of hosts hath sent 1697
8: 9 ye that hear in these days these **w** by 1697
Mal 2:17 Ye have wearied the LORD with your **w**. 1697
3:13 Your **w** have been stout against me, 1697
Mt 10:14 nor hear your **w**, when ye depart out of that *3056*
12:37 For by thy **w** thou shalt be justified, and *3056*
12:37 and by thy **w** thou shalt be condemned. *3056*
22:22 When they had heard *these w*, they NIG
24:35 pass away, but my **w** shall not pass away. *3056*
26:44 prayed the third time, saying the same **w**. *3056*
Mk 8:38 and of my **w** in this adulterous and *3056*
10:24 And the disciples were astonished at his **w**. *3056*
12:13 and of the Herodians, to catch him in *his* **w**. *3056*
13:31 pass away: but my **w** shall not pass away. *3056*
14:39 and prayed, and spake the same **w**. *3056*
Lk 1:20 because thou believest not my **w**, *3056*
3: 4 As it is written in the book of the **w** of *3056*
4:22 wondered at the gracious **w** which *3056*
9:26 shall be ashamed of me and of my **w**, *3056*
20:20 *men*, that they might take hold of his **w**, *3056*
20:26 And they could not take hold of his **w** *4487*
21:33 pass away: but my **w** shall not pass away. *3056*
23: 9 Then he questioned *with* him in many **w**; *3056*
24: 8 And they remembered his **w**, *4487*
24:11 And their **w** seemed to them as idle tales, *4487*
24:44 These *are* the **w** which I spake unto you, *3056*
Jn 3:34 For he whom God hath sent speaketh the **w** *4487*
5:47 his writings, how shall ye believe my **w**? *4487*
6:63 the **w** that I speak unto you, *they* are spirit, *4487*
6:68 shall we go? thou hast the **w** of eternal life. *4487*
7: 9 When he had said these *w* unto them, NIG
8:20 These **w** spake Jesus in the treasury, as he *4487*
8:30 As he spake these *w*, many believed on him. NIG
8:47 He that is of God heareth God's **w**: ye *4487*
9:22 These *w* spake his parents, because NIG
9:40 which were with him heard these *w*, NIG
10:21 These are not the **w** of him that hath a *4487*
12:47 And if any *man* hear my **w**, and believe not, *4487*
12:48 that rejecteth me, and receiveth not my **w**, *4487*
14:10 the **w** that I speak unto you, I speak not of *4487*
14:23 If a man love me, he will keep my **w**: *3056*
15: 7 If ye abide in me, and my **w** abide in you, *4487*
17: 1 These *w* spake Jesus, and lift up his eyes to NIG
17: 8 For I have given unto them the **w** which *4487*
18: 1 When Jesus had spoken these *w*, he went NIG
Ac 2:14 this known unto you, and hearken to my **w**: *4487*
2:22 Ye men of Israel, hear these **w**; Jesus of *3056*
2:40 And with many other **w** did he testify and *3056*
5: 5 And Ananias hearing these **w** fell down, *3056*
5:20 speak in the temple to the people all the **w** *4487*
6:11 We have heard him speak blasphemous **w** *4487*
6:13 blasphemous **w** against this holy place, *4487*
7:22 and was mighty in **w** and in deeds. *3056*
10:22 thee into his house, and to hear **w** of thee. *4487*
10:44 While Peter yet spake these **w**, the Holy *4487*
11:14 Who shall tell thee **w**, whereby thou and *4487*
13:42 the Gentiles besought that these **w** might be *4487*
15:15 And to this agree the **w** of the prophets; *3056*
15:24 went out from us have troubled you with **w**, *3056*
15:32 exhorted the brethren with many **w**, and *3056*
16:38 And the sergeants told these **w** unto *4487*
18:15 But if it be a question of **w** and names, and *3056*
20:35 and to remember the **w** of the Lord Jesus, *3056*
20:38 Sorrowing most *of all* for the **w** which he *3056*
24: 4 wouldest hear us of thy clemency a **few w**. *4935*
26:25 but speak forth *the* **w** of truth and *4487*
28:29 And when he had said these *w*, the Jews NIG
Ro 10:18 and their **w** unto the ends of the world. *4487*
16:18 and by **good w** and fair speeches deceive *5542*
1Co 1:17 not with wisdom of **w**, lest the cross of *3056*
2: 4 my preaching *was* not with enticing **w** of *3056*
2:13 not in the **w** which man's wisdom teacheth, *3056*
14: 9 except ye utter by the tongue **w** easy to be *3056*
14:19 Yet in the church I had rather speak five **w** *3056*
14:19 than ten thousand **w** in an *unknown* tongue. *3056*
2Co 12: 4 and heard unspeakable **w**, which *it is* not *4487*
Eph 3: 3 me the mystery; (as I wrote afore in few *w*, NIG
5: 6 Let no *man* deceive you with vain **w**: for *3056*
Col 2: 4 *man* should beguile you with **enticing w**. *4086*
1Th 2: 5 neither at any time used we flattering **w**, *3056*
4:18 comfort one another with these **w**. *3056*
1Ti 4: 6 nourished up in the **w** of faith and of good *3056*
6: 3 and consent not to wholesome **w**, *3056*
6: 3 *even* the *w* of our Lord Jesus Christ, and NIG
6: 4 but doting about questions and **strifes of w**, *3055*
2Ti 1:13 Hold fast the form of sound **w**, which thou *3056*
2:14 that *they* **strive** not **about w** to no profit, *3054*
4:15 for he hath greatly withstood our **w**. *3056*
Heb 12:19 the sound of a trumpet, and the voice of **w**; *4487*
13:22 I have written a letter unto you in few *w*. NIG
2Pe 2: 3 with feigned **w** make merchandise of you: *3056*
2:18 For when they speak great swelling *w* of NIG
3: 2 That *ye* may be mindful of the **w** which *4487*
3Jn 1:10 prating against us with malicious **w**: *3056*
Jude 1:16 their mouth speaketh great swelling *w*, NIG
1:17 remember ye the **w** which were spoken *4487*
Rev 1: 3 and they that hear the **w** of *this* prophecy, *3056*
17:17 until the **w** of God shall be fulfilled. *4487*
21: 5 Write: for these **w** are true and faithful. *3056*
22:18 heareth the **w** of the prophecy of this book, *3056*
22:19 And if any *man* shall take away from the **w** *3056*

WORK (419) [FELLOWWORKERS, HANDYWORK, NEEDLEWORK, NETWORK, NETWORKS, WORK'S, WORKER, WORKERS, WORKETH, WORKFELLOW, WORKING, WORKMAN, WORKMANSHIP, WORKMEN, WORKMEN'S, WORKS, WORKS']

Ge 2: 2 on the seventh day God ended his **w** which 4399
2: 2 he rested on the seventh day from all his **w** 4399
2: 3 that in it he had rested from all his **w** which 4399
5:29 *same* shall comfort us concerning our **w** 4639
Ex 5: 9 Let there more **w** be laid upon the men, 5656
5:11 not ought of your **w** *shall be* diminished. 5656
5:18 Go therefore now, *and* **w**; for there shall no 5647
12:16 no *manner of* **w** shall be done in them, 4399
14:31 Israel saw *that* great **w** which the LORD 3027
18:20 must walk, and the **w** that they must do. 4639
20: 9 days shalt thou labour, and do all thy **w**: 4399
20:10 *in it* thou shalt not do any **w**, thou, nor thy 4399
23:12 Six days thou shalt do thy **w**, and on 4639

W

Ex	24:10	as it were a paved w of a sapphire stone,	4639
	25:18	*of* **beaten w** shalt thou make them, in	4749
	25:31	*of* **beaten w** shall the candlestick be made:	4749
	25:36	all it *shall be* one **beaten w** *of* pure gold.	4749
	26: 1	*with* cherubims *of* cunning w shalt thou	4639
	26:31	scarlet, and fine twined linen *of* cunning w:	4639
	28: 6	fine twined linen, *with* cunning w.	4639
	28: 8	be of the same, according to the w thereof;	4639
	28:11	*With* the w of an engraver in stone, *like*	4639
	28:14	*of* wreathen w shalt thou make them, and	4639
	28:15	breastplate of judgment *with* cunning w;	4639
	28:15	after the w of the ephod thou shalt make it;	4639
	28:22	at the ends *of* wreathen w *of* pure gold.	4639
	28:32	it shall have a binding of woven w round	4639
	31: 4	to w in gold, and in silver, and in brass,	6213
	31: 5	to w in all *manner of* workmanship.	6213
	31:14	for whosoever doeth *any* w therein, that	4399
	31:15	Six days may w be done; but in the seventh	4399
	31:15	whosoever doeth *any* w in the sabbath day,	4399
	32:16	the tables *were* the w of God, and	4639
	34:10	thou *art* shall see the w of the LORD:	4639
	34:21	Six days thou shalt w, but on the seventh	5647
	35: 2	Six days shall w be done, but on	4399
	35: 2	whosoever doeth w therein shall be put to	4399
	35:21	the w of the tabernacle of the congregation,	4399
	35:24	shittim wood for any w of the service,	4399
	35:29	them willing to bring for all *manner of* w,	4399
	35:32	to w in gold, and in silver, and in brass,	6213
	35:33	to make any *manner of* cunning w.	4399
	35:35	to w all *manner of* work, of the engraver,	6213
	35:35	to work all *manner of* w, of the engraver,	4399
	35:35	*even* of them that do any w, and of those	4399
	35:35	and of **those that devise cunning w.**	2803+4284
	36: 1	understanding to know how to w all	6213
	36: 1	*of* w for the service of the sanctuary,	4399
	36: 2	stirred him up to come unto the w to do it:	4399
	36: 3	for the w of the service of the sanctuary,	4399
	36: 4	all the wise *men,* that wrought all the w of	4399
	36: 4	came every man from his w which they	4399
	36: 5	more than enough for the service of the w,	4399
	36: 6	more w for the offering of the sanctuary.	4399
	36: 7	*had* was sufficient for all the w to make it,	4399
	36: 8	w *of* the tabernacle made ten curtains *of*	4399
	36: 8	*with* cherubims *of* cunning w made he	4639
	36:35	*with* cherubims made he it *of* cunning w.	4639
	37:17	*of* **beaten w** made he the candlestick;	4749
	37:22	all of it *was* one **beaten w** *of* pure gold.	4749
	37:29	*according to* the w of the apothecary.	4639
	38:24	All the gold that was occupied for the w in	4399
	38:24	w of the holy *place,* even the gold of	4399
	39: 3	to w *it* in the blue, and in the purple, and	6213
	39: 3	in the fine linen, *with* cunning w.	4639
	39: 5	of the same, according to the w thereof;	4639
	39: 8	he made the breastplate *of* cunning w,	4639
	39: 8	*of* cunning work, like the w of the ephod;	4639
	39:15	at the ends, *of* wreathen w *of* pure gold.	4639
	39:22	he made the robe of the ephod *of* woven w,	4639
	39:27	they made coats *of* fine linen *of* woven w	4639
	39:32	Thus was all the w of the tabernacle of	5656
	39:42	so the children of Israel made all the w.	5656
	39:43	Moses did look upon all the w, and behold,	4399
	40:33	of the court gate. So Moses finished the w.	4399
Lev	11:32	whatsoever vessel *it be,* wherein *any* w is	4399
	13:51	in a skin, *or* in any w that is made of skin;	4399
	16:29	do no w *at all, whether it be* one of your	4399
	23: 3	Six days shall w be done: but the seventh	4399
	23: 3	ye shall do no w *therein:* it *is* the sabbath of	4399
	23: 7	ye shall do no servile w *therein.*	4399
	23: 8	ye shall do no servile w *therein.*	4399
	23:21	ye shall do no servile w *therein: it shall be*	4399
	23:25	Ye shall do no servile w *therein:* but	4399
	23:28	ye shall do no w in that same day: for it *is* a	4399
	23:30	whatsoever soul *it be* that doeth any w in	4399
	23:31	Ye shall do no *manner of* w: *it shall be* a	4399
	23:35	ye shall do no servile w *therein.*	4399
	23:36	*and* ye shall do no servile w *therein.*	4399
Nu	4: 3	to do the w in the tabernacle of	4399
	4:23	to do the w in the tabernacle of	5656
	4:30	to do the w of the tabernacle of	5656
	4:35	for the w in the tabernacle of	5656
	4:39	for the w in the tabernacle of	5656
	4:43	for the w in the tabernacle of	5656
	8: 4	this w of the candlestick *was of* beaten	4639
	8: 4	unto the flowers thereof, *was* **beaten w:**	4749
	28:18	ye shall do no *manner of* servile w *therein:*	4399
	28:25	holy convocation; ye shall do no servile w.	4399
	28:26	holy convocation; ye shall do no servile w:	4399
	29: 1	holy convocation; ye shall do no servile w:	4399
	29: 7	your souls: ye shall not do any w *therein:*	4399
	29:12	ye shall do no servile w, and ye shall keep a	4399
	29:35	ye shall do no servile w *therein:*	4399
	31:20	all w of goats' *hair,* and all things made of	4639
Dt	4:28	the w of men's hands, wood and stone,	4639
	5:13	days thou shalt labour, and do all thy w:	4399
	5:14	*in it* thou shalt not do any w, thou, nor thy	4399
	14:29	in all the w of thine hand which thou doest.	4639
	15:19	thou shalt **do** no w with the firstling of thy	5647
	16: 8	thy God: thou shalt do no w *therein.*	4399
	24:19	may bless thee in all the w of thine hands.	4639
	27:15	the w of the hands of the craftsman, and	4639
	28:12	and to bless all the w of thine hand:	4639
	30: 9	thee plenteous in every w of thine hand,	4639
	31:29	to provoke him to anger through the w of	4639
	32: 4	*He is* the Rock, his w *is* perfect: for all his	6467
	33:11	and accept the w of his hands:	6467
Jos	9: 4	They did w wilily, and went and made as if	6213
Jdg	19:16	there came an old man from his w out of	4639
Ru	2:12	The LORD recompense thy w, and a full	6467
1Sa	8:16	and your asses, and put *them* to his w.	4399
	14: 6	it may be that the LORD will w for us:	6213
1Ki	5:16	Solomon's officers which *were* over the w,	4399
	5:16	ruled over the people that wrought in the w.	4399
	6:35	*them* with gold fitted upon the **carved w.**	2707
	7: 8	within the porch, *which* was of the like w.	4639
	7:14	and cunning to w all works in brass.	6213
	7:14	to king Solomon, and wrought all his w.	4399
	7:17	*And* nets of checker w, *and* wreaths of	4639
	7:17	of checker work, *and* wreaths of chain w,	4639
	7:19	of the pillars *were* of lily w in the porch,	4639
	7:22	upon the top of the pillars *was* lily w: so	4639
	7:22	so was the w of the pillars finished.	4399
	7:28	the w of the bases *was on* this *manner:* they	4639
	7:29	oxen *were certain* additions made of thin w.	4639
	7:31	the mouth thereof *was* round *after* the w of	4639
	7:33	the w of the wheels *was* like the work of a	4639
	7:33	the work of the wheels *was* like the w of a	4639
	7:40	So Hiram made an end of doing all the w	4399
	7:51	So was ended all the w that king Solomon	4399
	9:23	of the officers that *were* over Solomon's w,	4399
	9:23	rule over the people that wrought in the w.	4399
	16: 7	in provoking him to anger with the w of his	4639
	21:20	thou hast sold thyself to w evil in the sight	6213
	21:25	which did sell himself to w wickedness in	6213
2Ki	12:11	into the hands of *them* that did the w,	4399
	19:18	but the w of men's hands, wood and stone:	4639
	22: 5	it into the hand of the doers of the w,	4399
	22: 5	let them give it to the doers of the w which	4399
	22: 9	it into the hand of them that do the w,	4399
	25:17	the **wreathen w,** and pomegranates upon	7639
	25:17	had the second pillar with **wreathen w.**	7639
1Ch	4:23	there they dwelt with the king for his w.	4399
	6:49	*were appointed* for all the w of the *place*	4399
	9:13	very able men *for* the w of the service of	4399
	9:19	*were* over the w of the service,	4399
	9:33	for they were employed in *that* w day and	4399
	16:37	ark continually, as every day's **w required:**	1697
	22:15	*of* cunning *men* for every *manner of* w.	4399
	23: 4	four thousand *were* to set forward the w of	4399
	23:24	that did the w for the service of the house	4399
	23:28	the w of the service of the house of God;	4639
	27:26	over them that did the w of the field for	4399
	28:13	for all the w of the service of the house of	4399
	28:20	until *thou* hast finished all the w for	4399
	29: 1	*is yet* young and tender, and the w *is* great:	4399
	29: 5	for all *manner of* w *to be made* by	4399
	29: 6	with the rulers over the king's w,	4399
2Ch	2: 7	therefore a man cunning to w in gold,	6213
	2:14	skilful to w in gold, and in silver, in brass,	6213
	2:18	six hundred overseers to **set** the people **a w.**	5647
	3:10	house he made two cherubims of image w,	4639
	4: 5	the brim of it like the w of the brim of a	4639
	4:11	Huram finished the w that he was to make	4399
	5: 1	Thus all the w that Solomon made for	4399
	8: 9	did Solomon make no servants for his w;	4399
	8:16	Now all the w of Solomon was prepared	4399
	15: 7	be weak: for your w shall be rewarded.	6468
	16: 5	off building of Ramah, and let his w cease.	4399
	24:12	Jehoiada gave it to such as did the w of	4399

2Ch	24:13	the w was perfected by them, and they set	4399
	29:34	till the w was ended, and until the *other*	4399
	31:21	in every w that he began in the service of	4639
	32:19	*which were* the w of the hands of man.	4639
	34:12	the men did the w faithfully: and	4399
	34:13	*were* overseers of all that wrought the w in	4399
Ezr	2:69	ability unto the treasure of the w threescore	4399
	3: 8	to set forward the w of the house of	4399
	4:24	ceased the w of the house of the God which	5673
	5: 8	this w goeth fast on, and prospereth in their	5673
	6: 7	Let the w of this house of God alone;	5673
	6:22	to strengthen their hands in the w of	4399
	10:13	neither *is this* a w of one day or two:	4399
Ne	2:16	to the rulers, nor to the rest that did the w.	4399
	2:18	strengthened their hands for *this* good *w*.	NIH
	3: 5	their nobles put not their necks to the w of	5656
	4: 6	for the people had a mind to w.	6213
	4:11	and slay them, and cause the w to cease.	4399
	4:15	all of us to the wall, every one unto his w.	4399
	4:16	the half of my servants wrought in the w,	4399
	4:17	*one* with one of his hands wrought in the w,	4399
	4:19	The w *is* great and large, and we *are*	4399
	4:21	So we laboured in the w: and half of them	4399
	5:16	Yea also I continued in the w of this wall,	4399
	5:16	servants *were* gathered thither unto the w.	4399
	6: 3	I *am* doing a great w, so that I cannot come	4399
	6: 3	why should the w cease, whilst I leave it,	4399
	6: 9	Their hands shall be weakened from the w,	4399
	6:16	for they perceived that this w was wrought	4399
	7:70	of the chief of the fathers gave unto the w.	4399
	7:71	of the w twenty thousand drams *of* gold,	4399
	10:33	and *for* all the w of the house of our God.	4399
	11:12	their brethren that did the w of the house	4399
	13:10	the Levites and the singers, that did the w,	4399
Job	1:10	thou hast blessed the w of his hands, and	4639
	7: 2	a hireling looketh for the **reward of** his w:	6467
	10: 3	that thou shouldest despise the w of thine	3018
	14:15	thou wilt have a desire to the w of thine	4639
	23: 9	where he doth w, but I cannot behold *him:*	6213
	24: 5	asses in the desert, go they forth to their w;	6467
	34:11	For the w of a man shall he render unto	6467
	34:19	for they all *are* the w of his hands.	4639
	36: 9	he sheweth them their w, and	6467
	36:24	Remember that thou magnify his w,	6467
	37: 7	every man; that all men may know his w.	4639
Ps	8: 3	the w of thy fingers, the moon and the stars,	4639
	9:16	the wicked is snared in the w of his own	6467
	28: 4	give them after the w of their hands;	4639
	44: 1	*what* w thou didst in their days, in the times	6467
	58: 2	Yea, in heart you w wickedness; you weigh	6466
	62:12	renderest to *every* man according to his w.	4639
	64: 9	shall fear, and shall declare the w of God;	6467
	74: 6	now they break down the **carved** w thereof	6603
	77:12	I will meditate also of all thy w, and talk of	6467
	90:16	Let thy w appear unto thy servants, and	6467
	90:17	establish thou the w of our hands upon us;	4639
	90:17	yea, the w of our hands establish thou it.	4639
	92: 4	LORD, hast made me glad through thy w:	6467
	95: 9	tempted me, proved me, and saw my w.	6467
	101: 3	I hate the w of them that turn aside; *it* shall	6213
	102:25	and the heavens *are* the w of thy hands.	4639
	104:23	Man goeth forth unto his w and to his	6467
	111: 3	His w *is* honourable and glorious: and	6467
	115: 4	*are* silver and gold, the w of men's hands.	4639
	119:126	*It is* time for *thee,* LORD, to w: *for* they	6213
	135:15	*are* silver and gold, the w of men's hands.	4639
	141: 4	to practise wicked works with men that w	6466
	143: 5	all thy works; I muse on the w of thy hands.	4639
Pr	11:18	The wicked worketh a deceitful w: but	6468
	16:11	all the weights of the bag *are* his w.	4639
	18: 9	He also that is slothful in his w *is* brother to	4399
	20:11	whether his w *be* pure, and whether *it be*	6467
	21: 8	strange: but *as for* the pure, his w *is* right.	6467
	24:27	Prepare thy w without, and make it fit for	4399
	24:29	I will render to the man according to his w.	6467
Ecc	2:17	the w that is wrought under the sun *is*	4639
	3:11	that no man can find out the w that God	4639
	3:17	there for every purpose and for every w.	4639
	4: 3	who hath not seen the evil w that is done	4639
	4: 4	I considered all travail, and every right w,	4639
	5: 6	and destroy the w of thine hands?	4639
	7:13	Consider the w of God: for who can make	4639
	8: 9	applied my heart unto every w that is done	4639
	8:11	Because sentence *against* an evil w is not	4639
	8:14	according to the w of the wicked;	4639
	8:14	according to the w of the righteous:	4639
	8:17	I beheld all the w of God, that a man cannot	4639
	8:17	that a man cannot find out the w that is	4639
	9:10	for *there is* no w, nor device,	4639
	12:14	For God shall bring every w into judgment,	4639
SS	7: 1	the w of the hands of a cunning workman.	4639
Isa	2: 8	they worship the w of their own hands,	4639
	5:12	they regard not the w of the LORD,	6467
	5:19	*and* hasten his w, that we may see *it:* and	4639
	10:12	performed his whole w upon mount Zion	4639
	17: 8	not look to the altars, the w of his hands,	4639
	19: 9	Moreover they that w in fine flax, and	5647
	19:14	they have caused Egypt to err in every w	4639
	19:15	Neither shall there be *any* w for Egypt,	4639
	19:25	Assyria the w of my hands, and Israel mine	4639
	28:21	that *he* may do his w, his strange work;	4639
	28:21	that *he* may do his work, his strange w;	4639
	29:14	I will proceed to **do a marvellous** w	6381
	29:14	*even* a **marvellous** w and a wonder:	6381
	29:16	for shall the w say of him that made it,	4639
	29:23	the w of mine hands, in the midst of him,	4639
	31: 2	against the help of them that w iniquity.	6466
	32: 6	his heart will w iniquity, to practise	6213
	32:17	the w of righteousness shall be peace; and	4639
	37:19	but the w of men's hands, wood and stone:	4639
	40:10	reward *is* with him, and his w before him.	6468
	41:24	ye *are* of nothing, and your w of nought:	6467
	43:13	of my hand: I will w, and who shall let it?	6466
	45: 9	makest thou? or thy w, He hath no hands?	6467
	45:11	concerning the w of my hands command ye	6467
	49: 4	with the LORD, and my w with my God.	6468
	54:16	that bringeth forth an instrument for his w;	4639
	60:21	the w of my hands, that *I* may be glorified.	4639
	61: 8	I will direct their w in truth, and I will	6468
	62:11	reward *is* with him, and his w before him.	6468
	64: 8	and we all *are* the w of thine hand.	4639
	65: 7	will I measure their former w into their	6468
	65:22	mine elect shall long enjoy the w of their	4639
Jer	10: 3	the w of the hands of the workman,	4639
	10: 9	the w of the workman, and of the hands of	4639
	10: 9	they *are* all the w of cunning *men.*	4639
	10:15	They *are* vanity, *and* the w of errors: in	4639
	17:22	neither do ye any w, but hallow ye	4399
	17:24	hallow the sabbath day, to do no w therein;	4399
	18: 3	and behold, he wrought a w on the wheels.	4399
	22:13	and giveth him not *for* his w;	6467
	31:16	for thy w shall be rewarded, saith	6468
	32:19	Great in counsel, and mighty in w: for thine	5950
	32:30	me to anger with the w of their hands,	4639
	48:10	Cursed *be* he that doeth the w of	4399
	50:25	for this *is* the w of the Lord GOD of hosts	4399
	50:29	recompense her according to her w;	6467
	51:10	let us declare in Zion the w of the LORD	4639
	51:18	They *are* vanity, the w of errors: in the time	4639
La	3:64	according to the w of their hands.	4639
	4: 2	the w of the hands of the potter!	4639
Eze	1:16	their w *was* like unto the colour of a beryl:	4639
	1:16	their w *was* as it were a wheel in the middle	4639
	15: 3	Shall wood be taken thereof to do *any* w?	4399
	15: 4	midst of it is burnt. Is it meet for *any* w?	4399
	15: 5	when it was whole, it was meet for no w:	4399
	15: 5	much less shall it be meet yet for *any* w,	4399
	16:10	I clothed thee also with **broidered** w, and	7553
	16:13	*of* fine linen, and silk, and **broidered** w;	7553
	16:30	seeing thou doest all these *things,* the w of	4639
	27: 7	Fine linen with **broidered** w from Egypt	7553
	27:16	**broidered** w, and fine linen, and coral, and	7553
	27:24	**broidered** w, and in chests of rich apparel,	7553
	33:26	ye w abomination, and ye defile every one	6213
Da	11:23	after the league *made* with him he shall w	6213
Hos	6: 8	Gilead *is* a city of them that w iniquity, *and*	6466
	13: 2	all of it the w of the craftsmen:	4639
	14: 3	neither will we say any more to the w of	4639
Mic	2: 1	devise iniquity, and w evil upon their beds!	6466
	5:13	thou shalt no more worship the w of thine	4639
Hab	1: 5	for *I will* w a work in your days, *which* ye	6466
	1: 5	for *I will* work a w in your days, *which* ye	6467
	2:18	that the maker of his w trusteth therein,	3336
	3: 2	revive thy w in the midst of the years,	6467
Zep	2:14	for he shall uncover the **cedar** w.	731
Hag	1:14	did w in the house of the LORD of hosts,	4399
	2: 4	of the land, saith the LORD, and w:	6213
	2:14	so *is* every w of their hands; and *that* which	4639

Mal 3:15 yea, they that w wickedness are set up; yea, 6213
Mt 7:23 depart from me, ye that w iniquity. *2038*
21:28 and said, Son, go w to day in my vineyard. *2038*
26:10 for she hath wrought a good w upon me. *2041*
Mk 6: 5 And he could there do no **mighty** w, *1411*
13:34 and to every man his w, and *2041*
14: 6 you her? she hath wrought a good w on me. *2041*
Lk 13:14 are six days in which *men* ought to w: *2038*
Jn 4:34 of him that sent me, and to finish his w. *2041*
5:17 My Father worketh hitherto, and I w. *2038*
6:28 we do, that we might w the works of God? *2038*
6:29 and said unto them, This is the w of God, *2041*
6:30 and believe thee? what dost thou w? *2038*
7:21 I have done one w, and ye all marvel. *2041*
9: 4 I must w the works of him that sent me, *2038*
9: 4 the night cometh, when no *man* can w. *2038*
10:33 saying, For a good w we stone thee not; *2041*
17: 4 I have finished the w which thou gavest me *2041*
Ac 5:38 for if this counsel or this w be of men, *2041*
13: 2 Saul for the w whereunto I have called *2041*
13:41 for I w a work in your days, a work which *2038*
13:41 for I work a w in your days, a work which *2041*
13:41 a w which you shall in no wise believe, *2041*
14:26 grace of God for the w which they fulfilled. *2041*
15:38 and went not with them to the w. *2041*
27:16 **had much** w to come by the boat: *2480+3433*
Ro 2:15 Which shew the w of the law written in *2041*
7: 5 did w in our members to bring forth fruit *1754*
8:28 And we know that all *things* w **together** for *4903*
9:28 For he will finish the w, and cut *it* short in *3056*
9:28 a short w will the Lord make upon *3056*
11: 6 more grace: otherwise w is no more work. *2041*
11: 6 more grace: otherwise work is no more w. *2041*
14:20 For meat destroy not the w of God. *2041*
1Co 3:13 Every man's w shall be made manifest: *2041*
3:13 the fire shall try every man's w of what sort *2041*
3:14 If any *man's* w abide which he hath built *2041*
3:15 If any *man's* w shall be burnt, he shall *2041*
9: 1 our Lord? are not you my w in the Lord? *2041*
15:58 always abounding in the w of the Lord, *2041*
16:10 for he worketh the w of the Lord, as I also *2041*
2Co 9: 8 in all *things,* may abound to every good w: *2041*
Gal 6: 4 But let every man prove his own w, and *2041*
Eph 4:12 For the perfecting of the saints for the w of *2041*
4:19 to w all uncleanness with greediness. *2039*
Php 1: 6 w in you will perform *it* until the day of *2041*
2:12 w **out** your own salvation with fear and *2716*
2:30 Because for the w of Christ he was nigh *2041*
Col 1:10 being fruitful in every good w, and *2041*
1Th 1: 3 Remembering without ceasing your w of *2041*
4:11 and to w with your own hands, *2038*
2Th 1:11 and the w of faith with power: *2041*
2: 7 For the mystery of iniquity doth already w: *1754*
2:17 and stablish you in every good word and w. *2041*
3:10 that if any would not w, neither should he *2038*
3:12 that with quietness they w, and eat their *2038*
1Ti 3: 1 the office of a bishop, he desireth a good w. *2041*
5:10 she have diligently followed every good w. *2041*
2Ti 2:21 *and* prepared unto every good w. *2041*
4: 5 do the w of an evangelist, make full proof *2041*
4:18 Lord shall deliver me from every evil w, *2041*
Tit 1:16 and unto every good w reprobate. *2041*
3: 1 to be ready to every good w, *2041*
Heb 6:10 For God *is* not unrighteous to forget your w *2041*
13:21 Make you perfect in every good w to do his *2041*
Jas 1: 4 But let patience have *her* perfect w, that ye *2041*
1:25 but a doer of the w, this *man* shall be *2041*
3:16 *is,* there *is* confusion and every evil w. *4229*
1Pe 1:17 judgeth according to every man's w, *2041*
Rev 22:12 to give every man according as his w shall *2041*

WORK'S (1) [WORK]

1Th 5:13 them very highly in love for their w sake. *2041*

WORKER (1) [WORK]

1Ki 7:14 his father *was* a man of Tyre, a w in brass: 2790

WORKERS (27) [WORK]

2Ki 23:24 Moreover the *w with* familiar spirits, and NIH
1Ch 22:15 hewers and w of stone and timber, and 2796
Job 31: 3 a strange punishment to the w of iniquity? 6466
34: 8 Which goeth in company with the w of 6466
34:22 where the w of iniquity may hide 6466
Ps 5: 5 in thy sight: thou hatest all w of iniquity. 6466
6: 8 Depart from me, all ye w of iniquity; 6466
14: 4 Have all the w of iniquity no knowledge? 6466
28: 3 with the wicked, and with the w of iniquity, 6466
36:12 There are the w of iniquity fallen: they are 6466
37: 1 neither be thou envious against the w of 6213
53: 4 Have the w of iniquity no knowledge? 6466
59: 2 Deliver me from the w of iniquity, and 6466
64: 2 from the insurrection of the w of iniquity: 6466
92: 7 and when all the w of iniquity do flourish; 6466
92: 9 all the w of iniquity shall be scattered. 6466
94: 4 *and* all the w of iniquity boast themselves? 6466
94:16 who will stand up for me against the w of 6466
125: 5 shall lead them forth with the w of iniquity: 6466
141: 9 for me, and the grins of the w of iniquity. 6466
Pr 10:29 but destruction *shall be* to the w of iniquity. 6466
21:15 but destruction *shall be* to the w of iniquity. 6466
Lk 13:27 depart from me, all *ye* w of iniquity. *2040*
1Co 12:29 *are* all teachers? *are* all w **of miracles**? *1411*
2Co 6: 1 *as* w **together** *with him,* beseech *you* also *4903*
11:13 For such *are* false apostles, deceitful w, *2040*
Php 3: 2 Beware of dogs, beware of evil w, *2040*

WORKETH (37) [WORK]

Job 33:29 all these *things* w God oftentimes with 6466
Ps 15: 2 w righteousness, and speaketh the truth in 6466
101: 7 He that w deceit shall not dwell within my 6213
Pr 11:18 The wicked w a deceitful work: but *to* him 6213
26:28 by it; and a flattering mouth w ruin. 6213
31:13 and flax, and w willingly with her hands. 6213
Ecc 3: 9 What profit *hath* he that w in *that* wherein 6213
Isa 44:12 The smith *with* the tongs both w in 6466
44:12 and w it with the strength of his arms: 6466
64: 5 him that rejoiceth and w righteousness, 6213
Da 6:27 he w signs and wonders in heaven and 5648
Jn 5:17 answered them, My Father w hitherto, *2038*
Ac 10:35 and w righteousness, is accepted with him. *2038*
Ro 2:10 and peace, to every *man* that w good, *2038*
4: 4 Now to him that w is the reward not *2038*
4: 5 But to him that w not, but believeth on him *2038*
4:15 Because the law w wrath: for where no law *2716*
5: 3 knowing that tribulation w patience; *2716*
13:10 Love w no ill to *his* neighbour: therefore *2038*
1Co 12: 6 but it is the same God which w all in all. *1754*
12:11 But all these w *that* one and the selfsame *1754*
16:10 for he w the work of the Lord, as I also *do.* *2038*
2Co 4:12 So then death w in us, but life in you. *1754*
4:17 w for us a far more exceeding *and* *2716*
7:10 For godly sorrow w repentance to salvation *2716*
7:10 but the sorrow of the world w death. *2716*
Gal 3: 5 you the Spirit, and w miracles among you, *1754*
5: 6 but faith which w by love. *1754*
Eph 1:11 w all *things* after the counsel of his own *1754*
2: 2 the spirit that now w in the children of *1754*
3:20 think, according to the power that w in us, *1754*
Php 2:13 For it is God which w in you both to will *1754*
Col 1:29 to his working, which w in me mightily. *1754*
1Th 2:13 which **effectually** w also in you that *1754*
Jas 1: 3 that the trying of your faith w patience. *2716*
1:20 For the wrath of man w not *2716*
Rev 21:27 neither *whatsoever* w abomination, or *4160*

WORKFELLOW (1) [FELLOW, WORK]

Ro 16:21 Timotheus my w, and Lucius, and Jason, *4904*

WORKING (20) [WORK]

Ps 52: 2 like a sharp rasor, w deceitfully. 6213
74:12 of old, w salvation in the midst of the earth. 6466
Isa 28:29 is wonderful in counsel, *and* excellent in w. 8454
Eze 46: 1 *toward* the east shall be shut the six w days; 4639
Mk 16:20 the Lord w **with** *them,* and confirming *4903*
Ro 1:27 men with men w that which is unseemly, *2716*
7:13 w death in me by that which is good; *2716*
1Co 4:12 And labour, w with our own hands: *2038*
9: 6 Barnabas, have not we power to forbear w? *2038*
12:10 To another the w of miracles; to another *1755*
Eph 1:19 according to the w of his mighty power, *1753*
3: 7 unto me by the **effectual** w of his power. *1753*
4:16 according to the **effectual** w in the measure *1753*
4:28 w with *his* hands the *thing which is* good, *2038*
Php 3:21 according to the w whereby he is able even *1753*
Col 1:29 I also labour, striving according to his w, *1753*
2Th 2: 9 *Even him,* whose coming is after the w of *1753*
3:11 w not at all, but are busybodies. *2038*
Heb 13:21 w in you *that which is* well pleasing in his *4160*

Rev 16:14 they are the spirits of devils, **w** miracles, *4160*

WORKMAN (10) [MAN, WORK]
Ex 35:35 of the **cunning w**, and of the embroiderer, 2803
38:23 a **cunning w**, and an embroiderer in blue, 2803
SS 7: 1 the work of the hands of a **cunning w**. 542
Isa 40:19 The **w** melteth a graven image, and 2796
40:20 he seeketh unto him a cunning **w** to prepare 2796
Jer 10: 3 the work of the hands of the **w**, with 2796
10: 9 the work of the **w**, and of the hands of 2796
Hos 8: 6 the **w** made it; therefore it *is* not God: but 2796
Mt 10:10 yet staves: for the **w** is worthy of his meat. *2040*
2Ti 2:15 a **w** that needeth not to be ashamed, *2040*

WORKMANSHIP (7) [MAN, WORK]
Ex 31: 3 and in knowledge, and in all *manner of* **w**, 4399
31: 5 of timber, to work in all *manner of* **w**. 4399
35:31 and in knowledge, and in all *manner of* **w**; 4399
2Ki 16:10 pattern of it, according to all the **w** thereof. 4639
1Ch 28:21 *there shall be* with thee for all *manner of* **w** 4399
Eze 28:13 the **w** of thy tabrets and of thy pipes was 4399
Eph 2:10 For we are his **w**, created in Christ Jesus *4161*

WORKMEN (11) [MAN, WORK]
2Ki 12:14 they gave that to the **w**, and 4399+6213
12:15 the money to be bestowed on **w**: 4399+6213
1Ch 22:15 Moreover *there are* **w** with thee in 4399+6213
25: 1 the number of the **w** according to their 376+4399
2Ch 24:13 So the **w** wrought, and 4399+6213+1886.1
34:10 **w** that had the oversight of 4399+6213+1886.1
34:10 they gave it *to* the **w** that 4399+6213+1886.1
34:17 and to the hand of the **w**. 4399+6213+1886.1
Ezr 3: 9 to set forward the **w** in the house of God: 6213
Isa 44:11 the **w**, they *are* of men: let them all be 2796
Ac 19:25 Whom he called together with the **w** of like *2040*

WORKMEN'S (1) [MAN, WORK]
Jdg 5:26 and her right hand to the **w** hammer; 6001

WORKS (236) [WORK]
Ex 5: 4 and Aaron, let the people from their **w**? 4639
5:13 Fulfil your **w**, *your* daily tasks, as when 4639
23:24 nor serve them, nor do after their **w**: 4639
31: 4 To devise **cunning w**, to work in gold, and 4284
35:32 to devise **curious w**, to work in gold, and 4284
Nu 16:28 the LORD hath sent me to do all these **w**; 4639
Dt 2: 7 hath blessed thee in all the **w** of thy hand: 4639
3:24 that can do according to thy **w**, and 4639
15:10 thy God shall bless thee in all thy **w**, 4639
16:15 in all the **w** of thine hands, therefore 4639
Jos 24:31 which had known all the **w** of the LORD, 4639
Jdg 2: 7 who had seen all the great **w** of 4639
2:10 nor yet the **w** which he had done for Israel. 4639
1Sa 8: 8 According to all the **w** which they have 4639
19: 4 his **w** *have been* to thee-ward very good: 4639
1Ki 7:14 and cunning to work all **w** in brass. 4399
13:11 told him all the **w** that the man of God had 4639
2Ki 22:17 me to anger with all the **w** of their hands; 4639
1Ch 16: 9 unto him, talk you of all his **wondrous w**. 6381
16:12 Remember his **marvellous w** that he hath 6381
16:24 his **marvellous w** among all nations. 6381
28:19 upon me, *even* all the **w** of *this* pattern. 4399
2Ch 20:37 the LORD hath broken thy **w**. 4639
32:30 And Hezekiah prospered in all his **w**. 4639
34:25 me to anger with all the **w** of their hands; 4639
Ne 6:14 and Sanballat according to these their **w**, 4639
9:35 neither turned they from their wicked **w**. 4611
Job 34:25 Therefore he knoweth their **w**, and 4566
37:14 and consider the **wondrous w** of God. 6381
37:16 the **wondrous w** of *him which is* perfect in 4652
Ps 8: 6 to have dominion over the **w** of thy hands; 4639
9: 1 I will shew forth all thy **marvellous w**. 6381
14: 1 are corrupt, they have done abominable **w**, 5949
17: 4 Concerning the **w** of men, by the word of 6468
26: 7 and tell of all thy **wondrous w**. 6381
28: 5 Because they regard not the **w** of 6468
33: 4 *is* right; and all his **w** *are done* in truth. 4639
33:15 their hearts alike; he considereth all their **w**. 4639
40: 5 *are* thy **wonderful w** *which* thou hast done, 6381
46: 8 Come, behold the **w** of the LORD, 4659
66: 3 unto God, How terrible *art thou in* thy **w**! 4639
66: 5 Come and see the **w** of God: *he is* terrible 4659
71:17 hitherto have I declared thy **wondrous w**. 6381
73:28 Lord GOD, that *I* may declare all thy **w**. 4399
75: 1 for *that* thy name *is* near thy **wondrous w** 6381
77:11 I will remember the **w** of the LORD: 4611
78: 4 and his **wonderful w** that he hath done. 6381
78: 7 not forget the **w** of God, but keep his 4611
78:11 forgat his **w**, and his wonders that he had 5949
78:32 and believed not for his **wondrous w**. 6381
86: 8 neither *are there any* **w** like unto thy works. NIH
86: 8 neither *are there any works* like unto thy **w**. 4639
92: 4 I will triumph in the **w** of thy hands. 4639
92: 5 O LORD, how great are thy **w**! *and* 4639
103:22 all his **w** in all places of his dominion: 4639
104:13 the earth is satisfied with the fruit of thy **w**. 4639
104:24 O LORD, how manifold are thy **w**! 4639
104:31 for ever: the LORD shall rejoice in his **w**. 4639
105: 2 unto him: talk ye of all his **wondrous w**. 6381
105: 5 Remember his **marvellous w** that he hath 6381
106:13 They soon forgat his **w**; they waited not for 4639
106:22 **Wondrous w** in the land of Ham, *and* 6381
106:35 among the heathen, and learned their **w**. 4639
106:39 Thus were they defiled with their own **w**, 4639
107: 8 *for* his **wonderful w** to the children of 6381
107:15 *for* his **wonderful w** to the children of 6381
107:21 *for* his **wonderful w** to the children of 6381
107:22 and declare his **w** with rejoicing. 4639
107:24 These see the **w** of the LORD, and 4639
107:31 *for* his **wonderful w** to the children of 6381
111: 2 The **w** of the LORD *are* great, sought out 4639
111: 4 He hath made his **wonderful w** to be 6381
111: 6 hath shewed his people the power of his **w**, 4639
111: 7 The **w** of his hands *are* verity and 4639
118:17 but live, and declare the **w** of the LORD. 4639
119:27 so shall I talk of thy **wondrous w**. 6381
138: 8 forsake not the **w** of thine own hands. 4639
139:14 marvellous *are* thy **w**; and *that* my soul 4639
141: 4 to practise wicked **w** with men that work 5949
143: 5 the days of old; I meditate on all thy **w**; 6467
145: 4 One generation shall praise thy **w** to 4639
145: 5 of thy majesty, and of thy wondrous **w**. 1697
145: 9 and his tender mercies *are* over all his **w**. 4639
145:10 All thy **w** shall praise thee, O LORD; and 4639
145:17 in all his ways, and holy in all his **w**. 4639
Pr 7:16 *with* carved **w**, *with* fine linen of Egypt. NIH
8:22 beginning of his way, before his **w** of old. 4659
16: 3 Commit thy **w** unto the LORD, and 4639
24:12 he render to *every* man according to his **w**? 6467
31:31 and let her own **w** praise her in the gates. 4639
Ecc 1:14 I have seen all the **w** that are done under 4639
2: 4 I made me great **w**; I builded me houses; 4639
2:11 I looked on all the **w** that my hands had 4639
3:22 that a man should rejoice in his own **w**; 4639
9: 1 the righteous, and the wise, and their **w**, 5652
9: 7 merry heart; for God now accepteth thy **w**. 4639
11: 5 thou knowest not the **w** of God who maketh 4639
Isa 26:12 for thou also hast wrought all our **w** in us. 4639
29:15 their **w** are in the dark, and they say, 4639
41:29 they *are* all vanity; their **w** *are* nothing: 4639
57:12 I will declare thy righteousness, and thy **w**; 4639
59: 6 shall they cover themselves with their **w**: 4639
59: 6 their **w** *are* works of iniquity, and the act of 4639
59: 6 their works *are* **w** of iniquity, and the act of 4639
66:18 For I *know* their **w** and their thoughts: 4639
Jer 1:16 and worshipped the **w** of their own hands. 4639
7:13 because ye have done all these **w**, 4639
21: 2 with us according to all his **wondrous w**, 6381
25: 6 provoke me not to anger with the **w** of your 4639
25: 7 with the **w** of your hands to your own hurt. 4639
25:14 and according to the **w** of their own hands. 4639
44: 8 me unto wrath with the **w** of your hands, 4639
48: 7 For because thou hast trusted in thy **w** and 4639
Eze 6: 6 be cut down, and your **w** may be abolished. 4639
Da 4:37 all whose **w** *are* truth, and his ways 4567
9:14 *is* righteous in all his **w** which he doeth: 4639
Am 8: 7 Surely I will never forget any of their **w**. 4639
Jnh 3:10 God saw their **w**, that they turned from 4639
Mic 6:16 all the **w** of the house of Ahab, and ye walk 4639
Mt 5:16 that they may see your good **w**, and *2041*
7:22 and in thy name done many **wonderful w**? *1411*
11: 2 had heard in the prison the **w** of Christ, *2041*
11:20 wherein most of his **mighty w** were done, *1411*
11:21 for if the **mighty w** which were done in *1411*
11:23 for if the **mighty w**, which have been done *1411*
13:54 this *man* this wisdom, and *these* **mighty w**? *1411*
13:58 And he did not many **mighty w** there, *1411*
14: 2 **mighty w** do shew forth themselves in him. *1411*

Mt 16:27 shall reward every man according to his **w**. *4234*
23: 3 and do; but do not ye after their **w**: *2041*
23: 5 But all their **w** they do for to be seen of *2041*
Mk 6: 2 that even such **mighty w** are wrought by *1411*
6:14 **mighty w** do shew forth themselves in him. *1411*
Lk 10:13 for if the **mighty w** had been done in Tyre *1411*
19:37 for all the **mighty w** that they had seen; *1411*
Jn 5:20 and he will shew him greater **w** than these, *2041*
5:36 for the **w** which the Father hath given me to *2041*
5:36 the same **w** that I do, bear witness of me, *2041*
6:28 we do, that we might work the **w** of God? *2041*
7: 3 that thy disciples also may see the **w** that *2041*
7: 7 I testify of it, that the **w** thereof are evil. *2041*
8:39 ye would do the **w** of Abraham. *2041*
9: 3 that the **w** of God should be made manifest *2041*
9: 4 I must work the **w** of him that sent me, *2041*
10:25 the **w** that I do in my Father's name, *2041*
10:32 Many good **w** have I shewed you from my *2041*
10:32 for which of those **w** do ye stone me? *2041*
10:37 If I do not the **w** of my Father, believe me *2041*
10:38 though ye believe not me, believe the **w**: *2041*
14:10 Father that dwelleth in me, he doeth the **w**. *2041*
14:12 on me, the **w** that I do shall he do also; *2041*
14:12 and greater *w* than these shall he do; NIG
15:24 If I had not done among them the **w** which *2041*
Ac 2:11 in our tongues the **wonderful w** of God. *3167*
7:41 and rejoiced in the **w** of their own hands. *2041*
9:36 this *woman* was full of good **w** and *2041*
15:18 Known unto God are all his **w** from *2041*
26:20 turn to God, and do **w** meet for repentance. *2041*
Ro 3:27 of **w**? Nay: but by the law of faith. *2041*
4: 2 For if Abraham were justified by **w**, he hath *2041*
4: 6 God imputeth righteousness without **w**, *2041*
9:11 not of **w**, but of him that calleth;) *2041*
9:32 by faith, but as *it were* by the **w** of the law. *2041*
11: 6 And if by grace, *then is it* no more of **w**: *2041*
11: 6 But if *it be* of **w**, *then* is it no more grace: *2041*
13: 3 For rulers are not a terror to good **w**, but *2041*
13:12 let us therefore cast off the **w** of darkness, *2041*
2Co 11:15 whose end shall be according to their **w**. *2041*
Gal 2:16 a man is not justified by the **w** of the law, *2041*
2:16 faith of Christ, and not by the **w** of the law: *2041*
2:16 for by the **w** of the law shall no flesh be *2041*
3: 2 Received ye the Spirit by the **w** of the law, *2041*
3: 5 *doeth he it* by the **w** of the law, or by *2041*
3:10 For as many as are of the **w** of the law are *2041*
5:19 Now the **w** of the flesh are manifest, *2041*
Eph 2: 9 Not of **w**, lest any *man* should boast. *2041*
2:10 created in Christ Jesus unto good **w**, *2041*
5:11 with the unfruitful **w** of darkness, *2041*
Col 1:21 and enemies in *your* mind by wicked **w**, *2041*
1Ti 2:10 women professing godliness) with good **w**. *2041*
5:10 Well reported of for good **w**; if she have *2041*
5:25 Likewise also the good **w** *of some* are *2041*
6:18 that *they* be rich in good **w**, ready to *2041*
2Ti 1: 9 not according to our **w**, but according to his *2041*
3:17 throughly furnished unto all good **w**. *2041*
4:14 the Lord reward him according to his **w**: *2041*
Tit 1:16 but in **w** they deny *him*, being abominable, *2041*
2: 7 *things* shewing thyself a pattern of good **w**: *2041*
2:14 a peculiar people, zealous of good **w**. *2041*
3: 5 Not by **w** of righteousness which we have *2041*
3: 8 God might be careful to maintain good **w**. *2041*
3:14 And let ours also learn to maintain good **w** *2041*
Heb 1:10 and the heavens are the **w** of thine hands: *2041*
2: 7 and didst set him over the **w** of thy hands: *2041*
3: 9 proved me, and saw my **w** forty years. *2041*
4: 3 although the **w** were finished from *2041*
4: 4 God did rest the seventh day from all his **w**. *2041*
4:10 he also hath ceased from his own **w**, as God *2041*
6: 1 the foundation of repentance from dead **w**, *2041*
9:14 purge your conscience from dead **w** to *2041*
10:24 to provoke unto love and to good **w**: *2041*
Jas 2:14 a man say *he* hath faith, and have not **w**? *2041*
2:17 Even so faith, if it hath not **w**, is dead, *2041*
2:18 may say, Thou hast faith, and I have **w**: *2041*
2:18 shew me thy faith without thy **w**, and I will *2041*
2:18 and I will shew thee my faith by my **w**. *2041*
2:20 O vain man, that faith without **w** is dead? *2041*
2:21 Was not Abraham our father justified by **w**, *2041*
2:22 Seest thou how faith wrought with his **w**, *2041*
2:22 and by **w** was faith made perfect? *2041*
2:24 then how that by **w** a man is justified, *2041*
2:25 was not Rahab the harlot justified by **w**, *2041*
2:26 is dead, so faith without **w** is dead also. *2041*
3:13 his **w** with meekness of wisdom. *2041*
1Pe 2:12 they may by *your* good **w**, *which* they shall *2041*
2Pe 3:10 and the **w** that are therein shall be burnt up. *2041*
1Jn 3: 8 that he might destroy the **w** of the devil. *2041*
3:12 Because his own **w** were evil, and his *2041*
Rev 2: 2 I know thy **w**, and thy labour, and *2041*
2: 5 art fallen, and repent, and do the first **w**; *2041*
2: 9 I know thy **w**, *2041*
2:13 I know thy **w**, and where thou dwellest, *2041*
2:19 I know thy **w**, and charity, and service, *2041*
2:19 and faith, and thy patience, and thy **w**; *2041*
2:23 unto every one of you according to your **w**. *2041*
2:26 and keepeth my **w** unto the end, *2041*
3: 1 I know thy **w**, that thou hast a name that *2041*
3: 2 for I have not found thy **w** perfect before *2041*
3: 8 I know thy **w**: behold, I have set before *2041*
3:15 I know thy **w**, that thou art neither cold nor *2041*
9:20 *yet* repented not of the **w** of their hands, *2041*
14:13 their labours; and their **w** do follow them. *2041*
15: 3 saying, Great and marvellous *are* thy **w**, *2041*
18: 6 double unto her double according to her **w**: *2041*
20:12 written in the books, according to their **w**. *2041*
20:13 judged every man according to their **w**. *2041*

WORKS' (1) [WORK]

Jn 14:11 or else believe me for the very **w** sake. *2041*

WORLD (287) [WORLD'S, WORLDLY, WORLDS]

1Sa 2: 8 and he hath set the **w** upon them. 8398
2Sa 22:16 the foundations of the **w** were discovered, 8398
1Ch 16:30 the **w** also shall be stable, that it be not 8398
Job 18:18 into darkness, and chased out of the **w**. 8398
34:13 or who hath disposed the whole **w**? 8398
37:12 them upon the face of the **w** in the earth. 8398
Ps 9: 8 he shall judge the **w** in righteousness, 8398
17:14 thy hand, O LORD, from men of the **w**, 2465
18:15 the foundations of the **w** were discovered at 8398
19: 4 and their words to the end of the **w**. 8398
22:27 All the ends of the **w** shall remember and 776
24: 1 the **w**, and they that dwell therein. 8398
33: 8 let all the inhabitants of the **w** stand in awe 8398
49: 1 give ear, all ye inhabitants of the **w**: 2465
50:12 for the **w** *is* mine, and the fulness thereof. 8398
73:12 *are* the ungodly, who prosper in the **w**; 5769
77:18 the lightnings lightened the **w**: the earth 8398
89:11 *as for* the **w** and the fulness thereof, 8398
90: 2 ever thou hadst formed the earth and the **w**, 8398
93: 1 the **w** also is stablished, *that* it cannot be 8398
96:10 the **w** also shall be established *that* it shall 8398
96:13 he shall judge the **w** with righteousness, 8398
97: 4 His lightnings enlightened the **w**: the earth 8398
98: 7 the **w**, and they that dwell therein. 8398
98: 9 with righteousness shall he judge the **w**, 8398
Pr 8:26 nor the highest part of the dust of the **w**. 8398
Ecc 3:11 also he hath set the **w** in their heart, so that 5769
Isa 13:11 I will punish the **w** for *their* evil, and 8398
14:17 *That* made the **w** as a wilderness, and 8398
14:21 nor fill the face of the **w** *with* cities. 8398
18: 3 All ye inhabitants of the **w**, and dwellers on 8398
23:17 of the **w** upon the face of the earth. 776
24: 4 the **w** languisheth *and* fadeth away, 8398
26: 9 the inhabitants of the **w** will learn 8398
26:18 neither have the inhabitants of the **w** fallen. 8398
27: 6 bud, and fill the face of the **w** *with* fruit. 8398
34: 1 the **w**, and all things that come forth of it. 8398
38:11 man no more with the inhabitants of the **w**. 2309
45:17 confounded **w without end**. 5703+5704+5769
62:11 hath proclaimed unto the end of the **w**, 776
64: 4 For **since the beginning of the w** 4480+5769
Jer 10:12 he hath established the **w** by his wisdom, 8398
25:26 with another, and all the kingdoms of the **w**, 776
51:15 he hath established the **w** by his wisdom, 8398
La 4:12 the earth, and all the inhabitants of the **w**, 8398
Na 1: 5 yea, the **w**, and all that dwell therein. 8398
Mt 4: 8 and sheweth him all the kingdoms of the **w**, *2889*
5:14 Ye are the light of the **w**. A city that is set *2889*
12:32 it shall not be forgiven him, neither in this **w**, *165*
12:32 in this world, neither in the *w* to come. NIG
13:22 and the care of this **w**, and the deceitfulness *165*
13:35 kept secret from the foundation of the **w**. *2889*
13:38 The field is the **w**; the good seed are *2889*
13:39 the harvest is the end of the **w**; and *165*
13:40 in the fire; so shall it be in the end of this **w**. *165*

W

Mt	13:49	So shall it be at the end of the w: the angels	*165*
	16:26	if he shall gain the whole w, and lose his	*2889*
	18: 7	Woe unto the w because of offences: for it	*2889*
	24: 3	sign of thy coming, and of the end of the w?	*165*
	24:14	in all the w for a witness unto all nations;	*3625*
	24:21	as was not since the beginning of the w	*2889*
	25:34	for you from the foundation of the w:	*2889*
	26:13	gospel shall be preached in the whole w,	*2889*
	28:20	with you alway, *even* unto the end of the w.	*165*
Mk	4:19	And the cares of this w, and	*165*
	8:36	if he shall gain the whole w, and lose his	*2889*
	10:30	and in the w to come eternal life.	*165*
	14: 9	shall be preached throughout the whole w,	*2889*
	16:15	Go ye into all the w, and preach the gospel	*2889*
Lk	1:70	which have been since the w began:)	*165*
	2: 1	that all the w should be taxed.	*3625*
	4: 5	shewed unto him all the kingdoms of the w	*3625*
	9:25	if he gain the whole w, and lose himself, or	*2889*
	11:50	was shed from the foundation of the w,	*2889*
	12:30	For all these *things* do the nations of the w	*2889*
	16: 8	for the children of this w are in their	*165*
	18:30	and in the w to come life everlasting.	*165*
	20:34	The children of this w marry, and are given	*165*
	20:35	shall be accounted worthy to obtain that w,	*165*
Jn	1: 9	lighteth every man *that* cometh into the w.	*2889*
	1:10	He was in the w, and the world was made	*2889*
	1:10	and the w was made by him, and the world	*2889*
	1:10	was made by him, and the w knew him not.	*2889*
	1:29	of God, which taketh away the sin of the w.	*2889*
	3:16	For God so loved the w, that he gave his	*2889*
	3:17	For God sent not his Son into the w to	*2889*
	3:17	his Son into the world to condemn the w;	*2889*
	3:17	but that the w through him might be saved.	*2889*
	3:19	that light is come into the w, and men loved	*2889*
	4:42	is indeed the Christ, the Saviour of the w.	*2889*
	6:14	*that* prophet that should come into the w.	*2889*
	6:33	from heaven, and giveth life unto the w.	*2889*
	6:51	which I will give for the life of the w.	*2889*
	7: 4	thou do these *things,* shew thyself to the w.	*2889*
	7: 7	The w cannot hate you; but me it hateth,	*2889*
	8:12	unto them, saying, I am the light of the w:	*2889*
	8:23	ye are of this w; I am not of this world.	*2889*
	8:23	ye are of this world; I am not of this w.	*2889*
	8:26	I speak to the w those *things* which I have	*2889*
	9: 5	As long as I am in the w, I am the light of	*2889*
	9: 5	I am in the world, I am the light of the w.	*2889*
	9:32	Since the w began was it not heard that any	*165*
	9:39	For judgment I am come into this w,	*2889*
	10:36	and sent into the w, Thou blasphemest;	*2889*
	11: 9	because he seeth the light of this w.	*2889*
	11:27	Son of God, which should come into the w.	*2889*
	12:19	behold, the w is gone after him.	*2889*
	12:25	he that hateth his life in this w shall keep it	*2889*
	12:31	Now is the judgment of this w: now shall	*2889*
	12:31	now shall the prince of this w be cast out.	*2889*
	12:46	I am come a light into the w,	*2889*
	12:47	for I came not to judge the w, but to save	*2889*
	12:47	not to judge the world, but to save the w.	*2889*
	13: 1	should depart out of this w unto the Father,	*2889*
	13: 1	having loved his own which were in the w,	*2889*
	14:17	whom the w cannot receive, because	*2889*
	14:19	a little while, and the w seeth me no more;	*2889*
	14:22	thyself unto us, and not unto the w?	*2889*
	14:27	not as the w giveth, give I unto you. Let not	*2889*
	14:30	for the prince of this w cometh, and	*2889*
	14:31	But that the w may know that I love	*2889*
	15:18	If the w hate you, ye know that it hated me	*2889*
	15:19	If ye were of the w, the world would love	*2889*
	15:19	of the world, the w would love his own:	*2889*
	15:19	but because ye are not of the w, but I have	*2889*
	15:19	but I have chosen you out of the w,	*2889*
	15:19	of the world, therefore the w hateth you.	*2889*
	16: 8	he will reprove the w of sin, and	*2889*
	16:11	because the prince of this w is judged.	*2889*
	16:20	and lament, but the w shall rejoice:	*2889*
	16:21	for joy that a man is born into the w.	*2889*
	16:28	from the Father, and am come into the w:	*2889*
	16:28	again, I leave the w, and go to the Father.	*2889*
	16:33	In the w ye shall have tribulation: but be of	*2889*
	16:33	be of good cheer; I have overcome the w.	*2889*
	17: 5	which I had with thee before the w was.	*2889*
	17: 6	the men which thou gavest me out of the w:	*2889*
	17: 9	I pray not for the w, but for *them* which	*2889*
	17:11	And *now* I am no more in the w, but	*2889*
	17:11	but these are in the w, and I come to thee.	*2889*
	17:12	While I was with them in the w, I kept	*2889*
	17:13	and these *things* I speak in the w, that they	*2889*
	17:14	and the w hath hated them, because	*2889*
	17:14	hated them, because they are not of the w,	*2889*
	17:14	not of the world, even as I am not of the w.	*2889*
	17:15	that thou shouldest take them out of the w,	*2889*
	17:16	They are not of the w, even as I am not of	*2889*
	17:16	not of the world, even as I am not of the w.	*2889*
	17:18	As thou hast sent me into the w, even *so*	*2889*
	17:18	even *so* have I also sent them into the w.	*2889*
	17:21	that the w may believe that thou hast sent	*2889*
	17:23	that the w may know that thou hast sent	*2889*
	17:24	lovedst me before the foundation of the w.	*2889*
	17:25	the w hath not known thee:	*2889*
	18:20	answered him, I spake openly to the w;	*2889*
	18:36	My kingdom is not of this w:	*2889*
	18:36	this world: if my kingdom were of this w,	*2889*
	18:37	I born, and for this cause came I into the w,	*2889*
	21:25	I suppose that even the w itself could not	*2889*
Ac	3:21	of all his holy prophets since the w began.	*165*
	11:28	should be great dearth throughout all the w:	*3625*
	15:18	all his works from the beginning of the w.	*165*
	17: 6	These that have turned the w upside down	*3625*
	17:24	God that made the w and all *things* therein,	*2889*
	17:31	in the which he will judge the w in	*3625*
	19:27	whom all Asia and the w worshippeth.	*3625*
	24: 5	among all the Jews throughout the w,	*3625*
Ro	1: 8	faith is spoken of throughout the whole w.	*2889*
	1:20	from the creation of the w are clearly seen,	*2889*
	3: 6	for then how shall God judge the w?	*2889*
	3:19	all the w may become guilty before God.	*2889*
	4:13	that he should be the heir of the w,	*2889*
	5:12	as by one man sin entered into the w, and	*2889*
	5:13	For until the law sin was in the w: but sin is	*2889*
	10:18	and their words unto the ends of the w.	*3625*
	11:12	if the fall of them *be* the riches of the w,	*2889*
	11:15	away of them *be* the reconciling of the w,	*2889*
	12: 2	And be not conformed to this w: but be ye	*165*
	16:25	was kept secret **since** the w **began,**	*166+5550*
1Co	1:20	where *is* the disputer of this w? hath not God	*165*
	1:20	God made foolish the wisdom of this w?	*2889*
	1:21	For after that in the wisdom of God the w	*2889*
	1:27	*things* of the w to confound the wise;	*2889*
	1:27	God hath chosen the weak *things* of the w	*2889*
	1:28	And base *things* of the w, and *things* which	*2889*
	2: 6	yet not the wisdom of this w, nor of	*165*
	2: 6	nor of the princes of this w, that come to	*165*
	2: 7	God ordained before the w unto our glory:	*165*
	2: 8	Which none of the princes of this w knew:	*165*
	2:12	not the spirit of the w, but the Spirit which	*2889*
	3:18	among you seemeth to be wise in this w,	*165*
	3:19	For the wisdom of this w is foolishness	*2889*
	3:22	or the w, or life, or death, or *things* present,	*2889*
	4: 9	for we are made a spectacle unto the w, and	*2889*
	4:13	we are made as the filth of the w, *and*	*2889*
	5:10	altogether with the fornicators of this w,	*2889*
	5:10	for then must ye needs go out of the w.	*2889*
	6: 2	not know that the saints shall judge the w?	*2889*
	6: 2	and if the w shall be judged by you, are ye	*2889*
	7:31	And they that use this w, as not abusing *it:*	*2889*
	7:31	as not abusing *it:* for the fashion of this w	*2889*
	7:33	careth for the *things that are* of the w,	*2889*
	7:34	is married careth for the *things* of the w,	*2889*
	8: 4	we know that an idol *is* nothing in the w,	*2889*
	8:13	I will eat no flesh while the w standeth, lest I	*165*
	10:11	upon whom the ends of the w are come.	*165*
	11:32	we should not be condemned with the w.	*2889*
	14:10	so many kinds of voices in the w, and	*2889*
2Co	1:12	we have had our conversation in the w, and	*2889*
	4: 4	In whom the god of this w hath blinded	*165*
	5:19	that God was in Christ reconciling the w	*2889*
	7:10	but the sorrow of the w worketh death.	*2889*
Gal	1: 4	he might deliver us from *this* present evil w,	*165*
	4: 3	in bondage under the elements of the w:	*2889*
	6:14	by whom the w is crucified unto me, and I	*2889*
	6:14	is crucified unto me, and I unto the w.	*2889*
Eph	1: 4	us in him before the foundation of the w,	*2889*
	1:21	not only in this w, but also in that which is to	*165*
	2: 2	walked according to the course of this w,	*2889*
	2:12	having no hope, and without God in the w:	*2889*
	3: 9	which from the **beginning of the** w hath	*165*
	3:21	all ages, w **without end.**	*165+165+3588+3588*
	6:12	against the rulers of the darkness of this w,	*165*

Php 2:15 among whom ye shine as lights in the **w**; *2889*
Col 1: 6 is come unto you, as *it is* in all the **w**; *2889*
2: 8 after the rudiments of the **w**, and not after *2889*
2:20 with Christ from the rudiments of the **w**, *2889*
2:20 why, as though living in the **w**, are ye *2889*
1Ti 1:15 that Christ Jesus came into the **w** to save *2889*
3:16 believed on in the **w**, received up into *2889*
6: 7 For we brought nothing into *this* **w**, *and* *2889*
6:17 Charge *them that are* rich in this **w**, that *they* *165*
2Ti 1: 9 us in Christ Jesus before the **w began**, *166+5550*
4:10 having loved *this* present **w**, and is departed *165*
Tit 1: 2 promised before the **w began**; *166+5550*
2:12 and godly, in *this* present **w**; *165*
Heb 1: 6 he bringeth in the firstbegotten into the **w**, *3625*
2: 5 hath he not put in subjection the **w** to come, *3625*
4: 3 were finished from the foundation of the **w**. *2889*
6: 5 of God, and the powers of the **w** to come, *165*
9:26 have suffered since the foundation of the **w**: *2889*
9:26 now once in the end of the **w** hath he *165*
10: 5 Wherefore when he cometh into the **w**, *2889*
11: 7 by the which he condemned the **w**, and *2889*
11:38 (Of whom the **w** was not worthy:) *2889*
Jas 1:27 *and* to keep himself unspotted from the **w**. *2889*
2: 5 Hath not God chosen the poor of this **w** rich *2889*
3: 6 And the tongue *is* a fire, a **w** of iniquity: so *2889*
4: 4 know ye not that the friendship of the **w** is *2889*
4: 4 will be a friend of the **w** is the enemy of *2889*
1Pe 1:20 before the foundation of the **w**, *2889*
5: 9 in your brethren that are in the **w**. *2889*
2Pe 1: 4 the corruption that is in the **w** through lust: *2889*
2: 5 And spared not the old **w**, but saved Noah *2889*
2: 5 bringing in the flood upon the **w** of *2889*
2:20 of the **w** through the knowledge of the Lord *2889*
3: 6 Whereby the **w** that then was, *2889*
1Jn 2: 2 but also for *the sins of* the whole **w**. *2889*
2:15 Love not the **w**, neither the *things* that are *2889*
2:15 neither the *things that are* in the **w**. *2889*
2:15 If any *man* love the **w**, the love of *2889*
2:16 For all that is in the **w**, the lust of the flesh, *2889*
2:16 of life, is not of the Father, but is of the **w**. *2889*
2:17 And the **w** passeth away, and the lust *2889*
3: 1 therefore the **w** knoweth us not, because *2889*
3:13 Marvel not, my brethren, if the **w** hate you. *2889*
4: 1 false prophets are gone out into the **w**. *2889*
4: 3 and *even* now already is it in the **w**. *2889*
4: 4 is he that is in you, than he that is in the **w**. *2889*
4: 5 They are of the **w**, therefore speak they of *2889*
4: 5 therefore speak they of the **w**, and *2889*
4: 5 they of the world, and the **w** heareth them. *2889*
4: 9 God sent his only begotten Son into the **w**, *2889*
4:14 sent the Son *to be* the Saviour of the **w**. *2889*
4:17 because as he is, so are we in this **w**. *2889*
5: 4 is born of God overcometh the **w**: *2889*
5: 4 this is the victory that overcometh the **w**, *2889*
5: 5 Who is he that overcometh the **w**, but he *2889*
5:19 and the whole **w** lieth in wickedness. *2889*
2Jn 1: 7 For many deceivers are entered into the **w**, *2889*
Rev 3:10 which shall come upon all the **w**, to try *3625*
11:15 The kingdoms of *this* **w** are become *2889*
12: 9 and Satan, which deceiveth the whole **w**: *3625*
13: 3 and all the **w** wondered after the beast. *1093*
13: 8 Lamb slain from the foundation of the **w**. *2889*
16:14 the kings of the earth and of the whole **w**, *3625*
17: 8 book of life from the foundation of the **w**, *2889*

WORLD'S (1) [WORLD]

1Jn 3:17 But whoso hath *this* **w** good, and seeth his *2889*

WORLDLY (2) [WORLD]

Tit 2:12 and **w** lusts we should live soberly, *2886*
Heb 9: 1 of divine service, and a **w** sanctuary. *2886*

WORLDS (2) [WORLD]

Heb 1: 2 of all *things*, by whom also he made the **w**; *165*
11: 3 Through faith we understand that the **w** were *165*

WORM (14) [CANKERWORM, PALMERWORM, WORMS, WORMWOOD]

Ex 16:24 not stink, neither was there any **w** therein. 7415
Job 17:14 to the **w**, *Thou art* my mother, and 7415
24:20 the **w** shall feed sweetly on him; 7415
25: 6 How much less man, *that is* a **w**? and 7415
25: 6 a worm? and the son of man, *which is* a **w**? 8438
Ps 22: 6 I *am* a **w**, and no man; a reproach of men, 8438
Isa 14:11 the **w** is spread under thee, and the worms 7415
41:14 thou **w** Jacob, *and* ye men of Israel; 8438
51: 8 and the **w** shall eat them like wool: 5580
66:24 for their **w** shall not die, neither shall their 8438
Jnh 4: 7 God prepared a **w** when the morning rose 8438
Mk 9:44 Where their **w** dieth not, and the fire is not *4663*
9:46 Where their **w** dieth not, and the fire is not *4663*
9:48 Where their **w** dieth not, and the fire is not *4663*

WORMS (8) [WORM]

Ex 16:20 until the morning, and it bred **w**, and stank: 8438
Dt 28:39 nor gather *the grapes;* for the **w** shall eat 8438
Job 7: 5 My flesh is clothed with **w** and clods of 7415
19:26 *though* after my skin **w** destroy this *body,* NIH
21:26 in the dust, and the **w** shall cover them. 7415
Isa 14:11 is spread under thee, and the **w** cover thee. 8438
Mic 7:17 they shall move out of their holes like **w** of 2119
Ac 12:23 and he was **eaten of w**, and gave up *4662*

WORMWOOD (9) [WOOD, WORM]

Dt 29:18 among you a root that beareth gall and **w**; 3939
Pr 5: 4 her end is bitter as **w**, sharp as a twoedged 3939
Jer 9:15 with **w**, and give them water of gall to 3939
23:15 I will feed them with **w**, and make them 3939
La 3:15 he hath made me drunken *with* **w**. 3939
3:19 and my misery, the **w** and the gall. 3939
Am 5: 7 *Ye* who turn judgment to **w**, and leave off 3939
Rev 8:11 And the name of the star is called **W**: and *894*
8:11 and the third *part* of the waters became **w**; *894*

WORSE (26) [BAD]

Ge 19: 9 now will we **deal w** with thee, than with 7489
2Sa 19: 7 that *will be* **w** unto thee than all the evil 7489
1Ki 16:25 and did **w** than all that *were* before him. 7489
2Ki 14:12 Judah was **put to the w** before Israel; and 5062
1Ch 19:16 that they were **put to the w** before Israel, 5062
19:19 that they were **put to the w** before Israel, 5062
2Ch 6:24 if thy people Israel be **put to the w** before 5062
25:22 Judah was **put to the w** before Israel, and 5062
33: 9 to err, *and* to do **w** than the heathen, 7451
Jer 7:26 their neck: they **did w** than their fathers. 7489
16:12 ye have done **w** than your fathers; 7489
Da 1:10 for why should he see your faces **w liking** 2196
Mt 9:16 from the garment, and the rent is made **w**. *5501*
12:45 the last *state* of that man is **w than** the first. *5501*
27:64 so the last error shall be **w than** the first. *5501*
Mk 2:21 away *from* the old, and the rent is made **w**. *5501*
5:26 was nothing bettered, but rather grew **w**, *5501*
Lk 11:26 the last *state* of that man is **w than** the first. *5501*
Jn 2:10 *men* have well drunk, then that which is **w**: *1640*
5:14 sin no more, lest a **w** *thing* come unto thee. *5501*
1Co 8: 8 neither, if we eat not, are we the **w**. *5302*
11:17 together not for the better, but for the **w**. *2276*
1Ti 5: 8 denied the faith, and is **w than** an infidel. *5501*
2Ti 3:13 shall wax **w and worse,** *1909+3588+5501*
3:13 shall wax **worse and w**, *1909+3588+5501*
2Pe 2:20 the latter *end* is **w** with them **than** *5501*

WORSHIP (108) [WORSHIPPED, WORSHIPPER, WORSHIPPERS, WORSHIPPETH, WORSHIPPING]

Ge 22: 5 I and the lad will go yonder and **w**, and 7812
Ex 24: 1 of the elders of Israel; and **w** ye afar off. 7812
34:14 For thou shalt **w** no other god: for 7812
Dt 4:19 shouldest be driven to **w** them, and 7812
8:19 other gods, and serve them, and **w** them, 7812
11:16 and serve other gods, and **w** them; 7812
26:10 and **w** before the LORD thy God: 7812
30:17 and **w** other gods, and serve them; 7812
Jos 5:14 did **w**, and said unto him, What saith my 7812
1Sa 1: 3 this man went up out of his city yearly to **w** 7812
15:25 again with me, that I may **w** the LORD. 7812
15:30 with me, that I may **w** the LORD thy God. 7812
1Ki 9: 6 but go and serve other gods, and **w** them: 7812
12:30 for the people went *to* **w** before the one, NIH
2Ki 5:18 goeth *into* the house of Rimmon to **w** there, 7812
17:36 him shall ye **w**, and to him shall ye do 7812
18:22 Ye shall **w** before this altar in Jerusalem? 7812
1Ch 16:29 **w** the LORD in the beauty of holiness. 7812
2Ch 7:19 shall go and serve other gods, and **w** them; 7812
32:12 Ye shall **w** before one altar, and 7812
Ps 5: 7 in thy fear will I **w** toward thy holy temple. 7812
22:27 all the kindreds of the nations shall **w** 7812
22:29 *they that be* fat upon earth shall eat and **w**: 7812
29: 2 **w** the LORD in the beauty of holiness. 7812

W

Ps 45:11 for he *is* thy Lord; and w thou him. 7812
66: 4 All the earth shall w thee, and shall sing 7812
81: 9 neither shalt thou w *any* strange god. 7812
86: 9 hast made shall come and w before thee, 7812
95: 6 O come, let us w and bow down: let us 7812
96: 9 O w the LORD in the beauty of holiness: 7812
97: 7 themselves of idols: w him, all ye gods. 7812
99: 5 LORD our God, and w at his footstool; 7812
99: 9 the LORD our God, and w at his holy hill; 7812
132: 7 his tabernacles: we will w at his footstool. 7812
138: 2 I will w toward thy holy temple, and 7812
Isa 2: 8 they w the work of their own hands, 7812
2:20 which they made *each one* for himself to w, 7812
27:13 shall w the LORD in the holy mount at 7812
36: 7 to Jerusalem, Ye shall w before this altar? 7812
46: 6 it a god: they fall down, yea, they w. 7812
49: 7 shall see and arise, princes also shall w, 7812
66:23 shall all flesh come to w before me, 7812
Jer 7: 2 that enter in at these gates to w the LORD. 7812
13:10 other gods, to serve them, and to w them, 7812
25: 6 to w them, and provoke me not to anger 7812
26: 2 which come to w *in* the LORD'S house, 7812
44:19 did we make her cakes to w her, and 6087
Eze 46: 2 and he shall w at the threshold of the gate: 7812
46: 3 Likewise the people of the land shall w *at* 7812
46: 9 w shall go out *by* the way of the south gate; 7812
Da 3: 5 w the golden image that Nebuchadnezzar 5457
3:10 shall fall down and w the golden image: 5457
3:12 nor w the golden image which thou hast set 5457
3:14 nor w the golden image which I have set 5457
3:15 and w the image which I have made; 5457
3:15 *well:* but if ye w not, ye shall be cast 5457
3:18 nor w the golden image which thou hast set 5457
3:28 that they might not serve nor w any god, 5457
Mic 5:13 thou shalt no more w the work of thine 7812
Zep 1: 5 them that w the host of heaven upon 7812
1: 5 them that w *and* that swear by the LORD, 7812
2:11 *men* shall w him, every one from his place, 7812
Zec 14:16 even go up from year to year to w the King, 7812
14:17 of the earth unto Jerusalem to w the King, 7812
Mt 2: 2 his star in the east, and are come to w him. *4352*
2: 8 that I may come and w him also. *4352*
4: 9 give thee, if thou wilt fall down and w me. *4352*
4:10 Thou shalt w the Lord thy God, and *4352*
15: 9 But in vain they do w me, teaching for *4576*
Mk 7: 7 Howbeit in vain do they w me, teaching for *4576*
Lk 4: 7 If thou therefore wilt w me, all shall be *4352*
4: 8 Thou shalt w the Lord thy God, and *4352*
14:10 shalt thou have w in the presence of them *1391*
Jn 4:20 is the place where *men* ought to w. *4352*
4:21 nor *yet* at Jerusalem, w the Father. *4352*
4:22 Ye w ye know not what: we know what we *4352*
4:22 we know what we w: for salvation is of *4352*
4:23 when the true worshippers shall w *4352*
4:23 for the Father seeketh such to w him. *4352*
4:24 they that w him must worship *him* in spirit *4352*
4:24 they that worship him must w *him* in spirit *4352*
12:20 among them that came up to w at the feast: *4352*
Ac 7:42 and gave them up to w the host of heaven; *3000*
7:43 figures which ye made to w them: *4352*
8:27 and had come to Jerusalem for to w, *4352*
17:23 Whom therefore ye ignorantly w, *2151*
18:13 This *fellow* persuadeth men to w God *4576*
24:11 days since I went up to Jerusalem for to w. *4352*
24:14 call heresy, so w I the God of my fathers, *3000*
1Co 14:25 so falling down on *his* face he will w God, *4352*
Php 3: 3 which w God in the spirit, and rejoice in *3000*
Col 2:23 have indeed a shew of wisdom in **will w**, *1479*
Heb 1: 6 And let all the angels of God w him. *4352*
Rev 3: 9 make them to come and w before thy feet, *4352*
4:10 and w him that liveth for ever and ever, and *4352*
9:20 that they should not w devils, and idols of *4352*
11: 1 and the altar, and them that w therein. *4352*
13: 8 And all that dwell upon the earth shall w *4352*
13:12 them which dwell therein to w the first *4352*
13:15 cause that as many as would not w *4352*
14: 7 and w him that made heaven, and earth, *4352*
14: 9 If any *man* w the beast and his image, and *4352*
14:11 who w the beast and his image, and *4352*
15: 4 all nations shall come and w before thee; *4352*
19:10 And I fell at his feet to w him. And he said *4352*
19:10 w God: for the testimony of Jesus is *4352*
22: 8 I fell down to w before the feet of *4352*
22: 9 keep the sayings of this book: w God. *4352*

WORSHIPPED (70) [WORSHIP]
Ge 24:26 bowed down his head, and w the LORD. 7812
24:48 w the LORD, and blessed the LORD 7812
24:52 he w the LORD, *bowing himself* to 7812
Ex 4:31 then they bowed their heads and w. 7812
12:27 And the people bowed the head and w. 7812
32: 8 have w it, and have sacrificed thereunto, 7812
33:10 all the people rose up and w, every man *in* 7812
34: 8 bowed his head toward the earth, and w. 7812
Dt 17: 3 w them, either the sun, or moon, or any of 7812
29:26 and served other gods, and w them, 7812
Jdg 7:15 that he w, and returned into the host of 7812
1Sa 1:19 w before the LORD, and returned, and 7812
1:28 to the LORD. And he w the LORD there. 7812
15:31 again after Saul; and Saul w the LORD. 7812
2Sa 12:20 came *into* the house of the LORD, and w: 7812
15:32 to the top *of the mount,* where he w God, 7812
1Ki 9: 9 and have w them, and served them: 7812
11:33 have w Ashtoreth the goddess of 7812
16:31 and went and served Baal, and w him. 7812
22:53 w him, and provoked to anger the LORD 7812
2Ki 17:16 w all the host of heaven, and served Baal. 7812
21: 3 w all the host of heaven, and served them. 7812
21:21 the idols that his father served, and w them: 7812
1Ch 29:20 and w the LORD, and the king. 7812
2Ch 7: 3 w, and praised the LORD, *saying,* For *he* 7812
7:22 other gods, and w them, and served them: 7812
29:28 all the congregation w, and the singers 7812
29:29 present with him bowed themselves, and w. 7812
29:30 and they bowed their heads and w. 7812
33: 3 w all the host of heaven, and served them. 7812
Ne 8: 6 w the LORD *with their* faces to 7812
9: 3 and w the LORD their God. 7812
Job 1:20 and fell down upon the ground, and w, 7812
Ps 106:19 a calf in Horeb, and w the molten image. 7812
Jer 1:16 and w the works of their own hands. 7812
8: 2 they have sought, and whom they have w: 7812
16:11 have w them, and have forsaken me, and 7812
22: 9 and w other gods, and served them. 7812
Eze 8:16 and they w the sun towards the east. 7812
Da 2:46 w Daniel, and commanded that *they* should 5457
3: 7 w the golden image that Nebuchadnezzar 5457
Mt 2:11 his mother, and fell down, and w him: *4352*
8: 2 there came a leper and w him, saying, Lord, *4352*
9:18 came a *certain* ruler, and w him, saying, *4352*
14:33 they that were in the ship came and w him, *4352*
15:25 Then came she and w him, saying, Lord, *4352*
18:26 fell down, and w him, saying, Lord, *4352*
28: 9 and held him by the feet, and w him. *4352*
28:17 And when they saw him, they w him: but *4352*
Mk 5: 6 he saw Jesus afar off, he ran and w him, *4352*
15:19 upon him, and bowing *their* knees w him. *4352*
Lk 24:52 And they w him, and returned to Jerusalem *4352*
Jn 4:20 Our fathers w in this mountain; and ye say, *4352*
9:38 he said, Lord, I believe. And he w him. *4352*
Ac 10:25 and fell down at *his* feet, and w *him.* *4352*
16:14 of the city of Thyatira, which w God, *4576*
17:25 Neither is w with men's hands, as though *2323*
18: 7 named Justus, one that w God, *4576*
Ro 1:25 and w and served the creature more than *4573*
2Th 2: 4 above all that is called God, or that is w; *4574*
Heb 11:21 and w, *leaning* upon the top of his staff. *4352*
Rev 5:14 and w him that liveth for ever and ever. *4352*
7:11 the throne on their faces, and w God, *4352*
11:16 fell upon their faces, and w God, *4352*
13: 4 And they w the dragon which gave power *4352*
13: 4 and they w the beast, saying, Who *is* like *4352*
16: 2 and *upon* them which w his image. *4352*
19: 4 fell down and w God that sat on the throne, *4352*
19:20 of the beast, and them that w his image. *4352*
20: 4 and which had not w the beast, neither his *4352*

WORSHIPPER (2) [WORSHIP]
Jn 9:31 but if any *man* be a **w of God**, and *2318*
Ac 19:35 is a w of the great goddess Diana, *3511*

WORSHIPPERS (7) [WORSHIP]
2Ki 10:19 to the intent that *he* might destroy the w of 5647
10:21 all the w of Baal came, so that there was 5647
10:22 Bring forth vestments for all the w of Baal. 5647
10:23 said unto the w of Baal, Search, and 5647
10:23 of the LORD, but the w of Baal only. 5647
Jn 4:23 when the true w shall worship the Father in *4353*
Heb 10: 2 that the w once purged should have had no *3000*

WORSHIPPETH (6) [WORSHIP]
Ne 9: 6 them all; and the host of heaven w thee. 7812
Isa 44:15 w *it;* he maketh it a graven image, and 7812
44:17 w *it,* and prayeth unto it, and saith, 7812
Da 3: 6 w shall the same hour be cast into the midst 5457
3:11 whoso falleth not down and w, *that* he 5457
Ac 19:27 whom all Asia and the world w. *4576*

WORSHIPPING (5) [WORSHIP]
2Ki 19:37 as he was w *in* the house of Nisroch his 7812
2Ch 20:18 fell before the LORD, w the LORD. 7812
Isa 37:38 as he was w *in* the house of Nisroch his 7812
Mt 20:20 w *him,* and desiring a certain *thing* of him. *4352*
Col 2:18 in a voluntary humility and w of angels, *2356*

WORST (1) [BAD]
Eze 7:24 Wherefore I will bring the w of 7451

WORTH (9) [THANKWORTHY, UNWORTHILY, UNWORTHY, WORTHIES, WORTHILY, WORTHY]
Ge 23: 9 for as much money as it is w he shall give it 4392
23:15 the land *is* w four hundred shekels of silver; NIH
Lev 27:23 the priest shall reckon unto him the w of 4373
Dt 15:18 for he hath been w a double hired servant *to* 7939
2Sa 18: 3 now *thou art* w ten thousand of us: 3644
1Ki 21: 2 I will give thee the w of it *in* money. 4242
Job 24:25 a liar, and make my speech nothing w? 3807.1
Pr 10:20 the heart of the wicked *is* **little** w. 4592+3509.1
Eze 30: 2 Lord GOD; Howl ye, Woe w the day! 3807.1

WORTHIES (1) [WORTH]
Na 2: 5 He shall recount his w: they shall stumble in 117

WORTHILY (1) [WORTH]
Ru 4:11 do thou w in Ephratah, and be famous in 2428

WORTHLESS See NOUGHT; VANITIES; VANITY

WORTHY (68) [WORTH]
Ge 32:10 I am **not** w of the least of all the mercies, 6994
Dt 17: 6 shall he that is *w* of death be put to death; NIH
19: 6 whereas he *was* not w of death, 4941
21:22 if a man have committed a sin w of death, 4941
22:26 *there is* in the damsel no sin *w* of death: NIH
25: 2 if the wicked *man be* w to be beaten, 1121
1Sa 1: 5 unto Hannah he gave a w portion; for he 639
26:16 ye *are* **w to die**, because ye have not 1121+4194
2Sa 22: 4 call on the LORD, who is *w* to be praised: NIH
1Ki 1:52 If he will shew himself a w man, 2428
2:26 thine own fields; for thou *art* w of death: 376
Ps 18: 3 upon the LORD, who is *w* to be praised: NIH
Jer 26:11 all the people, saying, This man *is* w to die; 4941
26:16 to the prophets; This man *is* not w to die: 4941
Mt 3:11 than I, whose shoes I am not w to bear: *2425*
8: 8 I am not w that thou shouldest come under *2425*
10:10 yet staves: for the workman is w of his meat. *514*
10:11 or town ye shall enter, inquire who in it is w; *514*
10:13 And if the house be w, let your peace come *514*
10:13 but if it be not w, let your peace return to *514*
10:37 or mother more than me is not w of me: *514*
10:37 or daughter more than me is not w of me. *514*
10:38 and followeth after me, is not w of me. *514*
22: 8 but they which were bidden were not w. *514*
Mk 1: 7 the latchet of whose shoes I am not w to *2425*
Lk 3: 8 Bring forth therefore fruits w of repentance, *514*
3:16 the latchet of whose shoes I am not w to *2425*
7: 4 That he was w for whom he should do this: *514*
7: 6 for I am not w that thou shouldest enter *2425*
7: 7 Wherefore neither **thought** I myself w to *515*
10: 7 for the labourer is w of his hire. Go not from *514*
12:48 and did commit *things* w of stripes, *514*
15:19 And am no more w to be called thy son: *514*
15:21 and am no more w to be called thy son. *514*
20:35 But they which shall be **accounted** w to *2661*
21:36 that ye may be **accounted** w to escape all *2661*
23:15 and lo, nothing w of death is done unto him. *514*
Jn 1:27 whose shoe's latchet I am not w to unloose. *514*
Ac 5:41 rejoicing that they were **counted** w to *2661*
13:25 whose shoes of *his* feet I am not w to loose. *514*
23:29 to have nothing laid to his charge w of death *514*
24: 2 that **very w deeds** are done unto this nation *2735*
25:11 or have committed any *thing* w of death, *514*
25:25 that he had committed nothing w of death, *514*
26:31 This man doeth nothing w of death or *514*
Ro 1:32 that they which commit such *things* are w of *514*
8:18 w to be compared with the glory which shall *514*
Eph 4: 1 beseech you that *ye* walk w of the vocation *516*
Col 1:10 That ye might walk w of the Lord unto all *516*
1Th 2:12 That ye would walk w of God, who hath *516*
2Th 1: 5 that ye may be **counted** w of the kingdom *2661*
1:11 that our God would **count** you w of *this* *515*
1Ti 1:15 *is* a faithful saying, and w of all acceptation, *514*
4: 9 *is* a faithful saying and w of all acceptation. *514*
5:17 Let the elders that rule well be **counted** w of *515*
5:18 And, The labourer *is* w of his reward. *514*
6: 1 count their own masters w of all honour, *514*
Heb 3: 3 For this *man* was **counted** w of more glory *515*
10:29 suppose ye, shall he be **thought** w, *515*
11:38 (Of whom the world was not w:) *514*
Jas 2: 7 Do not they blaspheme *that* w name by *2570*
Rev 3: 4 shall walk with me in white: for they are w. *514*
4:11 Thou art w, O Lord, to receive glory and *514*
5: 2 Who is w to open the book, and to loose *514*
5: 4 because no *man* was found w to open and *514*
5: 9 Thou art w to take the book, and to open *514*
5:12 W is the Lamb that was slain to receive *514*
16: 6 given them blood to drink; for they are w. *514*

WOT (10) [WIT]
Ge 21:26 I w not who hath done this thing: 3045
44:15 w ye not that such a man as I can certainly 3045
Ex 32: 1 of Egypt, we w not what is become of him. 3045
32:23 of Egypt, we w not what is become of him. 3045
Nu 22: 6 for I w that *he* whom thou blessest *is* 3045
Jos 2: 5 whither the men went I w not: pursue after 3045
Ac 3:17 I w that through ignorance ye did *it,* as *did* *1492*
7:40 of Egypt, we w not what is become of him. *1492*
Ro 11: 2 W ye not what the scripture saith of Elias? *1492*
Php 1:22 my labour: yet what I shall choose I w not. *1107*

WOTTETH (1) [WIT]
Ge 39: 8 my master w not what *is* with me in 3045

WOULD (451) [WILL, WOULDEST] See Index

WOULDEST (38) [WOULD] See Index

WOUND (25) [WIND, WOUNDED, WOUNDEDST, WOUNDETH, WOUNDING, WOUNDS]
Ex 21:25 for burning, w for wound, stripe for stripe. 6482
21:25 for burning, wound for w, stripe for stripe. 6482
Dt 32:39 I kill, and I make alive; I w, and I heal: 4272
1Ki 22:35 the blood ran out of the w into the midst of 4347
Job 34: 6 my w *is* incurable without transgression. 2671
Ps 68:21 God shall w the head of his enemies, *and* 4272
110: 6 he shall w the heads over many countries. 4272
Pr 6:33 A w and dishonour shall he get; and 5061
20:30 The blueness of a w cleanseth away evil: so 6482
Isa 30:26 and healeth the stroke of their w. 4347
Jer 10:19 my w *is* grievous: but I said, Truly this *is* a 4347
15:18 is my pain perpetual, and my w incurable, 4347
30:12 bruise *is* incurable, *and* thy w *is* grievous. 4347
30:14 for I have wounded thee *with* the w of an 4347
Hos 5:13 Judah *saw* his w, then went Ephraim to 4205
5:13 he not heal you nor cure you of your w. 4205
Ob 1: 7 *they that eat* thy bread have laid a w under 4204
Mic 1: 9 For her w *is* incurable; for it is come unto 4347
Na 3:19 no healing of thy bruise; thy w *is* grievous: 4347
Jn 19:40 and w it in linen clothes with the spices, *1210*
Ac 5: 6 w him **up**, and carried *him* out, and *4958*
1Co 8:12 the brethren, and w their weak conscience, *5180*
Rev 13: 3 to death; and his deadly w was healed: *4127*
13:12 the first beast, whose deadly w was healed. *4127*
13:14 which had the w by a sword, and did live. *4127*

WOUNDED (35) [WOUND]
Dt 23: 1 He that is w in the stones, or hath *his* privy 6481
Jdg 9:40 and many were overthrown *and* w, 2491
1Sa 17:52 the w of the Philistines fell down by 2491
31: 3 hit him; and he was sore w of the archers. 2342
2Sa 22:39 and w them, that they could not arise: 4272
1Ki 20:37 smote him, so that in smiting he w *him.* 6481
22:34 and carry me out of the host; for I am w. 2470
2Ki 8:28 in Ramoth-gilead; and the Syrians w Joram. 5221
1Ch 10: 3 hit him, and he was w of the archers. 2342
2Ch 18:33 mayest carry me out of the host; for I am w. 2470
35:23 Have me away; for I am sore w. 2470
Job 24:12 of the city, and the soul of the w crieth out: 2491
Ps 18:38 I have w them that they were not able to 4272

W

Ps 64: 7 *with* an arrow; suddenly shall they be w. 4347
69:26 talk to the grief of those whom thou hast w. 2491
109:22 and needy, and my heart is w within me. 2490
Pr 7:26 For she hath cast down many w: yea, 2491
18:14 his infirmity; but a w spirit who can bear? 5218
SS 5: 7 city found me, they smote me, they w me; 6481
Isa 51: 9 it that hath cut Rahab, *and* w the dragon? 2490
53: 5 he *was* w for our transgressions, *he was* 2490
Jer 30:14 for I have w thee *with* the wound of an 5221
37:10 there remained *but* w men among them, 1856
51:52 and through all her land the w shall groan. 2491
La 2:12 when they swooned as the w in the streets 2491
Eze 26:15 at the sound of thy fall, when the w cry, 2491
28:23 the w shall be judged in the midst of her by 2491
30:24 him *with* the groanings of a **deadly** w *man.* 2491
Joel 2: 8 fall upon the sword, they shall not be w. 1214
Zec 13: 6 *Those with* which I was w *in* the house of 5221
Mk 12: 4 and w *him* **in the head**, and sent *him* away *2775*
Lk 10:30 and w *him,* and departed, *2007+4127*
20:12 and they w him also, and cast *him* out. *5135*
Ac 19:16 *they* fled out of that house naked and w. *5135*
Rev 13: 3 And I saw one of his heads as *it were* w to *4969*

WOUNDEDST (1) [WOUND]
Hab 3:13 thou w the head out of the house of 4272

WOUNDETH (1) [WOUND]
Job 5:18 he w, and his hands make whole. 4272

WOUNDING (1) [WOUND]
Ge 4:23 for I have slain a man to my w, and 6482

WOUNDS (15) [WOUND]
2Ki 8:29 w which the Syrians had given him at 4347
9:15 of the w which the Syrians had given him, 4347
2Ch 22: 6 of the w which were given him at Ramah, 4347
Job 9:17 and multiplieth my w without cause. 6482
Ps 38: 5 My w stink *and* are corrupt because of my 2250
147: 3 the broken in heart, and bindeth up their w. 6094
Pr 18: 8 The words of a talebearer *are* as w, and 3859
23:29 who hath w without cause? who hath 6482
26:22 The words of a talebearer *are* as w, and 3859
27: 6 Faithful *are* the w of a friend; but the kisses 6482
Isa 1: 6 *but* w, and bruises, and putrifying sores: 6482
Jer 6: 7 in her; before me continually *is* grief and w. 4347
30:17 I will heal thee of thy w, saith the LORD; 4347
Zec 13: 6 unto him, What *are* these w in thine hands? 4347
Lk 10:34 And went to *him,* and bound up his w, *5134*

WOVE (1) [WEAVE]
2Ki 23: 7 where the women w hangings for the grove. 707

WOVEN (4) [WEAVE]
Ex 28:32 it shall have a binding of w work round 707
39:22 he made the robe of the ephod *of* w work, 707
39:27 they made coats *of* fine linen *of* w work for 707
Jn 19:23 without seam, w from the top throughout. *5307*

WRAP (2) [WRAPPED, WRAPT]
Isa 28:20 the covering narrower than that *he* can w 3664
Mic 7: 3 his mischievous desire: so they w it **up**. 5686

WRAPPED (9) [WRAP]
Ge 38:14 and w herself, and sat in an open place, 5968
1Ki 19:13 when Elijah heard *it,* that he w his face in 3874
Job 8:17 His roots are w about the heap, *and* 5440
Mt 27:59 the body, he w it in a clean linen cloth, *1794*
Mk 15:46 and w *him* **in** the linen, and laid him in a *1750*
Lk 2: 7 and w him **in swaddling clothes**, and *4683*
2:12 shall find *the* babe w **in swaddling clothes**, *4683*
23:53 and w it in linen, and laid it in a sepulchre *1794*
Jn 20: 7 but w **together** in a place by itself. *1794*

WRAPT (5) [WRAP]
1Sa 21: 9 it *is here* w in a cloth behind the ephod: 3874
2Ki 2: 8 w *it* **together**, and smote the waters, and 1563
Job 40:17 the sinews of his stones are w **together**. 8276
Eze 21:15 *is* made bright, *it is* w **up** for the slaughter. 4593
Jnh 2: 5 the weeds *were* w **about** my head. 2280

WRATH (198) [WRATHFUL, WRATHS, WROTH]
Ge 39:19 thy servant to me; that his w was kindled. 639
49: 7 *it was* fierce; and their w, for it was cruel: 5678
Ex 15: 7 thou sentest forth thy w, *which* consumed 2740
22:24 my w shall wax hot, and I will kill you with 639
32:10 that my w may wax hot against them, and 639
32:11 why doth thy w wax hot against thy people, 639
32:12 Turn from thy fierce w, and repent of *this* 639
Lev 10: 6 and lest w come upon all the people: 7107
Nu 1:53 that there be no w upon the congregation of 7110
11:33 the w of the LORD was kindled against 639
16:46 for there is w gone out from the LORD; 7110
18: 5 that there be no w any more upon 7110
25:11 hath turned my w away from the children 2534
Dt 9: 7 **provokedst** the LORD thy God **to w** in 7107
9: 8 in Horeb ye **provoked** the LORD **to** w, 7107
9:22 ye **provoked** the LORD **to** w. 7107
11:17 *then* the LORD'S w be kindled against you, 639
29:23 overthrew in his anger, and in his w: 2534
29:28 in w, and in great indignation, and 2534
32:27 Were it not that I feared the w of 3708
Jos 9:20 lest w be upon us, because of the oath 7110
22:20 and w fell on all the congregation of Israel? 7110
1Sa 28:18 nor executedst his fierce w upon Amalek, 639
2Sa 11:20 if so be that the king's w arise, and he say 2534
2Ki 22:13 for great *is* the w of the LORD that is 2534
22:17 my w shall be kindled against this place, 2534
23:26 turned not from the fierceness of his great w, 639
1Ch 27:24 because there fell w for it against Israel; 7110
2Ch 12: 7 my w shall not be poured out upon 2534
12:12 the w of the LORD turned from him, 639
19: 2 *is* w upon thee from before the LORD. 7110
19:10 *so* w come upon you, and upon your 7110
24:18 w came upon Judah and Jerusalem for this 7110
28:11 for the fierce w of the LORD *is* upon you. 639
28:13 is great, and *there is* fierce w against Israel. 639
29: 8 Wherefore the w of the LORD was upon 7110
29:10 that his fierce w may turn away from us. 639
30: 8 that the fierceness of his w may turn away 639
32:25 therefore there was w upon him, and 7110
32:26 that the w of the LORD came not upon 7110
34:21 for great *is* the w of the LORD that is 2534
34:25 my w shall be poured out upon this place, 2534
36:16 until the w of the LORD arose against his 2534
Ezr 5:12 had **provoked** the God of heaven **unto** w, 7265
7:23 for why should there be w against the realm 7109
8:22 his w *is* against all them that forsake him. 639
10:14 until the fierce w of our God for this matter 639
Ne 13:18 yet ye bring more w upon Israel by 2740
Est 1:18 *shall there arise* too much contempt and w. 7110
2: 1 when the w of king Ahasuerus was 2534
3: 5 him reverence, *then* was Haman full *of* w. 2534
7: 7 wine in his w *went* into the palace garden: 2534
7:10 Then was the king's w pacified. 2534
Job 5: 2 For w killeth the foolish man, and 3708
14:13 wouldest keep me secret, until thy w be past, 639
16: 9 He teareth *me in* his w, who hateth me: 639
19:11 He hath also kindled his w against me, and 639
19:29 for w *bringeth* the punishments of 2534
20:23 *God* shall cast the fury of his w upon him, 639
20:28 *goods shall* flow away in the day of his w. 639
21:20 and he shall drink of the w of the Almighty. 2534
21:30 they shall be brought forth to the day of w. 5678
32: 2 was kindled the w of Elihu the son of 639
32: 2 against Job was his w kindled, because 639
32: 3 Also against his three friends was his w 639
32: 5 of *these* three men, then his w was kindled. 639
36:13 the hypocrites in heart heap up w: they cry 639
36:18 Because *there is* w, *beware* lest he take thee 2534
40:11 Cast abroad the rage of thy w: and 639
42: 7 My w is kindled against thee, and against thy 639
Ps 2: 5 Then shall he speak unto them in his w, and 639
2:12 the way, when his w is kindled but a little: 639
21: 9 the LORD shall swallow them up in his w, 639
37: 8 Cease from anger, and forsake w: fret not 2534
38: 1 O LORD, rebuke me not in thy w: 7110
55: 3 iniquity upon me, and in w they hate me. 639
58: 9 with a whirlwind, both living, and in *his* w. 2740
59:13 Consume *them* in w, consume *them,* that 2534
76:10 Surely the w of man shall praise thee: 2534
76:10 the remainder of w shalt thou restrain. 2534
78:31 The w of God came upon them, and slew 639
78:38 anger away, and did not stir up all his w. 2534
78:49 w, and indignation, and trouble, 5678
79: 6 Pour out thy w upon the heathen that have 2534
85: 3 Thou hast taken away all thy w: thou hast 5678
88: 7 Thy w lieth hard upon me, and thou hast 2534
88:16 Thy **fierce** w goeth over me; thy terrors 2740
89:46 for ever? shall thy w burn like fire? 2534

W

Ps 90: 7 thine anger, and by thy w are we troubled. 2534
90: 9 For all our days are passed away in thy w: 5678
90:11 even according to thy fear, *so is* thy w. 5678
95:11 *Unto* whom I sware in my w that they should 639
102:10 Because of thine indignation and thy w: 7110
106:23 to turn away his w, lest *he* should destroy 2534
106:40 Therefore was the w of the LORD kindled 639
110: 5 shall strike through kings in the day of his w. 639
124: 3 when their w was kindled against us: 639
138: 7 thine hand against the w of mine enemies, 639
Pr 11: 4 Riches profit not in the day of w: but 5678
11:23 *but* the expectation of the wicked *is* w. 5678
12:16 A fool's w is presently known: but 3708
14:29 *He that is* slow to w *is* of great 639
14:35 but his w is *against* him that causeth shame. 5678
15: 1 A soft answer turneth away w: but 2534
16:14 The w of a king *is as* messengers of death: 2534
19:12 The king's w *is* as the roaring of a lion; but 2197
19:19 *A man* of great w *shall* suffer punishment: 2534
21:14 and a reward in the bosom strong w. 2534
21:24 *is* his name, who dealeth in proud w. 5678
24:18 and he turn away his w from him. 639
27: 3 but a fool's w *is* heavier than them both. 3708
27: 4 W *is* cruel, and anger *is* outrageous; but 2534
29: 8 city into a snare: but wise *men* turn away w. 639
30:33 so the forcing of w bringeth forth strife. 639
Ecc 5:17 *hath* much sorrow and w with his sickness. 7110
Isa 9:19 Through the w of the LORD of hosts is 5678
10: 6 against the people of my w will I give him 5678
13: 9 cruel both *with* w and fierce anger, to lay 5678
13:13 in the w of the LORD of hosts, and in 5678
14: 6 He who smote the people in w *with* a 5678
16: 6 of his haughtiness, and his pride, and his w: 5678
54: 8 In a little w I hid my face from thee for a 7110
60:10 for in my w I smote thee, but in my favour 7110
Jer 7:29 and forsaken the generation of his w. 5678
10:10 at his w the earth shall tremble, and 7110
18:20 *and* to turn away thy w from them. 2534
21: 5 even in anger, and in fury, and in great w. 7110
32:37 mine anger, and in my fury, and in great w; 7110
44: 8 In that *ye* **provoke** me **unto** w with 3707
48:30 I know his w, saith the LORD; but *it shall* 5678
50:13 Because of the w of the LORD it shall not 7110
La 2: 2 he hath thrown down in his w the strong 5678
3: 1 *that* hath seen affliction by the rod of his w. 5678
Eze 7:12 for w *is* upon all the multitude thereof. 2740
7:14 for my w *is* upon all the multitude thereof. 2740
7:19 them in the day of the w of the LORD: 5678
13:15 Thus will I accomplish my w upon 2534
21:31 I will blow against thee in the fire of my w, 5678
22:21 blow upon you in the fire of my w, and 5678
22:31 have consumed them with the fire of my w: 5678
38:19 *and* in the fire of my w have I spoken, 5678
Hos 5:10 I will pour out my w upon them like water. 5678
13:11 in mine anger, and took *him away* in my w. 5678
Am 1:11 tear perpetually, and he kept his w for ever: 5678
Na 1: 2 and he reserveth *w* for his enemies. NIH
Hab 3: 2 years make known; in w remember mercy. 7267
3: 8 *was* thy w against the sea, that thou didst 5678
Zep 1:15 That day *is* a day of w, a day of trouble and 5678
1:18 deliver them in the day of the LORD's w; 5678
Zec 7:12 came a great w from the LORD of hosts. 7110
8:14 when your fathers **provoked** me **to** w, 7107
Mt 3: 7 who hath warned you to flee from the w to *3709*
Lk 3: 7 who hath warned you to flee from the w to *3709*
4:28 they heard these *things*, were filled with w, *2372*
21:23 distress in the land, and w upon this people. *3709*
Jn 3:36 see life; but the w of God abideth on him. *3709*
Ac 19:28 heard *these sayings*, they were full of w, *2372*
Ro 1:18 For the w of God is revealed from heaven *3709*
2: 5 heart treasurest up unto thyself w *3709*
2: 5 up unto thyself wrath against the day of w *3709*
2: 8 obey unrighteousness, indignation and w, *3709*
4:15 Because the law worketh w: for where no *3709*
5: 9 we shall be saved from w through him. *3709*
9:22 willing to shew *his* w, and to make his *3709*
9:22 *the* vessels of w fitted to destruction: *3709*
12:19 but *rather* give place unto w: *3709*
13: 4 a revenger to *execute* w upon him that doeth *3709*
13: 5 not only for w, but also for conscience *3709*
Gal 5:20 emulations, w, strife, seditions, heresies, *2372*
Eph 2: 3 and were by nature the children of w, *3709*
4:26 let not the sun go down upon your w: *3950*
4:31 and w, and anger, and clamour, and *2372*
5: 6 of these *things* cometh the w of God upon *3709*
6: 4 ye fathers, **provoke** not your children **to** w: *3949*
Col 3: 6 For which *things'* sake the w of God *3709*
3: 8 w, malice, blasphemy, *2372*
1Th 1:10 which delivered us from the w to come. *3709*
2:16 for the w is come upon them to *3709*
5: 9 For God hath not appointed us to w, but *3709*
1Ti 2: 8 up holy hands, without w and doubting. *3709*
Heb 3:11 So I sware in my w, They shall not enter *3709*
4: 3 as *he* said, As I have sworn in my w, if they *3709*
11:27 not fearing the w of the king: *2372*
Jas 1:19 be swift to hear, slow to speak, slow to w: *3709*
1:20 For the w of man worketh not *3709*
Rev 6:16 on the throne, and from the w of the Lamb: *3709*
6:17 For the great day of his w is come; and *3709*
11:18 and thy w is come, and the time of *3709*
12:12 having great w, because he knoweth that he *2372*
14: 8 of the wine of the w of her fornication. *2372*
14:10 The same shall drink of the wine of the w *2372*
14:19 cast *it* into the great winepress of the w of *2372*
15: 1 for in them is filled up the w of God. *2372*
15: 7 seven golden vials full of the w of God, *2372*
16: 1 pour out the vials of the w of God upon *2372*
16:19 cup of the wine of the fierceness of his w. *3709*
18: 3 of the wine of the w of her fornication, *2372*
19:15 of the fierceness and w of Almighty God. *3709*

WRATHFUL (2) [WRATH]
Ps 69:24 and let thy w anger take hold of them. 2740
Pr 15:18 A w man stirreth up strife: but *he that is* 2534

WRATHS (1) [WRATH]
2Co 12:20 envyings, w, strifes, backbitings, *2372*

WREATH (1) [WREATHED, WREATHEN, WREATHS]
2Ch 4:13 two rows *of* pomegranates on each w, to 7639

WREATHED (1) [WREATH]
La 1:14 they are w, *and* come up upon my neck: 8276

WREATHEN (10) [WREATH]
Ex 28:14 *of* w work shalt thou make them, and 5688
28:14 and fasten the w chains to the ouches. 5688
28:22 chains at the ends *of* w work *of* pure gold. 5688
28:24 thou shalt put the two w *chains of* gold in 5688
28:25 *the other* two ends of the two w *chains* thou 5688
39:15 chains at the ends, *of* w work *of* pure gold. 5688
39:17 they put the two w *chains of* gold in 5688
39:18 the two ends of the two w *chains* they 5688
2Ki 25:17 the w **work**, and pomegranates upon 7639
25:17 these had the second pillar with w **work**. 7639

WREATHS (3) [WREATH]
1Ki 7:17 nets of checker work, *and* w of chain work, 1434
2Ch 4:12 the two w to cover the two pommels of 7639
4:13 four hundred pomegranates on the two w; 7639

WREST (5) [WRESTLE]
Ex 23: 2 cause to decline after many to w *judgment:* 5186
23: 6 Thou shalt not w the judgment of thy poor 5186
Dt 16:19 Thou shalt not w judgment; thou shalt not 5186
Ps 56: 5 Every day they w my words: all their 6087
2Pe 3:16 *they that are* unlearned and unstable w, *4761*

WRESTLE (1) [WREST, WRESTLED, WRESTLINGS]
Eph 6:12 For we w not against flesh and *1510+3823*

WRESTLED (3) [WRESTLE]
Ge 30: 8 With great wrestlings have I w with my 6617
32:24 there w a man with him until the breaking of 79
32:25 thigh was out of joint, as he w with him. 79

WRESTLINGS (1) [WRESTLE]
Ge 30: 8 With great w have I wrestled with my 5319

WRETCHED (2) [WRETCHEDNESS]
Ro 7:24 O w man that I am! who shall deliver me *5005*
Rev 3:17 and knowest not that thou art w, and *5005*

WRETCHEDNESS (1) [WRETCHED]
Nu 11:15 in thy sight; and let me not see my w. 7451

WRING (3) [WRINGED, WRINGING, WRUNG]
Lev 1:15 and w **off** his head, and burn *it* on the altar; 4454
5: 8 w **off** his head from his neck, but shall not 4454
Ps 75: 8 the wicked of the earth shall w *them* **out**, 4680

W

WRINGED (1) [WRING]
Jdg 6:38 w the dew out of the fleece, a bowl full *of* 4680

WRINGING (1) [WRING]
Pr 30:33 and the w of the nose bringeth forth blood: 4330

WRINKLE (1) [WRINKLES]
Eph 5:27 or w, or any such *thing;* but that it should *4512*

WRINKLES (1) [WRINKLE]
Job 16: 8 thou hast **filled** me **with** w, *which* is a 7059

WRITE (91) [HANDWRITING, WRITER, WRITER'S, WRITEST, WRITETH, WRITING, WRITINGS, WRITTEN, WROTE]
Ex 17:14 W this *for* a memorial in a book, and 3789
34: 1 I will w upon *these* tables the words that 3789
34:27 said unto Moses, W thou these words: 3789
Nu 5:23 the priest shall w these curses in a book, 3789
17: 2 w thou every man's name upon his rod. 3789
17: 3 thou shalt w Aaron's name upon the rod of 3789
Dt 6: 9 thou shalt w them upon the posts of thy 3789
10: 2 I will w on the tables the words that were in 3789
11:20 thou shalt w them upon the door posts of 3789
17:18 that he shall w him a copy of this law in a 3789
24: 1 let him w her a bill of divorcement, and 3789
24: 3 w her a bill of divorcement, and giveth *it* in 3789
27: 3 thou shalt w upon them all the words of this 3789
27: 8 thou shalt w upon the stones all the words 3789
31:19 Now therefore w ye this song for you, 3789
2Ch 26:22 did Isaiah the prophet, the son of Amoz, w. 3789
Ezr 5:10 that we might w the names of the men that 3790
Ne 9:38 w *it;* and our princes, Levites, *and* priests, 3789
Est 8: 8 W ye also for the Jews, as it liketh you, 3789
Pr 3: 3 w them upon the table of thine heart: 3789
7: 3 w them upon the table of thine heart. 3789
Isa 8: 1 w in it with a man's pen concerning 3789
10: 1 that w grievousness *which* they have 3789
10:19 shall be few, that a child may w them. 3789
30: 8 w it before them in a table, and note it in a 3789
Jer 22:30 saith the LORD, W ye this man childless, 3789
30: 2 W thee all the words that I have spoken 3789
31:33 their inward parts, and w it in their hearts; 3789
36: 2 w therein all the words that I have spoken 3789
36:17 How didst thou w all these words at his 3789
36:28 w in it all the former words that were in 3789
Eze 24: 2 Son of man, w thee the name of the day, 3789
37:16 w upon it, For Judah, and for the children 3789
37:16 another stick, and w upon it, For Joseph, 3789
43:11 w *it* in their sight, that they may keep 3789
Hab 2: 2 W the vision, and make *it* plain upon 3789
Mk 10: 4 Moses suffered to w a bill of divorcement, *1125*
Lk 1: 3 to w unto thee in order, most excellent *1125*
16: 6 thy bill, and sit down quickly, and w fifty. *1125*
16: 7 unto him, Take thy bill, and w fourscore. *1125*
Jn 1:45 and the prophets, did w, Jesus of Nazareth, *1125*
19:21 to Pilate, W not, The King of the Jews; *1125*
Ac 15:20 But that *we* w unto them, that *they* abstain *1989*
25:26 Of whom I have no certain *thing* to w unto *1125*
25:26 I might have somewhat to w. *1125*
1Co 4:14 I w not these *things* to shame you, but *1125*
14:37 let him acknowledge that *the things* that I w *1125*
2Co 1:13 For we w none other *things* unto you, *1125*
2: 9 For to this end also did I w, that I might *1125*
9: 1 it is superfluous for me to w to you: *1125*
13: 2 being absent now I w to them which *1125*
13:10 Therefore I w these *things* being absent, *1125*
Gal 1:20 Now *the things* which I w unto you, *1125*
Php 3: 1 To w the same *things* to you, to me indeed *1125*
1Th 4: 9 love ye need not that *I* w unto you: *1125*
5: 1 ye have no need that *I* w unto you. *1125*
2Th 3:17 which is the token in every epistle: so I w. *1125*
1Ti 3:14 These *things* w I unto thee, hoping to come *1125*
Heb 8:10 into their mind, and w them in their hearts: *1924*
10:16 and in their minds will I w them; *1924*
2Pe 3: 1 second epistle, beloved, I now w unto you; *1125*
1Jn 1: 4 And these *things* w we unto you, that your *1125*
2: 1 these *things* w I unto you, that ye sin not. *1125*
2: 7 I w no new commandment unto you, but *1125*
2: 8 Again, a new commandment I w unto you, *1125*
2:12 I w unto you, little children, because *1125*
2:13 I w unto you, fathers, because ye have *1125*
2:13 I w unto you, young men, because *1125*
2:13 I w unto you, little children, because *1125*
2Jn 1:12 Having many *things* to w unto you, I would *1125*
1:12 unto you, I would not *w* with paper and ink: NIG
3Jn 1:13 I had many *things* to w, *1125*
1:13 but I will not with ink and pen w unto thee: *1125*
Jude 1: 3 when I gave all diligence to w unto you of *1125*
1: 3 it was needful for me to w unto you, and *1125*
Rev 1:11 w in a book, and send *it* unto the seven *1125*
1:19 W *the things* which thou hast seen, and *1125*
2: 1 Unto the angel of the church of Ephesus w; *1125*
2: 8 unto the angel of the church in Smyrna w; *1125*
2:12 to the angel of the church in Pergamos w; *1125*
2:18 unto the angel of the church in Thyatira w; *1125*
3: 1 unto the angel of the church in Sardis w; *1125*
3: 7 the angel of the church in Philadelphia w; *1125*
3:12 and I will w upon him the name of my God, *1125*
3:12 and *I will w upon him* my new name. NIG
3:14 angel of the church of the Laodiceans w; *1125*
10: 4 had uttered their voices, I was about to w: *1125*
10: 4 the seven thunders uttered, and w them not. *1125*
14:13 a voice from heaven saying unto me, W, *1125*
19: 9 And he saith unto me, W, Blessed *are* they *1125*
21: 5 And he said unto me, W: for these words *1125*

WRITER (2) [WRITE]
Jdg 5:14 Zebulun they that handle the pen of the w. 5608
Ps 45: 1 *the* king: my tongue *is* the pen of a ready w. 5608

WRITER'S (2) [WRITE]
Eze 9: 2 *with* linen, with a w inkhorn by his side: 5608
9: 3 which *had* the w inkhorn by his side; 5608

WRITEST (2) [WRITE]
Job 13:26 For thou w bitter *things* against me, and 3789
Eze 37:20 the sticks whereon thou w shall be in thine 3789

WRITETH (1) [WRITE]
Ps 87: 6 shall count, when he w *up* the people, 3789

WRITING (38) [WRITE]
Ex 32:16 the w *was* the writing of God, graven upon 4385
32:16 the writing *was* the w of God, graven upon 4385
39:30 wrote upon it a w, *like to* the engravings of 4385
Dt 10: 4 according to the first w, the ten 4385
31:24 when Moses had made an end of w 3789
1Ch 28:19 me understand in w by *his* hand upon me, 3791
2Ch 2:11 Huram the king of Tyre answered in w, 3791
21:12 there came a w to him from Elijah 4385
35: 4 according to the w of David king of Israel, 3791
35: 4 and according to the w of Solomon his son. 4385
36:22 his kingdom, and *put it* also in w, saying, 4385
Ezr 1: 1 his kingdom, and *put it* also in w, saying, 4385
4: 7 the w of the letter *was* written in the Syrian 3791
Est 1:22 into every province according to the w 3791
3:12 every province according to the w thereof, 3791
3:14 The copy of the w for a commandment to 3791
4: 8 Also he gave him the copy of the w of 3791
8: 8 for the w which *is* written in the king's 3791
8: 9 *unto* every province according to the w 3791
8: 9 to the Jews according to their w, and 3791
8:13 The copy of the w for a commandment to 3791
9:27 keep these two days according to their w, 3791
Isa 38: 9 The w of Hezekiah, king of Judah, when he 4385
Eze 13: 9 neither shall they be written in the w of 3791
Da 5: 7 Whosoever shall read this w, and shew me 3792
5: 8 wise *men:* but they could not read the w, 3792
5:15 that they should read this w, and 3792
5:16 now if thou canst read the w, and 3792
5:17 yet I will read the w unto the king, and 3792
5:24 hand sent from him; and this w *was* written. 3792
5:25 this *is* the w that *was* written, MENE, 3792
6: 8 establish the decree, and sign the w, 3792
6: 9 Wherefore king Darius signed the w and 3792
6:10 Now when Daniel knew that the w *was* 3792
Mt 5:31 let him give her a **w of divorcement:** *647*
19: 7 then command to give a w of divorcement, *975*
Lk 1:63 And he asked for a w **table**, and wrote, *4093*
Jn 19:19 And the w was, JESUS OF NAZARETH *1125*

WRITINGS (1) [WRITE]
Jn 5:47 But if ye believe not his w, how shall ye *1121*

WRITTEN (291) [WRITE]
Ex 24:12 a law, and commandments which I have w; 3789
31:18 tables of stone, w with the finger of God. 3789
32:15 the tables *were* w on both their sides; on 3789
32:15 the one side and on the other *were* they w. 3789

W

Ex	32:32	out of thy book which thou hast **w**.	3789
Nu	11:26	they *were* of them that **were w**, but	3789
Dt	9:10	tables of stone **w** with the finger of God;	3789
	9:10	on them *was* **w** according to all the words,	NIH
	28:58	words of this law that are **w** in this book,	3789
	28:61	which *is* not **w** in the book of this law,	3789
	29:20	all the curses that are **w** in this book shall	3789
	29:21	covenant that are **w** in this book of the law:	3789
	29:27	to bring upon it all the curses that are **w** in	3789
	30:10	his statutes which are **w** in this book of	3789
Jos	1: 8	to do according to all that is **w** therein:	3789
	8:31	as it is **w** in the book of the law of Moses,	3789
	8:34	according to all that is **w** in the book of	3789
	10:13	*Is* not this **w** in the book of Jasher? So	3789
	23: 6	to do all that is **w** in the book of the law of	3789
2Sa	1:18	behold, *it is* **w** in the book of Jasher.)	3789
1Ki	2: 3	as *it is* **w** in the law of Moses,	3789
	11:41	*are* they not **w** in the book of the acts of	3789
	14:19	behold they *are* **w** in the book of	3789
	14:29	*are* they not **w** in the book of the chronicles	3789
	15: 7	*are* they not **w** in the book of the chronicles	3789
	15:23	*are* they not **w** in the book of the chronicles	3789
	15:31	*are* they not **w** in the book of the chronicles	3789
	16: 5	*are* they not **w** in the book of the chronicles	3789
	16:14	*are* they not **w** in the book of the chronicles	3789
	16:20	*are* they not **w** in the book of the chronicles	3789
	16:27	*are* they not **w** in the book of the chronicles	3789
	21:11	as *it was* **w** in the letters which she had sent	3789
	22:39	*are* they not **w** in the book of the chronicles	3789
	22:45	*are* they not **w** in the book of the chronicles	3789
2Ki	1:18	*are* they not **w** in the book of the chronicles	3789
	8:23	*are* they not **w** in the book of the chronicles	3789
	10:34	*are* they not **w** in the book of the chronicles	3789
	12:19	*are* they not **w** in the book of the chronicles	3789
	13: 8	*are* they not **w** in the book of the chronicles	3789
	13:12	*are* they not **w** in the book of the chronicles	3789
	14: 6	according unto that which is **w** in the book	3789
	14:15	*are* they not **w** in the book of the chronicles	3789
	14:18	*are* they not **w** in the book of the chronicles	3789
	14:28	*are* they not **w** in the book of the chronicles	3789
	15: 6	*are* they not **w** in the book of the chronicles	3789
	15:11	they *are* **w** in the book of the chronicles of	3789
	15:15	they *are* **w** in the book of the chronicles of	3789
	15:21	*are* they not **w** in the book of the chronicles	3789
	15:26	they *are* **w** in the book of the chronicles of	3789
	15:31	they *are* **w** in the book of the chronicles of	3789
	15:36	*are* they not **w** in the book of the chronicles	3789
	16:19	*are* they not **w** in the book of the chronicles	3789
	20:20	*are* they not **w** in the book of the chronicles	3789
	21:17	*are* they not **w** in the book of the chronicles	3789
	21:25	*are* they not **w** in the book of the chronicles	3789
	22:13	to do according unto all that which is **w**	3789
	23: 3	of this covenant that were **w** in this book.	3789
	23:21	as it is **w** in the book of this covenant.	3789
	23:24	**w** in the book that Hilkiah the priest found	3789
	23:28	*are* they not **w** in the book of the chronicles	3789
	24: 5	*are* they not **w** in the book of the chronicles	3789
1Ch	4:41	these **w** by name came in the days of	3789
	9: 1	they *were* **w** in the book of the kings of	3789
	16:40	*to do* according to all that is **w** in the law of	3789
	29:29	they *are* **w** in the book of Samuel the seer,	3789
2Ch	9:29	*are* they not **w** in the book of Nathan	3789
	12:15	*are* they not **w** in the book of Shemaiah	3789
	13:22	*are* **w** in the story of the prophet Iddo.	3789
	16:11	they *are* **w** in the book of the kings of Judah	3789
	20:34	behold they *are* **w** in the book of Jehu	3789
	23:18	as it is **w** in the law of Moses,	3789
	24:27	behold they *are* **w** in the story of the book	3789
	25: 4	*did* as it is **w** in the law in the book of	3789
	25:26	*are* they not **w** in the book of the kings of	3789
	27: 7	lo they *are* **w** in the book of the kings of	3789
	28:26	they *are* **w** in the book of the kings of Judah	3789
	30: 5	*it* of a long *time in such sort* as it was **w**.	3789
	30:18	eat the passover otherwise than it was **w**.	3789
	31: 3	as it is **w** in the law of the LORD.	3789
	32:32	they *are* **w** in the vision of Isaiah	3789
	33:18	they *are* **w** in the book of the kings of Israel.	NIH
	33:19	they *are* **w** among the sayings of the seers.	3789
	34:21	to do after all that is **w** in this book.	3789
	34:24	*even* all the curses that are **w** in the book	3789
	34:31	of the covenant which are **w** in this book.	3789
	35:12	as it is **w** in the book of Moses.	3789
	35:25	and behold, they *are* **w** in the lamentations.	3789
	35:26	according to that which was **w** in the law of	3789
	35:27	they *are* **w** in the book of the kings of Israel	3789
	36: 8	they *are* **w** in the book of the kings of Israel	3789
Ezr	3: 2	as it is **w** in the law of Moses the man of	3789
	3: 4	as it is **w**, and *offered* the daily burnt	3789
	4: 7	the writing of the letter *was* **w** in the Syrian	3789
	5: 7	sent a letter unto him, wherein *was* **w** thus:	3790
	6: 2	a roll, and therein *was* a record thus **w**:	3790
	6:18	as it is **w** in the book of Moses.	3792
	8:34	and all the weight was **w** at that time.	3789
Ne	6: 6	Wherein *was* **w**, *It is* reported among	3789
	7: 5	came up at the first, and found **w** therein,	3789
	8:14	they found **w** in the law which the LORD	3789
	8:15	of thick trees, to make booths, as it is **w**.	3789
	10:34	the LORD our God, as it is **w** in the law:	3789
	10:36	as it is **w** in the law, and the firstlings of	3789
	12:23	*were* **w** in the book of the chronicles,	3789
	13: 1	therein was found **w**, that the Ammonite	3789
Est	1:19	let it be **w** among the laws of the Persians	3789
	2:23	it was **w** in the book of the chronicles	3789
	3: 9	let it be **w** that they may be destroyed:	3789
	3:12	there was **w** according to all that Haman	3789
	3:12	in the name of king Ahasuerus was it **w**,	3789
	6: 2	it was found **w**, that Mordecai had told of	3789
	8: 5	let it be **w** to reverse the letters devised by	3789
	8: 8	for the writing which *is* **w** in the king's	3789
	8: 9	it was **w** according to all that Mordecai	3789
	9:23	and as Mordecai had **w** unto them;	3789
	9:32	matters of Purim; and *it was* **w** in the book.	3789
	10: 2	*are* they not **w** in the book of the chronicles	3789
Job	19:23	O that my words were now **w**! O that they	3789
	31:35	and *that* mine adversary had **w** a book.	3789
Ps	40: 7	in the volume of the book *it is* **w** of me,	3789
	69:28	the living, and not be **w** with the righteous.	3789
	102:18	This shall be **w** for the generation to come:	3789
	139:16	in thy book all *my members* were **w**,	3789
	149: 9	To execute upon them the judgment **w**:	3789
Pr	22:20	Have not I **w** to thee excellent things in	3789
Ecc	12:10	*that which was* **w** *was* upright, *even* words	3789
Isa	4: 3	*even* every one that is **w** among the living	3789
	65: 6	Behold, *it is* **w** before me: I will not keep	3789
Jer	17: 1	The sin of Judah *is* **w** with a pen of iron,	3789
	17:13	they that depart from me shall be **w** in	3789
	25:13	*even* all that is **w** in this book, which	3789
	36: 6	the roll, which thou hast **w** from my mouth,	3789
	36:29	Why hast thou **w** therein, saying,	3789
	45: 1	when he had **w** these words in a book at	3789
	51:60	*even* all these words that are **w** against	3789
Eze	2:10	and it *was* **w** within and without:	3789
	2:10	*there was* **w** therein lamentations, and	3789
	13: 9	neither shall they be **w** in the writing of	3789
Da	5:24	sent from him; and this writing *was* **w**.	7560
	5:25	this *is* the writing that *was* **w**, MENE,	7560
	9:11	the oath that *is* **w** in the law of Moses	3789
	9:13	As *it is* **w** in the law of Moses, all this evil	3789
	12: 1	every one that *shall* be found **w** in the book.	3789
Hos	8:12	I have **w** to him the great things of my law,	3789
Mal	3:16	a book of remembrance was **w** before him	3789
Mt	2: 5	of Judea: for thus it is **w** by the prophet,	*1125*
	4: 4	But he answered and said, It is **w**, Man	*1125*
	4: 6	for it is **w**, He shall give his angels charge	*1125*
	4: 7	Jesus said unto him, It is **w** again,	*1125*
	4:10	for it is **w**, Thou shalt worship the Lord thy	*1125*
	11:10	For this is *he,* of whom it is **w**, Behold,	*1125*
	21:13	And said unto them, It is **w**, My house shall	*1125*
	26:24	The Son of man goeth as it is **w** of him: but	*1125*
	26:31	for it is **w**, I will smite the shepherd, and	*1125*
	27:37	And set up over his head his accusation **w**,	*1125*
Mk	1: 2	As it is **w** in the prophets, Behold, I send	*1125*
	7: 6	as it is **w**, This people honoureth me with	*1125*
	9:12	and how it is **w** of the Son of man,	*1125*
	9:13	whatsoever they listed, as it is **w** of him.	*1125*
	11:17	he taught, saying unto them, Is it not **w**,	*1125*
	14:21	Son of man indeed goeth, as it is **w** of him:	*1125*
	14:27	for it is **w**, I will smite the shepherd, and	*1125*
	15:26	of his accusation was **w over**,	*1924*
Lk	2:23	(As it is **w** in the law of the Lord, Every	*1125*
	3: 4	As it is **w** in the book of the words of	*1125*
	4: 4	And Jesus answered him, saying, It is **w**,	*1125*
	4: 8	for it is **w**, Thou shalt worship the Lord thy	*1125*
	4:10	For it is **w**, He shall give his angels charge	*1125*
	4:17	he found the place where it was **w**,	*1125*
	7:27	This is *he,* of whom it is **w**, Behold, I send	*1125*
	10:20	because your names are **w** in heaven.	*1125*
	10:26	He said unto him, What is **w** in the law?	*1125*

Lk 18:31 all *things* that are **w** by the prophets *1125*
19:46 Saying unto them, It is **w**, My house is *1125*
20:17 and said, What is this then that is **w**, *1125*
21:22 that all *things* which are **w** may be fulfilled. *1125*
22:37 that this that is **w** must yet be accomplished *1125*
23:38 And a superscription also was **w** over him *1125*
24:44 which were **w** in the law of Moses, and *1125*
24:46 Thus it is **w**, and thus it behoved Christ to *1125*
Jn 2:17 his disciples remembered that it was **w**, *1125*
6:31 as it is **w**, He gave them bread from heaven *1125*
6:45 It is **w** in the prophets, And they shall be all *1125*
8:17 It is also **w** in your law, that the testimony *1125*
10:34 Is it not **w** in your law, I said, Ye are gods? *1125*
12:14 found a young ass, sat thereon; as it is **w**, *1125*
12:16 remembered they that these *things* were **w** *1125*
15:25 might be fulfilled that is **w** in their law, *1125*
19:20 and it was **w** in Hebrew, *and* Greek, *and* *1125*
19:22 What I have **w** I have written. *1125*
19:22 What I have written I have **w**. *1125*
20:30 his disciples, which are not **w** in this book: *1125*
20:31 But these are **w**, that ye might believe that *1125*
21:25 the which, if they should be **w** every one, *1125*
21:25 not contain the books that should be **w**. *1125*
Ac 1:20 For it is **w** in the book of Psalms, Let his *1125*
7:42 as it is **w** in the book of the prophets, O *ye* *1125*
13:29 And when they had fulfilled all that was **w** *1125*
13:33 as it is also **w** in the second psalm, Thou art *1125*
15:15 agree the words of the prophets; as it is **w**, *1125*
21:25 we have **w** and concluded that they observe *1989*
23: 5 for it is **w**, Thou shalt not speak evil of *1125*
24:14 believing all *things* which are **w** in the law *1125*
Ro 1:17 as it is **w**, The just shall live by faith. *1125*
2:15 Which shew the work of the law **w** in their *1123*
2:24 among the Gentiles through you, as it is **w**. *1125*
3: 4 as it is **w**, That thou mightest be justified in *1125*
3:10 As it is **w**, There is none righteous, no, *1125*
4:17 (As it is **w**, I have made thee a father of *1125*
4:23 Now it was not **w** for his sake alone, that it *1125*
8:36 As it is **w**, For thy sake we are killed all *1125*
9:13 As it is **w**, Jacob have I loved, *1125*
9:33 As it is **w**, Behold, I lay in Sion a *1125*
10:15 as it is **w**, How beautiful *are* the feet of *1125*
11: 8 (According as it is **w**, God hath given them *1125*
11:26 as it is **w**, There shall come out of Sion *1125*
12:19 for it is **w**, Vengeance *is* mine; I will repay, *1125*
14:11 For it is **w**, *As* I live, saith the Lord, every *1125*
15: 3 but, as it is **w**, The reproaches of them that *1125*
15: 4 For whatsoever *things* were **w aforetime** *4270*
15: 4 written aforetime were **w** for our learning, *4270*
15: 9 as it is **w**, For this cause I will confess to *1125*
15:15 I have **w** the more boldly unto you in some *1125*
15:21 But as it is **w**, To whom he was not spoken *1125*
16: S **W** to the Romans from Corinthus, *and* *1125*
1Co 1:19 For it is **w**, I will destroy the wisdom of *1125*
1:31 That, according as it is **w**, He that glorieth, *1125*
2: 9 But as it is **w**, Eye hath not seen, nor ear *1125*
3:19 For it is **w**, He taketh the wise in their own *1125*
4: 6 not to think *of men* above *that* which is **w**, *1125*
5:11 But now I have **w** unto you not to keep *1125*
9: 9 For it is **w** in the law of Moses, Thou shalt *1125*
9:10 For our sakes, no doubt, *this* is **w**: that he *1125*
9:15 have I **w** these *things*, that it should be *1125*
10: 7 as it is **w**, The people sat down to eat and *1125*
10:11 and they are **w** for our admonition, *1125*
14:21 In the law it is **w**, With *men* of other *1125*
15:45 And so it is **w**, The first man Adam was *1125*
15:54 be brought to pass the saying that is **w**, *1125*
16: S The first *epistle* to the Corinthians was **w** *1125*
2Co 3: 2 Ye are our epistle **w** in our hearts, known *1449*
3: 3 **w** not with ink, but with the Spirit of *1449*
3: 7 **w** *and* engraven in stones, *1121+1722*
4:13 according as it is **w**, I believed, *and* *1125*
8:15 As it is **w**, He that *had gathered* much had *1125*
9: 9 (As it is **w**, He hath dispersed abroad; *1125*
13: S to the Corinthians was **w** from Philippi, *1125*
Gal 3:10 for it is **w**, Cursed *is* every one that *1125*
3:10 are **w** in the book of the law to do them. *1125*
3:13 for it is **w**, Cursed *is* every one that hangeth *1125*
4:22 For it is **w**, that Abraham had two sons, *1125*
4:27 For it is **w**, Rejoice, *thou* barren that bearest *1125*
6:11 Ye see how large a letter I have **w** unto you *1125*
6: S Unto the Galatians **w** from Rome. *1125*
Eph 6: S **W** from Rome unto the Ephesians by *1125*
Php 4: S It was **w** to the Philippians from Rome by *1125*
Col 4: S **W** from Rome to the Colossians by *1125*
1Th 5: S unto the Thessalonians was **w** from Athens. *1125*
2Th 3: S to the Thessalonians was **w** from Athens. *1125*
1Ti 6: S The first to Timothy was **w** from Laodicea, *1125*
2Ti 4: S was **w** from Rome, when Paul was brought *1125*
Tit 3: S It was **w** to Titus, ordained the first bishop *1125*
Phm 1:19 I Paul have **w** *it* with mine own hand, I will *1125*
1: S **W** from Rome to Philemon, by Onesimus a *1125*
Heb 10: 7 I come (in the volume of the book it is **w** of *1125*
12:23 which are **w** in heaven, and to God the Judge *583*
13:22 for I have **w a letter** unto you in few *1989*
13: S **W** to the Hebrews from Italy by Timothy. *1125*
1Pe 1:16 Because it is **w**, Be ye holy; for I am holy. *1125*
5:12 I have **w** briefly, exhorting, and *1125*
2Pe 3:15 wisdom given unto him hath **w** unto you; *1125*
1Jn 2:14 I have **w** unto you, fathers, because ye have *1125*
2:14 I have **w** unto you, young men, because *1125*
2:21 I have not **w** unto you because ye know not *1125*
2:26 These *things* have I **w** unto you concerning *1125*
5:13 These *things* have I **w** unto you that believe *1125*
Rev 1: 3 and keep those *things* which are **w** therein: *1125*
2:17 and in the stone a new name **w**, *1125*
5: 1 him that sat on the throne a book **w** within *1125*
13: 8 whose names are not **w** in the book of life *1125*
14: 1 having his Father's name **w** in their *1125*
17: 5 And upon her forehead *was* a name **w**, *1125*
17: 8 whose names were not **w** in the book of life *1125*
19:12 and he had a name **w**, that no *man* knew, *1125*
19:16 on *his* vesture and on his thigh a name **w**, *1125*
20:12 of those *things* which were **w** in the books, *1125*
20:15 And whosoever was not found **w** in *1125*
21:12 gates twelve angels, and names **w** ***thereon***, *1924*
21:27 they which are **w** in the Lamb's book of *1125*
22:18 him the plagues that are **w** in this book: *1125*
22:19 *from* the *things* which are **w** in this book. *1125*

WRONG (26) [WRONGED, WRONGETH, WRONGFULLY]

Ge 16: 5 Sarai said unto Abram, My **w** *be* upon thee: 2555
Ex 2:13 he said to **him that did** the **w**, Wherefore 7563
Dt 19:16 man to testify against him *that which is* **w**; 5627
Jdg 11:27 but thou doest me **w** to war against me: 7451
1Ch 12:17 seeing *there is* no **w** in mine hands, the God 2555
16:21 He suffered no man to **do** them **w**: yea, 6231
Est 1:16 Vashti the queen hath not **done w** to 5753
Job 19: 7 Behold, I cry out *of* **w**, but I am not heard: 2555
Ps 105:14 He suffered no man to **do** them **w**: yea, 6231
Jer 22: 3 **do** no **w**, do no violence, to the stranger, 3238
22:13 his chambers by **w**; 3808+4941
La 3:59 O LORD, thou hast seen my **w**: 5792
Hab 1: 4 therefore **w** judgment proceedeth. 6127
Mt 20:13 one of them, and said, Friend, I do thee no **w**: *91*
Ac 7:24 And seeing one *of them* **suffer w**, *91*
7:26 ye are brethren; why do ye **w** one to another? *91*
7:27 But he that **did** his neighbour **w** thrust him *91*
18:14 If it were a matter of **w** or wicked lewdness, *92*
25:10 to the Jews have I **done** no **w**, as thou very *91*
1Co 6: 7 Why do ye not rather **take w**? why do ye not *91*
6: 8 you do **w**, and defraud, and that *your* brethren. *91*
2Co 7:12 *I did it* not for his cause that had **done** the **w**, *91*
7:12 nor for his cause that **suffered w**, but that our *91*
12:13 not burdensome to you? forgive me this **w**. *93*
Col 3:25 But he that **doeth w** shall receive *for* *91*
3:25 shall receive *for* the **w** which he hath **done**: *91*

WRONGED (2) [WRONG]

2Co 7: 2 we have **w** no *man*, we have corrupted no *91*
Phm 1:18 If he hath **w** thee, or oweth *thee* ought, *91*

WRONGETH (1) [WRONG]

Pr 8:36 he that sinneth *against* me **w** his own soul: 2554

WRONGFULLY (7) [WRONG]

Job 21:27 the devices *which* ye **w imagine** against 2554
Ps 35:19 Let not them that are mine enemies **w** 8267
38:19 and they that hate me **w** are multiplied. 8267
69: 4 *being* mine enemies **w**, are mighty: 8267
119:86 they persecute me **w**; help thou me. 8267
Eze 22:29 oppressed the stranger **w**. 3808+4941+871.1
1Pe 2:19 toward God endure grief, suffering **w**. *95*

WROTE (62) [WRITE]

Ex 24: 4 Moses **w** all the words of the LORD, and 3789
34:28 he **w** upon the tables the words of 3789
39:30 **w** upon it a writing, *like to* the engravings 3789

Nu 33: 2 Moses w their goings out according to their 3789
Dt 4:13 and he w them upon two tables of stone. 3789
5:22 he w them in two tables of stone, and 3789
10: 4 he w on the tables, according to the first 3789
31: 9 Moses w this law, and delivered it unto 3789
31:22 Moses therefore w this song the same day, 3789
Jos 8:32 he w there upon the stones a copy of 3789
8:32 which he w in the presence of the children 3789
24:26 Joshua w these words in the book of 3789
1Sa 10:25 w *it* in a book, and laid *it* up before 3789
2Sa 11:14 that David w a letter to Joab, and sent *it* by 3789
11:15 he w in the letter, saying, Set ye Uriah in 3789
1Ki 21: 8 So she w letters in Ahab's name, and 3789
21: 9 she w in the letters, saying, Proclaim a fast, 3789
2Ki 10: 1 Jehu w letters, and sent *to* Samaria, 3789
10: 6 he w a letter the second time to them, 3789
17:37 the commandment, which he w for you, 3789
1Ch 24: 6 w them before the king, and the princes, 3789
2Ch 30: 1 w letters also to Ephraim and Manasseh, 3789
32:17 He w also letters to rail on the LORD God 3789
Ezr 4: 6 w they *unto him* an accusation against 3789
4: 7 in the days of Artaxerxes w Bishlam, 3789
4: 8 Shimshai the scribe w a letter against 3790
4: 9 *w* Rehum the chancellor, and Shimshai NIH
Est 8: 5 which he w to destroy the Jews which *are* 3789
8:10 And he w in the king Ahasuerus' name, and 3789
9:20 Mordecai w these things, and sent letters 3789
9:29 and Mordecai the Jew, w with all authority, 3789
Jer 36: 4 Baruch w from the mouth of Jeremiah all 3789
36:18 and I w *them* with ink in the book. 3789
36:27 the words which Baruch w at the mouth of 3789
36:32 who w therein from the mouth of Jeremiah 3789
51:60 So Jeremiah w in a book all the evil that 3789
Da 5: 5 w over against the candlestick upon 3790
5: 5 the king saw the part of the hand that w. 3790
6:25 king Darius w unto all people, nations, 3790
7: 1 he w the dream, *and* told the sum of 3790
Mk 10: 5 For the hardness of your heart he w you *1125*
12:19 Master, Moses w unto us, If a man's *1125*
Lk 1:63 and w, saying, His name is John. *1125*
20:28 Saying, Master, Moses w unto us, If any *1125*
Jn 5:46 would have believed me: for he w of me. *1125*
8: 6 and with *his* finger w on the ground, *1125*
8: 8 he stooped down, and w on the ground. *1125*
19:19 And Pilate w a title, and put *it* on the cross. *1125*
21:24 and w these *things:* and we know that his *1125*
Ac 15:23 And they w *letters* by them after this *1125*
18:27 the brethren w, exhorting the disciples to *1125*
23:25 And he w a letter after this manner: *1125*
Ro 16:22 I Tertius, who w *this* epistle, salute you in *1125*
1Co 5: 9 I w unto you in an epistle not to company *1125*
7: 1 Now concerning *the things* whereof ye w *1125*
2Co 2: 3 And I w this same unto you, lest, when I *1125*
2: 4 anguish of heart I w unto you with many *1125*
7:12 Wherefore, though I w unto you, *I did it* not *1125*
Eph 3: 3 the mystery; (as I w **afore** in few *words,* *4270*
Phm 1:21 Having confidence in thy obedience I w *1125*
2Jn 1: 5 not as though I w a new commandment *1125*
3Jn 1: 9 I w unto the church: but Diotrephes, *1125*

WROTH (49) [WRATH]

Ge 4: 5 Cain was very w, and his countenance fell. 2734
4: 6 LORD said unto Cain, Why art thou w? 2734
31:36 Jacob was w, and chode with Laban: and 2734
34: 7 they were very w, because he had wrought 2734
40: 2 Pharaoh was w against two *of* his officers, 7107
41:10 Pharaoh was w with his servants, and 7107
Ex 16:20 and stank: and Moses was w with them. 7107
Nu 16:15 Moses was very w, and said unto 2734
16:22 wilt thou be w with all the congregation? 7107
31:14 Moses was w with the officers of the host, 7107
Dt 1:34 your words, and was w, and sware, saying, 7107
3:26 the LORD was w with me for your sakes, 5674
9:19 where*with* the LORD was w against you 7107
Jos 22:18 that to morrow he will be w with the whole 7107
1Sa 18: 8 Saul was very w, and the saying displeased 2734
20: 7 if he be **very** w, *then* be sure that evil 2734+2734
29: 4 the princes of the Philistines were w with 7107
2Sa 3: 8 was Abner very w for the words of 2734
13:21 heard of all these things, he was very w. 2734
22: 8 and shook, because he was w. 2734
2Ki 5:11 Naaman was w, and went away, and said, 7107
13:19 the man of God was w with him, and said, 7107
2Ch 16:10 Asa was w with the seer, and put him *in* a 3707
26:19 Uzziah was w, and *had* a censer in his hand 2196
26:19 while he was w with the priests, the leprosy 2196
28: 9 the LORD God of your fathers was w 2534
Ne 4: 1 he was w, and took great indignation, and 2734
4: 7 to be stopped, then they were very w, 2734
Est 1:12 therefore was the king very w, and 7107
2:21 were w, and sought to lay hand on the king 7107
Ps 18: 7 and were shaken, because he was w. 2734
78:21 the LORD heard *this,* and was w: 5674
78:59 When God heard *this,* he was w, and 5674
78:62 the sword; and was w with his inheritance. 5674
89:38 thou hast been w with thine anointed. 5674
Isa 28:21 he shall be w as *in* the valley of Gibeon, 7264
47: 6 I was w with my people, I have polluted 7107
54: 9 have I sworn that *I* would not be w with 7107
57:16 for ever, neither will I be always w: 7107
57:17 the iniquity of his covetousness was I w, 7107
57:17 was w, and he went on frowardly in 7107
64: 5 behold, thou art w; for we have sinned: 7107
64: 9 Be not w very sore, O LORD, 7107
Jer 37:15 Wherefore the princes were w with 7107
La 5:22 rejected us; thou art very w against us. 7107
Mt 2:16 was exceeding w, and sent forth, and *2373*
18:34 And his lord was w, and delivered him to *3710*
22: 7 But when the king heard *thereof,* he was w: *3710*
Rev 12:17 And the dragon was w with the woman, *3710*

WROUGHT (100) [WROUGHTEST]

Ge 34: 7 he had w folly in Israel in lying with 6213
Ex 10: 2 what things I have w in Egypt, and my 5953
26:36 twined linen, w **with needlework.** 4639+7551
27:16 fine twined linen, w with needlework: 4639
36: 1 w Bezaleel and Aholiab, and every wise 6213
36: 4 all the wise *men,* that w all the work of 6213
36: 8 every wise hearted *man* among them that w 6213
39: 6 they w onyx stones inclosed *in* ouches *of* 6213
Lev 20:12 they have w confusion; their blood *shall be* 6213
Nu 23:23 of Jacob and of Israel, What hath God w! 6466
31:51 took the gold of them, *even* all w jewels. 4639
Dt 13:14 *that* such abomination is w among you; 6213
17: 2 that hath w wickedness in the sight of 6213
17: 4 *that* such abomination is w in Israel: 6213
21: 3 which hath not been w with, *and* 5647
22:21 because she hath w folly in Israel, to play 6213
31:18 for all the evils which they shall have w, 6213
Jos 7:15 and because he hath w folly in Israel. 6213
Jdg 20:10 according to all the folly that they have w 6213
Ru 2:19 her mother in law with whom she had w, 6213
2:19 The man's name with whom I w to day *is* 6213
1Sa 6: 6 when he had w **wonderfully** among them, 5953
11:13 for to day the LORD hath w salvation in 6213
14:45 who hath w this great salvation in Israel? 6213
14:45 for he hath w with God this day. 6213
19: 5 the LORD w a great salvation for all 6213
2Sa 18:13 Otherwise I should have w falsehood 6213
23:10 the LORD w a great victory that day; 6213
23:12 and the LORD w a great victory. 6213
1Ki 5:16 which ruled over the people that w in 6213
7:14 came to king Solomon, and w all his work. 6213
7:26 the brim thereof was w like the brim of a 4639
9:23 which bare rule over the people that w in 6213
16:20 the acts of Zimri, and his treason that he w, 7194
16:25 Omri w evil in the eyes of the LORD, and 6213
2Ki 3: 2 he w evil in the sight of the LORD; but 6213
12:11 that w upon the house of the LORD, 6213
17:11 w wicked things to provoke the LORD to 6213
21: 6 he w much wickedness in the sight of 6213
1Ch 4:21 the families of the house of them that w 5656
22: 2 he set masons to hew w stones to build 1496
2Ch 3:14 and fine linen, and w cherubims thereon. 5927
21: 6 he w *that* which *was* evil in the eyes of 6213
24:12 also such as w iron and brass to mend 2796
24:13 So the workmen w, and the work was 6213
31:20 w *that* which *was* good and right and truth 6213
33: 6 he w much evil in the sight of the LORD, 6213
34:10 they gave it *to* the workmen that w in 6213
34:13 *were* overseers of all that w the work in any 6213
Ne 4:16 *that* the half of my servants w in the work, 6213
4:17 *every one* with one of his hands w in 6213
6:16 for they perceived that this work was w of 6213
9:18 out of Egypt, and had w great provocations; 6213
9:26 to thee, and they w great provocations. 6213
Job 12: 9 that the hand of the LORD hath w this? 6213
36:23 or who can say, Thou hast w iniquity? 6466

Ps 31:19 *which* thou hast w for them that trust in 6466
45:13 glorious within: her clothing *is* of w gold. 4865
68:28 O God, that which thou hast w for us. 6466
78:43 How he had w his signs in Egypt, and 7760
139:15 **curiously** w in the lowest parts of the earth. 7551
Ecc 2:11 on all the works that my hands had w, 6213
2:17 the work that is w under the sun *is* grievous 6213
Isa 26:12 for thou also hast w all our works in us. 6466
26:18 we have not w any deliverance *in* the earth; 6213
41: 4 Who hath w and done *it,* calling 6466
Jer 11:15 *seeing* she hath w lewdness *with* many, and 6213
18: 3 and behold, he w a work on the wheels. 6213
Eze 20: 9 I w for my name's sake, that *it* should not 6213
20:14 I w for my name's sake, that *it* should not 6213
20:22 mine hand, and w for my name's sake, 6213
20:44 when I have w with you for my name's 6213
29:20 because they w for me, saith the Lord 6213
Da 4: 2 wonders that the high God hath w toward 5648
Jnh 1:11 for the sea w, and was tempestuous. 1980
1:13 for the sea w, and was tempestuous against 1980
Zep 2: 3 of the earth, which have w his judgment; 6466
Mt 20:12 These last have w *but* one hour, and *4160*
26:10 for she hath w a good work upon me. *2038*
Mk 6: 2 that even such mighty works are w by his *1096*
14: 6 you her? she hath w a good work on me. *2038*
Jn 3:21 be made manifest, that they are w in God. *2038*
Ac 5:12 and wonders w among the people; *1096*
15:12 wonders God had w among the Gentiles by *4160*
18: 3 the same craft, he abode with them, and w: *2038*
19:11 And God w special miracles by the hands *4160*
21:19 had w among the Gentiles by his ministry. *4160*
Ro 7: 8 w in me all *manner of* concupiscence. *2716*
15:18 *things* which Christ hath not w by me, *2716*
2Co 5: 5 Now he that hath w us for the selfsame *2716*
7:11 what carefulness it w in you, yea, *2716*
12:12 Truly the signs of an apostle were w among *2716*
Gal 2: 8 (For he that w **effectually in** Peter to *1754*
Eph 1:20 Which he w in Christ, when he raised him *1754*
2Th 3: 8 but w with labour and travail night and day, *2038*
Heb 11:33 w righteousness, obtained promises, *2038*
Jas 2:22 Seest thou how faith w **with** his works, and *4903*
1Pe 4: 3 us to have w the will of the Gentiles, *2716*
2Jn 1: 8 we lose not *those things* which we have w, *2038*
Rev 19:20 with him the false prophet that w miracles *4160*

WROUGHTEST (1) [WROUGHT]

Ru 2:19 where w thou? blessed be he that did take 6213

WRUNG (4) [WRING]

Lev 1:15 the blood thereof shall be w **out** at the side 4680
5: 9 the rest of the blood shall be w **out** at 4680
Ps 73:10 and waters of a full *cup* are w **out** to them. 4680
Isa 51:17 of the cup of trembling, *and* w *them* **out**. 4680

X

XERXES See AHASUERUS

Y

YARN (4)

1Ki 10:28 horses brought out of Egypt, and **linen** y: 4723
10:28 the king's merchants received the **linen** y at 4723
2Ch 1:16 horses brought out of Egypt, and **linen** y: 4723
1:16 the king's merchants received the **linen** y at 4723

YE (3796) [YOU] See Index

YEA (340) See Index

YEAR (372) [YEAR'S, YEARLY, YEARS, YEARS']

Ge 7:11 In the six hundredth y of Noah's life, in 8141
8:13 to pass in the six hundredth and first y, 8141
14: 4 and *in* the thirteenth y they rebelled. 8141
14: 5 in the fourteenth y came Chedorlaomer, 8141
17:21 bear unto thee at this set time in the next y. 8141
26:12 received in the same y an hundredfold: 8141
47:17 with bread for all their cattle for that y. 8141
47:18 When that y was ended, they came unto 8141
47:18 they came unto him the second y, and 8141
Ex 12: 2 it *shall be* the first month of the y to you. 8141
12: 5 be without blemish, a male of the first y: 8141
13:10 keep this ordinance in his season from y to 3117
13:10 this ordinance in his season from year to y. 3117
23:11 the seventh *y* thou shalt let it rest and NIH
23:14 thou shalt keep a feast unto me in the y. 8141
23:16 of ingathering, *which is* in the end of the y, 8141
23:17 Three times in the y all thy males shall 8141
23:29 drive them out from before thee in one y; 8141
29:38 two lambs of the first y day by day 8141
30:10 y with the blood of the sin offering of 8141
30:10 once in the y shall he make atonement upon 8141
34:23 Thrice in the y shall all your men children 8141
34:24 before the LORD thy God thrice in the y. 8141
40:17 to pass in the first month in the second y, 8141
Lev 9: 3 a calf and a lamb, both of the first y, 8141
12: 6 she shall bring a lamb of the first y for a 8141
14:10 one ewe lamb of the first y without 8141
16:34 children of Israel for all their sins once a y. 8141
19:24 in the fourth y all the fruit thereof shall be 8141
19:25 in the fifth y shall ye eat of the fruit thereof, 8141
23:12 first y for a burnt offering unto the LORD. 8141
23:18 seven lambs without blemish of the first y, 8141
23:19 two lambs of the first y for a sacrifice of 8141
23:41 feast unto the LORD seven days in the y. 8141
25: 4 in the seventh y shall be a sabbath of rest 8141
25: 5 *for* it is a y of rest unto the land. 8141
25:10 ye shall hallow the fiftieth y, and 8141
25:11 A jubile shall that fiftieth y be unto you: 8141
25:13 In the y of this jubile ye shall return every 8141
25:20 shall say, What shall we eat the seventh y? 8141
25:21 my blessing upon you in the sixth y, 8141
25:22 ye shall sow the eighth y, and eat *yet* of old 8141
25:22 and eat *yet* of old fruit until the ninth y; 8141
25:28 him that hath bought it until the y of jubile: 8141
25:29 he may redeem it within a whole y after it 8141
25:29 it is sold; *within* a **full** y may he redeem it. 3117
25:30 not redeemed within the space of a full y, 8141
25:33 shall go out in the *y of* jubile: NIH
25:40 *and* shall serve thee unto the y of jubile: 8141
25:50 y that he was sold to him unto the year of 8141
25:50 that he was sold to him unto the y of jubile: 8141
25:52 but few years unto the y of jubile, 8141
25:54 then he shall go out in the y of jubile, 8141
27:17 If he sanctify his field from the y of jubile, 8141
27:18 *even* unto the y of the jubile, and it shall be 8141
27:23 *even* unto the y of the jubile: 8141
27:24 In the y of the jubile the field shall return 8141
Nu 1: 1 in the second y after they were come out of 8141
6:12 shall bring a lamb of the **first** y for a 1121+8141
6:14 one he lamb of the **first** y without 1121+8141
6:14 one ewe lamb of the **first** y without 1323+8141
7:15 one ram, one lamb of the **first** y, 1121+8141
7:17 he goats, five lambs of the **first** y: 1121+8141
7:21 one ram, one lamb of the **first** y, 1121+8141
7:23 he goats, five lambs of the **first** y: 1121+8141
7:27 one ram, one lamb of the **first** y, 1121+8141
7:29 he goats, five lambs of the **first** y: 1121+8141
7:33 one ram, one lamb of the **first** y, 1121+8141
7:35 he goats, five lambs of the **first** y: 1121+8141
7:39 one ram, one lamb of the **first** y, 1121+8141
7:41 he goats, five lambs of the **first** y: 1121+8141
7:45 one ram, one lamb of the **first** y, 1121+8141
7:47 he goats, five lambs of the **first** y: 1121+8141
7:51 one ram, one lamb of the **first** y, 1121+8141
7:53 he goats, five lambs of the **first** y: 1121+8141
7:57 one ram, one lamb of the **first** y, 1121+8141
7:59 he goats, five lambs of the **first** y: 1121+8141
7:63 one ram, one lamb of the **first** y, 1121+8141
7:65 he goats, five lambs of the **first** y: 1121+8141
7:69 one ram, one lamb of the **first** y, 1121+8141
7:71 he goats, five lambs of the **first** y: 1121+8141
7:75 one ram, one lamb of the **first** y, 1121+8141

Nu 7:77 he goats, five lambs of the **first y**: 1121+8141
7:81 one ram, one lamb of the **first y**, 1121+8141
7:83 he goats, five lambs of the **first y**: 1121+8141
7:87 the lambs of the **first y** twelve, 1121+8141
7:88 the lambs of the **first y** sixty. 1121+8141
9: 1 in the first month of the second y after they 8141
9:22 *it were* two days, or a month, or a y, 3117
10:11 *day* of the second month, in the second y, 8141
14:34 *even* forty days, each day for a y, shall ye 8141
15:27 he shall bring a she goat of the first y for a 8141
28: 3 two lambs of the **first y** without spot 1121+8141
28: 9 on the sabbath day two lambs of the first y 8141
28:11 lambs of the **first y** without spot; 1121+8141
28:14 month throughout the months of the y. 8141
28:19 and seven lambs of the **first y**: 1121+8141
28:27 one ram, seven lambs of the **first y**; 1121+8141
29: 2 lambs of the **first y** without blemish: 1121+8141
29: 8 *and* seven lambs of the **first y**; 1121+8141
29:13 *and* fourteen lambs of the **first y**; 1121+8141
29:17 lambs of the **first y** without spot: 1121+8141
29:20 fourteen lambs of the **first y** without 1121+8141
29:23 fourteen lambs of the **first y** without 1121+8141
29:26 lambs of the **first y** without spot: 1121+8141
29:29 fourteen lambs of the **first y** without 1121+8141
29:32 fourteen lambs of the **first y** without 1121+8141
29:36 lambs of the **first y** without blemish: 1121+8141
33:38 in the fortieth y after the children of Israel 8141
Dt 1: 3 it came to pass in the fortieth y, in 8141
11:12 from the beginning of the y even unto 8141
11:12 of the year even unto the end of the y. 8141
14:22 the field bringeth forth **y by year**. 8141+8141
14:22 the field bringeth forth **year by y**. 8141+8141
14:28 all the tithe of thine increase the same y, 8141
15: 9 saying, The seventh y, the year of release, 8141
15: 9 seventh year, the y of release, is at hand; 8141
15:12 in the seventh y thou shalt let him go free 8141
15:20 **y by year** in the place which 8141+8141+871.1
15:20 **year by y** in the place which 8141+8141+871.1
16:16 Three times in a y shall all thy males 8141
24: 5 *but* he shall be free at home one y, and 8141
26:12 all the tithes of thine increase the third y, 8141
26:12 *which is* the y of tithing, and hast given *it* 8141
31:10 in the solemnity of the y of release, in 8141
Jos 5:12 eat of the fruit of the land of Canaan that y. 8141
Jdg 10: 8 that y they vexed and oppressed 8141
11:40 of Jephthah the Gileadite four days in a y. 8141
17:10 will give thee ten *shekels* of silver by the y, 3117
1Sa 1: 7 *as* he did so y by year, when she went up to 8141
1: 7 *as* he did so year by y, when she went up to 8141
2:19 and brought *it* to him from y to year, 3117
2:19 and brought *it* to him from year to y, 3117
7:16 he went from y to year in circuit *to* Beth-el, 8141
7:16 he went from year to y in circuit *to* Beth-el, 8141
13: 1 Saul reigned one y; and when he had 8141
27: 7 in the country of the Philistines was a **full y** 3117
2Sa 11: 1 it came to pass, after the y was expired, 8141
21: 1 the days of David three years, y after year; 8141
21: 1 the days of David three years, year after y; 8141
1Ki 4: 7 each man *his* month in a y made provision. 8141
5:11 thus gave Solomon to Hiram y by year. 8141
5:11 thus gave Solomon to Hiram year by y. 8141
6: 1 eightieth y after the children of Israel were 8141
6: 1 in the fourth y of Solomon's reign over 8141
6:37 In the fourth y was the foundation of 8141
6:38 in the eleventh y, in the month Bul, 8141
9:25 three times in a y did Solomon offer burnt 8141
10:14 in one y was six hundred threescore 8141
10:25 spices, horses, and mules, a rate y by year. 8141
10:25 spices, horses, and mules, a rate year by y. 8141
14:25 it came to pass in the fifth y of king 8141
15: 1 Now in the eighteenth y of king Jeroboam 8141
15: 9 in the twentieth y of Jeroboam king of 8141
15:25 Israel in the second y of Asa king of Judah, 8141
15:28 Even in the third y of Asa king of Judah did 8141
15:33 In the third y of Asa king of Judah *began* 8141
16: 8 sixth y of Asa king of Judah *began* Elah 8141
16:10 and seventh y of Asa king of Judah, 8141
16:15 seventh y of Asa king of Judah did Zimri 8141
16:23 first y of Asa king of Judah *began* Omri to 8141
16:29 eighth y of Asa king of Judah *began* Ahab 8141
18: 1 of the LORD came to Elijah in the third y, 8141
20:22 for at the return of the y the king of Syria 8141
20:26 it came to pass at the return of the y, 8141
22: 2 it came to pass on the third y, that 8141
22:41 in the fourth y of Ahab king of Israel. 8141
22:51 y of Jehoshaphat king of Judah, 8141
2Ki 1:17 y of Jehoram the son of Jehoshaphat king 8141
3: 1 eighteenth y of Jehoshaphat king of Judah, 8141
8:16 in the fifth y of Joram the son of Ahab king 8141
8:25 In the twelfth y of Joram the son of Ahab 8141
8:26 to reign; and he reigned one y in Jerusalem. 8141
9:29 in the eleventh y of Joram the son of Ahab 8141
11: 4 the seventh y Jehoiada sent and fet 8141
12: 1 In the seventh y of Jehu Jehoash *began* to 8141
12: 6 twentieth y of king Jehoash the priests had 8141
13: 1 twentieth y of Joash the son of Ahaziah 8141
13:10 seventh y of Joash king of Judah *began* 8141
13:20 invaded the land *at* the coming in of the y. 8141
14: 1 In the second y of Joash son of Jehoahaz 8141
14:23 In the fifteenth y of Amaziah the son of 8141
15: 1 seventh y of Jeroboam king of Israel *began* 8141
15: 8 eighth y of Azariah king of Judah did 8141
15:13 thirtieth y of Uzziah king of Judah; 8141
15:17 thirtieth y of Azariah king of Judah *began* 8141
15:23 In the fiftieth y of Azariah king of Judah 8141
15:27 fiftieth y of Azariah king of Judah Pekah 8141
15:30 in the twentieth y of Jotham the son of 8141
15:32 In the second y of Pekah the son of 8141
16: 1 In the seventeenth y of Pekah the son of 8141
17: 1 In the twelfth y of Ahaz king of Judah 8141
17: 4 king of Assyria, as *he had done* y by year: 8141
17: 4 king of Assyria, as *he had done* year by y: 8141
17: 6 In the ninth y of Hoshea, the king of 8141
18: 1 Now it came to pass in the third y of 8141
18: 9 it came to pass in the fourth y of king 8141
18: 9 which *was* the seventh y of Hoshea son of 8141
18:10 *even* in the sixth y of Hezekiah, that *is* 8141
18:10 that *is* the ninth y of Hoshea king of Israel, 8141
18:13 Now in the fourteenth y of king Hezekiah 8141
19:29 Ye shall eat *this* y such things as grow of 8141
19:29 in the second y that which springeth of 8141
19:29 in the third y sow ye, and reap, and 8141
22: 3 it came to pass in the eighteenth y of king 8141
23:23 in the eighteenth y of king Josiah, 8141
23:36 and five y old when he *began* to reign; 8141
24:12 king of Babylon took him in the eighth y 8141
25: 1 it came to pass in the ninth y of his reign, 8141
25: 2 the city was besieged unto the eleventh y of 8141
25: 8 which *is* the nineteenth y of king 8141
25:27 thirtieth y of the captivity of Jehoiachin 8141
25:27 of Babylon, in the y that he *began* to reign, 8141
1Ch 20: 1 it came to pass, that after the y was expired, 8141
26:31 In the fortieth y of the reign of David they 8141
27: 1 month throughout all the months of the y, 8141
2Ch 3: 2 second month, in the fourth y of his reign. 8141
8:13 on the solemn feasts, three times in the y, 8141
9:13 came to Solomon in one y was six hundred 8141
9:24 spices, horses, and mules, a rate y by year. 8141
9:24 spices, horses, and mules, a rate year by y. 8141
12: 2 *that* in the fifth y of king Rehoboam 8141
13: 1 Now in the eighteenth y of king Jeroboam 8141
15:10 in the fifteenth y of the reign of Asa. 8141
15:19 the five and thirtieth y of the reign of Asa. 8141
16: 1 thirtieth y of the reign of Asa Baasha king 8141
16:12 ninth y of his reign was diseased in his feet, 8141
16:13 died in the one and fortieth y of his reign. 8141
17: 7 Also in the third y of his reign he sent to his 8141
22: 2 to reign, and he reigned one y in Jerusalem. 8141
23: 1 in the seventh y Jehoiada strengthened 8141
24: 5 the house of your God from y to year, 8141
24: 5 the house of your God from year to y, 8141
24:23 it came to pass at the end of the y, *that* 8141
27: 5 him the same y an hundred talents of silver, 8141
27: 5 unto him, both the second y, and the third. 8141
29: 3 He in the first y of his reign, in the first 8141
34: 3 For in the eighth y of his reign, while he 8141
34: 3 in the twelfth y he began to purge Judah 8141
34: 8 Now in the eighteenth y of his reign, 8141
35:19 In the eighteenth y of the reign of Josiah 8141
36:10 when the y was expired, king 8141
36:22 Now in the first y of Cyrus king of Persia, 8141
Ezr 1: 1 Now in the first y of Cyrus king of Persia, 8141
3: 8 Now in the second y of their coming unto 8141
4:24 So it ceased unto the second y of the reign 8140
5:13 in the first y of Cyrus the king of Babylon 8140
6: 3 In the first y of Cyrus the king *the same* 8140
6:15 which *was in* the sixth y of the reign of 8140
7: 7 in the seventh y of Artaxerxes the king. 8141

Ezr 7: 8 which *was in* the seventh y of the king. 8141
Ne 1: 1 *in* the twentieth y, as I was in Shushan 8141
2: 1 *in* the twentieth y of Artaxerxes the king, 8141
5:14 from the twentieth y even unto the two 8141
5:14 and thirtieth y of Artaxerxes the king, 8141
10:31 *that* we would leave the seventh y, and 8141
10:34 of our fathers, at times appointed y by year, 8141
10:34 of our fathers, at times appointed year by y, 8141
10:35 y by year, unto the house of the LORD: 8141
10:35 year by y, unto the house of the LORD: 8141
13: 6 thirtieth y of Artaxerxes king of Babylon 8141
Est 1: 3 In the third y of his reign, he made a feast 8141
2:16 month Tebeth, in the seventh y of his reign. 8141
3: 7 in the twelfth y of king Ahasuerus, 8141
9:27 time **every** y; 3605+8141+8141+2050.1
Job 3: 6 let it not be joined unto the days of the y, 8141
Ps 65:11 Thou crownest the y with thy goodness; 8141
Isa 6: 1 In the y that king Uzziah died I saw also 8141
14:28 In the y that king Ahaz died was this 8141
20: 1 In the y that Tartan came unto Ashdod, 8141
21:16 Within a y, according to the years of a 8141
29: 1 add ye y to year; let them kill sacrifices. 8141
29: 1 add ye year to y; let them kill sacrifices. 8141
34: 8 the y of recompences for the controversy of 8141
36: 1 Now it came to pass in the fourteenth y of 8141
37:30 Ye shall eat *this* y such as groweth of itself; 8141
37:30 the second y that which springeth of 8141
37:30 in the third y sow ye, and reap, and 8141
61: 2 To proclaim the acceptable y of 8141
63: 4 and the y of my redeemed is come. 8141
Jer 1: 2 of Judah, in the thirteenth y of his reign. 8141
1: 3 unto the end of the eleventh y of Zedekiah 8141
11:23 of Anathoth, *even* the y of their visitation. 8141
17: 8 shall not be careful in the y of drought, 8141
23:12 *even* the y of their visitation, saith 8141
25: 1 y of Jehoiakim the son of Josiah king of 8141
25: 1 that *was* the first y of Nebuchadrezzar king 8141
25: 3 From the thirteenth y of Josiah the son of 8141
25: 3 this day, that *is* the three and twentieth y, 8141
28: 1 it came to pass the same y, in the beginning 8141
28: 1 in the fourth y, *and* in the fifth month, 8141
28:16 *this* y thou *shalt* die, because thou hast 8141
28:17 So Hananiah the prophet died the same y in 8141
32: 1 in the tenth y of Zedekiah king of Judah, 8141
32: 1 which *was* the eighteenth y of 8141
36: 1 it came to pass in the fourth y of Jehoiakim 8141
36: 9 it came to pass in the fifth y of Jehoiakim 8141
39: 1 In the ninth y of Zedekiah king of Judah, 8141
39: 2 *And* in the eleventh y of Zedekiah, in 8141
45: 1 in the fourth y of Jehoiakim the son of 8141
46: 2 y of Jehoiakim the son of Josiah king of 8141
48:44 *even* upon Moab, the y of their visitation, 8141
51:46 a rumour shall both come *one* y, and 8141
51:46 after that in *another* y *shall come* a rumour, 8141
51:59 *into* Babylon in the fourth y of his reign. 8141
52: 1 and twenty y old when he *began* to reign, 8141
52: 4 it came to pass in the ninth y of his reign, 8141
52: 5 the city was besieged unto the eleventh y 8141
52:12 which *was* the nineteenth y of 8141
52:28 in the seventh y three thousand Jews and 8141
52:29 In the eighteenth y of Nebuchadrezzar he 8141
52:30 twentieth y of Nebuchadrezzar 8141
52:31 thirtieth y of the captivity of Jehoiachin 8141
52:31 y of his reign lifted up the head of 8141
Eze 1: 1 Now it came to pass in the thirtieth y, in 8141
1: 2 which *was* the fifth y of king Jehoiachin's 8141
4: 6 I have appointed thee each day for a y. 8141
8: 1 it came to pass in the sixth y, in the sixth 8141
20: 1 it came to pass in the seventh y, in the fifth 8141
24: 1 Again in the ninth y, in the tenth month, 8141
26: 1 it came to pass in the eleventh y, in the first 8141
29: 1 In the tenth y, in the tenth *month,* in 8141
29:17 came to pass in the seven and twentieth y, 8141
30:20 it came to pass in the eleventh y, in the first 8141
31: 1 it came to pass in the eleventh y, in 8141
32: 1 it came to pass in the twelfth y, in 8141
32:17 It came to pass also in the twelfth y, in 8141
33:21 it came to pass in the twelfth y of our 8141
40: 1 In the five and twentieth y of our captivity, 8141
40: 1 in the beginning of the y, in the tenth *day* of 8141
40: 1 in the fourteenth y after that the city was 8141
46:13 *of* a lamb of the first y without blemish: 8141
46:17 then it shall be his to the y of liberty; 8141
Da 1: 1 In the third y of the reign of Jehoiakim king 8141
1:21 Daniel continued *even* unto the first y of 8141
2: 1 in the second y of the reign of 8141
5:31 *being* about threescore and two y old. 8140
7: 1 In the first y of Belshazzar king of Babylon 8140
8: 1 In the third y of the reign of king 8141
9: 1 In the first y of Darius the son of 8141
9: 2 In the first y of his reign I Daniel 8141
10: 1 In the third y of Cyrus king of Persia a 8141
11: 1 Also I in the first y of Darius the Mede, 8141
Am 1: 1 king of Israel, **two** y before the earthquake. 8141
Mic 6: 6 with burnt offerings, with calves of a y old? 8141
Hag 1: 1 In the second y of Darius the king, in 8141
1:15 in the second y of Darius the king. 8141
2:10 the ninth *month,* in the second y of Darius, 8141
Zec 1: 1 the eighth month, in the second y of Darius, 8141
1: 7 the month Sebat, in the second y of Darius, 8141
7: 1 it came to pass in the fourth y of king 8141
14:16 go up from y to year to worship the King, 8141
14:16 go up from year to y to worship the King, 8141
Lk 2:41 Now his parents went to Jerusalem every y *2094*
3: 1 Now in the fifteenth y of the reign of *2094*
4:19 To preach the acceptable y of the Lord. *1763*
13: 8 Lord, let it alone this y also, till I shall dig *2094*
Jn 11:49 being the high priest that *same* y, said unto *1763*
11:51 but being high priest that y, he prophesied *1763*
18:13 which was the high priest that *same* y. *1763*
Ac 11:26 that a whole y they assembled themselves *1763*
18:11 And he continued *there* a y and six months, *1763*
Ro 4:19 when he was about an **hundred** y **old,** *1541*
2Co 8:10 to do, but also to be forward **a** y **ago.** *575+4070*
9: 2 that Achaia was ready **a** y **ago**; *575+4070*
Heb 9: 7 *went* the high priest alone once every y, *1763*
9:25 the holy *place* every y with blood of others; *1763*
10: 1 y **by year** continually make *1763+2596*
10: 1 **year by** y continually make *1763+2596*
10: 3 a remembrance *again made* of sins every y. *1763*
Jas 4:13 and continue there a y, and buy and sell, *1763*
Rev 9:15 and a day, and a month, and a y, for to slay *1763*

YEAR'S (2) [YEAR]
Ex 34:22 and the feast of ingathering *at* the y end. 8141
2Sa 14:26 (for it was at **every** y end 3117+3117+3807.1

YEARLING See FATLING

YEARLY (9) [YEAR]
Lev 25:53 *And* as a y hired servant shall 8141+8141+871.1
Jdg 11:40 y to lament 3117+3117+4480+1886.5
21:19 y *in a place* which *is* 3117+3117+4480+1886.5
1Sa 1: 3 his city y to worship 3117+3117+4480+1886.5
1:21 went up to offer unto the LORD the y 3117
2:19 up with her husband to offer the y sacrifice. 3117
20: 6 for *there is* a y sacrifice there for all 3117
Ne 10:32 to charge ourselves y with the third *part* of 8141
Est 9:21 of the same, y, 3605+8141+8141+871.1+2050.1

YEARN, YEARNED See YERN, YERNED

YEARS (532) [YEAR]
Ge 1:14 and for seasons, and for days, and y: 8141
5: 3 Adam lived an hundred and thirty y, and 8141
5: 4 he had begotten Seth were eight hundred y: 8141
5: 5 Adam lived were nine hundred and thirty y: 8141
5: 6 Seth lived an hundred and five y, and 8141
5: 7 he begat Enos eight hundred and seven y, 8141
5: 8 of Seth were nine hundred and twelve y: 8141
5: 9 And Enos lived ninety y, and begat Cainan: 8141
5:10 begat Cainan eight hundred and fifteen y, 8141
5:11 days of Enos were nine hundred and five y: 8141
5:12 Cainan lived seventy y, and 8141
5:13 begat Mahalaleel eight hundred and forty y, 8141
5:14 of Cainan were nine hundred and ten y: 8141
5:15 Mahalaleel lived sixty and five y, and 8141
5:16 he begat Jared eight hundred and thirty y, 8141
5:17 were eight hundred ninety and five y: 8141
5:18 Jared lived an hundred sixty and two y, 8141
5:19 lived after he begat Enoch eight hundred y, 8141
5:20 of Jared were nine hundred sixty and two y: 8141
5:21 Enoch lived sixty and five y, and 8141
5:22 after he begat Methuselah three hundred y, 8141
5:23 Enoch were three hundred sixty and five y: 8141
5:25 lived an hundred eighty and seven y, 8141
5:26 Lamech seven hundred eighty and two y, 8141
5:27 were nine hundred sixty and nine y: 8141
5:28 Lamech lived an hundred eighty and two y, 8141

Ge 5:30 begat Noah five hundred ninety and five **y**. 8141
5:31 were seven hundred seventy and seven **y**: 8141
5:32 Noah was five hundred **y** old: and 8141
6: 3 his days shall be an hundred and twenty **y**. 8141
7: 6 Noah *was* six hundred **y** old when the flood 8141
9:28 after the flood three hundred and fifty **y**. 8141
9:29 of Noah were nine hundred and fifty **y**: 8141
11:10 Shem *was* an hundred **y** old, and 8141
11:10 and begat Arphaxad **two y** after the flood: 8141
11:11 after he begat Arphaxad five hundred **y**, 8141
11:12 Arphaxad lived five and thirty **y**, and 8141
11:13 he begat Salah four hundred and three **y**, 8141
11:14 And Salah lived thirty **y**, and begat Eber: 8141
11:15 he begat Eber four hundred and three **y**, 8141
11:16 Eber lived four and thirty **y**, and 8141
11:17 he begat Peleg four hundred and thirty **y**, 8141
11:18 And Peleg lived thirty **y**, and begat Reu: 8141
11:19 after he begat Reu two hundred and nine **y**, 8141
11:20 Reu lived two and thirty **y**, and 8141
11:21 he begat Serug two hundred and seven **y**, 8141
11:22 And Serug lived thirty **y**, and begat Nahor: 8141
11:23 lived after he begat Nahor two hundred **y**, 8141
11:24 Nahor lived nine and twenty **y**, and 8141
11:25 he begat Terah an hundred and nineteen **y**, 8141
11:26 Terah lived seventy **y**, and begat Abram, 8141
11:32 days of Terah were two hundred and five **y**: 8141
12: 4 five **y** old when he departed out of Haran. 8141
14: 4 Twelve **y** they served Chedorlaomer, and 8141
15: 9 Take me a heifer of **three y old**, and a she 8027
15: 9 a she goat of **three y old**, and a ram of 8027
15: 9 a ram of **three y old**, and a turtle-dove, and 8027
15:13 and they shall afflict them four hundred **y**; 8141
16: 3 after Abram had dwelt ten **y** in the land of 8141
16:16 Abram *was* fourscore and six **y** old, 8141
17: 1 when Abram was ninety **y** old and nine, 8141
17:17 be born unto him that is an hundred **y** old? 8141
17:17 and shall Sarah, that is ninety **y** old, bear? 8141
17:24 Abraham *was* ninety **y** old and nine, 8141
17:25 Ishmael his son *was* thirteen **y** old, when he 8141
21: 5 Abraham *was* an hundred **y** old, when his 8141
23: 1 an hundred and seven and twenty **y old**: 8141
23: 1 *these were* the **y** of the life of Sarah. 8141
25: 7 these *are* the days of the **y** of Abraham's 8141
25: 7 an hundred threescore and fifteen **y**. 8141
25: 8 full *of* **y**; and was gathered to his people. NIH
25:17 these *are* the **y** of the life of Ishmael, 8141
25:17 an hundred and thirty and seven **y**: 8141
25:20 Isaac was forty **y** old when he took 8141
25:26 Isaac *was* threescore **y** old when she bare 8141
26:34 Esau was forty **y** old when he took to wife 8141
29:18 I will serve thee seven **y** for Rachel thy 8141
29:20 Jacob served seven **y** for Rachel; and 8141
29:27 thou shalt serve with me yet seven other **y**. 8141
29:30 and served with him yet seven other **y**. 8141
31:38 This twenty **y** *have* I *been* with thee; 8141
31:41 Thus have I been twenty **y** in thy house; 8141
31:41 I served thee fourteen **y** for thy two 8141
31:41 thy two daughters, and six **y** for thy cattle: 8141
35:28 of Isaac were an hundred and fourscore **y**. 8141
37: 2 Joseph, *being* seventeen **y** old, was feeding 8141
41: 1 came to pass at the end of **two full y**, 3117+8141
41:26 The seven good kine *are* seven **y**; and 8141
41:26 and the seven good ears *are* seven **y**: 8141
41:27 kine that came up after them *are* seven **y**; 8141
41:27 the east wind shall be seven **y** of famine. 8141
41:29 there come seven **y** of great plenty 8141
41:30 there shall arise after them seven **y** of 8141
41:34 the land of Egypt in the seven plenteous **y**. 8141
41:35 let them gather all the food of those good **y** 8141
41:36 to the land against the seven **y** of famine, 8141
41:46 Joseph *was* thirty **y** old when he stood 8141
41:47 in the seven plenteous **y** the earth brought 8141
41:48 he gathered up all the food of the seven **y**, 8141
41:50 born two sons before the **y** of famine came, 8141
41:53 the seven **y** of plenteousness, that was in 8141
41:54 the seven **y** of dearth began to come, 8141
45: 6 For these **two y** *hath* the famine *been* in 8141
45: 6 yet *there are* five **y**, *in* the which *there shall* 8141
45:11 for yet *there are* five **y** of famine; lest thou, 8141
47: 9 The days of the **y** of my pilgrimage *are* an 8141
47: 9 my pilgrimage *are* an hundred and thirty **y**: 8141
47: 9 evil have the days of the **y** of my life been, 8141
47: 9 have not attained unto the days of the **y** of 8141
47:28 lived in the land of Egypt seventeen **y**: 8141
47:28 of Jacob was an hundred forty and seven **y**. 8141
50:22 and Joseph lived an hundred and ten **y**. 8141
50:26 *being* an hundred and ten **y** old: 8141
Ex 6:16 the **y** of the life of Levi *were* an hundred 8141
6:16 of Levi *were* an hundred thirty and seven **y**. 8141
6:18 the **y** of the life of Kohath *were* an hundred 8141
6:18 Kohath *were* an hundred thirty and three **y**. 8141
6:20 the **y** of the life of Amram *were* an hundred 8141
6:20 *were* an hundred and thirty and seven **y**. 8141
7: 7 Moses *was* fourscore **y** old, and 8141
7: 7 Aaron fourscore and three **y** old, when they 8141
12:40 in Egypt, *was* four hundred and thirty **y**. 8141
12:41 at the end of the four hundred and thirty **y**, 8141
16:35 the children of Israel did eat manna forty **y**, 8141
21: 2 buy a Hebrew servant, six **y** he shall serve: 8141
23:10 six **y** thou shalt sow thy land, and 8141
30:14 from twenty **y** old and above, shall give an 8141
38:26 from twenty **y** old and upward, for six 8141
Lev 19:23 three **y** shall it be as uncircumcised unto 8141
25: 3 Six **y** thou shalt sow thy field, and six years 8141
25: 3 and six **y** thou shalt prune thy vineyard, and 8141
25: 8 thou shalt number seven sabbaths of **y** unto 8141
25: 8 of years unto thee, seven times seven **y**; 8141
25: 8 the space of the seven sabbaths of **y** shall 8141
25: 8 of years shall be unto thee forty and nine **y**. 8141
25:15 According to the number of **y** after 8141
25:15 according unto the number of **y** of the fruits 8141
25:16 According to the multitude of **y** thou shalt 8141
25:16 according to the fewness of **y** thou shalt 8141
25:16 for *according to* the number *of the* **y** of NIH
25:21 it shall bring forth fruit for three **y**. 8141
25:27 Then let him count the **y** of the sale thereof, 8141
25:50 shall be according unto the number of **y**, 8141
25:51 If *there be* yet many **y** *behind,* according 8141
25:52 but few **y** unto the year of jubile, 8141
25:52 according unto his **y** shall he give *him* 8141
25:54 if he be not redeemed in these *y*, then NIH
27: 3 of the male from twenty **y** old even unto 8141
27: 3 twenty years old even unto sixty **y** old, 8141
27: 5 if *it be* from five **y** old even unto twenty 8141
27: 5 from five years old even unto twenty **y** old, 8141
27: 6 if *it be* from a month old even unto five **y** 8141
27: 7 if *it be* from sixty **y** old and above; if *it be* a 8141
27:18 the money according to the **y** that remain, 8141
Nu 1: 3 From twenty **y** old and upward, all that *are* 8141
1:18 from twenty **y** old and upward, by their 8141
1:20 every male from twenty **y** old and upward, 8141
1:22 every male from twenty **y** old and upward, 8141
1:24 from twenty **y** old and upward, all that *were* 8141
1:26 from twenty **y** old and upward, all that *were* 8141
1:28 from twenty **y** old and upward, all that *were* 8141
1:30 from twenty **y** old and upward, all that *were* 8141
1:32 from twenty **y** old and upward, all that *were* 8141
1:34 from twenty **y** old and upward, all that *were* 8141
1:36 from twenty **y** old and upward, all that *were* 8141
1:38 from twenty **y** old and upward, all that *were* 8141
1:40 from twenty **y** old and upward, all that *were* 8141
1:42 from twenty **y** old and upward, all that *were* 8141
1:45 from twenty **y** old and upward, 8141
4: 3 From thirty **y** old and upward even until 8141
4: 3 years old and upward even until fifty **y** old, 8141
4:23 From thirty **y** old and upward until fifty 8141
4:23 upward until fifty **y** old shalt thou number 8141
4:30 From thirty **y** old and upward even unto 8141
4:30 upward even unto fifty **y** old shalt thou 8141
4:35 From thirty **y** old and upward even unto 8141
4:35 years old and upward even unto fifty **y** old, 8141
4:39 From thirty **y** old and upward even unto 8141
4:39 years old and upward even unto fifty **y** old, 8141
4:43 From thirty **y** old and upward even unto 8141
4:43 years old and upward even unto fifty **y** old, 8141
4:47 From thirty **y** old and upward even unto 8141
4:47 years old and upward even unto fifty **y** old, 8141
8:24 from twenty and five **y** old and 8141
8:25 from the age of fifty **y** they shall cease 8141
13:22 *were.* (Now Hebron was built seven **y** 8141
14:29 from twenty **y** old and upward, 8141
14:33 shall wander in the wilderness forty **y**, 8141
14:34 *even* forty **y**, and ye shall know my breach 8141
26: 2 from twenty **y** old and upward, throughout 8141
26: 4 *Take the sum of the people,* from twenty **y** 8141
32:11 from twenty **y** old and upward, shall see 8141
32:13 them wander in the wilderness forty **y**, 8141
33:39 and three **y** old when he died in mount Hor. 8141

Dt	2: 7	these forty y the LORD thy God *hath been*	8141
	2:14	the brook Zered, *was* thirty and eight y;	8141
	8: 2	led thee these forty y in the wilderness,	8141
	8: 4	neither did thy foot swell, these forty y.	8141
	14:28	At the end of three y thou shalt bring forth	8141
	15: 1	At the end of *every* seven y thou shalt make	8141
	15:12	be sold unto thee, and serve thee six y;	8141
	15:18	hired servant *to thee,* in serving thee six y:	8141
	29: 5	I have led you forty y in the wilderness:	8141
	31: 2	I *am* an hundred and twenty y old *this* day;	8141
	31:10	saying, At the end of *every* seven y,	8141
	32: 7	of old, consider the y of many generations:	8141
	34: 7	an hundred and twenty y old when he died:	8141
Jos	5: 6	For the children of Israel walked forty y in	8141
	13: 1	Now Joshua was old *and* stricken in y; and	3117
	13: 1	Thou art old *and* stricken in y, and	3117
	14: 7	Forty y old *was* I when Moses the servant	8141
	14:10	me alive, as he said, these forty and five y,	8141
	14:10	I *am this* day fourscore and five y old.	8141
	24:29	died, *being* an hundred and ten y old.	8141
Jdg	2: 8	died, *being* an hundred and ten y old.	8141
	3: 8	Israel served Chushan-rishathaim eight y.	8141
	3:11	the land had rest forty y. And Othniel	8141
	3:14	served Eglon the king of Moab eighteen y.	8141
	3:30	of Israel. And the land had rest fourscore y.	8141
	4: 3	twenty y he mightily oppressed the children	8141
	5:31	in his might. And the land had rest forty y.	8141
	6: 1	them into the hand of Midian seven y.	8141
	6:25	even the second bullock of seven y **old**, and	8141
	8:28	the country was in quietness forty y in	8141
	9:22	When Abimelech had reigned three y over	8141
	10: 2	he judged Israel twenty and three y, and	8141
	10: 3	and judged Israel twenty and two y.	8141
	10: 8	eighteen y, all the children of Israel that	8141
	11:26	by the coasts of Arnon, three hundred y?	8141
	12: 7	Jephthah judged Israel six y. Then died	8141
	12: 9	for his sons. And he judged Israel seven y.	8141
	12:11	judged Israel; and he judged Israel ten y.	8141
	12:14	ten ass colts: and he judged Israel eight y.	8141
	13: 1	into the hand of the Philistines forty y.	8141
	15:20	in the days of the Philistines twenty y.	8141
	16:31	his father. And he judged Israel twenty y.	8141
Ru	1: 4	and they dwelled there about ten y.	8141
1Sa	4:15	Now Eli *was* ninety and eight y old; and	8141
	4:18	heavy. And he had judged Israel forty y.	8141
	7: 2	for it was twenty y: and all the house of	8141
	13: 1	and when he had reigned two y over Israel,	8141
	29: 3	or these y, and I have found no *fault* in him	8141
2Sa	2:10	Ish-bosheth Saul's son *was* forty y old	8141
	2:10	to reign over Israel, and reigned two y.	8141
	2:11	over the house of Judah was seven y	8141
	4: 4	was five y old when the tidings came of	8141
	5: 4	David *was* thirty y old when he *began* to	8141
	5: 4	he *began* to reign, *and* he reigned forty y.	8141
	5: 5	In Hebron he reigned over Judah seven y	8141
	5: 5	and three y over all Israel and Judah.	8141
	13:23	it came to pass after **two full** y,	3117+8141
	13:38	and went to Geshur, and was there three y.	8141
	14:28	So Absalom dwelt **two full** y in	3117+8141
	15: 7	it came to pass after forty y, that Absalom	8141
	19:32	was a very aged man, *even* fourscore y old:	8141
	19:35	I *am this* day fourscore y old: *and* can I	8141
	21: 1	was a famine in the days of David three y,	8141
	24:13	Shall seven y of famine come unto thee in	8141
1Ki	1: 1	Now king David was old *and* stricken in y;	3117
	2:11	that David reigned over Israel *were* forty y:	8141
	2:11	seven y reigned he in Hebron, and thirty	8141
	2:11	thirty and three y reigned he in Jerusalem.	8141
	2:39	it came to pass at the end of three y,	8141
	6:38	of it. So was he seven y in building it.	8141
	7: 1	was building his own house thirteen y,	8141
	9:10	it came to pass at the end of twenty y,	8141
	10:22	once in three y came the navy of Tharshish,	8141
	11:42	in Jerusalem over all Israel *was* forty y.	8141
	14:20	Jeroboam reigned *were* two and twenty y:	8141
	14:21	and one y old when he *began* to reign,	8141
	14:21	and he reigned seventeen y in Jerusalem,	8141
	15: 2	Three y reigned he in Jerusalem. And his	8141
	15:10	and one y reigned he in Jerusalem.	8141
	15:25	of Judah, and reigned over Israel **two** y.	8141
	15:33	over all Israel in Tirzah, twenty and four y.	8141
	16: 8	to reign over Israel in Tirzah, **two** y.	8141
	16:23	*began* Omri to reign over Israel, twelve y:	8141
	16:23	twelve years: six y reigned he in Tirzah.	8141
	16:29	over Israel in Samaria twenty and two y.	8141
	17: 1	there shall not be dew nor rain these y, but	8141
	22: 1	they continued three y without war between	8141
	22:42	and five y old when he *began* to reign;	8141
	22:42	he reigned twenty and five y in Jerusalem.	8141
	22:51	of Judah, and reigned **two** y over Israel.	8141
2Ki	3: 1	king of Judah, and reigned twelve y.	8141
	8: 1	it shall also come upon the land seven y.	8141
	8: 2	in the land of the Philistines seven y.	8141
	8:17	two y old was he when he *began* to reign;	8141
	8:17	and he reigned eight y in Jerusalem.	8141
	8:26	twenty y old *was* Ahaziah when he *began*	8141
	10:36	Israel in Samaria *was* twenty and eight y.	8141
	11: 3	her hid *in* the house of the LORD six y.	8141
	11:21	Seven y old *was* Jehoash when he *began* to	8141
	12: 1	and forty y reigned he in Jerusalem.	8141
	13: 1	Israel in Samaria, *and reigned* seventeen y.	8141
	13:10	Israel in Samaria, *and reigned* sixteen y.	8141
	14: 2	and five y old when he *began* to reign,	8141
	14: 2	reigned twenty and nine y in Jerusalem.	8141
	14:17	son of Jehoahaz king of Israel fifteen y.	8141
	14:21	which *was* sixteen y old, and made him	8141
	14:23	in Samaria, *and reigned* forty and one y.	8141
	15: 2	Sixteen y old was he when he *began* to	8141
	15: 2	and he reigned two and fifty y in Jerusalem.	8141
	15:17	over Israel, *and reigned* ten y in Samaria.	8141
	15:23	over Israel in Samaria, *and reigned* **two** y.	8141
	15:27	Israel in Samaria, *and reigned* twenty y.	8141
	15:33	twenty y old was he when he *began* to	8141
	15:33	and he reigned sixteen y in Jerusalem.	8141
	16: 2	Twenty y old *was* Ahaz when he *began* to	8141
	16: 2	reigned sixteen y in Jerusalem, and did not	8141
	17: 1	Elah to reign in Samaria over Israel nine y.	8141
	17: 5	went up *to* Samaria, and besieged it three y.	8141
	18: 2	five y old was he when he *began* to reign;	8141
	18: 2	he reigned twenty and nine y in Jerusalem.	8141
	18:10	at the end of three y they took it: *even* in	8141
	20: 6	I will add unto thy days fifteen y; and I will	8141
	21: 1	Manasseh *was* twelve y old when he *began*	8141
	21: 1	and reigned fifty and five y in Jerusalem.	8141
	21:19	and two y old when he *began* to reign,	8141
	21:19	to reign, and he reigned two y in Jerusalem.	8141
	22: 1	Josiah *was* eight y old when he *began* to	8141
	22: 1	he reigned thirty and one y in Jerusalem.	8141
	23:31	and three y old when he *began* to reign;	8141
	23:36	and he reigned eleven y in Jerusalem.	8141
	24: 1	and Jehoiakim became his servant three y:	8141
	24: 8	Jehoiachin *was* eighteen y old when he	8141
	24:18	and one y old when he *began* to reign,	8141
	24:18	and he reigned eleven y in Jerusalem.	8141
1Ch	2:21	whom he married when he *was* threescore y	8141
	3: 4	there he reigned seven y and six months:	8141
	3: 4	in Jerusalem he reigned thirty and three y.	8141
	23: 3	were numbered from the age of thirty y	8141
	23:24	from the age of twenty y and upward.	8141
	23:27	the Levites *were* numbered from twenty y	8141
	27:23	not the number of them from twenty y old	8141
	29:27	time that he reigned over Israel *was* forty y;	8141
	29:27	seven y reigned he in Hebron, and thirty	8141
	29:27	thirty and three *y* reigned he in Jerusalem.	NIH
2Ch	8: 1	it came to pass at the end of twenty y,	8141
	9:21	every three y once came the ships of	8141
	9:30	reigned in Jerusalem over all Israel forty y.	8141
	11:17	the son of Solomon strong, three y:	8141
	11:17	for three y they walked in the way of David	8141
	12:13	and forty y old when he *began* to reign,	8141
	12:13	and he reigned seventeen y in Jerusalem,	8141
	13: 2	He reigned three y in Jerusalem.	8141
	14: 1	In his days the land was quiet ten y.	8141
	14: 6	land had rest, and he had no war in those y;	8141
	18: 2	after *certain* y he went down to Ahab to	8141
	20:31	and five y old when he *began* to reign,	8141
	20:31	he reigned twenty and five y in Jerusalem.	8141
	21: 5	and two y old when he *began* to reign,	8141
	21: 5	and he reigned eight y in Jerusalem.	8141
	21:19	in process of time, after the end of two y,	3117
	21:20	two *y* old was he when he *began* to reign,	NIH
	21:20	he reigned in Jerusalem eight y, and	8141
	22: 2	two y old *was* Ahaziah when he *began* to	8141
	22:12	with them hid in the house of God six y:	8141
	24: 1	Joash *was* seven y old when he *began* to	8141
	24: 1	and he reigned forty y in Jerusalem.	8141
	24:15	and thirty y old *was he* when he died.	8141
	25: 1	and five y old *when* he *began* to reign,	8141

2Ch 25: 1 he reigned twenty and nine y in Jerusalem. 8141
25: 5 he numbered them from twenty y old and 8141
25:25 son of Jehoahaz king of Israel fifteen y. 8141
26: 1 who *was* sixteen y old, and made him king 8141
26: 3 Sixteen y old *was* Uzziah when he *began* to 8141
26: 3 and he reigned fifty and two y in Jerusalem. 8141
27: 1 and five y old when he *began* to reign, 8141
27: 1 and he reigned sixteen y in Jerusalem. 8141
27: 8 and twenty y old when he *began* to reign, 8141
27: 8 and reigned sixteen y in Jerusalem. 8141
28: 1 Ahaz *was* twenty y old when he *began* to 8141
28: 1 and he reigned sixteen y in Jerusalem: 8141
29: 1 to reign *when he was* five and twenty y old, 8141
29: 1 he reigned nine and twenty y in Jerusalem. 8141
31:16 of males, from three y old and upward, 8141
31:17 the Levites from twenty y old and upward, 8141
33: 1 Manasseh *was* twelve y old when he *began* 8141
33: 1 he reigned fifty and five y in Jerusalem: 8141
33:21 and twenty y old when he *began* to reign, 8141
33:21 to reign, and reigned two y in Jerusalem. 8141
34: 1 Josiah *was* eight y old when he *began* to 8141
34: 1 he reigned in Jerusalem one and thirty y. 8141
36: 2 and three y old when he *began* to reign, 8141
36: 5 and five y old when he *began* to reign, 8141
36: 5 and he reigned eleven y in Jerusalem: 8141
36: 9 Jehoiachin *was* eight y old when he *began* 8141
36:11 and twenty y old when he *began* to reign, 8141
36:11 to reign, and reigned eleven y in Jerusalem. 8141
36:21 kept sabbath, to fulfil threescore and ten y. 8141
Ezr 3: 8 appointed the Levites from twenty y old 8141
5:11 house that was builded these many y ago, 8140
Ne 5:14 *that is,* twelve y, I and my brethren have 8141
9:21 forty y didst thou sustain them in 8141
9:30 Yet many y didst thou forbear them, and 8141
Job 10: 5 the days of man? *are* thy y as man's days, 8141
15:20 the number of y is hidden to the oppressor. 8141
16:22 When a few y are come, then I shall go 8141
32: 7 and multitude of y should teach wisdom. 8141
36:11 days in prosperity, and their y in pleasures. 8141
36:26 neither can the number of his y be searched 8141
42:16 After this lived Job an hundred and forty y, 8141
Ps 31:10 is spent with grief, and my y with sighing: 8141
61: 6 king's life: *and* his y as many generations. 8141
77: 5 the days of old, the y of ancient times. 8141
77:10 *I will remember* the y of the right hand of 8141
78:33 consume in vanity, and their y in trouble. 8141
90: 4 For a thousand y in thy sight *are but* 8141
90: 9 we spend our y as a tale *that is told.* 8141
90:10 The days of our y *are* threescore years and 8141
90:10 The days of our years *are* threescore y and 8141
90:10 if by reason of strength *they be* fourscore y, 8141
90:15 *and* the y *wherein* we have seen evil. 8141
95:10 Forty y long was I grieved with *this* 8141
102:24 thy y *are* throughout all generations. 8141
102:27 *art* the same, and thy y shall have no end. 8141
Pr 4:10 and the y of thy life shall be many. 8141
5: 9 unto others, and thy y unto the cruel: 8141
9:11 and the y of thy life shall be increased. 8141
10:27 but the y of the wicked shall be shortened. 8141
Ecc 6: 3 beget an hundred *children,* and live many y, 8141
6: 3 so that the days of his y be many, and 8141
6: 6 though he live a thousand y twice *told,* yet 8141
11: 8 if a man live many y, *and* rejoice in them 8141
12: 1 nor the y draw nigh, when thou shalt say, 8141
Isa 7: 8 and five y shall Ephraim be broken, 8141
15: 5 *shall flee* unto Zoar, a heifer of **three y old**: 7992
16:14 saying, Within three y, as the years of a 8141
16:14 as the y of a hireling, and the glory of 8141
20: 3 barefoot three y *for* a sign and wonder upon 8141
21:16 according to the y of a hireling, and all 8141
23:15 that Tyre shall be forgotten seventy y, 8141
23:15 after the end of seventy y shall Tyre sing as 8141
23:17 come to pass after the end of seventy y, 8141
32:10 Many days and y shall ye be troubled, 8141
38: 5 behold, I will add unto thy days fifteen y. 8141
38:10 I am deprived of the residue of my y. 8141
38:15 softly all my y in the bitterness of my soul. 8141
65:20 for the child shall die an hundred y old; but 8141
65:20 the sinner *being* an hundred y old shall be 8141
Jer 25:11 shall serve the king of Babylon seventy y. 8141
25:12 to pass, when seventy y are accomplished, 8141
28: 3 Within **two full** y *will* I bring again 3117+8141
28:11 within the space of **two full** y. 3117+8141
29:10 That after seventy y be accomplished at 8141

34:14 At the end of seven y let ye go every man 8141
34:14 when he hath served thee six y, thou shalt 8141
48:34 unto Horonaim, *as* a heifer of **three y old**: 7992
52: 1 and he reigned eleven y in Jerusalem. 8141
Eze 4: 5 For I have laid upon thee the y of their 8141
22: 4 to draw near, and art come *even* unto thy y: 8141
29:11 neither shall it be inhabited forty y. 8141
29:12 *that are* laid waste shall be desolate forty y: 8141
29:13 At the end of forty y will I gather 8141
38: 8 in the latter y thou shalt come into the land 8141
38:17 which prophesied in those days *many* y, 8141
39: 9 and they shall burn them with fire seven y: 8141
Da 1: 5 so nourishing them three y, that at the end 8141
9: 2 understood by books the number of the y, 8141
9: 2 that *he* would accomplish seventy y in 8141
11: 6 in the end of y they shall join themselves 8141
11: 8 he shall continue *more* y than the king of 8141
11:13 shall certainly come after certain y with a 8141
Joel 2: 2 after it, *even* to the y of many generations. 8141
2:25 I will restore to you the y that the locust 8141
Am 2:10 led you forty y through the wilderness, 8141
4: 4 *and* your tithes after three y: 3117
5:25 and offerings in the wilderness forty y, 8141
Hab 3: 2 revive thy work in the midst of the y, 8141
3: 2 in the midst of the y make known; 8141
Zec 1:12 had indignation these threescore and ten y? 8141
7: 3 as I have done these so many y? 8141
7: 5 and seventh *month,* even those seventy y, 8141
Mal 3: 4 as *in* the days of old, and as *in* former y. 8141
Mt 2:16 coasts thereof, from **two y old** and under, *1332*
9:20 diseased with an issue of blood twelve y, *2094*
Mk 5:25 which had an issue of blood twelve y, *2094*
5:42 walked; for she was *of the age* of twelve y. *2094*
Lk 1: 7 and they both were *now* well stricken in y. *2250*
1:18 an old man, and my wife well stricken in y. *2250*
2:36 had lived with a husband seven y from her *2094*
2:37 *was* a widow of about fourscore and four y, *2094*
2:42 And when he was twelve **y old**, they went *2094*
3:23 himself began *to be* about thirty **y of age**, *2094*
4:25 when the heaven was shut up three y and *2094*
8:42 about twelve **y of age**, and she lay a dying. *2094*
8:43 a woman having an issue of blood twelve y, *2094*
12:19 thou hast much goods laid up for many y; *2094*
13: 7 *these* three y I come seeking fruit on this *2094*
13:11 which had a spirit of infirmity eighteen y, *2094*
13:16 Satan hath bound, lo *these* eighteen y, *2094*
15:29 *his* father, Lo, these many y do I serve thee, *2094*
Jn 2:20 Forty and six y was this temple in building, *2094*
5: 5 which had an infirmity thirty *and* eight y. *2094*
8:57 Thou art not yet fifty **y old**, and hast thou *2094*
Ac 4:22 For the man was above forty **y old**, *2094*
7: 6 and entreat *them* evil four hundred y. *2094*
7:23 And when he was full **forty** y old, it came *5063*
7:30 And when forty y were expired, *2094*
7:36 the Red sea, and in the wilderness forty y. *2094*
7:42 sacrifices *by the space of* forty y in *2094*
9:33 which had kept his bed eight y, and was *2094*
13:18 And about the time of **forty** y suffered he *5063*
13:20 about *the space of* four hundred and fifty y, *2094*
13:21 tribe of Benjamin, *by the space of* forty y. *2094*
19:10 And this continued by the space of two y; *2094*
20:31 that *by the space of* **three** y I ceased not to *5148*
24:10 been of many y a judge unto this nation, *2094*
24:17 Now after many y I came to bring alms to *2094*
24:27 But after **two** y Porcius Festus came into *1333*
28:30 And Paul dwelt **two** whole y in his own *1333*
Ro 15:23 having a great desire these many y to come *2094*
2Co 12: 2 I knew a man in Christ above fourteen y *2094*
Gal 1:18 Then after three y I went up to Jerusalem to *2094*
2: 1 Then fourteen y after I went up again to *2094*
3:17 which was four hundred and thirty y after, *2094*
4:10 and months, and times, and y. *1763*
1Ti 5: 9 into the number under threescore **y old**, *2094*
Heb 1:12 thou art the same, and thy y shall not fail. *2094*
3: 9 proved me, and saw my works forty y. *2094*
3:17 But with whom was he grieved forty y? *2094*
11:24 By faith Moses, when he was **come to y**, *3173*
Jas 5:17 not on the earth *by the space of* three y *1763*
2Pe 3: 8 one day *is* with the Lord as a thousand y, *2094*
3: 8 and a thousand y as one day. *2094*
Rev 20: 2 and Satan, and bound him a thousand y, *2094*
20: 3 till the thousand y should be fulfilled: *2094*
20: 4 and reigned with Christ a thousand y. *2094*
20: 5 again until the thousand y were finished. *2094*

Rev 20: 6 and shall reign with him a thousand y. *2094*
20: 7 And when the thousand y are expired, *2094*

YEARS' (2) [YEAR]
2Ki 8: 3 it came to pass at the seven y end, that 8141
1Ch 21:12 Either three y famine; or three months to be 8141

YELL (1) [YELLED]
Jer 51:38 like lions: they shall y as lions' whelps, 5286

YELLED (1) [YELL]
Jer 2:15 *and* y, and they made his land waste: 5414+6963

YELLOW (4)
Lev 13:30 *there be* in it a y thin hair; then the priest 6669
13:32 there be in it no y hair, and the scall *be* not 6669
13:36 the skin, the priest shall not seek for y hair: 6669
Ps 68:13 with silver, and her feathers with y gold. 3422

YERN (1) [YERNED]
Ge 43:30 for his bowels did y upon his brother: 3648

YERNED (1) [YERN]
1Ki 3:26 for her bowels y upon her son, and she said, 3648

YES (4) See Index

YESTERDAY (9) [DAY]
Ex 5:14 fulfilled your task in making brick both y 8543
1Sa 20:27 son of Jesse to meat, neither y, nor to day? 8543
2Sa 15:20 *Whereas* thou camest *but* y, should I *this* 8543
2Ki 9:26 Surely I have seen y the blood of Naboth, 570
Job 8: 9 (For we *are but of* y, and know nothing, 8543
Ps 90: 4 thy sight *are but* as y when it is past, 865+3117
Jn 4:52 Y at the seventh hour the fever left him. *5504*
Ac 7:28 thou kill me, as thou didst the Egyptian y? *5504*
Heb 13: 8 Jesus Christ the same y, and to day, and *5504*

YESTERNIGHT (3) [NIGHT]
Ge 19:34 the younger, Behold, I lay y with my father: 570
31:29 but the God of your father spake unto me y, 570
31:42 the labour of my hands, and rebuked *thee* y. 570

YET (683) See Index

YIELD (30) [YIELDED, YIELDETH, YIELDING]
Ge 4:12 it shall not henceforth y unto thee her 5414
49:20 *shall be* fat, and he shall y royal dainties. 5414
Lev 19:25 that *it* may y unto you the increase thereof: 3254
25:19 the land shall y her fruit, and ye shall eat 5414
26: 4 the land shall y her increase, and the trees 5414
26: 4 and the trees of the field shall y their fruit. 5414
26:20 for your land shall not y her increase, 5414
26:20 neither shall the trees of the land y their 5414
Dt 11:17 be no rain, and *that* the land y not her fruit; 5414
2Ch 30: 8 *but* y yourselves unto the LORD, 3027+5414
Ps 67: 6 *Then* shall the earth y her increase; *and* 5414
85:12 *is* good; and our land shall y her increase. 5414
107:37 which may y fruits of increase. 6213
Pr 7:21 her much fair speech she **caused** him **to** y, 5186
Isa 5:10 ten acres of vineyard shall y one bath, and 6213
5:10 and the seed of a homer shall y an ephah. 6213
Eze 34:27 the tree of the field shall y her fruit, and 5414
34:27 the earth shall y her increase, and they shall 5414
36: 8 and y your fruit to my people of Israel; 5375
Hos 8: 7 the bud shall y no meal: if so be it yield, 6213
8: 7 if so be it y, *the* strangers shall swallow it 6213
Joel 2:22 the fig tree and the vine do y their strength. 5414
Hab 3:17 shall fail, and the fields shall y no meat; 6213
Mk 4: 8 and did y fruit that sprang up and *1325*
Ac 23:21 But do not thou y **unto** them: for there lie *3982*
Ro 6:13 Neither y ye your members *as* instruments *3936*
6:13 but y yourselves unto God, as *those that are* *3936*
6:16 that to whom ye y yourselves servants to *3936*
6:19 now y your members servants to *3936*
Jas 3:12 so *can* no fountain *both* y salt water and *4160*

YIELDED (8) [YIELD]
Ge 49:33 y **up the ghost**, and was gathered unto his 1478
Nu 17: 8 and bloomed blossoms, and y almonds. 1580
Da 3:28 the king's word, and y their bodies, 3052
Mt 27:50 cried again with a loud voice, y **up** the ghost. *863*
Mk 4: 7 grew up, and choked it, and it y no fruit. *1325*
Ac 5:10 straightway at his feet, and y **up the ghost**: *1634*
Ro 6:19 for as ye have y your members servants to *3936*
Rev 22: 2 *of* fruits, *and* y her fruit every month: *591*

YIELDETH (4) [YIELD]
Ne 9:37 it y much **increase** unto the kings whom 8393
Job 24: 5 the wilderness y food for them *and* for *their* NIH
Pr 12:12 but the root of the righteous y *fruit.* 5414
Heb 12:11 nevertheless afterward it y the peaceable *591*

YIELDING (7) [YIELD]
Ge 1:11 the herb y seed, *and* the fruit tree yielding 2232
1:11 *and* the fruit tree y fruit after his kind, 6213
1:12 *and* herb y seed after his kind, and the tree 2232
1:12 the tree y fruit, whose seed *was* in itself, 6213
1:29 in the which *is* the fruit of a tree y seed; 2232
Ecc 10: 4 not thy place; for y pacifieth great offences. 4832
Jer 17: 8 of drought, neither shall cease from y fruit. 6213

YOKE (59) [YOKED, YOKEFELLOW, YOKES]
Ge 27:40 that thou shalt break his y from off thy 5923
Lev 26:13 I have broken the bands of your y, and 5923
Nu 19: 2 no blemish, *and* upon which never came y: 5923
Dt 21: 3 *and* which hath not drawn in the y; 5923
28:48 and he shall put a y of iron upon thy neck, 5923
1Sa 6: 7 on which there hath come no y, and tie 5923
11: 7 he took a y of oxen, and hewed them in 6776
14:14 of land, *which* a y *of oxen might plow.* 6776
1Ki 12: 4 Thy father made our y grievous: now 5923
12: 4 his heavy y which he put upon us, lighter, 5923
12: 9 Make the y which thy father did put upon 5923
12:10 Thy father made our y heavy, but 5923
12:11 my father did lade you with a heavy y, 5923
12:11 you with a heavy yoke, I will add to your y: 5923
12:14 My father made your y heavy, and I will 5923
12:14 your yoke heavy, and I will add to your y: 5923
19:19 who *was* plowing *with* twelve y *of oxen* 6776
19:21 took a y of oxen, and slew them, and boiled 6776
2Ch 10: 4 Thy father made our y grievous: now 5923
10: 4 his heavy y that he put upon us, and we will 5923
10: 9 Ease somewhat the y that thy father did put 5923
10:10 Thy father made our y heavy, but 5923
10:11 For whereas my father put a heavy y upon 5923
10:11 yoke upon you, I will put more to your y: 5923
10:14 My father made your y heavy, but I will 5923
Job 1: 3 five hundred y of oxen, and five hundred 6776
42:12 a thousand y of oxen, and a thousand she 6776
Isa 9: 4 For thou hast broken the y of his burden, 5923
10:27 his y from off thy neck, and the yoke shall 5923
10:27 the y shall be destroyed because of 5923
14:25 shall his y depart from off them, and 5923
47: 6 ancient hast thou very heavily laid thy y. 5923
58: 6 go free, and *that* ye break every y? 4133
58: 9 take away from the midst of thee the y, 4133
Jer 2:20 For of old time I have broken thy y, *and* 5923
5: 5 these have altogether broken the y, *and* 5923
27: 8 that will not put their neck under the y of 5923
27:11 the nations that bring their neck under the y 5923
27:12 Bring your necks under the y of the king of 5923
28: 2 I have broken the y of the king of Babylon. 5923
28: 4 for I will break the y of the king of 5923
28:10 Hananiah the prophet took the y from off 4133
28:11 will I break the y of Nebuchadnezzar king 5923
28:12 y from off the neck of the prophet 4133
28:14 I have put a y of iron upon the neck of all 5923
30: 8 *that* I will break his y from off thy neck, 5923
31:18 as a bullock unaccustomed *to the* y; turn NIH
51:23 pieces the husbandman and his y **of oxen**; 6776
La 1:14 The y of my transgressions is bound by his 5923
3:27 *It is* good for a man that he bear the y in his 5923
Eze 34:27 when I have broken the bands of their y, 5923
Hos 11: 4 I was to them as they that take off the y on 5923
Na 1:13 For now will I break his y from off thee, 4132
Mt 11:29 Take my y upon you, and learn of me; for I *2218*
11:30 For my y *is* easy, and my burden is light. *2218*
Lk 14:19 I have bought five y of oxen, and I go to *2201*
Ac 15:10 to put a y upon the neck of the disciples, *2218*
Gal 5: 1 be not entangled again with the y of *2218*
1Ti 6: 1 Let as many servants as are under the y *2218*

YOKED (1) [YOKE]
2Co 6:14 Be ye not **unequally** y **together** with *2086*

YOKEFELLOW (1) [FELLOW, YOKE]
Php 4: 3 And I intreat thee also, true y, help those *4805*

YOKES (4) [YOKE]
Jer 27: 2 Make thee bonds and y, and put them upon 4133

Jer 28:13 Thou hast broken the **y** of wood; but 4133
28:13 but thou shalt make for them **y** of iron. 4133
Eze 30:18 when I shall break there the **y** of Egypt: 4133

YONDER (7)
Ge 22: 5 I and the lad will go **y** and worship, 3541+5704
Nu 16:37 of the burning, and scatter thou the fire **y**; 1973
23:15 burnt offering, while I meet *the* LORD **y**. 3541
32:19 For we will not inherit with them on *y* side NIH
2Ki 4:25 his servant, Behold, *y is* that Shunammite: NIH
Mt 17:20 this mountain, Remove hence **to y place**; *1563*
26:36 Sit ye here, while I go and pray **y**. *1563*

YOU (2802) [YE, YOU-WARD, YOU-WARDS, YOUR, YOURS, YOURSELVES] See Index

YOUNG (300) [YOUTH]
Ge 4:23 to my wounding, and a **y man** to my hurt. 3206
14:24 Save only that which the **y men** have eaten, 5288
15: 9 and a turtle-dove, and a **y pigeon**. 1469
18: 7 and good, and gave *it* unto a **y man**; 5288
19: 4 compassed the house round, both old and **y**, 5288
22: 3 took two of his **y men** with him, and Isaac 5288
22: 5 Abraham said unto his **y men**, Abide you 5288
22:19 So Abraham returned unto his **y men**, and 5288
31:38 and thy she goats have not **cast** their **y**, 7921
33:13 the flocks and herds with **y** *are* with me: 5763
34:19 And the **y man** deferred not to do the thing, 5288
41:12 *there was* there with us a **y man**, a Hebrew, 5288
Ex 10: 9 We will go with our **y** and with our old, 5288
23:26 There shall nothing **cast** their **y**, nor be 7921
24: 5 And he sent **y men** of the children of Israel, 5288
29: 1 Take one **y** bullock, and two rams without 1121
33:11 servant Joshua, the son of Nun, a **y man**, 5288
Lev 1:14 his offering of turtledoves, or of **y** pigeons. 1121
4: 3 a **y** bullock without blemish unto 1121
4:14 the congregation shall offer a **y** bullock for 1121
5: 7 two turtledoves, or two **y** pigeons, unto 1121
5:11 or two **y** pigeons, then he that sinned shall 1121
9: 2 Take thee a **y** calf for a sin offering, and 1121
12: 6 a **y** pigeon, or a turtledove, for a sin 1121
12: 8 shall bring two turtles, or two **y** pigeons; 1121
14:22 two turtledoves, or two **y** pigeons, such as 1121
14:30 or of the **y** pigeons, such as he can get; 1121
15:14 or two **y** pigeons, and come before 1121
15:29 or two **y** pigeons, and bring them unto 1121
16: 3 *place:* with a **y** bullock for a sin offering, 1121
22:28 shall not kill it and her **y** both in one day. 1121
23:18 first year, and one **y** bullock, and two rams: 1121
Nu 6:10 two turtles, or two **y** pigeons, to the priest, 1121
7:15 One **y** bullock, one ram, one lamb of 1121
7:21 One **y** bullock, one ram, one lamb of 1121
7:27 One **y** bullock, one ram, one lamb of 1121
7:33 One **y** bullock, one ram, one lamb of 1121
7:39 One **y** bullock, one ram, one lamb of 1121
7:45 One **y** bullock, one ram, one lamb of 1121
7:51 One **y** bullock, one ram, one lamb of 1121
7:57 One **y** bullock, one ram, one lamb of 1121
7:63 One **y** bullock, one ram, one lamb of 1121
7:69 One **y** bullock, one ram, one lamb of 1121
7:75 One **y** bullock, one ram, one lamb of 1121
7:81 One **y** bullock, one ram, one lamb of 1121
8: 8 let them take a **y** bullock with his meat 1121
8: 8 another **y** bullock shalt thou take for a sin 1121
11:27 there ran a **y man**, and told Moses, and 5288
11:28 *one* of his **y men**, answered and said, 979
15:24 that all the congregation shall offer one **y** 1121
23:24 a great lion, and lift up himself as a **y lion**: 738
28:11 two **y** bullocks, and one ram, seven lambs 1121
28:19 two **y** bullocks, and one ram, and 1121
28:27 two **y** bullocks, one ram, seven lambs of 1121
29: 2 one **y** bullock, one ram, *and* seven lambs of 1121
29: 8 one **y** bullock, one ram, *and* seven lambs of 1121
29:13 thirteen **y** bullocks, two rams, *and* 1121
29:17 on the second day *ye shall offer* twelve **y** 1121
Dt 22: 6 *whether they be* **y ones**, or eggs, and the dam 667
22: 6 the dam sitting upon the **y**, or upon the eggs, 667
22: 6 thou shalt not take the dam with the **y**: 1121
22: 7 wise let the dam go, and take the **y** to thee; 1121
28:50 person of the old, nor shew favour to the **y**: 5288
28:57 towards her **y one** that cometh out from 7988
32:11 fluttereth over her **y**, spreadeth abroad her 1469
32:25 shall destroy both the **y man** and the virgin, 970
Jos 6:21 **y** and old, and ox, and sheep, and ass, 5288
6:23 the **y men** that were spies went in, and 5288
Jdg 6:25 said unto him, Take thy father's **y** bullock, 6499
8:14 And caught a **y man** of the men of Succoth, 5288
9:54 he called hastily unto the **y man** his 5288
9:54 his **y man** thrust him through, and he died. 5288
14: 5 behold, a **y** lion roared against him. 3715
14:10 there a feast; for so used the **y men** to do. 970
17: 7 there was a **y man** out of Beth-lehem-judah 5288
17:11 the **y man** was unto him as one of his sons. 5288
17:12 the **y man** became his priest, and was in 5288
18: 3 they knew the voice of the **y man** 5288
18:15 came to the house of the **y man** the Levite, 5288
19:19 for the **y man** *which is* with thy servants: 5288
21:12 of Jabesh-gilead four hundred **y** virgins, 5291
Ru 2: 9 have I not charged the **y men** that *they* shall 5288
2: 9 drink of *that* which the **y men** have drawn. 5288
2:15 Boaz commanded his **y men**, saying, 5288
2:21 me also, Thou shalt keep fast by my **y men**, 5288
3:10 inasmuch as *thou* followedst not **y men**, 970
4:12 LORD shall give thee of this **y woman**. 5291
1Sa 1:24 the LORD *in* Shiloh: and the child *was* **y**. 5288
2:17 Wherefore the sin of the **y men** was very 5288
8:16 your goodliest **y men**, and your asses, and 970
9: 2 *was* Saul, a choice *y man*, and a goodly: NIH
9:11 they found **y maidens** going out to draw 5291
14: 1 said unto the **y man** that bare his armour, 5288
14: 6 Jonathan said to the **y man** that bare his 5288
17:58 to him, Whose son *art* thou, *thou* **y man**? 5288
20:22 if I say thus unto the **y man**, Behold, 5958
21: 4 if the **y men** have kept themselves at least 5288
21: 5 the vessels of the **y men** are holy, and 5288
25: 5 David sent out ten **y men**, and David said 5288
25: 5 David said unto the **y men**, Get you up to 5288
25: 8 Ask thy **y men**, and they will shew thee. 5288
25: 8 Wherefore let the **y men** find favour in 5288
25: 9 when David's **y men** came, they spake to 5288
25:12 So David's **y men** turned their way, and 5288
25:14 one of the **y men** told Abigail, 5288
25:25 I thine handmaid saw not the **y men** of my 5288
25:27 let it even be given unto the **y men** that 5288
26:22 let one of the **y men** come over and fetch it. 5288
30:13 he said, I *am* a **y man** of Egypt, servant to 5288
30:17 save four hundred **y men**, which rode 376+5288
2Sa 1: 5 David said unto the **y man** that told him, 5288
1: 6 the **y man** that told him said, As I 5288
1:13 David said unto the **y man** that told him, 5288
1:15 David called one of the **y men**, and said, 5288
2:14 Let the **y men** now arise, and play before 5288
2:21 lay thee hold on one of the **y men**, and 5288
4:12 David commanded *his* **y men**, and 5288
9:12 Mephibosheth had a **y** son, whose name 6996
13:32 have slain all the **y men** the king's sons; 5288
13:34 the **y man** that kept the watch lift up his 5288
14:21 bring the **y man** Absalom again. 5288
16: 2 and summer fruit for the **y men** to eat; 5288
18: 5 *Deal* gently for my sake with the **y man**, 5288
18:12 Beware *that* none *touch* the **y man** 5288
18:15 ten **y men** that bare Joab's armour 5288
18:29 the king said, *Is* the **y man** Absalom safe? 5288
18:32 unto Cushi, *Is* the **y man** Absalom safe? 5288
18:32 thee to do *thee* hurt, be as *that* **y man** *is*. 5288
1Ki 1: 2 Let there be sought for my lord the king a **y** 5291
11:28 Solomon seeing the **y man** that he was 5288
12: 8 consulted with the **y men** that were grown 3206
12:10 the **y men** that were grown up with him 3206
12:14 to them after the counsel of the **y men**, 3206
20:14 *Even* by the **y men** of the princes of 5288
20:15 he numbered the **y men** of the princes of 5288
20:17 the **y men** of the princes of the provinces 5288
20:19 So these **y men** of the princes of 5288
2Ki 4:22 one of the **y men**, and one of the asses, 5288
5:22 two **y men** of the sons of the prophets: 5288
6:17 the LORD opened the eyes of the **y man**; 5288
8:12 their **y** *men* wilt thou slay with the sword, 970
9: 4 So the **y man**, *even* the young man 5288
9: 4 young man, *even* the **y man** the prophet, 5288
1Ch 12:28 a **y man** mighty of valour, and *of* his 5288
22: 5 Solomon my son *is* **y** and tender, and 5288
29: 1 *is yet* **y** and tender, and the work *is* great: 5288
2Ch 10: 8 took counsel with the **y men** that were 3206
10:10 the **y men** that were brought up with him 3206
10:14 them after the advice of the **y men**, 3206
13: 7 when Rehoboam was **y** and tender hearted, 5288
13: 9 to consecrate himself with a **y** bullock 1121

Y

2Ch 34: 3 eighth year of his reign, while he was yet y, 5288
36:17 who slew their y **men** with the sword in 970
36:17 had no compassion upon y **man** or maiden, 970
Ezr 6: 9 both y bullocks, and rams, and lambs, 1123
Est 2: 2 Let there be fair y virgins sought for 5291
2: 3 that they may gather together all the fair y 5291
3:13 all Jews, both y and old, little children and 5288
8:10 on mules, camels, *and* y dromedaries: 1121
Job 1:19 it fell upon the y **men**, and they are dead; 5288
4:10 and the teeth of the y **lions**, are broken. 3715
19:18 Yea, y **children** despised me; I arose, and 5759
29: 8 The y **men** saw me, and hid themselves: 5288
32: 6 I *am* y, and ye *are* very old; 3117+6810+3807.1
38:39 the lion? or fill the appetite of the y **lions**, 3715
38:41 when his y **ones** cry unto God, they wander 3206
39: 3 they bring forth their y **ones**, 3206
39: 4 Their y **ones** are in good liking, they grow 1121
39:16 She is hardened against her y **ones**, 1121
39:30 Her y **ones** also suck up blood: and where 667
Ps 17:12 as it were a y **lion** lurking in secret places. 3715
29: 6 a calf; Lebanon and Sirion like a y unicorn. 1121
34:10 The y **lions** do lack, and suffer hunger: but 3715
37:25 I have been y, and *now* am old; yet have I 5288
58: 6 break out the great teeth of the y **lions**, 3715
78:63 The fire consumed their y **men**; and 970
78:71 From following the *ewes* **great with** y he 5763
84: 3 where she may lay her y, *even* thine altars, 667
91:13 the y **lion** and the dragon shalt thou trample 3715
104:21 The y **lions** roar after *their* prey, and seek 3715
119: 9 Wherewithal shall a y **man** cleanse his 5288
147: 9 his food, *and* to the y ravens which cry. 1121
148:12 Both y **men**, and maidens; old men, and 970
Pr 1: 4 to the y **man** knowledge and discretion. 5288
7: 7 the youths, a y **man** void of understanding, 5288
20:29 The glory of y **men** *is* their strength: and 970
30:17 pick it out, and the y eagles shall eat it. 1121
Ecc 11: 9 Rejoice, O y **man**, in thy youth; and let thy 970
SS 2: 9 My beloved *is* like a roe or a y hart: behold, 6082
2:17 or a y hart upon the mountains of Bether. 6082
4: 5 Thy two breasts *are* like two y roes *that are* 6082
7: 3 Thy two breasts *are* like two y roes *that are* 6082
8:14 or to a y hart upon the mountains of spices. 6082
Isa 5:29 *be* like a lion, they shall roar like y **lions**: 3715
7:21 *that* a man shall nourish a y **cow**, 1241+5697
9:17 the Lord shall have no joy in their y **men**, 970
11: 6 the calf and the y **lion** and the fatling 3715
11: 7 their y **ones** shall lie down together: 3206
13:18 *Their* bows also shall dash the y **men** to 5288
20: 4 y and old, naked and barefoot, 5288
23: 4 neither do I nourish up y **men**, *nor* bring up 970
30: 6 from whence *come* the y^{s} and old lion, 3833
30: 6 their riches upon the shoulders of y **asses**, 5895
30:24 the y **asses** that ear the ground shall eat 5895
31: 4 the lion and the y **lion** roaring on his prey, 3715
31: 8 and his y **men** shall be discomfited. 970
40:11 *and* shall gently lead those that are **with y**. 5763
40:30 be weary, and the y **men** shall utterly fall: 970
62: 5 For *as* a y **man** marrieth a virgin, *so* shall thy 970
Jer 2:15 The y **lions** roared upon him, *and* yelled, 3715
6:11 and upon the assembly of y **men** together: 970
9:21 *and* the y **men** from the streets. 970
11:22 the y **men** shall die by the sword; their sons 970
15: 8 mother of the y **men** a spoiler at noonday: 970
18:21 *let* their y **men** *be* slain by the sword in 970
31:12 and for the y of the flock and of the herd: 1121
31:13 in the dance, both y **men** and old together: 970
48:15 his chosen y **men** are gone down to 970
49:26 Therefore her y **men** shall fall in her streets, 970
50:30 Therefore shall her y **men** fall in the streets, 970
51: 3 spare ye not her y **men**; destroy ye utterly all 970
51:22 with thee will I break in pieces old and y; 5288
51:22 with thee will I break in pieces the y **man** 970
La 1:15 an assembly against me to crush my y **men**: 970
1:18 and my y **men** are gone into captivity. 970
2:19 toward him for the life of thy y **children**, 5768
2:21 The y and the old lie on the ground in 5288
2:21 and my y **men** are fallen by the sword; 970
4: 3 the breast, they give suck to their y **ones**: 1482
4: 4 the y **children** ask bread, *and* no man 5768
5:13 They took the y **men** to grind, and 970
5:14 from the gate, the y **men** from their musick. 970
Eze 9: 6 Slay utterly old *and* y, both maids, and 970
17: 4 He cropt off the top of his y **twigs**, and 3242
17:22 off from the top of his y **twigs** a tender one, 3127
19: 2 she nourished her whelps among y **lions**. 3715
19: 3 it became a y **lion**, and it learned to catch 3715
19: 5 of her whelps, *and* made him a y **lion**. 3715
19: 6 he became a y **lion**, and learned to catch 3715
23: 6 and rulers, all of them desirable y **men**, 970
23:12 upon horses, all of them desirable y **men**. 970
23:23 all of them desirable y **men**, captains and 970
30:17 The y **men** of Aven and of Phi-beseth shall 970
31: 6 the beasts of the field **bring forth** their y, 3205
32: 2 Thou art like a y **lion** of the nations, and 3715
38:13 with all the y **lions** thereof, shall say unto 3715
41:19 the face of a y **lion** toward the palm tree on 3715
43:19 Lord God, a y bullock for a sin offering. 1121
43:23 shalt offer a y bullock without blemish, 1121
43:25 they shall also prepare a y bullock, and 1121
45:18 thou shalt take a y bullock without blemish, 1121
46: 6 in the day of the new moon *it shall be* a y 1121
Hos 5:14 and as a y **lion** to the house of Judah: 3715
Joel 2:28 dream dreams, your y **men** shall see visions: 970
Am 2:11 and of your y **men** for Nazarites. 970
3: 4 will a y **lion** cry out of his den, if he have 3715
4:10 your y **men** have I slain with the sword, and 970
8:13 the fair virgins and y **men** faint for thirst. 970
Mic 5: 8 as a y **lion** among the flocks of sheep: 3715
Na 2:11 the feeding place of the y **lions**, where 3715
2:13 and the sword shall devour thy y **lions**: 3715
3:10 her y **children** also were dashed in pieces 5768
Zec 2: 4 unto him, Run, speak to this y **man**, saying, 5288
9:17 corn shall make the y **men** cheerful, and 970
11: 3 a voice of the roaring of y **lions**; for 3715
11:16 neither shall seek the y **one**, nor heal that 5289
Mt 2: 8 Go and search diligently for the y **child**; 3813
2: 9 and stood over where the y **child** was. 3813
2:11 they saw the y **child** with Mary his mother, 3813
2:13 and take the y **child** and his mother, and 3813
2:13 for Herod will seek the y **child** to destroy 3813
2:14 he took the y **child** and his mother by night, 3813
2:20 and take the y **child** and his mother, and 3813
2:20 they are dead which sought the y **child's** 3813
2:21 and took the y **child** and his mother, and 3813
19:20 The y **man** saith unto him, All these *things* 3495
19:22 But when the y **man** heard *that* saying, 3495
Mk 7:25 whose y **daughter** had an unclean spirit, 2365
10:13 And they brought y **children** to him, 3813
14:51 And there followed him a certain y **man**, 3495
14:51 and the y **men** laid hold on him: 3495
16: 5 they saw a y **man** sitting on the right side, 3495
Lk 2:24 A pair of turtledoves, or two y pigeons. 3502
7:14 And he said, Y **man**, I say unto thee, Arise. 3495
Jn 12:14 And Jesus, when he had found a y **ass**, 3678
21:18 verily, I say unto thee, When thou wast y, 3501
Ac 2:17 and your y **men** shall see visions, and 3495
5: 6 And the y **men** arose, wound him up, and 3501
5:10 and the y **men** came in, and found her dead, 3495
7:19 so that *they* cast out their y **children**, 1025
7:58 laid down their clothes at a y **man's** feet, 3494
20: 9 And there sat in a window a certain y **man** 3494
20:12 And they brought the y **man** alive, and 3816
23:17 Bring this y **man** unto the chief captain: 3494
23:18 prayed *me* to bring this y **man** unto thee, 3494
23:22 the chief captain then let the y **man** depart, 3494
Tit 2: 4 That they may teach the y *women* to be 3501
2: 6 Y *men* likewise exhort to be sober minded. 3501
1Jn 2:13 y **men**, because you have overcome 3495
2:14 y **men**, because ye are strong, and the word 3495

YOUNGER (31) [YOUTH]

Ge 9:24 knew what his y son had done unto him. 6996
19:31 the firstborn said unto the y, Our father *is* 6810
19:34 that the firstborn said unto the y, Behold, 6810
19:35 the y arose, and lay with him; and 6810
19:38 the y, she also bare a son, and called his 6810
25:23 and the elder shall serve the y. 6810
27:15 and put them upon Jacob her y son: 6996
27:42 she sent and called Jacob her y son, and 6996
29:16 and the name of the y *was* Rachel. 6996
29:18 thee seven years for Rachel thy y daughter. 6996
29:26 to give the y before the firstborn. 6810
43:29 and said, *Is* this your y brother, 6996
48:14 who *was* the y, and his left hand upon 6810
48:19 truly his y brother shall be greater than he, 6996
Jdg 1:13 the son of Kenaz, Caleb's y brother, took it: 6996
3: 9 the son of Kenaz, Caleb's y brother. 6996
15: 2 *is* not her y sister fairer than she? take her, 6996

1Sa 14:49 and the name of the y Michal: 6996
1Ch 24:31 fathers over against their y brethren. 6996
Job 30: 1 now *they that are* y than I have me in 3117+6810
Eze 16:46 thy y sister, that dwelleth at thy right hand, 6996
16:61 receive thy sisters, thine elder and thy y: 6996
Lk 15:12 And the y of them said to *his* father, Father, *3501*
15:13 And not many days after the y son gathered *3501*
22:26 is greatest among you, let him be as the y; *3501*
Ro 9:12 said unto her, The elder shall serve the y. *1640*
1Ti 5: 1 *him* as a father; *and* the y *men* as brethren; *3501*
5: 2 as mothers; the y as sisters, with all purity. *3501*
5:11 But the y widows refuse: for when they *3501*
5:14 I will therefore that the y *women* marry, *3501*
1Pe 5: 5 Likewise, *ye* y, submit yourselves unto *3501*

YOUNGEST (18) [YOUTH]
Ge 42:13 the y *is this* day with our father, and one *is* 6996
42:15 except your y brother come hither. 6996
42:20 bring your y brother unto me; so shall your 6996
42:32 the y *is this* day with our father in the land 6996
42:34 bring your y brother unto me: then shall I 6996
43:33 and the y according to his youth: 6810
44: 2 in the sack's mouth of the y, and his corn 6996
44:12 *and* began at the eldest, and left at the y: 6996
44:23 Except your y brother come down with 6996
44:26 if our y brother be with us, then will we go 6996
44:26 man's face, except our y brother *be* with us. 6996
Jos 6:26 in his y *son* shall he set up the gates of it. 6810
Jdg 9: 5 notwithstanding yet Jotham the y son of 6996
1Sa 16:11 There remaineth yet the y, and behold, 6996
17:14 David *was* the y: and the three eldest 6996
1Ki 16:34 set up the gates thereof in his y *son* Segub, 6810
2Ch 21:17 left him, save Jehoahaz, the y of his sons. 6996
22: 1 made Ahaziah his y son king in his stead: 6996

YOUR (1776) [YOU] See Index

YOURS (12) [YOU] See Index

YOURSELVES (191) [SELF, YOU] See Index

YOUTH (70) [YOUNG, YOUNGER, YOUNGEST, YOUTHFUL, YOUTHS]
Ge 8:21 of man's heart *is* evil from his y; 5271
43:33 and the youngest according to his y: 6812
46:34 about cattle from our y even until now, 5271
Lev 22:13 as *in* her y, she shall eat of her father's 5271
Nu 30: 3 a bond, *being* in her father's house in her y; 5271
30:16 *being yet* in her y *in* her father's house. 5271
Jdg 8:20 the y drew not his sword: for he feared, 5288
8:20 for he feared, because he *was* yet a y. 5288
1Sa 17:33 for thou *art but* a y, and he a man of war 5288
17:33 a youth, and he a man of war from his y. 5271
17:42 for he was *but* a y, and ruddy, and of a fair 5288
17:55 of the host, Abner, whose son *is* this y? 5288
2Sa 19: 7 evil that befell thee from thy y until now. 5271
1Ki 18:12 *I* thy servant fear the LORD from my y. 5271
Job 13:26 me to possess the iniquities of my y. 5271
20:11 His bones are full *of the sin of* his y, 5934
29: 4 As I was in the days of my y, when 2779
30:12 Upon *my* right hand rise the y; they push 6526
31:18 (For from my y he was brought up *with* me, 5271
33:25 he shall return to the days of his y: 5934
36:14 They die in y, and their life *is* among 5290
Ps 25: 7 Remember not the sins of my y, nor my 5271
71: 5 Lord GOD: *thou art* my trust from my y. 5271
71:17 O God, thou hast taught me from my y: and 5271
88:15 ready to die from *my* y *up: while* I suffer 5290
89:45 The days of his y hast thou shortened: 5934
103: 5 *so that* thy y is renewed like the eagle's. 5271
110: 3 of the morning: thou hast the dew of thy y. 3208
127: 4 of a mighty *man; so are* children of the y. 5271
129: 1 a time have they afflicted me from my y, 5271
129: 2 a time have they afflicted me from my y: 5271
144:12 sons *may be* as plants grown up in their y; 5271
Pr 2:17 Which forsaketh the guide of her y, and 5271
5:18 and rejoice with the wife of thy y. 5271
Ecc 11: 9 Rejoice, O young man, in thy y; and let thy 3208
11: 9 let thy heart cheer thee in the days of thy y, 979
11:10 thy flesh: for childhood and y *are* vanity. 7839
12: 1 now thy Creator in the days of thy y, 979
Isa 47:12 wherein thou hast laboured from thy y; 5271
47:15 *even* thy merchants, from thy y: 5271
54: 4 for thou shalt forget the shame of thy y, and 5934
54: 6 and grieved in spirit, and a wife of y, 5271
Jer 2: 2 I remember thee, the kindness of thy y, 5271
3: 4 My father, thou *art* the guide of my y? 5271
3:24 the labour of our fathers from our y; 5271
3:25 from our y even unto this day, and have not 5271
22:21 This *hath been* thy manner from thy y, 5271
31:19 because I did bear the reproach of my y. 5271
32:30 have only done evil before me from their y: 5271
48:11 Moab hath been at ease from his y, and 5271
La 3:27 for a man that he bear the yoke in his y. 5271
Eze 4:14 for from my y up even till now have I not 5271
16:22 thou hast not remembered the days of thy y, 5271
16:43 thou hast not remembered the days of thy y, 5271
16:60 my covenant with thee in the days of thy y, 5271
23: 3 they committed whoredoms in their y: 5271
23: 8 for in her y they lay with her, and 5271
23:19 calling to remembrance the days of her y, 5271
23:21 to remembrance the lewdness of thy y, 5271
23:21 teats by the Egyptians for the paps of thy y. 5271
Hos 2:15 as *in* the days of her y, and as *in* the day 5271
Joel 1: 8 with sackcloth for the husband of her y. 5271
Zec 13: 5 man taught me *to keep cattle* from my y. 5271
Mal 2:14 witness between thee and the wife of thy y, 5271
2:15 deal treacherously against the wife of his y. 5271
Mt 19:20 All these *things* have I kept from my y up: *3503*
Mk 10:20 all these have I observed from my y. *3503*
Lk 18:21 he said, All these have I kept from my y up. *3503*
Ac 26: 4 My manner of life from *my* y, which was at *3503*
1Ti 4:12 Let no *man* despise thy y; but be thou an *3503*

YOUTHFUL (1) [YOUTH]
2Ti 2:22 Flee also y lusts: but follow righteousness, *3512*

YOUTHS (2) [YOUTH]
Pr 7: 7 the simple ones, I discerned among the y, 1121
Isa 40:30 Even the y shall faint and be weary, and 5288

YOU-WARD (2) [YOU]
2Co 13: 3 which to y is not weak, but is mighty in *4771*
Eph 3: 2 of the grace of God which is given me to y: *4771*

YOU-WARDS (1) [YOU]
2Co 1:12 in the world, and more abundantly to y. *4771*

Z

ZAANAIM (1)
Jdg 4:11 pitched his tent unto the plain of Z, 6815

ZAANAN (1)
Mic 1:11 the inhabitant of Z came not forth *in* 6630

ZAANANNIM (1)
Jos 19:33 from Allon to Z, and Adami, Nekeb, and 6815

ZAAVAN (1)
Ge 36:27 of Ezer *are* these; Bilhan, and Z, and Akan. 2190

ZABAD (8)
1Ch 2:36 Attai begat Nathan, and Nathan begat Z, 2066
2:37 Z begat Ephlal, and Ephlal begat Obed, 2066
7:21 Z his son, and Shuthelah his son, and Ezer, 2066
11:41 Uriah the Hittite, Z the son of Ahlai, 2066
2Ch 24:26 Z the son of Shimeath an Ammonitess, and 2066
Ezr 10:27 Mattaniah, and Jeremoth, and Z, and Aziza. 2066
10:33 Z, Eliphelet, Jeremai, Manasseh, *and* 2066
10:43 Z, Zebina, Jadau, and Joel, Benaiah. 2066

ZABBAI (2)
Ezr 10:28 Jehohanan, Hananiah, Z, *and* Athlai. 2079
Ne 3:20 After him Baruch the son of Z earnestly 2079

ZABBUD (1)
Ezr 8:14 Uthai, and Z, and with them seventy males. 2072

ZABDI (6)
Jos 7: 1 of Carmi, the son of Z, the son of Zerah, 2067
7:17 the Zarhites man by man; and Z was taken: 2067
7:18 of Carmi, the son of Z, the son of Zerah, 2067

1Ch 8:19 And Jakim, and Zichri, and **Z**, 2067
27:27 for the wine cellars *was* **Z** the Shiphmite: 2067
Ne 11:17 of Micha, the son of **Z**, the son of Asaph, 2067

ZABDIEL (2)
1Ch 27: 2 first month *was* Jashobeam the son of **Z**: 2068
Ne 11:14 their overseer *was* **Z**, the son of *one of* 2068

ZABUD (1)
1Ki 4: 5 **Z** the son of Nathan *was* principal officer, 2071

ZABULON (3) [ZEBULUN]
Mt 4:13 in the borders of **Z** and Nephthalim: *2194*
4:15 The land of **Z**, and the land of Nephthalim, *2194*
Rev 7: 8 Of the tribe of **Z** *were* sealed twelve *2194*

ZACCAI (2)
Ezr 2: 9 The children of **Z**, seven hundred and 2140
Ne 7:14 The children of **Z**, seven hundred and 2140

ZACCHEUS (3)
Lk 19: 2 And behold, *there was* a man named **Z**, *2195*
19: 5 unto him, **Z**, make haste, and come down; *2195*
19: 8 And **Z** stood, and said unto the Lord; *2195*

ZACCHUR (1)
1Ch 4:26 Hamuel his son, **Z** his son, Shimei his son. 2139

ZACCUR (8)
Nu 13: 4 the tribe of Reuben, Shammua the son of **Z**. 2139
1Ch 24:27 Beno, and Shoham, and **Z**, and Ibri. 2139
25: 2 **Z**, and Joseph, and Nethaniah, and 2139
25:10 The third *to* **Z**, *he*, his sons, and 2139
Ne 3: 2 And next to them builded **Z** the son of Imri. 2139
10:12 **Z**, Sherebiah, Shebaniah, 2139
12:35 the son of **Z**, the son of Asaph: 2139
13:13 next to them *was* Hanan the son of **Z**, 2139

ZACHARIAH (4) [ZACHARIAS, ZECHARIAH]
2Ki 14:29 of Israel; and **Z** his son reigned in his stead. 2148
15: 8 eighth year of Azariah king of Judah did **Z** 2148
15:11 the rest of the acts of **Z**, behold, they *are* 2148
18: 2 name also *was* Abi, the daughter of **Z**. 2148

ZACHARIAS (11) [ZACHARIAH]
Mt 23:35 Abel unto the blood of **Z** son of Barachias, *2197*
Lk 1: 5 the king of Judea, a certain priest named **Z**, *2197*
1:12 And when **Z** saw *him*, he was troubled, and *2197*
1:13 But the angel said unto him, Fear not, **Z**: *2197*
1:18 And **Z** said unto the angel, Whereby shall I *2197*
1:21 And the people waited for **Z**, and *2197*
1:40 And entered into the house of **Z**, and *2197*
1:59 and they called him **Z**, after the name of his *2197*
1:67 And his father **Z** was filled with the Holy *2197*
3: 2 unto John the son of **Z** in the wilderness. *2197*
11:51 the blood of Abel unto the blood of **Z**, *2197*

ZACHER (1)
1Ch 8:31 And Gedor, and Ahio, and **Z**. 2144

ZADOK (52) [ZADOK'S]
2Sa 8:17 **Z** the son of Ahitub, and Ahimelech the son 6659
15:24 lo **Z** also, and all the Levites *were* with 6659
15:25 the king said unto **Z**, Carry back the ark of 6659
15:27 The king said also unto **Z** the priest, *Art not* 6659
15:29 **Z** therefore and Abiathar carried the ark of 6659
15:35 *hast thou* not there with thee **Z** and 6659
15:35 thou shalt tell *it* to **Z** and Abiathar 6659
17:15 said Hushai unto **Z** and to Abiathar 6659
18:19 said Ahimaaz the son of **Z**, Let me now 6659
18:22 said Ahimaaz the son of **Z** yet again to 6659
18:27 *is* like the running of Ahimaaz the son of **Z**. 6659
19:11 king David sent to **Z** and to Abiathar 6659
20:25 and **Z** and Abiathar *were* the priests: 6659
1Ki 1: 8 **Z** the priest, and Benaiah the son of 6659
1:26 **Z** the priest, and Benaiah the son of 6659
1:32 Call me **Z** the priest, and Nathan 6659
1:34 let **Z** the priest and Nathan the prophet 6659
1:38 So **Z** the priest, and Nathan the prophet, 6659
1:39 **Z** the priest took a horn of oil out of 6659
1:44 the king hath sent with him **Z** the priest, 6659
1:45 **Z** the priest and Nathan the prophet have 6659
2:35 **Z** the priest did the king put in the room of 6659
4: 2 he had; Azariah the son of **Z** the priest, 6659
4: 4 and **Z** and Abiathar *were* the priests: 6659
2Ki 15:33 name *was* Jerusha, the daughter of **Z**. 6659
1Ch 6: 8 Ahitub begat **Z**, and Zadok begat Ahimaaz, 6659
6: 8 Ahitub begat Zadok, and **Z** begat Ahimaaz, 6659
6:12 Ahitub begat **Z**, and Zadok begat Shallum, 6659
6:12 Ahitub begat Zadok, and **Z** begat Shallum, 6659
6:53 **Z** his son, Ahimaaz his son. 6659
9:11 the son of **Z**, the son of Meraioth, the son 6659
12:28 **Z**, a young man mighty of valour, and 6659
15:11 David called for **Z** and Abiathar the priests, 6659
16:39 **Z** the priest, and his brethren the priests, 6659
18:16 **Z** the son of Ahitub, and Abimelech the son 6659
24: 3 both **Z** of the sons of Eleazar, and 6659
24: 6 **Z** the priest, and Ahimelech the son of 6659
24:31 **Z**, and Ahimelech, and the chief of 6659
27:17 the son of Kemuel: of the Aaronites, **Z**: 6659
29:22 to be the chief governor, and **Z** to be priest. 6659
2Ch 27: 1 name also *was* Jerushah, the daughter of **Z**. 6659
31:10 Azariah the chief priest of the house of **Z** 6659
Ezr 7: 2 of Shallum, the son of **Z**, the son of Ahitub, 6659
Ne 3: 4 next unto them repaired **Z** the son of 6659
3:29 After them repaired **Z** the son of Immer 6659
10:21 Meshezabeel, **Z**, Jaddua, 6659
11:11 the son of **Z**, the son of Meraioth, the son 6659
13:13 **Z** the scribe, and of the Levites, Pedaiah: 6659
Eze 40:46 these *are* the sons of **Z** among the sons of 6659
43:19 priests the Levites that *be* of the seed of **Z**, 6659
44:15 the priests the Levites, the sons of **Z**, 6659
48:11 priests that are sanctified of the sons of **Z**; 6659

ZADOK'S (1) [ZADOK]
2Sa 15:36 Ahimaaz **Z** *son*, and 6659+3807.1

ZAHAM (1)
2Ch 11:19 him children; Jeush, and Shamariah, and **Z**. 2093

ZAIR (1)
2Ki 8:21 So Joram went over to **Z**, and all 6811

ZALAPH (1)
Ne 3:30 Hanun the sixth son of **Z**, another piece. 6764

ZALMON (2)
Jdg 9:48 Abimelech gat him up *to* mount **Z**, he and 6756
2Sa 23:28 **Z** the Ahohite, Maharai the Netophathite, 6756

ZALMONAH (2)
Nu 33:41 departed from mount Hor, and pitched in **Z**. 6758
33:42 they departed from **Z**, and pitched in 6758

ZALMUNNA (12)
Jdg 8: 5 I am pursuing after Zebah and **Z**, kings of 6759
8: 6 hands of Zebah and **Z** now in thine hand, 6759
8: 7 hath delivered Zebah and **Z** into mine hand, 6759
8:10 Now Zebah and **Z** *were* in Karkor, and 6759
8:12 when Zebah and **Z** fled, he pursued after 6759
8:12 and **Z**, and discomfited all the host. 6759
8:15 said, Behold Zebah and **Z**, with whom ye 6759
8:15 hands of Zebah and **Z** now in thine hand, 6759
8:18 said he unto Zebah and **Z**, What manner of 6759
8:21 Zebah and **Z** said, Rise thou, and fall upon 6759
8:21 slew Zebah and **Z**, and took away 6759
Ps 83:11 yea, all their princes as Zebah, and as **Z**: 6759

ZAMZUMMIMS (1)
Dt 2:20 old time; and the Ammonites call them **Z**; 2157

ZAMZUMMITES See ZAMZUMMIMS

ZANOAH (5)
Jos 15:34 **Z**, and En-gannim, Tappuah, and Enam, 2182
15:56 And Jezreel, and Jokdeam, and **Z**, 2182
1Ch 4:18 of Socho, and Jekuthiel the father of **Z**. 2182
Ne 3:13 repaired Hanun, and the inhabitants of **Z**; 2182
11:30 **Z**, Adullam, and *in* their villages, 2182

ZAPHENATH-PANEAH See ZAPHNATH-PAANEAH

ZAPHNATH-PAANEAH (1)
Ge 41:45 Pharaoh called Joseph's name **Z**; and 6847

ZAPHON (1)
Jos 13:27 and Beth-nimrah, and Succoth, and **Z**, 6829

ZARA (1) [ZARAH]
Mt 1: 3 And Judas begat Phares and **Z** of Thamar; *2196*

ZARAH (1) [ZARA]
Ge 38:30 upon his hand: and his name was called Z. 2226

ZAREAH (1)
Ne 11:29 at En-rimmon, and at Z, and at Jarmuth, 6881

ZAREATHITES (1)
1Ch 2:53 of them came the Z, and the Eshtaulites. 6882

ZARED (1)
Nu 21:12 and pitched in the valley of Z. 2218

ZAREPHATH (3) [SAREPTA]
1Ki 17: 9 Arise, get thee to Z, which *belongeth* to 6886
17:10 So he arose and went to Z. And when he 6886
Ob 1:20 *possess* that of the Canaanites, *even* unto Z; 6886

ZARETAN (1)
Jos 3:16 from the city Adam, that *is* beside Z: 6891

ZARETHAN See ZARETAN; ZARTANAH; ZARTHAN; ZEREDATHAH

ZARETH-SHAHAR (1)
Jos 13:19 Sibmah, and Z in the mount of the valley, 6890

ZARHITES (6)
Nu 26:13 Of Zerah, the family of the Z: of Shaul, 2227
26:20 the Pharzites: of Zerah, the family of the Z. 2227
Jos 7:17 of Judah; and he took the family of the Z: 2227
7:17 he brought the family of the Z man by man; 2227
1Ch 27:11 *was* Sibbecai the Hushathite, of the Z: 2227
27:13 *was* Maharai the Netophathite, of the Z: 2227

ZARTANAH (1)
1Ki 4:12 which *is* by Z beneath Jezreel, 6891

ZARTHAN (1)
1Ki 7:46 in the clay ground between Succoth and Z. 6891

ZATTHU (1)
Ne 10:14 Parosh, Pahath-moab, Elam, Z, Bani, 2240

ZATTU (3)
Ezr 2: 8 The children of Z, nine hundred forty and 2240
10:27 of the sons of Z; Elioenai, Eliashib, 2240
Ne 7:13 The children of Z, eight hundred forty and 2240

ZAVAN (1)
1Ch 1:42 The sons of Ezer; Bilhan, and Z, *and* Jakan. 2190

ZAZA (1)
1Ch 2:33 the sons of Jonathan; Peleth, and Z. 2117

ZEAL (16) [ZEALOUS, ZEALOUSLY]
2Sa 21: 2 Saul sought to slay them in his z to 7065
2Ki 10:16 with me, and see my z for the LORD. 7068
19:31 the z of the LORD *of hosts* shall do this. 7068
Ps 69: 9 For the z of thine house hath eaten me up; 7068
119:139 My z hath consumed me, because 7068
Isa 9: 7 The z of the LORD of hosts will perform 7068
37:32 the z of the LORD of hosts shall do this. 7068
59:17 *for* clothing, and was clad with z as a cloke. 7068
63:15 where *is* thy z and thy strength, 7068
Eze 5:13 that I the LORD have spoken *it* in my z, 7068
Jn 2:17 The z of thine house hath eaten me up. *2205*
Ro 10: 2 For I bear them record that they have a z of *2205*
2Co 7:11 yea, *what* z, yea, *what* revenge! *2205*
9: 2 and your z hath provoked very many. *2205*
Php 3: 6 Concerning z, persecuting the church; *2205*
Col 4:13 that he hath a great z for you, and them that *2205*

ZEALOT See ZELOTES

ZEALOUS (8) [ZEAL]
Nu 25:11 he was z for my sake among them, 7065+7068
25:13 because he was z for his God, and made an 7065
Ac 21:20 which believe; and they are all z of the law: *2207*
22: 3 and was z towards God, as ye all are this *2207*
1Co 14:12 forasmuch as ye are z of spiritual *gifts*, seek *2207*
Gal 1:14 being more exceedingly z of the traditions *2207*
Tit 2:14 himself a peculiar people, z of good works. *2207*
Rev 3:19 and chasten: be z therefore, and repent. *2206*

ZEALOUSLY (2) [ZEAL]
Gal 4:17 They **z affect** you, *but* not well; yea, *2206*
4:18 But *it is* good to be **z affected** always in a *2206*

ZEBADIAH (9)
1Ch 8:15 And Z, and Arad, and Ader, 2069
8:17 Z, and Meshullam, and Hezeki, and Heber, 2069
12: 7 Joelah, and Z, the sons of Jeroham of 2069
26: 2 Jediael the second, Z the third, Jathniel 2069
27: 7 brother of Joab, and Z his son after him: 2069
2Ch 17: 8 Z, and Asahel, and Shemiramoth, and 2069
19:11 Z the son of Ishmael, the ruler of the house 2069
Ezr 8: 8 Z the son of Michael, and with him 2069
10:20 And of the sons of Immer; Hanani, and Z. 2069

ZEBAH (12)
Jdg 8: 5 I am pursuing after Z and Zalmunna, 2078
8: 6 *Are* the hands of Z and Zalmunna now in 2078
8: 7 when the LORD hath delivered Z 2078
8:10 Now Z and Zalmunna *were* in Karkor, and 2078
8:12 when Z and Zalmunna fled, he pursued 2078
8:12 Z and Zalmunna, and discomfited all 2078
8:15 said, Behold Z and Zalmunna, with whom 2078
8:15 *Are* the hands of Z and Zalmunna now in 2078
8:18 said he unto Z and Zalmunna, 2078
8:21 Z and Zalmunna said, Rise thou, and 2078
8:21 slew Z and Zalmunna, and took away 2078
Ps 83:11 all their princes as Z, and as Zalmunna: 2078

ZEBAIM See POCHERETH OF ZEBAIM, POCHERETH ZEBAIM

ZEBEDEE (10) [ZEBEDEE'S]
Mt 4:21 James the *son* of Z, and John his brother, *2199*
4:21 his brother, in a ship with Z their father, *2199*
10: 2 the *son* of Z, and John his brother; *2199*
26:37 took with *him* Peter and the two sons of Z, *2199*
Mk 1:19 he saw James the *son* of Z, and John his *2199*
1:20 they left their father Z in the ship with *2199*
3:17 And James the *son* of Z, and John *2199*
10:35 And James and John, the sons of Z, *2199*
Lk 5:10 so *was* also James, and John, *the* sons of Z, *2199*
Jn 21: 2 and the *sons* of Z, and two other of his *2199*

ZEBEDEE'S (2) [ZEBEDEE]
Mt 20:20 Then came to him the mother of Z children *2199*
27:56 and Joses, and the mother of Z children. *2199*

ZEBIDAH See ZEBUDAH

ZEBINA (1)
Ezr 10:43 Zabad, Z, Jadau, and Joel, Benaiah. 2081

ZEBOIIM (2) [ZEBOIM]
Ge 14: 2 Shemeber king of Z, and the king of Bela, 6636
14: 8 the king of Z, and the king of Bela 6636

ZEBOIM (5) [ZEBOIIM]
Ge 10:19 Gomorrah, and Admah, and Z, even unto 6636
Dt 29:23 of Sodom, and Gomorrah, Admah, and Z, 6636
1Sa 13:18 to the valley of Z toward the wilderness. 6650
Ne 11:34 Hadid, Z, Neballat, 6650
Hos 11: 8 *how* shall I set thee as Z? mine heart is 6636

ZEBUDAH (1)
2Ki 23:36 his mother's name *was* Z, the daughter of 2080

ZEBUL (6)
Jdg 9:28 Z his officer? serve the men of Hamor 2083
9:30 when Z the ruler of the city heard 2083
9:36 Gaal saw the people, he said to Z, Behold, 2083
9:36 Z said unto him, Thou seest the shadow of 2083
9:38 said Z unto him, Where *is* now thy mouth, 2083
9:41 Z thrust out Gaal and his brethren, that *they* 2083

ZEBULONITE (2) [ZEBULUN]
Jdg 12:11 after him Elon, a Z, judged Israel; and 2075
12:12 Elon the Z died, and was buried in Aijalon 2075

ZEBULUN (45) [ZABULON, ZEBULONITE, ZEBULUNITES]
Ge 30:20 him six sons: and she called his name Z. 2074
35:23 and Levi, and Judah, and Issachar, and Z: 2074
46:14 the sons of Z; Sered, and Elon, and Jahleel. 2074
49:13 Z shall dwell at the haven of the sea; and 2074
Ex 1: 3 Issachar, Z, and Benjamin, 2074
Nu 1: 9 Of Z; Eliab the son of Helon. 2074
1:30 Of the children of Z, *by* their generations, 2074
1:31 *even* of the tribe of Z, *were* fifty and 2074
2: 7 *Then* the tribe of Z: and Eliab the son of 2074

Nu 2: 7 Helon *shall be* captain of the children of Z. 2074
7:24 prince of the children of Z, *did offer:* 2074
10:16 children of Z *was* Eliab the son of Helon. 2074
13:10 Of the tribe of Z, Gaddiel the son of Sodi. 2074
26:26 *Of* the sons of Z after their families: 2074
34:25 the prince of the tribe of the children of Z, 2074
Dt 27:13 Gad, and Asher, and Z, Dan, and Naphtali. 2074
33:18 of Z he said, Rejoice, Zebulun, in thy going 2074
33:18 he said, Rejoice, Z, in thy going out; 2074
Jos 19:10 the third lot came up for the children of Z 2074
19:16 This *is* the inheritance of the children of Z 2074
19:27 reacheth to Z, and to the valley of 2074
19:34 reacheth to Z on the south side, and 2074
21: 7 and out of the tribe of Z, twelve cities. 2074
21:34 the rest of the Levites, out of the tribe of Z, 2074
Jdg 1:30 Neither did Z drive out the inhabitants of 2074
4: 6 of Naphtali and of the children of Z? 2074
4:10 Barak called Z and Naphtali to Kedesh; 2074
5:14 out of Z they that handle the pen of 2074
5:18 Z and Naphtali *were* a people *that* 2074
6:35 unto Asher, and unto Z, and unto Naphtali; 2074
12:12 was buried in Aijalon in the country of Z. 2074
1Ch 2: 1 Simeon, Levi, and Judah, Issachar, and Z, 2074
6:63 and out of the tribe of Z, twelve cities. 2074
6:77 of Merari *were given* out of the tribe of Z, 2074
12:33 Of Z, such as went forth to battle, expert in 2074
12:40 *even* unto Issachar and Z and Naphtali, 2074
27:19 Of Z, Ishmaiah the son of Obadiah: 2074
2Ch 30:10 of Ephraim and Manasseh even unto Z: 2074
30:11 Manasseh and of Z humbled themselves, 2074
30:18 and Manasseh, Issachar, and Z, 2074
Ps 68:27 the princes of Z, *and* the princes of 2074
Isa 9: 1 at the first he lightly afflicted the land of Z 2074
Eze 48:26 east side unto the west side, Z a *portion.* 2074
48:27 by the border of Z, from the east side unto 2074
48:33 one gate of Issachar, one gate of Z. 2074

ZEBULUNITES (1) [ZEBULUN]

Nu 26:27 These *are* the families of the Z according to 2075

ZECHARIAH (39) [ZACHARIAH]

1Ch 5: 7 was reckoned, *were* the chief, Jeiel, and Z, 2148
9:21 *And* Z the son of Meshelemiah *was* porter 2148
9:37 And Gedor, and Ahio, and Z, and Mikloth. 2148
15:18 Z, Ben, and Jaaziel, and Shemiramoth, and 2148
15:20 Z, and Aziel, and Shemiramoth, and Jehiel, 2148
15:24 Amasai, and Z, and Benaiah, and Eliezer, 2148
16: 5 next to him Z, Jeiel, and Shemiramoth, and 2148
24:25 *was* Isshiah: of the sons of Isshiah; Z. 2148
26: 2 the sons of Meshelemiah *were,* Z 2148
26:11 the second, Tebaliah the third, Z the fourth: 2148
26:14 *for* Z his son, a wise counseller, they cast 2148
27:21 of Manasseh in Gilead, Iddo the son of Z: 2148
2Ch 17: 7 to Z, and to Nethaneel, and to Michaiah, 2148
20:14 upon Jahaziel the son of Z, the son of 2148
21: 2 Z, and Azariah, and Michael, and 2148
24:20 the spirit of God came upon Z the son of 2148
26: 5 he sought God in the days of Z, who had 2148
29: 1 name *was* Abijah, the daughter of Z. 2148
29:13 of the sons of Asaph; Z, and Mattaniah: 2148
34:12 Z and Meshullam, of the sons of 2148
35: 8 Hilkiah and Z and Jehiel, rulers of 2148
Ezr 5: 1 Haggai the prophet, and Z the son of Iddo, 2148
6:14 Haggai the prophet and Z the son of Iddo. 2148
8: 3 of Shechaniah, of the sons of Pharosh; Z: 2148
8:11 Z the son of Bebai, and with him twenty 2148
8:16 for Nathan, and for Z, and for Meshullam, 2148
10:26 Z, and Jehiel, and Abdi, and Jeremoth, and 2148
Ne 8: 4 and Hashbadana, Z, *and* Meshullam. 2148
11: 4 the son of Z, the son of Amariah, the son of 2148
11: 5 of Adaiah, the son of Joiarib, the son of Z, 2148
11:12 the son of Amzi, the son of Z, the son of 2148
12:16 Of Iddo, Z; of Ginnethon, Meshullam; 2148
12:35 *namely,* Z the son of Jonathan, the son of 2148
12:41 Michaiah, Elioenai, Z, *and* Hananiah, 2148
Isa 8: 2 the priest, and Z the son of Jeberechiah. 2148
Zec 1: 1 came the word of the LORD unto Z, 2148
1: 7 came the word of the LORD unto Z, 2148
7: 1 *that* the word of the LORD came unto Z 2148
7: 8 the word of the LORD came unto Z, 2148

ZEDAD (2)

Nu 34: 8 the goings forth of the border shall be to Z: 6657
Eze 47:15 the way of Hethlon, as *men* go to Z; 6657

ZEDEKIAH (61) [ZEDEKIAH'S]

1Ki 22:11 Z the son of Chenaanah made him horns of 6667
22:24 Z the son of Chenaanah went near, and 6667
2Ki 24:17 in his stead, and changed his name *to* Z. 6667
24:18 Z *was* twenty and one years old when he 6667
24:20 that Z rebelled against the king of Babylon. 6667
25: 2 besieged unto the eleventh year of king Z. 6667
25: 7 they slew the sons of Z before his eyes, 6667
25: 7 put out the eyes of Z, and bound him with 6667
1Ch 3:15 the third Z, the fourth Shallum. 6667
3:16 of Jehoiakim: Jeconiah his son, Z his son. 6667
2Ch 18:10 Z the son of Chenaanah had made him 6667
18:23 Z the son of Chenaanah came near, and 6667
36:10 made Z his brother king over Judah and 6667
36:11 Z *was* one and twenty years old when he 6667
Jer 1: 3 unto the end of the eleventh year of Z 6667
21: 1 when king Z sent unto him Pashur the son 6667
21: 3 Jeremiah unto them, Thus shall ye say to Z: 6667
21: 7 I will deliver Z king of Judah, and his 6667
24: 8 So will I give Z the king of Judah, and his 6667
27: 3 come *to* Jerusalem unto Z king of Judah; 6667
27:12 I spake also to Z king of Judah according to 6667
28: 1 in the beginning of the reign of Z king of 6667
29: 3 whom Z king of Judah sent unto Babylon 6667
29:21 of Kolaiah, and of Z, the son of Maaseiah, 6667
29:22 The LORD make thee like Z and 6667
32: 1 in the tenth year of Z king of Judah, 6667
32: 3 For Z king of Judah had shut him up, 6667
32: 4 Z king of Judah shall not escape out of 6667
32: 5 he shall lead Z *to* Babylon, and there shall 6667
34: 2 Go and speak to Z king of Judah, and 6667
34: 4 word of the LORD, O Z king of Judah; 6667
34: 6 words unto Z king of Judah in Jerusalem, 6667
34: 8 after that the king Z had made a covenant 6667
34:21 Z king of Judah and his princes will I give 6667
36:12 Z the son of Hananiah, and all the princes. 6667
37: 1 king Z the son of Josiah reigned instead of 6667
37: 3 Z the king sent Jehucal the son of 6667
37:17 Z the king sent, and took him *out:* and 6667
37:18 Moreover Jeremiah said unto king Z, 6667
37:21 Z the king commanded that they should 6667
38: 5 Z the king said, Behold, he *is* in your hand: 6667
38:14 Z the king sent, and took Jeremiah 6667
38:15 Jeremiah said unto Z, If I declare *it* unto 6667
38:16 So Z the king sware secretly unto Jeremiah, 6667
38:17 said Jeremiah unto Z, Thus saith 6667
38:19 Z the king said unto Jeremiah, I am afraid 6667
38:24 said Z unto Jeremiah, Let no man know of 6667
39: 1 In the ninth year of Z king of Judah, in 6667
39: 2 *And* in the eleventh year of Z, in the fourth 6667
39: 4 *that* when Z the king of Judah saw them, 6667
39: 5 and overtook Z in the plains of Jericho: 6667
39: 6 the king of Babylon slew the sons of Z in 6667
44:30 as I gave Z king of Judah into the hand of 6667
49:34 beginning of the reign of Z king of Judah, 6667
51:59 when he went with Z the king of Judah *into* 6667
52: 1 Z *was* one and twenty year old when he 6667
52: 3 that Z rebelled against the king of Babylon. 6667
52: 5 besieged unto the eleventh year of king Z. 6667
52: 8 and overtook Z in the plains of Jericho; 6667
52:10 the king of Babylon slew the sons of Z 6667
52:11 he put out the eyes of Z; and the king of 6667

ZEDEKIAH'S (1) [ZEDEKIAH]

Jer 39: 7 Moreover he put out Z eyes, and 6667

ZEEB (6)

Jdg 7:25 two princes of the Midianites, Oreb and Z; 2062
7:25 Z they slew at the winepress of Zeeb, and 2062
7:25 Zeeb they slew at the winepress of Z, and 2062
7:25 and Z to Gideon on the *other* side Jordan. 2062
8: 3 hands the princes of Midian, Oreb and Z: 2062
Ps 83:11 Make their nobles like Oreb, and like Z: 2062

ZEKER See ZACHER

ZELAH (2)

Jos 18:28 Z, Eleph, and Jebusi, which *is* Jerusalem, 6762
2Sa 21:14 they in the country of Benjamin in Z, 6762

ZELEK (2)

2Sa 23:37 Z the Ammonite, Naharai the Beerothite, 6768
1Ch 11:39 Z the Ammonite, Naharai the Berothite, 6768

ZELOPHEHAD (11)
Nu 26:33 Z the son of Hepher had no sons, but 6765
26:33 the names of the daughters of Z *were* 6765
27: 1 came the daughters of Z, the son of 6765
27: 7 The daughters of Z speak right: thou shalt 6765
36: 2 of Z our brother unto his daughters. 6765
36: 6 command concerning the daughters of Z, 6765
36:10 so did the daughters of Z: 6765
36:11 and Milcah, and Noah, the daughters of Z, 6765
Jos 17: 3 Z, the son of Hepher, the son of Gilead, 6765
1Ch 7:15 and the name of the second *was* Z: 6765
7:15 *was* Zelophehad: and Z had daughters. 6765

ZELOTES (2)
Lk 6:15 the *son* of Alpheus, and Simon called Z, *2208*
Ac 1:13 and Simon Z, and Judas *the brother* of *2208*

ZELZAH (1)
1Sa 10: 2 sepulchre in the border of Benjamin at Z; 6766

ZEMARAIM (2)
Jos 18:22 And Beth-arabah, and Z, and Beth-el, 6787
2Ch 13: 4 Abijah stood up upon mount Z, which *is* in 6787

ZEMARITE (2)
Ge 10:18 the Arvadite, and the Z, and the Hamathite: 6786
1Ch 1:16 the Arvadite, and the Z, and the Hamathite. 6786

ZEMIRA (1)
1Ch 7: 8 Z, and Joash, and Eliezer, and Elioenai, and 2160

ZENAN (1)
Jos 15:37 Z, and Hadashah, and Migdal-gad, 6799

ZENAS (1)
Tit 3:13 Bring Z the lawyer and Apollos on their *2211*

ZEPHANIAH (10)
2Ki 25:18 Z the second priest, and the three keepers 6846
1Ch 6:36 of Joel, the son of Azariah, the son of Z, 6846
Jer 21: 1 Z the son of Maaseiah the priest, saying, 6846
29:25 and to Z the son of Maaseiah the priest, and 6846
29:29 Z the priest read this letter in the ears of 6846
37: 3 Z the son of Maaseiah the priest to 6846
52:24 Z the second priest, and the three keepers 6846
Zep 1: 1 which came unto Z the son of Cushi, 6846
Zec 6:10 go *into* the house of Josiah the son of Z; 6846
6:14 and to Jedaiah, and to Hen the son of Z, 6846

ZEPHATH (1)
Jdg 1:17 they slew the Canaanites that inhabited Z, 6857

ZEPHATHAH (1)
2Ch 14:10 they set the battle in array in the valley of Z 6859

ZEPHI (1) [ZEPHO]
1Ch 1:36 Omar, Z, and Gatam, Kenaz, and Timna, 6825

ZEPHO (2) [ZEPHI]
Ge 36:11 Omar, Z, and Gatam, and Kenaz. 6825
36:15 duke Omar, duke Z, duke Kenaz, 6825

ZEPHON (1) [BAAL-ZEPHON, ZEPHONITES]
Nu 26:15 of Z, the family of the Zephonites: 6827

ZEPHONITES (1) [ZEPHON]
Nu 26:15 of Zephon, the family of the Z: of Haggi, 6831

ZER (1)
Jos 19:35 Z, and Hammath, Rakkath, and Chinnereth, 6863

ZERAH (20)
Ge 36:13 Nahath, and Z, Shammah, and Mizzah: 2226
36:17 duke Nahath, duke Z, duke Shammah, 2226
36:33 Jobab the son of Z of Bozrah reigned in his 2226
46:12 and Onan, and Shelah, and Pharez, and Z: 2226
Nu 26:13 Of Z, the family of the Zarhites: of Shaul, 2226
26:20 of Z, the family of the Zarhites. 2226
Jos 7: 1 of Carmi, the son of Zabdi, the son of Z, 2226
7:18 of Carmi, the son of Zabdi, the son of Z, 2226
7:24 took Achan the son of Z, and the silver, and 2226
22:20 Did not Achan the son of Z commit a 2226
1Ch 1:37 Nahath, Z, Shammah, and Mizzah. 2226
1:44 Jobab the son of Z of Bozrah reigned in his 2226
2: 4 his daughter in law bare him Pharez and Z. 2226
2: 6 the sons of Z; Zimri, and Ethan, and 2226
4:24 and Jamin, Jarib, Z, *and* Shaul: 2226
6:21 Joah his son, Iddo his son, Z his son, 2226
6:41 The son of Ethni, the son of Z, the son of 2226
9: 6 of the sons of Z; Jeuel, and their brethren, 2226
2Ch 14: 9 there came out against them Z 2226
Ne 11:24 of the children of Z the son of Judah, 2226

ZERAHIAH (5)
1Ch 6: 6 Uzzi begat Z, and Zerahiah begat Meraioth, 2228
6: 6 Uzzi begat Zerahiah, and Z begat Meraioth, 2228
6:51 Bukki his son, Uzzi his son, Z his son, 2228
Ezr 7: 4 The son of Z, the son of Uzzi, the son of 2228
8: 4 Elihoenai the son of Z, and with him two 2228

ZERAHITE See ZARHITES

ZERED (3)
Dt 2:13 *said I,* and get you over the brook Z. 2218
2:13 And we went over the brook Z. 2218
2:14 until we were come over the brook Z, 2218

ZEREDA (1)
1Ki 11:26 an Ephrathite of Z, Solomon's servant, 6868

ZEREDATHAH (1)
2Ch 4:17 in the clay ground between Succoth and Z. 6868

ZERERATH (1)
Jdg 7:22 the host fled to Beth-shittah in Z, *and* to 6888

ZERESH (4)
Est 5:10 and called for his friends, and Z his wife. 2238
5:14 said Z his wife and all his friends unto him, 2238
6:13 Haman told Z his wife and all his friends 2238
6:13 said his wise *men* and Z his wife unto him, 2238

ZERETH (1)
1Ch 4: 7 the sons of Helah *were,* Z, and Jezoar, and 6889

ZERETH SHAHAR See ZARETHSHAHAR

ZERI (1)
1Ch 25: 3 Gedaliah, and Z, and Jeshaiah, Hashabiah, 6874

ZEROR (1)
1Sa 9: 1 the son of Abiel, the son of Z, the son of 6872

ZERUAH (1)
1Ki 11:26 whose mother's name *was* Z, a widow 6871

ZERUBBABEL (22) [ZOROBABEL]
1Ch 3:19 the sons of Pedaiah *were,* Z, and Shimei: 2216
3:19 the son of Z; Meshullam, and Hananiah, 2216
Ezr 2: 2 Which came with Z: Jeshua, Nehemiah, 2216
3: 2 and Z the son of Shealtiel, and his brethren, 2216
3: 8 began Z the son of Shealtiel, and Jeshua 2216
4: 2 they came to Z, and to the chief of 2216
4: 3 Z, and Jeshua, and the rest of the chief of 2216
5: 2 rose up Z the son of Shealtiel, and 2217
Ne 7: 7 Who came with Z, Jeshua, Nehemiah, 2216
12: 1 the Levites that went up with Z the son of 2216
12:47 all Israel in the days of Z, and in the days 2216
Hag 1: 1 the prophet unto Z the son of Shealtiel, 2216
1:12 Z the son of Shealtiel, and Joshua the son 2216
1:14 the LORD stirred up the spirit of Z 2216
2: 2 Speak now to Z the son of Shealtiel, 2216
2: 4 Yet now be strong, O Z, saith the LORD; 2216
2:21 Speak to Z, governor of Judah, saying, 2216
2:23 will I take thee, O Z, my servant, the son of 2216
Zec 4: 6 This *is* the word of the LORD unto Z, 2216
4: 7 before Z *thou shalt* become a plain: and 2216
4: 9 The hands of Z have laid the foundation of 2216
4:10 shall see the plummet in the hand of Z *with* 2216

ZERUIAH (26)
1Sa 26: 6 to Abishai the son of Z, brother to Joab, 6870
2Sa 2:13 Joab the son of Z, and the servants of 6870
2:18 there were three sons of Z there, Joab, and 6870
3:39 these men the sons of Z *be* too hard for me: 6870
8:16 Joab the son of Z *was* over the host; and 6870
14: 1 Now Joab the son of Z perceived that 6870
16: 9 said Abishai the son of Z unto the king, 6870
16:10 What have I to do with you, ye sons of Z? 6870
17:25 of Nahash, sister to Z Joab's mother. 6870
18: 2 part under the hand of Abishai the son of Z, 6870
19:21 Abishai the son of Z answered and said, 6870

2Sa 19:22 What have I to do with you, ye sons of **Z**, 6870
21:17 Abishai the son of **Z** succoured him, and 6870
23:18 the brother of Joab, the son of **Z**, 6870
23:37 armourbearer to Joab the son of **Z**, 6870
1Ki 1: 7 he conferred with Joab the son of **Z**, and 6870
2: 5 also what Joab the son of **Z** did to me, 6870
2:22 the priest, and for Joab the son of **Z**. 6870
1Ch 2:16 Whose sisters *were* **Z**, and Abigail. And 6870
2:16 the sons of **Z**; Abishai, and Joab, and 6870
11: 6 So Joab the son of **Z** went first up, and 6870
11:39 the armourbearer of Joab the son of **Z**, 6870
18:12 Moreover Abishai the son of **Z** slew of 6870
18:15 Joab the son of **Z** *was* over the host; and 6870
26:28 and Joab the son of **Z**, had dedicated; 6870
27:24 Joab the son of **Z** began to number, but 6870

ZETHAM (2)
1Ch 23: 8 the chief *was* Jehiel, and **Z**, and Joel, three. 2241
26:22 **Z**, and Joel his brother, *which were* over 2241

ZETHAN (1)
1Ch 7:10 and **Z**, and Tharshish, and Ahishahar. 2133

ZETHAR (1)
Est 1:10 Bigtha, and Abagtha, **Z**, and Carcas, 2242

ZEUS See JUPITER

ZIA (1)
1Ch 5:13 Jorai, and Jachan, and **Z**, and Heber, seven. 2127

ZIBA (16)
2Sa 9: 2 house of Saul a servant whose name *was* **Z**. 6717
9: 2 the king said unto him, *Art* thou **Z**? 6717
9: 3 **Z** said unto the king, Jonathan hath yet a 6717
9: 4 **Z** said unto the king, Behold, he *is in* 6717
9: 9 the king called to **Z**, Saul's servant, and 6717
9:10 Now **Z** had fifteen sons and 6717
9:11 said **Z** unto the king, According to all that 6717
9:12 all that dwelt in the house of **Z** *were* 6717
16: 1 **Z** the servant of Mephibosheth met him, 6717
16: 2 the king said unto **Z**, What meanest thou by 6717
16: 2 **Z** said, The asses *be* for the king's 6717
16: 3 **Z** said unto the king, Behold, he abideth at 6717
16: 4 said the king to **Z**, Behold, thine *are* all that 6717
16: 4 **Z** said, I humbly beseech thee *that* I may 6717
19:17 **Z** the servant of the house of Saul, and 6717
19:29 I have said, Thou and **Z** divide the land. 6717

ZIBEON (8)
Ge 36: 2 of Anah the daughter of **Z** the Hivite; 6649
36:14 of Anah, daughter of **Z**, Esau's wife: 6649
36:20 Lotan, and Shobal, and **Z**, and Anah, 6649
36:24 these *are* the children of **Z**; both Aiah, and 6649
36:24 as he fed the asses of **Z** his father. 6649
36:29 duke Shobal, duke **Z**, duke Anah, 6649
1Ch 1:38 **Z**, and Anah, and Dishon, and Ezer, and 6649
1:40 Onam. And the sons of **Z**; Aiah, and Anah. 6649

ZIBIA (1)
1Ch 8: 9 and **Z**, and Mesha, and Malcham, 6644

ZIBIAH (2)
2Ki 12: 1 his mother's name *was* **Z** of Beer-sheba. 6645
2Ch 24: 1 His mother's name also *was* **Z** of 6645

ZICHRI (12)
Ex 6:21 sons of Izhar; Korah, and Nepheg, and **Z**. 2147
1Ch 8:19 And Jakim, and **Z**, and Zabdi, 2147
8:23 And Abdon, and **Z**, and Hanan, 2147
8:27 Jaresiah, and Eliah, and **Z**, the sons of 2147
9:15 of Micah, the son of **Z**, the son of Asaph; 2147
26:25 and **Z** his son, and Shelomith his son. 2147
27:16 of the Reubenites *was* Eliezer the son of **Z**: 2147
2Ch 17:16 next him *was* Amasiah the son of **Z**, 2147
23: 1 Elishaphat the son of **Z**, into covenant with 2147
28: 7 **Z**, a mighty *man* of Ephraim, slew 2147
Ne 11: 9 Joel the son of **Z** *was* their overseer: 2147
12:17 Of Abijah, **Z**; of Miniamin, of Moadiah, 2147

ZICRI See ZICHRI

ZIDDIM (1)
Jos 19:35 the fenced cities *are* **Z**, Zer, and Hammath, 6661

ZIDKIJAH (1)
Ne 10: 1 the Tirshatha, the son of Hachaliah, and **Z**, 6667

ZIDON (21) [SIDON, ZIDONIANS]
Ge 49:13 of ships; and his border *shall be* unto **Z**. 6721
Jos 11: 8 chased them unto great **Z**, and 6721
19:28 Hammon, and Kanah, *even* unto great **Z**; 6721
Jdg 1:31 nor the inhabitants of **Z**, nor of Ahlab, 6721
10: 6 the gods of **Z**, and the gods of Moab, and 6721
18:28 because it *was* far from **Z**, and they had no 6721
2Sa 24: 6 and they came to Dan-jaan, and about to **Z**, 6721
1Ki 17: 9 which *belongeth* to **Z**, and dwell there: 6721
1Ch 1:13 Canaan begat **Z** his firstborn, and Heth, 6721
Ezr 3: 7 oil, unto them of **Z**, and to them of Tyre, 6722
Isa 23: 2 thou whom the merchants of **Z**, that pass 6721
23: 4 Be thou ashamed, O **Z**: for the sea hath 6721
23:12 O thou oppressed virgin, daughter of **Z**: 6721
Jer 25:22 all the kings of **Z**, and the kings of the isles 6721
27: 3 to the king of Tyrus, and to the king of **Z**, 6721
47: 4 and **Z** every helper that remaineth: 6721
Eze 27: 8 The inhabitants of **Z** and Arvad were thy 6721
28:21 set thy face against **Z**, and prophesy against 6721
28:22 Behold, I *am* against thee, O **Z**; and I will 6721
Joel 3: 4 and **Z**, and all the coasts of Palestine? 6721
Zec 9: 2 and **Z**, though it be very wise. 6721

ZIDONIANS (10) [ZIDON]
Jdg 10:12 The **Z** also, and the Amalekites, and 6722
18: 7 after the manner of the **Z**, quiet and secure; 6722
18: 7 they *were* far from the **Z**, and had no 6722
1Ki 11: 1 Ammonites, Edomites, **Z**, *and* Hittites; 6722
11: 5 went after Ashtoreth the goddess of the **Z**, 6722
11:33 worshipped Ashtoreth the goddess of the **Z**, 6722
16:31 the daughter of Ethbaal king of the **Z**, 6722
2Ki 23:13 for Ashtoreth the abomination of the **Z**, 6722
1Ch 22: 4 for the **Z** and they of Tyre brought much 6722
Eze 32:30 of the north, all of them, and all the **Z**, 6722

ZIF (2)
1Ki 6: 1 in the month **Z**, which *is* the second month, 2099
6:37 house of the LORD laid, in the month **Z**: 2099

ZIHA (3)
Ezr 2:43 the children of **Z**, the children of Hasupha, 6727
Ne 7:46 the children of **Z**, the children of Hashupha, 6727
11:21 and **Z** and Gispa *were* over the Nethinims. 6727

ZIKLAG (15)
Jos 15:31 And **Z**, and Madmannah, and Sansannah, 6860
19: 5 **Z**, and Beth-marcaboth, and Hazar-susah, 6860
1Sa 27: 6 Achish gave him **Z** that day: wherefore 6860
27: 6 wherefore **Z** pertaineth unto the kings of 6860
30: 1 his men were come *to* **Z** on the third day, 6860
30: 1 **Z**, and smitten Ziklag, and burnt it with 6860
30: 1 and smitten **Z**, and burnt it with fire; 6860
30:14 south of Caleb; and we burnt **Z** with fire. 6860
30:26 when David came to **Z**, he sent of the spoil 6860
2Sa 1: 1 and David had abode two days in **Z**; 6860
4:10 I took hold of him, and slew him in **Z**, 6860
1Ch 4:30 And at Bethuel, and at Hormah, and at **Z**, 6860
12: 1 these *are* they that came to David to **Z**, 6860
12:20 As he went to **Z**, there fell to him of 6860
Ne 11:28 at **Z**, and at Mekonah, and in the villages 6860

ZILLAH (3)
Ge 4:19 one *was* Adah, and the name of the other **Z**. 6741
4:22 **Z**, she also bare Tubal-cain, an instructor of 6741
4:23 his wives, Adah and **Z**, Hear my voice; 6741

ZILLETHAI See ZILTHAI

ZILPAH (7)
Ge 29:24 Laban gave unto his daughter Leah **Z** his 2153
30: 9 she took **Z** her maid, and gave her Jacob to 2153
30:10 And **Z** Leah's maid bare Jacob a son. 2153
30:12 **Z** Leah's maid bare Jacob a second son. 2153
35:26 the sons of **Z**, Leah's handmaid; Gad, and 2153
37: 2 and with the sons of **Z**, his father's wives: 2153
46:18 These *are* the sons of **Z**, whom Laban gave 2153

ZILTHAI (2)
1Ch 8:20 And Elienai, and **Z**, and Eliel, 6769
12:20 Michael, and Jozabad, and Elihu, and **Z**, 6769

ZIMMAH (3)

1Ch	6:20	Libni his son, Jahath his son, **Z** his son,	2155
	6:42	The son of Ethan, the son of **Z**, the son of	2155
2Ch	29:12	Joah the son of **Z**, and Eden the son of	2155

ZIMRAN (2)

Ge	25: 2	she bare him **Z**, and Jokshan, and Medan,	2175
1Ch	1:32	she bare **Z**, and Jokshan, and Medan, and	2175

ZIMRI (15)

Nu	25:14	*was* **Z**, the son of Salu, a prince of a chief	2174
1Ki	16: 9	his servant **Z**, captain of half *his* chariots,	2174
	16:10	**Z** went in and smote him, and killed him,	2174
	16:12	Thus did **Z** destroy all the house of Baasha,	2174
	16:15	seventh year of Asa king of Judah did **Z**	2174
	16:16	**Z** hath conspired, and hath also slain	2174
	16:18	to pass, when **Z** saw that the city was taken,	2174
	16:20	Now the rest of the acts of **Z**, and	2174
2Ki	9:31	she said, *Had* **Z** peace, who slew his	2174
1Ch	2: 6	**Z**, and Ethan, and Heman, and Calcol, and	2174
	8:36	begat Alemeth, and Azmaveth, and **Z**;	2174
	8:36	and Zimri; and **Z** begat Moza,	2174
	9:42	begat Alemeth, and Azmaveth, and **Z**;	2174
	9:42	and Zimri; and **Z** begat Moza;	2174
Jer	25:25	all the kings of **Z**, and all the kings of	2174

ZIN (10)

Nu	13:21	searched the land from the wilderness of **Z**	6790
	20: 1	*into* the desert of **Z** in the first month:	6790
	27:14	my commandment in the desert of **Z**,	6790
	27:14	Meribah in Kadesh *in* the wilderness of **Z**.	6790
	33:36	pitched in the wilderness of **Z**, which *is*	6790
	34: 3	of **Z** along by the coast of Edom,	6790
	34: 4	the ascent of Akrabbim, and pass on to **Z**:	6790
Dt	32:51	of Meribah-Kadesh, *in* the wilderness of **Z**;	6790
Jos	15: 1	the wilderness of **Z** southward *was*	6790
	15: 3	passed along to **Z**, and ascended up on	6790

ZINA (1) [ZIZAH]

1Ch	23:10	*were*, Jahath, **Z**, and Jeush, and Beriah.	2126

ZION (153) [SION, ZION'S]

2Sa	5: 7	David took the strong hold of **Z**:	6726
1Ki	8: 1	out of the city of David, which *is* **Z**.	6726
2Ki	19:21	The virgin the daughter of **Z** hath despised	6726
	19:31	and they that escape out of mount **Z**:	6726
1Ch	11: 5	Nevertheless David took the castle of **Z**,	6726
2Ch	5: 2	out of the city of David, which *is* **Z**.	6726
Ps	2: 6	have I set my king upon my holy hill of **Z**.	6726
	9:11	to the LORD, which dwelleth in **Z**:	6726
	9:14	thy praise in the gates of the daughter of **Z**:	6726
	14: 7	the salvation of Israel *were come* out of **Z**!	6726
	20: 2	the sanctuary, and strengthen thee out of **Z**;	6726
	48: 2	*is* mount **Z**, *on* the sides of the north,	6726
	48:11	Let mount **Z** rejoice, let the daughters of	6726
	48:12	Walk about **Z**, and go round about her:	6726
	50: 2	Out of **Z**, the perfection of beauty,	6726
	51:18	Do good in thy good pleasure unto **Z**:	6726
	53: 6	the salvation of Israel *were come* out of **Z**!	6726
	65: 1	Praise waiteth for thee, O God, in **Z**: and	6726
	69:35	For God will save **Z**, and will build	6726
	74: 2	this mount **Z**, wherein thou hast dwelt.	6726
	76: 2	his tabernacle, and his dwelling place in **Z**.	6726
	78:68	tribe of Judah, the mount **Z** which he loved.	6726
	84: 7	*every one of them* in **Z** appeareth before	6726
	87: 2	The LORD loveth the gates of **Z** more	6726
	87: 5	of **Z** it shall be said, This and that man was	6726
	97: 8	**Z** heard, and was glad, and the daughters of	6726
	99: 2	The LORD *is* great in **Z**; and he *is* high	6726
	102:13	Thou shalt arise, *and* have mercy upon **Z**:	6726
	102:16	When the LORD shall build up **Z**, he shall	6726
	102:21	To declare the name of the LORD in **Z**,	6726
	110: 2	shall send the rod of thy strength out of **Z**:	6726
	125: 1	trust in the LORD *shall be* as mount **Z**,	6726
	126: 1	the LORD turned again the captivity of **Z**,	6726
	128: 5	The LORD shall bless thee out of **Z**: and	6726
	129: 5	be confounded and turned back that hate **Z**.	6726
	132:13	For the LORD hath chosen **Z**; he hath	6726
	133: 3	that descended upon the mountains of **Z**:	6726
	134: 3	made heaven and earth bless thee out of **Z**.	6726
	135:21	Blessed *be* the LORD out of **Z**,	6726
	137: 1	yea, we wept, when we remembered **Z**.	6726
	137: 3	*saying*, Sing us *one* of the songs of **Z**.	6726
	146:10	*even* thy God, O **Z**, unto all generations.	6726
	147:12	O Jerusalem; praise thy God, O **Z**.	6726
	149: 2	let the children of **Z** be joyful in their King.	6726
SS	3:11	O ye daughters of **Z**, and behold king	6726
Isa	1: 8	the daughter of **Z** is left as a cottage in a	6726
	1:27	**Z** shall be redeemed with judgment, and	6726
	2: 3	for out of **Z** shall go forth the law, and	6726
	3:16	Because the daughters of **Z** are haughty,	6726
	3:17	crown of the head of the daughters of **Z**,	6726
	4: 3	*that* he that is left in **Z**, and he that	6726
	4: 4	away the filth of the daughters of **Z**,	6726
	4: 5	upon every dwelling place of mount **Z**,	6726
	8:18	of hosts, which dwelleth in mount **Z**.	6726
	10:12	performed his whole work upon mount **Z**	6726
	10:24	O my people that dwellest in **Z**, be not	6726
	10:32	*against* the mount of the daughter of **Z**,	6726
	12: 6	Cry out and shout, thou inhabitant of **Z**:	6726
	14:32	That the LORD hath founded **Z**, and	6726
	16: 1	unto the mount of the daughter of **Z**.	6726
	18: 7	name of the LORD of hosts, the mount **Z**.	6726
	24:23	the LORD of hosts shall reign in mount **Z**,	6726
	28:16	Behold, I lay in **Z** for a foundation a stone,	6726
	29: 8	the nations be, that fight against mount **Z**.	6726
	30:19	For the people shall dwell in **Z** at	6726
	31: 4	of hosts come down to fight for mount **Z**,	6726
	31: 9	whose fire *is* in **Z**, and his furnace in	6726
	33: 5	he hath filled **Z** *with* judgment and	6726
	33:14	The sinners in **Z** are afraid; fearfulness hath	6726
	33:20	Look upon **Z**, the city of our solemnities:	6726
	34: 8	of recompences for the controversy of **Z**.	6726
	35:10	come *to* **Z** with songs and everlasting joy	6726
	37:22	The virgin, the daughter of **Z**, hath despised	6726
	37:32	and they that escape out of mount **Z**:	6726
	40: 9	O **Z**, that bringest good tidings, get thee up	6726
	41:27	The first *shall say* to **Z**, Behold,	6726
	46:13	I will place salvation in **Z** for Israel my	6726
	49:14	**Z** said, The LORD hath forsaken me, and	6726
	51: 3	For the LORD shall comfort **Z**: he will	6726
	51:11	shall return, and come with singing *unto* **Z**;	6726
	51:16	and say unto **Z**, Thou *art* my people.	6726
	52: 1	Awake, awake; put on thy strength, O **Z**;	6726
	52: 2	bands of thy neck, O captive daughter of **Z**.	6726
	52: 7	that saith unto **Z**, Thy God reigneth!	6726
	52: 8	when the LORD shall bring again **Z**.	6726
	59:20	the redeemer shall come to **Z**, and	6726
	60:14	The **Z** of the Holy One of Israel.	6726
	61: 3	To appoint unto them that mourn in **Z**,	6726
	62:11	Say ye to the daughter of **Z**, Behold,	6726
	64:10	**Z** is a wilderness, Jerusalem a desolation.	6726
	66: 8	for as soon as **Z** travailed, she brought forth	6726
Jer	3:14	two of a family, and I will bring you *to* **Z**:	6726
	4: 6	Set up the standard toward **Z**: retire,	6726
	4:31	the voice of the daughter of **Z**,	6726
	6: 2	I have likened the daughter of **Z** *to* a	6726
	6:23	men for war against thee, O daughter of **Z**.	6726
	8:19	*Is* not the LORD in **Z**? *is* not her king in	6726
	9:19	For a voice of wailing is heard out of **Z**,	6726
	14:19	hath thy soul lothed **Z**? why hast thou	6726
	26:18	**Z** shall be plowed *like* a field, and	6726
	30:17	called thee an Outcast, *saying*, This *is* **Z**,	6726
	31: 6	let us go up *to* **Z** unto the LORD our God.	6726
	31:12	they shall come and sing in the height of **Z**,	6726
	50: 5	They shall ask the way *to* **Z** with their faces	6726
	50:28	to declare in **Z** the vengeance of	6726
	51:10	let us declare in **Z** the work of the LORD	6726
	51:24	evil that they have done in **Z** in your sight,	6726
	51:35	shall the inhabitant of **Z** say;	6726
La	1: 4	The ways of **Z** do mourn, because	6726
	1: 6	from the daughter of **Z** all her beauty is	6726
	1:17	**Z** spreadeth forth her hands, *and there is*	6726
	2: 1	the daughter of **Z** with a cloud in his anger,	6726
	2: 4	in the tabernacle of the daughter of **Z**:	6726
	2: 6	and sabbaths to be forgotten in **Z**,	6726
	2: 8	to destroy the wall of the daughter of **Z**:	6726
	2:10	The elders of the daughter of **Z** sit upon	6726
	2:13	may comfort thee, O virgin daughter of **Z**?	6726
	2:18	unto the Lord, O wall of the daughter of **Z**,	6726
	4: 2	The precious sons of **Z**, comparable to fine	6726
	4:11	hath kindled a fire in **Z**, and it hath	6726
	4:22	iniquity is accomplished, O daughter of **Z**;	6726
	5:11	They ravished the women in **Z**, *and*	6726
	5:18	Because of the mountain of **Z**, which is	6726
Joel	2: 1	Blow ye the trumpet in **Z**, and sound an	6726
	2:15	Blow the trumpet in **Z**, sanctify a fast,	6726
	2:23	ye children of **Z**, and rejoice in the LORD	6726

Joel 2:32 for in mount **Z** and in Jerusalem shall be 6726
3:16 The LORD also shall roar out of **Z**, and 6726
3:17 I *am* the LORD your God dwelling in **Z**, 6726
3:21 not cleansed: for the LORD dwelleth in **Z**. 6726
Am 1: 2 The LORD will roar from **Z**, and utter his 6726
6: 1 Woe to them *that are* at ease in **Z**, and trust 6726
Ob 1:17 But upon mount **Z** shall be deliverance, and 6726
1:21 saviours shall come up on mount **Z** to 6726
Mic 1:13 beginning of the sin to the daughter of **Z**: 6726
3:10 They build up **Z** with blood, and 6726
3:12 Therefore shall **Z** for your sake be plowed 6726
4: 2 for the law shall go forth of **Z**, and 6726
4: 7 over them in mount **Z** from henceforth, 6726
4: 8 the strong hold of the daughter of **Z**, 6726
4:10 and labour to bring forth, O daughter of **Z**, 6726
4:11 her be defiled, and let our eye look upon **Z**. 6726
4:13 Arise and thresh, O daughter of **Z**: for I 6726
Zep 3:14 Sing, O daughter of **Z**; shout, O Israel; 6726
3:16 *and to* **Z**, Let not thine hands be slack. 6726
Zec 1:14 and for **Z** *with* a great jealousy. 6726
1:17 the LORD shall yet comfort **Z**, and 6726
2: 7 Deliver thyself, O **Z**, that dwellest *with* 6726
2:10 Sing and rejoice, O daughter of **Z**: for lo, 6726
8: 2 I was jealous for **Z** *with* great jealousy, and 6726
8: 3 I am returned unto **Z**, and will dwell in 6726
9: 9 Rejoice greatly, O daughter of **Z**; shout, 6726
9:13 O **Z**, against thy sons, O Greece, and 6726

ZION'S (1) [ZION]
Isa 62: 1 For **Z** sake will I not hold my peace, and 6726

ZIOR (1)
Jos 15:54 and Kirjath-arba, which *is* Hebron, and **Z**; 6730

ZIPH (10) [ZIPHIMS, ZIPHITES]
Jos 15:24 **Z**, and Telem, and Bealoth, 2128
15:55 Maon, Carmel, and **Z**, and Juttah, 2128
1Sa 23:14 in a mountain in the wilderness of **Z**. 2128
23:15 David *was* in the wilderness of **Z** in a 2128
23:24 they arose, and went to **Z** before Saul: but 2128
26: 2 and went down to the wilderness of **Z**, 2128
26: 2 to seek David in the wilderness of **Z**. 2128
1Ch 2:42 his firstborn, which *was* the father of **Z**; 2128
4:16 **Z**, and Ziphah, Tiria, and Asareel. 2128
2Ch 11: 8 And Gath, and Mareshah, and **Z**, 2128

ZIPHAH (1)
1Ch 4:16 Ziph, and **Z**, Tiria, and Asareel. 2129

ZIPHIMS (1) [ZIPH]
Ps 54: T when the **Z** came and said to Saul, 2130

ZIPHION (1)
Ge 46:16 **Z**, and Haggi, Shuni, and Ezbon, Eri, and 6837

ZIPHITES (2) [ZIPH]
1Sa 23:19 came up the **Z** to Saul to Gibeah, saying, 2130
26: 1 the **Z** came unto Saul to Gibeah, saying, 2130

ZIPHRON (1)
Nu 34: 9 the border shall go on to **Z**, and the goings 2202

ZIPPOR (7)
Nu 22: 2 Balak the son of **Z** saw all that Israel had 6834
22: 4 Balak the son of **Z** *was* king of 6834
22:10 Balak the son of **Z**, king of Moab, hath sent 6834
22:16 said to him, Thus saith Balak the son of **Z**, 6834
23:18 and hear; hearken unto me, thou son of **Z**: 6834
Jos 24: 9 Balak the son of **Z**, king of Moab, arose 6834
Jdg 11:25 any thing better than Balak the son of **Z**, 6834

ZIPPORAH (3)
Ex 2:21 and he gave Moses **Z** his daughter. 6855
4:25 **Z** took a sharp stone, and cut off 6855
18: 2 Moses' father in law, took **Z**, Moses' wife, 6855

ZITHRI (1)
Ex 6:22 of Uzziel; Mishael, and Elzaphan, and **Z**. 5644

ZIV See ZIF

ZIZ (1)
2Ch 20:16 behold, they come up by the cliff of **Z**; and 6732

ZIZA (2)
1Ch 4:37 **Z** the son of Shiphi, the son of Allon, 2124
2Ch 11:20 and Attai, and **Z**, and Shelomith. 2124

ZIZAH (1) [ZINA]
1Ch 23:11 Jahath was the chief, and **Z** the second: 2125

ZOAN (7)
Nu 13:22 was built seven years before **Z** in Egypt.) 6814
Ps 78:12 in the land of Egypt, *in* the field of **Z**. 6814
78:43 in Egypt, and his wonders in the field of **Z**: 6814
Isa 19:11 Surely the princes of **Z** *are* fools, 6814
19:13 The princes of **Z** are become fools, 6814
30: 4 For his princes were at **Z**, and 6814
Eze 30:14 will set fire in **Z**, and will execute 6814

ZOAR (10)
Ge 13:10 the land of Egypt, as thou comest unto **Z**. 6820
14: 2 and the king of Bela, which *is* **Z**. 6820
14: 8 and the king of Bela (the same *is* **Z**); 6820
19:22 the name of the city was called **Z**. 6820
19:23 upon the earth when Lot entered into **Z**. 6820
19:30 Lot went up out of **Z**, and dwelt in 6820
19:30 with him; for he feared to dwell in **Z**: 6820
Dt 34: 3 of Jericho, the city of palm trees, unto **Z**. 6820
Isa 15: 5 his fugitives *shall flee* unto **Z**, a heifer of 6820
Jer 48:34 from **Z** *even* unto Horonaim, *as* a heifer of 6820

ZOBA (2) [ZOBAH]
2Sa 10: 6 the Syrians of **Z**, twenty thousand footmen, 6678
10: 8 the Syrians of **Z**, and of Rehob, and 6678

ZOBAH (11) [ARAM-ZOBAH, HAMATH-ZOBAH, ZOBA]
1Sa 14:47 against the kings of **Z**, and against 6678
2Sa 8: 3 the son of Rehob, king of **Z**, 6678
8: 5 came to succour Hadadezer king of **Z**, 6678
8:12 of Hadadezer, son of Rehob, king of **Z**. 6678
23:36 Igal the son of Nathan of **Z**, Bani 6678
1Ki 11:23 fled from his lord Hadadezer king of **Z**: 6678
11:24 when David slew them *of* **Z**: and they went NIH
1Ch 18: 3 David smote Hadarezer king of **Z** unto 6678
18: 5 came to help Hadarezer king of **Z**, 6678
18: 9 smitten all the host of Hadarezer king of **Z**; 6678
19: 6 and out of Syria-maachah, and out of **Z**. 6678

ZOBEBAH (1)
1Ch 4: 8 **Z**, and the families of Aharhel the son of 6637

ZOHAR (4)
Ge 23: 8 and intreat for me to Ephron the son of **Z**, 6714
25: 9 in the field of Ephron the son of **Z** 6714
46:10 **Z**, and Shaul the son of a Canaanitish 6714
Ex 6:15 **Z**, and Shaul the son of a Canaanitish 6714

ZOHELETH (1)
1Ki 1: 9 and oxen and fat cattle by the stone of **Z**, 2120

ZOHETH (1)
1Ch 4:20 the sons of Ishi *were*, **Z**, and Ben-zoheth. 2105

ZOPHAH (2)
1Ch 7:35 **Z**, and Imna, and Shelesh, and Amal. 6690
7:36 The sons of **Z**; Suah, and Harnepher, and 6690

ZOPHAI (1)
1Ch 6:26 of Elkanah; **Z** his son, and Nahath his son, 6689

ZOPHAR (4)
Job 2:11 Bildad the Shuhite, and **Z** the Naamathite: 6691
11: 1 Then answered **Z** the Naamathite, and said, 6691
20: 1 Then answered **Z** the Naamathite, and said, 6691
42: 9 the Shuhite *and* **Z** the Naamathite went, 6691

ZOPHIM (1) [RAMATHAIM-ZOPHIM]
Nu 23:14 he brought him *into* the field of **Z**, to 6839

ZORAH (8)
Jos 19:41 the coast of their inheritance was **Z**, and 6881
Jdg 13: 2 there was a certain man of **Z**, of the family 6881
13:25 the camp of Dan, between **Z** and Eshtaol. 6881
16:31 buried him between **Z** and Eshtaol in 6881
18: 2 men of valour, from **Z** and from Eshtaol, 6881
18: 8 they came unto their brethren *to* **Z** and 6881
18:11 out of **Z** and out of Eshtaol, six hundred 6881
2Ch 11:10 **Z**, and Aijalon, and Hebron, which *are* in 6881

ZORATHITES (1)
1Ch 4: 2 and Lahad. These *are* the families of the **Z**. 6882

ZOREAH (1)
Jos 15:33 in the valley, Eshtaol, and Z, and Ashnah, 6881

ZORITES (1)
1Ch 2:54 and half of the Manahethites, the Z. 6882

ZOROBABEL (3) [ZERUBBABEL]
Mt 1:12 begat Salathiel; and Salathiel begat Z; *2216*
1:13 And Z begat Abiud; and Abiud begat *2216*
Lk 3:27 *the son* of Rhesa, which was *the son* of Z, *2216*

ZUAR (5)
Nu 1: 8 Of Issachar; Nethaneel the son of Z. 6686
2: 5 Nethaneel the son of Z *shall be* captain of 6686
7:18 On the second day Nethaneel the son of Z, 6686
7:23 *was* the offering of Nethaneel the son of Z. 6686
10:15 of Issachar *was* Nethaneel the son of Z. 6686

ZUPH (3)
1Sa 1: 1 son of Tohu, the son of Z, an Ephrathite: 6689
9: 5 *And* when they were come to the land of Z, 6689
1Ch 6:35 The son of Z, the son of Elkanah, the son 6689

ZUPHITE See RAMATHAIM-ZOPHIM

ZUR (5) [BETH-ZUR]
Nu 25:15 was slain *was* Cozbi, the daughter of Z; 6698
31: 8 and Rekem, and Z, and Hur, and Reba, 6698
Jos 13:21 Evi, and Rekem, and Z, and Hur, and Reba, 6698
1Ch 8:30 and Z, and Kish, and Baal, and Nadab, 6698
9:36 Z, and Kish, and Baal, and Ner, and Nadab, 6698

ZURIEL (1)
Nu 3:35 of Merari *was* Z the son of Abihail: 6700

ZURISHADDAI (5)
Nu 1: 6 Of Simeon; Shelumiel the son of Z. 6701
2:12 of Simeon *shall be* Shelumiel the son of Z. 6701
7:36 On the fifth day Shelumiel the son of Z, 6701
7:41 *was* the offering of Shelumiel the son of Z. 6701
10:19 of Simeon *was* Shelumiel the son of Z. 6701

ZUZIMS (1)
Ge 14: 5 the Z in Ham, and the Emims in Shaveh 2104

ZUZITES See ZUZIMS

INDEX OF ARTICLES, CONJUNCTIONS, PREPOSITIONS, PRONOUNS, ETC.

A [8718]

ABOUT [632]

ABOVE [223]

ACCORDING [793]

1:19; 3:8; 4:3; 9:21, 28; 10:3; **Job** 1:6; 2:1, 8; 15:19; 17:10; 18:19; 28:10; 30:5, 7; 33:23; 34:4; 36:14; 39:25; 41:6; 42:15; **Ps** 9:11; 12:1; 18:49; 21:10; 22:18, 28; 31:11, 11; 35:18; 44:11, 14, 14; 45:9, 12; 46:10; 55:15; 57:4, 4, 9, 9; 67:2; 68:13, 17, 18, 25; 74:9; 77:14; 78:45, 49, 60; 79:10; 80:6; 82:1; 86:8; 88:5; 89:6; 94:8; 96:3, 3, 10; 99:6, 6; 104:10, 12; 105:1, 27, 37; 106:27, 35, 47; 108:3, 3; 109:30; 110:6; 126:2; 136:11; **Pr** 1:14; 6:19; 7:7, 7; 14:9; 15:31; 17:2; 23:28; 27:22; 30:14, 30; 31:23; **Ecc** 6:1; 7:28, 28; 9:3, 17; **SS** 1:8; 2:2, 2, 3, 3, 16; 4:2, 5; 5:9, 10; 6:1, 3, 6; **Isa** 2:4; 4:3; 8:15, 16; 10:16; 12:4; 24:13; 29:19; 33:14; 39:4; 42:23; 43:9, 12; 44:4, 14; 48:14; 50:10; 51:18; 57:6; 61:9, 9; 65:4; 66:19, 19; **Jer** 3:19; 4:3; 5:26; 6:15, 18, 27; 8:12, 17; 9:16; 10:7; 11:9, 9; 12:14; 14:22; 18:13; 24:10; 25:16, 27; 29:18, 32; 31:7; 37:4, 10; 39:14; 40:1, 5, 6, 11; 41:8, 8; 44:8; 46:18; 48:27; 49:15, 15; 50:2, 23, 46; 51:27, 41; **La** 1:1, 1, 2, 3, 17; 2:9; 4:15, 20; **Eze** 1:1, 13; 2:5, 6; 3:15, 25; 4:13; 5:14; 6:8, 9, 13; 9:2; 11:1, 9, 16, 16; 12:10, 12, 15, 16; 13:19; 15:2, 6; 16:14; 18:18; 19:2, 2, 6, 11; 20:9, 23, 38; 22:15, 26, 30; 23:10; 25:10; 27:24, 36; 28:19, 25; 29:12, 12; 30:23, 26, 26; 31:3, 10, 14, 18; 32:9, 21; 33:6, 33; 34:12, 24; 36:19, 21, 22, 23, 24, 30; 37:21; 39:6, 21, 28; 40:46; 44:9; 47:22, 22, 22, 22; **Da** 1:6, 19; 4:35; 7:8; 11:24, 33; **Hos** 5:9; 7:7, 8; 8:8, 10; 9:17; 10:14; 13:15; **Joel** 2:17, 19, 25; 3:2, 9; **Am** 1:1; 2:16; 4:10; 9:9; **Ob** 1:1, 2, 4; **Mic** 3:11; 4:3; 5:2, 8, 8, 8; 7:2; **Na** 3:8; **Hab** 1:5; **Zep** 3:20; **Hag** 2:3, 5; **Zec** 1:8, 10, 11; 3:7; 7:14; 8:13; 10:9; 12:6, 8; 14:13; **Mal** 1:10, 11, 11, 14; **Mt** 2:6; 4:23; 9:35; 11:11; 12:11; 13:7, 22, 25, 32, 49; 16:7, 8; 20:26, 26, 27; 21:38; 23:11; 26:5; 27:35, 56; 28:15; **Mk** 1:27; 4:7, 18; 5:3; 6:4, 41; 8:16, 19, 20; 9:33, 34; 10:26, 43, 43; 13:10; 15:31, 40; 16:3; **Lk** 1:1, 25, 28, 42; 2:44; 4:36; 7:16, 28; 8:7, 14; 9:46, 48; 10:3, 30, 36; 19:2, 39; 20:14; 22:17, 23, 24, 26, 27, 37, 55; 24:5, 47; **Jn** 1:14, 26; 6:9, 43; 7:12, 35, 35, 43; 8:7; 9:16; 10:19; 11:54, 56; 12:19, 20, 42; 15:24; 16:17, 19; 19:24, 24; 21:23; **Ac** 1:21; 2:22; 3:23; 4:12, 15, 17, 34; 5:12, 34; 6:3, 8; 10:22; 12:18; 13:26; 14:14; 15:7, 12, 19, 22; 17:33, 34; 18:11; 20:25, 29, 32; 21:19, 21, 34; 23:10; 24:5, 21; 25:5, 6; 26:3, 4, 18; 27:22; 28:4, 25, 29; **Ro** 1:5, 6, 13, 13; 2:24; 12:3; 15:9; 16:7; **1Co** 1:10, 11; 2:2, 6; 3:3, 18; 5:1, 2, 13; 6:7; 11:18, 19, 19, 30; 15:12; **2Co** 1:19; 6:17; 10:1; 11:6, 26; 12:12, 21; **Gal** 1:16; 2:2; 3:1, 5; **Eph** 2:3; 3:8; **Php** 2:15; **Col** 1:27; **1Th** 1:5; 2:7, 10; 5:12, 13, 15; **2Th** 1:10; 3:7, 11; **2Ti** 2:2; **Heb** 5:1; **Jas** 1:26; 4:1; 5:13, 14; **1Pe** 2:12; 4:8; 5:1, 2; **2Pe** 2:1, 1, 8; **3Jn** 1:9; **Jude** 1:15; **Rev** 2:13; 7:15; 14:4

AMONGST [59]

Ge 3:8; 23:9, 10; 24:3; 30:33, 33, 35; 34:30; 47:6; **Ex** 9:20; 10:2; 12:31; 13:13; 17:7; 25:8; 29:45, 46; 30:12; 31:14; 32:25; 34:9, 19; 35:5; **Lev** 19:34; 26:11; **Nu** 11:21; 15:29; 25:7; **Dt** 14:6; 31:16, 17; **Jos** 7:11, 12; 23:7; 24:5; **Ru** 2:7; **1Ch** 4:23; **Job** 34:37; **Pr** 23:20, 20; **Isa** 5:27; 29:14; 33:14; 36:20; 41:28; **Jer** 32:20; **Eze** 35:11; **Mk** 12:7; **Lk** 16:15; **Jn** 6:52; **Ro** 8:29; 11:17; **1Co** 5:1; 6:5; **2Co** 10:12; **Eph** 5:3; **Col** 4:16; **Jas** 3:6, 13

AN [1267]

Ge 4:3, 22; 5:3, 6, 18, 25, 28; 6:3, 14; 7:24; 8:11, 20; 11:10, 25; 12:7, 8; 13:18; 16:1; 17:7, 8, 13, 17, 19; 21:5, 20; 22:9; 23:1; 25:7, 8, 17; 26:12, 25, 28; 27:30; 33:19, 20; 35:1, 3, 7, 8, 28; 37:33, 36; 38:14; 39:1, 1; 41:16; 42:23; 43:12, 32; 44:20; 46:34; 47:9, 28; 48:4; 49:9, 17, 33; 50:22, 25, 26; **Ex** 2:3, 11, 19; 4:20; 6:8, 16, 18, 20; 10:13; 12:14, 17, 24; 13:13; 15:25; 16:16, 18, 32, 33, 36, 36; 17:15; 18:3; 20:24, 25; 21:6, 28, 33, 33; 22:1, 1, 10, 10, 11, 25; 23:1, 20, 22, 22; 24:4; 25:2, 10; 27:1, 9, 11, 18; 28:4, 11, 18, 19, 19, 20, 32; 29:18, 25, 36, 37, 37, 41; 30:1, 10, 14, 15, 15, 16, 25, 25; 31:18; 32:5, 30; 33:2; 34:20; 35:5, 5, 22, 24; 38:9, 11, 23, 23, 25, 27; 39:11, 12, 12, 13, 23; 40:10, 15; **Lev** 1:2, 9, 13, 17; 2:2, 4, 9, 16; 3:3, 5, 9, 14; 4:20, 26, 31, 35; 5:2, 4, 6, 10, 11, 13, 16, 18; 6:7, 20; 7:5, 18, 25; 8:21, 28, 33, 34; 9:7, 7; 11:10, 11, 12, 13, 20, 23, 41, 42; 12:7, 8; 13:11, 28; 14:5, 18, 19, 20, 21, 29, 31, 40, 41, 45, 50, 53; 15:13, 15, 19, 25, 30, 32, 33; 16:6, 10, 11, 16, 17, 17, 18, 20, 24, 30, 33, 33, 33, 34, 34; 17:3, 4, 11, 11; 19:22; 20:13, 21; 22:12, 22, 27; 23:8, 13, 14, 18, 25, 27, 28, 36, 36, 37; 24:7, 8, 10, 10; 25:46; 26:8, 8; 27:9, 27; **Nu** 2:9, 16, 24, 24, 31; 4:15; 5:2, 8, 15, 15, 15, 17, 19, 21, 21; 6:11; 7:3, 13, 19, 25, 31, 37, 43, 49, 55, 61, 67, 73, 79, 85, 86; 8:11, 12, 13, 15, 19, 21, 21; 9:7; 10:5, 6, 6, 7, 8, 9; 12:1; 13:32; 14:7; 15:3, 10, 13, 14, 15, 25, 28, 28; 16:31, 46, 47; 18:8, 17, 21; 19:17; 20:16; 22:22; 23:22; 24:8; 25:13, 13; 26:53; 27:7; 28:5, 22, 30; 29:5; 30:2, 10; 31:50, 50; 32:14; 33:39, 54; 34:2; 35:16; 36:2, 8; **Dt** 4:21, 38; 7:25, 26; 10:1, 3; 14:21; 15:4, 17; 17:1; 18:10, 10, 12; 19:10; 20:9, 16, 19; 21:23; 22:10, 10, 14, 19, 19; 23:3, 7, 7; 24:4; 25:16, 19; 26:1, 8, 12; 27:5, 5, 15, 25; 28:22, 22, 37; 29:8; 31:2, 24; 32:11, 45; 34:7; **Jos** 1:6; 7:13; 8:2, 24, 30, 31; 10:20; 11:23; 13:6, 7; 14:13; 17:4, 4, 6; 19:49, 49, 51, 51; 22:10, 11, 16, 19, 23, 26, 29; 23:4; 24:25, 26, 29, 32; **Jdg** 2:1, 8; 3:18, 31; 6:11, 11, 19, 22, 22, 24, 26; 8:10, 27; 9:23, 48; 12:5; 13:6, 16, 21; 14:4; 15:15, 16, 16, 17; 17:5; 18:1, 14; 19:9, 16, 28; 20:10, 10, 35, 38; 21:4, 17; **Ru** 2:17; **1Sa** 1:1; 2:28, 31, 32, 32; 3:12; 4:18; 7:17; 9:6; 10:13; 13:10; 14:3, 28, 35; 16:14, 15, 20; 17:12, 17; 18:1, 25; 19:13, 16; 20:36; 21:7; 23:6; 24:16; 25:18, 42; 26:19; 28:14; 29:4, 9; 30:11, 13, 14, 25; **2Sa** 1:8, 13; 3:14, 29; 6:18; 8:4; 11:2, 19; 13:36; 14:17, 20; 15:19; 16:1, 1; 17:25; 18:10; 19:26, 27; 23:5, 21, 38, 38; 24:3, 18, 21, 25; **1Ki** 1:41, 41; 3:1, 9, 12; 4:23; 7:2, 40; 8:31, 36, 54, 63; 10:10, 29; 11:14, 25, 26; 12:21; 13:11, 14, 18; 14:21, 31; 15:13; 16:32; 18:4, 10, 13, 32; 19:5, 11; 20:25, 29, 30; 22:9, 25; **2Ki** 3:4, 4; 4:24, 43; 6:25; 9:2, 5; 10:25; 11:4; 16:10, 11; 18:31; 19:32, 35; 23:33; 25:19; **1Ch** 2:34; 5:21; 6:49; 8:40; 11:23; 12:14, 37; 15:5, 7, 10, 27; 16:2, 17, 29; 18:4; 21:3, 5, 15, 18, 22, 26; 22:14; 27:4; 28:8; **2Ch** 1:17; 2:4, 17; 3:4, 16; 4:1, 8; 5:12; 6:22, 27; 7:1, 5, 21; 9:9; 11:1; 12:13; 13:3, 13; 14:8; 15:16; 17:18; 18:24; 20:23; 21:18; 24:10, 15, 26; 25:6, 6; 26:13; 27:5; 28:6; 29:17, 24, 29, 32; 32:8, 21; 35:25; 36:3; **Ezr** 2:3, 18, 21, 23, 27, 30, 41, 42; 4:6, 17; 6:17; 7:22, 22, 22, 22; 8:3, 10, 12, 26, 26; 9:11, 12; 10:17; **Ne** 4:2; 5:12, 17; 6:5, 13; 7:8, 24, 26, 27, 31, 32, 44, 45; 10:29, 33; 11:14, 19; **Est** 1:1, 4; 8:9; **Job** 1:8; 2:3, 11; 4:16; 6:6; 7:1; 14:4; 16:3; 18:2; 19:15, 24; 26:10; 28:3; 31:6, 11, 28; 33:23; 40:9, 15; 42:11, 16; **Ps** 5:9; 7:9; 18:25; 26:12; 33:2; 41:8; 43:1; 48:7; 55:12; 64:5, 7; 69:8, 13, 31; 78:26, 55; 88:8; 92:3, 10; 96:8; 102:6; 105:10; 106:20; 119:96, 111, 142; 127:3; 135:12, 12; 136:21, 22; 140:11; 141:5; 144:9; 145:13; **Pr** 1:9; 4:9; 6:11, 16; 7:13, 22; 8:5, 7; 10:25; 13:22; 15:8, 9, 26; 16:5, 12, 19, 27; 17:10, 11, 27; 19:15, 28; 20:3, 21, 23; 21:19; 22:24; 23:5, 6, 18, 32; 24:9, 34; 25:12, 12, 12, 19, 23; 27:6; 28:10, 22; 29:6, 22, 27, 27; 30:19, 20, 23; **Ecc** 4:13; 5:6; 6:1, 2, 3, 3; 7:11; 8:3, 11, 12; 9:2, 3, 12, 12; 10:5, 5; **SS** 4:4, 13; 6:4, 10; **Isa** 1:13, 30; 5:10, 26; 6:13; 9:17; 11:10, 12; 14:19; 16:4; 17:6, 9; 18:3; 19:19; 24:13; 29:5, 21; 30:13, 17, 28; 33:1; 36:16; 37:33, 36; 38:12, 13; 41:24; 43:23; 44:14, 19; 45:17; 48:4; 49:8, 18; 53:10; 54:16; 55:3, 13; 56:5; 58:5; 60:15, 19; 61:8; 63:12; 64:6; 65:9, 20, 20, 20, 20; 66:3, 3, 3, 14, 20, 20, 24; **Jer** 1:11, 14, 18; 2:7, 19; 3:18; 4:7; 5:15, 16; 6:26; 9:2, 8, 11; 10:10; 11:19; 14:12; 18:17; 21:5; 22:19; 23:40; 25:9, 11, 18; 26:8, 9; 29:11, 18; 30:14, 17; 31:3; 32:14, 40; 33:9; 34:22; 42:18, 18; 43:1; 44:12, 12, 22, 22, 27; 46:19, 22; 47:2; 48:40; 49:2, 14; 50:9; 51:29, 34, 37, 37, 41, 63; 52:23, 25; **La** 1:15; 2:4, 4, 5; 5:10; **Eze** 1:10, 10; 3:9; 4:3; 5:15, 15; 7:2, 5, 5, 6; 10:14; 13:11, 13; 16:3, 24, 30, 45, 60; 17:13; 20:17; 21:25, 29; 23:24; 33:32; 35:5; 36:3; 37:10, 26; 38:10, 22; 40:19, 23, 27, 47, 47; 41:7, 13, 13, 14, 15; 42:2, 8, 15; 43:23; 44:28; 45:1, 13, 13, 24, 24, 24; 46:5, 5, 7, 7, 7, 11, 11, 11, 14; 47:22; **Da** 2:46; 3:1; 4:3, 34; 5:12; 6:1, 3; 7:14, 27; 9:24; 11:6, 7; **Hos** 3:1, 4, 4; 7:4, 6, 7; 8:1; 10:1; 13:13, 15; **Joel** 2:1; **Am** 3:11, 12, 15; 5:3, 3, 13; 7:2; 8:10; **Ob** 1:1; **Jnh** 3:3; **Mic** 1:15; 2:3, 8; **Na** 1:8, 8, 9; **Hab** 2:3, 9; **Zep** 3:12; **Zec** 5:6; 7:12; 9:9, 9, 16; **Mal** 1:10, 13; 2:11, 12; 3:3; 4:1; **Mt** 2:19; 4:8; 5:38, 38; 9:16, 20; 11:1; 12:35, 39; 13:8, 23, 28; 14:7; 16:23; 18:12, 28; 19:29; 21:2, 5, 5; 24:44, 50; 26:5, 7, 72; **Mk** 1:23; 2:21; 3:26, 30; 4:8, 20; 5:2, 25; 6:27; 7:22, 25, 32; 10:30; 14:2, 3; 15:43; **Lk** 1:11, 18; 4:33; 5:36; 6:7, 45; 7:37; 8:8, 15, 43; 9:28; 10:34; 11:12, 29; 12:1, 40, 46; 14:5, 5, 32; 15:4; 16:2, 6, 7; 19:21, 22; 22:37, 43, 44; **Jn** 1:22, 47; 5:4, 5; 12:15, 29; 13:15; 19:39; 21:11; **Ac** 1:13, 15; 2:30; 3:3; 6:15; 7:30; 8:27; 9:37; 10:3, 28; 11:13; 12:21; 14:5; 17:5, 23; 18:24; 19:40; 20:32; 21:16, 26, 29, 31, 38; 23:9, 21, 27; 25:11; **Ro** 1:1, 23; 2:20; 3:13; 4:19; 7:3; 11:1; 14:13; **1Co** 1:1; 5:9, 11, 11; 8:4, 7; 9:1, 2, 25; 12:17; 14:2, 4, 8, 13, 14, 19, 26, 27; 15:9, 52; **2Co** 1:1; 2:11; 6:15; 8:14; 11:7, 14; 12:12; **Gal** 1:1, 8; 2:5; 4:7, 14, 24; 5:13; **Eph** 1:1, 11; 5:2, 5; 6:20; **Php** 1:28; 3:17; 4:18; **Col** 1:1; **2Th** 3:9, 15; **1Ti** 1:1; 2:7; 4:12; 5:1, 8, 19, 19; **2Ti** 1:1, 11; 2:9; 4:5; **Tit** 1:1; **Heb** 3:12; 6:6, 16, 16, 17, 19; 7:16, 20, 21, 21, 24; 10:22, 29, 34; 11:7, 8; 12:22; 13:10; **Jas** 3:8; 5:10; **1Pe** 1:1, 4; 2:21; 3:15; 4:15; 5:1; **2Pe** 1:1, 11; 2:6, 6; **1Jn** 2:1, 7, 20; 5:20; **2Jn** 1:7; **Jude** 1:7; **Rev** 2:7, 11, 17, 29; 3:6, 8, 13, 22; 4:3; 7:4; 8:1, 5, 13; 9:15; 11:19; 13:9, 14; 14:1; 16:18; 19:17; 20:1; 21:17, 19, 20

AND [51713]

Ge 1:1, 2, 2, 2, 2, 3, 3, 4, 4, 5, 5, 5, 5, 6, 6, 7, 7, 7, 8, 8, 8, 9, 9, 9, 10, 10, 10, 11, 11, 11, 12, 12, 12, 12, 13, 13, 14, 14, 14, 14, 14, 15, 15, 16, 16, 17, 18, 18, 18, 18, 19, 19, 20, 20, 21, 21, 21, 21, 22, 22, 22, 22, 23, 23, 24, 24, 24, 24, 25, 25, 25, 25, 26, 26, 26, 26, 26, 26, 27, 28, 28, 28, 28, 28, 28, 28, 28, 29, 29, 30, 30, 30, 30, 31, 31, 31, 31; 2:1, 1, 2, 2, 3, 3, 3, 4, 4, 5, 5, 5, 6, 7, 7, 7, 8, 8, 9, 9, 9, 9, 10, 10, 10, 12, 12, 13, 14, 14, 15, 15, 15, 16, 17, 18, 19, 19, 19, 19, 20, 20, 20, 21, 21, 21, 21, 22, 22, 23, 23, 24, 24, 24, 25, 25, 25; 3:1, 2, 4, 5, 5, 6, 6, 6, 6, 6, 6, 7, 7, 7, 7, 8, 8, 8, 9, 9, 10, 10, 10, 11, 12, 12, 13, 13, 13, 14, 14, 14, 15, 15, 15, 15, 15, 16, 16, 16, 17, 17, 18, 18, 19, 20, 21, 21, 22, 22, 22, 22, 22, 22, 24, 24; 4:1, 1, 1, 1, 2, 2, 3, 4, 4, 4, 4, 5, 5, 5, 6, 6, 7, 7, 7, 8, 8, 8, 9, 9, 10, 11, 12, 13, 14, 14, 14, 14, 15, 15, 16, 16, 17, 17, 17, 17, 17, 18, 18, 18, 18, 19, 19, 20, 20, 21, 21, 22, 22, 22, 23, 23, 23, 24, 25, 25, 25, 26, 26; 5:2, 2, 2, 3, 3, 3, 3, 4, 4, 4, 5, 5, 5, 6, 6, 6, 7, 7, 7, 7, 8, 8, 8, 9, 9, 10, 10, 10, 10, 11, 11, 11, 12, 12, 13, 13, 13, 13, 14, 14, 14, 15, 15, 15, 16, 16, 16, 16, 17, 17, 17, 18, 18, 18, 19, 19, 19, 20, 20, 20, 21, 21, 21, 22, 22, 22, 23, 23, 24, 24, 25, 25, 25, 26, 26, 26, 26, 27, 27, 27, 28, 28, 28, 29, 29, 30, 30, 30, 30, 31, 31, 31, 32, 32, 32; 6:1, 1, 2, 3, 3, 4, 4, 5, 5, 6, 6, 7, 7, 7, 7, 9, 9, 10, 10, 11, 12, 12, 13, 13, 14, 14, 15, 15, 16, 16, 16, 17, 17, 18, 18, 18, 18, 19, 19, 20, 21, 21, 21, 21; 7:1, 1, 2, 2, 2, 3, 4, 4, 4, 5, 6, 7, 7, 7, 7, 8, 8, 8, 9, 9, 10, 11, 12, 12, 13, 13, 13, 13, 13, 14, 14, 14, 14, 15, 15, 16, 16, 16, 17, 17, 17, 17, 18, 18, 18, 19, 19, 20, 21, 21, 21, 21, 21, 23, 23, 23, 23, 23, 23, 23, 24, 24; 8:1, 1, 1, 1, 1, 2, 2, 3, 3, 3, 4, 5, 6, 7, 7, 9, 9, 9, 10, 10, 11, 11, 12, 12, 13, 13, 13, 13, 13, 14, 14, 15, 16, 16, 16, 17, 17, 17, 17, 18, 18, 18, 18, 19, 19, 20, 20, 20, 20, 21, 21, 22, 22, 22, 22, 22, 22, 22; 9:1, 1, 1, 1, 1, 2, 2, 2, 2, 5, 5, 7, 7, 7, 8, 8, 9, 9, 10, 10, 11, 12, 12, 12, 13, 13, 14, 15, 15, 15, 15, 16, 16, 16, 17, 17, 18, 18, 18, 18, 19, 20, 20, 21, 21, 21, 22, 22, 23, 23, 23, 23, 23, 23, 23, 24, 24, 25, 26, 26, 27, 27, 28, 28, 29, 29, 29; 10:1, 1, 2, 2, 2, 2, 2, 2, 3, 3, 3, 4, 4, 4, 6, 6, 6, 6, 7, 7, 7, 7, 7, 7, 7, 8, 10, 10, 10, 10, 11, 11, 11, 12, 12, 13, 13, 13, 13, 14, 14, 14, 15, 15, 16, 16, 16, 17, 17, 17, 18, 18, 18, 18, 19, 19, 19, 19, 20, 22, 22, 22, 22, 23, 23, 23, 23, 24, 24, 25, 25, 26, 26, 26, 26, 27, 27, 27, 28, 28, 28, 29, 29, 29, 30, 32; 11:1, 1, 2, 2, 3, 3, 3, 3, 4, 4, 4, 5, 5, 6, 6, 6, 6, 7, 8, 9, 10, 11, 11, 11, 12, 12, 12, 13, 13, 13, 13, 14, 14, 15, 15, 15, 15, 16, 16, 16, 17, 17, 17, 17, 18, 18, 19, 19, 19, 19, 20, 20, 20, 21, 21, 21, 21, 22, 22, 23, 23, 23, 24, 24, 24, 25, 25, 25, 25, 26, 26, 26, 27, 27, 28, 29, 29, 29, 29, 31, 31, 31, 31, 31, 31, 32, 32, 32; 12:1, 1, 2, 2, 2, 2, 3, 3, 3, 4, 4, 4, 5, 5, 5, 5, 5, 5, 6, 6, 7, 7, 7, 8, 8, 8, 8, 8, 9, 10, 10, 11, 12, 13, 14, 15, 15, 16, 16, 16, 16, 16, 16, 16, 16, 17, 17, 18, 18, 19, 20, 20, 20, 20; 13:1, 1, 1, 1, 2, 2, 3, 3, 4, 5, 5, 5, 6, 7, 7, 7, 7, 8, 8, 8, 8, 10, 10, 10, 11, 11, 12, 12, 13, 14, 14, 14, 14, 14, 15, 16, 17, 18, 18, 18; 14:1, 1, 2, 2, 2, 4, 5, 5, 5, 5, 5, 6, 7, 7, 7, 7, 8, 8, 8, 8, 8, 8, 9, 9, 9, 10, 10, 10, 10, 10, 11, 11, 11, 11, 12, 12, 12, 13, 13, 13, 13, 14, 14, 14, 15, 15, 15, 15, 16, 16, 16, 16, 16, 17, 17, 18, 18, 18, 19, 19, 19, 20, 20, 21, 21, 22, 22, 23, 24, 24; 15:1, 2, 2, 3, 3, 4, 5, 5, 5, 5, 6, 6, 7, 8, 9, 9, 9, 9, 9, 10, 10, 10, 11, 12, 12, 13, 13, 13, 14, 14, 15, 17, 17, 17, 19, 19, 20, 20, 20, 21, 21, 21, 21; 16:1, 2, 2, 3, 3, 4, 4, 4, 5, 5, 5, 6, 7, 8, 8, 8, 9, 9, 10, 11, 11, 11, 12, 12, 12, 13, 14, 15, 15, 16, 16; 17:1, 1, 1, 1, 2, 2, 2, 3, 3, 4, 6, 6, 6, 7, 7, 7, 7, 8, 8, 8, 9, 9, 10, 10, 11, 11, 11, 12, 13, 13, 14, 15, 16, 16, 16, 17, 17, 17, 18, 19, 19, 19, 19, 20, 20, 20, 20, 22, 22, 23, 23, 23, 23, 24, 24, 25, 26, 27, 27; 18:1, 1, 2, 2, 2, 2, 2, 3, 4, 4, 5, 5, 5, 6, 6, 6, 7, 7, 7, 7, 7, 8, 8, 8, 8, 8, 8, 9, 9, 10, 10, 10, 11, 11, 11, 13, 14, 15, 16, 16, 16, 17, 18, 18, 19, 19, 19, 20, 20, 20, 21, 21, 22, 22, 23, 23, 24, 25, 26, 27, 27, 27, 28, 28, 29, 29, 29, 30, 30, 30, 31, 31, 32, 32, 32, 33, 33; 19:1, 1, 1, 1, 2, 2, 2, 2, 2, 2, 3, 3, 3, 3, 3, 3, 4, 5, 5, 6, 6, 7, 8, 9, 9, 9, 9, 9, 10, 10, 11, 11, 12, 12, 12, 12, 13, 14, 14, 14, 15, 15, 16, 16, 16, 16, 16, 17, 18, 19, 19, 19, 20, 20, 21, 24, 24, 25, 25, 25, 25, 26, 27, 28, 28, 28, 28, 28, 29, 29, 30, 30, 30, 30, 30, 31, 31, 32, 33, 33, 33, 33, 34, 34, 34, 35, 35, 35, 35, 37, 37, 38, 38; 20:1, 1, 1, 1, 2, 2, 2, 3, 4, 5, 5, 6, 7, 7, 7, 7, 8, 8, 8, 9, 9, 9, 10, 11, 11, 12, 12, 13, 14, 14, 14, 14, 14, 14, 15, 16, 16, 17, 17, 17, 17; 21:1, 1, 2, 3, 4, 5, 6, 7, 8, 8, 8, 9, 10, 11, 12, 12, 13, 14, 14, 14, 14, 14, 14, 14, 14, 15, 15, 16, 16, 16, 16, 16, 17, 17, 17, 18, 19, 19, 19, 19, 19, 20, 20, 20, 20, 21, 21, 22, 22, 23, 24, 25, 26, 27, 27, 27, 27, 28, 29, 30, 32, 32, 33, 33, 34; 22:1, 1, 1, 2, 2, 2, 3, 3, 3, 3, 3, 3, 3, 4, 5, 5, 5, 5, 5, 6, 6, 6, 6, 6, 7, 7, 7, 7, 7, 8, 9, 9, 9, 9, 9, 10, 10, 11, 11, 11, 12, 13, 13, 13, 13, 13, 13, 14, 15, 16, 16, 17, 17, 17, 18, 19, 19, 19, 20, 21, 21, 22, 22, 22, 22, 22, 23, 24, 24, 24, 24; 23:1, 1, 1, 2, 2, 2, 3, 3, 4, 5, 7, 7, 8, 8, 10, 10, 11, 12, 13, 13, 14, 15, 16, 16, 17, 17, 17, 19, 20, 20; 24:1, 1, 1, 2, 3, 3, 4, 4, 5, 6, 7, 7, 7, 7, 8, 9, 9, 10, 10, 10, 10, 11, 12, 12, 13, 14, 14, 14, 14, 15, 16, 16, 16, 16, 17, 17, 18, 18, 18, 18, 19, 20, 20, 20, 20, 21, 22, 22, 23, 24, 25, 25, 26, 26, 27, 27, 28, 28, 29, 29, 29, 30, 30, 30, 30, 31, 31, 32, 32, 32, 32, 32, 32, 33, 33, 34, 35, 35, 35, 35, 35, 35, 35, 35, 35, 35, 36, 36, 37, 38, 38, 39, 40, 40, 40, 40, 41, 42, 42, 43, 43, 44, 44, 45, 45, 45, 45, 46, 46, 46, 46, 46, 47, 47, 47, 47, 47, 48, 48, 48, 49, 49, 49, 50, 50, 51, 51, 52, 53, 53, 53, 53, 53, 54, 54, 54, 54, 54, 54, 55, 55, 56, 57, 57, 58, 58, 58, 59, 59, 59, 59, 60, 60, 60, 61, 61, 61, 61, 61, 61, 62, 63, 63, 63, 63, 64, 64, 65, 65, 66, 67, 67, 67, 67, 67; 25:1, 2, 2, 2, 2, 2, 2, 3, 3, 3, 3, 3, 4, 4, 4, 4, 4, 5, 6, 7, 7, 8, 8, 8, 9, 9, 10, 11, 11, 13, 13, 13, 13, 14, 14, 14, 15, 15, 16, 16, 17, 17, 17, 17, 17, 17, 18, 18, 19, 20, 21, 21, 21, 22, 22, 22, 23, 23, 23, 23, 24, 25, 25, 26, 26, 26, 26, 27, 27, 27, 28, 29, 29, 29, 30, 31, 32, 32, 33, 33, 33, 34, 34, 34, 34, 34; 26:1, 1, 2, 2, 3, 3, 3, 3, 4, 4, 4, 5, 5, 6, 7, 7, 8, 8, 8, 9, 9, 9, 9, 10, 10, 11, 12, 12, 13, 13, 13, 14, 14, 14, 15, 16, 17, 17, 17, 18, 18, 19, 19, 20, 20, 21, 21, 21, 22, 22, 22, 22, 22, 22, 23, 24, 24, 24, 24, 25, 25, 25, 25, 26, 26, 27, 27, 28, 28, 28, 28, 29, 29, 30, 30, 30, 31, 31, 31, 31, 32, 32, 32, 33, 34, 34, 35; 27:1, 1, 1, 1, 2, 3, 3, 3, 4, 4, 5, 5, 5, 6, 7, 7, 9, 9, 10, 10, 11, 11, 12, 12, 12, 13, 13, 14, 14, 14, 14, 15, 15, 16, 16, 17, 17, 18, 18, 18, 19, 19, 20, 20, 21, 22, 22, 22, 23, 24, 24, 25, 25, 25, 25, 25, 25, 26, 26, 27, 27, 27, 27, 27, 28, 28, 28, 29, 29, 29, 30, 30, 31, 31, 31, 31, 32, 32, 33, 33, 33, 33, 33, 33, 34, 34, 34, 35, 35, 36, 36, 36, 37, 37, 37, 37, 37, 37, 38, 38, 38, 39, 39, 39, 40, 40, 40, 41, 41, 42, 42, 42, 42, 43, 44, 45, 45, 46; 28:1, 1, 1, 1, 2, 3, 3, 3, 4, 4, 5, 5, 5, 6, 6, 7, 7, 7, 8, 9, 10, 10, 11, 11, 11, 11, 11, 12, 12, 12, 12, 12, 13, 13, 13, 13, 14, 14, 14, 14, 14, 14, 14, 15, 15, 15, 16, 16, 16, 17, 17, 17, 18, 18, 18, 18, 19, 20, 20, 20, 20, 22, 22; 29:1, 2, 2, 2, 2, 3, 3, 3, 3, 4, 4, 5, 5, 6, 6, 6, 7, 7, 7, 8, 8, 9, 10, 10, 10, 10, 11, 11, 11, 12, 12, 12, 12, 13, 13, 13, 13, 13, 14, 14, 14, 15, 16, 16, 17, 18, 18, 19, 20, 20, 21, 22, 22, 23, 23, 23, 24, 25, 25, 26, 27, 28, 28, 28, 29, 30, 30, 30, 31, 32, 32, 32, 33, 33, 33, 33, 34, 34, 34, 35, 35, 35, 35; 30:1, 1, 2, 2, 3, 3, 4, 4, 5, 5, 6, 6, 6, 7, 7, 8, 8, 8, 9, 10, 11, 11, 12, 13, 13, 14, 14, 14, 15, 15, 15, 16, 16, 16, 16, 17, 17, 17, 18, 18, 19, 19, 20, 20, 21, 21, 22, 22, 22, 23, 23, 23, 24, 24, 25, 25, 26, 26, 27, 28, 28, 29, 29, 30, 30, 30, 31, 31, 31, 32, 32, 32, 32, 32, 33, 33, 34, 35, 35, 35, 35, 35, 35, 35, 36, 36, 36, 37, 37, 37, 37, 37, 38, 39, 39, 39, 40, 40, 40, 40, 40, 41, 42, 43, 43, 43, 43, 43, 43; 31:1, 1, 2, 2, 3, 3, 3, 4, 4, 4, 5, 6, 7, 7, 8, 9, 10, 10, 10, 10, 11, 11, 12, 12, 12, 13, 13, 14, 14, 14, 15, 16, 17, 17, 18, 18, 19, 19, 20, 21, 21, 21, 22, 23, 23, 23, 24, 24, 25, 26, 26, 27, 27, 27, 27, 28, 28, 30, 31, 31, 32, 33, 33, 33, 33, 34, 34, 34, 35, 35, 36, 36, 36, 36, 37, 38, 38, 40, 40, 41, 41, 42, 42, 42, 43, 43, 43, 43, 43, 43, 44, 44, 44, 45, 45, 46, 46, 46, 46, 47, 48, 48, 49, 49, 50, 51, 51, 51, 52, 52, 52, 53, 53, 54, 54, 54, 55, 55, 55, 55, 55, 55; 32:1, 1, 2, 2, 3, 4, 4, 5, 5, 5, 5, 5, 6, 6, 6, 7, 7, 7, 7, 7, 8, 8, 9, 9, 9, 9, 10, 10, 11, 11, 12, 12, 13, 13, 14, 14, 15, 15, 16, 16, 16, 16, 17, 17, 17, 17, 18, 19, 19, 19, 20, 20, 21, 22, 22, 22, 22, 22, 23, 23, 23, 24, 24, 25, 25, 26, 26, 27, 27, 28, 28, 28, 29, 29, 29, 29, 30, 30, 31, 31; 33:1, 1, 1, 1, 1, 1, 1, 2, 2, 2, 2, 2, 2, 3, 3, 4, 4, 4, 4, 4, 5, 5, 5, 5, 5, 6, 6, 7, 7, 7, 7, 7, 8, 8, 9, 10, 10, 11, 11, 11, 12, 12, 12, 13, 13, 13, 13, 14, 14, 15, 15, 17, 17, 17, 18, 18, 19, 20, 20; 34:1, 2, 2, 2, 3, 3, 3, 4, 5, 5, 6, 7, 7, 7, 8, 9, 9, 9, 10, 10, 10, 10, 11, 11, 11, 12, 12, 13, 13, 13, 14, 16, 16, 16, 17, 18, 18, 19, 19, 20, 20, 20, 21, 21, 23, 23, 23, 24, 24, 24, 25, 25, 25, 25, 26, 26, 26, 26, 27, 28, 28, 28, 28, 29, 29, 29, 29, 30, 30, 30, 30, 30, 30, 30, 31; 35:1, 1, 1, 2, 2, 2, 3, 3, 3, 3, 4, 4, 4, 5, 5, 5, 6, 7, 7, 8, 8, 9, 9, 10, 10, 11, 11, 11, 11, 12, 12, 12, 13, 14, 14, 14, 15, 16, 16, 16, 16, 17, 18, 19, 19, 20, 21, 21, 22, 22, 22, 23, 23, 23, 23, 23, 24, 25, 25, 26, 26, 27, 27, 28, 28, 29, 29, 29, 29, 29, 29; 36:2, 3, 4, 4, 5, 5, 5, 6, 6, 6, 6, 6, 6, 6, 6, 7, 9, 11, 11, 11, 12, 12, 13, 13, 13, 14, 14, 14, 14, 16, 17, 18, 19, 20, 20, 20, 21, 21, 21, 22, 22, 22, 23, 23, 23, 23, 24, 24, 25, 25, 26, 26, 26, 26, 27, 27, 28, 31, 32, 32, 33, 33, 34, 34, 35, 35, 35, 36, 36, 37, 37, 38, 38, 39, 39, 39, 39, 40; 37:1, 2, 2, 2, 3, 4, 4, 5, 5, 5, 6, 7, 7, 7, 7, 8, 8, 8, 9, 9, 9, 9, 9, 9, 10, 10, 10, 10, 10, 10, 11, 12, 13, 13, 13, 14, 14, 14, 14, 15, 15, 15, 16, 17, 17, 17, 18, 19, 20, 20, 20, 20, 21, 21, 21, 22, 22, 23, 24, 24, 24, 25, 25, 25, 25, 25, 25, 26, 26, 27, 27, 27, 27, 28, 28, 28, 28, 29, 29, 29, 30, 30, 30, 31, 31, 31, 32, 32, 32, 33, 33, 34, 34, 34, 35, 35, 35, 36, 36; 38:1, 1, 2, 2, 2, 3, 3, 3, 4, 4, 4, 5, 5, 5, 5, 6, 7, 7, 8, 8, 8, 9, 9, 10, 11, 11, 12, 12, 12, 12, 13, 14, 14, 14, 14, 14, 16, 16, 16, 17, 17, 18, 18, 18, 18, 18, 18, 18, 19, 19, 19, 19, 20, 21, 22, 22, 22, 23, 23, 24, 24, 24, 24, 25, 25, 25, 26, 26, 26, 27, 28, 28, 28, 29, 29, 30, 30; 39:1, 1, 2, 2, 2, 3, 3, 4, 4, 4, 4, 5, 5, 5, 5, 6, 6, 6, 6, 7, 7, 8, 8, 9, 10, 11, 11, 12, 12, 12, 12, 13, 13, 14, 14, 15, 15, 15, 15, 16, 17, 18, 18, 18, 19, 20, 20, 20, 21, 21, 22, 22, 23; 40:1, 1, 2, 2, 3, 4, 4, 4, 5, 5, 6, 6, 6, 7, 8, 8, 8, 9, 9, 10, 10, 10, 10, 11, 11, 11, 11, 12, 13, 13, 14, 14, 14, 15, 16, 17, 17, 18, 18, 19, 19, 20, 20, 20, 21, 21; 41:1, 1, 2, 2, 2, 3, 3, 3, 4, 4, 4, 5, 5, 5, 5, 6, 6, 7, 7, 7, 7, 8, 8, 8, 8, 8, 10, 10, 11, 11, 12, 12, 12, 13, 13, 14, 14, 14, 14, 14, 15, 15, 15, 16, 17, 18, 18, 18, 19, 19, 19, 20, 20, 21, 22, 22, 22, 23, 23, 24, 24, 25, 26, 27, 27, 27, 30, 30, 30, 31, 32, 32, 33, 33, 34, 34, 35, 35, 35, 36, 37, 37, 38, 39, 39, 40, 41, 42, 42, 42, 42, 43, 43, 43, 44, 44, 45, 45, 45, 46, 46, 46, 47, 48, 48, 49, 50, 51, 51, 52, 53, 54, 54, 55, 55, 56, 56, 56, 56, 57; 42:2, 2, 2, 3, 5, 6, 6, 6, 6, 7, 7, 7, 7, 7, 8, 9, 9, 10, 12, 13, 13, 13, 14, 16, 16, 17, 18, 18, 20, 20, 21, 21, 22, 22, 23, 24, 24, 24, 24, 24, 24, 25, 25, 25, 26, 26, 27, 28, 28, 28, 28, 29, 29, 30, 31, 32, 33, 33, 33, 34, 34, 35, 35, 35, 36, 36, 36, 37, 37, 38, 38; 43:1, 2, 3, 4, 6, 7, 7, 7, 8, 8, 8, 8, 8, 8, 9, 11, 11, 11, 11, 11, 12, 12, 13, 14, 14, 15, 15, 15, 15, 15, 16, 16, 16, 17, 17, 18, 18, 18, 18, 18, 19, 19, 20, 21, 21, 21, 22, 23, 23, 23, 24, 24, 24, 24, 25, 26, 26, 27, 27, 28, 28, 28, 29, 29, 29, 29, 30, 30, 30, 30, 31, 31, 31, 31, 32, 32, 32, 33, 33, 33, 34, 34, 34, 34; 44:1, 1, 2, 2, 2, 3, 4, 4, 4, 5,

ANOTHER [448]

ANOTHER'S [5]

Idx

ART [495]

AS [3520]

ASIDE [72]

ASK [109]

BEHOLD [1326]

Ge 1:29, 31; 3:22; 4:14; 6:12, 13, 17; 8:13; 9:9; 11:6; 12:11, 19; 15:3, 4, 17; 16:2, 6, 11, 14; 17:4, 20; 18:9, 27, 31; 19:2, 8, 19, 20, 34; 20:3, 15, 16, 16; 22:1, 7, 13, 20; 24:13, 15, 30, 43, 45, 51, 63; 25:24, 32; 26:8, 9; 27:1, 2, 6, 11, 36, 37, 39, 42; 28:12, 12, 13, 15; 29:2, 6, 25; 30:3, 34; 31:2, 10, 51, 51; 32:18, 20; 33:1; 34:21; 37:7, 7, 9, 9, 15, 19, 25, 29; 38:13, 23, 24, 27, 29; 39:8; 40:6, 9, 16; 41:1, 2, 3, 5, 6, 7, 17, 18, 19, 22, 23, 29; 42:2, 13, 22, 27, 35; 43:21; 44:8, 16; 45:12; 47:1, 23; 48:1, 2, 4, 21; 50:18; **Ex** 1:9; 2:6, 13; 3:2, 9, 13; 4:1, 6, 7, 14, 23; 5:5, 16; 6:12, 30; 7:16, 17; 8:2, 21, 29; 9:3, 7, 18; 10:4; 14:10, 17; 16:4, 10, 14; 17:6; 23:20; 24:8, 14; 31:6; 32:9, 34; 33:21; 34:10, 11, 30; 39:43; **Lev** 10:16, 18, 19; 13:5, 6, 8, 10, 13, 17, 20, 21, 25, 26, 30, 31, 32, 34, 36, 39, 43, 53, 55, 56; 14:3, 37, 39, 44, 48; 25:20; **Nu** 3:12; 12:8, 10, 10; 16:42, 47; 17:8, 12; 18:6, 8, 21; 20:16; 22:5, 5, 11, 32; 23:9, 11, 17, 20, 24; 24:10, 14, 17; 25:6, 12; 31:16; 32:1, 14, 23; **Dt** 1:8, 10, 21; 2:24, 31; 3:11, 27; 4:5; 5:24; 9:13, 16; 10:14; 11:26; 13:14; 17:4; 19:18; 26:10; 31:14, 16, 27; 32:49; **Jos** 2:2, 18; 3:11; 5:13; 7:21, 22; 8:4, 20; 9:12, 13, 25; 14:10; 22:11, 28; 23:4, 14; 24:27; **Jdg** 1:2; 3:24, 25, 25; 4:22, 22; 6:15, 28, 37; 7:13, 13, 17; 8:15; 9:31, 31, 33, 36, 43; 11:34; 13:3, 7, 10; 14:5, 8, 16; 16:10; 17:2; 18:9, 12; 19:9, 9, 16, 22, 24, 27; 20:7, 40; 21:8, 9, 19, 21; **Ru** 1:15; 2:4; 3:2, 8; 4:1; **1Sa** 2:31; 3:11; 5:3, 4; 8:5; 9:6, 7, 8, 12, 14, 17, 24; 10:8, 10, 11, 22; 11:5; 12:1, 2, 2, 3, 13, 13; 13:10; 14:7, 8, 11, 16, 17, 20, 26, 33; 15:12, 22; 16:11, 15, 18; 17:23; 18:17, 22; 19:16, 19, 22; 20:2, 5, 12, 21, 21, 22, 23; 21:9; 23:1, 3; 24:1, 4, 4, 9, 10, 20; 25:14, 19, 20, 36, 41; 26:7, 21, 22, 24; 28:7, 9, 21; 30:3, 16, 26; **2Sa** 1:2, 6, 18; 3:12, 22, 24; 4:8, 10; 5:1; 9:4, 6; 12:11, 18; 13:24, 34, 35, 36; 14:7, 21, 32; 15:15, 26, 32, 36; 16:1, 3, 4, 5, 8, 11; 17:9; 18:10, 11, 24, 26, 31; 19:1, 8, 20, 37, 41; 20:21; 24:22; **1Ki** 1:14, 18, 23, 25, 42, 51; 2:8, 29, 39; 3:12, 15, 21, 21; 5:5; 8:27; 10:7; 11:22, 31; 12:28; 13:1, 2, 3, 25; 14:2, 5, 10, 19; 15:19; 16:3; 17:9, 10, 12; 18:7, 8, 11, 14, 44; 19:5, 6, 9, 11, 13; 20:13, 13, 31, 36, 39; 21:18, 21; 22:13, 23, 25; **2Ki** 1:9, 14; 2:11, 16, 19; 3:20; 4:9, 13, 25, 32; 5:6, 11, 15, 20, 22; 6:1, 13, 15, 17, 20, 25, 30, 33, 33; 7:2, 2, 5, 10, 13, 13, 19, 19; 8:5; 9:5; 10:4, 9; 11:14; 13:21; 15:11, 15, 26, 31; 17:26; 18:21; 19:7, 9, 11, 35; 20:5, 17; 21:12; 22:16, 20; **1Ch** 9:1; 11:1, 25; 22:9, 14; 28:21; 29:29; **2Ch** 2:4, 8, 10; 6:18; 9:6; 13:12, 14; 16:3, 11; 18:12, 22, 24; 19:11; 20:2, 10, 11, 16, 24, 34; 21:14; 23:3, 13; 24:27; 25:26; 26:20; 28:9, 26; 29:19; 32:32; 33:18, 19; 34:24, 28; 35:25, 27; 36:8; **Ezr** 9:15; **Ne** 9:36, 36; **Est** 6:5; 7:9; 8:7; **Job** 1:12, 19; 2:6; 4:3, 18; 5:17; 8:19, 20; 9:12; 12:14, 15; 13:18; 15:15; 16:19; 19:7, 27; 20:9; 21:27; 22:12; 23:8, 9; 24:5; 25:5; 27:12; 28:28; 31:35; 32:11, 12, 19; 33:2, 6, 7, 10, 12; 34:29; 35:5; 36:5, 22, 24, 25, 26, 30; 39:29; 40:4, 11, 15, 23; 41:9; **Ps** 7:14; 11:4, 7; 17:2, 15; 27:4; 33:18; 37:37; 39:5; 46:8; 51:5, 6; 54:4; 59:4, 7; 66:7; 73:12, 15; 78:20; 80:14; 84:9; 87:4; 91:8; 102:19; 113:6; 119:18, 40; 121:4; 123:2; 128:4; 133:1; 134:1; 139:8; **Pr** 1:23; 7:10; 11:31; 23:33; 24:12; **Ecc** 1:14; 2:1, 11, 12; 4:1; 5:18; 7:27; 11:7; **SS** 1:15, 15, 16; 2:8, 9; 3:7, 11; 4:1, 1; **Isa** 3:1; 5:7, 7, 26, 30; 7:14; 8:7, 18, 22; 10:33; 12:2; 13:9, 17; 17:1, 14; 19:1; 20:6; 21:9; 22:13, 17; 23:13; 24:1; 26:10, 21; 28:2, 16; 29:8, 8, 8, 14; 30:27; 32:1; 33:7, 17; 34:5; 35:4; 37:7, 11, 36; 38:5, 8, 11, 17; 39:6; 40:9, 10, 10, 15, 15, 26; 41:11, 15, 23, 24, 27, 27, 29; 42:1, 9; 43:19; 44:11; 47:14; 48:7, 10; 49:12, 16, 18, 21, 22; 50:1, 2, 9, 11; 51:22; 52:6, 13; 54:11, 15, 16; 55:4, 5; 56:3; 58:3, 4; 59:1, 9; 60:2; 62:11, 11, 11; 63:15; 64:5, 9; 65:1, 1, 6, 13, 13, 13, 14, 17, 18; 66:12, 15; **Jer** 1:6, 9, 18; 2:35; 3:5, 22; 4:13, 16; 5:14; 6:10, 10, 19, 21, 22; 7:8, 11, 20, 32; 8:15, 17, 19; 9:7, 15, 25; 10:18, 22; 11:11, 22; 12:14; 13:7, 13, 20; 14:13, 18, 18, 19; 16:9, 12, 14, 16, 21; 17:15; 18:3, 6, 11; 19:3, 6, 15; 20:4, 4; 21:4, 8, 13; 23:2, 5, 7, 15, 19, 30, 31, 32, 39; 24:1; 25:9, 32; 26:14; 27:16; 28:16; 29:17, 21, 32, 32; 30:18, 23; 31:8, 27, 31, 38; 32:3, 4, 7, 17, 24, 24, 27, 28, 37; 33:6, 14; 34:2, 3, 17, 22; 35:17; 37:7; 38:5, 22; 39:16; 40:4, 4, 10; 42:2, 4; 43:10; 44:2, 11, 26, 27, 30; 45:4, 5; 46:25, 27; 47:2; 48:12, 40; 49:2, 5, 12, 19, 22, 35; 50:12, 18, 31, 41, 44; 51:1, 25, 36, 47, 52; **La** 1:9, 12, 18, 20; 2:20; 3:50, 63; 5:1; **Eze** 1:4, 15; 2:9; 3:8, 23, 25; 4:8, 14, 16; 5:8; 6:3; 7:5, 6, 10, 10; 8:4, 5, 7, 8, 9, 10, 14, 16; 9:2, 11; 10:1, 9; 11:1; 12:27; 13:8, 20; 14:22, 22; 15:4, 5; 16:8, 27, 37, 43, 44, 49; 17:7, 10, 12; 18:4; 20:47; 21:3, 7; 22:6, 13, 19; 23:22, 28; 24:16, 21; 25:4, 7, 8, 9, 16; 26:3, 7; 28:3, 7, 17, 18, 22; 29:3, 8, 10, 19; 30:22; 31:3; 34:10, 11, 17, 20; 35:3; 36:6, 9; 37:2, 5, 7, 11, 12, 19, 21; 38:3; 39:1, 8; 40:3, 4, 5, 24; 43:2, 5, 12; 44:4, 5; 46:19, 21; 47:1, 2, 7; **Da** 2:31; 4:10, 13; 7:2, 5, 7, 8, 8, 13; 8:3, 5, 15, 19; 9:18; 10:5, 10, 16; 11:2; 12:5; **Hos** 2:6, 14; **Joel** 2:19; 3:1, 7; **Am** 2:13; 3:9; 6:11, 14; 7:1, 4, 7, 8; 8:1, 11; 9:8, 13; **Ob** 1:2; **Mic** 1:3; 2:3; 7:9, 10; **Na** 1:15; 2:13; 3:5, 13; **Hab** 1:3, 5, 13; 2:4, 13, 19; **Zep** 3:19; **Zec** 1:8, 11, 18; 2:1, 3, 9; 3:4, 8, 9, 9; 4:2; 5:1, 7, 9; 6:1, 8, 12; 8:7; 9:4, 9; 12:2; 14:1; **Mal** 1:13; 2:3; 3:1, 1; 4:1, 5; **Mt** 1:20, 23; 2:1, 13, 19; 4:11; 6:26; 7:4; 8:2, 24, 29, 32, 34; 9:2, 3, 10, 18, 20, 32; 10:16; 11:8, 10, 19; 12:2, 10, 18, 41, 42, 46, 47, 49; 13:3; 15:22; 17:3, 5, 5; 18:10; 19:16, 27; 20:18, 30; 21:5; 22:4; 23:34, 38; 24:25, 26, 26; 25:6, 20, 22; 26:45, 46, 51, 65; 27:51; 28:2, 7, 9, 11; **Mk** 1:2; 2:24; 3:32, 34; 4:3; 5:22; 10:33; 11:21; 13:23; 14:41; 15:4, 35; 16:6; **Lk** 1:20, 31, 36, 38, 48; 2:10, 25, 34, 48; 5:12, 18; 6:23; 7:12, 25, 27, 34, 37; 8:41; 9:30, 38; 10:3, 19, 25; 11:31, 32, 41; 13:7, 11, 30, 32, 35; 14:2, 29; 17:21; 18:31; 19:2, 8, 20; 21:6, 29; 22:10, 21, 31, 38, 47; 23:14, 29, 50; 24:4, 13, 39, 49; **Jn** 1:29, 36, 47; 3:26; 4:35; 5:14; 11:3, 36; 12:15, 19; 16:32; 17:24; 18:21; 19:4, 5, 14, 26, 27; 20:27; **Ac** 1:10; 2:7; 4:29; 5:9, 25, 28; 7:31, 32, 56; 8:27; 9:10, 11; 10:17, 19, 21, 30; 11:11; 12:7; 13:11, 25, 41; 16:1; 20:22, 25; **Ro** 2:17; 9:33; 11:22; **1Co** 10:18; 15:51; **2Co** 3:7; 5:17; 6:2, 2, 9; 7:11; 12:14; **Gal** 1:20; 5:2; **Heb** 2:13; 8:8; **Jas** 3:3, 4, 5; 5:4, 7, 9, 11; **1Pe** 2:6, 12; 3:2; **1Jn** 3:1; **Jude** 1:14; **Rev** 1:7, 18; 2:10, 22; 3:8, 9, 9, 11, 20; 4:1, 2; 5:5; 6:2, 8; 9:12; 11:14; 12:3; 14:14; 15:5; 16:15; 17:8; 19:11; 21:3, 5; 22:7, 12

BEING [291]

Ge 18:12; 19:16; 21:4; 24:27; 34:30; 35:29; 37:2; 50:26; **Ex** 12:34; 13:15; 22:14; 28:16; 32:18; 39:9; **Lev** 21:4; 24:8; **Nu** 1:44; 22:24; 30:3, 16; 31:32; 32:38; **Dt** 3:13; 17:8; 22:24; 32:31; **Jos** 9:23; 21:10; 24:29; **Jdg** 2:8; 9:5; **1Sa** 2:18; 15:23, 26; 26:13; **2Sa** 8:13; 13:4, 14; 19:3; 21:16; **1Ki** 1:41; 2:27; 11:17; 15:13; 16:7; 20:15; **2Ki** 8:16; 10:6; 12:11; **1Ch** 9:19; 24:6; **2Ch** 5:12; 13:3; 15:16; 21:20; 26:21; **Ezr** 6:11; 10:19; **Ne** 6:11; **Est** 1:3, 7; 3:15; 8:14; **Job** 4:7; 21:23; 42:17; **Ps** 49:12; 65:6; 69:4; 78:9, 38; 83:4; 104:33; 107:10; 139:16; 146:2; **Pr** 3:26; 29:1; **SS** 3:8, 10; **Isa** 3:26; 17:1; 40:13; 65:20; **Jer** 2:25; 12:11; 17:16; 31:36; 34:9; 40:1; 48:2, 42; **Eze** 17:10; 23:42; 47:8; 48:22; **Da** 3:27; 5:31; 6:10; 8:22; 9:21; **Mt** 1:19, 23, 24; 2:12, 22; 7:11; 12:34; 14:8; **Mk** 3:5; 5:41; 8:1; 9:33; 14:3; 15:22, 34; **Lk** 1:74; 2:5; 3:1, 1, 2, 19, 21, 23; 4:1, 2, 15; 7:29, 30; 8:25; 11:13; 13:16; 14:21; 16:23; 20:36; 21:12; 22:3, 44; **Jn** 1:38, 41; 4:6, 9; 5:13; 6:71; 7:50; 8:9; 10:33; 11:49, 51; 13:2; 14:25; 18:26; 19:38; 20:19, 26; **Ac** 1:3, 4; 2:23, 30, 33; 3:1; 4:2, 23, 36; 5:2; 7:55; 13:4, 12; 14:8; 15:3, 21, 25, 32, 40; 16:18, 20, 21, 37; 17:28; 18:25; 19:40; 20:9; 22:11; 26:11; 27:2, 18, 22; **Ro** 1:20, 29; 2:18; 3:21, 24; 4:11, 12, 19, 21; 5:1, 9, 10; 6:9, 18, 22; 7:6; 9:11; 10:3; 11:17; 12:5; 15:16; **1Co** 4:12, 12, 13; 7:18, 21, 22, 22; 8:7; 9:21; 10:17; 12:12; **2Co** 5:3, 4; 8:17; 9:11; 10:1; 11:9; 12:16; 13:2, 10, 10; **Gal** 1:14; 2:3, 14; 3:13; **Eph** 1:11, 18; 2:11, 12, 20; 3:17; 4:18, 19; **Php** 1:6, 11; 2:2, 6, 8; 3:10; **Col** 1:10; 2:2, 13; **1Th** 2:8, 17; **1Ti** 2:14; 3:6, 10; **2Ti** 1:4; 3:13; **Tit** 1:16; 3:7, 11; **Phm** 1:9; **Heb** 1:3, 4; 2:18; 4:1, 2; 5:9; 7:2, 12; 9:11; 11:4, 7, 37; 13:3; **Jas** 1:25; 2:17; **1Pe** 1:7, 23; 2:8, 24; 3:5, 7, 18, 22; 5:3, 3; **2Pe** 3:6, 12, 17; **Rev** 1:12; 12:2; 14:4

BENEATH [28]

Ge 35:8; **Ex** 20:4; 26:24; 27:5; 28:33; 32:19; 36:29; 38:4; **Dt** 4:18, 39; 5:8, 8; 28:13; 33:13; **Jos** 2:11; **Jdg** 7:8; **1Ki** 4:12; 7:29; 8:23; **Job** 18:16; **Pr** 15:24; **Isa** 14:9; 51:6; **Jer** 31:37; **Am** 2:9; **Mk** 14:66; **Jn** 8:23; **Ac** 2:19

BESIDE [95]

Ge 31:50; **Ex** 12:37; 14:9; 29:12; **Lev** 1:16; 9:17; 10:12; 23:38, 38, 38, 38; **Nu** 5:8, 20; 11:6; 16:49; 24:6; 28:10, 23, 24; 29:6, 11, 16, 19, 22, 25, 28, 31, 34, 38; 31:8; **Dt** 3:5; 11:30; 18:8; 19:9; 29:1; **Jos** 3:16; 7:2; 12:9; 13:4; 17:5; 22:19; **Jdg** 6:37; 7:1; 8:26, 26; 11:34; 20:15, 17, 36; **Ru** 2:14; **1Sa** 2:2; 4:1; 19:3; **2Sa** 7:22; 13:23; 15:2, 18; **1Ki** 3:20; 4:23; 9:26; 10:19; 11:25; 13:31; **2Ki** 11:20; 12:9; 21:16; **1Ch** 3:9; **2Ch** 20:1; 26:19; 31:16; **Ezr** 1:6; 2:65; **Ne** 5:15; 7:67; 8:4; **Job** 1:14; **Ps** 23:2; 73:25; **SS** 1:8; **Isa** 32:20; 43:11; 45:21, 21; **Jer** 36:21; **Eze** 9:2; 10:6, 16; **Hos** 13:4; **Zep** 2:15; **Mt** 14:21; 15:38; **Mk** 3:21; **Lk** 24:21; **Ac** 26:24; **2Pe** 1:5

BESIDES [45]

Ge 19:12; 26:1; 46:26; **Lev** 6:10; 7:13; 18:18; **Nu** 6:21; 28:15, 31; 29:39; **Dt** 4:35; **Jos** 22:29; **Ru** 4:4; **1Ki** 5:16; 10:13, 15; 22:7; **1Ch** 17:20; **2Ch** 9:12, 14; 17:19; 18:6; **Ezr** 1:4; **Ne** 5:17; **Isa** 26:13; 44:6, 8; 45:5, 6; 47:8, 10; 56:8; 64:4; **Jer** 36:32; **Eze** 10:19; 11:22; 32:13; **Da** 11:4; **Mt** 25:20, 22; **Lk** 16:26; **1Co** 1:16; **2Co** 5:13; 11:28; **Phm** 1:19

BETWEEN [232]

Ge 3:15, 15; 9:12, 13, 15, 16, 17; 10:12; 13:3, 7, 8, 8; 15:17; 16:5, 14; 17:2, 7, 10; 20:1; 31:44, 48, 49; 48:12; 49:10, 14; **Ex** 8:23; 9:4; 11:7; 13:9, 16; 14:2, 20; 16:1; 18:16; 22:11; 25:22; 26:33; 28:33; 30:18; 31:13, 17; 39:25, 25; 40:7, 30; **Lev** 10:10, 10; 11:47, 47; 20:25, 25; 26:46; **Nu** 7:89; 11:33; 13:23; 16:48; 21:13; 26:56; 30:16, 16; 31:27, 27; 35:24; **Dt** 1:1, 16, 16, 39; 5:5; 6:8; 11:18; 14:1; 17:8, 8, 8; 19:17; 25:1; 28:57; 33:12; **Jos** 3:4; 8:9, 11, 12; 18:11; 22:25, 27, 28, 34; 24:7; **Jdg** 4:5, 17; 9:23; 11:10, 27; 13:25; 15:4; 16:25, 31; 20:38; **1Sa** 4:4; 7:12, 14; 14:4, 42; 17:1, 3, 6; 20:3, 23, 42, 42; 24:12, 15; 26:13; **2Sa** 3:1, 6; 6:2; 18:9, 24; 19:35; 21:7, 7; **1Ki** 3:9; 5:12; 7:28, 29, 46; 14:30; 15:6, 7, 16, 19, 19, 32; 18:6, 21, 42; 22:1, 34; **2Ki** 9:24; 11:17, 17; 16:14; 19:15; 25:4; **1Ch** 13:6; 21:16; **2Ch** 4:17; 12:15; 13:2; 16:3, 3; 18:33; 19:10, 10; 23:16, 16, 16; **Ne** 3:32; **Job** 41:16; **Ps** 80:1; 99:1; **Pr** 18:18; **Isa** 22:11; 37:16; 59:2; **Jer** 7:5; 34:18, 19; 42:5; 52:7; **La** 1:3; **Eze** 4:3; 8:3, 16; 10:2, 2, 6, 6, 7, 7; 18:8; 20:12, 20; 22:26, 26; 34:17, 17, 20, 20, 22; 40:7; 41:10, 18; 42:20; 43:8; 44:23, 23; 47:16; 48:22; **Da** 7:5; 8:5, 16, 21; 11:45; **Hos** 2:2; **Joel** 2:17; **Jnh** 4:11; **Zec** 5:9; 6:1, 13; 9:7; 11:14; **Mal** 2:14; 3:18, 18; **Mt** 18:15; 23:35; **Lk** 11:51; 16:26; 23:12; **Jn** 3:25; **Ac** 12:6; 15:9, 39; 23:7; 26:31; **Ro** 1:24; 10:12; **1Co** 6:5; 7:34; **Eph** 2:14; **1Ti** 2:5

BETWIXT [16]

Ge 17:11; 23:15; 26:28, 28; 30:36; 31:37, 50, 51, 53; 32:16; **Job** 9:33; 36:32; **SS** 1:13; **Isa** 5:3; **Jer** 39:4; **Php** 1:23

BEYOND [54]

Ge 35:21; 50:10, 11; **Lev** 15:25; **Nu** 22:18; 24:13; **Dt** 3:20, 25; 30:13; **Jos** 9:10; 13:8; 18:7; **Jdg** 3:26; 5:17; **1Sa** 20:22, 36, 37; **2Sa** 10:16; **1Ki** 4:12; 14:15; **1Ch** 19:16; **2Ch** 20:2; **Ezr** 4:17, 20; 6:6, 6, 8; 7:21, 25; **Ne** 2:7, 9; 12:38; **Isa** 7:20; 9:1; 18:1; **Jer** 22:19; 25:22; **Am** 5:27; **Zep** 3:10; **Mt** 4:15, 25; 19:1; **Mk** 3:8; 6:51; 7:37; **Jn** 1:28; 3:26; 10:40; **Ac** 7:43; **2Co** 8:3; 10:14, 16; **Gal** 1:13; **1Th** 4:6

BOTH [361]

Ge 2:25; 3:7; 6:7; 7:21, 23; 8:17; 9:23; 19:4, 11, 36; 21:27, 31; 22:6, 8; 24:25, 44; 27:45; 31:37; 36:24; 40:5; 41:10; 42:35; 43:8; 44:9, 16; 46:34; 47:3, 19; 48:13; 50:9; **Ex** 5:14; 7:19; 8:4; 9:25; 12:12, 31; 13:2, 15; 18:18; 22:9, 11; 26:24; 29:44; 32:15; 35:22, 25, 34; 36:29, 29; 37:26; **Lev** 6:28; 8:11; 9:3; 15:18; 16:21; 17:15; 20:11, 12, 13, 14, 18; 21:22; 22:28; 25:41, 44, 54; 27:28, 33; **Nu** 3:13; 5:3; 7:1, 13, 19, 25, 31, 37, 43, 49, 55, 61, 67, 73, 79; 8:17; 9:14; 12:5; 15:15, 29; 16:11; 25:8; 27:21; 31:11, 19, 26, 28, 47; 35:15; **Dt** 19:17; 21:15; 22:22, 22, 24; 23:18; 30:19; 32:25; **Jos** 6:21; 8:25; 11:21; 17:16; **Jdg** 5:30; 6:5; 8:22; 10:10; 15:5; 19:6, 8, 19; **Ru** 1:5; **1Sa** 2:26, 34; 3:11; 5:4, 9; 6:18; 9:26; 12:14, 25; 14:11; 15:3; 17:36; 20:11, 42; 22:19; 25:6, 16, 43; 26:25; **2Sa** 8:18; 9:13; 15:25; 16:23; 17:18; **1Ki** 3:13; 6:5, 15, 16, 25; 7:12, 50; **2Ki** 2:11; 3:17; 6:15; 17:41; 21:12; 23:2, 15; 25:26; **1Ch** 12:2, 15; 15:12; 16:3; 23:29; 24:3; 28:15; 29:12; **2Ch** 20:25; 24:16; 25:21; 26:10; 27:5; 31:17; 32:26; **Ezr** 3:5; 6:9; **Ne** 1:6; 4:16; 8:2; 10:9; 12:27, 28, 45; **Est** 1:5, 20; 2:23; 3:13; 8:11; 9:20; **Job** 9:33; 15:10; **Ps** 4:8; 49:2; 58:9; 64:6; 76:6; 104:25; 115:13; 135:8; 139:12; 148:12; **Pr** 17:15; 20:10, 12; 24:22; 26:10; 27:3; 29:13; **Ecc** 4:3, 6; 8:5; 11:6; **Isa** 1:31; 7:16; 8:14; 10:18; 13:9; 18:5; 31:3; 38:15; 44:12; **Jer** 5:24; 9:10; 14:18; 16:6; 21:6; 23:11; 26:5; 28:8; 31:13; 32:11, 14; 36:16; 44:25; 46:12; 50:3; 51:12, 46; **La** 3:26; **Eze** 9:6; 14:22; 15:4; 21:19; 23:13, 29; 34:11; 39:9; 42:11; **Da** 8:13; 11:27; **Mic** 5:8; 7:3; **Na** 3:3; **Zep** 2:14; **Zec** 6:13; 12:2; **Mt** 9:17; 10:28; 12:22; 13:30; 15:14; 22:10; **Mk** 6:30; 7:37; **Lk** 1:6, 7; 2:46; 5:7, 36, 38; 6:39; 7:42; 21:16; 22:33; **Jn** 2:2; 4:36; 7:28; 9:37; 11:48, 57; 12:28; 15:24, 24; 20:4; **Ac** 1:1, 8, 13; 2:29, 36; 4:27; 5:14; 8:12, 38, 38; 10:39; 14:1, 1, 5; 19:10; 20:21; 21:12; 22:4; 23:8; 24:15; 25:24; 26:16, 22, 29; 28:23; **Ro** 1:12, 14, 14; 3:9; 11:33; 14:9, 9; **1Co** 1:2, 24; 4:5, 11; 6:13, 14; 7:29, 34; **2Co** 9:10; **Eph** 1:10; 2:14, 16, 18; **Php** 1:7; 2:13; 4:9, 12, 12, 12; **1Th** 2:15; 5:15; **2Th** 3:4; **1Ti** 4:10, 16; **Tit** 1:9; **Phm** 1:16; **Heb** 2:4, 11; 5:1, 14; 6:19; 9:9, 19, 21; 10:33; 11:21; **Jas** 3:12; **2Pe** 3:1, 18; **2Jn** 1:9; **Jude** 1:25; **Rev** 13:15, 16; 19:5, 18, 18, 20

BRING [727]

Ge 1:11, 20, 24; 3:16, 18; 6:17, 19; 8:17; 9:7, 14; 18:16, 19; 19:5, 8, 12; 24:5, 6, 8; 27:4, 5, 7, 10, 12, 25; 28:15; 37:14; 38:24; 40:14; 41:32; 42:20, 34, 37, 37, 38; 43:7, 9, 16; 44:21, 29, 31, 32; 45:13, 19; 46:4; 48:9, 21; 50:20, 24; **Ex** 3:8, 10, 11, 17; 6:6, 8, 13, 26, 27; 7:4, 5; 8:3, 18; 10:4; 11:1; 12:51; 13:5, 11; 15:17; 16:5; 18:19, 22; 21:6, 6; 22:13; 23:4, 19, 20, 23; 25:2; 26:33; 27:20; 29:3, 4, 8; 32:2, 12; 33:12; 34:26; 35:5, 29; 36:5; 40:4, 4, 12, 14; **Lev** 1:2, 2, 5, 10, 13, 14, 15; 2:2, 4, 8, 8, 11; 4:3, 4, 5, 14, 16, 23, 28, 32, 32; 5:6, 7, 7, 8, 11, 11, 12, 15, 18; 6:6, 21; 7:29, 30, 30; 10:15; 12:6, 8, 8; 14:23; 15:29; 16:9, 11, 12, 15, 20; 17:5, 5; 18:3; 19:21; 20:22; 23:10, 17; 24:2, 14, 23; 25:21; 26:10, 21, 25, 31, 32; 27:9; **Nu** 3:6; 5:9, 15, 15, 16; 6:10, 12, 16; 8:9, 10; 11:16; 13:20; 14:8, 16, 24, 31, 37; 15:4, 9, 10, 18, 25, 27; 16:9, 17; 17:10; 18:2, 13, 15; 19:2, 3; 20:5, 8, 12, 25; 22:8; 23:27; 27:17; 28:26; 32:5; **Dt** 1:17, 22; 4:38; 6:23; 7:1, 26; 9:3, 28; 12:6, 11; 14:28; 17:5; 21:4, 12, 19; 22:1, 2, 8, 14, 15, 21, 24; 23:18; 24:11; 26:2; 28:36, 49, 60, 61, 63, 68; 29:27; 30:5, 12, 13; 31:23; 33:7; **Jos** 2:3, 18; 6:22; 10:22; 18:6; 23:15; **Jdg** 6:13, 18, 30; 7:4; 11:9; 19:3, 22, 24; **Ru** 3:15; **1Sa** 1:22; 4:4; 6:7; 9:7, 7, 23; 11:12; 13:9; 14:18, 34; 15:32; 16:17; 17:19; 19:15; 20:8; 23:9; 27:11; 28:8, 11, 11, 15; 30:7, 15, 15; **2Sa** 2:3; 3:12, 13; 6:2; 9:10; 12:23; 13:10; 14:10, 21; 15:8, 14, 25; 17:3, 13, 14; 19:11, 12; 22:28; **1Ki** 1:33; 2:9; 3:24; 5:9; 8:1, 4, 32, 34; 10:29; 12:21; 13:18; 14:10; 17:11, 13; 20:33; 21:21, 29, 29; **2Ki** 2:20; 3:15; 4:6, 41; 6:19; 10:22; 12:4; 19:3; 22:16, 20; 23:4; **1Ch** 9:28; 13:3, 5, 6, 12; 15:3, 12, 14, 25; 16:29; 21:2, 12; 22:19; **2Ch** 2:16; 5:2, 5; 6:25; 11:1; 24:6, 9, 19; 28:13; 29:31; 31:10; 34:24, 28; **Ezr** 1:8, 11; 3:7; 8:17, 30; **Ne** 1:9; 5:5; 8:1; 9:29; 10:31, 34, 35, 36, 37, 38, 39; 11:1; 12:27; 13:18, 18; **Est** 1:11; 3:9; 6:1, 9, 14; **Job** 6:22; 10:9; 14:4, 9; 15:35; 18:14; 30:23; 33:30; 38:32; 39:1, 2, 3, 12; 40:12, 20; **Ps** 18:27; 25:17; 37:5, 6; 38:T; 43:3; 55:23; 59:11; 60:9; 68:22, 22, 29; 70:T; 71:20; 72:3, 10; 76:11; 81:2; 92:14; 94:23; 96:8; 104:14; 108:10; 142:7; 143:11; 144:13; **Pr** 4:8; 19:24; 26:15; 27:1; 29:8, 23; **Ecc** 3:22; 11:9; 12:14; **SS** 8:2, 11; **Isa** 1:13; 5:2, 4; 7:17; 14:2; 15:9; 23:4, 4, 9; 25:5, 11, 12, 12; 28:21; 31:2; 33:11; 37:3; 38:8; 41:21, 22; 42:1, 3, 7, 16; 43:5, 6, 8, 9; 45:8, 21; 46:8, 11, 13; 49:5, 22; 52:8; 55:10; 56:7; 58:7; 59:4; 60:6, 9, 11, 17, 17; 63:6; 65:9, 23; 66:4, 8, 9, 9, 9, 20, 20; **Jer** 3:14; 4:6; 5:15; 6:19; 8:1; 10:24; 11:8, 11, 23; 12:2, 15; 15:19; 16:15; 17:18, 21, 24; 18:22; 19:3, 15; 23:3, 12, 40; 24:6; 25:9, 13, 29; 26:15; 27:11, 12, 22; 28:3, 4, 6; 29:14; 30:3, 18; 31:8, 23, 32; 32:37, 42; 33:6, 11; 35:2, 17; 36:31; 38:23; 39:16; 41:5; 42:17; 45:5; 48:44, 47; 49:5, 6, 8, 16, 32, 36, 37, 39; 50:19; 51:40, 44, 64; **La** 1:21; **Eze** 5:17; 6:3; 7:24; 11:7, 8, 9; 12:4, 13; 13:14; 14:17; 16:40, 53, 53; 17:8, 20, 23; 20:6, 15, 34, 35, 37, 38, 41, 42; 21:29; 23:22, 46; 24:6; 26:7, 19, 20; 28:7, 8, 18, 18; 29:4, 8, 14; 31:6; 32:3, 9; 33:2; 34:13, 13, 16; 36:11, 24; 37:6, 12, 21; 38:4, 16, 17; 39:2, 25; 47:12; **Da** 1:3, 18; 2:24; 3:13; 4:6; 5:2, 7; 9:24; **Hos** 2:14; 7:12; 9:12, 13, 16; **Joel** 3:1, 2; **Am** 3:11; 4:1, 4; 6:10; 8:10; 9:2, 14; **Ob** 1:3, 4; **Jnh** 1:13; **Mic** 1:15; 4:10; 7:9; **Zep** 1:17; 2:2; 3:5, 10, 20; **Hag** 1:6, 8; **Zec** 3:8; 4:7; 5:4; 8:8; 10:6, 10, 10; 13:9; **Mal** 3:10; **Mt** 1:21, 23; 2:8, 13; 3:8; 5:23; 7:18, 18; 14:18; 17:17; 21:2; 28:8; **Mk** 4:20; 7:32; 8:22; 9:19; 11:2; 12:15; 15:22; **Lk** 1:31; 2:10; 3:8; 5:18, 19; 6:43; 8:14, 15; 9:41; 12:11; 14:21; 15:22, 23; 19:27, 30; **Jn** 10:16; 14:26; 15:2, 16; 18:29; 19:4; 21:10; **Ac** 5:28; 7:6; 9:2, 21; 12:4; 17:5; 22:5; 23:10, 15, 17, 18, 20, 24; 24:17; **Ro** 7:4, 5; 10:6, 7, 15; **1Co** 1:19, 28; 4:5, 17; 9:27; 16:3, 6; **2Co** 11:20; **Gal** 2:4; 3:24; **Eph** 6:4; **1Th** 4:14; **2Ti** 4:11, 13; **Tit** 3:13; **1Pe** 3:18; **2Pe** 2:1, 1, 11; **2Jn** 1:10; **3Jn** 1:6; **Jude** 1:9; **Rev** 21:24, 26

BRINGERS [1]

2Ki 10:5

BRINGEST [5]

1Ki 1:42; **Job** 14:3; **Isa** 40:9, 9; **Ac** 17:20

BRINGETH [79]

Ex 6:7; **Lev** 11:45; 17:4, 9; **Dt** 8:7; 14:22; **1Sa** 2:6, 6, 7; **2Sa** 18:26; 22:48, 49; **Job** 12:6, 22; 19:29; 28:11; **Ps** 1:3; 14:7; 33:10; 37:7; 53:6; 68:6; 107:28, 30; 135:7; **Pr** 10:31; 16:30; 18:16; 19:26; 20:26; 21:27; 29:15, 21, 25; 30:33, 33, 33; 31:14; **Ecc** 2:6; **Isa** 8:7; 26:5, 5; 40:23, 26; 41:27; 43:17; 52:7, 7; 54:16; 61:11; **Jer** 4:31; 10:13; 51:16; **Eze** 29:16; **Hos** 10:1; **Na** 1:15; **Hag** 1:11; **Mt** 3:10; 7:17, 17, 19; 12:35, 35; 13:23, 52; 17:1; **Mk** 4:28; **Lk** 3:9; 6:43, 45, 45; **Jn** 12:24; 15:5; **Col** 1:6; **Tit** 2:11; **Heb** 1:6; 6:7; **Jas** 1:15, 15

BRINGING [24]

Ex 12:42; 36:6; **Nu** 5:15; 14:36; **2Sa** 19:10, 43; **1Ki** 10:22; **2Ki**

21:12; **2Ch** 9:21; **Ne** 13:15; **Ps** 126:6; **Jer** 17:26, 26; **Eze** 20:9; **Da** 9:12; **Mt** 21:43; **Mk** 2:3; **Lk** 24:1; **Ac** 5:16; **Ro** 7:23; **2Co** 10:5; **Heb** 2:10; 7:19; **2Pe** 2:5

BROUGHT [864]

Ge 1:12, 21; 2:19, 22; 4:3, 4; 14:16, 16, 18; 15:5, 7; 19:16, 17; 20:9; 24:53, 67; 26:10; 27:14, 20, 25, 25, 31, 33; 29:13, 23; 30:14, 39; 31:39; 33:11; 37:2, 28, 32; 38:25; 39:1, 1, 14, 17; 40:10; 41:14, 47; 43:2, 12, 17, 18, 18, 21, 22, 23, 24, 26; 44:8; 46:7, 32; 47:7, 14, 17; 48:10, 12, 13; 50:23; **Ex** 2:10; 3:12; 8:7, 12; 9:19; 10:8, 13, 13; 12:17, 39; 13:3, 9, 14, 16; 15:19, 22, 26; 16:3, 6, 32; 17:3; 18:1, 26; 19:4, 17; 20:2; 22:8; 29:10, 46; 32:1, 3, 4, 6, 8, 11, 21, 23; 33:1; 35:21, 22, 23, 24, 24, 25, 27, 29; 36:3, 3; 39:33; 40:21; **Lev** 6:30; 8:6, 13, 14, 18, 22, 24; 9:5, 9, 15, 16, 17; 10:18; 13:2, 9; 14:2; 16:27; 19:36; 22:27, 33; 23:14, 15, 43; 24:11; 25:38, 42, 55; 26:13, 41, 45; **Nu** 6:13; 7:3, 3; 9:13; 11:31; 12:15; 13:23, 26, 32; 14:3; 15:33, 36, 41; 16:10, 13, 14; 17:8, 9; 20:4, 16; 21:5; 22:41; 23:7, 14, 22, 28; 24:8; 25:6; 27:5; 31:12, 50, 54; 32:17; **Dt** 1:25, 25, 27; 4:20, 37; 5:6, 15; 6:10, 12, 21, 23; 7:8, 19; 8:14, 15; 9:4, 12, 26, 28; 11:29; 13:5, 10; 16:1; 20:1; 22:19; 26:8, 9, 10, 13; 29:25; 31:20, 21; 33:14; **Jos** 2:6; 6:23, 23; 7:7, 14, 16, 17, 17, 18, 23, 24; 8:23; 10:23, 24; 14:7; 22:32; 24:5, 6, 7, 8, 17, 32; **Jdg** 1:7; 2:1, 12; 3:17; 5:25; 6:8, 8, 19; 7:5, 25; 11:35; 14:11; 15:13; 16:8, 18, 21, 31; 18:3; 19:3, 21, 25; 21:12; **Ru** 1:21; 2:18; **1Sa** 1:24, 25; 2:14, 19; 5:1, 2, 10; 6:21; 7:1; 8:8; 9:22; 10:18, 27; 12:6, 8; 14:34; 15:15, 20; 16:12; 17:54, 57; 18:27; 19:7; 20:8; 21:8, 14, 15; 22:4; 23:5; 25:27, 35; 28:25; 30:7, 11, 16; **2Sa** 1:10; 2:8; 3:22, 26; 4:8, 10; 6:3, 4, 12, 15, 17; 7:6, 18; 8:2, 6, 7, 10; 10:16; 12:30, 31; 13:10, 11, 18; 14:23; 17:28; 19:41; 21:8, 13; 22:20; 23:16; **1Ki** 1:3, 38, 53; 2:30, 40; 3:1, 24; 4:21, 28; 5:17; 6:7; 7:51; 8:4, 6, 16, 21; 9:9, 9, 28; 10:11, 11, 25, 28; 12:28; 13:20, 23, 26, 29; 14:28; 15:15; 17:6, 20, 23; 18:40; 20:9, 39; 22:37; **2Ki** 2:20; 4:5, 20, 42; 5:2, 6, 20; 10:1, 6, 8, 22, 24, 26; 11:4, 12, 19; 12:4, 9, 13, 16; 14:20; 16:14; 17:4, 7, 24, 27, 36; 19:25; 20:11, 20; 22:4, 9, 20; 23:6, 8, 30; 24:16; 25:6, 20; **1Ch** 5:26; 10:12; 11:18, 19; 12:40; 13:13; 14:17; 15:28; 16:1; 17:5, 16; 18:2, 6, 7, 8, 11; 20:2, 3; 22:4; **2Ch** 1:4, 16, 17, 17; 5:1, 5, 7; 6:5; 7:22, 22; 8:11, 18; 9:10, 10, 12, 14, 14, 24, 28; 10:8, 10; 12:11; 13:18; 15:11, 18; 16:2; 17:5, 11, 11; 19:4; 22:9; 23:11, 14, 20; 24:10, 11, 14; 25:12, 14, 23, 28; 28:5, 8, 15, 19, 27; 29:4, 16, 21, 23, 31, 32; 30:15; 31:5, 5, 6, 12; 32:23, 30; 33:11, 13; 34:9, 14, 14, 16, 28; 35:24; 36:10, 17, 18; **Ezr** 1:7, 7, 11; 4:2, 10; 5:14; 6:5, 5; 8:18; **Ne** 4:15; 5:5; 8:2, 16; 9:18, 33; 12:31; 13:9, 12, 15, 16, 19; **Est** 1:17; 2:7, 8, 20; 6:8, 11; 9:11; **Job** 4:12; 10:18; 14:21; 21:30, 32; 24:24; 31:18; 42:11; **Ps** 7:14; 18:19; 20:8; 22:15; 30:3; 35:4, 26; 40:2; 45:14, 14, 15; 71:24; 73:19; 78:16, 26, 54, 71; 79:8; 80:8; 81:10; 85:1; 89:40; 90:2; 105:30, 37, 40, 43; 106:42, 43; 107:12, 14, 39; 116:6; 136:11; 142:6; **Pr** 6:26; 8:24, 25, 30; **Ecc** 12:4; **SS** 1:4; 2:4; 3:4; 8:5, 5; **Isa** 1:2; 2:12; 5:2, 4, 15; 14:11, 15; 15:1, 1; 18:7; 21:14; 23:13; 25:5; 26:18; 29:4, 20; 37:26; 43:14, 23; 45:10; 48:15; 49:21; 51:18, 18; 53:7; 59:16; 60:11; 62:9; 63:5, 11; 66:7, 8; **Jer** 2:6, 7, 27; 7:22; 10:9; 11:4, 7, 19; 15:8; 16:14, 15; 20:3, 15; 23:7, 8; 24:1; 26:23; 27:16; 32:21, 42; 34:11, 13, 16; 35:4; 37:14; 38:22; 39:5; 40:3; 41:16; 44:2; 50:25; 51:10; 52:26, 31; **La** 2:2, 22; 3:2; 4:5; **Eze** 8:3, 7, 14, 16; 11:1, 24; 12:7, 7; 14:22, 22, 22; 17:6, 24; 19:3, 4, 9, 9; 20:10, 14, 22, 28; 21:7; 23:8, 27, 42; 27:6, 15, 26; 29:5; 30:11; 31:18; 34:4; 37:13; 38:8, 8; 39:27; 40:1, 2, 3, 4, 17, 24, 28, 32, 35, 48, 49; 41:1; 42:1, 1, 15; 43:1, 5; 44:1, 4, 7; 46:19, 21; 47:1, 2, 3, 4, 4, 6, 8; **Da** 1:2, 9, 18; 2:25; 3:13; 5:3, 13, 13, 15, 23; 6:16, 17, 18, 24; 7:13; 9:14, 15; 11:6; **Hos** 12:13; **Am** 2:10; 3:1; 9:7; **Ob** 1:7; **Jnh** 2:6; **Mic** 5:3; 6:4; **Na** 2:7; **Hag** 1:9; 2:19; **Zec** 10:11; **Mal** 1:13, 13; **Mt** 1:12, 25; 4:24; 8:16; 9:2, 32; 10:18; 11:23; 12:22, 25; 13:8, 26; 14:11, 11, 35; 16:8; 17:16; 18:24; 19:13; 21:7; 22:19; 25:20; 27:3; **Mk** 1:32; 4:8, 21, 29; 6:27, 28; 9:17, 20; 10:13, 13; 11:7; 12:16; 13:9; **Lk** 1:57; 2:7, 22, 27; 3:5; 4:9, 16, 40; 5:11, 18; 7:37; 10:34; 11:17; 12:16; 18:15, 40; 19:35; 21:12; 22:54; 23:14; **Jn** 1:42; 4:33; 7:45; 8:3; 9:13; 18:16; 19:13, 39; **Ac** 4:34, 37; 5:2, 15, 19, 21, 26, 27, 36; 6:12; 7:36, 40, 45; 9:8, 27, 30, 39; 11:26; 12:6, 17; 13:1, 17; 14:13; 15:3; 16:16, 20, 30, 34, 39; 17:15, 19; 18:12; 19:12, 19, 24, 37; 20:12; 21:5, 16, 28, 29; 22:3, 24, 30; 23:18, 28, 31; 25:6, 17, 18, 23, 26; 27:24; **Ro** 15:24; **1Co** 6:12; 15:54; **2Co** 1:16; **Gal** 2:4; **1Th** 3:6; **1Ti** 5:10; 6:7; **2Ti** 1:10; 4:99; **Heb** 13:11, 20; **Jas** 5:18; **1Pe** 1:13; **2Pe** 2:19; **Rev** 12:5, 13

BROUGHTEST [13]

Ex 32:7; **Nu** 14:13; **Dt** 9:28, 29; **2Sa** 5:2; **1Ki** 8:51, 53; **1Ch** 11:2; **Ne** 9:7, 15, 23; **Ps** 66:11, 12

BUT [3994]

Ge 2:6, 17, 20; 3:3; 4:2, 5; 6:8, 18; 8:9; 9:4; 11:30; 12:12; 13:13; 15:4, 10, 16; 16:6; 17:5, 15, 21; 18:15, 22, 27, 32; 19:2, 4, 10, 14, 26; 20:3, 3, 4, 12; 21:23, 26; 22:7; 23:6, 13; 24:4, 33, 38; 25:6, 28; 26:29; 27:22, 38; 28:17, 19; 29:17, 20, 31; 30:42; 31:5, 7, 29, 33, 34, 35, 47; 32:28; 34:12, 15, 17; 35:8, 10, 16, 18; 37:11, 22, 35; 38:20; 39:8, 9, 21; 40:14, 22, 23; 41:8, 21, 24, 54; 42:4, 7, 8, 10, 12, 20, 34; 43:5, 34; 44:17; 45:8, 22; 46:12; 47:18, 30; 48:7, 19, 21; 49:19, 24; 50:20, 20; **Ex** 1:12, 16, 17, 17; 2:15, 17; 3:22; 4:1, 10, 21; 5:16, 17; 6:3, 9; 7:4, 12; 8:15, 18, 29; 9:6, 30, 32; 10:8, 20, 23, 27; 11:7; 12:9, 44; 13:15, 18; 14:9, 16, 20, 29; 15:19; 16:8, 20, 26; 17:12; 18:22, 26; 19:13, 24; 20:10, 19; 21:13, 14, 18, 28, 29, 29; 22:15; 23:11, 22, 24; 24:2; 29:14, 33; 31:15; 32:18; 33:11, 23; 34:13, 20, 21, 34; 35:2; 36:38; 40:37; **Lev** 1:9, 13, 17; 2:12; 5:8, 11; 6:28; 7:16, 17, 20, 24, 31; 8:17; 9:10; 10:6; 11:4, 5, 6, 11, 23, 36, 38; 12:5; 13:6, 7, 14, 21, 21, 23, 26, 26, 28, 33, 35, 37; 14:9, 53; 15:28; 16:10; 17:16; 19:14, 15, 18, 24, 34; 20:24; 21:2, 4, 14; 22:11, 13, 13, 20, 23, 32; 23:3, 8, 25; 25:4, 17, 28, 31, 34, 36, 40, 43, 46, 52; 26:14, 15, 23, 27, 45; 27:8, 13, 18, 21, 29; **Nu** 1:47, 50, 53; 2:33; 3:38; 4:15, 19, 20; 5:8, 20, 28; 6:12; 7:9; 8:26; 9:13, 22; 10:4, 7, 7, 30; 11:6, 20, 26, 26; 12:14; 13:31; 14:10, 21, 24, 31, 32, 38, 41, 44; 15:30; 16:9, 30, 41; 18:2, 17, 23, 24; 19:12, 20; 21:22, 23; 22:20, 24, 35; 23:13, 26; 24:1, 4, 11, 13, 16, 17, 17, 20; 26:33, 64; 27:3; 28:19, 27; 29:8, 36; 30:5, 8, 9, 12, 14, 15; 31:18; 32:17, 23, 27, 30; 33:55; 35:8, 20, 22, 26, 28, 30, 31, 33; 36:9; **Dt** 1:17, 26, 38, 40, 43, 45; 2:11, 12, 21, 30; 3:7, 19, 26, 28; 4:4, 9, 12, 20, 22, 22, 26, 29; 5:3, 14, 31; 7:5, 8, 15, 18, 23, 26; 8:3, 18; 9:4, 5, 19; 10:12; 11:7, 11, 28; 12:5, 10, 14, 18; 13:9; 14:7, 12, 20; 15:3, 6, 6, 8; 16:6; 17:6, 16; 18:14, 20, 22; 19:11, 13, 21; 20:12, 14, 16, 17; 21:14, 17, 23; 22:7, 20, 25, 26; 23:5, 11, 20, 22, 24, 25; 24:5, 18; 25:15; 26:14; 28:15, 38, 39, 40, 41, 65; 29:15, 20, 29; 30:14, 17, 17; 32:15, 52; 34:4, 6; **Jos** 1:8, 14; 2:4, 6, 22; 5:5, 12, 14; 6:13, 19, 22; 7:1, 3, 3, 12; 8:4, 9, 14; 9:12, 19, 21; 10:16, 19, 30, 37, 40; 11:13, 14, 20; 13:13, 33; 14:3, 8; 15:63; 16:10; 17:3, 3, 8, 12, 13, 14, 18; 18:7; 21:12; 22:3, 5, 7, 18, 19, 27, 28; 23:8, 9, 13; 24:4, 10, 12, 15, 21; **Jdg** 1:6, 19, 21, 25, 27, 29, 30, 32, 33, 35; 2:2, 3, 17, 17; 3:15, 16, 19; 4:8, 16; 5:31; 6:10, 13, 34, 39, 39; 7:6, 10, 19; 8:20; 9:9, 11, 20, 51; 11:16, 17, 17, 18, 20, 20, 27; 13:3, 6, 7, 9, 21, 23; 14:4, 6, 9, 13, 16, 20; 15:1, 1, 13, 13, 19; 16:21; 17:6; 19:10, 10, 16, 18, 24, 25, 28; 20:9, 13, 14, 32, 34, 40, 42, 47; **Ru** 1:14, 17; 2:8; 3:13, 13; 4:4; **1Sa** 1:2, 5, 5, 11, 13, 15, 22; 2:15, 16, 18, 25, 30; 4:20; 5:6; 6:3, 9; 7:10; 8:3, 6, 7, 19; 9:4, 4, 7, 27; 10:12, 16, 19, 27, 27; 12:10, 12, 15, 15, 20, 23, 25; 13:8, 14, 16, 20, 22; 14:1, 10, 26, 27, 37, 39, 41, 43; 15:3, 9, 9, 19, 21; 16:7, 7, 14; 17:9, 15, 33, 42, 45, 50, 54; 18:8, 8, 16, 17, 19, 25, 25; 19:2, 10; 20:2, 3, 3, 5, 7, 13, 15, 22, 39; 21:4, 6; 22:17, 23; 23:14, 24, 27; 24:7, 10, 12, 13, 22; 25:3, 14, 15, 19, 25, 29, 31, 37, 44; 26:3, 7, 11, 19, 23; 28:23, 23; 29:2, 8; 30:2, 6, 10, 24; 31:4; **2Sa** 2:8, 10, 21, 31; 3:1, 13, 22, 26; 4:12; 5:17, 23; 6:10; 7:2, 6, 15, 19; 8:4; 9:10; 10:11; 11:1, 9, 13, 27; 12:3, 4, 12, 17, 19, 21, 23, 23; 13:3, 9, 14, 16, 20, 21, 25, 27, 34, 37; 14:2, 6, 25, 29; 15:3, 10, 20, 26, 34; 16:18; 17:16, 18; 18:3, 3, 20, 20, 22, 23, 29; 19:4, 21, 27, 28, 37; 20:2, 3, 5, 10, 21; 21:2, 7, 8, 17; 22:19, 28, 42, 42; 23:6, 7, 12, 16, 21, 23; 24:3, 17, 24; **1Ki** 1:1, 4, 8, 10, 19, 26, 52; 2:7, 8, 9, 26, 30, 33; 3:7, 11, 21, 22, 22, 23, 26, 26; 5:4; 7:1, 31; 8:16, 19, 27, 41; 9:6, 6, 22, 22, 24; 11:1, 10, 12, 13, 22, 32, 34, 35, 39; 12:8, 10, 11, 14, 17, 20, 22; 13:18, 22, 33; 14:4, 9, 14; 15:14; 16:22, 25; 17:1, 12, 13; 18:12, 18, 21, 22, 25, 26; 19:4, 11, 11, 12; 20:9, 16, 23, 27, 28, 30; 21:5, 15, 25, 29; 22:8, 8, 16, 18, 24, 30, 31, 48, 49; **2Ki** 1:3, 4, 6, 16; 2:10, 17, 19; 3:2, 5, 11, 15, 18, 24, 26; 4:27, 31, 41; 5:1, 11, 15, 16, 16, 17, 20, 20, 25; 6:5, 12, 19, 32, 32; 7:2, 4, 10, 19; 8:13; 9:15, 18, 27, 35; 10:4, 9, 18, 19, 23, 31; 11:2, 15; 12:3, 6, 7, 9, 14; 13:6, 7, 11, 19, 22; 14:6, 6, 11, 19, 27; 15:25; 16:3, 5; 17:2, 14, 18, 19, 36, 39, 40; 18:6, 12, 20, 20, 22, 27, 36; 19:18, 27; 20:10; 21:9; 22:18; 23:9, 23, 35; 25:12, 25; **1Ch** 2:30, 34; 4:27; 5:1, 2; 6:49, 56; 7:14; 10:4; 11:18, 18, 25; 12:17, 19; 13:13; 15:2; 16:5, 19, 26; 17:1, 5, 14; 18:4; 19:3, 12, 18; 20:1, 7; 21:3, 6, 8, 13, 17, 17, 24, 30; 22:8; 23:11, 17, 22; 24:2; 27:23, 24; 28:3, 9; 29:1, 14; **2Ch** 1:4, 11; 2:6; 4:6; 5:9; 6:2, 6, 8, 9, 18, 32; 7:19; 8:8, 9, 9; 10:8, 10, 11, 14, 14, 17, 18; 11:2; 12:7; 13:10, 11, 13, 21; 15:2, 4, 5, 17; 16:12; 17:4; 18:6, 7, 7, 15, 17, 29, 31; 19:6; 20:10, 12, 15; 21:3, 13, 20; 22:10, 11; 23:6, 6, 7; 24:15, 19, 22, 25; 25:2, 4, 4, 4, 7, 8, 9, 13, 20, 27; 26:16, 18; 28:1, 9, 10, 20, 21, 23, 27; 29:34; 30:8, 10, 18; 32:8, 9, 25; 33:2, 10, 22, 23, 25; 35:13, 21, 21, 22; 36:13, 16; **Ezr** 2:59, 62; 3:6, 12; 4:3, 3; 5:5, 12, 13; 8:22; 9:9; 10:13; **Ne** 1:9; 2:2, 14, 19, 20; 3:3, 5, 14, 15; 4:1, 7; 5:15, 15; 6:2, 8, 12; 7:4, 61, 64; 9:16, 17, 17, 28, 29, 33; 11:3, 21; 13:2, 6, 24; **Est** 1:12, 16, 17; 2:15; 3:2, 15; 4:4, 11, 14; 5:9, 12; 6:12, 13; 7:4; 9:10, 15, 16, 16, 18, 25; **Job** 1:11; 2:5, 6, 10; 3:9, 21; 4:2, 5, 16; 5:3, 15; 6:1, 14, 25; 7:21; 8:9, 15, 15; 9:2, 11, 15, 18, 35; 11:5, 20; 12:2, 3, 7; 13:4, 15; 14:10, 21, 22; 16:5, 7, 12, 20; 17:10; 19:7, 7, 28; 20:5, 13; 21:1; 22:8, 18, 20; 23:6, 8, 8, 9, 10, 13; 24:24; 26:1, 14, 14; 27:17, 19; 28:12; 30:1; 31:32; 32:8, 16; 35:10, 12, 15; 36:6, 7, 12, 13, 17; 37:21; 38:11; 40:5, 5; 42:5; **Ps** 1:2, 4, 6; 2:12; 3:3; 4:3; 5:7, 11; 6:3; 7:9; 9:7, 20; 11:5; 13:5; 15:4; 16:3; 18:18, 27, 41, 41; 20:7, 8; 22:2, 3, 6, 9, 19, 24; 26:11; 28:3; 30:5, 5; 31:6, 11, 14; 32:10; 34:10, 19; 35:13, 15, 20; 37:9, 11, 17, 20, 21, 28, 36, 38, 39; 38:13, 19; 40:17; 41:10; 44:3, 7, 9; 49:15; 50:16, 21; 52:7, 8; 55:13, 21, 23, 23; 59:8, 16; 62:4; 63:9, 11, 11; 64:7; 66:12, 19; 68:3, 6, 21; 69:13, 20, 20, 29; 70:5; 71:7, 14; 73:2, 4, 25, 26, 28; 74:6; 75:7, 8, 9, 10; 77:10; 78:7, 30, 38, 39, 50, 52, 53, 57, 68; 81:11, 15; 82:7; 85:8; 86:15; 88:13; 89:24, 38; 90:4; 91:7; 92:8, 10; 94:15, 22; 96:5; 102:12, 26, 27; 103:17; 105:12; 106:7, 14, 15, 25, 35, 43; 109:4, 16, 21, 28, 28; 115:1, 3, 5, 5, 6, 6, 7, 7, 16, 18; 118:10, 11, 13, 17, 18; 119:23, 61, 67, 69, 70, 78, 81, 87, 95, 96, 113, 161, 163; 120:7; 125:1, 5; 127:1, 5; 130:4; 132:18; 135:16, 16, 17; 136:15; 138:6; 139:4, 12; 141:8; 142:4; 145:20; 146:9; **Pr** 1:7, 25, 28, 28, 33; 2:22; 3:1, 32, 33, 34, 35; 4:18; 5:4; 6:31, 32; 8:36; 9:12, 18; 10:1, 2, 3, 4, 5, 6, 7, 8, 9, 10, 11, 12, 13, 14, 17, 19, 21, 23, 24, 25, 27, 28, 29, 30, 31, 32; 11:1, 2, 3, 4, 5, 6, 9, 11, 12, 13, 14, 17, 18, 20, 21, 23, 24, 26, 27, 28; 12:1, 2, 3, 4, 5, 6, 7, 8, 10, 11, 12, 13, 15, 16, 17, 18, 19, 20, 21, 22, 23, 24, 25, 26, 27; 13:1, 2, 3, 4, 5, 6, 8, 9, 10, 11, 12, 13, 15, 16, 17, 18, 19, 20, 21, 23, 24, 25; 14:1, 2, 3, 4, 5, 6, 8, 9, 11, 12, 15, 16, 18, 20, 21, 22, 23, 24, 25, 28, 29, 30, 31, 32, 33, 34, 35; 15:1, 2, 4, 5, 6, 7, 8, 9, 13, 14, 15, 18, 19, 20, 21, 22, 25, 26, 27, 28, 29, 32; 16:2, 9, 14, 22, 25, 33; 17:3, 9, 22, 24; 18:2, 14, 17, 23; 19:4, 12, 16; 20:3, 5, 6, 14, 15, 17, 21, 22; 21:2, 5, 8, 12, 13, 15, 20, 26, 28, 29, 31; 22:3, 15; 23:7, 17; 24:16, 25; 25:2; 27:3, 4, 6, 7, 12; 28:1, 2, 4, 5, 7, 10, 11, 12, 13, 14, 16, 18, 19, 20, 25, 26, 27, 28; 29:2, 3, 4, 6, 7, 8, 10, 11, 15, 16, 18, 23, 25, 26; 30:24, 26; 31:29, 30; **Ecc** 1:4; 2:14, 26; 3:12; 4:1, 10, 11; 5:7, 12, 14; 6:2; 7:4, 12, 14, 23, 26, 28, 28, 29; 8:13; 9:5, 11, 18; 10:2, 10, 12, 19; 11:8, 9; **SS** 1:5, 6; 3:1, 2, 4, 4; 5:2, 6, 6, 6; 6:9; **Isa** 1:3, 6, 20, 21; 5:6, 7, 7, 12, 16, 25; 6:9, 9, 13; 7:1, 12, 13, 25; 8:14; 9:5, 10, 10, 13, 17, 21; 10:4, 7, 7, 20; 11:4, 14; 13:21; 14:19; 16:6, 12, 14; 17:11, 13; 22:11; 24:16; 26:11, 13; 28:7, 13, 27; 29:8, 8, 9, 9, 13, 23; 30:1, 1, 5, 16, 20; 31:1, 2, 8; 32:8; 33:21; 34:11, 12; 35:8, 9; 36:5, 5, 7, 12, 21; 37:19, 28; 38:17; 40:8, 31; 41:8; 42:19, 20, 20, 22; 43:1, 22, 22, 24; 45:17; 46:2; 47:9; 48:1, 10; 49:14, 25; 51:6, 8, 15, 21, 23; 53:5; 54:7, 8, 10, 15; 55:10, 11; 57:3, 13, 13, 20; 59:2, 9, 9, 11, 11; 60:2, 10, 18, 19; 61:6; 62:4, 9; 63:10, 18; 64:6, 8; 65:6, 11, 12, 13, 13, 13, 14, 18, 20; 66:2, 4, 5; **Jer** 1:7, 19; 2:7, 11, 25, 27, 28, 34; 3:1, 7, 8, 10, 19; 4:22; 5:3, 3, 5, 10, 23; 6:16, 17, 19; 7:12, 13, 13, 23, 24, 24, 26, 27, 27, 28, 32; 8:6, 7, 15; 9:3, 8, 14, 24; 10:5, 8, 10, 19, 24; 11:8, 8, 12, 19, 20; 12:3, 13, 13, 17; 13:11, 14, 17; 14:12, 13; 15:19, 20; 16:4, 15; 17:6, 8, 18, 18, 22, 23, 23, 24, 27; 18:12, 23; 19:6; 20:3, 9, 11, 12; 21:9, 14; 22:5, 10, 12, 17, 17, 21, 27; 23:8, 22, 38; 25:3, 4; 26:5, 15, 21; 27:11, 18; 28:13, 15; 29:19; 30:7, 9, 11; 31:30, 33; 32:4, 23, 34, 40; 33:5; 34:3, 5, 8, 11, 14, 16; 35:6, 7, 10, 11, 14, 14, 15, 16, 17, 17; 36:20, 25, 26, 26, 31; 37:2, 10, 14; 38:2, 4, 6, 18, 20, 21, 23, 25; 39:5, 10, 12, 17, 18; 40:4, 10, 14, 16; 41:8, 11, 15; 42:2, 13, 14, 21; 43:2, 5; 44:5, 14, 17, 18; 45:5; 46:17, 20, 27, 28, 28; 48:30, 45; 49:10, 12, 19, 39; 50:13, 44; 51:9, 26, 62; 52:8, 16; **La** 1:19; 2:14; 3:2, 32; 5:22; **Eze** 2:8; 3:5, 7, 14, 18, 19, 20, 25, 27; 7:4, 14, 16, 20, 26; 8:6; 9:6, 10; 10:11; 11:7, 11, 12, 21; 12:16, 23, 28; 14:11, 14, 16, 18, 20; 16:5, 15, 32, 33, 43, 47, 51, 61; 17:14, 15; 18:5, 7, 11, 16, 17, 24; 19:12; 20:8, 9, 13, 14, 16, 18, 24, 39; 21:23; 22:30; 24:23; 28:9; 29:4, 16; 30:24, 25; 32:27; 33:5, 6, 6, 8, 9, 11, 13, 17, 19, 24, 31, 31, 32; 34:3, 4, 8, 16, 18, 18, 28; 36:8, 21, 22; 37:8, 23; 38:8; 39:2, 28; 41:6; 42:6, 14; 44:8, 13, 14, 15, 22, 25; 46:1, 2, 9, 9, 17, 17, 18; 47:11; **Da** 1:4, 8; 2:6, 9, 9, 28, 30, 30, 41, 43, 44, 49; 3:15, 18; 4:7, 8, 18; 5:8, 15, 20, 23; 6:4, 13; 7:18, 26, 28; 8:3, 4, 7, 17, 18, 22, 24, 25, 27; 9:7, 18, 26; 10:1, 7, 13, 13, 21, 21; 11:6, 6, 7, 10, 11, 12, 14, 16, 17, 18, 19, 20, 21, 25, 27, 29, 32, 34, 38, 41, 43, 44; 12:4, 8, 10, 10, 13; **Hos** 1:6, 7; 2:7, 7; 5:6; 6:7; 7:16; 8:4, 6, 12, 13, 14; 9:3, 8, 10, 13; 10:11; 11:3, 5, 12; 13:1, 4, 9; 14:9; **Joel** 2:20; 3:16, 20; **Am** 1:4, 7, 10, 12, 14; 2:2, 5, 12; 3:7, 8; 4:8; 5:5, 11, 11, 24, 26; 6:6, 14; 7:13, 14; 8:11; **Ob** 1:12, 17; **Jnh** 1:3, 4, 5, 13; 2:9; 3:8; 4:1, 7; **Mic** 1:12; 3:4, 8; 4:1, 4, 12; 5:2; 6:8, 14, 14, 15, 15, 15; **Na** 1:8; 2:8, 8; 3:17; **Hab** 2:3, 4, 5, 20; **Zep** 1:13, 13, 18; 3:5, 7; **Hag** 1:6, 6, 6; 2:16, 16; **Zec** 1:4, 6, 15, 21; 4:6; 7:11, 14; 8:11, 13; 9:7; 11:6, 16; 13:5, 8; 14:7, 7, 11; **Mal** 1:4, 4, 12, 14; 2:8, 9; 3:2, 7, 8; 4:2; **Mt** 1:20; 2:19, 22; 3:7, 11, 12, 14; 4:4, 4; 5:13, 13, 15, 17, 19, 22, 22, 28, 32, 33, 34, 37, 39, 39, 44; 6:3, 6, 7, 13, 15, 17, 18, 20, 23, 33; 7:3, 15, 17, 21; 8:4, 8, 12, 20, 22, 24, 27; 9:6, 8, 12, 12, 13, 13, 14, 15, 17, 18, 21, 22, 24, 25, 31, 34, 36, 37; 10:6, 13, 17, 19, 20, 22, 23, 28, 28, 30, 33, 34; 11:8, 9, 16, 19, 22, 24, 27; 12:2, 3, 4, 6, 7, 15, 24, 24, 28, 31, 32, 36, 39, 39, 48; 13:8, 11, 12, 16, 20, 21, 23, 25, 26, 29, 30, 32, 38, 48, 57; 14:6, 16, 17, 24, 27, 30; 15:3, 5, 8, 9, 11, 13, 18, 20, 23, 24, 24, 26; 16:3, 4, 12, 15, 17, 23, 23; 17:12, 12, 21; 18:6, 7, 16, 17, 22, 25, 28, 30; 19:6, 8, 11, 14, 17, 17, 22, 26, 26, 30; 20:10, 12, 13, 16, 22, 23, 23, 25, 26, 26, 28, 31; 21:13, 19, 21, 26, 28, 29, 32, 37, 38, 44, 46; 22:5, 7, 8, 14, 18, 30, 31, 32, 34; 23:3, 4, 5, 8, 11, 13, 16, 18, 25, 27, 28; 24:6, 13, 20, 22, 35, 36, 36, 37, 43, 48; 25:4, 9, 9, 12, 18, 29, 33, 46; 26:5, 8, 11, 24, 29, 32, 39, 41, 54, 56, 58, 60, 63, 70; 27:20, 23, 24; 28:17; **Mk** 1:8, 30, 44, 45, 45; 2:6, 7, 10, 17, 17, 18, 20, 22, 26; 3:4, 7, 26, 29, 29; 4:6, 11, 15, 17, 22, 29, 32, 34; 5:6, 19, 26, 28, 33, 39, 40; 6:4, 4, 9, 16, 19, 49, 56; 7:5, 6, 11, 15, 19, 24, 27, 36; 8:28, 29, 33, 33, 35; 9:13, 22, 27, 29, 32, 34, 37, 39, 50; 10:6, 8, 14, 18, 24, 27, 30, 31, 38, 40, 40, 42, 43, 43, 45, 48; 11:13, 17, 23, 26, 32; 12:7, 12, 14, 15, 25, 27, 32, 44; 13:7, 9, 11, 11, 11, 13, 14, 17, 20, 23, 24, 31, 32, 32; 14:2, 7, 21, 28, 29, 31, 36, 38, 49, 56, 59, 61, 68, 71; 15:3, 5, 9, 11, 23; 16:7, 16; **Lk** 1:13, 60; 2:19, 37, 44, 51; 3:16, 17, 19; 4:4, 25, 26, 30; 5:2, 14, 15, 21, 22, 24, 30, 31, 32, 33, 35, 38; 6:4, 8, 24, 27, 35, 40, 41, 49; 7:7, 25, 26, 28, 30, 35, 44, 45, 46, 47; 8:10, 15, 16, 23, 27, 38, 42, 50, 52, 52, 56; 9:9, 13, 13, 19, 20, 24, 27, 32, 43, 45, 55, 56, 58, 59, 60, 61; 10:2, 10, 12, 14, 20, 22, 22, 29, 33, 40, 42; 11:4, 15, 17, 20, 22, 28, 29, 33, 34, 39, 41, 42; 12:5, 7, 9, 10, 20, 31, 45, 48, 50, 51, 56; 13:3, 5, 27; 14:10, 13, 34, 35; 15:20, 22, 30; 16:15, 25, 25, 30; 17:1, 7, 17, 25, 29; 18:4, 13, 15, 16, 39; 19:14, 27, 42, 46, 47; 20:6, 10, 14, 18, 21, 23, 35, 38; 21:4, 7, 9, 9, 12, 18, 23, 33; 22:21, 22, 26, 26, 27, 32, 36, 42, 48, 53, 56; 23:9, 21, 25, 28, 28, 40, 41; 24:6, 16, 21, 24, 29, 37, 49; **Jn** 1:8, 12, 13, 17, 20, 26, 31, 33; 2:9, 10, 21, 24; 3:8, 13, 15, 16, 17, 18, 21, 28, 29, 30, 36; 4:2, 14, 14, 23, 32; 5:7, 17, 18, 19, 22, 24, 30, 34, 34, 36, 42, 47; 6:9, 20, 22, 26, 27, 32, 36, 38, 39, 64; 7:6, 7, 10, 10, 12, 16, 18, 22, 24, 26, 27, 28, 29, 30, 39, 41, 44, 49; 8:5, 6, 10, 12, 14, 16, 26, 28, 35, 37, 40, 42, 49, 55, 55, 59; 9:3, 9, 18, 21, 28, 31, 41; 10:1, 2, 5, 6, 8, 10, 12, 18, 26, 33, 38, 39, 41; 11:4, 10, 11, 13, 20, 22, 30, 42, 46, 51, 52, 54; 12:2, 6, 8, 9, 10, 16, 24, 27, 30, 37, 42, 44, 47, 49; 13:7, 9, 10, 10, 18, 36; 14:6, 10, 17, 19, 24, 26, 31; 15:15, 16, 19, 21, 22, 24, 25, 26; 16:4, 5, 6, 7, 12, 13, 20, 20, 21, 22, 25, 25, 33; 17:9, 11, 12, 15, 20, 25; 18:16, 23, 28, 36, 39, 40; 19:9, 12, 13, 15, 15, 21, 24, 33, 34, 38; 20:7, 11, 17, 24, 25, 27, 31; 21:4, 4, 8, 18, 23; **Ac** 1:4, 5, 8; 2:14, 15, 16, 34; 3:6, 14, 18; 4:15, 17, 19, 20, 32; 5:1, 3, 4, 13, 19, 21, 22, 23, 39; 6:4; 7:9, 12, 17, 25, 27, 39, 47, 55; 8:9, 12, 20, 40; 9:7, 8, 15, 21, 22, 24, 26, 27, 29, 40; 10:10, 14, 26, 28, 35, 41; 11:4, 8, 9, 16, 19; 12:5, 9, 14, 15, 16, 17, 20, 24; 13:8, 14, 25, 30, 37, 45, 46, 50, 51; 14:2, 4; 15:5, 11, 20, 38; 16:1, 7, 18, 28, 37, 37; 17:5, 13, 14, 21, 30; 18:9, 15, 19, 21, 21; 19:9, 9, 15, 22, 26, 27, 34, 39; 20:20, 24; 21:13, 24, 39; 22:9, 28; 23:6, 8, 9, 21, 29; 24:7, 11, 14, 27; 25:4, 9, 11, 19, 21, 25; 26:16, 20, 25, 25, 29; 27:10, 14, 21, 22, 27, 39, 41, 43; 28:6, 16, 19, 22; **Ro** 1:13, 21, 32; 2:2, 5, 8, 8, 10, 13, 25, 29, 29; 3:4, 5, 21, 27; 4:2, 4, 5, 5, 10, 12, 13, 16, 20, 24; 5:3, 8, 11, 13, 15, 16, 20; 6:10, 11, 13, 14, 15, 17, 17, 22, 23; 7:2, 3, 6, 7, 8, 9, 13, 14, 15, 17, 18, 19, 20, 23, 25; 8:1, 4, 5, 6, 9, 9, 10, 11, 13, 15, 20, 23, 24, 25, 26, 32; 9:7, 8, 10, 11, 13, 16, 20, 24, 31, 32; 10:2, 6, 8, 16, 18, 19, 20, 21; 11:4, 6, 7, 11, 15, 18, 18, 20, 22, 28; 12:2, 3, 16, 19, 21; 13:1, 3, 4, 5, 8, 14; 14:1, 10, 13, 14, 15, 17, 20; 15:3, 21, 23, 25; 16:4, 18, 19, 26; **1Co** 1:10, 14, 17, 18, 23, 24, 27, 30; 2:4, 5, 7, 9, 10, 11, 12, 13, 14, 15, 16; 3:1, 5, 6, 7, 10, 15; 4:3, 4, 10, 10, 10, 14, 19, 19, 20; 5:3, 8, 11, 13; 6:6, 11, 11, 11, 12, 12, 13, 13, 17, 18; 7:4, 4, 6, 7, 9, 10, 11, 12, 14, 15, 15, 17, 19, 21, 28, 28, 29, 32, 33, 34, 35, 36, 37, 38, 39, 40; 8:1, 3, 4, 6, 6, 8, 9, 12; 9:12, 15, 17, 21, 24, 25, 27; 10:5, 13, 13, 13, 20, 23, 23, 24, 28, 29, 33; 11:3, 5, 6, 7, 8, 9, 12, 15, 16, 17, 28, 32; 12:3, 4, 5, 6, 7, 11, 14, 18, 20, 20, 24, 25, 31; 13:6, 8, 10, 11, 12, 12, 13; 14:1, 2, 3, 4, 5, 14, 17, 20, 22, 22, 24, 28, 33, 34, 35; 15:6, 10, 10, 10, 13, 20, 23, 27, 35, 37, 38, 39, 40, 46, 51, 57; 16:7, 8, 11, 12, 12; **2Co** 1:9, 9, 12, 18, 19, 24; 2:1, 2, 4, 5, 5, 13, 17, 17; 3:3, 3, 5, 6, 6, 7, 14, 15, 18; 4:2, 2, 3, 5, 7, 8, 9, 9, 12, 16, 17, 18, 18; 5:4, 11, 12, 15; 6:4, 12; 7:5, 7, 8, 9, 10, 12, 14; 8:5, 8, 10, 14, 16, 17, 19, 21, 22; 9:6, 12; 10:1, 2, 4, 10, 12, 13, 13, 15, 17, 18; 11:3, 6, 6, 12, 17; 12:5, 6, 14, 14, 16, 19; 13:3, 4, 6, 7, 8; **Gal** 1:1, 7, 8, 11, 12, 15, 17, 19, 23; 2:2, 3, 6, 7, 11, 12, 14, 16, 17, 20; 3:11, 12, 15, 16, 18, 20, 22, 23, 25; 4:2, 4, 7, 9, 14, 17, 18, 23, 23, 26, 29, 31; 5:6, 10, 13, 15, 18, 22; 6:4, 8, 13, 14, 15; **Eph** 1:21; 2:4, 13, 19; 4:7, 9, 15, 20, 28, 29; 5:3, 4, 8, 11, 13, 15, 17, 18, 27, 29, 32; 6:4, 6, 12, 21; **Php** 1:12, 17, 20, 22, 28, 29; 2:3, 4, 7, 12, 19, 22, 24, 25, 27, 27; 3:1, 7, 8, 8, 9, 12, 13; 4:6, 10, 10, 15, 17, 18, 19; **Col** 1:26; 2:17; 3:8, 11, 22, 25; **1Th** 1:5, 8; 2:2, 4, 4, 7, 8, 13, 17, 18; 3:6; 4:7, 8, 9, 10, 13; 5:1, 4, 6, 8, 9, 15; **2Th** 2:12, 13; 3:3, 8, 9, 11, 13, 15; **1Ti** 1:8, 9, 13; 2:10, 12, 12, 14; 3:3, 15; 4:7, 8, 12; 5:1, 4, 6, 8, 11, 13, 19, 23; 6:2, 4, 6, 9, 11, 17; **2Ti** 1:8, 9, 10, 17; 2:9, 14, 16, 20, 20, 22, 23, 24; 3:5, 9, 10, 11, 13, 14; 4:3, 5, 8, 13, 16, 20; **Tit** 1:3, 8, 15, 15, 16; 2:1, 10; 3:2, 4, 5, 9; **Phm** 1:11, 14, 14, 16, 16, 22; **Heb** 1:8, 11, 12, 13; 2:6, 8, 9, 16; 3:4, 6,

13, 17, 18; 4:2, 13, 15; 5:4, 5, 14; 6:8, 9, 12; 7:3, 6, 8, 16, 19, 21, 24, 28; 8:6; 9:7, 11, 12, 23, 24, 26, 27; 10:3, 5, 12, 25, 27, 32, 38, 39, 39; 11:6, 13, 16; 12:8, 10, 11, 13, 22, 26, 26; 13:4, 14, 16, 19; **Jas** 1:4, 6, 10, 11, 14, 22, 25, 25, 26; 2:6, 9, 20; 3:8, 14, 15, 17; 4:6, 6, 11, 11, 16; 5:12, 12; **1Pe** 1:12, 15, 19, 20, 23, 25; 2:4, 7, 9, 10, 10, 16, 18, 20, 23, 25; 3:4, 9, 12, 14, 15, 18, 21; 4:2, 6, 7, 13, 14, 15, 16; 5:2, 2, 3, 10; **2Pe** 1:9, 16, 21; 2:1, 4, 5, 10, 12, 16, 22; 3:7, 8, 9, 9, 10, 18; **1Jn** 1:7; 2:2, 5, 7, 11, 16, 17, 19, 19, 20, 21, 22, 23, 27, 27; 3:2, 17, 18; 4:1, 10, 18; 5:5, 6, 18; **2Jn** 1:1, 5, 8, 12; **3Jn** 1:9, 11, 11, 13, 14; **Jude** 1:6, 9, 10, 10, 17, 20; **Rev** 2:6, 9, 9, 14, 24, 25; 3:5, 9; 9:4, 5, 11; 10:7, 9; 11:2; 12:12; 14:3; 17:12; 19:12; 20:5, 6; 21:8, 27; 22:3

BY [2633]

Ge 7:2, 2, 3; 9:6, 11; 10:5, 32; 14:6, 15; 16:2, 7, 7; 18:2, 8; 19:36; 20:3; 21:23, 28, 29; 22:13, 16; 23:20; 24:3, 11, 13, 30, 43; 25:11, 13, 16, 16; 26:18; 27:40; 29:2; 30:3, 27, 40; 31:24, 31, 39, 39, 40, 53; 32:16; 33:8; 35:4; 36:37, 40; 37:28; 38:14, 16, 18, 19, 20, 21, 24, 25; 39:10, 10, 12, 16; 41:1, 3, 31, 32, 47; 42:15, 16, 23, 38; 43:32, 32, 32; 45:1, 7, 23, 24; 47:13; 48:7; 49:17, 22, 24, 25, 25; **Ex** 2:3, 5, 15, 23, 23; 3:7, 19; 4:4, 13, 24; 6:3, 3; 7:4, 15; 8:24; 9:35; 12:14, 17, 26, 31, 51; 13:3, 14, 16, 21, 21, 21, 22, 22; 14:2, 9, 20, 21; 15:16, 27; 16:3, 3; 18:8, 13, 14; 19:19; 20:26; 21:3, 3, 4; 22:25, 26; 23:30; 25:14; 26:9, 9; 28:28; 29:11, 18, 25, 28, 32, 38, 41, 43; 30:4, 6, 20; 31:2; 32:13, 27; 33:6, 12, 17, 21, 22, 22; 34:6, 7; 35:29, 30; 36:16, 16; 37:3, 5, 27; 38:21; 39:4, 21; 40:29, 38, 38; **Lev** 1:5, 9, 13, 16, 17; 2:2, 3, 9, 10, 11, 14, 16; 3:3, 4, 5, 9, 9, 10, 11, 14, 15, 16; 4:9, 35; 5:12, 15, 17; 6:2, 17, 18; 7:4, 5, 25, 30, 34, 35, 36; 8:21, 28, 36; 10:11, 12, 13, 15, 15; 16:21, 31; 19:12, 31; 20:25, 25, 25; 21:6, 9, 21; 22:4, 22, 27; 23:8, 13, 18, 25, 27, 36, 36, 37; 24:7, 8, 9, 9; 25:39, 47, 47, 47; 26:7, 8, 23, 23, 26, 46; 27:2; **Nu** 1:2, 2, 3, 17, 18, 18, 20, 20, 20, 22, 22, 22, 24, 24, 26, 26, 28, 28, 30, 30, 32, 32, 34, 34, 36, 36, 38, 38, 40, 40, 42, 45, 52, 52; 2:2, 12, 17, 20, 25, 27, 32, 34; 3:15, 17, 18, 19, 20, 26, 26, 43, 47, 49; 4:2, 22, 26, 26, 29, 32, 36, 37, 38, 40, 42, 45, 49; 5:2, 19; 6:9, 11; 7:84; 9:6, 7, 10, 16, 16, 21, 21, 23; 10:13, 34; 11:31; 12:2, 2; 13:3, 22, 29, 29; 14:3, 14, 14, 18, 25, 36, 37, 43; 15:3, 10, 13, 14, 23, 24, 25, 28; 16:40; 18:8, 8, 11, 17, 19, 32; 20:17, 18, 19, 23; 21:1, 4, 18, 22, 33; 22:1, 5; 23:3, 6, 15, 17; 24:6; 26:3, 55, 63, 63; 27:2, 23; 28:2, 3, 3, 6, 8, 13, 19, 24; 29:6, 13, 36; 30:3, 10; 31:12, 17, 18, 35; 33:2, 10, 48, 49, 50, 54; 34:3, 13, 18; 35:1, 20, 30, 33; 36:2, 2, 13, 13; **Dt** 1:2, 7, 19, 22, 33, 33, 33, 40; 2:1, 8, 8, 27, 30, 36, 36; 3:12; 4:34, 34, 34, 34, 34, 34, 34, 48; 5:5, 15, 31; 6:7, 13; 7:19, 22; 8:3, 3; 9:29, 29; 10:20; 11:19, 30; 12:30; 14:22; 15:20; 16:1; 18:1; 20:19; 21:5, 17; 22:4; 23:10, 10; 24:9; 25:2, 11, 17, 18; 27:16; 28:10, 20, 68; 29:16; 33:12, 14, 14, 29; **Jos** 2:12, 15, 18; 3:4, 4; 4:6; 5:1, 4, 5, 7, 13; 7:14, 14, 16, 17, 18; 8:3, 15; 9:13, 18, 19; 10:18; 11:7, 23; 13:6, 14, 16, 22, 29, 31, 32; 14:2, 2; 15:1, 6, 8; 16:1, 6, 8; 17:2, 2; 18:9, 20; 19:49, 51; 20:2, 8, 9; 21:2, 4, 5, 6, 7, 8, 8, 9, 40, 40; 22:9, 10; 23:4, 7; 24:26; **Jdg** 2:18; 3:1, 4, 4, 15, 19, 19; 4:11; 5:10, 19, 22; 6:11, 25, 27, 27, 28, 30, 36, 37; 7:1, 5, 7, 12; 8:11; 9:6, 9, 25, 32, 34, 37, 37; 11:18, 26; 16:5, 26; 17:10; 18:3, 16, 28; 19:11, 14; 20:5, 9; 21:7, 11, 12; **Ru** 2:8, 21, 23; 4:1; **1Sa** 1:7, 9, 26; 2:3, 9, 16, 23, 28; 3:21; 4:13, 18, 20; 5:2; 6:8, 9; 9:23; 10:2, 19, 19, 21; 11:7, 9; 14:4, 6, 6, 36; 16:9, 20; 17:2, 23, 26, 35, 43, 52; 18:25, 30; 20:7, 9, 19, 25, 25; 23:7; 24:3, 21; 25:13, 16, 20, 22, 34; 26:3, 7, 24, 24; 27:1; 28:6, 6, 6, 8, 8, 10, 15, 15, 17; 29:1, 2, 2; 30:15, 24; **2Sa** 1:6, 12; 2:13, 15, 16, 24; 3:5, 18; 6:2, 7; 10:2, 8; 11:14; 12:14, 25; 13:31, 32, 34; 15:30, 36; 16:2, 13; 17:11, 17, 22; 18:4, 4, 4, 23; 19:3, 7, 37; 20:9, 11, 12, 21; 21:10, 10, 22, 22; 22:9, 30, 30, 35; 23:2, 4, 15, 16; 24:16; **1Ki** 1:9, 9, 17, 27, 30; 2:8, 23, 25, 29, 42; 3:5; 4:12, 20; 5:9, 11, 14; 6:21, 22; 7:20; 8:38, 38, 43, 53, 56; 9:8; 10:5, 25, 29; 12:15; 13:1, 1, 2, 5, 9, 9, 10, 17, 17, 18, 24, 24, 24, 25, 25, 28, 32; 14:4, 18; 15:13, 29, 30; 16:7, 12, 13, 13, 34; 17:3, 5, 16, 20, 24; 18:4, 6, 6, 13, 24; 19:2, 11, 19; 20:14, 14, 38, 39, 39; 21:1, 23; 22:8, 19, 28; **2Ki** 2:1, 7, 11, 13, 23; 3:11, 20; 4:8, 9, 27; 5:1, 2; 6:14, 26, 30; 8:8, 21; 9:27, 27, 36; 10:6, 10, 33; 11:11, 14, 14, 16, 16, 19; 13:7, 25; 14:7, 9, 25, 27; 16:15; 17:4, 6, 13, 13, 13, 23; 18:11, 17, 31; 19:7, 11, 23, 28, 28, 33, 33; 20:11; 21:10; 23:3, 7, 11, 21; 24:2; 25:4, 4, 4; **1Ch** 1:48; 3:3; 4:38, 41; 5:7, 10, 17; 6:15, 61, 63, 65, 65, 78; 7:4, 5, 7, 9, 11, 29; 8:28; 9:1, 22, 23, 28; 11:3, 11, 14, 18; 12:22, 31; 14:11; 15:16; 16:41; 17:21; 18:3; 19:4, 9; 20:8, 8; 21:15, 25, 26; 23:3, 3, 24, 24, 27, 31; 24:5, 27; 26:16, 25; 27:1; 28:1, 12, 14, 14, 15, 15, 16, 17, 17, 18, 19; 29:5, 8; **2Ch** 1:17; 2:16; 3:3; 5:11, 14; 6:23, 23, 23, 23, 33, 34; 7:6, 12, 14, 20, 21; 8:14, 18; 9:4, 18, 24; 10:15; 12:7; 13:5; 16:14; 18:7, 27; 19:5; 20:15, 16; 21:9, 15, 15, 15, 19; 22:7; 23:10, 10, 13, 15, 18, 18; 24:11, 11, 13; 25:18; 26:11, 11, 15; 28:15; 29:9, 15, 25, 27; 30:12, 21; 31:6, 15, 17, 17, 19, 19; 32:11, 11; 33:8; 34:14; 35:4, 6, 20; 36:13, 15, 21, 22; **Ezr** 1:1, 8; 2:62; 3:4, 11; 4:16, 23; 5:5; 6:9; 7:23; 8:3, 18, 20, 31, 33, 34, 34; 9:11; 10:16, 17, 44; **Ne** 1:10, 10; 2:6, 13, 13, 15, 15; 3:15, 23, 25; 4:3, 12, 18, 18; 7:3, 5, 64; 8:14, 18; 9:9, 12, 12, 14, 19, 19, 30; 10:29, 34, 35; 12:37; 13:18, 25, 26; **Est** 1:12, 15; 2:14; 3:13, 15; 7:7; 8:5, 10, 14; 9:25; **Job** 4:9, 9; 6:16; 9:11; 11:7; 15:30; 16:12; 17:7; 18:8, 9; 20:29; 21:29; 22:30; 26:12, 13; 27:11; 28:8, 9, 25; 29:3, 19; 30:4, 18; 31:9, 11, 23, 28, 30, 33; 33:18; 35:9, 9; 36:12, 22, 31, 32; 37:10, 11, 12, 17, 19; 38:2, 24; 39:9, 26; 41:18, 25; 42:5; **Ps** 1:3; 5:10; 9:16; 10:10; 17:4, 7; 18:8, 29, 29, 34; 19:11; 30:7; 33:6, 6, 16, 16, 17; 37:23; 38:8; 39:10; 41:11; 44:3, 12, 16; 45:8; 48:4; 49:7; 50:5; 54:1, 1; 56:7; 59:11; 63:10, 11; 65:5, 6; 66:7; 68:4; 71:6; 72:3; 73:23; 74:7, 13; 77:20; 78:17, 18, 26, 49, 55, 64, 65, 72; 79:10; 80:12; 88:9; 89:35, 39, 41; 90:7, 7, 10; 91:5, 5; 94:20; 102:5; 104:8, 8, 12; 106:22; 107:7; 119:9; 121:6, 6; 128:3; 129:8; 134:1; 136:5, 8, 9; 137:1; 140:5; 147:4; **Pr** 3:19, 19, 20, 28, 29; 4:15; 6:26; 7:26; 8:2, 15, 16, 30; 9:11; 11:5, 11, 11; 12:3, 13, 14; 13:2, 10, 11, 11; 14:4; 15:13, 23; 16:6, 6, 12; 20:4, 11, 18, 28; 21:6; 22:4; 24:3, 4, 6, 30, 30; 25:15; 26:2, 2, 6, 17, 17, 26, 28; 27:9; 28:2, 8; 29:4, 19; 30:27; 31:18; **Ecc** 1:13; 5:3, 9, 14; 7:3, 11, 23, 26, 27; 9:1, 15; 10:3, 18; 12:11, 12; **SS** 1:7, 8; 2:7, 7; 3:1, 5, 5; 5:4, 12; 7:4; **Isa** 1:7; 3:5, 5, 25; 4:1, 4, 4, 5, 5; 7:20, 20; 9:1; 10:13, 13, 34; 13:15; 15:5; 18:2; 19:7, 7, 7; 20:2; 22:3, 5, 14; 23:3; 26:13; 27:7, 9, 12; 28:18, 19, 19, 19; 29:13; 32:8; 34:17; 36:2, 16; 37:7, 11, 24, 24, 29, 29, 34, 34; 38:8, 16; 40:26, 26, 26; 41:3; 42:16; 43:1, 7; 44:4, 5, 5, 24; 45:3, 4, 23; 46:3; 48:1, 1, 17; 49:10, 19; 50:4; 51:18, 19; 52:12; 53:11; 54:15; 60:19; 62:2, 8, 8; 63:12, 19; 64:4; 65:1, 5, 15, 16; 66:16, 16; **Jer** 2:8, 17, 34; 4:26; 5:7, 7, 22, 31; 6:5, 25; 7:10, 11, 14, 30; 8:3, 5; 10:12, 12, 12, 14; 11:21, 22, 22; 12:16, 16; 13:5, 16; 14:9, 12, 12, 12, 15; 15:16; 16:4, 4; 17:2, 8, 8, 11, 19, 20, 21; 18:21, 21; 19:2, 7, 7; 20:2, 4; 21:9, 9, 9; 22:2, 4, 5, 8, 13, 13; 23:27, 32, 32; 25:29; 27:3, 5, 5, 8, 13, 13, 13; 29:3, 19, 22; 31:9, 32, 35, 35; 32:17, 34, 36, 36, 36; 33:4, 4; 34:4, 15; 35:4; 37:2; 38:2, 2, 2, 11, 23; 39:4, 4, 4, 18; 41:12, 17; 42:17, 17, 17, 22, 22, 22; 44:12, 12, 12, 12, 13, 13, 13, 15, 18, 18, 26, 27, 27; 46:2, 6, 10, 18; 48:19; 49:3, 9, 13, 17; 50:1, 13; 51:14, 15, 15, 15, 17, 17; 52:7, 7, 7, 7; **La** 1:12, 14; 2:15, 21; 3:1; 5:12; **Eze** 1:1, 3, 15, 19; 3:15, 23; 4:10, 11, 16, 16; 5:12, 14; 6:11, 11, 11, 12, 12; 8:3; 9:2, 3, 11; 10:9, 9, 9, 15, 16, 20, 22; 11:10, 24; 12:3, 4, 7; 13:19, 22; 14:3, 7, 13, 14, 20; 16:6, 8, 15, 25, 36, 56, 61; 17:5, 7, 8, 9, 14, 17, 18, 21; 18:7, 12, 16, 18; 19:7, 10, 10; 20:3, 31, 31; 21:12; 22:7, 7, 12; 23:21, 25, 25; 24:6, 21; 25:12, 13, 14, 15; 26:6, 10, 11; 27:12, 16, 34; 28:5, 5, 10, 16, 17, 18, 18, 23; 29:7; 30:5, 6, 10, 12, 17; 31:7, 9, 12, 14; 32:12, 20, 21, 22, 23, 24, 25, 26, 29, 29, 30, 31; 33:27, 30; 34:13; 35:5; 36:17, 17, 34, 37; 37:2, 18; 38:17; 39:15, 23; 40:2, 5, 7, 18, 22, 28, 38, 41, 49, 49; 41:7, 17, 17; 42:20; 43:3, 4, 6, 7, 7, 8, 8, 8, 13; 44:2, 2, 3, 3; 45:1; 46:2, 2, 8, 8, 9, 9, 9, 9, 9, 14, 16, 18, 21; 47:2, 12, 16, 18, 22; 48:2, 3, 4, 5, 6, 7, 8, 12, 20, 24, 25, 26, 27, 28, 29; **Da** 4:17, 17, 27, 27, 30; 5:10; 7:2, 8, 16; 8:2, 11, 12, 24, 25; 9:2, 3, 5, 10, 11, 12, 18, 19; 10:4, 16; 11:2, 12, 16, 18, 21, 32, 33, 33, 33, 33; 12:7; **Hos** 1:2, 7, 7, 7, 7, 7, 7; 2:17; 4:2; 6:5, 5, 9; 7:4, 16; 8:4, 9; 11:3; 12:3, 3, 10, 10, 13, 13; 13:7, 16; 14:1; **Am** 2:8; 4:2; 5:3, 3; 6:8, 10, 13; 7:2, 4, 4, 5, 7, 8, 11, 17, 17; 8:2, 5, 7, 8, 14; 9:5, 10, 12; **Ob** 1:5, 9; **Jnh** 2:2; 3:7; **Mic** 2:2, 5, 8, 12, 13; 3:8; 7:18; **Na** 1:6; **Hab** 1:16; 2:4, 5, 10, 12; 3:10, 13; **Zep** 1:5, 5, 18; 2:12, 15; 3:6; **Hag** 1:1, 3; 2:1, 10, 13, 22; **Zec** 1:8; 3:5, 7; 4:3, 6, 6, 6, 14; 5:4; 7:7, 12; 8:9; 9:8, 11; **Mal** 1:1, 9; 2:10; **Mt** 1:22; 2:5, 14, 15, 17, 23; 3:3; 4:4, 4, 14, 15, 18; 5:21, 26, 27, 33, 34, 35, 35, 36; 6:27; 7:16, 20; 8:17, 28; 9:25; 11:12; 12:17, 24, 27, 27, 28, 33, 37, 37; 13:1, 4, 14, 19, 21, 21, 35; 14:13; 15:3, 5, 5, 6; 17:21; 18:7, 28; 20:30, 30; 21:4, 23, 24, 27; 22:1, 31; 23:16, 16, 18, 18, 20, 20, 20, 21, 21, 21, 22, 22, 22; 24:15; 26:4, 24, 63, 73; 27:9, 32, 35, 39, 64; 28:9, 13; **Mk** 1:16, 31; 2:13, 14; 3:22; 4:1, 1, 2, 4, 15; 5:4, 7, 21, 22, 41; 6:2, 7, 25, 25, 32, 39, 40, 40, 48; 7:11, 11, 26; 8:3, 23, 27; 9:2, 27, 29, 29, 33, 34; 10:1, 46; 11:4, 20, 28, 29, 33; 12:1, 36; 13:14; 14:1, 19, 21, 47, 69, 70; 15:21, 29, 35; **Lk** 1:61, 70, 77; 2:8, 18, 26, 27; 3:19; 4:1, 4, 4; 5:1, 2, 15, 17, 19; 6:44; 8:4, 5, 12, 20, 36, 54; 9:7, 14, 47; 10:4, 19, 31, 31, 32; 11:3, 19, 19; 13:17; 16:22; 17:6, 7, 7; 18:5, 31, 35, 36, 37; 19:8, 15, 24; 20:2, 8; 21:9, 9, 16, 24; 22:22, 56; 23:8; 24:4, 12, 32; **Jn** 1:3, 10, 17, 17, 42; 3:2, 34; 5:2; 6:15, 18, 57, 57; 7:50; 8:9, 9, 59; 9:1, 7, 21; 10:1, 2, 3, 9; 11:39, 42; 12:11, 29; 13:35; 14:6; 16:30; 18:22; 19:7, 25, 26, 39; 20:7; 21:19; **Ac** 1:3, 10, 16, 25; 2:16, 22, 22, 23, 23, 33, 43; 3:7, 12, 16, 18, 21; 4:7, 7, 9, 10, 10, 16, 25, 30, 30, 36; 5:10, 12, 15, 19; 6:10; 7:25, 35, 42, 53; 9:8, 13, 25, 25, 36, 39; 10:6, 22, 32, 36; 11:4, 5, 28, 30; 12:9, 20; 13:4, 8, 11, 19, 21, 36, 39, 39, 45; 14:3; 15:3, 7, 9, 12, 23, 27, 40; 16:2, 8, 13, 16; 17:10, 23, 29, 31; 18:3, 9, 21, 28; 19:10, 11, 13, 25; 20:16, 19, 31; 21:19; 22:11, 20, 24, 25; 23:2, 4, 10, 11, 19, 31; 24:2, 2, 8, 21; 25:14; 26:18; 27:2, 11, 12, 13, 16, 23; 28:16, 25; **Ro** 1:2, 4, 5, 10, 10, 12, 17, 20; 2:7, 12, 14, 16, 27, 27; 3:20, 20, 21, 22, 24, 27, 27, 28, 30; 4:2, 16; 5:1, 2, 2, 5, 9, 10, 10, 11, 12, 12, 15, 15, 16, 16, 17, 17, 17, 18, 18, 19, 19, 21; 6:4, 4; 7:2, 4, 5, 7, 8, 11, 11, 13, 13; 8:11, 14, 20, 24; 9:10, 10, 32, 32; 10:5, 17, 17, 19, 19; 11:6, 14, 20, 24; 12:1, 2; 14:14; 15:16, 18, 18, 19, 24, 28, 32; 16:18, 26, 99; **1Co** 1:4, 5, 9, 10, 11, 21, 21; 2:10; 3:5, 13, 15; 4:4; 6:2, 11, 14; 7:6, 14, 14, 39; 8:6, 6, 9; 9:22, 27; 10:30; 11:12; 12:3, 3, 8, 8, 9, 9, 13; 14:6, 6, 6, 6, 9, 19, 27, 27, 27, 30, 31; 15:2, 10, 21, 21, 31; 16:2, 3, 7, 99; **2Co** 1:1, 4, 5, 11, 11, 11, 12, 16, 19, 19, 20, 24; 2:2, 14; 3:3, 10, 18; 4:2, 14, 16; 5:7, 7, 18, 20; 6:6, 6, 6, 6, 6, 6, 7, 7, 7, 8, 8; 7:6, 7, 7, 9, 13; 8:5, 8, 8, 14, 19, 20; 9:12, 13, 14; 10:1, 9, 11, 12, 15; 11:3, 26, 26, 33; 12:17; 13:4, 4, 99; **Gal** 1:1, 1, 12, 15, 22; 2:2, 2, 5, 15, 16, 16, 16, 16, 16, 17, 20, 21; 3:2, 2, 3, 5, 5, 11, 11, 18, 19, 21, 22, 24, 26; 4:8, 22, 22, 23; 5:4, 5, 6, 13; 6:14; **Eph** 1:1, 5; 2:3, 5, 8, 11, 11, 13, 16, 18; 3:3, 5, 6, 7, 9, 10, 12, 16, 17, 21; 4:14, 16, 21; 5:13, 26; 6:99; **Php** 1:11, 14, 20, 20, 26, 28; 3:9, 11, 16; 4:6, 19, 99; **Col** 1:1, 16, 16, 17, 20, 20, 21; 2:11, 18, 19; 3:17; 4:18, 99; **1Th** 3:3, 5, 7; 4:1, 2, 15; 5:9, 27; **2Th** 2:1, 1, 2, 2, 2, 3, 14, 15, 15; 3:12, 14, 16; **1Ti** 1:1, 18; 4:5, 14; 5:21; **2Ti** 1:1, 6, 10, 14; 2:26; 3:16; 4:17; **Tit** 1:9; 3:5, 5, 7; **Phm** 1:6, 7, 99; **Heb** 1:1, 2, 2, 3, 3, 4; 2:2, 3, 3, 9, 10; 3:4, 16; 5:3, 8, 14; 6:7, 13, 13, 16, 17, 18; 7:2, 11, 19, 21, 22, 23, 25; 8:6, 9; 9:11, 12, 12, 15, 22, 26; 10:1, 8, 10, 14, 19, 20, 33, 38; 11:2, 3, 4, 4, 4, 5, 7, 7, 7, 8, 9, 12, 17, 20, 21, 22, 23, 24, 27, 29, 29, 30, 31; 13:11, 15, 99; **Jas** 2:7, 12, 18, 21, 22, 24, 24, 25; 5:4, 12, 12, 12, 17; **1Pe** 1:3, 5, 12, 18, 21, 23, 25; 2:5, 12, 14, 24; 3:1, 18, 19, 20, 21; 5:2, 10, 12; **2Pe** 1:4, 13, 21, 21; 2:2; 3:1, 2, 5, 7; **1Jn** 3:24; 5:2, 6, 6, 6; **3Jn** 1:14; **Jude** 1:1, 12, 23; **Rev** 1:1; 5:9; 8:13; 9:2, 18, 18, 18, 20; 10:6; 12:11, 11; 13:14, 14; 14:20; 18:15, 17, 19, 23; 21:25

CAME [2096]

Ge 4:3, 8; 6:1, 4; 7:10; 8:6, 11, 13; 10:14; 11:2, 5, 31; 12:5, 11, 14; 13:18; 14:1, 5, 7, 13; 15:1, 4, 11, 17; 19:1, 5, 8, 9, 9, 17, 29, 34; 20:3, 13; 21:22; 22:1, 9, 20; 23:2; 24:15, 15, 16, 22, 30, 30, 32, 42, 45, 52, 62; 25:11, 25, 26, 29; 26:8, 32, 32; 27:1, 18, 27, 30, 30, 35; 29:1, 9, 10, 13, 23, 25; 30:16, 25, 30, 38, 38, 41; 31:10, 24; 32:6, 13; 33:1, 3, 6, 7, 7, 18, 18; 34:7, 20, 25, 25, 27; 35:6, 9, 17, 18, 22, 27; 36:16, 17, 18, 29, 30, 40; 37:14, 18, 23, 25; 38:1, 9, 18, 24, 27, 28, 28, 29, 29, 30; 39:5, 7, 10, 11, 13, 14, 15, 16, 17, 18, 19; 40:1, 6, 20; 41:1, 2, 3, 5, 8, 13, 14, 18, 19, 22, 27, 50, 57; 42:5, 5, 6, 29, 35; 43:2, 19, 20, 21, 21, 25, 26; 44:14, 18, 24, 24; 45:4, 25; 46:1, 6, 8, 26, 26, 27, 28; 47:1, 15, 18; 48:1, 5, 7; 50:10; **Ex** 1:1, 5, 21; 2:5, 11, 16, 17, 18, 23, 23; 3:1; 4:24; 5:15, 20, 23; 6:28; 8:6, 24; 10:3; 12:29, 41, 41, 51; 13:3, 4, 8, 15, 17; 14:20, 20, 24, 28; 15:23, 27; 16:1, 10, 13, 13, 22, 22, 27, 35, 35; 17:8, 11; 18:5, 7, 12, 13; 19:1, 7, 16, 20; 21:3; 22:15; 24:3; 32:19, 19, 24, 30; 33:7, 8, 9; 34:29, 29, 29, 32, 34, 34; 35:21, 22; 36:4; 40:17, 32; **Lev** 9:1, 22, 23, 24; **Nu** 4:47; 7:1; 9:6; 10:11, 21, 35; 11:20, 25, 25; 12:4, 5, 5; 13:22, 23, 26, 27; 14:45; 16:27, 31, 35, 42, 43; 17:8; 19:2; 20:1, 11, 20, 22, 28; 21:1, 7, 9, 23; 22:7, 9, 16, 20, 39, 41; 23:17; 24:2; 25:6; 26:1; 27:1; 31:14, 48; 32:2, 11, 16; 33:9; 36:1; **Dt** 1:3, 19, 22, 24, 31, 44; 2:14, 16, 23, 32; 3:1; 4:11, 45; 5:23, 23; 9:7, 11, 15; 10:5; 11:5, 10; 22:14; 23:4; 29:7, 7, 16; 31:24; 32:17, 44; 33:2, 2, 21; **Jos** 1:1; 2:1, 2, 4, 5, 8, 10, 22, 23; 3:1, 2, 14, 16, 16; 4:1, 11, 18, 19, 22; 5:1, 4, 4, 5, 5, 6, 8, 13; 6:1, 8, 9, 11, 13, 15, 16, 20; 8:11, 14, 24; 9:1, 12, 16, 17; 10:1, 9, 11, 20, 24, 24, 27, 33; 11:1, 5, 7, 21; 14:6; 15:18, 18; 16:7; 17:4, 13; 18:9, 11, 11, 16; 19:1, 10, 17, 24, 32, 40; 21:1, 4, 45; 22:10, 15; 23:1; 24:6, 11, 29; **Jdg** 1:1, 14, 14, 28; 2:1, 4, 19; 3:10, 20, 22, 24, 27; 4:5, 22, 22; 5:14, 19, 23; 6:3, 3, 5, 5, 7, 11, 25, 34, 35; 7:9, 13, 19; 8:4, 15, 33; 9:25, 26, 42, 52, 57; 11:4, 13, 16, 16, 18, 18, 29, 34, 34, 35, 39; 13:6, 6, 9, 10, 11, 20; 14:2, 5, 6, 9, 11, 14, 14, 15, 17, 19; 15:1, 6, 14, 14, 17, 19, 19; 16:4, 5, 16, 18, 25, 31; 17:8; 18:2, 7, 8, 13, 15, 17, 27; 19:1, 5, 10, 16, 22, 26, 30; 20:4, 21, 24, 26, 33, 34, 42, 48, 48; 21:2, 4, 5, 5, 8, 8, 14; **Ru** 1:1, 2, 19, 19, 22; 2:3, 4, 6, 7; 3:7, 8, 14, 16; 4:1; **1Sa** 1:12, 19, 20; 2:13, 14, 15, 19, 27; 3:2, 10; 4:1, 5, 12, 13, 13, 16, 18, 19; 5:10, 10; 6:14; 7:1, 2, 11, 13; 8:1, 4; 9:12, 14, 15, 26; 10:9, 10, 10, 11, 13, 14; 11:1, 4, 5, 6, 7, 9, 9, 11, 11; 12:12; 13:5, 8, 10, 10, 17, 22; 14:1, 19, 20, 25; 15:2, 5, 6, 10, 12, 13, 32, 35; 16:4, 6, 13, 21, 23; 17:20, 22, 23, 34, 41, 48, 48; 18:1, 6, 6, 6, 10, 10, 13, 16, 19, 30; 19:18, 22, 23; 20:1, 27, 35, 38; 21:1, 5; 22:5, 11; 23:6, 6, 19, 25, 27; 24:1, 3, 5, 16; 25:9, 12, 20, 20, 36, 37, 38; 26:1, 3, 5, 7, 15; 27:9; 28:1, 4, 8, 21; 30:1, 3, 9, 12, 21, 21, 23, 26; 31:7, 8, 8, 12; **2Sa** 1:1, 2, 2, 2; 2:1, 4, 23, 23, 23, 29, 32; 3:6, 20, 22, 23, 24, 24, 25, 35; 4:4, 4, 5, 6, 7; 5:1, 3, 17, 18, 20, 22; 6:6, 16, 20; 7:1, 4, 4; 8:1, 5; 10:1, 2, 8, 14, 16, 17; 11:1, 2, 4, 4, 14, 16, 22, 23; 12:1, 4, 18, 20, 20; 13:1, 23, 24, 30, 30, 34, 36, 36; 14:31, 33, 33; 15:1, 2, 5, 6, 7, 13, 18, 32, 32, 37, 37; 16:5, 5, 5, 11, 14, 15, 16; 17:18, 20, 21, 21, 24, 27; 18:4, 25, 31; 19:5, 8, 15, 15, 16, 24, 24, 25, 31, 41; 20:3, 12, 15; 21:18; 22:10; 23:13; 24:6, 6, 7, 8, 11, 13, 18; **1Ki** 1:22, 28, 32, 40, 42, 47, 53; 2:7, 8, 13, 28, 30, 39; 3:15, 16, 18; 4:27, 34; 5:7; 6:1, 11; 7:14; 8:3, 9, 10; 9:1, 10, 12, 24, 28; 10:1, 2, 7, 10, 12, 14, 22, 29; 11:4, 15, 18, 18, 29; 12:2, 3, 12, 20, 22; 13:1, 4, 10, 11, 12, 20, 20, 21, 23, 25, 29, 31; 14:4, 6, 17, 17, 25, 25; 15:21, 29; 16:1, 7, 11, 18, 31; 17:2, 7, 8, 10, 17, 22; 18:1, 1, 17, 21, 27, 29, 30, 31, 36, 36, 44, 45; 19:3, 4, 7, 9, 9, 13; 20:5, 12, 13, 19, 22, 26, 28, 30, 32, 32, 33, 43; 21:1, 4, 5, 13, 15, 16, 17, 27, 28; 22:2, 2, 15, 21, 32, 33; **2Ki** 1:6, 7, 10, 12, 13, 14; 2:1, 3, 4, 5, 9, 11, 15, 18, 23, 24; 3:5, 15, 15, 20, 20, 24; 4:6, 7, 11, 25, 25, 27, 27, 38, 39, 40, 42; 5:7, 9, 13, 14, 15, 24; 6:4, 14, 18, 20, 23, 24, 30, 32, 33; 7:8, 8, 10, 10, 17, 18; 8:3, 5, 7, 9, 14, 15; 9:5, 11, 11, 17, 18, 19, 20, 22, 36; 10:7, 7, 8, 9, 12, 17, 21, 21, 21, 25; 11:9, 13, 16, 19; 12:10; 13:14, 21; 14:5, 13; 15:12, 14, 19, 29; 16:5, 6, 11; 17:3, 5, 28; 18:1, 9, 9, 17, 17, 18, 37; 19:1, 5, 33, 35, 37; 20:1, 4, 4, 14, 14; 21:15; 22:3, 9, 11; 23:9, 17, 18, 34; 24:1, 3, 7, 10, 11, 20; 25:1, 1, 8, 23, 25, 25, 26, 27; **1Ch** 1:12; 2:53, 55; 4:41; 5:2; 7:21, 22; 10:7, 8, 8; 11:3; 12:1, 16, 18, 19, 22, 23, 38; 13:9; 14:9, 11; 15:26, 29, 29; 17:1, 3, 3, 16; 18:1, 5; 19:1, 2, 7, 7, 9, 15, 17; 20:1, 1, 4; 21:4, 11, 21; 22:8; 24:7, 28; 25:9; 26:14, 16; 27:1; **2Ch** 1:13; 5:4, 10, 11, 13; 7:1, 3, 11; 8:1; 9:1, 6, 13, 21; 10:2, 3, 12; 11:2, 14, 16; 12:1, 2, 2, 3, 4, 5, 7, 9, 11; 13:15; 14:9, 9, 14; 15:1, 5; 16:1, 5, 7; 18:20, 23, 31, 32; 20:1, 1, 2, 4, 10, 14, 24, 25, 28; 21:12, 17, 19; 22:1, 8; 23:2, 12, 20; 24:4, 11, 11, 17, 18, 20, 23, 23, 23, 24; 25:3, 7, 14, 16, 20; 28:9, 12, 20; 29:15, 17; 30:11, 25, 25, 27; 31:5, 8; 32:1, 21, 26; 34:9, 19; 35:20, 22; 36:6; **Ezr** 2:1, 2, 68; 4:2, 12; 5:3, 5, 16; 7:8, 9; 8:32; 9:1; 10:6; **Ne** 1:1, 2, 4; 2:1, 9, 11; 4:1, 7, 12, 12, 15, 16; 5:17; 6:1, 10, 16, 17; 7:1, 5, 6, 7, 73; 13:3, 6, 7, 19, 21; **Est** 1:1, 17; 2:8, 13, 14; 3:4; 4:2, 3, 4, 9; 5:1, 5, 10; 6:6, 12, 14; 7:1; 8:1, 17; 9:25; **Job** 1:6, 6, 14, 16, 17, 18, 19, 21; 2:1, 1, 11; 3:11, 26; 4:14; 6:20; 26:4; 29:13; 30:14, 26, 26; 38:29; 42:11; **Ps** 18:6, 9; 27:2; 51:T; 52:T; 54:T; 78:21, 31; 88:17; 105:19, 23, 31, 34; **Pr** 7:15; **Ecc** 5:15, 15, 16; 9:14; **SS** 4:2; **Isa** 7:1; 11:16; 20:1; 30:4; 36:1, 1, 3, 22; 37:1, 5, 34, 38; 38:1, 4; 39:3, 3; 41:5; 48:3, 5; 50:2; 66:7; **Jer** 1:2, 3, 4, 11, 13; 2:1, 3:9; 7:1, 25, 31; 8:15; 11:1; 13:3, 6, 8; 14:1, 3; 16:1; 17:16; 18:1, 5; 19:5, 14; 20:3, 18; 21:1; 24:4; 25:1; 26:1, 8, 10; 27:1; 28:1, 12; 29:30; 30:1; 32:1, 6, 8, 23, 26, 35; 33:1, 19, 23; 34:1, 8, 12; 35:1, 11, 11, 12; 36:1, 1, 9, 9, 14, 16, 23, 27; 37:4, 6, 11; 38:27; 39:1, 3, 4, 15; 40:1, 8, 12, 13; 41:1, 1, 4, 5, 6, 7, 13; 42:1, 7, 7; 43:1, 7, 8; 44:1, 21; 46:1; 47:1; 49:34; 52:3, 4, 4, 12, 31; **La** 1:9; **Eze** 1:1, 3, 4, 5; 3:15, 16, 16; 4:14; 6:1; 7:1; 8:1; 9:2, 8; 10:6; 11:13, 14; 12:1, 8, 17, 21, 26; 13:1; 14:1, 2, 12; 15:1; 16:1, 23; 17:1, 3, 11; 18:1; 20:1, 1, 2, 45; 21:1, 8, 18; 22:1, 17, 23; 23:1, 17, 39, 40; 24:1, 15, 20; 25:1; 26:1, 1; 27:1; 28:1, 11, 20; 29:1, 17, 17; 30:1, 20, 20; 31:1, 1; 32:1, 1, 17, 17; 33:1, 21, 21, 22, 22, 23; 34:1; 35:1; 36:16; 37:7, 8, 10, 15; 38:1; 40:6; 43:2, 3, 4; 46:9; 47:1; **Da** 1:1; 2:2, 29; 3:8, 26, 26; 4:7, 8, 13, 28; 5:5, 8, 10; 6:12, 20, 24; 7:3, 8, 10, 13, 13, 16, 20, 22, 22; 8:2, 3, 5, 6, 8, 9, 15, 17; 9:2, 23; 10:3, 13, 18; **Hos** 1:1; 2:15; **Joel** 1:1; **Am** 6:1; 7:2; **Ob** 1:5, 5; **Jnh** 1:1, 6; 2:7; 3:1, 6; 4:8, 10; **Mic** 1:1, 11, 12; **Hab** 3:3, 14; **Zep** 1:1; **Hag** 1:1, 3, 9, 14; 2:1, 5, 10, 16, 16, 20; **Zec** 1:1, 7; 4:1; 5:9; 6:1, 9; 7:1, 1, 4, 8, 12; 8:1, 10, 16, 18; 10:4; 14:16; **Mt** 1:18; 2:1, 9, 21, 23; 3:1; 4:3, 11, 13; 5:1; 7:25, 27, 28; 8:2, 5, 19, 25, 34; 9:1, 10, 10, 14, 18, 20, 23, 28; 10:34; 11:1, 18, 19; 12:42, 44; 13:4, 10, 25, 27, 36, 53; 14:12, 15, 33, 34; 15:1, 12, 22, 23, 25, 29, 30, 39; 16:1, 13; 17:7, 9, 14, 19, 24; 18:1, 21, 31; 19:1, 1, 3, 16; 20:9, 10, 20, 28; 21:14, 19, 23, 28, 30, 32; 22:11, 23; 24:1, 3, 39; 25:10, 11, 20, 22, 24, 36, 39; 26:1, 7, 17, 43, 47, 49, 50, 60, 60, 69, 73; 27:32, 53, 57, 62; 28:1, 2, 9, 11, 13, 18; **Mk** 1:9, 9, 11, 14, 26, 31, 38, 40, 45; 2:15, 17, 23; 3:8, 13, 22, 31; 4:4, 4; 5:1, 27, 33, 35; 6:1, 22, 25, 29, 33, 34, 35, 53; 7:1, 1, 25, 31; 8:3, 10, 11; 9:7, 9, 14, 21, 25, 26, 33; 10:2, 17, 45, 46, 50; 11:1, 13, 13; 12:28, 42; 14:3, 16, 32; 15:41, 43; 16:2; **Lk** 1:8, 22, 23, 28, 41, 57, 59, 59, 65; 2:1, 9, 15, 16, 27, 46, 51; 3:2, 3, 7, 12, 21, 22; 4:16, 31, 35, 41, 42; 5:1, 7, 12, 15, 17, 26; 6:1, 6, 12, 17, 17; 7:4, 11, 12, 14, 16, 33, 45; 8:1, 19, 22, 23, 24, 35, 40, 41, 44, 47, 51, 55; 9:12, 18, 28, 33, 34, 35, 37, 51, 57; 10:31, 32, 33, 38, 40; 11:1, 14, 24, 27, 31; 13:6, 31; 14:1, 21; 15:17, 20, 25, 28; 16:21, 22; 17:11, 14, 27; 18:3, 35; 19:5, 6, 15, 16, 18, 20, 29; 20:1, 1, 27; 21:38; 22:7, 39, 66; 23:48, 55; 24:1, 4, 15, 23, 30, 51; **Jn** 1:7, 11, 17, 39; 3:2, 13, 22, 23, 26; 4:27, 30, 46; 6:23, 24, 38, 41, 42, 51, 58; 7:45, 50; 8:2, 2, 14, 42, 42; 9:7; 10:8, 24, 35; 11:17, 19, 29, 33, 44, 45; 12:1, 9, 20, 21, 27, 28, 30, 47; 16:27, 28; 17:8; 18:37; 19:5, 32, 33, 34, 38, 39, 39; 20:3, 4, 8, 18, 19, 24, 26; 21:8; **Ac** 2:6, 43; 4:1, 5; 5:5, 7, 10, 11, 16, 21, 22, 25; 6:12; 7:4, 11, 23, 31, 45; 8:7, 36, 40; 9:3, 21, 32, 32, 37, 43; 10:13, 29, 45; 11:5, 22, 23, 26, 27, 28; 12:7, 10, 12, 13, 20; 13:13, 14, 31, 44, 51; 14:1, 19, 20, 24; 15:1, 6, 30; 16:1, 8, 11, 16, 18, 29, 39; 17:1, 13; 18:1, 2, 19, 24; 19:1, 1, 6, 18; 20:2, 6, 7, 14, 15, 15, 18; 21:1, 7, 8, 10, 31, 33, 35; 22:6, 11, 13, 17, 27; 23:14, 27, 33; 24:7, 17, 24, 27; 25:7, 13; 27:5, 8, 44; 28:3, 8, 9, 13, 13, 15, 16, 17, 21, 23, 30; **Ro** 5:18, 18; 7:9; 9:5; **1Co** 2:1, 1; 14:36, 36; 15:21, 21; **2Co** 1:8, 23; 2:3, 12; 11:9; **Gal** 1:21; 2:4, 12; 3:23; **Eph** 2:17;

17:9; 18:23; 19:17; **1Sa** 15:7; 16:4; 17:43, 45; **2Sa** 1:3; 3:13; **1Ki** 2:13; 19:15; **2Ki** 5:25; 9:2; **Job** 1:7; 2:2; **Jer** 51:61; **Jnh** 1:8; **Mt** 3:14; **Lk** 23:42; **2Ti** 4:13

COMETH [282]

Ge 24:43; 29:6; 30:11; 32:6; 37:19; 48:2; **Ex** 4:14; 8:20; 13:12; 28:35; 29:30; **Lev** 11:34; **Nu** 1:51; 3:10, 38; 5:30; 12:12; 17:13; 18:7; 21:13; 26:5; **Dt** 18:8; 23:11, 13; 28:57; **Jdg** 11:31; 13:14; **1Sa** 4:3; 9:6; 11:7; 20:27, 29; 25:8; 28:14; **2Sa** 13:5; 18:27; **1Ki** 8:41; 14:5, 5; **2Ki** 4:10; 6:32; 9:18, 20; 10:2; 11:8, 8; 12:4, 9; **1Ch** 16:33; 29:16; **2Ch** 13:9; 20:2, 9, 12; 23:7, 7; **Job** 3:21, 24; 5:6, 21, 26; 14:2, 18; 20:25, 25; 21:17; 27:9; 28:5, 20; 36:32; 37:9, 22; **Ps** 30:5; 62:1; 75:6; 78:39; 96:13, 13; 98:9; 118:26; 121:1, 2; **Pr** 1:26, 27, 27, 27; 2:6; 3:25; 11:2, 2, 8; 13:5, 10, 12; 18:3, 3, 17; 29:26; **Ecc** 1:4; 2:12; 4:14; 5:3; 6:4; 11:8; **SS** 2:8; 3:6; 8:5; **Isa** 13:9; 21:1, 9, 12; 24:18; 26:21; 28:29; 30:13, 27; 42:5; 55:10; 62:11; 63:1; **Jer** 6:20, 22; 17:6, 8; 18:14; 43:11; 46:7, 20, 20; 47:4; 50:3; 51:54; **La** 3:37; **Eze** 4:12; 7:25; 14:4, 4, 7; 20:32; 21:7, 7; 24:24; 30:9; 33:30, 31, 33; 47:9; **Da** 11:16; 12:12; **Hos** 7:1; **Joel** 2:1; **Mic** 1:3; 5:6; 7:4; **Hab** 3:16; **Zec** 9:9; 14:1; **Mal** 4:1, 1; **Mt** 3:11, 13; 5:37; 8:9; 13:19; 15:11; 17:27; 18:7; 21:5, 9, 40; 23:39; 24:27, 44, 46; 25:6, 13, 19; 26:36, 40, 45; **Mk** 1:7; 3:20; 4:15; 5:22, 38; 6:48; 7:20; 8:22, 38; 9:12; 10:1; 11:9, 10; 13:35; 14:17, 37, 41, 43, 66; **Lk** 3:16; 6:47; 7:8; 8:12, 49; 11:25; 12:36, 37, 40, 43, 54, 55; 13:35; 14:10, 31; 15:6; 17:20; 18:8; 19:38; **Jn** 1:9, 15, 30; 3:8, 20, 21, 31, 31; 4:5, 7, 21, 23, 25, 35; 5:44; 6:33, 35, 37, 45, 50; 7:27, 31, 42; 9:4; 10:10; 11:38; 12:13, 15, 22; 13:6; 14:6, 30; 15:25; 16:2, 25, 32; 18:3; 20:1, 2, 6; 21:13; **Ac** 10:32; 13:25; 18:21; **Ro** 4:9; 10:17; **1Co** 15:24; **2Co** 11:4, 28; **Gal** 5:8; **Eph** 5:6; **Col** 3:6; **1Th** 5:2, 3; **1Ti** 6:4; **Heb** 6:7; 10:5; 11:6; **Jas** 1:17; **Jude** 1:14; **Rev** 1:7; 3:12; 11:14; 17:10

COMING [100]

Ge 24:63; 30:30; **Nu** 22:16; 33:40; **Jdg** 5:28; **1Sa** 10:5; 16:4; 22:9; 25:26, 33; 29:6, 6; **2Sa** 3:25; 24:20; **2Ki** 10:15; 13:20; 19:27; **2Ch** 22:7; **Ezr** 3:8; **Ps** 19:5; 37:13; 121:8; **Pr** 8:3; **Isa** 14:9; 32:19; 37:28; 44:7; **Jer** 8:7; **Da** 4:23; **Mic** 7:15; **Hab** 3:4; **Mal** 3:2; 4:5; **Mt** 8:28; 16:28; 24:3, 27, 30, 37, 39, 48; 25:27; 26:64; **Mk** 1:10; 6:31; 13:26, 36; 14:62; 15:21; **Lk** 2:38; 9:42; 12:45; 18:5; 19:23; 21:26, 27; 23:26, 29, 36; **Jn** 1:27, 29, 47; 5:7, 25, 28; 10:12; 11:20; 12:12; **Ac** 7:52; 9:12, 28; 10:3, 25; 13:24; 17:10; 27:33; **Ro** 15:22; **1Co** 1:7; 15:23; 16:17; **2Co** 7:6, 7; 13:1; **Php** 1:26; **1Th** 2:19; 3:13; 4:15; 5:23; **2Th** 2:1, 8, 9; **Jas** 5:7, 8; **1Pe** 2:4; **2Pe** 1:16; 3:4, 12; **1Jn** 2:28; **Rev** 13:11; 21:2

COMINGS [1]

Eze 43:11

CONCERNING [242]

Ge 5:29; 12:20; 19:21; 24:9; 26:32; 42:21; **Ex** 6:8; 24:8; **Lev** 4:2, 13, 22, 26, 27; 5:6, 18; 6:3, 18; 23:2; 27:32; **Nu** 8:20, 22; 9:8; 10:29; 14:30; 30:1, 12, 12; 32:28; 36:6; **Jos** 14:6; 23:14; **Jdg** 15:3; 21:5; **Ru** 4:7, 7; **1Sa** 3:12; 25:30; **2Sa** 3:8; 7:25, 25; 11:18; 13:39; 14:8; 18:5; **1Ki** 2:4, 27; 5:8, 8; 6:12; 8:41; 10:1; 11:2, 10; 22:8, 18, 23; **2Ki** 10:10; 17:15; 19:21, 32; 22:13, 13; **1Ch** 11:10; 17:23, 23; 19:2; 22:12, 13; 23:14; 24:21, 29; 26:1, 21; **2Ch** 6:32; 8:15, 15; 12:15; 15:16; 24:27; 31:6, 9; 34:21, 26; **Ezr** 5:5, 17; 6:3; 7:14; 10:2; **Ne** 1:2, 2; 9:23; 11:23, 24; 13:14, 22; **Est** 3:2; 9:26; **Job** 36:33, 33; **Ps** 7:T; 17:4; 73:8; 90:13; 106:34; 119:128, 152; 135:14; **Ecc** 1:13; 3:18; 7:10; **Isa** 1:1; 2:1; 8:1; 16:13; 23:5; 29:22; 30:7; 37:9, 22, 33; 45:11, 11; **Jer** 7:22; 14:1, 15; 16:3, 3, 3, 3; 18:7, 7, 9, 9; 22:18; 23:15; 25:1; 27:19, 19, 19, 19, 21; 29:31; 30:4, 4; 32:36; 33:4, 4; 39:11; 42:19; 44:1; 49:1, 7, 23, 28, 28; 52:21; **La** 1:17; **Eze** 13:16; 14:7, 22, 22; 18:2; 21:28, 28; 36:6; 44:5; 45:14; 47:14; **Da** 2:18; 5:29; 6:4, 5, 12, 17; 7:12; 8:13; **Am** 1:1; **Ob** 1:1; **Mic** 1:1; 3:5; **Na** 1:14; **Hag** 2:11; **Mt** 4:6; 11:7; 16:11; **Mk** 5:16; 7:17; **Lk** 2:17; 7:24; 18:31; 22:37; 24:19, 27, 44; **Jn** 7:12, 32; 9:18; 11:19; **Ac** 1:16; 2:25; 8:12; 13:34; 19:8, 39; 21:24; 22:18; 23:15; 24:24; 25:16; 28:21, 22, 23; **Ro** 1:3; 9:5, 27; 11:28; 16:19; **1Co** 5:3; 7:1, 25; 8:4; 12:1; 16:1; **2Co** 8:23; 11:21; **Eph** 4:22; 5:32; **Php** 3:6; 4:15; **1Th** 3:2; 4:13; 5:18; **1Ti** 1:19; 6:21; **2Ti** 2:18; 3:8; **Heb** 7:14; 11:20, 22; **1Pe** 4:12; **2Pe** 3:9; **1Jn** 2:26

COULD [166]

Ge 13:6; 27:1; 36:7; 37:4; 41:8, 21, 24; 43:7; 45:1, 3; 48:10; **Ex** 2:3; 7:21, 24; 8:18; 9:11; 12:39; 15:23; **Nu** 9:6; **Jos** 7:12; 15:63; 17:12; **Jdg** 1:19; 2:14; 3:22; 6:27; 12:6; 14:14; 17:8; 20:16; **Ru** 3:14; **1Sa** 3:2; 4:15; 10:21; 23:13; 30:10, 21; **2Sa** 1:10; 3:11; 17:20; 22:39; **1Ki** 5:3; 8:5, 11; 13:4; 14:4; **2Ki** 3:26; 4:40; 16:5; **1Ch** 12:2, 8, 33, 38; 21:30; **2Ch** 4:18; 5:6, 14; 7:2; 13:7; 14:13; 20:25; 25:5, 15; 29:34; 30:3; 32:14; 34:12; **Ezr** 2:59; 3:13; 5:5; **Ne** 7:61; 8:2, 3; 13:24; **Est** 6:1; 7:4; 9:2; **Job** 4:16; 16:4, 4; 31:23; **Ps** 37:30; 55:12; 73:7; 78:44; **SS** 5:6; **Isa** 5:4; 7:1; 30:5; 33:23, 23; 41:28; 46:2; **Jer** 6:15; 8:12; 15:1; 20:9; 24:2; 44:22; **La** 4:14, 17; **Eze** 31:8; 47:5, 5; **Da** 5:8, 15; 6:4; 8:4, 7; **Hos** 5:13; **Jnh** 1:13; **Mt** 17:16, 19; 26:40; 27:24; **Mk** 1:45; 2:4; 3:20; 5:3, 4; 6:5, 19; 7:24; 9:18, 28; 14:8; **Lk** 1:22; 5:19; 6:48; 8:19, 43; 9:40; 13:11; 14:6; 19:3, 48; 20:7, 26; **Jn** 9:33; 11:37; 12:39; 21:25; **Ac** 4:14; 11:17; 13:39; 21:34; 22:11; 25:7; 27:15, 43; **Ro** 8:3; 9:3; **1Co** 3:1; 13:2; **2Co** 3:7, 13; 11:1; **Gal** 3:21; **1Th** 3:1, 5; **Heb** 3:19; 6:13; 9:9; 12:20; **Rev** 7:9; 14:3

COULDEST [5]

Jer 3:5; **Eze** 16:28; **Da** 2:47; **Mk** 14:37; **Jn** 19:11

DID [1006]

Ge 3:6, 6, 12, 13, 21; 6:22, 22; 7:5, 20; 11:9, 9; 18:8, 13; 19:3, 3; 21:1; 22:1, 23; 24:54; 25:28, 34; 26:20, 30; 27:25; 29:25, 28; 30:40, 41; 31:46, 54; 35:5; 38:10, 11; 39:3, 6, 19, 22, 23; 40:17, 23; 41:4, 12, 20; 42:20, 25; 43:3, 17, 30, 32; 44:2; 45:5, 21; 47:22; 48:15; 50:12, 15, 16, 17; **Ex** 1:11, 17; 2:13; 4:30; 5:8, 19; 6:8; 7:6, 6, 10, 11, 20, 22, 22, 23; 8:7, 13, 17, 18, 24, 31; 9:6, 7; 10:11, 15; 11:10; 12:28, 28, 35, 50, 50, 51; 13:8; 14:4, 12, 31; 16:3, 17, 18, 24, 35, 35; 17:2, 6, 10; 18:7, 14, 24; 19:4; 24:11; 32:12, 21, 28; 33:4; 34:28; 35:24, 25; 36:22, 29; 39:3, 21, 32, 32, 43; 40:16, 16; **Lev** 4:20; 8:4, 9, 36; 9:14; 10:7; 16:15, 34; 24:23; 26:35; 27:24; **Nu** 1:54, 54; 2:34; 4:37, 41; 5:4, 4; 7:18, 24, 30, 36; 8:3, 20, 20, 22; 9:5; 10:21; 11:5, 25; 14:22, 37; 17:11, 11; 20:27; 21:14; 22:37; 23:2, 30; 25:2; 27:22; 31:31; 32:8; 36:10; **Dt** 1:30, 32; 2:12, 22, 29; 3:6; 4:3, 4, 33, 34; 5:23; 7:7, 18; 8:3, 4; 9:9, 18; 11:3, 4, 5, 6, 7; 12:30; 24:9; 25:17; 29:2; 31:4; 32:12, 38; 33:9; 34:9; **Jos** 2:10, 11, 11; 4:8, 18, 20, 23; 5:4, 11, 12, 14, 15; 6:14; 9:4, 9, 10, 26; 10:23, 28, 28, 30, 30, 39, 42; 11:9, 12, 13, 15, 15; 12:6; 13:12, 22, 32; 14:5; 17:13; 22:20, 33; 24:5, 13, 17; **Jdg** 1:21, 27, 28, 29, 30, 31, 32, 33; 2:7, 11, 17, 22; 3:7, 12, 16; 4:1; 5:17; 6:1, 13, 20, 27, 27, 40; 8:1, 15, 25; 9:27, 56, 57; 10:6, 11; 12:11; 7, 25, 25, 26, 39; 13:1, 19, 21; 14:9; 15:11; 16:21; 17:6; 19:4, 6, 8, 21; 21:22, 23, 25; **Ru** 2:14, 19; 3:6; 4:11; **1Sa** 1:7, 7, 18; 2:11, 14, 22, 27, 28, 28; 3:7, 19; 4:20; 6:6, 10; 7:4, 14; 9:24; 12:7; 13:6; 14:32, 43; 15:2; 16:4; 19:5; 20:34; 21:11; 22:15, 17, 18; 25:4; 27:11; 28:24, 25; 30:11; **2Sa** 1:2; 2:3; 3:36; 5:25; 7:17; 8:11; 9:6, 13; 11:7, 7, 13, 20, 21; 12:3, 6, 17, 20, 31; 13:8, 29; 14:4; 15:6; 17:15; 19:19, 28, 43; 20:6; 21:6; 22:7, 7, 11, 23, 37, 43, 43, 43; 23:17, 22; 24:23; **1Ki** 1:16, 31; 2:5, 5, 35, 42; 3:4, 14, 21; 5:18; 7:15, 18, 23, 46, 51; 8:4, 64; 9:21, 22, 24, 25; 10:29; 11:6, 6, 7, 8, 16, 25, 33, 38, 41; 12:9, 11, 32; 13:19, 22; 14:4, 16, 21, 22, 24, 29; 15:4, 5, 7, 11, 11, 23, 26, 28, 31, 34; 16:5, 7, 12, 14, 15, 19, 25, 27, 30, 33, 34; 17:5, 15, 15, 16; 18:13, 34, 34; 19:6, 8, 21; 20:25, 33, 33; 21:11, 13, 25, 26, 26; 22:18, 39, 52; **2Ki** 1:18; 2:18; 4:1, 28, 28, 44; 6:6, 29; 7:8; 8:2, 18, 18, 23, 25, 27, 27; 9:27, 34; 10:19, 34; 11:3, 9, 10; 12:2, 11, 19; 13:2, 7, 8, 11, 12, 25; 14:3, 3, 3, 4, 15, 24, 28; 15:3, 6, 8, 9, 18, 21, 24, 26, 28, 31, 34, 34, 36; 16:2, 16, 19; 17:2, 9, 11, 14, 22, 40, 40, 41; 18:3, 3, 4, 11, 13, 16; 21:2, 3, 9, 11, 17, 20, 20, 25; 22:2; 23:9, 12, 13, 19, 24, 28, 32, 37; 24:3, 5, 9, 11, 19; 25:11, 13, 27, 29; **1Ch** 4:27; 9:22; 11:19, 24; 14:16; 15:13, 24; 17:15; 23:24; 26:27; 27:26; 29:22; **2Ch** 1:7; 2:7; 4:2, 3, 16, 17; 5:5, 11; 8:8, 9; 10:9; 12:14; 13:20; 14:2; 15:4, 6; 18:16, 17; 19:8; 20:35, 35; 21:6, 10; 22:4; 23:8; 24:2, 7, 11, 12; 25:2, 4, 12, 27; 26:4, 4, 22; 27:2, 2, 5; 28:1, 16, 22; 29:2, 19, 34; 30:18, 22, 24; 31:20, 21; 32:3, 9, 33; 33:2, 17, 22, 22; 34:2, 6, 12, 32; 35:3, 12, 18; 36:5, 8, 9, 12; **Ezr** 1:8, 11; 5:14; 6:13, 21; 10:6, 16; **Ne** 2:16, 16; 3:3; 5:13, 15; 9:25, 28; 11:12; 13:7, 10, 18, 18, 26, 26; **Est** 1:8, 21; 2:4, 11, 20; 3:1, 2, 5; 4:17; 5:12; 8:1; 9:5; **Job** 1:5; 2:10; 3:11, 12; 6:22; 28:27; 30:25; 31:13, 15, 15, 32, 34, 34; 42:9, 11; **Ps** 14:2; 18:10, 10, 22, 36, 37, 42, 42; 31:11; 35:11, 15; 41:9; 44:3; 45:9; 51:5; 53:2, 2; 55:12; 66:6; 68:12; 78:12, 25, 29, 33, 36, 38, 40; 102:19; 105:35; 106:34, 43; 119:23, 23; 135:6; 139:16; 142:1; **Pr** 1:29; **Isa** 5:25; 6:2; 9:1; 10:10; 13:1; 14:16; 20:2; 22:12; 38:14, 14; 42:24; 48:3; 53:4; 58:2; 65:12, 12, 12, 12; 66:4, 4, 4; **Jer** 7:12, 26; 11:8; 14:6, 6; 15:4, 16; 22:15; 26:19, 19; 31:19; 36:8; 37:2; 38:12; 41:1; 44:19, 21; 46:15, 17, 21; 52:2, 21, 33; **La** 1:7, 7; 4:5; **Eze** 3:3; 6:13; 11:22; 12:7; 16:49; 17:7; 18:18; 20:8, 8, 17; 24:18; 27:25; 31:6; 34:6, 8; 43:22; 46:12; **Da** 1:15; 3:24; 4:7, 33; 6:10; 7:9; 8:4, 27; 10:3; **Hos** 2:8; 9:17; 10:9; 13:5; **Am** 1:11, 11, 11; 5:19; 7:4; **Ob** 1:14, 14; **Jnh** 3:10; 4:8; **Na** 2:12; **Hab** 1:1; 3:6, 7; **Hag** 1:9, 12, 14; **Zec** 1:4, 6, 21; 7:5, 6, 6, 6; 9:3; **Mal** 2:6, 15; **Mt** 1:24; 2:22; 9:19; 12:3, 4; 13:58; 14:20; 15:7, 37, 38; 17:2; 19:7; 20:5; 21:6, 15, 25, 31, 36, 42; 25:44, 45, 45; 26:12, 19, 21, 67; 27:9, 35, 51; 28:4, 8, 15; **Mk** 1:4, 6, 32; 2:25, 26; 3:8; 4:8; 5:20; 6:20, 42, 44; 8:6, 8; 10:3; 11:31; 12:44, 44; 14:18, 22, 59, 65; 15:19; **Lk** 4:2; 6:1, 3, 4, 10, 23, 26, 49; 7:38; 9:15, 17, 43, 53, 54; 11:40; 12:47, 48; 15:16; 17:9, 27, 28; 19:22; 24:32, 43; **Jn** 1:45; 2:11, 23, 24; 4:29, 39, 45, 54; 5:16; 6:2, 14, 23, 26, 31, 49, 58; 7:5, 19; 8:40; 9:2, 18, 22, 26, 27; 10:8, 41; 11:45; 12:36, 42; 15:24; 18:15, 26, 34; 19:24, 24; 20:4, 30; 21:7, 25; **Ac** 2:22, 26, 31, 40, 46; 3:17, 17; 4:25; 5:28; 6:8; 7:27, 35, 51; 8:6; 9:9, 36; 10:39, 41; 11:17, 30; 12:8; 14:17; 15:8, 14, 16; 16:18; 19:14; 21:9; 26:10, 10, 22; **Ro** 1:26, 28; 3:3; 5:20; 7:5; 8:29, 29, 30; 10:19; **1Co** 4:8; 10:3, 4; 15:27; **2Co** 1:17; 2:9; 5:20; 7:8, 12; 8:5; 12:16, 17, 18; **Gal** 2:12; 4:8; 5:7, 7; **Php** 4:14; **2Th** 3:8; **1Ti** 1:13; **2Ti** 4:14; **Heb** 3:16; 4:2, 4, 10; 7:19, 27; 9:9; **1Pe** 1:11, 12; 2:22; **Rev** 12:4; 13:14; 19:2; 21:23

DIDST [123]

Ge 12:18; 18:15; 20:6; 21:26; 31:27, 27, 39; **Ex** 15:10; 40:15; **Nu** 21:34; **Dt** 3:2; 9:7; 32:14; 33:8, 8; **Jos** 2:18; 8:2; **Jdg** 12:1; 13:8; **1Sa** 3:6, 8; 15:19, 19, 19; 19:5; 20:19; 25:25; **2Sa** 11:10; 12:12, 21, 21; 13:16; 18:11; 19:28; **1Ki** 1:13; 2:44; 8:18, 53; 20:9; 21:10; **1Ch** 17:22; **2Ch** 2:3, 3; 6:8; 16:8; 20:7; 34:27, 27; **Ne** 9:7, 9, 10, 11, 17, 21, 22, 28, 30, 31, 34; **Ps** 22:4, 9; 30:7; 39:9; 40:6; 44:1, 2, 2; 60:10; 68:7, 9, 9; 73:18; 74:13, 15; 76:8; 80:9; **Isa** 14:12; 22:8; 47:6, 7, 7; 48:6; 54:1, 1; 57:9, 9, 9; 63:14; 64:3; **Jer** 32:22; 36:17; 45:3; **La** 1:10; **Eze** 16:13, 13, 15, 16, 17, 36; 23:40; 27:33; 29:7; 35:15; **Da** 10:12; **Hos** 10:13; **Hab** 3:8, 9, 12, 14, 15; **Mt** 13:27; 14:31; 20:13; **Lk** 7:46; 19:21; **Jn** 17:8; **Ac** 7:28; 11:3; **1Co** 4:7, 7; **Heb** 2:7; **Rev** 17:7

DO [1368]

Ge 6:17; 9:13; 11:6, 6; 16:6; 18:5, 17, 19, 25, 25, 29, 30; 19:7, 8, 8, 22; 21:23; 22:12; 24:42; 25:32; 26:29; 27:37, 46; 30:31; 31:16, 29, 43; 32:12; 34:14, 19; 37:13; 39:9, 11; 40:8; 41:9, 25, 28, 34, 55; 42:1, 18, 22; 43:11; 44:7, 17; 45:17, 19; 47:30; **Ex** 1:16; 3:20; 4:15, 17, 21; 5:4, 17; 6:1; 8:8, 26; 9:5; 15:26; 17:2, 4; 18:16, 20, 23; 19:8; 20:9, 10; 21:7, 11; 22:30; 23:2, 12, 22, 24; 24:3, 7, 14; 29:1, 35, 41; 31:11; 32:14, 18; 33:5, 17; 34:10, 10, 15; 35:1, 19, 35; 36:2; 39:1, 41; **Lev** 4:2, 3, 20, 20; 5:1, 4, 4; 8:34; 9:6; 10:9; 16:15, 16, 29; 18:3, 3, 4, 5, 25; 19:15, 29, 35, 37; 20:4, 8, 22; 21:6, 15, 23; 22:9, 16, 31; 23:7, 7, 8, 21, 25, 28, 31, 35, 36; 25:18, 18, 45; 26:3, 14, 15, 16; 27:11; **Nu** 2:5; 3:7, 8; 4:3, 19, 23, 30, 37, 41, 47; 5:6; 6:21; 7:5; 8:7, 15, 19, 22, 26, 26; 9:14; 10:29, 32, 32; 11:27; 14:28, 35, 41; 15:12, 13, 14, 14, 20, 39, 40; 16:6, 9, 28; 18:6, 23; 21:34; 22:17, 18, 20, 30; 23:19, 26; 24:13, 14, 18; 28:18, 25, 26; 29:1, 7, 12, 35, 39; 30:2; 31:19; 32:20, 23, 24, 25, 31; 33:56, 56; **Dt** 1:14, 18, 44; 3:2, 21, 24; 4:1, 5, 6, 14, 25; 5:1, 13, 14, 27, 31, 32; 6:1, 3, 18, 24, 25; 7:11, 12, 19; 8:1, 16, 19; 11:22, 32; 12:1, 4, 8, 8, 14, 25, 30, 31, 32; 13:11, 18; 15:5, 17, 19; 16:8, 12; 17:10, 10, 11, 12, 13, 19; 18:7, 9, 12, 14; 19:9, 19; 20:3, 15, 18; 21:9; 22:3, 3, 3, 5, 26; 24:8, 8, 18, 22; 25:16, 16; 26:16, 16; 27:10, 26; 28:1, 13, 15, 20, 58, 63; 29:9, 9, 14, 29; 30:5, 8, 8, 12, 13, 14; 31:4, 5, 12, 29; 32:6, 46; 34:11; **Jos** 1:2, 7, 8, 16; 2:14, 24; 3:5; 6:3; 7:9; 8:2, 8; 9:20, 25, 25; 10:25; 22:5, 24, 27; 23:6, 12; 24:13, 20; **Jdg** 6:27; 7:17, 17, 17; 8:3; 9:33, 48, 48; 10:15; 11:10, 12, 36; 13:8, 12, 17; 14:10; 15:3, 10; 17:13; 18:14, 14, 18; 19:23, 23, 24, 24; 20:9, 10; 21:7, 11, 16; **Ru** 1:17; 2:9; 3:4, 5, 11, 13, 13, 13; 4:11; **1Sa** 1:23; 2:23, 35; 3:11, 17, 18; 5:8; 6:2, 6; 7:3; 8:8; 10:2, 7, 8; 11:10; 12:16, 25; 14:7, 36, 40, 44; 16:3; 20:2, 4, 13, 20; 22:3; 24:4, 6; 25:17, 22; 26:21, 25; 28:2, 15; 29:3; 30:23; **2Sa** 3:8, 9, 9, 18, 35; 7:3, 23, 25; 9:11; 10:12; 11:11; 12:9, 12; 13:2, 12, 12; 15:4, 5, 15, 26; 16:10, 11, 20; 17:6; 18:4, 32; 19:13, 18, 19, 22, 22, 27, 37, 38, 38; 20:6, 17; 21:3, 4; 23:17; 24:12; **1Ki** 1:30; 2:6, 9, 23, 31, 38; 3:28; 5:8; 8:32, 39, 43, 43; 9:1, 4; 10:9; 11:12, 33, 38; 12:6, 27; 14:8; 17:13, 18; 18:34, 34; 19:2; 20:9, 9, 10, 24; 22:22; **2Ki** 2:9; 3:13; 4:2, 16, 28; 5:13; 6:15, 27, 31; 7:9; 8:12, 13; 9:18, 19; 10:5, 5, 19; 11:5; 17:12, 15, 17, 34, 34, 36, 37, 41; 18:12; 19:31; 20:9; 21:8, 9; 22:9, 13; **1Ch** 11:19; 12:32; 13:4; 16:21, 22, 40; 17:2, 23; 19:13; 21:8, 10, 23; 28:7, 10, 20; 29:19; **2Ch** 6:23, 33; 7:17; 9:8; 14:4; 18:21; 19:6, 7, 9, 10; 20:12; 22:3; 23:4; 25:8, 9; 30:12; 32:10; 33:8, 9; 34:16, 21; 35:6, 21; **Ezr** 4:2, 2, 3, 22; 6:8; 7:10, 18, 18, 21, 26; 10:4, 5, 11, 12; **Ne** 1:9; 2:12, 19; 4:2; 5:9, 12, 12; 6:2, 13; 9:24, 29; 10:29; 13:17, 21, 27; **Est** 1:8, 15; 3:11; 4:11; 5:5, 8; 6:6, 10; 7:5; 9:13, 23; **Job** 6:24, 26; 7:20; 9:13; 10:2; 11:8; 13:2, 9, 10, 14, 20; 15:3, 12; 16:4; 17:10; 19:22; 20:2; 21:7, 29; 22:17; 24:1; 31:14; 32:9; 34:10, 12, 32; 36:28; 37:12, 24; 39:1; 41:8; 42:2; **Ps** 2:1; 7:1; 11:3; 12:2; 16:1; 25:1, 5; 31:1; 34:10, 14, 16; 36:3; 37:3, 8, 27; 38:15; 40:8; 41:7; 50:16; 51:18; 56:4, 11; 58:1, 1; 60:12; 64:4; 71:1; 75:1, 1; 80:12; 82:3; 83:9; 86:4; 89:50; 92:7; 95:10; 103:18, 20, 21; 104:20; 105:14, 15; 107:23; 108:13; 109:21; 111:10; 118:6; 119:3, 21, 35, 83, 109, 113, 132, 141, 153, 157, 163, 164, 176; 125:4; 129:8; 130:5; 131:1; 137:6; 139:21; 143:8, 10; **Pr** 2:14; 3:27; 6:3, 30; 8:13; 10:23; 14:22; 17:7; 19:7, 7, 19; 20:30; 21:3, 7, 15; 24:8, 29; 25:8; 28:12; 31:12; **Ecc** 2:3, 11, 12; 3:12; 4:8; 5:1; 6:6; 8:11, 12; 9:10, 10; 10:10; 11:5; **SS** 1:3; 8:8; **Isa** 1:16, 17; 5:5; 9:13; 10:3, 11; 14:21; 19:15, 21; 23:4; 24:4, 7, 18; 27:3; 28:21; 29:13, 14; 37:32; 38:7, 19; 41:23, 23; 42:9, 16; 43:19; 45:7; 46:10, 11; 48:11, 14; 55:2; 56:1; 57:4; 58:4; 64:6; 65:8; **Jer** 2:8, 18, 18; 4:22, 22, 30; 5:28, 31; 7:10, 14, 17, 19, 19; 8:8, 14; 9:7; 10:5, 5; 11:4, 6, 8, 15; 12:5; 13:12, 23, 23; 14:7, 21, 21; 17:22, 24; 18:6, 8, 10, 12; 19:12; 22:3, 3, 4, 15, 17; 23:24, 32; 25:6; 26:3, 14; 28:6; 29:32; 30:6; 31:20; 32:23, 35, 40, 41; 33:9, 18; 36:3; 38:5; 39:12, 12; 40:16; 42:2, 3, 5, 20; 44:4, 17; 50:15, 21, 29; 51:47, 52, 55; **La** 1:4, 22; 2:11; **Eze** 2:4; 5:9, 9; 6:10; 7:27; 8:6, 9, 12, 13; 11:20; 15:3; 16:5; 18:5, 21; 20:11, 13, 19, 21, 21; 21:24; 22:14; 23:30, 48; 24:14, 22, 24; 25:8, 14; 33:9, 14, 19, 31, 32; 34:2; 35:11, 15; 36:11, 22, 27, 32, 36, 37; 37:24, 28; 39:17; 43:11; 44:13; 45:20, 25; **Da** 3:14; 4:26; 9:18, 19; 11:3, 16, 17, 24, 27, 28, 30, 32, 32, 32, 36, 39; 12:10; **Hos** 4:18; 6:4, 4; 7:10, 15; 9:5; 10:3, 15; 12:1; 14:8; **Joel** 1:18; 2:21, 22, 22; 3:4; **Am** 3:7, 10; 4:12, 12; **Jnh** 1:11; 3:10; 4:9; **Mic** 2:3, 7, 7, 11; 6:8; 7:3; **Na** 1:9; **Zep** 1:12, 12; 3:5, 13; **Hag** 2:3, 12; **Zec** 1:5, 6, 21; 5:10; 8:15, 16; 9:12; 12:7; **Mal** 1:10; 2:2, 10; 4:1, 3; **Mt** 5:6, 15, 19, 44, 46, 47, 47; 6:1, 2, 2, 7, 20, 26, 28, 32; 7:12, 12, 16; 8:9, 29; 9:14, 17, 28; 11:3, 4; 12:2, 2, 12, 27, 50; 13:13, 41; 14:2; 15:2, 3, 9, 17; 16:9, 11, 13; 17:25; 18:10, 35; 19:16, 18; 20:13, 15, 32; 21:21, 24, 27, 40; 22:29; 23:3, 3, 3, 5; 26:72; 27:19, 22; **Mk** 1:24, 27; 2:18, 24; 3:4, 4, 35; 5:7; 6:5, 14; 7:7, 8, 12, 13, 18; 8:18, 21, 27; 9:22, 39; 10:17, 19, 19, 19, 19, 35, 36, 51; 11:3, 5, 26, 28, 29, 33, 33; 12:9, 24, 27; 13:11; 14:7; 15:8, 12; **Lk** 2:27; 3:10, 11, 12, 14, 14; 4:23, 34; 5:30, 33; 6:2, 2, 9, 9, 11, 27, 31, 31, 33, 33, 33, 35, 44, 46; 7:4, 8; 8:21, 28; 10:11, 25, 28, 37; 11:19, 39; 12:4, 17, 18, 26, 30, 56; 13:32; 15:29; 16:3, 4; 17:10; 18:18, 20, 20, 20, 41; 19:31, 48; 20:8, 13, 15; 22:19, 23; 23:31, 34; 24:38; **Jn** 2:4, 5; 3:2, 11; 4:34; 5:19, 19, 30, 36, 45; 6:6, 28, 38; 7:4, 17, 26, 31; 8:11, 28, 29, 38, 39, 41, 43, 44, 46, 49; 9:15, 16, 33; 10:25, 32, 37, 38; 11:12, 47; 13:7, 15, 17, 27; 14:12, 12, 12, 13, 14, 31; 15:5, 14, 21; 16:3, 19, 31; 17:4; 21:21; **Ac** 1:1; 2:11, 37; 4:16, 28; 5:35; 7:26, 51, 51; 9:6, 6; 10:6; 14:15; 15:29, 36; 16:20, 28, 30, 37; 17:7; 19:36; 21:23; 22:10, 10; 23:21; 24:10, 16; 25:9; 26:9, 20; **Ro** 1:28, 32, 32; 2:3, 8, 14; 3:8, 31; 7:15, 15, 15, 16, 17, 19, 19, 20, 20, 21; 8:3, 5, 13, 25; 12:8, 15; 13:3, 4; 15:31; **1Co** 5:12, 12; 6:2, 7, 7, 8; 7:36; 9:3, 13, 17, 23, 25; 10:22, 31, 31; 11:24, 25, 26; 12:30, 30; 15:29, 35; 16:1, 5, 10; **2Co** 1:17; 3:1; 5:4; 7:8; 8:1, 10, 23; 10:3, 7; 11:8, 12, 12; 12:19; 13:7, 7, 8; **Gal** 1:10, 10; 2:10, 14, 14, 21; 3:10; 4:21; 5:3, 11, 17, 21; 6:10; **Eph** 3:20; 6:9, 21; **Php** 1:18; 2:13, 14, 18; 3:8, 13; 4:9, 13; **Col** 1:9; 3:13, 17, 17, 23, 23; **1Th** 3:12; 4:10, 11; 5:6, 11, 24; **2Th** 3:4, 4; **1Ti** 1:4; 6:2, 18; **2Ti** 2:23; 3:8; 4:5, 9, 21; **Phm** 1:14, 19, 21; **Heb** 3:10; 4:3, 13; 6:3, 10, 11; 10:7, 9; 11:3, 29; 13:6, 16, 17, 19, 21; **Jas** 1:16; 2:6, 7, 8, 11, 11, 12; 4:5, 15, 17; 5:19; **1Pe** 1:21; 2:14, 20; 3:6, 11, 12; 4:11; **2Pe** 1:10, 19; 3:16; **1Jn** 1:6; 2:3; 3:22; 4:14; 5:16; **3Jn** 1:6; **Rev** 2:5; 3:9, 18; 9:19; 13:14; 14:13; 19:10; 21:24; 22:9, 14

DOEST [45]

Ge 4:7, 7; 21:22; **Ex** 18:14, 17; **Dt** 12:28; 14:29; 15:18; **Jdg** 11:27; **2Sa** 3:25; **1Ki** 2:3; 19:9, 13; 20:22; **Job** 9:12; 35:6, 6; **Ps** 49:18; 77:14; 86:10; 119:68; **Ecc** 8:4; **Jer** 11:15; 15:5; **Eze** 12:9; 16:30; 24:19; **Da** 4:35; **Jnh** 4:4, 9; **Mt** 6:2, 3; 21:23; **Mk** 11:28; **Lk** 20:2; **Jn** 2:18; 3:2; 7:3; 13:27; **Ac** 22:26; **Ro** 2:1, 3; **Jas** 2:19; **3Jn** 1:5, 5

DOETH [93]

Ge 31:12; **Ex** 31:14, 15; 35:2; **Lev** 4:27; 6:3; 23:30; **Nu** 15:30; 24:23; **Job** 5:9; 9:10; 23:13; 24:21; 37:5; **Ps** 1:3; 14:1, 3; 15:3, 5; 53:1, 3; 72:18; 106:3; 118:15, 16; 136:4; **Pr** 6:32; 11:17; 15:7; 17:21, 22; 28:17; **Ecc** 2:2; 3:14, 14; 7:20; 8:3; **Isa** 56:2; **Jer** 48:10; **Eze** 17:15; 18:10, 11, 14, 24, 24, 27; **Da** 4:35; 9:14; **Am** 9:12; **Mal** 2:17; **Mt** 6:3; 7:21, 24, 26; 8:9; **Lk** 6:47, 49; 7:8; **Jn** 3:20, 21; 5:19, 19, 20; 7:4, 51; 9:31; 11:47; 14:10; 15:15; 16:2; **Ac** 15:17; 26:31; **Ro** 2:9; 3:12; 10:5; 13:4; **1Co** 6:18; 7:37, 38, 38; **Gal** 3:5, 12; **Eph** 6:8; **Col** 3:25; **Jas** 4:17; **1Jn** 2:17, 29; 3:7, 10; **3Jn** 1:10, 11, 11; **Rev** 13:13

Idx

DOING [39]

DOINGS [51]

DONE [565]

DOST [56]

DOTH [210]

DOWN [1125]

EACH [51]

EITHER [41]

ELSE [48]

EVEN [1395]

EVERY [1238]

EXCEPT [74]

EXCEPTED [1]

FAR [173]

FOR [8985]

FORASMUCH [42]

FORSOMUCH [2]

FORTH [888]

FRO [25]

FROM [3660]

Idx

HAVING [193]

HE [10430]

HER [1993]

HERE [162]

HEREAFTER [14]

HEREBY [13]

HEREIN [9]

HERETOFORE [8]

HIMSELF [528]

HIS [8478]

Idx

HITHER [67]

HITHERTO [19]

HOW [543]

HOWBEIT [64]

HUNDRED [590]

HUNDREDS [28]

HUNDREDTH [3]

I [8851]

IF [1595]

Idx

IN [12674]

26, 26, 28, 29, 35; 14:8, 10, 10, 15, 21, 23; 15:4, 7, 10, 14, 14, 21, 25, 28; 16:8, 10, 10, 10, 10, 11, 12, 15, 19, 23, 23, 23, 24, 24, 25; 17:4, 4, 6, 24, 26, 26, 27, 28, 30, 31, 31, 31, 34, 34, 36; 18:2, 3, 9, 12, 17, 22, 30, 30; 19:17, 20, 30, 36, 38, 38, 38, 42, 43, 44, 47; 20:1, 31, 33, 34, 35, 42, 45, 46, 46, 46; 21:2, 3, 4, 4, 6, 8, 11, 14, 19, 21, 21, 21, 23, 23, 25, 25, 25, 27, 37, 37, 37, 38, 38; 22:6, 10, 16, 19, 20, 28, 30, 37, 44, 53, 55; 23:4, 9, 11, 14, 19, 22, 29, 31, 31, 38, 40, 43, 45, 53, 53, 53; 24:1, 3, 4, 6, 12, 18, 18, 19, 27, 29, 35, 35, 36, 38, 44, 44, 44, 47, 49, 53; **Jn** 1:1, 2, 4, 5, 10, 18, 23, 28, 45, 47; 2:1, 11, 14, 19, 20, 20, 23, 23, 23, 25; 3:13, 14, 15, 16, 18, 21, 23; 4:14, 18, 20, 20, 21, 23, 23, 24, 24, 31, 44, 53; 5:2, 3, 4, 6, 13, 14, 26, 26, 28, 28, 35, 38, 39, 42, 43, 43, 45; 6:10, 10, 31, 37, 45, 49, 53, 56, 56, 59, 59, 61; 7:1, 1, 4, 5, 9, 10, 18, 28, 37; 8:2, 3, 3, 4, 4, 5, 9, 12, 17, 20, 20, 21, 24, 24, 31, 33, 35, 37, 44, 44; 9:3, 5, 7, 34; 10:2, 9, 9, 23, 23, 25, 34, 38, 38; 11:6, 9, 9, 10, 10, 13, 17, 20, 24, 25, 26, 30, 31, 33, 38, 52, 56; 12:13, 25, 35, 36, 46, 48; 13:1, 21, 31, 32, 32; 14:1, 1, 2, 10, 10, 10, 11, 11, 13, 13, 14, 17, 20, 20, 20, 26, 30; 15:2, 4, 4, 4, 4, 5, 5, 6, 7, 7, 9, 10, 10, 11, 16, 25; 16:21, 23, 23, 24, 25, 25, 26, 33, 33; 17:10, 11, 11, 12, 12, 13, 13, 21, 21, 21, 23, 23, 23, 26, 26; 18:13, 15, 16, 20, 20, 20, 26, 38; 19:4, 6, 13, 13, 13, 17, 18, 20, 40, 41, 41; 20:5, 5, 7, 8, 12, 19, 25, 26, 30, 30; 21:2, 8; **Ac** 1:2, 7, 8, 8, 8, 10, 11, 13, 14, 15, 15, 18, 19, 20, 21; 2:1, 6, 8, 9, 9, 9, 10, 10, 11, 12, 17, 18, 19, 19, 22, 26, 27, 31, 37, 38, 42, 42, 42, 46; 3:6, 11, 13, 16, 16, 22, 25, 26; 4:3, 7, 12, 16, 17, 18, 19, 24; 5:4, 4, 7, 10, 12, 18, 20, 21, 22, 25, 25, 28, 34, 34, 37, 40, 42, 42; 6:1, 1, 7, 15; 7:2, 2, 4, 5, 6, 7, 7, 10, 12, 16, 17, 20, 20, 22, 22, 22, 29, 30, 30, 30, 34, 35, 36, 36, 36, 38, 38, 38, 39, 41, 41, 42, 42, 44, 45, 48, 51; 8:8, 9, 16, 21, 21, 23, 23, 25, 28, 33, 40; 9:10, 11, 12, 12, 17, 20, 21, 22, 25, 27, 27, 28, 29, 31, 31, 37, 37, 42, 43; 10:1, 3, 3, 17, 23, 25, 27, 30, 30, 31, 31, 32, 35, 39, 39, 43, 48; 11:1, 3, 5, 5, 13, 22, 26, 27, 28, 29; 12:4, 5, 7, 14, 21; 13:1, 5, 13, 14, 17, 18, 19, 27, 28, 29, 33, 33, 35, 40, 41, 41, 43; 14:1, 3, 8, 11, 11, 14, 16, 16, 17, 22, 23, 25; 15:21, 21, 23, 33, 35, 36; 16:3, 5, 5, 6, 9, 12, 18, 24, 29, 32, 34, 36; 17:2, 11, 11, 16, 17, 17, 21, 22, 22, 24, 28, 31, 31, 31; 18:2, 4, 5, 9, 10, 18, 21, 23, 24, 25, 25, 26; 19:5, 9, 10, 16, 21, 22, 27, 29, 30, 39, 40, 40; 20:6, 8, 9, 10, 13, 14, 16, 19, 22, 23, 29; 21:18, 27, 29, 31, 39, 40; 22:2, 3, 3, 3, 17, 17, 19; 23:1, 6, 6, 9, 10, 11, 16, 21, 35; 24:3, 12, 12, 12, 14, 18, 20, 21, 24; 25:3, 5, 6, 14; 26:3, 10, 10, 11, 13, 14, 16, 18, 21, 26; 27:12, 20, 21, 27, 31, 35, 37, 37, 39; 28:7, 8, 9, 11, 11, 18, 30, 30; **Ro** 1:2, 7, 9, 9, 15, 18, 19, 21, 27, 27, 28, 32; 2:7, 12, 14, 15, 16, 17, 19, 20, 28, 29, 29; 3:4, 9, 16, 20, 24, 25, 26; 4:10, 10, 10, 10, 12, 18, 19, 20; 5:2, 3, 5, 6, 8, 11, 13, 17; 6:1, 4, 5, 5, 10, 10, 12, 12, 21; 7:5, 5, 6, 6, 8, 13, 17, 18, 18, 20, 22, 23, 23; 8:1, 2, 3, 3, 3, 4, 8, 9, 9, 9, 10, 11, 11, 18, 20, 22, 37, 39; 9:1, 1, 2, 7, 17, 25, 26, 28, 33; 10:6, 8, 8, 9, 14, 14; 11:17, 19, 22, 23, 23, 23, 25, 25, 25, 30, 32; 12:4, 5, 10, 11, 11, 12, 12, 12, 16, 17, 18, 20; 13:4, 9, 13, 13, 13, 13; 14:1, 5, 13, 17, 18, 22; 15:12, 13, 13, 15, 15, 17, 23, 24, 27, 29, 30, 31; 16:2, 2, 3, 5, 7, 8, 9, 10, 11, 12, 12, 13, 22; **1Co** 1:2, 2, 5, 5, 5, 6, 7, 8, 10, 10, 13, 15, 21, 29, 30, 31; 2:3, 3, 3, 4, 5, 5, 7, 11, 13; 3:1, 16, 18, 19, 21; 4:2, 6, 6, 10, 15, 15, 17, 17, 17, 20, 20, 21, 21; 5:3, 3, 4, 5, 9; 6:4, 11, 19, 20, 20; 7:15, 17, 18, 20, 22, 28, 34, 34, 37, 37, 38, 38, 39; 8:4, 4, 5, 5, 6, 7, 10; 9:1, 2, 9, 10, 10, 18, 24, 25; 10:2, 2, 5, 8, 19, 25, 28, 33; 11:2, 11, 13, 17, 18, 21, 22, 22, 23, 24, 25, 25, 34; 12:6, 18, 25, 27, 28; 13:6, 6, 9, 9, 10, 12; 14:2, 2, 4, 7, 10, 13, 14, 19, 19, 20, 20, 20, 21, 23, 24, 25, 27, 28, 33, 34, 35, 40; 15:2, 2, 10, 17, 18, 19, 19, 22, 22, 23, 28, 30, 31, 41, 42, 42, 43, 43, 43, 43, 52, 52, 54, 58, 58, 58; 16:2, 11, 13, 19, 19, 24; **2Co** 1:1, 4, 4, 5, 6, 8, 9, 9, 9, 10, 12, 12, 14, 14, 15, 19, 20, 20, 21, 22; 2:1, 3, 5, 9, 10, 13, 14, 14, 15, 15, 17, 17; 3:2, 3, 3, 7, 9, 10, 14, 14, 18; 4:2, 2, 4, 6, 6, 7, 8, 10, 10, 11, 12, 12; 5:1, 2, 4, 6, 10, 11, 12, 12, 17, 19, 20, 21; 6:1, 2, 2, 3, 4, 4, 4, 4, 4, 5, 5, 5, 5, 5, 5, 12, 12, 13, 16, 16; 7:1, 3, 4, 7, 9, 11, 11, 11, 12, 13, 14, 16, 16; 8:2, 6, 7, 7, 7, 7, 7, 18, 20, 21, 21, 22, 22; 9:3, 3, 4, 7, 8, 11, 14; 10:1, 3, 6, 11, 11, 14, 16, 16, 17; 11:1, 3, 6, 6, 6, 7, 9, 10, 10, 17, 23, 23, 23, 23, 25, 26, 26, 26, 26, 26, 26, 26, 26, 26, 26, 26, 27, 27, 27, 27, 27, 32, 33; 12:2, 2, 3, 5, 7, 9, 9, 10, 10, 10, 10, 10, 11, 11, 12, 12, 18, 18, 19; 13:1, 3, 3, 4, 5, 5, 11; **Gal** 1:13, 13, 14, 14, 16, 22, 23, 24; 2:2, 4, 4, 4, 6, 8, 8, 16, 20, 20, 21; 3:3, 4, 4, 8, 10, 10, 11, 12, 17, 19, 26, 28; 4:3, 9, 11, 14, 18, 19, 19, 20, 25, 25; 5:1, 6, 10, 14, 14, 16, 21, 25, 25; 6:1, 1, 4, 4, 6, 6, 9, 9, 12, 13, 14, 15, 17; **Eph** 1:1, 3, 3, 4, 4, 6, 7, 8, 9, 10, 10, 10, 10, 10, 11, 12, 13, 13, 15, 16, 17, 18, 20, 20, 21, 21, 23; 2:1, 2, 2, 3, 3, 4, 5, 6, 6, 7, 7, 10, 10, 11, 11, 11, 12, 13, 15, 15, 15, 16, 21, 21, 22; 3:3, 4, 5, 6, 9, 10, 11, 12, 15, 16, 17, 17, 20, 21; 4:2, 3, 4, 6, 13, 14, 15, 15, 16, 16, 17, 17, 18, 21, 23, 24; 5:2, 5, 8, 9, 12, 19, 19, 20, 21, 24, 33; 6:1, 4, 5, 9, 10, 10, 12, 13, 18, 20, 21, 24; **Php** 1:1, 4, 5, 6, 7, 7, 7, 8, 9, 9, 13, 13, 13, 14, 18, 18, 20, 20, 22, 23, 24, 26, 27, 28, 29, 30, 30; 2:1, 3, 5, 5, 6, 7, 8, 10, 10, 12, 12, 13, 15, 15, 16, 16, 16, 19, 22, 24, 25, 29, 29; 3:1, 3, 3, 3, 4, 4, 6, 9, 14, 15, 19, 20; 4:1, 2, 3, 3, 4, 6, 9, 10, 11, 11, 12, 15, 16, 19, 21; **Col** 1:2, 4, 5, 5, 6, 6, 6, 8, 9, 10, 10, 12, 14, 16, 16, 18, 19, 20, 20, 21, 22, 22, 23, 24, 24, 27, 28, 28, 29; 2:1, 2, 3, 5, 5, 5, 6, 7, 7, 9, 10, 11, 11, 12, 13, 15, 16, 16, 16, 18, 20, 23, 23; 3:3, 4, 7, 7, 10, 11, 15, 15, 16, 16, 16, 16, 17, 17, 18, 20, 22, 22; 4:1, 2, 2, 3, 5, 7, 12, 12, 13, 13, 15, 15, 16, 17; **1Th** 1:1, 1, 2, 3, 3, 5, 5, 5, 5, 6, 7, 8, 8, 9; 2:1, 1, 2, 3, 4, 13, 13, 14, 14, 17, 17, 19; 3:2, 5, 7, 8, 10, 12, 13; 4:4, 5, 6, 10, 14, 16, 17, 17; 5:2, 4, 7, 7, 12, 13, 18, 18; **2Th** 1:1, 4, 4, 4, 8, 10, 10, 10, 12, 12; 2:2, 4, 6, 10, 12, 17; 3:4, 6, 13, 17; **1Ti** 1:2, 4, 13, 14, 16; 2:2, 2, 3, 6, 7, 7, 9, 9, 11, 12, 14, 15, 15; 3:4, 9, 11, 13, 13, 15, 16, 16, 16; 4:1, 2, 6, 6, 10, 12, 12, 12, 12, 12, 12, 14, 16, 16; 5:5, 5, 6, 7, 17; 6:9, 13, 15, 16, 17, 17, 17, 18, 19; **2Ti** 1:1, 3, 5, 5, 5, 6, 6, 9, 13, 13, 14, 15, 17, 18, 18; 2:1, 1, 7, 10, 14, 20, 25; 3:1, 12, 14, 15, 16; 4:2, 5; **Tit** 1:2, 3, 5, 5, 5, 13, 16; 2:2, 2, 2, 3, 7, 7, 9, 10, 12; 3:1, 3, 8, 15; **Phm** 1:2, 4, 6, 6, 7, 8, 10, 11, 13, 13, 16, 16, 20, 20, 21, 23; **Heb** 1:1, 1, 2, 6, 10; 2:5, 6, 8, 8, 8, 10, 12, 13, 17, 17, 18; 3:2, 5, 8, 8, 8, 10, 11, 12, 12, 15, 17, 19; 4:2, 3, 4, 5, 6, 7, 13, 15, 16; 5:1, 6, 7, 7, 13; 6:7, 10, 18; 7:9, 10, 19; 8:1, 5, 9, 9, 10, 13; 9:9, 10, 12, 23, 24, 26; 10:3, 6, 7, 16, 22, 32, 34, 34, 34, 38; 11:9, 9, 9, 12, 13, 18, 19, 26, 34, 37, 38, 38, 38; 12:3, 9, 23; 13:3, 3, 4, 18, 21, 21, 21, 22; **Jas** 1:6, 8, 9, 10, 11, 23, 25, 27; 2:2, 2, 2, 3, 4, 5, 10, 16; 3:2, 2, 3, 7, 14, 18; 4:1, 5, 5, 10, 16; 5:5, 5, 10, 14; **1Pe** 1:4, 5, 6, 8, 11, 14, 15, 17, 20, 21, 21, 22; 2:6, 6, 10, 12, 22, 24; 3:1, 4, 4, 5, 5, 5, 15, 15, 16, 18, 19, 20; 4:1, 1, 2, 3, 6, 6, 11, 15, 19; 5:6, 9, 9, 9, 14; **2Pe** 1:4, 8, 8, 12, 12, 13, 13, 15, 17, 18, 19, 19, 21; 2:1, 5, 8, 10, 11, 12, 13, 18, 19, 22; 3:1, 3, 5, 7, 10, 10, 11, 14, 16, 16, 16, 18, 18; **1Jn** 1:5, 6, 7, 7, 8, 10; 2:4, 5, 5, 6, 8, 8, 9, 9, 10, 10, 11, 11, 14, 15, 15, 16, 24, 24, 24, 24, 27, 27, 28; 3:3, 5, 6, 9, 10, 14, 15, 17, 18, 18, 18, 18, 22, 24, 24, 24; 4:2, 3, 3, 4, 4, 9, 12, 12, 13, 13, 15, 15, 16, 16, 16, 17, 17, 18, 18; 5:7, 8, 8, 10, 11, 14, 19, 20, 20; **2Jn** 1:1, 2, 3, 4, 6, 7, 9, 9; **3Jn** 1:1, 2, 3, 3, 4; **Jude** 1:1, 4, 5, 6, 7, 10, 11, 11, 12, 16, 18, 20, 21; **Rev** 1:4, 5, 9, 9, 9, 10, 11, 11, 13, 15, 16, 16, 20; 2:1, 1, 7, 8, 12, 13, 17, 18, 24; 3:1, 4, 4, 5, 7, 12, 18, 20, 21, 21; 4:1, 2, 2, 3, 4, 6; 5:1, 3, 3, 6, 6, 13, 13, 13; 6:5, 6, 15, 15; 7:3, 9, 13, 14, 15, 17; 8:1, 9; 9:4, 6, 10, 11, 11, 14, 17, 19, 19; 10:2, 7, 8, 9, 10; 11:3, 5, 6, 8, 9, 12, 13, 15, 19, 19; 12:1, 2, 3, 7, 8, 10, 12; 13:6, 6, 8, 13, 14, 16, 16; 14:1, 5, 6, 9, 9, 10, 10, 13, 14, 15, 16, 17, 18, 19; 15:1, 1, 5, 6; 16:3, 16, 19; 17:3, 4, 4, 8, 17; 18:6, 7, 8, 10, 16, 17, 17, 19, 19, 22, 22, 22, 23, 23, 24; 19:1, 8, 11, 13, 14, 14, 17, 17; 20:1, 4, 6, 8, 12, 13, 13, 15; 21:8, 10, 14, 23, 24, 27, 27; 22:2, 3, 4, 14, 16, 18, 19

INASMUCH [9]

Dt 19:6; **Ru** 3:10; **Mt** 25:40, 45; **Ro** 11:13; **Php** 1:7; **Heb** 3:3; 7:20; **1Pe** 4:13

INDEED [70]

Ge 17:19; 20:12; 37:8, 8, 10; 40:15; 43:20; 44:5; **Ex** 19:5; 23:22; **Lev** 10:18; **Nu** 12:2; 21:2; 22:37; **Dt** 2:15; 21:16; **Jos** 7:20; **1Sa** 1:11; 2:30; **2Sa** 14:5; 15:8; **1Ki** 8:27; **2Ki** 14:10; **1Ch** 4:10; 21:17; **Job** 19:4, 5; **Ps** 58:1; **Isa** 6:9, 9; **Jer** 22:4; **Mt** 3:11; 13:32; 20:23; 23:27; 26:41; **Mk** 1:8; 9:13; 10:39; 11:32; 14:21; **Lk** 3:16; 11:48; 23:41; 24:34; **Jn** 1:47; 4:42; 6:55, 55; 7:26; 8:31, 36; **Ac** 4:16; 11:16; 22:9; **Ro** 6:11; 8:7; 14:20; **1Co** 11:7; **2Co** 8:17; 11:1; **Php** 1:15; 2:27; 3:1; **Col** 2:23; **1Th** 4:10; **1Ti** 5:3, 5, 16; **1Pe** 2:4

INSOMUCH [20]

Ps 106:40; **Mal** 2:13; **Mt** 8:24; 12:22; 13:54; 15:31; 24:24; 27:14; **Mk** 1:27, 45; 2:2, 12; 3:10; 9:26; **Lk** 12:1; **Ac** 1:19; 5:15; **2Co** 1:8; 8:6; **Gal** 2:13

INSTEAD [39]

Ge 2:21; 4:25; 44:33; **Ex** 4:16, 16; 5:12; **Nu** 3:12, 41, 41, 45, 45; 5:19, 20, 29; 8:16, 16; 10:31; **Jdg** 15:2; **2Sa** 17:25; **1Ki** 3:7; **2Ki** 14:21; 17:24; **1Ch** 29:23; **2Ch** 12:10; **Est** 2:4, 17; **Job** 31:40, 40; **Ps** 45:16; **Isa** 3:24, 24, 24, 24, 24; 55:13, 13; **Jer** 22:11; 37:1; **Eze** 16:32

INTO [2015]

Ge 2:7, 10, 15; 6:18, 19; 7:1, 7, 9, 13, 15; 8:9, 9; 9:2; 11:31; 12:5, 5, 10, 11, 14, 15; 13:1; 14:20; 16:5; 18:6; 19:2, 3, 10, 23; 21:32; 22:2; 24:20, 32, 67; 26:2; 27:17; 28:15; 29:1; 30:35; 31:33, 33, 33, 33; 32:7, 16; 36:6; 37:20, 22, 24, 28, 35, 36; 39:4, 11, 20; 40:3, 11, 11, 13, 15, 21; 41:57; 42:17, 25, 37; 43:17, 18, 24, 26, 30; 45:4, 25; 46:3, 4, 6, 7, 8, 26, 27, 28; 47:14; 48:5, 16; 49:6, 33; 50:13, 14; **Ex** 1:1, 22; 3:18; 4:6, 6, 7, 7, 19, 21, 27; 5:3; 7:23; 8:3, 3, 3, 3, 3, 21, 24, 24, 24, 27; 9:20; 10:4, 19; 11:4; 13:5, 11; 14:22, 28; 15:1, 4, 5, 19, 21, 22, 25; 16:3; 18:5, 7, 27; 19:1, 12; 21:13; 23:19, 20, 31; 24:12, 13, 15, 18, 18; 25:14, 16; 26:11; 27:7; 29:3, 30; 30:20; 32:24; 33:5, 8, 9, 11; 37:5; 38:7; 39:3, 3; 40:20, 21, 32, 35; **Lev** 1:6, 12; 6:30; 8:20; 9:23; 10:9; 11:32; 12:4; 13:17; 14:7, 8, 15, 26, 34, 36, 40, 41, 45, 46, 53; 16:2, 3, 10, 21, 23, 23, 26, 28; 19:23; 23:10; 25:2; 26:25, 32, 36, 41; **Nu** 4:3, 30, 35, 39, 43; 5:17, 22, 24, 27; 7:89; 11:30; 13:17; 14:3, 4, 8, 16, 24, 25, 30, 40; 15:2, 18; 16:14, 30, 33, 47; 17:8; 19:6, 7, 14; 20:1, 4, 12, 15, 24, 27; 21:2, 22, 22, 23, 27, 29, 34; 22:13, 23, 23, 41; 23:14; 24:4, 16; 25:8; 27:12; 31:24, 27, 54; 32:7, 9, 32; 33:8, 38, 51; 34:2; 35:10, 28; 36:12; **Dt** 1:22, 24, 27, 31, 40, 41, 43; 2:1, 24, 29, 30; 3:2, 3, 27; 5:5, 30; 6:10; 7:1, 24, 26; 8:7; 9:9, 21, 28; 10:1, 3, 22; 11:5; 13:16; 14:6, 25; 17:8; 18:9; 19:3, 5, 11, 12; 20:13; 21:10; 23:1, 2, 2, 3, 3, 5, 8, 11, 18, 24, 25; 24:10; 26:5, 9; 28:25, 38, 41, 68; 29:12, 12, 28; 30:5; 31:20, 21, 23; 32:26, 49; **Jos** 2:1, 3, 18, 19, 24; 3:11; 4:5; 6:2, 11, 14, 19, 20, 22, 24; 7:7; 8:1, 7, 13, 18, 19; 10:8, 19, 19, 20, 27, 30, 32; 11:8; 13:5; 18:5, 6, 9; 20:4, 5; 21:44; 22:13; 24:4, 8, 8, 11; **Jdg** 1:2, 3, 3, 4, 16, 24, 25, 26, 34; 2:14, 14, 23; 3:8, 10, 21, 28; 4:2, 7, 9, 14, 18, 21, 21, 22; 5:15; 6:1, 5, 13; 7:2, 7, 9, 13, 14, 15, 15, 16; 8:3, 7; 9:27, 27, 42, 43, 46; 10:7, 7; 11:19, 21, 30, 32; 12:3; 13:1; 15:1, 5, 12, 13, 18, 18; 16:23, 24; 18:10, 18; 19:3, 11, 12, 15, 21, 22, 23, 29, 29, 29; 20:4, 8, 28; **Ru** 1:2; 2:18; 3:14, 15; 4:11; **1Sa** 2:14, 36; 4:3, 5, 6, 7, 10, 13; 5:2, 5; 6:14, 19; 7:1, 13; 9:13, 14, 14, 22, 25; 10:6; 11:11; 12:8, 9, 9, 9; 14:10, 12, 21, 26, 37; 17:22, 46, 47, 49; 19:10; 20:8, 11, 11, 35, 42; 21:15; 22:5, 5; 23:4, 7, 7, 11, 12, 14, 16, 20, 25; 24:4, 10, 18; 26:3, 8, 10, 23; 27:1; 28:19, 19; 29:11; 30:15, 23; 31:9; **2Sa** 2:1; 3:8, 34; 4:6, 7; 5:8, 19, 19; 6:10, 10, 12, 16; 10:2, 10, 14; 11:11, 23; 12:8, 20; 13:10, 10; 15:25, 27, 31, 37, 37; 16:8; 17:13, 13, 17; 18:6, 17; 19:2, 3, 5; 20:12; 21:9; 22:7, 20; 23:11; 24:14, 14; **1Ki** 1:15, 28; 3:1; 6:8, 8; 8:6; 11:17, 40; 13:18; 14:12, 28, 28; 15:15, 18; 16:18, 21; 17:19, 21, 22, 23; 18:5, 9; 19:4; 20:2, 13, 28, 30, 30, 30, 33, 39; 21:4; 22:6, 12, 15, 25, 30, 30, 35; **2Ki** 2:1, 11, 16; 3:10, 13, 18; 4:4, 11, 32, 39, 39, 41; 5:18; 6:5, 20, 23; 7:4, 8, 8, 12; 8:21; 9:6, 26; 10:15, 21, 23, 24; 11:4, 13, 16, 18; 12:4, 4, 4, 9, 9, 11, 13, 15, 16; 13:3, 3, 21; 17:6, 20; 18:21, 30; 19:1, 10, 14, 18, 23, 23, 25, 28, 32, 33, 37; 20:4, 8, 20; 21:14; 22:4, 5, 7, 9, 20; 23:2, 12; 24:15; **1Ch** 5:20; 6:15; 10:9; 11:15; 12:8; 13:13; 14:10, 10, 17; 16:7; 19:2, 15; 21:13, 13, 27; 22:18, 19; 23:6; 24:19; **2Ch** 5:7; 6:41; 7:2, 10, 11; 9:4; 12:11, 11; 13:16; 15:12, 18; 16:8; 18:5, 11, 14, 24; 20:20; 21:17, 17; 23:1, 6, 7, 12, 20; 24:10, 24; 25:20; 26:16; 27:2; 28:5, 5, 9, 27; 29:4, 16, 16, 16, 31; 30:8, 9, 14, 15; 31:1, 10, 16; 32:1, 21; 33:13; 34:7, 9, 14, 17, 30; 36:17; **Ezr** 5:8, 12, 12, 14, 15; 9:7; 10:6; **Ne** 2:7, 8; 5:5; 6:11; 7:5; 8:1; 9:11, 11, 22, 23, 24, 27, 30; 10:29, 29, 34, 38; 12:44; 13:1, 2, 15; **Est** 1:22, 22; 2:14, 16; 3:9, 13; 4:1, 2, 11; 6:4; 7:7, 8; 9:22; **Job** 3:6; 9:24; 10:9; 12:6; 14:3; 16:11; 17:12; 18:8, 18; 22:4; 30:3, 19, 31; 33:28; 34:23; 36:16; 37:8; 38:16, 22, 38; 39:12; 40:23; 41:2, 22, 28; **Ps** 4:2; 5:7; 7:15; 9:17; 10:9; 16:4; 18:6, 19; 22:15; 24:3; 28:1; 30:11; 31:5, 8; 32:4; 35:8, 13; 37:15, 20; 45:2, 15; 46:2; 55:15, 23; 56:8; 57:6; 60:9, 9; 63:9; 66:6, 11, 12, 13; 69:2, 27; 73:17, 18, 19; 74:7; 76:6; 78:44, 61, 61; 79:1, 12; 88:4, 18; 95:11; 96:8; 100:4, 4; 104:10; 105:23, 29; 106:15, 20, 41, 42; 107:33, 33, 34, 35, 35; 108:10, 10; 109:18, 18; 114:8, 8; 115:17; 118:19, 20; 122:1; 132:3, 3, 7, 8; 135:9; 136:13; 139:8; 140:10, 10; 141:10; 143:2, 7, 10; **Pr** 1:12; 2:10; 4:14; 6:3; 13:17; 16:29, 33; 17:10, 10, 20; 18:6, 8, 10; 19:15; 23:10; 24:16; 26:9, 22; 27:10; 28:10, 14; 29:8; 30:4; **Ecc** 1:7; 10:8; 11:9; 12:14; **SS** 1:4; 3:4, 4; 4:16; 5:1; 6:2, 11; 7:11; 8:2; **Isa** 2:4, 4, 10, 19, 19, 21, 21; 3:14; 5:13, 14; 9:8, 10; 13:2, 14; 14:7, 13; 19:1, 4, 8, 23, 23; 21:4; 22:18, 21; 23:9; 24:18; 26:20; 29:17; 30:2, 6, 20, 29; 34:9, 9; 36:6, 15; 37:1, 10, 19, 24, 26, 29, 33, 34, 38; 38:18; 40:9; 44:23; 46:2; 47:5, 6; 49:13; 51:23; 52:1, 4, 9; 54:1; 55:12; 57:2; 59:5; 63:14; 65:6, 7, 17; 66:20; **Jer** 2:7, 21; 4:5, 29; 6:9, 25; 7:31; 8:6, 14; 9:21, 21; 10:9; 12:7; 13:16; 14:18, 18, 18; 15:4, 14; 16:5, 8, 13, 15; 17:25; 19:5; 20:4, 4, 5, 6; 21:4, 7, 7, 7, 10, 13; 22:7, 22, 25, 25, 25, 25, 26, 28; 23:15; 24:5, 9; 26:21, 22, 22, 23, 24; 27:6; 28:3, 4, 6; 29:14, 16, 21; 30:6, 16; 31:13; 32:3, 4, 18, 24, 25, 28, 28, 35, 36, 43; 33:11; 34:2, 3, 10, 11, 16, 17, 20, 20, 21, 21, 21; 35:2, 2, 4, 4, 11; 36:5, 12, 12, 20, 23; 37:4, 7, 12, 16, 16, 17, 21; 38:3, 6, 9, 11, 11, 14, 16, 18, 19; 39:9, 17; 40:4, 4; 41:7, 7, 17; 42:14, 15, 17, 18, 19; 43:2, 3, 3, 7; 44:12, 14, 14, 21, 28, 28, 30, 30, 30; 46:11, 19, 24, 26, 26, 26; 47:6; 48:7, 11, 44; 49:3, 32; 51:9, 50, 51, 59, 63; 52:12; **La** 1:3, 5, 7, 10, 10, 13, 14, 18; 2:7, 9, 12; 3:2, 2, 13; 4:12, 22; 5:15; **Eze** 2:2; 3:22, 23, 24; 4:14; 5:4, 4, 6, 10, 12; 7:11, 21, 22; 8:16; 10:7; 11:5, 9, 24; 12:4, 11; 13:5, 9; 14:19; 15:4; 16:8, 13, 39; 17:4, 15; 19:9; 20:6, 10, 15, 28, 32, 35, 37, 38, 42, 42; 21:11, 14, 30, 31; 22:19, 20; 23:9, 9, 16, 17, 28, 28, 31, 39; 24:3, 4; 25:3; 26:10, 10, 20; 27:26, 27; 28:4, 23, 23; 29:5, 14, 14; 30:12, 17, 18, 25; 31:11, 16, 17; 32:9, 18, 24; 36:5, 24; 37:5, 10, 12, 17, 21, 22; 38:4, 8, 10; 39:23, 23, 28; 40:2, 17, 32; 41:6; 42:1, 1, 9, 12, 14; 43:4, 5; 44:7, 9, 12, 16, 19, 19, 21, 27; 46:19, 20, 21; 47:8, 8, 8; **Da** 1:2, 2, 2, 9; 2:29, 38; 3:6, 11, 15, 20, 21, 23, 24; 5:10; 6:7, 10, 12, 16, 24; 7:25; 10:8; 11:7, 8, 9, 9, 11, 28, 40, 41; **Hos** 2:14; 4:7; 9:4; 11:5, 9; 12:1, 12; **Joel** 1:14; 2:20, 31, 31; 3:2, 5, 8, 10, 10; **Am** 1:4, 5, 15; 2:1; 4:3; 5:5, 5, 8, 19, 27; 6:12, 12; 7:12, 17; 8:10, 10; 9:2, 4; **Ob** 1:11, 13; **Jnh** 1:3, 4, 5, 5, 12, 15; 2:3, 7; 3:4; **Mic** 1:6, 16; 3:5; 4:3, 3, 12; 5:5, 6; 7:19; **Na** 3:10, 12, 14; **Hab** 3:16; **Hag** 1:6; **Zec** 5:4, 4, 8; 6:6, 10; 10:10; 11:6, 6; 14:2; **Mal** 3:10; **Mt** 1:17, 17; 2:11, 12, 13, 14, 20, 21, 22; 3:10, 12; 4:1, 5, 8, 12, 12, 18; 5:1, 20, 25, 29, 30; 6:6, 13, 26, 30; 7:19, 21; 8:5, 12, 14, 23, 28, 31, 32, 32, 33; 9:1, 1, 17, 17, 23, 26, 28, 38; 10:5, 5, 11, 12, 23; 11:7; 12:4, 9, 11, 29, 44; 13:2, 8, 20, 23, 30, 36, 42, 47, 48, 50, 54; 14:13, 15, 22, 23, 32, 34, 35; 15:11, 14, 17, 17, 21, 29, 39; 16:13; 17:1, 15, 15, 22, 25; 18:3, 8, 8, 9, 9, 12, 30; 19:1, 17, 23, 24; 20:1, 2, 4, 7; 21:2, 10, 12, 17, 18, 21, 23, 31, 33; 22:9, 10, 13; 24:16, 38; 25:14, 21, 23, 30, 41, 46, 46; 26:18, 30, 32, 41, 45, 52, 71; 27:6, 27, 53; 28:7, 10, 11, 16, 16; **Mk** 1:12, 14, 16, 21, 21, 29, 35, 38, 45; 2:1, 11, 22, 22, 26; 3:1, 13, 19, 27; 4:1, 26, 37; 5:1, 12, 12, 13, 13, 18; 6:1, 10, 31, 32, 36, 36, 45, 46, 51, 53, 56; 7:15, 17, 18, 19, 19, 19, 24, 24, 33; 8:10, 10, 13, 26, 27; 9:2, 22, 22, 25, 28, 31, 42, 43, 43, 43, 45, 45, 45, 47, 47; 10:1, 17, 23, 24, 25; 11:2, 2, 11, 11, 15, 23; 12:1, 41, 43; 13:15; 14:13, 16, 26, 28, 38, 41, 54, 68; 15:16; 16:5, 7, 12, 15, 19; **Lk** 1:9, 39, 39, 40, 79; 2:3, 4, 15, 27, 39; 3:3, 9, 17; 4:1, 5, 14, 16, 37, 38, 42; 5:3, 4, 16, 19, 24, 37, 38; 6:4, 6, 12, 38, 39; 7:1, 11, 24, 36, 44; 8:22, 29, 30, 31, 32, 33, 33, 37, 41, 51; 9:4, 10, 12, 28, 34, 44, 44, 52; 10:1, 2, 5, 8, 10, 10, 38, 38; 11:4; 12:5, 28, 58; 13:19; 14:1, 5, 21, 23; 15:13, 15; 16:4, 9, 16, 22, 28; 17:2, 12, 27; 18:10, 24, 25; 19:4, 12, 23, 30, 45; 20:9; 21:1, 12, 24; 22:3, 10, 10, 33, 40, 46, 54, 66; 23:19, 25, 42, 46; 24:7, 26, 51; **Jn** 1:9, 43; 3:4, 5, 17, 19, 22, 24, 35; 4:3, 14, 28, 38, 43, 45, 46, 47, 54; 5:4, 7, 24; 6:3, 14, 15, 17, 21, 22; 7:3, 14; 8:2; 9:39; 10:1, 36, 40; 11:7, 27, 30, 54; 12:24, 46; 13:2, 3, 5, 27; 15:6; 16:13, 20, 21, 28; 17:18, 18; 18:1, 11, 15, 28, 33, 37; 19:9, 17; 20:6, 11, 25, 25, 27; 21:3, 7; **Ac** 1:11, 11, 11, 13; 2:20, 20, 34; 3:1, 2, 3, 8; 5:15, 21; 7:3, 4, 6, 9, 15, 16, 23, 34, 39, 45, 55; 8:3, 38; 9:6, 8, 11, 17, 39; 10:10, 16, 22, 24; 11:8, 10, 12; 12:17; 13:14; 14:1, 20, 22, 25; 16:7, 9, 10, 15, 19, 23, 24, 34, 37, 40; 17:10; 18:7, 18, 19, 27; 19:8, 22, 29, 31; 20:1, 2, 3, 4, 9, 18; 21:3, 8, 11, 26, 28, 29, 34, 37, 38; 22:4, 10, 11, 23, 24; 23:10, 16, 20, 28; 24:27; 25:1, 23; 27:1, 2, 6, 15, 17, 30, 38, 39, 41, 43; 28:5, 17, 23; **Ro** 1:23, 25, 26; 5:2, 12; 6:3, 3, 4; 7:23; 8:21; 10:6, 7, 18; 11:24, 24; 15:24, 28; **1Co** 2:9; 4:17; 9:27; 11:20; 12:13, 13; 14:9, 23; **2Co** 1:16; 2:13; 3:18; 7:5; 8:16; 10:5; 11:13, 14, 20; 12:4; **Gal** 1:6, 17, 21; 2:4; 3:27; 4:6; **Eph** 4:9, 15; **Col** 1:13; 2:18; **2Th** 3:5, 5; **1Ti** 1:3, 12, 15; 3:6, 7, 16; 5:9; 6:7, 9, 9; **2Ti** 3:6; **Heb** 1:6; 3:11, 18; 4:1, 3, 3, 5, 10, 11, 14; 6:19; 8:10; 9:6, 7, 8, 12, 24, 24, 25; 10:5, 16, 19, 31; 11:8; 13:11; **Jas** 1:2, 25; 4:13; 5:4, 12; **1Pe** 1:12; 2:9; 3:22; 5:10; **2Pe** 1:11; 2:4, 6; **1Jn** 4:1, 9; **2Jn** 1:7, 10; **Jude** 1:4; **Rev** 2:10, 22, 22; 5:6; 8:5, 8; 11:11; 12:6, 9, 14, 14; 13:10, 10; 14:10, 19, 19; 15:8; 16:16, 17, 19; 17:3, 8, 11; 18:21; 19:20; 20:3, 10, 14, 15; 21:24, 26, 27; 22:14

IS [6993]

Ge 1:11, 29, 29, 30; 2:9, 11, 11, 11, 12, 12, 13, 13, 14, 14, 14, 18, 23; 3:3, 13, 17, 22; 4:6, 9, 13; 5:1; 6:3, 13, 13, 15, 17, 17, 21; 7:15; 8:17, 21; 9:4, 10, 12, 12, 15, 16, 17, 17, 18; 10:9, 12; 11:6, 9; 12:12, 18, 19; 13:9, 18; 14:2, 3, 6, 7, 8, 15, 17, 23; 15:2, 3, 13, 16; 16:6, 14; 17:4, 10, 12, 12, 12, 13, 13, 14, 17, 17; 18:9, 14, 20, 20, 21; 19:8, 13, 20, 20, 20, 31, 31, 37, 38; 20:2, 3, 5, 5, 7, 11, 12, 12, 13, 13, 15, 16; 21:13, 17, 22; 22:7, 14, 17; 23:2, 9, 9, 11, 15, 15, 19, 20; 24:23, 35, 51, 65, 65; 25:9, 18; 26:7, 7, 9, 9, 10, 20, 33; 27:11, 20, 22, 27, 33, 36; 28:16, 17, 17, 17; 29:6, 6, 7, 7, 19, 25; 30:15, 30, 33; 31:5, 14, 16, 29, 32, 35, 36, 36, 43, 48, 50, 50; 32:2, 8, 18, 18, 20, 27, 29, 30, 32; 33:11, 17, 18; 34:14, 21; 35:6, 6, 10, 19, 20, 27; 36:1, 8, 19, 43; 37:10, 22, 26, 27, 30, 33, 33; 38:14, 18, 21, 24; 39:8, 9; 40:8, 12, 18; 41:15, 16, 25, 25, 26, 28, 28, 32, 32, 38, 38, 39; 42:2, 13, 13, 14, 21, 22, 28, 28, 28, 30, 32, 32, 36, 36, 38, 38; 43:7, 27, 27, 28, 28, 29, 32; 44:5, 10, 15, 16, 17, 20, 20, 28, 30, 31; 45:12, 20, 26, 26, 28, 28; 46:33, 34; 47:3, 4, 6, 18, 18, 23; 48:1, 7, 18; 49:9, 14, 21, 22, 24, 28, 29, 30, 30, 32; 50:10, 11, 11, 20; **Ex** 1:22; 2:6, 14, 18, 20, 20; 3:3, 5, 9, 13, 15, 15, 16; 4:2, 14, 22; 5:2, 16, 16, 22; 7:14, 17, 18; 8:10, 19, 26; 9:3, 3, 4, 14, 27, 28, 29; 10:5, 7, 10; 11:5; 12:11, 19, 22, 22, 27, 42, 42, 43, 44, 48, 49; 13:2, 8, 14; 14:12; 15:2, 2, 2, 3, 3, 6, 11, 11, 26; 16:1, 15, 15, 16, 23, 23, 25, 26, 32, 36; 17:3, 7; 18:11, 14, 17, 18, 18; 19:5; 20:4, 4, 4, 10, 10, 11, 17, 20; 21:21, 30; 22:16,

IT [6132]

ITSELF [50]

LEST [240]

LET [1511]

LIKE [669]

LIKEWISE [107]

Idx

MAYEST [114]

ME [4096]

MYSELF [118]

NAMELY [23]

NAY [55]

NEITHER [879]

NEVER [86]

NEVERTHELESS [97]

NEXT [60]

NO [1393]

NONE [358]

NOR [758]

NOT [6596]

Idx

Idx

ONE'S [2]

ONES [77]

ONLY [253]

OR [1130]

OTHER [465]

OTHER'S [1]

OTHERS [67]

OTHERWISE [15]

OUGHT [100]

13:14; 19:7; **Ac** 4:32; 5:29; 17:29; 19:36; 20:35; 21:21; 24:19, 19; 25:10, 24; 26:9; 28:19; **Ro** 8:26; 12:3; 15:1; **1Co** 8:2; 11:7, 10; **2Co** 2:3, 7; 12:11, 14; **Eph** 5:28; 6:20; **Col** 4:4, 6; **1Th** 4:1; **2Th** 3:7; **1Ti** 5:13; **Tit** 1:11; **Phm** 1:18; **Heb** 2:1; 5:3, 12; **Jas** 3:10; 4:15; **2Pe** 3:11; **1Jn** 2:6; 3:16; 4:11; **3Jn** 1:8

OUGHTEST [4]

1Ki 2:9; **Mt** 25:27; **Ac** 10:6; **1Ti** 3:15

OUR [1165]

Ge 1:26, 26; 5:29, 29; 19:31, 32, 32, 34; 23:6; 24:60; 29:26; 31:1, 1, 14, 15, 16, 16, 32; 33:12; 34:9, 14, 16, 17, 21, 31; 37:26, 27, 27, 27; 41:12; 42:13, 21, 32, 32; 43:4, 7, 7, 8, 18, 18, 21, 21, 21, 22, 22, 22, 28; 44:8, 25, 26, 26, 31; 46:34, 34; 47:3, 18, 18, 18, 18, 19, 19, 19, 25; **Ex** 1:10; 3:18; 5:3, 8, 21; 8:10, 26, 27; 10:9, 9, 9, 9, 9, 25, 26, 26; 12:27; 17:3, 3; 34:9, 9; **Lev** 25:20; **Nu** 11:6, 6; 13:33; 14:3, 3; 20:3, 4, 15, 15, 16; 21:5; 27:3, 4, 4; 31:49, 50; 32:16, 16, 17, 18, 19, 26, 26, 26, 26, 32; 36:2, 3, 3, 4; **Dt** 1:6, 19, 20, 25, 28, 28, 41; 2:1, 8, 29, 33, 36, 37; 3:3, 3; 4:7; 5:2, 3, 24, 25, 27, 27; 6:4, 20, 22, 23, 24, 24, 25, 25; 21:7, 7, 20, 20; 26:3, 7, 7, 7, 7, 7, 15; 29:15, 18, 29, 29; 31:17; 32:3, 27, 31, 31; **Jos** 2:11, 13, 14, 14, 19, 20, 24; 5:13; 7:9; 9:11, 11, 12, 12, 12, 13, 13, 24; 17:4; 18:6; 21:2; 22:19, 24, 25, 27, 27, 27, 27, 27, 28, 28, 29; 24:17, 17, 17, 18, 24; **Jdg** 6:13; 9:3; 10:10; 11:2, 6, 8, 24; 13:23; 16:23, 23, 23, 24, 24, 24, 24; 18:5; 19:19; 21:7, 18, 22; **Ru** 2:20; 3:2; 4:3; **1Sa** 2:2; 4:3; 5:7, 10, 11; 7:8; 8:20, 20; 9:6, 7, 8; 12:10, 19; 14:9, 10; 16:16; 17:9, 47; 20:29; 23:20; 25:14, 17; 30:23; **2Sa** 7:22; 10:12, 12; 12:18; 18:12; 19:9, 41, 43, 43; 22:32; **1Ki** 1:11, 43, 47; 8:21, 40, 53, 57, 57, 58, 58, 59, 61, 65; 12:4, 10; 20:31, 31; **2Ki** 7:9; 18:22; 19:19; 22:13; **1Ch** 12:17, 19; 13:2, 2, 3; 15:13; 16:14, 35; 17:20; 19:13, 13; 28:2, 8; 29:10, 13, 15, 15, 16, 18; **2Ch** 2:4, 5; 6:31; 10:4, 10; 13:10, 11, 12; 14:7, 11, 11; 19:7; 20:6, 7, 9, 12, 12; 28:13, 13, 13; 29:6, 6, 9, 9, 9, 9; 32:8, 8, 11; 34:21; **Ezr** 4:3; 5:12; 7:27; 8:17, 18, 21, 21, 21, 22, 23, 25, 30, 31, 33; 9:6, 6, 6, 7, 7, 7, 7, 8, 8, 8, 8, 9, 9, 9, 10, 13, 13, 13, 13, 15; 10:2, 3, 3, 14, 14, 14; **Ne** 4:4, 9, 9, 11, 15, 20, 23; 5:2, 2, 3, 4, 5, 5, 5, 5, 5, 5, 5, 8, 8, 9, 9; 6:1, 16, 16; 8:10; 9:9, 16, 32, 32, 32, 32, 32, 32, 34, 34, 34, 34, 36, 37, 37, 37, 38; 10:29, 30, 30, 32, 33, 34, 34, 34, 35, 36, 36, 36, 36, 36, 36, 37, 37, 37, 37, 37, 38, 39; 13:2, 4, 18, 27; **Job** 8:9; 17:16; 22:20; 28:22; 37:19; **Ps** 8:1, 9; 12:4, 4, 4; 17:11; 18:31; 20:5, 5, 7; 22:4; 33:20, 20, 20, 21; 35:21; 40:3; 44:1, 1, 5, 7, 9, 13, 18, 18, 20, 20, 24, 24, 25, 25, 26; 46:1, 7, 11; 47:3, 4, 6; 48:1, 8, 14, 14; 50:3; 59:11; 60:10, 12; 65:3, 5; 66:8, 9, 9, 11, 12; 67:6; 68:19, 20; 74:9; 77:13; 78:3, 5; 79:4, 9, 9, 10, 12; 80:6, 6; 81:1, 3; 84:9; 85:4, 9, 12; 89:17, 18, 18; 90:1, 8, 8, 9, 9, 10, 12, 12, 14, 17, 17, 17; 92:13; 94:23; 95:1, 6, 7; 98:3; 99:5, 8, 9, 9; 103:10, 10, 12, 14; 105:7; 106:6, 7, 47; 108:11, 13; 113:5; 115:3; 116:5; 118:23; 122:2, 9; 123:2, 2, 4; 124:1, 2, 4, 5, 7, 8; 126:2, 2, 4; 135:2, 5; 136:23, 24; 137:2; 141:7; 144:12, 12, 13, 13, 13, 14, 14; 147:1, 5, 7; **Pr** 1:13; 7:18; **SS** 1:16, 17, 17; 2:9, 12, 15; 7:13; 8:8; **Isa** 1:10; 3:6; 4:1, 1, 1; 20:6; 25:9; 26:8, 12, 13; 28:15; 33:2, 20, 22, 22, 22; 35:2; 36:7; 37:20; 38:20; 40:3, 8; 42:17; 47:4; 52:10; 53:1, 3, 4, 4, 5, 5, 5; 55:7; 58:3; 59:12, 12, 12, 12, 13; 61:2, 6; 63:16, 16, 16, 17, 18; 64:6, 6, 7, 8, 8, 11, 11, 11, 11; **Jer** 3:22, 23, 24, 24, 25, 25, 25, 25, 25, 25; 5:19, 24; 6:24; 8:14; 9:18, 18, 19, 21, 21; 11:21; 12:4; 14:7, 7, 20, 20, 22; 16:10, 10, 10, 19; 17:12; 18:12; 20:10; 21:13; 23:6, 36; 26:16, 19; 31:6; 33:16; 35:6, 8, 8, 8, 8, 8, 10; 36:15; 37:3; 42:2, 6, 6, 20, 20; 43:2; 44:17, 17, 17, 17, 19, 25; 46:16, 16; 50:28; 51:10, 10, 51; **La** 3:40, 41, 41, 44, 46; 4:17, 17, 17, 18, 18, 18, 18, 18, 19, 20, 20; 5:1, 2, 2, 3, 4, 4, 5, 7, 9, 9, 10, 15, 15, 16, 17, 17, 21; **Eze** 33:10, 10, 21; 37:11, 11, 11; 40:1; **Da** 1:13; 3:17; 9:6, 6, 6, 8, 8, 8, 9, 10, 12, 13, 13, 13, 14, 15, 16, 16, 17, 18, 18, 18; **Hos** 7:5; 14:2, 3, 3; **Joel** 1:16, 16; **Am** 6:13; **Mic** 2:4; 4:5, 11; 5:5, 5, 6, 6; 7:17, 19, 20; **Zec** 1:6, 6; 9:7; **Mal** 2:10; **Mt** 3:9; 6:9, 11, 12, 12; 8:17, 17; 20:33; 21:42; 23:30; 25:8; 27:25; **Mk** 9:40; 11:10; 12:11, 29; **Lk** 1:55, 71, 72, 73, 74, 75, 78, 79; 3:8; 7:5; 11:2, 3, 4; 13:26; 17:5, 10; 23:41; 24:20, 22, 32; **Jn** 3:11; 4:12, 20; 6:31; 7:51; 8:39, 53; 9:20; 11:11, 48; 12:38; 14:23; 19:7; **Ac** 2:8, 11, 39; 3:12, 13, 25; 5:30; 7:2, 11, 12, 15, 19, 19, 38, 39, 44, 45, 45; 13:17; 14:17; 15:10, 25, 26, 36; 16:20; 17:20, 28; 19:25, 27; 20:21; 21:5, 5, 6, 7, 15; 22:14; 24:6, 7; 26:5, 6, 7; 27:10, 19; 28:17, 25; **Ro** 1:3, 7; 3:5; 4:1, 12, 24, 25, 25; 5:1, 5, 11, 21; 6:6, 11, 23; 7:5, 25; 8:16, 23, 26, 39; 9:10; 10:16; 12:7; 13:11; 15:4, 6; 16:1, 9, 18, 20, 24; **1Co** 1:1, 2, 3, 7, 8, 9, 10; 2:7; 4:12; 5:4, 4, 7; 6:11; 9:1, 10, 10; 10:1, 6, 11; 12:23, 24; 15:3, 14, 31, 57; 16:12, 23; **2Co** 1:1, 2, 3, 4, 5, 7, 8, 11, 12, 12, 12, 18, 22; 3:2, 2, 5; 4:3, 6, 10, 11, 16, 17; 5:1, 2, 12; 6:11, 11; 7:3, 4, 5, 12, 14; 8:9, 22, 23, 24; 9:3; 10:4, 8, 13, 14, 15, 15, 16; 11:31; **Gal** 1:3, 4, 4; 2:4; 3:24; 6:14, 18; **Eph** 1:2, 3, 14, 17; 2:3, 3, 14; 3:11, 14; 5:20; 6:22, 24; **Php** 1:2; 3:20, 21; 4:20, 23; **Col** 1:1, 2, 3, 7; 3:4; **1Th** 1:1, 2, 3, 3, 5; 2:1, 2, 3, 4, 8, 9, 19, 19, 20; 3:2, 2, 5, 7, 9, 11, 11, 11, 13, 13; 5:9, 23, 28; **2Th** 1:1, 2, 8, 10, 11, 12, 12; 2:1, 1, 14, 14, 15, 16, 16; 3:6, 12, 14, 18; **1Ti** 1:1, 1, 2, 2, 12, 14; 2:3; 6:3, 14; **2Ti** 1:2, 8, 9, 10; 4:15; **Tit** 1:3, 4; 2:10, 13; 3:4, 6; **Phm** 1:1, 1, 2, 2, 3, 25; **Heb** 1:3; 3:1, 14; 4:14, 15; 7:14; 10:22, 22, 23; 12:2, 9, 10, 29; 13:15, 20, 23; **Jas** 2:1, 21; 3:6; **1Pe** 1:3; 2:24; 4:3; **2Pe** 1:1, 2, 8, 11, 14, 16; 3:15, 15, 18; **1Jn** 1:1, 1, 3, 9, 9; 2:2; 3:5, 16, 19, 20, 20, 21; 4:10, 17; 5:4; **2Jn** 1:12; **3Jn** 1:12, 14; **Jude** 1:4, 4, 17, 21, 25; **Rev** 1:5; 5:10; 6:10; 7:3, 10, 12; 11:8, 15; 12:10, 10, 10; 19:1, 5; 22:21

OURS [12]

Ge 26:20; 31:16; 34:23; **Nu** 32:32; **1Ki** 22:3; **Eze** 36:2; **Mk** 12:7; **Lk** 20:14; **1Co** 1:2; **2Co** 1:14; **Tit** 3:14; **1Jn** 2:2

OURSELVES [51]

Ge 37:10; 44:16; **Nu** 32:17; **Dt** 2:35; 3:7; **1Sa** 14:8; **1Ch** 19:13; **Ezr** 4:3; 8:21; **Ne** 10:32; **Job** 34:4; **Ps** 83:12; 100:3; **Pr** 7:18; **Isa** 28:15; 56:12; **Jer** 50:5; **Lk** 22:71; **Jn** 4:42; **Ac** 6:4; 23:14; **Ro** 8:23, 23, 23; 15:1; **1Co** 11:31; **2Co** 1:4, 9, 9; 3:1, 5, 5; 4:2, 5, 5; 5:12, 13; 6:4; 7:1; 10:12, 12, 14; 12:19; **Gal** 2:17; **1Th** 2:10; **2Th** 1:4; 3:7, 9; **Tit** 3:3; **Heb** 10:25; **1Jn** 1:8

OUT [2777]

Ge 2:9, 10, 19, 23; 3:19, 24; 4:14, 16; 8:10, 19; 9:10; 10:11, 14; 12:1, 4; 13:1; 14:8, 17; 15:4, 7, 14; 17:6; 19:5, 6, 8, 12, 14, 14, 24, 29, 30; 21:10, 17, 21; 22:11, 15; 23:4, 8; 24:11, 13, 15, 29, 44, 63; 25:25, 26; 26:8; 27:3, 30; 28:10, 16; 29:2; 30:16, 16; 31:13, 33; 32:25; 34:1, 6, 7, 24, 24, 26, 26; 35:9, 11; 37:14, 21, 22, 23, 28; 38:28, 28, 29, 30; 39:12, 15, 18; 40:14, 15, 17; 41:2, 3, 14, 18, 33, 45, 46; 43:2, 23, 31; 44:4, 8, 8, 16, 28; 45:1, 19, 24, 25; 46:26; 47:1, 10, 30; 48:12, 14, 22; 49:20; 50:24; **Ex** 1:5, 10, 10; 2:10, 11, 13, 19; 3:2, 4, 8, 8, 10, 11, 12, 17, 20; 4:6, 7, 9; 5:10; 6:1, 6, 6, 6, 7, 11, 13, 26, 27; 7:2, 4, 5, 15, 19; 8:6, 12, 13, 13, 13, 16, 17, 29, 30; 9:15, 29, 33; 10:5, 6, 11, 12, 18, 21; 11:1, 4, 8, 8, 8, 10; 12:5, 15, 17, 21, 22, 33, 39, 39, 41, 42, 46, 51; 13:3, 3, 3, 4, 8, 9, 14, 16, 18; 14:8, 10, 11, 16, 21, 26, 30; 15:12, 20, 22; 16:1, 4, 6, 27, 29; 17:3, 6, 9, 9, 14; 18:1, 7, 9, 10, 10, 21, 25; 19:1, 3, 17; 20:2, 2; 21:2, 3, 3, 4, 5, 7, 11, 27; 22:6, 7; 23:13, 15, 16, 28, 29, 30, 31; 24:16; 25:32, 32, 32, 33, 35; 28:35; 29:23, 46; 32:1, 1, 4, 7, 8, 8, 11, 12, 19, 23, 24, 27, 32, 33; 33:1, 2, 7, 8, 11; 34:11, 18, 24, 34, 34; 37:7, 8, 9, 18, 18, 18, 19, 21; **Lev** 1:1, 15; 2:14; 4:12, 12, 18, 25, 30, 34; 5:9, 15, 18; 6:6, 12, 13; 7:14, 35; 8:26, 33; 9:9, 23, 24; 10:2, 4, 5, 7, 14; 11:45; 13:12, 20, 25, 56, 56, 56, 56; 14:3, 8, 38, 41, 43, 45, 53; 15:2, 16, 25; 16:17, 18; 17:3, 13; 18:24, 25, 28, 28; 19:36; 20:22, 23; 21:12; 22:33; 23:17, 43; 24:10, 23; 25:12, 28, 30, 31, 33, 38, 42, 51, 54, 55; 26:6, 13, 33, 45; 27:21; **Nu** 1:1; 3:9; 5:2, 3, 4, 23, 25; 6:19; 9:1; 10:12, 33, 34; 11:15, 20, 20, 24, 26; 12:4, 4, 12, 14, 15; 13:16, 17; 14:44; 15:41; 16:13, 14, 27, 35, 37, 46; 17:9; 18:29, 29; 20:5, 8, 10, 11, 16, 18, 20; 21:5, 13, 23, 26, 28, 32, 32, 33; 22:5, 6, 11, 11, 23, 32, 36; 23:7, 22; 24:7, 8, 17, 17, 19; 26:4; 27:17, 17, 21; 28:26; 30:2, 6, 12; 31:5, 27, 28, 36; 32:11, 21, 23, 24; 33:1, 2, 2, 3, 12, 38, 52, 55; 34:5, 7, 8, 9, 10, 12; 35:26; **Dt** 1:22, 24, 27, 33, 44; 2:14, 23, 26, 32; 3:1, 8; 4:12, 15, 20, 20, 33, 34, 36, 36, 37, 37, 38, 45, 46; 5:4, 6, 15, 15, 22, 23, 24, 26; 6:12, 19, 21, 23; 7:1, 8, 8, 19, 19, 22; 8:3, 7, 9, 14, 15; 9:3, 4, 4, 5, 7, 10, 12, 12, 14, 16, 17, 21, 26, 28, 28, 29, 29; 10:4; 11:2, 10, 23, 28; 12:3, 5, 27; 13:5, 5, 5, 10, 13; 15:11, 13, 14, 14, 14; 16:1, 3, 3, 6; 17:18; 18:5, 6, 12; 20:1, 1; 21:19; 22:21, 24; 23:4, 10, 23; 24:1, 2, 3, 5, 9, 11; 25:4, 6, 11, 17, 19; 26:4, 8, 13; 27:18; 28:6, 7, 19, 25, 38, 57; 29:7, 20, 21, 25, 28; 30:4; 31:2, 21, 32:13, 13, 39; 33:18, 27; **Jos** 1:8; 2:1, 2, 3, 5, 7, 10, 19; 3:10, 12, 12; 4:2, 2, 3, 3, 4, 8, 16, 17, 18, 19, 20; 5:4, 4, 5, 5, 6; 6:1, 10, 22, 22, 23, 25; 7:23, 23; 8:3, 5, 6, 14, 17, 18, 18, 19, 19, 22, 26; 9:12, 26; 10:22, 22, 23, 24; 11:4; 13:6, 12; 14:7, 11, 12; 15:3, 4, 4, 7, 9, 11, 11, 11, 63; 16:2, 3, 6, 7, 8, 8, 10; 17:12, 13, 18; 18:4, 12, 14, 15, 15; 19:9, 12, 13, 17, 24, 27, 32, 34, 40, 47; 20:2, 8, 8, 8; 21:3, 4, 4, 4, 4, 5, 5, 5, 6, 6, 6, 6, 7, 7, 7, 9, 9, 16, 17, 20, 23, 25, 27, 28, 30, 32, 34, 36, 38; 22:9, 31, 32; 23:5, 9, 13; 24:5, 6, 10, 12, 17, 18, 32; **Jdg** 1:16, 19, 19, 21, 24, 27, 28, 29, 30, 31, 32, 33; 2:1, 3, 12, 15, 16, 17, 18, 21, 23; 3:10, 19, 20, 22, 22, 24; 4:6, 14, 18, 22; 5:4, 4, 14, 14, 14, 28; 6:8, 9, 9, 9, 19, 20, 21, 21, 30, 38; 7:23, 23, 23; 8:34; 9:4, 15, 17, 20, 20, 27, 29, 33, 35, 38, 39, 41, 42, 43; 10:12; 11:2, 3, 5, 7, 13, 24, 34, 36; 12:2; 13:5; 14:9, 12, 14, 14, 18; 15:17; 16:14, 20, 20, 21, 25; 17:7, 8; 18:2, 11, 11, 14, 17; 19:1, 16, 23, 24, 27, 30; 20:1, 10, 14, 14, 15, 20, 21, 25, 28, 31, 33, 33, 33, 34, 38, 40, 42; 21:16, 17, 21, 21, 24; **Ru** 1:7, 13, 21, 22; 2:6, 17, 22; 4:3; **1Sa** 1:3, 15, 16; 2:3, 5, 8, 10, 28; 3:3; 4:1, 3, 3, 8, 12, 13, 16, 16; 5:10; 7:3, 6, 8, 11, 14; 8:8, 18, 20; 9:11, 14, 16, 16, 26; 10:18, 18, 18, 19; 11:2, 3, 5, 7, 10; 12:6, 8, 10, 11; 13:10, 17, 23; 14:11, 48; 15:6; 16:16; 17:4, 4, 8, 23, 34, 35, 35, 37, 37, 37, 40, 51; 18:5, 6, 11, 13, 16; 19:3, 8, 10; 20:11, 11, 21, 35, 36, 41; 21:5; 23:13, 15, 23; 24:2, 7, 8, 14, 15, 21; 25:5, 14, 29, 29, 37; 26:4, 19, 20, 24; 27:1; 28:1, 3, 9, 13, 17; 29:6; 30:16, 16; **2Sa** 1:2, 3; 2:12, 13, 23; 3:18, 18, 25, 26; 4:4, 9; 5:2, 13, 24; 6:3, 4, 20; 7:6, 9, 12; 8:1; 9:5; 10:3, 8, 16; 11:8, 13, 17, 23; 12:7, 11; 13:9, 9, 9, 17, 18; 14:16, 16; 15:11, 24, 35; 16:5, 7, 7; 17:1, 21; 18:3, 4, 6; 19:9, 9, 9, 19; 20:7, 7, 8, 10, 12, 13, 16, 22; 21:10, 17; 22:1, 7, 9, 9, 15, 17, 46; 23:4, 16, 16, 21, 29; 24:4, 7, 16, 20; **1Ki** 1:29, 39; 2:27, 37, 42, 46; 3:7; 4:23, 33; 5:6, 13; 6:1, 8; 7:13, 47; 8:1, 8, 8, 9, 10, 16, 16, 19, 21, 41, 42, 44, 51, 53; 9:7, 7, 9, 12, 24; 10:28, 29, 29; 11:12, 18, 18, 29, 31, 32, 34, 35; 12:25, 28; 13:1, 3, 5; 14:15, 21, 24; 15:12, 17; 16:2; 17:19, 23; 18:28, 44; 19:13; 20:16, 17, 17, 17, 18, 18, 19, 21, 24, 31, 39, 42; 21:10, 13, 26; 22:3, 32, 34, 35, 46; **2Ki** 2:23, 24; 3:6; 4:4, 5, 18, 21, 37, 39, 40, 40, 41; 5:2, 2, 11, 27; 6:7, 27, 27; 7:12, 12, 16, 20; 8:3; 9:2, 15, 19, 21, 21, 24, 30, 32; 10:3, 9, 25, 26, 28; 11:8, 9; 12:11, 12; 13:5, 25, 25; 14:27; 16:3, 7, 7; 17:7, 8, 18, 20, 23, 23, 36, 36, 39; 18:18, 29, 31, 33, 34, 35, 35; 19:9, 19, 27, 31, 31, 35; 20:4, 6; 21:2, 7, 8, 15; 23:4, 6, 8, 16, 18, 27; 24:3, 7, 12, 13, 20; 25:7, 19, 21, 27; **1Ch** 5:18; 6:60, 61, 61, 62, 62, 62, 63, 63, 63, 65, 65, 65, 66, 70, 71, 72, 74, 76, 77, 78, 80; 7:11; 9:28; 11:2, 18, 18, 23; 12:2, 17; 13:7; 14:8, 15, 17; 15:25, 29; 16:33; 17:21, 21; 18:1; 19:3, 6, 6, 6, 9, 10; 20:1, 2, 3; 21:16, 21; 26:14, 27; 27:1; 28:18; **2Ch** 1:10, 16, 17, 17; 2:2, 8, 14, 16; 4:18; 5:2, 9, 10, 11; 6:5, 9, 32, 34; 7:20, 20, 22; 8:11; 9:28, 28; 10:2; 11:13, 16; 12:3, 7, 13; 13:9; 14:5, 8, 8, 9, 10; 15:2, 5, 8, 8, 9, 9, 9, 17; 16:1, 2, 2, 7; 17:6; 18:20, 21, 21, 31, 33; 19:2, 3, 4; 20:4, 7, 10, 11, 17, 21; 21:15, 19; 22:7; 23:2, 7, 8, 11, 14; 24:5, 6, 6; 25:6, 10, 15; 26:11, 18, 20, 20; 28:3, 9, 21, 21; 29:5, 7, 16, 16; 30:6, 25, 25; 31:1, 1; 32:11, 13, 14, 14, 15, 15, 15, 15, 17, 17; 33:2, 8, 15, 15; 34:14, 21, 25, 33; 35:20, 24; **Ezr** 1:7; 2:1; 3:8; 5:14, 14; 6:4, 5, 21; 7:20, 28; 8:35; 9:5; 10:1; **Ne** 1:9; 2:13; 3:25, 26, 27; 4:2, 5; 5:13, 13; 6:8; 7:6; 8:17; 9:7, 15, 18, 27; 12:27, 28, 29, 44; 13:8, 14; **Est** 2:9, 13, 23; 3:15; 4:1, 11; 5:2; 7:8, 8; 8:4, 14, 15; 9:4; **Job** 1:17, 21; 3:11, 24; 5:5, 6; 6:17; 8:10, 19; 9:6, 8, 10, 14; 10:7, 10, 18; 11:7, 7, 13; 12:15, 22, 22; 13:9; 14:4, 12, 18, 19; 15:13, 22, 25, 30; 16:13, 20; 18:4, 5, 6, 14, 18; 19:7; 20:15, 25, 25; 21:17; 22:16; 24:4, 12, 12, 24; 26:7; 27:21, 22, 23; 28:2, 2, 3, 4, 5, 10, 27; 29:6, 7, 16, 17, 19, 25; 30:16, 24; 31:7, 8, 12, 34; 32:11, 13; 33:6, 21; 35:9; 36:16, 26; 37:1, 2, 9, 9, 18, 22, 23; 38:1, 8, 13, 29; 39:3, 5; 40:6; 41:1, 19, 19, 20, 20, 21; **Ps** 3:4; 5:10; 8:2; 9:5; 10:5, 15, 16; 14:7; 15:5; 17:1; 18:6, 8, 14, 14, 16, 42, 45; 19:4, 5; 20:2; 21:8, 8; 22:7, 9, 14, 14; 25:15, 17, 22; 27:12; 31:4, 12; 34:6, 17, 19; 35:3; 37:14; 40:2, 2; 42:4; 43:3; 44:2, 2, 20, 21; 45:8; 50:2, 9, 9; 51:1, 9; 52:5, 5; 53:6; 54:7; 55:23; 58:6; 59:7; 60:6, 8, 10; 62:8; 64:6; 66:12; 68:6, 31, 31, 33, 35; 69:14, 14, 24, 28; 71:4, 4, 6; 73:7, 10; 74:11; 75:8, 8; 77:17, 17; 78:15, 16, 20, 55, 65; 79:6; 80:8, 8, 11, 13; 81:5, 10, 16; 82:4, 5; 84:2; 85:5, 11; 88:9; 89:19, 34; 94:12; 97:10; 102:T; 104:2, 14, 35; 105:41; 107:3, 6, 13, 14, 19, 28; 108:7, 9; 109:10, 13, 14; 110:2; 111:2; 113:7, 7; 114:1; 118:26; 119:18, 43; 121:8; 124:7; 128:5; 130:1; 132:5; 134:3; 135:7, 21; 136:6, 11, 12; 142:2, 7; 143:11; 144:6, 7, 14; 147:18; **Pr** 1:23, 24; 2:6, 22; 3:10; 4:23; 5:15, 15; 6:9; 8:12; 9:1; 10:31; 11:8; 12:13; 13:9; 15:2, 28; 17:14, 23; 20:5, 20; 21:16; 22:10, 10; 24:20; 25:1, 2, 19; 26:20; 28:11; 30:17; 31:18, 20; **Ecc** 1:13; 3:11; 4:14; 7:24, 25, 27, 29; 8:3, 17, 17; 12:3, 9, 10; **SS** 3:6; 4:16; 8:11; **Isa** 2:3; 5:2, 25; 8:8; 9:12, 17, 21; 10:4; 11:1, 1, 16; 12:3, 6; 13:9, 13; 14:19, 26, 27, 29; 15:4, 5; 16:2, 4, 8, 10, 10; 18:2, 7; 19:23; 21:11; 22:16, 16; 23:11; 24:18; 26:16, 17, 19, 21; 28:7, 7, 27; 29:4, 4, 4, 4, 9, 10, 18, 18; 30:11, 11, 13, 14; 31:3; 34:3, 3, 11, 16; 35:6; 36:16, 18, 19, 20, 20; 37:28, 32, 32; 38:6; 40:12, 22, 22, 26; 42:5, 5, 7, 7; 43:13, 25; 44:13, 13, 13, 22; 45:12, 23; 46:6, 7; 48:1, 3, 21, 21; 51:17, 22; 52:11, 11, 12; 53:2, 8, 12; 55:11, 12; 57:4, 14; 58:7, 10; 59:5, 21, 21, 21; 62:10, 12; 63:11; 65:2, 9, 9; 66:5, 11, 20; **Jer** 1:5, 10, 14; 2:6, 13; 3:18; 4:1, 16; 5:6, 6; 6:1, 1, 4, 7, 7, 11, 12; 7:15, 15, 18, 20, 22, 25; 8:1, 1; 9:8, 18, 19, 19; 10:3, 12, 13, 17, 18, 22, 25; 11:4, 7; 12:3, 8, 14, 14, 15; 14:16; 15:1, 6, 21, 21; 16:9, 13, 14, 16; 17:8, 16, 19, 22; 18:21, 23; 19:13; 20:3, 8, 18; 21:9, 12, 12; 22:3, 11, 14, 26, 28; 23:3, 7, 8, 16, 39; 24:5; 26:23; 27:10, 15; 30:7, 19; 31:32, 37; 32:4, 17, 21, 21, 29, 37; 34:3, 13, 13; 36:6, 11, 21, 30; 37:4, 5, 12, 17, 21; 38:8, 10, 13, 18, 23, 23; 39:4, 4, 7, 14; 40:12; 44:7, 17, 17, 18, 19, 19, 25, 28; 46:20; 47:2; 48:15, 31, 44, 45; 49:5, 20; 50:3, 8, 8, 28, 45; 51:6, 15, 16, 25, 34, 44, 45, 55; 52:3, 7, 11, 25, 27, 31; **La** 1:10; 2:4, 8, 12, 19, 19; 3:7, 8, 38, 55; 4:1, 3, 11; 5:8; **Eze** 1:4, 4, 4, 5, 13; 3:25; 4:12; 5:2, 12; 6:14; 7:8; 9:8; 10:7, 19; 11:7, 9, 17, 19; 12:5, 12, 14; 13:2, 17, 21, 23; 14:9, 13, 19; 15:7; 16:5, 15, 27, 36; 19:14; 20:8, 9, 10, 13, 14, 21, 28, 33, 33, 34, 34, 34, 34, 38, 38, 41, 41; 21:3, 4, 5, 19, 31; 22:15, 22, 31; 23:26, 34, 48; 24:6, 6, 12; 25:7, 7, 13, 16; 27:6, 33; 28:16; 29:4, 8; 30:13, 22, 25; 31:4, 11; 32:3, 7, 21; 33:21; 34:11, 12, 12, 12, 13, 25, 27; 35:3, 7, 11; 36:5, 20, 24, 26; 37:1, 12, 13, 23; 38:8, 8, 12, 15; 39:3, 3, 10, 10, 14, 27, 29; 42:11, 14; 43:6, 11, 23, 25; 44:3; 45:14, 15, 15, 15; 46:9, 18, 18, 20; 47:1, 2, 2, 8, 12; 48:19, 30; **Da** 2:34, 45; 3:15, 17; 5:2, 3, 3, 13; 6:23, 23; 7:17, 24, 25; 8:4, 7, 9, 22; 9:15; 11:7, 41, 44, 44; **Hos** 1:11; 2:2, 10, 15, 17, 18; 4:2; 5:10; 7:5; 9:15; 10:11; 11:1, 1, 11, 11; 12:8, 13; 13:3, 3; **Joel** 2:16, 28, 29; 3:7, 16; **Am** 3:4, 12, 12; 4:3, 11; 5:3, 6, 8; 6:4, 4, 10, 10; 7:11; 8:8; 9:3, 6, 7, 15; **Ob** 1:6, 8, 8; **Jnh** 1:4; 2:1, 2, 4, 10; 4:5; **Mic** 1:3; 2:9, 13; 4:6, 9, 10; 5:2, 10, 12, 13, 14; 6:4, 4; 7:2, 15, 17; **Na** 1:6, 11, 14; 2:2, 9; **Hab** 1:2; 2:11, 11; 3:4, 13, 14; **Zep** 1:4, 17; 2:4, 13; 3:11, 15, 19; **Hag** 2:5, 16, 16; **Zec** 1:21; 2:3, 13; 3:2; 4:1, 12; 5:9; 6:1, 12; 8:10, 23; 9:4, 7, 11; 10:4, 4, 4, 4, 10, 10; 11:6; 13:2, 2; 14:8; **Mal** 2:8, 12, 13; 3:10; **Mt** 2:6, 15; 3:5, 16; 4:4; 5:13, 26, 29; 7:4, 4, 5, 5, 5, 22; 8:12, 16, 28, 29, 31, 32, 34, 34; 9:17, 32, 33, 34; 10:1, 8, 14; 11:7, 8, 9; 12:11, 14, 24, 26, 27, 27, 28, 34, 35, 35, 43, 44; 13:1, 41, 52; 14:13, 26, 29, 35; 15:11, 17, 18, 19, 22; 17:5, 18, 19, 21; 18:9, 28; 20:1, 3, 5, 6, 30; 21:12, 16, 17, 33, 39, 41; 22:10, 16; 23:24; 24:1, 17, 27; 25:6, 8; 26:30, 51, 55, 71, 75; 27:23, 32, 53, 60; **Mk** 1:5, 10, 23, 25, 26, 29, 34, 35, 39, 45; 3:5, 15, 21, 22, 23; 4:3, 32; 5:2, 2, 8, 10, 13, 14, 17, 30, 40; 6:1, 12, 13, 33, 34, 49, 54; 7:15, 19, 20, 21, 26, 29, 30; 8:23, 27; 9:7, 18, 24, 25, 26, 28, 38, 47; 10:26, 46, 47; 11:11, 15, 19; 12:1, 8, 8; 13:1, 15; 14:26, 48, 68; 15:13, 14, 20, 21, 39, 46; 16:8, 9, 17; **Lk** 1:22, 42, 74; 2:1, 4; 4:14, 22, 29, 33, 35, 35, 36, 37, 38, 41, 41; 5:2, 3, 3, 4, 17, 36; 6:12, 17, 19, 22, 42, 42, 42, 45, 45; 7:12, 24, 25, 26; 8:2, 4, 5, 12, 27, 28, 29, 31, 33, 35, 35, 38, 46, 54; 9:5, 35, 38, 39, 40, 49; 10:10, 35; 11:14, 14, 15, 18, 19, 19, 20, 24, 24, 54; 12:54; 13:28, 31, 32, 33; 14:5, 7, 21, 23, 35; 15:28; 16:4; 17:24, 29; 19:22, 40, 45; 20:12, 15; 21:21, 37; 22:39, 52, 62; 23:18, 26; 24:31, 50; **Jn** 1:46; 2:8, 15, 15; 4:30, 47, 54; 6:37; 7:38, 41, 42, 52; 8:59; 9:22, 34, 35; 10:3, 9, 28, 29, 39; 11:11, 31, 55; 12:17, 31, 34, 42; 13:1, 30, 31; 15:19; 16:2, 27; 17:6, 8, 15; 18:16, 29, 38; 19:6, 12, 15, 34; 20:2; **Ac** 1:9, 18, 21; 2:5, 17, 18; 3:19; 4:15; 5:6, 9, 16; 6:3; 7:3, 4, 10, 19, 21, 36, 40, 45, 57, 58; 8:7, 9, 39; 9:1, 28; 10:45; 12:9, 10, 11, 17; 13:17, 42, 50; 14:14, 19; 15:14, 24; 16:13, 18, 27, 27, 30, 37, 37, 39, 39, 40; 17:2, 5; 19:12, 16, 28, 33, 34; 21:5, 28, 30, 38; 22:18, 23; 23:6; 24:7; 27:19, 29, 30, 30, 38, 42; 28:3, 21, 23, 23; **Ro** 2:18; 3:12; 11:24, 26, 33; 13:11; **1Co** 5:7, 10; 9:9; 14:36; 15:8; **2Co** 1:8; 2:4; 4:6; 6:17; 8:11; 12:2, 3; **Gal** 2:4; 4:15, 30; **Eph** 4:29; **Php** 1:12; 2:12; **Col** 2:14, 14; 3:8; **1Th** 1:8; **2Th** 2:7; **1Ti** 1:5; 5:18; 6:7; **2Ti** 1:17; 2:22, 26; 3:11; 4:2, 17; **Heb** 3:16; 5:2; 7:5, 14; 8:9; 11:8, 8, 15, 34; 12:13; **Jas** 2:25; 3:10, 13; **1Pe** 2:9; **2Pe** 2:9; 3:5; **1Jn** 2:19, 19; 4:1, 18; **3Jn** 1:10; **Jude** 1:5, 13, 23; **Rev** 1:16; 2:5; 3:5, 5, 12, 12, 16; 4:5; 5:7, 9; 6:4, 14; 7:14; 8:4; 9:2, 3, 17, 18; 10:10; 11:2, 5, 7, 12:9, 9, 9, 15, 16; 13:1, 11; 14:10, 15, 17, 18, 20; 15:6; 16:1, 1, 2, 3, 4, 7, 8, 10, 12, 13, 13, 13, 17, 17, 21; 17:8; 18:4; 19:5, 15, 21; 20:7, 8, 9, 12; 21:2, 3, 10; 22:1, 19, 19

OVER [1009]

Ge 1:18, 18, 26, 26, 26, 26, 26, 28, 28, 28; 3:16; 4:7; 8:1; 9:14; 21:16, 16; 24:2; 25:25; 27:29; 31:21, 52, 52; 32:10, 16, 21, 22, 23, 23, 31; 33:3, 14; 36:31; 37:8, 8; 39:4, 5; 41:33, 34, 40, 41, 43, 45, 56; 42:6; 45:26; 47:6, 20, 26; 49:22; **Ex** 1:8, 11; 2:14; 5:14; 8:5, 5, 5, 6, 9; 10:12, 13, 14, 21; 12:13, 23, 27; 14:2, 7, 16, 21, 26, 27; 15:16, 16; 16:18, 23; 18:21, 25; 25:27, 37; 26:12, 13, 35; 28:27; 30:6; 36:14; 37:9, 14; 39:20; 40:19, 24, 36; **Lev** 14:5, 6, 50; 16:21; 25:43, 46, 46, 53; 26:16, 17; **Nu** 1:50, 50, 50; 3:32, 49; 4:6; 5:30; 7:2; 8:2, 3; 10:10, 10, 14, 15, 16, 18, 19, 20, 22, 23, 24, 25, 26, 27; 11:16; 14:14; 16:13; 22:5; 25:15; 27:16; 31:14, 14, 48; 32:5, 7, 21, 27, 29, 30, 32; 33:51; 35:10; **Dt** 1:1, 13, 15, 15, 15, 15, 15; 2:13, 13, 14, 18, 19, 24, 29; 3:18, 25, 27, 28, 29; 4:14, 21, 22, 22, 26, 46; 9:1, 3; 11:30, 31; 12:10; 15:6, 6; 17:14, 15, 15, 15; 21:6; 24:20; 27:2, 3, 4, 12; 28:23, 36, 63, 63; 30:9, 9, 13, 18; 31:2, 3, 3, 13, 15; 32:11, 47, 49; 34:1, 4, 6; **Jos** 1:2, 11; 2:23; 3:1, 6, 11, 14, 16, 17, 17; 4:1, 3, 5, 7, 8, 10, 11, 11, 12, 13, 18, 22, 23, 23; 5:1, 13; 7:7, 26; 8:31, 33, 33; 9:1; 18:13, 17, 18; 22:11, 19; 24:11; **Jdg** 3:28; 5:13, 13; 6:33; 8:4, 22, 23, 23, 23; 9:2, 2, 8, 8, 9, 10, 11, 12, 13, 14, 15, 18, 22, 26; 10:9, 18; 11:8, 11, 29, 29, 29, 32; 12:1, 3, 5; 14:4; 15:11; 19:10, 12; 20:43; **Ru** 2:5, 6; 3:9; **1Sa** 2:1; 8:1, 7, 9, 11, 12, 12, 19; 9:16, 17; 10:1, 19; 11:12; 12:1, 12, 13, 14; 13:1, 7, 14; 14:1, 4, 5, 5, 6, 8, 23, 47; 15:1, 1, 7, 17, 26, 35; 16:1; 17:50; 18:5, 13; 19:20; 22:2, 9; 23:17; 25:30; 26:13, 22; 27:2; 30:10; **2Sa** 1:17, 17, 24; 2:4, 7, 8, 9, 9, 9, 9, 9, 10, 11, 15, 29; 3:10, 10, 17, 21, 33, 34; 4:12; 5:2, 2, 3, 5, 5, 12, 17, 23; 6:21, 21; 7:8, 8, 11, 26; 8:15, 16, 18; 10:17; 12:7; 15:22, 22, 23, 23, 23; 16:9, 13; 17:16,

19, 20, 21, 22, 22, 24; 18:1, 8, 24, 33; 19:10, 15, 17, 18, 18, 18, 22, 31, 31, 33, 36, 37, 38, 39, 39, 41; 20:21, 23, 23, 23, 24; 22:30; 23:3, 23; 24:5; **1Ki** 1:34, 35, 35; 2:11, 35, 37; 4:1, 4, 5, 6, 6, 7, 21, 24, 24; 5:7, 14, 16, 16; 6:1; 7:20, 39; 8:7, 16; 9:23, 23; 11:24, 25, 28, 37, 42; 12:17, 18, 20; 13:30; 14:2, 7, 14; 15:1, 9, 25, 25, 33; 16:2, 8, 16, 18, 23, 29, 29; 19:15, 16; 20:29; 22:31, 41, 51, 51; **2Ki** 2:8, 9, 14; 3:1; 5:11; 8:13, 20, 21; 9:3, 6, 6, 12, 29; 10:5, 5, 22, 36; 11:3, 4, 9, 10, 18, 19; 13:1, 10, 14; 15:5, 8, 17, 23, 27; 17:1; 18:18, 37; 19:2; 21:13; 25:19, 22; **1Ch** 1:43; 5:11; 6:31; 8:32; 9:19, 19, 20, 26, 31, 32, 38; 11:2, 3, 25; 12:4, 14, 14, 15, 38; 14:2, 8, 14; 15:25; 17:7, 10; 18:14, 15, 17; 19:17; 21:16; 22:10; 23:1; 24:31, 31; 26:20, 20, 22, 26, 26, 29, 32; 27:2, 4, 16, 25, 25, 26, 27, 27, 28, 28, 29, 29, 30, 30, 31; 28:1, 1, 1, 4, 4, 5; 29:3, 6, 12, 26, 27, 30, 30, 30; **2Ch** 1:9, 11, 13; 2:11; 4:10; 5:8; 6:5, 6, 36; 8:10; 9:8, 26, 30; 10:17, 18; 13:1, 5; 19:11; 20:6, 27, 31; 22:12; 23:14; 25:5, 5; 26:21; 31:12, 14; 32:6, 11; 34:13; 36:4, 10; **Ezr** 4:10, 20, 20; 9:6; **Ne** 2:7; 3:10, 16, 19, 23, 25, 26, 27, 28, 29, 30, 31; 5:15; 7:2, 3; 9:28, 37, 37, 37; 11:9, 21, 22; 12:8, 9, 24, 24, 37, 38, 44; 13:13, 26; **Est** 1:1; 3:12; 5:1, 1; 8:2; 9:1, 1; **Job** 6:5; 7:12; 14:16; 16:11; 26:7; 34:13; 41:34; 42:11; **Ps** 8:6; 12:4; 13:2; 18:29; 19:13; 23:5; 25:2; 27:12; 30:1; 35:19, 24; 38:4, 16; 41:11; 42:7; 47:2, 8; 49:14; 60:8; 65:13; 66:12; 68:34; 78:50, 62; 83:18; 88:16; 91:11; 103:16, 19; 104:9; 106:41; 108:9, 9; 109:6; 110:6; 118:18; 119:133; 124:4, 5; 145:9; **Pr** 17:2; 19:10, 11; 20:26; 22:7; 24:31; 25:28; 28:15; **Ecc** 1:12; 2:19; 7:14, 16, 16, 17; 8:8, 9; **SS** 2:4, 11; **Isa** 3:4, 12; 8:7, 7, 8; 10:29; 11:15, 15; 14:2; 15:2, 2; 16:8; 19:4, 4, 16; 22:15; 23:2, 6, 11, 12; 25:7, 7; 26:13; 28:19; 31:5, 9; 35:8; 36:3, 22; 37:2; 40:19, 27; 41:2; 45:14, 14; 47:2; 51:10, 23, 23; 52:5; 54:9; 62:5, 5; 63:19; **Jer** 1:10, 10; 2:10; 5:6, 22; 6:17; 13:21; 15:3; 23:4; 31:28, 28, 39; 32:41; 33:26; 40:5, 11; 41:2, 10; 43:10; 44:27; 48:32, 40; 49:19, 22; 50:44; **La** 2:17; 3:54; 5:8; **Eze** 1:20, 21, 22, 25, 26; 3:13; 9:1; 10:1, 2, 4, 18, 19; 11:22; 16:8, 27; 19:8; 20:33; 27:32; 29:15; 32:3, 8, 31; 34:23; 37:24; 40:18, 23; 41:6, 15, 16; 42:1, 3, 3, 7, 10, 10; 45:6, 7; 46:9; 47:5, 5, 20; 48:13, 15, 18, 18, 21, 21, 21; **Da** 1:11; 2:38, 39, 48, 48, 49; 3:12; 4:16, 17, 23, 25, 32; 5:5, 21; 6:1, 1, 2, 3; 9:1; 11:39, 40, 43, 43; **Hos** 10:5, 11; 12:4; **Joel** 2:17; **Ob** 1:12; **Jnh** 2:3; 4:6, 6; **Mic** 3:6, 6; 4:7; **Na** 3:19; **Hab** 1:11, 14; 2:19; **Zep** 3:17, 17; **Hag** 1:10; **Zec** 1:21; 5:3; 9:14; 14:9; **Mt** 2:9; 9:1; 10:23; 14:34; 20:25; 21:2; 24:45, 47; 25:21, 21, 23, 23; 27:37, 45, 61; **Mk** 4:35; 5:1, 21; 6:7, 53; 10:42, 42; 11:2; 12:41; 13:3; 15:26, 33, 39; **Lk** 1:33; 2:8; 4:10, 39; 6:38; 8:22, 26; 9:1; 10:19; 11:42, 44; 12:14, 42, 44; 15:7, 7, 10; 19:14, 17, 19, 27, 30, 41; 22:25; 23:38, 44; **Jn** 6:1, 13, 17; 17:2; 18:1; **Ac** 6:3; 7:10, 11, 16, 27; 8:2; 16:9; 18:23; 19:13; 20:2, 15, 28; 21:2; 27:5, 7, 7; **Ro** 1:28; 5:14; 6:9, 14; 7:1; 9:5, 21; 10:12; 15:12; **1Co** 7:37; 9:12; **2Co** 1:24; 3:13; 8:15; 11:2; **Eph** 1:22; 4:19; **Col** 2:15; **1Th** 3:7; 5:12; **1Ti** 2:12; **Heb** 2:7; 3:6; 9:5; 10:21; 13:7, 17, 24; **Jas** 5:14; **1Pe** 3:12; 5:3; **Jude** 1:7; **Rev** 2:26; 6:8; 9:11; 11:6, 10; 13:7; 14:18; 15:2, 2, 2, 2; 16:9; 17:18; 18:11, 20

PASS [830]

Ge 4:3, 8, 14; 6:1; 7:10; 8:1, 6, 13; 9:14; 11:2; 12:11, 12, 14; 14:1; 15:17; 18:3, 5; 19:17, 29, 34; 20:13; 21:22; 22:1, 20; 24:14, 15, 22, 30, 43, 52; 25:11; 26:8, 32; 27:1, 30, 40; 29:10, 13, 23, 25; 30:25, 32, 41; 31:10, 52, 52; 32:16; 33:14; 34:25; 35:17, 18, 22; 37:23; 38:1, 9, 24, 27, 28, 29; 39:5, 7, 10, 11, 13, 15, 18, 19; 40:1, 20; 41:1, 8, 13, 32; 42:35; 43:2, 21; 44:24, 31; 46:33; 47:24; 48:1; 50:20; **Ex** 1:10, 21; 2:11, 23; 3:21; 4:8, 9, 24; 6:28; 12:12, 13, 23, 23, 25, 26, 29, 41, 41, 51; 13:15, 17; 14:24; 15:16, 16; 16:5, 10, 13, 22, 27; 17:11; 18:13; 19:16; 22:27; 32:19, 30; 33:7, 8, 9, 19, 22, 22; 34:29; 40:17; **Lev** 9:1; 18:21; **Nu** 5:27; 7:1; 10:11, 35; 11:23, 25; 16:31, 42; 17:5, 8; 20:17, 17, 18; 21:8, 9, 22, 23; 22:41; 26:1; 27:7, 8; 32:27, 29, 30, 32; 33:55, 56; 34:4, 4; **Dt** 1:3; 2:4, 16, 18, 24, 27, 28, 29, 30; 3:18; 5:23; 7:12; 9:1, 11; 11:13, 29, 31; 13:2; 18:10, 19, 22; 24:1; 27:2; 28:1, 15, 63; 29:19; 30:1; 31:21, 24; **Jos** 1:1, 11, 11, 14; 2:5; 3:2, 6, 13, 14, 14; 4:1, 5, 11, 18; 5:1, 8, 13; 6:5, 7, 7, 8, 15, 16, 20; 8:5, 14, 24; 9:1, 16; 10:1, 11, 20, 24, 27; 11:1; 15:18; 17:13; 21:45; 22:19; 23:1, 14, 15; 24:29; **Jdg** 1:1, 14, 28; 2:4, 19; 3:27, 28; 6:7, 25; 7:9; 8:33; 9:42; 11:4, 17, 19, 20, 35, 39; 13:12, 17, 20; 14:11, 15, 17; 15:1, 17; 16:4, 16, 25; 19:1, 5, 12; 21:3, 4; **Ru** 1:1, 19; 3:8; **1Sa** 1:12, 20; 2:36; 3:2; 4:18; 5:10; 7:2; 8:1; 9:6, 26, 27; 10:5, 9, 11; 11:11; 13:10, 22; 14:1, 8, 19; 16:6, 8, 9, 10, 16, 23; 17:48; 18:1, 6, 10, 19, 30; 20:27, 35; 23:6, 23; 24:1, 5, 16; 25:30, 37, 38; 28:1; 30:1; 31:8; **2Sa** 1:1, 2; 2:1, 23; 3:6; 4:4; 7:1, 4; 8:1; 10:1; 11:1, 2, 14, 16; 12:18, 31; 13:1, 23, 30, 36; 15:1, 7, 22, 32; 16:16; 17:9, 16, 21, 21, 27; 19:25; 21:18; **1Ki** 1:21; 2:39; 3:18; 5:7; 6:1; 8:10; 9:1, 10; 11:4, 15, 29; 12:2, 20; 13:4, 20, 23, 31, 32; 14:25; 15:21, 29; 16:11, 18, 31; 17:7, 17; 18:1, 6, 12, 17, 27, 29, 36, 44, 45; 19:17; 20:12, 26; 21:1, 15, 16, 27; 22:2, 32, 33; **2Ki** 2:1, 9, 11; 3:5, 15, 20; 4:6, 25, 40; 5:7; 6:9, 20, 24, 30; 7:18; 8:3, 5, 15; 9:22; 10:7, 9, 25; 13:21; 14:5; 15:12; 16:3; 17:17; 18:1, 9; 19:1, 25, 35, 37; 20:4; 21:6; 22:3, 11; 23:10; 24:20; 25:1, 25, 27; **1Ch** 10:8; 15:26, 29; 17:1, 3, 11; 18:1; 19:1; 20:1, 4; **2Ch** 5:11, 13; 8:1; 10:2; 12:1, 2; 13:15; 16:5; 18:31, 32; 20:1; 21:19; 22:8; 24:4, 11, 23; 25:3, 14, 16; 33:6; 34:19; **Ne** 1:1, 4; 2:1, 14; 4:1, 7, 12, 15, 16; 6:1, 16; 7:1; 13:3, 19; **Est** 1:1; 2:8; 3:4; 5:1; **Job** 6:15; 11:16; 14:5; 19:8; 34:20; **Ps** 37:5, 7; 58:8; 78:13; 80:12; 89:41; 104:9; 136:14; 148:6; **Pr** 4:15, 15; 8:29; 16:30; 19:11; 22:3; 27:12; **Isa** 2:2; 3:24; 4:3; 7:1, 7, 18, 21, 22, 23; 8:8, 21, 21; 10:12, 20, 27; 11:11; 14:3, 24; 16:12; 17:4; 21:1; 22:7, 20; 23:2, 6, 10, 12, 15, 17; 24:18, 21; 27:12, 13; 28:15, 18, 19, 21; 30:32; 31:9; 33:21; 34:10; 35:8; 36:1; 37:1, 26, 38; 42:9; 46:11; 47:2; 48:3, 5; 51:10; 65:24; 66:23; **Jer** 2:10; 3:9, 16; 4:9; 5:19, 22, 22; 8:13; 9:10; 12:15, 16; 13:6; 15:2, 14; 16:10; 17:24; 20:3; 22:8; 25:12; 26:8; 27:8; 28:1, 9; 30:8; 31:28; 32:24, 35; 33:13; 35:11; 36:1, 9, 16, 23; 37:11; 39:4; 41:1, 4, 6, 13; 42:4, 7, 16; 43:1; 49:39; 51:43; 52:3, 4, 31; **La** 1:12; 2:15; 3:37, 44; 4:21; **Eze** 1:1; 3:16; 5:1, 14, 17; 8:1; 9:8; 10:6; 11:13; 12:25; 14:15, 15; 16:21, 23; 20:1, 26, 31, 37; 21:7; 23:37; 24:14; 26:1; 29:11, 11, 17; 30:20; 31:1; 32:1, 17, 19; 33:21, 28, 33; 37:2; 38:10, 18; 39:11, 15; 44:17; 46:21; 47:5, 9, 10, 22, 23; **Da** 2:29, 29, 45; 4:16, 23, 25, 32; 7:14; 8:2, 15; 11:10, 40; **Hos** 1:5, 10; 2:21; **Joel** 2:28, 32; 3:17, 18; **Am** 5:5, 17; 6:2, 9; 7:2, 8; 8:2, 9; **Jnh** 4:8; **Mic** 1:11; 2:8, 13; 4:1; 5:10; **Na** 1:12, 15; 3:7; **Hab** 1:11; **Zep** 1:8, 10, 12; 2:2; **Zec** 3:4; 6:15; 7:1, 13; 8:13, 20, 23; 9:8; 10:11; 12:9; 13:2, 2, 3, 4, 8; 14:6, 7, 13, 16; **Mt** 5:18, 18; 7:28; 8:28; 9:10; 11:1; 13:53; 19:1; 24:6, 34, 35, 35; 26:1, 39, 42; **Mk** 1:9; 2:15, 23; 4:4, 35; 11:23; 13:29, 30, 31, 31; 14:35; **Lk** 1:8, 23, 41, 59; 2:1, 15, 15, 46; 3:21; 5:1, 12, 17; 6:1, 6, 12; 7:11; 8:1, 22, 40; 9:18, 28, 33, 37, 51, 57; 10:38; 11:1, 14, 27, 42; 12:55; 14:1; 16:17, 22, 26, 26; 17:11, 14; 18:35, 36; 19:4, 15, 29; 20:1; 21:7, 9, 28, 31, 32, 33, 33, 36; 24:4, 12, 15, 18, 30, 51; **Jn** 13:19; 14:29, 29; 15:25; **Ac** 2:17, 21; 3:23; 4:5; 9:32, 37, 43; 11:26, 28; 14:1; 16:16; 18:27; 19:1; 21:1; 22:6, 17; 27:44; 28:8, 17; **Ro** 9:26; **1Co** 7:36; 15:54; 16:5, 5; **2Co** 1:16; **1Th** 3:4; **Jas** 1:10; **1Pe** 1:17; **2Pe** 3:10; **Rev** 1:1

PASSED [161]

Ge 12:6; 15:17; 31:21; 32:10, 22, 31; 33:3; 37:28; **Ex** 12:27; 34:6; **Nu** 14:7; 20:17; 33:8, 51; **Dt** 2:8, 8; 27:3; 29:16; **Jos** 2:23; 3:1, 4, 16, 17, 17; 4:1, 7, 10, 11, 11, 12, 13, 23; 5:1; 6:8; 10:29, 31, 34; 15:3, 3, 4, 6, 7, 10, 10, 11; 16:6; 18:9, 18, 19; 24:17; **Jdg** 3:26; 8:4; 10:9; 11:29, 29, 29, 32; 12:3; 18:13; 19:14; **1Sa** 9:4, 4, 4, 4, 27; 14:23; 15:12; 27:2; 29:2, 2; **2Sa** 2:29; 10:17; 15:18, 18, 22, 23, 23, 23; 17:22, 24; 24:5; **1Ki** 13:25; 19:11, 19; 20:39; **2Ki** 4:8, 8, 31; 6:30; 14:9; **1Ch** 19:17; **2Ch** 9:22; 25:18; 30:10; **Job** 4:15; 9:26; 15:19; 28:8; **Ps** 18:12; 37:36; 48:4; 90:9; **SS** 3:4; **Isa** 10:28; 40:27; 41:3; **Jer** 2:6; 11:15; 34:18, 19; 46:17; **Eze** 16:6, 8, 15, 25; 36:34; 47:5; **Da** 3:27; 6:18; **Hos** 10:11; **Jnh** 2:3; **Mic** 2:13; **Na** 3:19; **Hab** 3:10; **Zec** 7:14; **Mt** 9:1, 9; 20:30; 27:39; **Mk** 2:14; 5:21; 6:35, 48, 53; 9:30; 11:20; 15:21, 29; **Lk** 10:31, 32; 17:11; 19:1; **Jn** 5:24; 8:59; 9:1; **Ac** 9:32; 12:10; 14:24; 15:3; 17:1, 23; 19:1, 21; **Ro** 5:12; **1Co** 10:1; **Eph** 2:11; **Heb** 4:14; 11:29; **1Jn** 3:14; **Rev** 21:1, 4

PASSEDST [1]

Jdg 12:1

PASSEST [5]

Dt 3:21; 30:18; **2Sa** 15:33; **1Ki** 2:37; **Isa** 43:2

PASSETH [38]

Ex 30:13, 14; 33:22; **Lev** 27:32; **Jos** 3:11; 16:2; 19:13; **1Ki** 9:8; **2Ki** 4:9; 12:4; **2Ch** 7:21; **Job** 9:11; 14:20; 30:15; 37:21; **Ps** 8:8; 78:39; 103:16; 144:4; **Pr** 10:25; 26:17; **Ecc** 1:4; **Isa** 29:5; **Jer** 9:12; 13:24; 18:16; 19:8; **Eze** 35:7; **Hos** 13:3; **Mic** 7:18; **Zep** 2:15; 3:6; **Zec** 9:8; **Lk** 18:37; **1Co** 7:31; **Eph** 3:19; **Php** 4:7; **1Jn** 2:17

PASSING [13]

Jdg 19:18; **2Sa** 1:26; 15:24; **2Ki** 6:26; **Ps** 84:6; **Pr** 7:8; **Isa** 31:5; **Eze** 39:14; **Lk** 4:30; **Ac** 5:15; 8:40; 16:8; 27:8

PLACE [721]

Ge 1:9; 12:6; 13:3, 4, 14; 18:24, 26, 33; 19:12, 13, 14, 27; 20:11, 13; 21:31; 22:3, 4, 9, 14; 26:7, 7; 28:11, 11, 11, 16, 17, 19; 29:3, 22; 30:25; 31:55; 32:2, 30; 33:17; 35:7, 13, 14, 15; 38:14, 21, 21, 22, 22; 39:20; 40:3, 13; 48:9; 50:19; **Ex** 3:5, 8; 10:23; 13:3; 15:17; 16:29, 29; 17:7; 18:21, 23; 21:13; 23:20; 26:33, 34; 28:29, 35, 43; 29:30, 31; 31:11; 32:34; 33:21; 35:19; 38:24; 39:1, 41; **Lev** 1:16; 4:12, 24, 29, 33; 6:11, 16, 25, 26, 27, 30; 7:2, 6; 10:13, 14, 17, 18, 18; 13:19, 23, 28; 14:13, 13, 28, 40, 41, 42, 45; 16:2, 3, 16, 17, 20, 23, 24, 27; 24:9; **Nu** 2:17; 9:17; 10:14, 29, 33; 11:3, 34; 13:24; 14:40; 18:10, 31; 19:9; 20:5, 5; 21:3; 22:26; 23:3, 13, 27; 24:11, 21, 25; 28:7; 32:1, 1, 17; 33:54; **Dt** 1:31, 33; 2:37; 9:7; 11:5, 24; 12:3, 5, 11, 13, 14, 18, 21, 26; 14:23, 23, 24, 25; 15:20; 16:2, 2, 6, 6, 7, 11, 11, 15, 16; 17:8, 10; 18:6; 21:19; 23:12, 16; 26:2, 2, 9; 27:15; 29:7; 31:11; **Jos** 1:3; 3:3; 4:3, 3, 8, 9, 18; 5:9, 15; 7:26; 8:19; 9:27; 20:4; **Jdg** 2:5; 6:26; 7:7, 21; 9:55; 11:19; 15:17, 19; 17:8, 9; 18:3, 10, 12; 19:16, 28; 20:22, 33, 36; 21:19; **Ru** 1:7; 3:4; 4:10; **1Sa** 3:2, 9; 5:3, 11; 6:2; 9:12, 13, 14, 19, 22, 25; 10:5, 12, 13; 12:8; 14:9, 46; 15:12; 19:2; 20:19, 25, 27, 37, 41; 21:2; 23:22, 28; 26:5, 5, 25; 27:5; 29:4; **2Sa** 2:16, 23, 23; 5:20; 6:8, 17; 7:10, 10; 11:16; 15:17, 19, 21; 17:9, 12; 18:18; 19:39; 22:20; 23:7; **1Ki** 3:4; 4:12, 28; 5:9; 6:16; 7:50; 8:6, 6, 7, 8, 10, 13, 21, 29, 29, 30, 30, 35, 39, 43, 49; 10:19; 11:7; 13:8, 16, 22; 20:24; 21:19; 22:10; **2Ki** 5:11; 6:1, 2, 6, 8, 9, 10; 18:25; 22:16, 17, 19, 20; 23:15, 15, 15; **1Ch** 6:32, 49; 13:11; 14:11; 15:1, 3, 12; 16:27, 39; 17:9, 9; 21:22, 25, 29; 23:32; 28:11; **2Ch** 1:3, 4, 13; 3:1; 4:22; 5:7, 7, 8, 11; 6:2, 20, 20, 21, 21, 26, 30, 33, 39, 40, 41; 7:12, 15; 9:18; 18:9; 20:26; 24:11; 29:5, 7; 30:16, 27; 34:24, 25, 27, 28, 31; 35:5, 10, 15; 36:15; **Ezr** 1:4, 4; 2:68; 5:15; 6:3, 5, 5, 7; 8:17, 17; 9:8; **Ne** 1:9; 2:3, 14; 3:16, 26, 31; 4:20; 8:7; 9:3; 13:11; **Est** 2:9; 4:14; 7:8; **Job** 2:11; 6:17; 7:10; 8:17, 18, 22; 9:6; 14:18; 16:18; 18:4, 21; 20:9; 26:7; 27:21, 23; 28:1, 6, 12, 20, 23; 36:16, 20; 37:1; 38:10, 12, 19; 39:28; 40:12; **Ps** 18:11, 19; 24:3; 26:8, 12; 32:7; 33:14; 37:10; 44:19; 46:4; 52:5; 66:12; 68:17; 74:7; 76:2; 79:7; 81:7; 90:1; 91:1; 103:16; 104:8; 118:5; 119:114; 132:5; **Pr** 1:21; 14:26; 15:3; 24:15; 25:6; 27:8; **Ecc** 1:5, 7; 3:16, 16, 20; 6:6; 8:10; 10:4, 6; 11:3; **Isa** 4:5, 6; 5:8; 7:23; 13:13; 14:2; 16:12; 18:4, 7; 22:23, 25; 25:5; 26:21; 28:8, 17, 25; 30:32; 32:2, 2, 19; 33:16, 21; 34:14; 35:1; 45:19; 46:7, 7, 13; 49:20, 20; 54:2; 56:5; 57:15; 60:13, 13; 65:10; 66:1; **Jer** 4:7, 26; 6:3; 7:3, 6, 7, 12, 14, 20, 32; 9:2; 13:7; 14:13; 16:2, 3, 9; 17:12; 18:14; 19:3, 4, 4, 6, 7, 11, 12, 13; 22:3, 11, 12; 24:5; 27:22; 28:3, 3, 4, 6; 29:10, 14; 32:37; 33:10, 12; 38:9; 40:2; 42:18, 22; 44:29; 50:6; 51:37, 62; **Eze** 3:12; 6:13; 7:22; 10:11; 12:3, 3; 16:24, 24, 25, 31, 31, 39; 17:16; 20:29; 21:19, 30; 25:5; 26:5, 14; 37:14, 26; 38:15; 39:11; 41:4, 9, 11, 11, 12, 13, 14, 15; 42:1, 10, 13, 13, 14, 20; 43:7, 7, 13, 21; 44:13; 45:3, 4, 4; 46:19, 20; 47:10; 48:15; **Da** 2:35; 8:11; 11:31; **Hos** 1:10; 4:16; 5:15; 9:13; 11:11; 13:13; **Joel** 3:7; **Am** 8:3; **Mic** 1:3, 4; **Na** 1:8; 2:11; 3:17; **Zep** 1:4; 2:11, 15; **Hag** 2:9; **Zec** 6:12; 10:6, 10; 12:6; 14:10, 10; **Mal** 1:11; **Mt** 8:32; 9:24; 12:6; 14:13, 15, 35; 17:20; 24:15; 26:36, 52; 27:33, 33; 28:6; **Mk** 1:35; 5:13; 6:10, 10, 31, 32, 35; 11:4; 12:1; 14:32; 15:22, 22; 16:6; **Lk** 4:17, 37, 42; 8:33; 9:10, 12; 10:1, 32; 11:1, 33; 14:9; 16:28; 19:5; 22:40; 23:5, 33; **Jn** 4:20; 5:13; 6:10, 23; 8:37; 10:40; 11:6, 30, 41, 48; 14:2, 3; 18:2; 19:13, 17, 17, 20, 41; 20:7; **Ac** 1:25; 2:1; 4:31; 6:13, 14; 7:7, 33, 49; 8:32; 12:17; 21:12, 28, 28; 25:23; 27:8, 41; **Ro** 9:26; 12:19; 15:23; **1Co** 1:2; 4:11; 11:20; 14:23; **2Co** 2:14; **Gal** 2:5; **Eph** 4:27; **1Th** 1:8; **Heb** 2:6; 4:4, 5; 5:6; 8:7; 9:12, 25; 11:8; 12:17; **Jas** 2:3; 3:11; **2Pe** 1:19; **Rev** 2:5; 12:6, 8, 14; 16:16; 20:11

PLACED [14]

Ge 3:24; 47:11; **1Ki** 12:32; **2Ki** 17:6, 24, 26; **2Ch** 1:14; 4:8; 17:2; **Job** 20:4; **Ps** 78:60; **Isa** 5:8; **Jer** 5:22; **Eze** 17:5

PLACES [220]

Ge 28:15; 36:40; **Ex** 20:24; 25:27; 26:29; 30:4; 36:34; 37:14, 27; 38:5; **Lev** 26:30; **Nu** 21:28; 22:41; 33:52; **Dt** 1:7; 12:2; 32:13; 33:29; **Jos** 5:8; **Jdg** 5:11, 18; 19:13; 20:33; **1Sa** 7:16; 13:6; 23:23; 30:31; **2Sa** 1:19, 25; 7:7; 22:34, 46; **1Ki** 3:2, 3; 12:31, 32; 13:2, 32, 33, 33; 14:23; 15:14; 22:43, 43; **2Ki** 12:3, 3; 14:4, 4; 15:4, 4, 35, 35; 16:4; 17:9, 11, 29, 32, 32; 18:4, 22; 19:24; 21:3; 23:5, 5, 8, 8, 9, 13, 14, 19, 20; **1Ch** 6:54; **2Ch** 8:11; 11:15; 14:3, 5; 15:17; 17:6; 20:33; 21:11; 28:4, 25; 31:1; 32:12; 33:3, 17, 19, 19; 34:3; **Ne** 4:12, 13, 13; 12:27; **Job** 3:14; 20:26; 21:28; 25:2; 37:8; **Ps** 10:8, 8; 16:6; 17:12; 18:33, 45; 49:11; 68:35; 73:18; 74:20; 78:58; 95:4; 103:22; 105:41; 109:10; 110:6; 135:6; 141:6; **Pr** 8:2, 2; 9:3, 14; **SS** 2:14; **Isa** 5:17; 15:2; 32:18; 36:7; 37:25; 40:4; 41:18; 44:26; 45:2, 3; 49:9, 19; 51:3; 52:9; 58:12, 14; 59:10; **Jer** 3:2, 21; 4:11, 12; 5:1; 7:29, 31; 8:3; 12:12; 13:17; 14:6; 17:3, 6, 26; 19:5; 23:10, 24; 24:9; 26:18; 29:14; 30:18; 32:35, 44; 33:13; 40:12; 45:5; 48:35; 49:10; 51:30; **La** 2:6; 3:6, 10; **Eze** 6:3, 6, 6; 7:24; 16:16, 39; 21:2; 26:20; 34:12, 13, 26; 36:2, 36; 37:23; 38:12, 20; 43:7; 46:23, 24; 47:11; **Da** 11:24; **Hos** 9:6; 10:8; **Am** 4:6, 13; 7:9; **Mic** 1:3, 5; 3:12; **Hab** 1:6; 3:19; **Zec** 3:7; **Mal** 1:4; **Mt** 12:43; 13:5, 20; 24:7; **Mk** 1:45; 13:8; **Lk** 11:24; 21:11; **Ac** 24:3; **Eph** 1:3, 20; 2:6; 3:10; 6:12; **Php** 1:13; **Heb** 9:24; **Rev** 6:14

PUT [911]

Ge 2:8, 15; 3:15, 22; 8:9; 19:10; 24:2, 9, 47; 26:11; 27:15, 16; 28:11, 18, 20; 29:3; 30:40, 40, 42; 31:34; 32:16; 33:2; 35:2; 37:34; 38:14, 19, 28; 39:4, 20; 40:3, 15; 41:10, 42, 42; 42:17; 43:22; 44:1, 2; 46:4; 47:29; 48:18; 50:26; **Ex** 2:3; 3:5, 22; 4:4, 4, 6, 6, 7, 7, 15, 21; 5:21; 8:23; 11:7; 12:15; 15:26; 16:33; 17:12, 14; 19:12; 21:12, 15, 16, 17, 29; 22:5, 8, 11, 19; 23:1; 24:6; 25:12, 14, 16, 21, 21, 26; 26:11, 34, 35; 27:5, 7; 28:12, 23, 24, 25, 26, 27, 30, 37, 41; 29:3, 5, 6, 6, 8, 9, 10, 12, 15, 17, 19, 20, 24, 30; 30:6, 18, 18, 36; 31:6, 14, 15; 32:27; 33:4, 5, 22; 34:33, 35; 35:2, 34; 36:1, 2; 37:5, 13; 38:7; 39:7, 16, 17, 18, 19, 20, 25; 40:3, 5, 7, 13, 18, 19, 20, 20, 22, 24, 26, 29, 30; **Lev** 1:4, 7; 2:1, 15; 4:7, 18, 25, 30, 34; 5:11, 11; 6:10, 10, 10, 11, 11, 12; 8:7, 7, 8, 8, 9, 9, 13, 13, 15, 23, 24, 26, 27; 9:9, 20; 10:1, 1, 10; 11:32, 38; 13:45; 14:14, 17, 25, 28, 29, 34, 42; 15:19; 16:4, 4, 13, 18, 23, 23, 24, 32; 18:19; 19:14, 20; 20:2, 9, 10, 11, 12, 13, 15, 16, 25, 27; 21:7, 10; 22:14; 24:7, 12, 16, 16, 17, 21; 26:8; 27:29; **Nu** 1:51; 3:10, 38; 4:6, 6, 7, 8, 10, 10, 11, 12, 12, 14, 14; 5:2, 3, 3, 4, 15, 17, 18; 6:18, 19, 27; 8:10; 11:17, 29; 15:34, 35, 38; 16:7, 7, 14, 17, 18, 46, 46, 47; 18:7; 19:17; 20:26, 28; 21:9; 23:5, 12, 16; 27:20; 35:16, 17, 18, 21, 30, 31; 36:3, 4; **Dt** 2:25; 7:15, 22; 10:2, 5; 11:29; 12:5, 7, 21; 13:5, 5, 9; 16:9; 17:6, 6, 7, 7, 12; 18:18; 19:13, 19; 21:9, 13, 21, 22; 22:5, 19, 21, 22, 24, 29; 23:24; 24:7, 16, 16, 16; 25:6; 26:2; 28:48; 30:7; 31:19, 26; 32:30; 33:10, 14; **Jos** 1:18; 6:24; 7:6, 11; 10:24, 24; 17:13; 24:7, 14, 23; **Jdg** 1:28; 3:21; 5:26; 6:19, 19, 21, 31, 37; 7:16; 8:27; 9:15, 26, 49; 10:16; 12:3; 14:12, 13, 16; 15:4, 15; 16:3, 21; 18:7, 21; 20:13, 13, 20, 22, 30, 33; 21:5; **Ru** 3:3; **1Sa** 1:14; 2:36; 4:2; 6:8, 15; 7:3, 4; 8:16; 11:11, 12, 13; 14:26, 27, 27; 17:21, 38, 39, 40, 49, 54; 19:5, 13; 21:6; 22:17; 24:10; 28:3, 8, 21; 31:10; **2Sa** 1:24; 3:34; 6:6; 7:15; 8:2, 6, 14, 14; 10:8, 9, 10; 12:13, 31; 13:17, 19; 14:2, 3, 19; 15:5; 17:23; 18:12; 19:21, 22; 20:3, 8; 21:9; **1Ki** 2:5, 8, 24, 26, 35, 35; 5:3; 7:39, 51; 8:9; 9:3; 10:17, 24; 11:36; 12:4, 9, 29; 13:4, 4; 14:21; 18:23, 23, 25, 33, 42; 20:6, 24, 31, 32; 21:27; 22:10, 23, 27, 30; **2Ki** 2:20; 3:2, 21; 4:34; 6:7; 9:13; 10:7; 11:12; 12:9, 10; 13:16, 16, 16; 14:6, 6, 6, 12; 16:14, 17; 17:29; 18:11, 24; 19:28; 21:4, 7; 23:5, 24, 33, 33; 25:7; **1Ch** 1:8; 5:20; 10:10; 11:19; 12:15; 13:9, 10; 18:6, 13; 19:9, 10, 16, 17, 19; 21:27; 27:24; **2Ch** 1:5; 2:14; 3:16, 16; 4:6; 5:1, 10; 6:11, 20, 24; 9:16, 23; 10:4, 9, 11, 11; 11:11, 12; 12:13; 15:8, 13; 16:10; 17:19; 18:22, 26, 29; 22:11; 23:7, 11; 25:22; 29:7; 33:7, 14; 34:10; 35:3, 24; 36:3, 7, 22; **Ezr** 1:1, 7; 2:62; 6:12; 7:27; 10:3, 19; **Ne** 2:12; 3:5; 4:23, 23; 6:14, 19; 7:5, 64; **Est** 4:1, 11; 5:1; 8:3; 9:1; **Job** 1:11, 12; 2:5; 4:18; 11:14; 13:14; 17:3; 18:5, 6; 19:13; 21:17; 22:23; 23:6; 27:17; 29:14; 38:36; 41:2; **Ps** 2:12; 4:5, 7; 5:11; 7:1; 8:6; 9:5, 10, 20; 11:1; 16:1; 17:7; 18:22; 25:20; 27:9; 30:11; 31:1, 18; 35:4; 36:7; 40:3, 14; 44:7, 9; 53:5; 55:20; 56:4, 8, 11; 70:2; 71:1, 1; 73:28; 78:66; 83:17; 88:8, 18; 118:8, 9; 119:31; 125:3; 146:3; **Pr** 4:24, 24; 8:1; 13:9; 20:20; 23:2; 24:20; 25:6, 7, 8, 10; 30:5; **Ecc** 3:14; 10:10; 11:10; **SS** 5:3, 3, 4; **Isa** 1:16; 5:20, 20; 10:13; 11:8; 20:2; 36:9; 37:29; 42:1; 43:26; 47:11; 50:1, 1; 51:9, 16, 23; 52:1, 1; 53:10; 54:4; 59:17, 17, 21; 63:11; **Jer** 1:9, 9; 3:1, 8, 19; 4:1; 7:21; 8:14; 12:13; 13:1, 1, 2; 18:21; 20:2; 26:15, 19, 21, 24; 27:2, 8; 28:14; 29:26; 31:33; 32:14, 40; 37:4, 15, 18; 38:4, 7, 12, 15, 16, 25; 39:7, 18; 40:10; 43:3; 46:4; 47:6; 50:14, 42; 52:11, 11, 27; **Eze** 3:25; 4:9; 8:3, 17; 10:7; 11:19; 14:3; 16:11, 12, 14; 17:2; 19:9; 22:26; 23:42; 24:17; 26:16; 29:4; 30:13, 21, 24, 25; 32:7, 25; 36:26, 27; 37:6, 14, 19; 38:4; 42:14; 43:9, 20; 44:19, 19, 22; 45:19; **Da** 5:19, 29; **Hos** 2:2; **Joel** 3:13; **Am** 6:3; **Jnh** 3:5; **Mic** 2:12; 7:5; **Na** 3:9; **Zep** 3:19; **Hag** 1:6; **Mt** 1:19; 5:15, 31, 32; 6:25; 8:3; 9:16, 17, 17, 25; 10:21; 12:18; 13:24, 31; 14:3, 5; 19:3, 6, 7, 8, 9, 9, 13; 21:7; 22:34; 25:27; 26:52, 59; 27:1, 6, 28, 29, 31, 48; **Mk** 1:14, 41; 2:22; 4:21; 5:40; 6:9; 7:32, 33; 8:23, 25; 10:2, 4, 9, 11, 12, 16; 13:12; 14:1, 55; 15:17, 20, 36; **Lk** 1:52; 5:13, 38; 8:54; 9:62; 12:22; 14:7; 15:22, 22; 16:4, 18; 18:33; 21:16; 23:32; **Jn** 5:7; 9:15, 22; 11:53; 12:6, 10, 42; 13:2; 16:2; 18:11, 31; 19:2, 2, 19, 29, 29; 20:25; **Ac** 1:7; 4:3; 5:18, 25, 34; 7:33; 9:40; 12:4, 19; 13:46; 15:9, 10; 26:10; 27:6; **Ro** 13:12, 14; 14:13; **1Co** 5:13; 7:11, 12; 13:11; 15:24, 25, 27, 27, 27, 28, 53, 53, 54, 54; **2Co** 3:13; 8:16; **Gal** 3:27; **Eph** 1:22; 4:22, 24, 31; 6:11; **Col** 3:8, 9, 10, 12, 14; **1Th** 2:4; **1Ti** 1:19; 4:6; **2Ti** 1:6; 2:14; **Tit** 3:1; **Phm** 1:18; **Heb** 2:5, 8, 8, 8, 8, 13; 6:6; 8:10; 9:26; 10:16; **Jas** 3:3; **1Pe** 2:15; 3:18; **2Pe** 1:12, 14; **Jude** 1:5; **Rev** 2:24; 11:9; 17:17

PUTTEST [7]

PUTTETH [30]

PUTTING [17]

RATHER [62]

SAID [4001]

SAIDST [22]

SAITH [1262]

SAME [332]

SAW [548]

SAWEST [21]

SAY [1057]

SAYEST [40]

SAYING [1445]

SHALT [1616]

SHE [981]

Ge 2:23, 23; 3:6, 12, 20; 4:1, 2, 17, 22, 25, 25; 8:9; 11:30; 12:14, 16, 18, 19; 15:9; 16:1, 4, 4, 4, 5, 5, 6, 8, 13, 13; 17:16; 18:15; 19:26, 33, 33, 35, 35, 38; 20:2, 3, 5, 5, 5, 12, 12, 12, 16; 21:7, 9, 10, 14, 15, 16, 16, 16, 19, 19; 22:20, 24; 24:14, 14, 16, 18, 18, 19, 19, 20, 24, 24, 25, 36, 44, 45, 46, 47, 55, 58, 64, 64, 65, 65, 67; 25:2, 21, 22, 22, 26; 26:7, 7, 7, 9, 9; 27:16, 17, 17, 42; 29:9, 12, 32, 32, 33, 33, 34, 35, 35, 35; 30:1, 3, 3, 4, 6, 8, 9, 9, 11, 13, 15, 17, 18, 20, 21, 23, 24, 35; 31:35, 38; 32:14, 15; 34:1; 35:8, 16, 17, 18, 18; 36:12, 14; 38:3, 4, 4, 5, 5, 14, 14, 14, 15, 16, 16, 17, 18, 18, 19, 24, 25, 25, 25, 26, 28, 29; 39:7, 10, 12, 13, 14, 16, 17, 19; 45:23; 46:15, 18, 25; **Ex** 1:16; 2:2, 2, 3, 3, 3, 5, 5, 6, 6, 6, 7, 10, 10, 10, 22; 4:26; 6:20, 23, 25; 21:4, 7, 8, 11; **Lev** 12:2, 2, 4, 4, 5, 5, 5, 6, 7, 8, 8, 8; 15:19, 20, 20, 22, 23, 25, 26, 26, 28, 28, 28, 29; 18:7, 9, 11, 12, 13, 14, 15, 19; 19:20, 20; 20:17, 18; 21:9, 9, 9; 22:12, 13; 26:43; **Nu** 5:13, 13, 14, 14, 27, 28; 12:10, 14; 15:27; 22:25, 27, 28, 33; 26:59; 30:4, 4, 5, 6, 6, 6, 7, 8, 8, 8, 10, 11; **Dt** 21:12, 13, 13, 14; 22:19, 21, 21, 24, 29; 24:1, 2, 2, 4; 25:6; 28:57, 57; **Jos** 2:6, 6, 8, 9, 15, 15, 16, 21, 21, 21; 6:17, 17, 22, 23, 25, 25, 25; 15:18, 18, 18; **Jdg** 1:14, 14, 14, 15; 4:4, 5, 6, 9, 18, 19; 5:24, 25, 25, 26, 26, 26, 26, 29; 8:31; 11:34, 36, 37, 38, 39, 39; 13:9, 14; 14:3, 7, 17, 17, 17; 15:2; 16:8, 9, 14, 15, 16, 18, 19, 19, 19, 19, 20; 19:3; 20:5; **Ru** 1:3, 6, 6, 6, 7, 7, 9, 15, 18, 18, 18, 20; 2:2, 3, 7, 7, 7, 10, 13, 14, 14, 15, 16, 17, 17, 18, 18, 18, 18, 18, 19, 19, 23; 3:5, 6, 7, 9, 14, 14, 15, 16, 16, 16, 17, 18; 4:13, 13; **1Sa** 1:7, 7, 7, 10, 11, 12, 13, 13, 18, 20, 22, 23, 24, 24, 26; 2:5, 19, 21; 4:19, 19, 20, 20, 21, 22; 18:19, 21; 19:14; 25:3, 19, 19, 20, 20, 20, 23, 35, 36, 41, 42; 28:12, 14, 24, 25; **2Sa** 4:4; 6:16; 11:4, 4, 4, 26, 27; 12:24; 13:2, 8, 9, 10, 11, 12, 14, 16, 18; 14:4, 5, 11, 27; 20:17, 18; 21:8, 8; **1Ki** 1:17, 22, 28; 2:13, 14, 16, 19, 20, 21; 3:19, 20, 26, 27; 10:1, 2, 2, 2, 6, 10, 13, 13, 13; 14:5, 5, 6, 17; 15:13; 17:11, 12, 15, 15, 18; 21:8, 9, 11; **2Ki** 2:24; 4:2, 5, 5, 6, 7, 8, 9, 12, 13, 14, 15, 16, 21, 22, 23, 24, 25, 25, 26, 27, 27, 28, 36, 37; 5:2, 3; 6:28, 29; 8:2, 3, 6, 6; 9:30, 31, 34; 11:1, 13, 14, 16, 16; 22:14, 15; **1Ch** 1:32; 2:21, 26, 29, 35, 49; 4:17; 7:14, 16, 23; 15:29; **2Ch** 9:1, 1, 1, 5, 9, 12, 12, 12, 12; 15:16; 22:10, 11, 11; 23:12, 13, 15; 34:22, 23; 36:21, 21; **Est** 1:11, 15, 17, 19; 2:1, 7, 9, 10, 12, 13, 14, 14, 14, 14, 15, 17, 20; 4:4, 8; 5:2, 12; **Job** 1:3; 39:16, 18, 18, 28, 29, 30; 42:12; **Ps** 45:14; 46:5; 68:12; 80:11; 84:3; **Pr** 1:20, 21, 21; 3:15, 18; 4:6, 6, 8, 8, 9, 9, 13; 7:11, 12, 13, 21, 21, 26; 8:2, 3; 9:1, 2, 2, 2, 3, 3, 4, 13, 14, 16; 12:4; 23:22, 25, 28; 30:20, 23; 31:12, 13, 14, 14, 15, 16, 16, 17, 18, 19, 20, 20, 21, 22, 24, 25, 26, 27, 30; **SS** 6:9, 9, 10; 8:5, 8, 8, 9, 9; **Isa** 3:26; 8:3; 23:3, 17; 40:2; 49:15; 51:18, 18; 66:7, 7, 7, 8; **Jer** 3:1, 6, 7, 7, 9; 4:17; 6:6, 7; 11:15; 15:9, 9, 9; 33:16; 46:24; 50:9, 12, 14, 15, 15, 29, 29; 51:8, 9, 42, 53; **La** 1:1, 1, 1, 2, 2, 3, 3, 4, 7, 8, 8, 9, 9, 9, 10; **Eze** 5:6; 16:46, 48, 49; 19:2, 2, 3, 5, 5, 5, 10, 11, 11, 12, 12, 13, 14; 23:5, 5, 7, 7, 7, 8, 9, 10, 11, 11, 12, 13, 14, 14, 16, 16, 17, 18, 19, 19, 20, 43; 24:7, 7, 12; 26:2, 2, 2, 17; 32:20; **Da** 11:6, 6, 17; **Hos** 1:6, 8, 8; 2:2, 3, 5, 5, 6, 7, 7, 7, 7, 8, 12, 13, 13, 13, 15, 15; 13:16; **Am** 5:2, 2; **Mic** 1:7, 13; 5:3; 7:10, 10; **Na** 2:7, 10; 3:10, 10; **Zep** 2:15; 3:2, 2, 2, 2; **Zec** 9:4; **Mal** 2:14; **Mt** 1:18, 21, 25; 8:15; 9:18, 21; 12:42; 14:7, 8, 11; 15:23, 25, 27; 20:21; 22:28; 26:10, 12, 12; **Mk** 1:31; 5:23, 23, 26, 27, 28, 29, 29, 42; 6:19, 24, 24, 25; 7:26, 28, 30, 30; 10:12; 12:23, 42, 44, 44; 14:3, 6, 8, 8, 8, 9, 67, 67; 16:10; **Lk** 1:29, 29, 36, 42, 45, 57, 57; 2:6, 7, 36, 37, 38; 4:39; 7:12, 37, 39, 44, 47; 8:42, 47, 47, 47, 47, 47, 50, 52, 53, 55; 10:39, 40; 11:31; 13:13; 15:8, 8, 9, 9; 18:3, 5; 20:33; 21:4, 4; **Jn** 8:11; 11:20, 27, 28, 28, 29, 29, 31, 31, 32; 12:7; 16:21, 21, 21; 20:2, 11, 11, 13, 14, 14, 15, 16, 18; **Ac** 5:8, 10; 9:36, 37, 39, 40, 40, 40; 12:14, 14, 15; 16:14, 15, 15, 15, 18; **Ro** 7:2, 3, 3, 3, 3, 3; 16:2, 2; **1Co** 7:11, 12, 28, 34, 34, 34, 36, 39, 39, 40, 40; 11:5; **Gal** 4:27; **Eph** 5:33; **1Ti** 2:15; 5:5, 6, 6, 10, 10, 10, 10, 10; **Heb** 11:11, 11, 31; **Jas** 2:25; **Rev** 2:21; 6:13; 12:2, 5, 6, 14, 14; 14:8; 18:6, 6, 7, 7, 8, 19; 19:8

SHOULD [783]

Ge 2:18; 4:15; 18:25; 21:7; 23:8; 26:7; 27:45; 29:7, 19; 30:38; 33:13; 34:31; 38:9, 9; 40:15; 43:25; 44:7, 8, 17, 22; 47:15, 26; **Ex** 3:11, 11; 5:2; 14:12; 22:3; 32:12; 35:1; 39:7, 23; **Lev** 4:13, 22; 9:6; 10:18, 19; 11:43; 20:26; 24:23; 26:13; 27:26; **Nu** 7:9; 9:4; 11:13; 12:14; 14:3, 31; 15:34; 20:4; 23:19, 19; 27:4; 32:9; 35:28, 32; **Dt** 1:18, 33, 39; 4:5, 21, 21, 42; 5:25; 17:16; 20:18; 25:3, 3; 29:18, 18; 32:27, 27, 30; **Jos** 8:29, 33; 9:27; 11:20; 22:28, 29; 24:16; **Jdg** 8:6, 15; 9:9, 11, 13, 28, 28, 38, 41; 20:38; 21:3, 22; **Ru** 1:12, 12, 12; **1Sa** 2:30; 8:7; 9:6; 10:22; 12:21, 23; 15:21, 29; 17:26; 18:18, 19; 19:1, 17; 20:2, 5; 22:13; 24:6; 26:11; 27:1, 5, 11; 29:4, 4; **2Sa** 2:22, 22; 12:23; 13:26; 15:20; 16:9, 19, 19; 18:12, 13; 19:19, 22, 34, 35, 36, 43; 20:20; 21:5; 23:17; **1Ki** 1:27; 2:1, 15; 6:6; 8:36; 11:10; 14:2; 21:3; **2Ki** 3:27; 4:43; 6:33; 7:19; 8:13; 11:9, 17; 17:15, 28; 18:35; 22:19; **1Ch** 9:28; 11:19; 16:42; 21:17, 18; 23:13, 32; 25:1; 29:14; **2Ch** 2:6; 4:20; 6:27; 15:13; 20:21; 23:16, 19; 25:13; 29:11, 24; 30:1, 5; 32:4, 14; **Ezr** 2:63; 4:22; 7:23; 8:17, 17; 9:14, 14; 10:5, 7, 8; **Ne** 2:3; 5:12; 6:3, 11, 13; 7:65; 8:14, 15; 9:12, 15, 19, 23; 10:37; 11:23; 13:1, 2, 19, 19, 19, 22, 22; **Est** 1:8, 22, 22; 2:10, 11; 3:14; 4:8; 8:13; 9:21, 22, 25, 25, 27, 28, 28; **Job** 3:12, 13, 13; 6:10, 11, 11, 14; 8:7; 9:2, 32, 32; 10:19, 19; 11:2, 2, 3; 13:5, 9; 15:2, 3, 14, 14; 16:5; 19:28; 21:4, 15, 15; 23:7; 27:5; 31:1, 28; 32:7, 7, 13; 34:6, 9, 10, 10, 23, 33; 36:16, 16; 41:11; **Ps** 27:3, 3; 30:3; 38:16; 49:5, 9; 69:22; 73:15; 78:5, 6, 6; 79:10; 81:14, 15, 15, 16, 16; 95:11; 104:5; 106:23; 115:2; 119:92; 139:18; 143:8; **Pr** 8:29; 22:6, 27; **Ecc** 2:3, 18, 24, 24; 3:13, 14, 22; 5:6; 7:14; **SS** 1:7; 8:1, 1, 3, 3; **Isa** 1:5, 9, 9; 5:2, 4; 8:11, 19; 10:15, 15; 36:20; 41:7; 48:11, 19; 49:15; 50:4; 51:14, 14; 53:2; 54:9; 57:6, 16; 63:13; **Jer** 5:17; 20:18; 23:22; 25:29; 26:24; 27:10, 10, 17; 29:26; 32:31, 35; 33:20, 21, 24; 34:9, 9, 10, 10; 37:10, 21, 21; 39:14; 40:15, 15; 44:14; 46:13; 51:53, 53, 60; **La** 1:10, 16, 17; 3:26, 44; 4:12; **Eze** 8:6; 13:19, 19, 22; 14:3, 14; 18:23, 23; 19:9; 20:9, 14, 22, 25; 21:10; 22:30, 30; 24:8; 33:10; 34:2; **Da** 1:3, 10, 16, 18; 2:13, 18, 29, 46; 3:11, 19; 5:15, 29; 6:1, 2, 23; 7:14; **Hos** 10:3, 10; 13:13; **Joel** 2:17, 17; **Jnh** 4:11; **Mic** 6:16; **Zep** 3:7; **Hag** 1:2; **Zec** 7:3, 7, 11, 12; 8:6; **Mal** 1:13; 2:7, 7; **Mt** 2:4, 12; 5:29, 29, 30, 30; 7:12; 11:3; 12:16; 13:15, 15, 15, 15; 15:33; 16:11, 20; 17:27; 18:14, 30, 34; 19:13; 20:10, 31; 24:22, 22; 25:27; 26:35; 27:20; **Mk** 3:9, 9, 12, 14; 4:12, 12, 22, 26, 27, 27; 5:43, 43; 6:8, 12; 7:36; 8:30; 9:9, 10, 18, 30, 34; 10:13, 32, 36, 48, 51; 11:16; 12:19; 13:20; 14:31; 15:11, 24; **Lk** 1:29, 43, 57, 71; 2:1, 6, 26; 4:42; 5:7; 6:31; 7:4, 19, 20; 8:12, 56; 9:13, 31, 46, 51; 15:32; 17:2, 6, 20; 18:39; 19:11, 27, 40; 20:10, 20, 28; 22:23, 24; 23:24; 24:16, 21, 47; **Jn** 1:31; 2:25; 3:15, 16, 20; 5:23; 6:14, 39, 39, 64, 71; 7:23, 39; 8:5, 19, 55; 9:3, 22, 41; 11:27, 37, 50, 51, 52, 57; 12:4, 23, 33, 40, 40, 42, 46, 49, 49; 13:1, 11, 15, 24, 24, 29; 14:7; 15:16, 16; 16:1, 30; 17:2; 18:4, 14, 28, 32, 36, 37, 39; 19:31, 36; 21:19, 23, 25, 25; **Ac** 1:4; 2:24, 25, 47; 3:18; 5:26, 28, 40; 6:2; 7:6, 6, 44; 8:31; 10:17, 28, 47; 11:22, 28; 12:19; 13:28, 46; 14:15; 15:2, 7; 17:27; 18:14; 19:4, 4, 27, 27; 20:38; 21:4, 16, 26; 22:22, 24, 29; 23:10, 27; 24:23, 26; 25:4; 26:8, 8, 20, 22, 23, 23, 23, 23; 27:1, 17, 20, 21, 29, 42, 43; 28:6, 27, 27, 27; **Ro** 2:21, 22; 4:13; 6:4, 6, 12; 7:4, 4, 6; 8:26; 11:8, 8, 11, 25, 25; 15:16, 20; **1Co** 1:15, 17, 29; 2:5; 4:3; 5:1; 9:10, 10, 12, 14, 15, 15, 27; 10:1, 6, 20; 11:31, 32; 12:25, 25; **2Co** 1:9, 17; 2:3, 4, 7, 11; 4:4; 5:15; 8:20; 9:3, 4; 10:8, 8; 11:3; 12:6, 7, 7; 13:7, 7, 10; **Gal** 1:10; 2:2, 9, 10; 3:1, 17, 19, 21, 23; 5:7; 6:12, 14; **Eph** 1:4, 12; 2:9, 10; 3:6, 8; 5:27; **Php** 1:12; 2:10, 11, 27; **Col** 1:19; 2:4; **1Th** 3:3, 4; 4:3, 4; 5:4, 10; **2Th** 2:11; 3:10; **1Ti** 1:16; **Tit** 2:12; 3:7; **Phm** 1:14; **Heb** 2:1, 9; 3:18; 4:1; 7:11; 8:4, 7; 9:23, 25; 10:2, 4; 11:5, 8, 28, 40; 12:19; **Jas** 1:18; **1Pe** 1:10, 11; 2:9, 21, 24; 3:9; 4:2; **2Pe** 2:6; 3:9, 9; **1Jn** 3:1, 11, 23; 4:3; **2Jn** 1:6; **Jude** 1:3, 18, 18; **Rev** 6:4, 11, 11, 11; 7:1; 8:3; 9:4, 5, 5, 20; 10:6, 7; 11:18; 12:6; 13:14, 15, 15; 19:8, 15; 20:3, 3

SHOULDEST [73]

Ge 3:11; 14:23; 26:10; 29:15; **Nu** 11:12; **Dt** 4:19; 26:18; 29:12; 30:12, 13; **Jdg** 11:23; **Ru** 2:10; **1Sa** 20:8; **2Sa** 9:8; **1Ki** 1:20; **2Ki** 8:14; 13:19; 14:10, 10; 19:25; **1Ch** 17:7; **2Ch** 19:2; 25:16, 19, 19; **Job** 7:17, 17, 18; 10:3, 3; 38:20, 20; **Ps** 50:16; 130:3; **Pr** 5:6; 25:7; 27:22; **Ecc** 5:5, 5; 7:16, 17, 18; **Isa** 37:26; 48:5, 7, 17; 49:6; 51:12; **Jer** 14:8, 9; 29:26; 49:16; **Ob** 1:12, 12, 12, 13, 13, 14, 14; **Mt** 8:8; 18:33; **Mk** 10:35; **Lk** 7:6; **Jn** 11:40; 17:15, 15; **Ac** 13:47; 22:14, 14; **Tit** 1:5; **Phm** 1:15; **Rev** 11:18, 18

SO [1689]

Ge 1:7, 9, 11, 15, 24, 27, 30; 3:24; 6:22; 8:11; 11:8; 12:4, 19; 13:6, 16; 15:5; 18:5; 19:7, 11, 18; 20:17; 21:6; 22:8, 19; 24:46; 25:22; 27:1, 20, 23; 28:21; 29:26, 28; 30:33, 42; 31:21, 28, 36; 32:19, 21; 33:16; 34:12; 35:6; 37:14; 40:7; 41:4, 13, 21, 39, 57; 42:20, 20, 34; 43:6, 11, 34; 44:5, 17; 45:8, 21, 24; 47:13, 20, 28; 48:10, 18; 49:17; 50:3, 17, 26; **Ex** 1:10; 2:18; 4:26; 5:12, 22; 6:9; 7:6, 10, 20, 22; 8:7, 17, 18, 18, 24, 26; 9:24; 10:10, 11, 15, 20; 11:10; 12:28, 36, 50; 14:4, 20, 25, 28; 15:22; 16:17, 30, 34; 17:6, 10; 18:22, 23, 24; 19:16, 25; 21:12, 22; 22:6; 25:9, 33; 27:8; 28:7; 30:21, 23; 32:21, 24; 33:16; 36:6, 13; 37:19; 39:32, 42, 43; 40:16, 33; **Lev** 4:20; 7:7; 8:34, 35, 36; 10:5, 13; 11:32; 14:13, 21; 16:4, 16; 24:19, 20; 26:15; 27:12, 14; **Nu** 1:19, 45, 54; 2:17, 34, 34; 4:26; 5:4, 4; 6:21; 8:3, 4, 7, 20, 22; 9:5, 14, 16, 20, 21; 12:7; 13:21, 33; 14:28; 15:12, 14, 15, 20; 16:27; 17:11, 11; 20:8; 21:35; 22:30, 35; 25:8; 31:5; 32:23, 28, 31; 35:7, 16, 29, 33; 36:3, 4, 7, 10; **Dt** 1:11, 15, 43, 46; 2:5, 16; 3:3, 21, 29; 4:5, 7, 7, 8, 8; 7:4, 19; 8:5, 20; 9:3, 8, 15; 12:4, 10, 22, 30, 31; 13:5; 14:24; 17:7; 18:14; 19:10, 19; 20:18; 21:9, 21; 22:3, 5, 21, 22, 24, 26; 24:8; 25:9; 28:34, 54, 55, 63; 29:22; 30:17; 31:17; 32:12; 33:25; 34:5, 8; **Jos** 1:5, 17; 2:21, 23; 3:7; 4:8; 5:15; 6:11, 14, 20, 20, 27; 7:4, 16, 22, 26; 8:3, 22, 22, 25; 9:26; 10:1, 7, 13, 23, 39, 40; 11:7, 15, 15, 16, 23; 14:5, 11, 12; 15:7; 16:4; 19:51; 21:40; 22:6, 25, 28; 23:15; 24:10, 25, 28; **Jdg** 1:3, 7, 35; 2:14, 17; 3:14, 22, 30; 4:14, 15, 21, 23; 5:28, 31; 6:3, 20, 27, 38, 40; 7:1, 5, 8, 15, 17, 19; 8:18, 21, 28; 9:49; 10:9; 11:5, 10, 21, 23, 24, 32; 12:5; 13:19; 14:10, 10, 15; 15:11; 16:9, 16, 30; 17:10; 18:21; 19:4, 21, 23, 24, 25, 30; 20:11, 36, 46; 21:14, 23; **Ru** 1:17, 19, 22; 2:7, 17, 23; 4:8, 13; **1Sa** 1:7, 7, 9, 18, 23; 2:3, 5, 14, 21; 3:9, 17; 4:4, 5; 5:7, 9, 11; 6:10; 7:13; 8:8; 9:10, 21, 24; 10:9; 11:7, 11, 11; 12:18; 13:22; 14:15, 23, 24, 44, 45, 47; 15:6, 31, 33; 16:13, 23; 17:27, 50; 18:30; 19:12, 17, 18; 20:2, 13, 16, 24, 34; 21:6; 22:14; 23:5, 5; 24:7; 25:12, 20, 21, 22, 25, 35; 26:7, 12, 24, 25; 27:1, 11, 11; 28:23; 29:8, 11; 30:3, 9, 10, 21, 23, 24, 25; 31:6; **2Sa** 1:2, 10; 2:2, 16, 28, 31; 3:9, 9, 20, 30, 34, 35; 5:3, 9, 25; 6:10, 12, 13, 15, 19; 7:8, 17; 8:2; 9:11, 13; 10:14, 19; 11:12, 20, 20, 22; 12:31; 13:2, 6, 8, 15, 20, 35, 38; 14:3, 7, 17, 23, 24, 25, 28, 33; 15:2, 5, 6, 9, 34, 37; 16:10, 10, 19, 22, 23; 17:3, 12, 12, 26; 18:6; 19:13, 14, 15; 20:2, 3, 5, 10, 10, 18, 21; 22:4, 35, 37; 23:5; 24:8, 13, 15, 24, 25; **1Ki** 1:3, 6, 30, 36, 37, 38, 40, 45, 53; 2:7, 10, 23, 27, 34, 38, 46; 3:9, 12, 13; 4:1; 5:4, 10, 18; 6:7, 9, 14, 20, 21, 26, 27, 33, 38; 7:9, 18, 22, 40, 51; 8:11, 25, 46, 48, 54, 63; 9:25; 10:13, 23, 29; 11:19; 12:12, 16, 16, 19, 32, 33; 13:4, 9, 10, 13, 19; 14:4, 6, 28; 15:20; 16:6, 22, 28; 17:5, 10, 17; 18:4, 6, 12, 16, 20, 42; 19:2, 13, 19; 20:10, 19, 25, 29, 32, 34, 37, 38, 40; 21:5, 8; 22:8, 12, 15, 22, 29, 37, 40; **2Ki** 1:17; 2:2, 4, 8, 10, 10, 22; 3:9, 12, 24; 4:5, 8, 25, 36, 40, 44; 5:8, 9, 12, 19, 21; 6:4, 23, 29, 31; 7:10, 16, 20; 8:6, 9, 14, 15, 21; 9:4, 14, 16, 18, 22, 22, 27, 33, 37; 10:11, 16, 21; 11:2, 6; 12:6, 10; 13:5, 24; 15:5, 7, 12, 20; 16:7, 11; 17:4, 7, 23, 25, 32, 41, 41; 18:5, 21; 19:5, 8, 36; 22:14; 23:18; 24:6; 25:6, 21; **1Ch** 9:1, 23; 10:4, 6, 13; 11:6, 9; 13:4, 5, 13; 14:11; 15:14, 17, 19, 25; 16:1, 37; 17:15; 18:14; 19:2, 7, 14, 17; 20:3; 21:3, 11, 14, 25; 22:5; 23:1; 25:7; 29:14; **2Ch** 1:3, 10, 17; 2:3; 5:14; 6:16, 31; 7:5, 21; 8:14, 16; 9:12; 10:3, 12, 15, 16; 11:17; 12:9, 13; 13:9, 13, 17; 14:1, 7, 12; 15:10; 17:10; 18:7, 11, 21, 28, 29; 19:10; 20:6, 20, 20, 25, 30; 21:10, 17, 19; 22:1, 9, 11, 11; 23:8, 15; 24:13, 24; 25:21; 26:23; 27:5, 6; 28:14; 29:17, 22, 25, 34, 35; 30:5, 6, 9, 10, 26; 32:4, 17, 21, 23, 26; 33:8, 9, 20; 34:6, 26, 28; 35:6, 10, 12, 16; **Ezr** 2:70; 3:13; 4:13, 15, 24; 5:17; 6:13; 8:23, 30; 9:2, 14; 10:12, 16; **Ne** 2:4, 6, 11, 15, 18; 4:6, 10, 18, 21, 23; 5:12, 13, 15; 6:3, 13, 15; 7:73; 8:8, 11, 16, 17; 9:10, 11, 21, 22, 24, 25, 28; 12:40, 43; 13:20, 21; **Est** 1:8, 13, 17; 2:4, 8, 12, 16, 17; 3:2; 4:4, 6, 16, 17; 5:2, 2, 5, 13; 6:6, 10; 7:1, 5, 10; 8:4, 14; 9:14, 27; **Job** 1:3, 5, 12; 2:7, 13; 5:12, 16, 27; 7:3, 9, 15, 20; 8:13; 9:2, 30, 35; 13:9; 14:12; 21:4; 23:7; 24:19, 25; 27:6; 32:1, 22; 33:20; 34:25, 28; 35:15; 36:16; 41:10, 16; 42:7, 9, 12, 15, 17; **Ps** 1:4; 7:7; 18:3, 34; 21:13; 22:1; 26:6; 35:25; 37:3; 40:12; 42:1; 45:11; 48:5, 8, 10; 58:5, 11; 61:8; 63:2; 64:8; 65:9; 68:2, 2; 72:7; 73:20, 22; 77:4, 13; 78:21, 29, 53, 60, 72; 79:13; 80:12, 18; 81:12; 83:15; 90:11, 12; 102:4, 15; 103:5, 11, 12, 13, 15; 104:25; 106:9, 30, 32, 33; 107:2, 29, 30, 38; 109:17, 17, 18; 115:8; 119:27, 42, 44, 88, 134; 123:2; 125:2; 127:2, 4; 135:18; 147:20; **Pr** 1:19; 2:2; 3:4, 10, 22; 6:11, 29; 7:13; 10:25, 26; 11:19, 22; 15:7; 19:24; 20:30; 23:7; 24:14, 29, 34; 25:12, 13, 16, 17, 20, 23, 25, 27; 26:1, 2, 7, 8, 9, 11, 14, 19, 20, 21; 27:8, 17, 18, 19, 20, 21; 28:15; 30:33; 31:11; **Ecc** 2:9, 15; 3:11, 19, 19; 4:1; 5:16; 6:2, 3; 7:6; 8:10, 10; 9:2, 12; 10:1; 11:5; **SS** 2:2, 3; 5:9; **Isa** 5:24; 6:13; 10:7, 7, 11, 26; 14:24, 24; 16:2, 6; 18:4; 20:2, 4; 21:1; 22:22; 23:1, 5; 24:2, 2, 2, 2, 2, 2; 26:17; 28:8; 29:8; 30:14; 31:4, 5; 36:6; 37:5, 8, 37; 38:8, 13, 14, 16; 40:20; 41:7; 47:7, 12, 12; 52:14, 15; 53:7; 54:9; 55:9, 11; 59:19; 60:15; 61:11; 62:5, 5; 63:8, 14; 65:8; 66:13, 22; **Jer** 2:26, 36; 3:20; 5:19, 27, 31; 6:7; 9:10; 10:18; 11:4, 5; 13:2, 5, 11; 17:11; 18:4, 6; 19:11; 21:2; 24:2, 3, 5, 8, 8; 26:3, 7; 28:6, 11, 17; 29:17; 30:7; 31:28; 32:8, 11, 42; 33:22, 26; 34:5; 35:11; 36:14, 15, 21; 37:14; 38:6, 11, 12, 13, 16, 20, 23, 27, 28; 39:13, 14; 40:5; 41:7, 8, 14; 42:17, 18, 20; 43:4, 7; 44:14, 22; 46:18; 48:30, 30, 39; 50:40; 51:8, 49, 60; 52:5, 6, 26; **La** 2:22; 3:29; 4:14; 5:20; **Eze** 1:18, 28; 3:2, 14; 4:5; 5:15, 17; 6:14; 8:5, 10; 11:24; 12:7, 11; 13:14, 14; 14:15, 17; 15:6; 16:16, 42, 44; 17:6; 18:4, 30; 19:14; 20:36; 21:24; 22:20, 22; 23:18, 27, 44; 24:18, 19; 28:14; 31:9; 33:7; 34:12; 35:15; 36:38; 37:7, 10, 23; 38:20; 39:7, 10, 22, 23; 40:5, 47; 41:4, 7, 13, 18, 19; 43:5, 15, 27; 45:20, 20; 47:21; **Da** 1:5, 14; 2:2, 15, 42; 3:17; 5:6; 6:23, 28; 7:16; 8:4, 17; 10:7; 11:9, 15, 30; **Hos** 1:3; 3:2, 3; 4:7; 6:9; 8:7; 10:15; 11:2; 13:6; 14:2; **Joel** 2:4; 3:17; **Am** 3:12; 4:8; 5:9, 14; **Ob** 1:16; **Jnh** 1:3, 4, 6, 6, 7, 12, 15; 3:3, 5; 4:5, 6; **Mic** 2:2; 5:14; 7:3; **Zep** 3:6, 7; **Hag** 2:5, 14, 14, 14; **Zec** 1:6, 14, 21; 3:5; 4:4; 6:7; 7:3, 13; 8:13, 15; 10:1; 11:11, 12; 14:15; **Mal** 3:13; **Mt** 1:17; 3:15; 5:12, 16, 19, 47; 6:30; 7:12, 17; 8:10, 13, 28, 31; 9:19, 33; 11:26, 26; 12:40, 45; 13:2, 27, 32, 40, 49; 15:33, 33; 18:13, 14, 31, 35; 19:8, 10, 12; 20:8, 16, 26, 34; 22:10; 23:28; 24:27, 33, 37, 39, 46; 25:9, 20; 27:64, 66; 28:15; **Mk** 2:2, 8; 3:20, 20; 4:1, 17, 26, 32, 37, 40; 6:31; 7:18, 36; 8:8; 9:3; 10:8, 43; 13:29; 14:59; 15:5, 15, 39; 16:19; **Lk** 1:21, 60; 2:6, 21; 5:7, 10, 15; 6:3, 10, 26; 7:9; 9:15; 10:21, 21; 11:2, 30; 12:21, 28, 38, 43, 54; 14:21, 33; 16:5, 26; 17:10, 24, 26; 18:13, 39; 20:15, 20; 21:31, 34; 22:26; 24:24; **Jn** 3:8, 14, 16; 4:40, 46, 53; 5:21, 26; 6:9, 10, 19, 57; 7:43; 8:7, 59; 10:15; 11:28; 12:37, 50; 13:12, 13, 33; 14:2, 9, 31; 15:8, 9; 17:18; 18:15, 22; 20:4, 20, 21; 21:11, 15; **Ac** 1:11; 3:12, 18; 4:21; 5:8, 32; 7:1, 5, 8, 15, 19, 51; 8:32; 10:14; 11:8; 12:8, 15; 13:4, 8, 47; 14:1; 15:30, 39, 39; 16:5, 26; 17:11, 33; 19:2, 10, 12, 14, 16, 20, 22, 27; 20:11, 13, 24, 35; 21:11, 35; 22:24; 23:7, 11, 18, 22; 24:9, 14; 27:17, 44; 28:9, 14; **Ro** 1:15, 20; 4:18; 5:3, 11, 12, 15, 16, 18, 19, 21; 6:3, 4, 19; 7:2, 3, 3, 25; 8:8, 9, 17; 9:16; 10:17; 11:5, 16, 26, 31; 12:5, 20; 14:12; 15:19, 20; **1Co** 1:7; 2:11; 3:7, 15; 4:1; 5:1, 3; 6:5; 7:17, 17, 26, 36, 37, 38, 40; 8:12; 9:14, 15, 24, 26, 26; 11:12, 28; 12:12; 13:2; 14:9, 10, 12, 25; 15:11, 11, 15, 22, 42, 45, 54; 16:1; **2Co** 1:5, 7, 10; 2:7; 3:7; 4:12; 5:3; 7:7, 14; 8:6, 11; 9:7; 10:7; 11:3, 9, 22, 22, 22; 12:16; **Gal** 1:6, 9; 3:3, 4, 9; 4:3, 29, 31; 5:17; 6:2; **Eph** 2:15; 4:20, 21; 5:24, 28, 33; **Php** 1:13, 20; 2:23; 3:17; 4:1; **Col** 2:6; 3:13; **1Th** 1:7, 8; 2:4, 8; 4:1, 14, 17; 5:2; **2Th** 1:4; 2:4; 3:17; **1Ti** 1:4; 3:11; 6:20; **2Ti** 3:8; **Heb** 1:4; 2:3; 3:11, 19; 4:7; 5:3, 5; 6:15; 7:9, 22; 9:28; 10:25, 33; 11:3, 12; 12:1, 1, 20, 21; 13:6; **Jas** 1:11; 2:12, 12, 17, 26; 3:4, 5, 6, 10, 12; **1Pe** 1:15; 2:3, 15; 3:17; 4:10; 5:13; **2Pe** 1:11; **1Jn** 2:6; 4:11, 17; **Rev** 1:7; 2:15; 3:16; 8:12; 13:13; 16:7, 18, 18; 17:3; 18:7, 17; 22:20

SOME [231]

Ge 19:19; 27:3; 30:35; 33:15; 37:20, 20; 47:2; **Ex** 16:17, 17, 20, 27; 30:36; **Lev** 4:7, 17, 18; 14:14, 15, 25, 27; 25:25; 27:16; **Nu** 5:20; 21:1; 27:20; 31:3; **Dt** 24:1; **Jos** 8:22, 22; **Jdg** 21:13; **Ru** 2:16; **1Sa** 8:11; 13:7; 24:10; 27:5; **2Sa** 11:17, 24; 17:9, 9, 9, 12; **1Ki** 14:13; **2Ki** 2:16, 16; 5:13; 7:9, 13; 9:33; 17:25; **1Ch** 4:42; 9:29, 30; 12:19; **2Ch** 12:7; 16:10; 17:11; 20:2; **Ezr** 2:68; 7:7; 10:44; **Ne** 2:12; 5:3, 5; 6:2; 7:70, 71, 73; 11:25; 12:44; 13:15, 19; **Job** 24:2; **Ps** 20:7, 7; 69:20; **Pr** 4:16; **Jer** 49:9; **Eze** 6:8; **Da** 8:10; 11:35; 12:2, 2; **Am** 4:11; **Ob** 1:5; **Mt** 13:4, 5, 7, 8, 8, 8, 23, 23, 23; 16:14, 14, 28; 19:12, 12; 23:34, 34; 27:47; 28:11, 17; **Mk** 2:1; 4:4, 5, 7, 8, 8, 8, 20, 20, 20; 7:2; 8:28; 9:1; 12:5, 5; 14:4, 65; 15:35; **Lk** 8:5, 6, 7; 9:7, 8, 19, 27; 11:15, 49; 13:1; 19:39; 21:5, 16; 23:8; **Jn** 3:25; 6:64; 7:12, 25, 41, 44; 9:16, 40; 10:1; 11:37, 46; 13:29; 16:17; **Ac** 5:15; 8:9, 31, 34; 11:20; 13:11; 15:36; 17:4, 18, 18, 21, 32; 18:23; 19:32, 32; 21:34, 34; 27:27, 34, 36, 44, 44; 28:24, 24; **Ro** 1:11, 13; 3:3, 8; 5:7; 11:14, 17; 15:15; **1Co** 4:18; 6:11; 8:7; 9:22; 10:7, 8, 9, 10; 12:28; 15:6, 12, 34, 35, 37; **2Co** 3:1; 10:2, 12; **Gal** 1:7; **Eph** 4:11, 11, 11, 11; **Php** 1:15, 15; **1Th** 3:5; **2Th** 3:11; **1Ti** 1:3, 6, 19; 4:1; 5:15, 24, 24, 25; 6:10, 21; **2Ti** 2:18, 20, 20; **Heb** 3:4, 16; 4:6; 10:25; 11:40; 13:2; **1Pe** 4:12; **2Pe** 3:9, 16; **Jude** 1:22; **Rev** 2:10

SOMEBODY [2]

Lk 8:46; **Ac** 5:36

SOMETHING [8]

1Sa 20:26; **Mk** 5:43; **Lk** 11:54; **Jn** 13:29; **Ac** 3:5; 23:15, 18; **Gal** 6:3

SOMETIME [3]

Col 1:21; 3:7; **1Pe** 3:20

SOMETIMES [3]

Eph 2:13; 5:8; **Tit** 3:3

SOMEWHAT [25]

Lev 4:13, 22, 27; 13:6, 19, 21, 24, 26, 28, 56; **1Ki** 2:14; **2Ki** 5:20; **2Ch** 10:4, 9, 10; **Lk** 7:40; **Ac** 23:20; 25:26; **Ro** 15:24; **2Co** 5:12; 10:8; **Gal** 2:6, 6; **Heb** 8:3; **Rev** 2:4

SOON [65]

Ge 18:33; 27:30; 44:3; **Ex** 2:18; 9:29; 32:19; **Dt** 4:26; **Jos** 2:7, 11; 3:13; 8:19, 29; **Jdg** 8:33; 9:33; **1Sa** 9:13; 13:10; 20:41; 29:10; **2Sa**

Idx

THE [64039]

Idx

THEE [3826]

THEIR [3931]

THEIRS [21]

THEM [6429]

THEMSELVES [409]

THEN [2168]

THENCE [145]

THENCEFORTH [4]

THERE [2299]

THEREABOUT [1]

THEREBY [21]

THEREFORE [1237]

THINE [933]

THING [548]

THINGS [1161]

THINGS' [1]

THIS [2786]

THITHER [95]

THITHERWARD [3]

THOSE [465]

THOU [5474]

THOUGH [233]

THROUGH [463]

THROUGHOUT [162]

THUS [737]

THY [4607]

THYSELF [215]

TILL [169]

TO [13641]

TOGETHER [484]

TOLD [283]

TOO [51]

TOOK [752]

TOOKEST [2]

TOWARD [265]

TOWARDS [81]

UNDER [392]

UNDERNEATH [3]

UNTIL [366]

UNTO [9005]

UP [2381]

UPON [2763]

UPWARD [61]

US [1449]

VERILY [140]

VERY [257]

WAS [4531]

WAST [66]

WE [1844]

WENT [1400]

WENTEST [14]

WERE [2776]

WERT [6]

WHAT [984]

WHATSOEVER [152]

WHEN [2848]

WHEREWITH [100]

Ge 27:41; **Ex** 3:9; 4:17; 16:32; 17:5; 29:33; **Nu** 3:31, 48; 4:9, 12, 14; 16:39; 25:18; 30:4, 4, 5, 6, 7, 8, 9, 11; 35:17, 18, 23; **Dt** 22:12; 28:53, 55, 57; 33:1; **Jos** 8:26; **Jdg** 6:15; 9:4, 9, 38; 16:6, 10, 13; **1Sa** 6:2; 8:8; 29:4; **2Sa** 13:15, 15; 21:3; **1Ki** 8:59; 15:26, 34; 16:26; 21:22; 22:22; **2Ki** 25:14; **1Ch** 18:8; **2Ch** 18:20; 35:21; **Job** 15:3; **Ps** 79:12; 89:51, 51; 93:1; 119:42; **Isa** 28:12; **Jer** 18:10; 19:9; 21:4; 33:16; 52:18; **La** 1:12; **Eze** 16:19; 29:20; 32:16; 36:18; 40:42; **Da** 2:1; **Mic** 6:6; **Mal** 2:5; **Mt** 5:13; **Mk** 3:28; 9:50; **Lk** 14:34; 17:8; **Jn** 13:5; **Ro** 14:19; **2Co** 1:4; 7:7; 10:2; **Gal** 5:1; **Eph** 2:4; 4:1; 6:16; **1Th** 3:9; **Heb** 10:29

WHETHER [171]

Ge 18:21; 24:21; 27:21; 31:39; 37:14, 32; 42:16; 43:6; **Ex** 4:18; 12:19; 16:4; 19:13; 21:31; 22:4, 8, 9; 34:19; **Lev** 3:1; 5:1, 2; 7:26; 11:32, 35; 13:47, 48, 48, 52, 55; 15:3; 16:29; 17:15; 18:9; 22:28; 27:12, 14, 26, 30, 33; **Nu** 9:21, 22; 11:23; 13:18, 19, 19, 20, 20; 15:30; 18:15; **Dt** 4:32; 8:2; 13:3; 18:3; 22:6; 24:14; **Jos** 24:15; **Jdg** 2:22; 3:4; 9:2; 18:5; **Ru** 3:10; **2Sa** 12:22; 15:21; **1Ki** 20:18, 18, 33; **2Ki** 1:2; **2Ch** 14:11; 15:13, 13; **Ezr** 2:59; 5:17; 7:26; **Ne** 7:61; **Est** 3:4; 4:11, 14; **Job** 34:29, 33, 33; 37:13; **Pr** 20:11, 11; 29:9; **Ecc** 2:19; 5:12; 11:6, 6; 12:14, 14; **SS** 6:11; 7:12; **Jer** 30:6; 42:6, 6; **Eze** 2:5, 5, 7, 7; 3:11, 11; 44:31; **Mt** 9:5; 21:31; 23:17, 19; 26:63; 27:21, 49; **Mk** 2:9; 3:2; 15:36, 44; **Lk** 3:15; 5:23; 6:7; 14:28, 31; 22:27; 23:6; **Jn** 7:17, 17; 9:25; **Ac** 1:24; 4:19; 5:8; 9:2; 10:18; 17:11; 19:2; 25:20; **Ro** 6:16; 12:6; 14:8, 8, 8; **1Co** 1:16; 3:22; 7:16, 16; 8:5; 10:31; 12:13, 13, 26; 13:8, 8, 8; 14:7; 15:11; **2Co** 1:6, 6; 2:9; 5:9, 10, 13, 13; 8:23; 12:2, 2, 3; 13:5; **Eph** 6:8; **Php** 1:18, 20, 27; **Col** 1:16, 20; **1Th** 5:10; **2Th** 2:15; **1Pe** 2:13; **1Jn** 4:1

WHICH [4419]

Ge 1:7, 7, 21, 29, 29; 2:2, 2, 3, 11, 14, 22; 3:1, 3, 17, 24; 4:11; 5:29; 6:2, 4, 15; 7:23; 8:6, 7, 12; 9:4, 12, 15, 17; 11:5, 6; 13:4, 5, 15, 18; 14:2, 3, 6, 7, 15, 17, 20, 24, 24; 16:15; 17:10, 12, 21; 18:8, 10, 13, 17, 19, 21, 27; 19:5, 8, 14, 15, 19, 21, 25, 29; 20:3, 13; 21:2, 9, 25, 29; 22:2, 3, 9, 17; 23:9, 9, 16, 17, 17, 17; 24:7, 7, 24, 42, 48, 60; 25:6, 7, 9, 10; 26:2, 3, 15, 18, 18, 32, 35; 27:8, 15, 17, 27, 45, 46; 28:4, 9, 15, 22; 29:27; 30:26, 30, 37, 38; 31:1, 10, 12, 16, 18, 18, 39, 43, 51; 32:8, 9, 10, 12, 13, 32, 32; 33:5, 8, 18; 34:1, 7, 28, 28; 35:3, 4, 4, 4, 6, 12, 19, 26, 27; 36:5, 6; 37:6; 38:10, 14; 39:1, 6, 17, 19, 23; 40:5, 20; 41:28, 36, 43, 48, 48, 50; 42:9, 38; 43:2, 26, 32; 44:5, 8; 45:6, 27, 27; 46:5, 6, 8, 15, 20, 22, 25, 26, 27, 27, 31; 47:14, 22, 26; 48:5, 6, 15, 16, 22; 49:1, 30, 30; 50:3, 5, 10, 11, 13, 15, 24; **Ex** 1:1, 8, 15; 3:7, 16, 20; 4:9, 18, 19, 21, 28, 30; 5:8, 14; 6:7, 8, 27; 7:15, 17; 8:3, 12, 22; 9:3, 19; 10:2, 5, 5, 5, 6, 15, 19, 21; 12:10, 16, 19, 25, 39; 13:3, 5, 8, 12; 14:13, 19, 31; 15:7, 13, 16, 17, 17, 25, 26, 26; 16:1, 5, 8, 15, 16, 16, 23, 23, 23, 26, 32; 18:3, 9; 19:6, 7, 22; 20:2, 12; 21:1; 22:9, 13; 23:16, 16, 20, 28; 24:3, 5, 8, 12; 25:3, 16, 22, 22, 40; 26:10, 13, 30; 27:21; 28:4, 8, 24, 26, 38; 29:27, 27, 27, 27, 35, 38; 30:37; 32:1, 2, 3, 4, 7, 8, 8, 11, 14, 20, 23, 32, 34, 35; 33:1, 1, 7, 7; 34:1, 10, 11, 34; 35:1, 4, 25, 29; 36:3, 4, 5, 12, 17, 25; 37:16; 38:8; 39:19; **Lev** 1:8, 12; 2:10, 11; 3:4, 5, 10, 15; 4:2, 3, 7, 7, 9, 13, 14, 18, 18, 22, 27, 28, 28; 5:6, 7, 8, 10, 17; 6:2, 3, 4, 4, 4, 4, 5, 10, 15, 20; 7:4, 8, 11, 21, 24, 25, 36, 38; 8:5, 30, 32, 36; 9:5, 6, 8, 12, 15, 18, 18, 19, 24; 10:1, 6, 11, 14, 16; 11:2, 10, 13, 21, 23, 26, 34, 34, 36, 37, 39; 13:18, 58; 14:32, 34, 37, 40; 15:12, 33; 16:2, 6, 9, 10, 11, 11, 23; 17:2, 5, 8, 13, 15, 15; 18:5, 24, 27, 30; 19:22, 22, 36; 20:8, 23, 24, 25; 21:3, 8; 22:2, 3, 6, 8, 15, 18, 24, 32; 23:2, 4, 10, 37, 38; 25:2, 5, 11, 25, 28, 31, 38, 42, 44, 45; 26:13, 22, 32, 40, 46; 27:11, 22, 22, 26, 29, 34; **Nu** 1:17, 44; 2:12, 32; 3:3, 26, 39, 46; 4:26, 37; 5:7, 9, 18; 6:5, 18, 21; 8:4; 10:4, 25, 29; 11:5, 12, 17, 20; 12:3; 13:2, 16, 24, 32, 32, 33; 14:6, 7, 8, 11, 15, 16, 22, 22, 23, 27, 27, 29, 30, 31, 31, 34, 36, 38, 40, 45; 15:2, 22, 39, 41; 16:11, 12, 40; 18:9, 12, 13, 15, 16, 19, 21, 24, 26, 28; 19:2, 2, 15; 20:12, 24; 21:1, 11, 13, 20, 30, 34; 22:5, 11, 20, 30, 36, 36; 23:12; 24:4, 4, 6, 12, 16, 16; 25:18; 26:4, 9; 27:12, 17, 17, 17, 17, 17; 28:3, 6, 23; 30:1, 8, 8, 14, 16; 31:12, 14, 21, 21, 28, 30, 32, 36, 38, 39, 40, 41, 42, 47, 48, 49; 32:4, 7, 9, 11, 24, 38, 39; 33:1, 4, 6, 7, 36, 40, 55; 34:13, 13, 17; 35:4, 6, 6, 7, 8, 8, 11, 13, 14, 25, 31, 34; 36:6, 13; **Dt** 1:1, 4, 4, 8, 14, 18, 19, 20, 25, 30, 35, 38, 39, 39, 44; 2:4, 8, 11, 12, 14, 22, 23, 23, 29, 29, 29, 35, 36; 3:2, 4, 9, 12, 12, 13, 16, 19, 20, 20, 28; 4:1, 1, 2, 2, 6, 8, 9, 13, 19, 21, 23, 23, 28, 31, 32, 40, 40, 42, 44, 45, 47, 48, 48; 5:1, 6, 16, 28, 31, 31, 33, 33; 6:1, 2, 6, 10, 10, 11, 11, 11, 12, 14, 17, 18, 18, 20, 23; 7:8, 9, 11, 12, 13, 15, 16, 19; 8:1, 1, 2, 3, 10, 11, 14, 16, 18, 20; 9:3, 5, 9, 10, 12, 12, 16, 18, 21, 23, 26, 26, 28, 29; 10:2, 4, 5, 11, 13, 17, 21; 11:2, 2, 3, 7, 8, 9, 12, 13, 17, 21, 22, 27, 28, 28, 30, 31, 32; 12:1, 1, 2, 5, 9, 10, 11, 11, 14, 15, 17, 18, 21, 21, 25, 26, 26, 28, 28, 31; 13:2, 5, 5, 6, 6, 7, 10, 12, 13, 18, 18; 14:4, 12, 23, 24, 25, 29, 29; 15:3, 4, 5, 7, 8, 20; 16:2, 4, 5, 6, 7, 10, 11, 15, 16, 17, 18, 20, 20, 21, 22; 17:2, 3, 5, 8, 10, 10, 11, 11, 11, 14, 15, 18; 18:6, 7, 8, 9, 14, 17, 19, 20, 20, 21, 22; 19:2, 3, 4, 8, 9, 10, 14, 14, 16, 17, 20; 20:1, 14, 15, 15, 16, 18, 20; 21:1, 2, 3, 3, 3, 4, 9, 16, 16, 18, 23; 22:3, 5, 9, 28; 23:13, 15, 16, 23, 23; 24:3, 4, 4, 5; 25:6, 6, 15, 19; 26:1, 2, 2, 3, 10, 11, 12, 13, 15, 19; 27:1, 2, 3, 4, 10; 28:1, 8, 11, 13, 14, 15, 33, 34, 36, 36, 45, 48, 50, 51, 52, 53, 54, 56, 57, 60, 61, 64, 67; 29:1, 1, 3, 12, 16, 17, 22, 23, 25, 29; 30:1, 5, 7, 8, 10, 11, 20; 31:5, 7, 9, 11, 13, 16, 18, 20, 21, 21, 23, 25, 29; 32:15, 21, 21, 38, 46, 46, 49, 49, 52; 34:4, 11, 12; **Jos** 1:2, 6, 7, 11, 13, 14, 15, 15; 2:3, 6, 7, 17, 18, 20; 3:4, 16; 4:9, 10, 20, 23; 5:1, 1, 6, 6; 6:25; 7:2, 11, 14, 14, 14; 8:27, 31, 32, 33, 35; 9:1, 10, 13, 20, 27; 10:11, 20, 24, 27, 32; 12:1, 2, 2, 4, 7, 7, 9; 13:3, 3, 8, 10, 12, 21, 21, 30, 32; 14:1, 1, 15; 15:7, 8, 9, 10, 13, 25, 49, 54, 60; 17:5; 18:2, 3, 7, 13, 14, 16, 17, 28; 19:50, 51; 20:7; 21:4, 9, 10, 11, 20, 40, 43, 45; 22:4, 5, 9, 17, 28, 30; 23:13, 14, 15, 15, 16, 16; 24:5, 8, 12, 13, 13, 13, 14, 15, 17, 18, 23, 27, 30, 31, 32, 32, 33; **Jdg** 1:16, 26; 2:1, 10, 10, 12, 16, 17, 20, 21; 3:1, 4, 16, 20, 31; 4:2, 11, 11, 14; 6:2, 8, 11, 13, 26; 8:27, 35; 9:2, 4, 13, 24, 24, 56; 10:4, 4, 8, 14; 11:24, 28, 36, 39; 12:5; 13:8; 14:19; 15:19; 16:8, 24, 29, 29, 30, 30; 17:2, 6; 18:5, 16, 24, 27, 27, 31; 19:10, 14, 16, 19; 20:9, 13, 15, 18, 31, 36, 42, 46; 21:12, 14, 19, 25; **Ru** 1:22; 2:9, 11; 4:3, 11, 12, 14, 15, 15; **1Sa** 1:27; 2:20, 29, 32, 35; 3:11, 12, 13; 4:4; 6:4, 7, 8, 17, 18; 7:14; 8:8, 18; 9:22, 23, 23, 24, 24; 10:2, 4; 11:11; 12:7, 8, 16, 17, 21; 13:5, 13, 14; 14:2, 4, 14, 14, 21, 22, 30, 39; 15:2, 14, 20, 21; 16:4, 16, 19; 17:1, 31, 40; 20:23, 27, 36, 37; 22:9, 14; 23:13, 19; 24:4; 25:7, 27, 32, 33, 34, 35, 44; 26:1, 3; 28:21; 29:1, 3, 4; 30:10, 14, 17, 20, 21, 23, 27, 27, 27, 28, 28, 28, 29, 29, 29, 30, 30, 30, 31; 31:11; **2Sa** 2:15, 16, 32; 3:8, 14, 26; 4:8; 5:6; 6:4, 21, 22; 7:12, 23; 8:11, 11; 9:3; 10:12; 12:3; 13:10, 23; 14:7, 13, 14; 15:4, 7, 16, 18; 16:11, 21, 23; 17:10, 18, 25; 18:18, 28; 19:5, 16, 19, 38; 20:5, 8; 21:12, 16, 18; 22:44; 23:15; 24:2, 24; **1Ki** 1:8, 9, 48; 2:4, 8, 24, 27, 31, 44, 46; 3:8, 13, 21, 28; 4:2, 7, 11, 12, 13, 13, 19, 20, 34; 5:3, 7, 8, 16, 16; 6:1, 2, 12, 12, 20, 38; 7:8, 17, 20, 41, 45, 51; 8:1, 2, 9, 15, 21, 26, 28, 29, 29, 34, 36, 38, 40, 43, 44, 48, 48, 48, 48, 51, 56, 58, 63; 9:1, 3, 6, 7, 7, 8, 12, 13, 15, 19, 20, 23, 24, 25, 26; 10:3, 5, 7, 8, 9, 10, 13, 24; 11:2, 8, 9, 10, 11, 13, 18, 23, 32, 33, 36; 12:4, 8, 8, 9, 15, 17, 21, 28, 31, 32, 33, 33; 13:3, 4, 4, 5, 11, 12, 21, 22, 26, 26, 32, 32; 14:2, 8, 15, 18, 20, 21, 22, 24, 26, 27; 15:3, 5, 11, 15, 15, 20, 23, 27, 29, 30, 30; 16:12, 13, 13, 15, 19, 19, 24, 27, 32, 34; 17:9, 16; 18:3, 19, 26, 26; 19:3, 18, 18; 20:19, 34; 21:1, 4, 11, 15, 18, 25; 22:13, 16, 24, 38, 39, 43, 46; **2Ki** 1:4, 6, 7, 16, 17, 18; 2:15, 22; 3:3, 8, 11; 4:4, 9; 5:20; 6:10, 11; 7:13, 15; 8:21, 29; 9:5, 15, 19, 27, 36; 10:5, 6, 10, 10, 17, 30, 31, 33; 11:2, 16; 12:2, 20; 13:2, 2, 11, 25; 14:3, 5, 6, 11, 15, 21, 24, 25, 25, 28; 15:3, 9, 12, 15, 18, 24, 28, 34; 16:2, 7, 14, 19; 17:2, 7, 8, 13, 13, 15, 19, 22, 25, 26, 29, 32, 34, 37; 18:3, 6, 9, 14, 16, 17, 18, 21, 27, 37; 19:2, 4, 6, 6, 12, 12, 15, 16, 20, 28, 29; 20:3, 11, 17, 18, 19; 21:2, 3, 4, 7, 7, 8, 11, 15, 16, 20, 25; 22:2, 4, 4, 5, 13, 16, 18, 18, 20; 23:2, 8, 10, 11, 12, 12, 13, 13, 15, 16, 17, 19, 24, 27, 27, 32, 37; 24:2, 4, 9, 13, 19; 25:4, 8, 16, 19, 19; **1Ch** 1:46; 2:3, 19, 42, 55; 3:1; 4:10, 11, 18; 6:61, 65; 9:22, 25; 10:13, 13; 11:4, 5; 12:31, 32, 33; 13:2, 6; 14:4; 15:3; 16:15, 16, 40; 17:11; 19:13, 18; 20:4; 21:19, 23, 24, 29; 22:13; 23:4, 5, 29, 29; 25:2; 26:22, 26, 26; 27:1, 31; 29:3, 17, 19; **2Ch** 1:3, 4, 6, 14; 2:5, 9, 11, 14, 15; 3:5; 4:3, 12, 12, 13; 5:2, 3, 6, 10, 12; 6:4, 9, 14, 15, 15, 16, 17, 18, 19, 20, 21, 25, 27, 31, 32, 33, 34, 34, 36, 38, 38, 38, 39; 7:6, 7, 14, 19, 20, 20, 21, 22; 8:2, 4, 7, 12; 9:2, 4, 5, 7, 8, 10, 12, 14, 18; 10:8, 9, 15; 11:1, 10, 15, 19, 20; 12:4, 9, 10, 13; 13:4, 8, 10; 14:2; 15:8, 11; 16:14, 14; 17:2; 18:23; 20:2, 11, 22, 25, 32; 21:6, 9, 13; 22:6; 23:9, 19; 24:2, 20, 22; 25:2, 9, 13, 15, 15, 21; 26:4, 23; 27:2; 28:1, 6, 11, 15, 23; 29:2, 6, 19, 32; 30:7, 8, 16; 31:6, 10, 12, 19, 20; 32:3, 19, 21; 33:2, 3, 7, 7, 7, 8, 11, 22, 22; 34:2, 9, 11, 24, 26, 31; 35:3, 3, 26; 36:5, 8, 8, 9, 12, 14, 23; **Ezr** 1:2, 3, 3, 5, 7; 2:1, 2, 59, 61, 68; 4:2, 12, 15, 18, 20, 24; 5:2, 6, 8, 11, 14, 16, 17; 6:5, 5, 5, 6, 9, 9, 12, 13, 15, 18, 21; 7:6, 8, 13, 14, 15, 16, 17, 20, 21, 25, 27, 27; 8:25, 35; 9:11, 11, 11; 10:14; **Ne** 1:2, 6, 6, 7; 2:8, 13, 18; 3:25; 4:2, 3, 12, 14, 17, 23; 5:8, 18; 6:6; 7:5, 61, 63, 72; 8:1, 4, 9, 14; 9:5, 15, 23, 26, 29, 35; 10:29; 12:8, 37; 13:5, 15, 16; **Est** 1:1, 2, 9, 13, 14, 14, 18, 20; 2:4, 6, 9, 14, 16, 21; 3:3, 13; 4:6, 16; 6:8, 8; 7:9; 8:2, 5, 5, 8, 9, 11, 12; 9:13, 22, 25, 26, 26; **Job** 3:3, 14, 16, 21, 22, 25, 25; 4:14, 19, 21; 5:1, 9, 11; 6:6, 16, 26; 9:5, 5, 6, 7, 8, 9, 10; 11:6; 14:19; 15:9, 14, 16, 17, 18, 28, 28; 16:8; 20:7, 9, 11, 18, 19, 20; 21:27; 22:15, 16, 17; 23:5; 24:11, 16, 19; 25:6; 27:11, 13; 28:7, 7; 29:16; 32:19; 33:27; 34:8, 32; 35:5; 36:16, 24, 28; 37:5, 16, 18, 21; 38:23, 24; 39:14; 40:15; 41:1; 42:3, 8; **Ps** 1:4; 3:2; 7:T, 10, 15; 8:3; 9:11, 13, 15, 16; 17:7, 13, 14, 14; 18:17; 19:5; 21:11; 25:3; 28:3; 31:18, 19, 19; 32:8, 9; 35:7, 10, 27; 40:5, 5; 41:9; 44:10; 45:1; 51:8; 58:5, 7, 8; 59:12; 60:10, 10; 61:7; 65:6, 7, 9; 66:9, 14, 20; 68:6, 16, 28, 33; 69:4, 22; 71:20, 23; 74:2, 2; 78:3, 5, 6, 45, 45, 54, 60, 68, 69; 79:10; 80:12, 15; 81:10; 83:10; 85:12; 86:17; 89:49; 90:5; 91:9; 94:20; 102:18; 104:8, 10, 12, 15, 16; 105:8, 9; 106:21, 36; 107:25, 37; 109:19; 114:8; 115:15; 118:20, 22, 24, 27; 119:21, 39, 47, 48, 49, 85, 165; 121:2; 125:1; 129:6, 8; 134:1; 135:21; 136:13, 16, 17; 138:8; 139:16; 140:2; 141:5, 9; 144:1; 146:6, 6, 7, 7; 147:9; 148:6; **Pr** 1:19; 2:16, 17; 6:7; 7:5; 9:5; 11:22; 12:27; 14:12, 33; 19:17; 20:25; 22:28; 23:5, 8; 24:13; 25:1; 27:16; 28:3; 30:18, 18, 21, 24, 29, 30; 31:3; **Ecc** 1:3, 9, 9, 9, 10, 15, 15; 2:3, 12, 16, 18, 20; 3:2, 10, 15, 15, 15, 19; 4:2, 2, 3, 15; 5:4, 13, 15, 18, 18; 6:1, 10, 12; 7:13, 19, 24, 28; 8:7, 12, 13, 14, 15; 9:9, 9; 10:5, 5, 20; 12:5, 10, 11; **SS** 1:1; 3:7; 4:2, 5; 6:6; 7:2, 4, 13; 8:6, 12; **Isa** 1:1, 29; 2:8, 20; 3:12; 5:23; 6:6; 8:18; 10:1, 3; 11:10, 11, 16; 13:1, 17; 14:12; 15:7; 17:2, 8, 9, 12; 18:1; 19:15, 16, 17; 21:10; 22:3, 15; 26:2; 27:13; 28:1, 2, 4, 4, 14, 29; 29:11; 30:10, 24, 31, 32; 31:7; 36:3; 37:4, 12, 12, 17, 22, 29, 30; 38:3, 8, 8; 39:6, 7, 8; 42:5; 43:16, 17; 44:2, 14; 45:3; 46:3, 3; 47:11; 48:1, 1, 14, 17, 17; 49:20; 50:1; 51:10, 12, 17, 23; 52:15, 15; 55:2, 2, 2, 11; 56:8, 11; 57:16; 59:5, 21; 61:9; 62:2, 6, 8; 63:7; 64:3; 65:2, 4, 4, 5, 7, 18; 66:4, 22; **Jer** 2:11, 11; 3:6, 15; 5:17, 21, 21, 22; 7:10, 11, 12, 14, 14, 30, 31, 31; 8:3, 17; 9:13, 14, 24, 25; 10:1; 11:4, 4, 5, 8, 10, 10, 11, 17; 12:14; 13:4, 6, 10, 10, 10; 15:4, 14, 14, 18; 17:4, 4, 16, 19; 18:1, 14; 19:2, 3, 5; 20:2, 5, 16; 21:1, 4, 13; 22:6, 11, 11, 28; 23:4, 7, 8, 8, 27, 27, 40; 24:2, 8; 25:2, 13, 13, 22, 26, 27, 29; 26:2, 3, 4, 19; 27:3, 8, 9, 18, 20; 28:1, 6, 9; 29:1, 8, 19, 21, 22, 23, 27; 31:2, 21, 32, 35, 35; 32:1, 2, 8, 11, 11, 14, 14, 20, 22, 32, 34, 35, 35; 33:3, 4, 9, 10, 12, 14, 24; 34:1, 5, 8, 10, 14, 15, 18, 18, 19, 21; 35:1, 4, 4, 15, 16; 36:3, 4, 6, 21, 27, 28, 32; 37:2, 7, 19; 38:3, 7, 20; 39:10; 40:1, 1, 4, 7, 10, 15; 41:9, 13, 17; 42:5, 8, 16, 21; 43:1, 9; 44:1, 1, 3, 9, 14, 14, 15, 20, 22; 45:4, 4; 46:1, 2, 2; 49:28, 31, 31; 50:3; 51:12, 25, 44, 59; 52:2, 7, 12, 12, 19, 19, 20, 25, 25; **La** 1:12; 2:3, 17; 5:18; **Eze** 1:2, 23, 23; 3:20, 23; 4:10, 14; 5:9, 16, 16; 6:9, 9, 9; 7:13, 13; 8:3, 14, 17; 9:2, 3, 6, 11; 10:22; 11:1, 3, 23; 12:2, 28; 13:11, 16, 16, 17; 14:7; 15:2, 6; 16:14, 17, 19, 27, 32, 36, 45, 51, 52, 57, 59; 17:3; 18:5, 14, 18, 19, 21, 27; 19:14; 20:6, 11, 13, 15, 15, 21, 28, 32, 42; 21:14; 22:4, 5, 13, 13; 23:6, 24, 42; 24:21, 27; 25:9; 26:6, 17, 17; 27:3, 7, 7, 27; 29:3, 16; 30:22; 32:9, 23, 24, 24, 27, 29, 30; 33:14, 16, 19, 29; 34:4, 4, 4, 4, 16, 16, 16, 16, 19, 19; 35:11, 12; 36:4, 5, 21, 22, 23, 23; 37:1, 19; 38:8, 12, 17; 39:19, 28; 40:2, 6, 6, 6, 40, 44, 46; 41:1, 6, 9, 9, 15; 42:1, 3, 3, 11, 13, 14; 43:3, 19; 44:1, 10, 13; 45:4, 14; 46:19, 19; 47:8, 9, 14, 16, 16, 22; 48:8, 11, 11, 22, 29; **Da** 1:2, 5, 8, 10, 15; 2:14, 26, 27, 34, 39, 44; 3:2, 12, 14, 15, 18, 29; 4:5, 20, 21, 24; 5:2, 2, 3, 13, 23; 6:1, 8, 12, 13, 15, 24, 26; 7:6, 11, 14, 14, 17, 17, 19, 19, 20, 23; 8:1, 2, 3, 6, 9, 13, 16, 20, 26; 9:1, 6, 10, 12, 14, 18; 10:4, 10, 21; 11:4, 7, 16, 24; 12:1, 6, 7; **Hos** 1:3, 10; 2:8, 23; 5:9; **Joel** 1:4, 4, 4; 2:25; **Am** 1:1, 4, 7, 10, 12; 2:4; 3:1; 4:1, 1, 1, 3; 5:1, 3, 26; 6:1, 13, 13; 9:10, 12, 15; **Ob** 1:20; **Jnh** 1:9; 4:10, 10; **Mic** 1:1; 2:3; 5:3; 6:14; 7:10, 14, 20; **Na** 3:17; **Hab** 1:1, 5, 6; 2:4, 6, 17; **Zep** 1:1, 9; 2:3; **Hag** 1:11; 2:14; **Zec** 1:6, 7, 12, 19, 21, 21; 2:8; 4:2, 10, 12; 6:5, 6, 10; 7:3, 7, 12; 8:9; 10:5; 11:10, 16; 12:1; 13:6; 14:4, 7, 16; **Mal** 1:13, 14; 2:11; 4:4; **Mt** 1:20, 22, 23; 2:9, 15, 16, 17, 20, 23; 3:10; 4:13, 14, 16, 16, 24, 24; 5:6, 10, 12, 16, 44, 45, 46, 48; 6:1, 4, 6, 6, 9, 18, 18, 27, 30; 7:6, 11, 13, 14, 15, 21, 24, 26; 8:17; 9:8, 16, 20; 10:20, 28, 28, 32, 33; 11:4, 10, 14, 21, 23, 23; 12:2, 4, 4, 10, 17, 50; 13:14, 17, 17, 19, 19, 23, 24, 31, 32, 33, 35, 35, 41, 44, 48, 52, 52; 14:9; 15:1, 11, 11, 13, 18, 20, 27; 16:8, 17, 28; 17:5; 18:6, 10, 11, 12, 13, 14, 19, 23, 24, 28; 19:4, 9, 12, 12, 12, 18, 28; 20:1, 12; 21:4, 21, 24, 33, 41, 42; 22:2, 4, 8, 11, 21, 23, 31, 35, 36; 23:9, 16, 24, 26, 27, 31, 37; 24:16, 17, 18; 25:1, 24, 28, 29; 26:25, 28, 51, 62, 75; 27:3, 9, 17, 22, 35, 44, 52, 55, 56, 60; 28:5; **Mk** 1:2, 44; 2:3, 24, 26, 26; 3:1, 3, 17, 19, 22, 34; 4:16, 18, 20, 22, 25, 31; 5:25, 35, 41; 6:2, 26; 7:1, 4, 13, 15, 20; 9:1, 17, 39; 10:42; 11:21, 23, 25, 26; 12:10, 18, 25, 28, 38, 40, 42, 43; 13:19, 32; 14:18, 24, 32, 60; 15:7, 22, 28, 34, 39, 41, 43, 46; 16:6, 14; **Lk** 1:1, 2, 20, 35, 45, 70, 73; 2:4, 10, 11, 15, 15, 17, 18, 21, 24, 31, 33, 34, 37, 50; 3:9, 13, 19, 22, 23, 24, 24, 24, 24, 24, 25, 25, 25, 25, 25, 26, 26, 26, 26, 26, 27, 27, 27, 27, 27, 28, 28, 28, 28, 28, 29, 29, 29, 29, 29, 30, 30, 30, 30, 30, 31, 31, 31, 31, 31, 32, 32, 32, 32, 32, 33, 33, 33, 33, 33, 34, 34, 34, 34, 34, 35, 35, 35, 35, 35, 36, 36, 36, 36, 36, 37, 37, 37, 37, 37, 38, 38, 38, 38; 4:22, 33; 5:3, 7, 9, 10, 17, 18, 21; 6:2, 3, 4, 8, 16, 17, 27, 27, 28, 32, 33, 45, 45, 46, 48, 49; 7:25, 27, 37, 39, 41, 42, 47; 8:2, 3, 13, 13, 14, 14, 15, 16, 18, 20, 21, 26, 27, 36, 43; 9:27, 30, 31, 36, 43, 46, 61; 10:11, 13, 15, 23, 24, 24, 30, 36, 39, 42; 11:2, 5, 27, 33, 35, 40, 40, 44, 50, 51; 12:1, 3, 5, 15, 20, 24, 25, 26, 28, 33, 47; 13:11, 14, 19, 21, 30, 30, 34; 14:2, 5, 7, 24, 28; 15:4, 6, 7, 9, 30; 16:1, 10, 12, 12, 15, 15, 19, 20, 21, 26; 17:7, 10, 10, 12, 31; 18:2, 7, 9, 27, 34, 39; 19:2, 10, 20, 26, 27, 30, 42; 20:17, 20, 25, 25, 27, 35, 46, 47; 21:6, 6, 15, 21, 21, 22, 26; 22:1, 19, 20, 23, 24, 28, 49, 52; 23:27, 29, 29, 33, 39, 48, 55; 24:1, 10, 12, 13, 14, 18, 19, 21, 22, 23, 24, 44, 44; **Jn** 1:9, 13, 18, 24, 29, 30, 33, 38, 40, 41, 42; 2:9, 10, 22, 23; 3:6, 6, 13, 29; 4:5, 9, 12, 25, 29, 39, 53; 5:2, 5, 12, 15, 23, 28, 30, 32, 36, 37, 39, 44; 6:1, 2, 9, 13, 22, 27, 27, 27, 33, 39, 39, 40, 41, 44, 46, 50, 51, 51, 58; 7:31, 39; 8:9, 26, 31, 38, 38, 40, 46, 53; 9:1, 7, 8, 39, 39, 40; 10:6, 16, 29, 32; 11:2, 16, 27, 31, 33, 37, 42, 45, 45; 12:1, 4, 21, 38, 49; 13:1; 14:24, 24, 26; 15:3, 24, 26; 17:4, 5, 6, 8, 9, 20, 22, 24; 18:1, 2, 5, 9, 9, 11, 13, 14, 16, 21, 22, 32; 19:17, 24, 32, 39; 20:8, 16, 30; 21:10, 20, 20, 24, 25, 25; **Ac** 1:2, 4, 7, 11, 11, 12, 16, 16, 21, 24, 25; 2:7, 16, 22, 33; 3:2, 10, 10, 11, 16, 18, 20, 21, 23, 25; 4:4, 11, 11, 14, 20, 21, 24, 32, 36; 5:9, 16, 17; 6:9, 10, 11, 13, 14; 7:3, 17, 18, 20, 34, 35, 37, 38, 40, 43, 45, 52, 52; 8:1, 6, 6, 9, 13, 14, 24, 26, 32; 9:7, 11, 19, 21, 22, 30, 32, 33, 36, 36, 39; 10:2, 7, 17, 17, 18, 21, 36, 37, 37, 39, 42, 44, 45, 47; 11:6, 13, 19, 20, 22, 28, 29, 30; 12:9, 10; 13:1, 7, 22, 27, 31, 32, 39, 40, 41, 45; 14:3, 13, 14, 15, 26; 15:1, 5, 8, 10, 16, 19, 23, 24, 29, 31; 16:1, 2, 3, 4, 12, 13, 14, 14, 16, 17, 21; 17:5, 12, 21, 31, 34; 18:27; 19:4, 10, 13, 14, 19, 24, 26, 31, 35, 37, 38; 20:19, 24, 28, 28, 32, 32, 38; 21:8, 9, 20, 21, 23, 25, 27, 38, 39; 22:1, 3, 5, 10, 12, 29; 23:13, 21; 24:14, 14, 15, 24; 25:5, 7, 7, 16, 19, 24; 26:3, 4, 5, 7, 7, 10, 13, 16, 16, 18, 22; 27:8, 11, 12, 16, 17, 39, 43; 28:9, 11, 24, 31; **Ro** 1:2, 3, 19, 26, 27, 27, 28, 32; 2:2, 3, 14, 15, 19, 20, 21, 27, 28, 28, 29; 3:22, 26, 30; 4:11, 12, 14, 16, 16, 17, 18; 5:5, 15, 17; 6:17; 7:2, 5, 10, 13, 13, 15, 16, 18, 19, 23; 8:1, 18, 23, 26, 39; 9:6, 8, 23, 25, 25, 30, 30, 31; 10:5, 5, 6, 8; 11:2, 7, 14, 22, 24, 24; 12:1, 9, 9, 14; 13:3, 4; 14:3, 19, 22; 15:17, 18, 22, 26, 31; 16:1, 1, 10, 11, 12, 14, 15, 17, 17, 19, 25; **1Co** 1:2, 4, 11, 18, 24, 27, 28, 28; 2:7, 8, 9, 11, 12, 13, 13, 13; 3:10, 11, 14, 17; 4:6, 17, 19; 6:16, 19, 19, 20; 7:13, 35; 8:10, 10, 10; 9:13, 13, 14, 24; 10:16, 16, 18, 19, 20, 30; 11:19, 23, 23, 24; 12:6, 22, 23, 24; 13:10, 10; 14:22; 15:1, 1, 2, 3, 10, 10, 18, 27, 29, 31, 36, 37, 46, 46, 46, 57; 16:17; **2Co** 1:1, 1, 4, 6, 6, 8, 9, 21; 2:2, 4, 6, 14, 17; 3:7, 10, 11, 11, 13, 13, 14; 4:4, 11, 14, 16, 17, 18, 18, 18, 18; 5:2, 12, 15, 15; 7:14; 8:11, 16, 19, 20, 22; 9:2, 6, 6, 11, 14; 10:2, 8, 13; 11:4, 4, 9, 9, 12, 17, 28, 30, 31; 12:4, 6, 21, 21; 13:2, 3, 7, 10; **Gal** 1:2, 7, 8, 11, 17, 20, 22, 23, 23; 2:2, 2, 4, 10, 12, 18, 20; 3:7, 9, 10, 16, 17, 21, 23; 4:8, 14, 24, 24, 24, 25, 26, 26, 27; 5:6, 12, 19, 21, 21; 6:1; **Eph** 1:1, 9, 10, 10, 14, 20, 21, 23; 2:10, 11, 17; 3:2, 5, 9, 11, 13, 19; 4:15, 16, 22, 24, 28, 29; 5:4, 12; 6:2, 17, 20; **Php** 1:1, 6, 11, 12, 23, 28, 30; 2:5, 9, 13, 21; 3:3, 6, 9, 9, 9, 12, 13, 13, 17; 4:3, 7, 9, 13, 18, 21; **Col** 1:2, 4, 5, 6, 12, 23, 23, 23, 24, 24, 25, 26, 27, 29; 2:10, 14, 17, 18, 19, 22, 23; 3:1, 5, 5, 6, 7, 10, 14, 15, 25; 4:1, 3, 9, 11, 11, 15, 15, 17; **1Th** 1:1, 10; 2:4, 13, 13, 14; 3:10; 4:5, 10, 13, 13, 14, 15, 15, 17; 5:12, 15, 21; **2Th** 1:5, 5; 2:15, 16; 3:4, 6, 11, 17; **1Ti** 1:1, 4, 4, 6, 11, 14, 16, 18, 19; 2:10; 3:7, 13, 15; 4:3, 3, 8, 14; 5:13; 6:3, 9, 10, 15, 16, 20, 21, 99; **2Ti** 1:1, 5, 6, 9, 12, 12, 13, 13, 14, 14, 15; 2:10; 3:6, 11, 14, 15, 15; 4:8; **Tit** 1:1, 2, 3, 11; 2:1; 3:5, 6, 8; **Phm** 1:5, 6, 8, 11; **Heb** 1:5, 13; 2:1, 3, 11, 13; 3:5; 4:3, 15; 5:8, 12; 6:7, 8, 10, 18, 19, 19; 7:2, 13, 14, 19, 28, 28; 8:1, 2, 6, 13; 9:2, 3, 4, 5, 7, 9, 9, 10, 15, 20, 24; 10:1, 8, 10, 11, 20, 27, 32, 35; 11:3, 3, 4, 7, 7, 8, 10, 12, 29; 12:1, 5, 9, 11, 12, 13, 14, 19, 20, 23, 27, 28; 13:3, 7, 9, 10, 21; **Jas** 1:1, 12, 21; 2:5, 7, 16, 23; 3:4, 9; 5:4, 4, 4, 11, 20; **1Pe** 1:3, 10, 11, 12, 12, 15, 23, 25; 2:7, 7, 7, 8, 10, 10, 11, 12; 3:4, 4, 13, 19, 20; 4:11, 12; 5:1, 2; **2Pe** 1:18; 2:11, 15; 3:1, 2, 7, 10, 16, 16; **1Jn** 1:1, 1, 1, 1, 2, 3, 5; 2:7, 7, 8, 24, 24, 27, 29; 3:24; 5:9, 16; **2Jn** 1:2, 5, 8; **3Jn** 1:6, 10, 11, 11; **Jude** 1:3, 6, 10, 15, 15, 17; **Rev** 1:1, 1, 3, 4, 4, 4, 4, 4, 7, 8, 8, 8, 11, 19, 19, 19, 20, 20; 2:2, 2, 6, 7, 8, 9, 10, 12, 15, 17, 20, 23, 24, 25; 3:2, 4, 9, 10, 11, 12, 12; 4:1, 1, 1, 5, 8; 5:6, 8, 13; 6:9; 7:4, 9, 10, 13, 14, 17; 8:2, 3, 4, 6, 9, 13; 9:4, 11, 13, 14, 14, 15, 18, 20, 20; 10:4, 5, 6, 8, 8, 8; 11:2, 8, 11, 16, 17, 18; 12:4, 9, 10, 13, 16, 17; 13:2, 4, 12, 14, 14; 14:3, 4, 4, 10, 13, 17, 18; 16:2, 2, 5, 9, 14; 17:1, 7, 9, 9, 12, 12, 15, 16, 18, 18; 18:6, 14, 15; 19:2, 9, 14, 20, 21; 20:2, 4, 8, 12, 12, 13, 13; 21:8, 8, 9, 12, 24, 27; 22:2, 6, 8, 9, 11, 19, 20

WHILE [210]

Ge 8:22; 19:16; 25:6; 29:9; 45:1; 46:29; **Ex** 33:22, 22; 34:29; **Lev** 4:27; 14:46; 26:43; **Nu** 11:33; 15:32; 23:15; 25:11; **Dt** 19:6; 31:27; **Jos** 14:10; **Jdg** 3:26; 11:26; 14:17; 15:1; 16:27; **1Sa** 2:13; 7:2; 9:27; 14:19; 20:14; 22:4; 25:7, 16; 27:11; **2Sa** 3:6, 35; 7:19; 12:18, 21, 22; 13:30; 15:8, 12; 17:2; 18:14; 19:32; 24:13; **1Ki** 1:14, 22, 42; 3:20; 6:7; 12:6; 17:7; 18:45; **2Ki** 6:33; **1Ch** 12:1; 17:17; 21:12; **2Ch** 10:6; 14:7; 15:2; 26:19; 34:3; **Ne** 7:3; **Est** 2:21; 6:14; **Job** 1:16, 17, 18; 20:23; 24:24; 27:3; **Ps** 7:2; 31:13; 37:10; 39:1, 3; 42:3, 10; 63:4; 69:3; 78:30; 88:15; 104:33; 146:2, 2; **Pr** 8:26; 19:18; 31:15; **Ecc** 9:3; 12:1, 2; **SS** 1:12; **Isa** 10:25; 28:4; 29:17; 55:6, 6; 63:18; **Jer** 13:16; 15:9; 33:1; 39:15; 40:5; 51:33; **La** 1:19; **Eze** 9:8; **Da** 4:31; **Hos** 1:4; **Na** 1:10, 10; **Hag** 2:6; **Zec** 14:12; **Mt**

Idx

WHILES [12]

WHILST [12]

WHITHER [124]

WHITHERSOEVER [29]

WHO [969]

WHOM [763]

WHOMSOEVER [20]

WHOSE [314]

WHOSO [54]

WHOSOEVER [183]

WHY [282]

WILL [3837]

33:16; 34:4; **Jos** 1:5, 5, 16, 16, 17, 18; 2:12, 13, 14, 17, 19, 20; 3:5, 7, 7, 10; 7:12; 8:5, 5, 6, 6, 6, 7, 18; 9:20, 20; 11:6; 13:6; 14:12; 15:16; 18:4; 22:18, 18; 23:13; 24:15, 15, 18, 19, 20, 21, 24, 24; **Jdg** 1:3, 12, 24; 2:1, 3, 21, 22; 4:7, 7, 8, 8, 9, 22; 5:3, 3; 6:16, 18, 31, 31, 31, 37, 39; 7:4, 7; 8:7, 9, 23, 25; 10:13, 18; 11:24, 31; 12:1; 13:16; 14:12, 12; 15:1, 7, 7, 12, 13, 13; 16:5, 17, 20; 17:3, 10, 13; 19:12, 12, 24; 20:8, 8, 9, 9, 10, 28; 21:7, 22; **Ru** 1:10, 11, 16, 16, 17, 17; 3:4, 5, 11, 13, 13, 13, 18, 18; 4:4; **1Sa** 1:11, 22, 22; 2:9, 15, 16, 30, 31, 35, 35; 3:11, 12, 12, 13; 6:5; 7:3, 5, 8; 8:11, 11, 12, 12, 13, 14, 15, 16, 17, 18, 19; 9:8, 13, 16, 19, 19; 10:2, 4, 6, 8; 11:1, 2, 3, 10; 12:3, 10, 14, 15, 16, 17, 22, 23; 13:12; 14:6, 8, 8, 9, 9, 10, 12, 40; 15:16, 26, 29; 16:1, 2, 3, 11; 17:9, 25, 25, 32, 37, 44, 46, 46, 46, 47; 18:11, 17, 21; 19:3, 3, 3; 20:2, 2, 4, 13, 18, 20, 21; 22:3, 7; 23:4, 11, 11, 11, 12, 12, 23, 23; 24:4, 10, 19; 25:8, 28; 26:6, 6, 8, 21; 27:11; 28:2, 19, 23; 30:15, 22, 24; **2Sa** 2:6, 26; 3:13, 18, 21, 21; 5:19; 6:21, 22, 22; 7:10, 10, 11, 12, 12, 13, 14, 14, 27; 9:7, 7; 10:2, 11; 11:11, 12; 12:11, 11, 12, 18, 22; 13:13; 14:7, 8, 15, 15, 16, 17; 15:8, 21, 25, 28, 34, 34; 16:12, 12, 18, 18, 19; 17:1, 2, 2, 2, 3, 8, 9, 9, 12, 13; 18:2, 3, 3, 4; 19:7, 7, 26, 33, 36, 38, 38; 20:21; 21:4, 4, 6, 6; 22:3, 4, 29, 50, 50; 24:24, 24; **1Ki** 1:5, 14, 30, 51, 52; 2:8, 17, 18, 20, 26, 30, 38; 3:14; 5:5, 6, 8, 9, 9; 6:12, 13, 13; 8:27; 9:5, 6, 7, 7; 11:2, 11, 11, 12, 12, 13, 13, 31, 31, 34, 34, 35, 35, 36, 37, 37, 38, 38, 39; 12:4, 7, 11, 11, 14, 14; 13:7, 8, 8, 16; 14:10, 10, 10; 16:3, 3; 18:1, 15, 23, 24; 19:20; 20:6, 9, 13, 22, 25, 28, 31, 34, 34; 21:2, 2, 4, 6, 6, 7, 21, 21, 21, 22, 29, 29; 22:14, 21, 22, 22, 30; **2Ki** 2:2, 3, 4, 5, 6; 3:7, 18; 4:30; 5:5, 11, 16, 17, 20; 6:3, 11, 19, 28; 7:4, 9, 12; 9:8, 9, 26; 10:5, 5, 6; 18:14, 21, 23, 30, 32; 19:4, 4, 7, 7, 23, 23, 28, 28, 34; 20:5, 6, 6, 6, 8, 9; 21:4, 7, 8, 8, 13, 13, 14; 22:16, 20, 20; 23:27, 27; **1Ch** 12:19; 14:10; 16:18; 17:9, 9, 10, 10, 11, 11, 12, 13, 13, 14; 19:2, 12; 21:3, 24, 24; 22:5, 9, 9, 10, 10; 28:6, 7, 9, 9, 20, 20, 21; **2Ch** 1:12; 2:10, 16, 16; 6:18; 7:14, 14, 14, 18, 20, 20, 20; 10:4, 7, 11, 11, 14, 14; 12:7, 7; 15:2, 2; 18:3, 5, 13, 20, 21, 29, 29; 20:17; 21:14; 28:23; 30:6, 9; 33:7, 8, 8; 34:24, 28, 28; **Ezr** 4:3, 13; 7:18, 26; 10:4; **Ne** 1:8, 9, 9; 2:19, 20, 20; 4:2, 2, 2, 2, 12; 5:8, 12, 12; 6:10, 10, 11; 10:39; 13:21; **Est** 3:9; 4:16, 16; 5:8; 7:8; **Job** 1:11; 2:4, 5; 5:1; 6:24; 7:11, 11, 11; 8:20, 20; 9:3, 12, 13, 18, 23, 27, 27; 10:1, 1, 2, 15; 11:11; 13:7, 8, 8, 10, 13, 15, 15, 19, 20, 22; 14:7, 7, 9, 14, 15; 15:17, 17; 17:3; 18:2, 2; 19:2, 5; 22:4, 4; 23:6; 24:25; 27:5, 6, 9, 10, 10, 11, 11; 30:24; 32:10, 14, 17, 17, 20, 20; 33:12, 26, 26, 28, 31; 34:12, 12, 23, 31, 32, 33; 35:3, 4, 13, 13; 36:2, 3, 3, 19; 37:4, 23; 38:3; 39:9, 10, 12; 40:4, 5, 5, 7, 14; 41:3, 3, 4, 12; 42:4, 4, 8; **Ps** 2:7; 3:6; 4:2, 2, 3, 6, 8; 5:2, 3, 3, 6, 7, 7; 6:9; 7:12, 17, 17; 9:1, 1, 2, 2, 9, 10, 14; 10:4, 11; 12:4, 5, 5; 13:6; 16:4, 7; 17:15; 18:1, 2, 3, 28, 49; 20:5, 5, 6, 7; 21:13; 22:22, 22, 25; 23:4, 6; 25:8, 9, 9, 14; 26:4, 5, 6, 6, 11, 12; 27:3, 4, 6, 6, 8, 10, 12; 28:1, 7; 29:11, 11; 30:1, 12; 31:7; 32:5, 8, 8; 34:1, 11; 35:18, 18; 37:33; 38:18, 18; 39:1, 1; 40:8; 41:2, 2, 3; 42:6, 8, 9; 43:4, 4; 44:5, 5, 6; 45:17; 46:2, 10, 10; 48:8, 14; 49:4, 4, 15, 18; 50:7, 7, 8, 9, 13, 15, 21, 23; 51:13; 52:9, 9; 54:6, 6; 55:16, 17, 23; 56:3, 4, 4, 4, 10, 10, 11, 12; 57:1, 2, 7, 8, 9, 9; 58:5; 59:9, 16, 16, 17; 60:6, 6, 8, 9, 9; 61:2, 4, 4, 8; 62:3; 63:1, 4, 4, 7; 66:13, 13, 15, 15, 16, 18; 68:16, 22, 22; 69:30, 30, 35, 35; 71:14, 14, 16, 16, 22, 22; 73:15; 75:2, 9, 9, 10; 77:7, 7, 10, 11, 11, 12; 78:2, 2, 4; 79:13, 13; 80:18, 18; 81:8, 10; 82:2, 5; 84:4, 11, 11; 85:8, 8, 8; 86:7, 11, 12, 12; 87:4; 89:1, 1, 4, 23, 25, 27, 28, 29, 32, 33, 34, 35; 91:2, 2, 14, 14, 15, 15, 15, 16; 92:4; 94:8, 14, 14, 16, 16; 95:7; 101:1, 1, 2, 2, 3, 4, 5, 5, 8; 102:17; 103:9, 9; 104:33, 33, 34; 105:11; 107:43; 108:1, 2, 3, 3, 7, 7, 9, 9, 10, 10; 109:30, 30; 110:4; 111:1, 5; 112:5; 115:12, 12, 12, 13, 18; 116:2, 9, 13, 14, 17, 17, 18; 118:6, 10, 11, 12, 19, 19, 21, 24, 28, 28; 119:7, 8, 15, 16, 16, 32, 45, 46, 46, 47, 48, 48, 62, 69, 74, 78, 93, 95, 106, 106, 115, 117, 134, 145; 121:1, 3, 3; 122:8, 9; 132:3, 4, 7, 7, 11, 11, 12, 14, 15, 15, 16, 17, 18; 135:14, 14; 138:1, 1, 2, 8; 139:14; 140:12; 143:10; 144:9, 9; 145:1, 1, 2, 2, 5, 6, 19, 19, 19, 20; 146:2, 2; 149:4; **Pr** 1:5, 5, 22, 23, 23, 26, 26, 28; 3:28; 6:26, 34, 35, 35; 7:20; 8:6, 21; 9:8, 9, 9; 10:3, 8; 12:2; 14:5, 5; 15:12, 25, 25; 16:14; 18:14; 19:6, 17, 24, 25, 25; 20:3, 4, 5, 6, 22; 21:1; 22:6, 23; 23:9, 35; 24:29, 29; 26:27; 27:22; 28:8, 21; 29:19, 19; 31:12; **Ecc** 2:1, 4:10, 13; 5:12; 7:2, 23; 10:11, 12; 11:9; **SS** 1:4, 4, 4, 11; 3:2, 2; 4:6; 6:13; 7:8, 8, 12; 8:9, 9; **Isa** 1:5, 15, 15, 24, 25, 26; 2:3, 3; 3:4, 7, 14, 17, 17, 18; 4:1, 5; 5:1, 5, 5, 5, 6, 6, 26, 26; 6:8; 7:9, 12, 12, 13; 8:17, 17; 9:7, 10, 10, 14; 10:3, 3, 3, 6, 12; 12:1, 2; 13:11, 11, 11, 12, 13, 17; 14:1, 1, 13, 13, 13, 14, 14, 22, 23, 23, 25, 30; 15:9; 16:9, 9; 18:4, 4; 19:2, 3, 4; 21:12; 22:4, 17, 17, 18, 19, 20, 21, 21, 22, 23; 23:17; 25:1, 1, 7, 8, 8, 9, 9; 26:1, 9, 9, 10, 10, 10, 11, 13; 27:3, 3, 11, 11; 28:11, 17, 28; 29:2, 3, 3, 3, 14; 30:6, 9, 16, 16, 18, 18, 19, 19, 32; 31:2, 2, 2, 4, 5, 5, 5; 32:6, 6, 6; 33:10, 10, 10, 21, 22; 35:4, 4; 36:6, 8, 15, 18; 37:4, 4, 7, 7, 24, 24, 29, 29, 35; 38:5, 6, 6, 7, 8, 12, 13, 20; 40:10, 18, 18, 20, 25; 41:10, 10, 10, 13, 13, 14, 15, 17, 17, 18, 18, 19, 19, 27; 42:6, 6, 8, 14, 14, 15, 15, 15, 16, 16, 16, 21, 23, 23; 43:2, 4, 5, 6, 13, 19, 19, 25; 44:2, 3, 3, 15, 26, 27; 45:1, 2, 2, 3, 13; 46:4, 4, 4, 4, 5, 10, 11, 11, 13; 47:3, 3; 48:6, 9, 9, 11, 11, 14; 49:3, 6, 8, 11, 13, 15, 22, 25, 25, 26; 50:7, 8, 9; 51:3, 3, 4, 23; 52:12, 12; 53:12; 54:7, 8, 11, 12; 55:3, 7, 7; 56:5, 5, 7, 8, 12, 12; 57:12, 16, 16, 18, 18, 19; 58:14; 59:2, 18, 18; 60:7, 12, 13, 15, 17, 17, 17, 22; 61:8, 8, 10, 11; 62:1, 1, 8; 63:3, 3, 6, 6, 7, 8; 65:6, 6, 7, 8, 9, 12, 19, 24, 24; 66:2, 4, 4, 12, 13, 15, 16, 18, 19, 19, 21, 22; **Jer** 1:12, 15, 16; 2:9, 9, 20, 24, 25, 27, 29, 31, 35; 3:5, 5, 12, 12, 14, 14, 15, 22; 4:6, 12, 27, 28, 28, 30, 30; 5:1, 5, 5, 14, 15, 18, 22, 31; 6:11, 12, 16, 17, 19, 21; 7:3, 7, 9, 14, 15, 16, 23, 27, 27, 34; 8:10, 13, 17, 17; 9:4, 4, 5, 5, 7, 10, 11, 11, 15, 16, 16, 25; 10:18, 18; 11:4, 8, 11, 11, 14, 22, 23; 12:14, 15, 15, 16, 17, 17; 13:9, 13, 14, 14, 17, 24, 26; 14:10, 12, 12, 12, 13, 16, 22; 15:3, 4, 6, 7, 7, 7, 9, 11, 13, 14, 19, 20, 21, 21; 16:9, 13, 13, 15, 16, 16, 18, 21, 21; 17:3, 4, 27, 27; 18:2, 8, 10, 12, 12, 14, 17, 17; 19:3, 7, 7, 7, 8, 9, 11, 12, 15; 20:4, 4, 5, 5, 9, 10, 10; 21:2, 4, 4, 5, 6, 7, 14, 14; 22:5, 6, 7, 14, 21, 25, 26; 23:2, 3, 3, 4, 5, 12, 15, 33, 34, 39, 39, 40; 24:5, 6, 6, 6, 6, 7, 7, 8, 9, 10; 25:6, 9, 9, 9, 10, 12, 12, 13, 14, 16, 27, 29, 31, 31; 26:3, 4, 6, 6, 13; 27:8, 8, 8, 11, 13, 13, 22; 28:3, 4, 4, 11, 16; 29:10, 12, 14, 14, 14, 14, 17, 17, 18, 18, 21, 32, 32; 30:3, 3, 8, 8, 9, 10, 11, 11, 11, 16, 17, 17, 18, 19, 19, 20, 21, 22; 31:1, 4, 8, 9, 9, 10, 13, 13, 14, 20, 27, 28, 31, 33, 33, 33, 34, 34, 37; 32:3, 28, 37, 37, 37, 38, 39, 40, 40, 40, 41, 41, 42, 44; 33:3, 6, 6, 6, 7, 7, 8, 8, 11, 14, 15, 22, 26, 26, 26; 34:2, 5, 17, 18, 20, 21, 22, 22; 35:6, 13, 17; 36:3, 7, 7, 16, 31, 31; 38:14, 16, 16, 25; 39:16, 17, 18; 40:4, 10, 10, 15; 42:4, 4, 4, 6, 10, 10, 10, 12, 13, 14, 14, 17, 20; 43:10, 10, 12; 44:11, 12, 13, 16, 17, 25, 25, 27, 29, 30; 45:4, 4, 5, 5; 46:8, 8, 8, 25, 26, 27, 28, 28, 28; 47:4, 6; 48:12, 31, 31, 32, 35, 44, 47; 49:2, 5, 6, 8, 8, 9, 11, 15, 16, 19, 19, 19, 27, 32, 32, 35, 36, 36, 37, 37, 37, 38, 38, 39; 50:9, 18, 19, 20, 31, 32, 42, 44, 44, 44; 51:1, 2, 6, 14, 20, 20, 21, 21, 22, 22, 22, 23, 23, 23, 24, 25, 25, 36, 36, 39, 39, 40, 44, 44, 47, 52, 57, 64; **La** 3:24, 31, 32; 4:16, 22, 22, 22; **Eze** 2:1, 5, 5, 7, 7; 3:7, 7, 11, 11, 18, 20, 22, 26, 27; 4:8, 13, 16; 5:2, 8, 9, 9, 10, 10, 11, 11, 12, 12, 13, 13, 14, 16, 16, 16, 17, 17; 6:3, 3, 4, 5, 5, 8, 12, 14; 7:3, 3, 3, 4, 4, 8, 8, 8, 9, 9, 21, 22, 24, 24, 27, 27; 8:18, 18, 18; 9:10, 10; 11:7, 8, 9, 9, 10, 11, 16, 17, 17, 19, 19, 19, 19, 20, 21; 12:3, 13, 13, 14, 14, 16, 23, 25, 25, 25; 13:13, 14, 15, 15, 18, 18, 19, 20, 20, 21, 23; 14:4, 7, 8, 8, 9, 9, 13, 13, 13, 13; 15:3, 6, 7, 8; 16:27, 37, 37, 37, 38, 38, 39, 41, 42, 42, 42, 43, 53, 59, 60, 60, 61, 62; 17:19, 20, 20, 20, 22, 22, 22, 22, 23; 18:21, 30, 31; 20:3, 8, 31, 32, 33, 34, 34, 35, 35, 36, 37, 37, 38, 38, 39, 40, 40, 41, 41, 47; 21:3, 3, 4, 17, 17, 23, 27, 27, 30, 31, 31; 22:14, 15, 15, 19, 20, 20, 21; 23:22, 22, 24, 25, 27, 28, 30, 31, 43, 46, 46, 48; 24:9, 14, 14, 14, 14, 21; 25:4, 5, 7, 7, 7, 7, 7, 9, 10, 11, 13, 13, 13, 14, 16, 16, 17; 26:3, 4, 7, 13, 14, 21; 28:7, 16, 16, 17, 17, 18, 18, 22, 23; 29:4, 4, 4, 5, 8, 10, 12, 12, 12, 13, 14, 14, 15, 19, 21, 21; 30:10, 12, 12, 13, 13, 13, 14, 14, 14, 15, 15, 16, 19, 22, 22, 23, 23, 24, 24, 25, 26; 32:3, 4, 4, 4, 5, 6, 7, 7, 8, 9, 10, 12, 13, 14; 33:6, 8, 11, 20, 27, 28, 31, 33; 34:10, 10, 11, 12, 12, 13, 13, 14, 15, 15, 16, 16, 16, 16, 20, 22, 22, 23, 24, 25, 25, 26, 26, 29; 35:3, 3, 4, 6, 7, 8, 9, 10, 11, 11, 14, 15; 36:9, 10, 11, 11, 11, 12, 15, 23, 24, 24, 25, 25, 26, 26, 26, 26, 27, 28, 29, 29, 30, 33, 36, 37, 37; 37:5, 6, 6, 12, 19, 19, 21, 21, 22, 23, 23, 23, 26, 26, 26, 27; 38:4, 4, 11, 11, 16, 21, 22, 22, 23, 23; 39:2, 2, 2, 3, 3, 4, 6, 7, 7, 11, 21, 25, 25, 29; 43:7, 9, 27; 44:14; **Da** 2:4, 5, 7, 9, 24, 25, 36; 3:17, 18; 4:17, 25, 32, 35; 5:12, 17, 21; 6:16; 8:4, 19; 10:20, 21; 11:2, 3, 16, 36; **Hos** 1:4, 4, 5, 6, 6, 7, 7, 7, 9; 2:4, 5, 6, 7, 9, 9, 10, 11, 12, 12, 13, 14, 15, 17, 18, 18, 18, 19, 19, 20, 21, 21, 23, 23, 23; 3:3; 4:5, 6, 6, 7, 9, 14, 16; 5:4, 10, 12, 14, 14, 15, 15; 6:1, 1, 2, 2; 7:12, 12, 12; 8:5, 10, 13, 14; 9:5, 9, 9, 12, 15, 15, 16, 17; 10:11; 11:9, 9, 9, 11; 12:2, 2, 9; 13:7, 7, 8, 8, 10, 14, 14, 14, 14; 14:2, 3, 3, 4, 4, 5; **Joel** 1:19; 2:14, 18, 19, 19, 19, 20, 20, 21, 23, 25, 28, 29, 30; 3:2, 2, 2, 4, 4, 7, 7, 8, 12, 16, 21; **Am** 1:2, 3, 4, 5, 6, 7, 8, 8, 9, 10, 11, 12, 13, 14; 2:1, 2, 3, 3, 4, 5, 6, 7; 3:2, 4, 4, 7, 8, 14, 15; 4:2, 12, 12; 5:15, 17, 21, 22, 22, 23, 27; 6:8, 11, 12, 14; 7:8, 8, 9; 8:2, 5, 7, 9, 9, 10, 10, 10, 11; 9:1, 2, 3, 3, 4, 4, 8, 8, 9, 9, 11, 11, 11, 14, 15; **Ob** 1:4; **Jnh** 1:6; 2:4, 9, 9; 3:9; **Mic** 1:3, 6, 6, 6, 7, 8, 8, 8, 15; 2:11, 12, 12, 12; 3:4, 4, 11; 4:2, 2, 5, 5, 6, 6, 7, 13, 13, 13; 5:3, 10, 10, 11, 12, 13, 14, 14, 15; 6:2, 7, 13, 14; 7:7, 7, 7, 9, 9, 15, 19, 19, 19; **Na** 1:2, 3, 8, 9, 12, 13, 13, 14, 14; 2:13, 13; 3:5, 5, 6, 6, 7; **Hab** 1:5, 5; 2:1, 1, 1, 3, 3; 3:16, 18, 18, 19, 19; **Zep** 1:2, 3, 3, 3, 4, 4, 8, 9, 12, 12, 12, 17; 2:5, 11, 11, 13, 13; 3:5, 9, 11, 12, 17, 17, 17, 17, 18, 19, 19, 19, 20, 20; **Hag** 1:8, 8; 2:6, 7, 7, 9, 19, 21, 22, 22, 22, 23, 23; **Zec** 1:3, 9; 2:5, 5, 9, 10, 11; 3:4, 7, 8, 9, 9; 5:4; 6:15; 8:3, 7, 8, 8, 11, 12, 13, 21, 23; 9:4, 4, 6, 7, 8, 10, 12; 10:6, 6, 6, 6, 8, 9, 10, 10, 12; 11:6, 6, 6, 7, 9, 16; 12:2, 3, 3, 4, 4, 4, 6, 9, 10; 13:2, 2, 7, 9, 9, 9, 9, 9; 14:2, 12, 17, 18; **Mal** 1:4, 4, 5, 8, 9, 9, 10; 2:2, 2, 2, 2, 3, 12, 13; 3:1, 5, 5, 7, 8, 10, 11, 17; 4:5; **Mt** 2:13; 3:12, 12; 4:9, 19; 5:40; 6:10, 14, 15, 21, 24, 24; 7:9, 10, 21, 22, 23, 24; 8:3, 7, 19; 9:13, 15, 38; 10:17, 17, 32, 33; 11:14, 27, 28; 12:7, 11, 18, 29, 44, 50; 13:30, 35, 35; 15:32; 16:2, 3, 18, 19, 24, 25, 25; 18:14, 16, 26, 29; 20:4, 14, 15, 26, 27, 32; 21:3, 24, 24, 25, 29, 31, 37, 40, 41, 41, 44; 23:4; 24:28; 25:21, 23; 26:15, 15, 18, 29, 31, 32, 33, 35, 39, 42; 27:17, 21, 42, 43, 49, 63; 28:14; **Mk** 1:17, 41; 2:20, 22; 3:27, 27, 35; 4:13; 6:22, 23, 25; 8:3, 34, 35; 9:50; 10:43, 44; 11:3, 26, 29, 29, 31; 12:6, 9, 9; 14:7, 15, 25, 27, 28, 29, 31, 36, 58, 58; 15:9, 12, 36; **Lk** 2:14; 3:17, 17, 17; 4:6, 6, 23; 5:5, 13, 35, 37; 6:9, 47; 7:42; 9:5, 23, 24, 24, 57, 61; 10:22, 35; 11:2, 8, 8, 11, 11, 12, 24, 49; 12:5, 18, 18, 18, 19, 28, 34, 36, 37, 44, 46, 46, 46, 47, 47, 48, 49, 55; 13:24, 31; 14:5; 15:18, 18; 16:11, 13, 13, 30, 31; 17:1, 7, 8, 22, 37; 18:5, 8; 19:14, 22; 20:3, 5, 6, 13, 13, 18; 21:6, 7, 15; 22:16, 18, 42, 67, 68; 23:16, 22, 25; **Jn** 1:13, 13; 2:19; 4:25, 34, 48; 5:20, 21, 30, 30, 40, 43, 45; 6:37, 38, 38, 39, 40, 40, 44, 51, 51, 54, 67; 7:17, 17, 31, 35, 35; 8:22, 44; 9:27, 31; 10:5, 5; 11:22, 48, 56; 12:26, 28, 32; 13:37; 14:3, 13, 14, 16, 18, 18, 21, 21, 23, 23, 23, 26, 30; 15:7, 20, 20, 21, 26; 16:2, 3, 7, 7, 8, 13, 13, 22, 23, 26; 17:24, 26; 18:39; 20:15, 25; 21:22, 23; **Ac** 2:17, 18, 19; 3:23; 5:38; 6:4; 7:7, 34, 43, 49; 9:16; 13:22, 34, 36; 15:16, 16, 16, 16; 17:18, 31, 32; 18:6, 15, 21, 21; 21:14, 22; 22:14, 18, 21; 23:14, 21, 35; 24:22, 25; 26:16; 27:10; 28:28; **Ro** 1:10; 2:6, 18; 4:8; 5:7; 7:18; 8:27; 9:9, 15, 15, 15, 15, 18, 18, 19, 25, 28, 28; 10:19, 19; 12:2, 19; 15:9, 18, 24, 28, 32; **1Co** 1:1, 19, 19; 4:5, 5, 19, 19, 19, 21; 6:12, 14; 7:36, 37, 37, 39; 8:13; 9:17; 10:13, 13; 11:34; 12:11; 14:15, 15, 15, 15, 21, 21, 23, 25, 35; 15:35; 16:3, 5, 6, 7, 8, 12, 12; **2Co** 1:1, 10; 6:16, 16, 17, 18; 8:5, 11; 10:11, 13; 11:9, 12, 18, 30; 12:1, 5, 5, 6, 9, 14, 15, 21; 13:2; **Gal** 1:4; 5:10; **Eph** 1:1, 5, 9, 11; 5:17; 6:6, 7; **Php** 1:6, 15, 18; 2:13, 20, 23; **Col** 1:1, 9; 2:23; 4:12; **1Th** 4:3, 14; 5:18, 24; **2Th** 2:7; 3:4; **1Ti** 2:4, 8; 5:11, 14; 6:9; **2Ti** 1:1; 2:12, 16, 17, 25, 26; 3:12; 4:3, 3, 18; **Tit** 3:8; **Phm** 1:19; **Heb** 1:5; 2:4, 12, 12, 13; 3:7, 15; 4:7; 6:3, 14, 14; 7:21; 8:8, 10, 10, 10, 12, 12; 10:7, 9, 10, 16, 16, 16, 17, 30, 36, 37, 37; 13:4, 5, 6, 21, 23; **Jas** 1:18; 2:18; 4:4, 7, 8, 13, 15; **1Pe** 2:15; 3:10, 13, 17; 4:2, 3, 19; **2Pe** 1:12, 15, 21; 3:10; **1Jn** 2:17; 5:14; **3Jn** 1:10, 13; **Jude** 1:5; **Rev** 2:5, 5, 7, 10, 16, 16, 17, 17, 22, 23, 23, 24, 26, 28; 3:3, 3, 5, 5, 9, 9, 10, 12, 12, 12, 16, 20, 20, 21; 4:1; 11:3, 5, 5, 6; 17:1, 7, 17; 21:3, 6, 7, 9; 22:17

WILT [245]

Ge 13:9; 15:2; 16:8; 18:23, 24, 28; 20:4; 21:23; 23:13; 24:58; 26:29; 30:31; 38:16, 17; 43:4, 5; **Ex** 4:13; 8:21; 9:2, 17; 10:3; 13:13; 15:26, 26, 26; 18:18; 20:25; 32:32; 33:12; **Nu** 16:14, 22; 21:2; **Dt** 23:13; 28:15, 58; 30:17; **Jos** 7:9; **Jdg** 1:14; 4:8, 8; 6:36, 37; 11:24; 13:16; **Ru** 4:4, 4; **1Sa** 1:11, 11, 14; 14:37; 16:1; 19:5; 21:9; 24:21, 21; 25:17; 30:15; **2Sa** 5:19; 13:4; 18:22; 20:19; 22:26, 26, 27, 27, 28; 24:13; **1Ki** 3:14; 6:12; 9:4, 4; 11:38, 38; 12:7, 7; 13:8; 22:4; **2Ki** 3:7; 4:23; 8:12, 12, 12, 12; 18:24; **1Ch** 14:10; 17:25; **2Ch** 7:17; 18:3; 20:9, 12; 25:8; **Ne** 2:6; **Est** 5:3; **Job** 4:2; 5:1; 7:19; 8:2; 9:28; 10:9, 14; 13:25, 25; 14:15; 30:23; 34:17; 38:39; 39:11, 11, 12; 40:8, 8; 41:4, 5, 5; **Ps** 5:12, 12; 10:13, 17, 17; 13:1, 1; 16:10, 10, 11; 17:6; 18:25, 25, 26, 26, 27, 27, 28; 35:17; 38:15; 41:2, 3; 51:17; 56:13; 60:10; 61:6; 65:5; 79:5; 80:4; 81:8; 85:5, 5, 6; 86:7; 88:10; 89:46; 101:2; 108:11, 11; 119:82, 84; 138:7; 139:19; **Pr** 2:1; 5:20; 6:9, 9; 23:5; **Isa** 26:3, 12; 27:8; 36:9; 38:12, 13, 16; 58:5; 64:12, 12; **Jer** 3:4; 4:1, 1, 30; 12:5; 13:21, 27; 15:18; 31:22; 38:15, 15, 17, 18; 47:5; **La** 1:21; **Eze** 9:8; 11:13; 20:4, 4; 22:2, 2; 23:36; 24:19; 28:9; 37:18; **Hos** 9:14; **Mic** 7:19, 20; **Hab** 1:2, 2; **Zep** 3:7, 7; **Zec** 1:12; 3:7, 7; **Mt** 4:9; 7:4; 8:2; 13:28; 15:28; 17:4; 19:17, 21; 20:21; 26:17, 39; **Mk** 1:40; 6:22; 10:51; 14:12, 36; **Lk** 4:7; 5:12; 9:54; 18:41; 22:9; **Jn** 2:20; 5:6; 11:22; 13:38; 14:22; **Ac** 1:6; 2:27, 27; 7:28; 9:6; 13:10; 25:9; **Ro** 9:19; 11:19; 13:3; **Phm** 1:21; **Jas** 2:20

WITH [6016]

Ge 3:6, 12; 4:8; 5:22, 24; 6:3, 9, 11, 13, 13, 14, 16, 18, 18, 19; 7:7, 13, 23; 8:1, 16, 17, 17, 18; 9:4, 8, 9, 9, 10, 10, 10, 11, 12; 11:31; 12:4, 13, 17; 13:1, 5; 14:2, 2, 5, 8, 9, 9, 9, 13, 17, 24; 15:14, 18; 16:6, 11; 17:3, 4, 12, 13, 19, 19, 21, 22, 23, 27, 27; 18:11, 16, 23, 25, 33; 19:1, 9, 9, 11, 30, 32, 33, 34, 34, 35, 36; 20:16, 16; 21:6, 10, 10, 19, 20, 22, 23, 23, 23; 22:3, 5; 23:4, 4, 8, 16; 24:15, 32, 40, 45, 49, 54, 55, 58; 25:30; 26:3, 8, 10, 15, 20, 20, 24, 28, 28; 27:15, 34, 35, 37, 44; 28:4, 15, 20; 29:6, 9, 9, 14, 19, 25, 27, 30; 30:8, 8, 15, 16, 16, 20, 20, 29, 33; 31:3, 5, 6, 21, 23, 25, 26, 27, 27, 27, 27, 32, 32, 36, 38, 42, 50; 32:4, 6, 7, 9, 10, 11, 15, 20, 24, 25, 28, 28; 33:1, 5, 7, 10, 11, 13, 13, 15, 15; 34:2, 5, 6, 7, 8, 9, 10, 16, 20, 21, 22, 23, 26, 31, 31; 35:2, 3, 6, 13, 14, 15, 22; 37:2, 2, 2, 14, 14, 25; 38:14, 24, 25; 39:2, 3, 7, 8, 10, 12, 14, 14, 15, 18, 21, 23; 40:4, 7, 14; 41:6, 10, 12, 23, 27; 42:4, 6, 13, 24, 25, 26, 32, 33, 38, 38; 43:3, 4, 5, 6, 8, 16, 16, 19, 32, 32, 34; 44:1, 9, 10, 16, 23, 26, 26, 29, 30, 31, 31, 33, 34; 45:1, 5, 15, 23, 23; 46:1, 4, 6, 7, 7, 15, 26; 47:12, 17, 29, 30; 48:1, 12, 21, 22, 22; 49:12, 12, 25, 29, 30; 50:7, 9, 10, 13, 14; **Ex** 1:1, 7, 10, 11, 13, 14, 14, 20; 2:3, 3, 21, 24, 24, 24; 3:2, 8, 12, 17, 18, 20; 4:12, 15, 15; 5:3, 3, 3, 15; 6:1, 1, 4, 6, 6; 7:11, 17, 22; 8:2, 5, 7, 17, 18; 9:9, 10, 15, 24; 10:9, 9, 9, 9, 9, 9, 10, 24, 26, 26; 12:8, 8, 9, 9, 9, 9, 10, 11, 22, 38, 48; 13:5, 7, 7, 9, 13, 19, 19; 14:6, 8, 11; 15:8, 10, 19, 19, 20, 20; 16:3, 12, 18, 20, 31; 17:2, 2, 3, 5, 8, 9, 9, 10, 13, 16; 18:5, 6, 12, 18, 19, 22; 19:9, 17, 24; 20:19, 19, 22, 23; 21:3, 6, 8, 9, 14, 18, 18, 20, 22, 29; 22:14, 15, 16, 19, 24, 30, 30, 30; 23:1, 5, 11, 11, 18, 32, 32; 24:2, 3, 8, 14; 25:2, 11, 13, 14, 20, 22, 22, 24, 28, 28, 33, 33, 34, 39; 26:1, 1, 6, 29, 29, 31, 32, 36, 37; 27:2, 6, 8, 16, 17; 28:1, 3, 6, 11, 11, 15, 21, 21, 28, 41; 29:2, 2, 3, 4, 5, 9, 12, 14, 21, 21, 34, 40, 40, 43; 30:3, 5, 6, 10, 20, 28, 34, 36; 31:3, 6, 8, 9, 18, 18; 32:4, 11, 11; 33:3, 9, 12, 14, 15, 16, 22; 34:3, 5, 10, 12, 15, 20, 25, 27, 27, 28, 29, 29, 31, 32, 33, 34, 35; 35:12, 14, 16, 23, 24, 25, 31, 35; 36:8, 13, 34, 34, 35, 36, 38, 38; 37:2, 4, 9, 9, 11, 15, 26, 28; 38:2, 6, 7, 17, 23; 39:3, 6, 14, 21, 23, 37, 37; 40:3, 12, 14; **Lev** 1:12, 13, 16, 17; 2:2, 4, 4, 5, 7, 11, 13, 13, 16; 3:4, 10, 15; 4:9, 11, 11, 12, 20, 20, 20, 25, 30, 34; 5:4, 4, 15, 16, 18; 6:6, 10, 16, 17, 21; 7:4, 10, 12, 12, 12, 12, 13, 17, 19, 24, 30; 8:2, 6, 7, 7, 7, 13, 15, 17, 30, 30, 31, 32; 9:4, 11, 13; 10:9, 14, 15, 15, 16; 11:43, 43, 44; 13:57; 14:10, 16, 21, 27, 31, 37, 52, 52, 52, 52, 52, 52; 15:3, 17, 18, 18, 24, 33; 16:3, 4, 4, 10, 14, 14, 15, 15, 19, 24; 17:13, 15; 18:20, 20, 22, 22, 23; 19:13, 19, 19, 20, 22, 26, 33, 34; 20:2, 5, 10, 10, 11, 12, 13, 13, 14, 15, 18, 20, 24, 27; 21:9; 22:6, 8, 11, 14; 23:13, 17, 18, 18, 20, 20; 24:23; 25:6, 23, 35, 35, 36, 40, 41, 43, 45, 46, 50, 50, 52, 53, 53, 54; 26:9, 39, 40, 42, 42, 42, 44; **Nu** 1:2, 4, 5; 2:2, 17, 31; 3:1; 4:5, 8, 11, 12, 32, 32; 5:7, 13, 13, 19, 19, 20, 21, 23; 6:15, 15, 17, 20; 7:13, 19, 25, 31, 37, 43, 49, 55, 61, 67, 73, 79, 87, 89; 8:8, 8, 26; 9:11; 10:3, 4, 8, 9, 10, 29, 32; 11:15, 16, 17, 17, 18, 33; 12:8; 13:23, 27, 31; 14:8, 9, 10, 12, 21, 24, 27, 43; 15:4, 5, 6, 9, 9, 14, 15, 16, 24, 35, 36; 16:2, 10, 13, 14, 18, 22, 30; 17:4, 13; 18:1, 1, 2, 2, 7, 11, 11, 19, 19; 19:4, 5, 12, 16; 20:3, 11, 13, 18, 20, 20; 21:18, 24; 22:7, 8, 9, 12, 13, 14, 20, 21, 22, 27, 35, 35, 39, 40; 23:13, 17, 21; 24:8; 25:1, 14, 18; 26:3, 10; 27:21; 28:5, 9, 12, 12, 13, 20, 28; 29:3, 9, 14; 30:2, 8, 10; 31:6, 8, 10, 14, 14, 17, 18, 23, 35; 32:19, 29, 30, 33; 33:1, 3; 34:2, 12; 35:7, 16, 17, 18, 21, 23, 25; **Dt** 1:16, 37; 2:5, 7, 9, 19, 24, 26; 3:5, 13, 26, 27; 4:11, 11, 21, 23, 29, 29, 37, 40, 40; 5:2, 3, 3, 4, 16, 22, 23, 24, 29, 29, 33; 6:3, 3, 5, 5, 5, 18, 21; 7:2, 3, 5, 5, 8, 9, 23, 25; 8:3, 16; 9:8, 9, 10, 15, 19, 20, 21, 26; 10:9, 12, 12, 14, 22; 11:2, 9, 10, 13, 13; 12:3, 12, 23, 25, 25, 28, 28; 13:3, 3, 10, 15, 15, 16; 14:27, 29; 15:3, 14, 16, 19; 16:3, 4, 10, 18; 17:5, 19; 18:1, 13, 13; 19:5, 5, 13; 20:1, 4, 12, 13, 20; 21:3, 21; 22:2, 3, 3, 3, 6, 7, 9, 10, 21, 22, 22, 23, 24, 25, 25, 28, 29; 23:4, 4, 11, 16, 23, 25; 24:5, 12; 25:3, 11; 26:5, 8, 8, 8, 8, 8, 9, 15, 16, 16; 27:1, 2, 3, 4, 14, 20, 21, 22, 23; 28:22, 22, 22, 22, 22, 22, 27, 27, 27, 27, 28, 30, 32, 35, 40, 47, 47, 67, 68; 29:1, 1, 10, 12, 12, 14, 15, 15, 15, 25; 30:2, 2, 6, 6, 10, 10; 31:6, 7, 8, 16, 16, 20, 23, 27; 32:12, 14, 14, 15, 16, 16, 21, 21, 21, 21, 22, 24, 24, 24, 24, 25, 34, 39, 42, 42, 43; 33:2, 8, 8, 17, 20, 21, 21, 23, 23, 24; 34:4; **Jos** 1:5, 5, 9, 17, 17; 2:6, 14, 19; 3:7, 7; 4:3, 8; 5:6, 13; 6:4, 5, 5, 8, 9, 9, 10, 13, 13, 16, 17, 20, 20, 21, 24, 27; 7:12, 15, 15, 24, 25, 25, 25; 8:1, 5, 11, 24, 35; 9:2, 2, 2, 6, 7, 11, 11, 15, 15, 16; 10:1, 4, 4, 7, 10, 11, 11, 15, 20, 24, 28, 29, 30, 31, 32, 34, 35, 36, 37, 38, 39, 43; 11:4, 4, 6, 7, 9, 10, 11, 11, 12, 14, 18, 19, 21; 13:8, 21, 22; 14:4, 8, 12; 15:32, 36, 41, 44, 45, 46, 47, 47, 51, 54, 57, 59, 60, 62, 63; 16:9; 18:24, 28; 19:15, 16, 22, 30, 31, 38, 46, 47, 48; 21:2, 8, 11, 13, 13, 14, 14, 15, 15, 16, 16, 17, 17, 18, 18, 19, 21, 21, 22, 22, 23, 23, 24, 24, 25, 25, 26, 27, 27, 28, 28, 29, 29, 30, 30, 31, 31, 32, 32, 32, 33, 34, 34, 35, 35, 36, 36, 37, 37, 38, 38, 39, 39, 41, 42; 22:5, 5, 8, 8, 8, 8, 8, 8, 8, 14, 15, 18, 24, 27, 27, 27, 30; 23:4, 12; 24:6, 8, 12, 12, 25; **Jdg** 1:3, 3, 8, 16, 17, 18, 18, 19, 21, 22, 25; 2:1, 2, 18; 3:27, 31; 4:6, 7, 8, 8, 9, 9, 10, 10, 13, 15, 18; 5:15, 26; 6:5, 12, 13, 16, 17, 26, 39; 7:1, 2, 4, 4, 4, 5, 10, 11, 16, 18, 18, 19; 8:1, 1, 4, 7, 7, 10, 15, 16; 9:1, 1, 16, 19, 19, 23, 26, 32, 33, 34, 35, 38, 39, 44, 45, 48, 48, 52; 11:3, 6, 8, 11, 12, 33, 34, 34, 38, 39; 12:1, 1, 2, 4; 13:9, 19; 14:7, 11, 15, 18; 15:1, 5, 6, 8, 13, 14, 16, 16; 16:3, 7, 8, 9, 11, 13, 14, 14, 14, 15, 16, 21, 29, 29, 30, 30; 17:2, 10, 11; 18:4, 7, 11, 16, 17, 17, 19, 23, 25, 27, 27, 28; 19:3, 4, 5, 10, 10, 19, 20, 24, 29; 20:1, 37, 38, 40, 43, 48; 21:5, 10, 10, 12; **Ru** 1:6, 7, 8, 8, 8, 10, 11, 18, 20, 22; 2:4, 6, 19, 19, 22, 23; 3:1, 2; **1Sa** 1:24, 24; 2:4, 13, 13, 18, 19, 22, 26, 26, 29; 3:14, 19; 4:4, 5, 8, 12, 12, 19; 5:6, 7, 8, 9, 12; 6:11, 15, 19; 7:3, 10; 9:3, 5, 19, 24, 25; 10:5, 6, 7, 26; 11:1, 2, 7, 10; 12:2, 7, 20, 24; 13:2, 2, 4, 5, 15, 16, 22, 22, 22; 14:2, 7, 17, 18, 20, 21, 21, 21, 21, 27, 28, 32, 33, 34, 34, 43, 45; 15:6, 8, 25, 26, 30; 16:1, 2, 5, 16, 18, 19, 20, 23; 17:5, 9, 19, 20, 23, 25, 28, 32, 33, 37, 38, 38, 39, 43, 45, 45, 47, 50, 50, 57; 18:1, 6, 6, 10, 11, 12, 14, 22, 28; 19:3, 8, 8, 9, 9, 10, 13, 16; 20:5, 8, 8, 13, 13, 16, 35, 35, 41; 21:1, 8; 22:2, 3, 4, 6, 8, 17, 19, 19, 23, 23; 23:5, 5, 6, 19, 23, 23; 24:7, 8, 18; 25:7, 15, 16, 25, 26, 29, 31, 33, 39, 42;

WITHAL [33]

WITHIN [186]

WITHOUT [426]

2Co 7:5; 10:13, 15; 11:28; **Eph** 1:4; 2:12, 12; 3:21; 5:27; **Php** 1:10, 14; 2:14, 15; **Col** 2:11; 4:5; **1Th** 1:3; 2:13; 4:12; 5:17; **1Ti** 2:8; 3:7, 16; 5:21; 6:14; **2Ti** 1:3; 3:3; **Phm** 1:14; **Heb** 4:15; 7:3, 3, 3, 7, 20, 21; 9:7, 14, 18, 22, 28; 10:23, 28; 11:6, 40; 12:8, 14; 13:5, 11, 12, 13; **Jas** 2:13, 18, 20, 26, 26; 3:17, 17; **1Pe** 1:17, 19, 19; 3:1; 4:9; **2Pe** 2:17; 3:14; **Jude** 1:12, 12, 12; **Rev** 11:2; 14:5, 10, 20; 22:15

WOULD [451]

Ge 2:19; 21:7; 30:34; 42:21, 22; 43:7; 44:22; **Ex** 2:4; 8:32; 9:35; 10:20, 27; 11:10; 13:15; 16:3; **Nu** 11:29, 29; 14:2, 2; 20:3; 21:23; 22:18, 29, 29; 24:13; **Dt** 1:26, 43, 45; 2:30; 3:26; 5:29; 7:8; 8:20; 9:25; 10:10; 23:5, 21; 28:56, 67, 67; 32:26, 26, 29; **Jos** 5:6, 6; 7:7; 17:12; 24:10; **Jdg** 1:27, 34, 35; 2:17; 3:4; 8:19, 24, 24; 9:29, 29; 11:17, 17; 13:23, 23, 23; 14:6; 15:1; 19:10, 25; 20:13; **Ru** 1:13, 13; **1Sa** 2:16, 25; 13:13; 15:9; 18:2; 20:9; 22:17, 22; 26:23; 31:4; **2Sa** 2:21; 4:6, 10; 6:10; 11:20; 12:8, 17, 18; 13:14, 16, 25; 14:16, 29, 29; 15:4; 18:11, 12, 33; 23:15, 16, 17; **1Ki** 8:12; 13:33; 18:32; 20:33; 21:4; 22:18, 49; **2Ki** 2:1; 3:14; 5:3, 3; 7:2; 8:19; 13:23; 14:11, 27; 17:14; 18:12; 24:4; **1Ch** 10:4; 11:17, 18, 19; 13:4; 19:19; 27:23; **2Ch** 6:1; 10:16; 12:12; 15:13; 18:17; 21:7; 24:19; 25:20; 33:10; 35:22; **Ezr** 10:8, 19; **Ne** 6:11, 14; 9:24, 29, 30; 10:30, 31, 31; **Est** 3:4; 6:6; 8:11; 9:5, 27; **Job** 5:8, 8; 6:3, 8, 9, 9, 10; 7:16; 8:6; 9:15, 15, 16, 21, 21, 35; 11:5, 6, 12; 13:3, 5; 16:5; 23:4, 5, 5, 5, 6; 27:22; 30:1; 31:12, 35, 35, 36, 37, 37; 32:22; 34:27; 36:16; 41:32; **Ps** 22:8; 35:25; 40:5; 50:12; 51:16; 55:6, 7, 8, 12; 56:1, 2; 57:3; 69:4; 81:11, 11; 106:23; 107:8, 15, 21, 31; 119:57; 142:4; **Pr** 1:25, 30; **SS** 3:4; 8:1, 2, 2, 2, 7, 7; **Isa** 27:4, 4, 4; 28:12; 30:15; 42:24; 54:9; **Jer** 8:18; 10:7; 13:11; 18:10; 22:24; 29:19; 36:25, 25; 38:26; 49:9; 51:9; **La** 4:12; **Eze** 3:6; 6:10; 13:6; 20:8, 13, 15, 21, 23; 38:17; **Da** 1:8; 2:8, 16, 16, 18; 5:19, 19, 19, 19; 7:19; 9:2; **Hos** 7:1; 11:7; **Ob** 1:5, 5; **Jnh** 3:10; 4:5; **Zec** 7:13, 13; **Mal** 1:10; **Mt** 2:18; 5:42; 7:12; 8:34; 11:21, 23; 12:7, 38; 14:5, 7; 16:1; 18:23, 30; 22:3; 23:30, 37, 37; 24:43, 43, 43; 27:15, 34; **Mk** 3:2, 13; 5:10; 6:19, 26, 48; 7:24, 26; 9:30; 10:35, 36; 11:16; **Lk** 1:62, 74; 5:3; 6:7, 31; 7:3, 36, 39; 8:31, 32, 41; 9:53; 10:1, 2; 12:39, 39; 13:34, 34; 15:16, 28; 16:26, 26; 18:4, 13, 15; 19:27, 40; 22:49; 24:28; **Jn** 1:43; 4:10, 40, 47; 5:46; 6:6, 11, 15; 7:1, 44; 8:39, 42; 9:27; 12:21; 14:2, 28; 15:19; 18:30, 36; **Ac** 2:30; 5:24; 7:5, 25, 25, 26, 39; 8:31; 9:38; 10:10; 11:23; 12:6; 14:13; 16:3, 27; 17:20; 18:14; 19:30, 31, 33; 20:16; 21:14; 22:30; 23:12, 15, 20, 28; 24:6; 25:3, 4, 20, 22; 26:5, 29; 27:30; 28:18; **Ro** 1:13; 5:7; 7:15, 16, 19, 19, 20, 21; 11:25; 16:19; **1Co** 2:8; 4:8, 18; 7:7, 32; 10:1, 20; 11:3, 31; 12:1; 14:5; **2Co** 1:8; 2:1, 8; 5:4; 8:4, 6; 9:5; 10:9; 11:1; 12:6, 20, 20; **Gal** 1:7; 2:10; 3:2, 8; 4:15, 17; 5:12, 17; **Eph** 3:16; **Php** 1:12; **Col** 1:27; 2:1; 4:3; **1Th** 2:9, 12, 18; 4:1, 13; **2Th** 1:11; 3:10; **Phm** 1:13, 14; **Heb** 4:8; 10:2; 11:32; 12:17; **1Jn** 2:19; **2Jn** 1:12; **3Jn** 1:10; **Rev** 3:15; 13:15

WOULDEST [38]

Ge 30:15; 31:30, 31; **Ex** 7:16; 23:5; **Dt** 8:2; 21:11; 28:62; **Jos** 15:18; **2Sa** 14:11; 18:13; **1Ki** 1:16; 18:9; **2Ki** 4:13; 5:13; 6:22; **1Ch** 4:10, 10; **2Ch** 6:20; 20:10; **Ezr** 9:14; **Ne** 2:5; **Job** 8:5; 14:13, 13, 13; **Isa** 48:8; 64:1, 1; **Lk** 16:27; **Jn** 4:10; 11:40; 21:18, 18; **Ac** 23:20; 24:4; **Heb** 10:5, 8

YE [3796]

Ge 3:1, 3, 3, 3, 4, 5, 5; 4:23; 9:7; 17:10, 11; 18:5; 19:2, 8, 14; 24:49; 26:27, 27; 29:4, 5, 7; 31:6; 32:4, 20; 34:9, 10, 11, 12, 15, 17, 30; 40:7; 42:1, 7, 9, 14, 15, 15, 16, 16, 19, 19, 20, 22, 33, 34, 34, 34, 36, 36, 38, 38; 43:3, 5, 6, 6, 7, 27, 29; 44:4, 5, 10, 15, 15, 19, 23, 27, 29, 29; 45:4, 5, 13, 17, 18, 19, 24; 46:34, 34; 47:23; 49:2; 50:17, 20, 21, 25; **Ex** 1:16, 16, 18, 22, 22; 2:20; 3:12, 21, 21, 22, 22; 4:15; 5:4, 7, 11, 14, 17, 17, 17, 18, 19; 6:7; 8:25, 28; 9:28, 30; 10:2, 11, 24; 11:7; 12:3, 5, 6, 10, 10, 11, 11, 15, 15, 17, 17, 18, 20, 20, 22, 24, 25, 25, 27, 31, 32, 46; 13:3, 4, 19; 14:2, 13, 13, 13, 14; 15:21; 16:3, 6, 7, 7, 8, 12, 12, 12, 16, 23, 25, 26, 28, 29; 17:2; 19:4, 5, 5, 6, 12; 20:20, 22, 23, 23; 22:21, 22, 31, 31, 31; 23:9, 9, 25; 24:1, 14; 25:2, 3, 9, 19; 30:9, 9, 32; 31:13, 13, 14; 32:30; 33:5; 34:13; 35:1, 3, 5; **Lev** 1:2; 2:11, 11, 12; 3:17; 7:23, 24, 26, 32; 8:32, 33, 35, 35; 9:3, 6; 10:7, 9, 9, 10, 11, 13, 14, 17, 18; 11:2, 3, 4, 8, 8, 9, 9, 11, 13, 21, 22, 24, 33, 39, 42, 43, 43, 43, 44, 44, 44, 45; 14:34; 15:31; 16:29, 30, 31; 17:14; 18:3, 3, 3, 3, 4, 5, 26, 28, 30, 30, 30; 19:2, 3, 4, 5, 5, 6, 9, 11, 12, 15, 19, 23, 23, 25, 26, 26, 27, 28, 30, 33, 34, 35, 36, 37; 20:7, 8, 15, 22, 23, 24, 25, 25, 26, 26; 22:19, 20, 22, 24, 25, 28, 29, 30, 31, 32; 23:2, 3, 4, 6, 7, 7, 8, 8, 10, 10, 12, 12, 14, 14, 15, 15, 16, 16, 17, 18, 19, 21, 21, 22, 24, 25, 25, 27, 28, 31, 32, 32, 35, 36, 36, 36, 37, 38, 39, 39, 40, 40, 41, 41, 42; 24:22; 25:2, 9, 10, 10, 10, 11, 12, 13, 14, 17, 18, 18, 19, 20, 22, 22, 23, 24, 44, 45, 46, 46; 26:1, 1, 2, 3, 5, 6, 7, 10, 12, 13, 14, 15, 15, 15, 16, 17, 17, 18, 21, 23, 25, 25, 26, 27, 29, 29, 34, 35, 37, 38; **Nu** 1:2; 4:18, 27, 32; 5:3, 3; 6:23; 9:3, 3, 14; 10:5, 9, 9, 9, 9, 10; 11:18, 18, 19, 20; 12:4, 8; 13:2, 20; 14:9, 9, 28, 30, 31, 31, 34, 34, 34, 41, 42, 43, 43; 15:2, 12, 12, 14, 15, 18, 19, 19, 20, 20, 20, 21, 22, 39, 39, 39, 40; 16:3, 7, 7, 8, 10, 11, 17, 26, 28, 30, 41; 18:5, 7, 26, 26, 28, 28, 29, 30, 31, 31, 32, 32, 32, 32; 19:3; 20:4, 5, 8, 10, 12, 12, 24; 21:5, 17; 22:19; 25:5; 27:8, 9, 10, 11, 14; 28:2, 3, 11, 18, 19, 20, 23, 24, 25, 25, 26, 26, 26, 27, 31; 29:1, 1, 2, 7, 7, 7, 8, 12, 12, 12, 13, 17, 35, 35, 36, 39; 31:4, 15, 19, 23, 23, 24, 24, 24; 32:6, 7, 14, 15, 15, 20, 20, 22, 23, 23, 24, 29; 33:51, 52, 53, 54, 54, 54, 54, 55, 55, 55; 34:2, 8, 10, 13, 18; 35:2, 4, 5, 6, 6, 6, 7, 7, 8, 8, 8, 10, 11, 13, 13, 14, 14, 31, 32, 33, 33, 34; **Dt** 1:6, 11, 13, 14, 17, 18, 20, 22, 26, 27, 31, 31, 32, 33, 39, 40, 41, 41, 41, 42, 45, 46, 46; 2:3, 4, 4, 6, 6, 6, 6, 24; 3:18, 19, 20, 22; 4:1, 2, 2, 4, 5, 5, 11, 12, 12, 14, 14, 15, 15, 16, 20, 22, 23, 25, 26, 26, 27, 28; 5:1, 5, 23, 23, 24, 28, 32, 32, 33, 33, 33; 6:1, 1, 3, 14, 16, 16; 7:5, 5, 7, 7, 12, 25; 8:1, 1, 19, 20, 20; 9:7, 7, 8, 16, 16, 18, 21, 22, 23; 10:19, 19; 11:5, 8, 8, 8, 9, 10, 11, 16, 17, 18, 19, 22, 23, 25, 27, 28, 28, 31, 31, 32; 12:1, 1, 2, 2, 4, 5, 6, 7, 7, 7, 8, 9, 10, 10, 11, 11, 12, 12, 16, 16; 13:4, 13; 14:1, 1, 4, 6, 7, 8, 9, 9, 10, 11, 12, 20, 21; 17:16; 18:15; 19:19; 20:2, 3, 18; 22:24, 24; 23:4; 24:8, 9; 25:17; 27:4, 4, 12; 28:62, 62, 63, 68; 29:2, 6, 6, 7, 9, 9, 10, 16, 16, 17; 30:18, 18; 31:5, 13, 13, 19, 27, 29, 29; 32:1, 3, 6, 43, 46, 47, 47, 51, 51; **Jos** 1:11, 14, 15; 2:5, 10, 12, 13, 14, 16; 3:3, 3, 4, 4, 4, 8, 8, 10, 12; 4:3, 5, 7, 17, 22, 23, 24; 6:3, 3, 4, 5, 10, 10, 18, 18, 22; 7:12, 13, 14; 8:2, 4, 4, 7, 8, 8, 8; 9:6, 7, 8, 8, 11, 22, 22, 23; 10:25; 18:6; 22:2, 3, 4, 4, 16, 16, 16, 18, 18, 19, 25, 25, 27, 31, 31; 23:3, 5, 6, 6, 7, 8, 11, 12, 13, 14, 16, 16; 24:7, 8, 11, 13, 13, 13, 13, 13, 14, 15, 19, 20, 22, 22, 27; **Jdg** 2:2, 2, 2; 5:2, 3, 3, 9, 10, 10, 23, 23; 6:10, 10, 31, 31; 7:17, 18; 8:15, 18, 19; 9:15, 16, 16, 16, 18, 19, 19, 48; 10:12, 13, 14; 11:7, 7, 7, 9, 26; 12:2, 3, 3, 4; 14:13, 13, 15, 18, 18; 15:7, 10, 12; 18:6, 8, 9, 10, 10, 14, 14, 18, 24, 24, 24; 19:24; 20:7; 21:11, 11, 21, 22; **Ru** 1:8, 13, 13, 21; 4:2, 9, 10; **1Sa** 2:23, 24, 29; 4:9, 9; 6:3, 3, 5, 5, 6, 8, 21; 7:3; 8:17, 18, 18, 22; 9:13, 13, 13, 19; 10:14, 19, 19, 24; 11:9, 9, 10; 12:1, 5, 11, 12, 12, 13, 13, 14, 14, 15, 17, 17, 20, 21, 21, 25, 25, 25; 14:33, 38, 40; 15:6; 17:8, 9, 25; 18:25; 21:14, 15; 22:7, 13; 23:21, 21, 23; 25:6; 26:16, 16; 27:10; 29:10; 30:23; **2Sa** 1:21, 24; 2:5, 5, 6, 7; 3:17, 38; 7:7; 11:15, 15, 20, 20, 20, 21; 13:28; 15:10, 10, 36, 36; 16:10; 19:10, 11, 12, 12, 12, 13, 22, 22, 42, 43, 43; 21:3; 24:2; **1Ki** 1:34, 35, 45; 11:2; 12:9, 24; 18:18, 21, 24, 25; 20:28, 33; 22:3; **2Ki** 1:3, 5; 2:16; 3:17, 17, 17, 17, 19; 6:2, 11, 19, 32; 7:1; 9:11; 10:6, 6, 6, 8, 9, 13; 11:5, 6, 8, 8; 12:7; 17:12, 13, 27, 35, 36, 36, 36, 37, 37, 38, 38, 39; 18:19, 22, 22, 31, 31, 32; 19:6, 10, 29, 29; 22:13, 18; **1Ch** 12:17, 17; 15:12, 12, 13; 16:10, 13, 13, 15, 19, 28, 35; 17:6; 22:19; 28:8; **2Ch** 7:19; 10:6, 9; 11:4; 12:5; 13:8, 8, 9, 11, 12; 15:2, 2, 2, 2, 7; 18:14, 25, 27, 30; 19:6, 6, 9, 10, 10; 20:15, 15, 16, 16, 17, 17, 20, 20; 23:4; 24:5, 20, 20, 20; 28:9, 10, 11, 13, 13; 29:5, 8, 31; 30:6, 7, 7, 8, 9, 9; 32:10, 10, 12, 13; 34:23, 26; **Ezr** 4:2, 18, 21, 22; 6:6, 8; 7:25; 8:28, 29, 29; 9:11, 12; 10:10; **Ne** 1:8, 9; 2:17, 19, 19; 4:12, 14, 20, 20; 5:9, 9, 11; 8:10, 11; 13:17, 18, 21, 21, 25; **Est** 4:16; 8:8; **Job** 6:21, 21, 26, 27; 12:2; 13:2, 4, 4, 8, 8, 9, 10; 16:2, 4; 19:2, 3, 5, 21, 22, 28, 29, 29; 21:27, 28, 29, 29, 34; 27:12, 12; 32:6, 13; 34:2, 2, 10, 18; 42:7, 8; **Ps** 2:10, 10, 12; 4:2, 2, 2; 6:8; 11:1; 22:23, 23, 23; 24:7, 7, 7, 9, 9; 27:8; 29:1; 30:4; 31:23, 24; 32:9, 11, 11; 33:1; 34:9, 11; 47:1, 7; 48:13, 13; 49:1, 1; 50:22; 58:1, 1, 1; 62:3, 3, 3, 8; 66:1, 8, 16; 68:13, 13, 16, 16, 26, 32, 34; 82:2, 6, 7; 90:3; 94:8, 8, 8; 95:7; 96:7; 97:7, 10, 12; 99:5; 100:1, 3; 103:20, 21, 21, 21; 104:35; 105:2, 3, 6, 6, 45; 106:1, 48; 111:1; 112:1; 113:1, 1, 9; 114:6, 6, 6; 115:11; 116:19; 117:1, 1, 2; 119:115; 134:1, 1; 135:1, 1, 1, 2, 20, 21; 139:19; 146:1, 10; 147:1, 20; 148:1, 1, 2, 2, 3, 3, 4, 4, 7, 14; 149:1, 9; 150:1, 6; **Pr** 1:22, 22, 24, 25; 4:1; 5:7; 7:24; 8:5, 5, 5, 32; **SS** 1:5; 2:7, 7; 3:3, 5, 5, 11; 5:8, 8; 6:13; 8:4; **Isa** 1:5, 5, 10, 10, 12, 15, 15, 16, 19, 19, 20, 20, 29, 29, 29, 30; 2:3, 5, 22; 3:10, 14, 15, 15; 6:9, 9; 7:9, 9, 13, 13; 8:9, 9, 9, 9, 9, 12, 12; 10:3, 3, 3; 12:3, 4; 13:2, 6; 16:1, 7; 18:2, 3, 3, 3; 19:11; 21:5, 12, 12, 13, 13; 22:9, 9, 10, 10, 11, 11, 14; 23:1, 2, 6, 6, 14; 24:15; 26:2, 4, 19; 27:2, 12, 12; 28:12, 14, 15, 18, 22, 23; 29:1, 9; 30:11, 12, 15, 15, 16, 16, 17, 17, 21, 21, 21, 22, 29; 31:6; 32:9, 9, 10, 10, 11, 11, 11, 11, 20; 33:11, 11, 13, 13; 34:1, 1, 16; 35:3; 36:4, 7, 13, 16, 16; 37:6, 10, 30, 30; 40:1, 1, 2, 3, 18, 18, 21, 21, 21, 25; 41:14, 23, 24; 42:10, 17, 18, 18, 18; 43:10, 10, 12, 18, 19; 44:8, 8, 23, 23, 23, 26; 45:8, 11, 17, 19, 20, 21, 22; 46:5, 8, 12; 48:1, 6, 14, 16, 16, 20, 20, 20, 20; 49:1; 50:11, 11, 11, 11; 51:1, 1, 1, 1, 7, 7, 7; 52:3, 3, 9, 11, 11, 11, 11, 11, 12; 55:1, 1, 2, 2, 6, 6, 12; 56:1, 9, 9, 12; 57:3, 4, 4, 4, 14, 14; 58:4, 4, 4, 6; 61:6, 6; 62:6, 11; 65:11, 12, 12, 12, 13, 13, 13, 14, 15; 66:1, 5, 10, 10, 10, 11, 11, 12, 12, 13, 14; **Jer** 2:4, 7, 7, 12, 12, 29, 29, 31; 3:13, 16, 22; 4:4, 5, 5, 10, 16; 5:1, 1, 10, 14, 19, 19, 19, 22, 22, 31; 6:1, 4, 6, 16, 16, 18; 7:2, 4, 6, 8, 9, 9, 12, 13, 13, 13, 14, 23, 23; 8:8; 9:4, 4, 17, 20; 10:1, 11; 11:2, 4, 6, 13; 12:9; 13:15, 16, 17, 23; 14:13, 13; 16:12, 12, 13, 13, 13; 17:4, 20, 20, 22, 22, 24; 18:6, 11, 13; 19:3; 20:13; 21:3, 4, 11; 22:3, 4, 5, 10, 26, 26, 30; 23:2, 17, 20, 35, 36, 36, 38, 38; 25:3, 4, 5, 7, 7, 8, 27, 28, 29, 29, 34, 34, 34; 26:4, 5, 11, 12, 15, 15, 15; 27:4, 9, 9, 10, 13, 14, 15, 15; 29:5, 6, 6, 7, 8, 12, 12, 13, 13, 15, 19, 20, 20, 26, 28; 30:6, 22, 24; 31:6, 7, 7, 10; 32:5, 5, 36, 43; 33:10; 34:14, 15, 15, 16, 16, 17; 35:5, 6, 6, 7, 7, 7, 7, 13, 14, 15, 15, 15, 18; 36:19; 37:7, 10, 18; 40:3, 10, 10, 10; 42:9, 10, 11, 13, 15, 15, 16, 16, 16, 18, 18, 18, 19, 19, 20, 20, 21, 22, 22; 44:2, 7, 8, 8, 8, 8, 9, 21, 21, 22, 23, 25, 25, 26, 29; 46:3, 4, 9, 9, 14, 14; 48:14, 17, 17, 20, 26, 28; 49:3, 3, 5, 8, 14, 28, 30; 50:2, 11, 11, 11, 11, 14, 29, 45; 51:3, 3, 27, 45, 45, 46, 50; **La** 1:12; 4:15; **Eze** 5:7; 6:3, 7, 8, 8, 13; 7:4, 9; 9:5, 5, 7; 11:5, 6, 6, 7, 8, 10, 10, 11, 12, 12, 15, 17; 12:20, 22; 13:2, 5, 7, 7, 7, 8, 9, 11, 12, 14, 14, 14, 18, 18, 19, 20, 20, 21, 22, 23, 23; 14:8, 22, 22, 23, 23; 15:7; 17:12, 21; 18:2, 2, 3, 19, 25, 31, 31, 32; 20:3, 7, 18, 20, 29, 30, 30, 31, 31, 31, 32, 34, 38, 39, 39, 39, 39, 41, 42, 43, 43, 43, 43, 44, 44; 21:24, 24, 24; 22:19, 21, 22, 22; 23:40, 49, 49; 24:21, 22, 22, 23, 23, 24, 24; 25:5; 30:2; 33:10, 11, 11, 11, 20, 20, 25, 25, 26, 26, 26, 26; 34:3, 3, 3, 3, 4, 4, 4, 4, 4, 4, 7, 9, 18, 18, 19, 19, 21, 21, 31; 35:9, 13; 36:1, 3, 3, 4, 6, 8, 8, 9, 11, 22, 22, 23, 25, 27, 28, 28, 30, 31; 37:4, 5, 6, 6, 13, 14, 14; 39:17, 18, 19, 19, 19, 20; 44:6, 7, 7, 8, 8, 28, 30; 45:1, 1, 6, 10, 13, 13, 14, 20, 21; 47:13, 14, 18, 21, 22, 23; 48:8, 9, 20, 29; **Da** 1:10; 2:5, 5, 6, 6, 8, 8, 9, 9, 9; 3:5, 5, 14, 15, 15, 15, 15, 15, 26; **Hos** 1:9, 10, 10; 2:1; 4:1, 15, 15, 18; 5:1, 1, 1, 1, 8; 9:5; 10:13, 13, 13; 14:3; **Joel** 1:2, 2, 3, 5, 5, 11, 11, 11, 13, 13, 13, 14; 2:1, 12, 19, 22, 23, 26, 27; 3:4, 4, 4, 5, 6, 6, 7, 9, 11, 13, 17; **Am** 2:11, 12; 3:13; 4:1, 3, 3, 5, 6, 8, 9, 10, 11, 11; 5:1, 4, 4, 6, 7, 11, 11, 11, 11, 11, 14, 14, 22, 25, 26, 26; 6:2, 2, 3, 12, 13; 8:4; 9:7; **Ob** 1:1, 16; **Mic** 1:2, 10, 10, 11; 2:3, 3, 6, 8, 9, 9, 10; 3:1, 6, 6, 9; 6:1, 2, 2, 5, 9, 16, 16; 7:5, 5; **Na** 1:9; 2:9; **Hab** 1:5, 5; **Zep** 1:11; 2:3, 3, 3, 12, 12; 3:8; **Hag** 1:4, 6, 6, 6, 6, 6, 6, 9, 9, 9; 2:3, 4, 5, 5, 17; **Zec** 1:3, 4, 4; 2:9; 3:10; 6:7, 15, 15; 7:5, 5, 6, 6, 6, 7; 8:9, 13, 13, 15, 16, 16; 9:12, 12; 10:1; 11:2, 12; 14:5, 5, 5; **Mal** 1:2, 5, 6, 7, 7, 7, 8, 8, 10, 12, 12, 13, 13, 13, 13; 2:1, 2, 2, 2, 4, 8, 8, 8, 9, 13, 14, 16, 17, 17, 17; 3:1, 1, 6, 7, 7, 8, 8, 9, 9, 10, 12, 13, 14, 18; 4:2, 3, 4; **Mt** 2:8; 3:2, 3; 5:11, 13, 14, 20, 21, 27, 33, 38, 39, 43, 45, 46, 46, 47, 47, 48; 6:1, 1, 7, 8, 8, 8, 9, 14, 15, 16, 24, 25, 25, 25, 26, 28, 30, 32, 33; 7:1, 2, 2, 2, 6, 7, 11, 12, 12, 13, 16, 20, 23; 8:26, 26; 9:4, 6, 13, 28, 38; 10:5, 7, 8, 11, 11, 12, 14, 16, 18, 19, 19, 20, 22, 23, 23, 27, 27, 27, 31, 31; 11:4, 7, 8, 9, 14, 17, 17, 28, 29; 12:3, 5, 7, 7, 34; 13:14, 14, 17, 17, 18, 29, 29, 30, 51; 14:16; 15:5, 6, 7, 16, 17, 34; 16:2, 3, 3, 3, 8, 8, 8, 9, 9, 10, 11, 11, 15; 17:5, 20, 20; 18:3, 3, 10, 12, 18, 18, 35; 19:4, 28, 28; 20:4, 6, 7, 7, 22, 22, 22, 23, 25, 32; 21:2, 3, 5, 13, 16, 21, 21, 21, 22, 22, 24, 25, 32, 32, 32, 32, 42; 22:9, 9, 18, 18, 29, 31, 42; 23:3, 8, 8, 10, 13, 13, 13, 14, 14, 15, 15, 16, 17, 19, 23, 23, 24, 25, 27, 28, 28, 29, 31, 31, 32, 33, 33, 33, 34, 34, 35, 37, 39, 39; 24:2, 6, 6, 9, 15, 20, 32, 33, 33, 42, 44; 25:6, 9, 13, 30, 34, 35, 35, 35, 36, 36, 36, 40, 40, 41, 42, 42, 43, 43, 43, 45, 45; 26:2, 10, 11, 11, 15, 27, 31, 36, 38, 40, 41, 55, 55, 64, 65, 66; 27:17, 21, 24, 65; 28:5, 5, 7, 13, 19; **Mk** 1:3, 15, 17; 2:8, 10, 25; 4:13, 13, 24, 40; 5:39; 6:10, 10, 11, 31, 37, 38; 7:8, 8, 9, 9, 11, 12, 13, 13, 18, 18; 8:5, 17, 17, 17, 17, 18, 18, 18, 19, 20, 21, 29; 9:16, 33, 41; 10:36, 38, 38, 38, 39, 39, 42; 11:2, 2, 3, 3, 5, 17, 24, 24, 24, 24, 25, 25, 26, 31; 12:10, 15, 24, 24, 26, 27; 13:7, 7, 9, 9, 11, 11, 11, 11, 13, 14, 18, 23, 28, 29, 29, 33, 33, 35, 35; 14:7, 7, 7, 7, 13, 14, 27, 32, 34, 38, 38, 48, 49, 62, 64, 64, 71; 15:9, 12, 12; 16:6, 7, 15; **Lk** 2:12, 49, 49; 3:4; 4:23; 5:22, 24, 30, 34; 6:2, 3, 20, 21, 21, 21, 21, 22, 23, 24, 25, 25, 31, 31, 32, 32, 33, 33, 34, 34, 34, 35, 35, 36, 37, 37, 37, 38, 46; 7:22, 24, 25, 26, 32, 32, 33, 34; 8:18; 9:4, 5, 13, 20, 55, 55; 10:2, 5, 8, 10, 11, 23, 24, 24; 11:2, 9, 13, 18, 39, 40, 42, 42, 43, 44, 46, 46, 46, 47, 48, 48, 48, 52, 52, 52; 12:1, 3, 3, 7, 11, 11, 11, 12, 22, 22, 24, 26, 26, 28, 29, 29, 29, 29, 30, 31, 33, 36, 40, 40, 51, 54, 54, 55, 55, 56, 56, 56, 57; 13:2, 3, 3, 4, 5, 5, 25, 26, 27, 28, 32, 34, 35, 35; 16:9, 11, 12, 13, 15; 17:6, 6, 10, 10, 22, 22; 19:30, 30, 31, 31, 33, 46; 20:5, 23; 21:6, 8, 8, 9, 14, 16, 17, 19, 20, 30, 31, 31, 31, 36, 36; 22:10, 11, 26, 28, 30, 35, 40, 46, 46, 51, 52, 53, 70; 23:14, 14; 24:5, 17, 17, 38, 39, 41, 48, 49, 49; **Jn** 1:26, 38, 51; 3:7, 11, 12, 12, 28; 4:20, 21, 22, 22, 32, 35, 38, 38, 48, 48; 5:20, 33, 34, 35, 37, 38, 38, 39, 39, 40, 40, 42, 43, 43, 44, 45, 46, 46, 47, 47; 6:26, 26, 26, 29, 36, 53, 53, 62, 67; 7:8, 19, 21, 22, 23, 28, 28, 28, 34, 34, 36, 36, 45, 47; 8:14, 15, 19, 19, 19, 21, 21, 22, 23, 23, 24, 24, 24, 28, 28, 31, 31, 32, 33, 36, 37, 37, 38, 38, 39, 39, 40, 41, 42, 43, 43, 44, 44, 45, 46, 47, 47, 49, 54, 55; 9:19, 27, 27, 30, 41, 41, 41; 10:20, 25, 26, 26, 32, 34, 36, 38, 38; 11:15, 34, 39, 49, 56; 12:8, 8, 19, 19, 35, 36, 36; 13:10, 11, 12, 13, 13, 14, 15, 17, 17, 17, 19, 33, 33, 34, 34, 35, 35; 14:1, 3, 4, 4, 7, 7, 7, 13, 14, 15, 17, 19, 19, 20, 28, 28, 28, 29; 15:3, 4, 4, 5, 5, 7, 7, 7, 8, 8, 9, 10, 10, 12, 14, 14, 16, 16, 17, 18, 19, 19, 27, 27; 16:1, 4, 10, 12, 16, 16, 17, 17, 19, 19, 19, 20, 20, 22, 23, 23, 24, 24, 26, 27, 31, 32, 33, 33; 18:4, 7, 8, 31, 39, 39; 19:4, 6, 35; 20:22, 23, 23, 31, 31; 21:5, 6, 10; **Ac** 1:4, 5, 8, 8, 11, 11, 11; 2:14, 14, 15, 22, 22, 23, 33, 36, 38; 3:12, 12, 12, 13, 14, 16, 17, 19, 22, 25; 4:7, 8, 10, 19; 5:8, 9, 25, 28, 30, 35, 35, 39, 39; 6:3; 7:4, 26, 26, 37, 42, 42, 43, 43, 49, 51, 51, 51, 52; 8:24, 24; 10:21, 21, 28, 29; 11:16; 13:15, 15, 16, 25, 39, 41, 46; 14:15, 15; 15:1, 1, 7, 10, 24, 29, 29, 29, 29; 16:15; 17:22, 22, 23; 18:14, 15; 19:2, 2, 3, 15, 25, 26, 35, 36, 37, 39; 20:18, 25, 34, 35; 21:13; 22:1, 3; 23:15, 15; 25:24; 27:21, 31, 33; 28:26, 26; **Ro** 1:6; 6:3, 11, 12, 13, 14, 16, 16, 16, 16, 17, 17, 18, 19, 20, 20, 21, 21, 22; 7:1, 4, 4; 8:9, 13, 13, 13, 13, 15, 15; 9:26; 11:2, 25, 25, 30; 12:1, 2, 2; 13:5, 14; 15:6, 7, 10, 11, 11, 13, 14, 30; 16:2, 2, 17; **1Co** 1:5, 7, 8, 9, 10, 10, 13, 26, 30; 3:2, 2, 3, 3, 4, 5, 9, 9, 16, 16, 17, 23; 4:6, 8, 8, 8, 8, 10, 10, 10, 15, 16, 21; 5:2, 4, 6, 7, 7, 10, 12; 6:2, 2, 3, 4, 7, 7, 7, 9, 11, 11, 11, 15, 16, 19, 19, 19, 20; 7:1, 5, 23, 23; 8:12, 12; 9:2, 13, 24, 24; 10:1, 7, 10, 13, 15, 20, 21, 21, 27, 31, 31; 11:1, 18, 20, 22, 22, 25, 25, 26, 26, 33, 34; 12:2, 2, 2, 27; 14:1, 5, 5, 9, 9, 12, 12, 12, 20, 23, 26, 31; 15:1, 2, 2, 2, 11, 17, 58; 16:1, 6, 13, 15, 16, 18, 20; **2Co** 1:7, 14, 24; 2:4, 7, 9, 10; 3:2, 3; 5:20; 6:1, 11, 12, 12, 13, 14, 16, 17, 18; 7:9, 9, 9, 9, 11, 11; 8:7, 7, 9, 9, 24; 9:3, 5, 8; 10:7; 11:4, 4, 4, 4, 19, 19, 20; 12:11, 13, 20; 13:3, 5, 5, 5, 6, 7, 7, 9; **Gal** 1:9, 13; 3:2, 3, 3, 4, 7, 26, 28, 29, 29; 4:6, 8, 8, 9, 9, 9, 10, 12, 12, 13, 14, 15, 21, 21; 5:2, 4, 7, 7, 13, 15, 15, 16, 17, 17, 18, 18; 6:1, 2, 11; **Eph** 1:13, 13, 13, 13, 18; 2:2, 5, 8, 11, 12, 13, 19; 3:2, 4, 4, 13, 17, 19; 4:1, 1, 4, 17, 20, 21, 22, 24, 26, 30, 32; 5:1, 5, 7, 8, 8, 15, 17; 6:4, 9, 11, 13, 16, 21, 22; **Php** 1:7, 10, 10, 12, 27, 30; 2:2, 2, 12, 15, 15, 18, 22, 26, 28, 28; 3:15, 17; 4:9, 10, 10, 14, 14, 15, 15, 16; **Col** 1:4, 5, 6, 7, 9, 10, 23, 23; 2:1, 6, 6, 7, 10, 11, 20, 20; 3:1, 3, 4, 7, 7, 9, 13, 15, 15, 17, 23, 24, 24; 4:1, 6, 10, 12, 16; **1Th** 1:5, 6, 7, 9; 2:2, 5, 8, 9, 10, 12, 13, 13, 13, 14, 14, 19, 20; 3:4, 6, 8; 4:1, 1, 1, 2, 3, 9, 9, 10, 10, 11, 12, 12, 13; 5:1, 4, 5, 11; **2Th** 1:4, 5, 5, 12; 2:2, 5, 6, 15; 3:4, 6, 7, 13; **Heb** 3:7, 15; 4:7; 5:11, 12, 12; 6:10, 10, 12; 10:25, 29, 32, 32, 33, 33, 34, 34, 36, 36, 36; 12:3, 4, 5, 7, 8, 8, 17, 18, 22, 25; 13:5, 23; **Jas** 1:2, 4, 22; 2:3, 4, 6, 7, 8, 8, 9, 9, 12, 16, 24; 3:14; 4:2, 2, 2, 2, 2, 3, 3, 3, 4, 4, 5, 8, 8, 13, 14, 15, 16; 5:1, 3, 5, 5, 6, 8, 9, 11, 12, 16; **1Pe** 1:6, 6, 8, 8, 8, 15, 16, 17, 18, 18, 22, 22; 2:2, 3, 5, 9, 9, 15, 20, 20, 20, 20, 21, 21, 24, 25; 3:1, 6, 6, 7, 8, 9, 9, 13, 14, 14, 17; 4:7, 13, 13, 14, 14; 5:4, 5, 10, 12, 14; **2Pe** 1:8, 10, 10, 12, 19, 19; 3:2, 11, 14, 14, 17, 17, 17; **1Jn** 1:3; 2:1, 7, 7, 13, 13, 14, 14, 14, 18, 20, 20, 21, 21, 24, 24, 24, 27, 27, 27, 29, 29; 3:5, 11, 15; 4:2, 4; 5:13, 13, 13; **2Jn** 1:6, 6; **3Jn** 1:12; **Jude** 1:3, 5, 17, 20; **Rev** 2:10, 10, 25; 12:12, 12; 18:4, 4, 20; 19:5, 5, 18

YEA [340]

Ge 3:1; 17:16; 20:6; 27:33; **Lev** 25:35; **Nu** 10:32; **Dt** 33:3; **Jdg** 5:29; **1Sa** 15:20; 21:5; 24:11; **2Sa** 19:30; 22:39; **2Ki** 2:3, 5; 16:3; **1Ch** 16:21; **2Ch** 26:20; **Ezr** 9:2; **Ne** 5:15, 16; 6:10; 9:18, 21; **Est** 5:12; **Job** 1:15, 17; 2:4; 5:19; 6:10, 27, 29; 9:10; 11:15, 18, 19; 12:3; 14:10; 15:4, 6, 15; 18:5; 19:18; 20:8, 25; 21:7; 22:25; 25:5; 28:27; 30:2, 8, 9; 31:8, 11; 32:12; 33:14, 22; 34:12; 36:7; 40:5; 41:24; **Ps** 7:4, 5; 8:7; 16:6; 18:10, 14, 48; 19:10; 23:4; 25:3; 27:6; 29:5, 10; 31:9; 35:10, 15, 21, 27; 37:10, 36; 40:8; 41:9; 43:4; 44:22; 57:1; 58:2; 59:16; 68:3, 16, 18; 72:11; 78:19, 38, 41; 83:11, 17; 84:2, 3; 85:12; 90:17; 93:4; 94:23; 102:13, 26; 105:12, 14; 106:24, 37; 109:30; 116:5; 118:11; 119:34, 103, 127; 128:6; 137:1; 138:5; 139:12; 144:15; **Pr** 2:3, 9; 3:24; 6:16; 7:26; 8:18, 19; 16:4; 22:10; 23:16, 34; 24:5; 29:17; 30:15, 18, 29; 31:20; **Ecc** 1:16; 2:18, 23; 3:19; 4:3, 8, 8; 6:6; 7:18; 8:17; 9:3; 10:3; 12:9; **SS** 1:16; 5:1, 16; 6:9; 8:1; **Isa** 1:15; 5:10, 29; 14:8; 19:21; 24:16; 26:8, 9, 11; 29:5; 30:33; 32:13; 40:24, 24, 24; 41:10, 10, 23, 26, 26, 26; 42:13; 43:7, 13; 44:8, 12, 15, 15, 16, 19; 45:21; 46:6, 7, 11; 47:3; 48:8, 8, 8, 15; 49:15; 55:1; 56:9, 11; 59:15; 60:12; 66:3; **Jer** 2:37; 5:28; 8:7; 12:2, 2, 6; 14:5, 18; 23:11, 26; 27:21; 31:3, 19; 32:41; 46:16; 51:44; **La** 1:8; **Eze** 6:14; 16:6, 8, 9, 28, 52; 17:10; 22:2, 21, 29; 23:36; 26:18; 28:26; 32:10, 28; 34:6; 36:12; 37:27; 39:13; **Da** 8:11; 9:11, 21; 10:19; 11:22, 24, 26; **Hos** 2:19; 4:3; 7:9; 8:10; 9:12, 16; 12:4, 11; **Joel** 1:16, 18; 2:3, 19; 3:4; **Am** 8:6; **Ob** 1:13, 16; **Jnh** 3:8; **Mic** 3:7; **Na** 1:5; **Hab** 2:5; **Zep** 2:1; **Hag** 2:19; **Zec** 7:12; 8:22; 10:7; 14:5, 21; **Mal** 2:2; 3:15, 15; 4:1; **Mt** 5:37, 37; 9:28; 11:9; 13:51; 21:16; 26:60; **Lk** 2:35; 7:26; 11:28; 12:5, 57; 14:26; 24:22; **Jn** 11:27; 16:2, 32; 21:15, 16; **Ac** 3:16, 24; 5:8; 7:43; 20:34; 22:27; **Ro** 3:4, 31; 8:34; 14:4; 15:20; **1Co** 1:28; 2:10; 4:3; 9:16; 15:15; 16:6; **2Co** 1:17, 17, 18, 19, 19, 20; 5:16; 7:11, 11, 11, 11, 11, 11, 13; 8:3; **Gal** 4:17; **Php** 1:18; 2:17; 3:8; **2Ti** 3:12; **Phm** 1:20; **Heb** 11:36; **Jas** 2:18; 5:12, 12; **1Pe** 5:5; **2Pe** 1:13; **3Jn** 1:12; **Rev** 14:13

YES [4]

YET [683]

YOU [2802]

YOUR [1776]

1:4, 5, 7; 2:3, 17; **Zec** 1:2, 4, 4, 4, 5, 6; 6:15; 7:10; 8:9, 13, 14, 16, 17; **Mal** 1:5, 9, 9, 10, 13; 2:2, 3, 3, 3, 13, 15, 16, 17; 3:7, 11, 11, 11, 13; 4:3; **Mt** 5:12, 16, 16, 16, 20, 37, 44, 45, 47, 48; 6:1, 1, 8, 14, 15, 15, 21, 21, 25, 25, 26, 32; 7:6, 11, 11; 9:4, 11, 29; 10:9, 10, 13, 13, 14, 14, 20, 29, 30; 11:29; 12:27, 27; 13:16, 16; 15:3, 6; 17:20, 24; 18:14, 35; 19:8, 8; 20:26, 27; 23:8, 9, 9, 10, 11, 32, 34, 38; 24:20, 42; 25:8; 26:45; 27:65; **Mk** 2:8; 6:11; 7:9, 13; 8:17; 10:5, 43; 11:2, 25, 25, 26, 26; 13:18; 14:41; 16:7; **Lk** 3:14; 4:21; 5:4, 22; 6:22, 23, 24, 27, 35, 35, 36, 38; 7:22; 8:25; 9:3, 5, 44; 10:3, 6, 10, 11, 20; 11:13, 13, 19, 19, 39, 46, 47, 48; 12:7, 22, 30, 32, 34, 34, 35, 35; 13:35; 16:11, 12, 15; 19:30; 21:14, 15, 18, 19, 19, 28, 28, 30, 34; 22:53; 23:28; 24:38; **Jn** 4:35; 6:49, 58; 7:6; 8:17, 21, 24, 24, 38, 41, 42, 44, 44, 54, 56; 9:19, 41; 10:34; 11:15; 12:30; 13:14, 14; 14:1, 26, 27; 15:11, 16; 16:6, 20, 22, 22, 24; 18:31; 19:14, 15; 20:17, 17; **Ac** 2:17, 17, 17, 17, 39; 3:17, 19, 22, 22; 5:28; 7:37, 37, 43, 51, 52; 13:41; 15:24; 17:23, 28; 18:6, 6, 15; 19:37; 20:30; 24:22; 27:34; **Ro** 1:8; 6:12, 13, 13, 19, 19, 19, 22; 8:11; 11:25, 28, 31; 12:1, 1, 2, 16; 14:16; 15:24, 30; 16:19, 19, 20; **1Co** 1:4, 26; 2:5; 4:6; 5:6; 6:5, 8, 15, 19, 19, 20, 20; 7:5, 14, 35; 9:11; 14:34; 15:14, 17, 17, 31, 34, 58; 16:3, 3, 14, 17; **2Co** 1:6, 6, 14, 24, 24; 2:8, 10; 4:5, 15; 5:11, 13; 6:12; 7:7, 7, 7, 13; 8:7, 8, 9, 14, 14, 19, 24, 24; 9:2, 2, 5, 10, 10, 10, 13, 13; 10:6, 8, 15; 11:3; 12:19; 13:5, 5, 9; **Gal** 4:6, 15, 16; 6:13, 18; **Eph** 1:13, 15, 18; 3:13, 17; 4:4, 23, 26, 29; 5:19, 22, 25; 6:1, 4, 5, 5, 9, 14, 15, 22; **Php** 1:5, 9, 19, 25, 26, 27, 27, 28; 2:12, 17, 19, 20, 25, 30; 4:5, 6, 7, 10, 17, 19; **Col** 1:4, 8, 21; 2:5, 5, 13, 13, 18; 3:2, 3, 5, 8, 15, 16, 18, 19, 20, 21, 22; 4:1, 6, 8, 8; **1Th** 1:3, 4, 5, 8; 2:14, 17; 3:2, 5, 6, 7, 9, 10, 10, 13; 4:3, 11, 11; 5:23; **2Th** 1:3, 4, 4; 2:17; 3:5; **Phm** 1:22, 25; **Heb** 3:8, 9, 15; 4:7; 6:10; 9:14; 10:34, 35; 12:3, 13; 13:5, 17; **Jas** 1:3, 21, 22; 2:2; 3:14; 4:1, 1, 3, 8, 8, 9, 9, 14, 16; 5:1, 2, 2, 3, 3, 4, 5, 8, 12, 12, 16; **1Pe** 1:7, 9, 9, 13, 14, 17, 18, 18, 21, 22; 2:12, 12, 16, 18, 20, 25; 3:1, 2, 7, 15, 16; 4:14; 5:7, 8, 9; **2Pe** 1:5, 10, 19; 3:1, 17; **1Jn** 1:4; 2:12; **2Jn** 1:10; **Jude** 1:12, 20; **Rev** 1:9; 2:23; 16:1

YOURS [12]

Ge 45:20; **Dt** 11:24; **Jos** 2:14; **2Ch** 20:15; **Jer** 5:19; **Lk** 6:20; **Jn** 15:20; **1Co** 3:21, 22; 8:9; 16:18; **2Co** 12:14

YOURSELVES [191]

Ge 18:4; 45:5; 49:1, 2; **Ex** 19:12; 30:37; 32:29; **Lev** 11:43, 43, 44, 44; 18:24, 30; 19:4; 20:7; **Nu** 11:18; 16:3, 21; 31:3, 18, 19; **Dt** 2:4; 4:15, 16, 23, 25; 11:16, 23; 14:1; 31:14, 29; **Jos** 2:16; 3:5; 6:18, 18; 7:13; 8:2; 23:7, 11, 16; 24:22; **Jdg** 15:12; **1Sa** 2:29; 4:9, 9; 10:19; 14:34; 16:5; **1Ki** 18:25; 20:12; **2Ki** 17:35; **1Ch** 15:12; **2Ch** 20:17; 29:5, 31; 30:8; 32:11; 35:4, 6; **Ezr** 10:11; **Ne** 13:25; **Job** 19:3, 5; 27:12; 42:8; **Isa** 8:9, 9, 9; 29:9; 45:20; 46:8; 48:14; 49:9; 50:1, 11; 52:3; 57:4, 5; 61:6; **Jer** 4:4, 5; 6:1; 8:14; 13:18; 17:21; 25:34; 26:15; 37:9; 44:8; 50:14; **Eze** 14:6; 18:30, 32; 20:7, 18, 31, 43; 36:31; 39:17, 17; 44:8; **Hos** 10:12; **Joel** 1:13; 3:11, 11; **Am** 3:9; 5:26; **Zep** 2:1; **Zec** 7:6, 6; **Mt** 3:9; 6:19, 20; 16:8; 23:13, 15, 31; 25:9; **Mk** 6:31; 9:33, 50; 13:9; **Lk** 3:8; 11:46, 52; 12:33, 36, 57; 13:28; 16:9, 15; 17:3, 14; 21:34; 22:17; 23:28; **Jn** 3:28; 6:43; 16:19; **Ac** 2:22, 40; 5:35; 13:46; 15:29; 20:10, 28, 34; **Ro** 6:11, 13, 16; 12:19; **1Co** 5:13; 6:7; 7:5; 11:13; 16:16; **2Co** 7:11, 11; 11:19; 13:5; **Eph** 2:8; 5:19, 21, 22; **Col** 3:18; **1Th** 2:1; 3:3; 4:9; 5:2, 11, 13, 15; **2Th** 3:6, 7; **Heb** 10:34; 13:3, 17; **Jas** 2:4; 4:7, 10; **1Pe** 1:14; 2:13; 4:1, 8; 5:5, 6; **1Jn** 5:21; **2Jn** 1:8; **Jude** 1:20, 21; **Rev** 19:17

HEBREW-ARAMAIC DICTIONARY-INDEX TO THE OLD TESTAMENT

FEATURES OF THE HEBREW-ARAMAIC TO ENGLISH DICTIONARY-INDEX

STRONG NUMBER
Matches the number at the end of context lines; one- to four-digit numbers in non-italic type are Hebrew and Aramaic (see the introduction, pages xii–xiv).

LEXICAL FORM AND TRANSLITERATION
See the table below. Note that the lexical forms conform to modern resources and sometimes differ from Strong's original spelling.

PART OF SPEECH
The part of speech is abbreviated (see below and introduction, page xiv).

G/K NUMBER
Cross reference to the G/K numbering system, widely used in up-to-date word study reference resources (see the introduction, page xiv).

122 אָדֹם *'ādōm,* a. GK: 137 [→ 131; cf. 119]. ← **RELATED WORDS LIST**: Hebrew and Aramaic words related by cognate are listed by Strong number (see the introduction, pages xiv–xv).

red, ruddy (skin):– ← **DEFINITION AND ETYMOLOGY**: Words are defined, often with expanded explanations, and if a proper name, the possible definition (etymology) is given in italics (see the introduction, pages xiv–xv).

red [7], ruddy [1] ← **KJV WORD AND (FREQUENCY COUNT)**: Following the symbol :– KJV words are listed according to their exact textual spelling and are organized according to frequency (see the introduction, page xiv).

displeased (+7451+871.1) [1], ← **MULTIPLE WORDS / MULTIPLE NUMBERS**: More than one KJV word and/or more than one Strong number indicate multiple-word translations (see the introduction, pages xiii–xiv).

same^{S} [1] ← **SUPERSCRIPT "S"**: Indicates "substitution" translation (see the introduction, pages xiii-xv).

HEBREW-ARAMAIC SIMPLIFIED TRANSLITERATION AND PRONUNCIATION TABLE

Heb

Consonants

א	'	[no sound]
ב, בּ	*b*	*b*oy
ג, גּ	*g*	*g*irl
ד, דּ	*d*	*d*og
ה	*h*	*h*ot
ו	*w*	*v*ote
ז	*z*	*z*ip
ח	*ḥ*	Ba*ch*
ט	*ṭ*	*t*ip
י	*y*	*y*es
ך, כ, כּ	*k*	*k*it
ל	*l*	*l*et
ם, מ	*m*	*m*other
ן, נ	*n*	*n*ot
ס	*s*	*s*ip
ע	'	[no sound]
ף, פ, פּ	*p*	*p*et
ץ, צ	*ṣ*	si*ts*
ק	*q*	tor*q*ue
ר	*r*	*r*ot
שׂ	*ś*	*s*ip
שׁ	*š*	*sh*ip
ת, תּ	*t*	*t*ip

Vowels

ָה	*â*	f*a*ther
ָ	*ā*	f*a*ther
ַ	*a*	f*a*ther
ֲ	^{a}	b*a*ton
וּ	*û*	t*u*ne
ֻ	*u*	s*u*re
ֵי	*ê*	th*ey*
ֵ	*ē*	th*ey*
ֶ	*e*	g*e*t
ְ if (vocal)	^{e}	s*e*lect
ֱ	^{e}	s*e*lect
ִי	*î*	mach*i*ne
ִ	*i*	p*i*n
וֹ	*ô*	ph*o*ne

HEBREW-ARAMAIC DICTIONARY ABBREVIATIONS

&	and
+	plus: in combination with
?	uncertain
[ ]	uncertain part of speech
→	see these related words
√	see this organizing word
1	first person
2	second person
3	third person
a.	adjective
abst.	abstract
adv.	adverb
art.	article
c.	conjunction
col.	collective
com.	common gender
demo.	demonstrative
den.	denominative
du.	dual number
emph.	emphatic
excl.	exclamation
f.	feminine
fig.	figurative(ly)
g.	gentilic
indecl.	indeclinable
indef.	indefinite
inf.	infinitive
intens.	intensive
inter.	interrogative
interj.	interjection
l.	loanword
loc.	location
m.	masculine
n.	noun
neg.	negative
num.	numeral
ord.	ordinal
p.	pronoun
pl.	plural
poss.	possibly
pp.	preposition
pr.	proper [noun]
pref.	prefix
prob.	probably
pt.	particle
ptcp.	participle
rel.	relative
s.	singular
subst.	substantive
suf.	suffix
temp.	temporal
tt.	technical term in Psalm title
v.	verb
var.	variant
vbl.	verbal

Hebrew Verbal Stems

[H]	Hiphil
[Ho]	Hophal
[Hotpaal]	Hotpaal
[Hotpael]	Hotpael
[Hsh]	Histaphel
[Ht]	Hitpael
[Htpal]	Hitpalpel
[Htpalpal]	Hitpalpal
[Htpo]	Hitpoel
[Htpoal]	Hitpoal
[Htpol]	Hitpolel
[Htpolal]	Hitpolal
[N]	Niphal
[P]	Piel
[Pilal]	Pilal
[Pilel]	Pilel
[Pilpal]	Pilpal
[Pil]	Pilpel
[Po]	Poel
[Poal]	Poal
[Poalal]	Poalal
[Pol]	Polel
[Polal]	Polal
[Pu]	Pual
[Pualal]	Pualal
[Pul]	Pulal
[Pulpal]	Pulpal
[Q]	Qal
[Qp]	Qal passive

Aramaic Verbal Stems

[A]	Aphel
[H]	Haphel
[Ho]	Hophal
[Hp]	Haphel passive
[Hsh]	Hishtaphel
[Hth]	Hithaphal
[Htpa]	Hitpaal
[Htpe]	Hitpeel
[Htpol]	Hitpolel
[Htt]	Ettaphal
[Itpa]	Itpaal
[Itpe]	Itpeel
[Itpo]	Itpoal
[P]	Peal
[Pa]	Pael
[Pap]	Pael passive
[Peil]	Peil
[Po]	Poel
[Pol]	Polel
[Pp]	Peal passive (participle)

0.1 אָ- ***-ā'***, p.suf.3.f.s. GK: 2 [cf. 1886.3]. she, her:– *not translated* [1]

0.2 אָ- ***-ā'*** (Aram.), art.suf. GK: 10002 [→ 1886.7]. the, a; indicates vocative: O; indicates emphatic state:– the [503], *usually untranslated* [258], O [24], a [13], that [5], continually (+8411+871.2) [2], the same [2], this [2], an [1], at what time (+1768+5732+871.2) [1], ever (+5705+5957) [1], ever (+5957) [1], for ever (+5957) [1], the same [1]

1 אָב ***'āb***, n.m. GK: 3 [cf. 2 (also used with compound proper names)]. father, grandfather, forefather, ancestor; (pl.) ancestors (of both genders); by extension: originator, founder (of a city or profession); a title of respect referring to humans or god. The "house of a father" is a subdivision of a clan:– father [593], fathers [475], father's [118], fathers' [13], father's (+3807.1) [6], chief [2], families (+1004) [2], fatherless (+369) [1], forefathers (+7223) [1], patrimony [1], prince [1], principal [1]

2 אַב ***'ab*** (Aram.), n.m. GK: 10003 [cf. 1]. father, predecessor, ancestor (not necessarily male):– father [6], fathers [3]

3 אֵב ***'ēb***, n.[m.]. GK: 4 [cf. 768; cf. 4]. new (plant) growth, shoot:– fruits [1], greenness [1]

4 אֵב ***'ēb*** (Aram.), n.m. GK: 10004 [cf. 3]. fruit:– fruit [3]

אֹב ***'ōb***. See 178.

5 אֲבַגְתָא ***'^{a}bagtā'***, n.pr.m. GK: 5. Abagtha:– Abagtha [1]

6 אָבַד ***'ābad***, v. GK: 6 [→ 8, 9, 10, 11, 12, 13; cf. 7]. [Q] perish, [P, H] destroy, demolish, annihilate; "to destroy the heart" means "to lose courage":– perish [65], destroy [39], destroyed [17], perished [17], lost [9], perisheth [6], destroyeth [4], surely perish (+6) [4], cause to perish [3], ready to perish [3], utterly destroy (+6) [2], utterly perish (+6) [2], broken [1], destroyest [1], destruction [1], failed (+4480) [1], faileth [1], have no (+4480) [1], lose [1], made to perish [1], not (+4480) [1], spendeth [1], take [1], undone [1], void [1]

7 אֲבַד ***'^{a}bad*** (Aram.), v. GK: 10005 [cf. 6]. [P] to perish; [H] to execute; [Ho] to be destroyed:– destroy [4], perish [2], destroyed [1]

8 אֹבֵד ***'ōbēd***, n.[m.]. GK: 7 [→ 6]. ruin:– perish [2]

9 אֲבֵדָה ***'^{a}bēdâ***, n.f. GK: 8 [→ 6]. lost item:– lost [3], that which was lost [1]

10 אֲבַדֹּה ***'^{a}baddōh***, n.f. GK: 9 [→ 11; cf. 6]. destruction; this can refer to the nether world of the dead, with a focus that this is the place of decay:– destruction [1]

11 אֲבַדּוֹן ***'^{a}baddôn***, n.f. GK: 10 & 11 [→ 10; cf. 6]. destruction; some translate as a proper noun, the Place of Destruction (the realm of the dead):– destruction [5]

12 אַבְדָן ***'abdān***, n.[m.]. GK: 12 [→ 6]. destruction:– destruction [1]

13 אָבְדָן ***'obdān***, n.[m.]. GK: 13 [→ 6]. destruction:– destruction [1]

14 אָבָה ***'ābâ***, v. GK: 14 [→ 17, 15?, 34?; cf. 2968, 8373?]. [Q] to be willing, consent, yield; with the negative, to be unwilling, refuse:– would [39], will [6], consent [4], willing [4], rest content [1]

15 אֲבִי ***'ābî***, interj. GK: 20 [→ 14?]. Oh, that!:– my desire [1]

16 אֵבֶה ***'ēbeh***, n.[m.]. GK: 15. papyrus or reed (boat):– swift [1]

17 אֲבוֹי ***'^{a}bôy***, interj. GK: 16 [→ 14]. sorrow (uneasiness); some parse as an interjection: woe!:– sorrow [1]

18 אֵבוּס ***'ēbûs***, n.m. GK: 17 [→ 75]. manger:– crib [3]

19 אִבְחָה ***'ibḥâ***, n.f. GK: 18 [cf. 2874]. slaughter:– point [1]

20 אֲבַטִּיחַ ***'^{a}baṭṭîaḥ***, n.[m.]. GK: 19 [→ 982]. melon:– melons [1]

21 אֲבִי ***'^{a}bî***, n.pr.m. GK: 23 [→ 29]. Abijah, Abiezrite, *"[my] father is Yahweh, Abi [my] father"*:– Abi [1]

22 אֲבִיאֵל ***'^{a}bî'ēl***, n.pr.m. GK: 24 [→ 410+1]. Abiel, *"[my] father is God [El]"*:– Abiel [3]

23 אֲבִיאָסָף ***'^{a}bî'āsāp***, n.pr.m. GK: 25 [→ 43]. Abiasaph, *"[my] father has gathered"*:– Abiasaph [1]

24 אָבִיב ***'ābîb***, n.m. GK: 26 [cf. 8512]. (month of) Abib, the first month of the Canaanite calendar equal to Nisan (March-April); head (of grain), already ripe but still soft:– Abib [6], green ears of corn [1], in the ear [1]

25 אֲבִי גִבְעוֹן ***'^{a}bî gib'ôn***, n.pr.m. GK: 3 + 1500 [→ 1+1391]. father of Gibeon (1 + 1391):–

26 אֲבִיגַיִל ***'^{a}bîgayil***, n.pr.f. GK: 28 [→ 1+1523?]. Abigail, *"[my] father rejoices* or *father [cause] of joy"*:– Abigail [17]

27 אֲבִידָן ***'^{a}bîdān***, n.pr.m. GK: 29 [→ 1+1777]. Abidan, *"[my] father is judge"*:– Abidan [5]

28 אֲבִידָע ***'^{a}bîdā'***, n.pr.m. GK: 30 [→ 1+3045]. Abida, *"[my] father knows"*:– Abidah [1], Abida [1]

29 אֲבִיָּה ***'^{a}biyyâ*** or אֲבִיָּהוּ ***'^{a}biyyāhû***, n.pr.m. & f. GK: 31 & 32 [→ 21]. Abijah, *"[my] father is Yahweh"*:– Abijah [20], Abiah [4], Abia [1]

30 אֲבִיהוּא ***'^{a}bîhû'***, n.pr.m. GK: 33 [→ 1+1931]. Abihu, *"he is [my] father"*:– Abihu [12]

31 אֲבִיהוּד ***'^{a}bîhûd***, n.pr.m. GK: 34 [→ 1+1935]. Abihud, *"[my] father has majesty"*:– Abihud [1]

32 אֲבִיהַיִל ***'^{a}bîhayil*** or אֲבִיחַיִל ***'^{a}bîḥayil***, n.pr.m. GK: 35 & 38 [→ 1+2428]. Abihail, *"[my] father has strength/wealth* or *cause of strength/wealth"*:– Abihail [6]

33 אֲבִי הָעֶזְרִי ***'^{a}bî 'ezrî***, a.g. GK: 49 [→ 44]. Abiezrite, *"of Abiezer"*:– Abi-ezrites [2], Abi-ezrite [1]

34 אֶבְיוֹן ***'ebyôn***, a. GK: 36 [→ 14?]. poor, needy, often as a class of persons with physical needs, of low status and little political power, with an associative meaning of oppression and misery:– needy [35], poor [24], beggar [1], poor man [1]

35 אֲבִיּוֹנָה ***'^{a}biyyônâ***, n.f. GK: 37. caper berry (that stimulates desire):– desire [1]

אֲבִיחַיִל ***'^{a}bîḥayil***. See 32.

36 אֲבִיטוּב ***'^{a}bîṭûb***, n.pr.m. GK: 39 [→ 1+2896]. Abitub, *"[my] father is good"*:– Abitub [1]

37 אֲבִיטַל ***'^{a}bîṭal***, n.pr.f. GK: 40 [→ 1+2919]. Abital, *"[my] father is [the] night dew"*:– Abital [2]

38 אֲבִיָּם ***'^{a}biyyām***, n.pr.m. GK: 41 [→ 1+3220]. Abiyam, *"[my] father is Yam [the sea]"*:– Abijam [5]

39 אֲבִימָאֵל ***'^{a}bîmā'ēl***, n.pr.m. GK: 42 [→ 1+410]. Abimael, *"[my] father is God [El]"*:– Abimael [2]

40 אֲבִימֶלֶךְ ***'^{a}bîmelek***, n.pr.m. GK: 43 [→ 1+4428]. Abimelech, *"[my] father is king* or *[my] father is Molech"*:– Abimelech [65], Abimelech's [2]

41 אֲבִינָדָב ***'^{a}bînādāb***, n.pr.m. GK: 44 [→ 1+5068]. Abinadab, *"[my] father is generous* or *[my] father is Nadab"*:– Abinadab [13]

42 אֲבִינֹעַם ***'^{a}bînō'am***, n.pr.m. GK: 45 [→ 1+5278]. Abinoam, *"[my] father is graciousness"*:– Abinoam [4]

אֲבִינֵר ***'^{a}bînēr***. See 74.

43 אֶבְיָסָף ***'ebyāsāp***, n.pr.m. GK: 47 [→ 23]. Ebiasaph, *"[my] father has gathered"*:– Ebiasaph [3]

44 אֲבִיעֶזֶר ***'^{a}bî'ezer***, n.pr.m. GK: 48 [→ 33]. Abiezer, *"[my] father is help"*:– Abi-ezer [7]

45 אֲבִי־עַלְבוֹן ***'^{a}bî-'albôn***, n.pr.m. GK: 50 [→ 1]. Abi-Albon, *"[my] father is Albon"*:– Abialbon [1]

46 אָבִיר ***'ābîr***, a. GK: 51 [→ 47, 82, 83, 84]. mighty, powerful; (as a divine title) the Mighty One:– mighty one [3], mighty [3]

47 אַבִּיר ***'abbîr***, a. GK: 52 [→ 46]. mighty, powerful; this can refer to strong animals, social leaders, and angelic beings:– bulls [4], mighty [4], stouthearted (+3820) [2], strong [2], valiant [2], angels' [1], chiefest [1], strong ones [1]

48 אֲבִירָם ***'^{a}bîrām***, n.pr.m. GK: 53 [→ 1+7311; cf. 87]. Abiram, *"[my] father is exalted"*:– Abiram [11]

49 אֲבִישַׁג ***'^{a}bîšag***, n.pr.f. GK: 54 [→ 1+7683]. Abishag, *"[my] father strays"*:– Abishag [5]

50 אֲבִישׁוּעַ ***'^{a}bîšûa'***, n.pr.m. GK: 55 [→ 1+7770]. Abishua, *"[my] father is salvation"*:– Abishua [5]

51 אֲבִישׁוּר ***'^{a}bîšûr***, n.pr.m. GK: 56 [→ 1+7794]. Abishur, *"[my] father is a wall"*:– Abishur [2]

52 אֲבִישַׁי ***'^{a}bîšay*** or אַבְשַׁי ***'abšay***, n.pr.m. GK: 57 & 93 [→ 1+7862]. Abishai, *"[my] father is Jesse* or *father exists"*:– Abishai [25]

53 אֲבִישָׁלוֹם ***'^{a}bîšālôm*** or אַבְשָׁלוֹם ***'abšālôm***, n.pr.m. GK: 58 & 94 [→ 1+7965]. Abishalom, *"[my] father is peace"*:– Absalom [104], Absalom's [5], Abishalom [2]

54 אֶבְיָתָר ***'ebyātār***, n.pr.m. GK: 59 [→ 1+3498]. Abiathar, *"[my] father gives abundance* or *the father is preeminent"*:– Abiathar [29], Abiathar's (+3807.1) [1]

55 אָבַךְ ***'ābak***, v. GK: 60 [cf. 2015]. [Ht] to roll upward, to be borne along:– mount up [1]

56 אָבַל ***'ābal***, v. GK: 61 & 62 [→ 57, 60]. [Q] to dry up, lie parched; to mourn, lament, grieve; [H] cause to mourn; mourning can be the emotion or attitude of sorrow, as well as the active observation of mourning rites and ceremonies; [Ht] to mourn, lament, grieve:– mourn [15], mourned [10], mourneth [8], caused a mourning [1], feign to be a mourner [1], lamented [1], lament [1], made to lament [1], mourning [1]

57 אָבֵל ***'ābēl***, a. GK: 63 [→ 56]. mourning, grieving, weeping:– mourn [3], mourners [2], mourning [2], mourneth [1]

58 אָבֵל ***'ābēl***, n.m. GK: 64 [→ 59, 62, 63, 64, 65, 66, 67, 180; cf. 2986]. meadow:– plain [1]

59 אָבֵל **ʾābēl**, n.pr.loc. GK: 64 [→ 58]. Abel, "*meadow*":– Abel [4], Abel-beth-maachah [2]

60 אֵבֶל **ʾēbel**, n.m. GK: 65 [→ 56]. ceremony of mourning, period of mourning; a mourning ceremony was a ritual for burial of the dead, with distinctive clothing, music, behaviors, and a set time period for the ritual, generally a longer period for more important people:– mourning [24]

61 אֲבָל **ʾᵃbāl**, adv. GK: 66 [→ 1077]. but; however, surely, indeed:– but [4], verily [3], indeed [2], nevertheless [2]

62 אָבֵל בֵּית מַעֲכָה **ʾābēl bêt maᵃkâ**, n.pr.loc. GK: 68 [→ 58+1004+4601]. Abel Beth Maacah, "*meadow of the house of Maacah [oppression]*":–

63 אָבֵל הַשִּׁטִּים **ʾābēl haššiṭṭîm**, n.pr.loc. GK: 69 [→ 58]. Abel Shittim, "*meadow of the acacia trees*":– Abel-shittim [1]

64 אָבֵל כְּרָמִים **ʾābēl kᵉrāmîm**, n.pr.loc. GK: 70 [→ 58]. Abel Keramim, "*meadow of vineyards*":–

65 אָבֵל מְחוֹלָה **ʾābēl mᵉḥôlâ**, n.pr.loc. GK: 71 [→ 58+4246; cf. 4259?]. Abel Meholah, "*meadow of the round dance*":– Abel-meholah [3]

66 אָבֵל מַיִם **ʾābēl mayim**, n.pr.loc. GK: 72 [→ 58+4325]. Abel Maim, "*meadow of waters*":– Abel-maim [1]

67 אָבֵל מִצְרַיִם **ʾābēl miṣrayim**, n.pr.loc. GK: 73 [→ 58+4714]. Abel Mizraim, "*meadow of Egypt* or *mourning of Egypt*":– Abel-mizraim [1]

68 אֶבֶן **ʾeben**, n.f. GK: 74 [→ 72, 70?; cf. 69]. stone, rock, natural or shaped, sometimes of specific size for use in a balance scale; a "precious stone" is a gem or jewel; by extension: hailstone. Rock is a title of God, with a focus of strength and stability, a place of refuge:– stones [142], stone [105], divers weights (+68+2050.1) [6], weight [4], great hailstones (+417) [3], weights [3], stony [2], carbuncles (+688) [1], chalkstones (+1615) [1], hailstones (+1259) [1], hailstones (+1259+1886.1) [1], headstone (+7222) [1], masons (+2796+7023) [1], plummet (+913) [1], slingstones (+7050) [1]

69 אֶבֶן **ʾeben** (Aram.), n.f. GK: 10006 [cf. 68]. rock, stone, including hewn or unhewn stones, stone slabs and bricks:– stone [6], stones [2]

70 אָבְנַיִם **ʾobnayim**, n.[m.]. GK: 78 [→ 68?]. potter's wheel; delivery stool:– stools [1], wheels [1]

71 אֲבָנָה **ʾᵃbānâ**, n.pr.loc. GK: 76 [cf. 549]. Abana:– Abana [1]

72 אֶבֶן הָעֵזֶר **ʾeben hāʿēzer**, n.pr.loc. GK: 75 [→ 68+5828]. Ebenezer, "*stone of help*":– Eben-ezer [3]

73 אַבְנֵט **ʾabnēṭ**, n.[m.]. GK: 77. (linen) sash, wrapped around the waist:– girdle [6], girdles [3]

74 אַבְנֵר or אֲבִינֵר **ʾabnēr** or **ʾᵃbînēr**, n.pr.m. GK: 46 & 79 [→ 1+5216]. Abner, "*[my] father is Ner [a lamp]*":– Abner [62], Abner's [1]

75 אָבַס **ʾābas**, v. GK: 80 [→ 18, 3965]. [Qp] to be fattened:– fatted [1], stalled [1]

76 אֲבַעְבֻּעֹת **ʾᵃbaʿbuʿōt**, n.f.pl. GK: 81 [→ 5042]. festers, blisters:– blains [2]

77 אֶבֶץ **ʾebeṣ**, n.pr.loc. GK: 82 [→ 78]. Ebez:– Abez [1]

78 אִבְצָן **ʾibṣān**, n.pr.m. GK: 83 [→ 77]. Ibzan, "*swift*":– Ibzan [2]

79 אָבַק **ʾābaq**, v.den. GK: 84 [cf. 3543?]. [N] to wrestle (with):– wrestled [2]

80 אָבָק **ʾābāq**, n.m. GK: 85 [→ 81]. fine dust, powder:– dust [4], powder [1], small dust [1]

81 אֲבָקָה **ʾᵃbāqâ**, n.f. GK: 86 [→ 80]. spice (scented powders):– powders [1]

82 אָבַר **ʾābar**, v.den. GK: 87 [→ 83; cf. 46]. [H] to take flight, soar upward:– fly [1]

83 אֵבֶר **ʾēber**, n.[m.]. GK: 88 [→ 82, 84; cf. 46]. feather, wing; other sources: the strong joint of the body to the wing, "pinion," with the associative meaning of strength that can bring freedom:– wings [2], longwinged (+750) [1]

84 אֶבְרָה **ʾebrâ**, n.f. GK: 89 [→ 83; cf. 46]. feather, pinion, wing; in some contexts may have the associative meaning of protection:– feathers [2], wings [2]

85 אַבְרָהָם **ʾabrāhām**, n.pr.m. GK: 90 [cf. 87]. Abraham, "*father of many*":– Abraham [161], Abraham's [14]

86 אַבְרֵךְ **ʾabrēk**, l.excl. GK: 91. Make way!; others: Kneel down! or Watch out!:– bow the knee [1]

87 אַבְרָם **ʾabrām**, n.pr.m. GK: 92 [→ 1+7311; cf. 48, 85]. Abram, "*exalted father*":– Abram [54], Abram's [7]

אַבְשַׁי **ʾabšay**. See 52.

אַבְשָׁלוֹם **ʾabšālôm**. See 53.

88 אֹבֹת **ʾōbōt**, n.pr.loc. GK: 95 [→ 2968?]. Oboth, "*fathers*":– Oboth [4]

89 אָגֵא **ʾāgēʾ**, n.pr.m. GK: 96. Agee, "[poss.] *fugitive*":– Agee [1]

90 אֲגַג **ʾᵃgag**, n.pr.m. GK: 97 [→ 91?]. Agag, "[poss.] *violent*":– Agag [8]

91 אֲגָגִי **ʾᵃgāgî**, a.g. GK: 98 [→ 90?]. Agagite, "*of Agag*":– Agagite [5]

92 אֲגֻדָּה **ʾᵃguddâ**, n.f. GK: 99. bunch, bundle; group, band; cord, bands; foundation, structure:– troop [2], bunch [1], burdens [1]

93 אֱגוֹז **ʾᵉgôz**, n.[m.]. GK: 100. nut tree:– nuts [1]

94 אָגוּר **ʾāgûr**, n.pr.m. GK: 101 [→ 103]. Agur, "*gatherer* [or poss.] *wage earner*":– Agur [1]

95 אֲגוֹרָה **ʾᵃgôrâ**, n.f. GK: 102 [→ 107]. fee, payment, a piece of precious metal used as a medium of exchange (but not a minted coin):– piece [1]

96 אֵגֶל **ʾēgel**, n.[m.]. GK: 103 [→ 97]. drop (of dew):– drops [1]

97 אֶגְלַיִם **ʾeglayim**, n.pr.loc. GK: 104 [→ 96]. Eglaim:– Eglaim [1]

98 אֲגַם **ʾᵃgam**, n.[m.]. GK: 106 [→ 100]. swamp, pond, marsh (with reeds):– ponds [2], pools [2], pool [2], standing [2], reeds [1]

99 אָגֵם **ʾāgēm**, a. GK: 108 [cf. 5701]. sick, grieved:– ponds [1]

100 אַגְמוֹן **ʾagmôn**, n.[m.]. GK: 109 [→ 98]. reed; cord (made of reeds):– rush [2], bulrush [1], caldron [1], hook [1]

101 אַגָּן **ʾaggān**, n.[m.]. GK: 110. (large and deep) bowl, goblet:– basons [1], cups [1], goblet [1]

102 אֲגַף **ʾᵃgap**, n.[m.]. GK: 111 [→ 1610]. troop, band:– bands [7]

103 אָגַר **ʾāgar**, v. GK: 112 [→ 94]. [Q] to gather (in):– gathereth [2], gather [1]

104 אִגְּרָה **ʾiggᵉrâ** (Aram.), n.f. GK: 10007 [cf. 107]. letter:– letter [3]

105 אֲגַרְטָל **ʾᵃgarṭāl**, n.m. GK: 113. dish; in context made of precious metals:– chargers [2]

106 אֶגְרֹף **ʾegrōp**, n.[m.]. GK: 114 [→ 1640?]. fist (the hand clenched to strike):– fist [2]

107 אִגֶּרֶת **ʾiggeret**, n.f. GK: 115 [→ 95; cf. 104]. letter, document:– letters [6], letter [4]

108 אֵד **ʾēd**, n.m. GK: 116. stream, fresh water that moves from a higher to lower place; in some contexts this may be an artesian spring:– mist [1], vapour [1]

109 אָדַב **ʾādab**, v. GK: 117 [→ 110]. [H] to grieve:– grieve [1]

110 אַדְבְּאֵל **ʾadbᵉʾēl**, n.pr.m. GK: 118 [→ 109+410]. Adbeel, "*[the] grief of God [El]*":– Adbeel [2]

111 אֲדַד **ʾᵃdad**, n.pr.m. GK: 119 [→ 1908]. Hadad, "*sharp*":– Hadad [1]

112 אִדּוֹ **ʾiddô**, n.pr.m. GK: 120. Iddo, "[prob.] *Yahweh has adorned*":– Iddo [2]

אֱדוֹם **ʾᵉdôm**. See 123.

אֱדוֹמִי **ʾᵉdômî**. See 30.

113 אָדוֹן **ʾādôn**, n.m. GK: 123 [→ 136, 137, 138, 138, 139, 140, 141]. lord, master, supervisor, one who has authority over another; husband; owner; the Lord, (with Yahweh [3068]) Sovereign. "Lord of lords" means the highest power or authority:– Lord/lord [216], master [77], master's [22], lord's [5], masters [5], lords [4], lord's (+3807.1) [3], masters' [1], owner [1], sir [1]

114 אַדּוֹן **ʾaddôn**, n.pr.loc. GK: 124 [cf. 135]. Addon:– Addon [1]

115 אֲדוֹרַיִם **ʾᵃdôrayim**, n.pr.m. GK: 126 [→ 1752?]. Adoraim, "[poss.] *pair of knolls*":– Adoraim [1]

116 אֱדַיִן **ʾᵉdayin** (Aram.), adv. GK: 10008 [cf. 227]. then, thus, so then:– then (+871.2) [28], then [26], now (+1768) [1], that time [1], then (+4481+6925+871.2) [1]

117 אַדִּיר **ʾaddîr**, a. GK: 129 [→ 142]. mighty, noble, majestic, splendid; (n.) any powerful or awesome person: noble, believer, elite soldier; (as a divine title) the Mighty One, with a focus on the power and splendor of God:– nobles [7], excellent [4], mighty [4], principal [3], famous [2], gallant [1], glorious [1], goodly [1], lordly [1], mightier [1], mighty one [1], worthies [1]

118 אֲדַלְיָא **ʾᵃdalyāʾ**, n.pr.m. GK: 130. Adalia, "[poss.] *honorable*":– Adalia [1]

119 אָדֵם **ʾādēm**, v. GK: 131 [→ 120, 121, 122, 123, 124, 125, 127, 130, 131, 132]. [Q] be ruddy; [Pu] be dyed red:– dyed red [5], red [3], made red [1], ruddy [1]

120 אָדָם **ʾādām**, n.m. GK: 132 & 133 & 135 [→ 119]. man, human being; humankind, people, often in contrast to animals; "son of man" means a human being (Nu 23:9), but often assumes messianic significance (Ps 8):– man [388], men [106], Adam [20], man's [16], men's [10], persons (+5315) [3], persons [3], man (+1121) [2], man (+5315) [2], men (+1121) [2], person [2], another [1], husbandman (+376+5647) [1], hypocrite (+2611) [1], low (+1121) [1], men (+5315) [1], men of low degree (+1121) [1], sort [1]

121 אָדָם **ʾādām**, n.pr.m. & loc. GK: 134 & 136 [→ 128; cf. 119]. Adam, "*[red] earth* or *[ruddy] skin color*":– Adam [2]

122 אָדֹם *'ādōm*, a. GK: 137 [→ 131; cf. 119]. red; ruddy (skin):– red [7], ruddy [1], same[s] [1]

123 אֱדוֹם *'edôm* or אֱדֹם *'edōm*, n.pr.m. GK: 121 & 139 [→ 130, 5654; cf. 119]. Edom, referring to a person and his ancestral territory S.E. of the Dead Sea, "*red*":– Edom [87], Edomites [9], Idumea [4]

124 אֹדֶם *'ōdem*, n.[f.]. GK: 138 [→ 119]. ruby:– sardius [3]

125 אֲדַמְדָּם *'adamdām*, a. GK: 140 [→ 119]. reddish, reddish-white:– reddish [4], somewhat reddish [2]

126 אַדְמָה *'admâ*, n.pr.loc. GK: 144. Admah, "*[red] earth*":– Admah [5]

127 אֲדָמָה *'adāmâ*, n.f. GK: 141 & 143 [→ 119]. earth, the entire surface of the place where humans dwell, as well as smaller regions: land; with a focus on the elements of the earth: ground, soil, dust. A "man of the soil" is a farmer; "fruit of the soil" are crops:– land [122], earth [52], ground [43], lands [3], country [1], dust [1], husbandman (+376+1886.1) [1], husbandry [1]

128 אֲדָמָה *'adāmâ*, n.pr.loc. GK: 142 [→ 121; cf. 119]. Adamah, "*[red] earth*":– Adamah [1]

אַדְמוֹנִי *'admônî*. See 132.

129 אֲדָמִי *'adāmî*, n.pr.loc. GK: 146 [→ 119]. Adami [with Nekeb 5346], "*ground [of piercing]*":– Adami [1]

130 אֲדוֹמִי *'adômî*, a.g. GK: 122 [→ 123; cf. 119; 726]. Edomite, "*of Edom*":– Edomite [7], Edomites [4]

131 אֲדֻמִּים *'adummîm*, n.pr.loc. GK: 147 [→ 122; cf. 119]. Adummim, "*red [streaks]*":– Adummim [2]

132 אַדְמוֹנִי *'admônî*, a. GK: 145 [→ 119]. red; ruddy (skin):– ruddy [2], red [1]

133 אַדְמָתָא *'admātā'*, n.pr.m. GK: 148. Admatha, "*unrestrained*":– Admatha [1]

134 אֶדֶן *'eden*, n.m. GK: 149. base, footing, pedestal:– sockets [54], foundations [1], socket [1]

אָדֹן *'ādōn*. See 113.

135 אַדָּן *'addān*, n.pr.loc. GK: 150 [cf. 114]. Addon:– Addan [1]

136 אֲדֹנָי *'adōnāy*, n.[pr.]m. GK: 151 [→ 113]. the Lord, a title of the one true God, with a focus on his majesty and authority:– Lord/lord [430], God [1], Lord's [1]

137 אֲדֹנִי בֶזֶק *'adōnî bezeq*, n.pr.m. GK: 152 [→ 113+966]. Adoni-Bezek, "*lord of Bezek*":– Adoni-bezek [3]

138 אֲדֹנִיָּה *'adôniyyâ* or אֲדֹנִיָּה *'adōniyyâ* or אֲדֹנִיָּהוּ *'adōniyyāhû*, n.pr.m. GK: 125 & 153 & 154 [→ 2899]. Adonijah, "*[my] lord is Yahweh*":– Adonijah [26]

139 אֲדֹנִי־צֶדֶק *'adōnî-ṣedeq*, n.pr.m. GK: 155 [→ 113+6664].Adoni-Zedek, "*[my] lord is righteousness*":– Adoni-zedek [2]

140 אֲדֹנִיקָם *'adōnîqām*, n.pr.m. GK: 156 [→ 113+6965]. Adonikam, "*[my] lord arises*":– Adonikam [3]

141 אֲדֹנִירָם *'adōnîrām*, n.pr.m. GK: 157 [→ 151]. Adoniram, "*[my] lord is exalted*":– Adoniram [2]

142 אָדַר *'ādar*, v. GK: 158 [→ 117, 145, 143, 155]. [N] to prove oneself majestic, powerful; [H] to make glorious, make powerful:– become glorious [1], glorious [1], make honourable [1]

143 אֲדָר *'adār*, n.pr.[m.]. GK: 160 [→ 142; cf. 144]. Adar, "[poss.] *dark, clouded*":– Adar [8]

144 אֲדָר *'adār* (Aram.), n.pr.month. GK: 10009 [cf. 143]. Adar, "[poss.] *dark, clouded*":– Adar [1]

145 אֶדֶר *'eder*, n.[m.]. GK: 159 [→ 142]. splendor, handsomeness, of obvious quality:– goodly [1], robe [1]

146 אַדָּר *'addār*, n.pr.m. & loc. GK: 161 & 162 [→ 2692, 5853]. Addar, "*glorious*":– Adar [1], Addar [1]

147 אִדַּר *'iddar* (Aram.), n.m. GK: 10010. threshing floor:– threshingfloors [1]

148 אֲדַרְגָּזַר *'adargāzar* (Aram.), n.m. GK: 10011. adviser, counselor, likely the king's "minister of information":– judges [2]

149 אַדְרַזְדָּא *'adrazdā'* (Aram.), adv. GK: 10012. with diligence, zealously:– diligently [1]

150 אֲדַרְכֹנִים *'adarkōnîm*, n.[m.pl.?]. GK: 163 [→ 1871]. darics, Persian gold coins:– drams [2]

151 אֲדוֹרָם *'adôrām* or אֲדֹרָם *'adōrām*, n.pr.m. GK: 127 & 164 [→ 141]. Adoram:– Adoram [2]

152 אַדְרַמֶּלֶךְ *'adrammelek*, n.pr.m. GK: 165 & 166. Adrammelech (pagan god and king), "*nobility of Molech [king]*":– Adrammelech [3]

153 אֶדְרָע *'edrā'* (Aram.), n.[f.]. GK: 10013 [→ 1872; cf. 248, 2220]. arm; fig., power, force:– force [1]

154 אֶדְרֶעִי *'edre'î*, n.pr.loc. GK: 167. Edrei, "*strong*":– Edrei [8]

155 אַדֶּרֶת *'adderet*, n.f. GK: 168 [→ 142]. cloak, royal robe, (hairy) garment:– mantle [5], garment [4], glory [1], goodly [1], robe [1]

156 אָדַשׁ *'ādaš*, v. GK: 169 [cf. 1758]. to thresh; see definitions at 1758:– threshing (+156) [2]

157 אָהַב *'āhab*, v. GK: 170 [→ 159, 158, 160]. [Q] to love, like, be a friend; [N] to be loved; [P] be a lover, an ally; love can refer to friendship, familial love, romantic love, or covenant loyalty:– love [75], loved [48], loveth [38], lovers [17], friends [8], lovest [7], beloved [5], friend [4], lover [2], liketh [1], lovedst [1], lovely [1], loving [1]

158 אַהַב *'ahab*, n.[m.]. GK: 172 [→ 157]. lover (negative); loving, charming (positive):– lovers [1], loving [1]

159 אֹהַב *'ōhab*, n.[m.]. GK: 171 [→ 157]. love; something loved:– loves [1]

160 אַהֲבָה *'ahabâ*, n.f. GK: 173 & 174 [→ 157]. love; friendship, familial love, romantic love, or covenant loyalty:– love [33], loved [7]

161 אֹהַד *'ōhad*, n.pr.m. GK: 176. Ohad:– Ohad [2]

162 אֲהָהּ *'ahāh*, interj. GK: 177. Ah!, Oh!, Alas!; an exclamation of emphasis, surprise, or sorrow:– ah [8], alas [7]

163 אַהֲוָא *'ahawā'*, n.pr.loc. GK: 178. Ahava:– Ahava [3]

164 אֵהוּד *'ēhûd*, n.pr.m. GK: 179 [cf. 261?]. Ehud, "*united*":– Ehud [9]

165 אֱהִי *'ehî*, adv. GK: 180. Where?:– be [2], where (+645) [1]

166 אָהַל *'āhal*, v. GK: 183 [→ 1984]. [H] to be bright:– shineth [1]

167 אָהַל *'āhal*, v.den. GK: 182 [→ 168]. [Q, P] to pitch a tent:– pitch tent [1], pitched tent [1], removed tent [1]

168 אֹהֶל *'ōhel*, n.m. GK: 185 [→ 167, 169, 170 (also used with compound proper names)]. tent, tent-dwelling; by extension: home, dwelling place, a permanent dwelling; family group. "The Tent of Meeting" was the worship tent built before the Temple:– tabernacle [187], tent [91], tents [50], tabernacles [11], dwelling place [2], covering [1], dwelling [1], home [1], places [1]

169 אֹהֶל *'ōhel*, n.pr.m. GK: 186 [→ 168]. Ohel, "*tent*":– Ohel [1]

170 אָהֳלָה *'ohºlâ*, n.pr.f. GK: 188 [→ 172, 173; cf. 168]. Oholah, "*she who has a tent*":– Aholah [5]

171 אָהֳלִיאָב *'ohºlî'āb*, n.pr.m. GK: 190 [→ 168+1]. Oholiab, "*tent of [my] father*":– Aholiab [5]

172 אָהֳלִיבָה *'ohºlîbâ*, n.pr.f. GK: 191 [→ 170+871.1+1886.3]. Oholibah, "*my tent is in her*":– Aholibah [6]

173 אָהֳלִיבָמָה *'ohºlîbāmâ*, n.pr.m. & f. GK: 192 [→ 168+1116?]. Oholibamah, "*[my] tent is a high place*":– Aholibamah [8]

174 אֲהָלוֹת *'ahālôt* or אֲהָלִים *'ahālîm*, n.[m.]. GK: 189 & 193. aloes; an aromatic wood from India:– aloes [3], trees of lign aloes [1]

175 אַהֲרֹן *'aharôn*, n.pr.m. GK: 195. Aaron:– Aaron [315], Aaron's [26], Aaron's (+3807.1) [4], Aaronites [2]

176 אוֹ *'ô*, c. GK: 196 [→ 194?]. or, or if, whether:– or [293], either [7], whether [7], and [2], nor [2], or if [2], also [1], at the least [1], if then (+227) [1], nor (+3808) [1], or else [1], otherwise [1], then [1]

177 אוּאֵל *'û'ēl*, n.pr.m. GK: 198 [→ 183?+410]. Uel, "[poss.] *will of God [El]*":– Uel [1]

178 אוֹב *'ôb*, n.m. GK: 199 & 200. wineskin, bag, a leather bag of goatskin turned inside out to hold fluids; medium, spiritist, one who communicates with and conjures ghosts or spirits:– familiar spirits [9], familiar spirit [7], bottles [1]

179 אוֹבִיל *'ôbîl*, n.pr.m. GK: 201 [→ 2986]. Obil, "*camel driver*":– Obil [1]

180 אֻבָל *'ubāl*, n.[m.]. GK: 67 [→ 58]. canal:– river [3]

181 אוּד *'ûd*, n.m. GK: 202 [→ 343]. burning stick:– brand [1], firebrands [1], firebrand [1]

182 אוֹדוֹת *'ôdôt*, n.f. GK: 128. on account of, because of, for the reason that:– because of (+5921) [5], concerning (+5921) [2], causes [1], cause [1], sake [1]

183 אָוָה *'āwâ*, v. GK: 203 [→ 185, 1942, 3970, 8378 (also used with compound proper names)]. [P, Ht] to crave, desire, yearn for, long for:– desireth [7], desired [5], desire [3], longed [2], coveteth greedily (+8378) [1], covet [1], desirous [1], fell a lusting (+8378) [1], greatly desire [1], longeth [1], lusted exceedingly (+8378) [1], lusted [1], lusteth after [1]

184 אָוָה *'āwâ*, v. GK: 204 [→ 226?; cf. 8376, 8379, 8427]. [Ht] to run a line, measure:– point out [1]

185 אַוָּה *'awwâ*, n.f. GK: 205 [→ 1942; cf. 183]. wanting, craving; earnestness:– desire [3], lusteth after [3], pleasure [1]

186 אוּזַי *'ûzay*, n.pr.m. GK: 206. Uzai, "*Yahweh has given ear, listened*":– Uzai [1]

187 אוּזָל ***'ûzāl***, n.pr.loc. [& m.]. GK: 207. Uzal, a person and a place:– Uzal [2]

188 אוֹי ***'ôy***, interj. GK: 208 [→ 190]. Woe! Alas!:– woe [23], alas [1]

189 אֱוִי ***'ᵉwî***, n.pr.m. GK: 209. Evi, "*desire*":– Evi [2]

אוֹיֵב ***'ôyēb***. See 341.

190 אוֹיָה ***'ôyâ***, interj. GK: 210 [→ 188]. Woe!, Alas!:– woe [1]

191 אֱוִיל ***'ᵉwîl***, a. GK: 211 [→ 196, 200; cf. 2973]. foolish; (n.) a fool:– fool [11], fools [7], foolish [5], fool's [2], foolish man [1]

192 אֱוִיל מְרֹדַךְ ***'ᵉwîl mᵉrōdak***, n.pr.m. GK: 213. Evil-Merodach, "*worshiper of Marduk[s]*; [corrupted to read] *fool of blessing*":– Evil-merodach [2]

193 אוּל ***'ûl***, n.[m.]. GK: 214 & 215 [→ 352; cf. 2974]. belly, sometimes referring to the whole body; leading man, noble; symbolic of strength:– strength [1]

194 אוּלַי ***'ûlay***, adv. GK: 218 [→ 176?+3808?]. what if, perhaps, maybe; this is in an expression of hope, pleading, or fear:– peradventure [23], if so be [8], it may be that [7], it may be [5], if so be that [1], unless [1]

195 אוּלַי ***'ûlay***, n.pr.loc. GK: 217. Ulai:– Ulai [2]

196 אֱוִלִי ***'ᵉwilî***, a. GK: 216 [→ 191]. foolish, without understanding:– foolish [1]

197 אוּלָם ***'ûlām***, n.m. GK: 221 [→ 361]. portico; hall; colonnade:– porch [33], porches [1]

198 אוּלָם ***'ûlām***, n.pr.m. GK: 220. Ulam, "*first, leader*":– Ulam [4]

199 אוּלָם ***'ûlām***, adv. GK: 219. but, however, on the other hand, nevertheless:– but (+2050.1) [6], truly [4], but [2], in very deed [2], surely [2], howbeit [1], wherefore (+2050.1) [1], would [1]

200 אִוֶּלֶת ***'iwwelet***, n.f. GK: 222 [→ 191]. foolishness, folly; in some contexts this may refer to thoughtless speech:– folly [13], foolishness [10], foolishly [1], foolish [1]

201 אוֹמָר ***'ômār***, n.pr.m. GK: 223 [→ 559]. Omar, "*speaker*":– Omar [3]

202 אוֹן ***'ôn***, n.m. GK: 226 [→ 203, 207, 208, 209]. power, strength, vigor, manhood; wealth:– strength [7], might [2], force [1], goods [1], substance [1]

203 אוֹן ***'ôn***, n.pr.m. GK: 227 [→ 208; cf. 202]. On, "*Sun [god] city*":– On [1]

204 אוֹן ***'ôn***, n.pr.loc. GK: 228. On, "*Sun [god] city*":– On [3]

205 אָוֶן ***'āwen***, n.m. GK: 224 & 230 [→ 578, 1007, 1126, 8383?]. evil, wickedness, iniquity; evildoer; an unfavorable circumstance: calamity, trouble, injustice; this can also refer to idols, with a focus that they are morally evil; mourning:– iniquity [47], vanity [6], wicked [6], affliction [3], mischief [3], Aven [2], unrighteous [2], wickedness [2], evil [1], false [1], idol [1], mourners [1], mourning [1], nought [1], sorrow [1], unjust [1], vain [1]

206 אָוֶן ***'āwen***, n.pr.loc. GK: 225. Heliopolis; (Valley of) Aven, "*evil power, wickedness*":– Aven [1]

207 אוֹנוֹ ***'ônô***, n.pr.loc. GK: 229 [→ 202]. Ono, "*strong*":– Ono [5]

208 אוֹנָם ***'ônām***, n.pr.m. GK: 231 [→ 203; cf. 202]. Onam, "*intense, strong*":– Onam [4]

209 אוֹנָן ***'ônān***, n.pr.m. GK: 232 [→ 202]. Onan, "*powerful, intense*":– Onan [8]

210 אוּפָז ***'ûpāz***, n.pr.loc. GK: 233. Uphaz:– Uphaz [2]

211 אוֹפִיר ***'ôpîr***, n.pr.m. & loc. GK: 234 & 235 [cf. 665]. Ophir:– Ophir [13]

212 אוֹפָן ***'ôpan***, n.m. GK: 236 [cf. 655?]. wheel (of a vehicle):– wheels [24], wheel [11], fitly (+5921) [1]

אוֹפִר ***'ôpir***. See 211.

213 אוּץ ***'ûṣ***, v. GK: 237. [Q] to be in haste, be eager; to press (for an answer); to be small, narrow; [H] to urge, insist upon:– hasted [2], hastened [2], hasty [2], hasteth [1], labour [1], maketh haste [1], narrow [1]

214 אוֹצָר ***'ôṣār***, n.m. GK: 238 [→ 686]. treasury, storehouse, storeroom, storage vault:– treasures [50], treasure [11], treasuries [7], treasury [3], cellars [2], storehouses [2], armoury [1], garners [1], storehouse (+1004) [1], store [1]

215 אוֹר ***'ôr***, v. GK: 239 [→ 216, 217, 218, 219, 221, 224?, 3974, 3975? (also used with compound proper names)]. [Q] to shine, be bright; [H] to give light, make shine, brighten; [N] to be resplendent with light, shine on; the fig. extension "to make the face shine" is to establish favorable circumstance, peace and relief from trouble:– give light [8], cause to shine [5], enlightened [4], lighten [2], light [2], make to shine [2], maketh to shine [2], at break of day [1], enlightening [1], gave light [1], give light (+216) [1], giveth light [1], glorious [1], have light [1], kindle [1], lightened [1], lighteneth [1], make shine [1], set on fire [1], shew light [1], shewed light [1], shined [1], shineth [1], shine [1]

216 אוֹר ***'ôr***, n.m. GK: 240 [→ 219; cf. 215]. light, contrasted with darkness; by extension: brightness; lightning; daylight, sunshine; the fig. extension "light of the face" is a positive, happy attitude, resulting from relief from trouble:– light [111], day [2], lights [2], bright [1], clear [1], give light (+215) [1], herbs [1], lightning [1], morning [1], sun [1]

217 אוּר ***'ûr***, n.m. GK: 241 [cf. 215]. light; east [the region of light], the direction of the sunrise:– fire [4], fires [1], light [1]

218 אוּר ***'ûr***, n.pr.m. & loc. GK: 243 & 244 [→ 215]. Ur, "*flame, light*":– Ur [5]

219 אוֹרָה ***'ôrâ***, n.f. GK: 245 & 246 [→ 216; cf. 215]. light, morning light; happiness, serenity, cheerfulness; herb, mallow, a tasty, edible plant:– herbs [2], light [2]

220 אֻרָוָה ***'ᵃwērâ***, n.f. GK: 774 [→ 723]. (animal) stall, pen, stable; cf. 723:– cotes [1]

221 אוּרִי ***'ûrî*** or אֻרִי ***'uri***, n.pr.m. GK: 247 & 788 [→ 215, 738]. Uri, "*Yahweh is [my] flame, light*":– Uri [8]

222 אוּרִיאֵל ***'ûrî'ēl***, n.pr.m. GK: 248 [→ 215+410]. Uriel, "*God [El] is [my] flame, light*":– Uriel [4]

223 אוּרִיָּה ***'ûriyyâ*** or אוּרִיָּהוּ ***'ûriyyāhû***, n.pr.m. GK: 249 & 250. Uriah, "*Yahweh is [my] flame, light*":– Uriah [26], Urijah [12], Uriah's [1]

224 אוּרִים ***'ûrîm***, n.m.[pl.]. GK: 242 & 251 [→ 215? *or* 717? *or* 779?]. Urim, devices used by the high priest to make God's will known, possibly related to radiating or reflecting light:– Urim [7]

אוֹרְנָה ***'ôrenâ***. See 728.

225 אוּת ***'ût***, v. GK: 252. [N] to consent, agree:– consent [3], consented [1]

226 אוֹת ***'ôt***, n.m. & f. GK: 253 [→ 184?; cf. 852]. sign, mark, symbol, a signal or event that communicates; a supernatural event or miracle as a sign from God:– sign [33], signs [27], token [10], tokens [4], miracles [2], ensigns [1], ensign [1], mark [1]

227 אָז ***'āz***, adv. GK: 255 [→ 233; cf. 116]. then, at that time, meanwhile:– then [114], since (+4480) [6], that time [3], the beginning [3], old [2], time [2], also [1], at which time [1], even from (+4480) [1], for [1], hitherto (+4480) [1], if then (+176) [1], now [1], than (+4480) [1], then (+3588) [1], when once (+4480) [1], yet [1]

228 אֲזָא ***'ᵃzâ*** (Aram.), v. GK: 10015. [P] to heat; [Pp] to be heated:– heat [2], hot [1]

229 אֶזְבַי ***'ezbāy***, n.pr.m. GK: 256 [→ 231?]. Ezbai:– Ezbai [1]

230 אַזְדָּא ***'azdā'*** (Aram.), a. GK: 10014. firm, assured:– gone [2]

231 אֵזוֹב ***'ēzôb***, n.m. GK: 257 [→ 229?]. hyssop:– hyssop [10]

232 אֵזוֹר ***'ēzôr***, n.m. GK: 258 [→ 247]. garments that are wrapped: belt, sash, loincloth:– girdle [13], girdles [1]

233 אֲזַי ***'ᵃzay***, adv. GK: 259 [→ 227]. (if not ...) then:– then [3]

234 אַזְכָּרָה ***'azkārâ***, n.f. GK: 260 [→ 2142]. memorial offering, memorial portion; the portion of the meal burnt as a token of honor to the Lord:– memorial [7]

235 אָזַל ***'āzal***, v. GK: 261 [cf. 236]. [Q] to go about, go away; disappear:– fail [1], gaddest about [1], going to and fro (+4480) [1], gone way [1], gone [1], spent [1]

236 אֲזַל ***'ᵃzal*** (Aram.), v. GK: 10016 [cf. 235]. [P] to go, return:– went [5], go [1], went up [1]

237 אֶזֶל ***'ezel***, n.pr.loc. GK: 262. Ezel:– Ezel [1]

238 אָזַן ***'āzan***, v.den. GK: 263 [→ 241]. [H] to listen, pay attention, give ear:– give ear [29], hearken [5], gave ear [2], hear [2], giveth ear [1], hearkened [1], perceived by the ear [1]

239 אָזַן ***'āzan***, v. GK: 264. [P] to ponder, give serious thought, an extension of weighing and testing on scales:– gave good heed [1]

240 אָזֵן ***'āzēn***, n.[m.]. GK: 266 [cf. 241?]. equipment, tools, specifically a digging tool:– weapon [1]

241 אֹזֶן ***'ōzen***, n.f. GK: 265 [→ 238, 244, 245; cf. 240?]. ear: the organ for hearing; by extension: listening, and hence, responding, obeying. "To be in the ear" shows close proximity; "to reveal to the ear" means "to inform":– ears [100], ear [63], audience [7], hearing [5], shew (+1540) [4], advertise (+1540) [1], displeased (+7451+871.1) [1], hear (+8085) [1], revealed (+1540) [1], sheweth (+1540) [1], sheweth unto (+1540) [1], theyˢ [1], told (+1540) [1]

242 אֻזֵּן שֶׁאֱרָה ***'uzzēn šeᵉrâ***, n.pr.loc. GK: 267 [cf. 7609]. Uzzen Sheerah, "[perhaps] *ear of Sheerah*":– Uzzen-sherah [1]

243 אַזְנוֹת תָּבוֹר ***'aznôt tābôr***, n.pr.loc. GK: 268 [cf. 8396]. Aznoth Tabor, "[poss.] *peaks of Tabor*":– Aznoth-tabor [1]

244 אָזְנִי ***'oznî***, n.pr.m. & a.g. GK: 269 & 270 [cf. 241]. Ozni, "*my ear, my hearing*"; Oznite, "*belonging to Ozni*":– Oznites [1], Ozni [1]

245 אֲזַנְיָה ***'ᵃzanyâ***, n.pr.m. GK: 271 [→ 241+3068]. Azaniah, "*Yahweh has listened*":– Azaniah [1]

246 אֲזִקִּים ***'ᵃziqqîm***, n.[m.]. GK: 272 [cf. 2131]. chains, which in context refer to manacles or wrist cuffs:– chains [2]

247 אָזַר ***'āzar***, v. GK: 273 [→ 232]. [Q] to gird up, belt on; [P] to gird someone; [N, Ht] to gird oneself; the action of wrapping a belt or sash around the waist; by extension "to take action" of various kinds: working, providing, going to battle:– girded [6], gird up [3], gird [2], girt [2], bindeth about [1], compass about [1], girdeth [1]

248 אֶזְרוֹעַ ***'ezrôa'***, n.f. GK: 274 [cf. 2220; cf. 153]. arm, with the associative meaning of power and potency:– arm [2]

249 אֶזְרָח ***'ezrāḥ***, n.m. GK: 275 [→ 2224]. native-born:– born [3], your own country [2], bay tree [1], born among [1], born in the country [1], born in the land [1], born of the country [1], homeborn [1], one born amongst [1], one of own country [1], that is born in land [1], that is born [1], that was born [1], your own nation [1]

250 אֶזְרָחִי ***'ezrāḥî***, a.g. GK: 276 [→ 2226; cf. 2224]. Ezrahite, "*of Ezrah*":– Ezrahite [3]

251 אָח ***'āḥ***, n.m. GK: 278 [→ 264, 269, 277; cf. 252 (also used with compound proper names)]. brother; by extension: family, kinsman, relative (of either gender); a term of endearment; anyone of the same race or large social group: countryman; associate. "Each to his brother" is usually translated "to each other" or "one to another.":– brethren [331], brother [244], brother's [24], another[s] [24], brethren's [1], brother's (+3807.1) [1], brotherly [1], kindred [1], like [1], other[s] [1]

252 אַח ***'aḥ*** (Aram.), n.m. GK: 10017 [cf. 251]. brother:– brethren [1]

253 אָהּ ***'āh***, interj. GK: 277. Alas!, Oh!:– ah [1], alas [1]

254 אָח ***'aḥ***, n.f. GK: 279. firepot:– hearth [3]

255 אֹחַ ***'ōaḥ***, n.[m.]. GK: 280. a howling animal: jackal, hyena, eagle owl:– doleful creatures [1]

256 אַחְאָב ***'aḥ'āb*** or אֶחָב ***'eḥāb***, n.pr.m. GK: 281 & 282 [→ 251+1]. Ahab, "*brother of father*":– Ahab [91], Ahab's [2]

257 אַחְבָּן ***'aḥbān***, n.pr.m. GK: 283. Ahban, "*brother of intelligent one*":– Ahban [1]

258 אָחַד ***'āḥad***, v. GK: 284 [→ 2300]. prob. same as 2300: [Ht] to slash; to go one way or another:– go one way or other [1]

259 אֶחָד ***'eḥād***, a.num. GK: 285 [→ 261; cf. 2297; 2300; cf. 2298]. one; a certain one; first:– one [681], a [60], first [37], another [35], other [31], any [15], once [11], certain [9], eleven (+6240) [9], each [8], every [7], some [7], an [5], together (+3509.1) [5], alone [4], eleventh (+6240) [4], every one [3], few [3], once (+6471) [3], somewhat [3], at once (+6471) [2], only [2], alike (+3509.1) [1], altogether (+871.1) [1], any (+3605) [1], apiece (+5982) [1], apiece [1], at once [1], daily (+3117+3807.1) [1], each man [1], each one [1], fro (+2008) [1], man [1], none (+369) [1], none (+3808) [1], once (+871.1) [1], one manner [1], one tenth deal (+6241) [1], one thing [1], the [1], threescore and one (+8346+2050.1) [1], to[s] (+2008) [1]

260 אָחוּ ***'āḥû***, n.m.col. GK: 286. reeds:– meadow [2], flag [1]

261 אֵהוּד ***'ēhûd***, n.pr.m. GK: 287 [→ 259; cf. 164?]. Ehud, "*united*":– Ehud [1]

262 אַחְוָה ***'aḥwâ***, n.f. GK: 289 [→ 2331]. what is said, declaration:– declaration [1]

263 אַחֲוָיָה ***'aḥᵃwāyâ*** (Aram.), n.f. GK: 10018 [→ 2324]. declaring:– shewing [1]

264 אַחֲוָה ***'aḥᵃwâ***, n.f. GK: 288 [→ 251]. brotherhood, community:– brotherhood [1]

265 אֲחוֹחַ ***'ᵃḥôaḥ***, n.pr.m. GK: 291 [→ 266]. Ahoah, "*brotherly*":– Ahoah [1]

266 אֲחוֹחִי ***'ᵃḥôḥî***, a.g. GK: 292 [→ 265]. Ahohite:– Ahohite [4], Ahohite (+1121) [1]

267 אֲחוּמַי ***'ᵃḥûmay***, n.pr.m. GK: 293. Ahumai:– Ahumai [1]

268 אָחוֹר ***'āḥôr***, subst. GK: 294 [→ 322; cf. 309]. back (of the body), rear, hindquarters; backward, from behind; west, as a compass point, because east (the direction of the sunrise) is the direction of orientation:– back [15], backward [10], behind [3], hinder parts [3], behind (+4480) [2], afterwards [1], back parts [1], backside [1], backs [1], backward (+3807.1) [1], hereafter [1], time to come [1], without [1]

269 אָחוֹת ***'āḥôt***, n.f. GK: 295 [→ 251]. sister, by extension: half-sister, any female blood-relative; a term of endearment. "Each to her sister" is a marker of reciprocal reference: one to another:– sister [90], sisters [11], another[s] [6], sister's [5], other[s] [1], together (+413+802) [1]

270 אָחַז ***'āḥaz***, v. GK: 296 & 297 [→ 271, 272, 275, 276; (also used with compound proper names)]. [Q] grasp, seize, hold; to attach, cover, panel; [Qp] to be fastened; [N] to be caught, acquire; [Ho] be attached; [P] to cover:– take hold [7], hold [6], took [6], taken [5], take [4], caught [3], fastened [3], held [3], taken hold upon [3], took hold [3], lay hold [2], portion [2], affrighted (+8178) [1], bar [1], caught hold [1], come upon [1], get possessions [1], had possession [1], handle [1], have possessions [1], hold on [1], holden [1], holdest [1], holdeth back [1], lay hold on [1], possessed [1], rested [1], surprised [1], take possession [1], taketh hold on [1], taketh [1], took hold upon [1]

271 אָחָז ***'āḥāz***, n.pr.m. GK: 298 [→ 274; cf. 270]. Ahaz, "*he has grasped*":– Ahaz [41]

272 אֲחֻזָּה ***'ᵃḥuzzâ***, n.f. GK: 299 [→ 270]. property, possession:– possession [64], possessions [2]

273 אַחְזַי ***'aḥzay***, n.pr.m. GK: 300 [→ 274]. Ahzai, "*Yahweh has grasped*":– Ahasai [1]

274 אֲחַזְיָה ***'ᵃḥazyâ*** or אֲחַזְיָהוּ ***'ᵃḥazyāhû***, n.pr.m. GK: 301 & 302 [→ 271, 273, 276]. Ahaziah, "*Yahweh has upheld*":– Ahaziah [37]

275 אֲחֻזָּם ***'ᵃḥuzzām***, n.pr.m. GK: 303 [→ 270]. Ahuzzam, "*possessor*":– Ahuzam [1]

276 אֲחֻזַּת ***'ᵃḥuzzat***, n.pr.m. GK: 304 [→ 274; cf. 270]. Ahuzzath, "*possession*":– Ahuzzath [1]

277 אֲחִי ***'ᵃḥî***, n.pr.m. GK: 306 [→ 251]. Ahi, "*my brother,* [poss.] *Yahweh is [my] brother*":– Ahi [2]

278 אֵחִי ***'ēḥî***, n.pr.m. GK: 305 [→ 297]. Ehi, "*my brother [is exalted]*":– Ehi [1]

279 אֲחִיאָם ***'ᵃḥî'ām***, n.pr.m. GK: 307 [→ 251+3963.1?]. Ahiam, "*brother of mother*":– Ahiam [2]

280 אֲחִידָה ***'ᵃḥîdâ*** (Aram.), n.f. GK: 10019 [cf. 2420]. riddle:– hard sentences [1]

281 אֲחִיָּה ***'ᵃḥiyyâ*** or אֲחִיָּהוּ ***'ᵃḥiyyāhû***, n.pr.m. GK: 308 & 309 [→ 251+3068]. Ahijah, "*[my] brother is Yahweh*":– Ahijah [20], Ahiah [4]

282 אֲחִיהוּד ***'ᵃḥîhûd***, n.pr.m. GK: 310 [→ 251+1935]. Ahihud, "*[my] brother has majesty*":– Ahihud [1]

283 אַחְיוֹ ***'aḥyô***, n.pr.m. GK: 311 [→ 251+3068]. Ahio, "*[my] brother is Yahweh*":– Ahio [6]

284 אֲחִיחֻד ***'ᵃḥîḥud***, n.pr.m. GK: 312 [→ 251+1935]. Ahihud, "*[my] brother has majesty*":– Ahihud [1]

285 אֲחִיטוּב ***'ᵃḥîṭûb***, n.pr.m. GK: 313 [→ 251+2896]. Ahitub, "*[my] brother is goodness*":– Ahitub [15]

286 אֲחִילוּד ***'ᵃḥîlûd***, n.pr.m. GK: 314 [→ 251+3205?]. Ahilud, "*[my] brother is born*":– Ahilud [5]

287 אֲחִימוֹת ***'ᵃḥîmôt***, n.pr.m. GK: 315 [→ 251+4191]. Ahimoth, "*[my] brother is my support* [or poss.] *[my] brother is Mot*":– Ahimoth [1]

288 אֲחִימֶלֶךְ ***'ᵃḥîmelek***, n.pr.m. GK: 316 [→ 251+4428]. Ahimelech, "*[my] brother is king*":– Ahimelech [16], Ahimelech's [1]

289 אֲחִימַן ***'ᵃḥîman***, n.pr.m. GK: 317 [→ 251+?]. Ahiman, "[poss.] *[my] brother is a gift*":– Ahiman [4]

290 אֲחִימַעַץ ***'ᵃḥîma'aṣ***, n.pr.m. GK: 318 [→ 251+4619]. Ahimaaz, "*[my] brother is fury*":– Ahimaaz [15]

291 אַחְיָן ***'aḥyān***, n.pr.m. GK: 319 [→ 251+4993.1?]. Ahian, "*little brother*":– Ahian [1]

292 אֲחִינָדָב ***'ᵃḥînādāb***, n.pr.m. GK: 320 [→ 251+5068]. Ahinadab, "*[my] brother is willing*":– Ahinadab [1]

293 אֲחִינֹעַם ***'ᵃḥînō'am***, n.pr.f. GK: 321 [→ 251+5278]. Ahinoam, "*[my] brother is pleasant*":– Ahinoam [7]

294 אֲחִיסָמָךְ ***'ᵃḥîsāmāk***, n.pr.m. GK: 322 [→ 251+5564]. Ahisamach, "*[my] brother is a support*":– Ahisamach [3]

295 אֲחִיעֶזֶר ***'ᵃḥî'ezer***, n.pr.m. GK: 323 [→ 251+5828]. Ahiezer, "*[my] brother is a help*":– Ahiezer [6]

296 אֲחִיקָם ***'ᵃḥîqām***, n.pr.m. GK: 324 [→ 251+6965]. Ahikam, "*[my] brother stands*":– Ahikam [20]

297 אֲחִירָם ***'ᵃḥîrām***, n.pr.m. GK: 325 [→ 278, 298, 2361, 2438]. Ahiram, "*[my] brother is exalted*":– Ahiram [1]

298 אֲחִירָמִי ***'ᵃḥîrāmî***, a.g. GK: 326 [→ 297]. Ahiramite, "*of Ahiram*":– Ahiramites [1]

299 אֲחִירַע ***'ᵃḥîra'***, n.pr.m. GK: 327 [→ 251+7452 *or* 7453 *or* 7454]. Ahira, "*[my] brother is my friend* or *my brother is evil*":– Ahira [5]

300 אֲחִישַׁחַר ***'ᵃḥîšāḥar***, n.pr.m. GK: 328 [→ 251+7835]. Ahishahar, "*[my] brother was born at early dawn*":– Ahishahar [1]

301 אֲחִישָׁר ***'ᵃḥîšār***, n.pr.m. GK: 329. Ahishar, "*[my] brother is upright* or *[my] brother has sung*":– Ahishar [1]

Heb

302 אֲחִיתֹפֶל **'ᵃḥîtōpel**, n.pr.m. GK: 330 [→ 251+8603?]. Ahithophel, "[poss.] *[my] brother is in the desert* or *[my] brother is foolishness*":– Ahithophel [20]

303 אַחְלָב **'aḥlāb**, n.pr.loc. GK: 331. Ahlab, "*fat, fruitful, healthy*":– Ahlab [1]

304 אַחְלָי **'aḥlāy**, n.pr. GK: 333 [→ 251+410]. Ahlai, "*Alas! I wish that!*":– Ahlai [2]

305 אַחֲלַי **'aḥᵃlay**, subst. GK: 332. Oh that!; If only!:– O that [1], would God [1]

306 אַחְלָמָה **'aḥlāmâ**, n.f. GK: 334. amethyst (exact identification uncertain):– amethyst [2]

307 אַחְמְתָא **'aḥmᵉtā'** (Aram.), n.pr.loc. GK: 10020. Ecbatana, "[perhaps] *place of gathering*":– Achmetha [1]

308 אֲחַסְבַּי **'ᵃḥasbay**, n.pr.m. GK: 335 [→ 2620+871.1?+3068?]. Ahasbai, "*I seek refuge in Yahweh*":– Ahasbai [1]

309 אָחַר **'āḥar**, v. GK: 336 [→ 268, 310, 314, 319, 322, 4279, 4283; cf. 3186]. [Q] to remain, stay on; [P] to detain, delay, slow down; [H] to take longer (than a set time), come late:– tarry [3], defer [2], make tarrying [2], slack [2], continue [1], deferred [1], delay [1], hinder [1], late [1], stayed [1], tarried longer [1], tarry long [1]

310 אַחַר **'aḥar**, subst. & adv. & pp. GK: 339 & 343 [cf. 309; cf. 311]. (temporal) after, afterward, later, some time later; (spatial) back, behind, following:– after [477], behind [35], following [26], afterward [22], followed (+1980) [16], followed [16], afterward (+3651) [15], from (+4480) [12], behind (+4480) [11], follow (+1980) [9], afterwards [5], follow [5], after (+4480) [4], afterwards (+3651) [4], posterity [4], after that (+3651) [2], at [2], behind (+413) [2], followed (+1961) [2], followeth (+935) [2], following (+1980) [2], forasmuch [2], pursuing [2], since [2], when [2], after (+413) [1], after that (+3651+2050.1) [1], afterward (+3651+4480) [1], again [1], away from (+4480) [1], backside [1], back [1], behind (+5921) [1], beside [1], by [1], follow (+1961) [1], follow (+935) [1], followed (+3318) [1], followedst (+1980) [1], followeth [1], following (+3651) [1], following after [1], forasmuch as [1], hereafter [1], hinder end [1], outlived (+748+3117) [1], overlived (+748+3117) [1], pursue (+1980) [1], remnant [1], seeing that (+834) [1], thenceforth (+3651) [1], when (+4970) [1], when (+834) [1], with [1]

311 אַחַר **'aḥar** (Aram.), pp. GK: 10021 [→ 320, 318; cf. 310]. after, in the future:– hereafter (+1836) [2], after [1]

312 אַחֵר **'aḥēr**, a. GK: 337 [→ 313]. other, another, different; next, additional, more, extra:– other [96], another [55], others [9], next [2], another man's [1], following [1], other men [1], strange [1]

313 אַחֵר **'aḥēr**, n.pr.m. GK: 338 [→ 312]. Aher, "*another, substitute*":– Aher [1]

314 אַחֲרוֹן **'aḥᵃrôn**, a.f. GK: 340 [→ 309]. (temporal) next, later, last, end; (spatial) at the back, behind, west, as a compass point, because east (the direction of the sunrise) is the direction of orientation:– last [19], latter [6], come [4], to come [3], after [2], come after [2], latter end [2], utmost [2], after (+871.1+1886.1) [1], afterward (+871.1+1886.1) [1], afterwards [1], afterward [1], following [1], hindermost [1], hinder [1], hindmost [1], last (+871.1+1886.1) [1], rereward [1], uttermost [1]

315 אַחְרַח **'aḥraḥ**, n.pr.m. GK: 341. Aharah, "*brother of Rah*":– Aharah [1]

316 אֲחַרְחֵל **'ᵃḥarḥēl**, n.pr.m. GK: 342. Aharhel, "*brother of Rachel*":– Aharhel [1]

317 אָחֳרִי **'oḥᵒrî** (Aram.), a.f. GK: 10023 [→ 321]. other, another:– another [5], other [1]

318 אָחֳרֵין **'oḥᵒrên** (Aram.), adv. GK: 10024 [→ 311]. finally, at last:– last [1]

319 אַחֲרִית **'aḥᵃrît**, n.f. GK: 344 [→ 309; cf. 320]. (spatial) the far side, the other side; (temporal) at the last, at the end, (in days) to come:– end [21], latter [11], latter end [8], last [6], last end [4], posterity [3], reward [2], hindermost [1], latter time [1], length [1], remnant [1], residue [1], uttermost parts [1]

320 אַחֲרִי **'aḥᵃrî** (Aram.), n.f.constr. GK: 10022 [→ 311; cf. 319]. end (of days), (days) to come:– latter [1]

321 אָחֳרָן **'oḥᵒrān** (Aram.), a.m. GK: 10025 [→ 317]. other, another, someone else:– other [3], another [2]

אָחֳרֵן **'oḥᵒrēn**. See 318.

322 אֲחֹרַנִּית **'ᵃḥōrannît**, adv. GK: 345 [→ 268; cf. 309]. backwardly, by turning around, in turning back:– backward [6], again [1]

323 אֲחַשְׁדַּרְפָּן **'ᵃḥašdarpān**, n.m.pl. GK: 346 [cf. 324]. satraps, an administrative governor of a Persian province:– lieutenants [4]

324 אֲחַשְׁדַּרְפַּן **'ᵃḥašdarpan** (Aram.), n.m. GK: 10026 [cf. 323]. satrap, a viceroy or governor having considerable power:– princes [9]

325 אֲחַשְׁוֵרוֹשׁ **'ᵃḥašwērôš** or אֲחַשְׁרֹשׁ **'ᵃḥašērōš**, n.pr.m. GK: 347 & 348. Ahaseurus, Xerxes:– Ahasuerus [30], Ahasuerus' [1]

326 אֲחַשְׁתָּרִי **'ᵃḥaštārî** or הָאֲחַשְׁתָּרִי **hā'ᵃḥaštārî**, n.pr.m. *or* a.g. GK: 349 & 2028. Ahashtari; Haahashtari, "*the Ahashtarites*":– Haahashtari [1]

327 אֲחַשְׁתְּרָן **'ᵃḥašᵗᵉrān**, a. GK: 350. royal, belonging to the king and used in the king's service:– camels [2]

328 אַט **'aṭ**, subst. & n.m. GK: 351 & 356. spirits of the dead; (adv.) gently, meekly, slowly:– softly (+3807.1) [2], charmers [1], gently (+3807.1) [1], secret [1], softly [1]

329 אָטָד **'āṭād** or אָטָד **'āṭād**, n.m. & n.pr.loc. GK: 353 & 354. thornbush; Atad, "*of the thorns [?]*":– bramble [3], Atad [2], thorns [1]

330 אֵטוּן **'ēṭûn**, n.[m.]. GK: 355. linen, possibly red in color:– fine linen [1]

331 אָטַם **'āṭam**, v. GK: 357. [Q] to stop up (one's ears); to hold (one's tongue); [Qp] to be narrow:– narrow [4], stoppeth [3], shutteth [1]

332 אָטַר **'āṭar**, v. GK: 358 [→ 333, 334]. [Q] to close:– shut [1]

333 אָטֵר **'āṭēr**, n.pr.m. GK: 359 [→ 332]. Ater, "[poss.] *crippled one, left-handed one*, or *Etir*":– Ater [5]

334 אִטֵּר **'iṭṭēr**, a. GK: 360 [→ 332]. hindered on the right hand, (thus) left-handed; other sources: ambidextrous:– lefthanded (+3027+3225) [2]

335 אֵי **'ê**, adv.inter. GK: 361 [→ 346, 349, 351, 370, 375, 645?]. where?, which way?:– where [11], where (+2088) [10], whence (+2088+4480) [5], from whence (+2088+4480) [2], which (+2088) [2], by what (+2088) [1], how [1], of what (+2088+4480) [1], what (+2088) [1], what [1], whether (+2088) [1], which way (+2088) [1]

336 אִי **'î**, adv. GK: 364 [→ 348?, 350]. not:– island [1]

337 אִי **'î**, interj. GK: 365. Woe!:– woe [2]

338 אִי **'î**, n.m. GK: 363 [cf. 339?]. hyena, jackals; some understand this to be a spirit or demon:– wild beasts of the islands [2], wild beasts of the island [1]

339 אִי **'î**, n.m. & f. GK: 362 [cf. 338?]. island; coastland; distant shores:– isles [27], islands [5], isle [3], country [1]

340 אָיַב **'āyab**, v. GK: 366 [→ 341, 342, 347]. [Q] to be an enemy, be hostile towards:– enemy [1]

341 אֹיֵב **'ōyēb**, n.m. *or* v.ptcp. GK: 367 [→ 340]. enemy, foe:– enemies [199], enemy [77], enemies' [3], foes [2], enemy's [1]

342 אֵיבָה **'êbâ**, n.f. GK: 368 [→ 340]. hostility, enmity:– enmity [3], hatred [2]

343 אֵיד **'êd**, n.m. GK: 369 [→ 181]. disaster, calamity, destruction:– calamity [16], destruction [7], calamities [1]

344 אַיָּה **'ayyâ**, n.f. GK: 370 [→ 345]. black kite; falcon; vulture:– kite [2], vulture's [1]

345 אַיָּה **'ayyâ**, n.pr.m. GK: 371 [→ 344]. Aiah, "*black kite*":– Aiah [6]

346 אַיֵּה **'ayyēh**, adv.inter. GK: 372 [→ 335]. Where?:– where [45]

347 אִיּוֹב **'iyyôb**, n.pr.m. GK: 373 [→ 340]. Job, "*where is my father,* [or perhaps] *Where is my father, O God?*":– Job [57], Job's [1]

348 אִיזֶבֶל **'îzebel**, n.pr.f. GK: 374 [→ 336?+2073?]. Jezebel, "[poss.] *unhusbanded, unexalted*":– Jezebel [21], Jezebel's [1]

349 אֵיךְ **'êk** or אֵיכָה **'êkâ** or אֵיכָכָה **'êkākâ**, adv.inter. & excl. GK: 375 & 377 & 379 [→ 335; cf. 1963]. How? Why? How! Also!:– how [78], where [2], how can [1], what [1]

350 אִיכָבוֹד **'îkābôd** or אִי־כָבוֹד **'î-kābôd**, n.pr.m. GK: 376 [→ 336+3519]. Ichabod, "*where is the glory?*":– Ichabod's [1], Ichabod [1]

351 אֵיכֹה **'êkōh**, adv.inter. & excl. GK: 378 [→ 335]. Where?:– where [1]

אֵיכָה **'êkâ**; אֵיכָכָה **'êkākâ**. See 349.

352 אַיִל **'ayil**, n.m. GK: 380 & 381 & 382 & 383 & 442 & 443 & 444 [→ 193, 354, 356, 358, 359?, 362, 424, 425, 427, 436, 437, 438, 439, 879]. ram, a male sheep generally more aggressive and protective of the flock; by extension: leading man, ruler; oaks; or any large, mighty tree without reference to a specific species; projecting wall; jamb:– ram [90], rams [61], posts [17], rams' [5], post [4], mighty [3], trees [2], lintel [1], mighty men [1], oaks [1]

353 אֱיָל **'ᵉyāl**, n.m. GK: 384 [→ 360; cf. 352]. strength:– strength [1]

354 אַיָּל **'ayyāl**, n.[m.] & f. GK: 385 [→ 355, 365, 357; cf. 352]. deer, young stag:– hart [9], harts [2]

355 אַיָּלָה **'ayyālâ**, n.f. GK: 387 [→ 354]. deer, doe:– hinds [4], hinds' [3], hind [1]

356 אֵילֹן **'ēlôn** or אֵילוֹן **'êlôn**, n.pr.m. & loc. GK: 390 & 391 & 472 [→ 436, 440; cf. 352]. Elon, "*species of a mighty tree*":– Elon [6]

357 אַיָּלוֹן **'ayyālôn**, n.pr.loc. GK: 389 [→ 354]. Aijalon, "*place of the deer*":– Aijalon [8], Ajalon [2]

358 אֵילוֹן בֵּית חָנָן **'êlôn bêt ḥānān**, n.pr.loc. GK: 392 [→ 352+1004+2605]. Elon Bethhanan, *"tree of Bethhanan"*:– Elon-beth-hanan [1]

359 אֵילוֹת or אֵילַת **'êlôt** or **'êlat**, n.pr.loc. GK: 393 & 397 [→ 352?]. Eloth, Elath, *"grove of large trees"*:– Elath [5], Eloth [3]

360 אֱיָלוּת **'eyālût**, n.m. GK: 394 [→ 353; cf. 352]. Strength, Power, a title of the one true God, with a focus that he is potent to help:– strength [1]

361 אֵילָם **'êlām**, n.m. GK: 395 [→ 197]. portico, porch, hall:– arches [15]

362 אֵילִם **'êlim**, n.pr.loc. GK: 396 [→ 352; cf. 352]. Elim, *"big trees"*:– Elim [6]

363 אִילָן **'îlān** (Aram.), n.m. GK: 10027 [cf. 436]. tree:– tree [6]

364 אֵיל פָּארָן **'êl pā'rān**, n.pr.loc. GK: 386 [→ 352+6290]. El Paran, *"tree of Paran"*:– El-paran [1]

אֵילֹן **'êlōn**. See 356.

365 אַיֶּלֶת **'ayyelet**, n.f. GK: 387 [→ 354]. deer, doe:– hind [2], Aijeleth [1]

אֵים **'ayim**. See 368.

366 אָיֹם **'āyōm**, a. GK: 398 [→ 367]. fearful; majestic, with an implication that this majesty instills awe that borders on fear:– terrible [3]

367 אֵימָה or אֵמָה **'êmâ** or **'ēmâ**, n.f. GK: 399 & 568 [→ 366, 368; cf. 520; cf. 574]. terror, dread, fear:– fear [5], terror [4], terrors [3], terrible [2], dread [1], horror [1], idols [1]

368 אֵימִים **'êmîm**, n.pr.m.pl. GK: 400 [→ 367]. Emites, *"frightening beings"*:– Emims [3]

369 אַיִן **'ayin**, subst.neg. GK: 401 [cf. 371]. there is no, not, none, without:– no [243], not [188], none [141], neither (+2050.1) [27], nothing [26], without [26], without (+4480) [18], no man [17], nor (+2050.1) [17], neither [13], nor any (+2050.1) [5], gone [4], never [4], nothing (+3972) [4], cannot [3], innumerable (+4557) [3], unsearchable (+2714) [3], without (+871.1) [3], neither any (+2050.1) [2], no (+3605) [2], no more [2], none (+376) [2], none (+4480) [2], nothing (+3605) [2], without (+5704) [2], abundance (+4557) [1], any [1], come to nought [1], else [1], except [1], faileth [1], fatherless (+1) [1], incurable (+4832) [1], infinite (+4557) [1], infinite (+7093) [1], infinite (+7097) [1], innumerable (+4557+5704) [1], more than (+3807.1) [1], neither (+637) [1], no (+1097) [1], no (+3605+3807.1) [1], no (+4480) [1], no where [1], none (+259) [1], none other [1], nor any thing (+2050.1) [1], nothing else (+1115) [1], past (+5704) [1], there be no [1], there is none [1], there is not [1], well nigh (+3509.1) [1], without any (+4480) [1]

370 אַיִן **'ayin**, adv. GK: 402 [cf. 335]. where (from)?:– whence (+4480) [12], whence [4], where (+4480) [1]

371 אִין **'în**, subst.neg. GK: 403 [cf. 369]. there is not:– not [1]

372 אִיעֶזֶר **'î'ezer**, n.pr.m. GK: 404 [→ 373]. Iezer, *"my [father] is help"*:– Jeezer [1]

373 אִיעֶזְרִי **'î'ezrî**, a.g. GK: 405 [→ 372]. Iezerite, *"of Iezer"*:– Jeezerites [1]

374 אֵיפָה **'êpâ**, n.f. GK: 406. ephah (dry measure, about three-fifths of a bushel (22 liters); also a large basket of unspecified measure; "ephah and ephah" means "two differing measures," as a measure that is not standardized:– ephah [34], divers measures (+374+2050.1) [4], measure [2]

375 אֵיפֹה **'êpōh**, adv. GK: 407 [→ 335+6311]. where?:– where [9], what manner [1]

376 אִישׁ **'îš**, n.m. GK: 408 [→ 380, 792, 802 (also used with compound proper names)]. man, sometimes in contrast to woman, human, sometimes in contrast to animal (without gender distinction); by extension: husband, in contrast to wife; (p.) each, every, someone, a certain one, anyone, whoever. This word is often used in phrases meaning "one of a kind," so a "man of war" is a soldier; a "man of bow" is an archer, etc:– man [763], men [679], every man [163], every one [112], one [71], husband [66], man's [31], any [24], any man [17], certain [14], persons [10], every one (+376) [8], each man [7], another[s] [6], every man's [6], he[s] [6], none (+3808) [6], whatsoever man (+376) [6], each [5], whosoever (+834) [5], every man (+376) [4], footmen (+7273) [4], husbands [4], none (+408) [4], person [4], what man soever (+376) [4], whosoever [4], any man's [3], him[s] [3], some [3], Benjamite (+3227) [2], Israel (+3478) [2], any man (+376) [2], an [2], champion (+1143+1886.1) [2], each (+376) [2], either[s] [2], every man's (+376+2050.1) [2], husband's [2], male [2], men's [2], none (+1115) [2], none (+369) [2], none (+376+3808) [2], one man [2], people [2], stranger (+2214) [2], stranger (+5237) [2], they[s] [2], those[s] [2], whosoever (+376) [2], whoso [2], Amalekite (+6003) [1], Benjamite (+1121+3227) [1], Egyptian (+4713) [1], Egyptian (+4713+1886.1) [1], Ishi [1], Israelite (+3478) [1], adulteress (+802) [1], adversary (+6862) [1], adversary (+7379) [1], all (+3605) [1], also [1], archers (+3384+7198+871.1+1886.1) [1], a [1], bear[s] [1], bloodthirsty (+1818) [1], chapmen (+1886.1) [1], consent [1], counseller (+6098) [1], counsellers (+6098) [1], destroyer (+4889) [1], divers [1], each one [1], eloquent (+1697) [1], every man's (+3807.1) [1], every [1], evil speaker (+3956) [1], familiar friend (+7965) [1], famous (+8034) [1], fellows [1], fellow [1], friends (+7965) [1], goodman [1], had war with (+1961+4421) [1], had wars with (+1961+4421) [1], high (+1121) [1], hunter (+6718) [1], husbandman (+120+5647) [1], husbandman (+127+1886.1) [1], in the flower of age [1], lender (+3867) [1], liar (+3577) [1], man carnally (+2233+7902) [1], mankind (+1320) [1], master (+1167) [1], men (+1121) [1], men of high degree (+1121) [1], merchantmen (+5503) [1], merchantmen [1], none (+1097) [1], none (+3808+3807.1) [1], one man's [1], oppressor (+2555) [1], reprover [1], servants [1], shipmen (+591) [1], slothful (+6102) [1], steward (+834+5921) [1], stranger (+1616) [1], stranger (+2114) [1], strangers (+1616) [1], them[s] [1], this[s] [1], trade about cattle (+4735) [1], trade to feed cattle (+4735) [1], whatsoever [1], whosoever (+3605) [1], whosoever (+834+3605) [1], workmen (+4399) [1], worthy [1], young men (+5288) [1]

377 אָשַׁשׁ or אִישׁ **'āšaš** or **'îš**, v. GK: 899 [→ 809?; cf. 787]. [Htpol] to fix in one's mind:– shew yourselves men [1]

378 אִישׁ־בֹּשֶׁת **'îš-bōšet**, n.pr.m. GK: 410 [→ 376+1322]. Ish-Bosheth, *"man of shame"*:– Ish-bosheth [11]

379 אִישְׁהוֹד **'îšhôd**, n.pr.m. GK: 412 [→ 376+1935]. Ishhod, *"man of grandeur"*:– Ishod [1]

380 אִישׁוֹן **'îšôn**, n.[m.]. GK: 413 & 854 [→ 376]. pupil, the black center of the eyeball, formally, "the little man (of the eye)," often translated as "the apple of the eye," an idiom of care and love:– apple [2], apple (+1323) [1], black [1], obscure [1]

אִישׁ־חַי **'îš-ḥay**. See 381.

381 אִישׁ־חַיִל **'îš-ḥayil**, n.m. GK: 408 + 2657 [→ 376+2428]. valiant man (376 + 2428):–

382 אִישׁ־טוֹב **'îš-ṭôb**, n.pr.m. GK: 411 [→ 376+2896]. Ish-Tob, *"man from Tob"*:– Ish-tob [2]

אִישַׁי **'îšay**. See 3448.

אִיתוֹן **'îtôn**. See 2978.

383 אִיתַי **'îtay** (Aram.), pt. GK: 10029 [cf. 3426]. there is, there are; a marker of existence often called a "quasi-verb":– there is [5], be [3], have [2], art [1], have (+3807.2) [1], is [1], none (+1768+3809) [1], there are [1], will [1]

384 אִיתִיאֵל **'îtî'ēl**, n.pr.m. GK: 417 [cf. 863]. Ithiel, *"God [El] is with me"*:– Ithiel [3]

385 אִיתָמָר **'îtāmār**, n.pr.m. GK: 418. Ithamar, "[poss.] *[is]land of palms; [father] of Tamar"*:– Ithamar [21]

386 אֵיתָן **'êtān**, a. GK: 419 [→ 387, 388, 3496, 3497]. ever-flowing, of a stream that is always filled with water; by extension: never-failing, steady, established, eternal:– strong [5], mighty [4], strength [2], hard [1], rough [1]

387 אֵיתָן **'êtān**, n.pr.m. GK: 420 [→ 386]. Ethan, *"long lived, ever-flowing [streams]"*:– Ethan [8]

388 אֵתָנִים **'ētānîm**, n.pr.[m.]. GK: 923 [→ 386]. Ethanim, *"ever-flowing [streams]"*:– Ethanim [1]

389 אַךְ **'ak**, adv. GK: 421 [→ 403]. but, surely, only, however:– only [35], surely [34], but [33], yet [12], nevertheless [11], notwithstanding [6], verily [6], also [4], howbeit [4], even [3], truly [3], at least [1], certainly [1], howbeit yet (+3588) [1], in any wise [1], indeed only (+7535) [1], notwithstanding (+2050.1) [1], of a surety [1], save [1], wherefore (+3588) [1], yet but [1]

390 אַכַּד **'akkad**, n.pr.loc. GK: 422. Akkad:– Accad [1]

391 אַכְזָב **'akzāb**, a. GK: 423 [→ 3576]. deceptive, deceitful, referring to a stream or a person:– liar [1], lie [1]

392 אַכְזִיב **'akzîb**, n.pr.loc. GK: 424 [→ 3576?]. Aczib, *"deceit"*:– Achzib [4]

393 אַכְזָר **'akzār**, a. GK: 425 [→ 394, 395]. deadly, ruthless, fierce, heartless:– cruel [3], fierce [1]

394 אַכְזָרִי **'akzārî**, a. GK: 426 [→ 393]. cruel, merciless:– cruel [7], cruel one [1]

395 אַכְזְרִיּוּת **'akzeriyyût**, n.f. GK: 427 [→ 393]. cruelty:– cruel [1]

396 אֲכִילָה **'akîlâ**, n.f. GK: 428 [→ 398]. food:– meat [1]

397 אָכִישׁ **'ākîš**, n.pr.m. GK: 429. Achish, *"the king gives"*:– Achish [21]

Heb

398 אָכַל **'ākal**, v. GK: 430 [→ 396, 400, 402, 3978, 3979, 3980, 4361; cf. 399]. [Q] to eat; [N] to be eaten; [Pu] be consumed, be destroyed; [H] to give to eat, feed; from the base meaning of eating food is the fig. extension of consuming and destroying something:– eat [471], eaten [74], devour [57], devoured [41], eateth [29], consumed [20], eat up [16], eating [13], consume [9], feed [8], devoureth [6], eaten at all (+398) [6], devouring [5], fed [5], meat [5], eaten up [4], eater [3], eatest [3], give to eat [3], ate [2], cause to eat [2], consumeth [2], consuming [2], eat in plenty (+398) [2], eaten freely (+398) [2], eateth up [2], freely eat (+398) [2], in no wise eat (+398+3808) [2], indeed eaten (+398) [2], quite devoured (+398) [2], burnt up [1], caused to eat [1], devourer [1], devourest up [1], dine [1], feedest [1], food [1], gave to eat [1], higher [1], moth-eaten (+6211) [1]

399 אֲכַל **'akal** (Aram.), v. GK: 10030 [cf. 398]. [P] to eat (food); to destroy, devastate, devour (an object):– accused (+7170) [2], devoured [2], devour [2], eat [1]

400 אֹכֶל **'ōkel**, n.m. GK: 431 [→ 398]. food; a general word for food as anything edible:– meat [18], food [16], eating [4], victuals [3], prey [2], mealtime (+6256+1886.1) [1]

401 אֻכָל **'ukāl**, n.pr.m. GK: 432 [→ 3615]. Ucal, "[poss.] *I am consumed* or *I cease*":– Ucal [1]

402 אָכְלָה **'oklâ**, n.f. GK: 433 [→ 398]. what is consumed, food, fuel:– meat [8], fuel [3], devour [2], eat [2], consume [1], devoured [1], food [1]

403 אָכֵן **'ākēn**, adv. GK: 434 & 435 [→ 389+2005]. Surely! Truly!, an exclamation to emphasize the unexpected:– surely [9], but [3], truly [2], verily [2], certainly [1], nevertheless [1]

404 אָכַף **'ākap**, v. GK: 436 [→ 405]. [Q] to drive, press hard:– craveth [1]

405 אֶכֶף **'ekep**, n.m. GK: 437 [→ 404]. hand, with a focus that this part of the body that can exert pressure or press hard:– hand [1]

406 אִכָּר **'ikkār**, n.m. GK: 438. farmer, people who work in fields and vineyards:– husbandmen [3], husbandman [2], plowmen [2]

407 אַכְשָׁף **'akšāp**, n.pr.loc. GK: 439 [→ 3784]. Acshaph, "*fascination*":– Achshaph [3]

408 אַל **'al**, adv.neg. GK: 440 [cf. 409]. no, not:– not [558], neither (+2050.1) [61], no [42], nor (+2050.1) [24], nay [8], neither [6], none [6], none (+376) [4], nothing (+1697) [3], nothing [3], never (+5769+3807.1) [2], cannot [1], neither (+1571) [1], neither (+1571+2050.1) [1], neither yet (+2050.1) [1], no (+3972) [1], none (+3605+871.1) [1], nothing (+3605) [1], than [1], whither [1]

409 אַל **'al** (Aram.), neg.adv. GK: 10031 [cf. 408]. not:– not [3], nor (+2050.3) [1]

410 אֵל **'ēl**, n.m. GK: 445 & 446 [→ 430, 433 (also used with compound proper names)]. God, the Mighty One, as a title of majesty and power, often used in combination with other titles; also any false god, gods; any person who is strong and capable: mighty one; strength:– God/god [229], mighty [3], power [3], God's [2], gods [2], goodly [1], great [1], idols [1], mighty (+1121) [1], mighty one [1], might [1], power (+3027) [1], strong [1]

411 אֵל **'ēl**, pr.pl.m. & f. GK: 447 [→ 428; cf. 412]. these:– these [7], those [2]

412 אֵל **'ēl** (Aram.), p.demo.pl. GK: 10032 [→ 1836; cf. 411]. these:– these [1]

413 אֶל **'el**, pp. GK: 448 [→ 454, 454]. to, toward; in, into; with regard to:– unto [2855], to [1183], into [308], upon [169], against [148], in [87], for [57], at [51], toward [49], on [44], with [44], by [27], of [26], over [23], concerning [17], towards [16], before (+6440) [15], before [8], after [7], among [6], over against (+6440) [4], under (+8478) [4], straight forward (+5676+6440) [3], whithersoever (+834+3605) [3], within [3], according to [2], among (+996) [2], because of [2], before (+4136+6440) [2], behind (+310) [2], beside [2], hands together (+3709+3709) [2], over against (+4136+6440) [2], regard (+6437) [2], therein (+1886.3) [2], through [2], touching [2], under [2], whereupon (+1992.1) [2]*

414 אֵלָא **'ēlā'**, n.pr.m. GK: 452 [cf. 425]. Ela:– Elah [1]

415 אֵל אֱלֹהֵי יִשְׂרָאֵל **'ēl 'elōhê yiśrā'ēl**, n.pr.loc. GK: 449 [→ 410+430+3478]. El Elohe Israel, "*God, the God of Israel*":– El-Elohe-Israel [1]

416 אֵל בֵּית־אֵל **'ēl bêt-'ēl**, n.pr.loc. GK: 450 [→ 410+1004+410]. El Bethel, "*God [El] of Bethel*":– El-beth-el [1]

417 אֶלְגָּבִישׁ **'elgābîš**, n.[m.]. GK: 453 [cf. 1378]. hail(stone) or clump of ice:– great hailstones (+68) [3]

418 אַלְגּוּמִּים **'algûmmîm**, n.[m.]pl. GK: 454 [cf. 484]. algum (wood); a transliteration of the Hebrew, the exact identification of which is uncertain:– algum [2], algum trees [1]

419 אֶלְדָּד **'eldād**, n.pr.m. GK: 455 [→ 410+1730]. Eldad, "*beloved of God [El]*; [poss.] *Dadi is god*":– Eldad [2]

420 אֶלְדָּעָה **'eldā'â**, n.pr.m. GK: 456 [→ 410]. Eldaah, "*God [El] is [my] desire*":– Eldaah [2]

421 אָלָה **'ālâ**, v. GK: 458. [Q] to mourn, wail:– lament [1]

422 אָלָה **'ālâ**, v. GK: 457 [→ 423, 8381]. [Q] to utter a curse, swear an oath; [H] to bind under oath, take an oath:– swearing [2], adjured [1], cause to swear [1], cursedst [1], make swear [1]

423 אָלָה **'ālâ**, n.f. GK: 460 [→ 422]. curse, oath; sworn agreement; public charge:– oath [14], curse [9], curses [5], cursing [4], execration [2], swearing [2]

424 אֵלָה **'ēlâ**, n.f. GK: 461 [→ 425; cf. 352; cf. 363]. oak, terebinth, or any species of large tree:– oak [11], elms [1], teil tree [1]

425 אֵלָה **'ēlâ**, n.pr.m. & loc. GK: 462 & 463 [→ 352, 424; cf. 414]. Elah, "*a mighty tree*":– Elah [16]

426 אֱלָהּ **'elāh** (Aram.), n.m. GK: 10033 [cf. 433]. God, in the singular usually the true God, but see Da 4:8; 6:7 for a pagan god; gods, in the plural:– God/god [81], gods [14]

427 אַלָּה **'allâ**, n.f. GK: 464 [→ 352]. oak, or any species of large tree:– oak [1]

428 אֵלֶּה **'ēlleh**, pr.pl.m. & f. GK: 465 [→ 411; cf. 429]. these:– these [647], those [39], them [10], this [10], some [6], such [4], they [4], one [3], other [3], such (+3509.1) [3], the same [2], whom [2], another [1], others [1], so [1], these things [1], the [1], things [1], thus [1], which [1], who [1]

429 אֵלֶּה **'ēlleh** (Aram.), p.demo.pl. GK: 10034 [→ 1836; cf. 428]. these:– these [1]

אֱלֹהַּ **'elōah**. See 433.

430 אֱלֹהִים **'elōhîm**, n.pl.m. & f. GK: 466 [→ 433; cf. 410]. God (plural of majesty: plural in form but singular in meaning, with a focus on great power); gods (true grammatical plural); any person characterized by greatness or power: mighty one, great one, judge:– God/god [2363], gods [216], God's [6], judges [4], goddess [2], mighty [2], God's (+3807.1) [1], angels [1], exceeding (+3807.1) [1], godly [1], great [1], judge [1], to God-ward (+4136+1886.1) [1], very great [1]

431 אֲלוּ **'alû** (Aram.), interj. GK: 10035 [→ 718]. there!, behold!; a discourse marker of transition, emphasis, or attention:– behold [5]

432 אִלּוּ **'illû**, c. GK: 467 [→ 518+3863]. if:– if [1], though [1]

433 אֱלוֹהַּ **'elôah**, n.m. GK: 468 [→ 430; cf. 410; cf. 426]. God; god; idol:– God/god [56], God's [1]

434 אֱלוּל **'elûl**, n.m.?. GK: 470 [→ 457]. idols, images, gods:–

435 אֱלוּל **'elûl**, n.pr. GK: 469. Elul:– Elul [1]

436 אֵלוֹן **'ēlôn**, n.[f.]. GK: 471 [→ 356; cf. 352; cf. 363]. great tree, large tree of an unspecified species:– plain [7], plains [2]

437 אַלּוֹן **'allôn**, n.m. GK: 473 [→ 438; cf. 352]. oak tree, large tree of an unspecified species:– oaks [5], oak [3]

438 אַלּוֹן **'allôn**, n.pr.m. GK: 474 [→ 437; cf. 352]. Allon, "*oak*":– Allon [2]

439 אַלּוֹן בָּכוּת **'allôn bākût**, n.pr.loc. GK: 475 [→ 352+1058]. Allon Bacuth, "*oak of weeping*":– Allon-bachuth [1]

440 אֵלֹנִי **'ēlōnî**, a.g. GK: 533 [→ 356]. Elonite, "*of Elon*":– Elonites [1], Elon [1]

441 אַלּוּף **'allûp**, a. & n.m. GK: 476 & 477 [→ 502, 503]. close friend, partner, ally, companion; chief, leader:– duke [43], dukes [14], guide [4], governors [2], captains [1], chief friends [1], governor [1], oxen [1], ox [1], very friends [1]

442 אָלוּשׁ **'ālûš**, n.pr.loc. GK: 478. Alush:– Alush [2]

443 אֶלְזָבָד **'elzābād**, n.pr.m. GK: 479 [→ 410+2064]. Elzabad, "*God [El] has given*":– Elzabad [2]

444 אָלַח **'ālah**, v. GK: 480. [N] to be, become (morally) corrupt, a fig. extension of milk turning sour, not found in the OT:– filthy [3]

445 אֶלְחָנָן **'elhānān**, n.pr.m. GK: 481 [→ 410+2605]. Elhanan, "*God [El] is gracious*":– Elhanan [4]

אֵלִי **'ēlî**. See 1017.

446 אֱלִיאָב **'elî'āb**, n.pr.m. GK: 482 [→ 410+1]. Eliab, "*God [El] is [my] father*":– Eliab [20], Eliab's [1]

447 אֱלִיאֵל **'elî'ēl**, n.pr.m. GK: 483 [→ 410+2967.1+410]. Eliel, "*God [El] is [my] God*":– Eliel [10]

448 אֱלִיאָתָה **'elî'ātâ** or אֱלִיָּתָה **'eliyyātâ**, n.pr.m. GK: 484 & 517 [→ 410+857]. Eliathah, "*God [El] comes*":– Eliathah [2]

449 אֱלִידָד ***'ᵉlîdād***, n.pr.m. GK: 485 [→ 410+1730]. Elidad, *"God [El] is [my] beloved"*:– Elidad [1]

450 אֶלְיָדָע ***'elyādā'***, n.pr.m. GK: 486 [→ 410+3045]. Eliada, *"God [El] knows"*:– Eliada [3], Eliadah [1]

451 אַלְיָה ***'alyâ***, n.f. GK: 487. fat tail (of a sheep):– rump [5]

452 אֵלִיָּה ***'ēliyyâ*** or אֵלִיָּהוּ ***'ēliyyāhû***, n.pr.m. GK: 488 & 489 [→ 410+3068]. Elijah, *"Yahweh is [my] God"*:– Elijah [69], Eliah [2]

453 אֱלִיהוּ ***'ᵉlîhû*** or אֱלִיהוּא ***'ᵉlîhû'***, n.pr.m. GK: 490 & 491 [→ 410+1931]. Elihu, *"Yahweh is [my] God"*:– Elihu [11]

454 אֶלְיְהוֹעֵינַי ***'elyᵉhô'ênay*** or אֶלְיוֹעֵינַי ***'elyô'ênay***, n.pr.m. GK: 492 & 493 [→ 413+3068+5869]. Eliehoenai, Elioenai, *"my eyes [look] to Yahweh"*:– Elioenai [8], Elihoenai [1]

455 אֶלְיַחְבָּא ***'elyaḥbā'***, n.pr.m. GK: 494 [→ 410+2244]. Eliahba, *"God [El] hides"*:– Eliahba [2]

456 אֱלִיחֹרֶף ***'ᵉlîḥōrep***, n.pr.m. GK: 495. Elihoreph:– Elihoreph [1]

457 אֱלִיל ***'ᵉlîl***, n.m. GK: 496 [→ 434]. idols, images, gods:– idols [16], idol [1], images [1], of no value [1], thing of nought [1]

458 אֱלִימֶלֶךְ ***'ᵉlîmelek***, n.pr.m. GK: 497 [→ 410+4428]. Elimelech, *"God [El] is [my] king"*:– Elimelech [4], Elimelech's [2]

459 אִלֵּין ***'illên*** (Aram.), p.demo.pl. GK: 10036 [→ 1836]. these:– these [4]

460 אֶלְיָסָף ***'elyāsāp***, n.pr.m. GK: 498 [→ 410+3254]. Eliasaph, *"God [El] has added"*:– Eliasaph [6]

461 אֱלִיעֶזֶר ***'ᵉlî'ezer***, n.pr.m. GK: 499 [→ 410+5828]. Eliezer, *"God [El] is [my] help"*:– Eliezer [14]

462 אֱלִיעֵינַי ***'ᵉlî'ênay***, n.pr.m. GK: 501 [→ 413+3068+5869]. Elienai, *"my eyes [look] to Yahweh"*:– Elienai [1]

463 אֱלִיעָם ***'ᵉlî'ām***, n.pr.m. GK: 500 [→ 410+5971]. Eliam, *"God [El] is [my] kinsman"*:– Eliam [2]

464 אֱלִיפַז ***'ᵉlîpaz***, n.pr.m. GK: 502 [→ 410+6337]. Eliphaz, *"God [El] is fine gold* or *God crushes"*:– Eliphaz [15]

465 אֱלִיפַל ***'ᵉlîpal***, n.pr.m. GK: 503 [→ 410+6419]. Eliphal, *"[my] God [El] sit in judgment"*:– Eliphal [1]

466 אֱלִיפְלֵהוּ ***'ᵉlîpᵉlēhû***, n.pr.m. GK: 504 [→ 410+6381?]. Eliphelehu, *"God [El] distinguish him!"*:– Elipheleh [2]

467 אֱלִיפֶלֶט ***'ᵉlîpeleṭ*** or אֶלְפֶּלֶט ***'elpeleṭ***, n.pr.m. GK: 505 & 550 [→ 410+6404]. Eliphelet, Elpelet, *"God [El] is [my] deliverance"*:– Eliphelet [6], Eliphalet [2], Elpalet [1]

468 אֱלִיצוּר ***'ᵉlîṣûr***, n.pr.m. GK: 506 [→ 410+6697]. Elizur, *"God [El] is [my] Rock"*:– Elizur [5]

469 אֱלִיצָפָן ***'ᵉlîṣāpān*** or אֶלְצָפָן ***'elṣāpān***, n.pr.m. GK: 507 & 553 [→ 410+6845]. Elizaphan, Elzaphan, *"God [El] is [my] hiding place"*:– Elizaphan [4], Elzaphan [2]

470 אֱלִיקָא ***'ᵉlîqā'***, n.pr.m. GK: 508 [→ 410+6965?]. Elika:– Elika [1]

471 אֶלְיָקִים ***'elyāqîm***, n.pr.m. GK: 509 [→ 410+6965]. Eliakim, *"God [El] establishes"*:– Eliakim [12]

472 אֱלִישֶׁבַע ***'ᵉlîšeba'***, n.pr.f. GK: 510 [→ 410; cf. 7652]. Elisheba, *"God [El] is an oath; God [El] is my fill"*:– Elisheba [1]

473 אֱלִישָׁה ***'ᵉlîšâ***, n.pr.loc. GK: 511. Elishah, *"God [El] saves"*:– Elishah [3]

474 אֱלִישׁוּעַ ***'ᵉlîšûa'***, n.pr.m. GK: 512 [→ 410+7768]. Elishua, *"God [El] is my salvation"*:– Elishua [2]

475 אֶלְיָשִׁיב ***'elyāšîb***, n.pr.m. GK: 513 [→ 410+7725]. Eliashib, *"God [El] restores"*:– Eliashib [17]

476 אֱלִישָׁמָע ***'ᵉlîšāmā'***, n.pr.m. GK: 514 [→ 410+8085]. Elishama, *"God [El] has heard"*:– Elishama [17]

477 אֱלִישָׁע ***'ᵉlîšā'***, n.pr.m. GK: 515 [→ 410+3467?]. Elisha, *"God [El] is [my] salvation"*:– Elisha [58]

478 אֱלִישָׁפָט ***'ᵉlîšāpāṭ***, n.pr.m. GK: 516 [→ 410+8199]. Elishaphat, *"God [El] is [my] judge"*:– Elishaphat [1]

אֱלִיתָה ***'ᵉlîtâ***. See 448.

479 אִלֵּךְ ***'illēk*** (Aram.), p.demo.pl. GK: 10037 [→ 1836]. these:– these [11], those [3]

480 אַלְלַי ***'allay***, interj. GK: 518. Woe!, What misery!, Alas!:– woe [2]

481 אָלַם ***'ālam*** or אָלַם ***'ālam***, v. GK: 519 & 520 [→ 483, 485, 492; cf. 481?]. [N] to be silenced, be speechless; [P] to bind:– dumb [6], became dumb [1], binding [1], put to silence [1]

482 אֵלֶם ***'ēlem***, n.[m.]. GK: 521 [cf. 481?]. silence [?]:– congregation [1]

אֵלָם ***'ēlām***. See 361.

אֻלָם ***'ulam***. See 485.

483 אִלֵּם ***'illēm***, a. GK: 522 [→ 481]. mute, unable to speak:– dumb [6]

484 אַלְמֻגִּים ***'almuggîm***, n.[m.]pl. GK: 523 [cf. 418]. almugwood; a transliteration of the Hebrew, the exact identification of which is uncertain:– almug [3]

485 אֲלֻמָּה ***'ᵃlummâ***, n.f. GK: 524 [→ 481]. sheaf:– sheaves [3], sheaf [2]

486 אַלְמוֹדָד ***'almôdād***, n.pr. GK: 525. Almodad, *"God [El] is loved"*:– Almodad [2]

487 אַלַּמֶּלֶךְ ***'allammelek***, n.pr.loc. GK: 526 [→ 427?+4428]. Allammelech, *"oak of the king* or *oak of Molech"*:– Alammelech [1]

488 אַלְמָן ***'almān***, a. & n.[f.]. GK: 527 & 528 [→ 490; cf. 759]. widowed (one forsaken); stronghold:– forsaken [1]

489 אַלְמֹן ***'almōn***, n.[m.]. GK: 529 [→ 490]. widowhood:– widowhood [1]

490 אַלְמָנָה ***'almānâ***, n.f. GK: 530 [→ 488, 489, 491]. widow:– widow [37], widows [12], widow's [3], desolate houses [1], desolate palaces [1], widow's (+802) [1]

491 אַלְמָנוּת ***'almānût***, n.f. GK: 531 [→ 490]. widowhood:– widowhood [3], widow's [1]

492 אַלְמֹנִי ***'almōnî***, a. GK: 532 [→ 481; cf. 6422, 6423]. a certain so-and-so, whoever, wherever, with a focus that this is not named or spoken out loud:– such a one (+6423) [1], such and such (+6423) [1], such [1]

אִלֵּן ***'illēn***. See 459.

אֵלֹנִי ***'ēlōnî***. See 440.

493 אֶלְנַעַם ***'elnā'am***, n.pr.m. GK: 534 [→ 410+5278]. Elnaam, *"God [El] is pleasantness"*:– Elnaam [1]

494 אֶלְנָתָן ***'elnātān***, n.pr.m. GK: 535 [→ 410+5414]. Elnathan, *"God [El] is given"*:– Elnathan [7]

495 אֶלָּסָר ***'ellāsār***, n.pr.loc. GK: 536. Ellasar:– Ellasar [2]

496 אֶלְעָד ***'el'ād***, n.pr.m. GK: 537 [→ 410+5749]. Elead, *"God [El] has testified"*:– Elead [1]

497 אֶלְעָדָה ***'el'ādâ***, n.pr.m. GK: 538 [→ 410+5710]. Eleadah, *"God [El] has adorned"*:– Eladah [1]

498 אֶלְעוּזַי ***'el'ûzay***, n.pr.m. GK: 539 [→ 410+5797?]. Eluzai, *"God [El] is my strength"*:– Eleuzai [1]

499 אֶלְעָזָר ***'el'āzār***, n.pr.m. GK: 540 [→ 410+5826]. Eleazar, *"God [El] is a help"*:– Eleazar [72]

500 אֶלְעָלֵא ***'el'ālē'*** or אֶלְעָלֵה ***'el'ālēh***, n.pr.loc. GK: 541 & 542 [→ 410+5927]. Elealeh, *"God [El] is high"*:– Elealeh [5]

501 אֶלְעָשָׂה ***'el'āśâ***, n.pr.m. GK: 543 [→ 410+6213]. Eleasah, *"God [El] has fashioned"*:– Eleasah [4], Elasah [2]

502 אָלַף ***'ālap***, v. GK: 544 [→ 441]. [Q] to learn, become familiar with; [P] to teach, instruct:– learn [1], teacheth [1], teach [1], uttereth [1]

503 אָלַף ***'ālap***, v.den. GK: 545 [→ 441, 505; cf. 504]. [H] to increase by thousands, produce in abundance:– bring forth thousands [1]

504 אֶלֶף ***'elep***, n.m. GK: 546 [→ 441, 505; cf. 502]. cattle herd; oxen:– kine [4], oxen [3], family [1]

505 אֶלֶף ***'elep***, n.m. GK: 547 & 548 [→ 503; cf. 506]. thousand; by extension from "thousand," this refers to any large unit or group: (family) clan, (military) unit:– thousand [418], thousands [46], two thousand [29], eleven hundred (+3967+2050.1) [3], forty two thousand (+702+7239) [2], eighteen thousand (+7239+8083+2050.1) [1], four [1], threescore and one thousand (+7239+8337+2050.1) [1], twelve hundred (+3967+2050.1) [1]

506 אֲלַף ***'ᵃlap*** (Aram.), n.m. GK: 10038 [cf. 505]. thousand; the phrase "thousands upon thousands" is an indefinitely large number:– thousand [3], thousands [1]

507 אֶלֶף ***'elep***, n.pr.loc. GK: 549. Eleph:– Eleph [1]

אַלֻּף ***'allup***. See 441.

אֶלְפֶּלֶט ***'elpeleṭ***. See 467.

508 אֶלְפַּעַל ***'elpa'al***, n.pr.m. GK: 551 [→ 410+6466]. Elpaal, *"God [El] creates"*:– Elpaal [3]

509 אָלַץ ***'ālaṣ***, v. GK: 552. [P] to prod, urge, a fig. extension of pressing one object hard against another, not found in the OT:– urged [1]

אֶלְצָפָן ***'elṣāpān***. See 469.

510 אַלְקוּם ***'alqûm***, n.[m.]?. GK: 554. army:– no rising up [1]

511 אֶלְקָנָה ***'elqānâ***, n.pr.m. GK: 555 [→ 410+7069]. Elkanah, *"God [El] has possessed"*:– Elkanah [21]

512 אֶלְקֹשִׁי ***'elqōšî***, a.g. GK: 556. Elkoshite, *"of Elkosh"*:– Elkoshite [1]

513 אֶלְתּוֹלַד ***'eltôlad***, n.pr.loc. GK: 557 [cf. 8434]. Eltolad, *"generation; kindred of God [El]; place where God [El] gives children"*:– Eltolad [2]

514 אֶלְתְּקֵא ***'eltᵉqē'*** or אֶלְתְּקֵה ***'eltᵉqēh***, n.pr.loc. GK: 558 & 559. Eltekeh, *"meeting place"*:– Eltekeh [2]

515 אֶלְתְּקֹן ***'eltᵉqôn***, n.pr.loc. GK: 560. Eltekon, *"God [El] has arranged"*:– Eltekon [1]

516 אַל תַּשְׁחֵת ***'al tašḥēt***, adv.neg.+v. GK: 440 + 8845 [→ 408+7843]. Al-taschith (408 + 7843), "Do not destroy":– Al-taschith [4]

517 אֵם ***'ēm***, n.f. GK: 562. mother, grandmother, ancestress; by extension: a term of endearment; caregiver; fork (in a road):– mother [143], mother's [67], dam [5], mothers [3], mothers' [1], parting [1]

518 אִם ***'im***, c. & pt.inter. GK: 561 [→ 432]. if, whether, or; whenever, as often as:– if [587], but (+3588) [86], or [43], not [35], though [33], whether [28], surely (+3808) [23], when [20], save (+3588) [13], that [9], or (+2050.1) [8], nor (+2050.1) [7], except (+3588) [6], except (+3808) [5], no [5], surely not [4], surely [4], though (+3588) [4], neither [3], until (+5704) [3], until (+834+5704) [3], and (+3588) [2], either [2], for (+3588) [2], none [2], nor [2], sith [2], surely (+3588) [2], than (+3588) [2], verily (+3808) [2], will (+3808) [2], yet (+3588) [2]*

519 אָמָה ***'āmâ***, n.f. GK: 563. slave woman; female servant, maidservant:– handmaid [22], maidservant [13], maid [5], bondwoman [4], maidservants [4], bondmaids [2], maids [2], handmaids [1], maidens [1], maidservant's [1], maidservants' [1]

אֵמָה ***'ēmâ***. See 367.

520 אַמָּה ***'ammâ***, n.f. GK: 564 & 567 [cf. 521]. cubit (measurement of length, from the elbow to end of fingers, about 18 to 22 inches [about half a meter]); an unspecified unit of time; pivot (of a door):– cubits [191], cubit [42], two cubits [9], measure [1], posts [1]

521 אַמָּה ***'ammâ*** (Aram.), n.f. GK: 10039 [cf. 520]. cubit (measurement of distance from the elbow to the end of the fingers, about 18 to 22 inches):– cubits [4]

522 אַמָּה ***'ammâ***, n.pr.loc. GK: 565. Ammah, *"cubit"*:– Ammah [1]

523 אֻמָּה ***'ummâ***, n.f. GK: 569 [cf. 524]. tribe, clan:– people [2], nations [1]

524 אֻמָּה ***'ummâ*** (Aram.), n.f. GK: 10040 [cf. 523]. nation, people:– nations [7], nation [1]

525 אָמוֹן ***'āmôn***, n.m. GK: 570 [→ 542]. one brought up:– one brought up [1]

526 אָמוֹן ***'āmôn***, n.pr.m. GK: 571 [→ 532; cf. 527, 539]. Amon, *"trustworthy"*:– Amon [17]

527 אָמוֹן ***'āmôn***, n.pr.[m.]. GK: 572 [→ 528; cf. 526, 539]. multitude, crowd; see also 1995:– multitude [2], populous [1]

528 אָמוֹן ***'āmôn***, n.pr.[m.]. GK: 572 [→ 527+4996; cf. 526, 539]. Amon (pagan god), *"trustworthy"*:–

529 אֵמוּן ***'ēmûn***, n.[m.]. GK: 573 & 574 [→ 539]. faithful, trustworthy:– faithful [4], faith [1], truth [1]

530 אֱמוּנָה ***'ᵉmûnâ***, n.f. GK: 575 [→ 539]. faithfulness, steadiness, trustworthiness:– faithfulness [18], truth [13], faithfully (+871.1) [5], set office [5], faithful [3], faith [1], stability [1], steady [1], truly [1], verily [1]

531 אָמוֹץ ***'āmôṣ***, n.pr.m. GK: 576 [→ 553]. Amoz, *"strong"*:– Amoz [13]

532 אָמִי ***'āmî***, n.pr.m. GK: 577 [→ 526; cf. 539]. Ami, *"trustworthy, reliable, faithful"*:– Ami [1]

אֲמִינוֹן ***'ᵃmînôn***. See 550.

533 אַמִּיץ ***'ammîṣ***, a. GK: 579 [→ 553]. strong, mighty, brave:– strong [4], courageous (+3820) [1], mighty [1]

534 אָמִיר ***'āmîr***, n.m. GK: 580 [→ 559]. branch:– branch [1], uppermost bough [1]

535 אָמַל ***'āmal***, v. GK: 581 & 582 [→ 536, 537]. [Qp] to be weak-willed; to be hot, feverish; [Pul] to wither, languish, fade away:– languisheth [8], languish [5], languished [1], waxed feeble [1], weak [1]

536 אֻמְלַל ***'umlal***, a. GK: 583 [→ 535]. faint, fading away:– weak [1]

537 אֲמֵלָל ***'ᵃmēlāl***, a. GK: 584 [→ 535]. feeble, fading:– feeble [1]

538 אֲמָם ***'ᵃmām***, n.pr.loc. GK: 585 [→ 4965]. Amam:– Amam [1]

539 אָמַן ***'āman***, v. GK: 586 & 587 [→ 526, 527, 529, 530, 532, 543, 544, 545, 548, 546, 547, 550, 551, 1968?; cf. 540, cf. 3330]. [Q] to nurse, nurture, care for; to be a trustee, be a guardian; [Qp, N] to be nurtured, cared for; to be faithful, be trustworthy, be established; [H] to believe, trust, have confidence:– believed [21], believe [19], faithful [19], sure [11], established [6], believeth [4], brought up [3], verified [3], long continuance [2], nurse [2], stedfast [2], trust [2], assurance [1], bringers up [1], fail (+3808) [1], nursed [1], nursing fathers [1], nursing father [1], put trust [1], putteth trust [1], stablished [1], stand fast [1], surely [1], trusted [1], trusty [1]

540 אֲמַן ***'ᵃman*** (Aram.), v. GK: 10041 [cf. 539]. [H] to trust in; [Hp] be trustworthy:– believed [1], faithful [1], sure [1]

541 אָמַן ***'āman***, v. GK: 3554 [→ 3225, 3231]. [H] to turn to the right; cf. 3231:– turn to the right hand [1]

542 אָמָּן ***'ommān***, n.m. GK: 588 [→ 525]. craftsman:– cunning workman [1]

543 אָמֵן ***'āmēn***, adv. GK: 589 [→ 539]. amen, surely; truth:– amen [27], truth [2], so be it [1]

544 אֹמֶן ***'ōmen***, n.[m.]. GK: 590 [→ 551, 552; cf. 539]. faithfulness:– truth [1]

545 אָמְנָה ***'omnâ***, n.f. GK: 594 [→ 539]. bringing up, caring, tending, fostering:– brought up [1]

546 אָמְנָה ***'omnâ***, adv. GK: 593 [→ 539]. really, truly, indeed:– indeed [2]

547 אֹמְנָה ***'ōmᵉnâ***, subst. GK: 595 [→ 539?]. doorpost:– pillars [1]

548 אֲמָנָה ***'ᵃmānâ***, n.f. GK: 591 [→ 539]. binding agreement, trustworthy agreement:– certain portion [1], sure [1]

549 אֲמָנָה ***'ᵃmānâ***, n.pr.loc. GK: 592 [cf. 71]. Amana, *"constant"*:– Amana [1]

אֲמֻנָה ***'ᵃmunâ***. See 530.

550 אֲמִינוֹן ***'ᵃmînôn*** or אַמְנוֹן ***'amnôn***, n.pr.m. GK: 578 & 596 [cf. 539]. Amnon, *"trustworthy"*:– Amnon [25], Amnon's [3]

551 אָמְנָם ***'omnām***, adv. GK: 597 [→ 552; cf. 544, 539]. indeed, truly, assuredly:– of a truth [3], indeed [2], no doubt [1], surely [1], true [1], truly [1]

552 אֻמְנָם ***'umnām***, adv. GK: 598 [→ 551; cf. 544, 539]. really, indeed; used in interrogative sentences:– indeed [3], in very deed [1], of a surety (+637) [1]

553 אָמֵץ ***'āmēṣ***, v. GK: 599 [→ 531, 533, 554, 555, 556, 3981 (also used with compound proper names)]. [Q] to be strong, courageous; [P] to strengthen, support, establish; harden; [Ht] to persist, determine:– of good courage [9], strengthen [7], strengthened [3], courageous [2], made speed [2], madest strong [2], strengtheneth [2], stronger [2], strong [2], confirm [1], established [1], fortify [1], hardened [1], harden [1], increaseth [1], made obstinate [1], made strong [1], prevailed [1], stedfastly minded [1]

554 אָמֹץ ***'āmōṣ***, a. GK: 600 [→ 553]. powerful, strong:– bay [2]

555 אֹמֶץ ***'ōmeṣ***, n.[m.]. GK: 601 [→ 553]. strength:– stronger and stronger (+3254) [1]

אַמִּץ ***'ammiṣ***. See 533.

556 אַמְצָה ***'amṣâ***, n.f. GK: 602 [→ 553]. strength:– strength [1]

557 אַמְצִי ***'amṣî***, n.pr.m. GK: 603 [→ 553; cf. 558?]. Amzi, "[poss.] *[Yahweh is] my strength"*:– Amzi [2]

558 אֲמַצְיָה ***'ᵃmaṣyâ*** or אֲמַצְיָהוּ ***'ᵃmaṣyāhû***, n.pr.m. GK: 604 & 605 [→ 557]. Amaziah, *"Yahweh is powerful"*:– Amaziah [40]

559 אָמַר ***'āmar***, v. GK: 606 & 607 [→ 201, 534, 561, 562, 565, 3982, 8560; cf. 560 (also used with compound proper names)]. [Q, H] to say, speak, think (say to oneself); [Qp, N] to be said; [Ht] to boast:– said [2776], saying [915], saith [581], say [560], spake [110], answered [91], speak [47], tell [29], commanded [25], saidst [19], sayest [18], spoken [15], told [14], answer [8], thought [8], speaketh [7], bade [6], bid [6], promised [5], called [4], call [3], commandeth [3], think [3], appointed [2], avouched [2], command [2], expressly say (+559) [2], intend [2], name [2], plainly say (+559) [2], purpose [2], reported [2], said indeed (+559) [2], say still (+559) [2], termed [2], verily thought (+559) [2], yet say (+559) [2], appoint [1], bidden [1], boast [1], certified [1], challengeth [1], charged [1], commandment [1], commune [1], consider [1], declared [1], demanded [1], desired [1], desireth [1], determined [1], gave a commandment [1], intendest [1], is [1], named [1], promisedst [1], published [1], requirest [1], spakest [1], suppose [1], talked [1], thinking [1], uses [1], uttereth [1]

560 אֲמַר ***'ᵃmar*** (Aram.), v. GK: 10042 [→ 3983; cf. 559]. [P] to say, tell; to command:– said [41], commanded [12], tell [5], told [4], saying [2], say [2], speak [2], declare [1], spake [1], spoken [1]

561 אֵמֶר ***'ēmer***, n.m. GK: 609 & 610 & 611 [→ 559, 564; cf. 563]. word, saying; branched antlers; fawn, lamb:– words [43], sayings [2], speeches [2], answer [1], appointed unto [1]

562 אֹמֶר ***'ōmer***, n.m. GK: 608 [→ 559]. saying, word:– speech [2], word [2], promise [1], thing [1]

563 אִמַּר ***'immar*** (Aram.), n.m. GK: 10043. male lamb:– lambs [3]

564 אִמֵּר ***'immēr***, n.pr.m. & loc. GK: 612 & 613 [→ 561]. Immer, *"lamb"*:– Immer [10]

565 אִמְרָה **'imrâ** or אֶמְרָה **'emrâ**, n.f. GK: 614 & 615 [→ 559]. word, saying, utterance:– word [26], speech [7], words [3], commandment [1]

566 אִמְרִי **'imrî**, n.pr.m. GK: 617 [→ 559+3068]. Imri, "*Yahweh spoke*":– Imri [2]

567 אֱמֹרִי **'emōrî**, a.g. GK: 616. Amorite, "[poss.] *hill dwellers; westerners*":– Amorites [73], Amorite [14]

568 אֲמַרְיָה **'amaryâ** or אֲמַרְיָהוּ **'amaryāhû**, n.pr.m. GK: 618 & 619. Amariah, "*Yahweh has said*":– Amariah [16]

569 אַמְרָפֶל **'amrāpel**, n.pr.m. GK: 620. Amraphel:– Amraphel [2]

570 אֶמֶשׁ **'emeš**, adv. GK: 621 [cf. 4871?]. last night; yesterday (evening):– yesternight [3], in former time [1], yesterday [1]

571 אֱמֶת **'emet**, n.f. GK: 622 [→ 573; cf. 539]. faithfulness, reliability, trustworthiness; truth, what conforms to reality in contrast to what is false; "the book of truth" is a reliable book, referring to heavenly scroll detailing future things:– truth [90], true [18], truly [4], right [3], truly (+871.1) [3], faithfully [2], assuredly (+871.1) [1], assured [1], establishment [1], faithful [1], sure [1], truth's [1], verity [1]

572 אַמְתַּחַת **'amtaḥat**, n.f. GK: 623 [→ 4969]. sack:– sacks [6], sack [5], sack's [3], sacks' [1]

573 אֲמִתַּי **'amittay**, n.pr.m. GK: 624 [→ 571; cf. 539]. Amittai, "*true*":– Amittai [2]

574 אֵימְתָן **'ēmetān** (Aram.), a. GK: 10028. frightening, terrible:– terrible [1]

575 אָן **'ān**, adv. GK: 625. how long?; where?:– whither (+1886.5) [16], how long (+5704+1886.5) [13], any whither (+575+1886.5+1886.5+2050.1) [4], where (+1886.5) [3], whither (+575+1886.5+1886.5+2050.1) [2], how long (+5704) [1], whithersoever (+1886.5) [1], whither [1]

אֹן **'ōn**. See 204.

576 אֲנָה **'anâ** (Aram.), p.1.com.s. GK: 10044 [cf. 589]. I:– I [14], me [2]

577 אָנָּא **'onnā'** or אָנָּה **'onnâ**, interj. GK: 626 & 629 [cf. 4994]. I ask you!, O! (preceding a request):– I beseech thee [5], beseech [2], oh [2], I pray thee [1], O [1], now [1], pray [1]

אֲנָה **'anâ**. See 576.

אָנָה **'ānâ**. See 575.

578 אָנָה **'ānâ**, v. GK: 627 [→ 205, 592, 3123, 8386; cf. 584, 596]. [Q] to mourn, lament, groan:– lament [1], mourn [1]

579 אָנָה **'ānâ**, v. GK: 628 [→ 8385]. [P] to make happen; [Pu] to befall, have happen to; [Ht] to pick a quarrel against:– befall (+413) [1], deliver [1], happen [1], seeketh a quarrel [1]

אָנָּה **'annâ**. See 577.

580 אֲנוּ **'anû**, p.com.pl. GK: 630 [→ 587]. we:– we [1]

אֹנוֹ **'ōnô**. See 207.

581 אִנּוּן **'innûn** (Aram.), p.3.m.pl. GK: 10045 [→ 1932]. they; those:– are [1], them [1], these [1], which [1]

582 אֱנוֹשׁ **'enôš**, n.m. GK: 632 [→ 583; cf. 605; cf. 606]. man, humankind, mortal, with an emphasis on frailty; "a man of peace" is a "friend":– man [29], men [7], man's [3], another[s] [1], familiars (+7965) [1], mortal man [1]

583 אֱנוֹשׁ **'enôš**, n.pr.m. GK: 633 [→ 582; cf. 605]. Enosh, "*[mortal] man*":– Enos [6], Enosh [1]

584 אָנַח **'ānaḥ**, v. GK: 634 [→ 585; cf. 578, 596, 5117]. [N] to groan, moan:– sigh [7], groan [1], mourn [1], sighed [1], sighest [1], sigheth [1]

585 אֲנָחָה **'anāḥâ**, n.f. GK: 635 [→ 584]. groaning, sighing:– sighing [5], groaning [4], mourning [1], sighs [1]

586 אֲנַחְנָא **'anaḥnā'** (Aram.), p.1.com.pl. GK: 10047 [cf. 587]. we:– we [4]

587 אֲנַחְנוּ **'anaḥnû**, p.com.pl. GK: 636 [→ 580, 589, 595, 5168; cf. 586]. we:– we [111], us [3], we ourselves [3]

588 אֲנָחֲרַת **'anāḥarat**, n.pr.loc. GK: 637. Anaharath:– Anaharath [1]

589 אֲנִי **'anî**, p.com.s. GK: 638 [→ 587; cf. 576]. I:– I [839], me [24], myself [2], I myself [1], mine [1], my [1], we [1], who [1]

590 אֳנִי **'onî**, n.m. GK: 639 [→ 591]. ships, fleet of ships:– navy [6], galley [1]

591 אֳנִיָּה **'oniyyâ**, n.f. GK: 641 [→ 590]. ship, trading ship; (pl.) fleet of ships:– ships [26], ship [4], shipmen (+376) [1]

592 אֲנִיָּה **'aniyyâ**, n.f. GK: 640 [→ 578]. lamentation, mourning:– lamentation [1], sorrow [1]

אִנִּין **'innîn**. See 581.

593 אֲנִיעָם **'anî'ām**, n.pr.m. GK: 642. Aniam, "*I am kinsman*":– Aniam [1]

594 אֲנָךְ **'anāk**, n.[m.]. GK: 643. plummet, weight for a plumb line:– plumbline [4]

595 אָנֹכִי **'ānōkî**, p.com.s. GK: 644 [→ 587]. I:– I [354], me [4], my [1]

596 אָנַן **'ānan**, v. GK: 645 [cf. 578 *or* 584]. [Htpol] to complain:– complained [1], complain [1]

597 אָנַס **'ānas**, v. GK: 646 [cf. 598]. [Q] to compel; "there is no compelling" means "to allow":– compel [1]

598 אֲנַס **'anas** (Aram.), v. GK: 10048 [cf. 597]. [P] to oppress, make difficult:– troubleth [1]

599 אָנַף **'ānap**, v. GK: 647 [→ 639, 649, 2739; cf. 600]. [Q] to be, become angry; [Ht] to feel angry:– angry [13], displeased [1]

600 אֲנַף **'anap** (Aram.), n.m. GK: 10049 [cf. 599]. face; "to fall on the face" is to assume a position of honor or reverence:– face [1], visage [1]

601 אֲנָפָה **'anāpâ**, n.f. GK: 649. heron, an unclean bird:– heron [2]

602 אָנַק **'ānaq**, v. GK: 650 [→ 603; cf. 5008, 5009]. [Q, N] to groan, lament, sigh:– cry [3], groan [1]

603 אֲנָקָה **'anāqâ**, n.f. GK: 651 [→ 602]. groaning, sighing:– sighing [2], crying out [1], groaning [1]

604 אֲנָקָה **'anāqâ**, n.f. GK: 652. gecko:– ferret [1]

605 אָנַשׁ **'ānaš**, v. GK: 631 & 653 [→ 605, 582, 583; cf. 5136]. [N] be ill, sickly; incurable, beyond cure; despairing:– incurable [5], desperately wicked [1], desperate [1], very sick [1], woeful [1]

606 אֱנָשׁ **'enāš** (Aram.), n.m. GK: 10050 [cf. 582]. man, human being; humankind, people, often in contrast to animals; "son of man" often means a human being, but in Da 7:13 assumes messianic significance:– men [12], man [8], man's [3], whosoever (+1768+1768+3606) [1], whosoever (+3606) [1]

אַנְתְּ **'ant**. See 859.

607 אַנְתְּ **'ant** or אַנְתָּה **'antâ** (Aram.), p.2.m.s. GK: 10051 & 10052 [cf. 859]. you, your:– thou [14], thee [1]

608 אַנְתּוּן **'antûn** (Aram.), p.2.m.pl. GK: 10053 [cf. 859]. you (all):– ye [1]

609 אָסָא **'āsā'**, n.pr.m. GK: 654. Asa, "[poss.] *healer; myrtle*":– Asa [57], Asa's [1]

610 אָסוּךְ **'āsûk**, n.[m.]. GK: 655 [→ 5480]. small (oil) jar, flask:– pot [1]

611 אָסוֹן **'āsôn**, n.m. GK: 656. serious injury, harm:– mischief [5]

612 אֵסוּר **'ēsûr**, n.m. GK: 657 [→ 631; cf. 613]. bindings, chains, fetters, shackles:– bands [2], prison (+1004+1886.1) [1]

613 אֱסוּר **'esûr** (Aram.), n.[m.]. GK: 10054 [→ 633; cf. 612]. bond, fetter; (pl.) imprisonment:– band [2], imprisonment [1]

614 אָסִיף **'āsîp**, n.[m.]. GK: 658 [→ 622]. (Feast of) Ingathering; harvest (from a threshing floor and winepress before the rainy season):– ingathering [2]

615 אָסִיר **'āsîr**, n.m. GK: 659 [→ 631]. prisoner, captive:– prisoners [8], bound [2], prisoner [2]

616 אַסִּיר **'assîr**, n.m.[col.]. GK: 660 [→ 617; cf. 631]. captive, prisoner:– prisoners [3]

617 אַסִּיר **'assîr**, n.pr.m. GK: 661 [→ 616; cf. 631]. Assir, "*prisoner*":– Assir [5]

618 אָסָם **'āsām**, n.m. GK: 662. barn, storehouse:– barns [1], storehouses [1]

619 אַסְנָה **'asnâ**, n.pr.m. GK: 663. Asnah, "[poss.] *thornbush; he who belongs to Nah*":– Asnah [1]

620 אָסְנַפַּר **'āsenappar** (Aram.), n.pr.m. GK: 10055. Ashurbanipal, "*Ashur creates a son*":– Asnappar [1]

621 אָסְנַת **'āsenat**, n.pr.f. GK: 664. Asenath, "*[belonging to] Neith*":– Asenath [3]

622 אָסַף **'āsap**, v. GK: 665 [→ 614, 623, 624, 625, 626, 627, 628]. [Q] to store, gather, harvest; [Qp] to be a victim; [N] to be gathered, assembled; [P] to be a rear guard, to bring in, gather; [Pu] to be gathered, collected; [Ht] to assemble; [H] to bring together:– gathered [49], gathered together [43], gather [25], assemble [9], taken away [7], gather together [6], assembled [5], rereward [5], gathereth [4], recover [4], withdraw [4], gather in [3], bring [2], gather up [2], gathered in [2], gathered up [2], generally gathered (+622) [2], surely assemble (+622) [2], took [2], assembled together [1], brought in [1], brought together [1], brought [1], consumed [1], destroy [1], fet [1], gathered together (+626) [1], gat [1], gotten [1], lose [1], put all together [1], put up [1], received in [1], receiveth [1], surely consume (+5486) [1], take away [1], take up [1], taken [1], takest away [1], take [1], utterly [1]

623 אָסָף **'āsāp**, n.pr.m. GK: 666 [→ 622]. Asaph, "*gatherer*":– Asaph [45], Asaph's [1]

אָסִף **'āsip**. See 614.

624 אָסֹף **'āsōp**, n.[m.]. GK: 667 [→ 622]. storehouse, storeroom:– Asuppim [2], thresholds [1]

625 אֹסֶף *'ōsep*, n.m. GK: 668 [→ 622]. harvest (of fruit), gathering:– gathering [2], gathered [1]

626 אֲסֵפָה *'ᵃsēpâ*, n.f.vbl. GK: 669 [→ 622]. gathering (prisoners); imprisonment:– gathered together (+622) [1]

627 אֲסֻפָּה *'ᵃsuppâ*, n.f. GK: 670 [→ 622]. collection (of sayings):– assemblies [1]

628 אֲסַפְסֻף *'ᵃsapsup*, n.[m.]. GK: 671 [→ 622]. rabble, collection (of grumblers):– mixt multitude [1]

629 אָסְפַּרְנָא *'osparnā'* (Aram.), adv. GK: 10056. with diligence, surely, fully:– speedily [4], fast [1], forthwith [1], with speed [1]

630 אַסְפָּתָא *'aspātā'*, n.pr.m. GK: 672. Aspatha, "[poss.] *given from a sacred horse*":– Aspatha [1]

631 אָסַר *'āsar*, v. GK: 673 [→ 612, 615, 616, 617, 632, 4147, 4149?, 4562?]. [Q] to bind, tie up; to obligate; [Qp] to be confined, be bound; [N] to be tied, be kept in prison; [Pu] to be captured, be taken prisoner:– bound [33], bind [11], bind fast (+631) [4], made ready [3], tied [3], prisoners [2], prison [2], bindeth [1], binding [1], girded [1], girdeth [1], harness [1], held [1], kept in prison [1], make ready [1], order [1], prepare [1], prison (+1004+1886.1) [1], put in bands [1], set in array [1], tie [1]

632 אִסָּר *'issār*, n.m. GK: 674 [→ 631; cf. 633]. pledge, a binding obligation:– bond [7], bonds [3], binding [1]

633 אֱסָר *'ᵉsār* (Aram.), n.m. GK: 10057 [→ 613; cf. 632]. (enforced) decree, i.e., a legally binding edict, a fig. extension of a bond or fetter that inhibits or controls:– decree [7]

634 אֵסַר־חַדֹּן *'ēsar-ḥaddōn*, n.pr.m. GK: 675. Esarhaddon, "*Ashur has given a brother [for a lost son]*":– Esar-haddon [3]

635 אֶסְתֵּר *'estēr*, n.pr.f. GK: 676. Esther, "[Persian] *star* [poss.] *Ishtar*":– Esther [52], Esther's [3]

636 אָע *'ā'* (Aram.), n.m. GK: 10058 [cf. 6086]. wood, timber:– timber [3], wood [2]

637 אַף *'ap*, c. GK: 677 [cf. 638]. how much (better, worse; more, less); really, truly; too, also, even more:– also [53], yea [36], even [7], how much more (+3588) [7], how much less (+3588) [5], and [3], how much more [2], also (+518) [1], although (+3588) [1], and (+2050.1) [1], and when [1], but [1], furthermore [1], how much less (+3588+3808) [1], how much less [1], how much more then (+3588) [1], how much rather [1], moreover [1], much less (+3588) [1], much less for (+3588) [1], much more (+3588) [1], neither (+369) [1], of a surety (+552) [1], so [1], though (+3588) [1], with [1], yea (+3588) [1], yet [1]

638 אַף *'ap* (Aram.), c. GK: 10059 [cf. 637]. even, also:– also [3], also (+2050.3) [1]

639 אַף *'ap*, n.m. GK: 678 [→ 649; cf. 599; cf. 600]. nose (representing the face or some part of the face); "hot of nose" signifies anger; "long of nose" signifies patience; "high of nose" signifies arrogance:– anger [171], wrath [42], face [19], nostrils [13], nose [11], angry [4], longsuffering (+750) [4], faces [3], before (+3807.1) [1], before (+871.1) [1], countenance [1], forbearing [1], forehead [1], noses [1], provocation of anger [1], snout [1], worthy [1]

640 אָפַד *'āpad*, v.den. GK: 679 [→ 642]. [Q] to fasten:– bound [1], gird [1]

אֵפֹד *'ēpōd*. See 646.

641 אֵפֹד *'ēpōd*, n.pr.m. GK: 681 [→ 646?; cf. 640]. Ephod, "*ephod*":– Ephod [1]

642 אֲפֻדָּה *'ᵃpuddâ*, n.f. GK: 682 [→ 640]. skillfully woven covering:– ephod [2], ornament [1]

643 אַפֶּדֶן *'appeden*, n.[m.]. GK: 683. palace tent, royal tent:– palace [1]

644 אָפָה *'āpâ*, v. GK: 684 & 685 [→ 3989; cf. 8601?]. [Q] to bake; [N] to be baked:– baker [8], bake [7], baken [3], baked [2], bakers [2], bakemeats (+3978+4639) [1], bakers' [1], baketh [1]

אֵפָה *'ēpâ*. See 374.

645 אֵפוֹא *'ēpô'*, pt. GK: 686 [→ 335?+6311?]. then, so then:– now [10], where [3], here [1], where (+165) [1]

646 אֵפֹד *'ēpōd*, n.m. GK: 680 [→ 641?; cf. 640]. ephod, a garment of a priest used for adornment and as an aid in priestly service:– ephod [49]

647 אֲפִיחַ *'ᵃpîaḥ*, n.pr.m. GK: 688. Aphiah:– Aphiah [1]

648 אָפִיל *'āpîl*, a. GK: 689 [→ 652]. late-ripening, late in the season:– not grown up [1]

649 אַפַּיִם *'appayim*, n.pr.m. GK: 691 [cf. 639, 599]. Appaim, "*[pair of] nostrils*":– Appaim [2]

650 אָפִיק *'āpîq*, n.m. GK: 692 & 693 [→ 662]. stream, water channel; valley, ravine, the deepest part of a valley flowing with water; mighty, strong:– rivers [10], channels [3], brooks [1], mighty [1], scales (+4043) [1], streams [1], stream [1], strong pieces [1]

אוֹפִיר *'ōpîr*. See 211.

651 אָפֵל *'āpēl*, a. GK: 695 [→ 652]. dark, gloomy:– very dark [1]

652 אֹפֶל *'ōpel*, n.m. GK: 694 [→ 648, 651, 653, 3990?, 3991?]. darkness, the absence of light, often with the associative meaning of gloom, despair; shadows:– darkness [7], obscurity [1], privily (+1119) [1]

653 אֲפֵלָה *'ᵃpēlâ*, n.f. GK: 696 [→ 652]. the dark, darkness, with the associative meaning of mental gloom and despair:– darkness [6], gloominess [2], dark [1], thick [1]

654 אֶפְלָל *'eplāl*, n.pr.m. GK: 697 [→ 6419]. Ephlal, "*judgment, arbitration*":– Ephlal [2]

655 אֹפֶן *'ōpen*, n.[m.]. GK: 698 [cf. 212?]. (right) time; aptly:–

אֹפָן *'ōpān*. See 212.

656 אָפֵס *'āpēs*, v. GK: 699 [→ 657, 658]. [Q] to come to an end, cease:– at an end [1], brought [1], clean gone [1], faileth [1], fail [1]

657 אֶפֶס *'epes*, n.m. GK: 700 & 701 [→ 656; cf. 6446]. ends (of the earth); no, nothing; however, but, only, yet; an extremity of the body, which in context wades through shallow water: ankles, or possibly soles of the feet:– ends [13], none [4], no [4], nothing [3], none else [2], not [2], without (+871.1) [2], ankles [1], but [1], howbeit [1], nevertheless (+3588) [1], nor any (+2050.1) [1], not any [1], notwithstanding (+3588) [1], only [1], save [1], saving [1], thing of nought [1], uttermost parts [1], want [1], without cause (+871.1) [1]

658 אֶפֶס דַּמִּים *'epes dammîm*, n.pr.loc. GK: 702 [→ 656]. Ephes Dammim, "*border of Dammim [blood]*":– Ephes-dammim [1]

659 אֶפַע *'epa'*, n. *or* a. GK: 703. worthless:– nought [1]

660 אֶפְעֶה *'ep'eh*, n.[m.]. GK: 704 [→ 6463?]. snake, variously identified as an adder or viper:– viper [2], viper's [1]

661 אָפַף *'āpap*, v. GK: 705. [Q] to surround, entangle, engulf:– compassed [3], compassed about [2]

662 אָפַק *'āpaq*, v. GK: 706 [→ 650]. [Ht] to control oneself, restrain oneself; to feel compelled:– refrained [3], refrain [2], forced [1], restrained [1]

663 אֲפֵק *'ᵃpēq*, n.pr.loc. GK: 707 [→ 664]. Aphek, "*stronghold*":– Aphek [8], Aphik [1]

664 אֲפֵקָה *'ᵃpēqâ*, n.pr.loc. GK: 708 [→ 663]. Aphekah, "*fortress*":– Aphekah [1]

665 אֵפֶר *'ēper*, n.[m.]. GK: 709 [→ 211]. ashes, dust:– ashes [22]

666 אֲפֵר *'ᵃpēr*, n.[m.]. GK: 710. headband:– ashes [2]

667 אֶפְרֹחַ *'eprōaḥ*, n.m. GK: 711 [→ 6524]. young (of a bird), chick:– young ones [2], young [2]

668 אַפִּרְיוֹן *'appiryôn*, n.[m.]. GK: 712. carriage; other sources: sedan chair, litter, or palanquin, a vehicle carried on poles by porters:– chariot [1]

669 אֶפְרַיִם *'eprayim*, n.pr.m. GK: 713 [→ 6509?]. Ephraim, "*doubly fruitful*":– Ephraim [171], Ephraimites [5], Ephraim's [3], Ephraim's (+3807.1) [1]

670 אֲפָרְסָי *'ᵃpārᵉsāy* (Aram.), n.pr.pl.g. GK: 10060 [cf. 6539?]. Persian, from Persia:– Apharsites [1]

671 אֲפָרְסְכָי *'ᵃparsᵉkāy* (Aram.), n.m.pl.[pr.g.?]. GK: 10061 & 10062. officials; transliterated in the KJV and ASV as the proper name "Apharsachites":– Apharsachites [2], Apharsathchites [1]

672 אֶפְרָת *'eprāt* or אֶפְרָתָה *'eprātâ*, n.pr.f. & loc. GK: 714 & 715 & 716 & 717 [→ 673, 3613]. Ephrath, Ephrathah, "*fruitful land*":– Ephratah [5], Ephrath [5]

673 אֶפְרָתִי *'eprātî*, a.g. GK: 718 [→ 672]. Ephraimite, "*of Ephraim*":– Ephrathite [3], Ephraimite [1], Ephrathites [1]

674 אַפְּתֹם *'appᵉtōm* (Aram.), n.m. GK: 10063. revenue, treasury:– revenue [1]

675 אֶצְבֹּן *'eṣbōn*, n.pr.m. GK: 719. Ezbon:– Ezbon [2]

676 אֶצְבַּע *'eṣba'*, n.f. GK: 720 [cf. 677]. digit appendage of hand or foot: finger, toe; "four fingers" is a measurement of width (Jer 52:21):– finger [19], fingers [10], fingers and toes [1], toes [1]

677 אֶצְבַּע *'eṣba'* (Aram.), n.f. GK: 10064 [cf. 676]. toe, finger:– toes [2], fingers [1]

678 אָצִיל *'āṣîl*, n.[m.]. GK: 721 & 722 [→ 680, 682]. leader, with an implication of being noble and distinguished; far corner, the remote areas of the earth:– chief men [1], nobles [1]

679 אַצִּיל *'aṣṣîl*, n.[f.]. GK: 723 [→ 680]. joint (of shoulder or wrist); "a cubit of the joint" (Eze 41:8) is an unknown length, translated as a "long cubit":– armholes (+3027) [2], great [1]

680 אָצַל ***'āṣal***, v.den. GK: 724 [→ 678, 679, 681, 683]. [Q] to turn aside; to take away; [N] to be smaller:– kept [1], reserved [1], straitened [1], take [1], took [1]

681 אֵצֶל ***'ēṣel***, subst.pp. GK: 725 [→ 680]. beside, near, at the side:– by [33], beside [11], with [3], at [2], from (+4480) [2], near [2], unto [2], besides [1], by (+4480) [1], hard by [1], near unto [1], toward [1], to [1]

682 אָצֵל ***'āṣēl***, n.pr.m. & loc. GK: 727 & 728 [→ 678]. Azel, "*noble*":– Azel [6], Azal [1]

683 אֲצַלְיָהוּ ***'^{a}ṣalyāhû***, n.pr.m. GK: 729 [→ 680+3068]. Azaliah, "*Yahweh is keeping in reserve*":– Azaliah [2]

684 אֹצֶם ***'ōṣem***, n.pr.m. GK: 730. Ozem:– Ozem [2]

685 אֶצְעָדָה ***'eṣ'ādâ***, n.f. GK: 731 [→ 6805]. armlet, armband; an ornamental chain worn on the wrist or the ankle:– bracelet [1], chains [1]

686 אָצַר ***'āṣar***, v. GK: 732 [→ 214, 687?]. [Q] to store up; [N] be stored; [H] to be in charge of a storeroom:– laid up in store [2], made treasurers [1], store up [1], treasured [1]

687 אֵצֶר ***'ēṣer***, n.pr.m. GK: 733 [→ 686?]. Ezer, "*help*":– Ezer [5]

688 אֶקְדָּח ***'eqdāḥ***, n.[m.]. GK: 734 [→ 6919]. sparkling jewel; some sources: beryl stone:– carbuncles (+68) [1]

689 אַקּוֹ ***'aqqô***, n.m. GK: 735 [→ 3243]. wild goat:– wild goat [1]

690 אֲרָא ***'^{a}rā'***, n.pr.m. GK: 736. Ara:– Ara [1]

691 אֶרְאֵל ***'er'ēl***, n.[m.]. GK: 737 [→ 739?]. brave man, hero:– valiant ones [1]

692 אַרְאֵלִי ***'ar'ēlî***, a.g. GK: 739 & 740 [→ 692; cf. 8634?]. Areli; Arelite, "*of Areli*":– Areli [2], Arelites [1]

693 אָרַב ***'ārab***, v. GK: 741 [→ 695, 696, 698?, 3993]. [Q] to lay in wait against, hide in ambush; [P] to ambush, waylay; [H] to set an ambush:– lie in wait [9], liers in wait [8], laid wait [5], ambush [4], lieth in wait [4], lay wait [3], lying in wait [2], ambushes [1], ambushments [1], lay in wait [1], lie in ambush [1], lie in wait against [1], liers in ambush [1]

694 אֲרָב ***'^{a}rāb***, n.pr.loc. GK: 742 [cf. 701?]. Arab, "*desert* or *steppe*":– Arab [1]

695 אֶרֶב ***'ereb***, n.[m.]. GK: 743 [→ 693]. cover, hiding place, lair; hiding place (for an ambush):– dens [1], lie in wait [1]

696 אֹרֶב ***'ōreb***, n.[m.]. GK: 744 [→ 693]. trap, intrigue:– wait [1]

אַרְבֵּאל ***'arbē'l***. See 1009.

697 אַרְבֶּה ***'arbeh***, n.m. GK: 746 [→ 7235?]. locust, mature locust:– locusts [11], locust [9], grasshoppers [3], grasshopper [1]

698 אָרְבָּה ***'orbâ***, n.f. GK: 747 [→ 693?]. cleverness; other sources: nimble movements (of the hands), perhaps some concrete survival skill, such as swimming:– spoils [1]

699 אֲרֻבָּה ***'^{a}rubbâ***, n.f. GK: 748. floodgate; window; nest (nesting hole):– windows [8], chimney [1]

700 אֲרֻבּוֹת ***'^{a}rubbôt***, n.pr.loc. GK: 749. Arubboth:– Aruboth [1]

701 אַרְבִּי ***'arbî***, a.g. GK: 750 [cf. 694?]. Arbite:– Arbite [1]

702 אַרְבַּע ***'arba'***, n.m. & f. GK: 752 [→ 704, 705, 706, 7153, 7243, 7251, 7253?, 7255, 7256; cf. 703]. four, (pl.) forty; fourth, fortieth:– four [264], fourteenth (+6240) [23], fourteen (+6240) [19], fourth [5], forty two thousand (+505+7239) [2], four apiece (+702) [2], threescore and fourteen (+7657+2050.1) [2], fourfold [1], thousand [1]

703 אַרְבַּע ***'arba'*** (Aram.), n.m. & f. GK: 10065 [→ 7244; cf. 702]. four:– four [8]

704 אַרְבַּע ***'arba'***, n.pr.m. GK: 753 [→ 702]. Arba:– Arbah [2], Arba [1]

אַרְבָּעָה ***'arbā'â***. See 702.

705 אַרְבָּעִים ***'arbā'îm***, n.pl.indecl. GK: 754 [→ 702]. forty (pl. of "four"):– forty [131], fortieth [4], forty's [1]

706 אַרְבַּעְתַּיִם ***'arba'tayim***, n.m. & f. GK: 752 [→ 702]. dual of 702: fourfold:–

707 אָרַג ***'ārag***, v. GK: 755 [→ 708]. [Q] to weave, spin (a web):– weaver's [4], woven [3], weaver [2], weave [2], weavest [1], wove [1]

708 אֶרֶג ***'ereg***, n.[m.]. GK: 756 [→ 707]. weaver's loom, weaver's shuttle:– beam [1], weaver's shuttle [1]

709 אַרְגֹּב ***'argōb***, n.pr.m. & loc. GK: 758 & 759 [cf. 7263]. Argob, "*mound*":– Argob [5]

710 אַרְגְּוָן ***'arg^{e}wān***, n.[m.]. GK: 760 [cf. 713]. purple (yarn):– purple [1]

711 אַרְגְּוָן ***'arg^{e}wān*** (Aram.), n.m. GK: 10066 [cf. 713]. purple (clothing), a sign of rulership:– scarlet [3]

712 אַרְגַּז ***'argaz***, n.m. GK: 761 [→ 7264]. chest (containing objects); other sources: saddlebag:– coffer [3]

713 אַרְגָּמָן ***'argāmān***, n.[m.]. GK: 763 [cf. 710; cf. 711]. purple (yarn):– purple [38]

714 אַרְדְּ ***'ard***, n.pr.m. GK: 764 [→ 715?, 716, 720?]. Ard, "*hunchbacked*":– Ard [2]

715 אַרְדּוֹן ***'ardôn***, n.pr.m. GK: 765 [→ 714?]. Ardon, "*hunchbacked*":– Ardon [1]

716 אַרְדִּי ***'ardî***, a.g. GK: 766 [→ 714]. Ardite, "*of Ard*":– Ardites [1]

717 אָרָה ***'ārâ***, v. GK: 768 [→ 224?]. [Q] to gather, pick (fruit):– gathered [1], pluck [1]

718 אֲרוּ ***'^{a}rû*** (Aram.), interj. GK: 10067 [→ 431]. there!, behold!, i.e., a discourse marker of introduction, transition, or emphasis:– behold [4], lo [1]

719 אַרְוָד ***'arwād***, n.pr.loc. GK: 770 [→ 721]. Arvad:– Arvad [2]

720 אֲרוֹד ***'^{a}rôd***, n.pr.m. GK: 769 [→ 714?]. Arod, see 722:– Arod [1]

721 אַרְוָדִי ***'arwādî***, a.g. GK: 773 [→ 719]. Arvadite, "*of Arvad*":– Arvadite [2]

722 אֲרוֹדִי ***'^{a}rôdî***, n.pr.m. & a.g. GK: 771 & 772. Arodi, "*hunchbacked*"; Arodite, "*of Arodi*":– Arodites [1], Arodi [1]

723 אֻרְוָה ***'urwâ*** or אֻרְיָה ***'uryâ***, n.f. GK: 774 & 795 [→ 220]. (animal) stall, pen, stable, manger, crib:– stalls [3]

724 אֲרוּכָה ***'^{a}rûkâ***, n.f. GK: 776 [→ 748]. healing, health; repair:– health [4], made up (+5927) [1], perfected (+5927) [1]

725 אֲרוּמָה ***'^{a}rûmâ***, n.pr.loc. GK: 777 [cf. 7316]. Arumah, "*lofty*":– Arumah [1]

726 אֲרוֹמִי ***'^{a}rômî***, a.g. GK: 122 [cf. 130]. var. of 130: Edomite, "*of Edom*":– Syrians [1]

727 אֲרוֹן ***'^{a}rôn***, n.m. & f. GK: 778. ark, chest, box; coffin:– ark [195], chest [6], coffin [1]

728 אֲוַרְנָה ***'^{a}rawnâ*** or אֲרַנְיָה ***'^{a}ranyâ***, n.pr.m. GK: 779 & 819. Araunah, Aranyah, "*strong*":– Araunah [9]

729 אָרוּז ***'ārûz***, a. GK: 775 [→ 730?]. tight, solid:– made of cedar [1]

730 אֶרֶז ***'erez***, n.m. GK: 780 [→ 729?, 731]. cedar; other sources: fir:– cedar [43], cedars [24], cedar trees [5], cedar tree [1]

731 אַרְזָה ***'arzâ***, n.f.col. GK: 781 [→ 730]. beam of cedar; other sources: paneling (made of fir):– cedar work [1]

732 אָרַח ***'āraḥ***, v. GK: 782 [→ 733?, 734, 736, 737?]. [Q] to go, travel; (ptcp.) traveler, wanderer; (ptcp.pl.) caravans:– wayfaring man [2], goeth [1], wayfaring men [1], wayfaring [1]

733 אָרַח ***'āraḥ***, n.pr.m. GK: 783 [→ 732?]. Arah, "*he wanders*":– Arah [4]

734 אֹרַח ***'ōraḥ***, n.m. GK: 784 [→ 732; cf. 735]. road, way, path, thoroughfare; by extension: way of life, manner of conduct; "the way of a woman" means "childbirth":– way [18], paths [16], path [9], ways [8], byways (+6128) [1], highways [1], manner [1], race [1], ranks [1], traveller [1], troops [1], wayfaring man (+5674) [1]

735 אֲרַח ***'^{a}raḥ*** (Aram.), n.[m.?]. GK: 10068 [cf. 734]. road, way; fig., conduct or way of life (only used fig. in the Aramaic portion of the Bible):– ways [2]

736 אֹרְחָה ***'ōrḥâ***, n.f. GK: 785 [→ 732]. caravan:– company [1], travelling companies [1]

737 אֲרֻחָה ***'^{a}ruḥâ***, n.f. GK: 786 [→ 732?]. allowance, provision; portion:– allowance [2], diet [2], dinner [1], victuals [1]

738 אֲרִי ***'^{a}rî***, n.m. GK: 787 & 793 [→ 221, 745; cf. 744]. (the African) lion, with the associative meanings of strength, fierceness, and sometimes nobility; sometimes fig. of people who are destructive:– lion [55], lions [17], lion's [4], lions' [2], young lion [1]

739 אֲרִיאֵל ***'^{a}rî'ēl***, n.pr.m. GK: 738 [→ 691?]. best man, warrior, possibly "lionlike":– lion-like men [2]

740 אֲרִיאֵל ***'^{a}rî'ēl***, n.pr.m. & n.pr.f. GK: 790 & 791 [→ 741]. Ariel, "*lioness of God [El]*":– Ariel [6]

741 אֲרִיאֵל ***'^{a}rî'ēl***, n.m. GK: 789 [→ 739, 740; cf. 2025]. altar hearth:– altar [2]

742 אֲרִידַי ***'^{a}rîday***, n.pr.m. GK: 767. Aridai, "[perhaps] *delight of Hari*":– Aridai [1]

743 אֲרִידָתָא ***'^{a}rîdātā'***, n.pr.m. GK: 792. Aridatha, "[perhaps] *given by Hari*":– Aridatha [1]

אַרְיֵה ***'aryēh***. See 738.

744 אַרְיֵה ***'aryēh*** (Aram.), n.m. GK: 10069 [cf. 738]. lion, an animal with the associative meanings of being fierce and powerful, and so causing fear:– lions [8], lions' [1], lion [1]

745 אַרְיֵה ***'aryēh***, n.pr.m. GK: 794 [→ 738]. Arieh, "*lion*":– Arieh [1]

אֲרָיָה ***'^{a}rāyâ***. See 723.

746 אַרְיוֹךְ ***'aryôk***, n.pr.m. GK: 796 & 10070. Arioch; note this name is Hebrew twice in Genesis and Aramaic five times in Daniel:– Arioch [7]

747 אֲרִיסַי ***'^{a}rîsay***, n.pr.m. GK: 798. Arisai:– Arisai [1]

748 אָרַךְ ***'ārak***, v. GK: 799 [→ 724, 750, 752, 753; cf. 754]. [Q] to be, become long; [H] to lengthen, to have a long (life):–

prolong [12], prolonged [5], long [3], drew out [2], lengthen [2], deferreth [1], defer [1], draw out [1], lengthened [1], made long [1], outlived (+310+3117) [1], overlived (+310+3117) [1], prolongeth [1], tarried long [1], tarried [1]

749 אֲרִיךְ ***'ᵃrîk*** (Aram.), a.vbl. GK: 10071. proper, fitting:– meet [1]

750 אָרֵךְ ***'ārēk***, a. GK: 800 [→ 748]. slow (to anger), patient, long-suffering:– slow [9], longsuffering (+639) [4], longwinged (+83) [1], patient [1]

751 אֶרֶךְ ***'erek***, n.pr.loc. GK: 804 [cf. 756]. Erech:– Erech [1]

752 אָרֹךְ ***'ārōk***, a. GK: 801 [→ 748]. length (spatial and temporal):– long [2], longer [1]

753 אֹרֶךְ ***'ōrek***, n.[m.]. GK: 802 [→ 748]. length (spatial and temporal):– length [70], long [21], ever (+3117) [2], high [1], so long [1]

754 אַרְכָה ***'arkâ*** (Aram.), n.f. GK: 10073 [cf. 752]. continuing, prolongation, lengthening of time:– lengthening [1], prolonged [1]

755 אַרְכֻבָּה ***'arkubbâ*** (Aram.), n.f. GK: 10072 [cf. 1288]. knee; "knocking of the knees" indicates fear:– knees [1]

אֲרֻכָה ***'ᵃrukâ***. See 724.

756 אַרְכְּוָי ***'arkᵉwāy*** (Aram.), n.pr.g. GK: 10074 [cf. 751]. Erech:– Archevites [1]

757 אַרְכִּי ***'arkî***, a.g. GK: 805. Arkite:– Archite [5], Archi [1]

758 אֲרָם ***'ᵃrām***, n.pr.m. GK: 806 [→ 762, 761, 6307 (also used with compound proper names)]. Aram:– Syria [67], Syrians [56], Aram [7], Mesopotamia [1], Syria-damascus (+1834) [1], Syria-maachah [1]

759 אַרְמוֹן ***'armôn***, n.m. GK: 810 [→ 764; cf. 488, 7411]. fortress, citadel, palace, stronghold, a military defensive building usually small of base but many floors high:– palaces [27], palace [4], castle [1]

760 אֲרַם צוֹבָה ***'ᵃram ṣôbâ***, n.pr.loc. GK: 809 [→ 758+6678]. Aram Zobah:– Aram-zobah [1]

761 אֲרַמִּי ***'ᵃrammî***, a.g. GK: 812 [→ 758]. Aramean:– Syrian [7], Syrians [3], Aramitess [1]

762 אֲרָמִי ***'ᵃrāmî***, adv. GK: 811 [→ 758]. in Aramaic:– in the Syrian language [2], in the Syrian tongue [2], in Syriack [1]

763 אֲרַם נַהֲרַיִם ***'ᵃram nahᵃrayim***, n.loc. GK: 808 [→ 758]. Aram Naharaim:– Mesopotamia [4], Aram-naharaim [1]

764 אַרְמֹנִי ***'armōnî***, n.pr.m. GK: 813 [→ 759]. Armoni, *"one born in the dwelling tower, the palace"*:– Armoni [1]

765 אֲרָן ***'ᵃrān***, n.pr.m. GK: 814. Aran, *"wild goat"*:– Aran [2]

766 אֹרֶן ***'ōren***, n.[m.]. GK: 815 [→ 767, 769?]. pine tree; other sources: laurel, sweet laurel, fir, cedar:– ash [1]

767 אֹרֶן ***'ōren***, n.pr.m. GK: 816 [→ 766]. Oren, *"fir or cedar; laurel"*:– Oren [1]

אָרֹן ***'ārōn***. See 727.

768 אַרְנֶבֶת ***'arnebet***, n.f. GK: 817 [cf. 3]. rabbit; other sources: hare:– hare [2]

769 אַרְנוֹן ***'arnôn***, n.pr.loc. GK: 818 [→ 766?]. Arnon:– Arnon [25]

אֲרַנְיָה ***'arnîah***. See 728.

770 אַרְנָן ***'arnān***, n.pr.m. GK: 820. Arnan:– Arnan [1]

771 אׇרְנָן ***'ornān***, n.pr.m. GK: 821. Araunah, *"strong"*:– Ornan [12]

772 אֲרַע ***'ᵃra'*** (Aram.), n.[f.]. GK: 10075 [→ 773, 778; cf. 776]. earth, world, the dwelling place of all peoples; land, ground, the dwelling place of a specific people:– earth [20], inferior [1]

773 אַרְעִי ***'ar'î*** (Aram.), n.f.den. GK: 10076 [→ 772]. floor, bottom:– bottom [1]

774 אַרְפָּד ***'arpād***, n.pr.loc. GK: 822. Arpad:– Arpad [4], Arphad [2]

775 אַרְפַּכְשַׁד ***'arpakšad***, n.pr.m. GK: 823. Arphaxad:– Arphaxad [9]

776 אֶרֶץ ***'ereṣ***, n.f. & m. GK: 824 [cf. 772, cf. 778]. world, earth, all inhabited lands; parts of the earth, land (in contrast to water), ground, soil; country, region, territory; "heaven and earth" means the totality of creation; "the ends of the earth" means "a very distant place":– land [1508], earth [712], ground [98], country [92], countries [48], lands [34], world [4], way [2], common [1], field [1], little way (+3530+1886.1) [1], nations [1], wilderness (+4057) [1]

777 אַרְצָא ***'arṣā'***, n.pr.m. GK: 825. Arza, "[perhaps] *gracious"*:– Arza [1]

778 אֲרַק ***'ᵃraq*** (Aram.), n.[f.]. GK: 10077 [→ 772; cf. 776]. earth:– earth [1]

779 אָרַר ***'ārar***, v. GK: 826 [→ 224?, 3994]. [Q] to curse, place a curse; [Qp] to be cursed, be under a curse; [N] to be cursed; [P] to bring a curse; [Ho] to bring a curse upon one:– cursed [44], curse [9], causeth the curse [5], curseth [2], bitterly [1], causeth curse [1], cursest [1]

780 אֲרָרַט ***'ᵃrāraṭ***, n.pr.loc. GK: 827. Ararat:– Ararat [2], Armenia [2]

781 אָרַשׂ ***'āraś***, v. GK: 829. [P] to betroth, pledge to marriage; [Pu] to be betrothed, be pledged to be married:– betrothed [6], betroth [4], espoused [1]

782 אֲרֶשֶׁת ***'ᵃrešet***, n.f. GK: 830 [→ 4180]. request, desire:– request [1]

783 אַרְתַּחְשַׁשְׂתְּא ***'artaḥšast'*** or אַרְתַּחְשַׁשְׂתְּ ***'artaḥšaśt*** or אַרְתַּחְשַׁשְׂתָּא ***'artaḥšaśtā'***, n.pr.m. GK: 831 & 10078. Artaxerxes; note this name occurs nine times in Hebrew in Ezra and Nehemiah and six times in Aramaic in Ezra:– Artaxerxes [14], Artaxerxes' [1]

784 אֵשׁ ***'ēš***, n.f. & m. GK: 836 [→ 800, 801; cf. 785]. fire, flame; lightning; same as 800:– fire [372], fiery [2], burning [1], fire (+3956) [1], flaming [1], hot [1]

785 אֶשָּׁא ***'eššā'*** (Aram.), n.[f.]. GK: 10080 [cf. 784, 801]. fire:– flame [1]

786 אִשׁ ***'iš***, subst. GK: 838 [→ 3426]. there is:– are there [1], can [1]

787 אֹשׁ ***'ōš*** (Aram.), n.m. GK: 10079 [cf. 8357]. foundation:– foundations [2], foundation [1]

788 אַשְׁבֵּל ***'ašbēl***, n.pr.m. GK: 839 [→ 789; cf. 7640]. Ashbel, "[poss. a form of] *man of Baal; having a long upper lip"*:– Ashbel [3]

789 אַשְׁבֵּלִי ***'ašbēlî***, a.g. GK: 840 [→ 788; cf. 7640]. Ashbelite, *"of Ashbel"*:– Ashbelites [1]

790 אֶשְׁבָּן ***'ešbān***, n.pr.m. GK: 841. Eshban, *"man of understanding"*:– Eshban [2]

791 אַשְׁבֵּעַ ***'ašbēa'***, n.pr.loc. GK: 842 [→ 1004+791]. Ashbea:– Ashbea [1]

792 אֶשְׁבַּעַל ***'ešba'al***, n.pr.m. GK: 843 [→ 376+1167]. Esh-Baal, *"man of Baal"*:– Eshbaal [2]

793 אֶשֶׁד ***'ešed***, n.[m.]. GK: 845 [→ 794]. foundation, bottom, lower part (slope):– stream [1]

794 אֲשֵׁדָה ***'ăšēd***, n.f. GK: 844 [→ 793, 799]. slopes, mountain slopes:– springs [3]

795 אַשְׁדּוֹד ***'ašdôd***, n.pr.loc. GK: 846 [→ 796, 797]. Ashdod, "[perhaps] *fortress"*:– Ashdod [17]

796 אַשְׁדּוֹדִי ***'ašdôdî***, a.g. GK: 847 [→ 795]. from Ashdod:– Ashdodites [1], Ashdothites [1], of Ashdod [1], them of Ashdod [1], they of Ashdod [1]

797 אַשְׁדּוֹדִית ***'ašdôdît***, adv. GK: 848 [→ 795]. language of Ashdod:– in the speech of Ashdod [1]

798 אַשְׁדּוֹת הַפִּסְגָּה ***'ašdôt happisgâ***, n.pr.loc. GK: 849 [→ 794+1886.1+6449]. Ashdoth Pisgah:– Ashdoth-pisgah [3]

799 אֶשְׁדָּת ***'ešdāt***, n.f. GK: 850 [→ 794]. mountain slope:– *not translated* [1]

800 אֵשׁ ***'ēš***, n.f. & m. GK: 836 [→ 784]. fire, flame; lightning; same as 784:–

801 אִשֶּׁה ***'iššeh***, n.m. GK: 852 [→ 784; cf. 785]. offering made by fire:– offering made by fire [35], offerings made by fire [15], sacrifice made by fire [9], sacrifices made by fire [3], offering by fire [2], offering made by fire (+7133) [1]

802 אִשָּׁה ***'iššâ***, n.f. GK: 851 [→ 376; cf. 5389]. woman, in contrast to man; wife, in contrast to husband; "to take a woman" means "to marry":– wife [301], woman [211], wives [115], women [103], wife's [8], one [7], woman's [7], every one [3], each [2], female [2], married (+1961+3807.1) [2], marry (+1961+3807.1) [2], adulteress (+376) [1], every woman [1], every [1], married (+1167) [1], married (+3807.1) [1], none (+3808) [1], together (+269+413) [1], whore's (+2181) [1], widow's (+490) [1], wife (+3807.1) [1], womankind [1], women's [1]

803 אֻשְׁיָה ***'ᵃšûyâ*** or אֹשְׁיָה ***'ošyâ***, n.f. GK: 853 & 859. tower:– foundations [1]

804 אַשּׁוּר ***'aššûr***, n.pr.g. & loc. GK: 855 [→ 839]. Asshur, Assyria:– Assyria [118], Assyrian [13], Asshur [8], Assyrians [6], Assyrians (+1121) [4], Assur [2]

805 אֲשׁוּרִי ***'ᵃšûrî***, a.g. & n.pr.g.pl. GK: 856. Ashuri; Asshurite, *"of Asshur"*:– Ashurites [1], Asshurim [1]

806 אַשְׁחוּר ***'ašḥûr***, n.pr.m. GK: 858. Ashhur:– Ashur [2]

807 אֲשִׁימָא ***'ᵃšîmā'***, n.pr.[m.]. GK: 860. Ashima:– Ashima [1]

אֲשֵׁרָה ***'ᵃšērâ***. See 842.

808 אָשִׁישׁ ***'āšîš***, n.m. GK: 861. man:– foundations [1]

809 אֲשִׁישָׁה ***'ᵃšîšâ***, n.f. GK: 862 [→ 377?]. cake of raisins, made of dried, compressed grapes; used as food and as an offering:– flagons [2], flagon [2]

810 אֶשֶׁךְ ***'ešek***, n.[m.]. GK: 863. testicle:– stones [1]

811 אֶשְׁכּוֹל ***'eškôl***, n.m. GK: 864 [→ 812; cf. 7921]. cluster of grapes:– clusters [4], cluster [4], cluster of grapes [1]

812 אֶשְׁכֹּל ***'eškōl***, n.pr.m. & loc. GK: 865 & 866 [→ 811]. Eshcol, *"[grape] cluster"*:– Eshcol [6]

813 אַשְׁכְּנַז ***'ašk^{e}naz***, n.pr.m. GK: 867. Ashkenaz:– Aschenaz [2], Ashkenaz [1]

814 אֶשְׁכָּר ***'eškār***, n.[m.]. GK: 868. gifts; payment:– gifts [1], present [1]

815 אֵשֶׁל ***'ēšel***, n.m. GK: 869. tamarisk tree:– tree [2], grove [1]

816 אָשַׁם ***'āšam***, v. GK: 870 [→ 817, 818, 819]. [Q] to be guilty; to be in a state of liable for a wrongdoing, with an implication of that one will suffer or be punished for the guilt; [N] to be suffering; [H] to declare guilty:– guilty [12], desolate [4], offend [4], certainly trespassed (+816) [2], greatly offended (+816) [2], made desolate [2], trespass [2], acknowledge offence [1], destroy [1], found faulty [1], found guilty [1], hath trespassed [1], hold guilty [1], offended [1]

817 אָשָׁם ***'āšām***, n.m. GK: 871 [→ 816]. guilt offering, atoning sacrifice; guilt, penalty:– trespass offering [35], trespass [6], sin [2], guiltiness [1], offering for sin [1], trespasses [1]

818 אָשֵׁם ***'āšēm***, a. GK: 872 [→ 816]. guilty, bearing guilt:– guilty [2], which is faulty [1]

819 אַשְׁמָה ***'ašmâ***, n.f. GK: 873 [→ 816]. guilt, guiltiness:– trespass [9], sins [2], sin [2], cause of trespass [1], offended [1], trespass offering [1], trespassed [1], trespasses [1], trespassing [1]

אַשְׁמוּרָה ***'ašmûrâ***. See 821.

820 אַשְׁמָן ***'ašmān***, n.[m.]pl. GK: 875 [→ 8081?]. strong one:– desolate places [1]

821 אַשְׁמוּרָה ***'ašmûrâ***, n.f. GK: 874 [→ 8104]. watch of the night (middle or last):– watch [4], watches [3]

822 אֶשְׁנָב ***'ešnāb***, n.[m.]. GK: 876 [→ 5380]. lattice, a barred or grated window:– casement [1], lattice [1]

823 אַשְׁנָה ***'ašnâ***, n.pr.loc. GK: 877. Ashnah:– Ashnah [2]

824 אֶשְׁעָן ***'eš'ān***, n.pr.loc. GK: 878. Eshan, "*support*":– Eshean [1]

825 אַשָּׁף ***'aššāp***, n.m. GK: 879 [cf. 826]. enchanter, conjurer, one of the profession of the secret arts, in communication with the dead:– astrologers [2]

826 אָשַׁף ***'āšap*** (Aram.), n.m. GK: 10081 [cf. 825]. enchanter, conjurer:– astrologers [4], astrologer [1], astrologians [1]

827 אַשְׁפָּה ***'ašpâ***, n.f. GK: 880. quiver (for arrows):– quiver [6]

828 אַשְׁפְּנַז ***'ašp^{e}naz***, n.pr.m. GK: 881. Ashpenaz, "*guest*":– Ashpenaz [1]

829 אֶשְׁפָּר ***'ešpār***, n.m. GK: 882 [→ 7782]. cake of dates:– good piece [2]

830 אַשְׁפֹּת ***'ašpōt***, n.[m.]. GK: 883 [→ 8239]. ash heap; Dung (Gate):– dung [4], dunghill [2], dunghills [1]

831 אַשְׁקְלוֹן ***'ašq^{e}lôn***, n.pr.loc. GK: 884 [→ 832]. Ashkelon:– Ashkelon [9], Askelon [3]

832 אֶשְׁקְלוֹנִי ***'ešq^{e}lônî***, a.g. GK: 885 [→ 831]. Ashkelonite, "*of Ashkelon*":– Eshkalonites [1]

833 אָשַׁר ***'āšar***, v. GK: 886 & 887 [→ 835, 836, 837, 838, 843]. [Q] to walk (straight); [P] to lead, guide; reprove; to call blessed, pronounce happy, speak well of; [Pu] to be guided; to be blessed; in some contexts, to give a blessing is to act kindly and impart benefits to the one being blessed; to be blessed implies the happy state that results:– call blessed [4], blessed [3], go [2], call happy [1], guide [1], happy [1], leaders [1], lead [1], led [1], relieve [1]

834 אֲשֶׁר ***'^{a}šer***, pt.rel. GK: 889. (rel.) who, which, what; (c.) that, in order that, so that:– which [1819], that [1671], as (+3509.1) [382], whom [262], who [94], what [75], whose [69], where (+8033) [54], when (+3509.1) [47], wherewith [41], whither (+8033+1886.5) [38], because [36], whatsoever (+3605) [33], when [32], how [28], where [28], for [27], until (+5704) [27], whither (+8033) [27], because (+5921) [26], wherein [25], as [23], because (+3282) [19], whereof [19], according as (+3509.1) [16], wherein (+871.1) [15], such as [14], wherein (+871.1+1886.3) [14], whereby [12], whithersoever (+3605+871.1) [12], because (+8478) [11], like as (+3509.1) [11], wherewith (+871.1) [11], whereon (+5921) [10], till (+5704) [9], wherewith (+5921) [8], whosoever (+3605) [8], such [7], where (+8033+1886.5) [7], where (+871.1) [7], wherein (+8033) [7], as soon as (+3509.1) [6], forasmuch as (+3282) [5], how that [5], whatsoever [5], whither [5], whosoever (+376) [5], as when (+3509.1) [4], because (+1697+5921) [4], if [4], that (+4616+3807.1) [4], that when (+3509.1) [4], what soever (+3605) [4], wherein (+871.1+2050.2) [4], wherein (+871.1+3963.1) [4]*

835 אֶשֶׁר ***'ešer***, n.[m.]. GK: 890 & 897 [→ 833, 837]. fortune, blessedness, happiness; (interj.) blessed!, happy!, a heightened state of happiness and joy, implying very favorable circumstances, often resulting from the kind acts of God:– blessed [27], happy [18]

836 אָשֵׁר ***'āšēr***, n.pr.m. GK: 888 [→ 843; cf. 833]. Asher, "*Happy One!*":– Asher [43]

837 אֹשֶׁר ***'ōšer***, n.[m.]. GK: 891 [→ 835; cf. 833]. fortune, blessedness, happiness:– happy [1]

838 אָשֻׁר ***'āšur***, n.f. GK: 892 & 893 [→ 833]. steps, tracks:– steps [5], goings [2], going [1], step [1]

839 אַשֻּׁר ***'aššur***, n.pr.g. & loc. GK: 894 [→ 804]. Asshur, Asshurite; cf. 804:– Ashurites [1]

אַשֻּׁר ***'aššur***. See 804, 838.

840 אֲשַׂרְאֵל ***'^{a}śar'ēl***, n.pr.m. GK: 832 [→ 841, 844, 845]. Asarel:– Asareel [1]

841 אֲשַׂרְאֵלָה ***'^{a}śar'ēlâ***, n.pr.m. GK: 833 [→ 840; cf. 3480]. Asarelah:– Asarelah [1]

842 אֲשֵׁרָה ***'^{a}šērâ***, n.pr.f. GK: 895 [cf. 6252?]. Asherah (pagan god), Asherah pole:– groves [24], grove [16]

843 אָשֵׁרִי ***'āšērî***, a.g. GK: 896 [→ 836; cf. 833]. people of Asher:– Asherites [1]

844 אַשְׂרִיאֵל ***'aśrî'ēl***, n.pr.m. GK: 835 [→ 840]. Asriel, "*God has filled with joy* or *[the object of] joy is God*":– Asriel [2], Ashriel [1]

845 אַשְׂרִאֵלִי ***'aśri'ēlî***, a.g. GK: 834 [→ 840]. Asrielite, "*of Asriel*":– Asrielites [1]

846 אֻשַּׁרְנָא ***'uššarnā'*** (Aram.), n.m. GK: 10082. structure, a building or part of a building (various sources translate more specifically: "beams, roofing, paneling, scaffolding," etc.):– walls [1], wall [1]

847 אֶשְׁתָּאוֹל ***'eštā'ôl***, n.pr.loc. GK: 900 [→ 848; cf. 7592]. Eshtaol, "*[place of oracles,] inquiry*":– Eshtaol [7]

848 אֶשְׁתָּאֻלִי ***'eštā'ulî***, a.g. GK: 901 [→ 847]. Eshtaolite, "*of Eshtaol*":– Eshtaulites [1]

849 אֶשְׁתַּדּוּר ***'eštaddûr*** (Aram.), n.m. GK: 10083 [→ 7712]. rebellion, sedition, revolt:– sedition [2]

850 אֶשְׁתּוֹן ***'eštôn***, n.pr.m. GK: 902. Eshton, "[poss.] *hen-pecked [husband]* or *effeminate*":– Eshton [2]

851 אֶשְׁתְּמֹה ***'ešt^{e}mōh*** or אֶשְׁתְּמוֹעַ ***'ešt^{e}mōa'***, n.pr.m. & loc. GK: 903 & 904 [→ 8085]. Eshtemoa, Eshtemoh, "*[place where oracle is] heard*":– Eshtemoa [5], Eshtemoh [1]

אַתְּ ***'at***. See 859.

852 אָת ***'āt*** (Aram.), n.m. GK: 10084 [cf. 226]. miraculous sign:– signs [3]

853 אֵת ***'ēt***, pt. GK: 906 [cf. 3487]. usually not translated: marks the direct object:– *usually untranslated* [513], consecrated (+3027+4390) [5], consecrate (+3027+4390) [4], besought (+2470+6440) [3], aided (+2388+3027) [1]

854 אֵת ***'ēt***, pp. GK: 907 [→ 856]. with, to, upon, beside, among, against:– with [606], from (+4480) [81], of (+4480) [71], against [27], to [20], before (+6440) [16], unto [14], by (+4480) [10], by [9], among [7], in [7], upon [7], for [3], of [3], amongst [2], and (+2050.1) [2], before [2], from [2], hath [2], also [1], at the hand of (+4480) [1], beside (+2050.1) [1], beside [1], delivered to keep (+6485+6487) [1], doing (+4480) [1], for (+2050.1) [1], had [1], have [1], knoweth [1], lie with at all (+7901+7901) [1], lien with (+7901) [1], lieth carnally with (+2233+7901+7902) [1], on side [1], on the behalf of (+4480) [1], out of (+4480) [1], own [1], requite (+6213) [1], than (+4480) [1], therewith (+2050.2) [1], towards [1], undo (+6213) [1], with (+4480) [1]

855 אֵת ***'ēt***, n.[m.]. GK: 908. plowshare, mattock:– plowshares [3], coulters [1], coulter [1]

אַתָּ ***'attā***. See 859.

אָתָא ***'ātā'***. See 857.

856 אֶתְבַּעַל ***'etba'al***, n.pr.m. GK: 909 [→ 854+1167]. Ethbaal, "*with [him is] Baal*":– Ethbaal [1]

857 אָתָה ***'ātâ***, v. GK: 910 [→ 2978, 448; cf. 858]. [Q] to come; [H] to bring:– come [9], came [4], cometh [3], to come [2], brought (+7125) [1], come upon [1], coming [1]

858 אֲתָה ***'^{a}tâ*** (Aram.), v. GK: 10085 [cf. 857]. [P] to come, go; [H] to bring; [Hp] to be brought:– brought [6], came [4], come [3], bring [2], brought out [1]

859 אַתָּה ***'attâ***, p.m.s.; אַתְּ ***'att*** or אַתִּי ***'attî***, p.f.s.; אַתֶּם ***'attem***, p.m.pl.; אַתֵּן ***'attēn***, p.f.pl. GK: 905 & 911 & 914 & 917 & 920 [cf. 607; cf. 608]. all forms of the second person pronoun: you, your, yourself; you (all), yours, yourselves:– thou [777], ye [251], you [29], thee [15], thyself [5], yourselves [4], thine [1], thy [1]

860 אָתוֹן ***'ātôn***, n.f. GK: 912. female donkey:– ass [16], asses [12], she asses [5], ass's [1]

861 אַתּוּן ***'attûn*** (Aram.), n.m. [& f.?]. GK: 10086. furnace:– furnace [10]

862 אַתּוּק ***'attûq*** or אַתִּיק ***'attîq***, n.m. GK: 913 & 916. gallery, porch; other sources: street, passage:– galleries [3], gallery [2]

אַתִּי ***'attî***. See 859.

863 אִיתַי ***'îtay*** or אִתַּי ***'ittay***, n.pr.m. GK: 416 & 915 [cf. 384]. Ithai, Ittai, "[poss.] *with me*":– Ittai [8], Ithai [1]

864 אֵתָם ***'ētām***, n.pr.loc. GK: 918. Etham, "[poss.] *fort*":– Etham [4]

אַתֶּם ***'attem***. See 859.

865 אֶתְמוֹל ***'etmôl***, subst.adv. GK: 919 [→ 8543]. yesterday; (adv.) before, formerly, lately, in the past:– before that time (+8032+3509.1) [1], beforetime (+4480+8032) [1], heretofore (+8032) [1], in time past (+1571+8032) [1], in times past (+8032) [1], late [1], old [1], yesterday (+3117) [1]

אַתֵּן ***'atten***. See 859.

866 אֶתְנָה ***'etnâ***, n.f. GK: 921 [→ 869]. payment (of a prostitute):– rewards [1]

אַתֵּנָה ***'attēnâ*** or אַתֵּנָּה ***'attēnnâ***. See 859.

867 אֶתְנִי ***'etnî***, n.pr.m. GK: 922. Ethni, "*gift or hire*":– Ethni [1]

868 אֶתְנָן ***'etnān***, n.pr.m. GK: 925 [→ 869]. Ethnan, "*hire [of a prostitute]*":– hire [7], reward [3], hires [1]

869 אֶתְנַן ***'etnan***, n.m. GK: 924 [→ 866, 868, 8566; cf. 5414]. wages, payment (of a prostitute):– Ethnan [1]

870 אֲתַר ***'ᵃtar*** (Aram.), n.m. GK: 10087 & 10092 [→ 871.2; cf. 834]. site, place; after:– place [5], after [3]

871 אֲתָרִים ***'ᵃtārîm***, n.pr.loc. GK: 926. Atharim, "[trad.] *way of the spies*":– spies [1]

871.1 -בְּ ***bᵉ-***, pp.pref. GK: 928 [→ 1119, 1152, 1164, 1212; cf. 871.2]. in, on, among, over, through, against; when, whenever; a spatial, temporal, or logical marker to show relationship of objects, words, and phrases:– in [6850], with [1418], by [699], when [584], into [476], at [438], on [372], upon [340], against [335], among [299], of [274], for [248], through [152], to [151], among (+8432) [106], unto [104], therein (+1886.3) [86], over [71], throughout [64], after [51], according to [43], by (+3027) [42], among (+7130) [41], while [36], before (+2962) [35], therein (+2050.2) [35], within [35], as [34], under [31], obey (+8085) [26], within (+7130) [25], every morning (+1242+1242+871.1+1886.1+1886.1) [20], obeyed (+8085) [20], amongst [19], because of [19], in (+8432) [19], within (+8432) [18], without (+3808) [17], wherein (+834) [15], for sake (+5668) [14], wherein (+834+1886.3) [14], that [13], because [12], wherein (+4100) [12], whithersoever (+834+3605) [12], without (+2351+1886.1) [12], therewith (+1886.3) [11], wherewith (+834) [11], here (+2088) [10], that (+5668) [10], when (+3117) [10], wherein (+2050.2) [10], wherewith (+4100) [10], with (+3027) [10]*

871.2 -בְּ ***bᵉ-*** (Aram.), pp.pref. GK: 10089 [→ 870; cf. 871.1]. in, with, by:– in [103], then (+116) [28], at [18], with [15], by [6], into [4], over [4], aloud (+2429) [3], of [3], on [3], upon [3], concerning [2], continually (+0.2+8411) [2], without (+3809) [2], according to [1], at what time (+0.2+1768+5732) [1], for [1], more [1], then (+116+4481+6925) [1], therein (+1459+1886.9) [1], therein (+1886.9) [1], therein (+1952.1) [1], through [1], wherein (+1459) [1], wheresoever (+1768+3606) [1], whiles [1], within [1]

872 בִּאָה ***bi'â***, n.f. GK: 929 [→ 935]. entrance:– entry [1]

873 בִּאישׁ ***bi'yš*** (Aram.), a. GK: 10090 [→ 888]. wicked, evil, bad:– bad [1]

874 בָּאַר ***bā'ar***, v. GK: 930. [P] to make plain, make clear, expound:– declare [1], make plain [1], plainly [1]

875 בְּאֵר ***bᵉ'ēr***, n.f. GK: 931 [→ 876, 877, 879, 883, 884, 878, 880, 881, 882, 885, 953, 1269, 1269 (also used with compound proper names)]. well, a shaft in the ground for extraction of water; pit, a depression in the earth with no focus on water:– well [23], well's [6], pit [3], wells [3], full of slimepits (+875+2564) [2]

876 בְּאֵר ***bᵉ'ēr***, n.pr.loc. GK: 932 [→ 875]. Beer, "*cistern, well*":– Beer [2]

877 בֹּאר ***bō'r***, n.m. GK: 934 [→ 953; cf. 875]. pit, well, cistern; dungeon; a cistern is usually a shaft in the ground, hewn out of soft stone and plastered to hold water:–

878 בְּאֵרָא ***bᵉ'ērā'***, n.pr.m. GK: 938 [→ 875]. Beera, "*cistern, well*":– Beera [1]

879 בְּאֵר אֵילִים ***bᵉ'ēr 'êlîm***, n.pr.loc. GK: 935 [→ 875+352; cf. 352]. Beer Elim, "*cistern, well of Elim*":– Beer-elim [1]

880 בְּאֵרָה ***bᵉ'ērâ***, n.pr.m. GK: 939 [→ 875]. Beerah, "*cistern, well*":– Beerah [1]

881 בְּאֵרוֹת ***bᵉ'ērôt***, n.pr.loc. GK: 940 [→ 886; cf. 875]. Beeroth, "*cisterns, wells*":– Beeroth [6]

882 בְּאֵרִי ***bᵉ'ērî***, n.pr.m. GK: 941 [→ 875]. Beeri, "*[my] cistern, well*":– Beeri [2]

883 בְּאֵר לַחַי רֹאִי ***bᵉ'ēr laḥay rō'î***, n.pr.loc. GK: 936 [→ 875+3807.1+2421]. Beer Lahai Roi, "*well that belongs to the Living One seeing me*":– well Lahai-roi [2], Beer-lahai-roi [1]

884 בְּאֵר שֶׁבַע ***bᵉ'ēr šeba'***, n.pr.loc. GK: 937 [→ 875+7651]. Beersheba, "*seventh well*":– Beer-sheba [34]

885 בְּאֵרֹת בְּנֵי־יַעֲקָן ***bᵉ'ērōt bᵉnê-yaᵃqān***, n.pr.loc. GK: 942 [→ 875+1121+3292]. Beeroth Bene-Jaakan, "*wells of the sons of Jaakan*":–

886 בְּאֵרֹתִי ***bᵉ'ērōtî***, a.g. GK: 943 [→ 881; cf. 1307]. Beerothite, "*of Beeroth*":– Beerothite [4], Beerothites [1]

887 בָּאַשׁ ***bā'aš***, v. GK: 944 [→ 889, 891, 890; cf. 888]. [Q] to stink, smell; [N] to become a stench; [H] to make a stench, to cause a bad smell; [Ht] to make oneself a stench:– stank [3], stink [3], made utterly to abhor (+887) [2], abhorred [1], had in abomination [1], loathsome [1], made odious [1], made to be abhorred [1], make to stink [1], stinketh [1], stinking savour [1], stunk [1]

888 בְּאֵשׁ ***bᵉ'ēš*** (Aram.), v. GK: 10091 [→ 873; cf. 887]. [P] to be distressed:– displeased [1]

889 בְּאֹשׁ ***bᵉ'ōš***, n.m. GK: 945 [→ 887]. stench, stink:– stink [3]

890 בָּאְשָׁה ***bo'šâ***, n.f. GK: 947 [→ 887]. weeds, a plant of no value, variously identified:– cockle [1]

891 בְּאֻשִׁים ***bᵉ'uš***, n.[m.]pl. GK: 946 [→ 887]. bad (putrid) fruit, rotten grapes:– wild grapes [2]

892 בָּבָה ***bābâ***, n.f. GK: 949 [→ 893?]. apple (of the eye), eyeball, formally, "little child of the eye," a term of endearment:– apple [1]

893 בֵּבַי ***bēbay***, n.pr.m. GK: 950 [→ 892?]. Bebai, "*child*":– Bebai [6]

894 בָּבֶל ***bābel***, n.pr.loc. GK: 951 [cf. 3778; cf. 895]. Babel, Babylon, "*gate of god[s]; [Ge 11:9] confused*":– Babylon [249], Babylon's [8], Babylonians (+1121) [3], Babel [2]

895 בָּבֶל ***bābel*** (Aram.), n.pr.loc. GK: 10093 [→ 896; cf. 894]. Babylon, "*gate of god(s)*":– Babylon [25]

896 בָּבְלָי ***bābᵉlî*** (Aram.), a.g. GK: 10094 [→ 895]. Babylonian, from Babylon:– Babylonians [1]

897 בַּג ***bag***, var. GK: 952 [cf. 957, 6598?]. plunder, loot, despoiling:–

898 בָּגַד ***bāgad***, v. GK: 953 [→ 899, 900, 901]. [Q] to be unfaithful, be faithless; to betray, act treacherously:– dealt treacherously [10], transgressors [8], deal treacherously [6], treacherous [3], deal very treacherously (+898) [2], dealt deceitfully [2], dealt very treacherously (+898) [2], transgressor [2], treacherous dealers [2], deal very treacherously (+899) [1], dealest treacherously [1], dealeth treacherously [1], dealt unfaithfully [1], dealt very treacherously (+899) [1], offend [1], transgressed [1], transgresseth [1], transgress [1], treacherous dealer [1], treacherously [1], unfaithful [1]

899 בֶּגֶד ***beged***, n.m. GK: 954 & 955 [→ 898]. clothing, garment, cloak, robe; treachery:– clothes [73], garments [70], garment [37], raiment [12], cloth [9], apparel [4], robes [4], wardrobe [2], clothing [1], deal very treacherously (+898) [1], dealt very treacherously (+898) [1], lap [1], rags [1], vestures [1]

900 בֹּגְדוֹת ***bōgᵉdôt***, n.pl.abst. GK: 956 [→ 898]. treachery:– treacherous [1]

901 בָּגוֹד ***bāgôd***, a. GK: 957 [→ 898]. unfaithful, pertaining to being adulterous, with the implication that the actions were deceptive and treacherous:– treacherous [2]

902 בִּגְוַי ***bigway***, n.pr.m. GK: 958. Bigvai, "*fortunate*":– Bigvai [6]

903 בִּגְתָא ***bigtā'***, n.pr.m. GK: 960 [→ 904]. Bigtha, "*gift of God*":– Bigtha [1]

904 בִּגְתָן ***bigtān*** or בִּגְתָנָא ***bigtānā'***, n.pr.m. GK: 961 & 962 [→ 903]. Bigthana, "*gift of God*":– Bigthana [1], Bigthan [1]

905 בַּד ***bad***, n.m. GK: 963 & 964 [→ 909]. part, member, limb; pole, bar; (adv.) alone, apart, only; in addition to:– alone (+3807.1) [39], only (+3807.1) [39], staves [37], beside (+4480+3807.1) [30], besides (+4480+3807.1) [13], apart (+3807.1) [11], by themselves (+3807.1) [6], by themselves (+3807.1+3963.1) [4], beside (+3807.1) [3], branches [3], by himself (+2050.2+3807.1) [3], each a like (+905+871.1) [2], strength [2], alone (+2050.2+3807.1) [1], bars [1], beside (+5921+3807.1) [1], besides (+3807.1) [1], by himself (+3807.1) [1], by themselves (+2006.1+3807.1) [1], by themselves (+3807.1+5089.1) [1], except (+3807.1) [1], myself (+2967.1) [1]

906 בַּד ***bad***, n.[m.]. GK: 965 [→ 909]. formally, a "(cut) piece (of a garment)," likely linen of the flax plant:– linen [23]

907 בַּד ***bad***, n.m. GK: 966 & 967 [→ 908]. boasting, idle talk; false prophet, with a focus on empty, idle talk:– lies [3], liars [2], parts [1]

908 בָּדָא ***bādā'***, v. GK: 968 [→ 907]. [Q] to choose; to make up, devise:– devised [1], feignest [1]

909 בָּדַד ***bādad***, v. GK: 969 [→ 905, 906, 910]. [Q] to be alone, isolated:– alone [3]

910 בָּדָד ***bādād***, n.[m.]. GK: 970 [→ 909]. alone, by oneself, apart:– alone [6], alone (+3807.1) [1], desolate [1], only (+3807.1) [1], solitarily (+3807.1) [1], solitary [1]

911 בְּדַד ***bᵉdad***, n.pr.m. GK: 971. Bedad, "*solitary*":– Bedad [2]

912 בֵּדְיָה ***bēdᵉyâ***, n.pr.m. GK: 973. Bedeiah, "*servant of Yahweh*":– Bedeiah [1]

913 בְּדִיל ***bᵉdîl***, n.[m.]. GK: 974 & 975 [→ 914]. tin, an inexpensive metal that could be used as a medium of exchange; impurities, slag, the dross of the smelting process, used as a figure of moral and ceremonial impurities:– tin [5], plummet (+68) [1]

914 בָּדַל ***bādal***, v. GK: 976 [→ 913, 915, 3995]. [N] separate oneself, be expelled; [H] to separate, sever completely, distinguish between:– separated [17], separate [7], divide [4], put difference [3], divide asunder [2], divided [2], severed [2], utterly separated (+914) [2], make a difference [1], make a separation [1], sever out [1]

915 בָּדָל ***bādāl***, n.[m.]. GK: 977 [→ 914]. piece (of an ear):– piece [1]

916 בְּדֹלַח ***bᵉdōlaḥ***, n.[m.]. GK: 978. aromatic resin; some sources: bdellium-gum (an aromatic, yellowish gum):– bdellium [2]

917 בְּדָן ***bᵉdān***, n.pr.m. GK: 979. Bedan, "*son of judgment*":– Bedan [2]

918 בָּדַק ***bādaq***, v.den. GK: 980 [→ 919; cf. 1333]. [Q] to repair, mend:– repair [1]

919 בֶּדֶק ***bedeq***, n.m. GK: 981 [→ 918]. breach (of a temple or a ship):– breaches [7], calkers (+2388) [2], breach [1]

920 בִּדְקַר ***bidqar***, n.pr.m. GK: 982 [→ 1121?+1857?]. Bidkar, "*son of Deker [piercing]*":– Bidkar [1]

921 בְּדַר ***bᵉdar*** (Aram.), v. GK: 10095 [cf. 967, 6340]. [Pa] to scatter:– scatter [1]

922 בֹּהוּ ***bōhû***, n.[m.]. GK: 983. emptiness, desolation, a void associated with chaos; "empty and void" is a state of total chaos:– void [2], emptiness [1]

923 בַּהַט ***bahaṭ***, n.[m.]. GK: 985. porphyry (or some other precious stone):– red [1]

924 בְּהִילוּ ***bᵉhîlû*** (Aram.), n.f. GK: 10096 [→ 927; cf. 926]. hurry, haste; (as adv.) immediately:– haste [1]

925 בָּהִיר ***bāhîr***, a. GK: 986 [→ 934]. bright, brilliant:– bright [1]

926 בָּהַל ***bāhal***, v. GK: 987 [→ 928; cf. 1089; cf. 927, cf. 927]. [N] to be terrified, alarmed, dismayed, bewildered; [P] to make afraid, terrify; to make haste; [Pu] to be hastened, made to hurry; to cause terror; to cause to hurry:– troubled [13], vexed [3], afraid [2], amazed [2], hasty [2], troubleth [2], trouble [2], affrighted [1], dismayed [1], gotten hastily [1], hasted [1], hastened [1], hasteth [1], make afraid [1], make haste [1], rash [1], speedily [1], speedy [1], thrust out [1], vex [1]

927 בְּהַל ***bᵉhal*** (Aram.), v. GK: 10097 & 10218 [→ 924; cf. 926]. [Pa] to frighten, terrify; [Htpe] to hurry, be at once; [Htpa] to be frightened:– troubled [6], haste [3], trouble [2]

928 בֶּהָלָה ***behālâ***, n.f. GK: 988 [→ 926; cf. 924]. sudden terror; misfortune:– trouble [2], terrors [1], terror [1]

929 בְּהֵמָה ***bᵉhēmâ***, n.f. GK: 989 [→ 930?]. beast, animal, livestock, herds, cattle:– beast [84], cattle [53], beasts [51], beasts (+929+2050.1) [2]

930 בְּהֵמוֹת ***bᵉhēmôt***, n.m. GK: 990 [→ 929?]. behemoth; sources variously identify as hippopotamus, crocodile, elephant; the plural form may indicate this is the ultimate creature, a composite description of the strongest attributes of the animal kingdom:– behemoth [1]

931 בֹּהֶן ***bōhen***, n.[f.]. GK: 984 & 991 [→ 932?]. thumb, big toe:– great toe [6], thumb [6], thumbs (+3027) [2], great toes [1], thumbs [1]

932 בֹּהַן ***bōhan***, n.pr.m. GK: 992 [→ 931?]. Bohan, "*thumb, big toe*":– Bohan [2]

933 בֹּהַק ***bōhaq***, n.m. GK: 993. harmless rash:– freckled spot [1]

934 בַּהֶרֶת ***baheret***, n.f. GK: 994 [→ 925]. spot, bright spot (on the skin):– bright spot [9], bright spots [3]

935 בּוֹא ***bô'***, v. GK: 995 [→ 872, 3996, 3997, 4126, 8393]. [Q] to come, go; [H] to bring, take; [Ho] to be brought:– come [627], came [621], brought [234], bring [222], go [88], cometh [83], enter [66], went [59], go in [58], went in [53], come in [39], entered [35], came in [31], brought in [25], bring in [23], comest [20], coming [14], goest [12], enter in [11], put [11], entering [10], carried [9], camest [8], come to pass [8], carry [7], entereth [7], get [7], goeth [7], gone [7], bringeth [6], certainly come (+935) [6], going down [6], bringing [5], cometh in [5], coming in [5], entering in [5], goeth in [5], stricken [5], attained [4], came to pass [4], down [4], go down [4], went down [4], go into [3], goeth down [3], apply [2], besieged (+4692+871.1+1886.1) [2], brought to pass [2], broughtest in [2], broughtest [2], come in (+935) [2], come upon [2], comest in [2], cometh surely to pass (+935) [2], doubtless come again (+935) [2], entered in [2], entrance [2], followeth (+310) [2], gat [2], gone in [2], indeed come (+935) [2], led [2], surely come (+935) [2], well stricken [2], abide (+871.1) [1], abideth (+871.1) [1], befell (+5921) [1], bring forth [1], bring to pass [1], bringest [1], bringing in [1], brought into [1], brought up [1], called for [1], came unto [1], came up [1], carried into [1], cause to come [1], cause to enter [1], cause to go down [1], caused to enter [1], cometh to pass [1], departed [1], eaten (+413+7130) [1], eaten up (+413+7130) [1], employ (+4480+6440) [1], enter into [1], entered into [1], entereth into [1], entereth in [1], fallen [1], fetch [1], follow (+310) [1], gave [1], get in [1], go in to [1], goest in [1], going [1], gone down [1], granted [1], had (+413) [1], have [1], invade (+871.1) [1], invaded (+871.1) [1], laid [1], lifted [1], mentioned [1], pulled in [1], pulled [1], resort [1], run down [1], runneth [1], send [1], set [1], taken [1], take [1], took in [1], way [1], went forward [1]

בּוּב ***bûb***. See 892, 5014.

936 בּוּז ***bûz***, v. GK: 996 [→ 937, 938?, 939, 940, 941]. [Q] to despise, scorn, deride:– despiseth [4], despise [4], despised [2], utterly contemned (+936) [2]

937 בּוּז ***bûz***, n.m. GK: 997 [→ 936]. contempt:– contempt [7], despised [2], contemptuously [1], shamed [1]

938 בּוּז ***bûz***, n.pr.m. GK: 998 [→ 936?]. Buz, "*contempt*":– Buz [3]

939 בּוּזָה ***bûzâ***, n.f. GK: 999 [→ 936]. contempt:– despised [1]

940 בּוּזִי ***bûzî***, a.g. GK: 1000 [→ 941; cf. 936]. Buzite, "*of Buz*":– Buzite [2]

941 בּוּזִי ***bûzî***, n.pr.m. GK: 1001 [→ 940; cf. 936]. Buzi, "*contempt*":– Buzi [1]

942 בַּוַּי ***bawway***, n.pr.m. GK: 1002 [cf. 1131]. Bavvai, cf. 1131:– Bavai [1]

943 בּוּךְ ***bûk***, v. GK: 1003 [→ 3998]. [N] to wander around, mill about; to be bewildered:– perplexed [2], entangled [1]

944 בּוּל ***bûl***, n.[m.]. GK: 1005 & 1006 [→ 8398?]. piece of wood, in context likely referring to a block of wood that has been crafted into an idol; produce, in context produce as a gift or tribute:– food [1], stock [1]

945 בּוּל ***bûl***, n.[m.]. GK: 1004. Bul (month), the eighth month of the Canaanite calendar (modern October-November):– Bul [1]

בּוּם ***bûm***. See 1116.

946 בּוּנָה ***bûnâ***, n.pr.m. GK: 1007. Bunah:– Bunah [1]

בּוּנִי ***bûnî***. See 1138.

947 בּוּס ***bûs***, v. GK: 1008 [→ 4001, 8395]. [Q, P] to trample down; loathe; [Htpol] to kick about; [Ho] to be trodden down:– tread down [4], polluted [2], loatheth [1], tread under foot [1], tread under [1], trodden down [1], trodden under feet [1], trodden under foot [1]

948 בּוּץ ***bûṣ***, n.[m.]. GK: 1009 [→ 949?, 1000]. fine linen; white linen:– fine linen [7], white linen [1]

949 בּוֹצֵץ ***bôṣēṣ***, n.pr.loc. GK: 1010 [→ 948? *or* 1206?]. Bozez, "*oozing place*":– Bozez [1]

950 בּוּקָה ***bûqâ***, n.f. GK: 1011 [→ 4003, 5802?]. pillage, that which is made desolate and emptied:– empty [1]

951 בּוֹקֵר ***bôqēr***, n.m.den. GK: 1012 [→ 1241; cf. 1239]. herdsman, usually a shepherd:– herdman [1]

952 בּוּר ***bûr***, v. GK: 1013. [Q] to conclude:– declare [1]

953 בּוֹר ***bôr***, n.m. GK: 1014 [→ 877; cf. 875, 3565, 6228]. pit, well, cistern; dungeon; a cistern is usually a shaft in the ground, hewn out of soft stone and plastered to hold water:– pit [41], dungeon [11], well [6], cistern [4], wells [3], cisterns [2], dungeon (+1004) [1], dungeon (+1004+1886.1) [1], fountain [1], pits [1]

954 בּוֹשׁ ***bôš***, v. GK: 1017 & 1018 [→ 955, 1317, 1322, 4016]. [Q] to be put to shame, be ashamed, be disgraced; [Polal] to be delayed, be long; [Htpolal] to feel ashamed; [H] to bring shame, to cause disgrace, act shamefully:– ashamed [74], confounded [29], at all ashamed (+954) [4], causeth shame [4], put to shame [3], shamed [2], bringeth to shame [1], delayed [1], done shamefully [1], greatly ashamed (+1322) [1], long [1], maketh ashamed [1], put to confusion [1], shame [1]

955 בּוּשָׁה ***bûšâ***, n.f. GK: 1019 [→ 954]. shame:– shame [4]

956 בִּית ***bît*** (Aram.), v.den. GK: 10102 [→ 1005]. [P] to spend the night:– passed the night [1]

957 בַּז **baz**, n.[m.]. GK: 1020 [→ 4122; cf. 962]. plunder, loot, despoiling:– prey [15], spoil [4], spoiled [2], take a prey (+962) [2], booty [1], take prey (+962) [1]

958 בָּזָא **bāzā'**, v. GK: 1021. [Q] to divide, likely referring to the washing out of rivers by force of the waters:– spoiled [2]

959 בָּזָה **bāzâ**, v. GK: 1022 [→ 960, 963, 964, 5240]. [Q] to despise, scorn, ridicule, show contempt for; [Qp] to be despised; [N] to be despised, be contemptible; [H] to cause to despise:– despised [26], despise [6], despiseth [4], contemptible [3], contemned [1], disdained [1], scorn [1], vile person [1]

960 בָּזֹה **bāzōh**, v.inf. GK: 1022 [→ 959]. inf. of 959: to despise, scorn, ridicule, show contempt for:– despiseth [1]

961 בִּזָּה **bizzâ**, n.f. GK: 1023 [→ 962]. plunder, booty, spoils:– spoil [6], prey [4]

962 בָּזַז **bāzaz**, v. GK: 1024 [→ 957, 961]. [Q] to plunder, loot, carry off spoils; [Qp, N, Pu] to be plundered:– spoiled [5], spoil [5], took for a prey [4], robbed [3], rob [3], take [3], prey [2], take a prey (+957) [2], take the spoil [2], utterly spoiled (+962) [2], caught [1], gathering [1], make a prey [1], prey upon [1], robbers [1], take away [1], take for a prey [1], take prey (+957) [1], taken spoil [1], took away [1], took spoil [1], took [1]

963 בִּזָּיוֹן **bizzāyôn**, n.[m.]. GK: 1025 [→ 964; cf. 959]. disrespect, contempt:– contempt [1]

964 בִּזְיוֹתְיָה **bizyôt^{e}yâ**, n.pr.loc. GK: 1026 [→ 963+3068]. Biziothiah, "*contempt of Yahweh*":– Bizjothjah [1]

965 בָּזָק **bāzāq**, n.[m.]. GK: 1027. flashes of lightning, lightning:– flash of lightning [1]

966 בֶּזֶק **bezeq**, n.pr.loc. GK: 1028 [→ 137]. Bezek, "*scattering, sowing*":– Bezek [3]

967 בָּזַר **bāzar**, v. GK: 1029 [cf. 6340; cf. 921]. [Q] to distribute; [P] to scatter:– scatter [2]

968 בִּזְּתָא **bizz^{e}tā'**, n.pr.m. GK: 1030. Biztha, "[perhaps] *eunuch* or *bound*":– Biztha [1]

969 בָּחוֹן **bāḥôn**, n.[m.]. GK: 1031 [→ 974]. tester of metals, assayer:– tower [1]

970 בָּחוּר **bāḥûr**, n.m. GK: 1033 & 1037 [→ 979]. young man, able (fighting) man; bridegroom:– young men [35], young man [5], young [2], choice [1], chosen [1]

בְּחוּרוֹת **b^{e}ḥûrôt**. See 979.

בַּחוּרִים **baḥûrîm**. See 980.

971 בַּחוּן **baḥûn**, n.[m.]. GK: 1032 & 1039 [→ 975]. siege tower, a moveable military engine used to attack a walled city:– towers [1]

972 בָּחִיר **bāḥîr**, n.m. GK: 1040 [→ 977]. chosen one, one preferred or selected by God with an implication of receiving special favor:– chosen [8], elect [4], choose [1]

973 בָּחַל **bāḥal**, v. GK: 1041 & 1042. [Q] to detest, disdain, feel an attitude of loathing; [Pu] to be gotten by greed:– abhorred [1]

974 בָּחַן **bāḥan**, v. GK: 1043 [→ 969, 976]. [Q] to test, try, probe, examine; [Qp, N, Pu] to be tested; to test and learn the genuineness of an object, fig. of assaying a metal to determine its purity or nature:– try [8], proved [6], tried [4], trieth [4], triest [3], examine [1], prove [1], tempt [1], trial [1]

975 בַּחַן **baḥan**, n.[m.]. GK: 1044 [→ 971]. watchtower:– towers [1]

976 בֹּחַן **bōḥan**, n.[m.]. GK: 1046 [→ 974]. tested (stone):– tried [1]

977 בָּחַר **bāḥar**, v. GK: 1034 & 1047 & 1048 [→ 972, 2984, 4004, 4005, 4006]. [Q] to choose, select, desire, prefer; to enter into a covenant; [Qp, N] to be chosen, choice, the best, preferred; [Pu] be joined:– chosen [78], choose [50], chose [22], choice [6], choose out [3], chooseth [3], choosest [2], chose out [2], acceptable [1], appoint [1], excellent [1], rather [1], require [1]

בָּחֻר **bāḥur**. See 970.

978 בַּחֲרֻמִי **baḥ^{a}rûmî**, a.g. GK: 1049. Baharumite:– Baharumite [1]

979 בְּחוּרוֹת **b^{e}ḥûrôt** or בְּחוּרִים **b^{e}ḥûrîm**, n.f.&m.pl.abst. GK: 1035 & 1036 [→ 970]. youth, as a state of being:– youth [2], young men [1]

980 בַּחוּרִים **baḥûrîm**, n.pr.loc. GK: 1038 [cf. 1273]. Bahurim, "*young men*":– Bahurim [5]

981 בָּטָא **bāṭā'**, v. GK: 1051 [→ 4008]. [Q, P] to speak thoughtlessly, to speak rashly, recklessly:– pronounce [1], pronouncing [1], spake unadvisedly [1], speaketh [1]

982 בָּטַח **bāṭaḥ** or בָּטֵחַ **bāṭaḥ**, v. GK: 1053 & 1054 [→ 20, 983, 985, 987, 986, 4009]. [Q] to trust, rely on, put confidence in; to stumble, fall to the ground; [Qp] to be confident; [H] to lead to believe, make trust:– trust [46], trusted [18], trusteth [14], put trust [9], trustest [6], put confidence [4], secure [4], careless [3], trustedst [3], confident [2], make trust [2], putteth trust [2], bold [1], caused to trust [1], hoped [1], make hope [1], makest to trust [1], sure [1], trusting [1]

983 בֶּטַח **beṭaḥ**, n.[m.]. GK: 1055 [→ 982]. safety, security:– safely (+3807.1) [14], safety [8], carelessly (+3807.1) [3], safely [3], careless [2], safe [2], assurance [1], boldly [1], confidence [1], hope [1], in safety [1], securely (+3807.1) [1], securely [1], secure [1], surely [1], without care [1]

984 בֶּטַח **beṭaḥ**, n.pr.loc. GK: 1056 [cf. 2880]. Betah, cf. 2875:– Betah [1]

985 בִּטְחָה **biṭḥâ**, n.f. GK: 1057 [→ 982]. trust, confidence:– confidence [1]

986 בִּטָּחוֹן **biṭṭāḥôn**, n.m. GK: 1059 [→ 982]. confidence, hope:– confidence [2], hope [1]

987 בַּטֻּחָה **baṭṭuḥâ**, n.f.pl. GK: 1058 [→ 982]. security, safety:– secure [1]

988 בָּטַל **bāṭal**, v. GK: 1060 [cf. 989]. [Q] to cease (activity):– cease [1]

989 בְּטֵל **b^{e}ṭal** (Aram.), v. GK: 10098 [cf. 988]. [P] to come to a standstill; [Pa] to stop (another):– cause to cease [2], ceased [2], hindered [1], made to cease [1]

990 בֶּטֶן **beṭen**, n.f. GK: 1061. inmost part, viscera: abdomen, belly, stomach, womb; by extension: the inner person, the heart, the seat of emotion, thought, and desire:– womb [31], belly [30], body [8], as soon as born (+4480) [1], within (+871.1) [1], within [1]

991 בֶּטֶן **beṭen**, n.pr.loc. GK: 1062 [cf. 992?]. Beten, "*womb, bowels*":– Beten [1]

992 בָּטְנָה **boṭnâ**, n.[m.]pl. GK: 1063 [cf. 991?, 993?]. pistachio nut:– nuts [1]

993 בְּטֹנִים **b^{e}ṭōnîm**, n.pr.loc. GK: 1064 [cf. 992?]. Betonim, "*pistachio nuts*":– Betonim [1]

994 בִּי **bî**, pt.entreaty. GK: 1065. O!, please!:– O [11], alas [1]

995 בִּין **bîn**, v. GK: 1067 [→ 996, 998, 2985?, 8394]. [Q] to understand, discern, realize; be prudent; [N] to be discerning, be understanding; [Pol] to care for; to have skill, insight; to instruct, explain; [Htpolel/Htpolal] to look closely, consider with full attention, ponder:– understand [36], understanding [18], consider [17], understood [11], prudent [8], give understanding [5], hath understanding [5], understandeth [5], regard [4], make to understand [3], perceived [3], perceive [3], wise [3], caused to understand [2], consider diligently (+995) [2], considering [2], discern [2], discreet [2], giveth understanding [2], instructed [2], taught [2], understandest [2], attended [1], cause to understand [1], consider perfectly (+998) [1], considered (+413) [1], considereth [1], cunning [1], dealt wisely [1], diligently consider [1], directeth [1], discerned [1], eloquent [1], feel [1], had understanding [1], have understanding [1], having understanding [1], informed [1], instruct [1], intelligence [1], know [1], looketh well [1], make understand [1], mark [1], perceiveth [1], regardest [1], regardeth [1], skilful [1], skill [1], teacher [1], think [1], understand (+3045) [1], viewed [1]

996 בַּיִן **bayin**, subst. & pp. GK: 1068 [→ 1143; cf. 995; cf. 997]. between; separate from; whether ... or:– between [194], among [28], betwixt [14], at even (+6153+1886.1) [6], at [6], from [4], in [4], whether [3], among (+413) [2], with [2], among (+4480) [1], among (+5921) [1], among (+871.1) [1], amongst [1], asunder [1], midst [1], once in [1], out of (+4480) [1], part (+5337) [1], spake unto [1], within [1]

997 בֵּין **bên** (Aram.), pp. GK: 10099 [cf. 996]. between, among:– among [1], between [1]

998 בִּינָה **bînâ**, n.f. GK: 1069 [→ 995; cf. 999]. understanding, insight, discernment, good sense, wisdom, usually referring to the wisdom that responds to the Lord and his instruction:– understanding [30], wisdom [2], come to understanding (+3045) [1], consider perfectly (+995) [1], had understanding (+3045) [1], knowledge [1], meaning [1], understand [1]

999 בִּינָה **bînâ** (Aram.), n.f. GK: 10100 [cf. 998]. discernment, insight:– understanding [1]

1000 בֵּיצָה **bêṣâ**, n.f. GK: 1070 [→ 948]. egg:– eggs [6]

1001 בִּירָה **bîrâ** (Aram.), n.f. GK: 10101 [cf. 1002]. citadel, fortress:– palace [1]

1002 בִּירָה **bîrâ**, n.f. GK: 1072 [cf. 1003; cf. 1001]. citadel, fort, palatial structure:– palace [16]

1003 בִּירָנִיָּה **bîrāniyyâ**, n.f. GK: 1073 [cf. 1002]. fortified place:– castles [2]

1004 בַּיִת **bayit**, n.m. GK: 1074 & 1428 [→ 1006, 1055; cf. 1005]. house, home; of royalty: palace; of deity: temple; a specific part of a house: room; place; by extension: household, family, clan, tribe; woven garment:– house [1766], houses [118], household [47], home [25], within (+4480) [14], temple [11], places [9], prison (+5470+1886.1) [8], households [7], place [7], inward (+1886.5) [5], prison (+3608+1886.1) [4], families (+1) [2], families [2], prison (+3608) [2], prison (+3628+1886.1) [2], within (+4480+1886.1) [2], contain [1], court [1], door [1], dungeon (+953) [1], dungeon (+953+1886.1) [1], family [1], hangings [1], homeborn (+3211) [1], inside [1], inward (+4480+1886.1) [1], inward [1], palace [1], prison (+612+1886.1) [1], prison (+631+1886.1) [1], prison (+6486+1886.1) [1], steward (+834+5921) [1], storehouse (+214) [1], tablets (+5315) [1], ward (+4931) [1], web [1], winterhouse (+2779) [1], within (+1886.1+3807.1) [1], within (+1886.5) [1], within (+4480+1886.5) [1], within (+4480+3807.1) [1], within (+871.1+1886.1) [1], within [1], without (+413+4480) [1]

1005 בַּיִת **bayit** (Aram.), n.m. GK: 10103 [→ 956; cf. 1004]. a place of residence: house, home; residence of royalty: palace; residence of God or a god: temple:– house [42], houses [2]

1006 בַּיִת **bayit**, n.m. GK: 1074 [→ 1004]. same as 1004: Bayit, *"house"*:– Bajith [1]

1007 בֵּית אָוֶן **bêt 'āwen**, n.pr.loc. GK: 1077 [→ 1004+205]. Beth Aven, *"house of idolatry"*:– Beth-aven [7]

1008 בֵּית־אֵל **bêt-'ēl**, n.pr.loc. GK: 1078 [→ 1004+410]. Bethel, *"temple [house] of God [El]"*:– Beth-el [66]

1009 בֵּית אַרְבֵאל **bêt 'arbē'l**, n.pr.loc. GK: 1079 [→ 1004]. Beth Arbel, *"house of Arbel"*:– Beth-arbel [1]

1010 בֵּית בַּעַל מְעוֹן **bêt ba'al mᵉ'ôn** or בֵּית מְעוֹן **bêt mᵉ'ôn**, n.pr.loc. GK: 1081 & 1110 [→ 1004+1186]. Beth Baal Meon, *"house of Baal Meon"*; Beth Meon, *"house of habitation"*:– Beth-baal-meon [1], Beth-meon [1]

1011 בֵּית בִּרְאִי **bêt bir'î**, n.pr.loc. GK: 1082 [→ 1004]. Beth Biri, *"house of Biri* or *den of a lioness"*:– Beth-birei [1]

1012 בֵּית בָּרָה **bêt bārâ**, n.pr.loc. GK: 1083 [→ 1004]. Beth Barah, *"house of Barah [the river ford]"*:– Beth-barah [2]

1013 בֵּית־גָּדֵר **bêt-gādēr**, n.pr.loc. GK: 1084 [→ 1004+1445; cf. 1451]. Beth Gader, *"house of Gader* or *site of a stone hedge"*:– Beth-gader [1]

1014 בֵּית גָּמוּל **bêt gāmûl**, n.pr.loc. GK: 1085 [→ 1004+1580]. Beth Gamul, *"house of recompense"*:– Beth-gamul [1]

1015 בֵּית דִּבְלָתַיִם **bêt diblātayim**, n.pr.loc. GK: 1086 [→ 1004]. Beth Diblathaim, *"house of Diblathaim"*:– Beth-diblathaim [1]

1016 בֵּית־דָּגוֹן **bêt-dāgôn**, n.pr.loc. GK: 1087 [→ 1004+1712]. Beth Dagon, *"temple [house] of Dagon"*:– Beth-dagon [2]

1017 בֵּית הָאֱלִי **bêt hā'ᵉlî**, a.g. GK: 1088 [→ 1004+430; cf. 433]. the Bethelite, *"of Bethel"*:– Bethelite [1]

1018 בֵּית הָאֵצֶל **bêt hā'ēṣel**, n.pr.loc. GK: 1089 [→ 1004+1886.1]. Beth Ezel, *"house of Ezel* or *site nearby"*:– Beth-ezel [1]

1019 בֵּית הַגִּלְגָּל **bêt haggilgāl**, n.pr.loc. GK: 1090 [→ 1004+1886.1+1537]. Beth Gilgal:–

1020 בֵּית הַיְשִׁימוֹת **bêt hayᵉšîmôt**, n.pr.loc. GK: 1093 [→ 1004]. Beth Jeshimoth, *"house of Jeshimoth* or *site of desolation"*:– Beth-jeshimoth [3], Beth-jesimoth [1]

1021 בֵּית־הַכֶּרֶם **bêt-hakkerem**, n.pr.loc. GK: 1094 [→ 1004]. Beth Hakkerem, *"house of Hakkerem* or *site of vineyard"*:– Beth-haccerem [2]

1022 בֵּית־הַלַּחְמִי **bêt-hallaḥmî**, a.g. GK: 1095 [→ 1004]. the Bethlehemite, *"of Bethlehem"*:– Beth-lehemite [4]

1023 בֵּית הַמֶּרְחָק **bêt hammerḥāq**, n.pr.loc. GK: 1092 [→ 1004+1886.1+7368]. Beth Hamerhaq:–

1024 בֵּית־הַמַּרְכָּבוֹת **bêt-hammarkābôt** or בֵּית מַרְכָּבוֹת **bêt markābôt**, n.pr.loc. GK: 1096 & 1112 [→ 1004]. Beth Marcaboth, *"site [house] of Marcaboth [chariots]"*:– Beth-marcaboth [2]

1025 בֵּית הָעֵמֶק **bêt hā'ēmeq**, n.pr.loc. GK: 1097 [→ 1004+1886.1+6010]. Beth Emek, *"house of Emek* or *site of the valley"*:– Beth-emek [1]

1026 בֵּית הָעֲרָבָה **bêt hā'ᵃrābâ**, n.pr.loc. GK: 1098 [→ 1004]. Beth Arabah, *"house of Arabah [desert, plain]"*:– Beth-arabah [3]

1027 בֵּית הָרָם **bêt hārām**, n.pr.loc. GK: 1099 [→ 1004]. Beth Haram:– Beth-aram [1]

1028 בֵּית הָרָן **bêt hārān**, n.pr.loc. GK: 1100 [→ 1004+2039]. Beth Haran, *"house of the mountaineer"*:– Beth-haran [1]

1029 בֵּית הַשִּׁטָּה **bêt haššiṭṭâ**, n.pr.loc. GK: 1101 [→ 1004]. Beth Shittah, *"house of Shittah [acacias]"*:– Beth-shittah [1]

1030 בֵּית־שִׁמְשִׁי **bêt-šimšî**, a.g. GK: 1128 [→ 1004]. of Beth Shemesh:– Beth-shemite [2]

1031 בֵּית־חָגְלָה **bêt-ḥoglâ**, n.pr.loc. GK: 1102 [→ 1004+2295]. Beth Hoglah, *"house of Hoglah* or *site of the partridge"*:– Beth-hoglah [2], Beth-hogla [1]

1032 בֵּית־חוֹרוֹן **bêt-ḥôrôn**, n.pr.loc. GK: 1103 [→ 1004]. Beth Horon, *"house of Horon* or *site of ravine"*:– Beth-horon [14]

בֵּית חָנָן **bêt ḥānān**. See 358.

1033 בֵּית כָּר **bêt kār**, n.pr.loc. GK: 1105 [→ 1004]. Beth Car, *"site [house] of a lamb"*:– Beth-car [1]

1034 בֵּית לְבָאוֹת **bêt lᵉbā'ôt**, n.pr.loc. GK: 1106 [→ 1004+3822]. Beth Lebaoth, *"house of Lebaoth* or *den of the lioness"*:– Beth-lebaoth [1]

1035 בֵּית לֶחֶם **bêt leḥem**, n.pr.loc. GK: 1107 [→ 1004+3899]. Bethlehem, *"house of bread; [poss.] temple [house] of Lakhmu"*:– Beth-lehem [31], Beth-lehem-judah (+3063) [10]

1036 בֵּית לְעַפְרָה **bêt lᵉ'aprâ**, n.pr.loc. GK: 1108 [→ 1004]. Beth Ophrah, *"house of Ophrah* or *house of dust"*:– house of Aphrah [1]

1037 בֵּית מִלּוֹא **bêt millô'**, n.pr.loc. GK: 1109 [→ 1004+4390]. Beth Millo, *"house of Millo* or *site of earth fill"*:–

1038 בֵּית מַעֲכָה **bêt maᵃkâ**, n.pr.loc. GK: 1111 [→ 1004+4601]. Beth Maacah:– Beth-maachah [2]

1039 בֵּית נִמְרָה **bêt nimrâ**, n.pr.loc. GK: 1113 [→ 1004+5247]. Beth Nimrah, *"house of Nimrah [spotted leopard]; house of a basin of clear, limpid water"*:– Beth-nimrah [2]

1040 בֵּית עֶדֶן **bêt 'eden**, n.pr.loc. GK: 1114 [→ 1004+5729]. Beth Eden, *"house of Eden; garden place"*:–

1041 בֵּית־עַזְמָוֶת **bêt-'azmāwet**, n.pr.loc. GK: 1115 [→ 1004+5820]. Beth Azmaveth, *"strong of death; house of Azmaveth [camel fodder]"*:– Beth-azmaveth [1]

1042 בֵּית־עֲנוֹת **bêt-'ᵃnôt**, n.pr.loc. GK: 1116 [→ 1004+6067]. Beth Anoth, *"house of Anath [plural]"*:– Beth-anoth [1]

1043 בֵּית־עֲנָת **bêt-'ᵃnāt**, n.pr.loc. GK: 1117 [→ 1004+6067]. Beth Anath, *"house of Anath"*:– Beth-anath [3]

1044 בֵּית־עֵקֶד **bêt-'ēqed**, n.pr.loc. GK: 1118 [→ 1004]. Beth Eked:– shearing [2]

1045 בֵּית עַשְׁתָּרוֹת **bêt 'aštārôt**, n.pr.loc.?. GK: 1119 [→ 1004+6252]. Beth Ashtaroth, *"temple of the Ashtoreths"*:–

1046 בֵּית פֶּלֶט **bêt pelet**, n.pr.loc. GK: 1120 [→ 1004+6404]. Beth Pelet, *"house of Pelet [escape]"*:– Beth-palet [1], Beth-phelet [1]

1047 בֵּית פְּעוֹר **bêt pᵉ'ôr**, n.pr.loc. GK: 1121 [→ 1004+6465]. Beth Peor, *"house of Peor"*:– Beth-peor [4]

1048 בֵּית פַּצֵּץ **bêt paṣṣēṣ**, n.pr.loc. GK: 1122 [→ 1004]. Beth Pazzez:– Beth-pazzez [1]

1049 בֵּית־צוּר **bêt-ṣûr**, n.pr.loc. GK: 1123 [→ 1004+6697]. Beth Zur, *"cliff house"*:– Beth-zur [4]

1050 בֵּית־רְחוֹב **bêt-rᵉḥôb**, n.pr.loc. GK: 1124 [→ 1004+7339]. Beth Rehob, *"house of Rehob [main street, market]"*:– Beth-rehob [2]

1051 בֵּית רָפָא **bêt rāpā'**, n.pr.[loc.?]. GK: 1125 [→ 1004+7495]. Beth Rapha, *"house of Rapha [healing]"*:– Beth-rapha [1]

1052 בֵּית־שְׁאָן **bêt-šᵉ'ān**, n.pr.loc. GK: 1126 [→ 1004]. Beth Shan, *"site [house] of Shan [repose]"*:– Beth-shean [6], Beth-shan [3]

1053 בֵּית שֶׁמֶשׁ **bêt šemeš**, n.pr.loc. GK: 1127 [→ 1004+8121]. Beth Shemesh, *"temple [house] of Shemesh"*:– Beth-shemesh [21]

1054 בֵּית־תַּפּוּחַ **bêt-tappûaḥ**, n.pr.loc. GK: 1130 [→ 1004+8598]. Beth Tappuah, *"house of Tappuah [apricot; apple]"*:– Beth-tappuah [1]

1055 בִּיתָן **bîtān**, n.[m.]. GK: 1131 [→ 1004]. dwelling place, of royalty: palace, with a possible focus on the inner parts of the palace complex:– palace [3]

1056 בָּכָא **bākā'**, n.pr.loc. GK: 1133 [→ 1058]. Baca, *"balsam tree* or *weeping"*:– Baca [1]

1057 בָּכָא **bākā'**, n.[m.]. GK: 1132 [→ 1058]. balsam tree; some sources: baka-shrub:– mulberry trees [4]

1058 בָּכָה **bākâ**, v. GK: 1134 [→ 1057, 1056, 1059, 1065, 1068; cf. 1066]. [Q] to weep, wail, cry, sob, mourn; [P] to weep for, mourn for; this can refer to ritual mourning as well as personal sorrow:– wept [51], weep [26], weeping [8], bewail [3], weepeth [3], wept sore (+1065+1419) [3], mourned [2], weep at all (+1058) [2], weep more (+1058) [2], weep sore (+1058) [2], weepeth sore (+1058) [2], wept sore (+1058) [2], bewail (+5921) [1], bewailed [1], complain [1], made lamentation [1], tears [1], weepest [1], wept sore (+1059) [1], wept sore (+1065) [1]

1059 בֶּכֶה **bekeh**, n.[m.]. GK: 1135 [→ 1058]. weeping:– wept sore (+1058) [1]

1060 בְּכֹר **bᵉkōr**, n.m. GK: 1147 [→ 1069]. firstborn, first male offspring (human or animal), the oldest son, with associative meanings of honor, status, prominence, and privileges of inheritance to the firstborn; by extension: one in a special relationship with God:– firstborn [102], firstling [9], eldest [3], eldest son [2], firstlings [1]

1061 בִּכּוּרִים ***bikkûrîm***, n.m. GK: 1137 [→ 1069]. firstfruits, first ripened produce:– firstfruits [14], first ripe [2], firstripe figs [1], hasty fruit [1]

1062 בְּכֹרָה ***b^ekōrâ***, n.f. GK: 1148 [→ 1069]. birthright, rights of the firstborn:– birthright [9], firstlings [5], firstborn [1]

1063 בִּכּוּרָה ***bikkûrâ***, n.f. GK: 1136 [→ 1069, 1073]. same as 1073: early ripened fruit, usually ripening in June (late fruit ripens in August):– firstripe fruit [1], firstripe [1]

1064 בְּכוֹרַת ***b^ekôrat***, n.pr.m. GK: 1138 [→ 1069]. Becorath, *"firstborn"*:– Bechorath [1]

1065 בְּכִי ***b^ekî***, n.m. GK: 1140 [→ 1058]. weeping:– weeping [20], wept sore (+1058+1419) [3], continual weeping (+1065) [2], weep [2], overflowing [1], wept aloud (+5414+6963+871.1) [1], wept sore (+1058) [1]

1066 בֹּכִים ***bōkîm***, n.pr.loc. GK: 1141 [cf. 1058]. Bokim, *"weepings"*:– Bochim [2]

1067 בְּכִירָה ***b^ekîrâ***, n.f. GK: 1142 [→ 1069]. first born (daughter):– firstborn [6]

1068 בְּכִית ***b^ekît***, n.f. GK: 1143 [→ 1058]. mourning, weeping:– mourning [1]

1069 בָּכַר ***bākar***, v. GK: 1144 [→ 1061, 1063, 1064, 1067, 1070, 1071, 1060, 1062, 1072, 1074, 1076, 1075]. [P] bear early fruit; give the rights of the firstborn; [Pu] be made a firstborn (dedication); [H] to bear one's first child:– bring forth new fruit [1], bringeth forth first child [1], firstling [1], make firstborn [1]

1070 בֵּכֶר ***bēker***, n.f. GK: 1145 [→ 1071; cf. 1069]. young bull camel:– dromedaries [1]

1071 בֶּכֶר ***beker***, n.pr.m. GK: 1146 [→ 1070, 1076, 1075; cf. 1069]. Beker, *"young male camel"*:– Becher [5]

1072 בִּכְרָה ***bikrâ***, n.f. GK: 1149 [→ 1069]. young cow-camel (having given birth to her first calf):– dromedary [1]

בְּכֹרָה ***b^ekōrâ***. See 1062.

1073 בִּכּוּרָה ***bikkûrâ***, n.f. GK: 1136 [→ 1063]. same as 1063: early ripened fruit, usually ripening in June (late fruit ripens in August):– first ripe [1]

1074 בֹּכְרוּ ***bōk^erû***, n.pr.m. GK: 1150 [→ 1069]. Bokeru, *"his first born"*:– Bocheru [2]

1075 בִּכְרִי ***bikrî***, n.pr.m. *or* a.g. GK: 1152 [→ 1071; cf. 1069]. Bicri, *"firstborn"*:– Bichri [8]

1076 בַּכְרִי ***bakrî***, a.g. GK: 1151 [→ 1071; cf. 1069]. Bekerite, *"of Beker"*:– Bachrites [1]

1077 בַּל ***bal***, adv. GK: 1153 [→ 61, 1107; cf. 1086]. no, not, cannot, never:– not [52], nor (+2050.1) [3], no [3], cannot [2], neither (+2050.1) [2], lest [1], never (+5331+3807.1) [1], never (+5769+3807.1) [1], none [1], nothing (+4100) [1], nothing [1]

1078 בֵּל ***bēl***, n.pr.m. GK: 1155 [→ 1112, 1085, 1095, 1114]. Bel, *"Bel"*:– Bel [3]

1079 בָּל ***bāl*** (Aram.), n.[m.]. GK: 10104. heart, mind:– heart [1]

1080 בְּלָא ***b^elâ*** (Aram.), v. GK: 10106 [cf. 1086]. [Pa] to oppress, wear down:– wear out [1]

1081 בַּלְאֲדָן ***bal'^adān***, n.pr.m. GK: 1156 [→ 4757]. Baladan:– Baladan [2]

1082 בָּלַג ***bālag***, v. GK: 1158 [→ 1083, 1084]. [H] to flash (with a focus on suddenness); by extension: to smile, rejoice, gleam, have a cheerful attitude:– comfort [1], recover strength [1], strengtheneth [1], take comfort [1]

1083 בִּלְגָּה ***bilgâ***, n.pr.m. GK: 1159 [→ 1082]. Bilgah, *"gleam, smile"*:– Bilgah [3]

1084 בִּלְגַּי ***bilgay***, n.pr.m. GK: 1160 [→ 1082]. Bilgai, *"gleam, smile"*:– Bilgai [1]

1085 בִּלְדַּד ***bildad***, n.pr.m. GK: 1161 [→ 1078?+1730]. Bildad, *"Bel has loved"*:– Bildad [5]

1086 בָּלָה ***bālâ***, v. GK: 1162 [→ 61, 1077, 1087, 1094, 1097, 1107, 1115, 8399; cf. 1080]. [Q] to wear out, waste away; [P] to enjoy, use to the full; to decay; to grow old; to oppress:– waxed old [4], wax old [3], waxen old [2], become old [1], consumeth [1], consume [1], long enjoy [1], made old [1], waste [1]

1087 בָּלֶה ***bāleh***, a. GK: 1165 [→ 1086]. old, worn-out:– old [5]

1088 בָּלָה ***bālâ***, n.pr.loc. GK: 1163 [cf. 1090]. Balah, *"old, worn out"*:– Balah [1]

1089 בָּלַהּ ***bālah***, v. GK: 1164 [→ 1090?, 1091; cf. 926]. [P] to be troubled:–

1090 בִּלְהָה ***bilhâ***, n.pr.f. & loc. GK: 1167 & 1168 [→ 1089?, 1172; cf. 1088]. Bilhah:– Bilhah [11]

1091 בַּלָּהָה ***ballāhâ***, n.f. GK: 1166 [→ 1089]. sudden terror, horrible end; in some contexts a horrible end refers to death:– terrors [6], terror [3], trouble [1]

1092 בִּלְהָן ***bilhān***, n.pr.m. GK: 1169. Bilhan, *"foolish"*:– Bilhan [4]

1093 בְּלוֹ ***b^elô*** (Aram.), n.[m.]. GK: 10107. tribute, tax:– tribute [3]

1094 בְּלוֹי ***b^elôy***, n.[m.]. GK: 1170 [→ 1086]. old, worn-out (things):– old [3]

1095 בֵּלְטְשַׁאצַּר ***bēlṭ^eša'ṣṣar***, n.pr.m. GK: 1171 [→ 1078; cf. 1096]. Belteshazzar, *"protect his life"*:– Belteshazzar [2]

1096 בֵּלְטְשַׁאצַּר ***bēlṭ^eša'ṣṣar*** (Aram.), n.pr.m. GK: 10108 [cf. 1113; cf. 1095]. Belteshazzar, *"protect his life"*:– Belteshazzar [8]

1097 בְּלִי ***b^elî***, subst. GK: 1172 [→ 1099, 1100; cf. 1086]. lacking, without; nothing:– not [10], without [9], no [5], without (+4480) [5], lack [3], none [3], none (+4480) [2], unwittingly (+1847+871.1) [2], without (+3807.1) [2], base men (+8034) [1], cannot [1], corruption [1], for want of (+4480) [1], ignorantly (+1847+871.1) [1], never (+5769+3807.1) [1], no (+369) [1], no (+4480) [1], no man [1], none (+376) [1], nothing (+3605) [1], nothing (+4100) [1], so long as endureth (+5704) [1], so that (+834+4480) [1], unawares (+1847+871.1) [1], want [1], without (+3509.1) [1], without (+871.1) [1]

1098 בְּלִיל ***b^elîl***, n.m. GK: 1173. fodder, mash, fermented matter:– corn [1], fodder [1], provender [1]

1099 בְּלִימָה ***b^elîmâ***, n.[m.]. GK: 1174 [→ 1097+4100]. nothing:–

1100 בְּלִיַּעַל ***b^eliyya'al***, n.[m.]. GK: 1175 [→ 1097+3276]. wicked one, vile one, evil one, worthless one, transliterated "Belial"; A "son of Belial" or "man of Belial" is a troublemaker and scoundrel:– Belial [16], wicked [5], ungodly men [2], ungodly [2], evil [1], naughty [1]

1101 בָּלַל ***bālal***, v. GK: 1176 [→ 7642?, 8397, 8400; cf. 1104?]. [Q] to confuse; give fodder, feed; pour upon; [Qp] to mix (with); [Htpolal] to be thrown about, shaken back and forth:– mingled [37], confound [2], anointed [1], gave provender [1], mixed [1], tempered [1]

1102 בָּלַם ***bālam***, v. GK: 1178. [Q] to be controlled, in check:– held in [1]

1103 בָּלַס ***bālas***, v.den. GK: 1179. [Q] to nip (scratch open) unripe sycamore-fig fruit, so as to promote ripening and make more palatable:– gatherer [1]

1104 בָּלַע ***bāla'***, v. GK: 1180 & 1181 & 1182 [→ 1105, 1106, 1108, 1109, 2991?; cf. 1101?]. [Q] to swallow up; [N] to be swallowed; be befuddled, confused; [P] to swallow up, gulp down, devour, consume; to communicate, spread abroad; confuse, turn away; [Pu] be swallowed up, be devoured; be communicated; to be led astray; [Ht] to be confused thoroughly:– swallowed up [17], swallow up [11], destroy [7], devoured [2], devoureth [2], swallow down [2], at wit's end (+2451+3605) [1], covered [1], destroyed [1], destroying [1], eateth up [1], spendeth up [1], swallowed down [1], swallowed [1]

1105 בֶּלַע ***bela'***, n.[m.]. GK: 1183 & 1184 [→ 1104]. what is swallowed; harmful, with a likely focus on destruction, fig. of what is greedily swallowed up:– devouring [1], swallowed up [1]

1106 בֶּלַע ***bela'***, n.pr.m. & loc. GK: 1185 & 1186 [→ 1104]. Bela, *"swallower, devourer"*:– Bela [13], Belah [1]

1107 בַּלְעֲדֵי ***bal'^adê***, adv. GK: 1187 [→ 1077+5704]. apart from, except for, besides:– beside (+4480) [3], save (+4480) [3], without (+4480) [3], besides (+4480) [2], not [2], besides [1], else beside (+4480+5750) [1], save [1], without [1]

1108 בַּלְעִי ***bal'î***, a.g. GK: 1188 [→ 1104]. Belaite, *"of Bela"*:– Belaites [1]

1109 בִּלְעָם ***bil'ām*** or בִּלְעָם ***bil'ām***, n.pr.m. & loc. GK: 1189 & 1190 [→ 1104]. Balaam, "[poss.] *Baal [lord] of the people;* [poss.] *the clan brings forth; devourer, glutton"*; Bileam, *"[gift] brought to the people"*:– Balaam [57], Balaam's [3], Bileam [1]

1110 בָּלַק ***bālaq***, v. GK: 1191 [→ 1111]. [Q] to devastate; [Pu] to be stripped, devastated:– maketh waste [1], waste [1]

1111 בָּלָק ***bālāq***, n.pr.m. GK: 1192 [→ 1110]. Balak, *"devastator"*:– Balak [42], Balak's [1]

1112 בֵּלְשַׁאצַּר ***bēl'šaṣṣar***, n.pr.m. GK: 1157 [→ 1078; cf. 1113]. Belshazzar, *"Bel protect the king"*:– Belshazzar [1]

1113 בֵּלְאשַׁצַּר ***bēl'šaṣṣar*** (Aram.), n.pr.m. GK: 10105 & 10109 [cf. 1112]. Belshazzar, *"Bel protect the king"*:– Belshazzar [7]

1114 בִּלְשָׁן ***bilšān***, n.pr.m. GK: 1193 [→ 1078]. Bilshan, *"their Bel [lord]"*:– Bilshan [2]

1115 בִּלְתִּי ***biltî***, subst. & adv. & pp. GK: 1194 [→ 1086]. no, not, without; except for; besides:– not [56], none [10], no [6], beside [3], nothing [3], save [3], without [3], except [2], from (+3807.1) [2], lest (+3807.1) [2], none (+376) [2], nor (+2050.1+3807.1) [2], not (+3807.1) [2], but (+518) [1], but [1], cannot [1], continual (+5627) [1], except (+518) [1], lest that (+3807.1) [1], neither (+2050.1) [1], neither [1], no (+3605) [1], no (+3807.1) [1], no more [1], nothing else (+369) [1], that no more (+3807.1) [1], that not (+3807.1) [1], unsatiable (+7654) [1], without (+3807.1) [1]

1116 בָּמָה ***bāmâ***, n.f. GK: 1195 [→ 173?, 1117, 1120]. high place, worship shrine (an elevated place, often artificial, for the worship of a god); heights:– high places [83], high place [18], heights [1], waves [1]

1117 בָּמָה ***bāmâ***, n.pr.loc. GK: 1196 [→ 1116]. Bamah, "*high place*":– Bamah [1]

1118 בִּמְהָל ***bimhāl***, n.pr.m. GK: 1197 [→ 1121+4107]. Bimhal, "*son of circumcision*":– Bimhal [1]

1119 בְּמוֹ ***b^{e}mô***, pp. GK: 1198 [→ 871.1]. by, with, in:– in [2], with [2], for [1], into [1], privily (+652) [1], through [1]

1120 בָּמוֹת ***bāmôt*** or בָּמוֹת בַּעַל ***bāmôt baʿal***, n.pr.loc. GK: 1199 & 1200 [→ 1116+1167]. Bamoth, "*high places [for cultic worship]*", Bamoth Baal, "*high places for Baal [worship]*":– Bamoth [2], Bamoth-baal [1]

1121 בֵּן ***bēn***, n.m. GK: 1201 [→ 1122, 1150; cf. 1129, 1248; cf. 1247 (also used with compound proper names)]. son, child (of either gender), descendant (in any generation), offspring (human or animal); by extension: a term of endearment; one of a class or kind or nation or family. A "son of man" is a "human being" (Nu 23:9), a term that often assumes messianic significance (Ps 8):– son [1906], children [1543], sons [1030], old [135], young [52], first year (+8141) [42], son's [21], sons' [21], men [17], Ammonites (+5983) [15], children's [15], child [10], first [9], strangers (+5236) [6], people (+5971) [5], sons' (+3807.1) [5], stranger (+5236) [5], Assyrians (+804) [4], valiant (+2428) [4], Babylonians (+894) [3], age [3], bullock (+1241) [3], Beno [2], calf (+1241) [2], calves (+1241) [2], fruitful bough (+6509) [2], hostages (+8594) [2], in a night (+3915) [2], lambs (+6629) [2], man (+120) [2], man [2], men (+120) [2], nephews (+1121) [2], ones [2], surely die (+4194) [2], whelps [2], young ones [2], Ahohite (+266) [1], Benjamite (+376+3227) [1], Benjamite [1], Egyptians (+4714) [1], Gileadites (+1569) [1], Grecians (+3125) [1], Hachmonite (+2453) [1], Levites (+3878) [1], Muth-labben (+4192+1886.1+3807.1) [1], afflicted (+6040) [1], appointed to death (+8546) [1], appointed to destruction (+2475) [1], appointed to die (+8546) [1], arrow (+7198) [1], arrows[s] [1], born [1], branch [1], breed [1], calves (+1241) [1], children (+3807.1) [1], children's (+3807.1) [1], colts [1], colt [1], common [1], corn [1], father[s] [1], foal [1], high[s] (+376) [1], kids (+5795) [1], low[s] (+120) [1], meet for the war (+2428) [1], men (+376) [1], men of high degree (+376) [1], men of low degree (+120) [1], mighty (+410) [1], one born [1], one [1], people [1], rebels (+4805) [1], robbers (+6530) [1], soldiers [1], sparks (+7565) [1], steward (+4943) [1], stranger's (+5236) [1], strong (+2428) [1], them[s] [1], valiantest (+2428) [1], very fruitful (+8081) [1], worthy to die (+4194) [1], worthy [1], youths [1]

1122 בֵּן ***bēn***, n.pr.m. GK: 1202 [→ 1121]. Ben:– Ben [1]

1123 בֵּן ***bēn*** (Aram.), n.m. GK: 10110. a direct descendant, human or animal, male or of either gender: son, child; a distant descendant: grandson, grandchild, descendant; fig., one of a class or kind:– children [6], sons [3], captives (+1547) [1], young [1]

1124 בְּנָה ***b^{e}nâ*** (Aram.), v. GK: 10111 [→ 1147; cf. 1129]. [P] to build, construct, rebuild; [Pp] to be built; [Htpe] to be built, be constructed, be rebuilt:– builded [10], build [7], building [3], built [1], make [1]

1125 בֶּן־אֲבִינָדָב ***ben-'^{a}bînādāb***, n.pr.m. GK: 1203 [→ 1121+1+5068]. Ben-Abinadab, "*son of Abinadab*":–

1126 בֶּן־אוֹנִי ***ben-'ônî***, n.pr.m. GK: 1204 [→ 1121+205]. Ben-Oni, "*son of my sorrow*":– Ben-oni [1]

1127 בֶּן־גֶּבֶר ***ben-geber***, n.pr.m. GK: 1205 [→ 1121+1397]. Ben-Geber, "*son of strength*":–

1128 בֶּן־דֶּקֶר ***ben-deqer***, n.pr.[loc.?]. GK: 1206 [→ 1121+1856]. Ben-Deker, "*son of Deker [pierces]*":–

1129 בָּנָה ***bānâ***, v. GK: 1215 [→ 1131, 1137, 1138, 1140, 1146, 4011, 8403; cf. 1121, 1323; cf. 1124 (also used with compound proper names)]. [Q] to make, build, rebuild, establish; [Qp, N] to be built, established:– built [152], build [132], builded [35], building [13], builders [10], build up [7], buildeth [7], buildest [3], built up [3], made [3], in building [2], repaired [2], set up [2], surely built (+1129) [2], buildedst [1], have children [1], obtain children [1]

1130 בֶּן־הֲדַד ***ben-h^{a}dad***, n.pr.m. GK: 1207 [→ 1121+1908]. Ben-Hadad, "*son of Hadad*":– Ben-hadad [25]

1131 בִּנּוּי ***binnûy***, n.pr.m. GK: 1218 [→ 1129; cf. 942]. Binnui, "*son*":– Binnui [7]

1132 בֶּן־זוֹחֵת ***ben-zôḥēt***, n.pr.m. GK: 1209 [→ 1121+2105]. Ben-Zoheth, "*son of Zoheth*":– Ben-zoheth [1]

1133 בֶּן־חוּר ***ben-ḥûr***, n.pr.m. GK: 1210 [→ 1121+2354]. Ben-Hur, "*son of Hur*":–

1134 בֶּן־חַיִל ***ben-ḥayil***, n.pr.m. GK: 1211 [→ 1121+2428]. Ben-Hail, "*son of strength*":– Ben-hail [1]

1135 בֶּן־חָנָן ***ben-ḥānān***, n.pr.m. GK: 1212 [→ 1121+2605]. Ben-Hanan, "*son of grace*":– Ben-hanan [1]

1136 בֶּן־חֶסֶד ***ben-ḥesed***, n.pr.m. GK: 1213 [→ 1121+2617]. Ben-Hesed, "*son of Hesed [loyal love]*":–

1137 בָּנִי ***bānî***, n.pr.m. GK: 1220 [→ 1129]. Bani, "*descendant*":– Bani [15]

1138 בֻּנִּי ***bunnî***, n.pr.m. GK: 1221 [→ 1129]. Bunni:– Bunni [3]

1139 בְּנֵי־בְרַק ***b^{e}nê-b^{e}raq***, n.pr.loc. GK: 1222 [→ 1121]. Bene Berak, "*sons of Barak [lightning]*":– Bene-berak [1]

1140 בִּנְיָה ***binyâ***, n.f. GK: 1224 [→ 1129]. building, physical structure:– building [1]

1141 בְּנָיָה ***b^{e}nāyâ*** or בְּנָיָהוּ ***b^{e}nāyāhû***, n.pr.m. GK: 1225 & 1226 [→ 1129+3068]. Benaiah, "*Yahweh has built*":– Benaiah [42]

1142 בְּנֵי יַעֲקָן ***b^{e}nê ya^{a}qān***, n.pr.loc. GK: 1223. Bene Jaakan, "[poss.] *son of Jaakan*":– Bene-jaakan [2]

1143 בֵּנַיִם ***bēnayim***, subst.[du.]. GK: 1227 [→ 996]. champion, single fighter:– champion (+376+1886.1) [2]

1144 בִּנְיָמִין ***binyāmîn*** or בֶּן־יָמִין ***ben-yāmîn***, n.pr.m. GK: 1228 [→ 1145, 3227]. Benjamin, "*son of [the] right hand; southerner*":– Benjamin [158], Benjamin's [4], Benjamites [4]

1145 בֶּן־יְמִינִי ***ben-y^{e}mînî*** or בִּימִינִי ***biny^{e}mînî***, a.g. GK: 1229 [→ 1030]. Benjamite, of Benjamin, "*of Benjamin*":– Benjamite [5], Benjamites [3]

1146 בִּנְיָן ***binyān***, n.m. GK: 1230 [→ 1129; cf. 1147]. building, structure; outer wall:– building [7]

1147 בִּנְיָן ***binyān*** (Aram.), n.[m.]. GK: 10112 [→ 1124; cf. 1146]. building:– building [1]

1148 בְּנִינוּ ***b^{e}nînû***, n.pr.m. GK: 1231 [→ 1121]. Beninu, "*our son*":– Beninu [1]

1149 בְּנַס ***b^{e}nas*** (Aram.), v. GK: 10113. [P] to become angry:– angry [1]

1150 בִּנְעָא ***binʿā'***, n.pr.m. GK: 1232 [→ 1121]. Binea:– Binea [2]

1151 בֶּן־עַמִּי ***ben-ʿammî***, n.pr.m. GK: 1214 [→ 1121+5971+2967.1]. Ben-Ammi, "*son of my people*":– Ben-ammi [1]

1152 בְּסוֹדְיָה ***b^{e}sôd^{e}yâ***, n.pr.m. GK: 1233 [→ 871.1+5475+3068; cf. 1153?]. Besodeiah, "*in secret council of Yahweh*":– Besodeiah [1]

1153 בֵּסַי ***bēsay***, n.pr.m. GK: 1234 [cf. 1152?]. Besai, "*in secret council of Yahweh*":– Besai [2]

1154 בֶּסֶר ***beser***, n.m. GK: 1235 [→ 1155]. unripe grapes, sour grapes:– unripe grape [1]

1155 בֹּסֶר ***bōser***, n.m. GK: 1235 [→ 1154]. unripe grapes, sour grapes:– sour grape [3], sour grapes [1]

1156 בְּעָה ***b^{e}ʿâ*** (Aram.), v. GK: 10114 [→ 1159; cf. 1158]. [P] to ask for, request; when petitioning deity: pray for, plead for:– sought [3], ask [2], desired [2], asked [1], desire [1], maketh petition (+1159) [1], praying [1], requested [1]

1157 בַּעַד ***baʿad***, subst.pp. GK: 1237. behind; through, over; around; from; on behalf of, for (benefit of):– for [61], upon [9], about [7], through [7], at [4], within (+4480) [3], by means of [1], by [1], concerneth [1], in [1], out at [1], over [1], sealeth up (+2856) [1], to [1]

1158 בָּעָא ***bāʿā*** or בָּעָה ***bāʿâ***, v. GK: 1239 & 1240 [cf. 1156]. [Q] to ask, inquire; to boil; [N] to be pillaged; other sources: searched out, with an implication that what is found would be taken and so ransacked; to bulge, be swollen:– inquire [2], causeth to boil [1], sought up [1], swelling out [1]

1159 בָּעוּ ***bāʿû*** (Aram.), n.f. GK: 10115 [→ 1156]. prayer, petition, request:– maketh petition (+1156) [1], petition [1]

1160 בְּעוֹר ***b^{e}ʿôr***, n.pr.m. GK: 1242. Beor, "[perhaps] *a burning*":– Beor [10]

1161 בִּעוּת ***biʿût***, n.m.pl. GK: 1243 [→ 1204]. terror:– terrors [2]

1162 בֹּעַז ***bōʿaz***, n.pr.m. GK: 1244 & 1245. Boaz, "[prob.] *in him is strength*":– Boaz [24]

1163 בָּעַט ***bāʿaṭ***, v. GK: 1246. [Q] to kick (in scorn):– kicked [1], kick [1]

1164 בְּעִי ***b^{e}ʿî***, n.[m.]. GK: 1247 [→ 871.1+5856]. ?:–

1165 בְּעִיר ***b^{e}ʿîr***, n.m. GK: 1248 [→ 1197, 1198]. animals, livestock, cattle:– beasts [3], cattle [2], beast [1]

1166 בָּעַל ***bāʿal***, v. GK: 1241 & 1249. [Q] to rule over; to marry, be a husband; [Qp, N] to be married, have a husband; (ptcp.) Beulah:– married [6], husband [3], Beulah [1], dominion [1], had dominion over [1], married wife [1], marrieth [1], marry [1], wife [1]

Heb

1167 בַּעַל ***ba'al***, n.m. GK: 1251 [→ 1168, 1172, 1191, 4810; cf. 1166; cf. 1169 (also used with compound proper names)]. Baal (pagan god), "*master, owner, lord*"; husband, master, owner, citizen; used in many phrases to indicate mastery of an object: "lord of arrows" is a master archer; "lord of dreams" is an interpreter of dreams, etc.:– men [20], owner [10], husband [9], man [4], owners [4], having [2], him that hath [2], husbands [2], lords [2], master [2], adversary (+4941) [1], archers (+2671) [1], babbler (+3956+1886.1) [1], bird (+3671) [1], captain [1], chief man [1], confederate (+1285) [1], creditor (+3027+4874) [1], dreamer (+2472+1886.1) [1], furious (+2534) [1], had [1], him that is great [1], horsemen (+6571) [1], man's [1], married (+802) [1], master (+376) [1], master's [1], masters [1], person [1], sworn (+7621) [1], that which hath [1], them that have [1], them to whom is due [1], they^{s} [1], those that are given to [1]

1168 בַּעַל ***ba'al***, n.pr.m. GK: 1252 [→ 1167]. Baal, "*master, owner, lord*":– Baal [62], Baalim [18], Baal's [1]

1169 בְּעֵל ***b^{e}'ēl*** (Aram.), n.m. GK: 10116 [cf. 1167]. master, lord; with 2941: "lord of the decree" is "commanding officer":– chancellor (+2942) [3]

1170 בַּעַל בְּרִית ***ba'al b^{e}rît***, n.pr. GK: 1253 [→ 1167+1285]. Baal-Berith, "*Baal [lord] of the covenant*":– Baal-berith [2]

1171 בַּעַל גָּד ***ba'al gād***, n.pr.loc. GK: 1254 [→ 1167+1410]. Baal Gad, "*lord [Baal] of good luck*":– Baal-gad [3]

1172 בַּעֲלָה ***ba^{a}lâ***, n.f. GK: 1266 [→ 1090, 1173?, 1175; cf. 1167]. mistress (of sorceries); (female) owner:– hath [2], mistress [2]

1173 בַּעֲלָה ***ba^{a}lâ***, n.pr.loc. GK: 1267 [→ 1172?]. Baalah, "[fem. of Baal] *lady*":– Baalah [5]

1174 בַּעַל הָמוֹן ***ba'al hāmôn***, n.pr.loc. GK: 1255 [→ 1167+1995]. Baal Hamon, "*lord [Baal] of Hamon* or *possessor of abundance*":– Baal-hamon [1]

1175 בְּעָלוֹת ***b^{e}'ālôt***, n.pr.loc. GK: 1268 [→ 1172]. Bealoth, "[fem. pl. of Baal] *lady*":– Aloth [1], Bealoth [1]

1176 בַּעַל זְבוּב ***ba'al z^{e}bûb***, n.pr. GK: 1256 [→ 1167+2070]. Baal-Zebub, "*Baal [lord] of the flies*":– Baal-zebub [4]

1177 בַּעַל חָנָן ***ba'al ḥānān***, n.pr.m. GK: 1257 [→ 1167+2605]. Baal-Hanan, "*lord [Baal] is gracious*":– Baal-hanan [5]

1178 בַּעַל חָצוֹר ***ba'al ḥāṣôr***, n.pr.loc. GK: 1258 [→ 1167+2691]. Baal Hazor, "*lord [Baal] of Hazor*":– Baal-hazor [1]

1179 בַּעַל חֶרְמוֹן ***ba'al ḥermôn***, n.pr.loc. GK: 1259 [→ 1167+2768]. Baal Hermon, "*lord [Baal] of Hermon*":– Baal-hermon [2]

1180 בַּעֲלִי ***b^{a}'ālî***, n.m. GK: 1251 + 3276 [→ 1167+2967.1]. my husband; my Baal (1167 + 2967.1); translated as a proper name in the KJV: Baali:– Baali [1]

1181 בַּעֲלֵי בָמוֹת ***b^{a}'alê bāmôt***, n.pr.loc. GK: 1251 + 1195 [→ 1167+1116]. lords of the high places (1167 + 1116):–

1182 בְּעֶלְיָדָע ***b^{e}'elyādā'***, n.pr.m. GK: 1269 [→ 1167+3045]. Beeliada, "*the lord [Baal] knows*":– Beeliada [1]

1183 בְּעַלְיָה ***b^{e}'alyâ***, n.pr.m. GK: 1270 [→ 1167+3045+3068]. Bealiah, "*Yahweh is Lord*":– Bealiah [1]

1184 בַּעֲלֵי יְהוּדָה ***b^{a}'alê y^{e}hûdâ***, n.pr.m. GK: 1251 + 3373 [→ 1167+3063]. Baale of Judah (1167 + 3063):– Baale of Judah [1]

1185 בַּעֲלִיס ***ba^{a}lîs***, n.pr.m. GK: 1271. Baalis, "[poss.] *son of delight* or *Baals*":– Baalis [1]

1186 בַּעַל מְעוֹן ***ba'al m^{e}'ôn***, n.pr.loc. GK: 1260 [→ 1167+4583?]. Baal Meon:– Baal-meon [3]

1187 בַּעַל פְּעוֹר ***ba'al p^{e}'ôr***, n.pr.m. GK: 1261 [→ 1167+6465]. Baal Peor, "*lord [Baal] of Peor*":– Baal-peor [6]

1188 בַּעַל־פְּרָצִים ***ba'al-p^{e}rāṣîm***, n.pr.loc. GK: 1262 [→ 1167+6556]. Baal Perazim, "*lord [Baal] of making a breech, breaking through*":– Baal-perazim [4]

1189 בַּעַל צְפֹן ***ba'al ṣ^{e}pōn***, n.pr.loc. GK: 1263 [→ 1167+6828]. Baal Zephon, "*lord [Baal] of the north*":– Baal-zephon [3]

1190 בַּעַל שָׁלִשָׁה ***ba'al šālišâ***, n.pr.loc. GK: 1264 [→ 1167+8031]. Baal Shalishah:– Baal-shalisha [1]

1191 בַּעֲלַת ***ba^{a}lāt***, n.pr.loc. GK: 1272 [→ 1167]. Baalath, "*lady, goddess* [fem. of Baal]":– Baalath [3]

1192 בַּעֲלַת בְּאֵר ***ba^{a}lat b^{e}'ēr***, n.pr.loc. GK: 1273 [→ 1167+875]. Baalath Beer, "*lord [Baal] of the well*":– Baalath-beer [1]

1193 בַּעַל תָּמָר ***ba'al tāmār***, n.pr.loc. GK: 1265 [→ 1167+8558]. Baal Tamar, "*lord [Baal] of the palm tree*":– Baal-tamar [1]

1194 בְּעֹן ***b^{e}'ōn***, n.pr.loc. GK: 1274. Beon:– Beon [1]

1195 בַּעֲנָא ***ba^{a}nā'***, n.pr.m. GK: 1275 [→ 1196]. Baana, "*son of affliction*":– Baana [2], Baanah [1]

1196 בַּעֲנָה ***ba^{a}nâ***, n.pr.m. GK: 1276 [→ 1195]. Baanah, "*son of affliction*":– Baanah [9]

1197 בָּעַר ***bā'ar***, v. GK: 1277 & 1278 & 1279 [→ 1165, 1199, 1200, 8404]. [Q] to burn; to be senseless, to be brutal; [N] to be purged; to behave senselessly; [P] to light a fire, set a blaze; to purge, remove, get rid of; [Pu] to be burning; [Ht] to start a fire, consume with fire; [H] to graze:– burn [19], put away [13], kindled [9], brutish [7], burned [6], burning [6], burnt [6], burneth [4], kindle [4], take away [4], burnt up [2], eaten up [2], taken away [2], brought away [1], cause to be eaten [1], eaten [1], feed [1], heated [1], set on fire [1], set [1], taketh away [1], took out [1], wasted [1]

1198 בַּעַר ***ba'ar***, n.m. GK: 1280 [→ 1165]. senselessness, stupidity, ignorance, comparable to an animal:– brutish [3], brutish person [1], foolish [1]

1199 בַּעֲרָא ***ba^{a}rā'***, n.pr.f. GK: 1281 [→ 1200; cf. 1197]. Baara, "*passionate [burning] one*":– Baara [1]

1200 בְּעֵרָה ***b^{e}'ērâ***, n.f. GK: 1282 [→ 1199; cf. 1197]. fire:– fire [1]

1201 בַּעְשָׁא ***ba'šā'***, n.pr.m. GK: 1284. Baasha, "*boldness*":– Baasha [28]

1202 בַּעֲשֵׂיָה ***ba^{a}śēyâ***, n.pr.m. GK: 1283. Baaseiah, "*the* LORD *is bold*":– Baaseiah [1]

1203 בְּעֶשְׁתְּרָה ***b^{e}'ešt^{e}râ***, n.pr.loc. GK: 1285 [cf. 6252?]. Be Eshtarah:– Beeshterah [1]

1204 בָּעַת ***bā'at***, v. GK: 1286 [→ 1205, 1161]. [N] to be afraid, be terrified; [P] to torment, terrify, overwhelm:– make afraid [5], afraid [3], made afraid [2], terrify [2], affrighted [1], terrifiest [1], troubled [1], troubleth [1]

1205 בְּעָתָה ***b^{e}'ātâ***, n.f. GK: 1287 [→ 1204]. terror:– trouble [2]

1206 בֹּץ ***bōṣ***, n.[m.]. GK: 1288 [→ 949?, 1207, 8405?]. mud, silt:– mire [1]

1207 בִּצָּה ***biṣṣâ***, n.f. GK: 1289 [→ 1206]. marsh, swamp, waterlogged ground:– fens [1], mire [1], miry places [1]

1208 בָּצוּר ***bāṣûr***, a. GK: 1290 [→ 1219]. fortified:–

1209 בֵּצַי ***bēṣay***, n.pr.m. GK: 1291. Bezai:– Bezai [3]

1210 בָּצִיר ***bāṣîr***, n.m. GK: 1292 & 1293 [→ 1219]. grape harvest; grapes; vineyard; dense, inaccessible (forest):– vintage [8]

1211 בָּצָל ***bāṣāl***, n.m. GK: 1294 [→ 1213?]. onion:– onions [1]

1212 בְּצַלְאֵל ***b^{e}ṣal'ēl***, n.pr.m. GK: 1295 [→ 871.1+6738+410]. Bezalel, "*in the shadow of God [El]*":– Bezaleel [9]

1213 בַּצְלוּת ***baṣlût*** or בַּצְלִית ***baṣlît***, n.pr.m. GK: 1296 & 1297 [→ 1211?]. Bazluth, Bazlith:– Bazlith [1], Bazluth [1]

1214 בָּצַע ***bāṣa'***, v. GK: 1298 [→ 1215]. [Q] to cut off; to be greedy, make unjust gain; [P] to cut off; to finish; to make unjust gain:– cut off [2], greedy of gain (+1215) [2], coveteth [1], covetous [1], cut [1], finish [1], fulfilled [1], gained [1], get dishonest gain (+1215) [1], given to covetousness (+1215) [1], given [1], greedily gained [1], performed [1], wounded [1]

1215 בֶּצַע ***beṣa'***, n.m. GK: 1299 [→ 1214]. ill-gotten gain, dishonest gain; cutting off:– covetousness [9], gain [5], profit [3], greedy of gain (+1214) [2], dishonest gain [1], get dishonest gain (+1214) [1], given to covetousness (+1214) [1], lucre [1]

1216 בָּצֵק ***bāṣēq***, v. GK: 1301 [→ 1217, 1218]. [Q] to swell, become swollen:– swelled [1], swell [1]

1217 בָּצֵק ***bāṣēq***, n.[m.]. GK: 1302 [→ 1216]. dough made of flour, not yet leavened:– dough [4], flour [1]

1218 בָּצְקַת ***boṣqat***, n.pr.loc. GK: 1304 [→ 1216]. Bozkath, "*swollen* or *elevated spot*":– Boscath [1], Bozkath [1]

1219 בָּצַר ***bāṣar***, v. GK: 1305 & 1306 & 1307 [→ 1208, 1210, 1221, 1223, 1224, 1225, 1226, 4013, 4014]. [Q] to harvest, gather grapes; to humble, break (the spirit); [N] to be impossible, be thwarted; [P] to strengthen, fortify:– fenced [16], defenced [5], fortify [2], gather [2], grapegatherers [2], cut off [1], gathered [1], gatherest grapes [1], grapegatherer [1], mighty [1], restrained [1], strong [1], walled up [1], walled [1], withholden [1]

1220 בֶּצֶר ***beṣer***, n.[m.]. GK: 1309 [→ 1222]. same as 1222: gold ore:– defence [1], gold [1]

1221 בֶּצֶר ***beṣer***, n.pr.m. & loc. GK: 1310 & 1311 [→ 1219]. Bezer, "*[metallic] ore* or *place of refuge*":– Bezer [5]

1222 בְּצַר ***b^{e}ṣar***, n.[m.]. GK: 1309 [→ 1220]. same as 1220: gold ore:– gold [1]

1223 בָּצְרָה ***boṣrâ***, n.f. GK: 1312 [→ 1219]. pen, sheep-fold:– Bozrah [1]

1224 בָּצְרָה ***boṣrâ***, n.pr.loc. GK: 1313 [→ 1219]. Bozrah, "*enclosure (for sheep), fortress*":– Bozrah [8]

1225 בִּצָּרוֹן ***biṣṣārôn***, n.[m.]. GK: 1315 [→ 1219]. fortress, stronghold:– strong hold [1]

1226 בַּצָּרָה ***baṣṣārâ*** or בַּצֹּרֶת ***baṣṣōret***, n.f. GK: 1314 & 1316 [→ 1219]. drought; trouble:– dearth [1], drought [1]

1227 בַּקְבּוּק ***baqbûq***, n.pr.m. GK: 1317 [→ 1228]. Bakbuk, "*gurgling (sound coming out of a bottle)*":– Bakbuk [2]

1228 בַּקְבֻּק ***baqbuq***, n.[m.]. GK: 1318 [→ 1227, 1229, 1231, 1232]. jar; in some contexts a flask:– bottle [2], cruse [1]

1229 בַּקְבֻּקְיָה ***baqbuqyâ***, n.pr.m. GK: 1319 [→ 1228+3068]. Bakbukiah, "*Yahweh pours out*":– Bakbukiah [3]

1230 בַּקְבַּקַּר ***baqbaqqar***, n.pr.m. GK: 1320. Bakbakkar, "*investigator*":– Bakbakkar [1]

1231 בֻּקִּי ***buqqî***, n.pr.m. GK: 1321 [→ 1228; cf. 1232]. Bukki, "*proved of Yahweh; mouth [gurgle sounds] of Yahweh*":– Bukki [5]

1232 בֻּקִּיָּהוּ ***buqqiyyāhû***, n.pr.m. GK: 1322 [→ 1228+3068?; cf. 1231]. Bukkiah, "*proved of Yahweh*":– Bukkiah [2]

1233 בְּקִיעַ ***bāqîa'***, n.[m.]. GK: 1323 [→ 1234]. breach (in a defense); bits, debris:– breaches [1], clefts [1]

1234 בָּקַע ***bāqa'***, v. GK: 1324 [→ 1233, 1235, 1237]. [Q] to divide, split, tear open; [N] to be split, burst open; [P] to split open, burst forth; [Pu] to be cracked open, broken through, ripped open; [H] to break through, divide; [Ho] to be broken through; [Ht] to split apart:– rent [7], broken up [5], clave [5], cleave [3], ript up [3], brake [2], cleaveth [2], divided [2], divide [2], hatch [2], brake into [1], break forth [1], break out [1], break through [1], breaketh out [1], broken in pieces [1], clave asunder [1], cleft [1], cutteth out [1], dividing [1], made a breach [1], make a breach [1], ready to burst [1], rent asunder [1], rip up [1], tare [1], tear [1], win [1]

1235 בֶּקַע ***beqa'***, n.[m.]. GK: 1325 [→ 1234]. beka (half-shekel, one-fifth of an ounce [five or six grams]):– bekah [1], half a shekel [1]

1236 בִּקְעָה ***biq'â*** (Aram.), n.f. GK: 10117 [cf. 1237]. plain, (broad) valley:– plain [1]

1237 בִּקְעָה ***biq'â***, n.f. GK: 1326 [→ 1234; cf. 1236]. valley, plain:– valley [9], plain [7], valleys [4]

1238 בָּקַק ***bāqaq***, v. GK: 1327 & 1328 [cf. 2999?]. [Q] to lay waste, ruin, destroy; to grow abundantly, spread out; [N] to be laid waste; [P] to devastate:– empty [2], utterly emptied (+1238) [2], emptied out [1], emptiers [1], fail [1], make void [1], maketh empty [1]

1239 בָּקַר ***bāqar***, v. GK: 1329 [→ 1241, 1242, 1243, 1244; cf. 1240]. [P] to inspect, seek; look after; consider:– inquire [2], seek out [2], make inquiry [1], search [1], seek [1]

1240 בְּקַר ***b^{e}qar*** (Aram.), v. GK: 10118 [cf. 1239]. [Pa] to make a search, inquire; [Htpa] to let a search be made:– search made [4], inquire [1]

1241 בָּקָר ***bāqār***, n.m. GK: 1330 [→ 951; cf. 1239]. animal, cow, bull; cattle, oxen, herd:– oxen [75], herds [30], bullock (+6499) [28], herd [14], beeves [7], bullocks (+6499) [5], bullocks [4], bullock (+1121) [3], ox [3], calf (+1121) [2], heifer (+5697) [2], kine [2], bullock [1], bulls [1], calf (+5695) [1], calves (+1121) [1], cattle [1], cow's [1], great cattle [1], young cow (+5697) [1]

1242 בֹּקֶר ***bōqer***, n.m. GK: 1332 [→ 1239]. morning:– morning [178], every morning (+1242+871.1+871.1+1886.1+1886.1) [20], morrow [4], day [3], every morning (+1242+1886.1+1886.1+3807.1+3807.1) [2], to morrow [2], days (+6153) [1], early (+1886.1+3807.1) [1], early (+871.1+1886.1) [1], early [1], to morrow (+871.1+1886.1) [1]

1243 בַּקָּרָה ***baqqārâ***, n.f.vbl. GK: 1333 [→ 1239]. looking after, caring for:– seeketh out [1]

1244 בִּקֹּרֶת ***biqqōret***, n.f. GK: 1334 [→ 1239]. due punishment (after investigation):– scourged [1]

1245 בָּקַשׁ ***bāqaš***, v. GK: 1335 [→ 1246]. [P] to seek, search, look for, inquire about; [Pu] be sought, be investigated:– seek [103], sought [48], seeketh [19], require [10], seek after [7], seekest [7], sought for [6], make request [3], required [3], seek out [3], besought [2], asked [1], ask [1], begging [1], desire [1], get [1], inquired of (+6440) [1], inquired [1], inquirest [1], inquisition was made [1], procureth [1], requested [1], requireth [1], sought after [1], sought out [1]

1246 בַּקָּשָׁה ***baqqāšâ***, n.m. GK: 1336 [→ 1245]. request:– request [8]

1247 בַּר ***bar*** (Aram.), n.m. GK: 10120 [cf. 1248, 1121]. a direct descendant, human or animal, male or of either gender: son, child; a distant descendant: grandson, grandchild, descendant; fig., one of a class or kind:– son [7], old [1]

1248 בַּר ***bar***, n.m. GK: 1337 [→ 1302; cf. 1121; cf. 1247]. son (exclusively male in the OT); the phrase translated "Kiss the Son" (Ps 2:12) is an act of homage to a king:– son [4]

1249 בַּר ***bar***, a. GK: 1338 [→ 1305]. pure; empty; favorite; radiant, bright:– clean [3], pure [2], choice [1], clear [1]

1250 בַּר ***bar***, n.m. GK: 1339 & 1340 [→ 1305; cf. 1257?; cf. 1251]. grain, wheat, that has been cleansed and threshed; wilds, in the open field:– corn [9], wheat [5]

1251 בַּר ***bar*** (Aram.), n.[m.]. GK: 10119 [cf. 1250]. open field, the wild, an area not populated by people, the place of undomesticated animals:– field [8]

1252 בֹּר ***bōr***, n.m. GK: 1341 [→ 1305]. cleanness:– cleanness [4], pureness [1]

1253 בֹּר ***bōr***, n.m. GK: 1342 [→ 1305]. soda, potash, lye, used in making soap:– make never so clean (+2141+871.1) [1], purely (+1886.1+3509.1) [1]

1254 בָּרָא ***bārā'***, v. GK: 1343 & 1344 & 1345 [→ 1256, 1274, 1277, 1278; cf. 4806]. [Q] to create, Creator; [N] to be created; can refers to creating from nothing as well as to reforming existing materials, as in "create in me a pure heart" (Ps 51:10); [P] to cut, cut down, clear (a forest); [H] to fatten:– created [33], create [8], creator [3], choose [2], cut down [2], createth [1], dispatch [1], done [1], made [1], make fat [1], make [1]

1255 בְּרֹאדַךְ־בַּלְאֲדָן ***b^{e}rō'dak-bal'^{a}dān***, n.pr.m. GK: 1347 [→ 4757]. Berodach-Baladan; cf. 4757:– Berodach-baladan [1]

בִּרְאִי ***bir'î***. See 1011.

1256 בְּרָאיָה ***b^{e}rā'yâ***, n.pr.m. GK: 1349 [→ 1254+3068]. Beraiah, "*Yahweh has created*":– Beraiah [1]

1257 בַּרְבֻּר ***barbur***, n.m.pl. GK: 1350 [cf. 1250?]. fowl, bird (of various species):– fowl [1]

1258 בָּרַד ***bārad***, v.den. GK: 1351 [→ 1259]. [Q] to shower hail:– hail [1]

1259 בָּרָד ***bārād***, n.m. GK: 1352 [→ 1258]. hail, hailstones:– hail [25], hailstones [2], hailstones (+68) [1], hailstones (+68+1886.1) [1]

1260 בֶּרֶד ***bered***, n.pr.m. & loc. GK: 1354 & 1355. Bered, "[poss.] *freezing rain*":– Bered [2]

1261 בָּרֹד ***bārōd***, a. GK: 1353. spotted, dappled:– grisled [4]

1262 בָּרָה ***bārâ***, v. GK: 1346 & 1356 & 1357 [→ 1267, 1279, 1285]. [Q] to eat; [H] to give to eat, urge to eat:– eat [3], cause to eat [1], choose [1], give [1], meat [1]

1263 בָּרוּךְ ***bārûk***, n.pr.m. GK: 1358 [→ 1288]. Baruch, "*be blessed*":– Baruch [26]

1264 בְּרֹמִים ***b^{e}rōmîm***, n.[m.]. GK: 1394. multicolored, a fabric of two-color webbing:– rich apparel [1]

1265 בְּרוֹשׁ ***b^{e}rôš***, n.m. GK: 1360 [cf. 1266]. pine tree; some sources: cypress or fir:– fir trees [8], fir [7], fir tree [5]

1266 בְּרוֹת ***b^{e}rôt***, n.m. GK: 1361 [cf. 1265]. fir tree; some sources: juniper or cypress:– fir [1]

1267 בָּרוּת ***bārût***, n.f. GK: 1362 [→ 1262]. food:– meat [1]

1268 בֵּרוֹתָה ***bērôtâ*** or בֵּרֹתַי ***bērōtay***, n.pr.loc. GK: 1363 & 1408. Berothah, Berothai, "*well*":– Berothah [1], Berothai [1]

1269 בִּרְזָוִת ***birzāwit*** or בִּרְזָיִת ***birzāyit***, n.pr.f. GK: 1364 & 1365 [→ 875+2132]. Birzaith, Birzavith, "*well of olive oil*":– Birzavith [1]

1270 בַּרְזֶל ***barzel***, n.m. GK: 1366 [→ 1271; cf. 6523]. iron, iron (implements):– iron [73], axe head [1], head [1], smith (+2796) [1]

1271 בַּרְזִלַּי ***barzillay***, n.pr.m. GK: 1367 [→ 1270]. Barzillai, "*[made of] iron*":– Barzillai [12]

1272 בָּרַח ***bāraḥ***, v. GK: 1368 & 1369 & 1370 [→ 1280, 1281, 4015]. [Q] to flee, run away, escape; [H] to drive out, make flee; [H] to injure; to make impassable:– fled [39], flee [10], flee away [3], would fain flee (+1272) [2], chased [1], chaseth away [1], drove away [1], fleddest [1], fleeth [1], make flee [1], make haste [1], put to flight [1], ran away [1], reach [1], shoot [1]

בָּרִחַ ***bāriaḥ***. See 1281.

1273 בַּרְחֻמִי ***barḥumî***, a.g. GK: 1372 [cf. 980]. Barhumite:– Barhumite [1]

1274 בְּרִי ***b^{e}rî***, a. GK: 1374 [→ 1254, 1277; cf. 4806]. fat, choice, healthy:– fat [1]

1275 בֵּרִי ***bērî***, n.pr.m. GK: 1373. Beri, "*wisdom*":– Beri [1]

1276 בֵּרִים ***bērîm***, a.g. GK: 1379. Berite:– Berites [1]

1277 בָּרִיא ***bārî'***, a. GK: 1374 [→ 1274]. fat, choice, healthy:– fat [5], fatfleshed (+1320) [2], rank [2], fatter [1], fed [1], firm [1], plenteous [1]

1278 בְּרִיאָה ***b^{e}rî'â***, n.f. GK: 1375 [→ 1254]. created thing, with a possible implication that it is something new:– new thing [1]

1279 בִּרְיָה ***biryâ***, n.f. GK: 1376 [→ 1262]. food; in context it refers to food for sick people:– meat [3]

Heb

1280 בְּרִיחַ **b^{e}rîaḥ**, n.m. GK: 1378 [→ 1272]. bar, gate bar, crossbar:– bars [36], bar [4], fugitives [1]

1281 בָּרִחַ **bāriaḥ**, a. GK: 1371 [→ 1272]. gliding; fugitive:– crooked [1], nobles [1], piercing [1]

1282 בָּרִיחַ **bārîaḥ**, n.pr.m. GK: 1377. Bariah, "[poss.] *board, bar; fugitive; descendant*":– Bariah [1]

1283 בְּרִיעָה **b^{e}rî'â**, n.pr.m. GK: 1380 [→ 1284]. Beriah, "*prominent, excellent*":– Beriah [11]

1284 בְּרִיעִי **b^{e}rî'î**, a.g. GK: 1381 [→ 1283]. Beriite, "*of Beriah*":– Beriites [1]

1285 בְּרִית **b^{e}rît**, n.f. GK: 1382 [→ 1286, 1170, 1262]. covenant, treaty, compact, agreement, an association between two parties with various responsibilities, benefits, and penalties; "to cut a covenant" is "make a covenant," a figure of the act of ceremonially cutting an animal into two parts, with an implication of serious consequences for not fulfilling the covenant:– covenant [264], league [15], in league [2], confederacy [1], confederate (+1167) [1], confederate [1]

1286 בְּרִית **b^{e}rît**, n.pr.[loc.?]. GK: 451 [→ 410+1285]. Berith, "*covenant*":– Berith [1]

1287 בֹּרִית **bōrît**, n.f. GK: 1383 [→ 1305]. soap, made from soap plants or potash:– sope [2]

1288 בָּרַךְ **bārak**, v. GK: 1384 & 1385 [→ 1263, 1290, 1292, 1293, 3000; cf. 1289]. [Q] to kneel down; [P] to bless, pronounce blessings, give praise, give thanks, extol; [Qp, N, Pu] to be blessed, be praised; [Ht] to bless oneself, be blessed; this can mean to speak words invoking divine favor (bless), or speak of the excellence of someone (praise); [H] to make kneel:– blessed [173], bless [112], blesseth [8], salute [4], blessest [3], curse [3], abundantly bless (+1288) [2], altogether blessed (+1288) [2], blaspheme [2], bless at all (+1288) [2], bless indeed (+1288) [2], blessed altogether (+1288) [2], blessed still (+1288) [2], blessing [2], greatly bless (+1288) [2], congratulate [1], cursed [1], kneeled [1], kneel [1], made to kneel down [1], praised [1], praise [1], saluted [1], thanked [1]

1289 בְּרַךְ **b^{e}rak** (Aram.), v. GK: 10121 & 10122 [→ 1291; cf. 1288]. [P] to kneel, an act of reverence to authority, often referring to God; [Pp] to be praised; [Pa] to praise; [Pap] to be praised, to give or receive words of excellence:– blessed [4], kneeled [1]

1290 בֶּרֶךְ **berek**, n.f. GK: 1386 [→ 1288, 1296; cf. 755, cf. 1291]. knee, the "buckling of the knees" means to falter, implying great fear or despair; "to bow the knee" means to be reverent or submissive:– knees [24], knee [1]

1291 בְּרֵךְ **b^{e}rēk** (Aram.), n.[f.]. GK: 10123 [→ 1289; cf. 1290]. knee; "to kneel down on the knees" is to assume a position of reverence or worship:– knees [1]

1292 בָּרַכְאֵל **barak'ēl**, n.pr.m. GK: 1387 [→ 1288+410]. Barakel, "*God [El] blesses*":– Barachel [2]

1293 בְּרָכָה **b^{e}rākâ**, n.f. GK: 1388 [→ 1294; cf. 1288]. blessing; gift:– blessing [50], blessings [11], blessed [3], present [3], Berachah [2], liberal [1]

1294 בְּרָכָה **b^{e}rākâ**, n.pr.m. & loc. GK: 1389 & 1390 [→ 1293; cf. 1288]. Beracah, "*blessing*":– Berachah [1]

1295 בְּרֵכָה **b^{e}rēkâ**, n.f. GK: 1391. (man-made) pool, reservoir:– pool [15], pools [2], fishpools [1]

1296 בֶּרֶכְיָה **berekyâ** or בֶּרֶכְיָהוּ **berekyāhû**, n.pr.m. GK: 1392 & 1393 [→ 1290+3068]. Berekiah, "*Yahweh blesses*":– Berechiah [10], Berachiah [1]

1297 בְּרַם **b^{e}ram** (Aram.), adv.advers. GK: 10124. but, however, nevertheless:– but [2], yet [2], nevertheless [1]

1298 בֶּרַע **bera'**, n.pr.m. GK: 1396. Bera, "*gift*":– Bera [1]

1299 בָּרַק **bāraq**, v. GK: 1397 [→ 1300, 1301, 1303]. [Q] to flash lightning:– cast forth lightning (+1300) [1]

1300 בָּרָק **bārāq**, n.m. GK: 1398 [→ 1301, 1303; cf. 1299]. lightning bolt, flash of lightning:– lightnings [9], glittering [4], lightning [4], bright [1], cast forth lightning (+1299) [1], glistering sword [1], glitter [1]

1301 בָּרָק **bārāq**, n.pr.m. GK: 1399 [→ 1300; cf. 1299]. Barak, "*lightning*":– Barak [13]

1302 בַּרְקוֹס **barqôs**, n.pr.m. GK: 1401 [→ 1248]. Barkos, "*son of Kos*":– Barkos [2]

1303 בַּרְקָן **barqōn**, n.m.pl. GK: 1402 [→ 1300; cf. 1299]. brier, a thorny plant:– briers [2]

1304 בָּרֶקֶת **bāreqet** or בָּרְקַת **bār^{e}qat**, n.f. GK: 1403 & 1404. beryl (a green stone, exact identification uncertain):– carbuncle [3]

1305 בָּרַר **bārar**, v. GK: 1359 & 1405 & 1406 [→ 1249, 1250, 1252, 1253, 1287]. [Q] to purge; [Qp] to be chosen, be choice; to be sharpened, polished, [N] to keep clean, be pure; [P] purify; [H] to cleanse; to sharpen; [Ht] to show oneself pure:– pure [3], choice [2], chosen [2], shew pure [2], cleanse [1], clean [1], clearly [1], make bright [1], manifest [1], polished [1], purge out [1], purge [1], purified [1]

1306 בִּרְשַׁע **birša'**, n.pr.m. GK: 1407. Birsha, "*disagreeable in taste*":– Birsha [1]

1307 בֵּרֹתִי **bērōtî**, a.g. GK: 1409 [cf. 886]. Berothite, "*of Berothai [?]*":– Berothite [1]

1308 בְּשׂוֹר **b^{e}śôr**, n.pr.loc. GK: 1410. Besor:– Besor [3]

1309 בְּשֹׂרָה **b^{e}śōrâ**, n.f. GK: 1415 [→ 1319]. news, good news:– tidings [4], good tidings [1], reward for tidings [1]

1310 בָּשַׁל **bāšal**, v. GK: 1418 [→ 1311, 4018]. [Q] to ripen; boil; [P] to cook, boil, roast, bake; [Pu] to be cooked, be boiled; [H] ripen:– seethe [9], boil [4], sodden [4], boiled [2], baked [1], bake [1], brought forth ripe [1], ripe [1], roasted [1], roast [1], seething [1], sodden at all (+1311) [1], sod [1]

1311 בָּשֵׁל **bāšēl**, a. GK: 1419 [→ 1310]. cooked, boiled:– sodden at all (+1310) [1], sodden [1]

1312 בִּשְׁלָם **bišlām**, n.pr.m. GK: 1420. Bishlam, "*son of Shalom [peace]*":– Bishlam [1]

1313 בָּשָׂם **bāśām**, n.m. GK: 1411 [→ 1314, 1315, 3005]. same as 1314: spices, perfume, fragrance; this can refer to balsam oil or to perfume in general:– spice [1]

1314 בֹּשֶׂם **bōśem**, n.m. GK: 1411 [→ 1313]. same as 1313: spices, perfume, fragrance; this can refer to balsam oil or to perfume in general:– spices [22], spice [2], sweet odours [2], sweet [2], sweet smell [1]

1315 בָּשְׂמַת **bāś^{e}mat**, n.pr.f. GK: 1412 [→ 1313]. Basemath, "*fragrant*":– Bashemath [6], Basmath [1]

1316 בָּשָׁן **bāšān**, n.pr.loc. GK: 1421 & 1422. Bashan, "*fertile stoneless plain*":– Bashan [59], Bashan-havoth-jair (+2334) [1]

1317 בָּשְׁנָה **bošnâ**, n.f. GK: 1423 [→ 954]. disgrace, shame:– shame [1]

1318 בָּשַׁס **bāšas**, v. GK: 1424. [Po] to trample:– treading [1]

1319 בָּשַׂר **bāśar**, v. GK: 1413 [→ 1309]. [P] to bring (good) news, proclaim (good) news; [Ht] to hear news:– bringeth good tidings [4], bear tidings [3], shew forth [3], bringest good tidings [2], publish [2], bringest tidings [1], bringeth tidings [1], brought good tidings [1], brought tidings [1], carry tidings [1], messenger [1], preach good tidings unto [1], preached [1], published [1], tidings [1]

1320 בָּשָׂר **bāśār**, n.m. GK: 1414 [cf. 1321]. flesh, the soft tissue mass of any animal; the whole body; particular parts of the body: meat, skin, genitals, etc.; by extension: humankind, living things:– flesh [256], body [2], fatfleshed (+1277) [2], kin [2], leanfleshed (+1851) [2], leanfleshed (+7534) [1], mankind (+376) [1], myself (+2967.1) [1], nakedness (+6172) [1], skin [1], thereof[s] [1]

1321 בְּשַׂר **b^{e}śar** (Aram.), n.m. GK: 10125 [cf. 1320]. flesh (human or creatures):– flesh [3]

בְּשֹׂרָה **b^{e}sōrâ**. See 1309.

1322 בֹּשֶׁת **bōšet**, n.f. GK: 1425 [→ 378; cf. 954]. shame, disgrace, humiliation:– shame [20], confusion [7], ashamed [1], greatly ashamed (+954) [1], shameful thing [1]

1323 בַּת **bat**, n.f. GK: 1426 [→ 1337, 1339, 1340; cf. 1129]. daughter, female child of any generation (granddaughter, etc.); by extension: any female, girl, woman; a term of endearment; fig., outlying village or settlement (of a "mother" city):– daughter [280], daughters [245], towns [32], villages [12], owls (+3284) [6], daughter's [3], first [2], owl (+3284) [2], apple (+380) [1], apple [1], branches [1], company [1], first year (+8141) [1], old [1]

1324 בַּת **bat**, n.m. & f. GK: 1427 [cf. 1325]. bath (liquid measure, equal to an ephah, about six gallons [about 22 liters]; some sources: eight to nine gallons):– baths [7], bath [6]

1325 בַּת **bat** (Aram.), n.[m.]. GK: 10126 [cf. 1324]. bath (liquid measure):– baths [2]

1326 בָּתָה **bātâ**, n.f. GK: 1429 [→ 1327?]. wasteland:– waste [1]

1327 בַּתָּה **battā**, n.f. GK: 1431 [→ 1326?]. steep ravine, face of a cliff:– desolate [1]

1328 בְּתוּאֵל **b^{e}tû'ēl**, n.pr.m. & loc. GK: 1432 & 1433 [→ 4962+410; cf. 1329?]. Bethuel, "*man of God [El]*":– Bethuel [10]

1329 בְּתוּל **b^{e}tûl**, n.pr.loc. GK: 1434 [cf. 1328?]. Bethul:– Bethul [1]

1330 בְּתוּלָה **b^{e}tûlâ**, n.f. GK: 1435 [→ 1331]. virgin, maiden; a marriageable woman who has never had sexual intercourse and still under the authority of her father; (unmarried) young woman:– virgin [24], virgins [14], maid [4], maidens [3], maids [3], maiden [2]

1331 בְּתוּלִים ***b^{e}tûlîm***, n.f. GK: 1436 [→ 1330]. virginity; proof of virginity, referring to a cloth with blood from a virgin's first sexual encounter:– virginity [8], maid [2]

1332 בִּתְיָה ***bityâ***, n.pr.f. GK: 1437. Bithiah, "[poss.] *worshiper of Yahweh* or *queen*":– Bithiah [1]

1333 בָּתַק ***bātaq***, v. GK: 1438 [cf. 918]. [P] to hack to pieces, slaughter:– thrust through [1]

1334 בָּתַר ***bātar***, v. GK: 1439 [→ 1335, 1336, 1338]. [Q, P] to cut in pieces:– divided [2]

1335 בֶּתֶר ***beter***, n.m. GK: 1440 [→ 1334]. piece:– parts [2], Bether [1], piece [1]

1336 בֶּתֶר ***beter***, n.m. GK: 1441 [→ 1334]. ruggedness, referring to mountains with rugged ravines:–

1337 בַּת־רַבִּים ***bat-rabbîm***, n.pr.loc. GK: 1442 [→ 1323+7235]. Bath Rabbim, "*daughter of a multitude*":– Bath-rabbim [1]

1338 בִּתְרוֹן ***bitrôn***, n.[pr.loc.?]. GK: 1443 [→ 1334]. Bithron, "*gully*":– Bithron [1]

1339 בַּת־שֶׁבַע ***bat-šeba'***, n.pr.f. GK: 1444 [→ 1323; cf. 7652]. Bathsheba, "*seventh daughter* or *daughter of an oath*":– Bath-sheba [11]

1340 בַּת־שׁוּעַ ***bat-šûa'***, n.pr.f. GK: 1445 [→ 1323+7651?]. Bath-Shua:– Bath-shua [1]

1341 גֵּא ***gē'***, a. GK: 1447 [→ 1342]. proud, arrogant:– proud [1]

1342 גָּאָה ***gā'â***, v. GK: 1448 [→ 1341, 1344, 1343, 1346, 1347, 1348, 1349, 1466]. [Q] to grow tall, be high, to rise up; by extension: to be exalted:– triumphed gloriously (+1342) [4], grow up [1], increaseth [1], risen [1]

1343 גֵּאֶה ***gē'eh***, a. GK: 1450 [→ 1342]. proud, arrogant:– proud [8]

1344 גֵּאָה ***gē'â***, n.f. GK: 1449 [→ 1342]. pride, arrogance:– pride [1]

1345 גְּאוּאֵל ***g^{e}'û'ēl***, n.pr.m. GK: 1451 [→ 1341+410]. Geuel, "*splendor of God [El]*":– Geuel [1]

1346 גַּאֲוָה ***ga'^{a}wâ***, n.f. GK: 1452 [→ 1342]. surging; majesty, glory, triumph; pride, arrogance, conceit:– pride [10], excellency [3], haughtiness [2], highness [1], proudly (+871.1) [1], proud [1], swelling [1]

1347 גָּאוֹן ***gā'ôn***, n.m. GK: 1454 [→ 1342]. surging (waves), lush (high) thickets; majesty, splendor, glory; pride, arrogance:– pride [19], excellency [10], majesty [7], pomp [5], arrogancy [3], swelling [3], excellent [1], proud [1]

1348 גֵּאוּת ***gē'ût***, n.f. GK: 1455 [→ 1342]. surging (sea), rising (smoke); majesty, glory; pride, arrogance:– majesty [2], pride [2], excellent things [1], lifting up [1], proudly (+871.1) [1], raging [1]

1349 גַּאֲיוֹן ***ga'^{a}yôn***, a. GK: 1456 [→ 1342]. arrogant, proud:– proud [1]

1350 גָּאַל ***gā'al***, v. GK: 1453 & 1457 [→ 1353, 3008]. [Q] to redeem, deliver; (n.) avenger; kinsman-redeemer; [Qp] to be redeemed; [N] to be redeemed, redeem oneself; often this redemption is in the context of saving from danger or hostility, as a figure of purchasing a slave or indentured person. A "kinsman-redeemer" purchases a relative from slavery (actual or potential); a "kinsman-avenger" provides justice on behalf of a relative; both concepts are in the image of God as Redeemer:– redeemed [24], redeem [22], redeemer [18], kinsman [7], avenger [6], revenger [6], at all redeem (+1350) [4], do the part of a kinsman [2], in any wise redeem (+1350) [2], near kinsman [2], ransomed [2], deliver [1], do the kinsman's part [1], kinsfolks [1], next kinsmen [1], perform the part of a kinsman [1], purchase [1], redeemeth [1], revengers [1], stain [1]

1351 גָּאַל ***gā'al***, v. GK: 1458 [→ 1352; cf. 1602]. [N] to be stained, defiled; [P] to defile; [Pu] to be unclean, defiled; [H/Aphel] to stain; [Ht] to defile oneself:– polluted [7], defile [2], defiled [1], stain [1]

1352 גֹּאַל ***gō'al***, n.[m.]. GK: 1459 [→ 1351]. defilement:– defiled [1]

1353 גְּאֻלָּה ***g^{e}'ullâ***, n.f. GK: 1460 [→ 1350]. redemption (of a person or object); right of redemption; blood relatives:– redemption [3], price of redemption [2], redeem (+1961) [2], kindred [1], redeem (+4672) [1], redeemed (+1961) [1], redeemed [1], redeeming [1], redeem [1], right [1]

1354 גַּב ***gab***, n.m. & f. GK: 1461 & 1462 [cf. 1355]. eyebrow; rim (of a wheel); mound, back; defense:– eminent place [3], bodies [2], rings [2], backs [1], back [1], bosses [1], eyebrows (+5869) [1], higher place [1], naves [1]

1355 גַּב ***gab*** (Aram.), n.[m.]. GK: 10128 [→ 1358?]. the back (body part):– back [1]

1356 גֵּב ***gēb***, n.[m.]. GK: 1463 & 1464 [→ 1374; cf. 1358]. ditch; cistern; an architectural structure variously interpretated: beam, rafter, paneling:– full of ditches (+1356) [2], beams [1], pits [1]

1357 גֵּבָה ***gēbâ***, n.[m.]. GK: 1466 [→ 1462]. swarm (of locust):– locusts [1]

1358 גֹּב ***gōb*** (Aram.), n.m. GK: 10129 [→ 1355?; cf. 1356]. den, pit (of lions), often an excavated hole:– den [10]

1359 גּוֹב ***gôb***, n.pr.loc. GK: 1570 [→ 1461?]. Gob, "*cistern*":– Gob [2]

1360 גֶּבֶא ***gebe'***, n.m. GK: 1465. cistern; marsh:– marishes [1], pit [1]

1361 גָּבַהּ ***gābah***, v. GK: 1467 [→ 1362, 1364, 1363, 1365, 1405, 3011]. [Q] to be tall, tower high; to exalt; to be proud, haughty, arrogant; [H] to make high, grow tall; exalt; the attitude of pride or arrogance is a fig. extension the base meaning of being tall or high; something that is "too high" cannot be understood:– lifted up [6], exalted [5], haughty [5], higher [4], exalt [3], high [2], exalteth [1], height [1], lift up [1], make high [1], mount up [1], on high [1], proud [1], raised up a great height [1], upward [1]

1362 גָּבֵהַּ ***gābēah***, a. GK: 1468 [→ 1361]. high, towered; proud, haughty; the attitude of pride or arrogance is a fig. extension the base meaning of being tall or high:– high [2], proud [2]

1363 גֹּבַהּ ***gōbah***, n.m. GK: 1470 [→ 1361]. tallness, height; splendor, majesty; pride, haughtiness, conceit; the attitude of pride or arrogance is a fig. extension the base meaning of being tall or high:– height [9], high [3], pride [2], excellency [1], haughty [1], loftiness [1]

1364 גָּבֹהַּ ***gāb ōah***, a. GK: 1469 [→ 1361]. high, tall; proud, haughty; the attitude of pride or arrogance is a fig. extension the base meaning of being tall or high:– high [24], higher [5], exceeding proudly (+1364) [2], lofty [2], haughty [1], height [1], highest [1], proud [1]

1365 גַּבְהוּת ***gabhût***, n.f. GK: 1471 [→ 1361]. arrogance:– loftiness [1], lofty [1]

1366 גְּבוּל ***g^{e}bûl***, n.m. GK: 1473 [→ 1367, 1379]. territory, boundary, border:– border [138], coast [46], coasts [23], borders [20], bound [4], landmark [4], space [2], bounds [1], limit [1], quarters [1]

1367 גְּבוּלָה ***g^{e}bûlâ***, n.f. GK: 1474 [→ 1366]. boundary stone, border marker:– coasts [5], bounds [2], borders [1], landmarks [1], place [1]

1368 גִּבּוֹר ***gibbôr***, a. GK: 1475 [→ 1396; cf. 1401]. mighty one, mighty warrior, special guard:– mighty [133], strong [5], valiant [5], men [4], mighty ones [3], mighties [2], champion [1], chief [1], excel [1], giant [1], man [1], mightiest [1], strongest [1]

1369 גְּבוּרָה ***g^{e}bûrâ***, n.f. GK: 1476 [→ 1396; cf. 1370]. power, strength, might, achievement:– might [27], strength [17], power [8], mighty acts [4], force [1], mastery [1], mighty (+5973) [1], mighty power [1], mighty [1]

1370 גְּבוּרָה ***g^{e}bûrâ*** (Aram.), n.f. GK: 10130 [→ 1400; cf. 1369]. power, might, strength:– might [2]

1371 גִּבֵּחַ ***gibbēaḥ***, a. GK: 1477 [→ 1372]. bald forehead:– forehead bald [1]

1372 גַּבַּחַת ***gabbaḥat***, n.f. GK: 1478 [→ 1371]. bald spot on the forehead; bare spot on cloth:– bald forehead [3], without [1]

1373 גַּבַּי ***gabbay***, n.pr.m. GK: 1480. Gabbai, "*collector*":– Gabbai [1]

1374 גֵּבִים ***gēbîm***, n.pr.loc. GK: 1481 [→ 1356]. Gebim, "*ditches*":– Gebim [1]

1375 גָּבִיעַ ***gābîa'***, n.m. GK: 1483 [→ 1392, 4021?]. cup, (drinking) bowl:– bowls [8], cup [5], pots [1]

1376 גְּבִיר ***g^{e}bîr***, n.m. GK: 1484 [→ 1376; cf. 1396]. lord, master:– lord [2]

1377 גְּבִירָה ***g^{e}bîrâ***, n.f. GK: 1485 [→ 1376; cf. 1396]. mistress (female lord); queen:– queen [6]

1378 גָּבִישׁ ***gābîš***, n.m. GK: 1486 [cf. 417]. jasper:– pearls [1]

1379 גָּבַל ***gābal***, v.den. GK: 1487 [→ 1366]. [Q] to set up a boundary; [H] to put limits around (a geographical area):– border [2], set bounds about [1], set bounds [1], set [1]

1380 גְּבַל ***g^{e}bal***, n.pr.loc. GK: 1488 [→ 1382]. Gebal, "[poss.] *border; hill*":– Gebal [1]

1381 גְּבָל ***g^{e}bāl***, n.pr.loc. GK: 1489. Gebal, "[poss.] *border; hill*":– Gebal [1]

גְּבֻלָה ***g^{e}bulâ***. See 1367.

1382 גִּבְלִי ***giblî***, a.g. GK: 1490 [→ 1380]. Gebalite, "*of Gebal*":– Giblites [1], stonesquarers [1]

1383 גַּבְלֻת ***gablut***, n.f. GK: 1491 [→ 4020]. braided (gold chain):– at the ends [1], ends [1]

1384 גִּבֵּן ***gibbēn***, a. GK: 1492 [→ 1386; cf. 1385]. hunchbacked:– crookbackt [1]

1385 גְּבִינָה ***g^{e}bînâ***, n.f. GK: 1482 [cf. 1384]. cheese:– cheese [1]

1386 גַּבְנֹן ***gabnôn***, n.[m.]. GK: 1493 [→ 1384]. ruggedness; a many-peaked mountain range with an appearance that suggests wonder and majesty:– high [2]

1387 גֶּבַע ***geba'***, n.pr.loc. GK: 1494 [→ 1389]. Geba, *"hill"*:– Geba [13], Gibeah [4], Gaba [2]

1388 גִּבְעָא ***gib'ā'***, n.pr.m. GK: 1495 [→ 1389?]. Gibea, *"mound, hill"*:– Gibea [1]

1389 גִּבְעָה ***gib'â***, n.f. GK: 1496 [→ 1387, 1388?, 1390, 1391, 1394, 1533]. hill, hill top, height:– hills [35], hill [30], little hills [4]

1390 גִּבְעָה ***gib'â***, n.pr.loc. GK: 1497 [→ 1395; cf. 1389]. Gibeah, *"mound, hill"*:– Gibeah [44], Gibeath [1]

1391 גִּבְעוֹן ***gib'ôn***, n.pr.loc. GK: 1500 [→ 1393; cf. 1389]. Gibeon, *"mound, hill"*:– Gibeon [37]

1392 גִּבְעֹל ***gib'ōl***, n.[m.]. GK: 1499 [→ 1375]. bloom:– bolled [1]

1393 גִּבְעֹנִי ***gib'ônî***, a.g. GK: 1498 [→ 1391; cf. 1389]. Gibeonite, of Gibeon, *"of Gibeon"*:– Gibeonites [6], Gibeonite [2]

1394 גִּבְעַת ***gib'at***, n.pr.loc. GK: 1501 & 1502 [→ 1389]. same as 1390: Gibeath, *"mound, hill"*:–

1395 גִּבְעָתִי ***gib'ātî***, a.g. GK: 1503 [→ 1390]. Gibeathite, *"of Gibeah"*:– Gibeathite [1]

1396 גָּבַר ***gābar***, v. GK: 1504 [→ 1368, 1369, 1376, 1377, 1397, 1398, 1399, 1402, 1403, 1404]. [Q] to rise, flood; to be greater, stronger; to prevail, overwhelm; [P] to strengthen; [H] to cause to triumph, confirm (a covenant); [Ht] to show oneself as a victor:– prevailed [9], prevail [5], great [2], strengthen [2], confirm [1], exceeded [1], mighty [1], put to more [1], strengtheneth [1], stronger [1], valiant [1]

1397 גֶּבֶר ***geber***, n.m. GK: 1505 [→ 1127, 1398, 1399, 1403; cf. 1396; cf. 1400]. (strong, young) man; in some contexts an indefinite pronoun: certain ones:– man [53], men [6], man's [2], mighty [2], every one [1], man child [1]

1398 גֶּבֶר ***geber***, n.pr.m. GK: 1506 [→ 1397; cf. 1396]. Geber, *"[strong young] man"*:– Geber [2]

1399 גְּבַר ***g^{e}bar***, n.m. GK: 1505 [→ 1397]. (mighty) man; in some contexts an indefinite pronoun: certain ones:– man [1]

1400 גְּבַר ***g^{e}bar*** (Aram.), n.m. GK: 10131 [→ 1370, 1401; cf. 1397]. (mighty) man; in some contexts an indefinite pronoun: certain ones:– men [16], certain [2], man [2], most mighty men (+1401+2429) [1]

1401 גִּבָּר ***gibbar*** (Aram.), n.m. GK: 10132 [→ 1400; cf. 1368]. strong man, mighty one:– most mighty men (+1400+2429) [1]

1402 גִּבָּר ***gibbār***, n.pr.m. GK: 1507 [→ 1396]. Gibbar, *"[young vigorous] man, hero"*:– Gibbar [1]

גְּבוּרָה ***g^{e}burâ***. See 1369.

1403 גַּבְרִיאֵל ***gabrî'ēl***, n.pr.m. GK: 1508 [→ 1397+410]. Gabriel, *"[strong] man of God [El]"*:– Gabriel [2]

1404 גְּבֶרֶת ***g^{e}beret***, n.f. GK: 1509 [→ 1396]. queen:– mistress [7], lady [2]

1405 גִּבְּתוֹן ***gibb^{e}tôn***, n.pr.loc. GK: 1510 [→ 1361]. Gibbethon, *"mound, hill"*:– Gibbethon [6]

1406 גָּג ***gāg***, n.m. GK: 1511. roof, top:– roof [9], housetops [6], top [4], housetop [3], top of house [3], roof of house [2], roofs [2], tops of houses [1]

1407 גַּד ***gad***, n.m. GK: 1512. coriander:– coriander [2]

1408 גַּד ***gad***, n.[m.]. GK: 1513 [→ 1409, 1410, 1426, 1427]. same as 1409: good fortune; (as a pagan god) Fortune:–

1409 גַּד ***gad***, n.[m.]. GK: 1513 [→ 1408]. same as 1408: good fortune; (as a pagan god) Fortune:– troop [2]

1410 גָּד ***gād***, n.pr.m. GK: 1514 [→ 1171, 1425, 1424; cf. 1408]. Gad, *"fortune"*:– Gad [70]

1411 גְּדָבַר ***g^{e}dābar*** (Aram.), n.m. GK: 10133 [cf. 1490; cf. 1489]. treasurer:– treasurers [2]

1412 גֻּדְגֹּדָה ***gudgōdâ***, n.pr.loc. GK: 1516. Gudgodah, *"cleft"*:– Gudgodah [2]

1413 גָּדַד ***gādad***, v. GK: 1517 & 1518 [→ 1416, 1417, 1418, 1464?; cf. 1414]. [Q] to band together; [Htpolal] to band together against; to cut oneself, slash oneself:– cut [5], assembled by troops [1], gather in troops [1], gather together [1]

1414 גְּדַד ***g^{e}dad*** (Aram.), v. GK: 10134 [cf. 1413]. [P] to cut down:– hew down [2]

גְּדוּדָה ***g^{e}dudâ***. See 1417.

1415 גָּדָה ***gādâ***, n.f. GK: 1519 [→ 1428]. bank (of a river):– banks [4]

גַּדָּה ***gaddâ***. See 2693.

1416 גְּדוּד ***g^{e}dûd***, n.m. GK: 1522 [→ 1413]. band of raiders; band of rebels; bandits; troops, divisions:– bands [9], troop [7], band [5], army [4], company [3], troops [3], armies [1], companies [1]

1417 גְּדוּד ***g^{e}dûd***, n.m. & f. GK: 1521 [→ 1413]. ridge (of a furrow):– cuttings [1]

1418 גְּדוּדָה ***g^{e}dûdâ***, n.m. & f. GK: 1523 [→ 1413]. slash, cut (of the skin):– furrows [1]

1419 גָּדוֹל ***gādôl***, a. GK: 1524 & 2045 [cf. 1431]. great, large; much, more; this can refer to physical size, quantity, degree, and social status (great king, high priest):– great [412], high [22], greater [20], loud [19], greatest [9], elder [7], mighty [7], eldest [6], more [4], wept sore (+1058+1065) [3], aloud (+6963+871.1) [1], displeased exceedingly (+3415+7451) [1], elder (+4480) [1], exceeding glad (+8055+8057) [1], exceedingly afraid (+3372+3374) [1], exceedingly [1], far [1], feared exceedingly (+3372+3374) [1], great men [1], great multitude [1], greatness [1], grew great [1], grieved exceedingly (+7451+7489) [1], hated exceedingly (+3966+8130+8135) [1], long [1], loud (+6963+871.1) [1], nobles [1], proud [1], very (+3966) [1], very [1]

1420 גְּדוּלָּה ***g^{e}dûllâ***, n.f. GK: 1525 [→ 1431]. greatness, majesty, recognition, honor:– greatness [7], great things [3], dignity [1], majesty [1]

1421 גִּדּוּף ***giddûp*** or גִּדּוּפָה ***giddûpâ***, n.m. GK: 1526 & 1528 [→ 1442]. taunt, scorn, insult, reviling:– revilings [2], reproaches [1]

1422 גְּדוּפָה ***g^{e}dûpâ***, n.f. GK: 1527 [→ 1442]. taunt, scorn, reviling:– taunt [1]

גְּדוֹר ***g^{e}dôr***. See 1446.

1423 גְּדִי ***g^{e}dî***, n.m. GK: 1531 [→ 1429, 5872]. (male) young goat:– kid (+5795) [7], kid [6], kids [3]

1424 גָּדִי ***gādî***, n.pr.m. GK: 1533 [→ 1410]. Gadi, *"my fortune"*:– Gadi [2]

1425 גָּדִי ***gādî***, a.g. GK: 1532 [→ 1410]. Gadite, of Gad, *"of Gad"*:– Gadites [14], Gadite [1], Gad [1]

1426 גַּדִּי ***gaddî***, n.pr.m. GK: 1534 [→ 1408]. Gaddi, *"my fortune"*:– Gaddi [1]

1427 גַּדִּיאֵל ***gaddî'ēl***, n.pr.m. GK: 1535 [→ 1408+410]. Gaddiel, *"God [El] is my fortune; Gad is [my] God"*:– Gaddiel [1]

1428 גִּדְיָה ***gidyâ***, n.f. GK: 1536 [→ 1415]. bank (of a river):–

1429 גְּדִיָּה ***g^{e}diyyâ***, n.f. GK: 1537 [→ 1423]. (female) young goat:– kids [1]

1430 גָּדִישׁ ***gādîš***, n.m. GK: 1538 & 1539. shock of grain, sheaf of grain; tomb:– shock of corn [1], shocks [1], stacks of corn [1], tomb [1]

1431 גָּדַל ***gādal***, v. GK: 1540 [→ 1419, 1420, 1432, 1433, 1435, 1434?, 1437, 4024, 4026 (also used with compound proper names)]. [Q] to grow up; be great, exalted; [P] to grow long, make great; to exalt, honor, glorify; [Pu] to be well-nurtured; [H] to make great, cause greatness; [Ht] to magnify oneself, show greatness:– magnified [17], great [16], magnify [15], grew [7], brought up [6], grown [5], grown up [4], greater [3], make great [3], waxed great [3], great things [2], grew up [2], made great [2], make greater [2], much set by [2], waxen great [2], advanced [1], became great [1], boasted [1], bring up [1], come to great estate [1], exceeded (+4480) [1], exceeded [1], excellent [1], great giveth [1], great things done [1], grow [1], increased [1], lift up [1], madest grow [1], magnifical [1], nourish up [1], nourished [1], nourishing [1], nourish [1], passed (+4480) [1], promoted [1], promote [1], proudly [1]

1432 גָּדֵל ***gādēl***, a.vbl. *or* v.ptcp. GK: 1541 [→ 1431]. great, powerful:– great [2], grew [2]

1433 גֹּדֶל ***gōdel***, n.m. GK: 1542 [→ 1431]. greatness, majesty, strength; pride, arrogance:– greatness [11], stoutness [1], stout [1]

1434 גְּדִל ***gādil***, n.[m.]pl. GK: 1544 [→ 1431?]. tassel, festoon:– fringes [1], wreaths [1]

1435 גִּדֵּל ***giddēl***, n.pr.m. GK: 1543 [→ 1431]. Giddel, *"big"*:– Giddel [4]

גָּדֹל ***gādōl***. See 1419.

גְּדֻלָּה ***g^{e}dullâ***. See 1420.

1436 גְּדַלְיָה ***g^{e}dalyâ*** or גְּדַלְיָהוּ ***g^{e}dalyāhû***, n.pr.m. GK: 1545 & 1546 [→ 1431+3068]. Gedaliah, *"great is Yahweh"*:– Gedaliah [32]

1437 גִּדַּלְתִּי ***giddaltî***, n.pr.m. GK: 1547 [→ 1431]. Giddalti, *"I pronounce [God as] Great; I reared up"*:– Giddalti [2]

1438 גָּדַע ***gāda'***, v. GK: 1548 [→ 1439, 1440, 1441]. [Q] to cut short, cut off, break; [P] to cut down, cut to pieces; [Qp, N, Pu] to be cut off, be cut down:– cut down [9], cut off [7], cut asunder [3], cut in sunder [2], hew down [1], hewn down [1]

1439 גִּדְעוֹן ***gid'ôn***, n.pr.m. GK: 1549 [→ 1441; cf. 1438]. Gideon, *"one who cuts, hacks"*:– Gideon [39]

1440 גִּדְעֹם ***gid'ōm***, n.pr.loc. GK: 1550 [→ 1438]. Gidom, *"cutting off, stop pursuit"*:– Gidom [1]

1441 גִּדְעֹנִי ***gid'ōnî***, n.pr.m. GK: 1551 [→ 1439; cf. 1438]. Gideoni, *"one who cuts, hacks"*:– Gideoni [5]

1442 גָּדַף ***gādap***, v. GK: 1552 [→ 1421, 1422]. [P] to blaspheme, revile:– blasphemed [5], blasphemeth [1], reproacheth [1]

גִּדּוּף ***giddup***, and גִּדּוּפָה ***giddupâ***. See 1421.

Heb

1443 גָּדַר **gādar**, v. GK: 1553 [→ 1446, 1445, 1444, 1447, 1448, 1449, 1450, 1448, 1452, 1453]. [Q] to built a stone wall, heap up stones for a wall:– masons [2], close up [1], fenced up [1], hedged [1], inclosed [1], made up the hedge (+1447) [1], make a wall (+1447) [1], make up the hedge (+1447) [1], repairer [1]

1444 גֶּדֶר **geder**, n.m. GK: 1555 [→ 1443, 1447]. same as 1447: wall, fence, a wall made of loose stones from the field without mortar:– wall [2]

1445 גֶּדֶר **geder**, n.pr.loc. GK: 1554 [→ 1013; cf. 1013, 1443]. Geder, "*wall [of stones]*":– Geder [1]

1446 גְּדוֹר **g^e^dôr**, n.pr.m. & loc. GK: 1529 & 1530 [→ 1443]. Gedor, "*wall; pock-marked*":– Gedor [7]

1447 גָּדֵר **gādēr**, n.m. GK: 1555 [→ 1444]. same as 1444: wall, fence, a wall made of loose stones from the field without mortar:– wall [5], fence [1], hedges [1], hedge [1], made up the hedge (+1443) [1], make a wall (+1443) [1], make up the hedge (+1443) [1], walls [1]

1448 גְּדֵרָה **g^e^dērâ** or גְּדֶרֶת **g^e^deret**, n.f. GK: 1556 & 1560 [→ 1443, 1449, 1450, 1452, 1453; cf. 1443]. wall, pen (for sheep) made of stone walls:– hedges [4], folds [3], sheepcotes (+6629) [1], sheepfolds (+6629) [1], wall [1]

1449 גְּדֵרָה **g^e^dērâ**, n.pr.loc. GK: 1557 [→ 1448; cf. 1443]. Gederah, "*stone pen, sheep corral*":– Gederah [1]

1450 גְּדֵרוֹת **g^e^dērôt**, n.pr.loc. GK: 1558 [→ 1448; cf. 1443]. Gederoth, "*stone pens, sheep corrals*":– Gederoth [2]

1451 גְּדֵרִי **g^e^dērî**, a.g. GK: 1559 [cf. 1013]. Gederite, "*of Geder*":– Gederite [1]

1452 גְּדֵרָתִי **g^e^dērātî**, a.g. GK: 1561 [→ 1448; cf. 1443]. Gederathite, "*of Geder[ath]*":– Gederathite [1]

1453 גְּדֵרֹתַיִם **g^e^dērōtayim**, n.pr.loc. GK: 1562 [→ 1448; cf. 1443]. Gederothaim, "*two stone pens, two sheep corrals*":– Gederothaim [1]

1454 גֵּה **gēh**, var. GK: 1563. var. of 2088: this:– this [1]

1455 גָּהָה **gāhâ**, v. GK: 1564 [→ 1456, 4010]. [Q] to heal:– cure [1]

1456 גֵּהָה **gēhâ**, n.f. GK: 1565 [→ 1455]. healing, cure; that which promotes healing: medicine:– medicine [1]

1457 גָּהַר **gāhar**, v. GK: 1566. [Q] to bow down; stretch out in prostration:– stretched [2], cast down [1]

1458 גַּו **gaw**, n.[m.]. GK: 1567 [→ 1460]. back (of the body); "to thrust behind the back" means "to reject":– back [2], backs [1]

1459 גַּו **gaw** (Aram.), n.m. GK: 10135 [cf. 1460]. middle, interior:– midst [10], the same (+1886.9) [1], therein (+871.2+1886.9) [1], wherein (+871.2) [1]

1460 גֵּו **gēw**, n.[m.]. GK: 1568 & 1569 [→ 1458, 1465, 1471?, 1472; cf. 1459]. back (of the body); "to walk upon the back" is a sign of conquest and subjugation; "to send sin behind the back" is "to forgive"; among; fellow people, community:– back [5], among [1], body [1]

1461 גּוּב **gûb**, v. GK: 1572 [→ 1359?]. [Q] to dig:–

1462 גּוֹב **gôb** or גֹּבַי **gōbay**, n.m.[col]. GK: 1571 & 1479 [→ 1357]. locust, locust swarm:– great grasshoppers (+1462) [2], grasshoppers [1]

1463 גּוֹג **gôg**, n.pr.m. GK: 1573 [→ 1996, 4031]. Gog, "*precious golden object*":– Gog [10]

1464 גּוּד **gûd**, v. GK: 1574 [→ 1413?]. [Q] to attack, invade:– overcome [2], invade with troops [1]

1465 גֵּוָה **gēwâ**, n.f. GK: 1576 [→ 1460]. back (of the body):– body [1]

1466 גֵּוָה **gēwâ**, n.f. GK: 1575 [→ 1342; cf. 1467]. pride, lifting up:– pride [2], lifting up [1]

1467 גֵּוָה **gēwâ** (Aram.), n.f. GK: 10136 [cf. 1466]. pride:– pride [1]

1468 גּוּז **gûz**, v. GK: 1577. [Q] to pass along, pass away:– brought [1], cut off [1]

1469 גּוֹזָל **gôzāl**, n.m. GK: 1578. young bird, hatchling:– young pigeon [1], young [1]

1470 גּוֹזָן **gôzān**, n.pr.loc. GK: 1579. Gozan:– Gozan [5]

1471 גּוֹי **gôy**, n.m. GK: 1580 & 1582. people, nation; regularly in the OT, any people in contrast to Israel: the Gentiles, pagan, heathen, uncultured:– nations [265], heathen [143], nation [107], Gentiles [30], people [11], every nation (+1471) [4], another [1]

1472 גְּוִיָּה **g^e^wiyyâ**, n.f. GK: 1581 [→ 1460]. dead body, corpse; carcass:– bodies [5], body [3], carcase [2], corpses [2], dead bodies [1]

1473 גּוֹלָה **gôlâ**, n.f. GK: 1583 [→ 1540; cf. 1547]. exile, captive, people deported to another place:– captivity [26], those carried away [3], carried away captives [2], carried away [2], removing [2], away [1], captives [1], captive [1], carried away captive [1], go into captivity [1], remove [1], them carried away [1]

1474 גּוֹלָן **gôlān**, n.pr.loc. GK: 1584. Golan:– Golan [4]

1475 גּוּמָּץ **gûmmāṣ**, n.m. GK: 1585. pit:– pit [1]

1476 גּוּנִי **gûnî**, n.pr.m. GK: 1586 [→ 1477]. Guni, "*spotted sand grouse*":– Guni [4]

1477 גּוּנִי **gûnî**, a.g. GK: 1587 [→ 1476]. Gunite, "*of Guni*":– Gunites [1]

1478 גָּוַע **gāwa'**, v. GK: 1588. [Q] to perish, die, breath one's last:– die [7], gave up the ghost [4], died [3], give up the ghost [2], dead [1], dying [1], given up the ghost [1], giveth up the ghost [1], perished [1], perish [1], ready to die [1], yielded up the ghost [1]

1479 גּוּף **gûp**, v. GK: 1589. [H] to shut (a door):– shut [1]

1480 גּוּפָה **gûpâ**, n.f. GK: 1590 [→ 1610]. dead body, corpse:– bodies [1], body [1]

1481 גּוּר **gûr**, v. GK: 1591 & 1592 & 1593 [→ 1483?, 1616, 1628, 4032, 4033, 4034, 4036; cf. 1624, 1482?, 3025]. [Q] to live as an alien, dwell as a stranger, implying less social rights than a native; to be terrified, be afraid, fear, revere; to attack, stir up; [Htpol] to stay, gather together:– sojourn [31], sojourneth [15], dwell [11], sojourned [11], afraid [6], strangers [6], abide [2], fear [2], gather together [2], surely gather together (+1481) [2], assemble [1], dwelleth [1], feared [1], gathered together [1], gathered [1], inhabitant [1], remain [1], sojourners [1], sojourning [1], stand in awe [1]

1482 גּוּר **gûr**, n.m. GK: 1594 [→ 1484; cf. 1481?]. cub (young of lions, jackals):– whelps [3], whelp [3], young ones [1]

1483 גּוּר **gûr**, n.pr.loc. GK: 1595 [→ 1481?]. Gur:– Gur [1]

1484 גֹּור **gôr**, n.[m.]. GK: 1596 [→ 1482]. cub (of lion):– whelps [2]

1485 גּוּר־בַּעַל **gûr-bā'al**, n.pr.loc. GK: 1597 [cf. 3017]. Gur Baal, "*sojourn of Baal*":– Gur-baal [1]

1486 גּוֹרָל **gôrāl**, n.m. GK: 1598. lot, device by which a decision was made, often a pebble, stick, or pottery shard either thrown or blindly pulled from a container; by extension: what is decided by lot, allotment (of land):– lot [61], lots [16]

1487 גּוּשׁ **gûš**, n.[m.]. GK: 1599 & 1641. scab, something crusted:– clods [1]

1488 גֵּז **gēz**, n.[m.]. GK: 1600 [→ 1494]. fleece, sheared wool; grass mowed:– fleece [2], mowings [1], mown grass [1]

1489 גִּזְבָּר **gizbār**, n.m. GK: 1601 [cf. 1411, cf. 1490]. treasurer:– treasurer [1]

1490 גִּזְבַּר **gizbar** (Aram.), n.m. GK: 10139 [cf. 1411; cf. 1489]. treasurer:– treasurers [1]

1491 גָּזָה **gāzâ**, v. GK: 1602 [→ 1496]. [Q] to bring forth, cut off (the umbilical cord):– took [1]

1492 גִּזָּה **gizzâ**, n.f. GK: 1603 [→ 1494]. wool fleece:– fleece [7]

1493 גִּזוֹנִי **gizônî**, a.g. GK: 1604. Gizonite, "*of Gizon*":– Gizonite [1]

1494 גָּזַז **gāzaz**, v. GK: 1605 [→ 1488, 1492, 1495]. [Q] to shear sheep; to shave one's head (in mourning):– shear [4], shearers [3], sheepshearers [2], cut down [1], cut off [1], poll [1], shaved [1], shearing [1], sheepshearers (+6629) [1]

1495 גָּזֵז **gāzēz**, n.pr.m. GK: 1606 [→ 1494]. Gazez, "[poss.] *sheep shearer;* [poss.] *one born at the time of shearing*":– Gazez [2]

1496 גָּזִית **gāzît**, n.f. GK: 1607 [→ 1491]. dressed stone, stone hewn or cut for masonry:– hewed stones [3], hewn stone [3], hewed stone [1], hewed [1], hewn stones [1], hewn [1], wrought [1]

1497 גָּזַל **gāzal**, v. GK: 1608 [→ 1499, 1498, 1500]. [Q] to rob, seize, snatch, take way; [Qp, N] to be robbed, be forcibly taken from:– spoiled [7], violently taken away [3], rob [2], away [1], caught [1], consume [1], exercised robbery (+1498) [1], pluck off [1], plucked [1], pluckt [1], pluck [1], robbed [1], robbeth [1], spoileth [1], take away from [1], take by force [1], take by violence [1], taken away [1], took violently away (+1500) [1], torn [1], violently take away [1]

1498 גָּזֵל **gāzēl**, n.[m.]. GK: 1610 [→ 1500; cf. 1497]. stealing, robbery, implying violence:– robbery [2], exercised robbery (+1497) [1], thing taken away by violence [1]

1499 גֵּזֶל **gēzel**, n.[m.]. GK: 1609 [→ 1497]. denial of rights:– violence [1], violent perverting [1]

גֹּזָל **gōzāl**. See 1469.

1500 גְּזֵלָה **g^e^zēlâ**, n.f. GK: 1611 [→ 1498; cf. 1497]. plunder, spoil, stolen things:– violence [3], robbed [1], spoil [1], took violently away (+1497) [1]

1501 גָּזָם **gāzām**, n.m. GK: 1612 [→ 1502; cf. 3697]. locust swarm; some sources: caterpillar or a specific state in the development of a locust:– palmerworm [3]

1502 גַּזָּם **gazzām**, n.pr.m. GK: 1613 [→ 1501]. Gazzam, "*some kind of bird or insect*":– Gazzam [2]

1503 גֶּזַע **geza'**, n.m. GK: 1614. stump, root stock:– stock [2], stem [1]

1504 גָּזַר **gāzar**, v. GK: 1615 & 1616 [→ 1506, 1507?, 1508, 1509, 1511, 4037; cf. 1629; cf. 1505, cf. 1510]. [Q] to cut in two, divide, cut down; decide on; to disappear; to devour, eat, with a possible focus on carving or chewing up food; [N] to be cut off, be excluded:– cut off [6], divide [2], cut down [1], decreed [1], decree [1], divided [1], snatch [1]

1505 גְּזַר **g**^e^**zar** (Aram.), v. GK: 10140 [→ 1510; cf. 1504]. [P] to determine; (as noun) diviner, astrologer; note that a diviner determines the future through interpretations of omens, such as the movement of the stars (astrologer), or through interpreting the fissures in bodily organs of animals, such as livers; [Htpe] to cut out; [Itpe] to cut out:– soothsayers [4], cut out [2]

1506 גֶּזֶר **gezer**, n.[m.]. GK: 1617 [→ 1504]. pieces (something divided and cut up):– parts [1], pieces [1]

1507 גֶּזֶר **gezer**, n.pr.loc. GK: 1618 [→ 1511; cf. 1504?]. Gezer, "[poss.] *pieces*":– Gezer [13], Gazer [2]

1508 גִּזְרָה **gizrâ**, n.f. GK: 1619 [→ 1504]. courtyard; appearance:– separate place [7], polishing [1]

Heb

1509 גְּזֵרָה **g**^e^**zērâ**, n.f. GK: 1620 [→ 1504; cf. 1510]. solitary place, unfertile land:– not inhabited [1]

1510 גְּזֵרָה **g**^e^**zērâ** (Aram.), n.f. GK: 10141 [→ 1505; cf. 1509]. decree, decision:– decree [2]

1511 גִּזְרִי **gizrî** or גִּרְזִי **girzî**, a.g. GK: 1621 & 1747 [→ 1507; cf. 1504]. Gizrite, Girzite:– Gezrites [1]

גִּחוֹן **giḥôn**. See 1521.

1512 גָּחוֹן **gāḥôn**, n.m. GK: 1623. belly (of reptile):– belly [2]

גֵּחֲזִי **gēḥ**^a^**zî**. See 1522.

גָּחֹל **gāḥol**. See 1513.

1513 גַּחַל **gaḥal** or גַּחֶלֶת **gaḥelet**, n.f. GK: 1624 & 1625. burning coals, hot embers:– coals [11], burning coals [3], coal [2], coals of fire [1], hot coals [1]

1514 גַּחַם **gaḥam**, n.pr.m. GK: 1626. Gaham, "*burning brightly*":– Gaham [1]

1515 גַּחַר **gaḥar**, n.pr.m. GK: 1627. Gahar, "*[born in the] year of little rain*":– Gahar [2]

גֹּי **gōy**. See 1471.

1516 גַּיְא **gay'**, n.m. & f. GK: 1628 [→ 2798]. valley:– valley [52], valleys [8]

1517 גִּיד **gîd**, n.m. GK: 1630. sinew, tendon:– sinews [4], sinew [3]

1518 גִּיחַ **gîaḥ**, v. GK: 1622 & 1631 [→ 1520, 1521; cf. 1519]. [Q] to burst forth, surge, bring forth (a baby); [H] to charge; to thrash about:– brake forth [1], came forth [1], camest forth [1], draw up [1], labour to bring forth [1], took out [1]

1519 גּוּחַ **gûaḥ** (Aram.), v. GK: 10137 [cf. 1518]. [H] to churn up, stir up (the sea):– strove [1]

1520 גִּיחַ **gîaḥ**, n.pr.loc. GK: 1632 [→ 1518]. Giah, "*bubbling spring*":– Giah [1]

1521 גִּיחוֹן **gîḥôn**, n.pr.loc. GK: 1633 [→ 1518]. Gihon, "*to gush forth*":– Gihon [6]

1522 גֵּיחֲזִי **gêḥ**^a^**zî**, n.pr.m. GK: 1634. Gehazi, "[poss.] *valley of vision*":– Gehazi [12]

1523 גִּיל **gîl**, v. GK: 1635 [→ 26?, 1524, 1525]. [Q] to rejoice, be glad, be joyful, the attitude and action of favorable circumstance, often expressed in shouts and song:– rejoice [23], glad [10], joyful [4], joy [2], rejoiced [2], delight [1], greatly rejoice (+1524) [1], rejoiceth [1]

1524 גִּיל **gîl**, n.[m.]. GK: 1636 & 1637 [→ 1523]. gladness, delight, jubilance; age, stage in life:– joy [3], gladness [2], greatly rejoice (+1523) [1], rejoice exceedingly (+413+8056) [1], rejoice [1], rejoicing [1], sort [1]

1525 גִּילָה **gîlâ**, n.f. GK: 1638 [→ 1523]. rejoicing, delight:– joy [1], rejoicing [1]

גִּלֹה **gîlōh**. See 1542.

1526 גִּלֹנִי **gîlōnî**, a.g. GK: 1639 [→ 1542; cf. 1540]. Gilonite, "*of Gilon*":– Gilonite [2]

1527 גִּינַת **gînat**, n.pr.m. GK: 1640. Ginath, "*protector*":– Ginath [2]

1528 גִּיר **gîr** (Aram.), n.[m.]. GK: 10142 [cf. 1615]. plaster:– plaister [1]

גֵּיר **gêr**. See 1616.

1529 גֵּישָׁן **gêšān**, n.pr.m. GK: 1642. Geshan:– Geshan [1]

1530 גַּל **gal**, n.m. GK: 1643 & 1644 [→ 1554, 1556]. waves, breaker waves, surging waves; fountain; heap, pile (of rocks, rubble):– waves [14], heap [12], heaps [6], Gallim [1], billows [1], spring [1]

1531 גֹּל **gōl**, n.f.?. GK: 1646 [→ 1543]. same as 1543: bowl:– bowl [1]

גְּלָא **g**^e^**lā'**. See 1541.

1532 גַּלָּב **gallāb**, n.[m.]. GK: 1647. barber:– barber's [1]

1533 גִּלְבֹּעַ **gilbōa'**, n.pr.loc. GK: 1648 [→ 1389]. Gilboa, "*bubbling*":– Gilboa [8]

1534 גַּלְגַּל **galgal**, n.m. GK: 1649 & 1650 [cf. 1556; cf. 1535]. wheel; whirlwind; tumbleweed (a wheel-shaped plant):– wheels [6], wheel [3], heaven [1], rolling thing [1]

1535 גַּלְגַּל **galgal** (Aram.), n.m. GK: 10143 [→ 1560; cf. 1534, 1536]. wheel:– wheels [1]

1536 גִּלְגָּל **gilgāl**, n.[m.]. GK: 1651 [→ 1556; cf. 1535]. wheel:– wheel [1]

1537 גִּלְגָּל **gilgāl**, n.pr.loc. GK: 1652 [→ 1019; cf. 1556]. Gilgal, "*circle of stones*":– Gilgal [41]

1538 גֻּלְגֹּלֶת **gulgōlet**, n.f. GK: 1653 [→ 1556]. skull; individual, person:– polls [6], skull [2], every man [1], head [1], man [1], poll [1]

1539 גֶּלֶד **gēled**, n.m. GK: 1654. skin:– skin [1]

1540 גָּלָה **gālâ**, v. GK: 1655 [→ 1473, 1526, 1546, 1549, 1542; cf. 1541]. [Q] to tell, uncover, reveal; depart, leave, be exiled, banished; [Qp] to be opened, unseal; be made known; [N] to be revealed, be exposed; [P] to reveal, expose (nakedness) = sexual relations; [Pu] to be opened, exiled; [H] to deport, exile:– uncover [22], discovered [18], carried away [17], carried away captive [15], discover [10], revealed [10], uncovered [10], open [6], removed [4], shew (+241) [4], surely go into captivity (+1540) [4], departed [3], gone into captivity [3], opened [3], openeth [3], revealeth [3], carried captive [2], carry away [2], go captive [2], plainly appear (+1540) [2], published [2], remove [2], reveal [2], surely led away captive (+1540) [2], advertise (+241) [1], appeared [1], appeareth [1], bewray [1], brought [1], captives [1], captive [1], captivity [1], carry away captives [1], carry away into captivity [1], carry captive [1], carrying away captive [1], cause to go into captivity [1], caused to be carried away captives [1], caused to be carried away captive [1], caused to be carried away [1], caused to be led into captivity [1], depart [1], disclose [1], discovereth [1], exile [1], go into captivity [1], gone [1], led away captive [1], led captive [1], openly shewed [1], revealed (+241) [1], shamelessly uncovereth [1], shewed [1], sheweth (+241) [1], sheweth unto (+241) [1], shew [1], told (+241) [1], told in [1], uncovereth [1], went into captivity [1]

1541 גְּלָה **g**^e^**lâ** (Aram.), v. GK: 10144 [cf. 1540]. [P] to reveal (mysteries); [Peil] to be revealed (i.e., mysteries); [H] to deport:– revealeth [3], revealed [2], brought over [1], carried away [1], revealer [1], reveal [1]

גֹּלָה **gōlâ**. See 1473.

1542 גִּלֹה **gilōh**, n.pr.loc. GK: 1656 [→ 1526; cf. 1540]. Giloh:– Giloh [2]

1543 גֻּלָּה **gullâ**, n.f. GK: 1657 & 1684 [→ 1531]. spring (of water); bowl-shaped capital (of a pillar):– springs [6], bowls [3], pommels [3], bowl [2]

1544 גִּלּוּלִים **gillûlîm**, n.m. GK: 1658 [→ 1556]. (pl.) idols:– idols [47], images [1]

1545 גְּלוֹם **g**^e^**lôm**, n.[m.]. GK: 1659 [→ 1563?]. fabric:– clothes [1]

1546 גָּלוּת **gālût**, n.f. GK: 1661 [→ 1540; cf. 1547]. exile, captive:– captivity [10], captives [3], carried away captive [2]

1547 גָּלוּ **gālû** (Aram.), n.f. GK: 10145 [cf. 1546]. exile:– captivity [3], captives (+1123) [1]

1548 גָּלַח **gālaḥ**, v. GK: 1662. [P] to shave off, cut off; [Pu] be shaved off; [Ht] to have oneself shaven, shave oneself:– shave [7], shaven [5], shave off [4], polled [3], shaved [2], caused to shave off [1], shaved off [1]

1549 גִּלָּיוֹן **gillāyôn**, n.m. GK: 1663 [→ 1540]. scroll (some sources: wooden tablet with a wax cover); mirror:– glasses [1], roll [1]

1550 גָּלִיל **gālîl**, a. GK: 1664 [→ 1556]. turnable (door); rings; rods:– folding [2], rings [2]

1551 גָּלִיל **gālîl**, n.pr.loc. GK: 1665 [→ 1552, 1553; cf. 1556]. Galilee, "*ring, circle, hence region*":– Galilee [6]

1552 גְּלִילָה **g**^e^**lîlâ**, n.f. GK: 1666 [→ 1553; cf. 1551]. region, district:– borders [3], coasts [1], country [1]

1553 גְּלִילוֹת **g**^e^**lîlôt**, n.pr.loc. GK: 1667 [→ 1552]. Geliloth, "*region*":– Geliloth [1]

1554 גַּלִּים **gallîm**, n.pr.loc. GK: 1668 [→ 1530; cf. 1556]. Gallim, "*heaps*":– Gallim [1]

1555 גָּלְיָת **golyāt**, n.pr.m. GK: 1669. Goliath, "*exile*":– Goliath [6]

1556 גָּלַל **gālal**, v. GK: 1670 & 1671 [→ 1530, 1530, 1561, 1534, 1534, 1536,

1537, 1538, 1544, 1550, 1551, 1552, 1553, 1554, 1557, 1559, 4039; cf. 4038?; cf. 1560]. [Q] to roll down, roll away; to commit, turn over; [N] to be rolled; [P] to roll; [Polal] to be rolled; [Htpol] to roll about, wallow; "to commit, trust" is a figure of rolling care or responsibilty onto the Lord:– rolled [4], roll [3], commit [2], remove [1], roll down [1], rolled away [1], rolled together [1], rolleth [1], run down [1], seek occasion [1], trusted [1], wallowed [1]

1557 גָּלָל ***gālāl***, n.[m.]. GK: 1672 [→ 1556]. dung, filth:– dung [1]

1558 גָּלָל ***gālāl***, n.[m.]. GK: 1673. because of, on account of, for the sake of:– because of (+871.1) [4], sake [2], for (+871.1) [1], for sake (+871.1) [1], sakes [1], that for (+871.1) [1]

1559 גָּלָל ***gālāl***, n.pr.m. GK: 1674 [→ 1562; cf. 1556]. Galal, "[poss.] *tortoise; roll away*":– Galal [3]

1560 גְּלָל ***g^{e}lāl*** (Aram.), n.[m.]. GK: 10146 [→ 1535, 4040; cf. 1556]. (col.) stone blocks, formally, "stones of rolling" i.e., stones too large to carry:– great [2]

1561 גֵּל ***gēl***, n.m. GK: 1645 [→ 1556]. dung, excrement, used for fuel in some contexts:– dung [4]

1562 גִּלֲלַי ***gil^{a}lay***, n.pr.m. GK: 1675 [→ 1559]. Gilalai:– Gilalai [1]

1563 גָּלַם ***gālam***, v. GK: 1676 [→ 1545?, 1564]. [Q] to roll up (clothing in a tight ball):– wrapt together [1]

1564 גֹּלֶם ***gōlem***, n.[m.]. GK: 1677 [→ 1563]. unformed body, embryo:– substance yet being unperfect [1]

1565 גַּלְמוּד ***galmûd***, a. GK: 1678. barren, haggard:– desolate [2], solitary [2]

1566 גָּלַע ***gāla'***, v. GK: 1679. [Ht] to burst out (in quarrel); to defy:– intermeddleth [1], meddled with [1], meddling [1]

1567 גַּלְעֵד ***gal'ēd***, n.pr.loc. GK: 1681. Galeed; "*heap of [stones that are a] witness*":– Galeed [2]

1568 גִּלְעָד ***gil'ād***, n.pr.loc. [& m.?]. GK: 1680 [→ 1569, 3003, 7433]. Gilead, "[perhaps] *monument of stones*":– Gilead [100], Gileadites [2], Gilead's [1], Ramoth-gilead [1]

1569 גִּלְעָדִי ***gil'ādî***, a.g. GK: 1682 [→ 1568]. Gileadite, of Gilead, "*of Gilead*":– Gileadite [9], Gileadites (+1121) [1], Gileadites [1]

1570 גָּלַשׁ ***gālaš***, v. GK: 1683. [Q] to descend; some sources: to leap, frisk:– appear [2]

1571 גַּם ***gam***, adv. GK: 1685 [cf. 4041]. also, surely, too; and, but, yet, even, moreover:– also [438], yea [55], even [49], and [45], both [30], yet [14], likewise [13], moreover [12], moreover (+2050.1) [10], nor [7], neither (+3808) [6], neither [6], also (+2050.1) [5], neither (+3808+2050.1) [5], likewise (+2050.1) [3], so [3], therefore [3], again [2], and (+2050.1) [2], and also [2], for [2], in like manner [2], in times past (+1571+8032+8543) [2], nay [2], nevertheless (+2050.1) [2], nor (+3808) [2], not [2], yea (+2050.1) [2], alike [1], and so much as [1], and yet [1], any [1], as soon as [1], as [1], both (+2050.1) [1], but (+2050.1) [1], but [1], either [1], except (+3588) [1], further [1], heretofore (+4480+4480+8032+8543) [1], howbeit (+2050.1) [1], in time past (+865+8032) [1], indeed [1], more yea [1], moreover as for [1], neither (+408) [1], neither (+408+2050.1) [1], neither yet (+3808+2050.1) [1], no not [1], nor (+3808+2050.1) [1], or [1], so much as [1], surely [1], then [1], therefore (+2050.1) [1], though [1], together with (+2050.1) [1], what [1], with [1], yet (+2050.1) [1]

1572 גָּמָא ***gāmā'***, v. GK: 1686 [→ 1573?]. [P] to eat up, swallow up; [H] to give water (to sip):– drink [1], swalloweth [1]

1573 גֹּמֶא ***gōme'***, n.m. GK: 1687 [→ 1572?]. papyrus:– bulrushes [2], rushes [1], rush [1]

1574 גֹּמֶד ***gōmed***, n.m. GK: 1688 [→ 1575?]. unit of measure: short cubit (the length from the elbow to the knuckles, about 12 to 18 inches):– cubit [1]

1575 גַּמָּדִים ***gammādîm***, n.pr.g. GK: 1689 [→ 1574?]. men of Gammad, "[prob.] *valiant men*":– Gammadims [1]

1576 גְּמוּל ***g^{e}mûl***, n.m. GK: 1691 [→ 1580]. what is done; benefit; what is deserved, recompense:– recompence [10], reward [3], as^{s} [1], benefits [1], benefit [1], desert [1], deserving [1], given [1]

1577 גָּמוּל ***gāmûl***, n.pr.m. GK: 1690 [→ 1580]. Gamul, "*weaned*":– Gamul [1]

1578 גְּמוּלָה ***g^{e}mûlâ***, n.f. GK: 1692 [→ 1580]. what is done; retribution, recompense:– deeds [1], recompences [1], reward [1]

1579 גִּמְזוֹ ***gimzô***, n.pr.loc. GK: 1693. Gimzo, "*place of sycamore trees*":– Gimzo [1]

1580 גָּמַל ***gāmal***, v. GK: 1694 [→ 1014, 1577, 1576, 1578, 1581?, 1582, 1583, 8408]. [Q] to do, produce, deal fully; to wean; to repay (what is deserved); [Qp, N] to be weaned:– weaned [9], rewarded [7], bestowed on [2], deal bountifully [2], dealt bountifully [2], did [2], recompense [2], weaned child [2], child weaned [1], doeth good [1], done [1], do [1], requite [1], reward [1], ripening [1], served [1], yielded [1]

1581 גָּמָל ***gāmāl***, n.m. GK: 1695 [→ 1580?]. camel:– camels [45], camel [5], camels' [3], camel's [1]

1582 גְּמַלִּי ***g^{e}mallî***, n.pr.m. GK: 1696 [→ 1580]. Gemalli, "*my reward*":– Gemalli [1]

1583 גַּמְלִיאֵל ***gamlî'ēl***, n.pr.m. GK: 1697 [→ 1580+410]. Gamaliel, "*recompense of God [El]*":– Gamaliel [5]

1584 גָּמַר ***gāmar***, v. GK: 1698 [→ 1586, 1587; cf. 1585]. [Q] to bring to an end, fail; fulfill:– ceaseth [1], come to an end [1], fail [1], perfect [1], performeth [1]

1585 גְּמַר ***g^{e}mar*** (Aram.), v. GK: 10147 [cf. 1584]. [Pp] to be finished; (as an introduction in a letter) Greetings:– perfect [1]

1586 גֹּמֶר ***gōmer***, n.pr.m. & f. GK: 1699 & 1700 [→ 1584]. Gomer, "*complete*":– Gomer [6]

1587 גְּמַרְיָה ***g^{e}maryâ*** or גְּמַרְיָהוּ ***g^{e}maryāhû***, n.pr.m. GK: 1701 & 1702 [→ 1584+3068]. Gemariah, "*Yahweh has accomplished*":– Gemariah [5]

1588 גַּן ***gan***, n.m. GK: 1703 [→ 1593; cf. 1598]. garden:– garden [39], gardens [3]

1589 גָּנַב ***gānab***, v. GK: 1704 [→ 1590, 1591, 1592?]. [Q] to steal, be a thief, kidnap; to deceive; [Qp, N, Pu] to be stolen, forcibly carried off; [Ht] to steal oneself away, sneak in:– stolen [11], steal [9], indeed stolen away (+1589) [2], stealeth [2], stealing [2], stolen (+1589) [2], stole [2], carrieth away [1], secretly brought [1], stale away unawares (+3820) [1], stale [1], steal away from [1], steal away [1], stealeth away [1], stealth [1], stolen away unawares (+3824) [1], stolen away [1]

1590 גַּנָּב ***gannāb***, n.m. GK: 1705 [→ 1589]. thief; kidnapper:– thief [13], thieves [4]

1591 גְּנֵבָה ***g^{e}nēbâ***, n.f. GK: 1706 [→ 1589]. stolen possession:– theft [2]

1592 גְּנֻבַת ***g^{e}nubat***, n.pr.m. GK: 1707 [→ 1589?]. Genubath, "*thief*":– Genubath [2]

1593 גַּנָּה ***gannâ***, n.f. GK: 1708 [→ 1594, 1588; cf. 1598]. same as 1594: garden, grove:– gardens [9], garden [3]

1594 גִּנָּה ***ginnâ***, n.f. GK: 1708 [→ 1593]. same as 1593: garden, grove:– garden [4]

1595 גֶּנֶז ***genez***, n.[m.]. GK: 1709 & 1710 [→ 1597; cf. 1596]. (royal) treasury; rug, carpet:– treasuries [2], chests [1]

1596 גְּנַז ***g^{e}naz*** (Aram.), n.m. GK: 10148 [cf. 1595]. place of treasure and archived documents:– treasure [2], treasures [1]

1597 גַּנְזַךְ ***ganzak***, n.[m.]. GK: 1711 [→ 1595]. (temple) storeroom, where treasures are kept:– treasuries [1]

1598 גָּנַן ***gānan***, v. GK: 1713 [→ 1588, 1593, 1594, 4043]. [Q] to defend, shield, protect:– defend [7], defending [1]

1599 גִּנְּתוֹן ***ginn^{e}tôn*** or גִּנְּתוֹי ***ginn^{e}tôy***, n.pr.m. GK: 1715 & 1714. Ginnethon, Ginnethoi:– Ginnethon [2], Ginnetho [1]

1600 גָּעָה ***gā'â***, v. GK: 1716. [Q] to bellow, low (of cattle):– loweth [1], lowing [1]

1601 גֹּעָה ***gō'â***, n.pr.loc. GK: 1717. Goah:– Goath [1]

1602 גָּעַל ***gā'al***, v. GK: 1718 [→ 1604, 1603; cf. 1351]. [Q] to abhor, despise, loathe; [N] to be defiled; [H] to cause defiling = fail to impregnate:– abhor [4], lothed [2], abhorred [1], faileth [1], lotheth [1], vilely cast away [1]

1603 גַּעַל ***ga'al***, n.pr.m. GK: 1720 [→ 1602]. Gaal, "*loathing*":– Gaal [9]

1604 גֹּעַל ***gō'al***, n.m. GK: 1719 [→ 1602]. despising, loathing:– lothing [1]

1605 גָּעַר ***gā'ar***, v. GK: 1721 [→ 1606, 4045]. [Q] to rebuke, reprimand; prevent (insects):– rebuke [7], rebuked [4], corrupt [1], rebuketh [1], reproved [1]

1606 גְּעָרָה ***g^{e}'ārâ***, n.f. GK: 1722 [→ 1605]. rebuke; threat:– rebuke [12], reproof [2], rebuking [1]

1607 גָּעַשׁ ***gā'aš***, v. GK: 1723. [Q] to shake, tremble; [Pu] to be shaken; [Ht] to shake back and forth, stagger, surge, tremble back and forth:– moved [3], shook [3], shaken [1], toss [1], troubled [1]

1608 גַּעַשׁ ***ga'aš***, n.pr.loc. GK: 1724. Gaash, "*rumble, quake*":– Gaash [4]

1609 גַּעְתָּם ***ga'tām***, n.pr.m. GK: 1725. Gatam:– Gatam [3]

1610 גַּף ***gap***, n.m. GK: 1726 & 1727 [→ 102, 1480]. height, elevation; body; by oneself:– himself (+2050.2) [3], highest places (+4791) [1]

1611 גַּף ***gap*** (Aram.), n.f. GK: 10149. wing:– wings [3]

1612 גֶּפֶן ***gepen***, n.f. & m. GK: 1728. vine, grapevine:– vine [43], vines [9], plant of vine [1], tree [1], vine (+3196) [1]

Heb

1613 גֹּפֶר ***gōper***, n.[m.]. GK: 1729. cypress (wood); exact identity of the wood is uncertain; "gopher wood" is simply a transliteration of the Hebrew:– gopher [1]

1614 גָּפְרִית ***goprît***, n.f. GK: 1730. sulfur; older versions: brimstone:– brimstone [7]

1615 גִּר ***gir***, n.[m.]. GK: 1732 [cf. 1528]. chalk:– chalkstones (+68) [1]

1616 גֵּר ***gēr***, n.m. GK: 1731 [→ 1628; cf. 1481]. alien, stranger (in a foreign land):– stranger [69], strangers [18], alien [1], sojourner [1], stranger (+376) [1], stranger's [1], strangers (+376) [1]

גֻּר ***gur***. See 1482.

1617 גֵּרָא ***gērā'***, n.pr.m. GK: 1733. Gera, "[perhaps] *sojourner*":– Gera [9]

1618 גָּרָב ***gārāb***, n.[m.]. GK: 1734 [→ 1619]. festering sore:– scurvy [2], scab [1]

1619 גָּרֵב ***gārēb***, n.pr.m. & loc. GK: 1735 & 1736 [→ 1618]. Gareb, "*scabby*":– Gareb [3]

1620 גַּרְגַּר ***gargar***, n.m. GK: 1737. ripe olives:– berries [1]

1621 גַּרְגְּרוֹת ***garg^erôt***, n.f.pl. GK: 1738. neck, throat:– neck [4]

1622 גִּרְגָּשִׁי ***girgāšî***, a.g. GK: 1739. Girgashite:– Girgashites [5], Girgashite [2]

1623 גָּרַד ***gārad***, v. GK: 1740. [Ht] to scrape oneself (with a broken piece of pottery):– scrape [1]

1624 גָּרָה ***gārâ***, v. GK: 1741 [→ 8409; cf. 1481]. [P] to stir up (a dispute); [Ht] to provoke (to war), engage (to battle):– meddle [4], contend [3], stirred up [3], stirreth up [3], striven [1]

1625 גֵּרָה ***gērâ***, n.f. GK: 1742 [→ 1641]. cud:– cud [11]

1626 גֵּרָה ***gērâ***, n.f. GK: 1743. gerah (measure, one-twentieth of a shekel, about half a gram):– gerahs [5]

גֹּרָה ***gōrâ***. See 1484.

1627 גָּרוֹן ***gārôn***, n.m. GK: 1744 [→ 1641]. throat, neck; by extension: mouth; an "outstretched neck" is a sign of arrogance and possibly of sexual misconduct:– throat [4], aloud (+871.1) [1], mouth [1], necks [1], neck [1]

1628 גֵּרוּת ***gērût***, n.f.[pr.loc.] GK: 1745 [→ 1616]. habitation; place name: Geruth:– habitation [1]

1629 גָּרַז ***gāraz***, v. GK: 1746 [→ 1631; cf. 1504]. [N] to be cut off, implying destruction:– cut off [1]

1630 גְּרִזִים ***g^erizîm***, n.pr.loc. GK: 1748. Gerizim:– Gerizim [3], Gerizzim [1]

1631 גַּרְזֶן ***garzen***, n.m. GK: 1749 [→ 1629]. ax, chisel:– axe [4]

1632 גָּרֹל ***gārōl***, a.var. GK: 1754. var. of 1419: large, great:–

גּוֹרָל ***gōrāl***. See 1486.

1633 גָּרַם ***gāram***, v.den. GK: 1750 & 1751 [→ 1634]. [Q] to leave, reserve; [P] to break, to break bones:– break [2], gnaw bones [1]

1634 גֶּרֶם ***gerem***, n.[m.]. GK: 1752 [→ 1633, 1636?; cf. 1635]. bone, rawboned, bony; bareness:– bones [2], bone [1], strong [1], top [1]

1635 גְּרַם ***g^eram*** (Aram.), n.[m.]. GK: 10150 [cf. 1634]. bone:– bones [1]

1636 גַּרְמִי ***garmî***, a.g. GK: 1753 [→ 1634?]. Garmite:– Garmite [1]

1637 גֹּרֶן ***gōren***, n.m. GK: 1755. threshing floor:– threshingfloor [17], floor [10], void place [2], barnfloor [1], barn [1], cornfloor (+1715) [1], corn [1], floors [1], threshingfloors [1], threshingplace [1]

גָּרֹן ***gārōn***. See 1627.

1638 גָּרַס ***gāras***, v. GK: 1756. [Q] to be crushed; [H] to break, crush:– breaketh [1], broken [1]

1639 גָּרַע ***gāra'***, v. GK: 1757 & 1758 [→ 4052]. [Q] to take away, reduce, hinder; [Qp] to be cut off (of a beard); [N] to be reduced, be taken away, to disappear; [P] to draw up (drops of water):– diminish [6], taken [3], diminished [2], abated [1], clipt [1], done away [1], kept back [1], maketh small [1], minish [1], restrainest [1], restrain [1], taken away [1], withdraweth [1]

1640 גָּרַף ***gārap***, v. GK: 1759 [→ 106, 4053]. [Q] to sweep away (of a river):– swept away [1]

1641 גָּרַר ***gārar***, v. GK: 1760 [→ 1625, 1627, 4050; cf. 5064]. [Q] to chew; to drag away; [Polal] to be sawn; [Htpol] to drive, swirl:– catch [1], cheweth [1], continuing [1], destroy [1], sawed [1]

1642 גְּרָר ***g^erār***, n.pr.loc. GK: 1761. Gerar, "*circle, region*":– Gerar [10]

1643 גֶּרֶשׂ ***gereś***, n.[m.]. GK: 1762. (coarse) crushed grain, grits, groats:– beaten corn [1], beaten out [1]

1644 גָּרַשׁ ***gāraš***, v. GK: 1763 & 1764 [→ 1645, 1646, 4054]. [Q] to cast up, toss up; to drive out; [Qp] to be divorced; [N] to be tossed, stirred up; to be banished; [P] to drive out, expel [Pu] to be banished:– drive out [11], cast out [8], thrust out [5], driven out [4], divorced [3], drave out [3], drove away [2], put away [2], surely thrust out (+1644) [2], cast up [1], driven forth [1], drive [1], driving out [1], drove out [1], expel [1], troubled [1]

1645 גֶּרֶשׁ ***gereš***, n.[m.]. GK: 1765 [→ 1644]. yield, produce:– put forth [1]

1646 גְּרֻשָׁה ***g^erušâ***, n.f. GK: 1766 [→ 1644]. dispossession:– exactions [1]

1647 גֵּרְשֹׁם ***gēršōm***, n.pr.m. GK: 1768 [→ 1648]. Gershom, Gershon, "*temporary resident there*":– Gershom [14]

1648 גֵּרְשׁוֹן ***gēršôn***, n.pr.m. GK: 1767 [→ 1647, 1649]. Gershon, "*temporary resident there*":– Gershon [17]

1649 גֵּרְשֻׁנִּי ***gēršunnî***, a.g. GK: 1769 [→ 1648]. Gershonite, "*of Gershon*":– Gershonites [9], Gershonite [3], Gershon [1]

1650 גְּשׁוּר ***g^ešûr***, n.pr.m. GK: 1770 [→ 1651]. Geshur, "*bridge*":– Geshur [8], Geshurites [1]

1651 גְּשׁוּרִי ***g^ešûrî***, a.g. GK: 1771 [→ 1650]. Geshurite, people of Geshur, "*of Geshur*":– Geshurites [4], Geshuri [2]

1652 גָּשַׁם ***gāšam***, v.den. GK: 1772 [→ 1653, 1654, 1656]. [H] to bring rain:– cause rain [1]

1653 גֶּשֶׁם ***gešem***, n.m. GK: 1773 [→ 1654, 1656; cf. 1652]. rain, shower, downpour:– rain [29], shower [3], great rain [1], much rain [1], showers [1]

1654 גֶּשֶׁם ***gešem*** or גַּשְׁמוּ ***gašmû***, n.pr.m. GK: 1774 & 1776 [cf. 1652, 1653]. Geshem, Gashmu, "*rain shower*":– Geshem [3], Gashmu [1]

1655 גְּשֵׁם ***g^ešēm*** (Aram.), n.m. GK: 10151. body; the phrase "give up the body" is translated "to die":– body [3], bodies [2]

1656 גֹּשֶׁם ***gōšem***, n.[m.]. GK: 1775 [→ 1653; cf. 1652]. shower, rain:– rained upon [1]

גַּשְׁמוּ ***gašmû***. See 1654.

1657 גֹּשֶׁן ***gōšen***, n.pr.loc. GK: 1777. Goshen, "*mound of earth*":– Goshen [15]

1658 גִּשְׁפָּא ***gišpā'***, n.pr.m. GK: 1778. Gishpa, "*listener*":– Gispa [1]

1659 גָּשַׁשׁ ***gāšaš***, v. GK: 1779. [P] to grope along, feel one's way (as if blind):– grope [2]

1660 גַּת ***gat***, n.f. GK: 1780 [→ 1661, 1662, 1667, 1663, 1664, 1665]. winepress; also used as a hiding place:– winepress [2], press [1], wine presses [1], winefat [1]

1661 גַּת ***gat***, n.pr.loc. GK: 1781 [→ 1663, 1665; cf. 1660]. Gath, "*winepress*":– Gath [33], Gath-hepher [1], Gittah-hepher [1]

1662 גַּת הַחֵפֶר ***gat haḥēper*** or גַּת חֵפֶר ***gat ḥēper***, n.pr.loc. GK: 1783 [→ 1660+1886.1+2660]. Gath Hepher, "*winepress waterpit*":–

1663 גִּתִּי ***gittî***, a.g. GK: 1785 [→ 1661; cf. 1660]. Gittite, "*of Gath*":– Gittite [8], Gittites [2]

1664 גִּתַּיִם ***gittayim***, n.pr.loc. GK: 1786 [→ 1660]. Gittaim, "*two winepresses*":– Gittaim [2]

1665 גִּתִּית ***gittît***, tt. GK: 1787 [→ 1661; cf. 1660]. gittith: unknown musical term, possibly the name of the tune, or the name of the instrument that played it, or even related in some way to ceremonies associated with the winepress:– Gittith [3]

1666 גֶּתֶר ***geter***, n.pr.m. GK: 1788. Gether:– Gether [2]

1667 גַּת־רִמּוֹן ***gat-rimmôn***, n.pr.loc. GK: 1784 [→ 1660+7416]. Gath Rimmon, "*winepress of pomegranate*":– Gath-rimmon [4]

1668 דָּא ***dā'*** (Aram.), p.demo.f. GK: 10154 [cf. 2090, 2097, 2088]. this, this one:– another [2], one [2], this [2]

1669 דָּאַב ***dā'ab***, v. GK: 1790 [→ 1670, 1671]. [Q] to be dim (of eyes); to sorrow:– mourneth [1], sorrowful [1], sorrow [1]

1670 דְּאָבָה ***d^e'ābâ***, n.f. GK: 1791 [→ 1669]. dismay, despair:– sorrow [1]

1671 דְּאָבוֹן ***d^e'ābôn***, n.[m.]. GK: 1792 [→ 1669]. despair:– sorrow [1]

1672 דָּאַג ***dā'ag***, v. GK: 1793 [→ 1673, 1674]. [Q] to worry, dread, be troubled, be afraid:– afraid [3], careful [1], sorroweth [1], sorry [1], take thought [1]

1673 דֹּאֵג ***dō'ēg***, n.pr.m. GK: 1795 [→ 1672]. Doeg, "*anxious*":– Doeg [6]

1674 דְּאָגָה ***d^e'āgâ***, n.f. GK: 1796 [→ 1672]. fear, anxiety, restlessness:– carefulness [2], care [1], fear [1], heaviness [1], sorrow [1]

1675 דָּאָה ***dā'â***, v. GK: 1797 [→ 1676; cf. 1772]. [Q] to swoop down, pounce; to soar:– fly [3], flieth [1]

1676 דָּאָה ***dā'â***, n.f. GK: 1798 [→ 1675]. red kite (bird):– vulture [1]

1677 דֹּב ***dōb***, n.m. GK: 1800 [→ 1680; cf. 1678]. bear (animal):– bear [10], bears [2]

1678 דֹּב ***dōb*** (Aram.), n.[m.]. GK: 10155 [cf. 1677]. bear:– bear [1]

1679 דֹּבֶא ***dōbe'***, n.[m.]. GK: 1801. strength:– strength [1]

1680 דָּבַב ***dābab***, v. GK: 1803 [→ 1677, 1681?, 1686?]. [Q] to flow over gently:– causing to speak [1]

1681 דִּבָּה ***dibbâ***, n.f. GK: 1804 [→ 1680?]. bad report, slander, bad reputation, whisper:– slander [3], infamy [2], report [2], defaming [1], evil report [1]

1682 דְּבוֹרָה ***d^{e}bôrâ***, n.f. GK: 1805 [→ 1683; cf. 1696]. wild honey bee; (pl.) swarm of bees:– bees [3], bee [1]

1683 דְּבוֹרָה ***d^{e}bôrâ***, n.pr.f. GK: 1806 [→ 1682; cf. 1696]. Deborah, *"hornet, wasp, wild honey bee"*:– Deborah [10]

1684 דְּבַח ***d^{e}baḥ*** (Aram.), v. GK: 10156 [→ 1685, 4056; cf. 2076]. [P] to present a sacrifice as an act of worship:– offered [1]

1685 דְּבַח ***d^{e}baḥ*** (Aram.), n.[m.]. GK: 10157 [→ 1684; cf. 2077]. sacrifice (i.e., animal):– sacrifices [1]

1686 דִּבְיוֹנִים ***dibyōnîm***, n.[m.]. GK: 1807 [→ 1680?+3123]. seed pods or doves' dung:– dove's dung [1]

1687 דְּבִיר ***d^{e}bîr***, n.m. GK: 1808 [→ 1688; cf. 1696?]. inner sanctuary, referring to the Most Holy Place:– oracle [16]

1688 דְּבִיר ***d^{e}bîr***, n.pr.m. & loc. GK: 1809 [→ 1687; cf. 1696]. Debir, *"back room [of a shrine temple for oracle pronouncement]"*:– Debir [14]

1689 דִּבְלָה ***diblâ***, n.pr.loc. GK: 1812. Diblah:– Diblath [1]

1690 דְּבֵלָה ***d^{e}bēlâ***, n.f. GK: 1811 [→ 1691?]. pressed fig cakes; poultice of figs:– cakes [2], lump [2], cake [1]

1691 דִּבְלַיִם ***diblayim***, n.pr.m. GK: 1813 [→ 1690?]. Diblaim, *"lump of [two dried fig] cakes"*:– Diblaim [1]

דִּבְלָתַיִם ***diblātayim***. See 1015.

1692 דָּבַק ***dābaq***, v. GK: 1815 [→ 1695, 1694; cf. 1693]. [Q] to be united, hold fast, keep, cling to; [H] to overtake, cause to cleave, press hard upon; [Pu] to be joined fast, be stuck together; [Ho] be made to cleave, stick to; from the base joining or fastening objects together comes the figure of close association of people:– cleave [13], clave [6], cleaveth [6], cleaved [3], followed hard [3], overtook [3], keep [2], make cleave [2], abide fast [1], cause to stick [1], caused to cleave [1], cleave fast together [1], cleave to [1], follow close [1], followed hard after [1], followeth hard [1], joined together [1], joined [1], keep fast [1], kept fast [1], pursued hard [1], stick [1], stuck [1], take [1]

1693 דְּבַק ***d^{e}baq*** (Aram.), v. GK: 10158 [cf. 1692]. [P] to be united, having a very close association:– cleave [1]

1694 דֶּבֶק ***debeq***, n.m. GK: 1817 [→ 1692]. welding; sections (of armor):– joints [2], sodering [1]

1695 דָּבֵק ***dābēq***, a. GK: 1816 [→ 1692]. holding fast, sticking to:– cleave [1], joining [1], sticketh closer [1]

1696 דָּבַר ***dābar***, v. GK: 1818 & 1819 [→ 1682, 1683, 1687?, 1688, 1697, 1698, 1699, 1699', 1700, 1702, 1703, 1705, 4057]. [Q, P, Ht] to say, speak, tell, command, promise; [Qp, Pu] to be spoken (of); [N] to speak together; a general term for verbal communication, note the specific contextual translations in the KJV; [P] to depart; to destroy; [H] to subdue:– spake [318], speak [273], spoken [174], said [85], speaking [37], promised [29], talked [29], say [27], speaketh [22], told [15], communed [14], pronounced [13], speakest [11], talk [11], spakest [8], tell [7], saith [6], utter [5], commanded [4], commune [4], say on [4], gave [3], talking [3], bid [2], communing [2], promisedst [2], speak well (+1696) [2], talkest [2], taught [2], telleth [2], wont to speak (+1696) [2], answered [1], appointed [1], badest [1], bade [1], declared [1], declare [1], destroyed [1], give [1], named [1], pronounce [1], published [1], rehearsed [1], saidst [1], speak on [1], spokesman [1], subdueth [1], subdue [1], talketh [1], telling [1], thought [1], uttered [1], uttereth [1]

1697 דָּבָר ***dābār***, n.m. GK: 1821 [→ 1696]. what is said, word (or any unit of speech such as a clause, or the whole of communication); matter (any event); thing (any object):– word [434], words [372], thing [178], acts [51], things [49], matter [47], chronicles (+3117) [33], nothing (+3808) [20], saying [20], commandment [15], manner [15], matters [15], business [8], said [8], book [7], speech [7], answer [6], cause [6], promise [6], chronicles (+3117+1886.1) [5], commandments [5], sayings [5], because (+834+5921) [4], portion [4], tidings [4], because of (+5921) [3], concerning (+5921) [3], deed [3], errand [3], message [3], nothing (+408) [3], rate [3], sentence [3], advice [2], affairs [2], answered (+7725) [2], any thing [2], causes [2], certain rate [2], deeds [2], it^s [2], of [2], ought [2], questions [2], report [2], request [2], spoken [2], talk [2], answer (+7725) [1], answered [1], any^s [1], as the matter require [1], care [1], case [1], commune [1], communication [1], conferred (+1961) [1], counsel [1], dealings [1], decree [1], disease [1], due [1], duty required [1], duty [1], effect [1], eloquent (+376) [1], every thing [1], evil favouredness (+7451) [1], for (+5921) [1], for sake (+5921) [1], hurt [1], iniquities (+5771) [1], judgment (+4941) [1], language [1], lies (+3577) [1], lies (+8267) [1], lying (+8267) [1], no (+3808) [1], nothing (+3605+3808) [1], oracle [1], parts [1], provision [1], purpose [1], reason [1], sakes [1], sake [1], so (+2088+1886.1+1886.1+3509.1) [1], somewhat to say [1], some [1], song (+7892) [1], sort [1], spakest [1], such [1], tasks [1], task [1], that (+2088+1886.1+1886.1) [1], thing (+1886.1) [1], things concerning [1], thought [1], thus (+2088+1886.1+1886.1) [1], what (+4100+1886.1) [1], whatsoever (+4100) [1], what [1], wherewith [1], whit [1], word's [1], work required [1], works [1]

1698 דֶּבֶר ***deber***, n.m. GK: 1822 & 1823 [→ 1696]. plague, pestilence, disease, a pandemic occurrence of sickness and death; some sources identify specific diseases in specific contexts; thorn:– pestilence [47], murrain [1], plagues [1]

1699 דֹּבֶר ***dōber***, n.[m.]. GK: 1824 [→ 1696]. pasture, in a remote place:– fold [1], manner [1]

1699' דִּבֵּר ***dibbēr***, n.[m.]. GK: 1825 [→ 1696]. word (of God):– word [2]

דְּבִר ***d^{e}bir***. See 1687, 1688.

1700 דִּבְרָה ***dibrâ***, n.f. GK: 1826 [→ 1696; cf. 1701]. cause; order; therefore, because:– cause [1], end [1], estate [1], order [1], regard [1]

1701 דִּבְרָה ***dibrâ*** (Aram.), n.f. GK: 10159 [cf. 1700]. affair, matter:– intent [1], sakes [1]

דְּבֹרָה ***d^{e}bōrâ*** or דְּבוֹרָה ***d^{e}bōrâ***. See 1682, 1683.

1702 דֹּבְרוֹת ***dōb^{e}rôt***, n.f.pl. GK: 1827 [→ 1696]. raft, a collection of logs towed behind a ship:– flotes [1]

1703 דַּבֶּרֶת ***dabberet***, n.f. GK: 1830 [→ 1696]. instruction, word:– words [1]

1704 דִּבְרִי ***dibrî***, n.pr.m. GK: 1828. Dibri, "[poss.] *speak*":– Dibri [1]

1705 דָּבְרַת ***dāb^{e}rat***, n.pr.loc. GK: 1829 [→ 1696]. Daberath, *"pasture"*:– Daberath [2], Dabareh [1]

1706 דְּבַשׁ ***d^{e}baš***, n.m. GK: 1831 [→ 3031]. honey:– honey [52], honeycomb (+3295+1886.1) [1], honeycomb (+6688) [1]

1707 דַּבֶּשֶׁת ***dabbešet***, n.f. GK: 1832 [→ 1708?]. hump (of a camel):– bunches [1]

1708 דַּבֶּשֶׁת ***dabbešet***, n.pr.loc. GK: 1833 [→ 1707?]. Dabbesheth, *"hump"*:– Dabbasheth [1]

1709 דָּג ***dāg*** or דָּאג ***dā'g***, n.m. GK: 1834 & 1794 [→ 1711?, 1710, 1728, 1729, 1771; cf. 1770]. fish:– fish [11], fishes [8]

1710 דָּגָה ***dāgā***, n.f. GK: 1836 [→ 1709]. fish:– fish [14], fish's [1]

1711 דָּגָה ***dāgâ***, v. GK: 1835 [→ 1709?]. [Q] to increase, multiply:– grow [1]

1712 דָּגוֹן ***dāgôn***, n.pr.m. GK: 1837 [→ 1016, 1715]. Dagon (pagan god), *"[god of] grain; fish"*:– Dagon [12], Dagon's [1]

1713 דָּגַל ***dāgal***, v.den. GK: 1838 & 1839 [→ 1714]. [Q] to lift a banner; [Qp] to be outstanding, conspicuous; [N] be gathered around the banner(s), organized as troops:– banners [1], chiefest [1], set up banners [1], with banners [1]

1714 דֶּגֶל ***degel***, n.m. GK: 1840 [→ 1713]. standard, banner:– standard [10], standards [3], banner [1]

1715 דָּגָן ***dāgān***, n.m. GK: 1841 [→ 1712]. grain:– corn [37], wheat [2], cornfloor (+1637) [1]

1716 דָּגַר ***dāgar***, v. GK: 1842. [Q] to care for; hatch eggs:– gather [1], sitteth [1]

1717 דַּד ***dad***, n.m. GK: 1843. bosom, breast:– breasts [2], teats [2]

1718 דָּדָה ***dādâ***, v. GK: 1844. [Ht] to walk, lead:– go softly [1], went with [1]

1719 דְּדָן ***d^{e}dān***, n.pr.loc. & g. GK: 1847 [→ 1720]. Dedan:– Dedan [11]

1720 דְּדָנִי ***d^{e}dānî***, a.g. GK: 1848 [→ 1719]. Dedanite, *"of Dedan"*:– Dedanim [1]

1721 דֹּדָנִים ***dōdānîm*** or רֹדָן ***rōdān***, n.pr.g.pl. GK: 1849 & 8102. Dodanim; Rhodes, Rodanim, *"people of Rhodes"*:– Dodanim [2]

1722 דְּהַב ***d^{e}hab*** (Aram.), n.m. GK: 10160 [cf. 2091]. gold:– gold [14], golden [9]

1723 דְּהוּא ***d^{e}hû'*** (Aram.), pt. + pr. GK: 10161 & 10162 [→ 1768+1932]. that is (1768 + 1932):– Dehavites [1]

1724 דָּהַם ***dāham***, v. GK: 1850. [N] to be taken by surprise, be astounded:– astonied [1]

1725 דָּהַר ***dāhar***, v. GK: 1851 [→ 1726]. [Q] to gallop:– pransing [1]

1726 דַּהֲרָה ***dah^{a}râ***, n.f. GK: 1852 [→ 1725]. galloping:– pransings [2]

דּוֹאֵג ***dô'ēg***. See 1673.

1727 דּוּב ***dûb***, v. GK: 1853 [cf. 2100]. [H] to drain away, wear away; loss of life as a fig.

extension of draining liquid out of a container:– cause sorrow [1]

דּוֹב **dôb**. See 1677.

1728 דַּוָּג **dawwāg**, n.m. GK: 1854 [→ 1709]. fisherman:– fishers [1]

1729 דּוּגָה **dûgâ**, n.f. GK: 1855 [→ 1709]. fishing (hooks):– fishhooks (+5518) [1]

1730 דּוֹד **dôd**, n.m. GK: 1856 [→ 419, 449, 1085, 1732?, 1733, 1734?, 1737?]. uncle, cousin, relative; beloved one, lover; a term of endearment ranging from friendship and familial affection to romantic love:– beloved [32], uncle [10], love [7], uncle's [6], beloved's (+3807.1) [2], father's brothers' [1], father's brother [1], loves [1], well-beloved [1]

1731 דּוּד **dûd**, n.m. GK: 1857. basket; kettle, caldron, pot:– basket [2], baskets [1], caldrons [1], kettle [1], pots [1], pot [1]

1732 דָּוִד **dāwid**, n.pr.m. GK: 1858 [→ 1730?]. David, *"beloved one"*:– David [1022], David's [50], David's (+3807.1) [3]

1733 דּוֹדָה **dôdâ**, n.f. GK: 1860 [→ 1730]. aunt (father's sister):– aunt [1], father's sister [1], uncle's wife [1]

1734 דּוֹדוֹ **dôdô** or דֹּדַי **dōdî**, n.pr.m. GK: 1861 & 1846 [→ 1730?]. Dodo, Dodai, *"beloved"*:– Dodo [5]

1735 דֹּדָוָהוּ **dōdāwāhû**, n.pr.m. GK: 1845. Dodavahu, *"beloved of Yahweh"*:– Dodavah [1]

1736 דּוּדָאִים **dûdā'îm** or דּוּדַי **dûday**, n.m. GK: 1859 & 1863. mandrake plant, thought to be a fertility aid or aphrodisiac:– mandrakes [6], baskets [1]

1737 דּוֹדַי **dôday**, n.pr.m. GK: 1862 [→ 1730?]. Dodai, *"beloved"*:– Dodai [1]

1738 דָּוָה **dāwâ**, v. GK: 1864 [→ 1739, 1741, 1742, 1773?, 4064]. [Q] to have a monthly period, menstruate:– infirmity [1]

1739 דָּוֶה **dāweh**, a. GK: 1865 [→ 1738]. pertaining to the menstrual cycle; fainting:– faint [2], having sickness [1], menstruous cloth [1], sick [1]

1740 דּוּחַ **dûaḥ**, v. GK: 1866 [cf. 5080]. [H] to rinse, wash, cleanse:– washed [2], cast out [1], purged [1]

1741 דְּוַי **d^e way**, n.[m.]. GK: 1867 [→ 1738]. illness:– languishing [1], sorrowful [1]

1742 דַּוָּי **dawwāy**, a. GK: 1868 [→ 1738]. faint; afflicted:– faint [3]

דָּוִיד **dāwîd**. See 1732.

1743 דּוּךְ **dûk**, v. GK: 1870 [→ 4085; cf. 1790, 1792, 1794, 1854]. [Q] to crush (in a mortar):– beat [1]

1744 דּוּכִיפַת **dûkîpat**, n.f. GK: 1871. hoopoe:– lapwing [2]

1745 דּוּמָה **dûmâ**, n.f. GK: 1872 [→ 1826]. silence:– silence [2]

1746 דּוּמָה **dûmâ**, n.pr.loc. GK: 1873 & 1874. Dumah, *"silence"*:– Dumah [4]

1747 דּוּמִיָּה **dûmiyyâ**, n.f. GK: 1875 [→ 1826; cf. 1820]. silence, stillness; rest:– waiteth [2], silence [1], silent [1]

1748 דּוּמָם **dûmām**, n.[m.]. GK: 1876 [cf. 1826]. in silence, quietly; lifeless:– dumb [1], quietly wait [1], silent [1]

דּוּמֶשֶׂק **dûmešeq**. See 1833.

1749 דּוֹנַג **dônag**, n.m. GK: 1880. wax:– wax [4]

1750 דּוּץ **dûṣ**, v. GK: 1881. [Q] to leap:– turned into joy [1]

1751 דּוּק **dûq**, v. GK: 1882 [→ 1785]. [Q] to review:–

1752 דּוּר **dûr**, v. GK: 1883 & 1884 [→ 115, 1754, 1755, 4071; cf. 1756; cf. 1753]. [Q] to dwell; to pile logs (around, to burn):– burn [1], dwell [1]

1753 דּוּר **dûr** (Aram.), v. GK: 10163 [→ 1859, 4070, 8411; cf. 1752]. [P] to live, dwell:– dwell [3], dwelt [2], inhabitants [2]

1754 דּוּר **dûr**, n.[m.]. GK: 1885 [→ 1752; cf. 8411]. all around, encircling; ball:– ball [1], round about (+1886.1+3509.1) [1]

1755 דּוֹר **dôr**, n.m. GK: 1886 & 1887 [→ 1752; cf. 1859]. generation, generation to come; descendant; house, dwelling:– generation [57], generations [50], all generations (+1755+2050.1) [26], many generations (+1755+2050.1) [12], all generations (+1755) [4], age [2], all generations (+1755+3605+2050.1) [2], evermore (+1755+2050.1) [2], every generation (+1755+2050.1) [2], every generation (+1755+3605+2050.1) [2], generations (+1755+2050.1) [2], never (+1755+3808+2050.1) [2], throughout all generations (+1755) [2], another[s] [1], posterity [1]

1756 דּוֹר **dôr** or דֹּאר **dō'r**, n.pr.loc. GK: 1888 & 1799 [→ 2576, 5874; cf. 1752]. Dor:– Dor [7]

1757 דּוּרָא **dûrā'** (Aram.), n.pr.loc. GK: 10164. Dura:– Dura [1]

1758 דּוּשׁ **dûš**, v. GK: 1889 [→ 1786, 1788?, 4098; cf. 1759]. [Q] to tread, trample, thresh; [Qp, N, Ho] be trampled, be threshed:– thresh [3], threshed [2], threshing [2], trodden down [2], break [1], tear [1], tread out [1], treadeth out [1]

1759 דּוּשׁ **dûš** (Aram.), v. GK: 10165 [cf. 1758]. [P] to trample, tread down:– tread down [1]

1760 דָּחָה **dāḥâ** or דָּחַח **dāḥaḥ**, v. GK: 1890 & 1891 [→ 1762, 4072; cf. 5080; cf. 1761]. [Q] to push, push away; trip up; [Qp] to totter; [N] to be brought down; to be pushed, pushed out; [Pu] to be thrown down:– outcasts [3], thrust sore (+1760) [2], cast down [1], chase [1], driven away [1], driven on [1], overthrow [1], tottering [1]

1761 דַּחֲוָה **daḥ^a wâ** (Aram.), n.f. GK: 10166. entertainment, variously interpreted as musical, dancing, sexual, culinary, etc:– instruments of musick [1]

1762 דְּחִי **d^e ḥî**, n.[m.]. GK: 1892 [→ 1760]. stumbling:– falling [2]

1763 דְּחַל **d^e ḥal** (Aram.), v. GK: 10167 [cf. 2119]. [P] to fear, reverence; [Pp] to be terrified, be awesome; [Pa] to make afraid:– dreadful [2], feared [1], fear [1], made afraid [1], terrible [1]

1764 דֹּחַן **dōḥan**, n.m. GK: 1893. (sorghum) millet:– millet [1]

1765 דָּחַף **dāḥap**, v. GK: 1894 [→ 4073]. [Qp] to be spurred on, be in haste; [N] to be eager, be rushed, hurry:– hasted [2], hastened [1], pressed on [1]

1766 דָּחַק **dāḥaq**, v. GK: 1895. [Q] to afflict, oppress:– thrust [1], vexed [1]

1767 דַּי **day**, subst. GK: 1896 [→ 1838, 4078]. enough, sufficient:– enough [6], from (+4480) [5], since (+4480) [3], sufficient [3], when (+4480) [3], in (+871.1) [2], very [2], ability [1], able (+3027+4672) [1], able (+3027+5381+3509.1) [1], able to bring (+3027+4672) [1], able [1], according to (+3509.1) [1], after (+4480) [1], among (+871.1) [1], as oft as (+4480) [1], much [1], so much as is sufficient [1], sufficient for [1], time [1]

1768 דִּי **dî** (Aram.), pt.rel. & c. GK: 10168 [cf. 2088, 2098]. who, that, of:– that [100], of [64], which [54], whom [13], forasmuch as (+3606+6903) [8], till (+5705) [8], for [5], because (+3606+6903) [4], when (+3509.4) [4], whereas [4], whomsoever (+4479) [4], whose [4], who [3], because [2], until (+5705) [2], whatsoever (+1768+3606) [2], what [2], whoso (+4479) [2], whosoever (+3606) [2], whosoever (+606+1768+3606) [2], as (+3509.4) [1], as (+3606+6903) [1], at what time (+0.2+5732+871.2) [1], because (+4481) [1], but [1], none (+383+3809) [1], now (+116) [1], seeing [1], than [1], that which [1], therefore (+3606+6903) [1], those [1], though (+3606+6903) [1], what (+3964+3807.2) [1], whatsoever (+3606) [1], whatsoever (+4101) [1], wheresoever (+3606+871.2) [1], where [1]

1769 דִּיבֹן **dîbôn**, n.pr.loc. GK: 1897 [→ 1769+1410; cf. 1775, 1776]. Dibon:– Dibon [9], Dibon-gad [2]

1770 דִּיג **dîg**, v.den. GK: 1899 [cf. 1709]. [Q] to catch fish:– fish [1]

1771 דַּיָּג **dayyāg**, n.m. GK: 1900 [→ 1709]. fisherman:– fishers [2]

1772 דַּיָּה **dayyâ**, n.f. GK: 1901 [cf. 1675]. falcon:– vultures [1], vulture [1]

1773 דְּיוֹ **d^e yô**, n.m. GK: 1902 [→ 1738?]. ink, a writing substance made of soot or metal shavings mixed with oil or resin:– ink [1]

1774 דִּי זָהָב **dî zāhāb**, n.pr.loc. GK: 1903. Dizahab, *"that which has gold"*:– Dizahab [1]

1775 דִּימוֹן **dîmôn**, n.pr.loc. GK: 1904 [cf. 1769]. Dimon:– Dimon [2]

1776 דִּימוֹנָה **dîmônâ**, n.pr.loc. GK: 1905 [cf. 1769]. Dimonah:– Dimonah [1]

1777 דִּין **dîn**, v. GK: 1906 [→ 1779, 1781, 1783, 1835, 4066, 4068, 4079, 4082, 4090; cf. 1778 (also used with compound proper names)]. [Q] to judge, punish; to plead, defend, vindicate, contend for; [N] to argue:– judge [14], judged [2], at strife [1], contend [1], execute [1], judgeth [1], minister judgment [1], plead the cause [1], plead [1], strive [1]

1778 דִּין **dîn** (Aram.), v. GK: 10169 [→ 1780, 1782, 1784, 4083; cf. 1777]. [P] to administer justice, judge:– judge [1]

1779 דִּין **dîn**, n.[m.]. GK: 1907 [→ 1777; cf. 1780]. cause, legal case; judgment, justice:– judgment [9], cause [8], plea [2], strife [1]

1780 דִּין **dîn** (Aram.), n.m. GK: 10170 [→ 1778; cf. 1779]. judgment, court (place of judgment):– judgment [5]

1781 דַּיָּן **dayyān**, n.m. GK: 1908 [→ 1777; cf. 1782]. defender, judge:– judge [2]

1782 דַּיָּן **dayyān** (Aram.), n.m. GK: 10171 [→ 1778; cf. 1781]. judge:– judges [1]

1783 דִּינָה **dînâ**, n.pr.f. GK: 1909 [→ 1777]. Dinah, *"female judge"*:– Dinah [7], Dinah's [1]

1784 דִּינָיֵא **dînāyē'** (Aram.), n.pr.g. GK: 10172 [→ 1778]. judge:– Dinaites [1]

Heb

דִּיפַת ***dîpat***. See 7384.

1785 דָּיֵק ***dāyēq***, n.m. GK: 1911 [→ 1751]. siege works:– forts [3], fort [3]

1786 דַּיִשׁ ***dayiš***, n.m. GK: 1912 [→ 1758]. threshing (season):– threshing [1]

1787 דִּישׁוֹן ***dîšôn***, n.pr.m. GK: 1914 [→ 1788?]. Dishon, Dishan, *"ibex[?]"*:– Dishon [6]

1788 דִּישׁוֹן ***dîšôn***, n.[m.]. GK: 1913 [→ 1787?, 1789?; cf. 1758?]. ibex:– pygarg [1]

1789 דִּישָׁן ***dîšān***, n.pr.m. GK: 1915 [→ 1788?]. Dishan, *"ibex[?]"*:– Dishan [5], Dishon [1]

1790 דַּךְ ***dak***, a. GK: 1916 [→ 1795; cf. 1743, 1792, 1794, 1854]. oppressed:– oppressed [3], afflicted [1]

1791 דֵּךְ ***dēk*** (Aram.), p.demo.com. GK: 10173 [→ 1797]. this:– this [12], the same [1]

1792 דָּכָא ***dākā'***, v. GK: 1917 [→ 1793; cf. 1743, 1790, 1794, 1854]. [N] to be contrite; [P] to crush; [Pu] to be crushed, be dejected, be humbled; [Ht] to lie crushed:– break in pieces [3], broken [2], crushed [2], beat to pieces [1], broken in pieces [1], bruised [1], bruise [1], contrite ones [1], crush [1], destroyed [1], destroy [1], humbled [1], oppress [1], smitten down [1]

1793 דַּכָּא ***dakkā'***, a. & n.[m.]. GK: 1918 & 1919 [→ 1792]. crushed, contrite; dust:– contrite [2], destruction [1]

1794 דָּכָה ***dākâ***, v. GK: 1920 [→ 1796; cf. 1743, 1790, 1792, 1854]. [Q, P] to crush; [N] to be crushed, contrite:– broken [2], contrite [1], croucheth [1], sore broken [1]

1795 דַּכָּה ***dakkâ***, n.f. GK: 1921 [→ 1790]. crushing (of testicle):– stones [1]

1796 דֳּכִי ***dᵒkî***, n.[m.]. GK: 1922 [→ 1794]. pounding (waves):– waves [1]

1797 דִּכֵּן ***dikkēn*** (Aram.), p.demo.com. GK: 10174 [→ 1791]. that:– same [1], that [1], this [1]

1798 דְּכַר ***dᵉkar*** (Aram.), n.m. GK: 10175 [cf. 2145]. ram (male animal):– rams [3]

1799 דִּכְרוֹן ***dikrôn*** or דָּכְרָן ***dokrān*** (Aram.), n.[m.]. GK: 10176 & 10177 [cf. 2146]. memorandum, record:– records [2], record [1]

1800 דַּל ***dal***, a. GK: 1924 [→ 1803; cf. 1809]. poor, needy, humble; weak, haggard, scrawny:– poor [43], needy [2], lean [1], weaker [1]

1801 דָּלַג ***dālag***, v. GK: 1925. [Q, P] to scale, ascend, leap up over:– leaped over [2], leap [2], leaping [1]

1802 דָּלָה ***dālâ***, v. GK: 1926 & 1927 [→ 1805, 1806, 1808]. [Q, P] to draw up, draw water (from a well); [Q] to hang limp, dangle:– drew water enough (+1802) [2], draw out [1], drew water [1], lifted up [1]

1803 דַּלָּה ***dallâ***, n.f. GK: 1929 & 1930 [→ 1800, 1809]. poor, a class of people with little status, influence, and social value; threads remaining on the loom; flowing hair:– poor [5], hair [1], pining sickness [1], poorest sort [1]

1804 דָּלַח ***dālaḥ***, v. GK: 1931. [Q] to churn, stir up:– trouble [2], troubledst [1]

1805 דְּלִי ***dᵉlî***, n.[m.]. GK: 1932 [→ 1802]. (water) bucket, possibly made of leather:– buckets [1], bucket [1]

1806 דְּלָיָה ***dᵉlāyâ*** or דְּלָיָהוּ ***dᵉlāyāhû***, n.pr.m. GK: 1933 & 1934 [→ 1802+3068]. Delaiah, *"Yahweh draws up [like water in a bucket]"*:– Delaiah [6], Dalaiah [1]

1807 דְּלִילָה ***dᵉlîlâ***, n.pr.f. GK: 1935 [→ 1809]. Delilah, *"tease"*:– Delilah [6]

1808 דָּלִית ***dālît***, n.f. GK: 1936 [→ 1802]. branch, bough:– branches [8]

1809 דָּלַל ***dālal***, v. GK: 1937 & 1938 [→ 1800, 1803, 1807]. [Q] to be in need, be weak, fade; to dangle:– brought low [3], dried up [1], emptied [1], fail [1], impoverished [1], made thin [1], not equal [1]

1810 דִּלְעָן ***dil'ān***, n.pr.loc. GK: 1939. Dilean, *"cucumber; protrude"*:– Dilean [1]

1811 דָּלַף ***dālap***, v. GK: 1940 & 1941 [→ 1812, 1813, 3044]. [Q] to leak; to pour out; to be weary, be sleepless:– droppeth through [1], melteth [1], poureth out [1]

1812 דֶּלֶף ***delep***, n.m. GK: 1942 [→ 1811]. leaky roof:– continual dropping (+2956) [1], dropping [1]

1813 דַּלְפוֹן ***dalpôn***, n.pr.m. GK: 1943 [→ 1811]. Dalphon, *"crafty; sleepless"*:– Dalphon [1]

1814 דָּלַק ***dālaq***, v. GK: 1944 [→ 1816; cf. 1815]. [Q] to set on fire; to hunt, chase, pursue; [H] to inflame, kindle:– kindle [2], burning [1], chasing [1], hotly pursued [1], inflame [1], persecute [1], persecutors [1], pursued [1]

1815 דְּלַק ***dᵉlaq*** (Aram.), v. GK: 10178 [cf. 1814]. [P] to be ablaze, burn:– burning [1]

1816 דַּלֶּקֶת ***dalleqet***, n.f. GK: 1945 [→ 1814]. inflammation:– inflammation [1]

1817 דֶּלֶת ***delet***, n.f. [& m.?]. GK: 1923 & 1928 & 1946. door, gate; column, lid, leaf (of a door):– doors [48], door [21], gates [13], leaves [4], lid [1], two leaved gates [1]

1818 דָּם ***dām***, n.m. GK: 1947. blood, lifeblood; by extension: bloodshed, death; blood-colored fluids: grape juice, wine; "to pour out blood" is "to kill" since life is in the blood:– blood [342], bloody [15], bloodguiltiness [1], bloodthirsty (+376) [1], person[s] [1]

1819 דָּמָה ***dāmâ***, v. GK: 1948 [→ 1823, 1824, 1825; cf. 1821]. [Q] to be like, liken, resemble; [N] to be like; [P] to think, plan, intend; to liken; [Ht] to consider oneself equal to:– like [14], liken [4], thought [4], likened [2], compared [1], devised [1], meaneth [1], think [1], thoughtest [1], used similitudes [1]

1820 דָּמָה ***dāmâ***, v. GK: 1949 & 1950 [→ 1822?, 1824; cf. 1747, 1826]. [Q] to destroy; to cease; to be silent; [N] to perish, be ruined, be destroyed, be wiped out; to be silenced:– cut off [3], brought to silence [2], perish [2], utterly cut off (+1820) [2], ceaseth [1], cease [1], cut down [1], destroyed [1], destroy [1], undone [1]

1821 דְּמָה ***dᵉmâ*** (Aram.), v. GK: 10179 [cf. 1819]. [P] to look like, resemble:– like [2]

1822 דֻּמָה ***dumâ***, n.f. GK: 1951 [→ 1820?]. one silenced:– destroyed [1]

1823 דְּמוּת ***dᵉmût***, n.f. GK: 1952 [→ 1819]. likeness, figure, image, form:– likeness [19], similitude [2], fashion [1], like (+3509.1) [1], like as [1], manner [1]

1824 דְּמִי ***dᵉmî*** or דֳּמִי ***dᵒmî***, n.[m.]. GK: 1953 & 1954 [→ 1819, 1820]. silence, rest; prime (of life), a fig. extension of being at a midway point in a journey:– cutting off [1], keep silence [1], rest [1], silence [1]

1825 דִּמְיוֹן ***dimyôn***, n.[m.]. GK: 1955 [→ 1819]. likeness:– like [1]

1826 דָּמַם ***dāmam***, v. GK: 1957 & 1958 & 1959 [→ 1745, 1747, 1827; cf. 1748, 1820]. [Q] to perish; to be still, be silent, be quiet, rest; [N] to be laid waste, be silenced, be destroyed; [Po] to quiet; [H] to doom to perish:– silent [4], still [4], cut off [3], cut down [2], keep silence [2], kept silence [2], ceased [1], cease [1], forbear [1], held peace [1], keepeth silence [1], put to silence [1], quieted [1], rested [1], rest [1], stand still [1], stood still [1], tarry [1], wait [1]

1827 דְּמָמָה ***dᵉmāmâ***, n.f. GK: 1960 [→ 1826]. hush, whisper:– calm [1], silence [1], still [1]

1828 דֹּמֶן ***dōmen***, n.m. GK: 1961 [→ 4087]. refuse, dung:– dung [6]

1829 דִּמְנָה ***dimnâ***, n.pr.loc. GK: 1962. Dimnah, *"manure"*:– Dimnah [1]

1830 דָּמַע ***dāma'***, v. GK: 1963 [→ 1831, 1832]. [Q] to weep:– weep sore (+1830) [2]

1831 דֶּמַע ***dema'***, n.[m.]. GK: 1964 [→ 1830]. juice:– liquors [1]

1832 דִּמְעָה ***dim'â***, n.f. GK: 1965 [→ 1830]. tears, weeping:– tears [23]

1833 דְּמֶשֶׁק ***dᵉmešeq***, n.[m.?]. GK: 1967 [→ 1834?]. Damascus, damask [?]:– Damascus [1]

1834 דַּמֶּשֶׂק ***dammeśeq*** or דּוּמֶּשֶׂק ***dûmmeśeq*** or דַּרְמֶשֶׂק ***darmeśeq***, n.pr.loc. GK: 1877 & 1966 & 2008 [→ 1833?]. Damascus:– Damascus [44], Syria-damascus (+758) [1]

1835 דָּן ***dān***, n.pr.m. & loc. GK: 1968 [→ 1842, 1839; cf. 1777]. Dan, *"judge"*:– Dan [71]

1836 דְּנָה ***dᵉnâ*** (Aram.), p.demo.com. GK: 10180 [→ 412, 429, 459, 479]. this, that:– this [38], therefore (+3606+6903) [3], these [3], hereafter (+311) [2], thus (+3509.4) [2], wherefore (+3606+6903) [2], aforetime (+4481+6928) [1], another [1], for this cause (+3606+6903) [1], one [1], such (+3509.4) [1], that (+3606+6903) [1], therefore (+5922) [1], which [1]

1837 דַּנָּה ***dannâ***, n.pr.loc. GK: 1972 [→ 4091]. Dannah, *"stronghold"*:– Dannah [1]

1838 דִּנְהָבָה ***dinhābâ***, n.pr.loc. GK: 1973 [→ 1767+5107]. Dinhabah:– Dinhabah [2]

1839 דָּנִי ***dānî***, a.g. GK: 1974 [→ 1835]. Danite, men of Dan, *"of Dan"*:– Danites [4], Dan [1]

1840 דָּנִאֵל ***dāni'ēl*** or דָּנִיֵּאל ***dāniyyē'l***, n.pr.m. GK: 1971 & 1975 [→ 1777+410; cf. 1841]. Danel, Daniel; this can refer to four different persons, the most prominent being the sage and prophet of the captivity, *"God is [my] judge"*:– Daniel [29]

1841 דָּנִיֵּאל ***dāniyyē'l*** (Aram.), n.pr.m. GK: 10181 [cf. 1840]. Daniel, *"God (El) is my judge"*:– Daniel [52]

1842 דָּן יַעַן ***dān ya'an***, n.pr.loc. GK: 1970 [→ 1835]. Dan Jaan:– Dan-jaan [1]

1843 דֵּעַ ***dēa'***, n.[m.]. GK: 1976 [→ 1844; cf. 3045]. what is known, knowledge:– opinion [3], knowledge [2]

1844 דֵּעָה ***dē'â***, n.f. GK: 1978 [→ 1843; cf. 3045]. knowledge:– knowledge [6]

1845 דְּעוּאֵל ***dᵉ'û'ēl***, n.pr.m. GK: 1979 [→ 3045+410]. Deuel, *"known of God [El]"*:– Deuel [4]

1846 דָּעַךְ ***dā'ak***, v. GK: 1980 [cf. 2193]. [Q] to snuff out, extinguish; [N] to vanish; [Pu] to die out:– put out [6], consumed [1], extinct [1], quenched [1]

1847 דַּעַת ***da'at***, n.f. & m. GK: 1981 & 1982 & 1983 [→ 3045]. knowledge; understanding, learning; claim:– knowledge [80], know [4], unwittingly (+1097+871.1) [2], cunning [1], hath knowledge (+3045) [1], have knowledge (+3045) [1], ignorantly (+1097+871.1) [1], knew [1], knowest (+5921) [1], unawares (+1097+871.1) [1]

1848 דֳּפִי ***d^opî***, n.[m.]. GK: 1984. blemish, stain; slander:– slanderest (+5414) [1]

1849 דָּפַק ***dāpaq***, v. GK: 1985 [→ 1850]. [Q] to drive hard; to knock hard (= worry); [Ht] to pound (on a door):– beat [1], knocketh [1], overdrive [1]

1850 דָּפְקָה ***dopqâ***, n.pr.loc. GK: 1986 [→ 1849]. Dophkah, "*drive [sheep]*":– Dophkah [2]

1851 דַּק ***daq***, a. GK: 1987 [→ 1854]. gaunt, thin, dwarfed; finely ground (incense), fine (dust):– thin [5], small [4], leanfleshed (+1320) [2], beaten small [1], dwarf [1], very little thing [1]

1852 דֹּק ***dōq***, n.[m.]. GK: 1988 [→ 1854]. canopy, thin veil:– curtain [1]

1853 דִּקְלָה ***diqlâ***, n.pr.m.[loc.]. GK: 1989. Diklah, "*[place of] date palms*":– Diklah [2]

1854 דָּקַק ***dāqaq***, v. GK: 1990 [→ 1851, 1852; cf. 1743, 1790, 1792, 1794; cf. 1855]. [Q] to finely crush or grind; [H] to grind to powder, break to pieces; [Ho] to be ground (to make bread):– powder [2], stampt small [2], beat in pieces [1], beat small [1], bruised [1], bruise [1], made dust [1], small [1], stamped [1], stamp [1], very small [1]

1855 דְּקַק ***d^eqaq*** (Aram.), v. GK: 10182 [cf. 1854]. [P] to break to pieces; [H] to crush, smash, pulverize:– brake in pieces [5], break in pieces [3], breaketh in pieces [1], broken to pieces [1]

1856 דָּקַר ***dāqar***, v. GK: 1991 [→ 1128, 1857, 4094]. [Q] to drive through, pierce, stab; [Qp, N, Pu] to be pierced:– thrust through [8], pierced [1], stricken through [1], wounded [1]

1857 דֶּקֶר ***deqer***, n.pr.m. GK: 1992 [→ 1856]. Deker:– Dekar [1]

1858 דַּר ***dar***, n.[m.]. GK: 1993. mother-of-pearl:– white [1]

1859 דָּר ***dār*** (Aram.), n.[m.]. GK: 10183 [→ 1753; cf. 1755]. generation; the phrase "from generation to generation" indicates an unlimited span of time: "eternal, forever":– generation [4]

דֹּר ***dōr***. See 1755.

1860 דֵּרָאוֹן ***dērā'ôn***, n.m. GK: 1994. loathing, contempt, aversion:– abhorring [1], contempt [1]

1861 דָּרְבָן ***dorbān***, n.[m.]. GK: 1995 & 1996. (iron) goading stick:– goads [2]

1862 דַּרְדַּע ***darda'***, n.pr.m. GK: 1997 [cf. 1873]. Darda:– Darda [1]

1863 דַּרְדַּר ***dardar***, n.[m.]. GK: 1998. thistle:– thistles [1], thistle [1]

1864 דָּרוֹם ***dārôm***, n.m. GK: 1999. south; south wind:– south [17]

1865 דְּרוֹר ***d^erôr***, n.[m.]. GK: 2001 & 2002. freedom, liberty; an event required every fifty years to restore Israelite slaves to freedom and Israelite land to tribal allotments; oil of myrrh, stacte:– liberty [7], pure [1]

1866 דְּרוֹר ***d^erôr***, n.f. GK: 2000. a kind of bird, perhaps swallow or dove:– swallow [2]

1867 דָּרְיָוֶשׁ ***dār^eyāweš***, n.pr.m. GK: 2003 [cf. 1868]. Darius, "*he who upholds the good*":– Darius [10]

1868 דָּרְיָוֶשׁ ***dār^eyāweš*** (Aram.), n.pr.m. GK: 10184 [cf. 1867]. Darius, "*he who upholds the good*":– Darius [15]

1869 דָּרַךְ ***dārak***, v. GK: 2005 [→ 1870, 4096]. [Q] to go out, set out, march on, walk upon, trample; to bend (a bow); [Qp] to string (a bow), be bent (of a bow); [H] to shoot (a bow); to cause to tread, to enable to go; to lead, guide:– tread [12], bend [7], bent [7], trodden [6], treadeth [4], bendeth [2], lead [2], archers (+7198) [1], archer [1], come [1], drew [1], goeth [1], guide [1], leadeth [1], led forth [1], led [1], make go over [1], make to go [1], make to walk [1], shoot [1], thresh [1], tread out [1], tread upon [1], treaders [1], treader [1], treading [1], trodden down [1], trode down [1], trode [1], walk [1]

1870 דֶּרֶךְ ***derek***, n.m. GK: 2006 [→ 1869]. way, path, route, road, journey; by extension: conduct, way of life; a pagan god (Am 8:14):– way [460], ways [164], toward [29], journey [23], manner [8], conversation [2], towards [2], along by (+4480) [1], away (+871.1) [1], by [1], custom [1], eastward (+6921+1886.1) [1], high way [1], in the way go (+5921+6310) [1], journeyed (+6213) [1], pass by (+5674) [1], passengers (+5674) [1], pathway (+5410) [1], through [1], transgression (+6588) [1], way side [1], wayfaring men (+1980) [1], wayside (+3027) [1], whithersoever (+834+871.1+1886.1) [1]

1871 דַּרְכְּמוֹנִים ***dark^emônîm***, n.[m.]. GK: 2007 [→ 150]. (pl.) drachmas (Persian: a unit of weight used as a money, the value of which is uncertain):– drams [4]

1872 דְּרָע ***d^erā'*** (Aram.), n.[f.]. GK: 10185 [→ 153; cf. 2220]. arm:– arms [1]

1873 דָּרַע ***dāra'***, n.pr.m. GK: 2009 [cf. 1862]. Daraa:– Dara [1]

1874 דַּרְקוֹן ***darqôn***, n.pr.m. GK: 2010. Darkon, "[perhaps] *rough* or *stern*":– Darkon [2]

1875 דָּרַשׁ ***dāraš***, v. GK: 2011 [→ 4097]. [Q] to seek, inquire, consult; [Qp] to ponder, be sought after; [N] to let oneself be inquired of, to allow a search to be made:– seek [54], inquire [29], sought [19], require [10], inquired [5], seeketh [5], inquired of [4], inquire of [3], search [3], diligently sought (+1875) [2], inquired of at all (+1875) [2], required [2], searcheth [2], seeking [2], sought after [2], sought out [2], surely require (+1875) [2], ask [1], cared [1], careth for [1], examine [1], inquired for [1], make inquisition [1], maketh inquisition [1], necromancer (+413+1886.1) [1], questioned [1], regard [1], search for [1], searchest [1], seek after [1], seek out [1], seeketh after [1], sought for [1]

1876 דָּשָׁא ***dāšā'***, v. GK: 2012 [→ 1877]. [Q] to become green (of pastures); [H] to produce, cause to shoot forth:– bring forth [1], spring [1]

1877 דֶּשֶׁא ***deše'***, n.m. GK: 2013 [→ 1876; cf. 1883]. (new) green vegetation, (new) green grass:– grass [6], herb [4], tender grass [2], tender herb [2], green [1]

1878 דָּשֵׁן ***dāšēn***, v. GK: 2014 [→ 1879, 1880]. [Q] to thrive, grow fat; [P] to anoint, give health; to remove the (fat) ashes; [Pu] to prosper, be satisfied, be soaked (with fat); [Hotpaal] to be covered with fat:– made fat [5], accept [1], anointest [1], maketh fat [1], receive ashes [1], take away ashes [1], waxen fat [1]

1879 דָּשֵׁן ***dāšēn***, a. GK: 2015 [→ 1878]. rich (pertaining to food which is fresh and possibly juicy), fresh:– fat [3]

1880 דֶּשֶׁן ***dešen***, n.m. GK: 2016 [→ 1878]. fat; ashes (the burned wood of the altar fire soaked with fat); by extension: abundance, riches, choice food; in the ancient Near East fatness was a positive, enviable state, though extreme obesity could be denounced or ridiculed:– ashes [8], fatness [7]

1881 דָּת ***dāt***, n.f. GK: 2017 [cf. 1882]. command (either written or oral), prescription, custom, edict, law:– decree [9], law [6], laws [3], commandment [2], commissions [1], manner [1]

1882 דָּת ***dāt*** (Aram.), n.f. GK: 10186 [cf. 1881]. law, decree, usually a written, codified prescription by either human or deity; the "Law of God" can refer to the Torah, the first five books of the Hebrew Bible:– law [9], decree [3], laws [2]

1883 דֶּתֶא ***dete'*** (Aram.), n.[m.]. GK: 10187 [cf. 1877]. grass (of the open country):– tender grass [2]

1884 דְּתָבַר ***d^etābar*** (Aram.), n.m. GK: 10188 [cf. 1881]. judge:– counsellers [2]

1885 דָּתָן ***dātān***, n.pr.m. GK: 2018. Dathan, "*strong*":– Dathan [10]

1886 דֹּתָן ***dōtān***, n.pr.loc. GK: 2019. Dothan, "*two wells*":– Dothan [3]

1886.1 הַ- ***ha-***, art.pref. GK: 2021 [cf. 0.2 (also used with compound proper names)]. the, a, who, this, that; often not translated:– the [18118], that [957], a [767], which [269], an [87], who [55], O [53], to day (+3117) [50], every morning (+1242+1242+871.1+871.1+1886.1) [20], he [17], for ever (+3117+3605) [15], it [12], without (+2351+871.1) [12], daily (+3117+3605) [11], those [10]*

1886.2 הֲ- ***h^a-***, inter.pt.pref. GK: 2022 [cf. 1886.6]. introduces a question; usually translated as a question mark:– *usually untranslated* [711], whether [23], if [5], as if [1], either [1], not [1], or [1]

1886.3 הּ- ***-āh*** or הָ- ***-hā*** or הָ- ***-â*** or הָא- ***-hā'***, p.f.s.suf. GK: 2023 [→ 1886.4, 1930.2, 1958.1, 1992.1, 1993.1, 2006.1, 2009.1, 2050.2, 3963.1, 4123.1, 4993.1, 5089.1, 5105.2]. she, her; it, its:– her [1518], it [649], thereof [343], therein (+871.1) [86], his [81], she [44], their [24], the^s [18], them [15], wherein (+834+871.1) [14], that [13], whose [13], therewith (+871.1) [11], thereon (+5921) [10], whereof [10]*

1886.4 הֹ- ***-ōh***, p.m.s.suf. GK: 2024 [→ 1886.3]. he, his, him:– his [11], it [3], one [3], them [3], they [3], he [1], same [1], thereof [1]

1886.5 הָ- ***-â***, adv.suf. GK: 2025. to, toward; a suffixed adverb or remnant of an archaic case ending:– to [269], into [97], toward [58], thither (+8033) [50], unto [49], upward (+4605) [45], on [41], whither (+834+8033) [38], upon [32], there (+8033) [31], westward (+3220) [21],

Heb

northward (+6828) [20], above (+4480+4605+3807.1) [18], whither (+575) [16], eastward (+4217) [15], west (+3220) [15], east (+6921) [14], at [13], how long (+575+5704) [13], southward (+5045) [13], in [12], upward (+4605+3807.1) [12], eastward (+6924) [9], north (+6828) [9], towards [9], abroad (+2351) [8], southward (+8486) [8], where (+834+8033) [7], above (+4605+3807.1) [6], without (+2351) [6], east (+6924) [5], inward (+1004) [5], on high (+4605+3807.1) [5], therein (+8033) [5], above (+4605) [4], any whither (+575+575+1886.5+2050.1) [4], eastward (+6921) [4], out (+2351) [3], where (+575) [3], yearly (+3117+3117+4480) [3], exceedingly (+4605+3807.1) [2], exceedingly (+4605+5704+3807.1) [2], forward (+4605) [2], south (+5045) [2], south (+8486+1886.5) [2], still (+4605+3807.1) [2], upward (+4480+4605+3807.1) [2], very high (+4605+4605+1886.5) [2], whither (+575+575+1886.5+2050.1) [2], whither (+8033) [2], without (+2351+4480) [2], abroad (+413+2351+1886.1) [1], by [1], east (+4217+6924) [1], exceeding (+4605) [1], exceeding (+4605+3807.1) [1], for [1], hither (+2008) [1], in north (+6828) [1], north side (+6828) [1], northwards (+6828) [1], on high (+4480+4605+3807.1) [1], outward (+2351) [1], over (+4480+4605+3807.1) [1], over (+4605+3807.1) [1], over and above (+4480+4605+3807.1) [1], overturned (+2015+4605+3807.1) [1], south (+8486) [1], south [1], thitherward (+8033) [1], through [1], unto (+8033) [1], up (+4605+3807.1) [1], very (+4605+3807.1) [1], westward (+4628) [1], whereinto (+834+8033) [1], whereunto (+834+8033) [1], whithersoever (+575) [1], within (+1004) [1], within (+1004+4480) [1], without (+2351+1886.1) [1], without (+2435) [1]

1886.6 הֲ־ ***hᵃ-*** (Aram.), inter.pt. GK: 10190 [cf. 1886.2]. introduces a question, translated as a question mark rather than as a word:– *not translated* [6]

1886.7 ־ָה ***-â*** (Aram.), art.suf. GK: 10191 [→ 0.2]. the, a:– the [32], The[s] [1], a [1], it [1], thereof [1], this [1]

1886.8 ־ֵהּ ***-ēh*** (Aram.), p.suf.3.m.s. GK: 10192 [→ 1958.2; cf. 1886.4]. he, him, his; it, its:– his [61], him [29], thereof [25], whose [11], it [4], the[s] [2], their [2], whom [2], he [1], his (+3807.2) [1], his own [1], same [1]

1886.9 ־ַהּ ***-ah*** (Aram.), p.suf.3.f.s. GK: 10193 [cf. 1886.3]. she, her; it, its:– it [21], his [5], same [3], whom [2], whose [2], the same (+1459) [1], therein (+1459+871.2) [1], therein (+871.2) [1], thereof [1]

1887 הֵא ***hē'***, interj. GK: 2026 [cf. 1888]. surely! see!, a discourse marker of emphasis:– behold [1], lo [1]

1888 הָא ***hā'*** or הֵא ***hē'*** (Aram.), demo.pt. GK: 10194 & 10195 [cf. 1887]. just as; look!, there!:– even [1], lo [1]

1889 הֶאָח ***he'āḥ***, interj. GK: 2027. Ah!, Aha!:– aha [10], ah [1], ha [1]

הָאֲרָרִי ***hā'rārî***. See 2043.

1890 הַבְהָב ***habhab***, n.m. GK: 2037. gift:– offerings [1]

1891 הָבַל ***hābal***, v.den. GK: 2038 [→ 1892]. [Q] to be worthless, meaningless; be proud, vain; [H] to fill with false hopes, cause to become vain:– vain [2], become vain [1], make vain [1]

1892 הֶבֶל ***hebel***, n.m. GK: 2039 [→ 1891; cf. 1893]. breath; by extension: something with no substance, meaninglessness, worthlessness, vanity, emptiness, futility; idol:– vanity [49], vanities [12], in vain [7], vain [4], altogether vain [1]

1893 הֶבֶל ***hebel***, n.pr.m. GK: 2040 [cf. 1892?]. Abel, *"morning mist"*:– Abel [8]

1894 הָבְנִים ***hobnîm***, n.[m.]. GK: 2041. ebony:– ebeny [1]

1895 הָבַר ***hābar***, v. GK: 2042. [Q] (ptcp.) astrologer, one who divides (classifies) the night sky for the purpose of telling the future:– astrologers (+8064) [1]

1896 הֵגֵא ***hēgē'*** or הֵגַי ***hēgay***, n.pr.m. GK: 2043 & 2051. Hegai:– Hegai [3], Hege [1]

1897 הָגָה ***hāgâ***, v. GK: 2047 [→ 1899, 1900, 1902]. [Q] to utter a sound, moan, meditate; [H] to mutter; from the base meaning of uttering a sound of any kind comes figure of meditation, the act of thoughtful deliberation with the implication of speaking to oneself:– meditate [6], mourn [3], speak [3], imagine [2], mourn sore (+1897) [2], studieth [2], muttered [1], mutter [1], roaring [1], speaketh [1], talk [1], uttering [1], utter [1]

1898 הָגָה ***hāgâ***, v. GK: 2048 [cf. 3014]. [Q] to expel, remove:– take away [2], stayeth [1]

1899 הֶגֶה ***hegeh***, n.m. GK: 2049 [→ 1897]. moaning, mourning, rumbling:– mourning [1], sound [1], tale [1]

1900 הָגוּת ***hāgût***, n.f. GK: 2050 [→ 1897]. utterance, meditation, which can include thinking and planning:– meditation [1]

1901 הָגִיג ***hāgîg***, n.m. GK: 2052. sighing, meditation:– meditation [1], musing [1]

1902 הִגָּיוֹן ***higgāyôn***, n.m. GK: 2053 [→ 1897]. muttering (sounds spoken to no one in particular), meditation; Higgaion, melody:– Higgaion [1], device [1], meditation [1], solemn sound [1]

1903 הָגִין ***hāgîn***, a. GK: 2054. corresponding:– directly [1]

1904 הָגָר ***hāgār***, n.pr.f. GK: 2057 [→ 1905?]. Hagar, *"emigration, flight"*:– Hagar [12]

1905 הַגְרִי ***hagrî***, a.g. [& n.pr.m.?]. GK: 2058 [→ 1904?]. Hagrites, of Hagri, *"wanderer"*:– Hagarites [3], Hagarenes [1], Hagerite [1], Haggeri [1]

1906 הֵד ***hēd***, n.[m.]. GK: 2059 [→ 1959]. joyous shout:– sounding again [1]

1907 הַדָּבַר ***haddābar*** (Aram.), n.m. GK: 10196. royal adviser, official of the king:– counsellers [4]

1908 הֲדַד ***hᵃdad***, n.pr.m. GK: 2060 [→ 111, 1130, 1909, 1910, 1913, 2582]. Hadad, *"thunderer"*:– Hadad [12]

1909 הֲדַדְעֶזֶר ***hᵃdad'ezer***, n.pr.m. GK: 2061 [→ 1908+5828]. Hadadezer, *"Hadad is a help"*:– Hadadezer [9]

1910 הֲדַד־רִמּוֹן ***hᵃdad-rimmôn***, n.pr.m.[loc.?]. GK: 2062 [→ 1908+7417]. Hadad Rimmon:– Hadadrimmon [1]

1911 הָדָה ***hādâ***, v. GK: 2063. [Q] to put, stretch out:– put [1]

1912 הֹדּוּ ***hōddû***, n.pr.loc. GK: 2064. India:– India [2]

1913 הֲדוֹרָם ***hᵃdôrām***, n.pr.m. GK: 2066 & 2067 [→ 1908+7311]. Hadoram, *"Hadad is exalted"*:– Hadoram [4]

1914 הִדַּי ***hidday***, n.pr.m. GK: 2068 [cf. 2355]. Hiddai:– Hiddai [1]

1915 הָדַךְ ***hādak***, v. GK: 2070. [Q] to crush by treading upon:– tread down [1]

1916 הֲדֹם ***hᵃdōm***, n.m. GK: 2071. footstool:– footstool (+7272) [5], footstool (+7272+3807.1) [1]

1917 הַדָּם ***haddām*** (Aram.), n.[m.]. GK: 10197. pieces, members (of an execution by dismemberment):– pieces [2]

1918 הֲדַס ***hᵃdas***, n.m. GK: 2072 [→ 1919]. myrtle tree:– myrtle trees [3], myrtle [2], myrtle tree [1]

1919 הֲדַסָּה ***hᵃdassâ***, n.pr.f. GK: 2073 [→ 1918]. Hadassah, *"myrtle; [poss.] bride* or *myrtle"*:– Hadassah [1]

1920 הָדַף ***hādap***, v. GK: 2074. [Q] to shove, push, thrust, drive out:– thrust [3], cast out [2], drive [2], casteth away [1], driven [1], expel [1], thrust away [1]

1921 הָדַר ***hādar***, v. GK: 2075 & 2065 [→ 1926, 1925, 1927; cf. 1922]. [Q] to show favoritism; show respect; [Qp] to be in splendor; [N] to be shown respect; [Ht] to exalt oneself:– honour [2], countenance [1], crooked places [1], glorious [1], honoured [1], put forth [1]

1922 הֲדַר ***hᵃdar*** (Aram.), v. GK: 10198 [→ 1923; cf. 1921]. [Pa] to glorify, honor, to speak words that elevate the status of another:– glorified [1], honoured [1], honour [1]

1923 הֲדַר ***hᵃdar*** (Aram.), n.[m.]. GK: 10199 [→ 1922; cf. 1926, 1925]. splendor, honor, majesty:– honour [2], majesty [1]

1924 הֲדַר ***hᵃdar***, n.pr.m. GK: 2076 [→ 1928]. Hadar; cf. 1908:– Hadar [1]

1925 הֶדֶר ***heder***, n.[m.]. GK: 2078 [→ 1921; cf. 1923]. splendor; "the royal splendor" may refer to the land of Israel, with the focus that this land is an valued ornament of the king:– glory [1]

1926 הָדָר ***hādār***, n.m. GK: 2077 [→ 1921; cf. 1923]. majesty, splendor, glory, nobility; often related to the appearance of an object that is beautiful and instills awe:– glory [7], majesty [6], honour [5], beauty [3], comeliness [3], excellency [2], beauties [1], full of majesty [1], glorious [1], goodly [1]

1927 הֲדָרָה ***hᵃdārâ***, n.f. GK: 2079 [→ 1921]. splendor, glory:– beauty [4], honour [1]

הֲדֹרָם ***hᵃdōrām***. See 1913.

1928 הֲדַרְעֶזֶר ***hᵃdar'ezer***, n.pr.m. GK: 2080 [→ 1924+5828]. Hadarezer:– Hadarezer [12]

1929 הָהּ ***hāh***, interj. GK: 2081. Alas!:– woe [1]

1930 הוֹ ***hô***, interj. GK: 2082 [→ 1945]. ah! (doubled for emphasis), with a strong implication of mourning or sorrow:– alas [2]

1930.1 הוּ ***hû***, p.m.s. GK: 2083 [→ 1931]. he, she, it; that, which:– it [1]

1930.2 ־הוּ ***-hû***, p.m.s.suf. GK: 2084 [→ 1886.3]. he, his, him; it, its:– him [568], his [219], it [164], them [33], thereof [13], he [8], his own [4], that [3], their [3], they [3], which [3], whose [3], himself [2], the same [2], whom [2], her [1], himself (+4617) [1], man's[s] [1], me [1], she [1], thereof (+4480) [1], there [1], whereof [1]

1931 הוּא ***hû'***, p.m.s. or הִיא ***hî'***, p.f.s. GK: 2085 & 2115 [→ 1930.1, 1992, 2007;

Heb

cf. 1932 (also used with compound proper names)]. he, she, it; this, that:– he [623], that [432], it [245], she [103], this [63], which [63], the same [53], they [24], who [24], himself [16], same [14], him [13], the[s] [6], her [2], such [2], their [2], the [2], those [2], his own [1], his [1], one [1], she herself [1], this same [1], thou [1], very [1], what (+834) [1], whom [1], whose [1]

1932 הוּא ***hû'***, p.3.m.s. or הִיא ***hî'*** (Aram.), p.3.f.s. GK: 10200 & 10205 [→ 581; cf. 1931]. he, she, it:– *usually untranslated* [10], he [6], it [3], this [2], that [1]

1933 הָוָה ***hāwâ***, v. GK: 2092 & 2093 [→ 1942, 1943, 1962; cf. 1961; cf. 1934]. [Q] to be, become; to get, have:– be [5], hath (+3807.1) [1]

1934 הֲוָה ***h***^a^***wâ*** (Aram.), v. GK: 10201 [cf. 1961, 1933]. [P] to be, become, happen:– *usually untranslated* [34], be [21], was [5], come to pass [3], became [2], been [1], have [1], might [1], offer [1], shall [1], so (+2050.3) [1]

1935 הוֹד ***hôd***, n.m. GK: 2086 [→ 1936, 5989; cf. 3034 (also used with compound proper names)]. splendor, majesty, glory, strength:– glory [9], honour [6], majesty [4], beauty [1], comeliness [1], glorious [1], goodly [1], honourable [1]

1936 הוֹד ***hôd***, n.pr.m. GK: 2087 [→ 1935]. Hod, "*grandeur*":– Hod [1]

1937 הוֹדְוָה ***hôd***^e^***wâ***, n.pr.m. GK: 2088 [→ 1938, 1939]. Hodaviah, "*give thanks to Yahweh*":– Hodevah [1]

1938 הוֹדַוְיָה ***hôdawyâ***, n.pr.m. GK: 2089 [→ 1939, 1937]. Hodaviah, "*give thanks to Yahweh*":– Hodaviah [3]

1939 הוֹדַוְיָהוּ ***hôdawyāhû***, n.pr.m. GK: 2069 & 2090 [→ 1937, 1938]. Hodaviah, "*give thanks to Yahweh*":– Hodaiah [1]

1940 הוֹדִיָּה ***hôdiyyâ***, n.pr.m. GK: 2091 [→ 1935+3068, 1941]. same as 1941: Hodiah, "*grandeur is Yahweh*":– Hodiah [1]

1941 הוֹדִיָּה ***hôdiyyâ***, n.pr.m. GK: 2091 [→ 1940]. same as 1940: Hodiah, Hodijah, "*grandeur is Yahweh*":– Hodijah [5]

הָוָה ***hāwâ***. See 1933.

הֲוָה ***h***^a^***wâ***. See 1934.

1942 הַוָּה ***hawwâ***, n.f. GK: 2094 & 2095 [→ 185, 1962; cf. 183; 1933]. (evil) desire, craving; destruction, ruin, corruption:– calamity [3], wickedness [3], calamities [1], iniquity [1], mischiefs [1], mischievous things [1], mischievous [1], naughtiness [1], naughty [1], noisome [1], perverse things [1], substance [1]

1943 הֹוָה ***hōwâ***, n.f. GK: 2096 [→ 1933]. calamity, disaster:– mischief [3]

1944 הוֹהָם ***hôhām***, n.pr.m. GK: 2097. Hoham:– Hoham [1]

1945 הוֹי ***hôy***, interj. GK: 2098 [→ 1930]. woe!, ah!, oh!, alas!; (to invite) come!:– woe [36], ah [7], O [3], ho [3], alas [2]

1946 הוּךְ ***hûk*** (Aram.), v. GK: 10202 [→ 1981]. same as 1981: [P] to go, walk:– go [2], brought [1], came [1]

1947 הוֹלֵלוֹת ***hôlēlôt***, n.f. GK: 2099 [→ 1984]. madness, delusion, folly:– madness [4]

1948 הוֹלֵלוּת ***hôlēlût***, n.f. GK: 2100 [→ 1984]. madness, delusion, folly:– madness [1]

1949 הוּם ***hûm***, v. GK: 2101 [→ 4103; cf. 1993, 2000, 5098]. [Q] to throw into confusion; [N] to be stirred up, be shook; [H] to be distraught; to throng:– rang again [2], destroy [1], make a noise [1], make great noise [1], moved [1]

1950 הוֹמָם ***hômām***, n.pr.m. GK: 2102 [→ 1967]. Homam:– Homam [1]

1951 הוּן ***hûn***, v. GK: 2103 [→ 1952]. [H] to think it easy:– ready [1]

1952 הוֹן ***hôn***, n.m. GK: 2104 [→ 1951]. wealth, riches, possessions:– riches [10], substance [7], wealth [5], enough [2], nought (+3808) [1], rich [1]

1952.1 הוֹן- ***-hôn*** (Aram.), p.suf.3.m.pl. GK: 10203 [cf. 1992.1]. they, them, their:– their [21], them [16], the[s] [3], their own [1], therein (+871.2) [1], these [1], whom [1], whose [1], your [1]

1953 הוֹשָׁמָע ***hôšāmā'***, n.pr.m. GK: 2106 [→ 8085+3068]. Hoshama, "*Yahweh has heard*":– Hoshama [1]

1954 הוֹשֵׁעַ ***hôšēa'***, n.pr.m. GK: 2107 [→ 3467+410 *or* 3068]. Hoshea; Joshua, "*salvation*":– Hoshea [11], Hosea [3], Oshea [2]

1955 הוֹשַׁעְיָה ***hôša'yâ***, n.pr.m. GK: 2108 [→ 3467+3068]. Hoshaiah, "*Yahweh has saved*":– Hoshaiah [3]

1956 הוֹתִיר ***hôtîr***, n.pr.m. GK: 2110 [→ 3498]. Hothir, "*one who remains*":– Hothir [2]

1957 הָזָה ***hāzâ***, v. GK: 2111. [Q] to dream:– sleeping [1]

1958 הִי ***hî***, n.[m.]. GK: 2113. woe!, an exclamation of sorrow:– woe [1]

הִיא ***hî'***. See 1931, 1932.

1958.1 הִי- ***-hî***, p.m.s.suf. GK: 2114 [→ 1886.3]. his, him:– his [1]

1958.2 הִי- ***-hî*** (Aram.), p.suf.3.m.s. GK: 10204 [→ 1886.8; cf. 1958.1]. he, his, him; it, its:– his [37], him [20], it [3], thereof [3], which [2], whose [2], himself [1], the[s] [1], thereon (+5922) [1], ye [1]

1959 הֵידָד ***hêdād***, n.m. GK: 2116 [→ 1906]. shout (of joy):– shouting [5], give a shout (+6030) [1], shout [1]

1960 הֻיְּדוֹת ***huyy***^e^***dôt***, n.f.pl. GK: 2117 [→ 3034]. (pl.) songs of thanksgiving:– thanksgiving [1]

1961 הָיָה ***hāyâ***, v. GK: 2118 & 181 [cf. 1933; cf. 1934]. [Q] to be, become, happen; [N] to be done, happen; the common verb of being, referring to state of being, change of state, existence, and the occurring of events, or even possession:– be [1277], was [525], came to pass [389], were [228], came [146], come to pass [125], is [75], had (+3807.1) [72], have (+3807.1) [72], been [71], become [64], became [59], are [56], have [26], am [20], had [18], wast [15], come [10], done [8], shall [8], became (+3807.1) [7], hath (+3807.1) [6], become (+3807.1) [4], being [4], did [4], fell [4], hath (+871.1) [4], went [4], art [3], continued [3], endure [3], fell on [3], follow [3], should [3], abode [2], be (+3807.1) [2], be altogether (+1961) [2], becamest [2], been (+1961) [2], came expressly (+1961) [2], continue [2], escape (+6413) [2], followed (+310) [2], go [2], had at all (+1961+3807.1) [2], hadst (+3807.1) [2], hast (+3807.1) [2], having [2], made [2], married (+802+3807.1) [2], marry (+802+3807.1) [2], pertained [2], quit [2], received (+3807.1) [2], redeem (+1353) [2], seemed (+5869+871.1) [2], shew (+3807.1) [2], surely become (+1961) [2], surely come to pass (+1961) [2], was altogether (+1961) [2], accomplished [1], after that (+4480+7093) [1], be at all [1], brake [1], brought to pass [1], brought [1], came up [1], caused [1], cherish (+5532) [1], cherished (+5532) [1], come [1], cometh to pass [1], committed [1], conferred (+1697) [1], count (+3807.1) [1], coupled (+8535) [1], determined (+7760) [1], do [1], endured [1], enjoy (+3807.1) [1], escape (+6412) [1], fainted [1], follow (+310) [1], give (+413) [1], gone [1], had (+5973) [1], had before (+4480) [1], had wars with (+376+4421) [1], had with (+376+4421) [1], happened [1], hast [1], hath [1], have (+871.1) [1], having (+3807.1) [1], help (+3444) [1], help (+8668) [1], keep (+4931) [1], keep [1], lasted [1], lay [1], let [1], lived (+2416) [1], liveth [1], make [1], marry [1], order (+4941) [1], pass [1], pertaineth [1], reach [1], redeemed (+1353) [1], rejoice (+8056) [1], remained [1], remain [1], required [1], seem (+5869+871.1) [1], shalt [1], since (+4480) [1], surely be [1], take (+3807.1) [1], trembled (+2730) [1], use (+3807.1) [1], waited on (+6440+3807.1) [1], wear (+5921) [1], will [1], would [1]

1962 הַיָּה ***hayyâ***, n.f. GK: 2119 [→ 1942; cf. 1933]. destruction:–

1963 הֵיךְ ***hêk***, adv. GK: 2120 [cf. 349]. how?:– how [2]

1964 הֵיכָל ***hêkāl***, n.m. GK: 2121 [cf. 1965]. a building of some kind: temple, sanctuary, palace; main hall:– temple [68], palace [7], palaces [3], temples [2]

1965 הֵיכַל ***hêkal*** (Aram.), n.m. GK: 10206 [cf. 1964]. residence of a deity: temple; residence of royalty: palace:– temple [8], palace [5]

1966 הֵילֵל ***hêlēl***, n.m.[pr.?]. GK: 2122 [→ 1984]. from the base meaning "shining one," this refers to an object in the night sky, often translated "morning star," and possibly referring the planet Venus; fig. used as a title of the king of Babylon (Isa 14:12). The Latin "lucifer" also means "shining one," and has become a title of Satan due to a traditional equation of the king of Babylon with the devil:– Lucifer [1]

1967 הֵימָם ***hêmām***, n.pr.m. GK: 2123 [→ 1950]. Homam:– Hemam [1]

1968 הֵימָן ***hêmān***, n.pr.m. GK: 2124 [→ 3225? *or* 539?]. Homam:– Heman [17]

1969 הִין ***hîn***, n.m. GK: 2125. hin (liquid measure of volume, one-sixth of a bath, about one gallon [four liters]):– hin [22]

1970 הָכַר ***hākar***, v. GK: 2128 & 2686. [Q] to attack (vigorously) or to make oneself strange:– make strange [1]

1971 הַכָּרָה ***hakkārâ***, n.f. GK: 2129 [→ 5234]. look (on a face) as a non-verbal communication, which in context may refer to personal bias:– shew [1]

הַל ***hal***. See 1973.

1972 הָלָא ***hālā'***, v.den. GK: 2133. [N] to be driven away, be removed:– cast far off [1]

1973 הָלְאָה ***hāl***^e^***'â***, adv. GK: 2131 & 2134 [→ 1886.1+3807.1]. beyond; far (and wide), some distance away; out of the way!:– forward [5], beyond (+4480) [4], hitherto [2], back [1], beyond (+4480+2050.1) [1], henceforward [1], thenceforth [1], yonder [1]

1974 הלולים ***hillûlîm***, n.[m.]. GK: 2136 [→ 1984]. offering of praise; festival (related to a god):– merry [1], praise [1]

1975 הַלָּז ***hallāz***, p.com.s. GK: 2137 [→ 1976]. this:– this [4], that [2], other [1]

1976 הַלָּזֶה ***hallāzeh***, p.m. GK: 2138 [→ 1975, 1977; cf. 2098]. this:– this [2]

1977 הַלֵּזוּ ***hallēzû***, p.f. GK: 2139 [→ 1976]. this:– this [1]

1978 הָלִיךְ ***hālîk***, n.[m.]. GK: 2141 [→ 1980]. path, steps:– steps [1]

1979 הֲלִיכָה ***h^{a}lîkâ***, n.f. GK: 2142 [→ 1980]. procession, way, walk; traveling merchants; affairs:– goings [2], ways [2], companies [1], walk [1]

1980 הָלַךְ ***hālak***, v. GK: 2143 [→ 1978, 1979, 1982, 3212, 4108, 4109, 4447, 8418, 8437; cf. 1981]. [Q] to walk, go, travel; [N] to fade away; [P] to walk about, go about, [H] to drive back, get rid of; enable to walk; to lead; bring; [Ht] to move to and fro, wander, walk about; by extension: to walk as a lifestyle, a pattern of conduct:– go [417], went [348], walk [133], walked [97], come [78], departed [47], gone [35], walketh [34], goest [18], get [17], depart [16], followed (+310) [16], goeth [16], led [13], came [11], walking [11], going [10], follow (+310) [9], went away [9], brought [8], wentest [7], went on (+1980) [6], went on [5], bring [4], walkest [4], camest [3], carry [3], departed (+4480) [3], going on [3], march [3], passeth away [3], walk to and fro [3], went along [3], all along as went (+1980) [2], came apace (+1980) [2], came on (+1980) [2], carried [2], cause to go [2], cause to walk [2], come away [2], continually [2], conversant [2], departeth [2], flow [2], following (+310) [2], gat away [2], gat [2], go along [2], go away [2], go speedily (+1980) [2], go to [2], go up and down [2], goeth away [2], goeth forth (+1980) [2], leadeth away [2], lead [2], needs be gone (+1980) [2], quite gone (+1980) [2], ran [2], run [2], still went on (+1980) [2], surely depart (+1980) [2], surely go (+1980) [2], travelleth [2], walked to and fro [2], walking up and down [2], waxed greater (+1980) [2], weak [2], went forth on a time (+1980) [2], went on continually (+1980) [2], went out [2], went up and down [2], wrought [2], along [1], at the point [1], away [1], bear [1], behaved [1], carry away [1], cause to run [1], caused to go [1], cometh out [1], cometh [1], coming [1], continually (+7725+2050.1) [1], depart (+4480) [1], enter [1], exercise [1], flowed [1], follow (+7272+871.1) [1], followedst (+310) [1], followed [1], get away [1], go forward [1], go in [1], go up [1], goeth about [1], goeth on still [1], gone away [1], gone up [1], grow [1], lead forth [1], leadeth [1], let down [1], made go [1], may [1], moveth [1], on [1], pass away [1], passeth [1], prospered [1], pursue (+310) [1], ran along [1], return again (+7725) [1], run continually [1], running [1], sent [1], shineth more and more [1], sounded long [1], spread abroad [1], spread [1], take away [1], takest [1], take [1], talebearer (+7400) [1], travellers (+5410) [1], vanisheth away [1], walk on [1], walk up and down [1], walked up and down [1], wandered [1], wandering [1], waxed greater [1], waxed stronger [1], waxed weaker [1], waxed [1], wayfaring men (+1870) [1], went abroad [1], went forward [1], went way [1], whirleth about continually (+5437+5437) [1], wont to haunt [1]

1981 הֲלַךְ ***h^{a}lak*** (Aram.), v. GK: 10207 [→ 1983; cf. 1946; cf. 1980]. [P] to go; [Pa] to walk about; [H] to walk around:– walked [1], walking [1], walk [1]

1982 הֵלֶךְ ***hēlek***, n.m. GK: 2144 [→ 1980]. oozing, flowing; visitor:– dropped [1], traveller [1]

1983 הֲלָךְ ***h^{a}lāk*** (Aram.), n.[m.]. GK: 10208 [→ 1981]. duty, toll, tax:– custom [3]

1984 הָלַל ***hālal***, v. GK: 2145 & 2146 & 2147 & 2149 [→ 166, 1947, 1948, 1966, 1974, 1985, 4110, 8416 (also used with compound proper names)]. [Q] to be arrogant; [P] to praise; give thanks; cheer, extol; [Po] to make a fool of, to mock, rail against; [Pu] to be praised, be worthy of praise, be of renown; [Ht] to make one's boast in (the name of God); to act like a madman; act furiously; [H] to flash, radiate, shine; "Hallelujah" is a compound of the second person plural imperative and the personal name of God: hallelu-yah, praise Yah(weh):– praise [92], praised [19], glory [12], boast [5], mad [5], praising [4], boasteth [3], commended [2], foolish [2], maketh mad [2], rage [2], shined [2], boastest [1], celebrate [1], deal foolishly [1], feigned mad [1], fools [1], given to marriage [1], give [1], gloriest [1], glorieth [1], make boast [1], maketh fools [1], praises [1], praiseth [1], renowned [1], shine [1]

1985 הִלֵּל ***hillēl***, n.pr.m. GK: 2148 [→ 1984]. Hillel, "*he has praises*":– Hillel [2]

1986 הָלַם ***hālam***, v. GK: 2150 [→ 1989, 4112]. [Q] to strike, smash, beat, trample:– smote [2], beaten [1], beating down [1], break down [1], broken down [1], broken [1], overcome [1], smite [1]

1987 הֶלֶם ***hēlem***, n.pr.m. GK: 2152. Helem, "*health*":– Helem [1]

1988 הֲלֹם ***h^{a}lōm***, adv. GK: 2151. to here:– hither [6], here [2], hitherto (+5704) [2], thither [1]

1989 הַלְמוּת ***halmût***, n.f. GK: 2153 [→ 1986]. hammer:– hammer [1]

1990 הָם ***hām***, n.pr.loc. GK: 2154. Ham:– Ham [1]

1991 הָם ***hām***, n.[m.]. GK: 2155 [cf. 1998]. wealth:– *not translated* [1]

1992 הֵם ***hēm*** or הֵמָּה ***hēmmâ***, p.m.pl. GK: 2156 & 2160 [→ 1931; cf. 1994]. they, them:– they [368], those [52], these [26], them [20], who [7], themselves [5], same [4], that [3], their [3], which [3], it [2], whom (+834) [2], whom [2], the things [1], this [1], whereby (+834) [1], withal (+871.1) [1], ye [1]

1992.1 ־הֶם ***-hem*** or ־הֵם ***-hēm***, p.m.pl.suf. GK: 2157 [cf. 1886.3]. they, them, their:– them [1496], their [1187], they [90], their (+3807.1) [38], themselves [26], their own [23]*

1992.2 ־הֹם ***-hōm*** (Aram.), p.suf.3.m.pl. GK: 10209 [→ 2006.2; cf. 1992.1]. they, them, their:– them [7], their [4]

1993 הָמָה ***hāmâ***, v. GK: 2159 [→ 1995, 1997?, 1998, 1999?; cf. 1949, 2000, 5098]. [Q] to make a noise, be tumultuous:– roar [6], disquieted [4], make a noise [4], sound [3], troubled [2], clamorous [1], concourse [1], cry aloud [1], in an uproar [1], loud [1], make a tumult [1], maketh a noise [1], mourning [1], moved [1], noise [1], raged [1], raging [1], roared [1], roareth [1], tumultuous [1]

1993.1 ־הֵמָה ***-hēmâ***, p.m.pl.suf. GK: 2161 [→ 1886.3]. they, them:– their [1]

1994 הִמּוֹ ***himmô*** (Aram.), p.3.pl. GK: 10210 [cf. 1992]. they, them:– them [8], those [1]

1995 הָמוֹן ***hāmôn***, n.m. GK: 2162 & 2171 [→ 1174, 1996, 1997; cf. 1993]. commotion, tumult, confusion; many, populace, hoards, army:– multitude [59], noise [4], tumult [4], abundance [3], many [3], multitudes [3], Hamon-gog [2], company [1], great store [1], multiplied [1], riches [1], rumbling [1], sounding [1], store [1]

הַמֹּלֶכֶת ***ham-mōleket***. See 4447.

1996 הֲמוֹן גּוֹג ***h^{a}môn gôg***, n.pr.loc. GK: 2163 [→ 1995+1463]. Hamon Gog, "*multitude of Gog*":–

1997 הֲמוֹנָה ***h^{a}mônâ***, n.pr.loc. GK: 2164 [→ 1995?; cf. 1993]. Hamonah, "*multitude*":– Hamonah [1]

הֲמוּנֵךְ ***h^{a}mûnēk***. See 2002.

1998 הֶמְיָה ***hemyâ***, n.f. GK: 2166 [→ 1993; cf. 1991]. noise, sound, tone:– noise [1]

1999 הֲמֻלָּה ***h^{a}mullâ***, n.f. GK: 2167 [→ 1993?]. tumult, sound, noise:– speech [1], tumult [1]

הַמֶּלֶךְ ***ham-melek***. See 4429.

2000 הָמַם ***hāmam***, v. GK: 2169 & 2170 [cf. 1949, 1993, 5098]. [Q] to throw into confusion; to rout; to drain:– discomfited [5], destroy [3], break [1], consume [1], crushed [1], troubled [1], vex [1]

הָמֹן ***hāmōn***. See 1995.

2001 הָמָן ***hāmān***, n.pr.m. GK: 2172. Haman:– Haman [50], Haman's [3], he^{s} [1]

2002 המונכ ***hmwnk*** or הֲמְיָנַךְ ***hamyānak*** (Aram.), n.[m.]. GK: 10211 & 10212. chain, necklace:– chain [3]

2003 הֲמָסִים ***h^{a}māsîm***, n.[m.]. GK: 2173. twigs, brushwood:– melting [1]

2004 הֵן ***hēn***, p.f.pl. GK: 2177 [→ 1886.3]. they, them, their:–

2005 הֵן ***hēn***, adv.demo. *or* interj. GK: 2176 [→ 403, 2008, 2009, 5728; cf. 2006]. behold!, see!, surely!; if, yet, but, then:– behold [82], lo [11], if [5], though [1]

2006 הֵן ***hēn*** (Aram.), c. GK: 10213 [cf. 2005, cf. 518?]. if, then, whether:– if [12], or [2], whether [2]

2006.1 ־הֵן ***-hēn*** or ־הֶן ***-hen***, p.f.pl.suf. GK: 2177 [→ 1886.3]. they, them, their:– their [90], them [52], they [6], therein (+871.1) [4], thereof [4], their (+3807.1) [2], their own [2], withal (+871.1) [2], by themselves (+905+3807.1) [1], it [1], thereby (+871.1) [1], these [1], those [1], wherein (+834+871.1) [1], wherein (+871.1) [1], withal (+834+871.1) [1]

2006.2 ־הֵן ***-hēn*** (Aram.), p.suf.3.f.pl. GK: 10214 [→ 1992.2, 3861; cf. 1992.1]. they, them, their:– *usually untranslated* [6], the others [1], them [1]

2007 הֵנָּה ***hēnnâ***, p.f.pl. GK: 2179 [→ 1931]. they, these, those:– they [13], these [7], them [4], those [3], such (+3509.1) [2], such things (+3509.1) [1], such [1], that [1], the [1], theirs [1], thence (+4480) [1], therein (+871.1+1886.1) [1], this [1], thither [1], wherein (+834+871.1) [1]

2008 הֵנָּה ***hēnnâ***, adv. GK: 2178 [→ 5728; cf. 2005]. here, to here; on this side, on the opposite side:– hither [20], hitherto (+5704) [5], thither [3], here [2], hither

(+5704) [2], thus far (+5704) [2], fro (+259) [1], hither (+1886.5) [1], hitherto (+5704+2050.1) [1], in hither [1], now [1], on this side (+5704) [1], side [1], since (+5704) [1], that way [1], there [1], this side [1], this way [1], thitherward [1], to (+259) [1], yet (+5704) [1]

2009 הִנֵּה ***hinnēh***, pt.demo. GK: 2180 [→ 2005]. look!, now!, here, there, a marker used to enliven a narrative, change a scene, emphasize an idea, or call attention to detail:– behold [928], lo [110], here [17], see [2], behold (+2088) [1], behold as soon as [1], behold here [1]

2009.1 ־הֵנָה ***-hᵉnâ*** or ־הֶנָה ***-henâ***, p.f.pl.suf. GK: 2181 [→ 1886.3]. they, them:– them [2], their [1]

2010 הֲנָחָה ***hᵃnāḥâ***, n.f. GK: 2182 [→ 3240]. holiday, an official day of rest and celebration:– release [1]

2011 הִנֹּם ***hinnōm***, n.pr.m. & loc. GK: 2183. Hinnom:– Hinnom [13]

2012 הֵנַע ***hēnaʿ***, n.pr.loc. GK: 2184. Hena, *"Anath"*:– Hena [3]

2013 הָסָה ***hāsâ***, v.den. GK: 2187 & 2188. [H] to silence, cause to be still:– hold peace [2], keep silence [2], be silent [1], hold tongue [1], silence [1], stilled [1]

2014 הֲפֻגָה ***hᵃpugâ***, n.f. GK: 2198 [→ 6313]. relief, stopping:– intermission [1]

2015 הָפַךְ ***hāpak***, v. GK: 2200 [→ 2016, 2017, 2018, 2019, 4114, 4115, 8419; cf. 55]. [Q] to overthrow, overturn, turn around, change; [Qp] to be turned over; [N] to be changed, transformed, turned into; [Ho] to be overwhelmed; [Ht] to tumble around, flash back and forth, swirl; from the base meaning of turning an object over comes the fig. extension of "changing one's mind":– turned [48], turn [7], overthrow [5], overthrew [4], overthrown [4], overturneth [3], turneth [3], changed [2], become [1], came [1], change [1], converted [1], gave [1], make [1], overturned (+4605+1886.5+3807.1) [1], overturn [1], perverse [1], perverted [1], retired [1], tumbled [1], turned aside [1], turned back [1], turned every way [1], turned into [1], turned up [1], turning [1]

2016 הֵפֶךְ ***hēpek***, n.m. GK: 2201 [→ 2015, 2017]. opposite, turning of things upside down, perversion:– contrary [2]

2017 הֹפֶךְ ***hōpek***, n.m. GK: 2201 [→ 2016]. opposite, turning of things upside down, perversion:– turning upside down [1]

2018 הֲפֵכָה ***hᵃpēkâ***, n.f. GK: 2202 [→ 2015]. catastrophe, demolition:– overthrow [1]

2019 הֲפַכְפַּךְ ***hᵃpakpak***, a. GK: 2203 [→ 2015]. devious, crooked:– froward [1]

2020 הַצָּלָה ***haṣṣālâ***, n.f. GK: 2208 [→ 5337]. deliverance:– deliverance [1]

2021 הֹצֶן ***hōṣen***, n.[m.]. GK: 2210. weapon (variously interpreted):– chariots [1]

2022 הַר ***har***, n.m. GK: 2215 [→ 2023, 2042]. hill, mountain, range (of hills, mountains); referring to low hills as well as high mountains:– mount [224], mountains [156], mountain [105], hill [35], hills [23], hill country [1], hill's [1]

2023 הֹר ***hōr***, n.pr.loc. GK: 2216 [→ 2022]. Hor, "[perhaps] *mountain*":– Hor [12]

2024 הָרָא ***hārāʾ***, n.pr.loc. GK: 2217. Hara, *"hill, highland"*:– Hara [1]

2025 הַרְאֵל ***harʾēl***, n.[m.]. GK: 2219 [cf. 741]. altar hearth:– altar [1]

2026 הָרַג ***hārag***, v. GK: 2222 [→ 2027, 2028]. [Q] to kill, put to death, murder, slaughter; [Qp, N, Pu] to be slain, be put to death, be slaughtered:– slew [57], slay [41], slain [31], kill [15], killed [3], slaying [3], kill out of hand (+2026) [2], killedst [2], slayeth [2], surely kill (+2026) [2], destroyed [1], killeth [1], killing [1], murderers [1], murderer [1], murder [1], put to death (+4194) [1], slaughter made (+2027) [1], slayer [1]

2027 הֶרֶג ***hereg***, n.m. GK: 2223 [→ 2026]. slaughter, killing:– slaughter [3], slain [1], slaughter made (+2026) [1]

2028 הֲרֵגָה ***hᵃrēgâ***, n.f. GK: 2224 [→ 2026]. slaughter:– slaughter [5]

2029 הָרָה ***hārâ***, v. GK: 2225 [→ 2030, 2032]. [Q] to conceive, become pregnant, be with child; [Gp; Pu] to be conceived, born:– conceived [34], conceive [4], with child [2], bare [1], conceiving [1], progenitors [1]

2030 הָרֶה ***hāreh*** or הָרִיָּה ***hāriyyâ***, a.f. GK: 2226 & 2230 [→ 2029]. pregnant, expecting (child):– with child [7], women with child [4], conceive [3], child [1], great [1]

2031 הַרְהֹר ***harhōr*** (Aram.), n.[m.]. GK: 10217. mental image (in a dream-like state):– thoughts [1]

2032 הֵרוֹן ***hērôn*** or הֵרָיוֹן ***hērāyôn***, n.[m.]. GK: 2228 & 2231 [→ 2029]. childbearing, pregnancy:– conception [3]

2033 הֲרוֹרִי ***hᵃrôrî***, a.g. GK: 2229. Harorite:– Harorite [1]

2034 הֲרִיסָה ***hᵃrîsâ***, n.f. GK: 2232 [→ 2040]. ruin:– ruins [1]

2035 הֲרִיסוּת ***hᵃrîsût***, n.f. GK: 2233 [→ 2040]. waste, ruin, destruction:– destruction [1]

2036 הֹרָם ***hōrām***, n.pr.m. GK: 2235 [cf. 2037]. Horam, *"height"*:– Horam [1]

2037 הָרוּם ***hārûm***, n.pr.m. GK: 2227 [cf. 2036]. Harum, *"consecrated"*:– Harum [1]

2038 הַרְמוֹן ***harmôn***, n.pr.loc. GK: 2236. Harmon:– palace [1]

2039 הָרָן ***hārān***, n.pr.m. GK: 2237 [→ 1028]. Haran, *"mountaineer [perhaps sanctuary]"*:– Haran [7]

2040 הָרַס ***hāras***, v. GK: 2238 [→ 2034, 2035]. [Q] to tear down, break down, destroy; [Qp] to be in ruins; [N] to be destroyed, in ruins; [P] to destroy:– thrown down [7], throw down [6], break down [4], broken down [4], destroyed [3], pull down [3], break through [2], overthrown [2], ruined [2], utterly overthrow (+2040) [2], beat down [1], breaketh down [1], break [1], destroyers [1], destroy [1], overthroweth [1], overthrow [1], plucketh down [1]

2041 הֶרֶס ***heres***, n.[m.]. GK: 2239 [→ 5892+2041]. destruction (= Heliopolis):– destruction [1]

2042 הָרָר ***hārār***, n.m. GK: 2215 [→ 2022]. hill, mountain, range (of hills, mountains); referring to low hills as well as high mountains:– mountains [8], hills [2], mountain [2], mount [1]

2043 הֲרָרִי ***hᵃrārî*** or הָאֲרָרִי ***hāʾrārî***, a.g. GK: 2240 & 2034. Hararite:– Hararite [5]

2044 הָשֵׁם ***hāšēm***, n.pr.m. GK: 2244. Hashem:– Hashem [1]

2045 הַשְׁמָעוּת ***hašmāʿût***, n.f. GK: 2245 [→ 8085]. news, communication, information:– cause to hear [1]

2046 הִתּוּךְ ***hittûk***, n.[m.]. GK: 2247 [→ 5413]. melting:– melted [1]

2047 הֲתָךְ ***hᵃtāk***, n.pr.m. GK: 2251. Hathach, *"good"*:– Hatach [4]

2048 הָתַל ***hātal***, v. GK: 2252 & 9438 [→ 2049, 4123]. [P] to taunt, mock:– mocked [4], deceived [2], deal deceitfully [1], deceive [1], mocketh [1], mock [1]

2049 הֲתֻלִים ***hᵃtulîm***, n.[m.]pl. GK: 2253 [→ 2048]. mockery:– mockers [1]

2050 הָתַת ***hātat***, v. GK: 2109 & 2254. [Po] to overwhelm with reproaches:– imagine mischief [1]

2050.1 ־וְ ***wᵉ-***, c.pref. GK: 2256 [cf. 2050.3]. a marker showing the relationship between words, clauses, sentences, and sections; generally, coordinating: and, also; contrasting: but, yet, however; showing a logical relationship: because, so then; emphazing: even, indeed:– and [38504], but [1748], then [1316], that [991], so [597], also [592], therefore [524], neither (+3808) [415], and when [371], for [368], even [363], or [363], now [290], with [282], nor [254], nor (+3808) [242], yet [185], yea [151], when [142], moreover [120], so that [110], thus [81], wherefore [77], which [66], neither (+408) [61], both [58], again [36], nevertheless [33], though [31], seeing [28], neither (+369) [27], howbeit [26], as [24], nor (+408) [24], neither [23], but when [19], nor (+369) [17], as for [16], if [16], lest (+3808) [14], all generations (+1755+1755) [13], now when [13], likewise [11], notwithstanding [11], and as [10], moreover (+1571) [10], whereas [10], while [10]*

2050.2 ־וֹ ***-ô*** or ־ו ***-w*** or ־וּ ***-û***, p.m.s.suf. GK: 2257 [→ 1886.3]. he, him, his; it, its:– his [6106], him [2818], it [586], he [454], thereof [366], their [202], his own [152], them [138], his (+3807.1) [76], whose [72], himself [68], the[s] [49], therein (+871.1) [35], thereon (+5921) [31], whom [27], her [23], the same [11], their own [11], wherein (+871.1) [10]*

2050.3 ־וְ ***wᵉ-*** (Aram.), c.pref. GK: 10221 [cf. 2050.1]. (connecting) and; (contrasting) or, but, however; (furthering) then, now:– and [612], but [20], or [10], that [10], nor (+3809) [7], even [6], also [5], then [5], so [4], which [4], neither (+3809) [3], nor [3], now [3], for [2], therefore [2], to [2], with [2], also (+638) [1], and that [1], as concerning [1], both [1], moreover [1], nor (+409) [1], nor (+5922) [1], so (+1934) [1], so that [1], therefore (+4481) [1], thus [1], upharsin (+6537) [1], yet [1]

2051 וְדָן ***wᵉdān***, n.pr.loc.?. GK: 2258. Vedan; and Dan (2050.1 + 1835):–

2052 וָהֵב ***wāhēb***, n.pr.loc.?. GK: 2259. Waheb:– what he did [1]

2053 וָו ***wāw***, n.[m.]. GK: 2260. hook, peg:– hooks [13]

2054 וָזָר ***wāzār***, a. GK: 2261. guilty:– strange [1]

2055 וַיְזָתָא ***wayᵉzātāʾ***, n.pr.m. GK: 2262. Vaizatha, "[poss.] *given of the best one*":– Vajezatha [1]

2056 וָלָד ***wālād***, n.m. GK: 2263 [→ 3205]. child:– child [2]

2057 וַנְיָה **wanyâ**, n.pr.m. GK: 2264. Vaniah, "[poss.] *worthy of love*":– Vaniah [1]

2058 וָפְסִי **wopsî**, n.pr.m. GK: 2265. Vophsi:– Vophsi [1]

2059 וַשְׁנִי **wašnî**, n.pr.m.?. GK: 2266. Vashni:– Vashni [1]

2060 וַשְׁתִּי **waštî**, n.pr.f. GK: 2267. Vashti, "*one beautiful, desired*":– Vashti [10]

2061 זְאֵב **z^{e}'ēb**, n.m. GK: 2269 [→ 2062]. wolf:– wolf [4], wolves [3]

2062 זְאֵב **z^{e}'ēb**, n.pr.m. GK: 2270 [→ 2061]. Zeeb, "*wolf*":– Zeeb [6]

2063 זֹאת **zō't**, p.demo. & adv. GK: 2271 [→ 2088]. this, these:– this [15], herewith (+871.1) [2], it [2], she [2], so [2], that [2], these [2], thus [2], hereby (+871.1) [1], herein (+871.1) [1], so much [1], such (+1886.1+3509.1) [1], such [1], the one [1], the other [1], the same [1], therefore (+871.1+2050.1) [1], thus (+871.1) [1]

2064 זָבַד **zābad**, v. GK: 2272 [→ 2065, 2066, 2067, 2071, 2072, 2080 (also used with compound proper names)]. [Q] to give (a gift), bestow:– endued [1]

2065 זֶבֶד **zēbed**, n.m. GK: 2273 [→ 2064]. gift:– dowry [1]

2066 זָבָד **zābād**, n.pr.m. GK: 2274 [→ 2064]. Zabad, "*he bestows*":– Zabad [8]

2067 זַבְדִּי **zabdî**, n.pr.m. GK: 2275 [→ 2064]. Zabdi, "*Yahweh bestows*":– Zabdi [6]

2068 זַבְדִּיאֵל **zabdî'ēl**, n.pr.m. GK: 2276 [→ 2064+410]. Zabdiel, "*God [El] bestows*":– Zabdiel [2]

2069 זְבַדְיָה **z^{e}badyâ** or זְבַדְיָהוּ **z^{e}badyāhû**, n.pr.m. GK: 2277 & 2278. Zebadiah, "*Yahweh bestows*":– Zebadiah [9]

2070 זְבוּב **z^{e}bûb**, n.m. GK: 2279 [→ 1176]. fly (insect):– flies [1], fly [1]

2071 זָבוּד **zābûd**, n.pr.m. GK: 2280 [→ 2064]. Zabud, "*[he has] bestowed upon*":– Zabud [1]

2072 זַבּוּד **zabbûd**, n.pr.f. GK: 2281 [→ 2064; cf. 2080]. Zabbud, "*[he has] bestowed upon*":– Zabbud [1]

2073 זְבֻל **z^{e}bul**, n.[m.]. GK: 2292 [→ 348?, 2074, 2082, 2083]. magnificent dwelling, princely mansion, lofty dwelling:– habitation [3], dwell in [1], dwelling [1]

2074 זְבוּלוּן **z^{e}bûlûn**, n.pr.m. GK: 2282 [→ 2075; cf. 2073]. Zebulun, "*honor Ge 30:20*":– Zebulun [45]

2075 זְבוּלֹנִי **z^{e}bûlōnî**, a.g. GK: 2283 [→ 2074; cf. 2073]. Zebulunite, "*of Zebulun*":– Zebulonite [2], Zebulunites [1]

2076 זָבַח **zābaḥ**, v. GK: 2284 [→ 2077, 2078, 4196; cf. 1684]. [Q, P] to offer a sacrifice; to slaughter, butcher:– sacrifice [44], sacrificed [29], offer [19], offered [17], sacrificeth [6], do sacrifice [3], kill [3], slew [3], killed [2], sacrificing [2], slain [2], offer a sacrifice (+2077) [1], offereth [1], offering [1], sacrificedst [1]

2077 זֶבַח **zebaḥ**, n.m. GK: 2285 [→ 2078; cf. 2076; cf. 1685]. sacrifice, offering:– sacrifice [101], sacrifices [53], offerings [6], offer a sacrifice (+2076) [1], offer [1]

2078 זֶבַח **zebaḥ**, n.pr.m. GK: 2286 [→ 2077; cf. 2076]. Zebah, "*sacrifice*":– Zebah [12]

2079 זַבַּי **zabbay**, n.pr.m. GK: 2287. Zabbai, "[perhaps] *God has given*":– Zabbai [2]

2080 זְבִידָה **z^{e}bîdâ**, n.pr.f. GK: 2288 [→ 2064; cf. 2072]. Zebidah, "*given*":– Zebudah [1]

2081 זְבִינָא **z^{e}bînā'**, n.pr.m. GK: 2289. Zebina, "*one bought, purchased*":– Zebina [1]

2082 זָבַל **zābal**, v. GK: 2290 [cf. 2073, 5445]. [Q] to honor, exalt; from the base meaning of lifting up or carrying an object, especially bringing presents, not found in the OT:– dwell with [1]

2083 זְבֻל **z^{e}bul**, n.pr.m. GK: 2291 [→ 2073]. Zebul, "*elevation, height, lofty [temple]*":– Zebul [6]

זְבֻלֻן **z^{e}bulūn**. See 2074.

2084 זְבַן **z^{e}ban** (Aram.), v. GK: 10223. [P] to try to gain (time), buy (time):– gain [1]

2085 זָג **zāg**, n.[m.]. GK: 2293 [cf. 2212]. skin, peel (of grape):– husk [1]

2086 זֵד **zēd**, a. GK: 2294 [→ 2087; cf. 2102]. arrogant, proud, haughty:– proud [12], presumptuous [1]

2087 זָדוֹן **zādôn**, n.m. GK: 2295 [→ 2086]. pride, arrogance, contempt, presumption:– pride [6], presumptuously (+871.1) [2], proud [2], most proud [1]

2088 זֶה **zeh**, p.demo. & adv. GK: 2296 [→ 2063, 2090, 2097, 2098; cf. 2098]. this, these, such:– this [1418], that [42], these [37], it [12], thus (+3509.1) [12], another [10], here (+871.1) [10], one [10], where (+335) [10], he [9], the [9], thus [9], hence (+4480) [7], the other [7], hence [6], such [5], whence (+335+4480) [5], one side [4], other side [4], same [4], such (+3509.1) [4], wherefore (+4100+3807.1) [4], hereby (+871.1) [3], that side [3]*

2089 זֶה **zeh**, n.m. & f. GK: 8445 [→ 7716]. lamb; var. for 7716:–

2090 זֹה **zōh**, p.demo. & adv. GK: 2297 [→ 2097; cf. 2088; cf. 1668]. this:– this [7], thus (+3509.1) [3], it [1], one [1], that [1]

2091 זָהָב **zāhāb**, n.m. GK: 2298 [→ 4314; cf. 6668; cf. 1722]. gold, nugget of gold, gold piece or coin:– gold [348], golden [40], fair weather [1]

2092 זָהַם **zāham**, v. GK: 2299 [→ 2093]. [P] to make repulsive, loathsome (to someone):– abhorreth [1]

2093 זַהַם **zaham**, n.pr.m. GK: 2300 [→ 2092]. Zaham, "*putrid, loathsome*":– Zaham [1]

2094 זָהַר **zāhar**, v. GK: 2302 [cf. 2114; cf. 2095]. [N] to be warned, take warning; [H] to give warning, dissuade; to shine:– warn [8], warned [4], admonished [2], taketh warning [2], give warning [1], given warning [1], givest warning [1], shine [1], teach [1], took warning [1]

2095 זְהִיר **z^{e}hîr** (Aram.), v. GK: 10224 [cf. 2094]. careful, cautious:– take heed [1]

2096 זֹהַר **zōhar**, n.[m.]. GK: 2303. brightness, shining:– brightness [2]

2097 זוֹ **zô**, p.demo. GK: 2305 [→ 2090; cf. 2088]. this:– this [1]

2098 זוּ **zû**, p.demo. & rel. GK: 2306 [→ 2088; cf. 1976]. who, which, that:– this [4], that [3], wherein [2], which [2], that which [1], whom [1]

2099 זִו **ziw**, n.pr. GK: 2304 [cf. 2122]. Ziv, "*bright [as colorful flowers]*":– Zif [2]

2100 זוּב **zûb**, v. GK: 2307 [→ 2101; cf. 1727]. [Q] to flow, gush out; discharge (of body fluids); "flowing with milk and honey" is a figure of sweet abundance:– floweth [12], issue [11], flowing [9], gushed out [3], running issue [2], hath an issue [1], hath [1], have an issue (+2101) [1], pine away [1], run [1]

2101 זוֹב **zôb**, n.m. GK: 2308 [→ 2100]. discharge (of body fluids):– issue [12], have an issue (+2100) [1]

2102 זִיד **zîd**, v. GK: 2326 [→ 2121, 5138; cf. 2086; cf. 2103]. [Q] to treat arrogantly, defy; [H] to cook; to act arrogantly, be contemptuous:– dealt proudly [4], presumptuously [2], come presumptuously [1], presume [1], proud [1], sod [1]

2103 זוּד **zûd** (Aram.), v. GK: 10225 [cf. 2102]. [H] to act proudly, act haughtily:– pride [1]

2104 זוּזִים **zûzîm**, n.pr.g. GK: 2309. Zuzite, "*strong nations; babblers*":– Zuzims [1]

2105 זוֹחֵת **zôḥēt**, n.pr.m. GK: 2311 [→ 1132]. Zoheth, "*proud*":– Zoheth [1]

2106 זָוִית **zāwît**, n.f. GK: 2312 [cf. 4200]. corner (of a palace, altar), pillar:– corner stones [1], corners [1]

2107 זוּל **zûl**, v. GK: 2313 [→ 2108]. [Q] to pour out, weigh out:– despise [1], lavish [1]

2108 זוּלָה **zûlâ**, n.[f.] pp.c. GK: 2314 [→ 2107]. but, only, except; apart from, besides:– save [6], besides [5], beside [2], but [2], only [1]

2109 זוּן **zûn**, v. GK: 2315 & 3469 [→ 4202; cf. 2110, cf. 4203]. [Q] to feed; [Pu] to be fed; to be lusty, be in the rut:– fed [1]

2110 זוּן **zûn** (Aram.), v. GK: 10226 [→ 4203; cf. 2109]. [Htpe] to be fed, live on:– fed [1]

2111 זוּעַ **zûa'**, v. GK: 2316 & 2398 [→ 2113; cf. 2189; cf. 2112]. [Q] to show fear, tremble; [Pil] to make tremble; terrify:– moved [1], tremble [1], vex [1]

2112 זוּעַ **zûa'** (Aram.), v. GK: 10227 [cf. 2111]. [P] to dread, fear, to have an attitude of terror or worship, a fig. extension of "to shake, tremble.":– trembled [1], tremble [1]

2113 זְוָעָה **z^{e}wā'â**, n.f. GK: 2317 [→ 2111]. abhorrence, terror, object of dread:– vexation [1]

2114 זוּר **zûr**, v. GK: 2319 & 2320 & 2424 [cf. 2094]. [Q, N, Ho] to go astray, turn aside, be estranged; [Q] to stink; by extension: to be offensive:– strangers [25], strange [20], stranger [18], estranged [4], another [2], another place [1], fanners [1], gone away [1], stranger (+376) [1], strangers' [1]

2115 זוּר **zûr**, v. GK: 2318 [→ 2116]. [Q] to squeeze, press upon, crush; [Qp] to be crushed:– closed [1], crush [1], thrust together [1]

2116 זוּרֶה **zûreh**, v.ptcp. GK: 2318 [→ 2115]. ptcp. of 2115: that which is crushed:– crushed [1]

2117 זָזָא **zāzā'**, n.pr.m. GK: 2321. Zaza, "*form of a shortened nick name; term of endearment*":– Zaza [1]

2118 זָחַח **zāḥaḥ**, v. GK: 2310 & 2322. [N] to come loose, get out of place; to swing out:– loosed [2]

Heb

2119 זָחַל ***zāḥal***, v. GK: 2323 & 2324 [→ 2120; cf. 1763]. [Q] to be afraid; to crawl, glide (of a snake):– afraid [1], serpents [1], worms [1]

2120 זֹחֶלֶת ***zōḥelet***, n.pr.loc. GK: 2325 [→ 2119]. Zoheleth, "*crawling thing* or *fearsome thing*":– Zoheleth [1]

2121 זֵידוֹן ***zêdôn***, a. GK: 2327 [→ 2102]. raging (water), implying it is out of control:– proud [1]

2122 זִיו ***zîw*** (Aram.), n.m. GK: 10228. radiant appearance: dazzling, splendor; terrified appearance: flushed, pale:– countenance [4], brightness [2]

2123 זִיז ***zîz***, n.m. GK: 2328 & 2329. creatures; nipple (of a lactating breast):– abundance [1], wild beasts [1], wild beast [1]

2124 זִיזָא ***zîzā'***, n.pr.m. GK: 2330 [→ 2125?]. Ziza, "*(childish abbreviation, like "mama," as a name of endearment)*":– Ziza [2]

2125 זִיזָה ***zîzâ***, n.pr.m. GK: 2331 [→ 2124?]. Ziza, "*(childish abbreviation, like "mama," as a term of endearment)*":– Zizah [1]

2126 זִינָא ***zînā'***, n.pr.m. GK: 2332 [cf. 2124]. Zina; cf. 2124:– Zina [1]

2127 זִיעַ ***zîa'***, n.pr.m. GK: 2333. Zia, "[poss.] *trembler*":– Zia [1]

2128 זִיף ***zîp***, n.pr.m. & loc. GK: 2334 & 2335 [→ 2130]. Ziph:– Ziph [10]

2129 זִיפָה ***zîpâ***, n.pr.m. GK: 2336. Ziphah:– Ziphah [1]

2130 זִיפִי ***zîpî***, a.g. GK: 2337 [→ 2128]. Ziphite, "*of Ziph*":– Ziphites [2], Ziphims [1]

2131 זִיקוֹת ***zîqôt*** or זֵק ***zēq***, n.[m.]. GK: 2338 & 2414 & 2415 [cf. 246]. flaming torch, firebrand; chains, fetters:– chains [3], sparks [2], fetters [1], firebrands [1]

2132 זַיִת ***zayit***, n.m. GK: 2339 [→ 1269, 1269, 2133, 2241?]. olive (tree, grove, oil, leaf):– olive [13], olive tree [8], olive trees [6], oliveyards [5], olives [4], Olivet [1], oliveyard [1]

2133 זֵיתָן ***zêtān***, n.pr.m. GK: 2340 [→ 2132]. Zethan, "*olive tree* or *one who deals in olives*":– Zethan [1]

2134 זַךְ ***zak***, a. GK: 2341 [→ 2141]. pure, clear; flawless, innocent, upright:– pure [9], clean [2]

2135 זָכָה ***zākâ***, v. GK: 2342 [cf. 2141; cf. 2136]. [Q] to be pure; be justified, be acquitted; [P] to keep pure; [Ht] to make oneself clean, pure; usually referring to moral purity as a superior quality:– clean [2], cleansed [1], cleanse [1], clear [1], count pure [1], made clean [1], make clean [1]

2136 זָכוּ ***zākû*** (Aram.), n.f. GK: 10229 [cf. 2135]. innocence:– innocency [1]

2137 זְכוֹכִית ***z^e kôkît***, n.[f.]. GK: 2343 [→ 2141]. crystal, referring to a transparent ornament):– crystal [1]

2138 זָכוּר ***zākûr***, n.m. GK: 2344 & 2345 [→ 2142]. male:– males [2], male [1], men children [1]

2139 זַכּוּר ***zakkûr***, n.pr.m. GK: 2346 [→ 2142]. Zaccur, "*remembering*":– Zaccur [8], Zacchur [1]

2140 זַכַּי ***zakkay***, n.pr.m. GK: 2347 [→ 2142+3068?]. Zaccai, "*Yahweh has remembered*, [or perhaps] *Yahweh remember*":– Zaccai [2]

2141 זָכַךְ ***zākak***, v. GK: 2348 [→ 2134, 2137; cf. 2135]. [Q] to be pure, bright, clean:– clean [1], make never so clean (+1253+871.1) [1], purer [1], pure [1]

2142 זָכַר ***zākar***, v. GK: 2349 & 2350 & 4654 [→ 234, 2138, 2139, 2143, 2144, 2145, 2146 (also used with compound proper names)]. [Q] to remember, commemorate, consider; [Qp] to remember; [N] to be remembered, be mentioned; to be born male; [H] to bring to remembrance, remind, mention, record:– remember [117], remembered [46], make mention [12], recorder [9], mindful [6], call to remembrance [3], mentioned [3], remembereth [3], bring to remembrance [2], earnestly remember (+2142) [2], mention [2], record [2], still in remembrance (+2142) [2], think [2], well remember (+2142) [2], bringeth to remembrance [1], bringing to remembrance [1], burneth [1], calling to remembrance [1], come to remembrance [1], in remembrance [1], keep in remembrance [1], made mention of [1], made mention [1], made to be remembered [1], make to be remembered [1], maketh mention [1], male [1], mention made [1], put in remembrance [1], recount [1], rememberest [1], remembering [1], think on [1]

2143 זֵכֶר ***zēker*** or זֶכֶר ***zeker***, n.m. GK: 2352 & 2354 [→ 2142]. memory, memorial, remembrance (with an implication of honor, worship, and celebration); fame, renown:– remembrance [11], memorial [5], memory [5], remembered [1], sent [1]

2144 זֶכֶר ***zeker***, n.pr.m. GK: 2353 [→ 2142]. Zeker, "*memorial*":– Zacher [1]

2145 זָכָר ***zākār***, n.m. & a. GK: 2351 [→ 2142; cf. 1798]. male, man:– male [37], males [30], man [9], man child [2], mankind [2], him[s] [1], men [1]

2146 זִכָּרוֹן ***zikkārôn***, n.m. GK: 2355 [→ 2142; cf. 1799]. memorial, remembrance (with an implication of honor, worship, and celebration), commemoration, reminder:– memorial [17], remembrance [5], records [1], remembrances [1]

2147 זִכְרִי ***zikrî***, n.pr.m. GK: 2356 [→ 2142?+3068?]. Zicri, "*Yahweh remembers*":– Zichri [12]

2148 זְכַרְיָה ***z^e karyâ*** or זְכַרְיָהוּ ***z^e karyāhû***, n.pr.m. GK: 2357 & 2358 & 10230. Zechariah, "*Yahweh remembers*": note this name is Aramaic twice in Ezra:– Zechariah [39], Zachariah [4]

2149 זֻלּוּת ***zullût***, n.f. GK: 2359 [→ 2151]. vileness:– vilest [1]

2150 זַלְזַל ***zalzal***, n.[m.]. GK: 2360 [→ 2151; cf. 5550]. shoots, sprigs, tendrils:– sprigs [1]

2151 זָלַל ***zālal***, v. GK: 2361 & 2362 [→ 2149, 2150]. [Q] to profligate, be a glutton, to gorge oneself; [N] to tremble (of mountains); [H] to despise, treat contemptibly:– glutton [2], vile [2], flow down [1], flowed down [1], riotous eaters [1], riotous [1]

2152 זַלְעָפָה ***zal'āpâ***, n.f. GK: 2363 [→ 2196]. raging (wind); indignation; fits of hunger:– horrible [1], horror [1], terrible [1]

2153 זִלְפָּה ***zilpâ***, n.pr.f. GK: 2364. Zilpah, "*short nosed person*":– Zilpah [7]

2154 זִמָּה ***zimmâ***, n.f. GK: 2365. lewdness, shamelessness, evil:– lewdness [14], wickedness [4], mischief [3], lewd [2], heinous crime [1], lewdly (+871.1) [1], purposes [1], thought [1], wicked devices [1], wicked mind [1]

2155 זִמָּה ***zimmâ***, n.pr.m. GK: 2366. Zimmah, "*consider, plan*":– Zimmah [3]

2156 זְמוֹרָה ***z^e môrâ***, n.[f.]. GK: 2367 [→ 2168; cf. 2231]. vine branch:– branch [3], slips [1], vine branches [1]

2157 זַמְזֻמִּים ***zamzummîm***, n.pr.g. GK: 2368 [→ 2161?]. Zamzummite, "*babblers*":– Zamzummims [1]

2158 זָמִיר ***zāmîr***, n.m. GK: 2369 [→ 2167]. song, music and song:– songs [3], psalmist [1], psalms [1], singing [1]

2159 זָמִיר ***zāmîr***, n.[m.]. GK: 2370 [→ 2168]. pruning (of vines); vintage:– branch [1]

2160 זְמִירָה ***z^e mîrâ***, n.pr.m. GK: 2371 [→ 2172?; cf. 2167]. Zemirah, "[poss.] *song [with instrumental accompaniment];* [poss.] *Yahweh has helped*":– Zemira [1]

2161 זָמַם ***zāmam***, v. GK: 2372 [→ 2157?, 2162, 4209]. [Q] to determine, plan, plot, intend, resolve:– thought [4], devised [3], purposed [2], considereth [1], imagined [1], plotteth [1], thought evil [1]

2162 זָמָם ***zāmām***, n.[m.]. GK: 2373 [→ 2161]. plan, plot:– wicked device [1]

2163 זָמַן ***zāman***, v. GK: 2374 [→ 2165; cf. 2164]. [Pu] to be set, be designated, appointed:– appointed [3]

2164 זְמַן ***z^e man*** (Aram.), v.den. GK: 10231 [→ 2166; cf. 2163]. [Htpe] to conspire, agree to; [H] to decide:– prepared [1]

2165 זְמָן ***z^e mān***, n.m. GK: 2375 [→ 2163; cf. 2166]. time, appointed time:– time [2], season [1], times [1]

2166 זְמַן ***z^e man*** (Aram.), n.m. GK: 10232 [→ 2166; cf. 2165]. time, event, occurrence; a unit of time: indefinite period of time, set time, season:– time [6], times [3], seasons [1], season [1]

2167 זָמַר ***zāmar***, v. GK: 2376 [→ 2158, 2160?, 2172, 2176, 4210; cf. 2170, cf. 2171]. [P] to sing, sing praises, to make music, to chant, sing, or play instruments to worship God and proclaim his excellence:– sing [38], give praise [2], sing psalms [2], praise [1], sing forth [1], sing praises [1]

2168 זָמַר ***zāmar***, v. GK: 2377 [→ 2156, 2159, 4211, 4212]. [Q] to prune (vines); [N] to be pruned:– prune [2], pruned [1]

2169 זֶמֶר ***zemer***, n.[m.]. GK: 2378 [cf. 2173?]. mountain sheep; some sources: gazelle:– chamois [1]

2170 זְמָר ***z^e mār*** (Aram.), n.[m.]. GK: 10233 [→ 2171; cf. 2167]. music in general, or string music in particular:– musick [4]

זָמִר ***zāmir***. See 2158.

זְמֹרָה ***z^e mōr***. See 2156.

2171 זַמָּר ***zammār*** (Aram.), n.m. GK: 10234 [→ 2170; cf. 2167]. singer:– singers [1]

2172 זִמְרָה ***zimrâ***, n.f. GK: 2379 [→ 2160?; cf. 2167]. singing, song, (instrumental) music:– melody [2], psalm [2]

2173 זִמְרָה ***zimrâ***, n.f. GK: 2380 [→ 2174; cf. 2169?]. best product, having a high value:– best fruits [1]

זְמִרָה ***z^e mirâ***. See 2158.

זְמֹרָה ***z^e mōrâ***. See 2156.

2174 זִמְרִי ***zimrî***, n.pr.m. & loc. GK: 2381 & 2382 [→ 2173]. Zimri, "*wild goats, sheep;* [poss.] *awe of Yahweh*":– Zimri [15]

2175 זִמְרָן ***zimrān***, n.pr.m. GK: 2383. Zimran, "*wild goats, sheep*":– Zimran [2]

2176 זִמְרָת ***zimrāt***, n.f. GK: 2384 [→ 2167?]. song or strength:– song [3]

2177 זַן ***zan***, n.[m.]. GK: 2385 [cf. 2178]. kind, sort:– all manner of store (+413+2177+4480) [2], divers kinds [1]

2178 זַן ***zan*** (Aram.), n.[m.]. GK: 10235 [cf. 2177]. kind, sort:– kinds [4]

2179 זָנַב ***zānab***, v.den. GK: 2386 [→ 2180]. [P] to cut off from the rear position, attack from the rear, as a fig. extension of the base meaning "to cut off a tail":– smite the hindmost [1], smote the hindmost [1]

2180 זָנָב ***zānāb***, n.m. GK: 2387 [→ 2179]. tail; stump:– tail [9], tails [2]

2181 זָנָה ***zānâ***, v. GK: 2388 & 2389 [→ 2185, 2183, 2184, 8457]. [Q] to be, become a prostitute; to be sexually immoral, be promiscuous, commit adultery; to feel a dislike for; [Pu] to be solicited for prostitution; [H] to make a prostitute, to turn to prostitution:– harlot [18], go a whoring [8], played the harlot [8], commit whoredom [6], went a whoring [5], gone a whoring [4], whore [4], whorish [3], committed great whoredom (+2181) [2], committed whoredom continually (+2181) [2], committed whoredoms [2], harlot's [2], harlots [2], play the harlot [2], played the whore [2], playedst the harlot [2], playing the harlot [2], whores [2], cause to be a whore [1], caused to commit fornication [1], commit fornication [1], commit whoredoms (+8457) [1], commit whoredoms [1], committed fornication [1], committest whoredom [1], fall to whoredom [1], harlots' [1], made to go a whoring [1], make go a whoring [1], play the whore [1], playeth the harlot [1], playing the whore [1], whore's (+802) [1], whoredoms [1], whoredom [1]

2182 זָנוֹחַ ***zānôaḥ***, n.pr.m. & loc. GK: 2391 & 2392 [→ 2186]. Zanoah, "*rejected*":– Zanoah [5]

2183 זְנוּנִים ***zᵉnûnîm***, n.[m.]. GK: 2393 [→ 2181]. wanton lust, prostitution, adultery; by extension: idolatry, as unfaithfulness to God:– whoredoms [11], whoredom [1]

2184 זְנוּת ***zᵉnût***, n.f.abst. GK: 2394 [→ 2181]. prostitution, sexual immorality, unfaithfulness; by extension: idolatry, as unfaithfulness to God:– whoredom [7], whoredoms [2]

2185 זוֹנָה ***zōnâ***, n.f. *or* v. GK: 2390 [→ 2181]. prostitute, harlot; translated as "armor" in the KJV:– armour [1]

2186 זָנַח ***zānaḥ***, v. GK: 2395 & 2396 [→ 2182]. [Q] to reject, cast out; [H] to declare rejected; to remove; to stink:– cast off [16], cast away [1], castest off [1], removed far off [1], turn far away [1]

2187 זָנַק ***zānaq***, v. GK: 2397. [P] to spring out:– leap [1]

2188 זֵעָה ***zēʿâ***, n.f. GK: 2399 [→ 3154]. sweat; the "sweat of the brow" refers to do heavy manual labor:– sweat [1]

2189 זַעֲוָה ***zaᵃwâ***, n.f. GK: 2400 [→ 2190; cf. 2111]. thing of horror, terror:– removed [6], trouble [1]

2190 זַעֲוָן ***zaᵃwān***, n.pr.m. GK: 2401 [→ 2189+4993.1?]. Zaavan, "[poss.] *trembling, terror*":– Zaavan [1], Zavan [1]

2191 זְעֵיר ***zᵉʿēr***, n.[m.]. GK: 2402 [→ 4213; cf. 6819; cf. 2192]. little; a little longer:– little [5]

2192 זְעֵיר ***zᵉʿêr*** (Aram.), a. GK: 10236 [cf. 2191]. little, small; fig., insignificant, light in status:– little [1]

2193 זָעַךְ ***zāʿak***, v. GK: 2403 [cf. 1846]. [N] to be extinguished:– extinct [1]

2194 זָעַם ***zāʿam***, v. GK: 2404 [→ 2195]. [Q] to express wrath, show fury, denounce; [Qp] to be under wrath, be accursed; [N] to be scolded, be cursed:– indignation [4], angry [2], defy [2], abhorred [1], abhor [1], abominable [1], defied [1]

2195 זַעַם ***zaʿam***, n.m. GK: 2405 [→ 2194]. wrath, anger, indignation, insolence:– indignation [20], anger [1], rage [1]

2196 זָעַף ***zāʿap***, v. GK: 2406 & 2407 [→ 2152, 2197, 2198]. [Q] to rage against, become angry; to look dejected, look pitiful:– wroth [2], fretteth [1], sad [1], worse liking [1]

2197 זַעַף ***zaʿap***, n.m. GK: 2408 [→ 2196]. rage, wrath:– indignation [2], rage [2], raging [1], wrath [1]

2198 זָעֵף ***zāʿēp***, a. GK: 2409 [→ 2196]. angry, raging:– displeased [2]

2199 זָעַק ***zāʿaq***, v. GK: 2410 [→ 2201; cf. 6817; cf. 2200]. [Q] to cry out, call to, weep aloud, howl; [N] to be called, be summoned; be assembled; [H] to summon, cause to gather together, issue a proclamation:– cried [26], cry [20], cried out [5], cry out [5], called [3], assemble [2], criest [2], gathered together [2], gathered [2], assembled [1], caused to be proclaimed [1], comest with a company [1], crieth out [1], crying [1], make to cry [1]

2200 זְעִק ***zᵉʿiq*** (Aram.), v. GK: 10237 [cf. 3815, cf. 6817]. [P] to call out, shout:– cried [1]

2201 זְעָקָה ***zᵉʿāqâ***, n.f. GK: 2411 [→ 2199]. outcry, shout, lament, wail:– cry [17], crying [1]

2202 זִפְרוֹן ***ziprôn***, n.pr.loc. GK: 2412. Ziphron:– Ziphron [1]

2203 זֶפֶת ***zepet***, n.f. GK: 2413. pitch (resin):– pitch [3]

זִק ***ziq*** or זֵק ***zēq***. See 2131.

2204 זָקֵן ***zāqēn***, v. GK: 2416 [→ 2206]. [Q] to be old; [H] to grow old; this can refer to maturity in contrast to youth or to advanced age:– old [22], waxed old [2], aged man [1], old man [1], wax old [1]

2205 זָקֵן ***zāqēn***, a. GK: 2418 [→ 2206]. elder, old, aged, veteran; (n.) elder, leader, dignitary; "elder" can refer to a formal position as a community leader and arbiter:– elders [114], old [21], old men [11], ancients [9], old man [9], ancient [5], aged [3], ancient men [1], elder (+3117+3807.1) [1], eldest [1], old men's [1], old women [1], senators [1]

2206 זָקָן ***zāqān***, n.m. GK: 2417 [→ 2204, 2205, 2207, 2209, 2208]. beard, whiskers (a sign of maturity or age); chin:– beard [15], beards [4]

2207 זֹקֶן ***zōqen***, n.[m.]. GK: 2419 [→ 2206]. old age:– age [1]

2208 זְקֻנִים ***zᵉqunîm***, n.pl.[m.]. GK: 2421 [→ 2206]. old age:– old age [4]

2209 זִקְנָה ***ziqnâ***, n.f. GK: 2420 [→ 2206]. old age, growing old:– old age [3], old [3]

2210 זָקַף ***zāqap***, v. GK: 2422 [cf. 2211]. [Q] to lift up:– raiseth up [1], raiseth [1]

2211 זְקַף ***zᵉqap*** (Aram.), v. GK: 10238 [cf. 2210]. [Pp] to be lifted up:– set up [1]

2212 זָקַק ***zāqaq***, v. GK: 2423 [cf. 2085]. [Q] to refine, distill; [P] to refine; [Pu] to be refined, be purified:– refined [2], fine [1], pour down [1], purge [1], purified [1], well refined [1]

2213 זֵר ***zēr***, n.m. GK: 2425 [→ 2237]. molding:– crown [10]

2214 זָרָא ***zārāʾ***, n.[f.]. GK: 2426. loathsome thing:– stranger (+376) [2], loathsome [1], strangers [1]

2215 זָרַב ***zārab***, v. GK: 2427. [Pu] to become dry:– wax warm [1]

2216 זְרֻבָּבֶל ***zᵉrubbābel***, n.pr.m. GK: 2428 [→ 2232+894; cf. 2217]. Zerubbabel, "*offspring [seed] of Babylon; scion i.e., one grafted into the [plant of] Babylon*":– Zerubbabel [21]

2217 זְרֻבָּבֶל ***zᵉrubbābel*** (Aram.), n.pr.m. GK: 10239 [cf. 2216]. Zerubbabel, "*seed of Babylon* or *one grafted into Babylon*":– Zerubbabel [1]

2218 זֶרֶד ***zered***, n.pr.loc. GK: 2429. Zered, "*[valley of some kind of] plant*":– Zered [3], Zared [1]

2219 זָרָה ***zārâ***, v. GK: 2430 & 2431 [→ 2239, 4214, 4215]. [Q, P] to scatter, spread out; winnow; to measure off, discern; [N, Pu] to be scattered, spread out:– scatter [12], disperse [7], scattered [6], fan [4], scattereth [2], spread [2], cast away [1], compassest [1], dispersed [1], strawed [1], winnowed [1], winnoweth [1]

2220 זְרוֹעַ ***zᵉrôaʿ***, n.f. GK: 2432 [cf. 248; cf. 153, cf. 1872]. arm, forearm, shoulder; power, strength, force:– arm [59], arms [24], power [3], shoulder [2], holpen [1], mighty [1], strength [1]

2221 זֵרוּעַ ***zērûaʿ***, n.[m.]. GK: 2433 [→ 2232]. (plants from) seeds:– sowing [1], things that are sown [1]

2222 זַרְזִיף ***zarzîp***, n.[m.]. GK: 2434 & 2449. dripping:– water [1]

זְרֹעָה ***zᵉrôʿâ***. See 2220.

2223 זַרְזִיר ***zarzîr***, a. GK: 2435 [→ 2237?]. a strutting animal, variously interpreted: rooster, horse, greyhound:– greyhound (+4975) [1]

2224 זָרַח ***zāraḥ***, v. GK: 2436 [→ 249, 250, 2225, 2226, 2227, 4217 (also used with compound proper names)]. [Q] to rise, dawn (of the sun); by extension: to appear bright red (as with a skin disorder):– ariseth [4], arise [3], risen [2], riseth [2], rose up [2], arose [1], rise [1], rose [1], shone [1], up [1]

2225 זֶרַח ***zeraḥ***, n.[m.]. GK: 2437 [→ 2226, 2227; cf. 2224]. dawning (of light):– rising [1]

2226 זֶרַח ***zeraḥ***, n.pr.m. GK: 2438 [→ 250; cf. 2224, 2225]. Zerah, "*dawning, shining* or *flashing [red or scarlet] light*":– Zerah [20], Zarah [1]

2227 זַרְחִי ***zarḥî***, a.g. GK: 2439 [→ 2226; cf. 2224, 2225]. Zerahite, "*of Zerah*":– Zarhites [6]

Heb

2228 זְרַחְיָה ***z^eraḥyâ***, n.pr.m. GK: 2440 [→ 2224+3068]. Zerahiah, "*Yahweh shines brightly [red or scarlet]; Yahweh has risen [like the sun]*":– Zerahiah [5]

2229 זָרַם ***zāram***, v. GK: 2441 & 2442 [→ 2230]. [Q] to sweep away, put an end to; [Po] to pour down:– carriest away as with a flood [1], poured out [1]

2230 זֶרֶם ***zerem***, n.m. GK: 2443 [→ 2229]. rain, rainstorm, thunderstorm, torrent rains:– storm [3], tempest [3], flood [1], overflowing [1], showers [1]

2231 זִרְמָה ***zirmâ***, n.f. GK: 2444 [cf. 2156]. male genitals or emission:– issue [2]

2232 זָרַע ***zāra'***, v. GK: 2445 [→ 2221, 2233, 2235, 4218; cf. 2234 (also used with compound proper names)]. [Q] to sow seed, plant seed; [Qp] to be sown upon; [Pu] to be sown; [N] to be sown, be planted, to have children, have descendants; [H] to yield seed, to become pregnant; from the base meaning of scattering seed onto the ground comes the fig. extension "to have children":– sow [26], sown [14], yielding [3], sowed [2], sower [2], soweth [2], bearing [1], conceive seed (+2233) [1], conceived seed [1], set [1], sow seeds [1], sow with seed [1], sowedst [1]

2233 זֶרַע ***zera'***, n.m. GK: 2446 [→ 2232; cf. 2234]. seed, semen, that which propagates a species; by extension: that which is propagated, child, offspring, descendant, line, race:– seed [218], child [2], conceive seed (+2232) [1], fruitful [1], lie carnally (+5414+7903+3807.1) [1], lieth carnally with (+854+7901+7902) [1], man carnally (+376+7902) [1], seed (+7902) [1], seed's [1], seedtime [1], sowing time [1]

2234 זְרַע ***z^era'*** (Aram.), n.[m.]. GK: 10240 [cf. 2233]. seed, "seed" of a person is translated "descendant":– seed [1]

זֵרוּעַ ***z^erōa'***. See 2220.

2235 זֵרֹעִים ***zērō'îm*** or זֵרְעֹנִים ***zēr'ōnîm***, n.[m.]. GK: 2447 & 2448 [cf. 2232]. vegetables:– pulse [2]

זְרֹעָה ***z^erō'â***. See 2220.

2236 זָרַק ***zāraq***, v. GK: 2450 & 2451 [→ 4219]. [Q] to sprinkle, to scatter, to toss (in the air); to creep in; [Pu] to be sprinkled:– sprinkled [16], sprinkle [14], scatter [2], here and there [1], sprinkleth [1], strowed [1]

2237 זָרַר ***zārar***, v. GK: 2452 & 2453 [→ 2213, 2223?]. [Qp] to be pressed out; [Po] to sneeze:– neesed [1]

2238 זֶרֶשׁ ***zereš***, n.pr.f. GK: 2454. Zeresh, "[poss.] *Kirsha; gold; mop-headed*":– Zeresh [4]

2239 זֶרֶת ***zeret***, n.f. GK: 2455 [→ 2219]. handbreadth, span (of an open hand, a measure of about nine inches [23 cm]):– span [7]

2240 זַתּוּא ***zattû'***, n.pr.m. GK: 2456. Zattu:– Zattu [3], Zatthu [1]

2241 זֵתָם ***zētām***, n.pr.m. GK: 2457 [→ 2132?]. Zetham, "[poss.] *olive tree*":– Zetham [2]

2242 זֵתַר ***zētar***, n.pr.m. GK: 2458. Zethar, "[poss.] *conqueror; slayer*":– Zethar [1]

2243 חֹב ***ḥōb***, n.[m.]. GK: 2460 [→ 2245; cf. 2244]. heart:– bosom [1]

2244 חָבָא ***ḥābā'***, v. GK: 2461 [→ 455, 4224; cf. 2243, 2246?, 2247, 3160?]. [N] to be hidden, to hide oneself; [Pu] to keep oneself in hiding; [H] to hide (another); [Ho] to be hidden away; [Ht] to keep oneself hidden:– hid [24], hide [7], held peace (+6963) [1], hideth [1], secretly [1]

2245 חָבַב ***ḥābab***, v. GK: 2462 [→ 2243, 2246?, 3160?]. [Q] to love:– loved [1]

2246 חֹבָב ***ḥōbāb***, n.pr.m. GK: 2463 [→ 2245?; cf. 2244?]. Hobab, "*beloved;* [poss.] *deceit*":– Hobab [2]

2247 חָבָה ***ḥābâ***, v. GK: 2464 [→ 2252, 2253; cf. 2244]. [Q] to hide; [N] to conceal oneself:– hide [4]

2248 חֲבוּלָה ***ḥ^abûlâ*** (Aram.), n.f. GK: 10242 [→ 2255]. wrong, crime:– hurt [1]

2249 חָבוֹר ***ḥābôr***, n.pr.loc. GK: 2466. Habor:– Habor [3]

2250 חַבּוּרָה ***ḥabbûrâ***, n.f. GK: 2467 [→ 2266]. bruise, welt, wound, injury:– stripe [2], blueness [1], bruises [1], hurt [1], stripes [1], wounds [1]

2251 חָבַט ***ḥābaṭ***, v. GK: 2468. [Q] to thresh, beat out; [N] to be beaten:– beat off [1], beat out [1], beaten out [1], beatest [1], threshed [1]

2252 חֲבַיָּה ***ḥ^obayyâ***, n.pr.m. GK: 2469 [→ 2247+3068]. Hobaiah, "*Yahweh has hidden*":– Habaiah [2]

2253 חֶבְיוֹן ***ḥebyôn***, n.[m.]. GK: 2470 [→ 2247]. hiding, covering:– hiding [1]

2254 חָבַל ***ḥābal***, v. GK: 2471 & 2472 & 2473 [→ 2256, 2258; cf. 2255]. [Q] to require a pledge, demand a security; to act wickedly, to offend; [P] to destroy, ruin, work havoc; to conceive, be pregnant, be in labor; [Pu] to be broken:– destroy [5], take a pledge [3], at all take to pledge (+2254) [2], bands [2], brought forth [2], dealt very corruptly (+2254) [2], destroyed [2], take to pledge [2], corrupt [1], laid to pledge [1], offend [1], spoil [1], take for a pledge [1], taken a pledge [1], taketh to pledge [1], travaileth [1], withholden the pledge (+2258) [1]

2255 חֲבַל ***ḥ^abal*** (Aram.), v. GK: 10243 [→ 2248, 2257; cf. 2254]. [Pa] to destroy, hurt; [Htpa] to be destroyed:– destroyed [3], destroy [2], hurt [1]

2256 חֶבֶל ***ḥebel*** or חֵבֶל ***ḥēbel***, n.m. GK: 2474 & 2475 & 2476 & 2477 & 2482 [→ 2254, cf. 2259, 2260]. rope, cord, line, rigging; share, portion, region, district; procession, group, union; destruction, ruin; labor pains, anguish of birth pangs:– cords [12], sorrows [10], line [5], coast [4], cord [4], lot [3], region [3], ropes [3], company [2], lines [2], pangs [2], portions [2], portion [2], bands [1], country [1], destruction [1], pain [1], snare [1], tacklings [1]

2257 חֲבָל ***ḥ^abāl*** (Aram.), n.m. GK: 10244 [→ 2255]. physical harm, wound, hurt; fig., damage resulting from the lowering of status:– hurt [2], damage [1]

2258 חֲבֹל ***ḥ^abōl*** or חֲבֹלָה ***ḥ^abōlâ***, n.[m.]. GK: 2478 & 2481 [→ 2254]. pledge for a loan:– pledge [3], withholden the pledge (+2254) [1]

2259 חֹבֵל ***ḥōbēl***, n.m. GK: 2480 [cf. 2256]. seaman, sailor:– pilots [4], shipmaster (+7227+1886.1) [1]

2260 חִבֵּל ***ḥibbēl***, n.[m.]. GK: 2479 [→ 2256]. (ship's) rigging, mast:– mast [1]

2261 חֲבַצֶּלֶת ***ḥ^abaṣṣelet***, n.f. GK: 2483. rose; crocus:– rose [2]

2262 חֲבַצִּנְיָה ***ḥ^abaṣṣinyâ***, n.pr.m. GK: 2484. Habazziniah, "[poss.] *exuberant in Yahweh*":– Habaziniah [1]

2263 חָבַק ***ḥābaq***, v. GK: 2485 [→ 2264]. [Q] to hold in one's arms, embrace; to fold one's hands; [P] to embrace, hug:– embrace [8], embraced [3], embracing [1], foldeth together [1]

2264 חִבֻּק ***ḥibbuq***, n.[m.]. GK: 2486 [→ 2263]. folding (of idle hands):– folding [2]

2265 חֲבַקּוּק ***ḥ^abaqqûq***, n.pr.m. GK: 2487. Habakkuk, "*garden plant*":– Habakkuk [2]

2266 חָבַר ***ḥābar***, v. GK: 2248 & 2488 & 2489 [→ 2250, 2267, 2268, 2270, 2271, 2272, 2274, 5683, 2275, 2276, 2277, 2278, 2279, 4226, 4225]. [Q] to join, unite, be attached, to be touching; to cast spells, to enchant; [Qp] to be joined; [P] to fasten, join; [Pu] to be fastened, be closely compacted; [Ht] to make an alliance, become allies; [H] to make fine speeches:– joined [6], coupled [5], couple together [3], coupled together [2], couple [2], joined together [2], charmer (+2267) [1], charming (+2267) [1], compact [1], fellowship [1], heap up [1], join together [1], joined to [1], join [1], league [1]

2267 חֶבֶר ***ḥeber***, n.[m.]. GK: 2490 [→ 2266]. sharing; band, group; magic spell:– enchantments [2], wide [2], charmer (+2266) [1], charming (+2266) [1], company [1]

2268 חֶבֶר ***ḥeber***, n.pr.m. GK: 2491 [→ 2277; cf. 2266]. Heber, "*associate*":– Heber [10], Heber's [1]

2269 חֲבַר ***ḥ^abar*** (Aram.), n.m. GK: 10245 [→ 2273; cf. 2270]. friend, companion:– fellows [2], companions [1]

2270 חָבֵר ***ḥābēr***, a. & n.m. GK: 2492 [→ 2266; cf. 2269, cf. 2273]. companion, associate, partner, friend:– companions [5], fellows [3], companion [2], fellow [1], knit together [1]

2271 חַבָּר ***ḥabbār***, n.m. GK: 2493 [→ 2266]. (fellow) trader, one of a community of traders:– companions [1]

2272 חֲבַרְבֻּרוֹת ***ḥ^abarburôt***, n.f. GK: 2494 [→ 2266]. spots (of a leopard):– spots [1]

2273 חַבְרָה ***ḥabrâ*** (Aram.), n.f. GK: 10246 [→ 2269; cf. 2270]. companion (horn):– fellows [1]

2274 חֶבְרָה ***ḥebrâ***, n.f. GK: 2495 [→ 2266]. company, association:– company [1]

2275 חֶבְרוֹן ***ḥebrôn***, n.pr.m. & loc. GK: 2496 & 2497 [→ 2276; cf. 2266, 5683?]. Hebron, "*association*":– Hebron [71]

2276 חֶבְרוֹנִי ***ḥebrônî***, a.g. GK: 2498 [→ 2275; cf. 2266, 5683]. Hebronite, "*of Hebron*":– Hebronites [6]

2277 חֶבְרִי ***ḥebrî***, a.g. GK: 2499 [→ 2268; cf. 2266]. Heberite, "*of Heber*":– Heberites [1]

2278 חֲבֶרֶת ***ḥ^aberet***, n.f. GK: 2500 [→ 2266]. partner, (marriage) companion:– companion [1]

2279 חֹבֶרֶת ***ḥōberet***, n.f. GK: 2501 [→ 2266]. set (of curtains):– coupleth [2], coupling [2]

2280 חָבַשׁ ***ḥābaš***, v. GK: 2502 [cf. 2805]. [Q] to tie, bind, saddle; [Qp] to be saddled; to be twisted, wrapped around; [P] to bind up; [Pu] to be bound, bandaged:– saddled [10], bind up [3], bindeth up [3], bind [3], bound up [3], saddle [3], put [2], bindeth [1], bound [1], girded about [1], govern [1], healer [1], wrapt about [1]

2281 חֲבִתִּים ***ḥᵃbittîm***, n.[m.]pl. GK: 2503 [→ 4227]. offering bread (flat cakes, baked in a pan):– pans [1]

2282 חַג ***ḥag***, n.m. GK: 2504 [→ 2287]. religious feast, festival; festal procession:– feast [50], feasts [3], keep a feast (+2287) [2], sacrifice [2], solemn feasts [2], sacrifices [1], solemn feast [1], solemnity [1]

2283 חָגָּא ***ḥoggā'***, n.[f.]. GK: 2505. terror; some sources: confusion:– terror [1]

2284 חָגָב ***ḥāgāb***, n.m. GK: 2506 [→ 2285, 2286]. grasshopper, locust (in some cultures distinguished from a grasshopper and used as a food source):– grasshoppers [2], grasshopper [2], locusts [1]

2285 חָגָב ***ḥāgāb***, n.pr.m. GK: 2507 [→ 2286; cf. 2284]. Hagab, "*locust*":– Hagab [1]

2286 חֲגָבָא ***ḥᵃgābā'*** or חֲגָבָה ***ḥᵃgābâ***, n.pr.m. GK: 2508 & 2509 [→ 2285; cf. 2284]. Hagaba, Hagabah, "*locust*":– Hagabah [1], Hagaba [1]

2287 חָגַג ***ḥāgag***, v. GK: 2510 [→ 2282, 2291, 2292, 2293, 2294; cf. 2328]. [Q] to hold a festival, celebrate a festival; this can refer to a religious celebration or a revel:– keep [6], keep a feast (+2282) [2], celebrate [1], dancing [1], hold a feast [1], keep a feast [1], keep a solemn feast [1], keep feast [1], kept holyday [1], reel to and fro [1]

2288 חָגוּ ***ḥāgû***, n.m.pl. GK: 2511. clefts (of a rock) that can be used as a hiding place or retreat from danger:– clefts [3]

2289 חָגוֹר ***ḥāgôr***, a. GK: 2513 [→ 2296]. belted (around the waist):– girdle [2], girded with [1], girdles [1]

2290 חֲגוֹר ***ḥᵃgôr*** or חֲגוֹרָה ***ḥᵃgôrâ***, n.m. & f. GK: 2512 & 2514 [→ 2296]. covering; belt, sash:– girdle [3], aprons [1], gird [1], put on armour (+2296) [1]

2291 חַגִּי ***ḥaggî***, n.pr.m. & a.g. GK: 2515 [→ 2287]. Haggi, "*festal; born on the feast day*":– Haggi [2], Haggites [1]

2292 חַגַּי ***ḥaggay***, n.pr.m. GK: 2516 & 10247 [→ 2287]. Haggai, "*festal; born on the feast day*": note this name is Aramaic twice in Ezra:– Haggai [11]

2293 חַגִּיָּה ***ḥaggiyyâ***, n.pr.m. GK: 2517 [→ 2287+3068]. Haggiah, "*feast of Yahweh*":– Haggiah [1]

2294 חַגִּית ***ḥaggît***, n.pr.f. GK: 2518 [→ 2287]. Haggith, "*festal; born on the feast day*":– Haggith [5]

2295 חָגְלָה ***ḥoglâ***, n.pr.f. GK: 2519 [→ 1031; cf. 2728]. Hoglah, "*partridge*":– Hoglah [4]

2296 חָגַר ***ḥāgar***, v. GK: 2520 [→ 2289, 2290, 4228]. [Q] to tie, strap, fasten; to tuck (lower robe) into one's belt, gird; [Qp] to be tucked in, girded:– girded [13], gird with [7], gird [5], appointed [3], girded on [3], gird up [2], girded with [2], afraid [1], gird on [1], girdeth on [1], girdeth [1], girding with [1], on every side [1], put on armour (+2290) [1], restrain [1]

2297 חַד ***ḥad***, a. GK: 2522 [cf. 259]. one, each:– one [1]

2298 חַד ***ḥad*** (Aram.), a. & subst. GK: 10248 [cf. 259]. one, first, a; time, occurrence:– one [5], a [4], first [4], together (+3509.4) [1]

2299 חַד ***ḥad***, a. GK: 2521 [→ 2300]. sharp (sword):– sharp [4]

2300 חָדַד ***ḥādad*** or חָדָה ***ḥādâ***, v. GK: 2523 & 2527 [→ 258, 2299, 2303, 2307; cf. 2302]. [Q] to be fierce, sharp; to sharpen; [H] to sharpen; [Ho] to be sharpened; [Ht] to slash:– sharpened [3], sharpeneth [2], fierce [1]

2301 חֲדַד ***ḥᵃdad***, n.pr.m. GK: 2524. Hadad, "*sharp, fierce*":– Hadad [1]

2302 חָדָה ***ḥādâ***, v. GK: 2525 & 2526 [→ 2304, 3164, 3165; cf. 2300]. [Q] to be delighted; [N] to be seen; to be joined; [P] to make glad:– joined [1], made [1], rejoiced [1]

2303 חַדּוּד ***ḥaddûd***, a. GK: 2529 [→ 2300]. jagged, pointed:– sharp [1]

2304 חֶדְוָה ***ḥedwâ***, n.f. GK: 2530 [→ 2302; cf. 2305]. joy:– gladness [1], joy [1]

2305 חֶדְוָה ***ḥedwâ*** (Aram.), n.f. GK: 10250 [cf. 2304]. joy:– joy [1]

2306 חֲדֵה ***ḥᵃdēh*** (Aram.), n.m. GK: 10249 [cf. 2373]. chest, breast:– breast [1]

2307 חָדִיד ***ḥādîd***, n.pr.loc. GK: 2531 [→ 2300]. Hadid, "*sharp*":– Hadid [3]

2308 חָדַל ***ḥādal***, v. GK: 2532 & 2533 [→ 2310, 2311?]. [Q] to stop, cease, refrain, fail; to become fat, have success:– forbear [15], cease [12], ceased [6], left off [4], forbare [3], leave [3], left [2], alone (+4480) [1], alone [1], ceaseth [1], ceasing [1], endeth [1], failed [1], forbeareth [1], forborn [1], forsake [1], off [1], rest [1], unoccupied [1], wanteth [1]

2309 חֶדֶל ***ḥedel***, n.[m.]. GK: 2535. world (of the living); some sources: the Underworld, the realm of the dead:– world [1]

2310 חָדֵל ***ḥādēl***, a. GK: 2534 [→ 2308]. refused, rejected, fleeting:– forbeareth [1], frail [1], rejected [1]

2311 חַדְלָי ***ḥadlāy***, n.pr.m. GK: 2536 [→ 2220 *or* 2308]. Hadlai, "*resting; fat, stout*":– Hadlai [1]

2312 חֵדֶק ***ḥēdeq***, n.[m.]. GK: 2537. brier, thorn:– brier [1], thorns [1]

2313 חִדֶּקֶל ***ḥiddeqel***, n.pr.loc. GK: 2538. Hiddekel = Tigris, "*arrow*":– Hiddekel [2]

2314 חָדַר ***ḥādar***, v. GK: 2539 [→ 2315]. [Q] to close in on every side, surround:– entereth into privy chambers [1]

2315 חֶדֶר ***ḥeder***, n.m. GK: 2540 [→ 2314, 2316]. room, chamber, bedroom; shrine; "the chambers of the belly" means "the most inner parts"; "the chambers of death" means "Sheol":– chamber [10], inner chamber (+2315+871.1) [8], chambers [7], bedchamber (+4904) [4], bedchamber (+4296) [2], innermost parts [2], inward parts [2], parlours [1], south [1], within (+4480) [1]

2316 חֲדַר ***ḥᵃdar***, n.pr.m. GK: 2540 [→ 2315]. Hadar:– Hadar [1]

2317 חַדְרָךְ ***ḥadrāk***, n.pr.loc. GK: 2541. Hadrach:– Hadrach [1]

2318 חָדַשׁ ***ḥādaš***, v. GK: 2542 [→ 2319, 2320, 2321, 2322]. [Q] to renew, restore, repair, reaffirm; [Ht] to renew oneself:– renew [3], repair [3], renewed [2], renewest [2]

2319 חָדָשׁ ***ḥādāš***, a. GK: 2543 [→ 2318; cf. 2323]. new, recent, fresh:– new [52], fresh [1]

2320 חֹדֶשׁ ***ḥōdeš***, n.m. [& f.?]. GK: 2544 [→ 2321; cf. 2318]. month; new moon, new moon festival:– month [216], months [37], new moons [11], new moon [9], every month (+2320+871.1) [2], another[s] [1], monthly [1]

2321 חֹדֶשׁ ***ḥōdeš***, n.pr.f. GK: 2545 [→ 2320; cf. 2318]. Hodesh, "*new moon*":– Hodesh [1]

2322 חֲדָשָׁה ***ḥᵃdāšâ***, n.pr.loc. GK: 2546 [→ 2318]. Hadashah, "*new*":– Hadashah [1]

2323 חֲדַת ***ḥᵃdat*** (Aram.), a. GK: 10251 [cf. 2319]. new:– new [1]

2324 חֲוָה ***ḥᵃwâ*** (Aram.), v. GK: 10252 [→ 263; cf. 2331]. [Pa] to reveal, tell, show; [H, A] tell, explain, make known, interpret:– shew [14]

2325 חוּב ***ḥûb***, v. GK: 2549 [→ 2326]. [P] to forfeit (one's head):– make endanger [1]

2326 חוֹב ***ḥôb***, n.[m.]. GK: 2550 [→ 2325]. loan, debt:– debtor [1]

2327 חוֹבָה ***ḥôbâ***, n.pr.loc. GK: 2551. Hobah:– Hobah [1]

2328 חוּג ***ḥûg***, v. GK: 2552 [→ 2329, 4230; cf. 2287]. [Q] to encircle:– compassed with (+5921+6440) [1]

2329 חוּג ***ḥûg***, n.[m.]. GK: 2553 [→ 2328]. circle, horizon:– circle [1], circuit [1], compass [1]

2330 חוּד ***ḥûd***, v.den. GK: 2554 [→ 2420; cf. 258]. [Q] to tell a riddle, set forth an allegory:– put forth [3], put forth a riddle (+2420) [1]

2331 חָוָה ***ḥāwâ***, v. GK: 2555 [→ 262; cf. 263, cf. 2324]. [P] to tell, explain, show, display:– shew [5], sheweth [1]

2332 חַוָּה ***ḥawwâ***, n.pr.f. GK: 2558 [cf. 2421]. Eve, "*life*":– Eve [2]

2333 חַוָּה ***ḥawwâ***, n.f. GK: 2557. settlement, camp; an unwalled village, a tent camp of nomadic peoples, more or less permanent:– towns [3], small towns [1]

2334 חַוֹּת יָאִיר ***ḥawwōt yā'îr***, n.pr.m. & n.f. GK: 2596 [cf. 2971]. Havvoth Jair, "*villages of Jair*":– Havoth-jair [2], Bashan-havoth-jair (+1316) [1]

2335 חוֹזָי ***ḥôzāy***, n.m. GK: 2559 [→ 2374; cf. 2372]. Hozai:–

2336 חוֹחַ ***ḥôaḥ***, n.m. GK: 2560 [cf. 2397]. thicket, thistle, thornbush, bramble, briers; hook:– thistle [4], thorns [3], thorn [2], brambles [1], thistles [1]

2337 חוֹחַ ***ḥôaḥ***, n.m. GK: 2561. hollows, cleft in rock; thicket:– thickets [1]

2338 חוּט ***ḥûṭ*** (Aram.), v. GK: 10253. [H] to repair:– joined [1]

2339 חוּט ***ḥûṭ***, n.m. GK: 2562 [cf. 2338]. line, cord, ribbon, thread:– thread [4], cord [1], fillet [1], line [1]

2340 חִוִּי ***ḥiwwî***, a.g. GK: 2563. Hivite:– Hivites [16], Hivite [9]

2341 חֲוִילָה ***ḥᵃwîlâ***, n.pr.loc. GK: 2564 [→ 2344]. Havilah, "*stretch of sand*":– Havilah [7]

2342 חוּל ***ḥûl*** or חִיל ***ḥîl***, v. GK: 2565 & 2655 & 2656 [→ 2427, 2428, 2479, 4234, 4235, 4246, 4257?; cf. 2426]. [Q] to swirl, turn, fall, dance; to writhe, tremble, be in labor, give birth; to endure, prosper; [Pol] to wait; to dance (the round dance); to give birth; be in deep anguish, to twist; [Polal] to be brought forth, be given birth; [Htpalpal] be in distress; [Htpol] to be in torment; to wait patiently; to swirl down; in some contexts this refers to a whirlwind; [H] to shake; [Ho] to be born:– formed [5], in pain [4], brought forth [3], fear [2], grieved [2], grievous [2], have great pain (+2342) [2], shaketh [2], stayed [2], travailed [2], trembled [2], tremble [2], wounded [2], abide [1], afraid [1], bare [1], calve [1], danced [1], dance [1], driveth away [1], fall grievously [1], fall with pain [1], in anguish [1], look for [1], made to bring forth [1], made [1], maketh to calve [1], much pained [1], pained [1], rest [1], shapen [1], sore pained [1], sorely pained [1], sorrowful [1], sorrow [1], tarried [1], travail with child [1], travaileth with pain [1], travail [1], trust [1], wait patiently [1], waited carefully [1]

2343 חוּל **ḥûl**, n.pr.m. GK: 2566. Hul:– Hul [2]

2344 חוֹל **ḥôl**, n.m. GK: 2567 & 2568 [→ 2341]. sand, grains of sand, with the associative meanings that the sands are vast and innumerable; palm tree or phoenix bird:– sand [23]

2345 חוּם **ḥûm**, a. GK: 2569 [→ 2552]. dark-colored; some shade of gray:– brown [4]

2346 חוֹמָה חֹמָה **ḥômâ**, n.f. GK: 2570 [→ 3181]. wall, with various associative meanings: protection, safety, or impenetrability:– wall [92], walls [35], two walls [4], walled [2]

2347 חוּס **ḥûs**, v. GK: 2571. [Q] to show pity, mercy, have compassion, spare:– spare [12], pity [5], spare (+5921) [2], spared [2], had pity [1], pitied [1], regard (+5869) [1]

2348 חוֹף **ḥôp**, n.[m.]. GK: 2572 [→ 2653]. coast, seashore, haven (for ships):– haven [2], shore [2], coasts [1], coast [1], side [1]

2349 חוּפָם **ḥûpām**, n.pr.m. GK: 2573 [→ 2350]. Hupham:– Hupham [1]

2350 חוּפָמִי **ḥûpāmî**, a.g. GK: 2574 [→ 2349]. Huphamite, "*of Hupham*":– Huphamites [1]

2351 חוּץ **ḥûṣ**, n.[m.]. GK: 2575 [→ 2435; cf. 2434]. out, outside; street, market area; countryside, fields, outdoors:– without (+4480) [43], streets [35], without (+871.1+1886.1) [12], out (+4480) [9], street [9], abroad (+1886.5) [8], abroad [6], out [6], without (+1886.5) [6], out (+1886.5) [3], without [3], abroad (+4480) [2], fields [2], forth [2], outside [2], without (+1886.1+3807.1) [2], without (+4480+1886.5) [2], abroad (+1886.1+3807.1) [1], abroad (+413+1886.1+1886.5) [1], abroad (+4480+1886.1) [1], abroad (+871.1+1886.1) [1], highways [1], more [1], outward (+1886.5) [1], utter [1], without (+1886.1+1886.5) [1], without (+413+1886.1) [1], without (+4480+1886.1) [1]

חוֹק **ḥôq**. See 2436.

חוֹקֹק **ḥûqōq**. See 2712.

2352 חֻר **ḥur**, n.[m.]. GK: 2987 [→ 2356]. hole, pit:– holes [1], hole [1]

2353 חוּר **ḥûr**, n.[m.]. GK: 2580 [→ 2357]. white garments, white linen:– white [2]

2354 חוּר **ḥûr**, n.pr.m. GK: 2581 [→ 1133, 5991?]. Hur, "[perhaps] *child*":– Hur [16]

2355 חוֹרָי **ḥōray**, n.m. GK: 2583 [→ 2357]. fine linen:– networks [1]

2356 חֹר **ḥōr**, n.[m.]. GK: 2986 [→ 2352, 2735]. hole (in various forms):– holes [3], hole [3], caves [1]

2357 חָוַר **ḥāwar**, v. GK: 2578 [→ 2353, 2355, 2751; cf. 2358]. [Q] to grow pale:– wax pale [1]

2358 חִוָּר **ḥiwwār** (Aram.), a. GK: 10254. white, a color of purity and lack of defilement:– white [1]

חוֹרוֹן **ḥôrôn**. See 1032.

חוֹרִי **ḥôrî**. See 2753.

2359 חוּרִי **ḥûrî**, n.pr.m. GK: 2585. Huri, "*linen weaver*":– Huri [1]

2360 חוּרַי **ḥûray**, n.pr.m. GK: 2584. Hurai:– Hurai [1]

2361 חוּרָם **ḥûrām**, n.pr.m. GK: 2586 & 2587 [→ 297?+1]. Huram, Hiram, "*[my] brother is elevated*":– Huram [12]

2362 חַוְרָן **ḥawrān**, n.pr.loc. GK: 2588. Hauran, "*black*":– Hauran [2]

2363 חוּשׁ **ḥûš**, v. GK: 2590 & 2591 [→ 2439, 2440, 4122]. same as 2439: [Q] to go quickly, hasten, rush upon; to be greatly disturbed; to find enjoyment; [Qp] to be ready; [H] to make hurry, hasten; to be dismayed:– make haste [9], hasten [4], hasted [2], haste [2], hasteth [1], made haste [1], ready [1]

2364 חוּשָׁה **ḥûšâ**, n.pr.m. GK: 2592 [→ 2843]. Hushah, "[perhaps] *haste*":– Hushah [1]

2365 חוּשַׁי **ḥûšay**, n.pr.m. GK: 2593 [cf. 7862?]. Hushai:– Hushai [14]

2366 חוּשִׁים **ḥûšîm** or חֻשִׁים **ḥušîm** or חֻשִׁם **ḥušim**, n.pr.f. & m. GK: 2594 & 3123. Hushim, Hushite:– Hushim [4]

2367 חוּשָׁם **ḥûšām**, n.pr.m. GK: 2595 [cf. 2828]. Husham:– Husham [4]

2368 חוֹתָם **ḥôtām**, n.m. GK: 2597 [→ 2369; cf. 2856]. seal, signet ring:– signet [8], seal [5], signets [1]

2369 חוֹתָם **ḥôtām**, n.pr.m. GK: 2598 [→ 2368; cf. 2856]. Hotham, "*signet ring, seal*":– Hotham [1], Hothan [1]

2370 חֲזָה **ḥ^a^zâ** (Aram.), v. GK: 10255 [→ 2376, 2379; cf. 2372]. [P] to see, look, watch, realize; [Pp] to be usual, be customary:– saw [9], sawest [7], beheld [6], see [4], seen [3], had[s] [1], wont [1]

2371 חֲזָאֵל **ḥ^a^zā'ēl** or חֲזָהאֵל **ḥ^a^zāh'ēl**, n.pr.m. GK: 2599 & 2604 [→ 2372+410]. Hazael, "*God [El] sees*":– Hazael [23]

2372 חָזָה **ḥāzâ**, v. GK: 2600 [→ 2335, 2374, 2377, 2380, 2378, 2384, 4236, 4237, 4238; cf. 2370 (also used with compound proper names)]. [Q] to see, to look, observe, gaze; by extension: to choose (one thing over another); to have visions, to prophesy:– see [15], seen [9], saw [8], behold [7], look [3], seeth [3], prophesy [2], seest [2], provide [1], sawest [1]

2373 חָזֶה **ḥāzeh**, n.m. GK: 2601 [cf. 2306]. breast (portion of sacrifice):– breast [11], breasts [2]

2374 חֹזֶה **ḥōzeh**, n.m. GK: 2602 & 2603 [→ 2335, 3626; cf. 2372]. seer, one who receives a communication from God, with a possible focus that the message has a visual component; agreement:– seer [11], seers [5], see [2], agreement [1], prophets [1], seeing [1], stargazers (+3556+871.1+1886.1) [1]

חֲזָהאֵל **ḥ^a^zāh'ēl**. See 2371.

2375 חֲזוֹ **ḥ^a^zô**, n.pr.m. GK: 2605. Hazo:– Hazo [1]

2376 חֵזוּ **ḥ^e^zû** (Aram.), n.m. GK: 10256 [→ 2370]. vision, appearance:– visions [9], vision [2], look [1]

2377 חָזוֹן **ḥāzôn**, n.m. GK: 2606 [→ 2372]. vision, revelation, a message from God, with a possible focus on the visual aspects of the message:– vision [32], visions [3]

2378 חֲזוֹת **ḥ^a^zôt**, n.[f.]. GK: 2608 [→ 2372]. visions:– visions [1]

2379 חֲזוֹת **ḥ^a^zôt** (Aram.), n.f. GK: 10257 [→ 2370]. visible sight:– sight [2]

2380 חָזוּת **ḥāzût**, n.f. GK: 2607 [→ 2372]. vision; prominent appearance:– vision [2], agreement [1], notable ones [1], notable [1]

2381 חֲזִיאֵל **ḥ^a^zî'ēl**, n.pr.m. GK: 2609 [→ 2372+410]. Haziel, "*vision of God [El]*":– Haziel [1]

2382 חֲזָיָה **ḥ^a^zāyâ**, n.pr.m. GK: 2610 [→ 2372+3068]. Hazaiah, "*Yahweh sees*":– Hazaiah [1]

2383 חֶזְיוֹן **ḥezyôn**, n.pr.m. GK: 2611. Hezion, "*vision; one with floppy ears*":– Hezion [1]

2384 חִזָּיוֹן **ḥizzāyôn**, n.m. GK: 2612 [→ 2372]. vision, dream, revelation:– vision [6], visions [3]

2385 חֲזִיז **ḥ^a^zîz**, n.[m.]. GK: 2613. storm cloud, dark and producing lightning and thunder:– lightning [2], bright clouds [1]

2386 חֲזִיר **ḥ^a^zîr**, n.m. GK: 2614 [→ 2387, 3170]. pig, boar:– swine's [4], swine [2], boar [1]

2387 חֵזִיר **ḥēzîr**, n.pr.m. GK: 2615 [→ 2386]. Hezir, "*boar*":– Hezir [2]

2388 חָזַק **ḥāzaq**, v. GK: 2616 [→ 2389, 2390, 2391, 2392, 2393, 2394 (also used with compound proper names)]. [Q] to be strong, hard, harsh, severe; [P] to harden (one's heart); to give strength, repair, encourage; [H] to grasp, seize, hold; to make repairs; [Ht] to establish oneself firmly; to encourage, to rally strength; from the base meaning of physical hardness come by extension: physical and internal strength of character; (negative) hardness of the heart, failure to respond to a person or message:– repaired [39], strong [38], strengthened [28], strengthen [14], hardened [9], prevailed [8], repair [8], take hold [7], of good courage [6], caught [5], encouraged [5], held [5], hold [5], make strong [5], encourage [4], harden [4], laid hold [4], stronger [4], took hold [4], took [4], caught hold [3], hold fast [3], made strong [3], sore [3], taketh [3], calkers (+919) [2], confirm [2], courageous [2], fortified [2], lay hold [2], mend [2], prevail [2], taken hold [2], taken [2], withstand (+6440+3807.1) [2], aided (+853+3027) [1], became mighty [1], behave valiantly [1], clave [1], confirmed [1], constant [1], constrained [1], continued [1], courageously [1], established [1], fastened [1], fasten [1], force [1], fortify [1], give strength [1], good courage [1], held fast [1], help (+3027+871.1) [1], help [1], holden [1], holdeth fast [1], holdeth [1], lay hold on [1], layeth hold [1], leaneth [1], made harder [1], maintain [1], obtain [1], play the men [1], received [1], recovered [1], relieve [1], retained (+871.1) [1], retained [1], retaineth [1], retain [1], seized [1], shew strong [1], stout [1], stronger than [1], sure [1], take fast hold [1], taken hold on [1], taketh hold [1], took courage [1], urgent [1], waxed mighty [1], waxed sore [1], waxen strong [1]

2389 חָזָק **ḥāzāq**, a. GK: 2617 [→ 2388]. mighty, powerful, strong, hard, severe; from the base meaning of physical hardness come by extension: physical and internal strength of character; (negative) hardness of the heart, failure to respond to a person or message:–

strong [26], mighty [20], sore [3], stronger [2], harder [1], hottest [1], impudent (+4696) [1], loud [1], stiff [1]

2390 חָזֵק **ḥāzēq**, a.vbl. GK: 2618 [→ 2388]. strong, loud:– stronger [1], waxed louder and louder (+3966) [1]

2391 חֵזֶק **ḥēzeq**, n.[m.]. GK: 2619 [→ 2388]. strength:– strength [1]

2392 חֹזֶק **ḥōzeq**, n.m. GK: 2620 [→ 2388]. might, strength, power:– strength [5]

2393 חֶזְקָה **ḥezqâ**, n.f. GK: 2621 [→ 2388]. strength, power:– strong [2], mightily (+871.1) [1], strengthened [1], strength [1]

2394 חָזְקָה **ḥozqâ**, n.f. GK: 2622 [→ 2388]. force, harshness, urgency:– force [2], mightily (+871.1) [1], repair [1], sharply (+871.1) [1]

2395 חִזְקִי **ḥizqî**, n.pr.m. GK: 2623 [→ 2388+3068]. Hizki, *"Yahweh is [my] strength* or *my strength"*:– Hezeki [1]

2396 חִזְקִיָּה **ḥizqiyyâ** or חִזְקִיָּהוּ **ḥizqiyyāhû**, n.pr.m. GK: 2624 & 2625 [→ 2388+3068]. Hezekiah, *"Yahweh is [my] strength"*:– Hezekiah [85], Hizkiah [1], Hizkijah [1]

2397 חָח **ḥāḥ**, n.m. GK: 2626 [cf. 2336]. hook; brooch:– chains [2], hooks [2], hook [2], bracelets [1]

חָחִי **ḥāḥî**. See 2397.

2398 חָטָא **ḥāṭā'**, v. GK: 2627 [→ 2399, 2400, 2401, 2402, 2403]. [Q] to sin, do wrong, miss the way; [P] to purify, cleanse, to offer a sin offering; [H] to bring a sin upon, cause to commit a sin; [Ht] to purify oneself; "to sin," to willfully act contrary to the will and law of God, is a figure of missing or moving from a standard or mark:– sinned [101], sin [38], made to sin [20], sinneth [13], sinner [8], cleanse [7], purify [7], committed [5], cause to sin [4], made sin [4], offended [4], purified [3], bear the blame [2], done [2], make sin [2], sinning [2], bare loss [1], cleansing [1], fault [1], grievously sinned (+2399) [1], harm done [1], made reconciliation [1], make an offender [1], miss [1], offered for sin [1], offereth for sin [1], purge [1], purifieth [1], sin committed (+2403) [1], sinful [1], sinnest [1], trespass [1]

2399 חֵטְא **ḥēṭ'**, n.m. GK: 2628 [→ 2398; cf. 2408]. sin, action contrary to the will and law of God, with a strong implication that guilt follows, error:– sin [21], sins [7], committed a sin [1], faults [1], grievously sinned (+2398) [1], offences [1], punishment of sins [1]

2400 חַטָּא **ḥaṭṭā'**, a. & n.m. GK: 2629 [→ 2398]. sinful, guilty; (n.) sinner, wicked one:– sinners [16], offenders [1], sinful [1]

2401 חֲטָאָה **ḥ^aṭā'â**, n.f. GK: 2630 & 2631 [→ 2398]. sin, guilt, condemnation; sin offering:– sin [7], sin offering [1]

2402 חַטָּאָה **ḥaṭṭā'â**, n.f. GK: 2632 [→ 2398]. sin, wickedness, fault:–

2403 חַטָּאת **ḥaṭṭā't**, n.f. GK: 2633 [→ 2398; cf. 2409]. sin, wrong, iniquity; sin offering, purification offering:– sin offering [115], sin [100], sins [70], punishment [2], purification for sin [2], punishment of sin [1], purifying [1], sin committed (+2398) [1], sin offerings [1], sinful [1], sinner [1], sins committed [1]

2404 חָטַב **ḥāṭab**, v. GK: 2634. [Q] to cut, chop (wood); (n.) woodcutter, woodsman; [Pu] to carve:– hewers [5], cut down [1], hewer [1], hew [1], polished [1]

2405 חֲטֻבוֹת **ḥ^aṭubôt**, n.f.pl. GK: 2635. colored, embroidered (fabric):– carved [1]

2406 חִטָּה **ḥiṭṭâ**, n.f. GK: 2636 [→ 2590; cf. 2591]. wheat:– wheat [29], wheaten [1]

2407 חַטּוּשׁ **ḥaṭṭûš**, n.pr.m. GK: 2637. Hattush:– Hattush [5]

2408 חֲטַי **ḥ^aṭay** (Aram.), n.[m.]. GK: 10259 [→ 2409; cf. 2399]. sin:– sins [1]

2409 חַטָּיָא **ḥaṭṭāyā'** (Aram.), n.f. GK: 10260 [→ 2408; cf. 2403]. sin offering:– sin offering [1]

2410 חֲטִיטָא **ḥ^aṭîṭā'**, n.pr.m. GK: 2638. Hatita:– Hatita [2]

2411 חַטִּיל **ḥaṭṭîl**, n.pr.m. GK: 2639. Hattil, *"talkative"*:– Hattil [2]

2412 חֲטִיפָא **ḥ^aṭîpā'**, n.pr.m. GK: 2640 [→ 2414]. Hatipha, *"taken captive"*:– Hatipha [2]

2413 חָטַם **ḥāṭam**, v. GK: 2641 [→ 2748]. [Q] to hold back, restrain:– refrain [1]

2414 חָטַף **ḥāṭap**, v. GK: 2642 [→ 2412]. [Q] to seize, carry off (by force):– catch [3]

2415 חֹטֶר **ḥōṭer**, n.m. GK: 2643. rod, switch; shoot, twig:– rod [2]

2416 חַי **ḥay**, n.m. & a. GK: 2644 & 2645 & 2646 & 2651 & 2652 & 2653 [→ 2421; cf. 2417; cf. 2423]. life, state of living (in contrast to death), lifetime; "as I live" is a formula for an oath, implying death should follow if what is sworn is not true; family, kin; band, army; animal, beast, livestock, living creature; living, alive, with an implication that life has movement and vigor; "living meat" is "raw meat"; "living water" is "fresh, running water":– life [143], living [80], liveth [67], live [46], beasts [41], beast [34], alive [30], living creatures [9], running [7], living creature [6], raw [5], lived [4], living thing [4], quick [3], congregation [2], lives [2], troop [2], alive (+871.1+1886.1) [1], appetite [1], company [1], life (+5315) [1], lifetime [1], lived (+1961) [1], lively [1], livest [1], maintenance [1], maketh merry (+8055) [1], multitude [1], old (+3117+8141) [1], quick raw (+4241) [1], springing [1], whole age (+3117+8141) [1], wild beasts [1]

2417 חַי **ḥay** (Aram.), a. GK: 10261 [→ 2418; cf. 2416]. living, alive:– living [4], life [1], lives [1], liveth [1]

2418 חֲיָא **ḥ^ayâ** (Aram.), v. GK: 10262 [→ 2417, 2423; cf. 2421]. [P] to live; [H] to spare, let live:– live [5], kept alive [1]

2419 חִיאֵל **ḥî'ēl**, n.pr.m. GK: 2647 [→ 251+410]. Hiel, *"God [El] lives here"*:– Hiel [1]

חָיַב **ḥāyab**. See 2325.

2420 חִידָה **ḥîdâ**, n.f. GK: 2648 [→ 2330; cf. 280]. riddle, hard question, allegory; hidden things, intrigue; scorn (the asking of a riddle as a game could imply scorn and ridicule toward the person asked):– riddle [8], dark sayings [2], hard questions [2], dark saying [1], dark sentences [1], dark speeches [1], proverb [1], put forth a riddle (+2330) [1]

2421 חָיָה **ḥāyâ**, v. GK: 2649 [→ 2416, 2422, 2424, 2425, 4241; cf. 2332; cf. 2418 (also used with compound proper names)]. same as 2425: [Q] to live; recover, revive; [P] to keep alive, preserve life; [H] to keep alive, save a life, spare a life, restore a life:– live [113], lived [44], surely live (+2421) [18], quicken [12], save alive [10], God save [8], keep alive [8], revive [8], saved alive [8], recover [4], restored to life [4], revived [4], certainly recover (+2421) [2], kept alive [2], liveth [2], make alive [2], preserve alive [2], preserve [2], quickened [2], recovered [2], save life [2], surely recover (+2421) [2], given life [1], giveth life [1], left alive [1], make to live [1], maketh alive [1], nourished up [1], nourish [1], preservest [1], preserveth life [1], promising life [1], repaired [1], save lives [1], saved lives [1], save [1], saving [1], suffer to live [1], whole [1]

2422 חָיֶה **ḥāyeh**, a. GK: 2650 [→ 2421]. vigorous:– lively [1]

2423 חֵיוָה **ḥêwâ** (Aram.), n.f. GK: 10263 [→ 2418; cf. 2416]. beast, animal; this can refer to physical creatures of earth as well as to fig. creatures of visions and parables:– beasts [13], beast [6], beast's [1]

2424 חַיּוּת **ḥayyût**, n.f.abst. GK: 2654 [→ 2421]. lifetime:– living [1]

2425 חָיַי **ḥāyay**, v. GK: 2649 [→ 2421]. same as 2421: [Q] to live; recover, revive; [P] to keep alive, preserve life; [H] to keep alive, save a life, spare a life, restore a life:–

2426 חֵיל **ḥêl**, n.m. GK: 2658 [→ 2430; cf. 2342]. ramparts, outer fortification, defense walls:– host [2], rampart [2], army [1], bulwarks [1], trench [1], walls [1], wall [1]

חִיל **ḥîl**. See 2342.

2427 חִיל **ḥîl** or חִילָה **ḥîlâ**, n.m. GK: 2659 & 2660 [→ 2342]. pain, anguish, any kind of physical trauma, as a fig. extension of the labor pains of birth:– pain [3], pangs [2], sorrow [2]

2428 חַיִל **ḥayil**, n.m. GK: 2657 [→ 32, 1134; cf. 2342; cf. 2429]. strength, capability, skill, valor, wealth; army, troop, warrior:– army [51], valour [37], host [28], valiant [16], forces [14], strength [12], riches [11], wealth [10], power [9], substance [8], might [6], valiantly [5], armies [4], strong [4], valiant (+1121) [4], able [3], virtuous [3], goods [2], activity [1], army (+6635) [1], band of men [1], band [1], company [1], hosts [1], meet for the war (+1121) [1], mighty [1], strong (+1121) [1], train [1], valiantest (+1121) [1], very able [1], virtuously [1], war [1], worthily [1], worthy [1]

2429 חַיִל **ḥayil** (Aram.), n.m. GK: 10264 [cf. 2428]. strength, power; an army:– aloud (+871.2) [3], army [2], most mighty men (+1400+1401) [1], power [1]

2430 חֵילָה **ḥêlâ**, n.m. GK: 2658 [→ 2426]. ramparts, outer fortification, defense walls:– bulwarks [1]

2431 חֵילָם **ḥêlām** or חֵלָאם **ḥēlā'm**, n.pr.loc. GK: 2663 & 2691. Helam, *"health"*:– Helam [2]

2432 חִילֵן **ḥîlēn**, n.pr.loc. GK: 2664. Hilen:– Hilen [1]

2433 חִין **ḥîn**, n.[m.]. GK: 2665 [→ 2603]. gracefulness:– comely [1]

2434 חַיִץ **ḥayiṣ**, n.[m.]. GK: 2666 [cf. 2351]. flimsy wall, inner wall:– wall [1]

2435 חִיצוֹן **ḥîṣôn**, a. GK: 2667 [→ 2351]. outer, outside, exterior:– utter [13], outward [7], without [3], without (+1886.5) [1], without (+871.1+1886.1) [1]

2436 חֵיק **ḥêq** or חֹק **ḥôq**, n.[m.]. GK: 2668 & 2576 [→ 2710]. lap, bosom, the area to which one holds and cradles a loved one; by extension: the inner person, heart, seat of affection; fold of a cloak, gutter:– bosom [32],

Heb

bottom [3], lap [1], midst [1], within (+871.1) [1]

2437 חִירָה ***ḥîrâ***, n.pr.m. GK: 2669. Hirah:– Hirah [2]

2438 חִירוֹם ***ḥîrôm*** or חִירָם ***ḥîrām***, n.pr.m. GK: 2670 & 2671 [→ 297?]. Hiram, "*[my] brother is elevated*":– Hiram [22], Hiram's [1]

2439 חִישׁ ***ḥîš***, v. GK: 2590 [→ 2363]. same as 2363: [Q] to go quickly, hasten, rush upon; [Qp] to be ready; [H] to make hurry, hasten:–

2440 חִישׁ ***ḥîš***, adv. GK: 2673 [→ 2363]. quickly, in haste:– soon [1]

2441 חֵךְ ***ḥēk***, n.m. GK: 2674. (area of the) mouth: lips, tongue (taste), roof of the mouth:– mouth [9], roof of mouth [5], taste [4]

2442 חָכָה ***ḥākâ***, v. GK: 2675. [Q] to wait; [P] to lie in wait (ambush); hope for, long for:– wait [5], waiteth [3], tarry [2], waited [2], long for [1], wait for [1]

2443 חַכָּה ***ḥakkâ***, n.f. GK: 2676. fishhook:– angle [2], hook [1]

2444 חֲכִילָה ***ḥ***^a^***kîlâ***, n.pr.loc. GK: 2677 [→ 2447]. Hakilah:– Hachilah [3]

2445 חַכִּים ***ḥakkîm*** (Aram.), n.m. GK: 10265 [→ 2452; cf. 2450]. wise man (usually pertaining to a social class):– wise [14]

2446 חֲכַלְיָה ***ḥ***^a^***kalyâ***, n.pr.m. GK: 2678 [→ 2447+3068]. Hacaliah, "*dark*":– Hachaliah [2]

2447 חַכְלִילִי ***ḥaklîlî***, a. GK: 2679 [→ 2444, 2446, 2448]. darker; some sources: sparkling:– red [1]

2448 חַכְלִלוּת ***ḥaklilût***, n.f. GK: 2680 [→ 2447]. bloodshot (eyes); some sources: sparkling:– redness [1]

Heb

2449 חָכַם ***ḥākam***, v. GK: 2681 [→ 2450, 2451, 2454, 2453?; cf. 2445]. [Q] to be wise, be skillful, gain wisdom; [P] to make wiser, to teach wisdom; [Pu] to be skillful; [H] to make wise; [Ht] to deal shrewdly; to show oneself wise; to be wise implies understanding and acting in a manner that is effective and usually moral:– wise [15], wiser [2], deal wisely [1], exceeding wise (+2450) [1], made wiser [1], made wise [1], make wise [1], maketh wiser [1], making wise [1], shewed wise [1], teach wisdom [1], wisely [1]

2450 חָכָם ***ḥākām***, a. GK: 2682 [→ 2449; cf. 2445]. wise, skilled, shrewd, craftsman; (n.) wise person, sage, one who interprets divination or prophecy, one who has fear of the Lord and understanding that leads to effective (moral) action:– wise [120], cunning [10], unwise (+3808) [2], wise men [2], wiser [2], exceeding wise (+2449) [1], subtil [1]

2451 חָכְמָה ***ḥokmâ***, n.f. GK: 2683 [→ 2449; cf. 2452]. wisdom, skill, learning; this can refer to skill in life, trade, war, or spiritual things:– wisdom [144], at wit's end (+1104+3605) [1], skilful [1], wisdom (+2050.2) [1], wisely (+4480) [1], wisely (+871.1) [1]

2452 חָכְמָה ***ḥokmâ*** (Aram.), n.f. GK: 10266 [→ 2445; cf. 2451]. wisdom:– wisdom [8]

2453 חַכְמֹנִי ***ḥakmōnî***, n.pr.m.[g.?]. GK: 2685 [→ 2449?]. Hacmoni; Hacmonite, "*wise*":– Hachmonite (+1121) [1], Hachmoni [1]

2454 חָכְמוֹת ***ḥokmôt***, n.f.pl.abst. GK: 2684 [→ 2449]. wisdom; the plural form may imply in its essential or supreme condition:– wisdom [4]

חֵל ***ḥēl***. See 2426.

2455 חֹל ***ḥōl***, n.[m.]. GK: 2687 [→ 2490]. common use, not holy, ordinary:– profane [4], common [2], unholy [1]

2456 חָלָא ***ḥālā'***, v. GK: 2688 [→ 2457, 2458, 8463; cf. 2470]. [Q] to be ill:– diseased [1]

2457 חֶלְאָה ***ḥel'â***, n.f. GK: 2689 [→ 2458; cf. 2456]. deposit, encrustation, rust:– scum [5]

2458 חֶלְאָה ***ḥel'â***, n.pr.f. GK: 2690 [→ 2457; cf. 2456]. Helah, "*necklace; rust*":– Helah [2]

2459 חֵלֶב ***ḥēleb***, n.m. GK: 2693. fat, fat portions; by extension: finest, best part; callous (heart that is dull and unresponsive):– fat [79], best [5], fatness [4], finest [2], grease [1], marrow [1]

2460 חֵלֶב ***ḥēleb***, n.pr.m. GK: 2694 [cf. 2466]. Heleb, cf. 2466:– Heleb [1]

2461 חָלָב ***ḥālāb***, n.m. GK: 2692 [→ 2464]. milk:– milk [42], cheeses (+2757) [1], sucking [1]

2462 חֶלְבָּה ***ḥelbâ***, n.pr.loc. GK: 2695. Helbah, "*fertile region*":– Helbah [1]

2463 חֶלְבּוֹן ***ḥelbôn***, n.pr.loc. GK: 2696. Helbon, "*fertile*":– Helbon [1]

2464 חֶלְבְּנָה ***ḥelb***^e^***nâ***, n.f. GK: 2697 [→ 2461]. galbanum (aromatic gum resin used to make incense):– galbanum [1]

2465 חֶלֶד ***ḥeled***, n.[m.]. GK: 2698 [→ 2466, 2469]. life, duration of life; this world:– age [2], world [2], short time [1]

2466 חֵלֶד ***ḥēled***, n.pr.m. GK: 2699 [→ 2465]. Heled, "*mole*":– Heled [1]

2467 חֹלֶד ***ḥōled***, n.[m.]. GK: 2700 [→ 2468]. weasel; some sources: rat or mole:– weasel [1]

2468 חֻלְדָּה ***ḥuldâ***, n.pr.m. GK: 2701 [→ 2467]. Huldah, "*weasel*":– Huldah [2]

2469 חֶלְדַּי ***ḥelday***, n.pr.m. GK: 2702 [→ 2465]. Heldai, "*mole*":– Heldai [2]

2470 חָלָה ***ḥālâ***, v. GK: 2703 & 2704 [→ 2483, 4245, 4248?, 4249?, 4250?, 4251, 4257?; cf. 2456]. [Q] to be ill, be weak, be faint, become diseased, be wounded; [N] to be made sick, be incurable; [P] to afflict; to entreat, implore, seek favor, intercede; [Pu] to become weak; [H] to make ill, to cause to suffer; [Ho] to be wounded; [Ht] to pretend to be ill, to feel sick:– sick [24], fell sick [4], grievous [4], besought (+853+6440) [3], diseased [3], pray [3], weak [3], wounded [3], besought (+6440) [2], grieved [2], intreat [2], made sick [2], make sick [2], sore [2], become weak [1], beseech (+6440) [1], fallen sick [1], grief [1], in travail [1], infirmity [1], intreat favour (+6440) [1], intreated [1], laid [1], made prayer [1], made supplication [1], make suit [1], maketh sick [1], put to grief [1], put to pain [1], sorry [1]

2471 חַלָּה ***ḥallâ***, n.f. GK: 2705 [→ 2490]. (ring-shaped) bread cakes:– cakes [7], cake [7]

2472 חֲלוֹם ***ḥ***^a^***lôm***, n.m. GK: 2706 [→ 2492; cf. 2493]. dream, dreamer; this can refer to a supernatural revelation by God by words and images:– dream [44], dreams [19], dreamer (+1167+1886.1) [1], dreamers [1]

2473 חֹלוֹן ***ḥōlôn***, n.pr.loc. GK: 2708. Holon, "[perhaps] *sandy*":– Holon [3]

2474 חַלּוֹן ***ḥallôn***, n.m. & f. GK: 2707 & 2709 [→ 2490]. window, narrow openings, parapet openings:– windows [18], window [13]

2475 חֲלוֹף ***ḥ***^a^***lôp***, n.m. GK: 2710 [→ 2498]. destitute, vanishing:– appointed to destruction (+1121) [1]

2476 חֲלוּשָׁה ***ḥ***^a^***lûšâ***, n.f. GK: 2711 [→ 2522]. defeat:– overcome [1]

2477 חֲלַח ***ḥ***^a^***laḥ***, n.pr.loc. GK: 2712. Halah:– Halah [3]

2478 חַלְחוּל ***ḥalḥûl***, n.pr.loc. GK: 2713. Halhul:– Halhul [1]

2479 חַלְחָלָה ***ḥalḥālâ***, n.f. GK: 2714 [→ 2342]. anguish, pain, trembling:– great pain [2], much pain [1], pain [1]

2480 חָלַט ***ḥālaṭ***, v. GK: 2715. [Q] to accept a statement:– catch [1]

2481 חֲלִי ***ḥ***^a^***lî***, n.m. GK: 2717 [→ 2484]. ornament, jewel:– jewels [1], ornament [1]

2482 חֲלִי ***ḥ***^a^***lî***, n.pr.loc. GK: 2718. Hali, "*adornment*":– Hali [1]

2483 חֳלִי ***ḥ***^o^***lî***, n.m. GK: 2716 [→ 2470]. illness, sickness, affliction; wound, injury:– sickness [11], disease [7], grief [3], griefs [1], sicknesses [1], sick [1]

2484 חֶלְיָה ***ḥelyâ***, n.f. GK: 2719 [→ 2481]. jewelry, ornament:– jewels [1]

2485 חָלִיל ***ḥālîl***, n.m. GK: 2720 [→ 2490, 5155?]. flute:– pipes [3], pipe [3]

2486 חָלִיל ***ḥālîl***, subst. GK: 2721 [→ 2490]. far be it!, never!:– God forbid [8], far be it [4], be it far [3], forbid [3], that be far [2], forbid it [1]

2487 חֲלִיפָה ***ḥ***^a^***lîpâ***, n.f. GK: 2722 [→ 2498]. set, sequence, shift; renewal, relief:– changes [7], change [4], courses [1]

2488 חֲלִיצָה ***ḥ***^a^***lîṣâ***, n.f. GK: 2723 [→ 2502]. belongings, equipment:– armour [1], spoil [1]

2489 חֶלְכָה ***ḥelkâ***, a. GK: 2724. victim:– poor [3]

2490 חָלַל ***ḥālal***, v. GK: 2725 & 2726 & 2727 [→ 2455, 2471, 2474, 2485, 2486, 2491, 4247, 5155?, 8462]. [Q] to be wounded; to play the flute; [N] to defile oneself, be profaned, be desecrated; [P] to pierce, wound; to defile, profane, desecrate; to enjoy; to play the flute; [Pu] to be killed; to be defiled; [Pol] to pierce, wound; [Polal] to be wounded; [H] to begin, to proceed, launch; [Ho] to be begun:– began [33], profane [17], profaned [15], polluted [13], begin [12], pollute [8], begun [7], defiled [5], break [3], wounded [3], defile [2], polluting [2], profaning [2], beginnest [1], broken [1], cast as profane [1], defiledst [1], defileth [1], eat as common things [1], eaten [1], eat [1], first [1], gather the grapes [1], piped [1], players on instruments [1], profaneth [1], prostitute [1], slain [1], slayeth [1], sorrow [1], stain [1], take inheritance [1]

2491 חָלָל ***ḥālāl***, n.m. & a. GK: 2728 & 2729 [→ 2490]. dead, slain, casualty; defiled, profane (moral or ceremonial failure):– slain [73], wounded [9], slew [4], profane [3], kill [2], deadly wounded [1], that is slain [1], that were slain [1]

חֲלִלָה ***ḥālilâ***. See 2486.

2492 חָלַם ***ḥālam***, v. GK: 2730 & 2731 [→ 2472]. [Q] to grow strong; to dream; [H] to restore to health; to encourage one to have dreams:– dreamed [19], dreamer [3], dreameth [2], dream [2], cause to be dreamed [1], in good liking [1], recover [1]

2493 חֵלֶם **ḥēlem** (Aram.), n.m. GK: 10267 [cf. 2472]. dream:– dream [21], dreams [1]

2494 חֵלֶם **ḥēlem,** n.pr.m. GK: 2732 [cf. 2469]. Helem, cf. 2469:– Helem [1]

2495 חַלָּמוּת **ḥallāmût,** n.f. GK: 2733. egg or mallow:– egg [1]

2496 חַלָּמִישׁ **ḥallāmîš,** n.m. GK: 2734. flinty rock, hard rock:– flint [3], flinty [1], rock [1]

2497 חֵלֹן **ḥēlōn,** n.pr.m. GK: 2735. Helon, "*strength, power*":– Helon [5]

2498 חָלַף **ḥālap,** v. GK: 2736 [→ 2475, 2487, 2500, 4252?, 4253; cf. 2499]. [Q] to go by, pass on, sweep by; to be new; to pierce, cut through; [P] to change; [H] to change, exchange, replace, renew:– changed [6], change [4], groweth up [2], renew [2], abolish [1], alter [1], cut off [1], go on [1], over [1], pass through [1], passed away [1], passed [1], passeth on [1], pass [1], renewed [1], sprout [1], stricken through [1], strike through [1]

2499 חֲלַף **ḥ^a^lap** (Aram.), v. GK: 10268 [cf. 2498]. [P] to pass by, pass over:– pass [4]

2500 חֵלֶף **ḥēlep,** n.[m.]. GK: 2739 [→ 2498]. in return for:– for [2]

2501 חֵלֶף **ḥēlep,** n.pr.loc. GK: 2738. Heleph, "[poss.] *sharp, cutting*":– Heleph [1]

2502 חָלַץ **ḥālaṣ,** v. GK: 2740 & 2741 [→ 2488, 2503, 4254]. [Q] to take off; [Qp] to be taken off; to be armed (for battle); [N] to be delivered, be rescued; to arm oneself; [P] to rescue, deliver; to tear out, rob; [H] to strengthen:– armed [11], delivered [9], deliver [5], delivereth [2], go armed [2], ready armed [2], armed soldiers [1], army [1], arm [1], draw out [1], loosed [1], loose [1], make fat [1], prepared [1], put off [1], ready prepared for [1], take away [1], taken away [1], withdrawn [1]

2503 חֶלֶץ **ḥeleṣ,** n.pr.m. GK: 2742 [→ 2502]. Helez, "*vigor; he has saved*":– Helez [5]

2504 חֲלָצַיִם **ḥ^a^lāṣayim,** n.[f.]. GK: 2743 [cf. 2783]. waist, stomach, the area between the lowest ribs and the hip-bones; by extension: body, flesh; the inner person, heart:– loins [9], reins [1]

2505 חָלַק **ḥālaq,** v. GK: 2744 & 2745 & 2746 [→ 2506, 2509, 2510, 2511, 2512, 2513, 2514, 2515, 2517, 2518, 2519, 2520, 4256]. [Q] to be smooth, slippery; deceitful; to divide, apportion, assign; [N] to be divided, be dispersed, be distributed; [P] to divide, allot, apportion; to destroy; [Pu] to be divided; [Ht] to divide among themselves; [H] to speak deceit, flatter, be seductive; to get one's share:– divided [21], divide [18], flattereth [5], dealt [2], distributed [2], parted [2], part [2], distributeth [1], distribute [1], dividing [1], flatter [1], given [1], have part [1], imparted [1], partner [1], received [1], separate [1], smoother [1], smootheth [1], took away a portion [1]

2506 חֵלֶק **ḥēleq,** n.m. GK: 2749 & 2750 [→ 2505, 2513, 2520; cf. 2505; cf. 2508 (also used with compound proper names)]. smoothness; share, portion, allotment, plot of ground:– portion [36], part [18], parts [4], portions [4], flattering [1], flattery (+3807.1) [1], inheritance [1], partaker [1]

2507 חֵלֶק **ḥēleq,** n.pr.m. GK: 2751 [→ 2516; cf. 2518?]. Helek, "*portion, lot*":– Helek [2]

2508 חֲלָק **ḥ^a^lāq** (Aram.), n.[m.]. GK: 10269 [→ 4255; cf. 2506]. portion, lot in life:– portion [3]

2509 חָלָק **ḥālāq,** a. GK: 2747 [→ 2505, 2511]. smooth, slippery, pleasant, flattering:– flattering [2], smoother [1], smooth [1]

2510 חָלָק **ḥālāq,** n.pr.loc. GK: 2748 [→ 2505]. Halak:– Halak [2]

2511 חַלָּק **ḥallāq,** a. GK: 2747 [→ 2509]. smooth, slippery, pleasant, flattering:– smooth [1]

2512 חַלֻּק **ḥalluq,** a. GK: 2752 [→ 2505]. smooth (stones):– smooth [1]

2513 חֶלְקָה **ḥelqâ,** n.f. GK: 2753 & 2754 [→ 2505, 2506]. smoothness; plot, field, tract:– portion [6], parcel [5], field [3], piece [3], flattering [2], piece of land [2], plat [2], smooth [2], flattery [1], ground [1], part [1], slippery [1]

2514 חֲלַקָּה **ḥ^a^laqqâ,** n.f. GK: 2756 [→ 2505]. smoothness, flattery:– flatteries [1]

2515 חֲלֻקָּה **ḥ^a^luqqâ,** n.f. GK: 2755 [→ 2505]. part, portion, division:– division [1]

2516 חֶלְקִי **ḥelqî,** a.g. GK: 2757 [→ 2507]. Helekite, "*of Helek*":– Helekites [1]

2517 חֶלְקָי **ḥelqāy,** n.pr.m. GK: 2758 [→ 2506+3068?]. Helkai, "*Yahweh is [my] portion*":– Helkai [1]

2518 חִלְקִיָּה **ḥilqiyyâ** or חִלְקִיָּהוּ **ḥilqiyyāhû,** n.pr.m. GK: 2759 & 2760 [cf. 2507?]. Hilkiah, "*Yahweh is [my] portion*":– Hilkiah [33], Hilkiah's [1]

2519 חֲלַקְלַק **ḥ^a^laqlaq,** n.f.abst. GK: 2761 [→ 2505]. slippery, slick and hard to walk on; by extension: slippery words, intrigue, insincere:– flatteries [2], slippery [2]

2520 חֶלְקַת **ḥelqat,** n.pr.loc. GK: 2762 [→ 2521; cf. 2505, 2506]. Helkath, "*portion*":– Helkath [2]

2521 חֶלְקַת הַצֻּרִים **ḥelqat haṣṣurîm,** n.pr.loc. GK: 2763 [→ 2520]. Helkath Hazzurim, "[poss.] *portion [field] of rock* or *swords; portion [field] of snare*":– Helkath-hazzurim [1]

2522 חָלַשׁ **ḥālaš,** v. GK: 2764 & 2765 [→ 2476, 2523]. [Q] to be laid low; to overcome, defeat:– discomfited [1], wasteth away [1], weaken [1]

2523 חַלָּשׁ **ḥallāš,** a. GK: 2766 [→ 2522]. weak, weakling:– weak [1]

2524 חָם **ḥām,** n.m. GK: 2767 [→ 2537, 2545]. father-in-law:– father in law [4]

2525 חָם **ḥām,** a. GK: 2768 [→ 2552]. hot, sweltering:– hot [1], warm [1]

2526 חָם **ḥām,** n.pr.m. & loc. GK: 2769 [→ 2536, 2537]. Ham:– Ham [16]

2527 חֹם **ḥōm,** n.m. GK: 2770 [→ 2552]. heat:– heat [9], hot [4], warm [1]

2528 חֱמָה **ḥ^a^mâ** (Aram.), n.f. GK: 10270 [cf. 2534]. fury, rage; "to be in fury and rage" refers to anger of highest degree:– fury [2]

חֵמָא **ḥēmā'**. See 2534.

2529 חֶמְאָה **ḥem'â,** n.f. GK: 2772 [cf. 4260]. curds, curdled milk; butter, cream:– butter [10]

2530 חָמַד **ḥāmad,** v. GK: 2773 & 2776 [→ 2531, 2532, 2533, 4261, 4262]. [Q] to covet, lust, desire; delight in; [Qp] (n.) what is coveted: treasure, wealth; [N] to be pleasing, be desirable; [P] to delight; this can refer to proper delight and fondness, as well as to improper lust and desire:– desired [5], desire [4], covet [3], desireth [2], beauty [1], coveted [1], delectable [1], delight in [1], lust after [1], pleasant [1], with great delight [1]

2531 חֶמֶד **ḥemed,** n.[m.]. GK: 2774 [→ 2530]. fruitfulness, lushness; pleasantness; handsomeness:– desirable [3], pleasant [2]

2532 חֶמְדָּה **ḥemdâ,** n.f. GK: 2775 [→ 2530]. desirable, pleasant, fine, valuable (things):– pleasant [11], precious [4], desire [3], greatly beloved [3], goodly [2], desired [1], pleasant things [1]

2533 חֶמְדָּן **ḥemdān,** n.pr.m. GK: 2777 [→ 2530; cf. 2566]. Hemdan, "*desirable*":– Hemdan [1]

2534 חֵמָה **ḥēmâ** or חֵמָא **ḥēmā',** n.f. GK: 2779 & 2771 [→ 3179; cf. 2528]. anger, wrath, fury, rage, from the base meaning of heat (as in "hot-headed"); by extension: venom (poison that causes a burning sensation):– fury [67], wrath [34], poison [6], furious [4], hot displeasure [3], rage [2], anger [1], bottles [1], furious (+1167) [1], furiously (+871.1) [1], heat [1], indignation [1], wrathful [1], wroth [1]

2535 חַמָּה **ḥammâ,** n.f. GK: 2780 [→ 2552]. heat (of the sun):– sun [5], heat [1]

2536 חַמּוּאֵל **ḥammû'ēl,** n.pr.m. GK: 2781 [→ 2526+410; cf. 2537]. Hammuel, "*God [El] of Ham*":– Hamuel [1]

2537 חֲמוּטַל **ḥ^a^mûṭal** or חֲמִיטַל **ḥ^a^mîṭal,** n.pr.f. GK: 2782 & 2795 [→ 2524+2919; 2526]. Hamutal, Hamital, "*my husband's father is like dew*":– Hamutal [3]

2538 חָמוּל **ḥāmûl,** n.pr.m. GK: 2783 [→ 2539; cf. 2550]. Hamul, "*pitied*":– Hamul [3]

2539 חָמוּלִי **ḥāmûlî,** a.g. GK: 2784 [→ 2538; cf. 2550]. Hamulite, "*of Hamul*":– Hamulites [1]

2540 חַמּוֹן **ḥammôn,** n.pr.loc. GK: 2785 [→ 2552]. Hammon, "*hot springs*":– Hammon [2]

2541 חָמוֹץ **ḥāmôṣ,** n.[m.]. GK: 2787 [→ 2556]. oppressor; oppressed:– oppressed [1]

2542 חַמּוּק **ḥammûq,** n.m. GK: 2788 [→ 2559]. gracefulness, curve:– joints [1]

2543 חֲמוֹר **ḥ^a^môr,** n.m. GK: 2789 [→ 2544; cf. 2565, 2560]. donkey:– ass [55], asses [39], ass's [1], he asses [1]

2544 חֲמוֹר **ḥ^a^môr,** n.pr.m. GK: 2791 [→ 2543; cf. 2560]. Hamor, "*male donkey*":– Hamor [12], Hamor's [1]

2545 חָמוֹת **ḥāmôt,** n.f. GK: 2792 [→ 2524]. mother-in-law:– mother in law [11]

2546 חֹמֶט **ḥōmeṭ,** n.[m.]. GK: 2793. skink (lizard):– snail [1]

2547 חֻמְטָה **ḥumṭâ,** n.pr.loc. GK: 2794. Humtah, "*[unclean] reptile*":– Humtah [1]

2548 חָמִיץ **ḥāmîṣ,** a. GK: 2796 [→ 2556]. sour mash, sorrel-fodder:– clean [1]

2549 חֲמִישִׁי **ḥ^a^mîšî,** a.num.ord. GK: 2797 [→ 2568]. fifth:– fifth [45]

2550 חָמַל **ḥāmal,** v. GK: 2798 & 2800 [→ 2538, 2539, 2551, 2602, 4263?]. [Q] to spare, take pity on, have mercy on:– spare [13], have pity [8], pitied [4], pity [4], spared [4], had compassion [3], had pity [2], have compassion [2], spareth [1]

2551 חֶמְלָה **ḥemlâ,** n.f. GK: 2799 [→ 2550]. mercy:– merciful [1], pity [1]

Heb

2552 חָמַם ***ḥāmam***, v. GK: 2801 [→ 2345, 2525, 2527, 2535, 2540, 2553, 2575, 2578, 2577; cf. 3179]. [Q] to be hot, be warm; by extension: to be aroused; be in a rage; [N] to burn with lust; [P] to let warm; [Ht] to warm oneself:– warm [3], hot [2], warmeth [2], get heat [1], have heat [1], inflaming [1], warmed [1], waxed hot [1], waxed warm [1]

2553 חַמָּן ***ḥammān***, n.m. GK: 2802 [→ 2552]. incense altar:– images [7], idols [1]

2554 חָמַס ***ḥāmas***, v. GK: 2803 & 2804 [→ 2555, 8464?]. [Q] to do violence, harm, to lay waste; to be stripped off; to think up, devise; [N] to be mistreated:– do violence [1], done violence [1], made bare [1], shake off [1], violated [1], violently taken away [1], wrongeth [1], wrongfully imagine [1]

2555 חָמָס ***ḥāmās***, n.m. GK: 2805 [→ 2554]. violence, destruction, malice, ruthlessness, fierceness:– violence [39], violent [6], cruelty [4], wrong [3], false [2], cruel hatred (+8135) [1], damage [1], injustice [1], oppressor (+376) [1], unrighteous [1], violent dealing [1]

2556 חָמֵץ ***ḥāmēṣ***, v. GK: 2806 & 2807 & 2808 [→ 2541, 2548, 2557, 2558]. [Q] to have yeast added, be leavened; to be cruel, oppress; [Qp] to be stained crimson; [Ht] to be grieved, embittered:– leavened [4], cruel [1], dyed [1], grieved [1], that which is leavened [1]

2557 חָמֵץ ***ḥāmēṣ***, n.m. GK: 2809 [→ 2556]. something leavened, made with yeast:– leavened bread [5], leaven [5], leavened [1]

2558 חֹמֶץ ***ḥōmeṣ***, n.m. GK: 2810 [→ 2556]. vinegar, wine vinegar:– vinegar [6]

2559 חָמַק ***ḥāmaq***, v. GK: 2811 [→ 2542]. [Q] to leave, turn away; [Ht] to wander, turn here and there:– go about [1], withdrawn [1]

2560 חָמַר ***ḥāmar***, v. GK: 2812 & 2813 & 2814 [→ 2543, 2565, 2544, 2561, 2563, 2564, 3180]. [Q] to foam; to coat, cover, to apply pitch as a sealant; [Poalal] to be reddened, glow:– troubled [3], daubed [1], foul [1], red [1]

2561 חֶמֶר ***ḥemer***, n.[m.]. GK: 2815 [→ 2560; cf. 2562]. (foaming, fermenting) wine:– pure [1], red wine [1]

2562 חֲמַר ***ḥ^{a}mar*** (Aram.), n.m. GK: 10271 [cf. 2561]. wine:– wine [6]

חֲמֹר ***ḥ^{a}mōr***. See 2543.

2563 חֹמֶר ***ḥōmer***, n.[m.]. GK: 2816 & 2817 & 2818 [→ 2560]. churning, storming (sea waters); clay, mortar, mud; "defenses of clay" are weak arguments; homer (dry measure of volume, roughly the amount a donkey could carry, variously reckoned from six to eleven bushels [220 to 394 liters]):– clay [11], homer [10], morter [4], mire [2], upon heaps (+2563) [2], heap [1], homers [1]

2564 חֵמָר ***ḥēmār***, n.[m.]. GK: 2819 [→ 2560]. tar (used in waterproofing or mortar):– slime [2], full of slimepits (+875+875) [1]

2565 חֲמֹרָה ***ḥ^{a}mōrâ***, n.f. GK: 2790 [→ 2560; cf. 2543]. heap:– heaps [2]

2566 חַמְרָן ***ḥamrān***, n.pr.m. GK: 2820 [cf. 2533]. Hamran, cf. 2533:– Amram [1]

2567 חָמַשׁ ***ḥāmaš***, v.den. GK: 2821 [→ 2571; cf. 2568]. [Qp] to be organized for war; [P] to take a fifth:– take up the fifth [1]

2568 חָמֵשׁ ***ḥāmēš***, n.m. & f. GK: 2822 [→ 2549, 2567, 2569, 2571, 2572]. five, (pl.) fifty:– five [299], fifteenth (+6240) [17], fifteen (+6240) [16], fifth [6], five apiece (+2568) [2], threescore and fifteen (+7657+2050.1) [2], fifteen (+6235+2050.1) [1], threescore and fifteen (+7657+2050.1+2050.1) [1]

2569 חֹמֶשׁ ***ḥōmeš***, n.[m.]. GK: 2823 [→ 2568]. fifth:– fifth [1]

2570 חֹמֶשׁ ***ḥōmeš***, n.m. GK: 2824. stomach, belly:– fifth [4]

2571 חָמֻשׁ ***ḥāmuš***, v.ptcp. GK: 2821 & 2826 [→ 2567; cf. 2568]. organized for war, armed:– armed [3], harnessed [1]

חֲמִשָּׁה ***ḥ^{a}miššâ***. See 2568.

חֲמִשִׁי ***ḥ^{a}miššî***. See 2549.

2572 חֲמִשִּׁים ***ḥ^{a}miššîm***, n.pl. GK: 2825 [→ 2568]. fifty (pl. of "five"):– fifty [149], fifties [6], fiftieth [4], by fifty (+2572) [2], fifty every where (+2572+871.1+1886.1) [2]

2573 חֵמֶת ***ḥēmet***, n.[m.]. GK: 2827. skin (for water or wine):– bottle [4]

2574 חֲמָת ***ḥ^{a}māt***, n.pr.loc. GK: 2828 & 4217 [→ 2578, 2577]. Hamath, "*fortress*":– Hamath [34], Hemath [2], Hamath-zobah [1]

חֲמֹת ***ḥ^{a}mōt***. See 2545.

2575 חַמַּת ***ḥammat***, n.pr.m. & loc. GK: 2830 & 2829 [→ 2576; cf. 2552]. Hammath, "*hot springs*":– Hammath [1], Hemath [1]

2576 חַמֹּת דֹּאר ***ḥammōt dō'r***, n.pr.loc. GK: 2831 [→ 2575+1756]. Hammoth Dor, "*hot spring of Dor*":– Hammoth-dor [1]

2577 חֲמָתִי ***ḥ^{a}mātî***, a.g. GK: 2833 [→ 2574; cf. 2552]. Hamathite, "*of Hamath*":– Hamathite [2]

2578 חֲמַת צוֹבָה ***ḥ^{a}māt ṣôbâ***, n.pr.loc. GK: 2832 [→ 2574+6678]. Hamath Zobah:–

2579 חֲמַת רַבָּה ***ḥ^{a}māt rabbâ***, n.pr.loc. GK: 2828 + 8051 [→ 2574+7237]. Hamath Rabbah:–

2580 חֵן ***ḥēn***, n.m. GK: 2834 [→ 2582, 2584, 2600; cf. 2603 (also used with compound proper names)]. favor, grace; charm; grace is the moral quality of kindness, displaying a favorable disposition; "to find grace in someone's eyes" means to be in a state of favor:– grace [38], favour [26], gracious [2], pleasant [1], precious [1], wellfavoured (+2896) [1]

2581 חֵן ***ḥēn***, n.pr.m. GK: 2835 [→ 2603]. Hen, "*gracious*":– Hen [1]

2582 חֵנָדָד ***ḥēnādād***, n.pr.m. GK: 2836 [→ 2580+1908]. Henadad, "*favor of Hadad*":– Henadad [4]

2583 חָנָה ***ḥānâ***, v. GK: 2837 [→ 2588, 4264, 4266, 8466]. [Q] to set up camp, pitch camp, encamp:– pitched [67], encamped [33], encamp [10], pitch [9], abode in tents [3], camp [3], dwelt [2], encampeth [2], lie [2], pitch tents [2], pitched tent [2], rested in tents [2], abide [1], camped [1], encamp about [1], encamping [1], groweth to an end [1], pitched tents [1]

2584 חַנָּה ***ḥannâ***, n.pr.f. GK: 2839 [→ 2580; cf. 2603]. Hannah, "*favor*":– Hannah [13]

2585 חֲנוֹךְ ***ḥ^{a}nôk***, n.pr.m. & loc. GK: 2840 & 2841 [→ 2599; cf. 2593, 2596]. Enoch; Hanoch, "*initiated; follower*":– Enoch [9], Hanoch [5], Henoch [2]

2586 חָנוּן ***ḥānûn***, n.pr.m. GK: 2842 [→ 2603]. Hanun, "*favored*":– Hanun [11]

2587 חַנּוּן ***ḥannûn***, a. GK: 2843 [→ 2603]. gracious, compassionate:– gracious [13]

2588 חָנוּת ***ḥānût***, n.f. GK: 2844 [→ 2583]. vaulted cell:– cabins [1]

2589 חַנּוֹת ***ḥannôt***, v. GK: 2838. verbal forms of 2603: gracious, intreated:– gracious [1], intreated [1]

2590 חָנַט ***ḥānaṭ***, v. GK: 2845 & 2846 & 2847 [→ 2406]. [Q] to embalm; to ripen:– embalmed [3], embalm [1], putteth forth [1]

2591 חִנְטָה ***ḥinṭâ*** (Aram.), n.f. GK: 10272 [cf. 2406]. wheat:– wheat [2]

2592 חַנִּיאֵל ***ḥannî'ēl***, n.pr.m. GK: 2848 [→ 2603+410]. Hanniel, "*favored of God [El]*":– Haniel [1], Hanniel [1]

2593 חָנִיךְ ***ḥānîk***, a. GK: 2849 [→ 2596; cf. 2585]. trained (and trusted person):– trained [1]

2594 חֲנִינָה ***ḥ^{a}nînâ***, n.f. GK: 2850 [→ 2603]. favor, kindness:– favour [1]

2595 חֲנִית ***ḥ^{a}nît***, n.f. GK: 2851. spear:– spear [34], javelin [6], spears [6], spear's [1]

2596 חָנַךְ ***ḥānak***, v. GK: 2852 [→ 2585, 2593, 2598, 2599]. [Q] to dedicate, to devote an object to deity; to train (morally and religiously):– dedicated [3], dedicate [1], train up [1]

2597 חֲנֻכָּה ***ḥ^{a}nukkâ*** (Aram.), n.f. GK: 10273 [cf. 2598]. (ceremonial religious) dedication:– dedication [4]

2598 חֲנֻכָּה ***ḥ^{a}nukkâ***, n.f. GK: 2853 [→ 2596; cf. 2597]. dedication, offering for dedication:– dedication [6], dedicating [2]

2599 חֲנֹכִי ***ḥ^{a}nōkî***, a.g. GK: 2854 [→ 2585; cf. 2596]. Hanochite, "*of Hanoch*":– Hanochites [1]

2600 חִנָּם ***ḥinnām***, subst.adv. GK: 2855 [→ 2580; cf. 2603]. without cause, for no reason; for nothing:– without cause [10], for nought [6], without a cause [5], causeless [2], cost nothing [1], for nothing [1], freely [1], free [1], in vain [1], innocent [1], vain [1], without cost [1], without wages [1]

2601 חֲנַמְאֵל ***ḥ^{a}nam'ēl***, n.pr.m. GK: 2856 [→ 2580+410]. Hanamel, "*God [El] is gracious*":– Hanameel [4]

2602 חֲנָמָל ***ḥ^{a}nāmal***, n.[m.]. GK: 2857 [→ 2550]. sleet:– frost [1]

2603 חָנַן ***ḥānan***, v. GK: 2858 & 2859 [→ 2433, 2580, 2581, 2584, 2586, 2587, 2594, 2600, 2605, 8465?, 8467, 8468, 8469, 8470?; cf. 2604 (also used with compound proper names)]. [Q] to be gracious, to have mercy, to take pity, be kind; to be loathsome; [Pol] to move to pity, be kind, be charming; [Ho] to be shown compassion, mercy; [Ht] to plead for grace, beg for mercy; this word implies acts of kindness, not simply feelings of pity:– gracious [12], have mercy [12], merciful [12], make supplication [7], besought [3], favour [3], made supplication [3], hath mercy [2], have pity [2], shew favour [2], very gracious (+2603) [2], besought (+413) [1], dealt graciously [1], fair [1], favour shewed [1], favourable [1], favoured [1], findeth favour [1], graciously given [1], grant graciously [1], hath pity [1], intreated [1], pity [1], pray [1], shew mercy [1], sheweth favour [1], sheweth mercy [1]

2604 חֲנַן ***ḥ^{a}nan*** (Aram.), v. GK: 10274 [cf. 2603]. [P] to be kind, show mercy; [Htpa] to ask, implore:– making supplication [1], shewing mercy [1]

2605 חָנָן **ḥānān**, n.pr.m. GK: 2860 [→ 2603 (also used with compound proper names)]. Hanan, "*gracious*":– Hanan [12]

2606 חֲנַנְאֵל **ḥ^a^nan'ēl**, n.pr.m. GK: 2861 [→ 2603+410]. Hananel, "*God [El] is gracious*":– Hananeel [4]

2607 חֲנָנִי **ḥ^a^nānî**, n.pr.m. GK: 2862 [→ 2603+3068]. Hanani, "*gracious*":– Hanani [11]

2608 חֲנַנְיָה **ḥ^a^nanyâ** or חֲנַנְיָהוּ **ḥ^a^nanyāhû**, n.pr.m. GK: 2863 & 2864 & 10275 [→ 2603+3068]. Hananiah, "*Yahweh is gracious*": note this name is Aramaic once in Daniel:– Hananiah [29]

2609 חָנֵס **ḥānēs**, n.pr.loc. GK: 2865. Hanes:– Hanes [1]

2610 חָנֵף **ḥānēp**, v. GK: 2866 [→ 2611, 2612, 2613]. [Q] to be desecrated, be defiled; [H] to corrupt, defile, pollute:– defiled [3], greatly polluted (+2610) [2], polluted [2], corrupt [1], defileth [1], pollute [1], profane [1]

2611 חָנֵף **ḥānēp**, a. GK: 2867 & 2868 [→ 2610]. godless, ungodly; limping:– hypocrite [6], hypocrites [3], hypocritical [2], hypocrite (+120) [1], hypocrite's [1]

2612 חֹנֶף **ḥōnep**, n.[m.]. GK: 2869 [→ 2610]. ungodliness, godlessness:– hypocrisy [1]

2613 חֲנֻפָּה **ḥ^a^nuppâ**, n.f. GK: 2870 [→ 2610]. ungodliness, godlessness:– profaneness [1]

2614 חָנַק **ḥānaq**, v. GK: 2871 [→ 4267]. [N] to hang oneself; [P] to strangle:– hanged [1], strangled [1]

2615 חַנָּתֹן **ḥannātôn**, n.pr.loc. GK: 2872. Hannathon:– Hannathon [1]

2616 חָסַד **ḥāsad**, v. GK: 2873 & 2874 [→ 1136, 2617, 2618, 2623, 2624]. [P] to put to shame, reproach, with the strong implication of an insult; [Ht] to conduct oneself as faithful:– shew merciful [2], put to shame [1]

2617 חֶסֶד **ḥesed**, n.m. GK: 2875 & 2876 [→ 1136, cf. 2616, 2618, 2619?, 2623]. unfailing love, loyal love, devotion, kindness, often based on a prior relationship, especially a covenant relationship; disgrace:– mercy [137], kindness [38], lovingkindness [26], goodness [12], mercies [9], kindly [5], lovingkindnesses [4], favour [3], merciful [3], mercy's [3], merciful kindness [2], good deeds [1], goodliness [1], pity [1], reproach [1], wicked thing [1]

2618 חֶסֶד **ḥesed**, n.pr.m. GK: 2877 [→ 2617; cf. 2616]. Hesed:– Hesed [1]

2619 חֲסַדְיָה **ḥ^a^sadyâ**, n.pr.m. GK: 2878 [→ 2617+3068]. Hasadiah, "*Yahweh is faithful*":– Hasadiah [1]

2620 חָסָה **ḥāsâ**, v. GK: 2879 [→ 308, 2622, 4268 (also used with compound proper names)]. [Q] to take refuge in, to trust in:– trust [19], put trust [12], trusteth [2], hope [1], make refuge [1], putteth trust [1], trusted [1]

2621 חֹסָה **ḥōsâ**, n.pr.m. & loc. GK: 2880 & 2881. Hosah, "*refuge*":– Hosah [5]

2622 חָסוּת **ḥāsût**, n.f. GK: 2882 [→ 2620]. refuge:– trust [1]

2623 חָסִיד **ḥāsîd**, a.m. GK: 2883 [→ 2624; cf. 2616, 2617]. godly, saints, the people of God with a focus on their faithfulness; this can refer to a prominent individual, with messianic significance (Ps 16:10):– saints [19], godly [3], holy [3], merciful [3], holy one [2], good [1], ungodly (+3808) [1]

2624 חֲסִידָה **ḥ^a^sîdâ**, n.f. GK: 2884 [→ 2623; cf. 2616]. stork; some sources: heron:– stork [5], ostrich [1]

2625 חָסִיל **ḥāsîl**, n.m. GK: 2885 [→ 2628]. grasshoppers, locusts at a particular stage of development:– caterpillar [5], caterpillars [1]

2626 חֲסִין **ḥ^a^sîn**, a. GK: 2886 [→ 2634]. mighty, strong:– strong [1]

2627 חַסִּיר **ḥassîr** (Aram.), a. GK: 10276 [cf. 2638]. wanting, lacking in quality or quantity, deficient:– wanting [1]

2628 חָסַל **ḥāsal**, v. GK: 2887 [→ 2625]. [Q, H] to devour, consume:– consume [1]

2629 חָסַם **ḥāsam**, v. GK: 2888 [→ 4269]. [Q] to muzzle (an animal); to block (the way):– muzzle [1], stop [1]

2630 חָסַן **ḥāsan**, v.den. GK: 2889 [→ 2633; cf. 2631]. [N] to be stored up:– laid up [1]

2631 חֲסַן **ḥ^a^san** (Aram.), v. GK: 10277 [→ 2632; cf. 2630]. [H] to take possession of, occupy:– possessed [1], possess [1]

2632 חֱסֵן **ḥ^e^sēn** (Aram.), n.m. GK: 10278 [→ 2631; cf. 2633]. power, might, force:– power [2]

2633 חֹסֶן **ḥōsen**, n.m. GK: 2890 [→ 2630; cf. 2632]. stored treasure, riches, wealth:– strength [2], treasure [2], riches [1]

2634 חָסֹן **ḥāsōn**, a. GK: 2891 [→ 2626]. mighty, strong:– strong [2]

2635 חֲסַף **ḥ^a^sap** (Aram.), n.[m.]. GK: 10279. (formed, molded) clay, baked clay:– clay [9]

2636 חַסְפַּס **ḥaspas**, v. GK: 2892. [Pualal] to flake; some sources: to be scale-like, pertaining to the shape of an object; to crisp, crackle, pertaining to the brittleness of an object:– round thing [1]

2637 חָסֵר **ḥāsēr**, v. GK: 2893 [→ 2638, 2639, 2640, 2642, 4270]. [Q] to lack; to have nothing; to go down, recede; [P] to make lower; to deprive; [H] to cause to lack, withhold:– want [4], lack [3], fail [2], lacked [2], wanteth [2], abated [1], bereave [1], cause to fail [1], decreased [1], had lack [1], have need [1], made lower [1], wanted [1]

2638 חָסֵר **ḥāsēr**, a. GK: 2894 [→ 2637]. lacking; wanting:– void [6], wanteth [4], lacketh [3], destitute [1], faileth [1], fail [1], lacked [1], need [1], want [1]

2639 חֶסֶר **ḥeser**, n.m. GK: 2895 [→ 2637]. poverty, lack:– poverty [1], want [1]

2640 חֹסֶר **ḥōser**, n.[m.]. GK: 2896 [→ 2637]. poverty, lack:– want [3]

2641 חַסְרָה **ḥasrâ**, n.pr.m. GK: 2897 [cf. 2745]. Hasrah:– Hasrah [1]

2642 חֶסְרוֹן **ḥesrôn**, n.m. GK: 2898 [→ 2637]. what is lacking:– that which is wanting [1]

2643 חַף **ḥap**, a. GK: 2899 [→ 2653]. clean, pure:– innocent [1]

2644 חָפָא **ḥāpā'**, v. GK: 2901. [P] to do secretly:– secretly [1]

2645 חָפָה **ḥāpâ**, v. GK: 2902 [→ 2646, 2647; cf. 2653]. [Q] to cover; [Qp] to be covered; [N] to be sheathed, be covered; [P] to panel, overlay, cover:– covered [7], overlaid [4], cieled [1]

2646 חֻפָּה **ḥuppâ**, n.f. GK: 2903 [→ 2647; cf. 2645]. canopy, shelter; chamber, pavilion (of marriage ceremony):– chamber [1], closet [1], defence [1]

2647 חֻפָּה **ḥuppâ**, n.pr.m. GK: 2904 [→ 2646; cf. 2645]. Huppah, "*canopy*, hence *protection*":– Huppah [1]

2648 חָפַז **ḥāpaz**, v. GK: 2905 [→ 2649]. [Q] to hurry away (in alarm or terror):– haste [3], hasted away [2], made haste [2], hasteth [1], tremble [1]

2649 חִפָּזוֹן **ḥippāzôn**, n.[m.]. GK: 2906 [→ 2648]. haste:– haste [3]

2650 חֻפִּים **ḥuppîm**, n.pr.m. & a.g. GK: 2907. Huppim; Huppite, "*coast people*":– Huppim [3]

2651 חֹפֶן **ḥōpen**, n.[m.]. GK: 2908. hollow of the hand, handful (sometimes as a measure of volume):– hands [2], both hands [1], fists [1], handfuls (+4393) [1], hand [1]

2652 חָפְנִי **ḥopnî**, n.pr.m. GK: 2909. Hophni, "*tadpole*":– Hophni [5]

2653 חָפַף **ḥāpap**, v. GK: 2910 [→ 2348, 2643; cf. 2645]. [Q] to shield, shelter:– cover [1]

2654 חָפֵץ **ḥāpēṣ**, v. GK: 2911 & 2912 [→ 2655, 2656, 2657]. [Q] to desire, delight in, be pleased with, have pleasure in; to sway; some sources: to hang:– delight [15], delighteth [12], delighted [10], pleased [7], desire [6], please [5], will [3], any pleasure at all (+2654) [2], desirest [2], like [2], pleasure [2], delight in [1], desired [1], favourest [1], favoureth [1], moveth [1], pleaseth [1], take delight in [1], well pleased [1], would [1]

2655 חָפֵץ **ḥāpēṣ**, a.vbl. GK: 2913 [→ 2654]. desire, delight, pleasure:– desire [2], pleasure [2], delight [1], desireth [1], favour [1], please [1], willing [1], wish [1], would [1]

2656 חֵפֶץ **ḥēpeṣ**, n.m. GK: 2914 [→ 2654]. desire, delight, pleasure:– pleasure [16], desire [9], delight [3], purpose [3], desired [2], acceptable [1], delightsome [1], desireth [1], matter [1], pleasant [1], willingly (+871.1) [1]

2657 חֶפְצִי־בָהּ **ḥepṣî-bāh**, n.pr.f. GK: 2915 [→ 2654+871.1+1886.3]. Hephzibah, "*my pleasure is in her*":– Hephzi-bah [2]

2658 חָפַר **ḥāpar**, v. GK: 2916 [→ 1662, 2660, 2663, 2661, 6512]. [Q] to dig, scoop, to paw, to make a hole of any depth in soil; by extension: to spy out, search for, look about, seek out:– digged [13], dig [3], search out [3], diggeth [1], paweth [1], seeketh [1]

2659 חָפֵר **ḥāpar**, v. GK: 2917. [Q] to feel dismay, be disgraced, be humiliated, be in confusion; [H] to bring disgrace, be ashamed, be humiliated:– confounded [6], ashamed [4], brought to confusion [2], bringeth reproach [1], brought unto shame [1], cometh to shame [1], put to shame [1], shame [1]

2660 חֵפֶר **ḥēper**, n.pr.m. & loc. GK: 2918 & 2919 [→ 1662, 2662; cf. 2658]. Hepher, "[perhaps] *help*":– Hepher [9]

2661 חֲפַרְפָּרָה **ḥ^a^parpārâ**, n.f. GK: 2923 [→ 2658, 6512]. rodent (an object of worship):– moles (+6512) [1]

2662 חֶפְרִי **ḥeprî**, a.g. GK: 2920 [→ 2660]. Hepherite, "*of Hepher*":– Hepherites [1]

2663 חֲפָרַיִם **ḥ^a^pārayim**, n.pr.loc. GK: 2921 [→ 2658]. Hapharaim, "*place of two trenches*":– Hapharaim [1]

חֲפַרְפֵּרָה **ḥ^a^parpērâ**. See 2661.

2664 חָפַשׂ **ḥāpaś**, v. GK: 2924 [→ 2665]. [Q] to search for, examine, plot; [N] to be ransacked; [P] to search, look around, track down, hunt down; [Pu] to go into hiding, to

Heb

devise; [Ht] to disguise oneself, become like:– disguised [5], search [5], disguise [2], search out [2], searched [2], changed [1], diligent [1], hidden [1], made diligent search [1], searched out [1], searchest for [1], searching [1]

2665 חֵפֶשׂ ***ḥēpeś***, n.[m.]. GK: 2925 [→ 2664]. plan, plot:– search [1]

2666 חָפַשׁ ***ḥāpaš***, v. GK: 2926 [→ 2670]. [Pu] to be freed:– free [1]

2667 חֹפֶשׁ ***ḥōpeš***, n.[m.]. GK: 2927. material (for saddle blanket):– precious [1]

2668 חֻפְשָׁה ***ḥupšâ***, n.f. GK: 2928 [→ 2670]. freedom:– freedom [1]

2669 חָפְשׁוּת ***ḥopšût*** or חָפְשִׁית ***ḥopšît***, n.f. GK: 2929 & 2931 [→ 2670]. separation, exemption (from duties):– several [2]

2670 חָפְשִׁי ***ḥopšî***, a. GK: 2930 [→ 2666, 2668, 2669]. free; set apart, exempt:– free [16], liberty [1]

2671 חֵץ ***ḥēṣ***, n.m. GK: 2932 [→ 2678]. arrow; archer:– arrows [37], arrow [11], archers (+1167) [1], dart [1], shaft [1], wound [1]

חוּץ ***ḥuṣ***. See 2351.

2672 חָצַב ***ḥāṣēb***, v. GK: 2933 & 2934 & 2935 [→ 4274]. [Q] to dig; hew out, cut out; to strike (with lightning); [Qp, N, Pu] to be dug, be engraved, be cut out; [H] to cut in pieces:– hewers [4], digged [3], masons [3], hewed out [2], hew [2], cut [1], diggedst [1], dig [1], divideth [1], graven [1], hewed [1], heweth out [1], heweth [1], hewn out [1], hewn [1], made [1]

2673 חָצָה ***ḥāṣâ***, v. GK: 2936 [→ 2676, 2677, 2677, 3183, 3185, 4275, 4276; cf. 2686, 2687]. [Q] to divide; set apart; to rise up to; [N] to be divided, be parceled out:– divided [8], divide [2], divide into two parts [1], live out half [1], midst [1], parted [1], part [1]

2674 חָצוֹר ***ḥāṣôr***, n.pr.loc. GK: 2937 & 2938 [→ 2691, 5877]. Hazor, "*enclosure*":– Hazor [18]

2675 חָצוֹר חֲדַתָּה ***ḥāṣôr ḥ^{a}dattâ***, n.pr.loc. GK: 2939 [→ 2691]. Hazor Hadattah, "*new Hazor*":– Hazor Hadattah [1]

2676 חֲצוֹת ***ḥ^{a}ṣôt***, n.f. GK: 2940 [→ 2673]. middle (of the night), mid(night):– at midnight (+3915) [2], midnight (+3915+1886.1) [1]

2677 חֲצִי ***ḥ^{a}ṣî***, n.m. GK: 2942 & 2944 [→ 2673, 2679, 2680]. half, halfway, middle, midst:– half [107], midst [8], midnight (+3915+1886.1) [4], part [3], middle [1], one half [1], two parts [1]

2678 חֵצִי ***ḥēṣî***, n.m. GK: 2943 [→ 2671]. arrow:– arrow [4]

2679 חֲצִי הַמְּנֻחוֹת ***ḥ^{a}ṣî hamm^{e}nuḥôt***, n.m.+a.g. GK: 2942 [→ 2677]. half of the Manahethites:– Manahethites [1]

2680 חֲצִי הַמְּנַחְתִּי ***ḥ^{a}ṣî hamm^{e}naḥtî***, n.m.+a.g. GK: 2942 [→ 2677]. half of the Manahethites:– Manahethites [1]

2681 חָצִיר ***ḥāṣîr***, n.[m.]. GK: 2948. home, abode, haunt:– court [1]

2682 חָצִיר ***ḥāṣîr***, n.m. GK: 2945 & 2946 & 2947 [→ 2690, 2689, 2695, 2696]. (green) grass; hay; leeks; reed:– grass [17], hay [2], herb [1], leeks [1]

2683 חֵצֶן ***ḥēṣen***, n.m. GK: 2949 [→ 2684, 2785?]. bosom (of a garment):– bosom [1]

2684 חֹצֶן ***ḥōṣen***, n.m. GK: 2950 [→ 2683]. arms, folds of a robe:– arms [1], lap [1]

2685 חֲצַף ***ḥ^{a}ṣap*** (Aram.), v. GK: 10280. [H] to show harshness:– hasty [1], urgent [1]

2686 חָצַץ ***ḥāṣaṣ***, v. GK: 2951 & 2952 [cf. 2673]. [Q] to be in order, in ranks; [P] to divide, share; to sing; some sources: to distribute water; [Pu] to come to an end:– archers [1], by bands [1], cut off in the midst [1]

2687 חָצָץ ***ḥāṣāṣ***, n.[m.]. GK: 2953 [cf. 2673]. gravel:– arrows [1], gravel stones [1], gravel [1]

2688 חַצְצוֹן תָּמָר ***ḥaṣ^{e}ṣôn tāmār***, n.pr.loc. GK: 2954 [cf. 8558]. Hazazon Tamar, "*Hazazon of the palm trees*":– Hazazon-tamar [1], Hazezon-tamar [1]

2689 חֲצֹצְרָה ***ḥ^{a}ṣōṣ^{e}râ***, n.f. GK: 2956 [→ 2690; cf. 2682]. trumpet, a metal instrument used for signaling and music:– trumpets [26], trumpeters [2], trumpet [1]

2690 חִצְצֵר ***ḥaṣṣar*** or חָצַר ***ḥaṣar***, v.den. GK: 2955 & 2957 [→ 2689; cf. 2682]. [P] to sound a trumpet, play a trumpet:– sounded [2], blow [1], sounded trumpets [1], sounding [1], trumpeters [1]

2691 חָצֵר ***ḥāṣēr***, n.m. GK: 2958 [→ 1178, 2674, 2675, 2691, 2692, 2693, 2694, 2701, 2702, 2703, 2704, 2705, 2699, 2700; cf. 2691]. courtyard, court of a house, enclosed areas; village, a permanent settlement but without walls:– court [116], villages [47], courts [24], Hazar-hatticon [1], towns [1]

2692 חֲצַר־אַדָּר ***ḥ^{a}ṣar-'addār***, n.pr.loc. GK: 2960 [→ 146+2691]. Hazar Addar, "*settlement of Addar*":– Hazar-addar [1]

2693 חֲצַר גַּדָּה ***ḥ^{a}ṣar gaddâ***, n.pr.loc. GK: 2961 [→ 2691]. Hazar Gaddah, "*settlement of Gad*":– Hazar-gaddah [1]

2694 חָצֵר הַתִּיכוֹן ***ḥāṣēr hattîkôn***, n.pr.loc. GK: 2962 [→ 2691]. Hazer Hatticon, "*place of Hatticon*":–

2695 חֶצְרוֹ ***ḥeṣrô*** or חֶצְרַי ***ḥeṣray***, n.pr.m. GK: 2968 & 2974 [→ 2682]. Hezro, Hezrai:– Hezrai [1], Hezro [1]

2696 חֶצְרוֹן ***ḥeṣrôn***, n.pr.m. & loc. GK: 2969 & 2970 [→ 2697, 7152; cf. 2682]. Hezron, "*enclosure*":– Hezron [17], Hezron's [1]

2697 חֶצְרוֹנִי ***ḥeṣrônî***, a.g. GK: 2971 [→ 2696; cf. 2682]. Hezronite, "*of Hezron*":– Hezronites [2]

2698 חֲצֵרוֹת ***ḥ^{a}ṣērôt***, n.pr.loc. GK: 2972. Hazeroth, "*settlements*":– Hazeroth [6]

2699 חֲצֵרִים ***ḥ^{a}ṣērîm***, n.pr.loc. GK: 2973 [→ 2691]. Hazerim:– Hazerim [1]

2700 חֲצַרְמָוֶת ***ḥ^{a}ṣarmāwet***, n.pr.m. GK: 2975 [→ 2691+4194]. Hazarmaveth, "*village of Maveth*":– Hazarmaveth [2]

2701 חֲצַר סוּסָה ***ḥ^{a}ṣar sûsâ***, n.pr.loc. GK: 2963 [→ 2691+5484]. Hazar Susah, "*settlement of Susah [horse]*":– Hazar-susah [1]

2702 חֲצַר סוּסִים ***ḥ^{a}ṣar sûsîm***, n.pr.loc. GK: 2964 [→ 2691]. Hazar Susim, "*settlement of Susah [horse]*":– Hazar-susim [1]

2703 חֲצַר עֵינוֹן ***ḥ^{a}ṣar 'ênôn***, n.pr.loc. GK: 2965 [→ 2691]. Hazar Enan, "*settlement of Enan*":– Hazar-enan [1]

2704 חֲצַר עֵינָן ***ḥ^{a}ṣar 'ênān***, n.pr.loc. GK: 2966 [→ 2691+5881]. Hazar Enan, "*settlement of Enan*":– Hazar-enan [3]

2705 חֲצַר שׁוּעָל ***ḥ^{a}ṣar šû'āl***, n.pr.loc. GK: 2967 [→ 2691+7776]. Hazar Shual, "*settlement of Shual [jackal]*":– Hazar-shual [4]

חֵק ***ḥēq***. See 2436.

2706 חֹק ***ḥōq***, n.m. GK: 2976 [→ 2708, 2711; cf. 2710]. decree, statute, prescription, a clear communication of what someone should do; allotment, share, portion, prescribed amount of something:– statutes [74], statute [13], decree [7], ordinance [6], due [4], law [4], ordinances [3], portion [3], bounds [2], custom [2], commandments [1], convenient [1], decreed [1], measure [1], necessary [1], ordinary [1], set time [1], task [1], thing that is appointed [1]

2707 חָקָה ***ḥāqâ***, v. GK: 2977 [cf. 2710]. [Pu] to be carved, be portrayed; [Ht] mark for oneself; from the base meaning of carving or engraving is by extension of the act of writing; the communication itself, regulation:– pourtrayed [2], carved work [1], settest a print [1]

2708 חֻקָּה ***ḥuqqâ***, n.f. GK: 2978 [→ 2706; cf. 2710]. decree, ordinance, regulation, statute:– statutes [57], statute [20], ordinance [12], ordinances [10], customs [2], appointed [1], manners [1], rites [1]

2709 חֲקוּפָא ***ḥ^{a}qûpā'***, n.pr.m. GK: 2979. Hakupha, "*crooked*":– Hakupha [2]

2710 חָקַק ***ḥāqaq***, v. GK: 2980 [→ 2436, 2706, 2708; cf. 2707]. [Q] to mark out, inscribe, chisel, engrave; [Qp] to be portrayed; [Po] to command, be a leader, ruler; staff (of a commander); [Pu] to be decreed; [Ho] to be written:– lawgiver [6], decree [2], governors [2], appointed [1], graven [1], graveth [1], law [1], note [1], pourtrayed [1], pourtray [1], printed [1], set [1]

2711 חֵקֶק ***ḥēqeq***, n.m. GK: 2981 [→ 2706]. decree, statute, prescription:– decrees [1], thoughts [1]

2712 חֻקֹּק ***ḥuqqōq*** or חוּקֹק ***ḥûqōq***, n.pr.loc. GK: 2982 & 2577. Hukkok, Hukok:– Hukkok [1], Hukok [1]

2713 חָקַר ***ḥāqar***, v. GK: 2983 [→ 2714, 4278]. [Q] to explore, search out, probe; [N] to be determined, be searched; [P] to search out:– search [7], searched out [4], search out [3], searched [3], found out [2], searcheth out [2], make search [1], searcheth [1], seek [1], sought out [1], sounded [1], try [1]

2714 חֵקֶר ***ḥēqer***, n.m. GK: 2984 [→ 2713]. searching, finding out, often negatively stated: what cannot be search thoroughly or found out:– search [3], unsearchable (+369) [3], searching [2], finding out [1], number [1], searched out [1], searchings [1]

2715 חֹר ***ḥōr***, n.m. GK: 2985. noble, free person:– nobles [13]

חוּר ***ḥur***. See 2352.

2716 חֲרָאִים ***ḥ^{a}rā'îm***, n.[m.]. GK: 2989 [→ 4280; cf. 2755]. filth, excrement:–

2717 חָרֵב ***ḥārēb***, v. GK: 2990 & 2991 & 2993 [→ 2719, 2720, 2721, 2722?, 2723, 2724, 2725; cf. 2718]. [Q] to be dried up, be parched; be desolate, lay in ruins; to kill; [N] to be ruined, be desolate; to be slaughtered; [Pu] to be dried up; [H] to lay waste, devastate, cause to dry up; [Ho] to lie in ruins:– laid waste [8], dried up [6], desolate [3], dried [3], dry up [2], dry [2], made waste [2], surely slain (+2717) [2], utterly wasted (+2717) [2], wasted [2], decayeth [1], destroyed [1], destroyer [1], drieth up [1], lie waste [1], make waste [1], slay [1], waste [1]

2718 חֲרַב ḥ^{a}rab (Aram.), v. GK: 10281 [cf. 2717]. [Ho] to be destroyed, be devastated:– destroyed [1]

2719 חֶרֶב ḥereb, n.f. GK: 2995 [→ 2717]. sword; dagger; knife; cutting tool; by extension: battle, war; used fig. of God's judgment:– sword [385], swords [17], dagger [3], knives [3], knife [2], axes [1], mattocks [1], tool [1]

2720 חָרֵב ḥārēb, a. GK: 2992 [→ 2717]. dry, desolate, wasted, in ruins:– waste [6], desolate [2], dry [2]

2721 חֹרֶב ḥōreb or **חֹרֶב ḥōreb**, n.m. GK: 2996 & 2997 [→ 2717]. heat, dryness, drought, fever; waste, rubble, object of horror, desolation:– heat [6], drought [3], dry [3], waste [2], desolation [1], utterly waste (+2723) [1]

2722 חֹרֵב ḥōrēb, n.pr.loc. GK: 2998 [→ 2717?]. Horeb, "*dry, desolate*":– Horeb [17]

2723 חָרְבָּה ḥorbâ, n.f. GK: 2999 [→ 2717]. ruins, desolate place:– wastes [7], waste [7], desolation [5], desolate places [4], waste places [4], desolations [3], deserts [2], desolate [2], laid waste [2], decayed places [1], desert [1], destructions [1], places desolate [1], utterly waste (+2721) [1], wasted [1]

2724 חָרָבָה ḥārābâ, n.f. GK: 3000 [→ 2717]. dry land, dry ground:– dry [8]

2725 חֲרָבוֹן ḥ^{a}rābôn, n.m. GK: 3001 [→ 2717]. dry heat, implying a drought:– drought [1]

2726 חַרְבוֹנָא ḥarbônā' or **חַרְבוֹנָה ḥarbônâ**, n.pr.m. GK: 3002 & 3003. Harbona, "*donkey driver*":– Harbonah [1], Harbona [1]

2727 חָרַג ḥārag, v. GK: 3004. [Q] to come out trembling:– afraid [1]

2728 חַרְגֹּל ḥargōl, n.[m.]. GK: 3005 [cf. 2295]. cricket; some sources: locust, grasshopper:– beetle [1]

2729 חָרַד ḥārad, v. GK: 3006 [→ 2730, 2731, 2732?, 2733?]. [Q] to tremble, quake, shudder, be startled; [H] to make afraid, frighten, make tremble:– make afraid [10], afraid [8], tremble [6], trembled [4], fray away [2], made afraid [2], careful [1], discomfited [1], fray [1], quaked [1], trembled (+2731) [1], trembleth [1], trembling [1]

2730 חָרֵד ḥārēd, a.vbl. GK: 3007 [→ 2729]. trembling, fearful:– tremble [2], afraid [1], trembled (+1961) [1], trembled [1], trembleth [1]

2731 חֲרָדָה ḥ^{a}rādâ, n.f. GK: 3010 [→ 2729]. panic, fear, terror, horror:– trembling [4], fear [2], care [1], quaking [1], trembled (+2729) [1]

2732 חֲרָדָה ḥ^{a}rādâ, n.pr.loc. GK: 3011 [→ 2729?]. Haradah, "*place of fear*":– Haradah [2]

2733 חֲרֹדִי ḥ^{a}rōdî, a.loc. GK: 3012 & 3009 [→ 2729?]. Harodite:– Harodite [2]

2734 חָרָה ḥārâ, v. GK: 3013 [→ 2740, 2750, 8474; cf. 2787]. [Q] to be angry, be aroused; to burn with anger; [N] to rage; [H] to be jealous; [Tiphel] to compete, contend with; [Ht] to fret:– kindled [44], wroth [12], angry [8], hot [5], fret [4], wax hot [4], displeased [3], incensed [2], very wroth (+2734) [2], burn [1], displease (+5869+871.1) [1], earnestly [1], grieved [1], very angry [1], waxed hot [1]

2735 חֹר הַגִּדְגָּד ḥōr haggidgād, n.pr.loc. GK: 2988 [→ 2356]. Hor Haggidgad, "*cavern of the Gidgad*":– Hor-hagidgad [2]

2736 חַרְהֲיָה ḥarh^{a}yâ, n.pr.m. GK: 3015 & 3029. Harhaiah:– Harhaiah [1]

2737 חֲרוּזִים ḥ^{a}rûzîm, n.[m.]pl. GK: 3016. string of jewels; some sources: string of beads or shells:– chains [1]

2738 חָרוּל ḥārûl, n.[m.]. GK: 3017. weeds, undergrowth, variously identified:– nettles [3]

חֹרֹן **ḥōrôn**. See 1032, 2772.

2739 חֲרוּמַף ḥ^{a}rûmap, n.pr.m. GK: 3018 [→ 2763+639]. Harumaph, "*disfigured nose*":– Harumaph [1]

2740 חָרוֹן ḥārôn, n.m. GK: 3019 [→ 2734]. fierce (anger), burning (anger), wrath:– fierce [23], fierceness [9], wrath [5], fierce wrath [1], fury [1], sore displeasure [1], wrathful [1]

2741 חֲרוּפִי ḥ^{a}rûpî or **חֲרִיפִי ḥ^{a}rîpî**, a.g. GK: 3020 & 3042 [→ 2756; cf. 2778]. Haruphite, Hariphite:– Haruphite [1]

2742 חָרוּץ ḥārûṣ, n.m. & a. GK: 3021 & 3022 & 3023 & 3025 & 3026 [→ 2782]. gold; trench, ditch, moat, a military defense; threshing sledge, sharp instrument for harvest; decision; diligent, industrious:– diligent [5], gold [4], decision [2], fine gold [2], threshing [2], sharp pointed [1], sharp [1], wall [1]

2743 חָרוּץ ḥārûṣ, n.pr.m. GK: 3027 [→ 2782?]. Haruz, "[perhaps] *gold* or *eager*":– Haruz [1]

2744 חַרְחוּר ḥarḥûr, n.pr.m. GK: 3028 [→ 2746; cf. 2787]. Harhur, "[poss.] *fever;* [poss.] *raven; one born during mother's fever*":– Harhur [2]

2745 חַרְחַס ḥarḥas, n.pr.m. GK: 3030 [cf. 2641]. Harhas:– Harhas [1]

2746 חַרְחֻר ḥarḥur, n.m. GK: 3031 [→ 2744; cf. 2787]. scorching heat; some souces: fever:– extreme burning [1]

2747 חֶרֶט ḥereṭ, n.[m.]. GK: 3032. pen; fashioning tool, stylus:– graving tool [1], pen [1]

חָרִט **ḥāriṭ**. See 2754.

2748 חַרְטֹם ḥarṭōm, n.m. GK: 3033 [→ 2413; cf. 2749]. magician:– magicians [11]

2749 חַרְטֹם ḥarṭōm (Aram.), n.m. GK: 10282 [cf. 2748]. magician:– magicians [4], magician [1]

2750 חֳרִי ḥ^{o}rî, n.m. GK: 3034 [→ 2734]. hot, burning, fierce (anger):– fierce [3], great [2], heat [1]

חֲרִי **ḥ^{a}rî**. See 2716.

2751 חֹרִי ḥōrî, n.[m.]. GK: 3035 [→ 2357]. (white) bread or cake:– white [1]

2752 חֹרִי ḥōrî, n.pr.m. GK: 3036. Hori, "*cave-dweller*":– Horites [3], Horims [2], Horite [1]

2753 חֹרִי ḥōrî, a.g. GK: 3037. Horite, "*of Hor[i]*":– Hori [4]

2754 חָרִיט ḥārîṭ, n.m. GK: 3038. bag, purse:– bags [1], crisping pins [1]

2755 חִרְיוֹנִים ḥiryyônîm, n.[m.]. GK: 3039 [cf. 2716+3123]. dove's dung [?], see 2716:–

2756 חָרִיף ḥārîp, n.pr.m. GK: 3040 [→ 2741; cf. 2778]. Hariph, "*one born at harvest time*":– Hariph [2]

2757 חָרִיץ ḥārîṣ, n.m. GK: 3043 & 3044 [→ 2782]. portion, slice; pick, hoe, an iron tool:– harrows [2], cheeses (+2461) [1]

2758 חָרִישׁ ḥārîš, n.m. GK: 3045 [→ 2790]. plowing, time of plowing:– earing time [1], earing [1], ground [1]

2759 חֲרִישִׁי ḥ^{a}rîšî, a. GK: 3046 [→ 2790?]. scorching:– vehement [1]

2760 חָרַךְ ḥārak, v. GK: 3047. [Q] to roast; some sources: to capture:– roasteth [1]

2761 חֲרַךְ ḥ^{a}rak (Aram.), v. GK: 10283. [Htpa] to be singed (i.e., hair burnt):– singed [1]

2762 חֲרַכִּים ḥ^{a}rakkîm, n.[m.]pl. GK: 3048. lattice, a window covered by crossed strips of wood:– lattice [1]

חָרֻל **ḥārul**. See 2738.

2763 חָרַם ḥāram, v. GK: 3049 & 3050 [→ 1179, 2739, 2764, 2766?, 2767, 2768, 2769]. [Qp] to be disfigured, mutilated, any split portion of the face, possibly a cleft palate; [H] to completely destroy, devote to destruction, exterminate, annihilate [Ho] to be destroyed, be devoted to destruction; this can refer to anything which is under the ban from common use, some things are set apart for use by priests, other things are destroyed utterly as devoted to the LORD:– utterly destroyed [19], utterly destroy [9], destroyed utterly [4], utterly destroy (+2763) [4], destroy utterly [3], destroying utterly [3], utterly destroying [2], consecrate [1], devoted [1], devote [1], flat nose [1], forfeited [1], make accursed [1], utterly make away [1], utterly to slay [1]

2764 חֵרֶם ḥērem, n.m. GK: 3051 & 3052 [→ 2763]. devoted, set apart for destruction; this can refer to anything which is under the ban from common use, some things are set apart for use by priests, other things are destroyed utterly as devoted to the LORD; net, fishnet, trap:– accursed thing [9], net [5], curse [4], nets [4], accursed [3], cursed thing [3], devoted [3], devoted thing [2], appointed to utter destruction [1], dedicate thing [1], thing accursed [1], things utterly destroyed [1], utter destruction [1]

2765 חֳרֵם ḥ^{o}rēm, n.pr.loc. GK: 3054. Horem, "*consecrated*":– Horem [1]

2766 חָרִם ḥārim, n.pr.m. GK: 3053 [→ 2763?]. Harim, "*consecrated [to Yahweh]*":– Harim [11]

2767 חָרְמָה ḥormâ, n.pr.loc. GK: 3055 [→ 2763]. Hormah, "*consecration*":– Hormah [9]

2768 חֶרְמוֹן ḥermôn, n.pr.loc. GK: 3056 [→ 1179, 2769; cf. 2763]. Hermon, "*consecrated place*":– Hermon [13]

2769 חֶרְמוֹנִים ḥermônîm, n.pr.loc. GK: 3057 [→ 2768; cf. 2763]. heights of Hermon:– Hermonites [1]

2770 חֶרְמֵשׁ ḥermēš, n.[m.]. GK: 3058. sickle (for harvest of grain):– sickle [2]

2771 חָרָן ḥārān, n.pr.m. & loc. GK: 3059 & 3060. Haran, "*mountaineer* perhaps *sanctuary*":– Haran [12]

חָרֹן **ḥārōn**. See 2740.

2772 חֹרֹנִי ḥōrōnî, a.g. GK: 3061. Horonite:– Horonite [3]

2773 חוֹרֹנַיִם ḥôrōnayim, n.pr.loc. GK: 2589. Horonaim, "*twin hollows, twin caves*":– Horonaim [4]

2774 חַרְנֶפֶר ***ḥarneper***, n.pr.m. *or* loc. GK: 3062. Harnepher, "*Horus is merciful*":– Harnepher [1]

2775 חֶרֶס ***ḥeres*** or חַרְסָה ***harᵉsâ***, n.m. GK: 3063 & 3064 & 3066 [→ 2776, 8556]. sun; itch, any eruptive skin rash:– sun [3], itch [1]

2776 חֶרֶס ***ḥeres***, n.pr.loc. GK: 3065 [→ 2775, 8556]. Heres, "*sun*":– Heres [1]

2777 חַרְסוּת ***ḥarsût*** or חַרְסִית ***ḥarsît***, n.f.col. GK: 3067 & 3068 [→ 2789]. potsherd:– east [1]

2778 חָרַף ***ḥārap***, v. GK: 3069 & 3070 & 3071 & 3072 [→ 2756, 2741, 2779, 2780, 2781; cf. 2741?]. [Q] to treat with contempt, insult, reproach, taunt; to (spend the time of) winter; [N] to be promised to a man, engaged; [P] to defy, ridicule, taunt, mock, insult; to disillusion, confuse:– reproached [12], reproach [10], defied [5], reproacheth [5], defy [3], betrothed [1], blasphemed [1], jeoparded [1], rail [1], upbraid [1], winter [1]

2779 חֹרֶף ***ḥōrep***, n.m. GK: 3074 [→ 2778]. winter (the early time of the harvest cycle); prime (the early time of one's youth):– winter [4], cold [1], winterhouse (+1004) [1], youth [1]

2780 חָרֵף ***ḥārēp***, n.pr.m. GK: 3073 [→ 2778]. Hareph, "*autumn* or *sharp; scornful*":– Hareph [1]

2781 חֶרְפָּה ***ḥerpâ***, n.f. GK: 3075 [→ 2778]. disgrace, contempt, scorn, insult:– reproach [65], shame [3], rebuke [2], reproaches [1], reproacheth [1], reproachfully (+871.1) [1]

2782 חָרַץ ***ḥāraṣ***, v. GK: 3024 & 3076 & 3077 [→ 2742, 2743?, 2757]. [Q] to pronounce, determine; to pay attention, act quickly; [Qp, N] to be determined, be decreed; to be maimed, mutilated, pertaining to what has been cut:– determined [6], bestir [1], decided [1], decreed [1], maimed [1], moved [1], move [1]

2783 חֲרַץ ***ḥᵃraṣ*** (Aram.), n.[m.]. GK: 10284 [cf. 2504]. hips, hip joints:– loins [1]

חָרֻץ ***ḥāruṣ***. See 2742.

2784 חַרְצֹב ***ḥarṣōb***, n.[f.]. GK: 3078. struggle; chains:– bands [2]

חָרִיץ ***ḥāriṣ***. See 2757.

2785 חַרְצָן ***ḥarṣān***, n.m.pl. GK: 3079 [→ 2683?]. seeds (of grapes); some sources: unripe fruit:– kernels [1]

2786 חָרַק ***ḥāraq***, v. GK: 3080. [Q] to gnash, grind (teeth):– gnasheth [2], gnash [2], gnashed [1]

2787 חָרַר ***ḥārar***, v. GK: 3081 & 3082 [→ 2744, 2746, 2788; cf. 2734]. [Q] to burn; (heated metal) glow; [N] be parched, burned, charred; to be hoarse; [Pil] to kindle, cause to burn, glow; by extension: to have a fever:– burnt [5], burned [2], angry [1], burn [1], dried [1], kindle [1]

2788 חֲרֵרִים ***ḥᵃrērîm***, n.[m.]. GK: 3083 [→ 2787]. parched place, a hot, lifeless desert place:– parched places [1]

2789 חֶרֶשׂ ***ḥereś***, n.[m.]. GK: 3084 [→ 2777, 7025]. clay pot, earthenware; potsherd, fragment of pottery:– earthen [8], potsherd [4], earth [1], potsherds [1], sheards [1], sheard [1], stones [1]

2790 חָרֵשׁ ***ḥārēš***, v. GK: 3086 & 3087 [→ 2758, 2759?, 2791, 2792?, 2794, 2795, 2796, 2797?, 2798, 2799, 4281, 4282]. [Q] to plow; engrave; plan, plot; to be silent, be quiet; to become deaf; [Qp] to be inscribed; [N] to be plowed; [H] to be quiet, say nothing, be silent; [Ht] to make no moves, keep silent; [H] to plot against:– hold peace [11], held peace [8], plow [6], plowed [5], altogether hold peace (+2790) [4], devise [3], keep silence [3], altogether holdest peace (+2790) [2], deviseth [2], hold tongue [2], holdeth peace [2], kept silence [2], plowing [2], plowman [2], cease [1], conceal [1], deaf [1], ear [1], graven [1], held peace (+3509.1) [1], held tongue [1], holdest tongue [1], imagine [1], left off speaking [1], make hold peace [1], plowers [1], quiet [1], rest [1], secretly practised [1], silent [1], speak not a word [1], still [1], worker [1]

2791 חֶרֶשׁ ***ḥereš***, n.[m.] (used as adv.). GK: 3089 [→ 2790]. secretly, silently:– artificer [1], craftsmen [1], secretly [1]

2792 חֶרֶשׁ ***ḥereš***, n.pr.m. GK: 3090 [→ 2790?]. Heresh, "*deaf, silent*":– Heresh [1]

2793 חֹרֶשׁ ***ḥōreš***, n.m.[loc.] GK: 3091 & 3092 [→ 2796?; cf. 2800]. wooded place, forest, thicket; as place name: Horesh, "*woodsman* or *craftsman*":– wood [4], bough [1], forests [1], shrowd [1]

2794 חֹרֵשׁ ***ḥāraš***, v.ptcp. GK: 3086 [→ 2790]. ptcp. of 2790: one who plows; engraves; plans:– artificer [1]

2795 חֵרֵשׁ ***ḥērēš***, a. GK: 3094 [→ 2790]. deaf (person):– deaf [9]

2796 חָרָשׁ ***ḥārāš***, n.m. GK: 3088 & 3093 [→ 2790, 2793?]. skilled craftsman: blacksmith, carpenter, stonemason, gemcutter, idol-maker, etc.; the ironic phrase "craftsman of destruction" means people who are very good at destroying things (Eze 21:31); magic, sorcery:– carpenters [6], workman [5], craftsmen [4], carpenters (+6086) [3], engraver [3], artificers [2], smith [2], carpenter (+6086) [1], carpenter [1], craftsman [1], makers [1], masons (+68+7023) [1], masons (+7023) [1], skilful [1], smith (+1270) [1], workers [1], workmen [1], wrought [1]

2797 חַרְשָׁא ***haršā'***, n.pr.m. GK: 3095 [→ 8521; cf. 2790?]. Harsha, "*deaf*":– Harsha [2]

2798 חֲרָשִׁים ***ḥᵃrāšîm***, n.pr.loc. GK: 3096 & 1629 [→ 1516; cf. 2790]. Harashim; Ge Harashim, "*valley of the craftsmen*":– Charashim [1]

2799 חֲרֹשֶׁת ***ḥᵃrōšet***, n.f. GK: 3098 [→ 2790]. cutting (stone), working (wood):– carving [2], cutting [2]

2800 חֲרֹשֶׁת ***ḥᵃrōšet***, n.pr.loc. GK: 3099 [→ 1471; cf. 2793]. Harosheth:– Harosheth [3]

2801 חָרַת ***ḥārat***, v. GK: 3100. [Qp] to be engraved:– graven [1]

2802 חֶרֶת ***ḥeret***, n.pr.loc. GK: 3101. Hereth:– Hareth [1]

2803 חָשַׁב ***ḥāšab***, v. GK: 3108 & 3110 [→ 2807, 2808, 2809, 2810, 2811, 2815, 4284; cf. 2804]. [Q] to plan, plot, purpose, consider; to credit, account, impute; [N] to be thought, considered, regarded; be reckoned, accounted; [P] to determine, plan, plot; to compute, account; [Ht] to consider oneself:– counted [18], devise [12], cunning [9], thought [9], imagine [6], think [6], accounted [5], devised [5], deviseth [4], esteemed [4], purposed [4], reckoned [4], count [3], reckon [3], counteth [2], cunning workman [2], imagined [2], imputed [2], purpose [2], conceived [1], considered [1], esteemeth [1], esteem [1], find out [1], forecast against [1], forecast [1], holdest [1], imagineth [1], imputeth [1], impute [1], invent [1], like [1], makest account [1], meant [1], reckoning made [1], regardeth [1], regard [1], thinkest [1], thinketh [1], those that devise cunning work (+4284) [1], thought on [1]

2804 חֲשַׁב ***ḥᵃšab*** (Aram.), v. GK: 10285 [cf. 2803]. [Pp] to be regarded, be respected:– reputed [1]

2805 חֵשֶׁב ***ḥēšeb***, n.m. GK: 3109 [cf. 2280]. waistband:– curious girdle [8]

2806 חַשְׁבַּדָּנָה ***ḥašbaddānâ***, n.pr.m. GK: 3111 [cf. 2811]. Hashbaddanah, "[prob.] *Yahweh has considered me*":– Hashbadana [1]

2807 חֲשֻׁבָה ***ḥᵃšubâ***, n.pr.m. GK: 3112 [→ 2803]. Hashubah, "*consideration*":– Hashubah [1]

2808 חֶשְׁבּוֹן ***ḥešbôn***, n.m. GK: 3113 [→ 2803]. scheme, plan:– account [1], device [1], reason [1]

2809 חֶשְׁבּוֹן ***ḥešbôn***, n.pr.loc. GK: 3114 [→ 2803]. Heshbon, "*reckoning*":– Heshbon [38]

2810 חִשָּׁבוֹן ***ḥiššābôn***, n.m. GK: 3115 [→ 2803]. catapult machine (for hurling against ramparts); scheme:– engines [1], inventions [1]

2811 חֲשַׁבְיָה ***ḥᵃšabyâ*** or חֲשַׁבְיָהוּ ***ḥᵃšabyāhû***, n.pr.m. GK: 3116 & 3117 [→ 2803+3068; cf. 2806]. Hashabiah, "*Yahweh has reckoned*":– Hashabiah [15]

2812 חֲשַׁבְנָה ***ḥᵃšabnâ***, n.pr.m. GK: 3118. Hashabnah, "[prob.] *Yahweh has considered me*":– Hashabnah [1]

2813 חֲשַׁבְנְיָה ***ḥᵃšabnᵉyâ***, n.pr.m. GK: 3119. Hashabneiah, "[prob.] *Yahweh has considered me*":– Hashabniah [2]

2814 חָשָׁה ***ḥāšâ***, v. GK: 3120. [Q] to be silent, be hushed; [H] to keep silent; to do nothing, hesitate:– hold peace [5], still [3], held peace [2], hold my peace [1], holden peace [1], keep silence [1], silence [1], silent [1], stilled [1]

2815 חַשּׁוּב ***ḥaššûb***, n.pr.m. GK: 3121 [→ 2803]. Hasshub, "*considerate*":– Hashub [4], Hasshub [1]

2816 חֲשׁוֹךְ ***ḥᵃšôk*** (Aram.), n.[m.]. GK: 10286 [cf. 2822]. darkness:– darkness [1]

2817 חֲשׂוּפָא ***ḥᵃśûpā'***, n.pr.m. GK: 3102. Hasupha:– Hashupha [1], Hasupha [1]

חָשׁוּק ***ḥāšûq***. See 2838.

2818 חֲשַׁח ***ḥᵃšaḥ***, v. or חַשְׁחָה ***ḥašḥâ*** (Aram.), n.f. GK: 10287 & 10288 [→ 2819]. [P] to be in need; (n.) need:– careful [1], have need of [1]

2819 חַשְׁחוּ ***ḥašḥû*** (Aram.), n.f.col. GK: 10289 [→ 2818]. what is needed:– needful [1]

חֲשֵׁכָה ***ḥᵃšēkᵃh***. See 2825.

חֻשִׁים ***ḥušîm***. See 2366.

2820 חָשַׂךְ ***ḥāśak***, v. GK: 3104. [Q] to keep back, to withhold, halt, spare; [N] to be spared, be relieved:– spareth [3], spare [3], withheld [3], reserved [2], spared [2], aswwaged [1], asswage [1], forbear [1], held back [1], hindereth [1], keep back [1], keepeth back [1], kept back [1], kept [1], punished [1],

Heb

refrained [1], refraineth [1], refrain [1], withholdeth [1]

2821 חָשַׁךְ ***ḥāšak***, v. GK: 3124 [→ 2822, 2823, 2824, 2825, 4285]. [Q] to grow dark, be dim, be black; [H] to darken, make dark; often darkness has the associative meanings of gloom, despair, terror, ignorance, or hard to understand:– darkened [7], dark [3], blacker [1], cause darkness [1], darkeneth [1], darken [1], dim [1], hideth [1], made dark [1], maketh dark [1]

2822 חֹשֶׁךְ ***ḥōšek***, n.m. GK: 3125 [→ 2821; cf. 2816]. darkness, dark; blackness, gloom; often darkness has the associative meanings of gloom, despair, terror, ignorance, or hard to understand:– darkness [70], dark [7], obscurity [2], night [1]

2823 חָשֹׁךְ ***ḥāšōk***, a. GK: 3126 [→ 2821]. obscure, dark, unknown:– mean [1]

2824 חֶשְׁכָה ***ḥeškâ***, n.f. GK: 3128 [→ 2821, 2825]. same as 2825: darkness:– dark [1]

2825 חֲשֵׁכָה ***ḥ^{a}šēkâ***, n.f. GK: 3128 [→ 2824]. same as 2824: darkness:– darkness [5]

2826 חָשַׁל ***ḥāšal***, v. GK: 3129. [N] to lag (behind), be worn out:– feeble [1]

2827 חֲשַׁל ***ḥ^{a}šal*** (Aram.), v. GK: 10290. [P] to smash, pulverize:– subdueth [1]

2828 חָשֻׁם ***ḥāšum***, n.pr.m. GK: 3130 [→ 2829, 2832; cf. 2367]. Hashum, "*broad-nosed*":– Hashum [5]

חֻשָׁם ***ḥušām***. See 2367.

חֻשִׁים ***ḥušim***. See 2366.

2829 חֶשְׁמוֹן ***ḥešmôn***, n.pr.loc. GK: 3132 [→ 2828]. Heshmon:– Heshmon [1]

2830 חַשְׁמַל ***ḥašmal***, n.[m.]. GK: 3133. glowing metal; some sources: electrum:– amber [3]

2831 חַשְׁמַן ***ḥašman***, n.m. GK: 3134. envoy:– princes [1]

2832 חַשְׁמֹנָה ***ḥašmōnâ***, n.pr.loc. GK: 3135 [→ 2828]. Hashmonah:– Hashmonah [2]

2833 חֹשֶׁן ***ḥōšen***, n.m. GK: 3136. breastpiece:– breastplate [25]

2834 חָשַׂף ***ḥāśap***, v. GK: 3103 & 3106 & 3107 [→ 2835, 4286]. [Q] to strip bare, lay bare; to scoop out, draw out; [Qp] to be bared; [P] to bring to premature birth:– made bare [2], uncovered [2], bare [1], discovereth [1], discover [1], draw out [1], made clean [1], make bare [1], take [1]

2835 חָשִׂף ***ḥāśip***, n.m. GK: 3105 [→ 2834]. small flock:– little flocks [1]

2836 חָשַׁק ***ḥāšaq***, v. GK: 3137 & 3138 [→ 2837, 2838, 2839]. [Q] to set one's affection, desire, love, be attached to; [P] to make bands, make joints for binding; [Pu] to have bands:– filleted [3], desired (+2837) [2], set love [2], had delight [1], hast a desire [1], in love [1], longeth [1]

2837 חֵשֶׁק ***ḥēšeq***, n.m. GK: 3139 [→ 2836]. thing desired, thing longed for:– desired (+2836) [2], desire [1], pleasure [1]

2838 חָשׁוּק ***ḥāšûq***, n.[m.]. GK: 3122 [→ 2836]. band, binding:– fillets [8]

2839 חִשֻּׁק ***ḥiššuq***, n.[m.]. GK: 3140 [→ 2836]. spokes (of a wheel):– felloes [1]

2840 חִשֻּׁר ***ḥiššur***, n.[m.]. GK: 3141 [→ 2841]. hub (of a wheel):– spokes [1]

2841 חַשְׁרָה ***ḥašrâ***, n.f. GK: 3142 [→ 2840]. collection, mass:– dark [1]

חֲשֻׁפָא ***ḥ^{a}supā'***. See 2817.

2842 חֲשַׁשׁ ***ḥ^{a}šaš***, n.m. GK: 3143. chaff, dry grass:– chaff [2]

2843 חֻשָׁתִי ***ḥušātî***, a.g. GK: 3144 [→ 2364]. Hushathite:– Hushathite [5]

2844 חַת ***ḥat***, n.m. & a. GK: 3145 & 3146 [→ 2865]. fear, dread, terror; terrified, broken:– broken [1], dismayed [1], dread [1], fear [1]

2845 חֵת ***ḥēt***, n.pr.m. GK: 3147 [→ 2850]. Hittite, "*descendants of Heth*":– Heth [14]

2846 חָתָה ***ḥātâ***, v. GK: 3149 [→ 4289]. [Q] to get, snatch, take away:– take [2], heap [1], take away [1]

2847 חִתָּה ***ḥittâ***, n.f. GK: 3150 [→ 2865]. terror:– terror [1]

2848 חִתּוּל ***ḥittûl***, n.[m.]. GK: 3151 [→ 2853]. splint, bandage:– roller [1]

2849 חַתְחַת ***ḥatḥat***, n.[m.]. GK: 3152 [→ 2865]. horror, terror, danger:– fears [1]

2850 חִתִּי ***ḥittî***, a.g. GK: 3153 [→ 2845]. Hittite, "*descendants of Heth*":– Hittite [26], Hittites [22]

2851 חִתִּית ***ḥittît***, n.f. GK: 3154 [→ 2865]. terror:– terror [8]

2852 חָתַךְ ***ḥātak***, v. GK: 3155. [N] to be decreed:– determined [1]

2853 חָתַל ***ḥātal***, v. GK: 3156 [→ 2848, 2854]. [Pu, Ho] to be wrapped in strips of cloth:– swaddled at all (+2853) [2]

2854 חֲתֻלָּה ***ḥ^{a}tullâ***, n.f. GK: 3157 [→ 2853]. band (of cloth) for wrapping:– swaddling band [1]

2855 חֶתְלֹן ***ḥetlôn***, n.pr.loc. GK: 3158. Hethlon:– Hethlon [2]

2856 חָתַם ***ḥātam***, v. GK: 3159 [→ 2368, 2369, 2858; cf. 2857]. [Q] to seal (with a signet ring); to seal up; by extension: to be a model; [Qp] to be sealed, be enclosed; [N] to be sealed; [P] to seal in; [H] to block, obstruct:– sealed [12], seal [5], sealed up [2], marked [1], seal up [1], sealest up [1], sealeth up (+1157) [1], sealeth up [1], sealeth [1], stopped [1]

2857 חֲתַם ***ḥ^{a}tam*** (Aram.), v. GK: 10291 [cf. 2856]. [P] to seal (with a signet ring):– sealed [1]

חֹתָם ***ḥōtām***. See 2368.

2858 חֹתֶמֶת ***ḥōtemet***, n.f. GK: 3160 [→ 2856]. signet ring seal:– signet [1]

2859 חָתַן ***ḥātan***, v.den. GK: 3161 & 3162 & 3165 [→ 2860]. [Q, Ht] to intermarry; to become or have a son-in-law:– father in law [21], son in law [5], make marriages [3], join in affinity [1], joined affinity [1], made affinity [1], mother in law [1]

2860 חָתָן ***ḥātān***, n.m. GK: 3163 [→ 2859, 2861]. son-in-law; bridegroom:– bridegroom [8], son in law [8], husband [2], sons in law [2]

2861 חֲתֻנָּה ***ḥ^{a}tunnâ***, n.f. GK: 3164 [→ 2860]. wedding, marriage:– espousals [1]

2862 חָתַף ***ḥātap***, v. GK: 3166 [→ 2863]. [Q] to snatch away:– taketh away [1]

2863 חֶתֶף ***ḥetep***, n.[m.]. GK: 3167 [→ 2862]. bandit, robber:– prey [1]

2864 חָתַר ***ḥātar***, v. GK: 3168 [→ 4290]. [Q] to dig, break into; row (in rough seas):– dig [5], digged [2], rowed hard [1]

2865 חָתַת ***ḥātat***, v. GK: 3169 [→ 2844, 2847, 2849, 2851, 2866, 2867?, 4287?, 4288]. [Q] to be shattered, dismayed, terrified; [N] to be discouraged, terrified; [P] to frighten; break; [H] to shatter, terrify:– dismayed [26], afraid [5], broken in pieces [5], broken [3], broken down [2], abolished [1], affrighted [1], amazed [1], beaten down [1], broken to pieces [1], cause to be dismayed [1], chapt [1], confound [1], discouraged [1], go down [1], made afraid [1], scarest [1], terrify [1]

2866 חֲתַת ***ḥ^{a}tat***, n.[m.]. GK: 3170 [→ 2866; cf. 2865]. something dreadful, horrible:– casting down [1]

2867 חֲתַת ***ḥ^{a}tat***, n.pr.m. GK: 3171 [→ 2866?; cf. 2865?]. Hathath, "[poss.] *terror*; [poss.] *weakness*":– Hathath [1]

2868 טְאֵב ***ṭ^e'ēb*** (Aram.), v. GK: 10293 [→ 2869; cf. 3191; cf. 2895, 3190]. [P] to be good = to have joy:– glad [1]

2869 טָב ***ṭāb*** (Aram.), a. GK: 10294 [→ 2868; cf. 2896]. good, pleasing, pure:– fine [1], good [1]

2870 טָבְאַל ***ṭāb^e'al*** or טָבְאֵל ***ṭāb^e'ēl***, n.pr.m. GK: 3174 & 3175 [→ 2896+410]. Tabeal, Tabeel, "*God [El] is good*":– Tabeal [1], Tabeel [1]

2871 טְבוּלִים ***ṭ^{e}bûlîm***, n.m. GK: 3178. turban:– exceeding in dyed attire (+5628) [1]

2872 טַבּוּר ***ṭabbûr***, n.[m.]. GK: 3179. center (of the land), as a fig. extension of the navel of the body, not found in the OT:– middle [1], midst [1]

2873 טָבַח ***ṭābaḥ***, v. GK: 3180 [→ 2874, 2876, 2879, 2878, 4293]. [Q] to slaughter, butcher; [Qp] to be slaughtered:– killed [3], slaughter [3], slay [2], kill [1], slain [1], sore slaughter (+2874) [1]

2874 טֶבַח ***ṭebaḥ***, n.m. GK: 3181 [→ 2875; cf. 19, 2873]. slaughtering:– slaughter [9], beasts [1], sore slaughter (+2873) [1]

2875 טֶבַח ***ṭebaḥ***, n.pr.m. & loc. GK: 3182 & 3183 [→ 2874; cf. 2880]. Tebah, "[poss.] *one born at the time or place of the slaughtering*":– Tebah [1]

2876 טַבָּח ***ṭabbāḥ***, n.m. GK: 3184 [→ 2879; cf. 2873; cf. 2877]. cook, butcher; by extension: executioner; guard, imperial guard:– guard [29], cook [2], guard's [1]

2877 טַבָּח ***ṭabbāḥ*** (Aram.), n.m. GK: 10295 [cf. 2876]. (royal) body-guard, executioner; an elite unit guarding a king, execution only one of its functions:– guard [1]

2878 טִבְחָה ***ṭibḥâ***, n.f. GK: 3186 [→ 2873]. slaughtered meat, butchered meat:– slaughter [2], flesh [1]

2879 טַבָּחָה ***ṭabbāḥâ***, n.f. GK: 3185 [→ 2876; cf. 2873]. (female) cook (of meat):– cooks [1]

2880 טִבְחַת ***ṭibḥat***, n.pr.loc. GK: 3187 [cf. 984, 2875]. Tebah, "[poss.] *one born at the time or place of slaughtering*":– Tibhath [1]

2881 טָבַל ***ṭābal***, v. GK: 3188. [Q] to dip, plunge; bathe, soak; [N] to be dipped:– dip [9], dipped [3], dipt [3], plunge [1]

2882 טְבַלְיָהוּ ***ṭ^{e}balyāhû***, n.pr.m. GK: 3189 [→ 2919+3807.1?+3068?]. Tabaliah, "*Yahweh has dipped*":– Tebaliah [1]

2883 טָבַע ***ṭāba'***, v. GK: 3190 [→ 2884, 2885]. [Q] to sink down, to fall into; [Pu] to be drowned; [Ho] to be sunk, be settled into:– sunk [4], sink [2], drowned [1], fastened [1], settled [1], sunk down [1]

2884 טַבָּעוֹת ***ṭabbā'ôt***, n.pr.m. GK: 3191 [→ 2885; cf. 2883]. Tabbaoth, "*[ornamental or signet] ring*":– Tabbaoth [2]

2885 טַבַּעַת **ṭabba'at**, n.f. GK: 3192 [→ 2884; cf. 2883]. ring; signet ring:– rings [40], ring [9]

2886 טַבְרִמֹּן **ṭabrimmōn**, n.pr.m. GK: 3193 [→ 2896+7417]. Tabrimmon, "*Rimmon is good*":– Tabrimon [1]

2887 טֵבֵת **ṭēbēt**, n.pr. GK: 3194. Tebeth:– Tebeth [1]

2888 טַבָּת **ṭabbāt**, n.pr.loc. GK: 3195. Tabbath, "[poss.] *good*":– Tabbath [1]

2889 טָהוֹר **ṭāhôr**, a. GK: 3196 [→ 2891, 2890]. clean, pure, flawless, free from impurity; moral or ceremonial purity as a fig. extension of an object being free from defect or filth:– clean [51], pure [40], fair [2], pureness [1], purer [1]

2890 טְהוֹר **ṭ^{e}hôr**, n.m. GK: 3196 [→ 2889]. same as 2889: cleanness, purity, flawlessness:–

2891 טָהֵר **ṭāhēr**, v. GK: 3197 [→ 2889, 2890, 2892, 2893]. [Q] to be (ceremonially) clean, purified; [P] to pronounce clean, cleanse, make ceremonially clean, to purify; [Ht] to cleanse oneself, purify oneself; this can mean moral or ceremonial purity:– clean [26], cleansed [23], cleanse [16], pronounce clean [10], purged [4], purified [3], purify [3], made clean [2], pure [2], cleanseth [1], make clean [1], maketh clean [1], purge [1], purifier [1]

2892 טֹהַר **ṭōhar**, n.[m.]. GK: 3198 & 3199 [→ 2891]. purity; cleanness; clearness, brightness, splendor:– purifying [2], clearness [1], glory [1]

2893 טָהֳרָה **ṭoh^{o}râ**, n.f. GK: 3200 [→ 2891]. cleansing, purification; pronouncement of (ceremonial) cleansing:– cleansing [7], purifying [3], purification [2], cleansed [1]

2894 טֵאטֵא **ṭē'ṭē'**, v. GK: 3173 [→ 4292; cf. 2916]. [Pil] to sweep away:– sweep [1]

2895 טוֹב **ṭôb**, v. GK: 3201 [→ 2896, 2897, 2898; cf. 3190; cf. 2868, cf. 3191]. [Q] to be good, well, pleasing; [H] to do well, do good, prosper; this can refer to quality as well as to moral goodness:– well [8], good [5], please [4], do good [3], didst well [2], please (+5921) [2], better [1], cheer [1], do better [1], doest good [1], done well [1], do [1], goodly [1], made goodly [1]

2896 טוֹב **ṭôb**, a. & n.m. GK: 3202 & 3203 [→ 2895, 2897; cf. 2869 (also used with compound proper names)]. good, pleasing, desirable; goodness; this can refer to quality as well as to moral goodness:– good [361], better [72], well [20], goodness [16], goodly [8], merry [7], best [6], fair [6], prosperity [6], precious [4], wealth [3], any thing better (+2896) [2], fair (+4758) [2], fairer [2], fine [2], glad [2], goodliest [2], goods [2], kindly [2], pleasant [2], pleased (+5869+871.1) [2], pleaseth (+5869+871.1) [2], please [2], pleasure [2], beautiful (+4758) [1], beautiful [1], bountiful [1], cheerful [1], ease [1], favour (+5869+871.1) [1], fine (+6668) [1], good deeds [1], goodlier [1], goodly (+8389) [1], graciously [1], in favour [1], joyful [1], kindness [1], kind [1], liketh (+5869+871.1) [1], liketh best (+871.1+1886.1) [1], loving [1], most [1], pleaseth (+6440+3807.1) [1], pleasing [1], ready [1], sweet [1], think best (+5869+871.1) [1], welfare [1], wellfavoured (+2580) [1]

2897 טוֹב **ṭôb**, n.pr.loc. GK: 3204 [→ 2896; cf. 2895]. Tob, "*good*":– Tob [2]

2898 טוּב **ṭûb**, n.m. GK: 3206 [→ 2895]. good, best; goodness, prosperity; this can refer to quality as well as to moral goodness:– goodness [13], good [9], goods [3], fair [1], gladness [1], goeth well [1], good things [1], good thing [1], goodness' [1], joy [1]

2899 טוֹב אֲדוֹנִיָּה **ṭôb '^{a}dôniyyâ**, n.pr.m. GK: 3207 [→ 2897+138]. Tob-Adonijah, "*good is [my] Lord Yahweh*":– Tob-adonijah [1]

2900 טוֹבִיָּה **ṭôbiyyâ** or טוֹבִיָּהוּ **ṭôbiyyāhû**, n.pr.m. GK: 3209 & 3210 [→ 2896+3068]. Tobiah; Tobijah, "*Yahweh is good*":– Tobiah [15], Tobijah [3]

2901 טָוָה **ṭāwâ**, v. GK: 3211 [→ 4299]. [Q] to spin (yarn):– spin [1], spun [1]

2902 טוּחַ **ṭûaḥ** or טָחַח **ṭāḥaḥ**, v. GK: 3212 & 3220 [→ 2915]. [Q] to cover with whitewash; overlay with plaster; [N] to be plastered, be coated:– daubed [6], plaistered [2], daub [1], overlay [1], plaister [1], shut [1]

2903 טוֹטָפֹת **ṭôṭāpōt**, n.f.pl. GK: 3213 [→ 5197]. symbol, sign (later, phylactery, a small box of Scripture verses worn as a sign of obedience to the covenant):– frontlets [3]

2904 טוּל **ṭûl**, v. GK: 3214 [→ 2925]. [P] to hurl; [H] to thrown, hurl; [Ho] to be overpowered, be fallen, be hurled:– cast forth [4], cast [4], cast out [2], carry away [1], cast down [1], sent out [1], utterly cast down [1]

2905 טוּר **ṭûr**, n.m. GK: 3215 [→ 2918]. row, course:– row [14], rows [12]

2906 טוּר **ṭûr** (Aram.), n.m. GK: 10296 [cf. 6697]. mountain:– mountain [2]

2907 טוּשׂ **ṭûś**, v. GK: 3216. [Q] to swoop down; some sources: to flutter:– hasteth [1]

2908 טְוָת **ṭ^{e}wāt** (Aram.), adv. GK: 10297. without eating, in hunger, in fasting:– fasting [1]

2909 טָחָה **ṭāḥâ**, v. GK: 3217. [Pil] to shoot (an arrow the distance of a bowshot; the distance of a bowshot is still in sight, though it is out of hearing range):– bowshot (+7198) [1]

2910 טֻחוֹת **ṭuḥôt**, n.f.pl. GK: 3219. inner parts; heart, with a possible focus that this is a mysterious and unknowable part of a person:– inward parts [2]

2911 טְחוֹן **ṭ^{e}ḥôn**, n.[m.]. GK: 3218 [→ 2912]. hand-mill, grinding-mill:– grind [1]

2912 טָחַן **ṭāḥan**, v. GK: 3221 & 3223 [→ 2911, 2913]. [Q] to grind to flour, crush to powder:– grind [4], ground [2], grinders [1], ground very small [1]

2913 טַחֲנָה **ṭaḥ^{a}nâ**, n.f. GK: 3222 [→ 2912]. grinding-mill:– grinding [1]

2914 טְחֹרִים **ṭ^{e}ḥōrîm**, n.m. GK: 3224. tumor, hemorrhoids:– emerods [7]

2915 טִיחַ **ṭîaḥ**, n.[m.]. GK: 3225 [→ 2902]. coating (of whitewash); some sources: coating of clay:– daubing [1]

2916 טִיט **ṭîṭ**, n.m. GK: 3226 [→ 2894, 4292; cf. 2917]. mud, dirt, mire, clay:– mire [8], clay [3], dirt [2]

2917 טִין **ṭîn** (Aram.), n.[m.]. GK: 10298 [cf. 2916]. (wet) clay:– miry [2]

2918 טִירָה **ṭîrâ**, n.f. GK: 3227 [→ 2905; cf. 3195?]. camp (protected by stone walls); tower, battlement:– castles [2], goodly castles [1], habitation [1], palaces [1], palace [1], rows [1]

2919 טַל **ṭal**, n.m. GK: 3228 [→ 37, 2537, 2882; cf. 2920]. dew, night mist:– dew [31]

2920 טַל **ṭal** (Aram.), n.[m.]. GK: 10299 [cf. 2919]. dew:– dew [5]

2921 טָלָא **ṭālā'**, v. GK: 3229. [Qp] to be spotted; be variegated; [Pu] to be patched:– spotted [6], clouted [1], divers colours [1]

2922 טְלָא **ṭ^{e}lā'**, n.m. GK: 3231 [→ 2923, 2924]. same as 2924: lamb:– lambs [1]

2923 טְלָאִים **ṭ^{e}lā'îm**, n.pr.loc. GK: 3230 [→ 2922]. Telaim, "*lambs*":– Telaim [1]

2924 טָלֶה **ṭāleh**, n.m. GK: 3231 [→ 2922]. same as 2922: lamb:– lamb [2]

2925 טַלְטֵלָה **ṭalṭēlâ**, n.f. GK: 3232 [→ 2904]. hurling, throwing:– captivity [1]

2926 טָלַל **ṭālal**, v. GK: 3233 [cf. 6751]. [P] to cover with a roof:– covered [1]

2927 טְלַל **ṭ^{e}lal** (Aram.), v. GK: 10300 [cf. 6751]. [H] to find shelter:– shadow [1]

2928 טֶלֶם **ṭelem**, n.pr.m. & loc. GK: 3234 & 3235 [cf. 2929]. Telem, "*brightness*":– Telem [2]

2929 טַלְמוֹן **ṭalmôn**, n.pr.m. GK: 3236 [cf. 2928]. Talmon, "[perhaps] *brightness*":– Talmon [5]

2930 טָמֵא **ṭāmē'**, v. GK: 3237 & 3239 [→ 2931, 2932, 2933?]. [Q] to be unclean, defiled; [N] to be made unclean, become defiled, impure; [P] to make unclean, defile, desecrate; [Pu] to become defiled; [Ht] to make oneself unclean, defiled; [Hotpaal] to be defiled; this can mean to be ceremonially impure or to be immoral in action:– unclean [61], defiled [45], defile [24], polluted [12], pronounce unclean [10], pollute [2], pronounce utterly unclean (+2930) [2], defile yourselves [1], defileth [1], made unclean [1], make unclean [1], take uncleanness [1]

2931 טָמֵא **ṭāmē'**, a. GK: 3238 [→ 2930]. unclean, defiled, impure; this can mean to be ceremonial impurity or active immorality:– unclean [80], defiled [5], infamous (+8034+1886.1) [1], polluted [1], pollution [1]

2932 טֻמְאָה **ṭum'â**, n.f. GK: 3240 [→ 2930]. uncleanness, impurity, filthiness; this can mean ceremonial impurity or a physical impurity on the body or in an object:– uncleanness [25], filthiness [7], unclean [3], uncleannesses [1]

2933 טָמָה **ṭāmâ**, v. GK: 3241 [→ 2930?]. [N] to be considered stupid; some sources: to be regarded as unclean:– make unclean [1], reputed vile [1]

2934 טָמַן **ṭāman**, v. GK: 3243 [→ 4301]. [Q] to hide; bury; [Qp] to be hidden; [N] to hide oneself; [H] to keep hidden:– hid [17], hide [5], hideth [2], hidden [1], hiding [1], laid privily [1], laid [1], laying privily [1], privily laid [1], secret [1]

2935 טֶנֶא **ṭene'**, n.m. GK: 3244. basket:– basket [4]

2936 טָנַף **ṭānap**, v. GK: 3245. [P] to soil, make dirty:– defile [1]

2937 טָעָה **ṭā'â**, v. GK: 3246 [cf. 8582]. [H] to lead astray:– seduced [1]

2938 טָעַם **ṭā'am**, v. GK: 3247 [→ 2940, 4303; cf. 2939]. [Q] to taste; to see, discover by experience:– taste [5], did but taste (+2938) [2], tasted [2], perceiveth [1], tasteth [1]

Heb

2939 טְעֵם ***ṭᵉʿēm*** (Aram.), v. GK: 10301 [→ 2941; cf. 2938]. [Pa] to eat:– make to eat [2], fed [1]

2940 טַעַם ***ṭaʿam***, n.m. GK: 3248 [→ 2938; cf. 2941]. taste; discretion; discernment; decree, judgment; "to turn from discernment" means "to pretend to be insane" (1Sa 21:13):– taste [5], behaviour [2], advice [1], decree [1], discretion [1], judgment [1], reason [1], understanding [1]

2941 טַעַם ***ṭaʿam*** (Aram.), n.m. GK: 10302 [→ 2939, 2942; cf. 2940]. same as 2942: order, decree, command:– commandment [2], commanded [1], matter [1]

2942 טְעֵם ***ṭᵉʿēm*** (Aram.), n.m. GK: 10302 [→ 2941]. same as 2941: order, decree, command; tact, good sense; report, advice; with 2562 "under the command of wine" means "to be intoxicated"; with 1169, "lord of the decree" is translated "commanding officer":– decree [13], chancellor (+1169) [3], commanded (+7761) [3], commandment [2], accounts [1], regarded (+7761) [1], tasted [1], wisdom [1]

2943 טָעַן ***ṭāʿan***, v. GK: 3250. [Q] to load:– lade [1]

2944 טָעַן ***ṭāʿan***, v. GK: 3249. [Pu] to be pierced:– thrust through [1]

2945 טַף ***ṭap***, n.m. GK: 3251 & 3252 [→ 2952]. (little) children, women and children, those (as a class) not able or barely able to march; drops:– little ones [29], children [9], little children [3], families [i]

2946 טָפַח ***ṭāpaḥ***, v.den. GK: 3253 & 3254 [→ 2947, 2948, 2949, 4304]. [P] to spread out; to care for; some sources: to bear healthy children:– spanned [1], swaddled [1]

2947 טֶפַח ***ṭepaḥ*** or טְפָחָה ***ṭapḥâ***, n.[m.]. GK: 3255 & 3257 & 3258 [→ 2946, 2948]. span, handbreadth (the width of the hand at the base of the four fingers, about three inches (8 cm); a figure of a short unit of time, a few years; eaves:– handbreadth [3], coping [1]

2948 טֹפַח ***ṭōpaḥ***, n.m. GK: 3256 [→ 2947; cf. 2946]. handbreadth, span of the hand:– hand breadth [2], handbreadth [2], hand broad [1]

2949 טִפֻּחִים ***ṭippuḥîm***, n.[m.]pl.abst. GK: 3259 [→ 2946]. caring for (children):– span long [1]

2950 טָפַל ***ṭāpal***, v. GK: 3260 [cf. 8602]. [Q] to smear, cover:– forged [1], forgers [1], sewest up [1]

2951 טִפְסָר ***ṭipsār***, n.[m.]. GK: 3261. official, clerk:– captains [1], captain [1]

2952 טָפַף ***ṭāpap***, v. GK: 3262 [→ 2945]. [Q] to take little steps, trip along:– mincing [1]

2953 טְפַר ***ṭᵉpar*** (Aram.), n.m. GK: 10303 [cf. 6856]. finger and toe nails (of a human); claws (of an animal):– nails [2]

2954 טָפַשׁ ***ṭāpaš***, v. GK: 3263. [Q] to be unfeeling, insensible:– fat [1]

2955 טָפַת ***ṭāpat***, n.pr.f. GK: 3264. Taphath, "[poss.] *little child*":– Taphath [1]

2956 טָרַד ***ṭārad***, v. GK: 3265 [→ 4308; cf. 2957]. [Q] to constantly drip:– continual dropping (+1812) [1], continual [1]

2957 טְרַד ***ṭᵉrad*** (Aram.), v. GK: 10304 [cf. 2956]. [P] to drive away (as noun) one driven away; [Peil] to be driven away:– driven [2], drive [2]

2958 טְרוֹם ***ṭᵉrôm***, adv.temp. GK: 3266 [→ 2961, 2962]. before:–

2959 טָרַח ***ṭāraḥ***, v. GK: 3267 [→ 2960]. [H] to load down, burden with:– wearieth [1]

2960 טֹרַח ***ṭōraḥ***, n.m. GK: 3268 [→ 2959]. burden, problem, load:– cumbrance [1], trouble [1]

2961 טָרִי ***ṭārî***, a. GK: 3269 [→ 2958]. fresh (bone); open, moist (sore):– new [1], putrifying [1]

2962 טֶרֶם ***ṭerem***, adv.temp. & c. GK: 3270 [→ 2958]. a marker of time: before; negative: not, not yet:– before (+871.1) [35], before [11], not yet [3], before (+3808+871.1) [2], ere [2], but ere (+871.1) [1], ere (+871.1) [1], neither yet (+2050.1) [1]

2963 טָרַף ***ṭārap***, v. GK: 3271 [→ 2964, 2965, 2966]. [Q] to tear, mangle; [Qp, N, Pu] to be torn (to pieces); [H] to provide (to enjoy):– torn in pieces (+2963) [4], ravening [3], teareth [3], tear [3], catch [2], tear in pieces [2], without doubt rent in pieces (+2963) [2], feed [1], prey [1], ravin [1], teareth in pieces [1], torn in pieces [1], torn [1]

2964 טֶרֶף ***ṭerep***, n.m. GK: 3272 [→ 2963]. prey (food for wild animals):– prey [18], meat [3], leaves [1], spoil [1]

2965 טָרָף ***ṭārāp***, a. GK: 3273 [→ 2963]. fresh-picked (leaf or vegetation):– pluckt off [1]

2966 טְרֵפָה ***ṭᵉrēpâ***, n.f. GK: 3274 [→ 2963]. animal torn by wild beasts:– torn [4], that which was torn [2], ravin [1], that which is torn [1], torn in pieces [1]

2967 טַרְפְּלָי ***ṭarpᵉlāy*** (Aram.), n.pr.g. GK: 10305. from Tripolis (Tarpel):– Tarpelites [1]

2967.1 ־ִי ***-î***, p.s.com.suf. GK: 3276 [→ 447, 5105.1, 5204.1]. I, me, my:– my [3551], me [1946], mine [494], I [241], my (+3807.1) [64], mine (+3807.1) [50], mine own [30], myself [21], our [7], us [7], me (+5315) [3], mine own (+3807.1) [3], the^s [3], Ammi (+5971) [1], for my sake [1], me (+6440) [1], mine (+5978) [1], mine (+8478) [1], my (+871.1) [1], myself (+1320) [1], myself (+3820) [1], myself (+5315) [1], myself (+905) [1], we [1]

2967.2 ־ִי ***-î*** (Aram.), p.suf.1.com.s. GK: 10307 [→ 5204.2; cf. 2967.1]. I, me, my:– my [32], me [22], I [10], mine [5]

2968 יָאַב ***yāʾab***, v. GK: 3277 [→ 88?, 3053?; cf. 14?, 8373?]. [Q] to long for:– longed [1]

2969 יָאָה ***yāʾâ***, v. GK: 3278. [Q] to be fitting, be proper:– appertain [1]

יְאוֹר ***yᵉʾōr***. See 2975.

2970 יַאֲזַנְיָה ***yaʾᵃzanyâ*** or יַאֲזַנְיָהוּ ***yaʾᵃzanyāhû***, n.pr.m. GK: 3279 & 3280. Jaazaniah, "*Yahweh listens*":– Jaazaniah [4]

2971 יָאִיר ***yāʾîr***, n.pr.m. GK: 3281 [→ 2334, 2972]. Jair, "*he gives light*":– Jair [9]

2972 יָאִרִי ***yāʾîrî***, a.g. GK: 3285 [→ 2971]. Jairite, "*of Jair*":– Jairite [1]

2973 יָאַל ***yāʾal***, v. GK: 3282 [cf. 191]. [N] to become foolish, act foolish:– done foolishly [1], dote [1], foolish [1], fools [1]

2974 יָאַל ***yāʾal***, v. GK: 3283 [cf. 193, 4136]. [H] to begin; to determine; be intent upon; to agree to; to be content, be pleased; to be bold:– content [7], please [3], would [3], taken upon [2], assayed [1], began [1], pleased [1], willingly [1]

2975 יְאֹר ***yᵉʾōr***, n.m. GK: 3284. river, stream, the Nile river; likely the Tigris river in Daniel:– river [35], rivers [15], flood [6], brooks [5], river's [3], streams [1]

2976 יָאַשׁ ***yāʾaš***, v. GK: 3286. [N] to be despairing of, be without hope, give up; [P] to let despair:– no hope [3], cause to despair [1], despair [1], desperate [1]

2977 יֹאשִׁיָּה ***yōʾšiyyâ*** or יֹאשִׁיָּהוּ ***yōʾšiyyāhû***, n.pr.m. GK: 3287 & 3288 [cf. 3068]. Josiah, "*let or may Yahweh give*":– Josiah [53]

2978 יִאתוֹן ***yiʾtôn*** or אִיתוֹן ***ʾîtôn***, n.m. GK: 3289 & 415 [→ 857]. entrance:– entrance [1]

2979 יְאָתְרַי ***yᵉʾāᵗᵉray***, n.pr.m. GK: 3290. Jeatherai:– Jeaterai [1]

2980 יָבַב ***yābab***, v. GK: 3291 [→ 3103]. [P] to cry out, lament:– cried [1]

2981 יְבוּל ***yᵉbûl***, n.m. GK: 3292 [→ 2986]. crops, produce, harvest:– increase [10], fruit [3]

2982 יְבוּס ***yᵉbûs***, n.pr.loc. GK: 3293 [→ 2983]. Jebus:– Jebus [4]

2983 יְבוּסִי ***yᵉbûsî***, a.g. GK: 3294 [→ 2982]. Jebusite, "*of Jebus*":– Jebusites [25], Jebusite [14], Jebusi [2]

2984 יִבְחָר ***yibḥār***, n.pr.m. GK: 3295 [→ 977]. Ibhar, "*he chooses*":– Ibhar [3]

2985 יָבִין ***yābîn***, n.pr.m. GK: 3296 [→ 995]. Jabin, "*perceptive*":– Jabin [7], Jabin's [1]

יָבֵשׁ ***yābēš***. See 3003.

2986 יָבַל ***yābal***, v. GK: 3297 [→ 58, 179, 2981, 2988, 2989, 3105; cf. 2987]. [H] to bring, take (a gift); [Ho] to be brought, be led, be carried off:– brought [6], bring [5], carried [3], brought forth [1], carry [1], lead [1], led forth [1]

2987 יְבַל ***yᵉbal*** (Aram.), v. GK: 10308 [cf. 2986]. [H] to bring, take:– brought [2], carry [1]

יֹבֵל ***yōbēl***. See 3104.

2988 יָבָל ***yābāl***, n.[m.]. GK: 3298 [→ 2986]. stream, watercourse:– courses [1], streams [1]

2989 יָבָל ***yābāl***, n.pr.m. GK: 3299 [→ 2986]. Jabal:– Jabal [1]

יֹבֵל ***yōbēl***. See 3104.

2990 יַבֶּלֶת ***yabbelet***, a. GK: 3301 [→ 3104]. wart; some sources: running sore:– having a wen [1]

2991 יִבְלְעָם ***yiblᵉʿām***, n.pr.loc. GK: 3300 [→ 1104?]. Ibleam:– Ibleam [3]

2992 יָבַם ***yābam***, v.den. GK: 3302 [→ 2993]. [P] to fulfill the procreational duty of the brother-in-law:– marry [1], perform the duty of a husband's brother [1], perform the duty of husband's brother [1]

2993 יָבָם ***yābām***, n.m. GK: 3303 [→ 2992, 2994]. husband's brother:– husband's brother [2]

2994 יְבָמָה ***yᵉbāmâ***, n.f. GK: 3304 [→ 2993]. brother's widow; sister-in-law, husband's brother's widow:– brother's wife [3], sister in law [2]

2995 יַבְנְאֵל ***yabnᵉʾēl***, n.pr.loc. GK: 3305 [→ 1129+410; cf. 2996]. Jabneel, "*God [El] will build*":– Jabneel [2]

2996 יַבְנֵה ***yabnēh***, n.pr.loc. GK: 3306 [cf. 2995]. Jabneh:– Jabneh [1]

2997 יִבְנְיָה ***yibnᵉyâ***, n.pr.m. GK: 3307 [→ 1129+3068]. Ibneiah, "*Yahweh built*":– Ibneiah [1]

2998 יִבְנִיָּה ***yibniyyâ***, n.pr.m. GK: 3308 [→ 1129+3068]. Ibnijah, "*Yahweh built*":– Ibnijah [1]

2999 יַבֹּק ***yabbōq***, n.pr.loc. GK: 3309 [→ 1238? *or* 79?]. Jabbok, "*flowing* or *wrestling*":– Jabbok [7]

3000 יְבֶרֶכְיָהוּ ***y^{e}berekyāhû***, n.pr.m. GK: 3310 [→ 1288+3068]. Jeberekiah, "*Yahweh blesses*":– Jeberechiah [1]

3001 יָבֵשׁ ***yābēš***, v. GK: 3312 [→ 3002, 3003, 3004, 3006]. [Q] to dry up, be dry, be withered, be shriveled up; [P] to make wither, dry up; [H] to make wither, dry up:– dried up [18], withered [9], wither [7], dry up [6], withereth [5], dry [3], clean dried up (+3001) [2], dried [2], utterly wither (+3001) [2], withered away [2], ashamed [1], confounded [1], driedst up [1], drieth up [1], drieth [1], make dry [1], maketh dry [1]

3002 יָבֵשׁ ***yābēš***, a.vbl. *or* v.ptcp. GK: 3313 [→ 3001]. dry, withered, by extension: a paralyzed person (whose limbs have a shriveled appearance):– dry [7], dried away [1], dried [1]

3003 יָבֵשׁ ***yābēš***, n.pr.m. & loc. GK: 3314 & 3315 & 3316 [→ 3001+1568]. Jabesh, "*dry*":– Jabesh-gilead [12], Jabesh [12]

3004 יַבָּשָׁה ***yabbāšâ***, n.f. GK: 3317 [→ 3001; cf. 3007]. dry ground, dry land (in contrast to bodies of water):– dry [13], land [1]

3005 יִבְשָׂם ***yibśām***, n.pr.m. GK: 3311 [→ 1313]. Ibsam, "*fragrance*":– Jibsam [1]

3006 יַבֶּשֶׁת ***yabbešet***, n.f. GK: 3318 [→ 3001]. dry ground, dry land:– dry [2]

3007 יַבֶּשָׁה ***yabb^{e}šâ*** (Aram.), n.f. GK: 10309 [cf. 3004]. earth; dry land (in contrast to the sea):– earth [1]

3008 יִגְאָל ***yig'āl***, n.pr.m. GK: 3319 [→ 1350]. Igal, "*he redeems*":– Igal [2], Igeal [1]

3009 יָגַב ***yāgab***, v. GK: 3320 [→ 3010]. [Q] to work a field, do farm work:– husbandmen [2]

3010 יָגֵב ***yāgēb***, n.m. GK: 3321 [→ 3009]. field:– fields [1]

3011 יָגְבְּהָה ***yogb^{e}hâ***, n.pr.loc. GK: 3322 [→ 1361]. Jogbehah, "*height*":– Jogbehah [2]

3012 יִגְדַּלְיָהוּ ***yigdalyāhû***, n.pr.m. GK: 3323 [→ 1431+3068]. Igdaliah, "*Yahweh is great*":– Igdaliah [1]

3013 יָגָה ***yāgâ***, v. GK: 3324 [→ 3015, 8424; cf. 3014]. [N] to be grieved; [P] to bring grief; [H] to torment, bring grief:– afflicted [3], afflict [1], cause grief [1], grieve [1], sorrowful [1], vex [1]

3014 יָגָה ***yāgâ***, v. GK: 3325 [cf. 1898, 3013]. [H] to remove:– removed [1]

3015 יָגוֹן ***yāgôn***, n.[m.]. GK: 3326 [→ 3013]. sorrow, anguish, grief:– sorrow [12], grief [2]

3016 יָגוֹר ***yāgôr***, a.vbl. GK: 3328 [→ 3025]. fearing, filled with fear:– afraid [1], fearest [1]

3017 יָגוּר ***yāgûr***, n.pr.loc. GK: 3327 [cf. 1485]. Jagur:– Jagur [1]

3018 יְגִיעַ ***y^{e}gîa'***, n.m. GK: 3330 [→ 3021]. labor, heavy work; the result of labor: produce, gain:– labour [12], labours [3], work [1]

3019 יָגִיעַ ***yāgîa'***, a. GK: 3329 [→ 3021]. weary, exhausted:– weary (+3581) [1]

3020 יָגְלִי ***yoglî***, n.pr.m. GK: 3332. Jogli, "[perhaps] *may God reveal*":– Jogli [1]

3021 יָגַע ***yāga'***, v. GK: 3333 [→ 3019, 3018, 3024, 3022, 3023]. [Q] to labor, toil, be weary; [P] to make weary; [H] to make weary:– labour [7], weary [7], wearied [5], laboured [4], fainted [1], make to labour [1], wearieth [1]

3022 יָגָע ***yāgā'***, n.[m.]. GK: 3334 [→ 3021]. what is toiled for, the produce of labor:– that which laboured for [1]

3023 יָגֵעַ ***yāgēa'***, a. GK: 3335 [→ 3021]. worn out, weary, wearisome:– weary [2], full of labour [1]

3024 יְגִיעָה ***y^{e}gî'â***, n.f. GK: 3331 [→ 3021]. weariness:– weariness [1]

3025 יָגֹר ***yāgōr***, v. GK: 3336 [→ 3016; cf. 1481]. [Q] to fear, dread:– afraid [4], fear [1]

3026 יְגַר שָׂהֲדוּתָא ***y^{e}gar śāh^{a}dûtā'***, n.[m.] & n.m. GK: 3337. Jegar Sahadutha, the Aramaic name of a stone monument, "witness heap":– Jegar-sahadutha [1]

3027 יָד ***yād***, n.f. & m. GK: 3338 [cf. 3028]. hand, by extension: arm, finger; fig. of control, power, strength, direction, care:– hand [1087], hands [271], by (+871.1) [42], next unto (+5921) [13], power [11], with (+871.1) [10], place [8], tenons [6], coast [5], consecrate (+4390) [5], consecrated (+853+4390) [5], consecrate (+853+4390) [4], custody [4], means [4], next to (+5921) [4], parts [4], side [4], stays [4], beside (+5921) [3], large (+7342) [3], next (+5921) [3], able to get (+5381) [2], armholes (+679) [2], as able [2], axletrees [2], because of (+871.1) [2], by (+5921) [2], consecrated (+4390) [2], dominion [2], force [2], from (+4480) [2], ledges [2], lefthanded (+334+3225) [2], ministry [2], near (+5921) [2], of (+4480) [2], order [2], paw [2], service [2], state [2], thumbs (+931) [2], times [2], to (+871.1) [2], wide (+7342) [2], ability (+5381) [1], able (+1767+4672) [1], able (+1767+5381+3509.1) [1], able (+4979) [1], able (+5381) [1], able to bring (+1767+4672) [1], able to bring (+5381) [1], about (+3807.1) [1], aided (+853+2388) [1], as ordained by (+5921) [1], at (+3807.1) [1], beside (+3807.1) [1], borders [1], border [1], bounty [1], broad (+7342) [1], brokenhanded (+7667) [1], by side [1], by [1], can get (+5381) [1], charge [1], coasts [1], creditor (+1167+4874) [1], dominion (+4475) [1], drew with full strength (+4390+871.1) [1], exaction of debt (+4853) [1], fallen in decay (+4131) [1], fellowship (+8667) [1], for (+871.1) [1], get (+5381) [1], give (+5414+871.1) [1], hand is able to get (+5381) [1], handed [1], handstaves (+4731) [1], handywork (+4639) [1], he (+2050.2) [1], help (+2388+871.1) [1], in (+871.1) [1], labour [1], large enough (+7342) [1], near (+413) [1], occasion serve (+4672) [1], occupied (+5503) [1], of (+871.1) [1], ordained by (+5921) [1], ordinance [1], own [1], places [1], power (+410) [1], power (+871.1) [1], presumptuously (+7311+871.1) [1], sore [1], stroke [1], sware (+5375) [1], swear (+5375) [1], sworn (+3678+5921) [1], sworn [1], thee (+3509.2) [1], themselves [1], thou (+3509.2) [1], through (+871.1) [1], throwing [1], under (+871.1) [1], wait on [1], wax rich (+5381) [1], way side (+4570) [1], wayside (+1870) [1], where [1], work [1], yield (+5414) [1]

3028 יַד ***yad*** (Aram.), n.f. GK: 10311 [cf. 3027]. hand (of a human), paw (of an animal); fig., power, control, action:– hand [12], hands [4], power [1]

3029 יְדָה ***y^{e}dâ*** (Aram.), v. GK: 10312 [cf. 3034]. [H] to give thanks, confess praise:– gave thanks [1], thank [1]

3030 יִדְאֲלָה ***yid^{a}lâ***, n.pr.loc. GK: 3339. Idalah:– Idalah [1]

3031 יִדְבָּשׁ ***yidbāš***, n.pr.m. GK: 3340 [→ 1706]. Idbash, "*honey*":– Idbash [1]

3032 יָדַד ***yādad***, v. GK: 3341 [cf. 3034]. [Q] to cast (lots for decision making):– cast [3]

3033 יְדִדוּת ***y^{e}didût***, n.f. GK: 3342 [→ 3039]. loved one, beloved:– dearly beloved [1]

3034 יָדָה ***yādâ***, v. GK: 3343 & 3344 [→ 1935, 1937, 1938, 1939, 1960, 8426; cf. 3032; cf. 3029]. [Q] to shoot (a bow); [P] to throw (down); [H] to express praise, give thanks, extol, make a public confession, make an admission; to praise is to speak of the excellence of someone or something; to give thanks has a focus on the gratitude of the speaker:– praise [52], give thanks [31], confess [11], thank [4], confessed [3], thanksgiving [2], cast out [1], cast [1], confesseth [1], confessing [1], giving thanks [1], made confession [1], making confession [1], praised [1], shoot [1], thankful [1], thanking [1]

3035 יִדּוֹ ***yiddô*** or יַדַּי ***yadday***, n.pr.m. GK: 3345 & 3346 & 3350 [→ 3039?]. Iddo, Jaddai, "[prob.] *Yahweh has adorned*":– Iddo [1], Jadau [1]

3036 יָדוֹן ***yādôn***, n.pr.m. GK: 3347. Jadon, "*frail one* or *Yahweh rules*":– Jadon [1]

3037 יַדּוּעַ ***yaddûa'***, n.pr.m. GK: 3348 [→ 3045]. Jaddua, "*one known*":– Jaddua [3]

3038 יְדוּתוּן ***y^{e}dûtûn*** or יְדִיתוּן ***y^{e}dîtûn***, n.pr.m. GK: 3349 & 3357. Jeduthun:– Jeduthun [17]

3039 יָדִיד ***yādîd***, a. GK: 3351 & 3353 [→ 3033, 3035?, 3040, 3041]. lovely, beloved, love song (referring to a wedding song):– beloved [5], well-beloved [2], amiable [1], loves [1]

3040 יְדִידָה ***y^{e}dîdâ***, n.pr.f. GK: 3352 [→ 3039]. Jedidah, "*beloved; lovely, beloved*":– Jedidah [1]

3041 יְדִידְיָה ***y^{e}dîd^{e}yāh***, n.pr.m. GK: 3354 [→ 3039+3068]. Jedidiah, "*beloved of Yahweh*":– Jedidiah [1]

3042 יְדָיָה ***y^{e}dāyâ***, n.pr.m. GK: 3355. Jedaiah, "*Yahweh has favored* or *Yahweh knows*":– Jedaiah [2]

3043 יְדִיעֲאֵל ***y^{e}dî^a'ēl***, n.pr.m. GK: 3356 [→ 3045+410]. Jediael, "*known of God [El]*":– Jediael [6]

3044 יִדְלָף ***yidlāp***, n.pr.m. GK: 3358 [→ 1811]. Jidlaph, "*he weeps*":– Jidlaph [1]

3045 יָדַע ***yāda'***, v. GK: 3359 [→ 1843, 1844, 1847, 3037, 3049, 4093, 4129, 4130; cf. 3046 (also used with compound proper names)]. [Q] to know, recognize, understand; to have sexual relations; [Qp] to be respected; [N] to be known, make oneself known; [P] to cause to know; [Pu] to be well known; [H] to show, teach, make known; [Ho] to be made aware; [Ht] to make oneself known; this can range in meaning from the mere acquisition and understanding of information to intimacy in relationship, including sexual relations:– know [404], knew [83], known [80], knowest [66], knoweth [58], make known [14], shew [12], perceived [11], knowledge [10], made known [8], tell [8], wist [7], acquaintance [6], certainly know (+3045) [6], perceive [6], wot [6], acknowledge [5], cause to know [5], knewest [5], make know [5], shewed [5], teach [5], consider [4], cunning [4], know certainly (+3045) [4], know for certain (+3045) [4], sure [4], understood [4], declared [3], declare [3], ignorant (+3808) [3], learned (+5612) [3], make to know [3], mark [3], skill [3], taught [3], understand [3], aware [2], certainly knoweth (+3045) [2], come to knowledge [2], considereth [2], could [2], diligent to know (+3045) [2], discern [2], endued [2], feel [2], knew certainly (+3045) [2], know assuredly (+3045) [2], know for a certain (+3045) [2], know for a certainty (+3045) [2], know of a surety (+3045) [2], knowing [2], skilful [2], takest knowledge [2], wit [2], acknowledged [1], acquainted with [1], advise [1], answer [1], appointed [1], can skill [1], cannot (+3808) [1], cause to discern [1], caused to know [1], come to understanding (+998) [1], comprehend [1], discerneth [1], discovered [1], familiar friends [1], famous [1], felt [1], given knowledge [1], had knowledge [1], had respect unto [1], had understanding (+998) [1], hast [1], hath knowledge (+1847) [1], hath [1], have knowledge (+1847) [1], have knowledge [1], have [1], having knowledge [1], instructed [1], kinsfolks [1], know well [1], madest known [1], make to be known [1], making known [1], perceivest [1], privy [1], prognosticators [1], regardeth [1], take knowledge [1], unawares (+3808) [1], understand (+995) [1], will [1], wotteth [1]

3046 יְדַע ***y^{e}da'*** (Aram.), v. GK: 10313 [→ 4486; cf. 3045]. [P] to know, understand, acknowledge; [Pp] to be known; [H] to make known, tell, inform:– know [13], make known [12], known [5], made known [5], certify [3], knew [2], maketh known [2], certified [1], knewest [1], knoweth [1], made know [1], teach [1]

3047 יָדָע ***yādā'***, n.pr.m. GK: 3360. Jada, "*shrewd one; [God] has cared*":– Jada [2]

3048 יְדַעְיָה ***y^{e}da'yâ***, n.pr.m. GK: 3361 [→ 3045+3068]. Jedaiah, "*Yahweh has favored* or *Yahweh knows*":– Jedaiah [11]

3049 יִדְּעֹנִי ***yidd^{e}'ōnî***, n.m. GK: 3362 [→ 3045]. spiritist, soothsayer:– wizards [9], wizard [2]

3050 יָהּ ***yāh***, n.pr.m. GK: 3363 [→ 3068]. LORD (Yahweh):– the LORD* [45], LORD* [3], Jah [1]

3051 יָהַב ***yāhab***, v. GK: 2035 & 3364 [cf. 3052]. [Q] to give; (interj.) come!, give!, put!, ascribe!:– give [24], go to [4], bring [2], ascribe [1], come on [1], set [1], take [1]

3052 יְהַב ***y^{e}hab*** (Aram.), v. GK: 10314 [cf. 5415; cf. 3051]. [P] to give; [Pp] to be given; [Htpe] to be given as payment; be entrusted:– given [16], gave [4], give [2], delivered [1], giveth [1], laid [1], paid [1], were [1], yielded [1]

3053 יְהָב ***y^{e}hāb***, n.[m.]. GK: 3365 [→ 2968?]. care, burden:– burden [1]

3054 יָהַד ***yāhad***, v.den. GK: 3366 [→ 3064; cf. 3063]. [Ht] to become a Jew, this can mean to join the Jewish faith or simply to act like a Jew:– became Jews [1]

3055 יְהוּד ***y^{e}hûd***, n.pr.loc. GK: 3372. Jehud, "*declare*":– Jehud [1]

3056 יָהְדַי ***yāhday***, n.pr.m. GK: 3367. Jahdai, "*Yahweh lead*":– Jahdai [1]

3057 יְהֻדִיָּה ***y^{e}hudiyyâ***, a.g. GK: 3368 [→ 3063]. Jewish, Judean:– Jehudijah [1]

3058 יֵהוּא ***yēhû'***, n.pr.m. GK: 3369 [→ 3068+1931]. Jehu, "*Yahweh is he*":– Jehu [58]

3059 יְהוֹאָחָז ***y^{e}hô'āḥāz***, n.pr.m. GK: 3370 [→ 3068+270]. Jehoahaz, "*Yahweh holds*":– Jehoahaz [20]

3060 יְהוֹאָשׁ ***y^{e}hô'āš***, n.pr.m. GK: 3371 [→ 3068+376]. Joash; Jehoash, "*Yahweh bestows; man of Yahweh*":– Jehoash [17]

3061 יְהוּד ***y^{e}hûd*** (Aram.), n.pr.loc. GK: 10315 [→ 3062; cf. 3063]. Judah, "*praised*":– Judah [5], Jewry [1], Judea [1]

3062 יְהוּדָי ***y^{e}hûdāy*** (Aram.), n.g. GK: 10316 [→ 3061; cf. 3064]. Jew:– Jews [10]

3063 יְהוּדָה ***y^{e}hûdâ***, n.pr.m. & loc. GK: 3373 [→ 3054, 3057, 3064, 3065, 3066, 3067; cf. 3061]. Judah, of Judah, Judean, "*praised*":– Judah [804], Beth-lehem-judah (+1035) [10], Judah's [4]

3064 יְהוּדִי ***y^{e}hûdî***, a.g. GK: 3374 [→ 3054, 3065, 3067; cf. 3063; cf. 3062]. (person) of Judah, Judean, Jew, Jewish, "*of Judah*":– Jews [63], Jew [10], Jews' [2], Judah [1]

3065 יְהוּדִי ***y^{e}hûdî***, n.pr.m. GK: 3375 [→ 3064; cf. 3063]. Jehudi, Yaudi, "*of Judah*":– Jehudi [4]

3066 יְהוּדִית ***y^{e}hûdît***, a.g.f. (used as adv.). GK: 3376 [→ 3063]. in Hebrew (language), in the language of Judah:– in the Jews' language [5], in the Jews' speech [1]

3067 יְהוּדִית ***y^{e}hûdît***, n.pr.f. GK: 3377 [→ 3064; cf. 3063]. Judith, "*Jewess* or *Judahite*":– Judith [1]

3068 יהוה ***yhwh*** or יֱהוִה ***y^{e}hwih***, n.pr.m. GK: 3378 [→ 3050, 3069 (also used with compound proper names)]. LORD (Yahweh), the proper name of the one true God; knowledge and use of the name implies personal or covenant relationship; the name pictures God as the one who exists and/or causes existence:– the LORD* [6043], LORD* [365], GOD* [309], the LORD'S* [79], the LORD'S* (+3807.1) [28], Jehovah [4], LORD'S* [1], he[s] [1]

3069 יֱהוִה ***y^{e}hwih***, n.pr.m. GK: 3378 [→ 3068]. same as 3068: LORD (Yahweh), with vowels points used in combination with 136:–

3070 יהוה יִרְאֶה ***yhwh yir'eh***, n.pr.loc. GK: 3378 + 8011 [→ 3068+7200]. Yahweh yireh, "The LORD (Yahweh) will see" (3068 + 7200):– Jehovah-jireh [1]

3071 יהוה נִסִּי ***yhwh nissî***, n.pr.loc. GK: 3378 + 5812 + 3276 [→ 3068+5251+2967.1]. "LORD (Yahweh) is my banner" (3068 + 5251 + 2967.1):– Jehovah-nissi [1]

3072 יהוה צִדְקֵנוּ ***yhwh ṣidqēnû***, n.pr.m. GK: 3378 + 7406 + 5646 [→ 3068+6664+5105.1]. "LORD (Yahweh) is our righteousness" (3068 + 6664 + 5105.1):–

3073 יהוה שָׁלוֹם ***yhwh šālôm***, n.pr.loc. GK: 3378 + 8934 [→ 3068+7965]. "LORD (Yahweh) is peace" (3068 + 7965):– Jehovah-shalom [1]

3074 יהוה שָׁמָּה ***yhwh šāmmâ***, n.pr.loc. GK: 3378 + 9004 + 2025 [→ 3068+8033+1886.5]. "LORD (Yahweh) is there" (3068 + 8033 + 1886.5):–

3075 יְהוֹזָבָד ***y^{e}hôzābād***, n.pr.m. GK: 3379 [→ 3068+2064]. Jehozabad, "*Yahweh endows*":– Jehozabad [4]

3076 יְהוֹחָנָן ***y^{e}hôḥānān***, n.pr.m. GK: 3380 [→ 3068+2603]. Jehohanan, "*Yahweh has been gracious*":– Jehohanan [6], Johanan [3]

3077 יְהוֹיָדָע ***y^{e}hôyādā'***, n.pr.m. GK: 3381 [→ 3068+3045]. Jehoiada, "*Yahweh has known*":– Jehoiada [51]

3078 יְהוֹיָכִין ***y^{e}hôyākîn***, n.pr.m. GK: 3382 [→ 3204, 3659]. Jehoiachin, "*Yahweh supports*":– Jehoiachin [10]

3079 יְהוֹיָקִים ***y^{e}hôyāqîm***, n.pr.m. GK: 3383 [→ 3068+6965]. Jehoiakim, "*Yahweh lifts up, establishes*":– Jehoiakim [37]

3080 יְהוֹיָרִיב ***y^{e}hôyārîb***, n.pr.m. GK: 3384 [→ 3068+7378]. Jehoiarib, "*Yahweh argues [for me]*":– Jehoiarib [2]

3081 יְהוּכַל ***y^{e}hûkal***, n.pr.m. GK: 3385 [→ 3068+3201; cf. 3116]. Jehucal, "*Yahweh is capable*":– Jehucal [1]

3082 יְהוֹנָדָב ***y^{e}hônādāb***, n.pr.m. GK: 3386 [→ 3068+5068]. Jonadab; Jehonadab, "*Yahweh is generous, noble*":– Jonadab [5], Jehonadab [3]

3083 יְהוֹנָתָן ***y^{e}hônātān***, n.pr.m. GK: 3387 [→ 3068+5414]. Jonathan; Jehonathan, "*gift of Yahweh*":– Jonathan [76], Jehonathan [3], Jonathan's [3]

3084 יְהוֹסֵף ***y^{e}hôsēp***, n.pr.m. GK: 3388 [cf. 3254]. Joseph, "*he will add*":– Joseph [1]

3085 יְהוֹעַדָּה ***y^{e}hô'addâ***, n.pr.m. GK: 3389. Jehoaddah:– Jehoadah [2]

3086 יְהוֹעַדִּין ***y^{e}hô'addîn*** or יְהוֹעַדָּן ***y^{e}hô'addān***, n.pr.f. GK: 3390 & 3391. Jehoaddin, Jehoaddan, "[prob.] *Yahweh is delight*":– Jehoaddan [2]

3087 יְהוֹצָדָק ***y^{e}hôṣādāq***, n.pr.m. GK: 3392 [→ 3068+6663; cf. 3136]. Jehozadak, "*Yahweh is just*":– Josedech [6], Jehozadak [2]

3088 יְהוֹרָם ***y^{e}hôrām***, n.pr.m. GK: 3393 [→ 3068+7311]. Joram; Jehoram, "*Yahweh exalts*":– Jehoram [23], Joram [6]

3089 יְהוֹשֶׁבַע ***y^{e}hôšeba'***, n.pr.f. GK: 3394 [→ 3068; cf. 7652]. Jehosheba, "*Yahweh is an oath; Yahweh gives plenty, satisfies*":– Jehosheba [1]

3090 יְהוֹשַׁבְעַת ***y^{e}hôšab'at***, n.pr.f. GK: 3395 [→ 3068; cf. 7652]. Jehosheba, "*Yahweh is an oath; Yahweh gives plenty, satisfies*":– Jehoshabeath [2]

3091 יְהוֹשֻׁעַ ***y^{e}hôšua'***, n.pr.m. GK: 3397 [→ 3068+7768]. Joshua, "*Yahweh saves*":– Joshua [216], Jehoshua [2]

3092 יְהוֹשָׁפָט ***y^{e}hôšāpāṭ***, n.pr.m. & loc. GK: 3398 & 3399 [→ 3068+8199]. Jehoshaphat, "*Yahweh has judged*":– Jehoshaphat [84]

3093 יָהִיר ***yāhîr***, a. GK: 3400. arrogant, haughty:– haughty [1], proud [1]

3094 יְהַלֶּלְאֵל ***y^{e}hallel'ēl***, n.pr.[m.]. GK: 3401 [→ 3094+410]. Jehallelel, "*he shall praise God [El]; God [El] shines forth*":– Jehaleleel [1], Jehalelel [1]

3095 יַהֲלֹם ***yāh^{a}lōm***, n.[m.]. GK: 3402. emerald (precious stone, exact identification uncertain):– diamond [3]

3096 יַהַץ ***yahaṣ*** or יַהְצָה ***yahṣâ***, n.pr.loc. GK: 3403 & 3404. Jahaz, Jahzah, "[perhaps] *a trodden* or *open place*":– Jahaz [5], Jahazah [3], Jahzah [1]

3097 יוֹאָב ***yô'āb***, n.pr.m. GK: 3405 [→ 5854]. Joab, "*Yahweh is father*":– Joab [138], Joab's [8]

Heb

3098 יוֹאָח **yô'āḥ**, n.pr.m. GK: 3406 [→ 3068+251]. Joah, "*Yahweh is brother*":– Joah [11]

3099 יוֹאָחָז **yô'āḥāz**, n.pr.m. GK: 3407 [→ 3068+270]. Jehoahaz; Joahaz, "*Yahweh grips, holds*":– Jehoahaz [3], Joahaz [1]

3100 יוֹאֵל **yô'ēl**, n.pr.m. GK: 3408 [→ 3068+410]. Joel, "*Yahweh is God [El]*":– Joel [19]

3101 יוֹאָשׁ **yô'āš**, n.pr.m. GK: 3409 [→ 3068+376]. Joash; Jehoash:– Joash [47]

3102 יוֹב **yôb**, n.pr.m. GK: 3410. Job:– Job [1]

3103 יוֹבָב **yôbāb**, n.pr.m. GK: 3411 & 3412 [→ 2980]. Jobab, "*howl*":– Jobab [9]

3104 יוֹבֵל **yôbēl**, n.m. GK: 3413 [→ 2990]. ram's horn; (blowing of ram's horn) jubilee, (Year of) Jubilee:– jubile [21], rams' horns [4], ram's [1], trumpet [1]

3105 יוּבַל **yûbal**, n.[m.]. GK: 3414 [→ 2986]. stream, watercourse:– river [1]

3106 יוּבָל **yûbal**, n.pr.m. GK: 3415. Jubal:– Jubal [1]

3107 יוֹזָבָד **yôzābād**, n.pr.m. GK: 3416 [→ 3068+2064]. Jozabad, "*Yahweh bestowed*":– Jozabad [9], Josabad [1]

3108 יוֹזָכָר **yôzākār**, n.pr.m. GK: 3417. Jozakar:– Jozachar [1]

3109 יוֹחָא **yôḥā'**, n.pr.m. GK: 3418. Joha:– Joha [2]

3110 יוֹחָנָן **yôḥānān**, n.pr.m. GK: 3419 [→ 3068+2603]. Johanan, "*Yahweh is gracious*":– Johanan [24]

יוּטָּה **yûṭâ**. See 3194.

3111 יוֹיָדָע **yôyādā'**, n.pr.m. GK: 3421 [→ 3068+3045]. Joiada, "*Yahweh knows*":– Joiada [4], Jehoiada [1]

3112 יוֹיָכִין **yôyākîn**, n.pr.m. GK: 3422 [→ 3068+3559]. Jehoiachin, "*Yahweh supports*":– Jehoiachin's [1]

3113 יוֹיָקִים **yôyāqîm**, n.pr.m. GK: 3423 [→ 3068+6965]. Joiakim, "*Yahweh lifts up*":– Joiakim [4]

3114 יוֹיָרִיב **yôyārîb**, n.pr.m. GK: 3424 [→ 3068+7378]. Joiarib, "*Yahweh contends, pleads [your case]*":– Joiarib [5]

3115 יוֹכֶבֶד **yôkebed**, n.pr.f. GK: 3425 [→ 3068+3513]. Jochebed, "*Yahweh is glorious*":– Jochebed [2]

3116 יוּכַל **yûkal**, n.pr.m. GK: 3426 [cf. 3081]. Jehucal, "*Yahweh is capable*":– Jucal [1]

3117 יוֹם **yôm**, n.m. GK: 3427 & 3428 [→ 3119; cf. 3118]. day (24 hours), daytime (in contrast to night); by extension: an indefinite period of time, an era with a certain characteristic, such as "the day of the LORD" and the prophetic "on that day"; storm, wind; breath:– day [1217], days [666], time [54], to day (+1886.1) [50], chronicles (+1697) [33], for ever (+3605+1886.1) [15], days' [13], daily (+3117) [12], every day (+3117+871.1) [12], daily (+3605+1886.1) [11], daily (+3117+871.1) [10], when (+871.1) [10], continually (+3605+1886.1) [9], while [6], yearly (+3117+4480+1886.5) [6], year [6], age [5], as long as (+3605) [5], chronicles (+1697+1886.1) [5], daily (+1886.1+3807.1) [5], day's [5], two full years (+8141) [5], years [5], alway (+3605+1886.1) [4], two days [4], always (+3605+1886.1) [3], ever (+3605+1886.1) [3], life [3], season [3], space [3], times [3], whole [3], yearly [3], as long as (+834+3605+1886.1) [2], at all times (+3117+871.1) [2], at other times (+3117+871.1) [2], daily (+3117+2050.1) [2], daily [2], day by day (+1886.1+3807.1) [2], each day (+3117) [2], ever (+753) [2], every day (+3117+3605+2050.1) [2], every day's (+3117+871.1) [2], every sabbath (+3117+7676+7676+871.1+871.1+1886.1+1886.1) [2], every year's (+3117+3807.1) [2], for every day (+3117+871.1) [2], full month (+3391) [2], full year [2], in process of time (+3117+4480+3807.1) [2], live [2], now (+1886.1) [2], now [2], perpetually (+3605+1886.1) [2], prolong life (+3117+5921) [2], time (+4557) [2], upon day (+3117+871.1) [2], afternoon (+5186+1886.1) [1], ago [1], always (+3605) [1], any time [1], as long as (+3605+1886.1) [1], as long as (+871.1) [1], birthday (+3205) [1], continually (+3605) [1], continuance [1], daily (+259+3807.1) [1], daily (+3605+871.1) [1], day (+1886.1) [1], each[s] [1], elder (+2205+3807.1) [1], elder [1], everlasting (+5769) [1], evermore (+3605+1886.1) [1], for evermore (+3605+1886.1) [1], full weeks (+7620) [1], how long (+4100+8141+3509.1) [1], in process of time (+4480) [1], in process of time (+7235+1886.1) [1], in trouble (+7186) [1], livest[s] [1], midday (+4276+1886.1) [1], now a days (+1886.1) [1], old (+2416+8141) [1], old [1], outlived (+310+748) [1], overlived (+310+748) [1], presently (+1886.1+3509.1) [1], presently (+871.1+1886.1) [1], process of time (+7227+1886.1+1886.1) [1], remaineth [1], sabbath (+7676) [1], since (+4480) [1], since (+4480+1886.1+3807.1) [1], so long as (+3605+1886.1) [1], so long as (+4480) [1], then (+1886.1) [1], to morrow (+4279) [1], two[s] [1], weather [1], when [1], while (+1886.1+3509.1) [1], while (+4480) [1], whole age (+2416+8141) [1], whole weeks (+7620) [1], within a while after (+4480) [1], yesterday (+865) [1], young (+6810+3807.1) [1], younger (+6810) [1]

3118 יוֹם **yôm** (Aram.), n.m. GK: 10317 [cf. 3117]. a period of time which is indefinite in scope: it can range widely in meaning from "daytime" (in contrast to night); "day," a period of time approximately 24 hours; to longer periods (seasons or years). The title "Ancient of Days" is a title of God as old (eternal), emphasizing wisdom and power:– days [9], day [5], time [2]

3119 יוֹמָם **yômām**, subst. & adv. GK: 3429 [→ 3117]. day; in the daytime, by day:– day [24], by day [17], in daytime [4], daytime [3], daily [2], by day time [1]

3120 יָוָן **yāwān**, n.pr.g. GK: 3430 [→ 3125]. Javan; Greeks; Greece:– Javan [7], Grecia [3], Greece [1]

3121 יָוֵן **yāwēn**, n.[m.]. GK: 3431. mire, mud, sediment:– mire [1], miry [1]

3122 יוֹנָדָב **yônādāb**, n.pr.m. GK: 3432 [→ 3068+5068]. Jonadab, "*Yahweh is generous, noble*":– Jonadab [7]

3123 יוֹנָה **yônâ**, n.f. GK: 3433 [→ 1686, 3124; cf. 578, 2755]. dove; pigeon:– dove [14], pigeons [9], doves [5], doves' [2], pigeon [1]

3124 יוֹנָה **yônâ**, n.pr.m. GK: 3434 [→ 3123]. Jonah, "*dove*":– Jonah [19]

3125 יְוָנִי **y[e]wānî**, a.g. GK: 3436 [→ 3120]. Javanite = Greek:– Grecians (+1121) [1]

3126 יוֹנֵק **yônēq**, n.m. GK: 3437 [→ 3243]. infant, one nursing; tender shoot:– tender plant [1]

3127 יוֹנֶקֶת **yôneqet**, n.f. GK: 3438 [→ 3243]. new shoot, young shoot (of a plant):– branches [3], branch [1], tender branch [1], young twigs [1]

3128 יוֹנַת אֵלֶם רְחֹקִים **yônat 'ēlem r[e]ḥōqîm**, tt. GK: 3439 [→ 3123+352+7368]. Dove of the Distant Oaks:– Jonath-elem-rechokim [1]

3129 יוֹנָתָן **yônātān**, n.pr.m. GK: 3440 [→ 3068+5414]. Jonathan, "*gift of Yahweh*":– Jonathan [42]

3130 יוֹסֵף **yôsēp**, n.pr.m. GK: 3441 [→ 3254]. Joseph, "*he will add*":– Joseph [193], Joseph's [20]

3131 יוֹסִפְיָה **yôsipyâ**, n.pr.m. GK: 3442 [→ 3254+3068]. Josiphiah, "*Yahweh will add*":– Josiphiah [1]

3132 יוֹעֵאלָה **yô'ē'lâ**, n.pr.m. GK: 3443. Joelah, "*let him help*":– Joelah [1]

3133 יוֹעֵד **yô'ēd**, n.pr.m. GK: 3444 [→ 3068+5707]. Joed, "*Yahweh is witness*":– Joed [1]

3134 יוֹעֶזֶר **yô'ezer**, n.pr.m. GK: 3445 [→ 3068+5828]. Joezer, "*Yahweh is help*":– Joezer [1]

3135 יוֹעָשׁ **yô'āš**, n.pr.m. GK: 3447 [→ 3068+5789]. Joash, "*Yahweh has bestowed*":– Joash [2]

3136 יוֹצָדָק **yôṣādāq**, n.pr.m. GK: 3449 & 10318 [→ 3068+6663, 3087]. Jozadak, "*Yahweh is righteous*": note this name is Aramaic once in Ezra:– Jozadak [5]

3137 יוֹקִים **yôqîm**, n.pr.m. GK: 3451 [→ 3068?+6965]. Jokim, "*Yahweh lifts up*":– Jokim [1]

3138 יוֹרֶה **yôreh**, n.[m.]. GK: 3453 [→ 7301]. autumn (i.e., the time of the early rains, from the end of October to the beginning of December):– first rain [1], former [1]

3139 יוֹרָה **yôrâ**, n.pr.m. GK: 3454. Jorah, "*one born during harvest*":– Jorah [1]

3140 יוֹרַי **yôray**, n.pr.m. GK: 3455. Jorai, "[poss.] *Yahweh sees; whom Yahweh teaches*":– Jorai [1]

3141 יוֹרָם **yôrām**, n.pr.m. GK: 3456 [→ 3068+7311]. Joram; Jehoram, "*Yahweh is exalted*":– Joram [20]

3142 יוּשַׁב חֶסֶד **yûšab ḥesed**, n.pr.m. GK: 3457. Jushab-Hesed, "*loyal love will be returned*":– Jushabhesed [1]

3143 יוֹשִׁבְיָה **yôšibyâ**, n.pr.m. GK: 3458 [→ 3427+3068]. Joshibiah, "*Yahweh places*":– Josibiah [1]

3144 יוֹשָׁה **yôšâ**, n.pr.m. GK: 3459. Joshah, "*gift of Yahweh*":– Joshah [1]

3145 יוֹשַׁוְיָה **yôšawyâ**, n.pr.m. GK: 3460 [→ 3427+3068]. Joshaviah, "*Yahweh places*":– Joshaviah [1]

3146 יוֹשָׁפָט **yôšāpāṭ**, n.pr.m. GK: 3461 [→ 3068+8199]. Joshaphat, "*Yahweh judges*":– Jehoshaphat [1], Joshaphat [1]

3147 יוֹתָם **yôtām**, n.pr.m. GK: 3462 [→ 3068+8535]. Jotham, "*Yahweh will complete*":– Jotham [24]

3148 יוֹתֵר ***yôtēr***, n.m. *or* v.ptcp. GK: 3463 [→ 3498]. the rest; gain, advantage, profit; more than:– more [2], better [1], further [1], more than [1], moreover [1], over [1], profit [1]

3149 יְזוּאֵל ***yᵉzû'ēl*** or יְזִיאֵל ***yᵉzî'ēl***, n.pr.m. GK: 3464 & 3465 [cf. 3150?, 3151?]. Jeziel, Jezuel, *"may God sprinkle [in atonement]; God unites"*:– Jeziel [1]

3150 יִזִּיָּה ***yizziyyâ***, n.pr.m. GK: 3466 [cf. 3149?]. Izziah, *"may Yahweh sprinkle [in atonement]; Yahweh unites"*:– Jeziah [1]

3151 יָזִיז ***yāzîz***, n.pr.m. GK: 3467 [cf. 3149?]. Jaziz:– Jaziz [1]

3152 יִזְלִיאָה ***yizlî'â***, n.pr.m. GK: 3468. Izliah, *"long living, eternal; Yahweh delivers"*:– Jezliah [1]

3153 יְזַנְיָה ***yᵉzanyâ*** or יְזַנְיָהוּ ***yᵉzanyāhû***, n.pr.m. GK: 3470 & 3471. Jezaniah, Jaazaniah, *"Yahweh listens"*:– Jezaniah [2]

3154 יֶזַע ***yeza'***, n.[m.]. GK: 3472 [→ 2188]. perspiration, sweat:– sweat [1]

3155 יִזְרָח ***yizrāḥ***, a.g. GK: 3473. Izrahite:– Izrahite [1]

3156 יִזְרַחְיָה ***yizraḥyâ***, n.pr.m. GK: 3474 [→ 2224+3068]. Izrahiah; Jezrahiah, *"Yahweh shines* or *will arise"*:– Izrahiah [2], Jezrahiah [1]

3157 יִזְרְעֶאל ***yizrᵉ'e'l***, n.pr.m. & loc. GK: 3475 & 3476 [→ 3158, 3159]. Jezreel, *"God [El] will sow"*:– Jezreel [36]

3158 יִזְרְעֵאלִי ***yizrᵉ'ē'lî***, a.g. GK: 3477 [→ 3157, 3159]. Jezreelite, of Jezreel, *"of Jezreel"*:– Jezreelite [8]

3159 יִזְרְעֵאלִית ***yizrᵉ'ē'lît***, a.g. GK: 3477 [→ 3158]. f. of 3158: Jezreelite, of Jezreel, *"of Jezreel"*:– Jezreelitess [5]

3160 יְחֻבָּה ***yᵉḥubbâ***, n.pr.m. GK: 3478 & 2465 [→ 2245?; cf. 2244?]. Jehubbah, *"God has hidden [someone from danger]"*:– Jehubbah [1]

3161 יָחַד ***yāḥad***, v. GK: 3479 [→ 3162, 3173]. [Q] to join, be united; [P] to unite:– joined with [1], united [1], unite [1]

3162 יַחַד ***yaḥad***, n.[m.] or יַחְדָּו ***yaḥdāw***, adv. GK: 3480 & 3481 [→ 3161]. together, along with, in close proximity or concord either in space or time; by extension: close association in relationships, unity:– together [118], alike [5], altogether [5], at once [2], likewise [2], withal [2], at all [1], both [1], coupled together (+8535) [1], even as [1], knit (+3807.1) [1], only [1], together in unity [1]

3163 יַחְדּוֹ ***yaḥdô***, n.pr.m. GK: 3482. Jahdo, *"[God] gives joy"*:– Jahdo [1]

3164 יַחְדִּיאֵל ***yaḥdî'ēl***, n.pr.m. GK: 3484 [→ 2302+410]. Jahdiel, *"God [El] gives joy"*:– Jahdiel [1]

3165 יֶחְדְּיָהוּ ***yeḥdᵉyāhû***, n.pr.m. GK: 3485 [→ 2302+3068]. Jehdeiah, *"Yahweh rejoices [in his works]"*:– Jehdeiah [2]

יְחַוְאֵל ***yᵉḥaw'ēl***. See 3171.

3166 יַחֲזִיאֵל ***yaḥᵃzî'ēl***, n.pr.m. GK: 3487 [→ 2372+410]. Jahaziel, *"God [El] will see"*:– Jahaziel [6]

3167 יַחְזְיָה ***yaḥzᵉyâ***, n.pr.m. GK: 3488 [→ 2372+3068]. Jahzeiah, *"Yahweh sees"*:– Jahaziah [1]

3168 יְחֶזְקֵאל ***yᵉḥezqē'l***, n.pr.m. GK: 3489 [→ 2388+410]. Ezekiel; Jehezkel, *"God [El] gives strength"*:– Ezekiel [2], Jehezekel [1]

3169 יְחִזְקִיָּה ***yᵉḥizqiyyâ*** or יְחִזְקִיָּהוּ ***yᵉḥizqiyyāhû***, n.pr.m. GK: 3490 & 3491 [→ 2388+3068]. Hezekiah, *"Yahweh is [my] strength"*; Jehizkiah, *"Yahweh gives strength"*:– Hezekiah [43], Jehizkiah [1]

3170 יַחְזֵרָה ***yaḥzērâ***, n.pr.m. GK: 3492 [→ 2386]. Jahzerah, "[poss.] *prudent"*:– Jahzerah [1]

3171 יְחוּאֵל ***yᵉḥû'ēl*** or יְחִיאֵל ***yᵉḥî'ēl***, n.pr.m. GK: 3486 & 3493 [→ 3172]. Jehuel, Jehiel, *"God [El] lives"*:– Jehiel [14]

3172 יְחִיאֵלִי ***yᵉḥî'ēlî***, n.pr.m. GK: 3494 [→ 3171]. Jehieli, *"of Jehiel"*:– Jehieli [2]

3173 יָחִיד ***yāḥîd***, a. & subst. GK: 3495 [→ 3161]. only son, only child (special and unique to the parents); precious life; alone, solitary:– only [7], darling [2], child [1], desolate [1], solitary [1]

3174 יְחִיָּה ***yᵉḥiyyâ***, n.pr.m. GK: 3496 [→ 2421+3068]. Jehiah, *"Yahweh lives"*:– Jehiah [1]

3175 יָחִיל ***yāḥîl***, a.vbl. GK: 3497 [→ 3176]. waiting:– hope [1]

3176 יָחַל ***yāḥal***, v. GK: 3498 [→ 3175, 3177, 3178, 8431]. [N] to wait; [P] to wait for, put hope in, expect; [H] to wait, put hope in:– hope [17], waited [6], wait [5], hoped [3], tarry [2], trust [2], caused to hope [1], made to hope [1], stayed [1], tarried [1], waiteth [1]

3177 יַחְלְאֵל ***yaḥlᵉ'ēl***, n.pr.m. GK: 3499 [→ 3178]. Jahleel, *"wait for God [El];* [poss.] *may God [El] show himself friendly"*:– Jahleel [2]

3178 יַחְלְאֵלִי ***yaḥlᵉ'ēlî***, a.g. GK: 3500 [→ 3177]. Jahleelite, *"of Jahleel"*:– Jahleelites [1]

3179 יָחַם ***yāḥam***, v. GK: 3501 [→ 2534; cf. 2552]. [Q] to be in (breeding) heat, be in the rut; [P] to be in (breeding) heat, to mate, to conceive:– conceive [4], conceived [2], hot [2], gat heat [1], warm [1]

3180 יַחְמוּר ***yaḥmûr***, n.[m.]. GK: 3502 [→ 2560]. roebuck, the roe deer:– fallow deer [1], fallowdeer [1]

3181 יַחְמַי ***yaḥmay***, n.pr.m. GK: 3503 [→ 2346]. Jahmai, *"protect"*:– Jahmai [1]

3182 יָחֵף ***yāḥēp***, a. GK: 3504. barefoot:– barefoot [4], unshod [1]

3183 יַחְצְאֵל ***yaḥṣᵉ'ēl***, n.pr.m. GK: 3505 [→ 3184]. Jahziel, Jahzeel, *"God [El] apportions"*:– Jahzeel [2]

3184 יַחְצְאֵלִי ***yaḥṣᵉ'ēlî***, a.g. GK: 3506 [→ 3183]. Jahzeelite, *"of Jahzeel"*:– Jahzeelites [1]

3185 יַחֲצִיאֵל ***yaḥᵃṣî'ēl***, n.pr.m. GK: 3507 [→ 2673+410]. Jahziel:– Jahziel [1]

3186 יָחַר ***yāḥar***, v. GK: 3508 [cf. 309]. var. of 309: to wait, hesitate:–

3187 יָחַשׂ ***yāḥaś***, v. GK: 3509 [→ 3188]. [Ht] to enroll oneself in a genealogical record, be in a family register:– genealogy [5], reckoned by genealogies [5], reckoned by genealogy [5], genealogy reckoned [2], genealogies [1], number after genealogy [1], throughout genealogy [1]

3188 יַחַשׂ ***yaḥaś***, n.[m.]. GK: 3510 [→ 3187]. (book of) genealogy:– genealogy [1]

3189 יַחַת ***yaḥat***, n.pr.m. GK: 3511. Jahath, *"snatch up"*:– Jahath [8]

3190 יָטַב ***yāṭab***, v. GK: 3512 [→ 3192, 3193, 4105, 4315; cf. 2895; cf. 2868, cf. 3191]. [Q] to be good, go well; to be glad, pleased; [H] to do good, right; to make successful, cause to prosper; "to be good in the eyes" indicates pleasure in and acceptance of a person or situation:– well [20], do good [14], pleased (+5869+871.1) [8], go well [4], merry [4], amend [3], do well [3], accepted [2], dealt well [2], diligently [2], doeth good [2], good [2], pleased well (+5869+871.1) [2], surely do good (+3190) [2], throughly amend (+3190) [2], benefit [1], best [1], better [1], comely [1], content (+5869+871.1) [1], deal well [1], diligent [1], doest well [1], done good [1], do [1], dresseth [1], earnestly (+3807.1) [1], entreated well [1], found favour [1], give [1], glad [1], made better [1], make better [1], make good [1], make sweet [1], maketh cheerful [1], making merry [1], please (+413) [1], pleased (+6440+3807.1) [1], pleased [1], pleaseth (+5869+871.1) [1], please [1], shewed more [1], skilfully [1], throughly [1], tired [1], trimmest [1], useth aright [1], very [1]

3191 יְטַב ***yᵉṭab*** (Aram.), v. GK: 10320 [cf. 2868; cf. 3190]. [P] to seem best, be pleasing:– seem good [1]

3192 יָטְבָה ***yoṭbâ***, n.pr.loc. GK: 3513 [→ 3190]. Jotbah, *"good, pleasant"*:– Jotbah [1]

3193 יָטְבָתָה ***yoṭbātâ***, n.pr.loc. GK: 3514 [→ 3190]. Jotbathah, *"good, pleasant"*:– Jotbathah [2], Jotbath [1]

3194 יוּטָּה ***yûṭṭâ***, n.pr.loc. GK: 3420. Juttah, *"extended, inclined"*:– Juttah [2]

3195 יְטוּר ***yᵉṭûr***, n.pr.m. & g. GK: 3515 [cf. 2918?]. Jetur:– Jetur [3]

3196 יַיִן ***yayin***, n.m. GK: 3516. wine, an alcoholic beverage made of naturally fermented fruit juice (usually grapes), usually diluted with water for general consumption:– wine [137], banqueting [1], vine (+1612) [1], vine [1], winebibbers [1]

3197 יַךְ ***yak***, var. GK: 3517. var. of 3027: hand, side:–

יָכֹל ***yākôl***. See 3201.

יְכָנְיָה ***yᵉkônᵉyâ***. See 3204.

3198 יָכַח ***yākaḥ***, v. GK: 3519 [→ 8433]. [N] to reason together (in a legal case); to be vindicated; [H] to rebuke, discipline, punish; decide, argue, defend, judge; [Ho] to be chastened; [Ht] to lodge a charge against:– reprove [15], rebuke [7], reproved [4], plead [3], rebuketh [3], reproveth [3], correcteth [2], in any wise rebuke (+3198) [2], reason [2], surely reprove (+3198) [2], appointed out [1], appointed [1], arguing [1], chastened [1], chasten [1], convinced [1], correction [1], correct [1], daysman [1], dispute [1], judge [1], maintain [1], reason together [1], rebuked [1], reprover [1]

יְכִילְיָה ***yᵉkîlᵉyâ***. See 3203.

3199 יָכִין ***yākîn***, n.pr.m. GK: 3520 & 3521 [→ 3200, 3559]. Jakin, *"he establishes"*:– Jachin [8]

3200 יָכִינִי ***yākînî***, a.g. GK: 3522 [→ 3199; cf. 3559]. Jakinite, *"of Jakin"*:– Jachinites [1]

3201 יָכֹל ***yākōl***, v. GK: 3523 [→ 3203; cf. 3202 (also used with compound proper names)]. [Q] to be able, capable; overcome, prevail, have victory:– could [45], able [41], cannot (+3808) [35], prevail [12], may [11], can [10], prevailed [8], canst [5], mayest [5], any power at all (+3201) [2], any ways able (+3201) [2], endure [2], might [2], still prevail (+3201) [2], well able to overcome (+3201) [2], attain [1], can do [1], cannot away with (+3808) [1], canst do [1], could endure [1], couldest [1], prevailed against [1], suffer [1]

3202 יְכִל ***yᵉkil*** (Aram.), v. GK: 10321 [cf. 3201]. [P] to be able:– able [4], canst [2], can [2], couldest [1], could [1], prevailed [1]

3203 יְכָלְיָה ***yᵉkolyâ*** or יְכָלְיָהוּ ***yᵉkolyāhû***, n.pr.f. GK: 3524 & 3525 [→ 3201+3068]. Jecoliah, *"Yahweh is able"*:– Jecholiah [1], Jecoliah [1]

3204 יְכָנְיָה ***yᵉkônᵉyâ*** or יְכָנְיָה ***yᵉkonyâ*** or יְכָנְיָהוּ ***yᵉkonyāhû***, n.pr.m. GK: 3518 & 3526 & 3527 [→ 3078]. Jeconiah, *"Yahweh supports"*:– Jeconiah [7]

3205 יָלַד ***yālad***, v. GK: 3528 & 4256 [→ 2056, 3206, 3207, 3208, 3209, 3211, 4138, 4140, 8434?, 8435]. [Q] to give birth to, have a child, become the father of; [Qp, N, Pu, Ho] to be born, be a descendant; [P] to assist in childbirth, be a midwife; [H] to become the father of, cause to come to birth:– begat [179], bare [111], born [78], bear [17], bring forth [12], beget [10], brought forth [10], in travail [9], begotten [7], midwives [7], delivered [5], bearing [3], begetteth [3], borne [3], travailed [3], travaileth [3], beareth [2], begettest [2], birth [2], brought up [2], cause to bring forth [2], child [2], labour [2], midwife [2], bearest [1], birthday (+3117) [1], bring forth children [1], bring forth young [1], calved [1], children [1], come [1], declared pedigrees [1], delivered of a child [1], delivery [1], do the office of a midwife [1], gendered [1], hatcheth [1], maketh bring forth [1], son [1], travail with child [1], travaileth with child [1], travailing woman [1], travailing [1], travail [1]

Heb

3206 יֶלֶד ***yeled***, n.m. GK: 3529 [→ 3205]. male child, young boy; this can refer to a wide range of ages, from infant to young adult:– child [38], children [30], young men [6], sons [3], young ones [3], child's [2], men children [2], boys [1], boy [1], fruit [1], young man [1]

3207 יַלְדָּה ***yaldâ***, n.f. GK: 3530 [→ 3205]. female child, young girl; this can refer to a wide range of ages, from infant to young adult:– damsel [1], girls [1], girl [1]

3208 יַלְדוּת ***yaldût***, n.f. GK: 3531 [→ 3205]. youth, childhood:– youth [2], childhood [1]

3209 יִלּוֹד ***yillôd***, a. GK: 3533 [→ 3205]. born (children):– born [5]

3210 יָלוֹן ***yālôn***, n.pr.m. GK: 3534. Jalon:– Jalon [1]

3211 יָלִיד ***yālîd***, a. GK: 3535 [→ 3205]. born (child, slave child); (pl.) descendants, children:– children [4], born [2], sons [2], that is born [2], he that is born [1], homeborn (+1004) [1], that were born [1]

3212 יָלַךְ ***yālak***, v. GK: 2143 [→ 1980]. all forms of this assumed root are aligned with 1980:–

3213 יָלַל ***yālal***, v. GK: 3536 [→ 3214, 3215]. [H] to wail, howl:– howl [27], howled [1], howlings [1], make to howl [1]

3214 יְלֵל ***yᵉlēl***, n.[m.]. GK: 3537 [→ 3213]. howling, wailing-cry:– howling [1]

3215 יְלָלָה ***yᵉlālâ***, n.f. GK: 3538 [→ 3213]. wailing, lamentation, howling:– howling [5]

3216 לָעַע ***lā'a'*** or יָלַע ***yāla'***, v. GK: 4363 [→ 3930; cf. 5966]. [Q] to sip, lap, slurp:– devoureth [1]

3217 יַלֶּפֶת ***yallepet***, n.f. GK: 3539. running sore; some sources: scab, ringworm:– scabbed [2]

3218 יֶלֶק ***yeleq***, n.m. GK: 3540. locust, grasshopper; young locust, possibly some stage in the development of the locust:– cankerworm [6], caterpillars [3]

3219 יַלְקוּט ***yalqûṭ***, n.[m.]. GK: 3541 [→ 3950]. pouch:– scrip [1]

3220 יָם ***yām***, n.m. GK: 3542 [cf. 39; cf. 3221]. sea; seashore; the west (the direction of the Mediterranean Sea relative to the Near East); by extension: a large container for holding water; the recurring image of the sea as a terrifying danger and opponent of the LORD has its source in the Sea (Yamm) as a hostile Canaanite god:– sea [297], west [33], seas [24], westward (+1886.5) [21], west (+1886.5) [15], west side [3], seafaring [1], south [1], western [1]

3221 יַם ***yam*** (Aram.), n.m. GK: 10322 [cf. 3220]. a body of water usually referring to ocean, sea, or lake; fig., the nether regions of mystery, chaos, and monsters:– sea [2]

3222 יֵמִם ***yēmim***, n.[m.]. GK: 3553 [→ 3224?]. hot springs; traditionally: mules; others: adders:– mules [1]

3223 יְמוּאֵל ***yᵉmû'ēl***, n.pr.m. GK: 3543 [cf. 5241]. Jemuel:– Jemuel [2]

3224 יְמִימָה ***yᵉmîmâ***, n.pr.f. GK: 3544 [→ 3222?]. Jemimah, *"dove"*:– Jemima [1]

3225 יָמִין ***yāmîn***, n.f. GK: 3545 [→ 541, 1144, 1145, 1968?, 3226, 3228, 3233, 8486, 8488]. (direction) right; south, southward (south is right when facing east, the direction of orientation in the ancient Near East); the right is considered culturally to be stronger and of greater prestige than the left; to be seated on the right side of a ruler is a greater position than on the left side:– right hand [106], right [22], right side [6], south [3], lefthanded (+334+3027) [2]

3226 יָמִין ***yāmîn***, n.pr.m. GK: 3546 [→ 3228; cf. 3225]. Jamin, "[poss.] *right hand; south, an indication of [good] fortune"*:– Jamin [6]

3227 יְמִינִי ***yᵉmînî***, a.g. GK: 3549 [→ 1144]. Benjamite, *"of Benjamin"*:– Benjamite (+376) [2], Benjamite (+376+1121) [1]

3228 יָמִינִי ***yāmînî***, a.g. GK: 3547 [→ 3226; cf. 3225]. Jaminite, *"of Jamin"*:– Benjamites [1], Jaminites [1]

3229 יִמְלָא ***yimlā'*** or יִמְלָה ***yimlâ***, n.pr.m. GK: 3550 & 3551 [→ 4390]. Imla, Imlah, *"fullness"*:– Imlah [2], Imla [2]

3230 יַמְלֵךְ ***yamlēk***, n.pr.m. GK: 3552 [→ 4427?]. Jamlech, *"he will reign"*:– Jamlech [1]

3231 יָמַן ***yāman***, v.den. GK: 3554 [→ 541, 3225]. [H] to go the right; (ptcp.) right-handed:– go to the right [1], on the right hand [1], turn to the right hand [1], use the right hand [1]

3232 יִמְנָה ***yimnâ***, n.pr.m. GK: 3555 [→ 4487]. Imnah; Imnite, *"good fortune"*:– Imnah [2], Jimnah [1], Jimna [1], Jimnites [1]

3233 יְמָנִי ***yᵉmānî***, a. GK: 3556 & 3548 [→ 3225]. (direction) right:– right [32], right hand [1]

3234 יִמְנָע ***yimnā'***, n.pr.m. GK: 3557 [→ 4513]. Imna, "[poss.] *he is withheld; luck, fortune"*:– Imna [1]

3235 יָמַר ***yāmar***, v. GK: 3558. [H] to change, exchange:– boast [1], changed [1]

3236 יִמְרָה ***yimrâ***, n.pr.m. GK: 3559 [→ 4784]. Imrah, *"he rebels"*:– Imrah [1]

3237 יָמַשׁ ***yāmaš***, v. GK: 3560 [cf. 4184, 4959]. [H] to touch:–

3238 יָנָה ***yānâ***, v. GK: 3561 & 3435. [Q] to oppress, to crush; [H] to mistreat, take advantage of, oppress:– oppress [5], oppressed [3], oppressing [3], vexed [2], vex [2], destroy [1], do wrong [1], oppression [1], oppressor [1]

3239 יָנוֹחַ ***yānôaḥ*** or יָנוֹחָה ***yānôḥâ***, n.pr.loc. GK: 3562 & 3563 [→ 3240]. Janoah, Janohah, *"resting place"*:– Janohah [2], Janoah [1]

יָנוּם ***yānum***. See 3241.

3240 יָנַח ***yānaḥ***, v. GK: 5663 [→ 2010, 3239, 4494, 4495, 4496, 4506, 5117, 5118, 5119?, 5183, 5184, 5207]. same as 5117: [Q] to settle, rest, wait; [H] to put, keep, settle, rest; to leave, allow; [Ho] to be placed, find rest:– leave [13], left [11], set [6], lay up [5], lay [5], put [5], let alone [4], laid up [3], laid [3], suffer [3], placed [2], set down [2], suffered [2], bestowed [1], cast down [1], laid down [1], leave off [1], pacifieth [1], place [1], remain still [1], withdraw [1], withhold [1]

3241 יָנוּם ***yānûm*** or יָנִים ***yānîm***, n.pr.loc. GK: 3564 & 3565 [→ 5123?]. Janum, Janim:– Janum [1]

3242 יְנִיקָה ***yᵉnîqâ***, n.f. GK: 3566 [→ 3243]. shoot (of a plant):– young twigs [1]

3243 יָנַק ***yānaq***, v. GK: 3567 & 4787 [→ 689, 3126, 3127, 3242; cf. 5134]. [Q] to suck, be nursing; [H] to give nourishment, nurse:– nurse [7], suck [7], sucking child [3], sucklings [3], suckling [3], give suck [2], gave suck [1], given suck [1], made to suck [1], milch [1], nursing mothers [1], sucked [1], those that suck [1]

3244 יַנְשׁוּף ***yanšûp***, n.[m.]. GK: 3568 [→ 5398]. great owl (an unclean bird, variously identified):– great owl [2], owl [1]

3245 יָסַד ***yāsad***, v. GK: 3569 & 3570 [→ 3246, 3247, 3248, 4143, 4144, 4145, 4146, 4328, 4527; cf. 5475]. [Q] to lay a foundation, establish, ordain; [N] to be founded; to associate, conspire (together); [P] to lay a foundation, establish; [Pu, Ho] to be founded, have a foundation laid:– founded [8], foundation laid [7], laid foundation [5], established [2], foundation [2], laid foundations [2], lay foundations [2], lay foundation [2], appointed [1], instructed [1], laid [1], lay for a foundation [1], lay the foundation [1], layeth foundation [1], ordained [1], ordain [1], set [1], sure foundation (+4143) [1], take counsel [1], took counsel [1]

3246 יְסֻד ***yᵉsud***, n.[m.]. GK: 3571 [→ 3245]. foundation, beginning:– began [1]

3247 יְסוֹד ***yᵉsôd***, n.f. & m. GK: 3572 [→ 3245]. foundation; base (of an altar); foot (base of the body); by extension: what is firm or enduring:– bottom [9], foundation [7], foundations [3], repairing [1]

3248 יְסוּדָה ***yᵉsûdâ***, n.f. GK: 3573 [→ 3245]. foundation:– foundation [1]

3249 יָסוּר ***yāsûr***, var. GK: 6073 [→ 5627, 5493; cf. 5494, 5495]. one who departs:–

3250 יִסּוֹר **yissôr,** n.m. GK: 3574 [→ 3256]. corrector, fault-finder, reprover:– instruct [1]

3251 יָסַךְ **yāsak,** v. GK: 3575 [cf. 5258, 5480]. same as 5480: [Q] to anoint, to use oils or perfumes or lotions:– poured [1]

3252 יִסְכָּה **yiskâ,** n.pr.f. GK: 3576. Iscah:– Iscah [1]

3253 יִסְמַכְיָהוּ **yismakyāhû,** n.pr.m. GK: 3577 [→ 5564+3068]. Ismakiah, "*Yahweh sustains*":– Ismachiah [1]

3254 יָסַף **yāsap,** v. GK: 3578 [→ 23, 43, 460, 3130, 3131; cf. 3084, cf. 3255]. [Q] to add to, to do once more, to do again; [N] to be added to, to gain more, to be joined; [H] to increase, to cause to add to, to continue on, to add to, to happen again:– again [40], more [39], add [22], more (+5750) [10], any more [7], henceforth [6], again (+5750) [5], increaseth [5], yet again (+5750) [5], increased [4], increase [4], put [4], added [3], addeth [3], further [3], any more (+5750) [2], continued (+5375) [2], do more [2], exceed [2], make so many moe [2], more and more [2], yet the more (+5750) [2], added more [1], any more at all (+5750) [1], bring more [1], bring [1], came again [1], came more [1], can more (+5750) [1], caused again [1], cease [1], do again (+5750) [1], done [1], exceedest [1], exceedeth [1], gave [1], gotten more [1], increase (+5921) [1], increase more and more [1], increased more [1], join [1], longer [1], maketh [1], more (+5750+3807.1) [1], more also (+3541) [1], more also [1], more and more (+3605+5921) [1], moreover given [1], proceed further [1], proceeded [1], proceed [1], prolongeth [1], put more [1], set again [1], stronger and stronger (+555) [1], yet more (+5750) [1], yield [1]

3255 יְסַף **yᵉsap** (Aram.), v. GK: 10323 [cf. 3254]. [Ho] to be added:– added [1]

3256 יָסַר **yāsar,** v. GK: 3579 & 3580 & 3581 [→ 3250, 4148, 4561]. [Q] to correct, discipline; [N] to accept correction, be warned, be disciplined; [P] to punish, correct, discipline; to instruct, train; to strengthen; [H] to catch; [Nitpael] to let oneself take warning:– chastised [6], chastise [6], correct [6], instructed [5], chasten [3], instruct [3], chastened sore (+3256) [2], chasteneth [2], taught [2], bound [1], chastened [1], chastenest [1], chastiseth [1], corrected [1], punish [1], reformed [1], reproveth [1]

3257 יָע **yāʿ,** n.[m.]. GK: 3582 [→ 3261]. shovel (for altar fires):– shovels [9]

3258 יַעְבֵּץ **yaʿbēṣ,** n.pr.m. & loc. GK: 3583 & 3584. Jabez, "*to grieve*":– Jabez [4]

3259 יָעַד **yāʿad,** v. GK: 3585 [→ 4150, 4151, 4152, 5129; cf. 5712]. [Q] to select, appoint, set out; [N] to meet with, assemble, band together, join forces; [H] to summon, challenge; [Ho] to be set, be ordered:– meet [7], appointed [3], assembled [3], gathered together [3], appoint the time [2], betrothed [2], set [2], agreed [1], assemble [1], gather [1], made an appointment [1], meet together [1], met together [1], set a time [1]

יֶעְדּוֹ **yeʿdô.** See 3260.

3260 יֶעְדּוֹ **yeʿdô** or יֶעְדִּי **yeʿdî,** n.pr.m. GK: 3587 & 3588 [→ 5710 *or* 5716]. Iddo, Iddi, "[prob.] *Yahweh has adorned*":– Iddo [1]

3261 יָעָה **yāʿâ,** v. GK: 3589 [→ 3257, 3262?, 3273?]. [Q] to sweep away:– sweep away [1]

3262 יְעוּאֵל **yᵉʿûʾēl,** n.pr.m. GK: 3590 [→ 3273]. Jeuel, "*God [El] has preserved*":– Jeuel [1]

3263 יְעוּץ **yᵉʿûṣ,** n.pr.m. GK: 3591. Jeuz, "*he comes to help;* [poss.] *encouraged*":– Jeuz [1]

3264 יָעוֹר **yaʿôr,** n.m. GK: 3623 [→ 3293, 3295]. same as 3293: forest, woods, thicket:– wood [1]

3265 יָעוּר **yāʿûr** or יָעִיר **yāʿîr,** n.pr.m. GK: 3592 & 3600 [→ 5782]. Jaur, Jair, "*he gives light*":– Jair [1]

3266 יְעוּשׁ **yᵉʿûš,** n.pr.m. GK: 3593 [→ 5789; cf. 3274]. Jeush, "[perhaps] *may God aid*":– Jeush [8], Jehush [1]

3267 יָעַז **yāʿaz,** v. GK: 3594 [cf. 5810]. [N] to be arrogant, be insolent:– fierce [1]

3268 יַעֲזִיאֵל **yaᵃzîʾēl,** n.pr.m. GK: 3595. Jaaziel, "*God [El] strengthens*":– Jaaziel [1]

3269 יַעֲזִיָּהוּ **yaᵃziyyāhû,** n.pr.m. GK: 3596. Jaaziah, "*may Yahweh nourish*":– Jaaziah [2]

3270 יַעְזֵיר **yaʿzêr,** n.pr.loc. GK: 3597 [→ 5826]. Jazer, "*he helps*":– Jazer [11], Jaazer [2]

3271 יָעַט **yāʿaṭ,** v. GK: 3598 [cf. 5844]. [Q] to array, cover:– covered with [1]

3272 יְעַט **yᵉʿaṭ** (Aram.), v. GK: 10324 & 10325 [→ 5843; cf. 3289]. [Itpa] to take counsel together, implying mutual agreement and choices:– counsellers [2], consulted together [1]

3273 יְעִיאֵל **yᵉʿîʾēl,** n.pr.m. GK: 3599 [→ 3262]. Jeiel, "*God [El] has preserved;* [poss.] *God [El] sweeps up*":– Jeiel [11], Jehiel [2]

יָעִיר **yāʿîr.** See 3265.

3274 יְעִישׁ **yᵉʿîš,** n.pr.m. GK: 3601 [→ 5789; cf. 3266]. Jeish:–

3275 יַעְכָּן **yaʿkān,** n.pr.m. GK: 3602. Jacan:– Jachan [1]

3276 יָעַל **yāʿal,** v. GK: 3603 [→ 1100]. [H] to have value, have use, have value, have benefit:– profit [17], profit at all (+3276) [2], do good [1], profitable [1], profiteth [1], set forward [1]

3277 יָעֵל **yāʿēl,** n.[m.]. GK: 3604 [→ 3278, 3279, 3280]. mountain goat, wild goat:– wild goats [3]

3278 יָעֵל **yāʿēl,** n.pr.f. GK: 3605 [→ 3277]. Jael, "*mountain goat*":– Jael [6]

3279 יַעֲלָא **yaᵃlāʾ** or יַעֲלָה **yaᵃlâ,** n.pr.m. GK: 3606 & 3608 [→ 3280; cf. 3277]. Jaala:– Jaalah [1], Jaala [1]

3280 יַעֲלָה **yaᵃlâ,** n.f. GK: 3607 [→ 3279; cf. 3277]. (female) mountain goat, ibex; deer:– roe [1]

3281 יַעְלָם **yaʿlām,** n.pr.m. GK: 3609 [→ 5934]. Jalam:– Jaalam [4]

3282 יַעַן **yaʿan,** subst.pp.c. GK: 3610 [→ 6031]. for, because, since:– because [56], because (+834) [19], forasmuch as (+834) [5], because (+3588) [3], because (+3282+871.1) [2], because (+871.1) [2], because of [2], because that [2], as [1], forasmuch as (+3588) [1], forsomuch as (+3588) [1], seeing then [1], that (+834) [1], therefore [1], whereas (+834) [1]

3283 יָעֵן **yāʿēn,** n.[m.]. GK: 3612 [cf. 3284]. (male) ostrich:– ostriches [1]

3284 יַעֲנָה **yaᵃnâ,** n.f. GK: 3613 [cf. 3283]. owl; horned owl:– owls (+1323) [6], owl (+1323) [2]

3285 יַעְנַי **yaʿnay,** n.pr.m. GK: 3614 [→ 6030?]. Janai, "*he will answer*":– Jaanai [1]

3286 יָעֵף **yāʿēp,** v. GK: 3615 [→ 3287, 3288; cf. 5774, 5889]. [Q] to grow tired, be faint, exhaust oneself:– weary [4], faint [3], caused to fly [1], fainteth [1]

3287 יָעֵף **yāʿēp,** a. GK: 3617 [→ 3286]. weary, exhausted, fatigued:– faint [2], weary [2]

3288 יְעָף **yᵉʿāp,** n.[m.]. GK: 3618 & 3616. flight; some source: tiredness, weariness:– swiftly (+871.1) [1]

3289 יָעַץ **yāʿaṣ,** v. GK: 3619 & 3446 [→ 4156, 6098; cf. 5779; cf. 3272]. [Q] to give advise, give counsel; to purpose, plan, plot, determine; [Qp] to be determined; [N] to seek advise, consult; to confer, to plot (together); [Ht] to consult together, conspire against:– counsellers [12], counseller [10], consulted [7], purposed [5], took counsel [5], counselled [4], counsel [3], take counsel [3], taken counsel [3], counsel gave (+6098) [2], counsel given (+6098) [2], counsel give [2], determined [2], deviseth [2], give counsel (+6098) [2], give counsel [2], taken [2], took counsel with [2], advertise [1], advice give [1], advise [1], consulted with [1], consult [1], given counsel [1], guide [1], taken counsel (+6098) [1], took advice [1], well advised [1]

3290 יַעֲקֹב **yaᵃqōb,** n.pr.m. & g. GK: 3620 [cf. 6119?, 6120?]. Jacob, "*follower, replacer, one who follows at the heel*":– Jacob [332], Jacob's [16], Jacob's (+3807.1) [1]

3291 יַעֲקֹבָה **yaᵃqōbâ,** n.pr.m. GK: 3621. Jaakobah, "*may [deity] protect*":– Jaakobah [1]

3292 יַעֲקָן **yaᵃqān,** n.pr.loc. GK: 3622 [→ 885; cf. 6130?]. Jaakan:– Jaakan [1], Jakan [1]

3293 יַעַר **yaʿar,** n.m. & pr. GK: 3623 & 3624 & 3625 [→ 3264, 3295]. forest, woods, thicket; (cultivated) tree groves; honeycomb; as n.pr. Jaar:– forest [37], wood [18], forests [1], honeycomb [1], woods [1]

3294 יַעְרָה **yaʿrâ** or יַעְדָּה **yaʿdâ,** n.pr.m. GK: 3628 & 3586 [→ 5710?]. Jarah, Jadah, "*honeycomb*":– Jarah [2]

3295 יַעֲרָה **yaᵃrâ,** n.f. GK: 3626 & 3627 [→ 3264, 3293]. forest; honeycomb:– forests [1], honeycomb (+1706+1886.1) [1]

3296 יַעְרֵי אֹרְגִים **yaᵃrê ʾōrᵉgîm,** n.pr.m. GK: 3629. Jaare-Oregim:– Jaare-oregim [1]

3297 יְעָרִים **yᵉʿārîm,** n.pr.loc. GK: 3630 [→ 7157]. Jearim, "*timberlands*":– Jearim [1]

3298 יַעֲרֶשְׁיָה **yaᵃrešyâ,** n.pr.m. GK: 3631 [→ 3068]. Jaareshiah, "*Yahweh plants*":– Jaresiah [1]

3299 יַעֲשׂוּ **yaᵃśû** or יַעֲשַׂי **yaᵃśay,** n.pr.m. GK: 3632 & 3633 [→ 6213]. Jaasu, Jaasai:– Jaasau [1]

3300 יַעֲשִׂיאֵל **yaᵃśîʾēl,** n.pr.m. GK: 3634 [→ 6213+410]. Jaasiel, "*God [El] does*":– Jaasiel [1], Jasiel [1]

3301 יִפְדְיָה **yipdᵉyâ,** n.pr.m. GK: 3635. Iphdeiah, "*Yahweh redeems*":– Iphedeiah [1]

3302 יָפָה **yāpâ,** v. GK: 3636 [→ 3303, 3304, 3305?, 3308]. [Q] to be beautiful, delightful; [P] to adorn, make beautiful; [Ht] to adorn oneself:– fair [3], beautiful [2], deck [1], fairer [1], make fair [1]

3303 יָפֶה **yāpeh,** a. GK: 3637 [→ 3302]. beautiful, fair, lovely, handsome:– fair [20], beautiful [5], well [5], fairest [3], beautiful

(+8389) [2], fair one [2], beauty [1], comely [1], fair (+8389) [1], goodly (+8389) [1], pleasant [1]

3304 יְפֵה־פִיָּה y^e*pêpiyyâ* or יְפֵה־פִיָּה y^e*pēh-piyyâ*, a.f. GK: 3645 & 3638 [→ 3302]. beautiful, pretty:– very fair [1]

3305 יָפוֹ *yāpô*, n.pr.loc. GK: 3639 [→ 3302?]. Joppa, "*beautiful*":– Joppa [3], Japho [1]

3306 יָפַח *yāpaḥ*, v. GK: 3640 [→ 3307; cf. 6315]. [Ht] to gasp for breath:– bewaileth [1]

3307 יָפֵחַ *yāpēaḥ*, a. GK: 3641 [→ 3306]. breathing out, with a strong implication that this breath results in an action or communication:– breathe out [1]

3308 יֳפִי y^o*pî*, n.m. GK: 3642 [→ 3302]. beauty:– beauty [19]

3309 יָפִיעַ *yāpîa'*, n.pr.m. & loc. GK: 3644 [→ 3313]. Japhia, "[perhaps] *may the deity shine*":– Japhia [5]

3310 יַפְלֵט *yaplēṭ*, n.pr.m. GK: 3646 [→ 3311; cf. 6403]. Japhlet, "*he delivers;* [poss.] *he escapes*":– Japhlet [3]

3311 יַפְלֵטִי *yaplēṭî*, a.g. GK: 3647 [→ 3310; cf. 6403]. Japhletite, "*of Japhlet*":– Japhleti [1]

3312 יְפֻנֶּה y^e*punneh*, n.pr.m. GK: 3648 [→ 6437]. Jephunneh, "[perhaps] *may he [God] turn* or *turned*":– Jephunneh [16]

3313 יָפַע *yāpa'*, v. GK: 3649 [→ 3309, 3314]. [H] to shine forth, flash; smile:– shine [2], caused to shine [1], light [1], shew [1], shine forth [1], shined forth [1], shined [1]

3314 יִפְעָה *yip'â*, n.f. GK: 3650 [→ 3313]. shining splendor:– brightness [2]

3315 יֶפֶת *yepet*, n.pr.m. GK: 3651 [→ 6601]. Japheth, "*enlarge*":– Japheth [11]

3316 יִפְתָּח *yiptāḥ*, n.pr.m. & loc. GK: 3652 & 3653 [→ 6605]. Jephthah, Iphtah, "*Yahweh opens, frees*":– Jephthah [29], Jiphtah [1]

3317 יִפְתַּח־אֵל *yiptaḥ-'ēl*, n.pr.loc. GK: 3654 [→ 6605+410]. Iphtah El, "*God [El] opens*":– Jiphthah-el [2]

3318 יָצָא *yāṣā'*, v. GK: 3655 & 3448 [→ 3329, 4161, 4162, 4163, 6631, 6792, 8444]. [Q] to go out, come out; [H] to bring out, lead forth; produce; [Ho] to be brought out; emptied; by extension: to grow (of plants), to have offspring:– went out [162], go forth [92], go out [82], brought forth [70], came out [63], went forth [54], brought out [51], come out [48], bring forth [39], came forth [35], come forth [35], bring out [32], gone out [18], goeth out [13], bringeth forth [12], goeth forth [12], gone forth [12], cometh forth [10], departed [10], going out [10], carry forth [9], came [8], carry out [7], proceed [7], bringeth out [6], cometh out [6], proceedeth [6], goest out [5], broughtest out [4], camest forth [4], get out [4], goeth [4], issued out [4], broughtest forth [3], cometh [3], depart [3], going forth [3], go [3], lieth out [3], utter [3], assuredly go forth (+3318) [2], at any time come (+3318) [2], bring up [2], bring [2], brought up [2], brought [2], camest out [2], carried out [2], coming out [2], failed [2], go on [2], goest forth [2], got [2], have forth [2], issue [2], laid out [2], leddest out [2], proceeded [2], put away [2], scarce gone out (+3318) [2], surely come out (+3318) [2], surely go forth (+3318) [2], uttereth [2], wentest forth [2], appeared [1], bear out [1], begotten [1], be [1], break out [1], bringing forth [1], bringing out [1], bringing up [1], brought forth out of [1], brought forth out [1], brought of [1], camest [1], carried forth [1], carry forth out [1], carry [1], cause to go out [1], caused to go forth [1], come abroad [1], departing [1], departure [1], do[s] [1], draw forth [1], drawn forth [1], drew forth [1], end [1], escaped [1], escape [1], exacted [1], fall out [1], falleth [1], fell out [1], fell [1], fet forth [1], fetch [1], followed (+310) [1], get away [1], get forth [1], get hence [1], go away [1], go way forth [1], goeth on [1], grow [1], have out [1], in departing [1], issue out [1], lead out [1], out [1], pluck out [1], plucked out [1], proceed out [1], pull out [1], risen [1], shooteth forth [1], spread [1], spring out [1], springeth out [1], stand out [1], take forth [1], took out [1], to [1], uttered [1], wentest out [1], went [1]

3319 שֵׁיצִיא *šêṣî'* or שֵׁיצָא y^e*ṣā'* (Aram.), v. GK: 10707. [Sh] to complete, finish:– finished [1]

3320 יָצַב *yāṣab*, v. GK: 3656 [cf. 5324; cf. 3321]. [Ht] to stand one's ground, confront; to stand before, present oneself, commit oneself:– stand [16], stood [7], present [5], set [5], presented [4], stand still [2], stand up [2], able to withstand (+5973) [1], remaining [1], resorted [1], setteth [1], stand fast [1], stand forth [1], standing [1]

3321 יְצַב y^e*ṣab* (Aram.), v. GK: 10326 [→ 3330; cf. 3320]. [Pa] to make certain, to know the truth:– know the truth [1]

3322 יָצַג *yāṣag*, v. GK: 3657 [cf. 3332]. [H] to set, place, present; touch; [Ho] to be left behind:– set [8], made [2], put [2], establish [1], leave [1], presented [1], stayed [1]

3323 יִצְהָר *yiṣhār*, n.[m.]. GK: 3658 [→ 3324, 3325; cf. 6671]. olive oil:– oil [22], anointed [1]

3324 יִצְהָר *yiṣhār*, n.pr.m. GK: 3659 [→ 3323; cf. 6671]. Izhar, "*the shining one*":– Izhar [8], Izehar [1]

3325 יִצְהָרִי *yiṣhārî*, a.g. GK: 3660 [→ 3323; cf. 6671]. Izharite, "*of Izhar*":– Izharites [3], Izeharites [1]

3326 יָצוּעַ *yāṣûa'* or יָצִיעַ *yāṣîa'*, n.m. GK: 3661 & 3662 & 3666 [→ 3331]. bed, couch; structure, room, often referring to an annex, wing, or level of a building:– bed [3], chambers [2], bed (+6210) [1], chamber [1], couch [1]

3327 יִצְחָק *yiṣḥāq*, n.pr.m. GK: 3663 [→ 6711; cf. 3446]. Isaac, "*he laugh, he will laugh* or *mock; [God] laughs*":– Isaac [104], Isaac's [4]

3328 יִצְחַר *yiṣḥār*, n.pr.m. GK: 3664 [cf. 6714]. Jizhar:– Jezoar [1]

3329 יָצִיא *yāṣî'*, a. GK: 3665 [→ 3318]. coming forth:– came forth [1]

3330 יַצִּיב *yaṣṣîb* (Aram.), a. GK: 10327 [→ 3321]. certain, true, reliable:– true [2], certainty [1], certain [1], truth [1]

יָצִיעַ *yāṣîa'*. See 3326.

3331 יָצַע *yāṣa'*, v. GK: 3667 [→ 3326, 4702]. [H] to spread out bedding; [Ho] to be spread out:– spread [2], lay [1], make bed [1]

3332 יָצַק *yāṣaq*, v. GK: 3668 [→ 3333, 4164, 4166, 4690?, 6694?; cf. 3322]. [Q] to pour out, cast out; [Qp] be cast out, be poured out, be smelted; [H] to pour out, spread out; [Ho] to be poured out, be washed away; be anointed:– cast [11], pour [11], poured [9], molten [6], poured out [4], firm [2], pour out [2], cleaveth fast [1], groweth [1], hard [1], laid out [1], overflown [1], ran out [1], set down [1], steadfast [1]

3333 יְצֻקָה y^e*ṣuqâ*, n.f. GK: 3669 [→ 3332]. casting (of metal), with a focus that this is one piece:– cast [1]

3334 יָצַר *yāṣar*, v. GK: 7674 [→ 4712, 6862, 6869, 6872, 6887; cf. 6696]. same as 6887: [Q] to bind up, wrap up, tie up; to hamper, oppress, be in distress; [Qp] be bound, be confined; [Pu] to be mended; [H] to bring trouble, distress, oppress:– distressed [4], straitened [2], in straits [1], narrow [1], vexed [1]

3335 יָצַר *yāṣar*, v. GK: 3670 & 3450 [→ 3336, 3337, 3338, 3339, 3340]. [Q] to form, fashion, shape, create; (of God) the Maker, the Creator; [N] to be formed; [Pu] to be formed; [Ho] to be forged, be formed; usually from existing material; God as Creator or Maker, has its focus his planning and forming the creation as a skilled craftsman:– formed [23], potter [8], potter's [7], maker [4], fashioneth [3], fashioned [2], former [2], formeth [2], made [2], earthen [1], form [1], framed [1], frameth [1], frame [1], make [1], potters' [1], potters [1], purposed [1]

3336 יֵצֶר *yēṣer*, n.m. GK: 3671 [→ 3337; cf. 3335]. something formed, creation; inclination, disposition, motivation:– imagination [4], frame [1], imaginations [1], mind [1], thing framed [1], work [1]

3337 יֵצֶר *yēṣer*, n.pr.m. GK: 3672 [→ 3339, 3340; cf. 3335, 3336]. Jezer, "*formed, fashioned*":– Jezer [3]

3338 יְצֻרִים y^e*ṣurîm*, n.m.pl. GK: 3674 [→ 3335]. frame, body, limbs, that which gives visible form to a person:– members [1]

3339 יִצְרִי *yiṣrî*, a.g. & n.pr.m. GK: 3673 [→ 3337; cf. 3335]. same as 3340: Izri; Jezerite, "*Yahweh designs*":– Izri [1]

3340 יִצְרִי *yiṣrî*, a.g. & n.pr.m. GK: 3673 [→ 3337]. same as 3339: Izri; Jezerite, "*Yahweh designs*":– Jezerites [1]

3341 יָצַת *yāṣat*, v. GK: 3675 [cf. 6702]. [Q] to set ablaze; [N] to burn, be burned; [H] to kindle, set on fire:– kindle [8], burnt [7], set [6], kindled [4], burnt up [2], desolate [1], set on [1]

3342 יֶקֶב *yeqeb*, n.m. GK: 3676 [cf. 5344]. winepress; (wine or oil) vat:– winepress [7], fats [2], presses [2], winepresses [2], pressfat [1], wine presses [1], wine [1]

3343 יְקַבְצְאֵל y^e*qabṣ^e'ēl*, n.pr.loc. GK: 3677 [→ 6908+410]. Jekabzeel, "*God [El] gathers*":– Jekabzeel [1]

3344 יָקַד *yāqad*, v. GK: 3678 & 3683 [→ 3350, 4168, 4169; cf. 3345, cf. 3346]. [Q] to burn; to kindle a fire; [Qp or n.m.] hearth (of a fireplace); [Ho] to be burning, be kindled:– burning [3], burn [3], burneth [1], hearth [1], kindle [1]

3345 יְקַד y^e*qad* (Aram.), v. GK: 10328 [→ 3346; cf. 3344]. [P] to burn:– burning [8]

3346 יְקֵדָה y^e*qēdâ* (Aram.), n.f. GK: 10329 [→ 3345]. blazing, burning:– burning [1]

3347 יָקְדְעָם *yoqd^e'ām*, n.pr.loc. GK: 3680. Jokdeam:– Jokdeam [1]

3348 יָקֶה *yāqeh*, n.pr.m. GK: 3681. Jakeh, "*prudent*":– Jakeh [1]

3349 יְקָהָה y^e*qāhâ*, n.f. GK: 3682. obedience:– gathering [1], obey [1]

3350 יְקוֹד y^e*qōd*, n.[m.]. GK: 3679 [→ 3344]. blazing, burning:– burning [2]

3351 יְקוּם yeqûm, n.[m.]. GK: 3685 [→ 6965]. living thing, living creature:– living substance [2], substance [1]

3352 יָקוֹשׁ yāqôš, n.[m.]. GK: 3686 [→ 3369]. fowler, bait-layer:– fowler [1]

3353 יָקוּשׁ yāqûš, n.[m.]. GK: 3687 [→ 3369]. fowler, one who snares birds:– fowler [2], snares [1]

3354 יְקוּתִיאֵל yeqûtî'ēl, n.pr.m. GK: 3688. Jekuthiel, "*God [El] will nourish*":– Jekuthiel [1]

3355 יָקְטָן yoqṭān, n.pr.m. GK: 3690 [→ 3364]. Joktan, "*smaller*":– Joktan [6]

3356 יָקִים yāqîm, n.pr.m. GK: 3691 [→ 6965]. Jakim, "*he will establish*":– Jakim [2]

3357 יַקִּיר yaqqîr, a. GK: 3692 [→ 3365; cf. 3358]. dear, precious:– dear [1]

3358 יַקִּיר yaqqîr (Aram.), a. GK: 10330 [→ 3367; cf. 3366]. honorable; difficult, with an implication that such difficulty makes something unlikely or improbable:– noble [1], rare [1]

3359 יְקַמְיָה yeqamyâ, n.pr.m. GK: 3693 [→ 6965+3068]. Jekamiah, "*Yahweh will establish*":– Jekamiah [2], Jecamiah [1]

3360 יְקַמְעָם yeqam'ām, n.pr.m. GK: 3694 [→ 6965+5971]. Jekameam, "*[my] kinsman establishes*":– Jekameam [2]

3361 יָקְמְעָם yoqme'ām, n.pr.loc. GK: 3695 [→ 3362?]. Jokmeam, "*let the people arise*":– Jokmeam [1], Jokneam [1]

3362 יָקְנְעָם yoqne'ām, n.pr.loc. GK: 3696 [→ 3361?]. Jokneam:– Jokneam [3]

3363 יָקַע yāqa', v. GK: 3697 [cf. 5361]. [Q] to turn (away), wrench; [H] to kill and expose; [Ho] to be killed and exposed:– alienated [2], hang up [2], hanged [2], depart [1], out of joint [1]

3364 יָקַץ yāqaṣ, v. GK: 3699 [→ 3355; cf. 6972]. [Q] to wake up, awake:– awoke [6], awaked [4], awake [1]

יָקַף *yāqap*. See 5362.

3365 יָקַר yāqar, v. GK: 3700 [→ 3357, 3368, 3366]. [Q] to be precious, be costly; become well known; [H] to make scarce:– precious [7], make precious [1], prised [1], set by [1], withdraw [1]

3366 יְקָר yeqār, n.m. GK: 3702 [→ 3365; cf. 3367]. honor, splendor, riches, valuable things:– honour [12], precious things [2], precious thing [1], precious [1], price [1]

3367 יְקָר yeqār (Aram.), n.m. GK: 10331 [→ 3358; cf. 3366]. glory, honor, majesty:– glory [5], honour [2]

3368 יָקָר yāqār, a. GK: 3701 [→ 3365]. precious, valuable, quality, pertaining to items that are rare, beloved, or splendid:– precious [25], costly [4], excellent [2], brightness [1], clear [1], fat [1], honourable [1], reputation [1]

3369 יָקַשׁ yāqaš, v. GK: 3704 [→ 3352, 3353, 3370, 4170; cf. 5367, 6983]. [Q] to lay a bird snare, set a trap; [N, Pu] to be ensnared, be trapped:– snared [5], fowlers [1], laid a snare [1], laid [1]

3370 יָקְשָׁן yoqšān, n.pr.m. GK: 3705 [→ 3369]. Jokshan:– Jokshan [4]

3371 יָקְתְאֵל yoqte'ēl, n.pr.loc. GK: 3706 [→ 410]. Joktheel:– Joktheel [2]

יָרָא *yārā'*. See 3384.

3372 יָרֵא yārē', v. GK: 3707 [→ 3373, 3374, 4172]. [Q] to be afraid, be frightened; to revere, respect; [N] to be awesome, be dreadful, be feared; [P] to frighten, terrify, intimidate; in some contexts fear relates to terror and fright, in other contexts fear relates to honor, respect and awe, as in "the fear of the LORD":– fear [146], afraid [75], feared [36], terrible [28], dreadful [5], feareth [2], fearful [2], made afraid [2], put in fear [2], reverence [2], affright [1], dread [1], durst not [1], exceedingly afraid (+1419+3374) [1], feared exceedingly (+1419+3374) [1], fearest [1], fearfully [1], fearing [1], had in reverence [1], reverend [1], terrible acts [1], terrible things [1], terribleness [1]

3373 יָרֵא yārē', a.vbl. GK: 3710 [→ 3372]. fear; worship:– fear [35], feareth [11], feared [9], afraid [3], fearful [2], one that feareth [2], fearest [1], one that feared [1]

3374 יִרְאָה yir'â, n.f. GK: 3711 [→ 3372]. fear, reverence, piety:– fear [41], dreadful [1], exceedingly afraid (+1419+3372) [1], feared exceedingly (+1419+3372) [1], fearfulness [1]

3375 יִרְאוֹן yir'ôn, n.pr.loc. GK: 3712. Iron:– Iron [1]

3376 יִרְאִיָּה yir'iyyāyh, n.pr.m. GK: 3713 [→ 7200+3068]. Irijah, "*Yahweh sees*":– Irijah [2]

3377 יָרֵב yārēb, n.m. GK: 3714 [→ 7231]. great (king):– Jareb [2]

3378 יְרֻבַּעַל yerubba'al, n.pr.m. GK: 3715 [→ 7231+1167]. Jerub-Baal, "*Baal contends*":– Jerubbaal [14]

3379 יָרָבְעָם yārob'ām, n.pr.m. GK: 3716 [→ 7231+5971]. Jeroboam, "*the people increase*":– Jeroboam [102], Jeroboam's [2]

3380 יְרֻבֶּשֶׁת yerubbešet, n.pr.m. GK: 3717 [→ 7231+954]. Jerub-Besheth, "*Shame [Baal] contends*":– Jerubbesheth [1]

3381 יָרַד yārad, v. GK: 3718 [→ 3383, 4174]. [Q] to come down, go down, descend; [H] to bring down, lower; [Ho] to be brought down, be taken down:– go down [73], went down [63], come down [53], came down [41], bring down [26], brought down [17], gone down [14], descended [12], get down [9], descend [6], goeth down [5], let down [5], run down [5], took down [4], camest down [3], cast down [3], going down [3], take down [3], bringeth down [2], came indeed down (+3381) [2], carry down [2], cause to come down [2], coming down [2], down [2], fell [2], runneth down [2], abundantly [1], casteth down [1], caused to run down [1], cometh down [1], descending [1], goeth [1], hang down [1], let fall down [1], lighted down [1], lighted [1], put down [1], put off [1], ran down [1], sank [1], subdued [1], taken down [1], went [1]

3382 יֶרֶד yered, n.pr.m. GK: 3719. Jared; Jered, "*rose; servant*":– Jared [5], Jered [2]

3383 יַרְדֵּן yardēn, n.pr.loc. GK: 3720 [→ 3381]. Jordan, "*descending*":– Jordan [182]

3384 יָרָה yārâ, v. GK: 3721 & 3722 & 3723 & 3452 [→ 3385, 3406, 3412, 4175, 4176, 8451, 8452]. [Q] to throw, cast; shoot; [N] to be shot through; [H] to shoot (an arrow), to hurl; to water upon, rain, shower; to teach, instruct, give guidance, in a formal or informal setting, with an implied authority for the teacher and the content of what is taught; [Ho] to be refreshed:– teach [33], shoot [11], shot [6], taught [5], cast [4], archers [3], teachers [3], teacheth [3], shot through (+3384) [2], archers (+376+7198+871.1+1886.1) [1], casteth [1], direct [1], former rain [1], inform [1], instructed [1], laid [1], rain [1], shewed [1], teacher [1], teaching [1], watered [1]

3385 יְרוּאֵל yerû'ēl, n.pr.loc. GK: 3725 [→ 3384+410]. Jeruel, "*God [El] is a foundation*":– Jeruel [1]

3386 יָרוֹחַ yārôaḥ, n.pr.m. GK: 3726 [→ 3391]. Jaroah, "*soft, delicate*":– Jaroah [1]

3387 יָרוֹק yārôq, n.[m.]. GK: 3728 [→ 3418]. green plant:– green thing [1]

3388 יְרוּשָׁא yerûšā' or יְרוּשָׁה *yerûšâ*, n.pr.f. GK: 3729 & 3730 [→ 3423]. Jerusha, "*possession*":– Jerushah [1], Jerusha [1]

3389 יְרוּשָׁלַםִ yerûšālaim, n.pr.loc. GK: 3731 [cf. 3390]. Jerusalem, "*foundation of Shalem [peace]*":– Jerusalem [640], Jerusalem's [3]

3390 יְרוּשְׁלֶם yerûšelem (Aram.), n.pr.loc. GK: 10332 [cf. 3389]. Jerusalem, "*foundation of Shalem (peace)*":– Jerusalem [26]

3391 יֶרַח yeraḥ, n.m. GK: 3732 [→ 3386, 3392, 3394, 3405; cf. 732; cf. 3393]. moon; (lunar) month:– months [5], month [4], full month (+3117) [2], moon [2]

3392 יֶרַח yeraḥ, n.pr.m. GK: 3733 [→ 3391]. Jerah, "*moon [god?]*":– Jerah [2]

3393 יְרַח yeraḥ (Aram.), n.m. GK: 10333 [cf. 3391]. month:– months [1], month [1]

3394 יָרֵחַ yārēaḥ, n.m. GK: 3734 [→ 3391]. moon:– moon [26]

יְרֵחוֹ *yerēḥô*. See 3405.

3395 יְרֹחָם yerōḥām, n.pr.m. GK: 3736 [→ 7355]. Jeroham, "*he will be compassionate*":– Jeroham [10]

3396 יְרַחְמְאֵל yeraḥme'ēl, n.pr.m. GK: 3737 [→ 7355+410]. Jerahmeel, "*God [El] will have compassion*":– Jerahmeel [8]

3397 יְרַחְמְאֵלִי yeraḥme'ēlî, a.g. GK: 3738 [→ 7355+410]. Jerahmeelite, "*of Jerahmeel*":– Jerahmeelites [2]

3398 יַרְחָע yarḥā', n.pr.m. GK: 3739. Jarha:– Jarha [2]

3399 יָרַט yāraṭ, v. GK: 3740. [Q] to throw (into someone's custody); to be reckless, a fig. extension of going down a steep ravine:– perverse [1], turned over [1]

3400 יְרִיאֵל yerî'ēl, n.pr.m. GK: 3741 [cf. 3404]. Jeriel, "*founded of God [El]; God [El] will see*":– Jeriel [1]

3401 יָרִיב yārîb, n.[m.]. GK: 3742 [→ 7378]. contender, accuser, adversary, opponent:– contend with [1], contendeth with [1], strive with [1]

3402 יָרִיב yārîb, n.pr.m. GK: 3743. Jarib, "*Yahweh contends*":– Jarib [3]

3403 יְרִיבַי yerîbay, n.pr.m. GK: 3744 [→ 7380?]. Jeribai, "*Yahweh pleads*":– Jeribai [1]

3404 יְרִיָּה yeriyyâ or יְרִיָּהוּ *yeriyyāhû*, n.pr.m. GK: 3745 & 3746 [cf. 3400]. Jeriah, "*Yahweh founds*":– Jeriah [2], Jerijah [1]

3405 יְרִיחוֹ yerîḥô or יְרִיחֹה *yerîḥōh*, n.pr.loc. GK: 3735 & 3747 [→ 3391]. Jericho, "*moon city*":– Jericho [57]

3406 יְרִימוֹת yerîmôt or יְרָמוֹת *yerāmôt* or יְרֵמוֹת *yerēmôt*, n.pr.m. GK: 3748 & 3755 & 3756 [→ 3384+4191?]. Jeramoth, Jeremoth; Jerimoth, "*swollen* or *obese*":– Jerimoth [8], Jeremoth [5]

3407 יְרִיעָה ***yᵉrîʿâ***, n.f. GK: 3749 [→ 3415]. tent curtain; tent, shelter, dwelling:– curtains [31], curtain [23]

3408 יְרִיעוֹת ***yᵉrîʿôt***, n.pr.m. GK: 3750 [→ 3415]. Jerioth, "*tents*":– Jerioth [1]

3409 יָרֵךְ ***yārēk***, n.f. GK: 3751 [→ 3411; cf. 3410]. the area and components of the torso: thigh, hip, breast, leg, side; by extension: side, base, of any object:– thigh [19], side [7], shaft [3], loins [2], thighs [2], body [1]

3410 יַרְכָה ***yarkâ*** (Aram.), n.f. GK: 10334 [cf. 3409]. (upper) thigh; some sources translate as "loin" (the lower back, as the soft area between the lower ribs and the hip joints):– thighs [1]

3411 יְרֵכָה ***yᵉrēkâ***, n.[f.]. GK: 3752 [→ 3409]. far end, ends (of the earth); remote area: heights, depths:– sides [15], two sides [4], coasts [3], parts [2], side [2], border [1], quarters [1]

3412 יַרְמוּת ***yarmût***, n.pr.loc. GK: 3754 [→ 3384+4191?]. Jarmuth, "*height*":– Jarmuth [7]

יְרֵמוֹת ***yᵉrēmôt***. See 3406.

3413 יְרֵמַי ***yᵉrēmay***, n.pr.m. GK: 3757 [cf. 3414?]. Jeremai, "[poss.] *fat*":– Jeremai [1]

3414 יִרְמְיָה ***yirmᵉyâ*** or יִרְמְיָהוּ ***yirmᵉyāhû***, n.pr.m. GK: 3758 & 3759 [cf. 3413?]. Jeremiah, "*Yahweh loosens [the womb]; Yahweh lifts up;* [poss.] *Yahweh shoots, establishes*":– Jeremiah [146], Jeremiah's [1]

3415 יָרַע ***yāraʿ***, v. GK: 3760 [→ 3407, 3408]. [Q] to tremble, be faint-hearted:– displeased (+5869+871.1) [6], grieved [3], grievous [3], evil [2], displease (+7489+871.1) [1], displeased (+7489+871.1) [1], displeased exceedingly (+1419+7451) [1], do harm [1], go ill [1], ill [1], sad [1]

3416 יִרְפְּאֵל ***yirpᵉʾēl***, n.pr.loc. GK: 3761 [→ 7495+410]. Irpeel, "*God [El] heals*":– Irpeel [1]

3417 יָרַק ***yāraq***, v. GK: 3762 [cf. 7556]. [Q] to spit (in the face as an act of contempt):– but spit (+3417) [2], spit [1]

3418 יֶרֶק ***yereq***, n.m. GK: 3764 [→ 3387, 3419, 3420, 3422]. green (of plants, foliage, shoots, grass):– green [3], green thing [2], grass [1]

3419 יָרָק ***yārāq***, n.[m.]. GK: 3763 [→ 3418]. vegetables, vegetable greens:– herbs [3], green [2]

יַרְקוֹן ***yarqôn***. See 4313.

3420 יֵרָקוֹן ***yērāqôn***, n.m. GK: 3766 [→ 3418]. paleness (of face); mildew (of grain):– mildew [5], paleness [1]

3421 יָרְקְעָם ***yorqᵒʿām***, n.pr.m. GK: 3767 [→ 7554]. Jorkeam:– Jorkoam [1]

3422 יְרַקְרַק ***yᵉraqraq***, a. GK: 3768 [→ 3418]. yellowish-green, pale-green (mildew); shining-yellowish (gold):– greenish [2], yellow [1]

3423 יָרַשׁ ***yāraš***, v. GK: 3769 [→ 3388, 3424, 3425, 4180, 4181, 7558, 7568, 8492; cf. 7326]. [Q] to be an heir, gain an inheritance, have as a possession; [N] to become destitute, to be poor; [P] to take possession of; [H] to drive away, push out, destroy; to cause to inherit; many of these meanings have a common element of gaining (by right or violence) or losing possession (by force or circumstance):– possess [93], drive out [26], inherit [19], possessed [19], cast out [11], heir [9], utterly drive out (+3423) [4], come to poverty [3], succeeded [3], dispossessed [2], dispossess [2], drave out [2], driven out [2], enjoy [2], expelled [2], inherited [2], succeedest [2], take possession [2], without fail drive out (+3423) [2], consume [1], destroy [1], disinherit [1], drive [1], driving out [1], drove out [1], drove [1], given to inherit [1], giveth to possess [1], got in possession [1], have in possession [1], heirs [1], inheritor [1], leave an inheritance [1], magistrate (+6114) [1], makest to possess [1], maketh poor [1], poor [1], possessest [1], possesseth [1], seize upon [1], take in possession [1], take that have [1], taken possession [1]

3424 יְרֵשָׁה ***yᵉrēšâ***, n.f. GK: 3771 [→ 3423]. possession conquered:– possession [2]

3425 יְרֻשָּׁה ***yᵉruššâ***, n.f. GK: 3772 [→ 3423]. possession, inheritance:– possession [11], inheritance [2], heritage [1]

3426 יֵשׁ ***yēš***, subst. GK: 3780 [→ 786, 3449?; cf. 8454; cf. 383]. there is, it exists:– there is [35], there be [16], is there [13], be [12], is [9], have (+3807.1) [8], there were [6], have [4], had (+3807.1) [3], are [2], hast [2], hath (+3807.1) [2], it is [2], it was [2], there [2], wilt [2], are there [1], do [1], had [1], hast (+3807.1) [1], hath (+871.1) [1], hath [1], have (+5973) [1], is able [1], it be [1], substance [1], there was [1], were [1], will [1], wouldest [1]

3427 יָשַׁב ***yāšab***, v. GK: 3782 [→ 4186, 7675, 7871?, 8453; cf. 3488 (also used with compound proper names)]. [Q] to live, inhabit, dwell, stay; [N] to be settled, be inhabited; [P] to set up; to cause to settle, make dwell, to cause to sit; by extension: to marry, with a focus that the spouses live together:– inhabitants [190], dwell [184], dwelt [182], sat [72], sit [54], abode [33], inhabitant [31], abide [29], inhabited [28], sitteth [24], sat down [22], dwelleth [19], dwell in [16], dwelling [15], sitting [14], set [13], dwellest [12], tarry [12], remain [11], remained [10], inhabit [8], dwelled [6], sittest [6], tarried [6], placed [5], sit down [5], taken [5], abideth [4], dwelt in [4], continued [3], abiding [2], continue [2], dwellest in [2], endure [2], habitation [2], made to dwell [2], make to dwell [2], satest [2], sit still [2], situate [2], abide in [1], abodest [1], bring to place [1], cause to dwell in [1], cause to dwell [1], caused to dwell [1], downsitting [1], dwelleth in [1], dwelling in [1], dwelt amongst [1], dwelt at [1], dwelt with [1], ease [1], establish [1], haunt [1], inhabitest [1], inhabiteth [1], lurking [1], made dwell [1], made to abide [1], make to be inhabited [1], makest dwell [1], maketh to dwell [1], maketh to keep [1], married [1], marrying [1], not fail to sit [1], place [1], remainest [1], remaineth [1], setteth [1], settle [1], sit in [1], sit up [1], sitteth still [1], sitting down [1], still [1], tarrieth [1], tarry abroad [1]

3428 יֶשֶׁבְאָב ***yesebʾāb***, n.pr.m. GK: 3784 [→ 7725+1]. Jeshebeab, "*father lives*":– Jeshebeab [1]

3429 יֹשֵׁב בַּשֶּׁבֶת ***yōšēb baššebet***, n.pr.m. GK: 3783. Josheb-Basshebeth, "*one sitting in the seat*":–

3430 יִשְׁבּוֹ בְנֹב ***yišbô bᵉnōb*** or יִשְׁבִּי בְנֹב ***yišbî bᵉnōb***, n.pr.m. GK: 3785 & 3787. Ishbo-Benob, Ishbi-Benob:– Ishbi-benob [1]

3431 יִשְׁבָּח ***yišbāḥ***, n.pr.m. GK: 3786 [→ 7623]. Ishbah, "*he boasts, congratulates*":– Ishbah [1]

3432 יָשֻׁבִי ***yāšûbî***, a.g. GK: 3795 [→ 3437; cf. 7725]. Jashubite, "*of Jashub*":– Jashubites [1]

3433 יָשֻׁבִי לֶחֶם ***yāšubî leḥem***, n.pr.m. GK: 3788 [→ 3899]. Jashubi Lehem, "*[they] returned to Lehem*":– Jashubi-lehem [1]

3434 יָשָׁבְעָם ***yāšobʿām***, n.pr.m. GK: 3790. Jashobeam, "*the people return*":– Jashobeam [3]

3435 יִשְׁבָּק ***yišbāq***, n.pr.m. GK: 3791 [→ 7733]. Ishbak:– Ishbak [2]

3436 יָשְׁבְּקָשָׁה ***yošbᵉqāšâ***, n.pr.m. GK: 3792. Joshbekashah, "*one sitting in request [prayer?]*":– Joshbekashah [2]

3437 יָשׁוּב ***yāšûb*** or יָשִׁיב ***yāšîb***, n.pr.m. GK: 3793 & 3806 [→ 3432; cf. 7725]. Jashub, Jashib, "*he returns*":– Jashub [3]

3438 יִשְׁוָה ***yišwâ***, n.pr.m. GK: 3796 [→ 7737]. Ishvah, "*he will level*":– Ishuah [1], Ishuai [1]

3439 יְשׁוֹחָיָה ***yᵉšôḥāyâ***, n.pr.m. GK: 3797 [→ 3068+7817?]. Jeshohaiah, "[poss.] *Yahweh humbles*":– Jeshohaiah [1]

3440 יִשְׁוִי ***yišwî***, n.pr.m. GK: 3798 [→ 7737]. Ishvi:– Ishui [2], Isuah [1], Jesui [1]

3441 יִשְׁוִי ***yišwî***, a.g. GK: 3799 [→ 7737]. Ishvite, "*of Ishvi*":– Jesuites [1]

3442 יֵשׁוּעַ ***yēšûaʿ***, n.pr.m. & loc. GK: 3800 & 3801 [cf. 3467; cf. 3443]. Jeshua, "*Yahweh saves*":– Jeshua [29]

3443 יֵשׁוּעַ ***yēšûaʿ*** (Aram.), n.pr.m. GK: 10336 [cf. 3442]. Jeshua, "*Yahweh saves*":– Jeshua [1]

3444 יְשׁוּעָה ***yᵉšûʿâ***, n.f. GK: 3802 [→ 3467]. salvation, deliverance, help, rescue from a dangerous circumstance or harmful state by a savior; divine salvation usually has its focus on rescue from earthly enemies, occasionally referring to salvation from guilt, sin, and punishment:– salvation [65], deliverance [2], health [2], help [2], deliverances [1], help (+1961) [1], helping [1], save [1], saving health [1], saving [1], welfare [1]

3445 יֶשַׁח ***yešaḥ***, n.[m.]. GK: 3803. emptiness; some sources: filth, dung:– casting down [1]

3446 יִשְׂחָק ***yiśḥāq***, n.pr.m. GK: 3773 [→ 7832; cf. 3327]. Isaac, "*he laughs, he will laugh* or *mock*; *[God] laughs*":– Isaac [4]

3447 יָשַׁט ***yāšaṭ***, v. GK: 3804. [H] to extend; hold out:– held out [2], hold out [1]

3448 יִשַׁי ***yišay***, n.pr.m. GK: 3805. Jesse:– Jesse [42]

יָשִׁיב ***yāšîb***. See 3437.

3449 יִשִּׁיָּה ***yiššiyyâ*** or יִשִּׁיָּהוּ ***yiššiyyāhû***, n.pr.m. GK: 3807 & 3808 [→ 3426?+3068]. Isshiah; Ishijah, "*Yahweh forgets*":– Isshiah [3], Jesiah [2], Ishiah [1], Ishijah [1]

3450 יְשִׂימִאֵל ***yᵉśîmiʾēl***, n.pr.m. GK: 3774 [→ 7760+410]. Jesimiel, "*God [El] will establish*":– Jesimiel [1]

3451 יְשִׁימָה ***yᵉšîmâ*** or יַשִּׁמָוֶת ***yaššîmawet***, n.f. GK: 3809 & 3812 [→ 3456]. desolation, devastation:–

3452 יְשִׁימוֹן ***yᵉšîmôn***, n.m. GK: 3810 [→ 3456]. Jeshimon; wasteland:– Jeshimon [6], desert [4], wilderness [2], solitary [1]

Heb

יְשִׁימוֹת ***y^{e}šîmôt***. See 1020, 3451.

3453 יָשִׁישׁ ***yāšîš***, a. GK: 3813 [→ 3454?; cf. 3486]. old, aged:– aged [1], ancient [1], very aged men [1], very old [1]

3454 יְשִׁישַׁי ***y^{e}šîšay***, n.pr.m. GK: 3814 [→ 3453?]. Jeshishai, "*aged*":– Jeshishai [1]

3455 יָשַׂם ***yāśam***, v. GK: 3775 [cf. 7760]. prob. same as 7760: to place, set:– put [1]

3456 יָשַׁם ***yāšam***, v. GK: 3815 [→ 3451, 3452; cf. 8074]. [Q] to be desolate:– desolate [4]

3457 יִשְׁמָא ***yišmāʾ***, n.pr.m. GK: 3816 [→ 3458]. Ishma, "*desolate; God [El] he heard*":– Ishma [1]

3458 יִשְׁמָעֵאל ***yišmāʿēʾl***, n.pr.m. GK: 3817 [→ 3457, 3459]. Ishmael, "*God [El] he heard*":– Ishmael [47], Ishmael's [1]

3459 יִשְׁמְעֵאלִי ***yišm^{e}ʿēʾlî***, a.g. GK: 3818 [→ 3458]. Ishmaelite, "*of Ishmael*":– Ishmeelites [4], Ishmaelites [2], Ishmaelite [1], Ishmeelite [1]

3460 יִשְׁמַעְיָה ***yišmaʿyâ*** or יִשְׁמַעְיָהוּ ***yišmaʿyāhû***, n.pr.m. GK: 3819 & 3820 [→ 3461?]. Ishmaiah, "*Yahweh heard*":– Ishmaiah [1], Ismaiah [1]

3461 יִשְׁמְרַי ***yišm^{e}ray***, n.pr.m. GK: 3821 [→ 3460?]. Ishmerai, "*Yahweh guards*":– Ishmerai [1]

3462 יָשֵׁן ***yāšēn***, v. GK: 3822 & 3823 [→ 3463, 3464?, 3465, 8142]. [Q] to sleep, fall asleep; [N] to live a long time, be old, chronic; [P] to put to sleep:– sleep [9], slept [5], made sleep [1], old store (+3465) [1], old [1], remained long [1], sleepest [1]

3463 יָשֵׁן ***yāšēn***, a. GK: 3825 [→ 3462]. sleeping, pertaining to sleep:– sleep [3], asleep [2], sleepeth [2], sleeping [1], slept [1]

3464 יָשֵׁן ***yāšēn***, n.pr.m. GK: 3826 [→ 3462?]. Jashen, "[poss.] *asleep*":– Jashen [1]

3465 יָשָׁן ***yāšān***, a. GK: 3824 [→ 3466?; cf. 3462]. old; pertaining to last year:– old [7], old store (+3462) [1]

3466 יְשָׁנָה ***y^{e}šānâ***, n.pr.loc. GK: 3827 [→ 3465?]. Jeshanah, "*old*":– Jeshanah [1]

3467 יָשַׁע ***yāšaʿ***, v. GK: 3828 & 3830 & 4635 [→ 3444, 3468, 4190, 4338, 4337, 8668 (also used with compound proper names)]. [N] to be rescued, be delivered, be saved; [H] to save, rescue, deliver; divine salvation has its focus on rescue from earthly enemies, occasionally referring to salvation from guilt, sin, and punishment:– save [103], saved [35], saviour [13], help [10], delivered [8], saveth [7], preserved [4], deliver [3], savest [3], avenging [2], brought salvation [2], deliverer [2], helped [2], save at all (+3467) [2], saviours [2], avenged [1], defend [1], gotten victory [1], having salvation [1], preservest [1], rescue [1], safe [1]

3468 יֶשַׁע ***yešaʿ***, n.m. GK: 3829 [→ 3442; cf. 3467 (also used with compound proper names)]. salvation, deliverance, protection, often implying a victory is at hand; (of God) Savior, a title of God that focuses on rescue from earthly enemies, occasionally referring to salvation from guilt, sin, and punishment:– salvation [32], safety [3], saving [1]

3469 יִשְׁעִי ***yišʿî***, n.pr.m. GK: 3831 [→ 3467?+3068?]. Ishi, "*God has saved*":– Ishi [5]

3470 יְשַׁעְיָה ***y^{e}šaʿyâ*** or יְשַׁעְיָהוּ ***y^{e}šaʿyāhû***, n.pr.m. GK: 3832 & 3833 [→ 3467+3068]. Jeshaiah, "*Yahweh will save*":– Isaiah [31], Jeshaiah [5], Jesaiah [2], Esai [1]

3471 יָשְׁפֵה ***yāš^{e}pēh***, n.[m.]. GK: 3835. jasper (exact identification uncertain):– jasper [3]

3472 יִשְׁפָּה ***yišpâ***, n.pr.m. GK: 3834 [→ 8192]. Ishpah, "[poss.] *barren way, empty path*":– Ispah [1]

3473 יִשְׁפָּן ***yišpān***, n.pr.m. GK: 3836 [→ 8192?]. Ishpan, "[poss.] *may God judge*":– Ishpan [1]

3474 יָשַׁר ***yāšar***, v. GK: 3837 [→ 3475, 3476, 3477, 3483, 3484, 4334, 4339, 8289, 8290]. [Q] to do good, do right, be straight; [P] to make straight, make smooth; [Pu] to be evenly hammered; [H] to make straight, gaze straight; from the base meaning of straightening out a crooked object comes the fig. extension of doing an act that is not perverse, but right or just:– direct [3], make straight [3], pleased (+5869+871.1) [3], pleased well (+5869+871.1) [3], brought straight [1], directeth [1], esteem to be right [1], fitted [1], go right [1], good [1], look straight [1], meet [1], please (+5869+871.1) [1], pleaseth well (+5869) [1], right [1], took straight [1], uprightly [1], upright [1]

3475 יֵשֶׁר ***yēšer***, n.pr.m. GK: 3840 [→ 3474]. Jesher, "[perhaps] *the deity shows himself just*":– Jesher [1]

3476 יֹשֶׁר ***yōšer***, n.m. GK: 3841 [→ 3474]. uprightness, straightness, honesty, integrity:– uprightness [9], right [2], equity [1], meet [1], upright [1]

3477 יָשָׁר ***yāšār***, a. & n.pr.m. GK: 3838 & 3839 [→ 3474]. straight (not crooked or twisted); by extension, something morally straight: right, upright, innocent; (n.) upright person; as n.pr. Jashar:– right [53], upright [41], righteous [9], straight [3], Jasher [2], convenient for (+413+1886.1) [1], convenient [1], equity [1], just [1], meetest [1], meet [1], most upright [1], pleased well (+5869+871.1) [1], upright ones [1], uprightly [1], uprightness [1]

3478 יִשְׂרָאֵל ***yiśrāʾēl***, n.pr.m. & g. GK: 3776 [→ 415, 3481, 3482; cf. 8280; cf. 3479]. Israel, "*he struggles with God [El]*":– Israel [2476], Israelites [16], Israel's [10], Israel (+376) [2], Israelite (+376) [1]

3479 יִשְׂרָאֵל ***yiśrāʾēl*** (Aram.), n.pr.g. GK: 10335 [cf. 3478]. Israel, "*he struggles with God (El)*":– Israel [8]

3480 יְשַׂרְאֵלָה ***y^{e}śarʾēlâ***, n.pr.m. GK: 3777 [cf. 841]. Jesarelah:– Jesharelah [1]

3481 יִשְׂרְאֵלִי ***yiśr^{e}ʾēlî***, a.g. GK: 3778 [→ 3478, 3482]. Israelite, "*of Israel*":– Israelite [1], Israel [1]

3482 יִשְׂרְאֵלִית ***yiśr^{e}ʾēlît***, a.g. GK: 3778 [→ 3481]. f. of 3481: Israelite, "*of Israel*":– Israelitish [3]

3483 יִשְׁרָה ***yišrâ***, n.f. GK: 3842 [→ 3474]. uprightness:– uprightness [1]

3484 יְשֻׁרוּן ***y^{e}šurûn***, n.pr.m. GK: 3843 [→ 3474]. Jeshurun, "*upright*":– Jeshurun [4]

3485 יִשָּׂשכָר ***yiśśāśkār***, n.pr.m. GK: 3779 [→ 376+7939]. Issachar, "*there is reward* [Ge. 30:18]; *may [God] show mercy; hired hand*":– Issachar [43]

3486 יָשֵׁשׁ ***yāšēš***, a. GK: 3844 [→ 3453]. aged, decrepit:– him that stooped for age [1]

3487 יָת ***yāt*** (Aram.), pt. GK: 10337 [cf. 853]. not translated, indicates the direct object:–

3488 יְתִב ***y^{e}tib*** (Aram.), v. GK: 10338 [cf. 3427]. [P] to live in, dwell; to sit, be seated; [H] to cause to settle, cause to dwell in:– set [2], sit [2], dwell [1]

3489 יָתֵד ***yātēd***, n.f. GK: 3845. tent peg, stake, pin (of a loom); tool for digging:– pins [10], nail [8], pin [3], stakes [2], paddle [1]

3490 יָתוֹם ***yātôm***, n.[m.]. GK: 3846. fatherless, orphan:– fatherless [38], fatherless children [2], fatherless child [1], orphans [1]

3491 יְתוּר ***y^{e}tûr***, var. GK: 3847 [cf. 8446]. range, extent; poss. a form of 8446:– range [1]

3492 יַתִּיר ***yattîr***, n.pr.loc. GK: 3848 [→ 3498]. Jattir, "[poss.] *preeminence*":– Jattir [4]

3493 יַתִּיר ***yattîr*** (Aram.), a. GK: 10339 [cf. 3471]. exceptional, outstanding; (as adv.) so, very, exceedingly:– excellent [5], exceeding [2], exceedingly [1]

3494 יִתְלָה ***yitlâ***, n.pr.loc. GK: 3849 [→ 8518]. Ithlah, "*hanging, lofty place*":– Jethlah [1]

3495 יִתְמָה ***yitmâ***, n.pr.m. GK: 3850. Ithmah, "*fatherless; purity*":– Ithmah [1]

3496 יַתְנִיאֵל ***yatnîʾēl***, n.pr.m. GK: 3853 [→ 386+410]. Jathniel, "*God [El] hires; God [El] is forever*":– Jathniel [1]

3497 יִתְנָן ***yitnān***, n.pr.loc. GK: 3854 [→ 386]. Ithnan:– Ithnan [1]

3498 יָתַר ***yātar***, v. GK: 3855 [→ 1956, 3148, 3492?, 3499, 3500, 3501, 3502, 3503, 3504, 3505, 3506, 3508, 4195, 4340; cf. 3493 (also used with compound proper names)]. [N] to remain, be left over, the rest; [H] to have left over, spare, preserve:– left [46], remain [12], rest [12], leave [6], remained [5], remainder [4], remaineth [4], remnant [3], residue [3], make plenteous [2], reserved [2], come to remain [1], excel [1], had reserved [1], leave a remnant [1], left behind [1], preserve [1], remaining [1], too much [1]

3499 יֶתֶר ***yeter***, n.m. GK: 3856 & 3857 [→ 3323, 4340; cf. 3498]. remainder, remnant, the rest, what is left over; thong, cord, bowstring:– rest [63], remnant [14], residue [8], excellency [3], left [3], withs [3], abundant [1], cord [1], exceeding [1], excellent [1], leave [1], plentifully [1], string [1]

3500 יֶתֶר ***yeter***, n.pr.m. GK: 3858 [→ 3505; cf. 3498, 3499]. Jether; Jethro:– Jether [8], Jethro [1]

3501 יִתְרָא ***yitrāʾ***, n.pr.m. GK: 3859 [→ 3498]. Jether, "*abundance*":– Ithra [1]

3502 יִתְרָה ***yitrâ***, n.f. GK: 3860 [→ 3498]. wealth, abundance:– abundance [1], riches [1]

3503 יִתְרוֹ ***yitrô***, n.pr.m. GK: 3861 [→ 3498]. Jethro, "*remainder*":– Jethro [9]

3504 יִתְרוֹן ***yitrôn***, n.[m.]. GK: 3862 [→ 3498]. profit, gain, increase:– profit [5], excelleth [2], better [1], excellency [1], profitable [1]

3505 יִתְרִי ***yitrî***, a.g. GK: 3863 [→ 3500; cf. 3498]. Ithrite:– Ithrite [4], Ithrites [1]

3506 יִתְרָן ***yitrān***, n.pr.m. GK: 3864 [→ 3498]. Ithran, "*what is over, profit; excellent*":– Ithran [3]

3507 יִתְרְעָם ***yitr^{e}ʿām***, n.pr.m. GK: 3865 [→ 3499+5971]. Ithream, "*remainder of the people*":– Ithream [2]

3508 יֹתֶרֶת **yōteret**, n.f. GK: 3866 [→ 3498]. covering, lobe (of certain animal livers):– caul [11]

3509 יְתֵת **y^etēt**, n.pr.m. GK: 3867. Jetheth:– Jetheth [2]

3509.1 -כְּ **k^e-**, subst.pref. GK: 3869 [→ 3644; cf. 3509.4]. marker of comparison: as, like; marker of similarity or correspondence: according to; marker of time: when, as soon as, about:– as [1044], as (+834) [382], according to [367], like [361], when [164], after [75], about [47], when (+834) [47], according unto [29], like unto [23], as it were [20], according as (+834) [16], as soon as [13], so [13], thus (+2088) [12], like as (+834) [11]*

3509.2 ךָ- **-kā** or ךְ- **-āk** or כָה- **-kēh**, p.m.s.suf. GK: 3870 [→ 3509.3, 3641.1, 3654.1]. you, your:– thy [3403], thee [2501], thine [639], thou [282], thyself [46], thine own [45], you [34], thine (+3807.1) [29], thy (+3807.1) [24], your [8], ye [3], thine own (+3807.1) [2], his [1], of thy [1], the^s [1], thee (+3027) [1], thee (+3807.1) [1], thee-ward [1], thine own self [1], thou (+3027) [1], thyself (+3807.1) [1], whose [1]

3509.3 ךְ- **-k** or כִי- **-kî**, p.f.s.suf. GK: 3871 [→ 3509.2]. you, your:– thy [619], thee [458], thine [101], thou [63], thine own [9], thy (+3807.1) [7], thine (+3807.1) [3], thyself [3], thyself (+5315) [1], whom [1]

3509.4 -כְּ **k^e-** (Aram.), pp.pref. GK: 10341 [cf. 3509.1]. as, like, according to:– like [10], as [9], according to [5], when (+1768) [4], after [2], how (+4101) [2], thus (+1836) [2], about [1], after sort [1], as (+1768) [1], for [1], such (+1836) [1], together (+2298) [1], when [1]

3509.5 ךְ- **-k** (Aram.), p.suf.2.m.s. GK: 10342 [cf. 3509.2]. you, your:– thee [44], thy [44], thine [7], thou [3], thyself [1]

3510 כָּאַב **kā'ab**, v. GK: 3872 [→ 3511, 4341]. [Q] to feel pain, ache; [H] to bring pain:– sorrowful [2], grieving [1], have pain [1], made sad [1], maketh sore [1], mar [1], sore [1]

3511 כְּאֵב **k^e'ēb**, n.m. GK: 3873 [→ 3510]. pain, anguish, suffering:– sorrow [3], grief [2], pain [1]

3512 כָּאָה **kā'â**, v. GK: 3874 [cf. 3543]. [N] to be brokenhearted, lose heart; [H] to dishearten, cause to lose heart:– broken [1], grieved [1], made sad [1]

3513 כָּבֵד **kābēd**, v. GK: 3877 [→ 3514, 3515, 3516, 3517, 3519, 3520, 3520]. [Q] to be heavy; to be wealthy, honored, glorified; to be failing, dull; [N] to be glorified, honored, renowned; [P] to honor, glorify, reward; [Pu] to be honored; [H] to make heavy, make hard; [Ht] to make numerous; honor oneself. If the base meaning is "to be weighty or heavy," then by extension, negatively: hard, dull, stubborn, difficult in circumstance; positively: substantial, honored, glorious, wealthy:– honourable [15], honour [15], heavy [9], glorify [7], glorified [6], hardened [6], honoured [5], made heavy [5], glorious [4], honoureth [4], chargeable [2], heavier [2], make many [2], promote unto great honour (+3513) [2], promote unto honour (+3513) [2], went sore [2], abounding [1], boast [1], bring to honour [1], come to honour [1], dim [1], do honour [1], get honour [1], glorifieth [1], glory [1], gotten honour [1], grievous [1], had in honour [1], harden [1], heavily laid [1], honourest [1], ladeth with [1], made glorious [1], make glorious [1], make heavy [1], more grievously afflict [1], more laid [1], nobles [1], prevailed [1], promote to honour [1], rich [1], sore [1], stopped [1]

3514 כֹּבֶד **kōbed**, n.[m.]. GK: 3880 [→ 3513]. heaviness; heavy mass (density, piles):– heavy [2], great number [1], grievousness [1]

3515 כָּבֵד **kābēd**, a. GK: 3878 [→ 3513]. heavy, severe, difficult, an extended degree or amount, positive or negative:– heavy [9], great [8], grievous [8], sore [4], hard [2], much [2], slow [2], hardened [1], heavier [1], laden [1], thick [1]

3516 כָּבֵד **kābēd**, n.m. GK: 3879 [→ 3513]. liver; heart:– liver [14]

כָּבֹד **kābōd**. See 3519.

3517 כְּבֵדֻת **k^ebēdut**, n.f. GK: 3881 [→ 3513]. difficulty, awkwardness:– heavily (+871.1) [1]

3518 כָּבָה **kābâ**, v. GK: 3882. [Q] to be quenched, snuffed out; [P] to quench, put out, snuff out:– quenched [9], quench [8], put out [3], goeth out [2], go out [1], went out [1]

3519 כָּבוֹד **kābôd**, n.m. GK: 3883 [→ 350; cf. 3513]. glory, honor, splendor, wealth; while related words can be positive or negative in context, this word is almost exclusively positive in the OT; "the Glory" a title for God focuses on his splendor and high status; "my glory" means "myself" (Ge 49:8):– glory [156], honour [32], glorious [10], gloriously [1], honourable [1]

3520 כְּבוּדָּה **k^ebûddâ**, n.f. GK: 3884 & 3885 [→ 3513]. possession, valuable property; glorious, elegant:– carriage [1], glorious [1], stately [1]

3521 כָּבוּל **kābûl**, n.pr.loc. GK: 3886 [→ 3525]. Cabul, *"good for nothing"*:– Cabul [2]

3522 כַּבּוֹן **kabbôn**, n.pr.loc. GK: 3887. Cabbon:– Cabbon [1]

3523 כָּבִיר **kābîr**, n.[m.]. GK: 3889 [→ 3527]. something braided; in context referring to goat's hair:– pillow [2]

3524 כַּבִּיר **kabbîr**, a. GK: 3888 [→ 3527]. great, mighty (of God and humans), with a focus on potency or ability:– mighty [5], much [2], feeble (+3808) [1], most [1], strong [1]

3525 כֶּבֶל **kebel**, n.[m.]. GK: 3890 [→ 3521]. shackles, fetters:– fetters [2]

3526 כָּבַס **kābas**, v. GK: 3891 [cf. 3533]. [Q] (ptcp.) washer, fuller; [P] to wash, launder; [Pu] to be washed; [Hotpael] to be washed off:– wash [39], washed [7], fuller's [3], fullers' [1], washing [1]

3527 כָּבַר **kābar**, v. GK: 3892 [→ 3524, 3523, 3528, 3529, 3531, 3530, 4342, 4346]. [H] to multiply; provide in abundance:– multiplieth [1]

3528 כְּבָר **k^ebār**, adv. GK: 3893 [→ 3527]. already, before:– already [5], now [4]

3529 כְּבָר **k^ebār**, n.pr.loc. GK: 3894 [→ 3527]. Kebar:– Chebar [8]

3530 כִּבְרָה **k^ebārâ**, n.f. GK: 3896 [→ 3527]. (a certain) distance; some sources: as far as a horse can run; as far as one can see; about seven miles:– little [2], little way (+776+1886.1) [1]

3531 כְּבָרָה **k^ebārâ**, n.f. GK: 3895 [→ 3527]. sieve:– sieve [1]

3532 כֶּבֶשׂ **kebeś**, n.m. GK: 3897 [→ 3535; cf. 3775]. ram-lamb, young ram sheep:– lambs [59], lamb [41], he lamb [3], sheep [2], he lambs [1], lamb (+7716) [1]

3533 כָּבַשׁ **kābaš**, v. GK: 3899 [→ 3534, 3536; cf. 3526, 3728]. [Q] to subdue, overcome, enslave; [N] be subdued, be subject, be brought under control; [P] to subdue; [H] subdue, subjugate:– subdued [5], subdue [3], brought into subjection [2], bring into bondage [1], brought into bondage [1], force [1], keep under [1]

3534 כֶּבֶשׁ **kebeš**, n.[m.]. GK: 3900 [→ 3533]. footstool:– footstool [1]

3535 כִּבְשָׂה **kibśâ**, n.f. GK: 3898 [→ 3532]. ewe-lamb, young female sheep:– ewe lambs [3], ewe lamb [3], lamb [2]

3536 כִּבְשָׁן **kibšān**, n.m. GK: 3901 [→ 3533]. furnace, likely in context referring to a kiln or forge for making glass, pottery, smelting, etc:– furnace [4]

3537 כַּד **kad**, n.f. GK: 3902. jar, pitcher (of the size that could by carried on the shoulder):– pitcher [10], pitchers [4], barrel [3], barrels [1]

3538 כְּדַב **k^edab** (Aram.), a. GK: 10343 [cf. 3577]. misleading, false:– lying [1]

3539 כַּדְכֹּד **kadkōd**, n.[m.]. GK: 3905. ruby (exact identification unknown):– agates [1], agate [1]

3540 כְּדָרְלָעֹמֶר **k^edorlā'ōmer** or כְּדָר־לָעֹמֶר **k^edor-lā'ōmer**, n.pr.m. GK: 3906. Kedorlaomer, *"servant of [the deity] Lagamar"*:– Chedorlaomer [5]

3541 כֹּה **kōh**, adv.demo. GK: 3907 [→ 3602; cf. 3542]. this is what, thus:– thus [520], so [23], also [7], here [4], hitherto (+5704) [2], in the mean while (+3541+5704+5704+2050.1) [2], this [2], and (+2050.1) [1], and [1], more also (+3254) [1], much [1], on the other side [1], on this side [1], on this wise [1], such [1], that manner [1], that way [1], this manner [1], this way [1], yonder (+5704) [1], yonder [1]

3542 כָּה **kâ** (Aram.), adv. GK: 10345 [cf. 3541]. here, up to this point:– hitherto (+5705) [1]

3543 כָּהָה **kāhâ**, v. GK: 3908 & 3909 [→ 3544, 3545; cf. 3512]. [Q] to grow dim, be weak; [P] to fade, become faint; to rebuke, set (someone) right, with an implication that future bad behavior is curtailed:– dim [3], utterly darkened (+3543) [2], fail [1], faint [1], restrained [1]

3544 כֵּהֶה **kēheh**, a. GK: 3910 [→ 3543]. dull; weak; smoldering; despairing:– somewhat dark [5], darkish [1], dim [1], heaviness [1], smoking [1]

3545 כֵּהָה **kēhâ**, n.f. GK: 3911 [→ 3543]. healing, relief:– healing [1]

3546 כְּהַל **k^ehal** (Aram.), v. GK: 10346 [cf. 3202]. [P] to be able:– able [2], could [2]

3547 כָּהַן **kāhan**, v.den. GK: 3912 [→ 3548]. [P] to serve as a priest:– minister in the priest's office [15], executed the priest's office [2], ministered in the priest's office [2], decketh with [1], do the office of a priest [1], executing the priest's office [1], priest [1]

3548 כֹּהֵן **kōhēn**, n.m. GK: 3913 [→ 3547, 3550; cf. 3549]. priest, who not only had religious duties, but also examined persons and things for medical diagnosis, policed the unruly, and taught the word of God:– priest [421], priests [298], priest's [14], priests' [8], his[s] own (+1886.1) [2], priest's (+3807.1) [2], chief rulers [1], chief ruler [1], priests' (+3807.1) [1], princes [1], principal officer [1]

3549 כָּהֵן ***kāhēn*** (Aram.), n.m. GK: 10347 [cf. 3548]. priest:– priests [6], priest [2]

3550 כְּהֻנָּה ***k^ehunnâ***, n.f. GK: 3914 [→ 3548]. priesthood, priestly office:– priesthood [9], priest's office [4], priests' offices [1]

3551 כַּוָּה ***kawwâ*** (Aram.), n.f. GK: 10348. window:– windows [1]

3552 כּוּב ***kûb***, n.pr.g. GK: 3915. Kub:– Chub [1]

3553 כּוֹבַע ***kôba'***, n.m. GK: 3916 [cf. 6959]. helmet:– helmet [4], helmets [2]

3554 כָּוָה ***kāwâ***, v. GK: 3917 [→ 3555, 3587, 4348]. [N] to be burned, be scorched:– burnt [2]

כֹּחַ ***kōaḥ***. See 3581.

3555 כְּוִיָּה ***k^ewiyyâ***, n.f. GK: 3918 [→ 3458]. burn spot, scar (of a burn):– burning [2]

3556 כּוֹכָב ***kôkāb***, n.m. GK: 3919. star, planet, a luminary in the night sky; by extension: human power (such as a king), heavenly power (that serve God); stargazer, one who studies the movements of the stars to predict the future:– stars [34], star [2], stargazers (+2374+871.1+1886.1) [1]

3557 כּוּל ***kûl***, v. GK: 3920 [cf. 3634?]. [Q] to hold, seize; [Pil] to hold; to provide, supply, sustain; [H] to hold; to bear, endure:– sustain [4], contain [3], fed [3], feed [3], abide [2], contained [2], nourish [2], receive [2], able to abide [1], bear [1], comprehended [1], containeth [1], forbearing [1], guide [1], held [1], holding in [1], hold [1], made provision [1], nourished [1], nourisher [1], present [1], provided of sustenance [1], provided victuals [1], provided victual [1]

3558 כּוּמָז ***kûmāz***, n.[m.]. GK: 3921. ornament, necklace:– tablets [2]

3559 כּוּן ***kûn***, v. GK: 3922 & 5788 [→ 3078, 3112, 3199, 3562, 3651, 3663, 4349, 4350, 4368, 4369, 5225, 8498, 8499; cf. 3653]. [N] to be established, be steadfast, be firm, be prepared; [Pol] to establish, set in place, make secure; [Polal] to be made firm, be prepared; [H] to establish, make preparations, provide; [Ho] to be made ready, be established, be attached:– prepared [53], established [42], prepare [28], establish [12], ready [9], fixed [4], made ready [4], make ready [4], right [4], stablished [4], stablish [4], prepareth [3], set [3], certain [2], confirmed [2], fashioned [2], firm [2], order [2], provideth [2], provide [2], certainty [1], confirm [1], could frame [1], directed [1], directeth [1], direct [1], faithfulness [1], fashion [1], fastened [1], fitted [1], made provision [1], make preparation [1], meet [1], ordained [1], ordered [1], perfect [1], preparation [1], preparest [1], provided for [1], set aright [1], set forth [1], set in order [1], setteth fast [1], stable [1], stablisheth [1], standeth [1], stood [1], tarry [1], very deed [1]

3560 כּוּן ***kûn***, n.pr.loc. GK: 3923. Cun, *"chosen"*:– Chun [1]

3561 כַּוָּן ***kawwān***, n.[m.]. GK: 3924. cake of bread (presented as an offering):– cakes [2]

3561.1 כוֹן- ***-kôn*** (Aram.), p.suf.2.m.pl. GK: 10349 [→ 3641.2; cf. 3641.1]. you, your:– you [6], ye [2], your [2]

3562 כּוֹנַנְיָהוּ ***kônanyāhû***, n.pr.m. GK: 3925 [→ 3559+3068]. Conaniah:– Cononiah [2], Conaniah [1]

3563 כּוֹס ***kôs***, n.f. GK: 3926 & 3927. cup; little owl:– cup [30], little owl [2], cups [1], owl [1]

3564 כּוּר ***kûr***, n.[m.]. GK: 3929 [cf. 3600]. (little) furnace (for smelting metals); by extension: the testing and purification process:– furnace [9]

כּוֹר ***kôr***. See 3733.

3565 כּוֹר עָשָׁן ***kôr 'āšān***, n.pr.loc. GK: 3930 [cf. 953]. Kor Ashan:– Chor-ashan [1]

3566 כּוֹרֶשׁ ***kôreš***, n.pr.m. GK: 3931 [cf. 3567]. Cyrus:– Cyrus [15]

3567 כּוֹרֶשׁ ***kôreš*** (Aram.), n.pr.m. GK: 10350 [cf. 3566]. Cyrus:– Cyrus [8]

3568 כּוּשׁ ***kûš***, n.pr.m. & loc. GK: 3932 & 3933 [→ 3569, 3570, 3571]. Cush:– Ethiopia [19], Cush [8], Ethiopians [3]

3569 כּוּשִׁי ***kûšî***, a.g. GK: 3934 [→ 3568]. Cushite, *"of Cush"*:– Cushi [10], Ethiopians [9], Ethiopian [8]

3570 כּוּשִׁי ***kûšî***, n.pr.m. GK: 3935 [→ 3568]. Cushi:–

3571 כּוּשִׁית ***kûšît***, a.g. GK: 3934 [→ 3569]. f. of 3569: Cushite, *"of Cush"*:–

3572 כּוּשָׁן ***kûšān***, n.pr.loc. GK: 3936. Cushan:– Cushan [1]

3573 כּוּשַׁן רִשְׁעָתַיִם ***kûšan riš'ātayim***, n.pr.m. GK: 3937. Cushan-Rishathaim, *"man of Cush, doubly guilty"*:– Chushan-rishathaim [4]

3574 כּוֹשָׁרָה ***kôšārâ***, n.f. GK: 3938 [cf. 7891]. singing or prosperity, fortune:– chains [1]

3575 כּוּת ***kût*** or כּוּתָה ***kûtâ***, n.pr.loc. GK: 3939 & 3940. Cuthah:– Cuthah [1], Cuth [1]

3576 כָּזַב ***kāzab***, v. GK: 3941 [→ 391, 392?, 3577, 3578, 3580]. [Q] to lie; [N] to be proven a liar, be false; [P] to lie, deceive, prove false; to fail; [H] to prove someone a liar:– lie [8], lied [2], fail [1], found a liar [1], in vain [1], liars [1], lying [1], make a liar [1]

3577 כָּזָב ***kāzāb***, n.m. GK: 3942 [→ 3576; cf. 3538]. lie, falsehood; by extension: delusion; false god (worshiped by a deluded person):– lies [21], leasing [2], lie [2], lying [2], deceitful [1], false [1], liar (+376) [1], lies (+1697) [1]

3578 כֹּזֵבָא ***kōzēbā'***, n.pr.loc. GK: 3943 [→ 3576]. Cozeba, *"liar"*:– Chozeba [1]

3579 כָּזְבִּי ***kozbî***, n.pr.f. GK: 3944. Cozbi, *"deceitful; luxuriant"*:– Cozbi [2]

3580 כְּזִיב ***k^ezîb***, n.pr.loc. GK: 3945 [→ 3576]. Kezib, *"deceit"*:– Chezib [1]

3581 כֹּחַ ***kōaḥ***, n.m. GK: 3946 & 3947. strength, power, might, ability; often physical strength and the vigor of good health, sometimes simply ability to accomplish an action; monitor lizard; some sources: any kind of lizard:– strength [57], power [47], might [7], force [3], ability [2], able [2], able (+6113) [1], chameleon [1], fruits [1], in strength [1], powerful [1], substance [1], wealth [1], weary (+3019) [1]

3582 כָּחַד ***kāḥad***, v. GK: 3948. [N] to be hidden; be destroyed, perish; [P] to hide, conceal, keep from; [H] to hide; to destroy, annihilate, get rid of:– cut off [10], hide [10], hid [6], concealed [2], conceal [2], cut down [1], desolate [1]

3583 כָּחַל ***kāḥal***, v. GK: 3949. [Q] to paint (eyes):– paintedst [1]

3584 כָּחַשׁ ***kāḥaš***, v. GK: 3950 [→ 3585, 3586]. [Q] to be thin; [N] to cringe, feign obedience; [P] to lie, deceive; fail; to cringe, feign obedience; [Ht] to cringe, feign obedience:– deny [3], submit [3], denied [2], fail [2], lying [2], belied [1], deal falsely [1], deceive [1], dissembled [1], faileth [1], found liars [1], lied [1], lieth [1], lie [1], submitted [1]

3585 כַּחַשׁ ***kaḥaš***, n.m. GK: 3951 [→ 3584]. lie, deception; gauntness, thinness, leanness:– lies [4], leanness [1], lying [1]

3586 כֶּחָשׁ ***keḥāš***, a. GK: 3952 [→ 3584]. deceitful, untruthful:– lying [1]

3587 כִּי ***kî***, n.[m.]. GK: 3953 [→ 3554]. branding:– burning [1]

3588 כִּי ***kî***, c. GK: 3954. a marker that shows the relationship between clauses, sentences, or sections; logical: for, that, because; contrast: but, except; introducing a statement, often untranslated:– for [2322], that [696], because [442], when [237], but [173], if [168], but (+518) [86], surely [44], though [37], save (+518) [13], seeing [12], how [11], yet [10], although [9], yea [9], therefore [8], how much more (+637) [7], even [6], except (+518) [6], how much less (+637) [5], how that [5], because (+5921) [4], for (+5921) [4], nevertheless [4], so that [4], though (+518) [4], until (+5704) [4], whereas [4], assuredly [3], because (+3282) [3], else [3], in that [3], so [3], while [3], and (+518) [2], as [2], because (+3651+5921) [2], because (+6118) [2], because that [2], for (+518) [2], for if [2], forasmuch as [2], if not [2], or (+2050.1) [2], surely (+518) [2], than (+518) [2], to be [2], truly [2], whether [2], yet (+518) [2], also [1], although (+637) [1], and when [1], and [1], because (+8478) [1], because of [1], but (+518+3808) [1], but for (+518) [1], but that (+518) [1], but that [1], certainly [1], doubtless [1], either [1], even so [1], except (+1571) [1], except (+3884) [1], except (+518+3808) [1], except [1], for (+2088) [1], for (+4480) [1], for (+5973) [1], for surely (+518) [1], for that (+8478) [1], for then [1], for though (+518) [1], forasmuch as (+3282) [1], forasmuch as (+3651+5921) [1], forasmuch [1], forsomuch as (+3282) [1], how much less (+637+3808) [1], how much more then (+637) [1], howbeit yet (+389) [1], howbeit [1], inasmuch as [1], moreover [1], most [1], much less (+637) [1], much less for (+637) [1], much more (+637) [1], neither (+3808) [1], nevertheless (+518) [1], nevertheless (+657) [1], notwithstanding (+657) [1], now (+6258) [1], now [1], of a truth (+518) [1], rightly [1], save only (+518) [1], saving (+518) [1], seeing that [1], shall (+518) [1], since [1], than that [1], that (+518) [1], that when [1], then (+227) [1], then [1], thereof [1], though (+5973) [1], though (+637) [1], thus [1], till (+5704) [1], too [1], to [1], unless (+3884) [1], unless (+518) [1], until (+518) [1], wherefore (+389) [1], which [1], whom [1], whose [1], yea (+637) [1]

3589 כִּיד ***kîd***, n.[m.]. GK: 3957. destruction:– destruction [1]

3590 כִּידוֹד ***kîdôd***, n.m. GK: 3958. spark:– sparks [1]

3591 כִּידוֹן ***kîdôn***, n.[m.]. GK: 3959 [→ 3592?]. javelin, lance, spear:– spear [5], shield [2], lance [1], target [1]

3592 כִּידֹן ***kîdōn***, n.pr.m. GK: 3961 [→ 3591?]. Kidon:– Chidon [1]

3593 כִּידוֹר ***kîdôr***, n.[m.]. GK: 3960. attack, battle:– battle [1]

3594 כִּיּוּן ***kiyyûn***, n.m. GK: 3962. pedestal:– Chiun [1]

3595 כִּיּוֹר ***kiyyôr***, n.m. GK: 3963. basin, pan, firepot:– laver [15], lavers [5], hearth [1], pan [1], scaffold [1]

3596 כִּילַי ***kîlay***, n.m. GK: 3964 [→ 5230?]. scoundrel:– churl [2]

3597 כֵּילַפּוֹת ***kêlappôt***, n.[f.]. GK: 3965 [→ 3619?]. an iron-tipped tool: ax, crowbar, pickax, etc:– hammers [1]

3598 כִּימָה ***kîmâ***, n.f. GK: 3966. Pleiades (a constellation):– Pleiades [2], seven stars [1]

3599 כִּיס ***kîs***, n.m. GK: 3967. bag, purse:– bag [4], purse [1]

3600 כִּיר ***kîr***, n.[m.]. GK: 3968 [cf. 3564]. cooking pot, stove, a small portable cooking hearth, the form of the word suggesting it is large enough for a pair of pots:– ranges for pots [1]

כִּיֹּר ***kîōr***. See 3595.

3601 כִּישׁוֹר ***kîšôr***, n.[m.]. GK: 3969. distaff, spindle, whorl, the small disk at the bottom of a distaff to promote turning:– spindle [1]

3602 כָּכָה ***kākâ***, adv. GK: 3970 [→ 3541]. this is what, this is how, thus:– thus [17], so [8], after this manner [3], even so [3], after that manner [1], even thus [1], in such a case [1], this [1]

3603 כִּכָּר ***kikkār***, n.f. GK: 3971 [→ 3769; cf. 3604]. plain (geographical area); loaf of bread; cover (of lead); talent (unit of weight or value, about 75 pounds [34 kg]):– talents [35], plain [12], talent [10], two talents [3], loaf [2], loaves [2], piece [2], morsel [1], plain country [1]

3604 כַּכַּר ***kakkar*** (Aram.), n.[f.]. GK: 10352 [cf. 3603]. talent (unit of weight or value, probably about 75 lbs [34 k]):– talents [1]

3605 כֹּל ***kōl***, n.m. GK: 3972 [→ 3626; cf. 3634; cf. 3606, cf. 3635]. all, everyone, everything, totality of a mass or collective; every, any, a particular of a totality:– all [4291], every [362], any [169], whole [130], every one [95], no (+3808) [43], whosoever [34], whatsoever (+834) [33], whatsoever [23], for ever (+3117+1886.1) [15], none (+3808) [13], whithersoever (+834+871.1) [12], daily (+3117+1886.1) [11], continually (+3117+1886.1) [9], wholly [9], whosoever (+834) [8], any thing [7], as long as (+3117) [5], altogether [4], alway (+3117+1886.1) [4], every man [4], every province (+4082+4082+2050.1) [4], every thing [4], nothing (+3808) [4], what soever (+834) [4], all things [3], always (+3117+1886.1) [3], always (+6256+871.1) [3], as many as [3], ever (+3117+1886.1) [3], nothing (+3808+1886.1) [3], what [3], whatsoever (+871.1) [3], whithersoever (+413+834) [3], whomsoever (+834) [3], as long as (+834+3117+1886.1) [2], every city (+5892+5892+2050.1) [2], no (+369) [2], nothing (+369) [2], perpetually (+3117+1886.1) [2], that [2], throughout (+871.1) [2], whatsoever (+3807.1) [2], whatsoever (+834+3509.1) [2], whoso [2], all (+376) [1], all generations (+1755+1755+2050.1) [1], all manner [1], all over [1], always (+3117) [1], always (+871.1) [1], any (+259) [1], any manner [1], any thing (+3972) [1], as (+834+3509.1) [1], as long as (+3117+1886.1) [1], as long as [1], as many as (+834) [1], as much as (+3509.1) [1], as much as (+834) [1], at wit's end (+1104+2451) [1], continually (+3117) [1], continually (+6256+871.1) [1], daily (+3117+871.1) [1], enough [1], everlasting (+5769) [1], evermore (+3117+1886.1) [1], every day (+3117+3117+2050.1) [1], every generation (+1755+1755+2050.1) [1], every man's [1], every where [1], every year (+8141+8141+2050.1) [1], for evermore (+3117+1886.1) [1], generally [1], howsoever (+834) [1], many [1], more and more (+3254+5921) [1], no (+1115) [1], no (+369+3807.1) [1], none (+408+871.1) [1], nor (+2050.1) [1], nothing (+1097) [1], nothing (+1697+3808) [1], nothing (+408) [1], open [1], ought else (+3972) [1], ought [1], so long as (+3117+1886.1) [1], so long as (+871.1) [1], soever [1], the[s] [1], throughout all [1], utterly [1], whatsoever (+3509.1) [1], whatsoever (+3627+1886.1) [1], whensoever (+871.1) [1], wheresoever (+3807.1) [1], wheresoever (+413) [1], wheresoever (+834+871.1) [1], wheresoever any (+834+8033) [1], while (+5750) [1], whithersoever (+834+5921) [1], whithersoever (+834+8033) [1], whosoever (+2050.2) [1], whosoever (+376) [1], whosoever (+376+834) [1], withal [1], yearly (+8141+8141+871.1+2050.1) [1]

3606 כֹּל ***kōl*** (Aram.), n.m. GK: 10353 [→ 3635; cf. 3605]. all, totality, completion of an event; a part of a totality: any, every:– all [51], any [8], forasmuch as (+1768+6903) [8], whole [6], because (+1768+6903) [4], every [4], no (+3809) [3], therefore (+1836+6903) [3], wherefore (+1836+6903) [2], whosoever (+1768) [2], as (+1768+6903) [1], for this cause (+1836+6903) [1], manner [1], no[s] [1], none (+3809) [1], that (+1836+6903) [1], therefore (+1768+6903) [1], though (+1768+6903) [1], whatsoever (+1768) [1], whatsoever (+1768+1768) [1], wheresoever (+1768+871.2) [1], whosoever (+606) [1], whosoever (+606+1768+1768) [1]

3607 כָּלָא ***kālā'***, v. GK: 3973 & 3974 [→ 3608, 3628, 4356; cf. 3615, 3627]. [Q] to stop, withhold, contain; [Qp] to be confined; [N] to be restrained; [P] to finish:– shut up [4], stayed [3], refrained [2], restrained [2], withhold [2], finish [1], forbid [1], keep back [1], kept [1], retain [1]

3608 כֶּלֶא ***kele'***, n.[m.]. GK: 3975 [→ 3607; cf. 3628]. prison, (house of) imprisonment:– prison (+1004+1886.1) [4], prison [4], prison (+1004) [2]

3609 כִּלְאָב ***kil'āb***, n.pr.m. GK: 3976. Kileab:– Chileab [1]

3610 כִּלְאַיִם ***kil'ayim***, n.[m.]. GK: 3977. (things of) two kinds:– diverse kind [1], divers [1], mingled of linen and woollen (+8162) [1], mingled [1]

3611 כֶּלֶב ***keleb***, n.m. GK: 3978 [→ 3612; cf. 3619]. dog; by extension of a person of low status: a dead dog; an immoral person: male prostitute:– dogs [16], dog [14], dog's [2]

3612 כָּלֵב ***kālēb***, n.pr.m. GK: 3979 [→ 3613, 3614, 3619, 3621; cf. 3611]. Caleb, *"dog; snappish, warding off"*:– Caleb [31], Caleb's [4]

3613 כָּלֵב אֶפְרָתָה ***kālēb 'eprātâ***, n.pr.loc. GK: 3980 [→ 3612+672]. Caleb Ephrathah:– Caleb-ephratah [1]

3614 כָּלִבִּי ***kālibbî***, a.g. GK: 3981 & 3982 [→ 3612]. Calebite, *"of Caleb"*:– of the house of Caleb [1]

3615 כָּלָה ***kālâ***, v. GK: 3983 [→ 401, 3616, 3617, 3631, 3630, 4357, 8502, 8503; cf. 3607, 3627, 3634, 5239]. [Q] to finish, fulfill, complete; to fail, cease, perish; [P] to finish, complete, fulfill; to destroy, end, wipe out; [Pu] to be completed, be concluded:– made an end [41], consumed [36], consume [22], finished [19], fail [12], done [9], accomplished [7], ended [7], accomplish [5], determined [4], faileth [4], spend [4], spent [4], end [2], fainteth [2], fulfilled [2], left [2], make an end [2], bringeth to pass [1], caused to fail [1], ceaseth [1], cease [1], consumed away [1], destroy utterly [1], destroyeth [1], expired [1], failed [1], finish [1], fulfil [1], fully [1], left off [1], longed [1], make clean riddance [1], pluck [1], quite take away [1], utterly destroyed [1], wasted [1], waste [1], wholly reap (+3807.1) [1]

3616 כָּלֶה ***kāleh***, a. GK: 3985 [→ 3615]. failing with desire, longing:– fail [1]

3617 כָּלָה ***kālâ***, n.f. GK: 3986 [→ 3615]. destruction, complete destruction:– full end [8], altogether [3], consumption [2], utter end [2], consumed [1], consume [1], consummation [1], determined [1], end [1], riddance [1], utterly consume [1]

3618 כַּלָּה ***kallâ***, n.f. GK: 3987 [→ 3623]. (before marriage) bride; daughter-in-law:– daughter in law [14], bride [9], spouse [6], daughters in law [3], spouses [2]

כְּלוּא ***k^{e}lû'***. See 3628.

3619 כְּלוּב ***k^{e}lûb***, n.m. GK: 3990 [→ 3597?, 3611, 3612, 3619, 3620?]. (fruit) basket; (bird) cage:– basket [2], cage [1]

3620 כְּלוּב ***k^{e}lûb***, n.pr.m. GK: 3991 [→ 3619?]. Kelub, *"basket"*:– Chelub [2]

3621 כְּלוּבָי ***k^{e}lûbāy***, n.pr.m. GK: 3992 [→ 3612]. Caleb, *"dog; snappish warding off"*:– Chelubai [1]

3622 כְּלֻהַי ***k^{e}luhî*** or כְּלוּהוּ ***k^{e}lûhû***, n.pr.m. GK: 3988 & 3993. Keluhi:– Chelluh [1]

3623 כְּלוּלֹת ***k^{e}lûlōt***, n.f. GK: 3994 [→ 3618]. time of betrothal, state of betrothal:– espousals [1]

3624 כֶּלַח ***kelaḥ***, n.m. GK: 3995. full vigor:– full age [1], old age [1]

3625 כֶּלַח ***kelaḥ***, n.pr.loc. GK: 3996. Calah, *"strength, vigor"*:– Calah [2]

3626 כָּל־חֹזֶה ***kol-ḥōzeh***, n.pr.m. GK: 3997 [→ 3605+2374]. Col-Hozeh, *"every seer"*:– Col-hozeh [2]

3627 כְּלִי ***k^{e}lî***, n.m. GK: 3998 [cf. 3607?, 3615?]. article, utensil, thing; a general term that can be used of any object:– vessels [132], instruments [37], vessel [34], jewels [20], armourbearer (+5375) [18], weapons [17], stuff [14], thing [11], armour [10], furniture [7], weapon [4], bag [2], carriage [2], instrument [2], artillery [1], carriages [1], furnish (+6213) [1], jewel [1], one another[s] [1], pot [1], psaltery (+5035) [1], sacks [1], that is made [1], that which pertaineth [1], things made [1], tool [1], wares [1], whatsoever (+3605+1886.1) [1]

3628 כְּלוּא ***k^{e}lû'*** or כְּלִיא ***k^{e}lî'***, n.[m.]. GK: 3989 & 3999 [→ 3607; cf. 3608]. imprisonment:– prison (+1004+1886.1) [2]

Heb

3629 כִּלְיָה ***kilyâ***, n.f. GK: 4000. kidney; by extension: inmost being: heart, mind, spirit, the seat of thought and emotion of the inner person; kernel (of wheat):– kidneys [18], reins [13]

3630 כִּלְיוֹן ***kilyôn***, n.pr.m. GK: 4002 [→ 3615]. Kilion, "*annihilation*":– Chilion [2], Chilion's [1]

3631 כִּלָּיוֹן ***killāyôn***, n.m. GK: 4001 [→ 3615]. destruction, annihilation; weariness, failure (of the eyes):– consumption [1], failing [1]

3632 כָּלִיל ***kālîl***, a. & subst. GK: 4003 [→ 3634]. entire, whole, perfect; whole burnt offering:– wholly [4], perfect [3], all [2], whole [2], every whit [1], flame [1], perfection [1], utterly [1]

3633 כַּלְכֹּל ***kalkōl***, n.pr.m. GK: 4004 [→ 3634?]. Calcol:– Calcol [1], Chalcol [1]

3634 כָּלַל ***kālal***, v. GK: 4005 [→ 3605, 3626, 3632, 3633?, 3636, 4358, 4360, 4359; cf. 3557?, 3615; cf. 3606, cf. 3635]. [Q] to bring to perfection, make complete:– made perfect [1], perfected [1]

3635 כְּלַל ***k***e***lal*** (Aram.), v. GK: 10354 [→ 3606; cf. 3634]. [Sh] to finish, restore; [Hsh] to be finished:– set up [4], make up [2], finished [1]

3636 כְּלָל ***k***e***lāl***, n.pr.m. GK: 4006 [→ 3634]. Kelal, "*perfection, completeness*":– Chelal [1]

3637 כָּלַם ***kālam***, v. GK: 4007 [→ 3639, 3640]. [N] to be disgraced, be humiliated, be put to shame; [H] to disgrace, humble, bring to shame; [Ho] to be mistreated, be despairing:– ashamed [11], confounded [11], put to shame [5], blush [3], hurt [2], done shame [1], make ashamed [1], put to confusion [1], reproached [1], reproach [1], shameth [1]

3638 כִּלְמַד ***kilmad***, n.pr.loc. GK: 4008. Kilmad:– Chilmad [1]

3639 כְּלִמָּה ***k***e***limmâ***, n.f. GK: 4009 [→ 3637]. disgrace, shame, scorn:– shame [20], confusion [6], dishonour [3], reproach [1]

3640 כְּלִמּוּת ***k***e***limmût***, n.f. GK: 4010 [→ 3637]. shame, disgrace, insult:– shame [1]

3641 כַּלְנֵה or כַּלְנוֹ ***kalnēh*** or ***kalnô***, n.pr.loc. GK: 4011 & 4012. Calneh, Calno, "*all of them*":– Calneh [2], Calno [1]

3641.1 כֶם- ***-kem***, p.m.pl.suf. GK: 4013 [→ 3509.2]. you, your:– you [1209], your [1175], ye [145], your (+3807.1) [44], your own [22], yourselves [22], yourselves (+5315) [6], yours (+3807.1) [4], thee [2], thou [1], thy [1], your (+4480) [1], yours [1]

3641.2 כֹם- ***-kōm*** (Aram.), p.suf.2.m.pl. GK: 10355 [→ 3641.2; cf. 3641.1]. you, your:– you [3], your [2]

3642 כָּמַהּ ***kāmah***, v. GK: 4014 [→ 3643]. [Q] to long for, yearn for:– longeth [1]

3643 כִּמְהָם or כִּמְוֹהָם ***kimhām*** or ***kimwhām***, n.pr.m. GK: 4016 & 4018 [cf. 3642]. Kimham, Kimuham:– Chimham [4]

3644 כְּמוֹ ***k***e***mô***, adv. & c. GK: 4017 [→ 3509.1+4100]. like, as; for, with, when:– as [60], like [41], like unto [17], according to [2], as it were [2], as well as [2], like to [2], such as [2], and [1], both [1], even [1], in comparison of [1], like as [1], so [1], the like [1], thus [1], when [1], worth [1]

3645 כְּמוֹשׁ or כְּמִישׁ ***k***e***môš*** or ***k***e***mîš***, n.pr. GK: 4019 & 4020. Chemosh, Chemish (pagan god):– Chemosh [8]

3646 כַּמֹּן ***kammōn***, n.m. GK: 4021. cummin (a small, flavorful seed of the carrot family):– cummin [3]

3647 כָּמַס ***kāmas***, v. GK: 4022 [→ 4363]. [Qp] to be kept in reserve:– laid up in store [1]

3648 כָּמַר ***kāmar***, v. GK: 4023 [→ 3649]. [N] to become hot; become aroused, be excited (with compassion):– black [1], kindled [1], yerned [1], yern [1]

3649 כֹּמֶר ***kōmer***, n.m. GK: 4024 [→ 3648]. priest, in the OT always one who serves a foreign god, with a possible focus on manic rituals and altered states of awareness:– Chemarims [1], idolatrous priests [1], priests [1]

3650 כַּמְרִיר ***kamrîr***, n.m. GK: 4025. blackness, deep gloom:– blackness [1]

3651 כֵּן ***kēn***, a. & adv. GK: 4026 & 4027 [cf. 3559; cf. 3652]. honest; right, correct, orderly; (adv.) marker to show sequence of logic: so, thus, therefore; marker to show sequence of events: so, then:– so [283], therefore (+3807.1) [176], therefore (+5921) [125], wherefore (+5921) [22], thus [20], wherefore (+3807.1) [18], this [17], afterward (+310) [15], that [12], likewise [11], such [7], true [5], afterwards (+310) [4], right [4], as [3], because (+5921) [3], in like manner [3], like [3], well [3], after that (+310) [2], because (+3588+5921) [2], even so [2], surely (+3807.1) [2], according [1], after that (+310+2050.1) [1], afterward (+310+4480) [1], also [1], aright [1], as (+834+3509.1) [1], as yet (+5704) [1], certainly [1], even as (+834+3509.1) [1], following (+310) [1], for which cause (+3807.1) [1], for which cause (+5921) [1], forasmuch (+3807.1) [1], forasmuch as (+3588+5921) [1], howbeit (+2050.1) [1], if so (+518) [1], state [1], straightway [1], that (+5921) [1], the more [1], thenceforth (+310) [1], therefore [1], which thing [1]

3652 כֵּן ***kēn*** (Aram.), adv. GK: 10357 [cf. 3651]. this is what, thus:– thus [8]

3653 כֵּן ***kēn***, n.m. GK: 4029 & 4030 [→ 3662, 3663; cf. 3559]. position; place; stand (of a basin):– foot [8], estate [4], base [2], office [1], place [1], well [1]

3654 כֵּן ***kēn***, n.[m.]. GK: 4031 & 4038. gnats, flies:– lice [6], in manner [1]

3654.1 כֶן- or כֶנָה- ***-ken*** or ***-kenâ***, p.f.pl.suf. GK: 4032 [→ 3509.2]. you, your:– your [16], you [2], ye [1]

3655 כָּנָה ***kānâ***, v. GK: 4033. [P] to bestow a title or name of honor; to flatter by giving a name of honor:– give flattering titles [2], surnamed [1], surname [1]

3656 כַּנֵּה ***kannēh***, n.pr.loc. GK: 4034. Canneh:– Canneh [1]

3657 כַּנָּה ***kannâ***, n.f. GK: 4035. root:– vineyard [1]

3658 כִּנּוֹר ***kinnôr***, n.m. GK: 4036. a stringed instrument: harp, lyre, lute, zither:– harp [25], harps [17]

3659 כָּנְיָהוּ ***konyāhû***, n.pr.m. GK: 4037 [→ 3078]. Jehoiachin:– Coniah [3]

3660 כְּנֵמָא ***k***e***nēmā'*** (Aram.), adv. GK: 10358. as follows, thus:– thus [2], after this manner [1], in this sort [1], so [1]

3661 כָּנַן ***kānan***, var. GK: *. to plant a vineyard:–

3662 כְּנָנִי ***k***e***nānî***, n.pr.m. GK: 4039 [→ 3663]. Kenani, "*Yahweh strengthens*":– Chenani [1]

3663 כְּנַנְיָה or כְּנַנְיָהוּ ***k***e***nanyâ*** or ***k***e***nanyāhû*** or כָּנַנְיָהוּ ***kānanyāhû***, n.pr.m. GK: 4040 & 4041 & 4042 [→ 3068+3559, 3662]. Kenaniah, Conaniah, "*Yahweh strengthens*":– Chenaniah [3]

3664 כָּנַס ***kānas***, v. GK: 4043 [→ 4370; cf. 3673]. [Q, P] to assemble, gather, store up; [Ht] to wrap around:– gather together [3], gathered [2], gathereth together [2], gather [2], heap up [1], wrap [1]

3665 כָּנַע ***kāna'***, v. GK: 4044 [→ 3666]. [N] to be humbled, be subdued, be subjected; [H] to subdue, humble, subject:– humbled [13], subdued [9], bring down [2], humbleth [2], humble [2], bring low [1], brought down [1], brought into subjection [1], brought low [1], brought under [1], humbledst [1], subduedst [1], subdue [1]

3666 כִּנְעָה ***kin'â***, n.f. GK: 4045 [→ 3665]. bundle of belongings:– wares [1]

3667 כְּנַעַן ***k***e***na'an***, n.pr.m. & loc. GK: 4046 & 4047 [→ 3668?, 3669]. Canaan; Canaanite, "*land of purple*, hence *merchant, trader*"; merchant, trader:– Canaan [89], merchant [3], traffickers [1], traffick [1]

3668 כְּנַעֲנָה ***k***e***na***a***nâ***, n.pr.m. GK: 4049 [→ 3667?]. Kenaanah, "*toward Canaan*":– Chenaanah [5]

3669 כְּנַעֲנִי ***k***e***na***a***nî***, a.g. & n.m. GK: 4048 & 4050 & 4051 [→ 3667]. Canaanite, of Canaan, in Canaan, "*of Canaan*"; merchant, trader:– Canaanites [55], Canaanite [12], Canaanitess [1], Canaanitish woman [1], Canaanitish [1], Canaan [1], merchants [1], merchant [1]

3670 כָּנַף ***kānap***, v.den. GK: 4052 [→ 3671]. [N] to hide oneself, be hidden:– removed into a corner [1]

3671 כָּנָף ***kānāp***, n.f. GK: 4053 [→ 3670]. extreme part: wing (of creatures that fly); corner, hem (of garment); ends (of the earth):– wings [60], wing [13], skirt [12], borders [2], corners [2], ends [2], feathered [2], one another (+413+3671) [2], skirts [2], sort [2], winged [2], bird (+1167) [1], flying [1], other[s] [1], overspreading [1], quarters [1], two wings [1], uttermost part [1]

3672 כִּנְּרוֹת ***kinrôt*** or כִּנֶּרֶת ***kinneret*** or כִּנֲּרוֹת ***kin***a***rôt***, n.pr.loc. GK: 4054 & 4055. Kinnereth, Kinneroth, "*zithers, lyres*":– Chinnereth [3], Cinneroth [3], Cinnereth [1]

3673 כְּנַשׁ ***k***e***naš*** (Aram.), v. GK: 10359 [cf. 3664]. [P] to assemble (persons); [Htpa] to be assembled:– gathered together [2], gather together [1]

3674 כְּנָת ***k***e***nāt***, n.f. GK: 4056 [cf. 3675]. associate, companion:– companions [1]

3675 כְּנָת ***k***e***nāt*** (Aram.), n.m. GK: 10360 [cf. 3674]. associate, colleague:– companions [7]

3676 כֵּס ***k's***, var. GK: 4058 [→ 3678+3050; cf. 3764]. poss. short form of 3678: seat, throne:–

3677 כֶּסֶא ***kese'***, n.[m.]. GK: 4057 & 4060 [→ 3678]. full moon:– appointed [1], time appointed [1]

3678 כִּסֵּא ***kissē'*** or כִּסֵּה ***kissēh***, n.m. GK: 4058 & 4061 [→ 3676]. seat, chair; in a public or civic setting: place of authority, seat of honor; of royalty or deity: throne:– throne [123], seat [7], thrones [4], stool [1], sworn (+3027+5921) [1]

3679 כַּשְׂדָּי ***kasdāy*** (Aram.), n.pr.g. GK: 10361 [cf. 3779]. Chaldean:– Chaldean [1]

3680 כָּסָה ***kāsâ***, v. GK: 4059 [→ 3681, 3682, 4372, 4374]. [Qp] to be covered; [N] to be covered; [P] to cover, conceal; to decorate; to overwhelm; [Pu] to be covered, be shrouded; [Ht] to cover oneself, put on clothing:– covered [61], cover [50], covereth [21], concealeth [2], conceal [2], coveredst [2], covering [2], hide [2], hid [2], overwhelmed [2], clad [1], closed [1], clothed [1], coverest [1], flee to hide [1], hideth [1]

כֶּסֶה ***keseh***. See 3677.

כִּסֵּה ***kissēh***. See 3678.

3681 כָּסוּי ***kāsûy***, n.[m.]. GK: 4062 [→ 3680]. covering:– covering [2]

3682 כְּסוּת ***kᵉsût***, n.f. GK: 4064 [→ 3680]. covering, cloak, clothing:– covering [6], raiment [1], vesture [1]

3683 כָּסַח ***kāsaḥ***, v. GK: 4065. [Qp] to be cut down (of brush):– cut down [1], cut up [1]

3684 כְּסִיל ***kᵉsîl***, n.m. GK: 4067 [→ 3685; cf. 3688]. foolish, stupid, insolent; (n.) fool, insolent person:– fool [34], fools [22], foolish [9], fool's [4], fools' [1]

3685 כְּסִיל ***kᵉsîl***, n.m. GK: 4068 [→ 3684; cf. 3688]. Orion (and its adjoining constellations):– Orion [3], constellations [1]

3686 כְּסִיל ***kᵉsîl***, n.pr.loc. GK: 4069. Kesil:– Chesil [1]

3687 כְּסִילוּת ***kᵉsîlût***, n.f. GK: 4070 [→ 3688]. folly, stupidity, insolence, with a possible implication of rebellion:– foolish [1]

3688 כָּסַל ***kāsal***, v. GK: 4071 [→ 3694, 3684, 3685, 3687, 3689, 3690, 3693, 3692]. [Q] to be foolish, be stupid:– foolish [1]

3689 כֶּסֶל ***kesel***, n.m. GK: 4072 & 4073 [→ 3688, 3696?]. waist, back; (pl.) loins; trust, confidence; stupidity:– flanks [6], hope [3], folly [2], confidence [1], loins [1]

3690 כִּסְלָה ***kislâ***, n.f. GK: 4074 [→ 3688]. confidence; folly:– confidence [1], folly [1]

3691 כִּסְלֵו ***kislēw***, n.pr.[m.]. GK: 4075. Kislev:– Chisleu [2]

3692 כִּסְלוֹן ***kislôn***, n.pr.m. GK: 4077 [→ 3688]. Kislon, *"slow; strength"*:– Chislon [1]

3693 כְּסָלוֹן ***kᵉsālôn***, n.pr.loc. GK: 4076 [→ 3688]. Kesalon:– Chesalon [1]

3694 כְּסֻלּוֹת ***kᵉsûlôt***, n.pr.loc. GK: 4063 [→ 3688]. Kesulloth, *"loins* or *flanks [of Mt. Tabor]"*:– Chesulloth [1]

3695 כַּסְלֻחִים ***kasluḥîm***, n.pr.g. GK: 4078. Casluhite:– Casluhim [2]

3696 כִּסְלֹת תָּבֹר ***kislōt tābôr***, n.pr.loc. GK: 4079 [→ 3689?+8396]. Kisloth Tabor:– Chislothtabor [1]

3697 כָּסַם ***kāsam***, v. GK: 4080 [→ 3698; cf. 1501, 3765]. [Q] to trip, clip (hair):– only poll (+3697) [2]

3698 כֻּסֶּמֶת ***kussemet***, n.f. GK: 4081 [→ 3697]. spelt, emmer wheat:– rye [2], fitches [1]

3699 כָּסַס ***kāsas***, v. GK: 4082 [→ 4371, 4373]. [Q] to determine, reckon, compute:– make count [1]

3700 כָּסַף ***kāsap***, v. GK: 4083 [→ 3701]. [Q] to long for; be hungry; [N] to long for, yearn for; to be ashamed:– sore longedst (+3700) [2], desired [1], greedy [1], have desire [1], longeth [1]

3701 כֶּסֶף ***kesep***, n.m. GK: 4084 [→ 3700; cf. 3702]. silver, silver piece = money:– silver [287], money [112], price [3], silverlings [1]

3702 כְּסַף ***kᵉsap*** (Aram.), n.m. GK: 10362 [cf. 3701]. silver:– silver [12], money [1]

3703 כָּסִפְיָא ***kāsipyā'***, n.pr.loc. GK: 4085. Casiphia:– Casiphia [2]

3704 כֶּסֶת ***keset***, n.f. GK: 4086. magic charm band:– pillows [2]

3705 כְּעַן ***kᵉ'an*** (Aram.), adv. GK: 10363 [→ 3706]. now, furthermore, to the present:– now [13]

3706 כְּעֶנֶת ***kᵉ'enet*** or כְּעֶת ***kᵉ'et*** (Aram.), adv. GK: 10364 & 10365 [→ 3705]. (and) now, a marker to connect what follows; the phrase "Peace and now" is a formal greeting in a letter:– at such a time [3], such a time [1]

3707 כָּעַס ***kā'as***, v. GK: 4087 [→ 3708; cf. 3708]. [Q] to be angry, be vexed, be incensed; [P] to anger, provoke; [H] to provoke to anger:– provoke to anger [24], provoked to anger [14], provoking to anger [3], angry [2], provoked [2], grieved [1], provoke unto wrath [1], provoked sore (+3708) [1], provoketh to anger [1], provoke [1], sorrow [1], took indignation [1], vex [1], wroth [1]

3708 כַּעַס ***ka'as*** or כַּעַשׂ ***ka'aś***, n.m. GK: 4088 & 4089 [→ 3707, 3708]. general uneasiness and anxiety, inwardly focused: anguish, grief; focused toward an object: anger, resentment:– grief [7], wrath [4], provocation [3], sorrow [3], anger [2], angry [1], indignation [1], provocations [1], provoked sore (+3707) [1], provoking [1], spite [1]

כְּעֶת ***kᵉ'et***. See 3706.

3709 כַּף ***kap***, n.f. GK: 4090 [→ 3721]. hand (of a person), palm of the hand, sole of the foot, paw (of an animal); by extension: power, strength; something hollowed: socket, (shallow) dish; a measure of quantity: handful:– hands [69], hand [55], sole [12], spoons [12], spoon [12], soles [7], hands together (+413+3709) [4], hollow [4], palms [3], handful (+4393) [2], palm of hand [2], apiece (+1886.1) [1], branches [1], clouds [1], foot (+7272) [1], handled (+8610+871.1+1886.1) [1], handles [1], middle [1], palms of hands [1], paws [1], power [1], took a handful (+4390) [1]

3710 כֵּף ***kēp***, n.[m.]. GK: 4091. rock:– rocks [2]

3711 כָּפָה ***kāpâ***, v. GK: 4092. [Q] to soothe, avert (anger):– pacifieth [1]

3712 כִּפָּה ***kippâ***, n.f. GK: 4093 [→ 3721]. palm branch, palm frond:– branch [3]

3713 כְּפוֹר ***kᵉpôr***, n.m. GK: 4094 & 4095 [→ 3722]. bowl, dish (made of gold or silver); frost:– basons [4], every bason (+3713+2050.1) [4], hoar frost [1], hoarfrost [1], hoary frost [1]

3714 כָּפִיס ***kāpîs***, n.m. GK: 4096. beam (of woodwork); some sources: rafter:– beam [1]

3715 כְּפִיר ***kᵉpîr***, n.m. GK: 4097 & 4099 [→ 3722, 3723]. young lion; village:– young lions [12], young lion [12], lion [4], lions [2], villages [1], young [1]

3716 כְּפִירָה ***kᵉpîrâ***, n.pr.loc. GK: 4098 [→ 3723]. Kephirah, *"village"*:– Chephirah [4]

3717 כָּפַל ***kāpal***, v. GK: 4100 [→ 3718, 4375]. [Q] to fold double; [Qp] to be folded double; [N] to be doubled:– doubled [3], double [2]

3718 כֶּפֶל ***kepel***, n.[m.]. GK: 4101 [→ 3717]. double; two sides:– double [3]

3719 כָּפַן ***kāpan***, v. GK: 4102 [→ 3720]. [Q] to hunger, send out roots in hunger:– bend [1]

3720 כָּפָן ***kāpān***, n.[m.]. GK: 4103 [→ 3719]. hunger, famine:– famine [2]

3721 כָּפַף ***kāpap***, v. GK: 4104 [→ 3709, 3712]. [Q] to bow down in distress; [Qp] be bowed down; [N] bow down (before):– bowed down [3], bow down [1], bow [1]

3722 כָּפַר ***kāpar***, v. GK: 4105 & 4106 [→ 3713, 3715, 3724, 3725, 3727]. [Q] to coat, cover (with pitch); [Nitpael] to be atoned (for); [P] to make atonement; make amends, pardon, release, appease, forgive; [Pu] to be atoned for, be annulled; [Ht] to allow for atonement; atonement may be a figure of covering over and therefore forgetting (forgiving) sin:– make an atonement [58], make atonement [6], made an atonement [5], purged [5], make reconciliation [4], atonement made [2], merciful [2], purge away [2], purge [2], reconcile [2], appease (+6440) [1], cleansed [1], disannulled [1], forgave [1], forgiven [1], forgive [1], maketh an atonement [1], maketh atonement [1], pacified [1], pacify [1], pardon [1], pitch [1], put off [1], reconciling [1]

3723 כָּפָר ***kāpār***, n.m. GK: 4107 [→ 3716, 3715, 3724, 3726]. (unwalled) village:– villages [2]

3724 כֹּפֶר ***kōper***, n.m. GK: 4108 & 4109 & 4110 & 4111 [→ 3722, 3723]. pitch (used to cover and seal the ark of Noah); (unwalled) village; henna, henna blossom; ransom, compensation, payment; bribe:– ransom [8], bribe [2], camphire [2], satisfaction [2], pitch [1], sum of money [1], villages [1]

3725 כִּפֻּרִים ***kippurîm***, n.pl.abst. GK: 4113 [→ 3722]. atonement; atonement may be a figure of covering over and therefore forgetting (forgiving) sin; "day of Atonement" is an annual day of rest and with ceremonies accomplishing full atonement for the nation of Israel:– atonement [7], atonements [1]

3726 כְּפַר הָעַמֹּנִי ***kᵉpar hā'ammōnî***, n.pr.loc. GK: 4112 [→ 3723]. Kephar Ammoni, *"village of Ammonites"*:– Chephar-haammonai [1]

3727 כַּפֹּרֶת ***kappōret***, n. GK: 4114 [→ 3722]. atonement cover (traditionally: mercy seat); the golden cover on the ark of the covenant, the place where atonement is made:– mercy seat [26], mercy seatward [1]

3728 כָּפַשׁ ***kāpaš***, v. GK: 4115 [cf. 3533]. [H] to trample down:– covered [1]

3729 כְּפַת ***kᵉpat*** (Aram.), v. GK: 10366. [Peil] to be bound; [Pa] to tie up; [Pap] to be tied:– bound [3], bind [1]

3730 כַּפְתּוֹר ***kaptôr***, n.m. GK: 4117. bud; top of a pillar or column:– knop [10], knops [6], lintel of the door [1], upper lintels [1]

3731 כַּפְתּוֹר kaptôr, n.pr.loc. GK: 4116 [→ 3732]. Caphtor:– Caphtor [3]

3732 כַּפְתֹּרִי kaptōrî, a.g. GK: 4118 [→ 3731]. Caphtorite, "*of Caphtor*":– Caphthorim [1], Caphtorims [1], Caphtorim [1]

3733 כַּר kar, n.m. GK: 4119 & 4120 & 4121 [→ 3769]. (young) ram; battering ram; meadow, pastureland; saddle, saddle-bag:– lambs [9], pastures [2], rams [2], captains [1], furniture [1], lamb [1]

3734 כֹּר kōr, n.[m.]. GK: 4123 & 10367. cor (measure of dry or liquid volume, about 60 gallons [220 liters]): note this word is Aramaic once in Ezra:– measures [8], cor [1]

3735 כְּרָא k^{e}râ (Aram.), v. GK: 10369. [Itpe] to be troubled, distressed:– grieved [1]

3736 כִּרְבֵּל kirbēl, v.den. GK: 4124 [cf. 3737]. [Pu] to be clothed, be wrapped:– clothed [1]

3737 כַּרְבְּלָה karb^{e}lâ (Aram.), n.f. GK: 10368. headdress of some kind: turban, cap; the etymology suggests something wrapped around the head:– hats [1]

3738 כָּרָה kārâ, v. GK: 4125 & 4127 & 4128 [→ 3740, 3741, 4351, 4379]. [Q] to dig; to hew (stone); to hollow out; to prepare a feast; to tie together:– digged [8], dig [2], made [2], diggeth up [1], diggeth [1], opened [1], pierced [1]

3739 כָּרָה kārâ, v. GK: 4126. [Q] to barter; purchase:– bought [1], buy [1], make a banquet [1], prepared [1]

3740 כֵּרָה kērâ, n.f. GK: 4130 [→ 3738]. feast, banquet:– provision [1]

3741 כָּרָה kārâ, n.f. GK: 4129 [→ 3738]. cistern, well:– cottages [1]

3742 כְּרוּב k^{e}rûb, n.m. GK: 4131. cherub, (pl.) cherubim, a class of supernatural beings that serve in the presence of God; used as ornamental figures on the atonement cover of the ark of the covenant and in the temple as well as on the walls and doors of the temple:– cherubims [63], cherub [27], cherubims' [1]

3743 כְּרוּב k^{e}rûb, n.pr.loc. GK: 4132. Kerub:– Cherub [2]

3744 כָּרוֹז kārôz (Aram.), n.m. GK: 10370 [→ 3745]. herald, proclaimer:– herald [1]

3745 כְּרַז k^{e}raz (Aram.), v.den. GK: 10371 [→ 3744]. [H] to proclaim:– made a proclamation [1]

3746 כָּרִי kārî, a.g. GK: 4133. Carite:– captains [2]

3747 כְּרִית k^{e}rît, n.pr.loc. GK: 4134 [→ 3772]. Kerith, "*cut off, perish*":– Cherith [2]

3748 כְּרִיתוּת k^{e}rîtût, n.f. GK: 4135 [→ 3772]. divorce:– divorcement [3], divorce [1]

3749 כַּרְכֹּב karkōb, n.[m.]. GK: 4136. ledge, rim, edge:– compass [2]

3750 כַּרְכֹּם karkōm, n.[m.]. GK: 4137. saffron (plant):– saffron [1]

3751 כַּרְכְּמִישׁ kark^{e}mîš, n.pr.loc. GK: 4138. Carchemish:– Carchemish [3]

3752 כַּרְכַּס karkas, n.pr.m. GK: 4139. Carcas, "[perhaps] *vulture*":– Carcas [1]

3753 כִּרְכָּרָה kirkārâ, n.f. GK: 4140 [→ 3769]. (fast running) female camel:– swift beasts [1]

3754 כֶּרֶם kerem, n.m. GK: 4142 [→ 3755, 3756?, 3757?, 3759]. vineyard:– vineyards [45], vineyard [44], vines [3], vintage [1]

3755 כֹּרֵם kōrēm, n.[m.] *or* v.ptcp. GK: 4144 [→ 3754]. worker in the vineyard, vine growers, vinedressers:– vinedressers [5]

3756 כַּרְמִי karmî, n.pr.m. GK: 4145 [→ 3757; cf. 3754?]. Carmi, "[poss.] *[fruitful] vine, vineyard owner*":– Carmi [8]

3757 כַּרְמִי karmî, a.g. GK: 4146 [→ 3756; cf. 3754?]. Carmite, "*of Carmi*":– Carmites [1]

3758 כַּרְמִיל karmîl, n.[m.]. GK: 4147. crimson (yarn):– crimson [3]

3759 כַּרְמֶל karmel, n.m. GK: 4149 & 4152 [→ 3760, 3761, 3762; cf. 3754]. fertile land, fruitful land; this can refer to an orchard or plantation; new grain, newly ripe grain:– fruitful field [6], plentiful field [2], corn of full ears [1], fruitful place [1], full ears of corn [1], green ears [1], plentiful [1]

3760 כַּרְמֶל karmel, n.pr.loc. GK: 4150 & 4151 [→ 3759, 3761]. Carmel, "*orchard planted with vine and fruit trees*":– Carmel [26]

3761 כַּרְמְלִי karm^{e}lî, a.g. GK: 4153 [→ 3760, 3762; cf. 3759]. Carmelite, of Carmel, "*of Carmel*":– Carmelite [5], Carmelitess [2]

3762 כַּרְמְלִית karm^{e}lît, a.g. GK: 4153 [→ 3761]. f. of 3761: Carmelite, of Carmel, "*of Carmel*":–

3763 כְּרָן k^{e}rān, n.pr.m. GK: 4154. Keran:– Cheran [2]

3764 כָּרְסֵא korsēʾ (Aram.), n.m. GK: 10372 [cf. 3676]. seat, chair; of power and position: throne; "to come down from the throne" means to be deposed and so lose power:– throne [2], thrones [1]

3765 כִּרְסֵם kirsēm, v. GK: 4155 [cf. 3697]. [P] to ravage, eat away:– waste [1]

3766 כָּרַע kāraʿ, v. GK: 4156 [→ 3767]. [Q] to kneel down, crouch, often with the associative meaning of respect and honor or of readiness for action; [H] to make bow down, make kneel (an act of oppression), make miserable:– bowed [10], bow down [5], bow [4], boweth down [2], brought very low (+3766) [2], fell [2], subdued [2], bowed down [1], brought down [1], cast down [1], couched [1], feeble [1], kneeling [1], smote down [1], stooped down [1], sunk down [1]

3767 כְּרָע keraʿ, n.[f.]. GK: 4157 [→ 3766]. leg bone (the shank bone, between the knee and ankle):– legs [9]

3768 כַּרְפַּס karpas, n.m. GK: 4158. (fine) linen:– green [1]

3769 כָּרַר kārar, v. GK: 4159 [→ 3564?, 3603, 3733, 3753]. [Pil] to dance:– danced [1], dancing [1]

3770 כָּרֵשׂ kārēś, n.[m.]. GK: 4160. stomach, belly:– belly [1]

כֹּרֶשׁ **kōreš**. See 3567.

3771 כַּרְשְׁנָא karš^{e}nāʾ, n.pr.m. GK: 4161. Carshena, "[poss.] *black*":– Carshena [1]

3772 כָּרַת kārat, v. GK: 4162 [→ 3747?, 3748, 3773]. [Q] to cut off, cut down; to make (a covenant, agreement); [Qp] to be cut off, broken off; [N] to be cut off, be destroyed; [Pu] to be cut down; [H] to cut off, get rid of, destroy, kill; [Ho] to be cut off; "to cut a covenant" is "make a covenant," a figure of the act of ceremonially cutting an animal into two parts, with an implication of serious consequences for not fulfilling the covenant:– cut off [146], made [52], make [30], cut down [21], cut [6], fail [5], want [3], covenanted [2], destroyed [2], destroy [2], hew [2], utterly cut off (+3772) [2], are [1], chewed [1], cut out [1], cutteth [1], fail (+3807.1) [1], feller [1], freed [1], hew down [1], heweth down [1], leese [1], madest [1], make a covenant [1], maketh [1], making [1], perish [1]

3773 כְּרֻתוֹת k^{e}rutôt, n.[f.pl.]. GK: 4164 [→ 3772]. beams (trimmed and cut):– beams [3]

3774 כְּרֵתִי k^{e}rētî, a.g. GK: 4165 [cf. 6432?]. Kerethite:– Cherethites [9], Cherethims [1]

3775 כֶּשֶׂב keśeb, n.[m.]. GK: 4166 [→ 3776; cf. 3532]. ram-lamb, young sheep:– sheep [8], lamb [3], lambs [1], sheep (+7716) [1]

3776 כִּשְׂבָּה kiśbâ, n.f. GK: 4167 [→ 3775]. ewe-lamb, young sheep:– lamb [1]

3777 כֶּשֶׂד keśed, n.pr.m. GK: 4168 [→ 3778]. Kesed, "*Chaldean, Babylonian*":– Chesed [1]

3778 כַּשְׂדִּים kaśdîm, n.pr.g. GK: 4169 [→ 3777; cf. 894; cf. 3679, cf. 3779]. Chaldean, Babylonian, astrologers:– Chaldeans [59], Chaldees [13], Chaldea [7], Chaldeans' [1], Chaldees' [1]

3779 כַּשְׂדָּי kaśdāy (Aram.), n.pr.g. GK: 10373 [cf. 3679; cf. 3778]. Chaldean; Babylonian; (as a common noun) astrologer:– Chaldeans [6], Chaldean [1]

3780 כָּשָׂה kāśâ, v. GK: 4170. [Q] to become sleek, heavy; stubborn, headstrong:– covered [1]

3781 כַּשִּׁיל kaššîl, n.[m.]. GK: 4172 [→ 3782]. axe:– axes [1]

3782 כָּשַׁל kāšal, v. GK: 4173 [→ 3781, 3783, 4383, 4384]. [Q] to stumble, falter, fail; [N] be caused to stumble, be brought down; [H] to cause to stumble, overthrow, bring to ruin; [Ho] to be overthrown:– fall [17], stumble [13], feeble [4], cast down [3], stumbled [3], cause to fall [2], caused to stumble [2], fallen [2], overthrown [2], utterly fall (+3782) [2], decayed [1], faileth [1], falling [1], fell down [1], fell [1], made to fall [1], make fall [1], make to fall [1], ruined [1], ruin [1], stumbleth [1], weak [1]

3783 כִּשָּׁלוֹן kiššālôn, n.[m.]. GK: 4174 [→ 3782]. falling down, stumbling:– fall [1]

3784 כָּשַׁף kāšap, v.den. GK: 4175 [→ 407, 3785, 3786]. [P] to engage in witchcraft, be a sorcerer:– sorcerers [3], witch [2], used witchcraft [1]

3785 כֶּשֶׁף kešep, n.m. GK: 4176 [→ 3784]. witchcraft, sorcery, often with the associative meanings of rebellion and seduction into false religion:– witchcrafts [4], sorceries [2]

3786 כַּשָּׁף kaššāp, n.m. GK: 4177 [→ 3784]. sorcerer:– sorcerers [1]

3787 כָּשֵׁר kāšēr, v. GK: 4178 [→ 3788]. [Q] to be right, successful; [H] to bring success:– direct [1], prosper [1], seem right [1]

3788 כִּשְׁרוֹן kišrôn, n.[m.]. GK: 4179 [→ 3787]. skill, achievement; benefit:– equity [1], good [1], right [1]

3789 כָּתַב kātab, v. GK: 4180 [→ 3791, 3793, 4385; cf. 3790]. [Q] to write, engrave (on stone tablets); [Qp] to be written, be inscribed; [N] to be written down, be listed, be recorded; [P] to issue a written statement; writing can refer to ink on leather or papyrus, stylus on wax or clay, or carving in stone:–

written [137], write [35], wrote [34], describe [4], described [2], subscribed [2], subscribe [2], writest [2], prescribed [1], recorded [1], were written [1], writeth [1], writing [1]

3790 כְּתַב ***kᵉtab*** (Aram.), v. GK: 10374 [→ 3792; cf. 3789]. [P] to write; [Pp, Peil] to be written:– wrote [5], written [2], write [1]

3791 כְּתָב ***kᵉtāb***, n.m. GK: 4181 [→ 3789; cf. 3792]. written communication in various forms: script, text, record, book (as a scroll or tablet):– writing [14], register [2], scripture [1]

3792 כְּתָב ***kᵉtāb*** (Aram.), n.m. GK: 10375 [→ 3790; cf. 3791]. writing, inscription, decree:– writing [10], prescribing [1], written [1]

3793 כְּתֹבֶת ***kᵉtōbet***, n.f. GK: 4182 [→ 3789]. tattoo mark:– any [1]

3794 כִּתִּיִּים ***kittiyyîm***, a. & n.g. GK: 4183. Kittim, Cyprus; western coastlands:– Chittim [6], Kittim [2]

3795 כָּתִית ***kātît***, a. GK: 4184 [→ 3807]. beaten or pressed olives; in some contexts this refers to virgin olive oil:– beaten [4], pure [1]

3796 כֹּתֶל ***kōtel***, n.[m.]. GK: 4185 [cf. 3797]. wall (of a house):– wall [1]

3797 כְּתַל ***kᵉtal*** (Aram.), n.[m.]. GK: 10376. wall:– walls [1], wall [1]

3798 כִּתְלִישׁ ***kitlîš***, n.pr.loc. GK: 4186. Kitlish:– Kithlish [1]

3799 כָּתַם ***kātam***, v. GK: 4187. [N] be stained, be defiled:– marked [1]

3800 כֶּתֶם ***ketem***, n.m. GK: 4188 [cf. 4387?]. gold, pure gold:– fine gold [4], gold [3], golden wedge [1], most [1]

3801 כֻּתֹּנֶת ***kuttōnet***, n.f. GK: 4189. garment, robe, tunic:– coat [16], coats [7], garments [3], garment [2], robe [1]

3802 כָּתֵף ***kātēp***, n.f. GK: 4190. shoulder, the part an animal or human that carries a load; by extension: shoulder piece; slope (of a hill), side, wall (of a building):– side [30], shoulders [13], shoulder [9], shoulderpieces [4], sides [4], undersetters [4], corner [2], arm [1]

3803 כָּתַר ***kātar***, v. GK: 4192 & 4193 & 4194 [→ 3804, 3805]. [P] to bear with, have patience with; to surround, encircle; [H] to gather about; hem in; to crown, wear as a headdress:– compass about [2], beset round [1], crowned [1], inclosed round about [1], suffer [1]

3804 כֶּתֶר ***keter***, n.m. GK: 4195 [→ 3803]. crown (probably not jeweled), royal headdress, crest, high turban:– crown [3]

3805 כֹּתֶרֶת ***kōteret***, n.f. GK: 4196 [→ 3803]. capital (of a pillar or column):– chapiters [12], chapiter [12]

3806 כָּתַשׁ ***kātaš***, v. GK: 4197 [→ 4388]. [Q] to grind, pound (in a mortar):– bray [1]

3807 כָּתַת ***kātat***, v. GK: 4198 [→ 3795, 3796]. [Q] to crush, beat; [Qp] to be crushed, be shattered; [P] to beat, crush, break to pieces; [Pu] to be crushed; [H] to beat down; [Ho] to be battered to pieces:– beat [3], destroyed [3], beat down [1], beaten down [1], beaten to pieces [1], beaten [1], brake in pieces [1], broken in pieces [1], crushed [1], discomfited [1], smite [1], smitten [1], stamped [1]

3807.1 לְ- ***lᵉ-***, pp.pref. GK: 4200 [→ 1973, 2882?, 3815, 4192, 3926, 3927, 3942; cf. 3807.2]. to, toward; in, through; before, at, with; temporally: before, until, when; logically: so that, in order to; agency: by means of:– to [4509], unto [2352], for [2001], of [1133], before (+6440) [958], in [462], that [358], with [227], therefore (+3651) [176], that (+4616) [167], by [163], into [131], against [122], had [122], after [116], at [116], have [110], according to [102], why (+4100) [92], on [81], upon [81], his (+2050.2) [76], had (+1961) [72], have (+1961) [72], wherefore (+4100) [70], hath [64], my (+2967.1) [64], before [59], throughout [56], mine (+2967.1) [50], for sake (+4616) [45], your (+3641.1) [44], alone (+905) [39], only (+905) [39], their (+1992.1) [38], among [37], as [37], concerning [31], beside (+905+4480) [30], toward [30], thine (+3509.2) [29], the LORD'S* (+3068) [28], from [27], over [27], hast [26], thy (+3509.2) [24], to (+4616) [19], above (+4480+4605+1886.5) [18], before (+5048) [18], wherefore (+3651) [18], before (+4480+6440) [17], over against (+5980) [15], safely (+983) [14], and [13], besides (+905+4480) [13], our (+5105.1) [13], because of (+4616) [12], from (+4480) [12], upward (+4605+1886.5) [12], according to (+6310) [11], apart (+905) [11], when [10]*

3807.2 לְ- ***lᵉ-*** (Aram.), pp.pref. GK: 10378 [cf. 3807.1]. to, for, toward, into; belonging to, with regard to:– to [101], unto [54], for [21], into [16], of [10], had [6], at [5], against [4], that [4], before (+6903) [3], by [2], in [2], why (+4101) [2], according to (+6903) [1], according to [1], against (+6655) [1], hast [1], have (+383) [1], his (+1886.8) [1], never (+3809+5957) [1], on [1], over [1], upon [1], what (+1768+3964) [1]

3808 לֹא]לֹה ***lō'*** or ***lōh***, adv. GK: 4202 & 4257 [→ 194?, 3810, 3818, 3819; cf. 3809 (also used with compound proper names)]. no, not:– not [3448], no [490], neither (+2050.1) [415], nor (+2050.1) [242], none [71], neither [58], cannot [57], no (+3605) [43], cannot (+3201) [35], surely (+518) [23], nothing [21], nothing (+1697) [20], nay [18], never [17], without (+871.1) [17], lest (+2050.1) [14], nor [14], none (+3605) [13], never (+5769+3807.1) [9], without [9], neither (+1571) [6], none (+376) [6], except (+518) [5], neither (+1571+2050.1) [5], nothing (+3972) [5], ere [4], nothing (+3605) [4], ignorant (+3045) [3], neither any (+2050.1) [3], nothing (+3605+1886.1) [3], without (+3807.1) [3], before (+2962+871.1) [2], before (+871.1) [2], by no means [2], never (+5331+3807.1) [2], no more [2], nor (+1571) [2], nought [2], unequal (+8505) [2], unwise (+2450) [2], verily (+518) [2], will (+518) [2], afore [1], but (+518) [1], but (+518+3588) [1], but [1], cannot (+3045) [1], cannot (+518) [1], cannot away with (+3201) [1], else (+518) [1], except (+518+3588) [1], fail (+539) [1], feeble (+3524) [1], feeble (+6099) [1], forbidden [1], how much less (+637+3588) [1], in no wise eat (+398+398) [1], lest (+4616+3807.1) [1], lest (+834) [1], measured (+4058) [1], neither (+2050.2) [1], neither (+3588) [1], neither yet (+1571+2050.1) [1], never (+1755+1755+2050.1) [1], never (+4480+5769) [1], never (+5331+5704) [1], never (+5704+5769) [1], never (+8548) [1], never again (+5750) [1], nevertheless (+2050.1) [1], no (+1697) [1], no (+3972) [1], none (+2050.2) [1], none (+259) [1], none (+376+376) [1], none (+376+3807.1) [1], none (+4480) [1], none (+802) [1], none (+834) [1], nor (+1571+2050.1) [1], nor (+176) [1], not (+518) [1], not (+5704) [1], not even [1], nothing (+1697+3605) [1], notwithstanding (+2050.1) [1], nought (+1952) [1], nought (+3972) [1], of a truth (+518) [1], or ever (+834+5704) [1], or ever [1], otherwise than (+871.1+3509.1) [1], out of (+2050.1) [1], out of (+871.1) [1], unaccustomed (+3925) [1], unawares (+3045) [1], ungodly (+2623) [1], unless (+518) [1], unprofitable [1], unrighteousness (+6664) [1], want of [1], wanting [1], whether (+518) [1], without (+2050.1) [1], without any (+2050.1) [1], wrong (+4941) [1], wrongfully (+4941+871.1) [1], yet neither (+2050.1) [1]

3809 לָא ***lā'*** (Aram.), adv.neg. GK: 10379 & 10384 [cf. 3808]. no, not, never:– not [49], nor (+2050.3) [7], no [7], neither (+2050.3) [3], no (+3606) [3], nor [2], without (+871.2) [2], without [2], cannot [1], ever [1], never (+5957+3807.2) [1], none (+3606) [1], none (+383+1768) [1], none [1], nothing [1]

לוּא ***lu'***. See 3863.

3810 לֹא דְבָר or לֹא דְבַר]לוֹ דְבָר ***lō' dābār*** or ***lō' dᵉbār*** or ***lô dᵉbār***, n.pr.loc. GK: 4203 & 4274 [→ 3808+1696]. Lo Debar, *"no pasture"*:– Lodebar [3]

3811 לָאָה ***lā'â***, v. GK: 4206 [→ 8513; cf. 3856]. [Q] to be weary; [N] to wear oneself out, be weary; [H] to wear someone out, try one's patience, frustrate:– weary [9], wearied [5], faintest [1], grieved [1], grieveth [1], lothe [1], made weary [1]

3812 לֵאָה ***lē'â***, n.pr.f. GK: 4207. Leah, "[poss.] *wild-cow; wild cow, gazelle; cow*":– Leah [29], Leah's [5]

לְאוֹם ***lᵉ'owm***. See 3816.

3813 לָאַט ***lā'aṭ***, v. GK: 4209 [cf. 3874]. [Q] to cover:– covered [1]

3814 לָאט ***lā'ṭ***, n.[m.]. GK: 4319 [→ 3874, 3909]. same as 3909: quietly, privately, secretly, a fig. extension of the base meaning "no physical sound"; (pl.) secret arts, with a focus on mysterious and hidden elements of this magic:– softly (+871.1+1886.1) [1]

3815 לָאֵל ***lā'ēl***, n.pr.m. GK: 4210 [→ 3807.1+410]. Lael, *"[belonging] to God [El]"*:– Lael [1]

3816 לְאֹם ***lᵉ'ōm***, n.m. GK: 4211. people, nation:– people [24], nations [9], folk [1], nation [1]

3817 לְאֻמִּים ***lᵉ'ummîm***, n.pr.g. GK: 4212. Leummite:– Leummim [1]

3818 לֹא עַמִּי ***lō' 'ammî***, n.pr.m. GK: 4204 [→ 3808]. Lo-Ammi, *"not my people"*:– Lo-ammi [1]

3819 לֹא רֻחָמָה ***lō' ruḥāmâ***, n.pr.f. GK: 4205 [→ 3808]. Lo-Ruhamah, *"no compassion"*:– Lo-ruhamah [2]

3820 לֵב ***lēb***, n.m. GK: 4213 [→ 3823, 3824, 3834; cf. 3821]. heart; by extension: the inner person, self, the seat of thought and emotion: conscience, courage, mind, understanding:– heart [483], hearts [20], midst [12], mind [12], understanding [10], hearted [9], wisdom [6], comfortably (+5921) [4], double heart (+3820+2050.1) [4], care (+7760) [2], considered (+7760) [2], friendly (+5921) [2], heart's [2], mark well (+7760) [2], regard (+7896) [2], stouthearted (+47) [2], well [2], bethink (+413+7725) [1], broken-hearted (+7665) [1], consent [1], consider (+7760) [1], considered (+7896) [1], courageous (+533) [1], hardhearted (+7186) [1], kindly (+5921) [1], kindly [1], merryhearted (+8056) [1], minded (+5973) [1], myself (+2967.1) [1], regard (+7760) [1], regarded (+7760) [1], stale away unawares (+1589) [1], take heed (+5414) [1], very heart (+7023) [1], willingly (+4480) [1]

3821 לֵב ***lēb*** (Aram.), n.[m.]. GK: 10380 [→ 3825; cf. 3820]. heart, mind:– heart [1]

3822 לְבָאוֹת ***lᵉbāʼôt***, n.pr.loc. GK: 4219 [→ 1034; cf. 3833]. Lebaoth, "*lionesses*":– Lebaoth [1]

3823 לָבַב ***lābab***, v.den. GK: 4220 & 4221 [→ 3826, 3834; cf. 3820]. [N] to be made wise, be made intelligent; [P] to steal one's heart (from a lover's glance); to make special bread or pastry (heart-shaped?):– ravished heart [2], made cakes [1], make cakes (+3834) [1], wise [1]

3824 לֵבָב ***lēbāb***, n.m. & f. GK: 4222 [→ 3820; cf. 3825]. heart; by extension: the inner person, self, the seat of thought and emotion: conscience, courage, mind, understanding:– heart [208], hearts [23], consider (+7760) [5], mind [4], understanding [3], bethink (+413+7725) [1], breasts [1], comfortably (+5921) [1], courage [1], fainthearted (+7390+1886.1) [1], fainthearted (+7401) [1], hearted [1], midst [1], stolen away unawares (+1589) [1]

3825 לְבַב ***lᵉbab*** (Aram.), n.m. GK: 10381 [→ 3821; cf. 3824]. heart (a physical organ); fig., the inner person that thinks, feels, and chooses: mind, heart, will; "one's heart" can mean "oneself":– heart [7]

לְבִבָה ***lᵉbibâ***. See 3834.

3826 לִבָּה ***libbâ***, n.[f.]. GK: 4226 [→ 3823]. rage:– hearts [6], heart [2]

3827 לַבָּה ***labbâ***, n.f. GK: 4225 [cf. 3852]. flame:– flame [1]

3828 לְבוֹנָה ***lᵉbônâ*** or לְבֹנָה ***lᵉbōnâ***, n.f. GK: 4227 & 4247 [→ 3829, 3836]. frankincense:– frankincense [15], incense [6]

3829 לְבוֹנָה ***lᵉbônâ***, n.pr.loc. GK: 4228 [→ 3828]. Lebonah, "*frankincense*":– Lebonah [1]

3830 לְבוּשׁ ***lᵉbûš***, n.m. GK: 4229 & 4230 [→ 3847; cf. 3831]. clothing, garment, robe:– clothing [9], apparel [8], garment [7], garments [2], vesture [2], clothed [1], put on [1], raiment [1], vestments [1]

3831 לְבוּשׁ ***lᵉbûš*** (Aram.), n.m. GK: 10382 [→ 3848; cf. 3830]. clothing, garment:– garments [1], garment [1]

3832 לָבַט ***lābaṭ***, v. GK: 4231. [N] to come to ruin, be trampled:– fall [3]

לֻבִּי ***lubbî***. See 3864.

3833 לָבִיא ***lābîʼ*** or לְבִיָּא ***lᵉbiyyāʼ*** or לְבָאָה ***libʼâ*** or לְבָא ***lebeʼ***, n.m. & f. GK: 4216 & 4218 & 4233 & 4234 [→ 1034, 3822]. lion, lioness:– lion [4], great lion [3], old lion [2], lionesses [1], lioness [1], lions [1], stout lion's [1], young[s] [1]

3834 לְבִבָה ***lᵉbibâ***, n.f. GK: 4223 [→ 3823; cf. 3820]. special bread (heart-shaped?):– cakes [2], make cakes (+3823) [1]

3835 לָבַן ***lāban***, v. GK: 4235 & 4236 [→ 3828, 3829, 3836, 3837, 3838, 3839, 3840, 3841?, 3842, 3844]. [Q] to make bricks; [H] to make white, be whitened; [Ht] to show oneself spotless, purified:– made white [2], make brick (+3843) [2], make white [1], making brick [1], whiter [1], white [1]

3836 לָבָן ***lābān***, a. GK: 4237 [→ 3828, 3837, 3842; cf. 3835]. white:– white [29]

3837 לָבָן ***lābān***, n.pr.m. & loc. GK: 4238 & 4239 [→ 3836]. Laban, "*white*":– Laban [51], Laban's [4]

לַבֵּן ***labbēn***. See 4192.

3838 לְבָנָה ***lᵉbānâ*** or לְבָנָא ***lᵉbānāʼ***, n.pr.loc. GK: 4245 & 4241 [→ 3842]. Lebanah; Lebana, "*white*":– Lebanah [1], Lebana [1]

3839 לִבְנֶה ***libneh***, n.[m.]. GK: 4242 [→ 3835]. poplar tree; some sources: storax tree:– poplars [1], poplar [1]

3840 לִבְנָה ***libnâ***, n.f. GK: 4246 [→ 3835, 3843, 4404]. same as 3843: brick; tablet:– paved [1]

3841 לִבְנָה ***libnâ***, n.pr.loc. GK: 4243 [→ 3835?]. Libnah, "*white*":– Libnah [18]

3842 לְבָנָה ***lᵉbānâ***, n.f. GK: 4244 [→ 3838; cf. 3836]. bright (full) moon:– moon [3]

3843 לְבֵנָה ***lᵉbēnâ***, n.f. GK: 4246 [→ 3840]. same as 3840: brick; tablet:– bricks [4], brick [3], make brick (+3835) [2], altars of brick [1], tile [1]

לְבֹנָה ***lᵉbōnâ***. See 3828.

3844 לְבָנוֹן ***lᵉbānôn***, n.pr.loc. GK: 4248 [→ 3835]. Lebanon, "*white, snow*":– Lebanon [71]

3845 לִבְנִי ***libnî***, n.pr.m. GK: 4249 [→ 3846]. Libni, "*[descendant of] Libni* or *white*":– Libni [5]

3846 לִבְנִי ***libnî***, a.g. GK: 4250 [→ 3845]. Libnite, "*of Libni*":– Libnites [2]

3847 לָבַשׁ ***lābaš***, v. GK: 4252 [→ 3830, 4403, 8516; cf. 3848]. [Q] to put on clothing, dress, clothe; [Qp] to be dressed; [Pu] to be dressed; [H] to dress another, clothe someone:– put on [30], clothed with [20], clothed [15], clothe with [8], put upon [8], clothed in [4], clothe [4], wear [4], armed [3], arrayed [3], came upon [3], array [2], put [2], apparelled [1], apparel [1], arrayed in [1], clothest with [1], put on clothing (+8516) [1]

3848 לְבַשׁ ***lᵉbaš*** (Aram.), v. GK: 10383 [→ 3831; cf. 3847]. [P] to be clothed; [H] to clothe (another):– clothed with [3]

לְבֻשׁ ***lᵉbuš***. See 3830.

3849 לֹג ***lōg***, n.m. GK: 4253. log (liquid measure, about a third of a quart or liter):– log [5]

3850 לֹד ***lōd***, n.pr.loc. GK: 4254. Lod:– Lod [4]

לִדְבִר ***lidbir***. See 3810.

3851 לַהַב ***lahab***, n.m. GK: 4258 [→ 3852, 7957]. flame of fire; by extension: flash (of a blade), blade of a sword:– flame [6], blade [2], flames [2], bright [1], glittering [1]

3852 לֶהָבָה ***lehābâ***, n.f. GK: 4259 [→ 3851; cf. 3827]. flame, blaze, flash; (iron) point (of a blade):– flame [12], flaming [5], flames [1], head [1]

3853 לְהָבִים ***lᵉhābîm***, n.pr.g. GK: 4260. Lehabite:– Lehabim [2]

3854 לַהַג ***lahag***, n.m. GK: 4261. study, devotion to books:– study [1]

3855 לַהַד ***lāhad***, n.pr.m. GK: 4262. Lahad, "[perhaps] *slow, indolent*":– Lahad [1]

3856 לָהַהּ ***lāhah***, v. GK: 3532 & 4263 & 4264 & 4271 [cf. 3811]. [Q] to languish, faint; [Ht] to behave like a madman:– fainted [1], mad [1]

3857 לָהַט ***lāhaṭ***, v. GK: 4265 & 4266 [→ 3858; cf. 3938]. [Q] to burn, flame; to devour; (n.) ravenous beast; [P] to set afire, set ablaze, consume:– set on fire [3], burn up [1], burneth up [1], burneth [1], burnt up [1], burnt [1], flaming [1], kindleth [1], setteth on fire [1]

3858 לַהַט ***lahaṭ***, n.[m.]. GK: 4267 & 4268 [→ 3857; cf. 3874]. flame; referring to the supernatural blade of a sword; secret arts, sorceries:– enchantments [1], flaming [1]

3859 לָהַם ***lāham***, v. GK: 4269. [Ht] to let oneself swallow greedily; (ptcp.) choice morsels:– wounds [2]

3860 לָהֵן ***lāhēn***, c. GK: 4270 [cf. 3861]. therefore:–

3861 לָהֵן ***lāhēn*** (Aram.), c. GK: 10385 & 10386 [→ 3809; cf. 3860]. so then, therefore; except, but, unless:– except [3], but [2], save [2], therefore [2], wherefore [1]

3862 לַהֲקָה ***lahᵃqâ***, n.f. GK: 4272. group, community:– company [1]

לוֹא ***lôʼ***. See 3808.

3863 לוּ ***lû***, c. GK: 4273 [→ 432, 3884]. if! if only!; O that!:– if [6], O that [5], would God [2], I pray thee [1], I would [1], if haply [1], neither [1], oh that [1], peradventure [1], though (+2050.1) [1], would God that [1], would to God (+2050.1) [1], would [1]

3864 לוּב ***lûb***, n.g.pl. GK: 4275. Libya, Libyan:– Lubims [2], Libyans [1], Lubim [1]

3865 לוּד ***lûd***, n.pr.m. & g. GK: 4276 [→ 3866]. same as 3866: Lud, Ludite; Lydia, Lydians:– Lud [4], Ludim [2], Lydians [1], Lydia [1]

3866 לוּדִים ***lûdîm***, n.pr.m. & g. GK: 4276 [→ 3865]. same as 3865: Lud, Ludite; Lydia, Lydians:–

3867 לָוָה ***lāwâ***, v. GK: 4277 & 4278 [→ 3878, 3881, 3880, 3882; cf. 3924]. [Q] to accompany; to borrow; [N] to be joined, be attached, be bound to; [H] to lend:– joined [8], lend [4], lendeth [3], borrower [2], join [2], abide with [1], borrowed [1], borroweth [1], borrow [1], cleave [1], lender (+376) [1], lender [1]

3868 לוּז ***lûz***, v. GK: 4279 [→ 3891]. [Q] to depart (from one's sight); [N] to be devious, be perverse, be deceitful; [H] to depart (from one's sight):– depart [2], froward [2], perverseness [1], perverse [1]

3869 לוּז ***lûz***, n.[m.]. GK: 4280 [→ 3870]. almond tree (branch):– hazel [1]

3870 לוּז ***lûz***, n.pr.loc. GK: 4281 [cf. 3869]. Luz, "*almond tree*":– Luz [8]

3871 לוּחַ ***lûaḥ***, n.m. GK: 4283 [→ 3872; cf. 3892]. tablets (of stone); board, panel (of wood); plate (metal):– tables [34], boards [4], table [4], plates [1]

3872 לוּחִית **lûḥît** or לֻחוֹת **luḥôt**, n.pr.loc. GK: 4284 & 4304 [→ 3871; cf. 3892]. Luhith, Luhoth:– Luhith [2]

3873 לוֹחֵשׁ **lôḥēš** or הַלּוֹחֵשׁ **hallôḥēš**, n.pr.m. GK: 4285 & 2135 [→ 1886.1+3907]. Lohesh or Hallohesh, "*the whisperer*":– Hallohesh [2]

3874 לוּט **lûṭ**, v. GK: 4286 [→ 3875, 3814, 3909, 3910; cf. 3813, 3858]. [Q] to cover, enfold; [Qp] to be wrapped up; [H] to cover, wrap up:– cast [1], wrapped [1], wrapt [1]

3875 לוֹט **lôṭ**, n.m. GK: 4287 [→ 3874]. shroud, covering:– covering [1]

3876 לוֹט **lôṭ**, n.pr.m. GK: 4288 [→ 3877]. Lot:– Lot [32], Lot's [1]

3877 לוֹטָן **lôṭān**, n.pr.m. GK: 4289 [→ 3876]. Lotan, "*of Lot*":– Lotan [5], Lotan's [2]

3878 לֵוִי **lēwî**, n.pr.m. GK: 4290 [→ 3867; cf. 3879]. Levi; Levite, "*of Levi*":– Levi [64], Levites (+1121) [1]

3879 לֵוָי **lēwāy** (Aram.), n.g. GK: 10387 [cf. 3878, 3881]. Levite, "*of Levi*":– Levites [4]

3880 לִוְיָה **liwyâ**, n.f. GK: 4292 [→ 3867]. garland, wreath:– ornament [2]

3881 לֵוִי **lēwî**, a.g. GK: 4291 [→ 3867; cf. 3879]. Levite, of Levi, "*of Levi*":– Levites [259], Levite [26]

3882 לִוְיָתָן **liwyātān**, n.m. GK: 4293 [→ 3867]. Leviathan, sea-monster; this refers both to a serpent-like sea creature and to a mythological monster of chaos opposed to the true God:– leviathan [5], mourning [1]

3883 לוּל **lûl**, n.[m.]. GK: 4294. stairway; some sources: trap door:– winding stairs [1]

3884 לוּלֵא **lûlē'**, c. GK: 4295 [→ 3863]. if not, unless:– except [3], if not [3], unless [3], were it not that [2], except (+3588) [1], not [1], unless (+3588) [1]

3885 לוּן **lûn** or לִין **lîn**, v. GK: 4296 & 4328 [→ 4411, 4412, 8519; cf. 3915, 3917]. [Q] to spend the night, stay the night; [N] to grumble against, blame; [H] to grumble against, blame; to hold back overnight, leave overnight; [Htpolal] to stay for the night; by extension: to stay, dwell an indeterminate amount of time:– lodge [18], lodged [12], murmured [7], murmur [6], abideth [3], abide [3], remain [3], tarried all night [3], tarry all night [3], abide all night [2], lie all night [2], lodge in [2], remain all night [2], remaineth [2], tarry [2], all night [1], cause to lodge [1], continue [1], dwell [1], endure [1], grudge [1], lay all night [1], left [1], lodge all night [1], lodgest [1], lodging [1], made to murmur [1], tarry for a night [1], tarry night [1]

3886 לוּעַ **lûa'**, v. GK: 4362. [Q] to talk impetuously, to dedicate (something) rashly; a fig. extension of drinking in a hurried, careless manner:– swallow down [1], swallowed up [1]

3887 לוּץ **lûṣ** or לִיץ **lîṣ**, v. GK: 4329 & 4370 [→ 3944, 3945, 4426]. [Q] to mock, scorn, talk big; [H] to mock; [Htpolal] to show oneself a mocker:– scorner [11], scorners [3], interpreter [2], scorneth [2], ambassadors [1], had in derision [1], make a mock at [1], mockers [1], mocker [1], scornest [1], scornful [1], scorn [1], teachers [1]

3888 לוּשׁ **lûš**, v. GK: 4297. [Q] to knead (bread dough):– kneaded [3], knead [2]

3889 לָוִשׁ **lāwiš**, n.pr.m. GK: 4298 [→ 3918]. Lawish; var. of 3919:–

3890 לְוָת **l^ewāt** (Aram.), pp. GK: 10388 [cf. 3807.2]. near, beside:– from (+4481) [1]

לֻחוֹת **luḥôt**. See 3872.

לָז **lāz** and לָזֶה **lāzeh**. See 1975 and 1976.

3891 לָזוּת **lāzût**, n.f. GK: 4299 [→ 3868]. crookedness, perversity, referring to a kind of speech:– perverse [1]

3892 לַח **laḥ**, a. GK: 4300 [→ 3871, 3872, 3893]. fresh, fresh-cut, still moist:– green [5], moist [1]

3893 לֵחַ **lēaḥ**, n.m. GK: 4301 [→ 3892]. strength:– natural force [1]

לֻחַ **luaḥ**. See 3871.

3894 לְחוּם **l^eḥûm**, n.[m.]. GK: 4302 & 4303 [→ 3898]. entrails; blow, wound; act of eating:– eating [1], flesh [1]

3895 לְחִי **l^eḥî**, n.m. GK: 4305 [→ 3896?, 7437?]. jaw, jawbone; by extension: cheek, jowl:– cheek [5], cheeks [4], jaws [4], jawbone [3], jaw [3], cheek bone [1], two cheeks [1]

3896 לְחִי **l^eḥî**, n.pr.loc. GK: 4306 [→ 3895?]. Lehi, "*jawbone*":– Lehi [3]

3897 לָחַךְ **lāḥak**, v. GK: 4308. [Q] to lick up; [P] to lick up, subdue:– lick up [2], lick [2], licked up [1], licketh up [1]

3898 לָחַם **lāḥam**, v. GK: 4309 & 4310 [→ 3894, 3899, 3901, 4421]. [Q] to fight against, attack; to eat, dine; [Qp] to be consumed; [N] to fight against, attack:– fight [85], fought [57], warred [7], eat [5], made war [4], fighteth [3], ever fight (+3898) [2], fighting [2], make war [2], overcome [2], warring [2], devoured [1], fought against [1], maketh war [1], making war [1], prevail [1], war [1]

3899 לֶחֶם **leḥem**, n.m. & f. GK: 4312 [→ 1035, 3433, 3898; cf. 3900]. bread, bread loaf; any kind of food; time or act of eating, meal; "bread of the Presence" is a regular offering to the LORD presented on a designated table in the tabernacle and temple:– bread [238], food [21], meat [18], loaves [5], shewbread (+6440) [3], shewbread (+6440+1886.1) [3], shewbread (+4635+1886.1) [2], victuals [2], eat [1], feast [1], fruit [1], provision [1], shewbread (+4635) [1], shewbread [1]

3900 לְחֶם **l^eḥem** (Aram.), n.m. GK: 10389 [cf. 3899]. bread; banquet meal:– feast [1]

3901 לָחֶם **lāḥem**, n.[m.]. GK: 4311 [→ 3898]. war; other sources vary:– war [1]

לָחֻם **lāḥum**. See 3894.

3902 לַחְמִי **laḥmî**, n.pr.m. GK: 4313. Lahmi:– Lahmi [1]

3903 לַחְמָס **laḥmās**, n.pr.loc. GK: 4314. Lahmas:– Lahmam [1]

3904 לְחֵנָה **l^eḥēnâ** (Aram.), n.f. GK: 10390. concubine, a class of spouse generally of lower status than a wife (the exact marriage relationship of a concubine varied in different cultures), usually for status and pleasure of the husband, also translated "mistress, consort":– concubines [3]

3905 לָחַץ **lāḥaṣ**, v. GK: 4315 [→ 3906; cf. 5169]. [Q] to oppress, crush, confine; [N] to be pressed close:– oppressed [7], oppress [5], afflict [1], crusht [1], forced [1], hold fast [1], oppresseth [1], oppressors [1], thrust [1]

3906 לַחַץ **laḥaṣ**, n.m. GK: 4316 [→ 3905]. oppression, affliction; short ration (of bread or water):– oppression [7], affliction [5]

3907 לָחַשׁ **lāḥaš**, v. GK: 4317 [→ 3873, 3908; cf. 5172]. [P] to charm, enchant (i.e., whisper); [Ht] to whisper together:– charmers [1], whispered [1], whisper [1]

3908 לַחַשׁ **laḥaš**, n.[m.]. GK: 4318 [→ 3907]. charming, whispering; charm, enchanter:– charmed [1], earrings [1], enchantment [1], orator [1], prayer [1]

3909 לָט **lāṭ**, n.[m.]. GK: 4319 [→ 3814]. quietly, privately, secretly, a fig. extension of the base meaning "no physical sound"; (pl.) secret arts, with a focus on mysterious and hidden elements of this magic:– enchantments [3], privily (+871.1+1886.1) [1], secretly (+871.1+1886.1) [1], softly (+871.1+1886.1) [1]

3910 לֹט **lōṭ**, n.[m.]. GK: 4320 [→ 3874]. myrrh (a resinous, fragrant and slightly bitter to the taste); some sources: mastic bark (a resinous gum of the rockrose plant):– myrrh [2]

3911 לְטָאָה **l^eṭā'â**, n.f. GK: 4321. wall lizard; some sources: gecko:– lizard [1]

3912 לְטוּשִׁים **l^eṭûšîm**, n.pr.g. GK: 4322 [→ 3913]. Letushite, "*sharpened*":– Letushim [1]

3913 לָטַשׁ **lāṭaš**, v. GK: 4323 [→ 3912]. [Q] to sharpen; to forge, hammer; to pierce (with the eyes); [Pu] to be sharpened:– instructor [1], sharpeneth [1], sharpen [1], sharp [1], whet [1]

3914 לֹיָה **lōyâ**, n.f. GK: 4324 [cf. 3924]. wreath, garland; some translate as a technical architectural term: border, rim:– additions [2], addition [1]

3915 לַיִל **layil** or לַיְלָה **laylâ**, n.m. GK: 4325 & 4326 [→ 3917; cf. 3885; cf. 3916]. night; sometimes with the implication that it is the time of illicit, illegal, or immoral activity:– night [199], nights [15], midnight (+2677+1886.1) [4], to night (+1886.1) [4], at midnight (+2676) [2], in a night (+1121) [2], night season [2], in night [1], midnight (+2676+1886.1) [1], midnight (+8432+1886.1) [1], night seasons [1], to night [1]

3916 לֵילֵי **lêlê** (Aram.), n.[m.]. GK: 10391 [cf. 3915]. night:– night [5]

3917 לִילִית **lîlît**, n.f. GK: 4327 [→ 3915; cf. 3885]. night creature; Lilith, a female demon of the night:– shrich owl [1]

3918 לַיִשׁ **layiš**, n.m. GK: 4330 [→ 3889, 3919]. lion:– old lion [2], lion [1]

3919 לַיִשׁ **layiš** or לַיְשָׁה **lay^ešâ**, n.pr.m. & loc. GK: 4331 & 4332 & 4333 [→ 3918; cf. 3959]. Laish, Laishah, "*lion*":– Laish [7]

3920 לָכַד **lākad**, v. GK: 4334 [→ 3921, 4434]. [Q] to capture, seize, take as a possession; [N] to be taken captive, be seized, be taken:– taken [44], took [43], take [19], taketh [5], caught [3], catch [2], taken at all (+3920) [2], frozen [1], holden [1], stick together [1]

3921 לֶכֶד **leked**, n.[m.]. GK: 4335 [→ 3920]. snaring, capturing:– taken [1]

3922 לֵכָה **lēkâ**, n.pr.loc. GK: 4336. Lecah, "*to you*":– Lecah [1]

3923 לָכִישׁ **lākîš**, n.pr.loc. GK: 4337. Lachish:– Lachish [24]

3924 לֻלָאוֹת **lulā'ôt**, n.f. GK: 4339 [cf. 3867, 3914]. (pl.) loops:– loops [13]

3925 לָמַד **lāmad**, v. GK: 4340 [→ 3928, 4451, 8527]. [Q] to learn, train for; [Qp] to be trained; [P] to teach, instruct, cause to learn; [Pu] to be trained; with implication that the learning will be put to use:– teach [32], taught [17], learn [16], learned [5], teacheth [5], diligently learn (+3925) [2], instructed [2], expert [1], instruct [1], skilful [1], teachers [1], teachest [1], teaching [1], unaccustomed (+3808) [1]

לִמֻּד **limmud**. See 3928.

3926 לְמוֹ **l^emô**, pp. GK: 4344 [→ 3807.1]. for, in, over:– at [1], for [1], to [1], upon [1]

3927 לְמוּאֵל **l^emû'ēl**, n.pr.m. GK: 4345 [→ 3807.1+410]. Lemuel, "*[belonging] to God [El]*":– Lemuel [2]

3928 לִמֻּד **limmud**, a. GK: 4341 [→ 3925]. accustomed to; (n.) a disciple, one who is taught, a follower:– learned [2], accustomed to [1], disciples [1], taught [1], used to [1]

3929 לֶמֶךְ **lemek**, n.pr.m. GK: 4347. Lamech:– Lamech [11]

3930 לֹעַ **lōa'**, n.[m.]. GK: 4350 [→ 3216]. throat:– throat [1]

3931 לָעַב **lā'ab**, v. GK: 4351. [H] to mock, make sport of (someone), make a game of (someone):– mocked [1]

3932 לָעַג **lā'ag**, v. GK: 4352 [→ 3933, 3934; cf. 5926]. [Q] to mock, scoff, ridicule; [N] to stammer, speak as a foreigner; [H] to mock, ridicule:– laughed to scorn [3], mocketh [3], laugh to scorn [2], laugh [2], mocked [2], mock [2], derision [1], have in derision [1], mockest [1], stammering [1]

3933 לַעַג **la'ag**, n.[m.]. GK: 4353 [→ 3932]. scorn, ridicule, derision:– derision [3], scorning [2], scorn [2]

3934 לָעֵג **lā'ēg**, a. GK: 4354 [→ 3932]. people of stammering lips or foreign language:– mockers [1], stammering [1]

3935 לַעְדָּה **la'dâ**, n.pr.m. GK: 4355 [→ 3936]. Laadah, "[perhaps] *having a fat throat or neck*":– Laadah [1]

3936 לַעְדָּן **la'dān**, n.pr.m. GK: 4356 [→ 3935]. Ladan:– Laadan [7]

3937 לָעַז **lā'az**, v. GK: 4357. [Q] to speak a foreign tongue, speak an unintelligible language:– strange language [1]

3938 לָעַט **lā'aṭ**, v. GK: 4358 [cf. 3857]. [H] to let (someone) gulp down:– feed [1]

3939 לַעֲנָה **la^anâ**, n.f. GK: 4360. gall (bitter to the taste, possibly poisonous); by extension: bitterness as a concept:– wormwood [7], hemlock [1]

3940 לַפִּיד **lappîd**, n.m. GK: 4365 [→ 3941?]. torch, firebrand; by extension: lightning:– lamps [4], lamp [3], brands [1], burning lamps [1], firebrands [1], firebrand [1], lightnings [1], torches [1], torch [1]

3941 לַפִּידוֹת **lappîdôt**, n.pr.m. GK: 4366 [→ 3940?]. Lappidoth, "*flames*":– Lapidoth [1]

3942 לִפְנֵי **lipnê**, pp.+n.m. GK: 4367 [→ 3807.1+6437]. before, in front of, in the presence of (3807.1 + 6440):–

3943 לָפַת **lāpat**, v. GK: 4369. [Q] to reach toward; [N] be turned aside; in some contexts there is an implication of touching or grasping the object reached toward:– took hold [1], turned aside [1], turned [1]

3944 לָצוֹן **lāṣôn**, n.[m.]. GK: 4371 [→ 3887]. mockery, scoffing, hostile speech of fools:– scornful [2], scorning [1]

3945 לָצַץ **lāṣaṣ**, n.[m.] *or* v.ptcp. GK: 4372 [→ 3887]. mocker, scoffer, with an implication that this class of person is foolish and rebellious:– scorners [1]

3946 לַקּוּם **laqqûm**, n.pr.loc. GK: 4373. Lakkum:– Lakum [1]

3947 לָקַח **lāqaḥ**, v. GK: 4374 [→ 3948, 3949, 4455, 4457, 4727, 4728]. [Q] to take, receive; [Qp] to be led away; [N] to be captured, taken away; [Pu] to be taken away, brought; [Ht] to flash back and forth; by extension: to gain possession, exercise authority; "to take a woman" means "to marry a wife":– took [347], take [343], taken [72], receive [35], received [22], fetch [19], bring [17], take away [16], took away [12], taketh [10], brought [9], taken away [9], fetched [5], fet [5], get [5], married [4], receiveth [4], carried away [3], buy [2], carry away [2], fetcht [2], have [2], accept [1], buyeth [1], drawn unto [1], getteth [1], infolding [1], mingled [1], placed [1], put [1], receiving [1], reserved [1], seize [1], sent for [1], take out [1], take up [1], taken up [1], takest [1], taketh away [1], taking [1], tookest [1], use [1], winneth [1]

3948 לֶקַח **leqaḥ**, n.m. GK: 4375 [→ 3947]. teaching, instruction, learning:– doctrine [4], learning [4], fair speech [1]

3949 לִקְחִי **liqḥî**, n.pr.m. GK: 4376 [→ 3947]. Likhi, "*take, marry*":– Likhi [1]

3950 לָקַט **lāqaṭ**, v. GK: 4377 [→ 3219, 3951]. [Q] to gather; [P] to gather, pick up, glean; [Pu] to be gathered up; [Ht] to gather oneself about; this act of gathering is general, and can refer to the second or final gleanings of the field or orchard:– gather [13], gathered [9], glean [7], gleaned [5], gathered up [2], gathereth [1]

3951 לֶקֶט **leqeṭ**, n.[m.]. GK: 4378 [→ 3950]. gleanings (of a harvest):– gleanings [1], gleaning [1]

3952 לָקַק **lāqaq**, v. GK: 4379. [Q, P] to lap up, lick up:– lapped [2], lappeth [2], licked up [1], licked [1], lick [1]

3953 לָקַשׁ **lāqaš**, v.den. GK: 4380 [→ 3954, 4456]. [P] to glean:– gather [1]

3954 לֶקֶשׁ **leqeš**, n.[m.]. GK: 4381 [→ 3953]. second crop, late grass at spring time:– latter growth [2]

3955 לָשָׁד **lāšād**, n.m. GK: 4382. moist (food), strength:– fresh [1], moisture [1]

3956 לָשׁוֹן **lāšôn**, n.m. GK: 4383 [→ 3960; cf. 3961]. tongue; by extension: language, speech, noise (of an animal); something tongue-shaped: wedge (of precious metal), bay, gulf, flame of fire:– tongue [89], language [9], tongues [9], bay [3], wedge [2], babbler (+1167+1886.1) [1], evil speaker (+376) [1], fire (+784) [1], languages [1], talkers [1]

3957 לִשְׁכָּה **liškâ**, n.f. GK: 4384 [cf. 5393]. room, chamber; hall; storeroom:– chambers [31], chamber [15], parlour [1]

3958 לֶשֶׁם **lešem**, n.[m.]. GK: 4385. jacinth (exact identification is uncertain):– ligure [2]

3959 לֶשֶׁם **lešem**, n.pr.loc. GK: 4386 [cf. 3919]. Leshem, "*lion*":– Leshem [2]

3960 לָשַׁן **lāšan**, v.den. GK: 4387 [→ 3956]. [Po] to slander; [H] to slander:– accuse [1], slandereth [1]

3961 לִשָּׁן **liššān** (Aram.), n.m. GK: 10392 [cf. 3956]. language, tongue:– languages [6], language [1]

3962 לֶשַׁע **leša'**, n.pr.loc. GK: 4388. Lasha:– Lasha [1]

3963 לֶתֶךְ **lētek**, n.[m.]. GK: 4390. lethek (a dry measure, half a cor, about 6 bushels [220 liters]):– half homer [1]

מַ **ma-**, or מָ **mā-**. See 4100.

3963.1 ־ָם **-ām** or ־ֵם **-m**, p.m.pl.suf. GK: 4392 [→ 279?, 1886.3]. they, them, their:– them [1859], their [1501], they [263], their own [46], it [16], whose [15], whom [14], these [11], those [11], themselves [10], thereof [9], the^s [6], theirs [6], which [6], you [6], by themselves (+905+3807.1) [4], therein (+871.1) [4], wherein (+834+871.1) [4], themselves (+5315) [3], whom (+834) [3], his [2], thereby (+871.1) [2], ye [2], man's^s [1], others [1], the^s people [1], their the [1], they (+5315) [1], wherein (+871.1) [1], wherein [1], whereof (+834) [1], whereof [1], wherewith (+834+871.1) [1], wherewith (+871.1) [1]

3964 מָא **mā'** (Aram.), p.inter. & indef. GK: 10394 [→ 4101; cf. 4100]. what?:– what (+1768+3807.2) [1]

3965 מַאֲבוּס **ma^abûs**, n.[m.]. GK: 4393 [→ 75]. granary:– storehouses [1]

3966 מְאֹד **m^eōd**, n.m. (used as adv.). GK: 4394. a marker of great degree or quanity: very, greatly, exceedingly, much:– very [129], greatly [47], sore [20], great [12], exceeding [10], exceeding (+3966+871.1) [8], much [7], very (+5704) [7], exceeding (+3966) [6], exceedingly (+3966) [6], diligently [4], exceedingly (+3966+871.1) [4], exceedingly [4], good [3], far [2], greatly (+5704) [2], mightily [2], might [2], utterly (+5704) [2], very sore (+5704) [2], ask never so much (+7235) [1], diligent [1], especially [1], exceeding (+5704) [1], exceeding (+7235) [1], exceedingly (+7235) [1], far off [1], fast [1], hated exceedingly (+1419+8130+8135) [1], mighty [1], quickly [1], right well [1], so much [1], sore (+5704) [1], so [1], very (+1419) [1], very (+5704+3807.1) [1], very great [1], very much (+5704) [1], waxed louder and louder (+2390) [1], well [1]

Heb

3967 מֵאָה **mē'â**, n.f. GK: 4395 [→ 3968?; cf. 3969]. hundred:– hundred [465], two hundred [76], hundreds [27], eleven hundred (+505+2050.1) [3], hundredth [3], one hundred [3], hundredfold (+6471) [1], hundredfold (+8180) [1], sixscore (+6242+2050.1) [1], twelve hundred (+505+2050.1) [1]

3968 מֵאָה **mē'â**, n.pr.loc. GK: 4396 [→ 3967?; cf. 3969]. (the Tower of) the Hundred:– Meah [2]

3969 מְאָה **m^e'â** (Aram.), n.f. GK: 10395 [cf. 3967, 3968]. hundred; (dual) two hundred:– hundred [7], two hundred [1]

3970 מַאֲוַיִּים **ma^awiyyîm**, n.[m.pl.]. GK: 4397 [→ 183]. desires:– desires [1]

מוֹאל **mô'l**. See 4136.

3971 מְאוּם **m^e'ûm** or מוּם **mûm**, n.m. GK: 4398 & 4583 [→ 3972]. defect, blemish, flaw, injury; by extension: shame, defilement:– blemish [15], spot [3], blot [2], blemishes [1]

3972 מְאוּמָה **m^{e}'ûmâ**, p.indef. GK: 4399 [→ 3971]. something, anything; (with negation) nothing:– any thing [13], nothing (+3808) [5], nothing (+369) [4], ought [4], any thing (+3605) [1], no (+3808) [1], no (+408) [1], nought (+3808) [1], ought else (+3605) [1], somewhat [1]

3973 מָאוֹס **mā'ôs**, n.[m.]. GK: 4400 [→ 3988]. refuse, trash:– refuse [1]

3974 מָאוֹר **mā'ôr**, n.m. GK: 4401 [→ 215]. light source, luminary, light-bearer:– light [15], lights [3], bright [1]

3975 מְאוּרָה **m^{e}'ûrâ**, n.f. GK: 4402 [→ 215?]. nest hole (of a viper):– den [1]

3976 מֹאזְנַיִם **mō'znayim**, n.[m.]du. GK: 4404 [cf. 3977]. set of scales, (two) balance pans for weight measurement, with an emphasis on honesty and standardized measurements; by extension: righteous evaluation of motives and actions:– balances [8], balance [7]

3977 מֹאזְנֵא **mō'znē'** (Aram.), n.m.emph. GK: 10396 [cf. 3976]. scale, balance, with a focus that the device is an objective implement for judging truth:– balances [1]

מֵאָה **mē'yâ**. See 3967.

3978 מַאֲכָל **ma'^{a}kāl**, n.m. & f. GK: 4407 [→ 398]. food, supplies, something to eat:– meat [22], food [5], bakemeats (+644+4639) [1], fruit [1], victual [1]

3979 מַאֲכֶלֶת **ma'^{a}kelet**, n.f. GK: 4408 [→ 398]. (butcher) knife, sometimes with a ceremonial or sacrificial focus:– knife [3], knives [1]

3980 מַאֲכֹלֶת **ma'^{a}kōlet**, n.f. GK: 4409 [→ 398]. fuel (for a fire); a fig. extension of food that is consumed:– fuel [2]

3981 מַאֲמָץ **ma'^{a}māṣ**, n.[m.]. GK: 4410 [→ 553]. effort, exertion:– forces [1]

3982 מַאֲמָר **ma'^{a}mār**, n.m. GK: 4411 [→ 559; cf. 3983]. command, decree, instruction:– commandment [2], decree [1]

3983 מֵאמַר **mē'mar** (Aram.), n.[m.]. GK: 10397 [→ 560; cf. 3982]. declaration, request:– appointment [1], word [1]

3984 מָאן **mā'n** (Aram.), n.m. GK: 10398. article, container, goblet:– vessels [7]

3985 מָאֵן **mā'an**, v. GK: 4412 [→ 3986, 3987]. [P] to refuse, reject:– refused [24], refuse [9], refuseth [5], utterly refuse (+3985) [2], refusedst [1]

3986 מָאֵן **mā'ēn**, a.v. GK: 4413 [→ 3985]. refusing:– refuse [4]

3987 מֵאֵן **mē'ēn**, a. GK: 4414 [→ 3985]. refusing:– refuse [1]

3988 מָאַס **mā'as**, v. GK: 4415 & 4416 [→ 3973, cf. 4529, 4549]. [Q] to reject, despise, spurn, disdain; [N] to be rejected, become vile; to be festering, be dissolving; be vanishing:– rejected [16], despised [12], despise [9], cast away [7], refused [5], utterly rejected (+3988) [4], cast off [3], despiseth [3], refuse [3], abhorred [2], abhorreth [1], abhor [1], become loathsome [1], contemneth [1], contemn [1], disdained [1], loathe [1], melt away [1], refuseth [1], reject [1], reprobate [1], vile [1]

3989 מַאֲפֶה **ma'^{a}peh**, n.[m.]. GK: 4418 [→ 644]. something baked:– baken [1]

3990 מַאֲפֵל **ma'^{a}pēl**, n.[m.]. GK: 4419 [→ 652?]. darkness:– darkness [1]

3991 מַאְפֵלְיָה **ma'pēlyâ**, n.f. GK: 4420 [→ 652?]. great darkness:– darkness [1]

3992 מָאַר **mā'ar**, v. GK: 4421. [H] to be destructive; to be painful:– fretting [3], pricking [1]

מְאֹר **mā'ōr**. See 3974.

3993 מַאֲרָב **ma'^{a}rāb**, n.m. GK: 4422 [→ 693]. ambush; troops in an ambush:– ambushment [2], lie in ambush [1], lurking places [1], lying in wait [1]

3994 מְאֵרָה **m^{e}'ērâ**, n.f. GK: 4423 [→ 779]. curse:– curse [4], cursing [1]

מְאֹרָה **m^{e}'ōrâ**. See 3974.

3995 מִבְדָּלוֹת **mibdālôt**, n.f. GK: 4426 [→ 914]. set aside, selected, singled out:– separate [1]

3996 מָבוֹא **mābô'**, n.m. GK: 4427 [→ 3997, 4126; cf. 935]. entrance, entryway, gateway; "the place where the sun goes (sets)" is the direction west:– entry [5], going down [5], entrance [3], entering in [2], came [1], cometh [1], coming in [1], enter into [1], entering [1], goeth down [1], the west (+8121+1886.1) [1], westward (+8121+1886.1) [1]

3997 מְבוֹאָה **m^{e}bô'â**, n.m. GK: 4427 [→ 3996]. same as 3996: entrance, entryway, gateway:– entry [1]

3998 מְבוּכָה **m^{e}bûkâ**, n.f. GK: 4428 [→ 943]. confusion, confused terror:– perplexity [2]

3999 מַבּוּל **mabbûl**, n.m. GK: 4429 [→ 5035]. flood (waters):– flood [13]

4000 מְבוֹנִים **m^{e}bônîm**, v.ptcp. GK: 4430. ptcp. of 995: knowing, taught:–

4001 מְבוּסָה **m^{e}bûsâ**, n.f. GK: 4431 [→ 947]. trampling down, implying subjugation:– treading down [1], trodden down [1], trodden under foot [1]

4002 מַבּוּעַ **mabbûa'**, n.[m.]. GK: 4432 [→ 5042]. (a bubbling) spring (of water):– springs [2], fountain [1]

4003 מְבוּקָה **m^{e}bûqâ**, n.f. GK: 4433 [→ 950]. plundering, devastation, desertion:– void [1]

4004 מִבְחוֹר **mibḥôr**, n.[m.]. GK: 4435 [→ 977]. choicest (trees); major (towns):– choice [2]

4005 מִבְחָר **mibḥār**, n.[m.] & f. GK: 4436 [→ 4006; cf. 977]. choicest, best, elite, finest (persons or things):– choice [7], chosen [4], choicest [1]

4006 מִבְחָר **mibḥār**, n.pr.m. GK: 4437 [→ 4005; cf. 977]. Mibhar, "*choice*":– Mibhar [1]

4007 מַבָּט **mabbāṭ**, n.m. GK: 4438 [→ 5027]. hope, trust in, relying on:– expectation [3]

4008 מִבְטָא **mibṭā'**, n.[m.]. GK: 4439 [→ 981]. rash promise, rashness:– that which uttered [1], uttered ought out [1]

4009 מִבְטָח **mibṭāḥ**, n.[m.]. GK: 4440 [→ 982]. security, trust, confidence:– confidence [8], trust [4], confidences [1], hope [1], sure [1]

4010 מַבְלִיגִית **mablîgît**, n.f. GK: 4443 [→ 1455]. comfort, smile, cheerfulness:– comfort [1]

4011 מִבְנֶה **mibneh**, n.m. GK: 4445 [→ 1129]. building, structure:– frame [1]

4012 מְבֻנַּי **m^{e}bunnay**, n.pr.m. GK: 4446. Mebunnai, "*well built*":– Mebunnai [1]

4013 מִבְצָר **mibṣār**, n.m. GK: 4448 & 4450 [→ 4014; cf. 1219]. fortress, fortification, stronghold; ore:– fenced [11], strong holds [10], defenced [4], fortress [4], fortresses [2], strong hold [2], strong [2], holds [1], most fenced [1]

4014 מִבְצָר **mibṣār**, n.pr.m. GK: 4449 [→ 4013; cf. 1219]. Mibzar, "*bastion*":– Mibzar [2]

מִבְצָרָה **mibṣārâ**. See 4013.

4015 מִבְרָח **mibrāḥ**, n.m. GK: 4451 [→ 1272]. fleeing, refugee:– fugitives [1]

4016 מְבוּשִׁים **m^{e}bûšîm**, n.[m.]. GK: 4434 [→ 954]. private parts, (male) genitals, with a possible focus on shame if exposed:– secrets [1]

4017 מִבְשָׂם **mibśām**, n.pr.m. GK: 4452. Mibsam, "*sweet odor*":– Mibsam [3]

4018 מְבַשְּׁלוֹת **m^{e}baśś^{e}lôt**, n.f.pl. GK: 4453 [→ 1310]. places for fire, cooking-places:– boiling places [1]

מָג **māg**. See 7248, 7249.

4019 מַגְבִּישׁ **magbîš**, n.pr.m. GK: 4455. Magbish, "[perhaps] *thick*":– Magbish [1]

4020 מִגְבָּלוֹת **migbālôt**, n.f.pl. GK: 4456 [→ 1383]. (braided) chains, (twisted) cords:– ends [1]

4021 מִגְבָּעָה **migbā'â**, n.f.pl. GK: 4457 [→ 1375?]. headband:– bonnets [4]

4022 מֶגֶד **meged**, n.m. GK: 4458 [→ 4023, 4025, 4030]. choice things, best gifts:– precious things [4], pleasant [3], precious [1]

4023 מְגִדּוֹ **m^{e}giddô** or מְגִדּוֹן **m^{e}giddôn**, n.pr.loc. GK: 4459 & 4461 [cf. 4022]. Megiddo, "*place of troops*":– Megiddo [11], Megiddon [1]

4024 מִגְדּוֹל **migdôl** or מִגְדֹּל **migdōl**, n.m. & n.pr.loc. GK: 4460 & 4465 [→ 1431, 4026]. Migdol, "*tower*"; great:– Migdol [4], tower [3]

4025 מַגְדִּיאֵל **magdî'ēl**, n.pr.m. GK: 4462 [→ 4022+410]. Magdiel, "*choice gift of God [El]*":– Magdiel [2]

4026 מִגְדָּל **migdāl**, n.m. GK: 4463 [→ 4024, 4027, 4028, 4029; cf. 1431]. tower, watchtower, usually a tall, narrow building used for defense; high platform (made of wood and used for public speaking to crowds); an elevated area such as a garden with mounds, terraces:– tower [34], towers [13], castles [1], flowers [1], pulpit [1]

מִגְדֹּל **migdōl**. See 4024.

מִגְדָּלָה **migdālâ**. See 4026.

4027 מִגְדַּל־אֵל **migdal-'ēl**, n.pr.loc. GK: 4466 [→ 4026+410; cf. 1431]. Migdal El, "*tower of God [El]*":– Migdal-el [1]

4028 מִגְדַּל־גָּד **migdal-gad**, n.pr.loc. GK: 4467 [→ 4026+1410; cf. 1431]. Migdal Gad, "*tower of Gad*":– Migdal-gad [1]

4029 מִגְדַּל־עֵדֶר **migdal-'ēder**, n.pr.loc. GK: 4468 [→ 4026+5740]. Migdal Eder, "*tower of Eder [flock]*":–

4030 מִגְדָּנוֹת **migdānôt**, n.f.[pl.]. GK: 4469 [→ 4022]. costly gifts, articles of value:– precious things [3], presents [1]

4031 מָגוֹג **māgôg**, n.pr.loc. GK: 4470 [→ 1463]. Magog, "[perhaps] *land of Gog*":– Magog [4]

4032 מָגוֹר **māgôr**, n.m. GK: 4471 [→ 4034; cf. 1481]. terror, horror:– fear [6], terrors [1], terror [1]

4033 מָגוֹר **māgôr**, n.[m.]. GK: 4472 & 4473 [→ 1481, 4035, 4460]. to live as an alien, stay as a stranger; place to live, place to lodge; grain pit, storage chamber = heart, mind:–

pilgrimage [4], stranger [3], dwellings [2], sojourn [1], strangers [1]

4034 מְגוֹרָה m^{e}gôrâ, n.f. GK: 4475 [→ 4032; cf. 1481]. dread, fear:– fear [1]

4035 מְגוּרָה m^{e}gûrâ, n.f. GK: 4476 [→ 4033]. barn, grain-pit, storage chamber:– fears [2], barn [1]

4036 מָגוֹר מִסָּבִיב māgôr missābîb, n.pr.m. GK: 4474 [→ 1481]. Magor-Missabib, "*terror on every side*":– Magor-missabib [1]

4037 מַגְזֵרָה magzērâ, n.f. GK: 4477 [→ 1504]. ax:– axes [1]

4038 מַגָּל maggāl, n.[m.]. GK: 4478 [cf. 1556?]. sickle:– sickle [2]

4039 מְגִלָּה m^{e}gillâ, n.f. GK: 4479 [→ 1556; cf. 4040]. scroll (a rolled up document made of leather or papyrus):– roll [20], volume [1]

4040 מְגִלָּה m^{e}gillâ (Aram.), n.f. GK: 10399 [→ 1560; cf. 4039]. scroll:– roll [1]

4041 מְגַמָּה m^{e}gammâ, n.f. GK: 4480 [cf. 1571]. horde:– sup up [1]

4042 מָגַן māgan, v. GK: 4481 [→ 4043]. [P] to hand over, deliver to, present with:– deliver [2], delivered [1]

4043 מָגֵן māgēn, n.m. GK: 4482 & 4483 & 4484 [→ 1598, 4042, 4044]. (small) shield used for defense, usually of oiled leather; by extension: ruler, a leader who protects; fig. of the impregnable scales of leviathan; insolent; gift, present (gifts made in return):– shield [33], shields [15], buckler [6], bucklers [3], armed [2], defence [2], rulers [1], scales (+650) [1]

4044 מְגִנָּה m^{e}ginnâ, n.f. GK: 4485 [→ 4043]. veil, covering:– sorrow [1]

4045 מִגְעֶרֶת mig'eret, n.f. GK: 4486 [→ 1605]. rebuke, reproach:– rebuke [1]

4046 מַגֵּפָה maggēpâ, n.f. GK: 4487 [→ 5062]. plague; blow, strike, slaughter:– plague [20], slaughter [3], plagued [1], plagues [1], stroke [1]

4047 מַגְפִּיעָשׁ magpî'āš, n.pr.m. GK: 4488. Magpiash, "*moth killer*":– Magpiash [1]

4048 מָגַר māgar, v. GK: 4489 [cf. 4049]. [Qp] to be thrown; [P] to cast, throw down:– cast down [1], terrors [1]

4049 מְגַר m^{e}gar (Aram.), v. GK: 10400 [cf. 4048]. [Pa] to overthrow:– destroy [1]

4050 מְגֵרָה m^{e}gērâ, n.f. GK: 4490 [→ 1641]. saw (stone-cutting tool):– saws [3], axes [1]

4051 מִגְרוֹן migrôn, n.pr.loc. GK: 4491. Migron, "*precipice*":– Migron [2]

4052 מִגְרָעוֹת migrā'ôt, n.f. GK: 4492 [→ 1639]. offset ledge, recess, rebatement (of a wall):– narrowed rests [1]

4053 מֶגְרָפָה megrāpâ, n.f. GK: 4493 [→ 1640]. clods (of earth) or a digging instrument: hoe, spade, shovel:– clods [1]

4054 מִגְרָשׁ migrāš or **מִגְרְשׁוֹת migr^{e}šôt**, n.m. GK: 4494 & 4495 [→ 1644]. pastureland, untilled open land (belonging to a town):– suburbs [114], cast out [1]

4055 מַד mad, n.m. GK: 4496 [→ 4058; cf. 4063]. clothing, garment; measure, decree:– garment [3], armour [2], clothes [1], garments [1], judgment [1], measures [1], measure [1], raiment [1]

4056 מַדְבַּח madbaḥ (Aram.), n.[m.]. GK: 10401 [→ 1684; cf. 4196]. altar:– altar [1]

4057 מִדְבָּר midbār, n.m. GK: 4497 & 4498 [→ 1696]. desert, wasteland, barren wilderness, desolate land that supports little life; open country, suitable for grazing; mouth, instrument of speech:– wilderness [255], desert [13], south [1], speech [1], wilderness (+776) [1]

4058 מָדַד mādad, v. GK: 4499 [→ 4055, 4059, 4060, 4461]. [Q] to measure a distance; consider a plan; [N] to be measured; [P] to measure off; [Htpol] to stretch oneself out:– measured [39], measure [7], mete out [2], measured (+3808) [1], mete [1], stretched [1]

4059 מִדַּד middad, v. GK: 4499 [→ 4058]. same as 4058: [P] to measure off:– gone [1]

4060 מִדָּה middâ, n.f. GK: 4500 & 4501 [→ 4058; cf. 5414; cf. 4061]. measurement, size, length; section (of a wall), length of life; tax:– measure [15], measures [12], measuring [10], piece [7], size [3], stature [3], garments [1], great stature [1], meteyard [1], tribute [1], wide [1]

4061 מִדָּה middâ or **מִנְדָּה mindâ** (Aram.), n.f. GK: 10402 & 10429 [cf. 4060]. tax, revenue, tribute:– toll [3], tribute [1]

4062 מַדְהֵבָה madhēbâ, n.f. GK: 4502 [cf. 7292]. fury; others: golden:– golden city [1]

4063 מַדוּ madû or **מַדְוֶה madweh**, n.m. GK: 4503 [cf. 4055]. garment:– garments [2]

4064 מַדְוֶה madweh, n.m. GK: 4504 [→ 1738]. disease, sickness:– diseases [2]

4065 מַדּוּחִים maddûḥîm, n.[m.]. GK: 4505 [→ 5080]. misleading, able to deceive:– causes of banishment [1]

4066 מָדוֹן mādôn, n.m. GK: 4506 [→ 4067; cf. 1777]. dissension, quarrel, strife, contention:– strife [7], contentions [4], contention [3], contentious [3], brawling [2], discord [2], strifes [1]

4067 מִדְיָן midyān or **מָדוֹן mādôn**, n.m. GK: 4517 [→ 4066, 4079, 4080, 4084, 4090, 4092; cf. 1777]. quarrel, strife, contention:– stature [1]

4068 מָדוֹן mādôn, n.pr.loc. GK: 4507 [→ 1777]. Madon, "*contention*":– Madon [2]

4069 מַדּוּעַ maddûa', adv. GK: 4508. Why?, What is the meaning?:– why [43], wherefore [28], how [1]

4070 מְדוֹר m^{e}dôr or **מְדָר m^{e}dār** (Aram.), n.[m.]. GK: 10403 & 10407 [→ 1753]. living, dwelling:– dwelling [4]

4071 מְדוּרָה m^{e}dûrâ, n.f. GK: 4509 [→ 1752]. (circular) pile of wood, fire pit:– pile for fire [1], pile [1]

4072 מִדְחֶה midḥeh, n.m. GK: 4510 [→ 1760]. ruin, downfall:– ruin [1]

4073 מַדְחֵפָה madḥēpâ, n.f. GK: 4511 [→ 1765]. blow, thrust; (pl.) blow after blow:– overthrow [1]

4074 מָדַי māday, n.pr.g. & loc. GK: 4512 [→ 4075; cf. 4076]. Madai; Media, Medes:– Medes [8], Media [6], Madai [2]

4075 מָדִי mādî, a.g. GK: 4513 [→ 4074]. Mede:– Mede [1]

4076 מָדַי māday (Aram.), n.pr.g. GK: 10404 [cf. 4074, 4077]. same as 4077: Mede; Media:– Medes [5], Median [1]

4077 מָדַי māday (Aram.), n.pr.g. GK: 10404 [→ 4076]. same as 4076: Mede; Media:–

4078 מַדַּי madday, n.[m.]. GK: 1896 [→ 1767]. prob. same as 1767: sufficiently:– sufficiently (+3807.1) [1]

4079 מִדְיָן midyān, n.m. GK: 4506 [→ 4067; cf. 1777]. same as 4066: dissension, quarrel, strife, contention:–

4080 מִדְיָן midyān, n.pr.m. & loc. GK: 4518 [→ 4084; cf. 1777, 4067]. Midian, Midianite:– Midian [39], Midianites [20]

4081 מִדִּין middîn, n.pr.loc. GK: 4516. Middin:– Middin [1]

4082 מְדִינָה m^{e}dînâ, n.f. GK: 4519 [→ 1777; cf. 4083]. province, district, region:– provinces [27], every province (+4082+2050.1) [10], every province (+3605+4082+2050.1) [8], province [8]

4083 מְדִינָה m^{e}dînâ (Aram.), n.f. GK: 10406 [→ 1778; cf. 4082]. province, district:– province [8], provinces [3]

4084 מִדְיָנִי midyānî, a.g. GK: 4520 [→ 4080, 4092; cf. 1777, 4067]. Midianite, "*of Midian*":– Midianites [3], Midianitish [2], Medanites [1], Midianite [1], Midianitish woman [1]

4085 מְדֹכָה m^{e}dōkâ, n.f. GK: 4521 [→ 1743]. mortar:– mortar [1]

4086 מַדְמֵן madmēn, n.pr.loc. GK: 4522 [→ 4088, 4089]. Madmen, "*[sounds like] be silenced*":– Madmen [1]

4087 מַדְמֵנָה madmēnâ, n.f. GK: 4523 [→ 1828]. manure-pile, dung-heap:– dunghill [1]

4088 מַדְמֵנָה madmēnâ, n.pr.loc. GK: 4524 [→ 4086]. Madmenah, "*dunghill*":– Madmenah [1]

4089 מַדְמַנָּה madmannâ, n.pr.m. & loc. GK: 4525 & 4526 [→ 4086]. Madmannah, "*dung place*":– Madmannah [2]

4090 מְדָן m^{e}dān, n.m. GK: 4506 [→ 4067; cf. 1777]. same as 4066: dissension, quarrel, strife, contention:–

4091 מְדָן m^{e}dān, n.pr.m. GK: 4527 [→ 1837]. Medan, "*dissension*":– Medan [2]

4092 מְדָנִי m^{e}dānî, a.g. GK: 4520 [→ 4084]. same as 4084: Midianite, "*of Midian*":–

4093 מַדָּע maddā', n.m. GK: 4529 [→ 3045; cf. 4486]. knowledge:– knowledge [4], science [1], thought [1]

מֹדַע mōdā'. See 4129.

מַדֻּעַ madua'. See 4069.

4094 מַדְקֵרָה madqērâ, n.f. GK: 4532 [→ 1856]. piercing (of a sword):– piercings [1]

מְדֹר m^{e}dōr. See 4070.

4095 מַדְרֵגָה madrēgâ, n.f. GK: 4533. cliff, (steep) mountainside (with footholds and hiding places):– stairs [1], steep places [1]

מְדֻרָה m^{e}durâ. See 4071.

4096 מִדְרָךְ midrāk, n.[m.]. GK: 4534 [→ 1869]. foot-width, footprint:– breadth [1]

4097 מִדְרָשׁ midrāš, n.[m.]. GK: 4535 [→ 1875]. annotation, study, writing, exposition:– story [2]

4098 מְדֻשָׁה m^{e}dušâ, n.f. GK: 4536 [→ 1758]. that which is crushed (by trampling on a threshing floor):– threshing [1]

4099 הַמְּדָתָא hamm^{e}dātā' or **מְדָתָא m^{e}dātā'**, n.pr.m. GK: 2158. Hammedatha, "*given by the moon [god]*":– Hammedatha [5]

4100 מָה **mâ**, p.inter. & indef. GK: 4537 [→ 1099, 3644, 4972; cf. 4478; cf. 3964, cf. 4101]. why?, what?, how?; O!, who, whoever, whatever:– what [404], why (+3807.1) [92], wherefore (+3807.1) [70], how [51], why [28], wherein (+871.1) [12], wherefore (+5921) [10], wherewith (+871.1) [10], that [6], wherefore [6], how long (+5704) [4], wherefore (+2088+3807.1) [4], why (+5921) [3], how great [2], how long (+3509.1) [2], how many (+3509.1) [2], how many (+5704+3509.1) [2], how much [2], how oft (+3509.1) [2], howsoever [2], what (+3509.1) [2], what (+3807.1) [2], wherein [2], which [2], because (+3807.1) [1], how (+3509.1) [1], how long (+3117+8141+3509.1) [1], nor (+2050.1) [1], nothing (+1077) [1], nothing (+1097) [1], not [1], so many (+3509.1) [1], thing [1], to what end (+3807.1) [1], until (+5704) [1], what (+1697+1886.1) [1], what (+2088) [1], what aileth (+3807.1) [1], what good (+3807.1) [1], what profit (+3807.1) [1], whatsoever (+1697) [1], whatsoever [1], whereby (+871.1) [1], wherefore (+8478) [1], wherein (+871.1+1886.1) [1], whereon (+5921) [1], whereto (+3807.1) [1], whereupon (+5921) [1], wherewithal (+871.1) [1], whether [1], why (+2088+3807.1) [1], why (+871.1) [1], why then (+2088+3807.1) [1]

4101 מָה **mâ** (Aram.), p.inter. & indef. GK: 10408 [→ 2987; cf. 4479; cf. 4100]. why?, what?; that which, what:– what [6], how (+3509.4) [2], why (+3807.2) [2], that which [1], whatsoever (+1768) [1], why (+5922) [1]

4102 מָהַהּ **māhah**, v. GK: 4538. [Htpal] to wait, delay, linger, hesitate:– tarry [3], lingered [2], tarried [2], delayed [1], stay [1]

4103 מְהוּמָה **mᵉhûmâ**, n.f. GK: 4539 [→ 1949]. turmoil, confusion, panic, discomfiture:– destruction [3], trouble [3], discomfiture [1], tumults [1], tumult [1], vexations [1], vexation [1], vexed [1]

4104 מְהוּמָן **mᵉhûmān**, n.pr.m. GK: 4540. Mehuman:– Mehuman [1]

4105 מְהֵיטַבְאֵל **mᵉhêṭab'ēl**, n.pr.m. & f. GK: 4541 [→ 3190+410]. Mehetabel, "*God [El] does good*":– Mehetabel [2], Mehetabeel [1]

4106 מָהִיר **māhîr**, a. GK: 4542 [→ 4116]. skilled, well versed, experienced; speedy, prompt:– ready [2], diligent [1], hasting [1]

4107 מָהַל **māhal**, v. GK: 4543 [→ 1118; cf. 4135]. [Qp] to be diluted, changed to an adulterated state; referring to dilution by water:– mixt [1]

4108 מַהְלֵךְ **mahlēk**, n.m. GK: 4544 [→ 1980, 4109]. same as 4109: passageway; journey:– places to walk [1]

4109 מַהֲלָךְ **mahᵃlāk**, n.m. GK: 4544 [→ 4108]. same as 4108: passageway; journey:– journey [3], walk [1]

4110 מַהֲלָל **mahᵃlāl**, n.[m.]. GK: 4545 [→ 4111; cf. 1984]. praise, good reputation:– praise [1]

4111 מַהֲלַלְאֵל **mahᵃlal'ēl**, n.pr.m. GK: 4546 [→ 4110+410]. Mahalalel, "*praise of God [El]*":– Mahalaleel [7]

4112 מַהֲלֻמוֹת **mahᵃlumôt**, n.f.pl. GK: 4547 [→ 1986]. (pl.) beating, thrashing, repeated blows to the body:– stripes [1], strokes [1]

4113 מַהֲמֹרוֹת **mahᵃmōrôt**, n.f.[pl.]. GK: 4549. miry pits, pits filled with rain water:– deep pits [1]

4114 מַהְפֵּכָה **mahpēkâ**, n.f. GK: 4550 [→ 2015]. overthrow, destruction, demolishing:– overthrew [3], overthrow [2], overthrown [1]

4115 מַהְפֶּכֶת **mahpeket**, n.f. GK: 4551 [→ 2015]. stocks (confining a prisoner, suggesting in a crooked posture or distortion):– prison [2], stocks [2]

4116 מָהַר **māhar**, v. GK: 4554 [→ 4106, 4117, 4118, 4120, 4122]. [N] to be swept away; to be impetuous, rash, disturbed; [P] to be quick, hasten, hurry, do at once:– hasted [14], make haste [8], haste [5], made haste [5], soon [3], swift [3], hastened [2], hasten [2], hasteth [2], hastily [2], hasty [2], in haste [2], make speed [2], carried headlong [1], cause to make haste [1], fearful [1], fetch quickly [1], hasteneth [1], make ready quickly [1], quickly [1], rash [1], ready [1], shortly [1], speedily [1], straightway [1], suddenly [1]

4117 מָהַר **māhar**, v.den. GK: 4555 & 4556 [→ 4116, 4119]. [Q] to pay the purchase price for a bride:– surely endow (+4117) [2]

4118 מַהֵר **mahēr**, adv. GK: 4557 [→ 4116]. swiftly:– quickly [8], speedily [4], hastily [2], at once [1], hasteth [1], suddenly [1]

מָהִר **māhir**. See 4106.

4119 מֹהַר **mōhar**, n.m. GK: 4558 [→ 4117, 4121]. bride-price, compensation to the father of the bride:– dowry [3]

4120 מְהֵרָה **mᵉhērâ**, n.f. GK: 4559 [→ 4116]. haste, quickness, speed; (adv.) quickly, swiftly, soon, at once:– quickly [8], speedily [4], hastily [1], make speed [1], pass quickly [1], quickly (+871.1) [1], shortly [1], soon [1], speed [1], very swiftly (+5704) [1]

4121 מַהֲרַי **mahᵃray**, n.pr.m. GK: 4560 [→ 4119]. Maharai, "*impetuous*":– Maharai [3]

4122 מַהֵר שָׁלָל חָשׁ בַּז **mahēr šālāl ḥāš baz**, n.pr.m. GK: 4561 [→ 4116+7998+2363+957]. Maher-Shalal-Hash-Baz, "*quick to the plunder, swift to the spoil*":– Maher-shalal-hash-baz [2]

4123 מַהֲתַלָּה **mahᵃtallâ**, n.f. GK: 4562 [→ 2048]. illusion, deception:– deceits [1]

4123.1 מוֹ- **-mô** or מוּ- **-mû**, p.suf. GK: 4564 [→ 1886.3]. he, him; they, them:– them [58], their [22], their (+3807.1) [6], themselves [6], they [5], he [2], him [2], his (+3807.1) [2], their own [2], whom [2], himself [1], his [1], that [1], thereto (+3807.1) [1], those [1], wherein (+5921) [1], which (+3807.1) [1]

4124 מוֹאָב **mô'āb**, n.pr.m. & loc. GK: 4565 & 4566 [→ 4125, 6355]. Moab, Moabite:– Moab [166], Moabites [15]

4125 מוֹאָבִי **mô'ābî**, a.g. GK: 4567 [→ 4124]. Moabite, from Moab, "*of Moab*":– Moabitess [6], Moabites [4], Moabite [3], Moabitish [1], of Moab [1], women of Moab [1]

מוֹאל **mô'l**. See 4136.

4126 מוֹבָא **môbā'**, n.[m.]. GK: 4569 [→ 3996; cf. 935]. coming in; entrance (way):– coming in [1], comings in [1]

4127 מוּג **mûg**, v. GK: 4570. [Q] to melt, waste away; [N] to melt away (in fear), be disheartened; to collapse; [Pol] to soften; to toss about; [Htpol] to melt away, flow from; from the base meaning the melting of a substance is the fig. extension of the inner person melting is fear:– dissolved [3], faint [3], melt [3], melted [2], consumed [1], dissolvest [1], fainthearted [1], makest soft [1], melt away [1], melted away [1]

4128 מוֹד **môd**, v. GK: 4571. [Pol] to shake, convulse, set into motion:– measured [1]

4129 מֹדַע **mōdā'**, n.m. GK: 4530 [→ 4130; cf. 3045]. (distant) relative, kinsman:– kinsman [1], kinswoman [1]

4130 מֹדַעַת **mōda'at**, n.f. GK: 4531 [→ 4129; cf. 3045]. (distant) kinsman:– kindred [1]

4131 מוֹט **môṭ**, v. GK: 4572 [→ 4132, 4133]. [Q] to slip, fall, totter, stagger; [N] to be shaken, be caused to move, be toppled; [H] to bring down, to cause to fall; [Htpol] to be thoroughly shaken, be continually shaken:– moved [19], removed [5], moved exceedingly (+4131) [2], slippeth [2], carried [1], cast [1], fallen in decay (+3027) [1], falling down [1], fall [1], out of course [1], ready [1], shaketh [1], slide [1], slip [1]

4132 מוֹט **môṭ**, n.[m.]. GK: 4573 [→ 4131]. carrying frame; pole; yoke bar:– bar [2], moved [2], staff [1], yoke [1]

4133 מוֹטָה **môṭâ**, n.f. GK: 4574 [→ 4131]. yoke bar, pole, bar; by extension: oppression of subjected people:– yokes [4], yoke [4], bands [2], heavy [1], staves [1]

4134 מוּךְ **mûk**, v. GK: 4575 [cf. 4355]. [Q] to become poor:– waxen poor [3], poorer [1], wax poor [1]

4135 מוּל **mûl**, v. GK: 4576 & 4577 [→ 4139; cf. 4107, 5243]. [Q] to circumcise; [Qp] to be circumcised; [N] to be circumcised, undergo circumcision, circumcise oneself; "to circumcise the heart" means to commit to covenant obedience from within, not only formally; [H] to cut off, ward off:– circumcised [23], circumcise [5], destroy [3], must needs be circumcised (+4135) [2], circumcising [1], cut down [1], cut in pieces [1]

4136 מוּל **mûl** or מוֹאל **mô'l**, subst. & pp. GK: 4578 & 4568 [cf. 2974]. before, opposite, in front of:– over against [10], against [5], forefront (+6440) [3], over against (+4480) [3], before (+413+6440) [2], over against (+413+6440) [2], against (+413) [1], before (+413) [1], before [1], forepart (+6440) [1], from (+4480) [1], off (+4480) [1], over against (+413) [1], to God-ward (+430+1886.1) [1], towards (+413) [1], towards (+4480) [1], upon (+413) [1]

4137 מוֹלָדָה **môlādâ**, n.pr.loc. GK: 4579. Moladah, "*generation*":– Moladah [4]

4138 מוֹלֶדֶת **môledet**, n.f. GK: 4580 [→ 3205]. family, relatives, children; (land of) birth, native (land):– kindred [11], nativity [6], born [2], begotten [1], issue [1], native [1]

4139 מוּלָה **mûlâ**, n.f. GK: 4581 [→ 4135]. circumcision:– circumcision [1]

4140 מוֹלִיד **môlîd**, n.pr.m. GK: 4582 [→ 3205]. Molid, "*descendant*":– Molid [1]

מוּם **muwm**. See 3971.

מוּמְכָן **mômukān**. See 4462.

4141 מוּסָב **mûsāb**, v.ptcp. GK: 6015 [→ 4142, 4524, 5252, 5437, 5438, 5439]. ptcp. of 5437: turning, winding:–

4142 מוּסַבָּה **mûsabbâ**, v.ptcp. GK: 6015 [→ 4141]. ptcp. of 5437: turning, winding:–

4143 מוֹסָד **môsād**, n.m. GK: 4586 [→ 4145; cf. 3245]. foundation, laying the foundation stone:– foundation [1], sure foundation (+3245) [1]

4144 מוֹסָד **môsād**, n.m. GK: 4587 [→ 4146; cf. 3245]. foundation:– foundations [3]

4145 מוּסָדָה **mûsādâ**, n.f. GK: 4588 [→ 4143, 4328; cf. 3245]. foundation:– grounded [1]

4146 מוֹסָדָה **môsādâ**, n.m. GK: 4589 [→ 4144; cf. 3245]. foundation:– foundations [10]

4147 מוֹסֵר **môsēr** or מוֹסֵרָה **môsērâ**, n.m. GK: 4591 & 4593 [→ 4149; cf. 631]. bonds, shackles, straps, chains, fetters:– bands [6], bonds [5]

4148 מוּסָר **mûsār**, n.m. GK: 4592 [→ 4561; cf. 3256]. discipline, instruction, correction; wisdom and teaching that imply correcting errant behavior:– instruction [30], correction [8], chastening [3], chastisement [3], bond [1], chasteneth [1], check [1], discipline [1], doctrine [1], rebuker [1]

4149 מוֹסֵרָה **môsērâ** or מֹסֵרוֹת **mōsērôt**, n.pr.loc. GK: 4594 & 5035 [→ 631?]. Moserah, Moseroth, *"bond, prison [?]"*:– Moseroth [2], Mosera [1]

4150 מוֹעֵד **mô'ēd**, n.m. GK: 4595 [→ 3259]. (Tent of) Meeting; appointed time, designated time, season:– congregation [149], time appointed [9], solemn feasts [8], feasts [6], set time [6], season [5], set feasts [5], appointed season [4], appointed [3], seasons [3], solemnities [3], time [3], solemn feast [2], solemn [2], appointed feasts [1], appointed sign [1], appointed times [1], appointed time [1], assemblies [1], assembly [1], congregations [1], due season [1], feast [1], places of assembly [1], solemn assembly [1], solemn days [1], solemnity [1], synagogues [1], times [1]

4151 מוֹעָד **mô'ād**, n.[m.]. GK: 4596 [→ 3259]. ranks, appointed place of a soldier:– appointed times [1]

4152 מוּעָדָה **mû'ādâ**, n.f. GK: 4597 [→ 3259]. designation, appointment:– appointed [1]

4153 מוֹעַדְיָה **mô'adyâ**, n.pr.m. GK: 4598 [→ 4154+3068; cf. 4572]. Moadiah, "[perhaps] *Yahweh assembles* or *Yahweh promises*":– Moadiah [1]

4154 מוּעֶדֶת **mû'edet**, v.ptcp. GK: 5048 [→ 4153, 4571, 4572, 4573, 5976]. ptcp. of 4571: dislocated:– out of joint [1]

4155 מוּעָף **mû'āp**, n.[m.]. GK: 4599 [→ 4588, 6079; cf. 5890]. gloom, darkness; fig. of the emotional state of sadness and despondency:– dimness [1], foundations [1]

4156 מוֹעֵצָה **mô'ēṣâ**, n.f. GK: 4600 [→ 3289]. plan, scheme, device, intrigue:– counsels [6], devices [1]

4157 מוּעָקָה **mû'āqâ**, n.f. GK: 4601 [→ 5781?]. burden, misery, hardship:– affliction [1]

4158 מוֹפַעַת **môpa'at** or מֵיפַעַת **mêpa'at**, n.pr.loc. GK: 4602 & 4789. Mophaath, Mephaath, *"splendor"*:– Mephaath [4]

4159 מוֹפֵת **môpēt**, n.m. GK: 4603. wonder, sign, miracle, portent; symbol:– wonders [19], sign [8], wonder [6], miracles [1], miracle [1], wondered at [1]

4160 מֵץ **mēṣ** or מוּץ **mûṣ**, n.m. GK: 5160 [→ 4330]. oppressor:– extortioner [1]

4161 מוֹצָא **môṣā'**, n.m. GK: 4604 [→ 3318]. act of going out, springing out, exiting, moving on; by extension, (n.) what goes out: spring (of water), mine shaft, sunrise, east:– going forth [4], goings out [4], brought out [2], spring [2], watersprings (+4325) [2], bud [1], east [1], go forth [1], going out [1], outgoings [1], proceeded out [1], springs [1], that proceedeth out [1], that which came out of [1], that which is gone out [1], thing that is gone out [1], vein [1], watercourse (+4325) [1]

4162 מוֹצָא **môṣā'**, n.pr.m. GK: 4605 [→ 3318]. Moza, *"sunrise"*:– Moza [5]

4163 מוֹצָאָה **môṣā'â**, n.f. GK: 4606 [→ 3318]. origin, coming out; latrine:– goings forth [1]

4164 מוּצָק **mûṣāq**, n.m. GK: 4607 [→ 4166; cf. 3332]. casting (of metal):– straitened [1], straitness [1], vexation [1]

4165 מוּצָק **mûṣāq**, n.[m.]. GK: 4608 [→ 6693]. restriction, constraint; distress, hardship:– casting [1], hardness [1]

4166 מוּצָקָה **mûṣāqâ**, n.f. GK: 4609 [→ 4164; cf. 3332]. casting (into one piece); channel, spout or lip (of a lamp):– cast [1], pipes [1]

4167 מוּק **mûq**, v. GK: 4610. [H] to scoff:– corrupt [1]

4168 מוֹקֵד **môqēd**, n.[m.]. GK: 4611 [→ 4169; cf. 3344]. hearth, (place of) glowing embers, burning embers:– burnings [1], hearth [1]

4169 מוֹקְדָה **môqᵉdâ**, n.f. GK: 4612 [→ 4168; cf. 3344]. hearth, place of burning:– burning [1]

4170 מוֹקֵשׁ **môqēš**, n.m. GK: 4613 [→ 3369]. snare, trap, that which captures prey; by extension: ensnarement, entrapment (of a person):– snare [14], snares [6], grins [2], ensnared [1], gin [1], snared [1], traps [1], trap [1]

4171 מוּר **mûr**, v. GK: 4614 & 4615 [→ 8545]. [N] to be changed; to shake, quake; [H] to exchange, substitute, change:– changed [4], change [3], at all change (+4171) [2], change at all (+4171) [2], changeth [1], exchange [1], removed [1]

4172 מוֹרָא **môrā'** or מוֹרָה **môrâ**, n.m. GK: 4616 & 4624 [→ 3372]. fear, terror, respect, reverence; awesome deed:– fear [6], terror [2], dread [1], feared [1], terribleness [1], terrors [1]

4173 מוֹרַג **môrag**, n.m. GK: 4617. threshing sledge:– threshing instruments [2], threshing instrument [1]

4174 מוֹרָד **môrād**, n.[m.]. GK: 4618 [→ 3381]. slope, road going down; something hammered down:– going down [3], made thin [1], steep place [1]

4175 מוֹרֶה **môreh**, n.[m.] *or* v.ptcp. GK: 4619 & 4620 & 4621 [→ 3384]. archer; autumn rains; teacher:– former rain [2], archers (+7198+871.1+1886.1) [1], rain [1], shooters [1]

4176 מוֹרֶה **môreh**, n.pr.[loc.?]. GK: 4622 [→ 3384]. Moreh:– Moreh [3]

4177 מוֹרָה **môrâ**, n.m. GK: 4623 [→ 6168]. razor:– rasor [3]

4178 מוֹרָט **môrāṭ**, v.ptcp. GK: 5307 [→ 4803; cf. 4804, cf. 4873]. ptcp. of 4803: polished, rubbed; skinned:– peeled [2]

4179 מֹרִיָּה **mōriyyâ**, n.pr.loc. GK: 5317. Moriah:– Moriah [2]

4180 מוֹרָשׁ **môrāš**, n.[m.]. GK: 4625 & 4626 [→ 782, 4181; cf. 3423]. possession, inheritance; desire:– possessions [1], possession [1], thoughts [1]

4181 מוֹרָשָׁה **môrāšâ**, n.f. GK: 4627 [→ 4180; cf. 3423]. possession:– possession [6], inheritance [2], heritage [1]

4182 מוֹרֶשֶׁת גַּת **môrešet gat**, n.pr.loc. GK: 4628 [→ 4183]. Moresheth Gath, *"possession of Gath"*:– Moresheth-gath [1]

4183 מוֹרַשְׁתִּי **môraštî**, a.g. GK: 4629 [→ 4182]. of Moresheth:– Morasthite [2]

4184 מוּשׁ **mûš**, v. GK: 4630 [cf. 3237, 4959]. [Q] to touch, feel; [H] be able to feel, touch:– feel [2], handle [1]

4185 מוּשׁ **mûš**, v. GK: 4631. [Q] to depart, leave, move away, vanish; [H] to remove:– depart [8], remove [4], departed [2], removed [2], cease [1], departeth [1], gone back from [1], took away [1]

4186 מוֹשָׁב **môšāb**, n.m. GK: 4632 [→ 3427]. dwelling, settlement, place to live, place:– dwellings [8], habitations [8], seat [7], dwelling [4], habitation [4], dwelling places [3], dwelt [2], sitting [2], assembly [1], dwell in [1], dwelling place [1], inhabited places [1], situation [1], sojourning [1]

4187 מוּשִׁי **mûšî**, n.pr.m. GK: 4633 [→ 4188]. Mushi:– Mushi [8]

4188 מוּשִׁי **mûšî**, a.g. GK: 4634 [→ 4187]. Mushite, *"of Mushi"*:– Mushites [2]

4189 מֹשְׁכוֹת **mōšᵉkôt**, n.f. GK: 5436 [→ 4900]. cords, chains, fetters:– bands [1]

4190 מוֹשָׁעָה **môšā'â**, n.f. GK: 4636 [→ 3467]. act of salvation, act of helping:– salvation [1]

Heb

4191 מוּת **mût**, v. GK: 4637 [→ 4194, 4463, 8546 (also used with compound proper names)]. [Q] to die, be killed, be dead; [Pol] to kill, slay, put to death; [H] to kill, make die, put to death, assassinate; [Ho] to be put to death, be murdered:– die [232], died [153], dead [134], surely put to death (+4191) [56], put to death [44], slew [40], surely die (+4191) [40], slay [38], kill [23], slain [18], dieth [16], death [10], killed [6], in wise slay (+4191) [4], die (+4191) [2], killeth [2], must needs die (+4191) [2], put at all to death (+4191) [2], surely be put to death (+4191) [2], surely kill (+4191) [2], cause to die [1], crying [1], dead man [1], destroyers [1], destroy [1], diest [1], slayeth [1], slaying [1]

4192 מוּת לַבֵּן **mût labbēn**, tt. GK: 4240 [→ 3807.1+1886.1+1121]. t.t. in Ps 9, poss. "death of the son" (4637 + 3807.1 + 1886.1 + 1121):– Muth-labben (+1121+1886.1+3807.1) [1]

4193 מוֹת **môt** (Aram.), n.[m.]. GK: 10409 [cf. 4194]. death:– death [1]

4194 מָוֶת **māwet**, n.m. GK: 4638 [→ 2700; cf. 4191; cf. 4193]. death, dying:– death [126], dead [8], died [8], die [6], dieth [5], surely die (+1121) [2], deadly [1], deaths [1], put to death (+2026) [1], slay [1], worthy to die (+1121) [1]

מוּת לַבֵּן **mût lab-bēn**. See 4192.

4195 מוֹתָר **môtār**, n.m. GK: 4639 [→ 3498]. profit, advantage:– hath preeminence [1], plenteousness [1], profit [1]

4196 מִזְבֵּחַ **mizbēaḥ**, n.m. GK: 4640 [→ 2076; cf. 4056]. altar:– altar [349], altars [52]

4197 מֶזֶג ***mezeg***, n.m. GK: 4641. blended wine, mixed wine (likely spiced):– liquor [1]

4198 מָזֶה ***māzeh***, a. GK: 4642. empty (from hunger), implying an unhealthy loss of weight and breakdown in health:– burnt [1]

4199 מִזָּה ***mizzâ***, n.pr.m. GK: 4645. Mizzah, *"terror"*:– Mizzah [3]

4200 מָזוּ ***māzû***, n.m. GK: 4646 [cf. 2106]. barn, granary:– garners [1]

4201 מְזוּזָה ***m^{e}zûzâ***, n.f. GK: 4647. doorframe, doorpost, doorjamb:– posts [10], side posts [4], post [3], door posts [1], door post [1]

4202 מָזוֹן ***māzôn***, n.m. GK: 4648 [→ 2109]. provisions, food:– meat [1], victual [1]

4203 מָזוֹן ***māzôn*** (Aram.), n.[m.]. GK: 10410 [→ 2110; cf. 2109]. food:– meat [2]

4204 מָזוֹר ***māzôr***, n.m. GK: 4650. trap, ambush:– wound [1]

4205 מָזוֹר ***māzôr***, n.[m.]. GK: 4649. sore, boil, ulcer:– wound [2], bound up [1]

מְזֻזָה ***m^{e}zuzâ***. See 4201.

4206 מֵזַח ***mēzaḥ*** or מְזִיחַ ***māzîaḥ***, n.m. GK: 4651 & 4652 & 4653 [→ 4231]. belt, leather girdle worn next to the skin; harbor; an area in which wind and wave are restricted as a fig. extension of a girdle or belt that restrains:– strength [2], girdle [1]

4207 מַזְלֵג ***mazlēg*** or מִזְלָגָה ***mizlāgâ***, n.m. & f. GK: 4656 & 4657 & 4658. (three-tined) meat fork:– fleshhooks [5], fleshhook [2]

4208 מַזָּל ***mazzāl***, n.[f.]pl. GK: 4655 [cf. 4216]. constellation (possibly of the zodiac signs):– planets [1]

4209 מְזִמָּה ***m^{e}zimmâ***, n.f. GK: 4659 [→ 2161]. discretion; scheme, plan, purpose, intent:– discretion [4], wicked devices [3], devices [2], thoughts [2], device [1], intents [1], lewdness [1], mischievous device [1], mischievous [1], thought [1], wickedly (+3807.1) [1], witty inventions [1]

4210 מִזְמוֹר ***mizmôr***, n.[m.]. GK: 4660 [→ 2167]. psalm, melody:– psalm [57]

4211 מַזְמֵרָה ***mazmērâ***, n.f. GK: 4661 [→ 2168]. pruning hook, pruning knife, vine-knife:– pruninghooks [3], pruning hooks [1]

4212 מְזַמֶּרֶת ***m^{e}zammeret***, n.f. GK: 4662 [→ 2168]. wick trimmer (scissors, possibly also used as a snuffer):– snuffers [5]

4213 מִזְעָר ***miz'ār***, n.[m.]. GK: 4663 [→ 2191]. small matter, few:– very little while (+4592) [2], few [1], small [1]

מָזֹר ***māzōr***. See 4205.

4214 מִזְרֶה ***mizreh***, n.[m.]. GK: 4665 [→ 2219]. winnowing fork, shovel:– fan [2]

4215 מְזָרִים ***m^{e}zārîm***, n.m. *or* v.ptcp. GK: 4668 [→ 2219]. driving (north) winds:– north [1]

4216 מַזָּרוֹת ***mazzārôt***, n.[f.]pl. GK: 4666 [cf. 4208]. constellations, variously specified:– Mazzaroth [1]

4217 מִזְרָח ***mizrāḥ***, n.[m.]. GK: 4667 [→ 2224]. direction of the sunrise, east, eastern; the east was the direction of orientation in the ancient Near East:– east [32], eastward (+1886.5) [15], rising [7], sunrising (+8121) [6], eastward [3], the sunrising (+8121+1886.1) [2], east (+6924+1886.5) [1], east side (+8121) [1], east side [1], eastward (+1886.1+3807.1) [1], eastward (+8121+1886.1) [1], rising of the sun [1], sunrising (+8121+1886.1) [1], sunrising [1], the east side (+8121+1886.1) [1]

4218 מִזְרָע ***mizrā'***, n.[m.]. GK: 4669 [→ 2232]. seeded field, land sown:– sown [1]

4219 מִזְרָק ***mizrāq***, n.m. GK: 4670 [→ 2236]. sacred bowl used for sprinkling (the altar):– bowl [13], basons [11], bowls [8]

4220 מֵחַ ***mēaḥ***, n.[m.]. GK: 4671 [→ 4221; cf. 4229]. fat sheep; (representing) the rich:– fat ones [1], fatlings [1]

4221 מֹחַ ***mōaḥ***, n.m. GK: 4672 [→ 4220; cf. 4229]. marrow (of the bones):– marrow [1]

4222 מָחָא ***māḥā'***, v. GK: 4673 [→ 4232; cf. 4229; cf. 4223]. [Q] to clap (hands in joy):– clap [2], clapped [1]

4223 מְחָא ***m^{e}ḥā'*** (Aram.), v. GK: 10411 [cf. 4272]. [P] to strike; [Pa] to hold back, prevent; [Htpe] to be impaled:– smote [2], hanged [1], stay [1]

4224 מַחֲבֵא ***maḥ^{a}bē'*** or מַחֲבֹא ***maḥ^{a}bō'***, n.[m.]. GK: 4675 & 4676 [→ 2244]. shelter, hiding place (from wind):– hiding place [1], lurking places [1]

4225 מַחְבֶּרֶת ***maḥberet***, n.f. GK: 4678 [→ 2266]. place of joining, seam, set (of curtains):– coupling [8]

4226 מְחַבְּרוֹת ***m^{e}ḥabb^{e}rôt***, n.f. GK: 4677 [→ 2266]. fittings, braces (of iron), joists, truss (of timber):– couplings [1], joinings [1]

4227 מַחֲבַת ***maḥ^{a}bat***, n.f. GK: 4679 [→ 2281]. (metal) griddle or baking pan:– pan [5]

4228 מַחֲגֹרֶת ***maḥ^{a}gōret***, n.f. GK: 4680 [→ 2296]. girding (of sackcloth wrapped around the body):– girding [1], king [1]

4229 מָחָה ***māḥâ***, v. GK: 4681 & 4682 & 4683 [→ 4239, 8547?; cf. 4220, 4221, 4222; cf. 4223]. [Q] to wash off, wipe out, blot out, destroy; to continue along, stretch along; [N] be blotted out, be wiped out, be exterminated; [Pu] (choice food-dishes) to be filled with marrow; [H] to cause to blot out:– blot out [9], blotted out [5], destroyed [3], destroy [2], put out [2], utterly put out (+4229) [2], wipeth [2], abolished [1], blotteth out [1], blot [1], destroyeth [1], full of marrow [1], reach [1], wipe away [1], wipe out [1], wiped away [1], wipe [1], wiping [1]

4230 מְחוּגָה ***m^{e}ḥûgâ***, n.f. GK: 4684 [→ 2328]. compass (for making circles):– compass [1]

4231 מָחוֹז ***māḥôz***, n.[m.]. GK: 4685 [→ 4206]. haven, harbor, which might include a population center like a repair yard and city:– haven [1]

4232 מְחוּיָאֵל ***m^{e}ḥûyā'ēl*** or מְחִיָּיאֵל ***m^{e}ḥiyyāy'ēl***, n.pr.m. GK: 4686 & 4696 [→ 4222+410]. Mehujael, Mehijael:– Mehujael [2]

4233 מַחֲוִים ***maḥ^{a}wîm***, a.g. GK: 4687. Mahavite:– Mahavite [1]

4234 מָחוֹל ***māḥôl***, n.m. GK: 4688 [→ 4235, 4246; cf. 2342]. circle-dancing, round-dancing:– dance [4], dances [1], dancing [1]

4235 מָחוֹל ***māḥôl***, n.pr.m. GK: 4689 [→ 4234; cf. 2342]. Mahol, *"place of round dancing"*:– Mahol [1]

מְחוֹלָה ***m^{e}ḥôlâ***. See 65, 4246.

4236 מַחֲזֶה ***maḥ^{a}zeh***, n.[m.]. GK: 4690 [→ 2372]. vision:– vision [4]

4237 מֶחֱזָה ***meḥ^{e}zâ***, n.f. GK: 4691 [→ 2372]. light, place of seeing, in some contexts referring to a window:– light [4]

4238 מַחֲזִיאוֹת ***maḥ^{a}zî'ôt***, n.pr.m. GK: 4692 [→ 2372]. Mahazioth, *"visions"*:– Mahazioth [2]

4239 מְחִי ***m^{e}ḥî***, n.[m.]. GK: 4693 [→ 4229]. blow (of a battering ram):– engines [1]

4240 מְחִידָא ***m^{e}ḥîdā'***, n.pr.m. GK: 4694. Mehida, "[poss.] *bought as slave"*:– Mehida [2]

4241 מִחְיָה ***miḥyâ***, n.f. GK: 4695 [→ 2421]. saving of a life; raw flesh; food, sustenance; relief, recovering:– reviving [2], preserve life [1], quick raw (+2416) [1], quick [1], recover [1], sustenance [1], victuals [1]

מְחִיאֵל ***m^{e}ḥiyā'ēl***. See 4232.

4242 מְחִיר ***m^{e}ḥîr***, n.m. GK: 4697 [→ 4243]. price, cost, money:– price [11], gain [1], hire [1], sold (+871.1) [1], worth [1]

4243 מְחִיר ***m^{e}ḥîr***, n.pr.m. GK: 4698 [→ 4242]. Mehir, *"hired hand"*:– Mehir [1]

4244 מַחְלָה ***maḥlâ***, n.pr.f. [& m.?]. GK: 4702. Mahlah, "[perhaps] *weak one"*:– Mahlah [4], Mahalah [1]

4245 מַחֲלֶה ***maḥ^{a}leh*** or מַחֲלָה ***maḥ^{a}lâ***, n.m. & f. GK: 4700 & 4701 [cf. 2470]. sickness, disease:– sickness [3], diseases [1], disease [1], infirmity [1]

4246 מְחֹלָה ***m^{e}ḥōlâ***, n.f. GK: 4703 [→ 4234; cf. 65, 2342]. circle-dance, round-dance:– dances [5], dancing [2], company [1]

4247 מְחִלָּה ***m^{e}ḥillâ***, n.f. GK: 4704 [→ 2490]. hole:– caves [1]

4248 מַחְלוֹן ***maḥlôn***, n.pr.m. GK: 4705 [→ 2470?]. Mahlon:– Mahlon [3], Mahlon's [1]

4249 מַחְלִי ***maḥlî***, n.pr.m. GK: 4706 [→ 2470?]. Mahli, "[perhaps] *shrewd, cunning"*:– Mahli [11], Mahali [1]

4250 מַחְלִי ***maḥlî***, a.g. GK: 4707 [→ 2470?]. Mahlite, *"of Mahli"*:– Mahlites [2]

4251 מַחֲלֻיִים ***maḥ^{a}luyîm***, n.m. GK: 4708 [→ 2470]. sickness (caused by wounding):– diseases [1]

4252 מַחֲלָף ***maḥ^{a}lāp***, n.m. GK: 4709 [→ 2498?]. utensil, perhaps a pan:– knives [1]

4253 מַחְלָפָה ***maḥ^{a}lāpâ***, n.f. GK: 4710 [→ 2498]. braids (of hair):– locks [2]

4254 מַחֲלָצוֹת ***maḥ^{a}lāṣôt***, n.f.[pl.]. GK: 4711 [→ 2502]. fine robes, fine, white, festival garments:– change of raiment [1], changeable suits of apparel [1]

4255 מַחְלְקָה ***maḥl^{e}qâ*** (Aram.), n.f. GK: 10412 [→ 2508; cf. 4256]. group, division (of priests):– courses [1]

4256 מַחֲלֹקֶת ***maḥ^{a}lōqet***, n.f. GK: 4713 [→ 2505; cf. 4255]. portion, share (of land); division, group (of people):– course [18], courses [14], divisions [8], companies by course [1], portions [1]

4257 מָחֲלַת ***māḥ^{a}lat***, n.f. GK: 4714 [→ 2342? *or* 2470?]. mahalath (t.t. in the Psalms):– Mahalath [2]

4258 מָחֲלַת ***māḥ^{a}lat***, n.pr.f. GK: 4715. Mahalath, *"suffering of affliction NIV; sickness or suffering poem JB"*:– Mahalath [2]

4259 מְחֹלָתִי ***m^{e}ḥōlātî***, a.g. GK: 4716 [cf. 65?]. Meholathite, of Meholah, *"of Meholah"*:– Meholathite [2]

4260 מַחְמָאֹת ***maḥmā'ōt***, n.f.pl. GK: 4717 [cf. 2529]. butter; some sources: curds, yogurt:– butter [1]

4261 מַחְמָד **maḥmād**, n.m. GK: 4718 [→ 2530]. thing of value, something of delight, treasure; "the delight of the eyes" is someone or something especially cherished:– pleasant things [4], desire [3], pleasant [3], beloved [1], goodly [1], lovely [1]

4262 מַחְמֹד **maḥmōd**, n.[m.]. GK: 4719 [→ 2530]. treasure, something precious:– pleasant things [1]

4263 מַחְמָל **maḥmāl**, n.[m.]. GK: 4720 [→ 2550?]. yearning:– pitieth [1]

4264 מַחֲנֶה **maḥ^{a}neh**, n.m. & f. GK: 4722 [→ 4266; cf. 2583]. camp, group (military or civilian):– camp [129], host [57], camps [7], company [5], tents [5], hosts [4], armies [3], bands [2], battle [1], companies [1], drove [1], two armies [1]

4265 מַחֲנֵה־דָן **maḥ^{a}nēh-dān**, n.pr.loc. GK: 4723. Mahaneh Dan, "*camp of Dan*":– Mahaneh-dan [1]

4266 מַחֲנַיִם **maḥ^{a}nayim**, n.pr.loc. GK: 4724 [→ 4264; cf. 2583]. Mahanaim, "*double camp*":– Mahanaim [13]

4267 מַחֲנָק **maḥ^{a}nāq**, n.[m.]. GK: 4725 [→ 2614]. strangling, suffocation:– strangling [1]

4268 מַחְסֶה **maḥseh**, n.m. GK: 4726 [→ 4271; cf. 2620]. refuge, shelter:– refuge [13], hope [2], place of refuge [2], shelter [2], trust [1]

4269 מַחְסוֹם **maḥsôm**, n.m. GK: 4727 [→ 2629]. muzzle, a covering for the mouth to keep silence:– bridle [1]

4270 מַחְסוֹר **maḥsôr**, n.[m.]. GK: 4728 [→ 2637]. need, lack of, scarcity, hence poverty:– want [7], lack [1], need [1], penury [1], poor [1], poverty [1], wants [1]

4271 מַחְסֵיָה **maḥsēyâ**, n.pr.m. GK: 4729 [→ 4268+3068]. Mahseiah:– Maaseiah [2]

4272 מָחַץ **māḥaṣ**, v. GK: 4730 [→ 4273; cf. 4223]. [Q] to beat to pieces, crush, shatter:– wound [3], smite [2], wounded [2], dipped [1], pierce through [1], pierced [1], smiteth through [1], strike through [1], woundedst [1], woundeth [1]

4273 מַחַץ **maḥaṣ**, n.[m.]. GK: 4731 [→ 4272]. wound (from a blow):– stroke [1]

4274 מַחְצֵב **maḥṣēb**, n.[m.]. GK: 4732 [→ 2672]. dressed (stone), hewn (stone):– hewn [2], hewed [1]

4275 מֶחֱצָה **meḥ^{e}ṣâ**, n.f. GK: 4733 [→ 2673]. half:– half [2]

4276 מַחֲצִית **maḥ^{a}ṣît**, n.f. GK: 4734 [→ 2673]. half; noon, middle of the day:– half [14], half so much [1], midday (+3117+1886.1) [1]

4277 מָחַק **māḥaq**, v. GK: 4735. [Q] to crush, smash, pierce:– smote off [1]

4278 מֶחְקָר **meḥqār**, n.m. GK: 4736 [→ 2713]. (unexplored) depths (of the earth):– deep places [1]

4279 מָחָר **māḥār**, n.m. (used as adv.). GK: 4737 [→ 4283; cf. 309]. tomorrow, the next day, in the future:– to morrow [43], in time to come [7], to come [1], to morrow (+3117) [1]

4280 מַחֲרָאָה **maḥ^{a}rā'â**, n.f. GK: 4738 [→ 2716]. latrine:– draught house [1]

4281 מַחֲרֵשָׁה **maḥ^{a}rēšâ**, n.f. GK: 4739 [→ 2790, 4282]. same as 4282: plowshare:– mattocks [1], mattock [1]

4282 מַחֲרֶשֶׁת **maḥ^{a}rešet**, n.f. GK: 4739 [→ 4281]. same as 4281: plowshare:– share [1]

4283 מָחֳרָת **moḥ^{o}rāt**, n.f. GK: 4740 [→ 4279; cf. 309]. the next day, the day after:– morrow [26], morrow after [3], next day [2], next [1]

4284 מַחֲשָׁבָה **maḥ^{a}šābâ**, n.f. GK: 4742 [→ 2803]. thought, plan, scheme, plot, design:– thoughts [27], devices [8], device [4], imaginations [3], purposes [3], purpose [3], cunning works [1], cunning [1], curious works [1], devised [1], invented [1], means [1], those that devise cunning work (+2803) [1], thought [1]

4285 מַחְשָׁךְ **maḥšāk**, n.m. GK: 4743 [→ 2821]. place of darkness, hiding place:– darkness [4], dark places [2], dark [1]

4286 מַחְשֹׂף **maḥśōp**, n.m. GK: 4741 [→ 2834]. exposing, laying bare (of wood):– made appear [1]

4287 מַחַת **maḥat**, n.pr.m. GK: 4744 [→ 2865?]. Mahath, "[perhaps] *tough*":– Mahath [3]

4288 מְחִתָּה **m^{e}ḥittâ**, n.f. GK: 4745 [→ 2865]. ruin, undoing; terror, horror:– destruction [7], terror [2], dismaying [1], ruin [1]

4289 מַחְתָּה **maḥtâ**, n.f. GK: 4746 [→ 2846]. censer, firepan, tray:– censers [8], censer [7], firepans [4], snuffdishes [3]

4290 מַחְתֶּרֶת **maḥteret**, n.m. GK: 4747 [→ 2864]. (the act of) breaking into (a house) and so trespassing:– breaking up [1], secret search [1]

4291 מְטָא **m^{e}ṭā'** (Aram.), v. GK: 10413. [P] to reach out, extend towards:– came [4], reached [2], come [1], reacheth [1]

4292 מַטְאֲטֵא **maṭ^{a}ṭē'**, n.[m.]. GK: 4748 [→ 2894; cf. 2916]. broom:– besom [1]

4293 מַטְבֵּחַ **maṭbēaḥ**, n.[m.]. GK: 4749 [→ 2873]. place of slaughter, slaughter yard:– slaughter [1]

4294 מַטֶּה **maṭṭeh**, n.m. [& f.?]. GK: 4751 [→ 5186]. staff, rod, club, a stick used to assist in walking, discipline, and guidance, often highly individualized and used for identification; of royalty: scepter; by extension: tribe, as a major unit of national group or clan (fig. identified with or under authority of a leader's staff):– tribe [163], rod [42], tribes [20], staff [15], rods [8], staves [1]

4295 מַטָּה **maṭṭâ**, adv. GK: 4752 [→ 5186]. below, beneath, lower, bottom:– downward (+3807.1) [5], beneath (+4480+3807.1) [4], beneath [2], underneath (+4480+3807.1) [2], very low (+4295) [2], beneath (+3807.1) [1], down (+3807.1) [1], less [1], under [1]

4296 מִטָּה **miṭṭâ**, n.f. GK: 4753 [→ 5186]. bed, couch, a piece of furniture on which one reclines for rest or sleep; by extension: bier, to carry the dead; carriage or palanquin (a vehicle carried on poles by porters):– bed [23], bedchamber (+2315) [2], beds [2], bed's [1], bier [1]

4297 מֻטֶּה **muṭṭeh**, n.[m.]. GK: 4754 [→ 5186]. injustice, warping (of justice), crookedness (of law):– perverseness [1]

4298 מֻטָּה **muṭṭâ**, n.f. GK: 4755 [→ 5186]. outspreading (of wings):– stretching out [1]

4299 מַטְוֶה **maṭweh**, n.[m.]. GK: 4757 [→ 2901]. that which is spun, yarn:– spun [1]

4300 מְטִיל **māṭîl**, n.m. GK: 4758. (iron) rod:– bars [1]

4301 מַטְמוֹן **maṭmôn**, n.m. GK: 4759 [→ 2934]. (hidden) treasure, (hidden) riches:– hid treasures [2], hidden riches [1], treasures [1], treasure [1]

4302 מַטָּע **maṭṭā'**, n.m. GK: 4760 [→ 5193]. (the act or place of) planting:– planting [2], plantation [1], plantings [1], plants [1], plant [1]

4303 מַטְעָם **maṭ'ām**, n.m. GK: 4761 [→ 2938]. tasty food, delicacy:– savoury meat [6], dainties [1], dainty meats [1]

4304 מִטְפַּחַת **miṭpaḥat**, n.f. GK: 4762 [→ 2946]. cloak, shawl:– vail [1], wimples [1]

4305 מָטַר **māṭar**, v.den. GK: 4763 [→ 4306]. [N] to be rained upon; [H] to send rain down on; [Ho] to be rained upon; rain has a generally positive associations of growth and refreshment, though excessive or ill-timed rain is potentially destructive to crops and even life-threatening:– rained [5], rain [5], cause to rain [3], caused to rain [3], rained down [1]

4306 מָטָר **māṭār**, n.m. GK: 4764 [→ 4305, 4309]. rain, rain shower:– rain [35], great [1], showers [1], small [1]

4307 מַטָּרָה **maṭṭārâ**, n.f. GK: 4766 [→ 5201]. (the court of the) guard, i.e., place of confinement; (the Gate of the) Guard (a place); target:– prison [13], mark [3]

4308 מַטְרֵד **maṭrēd**, n.pr.f. GK: 4765 [→ 2956]. Matred, "[perhaps] *spear*":– Matred [2]

4309 מַטְרִי **maṭrî**, a.g. GK: 4767 [→ 4306]. Matri:– Matri [1]

4310 מִי **mî**, p.inter. GK: 4769 [→ 4316?, 4317, 4318, 4319, 4320, 4322, 4321, 4332]. who?, what?, which?; anyone, whoever:– who [284], whom [47], what [25], O that (+5414) [17], whose [11], whose (+3807.1) [7], which [6], oh that [3], whosoever [3], whoso [3], any [2], he [2], would God (+5414) [2], would to God (+5414) [2], him [1], none [1], that [1], what (+2088) [1], who else [1], whosoever (+834) [1], would God that (+5414) [1], would [1]

4311 מֵידְבָא **mêdᵉbā'**, n.pr.loc. GK: 4772. Medeba:– Medeba [5]

4312 מֵידָד **mêdād**, n.pr.m. GK: 4773. Medad, "*beloved*":– Medad [2]

4313 מֵי הַיַּרְקוֹן **mê hayyarqôn**, n.pr.loc. GK: 4770 [→ 4325]. Me Jarkon, "*waters of Jarkon [greenish?]*":– Me-jarkon [1]

4314 מֵי זָהָב **mê zāhāb**, n.pr.m. GK: 4771 [→ 4325+2091]. Me-Zahab, "*waters of gold*":– Mezahab [2]

4315 מֵיטָב **mêṭāb**, n.[m.]. GK: 4774 [→ 3190]. best (part of something):– best [6]

4316 מִיכָא **mîkā'**, n.pr.m. GK: 4775 [→ 4317?, 4318; cf. 4310?]. Mica, "*Who is like Yahweh?*":– Micha [4], Micah [1]

4317 מִיכָאֵל **mîkā'ēl**, n.pr.m. GK: 4776 [→ 4316?]. Michael, "*Who is like God [El]?*":– Michael [13]

4318 מִיכָה **mîkâ**, n.pr.m. GK: 4777 [→ 4316]. Micah; Mica; Micaiah, "*Who is like Yahweh?*":– Micah [24], Michah [4], Micah's [3], Micaiah [1]

4319 מִיכָהוּ **mîkāhû**, n.pr.m. GK: 4778 [→ 4310+3509.1+1930.2]. Micahu, cf. 4322:–

4320 מִיכָיָה **mîkāyâ**, n.pr.m. GK: 4779 [→ 4322, 4321]. Micaiah, "*Who is like Yahweh?*":– Michaiah [3]

Heb

4321 מִיכָיְהוּ ***mîkāy^e^hû***, n.pr.m. GK: 4781 [→ 4320]. Micaiah; Micah, "*Who is like Yahweh?*":– Micaiah [17], Micah [2], Michaiah [2]

4322 מִיכָיָהוּ ***mîkāyāhû***, n.pr.m. & f. GK: 4780 [→ 4320]. Micaiah, "*Who is like Yahweh?*":– Michaiah [2]

4323 מִיכָל ***mîkāl***, n.[m.]. GK: 4782 [→ 4324]. brook, stream; some sources: pool, reservoir:– brook [1]

4324 מִיכַל ***mîkal***, n.pr.f. GK: 4783 [→ 4323]. Michal, "*Who is like God [El]?*":– Michal [18]

4325 מַיִם ***mayim***, n.m. GK: 4784 [→ 66, 4313, 4314, 4956]. water; in nature: ocean, lake, flood, river; from the body: tears, urine:– water [306], waters [267], piss (+7272) [2], watersprings (+4161) [2], washing [1], watercourse (+4161) [1], waterflood (+7641) [1], watering [1]

4326 מִיָּמִין ***miyyāmîn***, n.pr.m. GK: 4785 [→ 4509]. Mijamin, "*from the right hand*":– Miamin [2], Mijamin [2]

4327 מִין ***mîn***, n.[m.]. GK: 4786 [→ 8544]. kind: genus or species:– kind [30], kinds [1]

4328 מְיֻסָּדָה ***m^e^yussādâ***, v.ptcp. GK: 4588 [→ 4145]. ptcp. of 3245: foundation:–

4329 מוּסָךְ ***mûsāk*** or מֵיסָךְ ***mêsāk***, n.m. GK: 4590 & 4788 [→ 5526]. canopy:– covert [1]

מֵיפַעַת ***mêpa'at***. See 4158.

4330 מִיץ ***mîṣ***, n.m. GK: 4790 [→ 4160]. pressing, squeezing:– churning [1], forcing [1], wringing [1]

4331 מֵישָׁא ***mêšā'***, n.pr.m. GK: 4791. Mesha:– Mesha [1]

4332 מִישָׁאֵל ***mîšā'ēl***, n.pr.m. GK: 4792 [→ 4310+7945+410; cf. 4333]. Mishael, "*Who belongs to God [El]?*":– Mishael [7]

4333 מִישָׁאֵל ***mîšā'ēl*** (Aram.), n.pr.m. GK: 10414 [cf. 4332]. Mishael, "*who belongs to God (El)?*":– Mishael [1]

4334 מִישׁוֹר ***mîšôr***, n.m. GK: 4793 [→ 3474]. (geographical) plateau, plain, level ground; (of ruling and right living) uprightness, justice, straightness:– plain [14], equity [2], even place [1], made straight [1], plains [1], righteously [1], right [1], straight [1], uprightness [1]

4335 מֵישַׁךְ ***mêšak***, n.pr.m. GK: 4794 [cf. 4336]. Meshach, "[perhaps] *I have become weak*":– Meshach [1]

4336 מֵישַׁךְ ***mêšak*** (Aram.), n.pr.m. GK: 10415 [cf. 4335]. Meshach, "[perhaps] *I have become weak*":– Meshach [14]

4337 מֵישָׁע ***mêšā'***, n.pr.m. GK: 4796 [→ 3467]. Mesha:– Mesha [1]

4338 מֵישַׁע ***mêša'***, n.pr.m. GK: 4795 [→ 3467]. Mesha:– Mesha [1]

4339 מֵישָׁרִים ***mêšārîm***, n.m. GK: 4797 [→ 3474]. uprightness, fairness, equity, justice; moral uprightness and justice are fig. extensions of an object that is straight rather than crooked:– equity [4], uprightly [3], uprightness [3], right things [2], agreement [1], aright (+871.1) [1], righteously (+871.1) [1], sweetly (+3807.1) [1], things that are equal [1], things that are right [1], upright [1]

4340 מֵיתָר ***mêtār***, n.m. GK: 4798 [→ 3499]. rope, cord; bow-string:– cords [8], laid up [2], strings [1]

4341 מַכְאֹב ***mak'ōb***, n.m. GK: 4799 [→ 3510]. pain, grief, sorrow, suffering:– sorrow [7], sorrows [5], grief [2], pain [2]

4342 מַכְבִּיר ***makbîr***, v.ptcp. GK: 3892 [→ 3527]. ptcp. of 3527: abundance:– abundance [1]

4343 מַכְבֵּנָה ***makbēnâ***, n.pr.loc. GK: 4800 [cf. 4344]. Macbenah, "*bond*":– Machbenah [1]

4344 מַכְבַּנַּי ***makbannay***, n.pr.m. GK: 4801 [cf. 4343]. Macbannai, "*clad with a cloak*":– Machbanai [1]

4345 מִכְבָּר ***mikbār***, n.m. GK: 4803 [→ 4346]. grating, lattice-work:– grate [6]

4346 מַכְבֵּר ***makbēr***, n.[m.]. GK: 4802 [→ 4345]. thick cloth, with a focus that it is twisted, braided, or woven:– thick cloth [1]

4347 מַכָּה ***makkâ***, n.f. GK: 4804 [→ 5221]. wound, injury, physical damage to the body; by extension: plague, affliction, calamity, disaster:– slaughter [13], plagues [9], wound [8], wounds [6], plague [2], stripes [2], stroke [2], beaten [1], blow [1], slaughter made (+5221) [1], smote [1], sores [1], wounded [1]

4348 מִכְוָה ***mikwâ***, n.f. GK: 4805 [→ 3554]. burn (on the skin), scar; in context this is not an intentional mark or tattoo:– burning [4], burneth [1]

4349 מָכוֹן ***mākôn***, n.m. GK: 4806 [→ 3559]. (established) place, site; foundation (of earth or throne):– place [11], dwelling place [2], habitation [2], foundations [1], settled place [1]

4350 מְכוֹנָה ***m^e^kônâ***, n.f. GK: 4807 [→ 3559, 4369]. movable stand; (established) place, foundation:– bases [16], base [8], every (+1886.1) [1]

4351 מְכוּרָה ***m^e^kûrâ***, n.f. GK: 4808 [→ 3738]. ancestry, origin, parentage:– birth [1], habitation [1], nativity [1]

4352 מָכִי ***mākî***, n.pr.m. GK: 4809. Maki, "[perhaps] *reduced* or *bought*":– Machi [1]

4353 מָכִיר ***mākîr***, n.pr.m. GK: 4810 [→ 4354]. Makir, Makirite, "*bought*":– Machir [22]

4354 מָכִירִי ***mākîrî***, a.g. GK: 4811 [→ 4353]. Makirite, "*of Makir*":– Machirites [1]

4355 מָכַךְ ***mākak***, v. GK: 4812 [cf. 4134]. [Q] to sink, go down, waste away; [N] to sag, be sunk down; [Ho] to be brought low:– brought low [2], decayeth [1]

4356 מִכְלָא ***miklā'***, n.[m.]. GK: 4813 [→ 3607]. pen, fold (for sheep or goats):– folds [1], fold [1], sheepfolds (+6629) [1]

4357 מִכְלוֹת ***miklôt***, n.[f.]. GK: 4816 [→ 3615]. solid (gold), purest (gold):– perfect [1]

4358 מִכְלוֹל ***miklôl***, n.m. GK: 4814 [→ 3634]. fullness, completeness, perfection:– all sorts [1], most gorgeously [1]

4359 מִכְלָל ***miklāl***, n.m. GK: 4817 [→ 3634]. perfection:– perfection [1]

4360 מַכְלוּל ***maklûl***, n.m. GK: 4815 [→ 3634]. beautiful garment, finery, with a focus the excellence of the item:– all sorts of things [1]

4361 מַכֹּלֶת ***makkōlet***, n.f. GK: 4818 [→ 398]. food:– food [1]

4362 מִכְמָן ***mikmān***, n.[m.]. GK: 4819. (hidden) treasure:– treasures [1]

4363 מִכְמָס ***mikmās*** or מִכְמָשׂ ***mikmāś***, n.pr.loc. GK: 4820 & 4825 [cf. 3647]. Micmas, Micmash, "[perhaps] *hidden place*":– Michmash [9], Michmas [2]

4364 מִכְמָר ***mikmār*** or מַכְמֹר ***makmōr***, n.[m.]. GK: 4821 & 4822 [cf. 4365]. net, snare (for capture of game):– nets [1], net [1]

4365 מִכְמֶרֶת ***mikmeret*** or מִכְמֹרֶת ***mikmōret***, n.f. GK: 4823 & 4824 [cf. 4364]. net, snare; fishing net, dragnet (for fish):– drag [2], nets [1]

מִכְמָשׁ ***mikmāš***. See 4363.

4366 מִכְמְתָת ***mikm^e^tāt***, n.pr.loc. GK: 4826. Micmethath:– Michmethah [2]

4367 מַכְנַדְבַי ***maknadbay***, n.pr.m. GK: 4827. Macnadebai, "[poss.] *possession of Nebo*":– Machnadebai [1]

מְכֹנָה ***m^e^kōnâ***. See 4350.

4368 מְכֹנָה ***m^e^kōnâ***, n.pr.loc. GK: 4828 [→ 3559]. Meconah, "*foundation*":– Mekonah [1]

4369 מְכֻנָה ***m^e^kunâ***, n.f. GK: 4807 [→ 4350]. same as 4350: movable stand; (established) place, foundation:–

4370 מִכְנָס ***miknās***, n.m. GK: 4829 [→ 3664]. undergarment, some kind of shorts or trousers:– breeches [5]

4371 מֶכֶס ***mekes***, n.m. GK: 4830 [→ 3699]. tribute, cultic dues or taxes:– tribute [6]

4372 מִכְסֶה ***mikseh***, n.[m.]. GK: 4832 [→ 3680]. covering:– covering [16]

4373 מִכְסָה ***miksâ***, n.f. GK: 4831 [→ 3699]. number (of persons); amount, valuation (of a thing):– number [1], worth [1]

4374 מְכַסֶּה ***m^e^kasseh***, n.m. GK: 4833 [→ 3680]. covering (of a body or building); layer of fat (on the kidneys):– clothing [1], covered [1], covereth [1], cover [1]

4375 מַכְפֵּלָה ***makpēlâ***, n.pr.loc. GK: 4834 [→ 3717]. Machpelah, "*double [cave]*":– Machpelah [6]

4376 מָכַר ***mākar***, v. GK: 4835 [→ 4377, 4378?, 4465, 4466]. [Q] to sell; [N] to be sold; [Ht] to sell oneself:– sold [44], sell [22], selleth [5], seller [3], sell at all (+4376) [2], sell ought (+4465) [1], sellers [1], sellest [1], sold (+4466) [1]

4377 מֶכֶר ***meker***, n.m. GK: 4836 [→ 4376]. worth, value; merchandise:– pay (+5414) [1], price [1], ware [1]

4378 מַכָּר ***makkār***, n.m. GK: 4837 [→ 4376?]. treasurer:– acquaintance [2]

4379 מִכְרֶה ***mikreh***, n.m. GK: 4838 [→ 3738]. (salt) pit:– saltpits (+4417) [1]

4380 מְכֵרָה ***m^e^kērâ***, n.[f.]. GK: 4839. sword, weapon:– habitations [1]

מְכֹרָה ***m^e^kōrâ***. See 4351.

4381 מִכְרִי ***mikrî***, n.pr.m. GK: 4840. Micri:– Michri [1]

4382 מְכֵרָתִי ***m^e^kērātî***, a.g. GK: 4841. Mekerathite:– Mecherathite [1]

4383 מִכְשׁוֹל ***mikšôl***, n.m. GK: 4842 [→ 3782]. stumbling block, obstacle; (occasion of) stumbling, downfall:– stumblingblock [7], offence [2], caused to fall [1], offend [1], ruins [1], ruin [1], stumblingblocks [1]

4384 מַכְשֵׁלָה ***makšēlâ***, n.f. GK: 4843 [→ 3782]. heap of ruins, heap of rubble:– ruin [1], stumblingblocks [1]

4385 מִכְתָּב ***miktāb***, n.m. GK: 4844 [→ 3789]. writing, inscription, letter:– writing [9]

4386 מְכִתָּה ***m^{e}kittâ***, n.f. GK: 4845 [→ 3807]. pieces, crushed fragments:– bursting [1]

4387 מִכְתָּם ***miktām***, n.[m.]. GK: 4846 [→ 3800?]. miktam (t.t. in the Psalms, of uncertain meaning):– Michtam [6]

4388 מַכְתֵּשׁ ***maktēš***, n.m. GK: 4847 [→ 3806, 4389]. hollow place; mortar; market district (at a hollow place in the city?):– hollow place [1], mortar [1]

4389 מַכְתֵּשׁ ***maktēš***, n.pr.m. GK: 4847 [→ 4388]. same as 4388 as n.pr.: Maktesh:– Maktesh [1]

מַל ***mul***. See 4136.

4390 מָלֵא ***mālē'*** or מָלָה ***mālâ***, v. GK: 4848 & 4862 [→ 3229, 4392, 4393, 4394, 4395, 4396, 4402, 4407; cf. 4391 (also used with compound proper names)]. [Q] to fill up, be full; [Qp] to be ordained, fulfilled; [N] to be filled, become filled up; [P] to fill up, satisfy; ordain, consecrate; [Pu] to be set; [Ht] to unite together; "to fill the hand" means to ordain or consecrate for service to God:– filled [72], full [46], fill [32], fulfilled [20], fulfil [8], accomplished [6], wholly [6], consecrate (+3027) [5], consecrated (+853+3027) [5], replenished [5], set [5], consecrate (+853+3027) [4], expired [3], consecrated (+3027) [2], filleth [2], replenish [2], accomplish [1], at an end [1], become full [1], confirm [1], consecrate [1], drew with full strength (+3027+871.1) [1], durst presume [1], fenced [1], filledst [1], fillest [1], fully set [1], fully [1], fulness [1], furnish unto [1], gather together [1], gathered [1], gather [1], gave in full tale [1], overfloweth (+5921) [1], overflown (+5921) [1], satisfied [1], satisfy [1], space [1], took a handful (+3709) [1], went fully [1]

4391 מְלָא ***m^{e}lā'*** (Aram.), v. GK: 10416 [cf. 4390]. [P] to fill; [Htpe] to be filled:– filled [1], full [1]

4392 מָלֵא ***mālē'***, a. GK: 4849 [→ 4390]. filled, full; "full of days" means "very old":– full [58], filled [2], all [1], fill [1], fully [1], multitude [1], with child [1], worth [1]

4393 מְלֹא ***m^{e}lō'***, n.m. GK: 4850 [→ 4390]. what fills, what makes something full; fullness, everything:– full [12], fulness [8], all that is therein [6], fill [2], handful (+3709) [2], multitude [2], take handful (+7061+7062) [2], all along (+6967) [1], all that is in [1], all that therein is [1], handfuls (+2651) [1]

מִלֹּא ***millō'***. See 4407.

4394 מִלֻּאִים ***millu'îm***, n.m. GK: 4854 [→ 4390]. ordination, consecration (of a priest); mounting, setting (of gem stones):– consecration [6], consecrations [5], set [4]

4395 מְלֵאָה ***m^{e}lē'â***, n.f. GK: 4852 [→ 4390]. full yield (of crops):– fruit [1], fulness [1], ripe fruits [1]

4396 מִלֻּאָה ***millu'â***, n.f. GK: 4853 [→ 4390]. mounting (of jewels), setting (of jewels):– inclosings [2], settings [1]

4397 מַלְאָךְ ***mal'āk***, n.m. GK: 4855 [→ 4399, 4400, 4401?; cf. 4398]. messenger, a human representative; angel, a supernatural representative of God, sometimes delivering messages, sometimes protecting God's people; the "angel of the LORD" sometimes shares divine characteristics and is sometimes thought to be an manifestation of God himself, or of the preincarnate Christ:– angel [101], messengers [74], messenger [24], angels [10], ambassadors [4]

4398 מַלְאַךְ ***mal'ak*** (Aram.), n.m. GK: 10417 [cf. 4397]. messenger; angel, a class of being that serves God, often to communicate with or rescue his faithful on earth:– angel [2]

4399 מְלָאכָה ***m^{e}lā'kâ***, n.f. GK: 4856 [→ 4397]. work, deed, duty, craft, service; thing, something:– work [126], business [12], workmanship [5], workmen (+6213+1886.1) [4], workmen (+6213) [3], works [3], goods [2], cattle [1], industrious (+6213) [1], labour [1], made [1], occupation [1], occupied (+6213) [1], officers (+6213+1886.1) [1], stuff [1], thing [1], use [1], workmen (+376) [1]

4400 מַלְאֲכוּת ***mal'ăkût***, n.f. GK: 4857 [→ 4397]. message (from a commissioned messenger):– message [1]

4401 מַלְאָכִי ***mal'ākî***, n.pr.m. GK: 4858 [→ 4397?]. Malachi, "*my messenger* or *messenger of Yahweh*":– Malachi [1]

4402 מִלֵּאת ***millē't***, n.f. GK: 4859 [→ 4390]. setting, mounting, the solid base in which a gem is set:– fitly [1]

4403 מַלְבּוּשׁ ***malbûš***, n.m. GK: 4860 [→ 3847]. clothing, robe, attire, garment:– apparel [4], raiment [3], vestments [1]

4404 מַלְבֵּן ***malbēn***, n.[m.]. GK: 4861 [→ 3840]. brickwork, brick pavement; (the act of) brickmaking:– brickkiln [3]

4405 מִלָּה ***millâ***, n.f. GK: 4863 [→ 4448; cf. 4406]. word, what is said; the act of speaking, speech:– words [21], speech [4], speaking [2], speeches [2], word [2], answer (+7725) [1], any thing to say [1], byword [1], matter [1], speak [1], talking [1], what to say [1]

4406 מִלָּה ***millâ*** (Aram.), n.f. GK: 10418 [→ 4449; cf. 4405]. word, command; matter, thing, affair; a general term like the English "thing":– thing [9], words [5], matter [4], things [2], word [2], commandment [1], matters [1]

מְלוֹ ***m^{e}lô*** or מְלוֹא ***m^{e}lô'***. See 4393.

4407 מִלּוֹא ***millô'*** or מִלֹּא ***millō'***, n.pr.loc. GK: 4864 & 4851 [cf. 4390]. Millo, "supporting terrace":– Millo [10]

4408 מַלּוּחַ ***mallûaḥ***, n.[m.]. GK: 4865 [→ 4417]. salt herb (collected by the destitute and banished):– mallows [1]

4409 מַלּוּךְ ***mallûk*** or מַלּוּכִי ***mallûkî*** or מְלִיכוּ ***m^{e}lîkû***, n.pr.m. GK: 4866 & 4868 & 4883 [→ 4428; cf. 4427]. Malluch, Melichu, "*counselor; king*":– Malluch [6], Melicu [1]

4410 מְלוּכָה ***m^{e}lûkâ***, n.f. GK: 4867 [→ 4427]. kingship, rulership, royalty:– kingdom [18], royal [4], king's [2]

4411 מָלוֹן ***mālôn***, n.m. GK: 4869 [→ 3885]. place of overnight lodging, place where one spends the night:– inn [3], lodging place [2], lodgings [1], place where lodged [1], taken up lodging [1]

4412 מְלוּנָה ***m^{e}lûnâ***, n.f. GK: 4870 [→ 3885]. hut, structure (of a watchman in the field):– cottage [1], lodge [1]

4413 מַלּוֹתִי ***mallôtî***, n.pr.m. GK: 4871 [→ 4448]. Mallothi, "*my expression*":– Mallothi [2]

4414 מָלַח ***mālaḥ***, v.den. GK: 4872 & 4873 [→ 4417, 4418]. [Q] to season with salt; [N] to vanish, be dispersed; [Pu] to be salted; [Ho] to be rubbed with salt:– salted at all (+4414) [2], season [1], tempered together [1], vanish away [1]

4415 מְלַח ***m^{e}laḥ*** (Aram.), v.den. GK: 10419 [→ 4416; cf. 4414]. [P] to eat salt (i.e., be under obligation to); "to eat the salt of the palace" is to be under the solemn obligation to the king's interests:– have maintenance (+4416) [1]

4416 מְלַח ***m^{e}laḥ*** (Aram.), n.m. GK: 10420 [→ 4415; cf. 4417]. salt, a condiment for food; also used in ceremonies:– salt [2], have maintenance (+4415) [1]

4417 מֶלַח ***melaḥ***, n.m. GK: 4875 [→ 4408, 4414, 4419, 4420, 5898, 8528; cf. 4415, cf. 4416]. salt, a staple of the ancient world; positively: for flavoring, as a nutrient, as a food preservative; as a medicine; for curing animal skins; negatively: used on fields to prevent or inhibit productive plant growth:– salt [28], saltpits (+4379) [1]

4418 מֶלַח ***melaḥ***, n.[m.]. GK: 4874 [→ 4414]. worn-out clothes, rags:– rotten rags [2]

4419 מַלָּח ***mallāḥ***, n.m. GK: 4876 [→ 4417]. sailor, mariner:– mariners [4]

4420 מְלֵחָה ***m^{e}lēḥâ***, n.f. GK: 4877 [→ 4417]. salt flat, salt waste-lands, barren country:– barrenness [1], barren [1], salt [1]

4421 מִלְחָמָה ***milḥāmâ***, n.f. GK: 4878 [→ 3898]. fighting, battle (a particular engagement), war (as an ongoing event):– war [150], battle [144], wars [8], battles [6], fight [5], warriors (+6213) [2], battle (+6635) [1], fighting (+6213) [1], had wars with (+376+1961) [1], had with (+376+1961) [1]

4422 מָלַט ***mālaṭ***, v. GK: 4880 & 4881 [→ 4423?, 4424; cf. 6403]. [N] to deliver oneself, escape, flee; [P] to save, deliver, rescue; [H] to rescue; to deliver (a child); [Ht] to shoot out (of sparks); to escape; to be bald:– escaped [25], escape [21], delivered [16], deliver [16], save [4], escapeth [3], speedily escape (+4422) [2], surely deliver (+4422) [2], get away [1], lay [1], leap out [1], let alone [1], preserve [1], saved [1]

4423 מֶלֶט ***meleṭ***, n.[m.]. GK: 4879 [→ 4422?]. clay flooring:– clay [1]

4424 מְלַטְיָה ***m^{e}laṭyâ***, n.pr.m. GK: 4882 [→ 4422+3068]. Melatiah, "*Yahweh sets free*":– Melatiah [1]

4425 מְלִילָה ***m^{e}lîlâ***, n.f. GK: 4884. (rubbed) kernels (of grain):– ears [1]

4426 מְלִיצָה ***m^{e}lîṣâ***, n.[f.]. GK: 4886 [→ 3887]. allusive saying, parable; ridicule:– interpretation [1], taunting [1]

4427 מָלַךְ ***mālak***, v.den. GK: 4887 & 4888 [→ 3230?, 4410, 4428, 4467, 4468; cf. 4431]. [Q] to reign as king; [N] to ponder, consider carefully within oneself; [H] to make one a king, have a coronation; [Ho] be made a king:– reigned [159], reign [115], made king [30], reigneth [11], make king [10], king [4], made a king (+4428) [3], indeed reign (+4427) [2], surely be king (+4427) [2], consulted [1], made queen [1], made to reign [1], made [1], make a king (+4428) [1], queen [1], reigned over (+4428) [1], reigning [1], rule [1], set a king (+4428) [1], set up kings [1], set up to be king (+4428) [1]

4428 מֶלֶךְ ***melek***, n.m. GK: 4889 [→ 4409, 4429, 4432, 4436, 4435, 4438, 4445, 4446; cf. 4427; cf. 4430 (also used with compound proper names)]. king, royal ruler, human and divine; "the great king" is the more prominent of the leaders in a convenant agreement and is used of God (Ps 48:2); the "king of kings" is the supreme sovereign and is not used of God in the OT:– king [1966], kings [282], king's [254], king's (+871.1) [4], kings' [3], made a king (+4427) [3], king's (+3807.1) [2], royal [2], make a king (+4427) [1], reigned over (+4427) [1], set a king (+4427) [1], set up to be king (+4427) [1]

4429 מֶלֶךְ ***melek***, n.pr.m. GK: 4890 [→ 4428; cf. 4427]. Melech, "*king*":– Hammelech [2], Melech [2], Moloch [1]

4430 מֶלֶךְ ***melek*** (Aram.), n.m. GK: 10421 [→ 4433, 4437; cf. 4428]. king, royal ruler:– king [147], king's [17], kings [15], royal [1]

4431 מְלַךְ ***m^e^lak*** (Aram.), n.m. GK: 10422 [cf. 4427]. advice, counsel:– counsel [1]

4432 מֹלֶךְ ***mōlek***, n.pr.[m.]. GK: 4891 [→ 4428]. Molech (pagan god), "*(shameful) king*":– Molech [8]

4433 מַלְכָּה ***malkâ*** (Aram.), n.f. GK: 10423 [→ 4430; cf. 4436]. queen, the wife of a king, with very high status but not likely equal status to the king; queen mother, mother or grandmother of a king:– queen [2]

4434 מַלְכֹּדֶת ***malkōdet***, n.f. GK: 4892 [→ 3920]. trap, snare:– trap [1]

4435 מִלְכָּה ***milkâ***, n.pr.f. GK: 4894 [→ 4428; cf. 4427]. Milcah, "*queen*":– Milcah [11]

4436 מַלְכָּה ***malkâ***, n.f. GK: 4893 [→ 4428; cf. 4427; cf. 4433]. queen (outside Israel), a female ruler of a kingdom; wife of a king, royalty but without much actual governmental power:– queen [33], queens [2]

4437 מַלְכוּ ***malkû*** (Aram.), n.f. GK: 10424 [→ 4430; cf. 4438]. kingdom, dominion, reign:– kingdom [47], reign [4], realm [3], kingdoms [2], kingly [1]

4438 מַלְכוּת ***malkût***, n.f. GK: 4895 [→ 4428; cf. 4427; cf. 4437]. kingdom, empire, realm; reign, royal power, position as a king:– kingdom [49], reign [21], royal [13], realm [4], kingdoms [2], empire [1], royal estate [1]

4439 מַלְכִּיאֵל ***malkî'ēl***, n.pr.m. GK: 4896 [→ 4440]. Malkiel, "*God [El] is [my] king*":– Malchiel [3]

4440 מַלְכִּיאֵלִי ***malkî'ēlî***, a.g. GK: 4897 [→ 4439]. Malkielite, "*of Malkiel*":– Malchielites [1]

4441 מַלְכִּיָּה or מַלְכִּיָּהוּ ***malkiyyâ*** or ***malkiyyāhû***, n.pr.m. GK: 4898 & 4899 [→ 4428+3068]. Malkijah, "*Yahweh is [my] king*":– Malchiah [9], Malchijah [6], Melchiah [1]

4442 מַלְכִּי־צֶדֶק ***malkî-ṣedeq***, n.pr.m. GK: 4900 [→ 4428+6664]. Melchizedek, "*[my] king is Zedek [just]*":– Melchizedek [2]

4443 מַלְכִּירָם ***malkîrām***, n.pr.m. GK: 4901 [→ 4428+7311]. Malkiram, "*[my] king is exalted*":– Malchiram [1]

4444 מַלְכִּי־שׁוּעַ ***malkî-šûa'***, n.pr.m. GK: 4902 [→ 4428+7768]. Malki-Shua, "*[my] king saves*":– Malchishua [4], Melchishua [1]

4445 מַלְכָּם or מִלְכֹּם ***malkām*** or ***milkōm***, n.pr.m. GK: 4903 & 4904 [→ 4428+3963.1]. Malcam, Milcom, Molech, "*their king* or *[servant of] Malk*":– Milcom [3], Malcham [2]

4446 מְלֶכֶת ***m^e^leket***, n.f. GK: 4906 [→ 4428]. Queen (of Heaven):– queen [5]

4447 מֹלֶכֶת or הַמֹּלֶכֶת ***mōleket*** or ***hammōleket***, n.pr.f. GK: 4907 & 2168 [→ 1980]. Moleketh, Hammoleketh, "*the queen*":– Hammoleketh [1]

4448 מָלַל ***mālal***, v. GK: 4910 & 4911 [→ 4405, 4413; cf. 4449]. [Q] to signal by rubbing or scraping; [P] to say, speak, proclaim:– utter [2], said [1], speaketh [1], speak [1]

4449 מְלַל ***m^e^lal*** (Aram.), v. GK: 10425 [→ 4406; cf. 4448]. [Pa] to speak:– spake [2], said [1], speaking [1], speak [1]

4450 מִלְלַי ***mil^a^lay***, n.pr.m. GK: 4912. Milalai:– Milalai [1]

4451 מַלְמָד ***malmād***, n.[m.]. GK: 4913 [→ 3925]. oxgoad, cattle prod, a (metal-tipped) poker used to guide animals, which could also be used as a weapon:– goad [1]

4452 מָלַץ ***mālaṣ***, v. GK: 4914. [N] to be smooth, pleasant, palatable, sweet:– sweet [1]

4453 מֶלְצַר ***melṣar***, n.m. GK: 4915 [→ 5341]. guard, guardian, official:– Melzar [2]

4454 מָלַק ***mālaq***, v. GK: 4916. [Q] to wring off, pinch off (the head of a bird):– wring off [2]

4455 מַלְקוֹחַ or מַלְקוֹחַיִם ***malqôaḥ*** or ***malqôḥayim***, n.m. GK: 4917 & 4918 [→ 3947]. spoils of war, plunder, war-booty; (du.) roof of the mouth, palate:– prey [6], booty [1], jaws [1]

4456 מַלְקוֹשׁ ***malqôš***, n.m. GK: 4919 [→ 3953]. spring rains, latter rains of March-April:– latter rain [6], latter [2]

4457 מֶלְקָחַיִם ***melqāḥayim***, n.[m.]du. GK: 4920 [→ 3947]. (pair of) wick trimmers; (pair of) tongs:– tongs [5], snuffers [1]

4458 מֶלְתָּחָה ***meltāḥâ***, n.f. GK: 4921. wardrobe:– vestry [1]

4459 מַלְתָּעוֹת ***maltā'ôt***, n.f.pl. GK: 4922 [→ 4973]. fangs, teeth; some sources: jawbone:– great teeth [1]

4460 מַמְּגֻרָה ***mamm^e^gûrâ***, n.f.pl. GK: 4923 [→ 4033]. granary, grain-pit:– barns [1]

4461 מֵמַד ***mēmād***, n.[m.]. GK: 4924 [→ 4058]. dimensions, measurement:– measures [1]

4462 מְמוּכָן or מוּמְכָן ***m^e^mûkān*** or ***m^e^wmukān***, n.pr.m. GK: 4925 & 4584. Memucan, Mumecan:– Memucan [3]

4463 מָמוֹת ***māmôt***, n.[m.]. GK: 4926 [→ 4191]. death:– deaths [2]

4464 מַמְזֵר ***mamzēr***, n.m. GK: 4927. one born of a forbidden marriage; foreigner; this can have the associative meaning of being an unprivileged or despised class:– bastard [2]

4465 מִמְכָּר ***mimkār***, n.m. GK: 4928 [→ 4376]. what is sold, goods, merchandise:– sale [2], sold [2], sell ought (+4376) [1], that was sold [1], that which cometh of sale [1], that which is sold [1], that which sold [1], ware [1]

4466 מִמְכֶּרֶת ***mimkeret***, n.f. GK: 4929 [→ 4376]. selling, sale:– sold (+4376) [1]

4467 מַמְלָכָה ***mamlākâ***, n.f. GK: 4930 [→ 4427]. kingdom, royal dominion, reign:– kingdom [62], kingdoms [48], royal [4], reign [2], king's [1]

4468 מַמְלָכוּת ***mamlākût***, n.f. GK: 4931 [→ 4427]. kingdom, realm, royal dominion:– kingdom [8], reign [1]

4469 מִמְסָךְ ***mimsāk***, n.m. GK: 4932 [→ 4537]. bowl of mixed wine, with a focus on the wine:– drink offering [1], mixt wine [1]

4470 מֶמֶר ***memer***, n.[m.]. GK: 4933 [→ 4843]. bitterness, annoyance:– bitterness [1]

4471 מַמְרֵא ***mamrē'***, n.pr.m. & loc. GK: 4934 & 4935 [→ 4806?]. Mamre, "*strength*":– Mamre [10]

4472 מַמְּרֹרִים ***mamm^e^rōrîm***, n.m.[pl.]. GK: 4936 [→ 4843]. misery, bitterness:– bitterness [1]

4473 מִמְשַׁח ***mimšaḥ***, n.[m.]. GK: 4937 [→ 4886]. anointing:– anointed [1]

4474 מִמְשָׁל ***mimšāl***, n.[m.]. GK: 4938 [→ 4910]. leader, ruler; power, dominion, sovereign authority:– dominion [2], ruled [1]

4475 מֶמְשָׁלָה ***memšālâ***, n.f. GK: 4939 [→ 4910]. dominion, power to govern, authority to rule:– dominion [10], rule [4], dominion (+3027) [1], government [1], power [1]

4476 מִמְשָׁק ***mimšāq***, n.[m.]. GK: 4940 [→ 4943]. place, ground (overgrown with weeds):– breeding [1]

4477 מַמְתַּקִּים ***mamtaqqîm***, n.m.[pl.]. GK: 4941 [→ 4985]. sweetness, sweet things:– most sweet [1], sweet [1]

4478 מָן ***mān***, n.m. GK: 4942 [cf. 4100]. manna, a food given by God to the generation of the Exodus: "the grain of heaven":– manna [14]

4479 מַן ***man*** (Aram.), p.inter. & indef. GK: 10426 [cf. 4101]. who? what?; anyone, whoever:– whomsoever (+1768) [4], who [3], whoso (+1768) [2], what [1]

4480 מִן or מִנִּי ***min*** or ***minnî***, pp. GK: 4946 & 4974 [→ 4648; cf. 4481]. marker of a source or extension from a source: from, out of, of; temporary: since, after; logically: because of; of degree: more than:– from [2335], of [1397], out of [970], than [227], on [204], from (+5921) [152], at [116], for [103], from (+854) [81], more than [73], of (+854) [71], by [62], with [57], because of (+6440) [54], before (+6440) [50], from (+5973) [46], without (+2351) [43], above [38], in [38], thence (+8033) [34], because of [32], from (+6440) [31], too [31], beside (+905+3807.1) [30], by reason of [25], among [24], because [24], since [23], of (+6440) [20], round about (+5439) [20], above (+4605) [19], not [19], out of (+5921) [19], above (+4605+1886.5+3807.1) [18], afar off (+7350) [18], without (+369) [18], after [17], before (+6440+3807.1) [17], both [17], thereof (+5105.2) [16], on every side (+5439) [15], from among [14], within (+1004) [14], beneath (+8478) [13], besides (+905+3807.1) [13], of (+5973) [13], under (+8478) [13], above (+5921) [12], because (+6440) [12], for (+6440) [12], from (+310) [12], from (+3807.1) [12], through [12], whence (+370) [12], against [11], before [11], behind (+310) [11], that [11], upon (+5921) [11], by (+854) [10]*

4481 מִן ***min*** (Aram.), pp. GK: 10427 [cf. 4480]. from, to, out of, more than:– from [31], of [27], out of [11], part [6], before (+6925) [4], of (+6925) [3], with [3], according to [2], after [2], for [2], aforetime (+1836+6928) [1], ago (+6928) [1], because (+1768) [1], because [1], by [1], concerning (+6655) [1], from (+3890) [1], from (+6925) [1], more than [1], of a truth (+7187) [1], over (+5924) [1], partly (+7118) [1], partly [1], since [1], than [1], then (+116+6925+871.2) [1], therefore (+2050.3) [1], to [1], upon [1], when [1]

4482 מֵן ***mēn***, n.[m.]. GK: 4944 & 4945 [→ 4487]. share, portion; (music of) stringed instruments:– in [1], stringed instruments [1], whereby [1]

4483 מְנָה ***m^{e}nâ*** (Aram.), v. GK: 10431 [→ 4484, 4510; cf. 4487]. [P] to number; [Pa] to appoint, set (over):– set [3], numbered [1], ordained [1]

4484 מְנֵא ***m^{e}nē'*** (Aram.), n.[m.]. GK: 10428 [→ 4483; cf. 4487]. mene (unit of weight, about 1.25 lbs. [0.6 kg]):– mene [3]

4485 מַנְגִּינָה ***mangînâ***, n.f. GK: 4947 [→ 5059]. mocking song:– musick [1]

מִנְדָּה ***mindâ***. See 4061.

4486 מַנְדַּע ***manda'*** (Aram.), n.[m.]. GK: 10430 [→ 3046; cf. 4093]. knowledge, understanding; in some contexts, sanity:– knowledge [2], reason [1], understanding [1]

מְנָה ***m^{e}nâ***. See 4483.

4487 מָנָה ***mānâ***, v. GK: 4948 [→ 3232, 4482, 4488, 4490, 4489, 4507, 4521, 8553?, 8554, 8556?; cf. 4483]. [Q] to count, number, take a census; [N] to be counted, be numbered; [P] to assign, appoint, provide; [Pu] to be assigned, be appointed:– numbered [7], number [7], appointed [4], prepared [4], telleth [2], count [1], prepare [1], set [1], told [1]

4488 מָנֶה ***māneh***, n.m. GK: 4949 [→ 4487; cf. 4484]. mina (unit of weight, about 1.25 pounds [0.6 kg]):– pound [4], maneh [1]

4489 מֹנֶה ***mōneh***, n.[m.]. GK: 4951 [→ 4487]. time, occurrence:– times [2]

4490 מָנָה ***mānâ***, n.f. GK: 4950 [→ 4487]. share, portion, piece:– portions [6], portion [4], part [3], such things as belonged [1]

4491 מִנְהָג ***minhāg***, n.m. GK: 4952 [→ 5090]. driving (of a chariot):– driving [2]

4492 מִנְהָרָה ***minhārâ***, n.f. GK: 4953. shelter, hole, cave (in mountain clefts):– dens [1]

4493 מָנוֹד ***mānôd***, n.[m.]. GK: 4954 [→ 5110]. shaking of the head (in scorn or derision):– shaking [1]

4494 מָנוֹחַ ***mānôaḥ***, n.m. GK: 4955 [→ 4495, 4496; cf. 3240]. resting place; the home of a person or the lair of an animal, with the focus that this is a place of rest, satisfaction, and contentment:– rest [6], place of rest [1]

4495 מָנוֹחַ ***mānôaḥ***, n.pr.m. GK: 4956 [→ 4494; cf. 3240]. Manoah, *"rest"*:– Manoah [18]

4496 מְנוּחָה ***m^{e}nûḥâ***, n.f. GK: 4957 [→ 4494; cf. 3240]. resting place:– rest [15], comfortable [1], quiet [1], resting places [1], resting place [1], still [1], with ease [1]

4497 מָנוֹן ***mānôn***, n.m. GK: 4959. grief:– son [1]

4498 מָנוֹס ***mānôs***, n.m. GK: 4960 [→ 4499; cf. 5127]. place to flee, place of escape, refuge:– refuge [4], escape [1], fled apace (+5127) [1], flight [1], way to flee [1]

4499 מְנוּסָה ***m^{e}nûsâ***, n.f. GK: 4961 [→ 4498; cf. 5127]. flight, fleeing:– fleeing [1], flight [1]

4500 מָנוֹר ***mānôr***, n.m. GK: 4962. (weaver's) rod, beam (of weavers):– beam [4]

4501 מְנֹרָה ***m^{e}nôrâ***, n.f. GK: 4963 [→ 5216]. lampstand (holding an oil lamp; not a candlestick, holding a wax candle):– candlestick [32], candlesticks [6], every candlestick (+4501+2050.1) [4]

4502 מִנְּזָר ***minn^{e}zār***, n.[m.]pl. GK: 4964 [cf. 5144]. guard, watchman, with a possible implication of status and rank:– crowned [1]

4503 מִנְחָה ***minḥâ***, n.f. GK: 4966 [cf. 4504]. grain offering; animal offering or sacrifice; gift, tribute, present:– meat offering [122], offering [29], present [22], meat offerings [10], gifts [6], presents [6], oblation [5], sacrifice [5], offerings [4], gift [1], oblations [1]

4504 מִנְחָה ***minḥâ*** (Aram.), n.f. GK: 10432 [cf. 4503]. offering, gift; grain offering:– meat offerings [1], oblation [1]

מְנֻחָה ***m^{e}nuḥâ***. See 4496.

מְנֻחוֹת ***m^{e}nuḥôt***. See 2679.

4505 מְנַחֵם ***m^{e}naḥēm***, n.pr.m. GK: 4968 [→ 5162]. Menahem, *"comforter"*:– Menahem [8]

4506 מָנַחַת ***mānaḥat***, n.pr.m. & loc. GK: 4969 & 4970 [→ 3240]. Manahath, *"resting place"*:– Manahath [3]

מְנַחְתִּי ***m^{e}naḥtî***. See 2680.

4507 מְנִי ***m^{e}nî***, n.pr. GK: 4972 [→ 4487]. Destiny (pagan god):– number [1]

מִנִּי ***minnî***. See 4480, 4482.

4508 מִנִּי ***minnî***, n.pr.loc. GK: 4973. Minni:– Minni [1]

מְנָיוֹת ***m^{e}nāyôt***. See 4521.

4509 מִנְיָמִין ***minyāmîn***, n.pr.m. GK: 4975 [→ 4326]. Miniamin, *"from the right, good, fortune"*:– Miniamin [3]

4510 מִנְיָן ***minyān*** (Aram.), n.[m.]. GK: 10433 [→ 4483]. number:– number [1]

4511 מִנִּית ***minnît***, n.pr.loc. GK: 4976. Minnith:– Minnith [2]

4512 מִנְלֶה ***minleh***, n.[m.]. GK: 4978 [cf. 5186]. possession, acquisition:– perfection [1]

מְנֻסָה ***m^{e}nusâ***. See 4499.

4513 מָנַע ***māna'***, v. GK: 4979 [→ 3234]. [Q] to keep from, withhold, deny, refuse; [N] to be kept from, be withheld, be denied:– withholden [8], withhold [5], withheld [3], kept back [2], refrain [2], denied [1], deny [1], hinder [1], keep back [1], keep still [1], keepeth back [1], restrained [1], withheldest [1], withholdeth [1]

4514 מַנְעוּל ***man'ûl***, n.[m.]. GK: 4980 [→ 5274]. bolt, lock (of a door):– locks [5], lock [1]

4515 מִנְעָל ***min'āl***, n.m. GK: 4981 [→ 5274]. bolt (on a gate):– shoes [1]

4516 מַנְעַמִּים ***man'ammîm***, n.[m.]pl. GK: 4982 [→ 5276]. (edible) delicacies:– dainties [1]

4517 מְנַעַנְעִים ***m^{e}na'an'îm***, n.[m.pl.]. GK: 4983 [→ 5128]. sistrum, rattle, percussion instrument not precisely identified:– cornets [1]

4518 מְנַקִּית ***m^{e}naqqît***, n.f. GK: 4984 [→ 5352]. bowl (used for drink offering):– bowls [3], cups [1]

מְנֹרָה ***m^{e}nōrâ***. See 4501.

4519 מְנַשֶּׁה ***m^{e}naššeh***, n.pr.m. GK: 4985 [→ 4520; cf. 5382]. Manasseh, *"one that makes to forget"*:– Manasseh [141], Manasseh's [3], Manasseh's (+3807.1) [1], Manassites [1]

4520 מְנַשִּׁי ***m^{e}naššî***, a.g. GK: 4986 [→ 4519; cf. 5382]. Manassite, of Manasseh, *"of Manasseh"*:– Manasseh [2], Manassites [2]

4521 מְנָת ***m^{e}nāt***, n.f. GK: 4987 [→ 4487]. portion, lot, assigned share:– portion [4], portions [3]

4522 מַס ***mas***, n.m. GK: 4989. forced labor, slave labor:– tribute [12], levy [4], tributaries [4], discomfited [1], taskmasters (+8269) [1], tributary [1]

4523 מָס ***mās***, a. GK: 4988 [→ 4549]. despairing (man):– afflicted [1]

4524 מֵסַב ***mēsab*** or מְסִבָּה ***m^{e}sibbâ***, n.[m.]. GK: 4990 & 4991 [cf. 4141]. surrounding; round table, circle of feasters; (adv.) around, round about:– round about [2], compass about [1], places round about [1], table [1]

מֻסַבָּה ***musabbâ***. See 4142.

4525 מַסְגֵּר ***masgēr***, n.[m.]. GK: 4993 & 4994 [cf. 5462]. prison, dungeon; artisan, craftsman; some sources: metalworker, locksmith:– smiths [4], prison [3]

4526 מִסְגֶּרֶת ***misgeret***, n.f. GK: 4995 [→ 5462]. side panels (of a building); rim (of a table and base); stronghold; den:– borders [8], border [6], close places [2], holes [1]

4527 מַסַּד ***massad***, n.[m.]. GK: 4996 [→ 3245]. foundation:– foundation [1]

מוֹסָדָה ***mōsādâ***. See 4146.

4528 מִסְדְּרוֹן ***misd^{e}rôn***, n.[m.]. GK: 4997 [→ 5468?]. porch, vestibule:– porch [1]

4529 מָסָה ***māsâ***, v. GK: 4998 [cf. 3988, 4549]. [H] to melt, dissolve; to consume; to drench (with tears):– made melt [1], makest to consume away [1], melteth [1], water [1]

4530 מִסָּה ***missâ***, n.f. GK: 5002. proportion, measure:– tribute [1]

4531 מַסָּה ***massâ***, n.f. GK: 4999 & 5000 [→ 4532, 4549; cf. 5254]. trial, test, temptation; despair:– temptations [3], temptation [1], trial [1]

4532 מַסָּה ***massâ***, n.pr.loc. GK: 5001 [→ 4531?; cf. 5254?]. Massah, *"test, try"*:– Massah [4]

4533 מַסְוֶה ***masweh***, n.[m.]. GK: 5003 [→ 5497]. veil, covering:– vail [3]

4534 מְסוּכָה ***m^{e}sûkâ***, n.f. GK: 5004 [→ 4881]. thorn hedge:– thorn hedge [1]

4535 מַסָּח ***massāḥ***, n.m. *or* adv. GK: 5005 [cf. 5255?]. in turn, taking turns:– not broken down [1]

4536 מִסְחָר ***misḥār***, n.m. GK: 5006 [cf. 5503]. revenue:– traffick [1]

4537 מָסַךְ ***māsak***, v. GK: 5007 [→ 4469, 4538]. [Q] to mingle, mix (substances into drinks):– mingled [4], mingle [1]

4538 מֶסֶךְ ***mesek***, n.[m.]. GK: 5008 [→ 4537]. mixture (of spices):– mixture [1]

4539 מָסָךְ ***māsāk***, n.[m.]. GK: 5009 [→ 5526]. curtain, covering; by extension: shield, defense:– hanging [17], covering [7], curtain [1]

4540 מְסֻכָּה ***m^{e}sukâ***, n.f. GK: 5010 [→ 5526]. (woven) covering:– covering [1]

4541 מַסֵּכָה ***massēkâ***, n.f. GK: 5011 & 5012 & 5013 [→ 5258, 5259]. image, idol (of cast metal); (woven) blanket, (interwoven) covering; alliance:– molten image [10], molten images [8], molten [7], covering [2], vail [1]

4542 מִסְכֵּן ***miskēn***, a. GK: 5014 [→ 4544; cf. 5533]. poor, needy (one):– poor [4]

4543 מִסְכְּנוֹת ***misk^{e}nôt***, n.f.pl. GK: 5016 [→ 5532]. storage places, warehouses:– store [5], storehouses [1], treasure [1]

4544 מִסְכֵּנֻת ***miskēnut***, n.f. GK: 5017 [→ 4542; cf. 5533]. scarcity, poverty:– scarceness [1]

4545 מַסֶּכֶת ***masseket***, n.f. GK: 5018 [→ 5259]. warp-threads (the lengthwise threads of a loom):– web [2]

4546 מְסִלָּה ***mᵉsillâ***, n.f. GK: 5019 [→ 5549]. main road; (raised) highway, ramp, stairs; by extension: lifestyle, conduct in life:– highway [14], highways [5], causeway [2], courses [1], high way [1], paths [1], path [1], terraces [1], ways [1]

4547 מַסְלוּל ***maslûl***, n.m. GK: 5020 [→ 5549]. highway:– highway [1]

4548 מַסְמֵר ***masmēr***, n.m. GK: 5021 [→ 5568]. nail:– nails [4]

4549 מָסַס ***māsas***, v. GK: 5022 [→ 4523, 4531, 8557; cf. 3988, 4529, 4885]. [Q] to waste away, dissolve; [N] to be melted, dissolved; [H] to cause to melt:– melted [6], melt [4], melteth [2], utterly melt (+4549) [2], discouraged [1], fainteth [1], faint [1], loosed [1], melt away [1], molten [1], refuse [1]

4550 מַסַּע ***massaʿ***, n.[m.]. GK: 5023 [→ 5265]. journey, travels from place to place:– journeys [9], journeyings [1], journeying [1], journey [1]

4551 מַסָּע ***massāʿ***, n.[m.]. GK: 5024 & 5025 [→ 5265]. quarry; a weapon probably thrown like a spear or javelin; dart:– brought [1], dart [1]

4552 מִסְעָד ***misʿād***, n.[m.]. GK: 5026 [→ 5582]. supports (for a building):– pillars [1]

4553 מִסְפֵּד ***mispēd***, n.m. GK: 5027 [→ 5594]. wailing, howling, weeping, mourning:– mourning [6], wailing [6], lamentation [3], mourneth [1]

4554 מִסְפּוֹא ***mispô'***, n.m. GK: 5028. fodder, animal feed:– provender [5]

4555 מִסְפָּחָה ***mispāḥâ***, n.f. GK: 5029 [→ 5596]. veil, (head) covering:– kerchiefs [2]

4556 מִסְפַּחַת ***mispaḥat***, n.f. GK: 5030 [→ 5597]. (uninfectious) breaking out of skin, rash or scab; referring to something relatively harmless:– scab [3]

4557 מִסְפָּר ***mispār***, n.m. GK: 5031 [→ 4558?, 4559?; cf. 5612]. number, quantity; listing, inventory, census:– number [109], few [5], all [3], innumerable (+369) [3], sum [2], time (+3117) [2], abundance (+369) [1], account [1], few (+4962) [1], infinite (+369) [1], innumerable (+369+5704) [1], numbered [1], numbers [1], tale [1], telling [1]

4558 מִסְפָּר ***mispār***, n.pr.m. GK: 5032 [→ 4559; cf. 4557?, 5612]. Mispar, "*number*":– Mizpar [1]

מֹסֵרוֹת ***mōsᵉrôt***. See 4149.

4559 מִסְפֶּרֶת ***misperet***, n.pr.m. GK: 5033 [→ 4558; cf. 4557?]. Mispereth:– Mispereth [1]

4560 מָסַר ***māsar***, v. GK: 5034 [→ 4562?]. [Q] to supply, deliver; [N] to be supplied:– commit [1], delivered [1]

4561 מֹסָר ***mōsār***, n.m. GK: 5036 [→ 4148; cf. 3256]. same as 4148: instruction:– instruction [1]

4562 מָסֹרֶת ***māsōret***, n.f. GK: 5037 [→ 631? *or* 4560?]. bond, obligation, duty:– bond [1]

4563 מִסְתּוֹר ***mistôr***, n.[m.]. GK: 5039 [→ 5641]. hiding place, shelter (from the elements):– covert [1]

4564 מַסְתֵּר ***mastēr***, n.[m.]. GK: 5040 [→ 5641]. (the act of) hiding:– hid [1]

4565 מִסְתָּר ***mistār***, n.[m.]. GK: 5041 [→ 5641]. hiding place, covered places (from which to ambush):– secret places [7], secretly (+871.1+1886.1) [2], secret [1]

מְעָא ***mᵉʿā'***. See 4577.

4566 מַעֲבָד ***maᵃbād***, n.[m.]. GK: 5042 [→ 5647; cf. 4567]. deed, action:– works [1]

4567 מַעְבָּד ***maᵃbād*** (Aram.), n.[m.]. GK: 10434 [→ 5648; cf. 4566]. what one does, work:– works [1]

4568 מַעֲבֶה ***maᵃbeh***, n.[m.]. GK: 5043 [→ 5666]. mold, foundry:– clay [1]

4569 מַעֲבָר ***maᵃbār*** or מַעְבָּרָה ***maʿbārâ***, n.[m.]. GK: 5044 & 5045 [→ 5674]. stroke (of a rod); (geographical) pass; ford (of a river):– passages [4], fords [3], passage [2], ford [1], pass [1]

4570 מַעְגָּל ***maʿgāl***, n.m. GK: 5046 & 5047 [→ 5696]. (rutted) path (of a cart or wagon); (circled) camp, encampment:– paths [6], path [3], trench [3], goings [2], way side (+3027) [1], ways [1]

4571 מָעַד ***māʿad***, v. GK: 5048 [→ 4154]. [Q] to slip, waver, wobble; [Pu] to become lame; [H] cause to wobble, to bend, wrench (one's back):– slip [3], slide [2], make to shake [1]

מוֹעֵד ***mōʿēd***. See 4150.

4572 מַעֲדַי ***maᵃday***, n.pr.m. GK: 5049 [→ 4573; cf. 4153]. Maadai, "*ornaments*":– Maadai [1]

4573 מַעַדְיָה ***maʿadyâ***, n.pr.m. GK: 5050 [→ 4572]. Moadiah, "[perhaps] *Yahweh assembles* or *Yahweh promises*":– Maadiah [1]

4574 מַעֲדַנִּים ***maᵃdannîm***, n.[m.pl.]. GK: 5052 [→ 5727]. delicacy; delight:– dainties [1], delicately (+3807.1) [1], delicately [1], delight [1]

4575 מַעֲדַנּוֹת ***maᵃdannôt***, n.[f.pl.]. GK: 5051 [→ 5727; cf. 6029]. beautiful; some sources: bands, cords used for binding; (adv.) confidently:– sweet influences [1]

4576 מַעְדֵּר ***maʿdēr***, n.[m.]. GK: 5053 [→ 5737]. hoe (to cultivate ground):– mattock [1]

4577 מְעֵה ***mᵉʿēh*** (Aram.), n.[m.]pl. GK: 10435 [cf. 4578]. belly:– belly [1]

4578 מֵעֶה ***mēʿeh***, n.m. GK: 5055 [cf. 4577]. viscera: stomach, heart, bowels, womb; (body as a whole); by extension: of the inner person, the seat of emotions: anguish, tenderness:– bowels [27], belly [3], heart [1], womb [1]

4579 מָעָה ***māʿâ***, n.f. GK: 5054. grain (of sand):– gravel [1]

4580 מָעוֹג ***māʿôg***, n.[m.]. GK: 5056 [→ 5746]. provision, supply; some sources: flat bread:– cake [1], feasts [1]

4581 מָעוֹז ***māʿôz***, n.m. GK: 5057 [cf. 5810]. refuge, stronghold, fortress, place of protection; (used with "head") helmet:– strength [24], fortress [3], strong [2], forces [1], fort [1], most strong [1], rock [1], strengthen [1], strong holds [1], strong hold [1]

4582 מָעוֹךְ ***māʿôk***, n.pr.m. GK: 5059 [cf. 4601]. Maoch, "*poor one*":– Maoch [1]

4583 מָעוֹן ***māʿôn***, n.[m.]. GK: 5060 & 5061 [→ 1010, 1186, 4584, 4585]. dwelling place; help:– habitation [9], dwelling place [3], dwelling [3], den [2], habitations [1], place [1]

4584 מָעוֹן ***māʿôn***, n.pr.m. & g. & loc. GK: 5062 & 5063 [→ 4583]. Maon; Maonite, "*dwelling*":– Maon [7], Maonites [1]

4585 מְעוֹנָה ***mᵉʿônâ***, n.f. GK: 5104 [→ 4583]. hiding place, refuge; dwelling place, (animal) den:– dens [4], den [1], dwelling place [1], habitations [1], places [1], refuge [1]

4586 מְעוּנִים ***mᵉʿûnîm***, n.pr.g. GK: 5064. Meunim, Meunite, "*people of Maon*":– Mehunims [1], Mehunim [1], Meunim [1]

4587 מְעוֹנֹתַי ***mᵉʿônōtay***, n.pr.m. GK: 5065. Meonothai, "*my dwellings*":– Meonothai [1]

4588 מָעוּף ***māʿûp***, n.[m.]. GK: 5066 [→ 4155]. gloom, darkness:– dimness [1]

4589 מָעוֹר ***māʿôr***, n.[m.]. GK: 5067 [→ 5783]. exposed genitals, nakedness:– nakedness [1]

מָעֹז ***māʿōz***. See 4581.

מָעֻז ***māʿuz***. See 4581.

4590 מַעַזְיָה ***maʿazyâ*** or מַעַזְיָהוּ ***maʿazyāhû***, n.pr.m. GK: 5068 & 5069. Maaziah, "*Yahweh is a refuge*":– Maaziah [2]

4591 מָעַט ***māʿaṭ***, v. GK: 5070 [→ 4592]. [Q] to dwindle, decrease, become few; [P] to become few; [H] to let reduce, make diminish, make collect little:– diminished [3], few [3], give less [3], diminish [2], little [2], bring to nothing [1], fewness [1], gathered least [1], gathered little [1], give few [1], less [1], make few in number [1], minished [1], suffereth to decrease [1]

4592 מְעַט ***mᵉʿaṭ***, subst. GK: 5071 [→ 4591]. little (of size), few (of quantity), short (of time):– little [47], few [22], almost (+3509.1) [4], little while [4], small thing [4], by little and little (+4592) [2], small matter [2], small [2], soon (+3509.1) [2], very little while (+4213) [2], almost (+5750) [1], few (+4962) [1], fewer [1], fewest [1], lightly (+3509.1) [1], little worth (+3509.1) [1], some (+3509.1) [1], very little (+6985) [1], very small (+3509.1) [1], very [1]

4593 מָעֹט ***māʿōṭ***, v.ptcp. GK: 6487 [→ 5844]. ptcp. of 5844: grasped, wrapped up:– wrapt up [1]

4594 מַעֲטֶה ***maᵃṭeh***, n.[m.]. GK: 5073 [→ 5844]. garment, mantle, wrap:– garment [1]

4595 מַעֲטֶפֶת ***maᵃṭepet***, n.f. GK: 5074 [→ 5848]. cape, outer garment:– mantles [1]

4596 מְעִי ***mᵉʿî***, n.[m.]. GK: 5075 [→ 5856]. heap (of ruins):– heap [1]

4597 מָעַי ***māʿay***, n.pr.m. GK: 5076. Maai, "*to be compassionate*":– Maai [1]

4598 מְעִיל ***mᵉʿîl***, n.m. GK: 5077. robe, cloak:– robe [17], mantle [7], robes [2], cloke [1], coat [1]

מֵעִים ***mēʿîm***. See 4578.

מְעִין ***mᵉʿîn*** (Aram.). See 4577.

4599 מַעְיָן ***maʿyān***, n.m. GK: 5078 [→ 5869]. spring, fountain, well; by extension: source of life (satisfaction, blessing):– fountain [9], fountains [7], wells [3], springs [2], well [2]

מְעִינַי ***mᵉʿînî***. See 4586.

4600 מָעַךְ ***māʿak***, v. GK: 5080. [Qp] be pressed (into the ground), be crushed, be bruised; [Pu] be fondled:– bruised [1], pressed [1], stuck [1]

4601 מַעֲכָה ***maᵃkâ*** or מַעֲכָת ***maᵃkāt***, n.pr.m. & f. & g. GK: 5081 & 5082 & 5083 [→ 4602; cf. 4582 (also used with compound proper names)]. Maacah, "[perhaps] *dull, stupid*":– Maachah [18], Maacah [3], Maachathites [1]

4602 מַעֲכָתִי ***maᵃkātî***, a.g. GK: 5084 [→ 4601]. Maacathite, of Maacah, "*of Maacah*":– Maachathite [4], Maachathites [3], Maachathi [1]

4603 מָעַל ***mā'al***, v. GK: 5085 [→ 4604]. [Q] to act unfaithfully, break faith, commit a violation:– trespassed [11], transgressed [5], commit a trespass (+4604) [4], committed a trespass (+4604) [3], transgress [2], committed trespass (+4604) [1], committed [1], do a trespass (+4604) [1], done trespass (+4604) [1], transgressed much (+4604) [1], transgressed sore (+4604) [1], transgresseth [1], transgression committed (+4604) [1], trespassing grievously (+4604) [1], trespass [1]

4604 מַעַל ***ma'al***, n.m. GK: 5086 [→ 4603]. unfaithfulness:– trespass [8], transgression [5], commit a trespass (+4603) [4], committed a trespass (+4603) [3], committed trespass (+4603) [1], do a trespass (+4603) [1], done trespass (+4603) [1], falsehood [1], transgressed much (+4603) [1], transgressed sore (+4603) [1], transgression committed (+4603) [1], trespasses [1], trespassing grievously (+4603) [1]

4605 מַעַל ***ma'al***, subst.adv. & pp. GK: 5087 [→ 5927]. above, beyond; this refer to spatial position, to degree, and to time (afterward):– upward (+1886.5) [45], above (+4480) [19], above (+4480+1886.5+3807.1) [18], upward (+1886.5+3807.1) [12], above (+1886.5+3807.1) [6], on high (+1886.5+3807.1) [5], above (+1886.5) [4], above [4], upon (+4480) [4], exceedingly (+1886.5+3807.1) [2], exceedingly (+5704+1886.5+3807.1) [2], forward (+1886.5) [2], still (+1886.5+3807.1) [2], upward (+4480+1886.5+3807.1) [2], very high (+4605+1886.5+1886.5) [2], above (+4480+3807.1) [1], exceeding (+1886.5) [1], exceeding (+1886.5+3807.1) [1], from above (+4480) [1], on high (+4480+1886.5+3807.1) [1], over (+1886.5+3807.1) [1], over (+4480+1886.5+3807.1) [1], over and above (+4480+1886.5 +3807.1) [1], overturned (+2015+1886.5+3807.1) [1], up (+1886.5+3807.1) [1], very (+1886.5+3807.1) [1]

מֵעַל ***mē'al***. See 5921.

4606 מֵעָל ***me'āl*** (Aram.), n.[m.]. GK: 10436 [→ 5954]. going in, (+ 8122) sunset:– going down [1]

4607 מֹעַל ***mō'al***, n.[m.]. GK: 5089 [→ 5927]. lifting (of hands):– lifting up [1]

4608 מַעֲלֶה ***maᵃleh***, n.m. GK: 5090 [→ 5927]. and ascent: hill, mount, (geographical) pass; stairs:– going up [9], ascent [2], chiefest [1], cliff [1], goeth up [1], hill [1], mounting up [1], stairs [1], up [1]

4609 מַעֲלָה ***maᵃlâ***, n.f. GK: 5091 & 5092 [→ 5927]. ascent: steps, stairway, paces; what goes through (or rises into) one's mind:– degrees [24], steps [11], stairs [5], dial [2], go up [1], high degree [1], stories [1], things that come into [1]

4610 מַעֲלֵה עַקְרַבִּים ***maᵃlēh 'aqrabbîm***, n.pr.loc. GK: 5091 + 6832 [→ 4609+6137]. Maaleh-akkrabim, the ascent of Akrabbim (or the Scorpions):– Maaleh-acrabbim [1]

4611 מַעֲלָל ***maᵃlāl***, n.m. GK: 5095 [→ 5953]. deeds, actions, practices, what is done:– doings [35], works [3], inventions [2], endeavours [1]

4612 מַעֲמָד ***maᵃmād***, n.[m.]. GK: 5096 [→ 5975]. attendance, serving; position of attendant:– attendance [2], office [1], place [1], state [1]

4613 מָעֳמָד ***moᵒmād***, n.[m.]. GK: 5097 [→ 5975]. foothold, firm ground:– standing [1]

4614 מַעֲמָסָה ***maᵃmāsâ***, n.f. GK: 5098 [→ 6006]. heavy stone, hard-to-lift rock:– burdensome [1]

4615 מַעֲמַקִּים ***maᵃmaqqîm***, n.m.pl. GK: 5099 [→ 6009]. depths (of waters or seas):– depths [3], deep [2]

4616 מַעַן ***ma'an***, subst.pp.c. GK: 5100 [→ 6031]. for the sake of, on account of, because; therefore, so that:– that (+3807.1) [167], for sake (+3807.1) [45], to (+3807.1) [19], because of (+3807.1) [12], for sakes (+3807.1) [5], for (+3807.1) [4], that (+834+3807.1) [4], to the end (+3807.1) [4], to the end that (+3807.1) [4], for that (+3807.1) [2], to the intent that (+3807.1) [2], lest (+3808+3807.1) [1], therefore (+3807.1) [1], to [1]

4617 מַעֲנֶה ***maᵃneh***, n.m. GK: 5101 & 5102 [→ 6030, 6031]. reply, answer, response; purpose:– answer [7], himself (+1930.2) [1]

4618 מַעֲנָה ***maᵃnâ***, n.f. GK: 5103 [cf. 6031]. furrow, plow path:– acre [1], furrows [1]

מְעֹנָה ***mᵉ'ōnâ***. See 4585.

4619 מַעַץ ***ma'aṣ***, n.pr.m. GK: 5106 [→ 290]. Maaz, "[perhaps] *angry* or *wrath*":– Maaz [1]

4620 מַעֲצֵבָה ***maᵃṣēbâ***, n.f. GK: 5107 [→ 6087]. place of torment, place of pain:– sorrow [1]

4621 מַעֲצָד ***maᵃṣād***, n.[m.]. GK: 5108. chiseling tool (for wood carving); some sources: ax, adze:– axe [1], tongs [1]

4622 מַעְצוֹר ***ma'ṣôr***, n.[m.]. GK: 5109 [→ 6113]. hindrance:– restraint [1]

4623 מַעְצָר ***ma'ṣār***, n.[m.]. GK: 5110 [→ 6113]. self-control:– rule [1]

4624 מַעֲקֶה ***maᵃqeh***, n.[m.]. GK: 5111. parapet, a short wall around the upper level of a house:– battlement [1]

4625 מַעֲקַשִּׁים ***maᵃqaššîm***, n.[m.]. GK: 5112 [→ 6140]. rough places, uneven terrain, rugged country:– crooked things [1]

4626 מַעַר ***ma'ar***, n.[m.]. GK: 5113 [→ 4629]. nakedness; available space:– nakedness [1], proportion [1]

4627 מַעֲרָב ***maᵃrāb***, n.m. GK: 5114 [→ 6148]. wares, goods (for trade, exchange, or barter):– merchandise [5], market [4]

4628 מַעֲרָב ***maᵃrāb***, n.[m.]. GK: 5115 [→ 6150]. west (the place of the sunset):– west [10], westward [2], westward (+1886.1+3807.1) [1], westward (+1886.5) [1]

4629 מַעֲרֶה ***maᵃreh***, n.[m.]. GK: 5116 [→ 4626]. approaches, vicinity:– meadows [1]

4630 מַעֲרָה ***maᵃrâ***, n.f. GK: 5120 [→ 4634, 6186]. var. of 4634: things arranged in a row: battle line, row of army ranks:–

4631 מְעָרָה ***mᵉ'ārâ***, n.f. GK: 5117. cave:– cave [32], caves [3], cave's [1], dens [1], den [1], holes [1]

4632 מְעָרָה ***mᵉ'ārâ***, n.f. GK: 5118 [→ 4638; cf. 6168]. wasteland, bare field:– Mearah [1]

4633 מַעֲרָךְ ***maᵃrāk***, n.[m.]. GK: 5119 [→ 6186]. plan, consideration, arrangement:– preparations [1]

4634 מַעֲרָכָה ***maᵃrākâ***, n.f. GK: 5120 [→ 4630]. things arranged in a row: battle line, row of army ranks; row, layer (of things); by extension: proper arrangement of something fitting and suitable:– army [8], armies [7], fight [1], ordered place [1], rank [1], rows [1], set in order [1]

4635 מַעֲרֶכֶת ***maᵃreket***, n.f. GK: 5121 [→ 6186]. (consecrated) bread set in rows:– shewbread [3], row [2], shewbread (+3899+1886.1) [2], in order [1], shewbread (+3899) [1]

4636 מַעֲרֹם ***maᵃrōm***, n.m. GK: 5122 [→ 6168]. nakedness, naked person:– naked [1]

4637 מַעֲרָצָה ***maᵃrāṣâ***, n.f. GK: 5124 [→ 6206]. terrifying power:– terror [1]

4638 מַעֲרָת ***maᵃrāt***, n.pr.loc. GK: 5125 [→ 4632?; cf. 6168]. Maarath, "*barren*":– Maarath [1]

4639 מַעֲשֶׂה ***maᵃśeh***, n.m. GK: 5126 [→ 4640, 4641; cf. 6213]. work, labor, deed; something made, something done:– work [116], works [73], acts [4], needlework (+7551) [4], art [3], doings [3], labours [3], wrought [3], deeds [2], network (+7568) [2], occupation [2], operation [2], wares of making [2], bakemeats (+644+3978) [1], business [1], deed [1], doing [1], do [1], handywork (+3027) [1], labour [1], possessions [1], purpose [1], things made [1], things offered [1], things that were made [1], well set hair (+4748) [1], working [1], workmanship [1], wrought with needlework (+7551) [1]

4640 מַעְשַׂי ***ma'śay***, n.pr.m. GK: 5127 [→ 4639+3068]. Maasai, "*work of Yahweh*":– Maasiai [1]

4641 מַעֲשֵׂיָה or מַעֲשֵׂיָהוּ ***maᵃśēyâ*** or ***maᵃśēyāhû***, n.pr.m. GK: 5128 & 5129 [→ 4639+3068; cf. 6213]. Maaseiah, "*Yahweh is a refuge*":– Maaseiah [23]

4642 מַעֲשַׁקּוֹת ***maᵃšaqqôt***, n.f. GK: 5131 [→ 6229]. (col.pl) extortion:– oppressions [1], oppressor [1]

4643 מַעֲשֵׂר ***maᵃśēr***, n.m. GK: 5130 [→ 6237]. tithe, setting aside a tenth:– tithes [16], tithe [11], tenth part [2], tenth [2], tithing [1]

4644 מֹף ***mōp***, n.pr.loc. GK: 5132 [cf. 5297]. Moph = Memphis:– Memphis [1]

מְפִבֹשֶׁת ***mᵉpibōšet***. See 4648.

4645 מִפְגָּע ***mipgā'***, n.[m.]. GK: 5133 [→ 6293]. target:– mark [1]

4646 מַפָּח ***mappāḥ***, n.[m.]. GK: 5134 [→ 5301]. (a dying) gasp, exhaling (of soul), with an implication of despair and affliction:– giving up of the ghost (+5315) [1]

4647 מַפֻּחַ ***mappuaḥ***, n.m. GK: 5135 [→ 5301]. bellows:– bellows [1]

4648 מְפִיבֹשֶׁת ***mᵉpîbōšet*** or מְפִי־בֹשֶׁת ***mᵉpî-bōšet***, n.pr.m. GK: 5136 [→ 4480+6310+1322]. Mephibosheth, "*from the mouth of Shame* [a derogatory name for Baal]":– Mephibosheth [15]

4649 מֻפִּים ***muppîm***, n.pr.m. GK: 5137. Muppim:– Muppim [1]

4650 מֵפִיץ ***mēpîṣ***, n.m. GK: 5138 [→ 6327]. war club:– maul [1]

4651 מַפָּל ***mappāl***, n.m. GK: 5139 [→ 4654; cf. 5307]. sweepings, waste, refuse (of wheat); (fleshy) folds (of the leviathan):– flakes [1], refuse [1]

4652 מִפְלָאוֹת ***miplā'ôt***, n.f.[pl.]. GK: 5140 [→ 6381]. wonders, marvelous works:– wondrous works [1]

4653 מִפְלַגָּה ***miplaggâ***, n.f. GK: 5141 [→ 6385]. division (of family groups), subgroup of a clan:– divisions [1]

4654 מַפָּלָה ***mappālâ*** or מַפֵּלָה ***mappēlâ***, n.f. GK: 5142 & 5143 [→ 4651; cf. 5307]. ruin, heap of rubble:– ruin [2], ruinous [1]

4655 מִפְלָט ***miplāṭ***, n.[m.]. GK: 5144 [→ 6403]. place of shelter, refuge, escape:– escape [1]

4656 מִפְלֶצֶת ***mipleṣet***, n.f. GK: 5145 [→ 6426]. repulsive image, disgraceful (idol):– idol [4]

4657 מִפְלָשׂ ***miplāś***, n.[m.]. GK: 5146. floating, hovering (clouds):– balancings [1]

4658 מַפֶּלֶת ***mappelet***, n.f. GK: 5147 [→ 5307]. downfall, collapse; (something downfallen) a shipwreck; carcass:– fall [5], ruin [2], carcase [1]

4659 מִפְעָל ***mip'āl*** or מִפְעָלָה ***mip'ālâ***, n.m. & f. GK: 5148 & 5149 [→ 6466]. deed, work:– works [3]

4660 מַפָּץ ***mappāṣ***, n.[m.]. GK: 5150 [→ 5310]. shattering, wrecking (weapon), implying death will follow its effective use:– slaughter [1]

4661 מַפֵּץ ***mappēṣ***, n.m. GK: 5151 [→ 5310]. war club:– battle axe [1]

4662 מִפְקָד ***mipqād***, n.m. & pr.loc. GK: 5152 [→ 4663, 6485]. appointment (by a king); number, counting (of the people); Inspection (Gate):– number [2], Miphkad [1], appointed place [1], commandment [1]

4663 מִפְקָד ***mipqād***, n.pr.loc. GK: 5152 [→ 4662]. same as 4662: Miphkad, "Inspection (Gate)":–

4664 מִפְרָץ ***mipraṣ***, n.[m.]. GK: 5153 [→ 6555]. cove, inlet, landing-place:– breaches [1]

4665 מַפְרֶקֶת ***mapreqet***, n.f. GK: 5154 [→ 6561]. neck:– neck [1]

4666 מִפְרָשׂ ***miprāś***, n.[m.]. GK: 5155 [→ 6566]. spreading (used of clouds and canvas sail):– spreadings [1], which spreadest forth [1]

4667 מִפְשָׂעָה ***mipśā'â***, n.f. GK: 5156 [cf. 6585]. buttocks, posterior area:– buttocks [1]

מֹפֵת ***mōpēt***. See 4159.

4668 מַפְתֵּחַ ***maptēaḥ***, n.m. GK: 5158 [→ 6605]. key:– key [2], opening [1]

4669 מִפְתָּח ***miptāḥ***, n.[m.]. GK: 5157 [→ 6605]. opening (of lips):– opening [1]

4670 מִפְתָּן ***miptān***, n.[m.]. GK: 5159 [cf. 6596]. threshold:– threshold [8]

4671 מֹץ ***mōṣ***, n.m. GK: 5161. chaff:– chaff [8]

4672 מָצָא ***māṣā'***, v. GK: 5162. [Q] to find, find out, discover, uncover; [N] to be found out; be caught; [H] to hand over, present; to bring upon, cause to encounter; "to find favor in the eyes" means to "be please":– found [261], find [82], present [17], find out [16], findeth [12], come upon [5], found out [5], befallen [3], met [3], presented [3], certainly found (+4672) [2], findest [2], finding [2], get [2], gotten [2], here [2], hit [2], left [2], meet [2], suffice [2], able (+1767+3027) [1], able to bring (+1767+3027) [1], befall [1], befell [1], came to hand [1], came to [1], catch [1], cause to find [1], causeth to come [1], come on [1], come unto [1], cometh [1], delivered [1], deliver [1], enough [1], find occasion [1], foundest [1], gat hold upon [1], hath (+3807.1) [1], lighted on [1], ligheth upon [1], occasion serve (+3027) [1], ready [1], received [1], redeem (+1353) [1], sped [1], sufficed [1], taken hold on [1]

מֹצָא ***mōṣā'***. See 4161.

4673 מַצָּב ***maṣṣāb***, n.m. GK: 5163 [→ 4675; cf. 5324]. standing place; office; outpost, garrison:– garrison [7], stood [2], station [1]

4674 מֻצָּב ***muṣṣāb***, n.[m.]. GK: 5164 [→ 5324]. pillar, tower:– mount [1]

4675 מַצָּבָה ***maṣṣābâ*** or מִצָּבָה ***miṣṣābâ***, n.f. GK: 5165 & 5166 [→ 4673, 5324]. guard, watch, outpost, garrison of soldiers on the perimeter of a guarded area:– army [1], garrison [1]

4676 מַצֵּבָה ***maṣṣēbâ***, n.f. GK: 5167 [→ 4678; cf. 5324]. sacred (upright) stone, stone pillar:– images [13], pillar [9], image [4], pillars [2], garrisons [1], standing images [1], standing image [1]

4677 מְצֹבָיָה ***m^{e}ṣōbāyâ***, a.g. GK: 5168. Mezobaite:– Mesobaite [1]

4678 מַצֶּבֶת ***maṣṣebet***, n.f. GK: 5169 & 5170 [→ 4676, 5324]. (tree) stump; sacred (upright) stone, stone pillar:– pillar [5], substance [2]

4679 מְצַד ***m^{e}ṣād***, n.f. GK: 5171 [→ 6679; cf. 4686]. stronghold, fortress (with difficult access):– strong holds [5], hold [2], castle [1], forts [1], holds [1], munitions [1]

מְצָדָה ***m^{e}ṣudā***. See 4686.

4680 מָצָה ***māṣâ***, v. GK: 5172 [cf. 4711]. [Q] to squeeze out; to drain dry; [N] to be drained out:– wrung out [4], suck out [1], wring out [1], wringed [1]

4681 מֹצָה ***mōṣâ***, n.pr.loc. GK: 5173. Mozah:– Mozah [1]

4682 מַצָּה ***maṣṣâ***, n.f. GK: 5174 [cf. 4711?]. unleavened bread, bread made without yeast; bread quickly made, without waiting for the dough to rise:– unleavened bread [34], unleavened [18], without leaven [1]

4683 מַצָּה ***maṣṣâ***, n.f. GK: 5175 [→ 5327]. quarrel, strife:– contention [1], debate [1], strife [1]

4684 מִצְהָלוֹת ***miṣhālôt***, n.f.[pl.]. GK: 5177 [→ 6670]. neighing:– neighings [1], neighing [1]

4685 מָצוֹד ***māṣôd*** or מְצוֹדָה ***m^{e}ṣôdâ***, n.m. & f. GK: 5178 & 5179 & 5182 & 5183 [→ 6679]. fortress, prison (a place difficult to access); plunder; stronghold; (hunting) snare, net:– net [2], bulwarks [1], holds [1], munition [1], snares [1]

4686 מְצוּדָה ***m^{e}ṣûdâ***, n.f. GK: 5180 & 5181 [→ 6679; cf. 4679]. stronghold, fortress, prison (a place difficult to access); (hunting) snare, net; prey:– fortress [6], hold [6], net [2], snare [2], castle [1], defence [1], fort [1], hunted [1], strong hold [1], strong place [1]

4687 מִצְוָה ***miṣwâ***, n.f. GK: 5184 [→ 6680]. command, order, prescription, instruction:– commandments [130], commandment [43], precepts [3], commanded [2], law [1], ordinances [1], precept [1]

4688 מְצוֹלָה ***m^{e}ṣôlâ*** or מְצֻלָה ***m^{e}ṣulâ***, n.f. GK: 5185 & 5198 [→ 4699, 6683]. depths, the deep:– deep [5], deeps [3], depths [2], bottom [1]

4689 מָצוֹק ***māṣôq***, n.[m.]. GK: 5186 [→ 4691; cf. 6693]. distress, suffering, stress, hardship:– straitness [4], anguish [1], distress [1]

4690 מָצוּק ***māṣûq***, n.m. GK: 5187 [→ 3332?]. foundation, pillar, support:– pillars [1], situate [1]

4691 מְצוּקָה ***m^{e}ṣûqâ***, n.f. GK: 5188 [→ 4689; cf. 6693]. distress, anguish, stress, affliction:– distresses [5], anguish [1], distress [1]

4692 מָצוֹר ***māṣôr***, n.[m.]. GK: 5189 & 5190 [→ 4694; cf. 6696]. stronghold, fortification, defense; siege; siege works, ramparts:– siege [13], besieged (+871.1+1886.1) [2], besieged (+935+871.1+1886.1) [2], strong [2], bulwarks [1], defence [1], fenced [1], fortress [1], strong hold [1], tower [1]

4693 מָצוֹר ***māṣôr***, n.pr.loc. GK: 5191 [→ 4714]. Egypt:– besieged [2], defence [1], fortified [1], fortress [1]

4694 מְצוּרָה ***m^{e}ṣûrâ*** or מַצָּרָה ***maṣṣārâ***, n.f. GK: 5193 & 5211 [→ 4692, 5341; cf. 6696]. fortification, defense, fortress; guard, watch:– fenced [5], forts [1], munition [1], strong holds [1]

4695 מַצּוּת ***maṣṣût***, n.f. GK: 5194 [→ 5327]. enemy, person of strife:– contended with [1]

4696 מֵצַח ***mēṣaḥ***, n.m. GK: 5195 [→ 4697; cf. 6705?]. forehead:– forehead [9], foreheads [2], brow [1], impudent (+2389) [1]

4697 מִצְחָה ***miṣḥâ***, n.f. GK: 5196 [→ 4696; cf. 6705?]. greaves (armor for the front or back of leg from ankle to knee):– greaves [1]

מְצֹלָה ***m^{e}ṣōlâ***. See 4688.

מְצֻלָה ***m^{e}ṣulâ***. See 4688.

4698 מְצִלָּה ***m^{e}ṣillâ***, n.f. GK: 5197 [→ 6750]. (small) bell (on a horse):– bells [1]

4699 מְצֻלָּה ***m^{e}ṣullâ***, n.f. GK: 5185 [→ 4688]. same as 4688: depths, the deep:– bottom [1]

4700 מְצִלְתַּיִם ***m^{e}ṣiltayim***, n.f.du. GK: 5199 [→ 6750]. (pair of) cymbals:– cymbals [13]

4701 מִצְנֶפֶת ***miṣnepet***, n.f. GK: 5200 [→ 6801]. turban, headband:– mitre [11], diadem [1]

4702 מַצָּע ***maṣṣā'***, n.m. GK: 5201 [→ 3331]. bed, couch:– bed [1]

4703 מִצְעָד ***miṣ'ād***, n.[m.]. GK: 5202 [→ 6805]. step; (position of submission in a) train:– steps [2], goings [1]

4704 מִצְּעִירָה ***miṣṣ^e'îrâ***, a. GK: 5203 [→ 4705, 6819]. form of 4705: small, little, lowly:– little [1]

4705 מִצְעָר ***miṣ'ār***, n.m. GK: 5203 [→ 4704]. small quantity, few:– little one [2], small [2], little while [1]

4706 מִצְעָר ***miṣ'ār***, n.pr.loc. GK: 5204 [→ 6819]. Mizar, "*small*":– Mizar [1]

4707 מִצְפֶּה ***miṣpeh***, n.m. GK: 5205 [→ 4708, 4709; cf. 6822]. watchtower (used for military defense and surveillance), any place that overlooks:– watch tower [1], watchtower [1]

4708 מִצְפֶּה ***miṣpeh***, n.pr.loc. GK: 5206 [→ 4707; cf. 6822]. Mizpah, "*lookout point*":– Mizpeh [9], Mizpah [5]

4709 מִצְפָּה ***miṣpâ***, n.pr.loc. GK: 5207 [→ 4707; cf. 6822]. Mizpah, "*lookout point*":– Mizpah [18], Mizpeh [14]

4710 מַצְפּוֹן ***maṣpôn***, n.[m.]. GK: 5208 [→ 6845]. hidden treasure, hiding place:– hid things [1]

4711 מָצַץ ***māṣaṣ***, v. GK: 5209 [cf. 4680?]. [Q] to drink deeply, quaff:– milk out [1]

מֻצָּקָה ***muṣāqâ***. See 4166.

4712 מֵצַר ***mēṣar***, n.[m.]. GK: 5210 [→ 3334]. anguish, distress, hardship:– distress [1], pains [1], straits [1]

מָצֻק ***māṣuq***. See 4690.

מְצֻקָה ***m***^e^***ṣuqâ***. See 4691.

מְצֻרָה ***m***^e^***ṣurâ***. See 4694.

4713 מִצְרִי ***miṣrî***, a.g. GK: 5212 [→ 4714]. Egyptian:– Egyptian [16], Egyptians [5], Egyptian's [4], Egyptian (+376) [1], Egyptian (+376+1886.1) [1], Egypt [1], of Egypt [1]

4714 מִצְרַיִם ***miṣrayim***, n.pr.loc. & g. GK: 5213 [→ 67, 4693, 4713]. Mizraim; Egypt, Egyptian:– Egypt [585], Egyptians [90], Mizraim [4], Egyptian [2], Egyptians (+1121) [1]

4715 מַצְרֵף ***maṣrēp***, n.[m.]. GK: 5214 [→ 6884]. crucible, melting pot for metal:– fining pot [2]

4716 מַק ***maq***, n.m. GK: 5215 [→ 4743]. stench, smell of decay:– rottenness [1], stink [1]

4717 מַקֶּבֶת ***maqqebet***, n.f. GK: 5216 [→ 5344]. hammer:– hammers [2], hammer [2]

4718 מַקֶּבֶת ***maqqebet***, n.f. GK: 5217 [→ 5344]. quarry:– hole [1]

4719 מַקֵּדָה ***maqqēdâ***, n.pr.loc. GK: 5218 [→ 5348]. Makkedah, "*locality of shepherds*":– Makkedah [9]

4720 מִקְדָּשׁ ***miqdāš***, n.m. GK: 5219 [→ 6942]. holy place, sanctuary, shrine:– sanctuary [64], sanctuaries [5], holy places [2], chapel [1], hallowed [1], holy place [1]

4721 מַקְהֵל ***maqhēl***, n.[m.]. GK: 5220 [→ 6951]. assembly, congregation:– congregations [2]

4722 מַקְהֵלֹת ***maqhēlôt***, n.pr.loc. GK: 5221 [→ 6951]. Makheloth, "*assemblies*":– Makheloth [2]

4723 מִקְוֶה ***miqweh***, n.[m.]. GK: 5223 & 5224 [→ 6960]. hope; collection (of water), reservoir; other sources: linen yarn:– hope [4], linen yarn [4], abiding [1], gathering together [1], plenty [1], pools [1]

4724 מִקְוָה ***miqwâ***, n.f. GK: 5225 [→ 6960]. reservoir:– ditch [1]

4725 מָקוֹם ***māqôm***, n.m. GK: 5226 [→ 6965]. place, site:– place [370], places [20], home [3], room [3], whithersoever (+834) [2], country [1], open [1], space [1]

4726 מָקוֹר ***māqôr***, n.m. GK: 5227 [→ 6979]. fountain, spring, source (of a flow), often with an implication of abundance or freshness:– fountain [11], spring [2], wellspring [2], issue [1], springs [1], well [1]

4727 מִקָּח ***miqqāḥ***, n.[m.]. GK: 5228 [→ 3947]. taking, accepting (a bribe):– taking [1]

4728 מַקָּחוֹת ***maqqāḥôt***, n.f. GK: 5229 [→ 3947]. (pl.) merchandise, wares:– ware [1]

4729 מִקְטָר ***miqṭār***, n.m. GK: 5230 [→ 6999]. burning:– burn [1]

מְקַטְּרָה ***m***^e^***qaṭṭ***^e^***râ***. See 6999.

4730 מִקְטֶרֶת ***miqṭeret***, n.f. GK: 5233 [→ 6999]. censer, incense burner:– censer [2]

4731 מַקֵּל ***maqqēl***, n.m. & f. GK: 5234. branch, stick; staff, a stick used to assist in walking, discipline, and guidance; war club:– staff [7], rods [6], rod [2], staves [2], handstaves (+3027) [1]

4732 מִקְלוֹת ***miqlôt***, n.pr.m. GK: 5235. Mikloth, "*rods*":– Mikloth [4]

4733 מִקְלָט ***miqlāṭ***, n.[m.]. GK: 5236 [→ 7038]. refuge, place of protection:– refuge [20]

4734 מִקְלַעַת ***miqla'at***, n.f. GK: 5237 [→ 7049]. carving, engraving (on wood):– carved figures (+6603) [1], carved [1], carvings [1], gravings [1]

מָקֹם ***māqōm***. See 4725.

מְקֹמָה ***m***^e^***qōmâ***. See 4725.

4735 מִקְנֶה ***miqneh***, n.m. GK: 5238 [→ 4737; cf. 7069]. livestock, (animals from) herds and flocks:– cattle [61], flocks [3], possession [3], possessions [2], substance [2], flocks (+6629) [1], herds [1], purchase [1], trade about cattle (+376) [1], trade to feed cattle (+376) [1]

4736 מִקְנָה ***miqnâ***, n.f. GK: 5239 [→ 7069]. something bought, purchased, acquisition:– bought [5], purchase [5], price [2], possession [1], that is bought [1], that were bought [1]

4737 מִקְנֵיָהוּ ***miqnēyāhû***, n.pr.m. GK: 5240 [→ 4735+3068; cf. 7069]. Mikneiah, "*Yahweh acquires*":– Mikneiah [2]

4738 מִקְסָם ***miqsām***, n.[m.]. GK: 5241 [→ 7080]. divination:– divination [2]

4739 מָקַץ ***māqaṣ***, n.pr.loc. GK: 5242. Makaz:– Makaz [1]

4740 מִקְצוֹעַ ***miqṣôa'***, n.m. GK: 5243 [→ 4742]. corner (of a base); angle of a wall:– corners [5], turning [5], every corner (+4740) [2]

4741 מַקְצֻעָה ***maqṣu'â***, n.[f.]. GK: 5244 [→ 7106]. (wood) chisel:– planes [1]

4742 מְקֻצְעָה ***m***^e^***quṣ'â***, v.ptcp. GK: 7910 [→ 4740, 7106]. ptcp. of 7106: made with corners:– corners [2]

4743 מָקַק ***māqaq***, v. GK: 5245 [→ 4716]. [N] to rot, waste away, fester; dissolve; [H] to cause to rot:– consume away [4], pine away [4], corrupt [1], dissolved [1]

מָקֹר ***māqōr***. See 4726.

4744 מִקְרָא ***miqrā'***, n.m. GK: 5246 [→ 7121]. assembly, calling the community together, usually for a religious ceremony:– convocation [16], convocations [3], assemblies [2], calling [1], reading [1]

4745 מִקְרֶה ***miqreh***, n.m. GK: 5247 [→ 7136]. happening by chance; fate, destiny:– befalleth [3], event [3], chance [1], happeneth [1], hap [1], something befallen [1]

4746 מְקָרֶה ***m***^e^***qāreh***, n.[m.]. GK: 5248 [→ 6982]. rafters, roof beams:– building [1]

4747 מְקֵרָה ***m***^e^***qērâ***, n.f. GK: 5249 [→ 6979]. coolness; cool room, summer home:– summer [2]

מֹקֵשׁ ***mōqēš***. See 4170.

4748 מִקְשֶׁה ***miqšeh***, n.[m.]. GK: 5250 [→ 4749]. well-dressed hair:– well set hair (+4639) [1]

4749 מִקְשָׁה ***miqšâ***, n.f. GK: 5251 [→ 4748]. hammered work; some sources: embossed metal work:– beaten work [6], beaten out of one piece [1], beaten [1], upright [1], whole piece [1]

4750 מִקְשָׁה ***miqšâ***, n.f. GK: 5252 [→ 7180]. melon field, cucumber field:– garden of cucumbers [1]

4751 מַר ***mar*** or מָרָה ***mārâ***, a. & subst. GK: 5253 & 5287 [cf. 4843]. bitter; bitterness, ranging from being merely disagreeable to the taste to being poisonous; by extension: anxiety, despair:– bitter [21], bitterness [9], bitterly [3], angry (+5315) [1], chafed [1], discontented (+5315) [1], great bitterness (+4843) [1], heavy [1]

4752 מַר ***mar***, n.[m.]. GK: 5254. drop (in a bucket):– drop [1]

4753 מֹר ***mōr***, n.m. GK: 5255 [→ 4843]. myrrh:– myrrh [12]

4754 מָרָא ***mārā'***, v. GK: 5256 & 5257 [cf. 4784]. [Q] to flap, spread the feathers as it runs; this can also refer to the feet kicking up dirt; [Ho] to be obstinate:– filthy [1], lifteth up [1]

4755 מָרָא ***mārā'***, n.pr.f. GK: 5259 [→ 4843]. Mara, "*bitter*":– Mara [1]

4756 מָרֵא ***mārē'*** (Aram.), n.m. GK: 10437. lord; (of God) the Lord; "Lord of kings" is one who is an authority over any and all other authorities:– Lord/lord [4]

מֹרָא ***mōrā'***. See 4172.

4757 מְרֹדַךְ־בַּלְאֲדָן ***m***^e^***rōdak-bal***^a^***dān***, n.pr.m. GK: 5282 [→ 4781+1081; cf. 1255]. Merodach-Baladan, "*Marduk has given a son*":– Merodach-baladan [1]

4758 מַרְאֶה ***mar'eh***, n.m. GK: 5260 [→ 7200]. what is seen with the eye, appearance; by extension: vision, supernatural revelation with a focus on visual communication, but can include verbal content:– appearance [33], vision [11], sight [10], countenance [9], favoured [8], in sight [8], look upon [4], appearances [2], countenances [2], fair (+2896) [2], apparently [1], appeareth [1], beautiful (+2896) [1], beauty [1], form [1], goodly [1], look on [1], look to [1], looketh (+5869) [1], pattern [1], saw [1], seem [1], see [1], visage [1]

4759 מַרְאָה ***mar'â***, n.f. GK: 5261 & 5262 [→ 7200]. vision; mirror:– vision [6], visions [5], looking-glasses [1]

4760 מֻרְאָה ***mur'â***, n.f. GK: 5263 [cf. 4784]. crop (of a bird):– crop [1]

מְראוֹן ***m***^e^***r'ôn***. See 8112.

4761 מַרְאֲשׁוֹת ***m***^e^***ra***^a^***šôt***, n.[f.]pl.den. GK: 5265 [→ 4762, 4763]. same as 4763: head rest, place near the head, headship:– principalities [1]

4762 מָרֵשָׁה ***mārēšâ***, n.pr.m. & loc. GK: 5358 & 5359 [→ 4761, 4763]. Mareshah, "[perhaps] *head place*":– Mareshah [8]

4763 מְרַאֲשׁוֹת ***m***^e^***ra***^a^***šôt***, n.[f.]pl.den. GK: 5265 [→ 4761]. same as 4761: head rest, place near the head:– bolster [6], pillows [2], head [1]

4764 מֵרַב ***mērab***, n.pr.f. GK: 5266 [→ 7231]. Merab, "*abundant*":– Merab [3]

4765 מַרְבַד ***marbad***, n.[m.]. GK: 5267 [→ 7234]. covering:– coverings of tapestry [2]

4766 מַרְבֶּה ***marbeh***, n.[m.]. GK: 5269 [→ 7235]. abundance, increase:– great [1], increase [1]

4767 מִרְבָּה ***mirbâ***, n.f. GK: 5268 [→ 7235]. so much:– much [1]

Heb

4768 מַרְבִּית ***marbît***, n.f. GK: 5270 [→ 7235]. great number; most, majority; profit:– increase [2], greatest part [1], greatness [1], multitude [1]

4769 מַרְבֵּץ ***marbēṣ***, n.[m.]. GK: 5271 [→ 7257]. lair, resting place, place to lie down:– couching place [1], place to lie down in [1]

4770 מַרְבֵּק ***marbēq***, n.[m.]. GK: 5272. fattening (of a calf):– stall [2], fatted [1], fat [1]

מֹרַג ***mōrag***. See 4173.

4771 מַרְגּוֹעַ ***margôaʿ***, n.[m.]. GK: 5273 [→ 7280]. resting place:– rest [1]

4772 מַרְגְּלוֹת ***margᵉlôt***, n.[f.]pl.den. GK: 5274 [→ 7272]. (place of) the feet:– feet [5]

4773 מַרְגֵּמָה ***margēmâ***, n.f. GK: 5275 [→ 7275]. sling:– sling [1]

4774 מַרְגֵּעָה ***margēʿâ***, n.f. GK: 5276 [→ 7280]. place of repose, resting-place:– refreshing [1]

4775 מָרַד ***mārad***, v. GK: 5277 [→ 4777, 4778?, 4780]. [Q] to rebel, revolt:– rebelled [12], rebel [8], rebellest [2], rebel against [1], rebellious [1], rebels [1]

4776 מְרַד ***mᵉrad*** (Aram.), n.[m.]. GK: 10438 [→ 4779; cf. 4777]. rebellion:– rebellion [1]

4777 מֶרֶד ***mered***, n.[m.]. GK: 5278 [→ 4778; cf. 4775; cf. 4776]. rebellion:– rebellion [1]

4778 מֶרֶד ***mered***, n.pr.m. GK: 5279 [→ 4777?; cf. 4775]. Mered, "*rebel*":– Mered [2]

4779 מָרָד ***mārād*** (Aram.), a. GK: 10439 [→ 4776]. rebellious:– rebellious [2]

4780 מַרְדּוּת ***mardût***, n.f. GK: 5280 [→ 4775]. rebellion, revolt:– rebellious [1]

4781 מְרֹדָךְ ***mᵉrōdāk***, n.pr. GK: 5281 [→ 4757, 4782]. Marduk, Merodak (pagan god):– Merodach [1]

4782 מָרְדֳּכַי ***mordᵒkay***, n.pr.m. GK: 5283 [→ 4781]. Mordecai, "*Marduk*":– Mordecai [58], Mordecai's [2]

4783 מֻרְדָּף ***murdāp***, n.f. & m. GK: 5284 [→ 7291]. aggression:– persecuted [1]

4784 מָרָה ***mārâ***, v. GK: 5286 [→ 3236, 4805, 4812?, 4850; cf. 4754, 4760]. [Q] to rebel, defy, become disobedient; some: to be bitter; [H] to act as a rebel, defy by one's action:– rebelled [14], rebellious [9], provoked [4], rebel [4], disobedient [2], grievously rebelled (+4784) [2], provoke [2], bitter [1], changed [1], disobeyed [1], provocation [1], provoking [1], rebelled against [1], rebels [1]

4785 מָרָה ***mārâ***, n.pr.f. GK: 5288 [→ 4796; cf. 4843]. Marah, "*bitter*":– Marah [5]

מֹרֶה ***mōreh***. See 4175.

4786 מֹרָה ***mōrâ***, n.f. GK: 5289 [→ 4843]. bitterness, grief:– grief [1]

4787 מָרָּה ***morrâ***, n.f. GK: 5285 [→ 4843]. bitterness:– bitterness [1]

4788 מָרוּד ***mārûd***, n.[m.]. GK: 5291 [→ 7300]. wandering; wanderer; homeless, with a focus on poverty:– cast out [1], miseries [1], misery [1]

4789 מֵרוֹז ***mērôz***, n.pr.loc. GK: 5292. Meroz:– Meroz [1]

4790 מָרוֹחַ ***mārôaḥ***, n.[m.]. GK: 5293 [→ 4799]. damaged (by pounding or grinding):– broken [1]

4791 מָרוֹם ***mārôm***, n.m. GK: 5294 [→ 7311]. heights, (place) on high, being in an elevated position; by extension: pride, haughtiness, arrogance, an improperly high opinion of oneself; exaltation, high in honor and status:– high [16], on high [11], height [9], above [4], high places [4], dignity [1], far above [1], haughty [1], heights [1], high ones [1], highest places (+1610) [1], loftily (+4480) [1], on high (+871.1+1886.1) [1], upward [1], very high (+5704) [1]

4792 מֵרוֹם ***mērôm***, n.pr.loc. GK: 5295 [→ 7311]. Merom, "*high place*":– Merom [2]

4793 מֵרוֹץ ***mērôṣ***, n.[m.]. GK: 5296 [→ 7323]. foot race, running:– race [1]

4794 מְרוּצָה ***mᵉrûṣâ***, n.f. GK: 5297 [→ 7323]. manner or mode of running; course of a race:– course [2], running [2]

4795 מְרוּקִים ***mᵉrûqîm***, n.[m.]. GK: 5299 [→ 4838]. beauty treatments (including massage and ointments):– purifications [1]

מְרוֹר ***mᵉrôr***. See 4844.

מְרוֹרָה ***mᵉrôrâ***. See 4846.

4796 מָרוֹת ***mārôt***, n.pr.loc. GK: 5300 [→ 4785; cf. 4843]. Maroth, "*bitterness*":– Maroth [1]

4797 מַרְזֵחַ ***marzēaḥ***, n.m. GK: 5301 [→ 4798]. same as 4798: funeral meal; cultic feast:– banquet [1]

4798 מַרְזֵחַ ***marzēaḥ***, n.m. GK: 5301 [→ 4797]. same as 4797: funeral meal; cultic feast:– mourning [1]

4799 מָרַח ***māraḥ***, v. GK: 5302 [→ 4790]. [Q] to apply by spreading on or rubbing in:– lay for a plaister [1]

4800 מֶרְחָב ***merḥāb***, n.[m.]. GK: 5303 [→ 4800+3050; cf. 7337]. spaciousness, wideness, with the associative meaning that such a wide area is comfortable, and possibly safe and free:– large place [4], breadth [1], large room [1]

4801 מֶרְחָק ***merḥāq***, n.m. GK: 5305 [→ 7368]. distance, far away:– far [11], afar off (+4480) [2], afar [1], far countries [1], far off (+4480) [1], far off [1], very far off [1]

4802 מַרְחֶשֶׁת ***marḥešet***, n.f. GK: 5306 [→ 7370]. cooking pan (with a lid):– fryingpan [2]

4803 מָרַט ***māraṭ***, v. GK: 5307 [→ 4178]. [Q] to pull out (hair); [Qp] to be polished, rubbed; [N] to lose one's hair, become bald; [Pu] to be polished, burnished, smooth (skinned):– furbished [5], hair fallen off [2], bright [1], peeled [1], plucked off hair [1], pluckt off hair [1], pluckt off [1]

4804 מְרַט ***mᵉraṭ*** (Aram.), v. GK: 10440 [cf. 4178]. [Peil] to be torn off, plucked out:– pluckt [1]

4805 מְרִי ***mᵉrî***, n.m. GK: 5308 [→ 4784]. rebellion; some: bitter:– rebellious [17], rebellion [4], bitter [1], rebels (+1121) [1]

4806 מְרִיא ***mᵉrîʾ***, n.[m.]. GK: 5309 [→ 1254, 1274, 1277, 4471?, 4813?]. fattened animal (choice for consumption):– fat cattle [3], fatlings [2], fat beasts [1], fatling [1], fed beasts [1]

4807 מְרִיב בַּעַל ***mᵉrîb baʿal***, n.pr.m. GK: 5311 [→ 1167; cf. 4810]. Merib-Baal, "*Baal contends*":– Merib-baal [3]

4808 מְרִיבָה ***mᵉrîbâ***, n.f. GK: 5312 [→ 4809; cf. 7378]. quarreling, strife; rebellion, with a focus on the feelings of enmity:– strife [5], provocation [1]

4809 מְרִיבָה ***mᵉrîbâ***, n.pr.loc. GK: 5313 [→ 4808; cf. 7378]. Meribah:– Meribah [6], Meribah-Kadesh [1]

4810 מְרִי־בַעַל ***mᵉrî-baʿal***, n.pr.m. GK: 5314 [→ 1167; cf. 4807]. Merib-Baal, "*Baal contends*":– Merib-baal [1]

4811 מְרָיָה ***mᵉrāyâ***, n.pr.m. GK: 5316. Meraiah, "*loved by Yahweh*":– Meraiah [1]

מֹרִיָּה ***mōrîâ***. See 4179.

4812 מְרָיוֹת ***mᵉrāyôt***, n.pr.m. GK: 5318 [→ 4784?]. Meraioth, "*rebellious*":– Meraioth [7]

4813 מִרְיָם ***miryām***, n.pr.f. & m. GK: 5319 [→ 4806?]. Miriam, "[variously] *bitterness; plump one; wished-for child; one who loves or is loved*":– Miriam [15]

4814 מְרִירוּת ***mᵉrîrût***, n.f. GK: 5320 [→ 4843]. bitterness:– bitterness [1]

4815 מְרִירִי ***mᵉrîrî***, a. GK: 5321 [→ 4843]. bitter, in context referring to something deadly:– bitter [1]

4816 מֹרֶךְ ***mōrek***, n.[m.]. GK: 5322 [→ 7401]. fearfulness, despondency:– faintness [1]

4817 מֶרְכָּב ***merkāb***, n.m. GK: 5323 [→ 7392]. seat, saddle, chariot:– chariots [1], covering [1], saddle [1]

4818 מֶרְכָּבָה ***merkābâ***, n.f. GK: 5324 [→ 7392]. chariot:– chariot [23], chariots [21]

4819 מַרְכֹּלֶת ***markōlet***, n.f. GK: 5326 [→ 7402]. marketplace, place of merchandising:– merchandise [1]

4820 מִרְמָה ***mirmâ***, n.f. GK: 5327 [→ 4821; cf. 7411]. deceit, deception, dishonesty, treachery:– deceit [19], deceitful [8], false [2], guile [2], craft [1], deceitfully (+3807.1) [1], deceitfully (+871.1) [1], deceitfully [1], deceits [1], feigned [1], subtilty [1], treachery [1]

4821 מִרְמָה ***mirmâ***, n.pr.m. GK: 5328 [→ 4820?; cf. 7411?]. Mirmah, "*deceit*":– Mirma [1]

4822 מְרֵמוֹת ***mᵉrēmôt***, n.pr.m. GK: 5329. Meremoth, "*elevations*":– Meremoth [6]

4823 מִרְמָס ***mirmās***, n.[m.]. GK: 5330 [→ 7429]. trampling down, running over:– trodden down [3], that which trodden [1], tread down (+7760) [1], treading [1], trodden under foot [1]

4824 מֵרֹנֹתִי ***mērōnōtî***, a.g. GK: 5331. Meronothite, of Meronoth, "*of Meronoth*":– Meronothite [2]

4825 מֶרֶס ***meres***, n.pr.m. GK: 5332. Meres, "*worthy*":– Meres [1]

4826 מַרְסְנָא ***marsᵉnāʾ***, n.pr.m. GK: 5333. Marsena:– Marsena [1]

4827 מֵרַע ***mēraʿ***, n.m. *or* v.ptcp. GK: 5334 [→ 7489]. evil, atrocity:– do mischief [1]

4828 מֵרֵעַ ***mērēaʿ***, n.[m.] *or* v.ptcp. GK: 5335 [→ 7462]. close friend, companion, personal adviser:– companion [3], friends [3], companions [1]

4829 מִרְעֶה ***mirʿeh***, n.m. GK: 5337 [→ 7462]. pasture, grazing place:– pasture [11], feeding place [1], pastures [1]

4830 מַרְעִית ***marʿît***, n.f. GK: 5338 [→ 7462]. pasture, place of grazing:– pasture [8], flocks [1], pastures [1]

4831 מַרְאֲלָה ***marᵃlâ***, n.pr.loc. GK: 5339 [→ 7477]. Maralah:– Maralah [1]

4832 מַרְפֵּא ***marpēʾ***, n.m. GK: 5340 & 5341 [→ 7503; cf. 7495]. healing, remedy; calmness, composure:– health [5], healing [3], remedy [3], cure [1], incurable (+369) [1], sound [1], wholesome [1], yielding [1]

Heb

4833 מִרְפָּשׂ ***mirpāś***, n.[m.]. GK: 5343 [→ 7511]. what is muddy, fouled (by trampling):– that which fouled [1]

4834 מָרַץ ***māraṣ***, v. GK: 5344. [N] to be painful, hurtful; [H] to provoke, irritate:– emboldeneth [1], forcible [1], grievous [1], sore [1]

4835 מְרוּצָה ***m^erûṣâ***, n.f. GK: 5298 [→ 7533]. extortion:– violence [1]

4836 מַרְצֵעַ ***marṣēa'***, n.[m.]. GK: 5345 [→ 7527]. awl (piercing tool):– aul [2]

4837 מַרְצֶפֶת ***marṣepet***, n.f. GK: 5346 [→ 7528]. (stone) base, stone-layer:– pavement [1]

4838 מָרַק ***māraq***, v. GK: 5347 [→ 4795, 4839, 8562]. [Q] to polish; [Qp] to be polished; [Pu] to be thoroughly scoured; [H] to cleanse:– bright [1], furbish [1], scoured [1]

4839 מָרָק ***mārāq***, n.m. GK: 5348 [→ 4838]. broth (juice stewed out of meat):– broth [3]

4840 מֶרְקָח ***merqāḥ***, n.[m.]. GK: 5349 [→ 7543]. aromatic herb, scented spice, perfume:– sweet [1]

4841 מֶרְקָחָה ***merqāḥâ***, n.f. GK: 5350 [→ 7543]. ointment jar, spice-pot:– pot of ointment [1], well [1]

4842 מִרְקַחַת ***mirqaḥat***, n.f. GK: 5351 [→ 7543]. mixture of fragrant spices, blend of perfumes:– apothecaries' [1], compound [1], ointment [1]

4843 מָרַר ***mārar***, v. GK: 5352 [→ 4470, 4472, 4751, 4753, 4755, 4787, 4785, 4786, 4796, 4814, 4815, 4844, 4845, 4846, 8563]. [Q] to be bitter; suffer anguish; [P] to make bitter, weep bitterly; [H] to make bitter; to grieve bitterly; [Htpal] to enrage oneself, be furious; from the base meaning "to taste bitter" come extensions of bitter feelings: anger, fury, anguish, rebellion:– in bitterness [2], moved with choler [2], vexed [2], bitterly [1], bitterness [1], bitter [1], dealt bitterly [1], great bitterness (+4751) [1], grieved [1], grieveth [1], made bitter [1], provoke [1], sorely grieved [1]

4844 מָרֹר ***mārōr***, n.m. GK: 5353 [→ 4843]. bitter things:– bitter [2], bitterness [1]

4845 מְרֵרָה ***m^erērâ***, n.f. GK: 5354 [→ 4843]. gall (bitter fluid from the gall bladder):– gall [1]

4846 מְרֹרָה ***m^erōrâ***, n.f. GK: 5355 [→ 4843]. gall bladder; venom, poison (of snakes):– bitter [2], gall [2]

4847 מְרָרִי ***m^erārî***, n.pr.m. GK: 5356 [→ 4848]. Merari; Merarite, "*bitter*":– Merari [39]

4848 מְרָרִי ***m^erārî***, a.g. GK: 5357 [→ 4847]. Merarite, "*of Merari*":– Merarites [1]

מָרֵשָׁה ***mārēšâ***. See 4762.

4849 מִרְשַׁעַת ***mirša'at***, n.f. GK: 5360 [→ 7561]. wickedness, of a person (that) wicked woman:– wicked woman [1]

4850 מְרָתַיִם ***m^erātayim***, n.pr.f. GK: 5361 [→ 4784]. Merathaim, "*double rebellion*":– Merethaim [1]

4851 מַשׁ ***maš***, n.pr.m. GK: 5390. prob. same as 4902: Mash, Meshech:– Mash [1]

4852 מֵשָׁא ***mēšā'***, n.pr.loc. GK: 5392 [→ 4854?]. Mesha:– Mesha [1]

4853 מַשָּׂא ***maśśā'***, n.m. GK: 5362 & 5363 [→ 4984]. burden, load, what is lifted and carried; by extension: oppression; singing (lifting the voice); oracle, prophetic utterance, pronouncement, with the focus on the content of the message:– burden [52], burdens [5], song [3], prophecy [2], carry away [1], exaction of debt (+3027) [1], set [1], tribute [1]

4854 מַשָּׂא ***maśśā'***, n.pr.g. & loc. GK: 5364 [→ 4852?]. Massa, "*burden, oracle*":– Massa [2]

4855 מַשָּׁא ***maššā'***, n.m. GK: 5391 [→ 5378]. debt; exacting of usury:– usury [2]

4856 מַשֹּׂא ***maśśō'***, n.m. GK: 5365 [→ 4984]. partiality:– respect [1]

4857 מַשְׁאָב ***maš'āb***, n.[m.]. GK: 5393 [→ 7579]. watering channel, place to draw water:– places of drawing [1]

מְשֹׂאָה ***m^ešō'â***. See 4875.

4858 מַשָּׂאָה ***maśśā'â***, n.f. GK: 5366 [→ 4984]. uplifted (clouds of smoke):– burden [1]

4859 מַשָּׁאָה ***maššā'â***, n.f. GK: 5394 [→ 5378]. (secured) loan:– debts [1], lend (+5383) [1]

מַשֻּׁאָה ***maššu'â***. See 4876.

4860 מַשָּׁאוֹן ***maššā'ôn***, n.[m.]. GK: 5396 [→ 5377]. deception:– deceit [1]

4861 מִשְׁאָל ***miš'āl***, n.pr.loc. GK: 5398 [cf. 4913]. Mishal:– Mishal [1], Misheal [1]

4862 מִשְׁאָלָה ***miš'ālâ***, n.f. GK: 5399 [→ 7592]. desire:– desires [1], petitions [1]

4863 מִשְׁאֶרֶת ***miš'eret***, n.f. GK: 5400 [→ 7603]. kneading trough:– kneadingtroughs [2], store [2]

4864 מַשְׂאֵת ***maś'ēt***, n.f. GK: 5368 [→ 4984]. what is lifted up: portion (of food), tax, tribute, gift, burden:– burdens [2], collection [2], flame [2], mess [2], burden [1], gifts [1], lifting up [1], messes [1], oblations [1], reward [1], sign of fire [1]

מֹשָׁב ***mōšāb***. See 4186.

מְשֻׁבָה ***m^ešubâ***. See 4878.

4865 מִשְׁבְּצוֹת ***mišb^eṣôt***, n.f.pl. GK: 5401 [→ 7660]. filigree settings (ornamental work with fine gold wire usually for setting jewels):– ouches [8], wrought [1]

4866 מַשְׁבֵּר ***mašbēr***, n.[m.]. GK: 5402 [→ 7665]. opening of the womb, the point where birth first occurs:– birth [2], breaking forth [1]

4867 מִשְׁבָּר ***mišbār***, n.[m.]. GK: 5403 [→ 7665]. breakers, waves:– waves [4], billows [1]

4868 מִשְׁבָּת ***mišbāt***, n.[m.]. GK: 5404 [→ 7673]. destruction, cessation, finish:– sabbaths [1]

4869 מִשְׂגָּב ***miśgāb***, n.m. & loc. GK: 5369 [→ 7682]. fortress, refuge, stronghold; Misgab:– defence [6], refuge [5], high tower [3], Misgab [1], high fort [1], place of defence [1]

4870 מִשְׁגֶּה ***mišgeh***, n.m. GK: 5405 [→ 7686]. inadvertent mistake, oversight:– oversight [1]

4871 מָשָׁה ***māšâ***, v. GK: 5406 [→ 4872; cf. 570?]. [Q] to draw out; [H] to cause to draw out:– drew out [2], drew [1]

4872 מֹשֶׁה ***mōšeh***, n.pr.m. GK: 5407 [→ 4871]. Moses, "*drawn out* [Ex 2:10]; Egyptian for *child*":– Moses [750], Moses' [15], Moses' (+3807.1) [1]

4873 מֹשֶׁה ***mōšeh*** (Aram.), n.pr.m. GK: 10441 [cf. 4872]. Moses, "*drawn out* [Ex 2:10]; [Egyptian for] *child*":– Moses [1]

4874 מַשֶּׁה ***maššeh***, n.m. GK: 5408 [→ 5378]. credit, loan; "the lord of the loan" is a "creditor":– creditor (+1167+3027) [1]

4875 מְשׁוֹאָה ***m^ešô'â***, n.f. GK: 5409. wasteland, desolate land:– waste [2], desolation [1]

4876 מַשּׁוּאָה or מַשּׁוּאוֹת ***maššû'â*** or ***maššu'ôt***, n.m. & f.[pl.]. GK: 5410 & 5397 [→ 5377]. ruin, rubble, desolation; deception:– desolations [1], destruction [1]

4877 מְשׁוֹבָב ***m^ešôbāb***, n.pr.m. GK: 5411 [→ 7725]. Meshobab:– Meshobab [1]

4878 מְשׁוּבָה ***m^ešûbâ***, n.f. GK: 5412 [→ 7725]. waywardness, backsliding, faithlessness, apostasy:– backsliding [7], backslidings [4], turning away [1]

4879 מְשׁוּגָה ***m^ešûgâ***, n.f. GK: 5413 [cf. 7683, 7686]. error:– error [1]

4880 מָשׁוֹט or מִשּׁוֹט ***māšôṭ*** or ***miššôṭ***, n.[m.]. GK: 5414 & 5415 [→ 7751]. oar:– oars [1], oar [1]

4881 מְשׂוּכָּה or מְשֻׂכָה ***m^eśûkkâ*** or ***m^eśukâ***, n.f. GK: 5372 & 5379 [→ 4534]. (thorn) hedge (which impedes movement):– hedge [2]

4882 מְשִׁסָּה ***m^ešiwssâ***, var. GK: 5416 [cf. 4933]. plunder, loot, booty; cf. 4934:–

4883 מַשּׂוֹר ***maśśôr***, n.m. GK: 5373. saw (cutting tool):– saw [1]

4884 מְשׂוּרָה ***m^eśûrâ***, n.f. GK: 5374. (liquid) measure of quantity, measure of capacity:– measure [4]

4885 מָשׂוֹשׂ ***māśôś***, n.m. GK: 5375 & 5376 [→ 7797; cf. 4549]. joy, delight, celebration; wasting away, rotting away:– joy [12], mirth [3], rejoiceth [1], rejoice [1]

4886 מָשַׁח ***māšaḥ***, v. GK: 5417 [→ 4473, 4888, 4899; cf. 4887]. [Q] to anoint; [Qp] to be spread, be anointed; [N] to be anointed; usually referring to pouring or smearing sacred oil on a person in a ceremony of dedication, possibly symbolizing divine empowering to accomplish the task or office:– anointed [42], anoint [25], anointedst [1], painted [1]

4887 מְשַׁח ***m^ešaḥ*** (Aram.), n.[m.]. GK: 10442 & 10443 [cf. 4888]. olive oil, used for food, lamp oil, and ceremonies; measure:– oil [2]

4888 מָשְׁחָה or מִשְׁחָה ***mošḥâ*** or ***mišḥâ***, n.f. GK: 5418 & 5419 & 5420 & 5421 [→ 4886]. portion; anointing (oil), usually referring to pouring or smearing sacred oil on a person in a ceremony of dedication, possibly symbolizing divine empowering to accomplish the task or office:– anointing [24], anointed [1], ointment [1]

4889 מַשְׁחִית ***mašḥît***, n.[m.]. GK: 5422 [→ 7843]. destroyer, one who destroys; destruction, corruption; bird trap:– destroy [4], corruption [2], destruction [2], destroyer (+376) [1], destroying [1], trap [1], utterly (+3807.1) [1]

4890 מִשְׂחָק ***miśḥāq***, n.[m.]. GK: 5377 [→ 7832]. (scoffing) laughter:– scorn [1]

4891 מִשְׁחָר ***mišḥār***, n.[m.]. GK: 5423 [→ 7835]. dawn, early morning light:– morning [1]

4892 מַשְׁחֵת ***mašḥēt***, n.[m.]. GK: 5424 [→ 7843]. destruction, annihilation:– destroying [1]

4893 מִשְׁחַת or מָשְׁחַת ***mišḥat*** or ***mošḥat***, n.[m.]. GK: 5425 & 5426 [→ 7843]. deformity, defect, corruption, disfigurement, implying ugliness and repulsion:– corruption [1], marred [1]

4894 מִשְׁטוֹחַ ***mišṭôaḥ***, n.[m.]. GK: 5427 [→ 7849]. place for spreading out nets, drying yard for nets:– place to spread forth [1], spread upon [1], spreading [1]

4895 מַשְׂטֵמָה ***maśṭēmâ***, n.f. GK: 5378 [→ 7852]. hostility, animosity, enmity:– hatred [2]

4896 מִשְׁטָר ***mišṭār***, n.m. GK: 5428 [→ 7860]. dominion, rule; some sources: heavenly writing (the starry sky as God's communication):– dominion [1]

4897 מֶשִׁי ***mešî***, n.[m.]. GK: 5429. costly fabric for garments; possibly referring to silk:– silk [2]

מֻשִׁי ***mušî***. See 4187.

4898 מְשֵׁיזַבְאֵל ***m***e***šêzab'ēl***, n.pr.m. GK: 5430 [cf. 7804]. Meshezabel, "*God [El] delivers*":– Meshezabeel [3]

4899 מָשִׁיחַ ***māšîaḥ***, n.m. GK: 5431 [→ 4886]. anointed (one), usually refers to pouring or smearing sacred oil on a person in a ceremony of dedication, possibly symbolizing divine empowering to accomplish the task or office; the Anointed One, the Messiah, God's ultimate chosen one, identified in the NT as Jesus:– anointed [37], Messiah [2]

4900 מָשַׁךְ ***māšak***, v. GK: 5432 [→ 4901, 4189]. [Q] to draw up, drag; to extend, spread out; [N] to be prolonged, delayed; [Pu] to be deferred; to be tall:– draw [7], drew [4], draw out [3], prolonged [3], draweth [2], drawn [2], scattered [2], continue [1], deferred [1], draw away [1], drew along [1], drew up [1], extend unto [1], forbear (+5921) [1], give [1], handle [1], make a long blast [1], soundeth long [1], soweth [1], stretched out [1]

4901 מֶשֶׁךְ ***mešek***, n.[m.]. GK: 5433 [→ 4900]. (leather) bag, pouch (= price):– precious [1], price [1]

4902 מֶשֶׁךְ ***mešek***, n.pr.g. GK: 5434. Meshech:– Meshech [8], Mesech [1]

4903 מִשְׁכַּב ***miškab*** (Aram.), n.[m.]. GK: 10444 [cf. 4904]. bed, formally "a place for lying," which can refer to simple mats and even outer cloaks, as well as to pieces of furniture:– bed [6]

4904 מִשְׁכָּב ***miškāb***, n.m. GK: 5435 [→ 7901; cf. 4903]. bed, couch, used as a place for sleep, meditation, convalescence, marital relations, and worship:– bed [28], beds [5], bedchamber (+2315) [4], lying with [4], couch [1], lay on a bed (+7901) [1], lien [1], lieth with [1]

מְשֻׂכָה ***m***e***sukâ***. See 4881.

4905 מַשְׂכִּיל ***maśkîl***, n.m. GK: 5380 [→ 7919]. maskil (t.t. in the Psalms, perhaps "wisdom song"):– Maschil [13]

מַשְׁכִּים ***maškîm***. See 7925.

4906 מַשְׂכִּית ***maśkît***, n.f. GK: 5381. carved image, sculpture, figurine; what is imagined, imagination:– pictures [2], conceit [1], imagery [1], image [1], wish [1]

4907 מִשְׁכַּן ***miškan*** (Aram.), n.[m.]. GK: 10445 [→ 7932; cf. 4908]. dwelling, abode:– habitation [1]

4908 מִשְׁכָּן ***miškān***, n.m. GK: 5438 [→ 7931; cf. 4907]. dwelling place, habitat, tent, tabernacle, the tent used as the central place of worship before the temple:– tabernacle [114], dwellings [6], tabernacles [5], dwelling places [4], habitation [3], dwelling place [2], habitations [2], dwelling [1], tents [1], where dwelleth [1]

4909 מַשְׂכֹּרֶת ***maśkōret***, n.f. GK: 5382 [→ 7936]. wage:– wages [3], reward [1]

4910 מָשַׁל ***māšal***, v. GK: 5440 [→ 4474, 4475, 4915]. [Q] to rule, govern, control; [H] make one a ruler, (n.) dominion:– rule [15], ruler [14], ruleth [7], ruled [5], reign [4], rulers [4], governor [3], have dominion [3], reigned [3], have power [2], have rule [2], indeed have dominion (+4910) [2], rule over [2], rulest [2], ruling [2], bare rule [1], barest rule [1], bear rule [1], beareth rule [1], cause to rule over [1], dominion [1], governors [1], had dominion [1], madest to have dominion [1], reignest [1], ruler's [1]

4911 מָשַׁל ***māšal***, v. GK: 5439 [→ 4912, 4915, 4914]. [Q] to quote (a proverb or saying), to make up a proverb; [N] to liken, be like; [P] to tell a proverb; [H] to liken, compare to; [Ht] to show oneself like:– become like [3], like [2], use proverb (+4912) [2], compare [1], like unto [1], speak a parable (+4912) [1], speak in proverbs [1], speak [1], use as a proverb [1], use proverb [1], useth proverbs [1], utter [1]

4912 מָשָׁל ***māšāl***, n.m. GK: 5442 [→ 4911]. wisdom sayings of various types: proverb, a short, pithy saying, easy to remember; parable, a brief story with a symbolic meaning; oracle, a discourse type of prophecy; taunt, ridicule, a stylized form for mocking an enemy:– parable [16], proverb [12], proverbs [5], use proverb (+4911) [2], byword [1], like unto [1], parables [1], speak a parable (+4911) [1]

4913 מָשָׁל ***māšāl***, n.pr.loc. GK: 5443 [cf. 4861]. Mashal:– Mashal [1]

4914 מְשֹׁל ***m***e***šōl***, n.[m.]. GK: 5446 [→ 4911]. byword:– byword [1]

4915 מֹשֶׁל ***mōšel***, n.[m.]. GK: 5444 & 5445 [→ 4910, 4911]. likeness, similarity; power, dominion:– dominion [2], like [1]

מִשְׁלוֹשׁ ***mišlôš***. See 7969.

4916 מִשְׁלוֹחַ ***mišlôaḥ*** or מִשְׁלַח ***mišlāḥ***, n.[m.]. GK: 5447 & 5448 [→ 7971]. giving, sending (presents); laying on (hands):– puttest unto [2], sending [2], settest unto [2], lay upon [1], put unto [1], sending forth [1], settest [1]

4917 מִשְׁלַחַת ***mišlaḥat***, n.f. GK: 5449 [→ 7971]. discharge (from military); band, company (of angels):– discharge [1], sending [1]

4918 מְשֻׁלָּם ***m***e***šullām***, n.pr.m. GK: 5450 [→ 4920; cf. 7999]. Meshullam, "*restitution*":– Meshullam [25]

4919 מְשִׁלֵּמוֹת ***m***e***šillēmôt***, n.pr.m. GK: 5451 [→ 4921; cf. 7999]. Meshillemoth, "*restitution*":– Meshillemoth [2]

4920 מְשֶׁלֶמְיָה ***m***e***šelemyâ*** or מְשֶׁלֶמְיָהוּ ***m***e***šelemyāhû***, n.pr.m. GK: 5452 & 5453 [→ 4918+3068]. Meshelemiah, "*Yahweh repays*":– Meshelemiah [4]

4921 מְשִׁלֵּמִית ***m***e***šillēmît***, n.pr.m. GK: 5454 [→ 4919; cf. 7999]. Meshillemith, "*restitution*":– Meshillemith [1]

4922 מְשֻׁלֶּמֶת ***m***e***šullemet***, n.pr.f. GK: 5455 [→ 7999]. Meshullemeth, "*restitution*":– Meshullemeth [1]

4923 מְשַׁמָּה ***m***e***šammâ***, n.f. GK: 5457 [→ 8074]. object of horror, desolate waste, dried up place:– desolate [3], most desolate (+8077+2050.1) [3], astonishment [1]

4924 מִשְׁמָן ***mišmān***, n.[m.]. GK: 5458 & 5460 [→ 8081]. fatness; by extension: sturdiness, stoutness; richness, fertility, abundance, prosperity; choice food, festive food, rich with oil or fat (rare and valued in the ancient Near East):– fatness [3], fat ones [1], fattest places [1], fattest [1], fat [1]

4925 מִשְׁמַנָּה ***mišmannâ***, n.pr.m. GK: 5459 [→ 8081]. Mishmannah, "*fatness*":– Mishmannah [1]

4926 מִשְׁמָע ***mišmā'***, n.[m.]. GK: 5461 [→ 4927; cf. 8085]. what one hears, rumor, hearsay:– hearing [1]

4927 מִשְׁמָע ***mišmā'***, n.pr.m. GK: 5462 [→ 4926; cf. 8085]. Mishma, "*rumor*":– Mishma [4]

4928 מִשְׁמַעַת ***mišma'at***, n.f. GK: 5463 [→ 8085]. bodyguard; subject, one obligated to allegiance:– guard [2], bidding [1], obey [1]

4929 מִשְׁמָר ***mišmār***, n.[m.]. GK: 5464 [→ 8104]. guard or guarding, custody, imprisonment:– ward [12], watch [4], guard [3], diligence [1], offices [1], prison [1]

4930 מַשְׂמְרָה ***maśmērâ***, n.m. GK: 5383 [cf. 5568]. nail (on the end of a goad):– nails [1]

4931 מִשְׁמֶרֶת ***mišmeret***, n.f. GK: 5466 [→ 8104]. responsibility, duty, service; requirement, obligation; guard, watch, what is cared for:– charge [45], kept [6], ward [5], watch [5], charges [4], ordinance [3], wards [3], watches [2], charge of [1], in safeguard [1], keep (+1961) [1], offices [1], ward (+1004) [1]

4932 מִשְׁנֶה ***mišneh***, n.[m.]. GK: 5467 [→ 8138]. second, next (in a series); twice, double:– second [9], double [8], next [6], college [2], copy [2], twice [2], fatlings [1], next to [1], second degree [1], second order [1], second sort [1], twice as much [1]

4933 מְשִׁסָּה ***m***e***šissâ***, n.f. GK: 5468 [→ 7601; cf. 4882]. plunder, loot, booty:– spoil [4], booties [1], booty [1]

4934 מִשְׁעוֹל ***miš'ôl***, n.m. GK: 5469 [→ 8168]. narrow path:– path [1]

4935 מִשְׁעִי ***miš'î***, n.f. GK: 5470. cleansing, implying cleansing by washing and rubbing:– supple [1]

4936 מִשְׁעָם ***miš'ām***, n.pr.m. GK: 5471. Misham:– Misham [1]

4937 מִשְׁעָן ***miš'ān*** or מַשְׁעֵן ***maš'ēn***, n.m. & f. GK: 5472 & 5473 [→ 8172]. support, supplies:– stay [5]

4938 מַשְׁעֵנָה ***maš'ēnâ*** or מִשְׁעֶנֶת ***miš'enet***, n.f. GK: 5474 & 5475 [→ 8172]. staff, stick; support, supply:– staff [11], staves [1]

4939 מִשְׂפָּח ***miśpāḥ***, n.[m.]. GK: 5384 [cf. 5596]. bloodshed, with a focus on violence:– oppression [1]

4940 מִשְׁפָּחָה ***mišpāḥâ***, n.f. GK: 5476 [→ 8198]. clan, family, people:– families [169], family [117], kindred [6], every family (+4940) [4], kindreds [3], every family (+4940+2050.1) [2], kinds [2]

4941 מִשְׁפָּט ***mišpāṭ***, n.m. GK: 5477 [→ 5880; cf. 8199]. justice, judgment; law, regulation, prescription, specification:– judgment [188], judgments [108], manner [34], right [18], cause [12], that which is lawful [7], ordinances [6], ordinance [5], worthy [4], after the manner [2], discretion [2], fashion [2], law [2], manners [2], measure [2], order [2], sentence [2], adversary (+1167) [1], as required [1], ceremonies [1], charge [1], crimes [1], custom [1], deserts [1], determination [1], disposing [1], due order [1], due [1], execute the judgment (+8199) [1], fashions [1], form [1], judged [1], judgment (+1697) [1], justice [1], justly [1], just [1], order (+1961) [1], order commanded [1], usest to do [1], wrong (+3808) [1], wrongfully (+3808+871.1) [1]

4942 מִשְׁפְּתַיִם **mišp^{e}tayim**, n.[m.]du. GK: 5478 [→ 8239]. (dual) campfires or two saddlebags:– sheepfolds [1], two burdens [1]

4943 מֶשֶׁק **mešeq**, n.[m.]. GK: 5479 [→ 4476]. inheritance, possession:– steward (+1121) [1]

4944 מַשָּׁק **maššāq**, n.[m.]. GK: 5480 [→ 8264]. onslaught, assault; formally "rushing," this is the sudden, aggressive movement of a swarm:– running to and fro [1]

4945 מַשְׁקֶה **mašqeh**, n.m. GK: 5482 & 5483 [→ 8248]. cupbearer; drink (liquid); drinking vessel; irrigation:– drinking [2], drink [2], butlership [1], fat pastures [1], well watered [1]

4946 מִשְׁקוֹל **mišqôl**, n.[m.]. GK: 5484 [→ 8254]. weight:– weight [1]

4947 מַשְׁקוֹף **mašqôp**, n.[m.]. GK: 5485 [→ 8259]. top (upper crosspiece of a door), lintel:– lintel [2], upper door post [1]

4948 מִשְׁקָל **mišqāl**, n.m. GK: 5486 [→ 8254]. weight:– weight [46], weigh [2], full weight [1]

4949 מִשְׁקֶלֶת **mišqelet**, n.f. GK: 5487 [→ 8254?]. plumb line, leveling instrument:– plummet [2]

4950 מִשְׁקָע **mišqā'**, n.[m.]. GK: 5488 [→ 8257]. clear (settled) water:– deep [1]

4951 מִשְׂרָה **miśrâ**, n.f. GK: 5385 [→ 7786]. dominion, rule:– government [2]

4952 מִשְׁרָה **mišrâ**, n.f. GK: 5489 [→ 8281]. (grape) juice:– liquor [1]

4953 מַשְׁרוֹקִי **mašrôqî** (Aram.), n.f. GK: 10446. flute, musical pipe, a cylinder-shaped instrument producing a high shrill sound, made of wood, reed, or bone:– flute [4]

4954 מִשְׁרָעִי **mišrā'î**, a.g. GK: 5490. Mishraite:– Mishraites [1]

4955 מִשְׂרָפוֹת **miśrāpôt**, n.[f.pl.]. GK: 5386 [→ 8313]. (complete) burning, funeral fire:– burnings [2]

4956 מִשְׂרְפוֹת מַיִם **miśr^{e}pôt mayim**, n.pr.loc. GK: 5387 [→ 8313+4325]. Misrephoth Maim, "*waters of Misrephoth [lime burning]*":– Misrephoth-maim [2]

4957 מַשְׂרֵקָה **maśrēqâ**, n.pr.loc. GK: 5388 [→ 8320]. Masrekah, "[perhaps] *vineyard*":– Masrekah [2]

4958 מַשְׂרֵת **maśrēt**, n.m. GK: 5389 [→ 7603]. cooking pan:– pan [1]

4959 מָשַׁשׁ **māšaš**, v. GK: 5491 [cf. 3237, 4184]. [Q] to touch, feel; [P] to grope, search thoroughly; [H] to let one feel:– grope [3], felt [2], searched [2], feel [1], gropeth [1]

4960 מִשְׁתֶּה **mišteh**, n.m. GK: 5492 [→ 8354; cf. 4961]. feast, banquet, dinner, with an focus on drinking:– feast [21], banquet [10], feasting [7], drink [3], drank [2], feasts [2], feasted (+6213) [1]

4961 מִשְׁתֵּא **mištē'** (Aram.), n.m. GK: 10447 [→ 8355; cf. 4960]. banquet (hall); feast (hall), a place of merriment and celebration, often associated with drinking bouts:– banquet [1]

4962 מֹת **mōt**, n.m. GK: 5493 [→ 1328, 4968]. men; few (people):– men [14], few [2], few (+4557) [1], few (+4592) [1], friends [1], number [1], persons [1], small [1]

4963 מַתְבֵּן **matbēn**, n.[m.]. GK: 5495 [→ 8401]. heap of straw:– straw [1]

4964 מֶתֶג **meteg**, n.m. GK: 5496 [→ 4965]. bridle or bit:– bridle [3], Metheg-ammah [1], bit [1]

4965 מֶתֶג הָאַמָּה **meteg hā'ammâ**, n.pr.loc. GK: 5497 [→ 4964+1886.1+538]. Metheg Ammah:–

4966 מָתוֹק **mātôq**, a. GK: 5498 [→ 4985]. sweet, sweetness; by extension: pleasant, delightful:– sweet [8], sweeter [2], sweetness [2]

4967 מְתוּשָׁאֵל **m^{e}tûšā'ēl**, n.pr.m. GK: 5499 [→ 4191+7945+410]. Methushael, "[perhaps] *man of God*":– Methusael [2]

4968 מְתוּשֶׁלַח **m^{e}tûšelaḥ**, n.pr.m. GK: 5500 [→ 4962+7971?]. Methuselah, "*man of the javelin*":– Methuselah [6]

4969 מָתַח **mātaḥ**, v. GK: 5501 [→ 572]. [Q] to spread out:– spreadeth out [1]

4970 מָתַי **mātay**, adv.inter. GK: 5503. How long?; When?:– how long (+5704) [28], when [12], for how long (+5704) [1], when (+310) [1], when (+3807.1) [1]

מְתִים **m^{e}tîm**. See 4962.

4971 מַתְכֹּנֶת **matkōnet**, n.f. GK: 5504 [→ 8505]. measure, formula:– composition [2], measure [1], state [1], tale [1]

4972 מַתְּלָאָה **matt^{e}lā'â**, p.indef.+n.f. GK: 5505 [→ 4100+8513]. what a burden! (4100 + 8513):– weariness [1]

4973 מְתַלְּעוֹת **m^{e}tall^e'ôt**, n.f.pl. GK: 5506 [→ 4459]. jaw; teeth:– cheek-teeth [1], jaw teeth [1], jaws [1]

4974 מְתֹם **m^{e}tōm**, n.[m.]. GK: 5507 [→ 8552]. health, soundness:– soundness [3], men [1]

מֶתֶן **meten**. See 4981.

4975 מָתְנַיִם **motnayim**, n.m.du. GK: 5516 [→ 4981?]. (dual) waist, lower back (lumbar region), loins; "girding the loins" involves tucking the skirt of a tunic or robe into the belt, thus preparing for action: running, working, fighting, etc:– loins [42], side [4], greyhound (+2223) [1]

4976 מַתָּן **mattān**, n.m.col. GK: 5508 [→ 4977, 4982, 4983; cf. 5414; cf. 4978]. gift, present:– gift [4], giveth gifts [1]

4977 מַתָּן **mattān**, n.pr.m. GK: 5509 [→ 4976; cf. 5414]. Mattan, "*gift*":– Mattan [3]

4978 מַתְּנָא **matt^{e}nâ** (Aram.), n.f. GK: 10448 [→ 5415; cf. 4976]. gift:– gifts [3]

4979 מַתָּנָה **mattānâ**, n.f. GK: 5510 [→ 4980; cf. 5414]. gift, something given, such as an offering to deity or a bribe:– gifts [11], gift [5], able (+3027) [1]

4980 מַתָּנָה **mattānâ**, n.pr.loc. GK: 5511 [→ 4979; cf. 5414]. Mattanah, "*gift*":– Mattanah [2]

4981 מִתְנִי **mitnî**, a.g. GK: 5512 [→ 4975?]. Mithnite:– Mithnite [1]

4982 מַתְּנַי **matt^{e}nay**, n.pr.m. GK: 5513 [→ 4976+3068]. Mattenai, "*gift*":– Mattenai [3]

4983 מַתַּנְיָה or מַתַּנְיָהוּ **mattanyâ** or **mattanyāhû**, n.pr.m. GK: 5514 & 5515 [→ 4976+3068]. Mattaniah, "*gift of Yahweh*":– Mattaniah [16]

מָתְנַיִם **motnayim**. See 4975.

4984 מִתְנַשֵּׂא **mitnaśśē'**, v.ptcp. GK: 5951 [→ 4853, 4853, 4856, 4858, 4864, 5375, 5379, 5385, 5387, 7613, 7721, 7863?, 7865?; cf. 5376]. ptcp. of 5375: lifted up, exalted:–

4985 מָתַק **mātaq**, v. GK: 5517 [→ 4477, 4966, 4986, 4987, 4988, 4989?]. same as 4988: [Q] to be, become sweet; [H] to taste sweet, enjoy sweetness:– sweet [3], made sweet [1], took sweet [1]

4986 מֶתֶק **māteq**, n.m. GK: 5518 [→ 4985]. sweetness; by extension: pleasantness:– sweetness [2]

4987 מֹתֶק **mōteq**, n.[m.]. GK: 5519 [→ 4985]. sweetness:– sweetness [1]

4988 מָתַק **mātaq**, v. GK: 5517 [→ 4985]. same as 4985: [Q] to be, become sweet:– feed sweetly on [1]

4989 מִתְקָה **mitqâ**, n.pr.loc. GK: 5520 [→ 4985?]. Mithcah, "*sweetness*":– Mithcah [2]

4990 מִתְרְדָת **mitr^{e}dāt**, n.pr.m. GK: 5521. Mithredath, "*gift to Mithra*":– Mithredath [2]

4991 מַתַּת **mattat**, n.f. GK: 5522 [→ 4993; cf. 5414]. gift, something given:– gift [3], give [2], reward [1]

4992 מַתַּתָּה **mattattâ**, n.pr.m. GK: 5523 [→ 5414]. Mattattah, "*gift*":– Mattathah [1]

4993 מַתִּתְיָה or מַתִּתְיָהוּ **mattityâ** or **mattityāhû**, n.pr.m. GK: 5524 & 5525 [→ 4991+3068]. Mattithiah, "*gift of Yahweh*":– Mattithiah [8]

4993.1 ןָ- **-ān** or ן- **-n**, p.f.pl.suf. GK: 5527 [→ 1886.3, 2190]. they, them, their:– their [14], them [11], they [8], thereof [1]

4994 נָא **nā'**, pt. GK: 5528 [→ 577]. often not translated, marks entreaty or exhortation: please!, I beg you!, now!:– now [167], I pray thee [150], I pray you [34], I beseech thee [22], we pray thee [10], we beseech thee [6], oh [5], go to [3], I pray [2], let [2], O [1]

4995 נָא **nā'**, a. GK: 5529. raw (meat):– raw [1]

4996 נֹא **nō'**, n.pr.loc. GK: 5530 [→ 527+4996]. No = Thebes:– no [5]

4996.1 נָא- **-nā'** (Aram.), p.suf.1.com.pl. GK: 10450 [cf. 5105.1]. we, our:– us [7], our [2], we [1]

4997 נֹאד **nō'd**, n.m. GK: 5532. skin vessel (skinned in one piece, the appendages tied or sewn, the neck the funnel, used to hold liquid):– bottle [4], bottles [2]

נֶאְדָּרִי **ne'dārî**. See 142.

4998 נָאָה **nā'â**, v. GK: 5533 [→ 5000; cf. 5115]. [Pilel] to be beautiful, adorn:– beautiful [1], becometh [1], comely [1]

4999 נָוָה **nāwâ**, n.f. GK: 5661 [→ 5380]. pasture, pastureland; (generally) abode, dwelling, camp, place:– habitations [5], pastures [5], houses [1], pleasant places [1]

5000 נָאוֶה **nā'weh**, a. GK: 5534 [→ 4998]. lovely, fitting, suited:– comely [6], seemly [2], becometh [1]

5001 נָאַם **nā'am**, v.den. GK: 5535 [→ 5002]. [Q] to declare as a prophet:– say [1]

5002 נְאֻם **n^e'um**, n.m. GK: 5536 [→ 5001]. declaration, oracle, utterance; often a marker introducing or punctuating prophetic discourse:– saith [366], said [9], spake [1]

5003 נָאַף **nā'ap**, v. GK: 5537 [→ 5005, 5004; cf. 5130]. [Q, P] to commit adultery; [ptcp.] adulterer, adulteress; by extension: to be unfaithful to God (by having illicit relations with other gods):– commit adultery [6], committed adultery [6], adulterers [5], committeth adultery [4], adulterer [3], adulteresses [2], adulteress [2], adulterous [1], break wedlock [1], committing adultery [1]

5004 נִאֻפִים ni'upîm, n.[m.]. GK: 5539 [→ 5003]. adultery:– adulteries [2]

5005 נַאֲפוּפִים na'ᵃpûpîm, n.[m.pl.]. GK: 5538 [→ 5003]. (marks of) unfaithfulness, adultery; such marks might refer to jewelry or adornments which signal that a woman is available for illicit sex:– adulteries [1]

5006 נָאַץ nā'aṣ, v. GK: 5540 [→ 5007]. [Q] to spurn, despise, reject; [P] to treat with contempt, revile, despise; [Htpo] be blasphemed, be reviled:– despised [6], abhorred [2], blasphemed [2], given great occasion to blaspheme (+5006) [2], provoked [2], provoke [2], abhorreth [1], abhor [1], blaspheme [1], contemned [1], contemn [1], despiseth [1], despise [1], provoked unto anger [1]

5007 נְאָצָה nᵉ'āṣâ or **נֶאָצָה ne'āṣâ**, n.f. GK: 5541 & 5542 [→ 5006]. disgrace, shame; contemptible things, blasphemies:– blasphemy [2], provocations [2], blasphemies [1]

5008 נָאַק nā'aq, v. GK: 5543 [→ 5009; cf. 602]. [Q] to groan:– groan [2]

5009 נְאָקָה nᵉ'āqâ, n.f. GK: 5544 [→ 5008; cf. 602]. groaning:– groanings [2], groaning [2]

5010 נָאַר nā'ar, v. GK: 5545. [P] to renounce, abandon:– abhorred [1], made void [1]

5011 נֹב nōb, n.pr.loc. GK: 5546. Nob:– Nob [6]

5012 נָבָא nābā', v.den. GK: 5547 [→ 5030; cf. 5013]. [N, Ht] to prophesy, speak as a prophet; prophecy has its focus on encouraging or restoring covenant faithfulness, the telling of future events encourages obedience or warns against disobedience:– prophesy [68], prophesied [40], prophesieth [3], maketh a prophet [2], prophesying [2]

5013 נְבָא nᵉbā' (Aram.), v. GK: 10451 [→ 5017, 5029; cf. 5012]. [Htpa] to prophesy, act as a prophet:– prophesied [1]

5014 נָבַב nābab, v. GK: 5554 & 5548. [Q] to hollow out; by extension: to be foolish:– hollow [3], vain [1]

5015 נְבוֹ nᵉbô, n.pr.m. & loc. GK: 5549 & 5550 & 5551 [→ (used with compound proper names)]. Nebo (pagan god), Nebo (loc.), *"height* or *Mount of Nabu [Nebo]"*:– Nebo [13]

5016 נְבוּאָה nᵉbû'â, n.f. GK: 5553 [→ 5030; cf. 5017]. prophecy, the word of the prophet; prophecy has its focus on encouraging or restoring covenant faithfulness, the telling of future events encourages obedience or warns against disobedience:– prophecy [3]

5017 נְבוּאָה nᵉbû'â (Aram.), n.f. GK: 10452 [→ 5013; cf. 5016]. prophesying, preaching:– prophesying [1]

5018 נְבוּזַרְאֲדָן nᵉbûzar'ᵃdān or **נְבוּזַר־אֲדָן nᵉbûzar-'ᵃdān**, n.pr.m. GK: 5555 [→ 5015+2232]. Nebuzaradan, *"Nebo [Nabu] has given seed [offspring]"*:– Nebuzar-adan [15]

5019 נְבוּכַדְנֶאצַּר nᵉbûkadne'ṣṣar or **נְבוּכַדְנֶצַּר nᵉbûkadneṣṣar** or **נְבוּכַדְנֶצּוֹר nᵉbûkadneṣṣôr** or **נְבוּכַדְרֶאצַּר nᵉbûkadre'ṣṣar** or **נְבוּכַדְרֶאצּוֹר nebûkadre'ṣṣôr**, n.pr.m. GK: 5556 & 5557 [→ 5015; cf. 5020]. Nebuchadnezzar, Nebuchadrezzar, *"Nebo protect my boundary stone; Nebo protect my son!"*:– Nebuchadrezzar [31], Nebuchadnezzar [29]

5020 נְבוּכַדְנֶצַּר nᵉbûkadneṣṣar (Aram.), n.pr.m. GK: 10453 [cf. 5019]. Nebuchadnezzar, *"Nebo protect my boundary stone* or *Nebo protect my son!"*:– Nebuchadnezzar [31]

5021 נְבוּשַׁזְבָּן nᵉbûšazbān or **נְבוּשַׁז־בָּן nᵉbûšaz-bān**, n.pr.m. GK: 5558 [→ 5015]. Nebushazban, *"Nebo [Nabu] save me!"*:– Nebushasban [1]

5022 נָבוֹת nābôt, n.pr.m. GK: 5559. Naboth, *"sprout"*:– Naboth [22]

5023 נְבִזְבָּה nᵉbizbâ (Aram.), n.f. GK: 10454. present, gift; this can be a gift given as a recompense for a proper service, a reward:– rewards [2]

5024 נָבַח nābaḥ, v. GK: 5560 [→ 5025?]. [Q] to bark:– bark [1]

5025 נֹבַח nōbaḥ, n.pr.m. & loc. GK: 5561 & 5562 [→ 5024?]. Nobah, *"barking"*:– Nobah [3]

5026 נִבְחַז nibḥaz, n.pr.[m.]. GK: 5563. Nibhaz (pagan god):– Nibhaz [1]

5027 נָבַט nābaṭ, v. GK: 5564 [→ 4007, 5028]. [P] to look at; [H] to look at, gaze at, consider:– look [21], looked [11], behold [9], consider [5], regard [4], see [4], looketh [3], have respect [2], look down [2], beheld (+413) [1], beheld [1], beholdest [1], cause to behold [1], look upon [1], looked about [1], lookest [1], respect [1]

5028 נְבָט nᵉbāṭ, n.pr.m. GK: 5565 [→ 5027]. Nebat, *"look to, regard [approvingly]"*:– Nebat [25]

5029 נְבִיא nᵉbî' (Aram.), n.m. GK: 10455 [→ 5013; cf. 5030]. prophet, one who speaks for God in inspired utterance, often including the application of the message:– prophets [2], prophet [2]

5030 נָבִיא nābî', n.m. GK: 5566 [→ 5012, 5016, 5031; cf. 5029]. prophet (true or false):– prophet [165], prophets [147], prophecy [1], prophesy [1], prophet's [1]

5031 נְבִיאָה nᵉbî'â, n.f. GK: 5567 [→ 5030]. prophetess (true or false):– prophetess [6]

5032 נְבָיוֹת nᵉbāyôt, n.pr.g. GK: 5568. Nebaioth:– Nebajoth [5]

5033 נֵבֶךְ nēbek, n.[m.]. GK: 5569. source springs (of the sea):– springs [1]

5034 נָבֵל nābēl, v. GK: 5570 & 5571 [→ 5036, 5037, 5038, 5039, 5040?]. [Q] to wither, shrivel, fade, decay; to play the fool, act disdainfully; [P] to treat with contempt, dishonor, reject:– fadeth [3], fade [3], fade away [2], fadeth away [2], fading [2], surely wear away (+5034) [2], wither [2], cometh to nought [1], disgrace [1], dishonoureth [1], done foolishly [1], fall down [1], falleth off [1], falling [1], lightly esteemed [1], make vile [1]

5035 נֵבֶל nēbel, n.m. GK: 5574 & 5575 [→ 3999]. (wine) skin; water jar, jug, pot (of clay); lyre, harp (stringed instrument):– psalteries [14], psaltery [8], bottle [5], bottles [3], viols [2], viol [2], flagons [1], pitchers [1], psaltery (+3627) [1], vessel [1]

5036 נָבָל nābāl, a. GK: 5572 [→ 5037; cf. 5034]. foolish, lacking understanding, (n.) fool; often pertaining to insolence, pride, and disobedience to God:– foolish [7], fool [7], fools [2], vile person [2]

5037 נָבָל nābāl, n.pr.m. GK: 5573 [→ 5036; cf. 5034]. Nabal, *"fool"*:– Nabal [18], Nabal's [4]

5038 נְבֵלָה nᵉbēlâ, n.f. GK: 5577 [→ 5034]. dead body, carcass:– carcase [28], carcases [7], dead body [3], dead bodies [2], dieth of itself [2], beast that dieth of itself [1], body [1], dead carcase [1], that is dead of itself [1], that which died of itself [1], that which dieth of itself [1]

5039 נְבָלָה nᵉbālâ, n.f. GK: 5576 [→ 5034]. (very) wicked thing, disgraceful thing; vileness, something a fool would do:– folly [10], villany [2], vile [1]

5040 נַבְלוּת nablût, n.f. GK: 5578 [→ 5034?]. (female) genitals:– lewdness [1]

5041 נְבַלָּט nᵉballāṭ, n.pr.loc. GK: 5579. Neballat:– Neballat [1]

5042 נָבַע nāba', v. GK: 5580 [→ 76, 4002]. [H] to gush forth, bubble out, spew forth:– utter [3], poureth out [2], abundantly utter [1], belch out [1], cause to send forth [1], flowing [1], pour out [1], uttereth [1]

5043 נֶבְרְשָׁא nebrᵉšā (Aram.), n.f.emph. GK: 10456. lampstand:– candlestick [1]

5044 נִבְשָׁן nibšān, n.pr.loc. GK: 5581. Nibshan:– Nibshan [1]

5045 נֶגֶב negeb, n.pr.[m.]. GK: 5582 [→ 7418]. south, the Negev:– south [88], southward (+1886.5) [13], south side [5], south (+1886.5) [2], south (+4480) [1], southward (+4480) [1], southward (+871.1+1886.1) [1], southward [1]

5046 נָגַד nāgad, v. GK: 5583 [→ 5048, 5057; cf. 5047]. [H] to tell, report, inform; [Ho] to be told, have reported to:– told [150], tell [66], declare [45], shew [34], shewed [18], declared [13], sheweth [5], surely tell (+5046) [4], declareth [3], utter [3], certainly declare (+5046) [2], certainly told (+5046) [2], fully been shewed (+5046) [2], messenger [2], report [2], shew forth [2], telleth [2], told plainly (+5046) [2], uttered [2], another^s [1], bewrayeth [1], certify [1], declaring [1], denounce [1], expounded [1], expound [1], profess [1], rehearsed [1], sheweth forth [1], speaketh [1]

5047 נְגַד nᵉgad (Aram.), v. GK: 10457 [→ 5049; cf. 5046]. [P] to flow:– issued [1]

5048 נֶגֶד neged, subst. & adv. & pp. GK: 5584 [→ 5046; cf. 5049]. before, in front of, opposite of, beyond:– before [59], before (+3807.1) [18], over against [16], against [6], in (+3807.1) [4], in the presence [4], over against (+3807.1) [4], presence [4], before (+4480) [3], from (+4480) [3], over against (+4480) [3], against (+4480) [2], meet for (+3509.1) [2], straight before [2], view (+4480) [2], about [1], afar off (+4480) [1], against (+3807.1) [1], aloof from (+4480) [1], before (+6440) [1], far (+4480) [1], far off (+4480) [1], in presence [1], in the sight [1], in [1], of (+4480) [1], on the other side (+4480) [1], other side [1], over (+3807.1) [1], over [1], right against [1], sight [1], withstand (+5975) [1], withstood (+5975+3807.1) [1]

5049 נֶגֶד neged (Aram.), pp. GK: 10458 [→ 5047; cf. 5048]. toward, before, facing:– toward [1]

5050 נָגַהּ nāgah, v. GK: 5585 [→ 5051, 5052, 5054]. [Q] to shine; [H] to cause to shine, give light:– shine [2], cause to shine [1], enlighten [1], lighten [1], shined [1]

5051 נֹגַהּ ***nōgah***, n.f. GK: 5586 [→ 5052; cf. 5050; cf. 5053]. brightness, radiance, splendor, brilliance:– brightness [11], shining [5], bright [1], clear shining [1], light [1]

5052 נֹגַהּ ***nōgah***, n.pr.m. GK: 5587 [→ 5051; cf. 5050]. Nogah, *"joy, splendor"*:– Nogah [2]

5053 נֹגַהּ ***n^egah*** (Aram.), n.[f.]. GK: 10459 [cf. 5051]. brightness (i.e., first light of dawn):– morning [1]

5054 נְגֹהָה ***n^egōhâ***, n.f. GK: 5588 [→ 5050]. brightness, luster:– brightness [1]

5055 נָגַח ***nāgaḥ***, v. GK: 5590 [→ 5056]. [Q] to gore (a bull into a person); [P] to gore, push back, butt; to engage in pushing back, butting, thrusting:– push [5], gored [2], gore [1], push down [1], pushing [1], pusht [1]

5056 נַגָּח ***naggāḥ***, a. GK: 5591 [→ 5055]. (the act of) goring (a bull into a person):– used to push [1], wont to push with his horn [1]

5057 נָגִיד ***nāgîd***, n.m. GK: 5592 [→ 5046]. leader, ruler, official, officer:– ruler [18], prince [8], captain [5], leader [3], captains [1], chief governor [1], chief ruler [1], chief [1], excellent things [1], governor [1], leaders [1], nobles [1], princes [1], rulers [1]

5058 נְגִינָה ***n^egînâ***, n.f. GK: 5593 [→ 5059]. stringed instrument; song that mocks, taunts:– Neginoth [6], song [4], Neginah [1], musick [1], songs [1], stringed instruments [1]

5059 נָגַן ***nāgan***, v. GK: 5594 [→ 4485, 5058]. [Q] to play a stringed instrument, (n.) musician; [P] to play a stringed instrument:– played [4], play [3], minstrel [2], melody [1], play on an instrument [1], players on instruments [1], player [1], playing [1], sing the stringed instruments [1]

5060 נָגַע ***nāga'***, v. GK: 5595 [→ 5061]. [Q] to touch; to strike; [Qp] to be plagued, be stricken; [N] to let oneself be driven back (in a battle); [P] to inflict, afflict; [Pu] to be plagued; [H] to extend, reach out, cause to touch; ranging in meaning from simple contact to violence:– toucheth [37], touch [31], touched [24], come [10], came [6], reacheth [4], reach [4], plagued [3], reaching [3], smote [3], bring [2], happeneth [2], beaten [1], bring down [1], bringeth [1], brought down [1], cast [1], come close [1], come nigh [1], cometh [1], draw near [1], draw nigh [1], draweth near [1], draweth nigh [1], drew near [1], getteth up [1], join [1], laid [1], near [1], reached [1], smitten [1], stricken [1], strike [1]

5061 נֶגַע ***nega'***, n.m. GK: 5596 [→ 5060]. plague, blow (of various kinds): mildew, infection, sores, scourge, disaster:– plague [64], sore [5], stroke [4], stripes [2], plagues [1], stricken [1], wound [1]

5062 נָגַף ***nāgap***, v. GK: 5597 [→ 4046, 5063]. [Q] to strike, afflict (with a plague); [N] to be defeated:– smitten [12], smite [9], smote [6], put to the worse [5], hurt [2], plagued [2], slain [2], smitten down (+5062) [2], smitten down [2], stumble [2], beaten [1], dash [1], plague [1], strake [1], struck [1]

5063 נֶגֶף ***negep***, n.m. GK: 5598 [→ 5062]. plague; stumbling (caused by a stone):– plague [6], stumbling [1]

5064 נָגַר ***nāgar***, v. GK: 5599 [cf. 1641]. [N] to be spilled, flow; [H] to pour out, hand over, deliver over; [Ho] to be poured down (a slope):– fall [1], flow away [1], pour down [1], pour out [1], poured [1], poureth out [1], ran [1], shed [1], spilt [1], trickleth down [1]

5065 נָגַשׂ ***nāgaś***, v. GK: 5601 [cf. 5066]. [Q] to oppress, exploit, (n.) a slave driver; [N] to be oppressed, be hard pressed:– oppressor [5], taskmasters [5], exact [3], distressed [2], oppressed [2], oppressors [2], driver [1], exacted [1], exactors [1], taxes [1]

5066 נָגַשׁ ***nāgaš***, v. GK: 5602 [cf. 5065]. [Q] to come near, approach; [N] to come near, approach; [H] to bring forth, present; [Ho] to be brought, be presented; [Ht] to draw near, assemble:– came near [17], come near [16], came [9], brought [8], come nigh [7], bring hither [6], come [6], drew near [6], draw near [5], approach [4], bring [4], offer [4], brought near [3], drew nigh [3], went near [3], bring forth [2], bring near [2], offered [2], overtake [2], approached nigh [1], brought forth [1], brought thither [1], came nigh [1], cause to come near [1], give place [1], go near [1], go [1], make to approach [1], near [1], offereth [1], presented [1], put [1], stand [1], went hard [1], went nigh [1]

5067 נֵד ***nēd***, n.m. GK: 5603. heap, wall, barrier, dam:– heap [6]

5068 נָדַב ***nādab***, v. GK: 5605 [→ 5070, 5071, 5081, 5082; cf. 5069 (also used with compound proper names)]. [Q] to be willing; to prompt, incite; [Ht] to willingly offer oneself, volunteer, give a freewill offering:– willingly offered [6], offered willingly [4], made willing [2], offer willingly [2], giveth willingly [1], offered freely [1], willing [1]

5069 נְדַב ***n^edab*** (Aram.), v. GK: 10461 [cf. 5068]. [Htpa] to be willing, to give freely; (as noun) a freewill offering:– freely offered [1], freewill offering [1], minded of own freewill [1], offering willingly [1]

5070 נָדָב ***nādāb***, n.pr.m. GK: 5606 [→ 5072; cf. 5068]. Nadab, *"volunteer, free will offering"*:– Nadab [20]

5071 נְדָבָה ***n^edābâ***, n.f. GK: 5607 [→ 5068]. free, voluntary; freewill offering:– freewill offering [8], freewill offerings [7], free offerings [2], freely (+871.1) [1], freely [1], plentiful [1], voluntarily [1], voluntary offering [1], voluntary [1], willing offering [1], willingly (+3807.1) [1], willing [1]

5072 נְדַבְיָה ***n^edabyâ***, n.pr.m. GK: 5608 [→ 5070]. Nedabiah, *"Yahweh volunteers"*:– Nedabiah [1]

5073 נִדְבָּךְ ***nidbāk*** (Aram.), n.m. GK: 10462. course (of timber or stone in building):– rows [1], row [1]

5074 נָדַד ***nādad***, v. GK: 5610 [→ 5076; cf. 5077, 5110; cf. 5075]. [Q] to flee, be a fugitive; to wander, stray; [Pol] to flee away; [H] to banish, put to flight; [Ho] to be banished, be cast aside:– fled [8], wandereth [4], flee apace (+5074) [2], flee away [2], chased away [1], chased [1], could not [1], departed [1], flee [1], moved [1], removed [1], thrust away [1], wanderers [1], wandereth abroad [1], wandering [1], wander [1]

5075 נְדַד ***n^edad*** (Aram.), v. GK: 10463 [cf. 5111; cf. 5074]. [P] to flee (i.e., sleep flees = insomnia):– went [1]

5076 נְדֻדִים ***n^edudîm***, n.[m.pl.]. GK: 5611 [→ 5074]. tossing and turning, restlessness (in bed in the night):– tossings to and fro [1]

5077 נָדָא ***nādā'*** or נָדָה ***nādâ***, v. GK: 5604 & 5612 [→ 5079, 5206; cf. 5074, 5110]. [P] to exclude; to put off thoughts, suppose to be far off; [H] detach, remove from:– cast out [1], put far away [1]

5078 נֵדֶה ***nēdeh***, n.m. GK: 5613. gift, reward; likely referring to a fee for service:– gifts [1]

5079 נִדָּה ***niddâ***, n.[m.]. GK: 5614 [→ 5206; cf. 5077]. period of menstruation; (water used in) cleansing, "unclean" water; (act of) impurity, corruption, defilement:– separation [14], filthiness [2], flowers [2], menstruous [2], put apart [2], far [1], removed woman [1], removed [1], that was set apart [1], unclean thing [1], uncleanness [1], unclean [1]

5080 נָדַח ***nādaḥ***, v. GK: 5615 & 5616 [→ 4065; cf. 1740, 1760]. [Q] to wield (an ax); (to have hand) be put (to the ax); [N] to be scattered, be exiled, be outcast; [Pu] be thrust into; [H] to cause to scatter, banish, drive out; to bring; [Ho] to be driven, be hunted:– driven [15], driven away [4], driven out [4], outcasts [4], cast out [3], drive [3], banished [2], drive out [2], bring [1], cast down [1], chased [1], compelled [1], drave [1], drawn away [1], expelled [1], fetcheth a stroke [1], forced [1], forcing [1], go astray [1], outcast [1], thrust away [1], thrust [1], withdrawn [1]

5081 נָדִיב ***nādîb***, a. (used as noun). GK: 5618 [→ 5082; cf. 5068]. willing, generous; prince, noble, ruler, official:– princes [10], nobles [4], prince [4], willing [3], free [2], liberal [2], prince's [1]

5082 נְדִיבָה ***n^edîbâ***, n.f. GK: 5619 [→ 5081; cf. 5068]. something noble; dignity, nobility:– liberal [2], soul [1]

5083 נָדָן ***nādān***, n.[m.]. GK: 5621 [cf. 5414]. gift, wages of illicit sexual favors:– gifts [1]

5084 נָדָן ***nādān***, n.[m.]. GK: 5620 [cf. 5085]. sheath (of a sword):– sheath [1]

5085 נִדְנֶה ***nidneh*** (Aram.), n.[m.]. GK: 10464. sheath (of the spirit = the body):– body [1]

5086 נָדַף ***nādap***, v. GK: 5622. [Q] to blow away, scatter; [N] to be windblown, be fleeting:– driven away [2], drive away [1], driven to and fro [1], driven [1], driveth away [1], shaken [1], thrusteth down [1], tossed to and fro [1]

5087 נָדַר ***nādar***, v. GK: 5623 [→ 5088; cf. 5144, 5145]. [Q] to make a vow:– vowed [16], vow [10], vowest [2], made [1], vowedst [1], voweth [1]

5088 נֶדֶר ***nēder***, n.m. GK: 5624 [→ 5087]. vow:– vows [30], vow [28], make a singular vow (+6381) [1], vowed [1]

5089 נֹהַּ ***nōah***, n.[m.]. GK: 5625. value, distinction:– wailing [1]

5089.1 נָה- ***-nâ***, p.f.s.suf. GK: 5626 [→ 1886.3]. her; it, its:– it [121], her [27], the same [11], them [9], she [5], thereof (+4480) [3], they [3], thence [2], therefrom (+4480) [2], thereof [2], by themselves (+905+3807.1) [1], their [1], therein [1], thereon [1], these things [1], this [1]

5090 נָהַג ***nāhag***, v. GK: 5627 & 5628 [→ 4491, cf. 5101]. [Q] to drive, lead, guide; [Qp] to be led; [P] to drive, lead forth, guide; to moan, sob, lament:– lead [7], drave [4], carried away [3], brought [2], lead away [2], led forth [2], led [2], acquainting [1], brought away [1], brought in [1], drive away [1], driveth [1], drive [1], guided [1], guide [1], leadest [1]

5091 נָהָה **nāhâ**, v. GK: 5629 & 5630 [→ 5092, 5093, 5204]. [Q] to mourn, wail; [N] to be taunted (with a mournful song); to keep close, stay loyal:– lamented [1], lament [1], wail [1]

5092 נְהִי **n**e**hî**, n.[m.]. GK: 5631 [→ 5204; cf. 5091]. wailing, mourning, often related to mournful songs: lamentation:– wailing [4], lamentation [2]

5093 נִהְיָה **nihyâ**, n.f. GK: 5632 [→ 5091]. wailing, lamentation, mourning:– doleful lamentation [1]

5094 נְהִיר **n**e**hîr** or נַהִירוּ **nahîrû** (Aram.), n.m. GK: 10466 & 10467 [cf. 5105]. light; insight, illumination (of the mind):– light [3]

5095 נָהַל **nāhal**, v. GK: 5633 [→ 5096, 5097]. [P] guide, bring along, lead; [Ht] to move along:– guide [3], guided [2], carried [1], fed [1], gently lead [1], lead on [1], leadeth [1]

5096 נַהֲלָל **nah**a**lāl** or נַהֲלֹל **nah**a**lōl**, n.pr.loc. GK: 5634 & 5636 [→ 5095, 5097]. Nahalal, Nahalol, "*watering place*":– Nahalal [1], Nahallal [1], Nahalol [1]

5097 נַהֲלֹל **nah**a**lōl**, n.m. GK: 5635 [→ 5096; cf. 5095]. watering hole:– bushes [1]

5098 נָהַם **nāham**, v. GK: 5637 [→ 5099, 5100; cf. 1949, 1993, 2000]. [Q] to growl, roar; to groan:– mourn [2], roar [2], roaring [1]

5099 נַהַם **naham**, n.[m.]. GK: 5638 [→ 5098]. roaring, growling:– roaring [2]

5100 נְהָמָה **n**e**hāmâ**, n.f. GK: 5639 [→ 5098]. roaring, growling; anguish, groaning:– disquietness [1], roaring [1]

5101 נָהַק **nāhaq**, v. GK: 5640 [cf. 5090]. [Q] to bray (of a donkey):– brayed [1], bray [1]

5102 נָהַר **nāhar**, v. GK: 5641 & 5642 [→ 5104, 5105; cf. 5216]. [Q] to stream to (like a river flow); to be radiant (with joy), beam (with joy):– flow [5], lightened [1]

5103 נְהַר **n**e**har** (Aram.), n.m. GK: 10468 [cf. 5104]. river, stream:– river [14], stream [1]

5104 נָהָר **nāhār**, n.m. GK: 5643 [→ 763, 5102; cf. 5103]. river, stream, canal; the River, which can refer to the Euphrates, Tigris, or Nile:– river [67], rivers [31], floods [10], flood [8], streams [2], river side [1]

5105 נְהָרָה **n**e**hārâ**, n.f. GK: 5644 [→ 5102; cf. 5094]. (beaming) light:– light [1]

5105.1 נוּ- **-nû**, p.com.pl.suf. GK: 5646 [→ 2967.1]. us, our:– us [775], our [749], we [67], our (+3807.1) [13], our own [8], ours (+3807.1) [5], ourselves [4], it [1], ours [1], thereof (+4480) [1], us-ward (+413) [1], we (+5315) [1]

5105.2 נוּ- **-nû** or נוֹ- **-nô**, p.m.s.suf. GK: 5647 [→ 1886.3]. him, his; it, its:– him [217], it [120], them [36], he [34], thereof (+4480) [16], thereof [12], the same [4], they [4], his [2], themselves [2], thereat (+4480) [2], every one of them [1], him (+5315) [1], himself [1], the[s] [1], their [1], thence [1], thereby [1], therefrom (+4480) [1], thereout (+4480) [1], therewith [1], which [1], whom (+834) [1], whom [1], whosoever (+834) [1]

5106 נוּא **nû'**, v. GK: 5648 [→ 8569]. [Q] to hinder; [H] to forbid, thwart, discourage:– disallowed [2], disallow [2], break [1], discouraged [1], discourage [1], maketh of none effect [1]

5107 נוּב **nûb**, v. GK: 5649 [→ 1838, 5108, 8570]. [Q] to bring forth, bear fruit, increase; [Pol] to make thrive:– bring forth fruit [1], bringeth forth [1], increase [1], make cheerful [1]

5108 נוֹב **nôb** or נִיב **nîb**, n.[m.]. GK: 5650 & 5762 [→ 5107]. fruit; "fruit of the lips" is praise:– fruit [2]

5109 נוֹבַי **nôbay** or נֵיבַי **nêbay**, n.pr.m. GK: 5651 & 5763. Nebai, Nobai, "*thrive*":– Nebai [1]

5110 נוּד **nûd**, v. GK: 5653 [→ 4493, 5112, 5113, 5205; cf. 5074, 5077; cf. 5111]. [Q] to sway, wander, be aimless, become homeless; to mourn, express sympathy (by shaking the head:– bemoan [5], remove [4], vagabond [2], bemoaned [1], bemoaning [1], flee [1], get [1], make move [1], mourn [1], removed [1], shaken [1], skippedst for joy [1], sorry [1], take pity [1], wag [1], wandering [1]

5111 נוּד **nûd** (Aram.), v. GK: 10469 [cf. 5075; cf. 5110]. [P] to flee:– get away [1]

5112 נוֹד **nôd**, n.[m.]. GK: 5654 [→ 5110]. lament; some sources: wandering, homelessness:– wanderings [1]

5113 נוֹד **nôd**, n.pr.loc. GK: 5655 [→ 5110]. Nod, "*wandering*":– Nod [1]

5114 נוֹדָב **nôdāb**, n.pr.g. GK: 5656. Nodab:– Nodab [1]

5115 נָוָה **nāwâ**, v. GK: 5657 & 5658 [→ 5116; cf. 4998]. [Q] to be at rest, reach one's aim; [H] to praise:– keepeth at home [1], prepare a habitation [1]

5116 נָוֶה **nāweh**, n.m. GK: 5659 & 5660 [→ 5115, 4999; cf. 4998]. dwelling, abiding; pasture, pastureland, with a possible focus that this is a place of rest and peace; (generally) abode, dwelling, house:– habitation [21], fold [3], dwelling [2], sheepcote [2], comely [1], dwelling place [1], dwellings [1], folds [1], habitations [1], pleasant place [1], stable [1], tarried [1]

5117 נוּחַ **nûaḥ**, v. GK: 5663 & 5664 [→ 3240; cf. 584]. [Q] to settle, rest, wait; to lament, wail; [H] to put, keep, settle, rest; to leave, allow; [Ho] to be placed, find rest:– rest [15], given rest [12], rested [7], cause to rest [4], give rest [4], at rest [3], caused to rest [3], gave rest [3], resteth [2], ceased [1], confederate [1], giveth rest [1], lay [1], let down [1], make to rest [1], quieted [1], quiet [1], remain [1], set down [1], set [1]

5118 נוֹחַ **nôaḥ**, n.f. GK: 5665 [→ 5119; cf. 3240]. resting place:– rested [2], resting place [1], rest [1]

5119 נוֹחָה **nôḥâ**, n.pr.m. GK: 5666 [→ 5118?; cf. 3240]. Nohah, "*rest*":– Nohah [1]

5120 נוּט **nûṭ**, v. GK: 5667. [Q] to shake, quake:– moved [1]

5121 נָוֹת **nāwôt** or נָוִית **nāwît**, n.pr.loc. GK: 5662 & 5668 & 5766. Navoth, Navith, Naioth, "*dwellings*":– Naioth [6]

5122 נְוָלוּ **n**e**wālû** (Aram.), n.f. GK: 10470. pile of rubble, garbage-heap:– dunghill [3]

5123 נוּם **nûm**, v. GK: 5670 [→ 3241?, 5124, 8572]. [Q] to sleep, slumber, implying detachment from activities and others; by extension: to be dead:– slumber [5], slept [1]

5124 נוּמָה **nûmâ**, n.f. GK: 5671 [→ 5123]. drowsiness:– drowsiness [1]

5125 נוּן **nûn**, v. GK: 5672 [cf. 5126?]. [N] to propagate, increase:– continued [1]

5126 נוּן **nûn**, n.pr.m. GK: 5673 [cf. 5125?]. Nun, "*fish hence fertile, productive*":– Nun [29], Non [1]

5127 נוּס **nûs**, v. GK: 5674 [→ 4498, 4499, 5211]. [Q] to flee away, escape; [Pol] to drive along; [H] to put to flight, get to safety:– fled [80], flee [52], flee away [8], fleeth [5], fled away [3], flee away (+5127) [2], abated [1], displayed [1], fled apace (+4498) [1], fleddest [1], fleeing [1], hide [1], lift up a standard [1], made flee [1], put to flight [1], ran away [1]

5128 נוּעַ **nûa'**, v. GK: 5675 [→ 4517]. [Q] to shake, sway, swagger, wander; [N] to be shaken; [H] to make wander, to set trembling, shake, toss:– moved [5], promoted [3], shaken [3], wandered [3], continually vagabonds (+5128) [2], fugitive [2], reel to and fro (+5128) [2], shake [2], stagger [2], wag [2], wander [2], gone away [1], made wander [1], make [1], moveable [1], move [1], removed [1], scatter [1], set [1], shaked [1], sifted [1], sift [1], wander up and down [1]

5129 נוֹעַדְיָה **nô'adyâ**, n.pr.m. & f. GK: 5676 [→ 3259+3068]. Noadiah, "*meet with Yahweh*":– Noadiah [2]

5130 נוּף **nûp**, v. GK: 5677 & 5678 [→ 5299, 5317, 8573; cf. 5003]. [Q] to sprinkle with myrrh (a bed); [Pol] to wave (the fist) threateningly; [H] to wave, present (an offering) by waving; to shake, wield, sweep; to cause (rain) to fall; [Ho] to be waved:– wave [11], shake [5], waved [5], lift up [4], offer [3], offered [2], shaketh [2], move [1], perfumed [1], send [1], sift [1], strike [1]

5131 נוֹף **nôp**, n.[m.]. GK: 5679 [→ 5299, 5316]. loftiness, elevation, height:– situation [1]

5132 נוּץ **nûṣ**, v. GK: 5680. [Q] to leave, go away:– fled away [1]

5133 נֹצָה **nôṣâ** or נוֹצָה **nôṣâ**, n.f. GK: 5901 & 5902 & 5681. contents (of a bird's crop); plumage, feathers; falcon or other bird:– feathers [4]

5134 נוּק **nûq**, v. GK: 5682 [cf. 3243]. [H] to suckle, nurse:– nursed [1]

5135 נוּר **nûr** (Aram.), n.f. & m. GK: 10471 [cf. 5216]. fire; used for heat, purification, and as a form of execution:– fiery [10], fire [7]

5136 נוּשׁ **nûš**, v. GK: 5683 [cf. 605]. [Q] to be sick:– full of heaviness [1]

5137 נָזָה **nāzâ**, v. GK: 5684 & 5685. [Q] to spatter; [H] to sprinkle; to leap, spring:– sprinkle [17], sprinkled [6], sprinkleth [1]

5138 נָזִיד **nāzîd**, n.[m.]. GK: 5686 [→ 2102]. stew, thick boiled food:– pottage [6]

5139 נָזִיר **nāzîr**, n.m. GK: 5687 [→ 5144]. Nazirite, with the designated meaning of separation; a class of people dedicated to God; untended vine, dedicated to God in the sabbatical year of rest:– Nazarite [9], Nazarites [3], vine undressed [2], separate from [1], separated from [1]

5140 נָזַל **nāzal**, v. GK: 5688 & 5689. [Q] to flow down, pour down, stream down; [H] to make flow:– floods [3], streams [2], caused to flow [1], distil [1], drop [1], flow out [1], flowing [1], flow [1], gush out [1], melted [1], pour down [1], pour [1], running waters [1]

5141 נֶזֶם **nezem**, n.m. GK: 5690. ring (in the nose or ear of male or female):– earrings [9], earring [5], jewel [2], jewels [1]

5142 נְזַק **n^e^zaq** (Aram.), v. GK: 10472 [cf. 5143]. [P] to suffer loss; [H] to cause to suffer, be a detriment, be troublesome:– damage [1], endamage [1], hurtful [1], hurt [1]

5143 נֵזֶק **nēzeq**, n.[m.]. GK: 5691 [cf. 5142]. burden, trouble:– damage [1]

5144 נָזַר **nāzar**, v. GK: 5692 & 5693 [→ 5139, 5145; cf. 4502, 5087]. [N] to separate oneself, consecrate oneself; [H] to keep separate; to abstain, separate as a Nazirite:– separate [4], separateth [3], consecrate [1], separated [1], separating [1]

5145 נֵזֶר **nēzer**, n.m. GK: 5694 [→ 5144; cf. 5087]. separation, dedication (to God); diadem, crown (as a sign of consecration); Nazirite, a class of people dedicated to God:– crown [11], separation [11], consecration [2], hair [1]

5146 נֹחַ **nōaḥ**, n.pr.m. GK: 5695 [→ 5162]. Noah, "*rest, comfort*":– Noah [44], Noah's [2]

5147 נַחְבִּי **naḥbî**, n.pr.m. GK: 5696. Nahbi, "[perhaps] *hidden* or *timid*":– Nahbi [1]

5148 נָחָה **nāḥâ**, v. GK: 5697. [Q, H] to lead, guide:– lead [16], guide [4], led [4], bringeth [2], brought [2], guided [2], leddest [2], bestowed [1], govern [1], leadeth [1], led forth [1], led on [1], put [1], straiteneth [1]

5149 נְחוּם **n^e^ḥûm**, n.pr.m. GK: 5700 [cf. 7348]. Nehum, "*comfort*":– Nehum [1]

5150 נִחֻמִים **niḥumîm**, n.m.[pl.]. GK: 5719 [→ 5162]. comfort, compassion:– comfortable [1], comforts [1], repentings [1]

5151 נַחוּם **naḥûm**, n.pr.m. GK: 5699 [→ 5162]. Nahum, "*comfort*":– Nahum [1]

5152 נָחוֹר **nāḥôr**, n.pr.m. GK: 5701. Nahor, "*the mound of Nahuru*":– Nahor [15], Nahor's [2], Nachor [1]

5153 נָחוּשׁ **nāḥûš**, a. GK: 5702 [→ 5178]. (made) of bronze:– brass [1]

5154 נְחוּשָׁה **n^e^ḥûšâ**, n.f. GK: 5703 [→ 5178; cf. 5174]. copper, bronze:– brass [7], steel [3]

5155 נְחִילוֹת **n^e^ḥîlôt**, n.f. GK: 5704 [→ 2485?; cf. 2490?]. flutes (a t.t. in Ps 5):– Nehiloth [1]

5156 נָחִיר **nāḥîr**, n.[m.]. GK: 5705 [→ 5170, 5170]. (dual) nostrils:– nostrils [1]

5157 נָחַל **nāḥal**, v.den. GK: 5706 [→ 5159]. [Q] to take as an appearance, take possession; [P] to assign an inheritance, allot; [H] to cause to inherit, give an inheritance; [Ho] to be allotted; [Ht] to obtain an inheritance for oneself; to distribute an inheritance:– inherit [16], cause to inherit [5], inherited [3], possess [3], giveth to inherit [2], have inheritance (+5159) [2], cause to possess [1], caused to inherit [1], distribute for inheritance [1], distributed for inheritance [1], divide an inheritance among [1], divide by inheritance [1], divide for an inheritance [1], divide inheritance unto [1], divided for an inheritance [1], divided inheritance [1], divide [1], dividing for inheritance [1], give inheritance [1], given for an inheritance [1], had [1], have inheritance [1], inheritance [1], inheriteth [1], leave for an inheritance [1], leaveth an inheritance [1], made to possess [1], make inherit [1], maketh to inherit [1], possession [1], take as inheritance [1], take for inheritance [1], taken as an heritage [1], took inheritance [1]

5158 נַחַל **naḥal** or נַחְלָה **naḥ^a^lâ**, n.m. & loc. GK: 5707 & 5711 [→ 5160]. river, stream, brook, torrent; ravine, gorge, valley; wadi (of Egypt):– river [46], brook [37], valley [18], brooks [9], rivers [8], stream [7], valleys [5], streams [4], flood [3], floods [2]

5159 נַחֲלָה **naḥ^a^lâ**, n.f. GK: 5709 [→ 5157]. inheritance, property:– inheritance [188], heritage [26], have inheritance (+5157) [2], inherit [2], river [2], have inheritance (+5307) [1], heritages [1], inheritances [1], possession [1]

5160 נַחֲלִיאֵל **naḥ^a^lî'ēl**, n.pr.loc. GK: 5712 [→ 5158+410]. Nahaliel, "*wadi of God [El]*":– Nahaliel [2]

5161 נֶחֱלָמִי **neḥ^e^lāmî**, a.g. GK: 5713. Nehelamite:– Nehelamite [3]

5162 נָחַם **nāḥam**, v. GK: 5714 [→ 4505, 5146, 5151, 5149, 5163, 5164, 5165, 5166, 5150, 5167, 8575, 8576]. [N] to relent, repent, change one's mind; be grieved; [P] to comfort, console, express sympathy; [Pu] to be comforted, be consoled; [Ht] to console oneself; to change one's mind; avenge oneself:– comfort [32], comforted [20], repent [19], repented [17], comforters [5], comforter [4], comforteth [3], repenteth [3], comfortedst [1], ease [1], receive comfort [1], repentest [1], repenting [1]

5163 נַחַם **naḥam**, n.pr.m. GK: 5715 [→ 5162]. Naham, "*repent, console*":– Naham [1]

5164 נֹחַם **nōḥam**, n.m. GK: 5716 [→ 5162]. compassion, pity:– repentance [1]

5165 נֶחָמָה **neḥāmâ**, n.f. GK: 5717 [→ 5162]. comfort, consolation:– comfort [2]

5166 נְחֶמְיָה **n^e^ḥemyâ**, n.pr.m. GK: 5718 [→ 5162+3068]. Nehemiah, "*Yahweh has comforted*":– Nehemiah [8]

5167 נַחֲמָנִי **naḥ^a^mānî**, n.pr.m. GK: 5720 [→ 5162]. Nahamani, "*Yahweh has consoled*":– Nahamani [1]

5168 נַחְנוּ **naḥnû**, p.com.pl. GK: 5721 [→ 587]. we:– we [6]

5169 נָחַץ **nāḥaṣ**, v. GK: 5722 [cf. 3905]. [Qp] to be urgent:– haste [1]

5170 נַחַר **naḥar** or נַחֲרָה **naḥ^a^râ**, n.m. & f. GK: 5724 & 5725 [→ 5156]. snorting (of a horse):– nostrils [1], snorting [1]

5171 נַחְרַי **naḥray**, n.pr.m. GK: 5726. Naharai:– Naharai [2]

5172 נָחַשׁ **nāḥaš**, v.den. GK: 5727 [→ 5173; cf. 3907]. [P] to practice divination, interpret omens and signs:– certainly divine (+5172) [2], indeed divineth (+5172) [2], used enchantments [2], diligently observe [1], enchanter [1], enchantments [1], learned by experience [1], use enchantment [1]

5173 נַחַשׁ **naḥaš**, n.[m.]. GK: 5728 [→ 5172]. sorcery, magic curse, spell:– enchantments [1], enchantment [1]

5174 נְחָשׁ **n^e^ḥāš** (Aram.), n.m. GK: 10473 [cf. 5154, 5178]. bronze material; "brass" is a copper alloy dating from Roman times:– brass [9]

5175 נָחָשׁ **nāḥāš**, n.m. GK: 5729 [→ 5176, 5177]. snake, serpent; by extension: a mythological creature of chaos opposed to God:– serpent [25], serpents [4], serpent's [2]

5176 נָחָשׁ **nāḥāš**, n.pr.m. GK: 5731 [→ 5175]. Nahash, "*viper* or *copper*":– Nahash [9]

נְחֻשָׁה **n^e^ḥušâ**. See 5154.

5177 נַחְשׁוֹן **naḥšôn**, n.pr.m. GK: 5732 [→ 5175]. Nahshon, "*small viper*":– Nahshon [9], Naashon [1]

5178 נְחֹשֶׁת **n^e^ḥōšet**, n.m. GK: 5733 & 5734 [→ 5153, 5154; cf. 5180; cf. 5174]. copper, bronze; this can refer to bronze as a medium of exchange; menstruation:– brass [101], brasen [28], fetters [3], chains [2], fetters of brass [2], chain [1], copper [1], filthiness [1], steel [1]

5179 נְחֻשְׁתָּא **n^e^ḥuštā'**, n.pr.f. GK: 5735. Nehushta, "*[strong as* or *color of] bronze*":– Nehushta [1]

5180 נְחֻשְׁתָּן **n^e^ḥuštān**, n.pr. GK: 5736 [cf. 5178]. Nehushtan, "*bronze viper*":– Nehushtan [1]

5181 נָחַת **nāḥat**, v. GK: 5737 [→ 5183, 5185; cf. 8478; cf. 5182]. [Q] to descend, go down; [N] to be pierced, penetrate; [P] to bend (a bow); to level off; [H] to bring down:– broken [2], cause to come down [1], come down [1], entereth [1], presseth sore (+5921) [1], settlest [1], stick fast [1]

5182 נְחַת **n^e^ḥat** (Aram.), v. GK: 10474 [cf. 5181]. [P] to come down; [H, A] to deposit, store; [Ho] to be deposed:– came down [1], carry [1], coming down [1], deposed [1], laid up [1], place [1]

5183 נַחַת **naḥat**, n.f. & m. GK: 5738 & 5739 [→ 5181, 5184; cf. 3240]. coming down, descending; rest, peace, tranquillity:– rest [4], lighting down [1], quietness [1], quiet [1], that which be set on [1]

5184 נַחַת **naḥat**, n.pr.m. GK: 5740 [→ 5183; cf. 3240]. Nahath, "*descent;* [poss.] *rest*":– Nahath [5]

5185 נָחֵת **nāḥēt**, a. GK: 5741 [→ 5181]. going down, descending:– come down [1]

5186 נָטָה **nāṭâ**, v. GK: 5742 [→ 4294, 4295, 4296, 4297, 4298]. [Q] to spread out, stretch out; [Qp] to be outstretched, be spread out, be extended; [N] to be spread out, be stretched out; [H] to turn aside, pervert, lead astray; [Ho] to be outspread:– stretched out [37], stretch out [22], incline [15], inclined [13], stretched forth [9], turn aside [9], turned [9], pitched [8], turn [7], bowed [5], spread [5], stretch forth [5], bow down [4], stretcheth out [4], declined [3], decline [3], outstretched [3], turned aside [3], turned away [3], wrest [3], bow [2], carried aside [2], declineth [2], extended [2], pervert [2], stretcheth forth [2], afternoon (+3117+1886.1) [1], apply [1], bowing down [1], bowing [1], caused to yield [1], deliver [1], extend [1], go down [1], goeth down [1], gone [1], intended [1], laid [1], lay down [1], let down [1], offer [1], overthrow [1], perverted [1], perverteth [1], prolong [1], put away [1], shewed [1], spread forth [1], spreadeth out [1], stretchedst out [1], stretched [1], stretchest out [1], stretch [1], took aside [1], turn away [1], turned in [1], turneth aside [1], turneth [1]

5187 נָטִיל **nāṭîl**, a. GK: 5744 [→ 5190]. weighing (of precious metals); by extension, trading: buying, selling, and bartering:– bear [1]

5188 נְטִיפָה **n^e^ṭîpâ**, n.[f.]. GK: 5755 [→ 5197]. pendant, a drop-shaped ornament:– chains [1], collars [1]

5189 נְטִישׁוֹת **n^e^ṭîšôt**, n.f. GK: 5746 [→ 5203]. spreading branches, tendrils:– battlements [1], branches [1], plants [1]

5190 נָטַל **nāṭal**, v. GK: 5747 [→ 5187, 5192; cf. 5191]. [Q] to lay upon; to weigh; [P] to lift:– bare [1], borne [1], offer [1], taketh up [1]

Heb

5191 נְטַל **nᵉṭal** (Aram.), v. GK: 10475 [cf. 5190]. [P] to raise up, lift up; [Peil] to be lifted up:– lift up [1], lifted up [1]

5192 נֵטֶל **nēṭel**, n.[m.]. GK: 5748 [→ 5190]. burden, load:– weighty [1]

5193 נָטַע **nāṭa'**, v. GK: 5749 [→ 4302, 5195, 5194, 5196]. [Q] to plant (seed or stock); by extension: to place, set, set up (any object on any surface):– plant [31], planted [21], plantedst [2], planteth [2], fastened [1], planters [1]

5194 נֶטַע **neṭa'**, n.[m.]. GK: 5750 [→ 5193]. garden, plants; young plant:– plant [3], plants [1]

5195 נָטִיעַ **nāṭîa'**, n.[m.]. GK: 5745 [→ 5193]. shoot (of a young plant):– plants [1]

5196 נְטָעִים **nᵉṭā'îm**, n.pr.loc. GK: 5751 [→ 5193]. Netaim:– plants [1]

5197 נָטַף **nāṭap**, v. GK: 5752 [→ 2903, 5188, 5198, 5199, 5200]. [Q] to pour down; gently fall, drip; [H] to (drip words) preach, prophesy:– drop [6], dropped [5], prophesy [4], drop down [1], dropping [1], prophet [1]

5198 נָטָף **nāṭāp**, n.[m.]. GK: 5753 & 5754 [→ 5197]. gum resin, drops of stacte (the resin of a shrub); drop (of water):– drops [1], stacte [1]

5199 נְטֹפָה **nᵉṭōpā**, n.pr.loc. GK: 5756 [→ 5200; cf. 5197]. Netophah, *"trickle, drip"*:– Netophah [2]

5200 נְטוֹפָתִי **nᵉṭôpātî**, a.g. GK: 5743 [→ 5199; cf. 5197]. Netophathite, *"of Netophah"*:– Netophathite [8], Netophathites [2], Netophathi [1]

5201 נָטַר **nāṭar**, v. GK: 5757 [→ 4307; cf. 5341]. [Q] to care for, tend; to be angry, harbor a grudge:– keep [3], bear any grudge against [1], keepers [1], keeper [1], kept [1], reserveth [1], reserve [1]

5202 נְטַר **nᵉṭar** (Aram.), v. GK: 10476 [cf. 5341]. [P] to keep (in one's mind or heart):– kept [1]

5203 נָטַשׁ **nāṭaš**, v. GK: 5759 [→ 5189]. [Q] to abandon, forsake, reject; [Qp] to be scattered; [N] to spread out; to be deserted; [Pu] to be abandoned:– forsake [7], left [7], forsaken [6], leave [5], spread [3], forsook [2], cast off [1], drawn [1], fall [1], joined [1], leave off [1], lie still [1], loosed [1], spread abroad [1], stretched out [1], suffered [1]

5204 נִי **nî**, n.[m.]. GK: 5760 [→ 5092; cf. 5091]. wailing:– wailing [1]

5204.1 נִי- **-nî**, p.com.s.suf. GK: 5761 [→ 2967.1]. I, me, my:– me [1072], I [217], my [7], us [3], myself [2], it [1], let me [1], mine (+4480) [1], mine [1], send me [1]

5204.2 נִי- **-nî** (Aram.), p.suf.1.com.s. GK: 10477 [→ 2967.2; cf. 5204.1]. I, me, my:– me [18]

5205 נִיד **nîd**, n.m. GK: 5764 [→ 5110]. comfort:– moving [1]

5206 נִידָה **nîdâ**, n.f. GK: 5765 [→ 5079; cf. 5077]. uncleanness, impurity:– removed [1]

5207 נִיחֹחַ **nîḥōaḥ**, n.[m.]. GK: 5767 [→ 3240; cf. 5208]. pleasing, soothing, appeasing:– sweet [42], sweet odours [1]

5208 נִיחוֹחַ **nîḥôaḥ** (Aram.), n.[m.]. GK: 10478 [cf. 5207]. incense, pleasing scent:– sweet odours [1], sweet savours [1]

5209 נִין **nîn**, n.[m.]. GK: 5769. offspring, children, posterity:– son [3]

5210 נִינְוֵה **nînᵉwēh**, n.pr.loc. GK: 5770. Nineveh:– Nineveh [17]

5211 נִיס **nîs**, n.m. *or* v. GK: 5771 [→ 5127]. flight, fleeing:–

5212 נִיסָן **nîsān**, n.pr. GK: 5772. Nisan:– Nisan [2]

5213 נִיצוֹץ **nîṣôṣ**, n.[m.]. GK: 5773 [→ 5340]. spark:– spark [1]

5214 נִיר **nîr**, v. GK: 5774 [→ 5215]. [Q] to break up, bring into cultivation:– break up [2]

5215 נִיר **nîr**, n.[m.]. GK: 5776 [→ 5214]. unplowed ground, likely referring to ground not plowed for the current season:– fallow ground [2], plowing [1], tillage [1]

5216 נִיר **nîr** or נֵר **nēr**, n.m. GK: 5775 & 5944 [→ 74, 4501, 5369, 5374; cf. 5102; cf. 5135]. lamp (fueled by olive oil); by extension: life (as a burning lamp); light (showing the way of truth):– lamps [26], lamp [9], candle [8], light [4], candles [1]

5217 נָכָא **nākā'**, v. GK: 5777 [→ 5218, 5219?; cf. 5221]. [N] to be driven out (by whipping or scourging):– viler [1]

5218 נָכָא **nākā'** or נָכֵא **nākē'**, a. GK: 5778 & 5779 [→ 5217]. crushed, beaten, broken; grieving (as one unmercifully beaten):– broken [2], stricken [1], wounded [1]

5219 נְכֹאת **nᵉkō't**, n.f. GK: 5780 [→ 5217?]. spices, resin:– spicery [1], spices [1]

5220 נֶכֶד **neked**, n.[m.]. GK: 5781. descendant, progeny:– nephew [2], son's son [1]

5221 נָכָה **nākâ**, v. GK: 5782 [→ 4347, 5223, 5222; cf. 5217]. [N] to be struck; [Pu] to be destroyed; [H] to kill, slaughter, destroy, defeat; [Ho] to be beat, be struck, be wounded, be killed:– smote [193], smite [95], slew [57], smitten [42], slain [21], killeth [11], smiteth [11], slay [8], slaughter [5], smiting [5], beaten [4], beat [4], kill [4], slay (+5315) [4], given [3], killed [3], stricken [3], wounded [3], indeed smitten (+5221) [2], killeth (+5315) [2], slaying [2], surely smite (+5221) [2], beatest [1], cast forth [1], clapt [1], murderers [1], punish [1], slaughter made (+4347) [1], slayer [1], slewest [1], smiters [1], smitest [1], smotest [1], strike [1], stripes give [1], stripes [1], strooke [1]

5222 נֵכֶה **nēkeh**, a. GK: 5784 [→ 5221]. attacker:– abjects [1]

5223 נָכֶה **nākeh**, a. GK: 5783 [→ 5221]. lame, crippled; contrite:– lame [2], contrite [1]

5224 נְכֹה **nᵉkōh** or נְכוֹ **nᵉkô**, n.pr.m. GK: 5785 & 5786. Neco:– Necho [3]

5225 נָכוֹן **nākôn**, n.pr.m. GK: 5789 [→ 3559]. Nacon, *"established"*:– Nachon's [1]

5226 נֵכַח **nēkaḥ**, subst. (used as pp. & adv.). GK: 5790 [→ 5227, 5228]. same as 5227: opposite, before, in front of:– before (+3807.1) [1], over against [1]

5227 נֹכַח **nōkaḥ**, subst. (used as pp. & adv.). GK: 5790 [→ 5226]. same as 5226: opposite, before, in front of:– before [7], over against [7], against [4], before (+3807.1) [1], directly (+413) [1], for (+3807.1) [1], right before (+6440) [1], right on (+3807.1) [1]

5228 נָכֹחַ **nākōaḥ**, a. & subst. GK: 5791 [→ 5226, 5229]. same as 5229: proper, right, honest, what is straight:– right [2], plain [1], uprightness [1]

5229 נְכֹחָה **nᵉkōḥâ**, a. & subst. GK: 5791 [→ 5228]. same as 5228: proper, right, honest, what is straight:– right [2], equity [1], uprightness [1]

5230 נָכַל **nākal**, v. GK: 5792 [→ 3596?, 5231]. [Q, P] to cheat, treat cunningly; [Ht] to conspire, plot:– beguiled [1], conspired against [1], deal subtilly [1], deceiver [1]

5231 נֵכֶל **nēkel**, n.[m.]. GK: 5793 [→ 5230]. deception, cunning:– wiles [1]

5232 נְכַס **nᵉkas** (Aram.), n.[m.]. GK: 10479 [cf. 5233]. treasury; fine:– goods [2]

5233 נְכָסִים **nᵉkāsîm**, n.m.[pl.]. GK: 5794 [cf. 5232]. riches, wealth, possessions:– wealth [4], riches [1]

5234 נָכַר **nākar**, v. GK: 5795 & 5796 [→ 1971, 5235, 5236, 5237]. [N] to disguise oneself, be not recognized; [P] to regard, consider; to favor; to misunderstand; to treat as foreign; [H] to recognize, acknowledge; [Ht] to pretend to be a stranger; to make known:– knew [8], know [8], acknowledge [6], discern [4], respect [4], discerned [2], known [2], take knowledge [2], acknowledged [1], behave strangely [1], could [1], delivered [1], dissembleth [1], estranged [1], feign to be another [1], feigneth to be another [1], knoweth [1], made strange [1], perceived [1], regardeth [1], took notice [1]

5235 נֵכֶר **nēker**, n.[m.]. GK: 5798 [→ 5234]. misfortune, disaster:– strange punishment [1], stranger [1]

5236 נֵכָר **nēkār**, n.[m.]. GK: 5797 [→ 5234]. (one from a foreign land) foreigner, alien, stranger:– strange [17], strangers (+1121) [6], stranger (+1121) [5], strangers [3], stranger [3], alien [1], stranger's (+1121) [1]

5237 נָכְרִי **nokrî**, a. GK: 5799 [→ 5234]. foreign, alien; (n.) foreigner:– strange [20], stranger [14], alien [3], stranger (+376) [2], strangers [2], aliens [1], foreigners [1], foreigner [1], outlandish [1]

5238 נְכֹת **nᵉkōt**, n.[f.]. GK: 5800. treasure, storage:– precious things [2]

5239 נָלָה **nālâ**, v. GK: 5801 [cf. 3615]. [H] to stop:– make an end [1]

5240 נְמִבְזֶה **nᵉmibzeh**, v.ptcp. GK: 1022 [→ 959]. ptcp. of 959: despised, contemptible:– vile [1]

5241 נְמוּאֵל **nᵉmû'ēl**, n.pr.m. GK: 5803 [→ 5242; cf. 3223, 5272?]. Nemuel:– Nemuel [3]

5242 נְמוּאֵלִי **nᵉmû'ēlî**, a.g. GK: 5804 [→ 5241]. Nemuelite, *"of Nemuel"*:– Nemuelites [1]

5243 נָמַל **nāmal** or מָלַל **mālal**, v. GK: 4909 [cf. 4135]. [Q] to circumcise; to wither away; [N] to be cut off; [Pol] to wither; [Htpol] be blunted (of arrows):– cut down [2], cut off [2], circumcise [1]

5244 נְמָלָה **nᵉmālâ**, n.f. GK: 5805. ant:– ants [1], ant [1]

5245 נְמַר **nᵉmar** (Aram.), n.[m.]. GK: 10480 [cf. 5246]. leopard, panther:– leopard [1]

5246 נָמֵר **nāmēr**, n.m. GK: 5807 [cf. 5245]. leopard:– leopard [4], leopards [2]

נִמְרֹד **nimrōd**. See 5248.

5247 נִמְרָה **nimrâ**, n.pr.loc. GK: 5809 [→ 1039, 5249]. Nimrah, *"spotted leopard; basin of limpid [clear] water"*:– Nimrah [1]

5248 נִמְרֹד ***nimrōd***, n.pr.m. GK: 5808. Nimrod, "[perhaps] *to rebel* or *the Arrow, the mighty hero*":– Nimrod [4]

5249 נִמְרִים ***nimrîm***, n.pr.loc. GK: 5810 [→ 5247]. Nimrim, "*limpid [clear] waters; wholesome waters;* [poss.] *waters of leopards*":– Nimrim [2]

5250 נִמְשִׁי ***nimšî***, n.pr.m. GK: 5811. Nimshi:– Nimshi [5]

5251 נֵס ***nēs***, n.[m.]. GK: 5812 [→ 5264; cf. 5263, 5264]. banner, standard, signal pole:– standard [7], ensign [6], banner [2], pole [2], sail [2], sign [1]

5252 נְסִבָּה ***n^{e}sibbâ***, n.f. GK: 5813 [→ 4141]. turn of events:– cause [1]

5253 נָסַג ***nāsag*** or סוּג ***sûg***, v. GK: 6047 [→ 5472, 7734; cf. 5473, 5509, 7873]. prob. same as 5472: [Q] to turn away, be faithless, be disloyal; [N] to be turned back, be disloyal, be faithless; [H] to move, displace; [Ho] to be driven back:– remove [4], departing away [1], removeth [1], take hold [1], take [1], turned away [1]

נְסָה ***n^{e}sâ***. See 5375.

5254 נָסָה ***nāsâ***, v. GK: 5814 [→ 4531, 4532?]. [P] to test (usually to prove character or faithfulness), to attempt; to test God implies a lack of confidence in his revealed character, thus is wicked:– prove [14], tempted [8], proved [5], tempt [4], adventure [1], assayed [1], assay [1], proveth [1], try [1]

5255 נָסַח ***nāsaḥ***, v. GK: 5815 [cf. 4535?; cf. 5256]. [Q] to tear down; [N] to be uprooted, be torn down:– destroy [1], plucked [1], pluck [1], rooted [1]

5256 נְסַח ***n^{e}saḥ*** (Aram.), v. GK: 10481 [cf. 5255]. [Htpe] to be pulled out:– pulled down [1]

5257 נָסִיךְ ***nāsîk***, n.m. GK: 5816 & 5817 [cf. 5258]. drink offering; metal image, idol; prince, leader:– princes [3], drink offerings [1], dukes [1], principal [1]

5258 נָסַךְ ***nāsak***, v. GK: 5818 & 5820 [→ 4541, 5257, 5262; cf. 3251, 5480; cf. 5260]. [Q] to pour out; to install, set; [N] to be poured out; to be appointed; [P] to pour out; [H] to pour out; [Ho] to be poured out; usually of pouring out a drink offering to deity:– poured out [7], pour out [5], cover [3], offer [2], poured [2], cause to be poured [1], melteth [1], molten [1], pour [1], set up [1], set [1]

5259 נָסַךְ ***nāsak***, v. GK: 5819 [→ 4541, 4545; cf. 5526, 7753]. [Qp] to be woven:– spread [1]

5260 נְסַךְ ***n^{e}sak*** (Aram.), v. GK: 10482 [→ 5261; cf. 5258]. [Pa] to present (an offering):– offer [1]

5261 נְסַךְ ***n^{e}sak*** (Aram.), n.[m.]. GK: 10483 [→ 5260; cf. 5262]. drink offering, libation:– drink offerings [1]

5262 נֶסֶךְ ***nesek***, n.m. GK: 5821 & 5822 [→ 5258; cf. 5261]. drink offering; metal image, idol:– drink offerings [30], drink offering [29], molten image [3], cover withal [1], molten images [1]

נִסְמָן ***nismān***. See 5567.

5263 נָסַס ***nāsas***, v. GK: 5823 [cf. 5251, 5264]. [Q] to falter:– standard-bearer [1]

5264 נָסַס ***nāsas***, v. GK: 5824 [→ 5251; cf. 5251, 5263]. [Htpol] to unfurl; to sparkle:– lifted up as an ensign [1]

5265 נָסַע ***nāsa'***, v. GK: 5825 [→ 4550, 4551]. [Q] to set out, move on, leave, travel on; [N] to be pulled up; [H] to lead, bring out; to pull out:– departed [30], journeyed [28], removed [26], set forward [13], went [8], took journey [7], take journey [5], go forward [3], brought [2], set forth [2], setteth forward [2], went away [2], brought out [1], caused to blow [1], get [1], go away [1], go forth [1], go [1], journeying [1], made to go forth [1], marched [1], on way [1], removeth [1], remove [1], set aside [1], still (+2050.1) [1], took [1], went forth [1], went onward [1], went out [1]

5266 נָסַק ***nāsaq*** or סָלַק ***sālaq***, v. GK: 5826. to go up:– ascend up [1]

5267 נְסַק ***n^{e}saq*** or סְלַק ***s^{e}laq*** (Aram.), v. GK: 10513 [→ 5559]. prob. same as 5559: [P] to come up, go up; [H] to lift up; [Ho] to be lifted up:– take up [1], taken up [1], took up [1]

5268 נִסְרֹךְ ***nisrōk***, n.pr.[m.]. GK: 5827. Nisroch (pagan god):– Nisroch [2]

5269 נֵעָה ***nē'â***, n.pr.loc. GK: 5828. Neah:– Neah [1]

5270 נֹעָה ***nō'â***, n.pr.f. GK: 5829. Noah, "*rest, comfort*":– Noah [4]

5271 נְעוּרִים ***n^e'ûrîm*** or נְעוּרוֹת ***n^e'ûrôt***, n.m. & f.pl. GK: 5830 & 5831 [→ 5286, 5288]. youth, childhood:– youth [46], childhood [1]

5272 נְעִיאֵל ***n^e'î'ēl***, n.pr.loc. GK: 5832 [cf. 5241?]. Neiel:– Neiel [1]

5273 נָעִים ***nā'îm***, a. GK: 5833 & 5834 [→ 5276]. pleasant, charming; singing, sweetly sounding, musical:– pleasant [9], pleasures [2], sweet [2]

5274 נָעַל ***nā'al***, v. GK: 5835 & 5836 [→ 4514, 4515, 5275]. [Q] to lock up, bolt; to put on a sandal; [Qp] to be locked up, be sealed; [H] to provide with sandals:– locked [2], shod [2], bolted [1], bolt [1], inclosed [1], shut up [1]

5275 נַעַל ***na'al***, n.f. GK: 5837 [→ 5274]. sandal (normal footware); not to wear sandals could have the associative meaning of being in poverty, misery, or disgrace:– shoes [11], shoe [9], dryshod [1], shoelatchet (+8288) [1]

5276 נָעֵם ***nā'ēm***, v. GK: 5838 [→ 42, 293, 493, 4516, 5273, 5277, 5278, 5279, 5279, 5281, 5280, 5283, 5282]. [Q] to be pleasant, be dear, be favored:– pleasant [5], delight [1], in beauty [1], sweet [1]

5277 נַעַם ***na'am***, n.pr.m. GK: 5839 [→ 5276]. Naam, "*pleasant*":– Naam [1]

5278 נֹעַם ***nō'am***, n.m. GK: 5840 [→ 42, 293, 493; cf. 5276]. pleasantness, favor:– beauty [4], pleasant [2], pleasantness [1]

5279 נַעֲמָה ***na^{a}mâ***, n.pr.f. & loc. GK: 5841 & 5842 [→ 5276]. Naamah, "*pleasant*":– Naamah [5]

5280 נַעֲמִי ***na^{a}mî***, a.g. GK: 5844 [→ 5281; cf. 5276]. Naamite, "*of Naaman*":– Naamites [1]

5281 נָעֳמִי ***no^{o}mî***, n.pr.f. GK: 5843 [→ 5276]. Naomi, "*my joy*":– Naomi [20], Naomi's [1]

5282 נַעֲמָנִים ***na^{a}mānîm***, n.[m.]. GK: 5846 [→ 5276]. finest (of Adonis [?]):– pleasant [1]

5283 נַעֲמָן ***na^{a}mān***, n.pr.m. GK: 5845 [→ 5280; cf. 5276]. Naaman, "*pleasantness*":– Naaman [15], Naaman's [1]

5284 נַעֲמָתִי ***na^{a}mātî***, a.g. GK: 5847. Naamathite:– Naamathite [4]

5285 נַעֲצוּץ ***na^{a}ṣûṣ***, n.[m.]. GK: 5848. thornbush:– thorns [1], thorn [1]

5286 נָעַר ***nā'ar***, v. GK: 5849 [→ 5271, 5289?, 5288?]. [Q] to growl:– yell [1]

5287 נָעַר ***nā'ar***, v. GK: 5850 [→ 5296]. [Q] to shake off; to refuse; [Qp] be shaken out; [N] to shake oneself free, be shaken off; [P] to shake off, sweep away; [Ht] to shake oneself free:– overthrew [2], shake [2], shake off [1], shake out [1], shaken out [1], shaken [1], shaketh [1], shook [1], tossed up and down [1]

5288 נַעַר ***na'ar***, n.m. GK: 5853 [→ 5271, 5290, 5291, 5292, 5294?; cf. 5286?]. young man, boy, child, ranging in age from infancy to young adulthood; by extension: servant, attendant, steward, with a possible focus on lower social status:– child [44], young men [39], young man [37], lad [32], servant [32], servants [22], young [14], children [7], youth [5], babe [1], boys [1], lads [1], men [1], young men (+376) [1], youths [1]

5289 נַעַר ***na'ar***, n.[m.]. GK: 5852 [→ 5286?]. scattering, shaking; (n.) scattered ones:– young one [1]

5290 נֹעַר ***nō'ar***, n.m. GK: 5854 [→ 5288]. youth:– youth [2], child's [1], child [1]

נָעֻר ***nā'ur***. See 5271.

5291 נַעֲרָה ***na^{a}râ***, n.f. GK: 5855 [→ 5292; cf. 5288]. young woman, girl, ranging in age from infancy to young adulthood; by extension: servant, maid, with a possible focus on lower social status:– damsel [24], maidens [12], damsel's [8], maid [4], young [4], maiden [3], damsels [2], every maid's (+5291+2050.1) [2], maids [2], young maidens [1], young woman [1]

5292 נַעֲרָה ***na^{a}râ***, n.pr.f. & loc. GK: 5856 & 5857 [→ 5291; cf. 5288, 5293?, 5295]. Naarah, "*[young] woman*":– Naarah [3], Naarath [1]

נְעֻרָה ***n^e'urâ***. See 5271.

5293 נַעֲרַי ***na^{a}ray***, n.pr.m. GK: 5858 [cf. 5292?]. Naarai, "*young man of Yahweh*":– Naarai [1]

5294 נְעַרְיָה ***n^e'aryâ***, n.pr.m. GK: 5859 [→ 5288?+3068]. Neariah, "*[young] man of Yahweh*":– Neariah [3]

5295 נַעֲרָן ***na^{a}rān***, n.pr.loc. GK: 5860 [cf. 5292]. Naaran:– Naaran [1]

5296 נְעֹרֶת ***n^e'ōret***, n.f. GK: 5861 [→ 5287]. tinder (broken fibers shaken off flax):– tow [2]

נַעֲרָתָה ***na^{a}rātâ***. See 5292.

5297 נֹף ***nōp***, n.pr.loc. GK: 5862 [cf. 4644]. Noph = Memphis:– Noph [7]

5298 נֶפֶג ***nepeg***, n.pr.m. GK: 5863. Nepheg, "*sprout, shoot*":– Nepheg [4]

5299 נָפָה ***nāpâ***, n.f. GK: 5864 & 5865 [→ 5130, 5131; cf. 5316]. height, yoke; sieve (winnowing device):– borders [1], coast [1], region [1], sieve [1]

5300 נְפוּשְׁסִים ***n^{e}pûssîm*** or נְפוּסִים ***n^{e}pûsîm*** or נְפִישְׁסִים ***n^{e}pîš^{e}sîm***, n.pr.g.?. GK: 5867 & 5866 & 5875 [→ 5304]. Nephushsim, Nephussim, Nephishsim:– Nephishesim [1], Nephusim [1]

5301 נָפַח ***nāpaḥ***, v. GK: 5870 [→ 4646, 4647, 8598; cf. 6315]. [Q] to blow upon, breathe upon; [Qp, Pu] to be blown upon; [H] to sniff out; to cause to breathe out:– blow [3], seething [2], bloweth [1], blown [1], breathed [1], breathe [1], caused to lose [1], given up the ghost (+5315) [1], snuffed [1]

5302 נֹפַח **nōpaḥ**, n.pr.loc. GK: 5871. Nophah:– Nophah [1]

5303 נְפִילִים **n^{e}pîlîm**, n.m.pl. GK: 5872 [→ 5307]. Nephilim:– giants [3]

5304 נְפִיסִים **n^{e}pîsîm**, n.pr.g.?. GK: 5873 [→ 5300]. Nephissim:–

5305 נָפִישׁ **nāpîš**, n.pr.m. GK: 5874 [→ 5314]. Naphish, *"refreshed"*:– Naphish [2], Nephish [1]

5306 נֹפֶךְ **nōpek**, n.[m.]. GK: 5876. turquoise (green semi-precious stone):– emerald [3], emeralds [1]

5307 נָפַל **nāpal**, v. GK: 5877 [→ 4651, 4654, 4658, 5303, 5309; cf. 5308]. [Q] to fall, fail; [Pilal?] to fall; [H] to cause to fall, to cast down, drop; (used of casting lots) to allocate; [Ht] to fall prostrate (to worship); to fall upon (to attack); by extension: to happen (of circumstance falling on a person):– fall [136], fell [98], fallen [52], fell down [20], cast [16], falleth [15], cast down [7], cause to fall [7], fall down [5], divide [4], failed [4], fallen down [3], falling [3], fell away [3], overthrown [3], present [3], rot [3], accepted [2], caused to fall [2], divided [2], fail [2], inferior [2], lay along [2], lighted [2], lost [2], overthrow [2], surely fall (+5307) [2], cast in [1], cast out [1], castedst down [1], casteth into [1], casting down [1], cause to lie down [1], ceased [1], died [1], fall away [1], fallest away [1], fell out [1], felled [1], fellest [1], felling [1], fugitives [1], have inheritance (+5159) [1], judged [1], keepeth [1], lay down [1], lay [1], liest [1], lighted down [1], lying [1], make fall [1], man^s [1], overwhelm (+5921) [1], perish [1], presented [1], presenting [1], slew [1], smite out [1], throw down [1]

Heb

5308 נְפַל **n^{e}pal** (Aram.), v. GK: 10484 [cf. 5307]. [P] to fall:– fall down [3], fell [3], falleth down [2], fell down [2], have occasion [1]

5309 נֵפֶל **nēpel**, n.m. GK: 5878 [→ 5307]. stillborn child, miscarriage:– untimely birth [3]

נְפִל **n^{e}pil**. See 5303.

5310 נָפַץ **nāpaṣ**, v. GK: 5879 & 5880 [→ 4660, 4661, 5311; cf. 6327]. [Q] to shatter; to scatter; [P] to shatter; (of log raft) to separate; [Pu] to be crushed:– break in pieces [9], scattered [2], beaten in sunder [1], brake [1], break [1], broken [1], cause to be discharged [1], dash in pieces [1], dasheth [1], dash [1], dispersed [1], overspread [1], scatter [1]

5311 נֶפֶץ **nepeṣ**, n.[m.]. GK: 5881 [→ 5310]. bursting, pelting (of rain):– scattering [1]

5312 נְפַק **n^{e}paq** (Aram.), v. GK: 10485 [→ 5313]. [P] to go out, come out; [H] to take out, remove:– came forth [3], taken out [2], come forth [1], gone forth [1], take [1], took forth [1], took [1], went forth [1]

5313 נִפְקָה **nipqâ** (Aram.), n.f. GK: 10486 [→ 5312]. expense, cost:– expences [2]

5314 נָפַשׁ **nāpaš**, v.den. GK: 5882 [→ 5305, 5315]. [N] to be refreshed, refresh oneself:– refreshed [3]

5315 נֶפֶשׁ **nepeš**, n.f. GK: 5883 [→ 5314]. breath; by extension: life, life force, soul, an immaterial part of a person, the seat of emotion and desire; a creature or person as a whole: self, body, even corpse:– soul [416], life [100], souls [58], lives [18], persons [13], person [13], heart [12], mind [11], creature [9], himself (+2050.2) [8], yourselves (+3641.1) [6], dead [5], dead body [4], minds [4], slay (+5221) [4], will [4], desire [3], man [3], me (+2967.1) [3], persons (+120) [3], pleasure [3], themselves (+3963.1) [3], any [2], beast [2], body [2], hearts [2], herself (+1886.3) [2], him (+2050.2) [2], killeth (+5221) [2], lust [2], man (+120) [2], thing [2], angry (+4751) [1], appetite [1], breath [1], deadly (+871.1) [1], desire (+5375) [1], discontented (+4751) [1], fish [1], given to appetite [1], given up the ghost (+5301) [1], giving up of the ghost (+4646) [1], greedy (+5794) [1], have a desire (+5375) [1], he (+2050.2) [1], heart's [1], hearty [1], her (+1886.3) [1], he [1], him (+5105.2) [1], him^s [1], his own (+2050.2) [1], life (+2416) [1], men (+120) [1], mortally [1], moving creature [1], myself (+2967.1) [1], one [1], soul's [1], tablets (+1004) [1], they (+3963.1) [1], thyself (+3509.3) [1], we (+5105.1) [1]

5316 נֶפֶת **nepet** or נָפוֹת **nāpôt**, n.f. or loc. GK: 5884 & 5868 [→ 5131; cf. 5299]. hill; or Nephet, Naphoth, *"heights"*:– countries [1]

5317 נֹפֶת **nōpet**, n.m. GK: 5885 [→ 5130]. honey of the honeycomb:– honeycomb [4], honeycomb (+6688) [1]

5318 נֶפְתּוֹחַ **neptôaḥ**, n.pr.loc. GK: 5886. Nephtoah, *"opening"*:– Nephtoah [2]

5319 נַפְתּוּלִים **naptûlîm**, n.[m.pl.]. GK: 5887 [→ 6617]. struggles, wrestlings:– wrestlings [1]

5320 נַפְתֻּחִים **naptuḥîm**, n.pr.loc. & a.g. GK: 5888. Naphtuhite:– Naphtuhim [2]

5321 נַפְתָּלִי **naptālî**, n.pr.m. GK: 5889 [→ 6617?]. Naphtali, *"wrestling"*:– Naphtali [50], Kedesh-naphtali (+6943) [1]

5322 נֵץ **nēṣ**, n.m. GK: 5890 & 5891 [→ 5323, 5340]. blossom; hawk or falcon (bird of prey):– hawk [3], blossoms [1]

5323 נָצָא **nāṣā'**, v. GK: 5892 [→ 5322]. [Q] to fly:– flee [1]

5324 נָצַב **nāṣab**, v. GK: 5893 & 5894 [→ 4673, 4674, 4675, 4676, 4678, 5325, 5333, 5334; cf. 3320]. [N] to stand oneself before; (n.) officer, official; to be wretched, exhausted; [H] to station, set up, establish; [Ho] to be set up, be decreed:– stood [17], set [11], stand [8], set up [7], officers [6], standing [4], standeth [3], stood upright [2], Huzzab [1], appointed [1], at best state [1], deputy [1], erected [1], establish [1], laid [1], made to stand [1], pillar [1], present [1], reared up [1], settest [1], settled [1], sharpen [1], stablish [1], standeth still [1], stoodest [1]

נְצִב **n^{e}ṣib**. See 5333.

5325 נִצָּב **niṣṣāb**, n.m. GK: 5896 [→ 5324]. handle, hilt (of sword, dagger or knife):– haft [1]

5326 נִצְבָּה **niṣbâ** (Aram.), n.f. GK: 10487. hardness, firmness, a quality of strength of a metal:– strength [1]

5327 נָצָה **nāṣâ**, v. GK: 5897 & 5898 [→ 4683, 4695]. [Q] to lie in ruins; [N] to fight (quarreling that can come to blows and struggles); to be laid waste, be desolate; [H] to rebel, engage in a struggle:– strove together [3], strove [3], ruinous [2], strive [2], laid waste [1]

נֹצָה **nōṣâ**. See 5133.

5328 נִצָּה **niṣṣâ**, n.f. GK: 5900 [→ 5340]. blossom:– flower [2]

נְצוּרָה **n^{e}ṣûrâ**. See 5341.

5329 נָצַח **nāṣaḥ**, v. GK: 5904 [→ 5331, 5335; cf. 5330]. [N] to be enduring, lasting; [P] to direct, supervise; (n.) director (of music, t.t. in the Psalms), supervisor:– chief Musician [55], set forward [4], overseers [2], chief singer [1], excel [1], oversee (+5921) [1], perpetual [1]

5330 נְצַח **n^{e}ṣaḥ** (Aram.), v. GK: 10488 [cf. 5329]. [Htpa] to distinguish oneself:– preferred [1]

5331 נֵצַח **nēṣaḥ**, n.m. GK: 5905 [→ 5329]. glory, majesty, splendor; forever, unending, everlasting, always; "the Glory of Israel" as a title of God probably emphasizes both glory and eternity:– ever [20], always (+3807.1) [2], end [2], ever (+3807.1) [2], for ever [2], never (+3808+3807.1) [2], perpetual [2], strength [2], victory [2], alway (+3807.1) [1], constantly (+3807.1) [1], for evermore [1], never (+1077+3807.1) [1], never (+3808+5704) [1], perpetual (+3807.1) [1], surely never (+518+3807.1) [1]

5332 נֵצַח **nēṣaḥ**, n.m. GK: 5906. juice (= blood):– blood [1], strength [1]

5333 נְצִיב **n^{e}ṣîb**, n.m. GK: 5907 [→ 5334; cf. 5324]. garrison, outpost; pillar:– garrisons [5], garrison [4], officer [1], pillar [1]

5334 נְצִיב **n^{e}ṣîb**, n.pr.loc. GK: 5908 [→ 5333; cf. 5324]. Nezib, *"pillar, garrison"*:– Nezib [1]

5335 נְצִיחַ **n^{e}ṣîaḥ**, n.pr.m. GK: 5909 [→ 5329]. Neziah, *"director [of worship]"*:– Neziah [2]

5336 נָצִיר **nāṣîr**, a. GK: 5910 [→ 5341]. preserved:–

5337 נָצַל **nāṣal**, v. GK: 5911 [→ 2020; cf. 5338]. [N] to be saved, be delivered, be spared; [P] to plunder, take away, tear away; [H] to deliver, save, rescue; [Ho] to be snatched; [Ht] to strip off oneself:– deliver [112], delivered [56], delivereth [7], delivered at all (+5337) [4], surely deliver (+5337) [4], rid [3], pluckt [2], recovered [2], recover [2], without fail recover (+5337) [2], defended [1], deliverer [1], deliverest [1], escape (+5869) [1], escaped [1], part (+996) [1], preserved [1], rescued [1], rescue [1], saved [1], spoiled [1], spoil [1], stript off [1], stript [1], taken away [1], taken out [1], taken [1], taketh [1], take [1]

5338 נְצַל **n^{e}ṣal** (Aram.), v. GK: 10489 [cf. 5337]. [H] to save, rescue, deliver:– deliver [2], rescueth [1]

5339 נִצָּנִים **niṣṣānîm**, n.[m.]. GK: 5912 [→ 5340]. blossoms:– flowers [1]

5340 נָצַץ **nāṣaṣ**, v. GK: 5913 & 5914 [→ 5213, 5322, 5328, 5339]. [Q] to gleam, sparkle; [H] to bloom, blossom:– bud forth [1], budded [1], flourish [1], sparkled [1]

5341 נָצַר **nāṣar**, v. GK: 5915 [→ 4453, 4694, 5336; cf. 5201; cf. 5202]. [Q] to guard, watch, protect, keep, preserve; [Qp] to be kept secret, be hidden:– keep [26], preserve [11], keepeth [7], kept [4], watchmen [3], besieged [2], hidden [1], keeper [1], keeping [1], monuments [1], observe [1], preserved [1], preserver [1], preserveth [1], subtil [1], watchers [1]

5342 נֵצֶר **nēṣer**, n.m. GK: 5916. branch, shoot (of a plant):– branch [4]

5343 נְקֵא **n^{e}qē'** (Aram.), a. GK: 10490 [cf. 5355]. pure, clean; this purity can be symbolized by the color white, as of lamb's wool:– pure [1]

5344 נָקַב ***nāqab***, v. GK: 5918 & 5919 [→ 4717, 4718, 5345, 5346, 5347; cf. 3342, 6895]. [Q] to bore (a hole), pierce; to designate, bestow; to blaspheme; [Qp] to have a hole; to be notable; [N] to be designated, be registered:– expressed [6], curse [4], blasphemeth [2], curse at all (+5344) [2], pierce [2], appoint [1], blasphemed [1], bore through [1], bored [1], cursed [1], holes [1], named [1], name [1], pierceth [1], strike through [1]

5345 נֶקֶב ***neqeb***, n.[m.]. GK: 5920 [→ 5344]. mounting (used in gold jewelry):– pipes [1]

5346 נֶקֶב ***neqeb***, n.pr.loc. GK: 5921 [→ 5344]. Nekeb:– Nekeb [1]

5347 נְקֵבָה ***n^{e}qēbâ***, n.f. GK: 5922 [→ 5344]. female, woman:– female [18], woman [2], maid child [1], women [1]

5348 נָקֹד ***nāqōd***, a. GK: 5923 [→ 4719, 5351, 5350]. speckled, spotted:– speckled [9]

5349 נֹקֵד ***nōqēd***, n.m. GK: 5924. shepherd, one who raises sheep:– herdmen [1], sheepmaster [1]

5350 נִקֻּדִים ***niqqudîm***, n.[m.]. GK: 5926 [→ 5348]. (small) cakes; crumbling (food supplies):– mouldy [2], cracknels [1]

5351 נְקֻדָּה ***n^{e}quddâ***, n.f. GK: 5925 [→ 5348]. point, drops (of silver on a gold earring):– studs [1]

5352 נָקָה ***nāqâ***, v. GK: 5927 [→ 4518, 5355, 5356]. [Q] to go unpunished; [N] be innocent, be released, go unpunished; [P] to leave unpunished, consider innocent, pardon:– unpunished [6], innocent [4], hold guiltless [3], altogether go unpunished (+5352) [2], at all acquit (+5352) [2], cleanse [2], clear (+5352) [2], clearing (+5352) [2], clear [2], cut off [2], free [2], guiltless [2], leave altogether unpunished (+5352) [2], leave wholly unpunished (+5352) [2], utterly unpunished (+5352) [2], acquit [1], blameless [1], cleansed [1], desolate [1], go unpunished [1], hold innocent [1], quit [1]

5353 נְקוֹדָא ***n^{e}qôdā'***, n.pr.m. GK: 5928. Nekoda:– Nekoda [4]

5354 נָקַט ***nāqaṭ*** or קוּט ***qûṭ***, v. GK: 7752 [→ 6900, 6962, cf. 6973, 8262]. prob. same as 6962: [Q] to feel anger, loathing; [N] to feel loathing; [Htpolal] to loathe, abhor:– weary [1]

5355 נָקִי ***nāqî*** or נָקִיא ***nāqî'***, a. GK: 5929 & 5930 [→ 5352; cf. 5343]. innocent, free of blame, not guilty:– innocent [29], guiltless [4], blameless [2], innocents [2], quit [2], clean [1], clear [1], exempted [1], free [1]

5356 נִקָּיוֹן ***niqqāyôn***, n.[m.]. GK: 5931 [→ 5352]. cleanness, purity; by extension: moral or ceremonial innocence, purity, cleanness; "cleanness of teeth" is a sign of lack of food in famine:– innocency [4], cleanness [1]

5357 נָקִיק ***nāqîq***, n.m. GK: 5932. crevice, cleft, crack:– holes [2], hole [1]

5358 נָקַם ***nāqam***, v. GK: 5933 [→ 5359, 5360]. [Q] to seek vengeance, avenge; [N] to be avenged, avenge oneself; [P] to avenge; [Ho or Qp] to be avenged; [Ht] to take one's own vengeance:– avenged [8], avenge [7], avenger [2], revengeth [2], surely punished (+5358) [2], take vengeance [2], avenge (+5360) [1], avenge the quarrel (+5359) [1], avenged (+5359) [1], punished [1], revenged [1], revenge [1], take vengeance (+5359) [1], take vengeance (+5360) [1], taken vengeance (+5359) [1], taking vengeance (+5359) [1], tookest vengeance [1], vengeance taken [1]

5359 נָקָם ***nāqām***, n.m. GK: 5934 [→ 5360; cf. 5358]. vengeance, revenge:– vengeance [12], avenge the quarrel (+5358) [1], avenged (+5358) [1], take vengeance (+5358) [1], taken vengeance (+5358) [1], taking vengeance (+5358) [1]

5360 נְקָמָה ***n^{e}qāmâ***, n.f. GK: 5935 [→ 5359; cf. 5358]. vengeance, revenge:– vengeance [18], avengeth (+5414) [2], revenge [2], avenge (+5358) [1], avenge (+5414) [1], avenged (+5414) [1], revenging [1], take vengeance (+5358) [1]

5361 נָקַע ***nāqa'***, v. GK: 5936 [cf. 3363]. [Q] to turn away in disgust:– alienated [3]

5362 נָקַף ***nāqap***, v. GK: 5937 & 5938 [→ 5363, 5364; cf. 8622]. [Q] to go through a yearly cycle; [P] to cut down; to be destroyed; [H] to surround, encircle, engulf:– compassed about [2], compassed [2], compassing [2], compass [2], go round about [2], compass about [1], cut down [1], destroy [1], going about [1], gone about [1], gone round about [1], inclosed [1], kill [1], round [1]

5363 נֹקֶף ***nōqep***, n.[m.]. GK: 5939 [→ 5362]. beating (fruit off olive tree in harvest):– shaking [2]

5364 נִקְפָּה ***niqpâ***, n.f. GK: 5940 [→ 5362]. rope (around waist):– rent [1]

5365 נָקַר ***nāqar***, v. GK: 5941 [→ 5366]. [Q] to gouge out, peck out (an eye); [P] to gouge out; to pierce; [Pu] to be hewn out (of quarry rock):– put out [2], digged [1], pick out [1], pierced [1], thrust out [1]

5366 נְקָרָה ***n^{e}qārâ***, n.f. GK: 5942 [→ 5365]. cleft; cavern:– clifts [1], clift [1]

5367 נָקַשׁ ***nāqaš***, v. GK: 5943 [cf. 3369, 6983; cf. 5368]. [N] to be ensnared; [P] to lay out snares; [Ht] to lay out traps, set a trap:– snared [2], catch [1], lay snares [1], layest a snare [1]

5368 נְקַשׁ ***n^{e}qaš*** (Aram.), v. GK: 10491 [cf. 5367]. [P] to knock (together):– smote [1]

נֵר ***nēr***, נִר ***nir***. See 5215, 5216.

5369 נֵר ***nēr***, n.pr.m. GK: 5945 [→ 5216]. Ner, "*lamp*":– Ner [16]

5370 נֵרְגַל ***nēr^{e}gal***, n.pr. GK: 5946 [→ 5371]. Nergal (pagan god):– Nergal [1]

5371 נֵרְגַל שַׂר־אֶצֶר ***nērgal śar-'eṣer***, n.pr.m. GK: 5947 [→ 5370+8272]. Nergal-Sharezer, "*Nergal protect the prince!*":– Nergal-sharezer [3]

5372 נִרְגָּן ***nirgān***, v.ptcp. GK: 8087 [→ 7279]. ptcp. of 7279: grumbling, gossiping:– talebearer [3], whisperer [1]

5373 נֵרְדְּ ***nērd***, n.m. GK: 5948. nard (aromatic ointment):– spikenard [3]

נֵרָה ***nērâ***. See 5216.

5374 נֵרִיָּה ***nēriyyâ*** or נֵרִיָּהוּ ***nēriyyāhû***, n.pr.m. GK: 5949 & 5950 [→ 4490]. Neriah, "*lamp of Yahweh*":– Neriah [10]

5375 נָשָׂא ***nāśā'***, v. GK: 5951 [→ 4984]. [Q] to bear, carry, lift up; forgive; [Qp] to be forgiven, honored, carried; [N] to be carried off, lifted up; [P] to elevate, carry along; [H] to cause to carry, to bring; [Ht] to exalt oneself, lift up oneself; from the base meaning of rise in elevation come fig. extensions "to exalt, honor," as the lifting up of a person in status, and "to forgive," as the removal of guilt and its penalties; "to lift up the eyes" means "to look up":– lift up [121], bear [96], lifted up [37], bare [33], take [30], took up [22], take up [20], armourbearer (+3627) [18], took [18], carry [14], borne [13], carried [13], brought [11], bearing [10], bring [8], forgive [8], take away [8], beareth [7], exalted [7], set up [7], accept [6], taken [5], took away [5], carry away [4], forgiven [4], honourable (+6440) [4], laid [4], obtained [4], suffer [4], bringing [3], carrying [3], pardon [3], receive [3], spare [3], stirred up [3], taken away [3], accept (+6440) [2], accepted (+6440) [2], advanced [2], bring forth [2], burnt [2], carried away [2], continued (+3254) [2], exalt [2], forgavest [2], forgiving [2], high [2], laden [2], lifteth up [2], must needs be borne (+5375) [2], regard [2], respect [2], set [2], taketh [2], utterly take away (+5375) [2], wear [2], able to bear [1], accepted [1], accepteth [1], arise [1], bare up [1], barest [1], bear up [1], been [1], brought forth [1], carrieth away [1], cast [1], contain [1], desire (+5315) [1], ease [1], exalted above [1], extolled [1], fetch [1], fet [1], furnished [1], furthered [1], gift [1], given [1], hadst [1], have a desire (+5315) [1], helped [1], help [1], hold up [1], laded [1], liftest up [1], lifting up [1], lofty [1], magnified [1], married (+3807.1) [1], offer [1], pardoneth [1], pluck up [1], raise up [1], raise [1], regard (+6440) [1], regard persons (+4480+6440) [1], regardeth [1], respected [1], setteth [1], suffer to bear [1], suffered [1], sware (+3027) [1], swear (+3027) [1], swear [1], taken up [1], takest [1], taketh up [1], wearing [1], went on journey (+7272) [1], yield [1]

5376 נְשָׂא ***n^{e}śā'*** (Aram.), v. GK: 10492 [cf. 4984]. [P] to take away, carry away; [Htpa] to revolt, rise up:– carried away [1], made insurrection [1], take [1]

5377 נָשָׁא ***nāšā'***, v. GK: 5958 [→ 4860, 4876]. [N] to be deceived; [H] to deceive:– deceive [7], deceived [4], greatly deceived (+5377) [2], beguiled [1], seize [1], utterly forget (+5382) [1]

5378 נָשָׁא ***nāšā'***, v. GK: 5957 [→ 4855, 4859, 4874, 5383, 5386; cf. 5392]. [Q] to give a loan, be a creditor; [H] to make a loan; to subject one to tribute:– exact [2], debt [1], taker of usury [1]

נָשִׂא ***nāsi'***. See 5387.

נְשֻׂאָה ***n^{e}su'â***. See 5385.

5379 נִשֵּׂאת ***niśśē't***, v.ptcp. GK: 5951 [→ 4984]. ptcp. of 5375: something lifted up, taken; gift:–

5380 נָשַׁב ***nāšab***, v. GK: 5959 [→ 822; cf. 5395, 5398]. [Q] to blow; [H] to cause to blow; to drive away:– bloweth [1], causeth to blow [1], drove away [1]

5381 נָשַׂג ***nāśag***, v. GK: 5952. [H] to overtake, catch up, attain; to reach, to be able to afford:– overtake [13], overtook [7], take hold [3], able to get (+3027) [2], obtain [2], reach unto [2], surely overtake (+5381) [2], ability (+3027) [1], able (+1767+3027+3509.1) [1], able (+3027) [1], able to bring (+3027) [1], attain unto [1], attained unto [1], can get (+3027) [1], get (+3027) [1], get [1], hand is able to get (+3027) [1], layeth [1], overtaken [1], overtaketh [1], put [1], remove [1], take hold on [1], taken hold upon [1], take [1], wax rich (+3027) [1]

5382 נָשָׁה ***nāšâ***, v. GK: 5960 [→ 4519, 4520, 5388; cf. 7876]. [Q] to forget; [N] to be forgotten; [P] to make forget; [H] to make one forget; to allow one to forget:– deprived [1],

Heb

exacteth [1], forgat [1], forgotten [1], made forget [1], utterly forget (+5377) [1]

5383 נָשָׁה nāšâ, v. GK: 5957 [→ 5378]. same as 5378: [Q] to give a loan, be a creditor; [H] to make a loan; to subject one to tribute:– exact [2], lent on usury [2], creditors [1], creditor [1], extortioner [1], giver of usury [1], lend (+4859) [1], lendeth [1], lend [1], usurer [1]

5384 נָשֶׁה nāšeh, n.[m.]. GK: 5962. tendon (attached to the hip), perhaps the sciatic nerve:– shrank [2]

5385 נְשׂוּאָה nᵉśû'â, n.f. GK: 5953 [→ 4984]. burden, load (of images that are carried about):– carriages [1]

5386 נְשִׁי nᵉšî, n.[m.]. GK: 5963 [→ 5378]. debt:– debt [1]

5387 נָשִׂיא nāśî', n.m. GK: 5954 & 5955 [→ 4984]. leader, ruler, chief, prince; cloud, rising mist, damp fog:– prince [55], princes [40], captain [12], chief [9], rulers [3], ruler [3], vapours [3], chief over [1], clouds [1], governor [1], prince's (+3807.1) [1], prince's [1]

5388 נְשִׁיָּה nᵉšiyyâ, n.f. GK: 5964 [→ 5382]. oblivion, place forgotten (by the LORD):– forgetfulness [1]

נָשִׁים nāšîm. See 802.

5389 נְשִׁין nᵉšîn (Aram.), n.f.pl. GK: 10493 [cf. 802]. wives, women:– wives [1]

5390 נְשִׁיקָה nᵉšîqâ, n.f. GK: 5965 [→ 5401]. kiss:– kisses [2]

5391 נָשַׁךְ nāšak, v. GK: 5966 & 5967 [→ 5392]. [Q] to bite; to earn interest; to claim interest against; [Qp] to be bitten; [P] to bite; [H] to charge interest:– bite [6], lend upon usury [3], biteth [2], bitten [2], bit [2], lent upon usury [1]

5392 נֶשֶׁךְ nešek, n.[m.]. GK: 5968 [→ 5391; cf. 5378]. interest, usury:– usury [12]

5393 נִשְׁכָּה niškâ, n.f. GK: 5969 [cf. 3957]. room (for various uses: living, storage, etc.):– chamber [2], chambers [1]

5394 נָשַׁל nāšal, v. GK: 5970. [Q] to take off, come off; to drive out:– cast out [1], cast [1], drave [1], loose [1], put off [1], put out [1], slippeth [1]

5395 נָשַׁם nāšam, v. GK: 5971 [→ 5397, 8580; cf. 5380, 5398]. [Q] to gasp, pant:– destroy [1]

5396 נִשְׁמָה nišmâ (Aram.), n.f. GK: 10494 [cf. 5397]. breath, air that enters and exhales the lungs; fig., that which is animate and conscious: life:– breath [1]

5397 נְשָׁמָה nᵉšāmâ, n.f. GK: 5972 [→ 5395; cf. 5396]. breath, blast of breath; by extension: life, life force, spirit:– breath [11], blast [3], breathed [2], breathe [2], spirit [2], breath (+7307) [1], breatheth [1], inspiration [1], souls [1]

5398 נָשַׁף nāšap, v. GK: 5973 [→ 3244, 5399; cf. 5380, 5395]. [Q] to blow:– blow [2]

5399 נֶשֶׁף nešep, n.m. GK: 5974 [→ 5398]. dusk, dawn (of morning); twilight (of evening):– twilight [6], night [3], dark [1], dawning of the day [1], dawning of the morning [1]

5400 נָשַׂק nāśaq, v. GK: 5956. [N] to be kindled; [H] to kindle a fire, burn:– burn [1], kindled [1], kindleth [1]

5401 נָשַׁק nāšaq, v. GK: 5975 & 5976 [→ 5390, 5402]. [Q] to be equipped, arm oneself; to kiss; [P] to kiss (repeatedly or intensely); a kiss can show familial or romantic affection, as well as homage and submission; [H] to brush against, touch up against:– kissed [21], kiss [9], armed [3], ruled [1], touched [1]

5402 נֶשֶׁק nešeq, n.[m.]. GK: 5977 [→ 5401]. weapon; armory:– armour [3], weapons [2], armed men [1], armoury [1], battle [1], harness [1], weapon [1]

5403 נְשַׁר nᵉšar (Aram.), n.m. GK: 10495 [cf. 5404]. eagle, vulture:– eagle's [1], eagles' [1]

5404 נֶשֶׁר nešer, n.m. GK: 5979 [cf. 5403]. eagle; vulture:– eagle [19], eagles [5], eagle's [1], eagles' [1]

5405 נָשַׁת nāšat, v. GK: 5980. [Q] to be dry, be parched; [N] to be dried up:– failed [1], faileth [1], fail [1]

נְתִיבָה nᵉtîbâ. See 5410.

5406 נִשְׁתְּוָן ništᵉwān, n.[m.]. GK: 5981 [cf. 5407]. letter, writing:– letter [2]

5407 נִשְׁתְּוָן ništᵉwān (Aram.), n.m. GK: 10496 [cf. 5406]. official letter, decree:– letter [3]

נָתוּן natûn. See 5411.

5408 נָתַח nātaḥ, v. GK: 5983 [→ 5409]. [P] to cut into pieces:– cut [4], cut in pieces [3], divided [1], hewed in pieces [1]

5409 נֵתַח nētaḥ, n.m. GK: 5984 [→ 5408]. piece (of butchered things or persons):– pieces [9], piece [3], parts [1]

5410 נָתִיב nātîb or **נְתִיבָה nᵉtîbâ**, n.m. & f. GK: 5985 & 5986. path, way, road; by extension: behavior, lifestyle:– paths [14], path [8], way [2], pathway (+1870) [1], travellers (+1980) [1]

5411 נָתִין nātîn, n.m. GK: 5987 [cf. 5414; cf. 5412]. temple servant:– Nethinims [17]

5412 נְתִין nᵉtîn (Aram.), n.m.pl. GK: 10497 [→ 5415; cf. 5411]. temple servant:– Nethinims [1]

5413 נָתַךְ nātak, v. GK: 5988 [→ 2046]. [Q] to pour out; [N] to be poured out, be melted; [H] to pour out (liquid or money); to melt; [Ho] to be melted:– poured out [7], poured forth [3], poured [3], melted [2], melt [2], dropped [1], gathered together [1], gathered [1], molten [1]

5414 נָתַן nātan, v. GK: 5989 [→ 866, 869, 868, 4976, 4977, 4979, 4980, 4991, 4992, 5411, 5416; cf. 4060, 5083; cf. 5415 (also used with compound proper names)]. [Q] to give, put; [Qp] to be given, dedicated; [N] to be given; [Ho or Qp] to be given; note the many contextual translations in the KJV:– give [471], gave [252], given [246], put [185], set [99], delivered [94], giveth [77], deliver [72], make [66], made [41], lay [22], gavest [21], O that (+4310) [17], yield [13], grant [12], laid [11], suffer [11], bring [10], granted [9], recompense [9], appointed [7], caused [7], givest [7], suffered [7], give up [6], send [6], cast [5], cause [5], committed [5], giving [5], shew [5], uttered [5], let [4], sent [4], surely give (+5414) [4], traded [4], utter [4], wholly given (+5414) [4], appoint [3], brought [3], fasten [3], occupied [3], place [3], putteth [3], set up [3], uttereth [3], add [2], applied [2], ascribed [2], ascribe [2], assigned [2], avengeth (+5360) [2], bestowed [2], bestow [2], bringeth [2], deliver up [2], delivered up [2], doubtless deliver (+5414) [2], fastened [2], given forth [2], hang up [2], indeed deliver (+5414) [2], laid up [2], maketh [2], offer [2], ordained [2], pay [2], surely given (+5414) [2], willingly give (+5414) [2], without fail deliver (+5414) [2], would God (+4310) [2], would to God (+4310) [2], God [1], appoint out [1], are delivered [1], avenge (+5360) [1], avenged (+5360) [1], be [1], bring forth [1], bringeth forth [1], causeth [1], charged [1], charge [1], cometh [1], commit [1], considered [1], count [1], cried [1], crieth out (+6963+871.1) [1], cry (+6963) [1], deliver over [1], deliveredst [1], delivereth [1], direct [1], distribute [1], done [1], frame [1], gave up [1], gift [1], give (+3027+871.1) [1], give forth [1], give leave [1], give out [1], give over [1], given over [1], given up [1], gotten [1], hang [1], hath [1], having the oversight (+871.1) [1], layeth up [1], leave [1], left [1], lend [1], let (+3807.1) [1], let out [1], lie (+7903) [1], lie carnally (+2233+7903+3807.1) [1], lie with (+7903) [1], lift up [1], liftest up [1], made sit [1], paid [1], pay (+4377) [1], perform [1], placed [1], planted [1], plant [1], pour [1], presented [1], print [1], pulled [1], put forth [1], put in [1], put on [1], put out [1], puttest [1], putteth out [1], putting [1], recompensed [1], recompensing [1], render [1], requite [1], restored [1], send out [1], sendeth forth [1], sendeth [1], sent out [1], set forth [1], setting [1], shewedst [1], shewed [1], shoot forth [1], shoot up [1], shot up [1], sing (+6963) [1], slanderest (+1848) [1], strike [1], submitted [1], suffereth [1], surely delivered [1], take heed (+3820) [1], taken up [1], thrust [1], tied [1], took [1], turned [1], turn [1], wept aloud (+1065+6963+871.1) [1], withdrew (+5637) [1], would God that (+4310) [1], yelled (+6963) [1], yield (+3027) [1], yieldeth [1]

5415 נְתַן nᵉtan (Aram.), v. GK: 10498 [→ 4978, 5412; cf. 3052; cf. 5414]. [P] to give, provide, supply:– giveth [3], bestow [2], give [1], pay [1]

5416 נָתָן nātān, n.pr.m. GK: 5990 [→ 5414]. Nathan, *"gift"*:– Nathan [42]

5417 נְתַנְאֵל nᵉtan'ēl, n.pr.m. GK: 5991 [→ 5321+410]. Nethanel, *"God [El] has given"*:– Nethaneel [14]

5418 נְתַנְיָה nᵉtanyâ or **נְתַנְיָהוּ nᵉtanyāhû**, n.pr.m. GK: 5992 & 5993 [→ 5414+3068]. Nethaniah, *"Yahweh has given"*:– Nethaniah [20]

5419 נְתַן־מֶלֶךְ nᵉtan-melek, n.pr.m. GK: 5994 [→ 5414+4428]. Nathan-Melech, *"gift of king* or *gift of Melek, Molech, Malk"*:– Nathan-melech [1]

5420 נָתַס nātas, v. GK: 5995 [cf. 5421, 5422, 5428]. [Q] to break up, tear up:– mar [1]

5421 נָתַע nāta', v. GK: 5996 [cf. 5420, 5422, 5428]. [N] to be broken down, be knocked out (of teeth):– broken [1]

5422 נָתַץ nātaṣ, v. GK: 5997 [cf. 5420, 5421, 5428]. [Q] to break down, tear down, demolish; [Qp] to be broken down; [N] to be shattered, lay in ruins; [P] to tear down, break down, shatter, destroy; [Pu] to be demolished; [Ho] to be broken up:– brake down [12], break down [5], broken down [5], destroy [4], beat down [3], cast down [3], thrown down [3], pull down [2], break out [1], destroyed [1], overthrow [1], threw down [1], throw down [1]

5423 נָתַק ***nātaq***, v. GK: 5998 [→ 5424]. [Q] to draw away, pull off; [Qp] to be torn; [N] to be lured away, be shattered, be torn, be broken; [P] to break, tear; [H] to lure away, drag off; [Ho] to be drawn away:– broken [6], burst [3], brake [2], drawn away [2], brake in sunder [1], break asunder [1], break [1], broken off [1], burst in sunder [1], drawn [1], draw [1], lift up [1], pluck off [1], plucked away [1], pluck [1], pull out [1], pull up [1], rooted out [1]

5424 נֶתֶק ***neteq***, n.m. GK: 5999 [→ 5423]. diseased area of skin: itch; some sources: ringworm, eczema:– scall [13], dry scall [1]

5425 נָתַר ***nātar***, v. GK: 6000 & 6001 & 6002. [Q] to leap up; [P] to hop up; [H] to make leap up, jump up; to let loose, set free, release, untie; withdraw:– drove asunder [1], leap [1], loosed [1], looseth [1], loose [1], maketh [1], moved [1], undo [1]

5426 נְתַר ***n^{e}tar*** (Aram.), v. GK: 10499. [H/A] to strip off, shake off:– shake off [1]

5427 נֶתֶר ***neter***, n.[m.]. GK: 6003. natron (a sodium carbonate for washing):– nitre [2]

5428 נָתַשׁ ***nātaš***, v. GK: 6004 [cf. 5420, 5421, 5422]. [Q] to uproot; [N] to be uprooted; [Ho] to be uprooted:– pluck up [6], plucked up [2], utterly pluck up (+5428) [2], destroyed [1], forsaken [1], pluck out [1], pluck up by the roots [1], plucked out [1], pluckt up [1], pluck [1], pulled up [1], root out [1], root up [1], rooted out [1]

5429 סְאָה ***s^e'â***, n.f. GK: 6006. seah (dry measure, one-third of an ephah, about seven quarts or liters):– two measures [4], measure [3], measures [2]

5430 סְאוֹן ***s^e'ôn***, n.m. GK: 6007 [→ 5431]. boot:– battle [1]

5431 סָאַן ***sā'an***, v.den. GK: 6008 [→ 5430]. [Q] to tramp along in boots:– warrior [1]

5432 סַאסְּאָה ***sa'ss^e'â***, n.f. GK: 6009. warfare, chasing away:– measure [1]

5433 סָבָא ***sābā'***, v. or סָבָא ***sābā'***, n.m. GK: 6010 [→ 5435]. [Q] to be a drunkard, drink too much; [Qp] to be drunk; others: bind-weed, shrub; others: Sabean, cf. 5434:– drunkard [2], drunken [1], fill [1]

5434 סְבָא ***s^{e}bā'***, n.pr.m. GK: 6013 [→ 5436]. Seba:– Seba [4]

5435 סֹבֶא ***sōbe'***, n.m. GK: 6011 [→ 5433]. wine, drink, implying drunkenness:– drink [1], drunkards [1], wine [1]

5436 סְבָאִי ***s^{e}bā'î***, n.pl.g. GK: 6014 [→ 5434]. Sabean:– Sabeans [2]

5437 סָבַב ***sābab***, v. GK: 6015 [→ 4141]. [Q] to go around, surround, encircle, engulf; [N] to change direction; to be surrounded; [P] to change; [Pol] to surround, shield, go about; [H] to turn about, circle around; [Ho] to be set, mounted, surrounded; to be changed:– turned [21], compassed [15], compassed about [10], turn [10], compass [9], compass about [7], turned about [6], went about [6], go about [5], carried about [3], compasseth [3], led about [3], beset round about [2], changed [2], compassed in [2], driven [2], fetch a compass [2], go round about [2], inclosed [2], remove [2], returned [2], turn away [2], turned away [2], whirleth about continually (+1980+5437) [2], winding about [2], about on every side [1], applied [1], avoided [1], beset about [1], besieged [1], bring about [1], bring again [1], brought about [1], came round about [1], cast about [1], caused about [1], circuit [1], closed round about [1], compass round about (+5439) [1], compass round about [1], compassed round [1], compasseth about [1], environ round [1], fetch about [1], fetched a compass [1], fetcht a compass [1], gone about [1], make about [1], occasioned [1], on every side [1], removed [1], round about compassing (+5439) [1], set [1], sit down [1], stood round about [1], turn aside [1], turn back [1], turned aside [1], turned back [1], turneth about [1], turneth [1], turning [1], walk about [1]

5438 סִבָּה ***sibbâ***, n.f. GK: 6016 [→ 4141]. turning, arrangement (of events):– cause [1]

5439 סָבִיב ***sābîb***, subst. (used as pp. & adv.). GK: 6017 [→ 4141]. all around, on all sides, surrounding, encircling:– round about [204], round about (+5439) [52], about [24], round about (+4480) [20], on every side (+4480) [15], on every side [7], every side [3], on every side (+5439) [2], about (+4480) [1], all about [1], circuits [1], compass round about (+5437) [1], compass [1], in compass [1], places round about [1], round about compassing (+5437) [1]

5440 סָבַךְ ***sābak***, v. GK: 6018 [→ 5442, 5441; cf. 7730]. [Qp, Pu] to be entangled, entwined:– folden together [1], wrapped [1]

5441 סְבֹךְ ***s^{e}bōk***, n.[m.]. GK: 6020 [→ 5440]. thicket, underbrush (where animals can live or hide):– thicket [1]

5442 סְבַךְ ***s^{e}bak***, n.[m.]. GK: 6019 [→ 5440]. thicket, underbrush:– thickets [2], thicket [1], thick [1]

5443 שַׂבְּכָא ***śabb^{e}kā'*** or סַבְּכָא ***sabb^{e}kā'*** (Aram.), n.[f.]. GK: 10676 & 10501 [cf. 7638]. lyre (triangular instrument with four strings):– sackbut [4]

5444 סִבְּכַי ***sibb^{e}kay***, n.pr.m. GK: 6021. Sibbecai:– Sibbecai [2], Sibbechai [2]

5445 סָבַל ***sābal***, v. GK: 6022 [→ 5447, 5448, 5449, 5450; cf. 2082; cf. 5446]. [Q] to bear, carry, sustain; [Pu] to be (heavy) laden; [Ht] to drag oneself along:– carry [3], bear [2], borne [1], burden [1], carried [1], strong to labour [1]

5446 סְבַל ***s^{e}bal*** (Aram.), v. GK: 10502 [cf. 5445]. [Po] to be laid:– strongly laid [1]

5447 סֵבֶל ***sēbel***, n.[m.]. GK: 6023 [→ 5445]. burden; forced labor:– burdens [1], burden [1], charge [1]

5448 סֹבֶל ***sōbel***, n.m. GK: 6024 [→ 5445]. burden:– burden [3]

5449 סַבָּל ***sabbāl***, n.[m.]. GK: 6025 [→ 5445]. carrier, burden-bearer:– bearers of burdens [3], burdens [2]

5450 סִבְלוֹת ***siblôt***, n.f. GK: 6026 [→ 5445]. forced labor, burden-bearer:– burdens [6]

5451 סִבֹּלֶת ***sibbōlet***, n.f. GK: 6027 [cf. 7641]. Sibboleth, "*ear of grain* or *torrent of water*":– sibboleth [1]

5452 סְבַר ***s^{e}bar*** (Aram.), v. GK: 10503 [cf. 7663]. [P] to try, strive, seek:– think [1]

5453 סִבְרַיִם ***sibrayim***, n.pr.loc. GK: 6028. Sibraim:– Sibraim [1]

5454 סַבְתָּא ***sabtā'*** or סַבְתָּה ***sabtâ***, n.pr.g. GK: 6029 & 6030. Sabta, Sabtah:– Sabtah [1], Sabta [1]

5455 סַבְתְּכָא ***sabt^{e}kā'***, n.pr.g. GK: 6031. Sabteca:– Sabtecha [2]

5456 סָגַד ***sāgad***, v. GK: 6032 [cf. 5457]. [Q] to bow down (in worship):– fall down [2], falleth down [2]

5457 סְגִד ***s^{e}gid*** (Aram.), v. GK: 10504 [cf. 5456]. [P] to worship, pay honor:– worship [8], worshipped [2], worshippeth [2]

5458 סְגוֹר ***s^{e}gôr***, n.[m.]. GK: 6033 [→ 5462]. enclosure, closing (of the heart):– caul [1], gold [1]

5459 סְגֻלָּה ***s^{e}gullâ***, n.f. GK: 6035. treasured possession, personal property:– peculiar treasure [3], peculiar [2], jewels [1], proper good [1], special [1]

5460 סְגַן ***s^{e}gan*** (Aram.), n.m. GK: 10505 [cf. 5461]. prefect, governor:– governors [5]

5461 סֶגֶן ***segen***, n.m. GK: 6036 [cf. 5532; cf. 5460]. official, officer, commander:– rulers [16], princes [1]

5462 סָגַר ***sāgar***, v. GK: 6037 & 6034 [→ 4525, 4526, 5458, 5474; cf. 5534; cf. 5463]. [Q] to shut, close; [Qp] to be shut; [N] to be confined, to be shut up, be imprisoned; [P] to deliver; [Pu] to be shut up, be barred, be closed; [H] to surrender, give over, deliver up; to put in isolation:– shut [30], shut up [23], pure [8], deliver up [5], deliver [5], delivered up [3], delivered [3], gave over [2], straitly shut up (+5462+2050.1) [2], closed up [1], closed [1], gave up [1], given up [1], inclosed [1], repaired [1], shut in [1], shutteth up [1], shutting [1], stop [1]

5463 סְגַר ***s^{e}gar*** (Aram.), v. GK: 10506 [cf. 5462]. [P] to shut, close up:– shut [1]

5464 סַגְרִיר ***sagrîr***, n.[m.]. GK: 6039. heavy rain, downpour of rain:– very rainy [1]

5465 סַד ***sad***, n.[m.]. GK: 6040 [cf. 7702]. shackles:– stocks [2]

5466 סָדִין ***sādîn***, n.[m.]. GK: 6041. linen garment:– fine linen [2], sheets [2]

5467 סְדֹם ***s^{e}dōm***, n.pr.loc. GK: 6042. Sodom:– Sodom [39]

5468 סֵדֶר ***sēder***, n.[m.]. GK: 6043 [→ 4528?; cf. 7713]. order, arrangement; "the land of disorder" refers to the Underworld, the region of darkness and chaos:– order [1]

5469 סַהַר ***sahar***, n.[m.]. GK: 6044 [→ 5470]. roundness; referring to the shape of a bowl:– round [1]

5470 סֹהַר ***sōhar***, n.[m.]. GK: 6045 [→ 5469]. prison:– prison (+1004+1886.1) [8]

5471 סוֹא ***sô'***, n.pr.m. GK: 6046. So:– So [1]

5472 סוּג ***sûg***, v. GK: 6047 [→ 5253]. [Q] to turn away, be faithless, be disloyal; [N] to be turned back, be disloyal, be faithless; [H] to move, displace; [Ho] to be driven back:– turned [6], turned away [3], backslider [1], driven [1], gone back [1], go [1], turned back [1]

5473 סוּג ***sûg***, v. GK: 6048 [cf. 5253; 7735?]. [Qp] to be encircled, be bordered (by lilies):– set about [1]

סוּג ***sûg***. See 5509.

5474 סוּגַר ***sûgar***, n.[m.]. GK: 6050 [→ 5462]. cage; some sources: neck-stock (of iron or wood):– ward [1]

5475 סוֹד ***sôd***, n.[m.]. GK: 6051 [→ 1152; cf. 3245]. confidential talk, conspiracy; council, confidant:– secret [7], assembly [5], counsel [5], secrets [2], inward [1], secret counsel [1]

5476 סוֹדִי **sôdî**, n.pr.m. GK: 6052. Sodi, "*Yahweh confides*":– Sodi [1]

5477 סוּחַ **sûaḥ**, n.pr.m. GK: 6053. Suah, "[poss.] *offal, dung, viscera*":– Suah [1]

5478 סוּחָה **sûḥâ**, n.f. GK: 6054 [→ 5501]. refuse, garbage, offal:– torn [1]

סוּט **sûṭ**. See 7750.

5479 סוֹטַי **sôṭay**, n.pr.m. GK: 6055. Sotai:– Sotai [2]

5480 סוּךְ **sûk**, v. GK: 6057 [→ 610; cf. 3251, 5258]. [Q] to anoint, to use oils or perfumes or lotions; [H] to put on lotions; [Ho] to be poured on; this can refer to the application of oils, perfumes, lotions, or resins to the body:– anoint [4], anointed [3], anoint at all (+5480) [2]

סוֹלְלָה **sôlᵉlâ**. See 5550.

5481 סוּמְפֹּנְיָה **sûmpōnᵉyâ** or סוּפֹּנְיָא **sûppōnᵉyā'** or סִיפֹּנְיָא **sîppōnᵉyā'** (Aram.), n.f. GK: 10507 & 10510 & 10512. musical instrument; sources vary widely: a wind instrument: pipe, bagpipe, double flute; a stringed instrument: dulcimer; a percussion instrument: drum, cymbal:– dulcimer [3]

5482 סְוֵנֵה **sᵉwēnēh**, n.pr.loc. GK: 6059. Syene = Aswan:– Syene [2]

5483 סוּס **sûs**, n.m. GK: 6061 & 6062 [→ 5484, 5485]. (male) horse, stallion; swallow, swift:– horses [97], horse [35], crane [2], horseback [2], on horseback (+7392) [2], horsehoofs (+6119) [1], horses' [1]

5484 סוּסָה **sûsâ**, n.f. GK: 6063 [→ 2701; cf. 5483]. (female) horse, mare:– company of horses [1]

5485 סוּסִי **sûsî**, n.f. GK: 6064 [→ 5483]. Susi, "*[my] horse*":– Susi [1]

5486 סוּף **sûp**, v. GK: 6066 [→ 5490, 5492; cf. 5487]. [Q] to come to an end; demolish; die; [H] to sweep away:– consume [3], consumed [2], have an end [1], perish [1], surely consume (+622) [1]

5487 סוּף **sûp** (Aram.), v. GK: 10508 [→ 5491; cf. 5486]. [P] to be fulfilled; [H] to bring to an end:– consume [1], fulfilled [1]

5488 סוּף **sûp**, n.m. GK: 6068 [→ 5489, 5492]. reed; Reed Sea (traditionally, Red Sea):– Red [24], flags [3], weeds [1]

5489 סוּף **sûp**, n.pr.loc. GK: 6069 [→ 5488]. Suph, "*reeds, bushes*":– Red [1]

5490 סוֹף **sôp**, n.m. GK: 6067 [→ 5486; cf. 5491]. end, conclusion, destiny; rear guard:– end [3], conclusion [1], hinder part [1]

5491 סוֹף **sôp** (Aram.), n.[m.]. GK: 10509 [→ 5487; cf. 5490]. end (of space, time, or circumstance):– end [5]

5492 סוּפָה **sûpâ**, n.f. & loc. GK: 6070 & 6071 [→ 5486, 5488]. storm wind, whirlwind, tempest, gale; Suphah, "*reeds, bushes*"; poss. Red (Reed) Sea:– whirlwind [10], storm [3], Red sea [1], tempest [1], whirlwinds [1]

5493 סוּר **sûr** or שׂוּר **śûr**, v. GK: 6073 & 8462 [→ 3249, 7795?]. [Q] to turn away, depart, leave; to saw; [Qp] to be rejected; [Pol] to drag from, turn aside; [H] to remove, get rid of, take off; [Ho] to be removed, be abolished; by extension: to forsake, reject:– depart [41], take away [41], departed [31], removed [20], taken away [18], put away [14], remove [14], turn aside [14], turned aside [14], took away [10], turn in [7], took off [4], turn away [4], turned in [4], turned [4], departeth [3], taken [3], took [3], turn [3], depart away [2], departing [2], escheweth [2], go aside [2], put off [2], take off [2], taketh away [2], take [2], beheaded (+7218) [1], brought [1], call back [1], declined [1], decline [1], eschewed [1], get out [1], go away [1], goeth [1], gone aside [1], gone away [1], go [1], grievous [1], laid by [1], lay away [1], left undone [1], past [1], pluck away [1], put away (+4480) [1], put down [1], put [1], rebel [1], removeth away [1], removing to and fro [1], removing [1], revolted [1], sour [1], turned away [1], turned back [1], turneth away [1], went [1], withdraw [1], without [1]

5494 סוּר **sûr**, a.vbl. GK: 6074 [cf. 3249]. corrupt:– degenerate [1]

5495 סוּר **sûr**, n.pr.loc. GK: 6075 [cf. 3249]. Sur:– Sur [1]

5496 סוּת **sût**, v. GK: 6077. [H] to incite, entice, urge, mislead:– moved [4], persuade [3], stirred up [2], entice [1], movedst [1], persuaded [1], persuadeth [1], provoked [1], removed [1], set on [1], setteth on [1], take away [1]

5497 סוּת **sût**, n.[m.]. GK: 6078 [→ 4533]. robe, garment:– clothes [1]

5498 סָחַב **sāḥab**, v. GK: 6079 [→ 5499]. [Q] to drag down:– draw out [2], drawn [1], draw [1], tear [1]

5499 סְחָבָה **sᵉḥābâ**, n.f. GK: 6080 [→ 5498]. rag:– cast clouts [2]

5500 סָחָה **sāḥâ**, v. GK: 6081 [cf. 5501]. [P] to scrape away:– scrape [1]

5501 סְחִי **sᵉḥî**, n.[m.]. GK: 6082 [→ 5478; cf. 5500]. scum, refuse:– offscouring [1]

סָחִישׁ **sāḥîš**. See 7823.

5502 סָחַף **sāḥap**, v. GK: 6085. [Q] to wash away (of rain); [N] to be washed away, be laid low:– sweeping [1], swept away [1]

5503 סָחַר **sāḥar**, v. GK: 6086 [→ 5504, 5505, 5506; cf. 4536]. [Q] to be a trader, a merchant; [Pealal] to pound, throb (of the heart):– merchants [9], merchant [4], trade [2], go about [1], merchant's [1], merchantmen (+376) [1], occupied (+3027) [1], panteth [1], traffick [1]

5504 סַחַר **saḥar**, n.m. GK: 6087 [→ 5503]. same as 5505: merchandise, profit (from merchandising in the marketplace):– merchandise [4]

5505 סָחַר **sāḥar**, v. GK: 6087 [→ 5503]. same as 5504: merchandise, profit (from merchandising in the marketplace):– merchandise [2], mart [1]

5506 סְחֹרָה **sᵉḥōrâ**, n.f. GK: 6088 [→ 5503]. customer:– merchandise [1]

5507 סֹחֵרָה **sōḥērâ**, n.f. GK: 6089. rampart, wall:– buckler [1]

5508 סֹחֶרֶת **sōḥeret**, n.f. GK: 6090. costly stone (not specifically defined):– black [1]

סֵט **sēṭ**. See 7750.

5509 סוּג **sûg** or סִיג **sîg**, n.[m.]. GK: 6049 & 6092 [cf. 5253, 7873]. dross (usually of silver):– dross [8]

5510 סִיוָן **sîwān**, n.pr. GK: 6094. Sivan:– Sivan [1]

5511 סִיחוֹן **sîḥôn**, n.pr.m. GK: 6095. Sihon:– Sihon [37]

5512 סִין **sîn**, n.pr.loc. GK: 6096 & 6097. Sin = Pelusium; Sin (a desert area between Sinai and Elim, having nothing to do with sinfulness), "*[desert] of clay* [or poss.] *[desert] of Sin*":– Sin [6]

5513 סִינִי **sînî**, a.g. GK: 6098. Sinite:– Sinite [2]

5514 סִינַי **sînay**, n.pr.loc. GK: 6099. Sinai, "*Sin; glare [from white chalk]*":– Sinai [35]

5515 סִינִים **sînîm**, a.g.pl. GK: 6100. Sinim, Chinese [?]:– Sinim [1]

5516 סִיסְרָא **sîsᵉrā'**, n.pr.m. GK: 6102. Sisera:– Sisera [21]

5517 סִיעָא **sî'ā'** or סִיעֲהָא **sî'ᵃhā'**, n.pr.m. GK: 6103 & 6104. Sia, Siaha, "*assembly*":– Siaha [1], Sia [1]

סִיפֹּנְיָא **sîponᵉyā'**. See 5481.

5518 סִיר **sîr** or סִירָה **sîrâ**, n.m. & f. GK: 6105 & 6106 [cf. 5626]. pot, pan, caldron, washbasin; thorn, thornbush; fishhook, barb:– pot [12], pots [9], thorns [4], caldron [3], caldrons [2], washpot (+7366) [2], fishhooks (+1729) [1], pans [1]

5519 סָךְ **sāk**, n.[m.]. GK: 6107 [→ 5526]. multitude, throng:– multitude [1]

5520 סֹךְ **sōk**, n.[m.]. GK: 6108 [→ 5521, 5523; cf. 7900]. covering, dwelling (of human or lion):– covert [1], den [1], pavilion [1], tabernacle [1]

5521 סֻכָּה **sukkâ**, n.f. GK: 6109 [→ 5523; cf. 5520]. tabernacle, shrine; booth, shelter, dwelling, tent:– booths [9], tabernacles [9], pavilions [3], tabernacle [3], booth [2], pavilion [2], cottage [1], covert [1], tents [1]

5522 סִכּוּת **sikkût**, n.pr.?. GK: 6110. Sikkut (pagan god?):– tabernacle [1]

5523 סֻכּוֹת **sukkôt**, n.pr.loc. GK: 6111 [→ 5521; cf. 5520]. Succoth, "*booths*":– Succoth [18]

5524 סֻכּוֹת בְּנוֹת **sukkôt bᵉnôt**, n.pr. GK: 6112. Succoth Benoth (pagan god):– Succoth-benoth [1]

5525 סֻכִּיִּים **sukkiyyîm**, n.pr.m.pl. GK: 6113. Sukkite:– Sukkiims [1]

5526 סָכַךְ **sākak**, v. GK: 6114 & 6115 [→ 4329, 4539, 4540, 5519, 5527; cf. 5259, 7753]. [Q] to cover, conceal, overshadow, shield; to knit together; [Pol] to knit together; [H] to cover, shield; to relieve oneself:– covered [8], cover [5], covereth [2], covering [2], defence [1], defendest (+5921) [1], hedged in [1], join together [1], set [1], shut up [1]

5527 סְכָכָה **sᵉkākâ**, n.pr.loc. GK: 6117 [→ 5526]. Secacah, "*thicket, cover*":– Secacah [1]

5528 סָכַל **sākal**, v. GK: 6118 [→ 5530, 5529, 5531]. [N] to do a foolish thing; [P] to turn into foolishness; [H] to act like a fool:– done foolishly [5], maketh foolish [1], played the fool [1], turn into foolishness [1]

5529 סֶכֶל **sekel**, n.m. GK: 6120 [→ 5528]. foolishness, fool:– folly [1]

5530 סָכָל **sākāl**, n.m. GK: 6119 [→ 5528]. foolish (one), senseless, stupid:– fool [4], foolish [2], sottish [1]

5531 סִכְלוּת **siklût** or שִׂכְלוּת **śiklût**, n.f. GK: 6121 & 8508 [→ 5528]. folly:– folly [5], foolishness [2]

5532 סָכַן **sākan**, v. GK: 6122 & 6125 [→ 4543; cf. 5461]. [Q] to be of use, benefit, profit; [H] to be in the habit; be familiar with; to get along well with:– ever wont (+5532) [2], profitable [2], acquainted [1], acquaint [1], advantage [1], cherish (+1961) [1], cherished (+1961) [1], profiteth [1], treasurer [1]

Heb

5533 סָכַן ***sākan***, v. GK: 6123 & 6124 [cf. 4542, 4544]. [N] to be endangered; [Pu] to be poor:– endangered [1], so impoverished [1]

5534 סָכַר ***sākar***, v. GK: 6126 & 6127 [cf. 5462]. [N] to be closed; be silent; [P] to hand over, deliver:– stopped [2], give over [1]

5535 סָכַת ***sākat***, v. GK: 6129. [H] to be silent, be still:– take heed [1]

סֻכֹּת *sukkōt*. See 5523.

5536 סַל ***sal***, n.m. GK: 6130. basket:– basket [13], baskets [2]

5537 סָלָא ***sālā'***, v. GK: 6131 [→ 5543, 5544?; cf. 5541]. [Pu] to be weighed (in correlation to gold):– comparable [1]

5538 סִלָּא ***sillā'***, n.pr.loc. GK: 6133. Silla, "*embankment*":– Silla [1]

5539 סָלַד ***sālad***, v. GK: 6134 [→ 5540?]. [P] to skip (for joy):– harden [1]

5540 סֶלֶד ***seled***, n.pr.m. GK: 6135 [→ 5539?]. Seled, "*jump for joy*":– Seled [2]

5541 סָלָה ***sālâ***, v. GK: 6136 & 6137 [cf. 5537]. [Q] to reject, toss aside; [P] to reject; [Pu] to be bought, be paid for:– valued [2], trodden down [1], trodden under foot [1]

5542 סֶלָה ***selâ***, n.[f.] GK: 6138 [cf. 5549?]. selah (t.t. in the Psalms):– Selah [74]

5543 סַלּוּא ***sallu'*** or סַלּוּ ***sallû*** or סָלוּא ***sālû'*** or סַלַּי ***sallay***, n.pr.m. GK: 6132 & 6139 & 6140 & 6144 [→ 5537]. Sallu, Salu, Sallai, "[poss.] *he restores*":– Sallu [3], Sallai [2], Salu [1]

5544 סִלּוֹן ***sillôn***, n.m. GK: 6141 [→ 5537?]. thorn, brier:– brier [1], thorns [1]

5545 סָלַח ***sālaḥ***, v. GK: 6142 [→ 5546, 5547]. [Q] to forgive, release, pardon; [N] to be forgiven:– forgive [18], forgiven [13], pardon [11], pardoned [2], forgiveth [1], spare [1]

5546 סַלָּח ***sallāḥ***, a. GK: 6143 [→ 5545]. forgiving:– ready to forgive [1]

סַלַּי *sallay*. See 5543.

5547 סְלִיחָה ***sᵉlîḥâ***, n.f. GK: 6145 [→ 5545]. forgiveness, pardon:– forgivenesses [1], forgiveness [1], ready to pardon [1]

5548 סַלְכָה ***salkâ***, n.pr.loc. GK: 6146. Salecah:– Salcah [2], Salchah [2]

5549 סָלַל ***sālal***, v. GK: 6147 & 6148 [→ 4546, 4547, 5550, 5551, 5552; cf. 5542?]. [Q] to build up, heap up (a highway), extol; to pile up; [Pil] to esteem, cherish; [Htpol] to behave haughtily, insolently:– cast up [6], raise up [2], exaltest [1], exalt [1], extol [1], made plain [1]

5550 סֹלְלָה ***sōlᵉlâ***, n.f. GK: 6149 [→ 5549; cf. 2150]. siege ramp, siege mound:– mount [5], bank [3], mounts [3]

5551 סֻלָּם ***sullām***, n.m. GK: 6150 [→ 5549]. stairway; some sources: ladder:– ladder [1]

5552 סַלְסִלָּה ***salsillâ***, n.[f.] GK: 6151 [→ 5549]. branch, shoot; some sources: basket:– baskets [1]

5553 סֶלַע ***selaʿ***, n.m. GK: 6152 [→ 5554, 5555, 5638?]. rock, stone; rock formation: cliff, crag; by extension: stronghold, fortress; God as a "Rock" focuses on stability, faithfulness, and protection:– rock [47], rocks [9], ragged rocks [1], stones [1], stony [1], strong hold [1]

5554 סֶלַע ***selaʿ***, n.pr.loc. GK: 6153 [→ 5553]. Sela, "*rock crags, cliffs*":– Selah [1], Sela [1]

5555 סֶלַע הַמַּחְלְקוֹת ***selaʿ hammaḥlᵉqôt***, n.pr.loc. GK: 6154 [→ 5553]. Sela Hammahlekoth:– Sela-hammahlekoth [1]

5556 סָלְעָם ***solʿām***, n.m. GK: 6155 [→ 5553?]. edible locust or katydid:– bald locust [1]

5557 סָלַף ***sālap***, v. GK: 6156 [→ 5558]. [P] to twist; to overthrow; to frustrate:– overthroweth [4], perverteth [2], pervert [1]

5558 סֶלֶף ***selep***, n.m. GK: 6157 [→ 5557]. duplicity, perversity, deceit:– perverseness [2]

5559 סְלִק ***sᵉlaq*** (Aram.), v. GK: 10513 [→ 5267]. [P] to come up, go up; [H] to lift up; [Ho] to be lifted up:– came up [4], came [1]

5560 סֹלֶת ***sōlet***, n.f. GK: 6159. fine flour (likely wheat flour):– fine flour [35], flour [17], fine [1]

5561 סַם ***sam***, n.m. GK: 6160. fragrant perfume:– sweet [13], sweet spices [3]

5562 סַמְגַּר־נְבוֹ ***samgar-nᵉbô***, n.pr.m. GK: 6162 [→ 5015]. Samgar-Nebo:– Samgar-nebo [1]

5563 סְמָדַר ***sᵉmādar***, n.m. GK: 6163. blossom (of a vine):– tender grape [2], tender grapes [1]

5564 סָמַךְ ***sāmak***, v. GK: 6164 [→ 294, 3253, 5565]. [Q] to sustain, uphold; to lay (one's hand upon); [Qp] to be braced, be steadfast; [N] to lean upon, rely upon, gain confidence; [P] to strengthen, refresh:– lay [12], laid [6], put [5], uphold [5], sustained [3], upholdeth [3], lean [2], stay [2], borne up [1], established [1], holden up [1], leaned [1], lieth hard [1], rested [1], set [1], stand fast [1], stayed [1], upheld [1]

5565 סְמַכְיָהוּ ***sᵉmakyāhû***, n.pr.m. GK: 6165 [→ 5564]. Semakiah, "*Yahweh sustains, consecrates*":– Semachiah [1]

5566 סֶמֶל ***semel***, n.m. GK: 6166. image, idol:– idol [2], image [2], figure [1]

5567 סָמַן ***sāman***, v. GK: 6168. [N] to be appointed, apportioned:– appointed [1]

5568 סָמַר ***sāmar***, v. GK: 6169 [→ 4548, 5569; cf. 4930]. [Q] to tremble, shudder (i.e., to have goose bumps, gooseflesh); [P] to bristle, stand on end (of hair):– stood up [1], trembleth [1]

5569 סָמָר ***sāmār***, a. GK: 6170 [→ 5568]. bristling (locust):– rough [1]

5570 סְנָאָה ***sᵉnā'â*** or הַסְּנָאָה ***hassᵉnā'â***, n.pr.m. GK: 6171 & 2189 [→ 1886.1, 8130, cf. 5574]. Hassenaah, Senaah, "*the hated one*":– Senaah [2], Hassenaah [1]

סְנוּאָה *sᵉnu'â*. See 5574.

5571 סַנְבַלַּט ***sanballaṭ***, n.pr.m. GK: 6172. Sanballat, "*Sin has given life*":– Sanballat [10]

5572 סְנֶה ***sᵉneh***, n.m. GK: 6174. bush, thorny shrub:– bush [6]

5573 סֶנֶּה ***senneh***, n.pr.loc. GK: 6175. Seneh, "*thorny*; [poss.] *[cliff shaped like] a tooth*":– Seneh [1]

סַנָּה *sannâ*. See 7158.

5574 סְנוּאָה ***sᵉnû'â*** or הַסְּנוּאָה ***hassᵉnu'â***, n.pr.m. GK: 6176 & 2190 [→ 1886.1+8130; cf. 5570]. Senuah, Hassenuah, "*the hated one*":– Hasenuah [1], Senuah [1]

5575 סַנְוֵרִים ***sanwērîm***, n.[m.pl.]. GK: 6177. blindness:– blindness [3]

5576 סַנְחֵרִיב ***sanḥērîb***, n.pr.m. GK: 6178. Sennacherib, "*Sin has increased the brothers; Sin replace the [lost] brothers!*":– Sennacherib [13]

5577 סַנְסִנָּה ***sansinnâ***, n.[m.]pl. GK: 6180. fruit cluster (of date tree):– boughs [1]

5578 סַנְסַנָּה ***sansannâ***, n.pr.loc. GK: 6179. Sansannah, "*palm branch*":– Sansannah [1]

5579 סְנַפִּיר ***sᵉnappîr***, n.[m.]. GK: 6181. fin:– fins [5]

5580 סָס ***sās***, n.m. GK: 6182. (garment) moth; some sources: worm:– worm [1]

סוּס *sus*. See 5483.

5581 סִסְמַי ***sismay***, n.pr.m. GK: 6183. Sismai, "[poss.] *belonging to Sisam*":– Sisamai [2]

5582 סָעַד ***sāʿad***, v. GK: 6184 [→ 4552; cf. 5583]. [Q] to sustain, support, refresh:– comfort [3], strengthen [2], held up [1], hold up [1], holden up [1], refresh [1], stablish [1], strengtheneth [1], upholden [1]

5583 סְעַד ***sᵉʿad*** (Aram.), v. GK: 10514 [cf. 5582]. [Pa] to help, support:– helping [1]

5584 סָעָה ***sāʿâ***, v. GK: 6185. [Q] to slander, defame, speak with malice:– storm [1]

5585 סָעִיף ***sāʿîp***, n.[m.]. GK: 6186 & 6187 [→ 5586, 5587, 5588, 5589, 5634]. cleft, crag; bough, branch:– branches [2], top [2], clifts [1], tops [1]

5586 סָעַף ***sāʿap***, v.den. GK: 6188 [→ 5585]. [P] to lop off, trim down:– lop [1]

5587 סְעִפִּים ***sᵉʿippîm*** or שְׂעִפִּים ***śᵉʿippîm***, n.f. GK: 6191 & 8546 [→ 5588, 8312; cf. 5585]. disquieted thoughts, troubled thoughts; division, divided opinion, a fig. extension of hobbling on crutches made of boughs:– thoughts [2], opinions [1]

5588 סֵעֵף ***sēʿēp***, a. GK: 6189 [→ 5587; cf. 5585]. double-minded, divided in heart:– thoughts [1]

5589 סְעַפָּה ***sᵉʿappâ***, n.f. GK: 6190 [→ 5585]. bough:– boughs [2]

5590 סָעַר ***sāʿar***, v. GK: 6192 [→ 5591; cf. 8175]. [Q] to grow stormier, rougher; [N] to be enraged; [P] to scatter in a wind; [Po] to scatter, swirl; [Pu] to be lashed by storms:– tempestuous [2], came out as a whirlwind [1], driven with a whirlwind [1], scattered with a whirlwind [1], sore troubled [1], tossed with tempest [1]

5591 סַעַר ***saʿar*** or סְעָרָה ***sᵉʿārâ***, n.m. GK: 6193 & 6194 [cf. 5590]. windstorm, tempest, gale:– whirlwind [11], tempest [6], stormy [4], storm [1], whirlwind (+7307) [1], whirlwinds [1]

5592 סַף ***sap***, n.m. GK: 6195 & 6196 & 6197 [→ 5605]. threshold, door frame, entrance, doorway; doorkeeper; basin, bowl; wool, hide, skin:– door [10], threshold [6], basons [2], bason [2], bowls [2], doors [2], gates [2], posts [2], thresholds [2], cup [1], door posts [1]

5593 סַף ***sap***, n.pr.m. GK: 6198 [cf. 5598]. Saph, "*basin, threshold*":– Saph [1]

5594 סָפַד ***sāpad***, v. GK: 6199 [→ 4553, 5636?]. [Q] to beat the breast, mourn, lament, weep; [N] to be mourned:– lament [9], mourn [9], mourned [6], lamented [4], mourners [1], wail [1]

5595 סָפָה ***sāpâ***, v. GK: 6200. [Q] to sweep away; take away; bring disaster; [N] to be swept away; be destroyed:– consumed [5], add [3], destroy [3], destroyed [2], perish [2], augment [1], consume [1], heap [1], joined [1], put [1]

5596 ספח **sāpaḥ** or שׂפח **śāpaḥ**, v. GK: 6202 & 6203 & 8558 [→ 4555, 5599; cf. 4939, 8198]. [Q] to associate, attach to; [N] to be attached, be united; [P] to pour out; to bring sores, make scabby; [Pu] be joined together; [Ht] to feel oneself attached to:– abiding [1], cleave [1], gathered together [1], puttest [1], put [1], smite with a scab [1]

5597 סַפַּחַת **sappaḥat**, n.f. GK: 6204 [→ 4556]. rash, skin eruption:– scab [2]

5598 סַפַּי **sippay**, n.pr.m. GK: 6205 [cf. 5593]. Sippai:– Sippai [1]

5599 סָפִיחַ **sāpîaḥ**, n.[m.]. GK: 6206 & 6207 [→ 5596]. what grows on its own, after-growth in a fallow year; torrent, downpour:– such as groweth of itself [1], such things as grow of themselves [1], that which growth of it own accord [1], that which growth of itself [1], things which grow [1]

5600 סְפִינָה **s**^e**pînâ**, n.f. GK: 6208 [→ 5603]. ship (with a covering or deck):– ship [1]

5601 סַפִּיר **sappîr**, n.[m.]. GK: 6209. sapphire; some sources: lapis lazuli:– sapphire [7], sapphires [3], sapphire stone [1]

5602 סֵפֶל **sēpel**, n.[m.]. GK: 6210. bowl (for water or curdled milk):– bowl [1], dish [1]

5603 סָפַן **sāpan**, v. GK: 6211 [→ 5600, 5604; cf. 8226]. [Q] to cover; [Qp] to be roofed, be paneled, be roofed:– covered [3], cieled [2], seated [1]

5604 סִפֻּן **sippun**, n.[m.]. GK: 6212 [→ 5603]. ceiling:– cieling [1]

5605 סָפַף **sāpap**, v.den. GK: 6214 [→ 5592]. [Htpol] to stand at the threshold:– doorkeeper [1]

5606 סָפַק **sāpaq** or שָׂפַק **śāpaq**, v. GK: 6215 & 6216 & 8562 & 8563 [→ 5607]. [Q] to clap hands (in derision); beat one's breast; to punish, slap; to wallow, splash; to be enough; [H] to clasp hands:– clap [2], clappeth [1], please [1], smite [1], smote together [1], smote [1], striketh [1], suffice [1], wallow [1]

5607 סֶפֶק **sepeq** or שֶׂפֶק **śēpeq**, n.[m.]. GK: 6217 & 8565 [→ 5606]. riches, abundance, plenty, sufficiency:– stroke [1], sufficiency [1]

5608 סָפַר **sāpar**, v. GK: 6218 & 6221 [→ 5612; cf. 5613]. [Q] to count, number, take a census; [N] to be counted, be recorded; by extension: [P] to tell, proclaim, recount (an event or principle); [Pu] to be told:– scribe [42], told [26], declare [20], tell [12], numbered [11], number [10], scribes [6], shew forth [5], count [4], declared [4], counted [2], scribe's [2], speak [2], writer's [2], writer [2], accounted [1], commune [1], numberest [1], numbering [1], penknife (+8593+1886.1) [1], reckon [1], shewing [1], talk [1], tellest [1], telling [1], told out [1]

5609 סְפַר **s**^e**par** (Aram.), n.m. GK: 10515 [→ 5613; cf. 5612]. record, archive, book (though not a book in the sense of a codex with bound pages); the phrase "book of Moses" means the first five books of the Bible:– book [3], books [1], rolls [1]

5610 סְפָר **s**^e**pār**, n.[m.]. GK: 6222 [→ 5612]. census:– numbering [1]

5611 סְפָר **s**^e**pār**, n.pr.loc. GK: 6223 [cf. 8234]. Sephar:– Sephar [1]

5612 סֵפֶר **sēper** or סִפְרָה **sipra**, n.m. GK: 6219 & 6225 [→ 4557, 4558?, 4559, 5608, 5610, 5615, 5618, 7158; cf. 5609]. book (as a scroll or tablet), scroll, letter, certificate, deed, dispatch:– book [136], letters [16], letter [13], evidence [6], bill [4], learned (+3045) [3], books [2], evidences [2], learning [2], register [1], scrole [1]

5613 סָפַר **sāpar** (Aram.), n.m. GK: 10516 [→ 5609; cf. 5608]. teacher of the Law; secretary (an official), scribe:– scribe [6]

5614 סְפָרַד **s**^e**pārad**, n.pr.loc. GK: 6224. Sepharad:– Sepharad [1]

סִפְרָה **siprâ**. See 5612.

5615 סְפֹרוֹת **s**^e**pōrôt**, n.f. GK: 6228 [→ 5612]. measure, number; some sources: art of writing:– numbers [1]

5616 סְפַרְוִים **s**^e**parwîm**, a.g. GK: 6227 [→ 5617]. Sepharvite, "*of Sepharvaim*":– Sepharvites [1]

5617 סְפַרְוַיִם **s**^e**parwayim**, n.pr.loc. GK: 6226 [→ 5616]. Sepharvaim:– Sepharvaim [6]

5618 סֹפֶרֶת **sōperet** or סוֹפֶרֶת **sôperet**, n.[pr.]m. GK: 6230 & 6072 [→ 5612]. (office of) scribes; as n.pr. Sophereth, "*scribe*":– Sophereth [2]

5619 סָקַל **sāqal**, v. GK: 6232. [Q] to stone (as an execution); [N] to be stoned; [P] to throw stones (out or away), pelt with stones; [Pu] to be stoned:– stone [7], stoned [6], surely stoned (+5619) [4], cast [1], gathered out stones [1], gather [1], stoning [1], threw [1]

5620 סַר **sar**, a. GK: 6234 [→ 5637]. sullen, dejected, discouraged:– heavy [2], so sad [1]

5621 סָרָב **sārāb**, n.m. GK: 6235. briers:– briers [1]

5622 סַרְבָּל **sarbāl** (Aram.), n.[m.]. GK: 10517. robe, garment; variously translated as "hose, trousers, tunic, mantle, coat, cloak":– coats [2]

5623 סַרְגוֹן **sargôn**, n.pr.m. GK: 6236. Sargon, "*firm, faithful king; the king is legitimate*":– Sargon [1]

5624 סֶרֶד **sered**, n.pr.m. GK: 6237 [→ 5625]. Sered:– Sered [2]

5625 סַרְדִּי **sardî**, a.g. GK: 6238 [→ 5624]. Seredite, "*of Sered*":– Sardites [1]

5626 סִרָה **sirâ**, n.pr.[loc.]. GK: 6241 [→ 953+5626; cf. 5518]. Sirah:– Sirah [1]

5627 סָרָה **sārâ**, n.f. GK: 6239 & 6240 [→ 3249, 5637]. ceasing, stopping; rebellion, revolt:– rebellion [2], revolt [2], continual (+1115) [1], revolted [1], turn away [1], wrong [1]

5628 סָרַח **sāraḥ**, v. GK: 6243 & 6244 & 6242 [→ 5629; cf. 8294]. [Q] to hang down, overhang, spread over; [Qp] to be overhanged; [N] to be decayed, be spoiled, become stinking:– hang [2], exceeding in dyed attire (+2871) [1], spreading [1], stretched [1], stretch [1], vanished [1]

5629 סֶרַח **seraḥ**, n.m. GK: 6245 [→ 5628]. overhang, what projects over:– remnant [1]

5630 סִרְיוֹן **siryôn**, n.[m.]. GK: 6246 [cf. 8302, 8303]. (scale) armor, coat of mail:– brigandines [1], brigandine [1]

5631 סָרִיס **sārîs**, n.m. GK: 6247 [→ 7249]. court official, palace officer, eunuch:– eunuchs [15], chamberlains [9], officers [7], officer [5], chamberlain [4], eunuch [2]

5632 סָרַךְ **sārak** (Aram.), n.m. GK: 10518. administrator:– presidents [5]

5633 סֶרֶן **seren**, n.[m.]. GK: 6248 & 6249. axle; ruler, prince:– lords [21], plates [1]

5634 סַרְעַפָּה **sar'appâ**, n.f. GK: 6250 [→ 5585]. bough:– boughs [1]

5635 סָרַף **sārap**, v. GK: 6251 [cf. 8313]. [P] to burn:– burneth [1]

5636 סִרְפָּד **sirpād**, n.[m.]. GK: 6252 [→ 5594?]. briers, stinging nettles:– brier [1]

5637 סָרַר **sārar**, v. GK: 6253 [→ 5620, 5627]. [Q] to be stubborn, be obstinate, be rebellious:– rebellious [6], stubborn [4], revolters [2], away [1], backsliding [1], revolting [1], slideth back [1], withdrew (+5414) [1]

5638 סְתָו **s**^e**tāw**, n.m. GK: 6255. winter, rainy season:– winter [1]

5639 סְתוּר **s**^e**tûr**, n.pr.m. GK: 6256 [→ 5641]. Sethur, "*concealed [by deity]*":– Sethur [1]

5640 סָתַם **sātam** or שָׂתַם **śātam**, v. GK: 6258 & 8608. [Q] to stop up, block off, seal; [Qp] to be closed up, (by extension) to be in a secret place; [N] to be closed; [P] to stop up:– stopped [5], shut up [2], stop [2], closed up [1], hidden [1], secret [1], shutteth out [1], stopt [1]

5641 סָתַר **sātar**, v. GK: 6259 [→ 4563, 4564, 4565, 5639, 5643; cf. 5642]. [Q] to be hidden, be concealed, have a refuge; [P] to hide; [Pu] to be hidden; [H] to hide, conceal; [Ht] to hide oneself, keep oneself hidden:– hide [32], hid [29], hidest [5], hideth [5], secret [3], kept close [2], surely hide (+5641) [2], absent [1], conceal [1], keep secret [1]

5642 סְתַר **s**^e**tar** (Aram.), v. GK: 10519 & 10520 [cf. 5641, cf. 8368]. [P] to destroy, demolish; [Pap] to be hidden; (as noun) hidden things:– destroyed [1], secret [1]

5643 סֵתֶר **sēter** or סִתְרָה **sitrâ**, n.[m.]. GK: 6260 & 6261 [cf. 5641]. hiding place, secret place, shelter; covering, veil; (adv.) secretly, in secret:– secretly (+871.1+1886.1) [9], secret [9], covert [5], secret place [4], hiding place [3], backbiting [1], covering [1], disguiseth [1], privily [1], protection [1], secret places [1]

5644 סִתְרִי **sitrî**, n.pr.m. GK: 6262. Sithri, "[poss.] *Yahweh is my hiding place*":– Zithri [1]

5645 עָב **'āb**, n.m. GK: 6265 & 6266 [→ 5743]. clouds; thicket:– clouds [15], cloud [7], thick clouds [5], thick cloud [2], clay [1], thickets [1], thick [1]

5646 עָב **'āb**, n.m. GK: 6264. overhang, overhanging roof:– thick beam [1], thick planks [1], thick [1]

5647 עָבַד **'ābad**, v. GK: 6268 [→ 4566, 5650, 5652, 5653, 5656, 5657, 5659, 5744 (also used with compound proper names); cf. 5648]. [Q] to work, serve, labor, do; to worship, minister, work in ministry; [N] to be plowed, be cultivated; [Pu] to be worked; [H] to reduce to servitude, enslave, cause to serve; [Ho] to be caused to serve, worship (a god):– serve [153], served [61], do [14], worshippers [5], servants [4], till [4], do service [3], made to serve [3], serveth [3], work [3], caused to serve [2], dress [2], labour [2], serving [2], tilled [2], tilleth [2], been[s] [1], bondmen [1], bondservice [1], bring to pass [1], cause to serve [1], compel to serve (+5656) [1], do work [1], done [1], eared [1], ear [1], execute [1], husbandman (+120+376) [1], keep in bondage [1], keep [1], labouring [1], made serve [1], servant [1], servedst [1], set a work [1], tiller [1], tillest [1], useth service [1], wrought [1]

5648 עֲבַד **^{a}bad** (Aram.), v. GK: 10522 [→ 4567, 5649, 5673; cf. 5647]. [P] to do, make; [Htpe] to be done, be made, be turned into; a general word of activity and occurrence; the context determines the best translation, "do, make, obey, happen," etc:– made [7], do [5], done [4], cut [2], did [2], doest [1], doeth [1], executed [1], goeth on [1], kept [1], moved [1], worketh [1], wrought [1]

5649 עֲבֵד **^{a}bēd** (Aram.), n.m. GK: 10523 [→ 5648; cf. 5650]. servant:– servants [6], servant [1]

5650 עֶבֶד **'ebed**, n.m. GK: 6269 [→ 5647, 5651, 5658, 5660, 5661; cf. 5649 (also used with compound proper names)]. servant, slave, attendant; indentured servants and owned slaves had varying levels of status and responsibilities; according to the OT Law, a Hebrew slave could be sold to a Hebrew master for only six years, but there was no time limit for Gentile slaves:– servants [370], servant [362], bondmen [15], manservant [12], bondage [10], menservants [9], servant's [8], bondman [6], servants' [4], bondservant [1], manservant's [1], manservants [1]

5651 עֶבֶד **'ebed**, n.pr.m. GK: 6270 [→ 5650]. Ebed, "*servant*":– Ebed [6]

5652 עֲבָד **^{a}bād**, n.m. GK: 6271 [→ 5647]. what is done, deed, act:– works [1]

5653 עַבְדָּא **'abdā'**, n.pr.m. GK: 6272 [→ 5647]. Abda, "*servant of Yahweh*":– Abda [2]

5654 עֹבֵד־אֱדוֹם **'ōbēd-^{e}dôm**, n.pr.m. GK: 6273 [→ 5647+123]. Obed-Edom, "*servant [worshiper] of Edom*":– Obed-edom [20]

5655 עַבְדְּאֵל **'abd^{e}'ēl**, n.pr.m. GK: 6274 [→ 5650+410; cf. 5661]. Abdeel, "*servant of God [El]*":– Abdeel [1]

5656 עֲבֹדָה **^{a}bōdâ**, n.f. GK: 6275 [→ 5647; cf. 5673]. work, service, labor, task, duty, job; special work and service to God: service, ministry; forced labor: slavery:– service [94], servile [12], work [10], bondage [8], act [2], all manner of service (+5656+2050.1) [2], any manner of service (+5656+2050.1) [2], every kind of service (+5656+2050.1) [2], servitude [2], tillage [2], compel to serve (+5647) [1], effect [1], labour [1], ministering [1], ministry [1], office [1], serveth [1], use [1], wrought [1]

5657 עֲבֻדָּה **^{a}buddâ**, n.f. GK: 6276 [→ 5647]. servant, slave:– household [1], servants [1]

5658 עַבְדּוֹן **'abdôn**, n.pr.m. & loc. GK: 6277 & 6278 [cf. 5650]. Abdon, "*servant*":– Abdon [8]

5659 עַבְדֻת **'abdut**, n.f. GK: 6285 [→ 5647]. slavery, servitude:– bondage [3]

5660 עַבְדִּי **'abdî**, n.pr.m. GK: 6279 [→ 5661?]. Abdi, "*servant of Yahweh* or *my servant*":– Abdi [3]

5661 עַבְדִּיאֵל **'abdî'ēl**, n.pr.m. GK: 6280 [→ 5655, 5660?; cf. 5655]. Abdiel, "*servant of God [El]*":– Abdiel [1]

5662 עֹבַדְיָה or עֹבַדְיָהוּ **'ōbadyâ** or **'ōbadyāhû**, n.pr.m. GK: 6281 & 6282 [→ 5647+3068]. Obadiah, "*servant [worshiper] of Yahweh*":– Obadiah [20]

5663 עֶבֶד־מֶלֶךְ **'ebed-melek**, n.pr.m. GK: 6283 [→ 5650+4428]. Ebed-Melech, "*servant of Melek [king] or Malk*":– Ebed-melech [6]

5664 עֲבֵד נְגוֹ **^{a}bēd n^{e}gô**, n.pr.m. GK: 6284 [→ 5650+5015; cf. 5665]. Abednego, "*servant of Nego* or *Nebo*":– Abed-nego [1]

5665 עֲבֵד נְגוֹ **^{a}bēd n^{e}gô** (Aram.), n.pr.m. GK: 10524 [→ 5649; cf. 5664]. Abednego, "*servant of Nego* or *Nebo*":– Abed-nego [14]

5666 עָבָה **'ābâ**, v. GK: 6286 [→ 4568, 5672]. [Q] to be thick:– thicker [2], grown thick [1]

5667 עֲבוֹט **^{a}bôṭ**, n.[m.]. GK: 6287 [→ 5670, 5671]. pledge, (garment) security (for a loan):– pledge [4]

5668 עֲבוּר **^{a}bûr**, pp. & c. GK: 6288. marker of cause or reason: for, because; marker of purpose or intent: on account of; in order to; a marker of result: then; benefit: for:– for sake (+871.1) [14], that (+871.1) [10], for (+871.1) [7], because of (+871.1) [5], to (+871.1) [3], because (+871.1) [2], for sakes (+871.1) [2], sake [2], and (+871.1) [1], for cause (+871.1) [1], for to (+871.1) [1], to (+871.1+3807.1) [1]

5669 עֲבוּר **^{a}bûr**, n.[m.]. GK: 6289 [→ 5674]. produce, yield:– old corn [2]

5670 עָבַט **'ābaṭ**, v.den. GK: 6292 & 6293 [→ 5667]. [Q] to borrow, i.e., take or receive a pledge; [P] to swerve, change (a course), implying a lack of purpose; [H] to lend on a pledge:– surely lend (+5670) [2], borrow [1], break [1], fetch [1], lend [1]

5671 עַבְטִיט **'abṭîṭ**, n.[m.]intens. GK: 6294 [→ 5667]. heavy pledges, excessive mortgage for a debt; there may be an implication of undue force being used to keep the pledge:– thick clay [1]

5672 עֳבִי **'^{o}bî**, n.[m.]. GK: 6295 [→ 5666]. thickness, density, mold:– thickness [2], thick [2]

5673 עֲבִידָה **^{a}bîdâ** (Aram.), n.f. GK: 10525 [→ 5648; cf. 5656]. work, service, administration:– work [3], affairs [2], service [1]

5674 עָבַר **'ābar**, v. GK: 6296 & 6297 [→ 4569, 5669, 5676, 5677, 5678, 5679, 5682]. [Q] to pass over, cross over, travel through; [N] to be crossed; [P] to extend; to breed; [H] to make pass through, let pass over, send over; by extensions: to forgive, as the passing over of guilt; [Ht] to be very angry, show oneself angry:– pass [46], passed over [43], pass over [40], passed [34], go over [29], passed by [17], went over [17], pass through [14], passeth [14], transgressed [12], went [11], gone over [10], passed on [10], come over [9], go [9], past [9], pass on [8], passed along [7], cause to pass [6], go through [6], gone [6], pass away [6], caused to pass [5], come [5], pass by [5], passeth by [5], wroth [5], goeth [4], passed through [4], passengers [4], passeth away [4], passing [4], put away [4], transgress [4], went on [4], caused to pass through [3], made pass [3], made to pass [3], make to pass [3], went through [3], at all brought over (+5674) [2], brought over [2], brought [2], carry over [2], cause to pass through [2], fail [2], go beyond [2], go by [2], go on [2], made a proclamation (+6963) [2], make go [2], overpast [2], passest over [2], passest [2], sent over [2], speedily pass over (+5674) [2], sweet smelling [2], take away [2], turn away [2], alienate [1], altered [1], beyond [1], bring over [1], brought through [1], came along [1], came by [1], came over [1], came [1], carried over [1], cause to sound [1], caused to be proclaimed (+6963) [1], charged (+5921) [1], cometh [1], coming on [1], conduct over [1], conducted [1], convey over [1], current [1], delivered [1], do away [1], enter [1], escape [1], gendereth [1], get over [1], go in [1], goeth forth [1], goeth over [1], going over [1], going [1], have away [1], have more than [1], laid [1], made a partition [1], made proclamation (+6963) [1], made to pass by [1], made to pass through [1], make pass [1], make proclamation (+6963) [1], make sound [1], make to transgress [1], maketh to pass through [1], meddleth [1], overcome [1], overpass [1], overran [1], overrunning [1], over [1], pass away from [1], pass by (+1870) [1], passage [1], passed away [1], passed beyond [1], passedst over [1], passengers (+1870) [1], passest on [1], passeth along [1], passeth on along [1], passeth out [1], passeth over [1], passeth through [1], passing by [1], passing through [1], perishing [1], perish [1], proclaim (+6963) [1], provoketh to anger [1], rageth [1], raiser [1], removed [1], set apart [1], shave (+8593) [1], taken [1], took away [1], took [1], transgressest [1], transgressing [1], transgressors [1], translate [1], wayfaring man (+734) [1], went away [1], went forth [1], went throughout (+871.1) [1]

5675 עֲבַר **^{a}bar** (Aram.), n.m. GK: 10526 [cf. 5676]. the opposite bank (of a river); Trans(-Euphrates) or "beyond (the River)" is to the east of Israel:– beyond [7], side [7]

5676 עֵבֶר **'ēber**, n.m. GK: 6298 [→ 5674; cf. 5675]. what is on the other side, what is beyond, across; i.e., east or west; Trans-Euphrates:– side [56], beyond (+871.1) [8], beyond [7], beyond (+4480) [6], sides [4], straight forward (+413+6440) [3], against (+6440) [1], by (+3807.1) [1], from (+4480) [1], over [1], passages [1], passage [1], quarter [1]

5677 עֵבֶר **'ēber**, n.pr.m. GK: 6299 [→ 5674]. Eber, "*[regions] beyond [the river]*":– Eber [13], Heber [2]

5678 עֶבְרָה **'ebrâ**, n.f. GK: 6301 [→ 5674]. wrath, anger, fury, rage; insolence:– wrath [31], rage [2], anger [1]

5679 עֲבָרָה **^{a}bārâ**, n.f. GK: 6302 [→ 5682; cf. 5674]. ford, crossing:– ferry boat [1]

5680 עִבְרִי **'ibrî**, a. & n.g. GK: 6303 [→ 5681]. Hebrew:– Hebrews [17], Hebrew [11], Hebrew women [2], Hebrew man [1], Hebrew woman [1], Hebrewess [1], Hebrews' [1]

5681 עִבְרִי **'ibrî**, n.pr.m. GK: 6304 [→ 5680]. Ibri, "*Hebrew*":– Ibri [1]

5682 עֲבָרִים **^{a}bārîm**, n.pr.loc. GK: 6305 [→ 5679; cf. 5674]. Abarim, "*geographical regions beyond*":– Abarim [4]

5683 עֶבְרֹן **'ebrōn**, n.pr.loc. GK: 6306 [→ 2266; cf. 5658]. Ebron, Hebron, "*association*":– Hebron [1]

5684 עַבְרֹנָה **'abrōnâ**, n.pr.loc. GK: 6307. Abronah:– Ebronah [2]

5685 עָבַשׁ **'ābaš**, v. GK: 6308. [Q] to shrivel, wither, dry up:– rotten [1]

5686 עָבַת **'ābat**, v. GK: 6309 [→ 5687, 5688]. [P] to conspire, twist:– wrap up [1]

5687 עָבֹת **'ābôt**, a. GK: 6290 [→ 5686]. leafy, dense, interwoven foliage:– thick [4]

5688 עֲבֹת **^{a}bōt**, n.m. GK: 6310 & 6291 [→ 5686]. rope, cord, chains, ties; fetters, harness; thick foliage:– wreathen [8], cords [5], bands [3], thick boughs [3], ropes [2], band [1], rope [1], thick branches [1]

Heb

5689 עָגַב **ʿāgab**, v. GK: 6311 [→ 5691, 5689; cf. 5748]. [Q] to lust, have sensual desire for:– doted [6], lovers [1]

5690 עֲגָבִים **^{a}gābîm**, n.[m.]. GK: 6313 [→ 5689]. devotion, love:– much love [1], very lovely [1]

5691 עֲגָבָה **^{a}gābâ**, n.f. GK: 6312 [→ 5689]. lust, sensual desire:– inordinate love [1]

5692 עֻגָה **ʿugâ**, n.f. GK: 6314 [→ 5746]. (round, flat) bread cakes:– cakes [4], cake [3]

עָגוֹל **ʿāgôl**. See 5696.

5693 עָגוּר **ʿāgûr**, n.[m.]. GK: 6315. (short footed) thrush (a bird):– swallow [2]

5694 עָגִיל **ʿāgîl**, n.[m.]. GK: 6316 [→ 5696]. earring:– earrings [2]

5695 עֵגֶל **ʿēgel**, n.m. GK: 6319 [→ 5696]. bull-calf; calf-shaped idol:– calf [20], calves [11], bullocks [1], bullock [1], calf (+1241) [1], calf's [1]

5696 עָגֹל **ʿāgōl**, a. GK: 6318 [→ 4570, 5694, 5696, 5695, 5697, 5698, 5699, 5700]. circular, round:– round [6]

5697 עֶגְלָה **ʿeglâ**, n.f. GK: 6320 [→ 5698; cf. 5696]. heifer-calf, young cow:– heifer [9], heifer (+1241) [2], calves [1], heifer's [1], young cow (+1241) [1]

5698 עֶגְלָה **ʿeglâ**, n.pr.f. GK: 6321 [→ 5697]. Eglah, "*heifer*":– Eglah [2]

5699 עֲגָלָה **^{a}gālâ**, n.f. GK: 6322 [→ 5696]. cart:– cart [15], wagons [8], chariot [1], wagon [1]

5700 עֶגְלוֹן **ʿeglôn**, n.pr.m. & loc. GK: 6323 & 6324 [→ 5696]. Eglon, "*circle; young bull*":– Eglon [13]

5701 עָגַם **ʿāgam**, v. GK: 6327 [cf. 99]. [Q] to grieve for, have pity on:– grieved [1]

5702 עָגַן **ʿāgan**, v. GK: 6328. [N] to keep withdrawn (from marital relations):– stay [1]

5703 עַד **ʿad**, n.m. GK: 6329. a unit of time, referring to the past: old, ancient; without limit: forever, eternal, for ever and ever; continual, always:– ever [39], everlasting [2], for ever [2], eternity [1], ever (+5769) [1], evermore [1], for ever (+5769+2050.1) [1], old [1], perpetually (+3807.1) [1], world without end (+5704+5769) [1]

5704 עַד **ʿad**, pp. GK: 6330 [→ 1107, 5728; cf. 5710?; cf. 5705]. until, up to, as far as:– unto [376], until [249], to [167], for [75], till [68], how long (+4970) [28], until (+834) [27], and [13], how long (+575+1886.5) [13], till (+834) [9], into [8], and (+2050.1) [7], both (+4480) [7], very (+3966) [7], by [5], even [5], hitherto (+2008) [5], or [5], how long (+4100) [4], toward [4], until (+3588) [4], until (+7945) [4], while [4]*

5705 עַד **ʿad** (Aram.), pp. & c. GK: 10527 [→ 5709?; cf. 5704]. up to, until:– till (+1768) [8], to [5], for [4], unto [4], till [3], until [3], until (+1768) [2], at [1], ever (+0.2+5957) [1], hitherto (+3542) [1], on [1], or [1], within [1]

5706 עַד **ʿad**, n.[m.]. GK: 6331 [→ 5710]. prey, plunder:– prey [3]

5707 עֵד **ʿēd**, n.m. GK: 6332 [→ 3133; cf. 5749]. witness, testimony; an object that serves as a memorial or a person giving of legal evidence:– witness [45], witnesses [21], take witnesses (+5749) [2], took witnesses (+5749) [1]

5708 עִדָּה **ʿiddâ**, n.f. GK: 6340. menstruation:– filthy [1]

עֹד **ʿōd**. See 5750.

5709 עֲדָה **^{a}dâ** (Aram.), v. GK: 10528 [→ 5705?; cf. 5710]. [P] to be taken, be repealed; [H] to take away:– altereth [2], departed [1], pass away [1], passed [1], removeth [1], take away [1], taken away [1], took [1]

עֹדֵד **ʿōdēd**. See 5752.

5710 עָדָה **ʿādâ**, v. GK: 6334 & 6335 [→ 497, 3260?, 3294?, 5704?, 5711, 5706, 5716; cf. 5709]. [Q] to adorn oneself, put on jewelry; to prowl; [H] to take away, remove:– decked [3], adorned [1], adorneth with [1], deckedst with ornaments (+5716) [1], deckest with [1], deck [1], passed [1], taketh away [1]

5711 עָדָה **ʿādâ**, n.pr.f. GK: 6336 [→ 5716; cf. 5710]. Adah, "*adornment*":– Adah [8]

5712 עֵדָה **ʿēdâ**, n.f. GK: 6337 [cf. 3259]. community, assembly, with a possible focus on the unity of the congregation; this can refer to good or evil groups; human or animal groups:– congregation [124], company [13], assembly [8], assemblies [1], multitude [1], people [1], swarm [1]

5713 עֵדָה **ʿēdâ**, n.f. GK: 6338 [→ 5749]. witness:– testimonies [21], witness [4], testimony [1]

5714 עִדֹּא **ʿiddōʾ** or עִדּוֹ **ʿiddô**, n.pr.m. GK: 6333 & 6341 & 6342 & 10529. Iddo, "[prob.] *Yahweh has adorned*": note this name is Aramaic twice in Ezra:– Iddo [10]

5715 עֵדוּת **ʿēdût**, n.f. GK: 6343 [→ 5749]. testimony, statute, stipulation, regulation; this can also mean "the Testimony" as a formal written copy of the precepts and stipulations of a covenant:– testimony [40], testimonies [15], witness [4], Shoshannim-Eduth (+7799) [1]

5716 עֲדִי **^{a}dî**, n.[m.]. GK: 6344 [→ 3260, 5711, 5717, 5718; cf. 5710 (also used with compound proper names)]. ornament, beautiful jewelry:– ornaments [7], excellent ornaments (+5716) [2], mouth [2], ornament [2], deckedst with ornaments (+5710) [1]

5717 עֲדִיאֵל **^{a}dîʾēl**, n.pr.m. GK: 6346 [→ 5716+410]. Adiel, "*adornment of God [El]*":– Adiel [3]

5718 עֲדָיָה **^{a}dāyâ** or עֲדָיָהוּ **^{a}dāyāhû**, n.pr.m. GK: 6347 & 6348 [→ 5716+3068]. Adaiah, "*adornment of Yahweh*":– Adaiah [9]

5719 עָדִין **ʿādîn**, a. GK: 6349 [→ 5727]. voluptuous, wantonness:– given to pleasures [1]

5720 עָדִין **ʿādîn**, n.pr.m. GK: 6350 [→ 5727]. Adin, "*voluptuous, luxurious*":– Adin [4]

5721 עֲדִינָא **^{a}dînāʾ**, n.pr.m. GK: 6351 [→ 5727]. Adina, "*adorned*":– Adina [1]

5722 עֲדִינוֹ **^{a}dînô**, n.pr.m. GK: 6352. Adino:– Adino [1]

5723 עֲדִיתַיִם **^{a}dîtayim**, n.pr.loc. GK: 6353. Adithaim, "*double [row] of adornments*":– Adithaim [1]

5724 עַדְלַי **ʿadlay**, n.pr.m. GK: 6354. Adlai, "*be just*":– Adlai [1]

5725 עֲדֻלָּם **^{a}dullām**, n.pr.loc. GK: 6355 [→ 5726]. Adullam, "*retreat* or *refuge; [poss.] [they are] just*":– Adullam [8]

5726 עֲדֻלָּמִי **^{a}dullāmî**, a.g. GK: 6356 [→ 5725]. Adullamite, of Adullam, "*of Adullam*":– Adullamite [3]

5727 עָדַן **ʿādan**, v.den. GK: 6357 [→ 4575, 4574, 5719, 5720, 5721, 5730; cf. 5734?]. [Ht] to revel in the good life, luxuriate:– delighted [1]

5728 עֲדֶן **^{a}den** or עֲדֶנָה **^{a}denâ**, adv. GK: 6362 & 6364 [→ 5704+2008]. yet, still:– yet [2]

5729 עֶדֶן **ʿeden**, n.pr.loc. GK: 6361 [→ 1040]. Eden, "*paradise, delight,* [poss.] *flat land*":– Eden [4]

5730 עֵדֶן **ʿēden** or עֶדְנָה **ʿednâ**, n.[m.]. GK: 6358 & 6366 [→ 5727, 5731, 5734; cf. 5733]. delight, delicacy; finery; (sexual) pleasure:– delicates [1], delights [1], pleasures [1], pleasure [1]

5731 עֵדֶן **ʿēden**, n.pr.m. & loc. GK: 6359 & 6360 [→ 5730]. Eden, "*paradise, delight,* [poss.] *flat land*":– Eden [16]

5732 עִדָּן **ʿiddān** (Aram.), n.m. GK: 10530. time (general or specific period); "time, times, and half a time" likely means three-and-one-half periods of time:– times [6], time [6], at what time (+0.2+1768+871.2) [1]

5733 עַדְנָא **ʿadnāʾ**, n.pr.m. GK: 6363 [cf. 5730, 5734]. Adna, "*delight*":– Adna [2]

5734 עַדְנָה **ʿadnâ**, n.pr.m. GK: 6365 & 6367 [→ 5730; cf. 5727?, 5733]. Adnah, "*delight*":– Adnah [2]

5735 עַדְעָדָה **ʿadʿādâ**, n.pr.loc. GK: 6368. Adadah:– Adadah [1]

5736 עָדַף **ʿādap**, v. GK: 6369. [Q] (ptcp.) what is left over, what is additional; [H] to have a surplus:– remaineth [3], had over [1], more [1], odd number [1], over and above (+5921) [1], overplus [1], remaineth over [1]

5737 עָדַר **ʿādar**, v. GK: 6370 & 6371 & 6372 [→ 4576, 5739; cf. 5826]. [Q] to help, serve; referring to a fighting unit that acts as a group; [N] to be cultivated, be weeded; to be missing; be lacking; [P] to let be lacking:– faileth [3], digged [2], lacked [2], fail [1], keep rank [1], keep [1], lacking [1]

5738 עֵדֶר **ʿeder**, n.pr.m. GK: 6376 [→ 5740]. Eder, "*flock*":– Ader [1]

5739 עֵדֶר **ʿēder**, n.m. GK: 6373 [→ 5737]. flock, herd:– flocks [16], flock [16], drove [2], every drove (+5739) [2], herds [2], droves [1]

5740 עֵדֶר **ʿēder**, n.pr.m. & loc. GK: 6374 & 6375 [→ 4029, 5738, 5741]. Eder, "*flock*":– Eder [3], Edar [1]

5741 עַדְרִיאֵל **ʿadrîʾēl**, n.pr.m. GK: 6377 [→ 5740+410]. Adriel, "*[my] help is God [El]*":– Adriel [2]

5742 עֲדָשִׁים **^{a}dāšîm**, n.f. GK: 6378. lentils:– lentiles [4]

עַוָּא **ʿawwāʾ**. See 5755.

5743 עוּב **ʿûb**, v.den. GK: 6380 [→ 5645]. [H] to cover with a cloud:– covered with a cloud [1]

5744 עוֹבֵד **ʿôbēd**, n.pr.m. GK: 6381 [→ 5647]. Obed, "*servant [worshiper]*":– Obed [10]

5745 עוֹבָל **ʿôbāl**, n.pr.g. GK: 6382 [cf. 5858]. Obal:– Obal [1]

5746 עוּג **ʿûg**, v.den. GK: 6383 [→ 4580, 5692]. [Q] to bake a (round, flat) cake of bread:– bake [1]

5747 עוֹג **ʿôg**, n.pr.m. GK: 6384. Og:– Og [22]

5748 עוּגָב **ʿûgāb**, n.m. GK: 6385 [cf. 5689]. flute:– organ [3], organs [1]

5749 עוּד *'ûd*, v.den. GK: 6386 & 6387 [→ 496, 5707, 5713, 5715, 5750, 5752, 8584]. [Q] to bear witness; [P] to surround (with ropes); [Pil] to sustain, relieve; [H] to admonish, warn, charge, declare; to testify, to call on a witness; [Ho] to be warned; [Htpol] to hold each other up; from the base meaning of binding (with ropes) come the fig. extensions of "to warn, charge, testify" (bind with words) and "to help, sustain" (bind oneself to another in aid and comfort):– testified [7], testify [6], call to record [2], earnestly protested (+5749) [2], protest solemnly (+5749) [2], protested [2], solemnly protest (+5749) [2], take witnesses (+5707) [2], testifiedst [2], admonished [1], bear witness against [1], call to witness [1], chargedst [1], charge [1], gave witness to [1], give warning [1], lifteth up [1], protesting [1], relieveth [1], robbed [1], stand upright [1], take to witness [1], took to record [1], took witnesses (+5707) [1], witnessed against [1], witness [1]

5750 עוֹד *'ôd*, subst. (used as adv.). GK: 6388 [→ 5749; cf. 5751]. longer, again, still, more:– yet [125], more [114], any more [72], again [44], still [21], while yet [12], else [10], more (+3254) [10], besides [6], again (+3254) [5], as yet [5], moreover [5], within (+871.1) [5], yet again (+3254) [5], moe [3], any longer [2], any more (+3254) [2], any more at all (+5750) [2], further [2], henceforth [2], longer [2], while have being (+871.1) [2], whiles [2], while [2], yet the more (+3254) [2], after [1], again (+2050.1) [1], all life long (+4480) [1], almost (+4592) [1], any more at all (+3254) [1], any [1], beside [1], but [1], can more (+3254) [1], do again (+3254) [1], else beside (+1107+4480) [1], ever since (+4480) [1], furthermore [1], good while [1], more (+3254+3807.1) [1], moreover (+2050.1) [1], mo [1], never again (+3808) [1], once [1], since [1], while (+3605) [1], while (+871.1) [1], whilst yet [1], within the space of (+871.1) [1], yet (+3807.1) [1], yet again [1], yet more (+3254) [1]

5751 עוֹד *'ôd* (Aram.), adv. GK: 10531 [cf. 5750]. still, yet:– while [1]

5752 עוֹדֵד *'ôdēd*, n.pr.m. GK: 6389 [→ 5749]. Oded, "*restorer*":– Oded [3]

5753 עָוָה *'āwâ*, v. GK: 6390 [→ 5754, 5771, 5773, 5856]. [Q] to do wrong; [N] to be perverse, be warped; [P] to ruin, make crooked; [H] to do wrong, pervert; from the base meaning of twisting an object comes the fig. extension of twisting morality: to be perverse, to do wrong:– commit iniquity [2], committed iniquity [2], perverse [2], perverted [2], bowed down [1], did perversely [1], done amiss [1], done perversely [1], done wickedly [1], done wrong [1], made crooked [1], troubled [1], turneth [1]

5754 עַוָּה *'awwâ*, n.f. GK: 6392 [→ 5857; cf. 5753]. ruin, wreckage, rubble:– overturn [3]

5755 עַוָּא *'awwā'* or עַוָּה *'awwâ* or עִוָּה *'iwwâ*, n.pr.loc. GK: 6379 & 6393 & 6394 [→ 5757, 5761]. Avva, Avvah, Ivvah:– Ivah [3], Ava [1]

עָוֹן *'āwôn*. See 5771.

5756 עוּז *'ûz*, v. GK: 6395 [→ 5797; cf. 5810]. [Q] to take refuge; [H] to bring to refuge, give shelter:– gather to flee [2], gather [1], retire [1]

5757 עַוִּים *'awwîm*, a.g. GK: 6398 [→ 5755]. Avvite:–

5758 עֲוָיָה *'ᵃwāyâ* (Aram.), n.f. GK: 10532. wickedness, iniquity:– iniquities [1]

5759 עֲוִיל *'ᵃwîl*, n.m. GK: 6396 [→ 5763]. little boys:– little ones [1], young children [1]

5760 עֲוִיל *'ᵃwîl*, n.m. GK: 6397 [→ 5765]. evil one, unjust one:– ungodly [1]

5761 עַוִּים *'awwîm*, n.pr.loc. GK: 6399 [→ 5755]. Avvim:– Avites [2], Avims [1], Avim [1]

5762 עֲוִית *'ᵃwît* or עֲיוֹת *'ᵃyôt*, n.pr.loc. GK: 6400 & 6511. Avith, Aioth:– Avith [2]

5763 עוּל *'ûl*, v. GK: 6402 [→ 5759, 5764, 5768]. [Q] to nurse, suckle:– milch [2], great with young [1], with young [1], young [1]

5764 עוּל *'ûl*, n.m. GK: 6403 [→ 5763]. nursing infant, baby:– infant [1], sucking child [1]

5765 עָוַל *'āwal*, v.den. GK: 6401 [→ 5760, 5766, 5767]. [P] to do evil, act wrong:– deal unjustly [1], unrighteous [1]

עוֹל *'ôl*. See 5923.

5766 עָוֶל *'āwel* or עַוְלָה *'awlâ* or עֹלָה *'ōlâ*, n.m. GK: 6404 & 6406 & 6593 [→ 5765]. wrong, evil, sin, injustice, what is morally perverted, warped, and twisted, an extension of the base meaning of a physically twisted, crooked object (not found in the OT):– iniquity [35], wickedness [7], unrighteousness [3], unjust [2], iniquities [1], perverseness [1], unjustly [1], unrighteously [1], wickedly [1], wicked [1]

5767 עַוָּל *'awwāl*, n.m. GK: 6405 [→ 5765]. wicked one, evil one, unjust one:– wicked [3], unjust [1], unrighteous [1]

עוֹלָה *'ôlâ*. See 5930.

5768 עוֹלֵל *'ôlēl* or עוֹלָל *'ôlāl*, n.m. GK: 6407 & 6408 [→ 5763]. child, little one:– children [10], young children [3], babes [2], infants [2], child [1], infant [1], little ones [1]

5769 עוֹלָם *'ôlām*, n.m. GK: 6409 [cf. 5865; cf. 5957]. everlasting, forever, eternity; from of old, ancient, lasting, for a duration:– ever [210], everlasting [59], for ever [47], perpetual [21], old [17], evermore [15], never (+3808+3807.1) [9], ever (+3807.1) [5], ancient [4], of old [4], everlasting (+3807.1) [3], alway (+3807.1) [2], always (+3807.1) [2], any more (+5704) [2], ever (+5704) [2], ever throughout [2], for ever (+3807.1) [2], long [2], never (+408+3807.1) [2], old time [2], world [2], always [1], ancient (+4480) [1], ancient times [1], any time [1], continuance [1], eternal [1], ever (+4480) [1], ever (+4480+1886.1) [1], ever (+5703) [1], ever of old (+4480) [1], everlasting (+3117) [1], everlasting (+3605) [1], for ever (+5703+2050.1) [1], lasting [1], long time [1], never (+1077+3807.1) [1], never (+1097+3807.1) [1], never (+3808+4480) [1], never (+3808+5704) [1], of old time (+3807.1) [1], of old time (+4480) [1], perpetual (+5704) [1], since the beginning of the world (+4480) [1], world without end (+5703+5704) [1]

5770 עָיַן *'āyan*, v.den. GK: 6523 [→ 5869]. [Q] to keep an eye on, look at (with suspicion or jealousy):– eyed [1]

5771 עָוֹן *'āwōn*, n.m. GK: 6411 [→ 5753; cf. 5758]. sin, wickedness, iniquity, often with a focus on the guilt or liability incurred, and the punishment to follow:– iniquity [167], iniquities [48], punishment of iniquity [5], punishment [4], fault [2], affliction [1], iniquities (+1697) [1], mischief [1], punishments [1], sin [1]

5772 עֹנָה *'ōnâ*, n.f. GK: 6703 [→ 6031?]. marital rights (of intercourse):– duty of marriage [1], furrows [1]

5773 עִוְעִים *'iw'îm*, n.pl.abst. GK: 6413 [→ 5753]. (col. pl.) dizziness, staggering, frenzy:– perverse [1]

5774 עוּף *'ûp*, v. GK: 6414 & 6545 & 6758 [→ 5775, 5888, 5889; cf. 3286]. [Q] to fly; to be faint, be exhausted; [Pol] to dart about (of a flying bird or a snake); to brandish; [H] to let (eyes) glance; [Ht] to fly away:– fly [8], flying [6], fly away [5], faint [2], flieth [2], brandish [1], flew [1], flieth away [1], set [1], shine forth [1], waxed faint [1], weary [1]

5775 עוֹף *'ôp*, n.m. GK: 6416 [→ 5774; cf. 5776]. bird, winged creatures, flying creatures:– fowls [36], fowl [23], birds [6], bird [3], flying [2], flieth [1]

5776 עוֹף *'ôp* (Aram.), n.[m.]. GK: 10533 [cf. 5775]. bird; a "bird of heaven" is any wild bird:– fowls [1], fowl [1]

5777 עֹפֶרֶת *'ōperet*, n.m. GK: 6769. lead (a mineral):– lead [9]

5778 עֵיפַי *'êpay* or עוֹפַי *'ôpay*, n.pr.m. GK: 6550 & 6417. Ephai, Ophai, "*my bird*":– Ephai [1]

5779 עוּץ *'ûṣ*, v. GK: 6418 [cf. 3289]. [Q] to consider, devise, plan:– take advice [1], take counsel together (+6098) [1]

5780 עוּץ *'ûṣ*, n.pr.m. & loc. GK: 6419 & 6420. Uz:– Uz [7], Huz [1]

5781 עוּק *'ûq*, v. GK: 6421 [→ 4157?, 6125]. [Q] to crush, totter; [H] to crush, cause to totter:– pressed [2]

5782 עוּר *'ûr*, v. GK: 6424 [→ 3265, 5892, 5895, 6147, 6179, 6180]. [Q] to awake; [N] to be aroused, stirred up, wakened; [Pol] to awaken, arouse, raise up; [Pil] to raise, keep up; [H] to stir up, rouse, waken; [Htpol] to rouse oneself:– awake [24], stir up [12], raised up [9], stirred up [5], raise up [4], stirreth up [4], lift up [3], raised [3], raise [2], wakened [2], wakeneth [2], arise [1], awake up [1], awakest [1], dare stir up [1], lifting up [1], master [1], raising [1], wake up [1], waked [1], waketh [1]

5783 עוּר *'ûr*, v. GK: 6423 [→ 4589, 5785?; cf. 6168]. [N] to be uncovered, be laid bare:– made quite naked (+6181) [1]

5784 עוּר *'ûr* (Aram.), n.[m.]. GK: 10534. chaff, the husk particles of threshed grain, used fig. to indicate something worthless:– chaff [1]

5785 עוֹר *'ôr*, n.m. GK: 6425 [→ 5783?]. skin, hide, leather:– skin [73], skins [23], hide [2], leather [1]

5786 עָוַר *'āwar*, v. GK: 6422 [→ 5787, 5788]. [P] to make blind:– put out [3], blindeth [1], blind [1]

5787 עִוֵּר *'iwwēr*, a. GK: 6426 [→ 5786]. blind:– blind [26]

עוֹרֵב *'ôrēb*. See 6159.

5788 עִוָּרוֹן *'iwwārôn* or עַוֶּרֶת *'awweret*, n.[m.]. GK: 6427 & 6428 [→ 5786]. blindness, blinding:– blindness [2], blind [1]

5789 עוּשׁ *'ûš*, v. GK: 6429 [→ 3135, 3266, 3274; cf. 5790]. [Q] to be quick or to help:– assemble [1]

5790 עוּת ***'ût***, v. GK: 6431 [→ 5793; cf. 5789]. [Q] to sustain, help:– speak in season [1]

5791 עָוַת ***'āwat***, v. GK: 6430 [→ 5792]. [P] to make crooked, pervert; [Pu] to be twisted, be made crooked; [Ht] to stoop down, bend over; from the base meaning of twisting an object comes the fig. extension of twisting morality: to pervert:– pervert [3], bow [1], crooked [1], dealt perversely with [1], falsifying [1], made crooked [1], overthrown [1], subvert [1], turneth upside down [1]

5792 עַוָּתָה ***'awwātâ***, n.f. GK: 6432 [→ 5791]. wrong:– wrong [1]

5793 עוּתַי ***'ûtay***, n.pr.m. GK: 6433 [→ 5790]. Uthai, "[poss.] *superiority of Yahweh;* [poss.] *[my] restoration*":– Uthai [2]

5794 עַז ***'az***, a. GK: 6434 & 6435 [→ 5810, 5815?]. strong, mighty, powerful, fierce:– strong [12], fierce [4], mighty [3], greedy (+5315) [1], power [1], roughly [1], stronger [1]

5795 עֵז ***'ēz***, n.m. GK: 6436 [→ 5810?; cf. 5796]. goat; goat hair:– goats [40], goats' [10], kid (+1423) [7], goat [5], she goats [3], he goat (+6842) [2], she goat [2], goat (+7716) [1], he goats (+6842) [1], kids (+1121) [1], kids [1], kid [1]

5796 עֵז ***'ēz*** (Aram.), n.[f.]. GK: 10535. goat (male and female):– he goats (+6841) [1]

5797 עֹז ***'ōz***, n.m. GK: 6437 [→ 5813, 5818; cf. 5756, 5810]. strength, power, might; stronghold, fortification; strong-willed, stubborn;:– strength [60], strong [17], power [11], might [2], boldness [1], loud [1], mighty [1]

5798 עֻזָּא ***'uzzā'*** or עֻזָּה ***'uzzâ***, n.pr.m. GK: 6438 & 6446 [→ 6560]. Uzza, Uzzah, "*strong, fierce one*":– Uzza [10], Uzzah [4]

5799 עֲזָאזֵל ***ᵃzā'zēl***, n.[m. *or* pr.]. GK: 6439. scapegoat, a goat sent into the wilderness of the Day of Atonement, symbolically carrying away the sin of the community; some see this word as the name of the desert spirit (Azazel) to whom the goat is sent:– scapegoat [4]

5800 עָזַב ***'āzab***, v. GK: 6440 & 6441 [→ 5801, 5805, 5806]. [Q] to leave, abandon, reject, desert; to restore, help; [Qp] be left, be abandoned, be freed; [N] be abandoned, be forsaken, be neglected; [Pu] be deserted, be abandoned:– forsaken [60], forsake [46], left [41], leave [28], forsook [16], forsaketh [5], faileth [2], forsookest [2], leave off [2], leaveth [2], left off [2], surely help (+5800) [2], committeth [1], fortified [1], fortify [1], help [1], left destitute [1], leftest [1], refuseth [1]

5801 עִזְבוֹנִים ***'izbônîm***, n.[m.]. GK: 6442 [→ 5800]. merchandise, goods:– fairs [6], wares [1]

5802 עַזְבּוּק ***'azbûq***, n.pr.m. GK: 6443 [→ 950?]. Azbuk:– Azbuk [1]

5803 עַזְגָּד ***'azgād***, n.pr.m. GK: 6444. Azgad, "*strong is Gad*":– Azgad [4]

5804 עַזָּה ***'azzâ***, n.pr.loc. GK: 6445 [→ 5841]. Gaza, "*strong*":– Gaza [18], Azzah [3]

5805 עֲזוּבָה ***ᵃzûbâ***, n.f. GK: 6447 [→ 5800]. forsaking, desolation:– forsaking [1]

5806 עֲזוּבָה ***ᵃzûbâ***, n.pr.f. GK: 6448 [→ 5800]. Azubah, "*adornment*":– Azubah [4]

5807 עֱזוּז ***ᵉzûz***, n.[m.]. GK: 6449 [→ 5810]. power, strength:– strength [2], might [1]

5808 עִזּוּז ***'izzûz***, a. GK: 6450 [→ 5810]. strong, powerful:– power [1], strong [1]

5809 עַזּוּר ***'azzur***, n.pr.m. GK: 6473. Azzur, "*help*":– Azur [2], Azzur [1]

5810 עָזַז ***'āzaz***, v. GK: 6451 [→ 4581, 5794, 5795?, 5807, 5808, 5811, 5812, 5815, 5819, 5821; cf. 3267, 5756, 5797]. [Q] to be strong, overpower; [H] to put on a bold face, be brazen:– strengthened [3], prevailed [2], strengthen [2], hardeneth [1], impudent [1], prevail [1], strengtheneth [1], strong [1]

5811 עָזָז ***'āzāz***, n.pr.m. GK: 6452 [→ 5810]. Azaz, "*strong*":– Azaz [1]

5812 עֲזַזְיָהוּ ***ᵃzazyāhû***, n.pr.m. GK: 6453 [→ 5810+3068]. Azaziah, "*Yahweh is strong*":– Azaziah [3]

5813 עֻזִּי ***'uzzî***, n.pr.m. GK: 6454 [→ 5797]. Uzzi, "*Yahweh is [my] strength*":– Uzzi [11]

5814 עֻזִּיָּא ***'uzziyyā'***, n.pr.m. GK: 6455 [cf. 5818]. Uzzia, "*[my] strength* or *Yahweh is [my] strength*":– Uzzia [1]

5815 עֲזִיאֵל ***ᵃzî'ēl***, n.pr.m. GK: 6456 [→ 5794?+410?]. Aziel, "*God is my strength*":– Aziel [1]

5816 עֻזִּיאֵל ***'uzzî'ēl***, n.pr.m. GK: 6457 [→ 5817]. Uzziel, "*God [El] is [my] strength*":– Uzziel [16]

5817 עָזִּיאֵלִי ***'ozzî'ēlî***, a.g. GK: 6458 [→ 5816]. Uzzielite, "*of Uzziel*":– Uzzielites [2]

5818 עֻזִּיָּה ***'uzziyyâ*** or עֻזִּיָּהוּ ***'uzziyyāhû***, n.pr.m. GK: 6459 & 6460 [→ 5797+3068; cf. 5814]. Uzziah, "*Yahweh is [my] strength*":– Uzziah [27]

5819 עֲזִיזָא ***ᵃzîzā'***, n.pr.m. GK: 6461 [→ 5810]. Aziza, "*powerful*":– Aziza [1]

5820 עַזְמָוֶת ***'azmāwet***, n.pr.m. & loc. GK: 6462 & 6463 [→ 1041]. Azmaveth, "*strong one of death; camel fodder, plant of the plumose family*":– Azmaveth [8]

5821 עַזָּן ***'azzān***, n.pr.m. GK: 6464 [→ 5810]. Azzan, "*strong*":– Azzan [1]

5822 עָזְנִיָּה ***'ozniyyâ***, n.f. GK: 6465. black vulture:– ospray [2]

5823 עָזַק ***'āzaq***, v. GK: 6466. [P] to dig:– fenced [1]

5824 עִזְקָה ***'izqâ*** (Aram.), n.f. GK: 10536. signet-ring, used to validate official business:– signet [2]

5825 עֲזֵקָה ***ᵃzēqâ***, n.pr.loc. GK: 6467. Azekah, "[poss.] *hoe [the ground]*":– Azekah [7]

5826 עָזַר ***'āzar***, v. GK: 6468 [→ 499, 3270, 5828, 5829, 5830, 5832, 5835, 5836, 5838; cf. 5737]. [Q] to help, support; [Qp] to be helped; [N] to be helped:– help [44], helped [17], helper [7], helpers [4], holpen [3], helpeth [2], succour [2], helped forward [1], succoured [1]

5827 עֵזֶר ***'ezer***, n.pr.m. GK: 6472 [→ 5828]. Ezer, "*help*":– Ezer [1]

5828 עֵזֶר ***'ēzer***, n.m. GK: 6469 [→ 5829, 5827, 5833, 5834; cf. 5826 (also used with compound proper names)]. help, helper:– help [21]

5829 עֵזֶר ***'ēzer***, n.pr.m. GK: 6470 [→ 5828; cf. 5826]. Ezer, "*help*":– Ezer [4]

עַזֻּר ***'azzur***. See 5809.

5830 עֶזְרָא ***'ezrā'***, n.pr.m. GK: 6474 [→ 5826; cf. 5831]. Ezra, "*help*":– Ezra [22]

5831 עֶזְרָא ***'ezrā'*** (Aram.), n.pr.m. GK: 10537 [cf. 5830]. Ezra, "*help*":– Ezra [3]

5832 עֲזַרְאֵל ***ᵃzar'ēl***, n.pr.m. GK: 6475 [→ 5826+410]. Azarel, "*God [El] has helped*":– Azareel [5], Azarael [1]

5833 עֶזְרָה ***'ezrâ***, n.f. GK: 6476 [→ 5834; cf. 5828]. help, aid, support; helper, ally:– help [24], helped [1], helpers [1]

5834 עֶזְרָה ***'ezrâ***, n.pr.m. GK: 6477 [→ 5833]. Ezrah:– Ezra [1]

5835 עֲזָרָה ***ᵃzārâ***, n.f. GK: 6478 [→ 5826]. court, enclosure; ledge, barrier:– settle [6], court [3]

5836 עֶזְרִי ***'ezrî***, n.pr.m. GK: 6479 [→ 5826+3068? *or* 2967.1?]. Ezri, "*my help*":– Ezri [1]

5837 עַזְרִיאֵל ***'azrî'ēl***, n.pr.m. GK: 6480 [→ 5828+410]. Azriel, "*God [El] is [my] help*":– Azriel [3]

5838 עֲזַרְיָה ***ᵃzaryâ*** or עֲזַרְיָהוּ ***ᵃzaryāhû***, n.pr.m. GK: 6481 & 6482 [→ 5826+3068; cf. 5839]. Azariah, "*Yahweh has helped*":– Azariah [48]

5839 עֲזַרְיָה ***ᵃzaryâ*** (Aram.), n.pr.m. GK: 10538 [cf. 5838]. Azariah, "*Yahweh has helped*":– Azariah [1]

5840 עַזְרִיקָם ***'azrîqām***, n.pr.m. GK: 6483 [→ 5828+6965]. Azrikam, "*[my] help arises*":– Azrikam [6]

5841 עַזָּתִי ***'azzātî***, a.g. GK: 6484 [→ 5804]. Gazite, "*of Gaza*":– Gazathites [1], Gazites [1]

5842 עֵט ***'ēṭ***, n.m. GK: 6485. (iron) engraving tool, stylus; (reed) pen:– pen [4]

5843 עֵטָא ***'ēṭâ*** (Aram.), n.f. GK: 10539 [→ 3272; cf. 6098]. counsel, wisdom:– counsel [1]

5844 עָטָה ***'āṭâ***, v. GK: 6486 & 6487 [→ 4593, 4594; cf. 3271]. [Q] to cover, wrap oneself; to grasp; [Pu] to be grasped; [H] cover, wrap another (thing):– cover [4], covered with [2], surely cover (+5844) [2], array with [1], clad with [1], covered [1], coverest [1], covereth [1], filleth [1], put a covering [1], putteth on [1], turneth aside [1]

5845 עֲטִין ***ᵃṭîn***, n.[m.]. GK: 6489. body, part of body; or pail, bucket:– breasts [1]

5846 עֲטִישָׁה ***ᵃṭîšâ***, n.f. GK: 6490. snorting, sneezing:– neesings [1]

5847 עֲטַלֵּף ***ᵃṭallēp***, n.[m.]. GK: 6491 [→ 5848+3807.1]. bat (animal):– bat [2], bats [1]

5848 עָטַף ***'āṭap***, v. GK: 6488 & 6493 & 6494 [→ 4595, 5847]. [Q] to clothe, mantle; to turn aside; to grow faint; [N] to be faint; [H] to be feeble; [Ht] to ebb away, grow faint:– overwhelmed [5], fainted [2], covered over [1], covereth [1], fail [1], faint [1], feebler [1], feeble [1], hideth [1], swooned [1], swoon [1]

5849 עָטַר ***'āṭar***, v. GK: 6496 & 6497 [→ 5850, 5851, 5852, 5853, 5854, 5855]. [Q] to surround, close in upon; [P] to crown, place a wreath (on the head); [H] to bestow a crown:– crowned [2], compassed round about [1], compass [1], crownest [1], crowneth [1], crowning [1]

5850 עֲטָרָה ***ᵃṭārâ***, n.f. GK: 6498 [→ 5849]. crown, wreath, placed on the head as a symbol of celebration or status; can be made of plants or precious metals:– crown [20], crowns [3]

5851 עֲטָרָה ***ᵃṭārâ***, n.pr.f. GK: 6499 [→ 5849]. Atarah, "*circlet, wreath*":– Atarah [1]

5852 עֲטָרוֹת **ʿᵃṭārôt**, n.pr.loc. GK: 6500 [→ 5853, 5854; cf. 5849]. Ataroth, "*circlets, wreaths*":– Ataroth [5]

5853 עַטְרוֹת אַדָּר **ʿaṭrôt ʾaddār**, n.pr.loc. GK: 6501 [→ 5852+146]. Ataroth Addar, "*wreaths of majesty*":– Ataroth-adar [1], Ataroth-addar [1]

5854 עַטְרוֹת בֵּית יוֹאָב **ʿaṭrôt bêt yôʾāb**, n.pr.loc. GK: 6502 [→ 5852+1004+3097]. Atroth Beth Joab, "*circlets, folds of the house of Joab*":–

5855 עַטְרוֹת שׁוֹפָן **ʿaṭrôt šôpān**, n.pr.loc. GK: 6503 [→ 5849]. Atroth Shophan, "*circlets, folds of Shophan*":– Atroth Shophan [1]

5856 עִי **ʿî**, n.[m.]. GK: 6505 [→ 1164, 4596, 5859, 5863, 5864; cf. 5753]. heap of rubble; (of a person) a broken man:– heaps [3], grave [1], heap [1]

5857 עַי **ʿay** or עַיָּת **ʿayyat** or עַיָּא **ʿayyâ**, n.pr.loc. GK: 6504 & 6509 & 6569 [cf. 5754]. Ai, Aiath, Ayyah; Aija, "*ruin, the heap*":– Ai [36], Hai [2], Aiath [1], Aija [1]

5858 עֵיבָל **ʿêbāl**, n.pr.m. & g. & loc. GK: 6506 & 6507 & 6508 [cf. 5745]. Ebal:– Ebal [8]

עַיָּה **ʿayâ**. See 5857.

5859 עִיּוֹן **ʿiyyôn**, n.pr.loc. GK: 6510 [→ 5856]. Ijon, "*place of heaps [of stone]*":– Ijon [3]

5860 עִיט **ʿîṭ**, v. GK: 6512 & 6513 [→ 5861, 5862?]. [Q] to hurl insults; to pounce upon (with shrieks and screams):– flew [1], fly [1], railed [1]

5861 עַיִט **ʿayiṭ**, n.m. GK: 6514 [→ 5862?; cf. 5860]. (coll) birds of prey, carrion birds:– fowls [3], birds [1], bird [1], fowl [1], ravenous bird [1], ravenous [1]

5862 עֵיטָם **ʿêṭām**, n.pr.loc. GK: 6515 [→ 5861?+3963.1?]. Etam, "[poss.] *place of birds of prey*":– Etam [5]

5863 עִיֵּי הָעֲבָרִים **ʿiyyê hāʿᵃbārîm**, n.pr.loc. GK: 6516 [→ 5856]. Iye Abarim, "*heaps of Abarim [regions beyond]*":– Ije-abarim [2]

5864 עִיִּים **ʿiyyîm**, n.pr.loc. GK: 6517 [→ 5856]. Iyim; Iim, "*heaps, ruins*":– Iim [2]

5865 עֵילוֹם **ʿêlôm**, n.m. GK: 6518 [cf. 5769]. forever:– ever [1]

5866 עִילַי **ʿîlay**, n.pr.m. GK: 6519. Ilai:– Ilai [1]

5867 עֵילָם **ʿêlām**, n.pr.m. & g. & loc. GK: 6520 & 6521 [cf. 5962]. Elam, "*highland*":– Elam [28]

5868 עַיָם **ʿᵃyām**, n.[m.]. GK: 6522. scorching (of wind):– mighty [1]

5869 עַיִן **ʿayin**, n.f. & m. GK: 6524 [→ 4599, 5770, 5871, 5879, 5881; cf. 5870 (also used with compound proper names)]. eye; by extension: sight; spring, fountain; to be "evil of eye" is to be displeased; to be "good of eye" is to be pleased; to be "good in one's eyes" is to be pleasing "right in one's eyes" means acceptable by one's personal standards:– eyes [420], sight [216], eye [77], colour [12], face [10], well [10], seemeth unto (+871.1) [9], pleased (+3190+871.1) [8], presence [8], fountain [7], before (+3807.1) [6], displeased (+3415+871.1) [6], seem unto (+871.1) [6], seemeth (+871.1) [6], conceit [4], fountains [4], looks [3], look [3], pleased (+3474+871.1) [3], pleased well (+3474+871.1) [3], seemed to (+871.1) [3], thought (+871.1) [3], before (+871.1) [2], displease (+7489+871.1) [2], look well (+7760) [2], pleased (+2896+871.1) [2], pleased well (+3190+871.1) [2], pleaseth (+2896+871.1) [2], seemed (+1961+871.1) [2], seemeth to (+871.1) [2], thinkest (+871.1) [2], content (+3190+871.1) [1], countenance [1], displease (+2734+871.1) [1], displease (+6213+7451+871.1) [1], displeased (+7489+871.1) [1], escape (+5337) [1], eye sight [1], eye's [1], eyebrows (+1354) [1], eyed [1], eyesight [1], favour (+2896+871.1) [1], for (+871.1) [1], humble person (+7807) [1], liketh (+2896+871.1) [1], looketh (+4758) [1], open place (+6607) [1], openly (+871.1+1886.1) [1], outward appearance [1], please (+3474+871.1) [1], please not (+7451+871.1) [1], pleased not (+7451+871.1) [1], pleased well (+3477+871.1) [1], pleaseth (+3190+871.1) [1], pleaseth well (+3474) [1], regard (+2347) [1], resemblance [1], seem (+1961+871.1) [1], seem (+871.1) [1], seem to (+871.1) [1], seem unto (+3807.1) [1], seemed unto (+871.1) [1], think (+871.1) [1], think best (+2896+871.1) [1], thinking (+871.1) [1], wells [1], with (+871.1) [1], without knowledge (+4480) [1]

5870 עַיִן **ʿayin** (Aram.), n.f. GK: 10540 [cf. 5869]. eye:– eyes [4], eye [1]

5871 עַיִן **ʿayin**, n.pr.loc. GK: 6526 [→ 5869]. Ain, "*eye[ball] or spring [of water]*":– Ain [5]

5872 עֵין גֶּדִי **ʿên gedî**, n.pr.loc. GK: 6527 [→ 5869+1423]. En Gedi, "*spring of young goat*":– En-gedi [6]

5873 עֵין גַּנִּים **ʿên gannîm**, n.pr.loc. GK: 6528 [→ 5869]. En Gannim, "*spring of gardens*":– En-gannim [3]

5874 עֵין־דֹּאר **ʿên-dōʾr** or עֵין־דּוֹר **ʿên-dôr**, n.pr.loc. GK: 6529 [→ 5869+1756]. Endor, "*spring of Dor*":– En-dor [3]

5875 עֵין הַקּוֹרֵא **ʿên haqqôrēʾ**, n.pr.loc. GK: 6530 [→ 5869]. En Hakkore, "*spring of the partridge* or *caller*":– En-hakkore [1]

עֵינוֹן **ʿênôn**. See 2703.

5876 עֵין חַדָּה **ʿên ḥaddâ**, n.pr.loc. GK: 6532 [→ 5869]. En Haddah, "*spring of gladness*":– En-haddah [1]

5877 עֵין חָצוֹר **ʿên ḥāṣôr**, n.pr.loc. GK: 6533 [→ 5869+2674]. En Hazor, "*spring of Hazor*":– En-hazor [1]

5878 עֵין חֲרֹד **ʿên ḥᵃrōd**, n.pr.loc. GK: 6534 [→ 5869]. En Harod, "*spring of Harod*":– Harod [1]

5879 עֵינַיִם **ʿênayim** or עֵינָם **ʿênām**, n.pr.loc. GK: 6542 & 6543 [→ 5869+3963.1]. Enam, Enaim, "*two springs*":– Enam [1]

5880 עֵין מִשְׁפָּט **ʿên mišpāṭ**, n.pr.loc. GK: 6535 [→ 5869+4941]. En Mishpat, "*spring of judgment*":– En-mishpat [1]

5881 עֵינָן **ʿênān**, n.pr.m. GK: 6544 [→ 2704]. Enan, "*spring*":– Enan [5]

5882 עֵין עֶגְלַיִם **ʿên ʿeglayim**, n.pr.loc. GK: 6536 [→ 5869]. En Eglaim, "*spring of two calves*":– En-eglaim [1]

5883 עֵין רֹגֵל **ʿên rōgēl**, n.pr.loc. GK: 6537 [→ 5869]. En Rogel, "*spring of the fuller* or *wanderer* or *spy*":– En-rogel [4]

5884 עֵין־רִמּוֹן **ʿên rimmôn**, n.pr.loc. GK: 6538 [→ 5869+7417]. En Rimmon, "*spring of Rimmon*":– En-rimmon [1]

5885 עֵין שֶׁמֶשׁ **ʿên šemeš**, n.pr.loc. GK: 6539 [→ 5869+8121]. En Shemesh, "*spring of Shemesh*":– En-shemesh [2]

5886 עֵין תַּנִּים **ʿên tannîm**, n.pr.loc. GK: 6524 + 9478 [→ 5869+8565]. En Tannim, "Well of the Jackal" (5869 + 8565):–

5887 עֵין תַּפּוּחַ **ʿên tappûaḥ**, n.pr.loc. GK: 6540 [→ 5869+8599]. En Tappuah, "*spring of apple*":– En-tappuah [1]

5888 עִיף **ʿîp**, v. GK: 6545 [→ 5774]. [Q] to be faint, be exhausted:– wearied [1]

5889 עָיֵף **ʿāyēp**, a. GK: 6546 [→ 5774; cf. 3286]. weary, faint; famished, parched:– weary [8], faint [6], thirsty [3]

5890 עֵיפָה **ʿêpâ**, n.f. GK: 6547 [→ 5891; cf. 4155]. darkness:– darkness [2]

5891 עֵיפָה **ʿêpâ**, n.pr.m. & f. & g. GK: 6548 & 6549 [cf. 5890]. Ephah, "*darkness*":– Ephah [5]

5892 עִיר **ʿîr**, n.f. GK: 6551 & 6552 [→ 5782, 6144? (also found with compound proper names)]. city, town, village, a general term for a population center; anguish, terror, wrath:– city [650], cities [421], several city (+5892+2050.1) [6], every city (+3605+5892+2050.1) [4], every city (+5892+2050.1) [4], town [4], towns [3], cities every one (+5892) [2]

5893 עִיר **ʿîr**, n.pr.m. GK: 6553 [→ 5895]. Ir, "[poss.] *stallion donkey*":– Ir [1]

5894 עִיר **ʿîr** (Aram.), n.m. GK: 10541 [cf. 5782]. messenger (of God), watcher, one who is a sentinel to guard and protect:– watcher [2], watchers [1]

5895 עַיִר **ʿayir**, n.m. GK: 6554 & 6555 [→ 5782, 5893, 5896, 5901, 5902]. (male) donkey:– ass colts [2], colt [2], young asses [2], foals [1], foal [1]

5896 עִירָא **ʿîrāʾ**, n.pr.m. GK: 6562 [→ 5895]. Ira, "[poss.] *stallion donkey*":– Ira [6]

5897 עִירָד **ʿîrād**, n.pr.m. GK: 6563 [→ 6171]. Irad:– Irad [2]

5898 עִיר הַמֶּלַח **ʿîr hammelaḥ**, n.pr.loc. GK: 6558 [→ 5892+1886.1+4417]. Ir Hammelak, "*the city of salt*":–

5899 עִיר הַתְּמָרִים **ʿîr hattᵉmārîm**, n.pr.loc. GK: 6559 [→ 5892+1886.1+8558]. Ir Hattemarim, "*the city of palms*":–

5900 עִירוּ **ʿîrû**, n.pr.m. GK: 6564. Iru:– Iru [1]

5901 עִירִי **ʿîrî**, n.pr.m. GK: 6565 [→ 5895]. Iri, "[perhaps] *donkey's colt*":– Iri [1]

5902 עִירָם **ʿîrām**, n.pr.m. GK: 6566 [→ 5895+3963.1]. Iram:– Iram [2]

5903 עֵירֹם **ʿêrōm**, a. (used as noun). GK: 6567 [→ 6168]. naked; nakedness:– naked [9], nakedness [1]

5904 עִיר נָחָשׁ **ʿîr nāḥāš**, n.pr.loc. GK: 6560 [→ 5892]. Ir Nahash, "*city of Nahash*":– Irnahash [1]

5905 עִיר שֶׁמֶשׁ **ʿîr šemeš**, n.pr.loc. GK: 6561 [→ 5892+8121]. Ir Shemesh, "*city of Shemesh*":– Ir-shemesh [1]

5906 עַיִשׁ **ʿayiš** or עָשׁ **ʿāš**, n.f. GK: 6568 & 6933 [→ 6211]. constellation: the Bear or the Lion, or some other constellation:– Arcturus [2]

עַיָּת **ʿayāt**. See 5857.

5907 עַכְבּוֹר **ʿakbôr**, n.pr.m. GK: 6570 [→ 5909]. Acbor, "*mouse or jerboa*":– Achbor [7]

Heb

5908 עַכָּבִישׁ **ʿakkābîš**, n.m. GK: 6571. spider:– spider's [2]

5909 עַכְבָּר **ʿakbār**, n.m. GK: 6572 [→ 5907]. (jumping) rat, jerboa:– mice [4], mouse [2]

5910 עַכּוֹ **ʿakkô**, n.pr.loc. GK: 6573. Acco:– Accho [1]

5911 עָכוֹר **ʿākôr**, n.pr.loc. GK: 6574 [→ 5916]. Achor, *"trouble"*:– Achor [5]

5912 עָכָן **ʿākān**, n.pr.m. GK: 6575. Achan, *"troubler"*:– Achan [6]

5913 עָכַס **ʿākas**, v.den. GK: 6576 [→ 5914, 5915]. [P] to jingle, rattle (of ankle ornaments):– making a tinkling [1]

5914 עֶכֶס **ʿekes**, n.[m.]. GK: 6577 [→ 5913]. bangle, ankle ornament:– stocks [1], tinkling ornaments [1]

5915 עַכְסָה **ʿaksâ**, n.pr.f. GK: 6578 [→ 5913]. Acsah, *"decorative anklet"*:– Achsah [5]

5916 עָכַר **ʿākar**, v. GK: 6579 [→ 5911, 5917, 5918]. [Q] to bring trouble, make trouble; [N] to be troubled, be anguished:– troubled [4], troubleth [4], trouble [4], stirred [1], troubler [1]

5917 עָכָר **ʿākār**, n.pr.m. GK: 6580 [→ 5916]. Achar, *"trouble"*:– Achar [1]

5918 עָכְרָן **ʿokrān**, n.pr.m. GK: 6581 [→ 5916]. Ocran, *"trouble"*:– Ocran [5]

5919 עַכְשׁוּב **ʿakšûb**, n.m. GK: 6582. (horned) viper; other sources: asp:– adder's [1]

5920 עַל **ʿal**, subst. GK: 6583 [→ 5927; cf. 5921; cf. 5943]. (the) Most High:– above [2], most high [2], above (+4480) [1], on high [1]

5921 עַל **ʿal**, pp. & c. GK: 6584 [→ 4480+5921; cf. 5920; cf. 5922]. marker of relationship: spatial: on, upon, over, against, toward; logical: because of, according to; temporal: on, when, during:– upon [1572], against [538], over [413], in [318], for [305], on [292], by [215], to [167], from (+4480) [152], unto [150], therefore (+3651) [125], with [106], at [87], concerning [79], off [63], above [56], of [55], into [47], before (+6440) [43], according to [32], thereon (+2050.2) [31], because (+834) [26], because of [26], because [25], upon (+6440) [23], wherefore (+3651) [22], after [20], out of (+4480) [19], toward [15], next unto (+3027) [13], about [12], above (+4480) [12], beside [12], before [11], upon (+4480) [11], thereon (+1886.3) [10], wherefore (+4100) [10], whereon (+834) [10]*

5922 עַל **ʿal** (Aram.), pp. GK: 10542 [→ 5924, 5928, 5943, 5952, 5946; cf. 5921]. upon, over, against, toward, concerning:– upon [19], unto [16], over [13], in [10], against [7], to [7], concerning [6], for [6], of [5], about [3], above [1], from [1], more [1], nor (+2050.3) [1], on [1], therefore (+1836) [1], thereon (+1958.2) [1], why (+4101) [1], with [1]

5923 עֹל **ʿōl**, n.m. GK: 6585 [→ 5953]. yoke, placed on draft animals; by extension: a figure of oppression or of proper training:– yoke [40]

5924 עֵלָּא **ʿēllāʾ** (Aram.), adv. GK: 10543 [→ 5922; cf. 5921]. over, above:– over (+4481) [1]

5925 עֻלָּא **ʿullāʾ**, n.pr.m. GK: 6587 [→ 5927]. Ulla:– Ulla [1]

5926 עִלֵּג **ʿillēg**, a. GK: 6589 [cf. 3932]. speaking inarticulately; (pl.n.) stammerers:– stammerers [1]

5927 עָלָה **ʿālâ**, v. GK: 6590 [→ 500, 4605, 4607, 4608, 4609, 5920, 5925, 5929, 5930, 5933, 5935, 5941, 5940, 5942, 5933, 5944, 5945, 8585]. [Q] to go up, ascend, rise; [N] to be lifted up, withdraw, be exalted; [H] to take up, set up, offer a sacrifice; [Ho] to be offered up, be carried away, be recorded; [Ht] to raise oneself up; from the base meaning of rise in elevation comes the fig. extension "to exalt, honor," as the lifting up of a person in status:– went up [156], go up [123], come up [81], came up [77], brought up [58], offered [35], bring up [32], offer [29], gone up [21], get up [18], come [11], goeth up [10], taken up [9], offering [8], brought [7], gat up [7], ascended [6], came [6], cause to come up [6], cheweth [6], cometh up [6], offer up [5], rise up [5], ascended up [4], ascend [4], carry up [4], going up [4], go [4], mount up [4], take up [4], went [4], bringeth up [3], bring [3], carried up [3], causeth to ascend [3], chew [3], climb up [3], cometh [3], increased [3], made to come up [3], offereth [3], took up [3], arose [2], ascending [2], cast up [2], cause to burn [2], depart [2], exalted [2], fell [2], go up at once (+5927) [2], lifteth up [2], lighted [2], light [2], offered up [2], put [2], raised [2], setteth up [2], spring [2], surely bring up (+5927) [2], wentest up [2], arise up [1], ariseth [1], arise [1], ascend up [1], breaketh [1], breaking [1], broken up [1], broughtest up [1], broughtest [1], burnt [1], cause come up [1], caused to come up [1], causeth to come up [1], climbed up [1], climb [1], cometh in [1], cut off [1], dawning [1], departed [1], excellest [1], fetch up [1], fetched up [1], fetcht up [1], getteth up [1], goest up [1], goeth [1], gone away [1], grow up [1], groweth [1], grown over [1], grow [1], increaseth [1], laid [1], leaped [1], leap [1], lift up [1], lightest [1], lighteth [1], made to go up [1], made up (+724) [1], make rise up [1], make to pay [1], mentioned [1], offering up [1], perfected (+724) [1], prefer [1], put on [1], raised up [1], recovered [1], restore [1], riseth up [1], rising [1], rose up [1], rose [1], scaleth [1], set up [1], set [1], shooting up [1], shot forth [1], spring up [1], stir up [1], take away [1], upon levy [1], vapour [1], went away [1], wrought [1]

5928 עֲלָוָה **ʿᵃlāwâ** (Aram.), n.f. GK: 10545 [→ 5922; cf. 5930]. burnt offering:– burnt offerings [1]

5929 עָלֶה **ʿāleh**, n.m. GK: 6591 [→ 5927]. leaves, foliage:– leaf [11], branches [4], branch [1], leaves [1]

5930 עֹלָה **ʿōlâ**, n.f. GK: 6592 [→ 5927; cf. 5928]. burnt offering, wholly dedicated to God:– burnt offering [183], burnt offerings [82], burnt sacrifice [17], burnt sacrifices [4], ascent [1], go up [1]

5931 עִלָּה **ʿillâ** (Aram.), n.f. GK: 10544 [cf. 5953]. grounds, basis, pretext (for charges):– occasion [3]

5932 עַלְוָה **ʿalwâ**, n.f. GK: 6594. evil, wickedness:– iniquity [1]

5933 עַלְוָה **ʿalwâ** or עַלְיָה **ʿalyâ**, n.pr.m. GK: 6595 & 6607 [→ 5927]. Alvah, Aliah:– Aliah [1], Alvah [1]

5934 עֲלוּמִים **ʿᵃlûmîm**, n.pl.abst. GK: 6596 [→ 3281, 5958, 5959, 5961]. (abst.pl.) youthfulness, (the vigor of) youth:– youth [4]

5935 עַלְוָן **ʿalwān** or עַלְיָן **ʿalyān**, n.pr.m. GK: 6597 & 6615 [→ 5927]. Alvan, Alian, "[poss.] *ascending one* or *tall*":– Alian [1], Alvan [1]

5936 עֲלוּקָה **ʿᵃlûqâ**, n.f. GK: 6598. leech:– horseleach [1]

5937 עָלַז **ʿālaz**, v. GK: 6600 [→ 5938, 5947; cf. 5965]. [Q] to rejoice, be jubilant:– rejoice [8], joyful [2], rejoiced [2], triumph [2], greatly rejoiceth [1], rejoicest [1]

5938 עָלֵז **ʿālēz**, a. (used as n.). GK: 6601 [→ 5937]. reveling, exultant; (n.) reveler:– rejoiceth [1]

5939 עֲלָטָה **ʿᵃlāṭâ**, n.f. GK: 6602. darkness, dusk:– twilight [3], dark [1]

5940 עֱלִי **ʿᵉlî**, n.[m.]. GK: 6605 [→ 5927]. pestle (of a mortar):– pestle [1]

5941 עֵלִי **ʿēlî**, n.pr.m. GK: 6603 [→ 3068 *or* 410+5927]. Eli, *"Yahweh is exalted; God [El] is exalted"*:– Eli [32], Eli's [1]

5942 עִלִּי **ʿillî**, a. GK: 6606 [→ 5927; cf. 5952]. upper:– upper [2]

5943 עִלַּי **ʿillāy** (Aram.), a. GK: 10546 [→ 5922]. highest, superior; the Most High, a title of God indicating his supreme status and power:– most high [9], high [1]

עַלְיָה **ʿalyâ**. See 5933.

5944 עֲלִיָּה **ʿᵃliyyâ**, n.f. GK: 6608 [→ 5927; cf. 5952]. upper room, upper parts:– chambers [4], chamber [4], parlour [4], going up [2], upper chambers [2], upper chamber [2], ascent [1], loft [1]

5945 עֶלְיוֹן **ʿelyôn**, a. GK: 6609 & 6610 [→ 5927; cf. 5943, cf. 5946]. upper, also used in place names; (the) Most High, a title of God with a focus on supremacy in status and power:– most high [27], high [9], upper [8], higher [4], highest [3], on high [1], uppermost [1]

5946 עֶלְיוֹן **ʿelyôn** (Aram.), a. GK: 10548 [→ 5922; cf. 5945]. highest, superior; (as a title) the Most High:– most high [4]

5947 עַלִּיז **ʿallîz**, a. GK: 6611 [→ 5937]. rejoicing, exulting; reveling, wild:– joyous [3], rejoice [3], rejoicing [1]

5948 עֲלִיל **ʿᵃlîl**, n.[m.]. GK: 6612 [→ 5953]. furnace:– furnace [1]

5949 עֲלִילָה **ʿᵃlîlâ**, n.f. GK: 6613 [→ 5953]. what is done, deed, action:– doings [13], works [3], deeds [2], occasions [2], actions [1], acts [1], doing [1], inventions [1]

5950 עֲלִילִיָּה **ʿᵃlîliyyâ**, n.f. GK: 6614. deed:– work [1]

עַלְיָן **ʿalyān**. See 5935.

5951 עֲלִיצֻת **ʿᵃlîṣut**, n.f. GK: 6617 [→ 5970; cf. 5965]. rejoicing, exaltation, including verbal expressions of joy and praise; from a negative perspective: haughtiness, presumption, gloating:– rejoicing [1]

5952 עִלִּי **ʿillî** (Aram.), n.f. GK: 10547 [→ 5922; cf. 5942]. upstairs room, a storage or guest room on the flat roof of a house:– chamber [1]

5953 עָלַל **ʿālal**, v. GK: 6618 & 6619 & 6620 & 6621 [→ 4611, 5923, 5948, 5949, 5955, 8586; cf. 5954]. [Po] to act or play the child; (n.) youths; to deal with; to glean, go over a second time; to thrust (in); [Poal] to be dealt with (in a way that causes suffering); [Ht] to deal harshly, abuse, mistreat; [Htpo] to take part in (wickedness):– done [3], abuse [2], glean [2], throughly glean (+5953) [2], abused [1], affecteth [1], children [1], defiled [1], do [1], gleaned [1], mocked [1], mock [1], practise [1], wrought wonderfully [1], wrought [1]

Heb

5954 עֲלַל ***ʿᵃlal*** (Aram.), v. GK: 10549 [→ 4606; cf. 5953]. [P] to go in; [H] to take in, bring before; [Ho] to be brought in, introduced before:– bring in [3], brought in [3], came in [3], went in [2], brought [1], came [1], went [1]

עֹלָל ***ʿōlāl***. See 5768.

עֲלִלָה ***ʿᵃlilâ***. See 5949.

5955 עֹלֵלוֹת ***ʿōlēlôt***, n.f.pl.intens. GK: 6622 [→ 5953]. gleanings:– gleaning grapes [3], gleaning of grapes [1], grapegleanings [1], grapes [1]

5956 עָלַם ***ʿālam***, v. GK: 6623 [→ 8587]. [Qp] to be in secret; [N] to be concealed, be hidden, be unaware; [H] to hide, shut off, conceal; [Ht] to hide oneself from, ignore:– hid [11], hide [7], any ways hide (+5956) [2], hideth [2], secret [2], blind [1], dissemblers [1], hidden [1], hidest [1]

5957 עָלַם ***ʿālam*** (Aram.), n.[m.]. GK: 10550 [cf. 5769]. forever, eternal, everlasting; ancient, a long time ago:– ever [10], everlasting [4], old [2], ever (+0.2) [1], ever (+0.2+5705) [1], for ever (+0.2) [1], never (+3809+3807.2) [1]

5958 עֶלֶם ***ʿelem***, n.m. GK: 6624 [→ 5934]. boy, young man:– stripling [1], young man [1]

עֹלָם ***ʿōlām***. See 5769.

5959 עַלְמָה ***ʿalmâ***, n.f. GK: 6625 [→ 5934; cf. 5961]. girl, young woman, (in certain contexts) virgin:– maid [2], virgins [2], virgin [2], damsels [1]

5960 עַלְמוֹן ***ʿalmôn***, n.pr.loc. GK: 6626 [→ 5963]. Almon:– Almon [1]

5961 עֲלָמוֹת ***ʿᵃlāmôt***, n.f. GK: 6628 [→ 5934; cf. 5959]. alamoth (t.t. in the Psalms):– Alamoth [2]

עַלְמוּת ***ʿalmût***. See 4192.

5962 עֵלְמָי ***ʿēlmāy*** (Aram.), n.g.pl. GK: 10551 [cf. 5867]. Elamite:– Elamites [1]

5963 עַלְמֹן דִּבְלָתָיְמָה ***ʿalmôn diblātayim***, n.pr.loc. GK: 6627 [→ 5960]. Almon Diblathaim, *"way of the double fig cakes"*:– Almon-diblathaim [2]

5964 עָלֶמֶת ***ʿālemet***, n.pr.m. & loc. GK: 6630 & 6631. Alemeth, *"concealment"*:– Alemeth [3], Alameth [1]

5965 עָלַס ***ʿālas***, v. GK: 6632 [cf. 5937, 5951, 5970]. [Q] to enjoy; [N] to appear glad; [Ht] to enjoy one another:– peacocks [1], rejoice [1], solace [1]

5966 עָלַע ***ʿālaʿ***, v. GK: 6633 [cf. 3216]. [Palpal] to drink, feast on:– suck up [1]

5967 עֲלַע ***ʿᵃlaʿ*** (Aram.), n.f. GK: 10552 [cf. 6763]. rib:– ribs [1]

5968 עָלַף ***ʿālap***, v. GK: 6634. [Pu] to faint; to be withered; be decorated, covered; [Ht] to disguise oneself; to grow faint:– fainted [2], faint [1], overlaid [1], wrapped [1]

5969 עֻלְפֶּה ***ʿulpeh***, var. GK: 6635. form of 5968: faint:– fainted [1]

5970 עָלַץ ***ʿālaṣ***, v. GK: 6636 [→ 5951; cf. 5965]. [Q] to rejoice, be jubilant:– rejoice [4], rejoiceth [2], joyful [1], triumph [1]

5971 עַם ***ʿam***, n.[m.]. GK: 6638 & 6639 [cf. 5972 (also used with compound proper names)]. people, nation, countrymen; army, troop; father's relatives, one's people:– people [1829], nations [15], every people (+5971+2050.1) [8], people (+1121) [5], each people (+5971+2050.1) [2], folk [2], nation [2], people's [2], Ammi (+2967.1) [1], men [1]

5972 עַם ***ʿam*** (Aram.), n.m. GK: 10553 [cf. 5971]. people, nation:– people [15]

5973 עִם ***ʿim***, pp. GK: 6640 [→ 6005; cf. 6004; cf. 5974]. marker of association or proximity: to, toward; with, among:– with [778], from (+4480) [46], against [36], unto [32], by [22], in [18], of (+4480) [13], among [11], to [11], and [7], for [5], of [5], before [4], by (+4480) [4], as [3], beside [3], at [2], towards [2], able to withstand (+3320) [1], accompanying [1], according to mind (+4480) [1], as long as [1], before (+4480) [1], besides [1], between [1], by reason of [1], for (+3588) [1], given of (+4480) [1], had (+1961) [1], had [1], have (+3426) [1], have [1], help [1], in the behalf of [1], lest (+2050.1) [1], lieth with (+7901) [1], like [1], mighty (+1369) [1], minded (+3820) [1], more than [1], near [1], on side [1], shew (+6213) [1], though (+3588) [1], to (+4480) [1], together with [1], toward [1], unto (+4480) [1], upon [1], withal [1]

5974 עִם ***ʿim*** (Aram.), pp. GK: 10554 [cf. 5973]. with, along with, to, for; a marker showing association in various meanings:– with [14], from [2], to [2], by [1], like [1], toward [1], unto [1]

5975 עָמַד ***ʿāmad***, v. GK: 6641 [→ 4612, 4613, 5977, 5978, 5979, 5982]. [Q] to stand, stand up, stand still; [H] to cause to stand, present; to appoint, assign; [Ho] to be presented, be caused to stand:– stood [175], stand [123], set [31], standeth [13], stand up [12], set up [11], stood still [11], appointed [10], standing [10], stay [8], stayed [7], present [6], stand still [6], continue [4], endureth [4], remained [4], standest [4], stood up [4], waited [4], endure [3], establish [3], made [3], remain [3], abideth [2], abide [2], appoint [2], at a stay [2], confirmed [2], left [2], set forth [2], setteth [2], standing up [2], stayed up [2], stoodest [2], withstand [2], able to stand [1], abode [1], arise [1], arose [1], caused to stand [1], ceased [1], continued [1], continueth [1], dwell [1], employed [1], enduring [1], established [1], made to serve [1], made to stand [1], ordained [1], over (+5921) [1], placed [1], presented [1], raised up [1], raiseth [1], remaineth [1], repair [1], served (+6440+3807.1) [1], serve [1], settled [1], settle [1], stablished [1], stablisheth [1], stand by [1], standeth (+3807.1) [1], stood fast [1], tarried [1], tarry [1], waited on [1], withstand (+5048) [1], withstand (+6440+3807.1) [1], withstood (+5048+3807.1) [1], withstood (+5921) [1]

5976 עָמַד ***ʿāmad*** for מָעַד ***māʿad***, v. GK: 5048 [→ 4154]. var. of 4571: [H] cause to wobble, to bend:– madest to be at a stand [1]

5977 עֹמֶד ***ʿōmed***, n.[m.]. GK: 6642 [→ 5975]. standing-place (a position, station, or post):– place [6], upright (+5921) [2], stood [1], where stood [1]

5978 עִמָּד ***ʿimmād***, pp. GK: 6643 [→ 5975]. with:– with [25], unto [7], against [1], by [1], from (+4480) [1], in [1], mine (+2967.1) [1], of (+4480) [1], take [1], upon [1], within [1]

עַמֻּד ***ʿammud***. See 5982.

5979 עֶמְדָּה ***ʿemdâ***, n.f. GK: 6644 [→ 5975]. place to stand, protection:– standing [1]

5980 עֻמָּה ***ʿummâ***, n.f. (used as pp.). GK: 6645 [→ 6004]. close by; alongside; adjoining:– over against (+3807.1) [15], against (+3807.1) [6], against [5], besides (+3807.1) [2], answerable (+3807.1) [1], at (+3807.1) [1], hard by (+3807.1) [1], points [1]

5981 עֻמָּה ***ʿummâ***, n.pr.loc. GK: 6646. Ummah:– Ummah [1]

5982 עַמּוּד ***ʿammûd***, n.m. GK: 6647 [→ 5975]. pillar, post, column; used fig. of the pillar-shaped cloud of God's presence:– pillars [80], pillar [29], apiece[s] (+259) [1], them[s] [1]

5983 עַמּוֹן ***ʿammôn***, n.pr.[loc.]. GK: 6648 [→ 5984; cf. 5971]. Ammonite; Ammon, *"my people [Ge 19:38]"*:– Ammon [90], Ammonites (+1121) [15], Ammonites [1]

5984 עַמּוֹנִי ***ʿammônî***, a.g. GK: 6649 [→ 5983, 5985]. Ammonite, from Ammon, *"of Ammon"*:– Ammonite [9], Ammonites [7], Ammonitess [4], of Ammon [1]

5985 עַמּוֹנִית ***ʿammônît***, a.g. GK: 6649 [→ 5984]. f. of 5984: Ammonite, from Ammon, *"of Ammon"*:–

5986 עָמוֹס ***ʿāmôs***, n.pr.m. GK: 6650 [→ 6006?]. Amos, *"burden bearer"*:– Amos [7]

5987 עָמוֹק ***ʿāmôq***, n.pr.m. GK: 6651 [→ 6009]. Amok, *"capable"*:– Amok [2]

5988 עַמִּיאֵל ***ʿammîʾēl***, n.pr.m. GK: 6653 [→ 5971+410]. Ammiel, *"God [El] is my kinsman"*:– Ammiel [6]

5989 עַמִּיהוּד ***ʿammîhûd***, n.pr.m. GK: 6654 [→ 5971+1935]. Ammihud, *"[my] people have majesty"*:– Ammihud [10]

5990 עַמִּיזָבָד ***ʿammîzābād***, n.pr.m. GK: 6655 [→ 5971+2064]. Ammizabad, *"[my] people have given a gift"*:– Ammizabad [1]

5991 עַמִּיחוּר ***ʿammîḥûr***, n.pr.m. GK: 6656 [→ 5971+2354?]. Ammihur, cf. 5989:–

5992 עַמִּינָדָב ***ʿammînādāb***, n.pr.m. GK: 6657 [→ 5971+5068]. Amminadab, *"[my] people are generous"*:– Amminadab [13]

5993 עַמִּי נָדִיב ***ʿammî Nādîb***, n.pr.m. GK: 6652 + 5618 [→ 5971+5081]. Amminadib, *"[my] people are generous"*:– Ammi-nadib [1]

5994 עַמִּיק ***ʿammîq*** (Aram.), a. GK: 10555 [cf. 6013]. deep; (as noun) the deep things, which are normally impenetrable and so secret and hidden, with the implication that such things are mysterious, profound, and valuable:– deep [1]

5995 עָמִיר ***ʿāmîr***, n.[m.]. GK: 6658 [→ 6014]. (newly) cut grain:– sheaves [2], handful [1], sheaf [1]

5996 עַמִּישַׁדָּי ***ʿammîšaddāy***, n.pr.m. GK: 6659 [→ 5971+7706]. Ammishaddai, *"Shaddai is [my] kinsman"*:– Ammishaddai [5]

5997 עָמִית ***ʿāmît***, n.m. GK: 6660 [→ 6004]. neighbor, countryman, associate (one in close, united relation):– neighbour [7], another[s] [2], neighbour's [2], fellow [1]

5998 עָמַל ***ʿāmal***, v. GK: 6661 [→ 5999, 6000, 6001]. [Q] to labor, toil, pour forth effort:– laboured [5], labour [2], taketh [2], laboureth [1], took [1]

5999 עָמָל ***ʿāmāl***, n.m. & f. GK: 6662 [→ 5998]. trouble, work, labor, toil:– labour [25], mischief [9], misery [3], travail [3], trouble [3], sorrow [2], grievance [1], grievousness [1], iniquity [1], miserable [1], painful [1], pain [1], perverseness [1], toil [1], wearisome [1], wickedness [1]

6000 עָמָל ***ʿāmāl***, n.pr.m. GK: 6663 [→ 5999; cf. 5998]. Amal, *"laborer, troubler"*:– Amal [1]

6001 עָמֵל *ʿāmēl,* n.m. GK: 6664 & 6665 [→ 5998]. misery; workman, laborer:– laboureth [2], in misery [1], laboured [1], labour [1], taken [1], takest [1], wicked [1], workmen's [1]

6002 עֲמָלֵק *ʿamālēq,* n.pr.m. GK: 6667 [→ 6003]. Amalek; Amalekite:– Amalek [24], Amalekites [15]

6003 עֲמָלֵקִי *ʿamālēqî,* a.g. GK: 6668 [→ 6002]. Amalekite, "*of Amalek*":– Amalekites [9], Amalekite [2], Amalekite (+376) [1]

6004 עָמַם *ʿāmam,* v. GK: 6669 & 6670 [→ 5973, 5980, 5997]. [Q] to be rival to, be equal to; to grow dark; [Ho] to lose luster, grow dark:– hide [2], become dim [1]

6005 עִמָּנוּ אֵל *ʿimmānû ʾēl,* n.pr.m. GK: 6672 [→ 5973+5105.1+410]. Immanuel, "*God with us*":– Immanuel [2]

6006 עָמַס *ʿāmas,* v. GK: 6673 [→ 4614, 5986?, 6007]. [Q] to load a burden, carry a burden; [Qp] to be burdensome, be upheld; [H] to lay a burden upon:– laded [2], borne [1], burden [1], heavy loaden [1], lade [1], lading (+5921) [1], loadeth [1], put [1]

6007 עֲמַסְיָה *ʿamasyâ,* n.pr.m. GK: 6674 [→ 6006+3068]. Amasiah, "*Yahweh carries a load*":– Amasiah [1]

6008 עַמְעָד *ʿamʿād,* n.pr.loc. GK: 6675. Amad:– Amad [1]

6009 עָמַק *ʿāmaq,* v. GK: 6676 [→ 1025, 4615, 5987, 6010, 6013, 6011, 6012, 7104]. [Q] to be profound; [H] to make deep (in various senses):– deep [3], deeply [2], depth [1], made deep [1], profound to make [1], seek deep [1]

6010 עֵמֶק *ʿēmeq,* n.m. GK: 6677 [→ 1025; cf. 6009]. valley; (low-lying) plain:– valley [54], valleys [9], vale [4], dale [2]

6011 עֹמֶק *ʿōmeq,* n.[m.]. GK: 6679 [→ 6009]. depth:– depth [1]

6012 עָמֵק *ʿāmēq,* a. GK: 6680 [→ 6009]. obscure, unintelligible, by extension of what is physically deep (not found in the OT):– strange [2], deeper [1], depths [1]

6013 עָמֹק *ʿāmōq,* a. GK: 6678 [→ 6009; cf. 5994]. deep; profound:– deeper [8], deep [7], exceeding deep (+6013) [2]

6014 עָמַר *ʿāmar,* v.den. GK: 6682 & 6683 [→ 5995, 6016, 6017, 6019, 6020, 6192, 6191; cf. 6192]. [P] to bind sheaves (of newly cut grain); [Ht] to treat brutally, deal tyrannically with:– bindeth sheaves [1], make merchandise [1], maketh merchandise [1]

6015 עֲמַר *ʿamar* (Aram.), n.m. GK: 10556 [cf. 6785]. wool:– wool [1]

6016 עֹמֶר *ʿōmer,* n.m. GK: 6684 & 6685 [→ 6014]. sheaf of grain; omer (dry measure, one-tenth of an ephah, about two quarts or liters):– sheaf [6], omer [5], sheaves [2], omers [1]

6017 עֲמֹרָה *ʿamōrâ,* n.pr.loc. GK: 6686 [→ 6014]. Gomorrah, "*to overwhelm with water*":– Gomorrah [19]

6018 עָמְרִי *ʿomrî,* n.pr.m. GK: 6687. Omri, "*thrive, live long*":– Omri [18]

6019 עַמְרָם *ʿamrām,* n.pr.m. GK: 6688 [→ 6020]. Amram, "*exalted people*":– Amram [13], Amram's [1]

6020 עַמְרָמִי *ʿamrāmî,* a.g. GK: 6689 [→ 6019]. Amramite, "*of Amram*":– Amramites [2]

עָמַשׂ *ʿamaś.* See 6006.

6021 עֲמָשָׂא *ʿamāśāʾ,* n.pr.m. GK: 6690 [→ 6022]. Amasa, "*[my] people are from Jesse*":– Amasa [16]

6022 עֲמָשַׂי *ʿamāśay,* n.pr.m. GK: 6691 [→ 6021]. Amasai, "*[my] people are from Jesse*":– Amasai [5]

6023 עֲמַשְׁסַי *ʿamašsay,* n.pr.m. GK: 6692. Amashai:– Amashai [1]

6024 עֲנָב *ʿanāb,* n.pr.loc. GK: 6693 [→ 6025]. Anab, "*grape*":– Anab [2]

6025 עֵנָב *ʿēnāb,* n.m. GK: 6694 [→ 6024]. cluster of grapes:– grapes [17], grape [1], wine [1]

6026 עָנַג *ʿānag,* v. GK: 6695 [→ 6027, 6028, 8588]. [Pu] to be delicate; [Ht] to delight oneself, enjoy, to mock:– delight [5], delicateness [1], delicate [1], delighted [1], have delight [1], sport [1]

6027 עֹנֶג *ʿōneg,* n.[m.]. GK: 6696 [→ 6026]. delight, luxury, enjoyment:– delight [1], pleasant [1]

6028 עָנֹג *ʿānōg,* a. GK: 6697 [→ 6026]. sensitive, delicate:– delicate [3]

6029 עָנַד *ʿānad,* v. GK: 6698 [cf. 4575]. [Q] to bind around, bind upon:– bind [1], tie [1]

6030 עָנָה *ʿānâ,* v. GK: 6699 & 6702 & 4361 [→ 3285?, 4617, 6031?, 6043; cf. 6032]. [Q] to answer, reply, respond; to sing; [N] to be answered; usually verbal, the response can involve action; [P] to sing to or sing about; (inf.) leannoth (t.t. in Ps 88):– answered [175], answer [54], hear [29], heard [11], testify [8], answereth [5], sing [5], speak [5], spake [3], testified [3], answeredst [2], answerest [2], bear [2], cry [2], gave answer [2], witness [2], beareth witness [1], beareth [1], brought low [1], give a shout (+1959) [1], give an answer [1], given answer [1], giveth account [1], giveth answer [1], heardest [1], hearest [1], lift up [1], make answer [1], said [1], sang [1], scholar [1], shout [1], sung [1], testifieth [1], utter [1]

6031 עָנָה *ʿānâ,* v. GK: 6700 & 6701 [→ 3282, 4616, 4617, 4618, 5772? 6030?, 6035, 6037, 6038, 6039, 6040, 6041, 6045, 6256, 6258, 6261, 6262, 8589]. [Q] to be afflicted; to stoop down; to be concerned about, be worried about; [N] to be afflicted, humbled, oppressed; [P] to afflict, oppress, subdue, humble, mistreat; [Pu] to be afflicted, deny oneself; [H] to afflict another, oppress; to keep occupied, keep oneself busy; [Ht] to humble oneself; humbling by force implies dishonor:– afflict [28], afflicted [21], humbled [7], forced [4], humble [4], afflict in any wise (+6031) [2], exercised [2], Leannoth [1], abase [1], afflictest [1], afflictions [1], answereth [1], chasten [1], dealt hardly with [1], defiled [1], force [1], gentleness [1], hurt [1], ravished [1], sing [1], submit [1], troubled [1], weakened [1]

6032 עֲנָה *ʿanâ* (Aram.), v. GK: 10558 [cf. 6030]. [P] to answer, reply; usually a reaction to a direct question, but can be a more general response:– answered [16], spake [14]

6033 עֲנֵה *ʿanēh* (Aram.), a. GK: 10559 [cf. 6041, 6035]. oppressed, needy, poor, implying that such persons are miserable in their life situation:– poor [1]

6034 עֲנָה *ʿanâ,* n.pr.m. GK: 6704 [→ 6067]. Anah:– Anah [12]

6035 עָנָו *ʿānāw* or עָנָיו *ʿānāyw,* n.m. GK: 6705 & 6718 [cf. 6031; cf. 6033]. humble, afflicted, poor, oppressed:– meek [13], humble [5], lowly [2], poor [1]

6036 עָנוּב *ʿānûb,* n.pr.m. GK: 6707. Anub, "*fruitful*":– Anub [1]

6037 עַנְוָה *ʿanwâ,* n.f. GK: 6709 [→ 6031]. humility:– gentleness [1], meekness [1]

6038 עֲנָוָה *ʿanāwâ,* n.f. GK: 6708 [→ 6031]. humility:– humility [3], meekness [1]

6039 עֱנוּת *ʿenût,* n.f. GK: 6713 [→ 6031]. suffering, affliction:– affliction [1]

6040 עֳנִי *ʿonî,* n.m. GK: 6715 [→ 6031]. affliction, suffering, misery:– affliction [32], trouble [3], afflicted (+1121) [1]

6041 עָנִי *ʿānî,* a. GK: 6714 [→ 6031; cf. 6033]. needy, poor, afflicted, oppressed, often referring to a class of persons of low status and lacking resources:– poor [59], afflicted [15], lowly [1]

6042 עֻנִּי *ʿunnî,* n.pr.m. GK: 6716. Unni, "*Yahweh has answered*":– Unni [3]

6043 עֲנָיָה *ʿanāyâ,* n.pr.m. GK: 6717 [→ 6030+3068]. Anaiah, "*Yahweh responds*":– Anaiah [2]

עָנִיו *ʿānāyw* See 6035.

6044 עָנִים *ʿānîm,* n.pr.loc. GK: 6719. Anim, "*springs*":– Anim [1]

6045 עִנְיָן *ʿinyān,* n.m. GK: 6721 [→ 6031]. task, work, labor; misfortune, cares, troubles:– travail [6], business [2]

6046 עָנֵם *ʿānēm,* n.pr.loc. GK: 6722. Anem, "*springs*":– Anem [1]

6047 עֲנָמִים *ʿanāmîm,* n.pr.g. GK: 6723. Anamite:– Anamim [2]

6048 עֲנַמֶּלֶךְ *ʿanammelek,* n.pr.[m.]. GK: 6724 [→ 6067+4428]. Anammelech (pagan god), "*Anath is king*":– Anammelech [1]

6049 עָנַן *ʿānan,* v.den. GK: 6725 & 6726 [→ 6031, 6051, 6052, 6053, 6054, 6055]. [P] to bring clouds; [Po] to practice sorcery, practice divination, cast spells:– observed times [2], soothsayers [2], Meonenim [1], bring a cloud (+6051) [1], enchanters [1], observe times [1], observer of times [1], observers of times [1], sorceress [1]

6050 עֲנָן *ʿanān* (Aram.), n.[m.]. GK: 10560 [cf. 6051]. cloud:– clouds [1]

6051 עָנָן *ʿānān,* n.m. GK: 6727 [→ 6053; cf. 6049; cf. 6050]. cloud, of moisture or smoke, natural or supernatural:– cloud [74], clouds [6], cloudy [6], bring a cloud (+6049) [1]

6052 עָנָן *ʿānān,* n.pr.m. GK: 6728 [→ 6051; cf. 6049]. Anan, "*cloud*":– Anan [1]

6053 עֲנָנָה *ʿanānâ,* n.f. GK: 6729 [→ 6051; cf. 6049]. cloud, likely referring to a dense rain cloud:– cloud [1]

6054 עֲנָנִי *ʿanānî,* n.pr.m. GK: 6730 [→ 6049+3068]. Anani, "*Yahweh is a covering*":– Anani [1]

6055 עֲנַנְיָה *ʿananyâ,* n.pr.m. & loc. GK: 6731 & 6732 [→ 6049+3068]. Ananiah, "*Yahweh is a covering*":– Ananiah [2]

6056 עֲנַף *ʿanap* (Aram.), n.[m.]. GK: 10561 [cf. 6057]. branch, bough:– branches [3], boughs [1]

6057 עָנָף *ʿānāp,* n.[m.]. GK: 6733 [→ 6058; cf. 6056]. branches:– boughs [3], branches [3], branch [1]

6058 עָנֵף **ʿānēp**, a. GK: 6734 [→ 6057]. full of branches:– full of branches [1]

6059 עָנַק **ʿānaq**, v.den. GK: 6735 [→ 6060]. [Q] to put on (as a necklace); [H] to supply, a fig. extension of putting an adornment around the neck:– furnish liberally (+6059) [2], compasseth about as a chain [1]

6060 עֲנָק **ᵃnāq**, n.m. GK: 6736 [→ 6059]. necklace chain:– chains [2], chain [1]

6061 עֲנוֹק **ᵃnôq**, n.pr.[m. *or* loc.]. GK: 6710 [→ 6062]. Anak, *"neck"*:– Anak [9]

6062 עֲנָק **ᵃnāq**, n.[m.] & g. GK: 6737 [→ 6061]. Anak, *"neck"*, Anakites:– Anakims [9]

6063 עָנֵר **ʿānēr**, n.pr.m. & loc. GK: 6738 & 6739. Aner:– Aner [3]

6064 עָנַשׁ **ʿānaš**, v.den. GK: 6740 & 6711 [→ 6066; cf. 6065]. [Q] to levy a fine (as a punishment or recompense); [N] to be fined, be punished:– punished [3], condemned [2], surely punished (+6064) [2], amerce [1], punish [1]

6065 עֲנָשׁ **ᵃnāš** (Aram.), n.[m.]. GK: 10562 [cf. 6066]. confiscation; some sources translate as "fine," a monetary penalty without the necessary confiscation of property:– confiscation [1]

6066 עֹנֶשׁ **ʿōneš**, n.[m.]. GK: 6741 [→ 6064]. levy, penalty, fine:– punishment [1], tribute [1]

עֶנֶת **ʿenet** See 3706.

6067 עֲנָת **ᵃnāt**, n.pr.m. GK: 6742 [→ 1042, 1043, 6034, 6048, 6068, 6069]. Anath, *"Semitic goddess"*:– Anath [2]

6068 עֲנָתוֹת **ᵃnātôt**, n.pr.f. & loc. GK: 6743 & 6744 [→ 6067]. Anathoth, *"plural of Anath"*:– Anathoth [15]

6069 עַנְּתֹתִי **ʿannᵉtōtî**, a.g. GK: 6745 [→ 6067]. Anathothite, from Anathoth, *"of Anathoth"*:– Antothite [2], Anathoth [1], Anethothite [1], Anetothite [1]

6070 עַנְתֹתִיָּה **ʿantōtiyyâ**, n.pr.m. GK: 6746. Anthothijah:– Antothijah [1]

6071 עָסִיס **ʿāsîs**, n.m. GK: 6747 [→ 6072]. new wine (relatively sweet); nectar:– new wine [2], sweet wine [2], juice [1]

6072 עָסַס **ʿāsas**, v. GK: 6748 [→ 6071]. [Q] to trample down:– tread down [1]

6073 עֳפִי **ºpî**, n.[m.]. GK: 6751 [cf. 6074]. branch:– branches [1]

6074 עֳפִי **ºpî** (Aram.), n.m. GK: 10564 [cf. 6073]. leaves, foliage:– leaves [3]

6075 עָפַל **ʿāpal**, v. GK: 6752 & 6753 [→ 6076, 6077]. [Pu] to be puffed up, be swelled; [H] to have presumption, to have the audacity to:– lifted up [1], presumed [1]

6076 עֹפֶל **ʿōpel**, n.m. GK: 6754 [→ 6075]. tumor, hemorrhoid, abscess:– emerods [1], forts [1], tower [1]

6077 עֹפֶל **ʿōpel**, n.[m.]. GK: 6755 [→ 6076]. hill; (as a proper name) the hill of Ophel:– Ophel [5], strong hold [1]

6078 עָפְנִי **ʿopnî**, n.pr.loc. GK: 6756. Ophni:– Ophni [1]

6079 עַפְעַפַּיִם **ʿapʿappayim**, n.m. GK: 6757 [→ 4155]. flashing rays (of dawn); glances or flitting of eyes or eyelids:– eyelids [9], dawning [1]

6080 עָפַר **ʿāpar**, v.den. GK: 6759 [→ 6083]. [P] to shower (with dust or dirt):– cast [1]

6081 עֵפֶר **ʿēper**, n.pr.m. GK: 6761 [→ 6085]. Epher, *"[small] gazelle"*:– Epher [4]

6082 עֹפֶר **ʿōper**, n.m. GK: 6762 [→ 6084; cf. 6083]. fawn (of a deer or gazelle):– young [5]

6083 עָפָר **ʿāpār**, n.m. GK: 6760 [→ 6080; cf. 6082]. dust, earth, soil in any form; used as a figure of something that cannot be counted:– dust [92], earth [8], powder [3], ashes [2], morter [2], rubbish [2], ground [1]

עָפְרָה **ʿaprâ**. See 1036.

6084 עָפְרָה **ʿoprâ**, n.pr.m. & loc. GK: 6763 & 6764 [cf. 6082]. Ophrah, *"young gazelle"*:– Ophrah [8]

6085 עֶפְרוֹן **ʿeprôn**, n.pr.m. & loc. GK: 6766 & 6767 [cf. 6081]. Ephron, *"gazelle"*:– Ephron [13], Ephrain [1]

עֹפֶרֶת **ʿōperet**. See 5777.

6086 עֵץ **ʿēṣ**, n.m. GK: 6770 [→ 6097; cf. 636]. tree; by extension, the product of the tree: wood, any wooden object:– wood [107], tree [84], trees [78], timber [23], stick [9], gallows [8], sticks [5], staff [4], carpenters (+2796) [3], stocks [2], stock [2], branches [1], carpenter (+2796) [1], helve [1], planks [1], stalks [1]

6087 עָצַב **ʿāṣab**, v. GK: 6771 & 6772 [→ 4620, 6089, 6090, 6091, 6092, 6093, 6094; cf. 6088]. [Q] to interfere with; [Qp] to be distressed; [N] to be grieved, be distressed; [P] to grieve; to shape; [H] to grieve; to make an image (of the Queen of Heaven); [Ht] to be filled with grief, be filled with pain:– grieved [8], grieve [2], displeased [1], hurt [1], made [1], sorry [1], vexed [1], worship [1], wrest [1]

6088 עֲצִיב **ᵃṣîb** (Aram.), v. GK: 10565. anguished, sorrowful:– lamentable [1]

6089 עֶצֶב **ʿeṣeb**, n.m. GK: 6775 & 6776 [→ 6087]. pot, vessel; pain, toil, hard work:– sorrow [2], grievous [1], idol [1], labours [1], labour [1], sorrows [1]

6090 עֹצֶב **ʿōṣeb**, n.m. GK: 6777 & 6778 [→ 6087]. idol; pain, toil:– sorrow [2], idol [1], wicked [1]

6091 עָצָב **ʿāṣāb**, n.[m.]. GK: 6773 [→ 6087]. idol, image, a crafted object believed to represent or even possess a spirit or god:– idols [16], images [1]

6092 עַצָּב **ʿaṣṣāb**, n.[m.]. GK: 6774 [→ 6087]. (hard) worker, toiler:– labours [1]

6093 עִצָּבוֹן **ʿiṣṣābôn**, n.[m.]. GK: 6779 [→ 6087]. pain, hardship, distress:– sorrow [2], toil [1]

6094 עַצֶּבֶת **ʿaṣṣebet**, n.f. GK: 6780 [→ 6087]. pain, sorrow, grief:– sorrows [2], sorrow [2], wounds [1]

6095 עָצָה **ʿāṣâ**, v. GK: 6781. [Q] to wink (the eye), as a non-verbal communication of what is evil, malicious, or lurid:– shutteth [1]

6096 עָצֶה **ʿāṣeh**, n.[m.]. GK: 6782. backbone, tailbone:– back bone [1]

6097 עֵצָה **ʿēṣâ**, n.f.col. GK: 6785 [→ 6086]. (coll.) wood; this can refer to wooden idols:– trees [1]

6098 עֵצָה **ʿēṣâ**, n.f. GK: 6783 [→ 3289; cf. 5843]. advice, counsel, plan, purpose, scheme:– counsel [72], counsel gave (+3289) [2], counsel given (+3289) [2], counsels [2], give counsel (+3289) [2], purpose [2], advice [1], advisement [1], counseller (+376) [1], counsellers (+376) [1], take counsel together (+5779) [1], taken counsel (+3289) [1]

6099 עָצוּם **ʿāṣûm**, a. GK: 6786 [→ 6110; cf. 6105]. strong, mighty, powerful:– strong [13], mighty [8], mightier [7], feeble (+3808) [1], great [1], much [1]

6100 עֶצְיוֹן גֶּבֶר **ʿeṣyôn geber**, n.pr.loc. GK: 6787. Ezion Geber, *"giant, the giant backbone"*:– Ezion-geber [4], Ezion-gaber [3]

6101 עָצַל **ʿāṣal**, v. GK: 6788 [→ 6102, 6103, 6104]. [N] to hesitate, be sluggish, be slow:– slothful [1]

6102 עָצֵל **ʿāṣēl**, a. GK: 6789 [→ 6101]. sluggish, slow, lazy; (n.) sluggard, one with no discipline or motivation, a moral failure:– slothful [7], sluggard [6], slothful (+376) [1]

6103 עַצְלָה **ʿaṣlâ**, n.f. GK: 6790 & 6792 [→ 6101]. laziness, slowness, sluggishness:– much slothfulness [1], slothfulness [1]

6104 עַצְלוּת **ʿaṣlût**, n.f. GK: 6791 [→ 6101]. idleness, sluggishness, laziness:– idleness [1]

6105 עָצַם **ʿāṣam**, v. GK: 6793 & 6794 [→ 6099, 6106, 6107, 6108, 6108, 6109, 6111, 8592]. [Q] to close (the eyes); to be vast, powerful, numerous; [P] to tightly shut (the eyes); to crush bones; [H] to make numerous, make powerful, make vast:– increased [4], strong [4], mighty [2], moe [2], waxed mighty [2], broken bones [1], closed [1], great [1], made stronger [1], mightier [1], shutteth [1]

6106 עֶצֶם **ʿeṣem**, n.f. GK: 6795 [→ 6107; cf. 6105]. bone; by extension: the whole body, any part of the body, limb; strength of the body, vigor; (adv.) that very (day); "one's bone and flesh" is a close relative:– bones [89], bone [15], selfsame [11], same [5], body [2], very [2], life [1], strength [1]

6107 עֶצֶם **ʿeṣem**, n.pr.loc. GK: 6796 [→ 6106; cf. 6105]. Ezem, *"bone [strength]"*:– Azem [2], Ezem [1]

6108 עֹצֶם **ʿōṣem**, n.[m.]. GK: 6797 & 6798 [→ 6105]. might, strength; framework (of bones of the human body):– might [1], strong [1], substance [1]

עָצֻם **ʿāṣum**. See 6099.

6109 עָצְמָה **ʿoṣmâ**, n.f. GK: 6800 [→ 6105]. power, potency, might:– strength [2], abundance [1]

6110 עֲצֻמוֹת **ᵃṣumôt**, n.f.[pl.]. GK: 6802 [→ 6099]. defensive arguments, strong words:– strong [1]

6111 עַצְמוֹן **ʿaṣmôn**, n.pr.loc. GK: 6801 [→ 6106; cf. 6105]. Azmon, *"strongly [built body]"*:– Azmon [3]

6112 עֶצְנִי **ʿeṣnî**, n.pr. *or* a.g.?. GK: 6804. Eznite:– Eznite [1]

6113 עָצַר **ʿāṣar**, v. GK: 6806 [→ 4622, 4623, 6114, 6115, 6116]. [Q] to refrain, hold back, restrain; [Qp] to be enslaved, be constrained; [N] to be stopped, be detained:– shut up [15], stayed [7], detain [2], fast closed up (+6113) [2], retained [2], able (+3581) [1], able [1], be [1], detained [1], keep still [1], kept close [1], kept [1], prevail [1], recover [1], refrained [1], reign [1], restrained [1], retain [1], shut [1], slack [1], stop [1], withholdeth [1], withhold [1]

6114 עֶצֶר **ʿeṣer**, n.[m.]. GK: 6807 [→ 6113]. restraint, oppression:– magistrate (+3423) [1]

6115 עֹצֶר **ʿōṣer**, n.[m.]. GK: 6808 [→ 6113]. oppression; barrenness:– barren [1], oppression [1], prison [1]

6116 עֲצָרָה **ᵃṣārâ**, n.f. GK: 6809 [→ 6113]. assembly, usually on a festive day:– solemn assembly [8], assembly [1], solemn assemblies [1], solemn meeting [1]

6117 עָקַב *ʿāqab*, v. GK: 6810 [→ 6120; cf. 6119, 6120, 6906]. [Q] to deceive; to grasp at the heel; [P] to hold the heel, to hold back:– utterly supplant (+6117) [2], stay [1], supplanted [1], took by the heel [1]

6118 עֵקֶב *ʿēqeb*, n.[m.] (used as adv. & c.). GK: 6813 [→ 6119]. (c.) because; (n.) a reward; unto the end:– because [3], reward [3], because (+3588) [2], because (+834) [2], end [2], by [1], for [1], if [1]

6119 עָקֵב *ʿāqēb*, n.m. GK: 6811 [→ 6118, 6121; cf. 3290, 6117, 6120]. heel, hoof; footstep, footprint; by extension: rear guard of a military formation; a euphemism for private parts:– heel [4], footsteps [3], heels [2], horsehoofs (+5483) [1], last [1], liers in wait [1], steps [1]

6120 עָקֵב *ʿāqēb*, a.vbl. GK: 6812 [→ 6117, 6121, 6122; cf. 3290, 6117, 6119, 6906]. deceiver:– heels [1]

6121 עָקֹב *ʿāqōb*, a. [& n.] GK: 6814 & 6815 [→ 6119, 6120]. deceitful; rough, bumpy; footprint:– crooked [1], deceitful [1], polluted [1]

6122 עָקְבָה *ʿoqbâ*, n.f. GK: 6817 [→ 6120]. deceptiveness, cunning, craftiness:– subtilty [1]

6123 עָקַד *ʿāqad*, v. GK: 6818 [→ 6124]. [Q] to bind (feet):– bound [1]

עֵקֶד *ʿēqed*. See 1044.

6124 עָקֹד *ʿāqōd*, a. GK: 6819 [→ 6123]. streaked, striped:– ringstraked [7]

6125 עָקָה *ʿāqâ*, n.f. GK: 6821 [→ 5781]. pressure; oppressive look, stare, or actions:– oppression [1]

6126 עַקּוּב *ʿaqqûb*, n.pr.m. GK: 6822. Akkub, "*guard*":– Akkub [8]

6127 עָקַל *ʿāqal*, v. GK: 6823 [→ 6128, 6129]. [Pu] to be perverted, be distorted, be crooked:– wrong [1]

6128 עֲקַלְקַל *^{a}qalqāl*, a.intens. GK: 6824 [→ 6127]. crooked, winding:– byways (+734) [1], crooked ways [1]

6129 עֲקַלָּתוֹן *^{a}qallātôn*, a. GK: 6825 [→ 6127]. coiling (serpent):– crooked [1]

6130 עֲקָן *^{a}qān*, n.pr.m. GK: 6826 [→ 3292?]. Akan:– Akan [1]

6131 עָקַר *ʿāqar*, v.den. GK: 6827 & 6828 [→ 6135, 6133, 6134; cf. 6132, cf. 6136]. [Q] to root up; [N] to be uprooted; [P] to hamstring (to cut the tendon and render helpless or useless):– houghed [3], digged down [1], hough [1], pluck up [1], rooted up [1]

6132 עֲקַר *^{a}qar* (Aram.), v.den. GK: 10566 [→ 6136; cf. 6131]. [Itpe] to be uprooted, plucked out:– pluckt up by roots [1]

6133 עֵקֶר *ʿēqer*, n.m. GK: 6830 [→ 6131]. offspring, as the fig. extension of a plant that grows up from a root:– stock [1]

6134 עֵקֶר *ʿēqer*, n.pr.m. GK: 6831 [→ 6131?]. Eker, "[poss.] *offspring*":– Eker [1]

6135 עָקָר *ʿāqār*, a. GK: 6829 [→ 6131]. barren, sterile, without children:– barren [10], female barren [1], male^{s} [1]

6136 עִקַּר *ʿiqqar* (Aram.), n.[m.]. GK: 10567 [→ 6132]. stump, root:– stump [3]

6137 עַקְרָב *ʿaqrāb*, n.m. GK: 6832 [→ 7128]. scorpion:– scorpions [6], Akrabbim [2]

6138 עֶקְרוֹן *ʿeqrôn*, n.pr.loc. GK: 6833 [→ 6139]. Ekron, "[*perhaps*] *barren place* or *fertile place*":– Ekron [22]

6139 עֶקְרוֹנִי *ʿeqrônî*, a.g. GK: 6834 [→ 6138]. Ekronite, of Ekron, "*of Ekron*":– Ekronites [2]

6140 עָקַשׁ *ʿāqaš*, v. GK: 6835 [→ 4625, 6141, 6142, 6143]. [N] to be perverse, be crooked; [P] to take crooked paths; to distort; [H] to pronounce guilty:– made crooked [1], perverse [1], perverteth [1], pervert [1], prove perverse [1]

6141 עִקֵּשׁ *ʿiqqēš*, a. GK: 6836 [→ 6142; cf. 6140]. perverse, crooked, warped:– froward [6], perverse [4], crooked [1]

6142 עִקֵּשׁ *ʿiqqēš*, n.pr.m. GK: 6837 [→ 6141; cf. 6140]. Ikkesh, "*crooked, perverted*":– Ikkesh [3]

6143 עִקְּשׁוּת *ʿiqq^{e}šût*, n.f. GK: 6838 [→ 6140]. perversion, corruption, crookedness:– froward [2]

עָר *ʿār*. See 5892.

6144 עָר *ʿār*, n.pr.loc. GK: 6840 [→ 5892?]. Ar, "[poss.] *city*":– Ar [6]

6145 עָר *ʿār*, n.m. GK: 6839 [→ 6209?]. enemy, adversary:– enemies [1], enemy [1]

6146 עָר *ʿār* (Aram.), n.m. GK: 10568 [cf. 6862]. adversary, foe:– enemies [1]

6147 עֵר *ʿēr*, n.pr.m. GK: 6841 [→ 5782; cf. 5894]. Er, "*watchful, watcher*":– Er [10]

6148 עָרַב *ʿārab*, v. GK: 6842 & 6843 [→ 4627, 6154, 6157, 6161, 6162, 8594; cf. 6150; cf. 6151]. [Q] to put up a security, make a guarantee, give a pledge; [Ht] to make a bargain, make a wager; to mingle, join in with, share with:– surety [4], give pledges [2], meddle [2], mingled [2], surety for [2], became surety [1], becometh surety (+6161) [1], engaged [1], intermeddle [1], mortgaged [1], occupiers [1], occupy [1], put in a surety [1], sureties [1], undertake [1]

6149 עָרַב *ʿārab*, v. GK: 6844 [→ 6156]. [Q] to be pleasing, be pleasant, be acceptable:– sweet [5], pleasant [1], pleasing [1], taken pleasure [1]

6150 עָרַב *ʿārab*, v.den. GK: 6845 [→ 4628, 6153; cf. 6148]. [Q] to become evening; (opposite of joy) turn to gloom; [H] to do something in the evening:– evening [2], darkened [1]

6151 עֲרַב *^{a}rab* (Aram.), v. GK: 10569 [cf. 6148]. [Pap] to be mixed; [Htpa] (ptcp.) mixture:– mixed [2], mingle [1], mixt [1]

6152 עֲרַב *^{a}rab*, n.pr.loc. & g. GK: 6851 [→ 6160]. Arabia, Arab:– Arabia [5]

6153 עֶרֶב *ʿereb*, n.[m.]. GK: 6847 [→ 6150]. evening, twilight, dusk, the fading of the day; twilight can extend into the dark of the night:– even [67], evening [47], at even (+996+1886.1) [6], every evening (+6153+871.1+871.1+1886.1+1886.1) [4], night [4], mingled people [3], eveningtide (+6256) [2], Arabia [1], days (+1242) [1], eventide (+6256+1886.1) [1], eventide (+6437) [1], eventide [1], people [1]

6154 עֵרֶב *ʿēreb*, n.[m.]. GK: 6849 & 6850 [→ 6148]. foreign people; knitted or woven material:– woof [9], mixed multitude [1], mixed [1]

6155 עֲרָבָה *^{a}rābâ*, n.[f.]. GK: 6857 [→ 6164]. poplar tree:– willows [5]

6156 עָרֵב *ʿārēb*, a. GK: 6853 [→ 6149]. pleasant, sweet (voice):– sweet [2]

6157 עָרֹב *ʿārōb*, n.m. GK: 6856 [→ 6148]. swarms of flies:– swarms [5], divers sorts [2], swarm [2]

6158 עֹרֵב *ʿōrēb*, n.m. GK: 6854 [→ 6159]. raven:– raven [6], ravens [4]

6159 עֹרֵב *ʿōrēb*, n.pr.m. GK: 6855 [→ 6158]. Oreb, "*raven*":– Oreb [7]

6160 עֲרָבָה *^{a}rābâ*, n.f. GK: 6858 [→ 6152, 6163]. plains (a geographical region of desert, wilderness or wasteland); (pr.n.) Arabah:– plain [22], plains [20], desert [8], wilderness [5], Arabah [2], champaign [1], deserts [1], evenings [1], heavens [1]

6161 עֲרֻבָּה *^{a}rubbâ*, n.f. GK: 6859 [→ 6148]. security, pledge; assurance:– becometh surety (+6148) [1], pledge [1]

6162 עֵרָבוֹן *ʿērābôn*, n.[m.]. GK: 6860 [→ 6148]. pledge, security:– pledge [3]

6163 עַרְבִי *ʿarbî* or עֲרָבִי *^{a}rābî*, a.g. GK: 6861 & 6862 [→ 6160]. Arab, of Arabia; may also refer to bedouin in general:– Arabians [5], Arabian [4]

6164 עַרְבָתִי *ʿarbātî*, a.g. GK: 6863 [→ 6155]. Arbathite, "*of Arabah*":– Arbathite [2]

6165 עָרַג *ʿārag*, v. GK: 6864 [→ 6170?]. [Q] to pant for, long for (as a thirsty animal):– panteth [2], cry [1]

6166 עֲרָד *^{a}rād*, n.pr.m. & loc. GK: 6865 & 6866 [→ 6171]. Arad, "*wild donkey*":– Arad [5]

6167 עֲרָד *^{a}rād* (Aram.), n.m. GK: 10570 [cf. 6171]. wild donkey:– wild asses [1]

6168 עָרָה *ʿārâ*, v. GK: 6867 [→ 4177, 4632, 4636, 5903, 6172, 6174, 6181, 6196, 8593; cf. 6209, 5783]. [N] to be poured; [P] to lay bare, empty, expose, strip; [H] to make exposed; to cause to pour out; to dishonor; [Ht] to show oneself naked:– emptied [2], rase [2], discovered [1], discovering [1], discover [1], leave destitute [1], make naked [1], poured out [1], poured [1], spreading [1], uncovered [1], uncovereth [1], uncover [1]

6169 עָרָה *ʿārâ*, n.f. GK: 6868. plants, bulrushes:– paper reeds [1]

6170 עֲרוּגָה *^{a}rûgâ*, n.f. GK: 6870 [→ 6165?]. garden bed, garden plot:– furrows [2], beds [1], bed [1]

6171 עָרוֹד *ʿārôd*, n.[m.]. GK: 6871 [→ 5897, 6166; cf. 6167]. wild donkey:– wild ass [1]

6172 עֶרְוָה *ʿerwâ*, n.f. GK: 6872 [→ 6168; cf. 6173]. nakedness (indecent or shameful in certain situations); "to expose the nakedness" is to have sexual relations:– nakedness [50], nakedness (+1320) [1], shame [1], uncleanness [1], unclean [1]

6173 עַרְוָה *ʿarwâ* (Aram.), n.f. GK: 10571 [cf. 6172]. nakedness; fig., dishonor, lowering of one's status in a community resulting in disgrace or shame:– dishonour [1]

6174 עָרוֹם *ʿārôm*, a. GK: 6873 [→ 6174]. naked, stripped:– naked [16]

6175 עָרוּם *ʿārûm*, a. GK: 6874 [→ 6191]. wise and understanding; with a positive connotation: prudent, clever; with a negative connotation: crafty:– prudent [8], crafty [2], subtil [1]

6176 עֲרוֹעֵר *^{a}rôʿēr*, n.[m.]. GK: 6875 [→ 6177; cf. 6209]. (juniper) bush:– heath [1]

6177 עֲרוֹעֵר *^{a}rôʿēr* or עַרְעוֹר *ʿarʿôr*, n.pr.loc. GK: 6876 & 6898 [→ 6200; cf. 6176, 6209]. Aroer, "*juniper*":– Aroer [16]

6178 עָרוּץ **'ārûṣ**, a. GK: 6877 [→ 6206]. dry or dreadful:– clifts [1]

6179 עֵרִי **'ērî**, n.pr.m. GK: 6878 [→ 6180; cf. 5782]. Eri, "*watcher*":– Eri [2]

6180 עֵרִי **'ērî**, a.g. GK: 6879 [→ 6179; cf. 5782]. Erite, "*of Eri*":– Erites [1]

6181 עֶרְיָה **'eryâ**, n.f. GK: 6880 [→ 6168]. bareness, nakedness, the state of being uncovered:– bare [4], made quite naked (+5783) [1], naked [1]

6182 עֲרִיסָה **ᵃrîsâ**, n.f. GK: 6881. ground meal (dough in the first phase of bread making):– dough [4]

6183 עֲרִיפִים **ᵃrîpîm**, n.[m.pl.]. GK: 6882 [→ 6201]. cloud:– heavens [1]

6184 עָרִיץ **'ārîṣ**, a. GK: 6883 [→ 6206]. ruthless, cruel, fierce:– terrible [8], terrible ones [3], oppressors [2], great power [1], mighty [1], oppressor [1], strong [1], terrible one to nought [1], terrible one [1], violent [1]

6185 עֲרִירִי **ᵃrîrî**, a. GK: 6884 [→ 6209]. childless, very undesireable and even shameful in the ancient Near East:– childless [4]

6186 עָרַךְ **'ārak**, v.[den.]. GK: 6885 [→ 6187, 4633, 4630, 4634, 4635]. [Q] to arrange in rows; put in order, take up (battle) positions; [Qp] to be arranged, be put in order, be put in formation; [H] to set a value:– put in array [14], set in array [12], order [6], set in order [5], lay in order [4], expert [3], value [3], equal [2], estimate [2], laid in order [2], ordained [2], ordered [2], prepared [2], prepare [2], compared [1], compare [1], directed [1], direct [1], esteem [1], furnished [1], furnish [1], handle [1], joined [1], preparest [1], put in order [1], reckoned up in order [1], set in order (+6187) [1], taxed [1]

6187 עֵרֶךְ **'ērek**, n.m. GK: 6886 [→ 6186]. proper estimated value:– estimation [23], equal (+3509.1) [1], estimations [1], price [1], proportion [1], set at [1], set in order (+6186) [1], set in order [1], suit [1], taxation [1], valuest [1]

6188 עָרֵל **'āral**, v.den. GK: 6887 [→ 6190]. [Q] to regard as forbidden, leave unharvested:– count as uncircumcised (+6190) [1], foreskin uncovered [1]

6189 עָרֵל **'ārēl**, a. GK: 6888 [→ 6190]. uncircumcised (i.e., having a foreskin of the penis):– uncircumcised [34], uncircumcised person [1]

6190 עָרְלָה **'orlâ**, n.f. GK: 6889 [→ 1394, 6188, 6189]. foreskin (of the penis):– foreskin [8], foreskins [5], uncircumcised [2], count as uncircumcised (+6188) [1]

6191 עָרַם **'āram**, v. GK: 6891 [→ 6175, 6193, 6195]. [Q] to be crafty, show prudence; [H] to initiate cunning plans:– dealeth very subtilly (+6191) [2], beware [1], prudent [1], taken crafty [1]

6192 עָרַם **'āram**, v. GK: 6890 [→ 6194; cf. 6014]. [N] to be piled up, be dammed up:– gathered together [1]

6193 עֹרֶם **'ōrem**, n.[m.]. GK: 6892 [→ 6191]. craftiness:– craftiness [1]

עֵרֹם **'ērōm**. See 5903.

עָרֹם **'ārōm**. See 6174.

6194 עֲרֵמָה **ᵃrēmâ**, n.f. GK: 6894 [→ 6192]. heap, mound (of grain):– heaps [5], heap [3], by heaps (+6194) [2], sheaves [1]

6195 עָרְמָה **'ormâ**, n.f. GK: 6893 [→ 6191]. prudence, cunning:– guile [1], prudence [1], subtilty [1], wilily (+871.1) [1], wisdom [1]

עֲרֵמָה **'arēmâ**. See 6194.

6196 עַרְמוֹן **'ermôn**, n.[m.]. GK: 6895 [→ 6168]. plane tree:– chesnut trees [1], chesnut tree [1]

6197 עֵרָן **'ērān**, n.pr.m. GK: 6896 [→ 6198]. Eran, "*watcher, watchful*":– Eran [1]

6198 עֵרָנִי **'ērānî**, a.g. GK: 6897 [→ 6197]. Eranite, "*of Eran*":– Eranites [1]

עַרְעוֹר **'ar'ôr**. See 6177.

6199 עַרְעָר **'ar'ār**, a. GK: 6899 [cf. 6209]. destitute, naked, stripped; (juniper) bush:– destitute [1], heath [1]

עֲרֹעֵר **ᵃrō'ēr**. See 6177.

6200 עֲרֹעֵרִי **ᵃrō'ērî**, a.g. GK: 6901 [→ 6177; cf. 6209]. Aroerite, "*of Aroer*":– Aroerite [1]

6201 עָרַף **'ārap**, v. GK: 6903 [→ 6183, 6205?; cf. 7491]. [Q] to trickle, drip:– drop down [1], drop [1]

6202 עָרַף **'ārap**, v.den. GK: 6904. [Q] to break; [Qp] be broken:– break neck [2], beheaded [1], break down [1], cut off neck [1], strike off neck [1]

6203 עֹרֶף **'ōrep**, n.m. GK: 6902 [→ 6204]. neck; to be "stiff of neck" is to be obstinate, stubborn, implying rebellion:– neck [11], necks [6], stiffnecked (+7186) [6], back [4], backs [3], stiffnecked (+7185) [1], stiffnecked [1], turn backs [1]

6204 עָרְפָּה **'orpâ**, n.pr.f. GK: 6905 [→ 6203]. Orpah, "*neck, the girl with the full mane[?]*":– Orpah [2]

6205 עֲרָפֶל **ᵃrāpel**, n.m. GK: 6906 [→ 6201?]. dark or thick clouds; deep gloom:– thick darkness [8], darkness [3], dark [2], gross darkness [2]

6206 עָרַץ **'āraṣ**, v. GK: 6907 [→ 4637, 6178, 6184]. [Q] to shake, to shake in terror; [N] to be feared; [H] to dread, stand in awe:– afraid [3], dread [2], fear [2], shake terribly [2], affrighted [1], break [1], feared [1], oppress [1], prevail [1], terrified [1]

6207 עָרַק **'āraq**, v. GK: 6908. [Q] to gnaw:– flying [1], sinews [1]

6208 עַרְקִי **'arqî**, a.g. GK: 6909. Arkite:– Arkite [2]

6209 עָרַר **'ārar**, v. GK: 6910 [→ 6145?, 6176, 6177, 6185, 6199, 6200; cf. 6168]. [Q] to strip off; [Po] to strip; [Pil] to level, demolish; [Htpal] to be laid utterly bare:– utterly broken (+6209) [2], make bare [1], raised up [1]

6210 עֶרֶשׂ **'ereś**, n.f. GK: 6911. bed, couch:– bed [4], bedstead [2], couch [2], bed (+3326) [1], couches [1]

6211 עָשׁ **'āš**, n.m. GK: 6931 & 6933 [→ 5906, 6244]. moth, which consumes some natural fabrics; Bear or Lion (a constellation):– moth [6], moth-eaten (+398) [1]

6211' עֲשַׂב **ᵃśab** (Aram.), n.[m.]. GK: 10572 [cf. 6212]. grass, (green) plants:– grass [5]

6212 עֵשֶׂב **'ēśeb**, n.m. GK: 6912 [cf. 6211']. green plant, vegetation, grass:– grass [16], herb [12], herbs [5]

6213 עָשָׂה **'āśâ**, v. GK: 6913 & 6914 [→ 501, 3299, 3300, 4639, 4640, 4641, 6214, 6221, 6222]. [Q] to do, make; [Qp] to be done; [N] to be done, be made; [P] to caress, squeeze; [Pu] to be made; a generic of action, seen in the many contextual translations of the KJV:– do [607], made [393], done [339], did [319], make [232], wrought [52], doeth [42], offer [41], keep [30], committed [27], execute [24], deal [23], maketh [23], prepare [22], work [22], shew [19], doest [18], kept [18], dealt [17], shewed [17], commit [16], executed [15], doing [14], maker [13], prepared [13], didst [12], perform [12], gotten [9], dealeth [7], dress [7], bring forth [6], maintain [6], offered [6], worketh [6], yield [6], dressed [5], executeth [5], performed [5], bear [4], brought forth [4], certainly make (+6213) [4], committeth [4], makest [4], workmen (+4399+1886.1) [4], bring to pass [3], doer [3], observe [3], ordained [3], practise [3], set [3], workmen (+4399) [3], yielding [3], accomplish [2], appointed [2], bruised [2], certainly do (+6213) [2], deal with [2], do great things (+6213) [2], do indeed (+6213) [2], doers [2], doth [2], fulfil [2], gat [2], get [2], holden [2], labour [2], made ready [2], meet [2], offering [2], procured [2], procure [2], sacrifice [2], sheweth [2], shewing [2], surely deal (+6213) [2], surely perform (+6213) [2], surely shew (+6213) [2], throughly execute (+6213) [2], used [2], warriors (+4421) [2], advanced [1], apt [1], at [1], become [1], bestow [1], bringeth to pass [1], bruising [1], busy [1], caused to be made [1], cause [1], charge [1], come to pass [1], committing [1], dealest [1], dealt with [1], deckedst [1], displease (+5869+7451+871.1) [1], effect [1], executedst [1], executest [1], executing [1], exercise [1], fashioned [1], feasted (+4960) [1], fighting (+4421) [1], fitteth [1], followed [1], fulfilled [1], fulfilling [1], furnish (+3627) [1], gathered [1], getteth [1], given [1], give [1], go about [1], govern [1], granted [1], held [1], hinder (+8442) [1], industrious (+4399) [1], journeyed (+1870) [1], laboured [1], madest [1], maintained [1], making [1], observed [1], occupied (+4399) [1], occupied [1], officers (+4399+1886.1) [1], pare [1], practised [1], preparest [1], preparing [1], provided [1], provide [1], put in execution [1], put [1], ready dressed [1], requite (+854) [1], sacrificed [1], served [1], shew (+5973) [1], shewest [1], sinneth through ignorance (+7684+871.1) [1], spendeth [1], surely [1], taken [1], take [1], trimmed [1], undo (+854) [1], used to do [1], vex (+7451) [1], workers [1], working [1], workmen [1], wroughtest [1]

6214 עֲשָׂהאֵל **ᵃśāh'ēl** or עֲשָׂה־אֵל **ᵃśāh-'ēl**, n.pr.m. GK: 6915 [→ 6213+410]. Asahel, "*God [El] has made*":– Asahel [18]

6215 עֵשָׂו **'ēśāw**, n.pr.m. GK: 6916. Esau, "*hairy*":– Esau [85], Esau's [12]

6216 עָשׁוֹק **'āšôq**, n.[m.]. GK: 6934 [→ 6231]. oppressor:– oppressor [1]

6217 עֲשׁוּקִים **ᵃšûqîm**, n.pl.abst. GK: 6935 [→ 6231]. oppression:– oppressions [2], oppressed [1]

6218 עָשׂוֹר **'āśôr**, n.[m.]. GK: 6917 [→ 6237]. (group of) ten:– tenth [12], instrument of ten strings [3], ten [1]

6219 עָשׁוֹת **'āšôt**, a. GK: 6936 [→ 6245]. wrought, fashioned (iron):– bright [1]

6220 עַשְׁוָת **'ašwāt**, n.pr.m. GK: 6937. Ashvath, "[poss.] *wrought iron*":– Ashvath [1]

6221 עֲשִׂיאֵל **ᵃśî'ēl**, n.pr.m. GK: 6918 [→ 6213+410]. Asiel, "*God [El] has made*":– Asiel [1]

6222 עֲשָׂיָה ***^{a}śāyâ***, n.pr.m. GK: 6919 [→ 6213+3068]. Asaiah, "*Yahweh has made*":– Asaiah [6], Asahiah [2]

6223 עָשִׁיר ***ʿāšîr***, a. (used as n.). GK: 6938 [→ 6238]. rich, wealthy; (n.) the rich, rich person:– rich [23]

6224 עֲשִׂירִי ***^{a}śîrî***, a.num.ord. GK: 6920 [→ 6237]. tenth:– tenth [29]

6225 עָשַׁן ***ʿāšan***, v.den. GK: 6939 [→ 6227, 6226]. [Q] to envelope in smoke, smolder:– smoke [5], angry [1]

6226 עָשֵׁן ***ʿāšēn***, a. GK: 6942 [→ 6225]. smoking, smoldering:– smoking [2]

6227 עָשָׁן ***ʿāšān***, n.m. GK: 6940 [→ 953+6228; cf. 6225]. smoke (billowing, ascending, blowing):– smoke [24], smoking [1]

6228 עָשָׁן ***ʿāšān***, n.pr.loc. GK: 6941 [cf. 953]. Ashan, "*smoke*":– Ashan [4]

6229 עָשַׂק ***ʿāśaq***, v. GK: 6921 [→ 4642]. [Ht] to dispute, quarrel:– strove [1]

6230 עֵשֶׂק ***ʿēśeq***, n.pr.loc. GK: 6922. Esek, "*dispute*":– Esek [1]

6231 עָשַׁק ***ʿāšaq***, v. GK: 6943 [→ 6216, 6217, 6232, 6233, 6234]. [Q] to oppress, mistreat; to defraud, extort; [Qp] to be oppressed, be tormented; [Pu] to be crushed:– oppressed [10], oppress [9], oppresseth [3], defrauded [2], do wrong [2], oppressors [2], oppressor [2], cruelly oppressed (+6233) [1], deceitfully gotten (+6233) [1], deceived [1], defraud [1], doeth violence [1], drinketh up [1], used oppression (+6233) [1]

6232 עֵשֶׁק ***ʿēšeq***, n.pr.m. GK: 6944 [→ 6231]. Eshek, "*oppressor*":– Eshek [1]

6233 עֹשֶׁק ***ʿōšeq***, n.m. GK: 6945 [→ 6231]. oppression, tyranny; extortion:– oppression [11], cruelly oppressed (+6231) [1], deceitfully gotten (+6231) [1], extortion [1], used oppression (+6231) [1]

עָשׁוּק ***ʿāšuq***. See 6217.

6234 עָשְׁקָה ***ʿošqâ***, n.f. GK: 6946 [→ 6233; cf. 6231]. trouble, oppression:– oppressed [1]

6235 עֶשֶׂר ***ʿeśer*** or עֲשָׂרָה ***^{a}śārâ***, n.m. & f. GK: 6924 & 6927 [→ 6237; cf. 6236]. ten:– ten [168], tens [3], fifteen (+2568+2050.1) [1], seventeen (+7651+2050.1) [1], ten's [1]

6236 עֲשַׂר ***^{a}śar*** (Aram.), n.m. & f. GK: 10573 [→ 6243; cf. 6235]. ten:– ten [4], twelve (+8648) [2]

6237 עָשַׂר ***ʿāśar***, v.den. GK: 6923 [→ 4643, 6218, 6224, 6235, 6240, 6241, 6242, 6240]. [Q] to take a tenth; [P] to give a tenth, set aside a tenth; [H] to give or receive a tenth:– surely give the tenth (+6237) [2], take the tenth [2], truly tithe (+6237) [2], take tithes [1], tithes [1], tithing [1]

6238 עָשַׁר ***ʿāšar***, v. GK: 6947 [→ 6223, 6239]. [Q] to be, become rich; [H] to make rich, bring wealth:– rich [6], maketh rich [3], enrich [2], made rich [2], become rich [1], enrichest [1], richer (+6239) [1], waxen rich [1]

6239 עֹשֶׁר ***ʿōšer***, n.m. GK: 6948 [→ 6238]. wealth, riches:– riches [36], richer (+6238) [1]

6240 עָשָׂר ***ʿāśār***, n. *or* a.num. GK: 6925 & 6926 & 6930 [→ 6237]. ten (always used in combined numbers):– twelve (+8147) [109], fourteenth (+702) [23], twelfth (+8147) [22], sixteen (+8337) [21], fourteen (+702) [19], eighteen (+8083) [18], fifteenth (+2568) [17], fifteen (+2568) [16], eleventh (+6249) [13], thirteen (+7969) [13], eighteenth (+8083) [11], thirteenth (+7969) [11], eleven (+259) [9], seventeen (+7651) [8], eleven (+6249) [6], seventeenth (+7651) [6], eleventh (+259) [4], nineteenth (+8672) [4], nineteen (+8672) [3], sixteenth (+8337) [3], sixscore (+8147) [1], ten [1]

עָשֹׂר ***ʿāśōr***. See 6218.

6241 עִשָּׂרוֹן ***ʿiśśārôn***, n.m. GK: 6928 [→ 6237]. tenth part:– tenth deals [18], several tenth deal (+6241) [10], tenth deal [3], one tenth deal (+259) [1], three tenth deals (+7969) [1]

6242 עֶשְׂרִים ***ʿeśrîm***, n.pl.indecl. GK: 6929 [→ 6237; cf. 6243]. twenty (pl. of "ten"):– twenty [277], twentieth [36], sixscore (+3967+2050.1) [1], twenty's [1]

6243 עֶשְׂרִין ***ʿeśrîn*** (Aram.), n.pl.indecl. GK: 10574 [→ 6236; cf. 6242]. twenty; note that this is the grammatical plural of "ten":– twenty [1]

6244 עָשֵׁשׁ ***ʿāšaš***, v. GK: 6949 [→ 6211]. [Q] to grow weak:– consumed [3]

6245 עָשַׁת ***ʿāšat***, v. GK: 6950 & 6951 [→ 6219, 6247, 6248, 6250; cf. 6246]. [Q] to grow sleek (i.e., smooth or shiny); [Ht] to take notice:– shine [1], think [1]

6246 עֲשִׁת ***^{a}šit*** (Aram.), v. GK: 10575 [cf. 6245]. [P] to plan, intend:– thought [1]

6247 עֶשֶׁת ***ʿešet***, n.[m.]. GK: 6952 [→ 6245]. polished piece, slab, plate:– bright [1]

6248 עַשְׁתּוּת ***ʿaštût***, n.f. GK: 6953 [→ 6245]. thought:– thought [1]

6249 עַשְׁתֵּי ***ʿaštê***, n. *or* a.num. GK: 6954. eleven, eleventh:– eleventh (+6240) [13], eleven (+6240) [6]

6250 עֶשְׁתֹּנֹת ***ʿeštōnet***, n.f. GK: 6955 [→ 6245]. plan, thought:– thoughts [1]

6251 עַשְׁתֶּרֶת ***ʿašteret***, n.f. GK: 6957. lamb or ewe:– flocks [4]

6252 עַשְׁתָּרֹת ***ʿaštārōt***, n.pr.loc. GK: 6958 [→ 1045, 6253, 6255, 6254; cf. 842, 1203?]. Ashtaroth:– Ashtaroth [10], Astaroth [1]

6253 עַשְׁתֹּרֶת ***ʿaštōret***, n.pr.f. GK: 6956 [→ 6252]. Ashtoreth (pagan god):– Ashtoreth [3], Ashtaroth [1]

6254 עַשְׁתְּרָתִי ***ʿašt^{e}rātî***, a.g. GK: 6960 [→ 6252]. Ashterathite:– Ashterathite [1]

6255 עַשְׁתְּרֹת קַרְנַיִם ***ʿašt^{e}rōt qarnayim***, n.pr.loc. GK: 6959 [→ 6252+7161]. Ashteroth Karnaim, "*Ashteroth of the pair of horns [twin peaks?]*":– Ashteroth Karnaim [1]

6256 עֵת ***ʿēt***, n.f. GK: 6961 [→ 6031]. time (in general); a unit of time (of various lengths), season:– time [233], times [24], season [8], due season [5], when (+871.1) [5], always (+3605+871.1) [3], eveningtide (+6153) [2], seasons [2], after (+3509.1) [1], after (+3807.1) [1], certain [1], continually (+3605+871.1) [1], due season (+2050.2) [1], eventide (+6153+1886.1) [1], long [1], mealtime (+400+1886.1) [1], noontide (+6672) [1], unto [1], when (+3807.1) [1], when [1]

6257 עָתַד ***ʿātad***, v. GK: 6963 [® 6259, 6260?, 6264]. [P] to make ready; [Ht] to be destined:– make fit [1], ready to become [1]

עַתֻּד ***ʿattud***. See 6260.

6258 עַתָּה ***ʿattâ***, adv. GK: 6964 [→ 6031]. now:– now [407], therefore [8], henceforth [6], this time forth [3], this time [2], I pray thee [1], as yet (+5704) [1], even now (+2088) [1], now (+3588) [1], straightway [1], whereas [1], yet (+5704) [1]

6259 עָתוּד ***ʿātûd***, a. GK: 6965 [→ 6257]. supply, treasure:– treasures [1]

6260 עַתּוּד ***ʿattûd***, n.m. GK: 6966 [→ 6257?]. male goat; (of humans) a leader:– he goats [15], goats [11], rams [2], chief ones [1]

6261 עִתִּי ***ʿittî***, a. GK: 6967 [→ 6031]. available:– fit [1]

6262 עַתַּי ***ʿattay***, n.pr.m. GK: 6968 [→ 6031]. Attai, "*timely,* [or perhaps] *an abbreviation of Athaiah*":– Attai [4]

6263 עֲתִיד ***^{a}tîd*** (Aram.), a. GK: 10577 [cf. 6264]. ready:– ready [1]

6264 עָתִיד ***ʿātîd***, a. GK: 6969 [→ 6257; cf. 6263]. ready, prepared:– ready [4], things that shall come [1]

6265 עֲתָיָה ***^{a}tāyâ***, n.pr.m. GK: 6970. Athaiah, "[poss.] *[the] superiority of Yahweh*":– Athaiah [1]

6266 עָתִיק ***ʿātîq***, a. GK: 6971 [→ 6275]. fine, choice, select:– durable [1]

6267 עַתִּיק ***ʿattîq***, a. GK: 6972 [→ 6275]. taken, removed (from place or time):– ancient [1], drawn [1]

6268 עַתִּיק ***ʿattîq*** (Aram.), a. GK: 10578. old, ancient; (as a title) the Ancient (of Days), a title of veneration and honor emphasizing wisdom and power:– ancient [3]

6269 עֲתָךְ ***^{a}tāk***, n.pr.loc. GK: 6973. Athach:– Athach [1]

6270 עַתְלַי ***ʿatlay***, n.pr.m. & f. GK: 6974 [→ 6271]. Athlai, "[poss.] *Yahweh is exalted; oldest of Yahweh*":– Athlai [1]

6271 עֲתַלְיָה ***^{a}talyâ*** or עֲתַלְיָהוּ ***^{a}talyāhû***, n.pr.m. & f. GK: 6975 & 6976 [→ 5830, 6270]. Athaliah, "[poss.] *Yahweh is exalted; oldest of Yahweh*":– Athaliah [17]

6272 עָתַם ***ʿātam***, v. GK: 6977. [N] to be destroyed; in context, to be scorched:– darkened [1]

6273 עָתְנִי ***ʿotnî***, n.pr.m. GK: 6978 [→ 6274]. Othni:– Othni [1]

6274 עָתְנִיאֵל ***ʿotnîʾēl***, n.pr.m. GK: 6979 [→ 6273+410]. Othniel:– Othniel [7]

6275 עָתַק ***ʿātaq***, v. GK: 6980 [→ 6266, 6267, 6277, 6276; cf. 6268]. [Q] to move; to grow old, grow weak; [H] to move on; to fail; to copy:– removed [4], become old [1], copied out [1], left off (+4480) [1], removeth [1], waxeth old [1]

6276 עָתֵק ***ʿātēq***, a. GK: 6982 [→ 6275]. enduring (wealth):– durable [1]

6277 עָתָק ***ʿātāq***, a. GK: 6981 [→ 6275]. arrogant, insolent, outstretched:– arrogancy [1], grievous things [1], hard [1], stiff [1]

6278 עֵת קָצִין ***ʿēt qāṣîn***, n.pr.loc. GK: 6962 [cf. 7101]. Eth Kazin:– Ittah-kazin [1]

6279 עָתַר ***ʿātar***, v. GK: 6983 [→ 6281?, 6282; cf. 6280?]. [Q] to pray; [N] to respond to prayer, be moved by an entreaty; [H] to pray, make entreaty:– intreated [12], intreat [6], make prayer [1], pray [1]

6280 עָתַר ***ʿātar***, v. GK: 6984 [→ 6283; cf. 6279?]. [N] to be multiplied; [H] to multiply:– deceitful [1], multiplied [1]

6281 עֶתֶר ***ʿeter***, n.pr.loc. GK: 6987 [→ 6279?]. Ether, "[perhaps] *perfume*":– Ether [2]

6282 עָתָר **ʿātār**, n.[m.]. GK: 6985 & 6986 [→ 6279]. worshiper; fragrance, perfume:– suppliants [1], thick [1]

6283 עֲתֶרֶת **ᵃteret**, n.f. GK: 6988 [→ 6280]. abundance:– abundance [1]

פֹּא **pōʾ**. See 6311.

6284 פָּאָה **pāʾâ**, v. GK: 6990 & 6991 [→ 6285]. [H] to split into pieces, scatter:– scatter into corners [1]

6285 פֵּאָה **pēʾâ**, n.f. GK: 6991 [→ 6284]. side, edge, boundary; forehead or crown of the head; piece, part:– side [63], corners [11], corner [5], quarter [3], end [1], part [1], quarter (+3807.1) [1], sides [1]

6286 פָּאַר **pāʾar**, v. GK: 6995 [→ 6287?, 8597]. [P] to honor, adorn, endow with splendor; to knock down olives a second time; [Ht] to glorify oneself, display one's splendor; (negatively) to boast:– glorified [6], beautify [3], boast [1], glorify [1], glory [1], go over the boughs [1], vaunt [1]

6287 פְּאֵר **pᵉʾēr**, n.m. GK: 6996 [→ 6286?]. turban, headdress:– bonnets [2], beauty [1], goodly [1], ornaments [1], tire of head [1], tires [1]

6288 פֹּארָה **pōʾrâ** or פֻּארָה **puʾrâ**, n.f. GK: 6997 & 6998. branch, leafy bough:– branches [4], boughs [1], bough [1], sprigs [1]

6289 פָּארוּר **pāʾrûr**, n.[m.]. GK: 6999 [→ 6517]. growing pale, turning pale; some sources: to burn, glow:– blackness [2]

6290 פָּארָן **pāʾrān**, n.pr.loc. GK: 7000 [→ 364; cf. 6501?]. Paran, *"plain"*:– Paran [11]

6291 פַּג **pag**, n.f. GK: 7001. early fruit, in context, unripe fig buds:– green figs [1]

6292 פִּגּוּל **piggûl**, n.m. GK: 7002. (ceremonially) unclean meat, kept too long after a sacrifice:– abominable [3], abomination [1]

6293 פֶּגַע **pāgaʿ**, n.m. GK: 7003 [→ 4645, 6294, 6295]. to strike, touch; intercede for, plead with; [H] to make intercession, intervene; strike; cause to encounter:– fall [6], meet [5], reacheth [5], fell [4], met [3], fall upon [2], intreat [2], made intercession [2], make intercession [2], meeteth [2], reached [2], came [1], cause to entreat [1], cometh betwixt [1], fell upon [1], intercessor [1], laid [1], lighted [1], meetest [1], met together [1], pray [1], run [1]

6294 פֶּגַע **pegaʿ**, n.m. GK: 7004 [→ 6293]. chance, occurrence:– chance [1], occurrent [1]

6295 פַּגְעִיאֵל **pagʿîʾēl**, n.pr.m. GK: 7005 [→ 6293+410]. Pagiel:– Pagiel [5]

6296 פָּגַר **pāgar**, v. GK: 7006 [→ 6297]. [P] to be exhausted:– faint [2]

6297 פֶּגֶר **peger**, n.m. GK: 7007 [→ 6296]. dead body, corpse; carcass; by extension: lifeless idol, with a focus that it is unclean and impotent:– carcases [12], dead bodies [6], corpses [2], carcase [1], dead carcases [1]

6298 פָּגַשׁ **pāgaš**, v. GK: 7008. [Q] to meet; to attack; [N] to have in common, to meet together; [P] to come upon, encounter:– met [6], meet [4], meet together [2], meeteth [1], met together [1]

6299 פָּדָה **pādâ**, v. GK: 7009 [→ 6302, 6303, 6304, 6306 (also used with compound proper names)]. [Q] to redeem, ransom, deliver, rescue, buy; [Qp] to be redeemed, be ransomed; [N] to be ransomed, be redeemed; [H] to let be ransomed; [Ho] to be brought to ransomed; this can mean to purchase a devoted animal from sacrifice or to purchase a person from slavery to freedom or new ownership; by extension: divine salvation from oppression, death, or sin:– redeemed [22], redeem [21], deliver [3], at all redeemed (+6299) [2], by any means redeem (+6299) [2], delivered [2], surely redeem (+6299) [2], ransomed [1], ransom [1], redeemedst [1], redeemeth [1], rescued [1]

6300 פְּדַהְאֵל **pᵉdahʾēl**, n.pr.m. GK: 7010 [→ 6299+410]. Pedahel, *"God [El] ransoms"*:– Pedahel [1]

6301 פְּדָהצוּר **pᵉdāhṣûr** or פְּדָה־צוּר **pᵉdāh-ṣûr**, n.pr.m. GK: 7011 [→ 6299+6697]. Pedahzur, *"the Rock ransoms"*:– Pedahzur [5]

6302 פְּדוּיִם **pᵉdûyim**, n.[m.]pl.abst. GK: 7012 [→ 6299]. redemption, ransom, paid to purchase firstborn Israelites from dedication to God:– redeemed [2], them that were redeemed [1], those that are redeemed [1]

6303 פָּדוֹן **pādôn**, n.pr.m. GK: 7013 [→ 6299]. Padon, *"ransom"*:– Padon [2]

6304 פְּדוּת **pᵉdût** or פְּלֻת **pᵉlut**, n.f. GK: 7014 & 7151 [→ 6299, 6395]. redemption, ransom, always of divine action; distinction:– redemption [2], division [1], redeem [1]

6305 פְּדָיָה **pᵉdāyâ** or פְּדָיָהוּ **pᵉdāyāhû**, n.pr.m. GK: 7015 & 7016 [→ 6299+3068]. Pedaiah, *"Yahweh ransoms"*:– Pedaiah [8]

6306 פִּדְיוֹם **pidyôm** or פִּדְיוֹן **pidyôn**, n.m. GK: 7017 & 7018 [→ 6299]. redemption, ransom; redemption money, ransom payment:– redemption [2], ransom [1]

6307 פַּדָּן **paddān** or פַּדַּן אֲרָם **paddan ʾᵃrām**, n.pr.loc. GK: 7019 & 7020 [→ 758]. Paddan, *"plain"*; Paddan Aram, *"plain of Aram"*:– Padan-aram [10], Padan [1]

6308 פָּדַע **pādaʿ**, v. GK: 7021. [Q] to spare, deliver:– deliver [1]

6309 פֶּדֶר **peder**, n.[m.]. GK: 7022. suet (the hard fat about kidney's and loins of animals):– fat [3]

פְּדֻת **pᵉdut**. See 6304.

6310 פֶּה **peh**, n.m. GK: 7023 [→ 6366, 6374; cf. 6433]. mouth (human or animal); by extension: speech, command, testimony; any opening; edge (of a sword):– mouth [329], commandment [37], edge [35], word [15], mouths [12], according to (+3807.1) [11], according to (+3509.1) [6], hole [6], according to (+5921) [4], another[s] [3], according unto (+3509.1) [2], appointment [2], one end [2], portion [2], tenor [2], according as (+834+3509.1) [1], according to (+834+5921) [1], according unto (+3807.1) [1], accord [1], after (+3807.1) [1], collar [1], command [1], eat (+871.1) [1], edges [1], end [1], entry [1], file (+6477) [1], in (+3807.1) [1], in the way go (+1870+5921) [1], mind [1], out of (+4480) [1], parts [1], saith (+871.1) [1], sayings [1], skirts [1], so that (+3509.1) [1], sound [1], speech [1], spoken [1], talk [1], to (+3807.1) [1], told (+7760+871.1) [1], twoedged [1], when (+3807.1) [1], wish [1], with assent [1]

6311 פֹּה **pōh**, adv.loc. GK: 7024 [→ 375, 645?]. here:– here [44], that side [13], this side [12], one side [5], other side [5], hither [2], hitherto (+5704) [1]

פּוֹא **pôʾ**. See 375.

6312 פּוּאָה **pûʾâ** or פּוּאָה **puûʾâ** or פֻּוָּה **puwwâ**, n.pr.m. GK: 7025 & 7026 & 7030 [→ 6324]. Puah, Puvah, "[perhaps] *girl*":– Puah [2], Phuvah [1], Pua [1]

6313 פּוּג **pûg**, v. GK: 7028 [→ 2014, 6314]. [Q] to grow numb, be feeble; [N] to be benumbed, be feeble:– ceased [1], fainted [1], feeble [1], slacked [1]

6314 פּוּגָה **pûgâ**, n.f. GK: 7029 [→ 6313]. relief, relaxation:– rest [1]

פֻּוָּה **puwwâ**. See 6312.

6315 פּוּחַ **pûaḥ**, v. GK: 7031 & 7032 [→ 6368; cf. 3306, 5301]. [Q] to blow, become dawn (of the day); to breathe out; [H] to blow (of wind); to breathe out, sneer, malign:– speaketh [5], blow [2], break [2], puffeth [2], bring into a snare [1], speak [1], utter [1]

6316 פּוּט **pûṭ**, n.pr.g. GK: 7033. Put:– Libya [2], Phut [2], Put [2], Libyans [1]

6317 פּוּטִיאֵל **pûṭîʾēl**, n.pr.m. GK: 7034 [→ 410]. Putiel, *"he whom God [El] gives"*:– Putiel [1]

6318 פּוֹטִיפַר **pôṭîpar**, n.pr.m. GK: 7035 [cf. 6319]. Potiphar, *"he whom Ra gives"*:– Potiphar [2]

6319 פּוֹטִי פֶרַע **pôṭî peraʿ**, n.pr.m. GK: 7036. Potiphera, *"he whom Ra gives"*:– Poti-pherah [3]

6320 פּוּךְ **pûk**, n.[m.]. GK: 7037. turquoise (stone); (eye) paint, possibly derived from turquoise:– fair colours [1], glistering [1], painting [1]

6321 פּוֹל **pôl**, n.[m.]col. GK: 7038. beans:– beans [2]

6322 פּוּל **pûl**, n.pr.m. GK: 7040 [→ 6467; cf. 6466]. Pul:– Pul [4]

6323 פּוּן **pûn**, v. GK: 7041. [Q] to be in despair:– distracted [1]

6324 פּוּאִי **pûʾî** or פּוּנִי **pûnî**, a.g. GK: 7027 & 7043 [→ 6312]. Puite, Punite, *"of Puah"*:– Punites [1]

6325 פּוּנֹן **pûnōn**, n.pr.loc. GK: 7044 [cf. 6373]. Punon:– Punon [2]

6326 פּוּעָה **pûʿâ**, n.pr.f. GK: 7045. Puah, "[perhaps] *girl*":– Puah [1]

6327 פּוּץ **pûṣ** or פָּצַץ **pāṣaṣ**, v. GK: 7046 & 7047 & 7207 [→ 1048, 4650, 6483, 8600; cf. 5310]. [Q] to be scattered; flow, overflow; [Qp] to be scattered; [N] to be scattered; [H] to cause to scatter; [Pol] to break to pieces, shatter; [Pil] to crush, smash; [Htpol] to be crumbled, be shattered:– scattered [31], scatter [16], scattered abroad [3], cast abroad [2], dispersed [2], scatter abroad [2], scattereth [2], spread abroad [2], breaketh in pieces [1], dasheth in pieces [1], disperse [1], drive [1], retired [1], scattereth abroad [1], shaken to pieces [1]

6328 פּוּק **pûq**, v. GK: 7048 [→ 6330; cf. 6329, 6375]. [Q] to stumble, totter; [H] to totter:– move [1], stumble [1]

6329 פּוּק **pûq**, v. GK: 7049 [cf. 6328]. [H] to bring out, furnish, promote:– obtaineth [2], affording [1], draw out [1], further [1], getteth [1], obtain [1]

6330 פּוּקָה **pûqâ**, n.f. GK: 7050 [→ 6328]. staggering, stumbling:– grief [1]

6331 פּוּר **pûr**, v. GK: 7051 [cf. 6565]. [H] to destroy:– bringeth to nought [1], broken [1], utterly take [1]

6332 פּוּר ***pûr***, n.m. GK: 7052. pur (the lot), pebbles, sticks, or pottery shards that were thrown to make decisions; (pl.) Purim, a Jewish festival celebrating God's control over the casting of lots:– Purim [5], Pur [3]

6333 פּוּרָה ***pûrâ***, n.f. GK: 7053. trough of the winepress; measure (equal to the filling of the winepress):– press [1], winepress [1]

פּוּרִים ***pûrîm***. See 6332.

6334 פּוֹרָתָא ***pôrātā'***, n.pr.m. GK: 7054. Poratha:– Poratha [1]

6335 פּוּשׁ ***pûš***, v. GK: 7055 & 7056. [Q] to leap, frolic, gallop; this may refer to the playful pawing action of a young animal; [N] to be scattered:– grow up [1], grown fat [1], scattered [1], spread [1]

6336 פּוּתִי ***pûtî***, a.g. GK: 7057. Puthite:– Puhites [1]

6337 פָּז ***paz***, n.m. GK: 7058 [→ 464, 6338]. pure gold:– fine gold [8], pure gold [1]

6338 פָּזַז ***pāzaz***, v. GK: 7059 [→ 6337]. [Ho] to be set with pure gold:– best [1]

6339 פָּזַז ***pāzaz***, v. GK: 7060. [Q] to be limber; [P] to leap:– leaping [1], made strong [1]

6340 פָּזַר ***pāzar***, v. GK: 7061 [cf. 967]. [Qp] to be scattered; [P] to scatter; [N] to be scattered; [Pu] to be dispersed:– scattered [6], scattereth [2], dispersed [1], scattered abroad [1]

6341 פַּח ***paḥ***, n.m. GK: 7062 & 7063 [→ 6351]. thin sheets (of hammered metal); snare, bird trap:– snare [18], snares [5], gin [1], grin [1], plates [1], thin plates [1]

6342 פָּחַד ***pāḥad***, v. GK: 7064 [→ 6343, 6345]. [Q] to tremble, be afraid; [P] to live in terror, fear; [H] to make shake, make tremble:– afraid [9], fear [8], feared [2], in great fear (+6343) [2], feareth [1], made to shake [1], standeth in awe [1]

6343 פַּחַד ***paḥad***, n.m. GK: 7065 [→ 6342; cf. 6765]. fear, terror, dread:– fear [40], dread [3], in great fear (+6342) [2], terror [2], dreadful [1], greatly feared [1]

6344 פַּחַד ***paḥad***, n.[m.]. GK: 7066. thigh:– stones [1]

6345 פַּחְדָּה ***paḥdâ***, n.f. GK: 7067 [→ 6342]. awe, dread:– fear [1]

6346 פֶּחָה ***peḥâ***, n.m. GK: 7068 [→ 6355?; cf. 6347]. governor, officer:– governor [10], captains [7], governors [7], captain [2], deputies [2]

6347 פֶּחָה ***peḥâ*** (Aram.), n.m. GK: 10580 [cf. 6346]. governor:– governor [6], captains [4]

6348 פָּחַז ***pāḥaz***, v. GK: 7069 [→ 6349, 6350]. [Q] to be arrogant, be insolent:– light [2]

6349 פַּחַז ***paḥaz***, n.[m.]. GK: 7070 [→ 6348]. turbulence, recklessness:– unstable [1]

6350 פַּחֲזוּת ***paḥ^{a}zût***, n.f. GK: 7071 [→ 6348]. insolence, arrogance, with an implication of recklessness:– lightness [1]

6351 פָּחַח ***pāḥaḥ***, v.den. GK: 7072 [→ 6341]. [H] to trap; [Ho] to be entrapped:– snared [1]

6352 פֶּחָם ***peḥām***, n.[m.]. GK: 7073. coal, charcoal:– coals [3]

6353 פֶּחָר ***peḥār*** (Aram.), n.m. GK: 10581. potter; sources translate "clay":– potter's [1]

6354 פַּחַת ***paḥat***, n.m. GK: 7074 [→ 6356]. pit, cave:– pit [8], hole's [1], snare [1]

6355 פַּחַת מוֹאָב ***paḥat mô'āb***, n.pr.m. GK: 7075 [→ 6346?+4124]. Pahath-Moab, "*supervisor of Moab*":– Pahath-moab [6]

6356 פְּחֶתֶת ***p^{e}ḥetet***, n.m. GK: 7076 [→ 6354]. mildew (that eats away at a garment):– fret [1]

6357 פִּטְדָה ***piṭdâ***, n.f. [*or* m.?]. GK: 7077. topaz; some sources: chrysolite:– topaz [4]

6358 פָּטַר ***pāṭar***, v.ptcp. GK: 7080 [→ 6359, 6362, 6363]. ptcp. of 6362: open:– open [4]

6359 פְּטִירִים ***p^{e}ṭîrîm***, var. GK: 7078 [→ 6358]. open, unoccupied:–

6360 פַּטִּישׁ ***paṭṭîš***, n.m. GK: 7079. (sledge-)hammer:– hammer [3]

6361 פַּטִּישׁ ***paṭṭîš*** (Aram.), n.[m.]. GK: 10582. trousers, leggings; some sources identify as other parts of clothing: coat, tunic, shirt, trousers, hose, hat, etc:– hosen [1]

6362 פָּטַר ***pāṭar***, v. GK: 7080 [→ 6358]. [Q] to elude, escape, release; [Qp] to be opened; [H] to open wide the mouth (as an insult):– dismissed [1], free [1], letteth out [1], shoot out [1], slipt away [1]

6363 פֶּטֶר ***peṭer***, n.m. or פִּטְרָה ***piṭrâ***, n.f. GK: 7081 & 7082 [cf. 6358]. first offspring, firstborn:– openeth [5], firstling [4], that openeth [2], open [1]

6364 פִּי־בֶסֶת ***pî-beset***, n.pr.loc. GK: 7083. Bubastis (Piy-Beset), "*house of the cat goddess Basht*":– Phi-beseth [1]

6365 פִּיד ***pîd***, n.[m.]. GK: 7085. misfortune, distress, calamity:– destruction [2], ruin [1]

6366 פִּיָה ***pîyâ***, n.m. GK: 7023 [→ 6310]. f. of 6310: mouth; by extension: edge (of a sword):–

6367 פִּי הַחִירֹת ***pî haḥîrôt***, n.pr.loc. GK: 7084. Pi Hahiroth, "*temple [house] of Hathor*":– Pi-hahiroth [4]

6368 פִּיחַ ***pîaḥ***, n.[m.]. GK: 7086 [→ 6315]. soot (from a furnace):– ashes [2]

6369 פִּיכֹל ***pîkōl***, n.pr.m. GK: 7087. Phicol:– Phichol [3]

6370 פִּלֶגֶשׁ ***pilegeš***, n.f. GK: 7108. concubine, a female consort generally with lower status and fewer rights than a wife, with the function of giving social status or pleasure to the husband; once this refers to a woman's male consorts (Eze 23:20):– concubine [22], concubines [14], paramours [1]

6371 פִּימָה ***pîmâ***, n.f. GK: 7089. fat, referring to an abundant life:– collops of fat [1]

6372 פִּינְחָס ***pîn^{e}ḥās***, n.pr.m. GK: 7090 [cf. 8471]. Phinehas, "*the black man*":– Phinehas [24], Phinehas' [1]

6373 פִּינֹן ***pînōn***, n.pr.m. GK: 7091 [cf. 6325]. Pinon, "*darkness* [name related to famous copper mines]":– Pinon [2]

6374 פִּיפִיּוֹת ***pîpiyyôt***, n.[f.pl.?]. GK: 7092 [→ 6310]. double-edged, with many teeth:– teeth [1], twoedged [1]

6375 פִּק ***piq***, n.[m.]. GK: 7211 [cf. 6328]. giving way, shaking (of knees):– smite together [1]

6376 פִּישׁוֹן ***pîšôn***, n.pr.loc. GK: 7093. Pishon:– Pison [1]

6377 פִּיתוֹן ***pîtôn***, n.pr.m. GK: 7094. Pithon:– Pithon [2]

6378 פַּךְ ***pak***, n.m. GK: 7095 [→ 6379]. flask, (small) jug:– box [2], vial [1]

6379 פָּכָה ***pākâ***, v. GK: 7096 [→ 6378]. [P] to trickle:– ran out [1]

6380 פֹּכֶרֶת הַצְּבָיִים ***pōkeret haṣṣ^{e}bāyîm***, n.pr.m. GK: 7097. Pokereth-Hazzebaim, "*pitfall of gazelles, i.e., gazelle hunter*":– Pochereth Zebaim [1], Pochereth of Zebaim [1]

6381 פָּלָא ***pālā'***, v.den. GK: 7098 [→ 466?, 4652, 6381, 6382, 6383, 6384, 6411, 6396; cf. 6395]. [N] to be wonderful, be marvelous, be amazing; to be hard, be amazing; [P] to fulfill; [H] to show a wonder, to cause to astound; [Ht] to show oneself marvelous:– wondrous works [10], wonders [9], marvellous [7], wonderful works [7], hard [5], wonderful [5], marvellous works [4], wondrous [4], marvellously [2], performing [2], accomplish [1], do a marvellous work [1], hidden [1], high [1], make a singular vow (+5088) [1], make wonderful [1], marvellous work [1], marvels [1], miracles [1], separate [1], shewed marvellous [1], shewest marvellous [1], wonderfully made [1], wonderfully [1], wondrously (+3807.1) [1], wondrously [1]

6382 פֶּלֶא ***pele'***, n.m. GK: 7099 [→ 6381]. wonder, miracle, astounding thing:– wonders [7], wonderful [2], marvellous things [1], wonderful things [1], wonderfully [1], wonder [1]

6383 פִּלְאִי ***pil'î***, a. GK: 7100 [→ 6381]. wonderful, beyond understanding:– secret [1], wonderful [1]

6384 פַּלֻּאִי ***pallu'î***, a.g. GK: 7101 [→ 6396; cf. 6381]. Palluite, "*wonderful*":– Palluites [1]

פְּלָאיָה ***p^{e}lā'yâ***. See 6411.

פִּלְאֶסֶר ***pil'eser***. See 8407.

6385 פָּלַג ***pālag***, v. GK: 7103 [→ 4653, 6388, 6390, 6391; cf. 6418; cf. 6386, cf. 6387]. [N] to be divided; [P] to cut open, divide:– divided [3], divide [1]

6386 פְּלַג ***p^{e}lag*** (Aram.), v. GK: 10583 [→ 6387, 6392; cf. 6385]. [Pp] to be divided:– divided [1]

6387 פְּלַג ***p^{e}lag*** (Aram.), n.[m.]. GK: 10584 [→ 6386; cf. 6388]. half:– dividing [1]

6388 פֶּלֶג ***peleg***, n.m. GK: 7104 [→ 6385]. stream, artificial irrigation canal:– rivers [8], river [1], streams [1]

6389 פֶּלֶג ***peleg***, n.pr.m. GK: 7105. Peleg, "*water canal*":– Peleg [7]

6390 פְּלַגָּה ***p^{e}laggâ***, n.f. GK: 7106 [→ 6385]. district, division; stream:– divisions [2], rivers [1]

6391 פְּלֻגָּה ***p^{e}luggâ***, n.f. GK: 7107 [→ 6385; cf. 6392]. division (of a clan or family):– divisions [1]

6392 פְּלֻגָּה ***p^{e}luggâ*** (Aram.), n.f. GK: 10585 [→ 6386; cf. 6391]. division (of priests):– divisions [1]

פִּלֶגֶשׁ ***pilegeš***. See 6370.

6393 פְּלָדֹת ***p^{e}lādōt***, n.f. GK: 7110. (polished) metal:– torches [1]

6394 פִּלְדָּשׁ ***pildāš***, n.pr.m. GK: 7109. Pildash, "*steely; spider*":– Pildash [1]

6395 פָּלָה ***pālâ***, v. GK: 7111 [→ 6397, 6411, 6423, 6304; cf. 6381]. [N] to be distinguished; [H] to deal differently, make a distinction:– sever [2], marvellous [1], put a difference [1], separated [1], set apart [1], shew marvellous [1]

6396 פַּלּוּא ***pallû'***, n.pr.m. GK: 7112 [→ 6384; cf. 6381]. Pallu, "*wonderful*":– Pallu [4], Phallu [1]

6397 פַּלּוֹנִי ***p^{e}lônî***, a.g. GK: 7113 [→ 6395]. Pelonite:– Pelonite [3]

6398 פָּלַח ***pālaḥ***, v. GK: 7114 [→ 6400, 6401; cf. 6399]. [Q] to plow; [P] to cut up, pierce; to bring forth (from the womb):– bring forth [1], cleaveth asunder [1], cutteth [1], shred [1], strike through [1]

6399 פְּלַח ***p^{e}laḥ*** (Aram.), v. GK: 10586 [→ 6402; cf. 6398?]. [P] to serve, worship, work for (deity or deities):– serve [7], servest [2], ministers [1]

6400 פֶּלַח ***pelaḥ***, n.f. GK: 7115 [→ 6398]. millstone; half (of a pomegranate); slice (of a cake):– piece [6]

6401 פִּלְחָא ***pilḥā'***, n.pr.m. GK: 7116 [→ 6398]. Pilha, "*millstone; plowman; harelip*":– Pileha [1]

6402 פָּלְחָן ***polḥān*** (Aram.), n.[m.]. GK: 10587 [→ 6399]. worship, service, work (for deity):– service [1]

6403 פָּלַט ***pālaṭ***, v. GK: 7117 [→ 3310, 3311, 4655, 6404, 6405, 6408, 6409, 6410, 6412, 6413; cf. 4422]. [Q] to escape; [P] to rescue, deliver; [H] to bring to safety:– deliver [11], deliverer [5], delivered [3], calveth [1], carry away safe [1], cause to escape [1], deliverest [1], delivereth [1], escape [1]

6404 פֶּלֶט ***peleṭ***, n.pr.m. GK: 7118 [→ 6407; cf. 6403 (also used with compound proper names)]. Pelet, "*rescue*":– Pelet [2]

פָּלֵט ***pālēṭ***. See 6412.

6405 פַּלֵּט ***pallēṭ***, n.[m.]. GK: 7119 [→ 6403]. deliverance:– escape [3], deliverance [1], escaped [1]

פְּלֵטָה ***p^{e}lēṭâ***. See 6413.

6406 פַּלְטִי ***palṭî***, n.pr.m. GK: 7120 [→ 6409]. Palti; Paltiel, "*God [El] is [my] deliverance*":– Palti [1], Phalti [1]

6407 פַּלְטִי ***palṭî***, a.g. GK: 7121 [→ 6404]. Paltite:– Paltite [1]

6408 פִּלְטַי ***pilṭāy***, n.pr.m. GK: 7122 [→ 6403]. Piltai, "*Yahweh rescues*":– Piltai [1]

6409 פַּלְטִיאֵל ***palṭî'ēl***, n.pr.m. GK: 7123 [→ 6406]. Paltiel, "*God [El] is [my] deliverance*":– Paltiel [1], Phaltiel [1]

6410 פְּלַטְיָה ***p^{e}laṭyâ*** or פְּלַטְיָהוּ ***p^{e}laṭyāhû***, n.pr.m. GK: 7124 & 7125 [→ 6403+3068]. Pelatiah, "*Yahweh rescues*":– Pelatiah [5]

פָּלִיא ***pālî'***. See 6383.

6411 פְּלָאיָה ***p^{e}lā'yâ*** or פְּלָיָה ***p^{e}lāyâ***, n.pr.m. GK: 7102 & 7126 [→ 6381+3068 *or* 6395+3068]. Pelaiah, "*Yahweh is spectacular*":– Pelaiah [3]

6412 פָּלִיט ***pālîṭ*** or פָּלֵיט ***pālêṭ***, n.m. GK: 7127 & 7128 [→ 6403]. fugitive, one who escapes:– escape [9], escaped [6], escapeth [2], escape (+1961) [1], fugitives [1], one that escaped [1], that escaped [1]

6413 פְּלֵיטָה ***p^{e}lêṭâ***, n.f. GK: 7129 [→ 6403]. fugitive, one who escapes, survivors, remnant:– deliverance [5], escaped [4], escape [4], escape (+1961) [2], that is escaped [2], they that escape [2], escaping [1], him that escapeth [1], remnant to escape [1], remnant [1], such as are escaped [1], that are escaped [1], them that are escaped [1], them that be escaped [1], which is escaped [1]

6414 פָּלִיל ***pālîl***, n.m. GK: 7130 [→ 6419]. judge:– judges [3]

6415 פְּלִילָה ***p^{e}lîlâ***, n.f. GK: 7131 [→ 6419]. decision:– judgment [1]

6416 פְּלִילִי ***p^{e}lîlî***, a. GK: 7132 [→ 6419]. for a judge, calling for judgment:– judge [1]

6417 פְּלִילִיָּה ***p^{e}lîliyyâ***, n.f. GK: 7133 [→ 6419]. rendering of a decision, the calling for a judgment:– judgment [1]

6418 פֶּלֶךְ ***pelek***, n.[m.]. GK: 7134 & 7135 [cf. 6385]. spindle-whorl, which could be used as a crutch; district:– part [8], distaff [1], staff [1]

6419 פָּלַל ***pālal***, v. GK: 7136 & 7137 [→ 654, 6414, 6415, 6416, 6417, 6420, 6421, 8605 (also used with compound proper names)]. [P] to mediate, intervene; to expect; to furnish justification; [Ht] to pray:– pray [35], prayed [30], praying [5], prayeth [4], executed judgment [1], intreat [1], judged [1], judge [1], made prayer [1], make supplication [1], make [1], prayer made [1], prayer make (+8605) [1], thought [1]

6420 פָּלָל ***pālāl***, n.pr.m. GK: 7138 [→ 6419]. Palal, "*he has judged*":– Palal [1]

6421 פְּלַלְיָה ***p^{e}lalyâ***, n.pr.m. GK: 7139 [→ 6419+3068]. Pelaliah, "*Yahweh intercedes in arbitration*":– Pelaliah [1]

6422 פַּלְמוֹנִי ***palmōnî***, p. GK: 7140 [cf. 492, 6423]. certain one:– certain [1]

פִּלְנְאֶסֶר ***piln^e'eser***. See 8407.

6423 פְּלֹנִי ***p^{e}lōnî***, p. GK: 7141 [→ 6395; cf. 492, 6422]. certain one:– such a one (+492) [1], such and such (+492) [1], such [1]

פִּלְנֶסֶר ***pilneser***. See 8407.

6424 פָּלַס ***pālas***, v.den. GK: 7142 & 7143 [→ 6425]. [P] to make level, make smooth, prepare; to examine, observe:– ponder [2], weigh [2], made [1], pondereth [1]

6425 פֶּלֶס ***peles***, n.[m.]. GK: 7144 [→ 6424]. balance, scale:– scales [1], weight [1]

פְּלֶסֶר ***p^{e}leser***. See 8407.

6426 פָּלַץ ***pālaṣ***, v. GK: 7145 [→ 4656, 6427, 8606]. [Ht] to tremble, shake:– tremble [1]

6427 פַּלָּצוּת ***pallāṣût***, n.f. GK: 7146 [→ 6426]. trembling, shuddering, shaking:– horror [2], fearfulness [1], trembling [1]

6428 פָּלַשׁ ***pālaš***, v. GK: 7147. [Ht] to roll oneself (in the dust or ash):– wallow [3], roll [1]

6429 פְּלֶשֶׁת ***p^{e}lešet***, n.pr.loc. GK: 7148 [→ 6430]. Philistia; Philistine:– Palestina [3], Philistia [3], Palestine [1], Philistines [1]

6430 פְּלִשְׁתִּי ***p^{e}lištî***, a.g. GK: 7149 [→ 6429]. Philistine:– Philistines [245], Philistine [33], Philistims [5], Philistines' [4], Philistim [1]

6431 פֶּלֶת ***pelet***, n.pr.m. GK: 7150. Peleth, "[perhaps] *swift* or *swiftness*":– Peleth [2]

6432 פְּלֵתִי ***p^{e}lētî***, a.g. GK: 7152 [cf. 3774?]. Pelethite:– Pelethites [7]

6433 פֻּם ***pum*** (Aram.), n.m. GK: 10588. mouth:– mouth [5], mouths [1]

6434 פֵּן ***pēn***, n.m. GK: 7157 [→ 6437, 6438]. same as 6438: corner (of a structure), cornerstone (as a crucial element); stronghold; by extension: leader:– corner [2]

6435 פֶּן ***pen***, c. GK: 7153 [→ 6437?]. lest, not:– lest [114], not [7], lest peradventure [5], that not [4], none [1], peradventure [1], that [1]

6436 פַּנַּג ***pannag***, n.[m.]. GK: 7154. food, confection:– Pannag [1]

6437 פָּנָה ***pānâ***, v. GK: 7155 [→ 3312, 3942, 6435?, 6440, 6434, 6438, 6439, 6441, 6442]. [Q] to turn (in various senses); [P] to prepare; to turn away; [H] to turn; [Ho] to be caused to turn:– turned [33], turn [16], looked [14], looking [9], look [9], looketh [8], prepare [4], look back [3], respect [3], turneth [3], have respect [2], regard (+413) [2], beholdeth [1], cast out [1], cometh on [1], corner [1], dawning [1], empty [1], eventide (+6153) [1], goeth away [1], lieth [1], look toward [1], looked back [1], looked toward [1], mark (+413) [1], passed away [1], preparedst [1], prepared [1], regardeth (+413) [1], regard [1], respecteth (+413) [1], return [1], right [1], turn away [1], turn back [1], turned aside [1], turned back [1], turned faces [1], turnest [1], turneth away [1], when appeared (+3807.1) [1]

פָּנֶה ***pāneh***. See 6440.

6438 פִּנָּה ***pinnâ***, n.f. GK: 7157 [→ 6434]. same as 6434: corner (of a structure), cornerstone (as a crucial element); stronghold; by extension: leader:– corner [16], corners [6], chief [2], towers [2], bulwarks [1], stay [1]

6439 פְּנוּאֵל ***p^{e}nû'ēl*** or פְּנִיאֵל ***p^{e}nî'ēl***, n.pr.m. & loc. GK: 7158 & 7159 & 7160 & 7161 [→ 6437]. Penuel, Peniel, "*face of God [El]*":– Penuel [8], Peniel [1]

פְּנִי ***pānî***. See 6443.

6440 פָּנֶה ***pāneh***, n.m. & f. GK: 7156 [→ 6753, 6441; cf. 6437]. face; by extension: appearance, presence; (pp.) before, in front of, in the presence of; to "show one's face" is a sign of favor; to "turn" or "hide one's face" is a sign of rejection:– before (+3807.1) [958], face [328], presence [70], before [67], faces [63], because of (+4480) [54], before (+4480) [50], before (+5921) [43], sight [33], from (+4480) [31], countenance [30], upon (+5921) [23], of (+4480) [20], before (+4480+3807.1) [17], before (+854) [16], before (+413) [15], open [13], because (+4480) [12], for (+4480) [12], persons [10], person [10], by reason of (+4480) [9], fear [7], before (+871.1) [6], prospect [6], toward (+5921) [6], with (+3807.1) [6], against (+3807.1) [5], over against (+5921) [5], sight (+3807.1) [5], forefront [4], from (+4480+3807.1) [4], honourable (+5375) [4], in (+5921) [4], over against (+413) [4], presence (+3807.1) [4], according to (+5921) [3], anger [3], at (+4480) [3], because [3], beforetime (+3807.1) [3], besought (+853+2470) [3], favour [3], for (+3807.1) [3], forefront (+4136) [3], forepart [3], meet [3], of (+3807.1) [3], of (+4480+3807.1) [3], say nay (+7725) [3], shewbread (+3899) [3], shewbread (+3899+1886.1) [3], straight forward (+413+5676) [3], unto (+3807.1) [3], accept (+5375) [2], accepted (+5375) [2], afore (+3807.1) [2], aforetime (+3807.1) [2], before (+413+4136) [2], besought (+2470) [2], from (+3807.1) [2], from off (+4480+5921) [2], looketh [2], looks [2], of old (+3807.1) [2], over against (+413+4136) [2], seemeth unto (+3807.1) [2], to (+3807.1) [2], unto [2], withstand (+2388+3807.1) [2], against (+413) [1], against (+5676) [1], appease (+3722) [1], as (+5921) [1], as long as (+3807.1) [1], at (+3807.1) [1], attend upon [1], because (+834+4480) [1], because of

Heb

(+4480+3807.1) [1], before (+5048) [1], before face [1], beforetime (+4480+3807.1) [1], beforetime [1], beseech (+2470) [1], by (+4480) [1], compassed with (+2328+5921) [1], deny (+7725) [1], disappoint (+6923) [1], edge [1], employ (+935+4480) [1], endure (+3807.1) [1], evident [1], first (+3807.1) [1], for (+4480+3807.1) [1], for fear of (+4480) [1], forefront (+3807.1) [1], forepart (+4136) [1], form [1], forward (+3807.1) [1], front [1], heaviness [1], himself (+2050.2) [1], impudent (+7186) [1], in former time (+3807.1) [1], in front (+5921) [1], in old time (+3807.1) [1], in presence (+7200) [1], in sight (+3807.1) [1], in the presence [1], in the sight (+3807.1) [1], in time past (+3807.1) [1], in times past (+3807.1) [1], inquired of (+1245) [1], intreat favour (+2470) [1], looked [1], look [1], me (+2967.1) [1], more than (+3807.1) [1], mouth [1], out of (+4480+5921) [1], over against [1], partial [1], pleased (+3190+3807.1) [1], pleaseth (+2896+3807.1) [1], purposed [1], regard (+5375) [1], regard persons (+4480+5375) [1], right before (+5227) [1], right forth (+3807.1) [1], send good speed (+7136+3807.1) [1], served (+5975+3807.1) [1], set [1], shewbread [1], state [1], themselves (+1992.1) [1], through (+4480) [1], throughout (+5921) [1], till (+3807.1) [1], towards (+3807.1) [1], towards (+4480) [1], toward [1], to [1], upside down (+5921) [1], upside down [1], waited on (+1961+3807.1) [1], whom (+834+4480) [1], with (+4480) [1], within (+4480+3807.1) [1], within [1], withstand (+5975+3807.1) [1]

6441 פְּנִימָה **pᵉnîmâ**, adv. *or* pp. GK: 7163 [→ 6442; cf. 6440, 6437]. inner, inside, within:– within (+4480) [3], within [3], inward (+3807.1) [2], within (+3807.1) [2], inner part [1], in [1], within (+413) [1]

6442 פְּנִימִי **pᵉnîmî**, a. GK: 7164 [→ 6441]. inner:– inner [30], inward (+413+1886.1) [1], within (+871.1+1886.1) [1]

6443 פְּנִינִים **pᵉnînîm**, n.[f.]pl. GK: 7165 [→ 6444]. rubies or corals:– rubies [6]

6444 פְּנִנָּה **pᵉninnâ**, n.pr.f. GK: 7166 [→ 6443]. Peninnah, "[poss.] *pearls, coral branches; woman with rich hair*":– Peninnah [3]

6445 פָּנַק **pānaq**, v. GK: 7167. [P] to pamper:– delicately bringeth up [1]

6446 פַּס **pas**, n.[m.]. GK: 7168 [→ 6450; cf. 657; cf. 6447]. ornamentation, many-colored or long-sleeved garment:– of many colours [3], divers colours [2]

6447 פַּס **pas** (Aram.), n.m. GK: 10589 [cf. 6446]. (palm of) hand; this may also refer to the entire hand:– part [2]

6448 פָּסַג **pāsag**, v. GK: 7170. [P] to look over or to walk among:– consider [1]

6449 פִּסְגָּה **pisgâ**, n.pr.loc. GK: 7171 [→ 798]. Pisgah:– Pisgah [5]

6450 פַּס דַּמִּים **pas dammîm**, n.pr.loc. GK: 7169 [→ 6446]. Pas Dammim, "*place of blood*":– Pas-dammim [1]

6451 פִּסָּה **pissâ**, n.f. GK: 7172. abundance, plenty:– handful [1]

6452 פָּסַח **pāsaḥ**, v. GK: 7173 & 7174 [→ 6453, 6454, 6455, 8607]. [Q] to pass over; to be limp; [N] to become crippled; to worship in a limping dance:– pass over [2], became lame [1], halt [1], leapt [1], passed over [1], passing over [1]

6453 פֶּסַח **pesaḥ**, n.m. GK: 7175 [→ 6452]. Passover; this can refer to the festival, the meal, or the lamb sacrificed at the festival:– passover [48], passovers [1]

6454 פָּסֵחַ **pāsēaḥ**, n.pr.m. GK: 7176 [→ 6452]. Paseah, "*hobbling one*":– Paseah [3], Phaseah [1]

6455 פִּסֵּחַ **pissēaḥ**, a. GK: 7177 [→ 6452]. lame, crippled:– lame [14]

6456 פָּסִיל **pāsîl**, n.m. GK: 7178 [→ 6458]. idol, carved image:– graven images [18], carved images [3], quarries [2]

6457 פָּסַךְ **pāsak**, n.pr.m. GK: 7179. Pasach, "*to divide*":– Pasach [1]

6458 פָּסַל **pāsal**, v. GK: 7180 [→ 6456, 6459]. [Q] to chisel out, carve (stone or wood):– hew [3], hewed [2], graven [1]

6459 פֶּסֶל **pesel**, n.m. GK: 7181 [→ 6458]. idol, usually an image carved of wood or stone:– graven image [26], carved image [2], graven images [2], graven [1]

6460 פְּסַנְתֵּרִין **pᵉsantērîn** (Aram.), n.[m.]. GK: 10590. harp (triangular stringed instrument):– psaltery [4]

6461 פָּסַס **pāsas**, v. GK: 7182. [Q] to vanish:– fail [1]

6462 פִּסְפָּה **pispâ**, n.pr.m. GK: 7183. Pispah:– Pispah [1]

6463 פָּעָה **pā'â**, v. GK: 7184 [→ 660?]. [Q] to cry out, groan (in childbirth):– cry [1]

6464 פָּעוּ **pā'û** or פָּעִי **pā'î**, n.pr.loc. GK: 7185 & 7187. Pau, Pai, "*groaning, bleating*":– Pai [1], Pau [1]

6465 פְּעוֹר **pᵉ'ôr**, n.pr.loc. GK: 7186 [→ 1047, 1187; cf. 6473?]. Peor, "*opening*":– Peor [4], Peor's [1]

פָּעִי **pā'î**. See 6464.

6466 פָּעַל **pā'al**, v. GK: 7188 [→ 508, 4659, 6322, 6467, 6468, 6469]. [Q] to do, make:– workers [19], work [7], wrought [7], do [5], worketh [4], done [3], made [3], commit [1], didst [1], doers [1], doest [1], maker [1], maketh [1], ordaineth [1], working [1]

6467 פֹּעַל **pō'al**, n.m. GK: 7189 [→ 6322; cf. 6466]. work, deed, labor:– work [27], deeds [2], done acts [2], works [2], act [1], do [1], getting [1], maker [1], reward of work [1]

6468 פְּעֻלָּה **pᵉ'ullâ**, n.f. GK: 7190 [→ 6469; cf. 6466]. work, deed, recompense:– work [8], labour [2], works [2], reward [1], wages [1]

6469 פְּעֻלְּתַי **pᵉ'ullᵉtay**, n.pr.m. GK: 7191 [→ 6468; cf. 6466]. Peullethai, "*worker, wage earner*":– Peulthai [1]

6470 פָּעַם **pā'am**, v. GK: 7192 [→ 6471, 6472]. [Q] to push, impel; [N] to be troubled; [Ht] to be troubled:– troubled [4], move at times [1]

6471 פַּעַם **pa'am**, n.f. GK: 7193 [→ 6472; cf. 6470]. step, foot; time, occurrence:– times [38], at other times (+6471+871.1) [12], time [12], once [8], feet [6], now [5], twice [5], steps [4], thrice (+7969) [4], corners [3], once (+259) [3], at once (+259) [2], now (+1886.1) [2], ranks [2], second time [2], anvil [1], footsteps [1], goings [1], hundredfold (+3967) [1], oftentimes (+7227) [1], oftentimes (+7969) [1], once (+871.1+1886.1) [1], order [1], two times [1], wheels [1]

6472 פַּעֲמֹן **paᵃmôn**, n.[m.]. GK: 7194 [→ 6471; cf. 6470]. bell (on a robe):– bell [4], bells [3]

6473 פָּעַר **pā'ar**, v. GK: 7196 [cf. 6465?, 6474?]. [Q] to open wide (mouth):– opened [2], gaped [1], opened wide [1]

6474 פַּעֲרַי **paᵃray**, n.pr.m. GK: 7197 [cf. 6473?]. Paarai, "*devotee of Peor*":– Paarai [1]

6475 פָּצָה **pāṣâ**, v. GK: 7198. [Q] to open (mouth); to deliver, set free:– opened [7], open [3], rid [2], delivereth [1], gaped [1], uttered [1]

6476 פָּצַח **pāṣaḥ**, v. GK: 7200. [Q] to break forth, burst forth; [P] to break (in pieces):– break forth [6], break [1], make a loud noise [1]

6477 פְּצִירָה **pᵉṣîrâ**, n.f. GK: 7201. sharpening (of plowshare):– file (+6310) [1]

6478 פָּצַל **pāṣal**, v. GK: 7202 [→ 6479]. [P] to peel (bark off boughs):– pilled [2]

6479 פְּצָלוֹת **pᵉṣālôt**, n.f.pl. GK: 7203 [→ 6478]. stripes (made by peeling bark):– strakes [1]

6480 פָּצַם **pāṣam**, v. GK: 7204. [Q] to tear open:– broken [1]

6481 פָּצַע **pāṣa'**, v. GK: 7205 [→ 6482]. [Q] to bruise, wound; [Qp] to be emasculated (by crushing):– wounded [3]

6482 פֶּצַע **peṣa'**, n.m. GK: 7206 [→ 6481]. wound, bruise:– wounds [4], wound [3], wounding [1]

פָּצֵץ **paṣṣēṣ**. See 1048.

6483 פִּצֵּץ **piṣṣēṣ** or הַפִּצֵּץ **happiṣṣēṣ**, n.pr.m. GK: 7209 & 2204 [→ 1886.1+6327]. Pizzez, Happizzez, "*one who breaks*":– Aphses [1]

6484 פָּצַר **pāṣar**, v. GK: 7210 [cf. 6555]. [Q] to insist on, bring pressure, persuade; [H] to be arrogant:– urged [4], pressed [2], stubbornness [1]

6485 פָּקַד **pāqad**, v. GK: 7212 & 7217 [→ 4662, 6486, 6487, 6488, 6489, 6490, 6496]. [Q] to pay attention, care for; to count, number; to punish; [Qp] to be counted, listed; [N] to be missing, empty; [P] to muster; [Pu] to be robbed; to be recorded; [H] to appoint, give a charge; [Ho] to be appointed; [Ht] be mustered, counted; [Hotpaal] to be counted:– numbered [103], visit [31], punish [27], visited [17], number [14], appoint [10], set [6], surely visit (+6485) [6], made governor [5], appointed [4], committed [4], officers [4], punished [4], visiting [4], charged [3], counted [3], empty [3], missed [3], at all miss (+6485) [2], by any means missing (+6485) [2], commit [2], do judgment [2], lacking [2], laid up [2], made overseer [2], made ruler [2], numberest [2], overseers [2], oversight [2], surely visited (+6485) [2], visitest [2], wanting [2], avenge [1], bestowed [1], calledst to remembrance [1], chargest [1], delivered to keep (+854+6487) [1], deprived [1], enjoined [1], given a charge [1], go see [1], had oversight [1], have oversight [1], hurt [1], lacked [1], lacketh [1], look [1], made rulers [1], make [1], missing [1], mustereth [1], reckon [1], remember [1], set over [1], sum [1], visiteth [1], want [1]

פִּקֻּד **piqqud**. See 6490.

6486 פְּקֻדָּה ***p^equddâ***, n.f. GK: 7213 [→ 6485]. positive: appointment, charge, visitation; negative: punishment:– visitation [13], office [3], officers [2], offices [2], oversight [2], account [1], charge [1], custody [1], numbers [1], orderings [1], prison (+1004+1886.1) [1], reckoning [1], that have charge over [1], that laid up [1]

6487 פִּקָּדוֹן ***piqqādôn***, n.m. GK: 7214 [→ 6485]. something entrusted, something in reserve:– delivered to keep (+854+6485) [1], store [1], that which was delivered to keep [1]

6488 פְּקִדֻת ***p^eqidut***, n.f. GK: 7215 [→ 6485]. (captain of the) guard:– ward [1]

6489 פְּקוֹד ***p^eqôd***, n.pr.loc. GK: 7216 [→ 6485]. Pekod, "*visitation*":– Pekod [2]

6490 פִּקּוּדִים ***piqqûdîm***, n.m.[pl.]. GK: 7218 [→ 6485]. precepts, directions, orders:– precepts [21], commandments [2], statutes [1]

6491 פָּקַח ***pāqaḥ***, v. GK: 7219 [→ 6492?, 6493, 6494, 6495]. [Q] to open; [Qp] to be opened; [N] to be opened:– open [10], opened [7], openeth [2], opening [1]

6492 פֶּקַח ***peqaḥ***, n.pr.m. GK: 7220 [→ 6491?]. Pekah, "*he has opened*":– Pekah [11]

6493 פִּקֵּחַ ***piqqēaḥ***, a. GK: 7221 [→ 6491]. (normal) sighted:– seeing [1], wise [1]

6494 פְּקַחְיָה ***p^eqaḥyâ***, n.pr.m. GK: 7222 [→ 6491+3068]. Pekahiah, "*Yahweh opens*":– Pekahiah [3]

6495 פְּקַח־קוֹחַ ***p^eqaḥ-qôaḥ***, n.[m.]. GK: 7223 [→ 6491]. opening (of eyesight); some sources: opening a prison house to release prisoners:– opening of the prison [1]

6496 פָּקִיד ***pāqîd***, n.m. GK: 7224 [→ 6485]. chief officer, supervisor, commissioner:– overseer [4], officers [3], officer [2], charge [1], governor [1], overseers [1], set [1]

6497 פְּקָעִים ***p^eqā'îm***, n.m.pl. GK: 7225 [→ 6498]. gourds:– knops [3]

6498 פַּקֻּעֹת ***paqqu'ōt***, n.[f.]pl. GK: 7226 [→ 6497]. gourds:– gourds [1]

6499 פַּר ***par***, n.m. GK: 7228 [→ 6510]. bull:– bullock [60], bullocks [31], bullock (+1241) [28], bullocks (+1241) [5], bullock's [3], bulls [2], oxen [2], calves [1], young [1]

6500 פָּרָא ***pārā'***, v. GK: 7229 [cf. 6509]. [H] to thrive in fruitfulness:– fruitful [1]

6501 פֶּרֶא ***pere'*** or פֶּרֶה ***pereh***, n.m. *or* f. GK: 7230 & 7241 [→ 6290?, 6502]. wild donkey; some sources: zebra, onager:– wild asses [4], wild ass [4], wild ass's [1], wild [1]

פֹּרָאה ***pōrā'h***. See 6288.

6502 פִּרְאָם ***pir'ām***, n.pr.m. GK: 7231 [→ 6501]. Piram, "[poss.] *wild donkey; indomitable;* [poss.] *zebra*":– Piram [1]

6503 פַּרְבָּר ***parbār*** or פַּרְוָר ***parwār***, n.[m.]. GK: 7232 & 7247. court (of the temple):– Parbar [2], suburbs [1]

6504 פָּרַד ***pārad***, v. GK: 7233 [→ 6505, 6506, 6507]. [Qp] to be spread out; [N] to be separated, be parted; [P] to consort with; [Pu] to be scattered; [H] to set apart, divide, separate; [Ht] to be scattered, be parted:– separated [8], divided [3], parted [2], separateth [2], separate [2], dispersed [1], out of joint [1], parteth [1], part [1], scattered abroad [1], scattered [1], severed [1], stretched [1], sundered [1]

6505 פֶּרֶד ***pered***, n.m. GK: 7234 [→ 6506; cf. 6504]. mule:– mules [8], mule [6], mules' [1]

6506 פִּרְדָּה ***pirdâ***, n.f. GK: 7235 [→ 6505]. (female) mule:– mule [3]

6507 פְּרֻדֹת ***p^erudōt***, n.f. GK: 7237 [→ 6504]. grain (of seed); some sources: dried fig:– seed [1]

6508 פַּרְדֵּס ***pardēs***, n.[m.]. GK: 7236. park, forest, orchard:– forest [1], orchards [1], orchard [1]

6509 פָּרָה ***pārâ***, v. GK: 7238 [→ 669?, 6513, 6529; cf. 6500]. [Q] to be fruitful, flourish; [H] to make fruitful:– fruitful [13], make fruitful [5], increased [3], fruitful bough (+1121) [2], beareth [1], bring forth [1], bring fruit [1], caused to be fruitful [1], grew [1], grow [1]

6510 פָּרָה ***pārâ***, n.f. GK: 7239 [→ 6499]. cow, heifer:– kine [18], heifer [6], cow [2]

6511 פָּרָה ***pārâ***, n.pr.loc. GK: 7240. Parah, "*cow*":– Parah [1]

פֶּרֶה ***pereh***. See 6501.

6512 פֵּרוֹת ***pērôt*** or חֲפַרְפָּרָה ***ḥ^aparpārâ***, n.f. GK: 7249 & 2923 [→ 2658, 2661]. rodent (an object of worship):– moles (+2661) [1]

6513 פֻּרָה ***purâ***, n.pr.m. GK: 7242 [→ 6509]. Purah, "*branch; imposing*":– Phurah [2]

6514 פְּרוּדָא ***p^erûdā'*** or פְּרִידָא ***p^erîdā'***, n.pr.m. GK: 7243 & 7263. Peruda, Perida, "*single, unique*":– Perida [1], Peruda [1]

פְּרוֹזִי ***p^erôzî***. See 6521.

6515 פָּרוּחַ ***pārûaḥ***, n.pr.m. GK: 7245 [→ 6524]. Paruah, "*blooming; cheerful*":– Paruah [1]

6516 פַּרְוַיִם ***parwayim***, n.pr.loc. GK: 7246. Parvaim:– Parvaim [1]

6517 פָּרוּר ***pārûr***, n.[m.]. GK: 7248 [→ 6289]. cooking pot:– pot [2], pans [1]

פַּרְוָר ***parwār***. See 6503.

6518 פָּרָז ***pāraz***, n.[m.]. GK: 7250. warrior:– villages [1]

6519 פְּרָזוֹת ***p^erāzôt***, n.f.[pl.]. GK: 7252 [→ 6520, 6521, 6522]. rural, open country:– towns without walls [1], unwalled villages [1], unwalled [1]

6520 פְּרָזוֹן ***p^erāzôn***, n.[m.]. GK: 7251 [→ 6519]. dwellers in the open country; warriors:– villages [2]

6521 פְּרָזִי ***p^erāzî***, n.[m.]. GK: 7253 [cf. 6519]. rural, open country:– country [1], unwalled [1], villages [1]

6522 פְּרִזִּי ***p^erizzî***, a.g. GK: 7254 [→ 6519]. Perizzite:– Perizzites [18], Perizzite [5]

6523 פַּרְזֶל ***parzel*** (Aram.), n.m. GK: 10591 [cf. 1270]. iron:– iron [20]

6524 פָּרַח ***pāraḥ***, v. GK: 7255 & 7256 & 7257 [→ 667, 6515, 6525, 6526?]. [Q] to sprout, blossom; break out, flourish; to fly; (n.) a bird; [H] to make flourish, bring to bud:– flourish [7], blossom [3], budded [3], blossom abundantly (+6524) [2], break out abroad (+6524) [2], breaking forth [2], broken out [2], bud [2], grow [2], make fly [2], break out [1], flourished [1], groweth [1], made to flourish [1], make to flourish [1], spreading [1], springeth up [1], spring [1], sprung up [1]

6525 פֶּרַח ***peraḥ***, n.m. GK: 7258 [→ 6524]. blossom, bud; floral work:– flowers [9], flower [5], blossom [1], buds [1], bud [1]

6526 פִּרְחַח ***pirḥaḥ***, n.m.col. GK: 7259 [→ 6524?]. offspring, brood, tribe, with a focus on energetic behavior:– youth [1]

6527 פָּרַט ***pāraṭ***, v. GK: 7260 [→ 6528?]. [Q] to strum, improvise (on a musical instrument):– chant [1]

6528 פֶּרֶט ***pereṭ***, n.[m.]col. GK: 7261 [→ 6527?]. fallen grapes:– grape [1]

6529 פְּרִי ***p^erî***, n.m. GK: 7262 [→ 6509]. fruit, produce, crops; by extension: offspring of any creature; result of any action; "fruit of the lips" is speech, praise; "fruit of the hand" is something earned:– fruit [107], fruits [7], fruitful [2], boughs [1], firstfruits (+7225) [1], reward [1]

פְּרִידָא ***p^erîdā'***. See 6514.

פּוּרִים ***purîm***. See 6332.

6530 פָּרִיץ ***pāriṣ***, n.m. GK: 7264 & 7265 [→ 6555]. ferocious (animal); robber; violent one:– robbers [2], destroyer [1], ravenous [1], robbers (+1121) [1], robber [1]

6531 פֶּרֶךְ ***perek***, n.[m.]. GK: 7266. ruthlessness, brutality, violence:– rigour [5], cruelty [1]

6532 פָּרֹכֶת ***pārōket***, n.f. GK: 7267. curtain:– vail [25]

6533 פָּרַם ***pāram***, v. GK: 7268. [Q] to tear; [Qp] to be torn:– rend [2], rent [1]

6534 פַּרְמַשְׁתָּא ***parmaš^etā'***, n.pr.m. GK: 7269. Parmashta, "*very first*":– Parmashta [1]

6535 פַּרְנָךְ ***parnāk***, n.pr.m. GK: 7270. Parnach:– Parnach [1]

6536 פָּרַס ***pāras***, v. GK: 7271 [→ 6538?, 6541; cf. 6537]. [Q] to offer food, share food; [H] to have a divided hoof:– divideth [5], divide [4], parteth [2], deal [1], hoofs [1], tear [1]

6537 פְּרַס ***p^eras***, v. and פְּרֵס ***p^erēs*** (Aram.), n.[m.]. GK: 10592 [cf. 6536]. [Peil] to be divided; parsin, peres (unit of measure and weight):– divided [1], peres [1], upharsin (+2050.3) [1]

6538 פֶּרֶס ***peres***, n.[m.]. GK: 7272 [→ 6536?]. vulture:– ossifrage [2]

6539 פָּרַס ***pāras***, n.pr.loc. GK: 7273 [→ 6542; cf. 6540, cf. 6543]. Persia; Persian:– Persia [27], Persians [1]

6540 פָּרַס ***pāras*** (Aram.), n.pr.loc. & g. GK: 10594 [→ 6543; cf. 6539]. Persia, Persian:– Persians [4], Persia [2]

6541 פַּרְסָה ***parsâ***, n.f. GK: 7274 [→ 6536]. hoof:– hoof [12], hoofs [5], claws [2], clovenfooted (+8156+8157) [2]

6542 פָּרְסִי ***pār^esî***, a.g. GK: 7275 [→ 6539; cf. 6543]. Persian:– Persian [1]

6543 פַּרְסָי ***parsāy*** (Aram.), a.g. GK: 10595 [→ 6540; cf. 6542]. Persian:– Persian [1]

6544 פָּרַע ***pāra'***, v.den. GK: 7276 & 7277 [→ 6546]. [Q] to take the lead; to be out of control, be unkempt; to ignore, avoid; [Qp] to be unkempt, be running wild; [N] be unrestrained; [H] to let neglect; to promote wickedness:– uncover [3], made naked [2], refuseth [2], avenging (+6546) [1], avoid [1], bare [1], go back [1], let [1], naked [1], perish [1], refuse [1], set at nought [1]

6545 פֶּרַע ***pera'***, n.[m.]. GK: 7279 [cf. 6546?]. long hair of head:– locks [2]

6546 פֶּרַע ***pera'***, n.[m.]. GK: 7278 [→ 6544; cf. 6545?]. leader, prince:– avenging (+6544) [1], revenges [1]

6547 פַּרְעֹה ***par'ōh***, n.m. GK: 7281 [→ 6548, 6549]. Pharaoh:– Pharaoh [222], Pharaoh's [43], Pharaoh's (+3807.1) [3]

6548 פַּרְעֹה חָפְרַע ***par'ōh ḥopra'***, n.pr.m. GK: 7281 + 2922 [→ 6547]. Pharaoh Hophra:– Pharaoh-hophra [1]

6549 פַּרְעֹה נְכֹה ***par'ōh n*^{e}*kōh***, n.pr.m. GK: 7281 + 5785 [→ 6547]. Pharaoh Neco:– Pharaoh-nechoh [4], Pharaoh-necho [1]

6550 פַּרְעֹשׁ ***par'ōš***, n.m. GK: 7282 [→ 6551]. flea:– flea [2]

6551 פַּרְעֹשׁ ***par'ōš***, n.pr.m. GK: 7283 [→ 6550]. Parosh, *"flea"*:– Parosh [5], Pharosh [1]

6552 פִּרְעָתוֹן ***pir'ātôn***, n.pr.loc. GK: 7284 [→ 6553]. Pirathon:– Pirathon [1]

6553 פִּרְעָתוֹנִי ***pir'ātônî***, a.g. GK: 7285 [→ 6552]. Pirathonite, from Pirathon, *"of Pirathon"*:– Pirathonite [5]

6554 פַּרְפַּר ***parpar***, n.pr.loc. GK: 7286. Pharpar:– Pharpar [1]

6555 פָּרַץ ***pāraṣ***, v. GK: 7287 [→ 1188, 4664, 6530, 6556, 6557, 6560, 6558, 6559; cf. 6484]. [Q] to break out, burst forth; [Qp] to be broken through; [N] to be spread abroad; [Pu] to be broken down; [Ht] to break oneself away:– broken down [5], increased [4], brake down [3], break down [3], break forth [3], breaketh [2], broken forth [2], broken up [2], broken [2], made a breach (+6556) [2], pressed [2], abroad every where [1], brake in [1], breaches [1], break away [1], break out [1], breaker [1], breaketh out [1], broken in upon [1], burst out [1], came abroad [1], compelled [1], dispersed [1], grew [1], increase [1], made a breach [1], open [1], scattered [1], spread abroad [1], urged [1]

6556 פֶּרֶץ ***pereṣ***, n.m. GK: 7288 [→ 1188, 7428; cf. 6555]. breech, break, gap caused by something breaking through; by extension: outburst of anger:– breach [9], breaches [3], breaking in [2], made a breach (+6555) [2], breaking forth [1], gaps [1], gap [1]

6557 פֶּרֶץ ***pereṣ***, n.pr.m. GK: 7289 [→ 6558; cf. 6555]. Perez, *"breaking out"*:– Pharez [12], Perez [3]

6558 פַּרְצִי ***parṣî***, a.g. GK: 7291 [→ 6557; cf. 6555]. Perezite:– Pharzites [1]

6559 פְּרָצִים ***p*^{e}*rāṣîm***, n.pr.loc. GK: 7292 [→ 6556; cf. 6555]. Perazim, *"breaking out"*:– Perazim [1]

6560 פֶּרֶץ עֻזָּא ***pereṣ 'uzzā'*** or פֶּרֶץ עֻזָּה ***pereṣ 'uzzâ***, n.pr.loc. GK: 7290 [→ 6556+5798]. Perez Uzzah, *"breaking out of Uzzah"*:– Perez-uzzah [1], Perez-uzza [1]

6561 פָּרַק ***pāraq***, v. GK: 7293 [→ 4665, 6563, 6564; cf. 6562]. [Q] to rip to pieces; to free (by tearing away); [P] to take off, tear off; [Ht] to take off from oneself, tear off from oneself:– break off [2], brake off [1], break [1], broken [1], deliver [1], redeemed [1], rending in pieces [1], rent [1], tear in pieces [1]

6562 פְּרַק ***p*^{e}*raq*** (Aram.), v. GK: 10596 [cf. 6561]. [P] to break off, tear away; to loosen, abolish; to renounce:– break off [1]

6563 פֶּרֶק ***pereq***, n.[m.]. GK: 7294 [→ 6561]. crossroad; plunder:– crossway [1], robbery [1]

6564 פָּרָק ***pārāq***, n.[m.]. GK: 7295 [→ 6561]. fragment:–

6565 פָּרַר ***pārar***, v. GK: 7296 & 7297 [cf. 6331]. [Q] to split asunder; [Pil] to shatter; [Pol] to split open; [Htpol] to split asunder; [H] to break, violate, nullify; [Ho] to be broken, revoked, thwarted:– break [13], broken [8], any ways make void (+6565) [2], brake [2], breaking [2], clean dissolved (+6565) [2], defeat [2], disannul [2], made void [2], utterly made void (+6565) [2], broken asunder [1], brought to nought [1], castest off [1], cause to cease [1], come to nought [1], disappointed [1], disappointeth [1], divide [1], fail [1], frustrateth [1], frustrate [1], make void [1], none effect [1]

6566 פָּרַשׂ ***pāraś***, v. GK: 7298 [→ 4666; cf. 6576]. [Q] to spread out, scatter; [Qp] to be spread out; [N] to be scattered; [P] to scatter, spread out:– spread [29], spread forth [10], spread out [6], spread abroad [4], spreadeth [3], scattered [2], spreadeth forth [2], stretch forth [2], breaketh [1], chop in pieces [1], layeth open [1], spreadeth abroad [1], stretch out [1], stretched forth [1], stretched out [1], stretcheth out [1], stretch [1]

6567 פָּרַשׁ ***pāraš***, v. GK: 7300 & 7301 [→ 6571, 6575; cf. 6569; cf. 6568]. [Q] to make clear; [N] to be given; [Pu] to be made clear; [H] to secrete poison:– declared [1], distinctly [1], scattered [1], shewed [1], stingeth [1]

6568 פְּרַשׁ ***p*^{e}*raš*** (Aram.), v. GK: 10597 [cf. 6566]. [Pap] to be translated, be made clear, with an implication that each and every element of the letter be read and made clear:– plainly [1]

6569 פֶּרֶשׁ ***pereš***, n.[m.]. GK: 7302 [→ 6570; cf. 6567]. offal, dung or intestinal contents of a butchered animal:– dung [7]

6570 פֶּרֶשׁ ***pereš***, n.pr.m. GK: 7303 [→ 6569]. Peresh, *"offal eviscerated; dung; contents of stomach [not intestine]"*:– Peresh [1]

6571 פָּרָשׁ ***pārāš***, n.m. GK: 7304 & 7305 [→ 6567]. horse; horseman:– horsemen [55], horseman [1], horsemen (+1167) [1]

6572 פַּרְשֶׁגֶן ***paršegen*** or פַּתְשֶׁגֶן ***patšegen***, n.m. GK: 7306 & 7358 [cf. 6573]. copy (of a text):– copy [4]

6573 פַּרְשֶׁגֶן ***paršegen*** (Aram.), n.m. GK: 10598 [cf. 6572]. copy (of a document):– copy [3]

6574 פַּרְשְׁדֹן ***parš*^{e}*dōn***, n.[m.]. GK: 7307. back (of a person), back door [?]:– dirt [1]

6575 פָּרָשָׁה ***pārāšâ***, n.f. GK: 7308 [→ 6567]. exact amount, exact statement:– declaration [1], sum [1]

6576 פַּרְשֵׂז ***paršēz***, a.vbl. *or* v. GK: 7299 [cf. 6566]. spreading:– spreadeth [1]

6577 פַּרְשַׁנְדָּתָא ***paršandātā'***, n.pr.m. GK: 7309. Parshandatha:– Parshandatha [1]

6578 פְּרָת ***p*^{e}*rāt***, n.pr.loc. GK: 7310. Euphrates (mighty river of Mesopotamia); Perath (small river or valley in the book of Jeremiah):– Euphrates [19]

פֹּרָת ***pōrāt***. See 6509.

6579 פַּרְתְּמִים ***part*^{e}*mîm***, n.m.pl. GK: 7312. nobles, princes:– most noble [1], nobles [1], princes [1]

6580 פַּשׁ ***paš***, n.[m.]. GK: 7317. wickedness or weakness, foolishness:– extremity [1]

6581 פָּשָׂה ***pāśâ***, v. GK: 7313. [Q] to spread:– spread [13], spread much abroad (+6581) [6], spread much (+6581) [2], spreadeth [1]

6582 פָּשַׁח ***pāšaḥ***, v. GK: 7318. [P] to mangle:– pulled in pieces [1]

6583 פַּשְׁחוּר ***pašḥûr***, n.pr.m. GK: 7319. Pashhur, "[perhaps] *be quiet* and *round about*":– Pashur [14]

6584 פָּשַׁט ***pāšaṭ***, v. GK: 7320. [Q] to take off, strip; to make a sudden dash, raid; [P] to strip; [H] to take off, strip off; [Ht] to strip oneself:– put off [6], strip [6], invaded [4], flay [3], stripped [3], fell [2], spoileth [2], stript [2], flayed [1], made a road [1], made an invasion [1], pull [1], ran [1], rushed forward [1], rushed [1], set [1], spoil [1], spread abroad [1], spread [1], strip out of [1], stripped off [1], stript off [1], stript out of [1]

6585 פָּשַׂע ***pāśa'***, v. GK: 7314 [→ 6587; cf. 4667]. [Q] to march, step forth:– go [1]

6586 פָּשַׁע ***pāša'***, v. GK: 7321 [→ 6588]. [Q] to rebel, revolt (against human or divine authority):– transgressed [13], transgressors [8], rebelled [6], revolted [5], transgress [3], offended [1], revolt [1], transgressing [1], transgression [1], transgressor [1], trespassed [1]

6587 פֶּשַׂע ***peśa'***, n.[m.]. GK: 7315 [→ 6585]. step:– step [1]

6588 פֶּשַׁע ***peša'***, n.m. GK: 7322 [→ 6586]. rebellion, revolt, sin, transgression (against human or divine authority):– transgressions [46], transgression [37], trespass [5], sins [2], rebellion [1], sin [1], transgression (+1870) [1]

6589 פָּשַׂק ***pāśaq***, v. GK: 7316. [Q] to open wide (the lips in talking or smirking); [P] to spread the feet or legs (in immorality):– opened [1], openeth wide [1]

6590 פְּשַׁר ***p*^{e}*šar*** (Aram.), v. GK: 10599 [→ 6591; cf. 6592, 6622]. [P] to give an interpretation; [Pa] to interpret; (as noun) an interpreter:– interpreting [1], make interpretations (+6591) [1]

6591 פְּשַׁר ***p*^{e}*šar*** (Aram.), n.m. GK: 10600 [→ 6590; cf. 6592]. interpretation, explanation, what something means:– interpretation [30], make interpretations (+6590) [1]

6592 פֵּשֶׁר ***pēšer***, n.[m.]. GK: 7323 [cf. 6590, cf. 6591]. explanation, interpretation:– interpretation [1]

6593 פֵּשֶׁת ***pēšet***, n.[m.]. GK: 7324 [→ 6594]. flax, linen (made of flax):– linen [9], flax [7]

6594 פִּשְׁתָּה ***pištâ***, n.f. GK: 7325 [→ 6593]. flax, wick (made of flax):– flax [3], tow [1]

6595 פַּת ***pat*** or פְּתוֹת ***p*^{e}*tôt***, n.f. GK: 7326 & 7336 [→ 6598, 6626]. little piece, morsel (of food):– morsel [8], pieces [2], piece [2], meat [1], morsels [1], part in pieces (+6626) [1]

6596 פֹּת ***pōt***, n.[f.]. GK: 7327 [cf. 4670]. scalp, forehead; socket (for doors):– hinges [1], secret parts [1]

פְּתָאִי ***p*^{e}*tā'î***. See 6612.

6597 פִּתְאֹם ***pit'ōm***, subst. (used as adv.). GK: 7328 [→ 6621]. suddenly, unexpectedly, all at once, in an instant:– suddenly [20], sudden [2], straightway [1], suddenly (+871.1) [1], very suddenly (+6621+871.1) [1]

6598 פַּת־בַּג ***pat-bag***, n.[m.]. GK: 7329 [→ 6595+897?]. (fine) food, choice provisions:– portion of meat [5], meat [1]

6599 פִּתְגָם ***pitgām***, n.m. GK: 7330 [cf. 6600]. edict, decree; sentence (for a crime):– decree [1], sentence [1]

6600 פִּתְגָם ***pitgām*** (Aram.), n.m. GK: 10601 [cf. 6599]. word: report, reply, edict, decision, decree:– answer [2], matter [2], letter [1], word [1]

6601 פָּתָה ***pātâ***, v.den. GK: 7331 & 7332 [→ 3315, 6612, 6615; cf. 6613]. [Q] to be simple, easily deceived, enticed; [P] to seduce, entice, deceive, allure; [N] to be enticed, deceived; [Pu] to be deceived, enticed, persuaded; [H] to provide ample space, make spacious:– entice [7], deceived [6], persuade [3], deceive [2], enticed [2], allure [1], enlarge [1], enticeth [1], flattereth [1], flatter [1], persuaded [1], silly one [1], silly [1]

6602 פְּתוּאֵל ***p^{e}tû'ēl***, n.pr.m. GK: 7333 [→ 6612+410]. Pethuel, *"God's opening"*:– Pethuel [1]

6603 פִּתּוּחַ ***pittûaḥ***, n.m. GK: 7334 [→ 6605]. engraving, inscription:– engravings [5], graving [2], carved figures (+4734) [1], carved work [1], grave (+3807.1) [1], graven [1]

6604 פְּתוֹר ***p^{e}tôr***, n.pr.loc. GK: 7335. Pethor:– Pethor [2]

6605 פָּתַח ***pātaḥ***, v. GK: 7337 & 7338 [→ 3316, 3317, 4669, 4668, 6603, 6607, 6608, 6609, 6610, 6611; cf. 6606]. [Q] to open; [Qp] to be opened; [N] to be opened; [P] to loosen, release, take off; to engrave, carve; [Pu] to be engraved; [Ht] to free oneself:– opened [51], open [47], loose [6], loosed [5], open wide (+6605) [4], openeth [4], grave [3], engrave [2], graved [2], openest [2], appear [1], break forth [1], drawn out [1], drawn [1], go free [1], graven [1], loose from [1], looseth [1], opening [1], put off [1], putteth off [1], set forth [1], set wide [1], spread out [1], ungirded [1], unstopped [1], vent [1]

6606 פְּתַח ***p^{e}taḥ*** (Aram.), v. GK: 10602 [cf. 6605]. [Pp, Peil] to be opened:– opened [1], open [1]

6607 פֶּתַח ***petaḥ***, n.m. GK: 7339 [→ 6605]. entrance, opening; of a building or city: door, gate:– door [116], entering [17], doors [11], entry [7], gate [4], gates [3], entrance [2], entrances [1], entries [1], open place (+5869) [1], openings [1]

6608 פֵּתַח ***pētaḥ***, n.m. GK: 7340 [→ 6605]. revelation, disclosure, an extension opening a door or gate:– entrance [1]

פָּתֻחַ ***pātuaḥ***. See 6603.

6609 פְּתִיחָה ***p^{e}tîḥâ***, n.[f.]. GK: 7347 [→ 6605]. drawn sword:– drawn swords [1]

6610 פִּתְחוֹן ***pittāḥôn***, n.[m.]. GK: 7341 [→ 6605]. opening (of mouth for communication):– opening [1], open [1]

6611 פְּתַחְיָה ***p^{e}taḥyâ***, n.pr.m. GK: 7342 [→ 6605+3068]. Pethahiah, *"Yahweh opens"*:– Pethahiah [4]

6612 פֶּתִי פְּתִי ***petî***, n.f. & a. GK: 7343 & 7344 [→ 6601, 6602]. simple, naive, someone easily deceived or persuaded; simple ways, simplemindedness:– simple [15], simple ones [2], foolish [1], simplicity [1]

6613 פְּתָי ***p^{e}tāy*** (Aram.), n.[m.]. GK: 10603. width, breadth:– breadth [2]

6614 פְּתִיגִיל ***p^{e}tîgîl***, n.[m.]. GK: 7345. fine clothing:– stomacher [1]

6615 פְּתַיּוּת ***p^{e}tayyût***, n.f. GK: 7346 [→ 6601]. undisciplined, deceptive:– simple [1]

6616 פָּתִיל ***pātîl***, n.m. GK: 7348 [→ 6617]. cord, strands, string:– lace [4], bracelets [2], bound [1], line [1], ribband [1], thread [1], wires [1]

6617 פָּתַל ***pātal***, v. GK: 7349 [→ 5319, 5321?, 6616, 6618]. [N] to have a struggle; to be wily, be crooked; [Ht] to show oneself shrewd:– froward [2], shew froward [1], shew unsavoury [1], wrestled [1]

6618 פְּתַלְתֹּל ***p^{e}taltōl***, a. GK: 7350 [→ 6617]. crooked, perverse:– crooked [1]

6619 פִּתֹם ***pitōm***, n.pr.loc. GK: 7351. Pithom, *"temple [house] of Atum"*:– Pithom [1]

6620 פֶּתֶן ***peten***, n.m. GK: 7352. cobra, serpent; some sources: viper:– asps [3], adder [2], asp [1]

6621 פֶּתַע ***peta'***, subst. (used as adv.). GK: 7353 [→ 6597]. instant; (adv.) suddenly, in an instant:– suddenly [3], instant [2], suddenly (+871.1) [1], very suddenly (+6597+871.1) [1]

6622 פָּתַר ***pātar***, v. GK: 7354 [→ 6623; cf. 6590, cf. 6591]. [Q] to interpret, give the meaning (of a dream):– interpret [4], interpreted [3], interpretation [1], interpreter [1]

6623 פִּתְרוֹן ***pittārôn***, n.m. GK: 7355 [→ 6622]. interpretation, meaning:– interpretation [4], interpretations [1]

6624 פַּתְרוֹס ***patrôs***, n.pr.loc. GK: 7356 [→ 6625]. Upper Egypt (Patros):– Pathros [5]

6625 פַּתְרֻסִים ***patrusîm***, a.g.pl. GK: 7357 [→ 6624]. Pathrusite:– Pathrusim [2]

פַּתְשֶׁגֶן ***patšegen***. See 6572.

6626 פָּתַת ***pātat***, v. GK: 7359 [→ 6595]. [Q] to crumble:– part in pieces (+6595) [1]

6627 צֵאָה ***ṣē'â***, n.f. GK: 7362. excrement, dung:– cometh from [1], cometh out [1]

צֹאָה ***ṣō'â***. See 6675.

צְאוֹן ***ṣ^{e}'ôn***. See 6629.

6628 צֶאֱלִים ***ṣe'^{e}lîm***, n.m.pl. GK: 7365. lotus plant:– shady trees [2]

6629 צֹאן ***ṣō'n***, n.col.f. *or* m. GK: 7366 [→ 6792; cf. 3318]. flock, sheep, goats (in contrast to larger mammals: cattle, donkeys, camels, etc.):– sheep [111], flock [84], flocks [53], cattle [14], lambs (+1121) [2], shepherds (+7462) [2], flocks (+4735) [1], lamb [1], sheepcotes (+1448) [1], sheepfolds (+1448) [1], sheepfolds (+4356) [1], sheepshearers (+1494) [1], shepherd (+7462) [1], small^{s} [1]

6630 צַאֲנָן ***ṣa'^{a}nān***, n.pr.loc. GK: 7367 [cf. 6799?]. Zaanan:– Zaanan [1]

6631 צֶאֱצָאִים ***ṣe'^{e}ṣā'îm***, n.m.[pl.]. GK: 7368 [→ 3318]. offspring, descendant:– offspring [9], that come forth [1], that which cometh out [1]

6632 צָב ***ṣāb***, n.[m.]. GK: 7369 & 7370 [→ 6637, 6638?]. (covered) wagon; some sources: litter without wheels; lizard (of unspecified species):– covered [1], litters [1], tortoise [1]

6633 צָבָא ***ṣābā'***, v. GK: 7371 [→ 6635]. [Q] to fight, do battle; to serve in (temple) corps:– fight [3], assembled [2], mustered [2], warred [2], assembling [1], fought [1], perform service (+6635) [1], wait (+6635) [1]

6634 צְבָה ***ṣ^{e}bâ*** (Aram.), v. GK: 10605 [→ 6640]. [P] to wish, desire, want, long for:– will [5], would [5]

6635 צָבָא ***ṣābā'***, n.m. & f. GK: 7372 [→ 6633]. army, host, divisions (of an army); as a title of God: of Hosts (the heavenly armies), the Almighty, with a focus on great power to conquer or rule, a fig. extension of the leader of an great army:– hosts [293], host [101], war [41], armies [22], army [7], battle [5], service [4], appointed time [2], warfare [2], army (+2428) [1], battle (+4421) [1], company [1], perform service (+6633) [1], soldiers [1], time appointed [1], wait (+6633) [1], waiting upon [1]

6636 צְבֹאִים ***ṣ^{e}bō'îm*** or צְבִיִּים ***ṣ^{e}bōyîm***, n.pr.loc. GK: 7375 & 7387 [cf. 6643]. Zeboiim, *"gazelles"*:– Zeboim [3], Zeboiim [2]

6637 צֹבֵבָה ***ṣōbēbâ***, n.pr.m. GK: 7376 [→ 6632]. Zobebah:– Zobebah [1]

6638 צָבָה ***ṣābâ***, v. GK: 7377 [→ 6632?, 6639]. [Q] to swell; [H] to cause to swell:– fight [1], make to swell [1], swell [1]

6639 צָבֶה ***ṣābeh***, a. GK: 7379 [→ 6638]. swollen:– swell [1]

צֹבָה ***ṣōbâ***. See 6678.

6640 צְבוּ ***ṣ^{e}bû*** (Aram.), n.f. GK: 10606 [→ 6634]. situation, matter, affair, thing:– purpose [1]

6641 צָבוּעַ ***ṣābûa'***, a. GK: 7380 [→ 6641, 6648; 6649, 6650]. speckled, variegated, pertaining to the pattern on a winged creature:– speckled [1]

6642 צָבַט ***ṣābaṭ***, v. GK: 7381 [cf. 6653]. [Q] to offer (food to another person):– reached [1]

6643 צְבִי ***ṣ^{e}bî***, n.m. GK: 7373 & 7374 & 7382 & 7383 [→ 6644, 6645, 6646; cf. 6636, 6719; cf. 6634]. ornament, beautiful (thing), glory; gazelle:– glory [8], roe [6], glorious [5], roebuck [4], roes [3], beauty [2], beautiful [1], goodly [1], pleasant [1], roebucks [1]

6644 צִבְיָא ***ṣibyā'***, n.pr.m. GK: 7384 [→ 6643]. Zibia, *"gazelle"*:– Zibia [1]

6645 צִבְיָה ***ṣibyâ***, n.pr.f. GK: 7385 [→ 6643]. Zibiah, *"gazelle"*:– Zibiah [2]

6646 צְבִיָּה ***ṣ^{e}biyyâ***, n.f. GK: 7386 [→ 6643]. (female) gazelle:– roes [2]

צְבִיִּים ***ṣ^{e}bîîm***. See 6636.

צְבָיִם ***ṣ^{e}bāyim***. See 6380.

6647 צְבַע ***ṣ^{e}ba'*** (Aram.), v. GK: 10607. [Pa] to drench, make wet; [Htpa] to be drenched, made wet:– wet [5]

6648 צֶבַע ***ṣeba'***, n.[m.]. GK: 7389 [→ 6641; cf. 6647]. colorful (dyed) garment:– divers colours [3]

6649 צִבְעוֹן ***ṣib'ôn***, n.pr.m. GK: 7390 [cf. 6641, 6650]. Zibeon, *"hyena"*:– Zibeon [8]

6650 צְבֹעִים ***ṣ^{e}bō'îm***, n.pr.loc. GK: 7391 [cf. 6641, 6649]. Zeboim, *"hyenas"*:– Zeboim [2]

6651 צָבַר ***ṣābar***, v. GK: 7392 [→ 6652]. [Q] to store up, heap up, pile up:– gathered together [1], gathered [1], heap up [1], heaped up [1], heapeth up [1], heap [1], lay up [1]

6652 צִבֻּר ***ṣibbur***, n.m. GK: 7393 [→ 6651]. pile, heap:– heaps [1]

6653 צֶבֶת ***ṣebet***, n.[m.]pl. GK: 7395 [cf. 6642]. bundle (of grain with the stalk):– handfuls [1]

6654 צַד ***ṣad***, n.m. GK: 7396 [→ 6657; cf. 6655]. side (of something):– side [20], sides [9], beside (+4480) [3], another^{s} [1]

6655 צַד ***ṣad*** (Aram.), n.[m.]. GK: 10608 [cf. 6654]. side:– against (+3807.2) [1], concerning (+4481) [1]

6656 צְדָא **ṣ^e^dā'** (Aram.), n.[m.]. GK: 10609. purpose, (with 1886.6) is it true?:– true [1]

6657 צְדָד **ṣādād**, n.pr.loc. GK: 7398 [→ 6654]. Zedad, *"side"*:– Zedad [2]

6658 צָדָה **ṣādâ**, v. GK: 7399 & 7400 [→ 6660]. [Q] to lie in wait, hunt down a person; [N] to be destroyed, be laid waste:– destroyed [1], huntest [1], lie in wait [1]

צֵדָה **ṣēdâ**. See 6720.

6659 צָדוֹק **ṣādôq**, n.pr.m. GK: 7401 [→ 6663]. Zadok, *"righteous one"*:– Zadok [52], Zadok's (+3807.1) [1]

6660 צְדִיָּה **ṣ^e^diyyâ**, n.f. GK: 7402 [→ 6658; cf. 6656]. ambush, lying-in-wait (with malicious intent):– laying of wait [2]

6661 צִדִּים **ṣiddîm**, n.pr.loc. GK: 7403. Ziddim, *"place on the sides or flanks [of the hill]"*:– Ziddim [1]

6662 צַדִּיק **ṣaddîq**, a. GK: 7404 [→ 6663]. righteous, upright, just, innocent; in accordance with a proper (God's) standard, and so implying innocence:– righteous [163], just [42], lawful [1]

צִדֹנִי **ṣidōnî**. See 6722.

6663 צָדַק **ṣādaq**, v.den. GK: 7405 [→ 3087, 3136, 6659, 6662, 6664, 6666, 6667]. [Q] to be righteous, be innocent, be vindicated; in accordance with a proper (God's) standard, and so implying innocence:– justified [12], righteous [10], justify [7], just [3], justifieth [2], justifying [2], cleansed [1], clear [1], do justice [1], justice [1], turn to righteousness [1]

6664 צֶדֶק **ṣedeq**, n.m. GK: 7406 [→ 139, 4442, 6667; cf. 6663]. righteousness, justice, rightness, acting according to a proper (God's) standard, doing what is right, being in the right:– righteousness [78], justice [10], just [10], righteous [8], righteously [3], right [3], altogether just (+6664) [2], even [1], righteous cause [1], righteousness' [1], unrighteousness (+3808) [1]

6665 צִדְקָה **ṣidqâ** (Aram.), n.f. GK: 10610 [cf. 6666]. what is right:– righteousness [1]

6666 צְדָקָה **ṣ^e^dāqâ**, n.f. GK: 7407 [→ 6663; cf. 6665]. righteousness, acting according to a proper (God's) standard, doing what is right, being in the right:– righteousness [124], justice [15], right [9], righteous acts [3], righteousnesses [3], moderately (+3807.1) [1], righteously [1], righteousness' [1]

6667 צִדְקִיָּה **ṣidqiyyâ** or צִדְקִיָּהוּ **ṣidqiyyāhû**, n.pr.m. GK: 7408 & 7409 [→ 6664+3068]. Zedekiah, *"Yahweh is [my] righteousness"*:– Zedekiah [61], Zedekiah's [1], Zidkijah [1]

6668 צָהַב **ṣāhab**, v. GK: 7410 [→ 6669, 6678; cf. 2091]. [Ho] to be polished, gleaming copper color:– fine (+2896) [1]

6669 צָהֹב **ṣāhōb**, a. GK: 7411 [→ 6668]. yellow, blond; some sources: gleaming red:– yellow [3]

6670 צָהַל **ṣāhal**, v. GK: 7412 & 7413 [→ 4684, cf. 6671]. [Q] to shout out, celebrate; to neigh (of a horse); [H] to make shine:– cry aloud [2], bellow [1], cry out [1], lift up [1], make to shine [1], neighed [1], rejoiced [1], shout [1]

6671 צָהַר **ṣāhar**, v.den. GK: 7414 [→ 3323, 3324, 3325, 6672; cf. 6670]. [H] to press olives; some sources: to spend the noontime:– make oil [1]

6672 צֹהַר **ṣōhar**, n.f. and צָהֳרַיִם **ṣoh^o^rayim**, n.[m.]. GK: 7415 [→ 6671]. roof, covering (for the ark of Noah); noon, noonday, midday:– noon [11], noonday [8], midday [1], noon day [1], noondays [1], noontide (+6256) [1], window [1]

6673 צַו **ṣaw**, n.[m.]. GK: 7417 [→ 7723? *or* 6680?]. worthless thing, an idol or utterance (perhaps a nonsense syllable, a mocking sound):– precept [8], commandment [1]

6674 צֹאִי **ṣō'î**, a. GK: 7364. filthy, befouled (with excrement):– filthy [2]

6675 צֹאָה **ṣō'â**, n.f. GK: 7363. filth, excrement, dung; by extension: moral filth:– dung [2], filthiness [2], filth [1]

6676 צַוַּאר **ṣawwa'r** (Aram.), n.m. GK: 10611 [cf. 6677]. neck:– neck [3]

6677 צַוָּאר **ṣawwā'r** or צַוְּרֹנִים **ṣaww^e^rōnîm**, n.m. GK: 7418 & 7454 [cf. 6676]. (back of) neck; necklace:– neck [32], necks [10]

6678 צוֹבָא **ṣôbā'** or צוֹבָה **ṣôbâ**, n.pr.loc. GK: 7419 & 7420 [→ 760, 2578; cf. 6668]. Zobah:– Zobah [10], Zoba [2]

6679 צוּד **ṣûd** or צִיד **ṣîd**, v. GK: 7421 & 7472 [→ 4679, 4685, 4686, 6718, 6719, 6720]. [Q] to hunt, stalk; [Pil] to ensnare; by extension to stalk people for capture or oppression; [Ht] to pack provisions for oneself:– hunt [10], chased sore (+6679) [2], hunt for [1], huntest [1], hunteth [1], taken [1], take [1], took provision [1]

6680 צָוָה **ṣāwâ**, v. GK: 7422 [→ 4687, 6673?]. [P] to command, order, instruct, give direction; [Pu] to be commanded, be directed, be ordered:– commanded [333], command [84], charged [23], commandeth [6], appointed [4], commandedst [4], gave a charge [4], bade [3], gave charge [3], give a charge [3], give charge [3], charge [2], commandest [2], gave commandment [2], given a commandment [2], set in order [2], appoint [1], commander [1], commanding [1], forbad [1], forbidden [1], gave a commandment [1], gave in commandment [1], give in commandment [1], given a charge [1], given commandment [1], given in commandment [1], put in order [1], sent a messenger [1], sent with commandment [1]

6681 צָוַח **ṣāwaḥ**, v. GK: 7423 [→ 6682]. [Q] to shout, cry aloud:– shout [1]

6682 צְוָחָה **ṣ^e^wāḥâ**, n.f. GK: 7424 [→ 6681]. cry of distress, wail:– cry [2], complaining [1], crying [1]

6683 צוּלָה **ṣûlâ**, n.f. GK: 7425 [→ 4688, 4699; cf. 6749]. the watery deep, the ocean abyss:– deep [1]

6684 צוּם **ṣûm**, v. GK: 7426 [→ 6685]. [Q] to fast, to voluntarily abstain from food as dedication to deity, as a sign of mourning, or possibly as a medical treatment:– fasted [11], fast [7], at all fast (+6684) [2], fasted (+6685) [1]

6685 צוֹם **ṣôm**, n.m. GK: 7427 [→ 6684]. fast, time of fasting, act of fasting:– fast [16], fasting [8], fasted (+6684) [1], fastings [1]

6686 צוּעָר **ṣû'ār**, n.pr.m. GK: 7428 [→ 6819]. Zuar, *"little one"*:– Zuar [5]

6687 צוּף **ṣûp**, v. GK: 7429 [→ 6688, 6689, 6824?]. [Q] to flow; [H] to make float; to overwhelm (with water):– flowed [1], made to overflow [1], swim [1]

6688 צוּף **ṣûp**, n.m. GK: 7430 [→ 6687]. honeycomb (dripping with honey):– honeycomb (+1706) [1], honeycomb (+5317) [1]

6689 צוּף **ṣûp** or צוֹפַי **ṣôpay** or צוּפִי **ṣûpî** or צִיף **ṣîp**, n.pr.m. & g. & loc. GK: 7431 & 7433 & 7434 & 7487 [→ 6687, 6688]. Zuph; Zuphite; Zophai; Ziph, *"[dripping, full] honeycomb"*:– Zuph [3], Zophai [1]

6690 צוֹפַח **ṣôpaḥ**, n.pr.m. GK: 7432 [→ 6838]. Zophah, *"bellied jug"*:– Zophah [2]

צוֹפַי **ṣôpay**. See 6689.

6691 צוֹפַר **ṣôpar**, n.pr.m. GK: 7436 [→ 6833?]. Zophar, "[poss.] *peep, twitter [as a bird]"*:– Zophar [4]

6692 צוּץ **ṣûṣ**, v. GK: 7437 & 7438 [→ 6731, 6733, 6734]. [Q] to bud, blossom; [H] to put forth blossoms; to cause to flourish; to peer at, look at:– flourish [3], flourisheth [2], bloomed [1], blossomed [1], blossom [1], shewing [1]

6693 צוּק **ṣûq**, v. GK: 7439 [→ 4165, 4689, 4691, 6695, 6695; cf. 6845]. [H] to oppress, compel, nag, inflict:– distress [5], oppressor [2], constraineth [1], lay sore upon [1], pressed [1], straiten [1]

6694 צוּק **ṣûq**, v. GK: 7440 [→ 3332?]. [Q] to pour out:– poured out [2], molten [1]

6695 צוֹק **ṣôq** or צוּקָה **ṣûqâ**, n.m. & f. GK: 7441 & 7442 [→ 6693]. trouble, distress, oppression:– anguish [3], troublous [1]

6696 צוּר **ṣûr**, v. GK: 7443 & 7444 & 7445 [→ 4692, 4694, 6699, 6736?; cf. 6737, 3334]. [Q] to siege, besiege, enclose; to oppose, harass; to fashion, shape:– besieged [14], besiege [6], distress [2], lay siege [2], adversary [1], assault [1], beset [1], besiege (+5921) [1], bind up [1], bind [1], bound [1], cast [1], distressed [1], fashioned [1], fortify [1], inclose [1], laid siege [1], put up [1]

6697 צוּר **ṣûr**, n.m. GK: 7446 & 7447 [→ 468, 1049, 6301, 6698, 6700, 6701, 6864; cf. 2906]. rock; pebble, flint; stone mass, rocky crag; a title of God, with a focus of stability, and possibly as a place of security and safety:– rock [57], rocks [7], strength [5], sharp [2], God [1], edge [1], mighty God [1], mighty one [1], stones [1], strong [1]

6698 צוּר **ṣûr**, n.pr.m. GK: 7448 [→ 6697]. Zur, *"rock"*:– Zur [5]

צוֹר **ṣôr**. See 6865.

צַוָּר **ṣawwār**. See 6677.

6699 צוּרָה **ṣûrâ**, n.f. GK: 7451 [→ 6696]. design, form:– forms [2], form [2], beauty [1]

צַוָּרֹן **ṣawwārōn**. See 6677.

6700 צוּרִיאֵל **ṣûrî'ēl**, n.pr.m. GK: 7452 [→ 6697+410]. Zuriel, *"God [El] is [my] rock"*:– Zuriel [1]

6701 צוּרִישַׁדַּי **ṣûrîšadday** or צוּרִי־שַׁדַּי **ṣûrî-šadday**, n.pr.m. GK: 7453 [→ 6697+7706]. Zurishaddai, *"Shaddai is [my] rock"*:– Zurishaddai [5]

6702 צוּת **ṣût**, v. GK: 7455 [cf. 3341]. [H] to set on fire:– burn [1]

6703 צַח **ṣaḥ**, a. GK: 7456 [→ 6705]. radiant, shimmering, scorching, clear:– clear [1], dry [1], plainly [1], white [1]

צִחָא **ṣiḥā'**. See 6727.

6704 צִחֶה **ṣiḥeh**, a. GK: 7457 [cf. 6705]. parched:– dried up [1]

6705 צָחַח **ṣāḥaḥ**, v. GK: 7458 [→ 4696?, 4697?, 6703, 6706, 6707, 6710; cf. 6704, 6708]. [Q] to be white:– whiter [1]

6706 צָחִיחַ *ṣāḥîaḥ*, n.[m.]. GK: 7460 [→ 6705; cf. 6708]. bare (rock or place in a wall):– top [4], higher places [1]

6707 צְחִיחָה *ṣᵉḥîḥā*, n.f. GK: 7461 [→ 6705]. bare, (sun-)scorched land:– dry [1]

6708 צְחִיחִי *ṣᵉḥîḥî*, n.[m.]. GK: 7459 [cf. 6705, 6706]. bare (rock or place in a wall):–

6709 צַחֲנָה *ṣaḥᵃnâ*, n.f. GK: 7462. putrid smell, stench:– ill savour [1]

6710 צַחְצָחוֹת *ṣaḥṣāḥôt*, n.[f.pl.]. GK: 7463 [→ 6705]. bare, (sun-)scorched land:– drought [1]

6711 צָחַק *ṣāḥaq*, v. GK: 7464 [→ 3327, 6712; cf. 7832]. [Q] to laugh; [P] to mock, make sport, caress; this can mean to laugh with delight or in scorn:– laughed [3], laugh [3], mock [2], made sport [1], mocked [1], mocking [1], play [1], sporting with [1]

6712 צְחֹק *ṣᵉḥōq*, n.[m.]. GK: 7465 [→ 6711]. laughter, scorn:– laughed to scorn [1], laugh [1]

6713 צַחַר *ṣāḥar*, n. & pr.m. GK: 7466 [→ 6715]. white; as n.pr. Zahar, *"yellowish red, tawny"*:– white [1]

6714 צֹחַר *ṣōḥar*, n.pr.m. GK: 7468 [→ 6715; cf. 3328]. Zohar, *"yellowish red, tawny"*:– Zohar [4]

6715 צָחֹר *ṣāḥōr*, a. GK: 7467 [→ 6713, 6714]. white, yellowish red, tawny:– white [1]

6716 צִי *ṣî*, n.m. GK: 7469. ship:– ships [3], ship [1]

6717 צִיבָא *ṣîbāʼ*, n.pr.m. GK: 7471. Ziba, *"gazelle"*:– Ziba [16]

6718 צַיִד *ṣayid*, n.m. GK: 7473 & 7474 [→ 6679]. food supply, provision; (hunting) game; hunter:– venison [8], hunter [2], provision [2], victuals [2], catcheth [1], food [1], hunter (+376) [1], hunting [1], took in hunting [1]

6719 צַיָּד *ṣayyād*, n.m. GK: 7475 [→ 6679]. hunter:– hunters [1]

6720 צֵידָה *ṣêdâ*, n.f. GK: 7476 [→ 6679]. food, provisions, supplies:– victuals [4], provision [2], victual [2], meat [1]

6721 צִידוֹן *ṣîdôn*, n.pr.loc. GK: 7477 [→ 6722]. Sidon, *"fishery"*:– Zidon [20], Sidon [2]

6722 צִידֹנִי *ṣîdōnî*, a.g. GK: 7479 [→ 6721]. Sidonian, people of Sidon:– Zidonians [10], Sidonians [5], Zidon [1]

6723 צִיָּה *ṣiyyâ*, n.f. GK: 7480 [→ 6728, 6724]. desert, parched land, dry land, waterless region:– dry [9], drought [2], wilderness [2], barren [1], dry land [1], solitary place [1]

6724 צָיוֹן *ṣāyôn*, n.[m.]. GK: 7481 [→ 6723]. desert, waterless country:– dry place [2]

6725 צִיּוּן *ṣiyyûn*, n.m. GK: 7483. sign, stone marker:– sign [1], title [1], waymarks [1]

6726 צִיּוֹן *ṣiyyôn*, n.pr.loc. GK: 7482. Zion, *"citadel"*:– Zion [153], Zion's [1]

6727 צִיחָא *ṣîḥāʼ*, n.pr.m. GK: 7484. Ziha:– Ziha [3]

6728 צִי *ṣî*, n.m. GK: 7470 [→ 6723]. desert creature, referring to known animals or presumed spirits or demons; tribe of the desert:– wild beasts of the desert [3], inhabiting the wilderness [1], that dwell in the wilderness [1], them that dwell in the wilderness [1]

6729 צִינֹק *ṣînōq*, n.[m.]. GK: 7485. neck-iron, iron collar:– stocks [1]

6730 צִיעֹר *ṣîʽōr*, n.pr.loc. GK: 7486 [→ 6819]. Zior, *"small, insignificant"*:– Zior [1]

צִיף *ṣîp*. See 6689.

6731 צִיץ *ṣîṣ*, n.m. GK: 7488 & 7490 [→ 6692, 6733, 6734]. flower, blossom; (ornamental) plate; salt:– flower [6], flowers [4], plate [3], blossoms [1], wings [1]

6732 צִיץ *ṣîṣ*, n.pr.loc. GK: 7489. Ziz, "[poss.] *ascent where the flowers grow*":– Ziz [1]

6733 צִיצָה *ṣîṣâ*, n.f. GK: 7491 [→ 6731; cf. 6692]. flower:– flower [1]

6734 צִיצִת *ṣîṣit*, n.f. GK: 7492 [→ 6731; cf. 6692]. tassel of threads; tuft of hair:– fringe [2], fringes [1], lock [1]

צִיקְלַג *ṣîqᵉlag*. See 6860.

6735 צִיר *ṣîr*, n.[m.]. GK: 7494 & 7495. hinge, (door-)pivot; pains, pangs, anguish; envoy, messenger:– ambassador [3], pangs [3], ambassadors [1], hinges [1], messengers [1], messenger [1], pains [1], sorrows [1]

6736 צִיר *ṣîr*, n.m. GK: 7497 [→ 6696?]. idol:– idols [1]

6737 צִיר *ṣîr*, v.den. GK: 7493 [cf. 6696]. [Ht] to act as a delegation:– made as if ambassadors [1]

6738 צֵל *ṣēl*, n.m. GK: 7498 [→ 1212, 6741, 6752, 6757, 6765; cf. 6751]. shadow, shade, protection:– shadow [45], defence [3], shade [1]

6739 צְלָה *ṣᵉlâ* (Aram.), v. GK: 10612. [Pa] to pray:– prayed [1], pray [1]

6740 צָלָה *ṣālâ*, v. GK: 7499 [→ 6748]. [Q] to roast (meat):– roasted [1], roasteth [1], roast [1]

6741 צִלָּה *ṣillâ*, n.pr.f. GK: 7500 [→ 6738; cf. 4980]. Zillah, *"[God is my] shadow*, i.e., *protection"*:– Zillah [3]

6742 צְלוּל *ṣᵉlûl* or צְלִיל ***ṣᵉlîl***, n.m. GK: 7501 & 7508. cake, round loaf:– cake [1]

6743 צָלַח *ṣālaḥ*, v. GK: 7502 & 7503 [cf. 6744]. [Q] to be powerful, come forcefully; to rush; to prosper, prevail, succeed, avail; [H] to make a success, grant prosperity, make victorious:– prosper [33], prospered [6], came [5], made to prosper [3], came mightily [2], make prosperous [2], prosperous [2], break out [1], cause to prosper [1], come [1], good [1], made prosperous [1], meet [1], profitable [1], prospereth [1], prosperously effected [1], prosperously [1], send prosperity [1], went over [1]

6744 צְלַח *ṣᵉlaḥ* (Aram.), v. GK: 10613 [cf. 6743]. [H] to cause to prosper; to promote; to make progress:– prospered [2], promoted [1], prospereth [1]

6745 צַלַּחַת *ṣallaḥat*, n.[f.]. GK: 7505 [→ 6746, 6747]. dish, pan:– pans [1]

6746 צְלֹחִית *ṣᵉlōḥît*, n.f. GK: 7504 [→ 6745]. (shallow) bowl; some sources: pan, cruse, dish:– cruse [1]

6747 צֵלָחַת *ṣēlaḥat*, n.[f.]. GK: 7506 [→ 6745]. pot for cooking:– bosom [2], dish [1]

6748 צָלִי *ṣālî*, a. GK: 7507 [→ 6740]. roasted (meat):– roast [3]

6749 צָלַל *ṣālal*, v. GK: 7510 [cf. 6683]. [Q] to sink down:– sank [1]

6750 צָלַל *ṣālal*, v. GK: 7509 [→ 4698, 4700, 6767]. [Q] to tingle; to quiver:– tingle [3], quivered [1]

6751 צָלַל *ṣālal*, v. GK: 7511 [→ 1212, 6738, 6741, 6752, 6753, 6757, 6765; cf. 2926; cf. 2927]. [Q] to grow dark; [H] to give shade:– dark [1], shadowing [1]

6752 צֵלֶל *ṣēlel*, n.m. GK: 7498 [→ 6738]. same as 6738: shadow, shade, protection:– shadows [3], shadow [1]

6753 הַצְּלֶלְפּוֹנִי *haṣṣᵉlelpônî*, n.pr.f. GK: 2209 [→ 1886.1+6751+6440+2967.1]. Hazzelelponi:– Hazelelponi [1]

6754 צֶלֶם *ṣelem*, n.m. GK: 7512 & 7513 [→ 6756?; cf. 6755]. image (usually referring to an object of worship), idol; phantom, fantasy, shadowy thing:– images [10], image [6], in a vain shew [1]

6755 צְלֵם *ṣᵉlēm* (Aram.), n.m. GK: 10614 [cf. 6754]. sculptured image, statue; this can refer to a statue, not necessarily worshiped, or to an idol, which is:– image [15], form [1], image's [1]

6756 צַלְמוֹן *ṣalmôn*, n.pr.m. & loc. GK: 7514 & 7515 [→ 6754?]. Zalmon, *"in his image, copy"* or *"black hill"*:– Zalmon [2], Salmon [1]

6757 צַלְמָוֶת *ṣalmāwet*, n.[m.]. GK: 7516 [→ 6738+4191]. shadow, darkness, gloom, blackness:– shadow of death [18]

6758 צַלְמֹנָה *ṣalmōnâ*, n.pr.loc. GK: 7517. Zalmonah, *"dark, gloomy, shaded place"*:– Zalmonah [2]

6759 צַלְמֻנָּע *ṣalmunnāʽ*, n.pr.m. GK: 7518. Zalmunna, *"protection refused"*:– Zalmunna [12]

6760 צָלַע *ṣālaʽ*, v. GK: 7519 [→ 6761]. [Q] to be lame, limp:– halted [2], halteth [2]

6761 צֶלַע *ṣelaʽ*, n.[m.]. GK: 7520 [→ 6760]. stumbling, falling, slipping:– adversity [1], halt [1]

6762 צֵלָע *ṣēlāʽ*, n.pr.loc. GK: 7522 [→ 6763]. Zela, Zelah, *"side, slope"*:– Zelah [2]

6763 צֵלָע *ṣēlāʽ*, n.f. & m. GK: 7521 [→ 6762; cf. 5967]. side:– side [15], side chambers [7], sides [4], boards [2], corners [2], side chamber [2], another[s] [1], beams [1], chambers [1], chamber [1], halting [1], leaves [1], one[s] [1], planks [1], ribs [1], rib [1]

6764 צָלָף *ṣālāp*, n.pr.m. GK: 7523. Zalaph, *"low, prickly shrub [caper plant]"*:– Zalaph [1]

6765 צְלָפְחָד *ṣᵉlopḥād*, n.pr.m. GK: 7524 [→ 6738+6343]. Zelophehad, *"shadow of dread, terror* i.e., *protection from terror or dread"*:– Zelophehad [11]

6766 צֶלְצַח *ṣelṣaḥ*, n.pr.loc. GK: 7525. Zelzah:– Zelzah [1]

6767 צְלָצַל *ṣᵉlāṣal* or צִלְצָל ***ṣilṣāl***, n.m. GK: 7526 & 7527 & 7528 & 7529 [→ 6750]. (swarm of) locust; some sources: cricket; whirring, buzzing; (fishing) spear; cymbals:– cymbals [3], locust [1], shadowing [1], spears [1]

6768 צֶלֶק *ṣeleq*, n.pr.m. GK: 7530. Zelek, *"cry aloud"*:– Zelek [2]

6769 צִלְּתַי *ṣillᵉtay*, n.pr.m. GK: 7531. Zillethai, *"shadow of Yahweh"*:– Zilthai [2]

צֹם *ṣōm*. See 6685.

6770 צָמֵא *ṣāmēʼ*, v. GK: 7532 [→ 6772, 6771, 6773, 6774]. [Q] to thirst, be thirsty:– athirst [2], thirsted [2], thirsteth [2], thirsty [2], suffer thirst [1], thirst [1]

Heb

6771 צָמֵא **ṣāmē'**, a. GK: 7534 [→ 6770]. thirsty, used of humans and animals; used fig. of parched ground:– thirsty [7], thirsteth [1], thirst [1]

6772 צָמָא **ṣāmā'**, n.[m.]. GK: 7533 [→ 6770]. thirst (of humans and animals); used fig. of parched ground:– thirst [16], thirsty [1]

6773 צִמְאָה **ṣim'â**, n.f. GK: 7535 [→ 6770]. thirst:– thirst [1]

6774 צִמָּאוֹן **ṣimmā'ôn**, n.[m.]. GK: 7536 [→ 6770]. thirsty ground:– drought [1], dry ground [1], thirsty land [1]

6775 צָמַד **ṣāmad**, v. GK: 7537 [→ 6776, 6781]. [N] to be joined together; [Pu] to be strapped on; [H] to harness, attach to:– joined [2], fastened [1], frameth [1], joined unto [1]

6776 צֶמֶד **ṣemed**, n.m. GK: 7538 [→ 6775]. yoke, team of two, pair; this can refer to a measurement of land, as the acreage a team of animals can plow:– yoke [6], couple [4], two [2], acres [1], together [1], yoke of oxen [1]

6777 צַמָּה **ṣammâ**, n.f. GK: 7539. veil:– locks [4]

6778 צִמּוּקִים **ṣimmûqîm**, n.m.[pl.]. GK: 7540 [→ 6784]. raisin cakes:– bunches of raisins [2], clusters of raisins [2]

6779 צָמַח **ṣāmaḥ**, v. GK: 7541 [→ 6780]. [Q] to sprout up, spring up; [P] to grow; [H] to cause to grow, bring to fruition:– grown [3], spring forth [3], cause to spring forth [2], grew [2], grow [2], spring up [2], beareth [1], bring forth [1], bringeth forth [1], bud [1], cause to bud forth [1], cause to grow up [1], causeth to grow [1], causeth to spring forth [1], grow up [1], groweth [1], grown up [1], made to grow [1], make to bud [1], make to grow [1], maketh to grow [1], sprang up [1], spring out [1], spring [1], sprung up [1]

6780 צֶמַח **ṣemaḥ**, n.m. GK: 7542 [→ 6779]. growth (which sprouts); (as a messianic title) the Branch:– branch [5], bud [3], grew [1], springing [1], spring [1], that which grew [1]

6781 צָמִיד **ṣāmîd**, n.m. GK: 7543 & 7544 [→ 6775]. bracelet; lid, cover:– bracelets [6], covering [1]

6782 צַמִּים **ṣammîm**, n.m. GK: 7545. snare:– robber [2]

6783 צְמִתֻת **ṣ^e^mitut**, n.f. GK: 7552 [→ 6789]. permanence, finality:– ever [2]

6784 צָמַק **ṣāmaq**, v. GK: 7546 [→ 6778]. [Q] to be dry, shriveled (of breasts):– dry [1]

6785 צֶמֶר **ṣemer**, n.m. GK: 7547 [→ 6787, 6788; cf. 6015]. wool:– wool [11], woollen [5]

6786 צְמָרִי **ṣ^e^mārî**, a.g. GK: 7548. Zemarite:– Zemarite [2]

6787 צְמָרַיִם **ṣ^e^mārayim**, n.pr.loc. GK: 7549 [→ 6785]. Zemaraim, "[poss.] *double peak*":– Zemaraim [2]

6788 צַמֶּרֶת **ṣammeret**, n.f. GK: 7550 [→ 6785]. top (of a tree):– top [3], highest branch [2]

6789 צָמַת **ṣāmat**, v. GK: 7551 [→ 6783]. [Q] to silence; [N] to be silenced; [Pil] to destroy; [P] to wear out; [H] to put to silence, destroy:– cut off [8], destroy [4], consumed [1], destroyed [1], vanish [1]

צְמִתֻת **ṣ^e^mitut**. See 6783.

6790 צִן **ṣin**, n.pr.loc. GK: 7554. Zin:– Zin [10]

6791 צֵן **ṣēn**, n.[m.]. GK: 7553 [→ 6793, 6796]. thorn; hook:– thorns [2]

6792 צֹנֶא **ṣōnā'** or צֹנֶה **ṣōneh**, [n.m.]. GK: 7555 & 7556 [→ 6629; cf. 3318]. flocks (of sheep and goats):– sheep [2]

6793 צִנָּה **ṣinnâ**, n.f. GK: 7557 & 7558 & 7559 [→ 6791]. coolness; (large) shield; hook:– shield [9], buckler [3], targets [3], bucklers [2], target [2], cold [1], hooks [1], shields [1]

6794 צִנּוֹר **ṣinnôr**, n.m. GK: 7562 [→ 6804]. water shaft; waterfall:– gutter [1], waterspouts [1]

6795 צָנַח **ṣānaḥ**, v. GK: 7563. [Q] to get down; to go down:– fastened [1], lighted off (+4480+5921) [1], lighted [1]

6796 צְנִינִים **ṣ^e^nînîm**, n.[m.pl.]. GK: 7564 [→ 6791]. thorns:– thorns [2]

6797 צָנוֹף **ṣānûp** or צָנִיף **ṣānîp** or צְנִיפָה **ṣ^e^nîpâ**, n.m. GK: 7561 & 7565 & 7566 [→ 6801]. turban, an ornamental head wrap:– diadem [2], mitre [2], hoods [1]

6798 צָנַם **ṣānam**, v. GK: 7567 & 7568. [Q] to dry up, harden, wither:– withered [1]

6799 צְנָן **ṣ^e^nān**, n.pr.loc. GK: 7569 [cf. 6630?]. Zenan, "*place of flocks*":– Zenan [1]

צְנָן **ṣānin**. See 6796.

6800 צָנַע **ṣāna'**, v. GK: 7570 & 7560 [→ 5204]. [H] to show a humble (walk with God), as an extension of acting in a cautious manner:– humbly [1], lowly [1]

6801 צָנַף **ṣānap**, v. GK: 7571 [→ 4701, 6797, 6802]. [Q] to wrap around, wind around:– surely violently turn and toss (+6801+6802) [2], attired [1]

6802 צְנֵפָה **ṣ^e^nēpâ**, n.f. GK: 7572 [→ 6801]. winding, wrapping:– surely violently turn and toss (+6801+6801) [1]

6803 צִנְצֶנֶת **ṣinṣenet**, n.f. GK: 7573. vessel, receptacle, likely referring to a jar:– pot [1]

6804 צַנְתָּרוֹת **ṣantārôt**, n.m.pl. GK: 7574 [→ 6794]. pipes:– pipes [1]

6805 צָעַד **ṣā'ad**, v. GK: 7575 [→ 685, 4703, 6806, 6807]. [Q] to step, march; [H] to make march:– bring [1], gone paces (+6806) [1], go [1], march through [1], marchedst [1], march [1], run [1], went [1]

6806 צַעַד **ṣa'ad**, n.m. GK: 7576 [→ 6805]. step, stride:– steps [11], goings [1], gone paces (+6805) [1], go [1]

6807 צְעָדָה **ṣ^e^'ādâ**, n.f. GK: 7577 & 7578 [→ 6805]. marching; ankle chains:– going [2], ornaments of the legs [1]

6808 צָעָה **ṣā'â**, v. GK: 7579. [Q] to lay down, stoop, incline; [P] to tip, pour out:– captive exile [1], cause to wander [1], travelling [1], wanderers [1], wanderest [1]

צָעוֹר **ṣā'ôr**. See 6810.

6809 צָעִיף **ṣā'îp**, n.[m.]. GK: 7581. veil:– vail [3]

6810 צָעִיר **ṣā'îr**, a. GK: 7582 [→ 6819; cf. 6812]. younger, small, little, lowly:– younger [7], least [4], youngest [3], little ones [2], little [2], small one [1], small [1], young (+3117+3807.1) [1], younger (+3117) [1]

6811 צָעִיר **ṣā'îr**, n.pr.loc. GK: 7583. Zair, "*small, insignificant,* hence *narrow pass*":– Zair [1]

6812 צְעִירָה **ṣ^e^'îrâ**, n.f. GK: 7584 [cf. 6810]. youth, youngest (offspring):– youth [1]

6813 צָעַן **ṣā'an**, v. GK: 7585. [Q] to pack up, move (a tent):– taken down [1]

6814 צֹעַן **ṣō'an**, n.pr.loc. GK: 7586. Zoan:– Zoan [7]

6815 צַעֲנַנִּים **ṣa^a^nannîm**, n.pr.loc. GK: 7588. Zaanannim:– Zaanaim [1], Zaanannim [1]

6816 צַעֲצֻעִים **ṣa^a^ṣu'îm**, n.[m.]pl. GK: 7589. sculptured work (by metal casting):– image [1]

6817 צָעַק **ṣā'aq**, v. GK: 7590 [→ 6818; cf. 2199; cf. 2200]. [Q] to cry; [N] to be called out, be summoned; [P] to keep crying; [H] to call together, summon:– cried [27], cry [13], gathered together [3], called together [2], cried out [2], crieth [2], cry at all (+6817) [2], criest [1], cry out [1], gathered themselves together [1], gathered [1]

6818 צְעָקָה **ṣ^e^'āqâ**, n.f. GK: 7591 [→ 6817]. cry of distress, outcry, wailing:– cry [19], crying [2]

6819 צָעַר **ṣā'ar**, v. GK: 7592 [→ 4704, 4705, 4706, 6686, 6730, 6810, 6820; cf. 2191]. [Q] to be trivial, insignificant, little:– brought low [1], little ones [1], small [1]

6820 צֹעַר **ṣō'ar**, n.pr.loc. GK: 7593 [→ 6819]. Zoar, "*small, insignificant*":– Zoar [10]

6821 צָפַד **ṣāpad**, v. GK: 7594. [Q] to shrivel:– cleaveth [1]

6822 צָפָה **ṣāpâ**, v. GK: 7595 [→ 4707, 4708, 4709, 6828, 6829, 6830, 6836, 6837?]. [Q] to keep watch, be a lookout; [Qp] to be spied out; [P] to watch, lookout:– watchman [14], watchmen [5], watch [4], beholding [1], behold [1], espy [1], kept watch [1], look up [1], looketh well [1], looketh [1], look [1], waited [1], watched [1], watcheth [1], watching [1], watchman's [1]

6823 צָפָה **ṣāpâ**, v. GK: 7596 [→ 6826, 6844, 6858, 6857?]. [Q] to arrange; [P] to overlay, cover, adorn; [Pu] to be overlaid, be coated:– overlaid [28], overlay [12], covered [5], garnished [1]

6824 צָפָה **ṣāpâ**, n.f. GK: 7597 [→ 6687?]. out-flow, discharge:– swimmest [1]

6825 צְפוֹ **ṣ^e^pô** or צְפִי **ṣ^e^pî**, n.pr.m. GK: 7598 & 7609. Zepho, Zephi, "[poss.] *gaze*":– Zepho [2], Zephi [1]

6826 צִפּוּי **ṣippûy**, n.[m.]. GK: 7599 [→ 6823]. overlaying, (metal) plating:– covering [3], overlaying [2]

6827 צְפוֹן **ṣ^e^pôn**, n.pr.m. GK: 7602 [→ 6831; cf. 6837]. Zephon, "[poss.] *gaze;* [poss.] *look out [tower], watch*":– Zephon [1]

6828 צָפוֹן **ṣāpôn**, n.f. GK: 7600 [→ 1189, 6829, 6830; cf. 6822]. north, northern:– north [105], northward (+1886.5) [20], north side [10], north (+1886.5) [9], northward (+4480) [2], in north (+1886.5) [1], north side (+1886.5) [1], north side (+4480) [1], north wind [1], northern (+4480) [1], northwards (+1886.5) [1], northward [1]

6829 צָפוֹן **ṣāpôn**, n.pr.loc. GK: 7601 [→ 6828; cf. 6822]. Zaphon, "[poss.] *North* or *[proper name of a god], Zephon*":– Zaphon [1]

6830 צְפוֹנִי **ṣ^e^pônî**, a. GK: 7603 [→ 6828; cf. 6822]. northern; (n.) northerner:– northern [1]

6831 צְפוֹנִי **ṣ^e^pônî** or צִפְיוֹנִי **ṣipyônî**, a.g. GK: 7604 & 7612 [→ 6827, 6837]. Zephonite, "*of Zephon*":– Zephonites [1]

6832 צָפוּעַ **ṣāpûa'** or צְפִיעַ **ṣāpîa'**, n.[m.]. GK: 7605 & 7616. manure, dung:– dung [1]

Heb

6833 צִפּוֹר ***ṣippôr***, n.f. & m. GK: 7606 [→ 6691?, 6834, 6855]. bird (individual and collective):– bird [21], birds [10], fowl [5], sparrow [2], bird's [1], fowls [1]

6834 צִפּוֹר ***ṣippôr***, n.pr.m. GK: 7607 [→ 6833; cf. 6853]. Zippor, "*bird, swallow*":– Zippor [7]

6835 צַפַּחַת ***ṣappaḥat***, n.f. GK: 7608 [→ 6838]. jug, jar (for liquid), a portable convex or spherical shape, with a lid or plug for transport:– cruse [7]

6836 צִפִּיָּה ***ṣippiyyâ***, n.f. GK: 7610 [→ 6822]. watchtower, lookout:– watching [1]

6837 צִפְיוֹן ***ṣipyôn***, n.pr.m. GK: 7611 [→ 6831; cf. 6822?, 6827]. Ziphion, cf. 6829:– Ziphion [1]

6838 צַפִּיחִת ***ṣappîḥit***, n.f. GK: 7613 [→ 6690, 6835]. wafer, flat-cake:– wafers [1]

6839 צֹפִים ***ṣōpîm***, n.pr.[loc.?]. GK: 7614. Zophim:– Zophim [1]

6840 צָפִין ***ṣāpîn***, n.[m.]. GK: 7615 [→ 6845]. hidden thing:–

6841 צְפִיר ***ṣᵉpîr*** (Aram.), n.m. GK: 10615 [cf. 6842]. male goat:– he goats (+5796) [1]

6842 צָפִיר ***ṣāpîr***, n.m. GK: 7618 [cf. 6841]. (male) goat:– goat [2], he goat (+5795) [2], he goats (+5795) [1], he goats [1]

6843 צְפִירָה ***ṣᵉpîrâ***, n.f. GK: 7619. crown, wreath; doom:– morning [2], diadem [1]

6844 צָפִית ***ṣāpît***, n.f. GK: 7620 [→ 6823]. rug, carpet:– watchtower [1]

6845 צָפַן ***ṣāpan***, v. GK: 7621 & 7636 [→ 4710, 6840; cf. 6693 (also used with compound proper names)]. [Q] to hide, conceal, store up; [Qp] to be treasured, be cherished; [N] to be stored up, be concealed; [H] to hide:– hid [8], hide [5], laid up [3], hidden [2], hideth [2], lay up [2], layeth up [2], lurk privily [2], esteemed [1], hidden ones [1], keep secretly [1], privily set [1], secret places [1], secret [1]

צָפֹן ***ṣāpōn***. See 6828.

6846 צְפַנְיָה ***ṣᵉpanyâ*** or צְפַנְיָהוּ ***ṣᵉpanyāhû***, n.pr.m. GK: 7622 & 7623 [→ 6845+3068]. Zephaniah, "*Yahweh has hidden [to shelter] or Yahweh has hidden [as a treasure]*":– Zephaniah [10]

6847 צָפְנַת פַּעְנֵחַ ***ṣāpᵉnat paʿnēaḥ***, n.pr.m. GK: 7624. Zaphenath-Paneah, "*the [pagan] god speaks and he [the newborn] lives*":– Zaphnath-paaneah [1]

6848 צֶפַע ***ṣepaʿ*** or צִפְעֹנִי ***ṣipʿōnî***, n.m. GK: 7625 & 7626. viper, serpent:– cockatrice' [2], adder [1], cockatrices [1], cockatrice [1]

6849 צְפִיעָה ***ṣᵉpîʿâ***, n.f. GK: 7617. offshoots, leaf:– issue [1]

צִפְעֹנִי ***ṣipʿōnî***. See 6848.

6850 צָפַף ***ṣāpap***, v. GK: 7627 [→ 6851]. [Pil] to chirp; to whisper:– chatter [1], peeped [1], peep [1], whisper [1]

6851 צַפְצָפָה ***ṣapṣāpâ***, n.f. GK: 7628 [→ 6850]. willow:– willow tree [1]

6852 צָפַר ***ṣāpar***, v. GK: 7629. [Q] to leave, depart:– depart early [1]

6853 צִפַּר ***ṣippar*** (Aram.), n.f. GK: 10616 [cf. 6834]. bird:– fowls [3], birds' [1]

צִפֹּר ***ṣippōr***. See 6833.

6854 צְפַרְדֵּעַ ***ṣᵉpardēaʿ***, n.f. GK: 7630. frogs:– frogs [13]

6855 צִפֹּרָה ***ṣippōrâ***, n.pr.f. GK: 7631 [→ 6833]. Zipporah, "*bird, swallow*":– Zipporah [3]

6856 צִפֹּרֶן ***ṣippōren***, n.[m.]. GK: 7632 [cf. 2953]. nail (of finger or toe); (flint or hard stone) point (of a stylus):– nails [1], point [1]

6857 צְפַת ***ṣᵉpat***, n.pr.loc. GK: 7634 [→ 6823?]. Zephath, "*watcher*":– Zephath [1]

6858 צֶפֶת ***ṣepet***, n.f. GK: 7633 [→ 6823]. capital (of a pillar):– chapiter [1]

6859 צְפָתָה ***ṣᵉpatâ***, n.pr.loc. GK: 7635. Zephathah, "*watchtower*":– Zephathah [1]

צִץ ***ṣiṣ***. See 6732.

6860 צִקְלַג ***ṣiqlag***, n.pr.loc. GK: 7637. Ziklag:– Ziklag [15]

6861 צִקְלוֹן ***ṣiqqālôn*** or בִּצְקָלוֹן ***biṣqālôn***, n.[m.]. GK: 7638 & 1303. head of grain; garment, bag:– husk [1]

6862 צַר ***ṣar***, a. & n.m. GK: 7639 & 7640 & 7641 [→ 3334, 6864, 6887; cf. 6146]. (n.) trouble, distress, anguish; (a.) narrow; enemy, foe, adversary, opponent; flint, known for its hardness:– enemies [26], adversaries [21], trouble [17], enemy [10], adversary [5], distress [4], affliction [3], strait [3], enemy's [2], foes [2], narrow [2], adversary (+376) [1], adversity [1], afflicted [1], anguish [1], close [1], distresses [1], small [1], sorrow [1], tribulation [1]

6863 צֵר ***ṣēr***, n.pr.loc. GK: 7643. Zer:– Zer [1]

6864 צֹר ***ṣōr***, n.[m.]. GK: 7644 [→ 6697, 6862, 6865, 6872, 6876]. flint knife:– flint [2], sharp stone [1]

6865 צֹר ***ṣōr*** or צוֹר ***ṣôr***, n.pr.loc. GK: 7645 & 7450 [→ 6876; cf. 6864]. Tyre, "*rocky place*":– Tyrus [22], Tyre [20]

צֻר ***ṣur***. See 6697.

6866 צָרַב ***ṣārab***, v. GK: 7646 [→ 6867]. [N] to be scorched:– burnt [1]

6867 צָרָב ***ṣārāb*** or צָרֶבֶת ***ṣārebet***, a. & n.f. GK: 7647 & 7648 [→ 6866]. scorching; scar:– burning [2], inflammation [1]

6868 צְרֵדָה ***ṣᵉrēdâ***, n.pr.loc. GK: 7649. Zeredah:– Zeredathah [1], Zereda [1]

6869 צָרָה ***ṣārâ***, n.f. GK: 7650 & 7651 [→ 6862, 6887; cf. 3334]. trouble, distress, calamity, anguish; rival-wife:– trouble [34], troubles [10], distress [8], affliction [7], anguish [5], adversity [4], tribulation [2], adversary [1], adversities [1], tribulations [1]

6870 צְרוּיָה ***ṣᵉrûyâ***, n.pr.f. GK: 7653. Zeruiah, "*perfumed resin*":– Zeruiah [26]

6871 צְרוּעָה ***ṣᵉrûʿâ***, n.pr.f. GK: 7654 [→ 6879]. Zeruah, "*one with skin disease*":– Zeruah [1]

6872 צְרוֹר ***ṣᵉrôr***, n.m. & pr. GK: 7655 & 7656 & 7657 [cf. 3334, 6864]. pouch, purse, sachet, bag; pebble; as n.pr. Zeror, "*money bag, pouch,* [or poss.] *pebbles*":– bag [3], bundle [3], Zeror [1], bindeth [1], bundles [1], least grain [1], small stone [1]

6873 צָרַח ***ṣāraḥ***, v. GK: 7658. [Q] to shout, cry out; [H] to raise the battle cry:– cry [1], roar [1]

6874 צְרִי ***ṣᵉrî***, n.pr.m. GK: 7662 [→ 6875]. Zeri, "*balsam*":– Zeri [1]

6875 צֳרִי ***ṣᵒrî***, n.[m.]. GK: 7661 [→ 6874]. balm, mastic (resin), usually obtained from processing from the bark of a tree:– balm [6]

6876 צֹרִי ***ṣōrî***, a.g. GK: 7660 [→ 6865]. Tyrian, of Tyre:– Tyre [2], of Tyre [2], men of Tyre [1]

6877 צְרִיחַ ***ṣᵉrîaḥ***, n.[m.]. GK: 7663. pit, (underground) stronghold, likely referring to a man-made pit:– hold [3], high places [1]

6878 צֹרֶךְ ***ṣōrek***, n.[m.]. GK: 7664. need:– need [1]

6879 צָרַע ***ṣāraʿ***, v.den. GK: 7665 [→ 6871, 6879?, 6883]. [Qp, Pu] to be leprous, afflicted with an infectious skin disease:– leper [13], leprous [6], lepers [1]

6880 צִרְעָה ***ṣirʿâ***, n.f.col. GK: 7667 [→ 6879?]. hornets or discouragement:– hornet [2], hornets [1]

6881 צָרְעָה ***ṣorʿâ***, n.pr.loc. GK: 7666 [→ 6882]. Zorah:– Zorah [8], Zareah [1], Zoreah [1]

6882 צָרְעִי ***ṣorʿî*** or צָרְעָתִי ***ṣārᵉʿātî***, a.g. GK: 7668 & 7670 [→ 6881]. Zorite; Zorathite, "*of Zorah*":– Zareathites [1], Zorathites [1], Zorites [1]

6883 צָרַעַת ***ṣāraʿat***, n.f. GK: 7669 [→ 6879]. infectious skin disease; (of clothing) mildew:– leprosy [35]

6884 צָרַף ***ṣārap***, v. GK: 7671 [→ 4715, 6885]. [Q] to smelt, refine (metals); (n.) (gold- or silver-)smith:– tried [8], founder [5], goldsmith [3], try [3], goldsmiths [2], pure [2], refined [2], casteth [1], finer [1], melteth [1], melt [1], purge away [1], refiner's [1], refiner [1], refine [1]

6885 צֹרְפִי ***ṣōrᵉpî***, n.[m.]col. GK: 7672 [→ 6884]. (member of the) goldsmiths:– goldsmith's [1]

6886 צָרְפַת ***ṣārᵉpat***, n.pr.loc. GK: 7673. Zarephath, "[poss.] *smelting place; place of pigmenting, staining*":– Zarephath [3]

6887 צָרַר ***ṣārar***, v. GK: 7674 & 7675 & 7677 [→ 3334, 6862, 6869]. [Q] to be a rival-wife; to be an enemy, adversary; to bind up, wrap up, tie up; to hamper, oppress, be in distress; [Qp] be bound, be confined; [Pu] to be mended; [H] to bring trouble, distress, oppress:– enemies [9], enemy [5], vex [5], besiege [4], bound up [4], adversaries [3], distress [3], afflicted [2], afflict [2], bound [2], distressed [2], in a strait [2], in pangs [2], affliction [1], bind up [1], bindeth up [1], bring distress [1], in distress [1], in trouble [1], narrower [1], oppresseth [1], shut up [1], strait [1], trouble [1], vexed [1]

6888 צְרֵרָה ***ṣᵉrērâ***, n.p.loc. GK: 7678. Zererah:– Zererath [1]

6889 צֶרֶת ***ṣeret***, n.pr.m. GK: 7679 [→ 6890]. Zereth, "*splendor*":– Zereth [1]

6890 צֶרֶת הַשַּׁחַר ***ṣeret haššaḥar***, n.pr.loc. GK: 7680 [→ 6889]. Zereth Shahar, "*glory of dawn*":– Zareth-shahar [1]

6891 צָרְתָן ***ṣārᵉtān***, n.pr.loc. GK: 7681. Zarethan:– Zaretan [1], Zartanah [1], Zarthan [1]

6892 קֵא ***qēʾ*** or קִיא ***qîʾ***, n.m. GK: 7683 & 7795 [→ 6958]. vomit:– vomit [4]

6893 קָאַת ***qāʾat***, n.[f.]. GK: 7684. desert owl:– pelican [3], cormorant [2]

6894 קַב ***qab***, n.[m.]. GK: 7685 [→ 6898]. cab (dry measure, one-eighteenth of an ephah, about one quart or liter):– kab [1]

6895 קָבַב ***qābab***, v. GK: 7686 [cf. 5344]. [Q] to curse:– curse [6], cursed [1]

6896 קֵבָה ***qēbâ***, n.f. GK: 7687 [→ 6897]. same as 6897: maw (4th stomach of cud-chewing animals); (of humans) belly, stomach area:– maw [1]

6897 קֹבָה ***qōbâ***, n.f. GK: 7687 [→ 6896]. same as 6896: maw (4th stomach of cud-chewing animals); (of humans) belly, stomach area:– belly [1]

6898 קֻבָּה ***qubbâ***, n.f. GK: 7688 [→ 6894]. woman's section (of a tent):– tent [1]

6899 קִבּוּץ ***qibbûṣ***, n.m. GK: 7689 [→ 6908]. collection (of idols):– companies [1]

6900 קְבוּרָה ***qᵉbûrâ***, n.f. GK: 7690 [→ 5354, 6912, 6962]. tomb, grave, burial:– sepulchre [5], burial [4], grave [4], buryingplace [1]

6901 קָבַל ***qābal***, v. GK: 7691 [→ 6904; cf. 6902]. [P] to receive, take; [H] to match, correspond:– received [3], receive [3], took [3], choose [1], held [1], take hold [1], undertook [1]

6902 קְבַל ***qᵉbal*** (Aram.), v.den. GK: 10618 [→ 6903; cf. 6901]. [Pa] to receive; to take over:– receive [1], take [1], took [1]

6903 קֳבֵל ***qᵒbēl*** (Aram.), subst. & pp. & c. GK: 10619 [→ 6902]. before, in front of; since, because of:– forasmuch as (+1768+3606) [8], because (+1768+3606) [4], before (+3807.2) [3], therefore (+1836+3606) [3], wherefore (+1836+3606) [2], according to (+3807.2) [1], against [1], as (+1768+3606) [1], for this cause (+1836+3606) [1], means [1], reason [1], that (+1836+3606) [1], therefore (+1768+3606) [1], though (+1768+3606) [1]

6904 קְבֹל ***qᵒbōl***, n.[m.]. GK: 7692 [→ 6901, 6905]. prob. same as 6905: (something) in front of, battering ram:– war [1]

6905 קְבֹל ***qᵒbōl***, n.[m.]. GK: 7692 [→ 6904]. prob. same as 6904: (something) in front of, battering ram:– before [1]

6906 קָבַע ***qāba'***, v. GK: 7693 [cf. 6117, 6120]. [Q] to rob, plunder:– robbed [3], rob [1], spoiled [1], spoil [1]

6907 קֻבַּעַת ***qubba'at***, n.f. GK: 7694. cup, goblet:– dregs [2]

6908 קָבַץ ***qābaṣ***, v. GK: 7695 [→ 6899, 6910, 6911 (also used with compound proper names)]. [Q] to collect, gather, assemble; [Qp] to be assembled; [N] to be gathered, be assembled, be joined; [P] to gather, assemble; [Pu] to be gathered; [Ht] to gather (themselves) together:– gather [43], gathered together [33], gathered [22], gather together [10], assemble [5], gathereth [4], gather up [2], surely gather (+6908) [2], assembled [1], brought together [1], gathered up [1], heapeth [1], resort [1], taketh up [1]

6909 קַבְצְאֵל ***qabṣᵉ'ēl***, n.pr.loc. GK: 7696 [→ 6908+410]. Kabzeel, "*God [El] collects*":– Kabzeel [3]

6910 קְבֻצָה ***qᵉbuṣâ***, n.f. GK: 7697 [→ 6908]. gathering:– gather [1]

6911 קִבְצַיִם ***qibṣayim***, n.pr.loc. GK: 7698 [→ 6908]. Kibzaim:– Kibzaim [1]

6912 קָבַר ***qābar***, v. GK: 7699 [→ 6900, 6913, 6914]. [Q] to store up, pile up, heap up:– buried [96], bury [32], burying [2], in any wise bury (+6912) [2], buriers [1]

6913 קֶבֶר ***qeber***, n.m. GK: 7700 [→ 6914]. burial site, tomb, grave:– grave [19], graves [16], sepulchre [14], sepulchres [12], buryingplace [6]

קְבֻרָה ***qᵉburâ***. See 6900.

6914 קִבְרוֹת הַתַּאֲוָה ***qibrôt hattaᵃwâ***, n.pr.loc. GK: 7701 [→ 6913]. Kibroth Hattaavah, "*graves of lust, greed*":– Kibroth-hattaavah [5]

6915 קָדַד ***qādad***, v. GK: 7702 [→ 6936?]. [Q] to bow low, bow down:– bowed down head [3], bowed heads [3], bowed down heads [2], bowed head [2], bowed [2], stooped [2], bowed the head [1]

6916 קִדָּה ***qiddâ***, n.f. GK: 7703. cassia (a spice):– cassia [2]

6917 קְדוּמִים ***qᵉdûmîm***, n.[m.pl.]. GK: 7704 [→ 6923]. age-old, ancient:– ancient [1]

6918 קָדוֹשׁ ***qādôš***, a. GK: 7705 [→ 6942; cf. 6922]. holy, sacred, consecrated, set apart as dedicated to God; by extension: pure, innocent, free from impurity; (n.) holy people of God, saints; as a title of God, "the Holy One" focuses on God as unique, wholly other:– holy [63], holy one [41], saints [9], saint [3]

6919 קָדַח ***qādaḥ***, v. GK: 7706 [→ 688, 6920]. [Q] to kindle, light (a fire):– kindled [3], burneth [1], kindle [1]

6920 קַדַּחַת ***qaddaḥat***, n.f. GK: 7707 [→ 6919]. fever, inflammation:– burning ague [1], fever [1]

6921 קָדִים ***qādîm***, n.m. GK: 7708 [→ 6923]. east, eastern, the direction of orientation in the ancient Near East (facing the sunrise); east is also the direction of the great desert, thus an east or desert wind is particularly hot:– east [36], east (+1886.5) [14], east wind [10], eastward (+1886.5) [4], eastward [3], east side [1], eastward (+1870+1886.1) [1]

6922 קַדִּישׁ ***qaddîš*** (Aram.), a. GK: 10620 [cf. 6918]. holy, ceremonial or moral purity; (as noun) holy one, saint, which can refer to human beings or angels:– saints [6], holy [4], holy one [2], holy ones [1]

6923 קָדַם ***qādam***, v.den. GK: 7709 [→ 6917, 6921, 6924, 6927, 6926, 6929, 6930, 6932, 6934, 6931, 6935; cf. 6925, cf. 6933]. [P] to be in front of, meet, confront:– prevented [8], prevent [6], come before [5], met [2], before [1], disappoint (+6440) [1], go before [1], preventest [1], went before [1]

6924 קֶדֶם ***qedem*** or קֵדְמָה ***qēdᵉmâ***, n.[m.]. GK: 7710 & 7711 & 7714 [→ 6923]. (as a direction) east, eastern; the direction of orientation in the ancient Near East (facing the sunrise); (used of time) ancient, eternal, long ago, possibly relating to east as the direction of origin (as the sunrise):– east [27], eastward (+1886.5) [9], old [9], of old [8], ancient [6], east (+1886.5) [5], east side [5], before [2], aforetime [1], ancient times [1], ancient time [1], before (+4480) [1], east (+4217+1886.5) [1], east country [1], east end [1], east parts [1], east part [1], eastward (+4480) [1], eastward [1], eternal [1], everlasting [1], forward [1], or ever was (+4480) [1], past [1]

6925 קֳדָם ***qᵒdām*** (Aram.), pp. GK: 10621 [→ 6928, 6933; cf. 6924]. before, in the presence of:– before [29], before (+4481) [4], of (+4481) [3], from (+4481) [1], in the presence [1], then (+116+4481+871.2) [1], thought [1]

קָדִם ***qādim***. See 6921.

6926 קִדְמָה ***qidmâ***, n.f. GK: 7713 [→ 6923]. east:– east [2], eastward [1], toward east [1]

6927 קַדְמָה ***qadmâ***, n.f. GK: 7712 [→ 6923; cf. 6928]. past, antiquity; ancient (city):– former estate [3], afore [1], antiquity [1], old estates [1]

6928 קַדְמָה ***qadmâ*** (Aram.), n.f. GK: 10622 [→ 6925; cf. 6927]. before times; (as adv.) formerly:– aforetime (+1836+4481) [1], ago (+4481) [1]

קֵדְמָה ***qēdmâ***. See 6924.

6929 קֵדְמָה ***qēdᵉmâ***, n.pr.m. GK: 7715 [→ 6923]. Kedemah, "*east*":– Kedemah [2]

6930 קַדְמוֹן ***qadmôn***, a. GK: 7716 [→ 6931, 6935; cf. 6923]. eastern:– east [1]

6931 קַדְמֹנִי ***qadmōnî***, a. GK: 7719 [→ 6930; cf. 6923]. (of a direction) eastern; (of time) old, former, past:– east [4], former [2], ancients [1], of old [1], old [1], they that went before [1]

6932 קְדֵמוֹת ***qᵉdēmôt***, n.pr.loc. GK: 7717 [→ 6923]. Kedemoth, "*east*":– Kedemoth [4]

6933 קַדְמָי ***qadmāy*** (Aram.), a. GK: 10623 [→ 6925; cf. 6924]. first; earlier, former:– first [3]

6934 קַדְמִיאֵל ***qadmî'ēl***, n.pr.m. GK: 7718 [→ 6923+410]. Kadmiel, "*[stand] before God [El]*":– Kadmiel [8]

קַדְמֹנִי ***qadmōnî***. See 6931.

6935 קַדְמֹנִי ***qadmōnî***, a.g. GK: 7720 [→ 6930; cf. 6923]. Kadmonite:– Kadmonites [1]

6936 קָדְקֹד ***qodqōd***, n.[m.]. GK: 7721 [→ 6915?]. top or crown of the head:– crown of the head [4], crown of head [2], crown [1], pate [1], scalp [1], top of head [1], top of the head [1]

6937 קָדַר ***qādar***, v. GK: 7722 [→ 6938, 6939, 6940, 6941]. [Q] to grow dark, be black; to mourn, wail, grieve; [H] to make dark, bring gloom; [Ht] to grow dark:– black [4], mourning [4], dark [2], make dark [2], blackish [1], caused to mourn [1], darkened [1], heavily [1], mourn [1]

6938 קֵדָר ***qēdār***, n.pr.g. GK: 7723 [→ 6937]. Kedar, "*mighty*":– Kedar [12]

6939 קִדְרוֹן ***qidrôn***, n.pr.loc. GK: 7724 [→ 6937]. Kidron:– Kidron [11]

6940 קַדְרוּת ***qadrût***, n.f. GK: 7725 [→ 6937]. darkness, blackness:– blackness [1]

6941 קְדֹרַנִּית ***qᵉdōrannît***, adv. GK: 7726 [→ 6937]. in mourner's attire, in an unkempt manner:– mournfully [1]

6942 קָדַשׁ ***qādaš***, v.den. GK: 7727 [→ 4720, 6918, 6943, 6944, 6945, 6946, 6947, 6948]. [Q] to be holy, sacred, consecrated; [N] to show oneself holy, be consecrated; [P] to consecrate, make holy; [Pu] to be dedicated, consecrated; [Ht] to consecrate oneself; [H] to set apart, consecrate, dedicate, regard as holy; to set apart as dedicated to God; by extension: pure, innocent, free from impurity:– sanctify [64], sanctified [45], hallow [15], hallowed [10], prepare [7], dedicated [5], holy [5], dedicate [4], consecrated [3], consecrate [2], wholly dedicated (+6942) [2], appointed [1], bid [1], defiled [1], holier [1], holy kept [1], holy places [1], keep holy [1], proclaim [1], purified [1], sanctified ones [1]

6943 קֶדֶשׁ ***qedeš***, n.pr.loc. GK: 7730 [→ 6942]. Kedesh, "*sacred place*":– Kedesh [11], Kedesh-naphtali (+5321) [1]

6944 קֹדֶשׁ ***qōdeš***, n.m. GK: 7731 [→ 6942]. holy or sacred thing, holy or sacred place, sanctuary; holiness, set apart as dedicated to God; the "holy of holies" is the most holy place, set apart exclusively for the Presence of God, with very limited high priestly access:– holy [256], most holy (+6944) [88], sanctuary [68], holiness [30], hallowed [9], dedicated [7], dedicate [5], consecrated [2], thing most holy (+6944) [2], holy dwelling [1], saints [1]

6945 קָדֵשׁ ***qādēš***, n.m. GK: 7728 [→ 6942, 6948]. (male or female) shrine prostitute:– sodomites [4], unclean [1], whore [1]

6946 קָדֵשׁ ***qādēš***, n.pr.loc. GK: 7729 [→ 4809+6946; cf. 6942]. Kadesh, "*sacred place*":– Kadesh [17]

קָדוֹשׁ ***qādôš***. See 6918.

6947 קָדֵשׁ בַּרְנֵעַ ***qādēš barnēaʿ***, n.pr.loc. GK: 7732 [→ 6942]. Kadesh Barnea, "*sacred place of Barnea*":– Kadesh-barnea [10]

6948 קְדֵשָׁה ***qᵉdēšâ***, n.m. GK: 7728 [→ 6945]. f. of 6945: female shrine prostitute:– harlot [3], harlots [1], sodomite [1]

6949 קָהָה ***qāhâ***, v. GK: 7733. [Q] to be dull, blunt (of teeth); [P] to be dull:– set on edge [3], blunt [1]

6950 קָהַל ***qāhal***, v.den. GK: 7735 [→ 6951]. [N] to be gathered, be assembled; [H] to summon, call together, cause to assemble:– gathered together [15], assembled [8], gather together [7], gathered [5], assembled together [3], gather [1]

6951 קָהָל ***qāhāl***, n.m. GK: 7736 [→ 4721, 4722, 6950, 6951, 6952, 6953, 6954, 7035; cf. 6963]. assembly, community, often of Israel assembled for religious ceremony:– congregation [86], assembly [17], company [16], multitude [3], companies [1]

6952 קְהִלָּה ***qᵉhillâ***, n.f. GK: 7737 [→ 6951]. assembly, meeting:– assembly [1], congregation [1]

6953 קֹהֶלֶת ***qōhelet***, n.m. GK: 7738 [→ 6951]. (as a title or name) the Teacher, one who calls together and instructs the assembly:– preacher [7]

6954 קְהֵלָתָה ***qᵉhēlātâ***, n.pr.loc. GK: 7739 [→ 6951]. Kehelathah, "*assembly*":– Kehelathah [2]

6955 קְהָת ***qᵉhāt***, n.pr.m. GK: 7740 [→ 6956]. Kohath, Kohathite:– Kohath [32]

6956 קְהָתִי ***qᵉhātî***, a.g. GK: 7741 [→ 6955]. Kohathite, "*of Kohath*":– Kohathites [15]

6957 קַו ***qāw***, n.m. GK: 7742 & 7744 [→ 6960?, 6978; cf. 6961]. measuring line, ruler; qav (a mocking sound, like blah-blah):– line [20], rule [1]

6958 קִיא ***qîʾ***, v. GK: 7794 [→ 6892, 7006]. same as 7006: [Q] to vomit; [H] to vomit out, spit out:– spue out [2], vomit up [2], spued out [1], vomited out [1], vomiteth out [1], vomit [1]

6959 קוֹבַע ***qôbaʿ***, n.[m.]. GK: 7746 [cf. 3553]. helmet:– helmet [2]

6960 קָוָה ***qāwâ***, v. GK: 7747 & 7748 [→ 4723, 4724, 6957?, 8615, 8616]. [Q] to hope in; [N] to be gathered; [P] to hope for, wait for, look for:– wait [13], looked [8], waited [6], look [4], wait for [4], wait on [4], wait upon [2], waited patiently for (+6960) [2], gathered together [1], gathered [1], looked for [1], looketh [1], tarrieth [1], waited for [1]

6961 קָוֶה ***qāweh***, n.m. GK: 7749 [cf. 6957]. measuring line, ruler:–

קוֹחַ ***qôaḥ***. See 6495.

6962 קוּט ***qûṭ***, v. GK: 7752 & 7753 [→ 5354, 6900, 6990]. [Q] to feel anger, loathing; to be fragile; [N] to feel loathing; [Htpolal] to loathe, abhor:– grieved [3], lothe [3]

6963 קוֹל ***qôl*** or קֹל ***qōl***, n.m. GK: 7754 & 7825 & 7826 [→ 6964?, 7043; cf. 6951; cf. 7032]. sound, voice, noise; lightness, (i.e., frivolity or light-heartedness):– voice [381], noise [49], sound [39], thunder [7], thunders [3], made a proclamation (+5674) [2], thunderings [2], voices [2], aloud (+1419+871.1) [1], bleating [1], caused to be proclaimed (+5674) [1], crackling [1], crieth out (+5414+871.1) [1], cry (+5414) [1], cry [1], fame [1], held peace (+2244) [1], lightness [1], loud (+1419+871.1) [1], lowing [1], made proclamation (+5674) [1], make proclamation (+5674) [1], proclaim (+5674) [1], proclamation [1], shouted aloud (+7311+8643+871.1+3807.1) [1], sing (+5414) [1], speaketh [1], wept aloud (+1065+5414+871.1) [1], yelled (+5414) [1]

6964 קוֹלָיָה ***qôlāyâ***, n.pr.m. GK: 7755 [→ 6963?]. Kolaiah, "*Yahweh's voice*":– Kolaiah [2]

6965 קוּם ***qûm***, v. GK: 7756 [→ 3351, 3356, 4725, 6967, 6968, 7009, 7012, 7054, 8617, 8618; cf. 6966 (also used with compound proper names)]. [Q] to get up, arise, stand, establish; [P] to establish, confirm, restore; [Pol] to raise up; [H] to set up, establish, restore; [Ho] to be set up, be raised up; [Htpol] to raise up against:– arise [103], arose [101], rose up [62], rise up [45], rise [28], raise up [26], stand [25], set up [23], establish [17], stood up [15], perform [13], performed [11], risen up [11], up [10], raised up [9], reared up [9], rose [8], established [7], riseth up [6], risen [5], confirm [4], raise [4], set [4], stand up [4], arose up [3], confirmeth [3], continue [3], riseth [3], stablish [3], stirred up [3], ariseth [2], confirmed [2], lift up [2], made sure [2], newly set (+6965) [2], raiseth up [2], rear up [2], risest up [2], rose up against [2], stablished [2], surely accomplish (+6965) [2], surely lift up again (+6965) [2], surely stand (+6965) [2], abide [1], arise up [1], arising [1], assured [1], clearer [1], decreed [1], dim [1], endure [1], enemies [1], enjoined (+5921) [1], establisheth [1], get up [1], help up [1], hold [1], made to stand [1], make arise up [1], make good [1], maketh [1], ordained [1], performeth [1], pitch [1], raised [1], rear [1], remain [1], rise again [1], rise up again [1], rising up [1], rising [1], rouse up [1], stir up [1], strengthen [1], succeed [1], upholden [1], uprising [1]

6966 קוּם ***qûm*** (Aram.), v. GK: 10624 [→ 7010?, 7011; cf. 6965]. [P] to stand, rise up; [Pa] to issue (a decree); [H, A] to set up, establish; [Ho] to be set up, be established; from the base meaning of "standing up" (in contrast to sitting or lying) comes fig. extension of causing something to be or come into existence, implying a lively, active state:– set up [10], arise [4], stood [4], set [3], establish [2], rose up [2], setteth up [2], appointeth [1], arose [1], establisheth [1], made stand [1], made [1], raised up [1], rise [1], stand [1]

6967 קוֹמָה ***qômâ***, n.f. GK: 7757 [→ 6965]. height:– height [30], stature [7], high [5], tall [2], all along (+4393) [1]

6968 קוֹמְמִיּוּת ***qômᵉmiyyût***, n.f. GK: 7758 [→ 6965]. (adv.) with head held high:– upright [1]

6969 קִין ***qîn***, v.den. GK: 7801 [→ 7015]. [Pol] to chant a lament, sing a dirge:– lament [4], lamented [3], mourning [1]

6970 קוֹעַ ***qôaʿ***, n.pr.g. GK: 7760 [cf. 7772]. Koa:– Koa [1]

6971 קוֹף ***qôp***, n.[m.]. GK: 7761. ape:– apes [2]

6972 קִיץ ***qîṣ*** or קוּץ ***qûṣ***, v. GK: 7810 [→ 7019; cf. 3364]. [Q] to pass the summer; [H] to rouse, awaken:– summer [1]

6973 קוּץ ***qûṣ***, v. GK: 7762 [→ 6975?; cf. 5354, 8262]. [Q] to detest, be disgusted, loathe:– abhorred [2], weary [2], abhorrest [1], distressed [1], grieved [1], loatheth [1], vex [1]

6974 קוּץ ***qûṣ***, v. GK: 7763. [H] to rouse, awaken; to tear apart:– awake [10], awaked [4], awaketh [3], wake [2], arise [1], awakest [1], watcheth [1]

6975 קוֹץ ***qôṣ***, n.m. GK: 7764 & 7765 [→ 6976?; cf. 6973?, 7093]. thorns, thornbush; shreds of a wick:– thorns [10], thorn [2]

6976 הַקּוֹץ ***haqqôṣ*** or קוֹץ ***qôṣ***, n.pr.m. GK: 2212 & 7766 [→ 1886.1+6975?]. Hakkoz, Koz, "*the thorn*":– Koz [4], Coz [1], Hakkoz [1]

6977 קְוֻצּוֹת ***qᵉwuṣṣôt***, n.f.pl. GK: 7767. locks of hair:– locks [2]

6978 קַו־קַו ***qaw-qaw***, n.m. GK: 7743 & 7744 [→ 6957]. strange speech; qav-qav (a mocking sound, like blah-blah):– meted out (+6978) [4]

6979 קוּר ***qûr*** or קָרַר ***qārar***, v. GK: 7769 & 7981 & 7982 [→ 4726, 4747, 7119, 7120, 7135]. [Q] to dig (a well or water hole); [Pil] to tear down:– casteth out [2], digged [2], breaking down [1], destroy [1]

6980 קוּר ***qûr***, n.m. GK: 7770. thread (of a spider cobweb):– webs [1], web [1]

6981 קֹרֵא ***qōrēʾ***, n.pr.m. GK: 7927 [→ 7124; cf. 7121]. Kore, "*proclaimer*":– Kore [3]

6982 קוֹרָה ***qôrâ***, n.f. GK: 7771 [→ 4746]. beam, pole, roof beams, tree:– beams [2], beam [2], roof [1]

6983 קוּשׁ ***qûš***, v. GK: 7772 [cf. 3369, 5367]. [Q] to set a snare:– lay a snare [1]

6984 קוּשָׁיָהוּ ***qûšāyāhû***, n.pr.m. GK: 7773 [cf. 7029]. Kushaiah:– Kushaiah [1]

6985 קַט ***qāṭ***, pt. GK: 7775. little; soon:– very little (+4592) [1]

6986 קֶטֶב ***qeṭeb***, n.m. GK: 7776 [→ 6987]. same as 6987: plague, destruction:– destruction [2], destroying [1]

6987 קֹטֶב ***qōṭeb***, n.m. GK: 7776 [→ 6986]. same as 6986: plague, destruction:– destruction [1]

6988 קְטוֹרָה ***qᵉṭôrâ***, n.m. GK: 7777 [→ 6999]. smoke (of sacrifice):– incense [1]

6989 קְטוּרָה ***qᵉṭûrâ***, n.pr.f. GK: 7778 [→ 6999]. Keturah, "*incense, scented one*":– Keturah [4]

6990 קוּט ***qûṭ*** or קָטַט ***qāṭaṭ***, v. GK: 7752 & 7753 [→ 6962]. [Q] to be fragile; cut off; cf. 6962:– cut off [1]

6991 קָטַל ***qāṭal***, v. GK: 7779 [→ 6993; cf. 6992]. [Q] to slay, kill:– slay [2], killeth [1]

6992 קְטַל ***qᵉṭal*** (Aram.), v. GK: 10625 [cf. 6991]. [P] to put to death, kill; [Peil] to be slain; [Htpe] to be put to death; [Pa] to kill;

[Htpa] to be put to death:– slain [4], slew [2], slay [1]

6993 קֶטֶל ***qeṭel***, n.[m.]. GK: 7780 [→ 6991]. slaughter:– slaughter [1]

6994 קָטֹן ***qāṭōn***, v. GK: 7781 [→ 6995, 6996, 6997]. [Q] to be unworthy, not enough, trifling; [H] to make a (measure) small:– small thing [2], making small [1], not worthy [1]

6995 קֹטֶן ***qōṭen***, n.m. GK: 7782 [→ 6994]. little finger; possibly a euphemism for penis:– little [2]

6996 קָטָן ***qāṭān*** or קָטֹן ***qāṭōn***, a. GK: 7783 & 7785 [→ 6994, 6997]. small (in size); few (in quantity); by extension, of status: lesser, insignificant; of age: young(est):– small [33], little [19], youngest [15], younger [14], least [10], less [3], lesser [2], little one [2], small quantity [1], smallest [1], young [1]

6997 קָטָן ***qāṭān*** or הַקָּטָן ***haqqāṭān***, n.pr.m. GK: 7784 & 2214 [→ 1886.1+6996; cf. 6994]. Katan, Hakkatan, "*the small one*":– Hakkatan [1]

6998 קָטַף ***qāṭap***, v. GK: 7786. [Q] to pick off (grain), break off (twigs); [N] to be picked off:– crop off [1], cropt off [1], cut down [1], cut up [1], pluck [1]

6999 קָטַר ***qāṭar***, v.den. GK: 7787 [→ 4729, 4730, 6988, 6989, 7002, 7003, 7004, 7008]. [P] to burn an offering (of incense smoke); [Pu] to be perfumed; [H] to make a burned smoking offering; [Ho] to be burned as an offering:– burn [34], burnt incense [25], burn incense [23], burnt [13], burned incense [3], burneth incense [2], not fail to burn (+6999) [2], offer [2], altars for incense [1], burn sacrifice [1], burned [1], burning incense [1], burnt incense (+7004) [1], incense [1], kindle [1], offer incense [1], offered incense [1], offered [1], offering incense [1], perfumed [1]

7000 קָטַר ***qāṭar***, v. GK: 7788. [Qp] to be enclosed:– joined [1]

7001 קְטַר ***qᵉṭar*** (Aram.), n.m. GK: 10626. joint (of the hip); difficult problem, "to solve a difficult problem" means to explain an enigma, as a fig. extension of untying a tight, hard-to-undo, knot:– doubts [2], joints [1]

7002 קִטֵּר ***qiṭṭēr***, n.f. GK: 7789 [→ 6999]. incense, often as or accompanying an offering to God:– incense [1]

7003 קִטְרוֹן ***qiṭrôn***, n.pr.loc. GK: 7790 [→ 6999]. Kitron, "*incense, [sacrificial] smoke*":– Kitron [1]

7004 קְטֹרֶת ***qᵉṭōret***, n.f. GK: 7792 [→ 6999]. incense, smoke offering, its pleasant fragrance symbolic of God's acceptance:– incense [56], perfume [3], burnt incense (+6999) [1]

7005 קַטָּת ***qaṭṭāt***, n.pr.loc. GK: 7793. Kattath:– Kattath [1]

7006 קִיא ***qî'*** or קָיָה ***qāyâ***, v. GK: 7794 & 7796 [→ 6958]. [Q] to vomit; [H] to vomit out, spit out:– spue [1]

7007 קַיִט ***qayiṭ*** (Aram.), n.[m.]. GK: 10627 [cf. 7019]. summer:– summer [1]

7008 קִיטוֹר ***qîṭôr***, n.m. GK: 7798 [→ 6999]. smoke:– smoke [3], vapour [1]

7009 קִים ***qîm***, n.m. GK: 7799 [→ 6965]. foe, adversary:– substance [1]

7010 קְיָם ***qᵉyām*** (Aram.), n.[m.]. GK: 10628 [→ 6966?]. edict, statute, decree:– statute [2]

7011 קַיָּם ***qayyām*** (Aram.), a. GK: 10629 [→ 6966]. enduring:– stedfast [1], sure [1]

7012 קִימָה ***qîmâ***, n.f. GK: 7800 [→ 6965]. standing up:– rising up [1]

קִימוֹשׂ ***qîmôš***. See 7057.

7013 קַיִן ***qayin***, n.[m.]. GK: 7802. spearhead, spear:– spear [1]

7014 קַיִן ***qayin***, n.pr.m. & g. & loc. GK: 7803 & 7804 & 7805 [→ 7017, 7018, 8423; cf. 7069]. Cain, "*metal worker; brought forth, acquired* [Ge 4:1]"; Kenite, "*metal workers*"; Kain, "*place of metal workers [?]*":– Cain [17], Kenites [1], Kenite [1]

7015 קִינָה ***qînâ***, n.f. GK: 7806 [→ 6969]. lament, mourning song, dirge:– lamentation [15], lamentations [3]

7016 קִינָה ***qînâ***, n.pr.loc. GK: 7807. Kinah, "*lament, dirge*":– Kinah [1]

7017 קֵינִי ***qênî***, a.g. GK: 7808 [→ 7014]. Kenite:– Kenites [7], Kenite [5]

7018 קֵינָן ***qênān***, n.pr.m. GK: 7809 [→ 7014]. Kenan:– Cainan [5], Kenan [1]

7019 קַיִץ ***qayiṣ***, n.m. GK: 7811 [→ 6972; cf. 7007]. summer; by extension, summer fruit, ripe fruit:– summer [11], summer fruits [6], summer fruit [3]

7020 קִיצוֹן ***qîṣôn***, a. GK: 7812 [→ 7093]. end, outermost:– uttermost [3], outmost [1]

7021 קִיקָיוֹן ***qîqāyôn***, n.m. GK: 7813. caster-oil vine; some sources: cucumber plant:– gourd [5]

7022 קִיקָלוֹן ***qîqālôn***, n.[m.]. GK: 7814 [→ 7043]. disgrace:– shameful spuing [1]

7023 קִיר ***qîr***, n.m. GK: 7815 [→ 7024; cf. 7176 (also used with compound proper names)]. wall (of a building or city); by extension, any surface of a construction: side, ceiling, surface; one who "urinates on a wall" is male:– wall [50], walls [16], sides [2], side [2], masons (+2796) [1], masons (+68+2796) [1], town [1], very heart (+3820) [1]

7024 קִיר ***qîr***, n.pr.loc. GK: 7816 & 7817 [→ 7023]. Kir, "*walled enclosure*":– Kir [5]

7025 קִיר־חֶרֶשׂ ***qîr-ḥereś*** or קִיר־חֲרֶשֶׂת ***qîr ḥᵃreśet***, n.pr.loc. GK: 7818 & 7819 [→ 7023+2789]. Kir Heres, Kir Hareseth, "*walled [city] of pottery fragments*":– Kir-heres [2], Kir-haraseth [1], Kir-hareseth [1], Kir-haresh [1]

7026 קֵירֹס ***qêrōs***, n.pr.m. GK: 7820. Keros:– Keros [2]

7027 קִישׁ ***qîš***, n.pr.m. GK: 7821. Kish, "*bow, power*":– Kish [21]

7028 קִישׁוֹן ***qîšôn***, n.pr.loc. GK: 7822. Kishon, "*cunning*":– Kishon [5], Kison [1]

7029 קִישִׁי ***qîšî***, n.pr.m. GK: 7823 [cf. 6984]. Kishi, "[poss.] *gift; snarer*":– Kishi [1]

7030 קִיתָרֹס ***qîtᵉrōs*** or קַתְרוֹס ***qatrôs*** (Aram.), n.[m.]. GK: 10630 & 10644. a stringed instrument, translated variously as "zither, lute, lyre," etc.:– harp [4]

7031 קַל ***qal***, a. GK: 7824 [→ 7043]. fleet-footed, swift, speedy:– swift [9], swiftly [2], light [1], swifter [1]

7032 קָל ***qāl*** (Aram.), n.m. GK: 10631 [cf. 6963]. sound, voice:– sound [4], voice [3]

קֹל ***qōl***. See 6963.

7033 קָלָה ***qālâ***, v. GK: 7828 [→ 7039]. [Q] to burn; [Qp] to be roasted; [N] to have a burning sensation:– dried [1], loathsome [1], parched [1], roasted [1]

7034 קָלָה ***qālâ***, v. GK: 7829 [→ 7036; cf. 7043]. [N] to lightly esteemed, to be a nobody, be degraded; [H] to dishonor, treat with contempt:– base [1], contemned [1], despised [1], lightly esteemed [1], setteth light [1], vile [1]

7035 קָלָה ***qālah***, v.den. GK: 7827 [→ 6951]. var. of 6950: [N] to be gathered:–

7036 קָלוֹן ***qālôn***, n.m. GK: 7830 [→ 7034]. shame, disgrace, dishonor:– shame [13], confusion [1], dishonour [1], ignominy [1], reproach [1]

7037 קַלַּחַת ***qallaḥat***, n.f. GK: 7831. caldron, (cooking) pot:– caldron [2]

7038 קָלַט ***qālaṭ***, v. GK: 7832 [→ 4733, 7042]. [Qp] to be stunted:– lacking in parts [1]

7039 קָלִי ***qālî***, n.m. GK: 7833 [→ 7033]. roasted grain, parched grain:– parched [6]

7040 קַלַּי ***qallāy***, n.pr.m. GK: 7834. Kallai, "*swift*":– Kallai [1]

7041 קֵלָיָה ***qēlāyâ***, n.pr.m. GK: 7835. Kelaiah, "[perhaps] *Yahweh has dishonored*":– Kelaiah [1]

7042 קְלִיטָא ***qᵉlîṭā'***, n.pr.m. GK: 7836 [→ 7038]. Kelita:– Kelita [3]

7043 קָלַל ***qālal***, v. GK: 7837 [→ 7022, 7031, 6963, 7044, 7045, 7052; cf. 7034]. [Q] to recede, grow smaller; to be vile, to disdain, despise; to be swift; [N] to be trivial, insignificant; to be swift; [P] to curse, blaspheme, revile; [Pu] to be accursed; [H] to lighten; to humble; to treat with contempt; [Htpal] to be shaken:– cursed [17], curse [17], curseth [6], swifter [5], light thing [4], make lighter [3], vile [3], abated [2], despised [2], ease somewhat [2], lighten [2], light [2], slightly (+5921) [2], accursed [1], bring into contempt [1], despise [1], easier (+4480) [1], easy [1], lightly afflicted [1], lightly esteemed [1], made bright [1], made vile [1], make somewhat lighter [1], moved lightly [1], revile [1], set light [1], swift [1], whet [1]

7044 קָלָל ***qālāl***, a. GK: 7838 [→ 7043]. burnished, polished:– burnished [1], polished [1]

7045 קְלָלָה ***qᵉlālâ***, n.f. GK: 7839 [→ 7043]. curse, condemnation:– curse [24], cursing [4], curses [3], accursed [1], cursings [1]

7046 קָלַס ***qālas***, v. GK: 7840 [→ 7047, 7048]. [P] to scorn; [Ht] to make fun of:– mocked [1], mock [1], scoff [1], scornest [1]

7047 קֶלֶס ***qeles***, n.[m.]. GK: 7841 [→ 7046]. derision, reproach:– derision [3]

7048 קַלָּסָה ***qallāsâ***, n.f. GK: 7842 [→ 7046]. laughingstock, object of derision:– mocking [1]

7049 קָלַע ***qāla'***, v. GK: 7843 & 7844 [→ 4734, 7050]. [Q] to hurl a stone (from a sling); to carve; [P] to hurl a stone (from a sling):– carved [3], sling out [2], slang [1], sling [1]

7050 קֶלַע ***qela'***, n.[m.]. GK: 7845 & 7846 [→ 7049, 7051]. sling (a weapon); curtains:– hangings [15], sling [4], leaves [1], slingstones (+68) [1], slings [1]

7051 קַלָּע ***qallā'***, n.m. GK: 7847 [→ 7050]. slinger (one who uses a sling):– slingers [1]

7052 קְלֹקֵל ***qᵉlōqēl***, a. GK: 7848 [→ 7043]. miserable (food), starvation (rations):– light [1]

7053 קִלְּשׁוֹן ***qillᵉšôn***, n.[m.]. GK: 7849. (sharp pointed, three-pronged) fork:– forks (+7969) [1]

Heb

7054 קָמָה ***qāmâ***, n.f. GK: 7850 [→ 6965]. standing grain:– standing corn [5], corn [2], grown up [2], stalk [1]

7055 קְמוּאֵל ***q^{e}mû'ēl***, n.pr.m. GK: 7851 [→ 6965+410]. Kemuel, "*God's [El's] mound*":– Kemuel [3]

7056 קָמוֹן ***qāmôn***, n.pr.loc. GK: 7852. Kamon:– Camon [1]

7057 קִמּוֹשׂ ***qimmôś***, n.m. GK: 7853 [→ 7063]. thorns, nettles, briers (weeds of all kinds):– nettles [2]

7058 קֶמַח ***qemaḥ***, n.[m.]. GK: 7854. flour:– meal [10], flour [4]

7059 קָמַט ***qāmaṭ***, v. GK: 7855. [Q] to seize; [Pu] to be seized:– cut down [1], filled with wrinkles [1]

7060 קָמַל ***qāmal***, v. GK: 7857. [Q] to wither:– hewn down [1], wither [1]

7061 קָמַץ ***qāmaṣ***, v. GK: 7858 [→ 7062]. [Q] to take a handful:– take handful (+4393+7062) [2], take a handful [1]

7062 קֹמֶץ ***qōmeṣ***, n.[m.]. GK: 7859 [→ 7061]. handful; (pl.) abundance:– take handful (+4393+7061) [2], handfuls [1], handful [1]

7063 קִמָּשׁוֹן ***qimmāšôn***, n.m. GK: 7853 [→ 7057]. same as 7057: thorns, nettles, briers (weeds of all kinds):– thorns [1]

7064 קֵן ***qēn***, n.m. GK: 7860 [→ 7077]. nest:– nest [12], rooms [1]

7065 קָנָא ***qānā'***, v.den. GK: 7861 [→ 7067, 7068, 7072]. [P] (of negative attitude) to be jealous, be envious; (of positive attitude) to be zealous:– jealous [8], envied [5], envious [4], very jealous (+7065) [4], envy [3], moved to jealousy [2], provoked to jealousy [2], enviest [1], move to jealousy [1], zealous (+7068) [1], zealous [1], zeal [1]

7066 קְנָה ***q^{e}nâ*** (Aram.), v. GK: 10632 [cf. 7069]. [P] to buy:– buy [1]

7067 קַנָּא ***qannā'***, a. GK: 7862 [→ 7072; cf. 7065]. jealous; an adjective or title used exclusively of God, focusing on his desire for exclusive relationships:– jealous [6]

7068 קִנְאָה ***qin'â***, n.f. GK: 7863 [→ 7065]. jealousy, envy, zeal:– jealousy [24], zeal [9], envy [7], envied [1], jealousies [1], zealous (+7065) [1]

7069 קָנָה ***qānâ***, v. GK: 7864 & 7865 [→ 511, 4735, 4736, 4737, 7075; cf. 7014, cf. 7066]. [Q] to buy, acquire, get; to create, bring forth; (as a title of God) Creator; [N] to be bought:– bought [21], buy [21], get [9], purchased [5], buyer [3], getteth [3], got [3], possessed [3], buyest [2], possessor [2], surely buy (+7069) [2], verily buy (+7069) [2], attain [1], buy (+7075) [1], gotten [1], owner [1], possessors [1], provoketh to jealousy [1], recover [1], redeemed [1], taught [1]

7070 קָנֶה ***qāneh***, n.m. GK: 7866 [→ 7071]. branch, rod; (calamus) reed, stalk, shaft, cane; by extension: a measure of length, variously reckoned:– reed [22], branches [19], reeds [6], branch [5], calamus [3], stalk [2], balance [1], bone [1], cane [1], spearmen [1], sweet cane [1]

7071 קָנָה ***qānâ***, n.pr.loc. GK: 7867 [→ 7070]. Kanah, "*reed*":– Kanah [3]

7072 קַנּוֹא ***qannô'***, a. GK: 7868 [→ 7067; cf. 7065]. jealous:– jealous [2]

7073 קְנַז ***q^{e}naz***, n.pr.m. GK: 7869 [→ 7074]. Kenaz, "*hunting*":– Kenaz [11]

7074 קְנִזִּי ***q^{e}nizzî***, a.g. GK: 7870 [→ 7073]. Kenizzite:– Kenezite [3], Kenizzites [1]

7075 קִנְיָן ***qinyān***, n.[m.]. GK: 7871 [→ 7069]. goods, property, possessions:– substance [4], getting [2], goods [2], buy (+7069) [1], riches [1]

7076 קִנָּמוֹן ***qinnāmôn***, n.m. GK: 7872. cinnamon (a spice from the far east):– cinnamon [3]

7077 קָנַן ***qānan***, v.den. GK: 7873 [→ 7064]. [P] to make a nest; [Pu] to be nestled, nested:– made nests [1], make nests [1], make nest [1], makest nest [1], maketh nest [1]

7078 קֶנֶץ ***qeneṣ***, n.[m.]. GK: 7874 [cf. 7093]. end, an extension of a snare or net that captures or restrains (not found in the OT):– end [1]

7079 קְנָת ***q^{e}nāt***, n.pr.loc. GK: 7875. Kenath, "*possession*":– Kenath [2]

7080 קָסַם ***qāsam***, v.den. GK: 7876 [→ 4738, 7081]. [Q] to practice divination, be a soothsayer, seek an omen:– diviners [7], divine [6], divination [1], divining [1], prudent [1], soothsayer [1], use divination (+7081) [1], used divination (+7081) [1], useth divination (+7081) [1]

7081 קֶסֶם ***qesem***, n.[m.]. GK: 7877 [→ 7080]. divination: pagan practice of determining the future by examining the position of stars, communication with the dead or with spirits, examining animal organs, or casting lots:– divination [4], divinations [1], divine sentence [1], rewards of divination [1], use divination (+7080) [1], used divination (+7080) [1], useth divination (+7080) [1], witchcraft [1]

7082 קָסַס ***qāsas***, v. GK: 7878 [cf. 7193]. [Pol] to strip off:– cut off [1]

7083 קֶסֶת ***qeset***, n.[f.]. GK: 7879. writing kit, writing-case:– inkhorn [3]

7084 קְעִילָה ***q^{e}'îlâ***, n.pr.loc. GK: 7881. Keilah:– Keilah [18]

7085 קַעֲקַע ***qa^{a}qa'***, n.[m.]. GK: 7882. tattoo:– marks [1]

7086 קְעָרָה ***q^{e}'ārâ***, n.f. GK: 7883 [→ 8258]. plate, dish:– charger [13], dishes [3], chargers [1]

קֹף ***qōp***. See 6971.

7087 קָפָא ***qāpā'***, v. GK: 7884. [Q, N] to congeal, thicken; [H] to curdle:– congealed [1], cruddled [1], dark [1], settled [1]

7088 קָפַד ***qāpad***, v. GK: 7886 [→ 7090, 7089; cf. 7091]. [P] to roll up:– cut off [1]

7089 קְפָדָה ***q^{e}pādâ***, n.[f.]. GK: 7888 [→ 7088]. terror, anguish:– destruction [1]

7090 קִפֹּד ***qippōd***, n.[m.]. GK: 7887 [→ 7088]. screech owl; some sources: hedgehog:– bittern [3]

7091 קִפּוֹז ***qippôz***, n.f. GK: 7889 [cf. 7088, 7092]. owl; some sources: tree snake:– great owl [1]

7092 קָפַץ ***qāpaṣ***, v. GK: 7890 [cf. 7091]. [Q] to draw together, shut; [N] to be gathered up; [P] to bound, leap:– shut [2], shut up [1], skipping [1], stoppeth [1], stop [1], taken out of the way [1]

7093 קֵץ ***qēṣ***, n.m. GK: 7891 [→ 7020; cf. 7078, 7112]. end, limit, boundary:– end [51], after (+4480) [6], after [2], after (+3807.1) [1], after that (+1961+4480) [1], borders [1], border [1], have an end [1], infinite (+369) [1], process [1], utmost border [1]

קֹץ ***qōṣ***. See 6975.

7094 קָצַב ***qāṣab***, v. GK: 7892 [→ 7095]. [Q] to cut off; [Qp] to be shorn, be cut off:– cut down [1], even shorn [1]

7095 קֶצֶב ***qeṣeb***, n.m. GK: 7893 [→ 7094]. shape, foundation:– size [2], bottoms [1]

7096 קָצָה ***qāṣâ***, v. GK: 7894 [→ 7097, 7098, 7099, 7117; cf. 7112]. [P] to cut off, reduce; [H] to scrape off:– cut short [1], cutteth off [1], cutting off [1], scrape off [1], scraped [1]

7097 קָצֶה ***qāṣeh*** or קֵצֶה ***qēṣeh***, n.[m.]. GK: 7895 & 7897 [→ 7096]. end, boundary, limit, outskirts, edge:– end [50], edge [6], ends [6], uttermost part [6], outside [3], border [2], other^{s} [2], utmost part [2], after (+4480) [1], borders [1], brim [1], brink [1], coasts [1], every quarter [1], frontiers [1], infinite (+369) [1], other^{s} (+8064) [1], outmost coast (+4480) [1], outmost parts [1], quarter [1], shore [1], side [1], some of (+4480) [1], utmost [1], uttermost (+4480) [1], uttermost part (+4480) [1], uttermost parts [1], uttermost [1]

7098 קָצָה ***qāṣâ***, n.f. & m.[pl.]. GK: 7896 [→ 7096]. end, fringe, edge:– ends [18], end [4], lowest [3], edges [2], selvedge [2], uttermost part [2], coasts [1], corners [1], parts [1], quarters [1]

7099 קָצוּ ***qāṣû***, n.[m.]. GK: 7898 [→ 7096]. ends, borders (of the earth):– ends [4], uttermost parts [1]

7100 קֶצַח ***qeṣaḥ***, n.m. GK: 7902. caraway, cummin:– fitches [3]

7101 קָצִין ***qāṣîn***, n.m. GK: 7903 [→ 6278]. commander, ruler, leader:– captain [2], princes [2], prince [2], rulers [2], ruler [2], captains [1], guide [1]

7102 קְצִיעָה ***q^{e}ṣî'â***, n.f. GK: 7904 [→ 7103; cf. 7106]. cassia:– cassia [1]

7103 קְצִיעָה ***q^{e}ṣî'â***, n.pr.f. GK: 7905 [→ 7102; cf. 7106]. Keziah, "*cassia [cinnamon]*":– Kezia [1]

7104 קְצִיץ ***q^{e}ṣîṣ***, n.pr.loc. GK: 7906 & 6681 [→ 6009; cf. 7093]. Keziz:– Keziz [1]

7105 קָצִיר ***qāṣîr***, n.m. GK: 7907 & 7908 [→ 7114]. harvest, time of reaping; branch, bough, twig, shoot:– harvest [46], boughs [3], branch [2], cuttest down harvest (+7114) [1], harvest time [1], harvestman [1]

7106 קָצַע ***qāṣa'***, v. GK: 7909 & 7910 [→ 4741, 4742, 7102, 7103]. [H] to scrape off; [Pu, Ho] to be made with corners:– cause to be scraped [1], corners [1]

7107 קָצַף ***qāṣap***, v. GK: 7911 [→ 7110; cf. 7108]. [Q] to be angry; [H] to provoke to anger; [Ht] to be enraged:– wroth [22], provoked to wrath [3], angry [2], sore displeased (+7110) [2], angered [1], displeased [1], fret [1], provokedst to wrath [1], wrath [1]

7108 קְצַף ***q^{e}ṣap*** (Aram.), v. GK: 10633 [→ 7109; cf. 7107]. [P] to become furious:– furious [1]

7109 קְצַף ***q^{e}ṣap*** (Aram.), n.[m.]. GK: 10634 [→ 7108; cf. 7110]. wrath, fury:– wrath [1]

7110 קֶצֶף ***qeṣep***, n.m. GK: 7912 & 7913 [→ 7107, 7111; cf. 7109]. wrath, anger, fury; twig (snapped off):– wrath [23], indignation [3], sore displeased (+7107) [2], foam [1]

7111 קְצָפָה ***q^{e}ṣāpâ***, n.f. GK: 7914 [→ 7110]. stump, splintering:– barked [1]

7112 קָצַץ ***qāṣaṣ***, v. GK: 7915 & 7899 [cf. 7093, 7096]. [Q] to cut off; [P] to cut off, take away; [Pu] to be cut off, maimed:– cut off [6], in the utmost [3], cut in pieces [2], cut asunder [1], cutteth in sunder [1], cut [1]

7113 קְצַץ ***q***^{e}***ṣaṣ*** (Aram.), v. GK: 10635 [cf. 7112]. [Pa] to trim off, cut off:– cut off [1]

7114 קָצַר ***qāṣar***, v. GK: 7917 & 7918 & 7900 [→ 7105, 7115, 7116]. [Q] to reap, harvest, gather; to be short; (by extension) to be impatient, angry; [P] to cut short; [H] to shorten, cut short:– reap [18], reapers [7], shortened [4], shortened at all (+7114) [2], shorter [2], cuttest down harvest (+7105) [1], discouraged [1], grieved [1], harvestman [1], lothed [1], mower [1], reaped [1], reaper [1], reapest [1], reapeth [1], reaping [1], straitened [1], troubled [1], vexed [1], waxed short [1]

7115 קֹצֶר ***qōṣer***, n.[m.]. GK: 7919 [→ 7114]. discouragement, despondency, an extension of shortness or lack (of spirit):– anguish [1]

7116 קָצֵר ***qāṣēr***, a. GK: 7920 [→ 7114]. shortened: quick-tempered, impatient:– small [2], few [1], hasty [1], soon [1]

7117 קְצָת ***q***^{e}***ṣāt***, n.f. GK: 7921 [→ 7096; cf. 7118]. end, extremity:– end [3], part (+4480) [1], some (+4480) [1]

7118 קְצָת ***q***^{e}***ṣāt*** (Aram.), n.f. GK: 10636 [cf. 7117]. part; the end:– end [2], partly (+4481) [1]

7119 קַר ***qar***, a. GK: 7922 [→ 6979]. cool, cold (water); cool-headed, even-tempered (of one's spirit):– cold [2]

קִר ***qir***. See 7023.

7120 קֹר ***qōr***, n.[m.]. GK: 7923 [→ 6979]. cold:– cold [1]

7121 קָרָא ***qārā'***, v. GK: 7924 [→ 4744, 7124, 6981, 7148, 7150; cf. 7123]. [Q] to call, summon, announce, proclaim; [Qp] to be invited as a guest, be appointed; [N] to be called, be summoned; [Pu] to be called; "to call on the name of the Lord" means to proclaim or praise the excellence of Yahweh, to worship Yahweh, or to summon Yahweh by name for help:– called [366], call [115], cried [51], cry [35], read [35], proclaim [20], call upon [14], calleth [13], proclaimed [11], called upon [10], named [5], crieth [4], guests [4], called for [3], calledst [3], calling [3], cried unto [3], gave [3], invited [3], renowned [3], bidden [2], criest [2], cry unto [2], named (+8034) [2], preach [2], proclaiming [2], reading [2], bewrayeth [1], call for [1], call on [1], called forth [1], crying [1], famous (+8034) [1], famous [1], made proclamation [1], mentioned [1], proclaim (+871.1) [1], proclaimed (+871.1) [1], proclaimeth [1], pronounced [1], publish [1], readeth [1], said [1]

7122 קָרָא ***qārā'***, v. GK: 7925 [→ 7125; cf. 7136]. [Q] to meet, encounter, happen; [N] to have met, have happened, [H] to cause to happen:– befall [4], met [2], befallen [1], came upon [1], caused to come upon [1], chance to be [1], come unto [1], come upon [1], falleth out [1], happened by chance [1], happened to be [1], happened unto [1]

7123 קְרָא ***q***^{e}***rā'*** (Aram.), v. GK: 10637 [cf. 7121]. [P] to call, proclaim, read out loud; [Pp, Peil] to be read out loud; [Htpe] to be called, be summoned:– read [7], cried [3], called [1]

7124 קֹרֵא ***qōrē'***, n.m. GK: 7926 [→ 6981; cf. 7121]. partridge:– partridge [2]

7125 קִרְאָה ***qir'â***, v.inf. GK: 7925 [→ 7122]. inf. of 7122: meeting, encounter, happening:– meet [69], against [39], met [4], brought (+857) [1], come against [1], come [1], coming [1], help [1], in the way (+3807.1) [1], meet with [1], meeting [1], seek [1]

7126 קָרַב ***qārab***, v. GK: 7928 [→ 6137, 7131, 7128, 7132, 7133, 7138; cf. 7127]. [Q] to come near, approach; [N] to present oneself, be brought near; [P] to bring near, approach; [H] to bring near, offer, present:– offer [79], bring [32], brought [24], come near [20], offered [16], came near [11], approach [9], offereth [9], came [6], come nigh [6], at hand [4], bring near [4], come [4], draw nigh [4], drew near [4], drew nigh [4], draw near [3], came nigh [2], cause to come near [2], cause to draw near [2], caused to come near [2], comest nigh [2], draweth near [2], go near [2], presented [2], went [2], approached [1], brought forth [1], brought near [1], came together [1], camest [1], cause to be brought [1], caused to draw near [1], causest to approach [1], draweth near the time [1], drewest near [1], goeth [1], go [1], joined [1], join [1], lay [1], made ready [1], near [1], offering [1], produce [1], stand [1], take [1], went near [1]

7127 קְרֵב ***q***^{e}***rēb*** (Aram.), v. GK: 10638 [→ 7129; cf. 7126]. [P] to come near, approach; [Pa] to offer (a sacrifice); [H] to bring near, offer (a sacrifice):– came near [4], brought near [1], came [1], offered [1], offer [1], sacrifices [1]

7128 קְרָב ***q***^{e}***rāb***, n.[m.]. GK: 7930 [→ 6137; cf. 7126, 7129]. war, battle:– battle [5], war [4]

7129 קְרָב ***q***^{e}***rāb*** (Aram.), n.[m.]. GK: 10639 [→ 7127; cf. 7128]. war:– war [1]

7130 קֶרֶב ***qereb***, n.[m.]. GK: 7931. inner parts; by extension: heart or mind as the seat of thought and emotion; interior, midst; (pp.) among, in the midst of:– midst [73], among (+871.1) [41], among [26], within (+871.1) [25], inwards [19], in (+871.1) [8], amongst (+871.1) [7], through (+871.1) [5], inward [3], out of (+4480) [3], amongst [2], into (+5921) [2], inward parts [2], before (+871.1) [1], bowels [1], charge [1], eaten (+413+935) [1], eaten up (+413+935) [1], heart [1], inwardly (+871.1) [1], purtenance [1], therein (+871.1) [1], therein (+871.1+1886.3) [1], within [1]

7131 קָרֵב ***qārēb***, a.v. GK: 7929 [→ 7126]. approaching, coming near:– cometh nigh [4], come near [2], cometh near (+7131) [2], drew near [2], approach [1], came [1]

קָרֹב ***qārōb***. See 7138.

7132 קִרְבָה ***qirbâ***, n.f. GK: 7932 [→ 7126]. nearness, approach:– approaching to [1], draw near [1]

7133 קָרְבָּן ***qorbān*** or קֻרְבָּן ***qurbān***, n.m. GK: 7933 & 7934 [→ 7126]. gift, offering, sacrifice; contribution, supply (of wood):– offering [65], oblation [11], oblations [1], offered [1], offering made by fire (+801) [1], offerings [1], sacrifice [1]

7134 קַרְדֹּם ***qardōm***, n.[m.]. GK: 7935. ax; some sources: adze:– axes [3], axe [2]

7135 קָרָה ***qārâ***, n.f. GK: 7938 [→ 6979]. cold:– cold [5]

7136 קָרָה ***qārâ***, v. GK: 7936 [→ 4745, 7137, 7147; cf. 7122]. [Q] to happen, meet, encounter; [N] to meet with, have happen; [P] to make beams, build beams; [H] to give success, to select oneself:– met [4], happeneth [3], befall [2], happen [2], laid beams [2], appoint [1], befallen [1], befell [1], brought [1], come to pass [1], come [1], floor [1], happened [1], layeth beams [1], light on [1], make beams [1], meet [1], send good speed (+6440+3807.1) [1]

7137 קָרֶה ***qāreh***, n.[m.]. GK: 7937 [→ 7136]. emission (at night):– chanceth [1]

קֹרָה ***qōrâ***. See 6982.

7138 קָרוֹב ***qārôb***, a. GK: 7940 [→ 7126]. near, close:– near [33], nigh [12], next [5], at hand [4], neighbours [3], approach [2], near of kin [2], neighbour [2], allied [1], come nigh [1], hand [1], kinsfolk [1], kinsmen [1], kin [1], near (+871.1) [1], near unto [1], nearer [1], newly (+4480) [1], nigh at hand [1], ready [1], short (+4480) [1], shortly (+4480) [1], short [1]

7139 קָרַח ***qāraḥ***, v. GK: 7942 [→ 7142, 7143, 7141, 7144, 7145, 7146]. [Q] to shave, make bald; [N] to shave oneself, make oneself bald; [H] to shave another, make bald; [Ho] to be rubbed bare, be make bald:– make bald [2], make utterly bald (+7139) [2], made bald [1], make baldness (+7144) [1]

7140 קֶרַח ***qeraḥ***, n.m. GK: 7943. ice, frost, hail:– frost [3], ice [3], crystal [1]

7141 קֹרַח ***qōraḥ***, n.pr.m. GK: 7946 [→ 7145; cf. 7139]. Korah, "*shaven, bald*":– Korah [37]

7142 קֵרֵחַ ***qērēaḥ***, a. GK: 7944 [→ 7139]. bald, bald-headed:– bald head [2], bald [1]

7143 קָרֵחַ ***qārēaḥ***, n.pr.m. GK: 7945 [→ 7139]. Kareah, "*bald head*":– Kareah [13], Careah [1]

7144 קָרְחָה ***qorḥâ***, n.f. GK: 7947 [→ 7139]. baldness, shaving the head:– baldness [8], bald [1], make baldness (+7139) [1]

7145 קָרְחִי ***qorḥî***, a.g. GK: 7948 [→ 7141; cf. 7139]. Korahite, "*of Korah*":– Korhites [4], Korahites [2], Korahite [1], Kore [1]

7146 קָרַחַת ***qāraḥat***, n.f. GK: 7949 [→ 7139]. bald spot (not the forehead area); bare spot (of articles):– bald head [3], bare within [1]

7147 קְרִי ***q***^{e}***rî***, n.[m.]. GK: 7950 [→ 7136]. hostile encounter, hostility:– contrary [7]

7148 קָרִיא ***qārî'***, a. GK: 7951 [→ 7121]. summoned, called:– famous [2]

7149 קִרְיָה ***qiryâ*** (Aram.), n.f. GK: 10640 [cf. 7151]. city, town:– city [8], cities [1]

7150 קְרִיאָה ***q***^{e}***rî'â***, n.f. GK: 7952 [→ 7121]. message, appeal:– preaching [1]

7151 קִרְיָה ***qiryâ*** or קִרְיַת ***qiryat***, n.f. [& pr.] GK: 7953 & 7956 [→ 7176; cf. 7149]. city, town; as n.pr. Kiriath:– city [32]

7152 קְרִיּוֹת ***q***^{e}***riyyôt***, n.pr.loc. GK: 7954 [→ 7176]. Kerioth, "*town*":– Kerioth [4]

7153 קִרְיַת אַרְבַּע ***qiryat 'arba'*** or קִרְיַת הָאַרְבַּע ***qiryat hā'arba'***, n.pr.loc. GK: 7957 & 7959 [→ 7176+702]. Kiriath Arba, "*city of four*":– Kirjath-arba [6]

7154 קִרְיַת־בַּעַל ***qiryat-ba'al***, n.pr.loc. GK: 7958 [→ 7176+1167]. Kiriath Baal:– Kirjath-baal [2]

7155 קִרְיַת חֻצוֹת ***qiryat ḥuṣôt***, n.pr.loc. GK: 7960 [→ 7176]. Kiriath Huzoth, "*city of Huzoth [outside spaces]*":– Kirjath-huzoth [1]

7156 קִרְיָתַיִם ***qiryātayim***, n.pr.loc. GK: 7964 [→ 7176]. Kiriathaim, "*two cities*":– Kiriathaim [3], Kirjathaim [3]

7157 קִרְיַת יְעָרִים ***qiryat yᵉ'ārîm***, n.pr.loc. GK: 7961 [→ 7176+3297]. Kiriath Jearim, "*city of timberlands*":– Kirjath-jearim [18], Kirjath-arim [1], Kirjath [1]

7158 קִרְיַת־סַנָּה ***qiryat-sannâ*** or קִרְיַת־סֵפֶר ***qiryat-sēper***, n.pr.loc. GK: 7962 & 7963 [→ 7176+5612]. Kiriath Sannah, "*city of Sannah*"; Kiriath Sepher, "*city of a scribe* or *book*":– Kirjath-sepher [4], Kirjath-sannah [1]

7159 קָרַם ***qāram***, v. GK: 7965. [Q] to cover with, spread; [N] to be spread over:– cover with [1], covered [1]

7160 קָרַן ***qāran***, v.den. GK: 7966 [→ 7161]. [Q] to be radiant; [H] to be with horns:– shone [3], horns [1]

7161 קֶרֶן ***qeren***, n.f. or קַרְנַיִם ***qarnayim***, n.pr.loc. GK: 7967 & 7969 [→ 6255, 7160, 7163; cf. 7162]. horn, (pair) of horns; something made of horns: wind instrument, container; horn often symbolizes strength and status, as in "horn of salvation"; as n.pr. Karnaim, "*horns*":– horns [43], horn [28], two horns [4], hill [1]

7162 קֶרֶן ***qeren*** (Aram.), n.f. GK: 10641 [cf. 7161]. horn (of an animal), also referring to a musical instrument:– horns [5], horn [5], cornet [4]

7163 קֶרֶן הַפּוּךְ ***qeren happûk***, n.pr.f. GK: 7968 [→ 7161]. Keren-Happuch, "*horn of [cosmetic] eye shadow;* i.e., *cosmetic case*":– Keren-happuch [1]

7164 קָרַס ***qāras***, v. GK: 7970 [→ 7165, 7166]. [Q] to stoop low, bend down:– stoopeth [1], stoop [1]

7165 קֶרֶס ***qeres***, n.[m.]. GK: 7971 [→ 7164]. clasp, hook (of curtains):– taches [10]

קֵרֹס ***qērōs***. See 7026.

7166 קַרְסֹל ***qarsōl***, n.[f.]. GK: 7972 [→ 7164]. (dual) ankles:– feet [2]

7167 קָרַע ***qāra'***, v. GK: 7973 [→ 7168]. [Q] to tear, rend, rip; [Qp] to be torn; [N] to be torn to pieces, be split apart:– rent [46], rend [5], tear [3], surely rend (+7167) [2], cutteth out [1], cut [1], rend away [1], rent away [1], rent in pieces (+7168) [1], rentest [1], tare [1]

7168 קְרָעִים ***qᵉrā'îm***, n.m.[pl.]. GK: 7974 [→ 7167]. torn pieces (of a garment), rags:– pieces [2], rags [1], rent in pieces (+7167) [1]

7169 קָרַץ ***qāraṣ***, v. GK: 7975 [→ 7171; cf. 7170]. [Q] to maliciously wink, purse (the lips); [Pu] to be shaped:– winketh [2], formed [1], moving [1], wink [1]

7170 קְרַץ ***qᵉraṣ*** (Aram.), n.[m.]. GK: 10642. piece, "to eat pieces" is slander, denouncement:– accused (+399) [2]

7171 קֶרֶץ ***qereṣ***, n.m. GK: 7976 [→ 7169]. gadfly; some sources: mosquito:– destruction [1]

7172 קַרְקַע ***qarqa'***, n.[m.]. GK: 7977 [→ 7173, 7174]. floor:– floor [6], bottom [1], other^{s} [1]

7173 קַרְקַע ***qarqa'***, n.pr.loc. GK: 7978 [→ 7172]. Karka, "*floor, ground*":– Karkaa [1]

7174 קַרְקֹר ***qarqōr***, n.pr.loc. GK: 7980 [→ 7172]. Karkor:– Karkor [1]

7175 קֶרֶשׁ ***qereš***, n.m. GK: 7983. frame:– boards [33], board [17], benches [1]

7176 קֶרֶת ***qeret***, n.f. GK: 7984 [→ 7151, 7152, 7156, 7177, 7178; cf. 7023 (also used with compound proper names)]. city, town:– city [5]

7177 קַרְתָּה ***qartâ***, n.pr.loc. GK: 7985 [→ 7176]. Kartah, "*city*":– Kartah [1]

7178 קַרְתָּן ***qartān***, n.pr.loc. GK: 7986 [→ 7176]. Kartan:– Kartan [1]

7179 קַשׁ ***qaš***, n.m. GK: 7990 [→ 7197]. stubble, chaff, straw:– stubble [15], gather stubble (+7197) [1]

7180 קִשֻּׁאָה ***qiššu'â***, n.f. GK: 7991 [→ 4750]. cucumber:– cucumbers [1]

7181 קָשַׁב ***qāšab***, v. GK: 7992 [→ 7182, 7183]. [Q] to listen; [H] to pay attention, give heed, listen:– hearken [21], attend [7], hearkened [5], give heed [2], attend to [1], attend unto [1], attended [1], cause to be heard [1], cause to hear [1], giveth heed [1], hearkened diligently (+7182) [1], incline [1], mark well [1], marked [1], regarded [1]

7182 קֶשֶׁב ***qešeb***, n.m. GK: 7993 [→ 7181]. paying attention, responding:– hearing [1], hearkened diligently (+7181) [1], heed [1], regarded [1]

7183 קַשָּׁב ***qaššāb*** or קַשֻּׁב ***qaššub***, a. GK: 7994 & 7995 [→ 7181]. attentive:– attentive [3], attent [2]

7184 קַשְׂוָה ***qaśwâ***, n.f. GK: 7987. pitcher, jar:– covers [3], cups [1]

7185 קָשָׁה ***qāšâ***, v. GK: 7996 [→ 7186, 7190]. [Q] to be hard, harsh, cruel; [N] to be distressed; [P] to have great difficulty (in labor); [H] to make stiff, harden, be difficult:– hardened [8], hard [4], hardeneth [2], harden [2], made grievous [2], cruel [1], fiercer [1], hard thing [1], hardly bestead [1], hardly [1], made stiff [1], sore [1], stiffened [1], stiffnecked (+6203) [1]

7186 קָשֶׁה ***qāšeh***, a. GK: 7997 [→ 7185]. hard, harsh, difficult, fierce; stubborn, stiff(-necked), obstinate:– hard [6], stiffnecked (+6203) [6], roughly [5], cruel [3], grievous [3], sore [2], churlish [1], hardhearted (+3820) [1], heavy [1], impudent (+6440) [1], in trouble (+3117) [1], obstinate [1], prevailed [1], rough [1], sorrowful [1], stiff [1], stubborn [1]

7187 קְשֹׁט ***qᵉšōṭ*** (Aram.), n.[m.]. GK: 10643 [cf. 7189]. truth; (as adv.) surely, truly, rightly:– of a truth (+4481) [1], truth [1]

7188 קָשַׁח ***qāšaḥ***, v. GK: 7998. [H] to harden:– hardened against [1], hardened [1]

7189 קֹשְׁט ***qōšṭ*** or קֹשֶׁט ***qōšeṭ***, n.m. GK: 7999 & 8000 [cf. 7198; cf. 7187]. truth; bow (weapon):– certainty [1], truth [1]

קשׁט ***qōšōṭ***. See 7187.

7190 קְשִׁי ***qᵉšî***, n.[m.]. GK: 8001 [→ 7185]. stubbornness:– stubbornness [1]

7191 קִשְׁיוֹן ***qišyôn***, n.pr.loc. GK: 8002. Kishion:– Kishion [1], Kishon [1]

7192 קְשִׂיטָה ***qᵉśîṭâ***, n.f. GK: 7988. piece of silver (unknown unit of weight or value):– piece of money [1], pieces of money [1], pieces of silver [1]

7193 קַשְׂקֶשֶׂת ***qaśqeśet***, n.f. GK: 7989 [cf. 7082]. scales (as on skin of marine creatures); scale armor:– scales [7], mail [1]

7194 קָשַׁר ***qāšar***, v. GK: 8003 [→ 7195, 7196]. [Q] to tie, bind; to plot, conspire; [Qp] to be bound up; be strong; [N] to be joined with; [P] to bind; [Pu] to be strong; [Ht] to conspire together:– conspired [18], bind [11], made a conspiracy (+7195) [4], bound [3], stronger [2], bound up [1], conspiracy made (+7195) [1], conspirators [1], joined together [1], knit [1], wrought [1]

7195 קֶשֶׁר ***qešer***, n.m. GK: 8004 [→ 7194]. conspiracy, treason:– treason [5], conspiracy [4], made a conspiracy (+7194) [4], confederacy [2], conspiracy made (+7194) [1]

7196 קִשֻּׁרִים ***qiššurîm***, n.[m.]pl. GK: 8005 [→ 7194]. sashes, wedding ornaments:– attire [1], headbands [1]

7197 קָשַׁשׁ ***qāšaš***, v.den. GK: 8006 & 8007 [→ 7179]. [Q] to gather together; [Pol] to gather; [Htpol] to gather together:– gathering [3], gather together [2], gather stubble (+7179) [1], gathered [1], gather [1]

7198 קֶשֶׁת ***qešet***, n.f. [& m.?]. GK: 8008 [→ 7199; cf. 7189]. bow (weapon); by extension, something bow shaped: rainbow:– bow [55], bows [13], archers [2], archers (+1869) [1], archers (+376+3384+871.1+1886.1) [1], archers (+4175+871.1+1886.1) [1], arrow (+1121) [1], bowmen (+7411) [1], bowshot (+2909) [1]

7199 קַשָּׁת ***qaššāt***, n.m. GK: 8009 [→ 7198]. archer:– archer (+7235) [1]

7200 רָאָה ***rā'â***, v. GK: 8011 [→ 7204, 4758, 4759, 7201?, 7202, 7203, 7203, 7207, 7209, 7210, 7212 (also used with compound proper names)]. [Q] to see, look, view; to realize, know, consider; [Qp] to be selected; [N] to become visible, appear, show oneself; [Pu] to be seen; [H] to cause to see, show; [Ho] to be shown; [Ht] to look at each other, meet with; a general word for visual perception; note the many contextual translations in the KJV:– see [349], saw [305], seen [161], behold [57], looked [53], look [50], appeared [39], shewed [37], seest [27], seeth [27], shew [27], appear [24], beheld [23], consider [15], seeing [11], seer [10], sawest [6], spied [5], considered [4], looketh [4], perceived [4], appeareth [3], enjoy [3], lo [3], respect [3], sheweth [3], beholdeth [2], considereth [2], foreseeth [2], indeed look (+7200) [2], look out [2], looked on [2], looked upon [2], provided [2], provide [2], regarded [2], saw certainly (+7200) [2], see indeed (+7200) [2], surely seen (+7200) [2], take heed [2], advise [1], approveth [1], beholding [1], caused to see [1], considerest [1], discern [1], espied [1], gaze [1], had experience [1], hath respect [1], in presence (+6440) [1], joyfully [1], make enjoy [1], mark [1], meet [1], near [1], perceive [1], presented [1], regardeth [1], regard [1], respecteth [1], seemeth [1], seer's [1], shewedst [1], sight [1], spy [1], stare [1], thinketh [1], view [1], visions [1]

7201 רָאָה ***rā'â***, n.f. GK: 8012 [→ 7200?]. red kite:– glede [1]

7202 רָאֶה ***rā'eh***, a. GK: 8013 [→ 7200]. seeing:–

7203 רֹאֶה ***rō'eh***, n.[m.]. GK: 8014 & 8015 [→ 7200]. seer; vision:– seers [1], vision [1]

7204 הָרֹאֶה ***hārō'eh*** or רֹאֶה ***rō'ēh***, n.pr.m. GK: 2218 [→ 7200]. Haroeh, "*the seer*":– Haroeh [1]

7205 רְאוּבֵן ***rᵉ'ûbēn***, n.pr.m. GK: 8017 [→ 7206]. Reuben, "*see, a son! [Ge 29:32]; substitute a son*":– Reuben [72]

7206 רְאוּבֵנִי **r^e'ûbēnî**, a.g. GK: 8018 [→ 7205]. Reubenite, of Reuben, "*of Reuben*":– Reubenites [16], Reubenite [1], Reuben [1]

7207 רַאֲוָה **ra'^{a}wâ**, n.f. GK: 8019 [→ 7200]. spectacle, sight:– beholding [1]

7208 רְאוּמָה **r^e'ûmâ**, n.pr.f. GK: 8020 [→ 7355? *or* 7214?]. Reumah:– Reumah [1]

7209 רְאִי **r^e'î**, n.m. GK: 8023 [→ 7200]. mirror:– looking glass [1]

7210 רֳאִי **r^o'î**, n.[m.]. GK: 8024 [→ 7200; cf. 7299]. appearance, spectacle:– seen [2], gazing-stock [1], look to [1], seest [1], seeth [1]

7211 רְאָיָה **r^e'āyâ**, n.pr.m. GK: 8025 [→ 7200+3068]. Reaiah, "*Yahweh has seen*":– Reaiah [3], Reaia [1]

7212 רְאִית **r^e'ît**, n.f. GK: 8026 [→ 7200]. look, sight:–

7213 רָאַם **rā'am**, v. GK: 8027 [→ 7216; cf. 7311]. [Q] to rise up high:– lifted up [1]

7214 רְאֵם **r^e'ēm**, n.m. GK: 8028 [→ 7208?]. wild oxen:– unicorn [6], unicorns [3]

7215 רָאמוֹת **rā'môt**, n.[f.pl.]. GK: 8029. coral:– coral [2]

7216 רָאמוֹת **rā'môt**, n.pr.loc. GK: 8030 [→ 7213; cf. 7311]. Ramoth, "*height*":– Ramoth [4]

7217 רֵאשׁ **rē'š** (Aram.), n.m. GK: 10646 [cf. 7218]. head (for functions of sight and thought as a crucial part of the body); fig., leader; or the very first part of an event, the beginning:– head [11], chief [1], heads [1], sum [1]

7218 רֹאשׁ **rō'š**, n.m. GK: 8031 [→ 7220, 7221, 7222, 7223, 7224, 7225, 7226; cf. 7217]. head (of the body); by extension: top (of an object); high in status or authority: leader, chief; source or origin: first, beginning; "to lift up the head" can mean to take a census, to behead, or to restore to a position:– head [263], chief [95], heads [85], top [67], beginning [12], sum [9], tops [8], companies [7], captains [6], first [6], company [5], principal [5], captain [4], chapiters [4], high [3], bands [2], beginnings [2], ends [2], rulers [2], beheaded (+5493) [1], chief place [1], chief things [1], chiefest [1], every [1], excellent [1], forefront [1], height [1], highest part [1], lead [1], of [1]

7219 רֹאשׁ **rō'š**, n.m. GK: 8032. poison; gall; bitterness:– gall [9], hemlock [1], poison [1], venom [1]

7220 רֹאשׁ **rō'š**, n.pr.m. & g. & loc. GK: 8033 & 8396 [→ 7218]. Rosh, "*head, leader*":– Rosh [1]

רֵאשׁ **rē'š**. See 7389.

7221 רִאשָׁה **ri'šâ**, n.f. GK: 8035 [→ 7218]. beginning, before:– beginnings [1]

7222 רֹאשָׁה **rō'šâ**, n.f. GK: 8036 [→ 7218]. uppermost, cap[stone]:– headstone (+68) [1]

7223 רִאשׁוֹן **ri'šôn**, a. GK: 8037 [→ 7224; cf. 7218]. (of position) first, foremost; (of time) former, beginning, earlier:– first [128], former [32], beginning [4], chief [3], foremost [3], before (+871.1+1886.1) [2], old time [2], aforetime (+871.1+1886.1) [1], ancestors [1], beforetime (+871.1+1886.1) [1], before [1], eldest [1], first (+871.1+1886.1) [1], forefathers (+1) [1], past [1]

7224 רִאשֹׁנִי **ri'šōnî**, a. GK: 8038 [→ 7223; cf. 7218]. first:– first [1]

7225 רֵאשִׁית **rē'šît**, n.f. GK: 8040 [→ 7218]. what is first; beginning:– beginning [18], firstfruits [10], first [10], chief [8], chiefest [1], first time [1], firstfruits (+6529) [1], firstfruit [1], principal thing [1]

7226 רַאֲשֹׁת **ra'^{a}šōt**, n.m. GK: 8031 [→ 7218]. pl. of 7218: place of the head:–

7227 רַב **rab**, a. & n. GK: 8041 & 8042 [→ 7237, 7248, 7249, 7262; cf. 7231; cf. 7229, cf. 7261]. many, much; great, abundant, numerous; commander, chief officer, high official:– many [191], great [117], much [33], captain [24], long [10], moe [8], enough [7], multitude [6], mighty [5], greater [4], more [4], greatly [3], manifold [3], plenteous [3], suffice [3], too much [3], abundantly [2], abundant [2], exceedingly [2], increased [2], long enough [2], many a time [2], princes [2], aboundeth [1], abound [1], common [1], elder [1], full [1], great men [1], great multitude [1], great one [1], great store [1], in abundance [1], in multitude [1], master [1], multiply [1], officers [1], oftentimes (+6471) [1], populous [1], process of time (+3117+1886.1+1886.1) [1], shipmaster (+2259+1886.1) [1], sufficient [1], too many [1]

7228 רַב **rab**, n.m. GK: 8043 [→ 7232]. archer:– archers [2]

7229 רַב **rab** (Aram.), a. GK: 10647 [→ 7236, 7260; cf. 7227]. great, large, many, chief; this can refer to a large object (great, large), a large amount of objects (many, much), or high status (chief):– great [9], master [2], captain [1], chief [1], lord [1], very great [1]

רִב **rib**. See 7378.

7230 רֹב **rōb**, n.m. GK: 8044 [→ 7231]. greatness, abundance; multitude:– multitude [69], abundance [32], greatness [9], great [9], much [7], abundantly (+3807.1) [3], many [3], abundance (+3807.1) [2], long [2], plenty [2], abundantly [1], all [1], common [1], excellent [1], great number (+3807.1) [1], great things [1], greatly (+3807.1) [1], huge (+3807.1) [1], in abundance (+3807.1) [1], increased [1], most [1], much (+3807.1) [1], number [1], plentifully (+3807.1) [1], plenty (+3807.1) [1], very [1]

7231 רָבַב **rābab**, v. GK: 8045 [→ 3377, 3378, 3379, 3380, 4764, 7227, 7230, 7233, 7237, 7239, 7241, 7245; cf. 7235]. [Q] to abound, increase, be great; [Pu] to increase by tens of thousands:– many [6], increased [3], multiplied [3], manifold [1], moe [1], more [1], multiply [1], ten thousands [1]

7232 רָבַב **rābab**, v. GK: 8046 [→ 7228; cf. 7235]. [Q] to shoot (an arrow):– shot out [1], shot [1]

7233 רְבָבָה **r^{e}bābâ**, n.f. GK: 8047 [→ 7231]. ten thousand, myriad; (virtually) countless number:– ten thousands [8], ten thousand [5], many [1], millions [1], multiply [1]

7234 רָבַד **rābad**, v. GK: 8048 [→ 4765, 7242]. [Q] to cover:– deckt [1]

7235 רָבָה **rābâ**, v. GK: 8049 & 8050 & 2221 [→ 697?, 1337, 4767, 4766, 4768, 8635, 8636; cf. 7231, 7232; cf. 7236]. [Q] to increase in number, multiply, grow large; to shoot; (ptcp.) archer; [P] to rear (offspring); to gain; make numerous; [H] to cause to increase, make numerous, enlarge:– multiply [38], multiplied [29], much [24], increase [19], many [19], increased [15], great [6], increaseth [5], more [5], give more [3], long [3], made many [3], greatly multiply (+7235) [2], made great [2], make many [2], much more [2], multiplieth [2], multiply exceedingly (+7235) [2], over much [2], very [2], abundance [1], abundantly [1], any more [1], archer (+7199) [1], ask never so much (+3966) [1], brought in abundance [1], brought up [1], continued [1], enlarge [1], exceeding (+3966) [1], exceedingly (+3966) [1], excelled [1], full [1], gathered much [1], give many [1], givest many [1], great store [1], greater [1], grow up [1], had many [1], heap [1], in authority [1], in process of time (+3117+1886.1) [1], increasest [1], make to multiply [1], many a time [1], more and more [1], much greater [1], multipliedst [1], multiplying [1], nourished [1], number [1], plenteous [1], plenty [1], so much as (+4480) [1], sore [1], store [1], take much [1], throughly [1], use many [1]

7236 רְבָה **r^{e}bâ** (Aram.), v. GK: 10648 [→ 7229, 7240?, 7238, 7260, 7261; cf. 7235]. [P] to become large, be great; [Pa] to place in a high position, make great:– grown [3], grew [2], made great [1]

7237 רַבָּה **rabbâ**, n.pr.loc. GK: 8051 [→ 7227; cf. 7231]. Rabbah, "*chief, capital [city]*":– Rabbah [13], Rabbath [2]

7238 רְבוּ **r^{e}bû** (Aram.), n.f. GK: 10650 [→ 7236]. greatness, high position:– majesty [3], greatness [2]

7239 רִבּוֹא **ribbô'**, n.f. GK: 8052 [→ 7231; cf. 7240]. ten thousand; myriad, (virtually) countless number:– thousand [3], forty two thousand (+505+702) [2], eighteen thousand (+505+8083+2050.1) [1], ten thousands [1], ten thousand [1], threescore and one thousand (+505+8337+2050.1) [1], twenty thousand [1]

7240 רִבּוֹ **ribbô** (Aram.), n.f. GK: 10649 [→ 7236?; cf. 7239]. ten thousand, myriad, (virtually) countless number:– ten thousand [2]

7241 רְבִיבִים **r^{e}bîbîm**, n.m. GK: 8053 [→ 7231]. rain shower, abundant rain, gentle rain:– showers [6]

7242 רָבִיד **rābîd**, n.[m.]. GK: 8054 [→ 7234]. necklace, ornamental chain:– chain [2]

7243 רְבִיעִי **r^{e}bî'î**, a.num.ord. GK: 8055 [→ 702; cf. 7244]. fourth:– fourth [55], foursquare [1]

7244 רְבִיעַי **r^{e}bî'āy** (Aram.), a.num.ord. GK: 10651 [→ 703; cf. 7243]. fourth:– fourth [6]

7245 רַבִּית **rabbît**, n.pr.loc. GK: 8056 [→ 7231]. Rabbith, "*great*":– Rabbith [1]

7246 רָבַךְ **rābak**, v. GK: 8057. [Ho] to be kneaded, mixed (of dough):– fried [2], baken [1]

7247 רִבְלָה **riblâ**, n.pr.loc. GK: 8058. Riblah:– Riblah [11]

7248 רַב מָג **rab māg**, n.m. GK: 8059 [→ 7227]. high official:– Rab-mag [2]

7249 רַב־סָרִיס **rab-sārîs**, n.m. GK: 8060 [→ 7227+5631]. chief officer:– Rab-saris [3]

7250 רָבַע **rāba'**, v.den. GK: 8061 [→ 7252; cf. 7257]. [Q] to lie down with, have sexual relations with; [H] to mate, cross-breed:– lie down [2], gender with [1]

7251 רָבַע **rāba'**, v.den. GK: 8062 [→ 702]. [Qp, P] to be squared, have four corners:– foursquare [8], square [3], squared [1]

7252 רֶבַע **reba'**, v.inf. GK: 8061 [→ 7250]. inf. of 7250: to lie down:– lying down [1]

7253 רֶבַע ***reba'***, n.m. GK: 8063 [→ 7254?; cf. 702?]. fourth-part, quarter; side (of a square thing):– sides [3], fourth part [2], squares [2]

7254 רֶבַע ***reba'***, n.pr.m. GK: 8064 [→ 7253?; cf. 702?]. Reba:– Reba [2]

7255 רֹבַע ***rōba'***, n.[m.]. GK: 8065 [→ 702]. fourth-part, quarter:– fourth part [2]

7256 רִבֵּעַ ***ribbēa'***, a. GK: 8067 [→ 702]. fourth; (n.) the fourth generation:– fourth [4]

רְבִיעִי *r^ebî'î*. See 7243.

7257 רָבַץ ***rābaṣ***, v. GK: 8069 [→ 4769, 7258; cf. 7250]. [Q] to lie down; [H] to make lie down; to cause to rest:– lie down [9], lieth [3], lie [3], lay down [2], lying [2], cause to lie down [1], causing to lie down [1], couched [1], coucheth [1], couching down [1], fell down [1], lay [1], make fold [1], makest to rest [1], maketh to lie down [1], sitting [1]

7258 רֵבֶץ ***rēbeṣ***, n.[m.]. GK: 8070 [→ 7257]. resting place:– resting place [2], place to lie down in [1], where lay [1]

7259 רִבְקָה ***ribqâ***, n.pr.f. GK: 8071. Rebekah, "[poss.] *choice calf*":– Rebekah [28], Rebekah's [2]

7260 רַבְרַב ***rabrab*** (Aram.), a. GK: 10647 [→ 7229]. same as 7229: great, large, many, chief; this can refer to a large object (great, large), a large amount of objects (many, much), or high status (chief):– great [7], stout [1]

7261 רַבְרְבָנִין ***rabr^ebānîn*** (Aram.), n.m.pl. GK: 10652 [→ 7236]. nobles, lords:– lords [6], princes [2]

7262 רַב־שָׁקֵה ***rab-šāqēh***, n.m. GK: 8072 [→ 7227+8248]. Assyrian officer: (field) commander, cupbearer:– Rab-shakeh [16]

7263 רֶגֶב ***regeb***, n.m. GK: 8073 [→ 709]. clod of dirt:– clods [2]

7264 רָגַז ***rāgaz***, v. GK: 8074 [→ 712, 7267, 7268, 7269; cf. 7265]. [Q] to quake, shake, tremble; to be angry, be in anguish; [H] to cause to shake, make tremble, cause a disturbance; [Ht] to enrage oneself (against):– tremble [8], rage [5], moved [4], trembled [3], troubled [3], disquieted [2], move [2], afraid [1], disquiet [1], fall out [1], fretted [1], made to tremble [1], much moved [1], provoke [1], quaked [1], quake [1], shaketh [1], shake [1], shook [1], stand in awe [1], wroth [1]

7265 רְגַז ***r^egaz*** (Aram.), v. GK: 10653 [→ 7266; cf. 7264]. [H] to anger, enrage:– provoked unto wrath [1]

7266 רְגַז ***r^egaz*** (Aram.), n.m. GK: 10654 [→ 7265; cf. 7267]. rage:– rage [1]

7267 רֹגֶז ***rōgez***, n.m. GK: 8075 [→ 7264; cf. 7266]. turmoil, excitement, tumult:– trouble [2], fear [1], noise [1], rage [1], troubling [1], wrath [1]

7268 רַגָּז ***raggāz***, a. GK: 8076 [→ 7264]. anxious, trembling:– trembling [1]

7269 רָגְזָה ***rogzâ***, n.f. GK: 8077 [→ 7264]. shuddering, agitation:– trembling [1]

7270 רָגַל ***rāgal***, v.den. GK: 8078 [→ 7272, 8637]. [Q] to slander; [P] to spy, explore:– spies [10], spy out [7], backbiteth [1], espy out [1], searched out [1], slandered [1], spied out [1], spy [1], taught to go [1], viewed [1], view [1]

7271 רְגַל ***r^egal*** (Aram.), n.[f.]. GK: 10655 [cf. 7272]. foot:– feet [7]

7272 רֶגֶל ***regel***, n.f. GK: 8079 [→ 4772, 7270, 7273, 8637; cf. 7271]. foot; by extension, body parts associated with the foot: sole, legs, big toe, ankle; a euphemism for the genitals; footing or base of an object; footstep, as a measure of length:– feet [152], foot [63], footstool (+1916) [5], times [4], after (+871.1) [3], follow (+871.1) [3], great toes [2], piss (+4325) [2], able to endure (+3807.1) [1], after (+3807.1) [1], brokenfooted (+7667) [1], coming [1], follow (+1980+871.1) [1], followed (+871.1) [1], foot (+3709) [1], footstool (+1916+3807.1) [1], goeth [1], haunt [1], legs [1], possession [1], went on journey (+5375) [1]

7273 רַגְלִי ***raglî***, a. GK: 8081 [→ 7272]. (persons) on foot (i.e., not riding):– footmen [7], footmen (+376) [4], on foot [1]

7274 רֹגְלִים ***rōg^elîm***, n.pr.loc. GK: 8082. Rogelim, "*[place of] treaders, fullers [one who cleans clothes by kneading with no soap]*":– Rogelim [2]

7275 רָגַם ***rāgam***, v. GK: 8083 [→ 4773, 7277]. [Q] to execute by hurling stones:– stone [9], stoned [5], certainly stone (+7275) [2]

7276 רֶגֶם ***regem***, n.pr.m. GK: 8084 [→ 7278; cf. 8638]. Regem, "*friend*":– Regem [1]

7277 רִגְמָה ***rigmâ***, n.f. GK: 8086 [→ 7275]. great throng, crowd, a bustling, noisy group:– council [1]

7278 רֶגֶם מֶלֶךְ ***regem melek***, n.pr.m. GK: 8085 [→ 7276+4428]. Regem-Melech, "*friend of the king;* [poss.] *chief of troops of the king*":– Regemmelech [1]

7279 רָגַן ***rāgan***, v. GK: 8087 [→ 5372]. [Q] to complain; [N] to be grumbling, be gossiping:– murmured [3]

7280 רָגַע ***rāga'***, v. GK: 8088 & 8089 & 8090 [→ 4771, 4774, 7281, 7282]. [Q] to stir up, churn up; to harden, crust over; [N] to cease; [H] to find repose, bring rest; to do something in an instant:– divideth [2], rest [2], suddenly [2], broken [1], cause to rest [1], divided [1], find ease [1], give rest [1], make to rest [1], moment [1]

7281 רֶגַע ***rega'***, n.m. GK: 8092 [→ 7280]. moment, instant; peace, tranquillity:– moment [13], in a moment [3], instant [2], every moment (+3807.1) [1], in a moment (+3509.1) [1], space [1], suddenly [1]

7282 רָגֵעַ ***rāgēa'***, a. GK: 8091 [→ 7280]. quiet, resting:– quiet [1]

7283 רָגַשׁ ***rāgaš***, v. GK: 8093 [→ 7285; cf. 7284]. [Q] to be restless, be in tumult, likely referring to a rebellious conspiracy:– rage [1]

7284 רְגַשׁ ***r^egaš*** (Aram.), v. GK: 10656 [cf. 7283]. [H] to go in as a group (causing an uproar), implying that those in the group are bumping into one another:– assembled [3]

7285 רֶגֶשׁ ***regeš*** or רִגְשָׁה ***rigšâ***, n.[m.]. GK: 8094 & 8095 [→ 7283]. crowd, throng:– company [1], insurrection [1]

7286 רָדַד ***rādad***, v. GK: 8096 [→ 7289]. [Q] to subdue, beat down; [H] to hammer out flat:– spent [1], spread [1], subdueth [1], subdue [1]

7287 רָדָה ***rādâ***, v. GK: 8097 & 8098 [→ 7288]. [Q] to rule over; to scoop out, scrape out; [H] to cause to dominate:– dominion [5], rule [5], ruled [3], bare rule [2], have dominion [2], made have dominion over [2], bear rule [1], made rule over [1], prevaileth [1], reign [1], rule over [1], ruler [1], taken [1], took [1]

7288 רַדַּי ***radday***, n.pr.m. GK: 8099 [→ 7287]. Raddai, "[poss.] *beating down; Yahweh rules*":– Raddai [1]

7289 רְדִיד ***r^edîd***, n.[m.]. GK: 8100 [→ 7286]. cloak, shawl, something wrapped around:– vails [1], vail [1]

7290 רָדַם ***rādam***, v. GK: 8101 [→ 8639]. [N] to be in a heavy sleep:– fast asleep [2], in a deep sleep [2], cast into a dead sleep [1], sleeper [1], sleepeth [1]

7291 רָדַף ***rādap***, v. GK: 8103 [→ 4783]. [Q] to pursue, chase, persecute; [N] to be pursued, be hounded; [P] to pursue, chase; [Pu] to be chased; [H] to chase:– pursued [35], pursue [28], persecute [15], chased [8], follow [8], persecutors [7], pursueth [7], chase [5], followeth after [5], persecuted [5], pursuers [5], pursuing [4], follow after [3], followed [2], followeth [1], hunt [1], past [1], persecution [1], pursuer [1], put to flight [1]

7292 רָהַב ***rāhab***, v. GK: 8104 [→ 7293, 7294, 7296, 7295; cf. 4062]. [Q] to rise up against; press one's plea; [H] to overwhelm; make bold:– behave proudly [1], make sure [1], overcome [1], strengthenedst [1]

7293 רַהַב ***rahab***, n.m. GK: 8105 [→ 7292]. same as 7294: pride, strength:– proud [2], strength [1]

7294 רַהַב ***rahab***, n.pr. GK: 8105 [→ 7292]. same as 7293: Rahab, a sea monster of chaos that opposes God; used of the land of Egypt, with a focus on affliction or arrogance:– Rahab [3]

7295 רָהָב ***rāhāb***, a. GK: 8107 [→ 7292]. proud, defiant:– proud [1]

7296 רֹהַב ***rōhab***, n.[m.]. GK: 8106 [→ 7292]. pride or hurry:– strength [1]

7297 רָהָה ***rāhâ*** or יָרָה ***yārah***, v. GK: 8109 & 3724. [Q] to fear:– afraid [1]

7298 רַהַט ***rahaṭ***, n.[m.]. GK: 8110 & 8111 [→ 7351]. tress, rafter; watering trough:– gutters [2], galleries [1], troughs [1]

7299 רֵו ***rēw*** (Aram.), n.m. GK: 10657. appearance:– form [2]

רוּב *rûb*. See 7378.

7300 רוּד ***rûd***, v. GK: 8113 [→ 4788]. [Q] to roam; [H] to grow restless, cause restlessness:– dominion [1], lords [1], mourn [1], ruleth [1]

7301 רָוָה ***rāwâ***, v. GK: 8115 [→ 3138, 7302, 7310, 7377]. [Q] to drink to satisfaction, quench the thirst; [P] to drench, refresh, satisfy; [H] to lavish upon, cause to refresh; from the base meaning of quenching thirst come the fig. extensions of refreshment, satisfaction, and fulfillment:– watereth [2], abundantly satisfied [1], bathed [1], filled [1], made drunken [1], made drunk [1], satiated [1], satiate [1], satisfy [1], soaked [1], take fill [1], waterest abundantly [1], water [1]

7302 רָוֶה ***rāweh***, a. GK: 8116 [→ 7301]. well-watered, drenched:– watered [2], drunkenness [1]

7303 רָהְגָּה ***rohgâ*** or רוֹהֲגָה ***rôh^agâ***, n.pr.m. GK: 8108 & 8117. Rohagah, Rohgah:– Rohgah [1]

7304 רָוַח ***rāwaḥ***, v. GK: 8118 [→ 7305, 7307, 7309, 7306, 7381]. [Q] to feel relief; [Pu] to be spacious:– refreshed [2], large [1]

7305 רֶוַח ***rewaḥ***, n.m. GK: 8119 [→ 7304]. relief; space:– enlargement [1], space [1]

7306 רִיחַ or רוּחַ ***rîaḥ*** or ***rûaḥ***, v. GK: 8193 [→ 7381; cf. 7304]. [H] to smell (an aroma or odor):– smell [5], smelled [2], accept [1], make of quick understanding [1], smelleth [1], toucheth [1]

7307 רוּחַ ***rûaḥ***, n.f. GK: 8120 [→ 7304; cf. 7308]. breath, wind; by extension: spirit, mind, heart, as the immaterial part of a person that can respond to God, the seat of life; spirit being, especially the Spirit of God:– spirit [227], wind [81], breath [27], winds [11], mind [5], side [5], spirits [5], blast [4], vain [2], air [1], anger [1], breath (+5397) [1], cool [1], courage [1], quarters [1], sides [1], spiritual [1], tempest [1], whirlwind (+5591) [1], windy [1]

7308 רוּחַ ***rûaḥ*** (Aram.), n.f. GK: 10658 [cf. 7382; cf. 7307]. wind, breath, spirit; from the base meaning of "wind" (or "breath") come the meaning of "spirit" as an immaterial supernatural being, and as the immaterial part of the inner person, with a possible focus on the reasoning and thinking faculty: "mind" or "heart":– spirit [8], mind [1], winds [1], wind [1]

7309 רְוָחָה ***r^{e}wāḥâ***, n.f. GK: 8121 [→ 7304]. relief, respite:– breathing [1], respite [1]

7310 רְוָיָה ***r^{e}wāyâ***, n.f. GK: 8122 [→ 7301]. place of abundance, overflowing:– runneth over [1], wealthy [1]

7311 רוּם or רָמַם ***rûm*** or ***rāmam***, v. GK: 8123 & 8249 & 8225 [→ 4791, 4792, 7213, 7312, 7315, 7316, 7317, 7318, 7319, 7410, 7415, 7427, 8641, 8642; cf. 7413, 7426; cf. 7313 (also used with compound proper names)]. [Q] to be high, raise up; to be proud, haughty; to be full of maggots, be wormy; [Pol] to exalt, lift high; [Polal] to be exalted, be lifted up; [H] to cause to lift up, present (an offering); to raise up against, rebel; [Ho] to be presented, be taken away; to exalt oneself; from the base meaning of being high in spatial position come the fig. extensions of being high in status: exalted, and high in attitude: proud, arrogant:– exalted [27], lift up [25], high [22], exalt [17], offer [11], lifted up [8], set up [6], take up [5], gave [4], exalteth [3], lifteth up [3], lofty [3], offer up [3], take off [3], take [3], tall [3], extol [2], heaved [2], held up [2], higher [2], liftest up [2], promotion [2], took up [2], bred [1], bring up [1], brought up [1], extolled [1], give [1], haughty [1], heaved up [1], heave [1], high ones [1], levy [1], lifted up on high [1], lifter up [1], lifteth [1], lifting up [1], loud [1], make on high [1], mount up [1], offered up [1], offered [1], presumptuously (+3027+871.1) [1], promote [1], proud [1], set up on high [1], setteth up [1], shouted aloud (+6963+8643+871.1+3807.1) [1], take away [1], taken away [1], taken off [1], taller [1], went up [1]

7312 רוּם ***rûm***, n.[m.]. GK: 8124 [→ 7311; cf. 7314]. height; haughtiness, pride:– haughtiness [3], high [2], height [1]

7313 רוּם ***rûm*** (Aram.), v. GK: 10659 [→ 7314; cf. 7311]. [P] to become arrogant; [Pol] to exalt, praise; [H] to promote, cause to rise (in rank); [Htpol] to rise up (against); all of these meanings are from the base meaning of "high":– lifted up [2], extol [1], set up [1]

7314 רוּם ***rûm*** (Aram.), n.m. GK: 10660 [→ 7313; cf. 7312?]. height; the top:– height [5]

7315 רוֹם ***rôm***, adv. GK: 8125 [→ 7311]. on high:– on high [1]

7316 רוּמָה ***rûmâ***, n.pr.loc. GK: 8126 [→ 7311; cf. 725]. Rumah, "*height*":– Rumah [1]

7317 רוֹמָה ***rômâ***, adv. GK: 8127 [→ 7311]. proudly, haughtily:– haughtily [1]

7318 רוֹמָם ***rômām***, n.[m.]. GK: 8128 [→ 7311]. praise, exaltation:–

7319 רוֹמֵמֻת ***rômēmut***, n.f. GK: 8129 [→ 7311, 7427]. rising up, lifting up:– high [1]

7320 רֹמַמְתִּי עֶזֶר ***rōmamtî 'ezer***, n.pr.m. GK: 8251 [→ 7311+5828]. Romamti-Ezer, "*[he is my] highest help*":– Romamti-ezer [2]

7321 רוּעַ ***rûa'***, v. GK: 8131 [→ 7452, 8643]. [H] to raise a battle cry; sound a trumpet blast; shout in triumph or exaltation:– shouted [10], shout [10], make a joyful noise [7], triumph [3], cried [2], sound an alarm [2], blow an alarm [1], cry alarm [1], cry aloud [1], cry out aloud (+7452) [1], cry out [1], cry [1], gave a shout [1], shout for joy [1], shouted for joy [1], shouting [1], smart (+7451) [1]

7322 רָפַף or רוּף ***rāpap*** or ***rûp***, v. GK: 8344. [Poal] to quake, shake:– tremble [1]

7323 רוּץ ***rûṣ***, v. GK: 8132 [→ 4793, 4794; cf. 7519?]. [Q] to run, hurry, be a messenger; [Pol] to dart about, run to and fro; [H] to chase; to bring quickly:– run [34], ran [28], guard [14], posts [6], running [6], runneth [4], make run [2], post [2], another^s [1], brake down [1], brought hastily [1], divided speedily [1], footmen [1], runnest [1], stretch out [1]

7324 רִיק or רוּק ***rîq*** or ***rûq***, v. GK: 8197 [→ 7385, 7386, 7387]. [H] to pour forth, empty out; to draw (a sword):– draw out [5], empty [4], draw [3], emptied [2], armed [1], cast out [1], make empty [1], pour out [1], poured forth [1]

7325 רִיר or רוּר ***rîr*** or ***rûr***, v. GK: 8201 [→ 7388]. [Q] to flow:– run [1]

7326 רוּשׁ ***rûš***, v. GK: 8133 [→ 7389; cf. 3423]. [Q] to be poor, be in poverty, be oppressed; [Htpol] to pretend to be poor:– poor [21], lack [1], maketh poor [1], needy [1]

רוֹשׁ ***rôš***. See 7219.

7327 רוּת ***rût***, n.pr.f. GK: 8134 [→ 7462?]. Ruth, "*friendship; refreshed [as with water]; [poss.] comrade, companion*":– Ruth [12]

7328 רָז ***rāz*** (Aram.), n.m. GK: 10661. mystery, secret:– secret [6], secrets [3]

7329 רָזָה ***rāzâ***, v. GK: 8135 [→ 7330, 7332, 7334]. [Q] to destroy; [N] to waste away:– famish [1], wax lean [1]

7330 רָזֶה ***rāzeh***, a. GK: 8136 [→ 7329]. lean; barren:– lean [2]

7331 רְזוֹן ***r^{e}zôn***, n.pr.m. GK: 8139 [→ 7336]. Rezon, "*prince; high official*":– Rezon [1]

7332 רָזוֹן ***rāzôn***, n.[m.]. GK: 8137 [→ 7329]. wasting disease; short, scrimped (ephah):– leanness [2], scant [1]

7333 רָזוֹן ***rāzôn***, n.m. GK: 8138 [→ 7336]. prince, dignitary:– prince [1]

7334 רָזִי ***rāzî***, n.[m.]. GK: 8140 [→ 7329]. wasting away, leanness:– leanness [2]

7335 רָזַם ***rāzam***, v. GK: 8141. [Q] to wink, flash the eyes:– wink [1]

7336 רָזַן ***rāzan***, v. GK: 8142 [→ 7333, 7331]. [Q] to be a ruler; (ptcp.) a prince, ruler:– princes [5], rulers [1]

7337 רָחַב ***rāḥab***, v. GK: 8143 [→ 4800, 7338, 7341, 7342, 7343, 7339, 7345, 7346]. [Q] to be wide; to swell (with joy); to boast; [N] to be roomy, be broad; [H] to enlarge, broaden, make wide:– enlarged [8], enlarge [7], enlargeth [2], large [2], enlarging [1], made room [1], make wide [1], maketh room [1], open wide [1], opened wide [1]

7338 רַחַב ***raḥab***, n.[m.]. GK: 8144 [→ 7337]. spacious place, vast expanse:– breadth [1], broad place [1]

7339 רְחֹב ***r^{e}ḥōb***, n.f. GK: 8148 [→ 1050, 7340, 7344; cf. 7337]. public square, open street:– street [21], streets [19], broad ways [2], broad places [1]

7340 רְחֹב ***r^{e}ḥōb***, n.pr.m. & loc. GK: 8149 & 8150 [→ 7339]. Rehob, "*broad, wide [place, market]*":– Rehob [10]

7341 רֹחַב ***rōḥab***, n.[m.]. GK: 8145 [→ 7337]. breadth, width:– breadth [74], broad [22], thickness [2], largeness [1], thick [1], wideness [1]

7342 רָחָב ***rāḥāb***, a. GK: 8146 [→ 7343?; cf. 7337]. spacious, broad, roomy:– broad [4], large [4], large (+3027) [3], proud [3], wide (+3027) [2], broad (+3027) [1], broader [1], large enough (+3027) [1], liberty [1], wide [1]

7343 רָחָב ***rāḥāb***, n.pr.f. GK: 8147 [→ 7342?; cf. 7337]. Rahab, "*spacious, broad*":– Rahab [5]

7344 רְחֹבוֹת ***r^{e}ḥōbôt***, n.pr.loc. GK: 8151 [→ 7339]. Rehoboth, "*broad, wide [places, markets]*":– Rehoboth [4]

7345 רְחַבְיָה or רְחַבְיָהוּ ***r^{e}ḥabyâ*** or ***r^{e}ḥabyāhû***, n.pr.m. GK: 8152 & 8153 [→ 7337+3068]. Rehabiah, "*Yahweh has enlarged*":– Rehabiah [5]

7346 רְחַבְעָם ***r^{e}ḥab'ām***, n.pr.m. GK: 8154 [→ 7337+5971]. Rehoboam, "*[my] people will enlarge, expand*":– Rehoboam [50]

רְחֹבֹת ***r^{e}ḥōbōt***. See 7344.

7347 רֵחַיִם ***rēḥayim***, n.[m.]. GK: 8160. handmill; pair of mill stones:– millstones [2], mills [1], mill [1], nether [1]

רְחוֹב ***r^{e}ḥôb***. See 7339, 7340.

7348 רְחוּם ***r^{e}ḥûm***, n.pr.m. GK: 8156 & 10662 [→ 7355; cf. 5149, 7359]. Rehum, "*[he] is compassionate*": note this name is Aramaic four times in Ezra:– Rehum [8]

7349 רַחוּם ***raḥûm***, a. GK: 8157 [→ 7355]. compassionate, merciful:– merciful [8], full of compassion [5]

7350 רָחוֹק ***rāḥôq***, a. (used as noun). GK: 8158 [→ 7368; cf. 7352]. far, distant; (n.) distance, afar:– far [31], afar off (+4480) [18], far off [13], afar off [4], afar [3], great while to come (+4480) [2], long ago (+4480+3807.1) [2], old [2], afar off (+4480+5704+3807.1) [1], afar off (+5704) [1], afar off (+871.1) [1], even afar off (+4480) [1], far abroad (+4480+5704+3807.1) [1], far off (+4480) [1], long (+4480) [1], long ago (+4480) [1], space [1]

7351 רָהִיט ***rāhîṭ***, n.m.col. GK: 8112 [→ 7298]. rafters:– rafters [1]

7352 רַחִיק ***raḥîq*** (Aram.), a. GK: 10663 [cf. 7350]. far away:– far [1]

7353 רָחֵל ***rāḥēl***, n.f. GK: 8161 [→ 7354]. ewe-sheep:– ewes [2], sheep [2]

7354 רָחֵל ***rāḥēl***, n.pr.f. GK: 8162 [→ 7353]. Rachel, "*ewe*":– Rachel [41], Rachel's [5], Rahel [1]

7355 רָחַם ***rāḥam***, v.den. GK: 8163 [→ 3395, 3396, 3397, 7208?, 7348, 7349, 7362; cf. 7358]. [Q] to love; [P] to have compassion on, show mercy, take pity on; [Pu] to find compassion, be loved; feelings of compassion are usually accompanied by acts of compassion:– have mercy [22], have compassion [7], shew mercy [3], hath mercy [2], pitieth [2], surely have mercy (+7355) [2], Ruhamah [1], findeth mercy [1], had compassion [1], had mercy [1], have pity [1], love [1], merciful [1], mercy [1], obtained mercy [1]

7356 רַחֲמִים ***raḥ^{a}mîm***, n.m.pl.abst. GK: 8171 [→ 7358; cf. 7359]. compassion, mercy, pity:– mercies [14], tender mercies [11], mercy [4], womb [4], bowels [2], compassions [2], compassion [2], damsel [1], mercies' [1], pitied [1], pity [1], tender love [1]

7357 רַחַם ***raḥam***, n.pr.m. GK: 8165 [→ 7360]. Raham, "*compassion*":– Raham [1]

7358 רֶחֶם ***reḥem***, n.m. GK: 8167 [→ 7361, 7356; cf. 7355]. womb; by extension: mother, any female, birth; an "open womb" is able to conceive; a "closed womb" cannot conceive:– womb [20], matrix [5], wombs [1]

7359 רַחֲמִין ***raḥ^{a}mîn*** (Aram.), n.[m.]pl.intens. GK: 10664 [cf. 7348; cf. 7356]. mercy, compassion:– mercies [1]

7360 רָחָם ***rāḥām*** or רָחָמָה ***rāḥāmâ***, n.[m.]. GK: 8164 & 8168 [→ 7357]. carrion-vulture; some sources: osprey:– gier eagle [2]

7361 רַחֲמָה ***raḥ^{a}mâ***, n.f. GK: 8169 [→ 7358]. womb; slang for woman:– two^s [1]

7362 רַחֲמָנִי ***raḥ^{a}mānî***, a. GK: 8172 [→ 7355]. compassionate:– pitiful [1]

7363 רָחַף ***rāḥap***, v. GK: 8173. [Q] to tremble, shake; [P] to hover:– fluttereth [1], moved [1], shake [1]

7364 רָחַץ ***rāḥaṣ***, v. GK: 8175 [→ 7366, 7367]. [Q] to wash, bathe; [Pu] to be cleansed; [Ht] to wash oneself:– wash [36], bathe [18], washed [16], washed away [1], washing [1]

7365 רְחַץ ***r^{e}ḥaṣ*** (Aram.), v. GK: 10665. [Htpe] to put one's trust in, rely on:– trusted [1]

7366 רַחַץ ***raḥaṣ***, n.[m.]. GK: 8176 [→ 7364]. washing:– washpot (+5518) [2]

7367 רַחְצָה ***raḥṣâ***, n.f. GK: 8177 [→ 7364]. washing:– washing [2]

7368 רָחַק ***rāḥaq***, v. GK: 8178 [→ 1023, 3128, 4801, 7350, 7369]. [Q] to be far off; to avoid, stand aloof; [P] to send far away, extend; [H] to remove far away, drive far off, go very far:– far [19], far off [4], remove far [4], put away far [3], put far [3], far removed [2], go far [2], removed far [2], very far away (+7368) [2], afar off [1], cast far off [1], drive far [1], far away [1], flee far [1], go far off [1], gone away far [1], gone far [1], good way off [1], good way [1], keep far [1], put far away [1], refrain [1], remove far off [1], removed far away [1], withdraw far [1]

7369 רָחֵק ***rāḥēq***, a.vbl. GK: 8179 [→ 7368]. one who is far away:– far from [1]

רָחֹק ***rāḥōq***. See 7350.

7370 רָחַשׁ ***rāḥaš***, v. GK: 8180 [→ 4802]. [Q] to be stirred up (one's heart):– inditing [1]

7371 רַחַת ***raḥat***, n.f. GK: 8181. winnowing fork, shovel:– shovel [1]

7372 רָטַב ***rāṭab***, v. GK: 8182 [→ 7373]. [Q] to be drenched, be wet:– wet [1]

7373 רָטֹב ***rāṭōb***, a. GK: 8183 [→ 7372]. well-watered (plant):– green [1]

7374 רֶטֶט ***reṭeṭ***, n.[m.]. GK: 8185 [cf. 7578]. panic:– fear [1]

7375 רֻטֲפַשׁ ***ruṭ^{a}paš***, v. GK: 8186. [Qp] to be renewed:– fresher [1]

7376 רָטַשׁ ***rāṭaš***, v. GK: 8187. [P] to dash to pieces; [Pu] to be dashed to pieces:– dashed in pieces [3], dash to pieces [1], dashed to pieces [1], dash [1]

7377 רִי ***rî***, n.[m.]. GK: 8188 [→ 7301]. moisture:– watering [1]

7378 רִיב ***rîb***, v. GK: 8189 [→ 3080, 3114, 3401, 4807, 4808, 4809, 7379]. [Q] to quarrel, contend, plead for:– plead [22], strive [7], contend [6], chide [4], contended [3], strove [3], chode [2], ever strive (+7378) [2], pleaded [2], throughly plead (+7378) [2], adversaries [1], complain [1], contend with [1], contendest [1], contendeth [1], debate with [1], debate [1], laid wait [1], plead for [1], pleadeth the cause [1], rebuked [1], strive together [1], striveth [1]

7379 רִיב ***rîb***, n.m. GK: 8190 & 8191 [→ 7378]. contention, grievance, strife, legal dispute:– cause [23], strife [14], controversy [12], contention [2], strivings [2], adversary (+376) [1], causes [1], chiding [1], contended [1], controversies [1], multitude [1], pleadings [1], strive with [1], suit [1]

7380 רִיבַי ***rîbay***, n.pr.m. GK: 8192 [→ 3403?]. Ribai, "*opponent*":– Ribai [2]

7381 רֵיחַ ***rêaḥ***, n.m. GK: 8194 [→ 7306; cf. 7304; cf. 7382]. aroma; pleasing and acceptable: fragrance; unpleasing and unacceptable: stench; both connotations are used of sacrifices as accepted or rejected by God:– savour [45], smell [11], sent [2]

7382 רֵיחַ ***rêaḥ*** (Aram.), n.f. GK: 10666 [cf. 7308; cf. 7381]. (singed, scorched) smell:– smell [1]

רֵים ***rêm***. See 7214.

רֵיעַ ***rêa'***. See 7453.

7383 רִיפוֹת ***rîpôt***, n.[f.]. GK: 8195. grain:– ground corn [1], wheat [1]

7384 רִיפַת ***rîpat*** or דִּיפַת ***dîpat***, n.pr.g. GK: 8196 & 1910. Riphath, Diphath:– Riphath [2]

7385 רִיק ***rîq***, n.[m.]. GK: 8198 [→ 7324]. emptiness, nothingness, vanity:– vain [8], vanity [2], empty [1], no purpose [1]

7386 רֵיק ***rêq***, a. GK: 8199 [→ 7324]. empty; idle, worthless:– vain [7], empty [6], emptied [1]

7387 רֵיקָם ***rêqām***, adv. GK: 8200 [→ 7324]. empty-handed, without cause or satisfaction:– empty [12], without cause [2], in vain [1], void [1]

7388 רִיר ***rîr***, n.m. GK: 8202 [→ 7325]. saliva; white (of an egg); some sources: a kind of plant juice:– spittle [1], white [1]

7389 רֵישׁ ***rêš***, n.m. GK: 8203 [→ 7326]. poverty:– poverty [7]

7390 רַךְ ***rak***, a. GK: 8205 [→ 7401]. gentle, tender, weak, soft:– tender [10], soft [3], fainthearted (+3824+1886.1) [1], tender one [1], weak [1]

7391 רֹךְ ***rōk***, n.[m.]. GK: 8204 [→ 7401]. gentleness, tenderness, softness:– tenderness [1]

7392 רָכַב ***rākab***, v. GK: 8206 [→ 4817, 4818, 7393, 7395, 7394, 7396, 7398]. [Q] to ride or mount an riding animal:– rode [15], riding [10], ride [8], rider [7], rideth [7], riders [5], carried [3], caused to ride [3], put [3], cause to ride [2], made ride [2], on horseback (+5483) [2], ride on [2], set [2], bring [1], brought on horseback [1], causest to ride [1], gat up [1], made to ride [1], make to ride [1], ridden [1]

7393 רֶכֶב ***rekeb***, n.m. GK: 8207 [→ 7392]. chariot; large upper mill stone:– chariots [86], chariot [29], millstone [2], upper millstone [1], wagons [1]

7394 רֵכָב ***rēkāb***, n.pr.m. GK: 8209 & 8211 [cf. 7392]. Recab, "[prob.] *rider* or *horseman* [from to ride, mount]":– Rechab [13]

7395 רַכָּב ***rakkāb***, n.m. GK: 8208 [→ 7392]. chariot driver, horseman:– chariot man [1], driver of chariot [1], horseman [1]

7396 רִכְבָּה ***rikbâ***, n.f. GK: 8210 [→ 7392]. act of riding:– chariots [1]

7397 רֵכָה ***rēkâ***, n.pr.loc. GK: 8212. Recah:– Rechabites [4], Rechah [1]

7398 רְכוּב ***r^{e}kûb***, n.[m.]. GK: 8213 [→ 7392]. chariot:– chariot [1]

7399 רְכוּשׁ ***r^{e}kûš***, n.m. GK: 8214 [→ 7408]. possessions, property, goods, equipment:– goods [12], substance [11], riches [5]

7400 רָכִיל ***rākîl***, n.[m.]. GK: 8215 [→ 7402?]. slanderer, gossip:– slanders [2], talebearer [2], carry tales [1], talebearer (+1980) [1]

7401 רָכַךְ ***rākak***, v. GK: 8216 [→ 4816, 7391, 7390]. [Q] to be soft, faint-hearted; [Pu] to be soothed; [H] to make faint:– faint [2], tender [2], fainthearted (+3824) [1], maketh soft [1], mollified [1], softer [1]

7402 רָכַל ***rākal***, v. GK: 8217 [→ 4819, 7400?, 7403?, 7404]. [Q] to do trade, act as a merchant; (n.) trader, merchant:– merchants [14], merchant [3]

7403 רָכָל ***rākāl***, n.pr.loc. GK: 8218 [→ 7402?]. Racal, "*trade*":– Rachal [1]

7404 רְכֻלָּה ***r^{e}kullâ***, n.f. GK: 8219 [→ 7402]. trading of merchandise:– merchandise [2], traffick [2]

7405 רָכַס ***rākas***, v. GK: 8220 [→ 7406, 7407?; cf. 7409]. [Q] to tie, bind:– bind [2]

7406 רֶכֶס ***rekes***, n.[m.]. GK: 8221 [→ 7405]. rugged place:– rough places [1]

7407 רֹכֶס ***rōkes***, n.[m.]. GK: 8222 [→ 7405?]. intrigue, plot, conspiracy:– pride [1]

7408 רָכַשׁ ***rākaš***, v. GK: 8223 [→ 7399]. [Q] to tie, bind:– gotten [3], gathered [1], got [1]

7409 רֶכֶשׁ ***rekeš***, n.m.col. GK: 8224 [cf. 7405]. team of horses; fast horses (for couriers):– mules [2], dromedaries [1], swift beast [1]

רְכֻשׁ ***r^{e}kuš***. See 7399.

רֵם ***rēm***. See 7214.

7410 רָם ***rām***, n.pr.m. GK: 8226 [→ 7311]. Ram, "*high, exalted*":– Ram [7]

רֻם ***rum***. See 7311.

7411 רָמָה ***rāmâ***, v. GK: 8227 & 8228 [→ 759, 3414, 4820, 4821, 7419, 7423, 8649; cf. 7503?; cf. 7412]. [Q] to hurl (horse and rider); to shoot (arrows); [P] to deceive, betray:– deceived [4], beguiled [2], thrown [2], betray [1], bowmen (+7198) [1], carrying [1], deceiveth [1]

Heb

7412 רְמָה ***r^e^mâ*** (Aram.), v. GK: 10667 [cf. 7411]. [P] to throw; to impose; [Peil] to be thrown, be set in place; [Htpe] to be thrown:– cast [11], impose [1]

7413 רָמָה ***rāmâ***, n.f. GK: 8229 [→ 7414, 7433, 7418, 7432, 7434, 7437, 7435; cf. 7311]. lofty shrine; height:– high place [3], high places [1]

7414 רָמָה ***rāmâ*** or רָמָתַיִם ***rāmātayim***, n.pr.loc. GK: 8230 & 8259 [→ 7413]. Ramah; Ramoth, *"elevated spot, height"*; Ramathaim, *"two heights"*:– Ramah [36], Ramath [1]

7415 רִמָּה ***rimmâ***, n.f. GK: 8231 [→ 7311]. worm, maggot:– worm [5], worms [2]

7416 רִמּוֹן ***rimmôn***, n.m. GK: 8232 [→ 1667, 7417, 7428]. pomegranate: the tree, its fruit, or decorative objects shaped like the fruit:– pomegranates [22], pomegranate [8], pomegranate tree [2]

7417 רִמּוֹן ***rimmôn*** or רִמּוֹנוֹ ***rimmônô***, n.pr.m. & loc. GK: 8233 & 8234 & 8235 & 8237 [→ 1910, 2886, 5884]. Rimmon, *"pomegranate* or pagan god *Rimmon"*; for Remmon-methoar, see also 1886.1 and 8388:– Rimmon [14], Remmon-methoar (+8388+1886.1) [1], Remmon [1]

רָמוֹת ***rāmôt***. See 7418, 7433.

7418 רָמוֹת־נֶגֶב ***rāmôt-negeb***, n.pr.loc. GK: 8241 [→ 7418+5045]. Ramoth Negev, *"heights of Negev [the south]"*:– Ramoth [1]

7419 רָמוּת ***rāmût***, n.f. GK: 8239 [→ 7411]. remains, refuse, rubbish:– height [1]

7420 רֹמַח ***rōmaḥ***, n.[m.]. GK: 8242. spear:– spears [9], spear [3], buckler [1], javelin [1], lancets [1]

7421 רַמִּי ***rammî***, n.pr.m. GK: 8246. Ramite or Aramean:– Syrians [1]

7422 רַמְיָה ***ramyâ***, n.pr.m. GK: 8243 [→ 7311?+3068?]. Ramiah, *"Yahweh is exalted"*:– Ramiah [1]

7423 רְמִיָּה ***r^e^miyyâ***, n.f. GK: 8244 & 8245 [→ 7411]. laziness, laxness, slackness; deceit:– deceitful [4], deceitfully [3], deceit [2], slothful [2], false [1], guile [1], idle [1], slack [1]

7424 רַמָּכָה ***rammākâ***, n.[f.]. GK: 8247. fast mare:– dromedaries [1]

7425 רְמַלְיָהוּ ***r^e^malyāhû***, n.pr.m. GK: 8248 [→ 3068]. Remaliah, *"Yahweh has adorned"*:– Remaliah [11], Remaliah's [2]

7426 רָמַם ***rāmam***, v. GK: 8250 [cf. 7311]. [Q] to be exalted; [N] to rise upward; to get away:– exalted [3], get up [1], lift up [1], lifted up [1], mounted up [1]

7427 רוֹמֵמֻת ***rômēmut***, n.f. GK: 8129 [→ 7319]. same as 7319: rising up, lifting up:– lifting up [1]

רִמֹּן ***rimmōn***. See 7416.

7428 רִמּוֹן פֶּרֶץ ***rimmôn pereṣ***, n.pr.loc. GK: 8236 [→ 7416+6556]. Rimmon Perez, *"pomegranate pass [breach]"*:– Rimmon-parez [2]

7429 רָמַס ***rāmas***, v. GK: 8252 [→ 4823]. [Q] to trample, tread upon; [N] to be trampled:– tread down [4], tread [2], trode down [2], trode upon [2], oppressors [1], stamped upon [1], stamped [1], trample under feet [1], trample [1], treadeth down [1], treadeth [1], trodden [1], trode under foot [1]

7430 רָמַשׂ ***rāmaś***, v. GK: 8253 [→ 7431]. [Q] to move along (ground or in the water):– creepeth [9], moveth [5], creep [2], moved [1]

7431 רֶמֶשׂ ***remeś***, n.m. GK: 8254 [→ 7430]. creatures that move along (ground or sea):– creeping things [7], creeping thing [7], moving thing [1], thing that creepeth [1], things creeping [1]

7432 רֶמֶת ***remet***, n.pr.loc. GK: 8255 [→ 7413]. Remeth, *"heights"*:– Remeth [1]

7433 רָמוֹת גִּלְעָד ***rāmôt gil'ād***, n.pr.loc. GK: 8240 [→ 7413+1568]. Ramoth Gilead, *"heights in Gilead"*:– Ramoth-gilead [18], Ramoth [3]

7434 רָמַת הַמִּצְפֶּה ***rāmat hammiṣpeh***, n.pr.loc. GK: 8256 [→ 7413]. Ramath Mizpah, *"height [hill] of Mizpah [watch tower]"*:– Ramath-mizpeh [1]

7435 רָמָתִי ***rāmātî***, a.g. GK: 8258 [→ 7413]. Ramathite, *"of Ramah"*:– Ramathite [1]

7436 רָמָתַיִם צוֹפִים ***rāmātayim ṣôpîm***, n.pr.loc. GK: 8259 + 7435 [→ 7413+6822]. Ramathaim Zophim:– Ramathaim-zophim [1]

7437 רָמַת לְחִי ***rāmat l^e^ḥî***, n.pr.loc. GK: 8257 [→ 7413+3895?]. Ramath Lehi, *"height [hill] of Lehi"*:– Ramath-lehi [1]

רָן ***rān***. See 1028.

7438 רֹן ***rōn***, n.[m.]. GK: 8260 [→ 7442]. (joyful) song:– songs [1]

7439 רָנָה ***rānâ***, v. GK: 8261 [→ 7440, 7441; cf. 7442]. [Q] to rattle:– rattleth [1]

7440 רִנָּה ***rinnâ***, n.f. GK: 8262 [→ 7441; cf. 7439, 7442]. shout of joy, song of joy; cry of pleading:– cry [12], singing [9], joy [3], rejoicing [3], gladness [1], proclamation [1], shouting [1], sing [1], songs [1], triumph [1]

7441 רִנָּה ***rinnâ***, n.pr.m. GK: 8263 [→ 7440; cf. 7439]. Rinnah, *"ringing cry [of joy] to Yahweh"*:– Rinnah [1]

7442 רָנַן ***rānan***, v. GK: 8264 [→ 7438, 7444, 7445, 7443; cf. 7439, 7440]. [Q] to shout for joy, sing for joy; to cry, plead; [P] to sing for joy; [Polal] to sing for joy; [H] to make sing, call for songs of joy:– sing [17], rejoice [9], shout for joy [4], sing aloud [4], crieth [2], caused to sing for joy [1], crieth out [1], cry out [1], greatly rejoice [1], into joy sing [1], joyful [1], makest to rejoice [1], sang [1], shout aloud for joy (+7444) [1], shouted [1], shouteth [1], shout [1], sing for joy [1], sing out [1], singing [1], triumph [1]

7443 רְנָנִים ***r^e^nānîm***, n.[m.]pl. GK: 8266 [→ 7442]. female ostrich:– goodly [1]

7444 רַנֵּן ***rannēn***, v.inf. GK: 8264 [→ 7442]. inf. of 7442: to shout for joy, sing for joy:– shout aloud for joy (+7442) [1], singing [1]

7445 רְנָנָה ***r^e^nānâ***, n.f. GK: 8265 [→ 7442]. shout of joy, joyful song:– joyful voice [1], joyful [1], singing [1], triumphing [1]

7446 רִסָּה ***rissâ***, n.pr.loc. GK: 8267 [→ 7450?]. Rissah, *"dew"*:– Rissah [2]

7447 רָסִיס ***rāsîs***, n.[m.]. GK: 8268 & 8269 [→ 7450]. broken piece (of rubble); drop (of moisture):– breaches [1], drops [1]

7448 רֶסֶן ***resen***, n.m. GK: 8270. bridle:– bridle [4]

7449 רֶסֶן ***resen***, n.pr.loc. GK: 8271. Resen:– Resen [1]

7450 רָסַס ***rāsas***, v. GK: 8272 [→ 7446?, 7447]. [Q] to moisten, sprinkle:– temper [1]

7451 רַע ***ra'***, a. & n. GK: 8273 & 8274 & 8288 [cf. 7489]. bad, disagreeable, inferior in quality; by extension: evil, wicked in ethical quality; what is disagreeable to God is ethically evil; God's actions of judgment are disagreeable to the wicked (Eze 14:21), but are not ethically evil:– evil [436], wickedness [58], wicked [25], hurt [20], mischief [19], bad [13], sore [9], trouble [9], evils [8], ill [6], affliction [5], harm [5], adversity [3], naught [3], grievous [2], ill favoured [2], mischiefs [2], noisome [2], sad [2], adversities [1], afflictions [1], calamities [1], displease (+5869+6213+871.1) [1], displeased (+241+871.1) [1], displeased exceedingly (+1419+3415) [1], displeasure [1], distress [1], doest evil [1], evil favouredness (+1697) [1], evil men [1], great wickedness (+7465) [1], grief [1], grieved exceedingly (+1419+7489) [1], heavy [1], hurtful [1], mischievous [1], misery [1], naughty [1], please not (+5869+871.1) [1], pleased not (+5869+871.1) [1], sadly [1], smart (+7321) [1], sorrow [1], troubles [1], vex (+6213) [1], wicked ones [1], wickedly (+871.1) [1], wickedly [1], worse [1], worst [1], wretchedness [1], wrong [1]

7452 רֵעַ ***rēa'***, n.m.vbl. GK: 8275 [→ 7321]. shouting, roar:– cry out aloud (+7321) [1], noise [1], shouted [1]

7453 רֵעַ ***rēa'***, n.m. GK: 8276 [→ 7462]. neighbor; friend, companion, associate:– neighbour [73], friend [28], neighbour's [26], another^s^ [21], friends [14], fellow [8], companion [3], neighbours [2], other^s^ [2], another's (+7794) [1], another's^s^ [1], brother [1], companions' [1], companions [1], fellow's [1], fellows [1], husband [1], lovers [1], neighbour's (+3807.1) [1], neighbours' [1]

7454 רֵעַ ***rēa'***, n.[m.]. GK: 8277. thought, intention:– thoughts [1], thought [1]

7455 רֹעַ ***rōa'***, n.[m.]. GK: 8278 [→ 7489]. bad, disagreeable, inferior in quality; by extension: evil, wicked in ethical quality:– evil [11], wickedness [3], badness [1], bad [1], naughtiness [1], sadness [1], sorrow [1]

7456 רָעֵב ***rā'ēb***, v. GK: 8279 [→ 7458, 7457, 7459]. [Q] to be hungry, be famished, be starving:– hungry [3], hunger [2], suffer hunger [2], famished [1], suffer to famish [1], suffered to hunger [1]

7457 רָעֵב ***rā'ēb***, a. GK: 8281 [→ 7456]. hungry:– hungry [22], hunger-bitten [1]

7458 רָעָב ***rā'āb***, n.m. GK: 8280 [→ 7456]. hunger, famine, starvation:– famine [87], hunger [8], dearth [5], famished [1]

7459 רְעָבוֹן ***r^e^'ābôn***, n.[m.]. GK: 8282 [→ 7456]. hunger, famine, starvation:– famine [3]

7460 רָעַד ***rā'ad***, v. GK: 8283 [→ 7461]. [Q, H] to tremble:– trembling [2], trembleth [1]

7461 רַעַד ***ra'ad*** or רְעָדָה ***r^e^'ādâ***, n.m. & f. GK: 8284 & 8285 [→ 7460]. trembling:– trembling [4], fearfulness [1], fear [1]

7462 רָעָה ***rā'â***, v. GK: 8286 & 8287 & 8289 [→ 4828, 4829, 4830, 7327?, 7453, 7463, 7464, 7466, 7467, 7468, 7469, 7471, 7472, 7473, 7474]. [Q] to be a companion, be a friend; to be a shepherd, to care for flocks, graze; by extension: to rule, with a focus on care and concern; [P] to be an attendant of the groom (of a wedding):– feed [55], shepherds [31], shepherd [27], fed [11], herdmen [7], pastors [7], feedeth on [3], feeding [3], kept [3], companion [2], feedeth

Heb

[2], shepherds (+6629) [2], broken [1], devour [1], eat up [1], eaten up [1], eat [1], evil entreateth [1], feedest [1], friend [1], keeper [1], keepeth company with [1], keepeth [1], keeping [1], make friendship [1], pastor [1], shepherd (+6629) [1], shepherd's [1], shepherds' [1], shew friendly [1], wander [1], waste [1]

7463 רֵעֶה ***rē'eh,*** n.m. GK: 8291 [→ 7462]. friend, personal advisor:– friend [3]

7464 רֵעָה ***rē'â,*** n.f. GK: 8292 [→ 7462]. companion, friend:– companions [2], fellows [1]

7465 רֹעָה ***rō'â,*** v.ptcp. GK: 8318 [→ 7489; cf. 7492, 7533]. ptcp. of 7489: broken:– broken [1], great wickedness (+7451) [1]

7466 רְעוּ ***r^{e}'û,*** n.pr.m. GK: 8293 [→ 7462; cf. 7472]. Reu, "*friend [of God]*":– Reu [4], Rehu [1]

7467 רְעוּאֵל ***r^{e}'û'ēl,*** n.pr.m. GK: 8294 [→ 7462+410]. Reuel, "*friend of God [El]*":– Reuel [10], Raguel [1]

7468 רְעוּת ***r^{e}'ût,*** n.f. GK: 8295 [→ 7462]. (female) neighbor; fellow (female):– another [2], mate [2], neighbour [2]

7469 רְעוּת ***r^{e}'ût,*** n.f. GK: 8296 [cf. 7470]. chasing after:– vexation [7]

7470 רְעוּ ***r^{e}'û*** (Aram.), n.f. GK: 10668 [→ 7476; cf. 7469]. will, decision:– pleasure [1], will [1]

7471 רְעִי ***r^{e}'î,*** n.[m.]. GK: 8297 [→ 7462]. pastured (cattle):– pastures [1]

7472 רֵעִי ***rē'î,*** n.pr.m. GK: 8298 [→ 7462; cf. 7466]. Rei, "*friendly* or *[my] friend*":– Rei [1]

7473 רֹעִי ***rō'î,*** v.ptcp. GK: 8286 [→ 7462]. ptcp. of 7462: shepherd:– shepherd's [1], shepherd [1]

7474 רַעְיָה ***ra'yâ,*** n.f. GK: 8299 [→ 7462]. darling, beloved, formally, companion, a woman who is the object of a man's love and affection:– love [9]

7475 רַעְיוֹן ***ra'yôn,*** n.[m.]. GK: 8301. chasing after, striving for:– vexation [3]

7476 רַעְיוֹן ***ra'yôn*** (Aram.), n.m. GK: 10669 [→ 7470; cf. 7475]. thought (in one's mind):– thoughts [5], cogitations [1]

7477 רָעַל ***rā'al,*** v. GK: 8302 [→ 4831, 7478, 7479, 8653]. [Ho] to be made to quiver:– terribly shaken [1]

7478 רַעַל ***ra'al,*** n.[m.]. GK: 8303 [→ 7477]. reeling:– trembling [1]

7479 רְעָלָה ***r^{e}'ālâ,*** n.[f.]. GK: 8304 [→ 7477]. veil:– mufflers [1]

7480 רְעֵלָיָה ***r^{e}'ēlāyâ,*** n.pr.m. GK: 8305 [cf. 7485]. Reelaiah:– Reelaiah [1]

7481 רָעַם ***rā'am,*** v.den. GK: 8306 & 8307 [→ 7482, 7485]. [Q] to be confused, distorted; to storm, thunder; [H] to irritate, agitate; to make thunder, make storm:– roar [3], thundered [3], thundereth [3], thunder [2], make fret [1], troubled [1]

7482 רַעַם ***ra'am,*** n.[m.]. GK: 8308 [→ 7481]. thunder; thunderous shout:– thunder [6]

7483 רַעְמָה ***ra'mâ,*** n.f. GK: 8310. mane (of a horse):– thunder [1]

7484 רַעְמָה ***ra'mâ*** or רַעְמָא ***ra'mā',*** n.pr.m. & loc. GK: 8311 & 8309. Raamah:– Raamah [5]

7485 רַעַמְיָה ***ra'amyâ,*** n.pr.m. GK: 8313 [→ 7481+3068; cf. 7480]. Raamiah, "*Yahweh has thundered*":– Raamiah [1]

7486 רַעְמְסֵס ***ra'm^{e}sēs,*** n.pr.loc. GK: 8314. Rameses, a town in Egypt and a region in the Nile Delta, "*Ra created him*":– Rameses [4], Raamses [1]

7487 רַעֲנָן ***ra^{a}nan*** (Aram.), a. GK: 10670 [cf. 7488?]. prosperous, flourishing:– flourishing [1]

7488 רָעַן ***rā'an,*** v. or רַעֲנָן ***ra^{a}nān,*** a. GK: 8316 [cf. 7487]. [Palel] to flourish; (n.) spreading (tree), verdant, luxuriant:– green [18], flourishing [1], fresh [1]

7489 רָעַע ***rā'a',*** v.den. GK: 8317 & 8318 [→ 4827, 7451, 7455, 7465]. [Q] to be distressed, be displeased; (by extension) to be bad, be evil; to break, shatter; [N] to suffer harm; [H] to do wickedness; bring trouble, mistreat; this refers to what is displeasing from a personal perspective; what is displeasing to God is ethically evil; [Htpol] to come to ruin:– evildoers [10], do evil [9], hurt [6], evil [4], wicked [4], afflicted [3], do harm [3], done evil [3], worse [3], afflict [2], break [2], displease (+5869+871.1) [2], done evil indeed (+7489) [2], done wickedly [2], evil entreated [2], still do wickedly (+7489) [2], utterly broken down (+7489) [2], associate [1], behaved ill [1], break in pieces [1], bring evil [1], broken [1], brought evil [1], deal worse [1], dealt ill [1], destroyed [1], did worse [1], displease (+3415+871.1) [1], displeased (+3415+871.1) [1], displeased (+5869+871.1) [1], do hurt [1], do wickedly [1], done mischief [1], evil doers [1], evildoer [1], grieved exceedingly (+1419+7451) [1], hurting [1], ill [1], punish [1], vexed [1], wicked doer [1], wickedly [1]

7490 רְעַע ***r^{e}'a'*** (Aram.), v. GK: 10671 [cf. 7533]. [P] to break, crush; [Pa] to break to pieces, shatter:– breaketh [1], bruise [1]

7491 רָעַף ***rā'ap,*** v. GK: 8319 [cf. 6201]. [Q] to drop, fall, overflow; [H] to cause to rain:– drop down [2], drop [2], distil [1]

7492 רָעַץ ***rā'aṣ,*** v. GK: 8320 [cf. 7465, 7533]. [Q] to shatter:– dashed in pieces [1], vexed [1]

7493 רָעַשׁ ***rā'aš,*** v. GK: 8321 [→ 7494]. [Q] to shake, quake, tremble; [N] to be made to quake; [H] to cause to shake, make to tremble:– shake [13], trembled [5], tremble [3], moved [2], shook [2], made to shake [1], made to tremble [1], make afraid [1], quake [1], remove [1]

7494 רַעַשׁ ***ra'aš,*** n.m. GK: 8323 [→ 7493]. commotion, rattling, earthquake; this can mean a quaking motion and the sounds from a quaking motion; by extension: any clamor, discord, or frenzy:– earthquake [6], rushing [3], shaking [3], commotion [1], confused noise [1], fierceness [1], quaking [1], rattling [1]

7495 רָפָא ***rāpā',*** v. GK: 8324 [→ 4832, 7498, 7500, 7505, 7499, 8644 (also used with compound proper names)]. [Q] to heal; [N] to be healed, be cured; [P] to heal, repair; [Ht] to recover:– healed [31], heal [21], healeth [4], physicians [4], cause to be thoroughly healed (+7495) [2], cure [1], made whole [1], make whole [1], physician [1], repaired [1]

7496 רְפָאִים ***r^{e}pā'îm,*** n.m. GK: 8327 [cf. 7503?]. dead, the spirits of the departed:– dead [7], deceased [1]

7497 רְפָאִים ***r^{e}pā'îm,*** n.pr.g. GK: 8328 & 8329 [cf. 7503?]. Rephaite, "*mighty*"; Rephaim, "*sunken, powerless ones [giants]; [poss.] shades, ghosts of the dead ones [giants]*":– giants [10], giant [7], Rephaim [6], Rephaims [2]

7498 רָפָא ***rāpā'*** or רָפָה ***rāpâ,*** n.pr.m. GK: 8325 & 8334 [→ 7495; cf. 7501]. Rapha, Raphah, "[poss.] *one healed*":– Rapha [2]

7499 רְפוּאָה ***r^{e}pû'â,*** n.f. GK: 8337 [→ 7495]. healing:– medicines [2], healed [1]

7500 רִפְאוּת ***rip'ût,*** n.f. GK: 8326 [→ 7495]. health, healing:– health [1]

7501 רְפָאֵל ***r^{e}pā'ēl,*** n.pr.m. GK: 8330 [→ 7495+410; cf. 7498]. Rephael, "*God [El] heals*":– Rephael [1]

7502 רָפַד ***rāpad,*** v. GK: 8331 [→ 7507, 7508]. [Q] to spread (mud, so as to leave a trail); [P] to spread out; to refresh:– comfort [1], made [1], spreadeth [1]

7503 רָפָה ***rāpâ,*** v. GK: 8332 [→ 4832, 7504, 7510; cf. 7411?, 7496?, 7497?]. [Q] to hang limp, sink down, be feeble; [N] to be lazy; [P] to lower; discourage; [H] to leave alone, abandon, withdraw; [Ht] to show oneself slack:– fail [4], let alone [4], feeble [3], idle [3], let go [3], slack [3], stay [3], faint [2], forsake [2], let down [2], waxed feeble [2], weakened [2], weakeneth [2], abated [1], cease [1], consumeth [1], draweth [1], give respite [1], go [1], leave [1], slothful [1], still [1], wax feeble [1], weak [1]

7504 רָפֶה ***rāpeh,*** a. GK: 8333 [→ 7503]. weak, feeble:– weak [4]

רָפָה ***rāpâ, rāpâ.*** See 7497, 7498.

רִפָּה ***ripâ.*** See 7383.

7505 רָפוּא ***rāpû',*** n.pr.m. GK: 8336 [→ 7495]. Raphu, "*healed*":– Raphu [1]

7506 רֶפַח ***repaḥ,*** n.pr.m. GK: 8338. Rephah, "[poss.] *rich; easy [life]*":– Rephah [1]

7507 רְפִידָה ***r^{e}pîdâ,*** n.f. GK: 8339 [→ 7502]. base (of a royal carriage); some sources: seat cover:– bottom [1]

7508 רְפִידִים ***r^{e}pîdîm,*** n.pr.loc. GK: 8340 [→ 7502]. Rephidim, "[poss.] *supports, rests; resting place*":– Rephidim [5]

7509 רְפָיָה ***r^{e}pāyâ,*** n.pr.m. GK: 8341 [cf. 7498?]. Rephaiah, "*Yahweh heals*":– Rephaiah [5]

7510 רִפָּיוֹן ***rippāyôn,*** n.[m.]. GK: 8342 [→ 7503]. hanging limp, possibly referring to despair:– feebleness [1]

7511 רָפַס ***rāpas*** or רָפַשׂ ***rāpaś,*** v. GK: 8346 [→ 4833, 7515; cf. 7512]. same as 7515: [Q] to muddy (a stream by trampling through); [N] to be muddied; [Ht] to be humbled, humble oneself:– humble [1], submit [1]

7512 רְפַס ***r^{e}pas*** (Aram.), v. GK: 10672 [cf. 7511]. [P] to trample down:– stamped [2]

7513 רַפְסֹדוֹת ***rapsōdôt,*** n.[f.pl.]. GK: 8343. (log) rafts:– flotes [1]

7514 רָפַק ***rāpaq,*** v. GK: 8345. [Ht] to lean oneself (upon):– leaning [1]

7515 רָפַשׂ ***rāpaś,*** v. GK: 8346 [→ 7511]. same as 7511: [Q] to muddy (a stream by trampling through); [N] to be muddied; [Ht] to be humbled, humble oneself:– fouledst [1], foul [1], troubled [1]

7516 רֶפֶשׁ ***repeš,*** n.[m.]. GK: 8347. mire (of the sea):– mire [1]

7517 רֶפֶת ***repet,*** n.[m.]. GK: 8348. stall, enclosure for cattle:– stalls [1]

7518 רַץ **raṣ**, n.[m.]. GK: 8349. bar (of silver):– pieces [1]

7519 רָצָא **rāṣāʾ**, v. GK: 8351 & 8352 [→ 7521; cf. 7323?]. [Q] to take pleasure in, accept; to run forth:– ran [1]

7520 רָצַד **rāṣad**, v. GK: 8353. [P] to gaze in hostility:– leap [1]

7521 רָצָה **rāṣâ**, v. GK: 8354 & 8355 [→ 7519, 7522, 7525?, 7526?, 8656]. [Q] to be pleased, delight in, accept; to pay for (sin); [Qp] to be favored, be esteemed; [N] to be accepted; to be paid for; [P] to make amends; [H] to enjoy; [Ht] to regain favor:– accept [13], accepted [7], enjoy [3], favourable [3], please [3], taketh pleasure [3], accepteth [2], delighteth [2], pleased with [2], pleased [2], take pleasure [2], acceptable [1], accomplish [1], approve [1], consentedst [1], delight in [1], delightest in [1], delight [1], enjoyed [1], hadst a favour [1], hast pleasure [1], liked [1], pardoned [1], reconcile [1], set affection [1]

7522 רָצוֹן **rāṣôn**, n.[m.]. GK: 8356 [→ 7521]. pleasure, acceptance, favor, will:– favour [15], will [9], acceptable [7], delight [5], accepted [4], pleasure [4], desire [3], good will [2], would [2], acceptable (+3807.1) [1], acceptance [1], good pleasure [1], selfwill [1], voluntary will [1]

7523 רָצַח **rāṣaḥ**, v. GK: 8357 [→ 7524]. [Q] to murder, kill; [N] to be murdered, killed; [P] to murder, kill:– slayer [17], murderer [13], kill [4], murder [3], slain [3], manslayer [2], killed [1], killing [1], murderers [1], put to death [1], slayeth [1]

7524 רֶצַח **reṣaḥ**, n.[m.]. GK: 8358 [→ 7523]. slaughter, murder, agony of death:– slaughter [1], sword [1]

7525 רִצְיָא **riṣyāʾ**, n.pr.m. GK: 8359 [→ 7521?]. Rizia, "[poss.] *pleasant one*":– Rezia [1]

7526 רְצִין **rᵉṣîn**, n.pr.m. GK: 8360 [→ 7521?]. Rezin:– Rezin [11]

7527 רָצַע **rāṣaʿ**, v. GK: 8361 [→ 4836]. [Q] to pierce (ear):– bore through [1]

7528 רָצַף **rāṣap**, v. GK: 8362 [→ 4837, 7531]. [Qp] to be inlaid, be fitted:– paved [1]

7529 רֶצֶף **reṣep**, n.f. GK: 8363 [→ 7530, 7531, 7532]. hot coals, live coals:– baken on the coals [1]

7530 רֶצֶף **reṣep**, n.pr.loc. GK: 8364 [→ 7529]. Rezeph, "*heated stones, live coals*":– Rezeph [2]

7531 רִצְפָּה **riṣpâ**, n.f. GK: 8365 & 8367 [→ 7528, 7529]. live coal, hot coal; (stone) pavement:– pavement [7], live coal [1]

7532 רִצְפָּה **riṣpâ**, n.pr.f. GK: 8366 [→ 7529]. Rizpah, "*heated stones, live coals*":– Rizpah [4]

7533 רָצַץ **rāṣaṣ**, v. GK: 8368 [→ 4835; cf. 7465, 7492; cf. 7490]. [Q] break, smash, oppress; [Qp] to be smashed, broken, splintered, oppressed; [N] to be broken, splintered; [P] to oppress, crush; [H] to crush to pieces; [Htpol] to jostle each other:– oppressed [6], broken [4], bruised [2], all to brake [1], brakest in pieces [1], break [1], crushed [1], crush [1], discouraged [1], struggled together [1]

7534 רַק **raq**, a. GK: 8369 [→ 7535, 7541, 7542, 7550, 7557]. lean, thin, lank:– leanfleshed (+1320) [1], lean [1], thin [1]

7535 רַק **raq**, adv. GK: 8370 [→ 7534]. only, but, however, except:– only [60], but [20], howbeit [5], nevertheless [5], surely [3], notwithstanding [2], save [2], yet [2], at the least [1], except [1], howsoever [1], in any wise [1], indeed only (+389) [1], nothing but [1], save only [1], save that [1], so that (+518) [1], so [1]

7536 רֹק **rōq**, n.[m.]. GK: 8371 [→ 7556]. spit, saliva; "to swallow one's spit" means a very brief time:– spitting [1], spittle [1], spit [1]

7537 רָקַב **rāqab**, v. GK: 8372 [→ 7538, 7539]. [Q] to rot, become worm-eaten:– rot [2]

7538 רָקָב **rāqāb**, n.[m.]. GK: 8373 [→ 7537]. rottenness, decay:– rottenness [4], rotten thing [1]

7539 רִקָּבוֹן **riqqābôn**, n.[m.]. GK: 8375 [→ 7537]. rottenness:– rotten [1]

7540 רָקַד **rāqad**, v. GK: 8376. [Q] to skip, dance; [P] to leap about, dance; [H] to make skip:– dance [3], skipped [2], dancing [1], jumping [1], leap [1], maketh to skip [1]

7541 רַקָּה **raqqâ**, n.f. GK: 8377 [→ 7534]. temple (of the head):– temples [5]

7542 רַקּוֹן **raqqôn**, n.pr.loc. GK: 8378 [→ 7534]. Rakkon, "*narrow place*":– Rakkon [1]

7543 רָקַח **rāqaḥ**, v. GK: 8379 [→ 4840, 4841, 4842, 7544, 7545, 7546, 7547, 7548]. [Q] to make perfume, mix spices; [Pu] to be blended (of perfume); [H] to mix spices:– apothecary [4], compoundeth [1], made [1], prepared [1], spice [1]

7544 רֶקַח **reqaḥ**, n.[m.]. GK: 8380 [→ 7545; cf. 7543]. (powdered) spice:– spiced [1]

7545 רֹקַח **rōqaḥ**, n.[m.]. GK: 8381 [→ 7544; cf. 7543]. fragrant blend, spice-blend:– confection [1], ointment [1]

7546 רַקָּח **raqqāḥ**, n.m. GK: 8382 [→ 7543]. perfume-maker, ointment-mixer:– apothecaries [1]

7547 רִקֻּחַ **riqquaḥ**, n.[m.]. GK: 8383 [→ 7543]. perfume, ointment:– perfumes [1]

7548 רַקָּחָה **raqqāḥâ**, n.f. GK: 8384 [→ 7543]. perfume-maker, ointment-mixer:– confectionaries [1]

7549 רָקִיעַ **rāqîaʿ**, n.m. GK: 8385 [→ 7554]. expanse (of the sky or heaven); the space above the earth that holds visible objects: clouds, planets, stars:– firmament [17]

7550 רָקִיק **rāqîq**, n.m. GK: 8386 [→ 7534]. wafer, (thin, flat) cake:– wafers [4], wafer [3], cakes [1]

7551 רָקַם **rāqam**, v. GK: 8387 [→ 7552?, 7553]. [Q] to embroider, weave colored thread; [Pu] to be woven together:– needlework (+4639) [4], embroiderer [2], curiously wrought [1], needlework [1], wrought with needlework (+4639) [1]

7552 רֶקֶם **reqem** or רָקֶם **rāqem**, n.pr.m. & loc. GK: 8388 & 8389 & 8390 [→ 7551?]. Rakem, Rekem, "*friendship*":– Rekem [5], Rakem [1]

7553 רִקְמָה **riqmâ**, n.f. GK: 8391 [→ 7551]. embroidered work; varied colored things:– broidered work [5], broidered [2], divers colours [2], needlework [2], raiment of needlework [1]

7554 רָקַע **rāqaʿ**, v. GK: 8392 [→ 3421, 7549, 7555]. [Q] to spread out; stamp upon, trample; [P] to hammer out thin, overlay (with precious metal); [Pu] to be hammered, be beaten thin; [H] to cause to spread out, make into plated metal:– beat [1], made broad [1], spread abroad [1], spread forth [1], spread into plates [1], spread out [1], spreadeth abroad [1], spreadeth over [1], stamped [1], stamp [1], stretched out [1]

7555 רִקֻּעַ **riqquaʿ**, n.[m.]. GK: 8393 [→ 7554]. sheet, something beaten thin:– broad [1]

7556 רָקַק **rāqaq**, v. GK: 8394 [→ 7536; cf. 3417]. [Q] to spit saliva:– spit [1]

7557 רַקַּת **raqqat**, n.pr.loc. GK: 8395 [→ 7534]. Rakkath, "*narrow place*":– Rakkath [1]

7558 רִשְׁיוֹן **rišyôn**, n.[m.]. GK: 8397 [→ 3423]. authorization, permission:– grant [1]

7559 רָשַׁם **rāšam**, v. GK: 8398 [cf. 7560]. [Qp] to be written, be inscribed:– noted [1]

7560 רְשַׁם **rᵉšam** (Aram.), v. GK: 10673 [cf. 7559]. [P] to put in writing, publish; [Peil] to be written, be published:– signed [4], written [2], sign [1]

7561 רָשַׁע **rāšaʿ**, v.den. GK: 8399 [→ 4849, 7562, 7563, 7564]. [Q] to do evil, act wickedly; to be guilty; [H] to declare guilty, condemn, inflict punishment; to do wrong:– condemn [11], do wickedly [4], done wickedly [4], wicked [4], condemneth [2], wickedly departed [2], committed wickedness [1], condemned [1], condemning [1], dealt wickedly [1], make trouble [1], very wickedly [1], vexed [1]

7562 רֶשַׁע **rešaʿ**, n.m. GK: 8400 [→ 7561]. evil, wickedness, wrongdoing:– wickedness [25], wicked [4], iniquity [1]

7563 רָשָׁע **rāšāʿ**, a. GK: 8401 [→ 7561]. wicked, evil, guilty:– wicked [252], ungodly [8], condemned [1], guilty [1], him that did wrong [1]

7564 רִשְׁעָה **rišʿâ**, n.f. GK: 8402 [→ 7561]. wickedness:– wickedness [13], fault [1], wickedly [1]

7565 רֶשֶׁף **rešep**, n.m. GK: 8404 [→ 7566]. flame:– coals [2], arrows [1], burning coals [1], burning heat [1], hot thunderbolts [1], sparks (+1121) [1]

7566 רֶשֶׁף **rešep**, n.pr.m. GK: 8405 [→ 7565]. Resheph, "*flame, flash of fire*":– Resheph [1]

7567 רָשַׁשׁ **rāšaš**, v. GK: 8406 [→ 8658?, 8659?]. [Pol] to destroy, shatter; [Pu] to be crushed, shattered:– impoverished [1], impoverish [1]

7568 רֶשֶׁת **rešet**, n.f. GK: 8407 [→ 3423]. net, snare, trap (for catching game); network (net-like metal grating):– net [20], network (+4639) [2]

7569 רַתּוֹק **rattôq**, n.[m.]. GK: 8408 [→ 7576]. chain:– chain [1]

7570 רָתַח **rātaḥ**, v. GK: 8409 [→ 7571]. [P] to bring to a boil; [Pu] to be caused to churn; [H] to make to churn:– boiled [1], make boil well (+7571) [1], maketh to boil [1]

7571 רֶתַח **retaḥ**, n.[m.]. GK: 8410 [→ 7570]. boiling:– make boil well (+7570) [1]

7572 רַתִּיקָה **rattîqâ**, n.[m.]. GK: 8411 [→ 7576]. chain:– chains [1]

7573 רָתַם **rātam**, v. GK: 8412 [→ 7574, 7575?]. [Q] to tie up, harness (horse team):– bind [1]

7574 רֹתֶם **rōtem**, n.m. GK: 8413 [→ 7575; cf. 7573?]. broom tree:– juniper tree [2], juniper [2]

7575 רִתְמָה ***ritmâ***, n.pr.loc. GK: 8414 [→ 7574; cf. 7573?]. Rithmah, "*[place of] broom plants*":– Rithmah [2]

7576 רָתַק ***rātaq***, v. GK: 8415 [→ 7569, 7572, 7577]. [Pu] to be bound with chains:– bound [1], loosed [1]

7577 רְתֻקוֹת ***rᵉtuqôt***, n.[f.pl.]. GK: 8416 [→ 7576]. chains:– chains [1]

7578 רְתֵת ***rᵉtēt***, n.[m.]. GK: 8417 [cf. 7374]. trembling, fright:– trembling [1]

7578.1 -שַׁ ***ša-***, pt.rel.pref. GK: 8611 [→ 4332, 4967, 7706]. who, that, because; see under 7945:–

7579 שָׁאַב ***šā'ab***, v. GK: 8612 [→ 4857]. [Q] to draw and carry water:– draw [9], drew [5], drawers [3], drawer [1], drawn [1]

7580 שָׁאַג ***šā'ag***, v. GK: 8613 [→ 7581]. [Q] to roar:– roar [10], roared [4], roaring [3], mightily roar (+7580) [2], roareth [1]

7581 שְׁאָגָה ***šᵉ'āgâ***, n.f. GK: 8614 [→ 7580]. roar, groan:– roaring [6], roarings [1]

7582 שָׁאָה ***šā'â***, v. GK: 8615 & 8616 [→ 7585, 7588, 7591, 7612, 7866?, 7898?, 8663]. [Q] to lie wasted; [N] to be ruined; to roar; [H] to turn into desolation:– lay waste [2], desolate [1], make a rushing [1], rush [1], wasted [1]

7583 שָׁאָה ***šā'â***, v. GK: 8617 [cf. 8159]. [Ht] to watch closely, gaze at:– wondering [1]

7584 שַׁאֲוָה ***ša'ᵃwâ***, n.f. GK: 8618. devastating storm:–

7585 שְׁאוֹל ***šᵉ'ôl***, n.f. & m. GK: 8619 [→ 7582; cf. 8040]. grave; by extension, realm of death, deepest depths, transliterated "Sheol":– hell [31], grave [30], pit [3], grave's [1]

7586 שָׁאוּל ***šā'ûl***, n.pr.m. GK: 8620 [→ 7587; cf. 7592]. Saul, Shaul, "*asked,* [poss.] *dedicated to God*":– Saul [368], Saul's [28], Shaul [7], Saul's (+3807.1) [3]

7587 שָׁאוּלִי ***šā'ûlî***, a.g. GK: 8621 [→ 7586]. Shaulite, "*of Shaul*":– Shaulites [1]

7588 שָׁאוֹן ***šā'ôn***, n.m. GK: 8623 [→ 7582]. roar, uproar, tumult, loud noise; waste, desolation:– noise [8], rushing [3], tumult [3], tumultuous [2], horrible [1], pomp [1]

7589 שְׁאָט ***šᵉ'āṭ***, n.[m.]. GK: 8624. malice:– despiteful [2], despite [1]

7590 שׁוּט ***šûṭ*** or שָׁאט ***šā'ṭ***, v. GK: 8764. [Q] to malign, act malicious:– despise [2], despised [1]

7591 שְׁאִיָּה ***šᵉ'iyyâ***, n.f. GK: 8625 [→ 7582]. desolation, ruin:– destruction [1]

7592 שָׁאַל ***šā'al***, v. GK: 8626 [→ 847, 848, 4862, 7586, 7587, 7956, 7957, 7961; cf. 7593 (also used with compound proper names)]. [Q] to ask, inquire, request; [Qp] to be given over; [N] to ask permission; [P] to ask intently, beg; [H] to give what is asked for:– asked [46], ask [38], inquired [15], inquire [7], asketh [4], borrow [4], desired [4], earnestly asked (+7592) [4], lent [4], required [4], asking [3], demand [3], requested [3], require [3], saluted (+7965+3807.1) [3], asked straitly (+7592) [2], beg [2], borrowed [2], desire [2], salute (+7965+3807.1) [2], surely ask (+7592) [2], ask on [1], ask petition (+7596) [1], askest [1], consulted [1], consulter [1], demanded [1], desire a request (+7596) [1], desiredst [1], desireth [1], greet (+7965+3807.1) [1], laid to charge [1], obtained [1], pray [1], wished [1], wishing [1]

7593 שְׁאֵל ***šᵉ'ēl*** (Aram.), v. GK: 10689 [→ 7595; cf. 7592]. [P] to ask, question:– asked [3], demanded [1], requireth [1], require [1]

7594 שְׁאָל ***šᵉ'āl***, n.pr.m. GK: 8627 [→ 7592]. Sheal, "*May God grant!, asking*":– Sheal [1]

שְׁאֹל ***šᵉ'ōl***. See 7585.

7595 שְׁאֵלָה ***šᵉ'ēlâ*** (Aram.), n.f. GK: 10690 [→ 7593; cf. 7596]. verdict, decision:– demand [1]

7596 שְׁאֵלָה ***šᵉ'ēlâ***, n.f. GK: 8629 [→ 7956; cf. 7592; cf. 7595]. petition, request:– petition [9], request [2], ask petition (+7592) [1], desire a request (+7592) [1], loan [1]

7597 שְׁאַלְתִּיאֵל ***šᵉ'altî'ēl*** or שַׁלְתִּיאֵל ***šaltî'ēl***, n.pr.m. GK: 8630 & 9003 [→ 7592+410]. Shealtiel, "*I have asked [him] of God [El];* [poss.] *God [El] is a shield, God [El] is a victor*":– Shealtiel [8], Salathiel [1]

7598 שְׁאַלְתִּיאֵל ***šᵉ'altî'ēl*** (Aram.), n.pr.m. GK: 10691 [cf. 7597]. Shealtiel:– Shealtiel [1]

7599 שָׁאַן ***šā'an***, v. GK: 8631 [→ 7600, 7946]. [Palpal] to be at ease, be at rest, be secure:– at ease [2], quiet [2], rest [1]

7600 שַׁאֲנָן ***ša'ᵃnān***, a. GK: 8633 [→ 7599]. at ease, complacent, secure; insolent, proud:– at ease [6], quiet [2], tumult [2]

7601 שָׁסַס ***šāsas*** or שָׁאַס ***šā'as***, v. GK: 9116 [→ 4933, 8155; cf. 8154]. same as 8155: [Q] to plunder, ransack; [N] to be looted, be ransacked:– spoil [1]

7602 שָׁאַף ***šā'ap***, v. GK: 8634 & 8635 [cf. 7779]. [Q] to pant after, long for, pursue; to trample, crush:– swallow up [4], desire [1], devour [1], earnestly desireth [1], hasteth [1], panted [1], pant [1], snuffed up [1], snuffeth up [1], swallowed up [1], swalloweth up [1]

7603 שְׂאֹר ***šᵉ'ōr***, n.m. GK: 8419 [→ 4958, 4863]. yeast, leaven:– leaven [4], leavened bread [1]

7604 שָׁאַר ***šā'ar***, v. GK: 8636 [→ 7605, 7610, 7609, 7611; cf. 7606]. [Q] to remain; [N] to be left, remain; [H] to leave, spare:– left [64], remained [23], remain [15], leave [12], remaineth [8], remnant [4], let [3], rest [2], left behind [1], reserve [1]

7605 שְׁאָר ***šᵉ'ār***, n.m. GK: 8637 [→ 7604; cf. 7606]. remainder, remnant, the rest:– remnant [11], rest [10], residue [4], other [1]

7606 שְׁאָר ***šᵉ'ār*** (Aram.), n.m. GK: 10692 [cf. 7605]. the rest, remainder:– rest [9], residue [2], more [1]

7607 שְׁאֵר ***šᵉ'ēr***, n.m. GK: 8638 [→ 7608]. flesh, meat; by extension: the body as a whole; blood relative, as one's "flesh and blood":– flesh [7], near kinswoman [2], body [1], food [1], kinsman [1], kin [1], near kin [1], near [1], that is nigh unto [1]

7608 שַׁאֲרָה ***ša'ᵃrâ***, var. GK: 8640 [→ 7607+1886.3]. blood relative, as one's "flesh and blood":– near kinswomen [1]

7609 שֶׁאֱרָה ***še'ᵉrâ***, n.pr.f. GK: 8641 [→ 7604; cf. 242]. Sheerah, "*blood relationship* or *female relative; remainder*":– Sherah [1]

7610 שְׁאָר יָשׁוּב ***šᵉ'ār yāšûb***, n.pr.m. GK: 8639 [→ 7604+3427]. Shear-Jashub, "*remnant will return*":– Shear-jashub [1]

7611 שְׁאֵרִית ***šᵉ'ērît***, n.f. GK: 8642 [→ 7604]. remnant, remainder, the rest:– remnant [44], residue [13], rest [3], remainder [2], escaped [1], left [1], posterity [1], remain [1]

7612 שֵׁאת ***šē't***, n.f. GK: 8643 [→ 7582]. ruin, desolation:– desolation [1]

7613 שְׂאֵת ***šᵉ'ēt***, n.f. GK: 8420 & 8421 [→ 4984, 7863?, 7865?; cf. 4984]. swelling; splendor, honor, loftiness, acceptance:– rising [7], dignity [2], excellency [2], accepted [1], highness [1], raiseth up [1]

7614 שְׁבָא ***šᵉbā'***, n.pr.m. & loc. GK: 8644 [→ 7615]. Sheba, "*seven* or *oath*":– Sheba [22], Sabeans [1]

7615 שְׁבָאִים ***šᵉbā'îm***, a.g. GK: 8645 [→ 7614]. Sabeans:– Sabeans [1]

7616 שְׁבָבִים ***šᵉbābîm***, n.[m.]pl. GK: 8646 [→ 7632]. broken pieces, splinters:– broken in pieces [1]

7617 שָׁבָה ***šābâ***, v. GK: 8647 [→ 7619, 7622, 7628, 7633, 7870]. [Q] to take captive; [Qp, N] to be taken captive:– carried away captive [7], carried captives [5], carry away captives (+7617) [4], captives [3], carried away [3], taken captives [3], taken captive [3], carried captive [2], carry away captive [2], lead captive [2], took captives [2], brought away captive [1], carried away captives (+7633) [1], carry away captives [1], driven away [1], led away captive [1], led captive [1], take captives [1], taken captive (+7628) [1], took away [1], took captive [1], took prisoners (+7628) [1]

7618 שְׁבוֹ ***šᵉbô***, n.[f.]. GK: 8648. agate (exact identification is uncertain):– agate [2]

7619 שׁוּבָאֵל ***šûbā'ēl*** or שְׁבוּאֵל ***šᵉbû'ēl***, n.pr.m. GK: 8742 & 8649 [→ 7617?+410]. Shubael, Shebuel, "[poss.] *captive of God [El]* or *God [El] restores*":– Shebuel [3], Shubael [3]

7620 שָׁבוּעַ ***šābûa'***, n.m. GK: 8651 [→ 7650]. week (a time period of seven); Feast of Weeks, a festival celebrating the first produce of the harvest; a unit of time used in the book of Daniel, possibly a "week" of seven years:– weeks [12], week [4], full weeks (+3117) [1], seven [1], two weeks [1], whole weeks (+3117) [1]

7621 שְׁבוּעָה ***šᵉbû'â***, n.f. GK: 8652 [→ 7650]. sworn oath:– oath [25], oaths [2], charge with an oath (+7650+871.1) [1], curse [1], sworn (+1167) [1]

7622 שְׁבוּת ***šᵉbût*** or שְׁבִית ***šᵉbît***, n.f. GK: 8654 & 8669 [→ 7617]. captivity, exile; fortunes:– captivity [31], captives [1]

7623 שָׁבַח ***šābaḥ***, v. GK: 8655 & 8656 [→ 3431; cf. 7624]. [P] to glorify, commend, extol; to keep still; [H] to cause stillness; [Ht] to glory in:– praise [4], commended [1], glory [1], keepeth [1], praised [1], stillest [1], stilleth [1], triumph [1]

7624 שְׁבַח ***šᵉbaḥ*** (Aram.), v. GK: 10693 [cf. 7623]. [Pa] to praise, honor:– praised [3], praise [2]

7625 שְׁבַט ***šᵉbaṭ*** (Aram.), n.m. GK: 10694 [cf. 7626]. tribe, a subgroup of a nation:– tribes [1]

7626 שֵׁבֶט ***šēbeṭ***, n.m. GK: 8657 [→ 8275; cf. 7625]. rod, staff, a stick used to assist in walking, discipline, and guidance, often highly individualized and used for identification; of royalty: scepter; by extension: tribe, as a major unit of national group or clan (fig. identified with or under authority of a leader's staff), people, clan, family:– tribes [84], tribe [57], rod [34], sceptre [9], staff [2], correction [1], darts [1], pen [1], sceptres [1]

7627 שְׁבָט ***šᵉbāṭ***, n.pr.m. GK: 8658. Shebat, "*[month of] destroying [rain]*":– Sebat [1]

7628 שְׁבִי ***šᵉbî***, n.m. GK: 8660 [→ 7617]. captivity, exile; captive, prisoner:– captivity [35], captives [6], captive [3], prisoners [1], taken away [1], taken captive (+7617) [1], taken [1], took prisoners (+7617) [1]

7629 שֹׁבִי ***šōbî***, n.pr.m. GK: 8661. Shobi, "[poss.] *captive* or *Yahweh returns*":– Shobi [1]

7630 שֹׁבַי ***šōbay***, n.pr.m. GK: 8662. Shobai, "[poss.] *captive* or *Yahweh returns*":– Shobai [2]

7631 שְׁבִיב ***šᵉbîb*** (Aram.), n.[m.]. GK: 10695 [cf. 7632]. flame:– flame [2]

7632 שָׁבִיב ***šābîb***, n.m. GK: 8663 [→ 7616; cf. 7631]. flame; some sources: spark:– spark [1]

7633 שִׁבְיָה ***šibyâ*** or שְׁבִיָּה ***šᵉbiyyâ***, n.f. GK: 8664 & 8665 [→ 7617]. captive, prisoner; captivity:– captives [7], captivity [1], carried away captives (+7617) [1]

7634 שָׁבְיָה ***šobyâ*** or שָׂכְיָה ***śākᵉyâ***, n.pr.m. GK: 8499 [→ 3068]. Shobia, "exile"; Sakia, "[poss.] *one who looks to Yahweh*":– Shachia [1]

7635 שְׁבִיל ***šᵉbîl***, n.[m.]. GK: 8666 [→ 7640]. way, path:– paths [1], path [1]

7636 שָׁבִיס ***šābîs***, n.[m.]. GK: 8667. headband:– cauls [1]

7637 שְׁבִיעִי ***šᵉbî'î***, a.num.ord. GK: 8668 [→ 7651]. seventh:– seventh [98]

שְׁבִית ***šᵉbît***. See 7622.

7638 שָׂבָךְ ***śābāk***, n.[m.]. GK: 8422 [→ 7639, 7730; cf. 5443]. same as 7639: network, lattice, interwoven mesh:–

שַׂבְּכָא ***sabbᵉkā'***. See 5443.

7639 שְׂבָכָה ***śᵉbākâ***, n.f. GK: 8422 [→ 7638]. same as 7638: network, lattice, interwoven mesh:– network [5], networks [2], wreathen work [2], wreaths [2], checker [1], lattice [1], nets [1], snare [1], wreath [1]

7640 שֹׁבֶל ***šōbel***, n.[m.]. GK: 8670 [→ 788, 789, 7635, 7641]. skirt, hem of skirt:– leg [1]

7641 שִׁבֹּלֶת ***šibbōlet***, n.f. GK: 8672 & 8673 [→ 7640; cf. 5451]. head of grain; flood, torrent, flow:– ears [11], ears of corn [3], branches [1], channel [1], floods [1], shibboleth [1], waterflood (+4325) [1]

7642 שַׁבְּלוּל ***šabbᵉlûl***, n.m. GK: 8671 [→ 1101?]. slug, snail; some sources: miscarriage:– snail [1]

שִׁבֹּלֶת ***šibbōlet***. See 7641.

7643 שְׂבָם ***śᵉbām*** or שִׂבְמָה ***śibmâ***, n.pr.loc. GK: 8423 & 8424. Sebam, Sibmah, "*sweet smell*":– Sibmah [4], Shebam [1], Shibmah [1]

7644 שֶׁבְנָא ***šebnā'*** or שֶׁבְנָה ***šebnâ***, n.pr.m. GK: 8674 & 8675 [→ 7645?]. Shebna, "*[Yahweh] return now*":– Shebna [9]

7645 שְׁבַנְיָה ***šᵉbanyâ*** or שְׁבַנְיָהוּ ***šᵉbanyāhû***, n.pr.m. GK: 8676 & 8677 [→ 7644?]. Shebaniah:– Shebaniah [7]

7646 שָׂבַע ***śāba'***, v. GK: 8425 [→ 7647, 7648, 7649, 7654, 7653]. [Q] to be satisfied, have enough, be satiated; the filling and even overfilling of appetites and desires:– satisfied [38], filled [21], full [14], satisfy [7], filleth [2], have enough [2], satisfieth [2], filled full [1], filledst [1], fill [1], had enough [1], had plenty [1], have plenty [1], satiate [1], satisfiest [1], sufficed [1], weary [1]

7647 שָׂבָע ***śābā'***, n.m. GK: 8426 [→ 7646]. abundance, overflowing:– plenty [4], plenteous [2], abundance [1], plenteousness [1]

7648 שֹׂבַע ***śōba'***, n.[m.]. GK: 8427 [→ 7646]. one's fill to contentment, all one wants:– full [3], fill [2], fulness [1], satisfying [1], sufficed [1]

7649 שָׂבֵעַ ***śābēa'***, a. GK: 8428 [→ 7646]. full, abounding:– full [8], satisfied [2]

7650 שָׁבַע ***šāba'***, v. GK: 8678 [→ 884, 7620, 7621, 7637, 7651, 7657, 7658, 7659]. [N] to swear an oath, make a sworn promise; [H] to make one swear an oath, give a charge:– sware [70], sworn [41], swear [32], sweareth [7], made swear [6], charge [5], swarest [5], took an oath [4], adjure [2], made to swear [2], straitly charged with an oath (+7650) [2], straitly sworn (+7650) [2], adjured [1], cause to swear [1], charge by an oath [1], charge with an oath (+7621+871.1) [1], charged with the oath [1], fed to the full [1], make swear [1], make to swear [1], swearers [1]

7651 שֶׁבַע ***šeba'***, n.m. & f. GK: 8679 [→ 884, 1340?, 7637, 7658; cf. 7650; cf. 7655]. seven; (pl.) seventy:– seven [360], seventh [12], seventeen (+6240) [8], seventeenth (+6240) [6], by sevens (+7651) [4], sevenfold [1], seventeen (+6235+2050.1) [1], seventy [1], threescore and seventeen (+7657+2050.1) [1], threescore and ten [1]

7652 שֶׁבַע ***šeba'***, n.pr.m. & loc. GK: 8680 & 8681 [cf. 472, 1339, 3089, 3090, 7656]. Sheba, "*seven* or *oath*":– Sheba [10]

שָׁבֻעַ ***šābua'***. See 7620.

7653 שִׂבְעָה ***śib'â***, n.f. GK: 8430 [→ 7646]. abundance, plenty:– fulness [1]

7654 שָׂבְעָה ***śob'â***, n.f. GK: 8429 [→ 7646]. abundance, satisfaction, enough:– enough [2], full [1], satisfieth [1], sufficiently (+3807.1) [1], unsatiable (+1115) [1]

שִׁבְעָה ***šib'â***. See 7651.

7655 שְׁבַע ***šᵉba'*** (Aram.), n.m. & f. GK: 10696 [cf. 7651]. seven; the phrase "seven times" (Da 3:19) likely means to be as hot as possible:– seven [6]

7656 שִׁבְעָה ***šib'â***, n.pr.loc. GK: 8683 [cf. 7652]. Shibah:– Shebah [1]

שְׁבֻעָה ***šᵉbu'â***. See 7620.

שְׁבִעִי ***šᵉbî'î***. See 7637.

7657 שִׁבְעִים ***šib'îm***, n.pl. GK: 8684 [→ 7650]. seventy (pl. of "seven"]):– seventy [57], threescore and ten [21], threescore and fifteen (+2568+2050.1) [2], threescore and fourteen (+702+2050.1) [2], threescore and twelve (+8147+2050.1) [2], seven [1], threescore and fifteen (+2568+2050.1+2050.1) [1], threescore and seventeen (+7651+2050.1) [1], threescore and sixteen (+8337+2050.1) [1], threescore and thirteen (+7969+1886.1+2050.1) [1], threescore and thirteen (+7969+2050.1) [1]

7658 שִׁבְעָנָה ***šib'ānâ***, n.m. GK: 8685 [→ 7651; cf. 7650]. seven:– seven [1]

7659 שִׁבְעָתַיִם ***šib'ātayim***, n.f.du. GK: 8686 [→ 7650]. seven-fold, seven times:– sevenfold [5], seven times [1]

7660 שָׁבַץ ***šābaṣ***, v. GK: 8687 [→ 4865, 7661, 8665]. [P] to weave; [Pu] to be woven (of fine metal), (n.) a filigree setting:– embroider [1], set [1]

7661 שָׁבָץ ***šābāṣ***, n.m. GK: 8688 [→ 7660]. seizure, cramp, referring to death throes:– anguish [1]

7662 שְׁבַק ***šᵉbaq*** (Aram.), v. GK: 10697. [P] to leave, have remain; [Htpe] to be left:– leave [3], alone [1], left [1]

7663 שָׂבַר ***śābar***, v. GK: 8431 & 8432 [→ 7664; cf. 5452]. [Q] to examine; [P] to wait for, hope for:– hoped [2], viewed [2], wait [2], hope [1], tarry [1]

7664 שֵׂבֶר ***śēber***, n.m. GK: 8433 [→ 7663]. hope:– hope [2]

7665 שָׁבַר ***šābar***, v. GK: 8689 & 8653 [→ 4866, 4867, 7667, 7669, 7670, 7671; cf. 8406]. [Q] to break, destroy, crush; [Qp] to be broken; [N] to be destroyed, be smashed, be broken; [P] to break, smash, shatter; [H] to bring to break through (of birth); [Ho] to be crushed:– broken [63], break [30], brake [15], destroyed [7], breaketh [5], brake in pieces [4], brakest [4], hurt [3], destroy [2], quite break down (+7665) [2], torn [2], brake down [1], brake up [1], break down [1], break in pieces [1], breakest [1], bring to the birth [1], broken down [1], broken off [1], broken-hearted (+3820) [1], crush [1], quench [1]

7666 שָׁבַר ***šābar***, v.den. GK: 8690 [→ 7668]. [Q] to buy grain or food; [H] to sell, allow to buy grain:– buy [14], sell [3], sold [2], bought [1], selleth [1]

7667 שֶׁבֶר ***šeber*** or שֵׁבֶר ***šēber***, n.m. GK: 8691 & 8694 [→ 7671; cf. 7665]. destruction, brokenness, injury; "destruction of spirit" is discouragement, and so lacking motivation and being faint-hearted; interpretation (of a dream):– destruction [21], breach [6], hurt [4], affliction [2], breaking [2], bruise [2], breaches [1], breakings [1], brokenfooted (+7272) [1], brokenhanded (+3027) [1], crashing [1], interpretation [1], vexation [1]

7668 שֶׁבֶר ***šeber***, n.[m.]. GK: 8692 [→ 7666]. grain:– corn [8], victuals [1]

7669 שֶׁבֶר ***šeber***, n.pr.m. GK: 8693 [→ 7667 *or* 7668]. Sheber, "[poss.] *lion;* [poss.] *breaking* or *crushing* or *roughly broken grain*":– Sheber [1]

7670 שִׁבָּרוֹן ***šibbārôn***, n.[m.]. GK: 8695 [→ 7665]. destruction, brokenness:– breaking [1], destruction [1]

7671 שְׁבָרִים ***šᵉbārîm***, n.m.[pl.]. GK: 8696 [→ 7667]. stone quarry:– Shebarim [1]

7672 שְׁבַשׁ ***šᵉbaš*** (Aram.), v. GK: 10698. [Htpa] to be baffled, be perplexed:– astonied [1]

7673 שָׁבַת ***šābat***, v. GK: 8697 [→ 4868, 7674, 7676, 7677, 7678]. [Q] to rest, observe the Sabbath; [N] to come to an end, disappear; [H] to put to an end, stop:– cause to cease [17], cease [9], ceased [6], rest [6], make to cease [5], ceaseth [4], rested [4], made to cease [3], caused to fail [1], causeth to cease [1], celebrate sabbath (+7676) [1], keep a sabbath (+7676) [1], kept sabbath [1], left without [1], make cease [1], make rest [1], make to fail [1], maketh to cease [1], put away [1], put down [1], puttest away [1], rid [1], still [1], suffer to be lacking [1], took away [1]

7674 שֶׁבֶת ***šebet***, n.f. GK: 8700 [→ 7673]. cessation, doing-nothing:– cease [1], loss of time [1], sit still [1]

7675 שֶׁבֶת ***šebet***, n.f. GK: 8699 [→ 3427]. place of sitting or settling, site, seat:– seat [3], habitation [1], place [1]

7676 שַׁבָּת **šabbāt**, n.f. & m. GK: 8701 [→ 7677, 7678; cf. 7673]. Sabbath, the seventh day of the week in the Hebrew calendar (modern Saturday) with a focus of this day as a day of rest and worship; by extension: sabbath, any day or year or period of rest:– sabbath [67], sabbaths [34], every sabbath (+3117+3117+7676+871.1+871.1+1886.1+1886.1) [2], every sabbath (+7676) [2], every sabbath (+7676+871.1) [2], another[s] [1], celebrate sabbath (+7673) [1], keep a sabbath (+7673) [1], sabbath (+3117) [1]

7677 שַׁבָּתוֹן **šabbātôn**, n.m. GK: 8702 [→ 7676]. (day of) rest:– rest [8], sabbath [3]

7678 שַׁבְּתַי **šabb**^{e}**tay**, n.pr.m. GK: 8703 [→ 7676]. Shabbethai, *"one born at Sabbath"*:– Shabbethai [3]

7679 שָׂגָא **śāgā'**, v. GK: 8434 [→ 7689; cf. 7685; cf. 7680]. [H] to make great, extol:– increaseth [1], magnify [1]

7680 שְׂגָא **ś**^{e}**gā'** (Aram.), v. GK: 10677 [→ 7690; cf. 7679, 7685]. [P] to grow great:– multiplied [2], grow [1]

7681 שָׁגֵה **šāgēh**, n.pr.m. GK: 8707 [→ 7686?]. Shagee, *"wanderer, meanderer [like grazing sheep]"*:– Shage [1]

7682 שָׂגַב **śāgab**, v. GK: 8435 [→ 4869, 7687]. [Q] to be too strong for; [N] to be lofty, be exalted; [P] to lift high; to protect; [Pu] to be kept safe; [H] to act exalted:– exalted [5], high [3], defend [2], safe [2], exalteth [1], excellent [1], lofty [1], set on high [1], set up on high [1], set up [1], setteth on high [1], strong [1]

7683 שָׁגַג **šāgag**, v. GK: 8704 [→ 49; cf. 4879, 7686]. [Q] to err unintentionally, go astray:– deceived [1], erred [1], sinneth ignorantly [1], went astray [1]

7684 שְׁגָגָה **š**^{e}**gāgâ**, n.f. GK: 8705 [cf. 7686]. unintentional wrong, accidental error:– ignorance [11], error [2], unawares (+871.1) [2], unawares [2], sinneth through ignorance (+6213+871.1) [1], unwittingly (+871.1) [1]

7685 שָׂגָה **śāgâ**, v. GK: 8436 [cf. 7679]. [Q] to be prosperous, thrive, grow; [H] to increase (in wealth):– grow [2], increase [2]

7686 שָׁגָה **šāgâ**, v. GK: 8706 [→ 4870; cf. 4879, 7683, 7684, 7681?, 7691]. [Q] to sin unintentionally, go astray, wander:– erred [6], err [4], ravisht [2], causeth to go astray [1], deceived [1], deceiver [1], erreth [1], go astray [1], maketh to wander [1], sin through ignorance [1], wandered [1], wander [1]

7687 שְׂגוּב **ś**^{e}**gûb** or שְׂגִיב **ś**^{e}**gîb**, n.pr.m. GK: 8437 & 8439 [→ 7682]. Segub, Sebig, *"exalted"*:– Segub [3]

7688 שָׁגַח **šāgaḥ**, v. GK: 8708. [H] to gaze, stare:– looketh [2], narrowly look [1]

7689 שַׂגִּיא **śaggî'**, a. GK: 8438 [→ 7679; cf. 7690]. exalted:– excellent [1], great [1]

7690 שַׂגִּיא **śaggî'** (Aram.), a. GK: 10678 [→ 7680; cf. 7689]. great, large, abundant:– much [4], great [3], many [2], exceeding [1], greatly [1], sore [1], very [1]

7691 שְׁגִיאָה **š**^{e}**gî'â**, n.f. GK: 8709 [cf. 7686]. error, mistake:– errors [1]

7692 שִׁגָּיוֹן **šiggāyôn**, tt. *or* n.m. GK: 8710. shiggaion, shigionoth:– Shiggaion [1], Shigionoth [1]

7693 שָׁגַל **šāgal**, v. GK: 8711 [→ 7694]. [Q] to ravish, sexually violate; [Qp, N, Pu] to be ravished, be raped:– lien [1]

7694 שֵׁגַל **šēgal**, n.f. GK: 8712 [→ 7693; cf. 7695]. queen, royal bride:– queen [2]

7695 שֵׁגַל **šēgal** (Aram.), n.f. GK: 10699 [cf. 7694?]. wife, concubine:– wives [3]

7696 שָׁגַע **šāga'**, v. GK: 8713 [→ 7697]. [Pu] to be mad, act like a maniac; [Ht] to carry on like a madman:– mad [5], mad men [1], play the mad man [1]

7697 שִׁגָּעוֹן **šiggā'ôn**, n.m. GK: 8714 [→ 7696]. madness:– madness [2], furiously (+871.1) [1]

7698 שֶׁגֶר **šeger**, n.f. GK: 8715. calf, offspring (of cattle):– increase [4], cometh [1]

7699 שַׁד **šad** or שֹׁד **šōd**, n.m. GK: 8716 & 8718 [→ 7705]. (female) breast:– breasts [19], breast [3], paps [1], teats [1]

7700 שֵׁד **šēd**, n.[m.]. GK: 8717. demon, evil spirit:– devils [2]

7701 שֹׁד **šōd**, n.m. GK: 8719 [→ 7703]. destruction, ruin, violence:– destruction [7], spoil [4], spoiled [3], spoiling [3], desolation [2], robbery [2], wasting [2], oppression [1], spoiler [1]

7702 שָׂדַד **śādad**, v. GK: 8440 [→ 7708; cf. 5465, 7713]. [P] to till, harrow, break up the ground:– break clods [1], break the clods [1], harrow [1]

7703 שָׁדַד **šādad**, v. GK: 8720 [→ 7701, 7736]. [Q] to destroy, devastate; [Qp] to be destroyed; [H] to be ruined; [P, Pol] to ravage, destroy; [Pu] to be destroyed, be ruined; [Ho] to be ruined:– spoiled [19], spoiler [8], spoil [8], laid waste [5], spoilers [3], robbers [2], utterly spoiled (+7703) [2], wasted [2], dead [1], destroyed [1], destroyer [1], destroy [1], oppress [1], spoilest [1], spoileth [1], wasteth [1]

7704 שָׂדֶה **śādeh** or שָׂדַי **śāday**, n.m. GK: 8441 & 8442. area of land, usually cultivated: field, open country, countryside:– field [245], fields [47], country [17], land [7], wild [7], ground [4], lands [4], soil [1], wild (+871.1+1886.1) [1]

7705 שִׁדָּה **šiddâ**, n.f. GK: 8721 [→ 7699]. lady, concubine; (pl.) harem:– musical instruments of all sorts (+7705) [2]

7706 שַׁדַּי **šadday**, n.[pr.m.]. GK: 8724 [→ 6701, 7707? (also used with compound proper names)]. Almighty:– Almighty [48]

7707 שְׁדֵיאוּר **š**^{e}**dê'ûr**, n.pr.m. GK: 8725 [→ 7706?+301]. Shedeur, *"Shaddai is light* or *Shaddai is fire"*:– Shedeur [5]

7708 שִׂדִּים **śiddîm**, n.pr.loc. GK: 8443 [→ 7702]. Siddim:– Siddim [3]

7709 שְׁדֵמָה **š**^{e}**dēmâ**, n.f. GK: 8727. (cultivated) field; terrace:– fields [5]

7710 שָׁדַף **šādap**, v. GK: 8728 [→ 7711; cf. 7805]. [Qp] to be scorched:– blasted [3]

7711 שְׁדֵפָה **š**^{e}**dēpâ** or שִׁדָּפוֹן **šiddāpôn**, n.f. & m. GK: 8729 & 8730 [→ 7710]. scorching; blight:– blasting [5], blasted [2]

7712 שְׁדַר **š**^{e}**dar** (Aram.), v. GK: 10700 [→ 849]. [Htpa] to make every effort, strive:– laboured [1]

7713 שְׂדֵרָה **ś**^{e}**dērâ**, n.f. GK: 8444 [cf. 5468, 7702]. ranks, rows; planks (architectural term):– ranges [3], boards [1]

7714 שַׁדְרַךְ **šadrak**, n.pr.m. GK: 8731 [cf. 7715]. Shadrach, *"servant of Aku"*:– Shadrach [1]

7715 שַׁדְרַךְ **šadrak** (Aram.), n.pr.m. GK: 10701 [cf. 7714]. Shadrach, *"servant of the (pagan moon god) Aku"*:– Shadrach [14]

7716 שֶׂה **śeh**, n.m. & f. GK: 8445 [→ 2089]. sheep, lamb:– sheep [17], lamb [16], cattle [8], ewe [1], goat (+5795) [1], lamb (+3532) [1], lesser cattle [1], sheep (+3775) [1], small cattle [1]

7717 שָׂהֵד **śāhēd**, n.[m.]. GK: 8446. witness:– record [1]

7718 שֹׁהַם **šōham**, n.m. GK: 8732 [→ 7719]. onyx (exact identification is uncertain):– onyx [11]

7719 שֹׁהַם **šōham**, n.pr.m. GK: 8733 [→ 7718]. Shoham, *"carnelian [precious stone]"*:– Shoham [1]

7720 שַׂהֲרֹנִים **śah**^{a}**rōnîm**, n.m. GK: 8448. ornamental crescent (or moon shaped) necklace:– ornaments [2], round tires like the moon [1]

שַׁו **šaw**. See 7723.

7721 שׂוֹא **śō'**, v.inf. GK: 5951 [→ 4984]. inf. of 5375: to lift up, arise:–

7722 שׁוֹא **šō'** or שׁוֹאָה **šō'â**, n.f. GK: 8738 & 8739. trouble, ruin, disaster, desolation; ravage:– desolation [5], desolate [2], destruction [2], destroy [1], destructions [1], storm [1], wasteness [1]

7723 שָׁוְא **šāw'**, n.[m.]. GK: 8736 [→ 6673?]. worthlessness, vanity, falseness:– vanity [22], vain [17], false [5], in vain [3], in vain (+1886.1+3807.1) [2], lying [2], falsely [1], lies [1]

7724 שְׁוָא **š**^{e}**wā'**, n.pr.m. GK: 8737 [→ 7737; cf. 7864]. Sheva, *"vanity, emptiness; one who will emulate"*:– Sheva [2]

7725 שׁוּב **šûb**, v. GK: 8740 [→ 3437, 3432, 4877, 4878, 7726, 7727, 7728, 7729, 8666; cf. 8421 (also used with compound proper names)]. [Q] to turn back, turn to, return; [Qp] to return; [Pol] to restore, bring back; [Polal] to be recovered; [H] to restore, recover, bring back; [Ho] to be returned, be brought back; from the base meaning of turning back comes the fig. extension of restoration of relationship, as when one returns in repentance to God:– return [223], returned [147], turn [71], bring again [54], turn away [36], turn again [32], turned [32], again [30], come again [30], brought again [25], restore [25], render [16], came again [15], restored [13], turned away [13], brought back [12], cause to return [12], turned back [12], answer [11], go again [11], turned again [10], turn back [9], turneth [9], bring back [6], bring [6], returneth [6], turneth away [6], recompensed [5], recovered [5], certainly return (+7725) [4], put again [4], went back [4], carry back [3], caused to return [3], cometh again [3], go back [3], recompense [3], relieve [3], rendered [3], repent [3], restored again [3], reverse [3], say nay (+6440) [3], answered (+1697) [2], answered [2], bring again indeed (+7725) [2], bringeth back [2], bringing back [2], brought [2], carried again [2], certainly requite (+7725) [2], deliver again [2], drew back [2], give again [2], gone back [2], hinder [2], in any case bring again (+7725) [2], in any case deliver again (+7725) [2], in any wise go back (+7725) [2], in any wise return (+7725) [2], may [2], must needs bring again (+7725) [2], restore again

Heb

[2], restorer [2], return at all (+7725) [2], reward [2], surely bring back again (+7725) [2], turnest [2], went again [2], withdrawn [2], answer (+1697) [1], answer (+4405) [1], answereth [1], at all turn [1], averse [1], back again [1], bethink (+413+3820) [1], bethink (+413+3824) [1], bring home [1], bringeth [1], call [1], came back [1], camest back [1], carry again [1], cause to answer [1], cause to turn [1], causing to return [1], cease [1], considereth [1], consider [1], continually (+1980+2050.1) [1], converted [1], converting [1], converts [1], convert [1], deliver [1], deny (+6440) [1], drawn [1], fetch again [1], fro [1], gave [1], get again [1], get back again [1], giveth [1], give [1], go home [1], let [1], make return [1], makest to turn [1], more [1], out [1], past [1], pay [1], perverted [1], pull in again [1], put up again [1], put [1], recall [1], recover [1], refresheth [1], rendered again [1], reported [1], requited [1], requite [1], requiting [1], rescue [1], restoreth [1], retire [1], return again (+1980) [1], return again [1], returned back [1], rewardeth [1], sent back [1], set again [1], slidden back [1], still [1], take back [1], taken off [1], take [1], turn back again [1], turn from [1], turneth back [1], turning away [1], turning [1], withdrawest [1], withdraw [1], withdrew [1]

שׁוּבָאֵל *šûbā'ēl*. See 7619.

7726 שׁוֹבָב ***šôbāb***, a. GK: 8743 [→ 7725]. faithless, rebellious, apostate:– backsliding [2], frowardly [1]

7727 שׁוֹבָב ***šôbāb***, n.pr.m. GK: 8744 [→ 7725]. Shobab, *"one who turns back, repents"*:– Shobab [4]

7728 שׁוֹבֵב ***šôbēb***, a. GK: 8745 [→ 7725]. unfaithful, traitorous, apostate:– backsliding [2]

7729 שׁוּבָה ***šûbâ***, n.f. GK: 8746 [→ 7725]. returning, i.e., repentance:– returning [1]

7730 שׂוֹבֶךְ ***śôbek***, n.[m.]. GK: 8449 [→ 7638; cf. 5440]. tangle of branches:– thick boughs [1]

7731 שׁוֹבָךְ ***šôbak***, n.pr.m. GK: 8747 [cf. 7780]. Shobach:– Shobach [2]

7732 שׁוֹבָל ***šôbāl***, n.pr.m. GK: 8748. Shobal, *"basket"*:– Shobal [9]

7733 שׁוֹבֵק ***šôbēq***, n.pr.m. GK: 8749 [→ 3435]. Shobek, *"victor"*:– Shobek [1]

7734 סוּג ***sûg*** or שׂוּג ***śûg***, v. GK: 6047 [→ 5253]. same as 5472: [N] to be turned back, be disloyal:– turned [1]

7735 שׂוּג ***śûg***, v. GK: 8451 [cf. 5473?]. [Pil] to cause growth, raise:– make to grow [1]

7736 שׁוּד ***šûd*** or שָׁדַד ***šādad***, v. GK: 8720 [→ 7703]. same as 7703: [Q] to destroy, devastate:– wasteth [1]

שׁוֹד *šôd*. See 7699, 7701.

7737 שָׁוָה ***šāwâ***, v. GK: 8750 & 8751 [→ 3438, 3440, 3441, 7724, 7740, 7741, 7862; cf. 7739]. [Q] to be like, be equal; to be appropriate, be deserved; [N] to be like; [P] to make smooth; to set, place, bestow; [H] to liken; to count as equal:– laid [3], compared [2], equal [2], maketh [2], alike [1], availeth [1], behaved [1], bringeth forth [1], countervail [1], like [1], made plain [1], make equal [1], profited [1], profit [1], reckoned [1], set [1]

7738 שָׁוָה ***šāwâ***, var. GK: *. to destroy:–

7739 שְׁוָה ***šᵉwâ*** (Aram.), v. GK: 10702 [cf. 7737]. [Peil] to be made like; [Pa] to make like; [Htpa] to be made into:– made [2]

7740 שָׁוֵה ***šāwēh***, n.pr.loc. GK: 8753 [cf. 7737]. Shaveh, *"level [valley]"*:– Shaveh [1]

7741 שָׁוֵה קִרְיָתַיִם ***šāwēh qiryātayim***, n.pr.loc. GK: 8754 [→ 7737+7176]. Shaveh Kiriathaim:– Shaveh Kiriathaim [1]

7742 שׂוּחַ ***śûaḥ***, v. GK: 8452. [Q] to meditate:– meditate [1]

7743 שׁוּחַ ***šûaḥ***, v. GK: 8755 [→ 7745, 7746?, 7845; cf. 7812, 7817]. [Q] sink down:– bowed down [1], humbled [1], inclineth [1]

7744 שׁוּחַ ***šûaḥ***, n.pr.m. GK: 8756 [→ 7747]. Shuah, *"depression, lowland [an Aramean land on the Euphrates River]"*:– Shuah [2]

7745 שׁוּחָה ***šûḥâ***, n.f. GK: 8757 [→ 7746?; cf. 7743, 7882]. pit, rift:– pit [3], ditch [1], pits [1]

7746 שׁוּחָה ***šûḥâ***, n.pr.[m.?]. GK: 8758 [→ 7745?; cf. 7743?]. Shuhah, *"pit, depression"*:– Shuah [1]

7747 שׁוּחִי ***šûḥî***, a.g. GK: 8760 [→ 7744]. Shuhite:– Shuhite [5]

7748 שׁוּחָם ***šûḥām***, n.pr.m. GK: 8761 [→ 7749]. Shuham:– Shuham [1]

7749 שׁוּחָמִי ***šûḥāmî***, a.g. GK: 8762 [→ 7748]. Shuhamite, *"of Shuham"*:– Shuhamites [2]

7750 שׂוּט ***śûṭ***, v. GK: 8454 [→ 7846?; cf. 7847]. [Q] to turn aside (to false gods):– turn aside [2]

7751 שׁוּט ***šûṭ***, v.den. GK: 8763 [→ 4880, 7752, 7850, 7885]. [Q] to roam, go about; to oar (a boat); [Pol] to wander, go here and there; [Htpol] to rush here and there:– run to and fro [6], going to and fro [2], gone [1], go [1], mariners [1], rowers [1], went about [1]

7752 שׁוֹט ***šôṭ***, n.m. GK: 8765 & 8867 [→ 7850; cf. 7751]. whip, lash, scourge:– scourge [5], whips [4], whip [2]

7753 שׂוּךְ ***śûk***, v. GK: 8455 [→ 7754, 7755; cf. 5259, 5526]. [Q] to block with thorn hedges:– fenced [1], hedge up [1], made a hedge [1]

7754 שׂוֹךְ ***śôk*** or שׂוֹכָה ***śôkâ***, n.f. GK: 8456 & 8457 [→ 7753]. branch or brushwood:– bough [2]

7755 שׂוֹכֹה ***śôkōh*** or שׂוֹכוֹ ***śôkô***, n.pr.loc. GK: 8458 & 8459 [→ 7753]. Soco, Socoh, "[poss.] *thorny place"*:– Shochoh [2], Socoh [2], Shocho [1], Shoco [1], Sochoh [1], Socho [1]

7756 שׂוּכָתִי ***śûkātî***, a.g. GK: 8460. Sucathite:– Suchathites [1]

7757 שׁוּל ***šûl***, n.m. GK: 8767 [cf. 7887]. hem (of a robe); skirt:– hem [5], skirts [4], hems [1], train [1]

7758 שׁוֹלָל ***šôlāl*** or שֵׁילָל ***šēlāl***, a. GK: 8768 & 8871 [→ 7997]. barefoot, stripped:– spoiled [2], stript [1]

7759 שׁוּלַמִּית ***šûlammît***, a.g.[f.]. GK: 8769. Shulammite:– Shulamite [2]

7760 שִׂים ***śîm*** or שׂוּם ***śûm***, v. GK: 8492 [→ 3450, 8667; cf. 3455; cf. 7761]. [Q] to place, put, establish, appoint; [Qp] to be placed, set upon; [H] to cause to place, put; [Ho] to be set:– put [142], set [114], make [64], made [48], laid [35], lay [23], appoint [11], set up [10], appointed [8], maketh [8], consider (+3824) [5], give [5], putteth [5], brought [4], gave [4], layeth [4], makest [3], put in [3], care (+3820) [2], considered (+3820) [2], disposed [2], in any wise set (+7760) [2], lay up [2], look well (+5869) [2], mark well (+3820) [2], ordained [2], painted (+7760+871.1+1886.1) [2], placed [2], put on [2], put to [2], puttest [2], set on [2], take [2], turneth [2], wholly set (+7760) [2], bring [1], called [1], cast [1], caused to be set [1], change [1], charged [1], commit [1], consider (+3807.1) [1], consider (+3820) [1], consider [1], convey [1], determined (+1961) [1], doeth [1], done [1], gavest [1], get [1], given [1], had [1], heap up [1], holdeth [1], impute [1], laid up [1], laidst [1], lay down [1], layest [1], leave [1], made out [1], named (+8034) [1], ordain [1], ordereth [1], place [1], preserve [1], purposed [1], putting [1], regard (+3820) [1], regarded (+3820) [1], regarding [1], rehearse [1], rewarded [1], settest [1], setteth [1], shed [1], shewed [1], shew [1], stedfastly [1], told (+6310+871.1) [1], took [1], tread down (+4823) [1], turned [1], turn [1], will[s] [1], wrought [1]

7761 שִׂים ***śîm*** (Aram.), v. GK: 10682 [cf. 7760]. [P] to place (an order), issue (a decree); [Peil] to be placed, be issued; [Htpe] to be put, be laid (to rubble):– made [10], make [5], commanded (+2942) [3], laid [2], given [1], give [1], named (+8036) [1], regarded (+2942) [1], regardeth [1], set [1]

7762 שׁוּמִים ***šûmîm***, n.[m.]. GK: 8770. garlic:– garlick [1]

7763 שֹׁמֵר ***šōmēr***, n.pr.m. GK: 9071 [→ 8116]. Shomer, *"guardian, watchman"*:– Shomer [2]

7764 שׁוּנִי ***šûnî***, n.pr.m. GK: 8771 [→ 7765]. Shuni:– Shuni [2]

7765 שׁוּנִי ***šûnî***, a.g. GK: 8772 [→ 7764]. Shunite, *"of Shuni"*:– Shunites [1]

7766 שׁוּנֵם ***šûnēm***, n.pr.loc. GK: 8773 [→ 7767]. Shunem:– Shunem [3]

7767 שׁוּנַמִּי ***šûnammî***, a.g. GK: 8774 [→ 7766]. Shunammite, *"of Shunem"*:– Shunammite [8]

7768 שָׁוַע ***šāwa'***, v. GK: 8775 [→ 7769, 7771, 7773, 7775 (also used with compound proper names)]. [P] to cry for help, plead:– cried [10], cry [6], crieth out [1], crieth [1], cry aloud [1], cry out [1], shout [1]

7769 שׁוּעַ ***šûa'***, n.[m.]. GK: 8780 & 8782 [→ 7768, 7770; cf. 7771]. cry for help; wealth:– cry [1], riches [1]

7770 שׁוּעַ ***šûa'***, n.pr.m. GK: 8781 [→ 7769; cf. 7771]. Shua, *"prosperity"*:– Shuah [2], Shua [1]

7771 שׁוֹעַ ***šôa'***, a. & n.m. GK: 8777 & 8779 [→ 50, 7768, 7770, 7769]. crying out; highly respected, noble; (n.) the rich:– bountiful [1], crying [1], rich [1]

7772 שׁוֹעַ ***šôa'***, n.pr.g. GK: 8778 [cf. 6970]. Shoa, *"rich"*:– Shoa [1]

7773 שֶׁוַע ***šewa'***, n.[m.]. GK: 8776 [→ 7768]. cry for help:– cry [1]

7774 שׁוּעָא ***šû'ā'***, n.pr.f. GK: 8783. Shua, *"prosperity"*:– Shua [1]

7775 שַׁוְעָה ***šaw'â***, n.f. GK: 8784 [→ 7768]. cry for help:– cry [11]

7776 שׁוּעָל ***šû'āl***, n.m. GK: 8785 [→ 2705, 7777]. fox; jackal:– foxes [6], fox [1]

7777 שׁוּעָל ***šû'āl***, n.pr.m. & loc. GK: 8786 & 8787 [→ 7776]. Shual, *"fox or jackal"*:– Shual [2]

7778 שֹׁעֵר ***šō'ēr***, n.m. GK: 8788 [→ 8179; cf. 8652]. gatekeeper, doorkeeper:– porters [31], porter [4], doorkeepers [2]

7779 שׁוּף **šûp**, v. GK: 8789 & 8790 [cf. 7602]. [Q] to strike; to crush; some sources: bruise, a wound that is not fatal:– bruise [2], breaketh [1], cover [1]

7780 שׁוֹפָךְ **šôpak**, n.pr.m. GK: 8791 [cf. 7731]. Shophach:– Shophach [2]

7781 שׁוּפָמִי **šûpāmî**, a.g. GK: 8793 [→ 8197]. Shuphamite, *"of Shupham"*:– Shuphamites [1]

שׁוֹפָן **šôpān**. See 5855.

7782 שׁוֹפָר **šôpār**, n.m. GK: 8795 [→ 829; cf. 8231]. trumpet, ram's horn:– trumpet [48], trumpets [20], cornet [3], cornets [1]

7783 שׁוּק **šûq**, v. GK: 8796 [→ 7785, 7784; cf. 8264?]. [H] to prove narrow, overflow; [Polel] to water abundantly:– overflow [2], waterest [1]

7784 שׁוּק **šûq**, n.m. GK: 8798 [→ 7783]. street:– streets [3], street [1]

7785 שׁוֹק **šôq**, n.[f.]. GK: 8797 [→ 7783; cf. 8243]. (lower) thigh; leg:– shoulder [13], legs [4], hip [1], thigh [1]

7786 שׂוּר **śûr**, v.den. GK: 8606 [→ 4951, 8269, 8323]. same as 8323: [Q] to rule, govern; [H] to choose a prince:– had power [1], made princes [1], reigned [1]

7787 שׂוּר **śûr**, v. GK: *. [Q] to saw:– cut [1]

7788 שׁוּר **šûr**, v. GK: 8801. [Q] to travel, descend:– sing [1], wentest [1]

7789 שׁוּר **šûr**, v. GK: 8800 [→ 7790, 7791, 7793?, 7791, 8284]. [Q] to see, look, view:– behold [5], see [4], lay wait [1], looketh [1], look [1], observed [1], observe [1], perceiveth [1], regard [1]

7790 שׁוּר **šûr**, n.[m.]. GK: 8803 [→ 7791, 7793; cf. 7789; cf. 7792]. enemy:– enemies [1]

7791 שׁוּר **šûr** or שׁוּרָה **šûrâ**, n.m. & f. GK: 8803 & 8805 [→ 7790, 8284; cf. 7789]. wall, supporting wall (of a terrace):– wall [3], walls [1]

7792 שׁוּר **šûr** (Aram.), n.m. GK: 10703 [cf. 7790]. wall:– walls [3]

7793 שׁוּר **šûr**, n.pr.loc. GK: 8804 [→ 7790; cf. 7789?]. Shur, *"wall"*:– Shur [6]

7794 שׁוֹר **šôr**, n.m. GK: 8802 [→ 51, 8670; cf. 8450]. bull, ox:– ox [54], bullock [11], oxen [8], cow [2], another's[s] (+7453) [1], bullocks [1], bull [1], wall [1]

7795 שׂוֹרָה **śôrâ**, n.[f.]. GK: 8463 [→ 5493?; cf. 8184?]. place, row or a type of grain:– principal [1]

שׂוֹרֵק **śôrēq**. See 8321.

7796 שֹׂרֵק **śôrēq**, n.pr.loc. GK: 8604 [→ 8320]. Sorek, *"blood red grapes"*:– Sorek [1]

7797 שׂוּשׂ **śûś**, v. GK: 8464 [→ 4885, 8342]. [Q] to rejoice, be pleased, be delighted:– rejoice [12], glad [4], rejoiced [3], rejoiceth [3], greatly rejoice (+7797) [2], exceedingly rejoice (+8057+871.1) [1], joy [1], make mirth [1]

7798 שַׁוְשָׁא **šawšā'**, n.pr.m. GK: 8807. Shavsha:– Shavsha [1]

7799 שׁוּשַׁן **šûšan**, n.m. GK: 8808. lily plant; some sources: lotus plant:– lilies [8], lily [5], Shoshannim [2], Shoshannim-Eduth (+5715) [1]

7800 שׁוּשַׁן **šûšan**, n.pr.loc. GK: 8809 [cf. 7801]. Susa:– Shushan [21]

7801 שׁוּשַׁנְכָי **šûšankāy** (Aram.), n.pr.g. & loc. GK: 10704 [cf. 7800]. of Susa:– Susanchites [1]

7802 שׁוּשַׁן עֵדוּת **šûšan 'ēdût**, t.t. GK: 8808 + 6343 [→ 7799+5715]. Shushan Eduth, "Lily of the covenant":– Shushan-eduth [1]

שׁוּשַׁק **šûšaq**. See 7895.

7803 שׁוּתֶלַח **šûtelaḥ**, n.pr.m. GK: 8811 [→ 8364]. Shuthelah:– Shuthelah [4]

7804 שֵׁיזִב **šêzib** (Aram.), v. GK: 10706. [Sh] to rescue, save:– deliver [6], delivered [2], delivereth [1]

7805 שָׁזַף **šāzap**, v. GK: 8812 [cf. 7710]. [Q] to see; to be darkened:– looked [1], saw [1], seen [1]

7806 שָׁזַר **šāzar**, v. GK: 8813. [Ho] to be finely twisted:– twined [21]

7807 שַׁח **šaḥ**, a. GK: 8814 [→ 7817]. downward, bent, low:– humble person (+5869) [1]

7808 שֵׂחַ **śēaḥ**, n.[m.]. GK: 8465 [→ 7878]. thoughts:– thought [1]

7809 שָׁחַד **šāḥad**, v. GK: 8815 [→ 7810]. [Q] to give a gift; pay a bribe; pay a ransom:– give a reward [1], hirest [1]

7810 שֹׁחַד **šōḥad**, n.m. GK: 8816 [→ 7809]. bribe, gift:– reward [7], gift [6], gifts [4], bribes [3], present [2], bribery [1]

7811 שָׂחָה **śāḥâ**, v. GK: 8466 [→ 7813]. [Q] to swim; [H] to make swim, flood:– make to swim [1], swimmeth [1], swim [1]

7812 שָׁחָה **šāḥâ**, v. GK: 8817 [cf. 7743, 7817]. [Q] to bow down; [H] to weigh down, cause to bow:– worship [54], worshipped [39], bowed [31], bow down [14], bowed down [4], made obeisance [4], bow [3], obeisance [3], reverence [3], worshippeth [3], worshipping [3], did obeisance [2], fall down [2], crouch [1], did reverence [1], fell down [1], fell flat [1], humbly beseech [1], maketh stoop [1], reverenced [1]

7813 שָׂחוּ **śāḥû**, n.[m.]. GK: 8467 [→ 7811]. water deep enough to swim in:– swim [1]

7814 שְׂחוֹק **ś^{e}ḥôq**, n.[m.]. GK: 8468 [→ 7832]. laughter, which can communicate joy or ridicule; object of ridicule: laughingstock:– laughter [6], derision [5], laughed to scorn [1], laughing [1], one mocked [1], sport [1]

7815 שְׁחוֹר **š^{e}ḥôr**, n.[m.]. GK: 8818 [→ 7835]. soot:– coal [1]

שִׁחוֹר **šiḥôr**. See 7883.

שָׁחוֹר **šāḥôr**. See 7838.

7816 שְׁחוּת **š^{e}ḥût**, n.f. GK: 8819 [→ 7825]. trap, pit:– pit [1]

7817 שָׁחַח **šāḥaḥ** or שִׁיחַ **šîaḥ**, v. GK: 8820 & 8863 [→ 7807; cf. 7743, 7812]. [Q] to bow down, bend low; [N] to be brought low; [H] to humble, bring low:– bowed down [4], cast down [4], bow [2], brought low [2], bending [1], boweth down [1], bring down [1], bringeth down [1], brought down [1], couch [1], humbleth [1], low [1], stoop [1]

7818 שָׂחַט **śāḥaṭ**, v. GK: 8469. [Q] to squeeze out (juice from grapes):– pressed [1]

7819 שָׁחַט **šāḥaṭ**, v. GK: 8821 & 8823 [→ 7821]. [Q] to slaughter, kill; [Qp, N] to be killed, be slaughtered:– kill [23], slew [21], killed [15], slay [9], slain [5], killeth [3], killing [1], offer [1], shot out [1], slaughter [1], slaying [1]

7820 שָׁחַט **šāḥaṭ**, v. GK: 8822. [Qp] to be hammered, beaten; some sources: to be alloyed, blended, referring to the mixing of metals:– beaten [5]

7821 שְׁחִיטָה **š^{e}ḥîṭâ**, n.f. GK: 8824 [→ 7819]. killing, slaughter:– killing [1]

7822 שְׁחִין **š^{e}ḥîn**, n.m. GK: 8825. boils, skin sores:– boil [9], boils [2], botch [2]

7823 שָׁחִיס **šāḥîs** or סָחִישׁ **sāḥîš**, n.[m.]. GK: 8826 & 6084. growth, what springs up on its own (in the second year):– that which springeth of the same [2]

7824 שָׂחִיף **śāḥîp**, a. GK: 8470. covered, paneled:– cieled [1]

7825 שְׁחִית **š^{e}ḥît**, n.f. GK: 8827 [→ 7816]. pit, trap, grave:– destructions [1], pits [1]

7826 שַׁחַל **šaḥal**, n.m. GK: 8828 [→ 7827]. lion:– lion [4], fierce lion [3]

7827 שְׁחֵלֶת **š^{e}ḥēlet**, n.f. GK: 8829 [→ 7826]. onycha (a fragrant spice):– onycha [1]

7828 שַׁחַף **šaḥap**, n.[m.]. GK: 8830. gull or possibly bat:– cuckow [2]

7829 שַׁחֶפֶת **šaḥepet**, n.f. GK: 8831. wasting disease, consumption:– consumption [2]

7830 שַׁחַץ **šaḥaṣ**, n.[m.]. GK: 8832 [→ 7831]. pride, dignity:– lion's [1], pride [1]

7831 שַׁחֲצוּמָה **šaḥ^{a}ṣûmâ** or שַׁחֲצִימָה **šaḥ^{a}ṣîmâ**, n.pr.loc. GK: 8833 & 8834 [→ 7830]. Shahazimah, Shahazumah, *"elevated place"*:– Shahazimah [1]

7832 שָׂחַק **śāḥaq**, v. GK: 8471 [→ 3446, 4890, 7814; cf. 6711]. [Q] to laugh, be amused; to laugh at, mock, scoff; [P] to celebrate, rejoice, frolic; [H] to scorn; this can communicate joy or ridicule:– laugh [8], play [5], played [3], make merry [2], playing [2], rejoicing [2], scorneth [2], deride [1], derision [1], in sport [1], laughed to scorn [1], laughed [1], laugheth [1], made sport [1], make sport [1], mockers [1], mocketh [1], mock [1], rejoice [1]

7833 שָׁחַק **šāḥaq**, v. GK: 8835 [→ 7834]. [Q] to grind, wear away:– beat small [2], beat [1], wear [1]

7834 שַׁחַק **šaḥaq**, n.m. GK: 8836 [→ 7833]. clouds, skies:– clouds [11], skies [5], heaven [2], sky [2], small dust [1]

שְׂחֹק **ś^{e}ḥōq**. See 7814.

7835 שָׁחַר **šāḥar**, v. GK: 8837 [→ 300, 4891, 7815, 7838, 7225, 7839, 7840, 7842]. [Q] to become black:– black [1]

7836 שָׁחַר **šāḥar**, v.den. GK: 8838 [→ 7841; cf. 7837?]. [Q] to seek, look; [P] to earnestly seek, search for:– seek early [4], betimes [1], diligently seeketh [1], diligently seek [1], early seek [1], inquired early after [1], rising betimes [1], seek betimes [1], seek in the morning [1]

7837 שַׁחַר **šaḥar**, n.m. GK: 8840 [→ 7223, 7842; cf. 7836?]. dawn, daybreak:– morning [12], day [5], early [2], Shahar [1], day began [1], dayspring [1], light [1], riseth [1]

שִׁחֹר **šiḥōr**. See 7883.

7838 שָׁחֹר **šāḥōr**, a. GK: 8839 [→ 7835]. black, dark:– black [6]

7839 שַׁחֲרוּת **šaḥ^{a}rût**, n.f. GK: 8841 [→ 7835]. vigor, prime of youth, an extension of dark hair color (or perhaps of the dawn):– youth [1]

7840 שְׁחַרְחֹר **š^{e}ḥarḥōr**, a. GK: 8842 [→ 7835]. dark, swarthy (complexion):– black [1]

7841 שְׁחַרְיָה **š^{e}ḥaryâ**, n.pr.m. GK: 8843 [→ 7836]. Shehariah, *"he seeks Yahweh"*:– Shehariah [1]

Heb

7842 שחרים ***šaḥ^{a}rayim***, n.pr.m. GK: 8844 [→ 7837; cf. 7835]. Shaharaim, *"one born at early [reddish] dawn"*:– Shaharaim [1]

7843 שחת ***šāḥat***, v. GK: 8845 [→ 4889, 4892, 4893; cf. 7844]. [N] to be corrupt, be ruined, be marred; [P] to corrupt, destroy, ruin; [H] to destroy, corrupt, bring to ruin:– destroy [68], destroyed [22], corrupted [11], corrupt [10], destroying [5], mar [4], marred [3], corrupters [2], destroyer [2], destroyeth [2], spoilers [2], utterly corrupt (+7843) [2], waster [2], battered [1], cast off [1], corrupting [1], corruptly [1], destroyers [1], destroyest [1], destruction [1], lose [1], perish [1], spilled [1], wasted [1]

7844 שחת ***š^{e}ḥat*** (Aram.), v. GK: 10705 [cf. 7843]. [Pp] to be corrupt, wicked; (as noun) corruption:– fault [2], corrupt [1]

7845 שחת ***šaḥat***, n.f. GK: 8846 [→ 7743]. pit, dungeon; corruption, decay:– pit [14], corruption [4], destruction [2], ditch [2], grave [1]

7846 שט ***śēṭ***, n.[m.]. GK: 8473 [→ 7750?]. rebel:– revolters [1]

7847 שטה ***śāṭâ***, v. GK: 8474 [cf. 7750]. [Q] to go astray:– gone aside [2], decline [1], go aside [1], goeth aside [1], turn [1]

7848 שטה ***šiṭṭâ***, n.f. GK: 8847 [→ 7851]. acacia wood:– shittim [27], shittah tree [1]

7849 שטח ***šāṭaḥ***, v. GK: 8848 [→ 4894]. [Q] to spread out, enlarge, scatter; [P] to spread out:– spread all abroad (+7849) [2], spread [2], enlargeth [1], stretched out [1]

7850 שטט ***šōṭēṭ***, n.[m.]. GK: 8849 [→ 7752; cf. 7751]. whip, scourge:– scourges [1]

7851 שטים ***šiṭṭîm***, n.pr.loc. GK: 8850 [→ 7848]. Shittim, *"acacia trees"*:– Shittim [5]

7852 שטם ***śāṭam***, v. GK: 8475 [→ 4895; cf. 7853]. [Q] to hold a grudge, hold hostility toward:– hated [2], hate [2], hateth [1], opposest [1]

7853 שטן ***śāṭan***, v.den. GK: 8476 [→ 7854, 7855, 7856; cf. 7852]. [Q] to accuse, slander:– adversaries [5], resist [1]

7854 שטן ***śāṭān***, n.m.[pr.]. GK: 8477 [→ 7853]. (human) adversary, accuser, one who opposes, slanderer; (as a proper name) Satan, the spirit being who is an opponent of God and slanderer of his creation:– Satan [19], adversary [6], adversaries [1], withstand [1]

7855 שטנה ***śiṭnâ***, n.f. GK: 8478 [→ 7856; cf. 7853]. accusation:– accusation [1]

7856 שטנה ***śiṭnâ***, n.pr.loc. GK: 8479 [→ 7855]. Sitnah, *"hostility"*:– Sitnah [1]

7857 שטף ***šāṭap***, v. GK: 8851 [→ 7858; cf. 8241]. [Q] to overflow, flood, wash away; [N] to be rinsed, be swept away; [Pu] to be rinsed:– overflow [10], overflowing [8], rinsed [3], drown [1], flowing [1], overflowed [1], overflown [1], overwhelmed [1], ran [1], rusheth [1], throughly washed away [1], washed [1], washest away [1]

7858 שטף ***šeṭep***, n.m. GK: 8852 [→ 7857; cf. 8241]. flood, torrents (of rain):– flood [3], floods [1], outrageous [1], overflowing of waters [1]

7859 שטר ***š^{e}ṭar*** (Aram.), n.m. GK: 10680. side:– side [1]

7860 שטר ***šāṭar***, n.m. GK: 8853 [→ 4896, 7861]. [Q] to keep a record; (n.) official, officer, foreman:– officers [23], overseer [1], ruler [1]

7861 שטרי ***šiṭray*** or שרטי ***širṭay***, n.pr.m. GK: 8855 & 9231 [→ 7860]. Shitrai, Shirtai, *"scribe, officer"*:– Shitrai [1]

7862 שי ***šay***, n.m. GK: 8856 [→ 52, 7737; cf. 2365?]. gift:– presents [2], present [1]

7863 שיא ***śî'***, n.m. GK: 8480 [→ 7865; cf. 4984; 7613?]. height:– excellency [1]

7864 שיא ***š^{e}yā'***, n.pr.m. GK: 8857 [cf. 7724]. Sheya, cf. 7724:–

7865 שיאן ***śî'ōn***, n.pr.loc. GK: 8481 [→ 7863; cf. 4984; 7613]. Siyon:– Sion [1]

7866 שיאן ***šî'ōn***, n.pr.loc. GK: 8858 [→ 7582?]. Shion:– Shion [1]

7867 שיב ***śîb***, v. GK: 8482 [→ 7869, 7872; cf. 7868]. [Q] to be gray(-haired); hence, old:– grayheaded [2]

7868 שיב ***śîb*** (Aram.), v. GK: 10681 [cf. 7867]. [P] to be gray-haired, (ptcp.) elder, a community leader with considerable political, social, and judicial authority, as a fig. extension of being gray-haired, implying wisdom and honor:– elders [5]

7869 שיב ***śēb***, n.[m.]. GK: 8483 [→ 7867]. gray-headedness, old age:– age [1]

7870 שיבה ***šîbâ***, n.f. GK: 8860 [→ 7617; cf. 7622]. captives:– captivity [1]

7871 שיבה ***šîbâ***, n.f. GK: 8859 [→ 3427?]. stay:– lay [1]

7872 שיבה ***śēbâ***, n.f. GK: 8484 [→ 7867]. gray-haired (person), old age:– old age [6], gray hairs [5], hoar head [2], hoary head [2], gray head [1], grayheaded [1], hoar hairs [1], hoary [1]

7873 שיג ***śîg***, n.[m.]. GK: 8485 [cf. 5253, 5509]. busyness; perhaps: bowel movement:– pursuing [1]

7874 שיד ***śîd***, v.den. GK: 8486 [→ 7875]. [Q] to coat with (a whitewash) plaster:– plaister [2]

7875 שיד ***śîd***, n.[m.]. GK: 8487 [→ 7874]. lime, plaster (used as a whitewash):– lime [2], plaister [2]

7876 שיה ***šāyâ***, v. GK: 8861 [cf. 5382]. [Q] to desert, forget:– unmindful [1]

7877 שיזא ***šîzā'***, n.pr.m. GK: 8862. Shiza:– Shiza [1]

7878 שיח ***śîaḥ***, v.den. GK: 8488 [→ 7808, 7879, 7881]. [Q] to meditate, muse on, consider, think on:– meditate [5], talk [5], speak [4], commune [1], complained [1], complain [1], declare [1], muse [1], pray [1]

7879 שיח ***śîaḥ***, n.m. GK: 8490 [→ 7878]. complaint, lament:– complaint [9], babbling [1], communication [1], meditation [1], prayer [1], talking [1]

7880 שיח ***śîaḥ***, n.[m.]. GK: 8489. bush, shrub:– bushes [2], plant [1], shrubs [1]

7881 שיחה ***śîḥâ***, n.f. GK: 8491 [→ 7878]. meditation:– meditation [2], prayer [1]

7882 שיחה ***šîḥâ***, n.f. GK: 8864 [cf. 7745]. pit, pitfall:– pits [1], pit [1]

7883 שיחור ***šîḥōr***, n.pr.loc. GK: 8865 [→ 7884]. Shihor, "[poss.] *black water*; [Egyptian] *Canal of Horus*":– Sihor [3], Shihor [1]

7884 שיחור לבנת ***šîḥôr libnāt***, n.pr.loc. GK: 8866 [→ 7883]. Shihor Libnath:– Shihor-libnath [1]

7885 שיט ***šayiṭ***, n.[m.]. GK: 8868 [→ 7751]. oar:– oars [1]

7886 שילה ***šîlōh***, n.pr.loc.?. GK: 8869 [→ 7887]. Shiloh:– Shiloh [1]

7887 שילו ***šîlô*** or שלו ***šilô*** or שלה ***šilōh***, n.pr.loc. GK: 8870 & 8926 & 8931 [→ 7886, 7888; cf. 7757, 8387]. Shiloh:– Shiloh [32]

7888 שילני ***šîlōnî***, a.g. GK: 8872 [→ 7887, 8023]. Shilonite, of Shiloh, *"of Shiloh"*:– Shilonite [5], Shilonites [1]

שילל ***šêlāl***. See 7758.

7889 שימון ***šîmôn***, n.pr.m. GK: 8873. Shimon:– Shimon [1]

7890 שין ***šayin***, n.[m.]. GK: 8875 [→ 8366]. urine:–

7891 שיר ***šîr***, v. GK: 8876 [→ 7892; cf. 3574]. [Q] to sing; [P ptcp.] singer, musician:– singers [36], sing [32], singing [9], sang [6], behold [1], singer [1], singeth [1], sung [1]

7892 שיר ***šîr***, n.m. & f. GK: 8877 & 8878 [→ 7891]. song, music:– song [62], songs [12], musick [7], singing [4], musical [2], singers [1], sing [1], song (+1697) [1]

שיש ***šîs***. See 7797.

7893 שיש ***šayiš***, n.[m.]. GK: 8880 [→ 8336]. alabaster:– marble [1]

7894 שישא ***šîšā'***, n.pr.m. GK: 8881. Shisha:– Shisha [1]

7895 שושק ***šûšaq*** or שישק ***šîšaq***, n.pr.m. GK: 8810 & 8882. Shushak, Shishak:– Shishak [7]

7896 שית ***šît***, v. GK: 8883 [→ 7897, 8351, 8352; cf. 8371]. [Q] to place, put, set; [Ho] to be demanded:– set [21], make [12], put [11], laid [8], lay [5], made [5], appoint [2], regard (+3820) [2], alone (+4480) [1], apply [1], appointed [1], bring [1], considered (+3820) [1], lay up [1], layeth up [1], look [1], make turn [1], makest [1], mark [1], set in array [1], settest [1], shew [1], stayed [1], take [1]

7897 שית ***šît***, n.m. GK: 8884 [→ 7896]. garment:– attire [1], garment [1]

7898 שית ***šayit***, n.[m.]. GK: 8885 [→ 7582?]. thorns, thorn-bushes:– thorns [7]

7899 שך ***śēk***, n.[m.]. GK: 8493. barb, splinter, thorn:– pricks [1]

7900 שך ***śōk***, n.[m.]. GK: 8494 [cf. 5520]. dwelling place:– tabernacle [1]

7901 שכב ***šākab***, v. GK: 8886 [→ 4904, 7902, 7903]. [Q] to lie down, rest; sleep with; (as a euphemism of sexual intercourse) to lie with, sleep with; [H] to make lie down; [Ho] to be laid down:– lie [41], slept [37], lay [32], lie down [15], lieth [15], lay down [11], sleep [10], laid down [9], laid [8], liest down [3], lieth down [3], lie with at all (+854+7901) [2], lien [2], lying [2], ravished [2], take rest [2], casting down [1], lain [1], lay down to sleep [1], lay on a bed (+4904) [1], lie together [1], lie with [1], lien with (+854) [1], liest [1], lieth carnally with (+854+2233+7902) [1], lieth with (+5973) [1], lodged [1], lying down [1], make to lie down [1], overlaid (+5921) [1], sleepest [1], stay [1], taketh rest [1]

7902 שכבה ***šikbâ***, n.f. GK: 8887 [→ 7901]. emission, discharge:– copulation [3], lay [2], lieth carnally with (+854+2233+7901) [1], man carnally (+376+2233) [1], seed (+2233) [1]

7903 שכבת ***š^{e}kōbet***, n.f. GK: 8888 [→ 7901]. sexual relations, sexual intercourse:– lain [1], lie (+5414) [1], lie carnally

(+2233+5414+3807.1) [1], lie with (+5414) [1]

7904 שָׂכָה ***śākâ***, v. GK: 8889. [H] to be well-fed; lusting:– morning [1]

7905 שֻׂכָּה ***śukkâ***, n.f. GK: 8496. harpoon:– barbed irons [1]

7906 שֵׂכוּ ***śekû***, n.pr.loc. GK: 8497. Secu, "*lookout point*":– Sechu [1]

7907 שֶׂכְוִי ***śekwî***, n.[m.]. GK: 8498. mind; some sources: mist:– heart [1]

7908 שְׁכוֹל ***šᵉkôl***, n.[m.]. GK: 8890 [→ 7921]. forlornness, loss of children:– loss of children [2], spoiling [1]

7909 שַׁכּוּל or שְׁכֻלָה ***šakkûl*** or ***šᵉkûlâ***, a. GK: 8891 & 8892 [→ 7921]. bereaved (of children):– barren [2], bereaved of children [1], bereaved of whelps [1], robbed of whelps [1], robbed [1]

7910 שִׁכּוֹר ***šikkôr***, a. GK: 8893 [→ 7937]. drunk, drunkenness; (n.) a drunkard:– drunken [6], drunkards [3], drunkard [2], drunk [2]

7911 שָׁכַח ***šākaḥ***, v. GK: 8894 [→ 7913; cf. 7912]. [Q] to forget; [N] to be forgotten; [P] to make forget; [H] to make forget; [Ht] to be forgotten:– forget [46], forgotten [39], forgat [7], forgetteth [3], do at all forget (+7911) [2], forgettest [2], cause to forget [1], caused to be forgotten [1], forgot [1]

7912 שְׁכַח ***šᵉkaḥ*** (Aram.), v. GK: 10708 [cf. 7911]. [H] to find; [Htpe] to be found:– found [12], find [6]

7913 שָׁכֵחַ ***šākēaḥ***, a. GK: 8895 [→ 7911]. forgetting:– forget [2]

7914 שְׂכִיָּה ***śᵉkiyyâ***, n.f. GK: 8500. marine vessel, ship:– pictures [1]

7915 שַׂכִּין ***śakkîn***, n.[m.]. GK: 8501. knife:– knife [1]

7916 שָׂכִיר ***śākîr***, a. GK: 8502 [→ 7917, 7936]. hired worker, servant under contract:– hired servant [8], hireling [6], him that is hired [1], hired men [1], hired [1]

7917 שְׂכִירָה ***śᵉkîrâ***, a. GK: 8502 [→ 7916]. f. of 7916: hired worker, servant under contract:– hired [1]

7918 שָׁכַךְ ***šākak***, v. GK: 8896. [Q] to recede, reside; [H] to get rid of:– appeased [1], asswaged [1], make to cease [1], pacified [1], setteth [1]

7919 שָׂכַל ***śākal***, v. GK: 8505 & 8506 [→ 4905, 7922; cf. 7920]. [Q] to have success; [P] to cross (the hands and arms in an extended motion); [H] to have insight, wisdom, understanding; to prosper, successful; the potent capacity to understand and so exercise skill in life, a state caused by proper training and teaching, enhanced by careful observation:– wise [11], understand [8], prosper [6], behaved wisely [4], understanding [4], instruct [2], prudent [2], understood [2], wisdom [2], behave wisely [1], considereth [1], consider [1], deal prudently [1], expert [1], give skill [1], guiding wittingly [1], handleth wisely [1], have good success [1], have understanding [1], instructed [1], made understand [1], make wise [1], prospered [1], prospereth [1], skilful [1], skill [1], taught knowledge (+7922) [1], teacheth [1], understandeth [1], wisely considereth [1], wisely consider [1]

7920 שְׂכַל ***śᵉkal*** (Aram.), v. GK: 10683 [→ 7924; cf. 7919]. [Htpa] to think about, consider:– considered [1]

7921 שָׁכֹל ***šākal***, v. GK: 8897 [→ 811, 7908, 7909, 7923]. [Q] to be bereaved (of children); [P] to make childless, bring bereavement, suffer miscarriage; [H] to miscarry:– bereave [3], barren [2], bereaved of children [2], bereaved [2], cast young [2], bereave of children [1], bereave of men [1], bereaveth [1], cast fruit before the time [1], casteth her calf [1], childless [1], deprived [1], destroy [1], lost children [1], made childless [1], miscarrying [1], rob of children [1], spoil [1]

7922 שֶׂכֶל ***śekel***, n.m. GK: 8507 [→ 7919; cf. 7924]. understanding, wisdom, discretion:– understanding [7], wisdom [3], discretion [1], policy [1], prudence [1], sense [1], taught knowledge (+7919) [1], wise [1]

שַׁכֻּל ***šakkul***. See 7909.

שִׂכְלוּת ***siklût***. See 5531.

7923 שִׁכֻּלִים ***šikkulîm***, n.[m.]pl.abst. GK: 8898 [→ 7921]. (state of) bereavement (of children):– lost [1]

7924 שָׂכְלְתָנוּ ***śoklᵉtānû*** (Aram.), n.f. GK: 10684 [→ 7920]. intelligence, understanding, insight:– understanding [3]

7925 שָׁכַם ***šākam***, v.den. GK: 8899 [→ 7926]. [H] to do early in the morning; to do again and again:– rose up early [18], rose early [9], arose early [8], rising early [6], rising up early [6], rise up early [5], early [4], be up early [1], early rose up [1], gat up early [1], get early [1], get up early [1], morning [1], rise early [1], rising up betimes [1], rose up betimes [1]

7926 שְׁכֶם ***šᵉkem***, n.m. GK: 8900 [→ 7925, 7927, 7928, 7929, 7930]. shoulder (upper part of the back); by extension: ridge of land:– shoulder [12], shoulders [5], back [2], consent [2], portion [1]

7927 שְׁכֶם ***šᵉkem***, n.pr.m. & loc. GK: 8901 & 8902 [→ 7926]. Shechem, "*shoulders [and upper part of the back];* [poss.] *shoulder [saddle of a hill]*":– Shechem [49], Sichem [1]

7928 שֶׁכֶם ***šekem***, n.pr.m. GK: 8903 [→ 7930; cf. 7926]. Shechem, "*shoulders [and upper part of the back]*":– Shechem [13], Shechem's [2]

7929 שִׁכְמָה ***šikmâ***, n.m. GK: 8900 [→ 7926]. f. of 7926: shoulder (upper part of the back); by extension: ridge of land:– shoulder blade [1]

7930 שִׁכְמִי ***šikmî***, a.g. GK: 8904 [→ 7928]. Shechemite, "*of Shechem*":– Shechemites [1]

7931 שָׁכַן ***šākan***, v. GK: 8905 [→ 4908, 7933, 7934, 7935; cf. 7932]. [Q] to dwell, abide, live among, stay; [P] to make to dwell, make a home; [H] to cause to dwell, settle in, set up a dwelling:– dwell [61], dwelleth [8], dwelt [8], abode [6], place [5], cause to dwell [3], dwell in [3], dwellest [3], dwelt in [3], habitation [2], inhabit [2], placed [2], remain [2], set [2], abide [1], abiding [1], at rest [1], cause to remain [1], continue [1], dwellers [1], dwelleth in [1], dwelling [1], inhabitants [1], inhabited [1], inhabiteth [1], lay [1], made to dwell [1], make dwell [1], remaineth [1], remaining [1], rested [1], rest [1], set up [1]

7932 שְׁכַן ***šᵉkan*** (Aram.), v. GK: 10709 [→ 4907; cf. 7931]. [P] to dwell; [Pa] to cause to dwell:– caused to dwell [1], habitation [1]

7933 שָׁכַן ***šākan***, v.inf. GK: 8905 [→ 7931]. inf. of 7931: to dwell, abide:–

7934 שָׁכֵן ***šākēn***, a. GK: 8907 [→ 7931]. neighbor; inhabitant:– neighbours [11], neighbour [6], inhabitants [1], inhabitant [1], nigh [1]

7935 שְׁכַנְיָה or שְׁכַנְיָהוּ ***šᵉkanyâ*** or ***šᵉkanyāhû***, n.pr.m. GK: 8908 & 8909 [→ 7931+3068]. Shecaniah, "*Yahweh has taken up his abode*":– Shechaniah [8], Shecaniah [2]

7936 שָׂכַר or סָכַר ***śākar*** or ***sākar***, v. GK: 8509 & 6128 [→ 3485, 4909, 7916, 7917, 7938, 7939, 7940]. [Q] to hire; [Qp] to be hired; [N] to hire oneself; [Ht] to earn wages for oneself:– hired [12], earneth wages [2], hire [2], rewardeth [2], surely hired (+7936) [2], hired out [1]

7937 שָׁכַר ***šākar***, v. GK: 8910 & 8912 [→ 7910, 7941, 7943]. [Q] to become drunk, drink to one's fill; [P] to make drunk; [H] to make drunk; [Ht] to behave drunken:– drunken [8], make drunk [3], make drunken [2], drink abundantly [1], filled with drink [1], made drunken [1], made drunk [1], makest drunken [1], merry [1]

7938 שֶׂכֶר ***śeker***, n.[m.]. GK: 8512 [→ 7936]. wage, reward:– reward [1], sluces [1]

7939 שָׂכָר ***śākār***, n.m. GK: 8510 [→ 7940; cf. 7936 (also used with compound proper names)]. wage, reward:– hire [9], reward [7], wages [6], price [2], rewarded [2], fare [1], worth [1]

7940 שָׂכָר ***śākār***, n.pr.m. GK: 8511 [→ 7939; cf. 7936]. Sacar, "*reward [given by God],* [poss.] *hired hand*":– Sacar [2]

7941 שֵׁכָר ***šēkār***, n.[m.]. GK: 8911 [→ 7937]. fermented drink, beer:– strong drink [21], drunkards (+8354) [1], strong wine [1]

שִׁכֹּר ***šikkōr***. See 7910.

7942 שִׁכְּרוֹן ***šikkārôn***, n.pr.loc. GK: 8914. Shikkeron, "[poss.] *drunkenness; hog bean plant*":– Shicron [1]

7943 שִׁכָּרוֹן ***šikkārôn***, n.[m.]. GK: 8913 [→ 7937]. drunkenness:– drunkenness [2], drunken [1]

7944 שַׁל ***šal***, n.[m.]. GK: 8915. irreverent act:– error [1]

7945 שֶׁל ***šel***, pt. GK: 8611 [→ 4332, 4967, 7706]. what, which, usually as prefix 7578.1:– that [54], which [20], whom [7], who [6], when [5], because [4], for [4], until (+5704) [4], wherein [3], whereof [3], till (+5704) [2], wherewith [2], as (+3509.1) [1], as [1], because (+871.1) [1], but (+5704) [1], by (+5921) [1], for cause (+871.1) [1], for sake (+871.1) [1], from whence [1], increase [1], it [1], of (+4480+3807.1) [1], when (+3509.1) [1], where [1], while (+5704) [1], whither (+8033) [1], whose (+2050.2) [1], whose [1]

7946 שַׁלְאֲנַן ***šalʾanan***, a. GK: 8916 [→ 7599]. secure:– at ease [1]

7947 שָׁלַב ***šālab***, v. GK: 8917 [→ 7948]. [Pu] to be joined, set parallel, dovetailed:– equally distant [1], set in order [1]

7948 שָׁלָב ***šālāb***, n.[m.]pl. GK: 8918 [→ 7947]. upright, crossbar:– ledges [3]

7949 שָׁלַג ***šālag***, v.den. GK: 8919 [→ 7950]. [H] to snow:– snow [1]

7950 שֶׁלֶג ***šeleg***, n.m. GK: 8920 & 8921 [→ 7949; cf. 8517]. snow; soap (processed from the soapwort plant):– snow [19], snowy [1]

7951 שָׁלָה ***šālâ***, v. GK: 8922 [→ 7961, 7959, 7962, 7968, 7987, 7988; cf. 7952]. [Q] to be at ease, have peace; [N] to give oneself to rest; [H] to raise hopes:– prosper [3], happy [1], in safety [1]

7952 שָׁלָה ***šālâ***, v. GK: 8923 [→ 7953, cf. 7951]. [Q] to take away, extract; to deceive:– deceive [1], negligent [1]

7953 שָׁלָה ***šālâ***, v. GK: 8923 [→ 7952]. prob. same as 7952: [Q] to take away, extract:– taketh away [1]

7954 שְׁלֵה ***šᵉlēh*** (Aram.), a. GK: 10710 [→ 7960, 7963; cf. 7961]. contented, at ease:– rest [1]

שִׁלֹה ***šilōh***. See 7887.

7955 שָׁלָה ***šillâ*** (Aram.), n.f. GK: 10685 [cf. 5541]. insolence, rebellion:–

שֵׁלָה ***šēlâ***. See 7596.

7956 שֵׁלָה ***šēlâ***, n.f. & pr.m. GK: 8924 & 8925 [→ 8024; cf. 7592]. petition; n.pr. Shelah, "*missile [a weapon], sprout*":– Shelah [8]

7957 שַׁלְהֶבֶת ***šalhebet***, n.f. GK: 8927 [→ 3851]. flame:– flame [2], most vehement flame [1]

שָׁלָו ***šālaw***. See 7951.

7958 שְׂלָו ***śᵉlāw***, n.f. GK: 8513. quail:– quails [4]

7959 שָׁלוּ ***šālû***, n.[m.]. GK: 8930 [→ 7951; cf. 7960]. secure feeling, ease:– prosperity [1]

שִׁלוֹ ***šilô***. See 7887.

7960 שָׁלוּ ***šālû*** (Aram.), n.f. GK: 10712 [→ 7954; cf. 7959]. negligence:– fail [2], any thing amiss [1], error [1]

7961 שָׁלֵו ***šālēw***, a. GK: 8929 [→ 7951; cf. 7954]. quiet, at ease, carefree:– at ease [2], peaceable [1], prosperity [1], prosper [1], quietness [1], quiet [1], wealthy [1]

7962 שַׁלְוָה ***šalwâ***, n.f. GK: 8932 [→ 7951; cf. 7963]. security, ease:– prosperity [3], abundance [1], peaceably (+871.1) [1], peaceably [1], peace [1], quietness [1]

7963 שְׁלֵוָה ***šᵉlēwâ*** (Aram.), n.f. GK: 10713 [→ 7954; cf. 7962]. prosperity:– tranquillity [1]

7964 שִׁלּוּחִים ***šillûḥîm***, n.[m.]pl. GK: 8933 [→ 7971]. parting gifts; sending away:– presents [1], present [1], sent [1]

7965 שָׁלוֹם ***šālôm***, n.m. GK: 8934 [→ 53, 8010, 8015, 8019; cf. 7999; cf. 8001]. peace, safety, prosperity, well-being; intactness, wholeness; peace can have a focus of security, safety which can bring feelings of satisfaction, well-being, and contentment:– peace [174], well [13], peaceably [7], welfare [5], prosperity [4], safe [3], saluted (+7592+3807.1) [3], how did (+3807.1) [2], peaceable [2], perfect peace (+7965) [2], salute (+7592+3807.1) [2], all is well [1], did [1], familiar friend (+376) [1], familiars (+582) [1], fare [1], favour [1], friends (+376) [1], greet (+7592+3807.1) [1], how doest (+3807.1) [1], how prospered (+3807.1) [1], in good health [1], in health [1], peaceably (+3807.1) [1], peaceably (+871.1) [1], prosperous [1], rest [1], safely [1], salute [1], wholly [1]

7966 שִׁלּוּם ***šillûm***, n.[m.]. GK: 8936 [→ 7999]. retribution, reckoning; bribe, gift:– recompences [1], recompence [1], reward [1]

7967 שַׁלּוּם ***šallûm***, n.pr.m. GK: 8935 [→ 7999]. Shallum, "*peace, well-being, prosperity*":– Shallum [27]

שְׁלוֹמִית ***šᵉlômît***. See 8019.

7968 שַׁלּוּן ***šallûn***, n.pr.m. GK: 8937 [→ 7951]. Shallun, "*recompense*":– Shallun [1]

7969 שָׁלוֹשׁ ***šālōš***, n.m. & f. GK: 8993 [→ 7991, 7992, 8027, 8028, 8030, 8032, 8029, 7970; cf. 8531]. three; (pl.) thirty:– three [389], thirteen (+6240) [13], thirteenth (+6240) [11], third [9], thrice (+6471) [4], forks (+7053) [1], oftentimes (+6471) [1], three tenth deals (+6241) [1], threescore and thirteen (+7657+1886.1+2050.1) [1], threescore and thirteen (+7657+2050.1) [1]

7970 שְׁלוֹשִׁים ***šᵉlōšîm***, n.indecl. GK: 9001 [→ 7969]. thirty (pl. of "three"):– thirty [163], thirtieth [9], captains [1]

שָׁלוּת ***šālût***. See 7960.

7971 שָׁלַח ***šālaḥ***, v. GK: 8938 [→ 4916, 4917, 7964, 7973, 7975, 7974, 7976, 7977; cf. 7972]. [Q] to send out; [Qp] to be sent away; [N] to be sent; [P] to send away, let go, release; [Pu] to be sent away, thrust out; [H] to send out; "to let go" from a marriage relationship is to divorce:– sent [405], send [140], let go [69], sent away [36], put forth [24], send away [10], put [9], sent forth [9], sending [8], sent out [8], cast out [7], lay [7], stretch forth [7], cast [6], laid [6], put away [6], sendeth [5], set [5], put out [4], go [3], send forth [3], sentest [3], shot forth [3], soweth [3], stretch out [3], depart [2], earnestly send (+7971) [2], in any wise let go (+7971) [2], let depart [2], let down [2], let go in any wise (+7971) [2], let loose [2], put in [2], putteth forth [2], sendest away [2], sendest [2], sendeth out [2], stretched forth [2], stretched out [2], appoint [1], away [1], bring on way [1], brought [1], cast away [1], conduct [1], forsaken [1], gave up [1], givest [1], layeth [1], left [1], let go away [1], letting go [1], loose [1], push away [1], putting away [1], putting forth [1], reacheth forth [1], send out [1], sendest forth [1], sendest out [1], sendeth forth [1], sending away [1], sent for [1], sentest forth [1], shoot out [1], shooteth forth [1], shot [1], spreadeth out [1], suffer to grow long [1]

7972 שְׁלַח ***šᵉlaḥ*** (Aram.), v. GK: 10714 [cf. 7971]. [P] to send out; [Pp, Peil] to be sent:– sent [12], put [1], send [1]

7973 שֶׁלַח ***šelaḥ*** or שְׁלָחִים ***šᵉlāḥîm***, n.[m.]. GK: 8939 & 8945 [→ 7971]. weapon, sword, javelin; shoots, sprouts of a plant (in a closed, private garden):– sword [3], weapon [2], darts [1], plants [1], put off [1]

7974 שֶׁלַח ***šelaḥ***, n.pr.m. GK: 8941 [→ 7973?; cf. 7971]. Shelah, "*missile [a weapon], sprout*":– Salah [6], Shelah [3]

7975 שֶׁלַח ***šelaḥ*** or שִׁלֹחַ ***šilōaḥ***, n.pr.loc. GK: 8940 & 8942 [→ 7971]. Siloam, Shiloah, "*sent*":– Shiloah [1], Siloah [1]

שִׁלֻּחַ ***šilluaḥ***. See 7964.

7976 שְׁלֻחוֹת ***šᵉluḥôt***, n.f. GK: 8943 [→ 7971]. shoot (of a vine):– branches [1]

7977 שִׁלְחִי ***šilḥî***, n.pr.m. GK: 8944 [→ 7971]. Shilhi, "[poss.] *[my] javelin [thrower?]*":– Shilhi [2]

7978 שִׁלְחִים ***šilḥîm***, n.pr.loc. GK: 8946. Shilhim:– Shilhim [1]

7979 שֻׁלְחָן ***šulḥān***, n.m. GK: 8947. table:– table [55], tables [14], every table (+7979+2050.1) [2]

7980 שָׁלַט ***šālaṭ***, v. GK: 8948 [→ 7983, 7986, 7989; cf. 7981]. [Q] to control, lord over; [H] to let rule, enable:– bare rule [1], given power [1], giveth power [1], have dominion [1], have power [1], have rule [1], ruleth [1], rule [1]

7981 שְׁלֵט ***šᵉlēṭ*** (Aram.), v. GK: 10715 [→ 7984, 7985, 7990; cf. 7980]. [P] to rule over, overpower; [H] to make rule over:– made ruler [2], ruler [2], bear rule [1], mastery [1], power [1]

7982 שֶׁלֶט ***šeleṭ***, n.m. GK: 8949. small (round) shield:– shields [7]

7983 שִׁלְטוֹן ***šilṭôn***, n.[m.]. GK: 8950 [→ 7980; cf. 7985]. supremacy:– power [2]

7984 שִׁלְטֹן ***šilṭōn*** (Aram.), n.m. GK: 10716 [→ 7981; cf. 7983]. high official:– rulers [2]

7985 שָׁלְטָן ***šolṭān*** (Aram.), n.m. GK: 10717 [→ 7981; cf. 7983?]. dominion, power, authority:– dominion [13], dominions [1]

7986 שַׁלֶּטֶת ***šalleṭet***, a. GK: 8951 [→ 7980]. brazen, domineering:– imperious [1]

7987 שְׁלִי ***šᵉlî***, n.[m.]. GK: 8952 [→ 7951]. privateness, uninterruptedness:– quietly (+871.1+1886.1) [1]

7988 שִׁלְיָה ***šilyâ***, n.f. GK: 8953 [→ 7951]. afterbirth:– young one [1]

שְׂלָיו ***śᵉlāyw***. See 7958.

שָׁלֵיו ***šalêw***. See 7961.

7989 שַׁלִּיט ***šallîṭ***, a. GK: 8954 [→ 7980; cf. 7990]. ruler, governor:– governor [1], mighty [1], power [1], ruler [1]

7990 שַׁלִּיט ***šallîṭ*** (Aram.), a. GK: 10718 [→ 7981; cf. 7989]. mighty, powerful, sovereign, ruling:– ruleth [3], ruled [2], ruler [2], captain [1], lawful [1], rule [1]

7991 שָׁלִשׁ ***šālîš*** or שָׁלִשִׁי ***šālîšî***, n.[m.]. GK: 8955 & 8956 & 8998 [→ 7969]. [the] Three, a rank of officer; bowlful, basketful (a unit of measure, probably of one-third of something); (three-stringed?) lute:– captains [8], lord [3], captain [2], measure [2], excellent things [1], great lords [1], instruments of musick [1], princes [1]

7992 שְׁלִישִׁי ***šᵉlîšî***, a.num.ord. GK: 8958 [→ 7969; cf. 8523, cf. 8532]. third:– third [97], third part [3], third time [3], three years old [2], third rank [1], three [1]

7993 שָׁלַךְ ***šālak***, v. GK: 8959 [→ 7994?, 7995]. [H] to throw, hurl, scatter; [Ho] to be thrown, be cast:– cast [77], cast out [13], cast away [11], cast down [11], cast forth [3], cast off [2], adventured [1], cast in [1], castest [1], casteth forth [1], hurl [1], pluckt [1], threwest [1], thrown [1]

7994 שָׁלָךְ ***šālāk***, n.[m.]. GK: 8960 [→ 7993?]. cormorant:– cormorant [2]

7995 שַׁלֶּכֶת ***šalleket***, n.f. GK: 8961 [→ 7993]. cutting down:– cast [1]

7996 שַׁלֶּכֶת ***šalleket***, n.pr.loc. GK: 8962. Shalleketh, "[poss.] *[gate of] sending forth*":– Shallecheth [1]

7997 שָׁלַל ***šālal***, v. GK: 8963 & 8964 [→ 7758, 7998]. [Q] to pull out; to plunder, loot; [Htpol] to be plundered:– spoiled [4], spoil [3], let fall of purpose (+7997) [2], take a spoil (+7998) [2], take [2], make a spoil [1], maketh prey [1], take spoil (+7998) [1]

7998 שָׁלָל **šālāl**, n.m. GK: 8965 [→ 4122; cf. 7997]. plunder, spoil, loot:– spoil [58], prey [10], take a spoil (+7997) [2], spoils won [1], spoils [1], take spoil (+7997) [1]

7999 שָׁלֵם **šālēm**, v. GK: 8966 [→ 4918, 4919, 4921, 4922, 7965, 7967, 7966, 8002, 8003, 8004, 8005, 8006, 8011, 8010, 8013, 8015, 8016, 8019, 8020, 8021 (also used with compound proper names)]. [Q] to be finished, be completed; be at peace; [Qp] to be at peace; [P] to repay, make restitution, fulfill (a vow); [Pu] be repaid, be fulfilled; [H] to make peace; cause to fulfill; [Ho] to be brought into peace:– pay [17], recompense [8], restore [8], render [7], made peace [6], make good [5], repay [5], perform [4], reward [4], at peace [3], finished [3], rewarded [3], rewardeth [3], ended [2], make an end [2], make full restitution (+7999) [2], make restitution [2], performeth [2], recompensed [2], requite [2], surely make good (+7999) [2], surely make restitution (+7999) [2], surely pay (+7999) [2], surely requite (+7999) [2], give again [1], make amends [1], make peace [1], make prosperous [1], maketh to be at peace [1], pay again [1], payed [1], payeth again [1], peaceable [1], perfect [1], performed [1], prospered [1], recompensest [1], renderest [1], rendereth [1], repayed [1], repayeth [1], requited [1]

8000 שְׁלִם **šᵉlim** (Aram.), v. GK: 10719 [→ 8001; cf. 7999]. [P] to be finished; [H] to (deliver) completely, bring to an end:– finished [2], deliver [1]

8001 שְׁלָם **šᵉlām** (Aram.), n.m. GK: 10720 [→ 8000; cf. 7965]. (as salutation) cordial greetings!; prosperity, well-being, good health:– peace [4]

8002 שֶׁלֶם **šelem**, n.[m.]. GK: 8968 [→ 7999]. fellowship (offering):– peace offerings [77], peace [6], peace offering [4]

8003 שָׁלֵם **šālēm**, a. GK: 8969 [→ 7999; cf. 8000]. safe, complete, whole:– perfect [16], whole [4], full [2], just [1], made ready [1], peaceable [1], perfected [1], quiet [1]

8004 שָׁלֵם **šālēm**, n.pr.loc. GK: 8970 [→ 7999]. Salem, *"peace"*:– Salem [2], Shalem [1]

שָׁלֹם **šālōm**. See 7965.

8005 שִׁלֵּם **šillēm**, n.pr.loc. GK: 8972 [→ 7999]. recompense:– recompence [1]

8006 שִׁלֵּם **šillēm**, n.pr.m. GK: 8973 [→ 8016; cf. 7999]. Shillem, *"recompense;* [poss.] *whole, healthy, complete"*:– Shillem [2]

שִׁלֻּם **šillum**. See 7966.

שַׁלֻּם **šallum**. See 7967.

8007 שַׂלְמָא **śalmā'**, n.pr.m. GK: 8514 [→ 8009, 8012]. Salma, *"little spark"*:– Salma [4]

8008 שַׂלְמָה **śalmâ**, n.f. GK: 8515 [cf. 8071]. clothing, garment, cloak, robe:– raiment [5], garments [4], garment [4], clothes [3]

8009 שַׂלְמָה **śalmâ**, n.pr.m. GK: 8516 [→ 8007]. Salmah:– Salmon [1]

8010 שְׁלֹמֹה **šᵉlōmōh**, n.pr.m. GK: 8976 [→ 7965; cf. 7999]. Solomon, *"peace, well-being"*:– Solomon [271], Solomon's [18], Solomon's (+3807.1) [4]

8011 שִׁלֻּמָה **šillumâ**, n.f. GK: 8974 [→ 7999]. punishment, retribution:– reward [1]

8012 שַׂלְמוֹן **śalmôn**, n.pr.m. GK: 8517 [→ 8007]. Salmon, *"little spark"*:– Salmon [1]

8013 שְׁלֹמוֹת **šᵉlōmôt**, n.pr.m. GK: 8977 [→ 7999]. Shelomoth, *"at peace"*:– Shelomoth [2]

8014 שַׁלְמַי **šalmay**, n.pr.m. GK: 8518 [cf. 8073]. Salmai, cf. 8073:– Shalmai [1]

8015 שְׁלֹמִי **šᵉlōmî**, n.pr.m. GK: 8979 [→ 8019; cf. 7965]. Shelomi, *"at peace"*:– Shelomi [1]

8016 שִׁלֵּמִי **šillēmî**, a.g. GK: 8980 [→ 8006]. Shillemite, *"of Shillem"*:– Shillemites [1]

8017 שְׁלֻמִיאֵל **šᵉlumî'ēl**, n.pr.m. GK: 8981 [→ 7999+410]. Shelumiel, *"God [El] is [my] peace"*:– Shelumiel [5]

8018 שֶׁלֶמְיָה **šelemyâ** or שֶׁלֶמְיָהוּ **šelemyāhû**, n.pr.m. GK: 8982 & 8983 [→ 7999+3068]. Shelemiah, *"Yahweh pays back* [poss.] *he restores peace offering of Yahweh"*:– Shelemiah [10]

8019 שְׁלֹמִית **šᵉlōmît**, n.pr.m. & f. GK: 8984 & 8985 [→ 8015; cf. 7999]. Shelomith, *"at peace"*:– Shelomith [9]

8020 שַׁלְמַן **šalman**, n.pr.m. GK: 8986 [→ 7999]. Shalman, "[abbreviation of] *Shalmaneser"*:– Shalman [1]

8021 שַׁלְמֹנִים **šalmōnîm**, n.[m.pl.]. GK: 8988 [→ 7999]. gifts:– rewards [1]

8022 שַׁלְמַנְאֶסֶר **šalman'eser**, n.pr.m. GK: 8987. Shalmaneser, *"Shulman is chief* or *Sulmanu is leader"*:– Shalmaneser [2]

8023 שִׁילֹנִי **šîlōnî**, a.g. GK: 8872 [→ 7888]. same as 7888: Shilonite, of Shiloh, *"of Shiloh"*:– Shiloni [1]

8024 שֵׁלָנִי **šēlānî**, a.g. GK: 8989 [→ 7956]. Shelanite, of Shelah, *"of Shelah"*:– Shelanites [1]

8025 שָׁלַף **šālap**, v. GK: 8990. [Q] to draw out (a sword); remove (a sandal); [Qp] to be drawn (sword):– drew [13], drawn [5], draw [4], drew off [1], groweth up [1], plucked off [1]

8026 שֶׁלֶף **šelep**, n.pr.m. GK: 8991. Sheleph, *"one plucked out, drawn out"*:– Sheleph [2]

8027 שָׁלַשׁ **šālaš**, v.den. GK: 8992 [→ 7969]. [P] to do a third time, on the third day; [Pu] to be three years old, in three parts:– three years old [3], did the third time [1], divide into three parts [1], do the third time [1], stayed three days [1], threefold [1], three [1]

8028 שֶׁלֶשׁ **šeleš**, n.pr.m. GK: 8994 [→ 7969]. Shelesh, *"triplet;* [poss.] *obedient* or *gentle"*:– Shelesh [1]

שָׁלֹשׁ **šālōš**. See 7969.

8029 שִׁלֵּשִׁים **šillēšîm**, a. GK: 9000 [→ 7969]. third (generation):– third [5]

8030 שִׁלְשָׁה **šilšâ**, n.pr.m. GK: 8996 [→ 7969]. Shilshah, "[poss.] *obedient* or *gentle; third [part, child?], triplet"*:– Shilshah [1]

8031 שָׁלִשָׁה **šālišâ**, n.pr.loc. GK: 8995 [→ 1190]. Shalisha, *"third part"*:– Shalisha [1]

שְׁלֹשָׁה **šālōšâ**. See 7969.

8032 שִׁלְשׁוֹם **šilšōm**, adv. GK: 8997 [→ 7969]. formally, three days ago; used with 8543: "yesterday and three days ago," as an adverb of time: formerly, previously:– heretofore (+8543) [4], in time past (+4480+8543) [4], before (+8543) [3], before that time (+865+3509.1) [1], beforetime (+4480+8543) [1], beforetime (+8543) [1], beforetime (+865+4480) [1], heretofore (+1571+4480+4480+8543) [1], heretofore (+4480+8543) [1], heretofore (+865) [1], in time past (+8543) [1], in time past (+865+1571) [1], in times past (+1571+1571+8543) [1], in times past (+4480+8543) [1], in times past (+865) [1], these three days (+8543) [1]

שְׁלֹשִׁים **šᵉlōšîm**. See 7970.

שַׁלְתִּיאֵל **šaltî'ēl**. See 7597.

8033 שָׁם **šām**, adv. GK: 9004 [cf. 8536]. there, where:– there [424], thence [66], where (+834) [54], thither (+1886.5) [50], whither (+834+1886.5) [38], thence (+4480) [34], there (+1886.5) [31], whither (+834) [27], where [22], thither [20], where (+834+1886.5) [7], wherein (+834) [7], therein (+1886.5) [5], therein [5], thereof (+4480) [4], on [3], whence [3], here [2], whence (+834) [2], whence (+834+4480) [2], whereunto (+834) [2], whither (+1886.5) [2], whither [2], in it [1], place where [1], the same place [1], thereout (+4480) [1], thitherward (+1886.5) [1], unto (+1886.5) [1], where (+834+871.1) [1], whereinto (+834+1886.5) [1], wherein [1], wheresoever any (+834+3605) [1], whereunto (+834+1886.5) [1], which[s] [1], whither (+7945) [1], whithersoever (+834+3605) [1], whithersoever (+834+5921) [1], whom (+834) [1], whom[s] [1]

8034 שֵׁם **šēm**, n.m. GK: 9005 [→ 8035?, 8050, 8061, 8062; cf. 8036]. name, a proper designation of a person, place, or thing; by extension: renown, fame; "to call on the name of the LORD" means to proclaim or praise the excellence of Yahweh, to worship Yahweh, or to summon Yahweh by name for help:– name [738], names [81], name's [19], renown [7], fame [4], named [3], famous [2], named (+7121) [2], other names (+8034) [2], base men (+1097) [1], famous (+376) [1], famous (+7121) [1], infamous (+2931+1886.1) [1], named (+7760) [1], report [1]

8035 שֵׁם **šēm**, n.pr.m. GK: 9006 [→ 8034?]. Shem, *"name, fame"*:– Shem [17]

8036 שֻׁם **šum** (Aram.), n.m. GK: 10721 [cf. 8034]. name, what someone is called:– name [8], names [3], named (+7761) [1]

8037 שַׁמָּא **šammā'**, n.pr.m. GK: 9007 [cf. 8048]. Shamma; Shammah, *"astonishment"*:– Shamma [1]

8038 שֵׁם־אֵבֶר **šem'ēber**, n.pr.m. GK: 9008. Shemeber:– Shemeber [1]

8039 שִׁמְאָה **šim'â**, n.pr.m. GK: 9009 [cf. 8043]. Shimeah, *"he has heard* or *he is obedient"*:– Shimeah [1]

8040 שְׂמֹאל **śᵉmō'l**, n.[m.]. GK: 8520 [→ 8041, 8042; cf. 7585]. left (opposite of right); north:– left [36], left hand [17], left side [1]

8041 שִׂמְאֵל **śim'ēl**, v.den. GK: 8521 [→ 8040]. [H] to go to the left; be left-handed:– left [2], go to the left [1], on the left [1], turn to the left [1]

8042 שְׂמָאלִי **śᵉmā'lî**, a. GK: 8522 [→ 8040]. on the left; northern:– left [9]

8043 שִׁמְאָם **šim'ām**, n.pr.m. GK: 9010 [cf. 8039]. Shimeam:– Shimeam [1]

8044 שַׁמְגַּר **šamgar**, n.pr.m. GK: 9011. Shamgar, *"Shimke gave [a son]"*:– Shamgar [2]

8045 שָׁמַד **šāmad**, v. GK: 9012 [cf. 8046]. [N] to be destroyed; [H] to destroy, demolish, annihilate:– destroyed [42], destroy [39], destroyed (+8045) [2], utterly destroy (+8045) [2], bring to nought [1], destruction

[1], overthrown [1], perished [1], quite pluck down [1]

8046 שְׁמַד **šᵉmad** (Aram.), v. GK: 10722 [cf. 8045]. [H] to completely destroy, exterminate:– consume [1]

שָׁמֶה **šāmeh**. See 8064.

8047 שַׁמָּה **šammâ**, n.f. GK: 9014 [→ 8074]. thing of horror; desolation, devastation, what is laid waste:– astonishment [13], desolation [11], desolate [10], waste [3], desolations [1], wonderful [1]

8048 שַׁמָּה **šammâ**, n.pr.m. GK: 9015 [→ 8049, 8054, 8060?; cf. 8037, 8085? *or* 8121?]. Shammah, "*waste*":– Shammah [8]

8049 שַׁמְהוּת **šamhût**, n.pr.m. GK: 9016 [→ 8054; cf. 8048]. Shamhuth, "[poss.] *one born at a time of a horrible event*":– Shamhuth [1]

8050 שְׁמוּאֵל **šᵉmûʾēl**, n.pr.m. GK: 9017 [→ 8034+410]. Samuel; Shemuel, "*his name is God [El]; heard of God; the unnamed god is El*":– Samuel [137], Shemuel [3]

שְׁמֹנֶה **šᵉmôneh**. See 8083.

שְׁמוֹנָה **šᵉmônâ**. See 8083.

שְׁמוֹנִים **šᵉmônîm**. See 8084.

8051 שַׁמּוּעַ **šammûaʿ**, n.pr.m. GK: 9018 [→ 8085+3068?]. Shammua, "[poss.] *[Yahweh] hears; rumor*":– Shammua [5]

8052 שְׁמוּעָה **šᵉmûʿâ**, n.f. GK: 9019 [→ 8085]. message, rumor, report:– rumour [9], tidings [8], report [4], fame [2], bruit [1], doctrine [1], mentioned [1], news [1]

8053 שָׁמוּר **šāmûr**, n.pr.m. GK: 9020 [cf. 8069]. Shamur, cf. 8069:–

8054 שַׁמּוֹת **šammôt**, n.pr.m. GK: 9021 [→ 8049; cf. 8048]. Shammoth, "*desolation*":– Shammoth [1]

8055 שָׂמַח **śāmaḥ**, v. GK: 8523 [→ 8056, 8057]. [Q] to rejoice, be glad, delight in:– rejoice [65], glad [33], rejoiced [19], make glad [4], maketh glad [4], rejoiceth [4], joy [3], made to rejoice [3], made glad [2], making very glad (+8055) [2], caused to rejoice [1], cheer up [1], cheereth [1], exceeding glad (+1419+8057) [1], hath joy [1], have joy [1], made joyful [1], made rejoice [1], make joyful [1], make rejoice [1], maketh merry (+2416) [1], merry [1], rejoicing [1]

8056 שָׂמֵחַ **śāmēaḥ**, a.vbl. GK: 8524 [→ 8055]. rejoicing, gladness, delight:– glad [4], rejoiced [4], rejoice [4], joyful [3], merry [2], making merry [1], merrily [1], merryhearted (+3820) [1], rejoice (+1961) [1], rejoice exceedingly (+413+1524) [1], rejoicing [1]

8057 שִׂמְחָה **śimḥâ**, n.f. GK: 8525 [→ 8055]. joy, gladness, pleasure, delight:– joy [43], gladness [32], mirth [8], rejoice [2], rejoicing [2], exceeding glad (+1419+8055) [1], exceedingly rejoice (+7797+871.1) [1], exceeding [1], glad [1], joyfulness [1], pleasure [1], rejoiced [1]

8058 שָׁמַט **šāmaṭ**, v. GK: 9023 [→ 8059]. [Q] to drop down, stumble; to lie unplowed; [N] to be thrown down; [H] to cancel a debt:– release [2], discontinue [1], overthrown [1], rest [1], shook [1], stumbled [1], threw down [1], throw down [1]

8059 שְׁמִטָּה **šᵉmiṭṭâ**, n.f. GK: 9024 [→ 8058]. canceling of debt:– release [5]

8060 שַׁמַּי **šammay**, n.pr.m. GK: 9025 [→ 8085? *or* 8048?]. Shammai, "*Yahweh has heard*":– Shammai [6]

8061 שְׁמִידָע **šᵉmîdāʿ**, n.pr.m. GK: 9026 [→ 8062]. Shemida, "[poss.] *the name knows;* [poss.] *Eshmun has known*":– Shemida [3]

8062 שְׁמִידָעִי **šᵉmîdāʿî**, a.g. GK: 9027 [→ 8061; cf. 8034]. Shemidaite, "*of Shemida*":– Shemidaites [1]

8063 שְׂמִיכָה **śᵉmîkâ**, n.f. GK: 8526. covering:– mantle [1]

8064 שָׁמַיִם **šāmayim**, n.m. GK: 9028 [cf. 8065]. region above the earth: the heavens: place of the stars, sky, air; heaven: the invisible realm of God:– heaven [289], heavens [109], air [21], astrologers (+1895) [1], other (+7097) [1]

8065 שְׁמַיִן **šᵉmayin** (Aram.), n.m.pl. GK: 10723 [cf. 8064]. the heavens (of this world), sky, air; heaven (the realm of God); "heaven" is also a euphemism for "God"; the phrase "heaven and earth" combine into one meaning "the universe," the totality of all that exists:– heaven [35], heavens [3]

8066 שְׁמִינִי **šᵉmînî**, a.num.ord. GK: 9029 [→ 8083]. eighth:– eighth [27], eight [1]

8067 שְׁמִינִית **šᵉmînît**, tt. GK: 9030 [→ 8083]. sheminith:– Sheminith [3]

8068 שָׁמִיר **šāmîr**, n.m. GK: 9031 & 9032 [→ 8104; cf. 8069?]. briers; hardest stone; (other contexts) flint or emery:– briers [8], adamant stone [1], adamant [1], diamond [1]

8069 שָׁמִיר **šāmîr**, n.pr.m. & loc. GK: 9033 & 9034 [cf. 8053, 8068?]. Shamir, "[poss.] *thorny* or *emery [flint]*":– Shamir [4]

8070 שְׁמִירָמוֹת **šᵉmîrāmôt** or שְׁמָרִימוֹת **šᵉmîrîmôt**, n.pr.m. GK: 9035 & 9082. Shemirimoth, Shemiramoth, "*heights, heavens;* [poss. pr.n. of pagan goddess]":– Shemiramoth [4]

8071 שִׂמְלָה **śimlâ**, n.f. GK: 8529 [→ 8072; cf. 8008]. clothing, garment, cloak:– raiment [11], clothes [6], garment [4], apparel [2], clothing [2], cloth [2], garments [2]

8072 שַׂמְלָה **śamlâ**, n.pr.m. GK: 8528 [→ 8071, 8073]. Samlah:– Samlah [4]

8073 שַׂמְלַי **śamlay** or שַׁלְמַי **šalmay** or שַׁמְלַי **šamlay**, n.pr.m. GK: 8530 & 8978 & 9036 [→ 8072; cf. 8014]. Samlai, Shalmai, Shamlai, "[perhaps] *Yahweh is well-being*":– Shalmai [1]

8074 שָׁמֵם **šāmēm**, v. GK: 9037 [→ 4923, 8047, 8076, 8077, 8078; cf. 3456; cf. 8075]. [Q] to be desolate, be appalled; [N] to become desolate, be appalled; [Pol] to cause desolation, be appalled; [H] to bring to devastation, cause to be appalled; [Ho] to lie desolate; [Htpol] to destroy oneself, be appalled:– desolate [31], astonished [14], astonied [6], make desolate [5], desolations [4], made desolate [4], lieth desolate [3], destroy [2], laid desolate [2], laid waste [2], maketh desolate [2], wondered [2], astonishment [1], bring into desolation [1], bring unto desolation [1], desolate places [1], desolation [1], destitute [1], destroyed [1], lay desolate [1], lie waste [1], make amazed [1], make waste [1], make [1], making desolate [1], waste [1]

8075 שְׁמַם **šᵉmam** (Aram.), v. GK: 10724 [cf. 8074]. [Itpo] to be greatly perplexed, implying one is in a state of severe distress, a fig. extension of destroying an object:– astonied [1]

8076 שָׁמֵם **šāmēm**, a. GK: 9038 [→ 8074]. desolate, deserted:– desolate [2]

8077 שְׁמָמָה **šᵉmāmâ** or שִׁמְמָה **šimᵉmâ**, n.f. GK: 9039 & 9040 [→ 8074]. desolation, ruin, wasteland:– desolate [36], desolation [12], most desolate (+4923+2050.1) [3], desolations [2], most desolate (+8077+2050.1) [2], utterly [1], waste [1]

8078 שִׁמָּמוֹן **šimmāmôn**, n.[m.]. GK: 9041 [→ 8074]. despair, which may border on feelings of horror and shuddering:– astonishment [2]

8079 שְׂמָמִית **śᵉmāmît**, n.f. GK: 8532. lizard; some sources: gecko:– spider [1]

8080 שָׁמֵן **šāmēn**, v. GK: 9042 [→ 8081]. [Q] to grow fat; [H] to show as well-fed; by extension: to be calloused, unresponsive of heart:– waxed fat [2], became fat [1], make fat [1], waxen fat [1]

8081 שֶׁמֶן **šemen**, n.m. GK: 9043 [→ 820?, 4924, 4925, 4924, 8080, 8082]. olive, the tree and its products: olive berry, olive oil, olive wood; olive oil was a staple of diet in biblical times, and was also used as a medicine, lamp fuel, and in religious offerings and ritual:– oil [165], ointment [11], olive [4], ointments [3], fat things [2], fat [2], oiled [2], anointing [1], fatness [1], pine [1], very fruitful (+1121) [1]

8082 שָׁמֵן **šāmēn**, a. GK: 9045 [→ 8081]. rich, fertile:– fat [8], lusty [1], plenteous [1]

8083 שְׁמֹנֶה **šᵉmōneh**, n.m. & f. GK: 9046 [→ 8066, 8067, 8084]. eight; (pl.) eighty:– eight [74], eighteen (+6240) [18], eighteenth (+6240) [11], eighth [5], eighteen thousand (+505+7239+2050.1) [1]

8084 שְׁמֹנִים **šᵉmōnîm**, n.pl.indecl. GK: 9047 [→ 8083]. eighty (pl. of "eight"):– fourscore [34], eighty [3], eightieth [1]

8085 שָׁמַע **šāmaʿ**, v. GK: 9048 [→ 851, 2045, 3458, 3460, 3461, 4926, 4927, 4928, 8048, 8049, 8052, 8060, 8087, 8088, 8089, 8090, 8093, 8094, 8095, 8096, 8097, 8099, 8100, 8101; cf. 1002]. [Q] to hear, listen, obey; [N] to be heard; [P] to summon, call together; [H] to proclaim, summon, make hear; from the base meaning of hearing come the extensions of understanding and obedience:– heard [362], hear [350], hearken [112], hearkened [73], heareth [26], obey (+871.1) [26], obeyed (+871.1) [20], obeyed [14], publish [12], heardest [11], obey [11], obedient [8], hearest [6], hearing [6], understand [6], cause to be heard [5], cause to hear [4], diligently hearken (+8085) [4], hear diligently (+8085) [4], heareth (+8085) [4], hearken diligently (+8085) [4], publisheth [4], shewed [4], make to be heard [3], call together [2], carefully hearken (+8085) [2], certainly heard (+8085) [2], diligently obey (+8085) [2], discern [2], hear indeed (+8085) [2], hearkeneth [2], indeed obey (+8085) [2], made to hear [2], obey indeed (+8085+871.1) [2], obeyedst (+871.1) [2], obeyeth (+871.1) [2], reported [2], shew [2], surely hear (+8085) [2], surely heard (+8085) [2], tell [2], told [2], called together [1], caused to be heard [1], caused to hear [1], consented [1], considered [1], content [1], declared [1], declareth [1], declare [1], gathered together [1], gave ear [1], hear (+241) [1], hear attentively [1], hearken diligently [1], hearken unto [1], hearkenedst [1], hearkening [1], listen [1], made a sound [1], made proclamation [1], make a sound [1], make hear [1], make noise [1], make to hear [1], making a noise [1], obeyeth [1], obeying (+871.1) [1], obeying [1], perceived [1], perceive [1], proclaimed [1], published [1], regardeth [1], sang loud [1], shew forth [1], sounding [1], sound [1], understandest [1], understanding [1], understood [1], witness [1]

8086 שְׁמַע *šᵉma'* (Aram.), v. GK: 10725 [cf. 8085]. [P] to hear; [Htpa] to obey:– heard [4], hear [4], obey [1]

8087 שֶׁמַע *šema'*, n.pr.m. GK: 9050. Shema, "*he hears*":– Shema [5]

8088 שֵׁמַע *šēma'*, n.[m.]. GK: 9051 [→ 8085]. what is heard, report, news, rumor:– fame [5], report [5], tidings [2], bruit [1], heard [1], hearing [1], hear [1], loud [1], speech [1]

8089 שֹׁמַע *šōma'*, n.m. GK: 9053 [→ 8085]. report; reputation:– fame [4]

8090 שְׁמַע *šᵉma'*, n.pr.loc. GK: 9054 [→ 8085]. Shema, "*he hears*":– Shema [1]

8091 שָׁמָע *šāmā'*, n.pr.m. GK: 9052 [→ 8085+3068?]. Shama, "*one obedient [to Yahweh]*":– Shama [1]

8092 שִׁמְעָא *šim'ā'*, n.pr.m. GK: 9055 [→ 8085+3068?]. Shimea; Shammua, "*he has heard* or *obedient one*":– Shimea [5], Shimma [1]

8093 שִׁמְעָה *šim'â*, n.pr.m. GK: 9056 [→ 8101]. Shimeah, "*he has heard* or *he is obedient*":– Shimeah [2]

8094 שְׁמָעָה *šᵉmā'â*, n.pr.m. GK: 9057 [→ 8085]. Shemaah, "[poss.] *Yahweh hears*":– Shemaah [1]

8095 שִׁמְעוֹן *šim'ôn*, n.pr.m. GK: 9058 [→ 8099; cf. 8085]. Simeon, Simeonite, "*he has heard* or *obedient one*":– Simeon [43], Shimeon [1]

8096 שִׁמְעִי *šim'î*, n.pr.m. GK: 9059 [→ 8097]. Shimei, "*Yahweh has heard* or *famous*":– Shimei [41], Shimhi [1], Shimi [1]

8097 שִׁמְעִי *šim'î*, a.g. GK: 9060 [→ 8096]. Shimeites, of Shimei, "*of Shimei*":– Shimei [1], Shimites [1]

8098 שְׁמַעְיָה *šᵉma'yâ* or שְׁמַעְיָהוּ *šᵉma'yāhû*, n.pr.m. GK: 9061 & 9062 [→ 8085+3068]. Shemaiah, "*Yahweh hears*":– Shemaiah [41]

8099 שִׁמְעֹנִי *šim'ōnî*, a.g. GK: 9063 [→ 8095]. Simeonite, of Simeon, "*of Simeon*":– Simeonites [3], Simeon [1]

8100 שִׁמְעָת *šim'āt*, n.pr.f. GK: 9064 [→ 8085]. Shimeath, "*guardian, watcher*":– Shimeath [2]

8101 שִׁמְעָתִי *šim'ātî*, a.g. GK: 9065 [→ 8093]. Shimeathite, "*of Shimeath*":– Shimeathites [1]

8102 שֶׁמֶץ *šēmeṣ*, n.[m.]. GK: 9066 [→ 8103?]. whisper:– little [2]

8103 שִׁמְצָה *šimṣâ*, v. GK: 9067 [→ 8102?]. laughingstock, derision:– shame [1]

8104 שָׁמַר *šāmar*, v. GK: 9068 [→ 821, 4929, 4931, 8068, 8105, 8106?, 8108, 8109, 8110, 8111, 8113, 8107, 8118, 8119 (also used with compound proper names)]. [Q] to keep, watch, observe, guard; [Qp] to be set aside, be secured; [N] to be careful, beware; [P] to cling to; [Ht] to keep oneself; to observe for oneself:– keep [183], kept [70], observe [41], take heed [31], keepeth [19], keepers [15], keeper [13], beware [9], preserve [9], keeping [7], preserved [6], preserveth [6], watch [5], diligently keep (+8104) [4], mark [4], watchman [4], watchmen [4], keepest [3], observed [3], regardeth [3], marked [2], regard [2], took heed [2], wait [2], circumspect [1], lay wait [1], lookest narrowly [1], markest [1], marketh [1], observest [1], observeth [1], reserveth [1], saved [1], save [1], spies [1], sure [1], takest heed [1], taking heed [1], wait on [1], waited [1], waiteth on [1], waiteth [1], waiting [1], watched [1], watcht [1]

8105 שֶׁמֶר *šemer*, n.m. GK: 9069 [→ 8106?; cf. 8104]. dregs (of wine); aged wine:– lees [2], wines on the lees [2], dregs [1]

8106 שֶׁמֶר *šemer*, n.pr.m. GK: 9070 [→ 8105?]. Shemer, "[poss.] *watch;* [poss.] *sediment of wine from which clear wine is made*":– Shamer [2], Shemer [2], Shamed [1]

8107 שִׁמֻּרִים *šimmurîm*, n.[m.pl.]. GK: 9081 [→ 8104]. vigil, night-watch:– much observed [1], observed [1]

שֹׁמֵר *šōmēr*. See 7763.

8108 שָׁמְרָה *šomrâ*, n.f. GK: 9072 [→ 8104]. guard, watch:– watch [1]

8109 שְׁמֻרָה *šᵉmurâ*, n.f. GK: 9073 [→ 8104]. eyelid (that covers and protects the eye):– waking [1]

8110 שִׁמְרוֹן *šimrôn*, n.pr.m. & loc. GK: 9074 & 9075 [→ 8104, 8117]. Shimron, "*guardian, watchman*":– Shimron [5]

8111 שֹׁמְרוֹן *šōmᵉrôn*, n.pr.m. GK: 9076 [→ 8118; cf. 8104; cf. 8115]. Samaria, the capital city of northern kingdom of Israel; by extension, the northern kingdom itself, "*belonging to the clan of Shemer [1Ki 16:24]*":– Samaria [109]

8112 שִׁמְרוֹן מְראוֹן *šimrôn mᵉr'ôn*, n.pr.loc. GK: 9077. Shimron Meron:– Shimron-meron [1]

8113 שִׁמְרִי *šimrî*, n.pr.m. GK: 9078 [→ 8104]. Shimri, "*Yahweh guards, preserves*":– Shimri [3], Simri [1]

8114 שְׁמַרְיָה *šᵉmaryâ* or שְׁמַרְיָהוּ *šᵉmaryāhû*, n.pr.m. GK: 9079 & 9080 [→ 8104+3068]. Shemariah, "*Yahweh guards, preserves*":– Shemariah [3], Shamariah [1]

שְׁמָרִימוֹת *šᵉmārîmôt*. See 8070.

8115 שָׁמְרַיִן *šāmᵉrayin* (Aram.), n.pr.loc. GK: 10726 [cf. 8111]. Samaria, "*belonging to the clan of Shemer*":– Samaria [2]

8116 שִׁמְרִית *šimrît*, n.pr.f. GK: 9083 [→ 7763]. Shimrith, "*guardianess, watch woman*":– Shimrith [1]

8117 שִׁמְרֹנִי *šimrōnî*, a.g. GK: 9084 [→ 8110]. Shimronite, "*of Shimron*":– Shimronites [1]

8118 שֹׁמְרֹנִי *šōmᵉrōnî*, a.g. GK: 9085 [→ 8111]. of Samaria, "*of Samaria*":– Samaritans [1]

8119 שִׁמְרָת *šimrāt*, n.pr.m. GK: 9086 [→ 8104]. Shimrath, "*guardian, watchman*":– Shimrath [1]

8120 שְׁמַשׁ *šᵉmaš* (Aram.), v. GK: 10727 [→ 8122?]. [Pa] to attend to, serve:– ministered [1]

8121 שֶׁמֶשׁ *šemeš*, n.f. & m. GK: 9087 [→ 1053, 1030, 5885, 5905, 8048, 8123; cf. 8122]. sun:– sun [119], sunrising (+4217) [6], the sunrising (+4217+1886.1) [2], east side (+4217) [1], eastward (+4217+1886.1) [1], sunrising (+4217+1886.1) [1], the east side (+4217+1886.1) [1], the west (+3996+1886.1) [1], westward (+3996+1886.1) [1], windows [1]

8122 שְׁמַשׁ *šᵉmaš* (Aram.), n.[m.]. GK: 10728 [→ 8120?, 8122; cf. 8121]. sun:– sun [1]

8123 שִׁמְשׁוֹן *šimšôn*, n.pr.m. GK: 9088 [→ 8121]. Samson, "*little one of Shemesh* or *strong*":– Samson [35], Samson's [3]

שִׁמְשִׁי *šimšî*. See 1030.

8124 שִׁמְשַׁי *šimšay* (Aram.), n.pr.m. GK: 10729 [→ 8122]. Shimshai, "*one given to (pagan sun god) Shemesh*":– Shimshai [4]

8125 שַׁמְשְׁרַי *šamšᵉray*, n.pr.m. GK: 9091. Shamsherai, "*may Shemesh guard*":– Shamsherai [1]

8126 שֻׁמָתִי *šumātî*, a.g. GK: 9092. Shumathite:– Shumathites [1]

8127 שֵׁן *šēn*, n.f. & m. GK: 9094 [→ 8143; cf. 8150; cf. 8128]. tooth (human or animal); by extension, anything tooth shaped: rocky crag; "cleanness of teeth" is a sign of lack of food in famine:– teeth [31], ivory [10], tooth [9], sharp [2], crag [1], forefront [1], tooth's [1]

8128 שֵׁן *šēn* (Aram.), n.[f.]. GK: 10730 [cf. 8127]. tooth; in the dual number it is a set of teeth, the upper and lower rows of teeth in a mouth:– teeth [3]

8129 שֵׁן *šēn*, n.pr.loc. GK: 9095 [→ 8150]. Shen, "*tooth, crag [of rock]*":– Shen [1]

8130 שָׂנֵא *śānē'*, v. GK: 8533 [→ 5570, 5574, 8135, 8146; cf. 8131]. [Q] to hate, be an enemy; [Qp] to be unloved; [N] to be hated, be shunned; [P] to be an adversary, be a foe; "hate" can be active, as an enemy or adversary; or passive, as someone unloved or shunned:– hate [68], hated [40], hateth [20], hatest [5], enemies [3], enemy [2], utterly hated (+8130) [2], foes [1], hated exceedingly (+1419+3966+8135) [1], hateful [1], haters [1], hating [1], odious [1]

8131 שְׂנֵא *śᵉnā'* (Aram.), v. GK: 10686 [cf. 8130]. [P] to hate; (as noun) an enemy:– hate [1]

8132 שָׁנָא *šānā'*, v. GK: 9096 [→ 8125?]. prob. same as 8138: [Q] to become dull; to change; [P] to change, alter; [Pu] to be changed:– changed [3]

8133 שְׁנָא *šᵉnâ* (Aram.), v. GK: 10731 [→ 8140; cf. 8138]. [P] to be changed, be different; [Pa] to change; defy; [Pap] to be different; [H] to change, alter; [Itpa] to be changed, be turned into:– changed [12], diverse [5], alter [2], changeth [1], change [1]

שֵׁנָא *šēnā'*. See 8142.

8134 שִׁנְאָב *šin'āb*, n.pr.m. GK: 9098. Shinab, "*Sin is his father*":– Shinab [1]

8135 שִׂנְאָה *śin'â*, n.f. GK: 8534 [→ 8130]. hatred, malice:– hatred [12], hated [2], cruel hatred (+2555) [1], hated exceedingly (+1419+3966+8130) [1], hatefully (+871.1) [1]

8136 שִׁנְאָן *šin'ān*, n.[m.]. GK: 9099 [→ 8125?]. high in rank or number:– angels [1]

8137 שֶׁנְאַצַּר *šen'aṣṣar*, n.pr.m. GK: 9100. Shenazzar, "*may Sin protect*":– Shenazzar [1]

8138 שָׁנָה *šānâ*, v. GK: 9101 [→ 4932, 8132?, 8136?, 8141, 8144?, 8145, 8147; cf. 8150; cf. 8133]. [Q] to repeat, do again; [N] to be repeated; [P] to change, alter; to pretend; [Pu] to be changed; [Ht] to disguise oneself:– changed [3], again [2], change [2], diverse [2], alter [1], changest [1], did the second time [1], disguise [1], do again [1], do the second time [1], doubled [1], given to change [1], pervert [1], preferred [1], repeateth [1], returneth [1], second time [1]

Heb

8139 שְׁנָה ***šᵉnâ*** (Aram.), n.f. GK: 10733 [cf. 8142]. sleep:– sleep [1]

8140 שְׁנָה ***šᵉnâ*** (Aram.), n.f. GK: 10732 [→ 8133; cf. 8141]. year:– year [6], years [1]

8141 שָׁנָה ***šānâ***, n.f. GK: 9102 [→ 8138; cf. 8140]. year:– years [446], year [288], first year (+1121) [42], two years [6], two full years (+3117) [5], every year (+3605+8141+2050.1) [2], year by year (+8141) [2], year by year (+8141+871.1) [2], yearly (+3605+8141+871.1+2050.1) [2], yearly (+8141+871.1) [2], years old [2], years' [2], first year (+1323) [1], how long (+3117+4100+3509.1) [1], long [1], old (+2416+3117) [1], two year [1], whole age (+2416+3117) [1], year's [1], yearly [1]

8142 שֵׁנָא ***šēnā'*** or שֵׁנָה ***šēnâ***, n.f. GK: 9097 & 9104 [→ 3462, 8153; cf. 8139]. sleep, with a focus of rest and inactivity, sometimes laziness; by extension: death:– sleep [23]

8143 שֶׁנְהַבִּים ***šenhabbîm***, n.m.[pl.]. GK: 9105 [→ 8127]. ivory:– ivory [2]

8144 שָׁנִי ***šānî***, n.[m.]. GK: 9106 [→ 8138?]. scarlet, crimson (thread):– scarlet (+8438) [31], scarlet [6], scarlet (+8438+1886.1) [2], scarlet thread [2], crimson [1]

8145 שֵׁנִי ***šēnî***, a.num.ord. GK: 9108 [→ 8147; cf. 8138; cf. 8578, cf. 8579]. second:– second [84], other [37], second time [16], again [7], another [7], more [3], either [1], second rank [1]

8146 שָׂנִיא ***śānî'***, a. GK: 8535 [→ 8130]. not loved, disdained:– hated [1]

8147 שְׁנַיִם ***šᵉnayim***, n.m. & f. GK: 9109 [→ 8145; cf. 8138; cf. 8648]. two:– two [528], twelve (+6240) [109], both [75], twelfth (+6240) [22], second [10], twain [6], double [5], twice [4], threescore and twelve (+7657+2050.1) [2], twenty [2], both twain [1], couple [1], sixscore (+6240) [1], twice (+871.1) [1]

8148 שְׁנִינָה ***šᵉnînâ***, n.f. GK: 9110 [→ 8150]. object of ridicule:– byword [3], taunt [1]

8149 שְׂנִיר ***śᵉnîr***, n.pr.loc. GK: 8536. Senir:– Senir [2], Shenir [2]

8150 שָׁנַן ***šānan***, v. GK: 9111 & 9112 [→ 8127, 8129, 8143, 8148; cf. 8138]. [Q] to sharpen; [Qp] be sharpened; [P] to impress, repeat; [Htpol] to be embittered:– sharp [4], whet [2], pricked [1], sharpened [1], teach diligently [1]

8151 שָׁנַס ***šānas***, v. GK: 9113. [P] to tuck up the cloak (into the belt):– girded up [1]

8152 שִׁנְעָר ***šin'ār***, n.pr.loc. GK: 9114. Shinar; Babylonia:– Shinar [7], Babylonish [1]

8153 שְׁנָת ***šᵉnāt***, n. GK: 9104 [→ 8142]. same as 8142: sleep:– sleep [1]

8154 שָׁסָה ***šāsâ***, v. GK: 9115 [cf. 7601]. [Q] to raid, loot, plunder; [Qp] to be looted:– spoiled [3], spoil [3], spoilers [2], destroyers [1], robbed [1], rob [1]

8155 שָׁסַס ***šāsas***, v. GK: 9116 [→ 7601]. same as 7601: [Q] to plunder, ransack; [N] to be looted, be ransacked:– spoiled [3], rifled [1], spoil [1]

8156 שָׁסַע ***šāsa'***, v. GK: 9117 [→ 8157]. [Q] to divide; [Qp] be divided; [P] to tear apart:– clovenfooted (+6541+8157) [2], rent [2], cleaveth [1], cleave [1], clovenfooted (+8157) [1], cloven [1], stayed [1]

8157 שֶׁסַע ***šesa'***, n.[m.]. GK: 9118 [→ 8156]. cleft (split hoof):– clovenfooted (+6541+8156) [2], cleft [1], clovenfooted (+8156) [1]

8158 שָׁסַף ***šāsap***, v. GK: 9119. [P] to hack to pieces (for execution):– hewed in pieces [1]

8159 שָׁעָה ***šā'â***, v. GK: 9120 [cf. 7583]. [Q] to look with favor, have regard for, pay attention to:– look [3], dismayed [2], respect [2], depart [1], dim [1], have respect [1], look away [1], looked [1], regard [1], spare [1], turn [1]

8160 שָׁעָה ***šā'â*** (Aram.), n.f. GK: 10734. moment, short time; (as adv.) immediately, suddenly, for a time:– hour [5]

שְׂעוֹר ***śᵉ'ôr***. See 8184.

שְׂעוֹרָה ***śᵉ'ôrâ***. See 8184.

8161 שַׁעֲטָה ***šᵉ'āṭâ***, n.f. GK: 9121. galloping, pounding (hooves):– stamping [1]

8162 שַׁעַטְנֵז ***ša'aṭnēz***, n.m. GK: 9122. woven cloth; likely referring to a wide mesh:– garment of divers sorts [1], mingled of linen and woollen (+3610) [1]

8163 שָׂעִיר ***śā'îr***, a. & n.m. GK: 8537 & 8538 & 8539 [→ 8166; cf. 8175]. hairy, shaggy; male goat; goat idol:– kid [26], goat [21], devils [2], goats [2], hairy [2], kids [2], he goats [1], rough [1], satyrs [1], satyr [1]

8164 שָׂעִיר ***śā'îr***, n.[m.]. GK: 8540. rain shower:– small rain [1]

8165 שֵׂעִיר ***śē'îr***, n.pr.m. & loc. GK: 8541 & 8542 & 8543 [→ 8167; cf. 8175]. Seir, "*hairy, shaggy, covered with trees;* [poss.] *the place of the goats* or *the place of Esau [Ge 25:25 BDB]; small forest, rich forest*":– Seir [39]

8166 שְׂעִירָה ***śᵉ'îrâ***, n.f. GK: 8544 [→ 8163]. female goat:– kid [2]

8167 שְׂעִירָה ***śᵉ'îrâ***, n.pr.loc. GK: 8545 [→ 8165]. Seirah, "*place of the goats;* [poss.] *woody hills; shaggy forest*":– Seirath [1]

8168 שֹׁעַל ***šō'al***, n.[m.]. GK: 9123 [→ 4934, 8171?]. hollow of the hand; handful, a measure of volume:– handfuls [2], hollow of hand [1]

שֻׁעָל ***šu'āl***. See 7776.

8169 שַׁעַלְבִים ***ša'albîm*** or שַׁעֲלַבִּין ***šaᵃlabbîn***, n.pr.loc. GK: 9124 & 9125. Shaalbim, Shaalabbin, "*site of foxes*":– Shaalbim [2], Shaalabbin [1]

8170 שַׁעַלְבֹנִי ***ša'albōnî***, a.g. GK: 9126. Shaalbonite:– Shaalbonite [2]

8171 שַׁעֲלִים ***šaᵃlîm***, n.pr.loc. GK: 9127 [→ 8168?]. Shaalim, "[poss.] *[land of] hollow depth*":– Shalim [1]

8172 שָׁעַן ***šā'an***, v. GK: 9128 [→ 4937, 4938]. [N] to lean oneself upon, rely on:– stay [5], leaned [4], lean [4], relied [3], rest [2], leaneth [1], lieth [1], rely [1], resteth [1]

8173 שָׁעַע ***šā'a'***, v. GK: 9129 & 9130 [→ 8191]. [Q] be blinded; [Pil] to take joy in, delight in; [Pulpal] to be dandled; [H] to make close the eyes; [Htpal] to blind oneself; a fig. extension of smearing over or pasting objects together; to delight oneself in:– delight [4], cry out [1], cry [1], dandled [1], play [1], shut [1]

שָׂעִף ***sā'ip***. See 5587.

8174 שַׁעַף ***ša'ap***, n.pr.m. GK: 9131. Shaaph:– Shaaph [2]

8175 שָׂעַר ***śā'ar***, v.den. GK: 8547 & 8548 & 8549 [→ 8163, 8165, 8166, 8167, 8178, 8181, 8183, 8184, 8185; cf. 5590]. [Q] to shudder, bristle with horror; to sweep away (by the wind); to know about, be acquainted with; [N] to be in a storm; [P] to sweep away (by a wind); [Ht] to storm against:– afraid [1], as a storm hurleth [1], come like a whirlwind [1], feared [1], horribly afraid [1], sore afraid (+8178) [1], take away as with a whirlwind [1], tempestuous [1]

8176 שָׁעַר ***šā'ar***, v. GK: 9132 [→ 8180]. [Q] to think, estimate, calculate:– thinketh [1]

8177 שְׂעַר ***śᵉ'ar*** (Aram.), n.m. GK: 10687 [cf. 8181]. hair (of the head or body):– hair [2], hairs [1]

8178 שַׂעַר ***śa'ar***, n.[m.]. GK: 8550 & 8551 [→ 8175]. horror, shudder, an extension of the bristling of hair (in excitement or fear); wind storm, gale:– affrighted (+270) [1], horribly [1], sore afraid (+8175) [1], storm [1]

8179 שַׁעַר ***ša'ar***, n.m. GK: 9133 [→ 7778, 8182, 8189; cf. 8651]. gate, gateway; often referring to the entrance to a city, a key point of the city's defense and a place for public hearings and decisions:– gate [249], gates [112], every gate (+8179+2050.1) [6], cities [2], city [1], doors [1], door [1], porters [1], port [1]

8180 שַׁעַר ***ša'ar***, n.[m.]. GK: 9134 [→ 8176]. measure (of grain):– hundredfold (+3967) [1]

שָׁעִר ***šā'ir***. See 8163.

8181 שֵׂעָר ***śē'ār***, n.m. GK: 8552 [→ 8175; cf. 8177]. hair:– hair [23], hairy [3], hairs [1], rough [1]

שֹׁעֵר ***šō'ēr***. See 7778.

8182 שֹׁעָר ***šō'ār***, a. GK: 9135 [→ 8179]. burst open, i.e., poor quality (figs):– vile [1]

8183 שְׂעָרָה ***śᵉ'ārâ***, n.f. GK: 8554 [→ 8175]. storm, gale:– storm [1], tempest [1]

8184 שְׂעֹרָה ***śᵉ'ōrâ***, n.f. GK: 8555 [→ 8175; cf. 7795?]. barley:– barley [34]

8185 שַׂעֲרָה ***śaᵃrâ***, n.f. GK: 8553 [→ 8175]. hair:– hair [5], hairs [2]

8186 שַׁעֲרוּר ***šaᵃrûr*** or שַׁעֲרוּרִי ***šaᵃrûrî***, n.f. GK: 9136 & 9137. something horrible, shocking thing:– horrible thing [4]

8187 שְׁעַרְיָה ***šᵉ'aryâ***, n.pr.m. GK: 9138 [→ 3068]. Sheariah, "[poss.] *Yahweh breaks*":– Sheariah [2]

8188 שְׂעֹרִים ***śᵉ'ōrîm***, n.pr.m. GK: 8556. Seorim, "*one born at the time of the barley [harvest]*":– Seorim [1]

8189 שַׁעֲרַיִם ***šaᵃrayim***, n.pr.loc. GK: 9139 [→ 8179]. Shaaraim, "*double gates*":– Shaaraim [2], Sharaim [1]

שַׁעֲרִירִיָּה ***šaᵃrîrîâ*** and שַׁעֲרֻרִת ***šaᵃrurit***. See 8186.

8190 שַׁעַשְׁגַז ***ša'ašgaz***, n.pr.m. GK: 9140. Shaashgaz:– Shaashgaz [1]

8191 שַׁעֲשׁוּעִים ***šaᵃšû'îm***, n.[m.]pl.intens. GK: 9141 [→ 8173]. delight:– delight [4], delights [3], pleasant [2]

8192 שָׁפָה ***šāpâ***, v. GK: 9142 [→ 3472, 3473?, 8194?, 8195?, 8205]. [N, Pu] to be swept bare:– high [1], stick out [1]

8193 שָׂפָה ***śāpâ***, n.f. & m. GK: 8557 [→ 8222]. lips (of the mouth); by extension: speech, language; edge of an object, rim, border; the "lip of the sea" is the seashore:– lips [110], bank [10], brim [8], edge [8], language [7], shore [6], speech [6], brink [5], border [3], side [3], lip [2], prating [2], vain [2], band [1], binding [1], full of talk [1], other [1]

8194 שְׁפוֹת ***šᵉpôt***, n.f. GK: 9147 [→ 8192?]. milk product: cream, curds, cheese, etc:– cheese [1]

8195 שְׁפוֹ ***šᵉpô*** or שְׁפִי ***šᵉpî***, n.pr.m. GK: 9143 & 9156 [→ 8192?, 8205?]. Shepho, Shephi, "[poss.] *barren way, empty path*":– Shephi [1], Shepho [1]

8196 שְׁפוֹט ***šᵉpôṭ***, n.m. GK: 9144 [→ 8199]. judgment, punishment:– judgment [2]

8197 שְׁפוּפָם ***šᵉpûpām*** or שְׁפוּפָן ***šᵉpûpān*** or שׁוּפָם ***šûpām***, n.pr.m. GK: 9145 & 9146 & 8792 [→ 7781, 8207?]. Shephupham, Shephuphan, Shupham; "[perhaps] *serpent*":– Shephuphan [1], Shupham [1]

8198 שִׁפְחָה ***šipḥâ***, n.f. GK: 9148 [→ 4940; cf. 5596]. maidservant, female slave:– handmaid [22], maid [12], handmaids [7], maidservants [5], bondwomen [3], maidservant [3], womenservants [3], handmaidens [2], maiden [2], bondmaid [1], maidens [1], servant [1], wench [1]

8199 שָׁפַט ***šāpaṭ***, v. GK: 9149 [→ 4941, 8195, 8196, 8201, 8202, 8204; cf. 8200 (also used with compound proper names)]. [Q] to judge, decide; lead, defend, vindicate; [N] to execute judgment, be brought to trial; to argue a matter; [Po] (ptcp.) judge:– judge [102], judges [37], judged [28], plead [7], judgeth [5], judging [4], avenged [2], judgest [2], needs be a judge (+8199) [2], plead with [2], condemn [1], contendeth [1], defend [1], deliver [1], execute the judgment (+4941) [1], execute [1], executing judgment [1], pleaded [1], pleadeth [1], reason [1], ruled [1]

8200 שְׁפַט ***šᵉpaṭ*** (Aram.), v. GK: 10735 [cf. 8199]. [P] to judge; (as noun) judge:– magistrates [1]

8201 שֶׁפֶט ***šepeṭ***, n.m. GK: 9150 [→ 8199]. judgment, punishment:– judgments [14], judgment [2]

8202 שָׁפָט ***šāpāṭ***, n.pr.m. GK: 9151 [→ 8199]. Shaphat, "*he judges*":– Shaphat [8]

8203 שְׁפַטְיָה ***šᵉpaṭyâ*** or שְׁפַטְיָהוּ ***šᵉpaṭyāhû***, n.pr.m. GK: 9152 & 9153 [→ 8199+3068]. Shephatiah, "*Yahweh has judged*":– Shephatiah [12], Shephathiah [1]

8204 שִׁפְטָן ***šipṭān***, n.pr.m. GK: 9154 [→ 8199]. Shiphtan, "*he has judged*":– Shiphtan [1]

8205 שְׁפִי ***šᵉpî***, n.m. GK: 9155 [→ 8195; cf. 8192]. barren height:– high places [8], high place [1]

8206 שֻׁפִּים ***šuppîm***, n.pr.m. & a.g. GK: 9157 & 9158 [→ 8221]. Shuppim; Shuppites:– Shuppim [3]

8207 שְׁפִיפֹן ***šᵉpîpōn***, n.[m.]. GK: 9159 [→ 8197?]. viper:– adder [1]

8208 שָׁפִיר ***šāpîr***, n.pr.loc. GK: 9160 [→ 8231]. Shaphir, "*lovely*":– Saphir [1]

8209 שַׁפִּיר ***šappîr*** (Aram.), a. GK: 10736 [→ 8232]. beautiful, fair, lovely:– fair [2]

8210 שָׁפַךְ ***šāpak***, v. GK: 9161 [→ 8211, 8212]. [Q] to pour out, shed, spill; [Qp, N, Pu] to be outpoured, be shed; [Ht] be scattered, ebb away; "to shed blood" means to kill:– shed [34], pour out [23], poured out [19], pour [10], cast [6], poured [6], poureth out [4], cast up [2], poureth [2], sheddeth [2], casting up [1], gushed out [1], pouredst out [1], pouring out [1], shed out [1], shedder [1], slipt [1]

8211 שֶׁפֶךְ ***šepek***, n.[m.]. GK: 9162 [→ 8210]. dump (for throwing out ash refuse):– poured out [2]

8212 שָׁפְכָה ***šopkâ***, n.f. GK: 9163 [→ 8210]. male organ (fluid duct):– privy member [1]

8213 שָׁפֵל ***šāpēl***, v. GK: 9164 [→ 8216, 8217, 8218, 8219, 8220; cf. 8214, cf. 8215]. [Q] to be humbled, be brought low; [H] to humble, bring low:– humbled [4], bring down [3], abase [2], brought down [2], humbleth [2], lay low [2], layeth low [2], made low [2], bring low [1], bringeth low [1], brought low [1], cast down [1], casteth down [1], debase [1], humble [1], low [1], put lower [1], putteth down [1]

8214 שְׁפַל ***šᵉpal*** (Aram.), v. GK: 10737 [→ 8215; cf. 8213]. [H] to humble, subdue, bring low:– abase [1], humbled [1], put down [1], subdue [1]

8215 שְׁפַל ***šᵉpal*** (Aram.), a. GK: 10738 [→ 8214; cf. 8217]. low; (as superlative) lowliest:– basest [1]

8216 שֵׁפֶל ***šēpel***, n.[m.]. GK: 9165 [→ 8213]. low estate, humble condition:– low estate [1], low place [1]

8217 שָׁפָל ***šāpāl***, a. GK: 9166 [→ 8213]. low, deep:– low [5], base [4], humble [4], lower [4], basest [1], lowly [1]

8218 שִׁפְלָה ***šiplâ***, n.f. GK: 9168 [→ 8213]. state of lowliness, condition of humiliation:– low place [1]

8219 שְׁפֵלָה ***šᵉpēlâ***, n.f. GK: 9169 [→ 8213]. (western) foothills, Shephelah, a major buffer area between the (Philistine) coastal plain and the highlands of Judah:– valley [6], vale [5], plain [3], low country [2], low plains [2], valleys [2]

8220 שִׁפְלוּת ***šiplût***, n.f. GK: 9170 [→ 8213]. idleness, inactivity, an extension of lowering the hands to a position of rest:– idleness [1]

8221 שְׁפָם ***šᵉpām***, n.pr.loc. GK: 9172 [→ 8225?]. Shepham, "*nakedness*":– Shepham [2]

8222 שָׂפָם ***śāpām***, n.[m.]. GK: 8559 [→ 8193]. (the area of the) mustache; lower part of the face:– lips [3], beard [1], upper lip [1]

8223 שָׁפָם ***šāpām***, n.pr.m. GK: 9171. Shapham:– Shapham [1]

8224 שִׂפְמוֹת ***śipmôt***, n.pr.loc. GK: 8560. Siphmoth:– Siphmoth [1]

8225 שִׁפְמִי ***šipmî***, a.g. GK: 9175 [→ 8221?]. Shiphmite:– Shiphmite [1]

8226 שָׂפַן ***śāpan***, v. GK: 8561 [cf. 5603]. [Qp] to be hidden:– treasures [1]

8227 שָׁפָן ***šāpān***, n.m. & n.pr.m. GK: 9176 & 9177. coney; n.pr. Shaphan, "*rock badger*":– Shaphan [30], conies [2], coney [1], cony [1]

8228 שֶׁפַע ***šepaʿ***, n.[m.]. GK: 9179. abundance:– abundance [1]

8229 שִׁפְעָה ***šipʿâ***, n.f. GK: 9180. (of water) flood; mass (of humans or animals):– abundance [3], company [2], multitude [1]

8230 שִׁפְעִי ***šipʿî***, n.pr.m. GK: 9181. Shiphi, "*flowing abundance*":– Shiphi [1]

שָׂפַק ***śāpaq***. See 5606.

8231 שָׁפַר ***šāpar***, v. GK: 9182 [→ 8208, 8233, 8235, 8236, 8237; cf. 7782; cf. 8232]. [Q] to be delightful, pleasing:– goodly [1]

8232 שְׁפַר ***šᵉpar*** (Aram.), v. GK: 10739 [→ 8209, 8238?; cf. 8231]. [P] to be pleased, have pleasure:– acceptable [1], good [1], pleased [1]

8233 שֶׁפֶר ***šeper***, n.m. GK: 9183 [→ 8231]. beauty, loveliness:– goodly [1]

8234 שֶׁפֶר ***šeper***, n.pr.loc. GK: 9184 [cf. 5611]. Shepher:– Shapher [2]

שֹׁפָר ***šōpār***. See 7782.

8235 שִׁפְרָה ***šiprâ***, n.f. GK: 9185 [→ 8231]. fairness, clearness (of skies):– garnished [1]

8236 שִׁפְרָה ***šiprâ***, n.pr.f. GK: 9186 [→ 8231]. Shiphrah, "*beautiful, fair*":– Shiphrah [1]

8237 שַׁפְרוּר ***šaprûr*** or שַׁפְרִיר ***šaprîr***, n.[m.]. GK: 9187 & 9188 [→ 8231]. royal canopy, pavilion:– royal pavilion [1]

8238 שְׁפַרְפָּר ***šᵉparpār*** (Aram.), n.[m.]. GK: 10740 [→ 8232?]. dawn:– very early [1]

8239 שָׁפַת ***šāpat***, v.den. GK: 9189 [→ 830, 4942, 8240]. [Q] to place, put:– set on [3], brought [1], ordain [1]

8240 שְׁפַתַּיִם ***šᵉpattayim***, n.[m.]du. GK: 9190 & 9191 [→ 8239]. double-pronged hooks; area of inactivity: (place of the) fireplaces; some sources: saddlebags or sheepfolds:– hooks [1], pots [1]

8241 שֶׁצֶף ***šeṣep***, n.m. GK: 9192 [cf. 7857, 7858]. surging, flooding (of anger):– little [1]

8242 שַׂק ***śaq***, n.m. GK: 8566. sackcloth; sack:– sackcloth [41], sack [4], sacks [2], sackclothes [1]

8243 שָׁק ***šāq*** (Aram.), n.[m.]. GK: 10741 [cf. 7785]. lower leg, shank:– legs [1]

8244 שָׂקַד ***śāqad***, v. GK: 8567. [N] to be bound:– bound [1]

8245 שָׁקַד ***šāqad***, v. GK: 9193 [→ 8246, 8247]. [Q] to be awake, watch, stand guard:– watch [6], watched [2], hasten [1], remain [1], waketh [1], watching [1]

8246 מְשֻׁקָּד ***mᵉšuqqād***, n.m. GK: 5481 [cf. 8245]. shape of almond flowers:– made like almonds [3], made like unto almonds [2], made after the fashion of almonds [1]

8247 שָׁקֵד ***šāqēd***, n.[m.]. GK: 9196 [cf. 8245]. almond tree, almond nuts:– almond tree [2], almonds [2]

8248 שָׁקָה ***šāqâ***, v. GK: 9197 [→ 4945, 8249, 8250, 8268; cf. 8354]. [N] to be given a drink; [Pu] to be moistened; [H] to give a drink to:– water [9], butler [8], give drink [7], give to drink [6], watered [6], gave drink [5], made drink [5], cause to drink [4], make drink [4], made to drink [3], cupbearers [2], drink [2], gave to drink [2], given to drink [2], butlers [1], cupbearer [1], givest to drink [1], giveth drink [1], giving drink [1], moistened [1], wateredst [1], watereth [1]

8249 שִׁקּוּ ***šiqquw***, n.[m.]. GK: 9198 [→ 8248]. same as 8250: drink; nourishing drink:– drink [1]

8250 שִׁקּוּי ***šiqqûy***, n.[m.]. GK: 9198 [→ 8248]. same as 8249: drink; nourishing drink:– drink [1], marrow [1]

8251 שִׁקּוּץ ***šiqqûṣ***, n.m. GK: 9199 [→ 8262]. detestable thing, vileness, abomination:– abominations [13], abomination [7], detestable things [5], abominable filth [1], abominable idols [1], detestable [1]

8252 שָׁקַט ***šāqaṭ***, v. GK: 9200 [→ 8253; cf. 8367]. [Q] to be at rest, be at peace; [H] to keep silent, remain quiet, remain calm:– quiet [14], rest [5], had rest [4], at rest [2], in rest [2], quietness [2], still [2], appeaseth [1], give rest [1], giveth quietness [1], idleness [1], in quietness [1], in quiet [1], quieteth [1], rested [1], settled [1], take rest [1]

8253 שֶׁקֶט **šeqeṭ**, n.[m.]. GK: 9201 [→ 8252]. quietness:– quietness [1]

8254 שָׁקַל **šāqal**, v. GK: 9202 [→ 4946, 4948, 4949?, 8255; cf. 8625]. [Q] to weigh out, make payment; [N] to be weighed:– weighed [11], pay [4], throughly weighed (+8254) [2], weigh [2], receiver [1], receive [1], spend [1]

8255 שֶׁקֶל **šeqel**, n.m. GK: 9203 [→ 8254; cf. 8625]. shekel (a unit of weight and value, about two-fifths of an ounce [11.5 grams]):– shekels [46], shekel [42]

8256 שִׁקְמָה **šiqmâ**, n.f. GK: 9204. sycamore-fig tree:– sycomore trees [5], sycomore fruit [1], sycomores [1]

8257 שָׁקַע **šāqa'**, v. GK: 9205 [→ 4950]. [Q] to sink down; [N] to sink; [H] to make sink down, make settle:– drowned [2], lettest down [1], make deep [1], quenched [1], sink [1]

8258 שְׁקַעֲרוּרָה **š^{e}qa^{a}rûrâ**, n.f. GK: 9206 [→ 7086]. depression, hollow:– hollow strakes [1]

8259 שָׁקַף **šāqap**, v. GK: 9207 [→ 4947, 8260?, 8261]. [N] to look down on, overlook; [H] to look down on:– looked [6], looked out [4], look down [3], looked down [3], looketh [3], appeareth [1], looketh forth [1], looking [1]

8260 שֶׁקֶף **šāqep**, n.[m.]. GK: 9208 [→ 8259?]. frame work (of a door):– windows [1]

8261 שְׁקֻפִים **š^{e}qupîm**, n.m. GK: 9209 [→ 8259]. clerestory window (a high place window):– lights [1], windows [1]

8262 שָׁקַץ **šāqaṣ**, v. GK: 9210 [→ 8251, 8263; cf. 5354, 6973]. [P] to detest, abhor, defile:– abomination [2], make abominable [2], utterly detest (+8262) [2], abhorred [1]

8263 שֶׁקֶץ **šeqeṣ**, n.m. GK: 9211 [→ 8262]. detestable thing:– abomination [9], abominable [2]

שִׁקּוּץ **šiqquṣ**. See 8251.

8264 שָׁקַק **šāqaq**, v. GK: 9212 [→ 4944; cf. 7783?]. [Q] to rush forth, charge forth; [Htpal] to rush back and forth:– appetite [1], justle against [1], longing [1], ranging [1], run to and fro [1], run [1]

8265 שָׂקַר **śāqar**, v. GK: 8568. [P] to flirt, ogle (with the eyes):– wanton [1]

8266 שָׁקַר **šāqar**, v.den. GK: 9213 [→ 8267]. [Q] to deal falsely with; [P] to deceive, lie, betray:– lie [3], deal falsely [1], dealt falsely [1], suffer to fail [1]

8267 שֶׁקֶר **šeqer**, n.m. GK: 9214 [→ 8266]. lie, falseness, deception; vanity:– lying [21], false [20], lies [18], falsehood [13], lie [10], falsely [7], falsely (+1886.1+3807.1) [4], wrongfully [4], vain [3], deceitful [2], deceit [1], falsely (+5921) [1], falsely (+871.1+1886.1) [1], feignedly (+871.1) [1], in vain (+1886.1+3807.1) [1], in vain [1], liar [1], lies (+1697) [1], lying (+1697) [1], vain thing [1], without a cause [1]

8268 שֹׁקֶת **šōqet**, n.f. GK: 9216 [→ 8248]. watering-trough:– troughs [1], trough [1]

8269 שַׂר **śar**, n.m. GK: 8569 [→ 5371, 8282, 8310; cf. 7786]. ruler of various spheres (military, religious, governmental): commander, official, prince, chief, leader; "Prince of Peace" is a title of the child who would rule on David's throne, referring to the Messiah:– princes [189], captains [80], captain [48], chief [33], rulers [23], prince [19], ruler [10], governor [4], chief captain [3], keeper [3], governors [2], principal [2], general [1], lords [1], master [1], stewards [1], taskmasters (+4522) [1]

8270 שֹׁר **šōr**, n.[m.]. GK: 9219 [→ 8307, 8326]. navel; umbilical cord:– navel [2]

8271 שְׁרָא **š^{e}râ** (Aram.), v. GK: 10742 [cf. 8281]. [P] to loosen, solve (a problem); [Pp] to be loosened; to dwell; [Pa] to begin; [Htpa] to be loose and shaking (of legs giving way):– began [1], dissolve [1], dissolving [1], dwelleth [1], loosed [1], loose [1]

8272 שַׂרְאֶצֶר **śar'eṣer**, שַׂר־אֶצֶר **śar-'eṣer**, n.pr.m. GK: 8570 [→ 5371]. Sharezer, "*[god] protect the king!*":– Sharezer [2], Sherezer [1]

8273 שָׁרָב **šārāb**, n.m. GK: 9220 [→ 8274?]. parching heat; burning hot sand:– heat [1], parched ground [1]

8274 שֵׁרֵבְיָה **šērēbyâ**, n.pr.m. GK: 9221 [→ 8273?+3068]. Sherebiah, "[poss.] *Yahweh has sent burning heat*":– Sherebiah [8]

8275 שַׁרְבִיט **šarbîṭ**, n.m. GK: 9222 [→ 7626]. scepter, staff:– sceptre [4]

8276 שָׂרַג **śārag**, v. GK: 8571 [→ 8299]. [Pu] to be close-knit, be intertwined; [Ht] to be woven together:– wrapt together [1], wreathed [1]

8277 שָׂרַד **śārad**, v. GK: 8572 [→ 8300]. [Q] to run away, escape:– remained [1]

8278 שְׂרָד **ś^{e}rād**, n.[m.]. GK: 8573 [→ 8279?]. woven material (with some kind of braiding woven in it):– service [4]

8279 שֶׂרֶד **śered**, n.[m.]. GK: 8574 [→ 8278?]. marker (for wood chiseling):– line [1]

8280 שָׂרָה **śārâ**, v. GK: 8575 [→ 415, 3478, 3481, 3482, 8304]. [Q] to struggle, contend:– as a prince hast power [1], had power [1]

8281 שָׁרָה **šārâ**, v. GK: 9223 [→ 4952, 8302; cf. 8271]. [Q] to unleash; to deliver, set free:– remnant [1]

8282 שָׂרָה **śārâ**, n.f. GK: 8576 [→ 8269, 8283; cf. 7786]. woman of nobility, lady of royal birth, queen:– ladies [2], princesses [1], princess [1], queens [1]

8283 שָׂרָה **śārâ**, n.pr.f. GK: 8577 [→ 8282; cf. 8297]. Sarah, "*princess*":– Sarah [36], Sarah's [2]

8284 שָׁרָה **šārâ**, n.[m.]. GK: 9224 [→ 7791; cf. 7789]. vineyard:– walls [1]

8285 שֵׁרָה **šērâ** or שֵׁר **šēr**, n.[f.]. GK: 9225 & 9217. bracelet:– bracelets [1]

8286 שְׂרוּג **ś^{e}rûg**, n.pr.m. GK: 8578. Serug, "*descendant* i.e., *younger branch*":– Serug [5]

8287 שָׁרוּחֶן **šārûḥen**, n.pr.loc. GK: 9226. Sharuhen:– Sharuhen [1]

8288 שְׂרוֹךְ **ś^{e}rôk**, n.[m.]. GK: 8579 [→ 8308]. thong (of a sandal):– latchet [1], shoelatchet (+5275) [1]

8289 שָׁרוֹן **šārôn** or לַשָּׁרוֹן **laššārôn**, n.pr.loc. GK: 9227 & 4389 [→ 8290; cf. 3474]. Sharon, "*plain, level country*"; Lasharon, "*[belonging to] Sharon*":– Sharon [6], Lasharon [1]

8290 שָׁרוֹנִי **šārônî**, a.g. GK: 9228 [→ 8289; cf. 3474]. Sharonite, "*of Sharon*":– Sharonite [1]

8291 שָׂרֹק **śārōq**, n.[m.]. GK: 8602 [→ 8320]. choice vines:– principal plants [1]

8292 שְׁרוּקָה **š^{e}rûqâ** or שְׁרִקָה **š^{e}riqâ**, n.[f.]. GK: 9229 & 9241 [→ 8319; cf. 8322]. whistling; scorn; some sources: flute playing:– bleatings [1], hissing [1]

8293 שֵׁרוּת **šērût**, var. GK: 9230 [cf. 8281]. freedom:–

8294 שֶׂרַח **śeraḥ**, n.pr.f. GK: 8580 [cf. 5628]. Serah, "*one who explains, opens, extends; abundance*":– Serah [2], Sarah [1]

8295 שָׂרַט **śāraṭ**, v. GK: 8581 [→ 8296]. [Q] to make a cut, incise the skin; [N] to make oneself incised, cut oneself:– cut in pieces (+8295) [2], make any cuttings (+8296) [1]

8296 שֶׂרֶט **śereṭ** or שָׂרֶטֶת **śāreṭet**, n.[m.]. GK: 8582 & 8583 [→ 8295]. cut, incision; this may refer to a tattoo:– cuttings [1], make any cuttings (+8295) [1]

8297 שָׂרַי **śāray**, n.pr.f. GK: 8584 [cf. 8283]. Sarai, "*princess*":– Sarai [16], Sarai's [1]

8298 שָׁרַי **šāray**, n.pr.m. GK: 9232. Sharai:– Sharai [1]

8299 שָׂרִיג **śārîg**, n.m. GK: 8585 [→ 8276]. branch, tendril (of grape vines and fig trees):– branches [3]

8300 שָׂרִיד **śārîd**, n.m. GK: 8586 [→ 8277]. survivor; those left:– remaining [9], remain [8], left [3], remaineth [3], remnant [2], alive [1], remained [1], rest [1]

8301 שָׂרִיד **śārîd**, n.pr.loc. GK: 8587. Sarid, "*survivor*":– Sarid [2]

8302 שִׁרְיָה **širyâ** or שִׁרְיוֹן **širyôn**, n.f. GK: 9233 & 9234 [→ 8281; cf. 5630]. coat of scale armor; a weapon that is thrown: javelin, lance, light spear; some sources: arrowhead:– coat [3], habergeons [2], harness [2], breastplate [1], habergeon [1]

8303 שִׂרְיוֹן **śiryôn**, n.pr.loc. GK: 8590 [cf. 5630]. Sirion, "*coat of mail*":– Sirion [2]

8304 שְׂרָיָה **ś^{e}rāyâ** or שְׂרָיָהוּ **ś^{e}rāyāhû**, n.pr.m. GK: 8588 & 8589 [→ 8280+3068]. Seraiah, "*Yahweh persists; Yahweh is prince; Yahweh contends*":– Seraiah [20]

8305 שָׂרִיק **śārîq**, a. GK: 8591. combed (flax, as a first step for making linen):– fine [1]

8306 שָׁרִיר **šārîr**, n.[m.]. GK: 9235 [→ 8307]. muscle:– navel [1]

8307 שְׁרִרוּת **š^{e}rirût**, n.f. GK: 9244 [→ 8270, 8306, 8325, 8326]. stubbornness:– imagination [9], lust [1]

8308 שָׂרַךְ **śārak**, v. GK: 8592 [→ 8288]. [P] to run here and there (aimlessly):– traversing [1]

8309 שְׁרֵמוֹת **š^{e}rēmôt**, var. GK: 9236. var. of 7709: field:–

8310 שַׂר־סְכִים **śar-s^{e}kîm**, n.pr.m. GK: 8593 [→ 8269]. Sarsekim:– Sarsechim [1]

8311 שָׂרַע **śāra'**, v. GK: 8594. [Qp] to be deformed; [Ht] to stretch oneself:– hath any thing superfluous [1], stretch [1], superfluous [1]

8312 שַׂרְעַפִּים **śar'appîm**, n.[m.]pl. GK: 8595 [→ 5587]. anxiety, anxious thoughts:– thoughts [2]

8313 שָׂרַף **śārap**, v. GK: 8596 [→ 4955, 4956, 8314, 8315, 8316; cf. 5635]. [Q] to burn, set a fire; [Qp, N, Pu] to be burned up:– burnt [64], burn [38], burneth [4], burned [3], utterly burnt (+8313) [2], burn thoroughly (+8316+3807.1) [1], burn up [1], burnt up [1], cause to be burnt [1], kindled [1], made a burning (+8316) [1]

8314 שָׂרָף **śārāp**, n.m. GK: 8597 [→ 8315; cf. 8313]. venomous snake; seraph (six-winged being):– fiery [3], fiery serpent [2], seraphims [2]

8315 שָׂרָף **śārāp**, n.pr.m. GK: 8598 [→ 8314; cf. 8313]. Saraph, *"burning one, serpent"*:– Saraph [1]

8316 שְׂרֵפָה **śᵉrēpâ**, n.f. GK: 8599 [→ 8313]. burning:– burning [8], burnt [2], burn thoroughly (+8313+3807.1) [1], burnt up [1], made a burning (+8313) [1]

8317 שָׁרַץ **šāraṣ**, v. GK: 9237 [→ 8318]. [Q] to teem, swarm, move about:– creepeth [4], bring forth abundantly [2], creep [2], breed abundantly [1], bring forth abundantly (+8318) [1], brought forth abundantly [1], brought forth in abundance [1], increased abundantly [1], moveth [1]

8318 שֶׁרֶץ **šereṣ**, n.m. GK: 9238 [→ 8317]. creatures that teem, swarm, move about:– creeping thing [7], creeping things [4], creep [2], bring forth abundantly (+8317) [1], move [1]

8319 שָׁרַק **šāraq**, v. GK: 9239 [→ 8322, 8292]. [Q] to whistle, hiss, scoff:– hiss [12]

8320 שָׂרֹק **śārōq**, a. GK: 8601 [→ 4957, 7796, 8291, 8321]. brown, dark red (color of grapes):– speckled [1]

8321 שֹׂרֵק **śōrēq** or שְׂרֵקָה **śᵉrēqâ**, n.m. & f. GK: 8603 & 8605 [→ 8320]. choice vines:– choicest vine [1], noble vine [1]

8322 שְׁרֵקָה **šᵉrēqâ**, n.f. GK: 9240 [→ 8319; cf. 8292]. object of scorn, thing of derision, something held in contempt; an extension of the act of whistling or shrieking in derision:– hissing [7], choice vine [1]

8323 שָׂרַר **śārar**, v.den. GK: 8606 [→ 7786]. [Q] to rule, govern; [H] to choose a prince; [Ht] to act out as a ruler:– make altogether a prince (+8323) [2], rule [2], bear rule [1]

8324 שׁוֹרֵר **šôrēr**, n.m. GK: 8806. enemy, adversary:– enemies [5]

8325 שָׁרָר **šārār**, n.pr.m. GK: 9243 [→ 8307]. Sharar, *"firm"*:– Sharar [1]

8326 שֹׁרֶר **šōrer**, n.m. GK: 9219 [→ 8270]. same as 8270: navel; umbilical cord:– navel [1]

8327 שָׁרַשׁ **šāraš**, v.den. GK: 9245 [→ 8328]. [P] to uproot; [Poel/Poal] to take root; [Pu] to be uprooted; [H] to take root:– root out [2], cause to take deep root (+8328) [1], cause to take root [1], rooted out [1], take root [1], taken root [1], taking root [1]

8328 שֹׁרֶשׁ **šōreš**, n.m. GK: 9247 [→ 8327, 8329; cf. 8330]. root of a plant; by extension: base or bottom of any object; source of a family line; "the Root of Jesse" is a messianic title, emphasizing Davidic origin:– root [16], roots [13], bottom [1], cause to take deep root (+8327) [1], heels [1], take root [1]

8329 שֶׁרֶשׁ **šereš**, n.pr.m. GK: 9246 [→ 8328]. Sheresh, *"root, rootstock, sucker [of a plant]"*:– Sheresh [1]

8330 שְׁרֹשׁ **šᵉrōš** (Aram.), n.m. GK: 10743 [→ 8332; cf. 8328]. root:– roots [3]

8331 שַׁרְשָׁה **šaršâ**, n.f. GK: 9248 [→ 8333]. chain:– chains [1]

8332 שְׁרֹשׁוּ **šᵉrōšû** or שְׁרֹשִׁי **šᵉrōšî** (Aram.), n.f. GK: 10744 & 10745 [→ 8330]. banishment, uprooting (from community):– banishment [1]

8333 שַׁרְשְׁרָה **šaršᵉrâ**, n.f. GK: 9249 [→ 8331]. chain:– chains [6], chain [1]

8334 שָׁרַת **šārat**, v. GK: 9250 [→ 8335]. [P] to minister, serve, attend:– minister [48], ministered [15], ministers [15], servant [4], served [4], serve [4], service [2], do service [1], ministering [1], servants [1], servitor [1], waited on [1]

8335 שָׁרֵת **šārēt**, n.m. GK: 9251 [→ 8334]. cultic service:– minister [1], ministry [1]

8336 שֵׁשׁ **šēš**, n.m. GK: 9253 & 9254 [→ 7893]. fine linen, byssus (processed from the flax plant); alabaster:– fine linen [37], marble [2], blue marble [1], silk [1]

8337 שֵׁשׁ **šēš**, n.m. GK: 9252 [→ 8345, 8346; cf. 8353]. six; (pl.) sixty:– six [187], sixteen (+6240) [21], sixteenth (+6240) [3], sixth [2], threescore and one thousand (+505+7239+2050.1) [1], threescore and sixteen (+7657+2050.1) [1]

8338 שָׁשָׁא **šāšāʼ**, v.intens. GK: 9255. [P] to lead along:– leave the sixth part [1]

8339 שֵׁשְׁבַּצַּר **šēšbaṣṣar**, n.pr.m. GK: 9256 [cf. 8339]. Sheshbazzar, *"may Sin protect [the father]"*:– Sheshbazzar [2]

8340 שֵׁשְׁבַּצַּר **šēšbaṣṣar** (Aram.), n.pr.m. GK: 10746 [cf. 8339]. Sheshbazzar, *"may (the pagan moon god) Sin protect (the father)"*:– Sheshbazzar [2]

שָׁשָׂה **šāsâ**. See 8154.

8341 שָׁשָׁה **šāšâ**, v.den. GK: 9257. [P] to give a sixth part:– give the sixth part [1]

8342 שָׂשׂוֹן **śāśôn**, n.m. GK: 8607 [→ 7797]. joy, gladness:– joy [15], gladness [3], mirth [3], rejoicing [1]

8343 שָׁשַׁי **šāšay**, n.pr.m. GK: 9258. Shashai, *"noble"*:– Shashai [1]

8344 שֵׁשַׁי **šēšay**, n.pr.m. GK: 9259. Sheshai, "[poss.] *sixth [child]*":– Sheshai [3]

8345 שִׁשִּׁי **šiššî**, a.num.ord. GK: 9261 [→ 8337]. sixth:– sixth [28]

8346 שִׁשִּׁים **šiššîm**, n.indecl. GK: 9262 [→ 8337; cf. 8361]. sixty (pl. of "six"):– threescore [46], sixty [12], threescore and one (+259+2050.1) [1]

8347 שֵׁשַׁךְ **šēšak**, n.pr.loc. GK: 9263. Sheshach, "[cryptogram for] *Babel*":– Sheshach [2]

8348 שֵׁשָׁן **šēšān**, n.pr.m. GK: 9264. Sheshan:– Sheshan [5]

שֹׁשָׁן **šōšān**. See 7799.

8349 שָׁשָׁק **šāšāq**, n.pr.m. GK: 9265. Shashak:– Shashak [2]

8350 שָׁשַׁר **šāšar**, n.[m.]. GK: 9266. red color (from lead, iron rust, or insects):– vermilion [2]

8351 שֵׁת **šēt**, n.pr.m. GK: 9269 [→ 7896, 8352]. same as 8352: Seth, Sheth, *"determined, granted, Ge 4:25; restitution"*:–

8352 שֵׁת **šēt**, n.pr.m. GK: 9269 [→ 8351]. same as 8353: Seth, Sheth, *"determined, granted, Ge 4:25; restitution"*:– Seth [7], Sheth [2]

8353 שֵׁת **šēt** (Aram.), n.m. & f. GK: 10747 [→ 8361; cf. 8337]. six:– sixth [1], six [1]

8354 שָׁתָה **šātâ**, v. GK: 9272 [→ 4960, 8358, 8360; cf. 8248; cf. 8355]. [Q] to drink; by extension: to be drunk; [N] to be drunken:– drink [160], drunk [17], drinking [12], drank [8], drinketh [6], drunken [3], assuredly drunken (+8354) [2], certainly drink (+8354) [2], drinketh up [2], surely drink (+8354) [2], banquet [1], drinkers [1], drunkards (+7941) [1]

8355 שְׁתָה **šᵉtâ** (Aram.), v. GK: 10748 [→ 4961; cf. 8354]. [P] to drink; this can refer to common consumption of liquid, or it can refer to drinking in worship to pagan gods and in insult to the true God (by drinking with his vessels):– drank [3], drink [1], drunk [1]

8356 שָׁתָה **šātâ**, n.m. GK: 9271 [→ 8354?, 8359]. worker in weaving:– foundations [1], purposes [1]

8357 שֵׁת **šēt**, n.[m.]. GK: 9268. foundation; buttocks:– buttocks [2]

8358 שְׁתִי **šᵉtî**, n.[m.]. GK: 9275 [→ 8354]. drunkenness, drinking:– drunkenness [1]

8359 שְׁתִי **šᵉtî**, n.m. GK: 9274 [→ 8356]. woven material, made on a loom; some sources: warp, the vertical threads on a loom:– warp [9]

8360 שְׁתִיָּה **šᵉtiyyâ**, n.f. GK: 9276 [→ 8354]. (manner of) drinking:– drinking [1]

שְׁתַּיִם **šᵉttayim**. See 8147.

8361 שִׁתִּין **šittîn** (Aram.), n.indecl. GK: 10749 [→ 8353; cf. 8346]. sixty:– threescore [4]

8362 שָׁתַל **šātal**, v. GK: 9278 [→ 8363]. [Q] to plant; [Qp] to be planted:– planted [8], plant [2]

8363 שָׁתִיל **šātîl**, n.[m.]. GK: 9277 [→ 8362]. slip, cutting (of a plant):– plants [1]

8364 שֻׁתַלְחִי **šutalḥî**, a.g. GK: 9279 [→ 7803]. Shuthelahite, *"of Shuthelah"*:– Shuthalhites [1]

שָׂתַם **śātam**. See 5640.

8365 שָׁתַם **šātam**, v. GK: 9280 & 9281. [Qp] to be opened:– open [2]

8366 שָׁתַן **šātan** or שִׁין **šîn**, v. GK: 9282 & 8874 [→ 7890]. [H, Hiphtil] to urinate (against a wall), i.e., a male:– pisseth [6]

8367 שָׁתַק **šātaq**, v. GK: 9284 [cf. 8252]. [Q] to become calm, die down:– calm [2], ceaseth [1], quiet [1]

8368 שָׂתַר **śātar**, v. GK: 8609 [cf. 5642]. [N] to be broken out (with tumors):– secret parts [1]

8369 שֵׁתָר **šētār**, n.pr.m. GK: 9285. Shethar:– Shethar [1]

8370 שְׁתַר בּוֹזְנַי **šᵉtar bôzᵉnay** (Aram.), n.pr.m. GK: 10750. Shethar-Bozenai:– Shethar-boznai [4]

8371 שָׁתַת **šātat**, v. GK: 9286 [cf. 7896]. [Q] to be destined, appoint, lay claim:– laid [1], set [1]

8372 תָּא **tāʼ**, n.m. GK: 9288. alcove for guards, guardroom:– little chambers [9], chamber [2], little chamber [2]

8373 תָּאַב **tāʼab**, v. GK: 9289 [→ 8375; cf. 14? *or* 2968?]. [Q] to long for, desire:– longed [2]

8374 תָּאַב **tāʼab**, v. GK: 9290 [cf. 8581]. [P] to abhor, loathe:– abhor [1]

8375 תַּאֲבָה **taʼᵃbâ**, n.f. GK: 9291 [→ 8373]. longing, desiring:– longing [1]

8376 תָּאָה **tāʼâ**, v. GK: 9292 [cf. 184, 8427]. [P] to draw a line, mark out (territory):– point out [2]

8377 תְּאוֹ **tᵉʼô**, n.m. GK: 9293. antelope; some sources: wild ox or sheep:– wild bull [1], wild ox [1]

8378 תַּאֲוָה ***ta'ᵃwâ***, n.f. GK: 9294 [→ 183]. longing, desire, craving:– desire [14], coveteth greedily (+183) [1], dainty [1], fell a lusting (+183) [1], lusted exceedingly (+183) [1], lust [1], pleasant [1]

8379 תַּאֲוָה ***ta'ᵃwâ***, n.f. GK: 9295 [→ 8427]. boundary:– utmost bound [1]

8380 תּוֹאֲמִים ***tô'ᵃmîm*** or תְּאֹמִים ***tᵉ'ômîm***, n.m. GK: 9339 & 9296 [→ 8382]. twins, (something) double:– twins [4]

8381 תַּאֲלָה ***ta'ᵃlâ***, n.f. GK: 9297 [→ 422]. curse:– curse [1]

8382 תָּאַם ***tā'am***, v.den. GK: 9298 [→ 8380]. [H] to have twins:– beareth twins [2], coupled together [1], coupled [1]

תָּאֹם ***tā'ōm***. See 8380.

8383 תְּאֻנִים ***tᵉ'unîm***, n.[m.]. GK: 9303 [→ 205?]. efforts, toil:– lies [1]

8384 תְּאֵנָה ***tᵉ'ēnâ***, n.f. GK: 9300. fig; fig tree:– fig tree [17], figs [15], fig trees [6], fig [1]

8385 תַּאֲנָה ***ta'ᵃnâ*** or תֹּאֲנָה ***tō'ᵃnâ***, n.f. GK: 9299 & 9301 [→ 579]. occasion, opportunity; (time of) heat, rut:– occasion [2]

8386 תַּאֲנִיָּה ***ta'ᵃniyyâ***, n.f. GK: 9302 [→ 578]. mourning:– heaviness [1], mourning [1]

8387 תַּאֲנַת שִׁלֹה ***ta'ᵃnat šilōh***, n.pr.loc. GK: 9304 [cf. 7887]. Taanath Shiloh, "[poss.] *approach to Shiloh*":– Taanath-shiloh [1]

8388 תָּאַר ***tā'ar***, v. GK: 9305 & 9306 [→ 8389; cf. 8446?]. [Q] to turn toward; [P] to mark out a form, make an outline; [Pu] to be turned toward:– drawn [5], marketh out [2], Remmon-methoar (+7417+1886.1) [1]

8389 תֹּאַר ***tō'ar***, n.m. GK: 9307 [→ 8388]. form, shape; beauty, fine-looking person:– form [3], beautiful (+3303) [2], favoured [2], comely [1], countenance [1], fair (+3303) [1], goodly (+2896) [1], goodly (+3303) [1], goodly [1], resembled (+3509.1) [1], visage [1]

8390 תַּאְרֵעַ ***ta'rēa'***, n.pr.m. GK: 9308 [cf. 8475]. Tarea:– Tarea [1]

8391 תְּאַשּׁוּר ***tᵉ'aššûr***, n.f. GK: 9309. cypress tree, cypress wood:– box tree [1], box [1]

8392 תֵּבָה ***tēbâ***, n.f. GK: 9310. box-shaped thing: chest, ark, basket:– ark [28]

8393 תְּבוּאָה ***tᵉbû'â***, n.f. GK: 9311 [→ 935]. harvest, crops, produce:– increase [22], fruit [7], fruits [6], revenues [3], revenue [2], gain [1], yieldeth increase [1]

8394 תְּבוּנָה ***tᵉbûnâ***, n.f. GK: 9312 [cf. 995]. understanding, insight; ability, skill, wisdom:– understanding [38], discretion [1], reasons [1], skilfulness [1], wisdom [1]

8395 תְּבוּסָה ***tᵉbûsâ***, n.f. GK: 9313 [→ 947]. downfall, ruin:– destruction [1]

8396 תָּבוֹר ***tābôr***, n.pr.loc. GK: 9314 [→ 3696; cf. 243]. Tabor:– Tabor [10]

8397 תֶּבֶל ***tebel***, n.[m.]. GK: 9316 [→ 1101]. perversion, abominable confusion:– confusion [2]

8398 תֵּבֵל ***tēbēl***, n.f. & m. GK: 9315 [→ 944?]. world, earth:– world [35], habitable part [1]

תֻּבַל ***tubal***. See 8422.

8399 תַּבְלִית ***tablît***, n.f. GK: 9318 [→ 1086]. destruction:– destruction [1]

8400 תְּבַלֻּל ***tᵉballul***, n.[m.]. GK: 9319 [→ 1101]. defect (obscuring vision); likely referring to a cataract:– blemish [1]

8401 תֶּבֶן ***teben***, n.m. GK: 9320 [→ 4963]. straw:– straw [15], chaff [1], stubble [1]

8402 תִּבְנִי ***tibnî***, n.pr.m. GK: 9321. Tibni:– Tibni [3]

8403 תַּבְנִית ***tabnît***, n.f. GK: 9322 [→ 1129]. image, form, shape:– pattern [9], likeness [5], form [3], similitude [2], figure [1]

8404 תַּבְעֵרָה ***tab'ērâ***, n.pr.loc. GK: 9323 [→ 1197]. Taberah, "*burning*":– Taberah [2]

8405 תֵּבֵץ ***tēbēṣ***, n.pr.loc. GK: 9324 [→ 1206?]. Thebez:– Thebez [3]

8406 תְּבַר ***tᵉbar*** (Aram.), v. GK: 10752 [cf. 7665]. [Pp] to be brittle, not to have flexibility, implying such an object is fragile and easy to break:– broken [1]

8407 תִּגְלַת פִּלְאֶסֶר ***tiglat pil'eser*** or תִּלְּגַת פִּלְנְאֶסֶר ***tillᵉgat pilnᵉ'eser*** or תִּלְּגַת פִּלְנֶסֶר ***tillᵉgat pilneser***, n.pr.m. GK: 9325 & 9433. Tiglath-Pileser, Tiglath-Pilneser, "*my trust is in the son of [the temple] Esharra*":– Tiglath-pileser [3], Tilgath-pilneser [3]

8408 תַּגְמוּל ***tagmûl***, n.m. GK: 9326 [→ 1580]. benefit, gracious act:– benefits [1]

8409 תִּגְרָה ***tigrâ***, n.f. GK: 9327 [→ 1624]. agitation, blow:– blow [1]

תֹּגַרְמָה ***tōgarmâ***. See 8425.

8410 תִּדְהָר ***tidhār***, n.[m.]. GK: 9329. fir tree; some sources: elm or ash tree:– pine tree [1], pine [1]

8411 תְּדִיר ***tᵉdîr*** (Aram.), n.f. GK: 10753 [→ 1753]. duration, encircling; (as adv.) continually:– continually (+0.2+871.2) [2]

8412 תַּדְמֹר ***tadmōr***, n.pr.loc. GK: 9330. Tadmor, "*palm tree*":– Tadmor [2]

8413 תִּדְעָל ***tid'āl***, n.pr.m. GK: 9331. Tidal:– Tidal [2]

8414 תֹּהוּ ***tōhû***, n.m. GK: 9332. formless, waste, empty; (of speech) useless, confused, vain:– vanity [4], confusion [3], in vain [2], vain [2], wilderness [2], without form [2], empty place [1], nothing [1], nought [1], thing of nought [1], waste [1]

8415 תְּהוֹם ***tᵉhôm***, n.f. & m. GK: 9333. the deep, depths, with the associative meanings of darkness and secrecy, controlled or inhabited by mysterious powers; "the depths of the earth" is the abode of the dead:– deep [19], depths [10], depth [5], deep places [1], deeps [1]

8416 תְּהִלָּה ***tᵉhillâ***, n.f. GK: 9335 [→ 1984]. praise, renown, glory; praise is proclaiming the excellence of a person or object:– praise [52], praises [5]

8417 תָּהֳלָה ***tohᵒlâ***, n.f. GK: 9334. error:– folly [1]

8418 תַּהֲלוּכָה ***tahᵃlûkâ***, n.f. GK: 9336 [→ 1980]. procession:– went [1]

תְּהֹם ***tᵉhōm***. See 8415.

8419 תַּהְפֻּכוֹת ***tahpukôt***, n.f. GK: 9337 [→ 2015]. perversity, confusing things:– frowardness [3], froward [3], froward things [2], perverse things [1], very froward [1]

8420 תָּו ***tāw***, n.m. GK: 9338 [→ 8427]. mark (on the forehead); signing (a document):– desire [1], mark [1], set a mark (+8427) [1]

8421 תּוּב ***tûb*** (Aram.), v. GK: 10754 [cf. 7725]. [P] to return, restore; [H] to give back, return, answer:– returned [4], answered [1], answer [1], restored [1], returned answer [1]

8422 תֻּבַל ***tubal***, n.pr.loc. GK: 9317. Tubal:– Tubal [8]

8423 תּוּבַל קַיִן ***tûbal qayin***, n.pr.m. GK: 9340 [→ 7014]. Tubal-Cain:– Tubal-cain [2]

תּוֹבֻנָה ***tôbunâ***. See 8394.

8424 תּוּגָה ***tûgâ***, n.f. GK: 9342 [→ 3013]. grief, sorrow:– heaviness [3], sorrow [1]

8425 תֹּגַרְמָה ***tōgarmâ***, n.pr.loc. GK: 9328. Togarmah:– Togarmah [4]

8426 תּוֹדָה ***tôdâ***, n.f. GK: 9343 [→ 3034]. thank offering; thanksgiving, confession of thankfulness; song of thanksgiving; thanks is the speaking of the excellence of a person or object, with a focus on the personal gratitude of the speaker:– thanksgiving [16], praise [4], thank offerings [3], thanks [3], confession [2], praises [1], sacrifice of praise [1], sacrifice of thanksgiving [1], thanksgivings [1]

8427 תָּוָה ***tāwâ***, v.den. GK: 9344 [→ 8379, 8420; cf. 184, 8376]. [P] to put a mark, place a sign:– scrabled [1], set a mark (+8420) [1]

8428 תָּוָה ***tāwâ***, v. GK: 9345. [H] to vex, bring pain:– limited [1]

8429 תְּוַהּ ***tᵉwah*** (Aram.), v. GK: 10755 [cf. 8539]. [P] to be amazed, be alarmed, an attitude or emotion that shows either fear or awe:– astonied [1]

8430 תּוֹחַ ***tôaḥ***, n.pr.m. GK: 9346 [cf. 8459]. Toah:– Toah [1]

8431 תּוֹחֶלֶת ***tôḥelet***, n.f. GK: 9347 [→ 3176]. hope, expectation:– hope [6]

תּוֹךְ ***tôk***. See 8496.

8432 תָּוֶךְ ***tāwek***, subst. GK: 9348 [→ 8484]. middle, midst, center, among, within:– midst [204], among (+871.1) [106], among [28], in (+871.1) [19], within (+871.1) [18], amongst (+871.1) [7], middle [6], midst (+871.1) [4], between (+871.1) [3], therein (+871.1+1886.3) [3], amongst [2], out of (+4480) [2], through (+871.1) [2], half [1], in (+413) [1], into (+413) [1], into (+871.1) [1], midnight (+3915+1886.1) [1], of (+871.1) [1], to (+413) [1], unto (+413) [1], wherein (+834+871.1) [1], whereinto (+413) [1], with (+871.1) [1], within (+413) [1], within [1]

8433 תּוֹכֵחָה ***tôkēḥâ*** or תּוֹכַחַת ***tôkaḥat***, n.f. GK: 9349 & 9350 [→ 3198]. rebuke, punishment, correction:– reproof [12], rebuke [4], rebukes [3], reproofs [2], reproved [2], arguments [1], chastened [1], correction [1], punishments [1], reasoning [1]

תּוּכִּי ***tûkkî***. See 8500.

8434 תּוֹלָד ***tôlād***, n.pr.loc. GK: 9351 [→ 3205?; cf. 513]. Tolad, "*birth, generation [?]*":– Tolad [1]

8435 תּוֹלֵדוֹת ***tôlēdôt***, n.f.pl. GK: 9352 [→ 3205]. account, record, genealogy, family line:– generations [38], birth [1]

8436 תּוֹלוֹן ***tôlôn*** or תִּילוֹן ***tîlôn***, n.pr.m. GK: 9353 & 9400. Tilon, Tolon:– Tilon [1]

8437 תּוֹלָל ***tôlāl***, n.m. GK: 9354 [→ 1980]. tormentor, oppressor:– wasted [1]

8438 תּוֹלָע ***tôlā'*** or תּוֹלֵעָה ***tôlē'â***, n.[m.]. GK: 9355 & 9357 [→ 8439, 8440, 8529]. (deep) red, purple; scarlet yarn, scarlet yarn; worm, maggot:– scarlet (+8144) [31], worm [5], worms [3], scarlet (+8144+1886.1) [2], crimson [1], scarlet [1]

8439 תּוֹלָע ***tôlā'***, n.pr.m. GK: 9356 [→ 8440; cf. 8438]. Tola:– Tola [6]

8440 תּוֹלָעִי ***tôlā'î***, a.g. GK: 9358 [→ 8439; cf. 8438]. Tolaite, *"of Tola"*:– Tolaites [1]

8441 תּוֹעֵבָה ***tô'ēbâ***, n.f. GK: 9359 [→ 8581?]. detestable thing, loathsome thing, abomination:– abominations [61], abomination [52], abominable [3], abominable things [1]

8442 תּוֹעָה ***tô'â***, n.f. GK: 9360 [→ 8582]. trouble, error:– error [1], hinder (+6213) [1]

8443 תּוֹעָפוֹת ***tô'āpôt***, n.f. GK: 9361. best, choice; strength; some sources: horns:– strength [3], plenty [1]

8444 תּוֹצָאוֹת ***tôṣā'ôt***, n.f. GK: 9362 [→ 3318]. end, limit, starting point:– goings out [11], outgoings [7], issues [2], borders [1], going forth [1], goings forth [1]

8445 תּוֹקְהַת ***towq^{e}hat***, n.pr.m. GK: 9363. Tokehath, Tavkehath:–

8446 תּוּר ***tûr***, v. GK: 9365 [cf. 3491, 8388?]. [Q] to explore, investigate, search out; [H] to send out to spy:– search [6], searched [4], search out [3], spy out [2], espied [1], excellent [1], searching [1], seek [1], sent to descry [1], sought [1]

8447 תּוֹר ***tôr***, n.m. GK: 9366 [→ 8448]. same as 8448: turning; earring:– turn [2], borders [1], rows [1]

8448 תּוֹר ***tôr***, n.m. GK: 9366 [→ 8447]. same as 8447: turning; earring:– estate [1]

8449 תּוֹר ***tôr***, n.f. & m. GK: 9367. dove:– turtle-doves [6], turtle-dove [3], turtles [3], turtle [2]

8450 תּוֹר ***tôr*** (Aram.), n.m. GK: 10756 [cf. 7794]. young bull or castrated bull, steer, ox, easier to handle for plowing, pulling, and threshing:– oxen [4], bullocks [3]

8451 תּוֹרָה ***tôrâ***, n.f. GK: 9368 [→ 3384, 8452]. law, regulation, teaching, instruction; often referring to the five books of Moses in whole and in part:– law [206], laws [13]

8452 תּוֹרָה ***tôrâ***, n.f. GK: 9368 [→ 8451]. same as 8451: manner, direction:– manner [1]

8453 תּוֹשָׁב ***tôšāb***, n.m. GK: 9369 [→ 3427]. temporary resident, stranger, alien:– sojourner [7], sojourners [2], stranger [2], foreigner [1], inhabitants [1], strangers [1]

8454 תּוּשִׁיָּה ***tûšiyyâ***, n.f. GK: 9370 [cf. 3426]. success, victory; sound judgment, wisdom:– wisdom [4], sound wisdom [3], enterprise [1], substance [1], that which is [1], thing as it is [1], working [1]

8455 תּוֹתָח ***tôtāḥ***, n.m. GK: 9371. (stout) club:– Darts [1]

8456 תָּזַז ***tāzaz***, v. GK: 9372. [H] to cut down:– cut down [1]

8457 תַּזְנוּת ***taznût***, n.f.abst. GK: 9373 [→ 2181]. promiscuity, prostitution, act of lust:– whoredoms [14], whoredom [3], commit whoredoms (+2181) [1], fornications [1], fornication [1]

8458 תַּחְבֻּלוֹת ***taḥbulôt***, n.f. GK: 9374. guidance, advice, giving direction:– counsels [2], counsel [1], good advice [1], wise counsels [1], wise counsel [1]

8459 תֹּחוּ ***tōḥû***, n.pr.m. GK: 9375 [cf. 8430]. Tohu:– Tohu [1]

8460 תְּחוֹת ***t^{e}ḥôt*** (Aram.), pp. GK: 10757 [→ 8479, cf. 8478]. under:– under [4]

8461 תַּחְכְּמֹנִי ***taḥk^{e}mōnî***, a.g. GK: 9376. Tahkemonite:– Tachmonite [1]

8462 תְּחִלָּה ***t^{e}ḥillâ***, n.f. GK: 9378 [→ 2490]. beginning, at first:– beginning [14], first [3], first (+871.1+1886.1) [2], first time [2], begin [1]

8463 תַּחֲלֻאִים ***taḥ^{a}lu'îm***, n.pl.m. GK: 9377 [→ 2456]. diseases:– diseases [2], grievous [1], sicknesses [1], them that are sick [1]

8464 תַּחְמָס ***taḥmās***, n.[m.]. GK: 9379 [→ 2554?]. screech owl:– night hawk [2]

8465 תַּחַן ***taḥan***, n.pr.m. GK: 9380 [→ 8470; cf. 2603?]. Tahan, "[poss.] *grace, favor*":– Tahan [2]

8466 תַּחֲנָה ***taḥ^{a}nâ***, n.f. GK: 9381 [→ 2583]. encampment:– camp [1]

8467 תְּחִנָּה ***t^{e}ḥinnâ***, n.f. GK: 9382 [→ 8468; cf. 2603]. plea, petition, request, supplication:– supplication [21], favour [1], grace [1], supplication made [1], supplications [1]

8468 תְּחִנָּה ***t^{e}ḥinnâ***, n.pr.m. GK: 9383 [→ 8467; cf. 2603]. Tehinnah, *"supplication for favor"*:– Tehinnah [1]

8469 תַּחֲנוּן ***taḥ^{a}nûn***, n.[m.]pl.abst. GK: 9384 [→ 2603]. plea for mercy, petition, supplication:– supplications [17], useth intreaties [1]

8470 תַּחֲנִי ***taḥ^{a}nî***, a.g. GK: 9385 [→ 8465; cf. 2603?]. Tahanite, *"of Tahan"*:– Tahanites [1]

8471 תַּחְפַּנְחֵס ***taḥpanḥēs***, n.pr.loc. GK: 9387 [cf. 6372]. Tahpanhes, *"fortress of Penhase [the black man]"*:– Tahpanhes [5], Tahapanes [1], Tehaphnehes [1]

8472 תַּחְפְּנֵיס ***taḥp^{e}nês***, n.pr.f. GK: 9388. Tahpenes, *"wife of the king"*:– Tahpenes [3]

8473 תַּחְרָא ***taḥrā'***, n.[m.]. GK: 9389. collar, edge around an opening in a garment:– habergeon [2]

8474 תַּחֲרָה ***taḥārâ***, v. GK: 3013 [→ 2734]. form of 2734: to be angry; to compete, contend with:– closest [1], contend [1]

8475 תַּחְרֵעַ ***taḥrēa'***, n.pr.m. GK: 9390 [cf. 8390]. Tahrea, "[poss.] *clever one*":– Tahrea [1]

8476 תַּחַשׁ ***taḥaš***, n.m. GK: 9391 [→ 8477]. (leather of) a sea cow:– badgers' [13], badgers' skins [1]

8477 תַּחַשׁ ***taḥaš***, n.pr.m. GK: 9392 [→ 8476]. Tahash, *"species of dolphin"*:– Thahash [1]

8478 תַּחַת ***taḥat***, n.[m.] & adv. & pp. GK: 9393 [→ 8480, 8481, 8482; cf. 5181; cf. 8460]. under, in place of, succeeding (on a sequence):– under [220], in stead [89], for [59], instead of [32], beneath (+4480) [13], under (+4480) [13], because (+834) [11], in place [11], in room [5], in the room of [5], beneath [4], under (+413) [4], in [3], place [3], flat [2], for sake [2], in rooms [2], in the stead of [2], instead [2], as [1], because (+3588) [1], because [1], for that (+3588) [1], in a place [1], in places [1], in steads [1], in the place of [1], in the place where [1], in the place [1], in the same place [1], mine (+2967.1) [1], on behalf [1], room [1], underneath (+4480) [1], unto [1], where (+1886.3) [1], whereas (+834) [1], whereas [1], wherefore (+4100) [1], with [1]

8479 תְּחוֹת ***t^{e}ḥōt*** (Aram.), pp. GK: 10757 [→ 8460]. same as 8460: under:– under [1]

8480 תַּחַת ***taḥat***, n.pr.m. & loc. GK: 9394 & 9395 [→ 8478]. Tahath, *"compensation"*:– Tahath [6]

תְּחֹת ***t^{e}ḥōt***. See 8460.

8481 תַּחְתּוֹן ***taḥtôn***, a. GK: 9396 [→ 8478]. lower:– lower [5], nether [5], lowest [2], nethermost [1]

8482 תַּחְתִּי ***taḥtî***, a. & subst. GK: 9397 [→ 8478]. lower; (n.) depths, below, sometimes referring to the underworld, the realm of the dead:– nether parts [5], lowest [3], nether [3], lower parts [2], lower [2], in low parts [1], lowest parts [1], low [1], nether part [1]

8483 תַּחְתִּים חָדְשִׁי ***taḥtîm ḥodšî***, n.pr.loc. GK: 9398. Tahtim Hodshi:– Tahtim-hodshi [1]

8484 תִּיכוֹן ***tîkôn***, a. GK: 9399 [→ 8432]. middle, center:– middle [8], middlemost [2], midst [1]

8485 תֵּימָא ***têmā'***, n.pr.loc. [& m.?]. GK: 9401. Tema, *"on the right [not left] side,* hence *south country"*:– Tema [5]

8486 תֵּימָן ***têmān***, n.f. GK: 9402 [→ 8487; cf. 3225]. south, southward, south wind:– south [10], southward (+1886.5) [8], south side [2], south (+1886.5) [1], south (+1886.5+1886.5) [1], south wind [1]

8487 תֵּימָן ***têmān***, n.pr.loc. GK: 9403 [→ 8489; cf. 3225, 8486]. Teman, *"on the right [not left] side,* hence *south country"*:– Teman [11]

8488 תֵּימְנִי ***têm^{e}nî***, n.pr.m. GK: 9405 [→ 3225]. Temeni, *"one from the right [not left],* hence *southerner"*:– Temeni [1]

8489 תֵּימָנִי ***têmānî***, a.g. GK: 9404 [→ 8487]. Temanite, *"of Teman"*:– Temanite [6], Temanites [1], Temani [1]

8490 תִּימָרָה ***tîmārâ***, n.f. GK: 9406 [→ 8560?, 8564; cf. 8558]. column (of smoke):– pillars [2]

8491 תִּיצִי ***tîṣî***, a.g. GK: 9407. Tizite:– Tizite [1]

8492 תִּירוֹשׁ ***tîrôš***, n.m. GK: 9408 [→ 3423]. new wine:– wine [26], new wine [11], sweet wine [1]

8493 תִּירְיָא ***tîr^{e}yā'***, n.pr.m. GK: 9409. Tiria:– Tiria [1]

8494 תִּירָס ***tîrās***, n.pr.loc. [& m.?]. GK: 9410. Tiras:– Tiras [2]

תִּרֹשׁ ***tîrōš***. See 8492.

8495 תַּיִשׁ ***tayiš***, n.m. GK: 9411. male goat:– he goats [3], he goat [1]

8496 תֹּךְ ***tōk***, n.m. GK: 9412 [→ 8501]. oppression, threat:– deceit [2], fraud [1]

8497 תָּכָה ***tākâ***, v. GK: 9413. [Pu] to bow down:– sat down [1]

8498 תְּכוּנָה ***t^{e}kûnâ***, n.f. GK: 9414 [→ 3559, 8499]. same as 8499: dwelling; arrangement, supply:– fashion [1], store [1]

8499 תְּכוּנָה ***t^{e}kûnâ***, n.f. GK: 9414 [→ 8498]. same as 8498: dwelling; arrangement, supply:– seat [1]

8500 תֻּכִּיִּים ***tukkiyyîm***, n.m.[pl.]. GK: 9415. baboons; some sources: monkeys, peacocks, poultry:– peacocks [2]

8501 תְּכָכִים ***t^{e}kākîm***, n.m.pl. GK: 9412 [→ 8496]. pl. of 8496: oppression, threat:– deceitful [1]

8502 תִּכְלָה ***tiklâ***, n.f. GK: 9416 [→ 3615]. perfection:– perfection [1]

8503 תַּכְלִית ***taklît***, n.f. GK: 9417 [→ 3615]. end, limit, boundary:– perfection [2], come to an end [1], end [1], perfect [1]

8504 תְּכֵלֶת ***t^{e}kēlet***, n.f. GK: 9418. blue material:– blue [49]

8505 תָּכַן ***tākan***, v. GK: 9419 [→ 4971, 8506, 8508; cf. 8626; cf. 8627]. [Q] to weigh, estimate; [N] to be just, be weighted; [P] to hold firm, mark off, understand; [Pu] to be determined:– equal [7], pondereth [2], unequal (+3808) [2], weigheth [2], bear up [1], directed [1], meted out [1], told [1], weighed [1]

8506 תֹּכֶן ***tōken***, n.m. GK: 9420 [→ 8505]. full quota, fixed measure; size, measurement:– measure [1], tale [1]

8507 תֹּכֶן ***tōken***, n.pr.loc. GK: 9421. Token, "*measure*":– Tochen [1]

8508 תָּכְנִית ***toknît***, n.f. GK: 9422 [→ 8505]. (perfect) example, design:– pattern [1], sum [1]

8509 תַּכְרִיךְ ***takrîk***, n.m. GK: 9423. robe, mantle:– garment [1]

8510 תֵּל ***tēl***, n.[m.]. GK: 9424 [→ 8512, 8521, 8528, 8524, 8534?]. mound, heap, ruin:– heap [4], strength [1]

8511 תָּלָא ***tālā'***, v. GK: 9428 [cf. 8518]. [Q] to hang; [Qp] to be suspended, be determined:– bent [1], hang in doubt [1], hanged [1]

8512 תֵּל אָבִיב ***tēl 'ābîb***, n.pr.loc. GK: 9425 [→ 8510+24]. Tel Abib, "*mound of barley; mound of storm tide; mound of flood*":– Tel-abib [1]

8513 תְּלָאָה ***tᵉlā'â***, n.f. GK: 9430 [→ 4972; cf. 3811]. hardship, burden:– travail [3], trouble [1]

8514 תַּלְאֻבוֹת ***tal'ubôt***, n.f. GK: 9429. burning heat:– great drought [1]

8515 תְּלַאשָּׂר ***tᵉla'śśār*** or תְּלַשָּׂר ***tᵉlaśśār***, n.pr.loc. GK: 9431 & 9445. Telassar, Tel Assar, "*ruined city, mound of Assar*":– Telassar [1], Thelasar [1]

8516 תִּלְבֹּשֶׁת ***tilbōšet***, n.f. GK: 9432 [→ 3847]. clothing, what is worn:– put on clothing (+3847) [1]

8517 תְּלַג ***tᵉlag*** (Aram.), n.[m.]. GK: 10758 [cf. 7950]. snow:– snow [1]

תִּלְגַת ***tilgat***. See 8407.

תּוֹלְדָה ***tōlᵉdâ***. See 8435.

8518 תָּלָה ***tālâ***, v. GK: 9434 [→ 3494, 8522; cf. 8511]. [Q, P] to hang, suspend; [Qp, N] to be hung:– hanged [16], hang [7], hanged up [2], hangeth [1], hanging [1]

8519 תְּלֻנּוֹת ***tᵉlunnôt***, n.f. GK: 9442 [→ 3885]. grumbling, complaint:– murmurings [8]

8520 תֶּלַח ***telaḥ***, n.pr.m. GK: 9436. Telah, "*fissure, split, fracture*":– Telah [1]

8521 תֵּל חַרְשָׁא ***tēl ḥaršā'***, n.pr.loc. GK: 9426 [→ 8510+2793 *or* 2796]. Tel Harsha, "*mound of the forest* or *craftsman*":– Tel-haresha [1], Tel-harsa [1]

8522 תְּלִי ***tᵉlî***, n.[m.]. GK: 9437 [→ 8518]. quiver (case to hold arrows that hangs or dangles):– quiver [1]

8523 תַּלְתַּי ***tᵉlîtāy*** (Aram.), a. GK: 10759 [→ 8531; cf. 7992]. third:– third [2]

8524 תָּלוּל ***tālûl***, a. GK: 9435 [→ 8510]. lofty, towering:– eminent [1]

8525 תֶּלֶם ***telem***, n.m. GK: 9439 [→ 8526]. furrow, plowed line:– furrows [3], furrow [1], ridges [1]

8526 תַּלְמַי ***talmay***, n.pr.m. GK: 9440 [→ 8525]. Talmai, "[poss.] *[my] furrow maker*":– Talmai [6]

8527 תַּלְמִיד ***talmîd***, n.[m.]. GK: 9441 [→ 3925]. student, pupil:– scholar [1]

8528 תֵּל מֶלַח ***tēl melaḥ***, n.pr.loc. GK: 9427 [→ 8510+4417]. Tel Melah, "*mound of salt*":– Tel-melah [2]

תְּלֻנָּה ***tᵉlunnâ***. See 8519.

8529 תָּלַע ***tāla'***, v.den. GK: 9443 [→ 8438]. [Pu] to be clad in scarlet material:– in scarlet [1]

תֹּלַעַת ***tōla'at***. See 8438.

8530 תַּלְפִּיּוֹת ***talpiyyôt***, n.f.pl. GK: 9444. elegance or courses of stones:– armoury [1]

תְּלַשָּׂר ***tᵉlassar***. See 8515.

8531 תְּלָת ***tᵉlāt*** (Aram.), n.m. GK: 10760 [→ 8523, 8532, 8533; cf. 7969]. three:– third [2]

8532 תַּלְתָּא ***taltā'*** (Aram.), a.den. GK: 10761 [→ 8531; 7992]. third highest; this can refer to ruling over a third of the kingdom, or ruling as third in command, or ruling in a triumvirate; some sources translate less specifically as a high official of indeterminate rank:– three [10], third [1]

תַּלְתִּי ***taltiy***. See 8523.

8533 תְּלָתִין ***tᵉlātîn*** (Aram.), n.indecl. GK: 10762 [→ 8531; cf. 7970]. thirty:– thirty [2]

8534 תַּלְתַּל ***taltāl***, n.f.?. GK: 9446 [→ 8510?]. wavy:– bushy [1]

8535 תָּם ***tām***, a. GK: 9447 [→ 3147; cf. 8552]. blameless, flawless, perfect:– perfect [9], undefiled [2], coupled (+1961) [1], coupled together (+3162) [1], plain [1], upright [1]

8536 תַּמָּה ***tammâ*** (Aram.), adv. GK: 10764 [cf. 8033]. there:– there [2], thence [1], where [1]

8537 תֹּם ***tōm***, n.[m.]. GK: 9448 [→ 8550; cf. 8552]. blamelessness, integrity, innocence:– integrity [11], uprightness [2], upright [2], venture [2], full [1], perfection [1], perfect [1], simplicity [1], uprightly (+871.1) [1], uprightly [1]

תְּמָא ***tēmā'***. See 8485.

8538 תֻּמָּה ***tummâ***, n.f. GK: 9450 [→ 8552]. integrity, blamelessness:– integrity [5]

8539 תָּמַהּ ***tāmah***, v. GK: 9449 [→ 8541; cf. 8429, cf. 8540]. [Q] to be astonished, be astounded, be stunned; [Htpal] to be stunned in oneself:– wonder [3], marvelled [2], amazed [1], astonished [1], marvellously [1], marvel [1]

8540 תְּמַהּ ***tᵉmah*** (Aram.), n.m. GK: 10763. wonder, miracle:– wonders [3]

8541 תִּמָּהוֹן ***timmāhôn***, n.[m.]. GK: 9451 [→ 8539]. confusion, panic:– astonishment [2]

8542 תַּמּוּז ***tammûz***, n.pr.[m.]. GK: 9452. Tammuz (pagan god):– Tammuz [1]

8543 תְּמוֹל ***tᵉmôl***, subst.adv. GK: 9453 [→ 865]. yesterday; (generally) before, in the past:– heretofore (+8032) [4], in time past (+4480+8032) [4], yesterday [4], before (+8032) [3], beforetime (+4480+8032) [1], beforetime (+8032) [1], heretofore (+1571+4480+4480+8032) [1], heretofore (+4480+8032) [1], in time past (+8032) [1], in times past (+1571+1571+8032) [1], in times past (+4480+8032) [1], these three days (+8032) [1]

8544 תְּמוּנָה ***tᵉmûnâ***, n.f. GK: 9454 [→ 4327]. form, image, likeness:– likeness [5], similitude [4], image [1]

8545 תְּמוּרָה ***tᵉmûrâ***, n.f. GK: 9455 [→ 4171]. substitution, transfer, exchange:– exchange [2], change [1], changing [1], recompence [1], restitution [1]

8546 תְּמוּתָה ***tᵉmûtâ***, n.f. GK: 9456 [→ 4191]. death:– appointed to death (+1121) [1], appointed to die (+1121) [1]

8547 תֶּמַח ***temaḥ***, n.pr.m. GK: 9457 [→ 4229?]. Temah:– Tamah [1], Thamah [1]

8548 תָּמִיד ***tāmîd***, n.m. (used as adv.). GK: 9458. (adv.) continually, constantly, regularly, daily:– continually [53], continual [26], daily [7], always [6], alway [4], ever [3], perpetual [2], continual employment [1], evermore [1], never (+3808) [1]

8549 תָּמִים ***tāmîm***, a. GK: 9459 [→ 8552]. without defect, blameless, perfect:– without blemish [44], perfect [18], upright [8], without spot [6], whole [4], uprightly [3], sincerely (+871.1) [2], complete [1], full [1], sincerity [1], sound [1], undefiled [1], uprightly (+871.1) [1]

8550 תֻּמִּים ***tummîm***, n.m.[pl.]. GK: 9460 [→ 8537; cf. 8552]. Thummim, formally "Perfections," devices used by the high priest to make God's will known, possibly related to the casting of lots:– Thummim [5]

8551 תָּמַךְ ***tāmak***, v. GK: 9461. [Q] to take hold of, grasp, hold secure; [N] to be seized:– uphold [3], holdeth [2], retaineth [2], retain [2], held up [1], hold up [1], holden [1], holding [1], hold [1], maintainest [1], stayed up [1], stay [1], take hold on [1], take hold [1], upholdest [1], upholdeth [1]

תְּמֹל ***tᵉmōl***. See 8543.

8552 תָּמַם ***tāmam***, v. GK: 9462 [→ 3147, 4974, 8535, 8537, 8538, 8549, 8550]. [Q] to complete, finish, perfect; [H] to end, stop, complete; [Ht] to show oneself blameless:– consumed [23], ended [5], finished [4], clean [3], spent [3], consume [2], done [2], end [2], failed [2], shew upright [2], wasted [2], accomplished [1], accomplish [1], all gone [1], all [1], cease [1], come to end [1], come to the full [1], make an end [1], makest perfect [1], perfect [1], sum [1], upright [1], utterly [1], whole [1]

תֵּמָן ***tēmān, tēmān***. See 8486, 8487.

8553 תִּמְנָה ***timnâ***, n.pr.loc. GK: 9463 [→ 8554; cf. 4487?]. Timnah, "*lot, portion*":– Timnath [8], Timnah [3], Thimnathah [1]

תְּמֻנָה ***tᵉmunâ***. See 8544.

8554 תִּמְנִי ***timnî***, a.g. GK: 9464 [→ 8553; cf. 4487?]. Timnite, "*of Timnah*":– Timnite [1]

8555 תִּמְנָע ***timna'***, n.pr.m. & f. GK: 9465. Timna, "*lot, portion*":– Timna [4], Timnah [2]

8556 תִּמְנַת־חֶרֶס ***timnat-ḥeres*** or תִּמְנַת־סֶרַח ***timnat-seraḥ***, n.pr.loc. GK: 9466 & 9467 [→ 4487?+2776]. Timnath Heres, Timnath Serah, "*place of the sun [worship]*":– Timnath-serah [2], Timnath-heres [1]

8557 תֶּמֶס ***temes***, n.m. GK: 9468 [→ 4549]. melting away:– melteth [1]

8558 תָּמָר ***tāmār***, n.m. GK: 9469 [→ 1193, 2688, 5899, 8559, 8560, 8561; cf. 8490]. palm tree:– palm trees [7], palm tree [4], palm [1]

8559 תָּמָר ***tāmār***, n.pr.f. & loc. GK: 9470 & 9471 [→ 8558]. Tamar, "*date palm*":– Tamar [24]

8560 תֹּמֶר **tōmer**, n.m. & loc. GK: 9472 & 9473 [→ 559, 8490?, 8558]. the Palm (of Deborah), "*date palm*"; scarecrow:– palm tree [2]

8561 תִּמֹרָה **timōrâ**, n.f. GK: 9474 [→ 8558]. palm tree:– palm trees [16], palm tree [3]

תַּמֹּר *tammōr*. See 8412.

תִּמָרָה *timārâ*. See 8490.

8562 תַּמְרוּק **tamrûq**, n.[m.]. GK: 9475 [→ 4838]. beauty treatment (including massages and cleansing rituals), cosmetics:– things for purification [2], cleanseth away [1], things for the purifying [1]

8563 תַּמְרוּרִים **tamrûrîm**, n.m. GK: 9476 [→ 4843]. bitterness:– bitter [2], most bitterly [1]

תַּמְרֻק *tamruq* and תַּמְרִיק *tamrîq*. See 8562.

8564 תַּמְרוּרִים **tamrûrîm**, n.m. GK: 9477 [→ 8490]. guidepost:– high heaps [1]

8565 תַּן **tan**, n.[m. & f.]. GK: 9478 [→ 8568, 8577]. jackal:–

8566 תָּנָה **tānâ**, v. GK: 9479 [→ 869]. [Q, H] to sell oneself as a prostitute:– hired [2]

8567 תָּנָה **tānâ**, v. GK: 9480. [P] to commemorate, recount:– lament [1], rehearse [1]

8568 תַּנָּה **tannâ**, n.[m. & f.]. GK: 9478 [→ 8565]. same as 8565: jackal:–

8569 תְּנוּאָה **tᵉnûʾâ**, n.f. GK: 9481 [→ 5106]. fault, opposition, what one has against another:– breach of promise [1], occasions [1]

8570 תְּנוּבָה **tᵉnûbâ**, n.f. GK: 9482 [→ 5107]. crop, produce:– fruit [2], increase [2], fruits [1]

8571 תְּנוּךְ **tᵉnûk**, n.[m.]. GK: 9483. lobe (of the ear):– tip [8]

8572 תְּנוּמָה **tᵉnûmâ**, n.f. GK: 9484 [→ 5123]. slumber, sleep:– slumber [4], slumberings [1]

8573 תְּנוּפָה **tᵉnûpâ**, n.f. GK: 9485 [→ 5130]. wave offering, what it waved:– wave offering [13], offering [7], wave [6], shaking [2], wave offerings [1], waved [1]

8574 תַּנּוּר **tannûr**, n.m. GK: 9486. oven, furnace, firepot (a portable oven for cooking bread):– oven [10], furnaces [2], furnace [2], ovens [1]

8575 תַּנְחוּמוֹת **tanḥûmôt** or תַּנְחוּמִים **tanḥûmîm**, n.pl.m. & f. GK: 9487 & 9488 [→ 5162]. consolation, comfort:– consolations [3], comforts [1], consolation [1]

8576 תַּנְחֻמֶת **tanḥumet**, n.pr.m. GK: 9489 [→ 5162]. Tanhumeth, "*comfort*":– Tanhumeth [2]

8577 תַּנִּין **tannîn**, n.m. GK: 9490 [→ 8565]. serpent, snake; monster of the deep; (pr.n.) Jackal (Well); can refer to large sea creatures as well as to mythological monsters of chaos opposed to God:– dragons [16], dragon [6], serpent [2], whale [2], sea monsters [1], serpents [1], whales [1]

8578 תִּנְיָן **tinyān** (Aram.), a. GK: 10765 [→ 8648]. second:– second [1]

8579 תִּנְיָנוּת **tinyānût** (Aram.), adv. GK: 10766 [→ 8648]. once more, in the second time:– again [1]

8580 תִּנְשֶׁמֶת **tinšemet**, n.f. GK: 9491 & 9492 [→ 5395]. white owl; chameleon:– swan [2], mole [1]

8581 תָּעַב **tāʿab**, v.den. GK: 9493 [→ 8441?; cf. 8374]. [N] to be repulsive, be vile, be rejected; [P] to detest, abhor, loathe, despise; [H] to behave in a vile manner:– abhor [8], abominable [4], abhorred [2], abhorreth [2], done abominable [2], utterly abhor (+8581) [2], abominably [1], made to be abhorred [1]

תֹּעֵבָה *tōʿēbâ*. See 8441.

8582 תָּעָה **tāʿâ**, v. GK: 9494 [→ 8442; cf. 2937]. [Q] to wander, go astray; [N] to deceive oneself; to stagger around (as a drunk); [H] to lead astray, make wander, mislead:– went astray [6], caused to err [4], cause to err [3], err [3], go astray [3], wandered [3], causeth to wander [2], erred [2], gone astray [2], made to err [2], out of the way [2], seduced [2], wander [2], caused to go astray [1], caused to wander [1], causing to err [1], deceived [1], dissembled [1], erreth [1], going astray [1], make err [1], maketh to stagger [1], panted [1], seduceth [1], staggereth [1], wandereth [1], wandering [1]

8583 תֹּעוּ **tōʿû** or תֹּעִי **tōʿî**, n.pr.m. GK: 9495 & 9497. Toi, Tou:– Toi [3], Tou [2]

8584 תְּעוּדָה **tᵉʿûdâ**, n.f. GK: 9496 [→ 5749]. testimony; method of legalizing transactions (sandal transaction):– testimony [3]

8585 תְּעָלָה **tᵉʿālâ**, n.f. GK: 9498 & 9499 [→ 5927]. trench, channel, aqueduct; healing:– conduit [4], trench [3], cured [1], healing [1], little rivers [1], watercourse [1]

8586 תַּעֲלוּלִים **taᵃlûlîm**, n.m.pl.abst. GK: 9500 [→ 5953]. wantonness; harsh treatment, referring to impulsive people:– babes [1], delusions [1]

8587 תַּעֲלֻמָה **taᵃlumâ**, n.f. GK: 9502 [→ 5956]. secret; hidden thing:– secrets [2], thing that is hid [1]

8588 תַּעֲנוּג **taᵃnûg**, n.[m.]. GK: 9503 [→ 6026]. delight, pleasure; living in luxury:– delights [2], delicate [1], delight [1], pleasant [1]

8589 תַּעֲנִית **taᵃnît**, n.f. GK: 9504 [→ 6031]. self-abasement, mortification:– heaviness [1]

8590 תַּעְנָךְ **taᵃnak**, n.pr.loc. GK: 9505. Taanach:– Taanach [6], Tanach [1]

8591 תָּעַע **tāʿaʿ**, v. GK: 9506 [→ 8595]. [Pil] to mock; [Htpal] to scoff at:– deceiver [1], misused [1]

8592 תַּעֲצֻמוֹת **taᵃṣumôt**, n.f.[pl.]. GK: 9508 [→ 6105]. strength, might:– power [1]

8593 תַּעַר **taʿar**, n.m. GK: 9509 [→ 6168]. razor, knife, scabbard:– sheath [6], rasor [4], penknife (+5608+1886.1) [1], scabbard [1], shave (+5674) [1]

8594 תַּעֲרֻבוֹת **taᵃrûbôt**, n.f.[pl.]. GK: 9510 [→ 6148]. hostage, formally "son of a pledge":– hostages (+1121) [2]

8595 תַּעְתֻּעִים **taʿtuʿîm**, n.[m.]pl.abst. GK: 9511 [→ 8591]. mockery:– errors [2]

8596 תֹּף **tōp**, n.m. GK: 9512 & 9513 [→ 8608]. tambourine, timbrel; setting, jewelry; some sources uncertain in meaning:– tabrets [5], timbrel [5], timbrels [4], tabret [3]

8597 תִּפְאֶרֶת **tipʾeret**, n.f. GK: 9514 [→ 6286]. glory, splendor, honor:– glory [22], beauty [10], beautiful [6], honour [4], fair [3], glorious [3], bravery [1], comely (+3807.1) [1], excellent [1]

8598 תַּפּוּחַ **tappûaḥ**, n.[m.]. GK: 9515 [→ 1054, 8599; cf. 5301]. apple, apple tree:– apple tree [3], apples [3]

8599 תַּפּוּחַ **tappûaḥ**, n.pr.m. & loc. GK: 9516 & 9517 [→ 5887, 8598; cf. 5301]. Tappuah, "*apple*":– Tappuah [6]

8600 תְּפוֹצָה **tᵉpûṣâ**, n.f.pl. GK: 9518 [→ 6327]. shattering, dispersing:– dispersions [1]

8601 תֻּפִינִים **tupînîm**, n.[m.]pl. GK: 9519 [cf. 644?]. broken into pieces:– baken [1]

8602 תָּפֵל **tāpēl**, n.[m.]. GK: 9521 & 9522 [→ 8604, cf. 2950]. tasteless (food); worthless (prophetic visions); whitewash:– untempered [5], foolish things [1], that which is unsavoury [1]

8603 תֹּפֶל **tōpel**, n.pr.loc. GK: 9523 [→ 302?]. Tophel, "*cement*":– Tophel [1]

8604 תִּפְלָה **tiplâ**, n.f. GK: 9524 [→ 8602]. repulsiveness, wrongdoing:– folly [2], foolishly [1]

8605 תְּפִלָּה **tᵉpillâ**, n.f. GK: 9525 [→ 6419]. prayer, plea, petition:– prayer [74], prayers [2], prayer make (+6419) [1]

8606 תִּפְלֶצֶת **tipleṣet**, n.f. GK: 9526 [→ 6426]. terror, horror, a state of great fear even to the point of shuddering:– terribleness [1]

8607 תִּפְסַח **tipsaḥ**, n.pr.loc. GK: 9527 [→ 6452]. Tiphsah:– Tiphsah [2]

8608 תָּפַף **tāpap**, v.den. GK: 9528 [→ 8596]. [Q] to tap (play) a tambourine; [Pol] to beat (the breast):– playing timbrels [1], tabring [1]

8609 תָּפַר **tāpar**, v. GK: 9529. [Q] to sew, mend; [P] to sew (together):– sew [2], sewed together [1], sewed [1]

8610 תָּפַשׂ **tāpaś**, v. GK: 9530. [Q] to take hold of, seize, capture; [Qp] to be covered; [N] to be seized, be caught, be captured; [P] to catch (a lizard):– took [17], taken [11], take [9], handle [5], caught [3], handleth [2], lay hold on [2], surely taken (+8610) [2], surprised [2], catch [1], handled (+3709+871.1+1886.1) [1], handling [1], holdest [1], hold [1], laid over [1], lay hold [1], stopped [1], take hold [1], taketh hold [1], taking [1], took hold [1]

8611 תֹּפֶת **tōpet**, n.f. GK: 9531. spitting:– tabret [1]

8612 תֹּפֶת **tōpet**, n.pr.loc. GK: 9532. Topheth:– Tophet [8], Topheth [1]

8613 תָּפְתֶּה **topteh**, n.pr.loc. GK: 9533. Topheth:– Tophet [1]

8614 תִּפְתָּי **tiptāy** (Aram.), n.m.pl. GK: 10767. magistrate, a general or legal authority such as a chief of police:– sheriffs [2]

תֹּצָאָה *tōṣāʾâ*. See 8444.

8615 תִּקְוָה **tiqwâ**, n.f. GK: 9535 & 9536 [→ 6960, 8616]. hope, expectation; cord:– hope [23], expectation [7], line [2], expected [1], thing long for [1]

8616 תִּקְוָה **tiqwâ**, n.pr.m. GK: 9537 [→ 8615; cf. 6960]. Tikvah, "*hope*":– Tikvah [2], Tikvath [1]

8617 תְּקוּמָה **tᵉqûmâ**, n.f. GK: 9538 [→ 6965]. ability to stand:– power to stand [1]

8618 תְּקוֹמֵם **tᵉqômēm**, v.ptcp. GK: 9539 [→ 6965]. ptcp. of 6965: to rise up against:– rise up [1]

8619 תָּקוֹעַ **tāqôaʿ**, n.[m.]. GK: 9540 [→ 8628]. trumpet, for battle signals:– trumpet [1]

8620 תְּקוֹעַ **tᵉqôaʿ**, n.pr.loc. GK: 9541 [→ 8621; cf. 8628]. Tekoa:– Tekoa [6], Tekoah [1]

8621 תְּקוֹעִי **tᵉqôʿî**, a.g. GK: 9542 [→ 8620]. Tekoite, of Tekoa, "*of Tekoa*":– Tekoite [3], Tekoah [2], Tekoites [2]

8622 תְּקוּפָה ***tᵉqûpâ***, n.f. GK: 9543 [cf. 5362]. turning, course:– end [2], circuit [1], come about (+3807.1) [1]

8623 תַּקִּיף ***taqqîp***, a. GK: 9544 [→ 8630; cf. 8624]. strong, mighty:– mightier [1]

8624 תַּקִּיף ***taqqîp*** (Aram.), a. GK: 10768 [→ 8631; cf. 8623]. strong, powerful, mighty:– strong [3], mighty [2]

8625 תְּקַל ***tᵉqal***, v. or תְּקֵל ***tᵉqēl*** (Aram.), n.[m.]. GK: 10769 & 10770 [cf. 8254, cf. 8255]. [Peil] to be weighed; (n.) tekel, (i.e., shekel of weight):– tekel [2], weighed [1]

8626 תָּקַן ***tāqan***, v. GK: 9545 [cf. 8505; cf. 8627]. [Q] to be straight; [P] to straighten, set in order:– made straight [1], make straight [1], set in order [1]

8627 תְּקַן ***tᵉqan*** (Aram.), v. GK: 10771 [cf. 8626, 8505]. [Ho] to be restored, be reestablished:– established [1]

8628 תָּקַע ***tāqaʿ***, v. GK: 9546 & 9364 [→ 8619, 8620, 8621, 8629]. [Q] to sound (a trumpet); to pitch, camp; to strike, clap; [Qp] to be driven; [N] to be sounded (a trumpet); to put up a security:– blow [22], blew [18], fastened [4], blown [3], blowing [2], clap [2], pitched [2], sounded [2], strike [2], thrust [2], blow up [1], bloweth [1], cast [1], fasten [1], pitch [1], smote [1], stricken [1], striketh [1], suretiship [1]

8629 תֵּקַע ***tēqaʿ***, n.[m.]. GK: 9547 [→ 8628]. sounding, blast (of a trumpet):– sound [1]

תְּקֹעִי ***tᵉqōʿî***. See 8621.

8630 תָּקַף ***tāqap***, v. GK: 9548 [→ 8623, 8633; cf. 8631]. [Q] to overpower, overwhelm:– prevail against [2], prevailest against [1]

8631 תְּקִף ***tᵉqip*** (Aram.), v. GK: 10772 [→ 8624, 8632; cf. 8630]. [P] to become strong, become hard; [Pa] to enforce, make hard:– strong [3], hardened [1], make firm [1]

8632 תְּקֹף ***tᵉqōp*** or תְּקָף ***tᵉqāp*** (Aram.), n.[m.]. GK: 10773 & 10774 [→ 8631; cf. 8633]. might, strength:– might [1], strength [1]

8633 תֹּקֶף ***tōqep***, n.m. GK: 9549 [→ 8630; cf. 8632]. power, strength, authority:– authority [1], power [1], strength [1]

תְּקֻפָה ***tᵉqupâ***. See 8622.

תֹּר ***tōr***. See 8447, 8449.

8634 תַּרְאֲלָה ***tarʾᵃlâ***, n.pr.loc. GK: 9550 [→ 692?]. Taralah:– Taralah [1]

8635 תַּרְבּוּת ***tarbût***, n.f. GK: 9551 [→ 7235]. a group of the same kind, brood:– increase [1]

8636 תַּרְבִּית ***tarbît***, n.f. GK: 9552 [→ 7235]. excessive interest, exorbitant interest:– increase [5], unjust gain [1]

8637 רָגַל ***rāgal*** or תִּרְגַּל ***tirgal***, v.den. GK: 8078 [→ 7270]. same as 7270: [Tiphil] to teach to walk:–

8638 תִּרְגֵּם ***tirgēm***, v. GK: 9553 [→ 7276]. [Pu] to be interpreted, be translated:– interpreted [1]

תֹּרָה ***tōrâ***. See 8451.

8639 תַּרְדֵּמָה ***tardēmâ***, n.f. GK: 9554 [→ 7290]. deep (supernatural) sleep, often a state of divine revelation and activity:– deep sleep [7]

8640 תִּרְהָקָה ***tirhāqâ***, n.pr.m. GK: 9555. Tirhakah:– Tirhakah [2]

8641 תְּרוּמָה ***tᵉrûmâ***, n.f. GK: 9556 [→ 7311]. offering, special gift, contribution:– heave offering [21], offering [19], oblation [17], offerings [8], heave [4], heave offerings [3], oblations [2], gifts [1], offered [1]

8642 תְּרוּמִיָּה ***tᵉrûmiyyâ***, n.f.den. GK: 9557 [→ 7311]. special gift, tribute:– oblation [1]

8643 תְּרוּעָה ***tᵉrûʿâ***, n.f. GK: 9558 [→ 7321]. trumpet blast, battle cry:– shout [10], shouting [8], alarm [6], joy [2], blowing of trumpets [1], blowing trumpets [1], blow [1], high sounding [1], joyful sound [1], jubile [1], loud noise [1], rejoicing [1], shouted aloud (+6963+7311+871.1+3807.1) [1], sounding [1]

8644 תְּרוּפָה ***tᵉrûpâ***, n.f. GK: 9559 [→ 7495]. healing:– medicine [1]

8645 תִּרְזָה ***tirzâ***, n.f. GK: 9560. cypress tree:– cypress [1]

8646 תֶּרַח ***teraḥ*** or תָּרַח ***tāraḥ***, n.pr.m. & loc. GK: 9561 & 9562. Terah, Tarah:– Terah [11], Tarah [2]

8647 תִּרְחֲנָה ***tirḥᵃnâ***, n.pr.[f.?]. GK: 9563. Tirhanah:– Tirhanah [1]

8648 תְּרֵין ***tᵉrên*** or תַּרְתֵּין ***tartên*** (Aram.), n.m. & f. GK: 10775 & 10778 [→ 8578, 8579; cf. 8147]. two:– twelve (+6236) [2], second [1], two [1]

8649 תַּרְמוּת ***tarmût*** or תַּרְמִית ***tarmît***, n.f. GK: 9566 & 9567 [cf. 7411]. deceitfulness, delusion:– deceit [4], deceitful [1], privily (+871.1) [1]

תְּרֻמָה ***tᵉrumâ***. See 8641.

8650 תֹּרֶן ***tōren***, n.m. GK: 9568. (sailing) mast; flagstaff (on top of hill):– beacon [1], masts [1], mast [1]

8651 תְּרַע ***tᵉraʿ*** (Aram.), n.[m.]. GK: 10776 [→ 8652; cf. 8179]. gate, door; opening (of a furnace); (royal) court, the entourage of a king:– gate [1], mouth [1]

8652 תָּרָע ***tārāʿ*** (Aram.), n.m. GK: 10777 [→ 8651; cf. 7778]. gatekeeper, doorkeeper:– porters [1]

8653 תַּרְעֵלָה ***tarʿēlâ***, n.f. GK: 9570 [→ 7477]. staggering, reeling:– trembling [2], astonishment [1]

8654 תִּרְעָתִים ***tirʿātîm***, n.pr.m.pl. GK: 9571. Tirathite:– Tirathites [1]

8655 תְּרָפִים ***tᵉrāpîm***, n.m.pl. GK: 9572. household god, idol:– teraphim [6], images [5], image [2], idolatry [1], idols [1]

8656 תִּרְצָה ***tirṣâ***, n.pr.f. & loc. GK: 9573 & 9574 [→ 7521]. Tirzah, "*pleasant one* or *compensation*":– Tirzah [18]

8657 תֶּרֶשׁ ***tereš***, n.pr.m. GK: 9575. Teresh, "[perhaps] *desire*":– Teresh [2]

8658 תַּרְשִׁישׁ ***taršîš***, n.m. GK: 9577 [→ 7567?]. chrysolite:– beryl [7]

8659 תַּרְשִׁישׁ ***taršîš***, n.pr.m. & loc. GK: 9576 & 9578 [→ 7567?]. Tarshish, "[poss.] *yellow jasper;* [poss.] *greedy one; foundry, refinery*"; ships of Tarshish = trading ships:– Tarshish [24], Tharshish [4]

8660 תִּרְשָׁתָא ***tiršātāʾ***, n.m. GK: 9579. governor:– Tirshatha [5]

תַּרְתֵּין ***tartên***. See 8648.

8661 תַּרְתָּן ***tartān***, n.m. GK: 9580 [cf. 8648]. supreme commander, second in command:– Tartan [2]

8662 תַּרְתָּק ***tartāq***, n.pr.[m.]. GK: 9581. Tartak (pagan god):– Tartak [1]

8663 תְּשֻׁאָה ***tᵉšuʾâ***, n.f. GK: 9583 & 9589 [→ 7582]. shouting, commotion, thundering, storm:– crying [1], noise [1], shoutings [1], stirs [1]

תֹּשָׁב ***tôšāb***. See 8453.

8664 תִּשְׁבִּי ***tišbî***, a.g. or תִּשְׁבֵּי ***tišbê***, n.pr.loc. GK: 9585. Tishbe; Tishbite, "*of Tishbe*":– Tishbite [6]

8665 תַּשְׁבֵּץ ***tašbēṣ***, n.[m.]. GK: 9587 [→ 7660]. woven or checkered fabric:– broidered [1]

8666 תְּשׁוּבָה ***tᵉšûbâ***, n.f. GK: 9588 [→ 7725]. spring [time of year]; answer:– expired [3], return [3], answers [2]

8667 תְּשׂוּמָה ***tᵉśûmâ***, n.f. GK: 9582 [→ 7760]. pledge, security:– fellowship (+3027) [1]

8668 תְּשׁוּעָה ***tᵉšûʿâ***, n.f. GK: 9591 [→ 3467]. deliverance, salvation, victory; divine salvation has its focus on rescue from earthly enemies, occasionally referring to salvation from guilt, sin, and punishment:– salvation [17], deliverance [5], help [4], safety [4], victory [3], help (+1961) [1]

8669 תְּשׁוּקָה ***tᵉšûqâ***, n.f. GK: 9592. desire, longing:– desire [3]

8670 תְּשׁוּרָה ***tᵉšûrâ***, n.f. GK: 9593 [→ 7794]. gift, present:– present [1]

תַּשְׁחֵת ***tašḥēt***. See 516.

תֻּשִׁיָּה ***tušîâ***. See 8454.

8671 תְּשִׁיעִי ***tᵉšîʿî***, a.num.ord. GK: 9595 [→ 8672]. ninth:– ninth [18]

תְּשֻׁעָה ***tᵉšuʿâ***. See 8668.

8672 תֵּשַׁע ***tēšaʿ***, n.m. & f. GK: 9596 [→ 8671, 8673]. nine, (pl.) ninety:– nine [45], ninth [6], nineteenth (+6240) [4], nineteen (+6240) [3]

8673 תִּשְׁעִים ***tišʿîm***, n.indecl. GK: 9597 [→ 8672]. ninety (pl. of "nine"):– ninety [20]

8674 תַּתְּנַי ***tattᵉnay*** (Aram.), n.pr.m. GK: 10779. Tattenai:– Tatnai [4]

GREEK DICTIONARY-INDEX TO THE NEW TESTAMENT

FEATURES OF THE GREEK TO ENGLISH DICTIONARY-INDEX

STRONG NUMBER
Matches the number at the end of context lines; Greek Strong numbers are in *italics* (see the introduction, pages xii, xiv).

LEXICAL FORM AND TRANSLITERATION
See the table below. Note that the lexical forms conform to modern resources and sometimes differ from Strong's original spelling.

PART OF SPEECH
The part of speech is abbreviated (see below and introduction, page xiv).

G/K NUMBER
Cross reference to the G/K numbering system, widely used in up-to-date word study reference resources (see the introduction, pages xiv).

223 ’Αλέξανδρος, ***Alexandros,*** n.pr. GK: *235* [→ *221, 222*].

RELATED WORDS LIST
Greek words related by common elements are listed by Strong number (see the introduction, page xiv, xv).

Alexander, “*defender of men*”:–

DEFINITION AND ETYMOLOGY
Words are defined, often with expanded explanations, and if a proper name, the possible definition (etymology) is given in italics (see the introduction, page xiv, xv).

Alexander [6],

KJV WORD AND (FREQUENCY COUNT)
Following the symbol :– KJV words are listed according to their exact textual spelling and are organized according to frequency (see the introduction, page xiv).

one another (+*1520*+*3588*) [2]

MULTIPLE WORDS / MULTIPLE NUMBERS
More than one KJV word and/or more than one Strong number indicate multiple-word translations (see the introduction, pages xii–xiv).

one another^S [2]

SUPERSCRIPT “S”
Indicates “substitution” translation (see the introduction, pages xiii, xiv).

GREEK TRANSLITERATION AND PRONUNCIATION TABLE

Α, α	*A, a*	f*a*ther	Κ, κ	*K, k*	*k*it	Τ, τ	*T, t*	*t*ip	γγ	*ng*	thi*ng*
Β, β	*B, b*	*b*oy	Λ, λ	*L, l*	*l*et	Υ, υ	*Y, y*	p*u*t	γκ	*nk*	thi*nk*
Γ, γ	*G, g*	*g*irl	Μ, μ	*M, m*	*m*other	Φ, φ	*Ph, ph*	*ph*one	γξ	*nx*	thi*nks*
Δ, δ	*D, d*	*d*og	Ν, ν	*N, n*	*n*ot	Χ, χ	*Ch, ch*	Ba*ch*	γχ	*nch*	thi*nk*
Ε, ϵ	*E, e*	g*e*t	Ξ, ξ	*X, x*	fo*x*	Ψ, ψ	*Ps, ps*	li*ps*			
Ζ, ζ	*Z, z*	a*dz*e	Ο, ο	*O, o*	h*o*t	Ω, ω	*Ō, ō*	ph*o*ne	αυ	*au*	kr*au*t
Η, η	*Ē, ē*	th*ey*	Π, π	*P, p*	*p*ot				ϵυ	*eu*	*you*
Θ, θ	*Th, th*	*th*ey	Ρ, ρ	*R, r*	*r*ot	‘Ρ, ῥ	*Rh, rh*	myr*rh*	ου	*ou*	thr*ou*gh
Ι, ι	*I, i*	p*i*n, mach*i*ne	Σ, σ, ς	*S, s, s*	*s*ip	‘	*H, h*	*h*ot	υι	*ui*	*we*

GREEK DICTIONARY ABBREVIATIONS

&	and	comp.	comparative	inter.	interrogative	pl.	plural
?	uncertain	cond.	conditional	interj.	interjection	poss.	possessive
+	plus: in combination with	contr.	contraction	intr.	intransitive	pp.	preposition
[ ]	uncertain part of speech	demo.	demonstrative	l.	loanword	pp.*	improper preposition
→	see these related words	disj.	disjunctive	letter	letter of the alphabet	pr.	proper [noun]
√	see this organizing word	emph.	emphatic	mid.	middle	pt.	particle
a.	adjective	excl.	exclamation	n.	noun	recip.	reciprocal
act.	active	fig.	figurative(ly)	neg.	negative	reflex.	reflexive
adv.	adverb	g.	gentilic	neu.	neuter	rel.	relative
adver.	adversative	imper.	impersonal	num.	numeral	super.	superlative
aff.	affirmative	indef.	indefinite	p.	pronoun	temp.	temporal
art.	article	infer.	inferential	pass.	passive	trans.	transitional
c.	conjunction	inten.	intensive	pers.	personal	v.	verb

1 α, **a**, letter. GK: *1 & 270* [→ *1;*   *4, 22, 35, 36, 46, 50, 51, 52, 56, 57, 62, 77, 82, 83, 84, 87, 88, 89, 90, 91, 92, 93, 94, 95, 96, 97, 101, 102, 106, 110, 112, 113, 114, 115, 120, 121, 167, 168, 169, 170, 171, 172, 175, 176, 177, 178, 179, 180, 181, 182, 183, 185, 186, 192, 193, 194, 208, 209, 210, 215, 216, 225, 226, 227, 228, 230, 249, 253, 255, 261, 262, 263, 267, 269, 272, 273, 274, 275, 276, 277, 278, 279, 280, 282, 283, 298, 299, 335, 338, 358, 361, 368, 369, 370, 371, 379, 382, 410, 411, 412, 413, 415, 418, 419, 421, 422, 423, 428, 434, 448, 449, 453, 454, 458, 459, 460, 462, 504, 505, 506, 512, 517, 521, 531, 532, 540, 543, 544, 545, 551, 552, 562, 563, 564, 569, 570, 571, 639, 640, 676, 677, 678, 679, 691, 692, 729, 731, 732, 761, 762, 763, 764, 765, 766, 767, 769, 770, 771, 772, 776, 777, 781, 784, 786, 790, 793, 794, 795, 799, 800, 801, 802, 803, 804, 805, 806, 807, 808, 809, 810, 811, 812, 813, 814, 815, 818, 819, 820, 821, 823, 824, 852, 853, 854, 855, 857, 858, 861, 862, 865, 866, 870, 877, 878, 880, 884, 886, 888, 889, 890, 893, 895, 1280, 1820, 2673;*   *12, 816;*   *79, 271?, 1811, 1872, 2628, 3877, 4870, 5359, 5360, 5361, 5569*]. 1) letter of the Greek alphabet, Alpha, "*First* or *Beginning*"; 2) inseparable prefix: alpha privative (as non- or un- in English),   prefix of intensity,   prefix of similarity, collectivity or association; also used as the numeral "1" in the superscriptions of some Greek manuscripts:– Alpha [4]

2 Ἀαρών, ***Aarōn***, n.pr. GK: *2*. Aaron (referring to both the person and his priesthood):– Aaron [4], Aaron's [1]

3 Ἀβαδδών, ***Abaddōn***, n.pr. GK: *3*. Abaddon, "*destruction*":– Abaddon [1]

4 ἀβαρής, ***abarēs***, a. GK: *4* [→ *1.1+922*]. not burdensome:– from being burdensome [1]

5 ἀββά, ***abba***, l.[n.]. GK: *5*. Aramaic for "father":– Abba [3]

6 Ἅβελ, ***Habel***, n.pr. GK: *6*. Abel, "*morning mist*":– Abel [4]

7 Ἀβιά, ***Abia***, n.pr. GK: *7*. Abijah, "*[my] father is Yahweh*":– Abia [3]

8 Ἀβιαθάρ, ***Abiathar***, n.pr. GK: *8*. Abiathar, "*[my] father gives abundance* or *the father is preeminent*":– Abiathar [1]

9 Ἀβιληνή, ***Abilēnē***, n.pr. GK: *9*. Abilene, a territory on the south end of the Ante-Lebanon mountain range, "[prob.] *meadow*":– Abilene [1]

10 Ἀβιούδ, ***Abioud***, n.pr. GK: *10*. Abiud, "*[my] father has majesty*":– Abiud [2]

11 Ἀβραάμ, ***Abraam***, n.pr. GK: *11*. Abraham, "*father of many*":– Abraham [68], Abraham's [5]

12 ἄβυσσος, ***abyssos***, n. GK: *12* [→ *1.2+1037*]. Abyss, the deep place, the underworld, the abode of the dead and demons, "*unfathomable depth*":– bottomless [7], deep [2]

13 Ἅγαβος, ***Hagabos***, n.pr. GK: *13*. Agabus:– Agabus [2]

14 ἀγαθοεργέω, ***agathoergeō***, v. GK: *14* [→ *18+2041*]. to do good:– do good [1]

15 ἀγαθοποιέω, ***agathopoieō***, v. GK: *16* [→ *18+4160*]. to do good, to do right:– do good [5], do well [2], well doing [2], did good [1], doeth good [1]

16 ἀγαθοποιΐα, ***agathopoiia***, n. GK: *17* [→ *18+4160*]. doing good:– well doing [1]

17 ἀγαθοποιός, ***agathopoios***, a. GK: *18* [→ *18+4160*]. one who does good, right:– do well [1]

18 ἀγαθός, ***agathos***, a. GK: *19* [→ *14, 15, 16, 17, 19, 865, 5358*]. good; good as a positive quality (vs. bad), good as a moral quality (vs. evil):– good [98], goods [2], benefit [1], well [1]

19 ἀγαθωσύνη, ***agathōsynē***, n. GK: *20* [→ *18*]. goodness:– goodness [4]

20 ἀγαλλίασις, ***agalliasis***, n. GK: *21* [→ *21*]. delight, great joy:– gladness [3], exceeding joy [1], joy [1]

21 ἀγαλλιάω, ***agalliaō***, v. GK: *22* [→ *20*]. to be filled with delight, with great joy:– rejoiced [4], rejoice [3], exceeding glad [1], exceeding joy [1], glad [1], greatly rejoice [1]

22 ἄγαμος, ***agamos***, n. GK: *23* [→ *1.1+1062*]. unmarried (man or woman):– unmarried [4]

23 ἀγανακτέω, ***aganakteō***, v. GK: *24* [→ *24*]. to be indignant:– had indignation [2], much displeased [2], indignation [1], moved with indignation [1], sore displeased [1]

24 ἀγανάκτησις, ***aganaktēsis***, n. GK: *25* [→ *23*]. indignation:– indignation [1]

25 ἀγαπάω, ***agapaō***, v. GK: *26* [→ *26, 27*]. to love; in the NT usually the active love of God for his Son and his people, and the active love his people are to have for God, each other, and even enemies:– love [73], loved [39], loveth [20], beloved [7], lovest [2], lovedst [1]

26 ἀγάπη, ***agapē***, n. GK: *27* [→ *25*]. love, in the NT usually the active love of God for his Son and his people, and the active love his people are to have for God, each other, and even enemies; love feast, the common meal shared by Christians in connection with church meetings:– love [85], charity [27], charitably (*+2596*) [1], dear [1], feasts of charity [1], love's [1]

27 ἀγαπητός, ***agapētos***, a. GK: *28* [→ *25*]. dearly loved one; the object of special affection and of special relationship, as with Jesus the beloved of the Father:– beloved [47], dearly beloved [9], dear [3], wellbeloved [3]

28 Ἁγάρ, ***Hagar***, n.pr. GK: *29*. Hagar:– Agar [2]

29 ἀγγαρεύω, ***angareuō***, v. GK: *30*. to force, compel, press into service in military or civil matters:– compel to go [1], compelled [1], compel [1]

30 ἀγγεῖον, ***angeion***, n. GK: *31*. jar, flask, a container for liquid, basket:– vessels [2]

31 ἀγγελία, ***angelia***, n. GK: *32* [→ *32*]. message:– message [1]

32 ἄγγελος, ***angelos***, n. GK: *34* [→ *31, 518, 312, 743, 1229, 1804, 1860, 1861, 1862, 2097, 2098, 2099, 2465, 2604, 2605, 3852, 3853, 4279, 4283, 4293; cf. 71*]. angel, messenger; this can refer to a human messenger, such as John the Baptist, or messengers sent by John the Baptist or Jesus, or to the supernatural class of being that serves God: the angel:– angel [96], angels [80], messenger [4], messengers [3], angel's [2]

33 ἄγε, ***agē***, v.imper. of *71*. GK: *72* [→ *71*]. look, pay attention, listen:–

34 ἀγέλη, ***agelē***, n. GK: *36* [→ *71*]. herd (of pigs):– herd [8]

35 ἀγενεαλόγητος, ***agenealogētos***, a. GK: *37* [→ *1.1+1096+3004*]. without genealogy:– without descent [1]

36 ἀγενής, ***agenēs***, a. GK: *38* [→ *1.1+1096*]. lowly, insignificant, implying low social standing:– base [1]

37 ἁγιάζω, ***hagiazō***, v. GK: *39* [→ *40*]. to sanctify, set apart, make holy; this can mean active dedication and service to God or the act of regarding or honoring as holy:– sanctified [16], sanctify [6], sanctifieth [4], hallowed [2], holy [1]

38 ἁγιασμός, ***hagiasmos***, n. GK: *40* [→ *40*]. holiness:– holiness [5], sanctification [5]

39 ἅγιον, ***hagion***, a.neut. of *40*. GK: *41* [→ *40*]. holy (moral quality), holy place = sanctuary:–

40 ἅγιος, ***hagios***, a. GK: *41* [→ *37, 38, 39, 41, 42; cf. 53*]. holy (moral quality), consecrated ([ceremonially] acceptable to God); holy person/people = saint(s), holy place = sanctuary:– holy [163], saints [60], holy one [4], sanctuary [4], holiest of all (*+40*) [2], holiest [2], holy thing [1], most holy [1], saints' [1], saint [1]

41 ἁγιότης, ***hagiotēs***, n. GK: *42* [→ *40*]. holiness, a characteristic of God, shared by his people, requiring a lifestyle acceptable to God:– holiness [1]

42 ἁγιωσύνη, ***hagiōsynē***, n. GK: *43* [→ *40*]. holiness, a characteristic of God, shared by his people, requiring a lifestyle acceptable to God:– holiness [3]

43 ἀγκάλη, ***ankalē***, n. GK: *44* [→ *1723*]. arm:– arms [1]

44 ἄγκιστρον, ***ankistron***, n. GK: *45* [→ *45*]. fish-hook, fish line with a hook on it:– hook [1]

45 ἄγκυρα, ***ankyra***, n. GK: *46* [→ *44*]. anchor; used fig. of security:– anchors [3], anchor [1]

46 ἄγναφος, ***agnaphos***, a. GK: *47* [→ *1.1+1102*]. unshrunk, new cloth that has not been laundered:– new [2]

47 ἁγνεία, ***hagneia***, n. GK: *48* [→ *53*]. purity, in the sense of moral purity and proper sexual conduct:– purity [2]

48 ἁγνίζω, ***hagnizō***, v. GK: *49* [→ *53*]. to purify, ceremonially cleanse:– purify [3], purified [2], purifieth [1], purifying [1]

49 ἁγνισμός, ***hagnismos***, n. GK: *50* [→ *53*]. purification:– purification [1]

50 ἀγνοέω, ***agnoeō***, v. GK: *51* [→ *1.1+1097*]. to be ignorant, not know, not understand:– ignorant [10], ignorantly [2], know not [2], understood not [2], unknown [2], have ignorant [1], knew not [1], not knowing [1], understand not [1]

51 ἀγνόημα, ***agnoēma***, n. GK: *52* [→ *1.1+1097*]. sin committed in ignorance:– errors [1]

52 ἄγνοια, ***agnoia***, n. GK: *53* [→ *1.1+1097*]. ignorance:– ignorance [4]

53 ἁγνός, ***hagnos***, a. GK: *54* [→ *47, 48, 49, 54, 55; cf. 40*]. pure (in some contexts morally pure), innocent:– pure [4], chaste [3], clear [1]

54 ἁγνότης, ***hagnotēs***, n. GK: *55* [→ *53*]. purity:– pureness [1]

55 ἁγνῶς, **hagnōs**, adv. GK: *56* [→ *53*]. sincerely, purely:– sincerely [1]

56 ἀγνωσία, **agnōsia**, n. GK: *57* [→ *1.1+1097*]. ignorance, with a focus on talk or action that opposes God:– ignorance [1], not knowledge [1]

57 ἄγνωστος, **agnōstos**, a. GK: *58* [→ *1.1+1097*]. unknown:– unknown [1]

58 ἀγορά, **agora**, n. GK: *59* [→ *59*]. marketplace (as a center of social and commercial life):– markets [4], marketplace [3], market [2], marketplaces [1], streets [1]

59 ἀγοράζω, **agorazō**, v. GK: *60* [→ *58, 60, 238, 1215, 1805; cf. 71*]. to buy, purchase; this refers to buying and acquiring possessions, as in a market place, and to setting a slave free through purchase, often to God's purchase (redemption) of sinners:– bought [13], buy [13], redeemed [3], buyeth [2]

60 ἀγοραῖος, **agoraios**, a. GK: *61* [→ *59*]. marketplace, place where the courts meet:– baser sort [1], law [1]

61 ἄγρα, **agra**, n. GK: *62* [→ *64, 69, 70, 2221*]. catch (of fish), a net full:– draught [2]

62 ἀγράμματος, **agrammatos**, a. GK: *63* [→ *1.1+1125*]. unschooled, probably in the sense of not having a formal rabbinic education:– unlearned [1]

63 ἀγραυλέω, **agrauleō**, v. GK: *64* [→ *68+833*]. to live outdoors, spend a night in the elements:– in country abiding [1]

64 ἀγρεύω, **agreuō**, v. GK: *65* [→ *61*]. to catch:– catch [1]

65 ἀγριέλαιος, **agrielaios**, n. GK: *66* [→ *68+1636*]. wild olive tree:– olive tree which is wild [1], wild olive tree [1]

66 ἄγριος, **agrios**, a. GK: *67* [→ *68*]. wild; undomesticated as well as uncontrolled:– wild [2], raging [1]

67 Ἀγρίππας, **Agrippas**, n.pr. GK: *68* [→ *68+2462*]. Agrippa, "*wild horse*":– Agrippa [12]

68 ἀγρός, **agros**, n. GK: *69* [→ *63, 65, 66, 67*]. field, countryside, both tilled and untilled ground:– field [21], country [8], lands [3], farm [1], fields [1], land [1], piece of ground [1]

69 ἀγρυπνέω, **agrypneō**, v. GK: *70* [→ *61+5258*]. to keep awake, keep alert:– watch [3], watching [1]

70 ἀγρυπνία, **agrypnia**, n. GK: *71* [→ *61+5258*]. sleeplessness, wakefulness:– watchings [2]

71 ἄγω, **agō**, v. GK: *72* [→ *33, 34, 72, 321, 411, 520, 747, 1236, 1334, 1335, 1396, 1521, 1555, 1806, 1834, 1863, 1877, 1898, 1996, 2023, 2024, 2230, 2231, 2232, 2233, 2519, 2609, 2723, 3329, 3594, 3595, 3807, 3831, 3855, 3919, 3920, 3931, 4013, 4254, 4285, 4316, 4317, 4318, 4755, 4812, 4863, 4864, 4879, 5217, 5468, 5496, 5497, 5524; cf. 32, 59, 514, 2723*]. to bring, lead; as a command: look, pay attention, listen:– brought [32], bring [13], led [10], go [8], bring out [1], bringing [1], carried [1], going [1], is [1], kept [1], leadeth [1], lead [1], led away [1], open [1]

72 ἀγωγή, **agōgē**, n. GK: *73* [→ *71*]. way of life, personal conduct:– manner of life [1]

73 ἀγών, **agōn**, n. GK: *74* [→ *74, 75, 464, 1864, 2610, 4865*]. struggle, fight, often an athletic contest:– conflict [2], fight [2], contention [1], race [1]

74 ἀγωνία, **agōnia**, n. GK: *75* [→ *73*]. anguish, anxiety:– agony [1]

75 ἀγωνίζομαι, **agōnizomai**, v. GK: *76* [→ *73*]. to fight, struggle, often an athletic contest:– fight [2], fought [1], labouring fervently [1], striveth for the mastery [1], strive [1], striving [1]

76 Ἀδάμ, **Adam**, n.pr. GK: *77*. Adam, "*[red] earth* or *[ruddy] skin color*":– Adam [8], Adam's [1]

77 ἀδάπανος, **adapanos**, a. GK: *78* [→ *1.1+1160*]. free of charge, without payment:– without charge [1]

78 Ἀδδί, **Addi**, n.pr. GK: *79*. Addi, "[poss.] *my witness* or *adorned*":– Addi [1]

79 ἀδελφή, **adelphē**, n. GK: *80* [→ *80; cf. 1.3*]. sister, fellow countrywoman; by extension a female believer, a sister in the family of faith:– sister [15], sisters [8], sister's [1]

80 ἀδελφός, **adelphos**, n. GK: *81* [→ *1.3, 79, 81, 5359, 5360, 5361, 5569*]. brother, fellow countryman, neighbor (often inclusive in gender); by extension a fellow believer in the family of faith; in the plural "brothers" regularly refers to men and women:– brethren [226], brother [113], brother's [7]

81 ἀδελφότης, **adelphotēs**, n. GK: *82* [→ *80*]. brotherhood, fellowship of believers (men and women):– brethren [1], brotherhood [1]

82 ἄδηλος, **adēlos**, a. GK: *83* [→ *1.1+1212*]. not clear:– appear not [1], uncertain [1]

83 ἀδηλότης, **adēlotēs**, n. GK: *84* [→ *1.1+1212*]. uncertainty:– uncertain [1]

84 ἀδήλως, **adēlōs**, adv. GK: *85* [→ *1.1+1212*]. aimlessly, uncertainly:– uncertainly [1]

85 ἀδημονέω, **adēmoneō**, v. GK: *86 & 194*. to be troubled, distressed:– very heavy [2], full of heaviness [1]

86 ᾅδης, **hadēs**, n. GK: *87*. Hades, the grave, the place of the dead, "*the underworld*":– hell [10], grave [1]

87 ἀδιάκριτος, **adiakritos**, a. GK: *88* [→ *1.1+1223+2919*]. impartial, free from prejudice:– without partiality [1]

88 ἀδιάλειπτος, **adialeiptos**, a. GK: *89* [→ *1.1+1223+3007*]. constant, unceasing:– continual [1], without ceasing [1]

89 ἀδιαλείπτως, **adialeiptōs**, adv. GK: *90* [→ *1.1+1223+3007*]. constantly, unceasingly:– without ceasing [4]

90 ἀδιαφθορία, **adiaphthoria**, n. GK: *91* [→ *1.1+1223+5351*]. sincerity, integrity:– uncorruptness [1]

91 ἀδικέω, **adikeō**, v. GK: *92* [→ *1.1+1349*]. to do wrong, mistreat:– hurt [10], wrong [3], done wrong [2], unjust [2], wronged [2], did wrong [1], doeth wrong [1], injured [1], offender [1], suffer wrong [1], suffered wrong [1], take wrong [1], wrong done [1]

92 ἀδίκημα, **adikēma**, n. GK: *93* [→ *1.1+1349*]. crime, unrighteous or unjust act:– evil doing [1], iniquities [1], wrong [1]

93 ἀδικία, **adikia**, n. GK: *94* [→ *1.1+1349*]. wickedness, evil, wrongdoing:– unrighteousness [16], iniquity [6], unjust [2], wrong [1]

94 ἄδικος, **adikos**, a. GK: *96* [→ *1.1+1349*]. unjust, unrighteous, used of things and persons; as a noun: unbeliever, wicked person:– unjust [8], unrighteous [4]

95 ἀδίκως, **adikōs**, adv. GK: *97* [→ *1.1+1349*]. unjustly:– wrongfully [1]

96 ἀδόκιμος, **adokimos**, a. GK: *99* [→ *1.1+1209*]. failing the test, rejected:– reprobates [3], reprobate [3], castaway [1], rejected [1]

97 ἄδολος, **adolos**, a. GK: *100* [→ *1.1+1388*]. pure, uncontaminated or tainted:– sincere [1]

98 Ἀδραμυττηνός, **Adramyttēnos**, a.pr.g. GK: *101*. of Adramyttium:– Adramyttium [1]

99 Ἀδρίας, **Adrias**, n.pr. GK: *102*. Adriatic Sea:– Adria [1]

100 ἁδρότης, **hadrotēs**, n. GK: *103*. liberal gift, liberality:– abundance [1]

101 ἀδυνατέω, **adynateō**, v. GK: *104* [→ *1.1+1410*]. to be impossible:– unpossible [2]

102 ἀδύνατος, **adynatos**, a. GK: *105* [→ *1.1+1410*]. impossible, powerless:– impossible [4], unpossible [2], could not do [1], impotent [1], not possible [1], weak [1]

103 ᾄδω, **adō**, v. GK: *106* [→ *5603*]. to sing:– singing [2], sung [2], sing [1]

104 ἀεί, **aei**, adv. GK: *107* [→ *126*]. always:– alway [4], always [3], ever [1]

105 ἀετός, **aetos**, n. GK: *108*. eagle (a noble, powerful bird), vulture (a carrion bird):– eagles [2], eagle [2]

106 ἄζυμος, **azymos**, a. GK: *109* [→ *1.1+2219*]. unleavened, (the Feast of) Unleavened Bread, made without yeast; fig. of purity:– unleavened bread [8], unleavened [1]

107 Ἀζώρ, **Azōr**, n.pr. GK: *110*. Azor:– Azor [2]

108 Ἄζωτος, **Azōtos**, n.pr. GK: *111*. Azotus, another name for Ashdod:– Azotus [1]

109 ἀήρ, **aēr**, n. GK: *113* [→ *822; cf. 143, 833*]. air, sky:– air [7]

ἀθά, **atha**. See **3134**.

110 ἀθανασία, **athanasia**, n. GK: *114* [→ *1.1+2348*]. immortality:– immortality [3]

111 ἀθέμιτος, **athemitos**, a. GK: *116*. unlawful, detestable:– abominable [1], unlawful [1]

112 ἄθεος, **atheos**, a. GK: *117* [→ *1.1+2316*]. without God, excluded from the heritage of Israel:– without God [1]

113 ἄθεσμος, **athesmos**, a. GK: *118* [→ *1.1+5087*]. lawless, unprincipled:– wicked [2]

114 ἀθετέω, **atheteō**, v. GK: *119* [→ *1.1+5087*]. to reject, set aside:– despiseth [6], reject [2], bring to nothing [1], cast off [1], despised [1], despise [1], disannulleth [1], frustrate [1], rejected [1], rejecteth [1]

115 ἀθέτησις, **athetēsis**, n. GK: *120* [→ *1.1+5087*]. setting aside, doing away with:– disannulling [1], put away [1]

116 Ἀθῆναι, **Athēnai**, n.pr. GK: *121* [→ *117*]. Athens:– Athens [6]

117 'Αθηναῖος, ***Athēnaios***, a.pr.g. GK: *122* [→ *116*]. Athenian, resident of Athens:– Athenians [1], of Athens [1]

118 ἀθλέω, ***athleō***, v. GK: *123* [→ *119, 4866*]. to compete in a contest:– strive for masteries [1], strive [1]

119 ἄθλησις, ***athlēsis***, n. GK: *124* [→ *118*]. contest, struggle:– fight [1]

120 ἀθυμέω, ***athymeō***, v. GK: *126* [→ *1.1+2372*]. to be discouraged, lose heart:– discouraged [1]

121 ἀθῷος, ***athōos***, a. GK: *127* [→ *1.1+5087*]. innocent:– innocent [2]

122 αἴγειος, ***aigeios***, a. GK: *128*. of a goat:– goatskins (*+1192*) [1]

123 αἰγιαλός, ***aigialos***, n. GK: *129* [→ *217*]. shore, beach:– shore [6]

124 Αἰγύπτιος, ***Aigyptios***, a.pr.g. GK: *130* [→ *125*]. Egyptian, person of Egypt:– Egyptian [3], Egyptians [2]

125 Αἴγυπτος, ***Aigyptos***, n.pr. GK: *131* [→ *124*]. Egypt:– Egypt [24]

126 ἀΐδιος, ***aidios***, a. GK: *132* [→ *104*]. eternal (referring to God's power, chains of punishment):– eternal [1], everlasting [1]

127 αἰδώς, ***aidōs***, n. GK: *133 & 1290* [→ *335, 1167, 1168, 1169, 1171, 1175, 1174*]. decency, modesty:– reverence [1], shamefastness [1]

128 Αἰθίοψ, ***Aithiops***, n.pr.g. GK: *134*. Ethiopian, person of Ethiopia:– Ethiopians [1], Ethiopia [1]

129 αἷμα, ***haima***, n. GK: *135* [→ *130, 131*]. blood; extended meanings: killing, death, sacrifice:– blood [99]

130 αἱματεκχυσία, ***haimatekchysia***, n. GK: *136* [→ *129+1632*]. shedding, pouring out of blood:– shedding of blood [1]

131 αἱμορροέω, ***haimorroeō***, v. GK: *137* [→ *129+4482*]. to be subject to bleeding, to experience loss of blood:– diseased with an issue of blood [1]

132 Αἰνέας, ***Aineas***, n.pr. GK: *138* [→ *136*]. Aeneas, "[poss.] *praise*":– Aeneas [2]

133 αἴνεσις, ***ainesis***, n. GK: *139* [→ *136*]. praise, speaking of the excellence of someone or something:– praise [1]

134 αἰνέω, ***aineō***, v. GK: *140* [→ *136*]. to praise; in the NT, speaking of the excellence of God:– praising [6], praise [3]

135 αἴνιγμα, ***ainigma***, n. GK: *141*. poor reflection, indistinct image:– darkly (*+1722*) [1]

136 αἶνος, ***ainos***, n. GK: *142* [→ *132, 133, 134, 1866, 1867, 1868, 3867*]. praise:– praise [2]

137 Αἰνών, ***Ainōn***, n.pr. GK: *143*. Aenon, "*spring*":– Aenon [1]

138 αἱρέομαι, ***haireomai***, v. GK: *145* [→ *139, 140, 141, 336, 337, 830, 851, 1243, 1244, 1807, 2506, 2507, 4014, 4255*]. to choose:– choose [1], choosing [1], chosen [1]

139 αἵρεσις, ***hairesis***, n. GK: *146* [→ *138*]. sect (religious party), faction, heresy:– sect [5], heresies [3], heresy [1]

140 αἱρετίζω, ***hairetizō***, v. GK: *147* [→ *138*]. to choose (for the purpose of showing special favor):– chosen [1]

141 αἱρετικός, ***hairetikos***, a. GK: *148* [→ *138*]. divisive:– heretick [1]

142 αἴρω, ***airō***, v. GK: *149* [→ *522, 1808, 1869, 3332, 4868, 5097, 5098, 5229*]. to take up, take away:– take up [14], take [14], took up [13], taken away [9], take away [7], taketh away [6], away with [5], taketh [5], taken [4], taken up [3], took [3], bear up [2], bear [2], lifted up [2], removed [2], took away [2], borne [1], carry [1], lift up [1], lift [1], loosing [1], make to doubt (*+3588+5590*) [1], put away [1], takest up [1], taking up [1]

143 αἰσθάνομαι, ***aisthanomai***, v. GK: *150* [→ *144, 145; cf. 109*]. to grasp, understand, to have the capacity to perceive something clearly:– perceived [1]

144 αἴσθησις, ***aisthēsis***, n. GK: *151* [→ *143*]. insight:– judgment [1]

145 αἰσθητήριον, ***aisthētērion***, n. GK: *152* [→ *143*]. sense, faculty:– senses [1]

146 αἰσχροκερδής, ***aischrokerdēs***, a. GK: *153* [→ *150+2771*]. pursuing dishonest gain:– greedy of filthy lucre [2], given to filthy lucre [1]

147 αἰσχροκερδῶς, ***aischrokerdōs***, adv. GK: *154* [→ *150+2771*]. in greediness for money:– for filthy lucre [1]

148 αἰσχρολογία, ***aischrologia***, n. GK: *155* [→ *150+3004*]. filthy language, vulgar speech:– filthy communication [1]

149 αἰσχρόν, ***aischron***, a.neut. of *150*. GK: *156* [→ *150*]. disgraceful, shameful:– shame [3]

150 αἰσχρός, ***aischros***, a. GK: *156* [→ *146, 147, 148, 149, 151, 152, 153, 422, 1870, 2617*]. disgraceful, shameful:– filthy [1]

151 αἰσχρότης, ***aischrotēs***, n. GK: *157* [→ *150*]. obscenity:– filthiness [1]

152 αἰσχύνη, ***aischynē***, n. GK: *158* [→ *150*]. shamefulness:– shame [5], dishonesty [1]

153 αἰσχύνομαι, ***aischynomai***, v. GK: *159* [→ *150*]. to be ashamed:– ashamed [5]

154 αἰτέω, ***aiteō***, v. GK: *160* [→ *155, 523, 1809, 1871, 3868, 4319*]. to ask, ask for (of other humans or God), demand:– ask [38], desired [10], asketh [5], desire [5], asked [3], begged [2], desiring [2], asked for [1], askest [1], called for [1], craved [1], require [1], requiring [1]

155 αἴτημα, ***aitēma***, n. GK: *161* [→ *154*]. request:– petitions [1], requests [1], required [1]

156 αἰτία, ***aitia***, n. GK: *162* [→ *157, 158, 159, 338, 4256*]. (legal) charge; reason, cause:– cause [9], accusation [3], fault [3], wherefore (*+1223+3739*) [3], case [1], crimes [1]

157 αἰτίαμα, ***aitiama***, n. GK: *163 & 166* [→ *156*]. charge, complaint:– complaints [1]

158 αἴτιον, ***aition***, a.neut. of *159*. GK: *165* [→ *156*]. basis, reason or cause (for legal charges), source:– cause [2], fault [2]

159 αἴτιος, ***aitios***, a. GK: *165* [→ *156*]. basis, reason or cause (for legal charges), source:– author [1]

160 αἰφνίδιος, ***aiphnidios***, a. GK: *167* [→ *869?, 1810, 1819*]. sudden, unexpected:– sudden [1], unawares [1]

161 αἰχμαλωσία, ***aichmalōsia***, n. GK: *168* [→ *164*]. captivity:– captivity [3]

162 αἰχμαλωτεύω, ***aichmalōteuō***, v. GK: *169* [→ *164*]. to take captive:– lead captive [1], led captive [1]

163 αἰχμαλωτίζω, ***aichmalōtizō***, v. GK: *170* [→ *164*]. to take captive, take prisoner:– bringing into captivity [2], led away captive [1]

164 αἰχμάλωτος, ***aichmalōtos***, n. GK: *171* [→ *161, 162, 163, 4869; cf. 259*]. prisoner:– captives [1]

165 αἰών, ***aiōn***, n. GK: *172* [→ *166*]. eternity, age (time period); "this age" can mean the universe or even the current world system, the "god of this age" refers to the devil:– ever [68], world [35], never (*+1519+3361+3588+3756*) [5], ages [2], eternal [2], ever (*+1519+3588*) [2], evermore (*+165*) [2], evermore [2], world without end (*+165+3588+3588*) [2], worlds [2], beginning of the world [1], course [1], ever (*+1519+3588+3956*) [1], ever (*+2250*) [1], never (*+1487+1519+3588+3756*) [1], never (*+1519+3588+3756*) [1]

166 αἰώνιος, ***aiōnios***, a. GK: *173* [→ *165*]. eternal, long ago:– eternal [42], everlasting [25], world began (*+5550*) [2], for ever [1], since world began (*+5550*) [1]

167 ἀκαθαρσία, ***akatharsia***, n. GK: *174* [→ *1.1+2513*]. impurity, a state of moral filthiness, especially in relation to sexual sin:– uncleanness [10]

168 ἀκαθάρτης, ***akathartēs***, n. GK: *175* [→ *1.1+2513*]. uncleanness:– filthiness [1]

169 ἀκάθαρτος, ***akathartos***, a. GK: *176* [→ *1.1+2513*]. unclean, evil:– unclean [28], foul [2]

170 ἀκαιρέομαι, ***akaireomai***, v. GK: *177* [→ *1.1+2540*]. to have no opportunity, have no time:– lacked opportunity [1]

171 ἀκαίρως, ***akairōs***, adv. GK: *178* [→ *1.1+2540*]. out of season, lack of a favorable opportunity:– out of season [1]

172 ἄκακος, ***akakos***, a. GK: *179* [→ *1.1+2556*]. blameless, innocent, unsuspecting:– harmless [1], simple [1]

173 ἄκανθα, ***akantha***, n. GK: *180* [→ *206*]. thorn, thornbush:– thorns [14]

174 ἀκάνθινος, ***akanthinos***, a. GK: *181* [→ *206*]. of thorns, thorny:– of thorns [2]

175 ἄκαρπος, ***akarpos***, a. GK: *182* [→ *1.1+2590*]. unfruitful, unproductive, something generally useless:– unfruitful [6], without fruit [1]

176 ἀκατάγνωστος, ***akatagnōstos***, a. GK: *183* [→ *1.1+2596+1097*]. not condemned, what cannot be criticized:– cannot be condemned [1]

177 ἀκατακάλυπτος, ***akatakalyptos***, a. GK: *184* [→ *1.1+2596+2572*]. uncovered:– uncovered [2]

178 ἀκατάκριτος, ***akatakritos***, a. GK: *185* [→ *1.1+2596+2919*]. uncondemned, without a proper trial:– uncondemned [2]

179 ἀκατάλυτος, ***akatalytos***, a. GK: *186* [→ *1.1+2596+3089*]. indestructible, unstoppable:– endless [1]

180 ἀκατάπαυστος, ***akatapaustos***, a. GK: *187 & 188* [→ *1.1+2596+3973*]. never stopping:– cannot cease from [1]

181 ἀκαταστασία, ***akatastasia***, n. GK: *189* [→ *1.1+2596+2476*]. disorder, rebellion, riot:– confusion [2], tumults [2], commotions [1]

182 ἀκατάστατος, ***akatastatos***, a. GK: *190* [→ *1.1+2596+2476*]. unstable, restless:– unstable [1]

183 ἀκατάσχετος, ***akataschetos***, a. GK: *191* [→ *1.1+2596+2192*]. uncontrollable:– unruly [1]

184 Ἀκελδαμάχ, ***Hakeldamach***, n.pr. GK: *192*. Akeldama (traditionally located south of the valley of Hinnom), "*field of blood*":– Aceldama [1]

185 ἀκέραιος, ***akeraios***, a. GK: *193* [→ *1.1+2767*]. innocent, pure, not mixed with evil:– harmless [2], simple [1]

186 ἀκλινής, ***aklinēs***, a. GK: *195* [→ *1.1+2827*]. unswerving, without wavering:– without wavering [1]

187 ἀκμάζω, ***akmazō***, v. GK: *196* [→ *206*]. to be or become ripe:– fully ripe [1]

188 ἀκμήν, ***akmēn***, adv. GK: *197* [→ *206*]. still, even yet:– yet [1]

189 ἀκοή, ***akoē***, n. GK: *198* [→ *191*]. (act of) hearing, what is heard:– hearing [10], ears [4], fame [3], report [2], rumours [2], audience [1], heard [1], preached [1]

190 ἀκολουθέω, ***akoloutheō***, v. GK: *199* [→ *1.3, 1811, 1872, 2628, 3877, 4870*]. to follow; accompany; fig., to follow or be a disciple of a leader's teaching:– followed [53], follow [30], followeth [5], following [3], reached [1]

191 ἀκούω, ***akouō***, v. GK: *201* [→ *189, 1251, 1522, 1873, 3876, 3878, 4257, 5218, 5219, 5255*]. to hear, pay attention, understand, obey:– heard [239], hear [141], heareth [23], hearing [13], hearken [6], hearest [4], gave audience [2], hearers [2], came [1], come to ears (+*1909*) [1], give audience [1], in audience [1], noised [1], reported [1], understandeth [1]

192 ἀκρασία, ***akrasia***, n. GK: *202* [→ *1.1+2904*]. lack of self-control:– excess [1], incontinency [1]

193 ἀκρατής, ***akratēs***, a. GK: *203* [→ *1.1+2904*]. without self-control:– incontinent [1]

194 ἄκρατος, ***akratos***, a. GK: *204* [→ *1.1+2767*]. undiluted (of wine not watered down):– without mixture [1]

195 ἀκρίβεια, ***akribeia***, n. GK: *205* [→ *198*]. thoroughness, strictness:– perfect manner [1]

196 ἀκριβέστατος, ***akribestatos***, a.super. GK: *206* [→ *198*]. strictest:– most straitest [1]

197 ἀκριβέστερον, ***akribesteron***, a.compar. GK: *206* [→ *198*]. more strict:– more perfectly [3], more perfect [1]

198 ἀκριβόω, ***akriboō***, v. GK: *208* [→ *195, 196, 197, 199*]. to find out exactly:– diligently inquired [1], inquired diligently [1]

199 ἀκριβῶς, ***akribōs***, adv. GK: *209* [→ *198*]. accurately, carefully, well:– diligently [2], circumspectly [1], perfectly [1], perfect [1]

200 ἀκρίς, ***akris***, n. GK: *210*. locust (in some cultures distinguished from a grasshopper and used as a food source):– locusts [4]

201 ἀκροατήριον, ***akroatērion***, n. GK: *211* [→ *202*]. audience room (of the procurator), in which hearings were held and justice was privately dispensed:– place of hearing [1]

202 ἀκροατής, ***akroatēs***, n. GK: *212* [→ *201, 1874*]. hearer:– hearers [2], hearer [2]

203 ἀκροβυστία, ***akrobystia***, n. GK: *213* [→ *206*]. uncircumcision, foreskin; fig., not of the Mosaic covenant, a Gentile:– uncircumcision [16], not circumcised [1], uncircumcised (+*1722*) [1], uncircumcised (+*2192*) [1], uncircumcised [1]

204 ἀκρογωνιαῖος, ***akrogōniaios***, a. GK: *214* [→ *206+1137*]. cornerstone, an essential stone in the construction of a building:– chief corner [2]

205 ἀκροθίνιον, ***akrothinion***, n. GK: *215* [→ *206*]. plunder, booty, fine spoils:– spoils [1]

206 ἄκρον, ***akron***, n. GK: *216* [→ *173, 174, 187, 188, 203, 204, 205, 891, 5230*]. end, top:– uttermost part [2], end [1], other[s] [1], tip [1], top [1]

207 Ἀκύλας, ***Akylas***, n.pr. GK: *217*. Aquila, "*eagle*":– Aquila [6]

208 ἀκυρόω, ***akyroō***, v. GK: *218* [→ *1.1+2964*]. to nullify, make void:– disannul [1], made of none effect [1], making of none effect [1]

209 ἀκωλύτως, ***akōlytōs***, adv. GK: *219* [→ *1.1+2967*]. without hinderance:– no forbidding [1]

210 ἄκων, ***akōn***, a. GK: *220* [→ *1.1+1635*]. not voluntary, unwilling:– against will [1]

211 ἀλάβαστρος, ***alabastros***, n. GK: *222 & 223*. alabaster jar; a long-necked flask, the top of which was broken off to empty its contents:– alabaster box [3], box [1]

212 ἀλαζονεία, ***alazoneia***, n. GK: *224* [→ *213, 214*]. boasting, pretension, arrogance:– boastings [1], pride [1]

213 ἀλαζών, ***alazōn***, n. GK: *225* [→ *212*]. boaster, braggart:– boasters [2]

214 ἀλαλάζω, ***alalazō***, v. GK: *226* [→ *212*]. to clang, wail:– tinkling [1], wailed [1]

215 ἀλάλητος, ***alalētos***, a. GK: *227* [→ *1.1+2980*]. inexpressible, unspeakable:– cannot be uttered [1]

216 ἄλαλος, ***alalos***, a. GK: *228* [→ *1.1+2980*]. mute, unable to speak:– dumb [3]

217 ἅλας, ***halas***, n. GK: *221 & 229* [→ *123, 231, 232, 233, 251, 252, 358, 1724, 3882; cf. 2281*]. salt; the impure salt of the ancient could become tasteless in adverse conditions, and its residue useless:– salt [8]

218 ἀλείφω, ***aleiphō***, v. GK: *230* [→ *1813*]. to pour on, anoint (usually with olive oil):– anointed [5], anoint [3], anointing [1]

219 ἀλεκτοροφωνία, ***alektorophōnia***, n. GK: *231* [→ *220+5456*]. crowing of a rooster; the third Roman watch of the night (about midnight to 3:00 a.m.):– cockcrowing [1]

220 ἀλέκτωρ, ***alektōr***, n. GK: *232* [→ *219*]. rooster:– cock [12]

221 Ἀλεξανδρεύς, ***Alexandreus***, n.pr.g. GK: *233* [→ *223*]. Alexandrian, person of Alexandria:– Alexandrians [1], at Alexandria [1]

222 Ἀλεξανδρῖνος, ***Alexandrinos***, a.pr.g. GK: *234* [→ *223*]. Alexandrian, of Alexandria:– Alexandria [2]

223 Ἀλέξανδρος, ***Alexandros***, n.pr. GK: *235* [→ *221, 222*]. Alexander, "*defender of men*":– Alexander [6]

224 ἄλευρον, ***aleuron***, n. GK: *236* [→ *229*]. flour:– meal [2]

225 ἀλήθεια, ***alētheia***, n. GK: *237* [→ *1.1+2990*]. truth, truthfulness; corresponding to reality:– truth [103], of a truth (+*1909*) [3], true [1], truly (+*1909*) [1], truth's [1], verity [1]

226 ἀληθεύω, ***alētheuō***, v. GK: *238* [→ *1.1+2990*]. to be truthful, tell the truth:– speaking the truth [1], tell the truth [1]

227 ἀληθής, ***alēthēs***, a. GK: *239* [→ *1.1+2990*]. true, genuine, reliable, trustworthy, valid:– true [23], truly [1], truth [1]

228 ἀληθινός, ***alēthinos***, a. GK: *240* [→ *1.1+2990*]. true, genuine:– true [27]

229 ἀλήθω, ***alēthō***, v. GK: *241* [→ *224*]. to grind grain (with a handmill operated by two women):– grinding [2]

230 ἀληθῶς, ***alēthōs***, adv. GK: *242* [→ *1.1+2990*]. truly, surely:– indeed [6], of a truth [6], surely [3], truly [2], in truth [1], of a surety [1], verily [1], very [1]

231 ἁλιεύς, ***halieus***, n. GK: *243* [→ *217*]. fisherman (by occupation):– fishers [4], fishermen [1]

232 ἁλιεύω, ***halieuō***, v. GK: *244* [→ *217*]. to catch fish, either by net or by line:– fishing [1]

233 ἁλίζω, ***halizō***, v. GK: *245* [→ *217*]. to salt, make salty:– salted [3]

234 ἀλίσγημα, ***alisgēma***, n. GK: *246*. pollution, ritually defiled:– pollutions [1]

235 ἀλλά, ***alla***, pt.adver. GK: *247* [→ *243*]. but, instead, yet, except:– but [573], yea [15], yet [11], nevertheless [10], howbeit [8], nay [4], therefore [3], and [2], save [2], also (+*2532*) [1], and (+*1065*) [1], howbeit (+*3303*) [1], moreover (+*2532*) [1], not so much as (+*3761*) [1], notwithstanding [1], no [1], than (+*2228*) [1], yet doubtless (+*1065*) [1]

236 ἀλλάσσω, ***allassō***, v. GK: *248* [→ *465, 525, 604, 1259, 2643, 2644, 3337, 3883; cf. 243*]. to change, exchange:– changed [4], change [2]

237 ἀλλαχόθεν, ***allachothen***, adv.pl. GK: *249* [→ *243*]. from another way:– some other way [1]

238 ἀλληγορέω, ***allēgoreō***, v. GK: *251* [→ *243+59*]. to take figuratively, speak allegorically, to employ an analogy or likeness in communication:– allegory [1]

239 ἀλληλουϊά, ***hallēlouia***, l.[v.+n.pr.]. GK: *252*. hallelujah; from Hebrew hallelu-yah, praise Yah(weh):– alleluia [4]

240 ἀλλήλων, ***allēlōn***, p.recip. GK: *253* [→ *243*]. one another, each other:– one another [74], themselves [12], yourselves [3], each other [2], one another's [2], one the other [2], mutual [1], one to the other [1], together (+*3326*) [1], together (+*4314*) [1], yourselves together [1]

241 ἀλλογενής, ***allogenēs***, a. GK: *254* [→ *243+1096*]. foreign:– stranger [1]

242 ἅλλομαι, ***hallomai***, v. GK: *256* [→ *1814, 2177; cf. 4531*]. to jump up, well up, quick movement of both humans and water:– leaped [1], leaping [1], springing up [1]

Grk

243 **ἄλλος**, ***allos***, a.&n. GK: *257* [→ *235, 237, 238, 240, 241, 244, 245, 246, 247, 526; cf. 236*]. another, other:– another [61], other [52], others [29], some [10], one [4], another (+*5100*) [1], moe [1], otherwise [1], some (+*3303*) [1]

244 **ἀλλοτριεπίσκοπος**, ***allotriepiskopos***, n. GK: *258* [→ *243+1909+4648*]. meddler, busybody; formally rendered "one who oversees what belongs to another" (in an unwarranted manner):– busybody in other men's matters [1]

245 **ἀλλότριος**, ***allotrios***, a. GK: *259* [→ *243*]. belonging to another:– another [4], strangers [3], other [2], strange [2], aliens [1], others [1], stranger [1]

246 **ἀλλόφυλος**, ***allophylos***, a. GK: *260* [→ *243+5443*]. Gentile, foreigner:– one of another nation [1]

247 **ἄλλως**, ***allōs***, adv. GK: *261* [→ *243*]. differently:– otherwise [1]

248 **ἀλοάω**, ***aloaō***, v. GK: *262* [→ *257, 3389, 3964*]. to tread, thresh, to separate grain kernels from the husks by beating or treading on:– treadeth out the corn [2], thresheth [1]

249 **ἄλογος**, ***alogos***, a. GK: *263* [→ *1.1+3004*]. unreasonable, without reason, brutish and living by instinct:– brute [2], unreasonable [1]

250 **ἀλόη**, ***aloē***, n. GK: *264*. aloes:– aloes [1]

251 **ἅλς**, ***hals***, n. GK: *265* [→ *217*]. salt:– salt [1]

252 **ἁλυκός**, ***halykos***, a. GK: *266* [→ *217*]. salt spring, salty:– salt [1]

253 **ἄλυπος**, ***alypos***, a. GK: *267* [→ *1.1+3077*]. free from anxiety; in the comparative, less anxiety:– less sorrowful [1]

254 **ἅλυσις**, ***halysis***, n. GK: *268*. chain (the state of imprisonment):– chains [7], chain [3], bonds [1]

255 **ἀλυσιτελής**, ***alysitelēs***, a. GK: *269* [→ *1.1+3089+5056*]. unadvantageous, without special benefit:– unprofitable [1]

256 **Ἀλφαῖος**, ***Halphaios***, n.pr. GK: *271*. Alphaeus:– Alpheus [5]

257 **ἅλων**, ***halōn***, n. GK: *272* [→ *248*]. threshing floor:– floor [2]

258 **ἀλώπηξ**, ***alōpēx***, n. GK: *273*. fox; this can refer to a wicked person with the probable implication of being cunning or treacherous:– foxes [2], fox [1]

259 **ἅλωσις**, ***halōsis***, n. GK: *274* [→ *355, 2654, 4321; cf. 164*]. capture, catch:– taken [1]

260 **ἅμα**, ***hama***, adv.&pp.*. GK: *275* [→ *537, 716; cf. 573*]. together, at the same time:– together [3], withal [3], also (+*2532*) [1], and [1], early in the morning (+*4404*) [1], with [1]

261 **ἀμαθής**, ***amathēs***, a. GK: *276* [→ *1.1+3129*]. ignorant, without a formal education:– unlearned [1]

262 **ἀμαράντινος**, ***amarantinos***, a. GK: *277* [→ *1.1+3133*]. unfading, without loss of pristine character:– fadeth not away [1]

263 **ἀμάραντος**, ***amarantos***, a. GK: *278* [→ *1.1+3133*]. never fading:– fadeth not away [1]

264 **ἁμαρτάνω**, ***hamartanō***, v. GK: *279* [→ *265, 266, 268, 361, 4258*]. to sin, do wrong; usually to do any act contrary to the will and law of God:– sin [16], sinned [15], sinneth [7], trespass [3], faults [1], offended [1]

265 **ἁμάρτημα**, ***hamartēma***, n. GK: *280* [→ *264*]. sin, wrongdoing; usually any act contrary to the will and law of God:– sins [3], sin [1]

266 **ἁμαρτία**, ***hamartia***, n. GK: *281* [→ *264*]. sin, wrongdoing; usually any act contrary to the will and law of God:– sin [94], sins [78], offence [1], sinful [1]

267 **ἀμάρτυρος**, ***amartyros***, a. GK: *282* [→ *1.1+3144*]. without testimony, without witness:– without witness [1]

268 **ἁμαρτωλός**, ***hamartōlos***, a. GK: *283* [→ *264*]. (a.) sinful, as an absolute moral failure; (n.) sinner, one who violates God's will or law; in some contexts, one who does not keep orthodox traditions and behaviors:– sinners [31], sinner [12], sinful [4]

269 **ἄμαχος**, ***amachos***, a. GK: *285* [→ *1.1+3163*]. peaceable, not quarrelsome, without conflict:– no brawlers [1], not a brawler [1]

270 **ἀμάω**, ***amaō***, v. GK: *286*. to mow, cut down:– reaped [1]

271 **ἀμέθυστος**, ***amethystos***, n. GK: *287* [→ *1.3?+3184*]. amethyst, usually purple or violet in color:– amethyst [1]

272 **ἀμελέω**, ***ameleō***, v. GK: *288* [→ *1.1+3199*]. to neglect, ignore:– neglect [2], made light of [1], negligent [1], regarded not [1]

273 **ἄμεμπτος**, ***amemptos***, a. GK: *289* [→ *1.1+3201*]. blameless, faultless:– blameless [3], faultless [1], unblameable [1]

274 **ἀμέμπτως**, ***amemptōs***, adv. GK: *290* [→ *1.1+3201*]. blamelessly:– blameless [1], unblameably [1]

275 **ἀμέριμνος**, ***amerimnos***, a. GK: *291* [→ *1.1+3308*]. free from concern, free from care:– secure (+*4160*) [1], without carefulness [1]

276 **ἀμετάθετος**, ***ametathetos***, a. GK: *292* [→ *1.1+3326+5087*]. unchangeable, unchanging:– immutability [1], immutable [1]

277 **ἀμετακίνητος**, ***ametakinētos***, a. GK: *293* [→ *1.1+3326+2795*]. not moveable, immovable:– unmoveable [1]

278 **ἀμεταμέλητος**, ***ametamelētos***, a. GK: *294* [→ *1.1+3326+3199*]. without regret, so, not revocable:– not repented of [1], without repentance [1]

279 **ἀμετανόητος**, ***ametanoētos***, a. GK: *295* [→ *1.1+3326+3563*]. unrepentant:– impenitent [1]

280 **ἄμετρος**, ***ametros***, a. GK: *296* [→ *1.1+3358*]. beyond limits, immeasurable:– without measure [2]

281 **ἀμήν**, ***amēn***, l.[adv.]. GK: *297*. amen, the truth; a formula of solemn expression of certainty. In the Gospel of John it is doubled in the sayings of Jesus for emphasis:– verily [101], amen [51]

282 **ἀμήτωρ**, ***amētōr***, a. GK: *298* [→ *1.1+3384*]. without a mother:– without mother [1]

283 **ἀμίαντος**, ***amiantos***, a. GK: *299* [→ *1.1+3392*]. pure:– undefiled [4]

284 **Ἀμιναδάβ**, ***Aminadab***, n.pr. GK: *300*. Amminadab, "*my people are generous*":– Aminadab [3]

285 **ἄμμος**, ***ammos***, n. GK: *302*. sand, often used as a figure of things that cannot be counted:– sand [5]

286 **ἀμνός**, ***amnos***, n. GK: *303*. lamb:– lamb [4]

287 **ἀμοιβή**, ***amoibē***, n. GK: *304*. repayment, recompense:– requite (+*591*) [1]

288 **ἄμπελος**, ***ampelos***, n. GK: *306* [→ *289, 290*]. vine, grapevine:– vine [9]

289 **ἀμπελουργός**, ***ampelourgos***, n. GK: *307* [→ *288+2041*]. one who takes care of a vineyard:– dresser of vineyard [1]

290 **ἀμπελών**, ***ampelōn***, n. GK: *308* [→ *288*]. vineyard:– vineyard [23]

291 **Ἀμπλίας**, ***Amplias***, n.pr. GK: *309*. Amplias:– Amplias [1]

292 **ἀμύνομαι**, ***amynomai***, v. GK: *310*. to defend, help, come to the aid of:– defended [1]

293 **ἀμφίβληστρον**, ***amphiblēstron***, n. GK: *312* [→ *906*]. casting net, fishing net (not a dragnet):– net [2]

294 **ἀμφιέννυμι**, ***amphiennymi***, v. GK: *313 & 314* [cf. *2439*]. to dress, clothe:– clothed [2], clothe [2]

295 **Ἀμφίπολις**, ***Amphipolis***, n.pr. GK: *315* [→ *4172*]. Amphipolis, "*a city surrounded* or *a city conspicuous*":– Amphipolis [1]

296 **ἄμφοδον**, ***amphodon***, n. GK: *316* [→ *3598*]. street, usually within a city:– place where two ways met [1]

297 **ἀμφότερος**, ***amphoteros***, a. GK: *317*. both, all:– both [14]

298 **ἀμώμητος**, ***amōmētos***, a. GK: *318* [→ *1.1+3201*]. blameless, unblemished:– blameless [1], without rebuke [1]

299 **ἄμωμος**, ***amōmos***, a. GK: *320* [→ *1.1+3201*]. unblemished, blameless:– without blemish [2], faultless [1], unblameable [1], without blame [1], without fault [1], without spot [1]

300 **Ἀμών**, ***Amōn***, n.pr. GK: *321*. Amon, "*trustworthy*":– Amon [2]

301 **Ἀμώς**, ***Amōs***, n.pr. GK: *322*. Amos, "*burden bearer*":– Amos [1]

302 **ἄν**, ***an***, pt. GK: *323* [→ *1437, 1875, 2579, 3752*]. not easily translated: indicates potential or condition:– whosoever (+*3739*) [32], till (+*2193*) [16], would have [15], would [8], should [7], whatsoever (+*3739*) [7], whatsoever (+*3745*) [6], until (+*2193*) [5], had [4], should have [4], whithersoever (+*3699*) [4], whomsoever (+*3739*) [4], as many as (+*3745*) [3], might [3], soever [3], that (+*3704*) [3], what (+*5101*) [3], whatsoever (+*3739+5100*) [3], whom (+*3739*) [3], whoso (+*3739*) [3], whosoever (+*3739+3956*) [3], whosoever (+*3748*) [3], as (+*5613*) [2], whatsoever (+*302+3739+5100*) [2], when (+*2259*) [2], wheresoever (+*3699*) [2], whosoever (+*3745*) [2], as (+*2530*) [1], as (+*3739+5100*) [1], as oft as (+*3740*) [1], as often as (+*3740*) [1], except (+*1509*) [1], he that (+*3739*) [1], how (+*1063+4459*) [1], howbeit whereinsoever (+*1161+1722+3739*) [1], if [1], may [1], might have [1], once (+*575+3739*) [1], so soon as (+*5613*) [1], soever (+*3739*) [1], that (+*3739*) [1], till (+*891+3739*) [1], whatsoever (+*3748*) [1], when (+*3704*) [1], when (+*5613*) [1], whereunto (+*5101*) [1], wherewith soever (+*3745*) [1], which (+*3748*) [1], which (+*5101*) [1], who

(+5101) [1], would (+2172) [1], wouldest have [1]

303 ἀνά, *ana*, pp. GK: *324* [→ *306, 308, 309, 310, 311, 508, 312, 313, 314, 319, 320, 321, 322, 323, 324, 325, 326, 327, 328, 329, 330, 331, 333, 336, 337, 339, 340, 341, 342, 343, 344, 345, 346, 347, 348, 349, 350, 351, 352, 353, 354, 355, 356, 357, 359, 360, 362, 363, 364, 365, 366, 372, 373, 374, 376, 375, 377, 378, 380, 381, 383, 384, 385, 386, 387, 388, 389, 390, 391, 392, 394, 396, 397, 398, 399, 400, 401, 402, 403, 404, 414, 420, 424, 425, 429, 430, 433, 447, 450, 456, 461, 463, 466, 1815, 1817, 1877, 1878, 1879, 1880, 1881, 1882, 2654, 4320, 4321, 4322, 4323, 4872, 4873, 4874, 4875, cf. 395, 426, 455, 507*]. each, in turn, among:– by [3], apiece [2], every man [2], among (+*3319*) [1], between (+*3319*) [1], by course (+*3313*) [1], in [1], several (+*1520*) [1], through [1]

304 ἀναβαθμός, *anabathmos*, n. GK: *325* [→ *305*]. step; (pl.) a flight of steps:– stairs [2]

305 ἀναβαίνω, *anabainō*, v. GK: *326* [→ *304, 307, 531, 576, 898, 939, 949, 950, 951, 952, 953, 968, 1041, 1224, 1226, 1545, 1684, 1687, 1688, 1910, 1913, 2597, 2600, 2601, 3327, 3845, 3847, 3848, 4260, 4262, 4263, 4264, 4320, 4782, 4819, 4822, 4872, 5233*]. to go up, rise:– went up [23], go up [9], come up [7], ascended up [5], ascended [4], ascend [3], ascending [2], coming up [2], entered [2], going up [2], gone up [2], arise [1], arose [1], ascend up [1], ascendeth up [1], ascendeth [1], ascending up [1], came unto [1], came up [1], came [1], climbed up [1], climbeth up [1], cometh up [1], goeth up [1], grew up [1], groweth up [1], rise up [1], rose up [1], sprang up [1], sprung up [1], went upon [1]

306 ἀναβάλλω, *anaballō*, v. GK: *327* [→ *303+906*]. to adjourn a proceeding (a legal term):– deferred [1]

307 ἀναβιβάζω, *anabibazō*, v. GK: *328* [→ *305*]. to pull up, bring up:– drew [1]

308 ἀναβλέπω, *anablepō*, v. GK: *329* [→ *303+991*]. to look up, receive sight:– received sight [8], receive sight [7], looked up [5], looking up [3], look up [1], looked [1], see [1]

309 ἀνάβλεψις, *anablepsis*, n. GK: *330* [→ *303+991*]. recovery of sight:– recovering of sight [1]

310 ἀναβοάω, *anaboaō*, v. GK: *331* [→ *303+995*]. to cry out:– cried out [1], cried [1], crying aloud [1]

311 ἀναβολή, *anabolē*, n. GK: *332* [→ *303+906*]. delay, postponement:– delay (+*4160*) [1]

312 ἀναγγέλλω, *anangellō*, v. GK: *334* [→ *303+32*]. to tell, report, announce:– shew [4], told [4], declare [2], shewed [2], tell [2], declared [1], rehearsed [1], reported [1], spoken [1]

313 ἀναγεννάω, *anagennaō*, v. GK: *335* [→ *303+1096*]. to give new birth, cause to be born again; used in the sense of spiritual rebirth, similar to being born again/from above:– begotten again [1], born again [1]

314 ἀναγινώσκω, *anaginōskō*, v. GK: *336* [→ *303+1097*]. to read, read aloud:– read [28], readeth [3], readest [2]

315 ἀναγκάζω, *anankazō*, v. GK: *337* [→ *318*]. to compel, force:– compelled [3], constrained [3], compellest [1], compel [1], constrain [1]

316 ἀναγκαῖος, *anankaios*, a. GK: *338* [→ *318*]. necessary, indispensable:– necessary [5], more needful [1], near [1], necessity [1]

317 ἀναγκαστῶς, *anankastōs*, adv. GK: *339* [→ *318*]. a must, by compulsion:– by constraint [1]

318 ἀνάγκη, *anankē*, n. GK: *340* [→ *315, 316, 317, 1876*]. necessity; distress, hardship:– necessity [7], distress [3], must needs [2], necessities [2], necessary [1], needeth (+*2250*) [1], needful (+*2192*) [1], needs [1]

319 ἀναγνωρίζω, *anagnōrizō*, v. GK: *341* [→ *303+1097*]. to tell, make known again:– made known [1]

320 ἀνάγνωσις, *anagnōsis*, n. GK: *342* [→ *303+1097*]. reading, public reading:– reading [3]

321 ἀνάγω, *anagō*, v. GK: *343* [→ *303+71*]. to lead up, bring up; (mid.) to put out to sea:– brought [3], launched [3], departed [2], loosed [2], sailed [2], bring forth [1], bring up again [1], brought again [1], depart [1], launched forth [1], led up [1], led [1], loosing [1], offered [1], sail [1], set forth [1], taking up [1]

322 ἀναδείκνυμι, *anadeiknymi*, v. GK: *344* [→ *303+1166*]. to show, appoint:– appointed [1], shew [1]

323 ἀνάδειξις, *anadeixis*, n. GK: *345* [→ *303+1166*]. public appearance:– shewing [1]

324 ἀναδέχομαι, *anadechomai*, v. GK: *346* [→ *303+1209*]. to receive, welcome:– received [2]

325 ἀναδίδωμι, *anadidōmi*, v. GK: *347* [→ *303+1325*]. to deliver, hand over:– delivered [1]

326 ἀναζάω, *anazaō*, v. GK: *348* [→ *303+2198*]. to become alive again:– alive again [2], revived [2], lived again [1]

327 ἀναζητέω, *anazēteō*, v. GK: *349* [→ *303+2212*]. to look for, search for:– seek [1], sought [1]

328 ἀναζώννυμι, *anazōnnymi*, v. GK: *350* [→ *303+2224*]. to gird (the loins), bind (to prepare for action); used fig. of "girding the loins of the mind" (1Pe 1:13) to prepare mentally for action:– gird up [1]

329 ἀναζωπυρέω, *anazōpyreō*, v. GK: *351* [→ *303+2198+4442*]. to fan a flame, rekindle:– stir up [1]

330 ἀναθάλλω, *anathallō*, v. GK: *352* [→ *303+2337*]. to renew, cause to grow or bloom again:– flourished again [1]

331 ἀνάθεμα, *anathema*, n. GK: *353* [→ *332, 334, 2652, 2653*]. curse, oath; one cursed:– accursed [4], anathema [1], bound under a great curse (+*332*) [1]

332 ἀναθεματίζω, *anathematizō*, v. GK: *354* [→ *331*]. to bind with an oath:– bound under a curse [1], bound under a great curse (+*331*) [1], bound with an oath [1], curse [1]

333 ἀναθεωρέω, *anatheōreō*, v. GK: *355* [→ *303+2334*]. to look carefully at:– beheld [1], considering [1]

334 ἀνάθημα, *anathēma*, n. GK: *356* [→ *331*]. gifts dedicated to God, devoted exclusively to the service of deity:– gifts [1]

335 ἀναίδεια, *anaideia*, n. GK: *357* [→ *1.1+127*]. boldness:– importunity [1]

336 ἀναίρεσις, *anairesis*, n. GK: *358* [→ *303+138*]. death:– death [2]

337 ἀναιρέω, *anaireō*, v. GK: *359* [→ *303+138*]. to kill, put to death; (mid.) take for oneself:– kill [6], killed [4], slain [3], slew [3], put to death [2], slay [2], didst [1], taketh away [1], took up [1]

338 ἀναίτιος, *anaitios*, a. GK: *360* [→ *1.1+156*]. innocent:– blameless [1], guiltless [1]

339 ἀνακαθίζω, *anakathizō*, v. GK: *361* [→ *303+2523*]. to sit up (from a reclining or lying position):– sat up [2]

340 ἀνακαινίζω, *anakainizō*, v. GK: *362* [→ *303+2537*]. to bring back, restore:– renew [1]

341 ἀνακαινόω, *anakainoō*, v. GK: *363* [→ *303+2537*]. to renew:– renewed [2]

342 ἀνακαίνωσις, *anakainōsis*, n. GK: *364* [→ *303+2537*]. renewal:– renewing [2]

343 ἀνακαλύπτω, *anakalyptō*, v. GK: *365* [→ *303+2572*]. to unveil, uncover:– open [1], untaken away (+*3361*) [1]

344 ἀνακάμπτω, *anakamptō*, v. GK: *366* [→ *303+2578*]. to return, come back:– return [2], returned [1], turn again [1]

345 ἀνάκειμαι, *anakeimai*, v. GK: *367* [→ *303+2749*]. to recline for a meal, dine (reclining was the normal posture at meals):– sat at meat [4], guests [2], sitteth at meat [2], leaning [1], lying [1], sat down [1], sat [1], set down [1], table [1]

346 ἀνακεφαλαιόω, *anakephalaioō*, v. GK: *368* [→ *303+2776*]. to bring together under one head, summarize:– briefly comprehended [1], gather together in one [1]

347 ἀνακλίνω, *anaklinō*, v. GK: *369* [→ *303+2827*]. to cause to lie down, recline (to eat):– sit down [3], laid [1], made sit down [1], make sit down to meat [1], make sit down [1], sat down to meat [1]

348 ἀνακόπτω, *anakoptō*, v. GK: *370* [→ *303+2875*]. to hinder, restrain:– hinder [1]

349 ἀνακράζω, *anakrazō*, v. GK: *371* [→ *303+2896*]. to cry out:– cried out [5]

350 ἀνακρίνω, *anakrinō*, v. GK: *373* [→ *303+2919*]. to examine, judge (in both a general and a legal sense):– examined [4], judged [3], asking question [2], judgeth [2], discerned [1], examine [1], examining [1], judge [1], searched [1]

351 ἀνάκρισις, *anakrisis*, n. GK: *374* [→ *303+2919*]. investigation:– examination [1]

352 ἀνακύπτω, *anakyptō*, v. GK: *376* [→ *303+2955*]. to straighten up, stand erect:– lift up [3], look up [1]

353 ἀναλαμβάνω, *analambanō*, v. GK: *377* [→ *303+2983*]. to take up, lift up, bring up:– received up [3], taken up [3], take in [1], take unto [1], take [1], taking [1], took in [1], took up [1], took [1]

354 ἀνάλημψις, *analēmpsis*, n. GK: *378* [→ *303+2983*]. taking up, ascension:– received up [1]

355 ἀναλίσκω, analiskō, v. GK: *379 & 384* [→ *303+259*]. to destroy, consume (with a possible implication of being used up):– consume [2], consumed [1]

356 ἀναλογία, analogia, n. GK: *381* [→ *303+3004*]. proportion, right relationship:– proportion [1]

357 ἀναλογίζομαι, analogizomai, v. GK: *382* [→ *303+3004*]. to consider, think carefully:– consider [1]

358 ἄναλος, analos, a. GK: *383* [→ *1.1+217*]. not salty:– lost saltness [1]

359 ἀνάλυσις, analysis, n. GK: *385* [→ *303+3089*]. departure (death):– departure [1]

360 ἀναλύω, analyō, v. GK: *386* [→ *303+3089*]. to depart (die), return:– depart [1], return [1]

361 ἀναμάρτητος, anamartētos, a. GK: *387* [→ *1.1+264*]. without sin:– without sin [1]

362 ἀναμένω, anamenō, v. GK: *388* [→ *303+3306*]. to wait for, expect:– wait for [1]

363 ἀναμιμνήσκω, anamimnēskō, v. GK: *389* [→ *303+3421*]. to remember, remind:– bring into remembrance [1], called to remembrance [1], called to mind [1], calling to remembrance [1], put in remembrance [1], remembereth [1]

364 ἀνάμνησις, anamnēsis, n. GK: *390* [→ *303+3421*]. reminder, remembrance:– remembrance [4]

365 ἀνανεόομαι, ananeoomai, v. GK: *391* [→ *303+3501*]. to be made new, renewed:– renewed [1]

366 ἀνανήφω, ananēphō, v. GK: *392* [→ *303+3525*]. to come to one's senses:– recover [1]

367 Ἀνανίας, Hananias, n.pr. GK: *393*. Ananias, "*Yahweh is gracious*":– Ananias [11]

368 ἀναντίρρητος, anantirrētos, a. GK: *394* [→ *1.1+473+4487*]. undeniable, indisputable:– cannot be spoken against [1]

369 ἀναντιρρήτως, anantirrētōs, adv. GK: *395* [→ *1.1+473+4487*]. without raising any objection, indisputable:– without gainsaying [1]

370 ἀνάξιος, anaxios, a. GK: *396* [→ *1.1+514*]. not competent, unworthy:– unworthy [1]

371 ἀναξίως, anaxiōs, adv. GK: *397* [→ *1.1+514*]. in an unworthy manner, possibly in a careless manner:– unworthily [2]

372 ἀνάπαυσις, anapausis, n. GK: *398* [→ *303+3973*]. rest, resting place:– rest [4], rest (+*2192*) [1]

373 ἀναπαύω, anapauō, v. GK: *399* [→ *303+3973*]. to rest, be refreshed; (act.) to give rest:– refreshed [3], rest [3], take rest [2], give rest [1], refresh [1], resteth [1], take ease [1]

374 ἀναπείθω, anapeithō, v. GK: *400* [→ *303+3982*]. to persuade, with an implication of inciting resistance:– persuadeth [1]

375 ἀναπέμπω, anapempō, v. GK: *402* [→ *303+3992*]. to send:– sent again [2], sent [2]

376 ἀνάπειρος, anapeiros, a. GK: *401* [→ *303*]. crippled:– maimed [2]

377 ἀναπίπτω, anapiptō, v. GK: *404* [→ *303+4098*]. recline, sit down, lie down (usually referring to the normal posture at meals):– sit down [4], sat down [3], leaned [1], sat down to meat [1], set down [1], sit down to meat [1]

378 ἀναπληρόω, anaplēroō, v. GK: *405* [→ *303+4137*]. to fulfill, make complete:– fill up [1], fulfilled [1], fulfil [1], occupieth [1], supplied [1], supply [1]

379 ἀναπολόγητος, anapologētos, a. GK: *406* [→ *1.1+575+3004*]. without excuse:– inexcusable [1], without excuse [1]

380 ἀναπτύσσω, anaptyssō, v. GK: *408* [→ *303+4428*]. to unroll (a scroll):– opened [1]

381 ἀνάπτω, anaptō, v. GK: *409* [→ *303+681*]. to set on fire:– kindled [2], kindleth [1]

382 ἀναρίθμητος, anarithmētos, a. GK: *410* [→ *1.1+706*]. countless:– innumerable [1]

383 ἀνασείω, anaseiō, v. GK: *411* [→ *303+4579*]. to stir up, incite:– moved [1], stirreth up [1]

384 ἀνασκευάζω, anaskeuazō, v. GK: *412* [→ *303+4632*]. to trouble, upset:– subverting [1]

385 ἀνασπάω, anaspaō, v. GK: *413* [→ *303+4685*]. to pull up, draw out:– drawn up [1], pull out [1]

386 ἀνάστασις, anastasis, n. GK: *414* [→ *303+2476*]. resurrection, rising to life; from the base meaning of the act of rising from a prone or sitting position to a standing position. In the NT it means returning to life after death, usually referring to the raising to life of Jesus Christ:– resurrection [39], raised to life again (+*1537*) [1], rise [1], rising again [1]

387 ἀναστατόω, anastatoō, v. GK: *415* [→ *303+2476*]. to cause trouble, start a revolt:– madest an uproar [1], trouble [1], turned upside down [1]

388 ἀνασταυρόω, anastauroō, v. GK: *416* [→ *303+4716*]. to crucify again:– crucify afresh [1]

389 ἀναστενάζω, anastenazō, v. GK: *417* [→ *303+4728*]. to sigh deeply:– sighed deeply [1]

390 ἀναστρέφω, anastrephō, v. GK: *418* [→ *303+4762*]. to conduct oneself, live (in a certain way); to return:– had conversation [2], live [2], abode [1], behave [1], overthrew [1], pass [1], returned [1], return [1], used [1]

391 ἀναστροφή, anastrophē, n. GK: *419* [→ *303+4762*]. way of life, behavior:– conversation [13]

392 ἀνατάσσομαι, anatassomai, v. GK: *421* [→ *303+5021*]. to draw up (an account), compile:– set forth in order [1]

393 ἀνατέλλω, anatellō, v. GK: *422* [→ *395*]. to rise, dawn:– up [2], arise [1], maketh to rise [1], rise out [1], risen [1], rising [1], sprang [1], sprung up [1]

394 ἀνατίθημι, anatithēmi, v. GK: *423* [→ *303+5087*]. to set before, declare before:– communicated [1], declared [1]

395 ἀνατολή, anatolē, n. GK: *424* [→ *393, 1816, cf. 303*]. east, rising of the sun; note that the east is the compass direction of orientation in the ancient Near East, just as the north is in the modern western world:– east [7], east (+*2246*) [2], dayspring [1]

396 ἀνατρέπω, anatrepō, v. GK: *426* [→ *303+5157*]. to overturn, destroy:– overthrow [1], subvert [1]

397 ἀνατρέφω, anatrephō, v. GK: *427* [→ *303+5142*]. to bring up, care for:– brought up [1], nourished up [1], nourished [1]

398 ἀναφαίνω, anaphainō, v. GK: *428* [→ *303+5316*]. to appear:– appear [1], discovered [1]

399 ἀναφέρω, anapherō, v. GK: *429* [→ *303+5342*]. to lead up, offer (a sacrifice), bear (sin):– offer up [2], bare [1], bear [1], bringeth up [1], carried up [1], leadeth up [1], offered up [1], offered [1], offer [1]

400 ἀναφωνέω, anaphōneō, v. GK: *430* [→ *303+5456*]. to exclaim, cry out loudly:– spake out [1]

401 ἀνάχυσις, anachysis, n. GK: *431* [→ *1632; cf. 303*]. flood, wide stream:– excess [1]

402 ἀναχωρέω, anachōreō, v. GK: *432* [→ *303+5562*]. to withdraw, leave:– departed [8], withdrew [2], give place [1], gone aside [1], turned aside [1], went aside [1]

403 ἀνάψυξις, anapsyxis, n. GK: *433* [→ *303+5594*]. refreshment, relaxation, relief:– refreshing [1]

404 ἀναψύχω, anapsychō, v. GK: *434* [→ *303+5594*]. to refresh, revive:– refreshed [1]

405 ἀνδραποδιστής, andrapodistēs, n. GK: *435* [→ *435+4228*]. slave trader, kidnapper:– menstealers [1]

406 Ἀνδρέας, Andreas, n.pr. GK: *436* [→ *435*]. Andrew, "*manly*":– Andrew [13]

407 ἀνδρίζομαι, andrizomai, v. GK: *437* [→ *435*]. to act courageously:– quit like men [1]

408 Ἀνδρόνικος, Andronikos, n.pr. GK: *438* [→ *435+3529*]. Andronicus, "*victor over men*":– Andronicus [1]

409 ἀνδροφόνος, androphonos, n. GK: *439* [→ *435+5408*]. murderer:– manslayers [1]

410 ἀνέγκλητος, anenklētos, a. GK: *441* [→ *1.1+1722+2564*]. blameless, free from accusation:– blameless [4], unreproveable [1]

411 ἀνεκδιήγητος, anekdiēgētos, a. GK: *442* [→ *1.1+1537+1223+71*]. indescribable, with the associative meanings of marvelous and wonderful:– unspeakable [1]

412 ἀνεκλάλητος, aneklalētos, a. GK: *443* [→ *1.1+1537+2980*]. inexpressible:– unspeakable [1]

413 ἀνέκλειπτος, anekleiptos, a. GK: *444* [→ *1.1+1537+3007*]. not exhaustible, unfailing:– faileth not [1]

414 ἀνεκτός, anektos, a. GK: *445* [→ *303+2192*]. bearable, tolerable; used only in the comparative: more bearable:– more tolerable [6]

415 ἀνελεήμων, aneleēmōn, a. GK: *446* [→ *1.1+1656*]. ruthless, merciless:– unmerciful [1]

416 ἀνεμίζω, anemizō, v. GK: *448* [→ *417*]. to be moved by the wind:– driven with the wind [1]

417 ἄνεμος, anemos, n. GK: *449* [→ *416*]. wind, gale:– wind [20], winds [11]

418 ἀνένδεκτος, anendektos, a. GK: *450* [→ *1.1+1722+1209*]. impossible:– impossible [1]

419 ἀνεξεραύνητος, anexeraunētos, a. GK: *451* [→ *1.1+1537+2045*]. unsearchable, inscrutable:– unsearchable [1]

420 ἀνεξίκακος, ***anexikakos***, a. GK: *452* [→ *303+2192+2556*]. not resentful, patient:– patient [1]

421 ἀνεξιχνίαστος, ***anexichniastos***, a. GK: *453* [→ *1.1+1537+2487*]. unsearchable, incomprehensible:– past finding out [1], unsearchable [1]

422 ἀνεπαίσχυντος, ***anepaischyntos***, a. GK: *454* [→ *1.1+1909+150*]. unashamed:– needeth not to be ashamed [1]

423 ἀνεπίλημπτος, ***anepilēmptos***, a. GK: *455* [→ *1.1+1909+2983*]. above reproach, not open to blame:– blameless [2], unrebukeable [1]

424 ἀνέρχομαι, ***anerchomai***, v. GK: *456* [→ *303+2064*]. to go up:– went up [3]

425 ἄνεσις, ***anesis***, n. GK: *457* [→ *863; cf. 303*]. rest, relaxation, relief:– rest [3], eased [1], liberty [1]

426 ἀνετάζω, ***anetazō***, v. GK: *458* [→ *1833; cf. 303*]. to question, examine, interrogate:– examined [2]

427 ἄνευ, ***aneu***, pp.*. GK: *459*. without, apart from:– without [3]

428 ἀνεύθετος, ***aneuthetos***, a. GK: *460* [→ *1.1+2095+5087*]. unsuitable, poor:– commodious [1]

429 ἀνευρίσκω, ***aneuriskō***, v. GK: *461* [→ *303+2147*]. to find:– finding [1], found [1]

430 ἀνέχομαι, ***anechomai***, v. GK: *462* [→ *303+2192*]. to put up with, endure:– suffer [7], bear with [4], endure [2], forbearing [2]

431 ἀνεψιός, ***anepsios***, n. GK: *463*. cousin:– sister's son [1]

432 ἄνηθον, ***anēthon***, n. GK: *464*. dill, a plant used for seasoning:– anise [1]

433 ἀνήκω, ***anēkō***, v. GK: *465* [→ *303+2240*]. to be fitting, proper; to do one's duty:– convenient [2], fit [1]

434 ἀνήμερος, ***anēmeros***, a. GK: *466* [→ *1.1*]. brutal, savage:– fierce [1]

435 ἀνήρ, ***anēr***, n. GK: *467* [→ *405, 406, 407, 408, 409, 3527, 5220, 5362*]. man, male, husband; usually an adult male, but in some contexts the emphasis is on maturity rather than gender (1Co 13:11; Eph 4:13; Jas 3:2):– men [79], man [75], husband [38], husbands [12], sirs [6], fellows [1], man's [1], murderer (*+5406*) [1]

436 ἀνθίστημι, ***anthistēmi***, v. GK: *468* [→ *473+2476*]. to resist, oppose, rebel, withstand:– resist [7], withstood [4], resisted [1], resisteth [1], withstand [1]

437 ἀνθομολογέομαι, ***anthomologeomai***, v. GK: *469* [→ *473+3670*]. to give thanks, praise:– gave thanks unto [1]

438 ἄνθος, ***anthos***, n. GK: *470*. flower, blossom:– flower [4]

439 ἀνθρακιά, ***anthrakia***, n. GK: *471* [→ *440*]. charcoal fire:– fire of coals [2]

440 ἄνθραξ, ***anthrax***, n. GK: *472* [→ *439*]. coal, charcoal:– coals [1]

441 ἀνθρωπάρεσκος, ***anthrōpareskos***, a. GK: *473* [→ *444+700*]. one who wins favor, who pleases people:– menpleasers [2]

442 ἀνθρώπινος, ***anthrōpinos***, a. GK: *474* [→ *444*]. human, common to mankind:– man's [3], after the manner of men [1], common to man [1], of mankind [1], of man [1]

443 ἀνθρωποκτόνος, ***anthrōpoktonos***, n. GK: *475* [→ *444+615*]. murderer:– murderer [3]

444 ἄνθρωπος, ***anthrōpos***, n. GK: *476* [→ *441, 442, 443, 5363, 5364*]. human being, person; humankind, people; man, husband; used of human beings in contrast to animals or deity; in some contexts it is used of male/husband in contrast to female/wife. "The Son of Man" is an OT phrase usually meaning "human being," that in the NT is used almost exclusively as a messianic title (see Da 7:13), emphasizing Jesus' humanity. "The outer person" is the corporeal body in contrast to "the inner (or hidden) person" of the spirit:– man [346], men [190], man's [10], men's [5], certain [2], Romans (*+4514*) [1], enemy (*+2190*) [1], householder (*+3617*) [1], men (*+3686*) [1], nobleman (*+2104*) [1]

445 ἀνθυπατεύω, ***anthypateuō***, v. GK: *477* [→ *446*]. to be proconsul:– deputy [1]

446 ἀνθύπατος, ***anthypatos***, n. GK: *478* [→ *445; cf. 473*]. proconsul:– deputy [3], deputies [1]

447 ἀνίημι, ***aniēmi***, v. GK: *479* [→ *863; cf. 303*]. loosen, untie; leave, abandon:– loosed [2], forbearing [1], leave [1]

448 ἀνίλεως, ***anileōs***, a. GK: *447 & 480* [→ *1.1+1656*]. merciless:– without mercy [1]

449 ἄνιπτος, ***aniptos***, a. GK: *481* [→ *1.1+3538*]. unwashed:– unwashen [3]

450 ἀνίστημι, ***anistēmi***, v. GK: *482* [→ *303+2476*]. to get up, stand up, come back to life:– arose [23], rise [14], arise [13], rose up [13], raise up [8], rise again [8], stood up [7], rose [5], raised up [4], risen again [4], rise up [2], risen [2], arise up [1], ariseth [1], lift up [1], raised up again [1], raised [1], rising up [1], rising [1], rose again [1], stand up [1], stand [1]

451 Ἄννα, ***Hanna***, n.pr. GK: *483*. Anna, *"grace"*:– Anna [1]

452 Ἄννας, ***Hannas***, n.pr. GK: *484*. Annas, *"grace"*:– Annas [4]

453 ἀνόητος, ***anoētos***, a. GK: *485 & 493* [→ *1.1+3563*]. foolish, senseless:– foolish [4], fools [1], unwise [1]

454 ἄνοια, ***anoia***, n. GK: *486* [→ *1.1+3563*]. folly, senselessness; fury:– folly [1], madness [1]

455 ἀνοίγω, ***anoigō***, v. GK: *487 & 1986* [→ *457, 1272, 455; cf. 303*]. to open:– opened [53], open [21], openeth [3]

456 ἀνοικοδομέω, ***anoikodomeō***, v. GK: *488* [→ *303+3624+1430*]. to rebuild:– build again [2]

457 ἄνοιξις, ***anoixis***, n. GK: *489* [→ *455*]. (the act of) opening:– open [1]

458 ἀνομία, ***anomia***, n. GK: *490* [→ *1.1+3551*]. wickedness, lawlessness, lawless deed:– iniquity [9], iniquities [3], transgresseth law (*+4160*) [1], transgression of law [1], unrighteousness [1]

459 ἄνομος, ***anomos***, a. GK: *491* [→ *1.1+3551*]. without law, transgressing law (by not regarding it); as a noun this can mean a Gentile (without God's covenant law); Paul uses the definite article to speak of "the lawless one" (1Th. 2:8), often considered a title of the antichrist:– without law [4], transgressors [2], wicked [2], lawless [1], unlawful [1]

460 ἀνόμως, ***anomōs***, adv. GK: *492* [→ *1.1+3551*]. apart from law, without law:– without law [2]

461 ἀνορθόω, ***anorthoō***, v. GK: *494* [→ *303+3717*]. to restore, rebuild, strengthen:– lift up [1], made straight [1], set up [1]

462 ἀνόσιος, ***anosios***, a. GK: *495* [→ *1.1+3741*]. unholy, wicked:– unholy [2]

463 ἀνοχή, ***anochē***, n. GK: *496* [→ *303+2192*]. tolerance, forbearance, clemency:– forbearance [2]

464 ἀνταγωνίζομαι, ***antagōnizomai***, v. GK: *497* [→ *473+73*]. to struggle against:– striving [1]

465 ἀντάλλαγμα, ***antallagma***, n. GK: *498* [→ *473+236*]. something given in exchange:– in exchange for [2]

466 ἀνταναπληρόω, ***antanaplēroō***, v. GK: *499* [→ *473+303+4137*]. to fill up, complete:– fill up [1]

467 ἀνταποδίδωμι, ***antapodidōmi***, v. GK: *500* [→ *473+575+1325*]. to repay, return:– recompense [3], recompensed [2], render again [1], repay [1]

468 ἀνταπόδομα, ***antapodoma***, n. GK: *501* [→ *473+575+1325*]. repayment, retribution:– recompence [2]

469 ἀνταπόδοσις, ***antapodosis***, n. GK: *502* [→ *473+575+1325*]. reward, repayment:– reward [1]

470 ἀνταποκρίνομαι, ***antapokrinomai***, v. GK: *503* [→ *473+575+2919*]. to talk back, answer (with implication of contradicting someone):– answer again [1], repliest against [1]

471 ἀντέπω, ***antepō***, v. GK: *515* [→ *473+3004*]. to speak against, talk back, contradict:– gainsay [1], say against [1]

472 ἀντέχω, ***antechō***, v. GK: *504* [→ *473+2192*]. to be devoted, hold firmly to; pay attention to:– hold to [2], holding fast [1], support [1]

473 ἀντί, ***anti***, pp. GK: *505* [→ *368, 369, 436, 437, 464, 465, 466, 467, 468, 469, 470, 471, 472, 474, 475, 476, 477, 478, 479, 480, 481, 482, 483, 484, 485, 486, 487, 488, 489, 492, 493, 494, 495, 496, 497, 498, 499, 500, 503, 528, 529, 1725, 2658, 4876, 4877, 4878, 5221, 5222; cf. 446, 1725*]. in exchange for (often as a sign of benefaction), in place of (often as a sign of contrast), instead of (often as a sign of an exchange of a relationship), one after another (often as a sign of purpose or result). Note that this preposition used in absolute does not mean to be "against" or "in opposition to" something:– for [14], because (*+3739*) [4], for cause [1], for that (*+3588*) [1], in the room of [1], therefore (*+3739*) [1]

474 ἀντιβάλλω, ***antiballō***, v. GK: *506* [→ *473+906*]. to discuss, exchange (words):– have [1]

475 ἀντιδιατίθημι, ***antidiatithēmi***, v. GK: *507* [→ *473+1223+5087*]. to oppose:– oppose themselves [1]

476 ἀντίδικος, ***antidikos***, n. GK: *508* [→ *473+1349*]. enemy, opponent (in battle or in court):– adversary [5]

477 ἀντίθεσις, ***antithesis***, n. GK: *509* [→ *473+5087*]. opposition, objection:– oppositions [1]

478 **ἀντικαθίστημι**, ***antikathistēmi***, v. GK: *510* [→ *473+2596+2476*]. to resist, oppose, contest against:– resisted [1]

479 **ἀντικαλέω**, ***antikaleō***, v. GK: *511* [→ *473+2564*]. to invite in reciprocation:– bid again [1]

480 **ἀντίκειμαι**, ***antikeimai***, v. GK: *512* [→ *473+2749*]. to be an opponent, in conflict:– adversaries [4], contrary [2], adversary [1], opposeth [1]

481 **ἄντικρυς**, ***antikrys***, adv. GK: *513* [→ *473*]. opposite of, in proximity to:– over against [1]

482 **ἀντιλαμβάνω**, ***antilambanō***, v. GK: *514* [→ *473+2983*]. to help, come to the aid of, benefit:– holpen [1], partakers [1], support [1]

483 **ἀντιλέγω**, ***antilegō***, v. GK: *515* [→ *473+3004*]. to speak against, talk back, contradict:– spake against [2], spoken against [2], answering again [1], contradicting [1], deny [1], gainsayers [1], gainsaying [1], speaketh against [1]

484 **ἀντίλημψις**, ***antilēmpsis***, n. GK: *516* [→ *473+2983*]. help, ability to aid:– helps [1]

485 **ἀντιλογία**, ***antilogia***, n. GK: *517* [→ *473+3004*]. argument, opposition, rebellion:– contradiction [2], gainsaying [1], strife [1]

486 **ἀντιλοιδορέω**, ***antiloidoreō***, v. GK: *518* [→ *473+3060*]. to retaliate:– reviled again [1]

487 **ἀντίλυτρον**, ***antilytron***, n. GK: *519* [→ *473+3089*]. ransom; the purchase price to bring liberation from oppression; it is the means to redemption. This refers to Jesus (in person and work) as the price of salvation:– ransom [1]

488 **ἀντιμετρέω**, ***antimetreō***, v. GK: *520* [→ *473+3358*]. to measure in return:– measured again [2]

489 **ἀντιμισθία**, ***antimisthia***, n. GK: *521* [→ *473+3408*]. an exchange; penalty:– recompence [2]

490 **Ἀντιόχεια**, ***Antiocheia***, n.pr. GK: *522* [→ *491*]. Antioch:– Antioch [18]

491 **Ἀντιοχεύς**, ***Antiocheus***, n.pr.g. GK: *523* [→ *490*]. from Antioch:– Antioch [1]

492 **ἀντιπαρέρχομαι**, ***antiparerchomai***, v. GK: *524* [→ *473+3844+2064*]. to pass by on the opposite side:– passed by on the other side [2]

493 **Ἀντιπᾶς**, ***Antipas***, n.pr. GK: *525* [→ *473+3962*]. Antipas:– Antipas [1]

494 **Ἀντιπατρίς**, ***Antipatris***, n.pr. GK: *526* [→ *473+3962*]. Antipatris:– Antipatris [1]

495 **ἀντιπέρα**, ***antipera***, adv. GK: *527* [→ *473+4008*]. across from, opposite of:– over against [1]

496 **ἀντιπίπτω**, ***antipiptō***, v. GK: *528* [→ *473+4098*]. to resist, oppose:– resist [1]

497 **ἀντιστρατεύομαι**, ***antistrateuomai***, v. GK: *529* [→ *473+4756*]. to wage war against:– warring against [1]

498 **ἀντιτάσσω**, ***antitassō***, v. GK: *530* [→ *473+5021*]. to oppose, rebel, resist:– resisteth [3], opposed [1], resist [1]

499 **ἀντίτυπος**, ***antitypos***, a. GK: *531* [→ *473+5180*]. copy, representation:– figures [1], like figure [1]

500 **ἀντίχριστος**, ***antichristos***, n. GK: *532* [→ *473+5547*]. antichrist:– antichrist [4], antichrists [1]

501 **ἀντλέω**, ***antleō***, v. GK: *533* [→ *502*]. to draw (water):– draw [2], draw out [1], drew [1]

502 **ἄντλημα**, ***antlēma***, n. GK: *534* [→ *501*]. container to draw water with:– draw with [1]

503 **ἀντοφθαλμέω**, ***antophthalmeō***, v. GK: *535* [→ *473+3788*]. to head into, face (the wind):– bear up into [1]

504 **ἄνυδρος**, ***anydros***, a. GK: *536* [→ *1.1+5204*]. arid, without water:– dry [2], without water [2]

505 **ἀνυπόκριτος**, ***anypokritos***, a. GK: *537* [→ *1.1+5259+2919*]. sincere, genuine, without hypocrisy; of good character, lacking pretense and prideful show:– unfeigned [4], without dissimulation [1], without hypocrisy [1]

506 **ἀνυπότακτος**, ***anypotaktos***, a. GK: *538* [→ *1.1+5259+5021*]. rebellious, disobedient; not made subject to, independent:– unruly [2], disobedient [1], not put under [1]

507 **ἄνω**, ***anō***, adv.pl. GK: *539* [→ *509, 510, 511, 1274, 1883, 5231; cf. 303*]. above, upward, heavenward, top:– above [5], up [2], high [1], the brim [1]

508 **ἀνάγαιον**, ***anagaion***, n. GK: *333* [→ *303+1093*]. upper room:– upper room [2]

509 **ἄνωθεν**, ***anōthen***, adv.pl. GK: *540* [→ *507*]. from above; from the beginning; again, anew:– from above [5], again [3], top [3], from beginning [1], from the very first [1]

510 **ἀνωτερικός**, ***anōterikos***, a. GK: *541* [→ *507*]. interior, upper (regions):– upper [1]

511 **ἀνώτερος**, ***anōteros***, a. GK: *542* [→ *507*]. higher, better in social standing; earlier, previously, first:– above [1], higher [1]

512 **ἀνωφελής**, ***anōphelēs***, a. GK: *543* [→ *1.1+5623*]. unprofitable, useless:– unprofitableness [1], unprofitable [1]

513 **ἀξίνη**, ***axinē***, n. GK: *544* [→ *2608*]. ax:– axe [2]

514 **ἄξιος**, ***axios***, a. GK: *545* [→ *370, 371, 515, 516, 2661; cf. 71*]. worthy, deserving, in keeping with, corresponding to:– worthy [35], meet for [2], meet [2], due reward [1], unworthy (+*3756*) [1]

515 **ἀξιόω**, ***axioō***, v. GK: *546* [→ *514*]. to consider worthy, consider wise or fitting:– counted worthy [2], thought worthy [2], count worthy [1], desire [1], thought good [1]

516 **ἀξίως**, ***axiōs***, adv. GK: *547* [→ *514*]. in a worthy manner, suitably:– worthy [3], becometh [2], after a sort [1]

517 **ἀόρατος**, ***aoratos***, a. GK: *548* [→ *1.1+3708*]. invisible, not seen:– invisible [5]

518 **ἀπαγγέλλω**, ***apangellō***, v. GK: *33 & 550* [→ *575+32*]. to tell, report, proclaim, announce, bring news, be a messenger:– told [19], shewed [6], tell [6], shew [4], declare [2], bring word again [1], bring word [1], declared [1], reported [1], report [1], shew again [1], told how [1]

519 **ἀπάγχω**, ***apanchō***, v. GK: *551*. to hang (oneself):– hanged [1]

520 **ἀπάγω**, ***apagō***, v. GK: *552* [→ *575+71*]. to lead away, bring before (an official):– led away [8], lead away [2], leadeth [2], bring [1], carried away [1], put to death [1], took away [1]

521 **ἀπαίδευτος**, ***apaideutos***, a. GK: *553* [→ *1.1+3816*]. stupid, uneducated:– unlearned [1]

522 **ἀπαίρω**, ***apairō***, v. GK: *554* [→ *575+142*]. to take away:– taken away [2], taken from [1]

523 **ἀπαιτέω**, ***apaiteō***, v. GK: *555* [→ *575+154*]. to demand back:– ask again [1], required [1]

524 **ἀπαλγέω**, ***apalgeō***, v. GK: *556*. to lose all sensitivity, become callous:– past feeling [1]

525 **ἀπαλλάσσω**, ***apallassō***, v. GK: *557* [→ *575+236*]. (act.) to set free, release; (pass.) to be reconciled, come to a settlement (in court); to be cured:– delivered [1], deliver [1], departed [1]

526 **ἀπαλλοτριόω**, ***apallotrioō***, v. GK: *558* [→ *575+243*]. to be excluded, separated, alienated:– alienated [2], aliens [1]

527 **ἁπαλός**, ***hapalos***, a. GK: *559*. tender (referring to sprouts):– tender [2]

528 **ἀπαντάω**, ***apantaō***, v. GK: *560* [→ *575+473*]. to meet, encounter:– met [5], meet [2]

529 **ἀπάντησις**, ***apantēsis***, n. GK: *561* [→ *575+473*]. (the act of) meeting, encountering:– meet [4]

530 **ἅπαξ**, ***hapax***, adv. GK: *562* [→ *2178*]. once, once more, once for all; the Greek idiom “once and yet twice” means to do something repeatedly, “again and again” (Php 4:16):– once [15]

531 **ἀπαράβατος**, ***aparabatos***, a. GK: *563* [→ *1.1+3844+305*]. permanent, unchangeable:– unchangeable [1]

532 **ἀπαρασκεύαστος**, ***aparaskeuastos***, a. GK: *564* [→ *1.1+3844+4632*]. unprepared, unready:– unprepared [1]

533 **ἀπαρνέομαι**, ***aparneomai***, v. GK: *565* [→ *575+720*]. to disown, deny, repudiate:– deny [11], denied [2]

534 **ἀπάρτι**, ***aparti***, adv. [pp.+adv.]. GK: *567* [→ *575+737*]. from now on, again:– henceforth [1]

535 **ἀπαρτισμός**, ***apartismos***, n. GK: *568* [→ *575+737*]. completion, finishing:– finish [1]

536 **ἀπαρχή**, ***aparchē***, n. GK: *569* [→ *575+757*]. firstfruits, the first of any crop or livestock offered to God before the rest could be used:– firstfruits [7], firstfruit [1]

537 **ἅπας**, ***hapas***, a. GK: *570* [→ *260+3956*]. all, every, whole:– all [39], whole [3], every one [1], every [1]

538 **ἀπατάω**, ***apataō***, v. GK: *572* [→ *539*]. to deceive, cheat, trick:– deceived [2], deceiveth [1], deceive [1]

539 **ἀπάτη**, ***apatē***, n. GK: *573* [→ *538, 1818, 5422, 5423*]. deception, deceitfulness:– deceitfulness [3], deceitful [1], deceit [1], deceivableness [1], deceivings [1]

540 **ἀπάτωρ**, ***apatōr***, a. GK: *574* [→ *1.1+3962*]. fatherless:– without father [1]

541 **ἀπαύγασμα**, ***apaugasma***, n. GK: *575* [→ *575+827*]. radiance, brilliance:– brightness [1]

542 **ἀπείδω**, ***apeidō***, v. GK: *927* [→ *575+3708*]. to fix one’s eyes; look away:– see [1]

543 **ἀπείθεια**, ***apeitheia***, n. GK: *577* [→ *1.1+3982*]. disobedience:– unbelief [4], disobedience [3]

544 ἀπειθέω, ***apeitheō***, v. GK: *578* [→ *1.1+3982*]. to disobey, be disobedient:– believed not [4], disobedient [4], not believed [2], obey not [2], believeth not [1], not believe [1], not obey [1], unbelieving [1]

545 ἀπειθής, ***apeithēs***, a. GK: *579* [→ *1.1+3982*]. disobedient:– disobedient [6]

546 ἀπειλέω, ***apeileō***, v. GK: *580* [→ *547*]. to threaten, warn:– straitly threaten [1], threatened [1]

547 ἀπειλή, ***apeilē***, n. GK: *581* [→ *546, 4324*]. threat:– threatenings [2], threatening [1]

548 ἄπειμι[1], ***apeimi***[1], v. GK: *582* [→ *575+1510*]. to be absent:– absent [7]

549 ἄπειμι[2], ***apeimi***[2], v. GK: *583* [→ *575*]. to go away:– went [1]

550 ἀπεῖπον, ***apeipon***, v. GK: *584* [→ *575+3004*]. to renounce, disown:– renounced [1]

551 ἀπείραστος, ***apeirastos***, a. GK: *585* [→ *1.1+3984*]. incapable of being tempted, without temptation:– cannot be tempted (*+1510*) [1]

552 ἄπειρος, ***apeiros***, a. GK: *586* [→ *1.1+3984*]. not acquainted with:– unskilful [1]

553 ἀπεκδέχομαι, ***apekdechomai***, v. GK: *587* [→ *575+1537+1209*]. wait eagerly for:– look for [2], wait for [2], waiting for [2], waiteth for [1]

554 ἀπεκδύομαι, ***apekdyomai***, v. GK: *588* [→ *575+1537+1416*]. to take off, disarm:– put off [1], spoiled [1]

555 ἀπέκδυσις, ***apekdysis***, n. GK: *589* [→ *575+1537+1416*]. removal, putting off:– putting off [1]

556 ἀπελαύνω, ***apelaunō***, v. GK: *590* [→ *575+1643*]. to eject from (court), drive away:– drave [1]

557 ἀπελεγμός, ***apelegmos***, n. GK: *591* [→ *575+1651*]. disrepute, discredit:– nought [1]

558 ἀπελεύθερος, ***apeleutheros***, n. GK: *592* [→ *575+1658*]. freedman, one no longer a slave:– freeman [1]

559 Ἀπελλῆς, ***Apellēs***, n.pr. GK: *593*. Apelles:– Apelles [1]

560 ἀπελπίζω, ***apelpizō***, v. GK: *594* [→ *575+1680*]. to expect nothing in return:– hoping for again [1]

561 ἀπέναντι, ***apenanti***, pp.*. GK: *595* [→ *575+1725*]. opposite, in front of, against (opposition to):– before [2], over against [2], contrary [1], in the presence [1]

ἀπέπω, *apepō*. See **550**.

562 ἀπέραντος, ***aperantos***, a. GK: *596* [→ *1.1+4008*]. endless, unlimited:– endless [1]

563 ἀπερισπάστως, ***aperispastōs***, adv. GK: *597* [→ *1.1+4012+4685*]. undivided, without distraction:– without distraction [1]

564 ἀπερίτμητος, ***aperitmētos***, a. GK: *598* [→ *1.1+4012+5114*]. uncircumcised (with a possible implication of being stubborn and obstinate):– uncircumcised [1]

565 ἀπέρχομαι, ***aperchomai***, v. GK: *599* [→ *575+2064*]. to go away, withdraw:– went [45], departed [23], go [17], went away [7], go away [4], come [3], depart [3], gone away [3], goest [2], past [2], came [1], depart out [1], go after [1], go aside [1], go out [1], goeth way [1], going [1], gone [1], passed away [1], went back (*+1519+3588+3694*) [1], went way [1]

566 ἀπέχει, ***apechei***, v.3.s. of *568*. GK: *600* [→ *575+2192*]. to receive (in full), have enough:–

567 ἀπέχομαι, ***apechomai***, v.mid. of *568*. GK: *600* [→ *575+2192*]. to abstain, avoid:–

568 ἀπέχω, ***apechō***, v. GK: *600* [→ *575+2192*]. to receive (in full); to be distant; (mid.) to abstain, avoid:– have [4], abstain from [3], abstain [3], from [3], enough [1], is from [1], off [1], received [1], receive [1]

569 ἀπιστέω, ***apisteō***, v. GK: *601* [→ *1.1+4103*]. to disbelieve, be faithless, unfaithful. In some contexts unbelief has no implication of faithlessness or hardheartedness (Lk 24:11); in other contexts unbelief is a moral failure, not acting like a true follower (2Ti 2:13):– believed not [4], believe not [1], believeth not [1], not believe [1]

570 ἀπιστία, ***apistia***, n. GK: *602* [→ *1.1+4103*]. unbelief, lack of faith (often with the implication of stubbornly refusing to believe or act in accord with God's will or law):– unbelief [12]

571 ἄπιστος, ***apistos***, a. GK: *603* [→ *1.1+4103*]. unbelieving, lacking in trust, doubting; as a noun: an unbeliever or outsider, one who does not believe the Gospel:– unbelieving [5], believe not [4], faithless [4], unbelievers [4], believeth not [3], infidel [2], incredible [1]

572 ἁπλότης, ***haplotēs***, n. GK: *605* [→ *573*]. Formally "the quality of singleness," translated "generosity," the state of giving things in a manner that shows liberality; "sincerity," the moral quality of honesty expressing singleness of purpose or motivation:– simplicity [3], singleness [2], bountifulness [1], liberality [1], liberal [1]

573 ἁπλοῦς, ***haplous***, a. GK: *606* [→ *572, 574; cf. 260*]. good in the sense of healthy, formally, "singleness." Some think "a good eye" means to be generous and liberal in giving.:– single [2]

574 ἁπλῶς, ***haplōs***, adv. GK: *607* [→ *573*]. generously, without reserve:– liberally [1]

575 ἀπό, ***apo***, pp. GK: *608* [→ *379, 467, 468, 469, 470, 518, 520, 522, 523, 525, 526, 528, 529, 533, 534, 535, 536, 541, 542, 548, 549, 550, 553, 554, 555, 556, 557, 558, 560, 561, 565, 566, 567, 568, 576, 577, 578, 579, 580, 581, 582, 583, 584, 585, 586, 587, 588, 589, 590, 591, 592, 593, 594, 595, 596, 597, 598, 599, 600, 601, 602, 603, 604, 605, 606, 607, 608, 609, 610, 611, 612, 613, 614, 616, 617, 618, 619, 620, 621, 622, 623, 626, 627, 628, 629, 630, 631, 632, 633, 634, 635, 636, 637, 638, 641, 642, 643, 644, 645, 646, 647, 648, 649, 650, 653, 654, 655, 656, 657, 658, 659, 660, 661, 662, 663, 664, 665, 666, 667, 668, 669, 670, 671, 672, 673, 674, 684, 851, 856, 864, 867, 868, 871, 872, 873, 874, 879, 3405, 3406, 4217, 4879, 4880, 4881; cf. 683, 863*]. from, away from; by means of; out of; against:– from [386], of [149], out of [25], for [10], at [9], by [9], off [6], afar off (*+3113*) [5], on [5], since [5], in [4], since (*+3739*) [4], with [4], from among [3], a year ago (*+4070*) [2], before [2], henceforth (*+737*) [2], hereafter (*+737*) [2], since began [2], a good while ago (*+744+2250*) [1], ago [1], away from [1], away [1], because of [1], forsake (*+646*) [1], from beginning [1], henceforth (*+3568+3588*) [1], hereafter (*+3568+3588*) [1], in that [1], now (*+737*) [1], once (*+302+3739*) [1], out [1], since the time (*+3739*) [1], somewhat (*+3313*) [1], some [1], space of [1], that (*+3739*) [1], upon [1]

576 ἀποβαίνω, ***apobainō***, v. GK: *609* [→ *575+305*]. to leave, get out; to result in, turn to, lead to:– come [1], gone out [1], turn to [1], turn [1]

577 ἀποβάλλω, ***apoballō***, v. GK: *610* [→ *575+906*]. to throw away:– cast away [1], casting away [1]

578 ἀποβλέπω, ***apoblepō***, v. GK: *611* [→ *575+991*]. to look ahead, pay attention:– respect [1]

579 ἀπόβλητος, ***apoblētos***, a. GK: *612* [→ *575+906*]. rejected (as unclean):– refused [1]

580 ἀποβολή, ***apobolē***, n. GK: *613* [→ *575+906*]. rejection; loss:– casting away [1], loss [1]

581 ἀπογίνομαι, ***apoginomai***, v. GK: *614* [→ *575+1096*]. to die:– dead [1]

582 ἀπογραφή, ***apographē***, n. GK: *615* [→ *575+1125*]. census, registration:– taxing [2]

583 ἀπογράφω, ***apographō***, v. GK: *616* [→ *575+1125*]. to take a census, register, record:– taxed [3], written [1]

584 ἀποδείκνυμι, ***apodeiknymi***, v. GK: *617* [→ *575+1166*]. to display, exhibit, proclaim; prove, accredit, attest:– approved [1], prove [1], set forth [1], shewing [1]

585 ἀπόδειξις, ***apodeixis***, n. GK: *618* [→ *575+1166*]. demonstration, proof:– demonstration [1]

586 ἀποδεκατόω, ***apodekatoō***, v. GK: *619 & 620* [→ *575+1176*]. to give a tenth, tithe; collect a tithe:– give tithes [1], pay tithe of [1], take tithes [1], tithe [1]

587 ἀπόδεκτος, ***apodektos***, a. GK: *621* [→ *575+1209*]. pleasing, pleasant:– acceptable [2]

588 ἀποδέχομαι, ***apodechomai***, v. GK: *622* [→ *575+1209*]. to welcome, accept, receive; acknowledge, acclaim:– received [3], accept [1], gladly received [1], receive [1]

589 ἀποδημέω, ***apodēmeō***, v. GK: *623* [→ *575+1218*]. to go away on a journey:– went into a far country [3], took journey [2], travelling into a far country [1]

590 ἀπόδημος, ***apodēmos***, a. GK: *624* [→ *575+1218*]. going away on a journey:– taking a far journey [1]

591 ἀποδίδωμι, ***apodidōmi***, v. GK: *625* [→ *575+1325*]. give, give away; pay, pay back:– give [8], render [8], pay [7], reward [6], sold [3], paid [2], delivered again [1], delivered [1], gave again [1], gave [1], payment made [1], perform [1], recompense [1], rendering [1], repay [1], requite (*+287*) [1], restore [1], rewarded [1], yielded [1], yieldeth [1]

592 ἀποδιορίζω, ***apodiorizō***, v. GK: *626* [→ *575+1223+3724*]. to divide, separate, cause a division:– separate [1]

593 ἀποδοκιμάζω, ***apodokimazō***, v. GK: *627* [→ *575+1209*]. to reject:– rejected [7], disallowed [2]

594 ἀποδοχή, ***apodochē***, n. GK: *628* [→ *575+1209*]. acceptance, approval:– acceptation [2]

595 ἀπόθεσις, ***apothesis***, n. GK: *629* [→ *575+5087*]. removal, putting aside, getting rid of; this can be a euphemism for death (2Pe 1:14):– put off [1], putting away [1]

596 ἀποθήκη, ***apothēkē***, n. GK: *630* [→ *575+2344*]. barn, storehouse:– barns [2], barn [2], garner [2]

597 ἀποθησαυρίζω, ***apothēsaurizō***, v. GK: *631* [→ *575+2344*]. to store up treasure:– laying up in store [1]

598 ἀποθλίβω, ***apothlibō***, v. GK: *632* [→ *575+2346*]. to press against, crowd up to:– press [1]

599 ἀποθνῄσκω, ***apothnēskō***, v. GK: *633* [→ *575+2348*]. to die (in a literal or fig. sense); to be about to die, be mortal:– die [41], died [32], dead [29], dying [4], dieth [2], death [1], perished [1], slain (+*5408*) [1]

600 ἀποκαθίστημι, ***apokathistēmi***, v. GK: *634 & 635* [→ *575+2596+2476*]. to (completely) restore, reestablish, cure:– restored [5], restore again [1], restoreth [1], restore [1]

601 ἀποκαλύπτω, ***apokalyptō***, v. GK: *636* [→ *575+2572*]. to reveal, disclose:– revealed [22], reveal [4]

602 ἀποκάλυψις, ***apokalypsis***, n. GK: *637* [→ *575+2572*]. revelation, what is revealed, disclosure, to make information known with an implication that the information can be understood. This refers in the NT to God making information known, especially to his close associates:– revelation [10], revealed [2], revelations [2], appearing [1], coming [1], lighten [1], manifestation [1]

603 ἀποκαραδοκία, ***apokaradokia***, n. GK: *638 & 2839* [→ *575+2898+1380*]. eager expectation:– earnest expectation [2]

604 ἀποκαταλλάσσω, ***apokatallassō***, v. GK: *639* [→ *575+2596+236*]. to reconcile, reunite:– reconcile [2], reconciled [1]

605 ἀποκατάστασις, ***apokatastasis***, n. GK: *640* [→ *575+2596+2476*]. restoration:– restitution [1]

606 ἀπόκειμαι, ***apokeimai***, v. GK: *641* [→ *575+2749*]. to be stored up, destined:– laid up [3], appointed [1]

607 ἀποκεφαλίζω, ***apokephalizō***, v. GK: *642* [→ *575+2776*]. to behead:– beheaded [4]

608 ἀποκλείω, ***apokleiō***, v. GK: *643* [→ *575+2808*]. to close:– shut to [1]

609 ἀποκόπτω, ***apokoptō***, v. GK: *644* [→ *575+2875*]. to cut off; emasculate:– cut off [6]

610 ἀπόκριμα, ***apokrima***, n. GK: *645* [→ *575+2919*]. sentence, verdict:– sentence [1]

611 ἀποκρίνομαι, ***apokrinomai***, v. GK: *646* [→ *575+2919*]. to answer, reply; sometimes used in the NT in the Hebraic sense of continuing a discourse:– answered [201], answering [29], answer [12], answerest [4], answereth [4]

612 ἀπόκρισις, ***apokrisis***, n. GK: *647* [→ *575+2919*]. answer:– answer [3], answers [1]

613 ἀποκρύπτω, ***apokryptō***, v. GK: *648* [→ *575+2928*]. to hide, conceal:– hid [3], hid from [2], hidden [1]

614 ἀπόκρυφος, ***apokryphos***, a. GK: *649* [→ *575+2928*]. concealed, hidden, secret:– hid [2], kept secret [1]

615 ἀποκτείνω, ***apokteinō***, v. GK: *650 & 651* [→ *443*]. to kill (either natural life or spiritual life):– kill [28], killed [21], slain [7], put to death [6], slew [4], killeth [3], slay [3], killest [2], killing [1]

616 ἀποκυέω, ***apokyeō***, v. GK: *652* [→ *575+2949*]. to give birth to, bring into being:– begat [1], bringeth forth [1]

617 ἀποκυλίω, ***apokyliō***, v. GK: *375 & 653* [→ *575+2947*]. to roll away, roll back:– rolled away [2], roll away [1], rolled back [1]

618 ἀπολαμβάνω, ***apolambanō***, v. GK: *655* [→ *575+2983*]. to receive, be repaid:– receive [7], receive again [1], receivedst [1], received [1], receiving [1], took [1]

619 ἀπόλαυσις, ***apolausis***, n. GK: *656* [→ *575*]. enjoyment, pleasure:– enjoy [1], pleasures [1]

620 ἀπολείπω, ***apoleipō***, v. GK: *657* [→ *575+3007*]. to leave behind:– left [3], remaineth [3]

621 ἀπολείχω, ***apoleichō***, v. GK: *658 & 2143 & 3314 & 4336* [→ *575*]. lick, lick off:– licked [1]

622 ἀπόλλυμι, ***apollymi***, v. GK: *660* [→ *575+3639*]. to destroy (an inanimate object), to kill (by taking a life), cause to lose (especially a life); to die or perish. Violence and strife is often the associative meaning related to this word:– perish [25], destroy [19], lose [17], lost [13], destroyed [7], perished [5], perisheth [3], die [1], loseth [1], marred [1]

623 Ἀπολλύων, ***Apollyōn***, n.pr. GK: *661* [→ *575+3639*]. Apollyon, *"destroyer"*:– Apollyon [1]

624 Ἀπολλωνία, ***Apollōnia***, n.pr. GK: *662* [→ *625*]. Apollonia:– Apollonia [1]

625 Ἀπολλῶς, ***Apollōs***, n.pr. GK: *663* [→ *624*]. Apollos:– Apollos [10]

626 ἀπολογέομαι, ***apologeomai***, v. GK: *664* [→ *575+3004*]. to defend oneself, speak in one's own behalf:– answer [3], answer for [1], answered for himself [1], answered for [1], excuse ourselves [1], excusing [1], made defence [1], spake for [1]

627 ἀπολογία, ***apologia***, n. GK: *665* [→ *575+3004*]. defense; answer or reply (of reason or accounting):– answer [3], defence [3], answer for [1], clearing [1]

628 ἀπολούω, ***apolouō***, v. GK: *666* [→ *575+3068*]. to wash away:– wash away [1], washed [1]

629 ἀπολύτρωσις, ***apolytrōsis***, n. GK: *667* [→ *575+3089*]. redemption, ransom, release:– redemption [9], deliverance [1]

630 ἀπολύω, ***apolyō***, v. GK: *668* [→ *575+3089*]. to release (forgive, grant clemency); divorce, send away:– let go [13], put away [13], release [13], sent away [7], send away [6], released [4], dismissed [2], loosed [2], set at liberty [2], departed [1], depart [1], divorced [1], forgiven [1], forgive [1], let depart [1], putteth away [1]

631 ἀπομάσσω, ***apomassō***, v. GK: *669* [→ *575+3146*]. to wipe off (this refers to an action of protest):– wipe off against [1]

632 ἀπονέμω, ***aponemō***, v. GK: *671* [→ *575+3551*]. to treat with, show, pay (respect):– giving [1]

633 ἀπονίπτω, ***aponiptō***, v. GK: *672* [→ *575+3538*]. to wash off:– washed [1]

634 ἀποπίπτω, ***apopiptō***, v. GK: *674* [→ *575+4098*]. to fall away, drop off:– fell [1]

635 ἀποπλανάω, ***apoplanaō***, v. GK: *675* [→ *575+4106*]. to deceive, mislead; (pass.) to wander:– erred [1], seduce [1]

636 ἀποπλέω, ***apopleō***, v. GK: *676* [→ *575+4126*]. to sail away from:– sailed [3], sail [1]

637 ἀποπλύνω, ***apoplynō***, v. GK: *677* [→ *575+4150*]. to wash off, wash out:– washing [1]

638 ἀποπνίγω, ***apopnigō***, v. GK: *678* [→ *575+4155*]. to choke, smother; (pass.) to be drowned, choked (with water):– choked [3]

639 ἀπορέω, ***aporeō***, v. GK: *679* [→ *1.1+4198*]. to be puzzled, at a loss, in wonder:– doubted [1], doubting [1], perplexed [1], stand in doubt [1]

640 ἀπορία, ***aporia***, n. GK: *680* [→ *1.1+4198*]. perplexity, consternation:– perplexity [1]

641 ἀπορίπτω, ***aporiptō***, v. GK: *681* [→ *575+4496*]. to jump into, throw oneself into:– cast [1]

642 ἀπορφανίζω, ***aporphanizō***, v. GK: *682* [→ *575+3737*]. to make an orphan of:– taken [1]

643 ἀποσκευάζω, ***aposkeuazō***, v. GK: *683 & 2171* [→ *575+4632*]. to pack up, get ready, make preparations:– took up carriages [1]

644 ἀποσκίασμα, ***aposkiasma***, n. GK: *684* [→ *575+4639*]. shadow:– shadow [1]

645 ἀποσπάω, ***apospaō***, v. GK: *685* [→ *575+4685*]. to draw out, draw away, attract; (pass.) to withdraw:– draw away [1], drew [1], gotten from [1], withdrawn [1]

646 ἀποστασία, ***apostasia***, n. GK: *686* [→ *575+2476*]. turning away, rebellion, abandonment, apostasy:– falling away [1], forsake (+*575*) [1]

647 ἀποστάσιον, ***apostasion***, n. GK: *687* [→ *575+2476*]. divorce:– divorcement [2], writing of divorcement [1]

648 ἀποστεγάζω, ***apostegazō***, v. GK: *689* [→ *575+4722*]. to make an opening in a roof, remove a roof:– uncovered [1]

649 ἀποστέλλω, ***apostellō***, v. GK: *690* [→ *651, 652, 1821, 4882, 5570*]. to send, send out, send away (especially used of the official sending out of the disciples):– sent [92], send [17], sent forth [8], send forth [5], sent away [3], sendeth forth [2], sent out [2], putteth in [1], send away [1], sendeth [1], set [1]

650 ἀποστερέω, ***apostereō***, v. GK: *691 & 935* [→ *575*]. to defraud, cheat, steal; deprive, deny, withhold, keep back:– defraud [3], defrauded [1], destitute [1], kept back by fraud [1]

651 ἀποστολή, ***apostolē***, n. GK: *692* [→ *649*]. apostleship, ministry / office of an apostle:– apostleship [4]

652 ἀπόστολος, ***apostolos***, n. GK: *693* [→ *649*]. apostle, representative, messenger, envoy; often used in a technical sense for the divinely appointed founders of the church:–

apostles [54], apostle [19], apostles' [5], he that is sent [1], messengers [1], messenger [1]

653 ἀποστοματίζω, **apostomatizō**, v. GK: *694* [→ *575+4750*]. to besiege with questions, interrogate closely:– provoke to speak [1]

654 ἀποστρέφω, **apostrephō**, v. GK: *695* [→ *575+4762*]. to turn away from, rebel, mislead; to desert, reject; to return, put back:– turn away [3], brought again [1], perverteth [1], put up again [1], turn away from [1], turn from [1], turned away from [1], turning away [1]

655 ἀποστυγέω, **apostygeō**, v. GK: *696* [→ *575+4767*]. to hate, abhor, loathe:– Abhor [1]

656 ἀποσυνάγωγος, **aposynagōgos**, a. GK: *697* [→ *575+4864*]. put out of the synagogue, excommunicated:– put out of the synagogue [2], out of the synagogues [1]

657 ἀποτάσσω, **apotassō**, v. GK: *698* [→ *575+5021*]. to say good-by, leave; give up, renounce, forsake:– bade farewell [1], bid farewell [1], forsaketh [1], sent away [1], taking leave of [1], took leave [1]

658 ἀποτελέω, **apoteleō**, v. GK: *699* [→ *575+5056*]. to bring to completion; (pass.) to be full-grown, mature, completed:– finished [1]

659 ἀποτίθημι, **apotithēmi**, v. GK: *700* [→ *575+5087*]. to put aside, get rid of:– put off [2], cast off [1], laid down [1], lay apart [1], lay aside [1], laying aside [1], putting away [1]

660 ἀποτινάσσω, **apotinassō**, v. GK: *701* [→ *1614; cf. 575*]. to shake off, stomp off:– shake off [1], shook off [1]

661 ἀποτίνω, **apotinō**, v. GK: *702* [→ *575+5099*]. to pay back, make restitution:– repay [1]

662 ἀποτολμάω, **apotolmaō**, v. GK: *703* [→ *575+5111*]. to bring forth boldly:– very bold [1]

663 ἀποτομία, **apotomia**, n. GK: *704* [→ *575+5114*]. sternness, severity:– severity [2]

664 ἀποτόμως, **apotomōs**, adv. GK: *705* [→ *575+5114*]. harshly, sharply, severely, rigorously:– sharply [1], sharpness [1]

665 ἀποτρέπω, **apotrepō**, v. GK: *706* [→ *575+5157*]. to have nothing to do with, turn away from completely, avoid:– from turn away [1]

666 ἀπουσία, **apousia**, n. GK: *707* [→ *575+1510*]. absence:– absence [1]

667 ἀποφέρω, **apopherō**, v. GK: *708* [→ *575+5342*]. to carry away, lead away:– carried away [3], bring [1], carried [1]

668 ἀποφεύγω, **apopheugō**, v. GK: *709* [→ *575+5343*]. to escape (from):– escaped [2], escaped from [1]

669 ἀποφθέγγομαι, **apophthengomai**, v. GK: *710* [→ *575+5350*]. to say, speak out, address, declare, in some contexts with the inference of urgency or boldness:– said [1], speak forth [1], utterance [1]

670 ἀποφορτίζομαι, **apophortizomai**, v. GK: *711* [→ *575+5342*]. to unload:– unlade [1]

671 ἀπόχρησις, **apochrēsis**, n. GK: *712* [→ *575+5530*]. using up, consumption:– using [1]

672 ἀποχωρέω, **apochōreō**, v. GK: *713* [→ *575+5562*]. to go away from, leave:– departeth [1], departing [1], depart [1]

673 ἀποχωρίζω, **apochōrizō**, v. GK: *714* [→ *575+5565*]. to part company, be separated; to recede, be split:– departed asunder [1], departed [1]

674 ἀποψύχω, **apopsychō**, v. GK: *715* [→ *575+5594*]. to faint (some translate "to die"):– hearts failing [1]

675 Ἄππιος, **Appios**, n.pr. GK: *716*. Appius:– Appii [1]

676 ἀπρόσιτος, **aprositos**, a. GK: *717* [→ *1.1+4314*]. unapproachable:– which no can approach unto [1]

677 ἀπρόσκοπος, **aproskopos**, a. GK: *718* [→ *1.1+4314+2875*]. blameless, clear; not causing one to stumble, not giving offense:– none offence [1], void of offence [1], without offence [1]

678 ἀπροσωπολήμπτως, **aprosōpolēmptōs**, adv. GK: *719* [→ *1.1+4383+2983*]. impartially, without prejudice:– without respect of persons [1]

679 ἄπταιστος, **aptaistos**, a. GK: *720* [→ *1.1+4417*]. without falling, without stumbling:– falling [1]

680 ἅπτομαι, **haptomai**, v.mid. of *681*. GK: *721* [→ *381, 681, 860, 2510, 681*]. to touch, hold, handle; "to touch a woman" means "to get married":–

681 ἅπτω, **haptō**, v. GK: *721 & 4312* [→ *680*]. to touch, hold, handle; (act.) to start a fire; "to touch a woman" means "to get married":– touched [21], touch [13], lighted [2], toucheth [2], kindled [1], light [1]

682 Ἀπφία, **Apphia**, n.pr. GK: *722*. Apphia:– Apphia [1]

683 ἀπωθέω, **apōtheō**, v. GK: *723* [→ *1856; cf. 575*]. to reject, repudiate, push aside:– cast away [2], put away [1], put from [1], thrust away [1], thrust from [1]

684 ἀπώλεια, **apōleia**, n. GK: *724* [→ *575+3639*]. destruction, ruin, waste:– perdition [8], destruction [5], waste [2], damnable [1], damnation [1], die [1], perish (*+1510+1519*) [1], pernicious ways [1]

685 ἀρά, **ara**, n. GK: *725* [→ *1944, 2671, 2672*]. curse:– cursing [1]

686 ἄρα, **ara**, pt.infer. GK: *726*. then, so, therefore, consequently:– then [14], therefore (*+3767*) [7], so [4], therefore [4], so then [2], else (*+1893*) [1], haply (*+1065*) [1], haply [1], if so be that (*+1512*) [1], no doubt [1], now [1], perhaps [1], then (*+1065*) [1], truly [1], wherefore (*+1065*) [1], wherefore [1]

687 ἆρα, **ara**, pt.inter. GK: *727*. difficult to translate directly: introduces direct questions, showing anxiety or impatience:– what (*+5101*) [2], therefore [1], what man (*+5101*) [1]

688 Ἀραβία, **Arabia**, n.pr. GK: *728* [→ *690*]. Arabia, "*desert* or *steppe*":– Arabia [2]

ἄραγε, **arage**. See **686** and **1065**.

689 Ἀράμ, **Aram**, n.pr. GK: *730*. Aram, Ram, "*high, exalted*":– Aram [3]

690 Ἄραψ, **Araps**, n.pr.g. GK: *732* [→ *688*]. Arab, "*desert dweller*":– Arabians [1]

691 ἀργέω, **argeō**, v. GK: *733* [→ *1.1+2041*]. to be idle, grow weary:– lingereth [1]

692 ἀργός, **argos**, a. GK: *734* [→ *1.1+2041*]. idle, lazy; useless, ineffective; careless:– idle [6], barren [1], slow [1]

693 ἀργύρεος, **argyreos**, a. GK: *735* [→ *696*]. (made of) silver:– silver [2], of silver [1]

694 ἀργύριον, **argyrion**, n. GK: *736* [→ *696*]. silver (always referring to money):– money [11], silver [9]

695 ἀργυροκόπος, **argyrokopos**, n. GK: *737* [→ *696+2875*]. silversmith:– silversmith [1]

696 ἄργυρος, **argyros**, n. GK: *738* [→ *693, 694, 695, 866, 5365, 5366*]. silver:– silver [5]

697 Ἄρειος πάγος, **Areios pagos**, n.pr. GK: *740 & 4076* [→ *698*]. meeting of the Areopagus; Mars' Hill, "*hill of the Greek god Ares*":– Areopagus [1], Mars' hill [1]

698 Ἀρεοπαγίτης, **Areopagitēs**, n.pr.g. GK: *741* [→ *697*]. member of the Areopagus:– Areopagite [1]

699 ἀρεσκεία, **areskeia**, n. GK: *742* [→ *700*]. pleasing, striving to please:– pleasing [1]

700 ἀρέσκω, **areskō**, v. GK: *743* [→ *441, 699, 701, 2100, 2101, 2102*]. to please, accommodate:– please [11], pleased [5], pleasing [1]

701 ἀρεστός, **arestos**, a. GK: *744* [→ *700*]. pleasing, desirable, right:– pleased (*+1510*) [1], please [1], pleasing [1], reason [1]

702 Ἀρέτας, **Haretas**, n.pr. GK: *745*. Aretas, "*virtuous*":– Aretas [1]

703 ἀρετή, **aretē**, n. GK: *746*. (moral) goodness, excellence, virtue:– virtue [4], praises [1]

704 ἀρήν, **arēn**, n. GK: *748* [→ *721*]. lamb:– lambs [1]

705 ἀριθμέω, **arithmeō**, v. GK: *749* [→ *706*]. to count:– numbered [2], number [1]

706 ἀριθμός, **arithmos**, n. GK: *750* [→ *382, 705, 2674*]. number:– number [18]

707 Ἀριμαθαία, **Harimathaia**, n.pr. GK: *751*. Arimathea:– Arimathea [4]

708 Ἀρίσταρχος, **Aristarchos**, n.pr. GK: *752* [→ *757*]. Aristarchus, "*best ruler*":– Aristarchus [5]

709 ἀριστάω, **aristaō**, v. GK: *753* [→ *712*]. to eat (breakfast):– dine [2], dined [1]

710 ἀριστερός, **aristeros**, a. GK: *754*. left side, left hand; the left is considered culturally to be weaker than the right; a weapon in the left hand is a defensive weapon; to be seated on the left side of a ruler is a lesser position than on the right side:– left [2], left hand [1]

711 Ἀριστόβουλος, **Aristoboulos**, n.pr. GK: *755* [→ *1014*]. Aristobulus, "*best advisor*":– Aristobulus' [1]

712 ἄριστον, **ariston**, n. GK: *756* [→ *709*]. meal, feast:– dinner [3]

713 ἀρκετός, **arketos**, a. GK: *757* [→ *714*]. enough, sufficient:– enough [1], suffice [1], sufficient [1]

714 ἀρκέω, **arkeō**, v. GK: *758* [→ *713, 841, 842, 1884*]. (mid./pass.) to be content, satisfied; (act.) to be sufficient:– content [4], sufficient [2], enough [1], sufficeth [1]

715 ἄρκος, ***arkos***, n. GK: *759 & 760*. bear:– bear [1]

716 ἅρμα, ***harma***, n. GK: *761* [→ *260*]. chariot, carriage (for traveling or military uses):– chariot [3], chariots [1]

717 Ἁρμαγεδών, ***Harmagedōn***, n.pr. GK: *762 & 3403*. Armageddon, "*Mount Megiddo*":– Armageddon [1]

718 ἁρμόζω, ***harmozō***, v. GK: *764* [→ *719, 4883*]. to promise for marriage, betroth:– espoused [1]

719 ἁρμός, ***harmos***, n. GK: *765* [→ *718*]. joint (where bones connect):– joints [1]

720 ἀρνέομαι, ***arneomai***, v. GK: *766* [→ *533*]. to deny, disown, renounce, repudiate:– denied [14], deny [7], denieth [4], denying [4], refused [2]

721 ἀρνίον, ***arnion***, n. GK: *768* [→ *704*]. lamb, sheep; the Lamb (a title of Christ):– lamb [27], lamb's [2], lambs [1]

722 ἀροτριάω, ***arotriaō***, v. GK: *769* [→ *723*]. to plow, furrow:– ploweth [1], plowing [1], plow [1]

723 ἄροτρον, ***arotron***, n. GK: *770* [→ *722*]. plow, furrow-maker:– plough [1]

724 ἁρπαγή, ***harpagē***, n. GK: *771* [→ *726*]. greediness, confiscation, robbery, plunder:– extortion [1], ravening [1], spoiling [1]

725 ἁρπαγμός, ***harpagmos***, n. GK: *772* [→ *726*]. something to hold onto:– robbery [1]

726 ἁρπάζω, ***harpazō***, v. GK: *773* [→ *724, 725, 727, 1283, 4884*]. to catch, steal, carry off:– caught up [4], take by force [3], pluck [2], catcheth away [1], catcheth [1], caught away [1], pulling [1]

727 ἅρπαξ, ***harpax***, a. GK: *774* [→ *726*]. swindling, robbing, implying violence in the process; (destructively) ferocious, ravenous; as a noun, a (violent) robber or swindler:– extortioners [3], extortioner [1], ravening [1]

728 ἀρραβών, ***arrabōn***, n. GK: *775*. deposit which guarantees, downpayment, pledge:– earnest [3]

729 ἄραφος, ***araphos***, a. GK: *731* [→ *1.1+4476*]. seamless:– without seam [1]

730 ἄρρην, ***arrēn***, n. GK: *776 & 781* [→ *733*]. male:– male [4], men [3], man [2]

731 ἄρρητος, ***arrētos***, a. GK: *777* [→ *1.1+4487*]. inexpressible, not to be spoken (in context, things or words too sacred to tell):– unspeakable [1]

732 ἄρρωστος, ***arrōstos***, a. GK: *778 & 779* [→ *1.1+4517*]. sick, ill:– sick [4], sickly [1]

733 ἀρσενοκοίτης, ***arsenokoitēs***, n. GK: *780* [→ *730+2749*]. one engaging in homosexual acts (likely referring to the active male partner), sexual deviant:– abusers with mankind [1], them that defile with mankind [1]

734 Ἀρτεμᾶς, ***Artemas***, n.pr. GK: *782* [→ *735+1325*]. Artemas, "*[given by] Artemis*":– Artemas [1]

735 Ἄρτεμις, ***Artemis***, n.pr. GK: *783* [→ *734*]. Artemis:– Diana [5]

736 ἀρτέμων, ***artemōn***, n. GK: *784*. foresail, sail:– mainsail [1]

737 ἄρτι, ***arti***, adv. GK: *785* [→ *534, 535, 738, 739, 1822, 2675, 2676, 2677, 4294*]. now, at once, immediately:– now [22], henceforth (+*575*) [2], hereafter (+*575*) [2], hitherto (+*2193*) [2], even now [1], henceforth [1], now (+*575*) [1], presently [1], present [1], this day [1], this hour [1], this present [1]

738 ἀρτιγέννητος, ***artigennētos***, a. GK: *786* [→ *737+1096*]. newborn:– newborn [1]

739 ἄρτιος, ***artios***, a. GK: *787* [→ *737*]. thorough, complete, capable, proficient, able to meet all demands:– perfect [1]

740 ἄρτος, ***artos***, n. GK: *788*. (loaf of) bread, food:– bread [72], loaves [22], shewbread (+*3588+4286*) [3], loaf [1], shewbread (+*4286*) [1]

741 ἀρτύω, ***artyō***, v. GK: *789*. to make salty, season:– seasoned [2], season [1]

742 Ἀρφαξάδ, ***Arphaxad***, n.pr. GK: *790*. Arphaxad:– Arphaxad [1]

743 ἀρχάγγελος, ***archangelos***, n. GK: *791* [→ *757+32*]. archangel:– archangel [2]

744 ἀρχαῖος, ***archaios***, a. GK: *792* [→ *757*]. ancient, of old:– old [8], of old time [3], a good while ago (+*575+2250*) [1]

745 Ἀρχέλαος, ***Archelaos***, n.pr. GK: *793* [→ *757+2992*]. Archelaus, "*ruler of people*":– Archelaus [1]

746 ἀρχή, ***archē***, n. GK: *794* [→ *757*]. beginning, origin, first; ruler, power, authority; position of authority, domain:– beginning [39], principalities [6], first [3], corners [2], principality [2], beginnings [1], first estate [1], magistrates [1], power [1], principles [1], rule [1]

747 ἀρχηγός, ***archēgos***, n. GK: *795* [→ *757+71*]. author, originator, founder; leader, ruler:– prince [2], author [1], captain [1]

748 ἀρχιερατικός, ***archieratikos***, a. GK: *796* [→ *757+2413*]. of the high priest:– high priest [1]

749 ἀρχιερεύς, ***archiereus***, n. GK: *797* [→ *757+2413*]. chief priest, high priest:– chief priests [63], high priest [51], high priest's [4], high priests [3], chief of the priests [1], priests [1]

750 ἀρχιποίμην, ***archipoimēn***, n. GK: *799* [→ *757+4166*]. chief shepherd:– chief shepherd [1]

751 Ἄρχιππος, ***Archippos***, n.pr. GK: *800* [→ *757+2462*]. Archippus, "*master of the horse*":– Archippus [2]

752 ἀρχισυνάγωγος, ***archisynagōgos***, n. GK: *801* [→ *757+4864*]. leader of the synagogue, an official whose duty it was to care for the physical needs for the worship service:– ruler of the synagogue [5], ruler of the synagogue's [2], rulers of the synagogue [2]

753 ἀρχιτέκτων, ***architektōn***, n. GK: *802* [→ *757+5078*]. expert builder:– masterbuilder [1]

754 ἀρχιτελώνης, ***architelōnēs***, n. GK: *803* [→ *757+5057*]. chief tax collector:– chief among publicans [1]

755 ἀρχιτρίκλινος, ***architriklinos***, n. GK: *804* [→ *757+5140+2827*]. master of the banquet, head waiter:– governor of the feast [2], ruler of the feast [1]

756 ἄρχομαι, ***archomai***, v.mid. of *757*. GK: *806* [→ *757*]. to begin:– began [64], begin [11], beginning [7], begun [1], from the beginning [1]

757 ἄρχω, ***archō***, v. GK: *806* [→ *536, 708, 743, 744, 745, 746, 747, 748, 749, 750, 751, 752, 753, 754, 755, 756, 758, 775, 1481, 1543, 1728, 1885, 3966, 3980, 4173, 4278, 4391, 4759, 5075, 5076, 5223, 5224, 5225, 5506*]. (act.) to rule; (mid.) to begin:– reign over [1], rule over [1]

758 ἄρχων, ***archōn***, n. GK: *807* [→ *757*]. ruler, leader, official:– rulers [14], prince [8], ruler [8], princes [3], chief [2], magistrate [1], ruler's [1]

759 ἄρωμα, ***arōma***, n. GK: *808*. spices, salves, scented oils, perfumes:– spices [4]

760 Ἀσά, ***Asa***, n.pr. GK: *809 & 811*. Asa, "[poss.] *healer; myrtle*":– Asa [2]

761 ἀσάλευτος, ***asaleutos***, a. GK: *810* [→ *1.1+4531*]. unshakable, immovable, fixed:– cannot be moved [1], unmoveable [1]

762 ἄσβεστος, ***asbestos***, a. GK: *812* [→ *1.1+4570*]. unquenchable, inextinguishable:– never be quenched [2], unquenchable [2]

763 ἀσέβεια, ***asebeia***, n. GK: *813* [→ *1.1+4576*]. ungodliness, godlessness, impiety (in thought and act):– ungodliness [4], ungodly [2]

764 ἀσεβέω, ***asebeō***, v. GK: *814* [→ *1.1+4576*]. to do ungodly acts, act impiously:– those that live ungodly [1], ungodly committed [1]

765 ἀσεβής, ***asebēs***, a. GK: *815* [→ *1.1+4576*]. ungodly, wicked, impious:– ungodly [9]

766 ἀσέλγεια, ***aselgeia***, n. GK: *816* [→ *1.1*]. debauchery, sensuality, lewdness:– lasciviousness [6], wantonness [2], filthy [1]

767 ἄσημος, ***asēmos***, a. GK: *817* [→ *1.1+4592*]. ordinary, obscure, insignificant:– mean [1]

768 Ἀσήρ, ***Asēr***, n.pr. GK: *818*. Asher, "*happy one*":– Aser [2]

769 ἀσθένεια, ***astheneia***, n. GK: *819* [→ *1.1+4599*]. weakness, illness, infirmity:– infirmities [10], infirmity [7], weakness [5], diseases [1], sickness [1]

770 ἀσθενέω, ***astheneō***, v. GK: *820* [→ *1.1+4599*]. to be weak, ill:– sick [17], weak [16], impotent [2], diseased [1]

771 ἀσθένημα, ***asthenēma***, n. GK: *821* [→ *1.1+4599*]. failing, weakness:– infirmities [1]

772 ἀσθενής, ***asthenēs***, a. GK: *822* [→ *1.1+4599*]. weak, ill (of physical weakness or illness, also of moral or spiritual weakness):– weak [13], sick [6], weakness [2], impotent [1], more feeble [1], weaker [1], without strength [1]

773 Ἀσία, ***Asia***, n.pr. GK: *823* [→ *774, 775*]. Asia:– Asia [19]

774 Ἀσιανός, ***Asianos***, n.pr.g. GK: *824* [→ *773*]. one from the Roman province of Asia:– of Asia [1]

775 Ἀσιάρχης, ***Asiarchēs***, n.pr. GK: *825* [→ *773+757*]. official of the province of Asia, Asiarch, a wealthy and influential man, probably connected with the Imperial cult:– chief of Asia [1]

776 ἀσιτία, ***asitia***, n. GK: *826* [→ *1.1+4621*]. going without food:– abstinence [1]

777 ἄσιτος, ***asitos***, a. GK: *827* [→ *1.1+4621*]. going without food:– fasting [1]

778 ἀσκέω, ***askeō***, v. GK: *828*. to strive, do one's best:– exercise [1]

779 ἀσκός, askos, n. GK: *829*. wineskin, leather bag holding wine:– bottles [12]

780 ἀσμένως, asmenōs, adv. GK: *830* [→ *2237*]. warmly, gladly:– gladly [2]

781 ἄσοφος, asophos, a. GK: *831* [→ *1.1+4680*]. unwise, foolish:– fools [1]

782 ἀσπάζομαι, aspazomai, v. GK: *571 & 832* [→ *783*]. to give greetings (hello or good-bye):– salute [32], greet [14], saluted [5], saluteth [5], embraced [2], greeteth [1], taken leave [1]

783 ἀσπασμός, aspasmos, n. GK: *833* [→ *782*]. greeting:– salutation [6], greetings [3], salutations [1]

784 ἄσπιλος, aspilos, a. GK: *834* [→ *1.1+4696*]. without spot, defect or blemish:– without spot [3], unspotted [1]

785 ἀσπίς, aspis, n. GK: *835*. viper, asp, cobra:– asps [1]

786 ἄσπονδος, aspondos, a. GK: *836* [→ *1.1+4689*]. unforgiving, not reconcilable:– implacable [1], trucebreakers [1]

787 ἀσσάριον, assarion, n. GK: *837*. assarion (coin worth one-sixteenth of a day's wage):– farthings [1], farthing [1]

788 ἆσσον, asson, adv. GK: *839*. nearer:– close by [1]

789 Ἄσσος, Assos, n.pr. GK: *840*. Assos:– Assos [2]

790 ἀστατέω, astateō, v. GK: *841* [→ *1.1+2476*]. to be homeless, a vagabond:– have no certain dwelling place [1]

791 ἀστεῖος, asteios, a. GK: *842*. not ordinary, beautiful, pleasing:– exceeding fair (*+2316+3588*) [1], proper [1]

792 ἀστήρ, astēr, n. GK: *843* [→ *798*]. star:– stars [13], star [11]

793 ἀστήρικτος, astēriktos, a. GK: *844* [→ *1.1+4741*]. unstable, weak:– unstable [2]

794 ἄστοργος, astorgos, a. GK: *845* [→ *1.1*]. without love, heartless:– without natural affection [2]

795 ἀστοχέω, astocheō, v. GK: *846* [→ *1.1*]. to wander away, miss the mark; to turn to, deviate from:– erred [2], swerved [1]

796 ἀστραπή, astrapē, n. GK: *847* [→ *797, 1823, 4015*]. lightning; light, ray of light:– lightnings [4], lightning [4], bright shining [1]

797 ἀστράπτω, astraptō, v. GK: *848* [→ *796*]. to flash, gleam like lightning:– lighteneth [1], shining [1]

798 ἄστρον, astron, n. GK: *849* [→ *792*]. star, constellation:– stars [3], star [1]

799 Ἀσύγκριτος, Asynkritos, n.pr. GK: *850* [→ *1.1+4862+2919*]. Asyncritus, "*incomparable*":– Asyncritus [1]

800 ἀσύμφωνος, asymphōnos, a. GK: *851* [→ *1.1+4862+5456*]. disagreeable, not harmonious:– agreed not (*+1510*) [1]

801 ἀσύνετος, asynetos, a. GK: *852* [→ *863*]. senseless, dull, without understanding, foolish:– without understanding [3], foolish [2]

802 ἀσύνθετος, asynthetos, a. GK: *853* [→ *1.1+4862+5087*]. faithless, untrustworthy:– covenantbreakers [1]

803 ἀσφάλεια, asphaleia, n. GK: *854* [→ *755; cf. 1.1*]. security, safety; certainty, truth:– safety [2], certainty [1]

804 ἀσφαλής, asphalēs, a. GK: *855* [→ *754, 757; cf. 1.1*]. safe, firm, certain; definite; the truth:– certainty [2], certain [1], safe [1], sure [1]

805 ἀσφαλίζω, asphalizō, v. GK: *856* [→ *755; cf. 1.1*]. to make secure; fasten:– made sure [2], made fast [1], make sure [1]

806 ἀσφαλῶς, asphalōs, adv. GK: *857* [→ *755; cf. 1.1*]. carefully, securely; under guard; assuredly, beyond a doubt:– safely [2], assuredly [1]

807 ἀσχημονέω, aschēmoneō, v. GK: *858* [→ *1.1+4976*]. to act improperly, dishonorably, indecently, rudely:– behave unseemly [1], behaveth uncomely [1]

808 ἀσχημοσύνη, aschēmosynē, n. GK: *859* [→ *1.1+4976*]. indecent act, shame:– shame [1], unseemly [1]

809 ἀσχήμων, aschēmōn, a. GK: *860* [→ *1.1+4976*]. unpresentable, shameful, indecent:– uncomely [1]

810 ἀσωτία, asōtia, n. GK: *861* [→ *1.1+4982*]. debauchery, dissipation, wildness:– riot [2], excess [1]

811 ἀσώτως, asōtōs, adv. GK: *862* [→ *1.1+4982*]. wildly, in debauchery, in dissipation:– riotous [1]

812 ἀτακτέω, atakteō, v. GK: *863* [→ *1.1+5021*]. to be idle, lazy:– behaved disorderly [1]

813 ἄτακτος, ataktos, a. GK: *864* [→ *1.1+5021*]. idle, lazy:– unruly [1]

814 ἀτάκτως, ataktōs, adv. GK: *865* [→ *1.1+5021*]. idly, irresponsibly:– disorderly [2]

815 ἄτεκνος, ateknos, a. GK: *866* [→ *1.1+5088*]. childless, without children:– without children [2], childless [1]

816 ἀτενίζω, atenizō, v. GK: *867* [→ *1614; cf. 1.2*]. to look intently, gaze, stare:– looked stedfastly [2], earnestly beholding [1], earnestly looked [1], fastened eyes [1], fastened [1], fastening eyes [1], look earnestly [1], looked [1], looking stedfastly [1], set eyes [1], stedfastly beholding [1], stedfastly behold [1], stedfastly look [1]

817 ἄτερ, ater, pp.*. GK: *868*. without, apart from:– in the absence of [1], without [1]

818 ἀτιμάζω, atimazō, v. GK: *869 & 870* [→ *1.1+5092*]. to dishonor, disgrace, treat shamefully, insult:– dishonour [2], despised [1], dishonourest [1], entreated shamefully [1], suffer shame [1]

819 ἀτιμία, atimia, n. GK: *871* [→ *1.1+5092*]. dishonor, disgrace, shame; common use:– dishonour [4], reproach [1], shame [1], vile [1]

820 ἄτιμος, atimos, a. GK: *872* [→ *1.1+5092*]. without honor, dishonored, despised:– without honour [2], despised [1], less honourable [1]

821 ἀτιμόω, atimoō, v. GK: *873* [→ *1.1+5092*]. to disgrace:– shamefully handled [1]

822 ἀτμίς, atmis, n. GK: *874* [→ *109*]. mist, vapor; billows (of smoke):– vapour [2]

823 ἄτομος, atomos, a. GK: *875* [→ *1.1+5114*]. in a flash, in a moment, an indivisible unit of time:– moment [1]

824 ἄτοπος, atopos, a. GK: *876* [→ *1.1+5117*]. wrong, wicked; unusual, surprising:– amiss [1], harm [1], unreasonable [1]

825 Ἀττάλεια, Attaleia, n.pr. GK: *877*. Attalia:– Attalia [1]

826 αὐγάζω, augazō, v. GK: *878 & 2964* [→ *827*]. to see; shine (forth):– shine [1]

827 αὐγή, augē, n. GK: *879* [→ *541, 826, 1306, 5081*]. daylight, dawn:– break of day [1]

828 Αὔγουστος, Augoustos, n.pr. GK: *880*. Augustus, "*reverant, holy*":– Augustus [1]

829 αὐθάδης, authadēs, a. GK: *881* [→ *846+2237*]. overbearing, arrogant, stubborn, self-willed:– selfwilled [2]

830 αὐθαίρετος, authairetos, a. GK: *882* [→ *846+138*]. on one's own initiative, of one's own accord:– of own accord [1], willing of themselves [1]

831 αὐθεντέω, authenteō, v. GK: *883* [→ *846*]. to have authority over:– usurp authority over [1]

832 αὐλέω, auleō, v. GK: *884* [→ *836*]. to play the flute:– piped [3]

833 αὐλή, aulē, n. GK: *885* [→ *63, 1886, 4259; cf. 109, 835*]. palace, house; courtyard, sheepfold:– palace [7], hall [2], court [1], fold [1], sheepfold (*+3588+4263*) [1]

834 αὐλητής, aulētēs, n. GK: *886* [→ *836*]. flute player:– minstrels [1], pipers [1]

835 αὐλίζομαι, aulizomai, v. GK: *887* [cf. *833*]. to spend the night, find lodging:– abode [1], lodged [1]

836 αὐλός, aulos, n. GK: *888* [→ *832, 834*]. flute:– pipe [1]

837 αὐξάνω, auxanō, v. GK: *889 & 891* [→ *838, 4885, 5232*]. to cause to grow; (intr.) to grow, increase:– grew [6], grow [5], increased [3], increase [2], gave increase [1], giveth increase [1], groweth [1], grown [1], increaseth [1], increasing [1]

838 αὔξησις, auxēsis, n. GK: *890* [→ *837*]. growth, increase:– increase [2]

839 αὔριον, aurion, adv. GK: *892* [→ *1887*]. tomorrow, the next day:– to morrow [9], morrow [4], next day [1], on morrow [1]

840 αὐστηρός, austēros, a. GK: *893* [→ *850*]. hard, severe, strict, exacting:– austere [2]

841 αὐτάρκεια, autarkeia, n. GK: *894* [→ *846+714*]. contentment, having all of one's needs, sufficiency:– contentment [1], sufficiency [1]

842 αὐτάρκης, autarkēs, a. GK: *895* [→ *846+714*]. content; (possibly) self-sufficient:– content [1]

843 αὐτοκατάκριτος, autokatakritos, a. GK: *896* [→ *846+2596+2919*]. self-condemned:– condemned of himself [1]

844 αὐτόματος, automatos, a. GK: *897* [→ *846*]. by itself, automatic:– of herself [1], of own accord [1]

845 αὐτόπτης, autoptēs, n. GK: *898* [→ *846+3708*]. eyewitness:– eyewitnesses [1]

846 αὐτός, autos, p.inten. GK: *899* [→ *829, 830, 831, 841, 842, 843, 844, 845, 847, 848, 849, 1438, 1683, 1763, 1824, 1888, 3910, 4572, 5024, 5367, 5615*]. he, she, it, they; also used as inten.p., himself, herself, itself, themselves; the same one; also an adv. of place: here, there, where:– him [1942], them [1145], his [1093], their [313], he [265], her [242], it [183], *usually untranslated* [166], they [134], same [77], himself [51], his own [30], thereof [29], therein (+*1722*) [16], their own [12], yourselves [12], myself [10], themselves [10], the same [9], she [8], itself [7], that [7], those [7], together (+*1909+3588*) [7], ourselves [6], this [5], therein (+*1519*) [4], there [4], very [4], ye [4], own [3], selfsame [3], theirs [3], thereof (+*1537*) [3], thereon (+*1722*) [3], thyself [3], whose [3], he himself [2], into one place (+*1909+3588*) [2], likeminded (+*3588+5426*) [2], thee [2], there (+*1722*) [2], thereby (+*1223*) [2], thereon (+*1883*) [2], thereon [2], therewith (+*1722*) [2], we [2], which [2], whom [2], who [2], I myself [1], I [1], Jesus[s] [1], and [1], even all one as if (+*1520+2532+3588*) [1], her own [1], here [1], herself [1], his own self [1], in one place (+*1909+3588*) [1], in the like manner (+*2596+3588*) [1], man's [1], myself (+*1473*) [1], nothing (+*1537+3361*) [1], one [1], own selves [1], so (+*2596+3588*) [1], the house[s] [1], the other[s] [1], the said [1], the same (+*3778*) [1], the very [1], their own company [1], thereat (+*1223*) [1], thereby (+*1722*) [1], thereinto (+*1519*) [1], therein [1], thereon (+*1909*) [1], thereunto (+*1519+3778*) [1], these [1], they themselves [1], the [1], things [1], together (+*2596+3588*) [1], we ourselves [1]

847 **αὐτοῦ**, ***autou***, p.gen. of *846*. GK: *899* [→ *846*]. as an adv. of place: here, there, where:–

848 **αὐτοῦ**, ***autou***, p.gen. of *846*. GK: *899* [→ *846*]. of him, her, it, them:–

849 **αὐτόχειρ**, ***autocheir***, a. or n. GK: *901* [→ *846+5495*]. with one's own hand:– with own hands [1]

850 **αὐχμηρός**, ***auchmēros***, a. GK: *903* [→ *840*]. dark:– dark [1]

851 **ἀφαιρέω**, ***aphaireō***, v. GK: *904* [→ *575+138*]. to take away from, remove; to cut (off):– take away [5], cut off [2], smote off [1], taken away [1], taketh away [1]

852 **ἀφανής**, ***aphanēs***, a. GK: *905* [→ *1.1+5316*]. hidden, invisible:– not manifest [1]

853 **ἀφανίζω**, ***aphanizō***, v. GK: *906* [→ *1.1+5316*]. to destroy, disfigure; to perish, vanish, disappear:– corrupt [2], disfigure [1], perish [1], vanisheth away [1]

854 **ἀφανισμός**, ***aphanismos***, n. GK: *907* [→ *1.1+5316*]. disappearance, destruction:– vanish away [1]

855 **ἄφαντος**, ***aphantos***, a. GK: *908* [→ *1.1+5316*]. disappearing, invisible:– vanished out of sight (+*1096*) [1]

856 **ἀφεδρών**, ***aphedrōn***, n. GK: *909* [→ *575+1476*]. latrine:– draught [2]

857 **ἀφειδία**, ***apheidia***, n. GK: *910* [→ *1.1+5339*]. harsh treatment, unsparing:– neglecting [1]

858 **ἀφελότης**, ***aphelotēs***, n. GK: *911* [→ *1.1*]. sincerity, simplicity:– singleness [1]

859 **ἄφεσις**, ***aphesis***, n. GK: *912* [→ *863*]. forgiveness, pardon, release, cancellation of a debt:– remission [9], forgiveness [6], deliverance [1], liberty [1]

860 **ἁφή**, ***haphē***, n. GK: *913* [→ *681*]. ligament, joint:– joints [1], joint [1]

861 **ἀφθαρσία**, ***aphtharsia***, n. GK: *914* [→ *1.1+5351*]. imperishableness, immortality:– incorruption [4], immortality [2], sincerity [2]

862 **ἄφθαρτος**, ***aphthartos***, a. GK: *915* [→ *1.1+5351*]. imperishable, immortal, lasting forever:– incorruptible [4], immortal [1], not corruptible [1], uncorruptible [1]

863 **ἀφίημι**, ***aphiēmi***, v. GK: *918 & 1889* [→ *425, 447, 801, 859, 1455, 3929, 3935, 4907, 4908, 4920; cf. 575*]. to forgive, pardon, remit, cancel; to leave, abandon; to allow, permit, tolerate:– left [36], forgive [23], forgiven [21], leave [9], let [8], suffer [8], let alone [6], suffered [6], forsook [4], leaving [3], forgave [2], forsaken [2], leave undone [2], leaveth [2], put away [2], sent away [2], cried [1], forgiveth [1], laying aside [1], let be [1], let go [1], let have [1], omitted [1], remitted [1], remit [1], yielded up [1]

864 **ἀφικνέομαι**, ***aphikneomai***, v. GK: *919* [→ *575+2425*]. to reach:– come abroad [1]

865 **ἀφιλάγαθος**, ***aphilagathos***, a. GK: *920* [→ *1.1+5384+18*]. not loving good:– despisers of good [1]

866 **ἀφιλάργυρος**, ***aphilargyros***, a. GK: *921* [→ *1.1+5384+696*]. not loving money, not greedy:– not covetous [1], without covetousness [1]

867 **ἄφιξις**, ***aphixis***, n. GK: *922* [→ *575+2425*]. leaving, departure:– departing [1]

868 **ἀφίστημι**, ***aphistēmi***, v. GK: *923* [→ *575+2476*]. to leave, withdraw, abandon; to revolt, mislead:– departed [6], depart [3], depart from [1], departing [1], drew away [1], fall away [1], refrain [1], withdraw [1]

869 **ἄφνω**, ***aphnō***, adv. GK: *924* [→ *160?*]. suddenly:– suddenly [3]

870 **ἀφόβως**, ***aphobōs***, adv. GK: *925* [→ *1.1+5401*]. fearlessly, without the slightest qualm, boldly:– without fear [4]

871 **ἀφομοιόω**, ***aphomoioō***, v. GK: *926* [→ *575+3664*]. (pass.) to be like, similar:– made like unto [1]

872 **ἀφοράω**, ***aphoraō***, v. GK: *927* [→ *575+3708*]. to fix one's eyes; look away:– looking [1]

873 **ἀφορίζω**, ***aphorizō***, v. GK: *928* [→ *575+3724*]. to separate, set apart, exclude:– separated [4], separate [4], divideth [1], sever [1]

874 **ἀφορμή**, ***aphormē***, n. GK: *929* [→ *575+3730*]. opportunity, opening, pretext:– occasion [7]

875 **ἀφρίζω**, ***aphrizō***, v. GK: *930* [→ *876*]. to foam at the mouth:– foameth [1], foaming [1]

876 **ἀφρός**, ***aphros***, n. GK: *931* [→ *875, 1890*]. foam, froth:– foameth (+*3326*) [1]

877 **ἀφροσύνη**, ***aphrosynē***, n. GK: *932* [→ *1.1+5424*]. foolishness, lack of sense:– foolishly (+*1722*) [2], folly [1], foolishness [1]

878 **ἄφρων**, ***aphrōn***, a. GK: *933* [→ *1.1+5424*]. foolish, ignorant:– fool [6], foolish [2], fools [2], unwise [1]

879 **ἀφυπνόω**, ***aphypnoō***, v. GK: *934* [→ *575+5258*]. to fall asleep:– fell asleep [1]

880 **ἄφωνος**, ***aphōnos***, a. GK: *936* [→ *1.1+5456*]. silent, mute, without speech; without meaning:– dumb [3], without signification [1]

881 **Ἀχάζ**, ***Achaz***, n.pr. GK: *937 & 941*. Ahaz, "*he has grasped*":– Achaz [2]

882 **Ἀχαΐα**, ***Achaia***, n.pr. GK: *938* [→ *883*]. Achaia:– Achaia [11]

883 **Ἀχαϊκός**, ***Achaikos***, n.pr. GK: *939* [→ *882*]. Achaicus, "*belonging to Achaia*":– Achaicus [2]

884 **ἀχάριστος**, ***acharistos***, a. GK: *940* [→ *1.1+5463*]. ungrateful:– unthankful [2]

885 **Ἀχίμ**, ***Achim***, n.pr. GK: *943*. Akim, "*Yahweh is my brother*":– Achim [2]

886 **ἀχειροποίητος**, ***acheiropoiētos***, a. GK: *942* [→ *1.1+5495+4160*]. not made by human hands, implying not of human origin:– made without hands [2], not made with hand [1]

887 **ἀχλύς**, ***achlys***, n. GK: *944*. mistiness, dimness of sight:– mist [1]

888 **ἀχρεῖος**, ***achreios***, a. GK: *945* [→ *1.1+5530*]. worthless, useless, unworthy:– unprofitable [2]

889 **ἀχρειόω**, ***achreioō***, v. GK: *946* [→ *1.1+5530*]. (pass.) to become worthless, depraved:– unprofitable [1]

890 **ἄχρηστος**, ***achrēstos***, a. GK: *947* [→ *1.1+5530*]. useless, worthless:– unprofitable [1]

891 **ἄχρι**, ***achri***, pp.*&c. GK: *948* [→ *206*]. until, up to, as far as, as long as:– until [12], unto [12], till (+*3739*) [4], till [4], until (+*3739*) [4], as far as [2], for [2], while (+*3739*) [2], even to [1], even unto [1], hitherto (+*1204+3588*) [1], into [1], in [1], till (+*302+3739*) [1], to [1]

892 **ἄχυρον**, ***achyron***, n. GK: *949*. chaff:– chaff [2]

893 **ἀψευδής**, ***apseudēs***, a. GK: *950* [→ *1.1+5574*]. not a liar, free from deceit, trustworthy:– cannot lie [1]

894 **ἄψινθος**, ***apsinthos***, n. GK: *951 & 952*. (m.) Wormwood, referring to a bitter herb (absinthe); (f.) bitterness:– wormwood [2]

895 **ἄψυχος**, ***apsychos***, a. GK: *953* [→ *1.1+5594*]. lifeless, inanimate:– without life [1]

896 **Βάαλ**, ***Baal***, n.pr. GK: *955*. Baal, "*master, owner, lord*":– Baal [1]

897 **Βαβυλών**, ***Babylōn***, n.pr. GK: *956*. Babylon, "*gate of god[s]*":– Babylon [12]

898 **βαθμός**, ***bathmos***, n. GK: *957* [→ *305*]. standing, rank:– degree [1]

899 **βάθος**, ***bathos***, n. GK: *958* [→ *901*]. depth, deep thing; extreme:– depth [4], deep (+*2596*) [1], deep things [1], deepness [1], deep [1], depths [1]

900 **βαθύνω**, ***bathynō***, v. GK: *959* [→ *901*]. to go down deep, dig deep:– deep [1]

901 **βαθύς**, ***bathys***, a. GK: *960* [→ *899, 900*]. deep; (as a time of day) early:– deep [2], very early in the morning (+*3722*) [1]

902 **βάϊον**, ***baion***, n. GK: *961*. (palm) branch:– branches [1]

903 **Βαλαάμ**, ***Balaam***, n.pr. GK: *962*. Balaam, "[poss.] *Baal [lord] of the people* or *the clan brings forth*":– Balaam [3]

904 **Βαλάκ**, ***Balak***, n.pr. GK: *963*. Balak, "*devastator*":– Balac [1]

905 **βαλλάντιον**, ***ballantion***, n. GK: *964*. purse, money-bag:– purse [3], bags [1]

906 **βάλλω**, ***ballō***, v. GK: *311 & 965* [→ *293, 306, 311, 474, 577, 579, 580, 956, 992,*

1000, 1001, 1002, 1225, 1228, 1544, 1546, 1685, 1911, 1915, 2598, 2602, 3036, 3328, 3846, 3850, 3925, 4016, 4018, 4261, 4820, 5146, 5234, 5235, 5236, 5260]. to throw, pour; to put, set:– cast [81], put [11], casting [6], laid [3], send [3], thrust [3], casteth [2], putteth [2], threw [2], thrust in [2], arose [1], cast in [1], dung (*+2874*) [1], lieth [1], lying [1], poured [1], poureth [1], put up [1], strike with the palms of hands (*+4475*) [1], thrown [1]

907 **βαπτίζω, *baptizō***, v. GK: *966* [→ *911*]. to baptize, wash; the baptizer:– baptized [61], baptize [9], baptizing [4], baptizeth [2], Baptist [1], baptizest [1], washed [1], wash [1]

908 **βάπτισμα, *baptisma***, n. GK: *967* [→ *911*]. baptism:– baptism [22]

909 **βαπτισμός, *baptismos***, n. GK: *968* [→ *911*]. baptism, ceremonial washing:– washing [2], baptisms [1], washings [1]

910 **βαπτιστής, *baptistēs***, n. GK: *969* [→ *911*]. Baptist, a surname of John:– Baptist [13], Baptist's [1]

911 **βάπτω, *baptō***, v. GK: *970* [→ *907, 908, 909, 910, 1686*]. to dip (in):– dipped [1], dipt [1], dip [1]

912 **Βαραββᾶς, *Barabbas***, n.pr. GK: *972*. Barabbas, "*son of a father* poss. *son of a rabbi*":– Barabbas [11]

913 **Βαράκ, *Barak***, n.pr. GK: *973*. Barak, "*lightning*":– Barak [1]

914 **Βαραχίας, *Barachias***, n.pr. GK: *974*. Berekiah, "*Yahweh blesses*":– Barachias [1]

915 **βάρβαρος, *barbaros***, a. GK: *975*. non-Greek, foreign, "barbarian"; someone who speaks an unintelligible language:– barbarian [3], barbarians [2], barbarous people [1]

916 **βαρέω, *bareō***, v. GK: *976* [→ *922*]. (pass.) to be burdened, under pressure:– heavy [3], burdened [1], charged [1], pressed [1]

917 **βαρέως, *bareōs***, adv. GK: *977* [→ *922*]. with difficulty:– dull [2]

918 **Βαρθολομαῖος, *Bartholomaios***, n.pr. GK: *978*. Bartholomew, "*son of Talmai*":– Bartholomew [4]

919 **Βαριησοῦς, *Bariēsous***, n.pr. GK: *979*. Bar-Jesus, "*son of Jesus [Joshua]*":– Barjesus [1]

920 **Βαριωνᾶς, *Bariōnas***, n.pr. GK: *980 & 981*. son of Jonah, Bar-Jona, "*son of Jonah* or *John*":– Barjona [1]

921 **Βαρναβᾶς, *Barnabas***, n.pr. GK: *982*. Barnabas, "*son of comfort*":– Barnabas [29]

922 **βάρος, *baros***, n. GK: *983* [→ *4, 916, 917, 925, 926, 927, 1912, 2599*]. burden, weight; this can refer either to difficulty or importance:– burden [3], burdensome (*+1722*) [1], burdens [1], weight [1]

923 **Βαρσαββᾶς, *Barsabbas***, n.pr. GK: *984*. Barsabbas, "*son of the Sabbath* or *son of Saba*":– Barsabas [2]

924 **Βαρτιμαῖος, *Bartimaios***, n.pr. GK: *985*. Bartimaeus, "*son of Timai* or *son of uncleanness*":– Bartimeus [1]

925 **βαρύνω, *barynō***, v. GK: *986 & 2852* [→ *922*]. to burden, grieve:– overcharged [1]

926 **βαρύς, *barys***, a. GK: *987* [→ *922*]. burdensome, heavy, important; savage, fierce:– grievous [3], heavy [1], weightier [1], weighty [1]

927 **βαρύτιμος, *barytimos***, a. GK: *988* [→ *922+5092*]. very expensive:– very precious [1]

928 **βασανίζω, *basanizō***, v. GK: *989* [→ *931*]. to torture, torment; (pass.) to be tortured, tormented, in pain:– tormented [5], torment [3], pained [1], toiling [1], tossed [1], vexed [1]

929 **βασανισμός, *basanismos***, n. GK: *990* [→ *931*]. torment, torture, agony:– torment [6]

930 **βασανιστής, *basanistēs***, n. GK: *991* [→ *931*]. torturer:– tormentors [1]

931 **βάσανος, *basanos***, n. GK: *992* [→ *928, 929, 930*]. torment, severe pain, torture:– torments [2], torment [1]

932 **βασιλεία, *basileia***, n. GK: *993* [→ *935*]. kingdom, kingship, royal rule:– kingdom [157], kingdoms [4], reigneth (*+2192*) [1]

933 **βασίλειον, *basileion***, a.neut. of *934*. GK: *994* [→ *935*]. as a noun, a residence of royalty: palace:– kings' courts [1]

934 **βασίλειος, *basileios***, a. GK: *994* [→ *935*]. royal, kingly; as a noun, a residence of royalty: palace:– royal [1]

935 **βασιλεύς, *basileus***, n. GK: *995* [→ *932, 933, 934, 936, 937, 938, 4821*]. king:– king [86], kings [29], king's [2], kings' [1]

936 **βασιλεύω, *basileuō***, v. GK: *996* [→ *935*]. to reign as a king, become king:– reign [13], reigned [5], kings [1], reigned as kings [1], reigneth [1]

937 **βασιλικός, *basilikos***, a. GK: *997 & 998* [→ *935*]. royal, noble, kingly; as a noun, royal official (possibly of the Herodian family):– nobleman [2], royal [2], king's [1]

938 **βασίλισσα, *basilissa***, n. GK: *999* [→ *935*]. queen:– queen [4]

939 **βάσις, *basis***, n. GK: *1000* [→ *305*]. foot:– feet [1]

940 **βασκαίνω, *baskainō***, v. GK: *1001*. to bewitch:– bewitched [1]

941 **βαστάζω, *bastazō***, v. GK: *1002* [→ *1419*]. to carry, bear up, carry off; to tolerate, help, support:– bear [11], bare [4], borne [4], bearing [3], bearest [1], carried [1], carrieth [1], carry [1], took up [1]

942 **βάτος[1], *batos*[1]**, n. GK: *1003*. bush, brier, thornbush:– bush [4], bramble bush [1]

943 **βάτος[2], *batos*[2]**, n. GK: *1004*. bath (a unit of liquid measure, between eight and nine gallons):– measures [1]

944 **βάτραχος, *batrachos***, n. GK: *1005*. frog:– frogs [1]

945 **βατταλογέω, *battalogeō***, v. GK: *1006* [→ *3004*]. to babble, prattle:– use vain repetitions [1]

946 **βδέλυγμα, *bdelygma***, n. GK: *1007* [→ *947, 948*]. abomination, something detestable:– abomination [4], abominations [2]

947 **βδελυκτός, *bdelyktos***, a. GK: *1008* [→ *946*]. detestable, abominable:– abominable [1]

948 **βδελύσσομαι, *bdelyssomai***, v. GK: *1009* [→ *946*]. (mid.) to abhor, detest; (pass.) to be vile, abhorrent:– abhorrest [1], abominable [1]

949 **βέβαιος, *bebaios***, a. GK: *1010* [→ *305*]. firm, sure, certain, binding:– stedfast [4], sure [2], firm [1], force [1], more sure [1]

950 **βεβαιόω, *bebaioō***, v. GK: *1011* [→ *305*]. to confirm; keep strong:– confirmed [2], confirm [2], confirming [1], established [1], stablished [1], stablisheth [1]

951 **βεβαίωσις, *bebaiōsis***, n. GK: *1012* [→ *305*]. confirmation:– confirmation [2]

952 **βέβηλος, *bebēlos***, a. GK: *1013* [→ *305*]. godless, irreligious, profane, worldly:– profane [5]

953 **βεβηλόω, *bebēloō***, v. GK: *1014* [→ *305*]. to desecrate, profane:– profane [2]

954 **Βεελζεβούλ, *Beelzeboul***, n.pr. GK: *1015*. Beelzebub, "*lord [baal] of the flies*":– Beelzebub [7]

955 **Βελίαλ, *Belial***, n.pr. GK: *1016*. Belial, "*wicked, without use*":– Belial [1]

956 **βέλος, *belos***, n. GK: *1018* [→ *906*]. arrow:– darts [1]

957 **βελτίων, *beltiōn***, a. GK: *1019*. having a detailed knowledge, translated "better, very well":– very well [1]

958 **Βενιαμίν, *Beniamin***, n.pr. GK: *1020 & 1021*. Benjamin, "*son of the right hand* or *Southerner*":– Benjamin [4]

959 **Βερνίκη, *Bernikē***, n.pr. GK: *1022* [→ *5342+3529*]. Bernice, "*victorious*":– Bernice [3]

960 **Βέροια, *Beroia***, n.pr. GK: *1023* [→ *961*]. Berea:– Berea [2]

961 **Βεροιαῖος, *Beroiaios***, a.pr.g. GK: *1024* [→ *960*]. Berean, person of Berea:– Berea [1]

962 **Βηθαβαρά, *Bēthabara***, n.pr. GK: *1028 & 1030*. Bethabara:– Bethabara [1]

963 **Βηθανία, *Bēthania***, n.pr. GK: *1029*. Bethany, "*House of Ananiah* [or *the poor* or *unripe figs*]":– Bethany [11]

964 **Βηθεσδά, *Bēthesda***, n.pr. GK: *1031 & 1032*. Bethesda, "*site [house] of mercy*":– Bethesda [1]

965 **Βηθλέεμ, *Bēthleem***, n.pr. GK: *1033*. Bethlehem, "*house of bread* poss. *temple of Lakhmu*":– Bethlehem [8]

966 **Βηθσαϊδά, *Bēthsaida***, n.pr. GK: *1034 & 1035*. Bethsaida, "*site [house] of fishing*":– Bethsaida [7]

967 **Βηθφαγή, *Bēthphagē***, n.pr. GK: *1036*. Bethphage, "*house of unripe figs*":– Bethphage [3]

968 **βῆμα, *bēma***, n. GK: *1037* [→ *305*]. judicial court, judge's seat; this can refer to human or divine judgment:– judgment seat [10], set on [1], throne [1]

969 **βήρυλλος, *bēryllos***, n. GK: *1039*. beryl, a semi-precious stone of sea-green color:– beryl [1]

970 **βία, *bia***, n. GK: *1040* [→ *971, 972, 973, 3849*]. force, violence, pounding (of surf):– violence [4]

971 **βιάζω, *biazō***, v. GK: *1041* [→ *970*]. (mid.) to force one's way:– presseth [1], suffereth violence [1]

972 **βίαιος, *biaios***, a. GK: *1042* [→ *970*]. violent, strong:– mighty [1]

973 **βιαστής, *biastēs***, n. GK: *1043* [→ *970*]. forceful one:– violent [1]

974 **βιβλαρίδιον, *biblaridion***, n. GK: *1044 & 1045* [→ *976*]. little scroll:– little book [4]

975 **βιβλίον, *biblion***, n. GK: *1046* [→ *976*]. scroll, book, certificate:– book [25], books [4], bill [1], scrole [1], writing [1]

976 βίβλος, *biblos*, n. GK: *1047* [→ *974, 975*]. book, scroll:– book [12], books [1]

977 βιβρώσκω, *bibrōskō*, v. GK: *1048* [→ *1033, 1034, 1035, 4598, 4662*]. to eat:– eaten [1]

978 Βιθυνία, *Bithynia*, n.pr. GK: *1049*. Bithynia:– Bithynia [2]

979 βίος, *bios*, n. GK: *1050* [→ *980, 981, 982, 3969*]. (everyday) life; what one lives on, property, possessions:– life [5], living [5], good [1]

980 βιόω, *bioō*, v. GK: *1051* [→ *979*]. to live:– live [1]

981 βίωσις, *biōsis*, n. GK: *1052* [→ *979*]. the way one lives:– manner of life [1]

982 βιωτικός, *biōtikos*, a. GK: *1053* [→ *979*]. (lesser things) of this life:– of life [1], pertaining to life [1], that pertain to life [1]

983 βλαβερός, *blaberos*, a. GK: *1054* [→ *984*]. harmful:– hurtful [1]

984 βλάπτω, *blaptō*, v. GK: *1055* [→ *983*]. to hurt, injure:– hurt [2]

985 βλαστάνω, *blastanō*, v. GK: *1056 & 1057* [→ *986*]. to sprout, bud:– brought forth [1], budded [1], spring [1], sprung up [1]

986 Βλάστος, *Blastos*, n.pr. GK: *1058* [→ *985*]. Blastus, "*sprout [of a vine or branch]*":– Blastus [1]

987 βλασφημέω, *blasphēmeō*, v. GK: *1059* [→ *988, 989; cf. 5346*]. to blaspheme, insult, slander, curse:– blasphemed [7], blaspheme [6], speak evil [5], evil spoken of [4], blasphemeth [2], blasphemers [1], blasphemest [1], blaspheming [1], blasphemously [1], defamed [1], railed on [1], railed [1], reviled [1], slanderously reported [1], speaking evil [1], spoken blasphemy [1]

988 βλασφημία, *blasphēmia*, n. GK: *1060* [→ *987*]. blasphemy, slander, malicious talk:– blasphemy [11], blasphemies [5], evil speaking [1], railings [1], railing [1]

989 βλάσφημος, *blasphēmos*, a. GK: *1061* [→ *987*]. blasphemous, slanderous, abusive, evil, hurtful (speech); as a noun, a reviler, blasphemer:– blasphemous [2], blasphemers [1], blasphemer [1], railing [1]

990 βλέμμα, *blemma*, n. GK: *1062* [→ *991*]. act of seeing:– seeing [1]

991 βλέπω, *blepō*, v. GK: *1063* [→ *308, 309, 578, 990, 1227, 1689, 1914, 4017, 4265*]. to see, look at; to watch out, beware, pay attention:– see [48], take heed [14], seeth [11], saw [9], seen [9], seeing [8], beware [7], seest [5], look [4], beholdest [3], behold [3], beheld [2], beholding [2], sight [2], lieth [1], look on [1], looked [1], looketh on [1], looking [1], perceive [1], regardest (*+1519*) [1], regardest [1]

992 βλητέος, *blēteos*, a. GK: *1064* [→ *906*]. must be put:– must be put [1], put [1]

993 Βοανηργές, *Boanērges*, l.[pr.n.]. GK: *1065*. Boanerges, "*sons of thunder*":– Boanerges [1]

994 βοάω, *boaō*, v. GK: *1066* [→ *995*]. to call, cry out, shout:– crying [6], cried [3], cry [2]

995 βοή, *boē*, n. GK: *1068* [→ *310, 994, 996, 997, 998, 1916*]. cry, shout:– cries [1]

996 βοήθεια, *boētheia*, n. GK: *1069* [→ *995*]. help; support (to hold something together with ropes or cables):– helps [1], help [1]

997 βοηθέω, *boētheō*, v. GK: *1070* [→ *995*]. to help, come to the aid of:– help [5], helped [1], succoured [1], succour [1]

998 βοηθός, *boēthos*, a. GK: *1071* [→ *995*]. helpful (one):– helper [1]

999 βόθυνος, *bothynos*, n. GK: *1072 & 1073*. pit, cistern:– ditch [2], pit [1]

1000 βολή, *bolē*, n. GK: *1074* [→ *906*]. throwing:– cast [1]

1001 βολίζω, *bolizō*, v. GK: *1075* [→ *906*]. to take a sounding (a nautical technical term):– sounded [2]

1002 βολίς, *bolis*, n. GK: *1076* [→ *906*]. missile, arrow, javelin:– dart [1]

1003 Βοόζ, *Booz*, n.pr. GK: *1067 & 1077 & 1078*. Boaz, "[perhaps] *in him is strength*":– Booz [3]

1004 βόρβορος, *borboros*, n. GK: *1079*. mud, filth, slime:– mire [1]

1005 βορρᾶς, *borras*, n. GK: *1080*. the north:– north [2]

1006 βόσκω, *boskō*, v. GK: *1081* [→ *1008*]. to feed, tend; (pass.) to eat, graze:– feeding [3], feed [3], fed [2], kept [1]

1007 Βοσόρ, *Bosor*, n.pr. GK: *1026 & 1027 & 1082*. Bosor:– Bosor [1]

1008 βοτάνη, *botanē*, n. GK: *1083* [→ *1006*]. crop (from any kind of plant or vegetation):– herbs [1]

1009 βότρυς, *botrys*, n. GK: *1084*. grape cluster, bunch of grapes:– clusters [1]

1010 βουλευτής, *bouleutēs*, n. GK: *1085* [→ *1014*]. member of a council (an advisory or legislative body):– counseller [2]

1011 βουλεύω, *bouleuō*, v. GK: *1086* [→ *1014*]. to make plans, consider, decide, plot:– minded [2], purpose [2], consulted [1], consulteth [1], determined [1], took counsel [1]

1012 βουλή, *boulē*, n. GK: *1087* [→ *1014*]. plan, purpose, will, decision:– counsel [9], advised (*+5087*) [1], counsels [1], will [1]

1013 βούλημα, *boulēma*, n. GK: *1088* [→ *1014*]. plan, will, choice:– purpose [1], will [1]

1014 βούλομαι, *boulomai*, v. GK: *1089* [→ *711, 1010, 1011, 1012, 1013, 1917, 2103, 3851, 4823, 4824, 4825*]. to wish, will, desire; to choose, determine, plan:– will [11], would [10], willing [5], minded [2], disposed [1], intending [1], intend [1], listeth (*+2116*) [1], of own will [1], would have [1]

1015 βουνός, *bounos*, n. GK: *1090*. hill:– hills [1], hill [1]

1016 βοῦς, *bous*, n. GK: *1091*. ox, cattle:– oxen [4], ox [4]

1017 βραβεῖον, *brabeion*, n. GK: *1092* [→ *1018*]. prize (from a contest or foot race):– prize [2]

1018 βραβεύω, *brabeuō*, v. GK: *1093* [→ *1017, 2603*]. to rule:– rule [1]

1019 βραδύνω, *bradynō*, v. GK: *1094* [→ *1021*]. to delay, hesitate:– slack [1], tarry long [1]

1020 βραδυπλοέω, *bradyploeō*, v. GK: *1095* [→ *1021+4126*]. to sail slowly:– sailed slowly [1]

1021 βραδύς, *bradys*, a. GK: *1096* [→ *1019, 1020, 1022*]. slow:– slow [3]

1022 βραδύτης, *bradytēs*, n. GK: *1097* [→ *1021*]. slowness:– slackness [1]

1023 βραχίων, *brachiōn*, n. GK: *1098* [→ *1024*]. arm; a figure of power and authority:– arm [3]

1024 βραχύς, *brachys*, a. GK: *1099* [→ *1023*]. little, short:– little [4], few [1], little space [1], little while [1]

1025 βρέφος, *brephos*, n. GK: *1100*. baby, infant:– babe [4], babes [1], child [1], infants [1], young children [1]

1026 βρέχω, *brechō*, v. GK: *1101* [→ *1028*]. to rain down (water or sulfur); to make wet:– rained [2], rain (*+5205*) [1], rain [1], sendeth rain [1], washed [1], wash [1]

1027 βροντή, *brontē*, n. GK: *1103*. thunder:– thunderings [4], thunders [4], thunder [3], thundered (*+1096*) [1]

1028 βροχή, *brochē*, n. GK: *1104* [→ *1026*]. rain:– rain [2]

1029 βρόχος, *brochos*, n. GK: *1105*. restriction, restraint (from the base meaning of a snare or noose, not found in the NT):– snare [1]

1030 βρυγμός, *brygmos*, n. GK: *1106* [→ *1031*]. gnashing, grinding:– gnashing [7]

1031 βρύχω, *brychō*, v. GK: *1107* [→ *1030*]. to gnash, grind:– gnashed [1]

1032 βρύω, *bryō*, v. GK: *1108*. to flow, pour forth:– send forth [1]

1033 βρῶμα, *brōma*, n. GK: *1109* [→ *977*]. food, what is eaten:– meat [10], meats [6], victuals [1]

1034 βρώσιμος, *brōsimos*, a. GK: *1110* [→ *977*]. eatable:– meat [1]

1035 βρῶσις, *brōsis*, n. GK: *1111* [→ *977*]. consumable, food, rust, corrosion:– meat [6], rust [2], eating [1], food [1], morsel of meat [1]

1036 βυθίζω, *bythizō*, v. GK: *1112* [→ *1037*]. (act.) to plunge; (pass.) to sink:– drown [1], sink [1]

1037 βυθός, *bythos*, n. GK: *1113* [→ *12, 1036*]. open sea, the deep:– deep [1]

1038 βυρσεύς, *byrseus*, n. GK: *1114*. tanner:– tanner [3]

1039 βύσσινος, *byssinos*, a. GK: *1115 & 3327* [→ *1040*]. made of fine linen, a product of the flax plant:– fine linen [4]

1040 βύσσος, *byssos*, n. GK: *1116* [→ *1039*]. fine linen:– fine linen [2]

1041 βωμός, *bōmos*, n. GK: *1117* [→ *305*]. altar:– altar [1]

1042 Γαββαθᾶ, *Gabbatha*, n.pr. GK: *1119*. Gabbatha, "[poss.] *height, ridge*":– Gabbatha [1]

1043 Γαβριήλ, *Gabriēl*, n.pr. GK: *1120*. Gabriel, "*[strong] man of God [El]*":– Gabriel [2]

1044 γάγγραινα, *gangraina*, n. GK: *1121*. gangrene:– canker [1]

1045 Γάδ, *Gad*, n.pr. GK: *1122*. Gad, "*fortune*":– Gad [1]

1046 Γαδαρηνός, *Gadarēnos*, a.pr.g. GK: *1123*. Gadarene, "*from Gadara*":– Gadarenes [3]

1047 γάζα^{2}, *gaza*^{2}, n. GK: *1125* [→ *1049*]. treasury:– treasure [1]

1048 **Γάζα[1]**, ***Gaza[1]***, n.pr. GK: *1124*. Gaza, "*strong*":– Gaza [1]

1049 **γαζοφυλάκιον**, ***gazophylakion***, n. GK: *1126* [→ *1047+5442*]. treasury, place where offerings are put:– treasury [5]

1050 **Γάϊος**, ***Gaios***, n.pr. GK: *1127* [→ *1093*]. Gaius:– Gaius [5]

1051 **γάλα**, ***gala***, n. GK: *1128*. milk:– milk [5]

1052 **Γαλάτης**, ***Galatēs***, n.pr.g. GK: *1129* [→ *1053*]. Galatian, "*from Galatia*":– Galatians [2]

1053 **Γαλατία**, ***Galatia***, n.pr. GK: *1130* [→ *1052, 1054*]. Galatia:– Galatia [4]

1054 **Γαλατικός**, ***Galatikos***, a.pr.g. GK: *1131* [→ *1053*]. Galatian:– of Galatia [2]

1055 **γαλήνη**, ***galēnē***, n. GK: *1132*. calm:– calm [3]

1056 **Γαλιλαία**, ***Galilaia***, n.pr. GK: *1133* [→ *1057*]. Galilee, "*ring, circle,* hence *region*":– Galilee [63]

1057 **Γαλιλαῖος**, ***Galilaios***, a.pr.g. GK: *1134* [→ *1056*]. Galilean, "*from Galilee*":– Galileans [5], Galilean [3], of Galilee [3]

1058 **Γαλλίων**, ***Galliōn***, n.pr. GK: *1136*. Gallio:– Gallio [3]

1059 **Γαμαλιήλ**, ***Gamaliēl***, n.pr. GK: *1137*. Gamaliel, "*recompense of God [El]*":– Gamaliel [2]

1060 **γαμέω**, ***gameō***, v. GK: *1138* [→ *1062*]. to marry:– marry [16], married [9], marrieth [3], marrying [1]

1061 **γαμίσκω**, ***gamiskō***, v. GK: *1139 & 1140* [→ *1062*]. to give in marriage, marry; (pass.) to be given in marriage:– given in marriage [1]

1062 **γάμος**, ***gamos***, n. GK: *1141* [→ *22, 1060, 1061, 1547, 1548, 1918*]. wedding banquet (a festive time in the community):– marriage [9], wedding [7]

1063 **γάρ**, ***gar***, c. GK: *1142* [→ *5105*]. shows inference or continuation: for, because, indeed, but:– for [1026], and [4], because [4], why [4], but [2], verily [2], yet (*+2532*) [2], as [1], even [1], how (*+302+4459*) [1], indeed [1], no doubt [1], seeing [1], that [1], then [1], therefore [1], when (*+5613*) [1], yet [1]

1064 **γαστήρ**, ***gastēr***, n. GK: *1143*. belly, womb, gluttony:– with child (*+1722+2192*) [5], child [2], bellies [1], womb [1]

1065 **γέ**, ***ge***, pt.emph. GK: *1145* [→ *2534, 2544, 3304, 3386*]. emphatic particle: indeed, surely:– yet [2], and (*+235*) [1], at least (*+2532*) [1], did [1], haply (*+686*) [1], then (*+686*) [1], wherefore (*+686*) [1], yet doubtless (*+235*) [1]

1066 **Γεδεών**, ***Gedeōn***, n.pr. GK: *1146*. Gideon, "*one who cuts, hacks*":– Gedeon [1]

1067 **γέεννα**, ***geenna***, n. GK: *1147*. Gehenna, hell, "*Valley of Hinnom*":– hell [12]

1068 **Γεθσημανῆ**, ***Gethsēmanē***, n.pr. GK: *1148 & 1149*. Gethsemane, "*olive oil press*":– Gethsemane [2]

1069 **γείτων**, ***geitōn***, n. GK: *1150*. neighbor:– neighbours [4]

1070 **γελάω**, ***gelaō***, v. GK: *1151* [→ *1071, 2606*]. to laugh:– laugh [2]

1071 **γέλως**, ***gelōs***, n. GK: *1152* [→ *1070*]. laughter:– laughter [1]

1072 **γεμίζω**, ***gemizō***, v. GK: *1153* [→ *1073*]. to fill:– filled [7], fill [1], full [1]

1073 **γέμω**, ***gemō***, v. GK: *1154* [→ *1072, 1117*]. to be full:– full [9], full of [2]

1074 **γενεά**, ***genea***, n. GK: *1155* [→ *1096*]. generation, one's own kind or race, descendant; fig., age, period of time (as in "to all generations"):– generation [31], generations [6], ages [2], nation [1], times [1], time [1]

1075 **γενεαλογέω**, ***genealogeō***, v. GK: *1156* [→ *1096+3004*]. to trace genealogical descent:– descent counted [1]

1076 **γενεαλογία**, ***genealogia***, n. GK: *1157* [→ *1096+3004*]. genealogy, lineage:– genealogies [2]

1077 **γενέσια**, ***genesia***, n. GK: *1158 & 1159 & 1160* [→ *1096*]. birthday (a day that was celebrated):– birthday [2]

1078 **γένεσις**, ***genesis***, n. GK: *1161* [→ *1096*]. birth; genealogy, descent; (course of one's) life:– generation [1], natural [1], nature [1]

1079 **γενετή**, ***genetē***, n. GK: *1162* [→ *1096*]. birth:– birth [1]

1080 **γεννάω**, ***gennaō***, v. GK: *1164* [→ *1096*]. to become the father of; to bear, give birth to; (pass.) to be conceived, born:– begat [42], born [39], begotten [7], bare [1], bear [1], brought forth [1], conceived [1], delivered [1], gendereth [1], gender [1], made [1], sprang [1]

1081 **γέννημα**, ***gennēma***, n. GK: *1163 & 1165* [→ *1096*]. fruit, product, yield, harvest; offspring, brood:– generation [4], fruit [3], fruits [2]

1082 **Γεννησαρέτ**, ***Gennēsaret***, n.pr. GK: *1166*. Gennesaret:– Gennesaret [2], Genesaret [1]

1083 **γέννησις**, ***gennēsis***, n. GK: *1167* [→ *1096*]. birth:– birth [2]

1084 **γεννητός**, ***gennētos***, a. GK: *1168* [→ *1096*]. pertaining to birth; "those born among women" means "all humankind":– born [2]

1085 **γένος**, ***genos***, n. GK: *1169* [→ *1096*]. family, offspring; nation, people, native (of a region); classification or kind:– kindred [3], kind [3], offspring [3], born [2], kinds [2], nation [2], stock [2], countrymen [1], diversities [1], generation [1], of the country of [1]

1086 **Γεργεσηνός**, ***Gergesēnos***, a.pr.g. GK: *1170 & 1171*. Gergesene, "*from Gergesa*":– Gergesenes [1]

1087 **γερουσία**, ***gerousia***, n. GK: *1172* [→ *1088*]. assembly of the elders:– senate [1]

1088 **γέρων**, ***gerōn***, n. GK: *1173* [→ *1087; cf. 1094*]. old person:– old [1]

1089 **γεύομαι**, ***geuomai***, v. GK: *1174*. to taste, eat, partake of (implying enjoyment of the experience):– taste [7], tasted [5], eaten [2], eat [1]

1090 **γεωργέω**, ***geōrgeō***, v. GK: *1175* [→ *1093+2041*]. to farm, cultivate:– dressed [1]

1091 **γεώργιον**, ***geōrgion***, n. GK: *1176* [→ *1093+2041*]. (farmer's) field:– husbandry [1]

1092 **γεωργός**, ***geōrgos***, n. GK: *1177* [→ *1093+2041*]. farmer, tenant farmer, share-cropper:– husbandmen [16], husbandman [3]

1093 **γῆ**, ***gē***, n. GK: *1178* [→ *508, 1050, 1090, 1091, 1092, 1919*]. earth, world, country, region; land, ground, soil:– earth [188], land [42], ground [18], country [2], earthly (*+1537+3588*) [1], world [1]

1094 **γῆρας**, ***gēras***, n. GK: *1179* [→ *1095; cf. 1088*]. old age:– old age [1]

1095 **γηράσκω**, ***gēraskō***, v. GK: *1180* [→ *1094*]. to grow old, age:– old [1], waxeth old [1]

1096 **γίνομαι**, ***ginomai***, v. GK: *1181* [→ *35, 36, 241, 313, 581, 738, 1074, 1075, 1076, 1077, 1078, 1079, 1080, 1081, 1083, 1084, 1085, 1103, 1104, 1118, 1230, 1549, 1920, 2104, 2225, 3439, 3824, 3854, 4266, 4269, 4772, 4773, 4836, 5041, 5042*]. to be, become, happen; to come into existence, be born. It is used in certain contexts to introduce a new section or paragraph in a narrative in Hebrew narrative style: and then, and it came to pass:– was [103], be [84], made [67], came to pass [65], done [63], come [27], were [26], become [21], came [21], is [20], became [17], God forbid (*+3361*) [15], come to pass [15], been [14], arose [11], are [5], have [5], become (*+1519*) [4], becometh [4], being [4], fulfilled [3], had [3], made (*+1519*) [3], married [3], ariseth [2], doing [2], grow [2], past [2], preferred before (*+1715*) [2], seemed [2], wrought [2], assembled [1], as [1], at even (*+3798*) [1], awaking out of sleep (*+1853*) [1], became (*+1519*) [1], befell [1], behaved [1], brought to pass [1], brought [1], came pass [1], camest [1], come by (*+4031*) [1], cometh to pass [1], cometh [1], continued [1], did [1], drawing [1], ended [1], falling headlong (*+4248*) [1], fell [1], finished [1], followed [1], found [1], give [1], happened [1], in [1], laid wait for (*+1917*) [1], obey (*+5255*) [1], ordained [1], partakest (*+4791*) [1], performed [1], preferred [1], published [1], purposed (*+1106*) [1], ran together (*+4890*) [1], require [1], shewed [1], sounded [1], spent [1], taken [1], there [1], thundered (*+1027*) [1], trembled (*+1719*) [1], trembled (*+1790*) [1], turned [1], used [1], vanished out of sight (*+855*) [1], was noised abroad (*+3588+5456*) [1], waxed (*+1519*) [1], waxed [1], wept (*+2805*) [1], were (*+1510*) [1]

1097 **γινώσκω**, ***ginōskō***, v. GK: *1182* [→ *50, 51, 52, 56, 57, 176, 314, 319, 320, 1106, 1107, 1108, 1109, 1110, 1231, 1232, 1233, 1921, 1922, 2589, 2607, 4267, 4268, 4774*]. to know, come to know, recognize, understand; to have sexual relations:– know [94], known [45], knew [30], knoweth [16], perceived [7], knowest [5], knowing [5], understood [4], understand [3], perceive [2], sure [2], allow [1], canst speak [1], can [1], felt [1], knewest [1], knowledge [1], resolved [1], understandest [1], ware of [1], ware [1]

1098 **γλεῦκος**, ***gleukos***, n. GK: *1183* [→ *1099*]. (sweet) wine:– new wine [1]

1099 **γλυκύς**, ***glykys***, a. GK: *1184* [→ *1098*]. sweet, fresh (water):– sweet [3], fresh [1]

1100 γλῶσσα, **glōssa**, n. GK: *1185* [→ *1101, 2084*]. tongue; language; sometimes refers to the supernatural gift of tongues:– tongues [26], tongue [24]

1101 γλωσσόκομον, **glōssokomon**, n. GK: *1186* [→ *1100+2889*]. container for money:– bag [2]

1102 γναφεύς, **gnapheus**, n. GK: *1187* [→ *46; cf. 2833*]. bleacher, fuller, one who cleans and sizes woolen cloth:– fuller [1]

1103 γνήσιος, **gnēsios**, a. GK: *1188* [→ *1096*]. true, loyal, sincere, genuine:– own [2], sincerity [1], true [1]

1104 γνησίως, **gnēsiōs**, adv. GK: *1189* [→ *1096*]. genuinely, sincerely:– naturally [1]

1105 γνόφος, **gnophos**, n. GK: *1190*. darkness:– blackness [1]

1106 γνώμη, **gnōmē**, n. GK: *1191* [→ *1097*]. purpose, resolve; judgment; consent:– judgment [3], mind [2], advice [1], agree (*+1520+4160*) [1], purposed (*+1096*) [1], will [1]

1107 γνωρίζω, **gnōrizō**, v. GK: *1192* [→ *1097*]. to make known, tell, reveal:– made known [9], make known [6], declare [3], certify [1], declared [1], give to understand [1], known [1], wit [1], wot [1]

1108 γνῶσις, **gnōsis**, n. GK: *1194* [→ *1097*]. knowledge, understanding:– knowledge [28], science [1]

1109 γνώστης, **gnōstēs**, n. GK: *1195* [→ *1097*]. one well acquainted with, expert in:– expert [1]

1110 γνωστός, **gnōstos**, a. GK: *1196* [→ *1097*]. known:– known [11], acquaintance [2], know (*+1510*) [1], notable [1]

1111 γογγύζω, **gongyzō**, v. GK: *1197* [→ *1112, 1113, 1234*]. to grumble, complain, mutter:– murmured [6], murmur [2]

1112 γογγυσμός, **gongysmos**, n. GK: *1198* [→ *1111*]. complaint, grumbling; whispering, private talk:– murmuring [2], grudging [1], murmurings [1]

1113 γογγυστής, **gongystēs**, n. GK: *1199* [→ *1111*]. grumbler, complainer:– murmurers [1]

1114 γόης, **goēs**, n. GK: *1200*. imposter:– seducers [1]

1115 Γολγοθᾶ, **Golgotha**, n.pr. GK: *1201*. Golgotha, "*skull*":– Golgotha [3]

1116 Γόμορρα, **Gomorra**, n.pr. GK: *1202*. Gomorrah, "*to overwhelm with water*":– Gomorrha [5]

1117 γόμος, **gomos**, n. GK: *1203* [→ *1073*]. cargo, freight:– merchandise [2], burden [1]

1118 γονεύς, **goneus**, n. GK: *1204* [→ *1096*]. (pl.) parents:– parents [19]

1119 γόνυ, **gony**, n. GK: *1205* [→ *1120*]. knee; "to bend the knee" means "to kneel (in submission or worship)":– kneeled down (*+3588+5087*) [5], knees [4], knee [3]

1120 γονυπετέω, **gonypeteō**, v. GK: *1206* [→ *1119+4098*]. to kneel (before in submission or worship):– kneeling down [2], bowed the knee [1], kneeled [1]

1121 γράμμα, **gramma**, n. GK: *1207* [→ *1125*]. letter (of the alphabet); document, Scriptures, written code; education:– letter [6], letters [3], bill [2], learning [1], scriptures [1], writings [1], written (*+1722*) [1]

1122 γραμματεύς, **grammateus**, n. GK: *1208* [→ *1125*]. teacher or expert in the law, scholar, scribe, city clerk:– scribes [62], scribe [4], townclerk [1]

1123 γραπτός, **graptos**, a. GK: *1209* [→ *1125*]. written:– written [1]

1124 γραφή, **graphē**, n. GK: *1210* [→ *1125*]. (s.) a passage of Scripture; (pl.) the collective whole of the Scriptures; holy, authoritative collection of writings:– scripture [31], scriptures [20]

1125 γράφω, **graphō**, v. GK: *1211 & 2863* [→ *62, 582, 583, 1121, 1122, 1123, 1124, 1449, 1923, 1924, 4270, 5261, 5498*]. to write:– written [135], write [50], wrote [21], describeth [1], writing [1]

1126 γραώδης, **graōdēs**, a. GK: *1212* [→ *1491*]. old wives' tale:– old wives' [1]

1127 γρηγορέω, **grēgoreō**, v. GK: *1213* [→ *1453*]. to keep watch, be on guard:– watch [16], watched [2], vigilant [1], wake [1], watcheth [1], watchful [1], watching [1]

1128 γυμνάζω, **gymnazō**, v. GK: *1214* [→ *1131*]. to train, exercise:– exercised [3], exercise [1]

1129 γυμνασία, **gymnasia**, n. GK: *1215* [→ *1131*]. training, exercise:– exercise [1]

1130 γυμνητεύω, **gymnēteuō**, v. GK: *1216 & 1217* [→ *1131*]. to be in ragged clothing, poorly dressed:– naked [1]

1131 γυμνός, **gymnos**, a. GK: *1218* [→ *1128, 1129, 1130, 1132*]. naked, without clothing; needing (more or better) clothing:– naked [14], bare [1]

1132 γυμνότης, **gymnotēs**, n. GK: *1219* [→ *1131*]. nakedness, insufficiently clothed:– nakedness [3]

1133 γυναικάριον, **gynaikarion**, n. GK: *1220* [→ *1135*]. weak-willed woman, "little woman":– silly women [1]

1134 γυναικεῖος, **gynaikeios**, a. GK: *1221* [→ *1135*]. feminine, weaker:– wife [1]

1135 γυνή, **gynē**, n. GK: *1222* [→ *1133, 1134*]. woman; wife:– woman [96], wife [80], women [33], wives [12]

1136 Γώγ, **Gōg**, n.pr. GK: *1223*. Gog:– Gog [1]

1137 γωνία, **gōnia**, n. GK: *1224* [→ *204, 5068*]. corner; cornerstone, capstone, keystone:– corner [6], corners [2], quarters [1]

1138 Δαβίδ, **Dabid**, n.pr. GK: *1226 & 1253*. David, "*beloved one*":– David [58], David's [1]

1139 δαιμονίζομαι, **daimonizomai**, v. GK: *1227* [→ *1140*]. to be demon-possessed:– possessed with devils [4], possessed with the devil [3], possessed of the devils [2], hath a devil [1], one possessed with a devil [1], possessed with a devil [1], vexed with a devil [1]

1140 δαιμόνιον, **daimonion**, n. GK: *1228* [→ *1139, 1141, 1142, 1175, 1174*]. demon, (pagan) god:– devils [41], devil [18], gods [1]

1141 δαιμονιώδης, **daimoniōdēs**, a. GK: *1229* [→ *1140+1491*]. of the devil, demonic:– devilish [1]

1142 δαίμων, **daimōn**, n. GK: *1230* [→ *1140*]. demon, evil spirit:– devils [4], devil [1]

1143 δάκνω, **daknō**, v. GK: *1231*. to bite:– bite [1]

1144 δάκρυον, **dakryon**, n. GK: *1232* [→ *1145*]. teardrop:– tears [11]

1145 δακρύω, **dakryō**, v. GK: *1233* [→ *1144*]. to weep, shed tears:– wept [1]

1146 δακτύλιος, **daktylios**, n. GK: *1234* [→ *1147*]. (finger) ring:– ring [1]

1147 δάκτυλος, **daktylos**, n. GK: *1235* [→ *1146, 5554; cf. 1166*]. finger:– finger [5], fingers [3]

1148 Δαλμανουθά, **Dalmanoutha**, n.pr. GK: *1236*. Dalmanutha:– Dalmanutha [1]

1149 Δαλματία, **Dalmatia**, n.pr. GK: *1237*. Dalmatia, "*deceitful*":– Dalmatia [1]

1150 δαμάζω, **damazō**, v. GK: *1238* [→ *1151*]. to tame, subdue, control:– tamed [2], tame [2]

1151 δάμαλις, **damalis**, n. GK: *1239* [→ *1150*]. heifer, young cow:– heifer [1]

1152 Δάμαρις, **Damaris**, n.pr. GK: *1240*. Damaris:– Damaris [1]

1153 Δαμασκηνός, **Damaskēnos**, a.pr.g. GK: *1241* [→ *1154*]. Damascene, "*from Damascus*":– Damascenes [1]

1154 Δαμασκός, **Damaskos**, n.pr. GK: *1242* [→ *1153*]. Damascus:– Damascus [15]

1155 δανείζω, **daneizō**, v. GK: *1244 & 1247* [→ *1156*]. to lend, (mid.) to borrow:– lend [3], borrow [1]

1156 δάνειον, **daneion**, n. GK: *1245 & 1249* [→ *1155, 1157*]. debt, loan:– debt [1]

1157 δανειστής, **daneistēs**, n. GK: *1246 & 1250* [→ *1156*]. moneylender, creditor:– creditor [1]

1158 Δανιήλ, **Daniēl**, n.pr. GK: *1248*. Daniel, "*God [El] is my judge*":– Daniel [2]

1159 δαπανάω, **dapanaō**, v. GK: *1251* [→ *1160*]. to spend; to pay expenses:– spent [2], charges [1], consume [1], spend [1]

1160 δαπάνη, **dapanē**, n. GK: *1252* [→ *77, 1159, 1550, 4325*]. cost, expense:– cost [1]

1161 δέ, **de**, pt.&c. GK: *1254* [→ *1847, 1848, 3365, 3366, 3367, 3368, 3369, 3760, 3761, 3762, 3763, 3764*]. but, and, then, rather:– and [1214], but [935], now [168], then [132], when [40], yet [20], for [19], so [15], howbeit [12], nevertheless [12], also [10], yea [10], moreover [9], notwithstanding [8], therefore [4], while [4], even [3], and yet [2], neither (*+3756*) [2], or [2], they (*+3588*) [2], though [2], wherefore [2], and forasmuch as [1], and part (*+3588*) [1], and partly (*+3778*) [1], and to [1], as for [1], as [1], but and [1], but though (*+1487+2532*) [1], but though [1], furthermore [1], howbeit whereinsoever (*+302+1722+3739*) [1], moreover (*+2089*) [1], moreover (*+3062+3739*) [1], neither any (*+3762*) [1], now about (*+2235*) [1], other (*+3588*) [1], so then [1], when (*+5613*) [1], who (*+3588*) [1]

1162 δέησις, **deēsis**, n. GK: *1255* [→ *1189*]. prayer, request, petition:– prayer [7], prayers [5], supplication [4], supplications [2], request [1]

1163 δεῖ, **dei**, v.imper. GK: *1256* [→ *1210*]. it is a must, it is necessary (one should, ought):– must [58], ought [25], must needs [5], ought to [3], meet [2], oughtest [2], should [2], behoved [1], must needs (*+3843*) [1], needful [1], need [1], ought to have [1], oughtest to have [1], should have [1], shouldest have [1]

1164 δεῖγμα, ***deigma***, n. GK: *1257* [→ *1165, 1730, 3856, 5262; cf. 1166*]. example:– example [1]

1165 δειγματίζω, ***deigmatizō***, v. GK: *1258* [→ *1164*]. to expose to public disgrace; to make a spectacle of:– made a shew [1]

1166 δεικνύω, ***deiknyō***, v. GK: *1259 & 1260* [→ *322, 323, 584, 585, 1731, 1732, 1925, 5263; cf. 1147, 1164*]. to show, point out, make known:– shew [20], shewed [8], sheweth [2], shewest [1]

1167 δειλία, ***deilia***, n. GK: *1261* [→ *127*]. timidity, cowardice:– fear [1]

1168 δειλιάω, ***deiliaō***, v. GK: *1262* [→ *127*]. to be afraid, cowardly, timid:– afraid [1]

1169 δειλός, ***deilos***, a. GK: *1264* [→ *127*]. afraid, cowardly, timid:– fearful [3]

1170 δεῖνα, ***deina***, n. GK: *1265*. a certain one, a person or thing one cannot or does not wish to name:– such a man [1]

1171 δεινῶς, ***deinōs***, adv. GK: *1267* [→ *127*]. terribly, fiercely:– grievously [1], vehemently [1]

1172 δειπνέω, ***deipneō***, v. GK: *1268* [→ *1173*]. to eat supper, dine:– sup [2], supped [1], supper [1]

1173 δεῖπνον, ***deipnon***, n. GK: *1270 & 1271* [→ *1172*]. banquet, supper, evening meal:– supper [13], feasts [3]

1174 δεισιδαίμων, ***deisidaimōn***, a. GK: *1273* [→ *127+1140*]. (compar.) very religious:– too superstitious [1]

1175 δεισιδαιμονία, ***deisidaimonia***, n. GK: *1272* [→ *127+1140*]. religion:– superstition [1]

1176 δέκα, ***deka***, n.num. GK: *1274* [→ *586, 586, 1177, 1178, 1179, 1180, 1181, 1182, 1183, 1427, 1428, 1429, 1733, 1734, 4003, 5065*]. ten:– ten [24], eighteen (+*2532+3638*) [3]

1177 δεκαδύο, ***dekadyo***, n.num. GK: *1275* [→ *1176+1417*]. twelve:– twelve [2]

1178 δεκαπέντε, ***dekapente***, n.num. GK: *1278* [→ *1176+4002*]. fifteen:– fifteen [3]

1179 Δεκάπολις, ***Dekapolis***, n.pr. GK: *1279* [→ *1176+4172*]. Decapolis, "*[league of] ten cities*":– Decapolis [3]

1180 δεκατέσσαρες, ***dekatessares***, n.num. GK: *1280* [→ *1176+5064*]. fourteen:– fourteen [5]

1181 δεκάτη, ***dekatē***, a.num.f. of *1182*. GK: *1281* [→ *1176*]. tenth in a series of things or events; as a noun, the tenth part, ten percent of something, tithe:– tenth [2], tithes [2]

1182 δέκατος, ***dekatos***, a.num. GK: *1281* [→ *1176*]. tenth in a series of things or events; as a noun, the tenth part, ten percent of something, tithe:– tenth [3]

1183 δεκατόω, ***dekatoō***, v. GK: *1282* [→ *1176*]. to collect a tenth; (pass.) to pay a tenth:– payed tithes [1], received tithes [1]

1184 δεκτός, ***dektos***, a. GK: *1283* [→ *1209*]. acceptable, favorable:– accepted [3], acceptable [2]

1185 δελεάζω, ***deleazō***, v. GK: *1284* [→ *1388*]. to entice, seduce, lure:– allure [1], beguiling [1], enticed [1]

1186 δένδρον, ***dendron***, n. GK: *1285*. tree:– tree [17], trees [9]

1187 δεξιολάβος, ***dexiolabos***, n. GK: *1286 & 1287* [→ *1188+2983*]. spearman; other sources: bowman, slinger, bodyguard:– spearmen [1]

1188 δεξιός, ***dexios***, a. GK: *1288* [→ *1187*]. the right hand or side in contrast to the left; the right is considered culturally to be stronger and of greater prestige than the left; to be seated on the right side of a ruler is a greater position than on the left side; to "give the right hand of fellowship" in Galatians is a sign of friendship, trust, and covenant:– right hand [38], right [12], right side [2], right hands [1]

1189 δέομαι, ***deomai***, v. GK: *1289* [→ *1162, 1729, 4326*]. to pray; ask, beg, plead:– pray [7], beseech [6], besought [3], prayed [2], praying [2], making request [1], prayed to [1]

δεόν, ***deon***. See ***1163***.

1190 Δερβαῖος, ***Derbaios***, a.pr.g. GK: *1291* [→ *1191*]. from Derbe, "*from Derbe*":– of Derbe [1]

1191 Δέρβη, ***Derbē***, n.pr. GK: *1292* [→ *1190*]. Derbe:– Derbe [3]

1192 δέρμα, ***derma***, n. GK: *1293* [→ *1194*]. skin, leather:– goatskins (+*122*) [1]

1193 δερμάτινος, ***dermatinos***, a. GK: *1294* [→ *1194*]. made of leather:– leathern [1], skin [1]

1194 δέρω, ***derō***, v. GK: *1296* [→ *1192, 1193*]. to beat up, strike, flog, slap:– beaten [5], beat [5], beateth [1], beating [1], smitest [1], smite [1], smote [1]

1195 δεσμεύω, ***desmeuō***, v. GK: *1297* [→ *1210*]. to tie up, bind; to arrest:– binding [1], bind [1]

1196 δεσμέω, ***desmeō***, v. GK: *1298* [→ *1210*]. to tie, bind:– bound [1]

1197 δέσμη, ***desmē***, n. GK: *1299* [→ *1210*]. bundle:– bundles [1]

1198 δέσμιος, ***desmios***, n. GK: *1300* [→ *1210*]. prisoner, one under arrest:– prisoner [11], prisoners [3], bonds [1], in bonds [1]

1199 δεσμός, ***desmos***, n. GK: *1301* [→ *1210*]. chain, fetter, imprisonment:– bonds [14], bands [3], bond [1], chains [1], string [1]

1200 δεσμοφύλαξ, ***desmophylax***, n. GK: *1302* [→ *1210+5442*]. jailer, warden:– keeper of the prison [2], jailor [1]

1201 δεσμωτήριον, ***desmōtērion***, n. GK: *1303* [→ *1210*]. prison, jail:– prison [4]

1202 δεσμώτης, ***desmōtēs***, n. GK: *1304* [→ *1210*]. prisoner:– prisoners [2]

1203 δεσπότης, ***despotēs***, n. GK: *1305* [→ *3616, 3617; cf. 1210*]. master; Sovereign Lord:– Lord/lord [5], masters [4], master's [1]

1204 δεῦρο, ***deuro***, adv.pl. GK: *1306* [→ *1205*]. come, come here:– come [6], hither [2], hitherto (+*891+3588*) [1]

1205 δεῦτε, ***deute***, adv. GK: *1307* [→ *1204*]. come, come here (pl. of *1204*):– come [12], follow (+*3694*) [1]

1206 δευτεραῖος, ***deuteraios***, a. GK: *1308* [→ *1417*]. on the following day, on the second day:– next day [1]

1207 δευτερόπρωτος, ***deuteroprōtos***, a. GK: *1310* [→ *1417+4413*]. lit: "second-first":– second after the first [1]

1208 δεύτερος, ***deuteros***, a. GK: *1309 & 1311* [→ *1417*]. second; (adv.) for the second time, secondly:– second [36], second time (+*1537*) [4], again (+*1537*) [2], second time [2], afterward [1], again [1], secondarily [1]

1209 δέχομαι, ***dechomai***, v. GK: *1312* [→ *96, 324, 418, 553, 587, 588, 593, 594, 1184, 1237, 1240, 1381, 1382, 1383, 1384, 1403, 1523, 1551, 1561, 1735, 1926, 2144, 3580, 3829, 3830, 3858, 4327, 5264*]. to welcome, receive, accept:– receive [24], received [16], receiveth [11], take [3], accepted [2], took [2]

1210 δέω, ***deō***, v. GK: *1313* [→ *1163, 1195, 1196, 1197, 1198, 1199, 1200, 1201, 1202, 1238, 2611, 4019, 4886, 4887, 5265, 5266; cf. 1203*]. to tie, bind, imprison:– bound [28], bind [9], tied [4], in bonds [1], knit [1], wound [1]

1211 δή, ***dē***, pt.emph. GK: *1314* [→ *1221, 1222, 1894, 1895*]. indeed, therefore; can show urgency or certainty:– also [1], doubtless [1], now [1], therefore [1]

1212 δῆλος, ***dēlos***, a. GK: *1316* [→ *82, 83, 84, 1213, 1552, 2612, 4271*]. clear, plain, evident:– bewrayeth (+*4160*) [1], certain [1], evident [1], manifest [1]

1213 δηλόω, ***dēloō***, v. GK: *1317* [→ *1212*]. to make clear, bring to light, show, point:– declared [2], declare [1], shewed [1], signifieth [1], signifying [1], signify [1]

1214 Δημᾶς, ***Dēmas***, n.pr. GK: *1318* [→ *1218 or* 1216]. Demas, "*common folks*":– Demas [3]

1215 δημηγορέω, ***dēmēgoreō***, v. GK: *1319* [→ *1218+59*]. to deliver a public address:– made an oration [1]

1216 Δημήτριος, ***Dēmētrios***, n.pr. GK: *1320* [→ *1214?*]. Demetrius, "*of Demeter*":– Demetrius [3]

1217 δημιουργός, ***dēmiourgos***, n. GK: *1321* [→ *1218+2041*]. builder, craftsman, maker:– maker [1]

1218 δῆμος, ***dēmos***, n. GK: *1322* [→ *589, 590, 1214?, 1215, 1217, 1219, 1553, 1736, 1927, 3530, 3927, 4898*]. people, crowd:– people [4]

1219 δημόσιος, ***dēmosios***, a. GK: *1323* [→ *1218*]. public, publicly:– publickly [2], common [1], openly [1]

1220 δηνάριον, ***dēnarion***, n. GK: *1324*. denarius [about a day's wage]:– penny [9], pence [5], pennyworth [2]

1221 δήποτε, ***dēpote***, adv. GK: *1325* [→ *1211+4226*]. whatever:–

1222 δήπου, ***dēpou***, adv. GK: *1327* [→ *1211+4226*]. surely, of course:– verily [1]

1223 διά, ***dia***, pp. GK: *1328* [→ *87, 88, 89, 90, 411, 475, 592, 1224, 1225, 1226, 1227, 1228, 1229, 1230, 1231, 1232, 1233, 1234, 1235, 1236, 1237, 1238, 1239, 1240, 1241, 1242, 1243, 1244, 1245, 1246, 1251, 1252, 1253, 1254, 1255, 1256, 1257, 1258, 1259, 1260, 1261, 1262, 1263, 1264, 1265, 1266, 1267, 1268, 1269, 1270, 1271, 1272, 1273, 1274, 1275, 1276, 1277, 1278, 1279, 1280, 1281, 1282, 1283, 1284, 1285, 1286, 1287, 1288, 1289, 1290, 1291, 1292, 1293, 1294, 1295, 1296, 1297, 1298, 1299, 1300, 1301, 1302, 1303, 1304, 1305, 1306, 1307, 1308, 1309, 1310, 1311, 1312, 1313, 1314, 1315, 1316, 1326, 1327, 1328, 1329, 1330, 1331, 1334, 1335, 1336, 1338, 1339, 1340, 1352,*

1353, 1355, 1357, 1358, 1360, 1368, 1555, 1928, 1930, 3859]. (gen.) through, by means of; (acc.) because of, for the sake of, therefore:– by [247], through [86], for [58], therefore (+*3778*) [43], for sake [35], because of [24], because (+*3588*) [21], with [17], for this cause (+*3778*) [14], for sakes [12], because [9], in [8], wherefore (+*3778*) [7], after [3], always (+*3956*) [3], by reason of [3], of [3], throughout [3], whereby (+*3739*) [3], wherefore (+*156*+*3739*) [3], at [2], thereby (+*846*) [2], thereby [2], wherefore (+*3739*) [2], among [1], avoid [1], because by reason of [1], because that (+*3588*) [1], briefly (+*3641*) [1], by (+*3588*) [1], by (+*5495*) [1], by occasion [1], by reason hereof (+*3778*) [1], by reason of (+*3588*) [1], by the means of [1], continually (+*3956*) [1], for (+*3588*) [1], from [1], glorious (+*1391*) [1], out of [1], that (+*3588*) [1], thereat (+*846*) [1], therefore [1], though [1], throughout (+*3650*) [1], to [1], wherein (+*3739*) [1], within [1]

Δία, *Dia*. See **2203**.

1224 διαβαίνω, ***diabainō***, v. GK: *1329* [→ *1223*+*305*]. to pass through, come over, cross:– come over [1], passed through [1], pass [1]

1225 διαβάλλω, ***diaballō***, v. GK: *1330* [→ *1223*+*906*]. (pass.) to have accusations brought upon someone:– accused [1]

1226 διαβεβαιόομαι, ***diabebaioomai***, v. GK: *1331* [→ *1223*+*305*]. to confidently affirm, stress, insist on:– affirm constantly [1], affirm [1]

1227 διαβλέπω, ***diablepō***, v. GK: *1332* [→ *1223*+*991*]. to see clearly; to open eyes wide:– see clearly [2]

1228 διάβολος, ***diabolos***, a. [used as n.]. GK: *1333* [→ *1223*+*906*]. devilish, malicious, slanderous; as a noun, the devil, Satan, or a wicked person who is like the devil:– devil [35], false accusers [2], slanderers [1]

1229 διαγγέλλω, ***diangellō***, v. GK: *1334* [→ *1223*+*32*]. to proclaim (throughout); to give notice:– declared [1], preach [1], signify [1]

1230 διαγίνομαι, ***diaginomai***, v. GK: *1335* [→ *1223*+*1096*]. to pass, elapse (of time):– after [1], past [1], spent [1]

1231 διαγινώσκω, ***diaginōskō***, v. GK: *1336* [→ *1223*+*1097*]. to determine, decide:– inquire [1], know the uttermost [1]

1232 διαγνωρίζω, ***diagnōrizō***, v. GK: *1337* [→ *1223*+*1097*]. to give an exact report:– made known abroad [1]

1233 διάγνωσις, ***diagnōsis***, n. GK: *1338* [→ *1223*+*1097*]. decision:– hearing [1]

1234 διαγογγύζω, ***diagongyzō***, v. GK: *1339* [→ *1223*+*1111*]. to mutter, grumble, complain:– murmured [2]

1235 διαγρηγορέω, ***diagrēgoreō***, v. GK: *1340* [→ *1223*+*1453*]. to become fully awake:– awake [1]

1236 διάγω, ***diagō***, v. GK: *1341* [→ *1223*+*71*]. to live, conduct one's life:– lead [1], living [1]

1237 διαδέχομαι, ***diadechomai***, v. GK: *1342* [→ *1223*+*1209*]. to receive (in turn):– came after [1]

1238 διάδημα, ***diadēma***, n. GK: *1343* [→ *1223*+*1210*]. crown, diadem:– crowns [3]

1239 διαδίδωμι, ***diadidōmi***, v. GK: *1344* [→ *1223*+*1325*]. to distribute, divide up:– distributed [1], distribute [1], distribution [1], divideth [1], give [1]

1240 διάδοχος, ***diadochos***, n. GK: *1345* [→ *1223*+*1209*]. successor:– came into room (+*2983*) [1]

1241 διαζώννυμι, ***diazōnnymi***, v. GK: *1346* [→ *1223*+*2224*]. to wrap around, tie around, put on:– girded [2], girt [1]

1242 διαθήκη, ***diathēkē***, n. GK: *1347* [→ *1223*+*5087*]. covenant, a solemn agreement between two parties; will, testament, a legal document by which property is transferred to heirs, usually upon death (Heb 9:16):– covenant [17], testament [13], covenants [3]

1243 διαίρεσις, ***diairesis***, n. GK: *1348* [→ *1223*+*138*]. difference, variety:– diversities [2], differences [1]

1244 διαιρέω, ***diaireō***, v. GK: *1349* [→ *1223*+*138*]. to divide, distribute, apportion:– divided [1], dividing [1]

1245 διακαθαρίζω, ***diakatharizō***, v. GK: *1350 & 1351* [→ *1223*+*2513*]. to clear out, clean out (with a possible implication that the cleaning is thorough):– throughly purge [2]

1246 διακατελέγχομαι, ***diakatelenchomai***, v. GK: *1352* [→ *1223*+*2596*+*1651*]. to refute (thoroughly):– convinced [1]

1247 διακονέω, ***diakoneō***, v. GK: *1354* [→ *1249*]. to serve, wait on, help, attend to; this often refers to spiritual and practical ministry in the Church. "To wait upon tables" (Ac 6:2) may mean to literally help in serving food, though some believe it refers (also) to the handling of finances:– ministered [14], minister [8], serve [7], administered [2], serveth [2], ministering [1], served [1], use the office of deacon [1], used the office of deacon [1]

1248 διακονία, ***diakonia***, n. GK: *1355* [→ *1249*]. ministry, service, this can refer to helps and service of various kinds which can range in meaning from "spiritual" biblical teaching (Ac 6:4) to the "practical" giving of provisions, supplies, support, and finances to those in need (2Co 9:12):– ministry [16], ministration [6], ministering [3], service [3], administrations [1], administration [1], minister [1], office [1], relief (+*1519*) [1], serving [1]

1249 διάκονος, ***diakonos***, n. GK: *1356* [→ *1247, 1248*]. servant, minister, a person who renders service and help to others, in some contexts with an implication of lower status; also transliterated as "deacon," a trusted officer of helps and service in the local church:– minister [14], ministers [6], servant [5], deacons [3], servants [3]

1250 διακόσιοι, ***diakosioi***, a.num. GK: *1357* [→ *1417*]. two hundred:– two hundred [8]

1251 διακούω, ***diakouō***, v. GK: *1358* [→ *1223*+*191*]. to give a (legal) hearing:– hear [1]

1252 διακρίνω, ***diakrinō***, v. GK: *1359* [→ *1223*+*2919*]. to make a distinction, judge a dispute; (mid./pass.) to doubt, hesitate, waver:– judge [3], doubting [2], doubt [2], contended [1], contending [1], discerning [1], discern [1], doubteth [1], maketh to differ [1], making a difference [1], partial [1], put difference [1], staggered [1], wavereth [1], wavering [1]

1253 διάκρισις, ***diakrisis***, n. GK: *1360* [→ *1223*+*2919*]. distinguishing, differentiation; passing judgment:– discerning [1], discern [1], disputations [1]

1254 διακωλύω, ***diakōlyō***, v. GK: *1361* [→ *1223*+*2967*]. to deter, prevent:– forbad [1]

1255 διαλαλέω, ***dialaleō***, v. GK: *1362* [→ *1223*+*2980*]. to talk about, discuss:– communed [1], noised abroad [1]

1256 διαλέγομαι, ***dialegomai***, v. GK: *1363* [→ *1223*+*3004*]. to reason, discuss, discourse; to argue, dispute:– reasoned [4], disputed [3], disputing [3], preached [1], preaching [1], speaketh [1]

1257 διαλείπω, ***dialeipō***, v. GK: *1364* [→ *1223*+*3007*]. to stop, cease:– ceased [1]

1258 διάλεκτος, ***dialektos***, n. GK: *1365* [→ *1223*+*3004*]. language, dialect, a communication code whether written or oral; in the NT this always refers to known languages commonly spoken in the ancient world:– tongue [5], language [1]

1259 διαλλάσσομαι, ***diallassomai***, v. GK: *1367* [→ *1223*+*236*]. to become reconciled:– reconciled [1]

1260 διαλογίζομαι, ***dialogizomai***, v. GK: *1368* [→ *1223*+*3004*]. to think, wonder about; to talk, discuss, argue:– reasoned [5], reason [5], cast in mind [1], consider [1], disputed [1], mused [1], reasoning [1], thought [1]

1261 διαλογισμός, ***dialogismos***, n. GK: *1369* [→ *1223*+*3004*]. thought, doubt; argument, dispute:– thoughts [8], disputings [1], doubtful [1], doubting [1], imaginations [1], reasoning [1], thought [1]

1262 διαλύω, ***dialyō***, v. GK: *1370* [→ *1223*+*3089*]. to disperse, break up:– scattered [1]

1263 διαμαρτύρομαι, ***diamartyromai***, v. GK: *1371* [→ *1223*+*3144*]. to (solemnly) warn or charge; to (solemnly) testify about:– testified [6], testify [4], charge [2], charging [1], testifying [1], witnesseth [1]

1264 διαμάχομαι, ***diamachomai***, v. GK: *1372* [→ *1223*+*3163*]. to argue vigorously, contend sharply:– strove [1]

1265 διαμένω, ***diamenō***, v. GK: *1373* [→ *1223*+*3306*]. to remain (constantly):– continue [2], continued [1], remained [1], remainest [1]

1266 διαμερίζω, ***diamerizō***, v. GK: *1374* [→ *1223*+*3313*]. to divide, distribute:– parted [5], divided [4], cloven [1], divide [1], parted among [1]

1267 διαμερισμός, ***diamerismos***, n. GK: *1375* [→ *1223*+*3313*]. division:– division [1]

1268 διανέμω, ***dianemō***, v. GK: *1376* [→ *1223*+*3551*]. (pass.) to be spread:– spread [1]

1269 διανεύω, ***dianeuō***, v. GK: *1377* [→ *1223*+*3506*]. to make signs, nod, beckon:– beckoned [1]

1270 διανόημα, ***dianoēma***, n. GK: *1378* [→ *1223*+*3563*]. thought:– thoughts [1]

1271 διάνοια, ***dianoia***, n. GK: *1379* [→ *1223*+*3563*]. mind, thinking, understanding; this is a part of the inner person that thinks and processes information into understanding, including the making of choices, the seat of which is the heart:–

mind [7], understanding [3], minds [2], imagination [1]

1272 **διανοίγω**, ***dianoigō***, v. GK: *1380* [→ *455; cf. 1223*]. to open; (pass.) to be opened; to explain:– opened [6], openeth [1], opening [1]

1273 **διανυκτερεύω**, ***dianyktereuō***, v. GK: *1381* [→ *1223+3571*]. to spend the (entire) night:– all night [1]

1274 **διανύω**, ***dianyō***, v. GK: *1382* [→ *1223+507*]. to continue:– finished [1]

1275 **διαπαντός**, ***diapantos***, adv. GK: *1383* [→ *1223+3956*]. always, continually, constantly:– always [3], alway [2], continually [1]

1276 **διαπεράω**, ***diaperaō***, v. GK: *1385* [→ *1223+4008*]. to cross over:– passed over [3], gone over [1], pass [1], sailing over [1]

1277 **διαπλέω**, ***diapleō***, v. GK: *1386* [→ *1223+4126*]. to sail across, sail through:– sailed over [1]

1278 **διαπονέομαι**, ***diaponeomai***, v. GK: *1387* [→ *1223+4192*]. to be greatly disturbed, troubled, annoyed:– grieved [2]

1279 **διαπορεύομαι**, ***diaporeuomai***, v. GK: *1388* [→ *1223+4198*]. to go through, travel through:– went through [2], in journey [1], pass by [1], went [1]

1280 **διαπορέω**, ***diaporeō***, v. GK: *1389* [→ *1223+1.1+4198*]. to be perplexed, puzzled, in wonder:– doubted [2], perplexed [2], doubt [1]

1281 **διαπραγματεύομαι**, ***diapragmateuomai***, v. GK: *1390* [→ *1223+4238*]. to gain, earn:– gained by trading [1]

1282 **διαπρίω**, ***diapriō***, v. GK: *1391* [→ *1223+4249*]. (pass.) to be furious:– cut [2]

1283 **διαρπάζω**, ***diarpazō***, v. GK: *1395* [→ *1223+726*]. to rob, carry off (many possessions):– spoil [4]

1284 **διαρήσσω**, ***diarēssō***, v. GK: *1392 & 1393 & 1396* [→ *1223+4486*]. to tear (clothes), break (chains):– rent [3], brake [2]

1285 **διασαφέω**, ***diasapheō***, v. GK: *1397* [→ *1223*]. to tell, explain (in detail):– told [1]

1286 **διασείω**, ***diaseiō***, v. GK: *1398* [→ *1223+4579*]. to extort money, as a fig. extension of a violent shaking motion:– violence [1]

1287 **διασκορπίζω**, ***diaskorpizō***, v. GK: *1399* [→ *1223+4650*]. to scatter:– scattered abroad [2], scattered [2], strawed [2], wasted [2], dispersed [1]

1288 **διασπάω**, ***diaspaō***, v. GK: *1400* [→ *1223+4685*]. (pass.) to be torn to pieces:– plucked asunder [1], pulled in pieces [1]

1289 **διασπείρω**, ***diaspeirō***, v. GK: *1401* [→ *1223+4687*]. (pass.) to be scattered:– scattered abroad [3]

1290 **διασπορά**, ***diaspora***, n. GK: *1402* [→ *1223+4687*]. scattering, dispersion, Diaspora:– dispersed among [1], scattered abroad (*+1722+3588*) [1], scattered throughout [1]

1291 **διαστέλλω**, ***diastellō***, v. GK: *1403* [→ *1223+4724*]. (mid.) to give orders, command, authorize; (pass.) what was commanded:– charged [6], commanded [1], gave commandment [1]

1292 **διάστημα**, ***diastēma***, n. GK: *1404* [→ *1223+2476*]. later time, interval:– space after [1]

1293 **διαστολή**, ***diastolē***, n. GK: *1405* [→ *1223+4724*]. difference, distinction:– difference [2], distinction [1]

1294 **διαστρέφω**, ***diastrephō***, v. GK: *1406* [→ *1223+4762*]. (act.) to subvert, pervert, make turn away; (pass.) to be perverted, depraved, turned from the truth:– perverse [4], perverting [1], pervert [1], turn [1]

1295 **διασῴζω**, ***diasōzō***, v. GK: *1407* [→ *1223+4982*]. save, spare, bring safely through a dangerous or distressing situation, with a focus that the rescue is complete or full; to heal, with a focus that the injured or sick person goes from the danger of ill health to the safety of a completely restored or healthy life:– escaped [2], bring safe [1], escaped safe [1], heal [1], made perfectly whole [1], saved [1], save [1]

1296 **διαταγή**, ***diatagē***, n. GK: *1408* [→ *1223+5021*]. putting into effect, institution:– disposition [1], ordinance [1]

1297 **διάταγμα**, ***diatagma***, n. GK: *1409* [→ *1223+5021*]. edict, command:– commandment [1]

1298 **διαταράσσω**, ***diatarassō***, v. GK: *1410* [→ *1223+5015*]. (pass.) to be greatly troubled, perplexed, confused:– troubled [1]

1299 **διατάσσω**, ***diatassō***, v. GK: *1411* [→ *1223+5021*]. (act./mid.) to command, order, direct; (pass.) to be required, ordered, put into effect:– commanded [6], appointed [4], ordained [2], commanding [1], given order [1], ordain [1], set in order [1]

1300 **διατελέω**, ***diateleō***, v. GK: *1412* [→ *1223+5056*]. to continue, remain:– continued [1]

1301 **διατηρέω**, ***diatēreō***, v. GK: *1413* [→ *1223+5083*]. to keep, treasure:– keep [1], kept [1]

1302 **διατί**, ***diati***, pt.inter. GK: *1414* [→ *1223+5101*]. why?:– why [23], wherefore [4]

1303 **διατίθεμαι**, ***diatithemai***, v. GK: *1415* [→ *1223+5087*]. to make a covenant or a will; to confer, assign; to decree, ordain:– make [2], testator [2], appointed [1], appoint [1], made [1]

1304 **διατρίβω**, ***diatribō***, v. GK: *1417* [→ *1223+5147*]. to stay, remain, spend some time:– abode [4], continued [2], tarried [2], abiding [1], been [1]

1305 **διατροφή**, ***diatrophē***, n. GK: *1418* [→ *1223+5142*]. food, sustenance:– food [1]

1306 **διαυγάζω**, ***diaugazō***, v. GK: *1419* [→ *1223+827*]. to dawn, shine through:– dawn [1]

1307 **διαφανής**, ***diaphanēs***, a. GK: *1420 & 1421* [→ *1223+5316*]. transparent:– transparent [1]

1308 **διαφέρω**, ***diapherō***, v. GK: *1422* [→ *1223+5342*]. (tr.) to carry, spread out; (intr.) to differ; to be more valuable than:– better than [3], differeth from [2], more value than [2], carry [1], driven up and down [1], excellent [1], maketh matter [1], more excellent [1], published [1]

1309 **διαφεύγω**, ***diapheugō***, v. GK: *1423* [→ *1223+5343*]. to escape, flee:– escape [1]

1310 **διαφημίζω**, ***diaphēmizō***, v. GK: *1424 & 5775* [→ *1223+5346*]. to spread news about, circulate:– blaze abroad [1], commonly reported [1], spread abroad fame [1]

1311 **διαφθείρω**, ***diaphtheirō***, v. GK: *1425* [→ *1223+5351*]. to destroy, corrupt:– destroy [2], corrupteth [1], corrupt [1], destroyed [1], perish [1]

1312 **διαφθορά**, ***diaphthora***, n. GK: *1426* [→ *1223+5351*]. decay:– corruption [6]

1313 **διάφορος**, ***diaphoros***, a. GK: *1427* [→ *1223+5342*]. different; superior, outstanding, excellent:– more excellent [2], differing [1], divers [1]

1314 **διαφυλάσσω**, ***diaphylassō***, v. GK: *1428* [→ *1223+5442*]. to guard carefully:– keep [1]

1315 **διαχειρίζω**, ***diacheirizō***, v. GK: *1429* [→ *1223+5495*]. (mid.) to kill, murder, formally, "to lay violent hands on":– kill [1], slew [1]

1316 **διαχωρίζω**, ***diachōrizō***, v. GK: *1431* [→ *1223+5565*]. (pass.) to be separated:– departed [1]

1317 **διδακτικός**, ***didaktikos***, a. GK: *1434* [→ *1321*]. able to teach, skillful at instructing:– apt to teach [2]

1318 **διδακτός**, ***didaktos***, a. GK: *1435* [→ *1321*]. taught, instructed:– teacheth [2], taught [1]

1319 **διδασκαλία**, ***didaskalia***, n. GK: *1436* [→ *1321*]. teaching, doctrine:– doctrine [15], doctrines [4], learning [1], teaching [1]

1320 **διδάσκαλος**, ***didaskalos***, n. GK: *1437* [→ *1321*]. teacher, instructor, one who provides instruction, implying authority over the students or followers:– master [46], teachers [6], teacher [4], doctors [1], masters [1]

1321 **διδάσκω**, ***didaskō***, v. GK: *1438* [→ *1317, 1318, 1319, 1320, 1322, 2085, 2312, 2567, 3547, 5572*]. to teach, instruct, to provide information in a manner intended to produce understanding, either in a formal or informal setting:– taught [40], teach [26], teaching [21], teachest [7], teacheth [3]

1322 **διδαχή**, ***didachē***, n. GK: *1439* [→ *1321*]. (the activity or content of) teaching, instruction:– doctrine [28], doctrines [1], taught [1]

1323 **δίδραχμον**, ***didrachmon***, n. GK: *1440* [→ *1417+1405*]. two-drachma (temple tax):– tribute money [1], tribute [1]

1324 **Δίδυμος**, ***Didymos***, n.pr. GK: *1441* [→ *1417*]. Didymus, "*twin*":– Didymus [3]

1325 **δίδωμι**, ***didōmi***, v. GK: *1442 & 1443* [→ *325, 467, 468, 469, 591, 734, 1239, 1390, 1394, 1395, 1431, 1432, 1433, 1434, 1554, 1560, 1929, 2130, 3330, 3405, 3406, 3860, 3862, 3970, 4272, 4273; cf. 1435*]. to give; that this can have many different specific meanings and referents depending on the context, as noted in the list of NIV translations:– give [141], given [123], gave [73], giveth [13], gavest [11], grant [7], put [5], giving [4], granted [3], shew [3], bestowed [2], delivered [2], had power [2], make [2], offer [2], suffer [2], adventure [1], brought forth [1], committed [1], deliver (*+4991*) [1], delivered up [1], gave forth [1], gave up [1], hinder (*+1464*) [1], minister [1], receive [1], set [1], shewed [1], smote with hands (*+4475*) [1], stroke with the palm of hand (+*4475*) [1], taking [1], utter [1], yielded [1], yield [1]

1326 **διεγείρω, *diegeirō***, v. GK: *1444* [→ *1223+1453*]. to get up, arouse, stimulate:– arose [2], stir up [2], awake [1], awoke [1], raised [1]

1327 **διέξοδος, *diexodos***, n. GK: *1447* [→ *1223+1537+3598*]. (street) corner:– highways (+*3588+3598*) [1]

1328 **διερμηνευτής, *diermēneutēs***, n. GK: *1449 & 2256* [→ *1223+2059*]. interpreter, translator:– interpreter [1]

1329 **διερμηνεύω, *diermēneuō***, v. GK: *1450* [→ *1223+2059*]. to interpret, translate, explain:– interpret [4], expounded [1], interpretation [1]

1330 **διέρχομαι, *dierchomai***, v. GK: *1451* [→ *1223+2064*]. to go through, travel throughout:– passed through [5], go through [3], passed [3], pass [3], go [2], pass through [2], passing through [2], walketh through [2], went through [2], come [1], departed [1], go over [1], going [1], gone over [1], gone throughout [1], gone through [1], gone [1], pass over [1], passed by [1], passed into [1], passed throughout [1], past [1], pierce through [1], travelled [1], went about [1], went abroad [1], went every where [1], went over [1]

1331 **διερωτάω, *dierōtaō***, v. GK: *1452* [→ *1223+2065*]. to find out, ask:– made inquiry [1]

1332 **διετής, *dietēs***, a. GK: *1453* [→ *1417+2094*]. two years old:– two years old [1]

1333 **διετία, *dietia***, n. GK: *1454* [→ *1417+2094*]. two years:– two years [2]

1334 **διηγέομαι, *diēgeomai***, v. GK: *1455* [→ *1223+71*]. to tell, report, describe:– declared [2], tell [2], told [2], declare [1], shew [1]

1335 **διήγησις, *diēgēsis***, n. GK: *1456* [→ *1223+71*]. account, narrative:– declaration [1]

1336 **διηνεκής, *diēnekēs***, a. GK: *1457* [→ *1223+5342*]. forever, endless, for all time:– continually (+*1519+3588*) [2], for ever (+*1519+3588*) [2]

1337 **διθάλασσος, *dithalassos***, a. GK: *1458* [→ *1417+2281*]. sandbar, sandbank (surrounded on both sides by sea):– where two seas met [1]

1338 **διϊκνέομαι, *diikneomai***, v. GK: *1459* [→ *1223+2425*]. to penetrate, pierce:– piercing [1]

1339 **διΐστημι, *diistēmi***, v. GK: *1460* [→ *1223+2476*]. to leave, pass:– gone further [1], parted [1], space after [1]

1340 **διϊσχυρίζομαι, *diischyrizomai***, v. GK: *1462* [→ *1223+2479*]. to assert, insist, maintain firmly:– confidently affirmed [1], constantly affirmed [1]

1341 **δικαιοκρισία, *dikaiokrisia***, n. GK: *1464* [→ *1349+2919*]. righteous judgment:– righteous judgment [1]

1342 **δίκαιος, *dikaios***, a. GK: *1465* [→ *1349*]. right, righteous, upright; in the NT this refers to God's proper standards and actions, expressed in the covenants; as a noun it refers to a person in accord with God's standards, in proper relationship with God:– righteous [41], just [31], right [5], just one [2], meet [2]

1343 **δικαιοσύνη, *dikaiosynē***, n. GK: *1466* [→ *1349*]. righteousness, what is right, justice, the act of doing what is in agreement with God's standards, the state of being in proper relationship with God:– righteousness [90], righteousness' [2]

1344 **δικαιόω, *dikaioō***, v. GK: *1467* [→ *1349*]. to justify, vindicate, declare righteous, to put someone in a proper relationship with another, usually referring to God's relationship to humankind, implying a proper legal or moral relationship:– justified [31], justify [4], justifieth [2], freed [1], justifier [1], righteous [1]

1345 **δικαίωμα, *dikaiōma***, n. GK: *1468* [→ *1349*]. regulation, requirement, commandment; act of righteousness:– righteousness [4], ordinances [3], judgments [1], judgment [1], justification [1]

1346 **δικαίως, *dikaiōs***, adv. GK: *1469* [→ *1349*]. justly, uprightly, righteously:– justly [2], righteously [2], righteousness [1]

1347 **δικαίωσις, *dikaiōsis***, n. GK: *1470* [→ *1349*]. justification:– justification [2]

1348 **δικαστής, *dikastēs***, n. GK: *1471* [→ *1349*]. judge:– judge [3]

1349 **δίκη, *dikē***, n. GK: *1472 & 2869* [→ *91, 92, 93, 94, 95, 476, 1341, 1342, 1343, 1344, 1345, 1346, 1347, 1348, 1556, 1557, 1558, 1738, 2613, 2993, 2994, 5267*]. punishment, with a focus that the penalty is justly deserved and right; this can also refer to a pagan Greek goddess, "Justice" (Ac 28:4), who would seek out the guilty and punish the wrongdoer:– vengeance [2], judgment [1], punished (+*5099*) [1]

1350 **δίκτυον, *diktyon***, n. GK: *1473*. (fish) net:– nets [6], net [6]

1351 **δίλογος, *dilogos***, a. GK: *1474* [→ *1417+3004*]. insincere, double-tongued:– doubletongued [1]

1352 **διό, *dio***, c.infer. GK: *1475* [→ *1223+3739*]. therefore, that is why, for this reason:– wherefore [39], therefore [9], for which cause [2], therefore (+*2532*) [1], wherefore (+*2532*) [1], wherefore seeing that [1]

1353 **διοδεύω, *diodeuō***, v. GK: *1476* [→ *1223+3598*]. to go through, travel through:– passed through [1], went throughout [1]

1354 **Διονύσιος, *Dionysios***, n.pr. GK: *1477*. Dionysius, "*belonging to Dionysus*":– Dionysius [1]

1355 **διόπερ, *dioper***, c.infer. GK: *1478* [→ *1223+3739+4007*]. therefore, for this reason:– wherefore [3]

1356 **διοπετής, *diopetēs***, a. GK: *1479* [→ *2203+4098*]. (the image) fallen from heaven (given by the pagan god Zeus):– fell down from Jupiter [1]

1357 **διόρθωσις, *diorthōsis***, n. GK: *1481* [→ *1223+3717*]. a new order:– reformation [1]

1358 **διορύσσω, *dioryssō***, v. GK: *1482* [→ *1223+3736*]. to break in:– break through [2], broken through [1], broken up [1]

Διός, *Dios*. See ***2203***.

1359 **Διόσκουροι, *Dioskouroi***, n.pr. GK: *1483* [→ *2203+2751*]. the twin gods Castor and Pollux, the Dioscuri, "*sons of Zeus*":– Castor and Pollux [1]

1360 **διότι, *dioti***, c. GK: *1484* [→ *1223+3739+5101*]. therefore, because:– because [11], for [8], because that [2], therefore [1]

1361 **Διοτρέφης, *Diotrephēs***, n.pr. GK: *1485* [→ *2203+5142*]. Diotrephes, "*nurtured by Zeus*":– Diotrephes [1]

1362 **διπλοῦς, *diplous***, a. GK: *1486 & 1487* [→ *1417*]. double, twice as much:– double [3], twofold more than [1]

1363 **διπλόω, *diploō***, v. GK: *1488* [→ *1417*]. to double, pay back double:– double [1]

1364 **δίς, *dis***, adv. GK: *1489* [→ *1417*]. twice, again:– twice [4], again [2]

Δίς, *Dis*. See ***2203***.

1365 **διστάζω, *distazō***, v. GK: *1491* [→ *1417*]. to doubt:– doubted [1], doubt [1]

1366 **δίστομος, *distomos***, a. GK: *1492* [→ *1417+4750*]. double-edged:– twoedged [2], with two edges [1]

1367 **δισχίλιοι, *dischilioi***, a.num. GK: *1493* [→ *1417+5507*]. two thousand:– two thousand [1]

1368 **διϋλίζω, *diylizō***, v. GK: *1494* [→ *1223+5208*]. to strain out, filter out:– strain out [1]

1369 **διχάζω, *dichazō***, v. GK: *1495* [→ *1417*]. to turn (one against another), cause a separation:– set at variance [1]

1370 **διχοστασία, *dichostasia***, n. GK: *1496* [→ *1417+2476*]. division, dissension:– divisions [2], seditions [1]

1371 **διχοτομέω, *dichotomeō***, v. GK: *1497* [→ *1417+5114*]. to cut to pieces, likely a figure for severe punishment rather than execution:– cut asunder [1], cut in sunder [1]

1372 **διψάω, *dipsaō***, v. GK: *1498* [→ *1373*]. to be thirsty:– thirst [10], athirst [3], thirsty [3]

1373 **δίψος, *dipsos***, n. GK: *1499* [→ *1372*]. thirst:– thirst [1]

1374 **δίψυχος, *dipsychos***, a. GK: *1500* [→ *1417+5594*]. double-minded:– double minded [2]

1375 **διωγμός, *diōgmos***, n. GK: *1501* [→ *1377*]. persecution:– persecutions [5], persecution [5]

1376 **διώκτης, *diōktēs***, n. GK: *1502* [→ *1377*]. persecutor:– persecutor [1]

1377 **διώκω, *diōkō***, v. GK: *1503* [→ *1375, 1376, 1559, 2614*]. to pursue, persecute, to systematically oppress and harass a person or group, as an extended meaning of pursuing a person on foot in a chase; also from the image of the chase comes the meaning of striving and pressing on to a goal with intensity: to press on:– persecuted [13], persecute [8], follow [7], persecutest [6], suffer persecution [3], followed [2], ensue [1], follow after [1], given to [1], persecuting [1], press [1]

1378 **δόγμα, *dogma***, n. GK: *1504* [→ *1380*]. decree, regulation:– decrees [2], ordinances [2], decree [1]

1379 **δογματίζω, *dogmatizō***, v. GK: *1505* [→ *1380*]. (pass.) to submit to a rule, regulation:– subject to ordinances [1]

1380 **δοκέω, *dokeō***, v. GK: *1506* [→ *603, 1378, 1379, 2106, 2107, 4328, 4329, 4909; cf. 1391*]. to think, consider, regard, an action of the mind and heart for processing information into understanding and choices,

Grk

sometimes with a focus on appearances. Often in the impersonal form translated, "it seems" (Ac 17:18):– think [22], seemeth [5], seem [5], thought [5], thinkest [4], seemed good [3], seemed [3], suppose [3], accounted [2], pleased [2], supposed [2], supposing [2], thinketh [2], of reputation [1], pleasure [1], trow [1]

1381 δοκιμάζω, ***dokimazō***, v. GK: *1507* [→ *1209*]. to test, try, examine; interpret:– prove [6], proved [3], approve [2], try [2], allowed [1], alloweth [1], approvest [1], discern (+*1492*) [1], discern [1], examine [1], like [1], proving [1], tried [1], trieth [1]

1382 δοκιμή, ***dokimē***, n. GK: *1509* [→ *1209*]. character, test, proof:– proof [3], experience [2], experiment [1], trial [1]

1383 δοκίμιον, ***dokimion***, n. GK: *1510* [→ *1209*]. testing, proved genuineness:– trial [1], trying [1]

1384 δόκιμος, ***dokimos***, a. GK: *1511* [→ *1209*]. approved by testing, genuine:– approved [6], tried [1]

1385 δοκός, ***dokos***, n. GK: *1512*. plank, beam of wood:– beam [6]

δόκω, *dokō*. See ***1380***.

1386 δόλιος, ***dolios***, a. GK: *1513* [→ *1388*]. deceitful, dishonest, tricky:– deceitful [1]

1387 δολιόω, ***dolioō***, v. GK: *1514* [→ *1388*]. to practice deceit, deceive:– used deceit [1]

1388 δόλος, ***dolos***, n. GK: *1515* [→ *97, 1185, 1386, 1387, 1389*]. deceit, slyness, trickery, as a fig. extension of the base meaning (not used in the NT) of trapping an animal by baiting or by cunning:– guile [7], deceit [2], subtilty [2], craft [1]

1389 δολόω, ***doloō***, v. GK: *1516* [→ *1388*]. to distort, falsify:– handling deceitfully [1]

1390 δόμα, ***doma***, n. GK: *1517* [→ *1325*]. gift:– gifts [3], gift [1]

1391 δόξα, ***doxa***, n. GK: *1518* [→ *1392, 1740, 1741, 2754, 2755, 3861, 4888; cf. 1380*]. This word has a wide range of meanings in the NT, corresponding closely the Hebrew 3883: glory, splendor, brilliance, from the base meaning of the awesome light that radiates from God's presence and is associated with his acts of power; honor, praise, speaking of words of excellence and assigning highest status to God:– glory [145], glorious [6], honour [6], praise [4], glorious (+*1722*) [3], dignities [2], glorious (+*1223*) [1], worship [1]

1392 δοξάζω, ***doxazō***, v. GK: *1519* [→ *1391*]. to glorify, give praise, honor:– glorified [34], glorify [17], glorifying [3], full of glory [1], had glory [1], have glory [1], honoured [1], honoureth [1], honour [1], made glorious [1], magnify [1]

1393 Δορκάς, ***Dorkas***, n.pr. GK: *1520*. Dorcas, "*gazelle*":– Dorcas [2]

1394 δόσις, ***dosis***, n. GK: *1521* [→ *1325*]. gift, act of giving:– gift [1], giving [1]

1395 δότης, ***dotēs***, n. GK: *1522* [→ *1325*]. giver:– giver [1]

1396 δουλαγωγέω, ***doulagōgeō***, v. GK: *1524* [→ *1401+71*]. to enslave, bring to subjection:– bring into subjection [1]

1397 δουλεία, ***douleia***, n. GK: *1525* [→ *1401*]. slavery, bondage:– bondage [5]

1398 δουλεύω, ***douleuō***, v. GK: *1526* [→ *1401*]. to serve (as a slave):– serve [13], in bondage [4], serving [3], did service [1], do service [1], doing service [1], served [1], serveth [1]

1399 δούλη, ***doulē***, n. GK: *1527* [→ *1401*]. female servant, female slave:– handmaidens [1], handmaiden [1], handmaid [1]

1400 δοῦλον, ***doulon***, a.neut. of *1401*. GK: *1529* [→ *1401*]. slavish, servile, completely controlled, as a fig. extension of a slavery system in the ancient world, see *1401*:–

1401 δοῦλος, ***doulos***, n. GK: *1528* [→ *1396, 1397, 1398, 1399, 1400, 1402, 2615, 3787, 4889*]. servant, slave; in the NT a person owned as a possession for various lengths of times (Hebrew slaves no more than seven years, Gentile slaves without time limit), of lower social status than free persons or masters; slaves could earn or purchase their freedom:– servant [66], servants [53], bond [6], bondman [1], servant's [1]

1402 δουλόω, ***douloō***, v. GK: *1530* [→ *1401*]. to enslave, to cause one to become a slave; (pass.) to become enslaved; see also *1401*:– servants [2], bring into bondage [1], brought in bondage [1], given [1], in bondage [1], made servant [1], under bondage [1]

1403 δοχή, ***dochē***, n. GK: *1531* [→ *1209*]. banquet:– feast [2]

1404 δράκων, ***drakōn***, n. GK: *1532*. dragon:– dragon [13]

1405 δράσσομαι, ***drassomai***, v. GK: *1533* [→ *1323, 1406*]. to catch, seize:– taketh [1]

1406 δραχμή, ***drachmē***, n. GK: *1534* [→ *1405*]. silver coin, drachma:– piece [2], silver [1]

δρέμω, *dremō*. See ***5143***.

1407 δρέπανον, ***drepanon***, n. GK: *1535*. sickle:– sickle [8]

1408 δρόμος, ***dromos***, n. GK: *1536* [→ *5143*]. race, course; course (in life), career:– course [3]

1409 Δρούσιλλα, ***Drousilla***, n.pr. GK: *1537*. Drusilla:– Drusilla [1]

δῦμι, *dumi*. See ***1416***.

1410 δύναμαι, ***dynamai***, v. GK: *1538* [→ *101, 102, 1411, 1412, 1413, 1414, 1415, 1743, 2616*]. to be able, have ability, to have the power to accomplish an action; humans have variously limited abilities, God is unlimited:– can [63], cannot (+*3756*) [45], able [41], could [29], canst [9], may [8], mayest [4], might [3], cannot (+*3361*) [2], might have [2], been [1], can do [1], possible [1], power [1]

1411 δύναμις, ***dynamis***, n. GK: *1539* [→ *1410*]. power, ability; miracle; ruler, an extended meaning of a person or supernatural being who has administrative power:– power [71], mighty works [10], miracles [7], strength [7], powers [6], might [4], virtue [3], mighty [2], ability [1], abundance [1], meaning [1], mightily [1], mighty deeds [1], mighty work [1], miracle [1], violence [1], wonderful works [1], workers of miracles [1]

1412 δυναμόω, ***dynamoō***, v. GK: *1540* [→ *1410*]. (pass.) to be strengthened:– strengthened [1]

1413 δυνάστης, ***dynastēs***, n. GK: *1541* [→ *1410*]. ruler, sovereign, (court) official:– mighty [1], of great authority [1], potentate [1]

1414 δυνατέω, ***dynateō***, v. GK: *1542* [→ *1410*]. to be able, powerful, strong:– mighty [1]

1415 δυνατός, ***dynatos***, a. GK: *1543* [→ *1410*]. possible (based on power); powerful, able, the Mighty One:– possible [13], able [10], mighty [7], strong [3], could [1], power [1]

1416 δύνω, ***dynō***, v. GK: *1544* [→ *554, 555, 1424, 1562, 1737, 1742, 1744, 1745, 1746, 1902, 1903, 1931, 3921*]. to set (of the sun):– setting [1], set [1]

1417 δύο, ***dyo***, n.num. GK: *1545* [→ *1177, 1206, 1207, 1208, 1250, 1323, 1324, 1332, 1333, 1337, 1351, 1362, 1363, 1364, 1365, 1366, 1367, 1369, 1370, 1371, 1374, 1427, 1428, 1429*]. two:– two [123], twain [10], both [2], two hundred thousand thousand (+*3461*) [1]

1418 δυσ-, ***dus-***, inseparable prefix. GK: * [→ *1419, 1420, 1421, 1422, 1423, 1425, 1426*]. prefix conveying the idea of difficulty, opposition, injuriousness:–

1419 δυσβάστακτος, ***dysbastaktos***, a. GK: *1546* [→ *1418+941*]. hard to carry:– grievous to be borne [2]

1420 δυσεντερία, ***dysenteria***, n. GK: *1547 & 1548* [→ *1418; cf. 1722*]. dysentery:– bloody flixe [1]

1421 δυσερμήνευτος, ***dysermēneutos***, a. GK: *1549* [→ *1418+2059*]. hard to explain:– hard [1]

1422 δύσκολος, ***dyskolos***, a. GK: *1551* [→ *1418, 1423; cf. 2967*]. hard, difficult:– hard [1]

1423 δυσκόλως, ***dyskolōs***, adv. GK: *1552* [→ *1418, 1422*]. hard, with difficulty:– hardly [3]

1424 δυσμή, ***dysmē***, n. GK: *1553* [→ *1416*]. west (setting of the sun):– west [5]

1425 δυσνόητος, ***dysnoētos***, a. GK: *1554* [→ *1418+3563*]. hard to understand:– hard to be understood [1]

1426 δυσφημία, ***dysphēmia***, n. GK: *1556* [→ *1418+5346*]. bad report, slander:– evil report [1]

δύω, *duō*. See ***1416***.

1427 δώδεκα, ***dōdeka***, n.num. GK: *1557* [→ *1417+1176*]. twelve:– twelve [72]

1428 δωδέκατος, ***dōdekatos***, a. GK: *1558* [→ *1417+1176*]. twelfth:– twelfth [1]

1429 δωδεκάφυλον, ***dōdekaphylon***, n. GK: *1559* [→ *1417+1176+5443*]. twelve tribes:– twelve tribes [1]

1430 δῶμα, ***dōma***, n. GK: *1560* [→ *456, 1739, 2026, 3618, 3619, 3620, 4925*]. roof, housetop:– housetop [4], housetops [2], house [1]

1431 δωρεά, ***dōrea***, n. GK: *1561* [→ *1325*]. gift:– gift [11]

1432 δωρεάν, ***dōrean***, adv. GK: *1562* [→ *1325*]. freely, free of charge, without payment:– freely [6], for nought [1], in vain [1], without a cause [1]

1433 δωρέομαι, ***dōreomai***, v. GK: *1563* [→ *1325*]. to give, confer, bestow:– given [2], gave [1]

1434 δώρημα, ***dōrēma***, n. GK: *1564* [→ *1325*]. gift:– gift [2]

1435 δῶρον, **dōron**, n. GK: *1565* [→ *2333; cf. 1325*]. gift, offering:– gift [10], gifts [8], offerings [1]

1436 ἔα, **ea**, pt.excl. GK: *1568*. ha!, aha!:– let alone [2]

1437 ἐάν, **ean**, c. GK: *1569* [→ *1487+302*]. if (usually used in general conditions or conditions that imply some doubt):– if [214], whosoever (*+3739*) [19], whatsoever (*+3739*) [15], though [12], whomsoever (*+3739*) [4], if (*+4007*) [3], wheresoever (*+3699*) [3], that (*+3739*) [2], whatsoever (*+3745*) [2], when [2], whether (*+5037*) [2], whom (*+3739*) [2], according to that (*+2526*) [1], and whether (*+5037*) [1], as many as (*+3745*) [1], as often as (*+3740*) [1], but (*+3361*) [1], except (*+3361*) [1], in what place soever (*+3699*) [1], or (*+5037*) [1], though (*+2532*) [1], what (*+3739*) [1], whatsoever (*+3739+5100*) [1], whatsoever (*+3748+3956+5100*) [1], whensoever (*+5613*) [1], whithersoever (*+3699*) [1], whithersoever (*+3757*) [1], whomsoever (*+5100*) [1], whoso (*+3739*) [1]

ἐάν μή, **ean mē**. See **3361** and **3362**.

1438 ἑαυτοῦ, **heautou**, p.reflex. GK: *1571* [→ *846*]. himself, herself, itself, themselves; (pl., in some contexts) reciprocal relationship, to one another:– himself [111], themselves [57], yourselves [36], ourselves [20], his [19], their [15], itself [9], his own [8], their own [7], them [7], one another [6], herself [5], you [5], her [4], your own selves [4], your own [4], him [3], her own [2], they [2], alone (*+2596*) [1], he himself [1], he [1], our own [1], she [1], their own home [1], their own selves [1], thine own [1], thyself [1], ye [1], your [1]

1439 ἐάω, **eaō**, v. GK: *1572* [→ *4330*]. to let, allow, permit:– suffered [5], suffer [2], committed [1], left [1], let alone [1], let [1], sufferest [1], suffereth [1]

1440 ἑβδομήκοντα, **hebdomēkonta**, n.num. GK: *1573* [→ *2033*]. seventy:– seventy [2], threescore and fifteen (*+4002*) [1], threescore sixteen (*+1803*) [1], threescore ten [1]

1441 ἑβδομηκοντάκις, **hebdomēkontakis**, adv. GK: *1574* [→ *2033*]. seventy times:– seventy times [1]

1442 ἕβδομος, **hebdomos**, a. GK: *1575* [→ *2033*]. seventh:– seventh [9]

1443 Ἔβερ, **Eber**, n.pr. GK: *1576*. Eber, "*[regions] beyond [the river]* or *source of the word "Hebrew"*":– Heber [1]

1444 Ἑβραϊκός, **Hebraikos**, a.pr. GK: *1577* [→ *1445*]. Hebrew:– Hebrew [1]

1445 Ἑβραῖος, **Hebraios**, n.pr.g. GK: *1578* [→ *1444, 1446, 1447*]. a Hebrew; a Hebraic Jew:– Hebrews [4], Hebrew [1]

1446 Ἑβραΐς, **Hebrais**, n.pr. GK: *1579* [→ *1445*]. Aramaic, Hebrew dialect:– in Hebrew [3]

1447 Ἑβραϊστί, **Hebraisti**, adv.pr. GK: *1580* [→ *1445*]. in Aramaic, in the Hebrew dialect:– in the Hebrew tongue [3], in the Hebrew [2], in Hebrew [1]

1448 ἐγγίζω, **engizō**, v. GK: *1581* [→ *1451*]. come near, draw near:– at hand [9], come nigh [6], drew nigh [6], drew near [4], come near [3], draw nigh [3], draweth nigh [3], came near [2], came nigh [2], nigh [2], approacheth [1], approaching [1], draweth near [1]

1449 ἐγγράφω, **engraphō**, v. GK: *1582* [→ *1722+1125*]. to write in, write on, record:– written [2]

1450 ἔγγυος, **engyos**, a. GK: *1583*. (n.) guarantee, guarantor:– surety [1]

1451 ἐγγύς, **engys**, adv. GK: *1584* [→ *1448, 1452, 4331*]. near, close:– nigh [12], at hand [6], nigh at hand [4], near [3], nigh to [2], from [1], near to [1], ready [1]

1452 ἐγγύτερον, **engyteron**, adv.comp. GK: *1585* [→ *1451*]. nearer, closer:– nearer [1]

1453 ἐγείρω, **egeirō**, v. GK: *1586* [→ *1127, 1235, 1326, 1454, 1825, 1892, 4891*]. to arise, to stand from a prone or sleeping position. From this base meaning are several fig. extended meanings: to wake from sleep; to restore from a dead or damaged state: to heal, raise to life; to cause something to exist: raise up (give birth to) a child:– raised [29], risen [20], raised up [16], rise [16], arise [13], arose [12], raise up [6], rise up [6], rose [4], awake [2], lift up [2], raise [2], risen up [2], ariseth [1], awoke [1], lift out [1], lifted up [1], raiseth up [1], raiseth [1], rear up [1], riseth [1], stand [1], took up [1]

1454 ἔγερσις, **egersis**, n. GK: *1587* [→ *1453*]. resurrection:– resurrection [1]

1455 ἐγκάθετος, **enkathetos**, a. GK: *1588* [→ *863*]. (n.) spy:– spies [1]

1456 ἐγκαίνια, **enkainia**, n. GK: *1589* [→ *1722+2537*]. Feast of Dedication (Hanukkah):– dedication [1]

1457 ἐγκαινίζω, **enkainizō**, v. GK: *1590* [→ *1722+2537*]. (pass.) to be put into effect, inaugurate; (act.) to open:– consecrated [1], dedicated [1]

1458 ἐγκαλέω, **enkaleō**, v. GK: *1592* [→ *1722+2564*]. to bring charges, accuse; (pass.) to be charged with, have an accusation brought to:– accused [4], called in question [1], implead [1], lay to the charge [1]

1459 ἐγκαταλείπω, **enkataleipō**, v. GK: *1593* [→ *1722+2596+3007*]. to forsake, leave, abandon:– forsaken [4], forsake [1], forsaking [1], forsook [1], leave [1], left [1]

1460 ἐγκατοικέω, **enkatoikeō**, v. GK: *1594* [→ *1722+2596+3624*]. to live among:– dwelling [1]

1461 ἐγκεντρίζω, **enkentrizō**, v. GK: *1596* [→ *1722+2759*]. to graft into:– graffed in [3], graff in [1], graffed into [1], graffed [1]

1462 ἔγκλημα, **enklēma**, n. GK: *1598* [→ *1722+2564*]. charge, accusation:– crime laid [1], laid to charge [1]

1463 ἐγκομβόομαι, **enkomboomai**, v. GK: *1599* [→ *1722*]. to clothe (oneself) with, put on:– clothed with [1]

1464 ἐγκοπή, **enkopē**, n. GK: *1600 & 1715* [→ *1722+2875*]. hinderance, restraint:– hinder (*+1325*) [1]

1465 ἐγκόπτω, **enkoptō**, v. GK: *1601* [→ *1722+2875*]. to hinder, stop, impede progress:– hindered from [1], hindered [1], tedious [1]

1466 ἐγκράτεια, **enkrateia**, n. GK: *1602* [→ *1722+2904*]. self-control:– temperance [4]

1467 ἐγκρατεύομαι, **enkrateuomai**, v. GK: *1603* [→ *1722+2904*]. to have control (of oneself):– contain [1], temperate [1]

1468 ἐγκρατής, **enkratēs**, a. GK: *1604* [→ *1722+2904*]. disciplined, self-controlled:– temperate [1]

1469 ἐγκρίνω, **enkrinō**, v. GK: *1605* [→ *1722+2919*]. to classify:– make of the number [1]

1470 ἐγκρύπτω, **enkryptō**, v. GK: *1606* [→ *1722+2928*]. to mix, put into:– hid [2]

1471 ἔγκυος, **enkyos**, a. GK: *1607* [→ *1722+2949*]. pregnant:– great with child [1]

1472 ἐγχρίω, **enchriō**, v. GK: *1608* [→ *1722+5548*]. to put on, rub on, anoint:– anoint [1]

1473 ἐγώ, **egō**, p.pers. GK: *1609* [→ *1683, 1691, 1698, 1699, 1700, 2248, 2249, 2251, 2254, 2257, 2504, 3165, 3365, 3427, 3450*]. I, me, my; we, us, our; often added for emphasis: myself, ourselves:– me [798], my [527], I [425], us [396], our [312], we [173], mine [24], mine own [4], ours [4], usward [2], myself (*+846*) [1], myself [1], ourselves [1], what have I to do (*+5101*) [1]

1474 ἐδαφίζω, **edaphizō**, v. GK: *1610* [→ *1475*]. to dash to the ground, raze:– lay even with the ground [1]

1475 ἔδαφος, **edaphos**, n. GK: *1611* [→ *1474*]. ground:– ground [1]

1476 ἑδραῖος, **hedraios**, a. GK: *1612* [→ *856, 1477, 1747, 1748, 1749, 2145, 2516, 4332, 4892; cf. 2516*]. firm, steadfast:– stedfast [2], settled [1]

1477 ἑδραίωμα, **hedraiōma**, n. GK: *1613* [→ *1476*]. foundation:– ground [1]

1478 Ἑζεκίας, **Hezekias**, n.pr. GK: *1614*. Hezekiah, "*God [El] strengthens*":– Ezekias [2]

1479 ἐθελοθρησκία, **ethelothrēskia**, n. GK: *1615* [→ *2309+2357*]. self-imposed religion:– will worship [1]

ἐθέλω, **ethelō**. See **2309**.

1480 ἐθίζω, **ethizō**, v. GK: *1616* [→ *1485*]. (pass.) to be accustomed, required:– custom [1]

1481 ἐθνάρχης, **ethnarchēs**, n. GK: *1617* [→ *1484+757*]. governor:– governor [1]

1482 ἐθνικός, **ethnikos**, a. GK: *1618* [→ *1484*]. pagan, Gentile:– heathen [2]

1483 ἐθνικῶς, **ethnikōs**, adv. GK: *1619* [→ *1484*]. like a Gentile, like a pagan:– after the manner of Gentiles [1]

1484 ἔθνος, **ethnos**, n. GK: *1620* [→ *1481, 1482, 1483*]. Gentile, pagan; (foreign) nation, a people:– Gentiles [93], nations [37], nation [27], heathen [5], people [2]

1485 ἔθος, **ethos**, n. GK: *1621* [→ *1480, 1486, 1486, 2239, 2550, 4914*]. custom, practice, habit:– customs [5], manner [4], custom [2], as wont (*+2596+3588*) [1]

1486 ἔθω, **ethō**, v. GK: *1622 & 1665* [→ *1485*]. to be accustomed; to have a custom:– wont [2], custom [1], manner [1]

1487 εἰ, **ei**, pt.cond. GK: *1623* [→ *1437, 3375, 1512, 1513, 1535, 2579, 5616, 5619*]. if, since:– if [270], whether [21], that [6], although (*+2532*) [1], but (*+1622+3361*) [1], but (*+3361*) [1], but though (*+1161+2532*) [1], except (*+1622+3361*) [1], forasmuch [1], had [1], if (*+3305*) [1], it may be (*+5177*) [1], it may chance (*+5177*) [1], never (*+165+1519+3588+3756*) [1], not [1], no [1], since [1], though (*+2532*) [1], unless (*+1622+3361*) [1], what if [1]

Grk

1488 εἶ, ***ei***, v.2.s of *1510*. GK: *1639* [→ *1510*]. you are, thou art; see *1510*:–

1489 εἴγε, ***eige***, pt.emph. GK: *1623 + 1145* [→ *1487+1065*]. if indeed, seeing that, unless; (with neg.) otherwise:– if [4], if so be that [1]

1490 εἰ δὲ μή (γε), ***ei de mē (ge)***, pt.emph. GK: *1623 + 1254 + 3590 (+ 1145)* [→ *1487+1161+3361+1065*]. but if not, or else, otherwise:– else [4], or else [4], if not [2], if otherwise [2], and if not [1], otherwise [1]

1491 εἶδος, ***eidos***, n. GK: *1626* [→ *1126, 1141, 2396, 2397, 2400, 3708, 4075, 5237; cf. 1497*]. form, appearance, sight:– shape [2], appearance [1], fashion [1], sight [1]

1492 εἴδω, ***eidō***; or οἶδα, ***oida***, v. GK: *3857* [→ *4893?, 4894?; cf. 2467*]. to know, to possess information; recognize, realize, to come to know; to understand, to be able to use knowledge:– saw [188], know [176], see [78], knowing [38], seen [34], knew [28], knoweth [22], knowest [15], beheld [10], tell [9], seeing [8], sawest [7], known [6], looked [6], wist [6], behold [4], knewest [3], perceive [3], perceiving [3], sure [3], wot [3], can [2], know how [2], aware [1], consider [1], discern (*+1381*) [1], knowledge [1], looked on [1], understandeth [1], understand [1]

1493 εἰδωλεῖον, ***eidōleion***, n. GK: *1627* [→ *1497*]. temple of an idol:– idol's temple [1]

1494 εἰδωλόθυτος, ***eidōlothytos***, a. GK: *1628* [→ *1497+2380*]. (food) sacrificed to idols:– things offered to idols [2], things sacrificed unto idols [2], meats offered to idols [1], offered in sacrifice to idols [1], offered in sacrifice unto idols [1], thing offered unto an idol [1], things offered in sacrifice unto idols [1], things offered unto idols [1]

1495 εἰδωλολατρία, ***eidōlolatria***, n. GK: *1630* [→ *1497+2999*]. idolatry, the reverence and worship of idols:– idolatry [3], idolatries [1]

1496 εἰδωλολάτρης, ***eidōlolatrēs***, n. GK: *1629* [→ *1497+2999*]. idolater, one who worships idols and so practices idolatry:– idolaters [5], idolater [2]

1497 εἴδωλον, ***eidōlon***, n. GK: *1631* [→ *1493, 1494, 1496, 1495, 2712; cf. 1491*]. idol, an object that is worshiped, formed by casting or carving (with the possible implication that a god or demon is intrinsic to the idol):– idols [7], idol [4]

1498 εἴην, ***eiēn***, v.subj. or opt. of *1510*. GK: *1639* [→ *1510*]. it may (could, might, should, would) be; see *1510*:–

1499 εἰ καί, ***ei kai***, conj. GK: *1623 + 2779* [→ *1487+2532*]. even if, although:– though [11], and if [1], if also [1], if that [1], though but [1]

1500 εἰκῇ, ***eikē***, adv. GK: *1632*. in vain, for nothing, to no purpose:– in vain [5], vainly [1], without a cause [1]

1501 εἴκοσι, ***eikosi***, n.num. GK: *1633*. twenty:– twenty [12]

1502 εἴκω, ***eikō***, v. GK: *1634* [→ *5226*]. to give in, yield:– gave place [1]

1503 ἔοικα, ***eoika***, v. GK: *2036* [→ *1504, 1932, 1933*]. to be like, resemble:– like [2]

1504 εἰκών, ***eikōn***, n. GK: *1635* [→ *1503*]. image, likeness, portrait:– image [23]

1505 εἰλικρίνεια, ***eilikrineia***, n. GK: *1636* [→ *1506*]. sincerity, the positive moral quality of purity (especially in motives), a fig. extension of an unadulterated or unmixed substance:– sincerity [3]

1506 εἰλικρινής, ***eilikrinēs***, a. GK: *1637* [→ *1505*]. pure, wholesome:– pure [1], sincere [1]

1507 εἱλίσσω, ***heilissō***, v. GK: *1813* [→ *1667*]. to roll up, roll together:– rolled together [1]

1508 εἰ μή, ***ei mē***, conj. GK: *1623 + 3590* [→ *1487+3361*]. if not, except, but:– but [52], save [17], except [7], saving [2], more than [1], save only [1], till (*+3752*) [1]

1509 εἰ μή τι, ***ei mē ti***, conj. GK: *1623 + 3590 + 5516* [→ *1508+5100*]. unless indeed, except, unless perhaps:– except [2], except (*+302*) [1]

1510 εἰμί, ***eimi***, v. GK: *1639* [→ *548, 666, 1488, 1498, 1511, 1526, 1751, 1762, 1832, 1849, 1967, 2070, 2071, 2075, 2076, 2077, 2252, 2258, 2277, 2468, 3689, 3776, 3918, 3952, 4041, 4840, 4895, 5123, 5600, 5607; cf. 1849*]. to be, exist, be present; all forms of this verb are indexed under *1510*:– is [829], be [366], was [349], are [345], were [155], am [139], art [85], being [37], been [24], have [23], had [16], be (*+1519*) [9], wast [6], come to pass [4], come [3], shall [3], meaneth [2], meant [2], mean [2], agree together (*+2470*) [1], agreed not (*+800*) [1], agreed together (*+2470*) [1], agree [1], belonged [1], belongeth [1], belong [1], cannot (*+3756*) [1], cannot be tempted (*+551*) [1], cometh [1], consisteth [1], continued [1], did [1], down [1], dureth [1], endure [1], exceedingly fear (*+1630*) [1], followed (*+3326*) [1], follow [1], for [1], give [1], hast [1], have being [1], having [1], held [1], know (*+1110*) [1], let [1], live long (*+3118*) [1], love husbands (*+5362*) [1], make [1], may [1], meaneth (*+2309*) [1], must [1], oweth [1], pass the flower of age (*+5230*) [1], perish (*+684+1519*) [1], please well (*+2101*) [1], pleased (*+701*) [1], profiteth (*+5624*) [1], remaineth (*+3062+3588*) [1], should [1], sojourn (*+3941*) [1], so [1], stand [1], used to [1], were (*+1096*) [1], were (*+4218*) [1], wert [1], while (*+1722+3588*) [1], wholly given to idolatry (*+2712*) [1], will [1], wrestle (*+3823*) [1]

1511 εἶναι, ***einai***, v.infin. of *1510*. GK: *1639* [→ *1510*]. to be, exist, be present; see *1510*:–

εἵνεκεν, ***heineken***. See **1752**.

1512 εἴπερ, ***eiper***, pt.cond. GK: *1642* [→ *1487+4007*]. if indeed, if in fact, since:– if so that [2], if so be that (*+686*) [1], if so [1], seeing [1], though (*+2532*) [1]

1513 εἴπως, ***eipōs***, pt. GK: *1643* [→ *1487+4226*]. if perhaps, if somehow:– if by any means [4]

1514 εἰρηνεύω, ***eirēneuō***, v. GK: *1644* [→ *1515*]. to live in peace, be at peace:– have peace [1], live in peace [1], live peaceably [1], peace [1]

1515 εἰρήνη, ***eirēnē***, n. GK: *1645* [→ *1514, 1516, 1517, 1518*]. peace, harmony, tranquility; safety, welfare, health; often with an emphasis on lack of strife or reconciliation in a relation, as when one has "peace with God." Often used as a verbal and written greeting. This word generally follows the meanings and usage of the Hebrew word 8934:– peace [89], quietness [1], rest [1], set at one (*+1519+4900*) [1]

1516 εἰρηνικός, ***eirēnikos***, a. GK: *1646* [→ *1515*]. peace-loving, peaceable, peaceful, with a focus of having freedom from emotional worry and frustration:– peaceable [2]

1517 εἰρηνοποιέω, ***eirēnopoieō***, v. GK: *1647* [→ *1515+4160*]. to make peace, to cause reconciliation between two parties, as in Christ causing the believer's peace with God:– made peace [1]

1518 εἰρηνοποιός, ***eirēnopoios***, a. GK: *1648* [→ *1515+4160*]. peacemaker, one who restores peace and reconciliation between persons and even nations:– peacemakers [1]

εἴρω, ***eirō***. See **1515**, **4483**, **5346**.

1519 εἰς, ***eis***, pp. GK: *1650* [→ *1521, 1522, 1523, 1524, 1525, 1528, 1529, 1530, 1531, 1532, 1533, 1898, 2072, 2080, 2081, 2082, 3919, 3920, 3921, 3922, 3923, 4897*]. to, toward, into; for. Spatially: movement toward or into an area (extending to a goal); logically: a marker of purpose or result; of time: extending to or up to a certain time:– into [543], to [316], unto [206], for [141], in [140], on [59], against [27], that (*+3588*) [27], to (*+3588*) [24], upon [24], at [21], among [18], towards [15], toward [14], be (*+1510*) [9], that [6], whereunto (*+3739*) [6], concerning [5], never (*+165+3361+3588+3756*) [5], throughout [5], become (*+1096*) [4], of [4], therein (*+846*) [4], to the end (*+3588*) [4], back (*+3588+3694*) [3], made (*+1096*) [3], therefore (*+3778*) [3], wherein (*+3739*) [3], abroad (*+5318*) [2], before [2], by [2], continually (*+1336+3588*) [2], ever (*+165+3588*) [2], for ever (*+1336+3588*) [2], for purpose [2], for this cause (*+3778*) [2], so that (*+3588*) [2], thereunto (*+3778*) [2], to this end (*+3778*) [2], why (*+5101*) [2], abundantly (*+4050*) [1], afar off (*+3112*) [1], after that (*+3195+3588*) [1], again (*+3588+3694*) [1], as concerning (*+3056*) [1], backward (*+3588+3694*) [1], became (*+1096*) [1], before (*+4383*) [1], by continual (*+5056*) [1], despised (*+3049+3762*) [1], ever (*+165+3588+3956*) [1], far more exceeding (*+2596+5236+5236*) [1], for to (*+3588*) [1], forth (*+3319+3588*) [1], from [1], grew (*+2064*) [1], hereunto (*+3778*) [1], home (*+2398+3588*) [1], in among [1], in no wise (*+3361+3588+3838*) [1], insomuch that (*+3588*) [1], lest (*+3361+3588*) [1], made ready to hand (*+2092*) [1], make mad (*+3130+4062*) [1], make war against (*+4171+4820*) [1], never (*+165+1487+3588+3756*) [1], never (*+165+3588+3756*) [1], peculiar (*+4047*) [1], perish (*+684+1510*) [1], regardest (*+991*) [1], relief (*+1248*) [1], set at one (*+1515+4900*) [1], thereinto (*+846*) [1], thereunto (*+846+3778*) [1], throughout (*+3837*) [1], till [1], to end [1], to make [1], to the intent (*+3588*) [1], took shipping (*+1684+3588+4143*) [1], until [1], waxed (*+1096*) [1], went back (*+565+3588+3694*) [1], wherefore (*+3739*) [1], wherefore (*+5101*) [1], whereinto (*+3739*) [1], whereto (*+3739*) [1], wherewith [1], while standeth [1], whither (*+3739*) [1], with [1]

1520* εἷς, *heis, n.num. GK: *1651* [→ *1733, 1734, 1775, 1847, 1848, 3367, 3391, 3762*]. one, single:– one [289], a [13], first [8], some [6], the other[s] [6], certain [5], any [2], an [2], man [2], one (+*5100*) [2], one another (+*1520+3588*) [2], agree (+*1106+4160*) [1], another [1], each (+*1538*) [1], even all one as if (+*846+2532+3588*) [1], every (+*1538+2596*) [1], every (+*1538*) [1], no not one (+*2193+3756*) [1], one by one (+*2596*) [1], only [1], other[s] [1], particularly (+*1538+2596*) [1], several (+*303*) [1], whether (+*3739*) [1]

1521* εἰσάγω, *eisagō, v. GK: *1652* [→ *1519+71*]. to bring in, take in:– brought into [4], brought in [3], bring in [1], bringeth in [1], led into [1]

1522* εἰσακούω, *eisakouō, v. GK: *1653* [→ *1519+191*]. (pass.) to be heard, listened to:– heard [4], hear [1]

1523* εἰσδέχομαι, *eisdechomai, v. GK: *1654* [→ *1519+1209*]. to receive, welcome:– receive [1]

1524* εἴσειμι, *eiseimi, v. GK: *1655* [→ *1519*]. to go in, enter:– entered [1], go [1], went in [1], went [1]

1525* εἰσέρχομαι, *eiserchomai, v. GK: *1656* [→ *1519+2064*]. to go in, enter:– enter [55], entered [48], went into [14], went in [11], come in [8], came in [7], enter in [7], go in [7], come into [6], entered in [5], coming in [3], entereth [3], entering [3], came into [2], come [2], go into [2], arose [1], came to [1], camest in [1], come to [1], come unto [1], cometh into [1], enter in through [1], entereth in [1], entering in [1], goeth into [1], gone [1], go [1], in [1], wentest in [1], went [1]

1526* εἰσί, *eisi, v.3.pl. of *1510*. GK: *1639* [→ *1510*]. they are; see *1510*.:–

1527* εἷς καθ' εἷς, *heis kath' heis, idiom. GK: *1651 + 2848* [→ *1520+2596+1520*]. one by one:– one by one [2], each [1]

1528* εἰσκαλέομαι, *eiskaleomai, v. GK: *1657* [→ *1519+2564*]. to invite into:– called in [1]

1529* εἴσοδος, *eisodos, n. GK: *1658* [→ *1519+3598*]. entering, entrance; reception, welcome:– coming [1], entering in [1], enter [1], entrance in [1], entrance [1]

1530* εἰσπηδάω, *eispēdaō, v. GK: *1659* [→ *1519*]. to rush in:– ran in [1], sprang in [1]

1531* εἰσπορεύομαι, *eisporeuomai, v. GK: *1660* [→ *1519+4198*]. to go in, enter:– entered [3], entereth [3], entereth in [2], entering [2], came in [1], come in [1], coming in [1], enter in [1], entering into [1], entering in [1], went into [1]

1532* εἰστρέχω, *eistrechō, v. GK: *1661* [→ *1519+5143*]. to run in:– ran in [1]

1533* εἰσφέρω, *eispherō, v. GK: *1662* [→ *1519+5342*]. to bring in, lead in:– bring in [2], brought [2], bringest [1], lead into [1], lead [1]

1534* εἶτα, *eita, adv. GK: *1663* [→ *1899, 3347*]. then, after that, next:– then [11], after that [3], afterward [1], furthermore (+*3303+3588*) [1]

1535* εἴτε, *eite, pt. GK: *1664* [→ *1487+5037*]. if, whether…or:– or [33], whether [28], or whether [3], if [1]

1536* εἴ τις, *ei tis, pt.cond.+p. GK: *1623 + 5516* [→ *1487+5100*]. if any, whoever, whatever:– if any [45], if a man [6], that [2], whosoever [2], if ought [1], that which [1], whether any [1]

1537* ἐκ, *ek, pp. GK: *1666* [→ *411, 412, 413, 419, 421, 553, 554, 555, 1327, 1544, 1545, 1546, 1547, 1548, 1549, 1550, 1551, 1552, 1553, 1554, 1555, 1556, 1557, 1558, 1559, 1560, 1561, 1562, 1567, 1568, 1569, 1570, 1571, 1572, 1573, 1574, 1575, 1576, 1577, 1578, 1579, 1580, 1581, 1582, 1583, 1584, 1585, 1586, 1587, 1588, 1589, 1590, 1591, 1592, 1593, 1594, 1597, 1598, 1599, 1600, 1601, 1602, 1603, 1604, 1605, 1606, 1607, 1608, 1609, 1610, 1611, 1612, 1613, 1615, 1620, 1622, 1624, 1625, 1626, 1627, 1628, 1629, 1630, 1631, 1633, 1634, 1804, 1805, 1806, 1807, 1808, 1809, 1810, 1811, 1813, 1814, 1815, 1816, 1817, 455, 1818, 1819, 1820, 1821, 1822, 1823, 1824, 1825, 1826, 1827, 1828, 1829, 1830, 1831, 1832, 1833, 1834, 1837, 1839, 1840, 1841, 1842, 1843, 1844, 1845, 1846, 1847, 1848, 1849, 1851, 1852, 1853, 1854, 1855, 1856, 1857, 2078, 2079, 3924, 4898, 4899, 5240; cf. 1614, 1632*]. of, out of; from, away from. Spatially: extension from a space to a goal outer in reference, separation; logically: the means or source of an activity, disassociation or separation:– of [441], from [185], out of [112], by [55], on [34], with [26], in [7], among [5], over [4], second time (+*1208*) [4], at [3], by reason of [3], from among [3], thereof (+*846*) [3], through [3], again (+*1208*) [2], because of [2], for [2], out [2], abundantly (+*4053*) [1], as much as lieth in [1], between [1], betwixt [1], beyond [1], by the means of [1], earthly (+*1093+3588*) [1], exceedingly (+*4053+5228*) [1], from thenceforth (+*3778*) [1], grudgingly (+*3077*) [1], heartily (+*5590*) [1], heavenly (+*3772*) [1], hereby (+*3778*) [1], highly (+*4053*) [1], nothing (+*846+3361*) [1], of company [1], off [1], over against (+*1727*) [1], raised to life again (+*386*) [1], since began [1], third time (+*5154*) [1], to [1], unto [1], vehemently (+*4053*) [1], whereof (+*3739*) [1], whereof [1], your (+*4771*) [1]

1538* ἕκαστος, *hekastos, a. GK: *1667* [→ *1539*]. each, every:– every man [34], every one [19], every [18], every man's [3], any man [1], both [1], daily (+*2250+2596*) [1], each (+*1520*) [1], each one [1], every (+*1520+2596*) [1], every (+*1520*) [1], every woman [1], particularly (+*1520+2596*) [1]

1539* ἑκάστοτε, *hekastote, adv. GK: *1668* [→ *1538+3739+5037*]. always, at any time:– always [1]

1540* ἑκατόν, *hekaton, n.num. GK: *1669* [→ *1541, 1542, 1543*]. hundred:– hundred [14], hundredfold [2], hundreds [1]

1541* ἑκατονταετής, *hekatontaetēs, a. GK: *1670* [→ *1540+2094*]. a hundred years old:– hundred year old [1]

1542* ἑκατονταπλασίων, *hekatontaplasiōn, a. GK: *1671* [→ *1540*]. a hundred times:– hundredfold [3]

1543* ἑκατοντάρχης, *hekatontarchēs, n. GK: *1672 & 1673* [→ *1540+757*]. centurion, officer:– centurion [17], centurions [3], centurion's [1]

1544* ἐκβάλλω, *ekballō, v. GK: *1675* [→ *1537+906*]. to take out, remove; to drive out, expel; bring out, send out:– cast out [46], bringeth forth [3], casteth out [3], casting out [3], cast [3], pull out [3], send forth [3], thrust out [3], put forth [2], cast forth [1], casteth [1], driveth [1], drove out [1], expelled [1], leave [1], pluck out [1], put out [1], putteth forth [1], put [1], sent away [1], sent out [1], took out [1]

1545* ἔκβασις, *ekbasis, n. GK: *1676* [→ *1537+305*]. way out; outcome, end, result:– end [1], way to escape [1]

1546* ἐκβολή, *ekbolē, n. GK: *1678* [→ *1537+906*]. throwing out (a ship's cargo), jettisoning:– lightened the ship (+*4160*) [1]

1547* ἐκγαμίζω, *ekgamizō, v. GK: *1679* [→ *1537+1062*]. to marry, give in marriage:– given in marriage [2], giveth in marriage [2], giving in marriage [1]

1548* ἐκγαμίσκω, *ekgamiskō, v. GK: *1680* [→ *1537+1062*]. to give in marriage:– given in marriage [2]

1549* ἔκγονος, *ekgonos, a. GK: *1681* [→ *1537+1096*]. (n.) grandchild:– nephews [1]

1550* ἐκδαπανάω, *ekdapanaō, v. GK: *1682* [→ *1537+1160*]. (pass.) to be completely expended, exhausted:– spent [1]

1551* ἐκδέχομαι, *ekdechomai, v. GK: *1683* [→ *1537+1209*]. to wait for, expect, look forward to:– expecting [1], look for [1], looked for [1], tarry for [1], waited for [1], waited [1], waiteth for [1], waiting for [1]

1552* ἔκδηλος, *ekdēlos, a. GK: *1684* [→ *1537+1212*]. clear, very evident, plain:– manifest [1]

1553* ἐκδημέω, *ekdēmeō, v. GK: *1685* [→ *1537+1218*]. to be away, absent:– absent [3]

1554* ἐκδίδωμι, *ekdidōmi, v. GK: *1686* [→ *1537+1325*]. (mid.) to rent, lease:– let out [3], let forth [1]

1555* ἐκδιηγέομαι, *ekdiēgeomai, v. GK: *1687* [→ *1537+1223+71*]. to tell:– declare [1], declaring [1]

1556* ἐκδικέω, *ekdikeō, v. GK: *1688* [→ *1537+1349*]. to avenge, take revenge; to grant justice, get justice:– avenge [4], avenged [1], revenge [1]

1557* ἐκδίκησις, *ekdikēsis, n. GK: *1689* [→ *1537+1349*]. justice; vengeance; punishment:– vengeance [4], avenge (+*3588+4160*) [1], avenged (+*4160*) [1], avenge [1], punishment [1], revenge [1]

1558* ἔκδικος, *ekdikos, a. GK: *1690* [→ *1537+1349*]. punishing, avenging:– avenger [1], revenger [1]

1559* ἐκδιώκω, *ekdiōkō, v. GK: *1691* [→ *1537+1377*]. to drive out, persecute (severely):– persecuted [1], persecute [1]

1560* ἔκδοτος, *ekdotos, a. GK: *1692* [→ *1537+1325*]. handed over, given up, delivered up:– delivered [1]

1561* ἐκδοχή, *ekdochē, n. GK: *1693* [→ *1537+1209*]. expectation:– looking for [1]

1562* ἐκδύω, *ekdyō, v. GK: *1694* [→ *1537+1416*]. to strip off clothing, unclothe:– stripped of raiment [1], stripped [1], took off from [1], took off [1], unclothed [1]

1563 ἐκεῖ, ***ekei***, adv. GK: *1695* [→ *1564, 1565, 1566, 1900, 2546, 2547, 2548, 5238*]. there, in a place where:– there [86], thither [7], thitherward [1], to yonder place [1], yonder [1]

1564 ἐκεῖθεν, ***ekeithen***, adv. GK: *1696* [→ *1563*]. from there, from that place:– thence [16], from thence [7], from that place [1], there [1]

1565 ἐκεῖνος, ***ekeinos***, p.demo. GK: *1697* [→ *1563*]. that, those; he, she, it:– that [105], he [40], those [40], they [15], the same [12], them [8], his [7], same [6], him [5], she [4], their [2], it [1], same (*+4012*) [1], selfsame [1], the other[s] [1], the same (*+2596*) [1], theirs [1], this [1]

1566 ἐκεῖσε, ***ekeise***, adv. GK: *1698* [→ *1563*]. there, a place where:– there [2]

1567 ἐκζητέω, ***ekzēteō***, v. GK: *1699* [→ *1537+2212*]. to seek out, seek earnestly; (pass.) to be held responsible:– required [2], after [1], diligently seek [1], inquired [1], seek after [1], sought carefully [1]

1568 ἐκθαμβέω, ***ekthambeō***, v. GK: *1701* [→ *1537+2285*]. (pass.) to be overwhelmed with wonder, distressed, alarmed:– affrighted [2], greatly amazed [1], sore amazed [1]

1569 ἔκθαμβος, ***ekthambos***, a. GK: *1702* [→ *1537+2285*]. (utterly) astonished:– greatly wondering [1]

1570 ἔκθετος, ***ekthetos***, a. GK: *1704* [→ *1537+5087*]. thrown out, exposed (to elements), abandoned:– cast out (*+4160*) [1]

1571 ἐκκαθαίρω, ***ekkathairō***, v. GK: *1705* [→ *1537+2513*]. to cleanse, clean out, get rid of:– purge out [1], purge [1]

1572 ἐκκαίω, ***ekkaiō***, v. GK: *1706* [→ *1537+2545*]. (pass.) to be inflamed, have a strong desire:– burned [1]

1573 ἐκκακέω, ***ekkakeō***, v. GK: *1591 & 1707* [→ *1537+2556*]. to give up, become discouraged, lose heart:– faint [4], weary [2]

1574 ἐκκεντέω, ***ekkenteō***, v. GK: *1708* [→ *1537+2759*]. to pierce:– pierced [2]

1575 ἐκκλάω, ***ekklaō***, v. GK: *1709* [→ *1537+2806*]. (pass.) to be broken off:– broken off [3]

1576 ἐκκλείω, ***ekkleiō***, v. GK: *1710* [→ *1537+2808*]. to alienate, shut out, exclude:– excluded [1], exclude [1]

1577 ἐκκλησία, ***ekklēsia***, n. GK: *1711* [→ *1537+2564*]. church, congregation, assembly; a group of people gathered together. It can refer to the OT assembly of believers (Ac 7:38), or a riotous mob (Ac 19:32), but usually to a Christian assembly, a church: as a totality (Eph 3:10), or in a specific locale (Col. 4:15). In the NT a church is never a building or meeting place:– church [78], churches [36], assembly [3], in every church (*+2596*) [1]

1578 ἐκκλίνω, ***ekklinō***, v. GK: *1712* [→ *1537+2827*]. to turn away, turn aside:– avoid [1], eschew [1], gone out of the way [1]

1579 ἐκκολυμβάω, ***ekkolymbaō***, v. GK: *1713* [→ *1537+2860*]. to swim away:– swim out [1]

1580 ἐκκομίζω, ***ekkomizō***, v. GK: *1714* [→ *1537+2889*]. to carry out:– carried out [1]

1581 ἐκκόπτω, ***ekkoptō***, v. GK: *1716* [→ *1537+2875*]. to cut off, cut down:– cut off [3], hewn down [3], cut down [2], cut off from [1], cut out [1], hindered [1]

1582 ἐκκρεμάννυμι, ***ekkremannymi***, v. GK: *1717* [→ *1537+2910*]. (mid.) to hang upon (words), to consider something seriously:– very attentive [1]

1583 ἐκλαλέω, ***eklaleō***, v. GK: *1718* [→ *1537+2980*]. to tell:– tell [1]

1584 ἐκλάμπω, ***eklampō***, v. GK: *1719* [→ *1537+2989*]. to shine:– shine forth [1]

1585 ἐκλανθάνομαι, ***eklanthanomai***, v. GK: *1720* [→ *1537+2990*]. to forget:– forgotten [1]

1586 ἐκλέγομαι, ***eklegomai***, v. GK: *1721* [→ *1537+3004*]. to chose, pick, select:– chosen [16], chose [3], chose out [1], made choice [1]

1587 ἐκλείπω, ***ekleipō***, v. GK: *1722* [→ *1537+3007*]. to fail, end, stop:– fail [3]

1588 ἐκλεκτός, ***eklektos***, a. GK: *1723* [→ *1537+3004*]. elect, chosen, the Chosen One:– elect [13], chosen [7], elect's [2], elects' [1]

1589 ἐκλογή, ***eklogē***, n. GK: *1724* [→ *1537+3004*]. election, choice, selection:– election [6], chosen [1]

1590 ἐκλύω, ***eklyō***, v. GK: *1725* [→ *1537+3089*]. (pass.) to lose heart; give up; collapse in weariness:– faint [5], fainted [1]

1591 ἐκμάσσω, ***ekmassō***, v. GK: *1726* [→ *1537+3146*]. to wipe off, dry off:– wiped [3], wipe [2]

1592 ἐκμυκτηρίζω, ***ekmyktērizō***, v. GK: *1727* [→ *1537+3456*]. to sneer at, ridicule:– derided [2]

1593 ἐκνεύω, ***ekneuō***, v. GK: *1728* [→ *1537+3506*]. to slip away, withdraw:– conveyed away [1]

1594 ἐκνήφω, ***eknēphō***, v. GK: *1729* [→ *1537+3525*]. to come to one's sense, become sober:– awake [1]

1595 ἑκούσιος, ***hekousios***, a. GK: *1730* [→ *1635*]. spontaneous, willing:– willingly (*+2596*) [1]

1596 ἑκουσίως, ***hekousiōs***, adv. GK: *1731* [→ *1635*]. willingly; deliberately, intentionally:– wilfully [1], willingly [1]

1597 ἔκπαλαι, ***ekpalai***, adv. GK: *1732* [→ *1537+3819*]. for a long time, long ago:– of a long time [1], of old [1]

1598 ἐκπειράζω, ***ekpeirazō***, v. GK: *1733* [→ *1537+3984*]. to test, put to a test, try, tempt:– tempt [3], tempted [1]

1599 ἐκπέμπω, ***ekpempō***, v. GK: *1734* [→ *1537+3992*]. to send away, send out:– sent away [1], sent forth [1]

ἐκπερισσοῦ, ***ekperissou***. See *1537* and *4053*.

1600 ἐκπετάννυμι, ***ekpetannymi***, v. GK: *1736* [→ *1537+4072*]. to hold out, spread out:– stretched forth [1]

1601 ἐκπίπτω, ***ekpiptō***, v. GK: *1738* [→ *1537+4098*]. to fall off; to fail; to run aground, be dashed to pieces:– fallen [2], fall [2], cast [1], faileth [1], fall from [1], fall off [1], fallen from [1], falleth away [1], falleth [1], fell off [1], taken none effect [1]

1602 ἐκπλέω, ***ekpleō***, v. GK: *1739* [→ *1537+4126*]. to sail (from):– sailed away [1], sailed thence [1], sailed [1]

1603 ἐκπληρόω, ***ekplēroō***, v. GK: *1740* [→ *1537+4137*]. to (utterly) fulfill:– fulfilled [1]

1604 ἐκπλήρωσις, ***ekplērōsis***, n. GK: *1741* [→ *1537+4137*]. end, completion:– accomplishment [1]

1605 ἐκπλήσσω, ***ekplēssō***, v. GK: *1742* [→ *1537+4141*]. (pass.) to be amazed, astonished:– astonished [10], amazed [3]

1606 ἐκπνέω, ***ekpneō***, v. GK: *1743* [→ *1537+4154*]. to breathe one's last breath, die:– gave up the ghost [3]

1607 ἐκπορεύομαι, ***ekporeuomai***, v. GK: *1744* [→ *1537+4198*]. to go out, come out, leave:– went out [6], cometh out [2], depart [2], goeth out [2], proceeded [2], proceedeth [2], proceed [2], came forth [1], come forth [1], come out [1], come [1], departed [1], go forth [1], going out [1], gone forth [1], issued out [1], issued [1], out goeth [1], proceed out [1], proceeded out [1], proceedeth out [1], proceeding out [1], went [1]

1608 ἐκπορνεύω, ***ekporneuō***, v. GK: *1745* [→ *1537+4204*]. to engage in sexual immorality:– giving over to fornication [1]

1609 ἐκπτύω, ***ekptyō***, v. GK: *1746* [→ *1537+4429*]. to scorn, spit out:– rejected [1]

1610 ἐκριζόω, ***ekrizoō***, v. GK: *1748* [→ *1537+4491*]. to uproot:– plucked up by the roots [1], plucked up by the root [1], root up [1], rooted up [1]

1611 ἔκστασις, ***ekstasis***, n. GK: *1749* [→ *1537+2476*]. amazement, astonishment, bewilderment; a trance:– trance [3], amazed (*+2983*) [1], amazed [1], amazement [1], astonishment [1]

1612 ἐκστρέφω, ***ekstrephō***, v. GK: *1750* [→ *1537+4762*]. (pass.) to be warped, perverted:– subverted [1]

1613 ἐκταράσσω, ***ektarassō***, v. GK: *1752* [→ *1537+5015*]. to throw into an uproar, into confusion:– exceedingly trouble [1]

1614 ἐκτείνω, ***ekteinō***, v. GK: *1753* [→ *660, 816, 1616, 1617, 1618, 1619, 1621, 1901, 2159, 3905, 4385, 4401, 5239, 5500; cf. 1537*]. to stretch out, reach out; point, motion:– stretched forth [5], stretch forth [4], put forth [3], stretched out [2], cast [1], stretching forth [1]

1615 ἐκτελέω, ***ekteleō***, v. GK: *1754* [→ *1537+5056*]. to finish, bring to a conclusion:– finish [2]

1616 ἐκτένεια, ***ekteneia***, n. GK: *1755* [→ *1614*]. earnestness:– instantly (*+1722*) [1]

1617 ἐκτενέστερον, ***ektenesteron***, adv.compar. of *1618*. GK: *1757* [→ *1614*]. more deeply, more earnestly:– more earnestly [1]

1618 ἐκτενής, ***ektenēs***, a. GK: *1756* [→ *1614*]. deep, earnest:– fervent [1], without ceasing [1]

1619 ἐκτενῶς, ***ektenōs***, adv. GK: *1757* [→ *1614*]. deeply, earnestly:– fervently [1]

1620 ἐκτίθημι, ***ektithēmi***, v. GK: *1758* [→ *1537+5087*]. (mid.) to explain; (pass.) to be placed out in the elements, exposed, abandoned:– expounded [3], cast out [1]

1621 ἐκτινάσσω, ***ektinassō***, v. GK: *1759* [→ *1614*]. to shake off, shake out:– shake off [2], shook off [1], shook [1]

1622 ἐκτός, **ektos**, adv. GK: *1760* [→ *1537*]. outside, beyond, except:– out of [2], but (+*1487+3361*) [1], except (+*1487+3361*) [1], excepted [1], other than [1], outside [1], unless (+*1487+3361*) [1], without [1]

1623 ἕκτος, **hektos**, a. GK: *1761* [→ *1803*]. sixth, noon (the sixth hour):– sixth [14]

1624 ἐκτρέπω, **ektrepō**, v. GK: *1762* [→ *1537+5157*]. to turn away, wander away from; be disabled:– turned aside [2], avoiding [1], turned out of the way [1], turned [1]

1625 ἐκτρέφω, **ektrephō**, v. GK: *1763* [→ *1537+5142*]. to feed, nourish; to bring up, rear (children):– bring up [1], nourisheth [1]

1626 ἔκτρωμα, **ektrōma**, n. GK: *1765* [→ *1537+5134*]. abnormal or untimely birth:– born out of due time [1]

1627 ἐκφέρω, **ekpherō**, v. GK: *1766* [→ *1537+5342*]. to bring out, carry out; to produce:– carry out [2], beareth [1], bring forth [1], brought forth [1], carried out [1], carrying forth [1]

1628 ἐκφεύγω, **ekpheugō**, v. GK: *1767* [→ *1537+5343*]. to escape:– escape [4], escaped [1], fled out [1], fled [1]

1629 ἐκφοβέω, **ekphobeō**, v. GK: *1768* [→ *1537+5401*]. to frighten, terrify:– terrify [1]

1630 ἔκφοβος, **ekphobos**, a. GK: *1769* [→ *1537+5401*]. frightened, terrified:– exceedingly fear (+*1510*) [1], sore afraid [1]

1631 ἐκφύω, **ekphyō**, v. GK: *1770* [→ *1537+5453*]. to come out, put forth:– putteth forth [2]

1632 ἐκχέω, **ekcheō**, v. GK: *1772 & 1773* [→ *130, 401, 2022, 2708, 4378, 4797, 4799, 5240, 5517, 5522; cf. 1537*]. to pour out, shed, scatter; (pass.) to be poured out, shed; to rush (for profit):– poured out [9], shed [9], pour out [3], spilled [2], gushed out [1], ran greedily after [1], runneth out [1], shed abroad [1], shed forth [1]

1633 ἐκχωρέω, **ekchōreō**, v. GK: *1774* [→ *1537+5562*]. to go out, go away:– depart out [1]

1634 ἐκψύχω, **ekpsychō**, v. GK: *1775* [→ *1537+5594*]. to die, expire:– gave up the ghost [2], yielded up the ghost [1]

1635 ἑκών, **hekōn**, a. GK: *1776* [→ *210, 1595, 1596*]. voluntarily, by one's own choice:– willingly [2]

1636 ἐλαία, **elaia**, n. GK: *1777* [→ *65, 1637, 1638, 2565*]. olive, olive tree; in the proper name "the Mount of Olives," a ridge on the east side of the Kidron Valley, overlooking Jerusalem and the Temple mount:– olives [11], olive tree [2], olive berries [1], olive trees [1]

1637 ἔλαιον, **elaion**, n. GK: *1778* [→ *1636*]. olive oil:– oil [11]

1638 ἐλαιών, **elaiōn**, n. GK: *1779* [→ *1636*]. Mount of Olives, olive grove:– Olivet [1]

1639 Ἐλαμίτης, **Elamitēs**, n.pr.g. GK: *1780*. Elamite, "*highland*":– Elamites [1]

1640 ἐλάσσων, **elassōn**, a. [also used as adv.]. GK: *1781 & 1784* [→ *1641, 1642, 1646, 1647*]. lesser, cheaper, younger:– less [1], under [1], worse [1], younger [1]

1641 ἐλαττονέω, **elattoneō**, v. GK: *1782* [→ *1640*]. to have too little:– had lack [1]

1642 ἐλαττόω, **elattoō**, v. GK: *1783* [→ *1640*]. to make lower than; (pass.) to be made lower than, become lesser, diminish:– decrease [1], made lower [1], madest lower [1]

1643 ἐλαύνω, **elaunō**, v. GK: *1785* [→ *556, 4900*]. to row (with oars); (pass.) to be driven:– driven [2], carried [1], rowed [1], rowing [1]

1644 ἐλαφρία, **elaphria**, n. GK: *1786* [→ *1645*]. lightness, levity:– lightness [1]

1645 ἐλαφρός, **elaphros**, a. GK: *1787* [→ *1644*]. light, not burdensome:– light [2]

1646 ἐλάχιστος, **elachistos**, a. GK: *1788* [→ *1640*]. least, very small, trivial:– least [9], very small [2], smallest matters [1], very little [1]

1647 ἐλαχιστότερος, **elachistoteros**, a.compar. of *1646*. GK: *1788* [→ *1640*]. far less, smallest:– least [1]

1648 Ἐλεάζαρ, **Eleazar**, n.pr. GK: *1789*. Eleazar, "*God [El] is a help*":– Eleazar [2]

1649 ἔλεγξις, **elenxis**, n. GK: *1792* [→ *1651*]. rebuke, reproof:– rebuked [1]

1650 ἔλεγχος, **elenchos**, n. GK: *1791 & 1793* [→ *1651*]. certainty, proof; rebuke, reproof:– evidence [1], reproof [1]

1651 ἐλέγχω, **elenchō**, v. GK: *1794* [→ *557, 1246, 1649, 1650, 1827*]. to expose; to rebuke, refute, show fault; to convince, convict:– rebuke [4], reproved [3], reprove [3], convinced [2], convicted [1], convinceth [1], convince [1], rebuked [1], tell fault [1]

1652 ἐλεεινός, **eleeinos**, a. GK: *1795* [→ *1656*]. pitiful:– miserable [1], most miserable [1]

1653 ἐλεέω, **eleeō**, v. GK: *1790 & 1796* [→ *1656*]. to have mercy on, pity; to show mercy to, show pity to another who is in serious need, usually with a focus on an act of kindness that will help meet the need:– have mercy [14], obtained mercy [6], had compassion [2], obtain mercy [2], sheweth mercy [2], had mercy [1], had pity [1], hath mercy [1], have compassion [1], received mercy [1]

1654 ἐλεημοσύνη, **eleēmosynē**, n. GK: *1797* [→ *1656*]. gift to the poor, alms, charitable gift; any act of generosity to someone in serious need, often referring to giving gifts of substance or money:– alms [13], almsdeeds [1]

1655 ἐλεήμων, **eleēmōn**, a. GK: *1798* [→ *1656*]. merciful, including feelings of pity, with a focus of showing compassion to those in serious need:– merciful [2]

1656 ἔλεος, **eleos**, n. GK: *1799* [→ *415, 448, 1652, 1653, 1654, 1655*]. mercy, pity; the moral quality of feeling compassion and especially of showing kindness toward someone in need. This can refer to a human kindness and to God's kindness to humankind:– mercy [27], tender mercy (+*4698*) [1]

1657 ἐλευθερία, **eleutheria**, n. GK: *1800* [→ *1658*]. freedom, liberty, not enslaved:– liberty [11]

1658 ἐλεύθερος, **eleutheros**, a. GK: *1801* [→ *558, 1657, 1659*]. free, released, liberated from various kinds of ownership, confinement, and distress: prison confinement, political domination and oppression, physical sickness, release from the marriage contract in death, and God's release of the sinner from sin. A free person is often contrasted to a slave:– free [19], freewoman [3], liberty [1]

1659 ἐλευθερόω, **eleutheroō**, v. GK: *1802* [→ *1658*]. to set free, liberate, cause someone to receive liberty or freedom:– made free [4], make free [2], delivered [1]

ἐλεύθω, **eleuthō**. See **2064**.

1660 ἔλευσις, **eleusis**, n. GK: *1803* [→ *2064*]. coming, advent:– coming [1]

1661 ἐλεφάντινος, **elephantinos**, a. GK: *1804*. made of ivory (derivative of the Greek word for "elephant," not found in the NT):– ivory [1]

1662 Ἐλιακείμ, **Eliakeim**, n.pr. GK: *1805 & 1806*. Eliakim, "*God [El] establishes*":– Eliakim [3]

1663 Ἐλιέζερ, **Eliezer**, n.pr. GK: *1808*. Eliezer, "*God [El] is [my] help*":– Eliezer [1]

1664 Ἐλιούδ, **Elioud**, n.pr. GK: *1809*. Eliud, "*God [El] is [my] grandeur*":– Eliud [2]

1665 Ἐλισάβετ, **Elisabet**, n.pr. GK: *1810*. Elizabeth, "*God [El] is [my] oath*":– Elisabeth [8], Elisabeth's [1]

1666 Ἐλισσαῖος, **Elissaios**, n.pr. GK: *1811 & 1812*. Elisha, "*God [El] is [my] salvation*":– Eliseus [1]

1667 ἑλίσσω, **helissō**, v. GK: *1813* [→ *1507*]. to roll up:– fold up [1]

1668 ἕλκος, **helkos**, n. GK: *1814* [→ *1669*]. sore, abscess:– sores [2], sore [1]

1669 ἑλκόω, **helkoō**, v. GK: *1815* [→ *1668*]. (pass.) to be covered with sores:– full of sores [1]

1670 ἑλκύω, **helkyō**, v. GK: *1816* [→ *1828*]. to drag, draw, pull in:– draw [4], drew [3], drew out [1]

1671 Ἑλλάς, **Hellas**, n.pr. GK: *1817* [→ *1672*]. Greece:– Greece [1]

1672 Ἕλλην, **Hellēn**, n.pr. GK: *1818* [→ *1671, 1673, 1674, 1675, 1676*]. Greek; Gentile, a class of person distinguished from the Jewish race and nation (not necessarily Greek):– Greeks [13], Greek [7], Gentiles [5], Gentile [2]

1673 Ἑλληνικός, **Hellēnikos**, a.pr. GK: *1819* [→ *1672*]. Greek (language):– Greek [2]

1674 Ἑλληνίς, **Hellēnis**, n.pr. GK: *1820* [→ *1672*]. Greek, Gentile, a class of person distinguished from the Jewish race and nation (not necessarily Greek):– Greeks [1], Greek [1]

1675 Ἑλληνιστής, **Hellēnistēs**, n.pr.g. GK: *1821* [→ *1672*]. Grecian Jew, Hellenist:– Grecians [3]

1676 Ἑλληνιστί, **Hellēnisti**, adv.pr. GK: *1822* [→ *1672*]. in Greek (language):– Greek [2]

1677 ἐλλογέω, **ellogeō**, v. GK: *1823 & 1824* [→ *1722+3004*]. to charge (to one's account):– imputed [1], put on account [1]

ἔλλομαι, **hellomai**. See **138**.

1678 Ἐλμωδάμ, **Elmōdam**, n.pr. GK: *1825 & 1826*. Elmodam:– Elmodam [1]

1679 ἐλπίζω, **elpizō**, v. GK: *1827* [→ *1680*]. to hope, hope for, put hope in, expect, an attitude of confidently looking forward to what is good and beneficial:– trust [15], hope [5], hoped [3], hope for [2], trusted [2], hoped for [1], hopeth [1], hoping [1], trusteth [1]

1680 ἐλπίς, elpis, n. GK: *1828* [→ *560, 1679, 4276*]. hope, expectation:– hope [53], hope's [1]

1681 Ἐλύμας, Elymas, n.pr. GK: *1829*. Elymas, "[poss.] *wise one* hence *magician*":– Elymas [1]

1682 ἐλωΐ, elōi, l.[n.+p.]. GK: *1830* [cf. *2241*]. Eloi [Aramaic: my God]:– eloi [2]

1683 ἐμαυτοῦ, emautou, p.reflex. GK: *1831* [→ *1473+846*]. myself, my own, of my own accord:– myself [30], me [4], mine own self [2], mine own [1]

1684 ἐμβαίνω, embainō, v. GK: *1832* [→ *1722+305*]. to get into, step into, embark:– entered [7], went [3], come [2], get [2], entering [1], stepped in [1], took shipping (+*1519+3588+4143*) [1], took [1]

1685 ἐμβάλλω, emballō, v. GK: *1833* [→ *1722+906*]. to throw into:– cast [1]

1686 ἐμβάπτω, embaptō, v. GK: *1834 & 1835* [→ *1722+911*]. to dip into:– dippeth [2], dipped [1]

1687 ἐμβατεύω, embateuō, v. GK: *1836* [→ *1722+305*]. to go into great detail about:– intruding into [1]

1688 ἐμβιβάζω, embibazō, v. GK: *1837* [→ *1722+305*]. to put on board (a vessel):– put [1]

1689 ἐμβλέπω, emblepō, v. GK: *1838* [→ *1722+991*]. to look (closely, directly) at, gaze at:– beheld [3], looked upon [2], looking upon [2], beholding [1], behold [1], gazing up [1], saw [1], see [1]

1690 ἐμβριμάομαι, embrimaomai, v. GK: *1839* [→ *1722*]. to warn sternly, rebuke harshly; to be deeply moved:– straitly charged [2], groaned [1], groaning [1], murmured against [1]

1691 ἐμέ, eme, p.pers.acc. of *1473*. GK: *1609* [→ *1473*]. me; see *1473*:–

1692 ἐμέω, emeō, v. GK: *1840*. to spit out:– spue [1]

1693 ἐμμαίνομαι, emmainomai, v. GK: *1841* [→ *1722+3105*]. to be enraged:– mad against [1]

1694 Ἐμμανουήλ, Emmanouēl, n.pr. GK: *1842*. Immanuel, "*God with us*":– Emmanuel [1]

1695 Ἐμμαοῦς, Emmaous, n.pr. GK: *1843*. Emmaus, "*hot springs*":– Emmaus [1]

1696 ἐμμένω, emmenō, v. GK: *1844* [→ *1722+3306*]. to remain in, stay in; remain faithful, continue in:– continue in [1], continued [1], continueth [1]

1697 Ἐμμώρ, Hemmōr, n.pr. GK: *1846*. Hamor, "*male donkey*":– Emmor [1]

1698 ἐμοί, emoi, p.pers.dat. of *1473*. GK: *1609* [→ *1473*]. in me; to me; my; see *1473*:–

1699 ἐμός, emos, a.poss. GK: *1847* [→ *1473*]. my, mine:– my [49], mine [12], mine own [11], me [4], I have [1]

1700 ἐμοῦ, ēmōu, p.pers.gen. of *1473*. GK: *1609* [→ *1473*]. my, mine; see *1473*.:–

1701 ἐμπαιγμός, empaigmos, n. GK: *1849* [→ *1722+3815*]. jeering, scoffing, mocking:– mockings [1]

1702 ἐμπαίζω, empaizō, v. GK: *1850* [→ *1722+3815*]. to mock, ridicule:– mocked [8], mock [3], mocking [2]

1703 ἐμπαίκτης, empaiktēs, n. GK: *1851* [→ *1722+3815*]. scoffer, mocker:– mockers [1], scoffers [1]

1704 ἐμπεριπατέω, emperipateō, v. GK: *1853* [→ *1722+4012+3961*]. to walk among:– walk in [1]

1705 ἐμπίπλημι, empiplēmi, v. GK: *1854 & 1855 & 1857 & 1858* [→ *1722+4130*]. (act.) to provide, fill, satisfy; (pass.) to be filled to satisfaction; to enjoy one's company:– filled [3], filling with [1], full [1]

1706 ἐμπίπτω, empiptō, v. GK: *1860* [→ *1722+4098*]. to fall into:– fall [5], fallen [1], fell [1]

1707 ἐμπλέκω, emplekō, v. GK: *1861* [→ *1722+4120*]. (mid./pass.) to be involved in, become entangled:– entangled [1], entangleth with [1]

ἐμπλήθω, *emplēthō*. See **1705**.

1708 ἐμπλοκή, emplokē, n. GK: *1862 & 4451* [→ *1722+4120*]. braiding (possibly associated with high fashion):– plaiting [1]

1709 ἐμπνέω, empneō, v. GK: *1863* [→ *1722+4154*]. to breath:– breathing out [1]

1710 ἐμπορεύομαι, emporeuomai, v. GK: *1864* [→ *1722+4198*]. to carry on business; exploit:– buy and sell [1], make merchandise [1]

1711 ἐμπορία, emporia, n. GK: *1865* [→ *1722+4198*]. business, trade:– merchandise [1]

1712 ἐμπόριον, emporion, n. GK: *1866* [→ *1722+4198*]. market, marketplace:– merchandise [1]

1713 ἔμπορος, emporos, n. GK: *1867* [→ *1722+4198*]. merchant:– merchants [4], merchant [1]

1714 ἐμπρήθω, emprēthō, v. GK: *1856 & 1859 & 1868* [→ *1722+4092*]. to burn, set on fire:– burnt up [1]

1715 ἔμπροσθεν, emprosthen, adv.&pp.*. GK: *1869* [→ *1722+4314*]. before, in front of, in the presence of:– before [38], in sight [2], preferred before (+*1096*) [2], against [1], at [1], in the presence [1], in the sight [1], of [1], went forth [1]

1716 ἐμπτύω, emptyō, v. GK: *1870* [→ *1722+4429*]. to spit on, spit at:– spit upon [2], spit [2], spit on [1], spitted on [1]

1717 ἐμφανής, emphanēs, a. GK: *1871* [→ *1722+5316*]. seen, revealed, visible:– manifest [1], openly [1]

1718 ἐμφανίζω, emphanizō, v. GK: *1872* [→ *1722+5316*]. to show; report; to present (legal) charges; petition; (pass.) to appear:– informed [3], manifest [2], appeared [1], appear [1], declare plainly [1], shewed [1], signify [1]

1719 ἔμφοβος, emphobos, a. GK: *1873* [→ *1722+5401*]. afraid, terrified:– afraid [3], affrighted [2], trembled (+*1096*) [1]

1720 ἐμφυσάω, emphysaō, v. GK: *1874* [→ *1722+5453*]. to breathe on:– breathed on [1]

1721 ἔμφυτος, emphytos, a. GK: *1875* [→ *1722+5453*]. implanted:– engrafted [1]

1722 ἐν, en, pp. GK: *1877* [→ *410, 418, 1449, 1455, 1456, 1457, 1458, 1459, 1460, 1461, 1462, 1463, 1464, 1465, 1466, 1467, 1468, 1469, 1470, 1471, 1472, 1677, 1684, 1685, 1686, 1687, 1688, 1689, 1690, 1693, 1696, 1701, 1702, 1703, 1704, 1705, 1714, 1706, 1707, 1708, 1709, 1710, 1711, 1712, 1713, 1714, 1715, 1716, 1717, 1718, 1719, 1720, 1721, 1723, 1724, 1725, 1728, 1729, 1730, 1731, 1732, 1735, 1736, 1737, 1738, 1739, 1740, 1741, 1742, 1743, 1744, 1745, 1746, 1747, 1748, 1749, 1750, 1751, 1753, 1754, 1755, 1756, 1757, 1758, 1759, 1760, 1761, 1762, 1764, 1765, 1770, 1771, 1772, 1773, 1774, 1776, 1777, 1779, 1780, 1782, 1783, 1784, 1786, 1787, 1788, 1789, 1790, 1791, 1792, 1793, 1794, 1795, 1796, 1797, 1798, 1799, 1801, 1902, 1903, 2714, 3925, 3926, 4278, 5241*; *cf. 1420, 1785*]. Spatially: in, inside, at, among, with; logically: by means of, with, because of; of time: during, while:– in [1877], with [145], by [141], at [110], among [104], on [46], through [38], wherein (+*3739*) [23], to [18], therein (+*846*) [16], as (+*3588*) [15], of [15], within [13], into [12], when (+*3588*) [12], unto [9], amongst [8], hereby (+*3778*) [8], as [7], herein (+*3778*) [7], for [6], whereby (+*3739*) [6], among (+*3319*) [5], throughout [5], while (+*3588*) [5], with child (+*1064+2192*) [5], shortly (+*5034*) [4], upon [4], when [4], where (+*3739*) [4], glorious (+*1391*) [3], in (+*3588*) [3], openly (+*5318*) [3], thereon (+*846*) [3], towards [3], wherewith (+*5101*) [3], while (+*3739*) [3], almost (+*3641*) [2], always (+*2540+3956*) [2], because of [2], foolishly (+*877*) [2], quickly (+*5034*) [2], there (+*846*) [2], therein (+*3778*) [2], therewith (+*846*) [2], under [2], when (+*3739*) [2], whereas (+*3739*) [2], whereupon (+*3739*) [2], wherewith (+*3739*) [2], about [1], accused (+*2724*) [1], after (+*1836+3588*) [1], afterward (+*2517+3588*) [1], after [1], against [1], age (+*2250+4260*) [1], all (+*3650*) [1], altogether (+*4183*) [1], at (+*3588*) [1], because [1], before (+*3319+3588*) [1], before [1], being [1], between [1], boldly (+*3954*) [1], burdensome (+*922*) [1], by (+*3588*) [1], by way of [1], darkly (+*135*) [1], first (+*4413*) [1], for sake [1], gorgeously (+*1741*) [1], howbeit whereinsoever (+*302+1161+3739*) [1], in that (+*3588*) [1], in the mean time (+*3739*) [1], instantly (+*1616*) [1], inwardly (+*2927+3588*) [1], known openly (+*3954*) [1], namely (+*3588*) [1], openly (+*3954*) [1], outward (+*3588+5318*) [1], outwardly (+*3588+5318*) [1], over [1], plainly (+*3954*) [1], scattered abroad (+*1290+3588*) [1], speedily (+*5034*) [1], that (+*3588*) [1], that (+*3739*) [1], that [1], thereby (+*846*) [1], thereby [1], therein [1], throughly (+*3956*) [1], uncircumcised (+*203*) [1], wherein (+*3739+3778*) [1], wherein [1], while (+*1510+3588*) [1], whilst (+*3588*) [1], wholly to [1], written (+*1121*) [1]

1723 ἐναγκαλίζομαι, enankalizomai, v. GK: *1878* [→ *1722+43*]. to take in one's arms:– taken in arms [1], took up in arms [1]

1724 ἐνάλιος, enalios, a. GK: *1879* [→ *1722+217*]. creatures pertaining to the sea:– in the sea [1]

1725 ἔναντι, enanti, adv. [used as pp.*]. GK: *1882* [→ *561, 1726, 1727, 2713, 5121, 5227*]. before (spatial); fig., in the eyes of:– before [1]

1726 ἐναντίον, enantion, adv. [used as pp.*]. GK: *1883* [→ *1725*]. before (spatial); fig., in the sight of:– before [4], in the sight [1]

1727 ἐναντίος, enantios, a. GK: *1885* [→ *1725*]. against, opposite, in hostility:– contrary [6], against [1], over against (+*1537*) [1]

1728 ἐνάρχομαι, ***enarchomai***, v. GK: *1887* [→ *1722+757*]. to begin:– begun [2]

1729 ἐνδεής, ***endeēs***, a. GK: *1890* [→ *1722+1189*]. needy, poor, impoverished:– lacked [1]

1730 ἔνδειγμα, ***endeigma***, n. GK: *1891* [→ *1722+1164*]. evidence, plain indication:– manifest token [1]

1731 ἐνδείκνυμι, ***endeiknymi***, v. GK: *1892* [→ *1722+1166*]. to show, display:– shew [6], shewing [2], did [1], shew forth [1], shewed [1]

1732 ἔνδειξις, ***endeixis***, n. GK: *1893* [→ *1722+1166*]. demonstration, proof, sign:– declare [2], evident token [1], proof [1]

1733 ἕνδεκα, ***hendeka***, n.num. GK: *1894* [→ *1520+1176*]. eleven:– eleven [6]

1734 ἑνδέκατος, ***hendekatos***, a. GK: *1895* [→ *1520+1176*]. eleventh:– eleventh [3]

1735 ἐνδέχομαι, ***endechomai***, v.imper. GK: *1896* [→ *1722+1209*]. it is possible:– cannot (+*3756*) [1]

1736 ἐνδημέω, ***endēmeō***, v. GK: *1897* [→ *1722+1218*]. to be at home:– present [2], at home [1]

1737 ἐνδιδύσκω, ***endidyskō***, v. GK: *1898* [→ *1722+1416*]. to put on, dress (another); (mid.) dress oneself:– clothed in [1], ware [1]

1738 ἔνδικος, ***endikos***, a. GK: *1899* [→ *1722+1349*]. just, deserved:– just recompence [1], just [1]

1739 ἐνδόμησις, ***endomēsis***, n. GK: *1900 & 1908* [→ *1722+1430*]. what something is made of, construction, material:– building [1]

1740 ἐνδοξάζομαι, ***endoxazomai***, v. GK: *1901* [→ *1722+1391*]. to be glorified, honored:– glorified [2]

1741 ἔνδοξος, ***endoxos***, a. GK: *1902* [→ *1722+1391*]. honored, having high status and so thought to be wonderful, a fig. extension of the feature of an object being radiant or expensive:– glorious [2], gorgeously (+*1722*) [1], honourable [1]

1742 ἔνδυμα, ***endyma***, n. GK: *1903* [→ *1722+1416*]. clothing, garment:– raiment [5], garment [2], clothing [1]

1743 ἐνδυναμόω, ***endynamoō***, v. GK: *1904* [→ *1722+1410*]. to give strength, strengthen; (mid./pass.) to be strong, strengthened:– strong [3], enabled [1], increased in strength [1], made strong [1], strengthened [1], strengtheneth [1]

1744 ἐνδύνω, ***endynō***, v. GK: *1905* [→ *1722+1416*]. to worm one's way, creep in:– creep [1]

1745 ἔνδυσις, ***endysis***, n. GK: *1906* [→ *1722+1416*]. putting on:– putting on [1]

1746 ἐνδύω, ***endyō***, v. GK: *1907* [→ *1722+1416*]. to clothe, dress; (mid.) clothe oneself:– put on [17], clothed in [2], clothed with [2], arrayed in [1], clothed with a garment [1], clothed [1], endued with [1], had on [1], having on [1], putting on [1]

ἐνέγκω, ***enegkō***. See *5342*.

1747 ἐνέδρα, ***enedra***, n. GK: *1909* [→ *1722+1476*]. plot, ambush:– laying wait (+*4160*) [1], lying in wait [1]

1748 ἐνεδρεύω, ***enedreuō***, v. GK: *1910* [→ *1722+1476*]. to wait in ambush, lie in wait for:– laying wait for [1], lie in wait for [1]

1749 ἔνεδρον, ***enedron***, n. GK: *1911* [→ *1722+1476*]. plot, ambush:–

1750 ἐνειλέω, ***eneileō***, v. GK: *1912* [→ *1722*]. to wrap in:– wrapped in [1]

1751 ἔνειμι, ***eneimi***, v. GK: *1913* [→ *1722+1510*]. to be inside; contents:– have [1]

1752 ἕνεκα, ***heneka***; or ἕνεκεν, ***heneken***; or εἵνεκεν, ***heineken***, pp.*. GK: *1914 & 1915 & 1641*. for the sake of; for this reason, because:– for sake [14], for cause [2], for this cause (+*3778*) [2], because (+*3739*) [1], because that [1], by reason of [1], for causes [1], for [1], that [1], wherefore (+*5101*) [1]

1753 ἐνέργεια, ***energeia***, n. GK: *1918* [→ *1722+2041*]. working, power, energy:– working [4], effectual working [2], operation [1], strong [1]

1754 ἐνεργέω, ***energeō***, v. GK: *1919* [→ *1722+2041*]. to be at work in; to produce:– worketh [10], work [2], do [1], effectual fervent [1], effectually worketh [1], effectual [1], mighty in [1], shew forth in [1], shew forth [1], wrought effectually in [1], wrought [1]

1755 ἐνέργημα, ***energēma***, n. GK: *1920* [→ *1722+2041*]. working, activity:– operations [1], working [1]

1756 ἐνεργής, ***energēs***, a. GK: *1921* [→ *1722+2041*]. active, effective:– effectual [2], powerful [1]

1757 ἐνευλογέω, ***eneulogeō***, v. GK: *1922* [→ *1722+2095+3004*]. (pass.) to be blessed:– blessed [2]

1758 ἐνέχω, ***enechō***, v. GK: *1923* [→ *1722+2192*]. to oppose, be hostile toward, bear a grudge against; (pass.) to be burdened:– entangled [1], had a quarrel against [1], urge [1]

1759 ἐνθάδε, ***enthade***, adv. GK: *1924* [→ *1722*]. here, in this place, to this place:– hither [4], here [3], there [1]

1760 ἐνθυμέομαι, ***enthymeomai***, v. GK: *1445 & 1926* [→ *1722+2372*]. to consider, reflect on:– think [1], thought on [1], thought [1]

1761 ἐνθύμησις, ***enthymēsis***, n. GK: *1927* [→ *1722+2372*]. thought, reflection; design, idea:– thoughts [3], device [1]

1762 ἔνι, ***eni***, v. GK: *1928* [→ *1722+1510*]. there is:– is [5]

1763 ἐνιαυτός, ***eniautos***, n. GK: *1929* [→ *846*]. year:– year [11], years [2], year by year (+*2596*) [1]

1764 ἐνίστημι, ***enistēmi***, v. GK: *1931* [→ *1722+2476*]. to be present, (ptcp.) the present:– present [5], at hand [1], come [1]

1765 ἐνισχύω, ***enischyō***, v. GK: *1932* [→ *1722+2479*]. to strengthen (another); to regain (one's own) strength:– strengthened [1], strengthening [1]

1766 ἔνατος, ***enatos***, a. GK: *1888* [→ *1767*]. ninth (ninth hour = three p.m.):– ninth [10]

1767 ἐννέα, ***ennea***, n.num. GK: *1933* [→ *1766, 1768*]. nine:– nine [5]

1768 ἐνενήκοντα, ***enenēkonta***, n.num. GK: *1916* [→ *1767*]. ninety:– ninety [4]

1769 ἐννεός, ***enneos***, a. GK: *1917 & 1934*. speechless:– speechless [1]

1770 ἐννεύω, ***enneuō***, v. GK: *1935* [→ *1722+3506*]. to make a sign, nod:– made signs [1]

1771 ἔννοια, ***ennoia***, n. GK: *1936* [→ *1722+3563*]. attitude, thought:– intents [1], mind [1]

1772 ἔννομος, ***ennomos***, a. GK: *1937* [→ *1722+3551*]. under law, subject to the law; legal (assembly):– lawful [1], under law [1]

1773 ἔννυχος, ***ennychos***, a. [used as adv.]. GK: *1939* [→ *1722+3571*]. while it is still dark, at night:– before day [1]

1774 ἐνοικέω, ***enoikeō***, v. GK: *1940* [→ *1722+3624*]. to live in, live with:– dwelleth [2], dwell [2], dwelt [1]

1775 ἑνότης, ***henotēs***, n. GK: *1942* [→ *1520*]. unity:– unity [2]

1776 ἐνοχλέω, ***enochleō***, v. GK: *1943* [→ *1722+3793*]. (act.) to cause trouble; (pass.) to be troubled:– trouble [1]

1777 ἔνοχος, ***enochos***, a. GK: *1944* [→ *1722+2192*]. subject to; guilty, liable for:– guilty [4], in danger [4], danger [1], subject [1]

1778 ἔνταλμα, ***entalma***, n. GK: *1945* [→ *1785*]. rule, commandment, precept:– commandments [3]

1779 ἐνταφιάζω, ***entaphiazō***, v. GK: *1946* [→ *1722+5028*]. to prepare (a corpse) for burial, bury:– burial [1], bury [1]

1780 ἐνταφιασμός, ***entaphiasmos***, n. GK: *1947* [→ *1722+5028*]. preparation for burial, burial:– burying [2]

1781 ἐντέλλω, ***entellō***, v. GK: *1948* [→ *1785*]. (mid.) to command, give orders, give instructions:– commanded [6], command [4], gave commandment [2], give charge [2], charged [1], enjoined [1], given commandments [1]

1782 ἐντεῦθεν, ***enteuthen***, adv. GK: *1925 & 1949* [→ *1722*]. from here, from this place:– hence [6], from hence [3], of either side (+*1782+2532*) [2], on either side one (+*1782+2532*) [2]

1783 ἔντευξις, ***enteuxis***, n. GK: *1950* [→ *1722+5177*]. prayer, intercession:– intercessions [1], prayer [1]

1784 ἔντιμος, ***entimos***, a. GK: *1952* [→ *1722+5092*]. highly valued, honored, precious:– precious [2], dear [1], more honourable than [1], reputation [1]

1785 ἐντολή, ***entolē***, n. GK: *1953* [→ *1778, 1781; cf. 1722*]. command, commandment, regulation, an order that has authority:– commandment [42], commandments [27], precept [2]

1786 ἐντόπιος, ***entopios***, a. GK: *1954* [→ *1722+5117*]. resident, local:– place [1]

1787 ἐντός, ***entos***, adv. GK: *1955* [→ *1722*]. inside, within:– within [2]

1788 ἐντρέπω, ***entrepō***, v. GK: *1956* [→ *1722+5157*]. to cause shame; (pass.) to be ashamed; (mid.) to care about, respect:– reverence [3], ashamed [2], gave reverence [1], regarded [1], regard [1], shame [1]

1789 ἐντρέφω, ***entrephō***, v. GK: *1957* [→ *1722+5142*]. (pass.) to be brought up, reared, trained:– nourished up [1]

1790 ἔντρομος, ***entromos***, a. GK: *1958* [→ *1722+5141*]. trembling:– quake [1], trembled (+*1096*) [1], trembling [1]

1791 ἐντροπή, ***entropē***, n. GK: *1959* [→ *1722+5157*]. shame, humiliation:– shame [2]

1792 **ἐντρυφάω, *entryphaō***, v. GK: *1960* [→ *1722+5172*]. to revel, carouse:– sporting [1]

1793 **ἐντυγχάνω, *entynchanō***, v. GK: *1961* [→ *1722+5177*]. to intercede, appeal, petition:– maketh intercession [3], dealt with [1], make intercession [1]

1794 **ἐντυλίσσω, *entylissō***, v. GK: *1962* [→ *1722*]. to wrap up (a body); (pass.) to be folded:– wrapped [2], wrapped together [1]

1795 **ἐντυπόω, *entypoō***, v. GK: *1963* [→ *1722+5180*]. (pass.) to be engraved, carved:– engraven [1]

1796 **ἐνυβρίζω, *enybrizō***, v. GK: *1964* [→ *1722+5196*]. to insult:– done despite unto [1]

1797 **ἐνυπνιάζομαι, *enypniazomai***, v. GK: *1965* [→ *1722+5258*]. to (have supernatural) dreams or visions:– dreamers [1], dream [1]

1798 **ἐνύπνιον, *enypnion***, n. GK: *1966* [→ *1722+5258*]. dream:– dreams [1]

1799 **ἐνώπιον, *enōpion***, pp.*. GK: *1967* [→ *1722+3708*]. before, in the presence of; in behalf of, by authority of:– before [62], in the sight [16], in the presence [6], in sight [5], in presence [2], before face [1], here before [1], presence [1], to [1]

1800 **Ἐνώς, *Enōs***, n.pr. GK: *1968*. Enosh, "*[mortal] man*":– Enos [1]

1801 **ἐνωτίζομαι, *enōtizomai***, v. GK: *1969* [→ *1722+3775*]. to listen carefully, pay attention to:– hearken [1]

1802 **Ἐνώχ, *Henōch***, n.pr. GK: *1970*. Enoch, "*initiated; follower*":– Enoch [3]

ἐξ, *ex*. See ***1537***.

1803 **ἕξ, *hex***, n.num. GK: *1971* [→ *1623, 1812, 1835*]. six:– six [11], threescore sixteen (*+1440*) [1]

1804 **ἐξαγγέλλω, *exangellō***, v. GK: *1972* [→ *1537+32*]. to declare, proclaim:– shew forth [1]

1805 **ἐξαγοράζω, *exagorazō***, v. GK: *1973* [→ *1537+59*]. (act.) to redeem, as a fig. extension of the act of purchasing something in the marketplace; (mid.) to make the most (of the time):– redeeming [2], redeemed [1], redeem [1]

1806 **ἐξάγω, *exagō***, v. GK: *1974* [→ *1537+71*]. to lead out, bring out, escort:– brought out [5], led out [3], brought forth [1], fetch out [1], lead out [1], leadeth out [1], leddest out [1]

1807 **ἐξαιρέω, *exaireō***, v. GK: *1975* [→ *1537+138*]. (act.) to gouge, take out, tear out; (mid.) to rescue, set free:– delivered [2], deliver [2], pluck out [2], delivering [1], rescued [1]

1808 **ἐξαίρω, *exairō***, v. GK: *1976* [→ *1537+142*]. to expel, remove, drive away:– put away [1], taken away [1]

1809 **ἐξαιτέω, *exaiteō***, v. GK: *1977* [→ *1537+154*]. (mid.) to ask for:– desired [1]

1810 **ἐξαίφνης, *exaiphnēs***, adv. GK: *1978 & 2005* [→ *1537+160*]. suddenly, unexpectedly:– suddenly [5]

1811 **ἐξακολουθέω, *exakoloutheō***, v. GK: *1979* [→ *1537+190; cf. 1.3*]. to follow, obey:– followed [1], following [1], follow [1]

1812 **ἑξακόσιοι, *hexakosioi***, a.num. GK: *1980* [→ *1803*]. six hundred:– six hundred [1]

1813 **ἐξαλείφω, *exaleiphō***, v. GK: *1981* [→ *1537+218*]. to wipe away, blot out, cancel:– wipe away [2], blot out [1], blotted out [1], blotting out [1]

1814 **ἐξάλλομαι, *exallomai***, v. GK: *1982* [→ *1537+242*]. to jump up:– leaping up [1]

1815 **ἐξανάστασις, *exanastasis***, n. GK: *1983* [→ *1537+303+2476*]. resurrection:– resurrection [1]

1816 **ἐξανατέλλω, *exanatellō***, v. GK: *1984* [→ *395; cf. 1537*]. to spring up:– sprang up [1], sprung up [1]

1817 **ἐξανίστημι, *exanistēmi***, v. GK: *1985* [→ *1537+303+2476*]. to raise up (seed) = have children; (intr.) to stand up:– raise up [2], rose up [1]

1818 **ἐξαπατάω, *exapataō***, v. GK: *1987* [→ *1537+539*]. to deceive, cheat:– deceive [3], beguiled [1], deceived [1]

1819 **ἐξάπινα, *exapina***, adv. GK: *1988* [→ *1537+160*]. suddenly:– suddenly [1]

1820 **ἐξαπορέω, *exaporeō***, v. GK: *1989* [→ *1537+1.1+4198*]. (mid.) to despair; (pass.) to be in despair:– despaired [1], in despair [1]

1821 **ἐξαποστέλλω, *exapostellō***, v. GK: *1990* [→ *1537+649*]. to send out, send away:– sent away [4], sent forth [4], send [1], sent out [1], sent [1]

1822 **ἐξαρτίζω, *exartizō***, v. GK: *1992* [→ *1537+737*]. to finish, complete; (pass.) to be equipped, furnished:– accomplished [1], throughly furnished [1]

1823 **ἐξαστράπτω, *exastraptō***, v. GK: *1993* [→ *1537+796*]. to flash like lightning:– glistering [1]

1824 **ἐξαυτῆς, *exautēs***, adv. GK: *1994* [→ *1537+846*]. immediately, at once, right now:– immediately [2], by and by [1], immediately already [1], presently [1], straightway [1]

1825 **ἐξεγείρω, *exegeirō***, v. GK: *1995* [→ *1537+1453*]. to raise, awaken (from the dead):– raise up [1], raised up [1]

1826 **ἔξειμι, *exeimi***, v. GK: *1996* [→ *1537*]. to leave, go out, go away:– departed [1], depart [1], get [1], gone out [1]

1827 **ἐξελέγχω, *exelenchō***, v. GK: *1998* [→ *1537+1651*]. to convict:– convince [1]

1828 **ἐξέλκω, *exelkō***, v. GK: *1999* [→ *1537+1670*]. (pass.) to be dragged away:– drawn away [1]

1829 **ἐξέραμα, *exerama***, n. GK: *2000* [→ *1537*]. vomit, what is disgorged:– vomit [1]

1830 **ἐξεραυνάω, *exeraunaō***, v. GK: *2001* [→ *1537+2045*]. to search intently, inquire carefully:– searched diligently [1]

1831 **ἐξέρχομαι, *exerchomai***, v. GK: *2002* [→ *1537+2064*]. to go out, leave:– went out [59], came out [30], departed [22], went forth [19], come out [18], gone out [10], go out [9], depart [6], came forth [5], went [5], come forth [4], go forth [4], get out [3], came [2], come [2], go [2], out [2], spread abroad [2], went abroad [2], came out of [1], camest forth [1], cometh out [1], coming out [1], depart out [1], departing [1], escaped [1], go thence [1], gone [1], out come [1], proceeded forth [1], proceedeth [1], proceed [1], went away [1], went from [1]

1832 **ἔξεστι, *exesti***, v.imper. GK: *1997 & 2003* [→ *1537+1510*]. it is legal, it is proper, it is permitted:– lawful [28], lawful for [1], let [1], mayest [1], may [1]

1833 **ἐξετάζω, *exetazō***, v. GK: *2004* [→ *426; cf. 1537*]. to make a search; to ask, inquire, question:– ask [1], inquire [1], search [1]

1834 **ἐξηγέομαι, *exēgeomai***, v. GK: *2007* [→ *1537+71*]. to tell, make known, describe, report:– declared [4], declaring [1], told [1]

1835 **ἑξήκοντα, *hexēkonta***, n.num. GK: *2008* [→ *1803*]. sixty:– threescore [4], sixty [3], sixtyfold [1]

1836 **ἑξῆς, *hexēs***, adv. GK: *2009* [→ *2192*]. next, afterward:– next [2], after (*+1722+3588*) [1], following [1], on morrow [1]

1837 **ἐξηχέω, *exēcheō***, v. GK: *2010* [→ *1537+2279*]. (pass.) to ring out, be caused to sound out:– sounded out [1]

1838 **ἕξις, *hexis***, n. GK: *2011* [→ *2192*]. constant use, practice:– use [1]

1839 **ἐξίστημι, *existēmi***, v. GK: *2012 & 2013 & 2014* [→ *1537+2476*]. to amaze, astound; confuse; (intr.) to be amazed, out of one's senses:– amazed [6], astonished [5], bewitched [2], beside himself [1], besides ourselves [1], made astonished [1], wondered [1]

1840 **ἐξισχύω, *exischyō***, v. GK: *2015* [→ *1537+2479*]. to have power, be strong enough:– able [1]

1841 **ἔξοδος, *exodos***, n. GK: *2016* [→ *1537+3598*]. exodus, departure:– decease [2], departing [1]

1842 **ἐξολεθρεύω, *exolethreuō***, v. GK: *2017* [→ *1537+3639*]. (pass.) to be completely cut off from:– destroyed [1]

1843 **ἐξομολογέω, *exomologeō***, v. GK: *2018* [→ *1537+3670*]. (act.) to consent; (mid.) to openly confess, admit, praise:– confess [5], confessing [2], thank [2], confessed [1], promised [1]

ἐξόν, *exon*. See ***1832***.

1844 **ἐξορκίζω, *exorkizō***, v. GK: *2019* [→ *1537+3727*]. to charge under oath, adjure:– adjure [1]

1845 **ἐξορκιστής, *exorkistēs***, n. GK: *2020* [→ *1537+3727*]. one driving out evil spirits, exorcist:– exorcists [1]

1846 **ἐξορύσσω, *exoryssō***, v. GK: *2021* [→ *1537+3736*]. to dig through, tear out:– broken up [1], plucked out [1]

1847 **ἐξουδενόω, *exoudenoō***, v. GK: *2022 & 2023* [→ *1537+3756+1161+1520*]. (pass.) to be rejected, treated with contempt:– set at nought [1]

1848 **ἐξουθενέω, *exoutheneō***, v. GK: *2024 & 2025* [→ *1537+3756+1161+1520*]. to treat with contempt, look down on, ridicule; (pass.) to be rejected, despised:– despised [3], despise [3], set at nought [3], contemptible [1], least esteemed [1]

1849 **ἐξουσία, *exousia***, n. GK: *2026* [→ *1850, 2715*]. authority, power, the right to control or govern; dominion, the area or sphere of jurisdiction; a ruler, human or supernatural:– power [57], authority [28], powers [8], power over [4], right [2], authorities [1], jurisdiction [1], liberty [1], strength [1]

1850 ἐξουσιάζω, exousiazō, v. GK: *2027* [→ *1849*]. to have power over; (pass.) to be mastered:– hath power [2], brought under power [1], exercise authority upon [1]

1851 ἐξοχή, exochē, n. GK: *2029* [→ *1537+2192*]. leading, prominent:– principal [1]

1852 ἐξυπνίζω, exypnizō, v. GK: *2030* [→ *1537+5258*]. to wake up, arouse:– awake out of sleep [1]

1853 ἔξυπνος, exypnos, a. GK: *2031* [→ *1537+5258*]. awake, aroused:– awaking out of sleep (+*1096*) [1]

1854 ἔξω, exō, adv. GK: *2032* [→ *1537*]. out, outside:– without [23], of [10], forth [6], out of [6], out [5], away [1], outward [1], strange [1]

1855 ἔξωθεν, exōthen, adv. GK: *2033* [→ *1537*]. from the outside:– without [4], from without [2], outside [2], outward [2], outwardly [1]

1856 ἐξωθέω, exōtheō, v. GK: *2034* [→ *683; cf. 1537*]. to drive out, expel; to run aground:– drave out [1], thrust in [1]

1857 ἐξώτερος, exōteros, a. GK: *2035* [→ *1537*]. outside, farthest out (as a superlative):– outer [3]

1858 ἑορτάζω, heortazō, v. GK: *2037* [→ *1859*]. to celebrate a festival:– keep the feast [1]

1859 ἑορτή, heortē, n. GK: *2038* [→ *1858*]. feast, festival, in the NT this refers the joyous gathering of people for the celebrations of the Jewish calendar year, having a focus on ceremonial eating, such as Passover, Pentecost, and New Moon:– feast [26], holyday [1]

1860 ἐπαγγελία, epangelia, n. GK: *2039* [→ *1909+32*]. promise:– promise [40], promises [12], message [1]

1861 ἐπαγγέλλομαι, epangellomai, v. GK: *2040* [→ *1909+32*]. to promise; to profess, lay claim to:– promised [10], professing [2], made promise [1], promise made [1], promise [1]

1862 ἐπάγγελμα, epangelma, n. GK: *2041* [→ *1909+32*]. promise:– promises [1], promise [1]

1863 ἐπάγω, epagō, v. GK: *2042* [→ *1909+71*]. to bring upon; to make guilty:– bring upon [1], bringing in [1], bring [1]

1864 ἐπαγωνίζομαι, epagōnizomai, v. GK: *2043* [→ *1909+73*]. to contend, fight:– earnestly contend for [1]

1865 ἐπαθροίζω, epathroizō, v. GK: *2044* [→ *1909; cf. 4867*]. (pass.) to increase; to be collected:– gathered thick together [1]

1866 Ἐπαίνετος, Epainetos, n.pr. GK: *2045* [→ *1909+136*]. Epenetus, "*praised*":– Epenetus [1]

1867 ἐπαινέω, epaineō, v. GK: *2046* [→ *1909+136*]. to praise, commend:– praise [4], commended [1], laud [1]

1868 ἔπαινος, epainos, n. GK: *2047* [→ *1909+136*]. praise, commendation:– praise [11]

1869 ἐπαίρω, epairō, v. GK: *2048* [→ *1909+142*]. to lift up; "to lift up the eyes" means "to look up"; "to lift up the voice" means "to shout" or "talk loudly"; "to lift up the heel" means "to oppose someone" (implying hostility):– lift up [13], exalteth [1], exalt [1], hoised up [1], lifted up [1], lifting up [1], taken up [1]

1870 ἐπαισχύνομαι, epaischynomai, v. GK: *2049* [→ *1909+150*]. to be ashamed of:– ashamed [11]

1871 ἐπαιτέω, epaiteō, v. GK: *2050* [→ *1909+154*]. to beg:– beg [1]

1872 ἐπακολουθέω, epakoloutheō, v. GK: *2051* [→ *1909+190; cf. 1.3*]. to follow after, accompany; be devoted to:– diligently followed [1], follow after [1], following [1], follow [1]

1873 ἐπακούω, epakouō, v. GK: *2052* [→ *1909+191*]. to hear, listen to:– heard [1]

1874 ἐπακροάομαι, epakroaomai, v. GK: *2053* [→ *1909+202*]. to listen to:– heard [1]

1875 ἐπάν, epan, c.temp. GK: *2054* [→ *1909+302*]. when, as soon as:– when [3]

1876 ἐπάναγκες, epanankes, adv. GK: *2055* [→ *1909+318*]. necessarily:– necessary [1]

1877 ἐπανάγω, epanagō, v. GK: *2056* [→ *1909+303+71*]. to put out (to sea); to return:– launch out [1], returned [1], thrust out [1]

1878 ἐπαναμιμνήσκω, epanamimnēskō, v. GK: *2057* [→ *1909+303+3421*]. to remind again:– putting in mind [1]

1879 ἐπαναπαύομαι, epanapauomai, v. GK: *2058* [→ *1909+303+3973*]. to rest on, rely on:– restest [1], rest [1]

1880 ἐπανέρχομαι, epanerchomai, v. GK: *2059* [→ *1909+303+2064*]. to return (home):– come again [1], returned [1]

1881 ἐπανίστημι, epanistēmi, v. GK: *2060* [→ *1909+303+2476*]. to rebel against, rise up (in rebellion):– rise up against [1], rise up [1]

1882 ἐπανόρθωσις, epanorthōsis, n. GK: *2061* [→ *1909+303+3717*]. correcting:– correction [1]

1883 ἐπάνω, epanō, adv. GK: *2062* [→ *1909+507*]. above, on, upon; more than:– over [6], on [4], above [3], upon [3], thereon (+*846*) [2], more than [1], thereon [1]

1884 ἐπαρκέω, eparkeō, v. GK: *2064* [→ *1909+714*]. to help, aid:– relieve [2], relieved [1]

1885 ἐπαρχεία, eparcheia, n. GK: *2065 & 2066* [→ *1909+757*]. province:– province [2]

1886 ἔπαυλις, epaulis, n. GK: *2068* [→ *1909+833*]. place to live, residence:– habitation [1]

1887 ἐπαύριον, epaurion, adv. GK: *2069* [→ *839; cf. 1909*]. the next day, tomorrow:– next day [7], on morrow [7], day following [2], morrow [1]

1888 ἐπαυτοφώρῳ, epautophōrō, a. GK: *2070* [→ *1909+846*]. pertaining to being caught in the act:– in the very act [1]

1889 Ἐπαφρᾶς, Epaphras, n.pr. GK: *2071*. Epaphras, "*handsome*":– Epaphras [3]

1890 ἐπαφρίζω, epaphrizō, v. GK: *576 & 2072* [→ *1909+876*]. to foam up:– foaming out [1]

1891 Ἐπαφρόδιτος, Epaphroditos, n.pr. GK: *2073*. Epaphroditus, "*handsome*":– Epaphroditus [3]

1892 ἐπεγείρω, epegeirō, v. GK: *2074* [→ *1909+1453*]. to stir up, arouse, excite:– raised [1], stirred up [1]

1893 ἐπεί, epei, c. GK: *2075* [→ *1909*]. since, because, for otherwise:– because [7], otherwise [4], seeing [3], else [2], then [2], else (+*686*) [1], for that [1], for then [1], forasmuch as [1], forasmuch [1], for [1], seeing that [1], since [1], when [1]

1894 ἐπειδή, epeidē, c. GK: *2076* [→ *1909+1211*]. when; since, because:– for [3], because [2], seeing [2], after that [1], forasmuch as [1], since [1]

1895 ἐπειδήπερ, epeidēper, c. GK: *2077* [→ *1909+1211+4007*]. inasmuch as, since, whereas:– forasmuch as [1]

1896 ἐπεῖδον, epeidon, v. GK: *2078 & 2393* [→ *1909+3708*]. to show favor, concern; to consider, look at:– behold [1], looked on [1]

1897 ἐπείπερ, epeiper, c. GK: *2080* [→ *1909+4007*]. since, indeed:– seeing [1]

1898 ἐπεισαγωγή, epeisagōgē, n. GK: *2081* [→ *1909+1519+71*]. introduction, bringing in:– bringing in [1]

1899 ἔπειτα, epeita, adv. GK: *2083* [→ *1909+1534*]. then, later, afterward:– then [9], after that [4], afterward [2], afterwards [1]

1900 ἐπέκεινα, epekeina, adv. GK: *2084* [→ *1909+1563*]. beyond, farther on:– beyond [1]

1901 ἐπεκτείνομαι, epekteinomai, v. GK: *2085* [→ *1614; cf. 1909*]. to strain toward, stretch out:– reaching forth [1]

1902 ἐπενδύομαι, ependyomai, v. GK: *2086* [→ *1909+1722+1416*]. to be clothed with:– clothed upon with [1], clothed upon [1]

1903 ἐπενδύτης, ependytēs, n. GK: *2087* [→ *1909+1722+1416*]. outer garment, coat:– fisher's coat [1]

1904 ἐπέρχομαι, eperchomai, v. GK: *2082 & 2088* [→ *1909+2064*]. to come, come upon, happen to, with a possible implication that it will happen suddenly and forcibly:– come upon [5], come [2], came thither [1], come on [1], coming on [1]

1905 ἐπερωτάω, eperōtaō, v. GK: *2089* [→ *1909+2065*]. to ask, question:– asked [44], ask [8], demanded [2], asked after [1], askest [1], asking [1], desired [1], questioned [1]

1906 ἐπερώτημα, eperōtēma, n. GK: *2090* [→ *1909+2065*]. pledge; some translate "request, appeal":– answer [1]

1907 ἐπέχω, epechō, v. GK: *2091* [→ *1909+2192*]. (tr.) hold out, hold fast; (intr.) to give attention, watch, notice; to stay, stop:– heed [1], holding forth [1], marked [1], stayed [1], take heed [1]

1908 ἐπηρεάζω, epēreazō, v. GK: *2092*. to mistreat, speak maliciously against:– despitefully use [2], falsely accuse [1]

1909 ἐπί, epi, pp. GK: *2093* [→ *244, 422, 423, 1860, 1861, 1862, 1863, 1864, 1865, 1866, 1867, 1868, 1869, 1870, 1871, 1872, 1873, 1874, 1875, 1876, 1877, 1878, 1879, 1880, 1881, 1882, 1883, 1884, 1885, 1886, 1887, 1888, 1890, 1892, 1893, 1894, 1895, 1896, 1966, 1897, 1898, 1899, 1900, 1901, 1902, 1903, 1904, 1905, 1906, 1907, 1910, 1911, 1912, 1913, 1914, 1915, 1916, 1917, 1918, 1919, 1920, 1921, 1922, 1923, 1924, 1925, 1926, 1927, 1928, 1929, 1930, 1931, 1932, 1933, 1934, 1935, 1936, 1937, 1938, 1939, 1940, 1941, 1942, 1943, 1944, 1945, 1970, 1946, 1947, 1948, 1949, 1950, 1951, 1952, 1953, 1954, 1955, 1956, 1957, 1958,*

1959, 1960, 1961, 1962, 1963, 1964, 1965, 1967, 1968, 1969, 1975, 1976, 1977, 1978, 1979, 1980, 1981, 1982, 1983, 1984, 1985, 1986, 1987, 1988, 1990, 1991, 1992, 1993, 1994, 1995, 1996, 1997, 1998, 1999, 2000, 2001, 2002, 2003, 2004, 2005, 2006, 2007, 2008, 2009, 2010, 2011, 2012, 2013, 2014, 2015, 2016, 2017, 2018, 2019, 2020, 2021, 2022, 2023, 2024, 2025, 2026, 2027, 2028, 2029, 2030, 2032, 2177, 2178, 2182, 2183, 2184, 2185, 2186, 2721, 3347, 3927, 4279, 4901, 4911; cf. 1971]. (gen.) on, over, when; (dat.) on, at, in, while; (acc.) across, over, on, to, for, while:– on [182], upon [148], in [122], over [49], unto [45], at [43], against [38], to [36], for [30], before [17], into [16], of [16], with [9], by [8], together (*+846+3588*) [7], above [5], toward [5], about [4], after [4], among [4], whereon (*+3739*) [4], as long as (*+3745+5550*) [3], besides [3], further (*+4183*) [3], of a truth (*+225*) [3], under [3], wherein (*+3739*) [3], as long as (*+3745*) [2], bountifully (*+2129*) [2], inasmuch as (*+3745*) [2], into one place (*+846+3588*) [2], throughout [2], through [2], towards [2], a great while (*+4183*) [1], about the time [1], as touching [1], because of [1], being [1], by the space of [1], chamberlain (*+2846+3588*) [1], charge of [1], come to ears (*+191*) [1], for the space of [1], in one place (*+846+3588*) [1], in the days of [1], in the time of [1], inasmuch as (*+3303+3745+3767*) [1], kept (*+2621*) [1], long (*+4183*) [1], long while (*+2425*) [1], longer (*+4183*) [1], on behalf [1], the space of [1], thereon (*+846*) [1], thereon [1], therewith (*+3778*) [1], three times (*+5151*) [1], thrice (*+5151*) [1], touching [1], truly (*+225*) [1], wherefore (*+3739*) [1], worse and worse (*+3588+5501*) [1]

1910 ἐπιβαίνω, *epibainō*, v. GK: *2094* [→ *1909+305*]. to go up, go upon, ride upon, board (a vessel):– came [1], come into [1], entering into [1], sitting [1], took [1], went aboard [1]

1911 ἐπιβάλλω, *epiballō*, v. GK: *2095* [→ *1909+906*]. (tr.) to throw over; to place; lay hold of, seize, arrest; to sew on; (intr.) to break over:– laid [6], lay on [2], putteth [2], beat [1], cast on [1], cast [1], falleth to [1], laid on [1], put to [1], stretched forth [1], thought thereon [1]

1912 ἐπιβαρέω, *epibareō*, v. GK: *2096* [→ *1909+922*]. to burden, weigh down excessively:– chargeable [2], overcharge [1]

1913 ἐπιβιβάζω, *epibibazō*, v. GK: *2097* [→ *1909+305*]. to put (someone) on (a mount):– set on [2], set thereon [1]

1914 ἐπιβλέπω, *epiblepō*, v. GK: *2098* [→ *1909+991*]. to look at, show special attention, consider, care about:– look upon [1], regarded [1], respect [1]

1915 ἐπίβλημα, *epiblēma*, n. GK: *2099* [→ *1909+906*]. patch:– piece [4]

1916 ἐπιβοάω, *epiboaō*, v. GK: *2100* [→ *1909+995*]. to cry out loudly:– crying [1]

1917 ἐπιβουλή, *epiboulē*, n. GK: *2101* [→ *1909+1014*]. plan, plot:– laid wait for (*+1096*) [1], laid wait [1], laying await [1], lying in wait [1]

1918 ἐπιγαμβρεύω, *epigambreuō*, v. GK: *2102* [→ *1909+1062*]. to marry (as next of kin):– marry [1]

1919 ἐπίγειος, *epigeios*, a. GK: *2103* [→ *1909+1093*]. being on the earth, earthly, that which is inferior when in contrast to heavenly or divine things:– earthly [4], terrestrial [2], in earth [1]

1920 ἐπιγίνομαι, *epiginomai*, v. GK: *2104* [→ *1909+1096*]. to come up, occur, happen:– blew [1]

1921 ἐπιγινώσκω, *epiginōskō*, v. GK: *2105* [→ *1909+1097*]. to know (fully), recognize, realize, come to understand:– knew [14], know [8], acknowledge [4], known [3], perceived [3], knoweth [2], knowing [2], acknowledged [1], had knowledge [1], knowest [1], knowledge [1], took knowledge [1], well known [1]

1922 ἐπίγνωσις, *epignōsis*, n. GK: *2106* [→ *1909+1097*]. knowledge, understanding, insight:– knowledge [16], acknowledging [3], acknowledgement [1]

1923 ἐπιγραφή, *epigraphē*, n. GK: *2107* [→ *1909+1125*]. inscription, superscription, written notice:– superscription [5]

1924 ἐπιγράφω, *epigraphō*, v. GK: *2108* [→ *1909+1125*]. (act.) to write; (pass.) to be written (upon), inscribed:– write [2], inscription [1], written over [1], written thereon [1]

1925 ἐπιδείκνυμι, *epideiknymi*, v. GK: *2109* [→ *1909+1166*]. to show, call attention to; to prove, point out:– shew [6], shewing [2], shewed [1]

1926 ἐπιδέχομαι, *epidechomai*, v. GK: *2110* [→ *1909+1209*]. to welcome, receive as a guest; to have to do with, accept, recognize:– receiveth [1], receive [1]

1927 ἐπιδημέω, *epidēmeō*, v. GK: *2111* [→ *1909+1218*]. to live as a visitor, foreigner:– strangers [1], were there [1]

1928 ἐπιδιατάσσομαι, *epidiatassomai*, v. GK: *2112* [→ *1909+1223+5021*]. to add to (a covenant):– added [1]

1929 ἐπιδίδωμι, *epididōmi*, v. GK: *2113* [→ *1909+1325*]. to give, deliver, hand over to:– give [5], delivered [2], gave [2], let drive (*+5342*) [1], offer [1]

1930 ἐπιδιορθόω, *epidiorthoō*, v. GK: *2114* [→ *1909+1223+3717*]. to straighten out, correct (in addition):– set in order [1]

1931 ἐπιδύω, *epidyō*, v. GK: *2115* [→ *1909+1416*]. to go down, set (of the sun):– go down [1]

1932 ἐπιείκεια, *epieikeia*, n. GK: *2116* [→ *1909+1503*]. gentleness, with an implication of tolerance and graciousness:– clemency [1], gentleness [1]

1933 ἐπιεικής, *epieikēs*, a. GK: *2117* [→ *1909+1503*]. gentle, considerate:– gentle [3], moderation [1], patient [1]

1934 ἐπιζητέω, *epizēteō*, v. GK: *2118* [→ *1909+2212*]. to look for, run after, seek earnestly:– seek [3], desire [2], seek after [2], seeketh after [2], after seek [1], desired [1], inquire [1], seeketh for [1], sought for [1]

1935 ἐπιθανάτιος, *epithanatios*, a. GK: *2119* [→ *1909+2348*]. condemned to die:– appointed to death [1]

1936 ἐπίθεσις, *epithesis*, n. GK: *2120* [→ *1909+5087*]. laying on:– laying on [3], putting on [1]

1937 ἐπιθυμέω, *epithymeō*, v. GK: *2121* [→ *1909+2372*]. to long for, desire; covet, lust:– desire [4], covet [2], desired [2], coveted [1], desireth [1], desiring [1], lust after [1], lusted [1], lusteth [1], lust [1], would fain [1]

1938 ἐπιθυμητής, *epithymētēs*, n. GK: *2122* [→ *1909+2372*]. one who desires, sets heart on (evil):– lust after [1]

1939 ἐπιθυμία, *epithymia*, n. GK: *2123* [→ *1909+2372*]. desire, longing (in contexts where the desire is positive and proper); coveting, craving, lusting (in contexts where the desire is immoral and sinful):– lusts [22], lust [9], concupiscence [3], desire [3], lusted after [1]

1940 ἐπικαθίζω, *epikathizō*, v. GK: *2125* [→ *1909+2523*]. to sit down (upon):– set [1]

1941 ἐπικαλέω, *epikaleō*, v. GK: *2126* [→ *1909+2564*]. (act./pass.) to call (upon), name, be named; (mid.) appeal to, call upon for aid:– surname [6], call on [5], surnamed [5], call upon [3], called [3], appeal unto [2], appealed unto [2], appealed to [1], appealed [1], call for [1], called on [1], calling on [1], calling upon [1]

1942 ἐπικάλυμμα, *epikalymma*, n. GK: *2127* [→ *1909+2572*]. cover-up, covering, veil:– cloke [1]

1943 ἐπικαλύπτω, *epikalyptō*, v. GK: *2128* [→ *1909+2572*]. (pass.) to be covered:– covered [1]

1944 ἐπικατάρατος, *epikataratos*, a. GK: *2063 & 2129* [→ *1909+2596+685*]. cursed:– cursed [3]

1945 ἐπίκειμαι, *epikeimai*, v. GK: *2130* [→ *1909+2749*]. to lay upon; to press, crowd upon, demand insistently:– imposed [1], instant [1], laid thereon [1], laid upon [1], lay on [1], lay [1], pressed upon [1]

1946 Ἐπικούρειος, *Epikoureios*, a.pr. or n.pr. GK: *2134* [→ *1909+2751*]. Epicurean, "*of Epicurus*":– Epicureans [1]

1947 ἐπικουρία, *epikouria*, n. GK: *2135* [→ *1909+2751*]. help:– help [1]

1948 ἐπικρίνω, *epikrinō*, v. GK: *2137* [→ *1909+2919*]. to decide, determine:– gave sentence [1]

1949 ἐπιλαμβάνομαι, *epilambanomai*, v. GK: *2138* [→ *1909+2983*]. to take hold, catch, trap, seize:– took [10], caught [2], lay hold on [2], take hold [2], took on [2], laid hold upon [1]

1950 ἐπιλανθάνομαι, *epilanthanomai*, v. GK: *2140* [→ *1909+2990*]. to forget:– forgotten [3], forget [2], forgetful [1], forgetteth [1], forgetting [1]

1951 ἐπιλέγω, *epilegō*, v. GK: *2141* [→ *1909+3004*]. (pass.) to be called; (mid.) to choose:– called [1], chose [1]

1952 ἐπιλείπω, *epileipō*, v. GK: *2142* [→ *1909+3007*]. to not have (time); to fail to have:– fail [1]

1953 ἐπιλησμονή, *epilēsmonē*, n. GK: *2144* [→ *1909+2990*]. forgetfulness:– forgetful [1]

1954 ἐπίλοιπος, *epiloipos*, a. GK: *2145* [→ *1909+3007*]. remaining, the rest:– rest [1]

1955 ἐπίλυσις, *epilysis*, n. GK: *2146* [→ *1909+3089*]. interpretation, explanation:– interpretation [1]

1956 ἐπιλύω, *epilyō*, v. GK: *2147* [→ *1909+3089*]. to explain; (pass.) to be settled, decided:– determined [1], expounded [1]

1957 ἐπιμαρτυρέω, *epimartyreō*, v. GK: *2148* [→ *1909+3144*]. to testify that, bear witness about:– testifying [1]

1958 ἐπιμέλεια, ***epimeleia***, n. GK: *2149* [→ *1909+3199*]. needs, care, attention:– refresh (*+5177*) [1]

1959 ἐπιμελέομαι, ***epimeleomai***, v. GK: *2150* [→ *1909+3199*]. to take care of, look after:– take care of [2], took care of [1]

1960 ἐπιμελῶς, ***epimelōs***, adv. GK: *2151* [→ *1909+3199*]. carefully, diligently:– diligently [1]

1961 ἐπιμένω, ***epimenō***, v. GK: *2152* [→ *1909+3306*]. to stay, remain; to continue in, keep on, persevere:– continue in [4], tarry [4], tarried [3], abide [2], continued [2], abode [1], bide still in [1], continue [1]

1962 ἐπινεύω, ***epineuō***, v. GK: *2153* [→ *1909+3506*]. to accept, give consent:– consented [1]

1963 ἐπίνοια, ***epinoia***, n. GK: *2154* [→ *1909+3563*]. thought, intention:– thought [1]

1964 ἐπιορκέω, ***epiorkeō***, v. GK: *2155* [→ *1909+3727*]. to break an oath, swear falsely:– forswear [1]

1965 ἐπίορκος, ***epiorkos***, a. GK: *2156* [→ *1909+3727*]. perjured; as a noun, perjurer:– perjured [1]

1966 ἔπειμι, ***epeimi***, v. GK: *2079* [→ *1909*]. (ptcp.) the next day (from a verb that means "to follow, approach"):– next [3], following [2]

1967 ἐπιούσιος, ***epiousios***, a. GK: *2157* [→ *1909+1510*]. what recurs on a day to day basis, daily:– daily [2]

1968 ἐπιπίπτω, ***epipiptō***, v. GK: *2158* [→ *1909+4098*]. to fall upon, come eagerly, embrace; to come on:– fell on [5], fell [4], fallen upon [1], fell upon [1], lying [1], pressed upon [1]

1969 ἐπιπλήσσω, ***epiplēssō***, v. GK: *2159* [→ *1909+4141*]. to rebuke, strike at:– rebuke [1]

1970 ἐπιπνίγω, ***epipnigō***, v. GK: *4464* [→ *1909+4155*]. to overgrow, throttle, choke:–

1971 ἐπιποθέω, ***epipotheō***, v. GK: *2160* [→ *1972, 1973, 1974; cf. 1909*]. to long for, crave, desire:– long after [2], desire [1], desiring greatly [1], earnestly desiring [1], greatly desiring [1], longed after [1], long [1], lusteth [1]

1972 ἐπιπόθησις, ***epipothēsis***, n. GK: *2161* [→ *1971*]. longing (for):– earnest desire [1], vehement desire [1]

1973 ἐπιπόθητος, ***epipothētos***, a. GK: *2162* [→ *1971*]. longed for:– longed for [1]

1974 ἐπιποθία, ***epipothia***, n. GK: *2163* [→ *1971*]. longing, desire:– great desire [1]

1975 ἐπιπορεύομαι, ***epiporeuomai***, v. GK: *2164* [→ *1909+4198*]. to come to, go to:– come out of [1]

1976 ἐπιράπτω, ***epiraptō***, v. GK: *2165 & 2193* [→ *1909+4476*]. to sew on:– seweth [1]

1977 ἐπιρίπτω, ***epiriptō***, v. GK: *2166* [→ *1909+4496*]. to throw on:– cast upon [1], casting [1]

1978 ἐπίσημος, ***episēmos***, a. GK: *2168* [→ *1909+4592*]. notorious, prominent, outstanding:– notable [1], note [1]

1979 ἐπισιτισμός, ***episitismos***, n. GK: *2169* [→ *1909+4621*]. food, something to eat:– victuals [1]

1980 ἐπισκέπτομαι, ***episkeptomai***, v. GK: *2170* [→ *1909+4648*]. to visit, show concern, care for, come to help:– visited [5], visit [4], look out [1], visitest [1]

1981 ἐπισκηνόω, ***episkēnoō***, v. GK: *2172* [→ *1909+4633*]. to rest upon, take up residence:– rest [1]

1982 ἐπισκιάζω, ***episkiazō***, v. GK: *2173* [→ *1909+4639*]. to cast a shadow, overshadow; to envelope with a cloud:– overshadowed [3], overshadow [2]

1983 ἐπισκοπέω, ***episkopeō***, v. GK: *2174* [→ *1909+4648*]. to see to, care for; to serve as an overseer:– looking diligently [1], taking the oversight [1]

1984 ἐπισκοπή, ***episkopē***, n. GK: *2175* [→ *1909+4648*]. coming, visitation, the coming of divine power for recompense; an office of responsibility and place of leadership referring to an office of apostle in Acts, and the office of overseer or bishop in the local church:– visitation [2], bishoprick [1], office of bishop [1]

1985 ἐπίσκοπος, ***episkopos***, n. GK: *2176* [→ *1909+4648*]. overseer or bishop, a leader in a local church, an extension of one who guards, supervises, and helps:– bishop [5], bishops [1], overseers [1]

1986 ἐπισπάομαι, ***epispaomai***, v. GK: *2177* [→ *1909+4685*]. to (attempt to) conceal circumcision, formally "to pull over (the foreskin to conceal circumcision)":– become uncircumcised [1]

1987 ἐπίσταμαι, ***epistamai***, v. GK: *2179* [→ *1909+2476*]. to understand, know, be aware:– know [9], knowing [3], knoweth [1], understand [1]

1988 ἐπιστάτης, ***epistatēs***, n. GK: *2181* [→ *1909+2476*]. master:– master [7]

1989 ἐπιστέλλω, ***epistellō***, v. GK: *2182* [→ *1992*]. to write a letter:– write [1], written a letter [1], written [1]

1990 ἐπιστήμων, ***epistēmōn***, a. GK: *2184* [→ *1909+2476*]. understanding, expert, learned:– knowledge [1]

1991 ἐπιστηρίζω, ***epistērizō***, v. GK: *2185* [→ *1909+4741*]. to strengthen:– confirming [2], confirmed [1], strengthening [1]

1992 ἐπιστολή, ***epistolē***, n. GK: *2186* [→ *1989*]. letter, epistle:– epistle [13], letters [6], letter [3], epistles [2]

1993 ἐπιστομίζω, ***epistomizō***, v. GK: *2187* [→ *1909+4750*]. to silence, formally, "to stop the mouth":– mouths stopped [1]

1994 ἐπιστρέφω, ***epistrephō***, v. GK: *2188* [→ *1909+4762*]. to turn (around, back, from), return:– converted [6], return [4], turned [4], turn [4], turn to [3], turned about [3], returned [2], turned to [2], came again [1], converteth [1], convert [1], go again [1], turn again [1], turn back [1], turn unto [1], turned again [1], turned unto [1], turning about [1], turning [1]

1995 ἐπιστροφή, ***epistrophē***, n. GK: *2189* [→ *1909+4762*]. conversion, a fig. extension of *turning* an object, not found in the NT:– conversion [1]

1996 ἐπισυνάγω, ***episynagō***, v. GK: *2190* [→ *1909+4862+71*]. to gather together:– gathered together [4], gather together [2], gathereth [1]

1997 ἐπισυναγωγή, ***episynagōgē***, n. GK: *2191* [→ *1909+4864*]. gathering, meeting, assembling:– assembling together [1], gathering together [1]

1998 ἐπισυντρέχω, ***episyntrechō***, v. GK: *2192* [→ *1909+4862+5143*]. to run together to:– came running together [1]

1999 ἐπίστασις, ***epistasis***, n. GK: *2180 & 2194* [→ *1909+4862+2476*]. stirring up, disturbance, insurrection, rebellion; pressure:– cometh upon [1], raising up (*+4160*) [1]

2000 ἐπισφαλής, ***episphalēs***, a. GK: *2195* [→ *1909; cf. 755*]. dangerous, unsafe:– dangerous [1]

2001 ἐπισχύω, ***epischyō***, v. GK: *2196* [→ *1909+2479*]. to insist:– more fierce [1]

2002 ἐπισωρεύω, ***episōreuō***, v. GK: *2197* [→ *1909+4987*]. to gather a great number, accumulate:– heap [1]

2003 ἐπιταγή, ***epitagē***, n. GK: *2198* [→ *1909+5021*]. command, order; authority:– commandment [6], authority [1]

2004 ἐπιτάσσω, ***epitassō***, v. GK: *2199* [→ *1909+5021*]. to command, order:– commanded [4], commandeth [3], charge [1], command [1], enjoin [1]

2005 ἐπιτελέω, ***epiteleō***, v. GK: *2200* [→ *1909+5056*]. to finish, complete, end; to perfect, attain a goal; (mid.) to undergo:– perform [2], accomplished [1], accomplishing [1], do [1], finish [1], made perfect [1], make [1], perfecting [1], performance [1], performed [1]

2006 ἐπιτήδειος, ***epitēdeios***, a. GK: *2201* [→ *1909+3588*]. needful, necessary, suitable:– needful [1]

2007 ἐπιτίθημι, ***epitithēmi***, v. GK: *2202* [→ *1909+5087*]. to place, lay upon, put on:– laid on [7], put [4], laid [3], lay on [3], put upon [3], add [2], laid upon [2], lay [2], put on [2], putting on [2], laded with [1], lay upon [1], layeth [1], on laid [1], on lay [1], set on [1], set up [1], setteth on [1], set [1], surnamed (*+3686*) [1], surnamed [1], wounded (*+4127*) [1]

2008 ἐπιτιμάω, ***epitimaō***, v. GK: *2203* [→ *1909+5092*]. to rebuke, warn:– rebuked [17], rebuke [6], charged [4], rebuking [1], straitly charged [1]

2009 ἐπιτιμία, ***epitimia***, n. GK: *2204* [→ *1909+5092*]. punishment:– punishment [1]

2010 ἐπιτρέπω, ***epitrepō***, v. GK: *2205* [→ *1909+5157*]. to let, allow, permit, give permission:– suffer [6], suffered [4], gave leave [2], permitted [2], permit [2], gave liberty [1], given licence [1], let [1]

2011 ἐπιτροπή, ***epitropē***, n. GK: *2207* [→ *1909+5157*]. commission, permission:– commission [1]

2012 ἐπίτροπος, ***epitropos***, n. GK: *2208* [→ *1909+5157*]. foreman, manager, guardian; derived from a Greek verb, "to instruct," not found in the NT:– steward [2], tutors [1]

2013 ἐπιτυγχάνω, ***epitynchanō***, v. GK: *2209* [→ *1909+5177*]. to obtain, receive, gain:– obtained [4], obtain [1]

2014 ἐπιφαίνω, ***epiphainō***, v. GK: *2210* [→ *1909+5316*]. (act.) to appear, make an appearance, show oneself; (pass.) shine:– appeared [3], give light [1]

2015 ἐπιφάνεια, ***epiphaneia***, n. GK: *2211* [→ *1909+5316*]. appearing, appearance; usually referring to the return of Christ, cf. the English word "epiphany":– appearing [5], brightness [1]

2016 ἐπιφανής, ***epiphanēs***, a. GK: *2212* [→ *1909+5316*]. glorious, splendid:– notable [1]

2017 ἐπιφαύσκω, ***epiphauskō***, v. GK: *2213* [→ *1909+5316*]. to shine on:– give light [1]

2018 ἐπιφέρω, ***epipherō***, v. GK: *2214* [→ *1909+5342*]. to bring upon, inflict:– brought [2], add [1], bring against [1], taketh [1]

2019 ἐπιφωνέω, ***epiphōneō***, v. GK: *2215* [→ *1909+5456*]. to shout, cry out loudly:– cried against [1], cried [1], gave a shout [1]

2020 ἐπιφώσκω, ***epiphōskō***, v. GK: *2216* [→ *1909+5316*]. to dawn, begin, shine forth:– dawn [1], drew on [1]

2021 ἐπιχειρέω, ***epicheireō***, v. GK: *2217* [→ *1909+5495*]. to attempt, try to:– taken in hand [1], took upon [1], went about [1]

2022 ἐπιχέω, ***epicheō***, v. GK: *2219* [→ *1632; cf. 1909*]. to pour on, pour over:– pouring in [1]

2023 ἐπιχορηγέω, ***epichorēgeō***, v. GK: *2220* [→ *1909+5525+71*]. to support, supply; (pass.) to be supported, receive:– ministereth [2], add [1], ministered [1], nourishment ministered [1]

2024 ἐπιχορηγία, ***epichorēgia***, n. GK: *2221* [→ *1909+5525+71*]. support, help:– supplieth [1], supply [1]

2025 ἐπιχρίω, ***epichriō***, v. GK: *2222* [→ *1909+5548*]. to put on, anoint on, spread on:– anointed [2]

2026 ἐποικοδομέω, ***epoikodomeō***, v. GK: *2224* [→ *1909+3624+1430*]. to build up, build on:– build [2], buildeth thereon [1], buildeth thereupon [1], building up [1], built thereupon [1], built up [1], built [1]

2027 ἐποκέλλω, ***epokellō***, v. GK: *2131 & 2225* [→ *1909+2753*]. to run aground:– ran aground [1]

2028 ἐπονομάζω, ***eponomazō***, v. GK: *2226* [→ *1909+3686*]. (pass.) to be called, named:– called [1]

2029 ἐποπτεύω, ***epopteuō***, v. GK: *2227* [→ *1909+3708*]. to see, observe:– behold [2]

2030 ἐπόπτης, ***epoptēs***, n. GK: *2228* [→ *1909+3708*]. eyewitness:– eyewitnesses [1]

2031 ἔπος, ***epos***, n. GK: *2229*. word:– so[s] [1]

2032 ἐπουράνιος, ***epouranios***, a. GK: *2230* [→ *1909+3772*]. heavenly, celestial; heavenly realms:– heavenly [16], celestial [2], high [1], in heaven [1]

2033 ἑπτά, ***hepta***, n.num. GK: *2231* [→ *1440, 1441, 1442, 2034, 2035*]. seven:– seven [86], seventh [1]

2034 ἑπτάκις, ***heptakis***, adv. GK: *2232* [→ *2033*]. seven times:– seven times [4]

2035 ἑπτακισχίλιοι, ***heptakischilioi***, a.num. GK: *2233* [→ *2033+5507*]. seven thousand:– seven thousand [1]

2036 ἔπω, ***epō***, v. GK: *3306* [→ *3004*]. to speak, say:–

2037 Ἔραστος, ***Erastos***, n.pr. GK: *2235*. Erastus, "*beloved*":– Erastus [3]

ἐραυνάω, ***eraunaō***. See ***2045***.

2038 ἐργάζομαι, ***ergazomai***, v. GK: *2237* [→ *2041*]. to work, be active, accomplish (something):– work [12], worketh [7], wrought [7], working [4], do [2], commit [1], doest [1], labouring [1], labour [1], minister [1], traded [1], trade [1]

2039 ἐργασία, ***ergasia***, n. GK: *2238* [→ *2041*]. trade, business, making money; indulgence:– gain [2], craft [1], diligence [1], gains [1], work [1]

2040 ἐργάτης, ***ergatēs***, n. GK: *2239* [→ *2041*]. worker, laborer, one who does (something):– labourers [8], workers [3], labourer [2], workman [2], workmen [1]

2041 ἔργον, ***ergon***, n. GK: *2240* [→ *14, 289, 691, 692, 1090, 1091, 1092, 1217, 1753, 1754, 1755, 1756, 2038, 2039, 2040, 2108, 2109, 2110, 2418, 2557, 2673, 2716, 3008, 3009, 3010, 3011, 3834, 3835, 4020, 4021, 4333, 4903, 4904, 4943; cf. 4468*]. work, deed, activity, task, job:– works [103], work [47], deeds [16], deed [6], doing [1], labour [1], work's [1], works' [1]

2042 ἐρεθίζω, ***erethizō***, v. GK: *2241*. to stir up, provoke, arouse; embitter, provoke, irritate:– provoked [1], provoke [1]

2043 ἐρείδω, ***ereidō***, v. GK: *2242*. to stick fast, make immovable, jam:– stuck fast [1]

2044 ἐρεύγομαι, ***ereugomai***, v. GK: *2243*. to utter, proclaim:– utter [1]

2045 ἐραυνάω, ***eraunaō***, v. GK: *2236* [→ *419, 1830; cf. 2065*]. to search, look into, try to find out:– searcheth [3], search [2], searching [1]

2046 ἐρέω, ***ereō***, v. GK: *3306* [→ *3004*]. to utter, speak say:–

2047 ἐρημία, ***erēmia***, n. GK: *2244* [→ *2048*]. remote place, desert, countryside, usually uninhabited areas:– wilderness [3], deserts [1]

2048 ἔρημος, ***erēmos***, a. GK: *2245* [→ *2047, 2049, 2050*]. deserted, remote, solitary; as a noun, desert, uninhabited wilderness, or grasslands, implying in some contexts to be a forsaken, desolate place:– wilderness [32], desert [12], desolate [4], deserts [1], solitary [1]

2049 ἐρημόω, ***erēmoō***, v. GK: *2246* [→ *2048*]. (pass.) to be brought to ruin, laid waste:– brought to desolation [2], come to nought [1], desolate [1], made desolate [1]

2050 ἐρήμωσις, ***erēmōsis***, n. GK: *2247* [→ *2048*]. desolation, devastation, destruction. "The Abomination of Desolation" is a phrase derived from Hebrew, formally, "the detestable thing of desolation." This abomination is a person, thing, or event that defiles a holy place and thus causes it to be abandoned, implying God detests this thing or action. Many refer this to desecration of the temple by Antiochus Epiphanes as analogous to a future event predicted by Jesus:– desolation [3]

2051 ἐρίζω, ***erizō***, v. GK: *2248* [→ *2054*]. to quarrel:– strive [1]

2052 ἐριθεία, ***eritheia***, n. GK: *2249* [→ *2054*]. selfish ambition, faction, strife:– strife [4], contention [1], contentious [1], strifes [1]

2053 ἔριον, ***erion***, n. GK: *2250*. wool:– wool [2]

2054 ἔρις, ***eris***, n. GK: *2251* [→ *2051, 2052*]. quarrel, strife, dissension, discord:– strife [4], contentions [2], debates [1], debate [1], variance [1]

2055 ἐρίφιον, ***eriphion***, n. GK: *2252* [→ *2056*]. goat:– goats [1]

2056 ἔριφος, ***eriphos***, n. GK: *2253* [→ *2055*]. (young) goat:– goats [1], kid [1]

2057 Ἑρμᾶς, ***Hermas***, n.pr. GK: *2254*. Hermas:– Hermas [1]

2058 ἑρμηνεία, ***hermēneia***, n. GK: *1448 & 2255* [→ *2059*]. interpretation, translation of meaning from one language to another, in the NT a gift of the Spirit necessary for understanding the gift of tongues in assembly:– interpretation [2]

2059 ἑρμηνεύω, ***hermēneuō***, v. GK: *2257* [→ *1328, 1329, 1421, 2058, 3177*]. to translate, give the meaning, interpret, explain:– by interpretation [3], interpreted [1]

2060 Ἑρμῆς, ***Hermēs***, n.pr. GK: *2258*. Hermes, "[poss.] *rock, cairn*":– Hermes [1], Mercurius [1]

2061 Ἑρμογένης, ***Hermogenēs***, n.pr. GK: *2259*. Hermogenes, "*born of Hermes*":– Hermogenes [1]

2062 ἑρπετόν, ***herpeton***, n. GK: *2260*. reptile:– creeping things [3], serpents [1]

2063 ἐρυθρός, ***erythros***, a. GK: *2261*. red:– Red [2]

2064 ἔρχομαι, ***erchomai***, v. GK: *2262* [→ *424, 492, 565, 1330, 1525, 1660, 1831, 1880, 1904, 2718, 3922, 3928, 4022, 4281, 4334, 4339, 4897, 4905*]. to come, go:– come [289], came [197], cometh [98], coming [27], went [11], comest [3], entered [2], go [2], resorted [2], accompanied (*+4862*) [1], appear [1], be [1], brought [1], camest [1], fallen out [1], for to come (*+3195*) [1], grew (*+1519*) [1], lighting [1], next [1], passing by [1], set [1]

2065 ἐρωτάω, ***erōtaō***, v. GK: *2263* [→ *1331, 1905, 1906; cf. 2045*]. to ask; beg, urge; pray:– ask [11], asked [10], pray [10], besought [9], beseech [4], desired [4], prayed [4], asketh [1], asking [1], beseeching [1], desireth [1], desire [1], intreat [1]

2066 ἐσθής, ***esthēs***, n. GK: *2264* [→ *2439*]. clothing, robe:– apparel [3], clothing [2], raiment [1], robe [1]

2067 ἔσθησις, ***esthēsis***, n. GK: *2265* [→ *2439*]. government:– garments [1]

2068 ἐσθίω, ***esthiō***, v. GK: *2266 & 2267* [→ *2068, 2719, 4906, 5315; cf. 3521, 5314*]. to eat, consume, devour:– eat [39], eateth [17], eating [6], devour [1], eaten [1], live [1]

2069 Ἑσλί, ***Hesli***, n.pr. GK: *2268*. Esli, "*Yahweh sets apart*":– Esli [1]

2070 ἐσμέν, ***esmen***, v.1.pl. of *1510*. GK: *1639* [→ *1510*]. we are; see *1510*:–

2071 ἔσομαι, ***esomai***, v.1.s.fut. of *1510*. GK: *1639* [→ *1510*]. will be; see *1510*:–

2072 ἔσοπτρον, ***esoptron***, n. GK: *2269* [→ *1519+3708*]. mirror:– glass [2]

2073 ἑσπέρα, ***hespera***, n. GK: *2270*. evening:– evening [2], eventide [1]

2074 Ἑσρώμ, ***Hesrōm***, n.pr. GK: *2272*. Hezron, "*enclosure*":– Esrom [3]

2075 ἐστέ, ***este***, v.2.pl. of *1510*. GK: *1639* [→ *1510*]. you are; see *1510*:–

2076 **ἐστί, *esti***, v.3.s. of *1510*. GK: *1639* [→ *1510*]. he, she, it is; see *1510*:–

2077 **ἔστω, *estō***, v.2.s.imper. of *1510*. GK: *1639* [→ *1510*]. be; see *1510*:–

2078 **ἔσχατος, *eschatos***, a. GK: *2274* [→ *1537*]. last (of a series), least, final:– last [48], lowest [2], ends [1], latter [1], uttermost part [1], uttermost [1]

2079 **ἐσχάτως, *eschatōs***, adv. GK: *2275* [→ *1537*]. finally; at the point of death:– lieth at the point of death (+*2192*) [1]

2080 **ἔσω, *esō***, adv. GK: *2276* [→ *1519*]. in, inner, inside, inwardly:– within [3], into [2], inner [1], inward [1]

2081 **ἔσωθεν, *esōthen***, adv. GK: *2277* [→ *1519*]. from within, from inside, inwardly:– within [7], from within [3], inward part [1], inwardly [1], inward [1], out [1]

2082 **ἐσώτερος, *esōteros***, a. GK: *2278* [→ *1519*]. inner:– inner [1], within [1]

2083 **ἑταῖρος, *hetairos***, n. GK: *2279*. friend, comrade, companion:– friend [3], fellows [1]

2084 **ἑτερόγλωσσος, *heteroglōssos***, a. GK: *2280* [→ *2087+1100*]. speaking in a foreign language:– other tongues [1]

2085 **ἑτεροδιδασκαλέω, *heterodidaskaleō***, v. GK: *2281* [→ *2087+1321*]. to teach false doctrine, teach heresy:– teach other doctrine [1], teach otherwise [1]

2086 **ἑτεροζυγέω, *heterozygeō***, v. GK: *2282* [→ *2087+2218*]. to yoke together in a mismatch:– unequally yoked together [1]

2087 **ἕτερος, *heteros***, a. GK: *2283* [→ *2084, 2085, 2086, 2088, 4220*]. other, different:– another [44], other [35], others [10], next [2], some [2], altered [1], another's [1], else [1], one [1], other's [1], strange [1]

2088 **ἑτέρως, *heterōs***, adv. GK: *2284* [→ *2087*]. differently, other, otherwise:– otherwise [1]

2089 **ἔτι, *eti***, adv. GK: *2285* [→ *3371, 3765*]. still, yet, again:– yet [42], more [16], while yet [7], any more [5], still [4], any further [3], further [3], longer [2], any longer [1], as yet [1], even [1], moreover (+*1161*) [1], moreover [1], no more (+*3367*) [1], now (+*3568*) [1], thenceforth [1], while as yet [1], yea (+*5037*) [1], yet a while [1]

2090 **ἑτοιμάζω, *hetoimazō***, v. GK: *2286* [→ *2092*]. to prepare, be ready:– prepared [18], prepare [11], make ready [6], made ready [4], provided [1]

2091 **ἑτοιμασία, *hetoimasia***, n. GK: *2288* [→ *2092*]. readiness, preparation:– preparation [1]

2092 **ἕτοιμος, *hetoimos***, a. GK: *2289* [→ *2090, 2091, 2093, 4282*]. ready, prepared:– ready [14], made ready to hand (+*1519*) [1], prepared [1], readiness [1]

2093 **ἑτοίμως, *hetoimōs***, adv. GK: *2290* [→ *2092*]. readily:– ready [3]

2094 **ἔτος, *etos***, n. GK: *2291* [→ *1332, 1333, 1541, 5063, 5148*]. year:– years [40], years old [4], year [3], years of age [2]

2095 **εὖ, *eu***, adv. GK: *2292* [→ *428, 1757, 2097, 2098, 2099, 2100, 2101, 2102, 2103, 2104, 2105, 2106, 2107, 2108, 2109, 2110, 2111, 2114, 2115, 2119, 2120, 2121, 2122, 2123, 2124, 2125, 2126, 2127, 2128, 2129, 2130, 2131, 2132, 2133, 2136, 2137, 2138, 2139, 2140, 2141, 2142, 2143, 2144, 2145, 2146, 2150, 2151, 2152, 2153, 2154, 2155, 2156, 2157, 2158, 2159, 2160, 2161, 2162, 2163, 2164, 2165, 2168, 2169, 2170, 2173, 2174, 2175, 2176, 4283, 4909, 4910*]. well; well done!:– well [5], good [1]

2096 **Εὕα, *Heua***, n.pr. GK: *2293*. Eve, *"life"*:– Eve [2]

2097 **εὐαγγελίζω, *euangelizō***, v. GK: *2294* [→ *2095+32*]. to preach (bring) the good news (gospel), often with a focus on the content of the message which is brought. In the NT it always refers to the death, burial, resurrection, and witness about Jesus Christ, including its implications for humankind's relationship to God:– preached [12], preach the gospel [10], preached the gospel [6], preach [6], preaching [5], the gospel preached [3], gospel preached [2], preach gospel [2], bring glad tidings [1], bring good tidings [1], brought good tidings [1], declare glad tidings [1], declared [1], preacheth [1], preaching the gospel [1], shew glad tidings [1], shewing the glad tidings [1]

2098 **εὐαγγέλιον, *euangelion***, n. GK: *2295* [→ *2095+32*]. gospel, good news; see also *2097*:– gospel [74], gospel's [3]

2099 **εὐαγγελιστής, *euangelistēs***, n. GK: *2296* [→ *2095+32*]. evangelist, preacher of the gospel:– evangelist [2], evangelists [1]

2100 **εὐαρεστέω, *euaresteō***, v. GK: *2297* [→ *2095+700*]. to please:– pleased [1], please [1], well pleased [1]

2101 **εὐάρεστος, *euarestos***, a. GK: *2298* [→ *2095+700*]. pleasing, acceptable:– acceptable [4], well pleasing [3], accepted [1], please well (+*1510*) [1]

2102 **εὐαρέστως, *euarestōs***, adv. GK: *2299* [→ *2095+700*]. in an acceptable or pleasing manner:– acceptably [1]

2103 **Εὔβουλος, *Euboulos***, n.pr. GK: *2300* [→ *2095+1014*]. Eubulus, *"good counsel"*:– Eubulus [1]

2104 **εὐγενής, *eugenēs***, a. GK: *2302* [→ *2095+1096*]. of noble birth, of noble character:– more noble than [1], nobleman (+*444*) [1], noble [1]

2105 **εὐδία, *eudia***, n. GK: *2304* [→ *2095+2203*]. fair weather:– fair weather [1]

2106 **εὐδοκέω, *eudokeō***, v. GK: *2305* [→ *2095+1380*]. to be well pleased, delight:– well pleased [7], pleased [5], pleasure [2], willing [2], good pleasure [1], had pleasure [1], have pleasure [1], take pleasure [1], thought good [1]

2107 **εὐδοκία, *eudokia***, n. GK: *2306* [→ *2095+1380*]. goodwill, good purpose, favor, pleasure, desire:– good pleasure [4], good will [2], good [2], desire [1]

2108 **εὐεργεσία, *euergesia***, n. GK: *2307* [→ *2095+2041*]. act of kindness, good deed:– benefit [1], good deed [1]

2109 **εὐεργετέω, *euergeteō***, v. GK: *2308* [→ *2095+2041*]. to do good to:– doing good [1]

2110 **εὐεργέτης, *euergetēs***, n. GK: *2309* [→ *2095+2041*]. benefactor; in context this is a title:– benefactors [1]

2111 **εὔθετος, *euthetos***, a. GK: *2310* [→ *2095+5087*]. fit, fit for service, useable, suitable:– fit [2], meet [1]

2112 **εὐθέως, *eutheōs***, adv. GK: *2311* [→ *2117*]. immediately, at once:– immediately [38], straightway [34], forthwith [8], by and by [3], anon [2], as soon as [2], shortly [1]

2113 **εὐθυδρομέω, *euthydromeō***, v. GK: *2312* [→ *2117+5143*]. to sail straight, run a straight course:– came with a straight course [1], straight course [1]

2114 **εὐθυμέω, *euthymeō***, v. GK: *2313* [→ *2095+2372*]. to keep up one's courage; to be happy, cheerful:– be of good cheer [2], merry [1]

2115 **εὔθυμος, *euthymos***, a. GK: *2314 & 2315* [→ *2095+2372*]. encouraged, cheerful, in good spirits:– more cheerfully [1], of good cheer [1]

2116 **εὐθύνω, *euthynō***, v. GK: *2316* [→ *2117*]. to make straight, straighten; to go straight:– listeth (+*1014*) [1], make straight [1]

2117 **εὐθύς, *euthys***, a. GK: *2317 & 2318* [→ *2112, 2113, 2116, 2118, 2720*]. straight, not crooked; by extension: right, upright, the moral quality of not being wrong or perverse to truth or purity:– straight [5], right [3]

2118 **εὐθύτης, *euthytēs***, n. GK: *2319* [→ *2117*]. righteousness, uprightness, a fig. extension of a straight (not crooked) object, not found in the NT:– righteousness [1]

2119 **εὐκαιρέω, *eukaireō***, v. GK: *2320* [→ *2095+2540*]. to have a chance to, have the opportunity to; to spend one's time:– had leisure [1], have convenient time [1], spent time [1]

2120 **εὐκαιρία, *eukairia***, n. GK: *2321* [→ *2095+2540*]. opportunity, the right moment:– opportunity [2]

2121 **εὔκαιρος, *eukairos***, a. GK: *2322* [→ *2095+2540*]. opportune, well timed, suitable; time of need:– convenient [1], time of need [1]

2122 **εὐκαίρως, *eukairōs***, adv. GK: *2323* [→ *2095+2540*]. opportunely, in season:– conveniently [1], in season [1]

2123 **εὔκοπος, *eukopos***, a. GK: *2324* [→ *2095+2875*]. easy; (compar.) easier:– easier [7]

2124 **εὐλάβεια, *eulabeia***, n. GK: *2325* [→ *2095+2983*]. reverence, reverent submission:– feared [1], godly fear [1]

2125 **εὐλαβέομαι, *eulabeomai***, v. GK: *2326* [→ *2095+2983*]. to have holy fear, reverence:– fearing [1], moved with fear [1]

2126 **εὐλαβής, *eulabēs***, a. GK: *2327* [→ *2095+2983*]. devout, godly, God-fearing:– devout [3]

2127 **εὐλογέω, *eulogeō***, v. GK: *2328* [→ *2095+3004*]. to praise, give thanks to, speak well of, extol; (pass.) to be blessed, receive blessing; in some contexts, to give a blessing is to act kindly and impart benefits to the one being blessed:– blessed [30], bless [10], blessing [3], praised [1]

2128 **εὐλογητός, *eulogētos***, a. GK: *2329* [→ *2095+3004*]. worthy of being praised, blessed, or commended:– blessed [8]

2129 **εὐλογία, *eulogia***, n. GK: *2330* [→ *2095+3004*]. blessing, praise, thanksgiving, the extolling of another; in some contexts, excessive praise is improper: flattery; by extention, generosity and (giving of) gifts:–

blessing [10], bountifully (*+1909*) [2], bounty [2], blessings [1], fair speeches [1]

2130 εὐμετάδοτος, *eumetadotos*, a. GK: *2331* [→ *2095+3326+1325*]. generous:– ready to distribute [1]

2131 Εὐνίκη, *Eunikē*, n.pr. GK: *2332* [→ *2095+3529*]. Eunice, "*good victory*":– Eunice [1]

2132 εὐνοέω, *eunoeō*, v. GK: *2333* [→ *2095+3563*]. to settle matters by coming to terms:– agree with [1]

2133 εὔνοια, *eunoia*, n. GK: *2334* [→ *2095+3563*]. wholeheartedness, enthusiasm, eagerness:– benevolence [1], good will [1]

2134 εὐνουχίζω, *eunouchizō*, v. GK: *2335* [→ *2135; cf. 2192*]. to emasculate, make (oneself) a eunuch; to be celibate, renounce marriage:– made eunuchs [2]

2135 εὐνοῦχος, *eunouchos*, n. GK: *2336* [→ *2134*]. eunuch, court official:– eunuch [5], eunuchs [3]

2136 Εὐοδία, *Euodia*, n.pr. GK: *2337* [→ *2095+3598*]. Euodia, "*good way* poss. *good fragrance*":– Euodias [1]

2137 εὐοδόω, *euodoō*, v. GK: *2338* [→ *2095+3598*]. (pass.) to get along with; to have a way opened; to prosper, get along well:– have a prosperous journey [1], prospered [1], prospereth [1], prosper [1]

2138 εὐπειθής, *eupeithēs*, a. GK: *2340* [→ *2095+3982*]. submissive, obedient, compliant:– easy to be intreated [1]

2139 εὐπερίστατος, *euperistatos*, a. GK: *2341 & 2342* [→ *2095+4012+2476*]. easily entangling, constricting, obstructing:– easily beset [1]

2140 εὐποιΐα, *eupoiia*, n. GK: *2343* [→ *2095+4160*]. doing good:– do good [1]

2141 εὐπορέω, *euporeō*, v. GK: *2344* [→ *2095+4198*]. to have (financial) ability, have plenty, be well off:– ability [1]

2142 εὐπορία, *euporia*, n. GK: *2345* [→ *2095+4198*]. prosperity, prosperous income:– wealth [1]

2143 εὐπρέπεια, *euprepeia*, n. GK: *2346* [→ *2095+4241*]. beauty:– grace [1]

2144 εὐπρόσδεκτος, *euprosdektos*, a. GK: *2347* [→ *2095+4314+1209*]. acceptable, favorable:– accepted [3], acceptable [2]

2145 εὐπρόσεδρος, *euprosedros*, a. GK: *2348* [→ *2095+4314+1476*]. devoted, constant:– attend upon [1]

2146 εὐπροσωπέω, *euprosōpeō*, v. GK: *2349* [→ *2095+4383*]. to make a good impression, make a good showing:– make a fair shew [1]

2147 εὑρίσκω, *heuriskō*, v. GK: *2351* [→ *429, 2182*]. (act.) to find, discover, meet; (mid.) to obtain; (pass.) to be found:– found [112], find [46], findeth [12], finding [4], get [1], obtained [1], perceived [1]

2148 εὐροκλύδων, *euroklydōn*, n. GK: *2352* [→ *2830*]. southeast wind, Euroclydon:– Euroclydon [1]

2149 εὐρύχωρος, *eurychōros*, a. GK: *2353* [→ *5562*]. broad, spacious:– broad [1]

2150 εὐσέβεια, *eusebeia*, n. GK: *2354* [→ *2095+4576*]. godliness, piety:– godliness [14], holiness [1]

2151 εὐσεβέω, *eusebeō*, v. GK: *2355* [→ *2095+4576*]. to worship; to put religion into practice, show piety toward:– shew piety [1], worship [1]

2152 εὐσεβής, *eusebēs*, a. GK: *2356* [→ *2095+4576*]. devout, godly, pious, reverent:– devout [3], godly [1]

2153 εὐσεβῶς, *eusebōs*, adv. GK: *2357* [→ *2095+4576*]. in a godly manner:– godly [2]

2154 εὔσημος, *eusēmos*, a. GK: *2358* [→ *2095+4592*]. intelligible, clear, distinct, easily recognizable:– easy to be understood [1]

2155 εὔσπλαγχνος, *eusplanchnos*, a. GK: *2359* [→ *2095+4698*]. compassionate, tenderhearted:– pitiful [1], tenderhearted [1]

2156 εὐσχημόνως, *euschēmonōs*, adv. GK: *2361* [→ *2095+4976*]. decently, fittingly, becomingly, properly:– honestly [2], decently [1]

2157 εὐσχημοσύνη, *euschēmosynē*, n. GK: *2362* [→ *2095+4976*]. modesty, presentability:– comeliness [1]

2158 εὐσχήμων, *euschēmōn*, a. GK: *2363* [→ *2095+4976*]. presentable, proper, right; prominent, of high standing:– honourable [3], comely [2]

2159 εὐτόνως, *eutonōs*, adv. GK: *2364* [→ *1614; cf. 2095*]. vehemently, vigorously:– mightily [1], vehemently [1]

2160 εὐτραπελία, *eutrapelia*, n. GK: *2365* [→ *2095+5157*]. coarse joking, vulgar jesting:– jesting [1]

2161 Εὔτυχος, *Eutychos*, n.pr. GK: *2366* [→ *2095+5177*]. Eutychus, "*fortunate*":– Eutychus [1]

2162 εὐφημία, *euphēmia*, n. GK: *2367* [→ *2095+5346*]. good report:– good report [1]

2163 εὔφημος, *euphēmos*, a. GK: *2368* [→ *2095+5346*]. admirable, appealing, praiseworthy:– good report [1]

2164 εὐφορέω, *euphoreō*, v. GK: *2369* [→ *2095+5342*]. to produce a good crop, be fruitful:– brought forth plentifully [1]

2165 εὐφραίνω, *euphrainō*, v. GK: *2370* [→ *2166, 2167*]. (act.) to cause celebration, make glad; (mid./pass.) to celebrate, rejoice, be glad:– rejoice [5], make merry [3], merry [3], fared [1], maketh glad [1], rejoiced [1]

2166 Εὐφράτης, *Euphratēs*, n.pr. GK: *2371* [→ *2165*]. Euphrates:– Euphrates [2]

2167 εὐφροσύνη, *euphrosynē*, n. GK: *2372* [→ *2165*]. joy, gladness, cheerfulness:– gladness [1], joy [1]

2168 εὐχαριστέω, *eucharisteō*, v. GK: *2373* [→ *2095+5463*]. to thank, give thanks, render gratitude; this can mean words that express gratitude or the emotion of gratitude:– thank [11], give thanks [8], gave thanks [6], given thanks [4], giving thanks [4], giveth thanks [2], givest thanks [1], thanked [1], thankful [1], thanks given [1]

2169 εὐχαριστία, *eucharistia*, n. GK: *2374* [→ *2095+5463*]. expression of thanks, thanksgiving, gratitude:– thanksgiving [8], giving thanks [2], thanks [2], giving of thanks [1], thankfulness [1], thanksgivings [1]

2170 εὐχάριστος, *eucharistos*, a. GK: *2375* [→ *2095+5463*]. thankful (in word and attitude):– thankful [1]

2171 εὐχή, *euchē*, n. GK: *2376* [→ *2172*]. vow, oath; prayer:– vow [2], prayer [1]

2172 εὔχομαι, *euchomai*, v. GK: *2377* [→ *2171, 4335, 4336*]. to pray for; wish for:– wish [3], pray [2], wished for [1], would (*+302*) [1]

2173 εὔχρηστος, *euchrēstos*, a. GK: *2378* [→ *2095+5530*]. useful, helpful, serviceable:– profitable [2], meet for use [1]

2174 εὐψυχέω, *eupsycheō*, v. GK: *2379* [→ *2095+5594*]. to be cheerful, glad:– of good comfort [1]

2175 εὐωδία, *euōdia*, n. GK: *2380* [→ *2095+3605*]. aroma, fragrance:– sweet savour [1], sweet smell [1], sweetsmelling [1]

2176 εὐώνυμος, *euōnymos*, a. GK: *2381* [→ *2095+3686*]. left (direction), south:– left [6], left hand [4]

2177 ἐφάλλομαι, *ephallomai*, v. GK: *2383* [→ *1909+242*]. to jump on, leap upon:– leapt on [1]

2178 ἐφάπαξ, *ephapax*, adv. GK: *2384* [→ *1909+530*]. once for all; at the same time:– once [3], at once [1], once for all [1]

2179 Ἐφεσῖνος, *Ephesinos*, a.pr.g. GK: *2385* [→ *2181*]. Ephesian:– Ephesus [1]

2180 Ἐφέσιος, *Ephesios*, a.pr.g. GK: *2386* [→ *2181*]. Ephesian, person of Ephesus:– Ephesians [5], Ephesian [1], of Ephesus [1]

2181 Ἔφεσος, *Ephesos*, n.pr. GK: *2387* [→ *2179, 2180*]. Ephesus:– Ephesus [15]

2182 ἐφευρετής, *epheuretēs*, n. GK: *2388* [→ *1909+2147*]. inventor, contriver:– inventors [1]

2183 ἐφημερία, *ephēmeria*, n. GK: *2389* [→ *1909+2250*]. (priestly) division, group, class:– course [2]

2184 ἐφήμερος, *ephēmeros*, a. GK: *2390* [→ *1909+2250*]. daily, for the day:– daily [1]

2185 ἐφικνέομαι, *ephikneomai*, v. GK: *2391* [→ *1909+2425*]. to come (to), reach (to):– reached [1], reach [1]

2186 ἐφίστημι, *ephistēmi*, v. GK: *2392* [→ *1909+2476*]. to approach, come near, stand beside, stop; to be imminent, at hand:– came upon [5], stood by [2], stood [2], assaulted [1], at hand [1], came to [1], came [1], come upon [1], cometh upon [1], come [1], coming in [1], instant [1], present [1], standing by [1], stood before [1]

2187 Ἐφραίμ, *Ephraim*, n.pr. GK: *2394*. Ephraim, "*doubly fruitful*":– Ephraim [1]

2188 ἐφφαθά, *ephphatha*, l.[v.]. GK: *2395*. ephphatha!, be opened!:– ephphatha [1]

2189 ἔχθρα, *echthra*, n. GK: *2397* [→ *2190*]. hostility, hatred, antagonism:– enmity [5], hatred [1]

2190 ἐχθρός, *echthros*, a. GK: *2398* [→ *2189*]. (n.) enemy:– enemies [19], enemy [10], foes [2], enemy (*+444*) [1]

2191 ἔχιδνα, *echidna*, n. GK: *2399*. viper, snake:– vipers [4], viper [1]

2192 ἔχω, *echō*, v. GK: *2400* [→ *183, 414, 420, 430, 463, 472, 566, 567, 568, 1758, 1777, 1836, 1838, 1851, 1907, 2517, 2558, 2697, 2722, 3348, 3352, 3353, 3562, 3794, 3930, 4023, 4042, 4122, 4123, 4124, 4284, 4337, 4465, 4778, 4830, 4910, 4912, 4928, 4975, 5242, 5247, 5254; cf. 2134, 4976*]. (tr.) to have, hold, keep; (intr.) to be:– have [262], hath [131], had [111], having [84], hast [27], need (*+5532*) [10],

Grk

are [5], were [5], with child (*+1064+1722*) [5], sick (*+2560*) [4], next [3], thank (*+5485*) [3], was [3], am [2], counted [2], count [2], holding [2], hold [2], is [2], must [2], needeth (*+5532*) [2], accompany [1], art [1], been [1], began to amend (*+2866*) [1], being [1], be [1], cannot (*+3756*) [1], could [1], diseased (*+2560*) [1], do [1], eat (*+3542*) [1], enjoy [1], fear (*+5401*) [1], following [1], go to law (*+2917*) [1], held [1], hold fast [1], is of [1], kept [1], lacked (*+3361*) [1], lieth at the point of death (*+2079*) [1], needed (*+5532*) [1], needest (*+5532*) [1], needful (*+318*) [1], possessed with [1], possessed [1], recover (*+2573*) [1], reigneth (*+932*) [1], rest (*+372*) [1], retain [1], sabbath day's journey (*+3598+4521*) [1], sick people (*+2560*) [1], took [1], trembled (*+5156*) [1], uncircumcised (*+203*) [1], using [1], with [1]

2193 **ἕως**, ***heōs***, c.&pp.*. GK: *2401*. up to, until:– unto [31], until [23], till (*+302*) [16], to [16], till [14], till (*+3739*) [9], how long (*+4219*) [7], until (*+302*) [5], until (*+3739*) [5], while [5], as far as [3], hitherto (*+737*) [2], till (*+3748*) [2], until (*+3748*) [2], while (*+3739*) [2], even (*+2532*) [1], even [1], no not one (*+1520+3756*) [1], thus far (*+3778*) [1], up to [1], whiles (*+3748*) [1]

2194 **Ζαβουλών**, ***Zaboulōn***, n.pr. GK: *2404*. Zebulun, "*honor*":– Zabulon [3]

2195 **Ζακχαῖος**, ***Zakchaios***, n.pr. GK: *2405*. Zacchaeus, "*righteous one, pure one*":– Zaccheus [3]

2196 **Ζάρα**, ***Zara***, n.pr. GK: *2406*. Zerah, "*dawning, shining* or *flashing [red or scarlet] light*":– Zara [1]

2197 **Ζαχαρίας**, ***Zacharias***, n.pr. GK: *2408*. Zechariah, "*Yahweh remembers*":– Zacharias [11]

2198 **ζάω**, ***zaō***, v. GK: *2409* [→ *326, 329, 2221, 2222, 2225, 2226, 2227, 4800, 4806*]. to be alive, to live a life; in the NT this can also refer to the resurrection life, Jesus Christ is then "the Living One":– live [54], living [34], liveth [24], alive [15], lived [4], quick [4], lively [3], livest [2], lifetime [1], life [1]

2199 **Ζεβεδαῖος**, ***Zebedaios***, n.pr. GK: *2411*. Zebedee, "*Yahweh bestows*":– Zebedee [10], Zebedee's [2]

2200 **ζεστός**, ***zestos***, a. GK: *2412* [→ *2204*]. hot:– hot [3]

2201 **ζεῦγος**, ***zeugos***, n. GK: *2414* [→ *2218*]. yoke; by extension: a pair:– pair [1], yoke [1]

2202 **ζευκτηρία**, ***zeuktēria***, n. GK: *2415* [→ *2218*]. rope, band:– bands [1]

2203 **Ζεύς**, ***Zeus***, n.pr. GK: *2416* [→ *1356, 1359, 1361, 2105, 2211*]. Zeus, "*shine, bright*":– Jupiter [2]

2204 **ζέω**, ***zeō***, v. GK: *2417* [→ *2200; cf. 2205, 2219*]. to have great fervor, as a fig. extension something boiling or seething, not found in the NT:– fervent [2]

2205 **ζῆλος**, ***zēlos***, n. GK: *2419* [→ *2206, 2207, 2208, 3863; cf. 2204*]. zeal, ardent concern, enthusiasm, an attitude or emotion of deep, earnest concern; jealousy, envy, rage, morally corrupt zealous ill will:– zeal [6], envying [4], indignation [2], emulations [1], envyings [1], envy [1], fervent mind [1], jealousy [1]

2206 **ζηλόω**, ***zēloō***, v. GK: *2418 & 2420* [→ *2205*]. to desire, eagerly desire, show zeal, feel an attitude or emotion of deep concern; to be jealous, envious, to experience morally corrupt zealous ill will; covet, as a negative attitude of lust and desire for another's possessions:– desire [2], moved with envy [2], affect [1], covet earnestly [1], covet [1], envieth [1], jealous [1], zealously affected [1], zealously affect [1], zealous [1]

2207 **ζηλωτής**, ***zēlōtēs***, n. GK: *2421* [→ *2205*]. zealot, enthusiast, adherent, one who has the feelings or attitudes of deep commitment to a person or cause; in the NT this can technically refer to a person who belonged to a nationalist Jewish group that sought independence from Rome:– zealous [5]

2208 **Ζηλωτής**, ***Zēlōtēs***, n. GK: *2421* [→ *2205*]. same as *2207*; zealot, enthusiast, adherent, one who has the feelings or attitudes of deep commitment to a person or cause; in the NT this can technically refer to a person who belonged to a nationalist Jewish group that sought independence from Rome:– Zelotes [2]

2209 **ζημία**, ***zēmia***, n. GK: *2422* [→ *2210*]. loss, damage:– loss [3], damage [1]

2210 **ζημιόω**, ***zēmioō***, v. GK: *2423* [→ *2209*]. (pass.) to forfeit, suffer loss or damage:– lose [2], cast away [1], receive damage [1], suffer loss [1], suffered loss [1]

2211 **Ζηνᾶς**, ***Zēnas***, n.pr. GK: *2424* [→ *2203*]. Zenas, "*gift of Zeus*":– Zenas [1]

2212 **ζητέω**, ***zēteō***, v. GK: *2426* [→ *327, 1567, 1934, 2213, 2214, 4802, 4803, 4804*]. to look for, seek out; to try to obtain, desire to possess, strive for:– seek [44], sought [31], seeking [11], seeketh [9], seek for [3], sought for [3], desiring [2], inquire [2], required [2], seekest [2], about [1], desired [1], endeavoured [1], go about [1], goeth about [1], going about [1], seek after [1], seeking for [1], sought out [1], went about [1]

2213 **ζήτημα**, ***zētēma***, n. GK: *2427* [→ *2212*]. question for discussion, point of dispute, controversy:– questions [3], question [2]

2214 **ζήτησις**, ***zētēsis***, n. GK: *1700 & 2428* [→ *2212*]. argument, debate, controversy, discussion:– questions [5], question [1]

2215 **ζιζάνιον**, ***zizanion***, n. GK: *2429*. weed, darnel, or some other troublesome weed:– tares [8]

2216 **Ζοροβαβέλ**, ***Zorobabel***, n.pr. GK: *2431*. Zerubbabel, "*offspring of Babylon*":– Zorobabel [3]

2217 **ζόφος**, ***zophos***, n. GK: *2432*. blackness, darkness, gloom:– darkness [2], blackness [1], mist [1]

2218 **ζυγός**, ***zygos***, n. GK: *2433* [→ *2086, 2201, 2202, 4801, 4805, 5268*]. yoke, a frame and cross bar placed on draft animals to pull various objects; pair of scales, ancient balance-pan scales. "To be under a yoke" means to be in an oppressed condition such as slavery:– yoke [5], pair of balances [1]

2219 **ζύμη**, ***zymē***, n. GK: *2434* [→ *106, 2220; cf. 2204*]. yeast, leaven:– leaven [13]

2220 **ζυμόω**, ***zymoō***, v. GK: *2435* [→ *2219*]. to leaven, ferment, work as yeast:– leavened [2], leaveneth [2]

2221 **ζωγρέω**, ***zōgreō***, v. GK: *2436* [→ *2198+61*]. to capture (alive):– catch [1], taken captive [1]

2222 **ζωή**, ***zōē***, n. GK: *2437* [→ *2198*]. life, physical or spiritual; with *166*, "eternal life":– life [133], lifetime [1]

2223 **ζώνη**, ***zōnē***, n. GK: *2438* [→ *2224*]. belt, sash:– girdle [5], girdles [1], purses [1], purse [1]

2224 **ζώννυμι**, ***zōnnymi***, v. GK: *2439 & 2440* [→ *328, 1241, 2223, 4024, 5269*]. to dress, clothe oneself, put on a belt or sash:– girdedst [1], gird [1]

2225 **ζωογονέω**, ***zōogoneō***, v. GK: *2441* [→ *2198+1096*]. to give life, make alive; to preserve life, keep alive:– live [1], preserve [1]

2226 **ζῷον**, ***zōon***, n. GK: *2442* [→ *2198*]. living creature, animal:– beasts [16], beast [7]

2227 **ζωοποιέω**, ***zōopoieō***, v. GK: *2443* [→ *2198+4160*]. to make alive, give life to:– quickeneth [5], quickened [2], given life [1], giveth life [1], made alive [1], quickening [1], quicken [1]

2228 **ἤ**, ***ē***, pt.disj. or comp. GK: *2445* [→ *2260, 2273*]. or; (in a series) either…or; (in comparison) than:– or [260], than [36], either [8], before (*+4250*) [6], nor [5], or else [5], and [4], neither [3], what [3], but [2], rather than [2], but (*+3756+4183*) [1], except [1], rather [1], save [1], than (*+235*) [1], than (*+3123*) [1], yea [1]

2229 **ἦ**, ***ē***, adv. GK: *2446*. truly:– surely (*+3375*) [1]

ἡ, ***hē***. See **3588**.

ἥ, ***hē***. See **3739**.

ἦ, ***ēi***. See **5600**.

2230 **ἡγεμονεύω**, ***hēgemoneuō***, v. GK: *2448* [→ *71*]. to govern, lead, rule:– governor [2]

2231 **ἡγεμονία**, ***hēgemonia***, n. GK: *2449* [→ *71*]. reign, leadership, rulership:– reign [1]

2232 **ἡγεμών**, ***hēgemōn***, n. GK: *2450* [→ *71*]. ruler, prince, governor, prefect, procurator:– governor [16], governors [2], rulers [2], governor's [1], princes [1]

2233 **ἡγέομαι**, ***hēgeomai***, v. GK: *2451* [→ *71*]. to lead, rule, guide; to consider, think, regard:– count [7], chief [3], counted [3], have the rule over [3], esteem [2], governor [2], think [2], thought [2], account [1], esteeming [1], judged [1], supposed [1]

2234 **ἡδέως**, ***hēdeōs***, adv. GK: *2452* [→ *2237*]. gladly, with delight; in the superlative, most gladly, with utter delight:– gladly [3]

2235 **ἤδη**, ***ēdē***, adv. GK: *2453*. already, by this time, even now:– now [35], already [17], yet [2], by this time [1], far spent (*+2827*) [1], now about (*+1161*) [1], now already [1], now high time (*+5610*) [1], now ready [1]

2236 **ἥδιστα**, ***hēdista***, adv.super. of *2234*. GK: *2452* [→ *2237*]. most gladly, with utter delight:– most gladly [1], very gladly [1]

2237 **ἡδονή**, ***hēdonē***, n. GK: *2454* [→ *780, 829, 2234, 2236, 2238, 4913, 5369*]. pleasure, desire, enjoyment, usually with a negative sense:– lusts [2], pleasures [2], pleasure [1]

2238 **ἡδύοσμον**, ***hēdyosmon***, n. GK: *2455* [→ *2237+3605*]. mint:– mint [2]

2239 **ἦθος**, ***ēthos***, n. GK: *2456* [→ *1485*]. character, habit and custom:– manners [1]

2240 ἥκω, ***hēkō***, v. GK: *2457* [→ *433, 2520*]. to come, to have come, be present:– come [24], came [3]

2241 ἠλί[1], ***ēli***[1], l.[n.+p.]. GK: *2458* [cf. *1682*]. Eli [Hebrew: my God]:– eli [2]

2242 Ἠλί[2], ***Ēli***[2], n.pr. GK: *2459*. Heli, "*ascent [to God]*":– Heli [1]

2243 Ἠλίας, ***Ēlias***, n.pr. GK: *2460*. Elijah, "*Yahweh is [my] God*":– Elias [30]

2244 ἡλικία, ***hēlikia***, n. GK: *2461* [→ *2245*]. life, time in life, age; stature, height:– stature [5], age [2], age (*+2540*) [1]

2245 ἡλίκος, ***hēlikos***, a. GK: *2462* [→ *2244, 4080, 4915, 5082*]. how much, how great, how large:– how great [1], what great [1]

2246 ἥλιος, ***hēlios***, n. GK: *2463* [cf. *1506*]. sun:– sun [30], east (*+395*) [2]

2247 ἧλος, ***hēlos***, n. GK: *2464* [→ *4338*]. nail (used in crucifixion):– nails [2]

2248 ἡμᾶς, ***hēmas***, p.pers.acc.pl. of *1473* GK: *1609* [→ *1473*]. us, to us; see *1473*:–

2249 ἡμεῖς, ***hēmeis***, p.pers.nom.pl. of *1473* GK: *1609* [→ *1473*]. we, us, ourselves; see *1473*:–

2250 ἡμέρα, ***hēmera***, n. GK: *2465* [→ *2183, 2184, 2522, 3314, 3574, 3637, 4594*]. day, time of the day, time, indefinite period of time. "The children of the day" means "God's people," who walk in light. "The day of the Lord" and "the day of Christ" are periods of judgment and vindication, longer than twenty-four hours:– day [199], days [154], daily (*+2596*) [15], this day (*+4594*) [3], time [3], years [2], a good while ago (*+575+744*) [1], age (*+1722+4260*) [1], alway (*+3588+3956*) [1], another[s] [1], at midday (*+3319*) [1], daily (*+1538+2596*) [1], daily (*+2596+3956*) [1], daily (*+3956*) [1], day by day (*+2596*) [1], day time [1], day's [1], ever (*+165*) [1], good while (*+2425*) [1], judgment [1], needeth (*+318*) [1]

2251 ἡμέτερος, ***hēmeteros***, a. GK: *2466* [→ *1473*]. our, our own:– our [6], ours [2]

2252 ἤμην, ***ēmēn***, v.1.imperf. of *1510*. GK: *1639* [→ *1510*]. I was; see *1510*:–

2253 ἡμιθανής, ***hēmithanēs***, a. GK: *2467* [→ *2255+2348*]. half dead:– half dead [1]

2254 ἡμῖν, ***hēmin***, p.pers.dat.pl. of *1473*. GK: *1609* [→ *1473*]. for us, to us, our; see *1473*:–

2255 ἥμισυς, ***hēmisys***, a. GK: *2468* [→ *2253, 2256, 2256*]. half (temporal and spacial):– half [5]

2256 ἡμιώριον, ***hēmiōrion***, n. GK: *2469 & 2470* [→ *2255+5610*]. half an hour:– half an hour [1]

2257 ἡμῶν, ***hēmōn***, p.pers.gen.pl. of *1473*. GK: *1609* [→ *1473*]. our; see *1473*:–

2258 ἦν, ***ēn***, v.3.imperf. of *1510*. GK: *1639* [→ *1510*]. he, she, it was; see *1510*:–

2259 ἡνίκα, ***hēnika***, pt. GK: *2471*. when, whenever, at the time when:– when (*+302*) [2]

2260 ἤπερ, ***ēper***, pt.comp. GK: *2472* [→ *2228+4007*]. than:– than [1]

2261 ἤπιος, ***ēpios***, a. GK: *2473*. gentle, kind:– gentle [2]

2262 Ἤρ, ***Ēr***, n.pr. GK: *2474*. Er, "*watcher, watchful*":– Er [1]

2263 ἤρεμος, ***ēremos***, a. GK: *2475*. peaceful, quiet, tranquil:– quiet [1]

2264 Ἡρῴδης, ***Hērōdēs***, n.pr. GK: *2476* [→ *2265, 2266, 2267*]. Herod:– Herod [40], Herod's [4]

2265 Ἡρῳδιανοί, ***Hērōdianoi***, n.pr.g. GK: *2477* [→ *2264*]. Herodians:– Herodians [3]

2266 Ἡρῳδιάς, ***Hērōdias***, n.pr. GK: *2478* [→ *2264*]. Herodias:– Herodias [4], Herodias' [2]

2267 Ἡρῳδίων, ***Hērōdiōn***, n.pr. GK: *2479* [→ *2264*]. Herodion:– Herodion [1]

2268 Ἠσαΐας, ***Ēsaias***, n.pr. GK: *2480*. Isaiah, "*Yahweh saves*":– Esaias [21]

2269 Ἠσαῦ, ***Ēsau***, n.pr. GK: *2481*. Esau, "*hairy*":– Esau [3]

2270 ἡσυχάζω, ***hēsychazō***, v. GK: *2483* [→ *2271, 2272*]. to be silent, have no objection; to rest; to lead a quiet life; to give up:– held peace [2], ceased [1], quiet [1], rested [1]

2271 ἡσυχία, ***hēsychia***, n. GK: *2484* [→ *2270*]. quietness, silence; settling down, lack of disturbance:– silence [3], quietness [1]

2272 ἡσύχιος, ***hēsychios***, a. GK: *2485* [→ *2270*]. quiet:– peaceable [1], quiet [1]

2273 ἤτοι, ***ētoi***, pt.disj. GK: *2486* [→ *2228+5104*]. (in a series) whether…or:– whether [1]

2274 ἡττάομαι, ***hēttaomai***, v. GK: *2273 & 2487* [→ *2276*]. to be inferior, lesser, worse off, with a focus on the manner in which someone is treated:– overcome [2], inferior [1]

2275 ἥττημα, ***hēttēma***, n. GK: *2488* [→ *2276*]. loss, defeat:– diminishing [1], fault [1]

2276 ἥττων, ***hēttōn***, a. GK: *2482 & 2489* [→ *2274, 2275*]. for the worse; (adv.) less:– less [1], worse [1]

2277 ἤτω, ***ētō***, v.3.s.imper. of *1510*. GK: *1639* [→ *1510*]. let it be:–

2278 ἠχέω, ***ēcheō***, v. GK: *2490* [→ *2279*]. to resound, ring out:– roaring [1], sounding [1]

2279 ἦχος[1], ***ēchos***[1], n. GK: *2491 & 2492 & 2493* [→ *1837, 2278, 2727*]. sound, tone, blast (of a trumpet); news, report:– sound [2], fame [1]

2280 Θαδδαῖος, ***Thaddaios***, n.pr. GK: *2497* [cf. *3002*]. Thaddaeus, "[poss.] *nipple*":– Thaddeus [2]

2281 θάλασσα, ***thalassa***, n. GK: *2498* [→ *1337, 3864; cf. 217*]. sea, lake, a general term for any natural body of water:– sea [92]

2282 θάλπω, ***thalpō***, v. GK: *2499*. to care for, cherish, comfort:– cherisheth [2]

2283 Θαμάρ, ***Thamar***, n.pr. GK: *2500*. Tamar, "*date palm*":– Thamar [1]

2284 θαμβέω, ***thambeō***, v. GK: *2501* [→ *2285*]. (pass.) to be amazed, astounded:– amazed [2], astonished [2]

2285 θάμβος, ***thambos***, n. GK: *2502* [→ *1568, 1569, 2284*]. amazement, astonishment, wonder:– amazed [1], astonished (*+4023*) [1], wonder [1]

2286 θανάσιμος, ***thanasimos***, a. GK: *2503* [→ *2348*]. deadly:– deadly [1]

2287 θανατηφόρος, ***thanatēphoros***, a. GK: *2504* [→ *2348+5342*]. deadly:– deadly [1]

2288 θάνατος, ***thanatos***, n. GK: *2505* [→ *2348*]. death:– death [116], deadly [2], deaths [1]

2289 θανατόω, ***thanatoō***, v. GK: *2506* [→ *2348*]. to put to death, kill:– put to death [7], killed [2], dead [1], mortify [1]

θάνω, ***thanō***. See ***2348***.

2290 θάπτω, ***thaptō***, v. GK: *2507* [→ *4916; cf. 5028*]. to bury, entomb:– buried [7], bury [4]

2291 Θάρα, ***Thara***, n.pr. GK: *2508*. Terah:– Thara [1]

2292 θαρρέω, ***tharreō***, v. GK: *2509* [→ *2294*]. to have confidence, be bold:– bold [2], confident [2], boldly [1], have confidence [1]

2293 θαρσέω, ***tharseō***, v. GK: *2510* [→ *2294*]. take heart!, take courage!, cheer up!:– be of good cheer [5], be of good comfort [3]

2294 θάρσος, ***tharsos***, n. GK: *2511* [→ *2292, 2293*]. encouragement, courage:– courage [1]

2295 θαῦμα, ***thauma***, n. GK: *2512* [→ *2296*]. wonder, marvel, astonishment:– admiration [1]

2296 θαυμάζω, ***thaumazō***, v. GK: *1703 & 2513* [→ *2295, 2297, 2298; cf. 2300*]. to be amazed (at), in wonder, astonished, surprised:– marvelled [21], wondered [11], marvel [9], wonder [2], admired [1], having in admiration (*+4383*) [1], wondering [1]

2297 θαυμάσιος, ***thaumasios***, a. GK: *2514* [→ *2296*]. wonderful, remarkable:– wonderful [1]

2298 θαυμαστός, ***thaumastos***, a. GK: *2515* [→ *2296*]. wonderful, marvelous, remarkable:– marvellous [6], marvel [1]

2299 θεά, ***thea***, n. GK: *2516* [→ *2316*]. goddess:– goddess [3]

2300 θεάομαι, ***theaomai***, v. GK: *2517* [cf. *2296, 2302, 2334*]. to see, look at; visit:– saw [8], seen [8], see [4], beheld [2], look on [1], looked upon [1]

2301 θεατρίζω, ***theatrizō***, v. GK: *2518* [→ *2302*]. to publicly expose:– made a gazingstock [1]

2302 θέατρον, ***theatron***, n. GK: *2519* [→ *2301; cf. 2300*]. theatre, spectacle, theatrical play:– theatre [2], spectacle [1]

2303 θεῖον, ***theion***, n. GK: *2520* [→ *2306; cf. 2316 or 2380*]. sulfur:– brimstone [7]

2304 θεῖος, ***theios***, a. GK: *2521* [→ *2316*]. divine:– divine [2], Godhead [1]

2305 θειότης, ***theiotēs***, n. GK: *2522* [→ *2316*]. divine nature, divinity:– Godhead [1]

2306 θειώδης, ***theiōdēs***, a. GK: *2523* [→ *2303*]. (yellow) as sulfur:– brimstone [1]

θελέω, ***theleō***. See ***2309***.

2307 θέλημα, ***thelēma***, n. GK: *2525* [→ *2309*]. will, decision, desire:– will [62], desires [1], pleasure [1]

2308 θέλησις, ***thelēsis***, n. GK: *2526* [→ *2309*]. will, decision:– will [1]

2309 θέλω, ***thelō***, v. GK: *2527* [→ *1479, 2307, 2308*]. to will, decide, want to; wish, desire:– would [69], will [68], wilt [21], desire [9], willing [8], have [5], wouldest [4], desirous [3], desiring [2], listed [2], willingly [2], desired [1], desireth [1], disposed [1], forward [1], had rather [1], intending [1], it hath pleased [1], listeth [1], love [1], meaneth (*+1510*) [1], mean [1], pleased [1], so[s] [1], voluntary [1], will have [1], willeth [1], would have [1], would that [1]

2310 θεμέλιος, ***themelios***, n. GK: *2528 & 2529* [→ *2311; cf. 5087*]. foundation:– foundation [12], foundations [4]

2311 θεμελιόω, ***themelioō***, v. GK: *2530* [→ *2310*]. to lay a foundation; to make steadfast:– founded [2], grounded [2], laid the foundation [1], settle [1]

2312 θεοδίδακτος, ***theodidaktos***, a. GK: *2531* [→ *2316+1321*]. taught by God:– taught of God [1]

2312' θεολόγος, ***theologos***, n. GK: *2532* [→ *2316+3004*]. one who speaks of God or divine things:–

2313 θεομαχέω, ***theomacheō***, v. GK: *2533* [→ *2316+3163*]. to fight against God:– fight against God [1]

2314 θεομάχος, ***theomachos***, a. GK: *2534* [→ *2316+3163*]. fighting against God:– fight against God [1]

2315 θεόπνευστος, ***theopneustos***, a. GK: *2535* [→ *2316+4154*]. God-breathed, inspired by God, referring to a communication from deity:– given by inspiration of God [1]

2316 θεός, ***theos***, n. GK: *2536* [→ *112, 2299, 2304, 2305, 2312, 2312', 2313, 2314, 2315, 2317, 2318, 2319, 2320, 2321, 2333, 5095, 5377; cf. 2303*]. God, usually refers to the one true God; in a very few contexts it refers to a (pagan) god or goddess. The "Son of God" as a title of Jesus emphasizes his unique relationship to the Father. "The god of this age" refers to the devil:– God/god [1309], God's [15], gods [8], godly [6], Godward [2], exceeding fair (*+791+3588*) [1], godly (*+2596*) [1]

2317 θεοσέβεια, ***theosebeia***, n. GK: *2537* [→ *2316+4576*]. worship of God, reverence for God:– godliness [1]

2318 θεοσεβής, ***theosebēs***, a. GK: *2538* [→ *2316+4576*]. godly, God-fearing, devout:– worshipper of God [1]

2319 θεοστυγής, ***theostygēs***, a. GK: *2539* [→ *2316+4767*]. God-hating:– haters of God [1]

2320 θεότης, ***theotēs***, n. GK: *2540* [→ *2316*]. Deity, Divinity:– Godhead [1]

2321 Θεόφιλος, ***Theophilos***, n.pr. GK: *2541* [→ *2316+5384*]. Theophilus, "*friend of God*":– Theophilus [2]

2322 θεραπεία, ***therapeia***, n. GK: *2542* [→ *2324*]. service, care; (hence) healing:– healing [2], household [2]

2323 θεραπεύω, ***therapeuō***, v. GK: *2543* [→ *2324*]. to serve, to give help, take care of another; by extension: to heal, cure; (pass.) to be healed:– healed [25], heal [10], cured [3], healing [3], cure [2], worshipped [1]

2324 θεράπων, ***therapōn***, n. GK: *2544* [→ *2322, 2323*]. servant, a person who renders service:– servant [1]

2325 θερίζω, ***therizō***, v. GK: *2545* [→ *2329*]. to reap, harvest:– reap [13], reapeth [3], reaped [2], reaping [2], reapest [1]

2326 θερισμός, ***therismos***, n. GK: *2546* [→ *2329*]. harvest:– harvest [13]

2327 θεριστής, ***theristēs***, n. GK: *2547* [→ *2329*]. harvester, reaper:– reapers [2]

2328 θερμαίνω, ***thermainō***, v. GK: *2548* [→ *2329*]. (mid.) to keep warm, warm (oneself):– warmed [5], warming [1]

2329 θέρμη, ***thermē***, n. GK: *2549* [→ *2325, 2326, 2327, 2328, 2330*]. heat:– heat [1]

2330 θέρος, ***theros***, n. GK: *2550* [→ *2329*]. summer:– summer [3]

2331 Θεσσαλονικεύς, ***Thessalonikeus***, n.pr.g. GK: *2552* [→ *2332*]. Thessalonian, "*from Thessalonica*":– Thessalonians [5], Thessalonica [1]

2332 Θεσσαλονίκη, ***Thessalonikē***, n.pr. GK: *2553* [→ *2331*]. Thessalonica:– Thessalonica [5]

2333 Θευδᾶς, ***Theudas***, n.pr. GK: *2554* [→ *2316+1435*]. Theudas, "*gift of God*":– Theudas [1]

θέω, ***theō***. See ***5087***.

2334 θεωρέω, ***theōreō***, v. GK: *2555* [→ *333, 2335, 3865; cf. 2300*]. to see, look at, watch closely; perceive, experience:– see [17], seeth [10], saw [9], beheld [4], beholding [4], perceive [4], behold [3], seen [2], consider [1], looking on [1], seeing [1], seest [1]

2335 θεωρία, ***theōria***, n. GK: *2556* [→ *2334*]. sight, spectacle:– sight [1]

2336 θήκη, ***thēkē***, n. GK: *2557* [→ *5087*]. sheath, scabbard:– sheath [1]

2337 θηλάζω, ***thēlazō***, v. GK: *2558* [→ *330, 2338*]. to nurse a baby; (n.) nursing infant:– give suck [3], gave suck [1], sucked [1], sucklings [1]

2338 θῆλυς, ***thēlys***, a. GK: *2559* [→ *2337*]. female, pertaining to women:– female [3], woman [1], women [1]

2339 θήρα, ***thēra***, n. GK: *2560* [→ *2342*]. trap, net:– trap [1]

2340 θηρεύω, ***thēreuō***, v. GK: *2561* [→ *2342*]. to catch in a mistake, a fig. extension of catching hunted prey, not found in the NT:– catch [1]

2341 θηριομαχέω, ***thēriomacheō***, v. GK: *2562* [→ *2342+3163*]. to fight wild animals:– fought with beasts [1]

2342 θηρίον, ***thērion***, n. GK: *2563* [→ *2339, 2340, 2341*]. (wild) animal, (fiendish) beast, snake:– beast [40], beasts [3], wild beasts [3]

2343 θησαυρίζω, ***thēsaurizō***, v. GK: *2564* [→ *2344*]. to store up, gather, reserve:– lay up [3], heaped treasure together [1], in store [1], kept in store [1], layeth up treasure [1], treasurest up [1]

2344 θησαυρός, ***thēsauros***, n. GK: *2565* [→ *596, 597, 2343; cf. 5087*]. treasure, what is stored up; storeroom:– treasure [13], treasures [5]

2345 θιγγάνω, ***thinganō***, v. GK: *2566*. to touch:– touch [2], handle [1]

2346 θλίβω, ***thlibō***, v. GK: *2567* [→ *598, 2347, 4918*]. (act.) to press upon, crowd up to; cause trouble; (pass.) to be narrow; to be pressed, troubled, persecuted:– afflicted [3], troubled [3], narrow [1], suffer tribulation [1], throng [1], trouble [1]

2347 θλῖψις, ***thlipsis***, n. GK: *2568* [→ *2346*]. trouble, distress, oppression, tribulation:– tribulation [18], affliction [11], afflictions [6], tribulations [3], trouble [3], afflicted [1], anguish [1], burdened [1], persecution [1]

2348 θνήσκω, ***thnēskō***, v. GK: *2569* [→ *110, 599, 1935, 2253, 2286, 2287, 2288, 2289, 2349, 4880*]. (perf.) to have died, be dead:– dead [11], dead man [1], died [1]

2349 θνητός, ***thnētos***, a. GK: *2570* [→ *2348*]. mortal:– mortal [5], mortality [1]

2350 θορυβέω, ***thorybeō***, v. GK: *2572* [→ *2351*]. to start a riot, throw into disorder; (pass.) to be alarmed, in commotion, distressed:– make ado [1], making noise [1], set on an uproar [1], trouble [1]

2351 θόρυβος, ***thorybos***, n. GK: *2573* [→ *2350*]. uproar, riot, commotion, disturbance:– tumult [4], uproar [3]

2352 θραύω, ***thrauō***, v. GK: *2575*. (pass.) to be oppressed, downtrodden, a fig. extension of an object broken in pieces:– bruised [1]

2353 θρέμμα, ***thremma***, n. GK: *2576* [→ *5142*]. livestock, domestic animal (usually a sheep or goat):– cattle [1]

2354 θρηνέω, ***thrēneō***, v. GK: *2577* [→ *2355, 2360*]. to sing a funeral dirge, lament, mourn:– mourned [2], lamented [1], lament [1]

2355 θρῆνος, ***thrēnos***, n. GK: *2578* [→ *2354*]. dirge, funeral song:– lamentation [1]

2356 θρησκεία, ***thrēskeia***, n. GK: *2579* [→ *2357*]. religion, worship:– religion [3], worshipping [1]

2357 θρησκός, ***thrēskos***, a. GK: *2580* [→ *1479, 2356*]. religious:– religious [1]

2358 θριαμβεύω, ***thriambeuō***, v. GK: *2581*. to lead in a triumphal procession:– causeth to triumph [1], triumphing over [1]

2359 θρίξ, ***thrix***, n. GK: *2582* [→ *5155*]. hair, a hair:– hair [10], hairs [5]

2360 θροέω, ***throeō***, v. GK: *2583* [→ *2354*]. (pass.) to be alarmed, disturbed:– troubled [3]

2361 θρόμβος, ***thrombos***, n. GK: *2584*. drop:– drops [1]

2362 θρόνος, ***thronos***, n. GK: *2585*. throne:– throne [50], seats [4], thrones [4], seat [3]

2363 Θυάτειρα, ***Thyateira***, n.pr. GK: *2587*. Thyatira:– Thyatira [4]

2364 θυγάτηρ, ***thygatēr***, n. GK: *2588* [→ *2365*]. daughter, by extension a term of endearment toward (younger) woman:– daughter [24], daughters [5]

2365 θυγάτριον, ***thygatrion***, n. GK: *2589* [→ *2364*]. little daughter:– little daughter [1], young daughter [1]

2366 θύελλα, ***thyella***, n. GK: *2590* [→ *2372*]. storm:– tempest [1]

2367 θύϊνος, ***thyinos***, a. GK: *2591* [→ *2380*]. citron, from the citron tree (a scented wood):– thyine [1]

2368 θυμίαμα, ***thymiama***, n. GK: *2592* [→ *2380*]. incense; burning incense, offering of incense:– incense [4], odours [2]

2369 θυμιατήριον, ***thymiatērion***, n. GK: *2593* [→ *2380*]. incense altar:– censer [1]

2370 θυμιάω, ***thymiaō***, v. GK: *2594* [→ *2380*]. to burn incense, offer incense:– burn incense [1]

2371 θυμομαχέω, ***thymomacheō***, v. GK: *2595* [→ *2372+3163*]. to quarrel, be fighting mad:– highly displeased [1]

2372 θυμός, ***thymos***, n. GK: *2596* [→ *120, 1760, 1761, 1937, 1938, 1939, 2114, 2115, 2366, 2371, 2373, 3114, 3115, 3116, 3661, 4288, 4289, 4290*]. wrath, fury, anger, rage, a state of intense displeasure based in some real or perceived wrong. "The anger of God" is due to moral offense and has a focus on righteous punishment:– wrath [14], fierceness [2], indignation [1], wraths [1]

2373 θυμόω, ***thymoō***, v. GK: *2597* [→ *2372*]. (pass.) to become angry:– wroth [1]

2374 θύρα, ***thyra***, n. GK: *2598* [→ *2375, 2376, 2377*]. door, gate, entrance:– door [29], doors [9], gate [1]

2375 θυρεός, ***thyreos***, n. GK: *2599* [→ *2374*]. (long, oblong) shield:– shield [1]

2376 θυρίς, ***thyris***, n. GK: *2600* [→ *2374*]. window:– window [2]

2377 θυρωρός, ***thyrōros***, n. GK: *2601* [→ *2374*]. doorkeeper, watcher (at door or gate):– kept the door [2], porter [2]

2378 θυσία, ***thysia***, n. GK: *2602* [→ *2380*]. sacrifice, offering:– sacrifice [17], sacrifices [12]

2379 θυσιαστήριον, ***thysiastērion***, n. GK: *2603* [→ *2380*]. altar:– altar [22], altars [1]

2380 θύω, ***thyō***, v. GK: *2124 & 2604* [→ *1494, 2367, 2368, 2369, 2370, 2378, 2379; cf. 2303*]. to kill, butcher; to offer sacrifice:– killed [5], kill [3], sacrifice [3], done sacrifice [1], sacrificed [1], slay [1]

2381 Θωμᾶς, ***Thōmas***, n.pr. GK: *2605*. Thomas, "*twin*":– Thomas [12]

2382 θώραξ, ***thōrax***, n. GK: *2606*. breastplate:– breastplates [3], breastplate [2]

2383 Ἰάϊρος, ***Iairos***, n.pr. GK: *2608*. Jairus, "*he gives light*":– Jairus [2]

2384 Ἰακώβ, ***Iakōb***, n.pr. GK: *2609* [→ *2385*]. Jacob, "*follower, replacer, one who follows the heel*":– Jacob [26], Jacob's [1]

2385 Ἰάκωβος, ***Iakōbos***, n.pr. GK: *2610* [→ *2384*]. James, "*follower, replacer, one who follows the heel*":– James [42]

2386 ἴαμα, ***iama***, n. GK: *2611* [→ *2390*]. healing:– healing [2], healings [1]

2387 Ἰαμβρῆς, ***Iambrēs***, n.pr. GK: *2612*. Jambres:– Jambres [1]

2388 Ἰανναί, ***Iannai***, n.pr. GK: *2613*. Jannai:– Janna [1]

2389 Ἰάννης, ***Iannēs***, n.pr. GK: *2614*. Jannes:– Jannes [1]

2390 ἰάομαι, ***iaomai***, v. GK: *2615* [→ *2386, 2392, 2395*]. (mid.) to heal; (pass.) to be healed, freed:– healed [18], heal [7], healing [1], made whole [1], maketh whole [1]

2391 Ἰάρετ, ***Iaret***, n.pr. GK: *2616*. Jared, "*servant*":– Jared [1]

2392 ἴασις, ***iasis***, n. GK: *2617* [→ *2390*]. healing, cure:– cures [1], healing [1], heal [1]

2393 ἴασπις, ***iaspis***, n. GK: *2618*. jasper:– jasper [4]

2394 Ἰάσων, ***Iasōn***, n.pr. GK: *2619*. Jason, "*to heal*":– Jason [5]

2395 ἰατρός, ***iatros***, n. GK: *2620* [→ *2390*]. doctor, physician:– physician [5], physicians [2]

2396 ἴδε, ***ide***, pt. GK: *2623* [→ *1491*]. see!, look!; here, there:– behold [24], lo [3], look [1], see [1]

2397 ἰδέα, ***idea***, n. GK: *1624 & 2624* [→ *1491*]. appearance (usually implies a condition of reality):– countenance [1]

2398 ἴδιος, ***idios***, a. GK: *2625* [→ *2399*]. one's own, private:– his own [47], their own [14], privately (*+2596*) [8], apart (*+2596*) [7], own [6], your own [6], his [5], due [3], her own [2], our own [2], their [2], acquaintance [1], alone (*+2596*) [1], aside (*+2596*) [1], his proper [1], his several [1], home (*+1519+3588*) [1], private [1], proper [1], severally [1], thine own [1]

2399 ἰδιώτης, ***idiōtēs***, n. GK: *2626* [→ *2398*]. ordinary, untrained person, one who does not understand, an inquirer:– unlearned [3], ignorant [1], rude [1]

2400 ἰδού, ***idou***, pt. GK: *2627* [→ *1491*]. look!, suddenly, now; here, there; this particle is used to enliven a Hebrew narrative style, by marking the change of a scene, or emphasize some detail or idea, and is not always translated:– behold [181], lo [29], see [3]

2401 Ἰδουμαία, ***Idoumaia***, n.pr. GK: *2628*. Idumea, "*[land of] Edom*":– Idumea [1]

2402 ἱδρώς, ***hidrōs***, n. GK: *2629*. sweat, perspiration:– sweat [1]

2403 Ἰεζάβελ, ***Iezabel***, n.pr. GK: *2630*. Jezebel, "[poss.] *unexalted, without a husband*":– Jezebel [1]

2404 Ἱεράπολις, ***Hierapolis***, n.pr. GK: *2631* [→ *2413+4172*]. Hierapolis, "*[pagan] sacred city*":– Hierapolis [1]

2405 ἱερατεία, ***hierateia***, n. GK: *2632* [→ *2413*]. priestly office, priesthood:– office of priesthood [1], priest's office [1]

2406 ἱεράτευμα, ***hierateuma***, n. GK: *2633* [→ *2413*]. priesthood:– priesthood [2]

2407 ἱερατεύω, ***hierateuō***, v. GK: *2634* [→ *2413*]. to serve as a priest:– executed the priest's office [1]

2408 Ἰερεμίας, ***Ieremias***, n.pr. GK: *2635*. Jeremiah, "*Yahweh loosens [the womb]; Yahweh lifts up, establishes*":– Jeremie [2], Jeremias [1]

2409 ἱερεύς, ***hiereus***, n. GK: *2636* [→ *2413*]. priest:– priest [17], priests [15]

2410 Ἰεριχώ, ***Ierichō***, n.pr. GK: *2637*. Jericho, "*moon city*":– Jericho [7]

2411 ἱερόν, ***hieron***, n. GK: *2639* [→ *2413*]. temple, sanctuary; of the temple in Jerusalem, it can denote the entire temple complex:– temple [71]

2412 ἱεροπρεπής, ***hieroprepēs***, a. GK: *2640* [→ *2413+4241*]. reverent, pertaining to proper reverence, worthy of reverence:– as becometh holiness [1]

2413 ἱερός, ***hieros***, a. GK: *2641* [→ *748, 749, 2404, 2405, 2406, 2407, 2409, 2411, 2412, 2416, 2417, 2418, 2420*]. sacred, holy, set apart for God; (pl.) the holy things:– holy [2]

2414 Ἱεροσόλυμα, ***Hierosolyma***, n.pr. GK: *2642* [→ *2419*]. Jerusalem:– Jerusalem [59]

2415 Ἱεροσολυμίτης, ***Hierosolymitēs***, n.pr.g. GK: *2643* [→ *2419*]. inhabitant of Jerusalem:– Jerusalem [1], of Jerusalem [1]

2416 ἱεροσυλέω, ***hierosyleō***, v. GK: *2644* [→ *2413+4813*]. to rob temples:– commit sacrilege [1]

2417 ἱερόσυλος, ***hierosylos***, a. GK: *2645* [→ *2413+4813*]. temple robber:– robbers of churches [1]

2418 ἱερουργέω, ***hierourgeō***, v. GK: *2646* [→ *2413+2041*]. to perform priestly duty, serve as a priest:– ministering [1]

2419 Ἰερουσαλήμ, ***Ierousalēm***, n.pr. GK: *2647* [→ *2414, 2415*]. Jerusalem, "*foundation of Shalem [peace]*":– Jerusalem [83]

2420 ἱερωσύνη, ***hierōsynē***, n. GK: *2648* [→ *2413*]. priesthood:– priesthood [4]

2421 Ἰεσσαί, ***Iessai***, n.pr. GK: *2649*. Jesse:– Jesse [5]

2422 Ἰεφθάε, ***Iephthae***, n.pr. GK: *2650*. Jephthah, "*Yahweh opens, frees*":– Jephthae [1]

2423 Ἰεχονίας, ***Iechonias***, n.pr. GK: *2651*. Jeconiah, "*Yahweh supports*":– Jechonias [2]

2424 Ἰησοῦς, ***Iēsous***, n.pr. GK: *2652*. Jesus, Joshua, "*Yahweh saves*":– Jesus [964], Jesus' [10], him[s] [1]

2425 ἱκανός, ***hikanos***, a. GK: *2653* [→ *864, 867, 1338, 2185, 2426, 2427, 2428*]. sufficient, considerable, much; appropriate, competent, worthy, deserving:– many [11], much [6], long [5], worthy [5], sufficient [3], able [1], content (*+4160*) [1], enough [1], good while (*+2250*) [1], great number [1], great [1], large [1], long while (*+1909*) [1], meet [1], security [1], sore [1]

2426 ἱκανότης, ***hikanotēs***, n. GK: *2654* [→ *2425*]. competence, fitness, capability:– sufficiency [1]

2427 ἱκανόω, ***hikanoō***, v. GK: *2655* [→ *2425*]. to make competent, qualify one for, authorize:– made able [1], made meet [1]

2428 ἱκετηρία, ***hiketēria***, n. GK: *2656* [→ *2425*]. petition, supplication:– supplications [1]

2429 ἰκμάς, ***ikmas***, n. GK: *2657*. moisture:– moisture [1]

2430 Ἰκόνιον, ***Ikonion***, n.pr. GK: *2658*. Iconium:– Iconium [6]

2431 ἱλαρός, ***hilaros***, a. GK: *2659* [→ *2433*]. cheerful, without grudging, with an implication of a gracious attitude; note that the transliteration "hilarious" does not communicate the meaning of this attitude:– cheerful [1]

2432 ἱλαρότης, ***hilarotēs***, n. GK: *2660* [→ *2433*]. cheerfully, not grudgingly, with an implication of a gracious attitude:– cheerfulness [1]

2433 ἱλάσκομαι, ***hilaskomai***, v. GK: *2661* [→ *2431, 2432, 2434, 2435, 2436*]. (mid.) to make atonement for, with a focus on the means for accomplishing forgiveness, resulting in reconciliation; (pass.) to have mercy on, be merciful to:– make reconciliation [1], merciful [1]

2434 ἱλασμός, ***hilasmos***, n. GK: *2662* [→ *2433*]. atoning sacrifice, the means of forgiveness; traditionally propitiation:– propitiation [2]

2435 ἱλαστήριον, ***hilastērion***, n. GK: *2663* [→ *2433*]. atoning sacrifice; atonement cover, the place where sins are forgiven; traditionally propitiation or mercy seat:– mercy seat [1], propitiation [1]

2436 ἵλεως, ***hileōs***, a. GK: *2664* [→ *2433*]. forgiving, gracious; (may God be) gracious!, God forbid!:– be it far from [1], merciful [1]

2437 Ἰλλυρικόν, ***Illyrikon***, n.pr. GK: *2665*. Illyricum:– Illyricum [1]

2438 ἱμάς, ***himas***, n. GK: *2666*. (leather) thong, strap:– latchet [3], thongs [1]

2439 **ἱματίζω, *himatizō***, v. GK: *2667* [→ *2066, 2067, 2440, 2441; cf. 294*]. (pass.) to be dressed, clothed:– clothed [2]

2440 **ἱμάτιον, *himation***, n. GK: *2668* [→ *2439*]. clothing, cloak, robe:– garments [15], garment [15], clothes [12], raiment [12], cloke [2], robe [2], vesture [2], apparel [1]

2441 **ἱματισμός, *himatismos***, n. GK: *2669* [→ *2439*]. clothing:– vesture [2], apparelled [1], apparel [1], array [1], raiment [1]

2442 **ἱμείρομαι, *himeiromai***, v. GK: *2670*. to desire, long for:– affectionately desirous [1]

2443 **ἵνα, *hina***, c. GK: *2671* [→ *2444*]. a marker that shows purpose or result: in order that, in order to, so that, then; it can focus on the introduction of a discourse or on the content itself:– that [537], to [71], for to [5], after [1], albeit [1], because [1], must [1], so as [1], so that [1], to the intent that [1], to the intent [1], would [1]

ἵνα μή, *hina mē*. See *3363*.

2444 **ἱνατί, *hinati***, pt.inter. GK: *2672* [→ *2443+5101*]. why?:– why [5], wherefore [1]

2445 **Ἰόππη, *Ioppē***, n.pr. GK: *2673*. Joppa, "*beautiful*":– Joppa [10]

2446 **Ἰορδάνης, *Iordanēs***, n.pr. GK: *2674*. Jordan, "*descending*":– Jordan [15]

2447 **ἰός, *ios***, n. GK: *2675* [→ *2728*]. poison, venom; corrosion, rust:– poison [2], rust [1]

2448 **Ἰουδά, *Iouda***, n.pr. GK: *2676* [→ *2455*]. Judah, "*praised*":– Juda [3]

2449 **Ἰουδαία, *Ioudaia***, n.pr. GK: *2677* [→ *2455*]. Judea, Judean, "*land of the Judahites*":– Judea [41], Jewry [2]

2450 **ἰουδαΐζω, *ioudaizō***, v. GK: *2678* [→ *2455*]. to follow Jewish customs, live as a Jew:– live as do the Jews [1]

2451 **Ἰουδαϊκός, *Ioudaikos***, a.pr. GK: *2679* [→ *2455*]. Jewish, "*Jewish*":– Jewish [1]

2452 **Ἰουδαϊκῶς, *Ioudaikōs***, adv.pr. GK: *2680* [→ *2455*]. like a Jew, in a Jewish manner, "*Jewish*":– as do the Jews [1]

2453 **Ἰουδαῖος, *Ioudaios***, a.pr.g. GK: *2681* [→ *2455*]. Jewish (people), "*Jewish*":– Jews [167], Jew [22], Jews' [4], Jewess [2], Judea [2]

2454 **Ἰουδαϊσμός, *Ioudaismos***, n.pr. GK: *2682* [→ *2455*]. Judaism, "*Judaism*":– Jews' religion [2]

2455 **Ἰούδας, *Ioudas***, n.pr. GK: *2683* [→ *2448, 2449, 2450, 2451, 2452, 2453, 2454*]. Judah, Judas, Jude, "*praised*":– Judas [33], Juda [8], Jude [1]

2456 **Ἰουλία, *Ioulia***, n.pr. GK: *2684* [→ *2457*]. Julia, "*of Julian [the family of Julius Caesar]*":– Julia [1]

2457 **Ἰούλιος, *Ioulios***, n.pr. GK: *2685* [→ *2456*]. Julius, "*of Julian [the family of Julius Caesar]*":– Julius [2]

2458 **Ἰουνιᾶς, *Iounias***, n.pr. GK: *2687*. Junias:– Junia [1]

2459 **Ἰοῦστος, *Ioustos***, n.pr. GK: *2688*. Justus, "*just*":– Justus [3]

2460 **ἱππεύς, *hippeus***, n. GK: *2689* [→ *2462*]. horseman, cavalryman:– horsemen [2]

2461 **ἱππικός, *hippikos***, a. GK: *2690* [→ *2462*]. mounted (troops), pertaining to a horseman:– horsemen [1]

2462 **ἵππος, *hippos***, n. GK: *2691* [→ *67, 751, 2460, 2461, 5374, 5375, 5376*]. horse:– horse [8], horses [7], horses' [1]

2463 **ἶρις, *iris***, n. GK: *2692*. rainbow; some translate as a brilliant halo or circle of light:– rainbow [2]

2464 **Ἰσαάκ, *Isaak***, n.pr. GK: *2693*. Isaac, "*he [God] laughs*":– Isaac [20]

2465 **ἰσάγγελος, *isangelos***, a. GK: *2694* [→ *2470+32*]. like an angel:– equal unto angels [1]

2466 **Ἰσαχάρ, *Isachar***, n.pr. GK: *2695 & 2704*. Issachar, "*there is a reward [Ge. 30:18]; may [God] show mercy; hired hand*":– Isachar [1]

2467 **ἴσημι, *isēmi***, v. GK: *3857* [cf. *1492*]. to know; presumed to be related to *1492*.:– know [2]

2468 **ἴσθι, *isthi***, v.2.s.imper. of *1510*. GK: *1639* [→ *1510*]. be; see *1510*:–

2469 **Ἰσκαριώτης, *Iskariōtēs***, n.pr.[g.?]. GK: *2696 & 2697*. Iscariot, "*man of Kerioth* or *of the assassins*":– Iscariot [11]

2470 **ἴσος, *isos***, a. GK: *2698* [→ *2465, 2471, 2472, 2473, 2481*]. equal, same; agreeable:– equal [4], agree together (*+1510*) [1], agreed together (*+1510*) [1], as much (*+3588*) [1], like [1]

2471 **ἰσότης, *isotēs***, n. GK: *2699* [→ *2470*]. equality, fairness:– equality [2], equal [1]

2472 **ἰσότιμος, *isotimos***, a. GK: *2700* [→ *2470+5092*]. as precious as, of equal value:– like precious [1]

2473 **ἰσόψυχος, *isopsychos***, a. GK: *2701* [→ *2470+5594*]. like, of like soul, heart or mind:– likeminded [1]

2474 **Ἰσραήλ, *Israēl***, n.pr. GK: *2702* [→ *2475*]. Israel, "*he struggles with God [El]*":– Israel [70]

2475 **Ἰσραηλίτης, *Israēlitēs***, n.pr.g. GK: *2703* [→ *2474*]. Israelite, (one) of Israel:– of Israel [5], Israelites [2], Israelite [2]

2476 **ἵστημι, *histēmi***, v. GK: *2705* [→ *181, 182, 386, 387, 436, 450, 478, 600, 605, 646, 647, 790, 868, 1292, 1339, 1370, 1611, 1764, 1815, 1817, 1839, 1881, 1987, 1988, 1990, 1999, 2139, 2186, 2525, 2688, 2721, 3179, 3936, 4026, 4291, 4368, 4414, 4712, 4713, 4714, 4715, 4739, 4911, 4921, 4955, 4956, 5287; cf. 4716, 4745*]. (intr.) to stand, to stand (firm), be present; to stop; (tr.) to make stand, place, put, establish:– stood [57], stand [34], standing [22], set [10], standeth [8], establish [3], stood still [3], appointed [2], established [2], standest [2], abode [1], brought [1], continue [1], covenanted [1], holden up [1], lay to charge [1], make stand [1], present [1], set up [1], setteth [1], stanched [1], stand still [1], standing up [1]

2477 **ἱστορέω, *historeō***, v. GK: *2707*. to get acquainted with, visit:– see [1]

2478 **ἰσχυρός, *ischyros***, a. GK: *2708* [→ *2479*]. powerful, strong, forceful:– strong [11], mighty [7], mightier than [3], stronger than [3], boysterous [1], powerful [1], valiant [1]

2479 **ἰσχύς, *ischys***, n. GK: *2709* [→ *1340, 1765, 1840, 2001, 2478, 2480, 2729*]. strength, power:– strength [4], power [3], might [2], ability [1], mightily [1]

2480 **ἰσχύω, *ischyō***, v. GK: *2710* [→ *2479*]. to be strong, powerful, able:– could [8], able [6], availeth [3], prevailed [3], whole [2], can do [1], cannot (*+3756*) [1], couldest [1], good [1], had much work (*+3433*) [1], might [1], strength [1]

2481 **ἴσως, *isōs***, adv. GK: *2711* [→ *2470*]. perhaps:– it may be [1]

2482 **Ἰταλία, *Italia***, n.pr. GK: *2712* [→ *2483*]. Italy:– Italy [5]

2483 **Ἰταλικός, *Italikos***, a.pr.g. GK: *2713* [→ *2482*]. Italian:– Italian [1]

2484 **Ἰτουραῖος, *Itouraios***, a.pr. GK: *2714*. Iturea, "*pertaining to Jetur*":– Iturea [1]

2485 **ἰχθύδιον, *ichthydion***, n. GK: *2715* [→ *2486*]. little fish:– little fishes [1], small fishes [1]

2486 **ἰχθύς, *ichthys***, n. GK: *2716* [→ *2485*]. fish:– fishes [15], fish [5]

2487 **ἴχνος, *ichnos***, n. GK: *2717* [→ *421*]. step, footstep; course of action:– steps [3]

2488 **Ἰωαθάμ, *Iōatham***, n.pr. GK: *2718*. Jotham, "*Yahweh will complete*":– Joatham [2]

2489 **Ἰωαννά, *Iōanna***, n.pr. GK: *2720* [cf. *2491*]. Joanna, "[prob.] *Yahweh is gracious*":– Joanna [2]

2490 **Ἰωαννᾶς, *Iōannas***, n.pr. GK: *2721* [cf. *2491*]. Joannas, "[prob.] *Yahweh is gracious*":– Joanna [1]

2491 **Ἰωάννης, *Iōannēs***, n.pr. GK: *2722* [cf. *2489, 2490*]. John, "*Yahweh is gracious*":– John [131], John's [2]

2492 **Ἰώβ, *Iōb***, n.pr. GK: *2724*. Job, "*where is my father* poss. *where is my father, O God?*":– Job [1]

2493 **Ἰωήλ, *Iōēl***, n.pr. GK: *2727*. Joel, "*Yahweh is God*":– Joel [1]

2494 **Ἰωνάμ, *Iōnam***; or **Ἰωνάν, *Iōnan***, n.pr. GK: *2729 & 2730*. Jonam, Jonan:– Jonan [1]

2495 **Ἰωνᾶς, *Iōnas***, n.pr. GK: *2731*. Jonah, "*dove*":– Jonas [12], Jona [1]

2496 **Ἰωράμ, *Iōram***, n.pr. GK: *2732*. Jehoram, "*Yahweh exalts*":– Joram [2]

2497 **Ἰωρίμ, *Iōrim***, n.pr. GK: *2733*. Jorim:– Jorim [1]

2498 **Ἰωσαφάτ, *Iōsaphat***, n.pr. GK: *2734*. Jehoshaphat, "*Yahweh has judged*":– Josaphat [2]

2499 **Ἰωσή, *Iōsē***, n.pr. GK: *2735* [cf. *2500*]. Jose, "*he will add*":– Jose [1]

2500 **Ἰωσῆς, *Iōsēs***, n.pr. GK: *2736* [cf. *2499*]. Joses, Joseph, "*he will add*":– Joses [6]

2501 **Ἰωσήφ, *Iōsēph***, n.pr. GK: *2737*. Joseph, "*he will add*":– Joseph [33], Joseph's [2]

2502 **Ἰωσίας, *Iōsias***, n.pr. GK: *2739*. Josiah, "*let or may Yahweh give*":– Josias [2]

2503 **ἰῶτα, *iōta***, n. GK: *2740*. smallest letter (of the Greek alphabet), which corresponds to the smallest letter of the Hebrew alphabet, *yodh*:– jot [1]

2504 **κἀγώ, *kagō***, contr. [c.+p.]. GK: *2743* [→ *2532+1473*]. and I, I also, but I:– and I [43], I also [19], I [5], even I [5], me also [3], so I [3], and me [2], I in like wise [1], also [1], both me [1], but me [1], even I also [1], that I [1], when I [1]

2505 καθά, katha, c. or adv. GK: *2745* [→ *2596+3739*]. (just) as:– as [1]

2506 καθαίρεσις, kathairesis, n. GK: *2746* [→ *2596+138*]. tearing down, demolishment, destruction:– destruction [2], pulling down [1]

2507 καθαιρέω, kathaireō, v. GK: *2747* [→ *2596+138*]. to take down, demolish, overthrow; (pass.) to be robbed of, suffer the loss of:– took down [3], destroyed [2], casting down [1], pull down [1], put down [1], take down [1]

2508 καθαίρω, kathairō, v. GK: *2748* [→ *2513*]. to prune, clear unproductive wood, cleanse:– purged [1], purgeth [1]

2509 καθάπερ, kathaper, c. or adv. GK: *2749* [→ *2596+3739+4007*]. as, just as, like:– as [10], even as [2], as well [1]

2510 καθάπτω, kathaptō, v. GK: *2750* [→ *2596+681*]. to fasten, attach, take hold of, seize:– fastened [1]

2511 καθαρίζω, katharizō, v. GK: *2751 & 2760* [→ *2513*]. to make clean, cleanse, purify:– cleansed [9], cleanse [6], make clean [5], clean [3], cleanseth [1], purged [1], purge [1], purging [1], purified [1], purifying [1], purify [1]

2512 καθαρισμός, katharismos, n. GK: *2752* [→ *2513*]. cleansing, purification, washing:– cleansing [2], purifying [2], purged (+*4160*) [1], purged [1], purification [1]

2513 καθαρός, katharos, a. GK: *2754* [→ *167, 168, 169, 1245, 1571, 2508, 2511, 2512, 2514, 4027*]. clean, pure, clear of responsibility, innocent:– pure [17], clean [10], clear [1]

2514 καθαρότης, katharotēs, n. GK: *2755* [→ *2513*]. cleanness, purity:– purifying [1]

2515 καθέδρα, kathedra, n. GK: *2756* [→ *2516*]. seat, bench:– seats [2], seat [1]

2516 καθέζομαι, kathezomai, v. GK: *2757* [→ *2515, 2521, 4410, 4775*]. to sit down, be seated:– sat [4], sitting [2]

2517 καθεξῆς, kathexēs, adv. GK: *2759* [→ *2596+2192*]. in order, in a sequence:– in order [2], afterward (+*1722+3588*) [1], by order [1], follow after [1]

2518 καθεύδω, katheudō, v. GK: *2761* [→ *2596*]. to sleep, fall asleep:– sleep [8], asleep [5], sleepeth [3], sleepest [2], sleeping [2], slept [2]

2519 καθηγητής, kathēgētēs, n. GK: *2762* [→ *2596+71*]. teacher; derivative of a verb "to guide, to explain," not found in the NT:– master [2], masters [1]

2520 καθήκω, kathēkō, v. GK: *2763* [→ *2596+2240*]. to be fitting; (pcpl.) things that ought to be, that are proper:– convenient [1], fit [1]

2521 κάθημαι, kathēmai, v. GK: *2764* [→ *2516*]. to sit, seat, ride; to live, stay, reside:– sat [41], sitting [20], sit [12], sitteth [10], sat down [2], dwell [1], set down [1], sittest [1], sitting down [1]

2522 καθημερινός, kathēmerinos, a. GK: *2766* [→ *2596+2250*]. daily:– daily [1]

2523 καθίζω, kathizō, v. GK: *2767* [→ *339, 1940, 3869, 4776*]. (tr.) to place, seat (someone), appoint; (intr.) to sit down, come to rest upon; stay, live. "To sit on the right side" means to be in a position of high status, "to sit on the left" is a lesser position. "To sit on the seat of Moses" means to have the capacity to interpret the Law of Moses with authority:– sit [14], sat down [11], sat [10], set [3], set down [2], sitteth down [2], continued [1], set to judge [1], sit down [1], sitteth [1], sitting [1], tarry [1]

2524 καθίημι, kathiēmi, v. GK: *2768* [→ *2596*]. to let down, lower:– let down [3], let down (+*5465*) [1]

2525 καθίστημι, kathistēmi, v. GK: *2769 & 2770* [→ *2596+2476*]. to put in charge, appoint; to escort, bring, take; (pass.) to be made, become, be appointed:– made [6], make ruler [5], is [2], ordained [2], appoint [1], conducted [1], made ruler [1], maketh [1], make [1], ordain [1], set [1]

2526 καθό, katho, adv. GK: *2771* [→ *2596+3739*]. insofar as, to the degree that:– according to that (+*1437*) [1], according to that [1], as we [1], inasmuch as [1]

2526′ καθολικός, katholikos, a. GK: *2772* [→ *2596+3650*]. general, universal:–

2527 καθόλου, katholou, adv. GK: *2773* [→ *2596+3650*]. at all, entirely, completely:– at all [1]

2528 καθοπλίζω, kathoplizō, v. GK: *2774* [→ *2596+3696*]. (mid.) to fully arm or equip (oneself):– armed [1]

2529 καθοράω, kathoraō, v. GK: *2775* [→ *2596+3708*]. (pass.) to be clearly seen, perceived:– clearly seen [1]

2530 καθότι, kathoti, c. GK: *2776* [→ *2596+3739+5101*]. as, to the degree that; because:– according as [1], as (+*302*) [1], because that [1], because [1], forsomuch as [1]

2531 καθώς, kathōs, adv. GK: *2777* [→ *2596+5613*]. as, just as, even as; in accordance with:– as [142], even as [27], according as [5], even [3], according to [1], as well as [1], how [1], seeing as [1], when [1]

2532 καί, kai, c. GK: *2779* [→ *2504, 2534, 2539, 2543, 2544, 2546, 2547, 2548, 2579, 4003, 5065*]. (as a connective) and; (connecting and continuing) and then, then; (as a disjuntive) but, yet, however; (as an adv.) also, even, likewise:– and [8167], also [517], even [100], both [47], but [41], then [25], so [18], neither (+*3756*) [16], likewise [12], or [12], that [12], nor [11], yet [10], when [9], for [8], neither [8], with [6], yea [5], as [4], indeed [4], neither (+*3361*) [4], and also [3], eighteen (+*1176+3638*) [3], moreover [3], though [3], very [3], and yet [2], nor (+*3756*) [2], now [2], therefore [2], yet (+*1063*) [2], also (+*235*) [1], also (+*260*) [1], although (+*1487*) [1], and (+*5119*) [1], and again [1], and no so much as (+*3761*) [1], and when [1], as well [1], at least (+*1065*) [1], beside [1], but though (+*1161+1487*) [1], by [1], else [1], even (+*2193*) [1], even all one as if (+*846+1520+3588*) [1], if [1], insomuch [1], moreover (+*235*) [1], neither (+*3364*) [1], neither (+*3761*) [1], neither any (+*3762*) [1], neither at any time (+*3763*) [1], nevertheless (+*4133*) [1], of either side (+*1782+1782*) [1], on either side one (+*1782+1782*) [1], so in like manner (+*3779*) [1], so that (+*5620*) [1], so that [1], therefore (+*1352*) [1], though (+*1437*) [1], though (+*1487*) [1], though (+*1512*) [1], thus [1], verily [1], wherefore (+*1352*) [1], wherefore (+*5620*) [1], which [1]

2533 Καϊάφας, Kaiaphas, n.pr. GK: *2780*. Caiaphas:– Caiaphas [9]

2534 καίγε, kaige, pt. GK: *2781* [→ *2532+1065*]. even, even though:–

2535 Κάϊν, Kain, n.pr. GK: *2782*. Cain, "*metal worker; brought forth, acquired [Ge. 4:1]*":– Cain [3]

2536 Καϊνάμ, Kainam; or **Καϊνάν, Kainan**, n.pr. GK: *2783 & 2784*. Cainam, Cainan, Kenan, "*worker in iron, metal worker*":– Cainan [2]

2537 καινός, kainos, a. GK: *2785* [→ *340, 341, 342, 1456, 1457, 2538*]. new, latest, anew; in some contexts new is superior to old (Mt 9:17; Heb 8):– new [44]

2538 καινότης, kainotēs, n. GK: *2786* [→ *2537*]. newness:– newness [2]

2539 καίπερ, kaiper, c. GK: *2788* [→ *2532+4007*]. though, even though, although:– though [5], and yet [1]

2540 καιρός, kairos, n. GK: *2789* [→ *170, 171, 2119, 2120, 2121, 2122, 4340*]. time (particular and general); right time, opportune time, proper time, appointed time:– time [53], times [11], season [8], seasons [4], always (+*1722+3956*) [2], due season [2], opportunity [2], age (+*2244*) [1], convenient season [1], due time [1], while [1]

2541 Καῖσαρ, Kaisar, n.pr. GK: *2790* [→ *2542*]. Caesar:– Cesar [21], Cesar's [9]

2542 Καισάρεια, Kaisareia, n.pr. GK: *2791* [→ *2541*]. Caesarea:– Cesarea [17]

2543 καίτοι, kaitoi, pt. GK: *2792* [→ *2532+5104*]. and yet:– although [1]

2544 καίτοιγε, kaitoige, pt. GK: *2793* [→ *2532+5104+1065*]. although, and yet:– though [2], nevertheless [1]

2545 καίω, kaiō, v. GK: *2794* [→ *1572, 2575, 2618, 2738, 2739, 2740, 2741, 2742, 2743, 3646*]. to light (a wick), keep burning:– burning [6], burned [3], burneth [1], burn [1], light [1]

2546 κἀκεῖ, kakei, contr. [c.+adv.]. GK: *2795* [→ *2532+1563*]. and there, and where:– and there [9], there also [1], thither also [1]

2547 κἀκεῖθεν, kakeithen, contr. [c.+adv.]. GK: *2796* [→ *2532+1563*]. and from there:– and from thence [6], and thence [3], and afterward [1], thence also [1]

2548 κἀκεῖνος, kakeinos, contr. [c.+p.demo.]. GK: *2797* [→ *2532+1563*]. and that one:– and he [4], and they [3], he also [3], and him [2], and the other [2], and them [2], they also [2], as them [1], even he [1], even they [1], him also [1], them also [1]

2549 κακία, kakia, n. GK: *2798* [→ *2556*]. evil, wickedness, depravity, malice; in some contexts an "evil" situation means a difficult and hard circumstance rather than a morally corrupt circumstance (Mt 6:34):– malice [6], maliciousness [2], evil [1], naughtiness [1], wickedness [1]

2550 κακοήθεια, kakoētheia, n. GK: *2799* [→ *2556+1485*]. malice:– malignity [1]

2551 κακολογέω, kakologeō, v. GK: *2800* [→ *2556+3004*]. to curse, malign, speak evil of:– curseth [2], spake evil [1], speak evil [1]

2552 κακοπάθεια, kakopatheia, n. GK: *2801* [→ *2556+3958*]. suffering:– suffering affliction [1]

2553 **κακοπαθέω**, ***kakopatheō***, v. GK: *2802* [→ *2556+3958*]. to suffer trouble, endure hardship:– afflicted [1], endure afflictions [1], endure hardness [1], suffer trouble [1]

2554 **κακοποιέω**, ***kakopoieō***, v. GK: *2803* [→ *2556+4160*]. to do evil, do what is wrong:– do evil [2], doeth evil [1], evil doing [1]

2555 **κακοποιός**, ***kakopoios***, a. GK: *2804* [→ *2556+4160*]. wrongdoing:– evildoers [3], evildoer [1], malefactor [1]

2556 **κακός**, ***kakos***, a. GK: *2805* [→ *172, 420, 1573, 2549, 2550, 2551, 2552, 2553, 2554, 2555, 2557, 2558, 2559, 2560, 2561, 4777, 4778*]. evil, wicked, wrong, bad, a perversion of what pertains to goodness; as a noun, an evil thing can refer to any crime, harm, or moral wrong:– evil [45], harm [2], bad [1], ill [1], noisome [1], wicked [1]

2557 **κακοῦργος**, ***kakourgos***, a. GK: *2806* [→ *2556+2041*]. criminal, evildoer:– malefactors [3], evil doer [1]

2558 **κακουχέω**, ***kakoucheō***, v. GK: *2807* [→ *2556+2192*]. (pass.) to be mistreated, maltreated, tormented:– suffer adversity [1], tormented [1]

2559 **κακόω**, ***kakoō***, v. GK: *2808* [→ *2556*]. to harm, mistreat, oppress, persecute; poison, embitter:– entreat evil [1], evil entreated [1], harm [1], hurt [1], made evil affected [1], vex [1]

2560 **κακῶς**, ***kakōs***, adv. GK: *2809* [→ *2556*]. badly, wrongly, terribly:– sick (*+2192*) [4], sick [3], evil [2], amiss [1], diseased (*+2192*) [1], diseased [1], grievously [1], miserably [1], sick people (*+2192*) [1], sore [1]

2561 **κάκωσις**, ***kakōsis***, n. GK: *2810* [→ *2556*]. oppression, mistreatment:– affliction [1]

2562 **καλάμη**, ***kalamē***, n. GK: *2811* [→ *2563*]. straw; note some translate "stubble":– stubble [1]

2563 **κάλαμος**, ***kalamos***, n. GK: *2812* [→ *2562*]. reed, staff, stick, measuring rod, pen:– reed [11], pen [1]

2564 **καλέω**, ***kaleō***, v. GK: *2813* [→ *410, 479, 1458, 1462, 1528, 1577, 1941, 2821, 2822, 3333, 3870, 3874, 3875, 4292, 4341, 4779, 4837*]. to call, invite, summon. The authority of the speaker dictates the nature of the calling (friends invite; kings summon). This is also translated "to name," the giving of attribution to someone or something:– called [103], call [16], bidden [10], calleth [6], bade [4], bid [2], calling [1], named [1], name [1], surname [1]

2565 **καλλιέλαιος**, ***kallielaios***, n. GK: *2814* [→ *2570+1636*]. cultivated olive tree:– good olive tree [1]

2566 **κάλλιον**, ***kallion***, a.neut. of *2570*. GK: *2819* [→ *2570*]. good, right; beautiful, fine, excellent:–

2567 **καλοδιδάσκαλος**, ***kalodidaskalos***, a. GK: *2815* [→ *2570+1321*]. teaching what is good:– teachers of good things [1]

2568 **Καλοὶ λιμένες**, ***Kaloi limenes***, n.pr. GK: *2816* [→ *2570+3040*]. Fair Havens, "*fair havens*":– fair havens [1]

2569 **καλοποιέω**, ***kalopoieō***, v. GK: *2818* [→ *2570+4160*]. to do what is right or good:– well doing [1]

2570 **καλός**, ***kalos***, a. GK: *2819* [→ *2565, 2566, 2567, 2568, 2569, 2573*]. good, right; beautiful, fine, excellent:– good [82], better [6], honest [5], goodly [2], meet [2], better (*+3123*) [1], good thing [1], well [1], worthy [1]

2571 **κάλυμμα**, ***kalymma***, n. GK: *2820* [→ *2572*]. veil, covering:– vail [4]

2572 **καλύπτω**, ***kalyptō***, v. GK: *2821* [→ *177, 343, 601, 602, 1942, 1943, 2571, 2619, 3871, 4028, 4780*]. cover, veil, hide:– covered [2], cover [2], hid [2], covereth [1], hide [1]

2573 **καλῶς**, ***kalōs***, adv. GK: *2822* [→ *2570*]. rightly, well, sometimes with an implication of correctness:– well [30], good [3], full well [1], honestly [1], recover (*+2192*) [1], very well [1]

2574 **κάμηλος**, ***kamēlos***, n. GK: *2823*. camel:– camel [4], camel's [2]

2575 **κάμινος**, ***kaminos***, n. GK: *2825* [→ *2545*]. furnace, oven:– furnace [4]

2576 **καμμύω**, ***kammyō***, v. GK: *2826*. close, shut (the eyes):– closed [2]

2577 **κάμνω**, ***kamnō***, v. GK: *2827*. to grow weary; be sick:– fainted [1], sick [1], wearied [1]

2578 **κάμπτω**, ***kamptō***, v. GK: *2828* [→ *344, 4781*]. to bend, bow (on a knee):– bow [3], bowed [1]

2579 **κἄν**, ***kan***, contr. [c.+pt.]. GK: *2829* [→ *2532+1487+302*]. and if, even if:– and if [5], though [4], if but [2], also if [1], and though [1], at the least [1], yet [1]

2580 **Κανά**, ***Kana***, n.pr. GK: *2830* [→ *2581*]. Cana, "*reed*":– Cana [4]

2581 **Κανανίτης**, ***Kananitēs***, n.pr.g. GK: *2832* [→ *2580*]. Canaanite, from Cana:– Canaanite [2]

2582 **Κανδάκη**, ***Kandakē***, n.pr. GK: *2833*. Candace, "[title?] *queen*":– Candace [1]

2583 **κανών**, ***kanōn***, n. GK: *2834*. rule, standard; sphere of activity, limit:– rule [4], line [1]

2584 **Καπερναούμ**, ***Kapernaoum***, n.pr. GK: *2835 & 3019*. Capernaum, "*village of Nahum*":– Capernaum [16]

2585 **καπηλεύω**, ***kapēleuō***, v. GK: *2836*. to act as a peddler, trade in for profit:– corrupt [1]

2586 **καπνός**, ***kapnos***, n. GK: *2837*. smoke:– smoke [13]

2587 **Καππαδοκία**, ***Kappadokia***, n.pr. GK: *2838*. Cappadocia:– Cappadocia [2]

2588 **καρδία**, ***kardia***, n. GK: *2840* [→ *2589, 4641*]. heart, mind (seat of thought and emotion). The heart was thought to be the seat of the inner self (composed of life, soul, mind, and spirit). "Heart" is similar in meaning to "soul," but often the "heart" has a focus on thinking and understanding (Mk 2:8; Lk 1:51; 24:38):– heart [101], hearts [57], heart's [1]

2589 **καρδιογνώστης**, ***kardiognōstēs***, n. GK: *2841* [→ *2588+1097*]. knower of the heart:– knowest hearts [1], knoweth hearts [1]

2590 **καρπός**, ***karpos***, n. GK: *2843* [→ *175, 2591, 2592, 2593*]. fruit, crop, harvest, produce of vegetation; by extension: deed, activity, produce of a person:– fruit [54], fruits [12]

2591 **Κάρπος**, ***Karpos***, n.pr. GK: *2842* [→ *2590*]. Carpus, "*fruit(ful)*":– Carpus [1]

2592 **καρποφορέω**, ***karpophoreō***, v. GK: *2844* [→ *2590+5342*]. to produce a crop, bear fruit:– bring forth fruit [4], bringeth forth fruit [2], beareth fruit [1], fruitful [1]

2593 **καρποφόρος**, ***karpophoros***, a. GK: *2845* [→ *2590+5342*]. crop, fruitbearing:– fruitful [1]

2594 **καρτερέω**, ***kartereō***, v. GK: *2846* [→ *4342, 4343; cf. 2904*]. to persevere, endure:– endured [1]

2595 **κάρφος**, ***karphos***, n. GK: *2847*. speck, chip, particle:– mote [6]

2596 **κατά**, ***kata***, pp. GK: *2848* [→ *176, 177, 178, 179, 180, 181, 182, 183, 478, 600, 604, 605, 843, 1246, 1455, 1459, 1460, 1944, 2505, 2506, 2507, 2509, 2510, 2516, 2517, 2518, 2519, 2520, 2522, 2524, 2525, 2526, 2526', 2527, 2528, 2529, 2530, 2531, 2597, 2598, 2599, 2600, 2601, 2602, 2603, 2604, 2605, 2606, 2607, 2609, 2610, 2611, 2612, 2613, 2614, 2615, 2616, 2653, 2617, 2618, 2619, 2620, 2621, 2622, 2623, 2624, 2625, 2626, 2627, 2628, 2629, 2630, 2631, 2632, 2633, 2634, 2635, 2636, 2637, 2638, 2639, 2640, 2641, 2642, 2643, 2644, 2645, 2646, 2647, 2648, 2649, 2650, 2651, 2652, 2653, 2654, 2655, 2656, 2657, 2658, 2659, 2660, 2661, 2662, 2663, 2664, 2665, 2666, 2667, 2668, 2669, 2670, 2671, 2672, 2673, 2674, 2675, 2676, 2677, 2678, 2679, 2680, 2681, 2682, 2683, 2684, 2685, 2686, 2687, 2688, 2689, 2690, 2691, 2692, 2693, 2694, 2695, 2696, 2697, 2698, 2699, 2700, 2701, 2702, 2703, 2704, 2705, 2706, 2708, 2709, 2710, 2711, 2712, 2713, 2714, 2715, 2716, 2718, 2719, 2720, 2721, 2722, 2723, 2726, 2727, 2728, 2729, 2730, 2731, 2732, 2733, 2734, 2735, 2736, 2737, 3872, 4293, 4294, 4782, 4783, 4784, 4785, 5270; cf. 2608*]. (gen.) against, contrary to, opposed; down, throughout; (acc.) in, by, with, in accordance with, for:– according to [104], after [59], against [58], in [32], by [28], daily (*+2250*) [15], as [10], every [10], at [8], of [8], privately (*+2398*) [8], apart (*+2398*) [7], throughout [7], through [4], to [4], about [3], according [3], concerning [3], down [3], every (*+3956*) [3], in divers [3], toward [3], with [3], after the manner [2], among [2], as concerning [2], as touching [2], before [2], from house to house (*+3624*) [2], inasmuch as (*+3745*) [2], into [2], natural (*+5449*) [2], on part [2], on [2], over against [2], upon [2], according as [1], affairs (*+3588*) [1], after a manner [1], after a sort [1], after the manner of [1], alone (*+1438*) [1], alone (*+2398*) [1], alone (*+3441*) [1], as (*+3739+5158*) [1], as (*+3745*) [1], as much as [1], as pertaining to [1], as wont (*+1485+3588*) [1], aside (*+2398*) [1], beyond measure (*+5236*) [1], cause [1], charitably (*+26*) [1], covered [1], daily (*+1538+2250*) [1], daily (*+2250+3956*) [1], day by day (*+2250*) [1], deep (*+899*) [1], even as (*+3739+3779+5158*) [1], even thus (*+5024*) [1], every (*+1520+1538*) [1], every (*+3588*) [1], every house (*+3624*) [1], exceeding (*+5236*) [1], face to face (*+4383*) [1], far more exceeding (*+1519+5236+5236*) [1], for [1], godly (*+2316*) [1], in due [1], in every church (*+1577*) [1], in every house (*+3624*) [1], in every [1], in respect of [1], in the like manner (*+846+3588*) [1], in the presence (*+4383*) [1], like as (*+3665*) [1], matter (*+3588*) [1], mightily (*+2904*) [1], more excellent (*+5236*) [1], one by one

(+*1520*) [1], out of measure (+*5236*) [1], particularly (+*1520*+*1538*) [1], particularly (+*3313*) [1], particular [1], pertaining to [1], reason (+*3056*) [1], so (+*846*+*3588*) [1], state [1], the same (+*1565*) [1], together (+*846*+*3588*) [1], touching [1], unto [1], whereby (+*5101*) [1], where [1], willingly (+*1595*) [1], year by year (+*1763*) [1], your (+*4771*) [1], your own (+*4771*) [1]

2597 καταβαίνω, ***katabainō***, v. GK: *2849* [→ *2596*+*305*]. to go down, descend:– come down [20], came down [16], went down [13], descended [7], descending [7], cometh down [4], descend [4], go down [2], coming down [1], falling down [1], fell [1], get down [1], goeth down [1], going down [1], steppeth down [1]

2598 καταβάλλω, ***kataballō***, v. GK: *2850* [→ *2596*+*906*]. (pass.) to be struck down; (mid.) to lay (a foundation):– cast down [2], laying [1]

2599 καταβαρέω, ***katabareō***, v. GK: *2851* [→ *2596*+*922*]. to burden, be a burden:– burden [1]

2600 κατάβασις, ***katabasis***, n. GK: *2853* [→ *2596*+*305*]. place that goes down, slope, down-grade:– descent [1]

2601 καταβιβάζω, ***katabibazō***, v. GK: *2854* [→ *2596*+*305*]. to bring down:– brought down [1], thrust down [1]

2602 καταβολή, ***katabolē***, n. GK: *2856* [→ *2596*+*906*]. creation (of the world), beginning, foundation:– foundation [10], conceive [1]

2603 καταβραβεύω, ***katabrabeuō***, v. GK: *2857* [→ *2596*+*1018*]. to disqualify for a prize, decide against:– beguile of reward [1]

2604 καταγγελεύς, ***katangeleus***, n. GK: *2858* [→ *2596*+*32*]. advocate, proclaimer:– setter forth [1]

2605 καταγγέλλω, ***katangellō***, v. GK: *2859* [→ *2596*+*32*]. to preach, proclaim, advocate, report:– preached [6], preach [4], shew [3], declare [1], declaring [1], spoken of [1], teach [1]

2606 καταγελάω, ***katagelaō***, v. GK: *2860* [→ *2596*+*1070*]. to laugh at, mock:– laughed to scorn [3]

2607 καταγινώσκω, ***kataginōskō***, v. GK: *2861* [→ *2596*+*1097*]. to condemn, convict; (pass.) to be in the wrong, condemned:– condemn [2], blamed [1]

2608 κατάγνυμι, ***katagnymi***, v. GK: *2862* [→ *513, 3489; cf. 2596*]. to break:– brake [2], break [1], broken [1]

2609 κατάγω, ***katagō***, v. GK: *2864* [→ *2596*+*71*]. to bring, bring down, land (on shore):– bring down [3], brought down [2], brought forth [1], brought [1], landed [1], landing [1], touched [1]

2610 καταγωνίζομαι, ***katagōnizomai***, v. GK: *2865* [→ *2596*+*73*]. (mid.) to conquer, defeat, overcome:– subdued [1]

2611 καταδέω, ***katadeō***, v. GK: *2866* [→ *2596*+*1210*]. to bandage, bind up:– bound up [1]

2612 κατάδηλος, ***katadēlos***, a. GK: *2867* [→ *2596*+*1212*]. clear, quite plain:– evident [1]

2613 καταδικάζω, ***katadikazō***, v. GK: *1463 & 2868* [→ *2596*+*1349*]. to judge, condemn:– condemned [4], condemn [1]

2614 καταδιώκω, ***katadiōkō***, v. GK: *2870* [→ *2596*+*1377*]. to look for, search for:– followed after [1]

2615 καταδουλόω, ***katadouloō***, v. GK: *2871* [→ *2596*+*1401*]. to make a slave, enslave:– bring into bondage [2]

2616 καταδυναστεύω, ***katadynasteuō***, v. GK: *2872* [→ *2596*+*1410*]. (act.) to exploit, oppress, dominate; (pass.) to be under the power of, oppressed by:– oppressed [1], oppress [1]

2617 καταισχύνω, ***kataischynō***, v. GK: *2875* [→ *2596*+*150*]. to dishonor, humiliate, shame, disappoint:– ashamed [6], confound [2], dishonoureth [2], confounded [1], maketh ashamed [1], shame [1]

2618 κατακαίω, ***katakaiō***, v. GK: *2876* [→ *2596*+*2545*]. to burn up, consume:– burnt up [3], burnt [3], burn [3], burn up [1], burned [1], utterly burnt [1]

2619 κατακαλύπτω, ***katakalyptō***, v. GK: *2877* [→ *2596*+*2572*]. (mid.) to cover (the head):– covered [2], cover [1]

2620 κατακαυχάομαι, ***katakauchaomai***, v. GK: *1595 & 2878* [→ *2596*+*2744*]. to boast about; to triumph over:– boast against [1], boast [1], glory [1], rejoiceth against [1]

2621 κατάκειμαι, ***katakeimai***, v. GK: *2879* [→ *2596*+*2749*]. to lie down (in bed); to recline (at dinner):– lay [5], sat at meat [2], kept (+*1909*) [1], lie [1], sat [1], sit at meat [1]

2622 κατακλάω, ***kataklaō***, v. GK: *2880* [→ *2596*+*2806*]. to break in pieces:– brake [2]

2623 κατακλείω, ***katakleiō***, v. GK: *1597 & 2881* [→ *2596*+*2808*]. to lock up:– shut up [2]

2624 κατακληροδοτέω, ***kataklērodoteō***, v. GK: *2882 & 2883* [→ *2596*+*2819*+*3551*]. to parcel out by lot:– divided by lot [1]

2625 κατακλίνω, ***kataklinō***, v. GK: *2884* [→ *2596*+*2827*]. (act.) to cause to sit; (pass.) to recline (at a table):– make sit down [1], sat at meat [1], sit down [1]

2626 κατακλύζω, ***kataklyzō***, v. GK: *2885* [→ *2596*+*2830*]. (pass.) to be deluged, flooded:– overflowed [1]

2627 κατακλυσμός, ***kataklysmos***, n. GK: *2886* [→ *2596*+*2830*]. flood, deluge:– flood [4]

2628 κατακολουθέω, ***katakoloutheō***, v. GK: *2887* [→ *2596*+*190; cf. 1.3*]. to follow:– followed after [1], followed [1]

2629 κατακόπτω, ***katakoptō***, v. GK: *2888* [→ *2596*+*2875*]. to cut:– cutting [1]

2630 κατακρημνίζω, ***katakrēmnizō***, v. GK: *2889* [→ *2596*+*2910*]. to throw down a cliff:– cast down headlong [1]

2631 κατάκριμα, ***katakrima***, n. GK: *2890* [→ *2596*+*2919*]. condemnation:– condemnation [3]

2632 κατακρίνω, ***katakrinō***, v. GK: *2891* [→ *2596*+*2919*]. to condemn:– condemned [8], condemn [7], damned [2], condemnest [1], condemneth [1]

2633 κατάκρισις, ***katakrisis***, n. GK: *2892* [→ *2596*+*2919*]. condemnation:– condemnation [1], condemn [1]

2634 κατακυριεύω, ***katakyrieuō***, v. GK: *2894* [→ *2596*+*2962*]. to lord it over, gain dominion over, subdue; in some contexts there is an implication that this exercise of authority is harsh:– exercise dominion over [1], exercise lordship over [1], lords over [1], overcame [1]

2635 καταλαλέω, ***katalaleō***, v. GK: *2895* [→ *2596*+*2980*]. to speak against, slander, accuse:– speak evil [2], speaketh evil [2], speak against [1]

2636 καταλαλιά, ***katalalia***, n. GK: *2896* [→ *2596*+*2980*]. slander, defamation, evil speech:– backbitings [1], evil speakings [1]

2637 κατάλαλος, ***katalalos***, a. GK: *2897* [→ *2596*+*2980*]. slanderous, defamatory:– backbiters [1]

2638 καταλαμβάνω, ***katalambanō***, v. GK: *2898* [→ *2596*+*2983*]. to obtain, attain, take hold of; seize, overtake; (mid.) to grasp, understand, realize, find out:– apprehended [2], taken [2], apprehend [1], attained [1], come upon [1], comprehended [1], comprehend [1], found [1], obtain [1], overtake [1], perceived [1], perceive [1], taketh [1]

2639 καταλέγω, ***katalegō***, v. GK: *2899* [→ *2596*+*3004*]. to put on a list, enroll, select:– taken into the number [1]

2640 κατάλειμμα, ***kataleimma***, n. GK: *2900 & 5698* [→ *2596*+*3007*]. remnant:– remnant [1]

2641 καταλείπω, ***kataleipō***, v. GK: *2901* [→ *2596*+*3007*]. to leave (behind), neglect; (pass.) remain (behind):– left [15], leave [6], forsaken [1], forsook [1], leaving [1], reserved [1]

2642 καταλιθάζω, ***katalithazō***, v. GK: *2902* [→ *2596*+*3037*]. to stone to death:– stone [1]

2643 καταλλαγή, ***katallagē***, n. GK: *2903* [→ *2596*+*236*]. reconciliation:– reconciliation [2], atonement [1], reconciling [1]

2644 καταλλάσσω, ***katallassō***, v. GK: *2904* [→ *2596*+*236*]. to reconcile (among human beings or between human beings and God):– reconciled [5], reconciling [1]

2645 κατάλοιπος, ***kataloipos***, a. GK: *2905* [→ *2596*+*3007*]. remaining, left over; (n.) remnant, the rest:– residue [1]

2646 κατάλυμα, ***katalyma***, n. GK: *2906* [→ *2596*+*3089*]. guest room; inn:– guestchamber [2], inn [1]

2647 καταλύω, ***katalyō***, v. GK: *2907* [→ *2596*+*3089*]. (tr.) throw down, abolish, destroy; (intr.) to be a guest, rest, find lodging:– destroy [6], thrown down [3], destroyest [2], come to nought [1], destroyed [1], dissolved [1], guest [1], lodge [1], overthrow [1]

2648 καταμανθάνω, ***katamanthanō***, v. GK: *2908* [→ *2596*+*3129*]. notice carefully, consider closely:– consider [1]

2649 καταμαρτυρέω, ***katamartyreō***, v. GK: *2909* [→ *2596*+*3144*]. to bring testimony against, bear testimony against:– witness against [4]

2650 καταμένω, ***katamenō***, v. GK: *2910* [→ *2596*+*3306*]. to stay, live:– abode [1]

2651 καταμόνας, ***katamonas***, a. GK: *2911* [→ *2596*+*3441*]. in private, alone:– alone [1]

2652 κατανάθεμα, ***katanathema***, n. GK: *2873 & 2912* [→ *2596*+*331*]. curse, that which is under the ban (devoted exclusively to God):– curse [1]

2653 καταναθεματίζω, ***katanathematizō***, v. GK: *2874 & 2913* [→ *2596+331*]. to (call down a) curse:– curse [1]

2654 καταναλίσκω, ***katanaliskō***, v. GK: *2914* [→ *2596+303+259*]. to consume:– consuming [1]

2655 καταναρκάω, ***katanarkaō***, v. GK: *2915* [→ *2596*]. to burden, be a burden:– burdensome [2], chargeable to [1]

2656 κατανεύω, ***kataneuō***, v. GK: *2916* [→ *2596+3506*]. to signal, nod:– beckoned [1]

2657 κατανοέω, ***katanoeō***, v. GK: *2917* [→ *2596+3563*]. to pay attention, notice, observe; consider, contemplate; this word has a strong implication that the attention paid is intense, and the contemplation is broad and thorough, resulting in complete understanding:– consider [4], behold [2], considered [2], beholdeth [1], beholding [1], considerest [1], discovered [1], perceived [1], perceivest [1]

2658 καταντάω, ***katantaō***, v. GK: *2918* [→ *2596+473*]. to come to, arrive at; attain, reach:– came [8], come [3], attain [2]

2659 κατάνυξις, ***katanyxis***, n. GK: *2919* [→ *2596+3572*]. stupor, bewilderment, unable to think:– slumber [1]

2660 κατανύσσομαι, ***katanyssomai***, v. GK: *2920* [→ *2596+3572*]. to be pierced, stabbed:– pricked [1]

2661 καταξιόω, ***kataxioō***, v. GK: *2921* [→ *2596+514*]. (pass.) to be counted worthy, considered worthy:– accounted worthy [2], counted worthy [2]

2662 καταπατέω, ***katapateō***, v. GK: *2922* [→ *2596+3961*]. to trample (an action that can show disdain):– trodden under foot [2], trample [1], trodden down [1], trode upon [1]

2663 κατάπαυσις, ***katapausis***, n. GK: *2923* [→ *2596+3973*]. rest:– rest [9]

2664 καταπαύω, ***katapauō***, v. GK: *2924* [→ *2596+3973*]. to keep from, restrain; to give rest; to rest, cease:– ceased [1], given rest [1], restrained [1], rest [1]

2665 καταπέτασμα, ***katapetasma***, n. GK: *2925* [→ *2596+4072*]. curtain:– vail [6]

2666 καταπίνω, ***katapinō***, v. GK: *2927* [→ *2596+4095*]. to swallow, devour; (pass.) to be swallowed up, overwhelmed, drowned:– swallowed up [4], devour [1], drowned [1], swallow [1]

2667 καταπίπτω, ***katapiptō***, v. GK: *2928* [→ *2596+4098*]. to fall down:– fallen down [1], fallen [1]

2668 καταπλέω, ***katapleō***, v. GK: *2929* [→ *2596+4126*]. to sail to:– arrived [1]

2669 καταπονέω, ***kataponeō***, v. GK: *2930* [→ *2596+4192*]. (pass.) to be oppressed, distressed:– oppressed [1], vexed [1]

2670 καταποντίζω, ***katapontizō***, v. GK: *2931* [→ *2596*]. (pass.) to be drowned; to sink:– drowned [1], sink [1]

2671 κατάρα, ***katara***, n. GK: *2932* [→ *2596+685*]. curse, imprecation:– curse [3], cursing [2], cursed [1]

2672 καταράομαι, ***kataraomai***, v. GK: *2933* [→ *2596+685*]. (mid.) to curse:– curse [4], cursedst [1], cursed [1]

2673 καταργέω, ***katargeō***, v. GK: *2934* [→ *2596+1.1+2041*]. to nullify, abolish, make ineffective; (pass.) cease, pass away:– done away [4], abolished [3], destroy [3], destroyed [2], become of no effect [1], bring to nought [1], ceased [1], come to nought [1], cumbereth [1], delivered [1], fail [1], loosed [1], made of none effect [1], make of none effect [1], make void [1], make without effect [1], put away [1], put down [1], vanish away [1]

2674 καταριθμέω, ***katarithmeō***, v. GK: *2935* [→ *2596+706*]. (pass.) to be numbered among, belong to:– numbered [1]

2675 καταρτίζω, ***katartizō***, v. GK: *2936* [→ *2596+737*]. to restore, put in order, mend; to make complete, equip, train; to prepare, ordain:– perfect [3], make perfect [2], mending [2], fitted [1], framed [1], perfected [1], perfectly joined together [1], prepared [1], restore [1]

2676 κατάρτισις, ***katartisis***, n. GK: *2937* [→ *2596+737*]. perfection, completion:– perfection [1]

2677 καταρτισμός, ***katartismos***, n. GK: *2938* [→ *2596+737*]. preparation, training, equipping:– perfecting [1]

2678 κατασείω, ***kataseiō***, v. GK: *2939* [→ *2596+4579*]. to motion, signal by waving or shaking:– beckoned [2], beckoning [2]

2679 κατασκάπτω, ***kataskaptō***, v. GK: *2940* [→ *2596+4626*]. (act.) to tear down; (pass.) to be ruined:– digged down [1], ruins [1]

2680 κατασκευάζω, ***kataskeuazō***, v. GK: *2941* [→ *2596+4632*]. to prepare, make ready; to build, construct; to set up, arrange, furnish; there is a strong implication that the preparation is thorough, and a possible implication that the act of building may be for a special purpose:– prepare [3], builded [2], prepared [2], built [1], made [1], ordained [1], preparing [1]

2681 κατασκηνόω, ***kataskēnoō***, v. GK: *2942* [→ *2596+4633*]. to perch, nest; to live, dwell:– lodge [2], lodged [1], rest [1]

2682 κατασκήνωσις, ***kataskēnōsis***, n. GK: *2943* [→ *2596+4633*]. nest:– nests [2]

2683 κατασκιάζω, ***kataskiazō***, v. GK: *2944* [→ *2596+4639*]. to overshadow:– shadowing [1]

2684 κατασκοπέω, ***kataskopeō***, v. GK: *2945* [→ *2596+4648*]. to spy on, lie in wait for:– spy out [1]

2685 κατάσκοπος, ***kataskopos***, n. GK: *2946* [→ *2596+4648*]. spy:– spies [1]

2686 κατασοφίζομαι, ***katasophizomai***, v. GK: *2947* [→ *2596+4680*]. to deal treacherously with:– dealt subtilly with [1]

2687 καταστέλλω, ***katastellō***, v. GK: *2948* [→ *2596+4724*]. (act.) to quiet, restrain:– appeased [1], quiet [1]

2688 κατάστημα, ***katastēma***, n. GK: *2949* [→ *2596+2476*]. the way one lives, behavior:– behaviour [1]

2689 καταστολή, ***katastolē***, n. GK: *2950* [→ *2596+4724*]. appearance, behavior:– apparel [1]

2690 καταστρέφω, ***katastrephō***, v. GK: *2951* [→ *2596+4762*]. to overturn, upset:– overthrew [2]

2691 καταστρηνιάω, ***katastrēniaō***, v. GK: *2952* [→ *2596+4764*]. to be filled with desires that conflict with dedication to someone:– wax wanton against [1]

2692 καταστροφή, ***katastrophē***, n. GK: *2953* [→ *2596+4762*]. ruin, destruction:– overthrow [1], subverting [1]

2693 καταστρώννυμι, ***katastrōnnymi***, v. GK: *2954* [→ *2596+4766*]. (pass.) to be scattered:– overthrown [1]

2694 κατασύρω, ***katasyrō***, v. GK: *2955* [→ *2596+4951*]. to drag away (by considerable force):– hale [1]

2695 κατασφάττω, ***katasphattō***, v. GK: *2956 & 2957* [→ *2596+4969*]. to kill, slaughter, strike down:– slay [1]

2696 κατασφραγίζω, ***katasphragizō***, v. GK: *2958* [→ *2596+4973*]. (pass.) to be sealed up:– sealed [1]

2697 κατάσχεσις, ***kataschesis***, n. GK: *2959* [→ *2596+2192*]. possession, taking into possession:– possession [2]

2698 κατατίθημι, ***katatithēmi***, v. GK: *2960* [→ *2596+5087*]. (mid.) to grant a favor, do a favor:– do [1], laid [1], shew [1]

2699 κατατομή, ***katatomē***, n. GK: *2961* [→ *2596+5114*]. mutilation, cutting away:– concision [1]

2700 κατατοξεύω, ***katatoxeuō***, v. GK: *2962* [→ *2596+5115*]. to shoot down:– thrust through [1]

2701 κατατρέχω, ***katatrechō***, v. GK: *2963* [→ *2596+5143*]. to run down:– ran down [1]

καταφάγω, ***kataphagō***. See ***2719***.

2702 καταφέρω, ***katapherō***, v. GK: *2965* [→ *2596+5342*]. to cast (a vote) against; to bring (charges); (pass.) to be overwhelmed (by sleep):– fallen into [1], gave [1], sunk down [1]

2703 καταφεύγω, ***katapheugō***, v. GK: *2966* [→ *2596+5343*]. to flee, take refuge:– fled for refuge [1], fled [1]

2704 καταφθείρω, ***kataphtheirō***, v. GK: *2967* [→ *2596+5351*]. (pass.) to be depraved, corrupt:– corrupt [1], utterly perish [1]

2705 καταφιλέω, ***kataphileō***, v. GK: *2968* [→ *2596+5384*]. to kiss:– kissed [5], kiss [1]

2706 καταφρονέω, ***kataphroneō***, v. GK: *2969* [→ *2707*]. to despise, look down on, scorn, show contempt:– despise [7], despisest [1], despising [1]

2707 καταφρονητής, ***kataphronētēs***, n. GK: *2970* [→ *2706*]. scoffer, despiser:– despisers [1]

2708 καταχέω, ***katacheō***, v. GK: *2972* [→ *1632; cf. 2596*]. to pour out, pour down:– poured [2]

2709 καταχθόνιος, ***katachthonios***, a. GK: *2973* [→ *2596*]. under the earth, subterranean; this may refer to the dead as a class of people, which generally are regarded as inhabiting the underworld. It is likely a more general term than the specific names for the abode of the dead: Hades, Gehenna, Tartaros, etc:– under the earth [1]

2710 καταχράομαι, ***katachraomai***, v. GK: *2974* [→ *2596+5530*]. to make full use of; to be engrossed in:– abuse [1], abusing [1]

2711 καταψύχω, ***katapsychō***, v. GK: *2976* [→ *2596+5594*]. to cool off, refresh with:– cool [1]

2712 κατείδωλος, ***kateidōlos***, a. GK: *2977* [→ *2596+1497*]. full of idols / images:– wholly given to idolatry (+*1510*) [1]

κατελεύθω, ***kateleuthō***. See ***2718***.

2713 κατέναντι, ***katenanti***, adv. GK: *2978* [→ *2596+1725*]. ahead, before, in the sight of; opposite of:– over against [4], before [1]

κατενέγκω, *katenegkō*. See *2702*.

2714 κατενώπιον, ***katenōpion***, adv.&pp.*. GK: *2979* [→ *2596+1722+3708*]. in the sight of, in the presence of; before:– before [2], before the presence [1], in the sight [1], sight [1]

2715 κατεξουσιάζω, ***katexousiazō***, v. GK: *2980* [→ *1849; cf. 2596*]. to exercise authority over:– exercise authority upon [2]

2716 κατεργάζομαι, ***katergazomai***, v. GK: *2981* [→ *2596+2041*]. to produce, accomplish, bring about, do:– worketh [7], wrought [6], do [3], done [2], working [2], causeth [1], doeth [1], perform [1], work out [1]

2717 , Not used in Strong's numbering system.

2718 κατέρχομαι, ***katerchomai***, v. GK: *2982* [→ *2596+2064*]. to go down, come down:– came down [4], came [2], went down [2], come down [1], come [1], departed [1], descendeth [1], landed [1]

2719 κατεσθίω, ***katesthiō***, v. GK: *2983 & 2984* [→ *2596+2068*]. to eat up, consume:– devour [6], devoured [3], devoured up [2], ate up [1], devoureth [1], eat up [1], eaten up [1]

2720 κατευθύνω, ***kateuthynō***, v. GK: *2985* [→ *2596+2117*]. to guide, direct, lead:– direct [2], guide [1]

2721 κατεφίσταμαι, ***katephistamai***, v. GK: *2987* [→ *2596+1909+2476*]. to make an attack upon, rise up against:– made insurrection against [1]

2722 κατέχω, ***katechō***, v. GK: *2988* [→ *2596+2192*]. to hold back, suppress, restrain; hold fast, possess; (pass.) to be bound:– hold fast [3], hold [2], keep [2], had [1], held [1], keep in memory [1], letteth [1], made [1], possessed [1], possessing [1], retained [1], seize [1], stayed [1], take [1], withholdeth [1]

2723 κατηγορέω, ***katēgoreō***, v. GK: *2989* [→ *2724, 2725*]. to accuse, bring charges against:– accuse [13], accused [6], accuseth [1], accusing [1], object [1]

2724 κατηγορία, ***katēgoria***, n. GK: *2990* [→ *2723*]. (legal) charge, accusation:– accusation [2], accusation against [1], accused (+*1722*) [1]

2725 κατήγορος, ***katēgoros***, n. GK: *2991 & 2992* [→ *2723*]. accuser:– accusers [6], accuser [1]

2726 κατήφεια, ***katēpheia***, n. GK: *2993* [→ *2596+5316*]. gloominess, a feeling of dejection:– heaviness [1]

2727 κατηχέω, ***katēcheō***, v. GK: *2994* [→ *2596+2279*]. (act.) to instruct; (pass.) to be instructed, informed:– informed [2], instructed [2], instructed in [1], taught [1], teacheth [1], teach [1]

2728 κατιόω, ***katioō***, v. GK: *2995* [→ *2596+2447*]. (pass.) to become corroded, tarnished:– cankered [1]

2729 κατισχύω, ***katischyō***, v. GK: *2996* [→ *2596+2479*]. to overcome, prevail; to be able:– prevail against [1], prevailed [1]

2730 κατοικέω, ***katoikeō***, v. GK: *2997 & 3001* [→ *2596+3624*]. to live in, reside in, settle:– dwell [19], dwelt [11], dwelleth [7], inhabiters [3], dwellers [2], dwelling [2], dwellest [1], dwelling at [1], dwelt in [1]

2731 κατοίκησις, ***katoikēsis***, n. GK: *2998* [→ *2596+3624*]. where one lives, residence:– dwelling [1]

2732 κατοικητήριον, ***katoikētērion***, n. GK: *2999* [→ *2596+3624*]. dwelling place, home:– habitation [2]

2733 κατοικία, ***katoikia***, n. GK: *3000* [→ *2596+3624*]. where one lives, dwelling place:– habitation [1]

2734 κατοπτρίζω, ***katoptrizō***, v. GK: *3002* [→ *2596+3708*]. (mid.) to reflect or to look at, contemplate:– beholding as in a glass [1]

2735 κατόρθωμα, ***katorthōma***, n. GK: *3003* [→ *2596+3717*]. success, prosperity, good order:– very worthy deeds [1]

2736 κάτω, ***katō***; or κατωτέρω, ***katōterō***, adv. GK: *3004 & 3006* [→ *2596*]. below; down, downward; bottom, under, lower:– down [5], beneath [3], bottom [2], under [1]

2737 κατώτερος, ***katōteros***, a. GK: *3005* [→ *2596*]. lower:– lower [1]

2738 καῦμα, ***kauma***, n. GK: *3008* [→ *2545*]. (scorching) heat:– heat [2]

2739 καυματίζω, ***kaumatizō***, v. GK: *3009 & 3010* [→ *2545*]. (act.) to scorch by heat, burn; (pass.) to be scorched, seared:– scorched [3], scorch [1]

2740 καῦσις, ***kausis***, n. GK: *3011* [→ *2545*]. burning:– burned [1]

2741 καυσόω, ***kausoō***, v. GK: *3012* [→ *2545*]. (pass.) to be consumed by fire, burned up:– fervent heat [2]

2742 καύσων, ***kausōn***, n. GK: *3014* [→ *2545*]. (scorching) heat, hot day:– heat [2], burning heat [1]

2743 καυτηριάζω, ***kautēriazō***, v. GK: *3013 & 3015* [→ *2545*]. (pass.) to be seared with a hot iron:– seared with a hot iron [1]

2744 καυχάομαι, ***kauchaomai***, v. GK: *3016* [→ *2620, 2745, 2746*]. to boast, brag about; to rejoice in, glory in; this can refer to proper or improper boasting, depending on the object of the boast:– glory [20], boast [6], rejoice [4], glorieth [2], makest boast [2], boasted [1], boasting [1], glorying [1], joy [1]

2745 καύχημα, ***kauchēma***, n. GK: *3017* [→ *2744*]. something to boast about, boasting; pride, joy:– rejoicing [4], glory [3], glorying [2], boasting [1], rejoice [1]

2746 καύχησις, ***kauchēsis***, n. GK: *3018* [→ *2744*]. boasting, pride; glorying in; this can refer to proper or improper boasting, depending on the object of the boast:– boasting [6], rejoicing [4], glorying [1], glory [1]

2747 Κεγχρεαί, ***Kenchreai***, n.pr. GK: *3020*. Cenchrea:– Cenchrea [3]

2748 Κεδρών, ***Kedrōn***, n.pr. GK: *3022*. Kidron:– Cedron [1]

2749 κεῖμαι, ***keimai***, v. GK: *3023* [→ *345, 480, 606, 733, 1945, 2621, 2837, 2838, 2845, 2846, 3873, 4029, 4295, 4873*]. to lay, lie, be laid, laid out; be destined, appointed:– laid [6], set [6], lying [4], lieth [2], appointed [1], is [1], laid up [1], lain [1], lay [1], lie [1], made [1], there [1]

2750 κειρία, ***keiria***, n. GK: *3024* [→ *2751*]. strip of linen, bandage, graveclothes:– graveclothes [1]

2751 κείρω, ***keirō***, v. GK: *3025* [→ *1359, 1946, 1947, 2750, 2772, 2773, 2877*]. (act.) to shear (another); (mid.) to have one's hair cut:– shorn [3], shearer [1]

2752 κέλευσμα, ***keleusma***, n. GK: *3026* [→ *2753*]. (loud) command, signal:– shout [1]

2753 κελεύω, ***keleuō***, v. GK: *3027* [→ *2027, 2752*]. to order, direct, command:– commanded [21], bid [1], commandest [1], commanding [1], commandment [1], command [1], gave commandment [1]

2754 κενοδοξία, ***kenodoxia***, n. GK: *3029* [→ *2756+1391*]. vain conceit, empty conceit, a state of pride that has no proper basis:– vainglory [1]

2755 κενόδοξος, ***kenodoxos***, a. GK: *3030* [→ *2756+1391*]. conceited, a state of pride that has no proper basis:– vain glory [1]

2756 κενός, ***kenos***, a. GK: *3031* [→ *2754, 2755, 2757, 2758, 2761*]. empty, empty-handed; by extension: vain, ineffective, useless, foolish:– vain [12], empty [4], in vain [2]

2757 κενοφωνία, ***kenophōnia***, n. GK: *3032* [→ *2756+5456*]. chatter, empty talk:– vain babblings [2]

2758 κενόω, ***kenoō***, v. GK: *3033* [→ *2756*]. to empty, deprive; (pass.) to be hollow, emptied, of no value:– in vain [1], made of no reputation [1], made of none effect [1], made void [1], make void [1]

2759 κέντρον, ***kentron***, n. GK: *3034* [→ *1461, 1574*]. sting, goad:– pricks [2], sting [2], stings [1]

2760 κεντυρίων, ***kentyriōn***, n. GK: *3035*. centurion, technically the commander of one hundred:– centurion [3]

2761 κενῶς, ***kenōs***, adv. GK: *3036* [→ *2756*]. without reason, in vain, to no purpose:– in vain [1]

2762 κεραία, ***keraia***, n. GK: *3037* [→ *2768*]. least stroke of a pen, projection [a portion of a letter of the alphabet], referring to the smallest detail of the Law:– tittle [2]

2763 κεραμεύς, ***kerameus***, n. GK: *3038* [→ *2766*]. potter:– potter's [2], potter [1]

2764 κεραμικός, ***keramikos***, a. GK: *3039* [→ *2766*]. pertaining to a potter:– potter [1]

2765 κεράμιον, ***keramion***, n. GK: *3040* [→ *2766*]. clay jar:– pitcher [2]

2766 κέραμος, ***keramos***, n. GK: *3041* [→ *2763, 2764, 2765*]. clay roof tile:– tiling [1]

2767 κεράννυμι, ***kerannymi***, v. GK: *3042* [→ *185, 194, 4786*]. to mix; (pass.) to be poured:– filled [1], fill [1], poured out [1]

2768 κέρας, ***keras***, n. GK: *3043* [→ *2762, 2769*]. horn, often a figure of power and position:– horns [10], horn [1]

2769 κεράτιον, ***keration***, n. GK: *3044* [→ *2768*]. carob pod:– husks [1]

κεράω, *keraō*. See *2767*.

2770 κερδαίνω, ***kerdainō***, v. GK: *2132 & 3045* [→ *2771*]. to gain; make money; win over; spare:– gain [8], gained [5], get gain [1], win [1], won [1]

2771 κέρδος, ***kerdos***, n. GK: *3046* [→ *146, 147, 2770*]. gain, profit:– gain [2], lucre's [1]

2772 κέρμα, ***kerma***, n. GK: *3047* [→ *2751*]. coin:– money [1]

2773 κερματιστής, ***kermatistēs***, n. GK: *3048* [→ *2751*]. money exchanger:– changers of money [1]

2774 **κεφάλαιον, *kephalaion***, n. GK: *3049* [→ *2776*]. the (main) point; price, sum of money:– sum [2]

2775 **κεφαλαιόω, *kephalaioō***, v. GK: *3050 & 3052* [→ *2776*]. to strike on the head:– wounded in the head [1]

2776 **κεφαλή, *kephalē***, n. GK: *3051* [→ *346, 607, 2774, 2775, 2777, 4030, 4344*]. head (of a body); top (stone in a building); by extension: someone or something in the primary place, the point of origin:– head [57], heads [19]

2777 **κεφαλίς, *kephalis***, n. GK: *3053* [→ *2776*]. section of a scroll:– volume [1]

2778 **κῆνσος, *kēnsos***, n. GK: *3056*. (poll) tax:– tribute [4]

2779 **κῆπος, *kēpos***, n. GK: *3057* [→ *2780*]. garden, grove:– garden [5]

2780 **κηπουρός, *kēpouros***, n. GK: *3058* [→ *2779*]. gardener:– gardener [1]

2781 **κηρίον, *kērion***, n. GK: *3059*. wax, honeycomb:–

2782 **κήρυγμα, *kērygma***, n. GK: *3060* [→ *2783*]. preaching, proclamation, message, with a focus on the content of what is preached:– preaching [8]

2783 **κῆρυξ, *kēryx***, n. GK: *3061* [→ *2782, 2784, 4296*]. herald, preacher, proclaimer:– preacher [3]

2784 **κηρύσσω, *kēryssō***, v. GK: *3062* [→ *2783*]. to preach, proclaim, tell, often urging acceptance of the message, with warnings of consequences for not doing so:– preach [22], preached [20], preaching [8], published [3], preacheth [2], publish [2], preacher [1], preachest [1], proclaimed [1], proclaiming [1]

2785 **κῆτος, *kētos***, n. GK: *3063*. huge fish:– whale's [1]

2786 **Κηφᾶς, *Kēphas***, n.pr. GK: *3064*. Cephas (Aramaic for Peter), "*rock*":– Cephas [6]

2787 **κιβωτός, *kibōtos***, n. GK: *3066*. ark, box, chest:– ark [6]

2788 **κιθάρα, *kithara***, n. GK: *3067* [→ *2789, 2790*]. harp, lyre:– harps [3], harp [1]

2789 **κιθαρίζω, *kitharizō***, v. GK: *3068* [→ *2788*]. to play the harp or lyre:– harped [1], harping [1]

2790 **κιθαρῳδός, *kitharōdos***, n. GK: *3069* [→ *2788+5603*]. harpist, lyre player:– harpers [2]

2791 **Κιλικία, *Kilikia***, n.pr. GK: *3070*. Cilicia:– Cilicia [8]

2792 **κινάμωμον, *kinamōmon***, n. GK: *3072 & 3077*. cinnamon:– cinnamon [1]

2793 **κινδυνεύω, *kindyneuō***, v. GK: *3073* [→ *2794*]. to be in danger:– in danger [2], in jeopardy [1], stand in jeopardy [1]

2794 **κίνδυνος, *kindynos***, n. GK: *3074* [→ *2793*]. danger, risk:– perils [8], peril [1]

2795 **κινέω, *kineō***, v. GK: *3075* [→ *277, 2796, 3334, 4787*]. to move, remove; to shake, stir up; (pass.) to be moved, removed; be aroused:– moved [2], move [2], wagging [2], mover [1], remove [1]

2796 **κίνησις, *kinēsis***, n. GK: *3076* [→ *2795*]. motion:– moving [1]

2797 **Κίς, *Kis***, n.pr. GK: *3078*. Kish, "*bow, power*":– Cis [1]

κίχρημι, *kichrēmi*. See ***5531***.

2798 **κλάδος, *klados***, n. GK: *3080* [→ *2806*]. branch, twig:– branches [9], branch [2]

2799 **κλαίω, *klaiō***, v. GK: *3081* [→ *2805*]. to weep, cry, wail, mourn:– weep [16], wept [11], weeping [9], weepest [2], bewail [1], weep (+*4160*) [1]

2800 **κλάσις, *klasis***, n. GK: *3082* [→ *2806*]. breaking:– breaking [2]

2801 **κλάσμα, *klasma***, n. GK: *3083* [→ *2806*]. broken piece, fragment:– fragments [7], broken [2]

2802 **Κλαύδα, *Klauda***; or **Καῦδα, *Kauda***, n.pr. GK: *3007 & 3084 & 3085*. Clauda, Cauda:– Clauda [1]

2803 **Κλαυδία, *Klaudia***, n.pr. GK: *3086* [→ *2804*]. Claudia, "[poss.] *lame*":– Claudia [1]

2804 **Κλαύδιος, *Klaudios***, n.pr. GK: *3087* [→ *2803*]. Claudius:– Claudius [3]

2805 **κλαυθμός, *klauthmos***, n. GK: *3088* [→ *2799*]. weeping, crying:– weeping [6], wailing [2], wept (+*1096*) [1]

2806 **κλάω, *klaō***, v. GK: *3089* [→ *1575, 2622, 2798, 2800, 2801, 2814*]. to break:– brake [9], broken [3], break [2], breaking [1]

2807 **κλείς, *kleis***, n. GK: *3090* [→ *2808*]. key:– key [4], keys [2]

2808 **κλείω, *kleiō***, v. GK: *3091* [→ *608, 1576, 2623, 2807, 4788*]. to close, shut, lock:– shut [10], shut up [3], shutteth [2], shutteth up [1]

2809 **κλέμμα, *klemma***, n. GK: *3092* [→ *2813*]. theft, stealing:– thefts [1]

2810 **Κλεοπᾶς, *Kleopas***, n.pr. GK: *3093* [→ *2811+3962*]. Cleopas, "*renowned father*":– Cleopas [1]

2811 **κλέος, *kleos***, n. GK: *3094* [→ *2810*]. credit, honor:– glory [1]

2812 **κλέπτης, *kleptēs***, n. GK: *3095* [→ *2813*]. thief:– thief [12], thieves [4]

2813 **κλέπτω, *kleptō***, v. GK: *3096* [→ *2809, 2812, 2829*]. steal:– steal [11], stole [2]

2814 **κλῆμα, *klēma***, n. GK: *3097* [→ *2806*]. branch (in context, vine branches):– branch [3], branches [1]

2815 **Κλήμης, *Klēmēs***, n.pr. GK: *3098*. Clement, "*mild*":– Clement [1]

2816 **κληρονομέω, *klēronomeō***, v. GK: *3099* [→ *2819+3551*]. to inherit, acquire; see also *2817*:– inherit [14], heirs [1], heir [1], inheritance obtained [1], inherited [1]

2817 **κληρονομία, *klēronomia***, n. GK: *3100* [→ *2819+3551*]. inheritance, transfer of property and possessions from one generation to another, usually within a family or clan and usually upon the death of the owner. This word often has an implication of a legitimate, historic right to the objects inherited. In some contexts this refers to salvation, an inheritance shared with Jesus Christ, the true heir:– inheritance [14]

2818 **κληρονόμος, *klēronomos***, n. GK: *3101* [→ *2819+3551*]. heir, one who inherits:– heir [8], heirs [7]

2819 **κλῆρος, *klēros***, n. GK: *3102* [→ *2624, 2816, 2817, 2818, 2820, 3490, 3647, 3648, 4345, 4789*]. (casting) lots; share, place, inheritance:– lots [6], inheritance [2], lot [2], part [2], heritage [1]

2820 **κληρόω, *klēroō***, v. GK: *3103* [→ *2819*]. (pass.) to be chosen, appointed:– obtained an inheritance [1]

2821 **κλῆσις, *klēsis***, n. GK: *3104* [→ *2564*]. call, calling; situation, station in life:– calling [10], vocation [1]

2822 **κλητός, *klētos***, a. GK: *3105* [→ *2564*]. called, invited:– called [11]

2823 **κλίβανος, *klibanos***, n. GK: *3106*. (fire of a) furnace, oven:– oven [2]

2824 **κλίμα, *klima***, n. GK: *3107* [→ *2827*]. region:– regions [2], parts [1]

2825 **κλίνη, *klinē***, n. GK: *3109* [→ *2827*]. bed, mat, stretcher:– bed [8], beds [1], tables [1]

2826 **κλινίδιον, *klinidion***, n. GK: *3110* [→ *2827*]. bed, mat, stretcher (smaller and more temporary than a bed found in a home):– couch [2]

2827 **κλίνω, *klinō***, v. GK: *3111* [→ *186, 347, 755, 1578, 2625, 2824, 2825, 2826, 2828, 4346, 4411*]. to bow down, lay down; to be over (late in the day):– lay [2], bowed down [1], bowed [1], far spent (+*2235*) [1], turned to flight [1], wear away [1]

2828 **κλισία, *klisia***, n. GK: *3112* [→ *2827*]. group reclining for a meal:– company [1]

2829 **κλοπή, *klopē***, n. GK: *3113* [→ *2813*]. theft, stealing:– thefts [2]

2830 **κλύδων, *klydōn***, n. GK: *3114* [→ *2148, 2626, 2627, 2831*]. raging waters, waves:– raging [1], wave [1]

2831 **κλυδωνίζομαι, *klydōnizomai***, v. GK: *3115* [→ *2830*]. to be tossed back and forth by waves:– tossed to and fro [1]

2832 **Κλωπᾶς, *Klōpas***, n.pr. GK: *3116*. Clopas:– Cleophas [1]

2833 **κνήθω, *knēthō***, v. GK: *3117* [cf. *1102*]. (pass.) to feel an itch:– itching [1]

2834 **Κνίδος, *Knidos***, n.pr. GK: *3118*. Cnidus, "*age*":– Cnidus [1]

2835 **κοδράντης, *kodrantēs***, n. GK: *3119*. penny, small Roman coin, about one-sixty-fourth of a denarius (a day's wage):– farthing [2]

2836 **κοιλία, *koilia***, n. GK: *3120*. any and all internal organs, translated in context as: belly, stomach, womb, etc.; by extension: the source of feelings and emotions. "The fruit of the womb" means "a child.":– belly [11], womb [11], wombs [1]

2837 **κοιμάω, *koimaō***, v. GK: *3121* [→ *2749*]. (pass.) to fall asleep, sleep; die:– sleep [4], slept [3], asleep [2], fallen asleep [2], fell asleep [2], sleeping [2], dead [1], fell on sleep [1], sleepeth [1]

2838 **κοίμησις, *koimēsis***, n. GK: *3122* [→ *2749*]. (noun) sleep:– taking of rest [1]

2839 **κοινός, *koinos***, a. GK: *3123* [→ *2840, 2841, 2842, 2843, 2844, 4790, 4791*]. common; (ceremonially) unclean, impure, unholy:– common [7], unclean [3], defiled [1], unholy [1]

2840 **κοινόω, *koinoō***, v. GK: *3124* [→ *2839*]. to make (ceremonially) unclean, impure; to defile:– defile [6], defileth [5], call common [2], polluted [1], unclean [1]

2841 **κοινωνέω, *koinōneō***, v. GK: *3125* [→ *2839*]. to share in, participate in:– partakers [2], partaker [2], communicated with [1], communicate [1], distributing [1], made partakers [1]

2842 κοινωνία, ***koinōnia***, n. GK: *3126* [→ *2839*]. fellowship, the close association between persons, emphasizing what is common between them; by extension: participation, sharing, contribution, gift, the outcome of such close relationships:– fellowship [12], communion [4], communicate [1], communication [1], contribution [1], distribution [1]

2843 κοινωνικός, ***koinōnikos***, a. GK: *3127* [→ *2839*]. willing to share, generous:– willing to communicate [1]

2844 κοινωνός, ***koinōnos***, n. GK: *3128* [→ *2839*]. partner, participant, one who joins in with another in some enterprise or activity, in business or ministry:– partakers [4], partner [2], companions [1], fellowship [1], partaker [1], partners [1]

2845 κοίτη, ***koitē***, n. GK: *3130* [→ *2749*]. (marriage) bed; conception; sexual immorality:– bed [2], chambering [1], conceived [1]

2846 κοιτών, ***koitōn***, n. GK: *3131* [→ *2749*]. bedroom; trusted personal servant, chamberlain:– chamberlain (+*1909+3588*) [1]

2847 κόκκινος, ***kokkinos***, a. GK: *3132* [→ *2848*]. scarlet, (bright) red; in some contexts, cloth that is scarlet or (bright) red (Rev 18:12,16):– scarlet [4], scarlet coloured [1], scarlet colour [1]

2848 κόκκος, ***kokkos***, n. GK: *3133* [→ *2847*]. seed, kernel of grain:– grain of seed [5], corn [1], grain [1]

2849 κολάζω, ***kolazō***, v. GK: *3134* [→ *2967*]. to punish:– punished [1], punish [1]

2850 κολακεία, ***kolakeia***, n. GK: *3135*. flattery:– flattering [1]

2851 κόλασις, ***kolasis***, n. GK: *3136* [→ *2967*]. punishment:– punishment [1], torment [1]

2852 κολαφίζω, ***kolaphizō***, v. GK: *3139*. to strike with the fists, beat, torment; (pass.) receive a beating, be brutally treated:– buffeted [3], buffet [2]

2853 κολλάω, ***kollaō***, v. GK: *3140* [→ *4347*]. (mid.) to join, associate with, cling to; (pass.) to be united, stuck to, piled up; to stay near, follow; to be hired out:– joined to [2], join [2], clave [1], cleaveth on [1], cleave [1], join to [1], joined [1], keep company [1]

2854 κολλούριον, ***kollourion***, n. GK: *3141*. eye salve:– eyesalve [1]

2855 κολλυβιστής, ***kollybistēs***, n. GK: *3142*. money exchanger:– moneychangers [2], changers' [1]

2856 κολοβόω, ***koloboō***, v. GK: *3143* [→ *2967*]. to cut short, shorten:– shortened [4]

2857 Κολοσσαί, ***Kolossai***, n.pr. GK: *3138 & 3145* [→ *2858*]. Colosse, "*punishment*":– Colosse [1]

2858 Κολοσσαεύς, ***Kolossaeus***, n.pr.g. GK: *3137 & 3144* [→ *2857*]. Colossian:– Colossians [1]

2859 κόλπος, ***kolpos***, n. GK: *3146*. lap area: side, bosom, chest; bay:– bosom [5], creek [1]

2860 κολυμβάω, ***kolymbaō***, v. GK: *3147* [→ *1579, 2861*]. to swim:– swim [1]

2861 κολυμβήθρα, ***kolymbēthra***, n. GK: *3148* [→ *2860*]. pool:– pool [5]

2862 κολωνία, ***kolōnia***, n. GK: *3149*. Roman colony:– colony [1]

2863 κομάω, ***komaō***, v. GK: *3150* [→ *2864*]. to have long hair:– have long hair [2]

2864 κόμη, ***komē***, n. GK: *3151* [→ *2863*]. (long) hair:– hair [1]

2865 κομίζω, ***komizō***, v. GK: *3152* [→ *2889*]. (act.) to bring; (mid.) to receive (what is due), reward, be repaid:– receive [6], received [3], brought [1], receiving [1]

2866 κομψότερον, ***kompsoteron***, adv.comp. GK: *3153* [→ *2889*]. better:– began to amend (+*2192*) [1]

2867 κονιάω, ***koniaō***, v. GK: *3154* [→ *2868*]. (pass.) to be whitewashed:– whited [2]

2868 κονιορτός, ***koniortos***, n. GK: *3155* [→ *2867+3730*]. dust:– dust [5]

2869 κοπάζω, ***kopazō***, v. GK: *3156* [→ *2875*]. to die down, abate:– ceased [3]

2870 κοπετός, ***kopetos***, n. GK: *3157* [→ *2875*]. mourning, sorrowing, lamentation:– lamentation [1]

2871 κοπή, ***kopē***, n. GK: *3158* [→ *2875*]. defeat, cutting down:– slaughter [1]

2872 κοπιάω, ***kopiaō***, v. GK: *3159* [→ *2875*]. to work, labor, give effort; to become tired, grow weary:– labour [8], laboured [5], bestowed labour [3], laboureth [2], toil [2], labouring [1], toiled [1], wearied [1]

2873 κόπος, ***kopos***, n. GK: *3160* [→ *2875*]. labor, work; bother, trouble, difficulty:– labour [8], labours [5], trouble (+*3930*) [4], troubleth (+*3930*) [1], weariness [1]

2874 κοπρία, ***kopria***, n. GK: *3161 & 3162 & 3163*. manure pile, rubbish pile:– dung (+*906*) [1], dunghill [1]

2875 κόπτω, ***koptō***, v. GK: *3164* [→ *348, 609, 677, 695, 1464, 1465, 1581, 2123, 2629, 2869, 2870, 2871, 2872, 2873, 2974, 4297, 4298, 4348, 4349, 4350*]. to cut; (mid.) to mourn, beat one's breast:– bewailed [2], cut down [2], lamented [1], lament [1], mourn [1], wail [1]

2876 κόραξ, ***korax***, n. GK: *3165*. raven, crow:– ravens [1]

2877 κοράσιον, ***korasion***, n. GK: *3166* [→ *2751*]. (little) girl:– damsel [6], maid [2]

2878 κορβᾶν, ***korban***; or κορβανᾶς, ***korbanas***, n. GK: *3167 & 3168*. Corban, a gift dedicated to God, temple treasury:– Corban [1], treasury [1]

2879 Κόρε, ***Kore***, n.pr. GK: *3169*. Korah, "*shaven, bald*":– Core [1]

2880 κορέννυμι, ***korennymi***, v. GK: *3170*. (pass.) to be filled to the full, have enough:– eaten enough (+*5160*) [1], full [1]

2881 Κορίνθιος, ***Korinthios***, n.pr.g. GK: *3171* [→ *2882*]. Corinthian:– Corinthians [4]

2882 Κόρινθος, ***Korinthos***, n.pr. GK: *3172* [→ *2881*]. Corinth, "*decoration*":– Corinth [6], Corinthus [1]

2883 Κορνήλιος, ***Kornēlios***, n.pr. GK: *3173*. Cornelius, "*of a horn*":– Cornelius [10]

2884 κόρος, ***koros***, n. GK: *3174*. cor (dry measure between ten and twelve bushels):– measures [1]

2885 κοσμέω, ***kosmeō***, v. GK: *3175* [→ *2889*]. to make beautiful, decorate, dress; trim (a lamp); (pass.) to put in order; be adorned, decorated, beautifully dressed:– adorned [3], garnished [3], adorn [2], garnish [1], trimmed [1]

2886 κοσμικός, ***kosmikos***, a. GK: *3176* [→ *2889*]. earthly, worldly:– worldly [2]

2887 κόσμιος, ***kosmios***, a. GK: *3177 & 3178* [→ *2889*]. respectable, honorable:– good behaviour [1], modest [1]

2888 κοσμοκράτωρ, ***kosmokratōr***, n. GK: *3179* [→ *2889+2904*]. (pl.) powers of the world:– rulers [1]

2889 κόσμος, ***kosmos***, n. GK: *3180* [→ *1101, 1580, 2865, 2866, 2885, 2886, 2887, 2888, 4792*]. world: earth, world system, whole universe; adornment. In some contexts, the world is simply the place where people live, in other contexts (especially in John), the world is a system opposed to God:– world [185], adorning [1], world's [1]

2890 Κούαρτος, ***Kouartos***, n.pr. GK: *3181*. Quartus, "*fourth [born]*":– Quartus [1]

2891 κοῦμι, ***koumi***, l.[v.]. GK: *3182 & 3183*. koumi (Aramaic: stand up!):– cumi [1]

2892 κουστωδία, ***koustōdia***, n. GK: *3184*. guard:– watch [3]

2893 κουφίζω, ***kouphizō***, v. GK: *3185*. to lighten, make lighter:– lightened [1]

2894 κόφινος, ***kophinos***, n. GK: *3186*. basket of various sizes and considered typical of the Jews:– baskets [6]

2895 κράβαττος, ***krabbatos***, n. GK: *3187 & 3188*. bed, (sleeping) mat:– bed [10], beds [1], couches [1]

2896 κράζω, ***krazō***, v. GK: *3189* [→ *349, 2905, 2906*]. call out, cry out, shout, exclaim:– cried [30], cried out [13], crying [6], crieth [3], crying out [3], cry out [2], crieth out [1], cry [1], out [1]

2897 κραιπάλη, ***kraipalē***, n. GK: *3190*. dissipation:– surfeiting [1]

2898 κρανίον, ***kranion***, n. GK: *3191* [→ *603*]. skull:– skull [3], Calvary [1]

2899 κράσπεδον, ***kraspedon***, n. GK: *3192*. edge, border, hem; tassel:– border [2], hem [2], borders [1]

2900 κραταιός, ***krataios***, a. GK: *3193* [→ *2904*]. mighty, powerful:– mighty [1]

2901 κραταιόω, ***krataioō***, v. GK: *3194* [→ *2904*]. (pass.) to be strong, become strong:– waxed strong [2], strengthened [1], strong [1]

2902 κρατέω, ***krateō***, v. GK: *3195* [→ *2904*]. to arrest, seize into custody; to take, grab, hold onto, obtain; (pass.) to be kept from, held:– took [10], hold [5], hold fast [3], holding [3], laid hold on [3], lay hold on [3], take [3], held [2], holden [2], laid hold [2], fast [1], holdest fast [1], holdeth [1], kept [1], laid hands on [1], laid hold upon [1], lay hands on [1], lay hold upon [1], obtained [1], retained [1], retain [1]

2903 κράτιστος, ***kratistos***, a. GK: *3196* [→ *2904*]. most excellent, "your Excellency":– most excellent [2], most noble [2]

2904 κράτος, ***kratos***, n. GK: *3197* [→ *192, 193, 1466, 1467, 1468, 2888, 2900, 2901,*

2902, 2903, 2908, 2909, 3841, 4031; cf. 2594]. power, strength:– power [5], dominion [4], mightily (*+2596*) [1], mighty [1], strength [1]

***2905* κραυγάζω, *kraugazō*,** v. GK: *3198* [→ *2896*]. to shout, cry out:– cried out [3], cried [3], cry [1]

***2906* κραυγή, *kraugē*,** n. GK: *3199* [→ *2896*]. crying out, shouting, verbal brawling:– cry [3], crying [2], clamour [1]

***2907* κρέας, *kreas*,** n. GK: *3200*. meat:– flesh [2]

***2908* κρεῖσσον, *krēisson*,** a.neut. of a form of *2909*. GK: *3201* [→ *2904*]. better, superior, greater:– better [1]

***2909* κρείττων, *kreittōn*,** a. GK: *3202* [→ *2904*]. better, superior, greater:– better [17], best [1], better than [1]

***2910* κρεμάννυμι, *kremannymi*,** v. GK: *3203* [→ *1582, 2630, 2911*]. to hang on, hang upon:– hanged [4], hang [2], hangeth [1]

***2911* κρημνός, *krēmnos*,** n. GK: *3204* [→ *2910*]. steep bank, cliff:– steep place [3]

***2912* Κρής, *Krēs*,** n.pr.g. GK: *3205* [→ *2914*]. Cretan:– Cretians [2], Cretes [1]

***2913* Κρήσκης, *Krēskēs*,** n.pr. GK: *3206*. Crescens, "*increasing*":– Crescens [1]

***2914* Κρήτη, *Krētē*,** n.pr. GK: *3207* [→ *2912*]. Crete:– Crete [5]

***2915* κριθή, *krithē*,** n. GK: *3208* [→ *2916*]. barley; barley flour was used in the preparation of cheaper kinds of bread:– barley [1]

***2916* κρίθινος, *krithinos*,** a. GK: *3209* [→ *2915*]. made of barley (flour):– barley [2]

***2917* κρίμα, *krima*,** n. GK: *3210* [→ *2919*]. judgment, condemnation; sentence, punishment:– judgment [12], damnation [7], condemnation [5], avenged (*+2919*) [1], condemned [1], go to law (*+2192*) [1], judgments [1]

***2918* κρίνον, *krinon*,** n. GK: *3211*. lily:– lilies [2]

***2919* κρίνω, *krinō*,** v. GK: *3212* [→ *87, 178, 350, 351, 470, 505, 610, 611, 612, 799, 843, 1252, 1253, 1341, 1469, 1506, 1948, 2631, 2632, 2633, 2917, 2920, 2922, 2923, 2924, 4299, 4793, 4942, 5271, 5272, 5273; cf. 1506*]. to decide, consider, as preferring one thing over another or determining the correctness of a matter; by extension: to judge, pass judgment on, condemn in a legal sense:– judge [45], judged [26], judgeth [9], determined [7], judgest [6], called in question [2], condemned [2], esteemeth [2], judging [2], avenged (*+2917*) [1], concluded [1], condemneth [1], condemning [1], condemn [1], damned [1], decreed [1], go to law [1], goeth to law [1], ordained [1], sentence [1], sue at the law [1], thought [1]

***2920* κρίσις, *krisis*,** n. GK: *3213* [→ *2919*]. judgment (human or divine), justice, the concept of determining the correctness of a matter; negatively, punishment, condemnation:– judgment [39], condemnation [3], damnation [3], accusation [2], judgments [2]

***2921* Κρίσπος, *Krispos*,** n.pr. GK: *3214*. Crispus, "*curled*":– Crispus [2]

***2922* κριτήριον, *kritērion*,** n. GK: *3215* [→ *2919*]. court of law; legal dispute, lawsuit:– judge [1], judgment seats [1], judgments [1]

***2923* κριτής, *kritēs*,** n. GK: *3216* [→ *2919*]. judge:– judge [13], judges [4]

***2924* κριτικός, *kritikos*,** a. GK: *3217* [→ *2919*]. able to discern or judge:– discerner [1]

***2925* κρούω, *krouō*,** v. GK: *3218*. to knock (on a gate or door):– knock [4], knocketh [3], knocked [1], knocking [1]

***2926* κρύπτη, *kryptē*,** n. GK: *3219* [→ *2928*]. hidden place:– *untranslated* [1]

***2927* κρυπτός, *kryptos*,** a. GK: *3220 & 3224 & 3226* [→ *2928*]. hidden, unseen, secret:– secret [10], hidden [3], hid [3], secrets [2], inwardly (*+1722+3588*) [1], secret place [1]

***2928* κρύπτω, *kryptō*,** v. GK: *3221* [→ *613, 614, 1470, 2926, 2927, 2931, 4032*]. to hide:– hid [10], hide [2], hidden [1], hideth [1], kept secret [1], secretly [1]

***2929* κρυσταλλίζω, *krystallizō*,** v. GK: *3222* [→ *2930*]. to be clear as crystal:– clear as crystal [1]

***2930* κρύσταλλος, *krystallos*,** n. GK: *3223* [→ *2929*]. rock crystal; some translate "ice":– crystal [2]

***2931* κρυφῇ, *kryphē*,** adv. GK: *3225* [→ *2928*]. in secret:– secret [1]

***2932* κτάομαι, *ktaomai*,** v. GK: *3227* [→ *2933, 2934, 2935*]. to get, gain, buy; take along; to control:– possess [3], purchased [2], obtained [1], provide [1]

***2933* κτῆμα, *ktēma*,** n. GK: *3228* [→ *2932*]. wealth, possessions; piece of property, field:– possessions [3], possession [1]

***2934* κτῆνος, *ktēnos*,** n. GK: *3229* [→ *2932*]. (domestic) animal: donkey, horse, cattle:– beasts [3], beast [1]

***2935* κτήτωρ, *ktētōr*,** n. GK: *3230* [→ *2932*]. (land) owner:– possessors [1]

***2936* κτίζω, *ktizō*,** v. GK: *3231* [→ *2937, 2938, 2939*]. to create; (ptcp.) Creator:– created [12], creator [1], made [1], make [1]

***2937* κτίσις, *ktisis*,** n. GK: *3232* [→ *2936*]. creation, created thing, creature; governmental institution:– creature [11], creation [6], building [1], ordinance [1]

***2938* κτίσμα, *ktisma*,** n. GK: *3233* [→ *2936*]. creature, created thing:– creatures [2], creature [2]

***2939* κτίστης, *ktistēs*,** n. GK: *3234* [→ *2936*]. Creator:– creator [1]

***2940* κυβεία, *kybeia*,** n. GK: *3235*. cunning, craftiness, trickery:– sleight [1]

***2941* κυβέρνησις, *kybernēsis*,** n. GK: *3236* [→ *2942*]. administration; derived from a Greek verb meaning "to steer a ship, to guide," not found in the NT:– governments [1]

***2942* κυβερνήτης, *kybernētēs*,** n. GK: *3237* [→ *2941*]. sea captain, pilot:– master [1], shipmaster [1]

***2943* κυκλόθεν, *kyklothen*,** adv. GK: *3239* [→ *2945*]. (all) around; from all sides:– round about [3], about [1]

κυκλός, *kuklos*. See ***2945***.

***2944* κυκλόω, *kykloō*,** v. GK: *3238 & 3240* [→ *2945*]. to surround: gather around, march around:– compassed about [2], came round about [1], compassed [1], stood round about [1]

***2945* κύκλῳ, *kyklō*,** adv. GK: *3241* [→ *2943, 2944, 4033*]. all around, in a circle, surrounding:– round about [7]

***2946* κύλισμα, *kylisma*,** n. GK: *3242 & 3243* [→ *2947*]. wallowing, rolling:– wallowing [1]

***2947* κυλίω, *kyliō*,** v. GK: *3244* [→ *617, 2946, 4351*]. (mid.) to roll around:– wallowed [1]

***2948* κυλλός, *kyllos*,** a. GK: *3245*. crippled, maimed:– maimed [4]

***2949* κῦμα, *kyma*,** n. GK: *3246* [→ *616, 1471*]. waves, surf:– waves [5]

***2950* κύμβαλον, *kymbalon*,** n. GK: *3247*. cymbal:– cymbal [1]

***2951* κύμινον, *kyminon*,** n. GK: *3248*. cummin:– cummin [1]

***2952* κυνάριον, *kynarion*,** n. GK: *3249* [→ *2965*]. (little or domesticated) dog:– dogs [4]

***2953* Κύπριος, *Kyprios*,** n.pr.g. GK: *3250* [→ *2954*]. from Cyprus:– Cyprus [3]

***2954* Κύπρος, *Kypros*,** n.pr. GK: *3251* [→ *2953*]. Cyprus, "*copper*":– Cyprus [5]

***2955* κύπτω, *kyptō*,** v. GK: *3252* [→ *352, 3879, 4794*]. to stoop down, bend down:– stooped [2], stoop down [1]

***2956* Κυρηναῖος, *Kyrēnaios*,** n.pr.g. GK: *3254* [→ *2957*]. from Cyrene:– Cyrenian [2], of Cyrene [2], Cyrene [1], Cyrenians [1]

***2957* Κυρήνη, *Kyrēnē*,** n.pr. GK: *3255* [→ *2956*]. Cyrene, "*wall*":– Cyrene [1]

***2958* Κυρήνιος, *Kyrēnios*,** n.pr. GK: *3256 & 3260*. Quirinius:– Cyrenius [1]

***2959* κυρία, *kyria*,** n. GK: *3257* [→ *2962*]. lady (female "lord"):– lady [2]

***2960* κυριακός, *kyriakos*,** a. GK: *3258* [→ *2962*]. pertaining to the Lord, the Lord's:– Lord's [2]

***2961* κυριεύω, *kyrieuō*,** v. GK: *3259* [→ *2962*]. to lord over, be master of, have authority over, one who rules or exercises authority; note in some contexts there is an implication that the authority exercised is harsh:– Lord/lord [1], dominion over [1], exercise lordship over [1], hath dominion over [1], have dominion over [1], lords [1], over [1]

***2962* κύριος, *kyrios*,** n. GK: *3261* [→ *2634, 2959, 2960, 2961, 2963; cf. 2964*]. lord, master. This can be a title of address to a person of higher status, "lord, sir"; a master of property or slaves; or a NT translation of the Hebrew 151 "Lord" or 3378 "LORD," that is "Yahweh," the proper name of God in the OT:– Lord/lord [703], Lord's/lord's [15], sir [11], masters [8], master [4], lords [3], God [1], masters' [1], owners [1], sirs [1]

***2963* κυριότης, *kyriotēs*,** n. GK: *3262* [→ *2962*]. authority, dominion, power, lordship:– dominion [2], dominions [1], government [1]

***2964* κυρόω, *kyroō*,** v. GK: *3263* [→ *208, 4300; cf. 2962*]. to reaffirm; to establish a covenant, ratify, validate:– confirmed [1], confirm [1]

***2965* κύων, *kyōn*,** n. GK: *3264* [→ *2952*]. dog:– dogs [4], dog [1]

***2966* κῶλον, *kōlon*,** n. GK: *3265*. dead body, corpse:– carcases [1]

***2967* κωλύω, *kōlyō*,** v. GK: *3266* [→ *209, 1254, 2849, 2851, 2856; cf. 1422*]. to hinder, stop, restrain, forbid; oppress; (pass.)

to be prevented, kept from:– forbid [9], forbad [3], forbidding [3], forbidden [1], forbiddeth [1], hindered [1], hinder [1], kept from [1], let [1], not suffered [1], withstand [1]

2968 **κώμη, *kōmē***, n. GK: *3267* [→ *2969, 2970*]. village, town:– village [10], town [8], villages [7], towns [3]

2969 **κωμόπολις, *kōmopolis***, n. GK: *3268* [→ *2968+4172*]. village, market town:– towns [1]

2970 **κῶμος, *kōmos***, n. GK: *3269* [→ *2968*]. orgy, revelry, carousing:– revellings [2], rioting [1]

2971 **κώνωψ, *kōnōps***, n. GK: *3270*. gnat, mosquito:– gnat [1]

2972 **Κῶς, *Kōs***, n.pr. GK: *3271*. Cos, "*summit*":– Cos [1]

2973 **Κωσάμ, *Kōsam***, n.pr. GK: *3272*. Cosam, "*diviner*":– Cosam [1]

2974 **κωφός, *kōphos***, a. GK: *3273* [→ *2875*]. unable to talk or speak, mute; deaf:– dumb [8], deaf [5], speechless [1]

2975 **λαγχάνω, *lanchanō***, v. GK: *3275*. to choose by lot, decide by lot; receive (by lot or divine will):– obtained [2], cast lots [1], lot [1]

2976 **Λάζαρος, *Lazaros***, n.pr. GK: *3276*. Lazarus, "*one whom God helps*":– Lazarus [15]

2977 **λάθρα, *lathra***, adv. GK: *3277* [→ *2990*]. secretly, quietly:– privily [3], secretly [1]

2978 **λαῖλαψ, *lailaps***, n. GK: *3278*. storm, hurricane, whirlwind:– storm [2], tempest [1]

2979 **λακτίζω, *laktizō***, v. GK: *3280*. to kick:– kick [2]

2980 **λαλέω, *laleō***, v. GK: *3281* [→ *215, 216, 412, 1255, 1583, 2635, 2636, 2637, 2981, 3424, 4354, 4814*]. to speak, talk:– speak [103], spake [72], spoken [33], speaketh [23], speaking [11], told [10], talked [8], said [7], say [6], preached [4], speakest [4], uttered [3], saith [2], tell [2], preaching [1], preach [1], talkest [1], talketh [1], talking [1], talk [1], utter [1]

2981 **λαλιά, *lalia***, n. GK: *3282* [→ *2980*]. speech, a way of speaking, language:– speech [3], saying [1]

2982 **λαμά, *lama***; or **λεμά, *lema***, l.[pp.+p.inter.]. GK: *3283 & 3316*. lama (Hebrew: why?):– lama [2]

2983 **λαμβάνω, *lambanō***, v. GK: *3284* [→ *353, 354, 423, 482, 484, 618, 678, 1187, 1949, 2124, 2125, 2126, 2638, 3028, 3335, 3336, 3880, 4301, 4355, 4356, 4380, 4381, 4382, 4815, 4838, 4843, 4878, 5274*]. to take, receive; (pass.) to be received, selected:– receive [61], received [57], took [55], take [32], receiveth [15], taken [12], taketh [4], taking [4], caught [3], had [2], obtain [2], took up [2], acceptest [1], accepteth [1], amazed (+*1611*) [1], attained [1], began [1], brought [1], call [1], came into room (+*1240*) [1], came [1], do [1], forgotten (+*3024*) [1], have [1], held [1], receiving [1]

2984 **Λάμεχ, *Lamech***, n.pr. GK: *3285*. Lamech:– Lamech [1]

λαμμᾶ, *lamma*. See ***2982***.

2985 **λαμπάς, *lampas***, n. GK: *3286* [→ *2989*]. lamp, lantern, torch:– lamps [6], lamp [1], lights [1], torches [1]

2986 **λαμπρός, *lampros***, a. GK: *3287* [→ *2989*]. bright, shining, splendorous, elegant:– bright [2], goodly [2], white [2], clear [1], gay [1], gorgeous [1]

2987 **λαμπρότης, *lamprotēs***, n. GK: *3288* [→ *2989*]. brightness:– brightness [1]

2988 **λαμπρῶς, *lamprōs***, adv. GK: *3289* [→ *2989*]. in luxury, splendidly:– sumptuously [1]

2989 **λάμπω, *lampō***, v. GK: *3290* [→ *1584, 2985, 2986, 2987, 2988, 4034*]. to give light, shine:– shine [3], shined [2], giveth light [1], shineth [1]

2990 **λανθάνω, *lanthanō***, v. GK: *3291* [→ *225, 226, 227, 228, 230, 1585, 1950, 1953, 2977, 3024*]. to keep secret, escape notice, be hidden:– hid [2], ignorant [2], hidden [1], unawares [1]

2991 **λαξευτός, *laxeutos***, a. GK: *3292*. cut in rock:– hewn in stone [1]

2992 **λαός, *laos***, n. GK: *3295* [→ *745, 2993, 2994, 3008, 3009, 3010, 3011, 3531, 3532*]. people, crowd; often denotes the people of God (either Israel or, by extension, the Christian church):– people [139], people's [2], peoples [2]

2993 **Λαοδίκεια, *Laodikeia***, n.pr. GK: *3293* [→ *2992+1349*]. Laodicea:– Laodicea [6]

2994 **Λαοδικεύς, *Laodikeus***, n.pr.g. GK: *3294* [→ *2992+1349*]. Laodicean:– Laodiceans [2]

2995 **λάρυγξ, *larynx***, n. GK: *3296*. throat:– throat [1]

2996 **Λασαία, *Lasaia***, n.pr. GK: *3297 & 3298*. Lasea:– Lasea [1]

2997 **λάσκω, *laskō***, v. GK: *3279 & 3299*. to burst open:– burst asunder [1]

2998 **λατομέω, *latomeō***, v. GK: *3300*. to cut, hew (rock):– hewn out [1], hewn [1]

2999 **λατρεία, *latreia***, n. GK: *3301* [→ *1496, 1495, 3000*]. worship, ministry, service (to God):– service [4], divine service [1]

3000 **λατρεύω, *latreuō***, v. GK: *3302* [→ *2999*]. to serve, minister (in religious duties):– serve [13], worship [3], served [2], service [1], serving [1], worshippers [1]

3001 **λάχανον, *lachanon***, n. GK: *3303*. plant, herb, vegetable:– herbs [4]

3002 **Λεββαῖος, *Lebbaios***, n.pr. GK: *3304* [cf. *2280*]. Lebbaeus, "*[one near to] my heart*":– Lebbeus [1]

3003 **λεγιών, *legiōn***, n. GK: *3305*. legion, technically an army unit of 6,000 with 6,000 support troops. Twice in the NT it is the proper name of a collective of demons (Mk 5:9; Lk 8:30):– legion [3], legions [1]

3004 **λέγω, *legō***, v. GK: *3306* [→ *35, 148, 249, 356, 357, 379, 471, 483, 485, 550, 626, 627, 945, 1075, 1076, 1256, 1258, 1260, 1261, 1351, 1586, 1588, 1589, 1677, 1757, 1951, 2036, 2046, 2127, 2128, 2129, 2312, 2551, 2639, 3048, 3049, 3050, 3051, 3052, 3053, 3054, 3055, 3056, 3150, 3151, 3473, 3670, 3881, 3884, 4086, 4180, 4277, 4280, 4302, 4691, 4758, 4816, 4817, 4883, 4899, 5378, 5542, 5573; cf. 3670*]. say, said, the most general term for speaking in the NT, translated contextually with more specific words such as say, tell; ask, answer:– said [995], saying [403], say [398], saith [298], tell [59], spake [50], spoken [45], called [39], speak [38], sayest [21], told [18], commanded [6], speaketh [6], calleth [4], call [4], bade [3], bid [3], callest [3], command [3], named [2], speakest [2], answer [1], asked [1], biddeth [1], boasting [1], bring word [1], describeth [1], giving out [1], grant [1], made [1], put forth [1], saidst [1], sayings [1], seen [1], shew [1], speaking [1], telleth [1], uttered [1]

3005 **λεῖμμα, *leimma***, n. GK: *3307* [→ *3007*]. remnant:– remnant [1]

3006 **λεῖος, *leios***, a. GK: *3308*. smooth, level:– smooth [1]

3007 **λείπω, *leipō***, v. GK: *3309* [→ *88, 89, 413, 620, 1257, 1459, 1587, 1952, 1954, 2640, 2641, 2645, 3005, 3062, 3063, 3064, 4035, 5275, 5277*]. to lack, fall short:– wanting [3], destitute [1], lackest [1], lack [1]

3008 **λειτουργέω, *leitourgeō***, v. GK: *3310* [→ *2992+2041*]. to perform religious duties; serve:– ministered [1], ministering [1], minister [1]

3009 **λειτουργία, *leitourgia***, n. GK: *3311* [→ *2992+2041*]. religious service, ceremony; service, ministry, help:– service [3], ministry [2], ministration [1]

3010 **λειτουργικός, *leitourgikos***, a. GK: *3312* [→ *2992+2041*]. ministering, engaged in holy service:– ministering [1]

3011 **λειτουργός, *leitourgos***, n. GK: *3313* [→ *2992+2041*]. servant, minister, one who cares for (another), often with a focus on a specific task or duty, which can be practical or spiritual:– ministers [2], minister [2], ministered [1]

3012 **λέντιον, *lention***, n. GK: *3317*. towel, likely made of linen:– towel [2]

3013 **λεπίς, *lepis***, n. GK: *3318* [→ *3014, 3015, 3016*]. scale, flake:– scales [1]

3014 **λέπρα, *lepra***, n. GK: *3319* [→ *3013*]. leprosy:– leprosy [4]

3015 **λεπρός, *lepros***, a. GK: *3320* [→ *3013*]. leprous; (n.) leper:– lepers [5], leper [4]

3016 **λεπτός, *leptos***, a. GK: *3321* [→ *3013*]. very small copper coin, worth about 1/128th of a denarius (a day's wage):– mites [2], mite [1]

3017 **Λευί, *Leui***, n.pr. GK: *3322* [→ *3018, 3019, 3020*]. Levi, "[perhaps] *wild cow* or *person pledged for a debt or vow*":– Levi [5]

3018 **Λευίς, *Leuis***, n.pr. GK: *3323* [→ *3017*]. Levi, "[perhaps] *wild cow* or *person pledged for a debt or vow*":– Levi [3]

3019 **Λευίτης, *Leuitēs***, n.pr.g. GK: *3324* [→ *3017*]. Levite:– Levite [2], Levites [1]

3020 **Λευιτικός, *Leuitikos***, a.pr.g. GK: *3325* [→ *3017*]. Levitical:– Levitical [1]

3021 **λευκαίνω, *leukainō***, v. GK: *3326* [→ *3022*]. to bleach, whiten:– made white [1], white [1]

3022 **λευκός, *leukos***, a. GK: *3328* [→ *3021*]. white; bright, gleaming:– white [25]

3023 **λέων, *leōn***, n. GK: *3329*. lion:– lion [6], lions [3]

3024 **λήθη, *lēthē***, n. GK: *3330* [→ *2990*]. forgetfulness:– forgotten (+*2983*) [1]

3025 **ληνός, *lēnos***, n. GK: *3332* [→ *5276*]. winepress:– winepress [4], winepress (+*3631*) [1]

3026 **λῆρος, *lēros***, n. GK: *3333*. nonsense, idle talk:– idle tales [1]

3027 **λῃστής, *lēstēs***, n. GK: *3334*. robber, bandit; rebel, revolutionary; this word is derived from the Greek verb, "to practice robbery or piracy," not found in the NT:– thieves [8], thief [3], robbers [2], robber [2]

3028 **λῆμψις, *lēmpsis***, n. GK: *3331 & 3335* [→ *2983*]. receiving:– receiving [1]

3029 **λίαν, *lian***, adv. GK: *3336*. very much, greatly, completely:– exceeding [5], greatly [4], chiefest [2], great while [1], sore [1], very [1]

3030 **λίβανος, *libanos***, n. GK: *3337* [→ *3031*]. frankincense, incense, an aromatic resinous gum:– frankincense [2]

3031 **λιβανωτός, *libanōtos***, n. GK: *3338* [→ *3030*]. censer (bowl for burning incense):– censer [2]

3032 **Λιβερτῖνος, *Libertinos***, n.pr. GK: *3339*. Freedman, "*Freedman*":– Libertines [1]

3033 **Λιβύη, *Libyē***, n.pr. GK: *3340*. Libya:– Libya [1]

3034 **λιθάζω, *lithazō***, v. GK: *3342* [→ *3037*]. to stone:– stoned [4], stone [4]

3035 **λίθινος, *lithinos***, a. GK: *3343* [→ *3037*]. made of stone:– stone [2], of stone [1]

3036 **λιθοβολέω, *lithoboleō***, v. GK: *3344* [→ *3037+906*]. to throw stones:– stoned [5], stonest [2], cast stones [1], stone [1]

3037 **λίθος, *lithos***, n. GK: *3345* [→ *2642, 3034, 3035, 3036, 3038, 5555*]. stone, boulder; this can refer to stone as a material or substance, and to a stone as a piece of rock. A "precious stone" is a "gem.":– stone [37], stones [15], another[s] [4], stumblingstone (+*4348*) [2], millstone (+*3457*) [1], stone's [1]

3038 **λιθόστρωτος, *lithostrōtos***, a. GK: *3346* [→ *3037+4766*]. (n.) stone pavement; translated in the NIV as a place name:– pavement [1]

3039 **λικμάω, *likmaō***, v. GK: *3347*. to crush:– grind to powder [2]

3040 **λιμήν, *limēn***, n. GK: *3348* [→ *2568, 3041*]. harbor:– haven [2]

3041 **λίμνη, *limnē***, n. GK: *3349* [→ *3040*]. lake:– lake [10]

3042 **λιμός, *limos***, n. GK: *3350*. hunger, famine, starvation:– famine [4], famines [3], hunger [3], dearth [2]

3043 **λίνον, *linon***, n. GK: *3351*. linen (garment); wick of a lamp:– flax [1], linen [1]

3044 **Λίνος, *Linos***, n.pr. GK: *3352*. Linus:– Linus [1]

3045 **λιπαρός, *liparos***, a. GK: *3353*. costly, rich; (n.) riches:– dainty [1]

3046 **λίτρα, *litra***, n. GK: *3354*. (Roman) pound (about 12 oz. or 327 gr.):– pound [2]

3047 **λίψ, *lips***, n. GK: *3355*. southwest:– south west [1]

3048 **λογεία, *logeia***, n. GK: *3356* [→ *3004*]. collection:– collection [1], gatherings [1]

3049 **λογίζομαι, *logizomai***, v. GK: *3357* [→ *3004*]. to credit, count, reckon; regard, think, consider:– think [7], imputed [5], counted [4], reckoned [4], accounted [2], reckon [2], suppose [2], accounting [1], account [1], conclude [1], count [1], despised (+*1519+3762*) [1], esteemeth [1], imputeth [1], impute [1], imputing [1], laid to charge [1], numbered [1], reasoned [1], thinkest [1], thinketh [1], thought [1]

3050 **λογικός, *logikos***, a. GK: *3358* [→ *3004*]. spiritual, logical:– reasonable [1], word [1]

3051 **λόγιον, *logion***, n. GK: *3359* [→ *3004*]. (pl.) words, sayings, oracles:– oracles [4]

3052 **λόγιος, *logios***, a. GK: *3360* [→ *3004*]. learned, eloquent:– eloquent [1]

3053 **λογισμός, *logismos***, n. GK: *3361* [→ *3004*]. thought; argument, reasoning:– imaginations [1], thoughts [1]

3054 **λογομαχέω, *logomacheō***, v. GK: *3362* [→ *3004+3163*]. to quarrel about words:– strive about words [1]

3055 **λογομαχία, *logomachia***, n. GK: *3363* [→ *3004+3163*]. quarrel about words:– strifes of words [1]

3056 **λόγος, *logos***, n. GK: *3364* [→ *3004*]. word, spoken or written, often with a focus on the content of a communication (note the many contextual translations in NIV); matter, thing. "The Word" is a title of Christ (Jn 1:1), emphasizing his own deity and communication of who God is and what he is like:– word [175], words [48], saying [34], sayings [16], account [8], speech [8], matter [4], utterance [4], communication [2], things [2], thing [2], work [2], as concerning (+*1519*) [1], cause [1], communications [1], doctrine [1], fame [1], given exhortation (+*3870*) [1], have to do [1], intent [1], mouth [1], none (+*3762*) [1], preaching [1], question [1], reason (+*2596*) [1], reason [1], reckoneth (+*4868*) [1], rumour [1], say [1], shew [1], speaker [1], talk [1], tidings [1], treatise [1], word spoken [1], word's [1]

3057 **λόγχη, *lonchē***, n. GK: *3365*. spear, lance:– spear [1]

3058 **λοιδορέω, *loidoreō***, v. GK: *3366* [→ *3060*]. to insult, curse:– reviled [3], revilest [1]

3059 **λοιδορία, *loidoria***, n. GK: *3367* [→ *3060*]. insult, slander, verbal abuse:– railing [2], speak reproachfully [1]

3060 **λοίδορος, *loidoros***, n. GK: *3368* [→ *486, 3058, 3059*]. slanderer, verbal abuser:– railer [1], revilers [1]

3061 **λοιμός, *loimos***, n.&a. GK: *3369*. pestilence; troublemaker, public menace:– pestilences [2], pestilent [1]

3062 **λοιπός, *loipos***, a. GK: *3370* [→ *3063*]. remaining, left over, the rest; in some contexts a marker for a conclusion, "finally," or an adverb of time, "from now on," or "henceforth":– other [17], rest [12], others [6], finally (+*3588*) [4], remnant [4], now (+*3588*) [2], besides [1], finally [1], from henceforth (+*3588*) [1], furthermore [1], henceforth (+*3588*) [1], henceforth [1], moreover (+*1161+3739*) [1], remaineth (+*1510+3588*) [1], remain [1], residue [1], then [1]

3063 **λοιπόν, *loipon***, a.neut.s. of *3062*. GK: *3370* [→ *3007, 3062, 3064*]. remaining, left over, the rest; see *3062*:–

3064 **λοιποῦ, *loipou***, a.gen.s. of *3062*. GK: *3370* [→ *3063*]. remaining, left over, the rest; see *3062*:–

3065 **Λουκᾶς, *Loukas***, n.pr. GK: *3371* [→ *3066*]. Luke:– Lucas [2], Luke [2]

3066 **Λούκιος, *Loukios***, n.pr. GK: *3372* [→ *3065*]. Lucius:– Lucius [2]

3067 **λουτρόν, *loutron***, n. GK: *3373* [→ *3068*]. washing, bath:– washing [2]

3068 **λούω, *louō***, v. GK: *3374* [→ *628, 3067*]. to wash, have a bath:– washed [6]

3069 **Λύδδα, *Lydda***, n.pr. GK: *3375*. Lydda:– Lydda [3]

3070 **Λυδία, *Lydia***, n.pr. GK: *3376*. Lydia:– Lydia [2]

3071 **Λυκαονία, *Lykaonia***, n.pr. GK: *3377* [→ *3072*]. Lycaonia:– Lycaonia [1]

3072 **Λυκαονιστί, *Lykaonisti***, adv.pr. GK: *3378* [→ *3071*]. in (the) Lycaonian (language):– in the speech of Lycaonia [1]

3073 **Λυκία, *Lykia***, n.pr. GK: *3379*. Lycia:– Lycia [1]

3074 **λύκος, *lykos***, n. GK: *3380*. wolf:– wolves [4], wolf [2]

3075 **λυμαίνω, *lymainō***, v. GK: *3381*. to destroy, damage, ruin:– made havock [1]

3076 **λυπέω, *lypeō***, v. GK: *3382* [→ *3077*]. (act.) to cause sorrow, grief; (pass.) to be sorrowful, sad, distressed:– sorrowful [6], grieved [5], made sorry [5], sorry [3], sorrowed [2], caused grief [1], grieve [1], heaviness [1], make sorry [1], sorrow [1]

3077 **λύπη, *lypē***, n. GK: *3383* [→ *253, 3076, 4036, 4818*]. sorrow, grief, pain:– sorrow [11], heaviness [2], grief [1], grievous [1], grudgingly (+*1537*) [1]

3078 **Λυσανίας, *Lysanias***, n.pr. GK: *3384*. Lysanias:– Lysanias [1]

3079 **Λυσίας, *Lysias***, n.pr. GK: *3385*. Lysias:– Lysias [3]

3080 **λύσις, *lysis***, n. GK: *3386* [→ *3089*]. divorce:– loosed [1]

3081 **λυσιτελέω, *lysiteleō***, v. GK: *3387* [→ *3089+5056*]. to be advantageous, (imper. form) it is better:– better [1]

3082 **Λύστρα, *Lystra***, n.pr. GK: *3388*. Lystra:– Lystra [6]

3083 **λύτρον, *lytron***, n. GK: *3389* [→ *3089*]. ransom, the price of release, thus making redemption possible:– ransom [2]

3084 **λυτρόω, *lytroō***, v. GK: *3390* [→ *3089*]. to redeem, free a slave by paying a ransom; from the base meaning of slave redemption in the marketplace comes the figure of sinners redeemed by God from slavery to sin and death:– redeemed [2], redeem [1]

3085 **λύτρωσις, *lytrōsis***, n. GK: *3391* [→ *3089*]. redemption, ransoming, releasing:– redemption [2], redeemed (+*4160*) [1]

3086 **λυτρωτής, *lytrōtēs***, n. GK: *3392* [→ *3089*]. deliverer, redeemer:– deliverer [1]

3087 **λυχνία, *lychnia***, n. GK: *3393* [→ *3088*]. lampstand (not a candlestick):– candlesticks [6], candlestick [6]

3088 **λύχνος, *lychnos***, n. GK: *3394* [→ *3087*]. lamp, usually of clay or metal, with olive oil to fuel its wick (not a candle):– candle [8], light [5], lights [1]

3089 **λύω, *lyō***, v. GK: *3395* [→ *179, 255, 359, 360, 487, 629, 630, 1262, 1590, 1955, 1956, 2646, 2647, 3080, 3081, 3083, 3084, 3085, 3086, 3885, 3886*]. to loose, release, untie; to break, destroy:– loose [15], loosed [10], broken [4], unloose [3], destroy [2], dissolved [2], loosing [2], break [1], broken down [1], broken up [1], melt [1], put off from [1]

3090 **Λωΐς**, ***Lōis***, n.pr. GK: *3396*. Lois, "[perhaps] *more desirable, better*":– Lois [1]

3091 **Λώτ**, ***Lōt***, n.pr. GK: *3397*. Lot:– Lot [3], Lot's [1]

3092 **Μάαθ**, ***Maath***, n.pr. GK: *3399*. Maath, "*to be small*":– Maath [1]

3093 **Μαγδαλά**, ***Magdala***, n.pr. GK: *3400 & 3401* [cf. *3094*]. Magdala:– Magdala [1]

3094 **Μαγδαληνή**, ***Magdalēnē***, n.pr.g. GK: *3402* [cf. *3093*]. Magdalene, "*from Magdala*":– Magdalene [12]

3095 **μαγεία**, ***mageia***, n. GK: *3404 & 3406* [→ *3096*]. magic:– sorceries [1]

3096 **μαγεύω**, ***mageuō***, v. GK: *3405* [→ *3095, 3097*]. to practice sorcery, magic:– used sorcery [1]

3097 **μάγος**, ***magos***, n. GK: *3407* [→ *3096*]. sorcerer; (pl.) Magi:– wise men [4], sorcerer [2]

3098 **Μαγώγ**, ***Magōg***, n.pr. GK: *3408*. Magog, "[perhaps] *land of Gog*":– Magog [1]

3099 **Μαδιάμ**, ***Madiam***, n.pr. GK: *3409*. Midian:– Madian [1]

3100 **μαθητεύω**, ***mathēteuō***, v. GK: *3411* [→ *3129*]. (act./tr.) to teach; to make a disciple; (pass./intr.) to become a disciple:– disciple [1], instructed [1], taught [1], teach [1]

3101 **μαθητής**, ***mathētēs***, n. GK: *3412* [→ *3129*]. disciple, student, follower; a committed learner and follower, in the NT usually of Jesus Christ:– disciples [240], disciple [27], disciples' [1]

3102 **μαθήτρια**, ***mathētria***, n. GK: *3413* [→ *3129*]. (female) disciple, student, follower:– disciple [1]

3103 **Μαθουσαλά**, ***Mathousala***, n.pr. GK: *3417*. Methuselah, "*man of the javelin*":– Mathusala [1]

3104 **Μαϊνάν**, ***Mainan***, n.pr. GK: *3418*. Mainan:– Menan [1]

3105 **μαίνομαι**, ***mainomai***, v. GK: *3419* [→ *1693, 3130, 3132*]. to rave, be insane, out of one's mind, to think or reason in an irrational manner manifested by erratic actions or lack of reasonable speech:– mad [4], beside thyself [1]

3106 **μακαρίζω**, ***makarizō***, v. GK: *3420* [→ *3107, 3108*]. to call blessed; to consider blessed:– call blessed [1], count happy [1]

3107 **μακάριος**, ***makarios***, a. GK: *3421* [→ *3106*]. blessed (receiving God's favor), fortunate, good (in a position of favor), happy (feelings associated with receiving God's favor):– blessed [44], happy [5], happier [1]

3108 **μακαρισμός**, ***makarismos***, n. GK: *3422* [→ *3106*]. blessedness, joy:– blessedness [3]

3109 **Μακεδονία**, ***Makedonia***, n.pr. GK: *3423* [→ *3110*]. Macedonia:– Macedonia [24]

3110 **Μακεδών**, ***Makedōn***, n.pr.g. GK: *3424* [→ *3109*]. Macedonian, "*from Macedonia*":– Macedonia [3], Macedonian [1], of Macedonia [1]

3111 **μάκελλον**, ***makellon***, n. GK: *3425*. meat market, food market:– shambles [1]

3112 **μακράν**, ***makran***, adv.&pp.*. GK: *3426* [→ *3372*]. far away, distant, long way off:– far [4], afar off (*+1519*) [1], afar off [1], far hence [1], far off [1], good way off [1], great way [1]

3113 **μακρόθεν**, ***makrothen***, adv. GK: *3427* [→ *3372*]. from a distance, from far away:– afar off (*+575*) [5], afar [5], afar off [3], from far [1]

3114 **μακροθυμέω**, ***makrothymeō***, v. GK: *3428* [→ *3372+2372*]. to have patience; to be patient; to exhibit internal and external control in a difficult circumstance, which control could exhibit itself by delaying an action:– patient [3], have patience [2], bear long [1], hath long patience [1], longsuffering [1], patiently endured [1], suffereth long [1]

3115 **μακροθυμία**, ***makrothymia***, n. GK: *3429* [→ *3372+2372*]. patience, forbearance, internal and external control in a difficult circumstance, which control could exhibit itself by delaying an action:– longsuffering [12], patience [2]

3116 **μακροθύμως**, ***makrothymōs***, adv. GK: *3430* [→ *3372+2372*]. patiently:– patiently [1]

3117 **μακρός**, ***makros***, a. GK: *3431* [→ *3372*]. lengthy, long; distant, far away:– long [3], far [2]

3118 **μακροχρόνιος**, ***makrochronios***, a. GK: *3432* [→ *3372+5550*]. pertaining to having a long life:– live long (*+1510*) [1]

3119 **μαλακία**, ***malakia***, n. GK: *3433* [→ *3120*]. sickness, ailment:– disease [3]

3120 **μαλακός**, ***malakos***, a. GK: *3434* [→ *3119*]. fine, soft; (n.) male prostitute, a male homosexual who is the passive sex partner:– soft [3], effeminate [1]

3121 **Μαλελεήλ**, ***Maleleēl***, n.pr. GK: *3435*. Mahalalel, "*praise of God [El]*":– Maleleel [1]

3122 **μάλιστα**, ***malista***, adv.super. GK: *3436* [→ *3123*]. especially:– specially [5], especially [4], chiefly [2], most [1]

3123 **μᾶλλον**, ***mallon***, adv.comp. GK: *3437* [→ *3122*]. more, more than; rather, instead:– more [42], rather [34], better (*+2570*) [1], far (*+4183*) [1], more than [1], much more [1], much [1], than (*+2228*) [1]

3124 **Μάλχος**, ***Malchos***, n.pr. GK: *3438*. Malchus, "*king*":– Malchus [1]

3125 **μάμμη**, ***mammē***, n. GK: *3439*. grandmother:– grandmother [1]

3126 **μαμωνᾶς**, ***mamōnas***, n. GK: *3440*. wealth, assets:– mammon [4]

3127 **Μαναήν**, ***Manaēn***, n.pr. GK: *3441*. Manaen, "*comforter*":– Manaen [1]

3128 **Μανασσῆς**, ***Manassēs***, n.pr. GK: *3442*. Manasseh, "*one that makes to forget*":– Manasses [3]

3129 **μανθάνω**, ***manthanō***, v. GK: *3443* [→ *261, 2648, 3100, 3101, 3102, 4827*]. to learn, study, be instructed:– learn [13], learned [10], learning [1], understood [1]

3130 **μανία**, ***mania***, n. GK: *3444* [→ *3105*]. insanity, madness:– make mad (*+1519+4062*) [1]

3131 **μάννα**, ***manna***, n. GK: *3445*. manna, a food given by God to the generation of the Exodus: "the bread of heaven":– manna [5]

3132 **μαντεύομαι**, ***manteuomai***, v. GK: *3446* [→ *3105*]. to fortune-tell, divine:– soothsaying [1]

3133 **μαραίνω**, ***marainō***, v. GK: *3447* [→ *262, 263*]. (pass.) to fade away, disappear:– fade away [1]

3134 **μαράνα θά**, ***marana tha***, l.[n.+v.]. GK: *3448*. maranatha (Aramaic: "Come, Lord!"):– Maranatha [1]

3135 **μαργαρίτης**, ***margaritēs***, n. GK: *3449*. pearl:– pearls [7], pearl [2]

3136 **Μάρθα**, ***Martha***, n.pr. GK: *3450*. Martha, "*lady [female lord]*":– Martha [13]

3137 **Μαρία**, ***Maria***; or **Μαριάμ**, ***Mariam***, n.pr. GK: *3451 & 3452*. Mary, "[perhaps] *beloved* or *plump*":– Mary [54]

3138 **Μᾶρκος**, ***Markos***, n.pr. GK: *3453*. Mark, "*[Latin] large hammer*":– Mark [5], Marcus [3]

3139 **μάρμαρος**, ***marmaros***, n. GK: *3454*. marble:– marble [1]

μάρτυρ, ***martur***. See **3144**.

3140 **μαρτυρέω**, ***martyreō***, v. GK: *3455* [→ *3144*]. to testify, give testimony; commend, speak well of, vouch for:– bear witness [15], testify [8], bear record [7], testified [6], bare record [5], bare witness [4], testifieth [4], beareth witness [3], witnessed [3], borne witness [2], gave testimony [2], obtained a good report [2], barest witness [1], bearest record [1], gave [1], give witness [1], good report [1], hath good report [1], having a good report [1], obtained witness [1], of honest report [1], testifying [1], testimony [1], well reported of [1], well reported [1], witnesses [1], witnesseth [1], witnessing [1], witness [1]

3141 **μαρτυρία**, ***martyria***, n. GK: *3456* [→ *3144*]. testimony, evidence; (good) reputation:– witness [15], testimony [14], record [7], report [1]

3142 **μαρτύριον**, ***martyrion***, n. GK: *3457* [→ *3144*]. testimony, proof:– testimony [15], witness [4], testified [1]

3143 **μαρτύρομαι**, ***martyromai***, v. GK: *3458* [→ *3144*]. to testify, declare; to insist on, urge:– testify [2], charged [1], take to record [1]

3144 **μάρτυς**, ***martys***, n. GK: *3459* [→ *267, 1263, 1957, 2649, 3140, 3141, 3142, 3143, 4303, 4828, 4901, 5576, 5577, 5575*]. witness, testimony; martyr (one who witnessed unto death):– witnesses [21], witness [8], martyr [2], record [2], martyrs [1]

3145 **μασσάομαι**, ***massaomai***, v. GK: *3460 & 3462* [→ *3146*]. to gnaw, bite:– gnawed [1]

3146 **μαστιγόω**, ***mastigoō***, v. GK: *3463* [→ *631, 1591, 3145, 3147, 3148*]. to flog, whip, scourge; to punish, chastise:– scourge [5], scourged [1], scourgeth [1]

3147 **μαστίζω**, ***mastizō***, v. GK: *3464* [→ *3146*]. to flog, scourge:– scourge [1]

3148 **μάστιξ**, ***mastix***, n. GK: *3465* [→ *3146*]. flogging device, whip; suffering; disease, sickness:– plagues [2], plague [2], scourgings [1], scourging [1]

3149 **μαστός**, ***mastos***, n. GK: *3410 & 3461 & 3466*. breast, chest:– paps [3]

3150 **ματαιολογία**, ***mataiologia***, n. GK: *3467* [→ *3152+3004*]. meaningless talk, empty talk:– vain jangling [1]

3151 **ματαιολόγος**, ***mataiologos***, a. GK: *3468* [→ *3152+3004*]. (n.) idle talker:– vain talkers [1]

3152 **μάταιος**, ***mataios***, a. GK: *3469* [→ *3150, 3151, 3153, 3154, 3155*]. worthless, futile, useless, empty:– vain [5], vanities [1]

3153 ματαιότης, ***mataiotēs***, n. GK: *3470* [→ *3152*]. emptiness, futility, frustration:– vanity [3]

3154 ματαιόω, ***mataioō***, v. GK: *3471* [→ *3152*]. (pass.) to become futile, given over to worthlessness:– vain [1]

3155 μάτην, ***matēn***, adv. GK: *3472* [→ *3152*]. in vain, to no end:– in vain [2]

3156 Ματθαῖος, ***Matthaios***; or Μαθθαῖος, ***Maththaios***, n.pr. GK: *3414 & 3473*. Matthew, "*gift of Yahweh*":– Matthew [5]

3157 Ματθάν, ***Matthan***, n.pr. GK: *3474*. Matthan, "*gift*":– Matthan [2]

3158 Ματθάτ, ***Matthat***; or Μαθθάτ, ***Maththat***, n.pr. GK: *3415 & 3475*. Mathat, "*gift*":– Matthat [2]

3159 Ματθίας, ***Matthias***, n.pr. GK: *3416 & 3476*. Matthias, "*gift of Yahweh*":– Matthias [2]

3160 Ματταθά, ***Mattatha***, n.pr. GK: *3477*. Mattatha, "*gift*":– Mattatha [1]

3161 Ματταθίας, ***Mattathias***, n.pr. GK: *3478*. Mattathias, "*gift of Yahweh*":– Mattathias [2]

3162 μάχαιρα, ***machaira***, n. GK: *3479* [→ *3163*]. (short) sword:– sword [23], swords [6]

3163 μάχη, ***machē***, n. GK: *3480* [→ *269, 1264, 2313, 2314, 2341, 2371, 3054, 3055, 3162, 3164*]. quarrel, conflict, fighting:– fightings [2], strifes [1], strivings [1]

3164 μάχομαι, ***machomai***, v. GK: *3481* [→ *3163*]. to fight, quarrel, argue:– strove [2], fight [1], strive [1]

3165 μέ, ***me***, p.pers.acc. of *1473*. GK: *1609* [→ *1473*]. me; see *1473*:–

3166 μεγαλαυχέω, ***megalaucheō***, v. GK: *3482* [→ *3173*]. to become proud, boast:– boasteth [1]

3167 μεγαλεῖος, ***megaleios***, a. GK: *3483* [→ *3173*]. (pl. n.) wonders, mighty deeds:– great things [1], wonderful works [1]

3168 μεγαλειότης, ***megaleiotēs***, n. GK: *3484* [→ *3173*]. majesty, greatness, grandeur:– magnificence [1], majesty [1], mighty power [1]

3169 μεγαλοπρεπής, ***megaloprepēs***, a. GK: *3485* [→ *3173+4241*]. majestic, magnificent:– excellent [1]

3170 μεγαλύνω, ***megalynō***, v. GK: *3486* [→ *3173*]. to glorify, regard highly, praise, exalt; to lengthen, expand:– magnified [3], magnify [2], enlarged [1], enlarge [1], shewed great [1]

3171 μεγάλως, ***megalōs***, adv. GK: *3487* [→ *3173*]. greatly:– greatly [1]

3172 μεγαλωσύνη, ***megalōsynē***, n. GK: *3488* [→ *3173*]. majesty:– majesty [3]

3173 μέγας, ***megas***, a. GK: *3489* [→ *3166, 3167, 3168, 3169, 3170, 3171, 3172, 3174, 3175, 3176, 3185, 3186, 3187*]. great; spatially: large; of quantity or degree: loud, intense, violent; of time: long (time); of position: great, important:– great [148], loud [33], greatest [2], high [2], large [2], come to years [1], exceedingly [1], great ones [1], great one [1], great things [1], mighty [1], sore [1], strong [1]

3174 μέγεθος, ***megethos***, n. GK: *3490* [→ *3173*]. greatness:– greatness [1]

3175 μεγιστάν, ***megistan***, n. GK: *3491* [→ *3173*]. great man, prince, high official:– great men [2], lords [1]

3176 μέγιστος, ***megistos***, a.super. GK: *3492* [→ *3173*]. very great:– exceeding great [1]

3177 μεθερμηνεύω, ***methermēneuō***, v. GK: *3493* [→ *3326+2059*]. to translate, give the meaning:– interpreted [6], by interpretation [1]

3178 μέθη, ***methē***, n. GK: *3494* [→ *3184*]. drunkenness:– drunkenness [3]

3179 μεθίστημι, ***methistēmi***; or μεθιστάνω, ***methistanō***, v. GK: *3495 & 3496* [→ *3326+2476*]. to move, remove; bring, lead astray; (pass.) to lose, be discharged:– put out [1], removed [1], remove [1], translated [1], turned away [1]

3180 μεθοδεία, ***methodeia***, n. GK: *3497* [→ *3326+3598*]. scheming, craftiness, strategy:– lie in wait [1], wiles [1]

3181 μεθόριον, ***methorion***, n. GK: *3498* [→ *3326+3724*]. boundary; (pl.) region:– borders [1]

3182 μεθύσκω, ***methyskō***, v. GK: *3499* [→ *3184*]. (pass.) to be or become drunk, intoxicated:– drunken [2], drunk [1], well drunk [1]

3183 μέθυσος, ***methysos***, n. GK: *3500* [→ *3184*]. drunkard:– drunkards [1], drunkard [1]

3184 μεθύω, ***methyō***, v. GK: *3501* [→ *271, 3178, 3182, 3183*]. to get drunk:– drunken [5], made drunk [1]

3185 μεῖζον, ***mēizon***, a.comp.n. of *3187*. GK: *3505* [→ *3173*]. greater, larger; older; louder; more:–

3186 μειζότερος, ***meizoteros***, a.comp. GK: *3504* [→ *3173*]. greater:– greater than [1]

3187 μείζων, ***meizōn***, a.comp. GK: *3505* [→ *3173*]. greater, larger; older; louder; more:– greater than [21], greater [13], greatest [9], more [2], elder [1]

3188 μέλαν, ***melan***, a.neut. of *3189*. GK: *3506* [→ *3189*]. the color black; ink, made of soot or other carbon source mixed with oil or resin:– ink [3]

3189 μέλας, ***melas***, a. GK: *3506* [→ *3188*]. the color black; ink, made of soot or other carbon source mixed with oil or resin:– black [3]

3190 Μελεᾶς, ***Meleas***, n.pr. GK: *3507*. Meleas:– Melea [1]

μέλει, ***melei***. See ***3199***.

3191 μελετάω, ***meletaō***, v. GK: *3509* [→ *3199*]. to plot, think about, meditate on; to give oneself wholly to, practice, cultivate:– imagine [1], meditate upon [1], premeditate [1]

3192 μέλι, ***meli***, n. GK: *3510* [→ *3193*]. honey:– honey [4]

3193 μελίσσιος, ***melissios***, a. GK: *3511 & 3512 & 3513* [→ *3192*]. pertaining to the bee, honeycomb:– honeycomb [1]

3194 Μελίτη, ***Melitē***, n.pr. GK: *3514 & 3515*. Melita:– Melita [1]

3195 μέλλω, ***mellō***, v. GK: *3516*. to be about to, on the point of; to be destined, must; to intend to; (what is) to come, the future:– should [21], shall [20], to come [14], will [7], would [7], about to [5], be [3], ready to [3], after [2], come [2], was to [2], would have [2], after that (*+1519+3588*) [1], afterwards [1], almost [1], at the point of [1], begin to [1], coming on [1], for to come (*+2064*) [1], hereafter [1], intending to [1], intend [1], meaning to [1], minding [1], ready [1], shall be [1], shalt [1], tarriest [1], time to come [1], to be [1], to [1], wilt [1], yet to [1]

3196 μέλος, ***melos***, n. GK: *3517*. part, member, limb:– members [29], member [5]

3197 Μελχί, ***Melchi***, n.pr. GK: *3518*. Melki, "*my king*":– Melchi [2]

3198 Μελχισέδεκ, ***Melchisedek***, n.pr. GK: *3519*. Melchizedek, "*[my] king is Zedek [just]*":– Melchisedec [9]

3199 μέλω, ***melō***, v. GK: *3508 & 3520* [→ *272, 278, 1958, 1959, 1960, 3191, 3338, 4304*]. to care, be concerned; (imper.) it is a care, it is a concern; (pers.) to trouble; to concern:– carest [3], careth [2], care for [1], cared for [1], cared [1], care [1], take care for [1]

3200 μεμβράνα, ***membrana***, n. GK: *3521*. parchment, a fine animal leather specially prepared for use in making scrolls:– parchments [1]

3201 μέμφομαι, ***memphomai***, v. GK: *3522* [→ *273, 274, 298, 299, 3202, 3437, 3469, 3470*]. to find fault with, blame:– find fault [1], finding fault with [1], found fault [1]

3202 μεμψίμοιρος, ***mempsimoiros***, a. GK: *3523* [→ *3201*]. fault-finding, complaining:– complainers [1]

3203 through ***3302*** are not used in Strong's numbering system.

3303 μέν, ***men***, pt.aff. GK: *3525* [→ *3304, 3305; cf. 3376*]. often untranslated; used with other particles to show contrast: on the one hand, one…or the other:– *usually untranslated* [121], indeed [22], verily [14], truly [12], some (*+3588*) [2], another (*+3739*) [1], as [1], even [1], for [1], furthermore (*+1534+3588*) [1], howbeit (*+235*) [1], inasmuch as (*+1909+3745+3767*) [1], one (*+3739*) [1], one [1], part (*+3588*) [1], partly (*+3778*) [1], some (*+243*) [1], some (*+3739*) [1], then [1]

3304 μενοῦν, ***menoun***; or μενοῦνγε, ***menounge***, pt. GK: *3528 & 3529* [→ *3303+3767+1065*]. rather, on the contrary, indeed:– doubtless [1], nay but [1], yea rather [1], yes verily [1]

3305 μέντοι, ***mentoi***, pt. GK: *3530* [→ *3303+5104*]. but, yet, nevertheless, really:– yet [2], but [1], howbeit [1], if (*+1487*) [1], likewise (*+3668*) [1], nevertheless (*+3676*) [1], nevertheless [1]

3306 μένω, ***menō***, v. GK: *3531* [→ *362, 1265, 1696, 1961, 2650, 3438, 3887, 4037, 4357, 4839, 5278, 5281*]. to stay, remain, live, dwell, abide; to be in a state that begins and continues, yet may or may not end or stop. "To abide in Christ" is to follow his example of a life obedient to the will of God:– abide [27], abideth [20], abode [12], dwelleth [10], remain [8], continue [7], tarry [7], remaineth [5], remained [3], abiding [2], continued [2], dwell [2], dwelt [2], endureth [2], tarried [2], continueth [1], continuing [1], dwellest [1], enduring [1], present [1], remaining [1], stand [1], tarried for [1]

3307 μερίζω, ***merizō***, v. GK: *3532* [→ *3313*]. to give, assign; (mid.) to divide, share; (pass.) to be divided:– divided [8], distributed [2], dealt [1], difference between [1], divide [1], gave [1]

3308 μέριμνα, *merimna*, n. GK: *3533* [→ *275, 3309, 4305; cf. 3313*]. worry, concern, anxiety:– cares [3], care [3]

3309 μεριμνάω, *merimnaō*, v. GK: *3534* [→ *3308*]. to worry, have anxiety, be concerned:– take thought [9], careth for [4], careful [2], taking thought [2], care for [1], have care [1]

3310 μερίς, *meris*, n. GK: *3535* [→ *3313*]. district; part, share, what is common between:– part [4], partakers [1]

3311 μερισμός, *merismos*, n. GK: *3536* [→ *3313*]. dividing, separation; distribution, apportionment:– dividing asunder [1], gifts [1]

3312 μεριστής, *meristēs*, n. GK: *3537* [→ *3313*]. arbiter:– divider [1]

3313 μέρος, *meros*, n. GK: *3538* [→ *1266, 1267, 3307, 3310, 3311, 3312, 4181, 4829; cf. 3308*]. part, share, portion; (pl.) district, region:– part [17], parts [7], coasts [3], portion [3], behalf [2], respect [2], by course (+*303*) [1], craft [1], particularly (+*2596*) [1], particular [1], partly (+*5100*) [1], piece [1], side [1], somewhat (+*575*) [1], sort [1]

3314 μεσημβρία, *mesēmbria*, n. GK: *3540* [→ *3319+2250*]. (of time) noon, midday; (of place) south:– noon [1], south [1]

3315 μεσιτεύω, *mesiteuō*, v. GK: *3541* [→ *3319*]. to confirm, guarantee:– confirmed [1]

3316 μεσίτης, *mesitēs*, n. GK: *3542* [→ *3319*]. mediator:– mediator [6]

3317 μεσονύκτιον, *mesonyktion*, n. GK: *3543* [→ *3319+3571*]. midnight:– midnight [3], at midnight [1]

3318 Μεσοποταμία, *Mesopotamia*, n.pr. GK: *3544* [→ *3319+4215*]. Mesopotamia, "*[land] between rivers*":– Mesopotamia [2]

3319 μέσος, *mesos*, a. GK: *3545* [→ *3314, 3315, 3316, 3317, 3318, 3320, 3321, 3322*]. middle, center, among; between; in front of, before:– midst [39], among [6], among (+*1722*) [5], in the midst [2], way [2], among (+*303*) [1], at midday (+*2250*) [1], at midnight (+*3571*) [1], before (+*1722+3588*) [1], between (+*303*) [1], forth (+*1519+3588*) [1], midnight (+*3571+3588*) [1]

3320 μεσότοιχον, *mesotoichon*, n. GK: *3546* [→ *3319+5038*]. dividing wall:– middle wall [1]

3321 μεσουράνημα, *mesouranēma*, n. GK: *3547* [→ *3319+3772*]. midair:– midst of heaven [3]

3322 μεσόω, *mesoō*, v. GK: *3539 & 3548* [→ *3319*]. to be halfway through, at midpoint:– midst [1]

3323 Μεσσίας, *Messias*, n.pr. GK: *3549*. Messiah, Anointed One; see also *5547*, "*anointed*":– Messias [2]

3324 μεστός, *mestos*, a. GK: *3550* [→ *3325*]. full:– full [8]

3325 μεστόω, *mestoō*, v. GK: *3551* [→ *3324*]. (pass.) to be filled:– full [1]

3326 μετά, *meta*, pp. GK: *3552* [→ *276, 277, 278, 279, 2130, 3177, 3179, 3180, 3181, 3327, 3328, 3329, 3330, 3331, 3332, 3333, 3334, 3335, 3336, 3337, 3338, 3339, 3340, 3341, 3342, 3343, 3344, 3345, 3346, 3347, 3348, 3350, 3351, 3352, 3353, 3359, 4830*]. (gen.) with, among, a marker of association of various kinds and meanings; (acc.) after, later, a marker of time:– with [345], after [76], after (+*3588*) [12], among [5], afterward (+*3778*) [4], against [4], hereafter (+*3778*) [4], in [2], and [1], boldly (+*3954*) [1], foameth (+*876*) [1], followed (+*1510*) [1], freely (+*3954*) [1], hence (+*3778*) [1], joyfully (+*5479*) [1], of [1], on [1], setting [1], since [1], that should follow (+*3778*) [1], together (+*240*) [1], to [1], unto [1], upon [1], when (+*3588*) [1], when [1], without (+*3756*) [1]

3327 μεταβαίνω, *metabainō*, v. GK: *3553* [→ *3326+305*]. to go on, leave, move from:– departed [4], depart [3], passed [2], remove [2], go [1]

3328 μεταβάλλω, *metaballō*, v. GK: *3554* [→ *3326+906*]. (mid.) to change one's mind:– changed [1]

3329 μετάγω, *metagō*, v. GK: *3555* [→ *3326+71*]. to turn, steer:– turn about [1], turned about [1]

3330 μεταδίδωμι, *metadidōmi*, v. GK: *3556* [→ *3326+1325*]. to impart, share, contribute to needs:– impart [2], giveth [1], give [1], imparted [1]

3331 μετάθεσις, *metathesis*, n. GK: *3557* [→ *3326+5087*]. removal, taking up; change, transformation:– change [1], removing [1], translation [1]

3332 μεταίρω, *metairō*, v. GK: *3558* [→ *3326+142*]. to move on, leave:– departed [2]

3333 μετακαλέω, *metakaleō*, v. GK: *3559* [→ *3326+2564*]. (mid.) to send for, summon, call to oneself:– called [2], call for [1], call hither [1]

3334 μετακινέω, *metakineō*, v. GK: *3560* [→ *3326+2795*]. (pass.) to be moved, removed, shifted from:– moved away [1]

3335 μεταλαμβάνω, *metalambanō*, v. GK: *3561* [→ *3326+2983*]. to share in, receive a share:– eat [1], have [1], partakers [1], partaker [1], receiveth [1], take [1]

3336 μετάλημψις, *metalēmpsis*, n. GK: *3562* [→ *3326+2983*]. receiving, sharing with:– received [1]

3337 μεταλλάσσω, *metallassō*, v. GK: *3563* [→ *3326+236*]. to exchange:– changed [1], change [1]

3338 μεταμέλομαι, *metamelomai*, v. GK: *3564* [→ *3326+3199*]. (mid.) to regret, repent; (pass.) to be repentant, changed of mind, remorseful:– repented [3], repent [3]

3339 μεταμορφόω, *metamorphoō*, v. GK: *3565* [→ *3326+3444*]. (pass.) to be transformed, transfigured, changed in form:– transfigured [2], changed [1], transformed [1]

3340 μετανοέω, *metanoeō*, v. GK: *3566* [→ *3326+3563*]. to repent, to change any or all of the elements composing one's life: attitude, thoughts, and behaviors concerning the demands of God for right living:– repent [21], repented [11], repenteth [2]

3341 μετάνοια, *metanoia*, n. GK: *3567* [→ *3326+3563*]. change of mind, repentance, the state of changing any or all of the elements composing one's life: attitude, thoughts, and behaviors concerning the demands of God for right living; note that this state can refer to the foundational salvation event in Christ, or to on-going repentance in the Christian life:– repentance [24]

3342 μεταξύ, *metaxy*, adv. GK: *3568* [→ *3326+4862*]. (spacial) between; (temporal) meanwhile, next:– between [6], mean while [1], next [1]

3343 μεταπέμπω, *metapempō*, v. GK: *3569* [→ *3326+3992*]. to summon, send for:– sent for [4], call for [2], send for [2]

3344 μεταστρέφω, *metastrephō*, v. GK: *3570* [→ *3326+4762*]. to pervert; to turn into, change:– turned [2], pervert [1]

3345 μετασχηματίζω, *metaschēmatizō*, v. GK: *3571* [→ *3326+4976*]. (act.) to transform, change (the form); (mid.) to masquerade, disguise (oneself):– transformed [2], change [1], in a figure transferred [1], transforming [1]

3346 μετατίθημι, *metatithēmi*, v. GK: *3572* [→ *3326+5087*]. to change (from one place or position to another); to bring back; to take away:– translated [2], carried over [1], changed [1], removed [1], turning [1]

3347 μετέπειτα, *metepeita*, adv. GK: *3575* [→ *3326+1909+1534*]. afterward:– afterward [1]

3348 μετέχω, *metechō*, v. GK: *3576* [→ *3326+2192*]. to share in, partake in, take part in:– partakers [3], partaker [2], pertaineth to [1], took part [1], useth [1]

3349 μετεωρίζομαι, *meteōrizomai*, v. GK: *3577*. to worry about, be anxious:– doubtful mind [1]

3350 μετοικεσία, *metoikesia*, n. GK: *3578* [→ *3326+3624*]. exile, deportation:– carrying away [2], brought [1], carried away [1]

3351 μετοικίζω, *metoikizō*, v. GK: *3579* [→ *3326+3624*]. to send to another place, exile, deport:– carry away [1], removed [1]

3352 μετοχή, *metochē*, n. GK: *3580* [→ *3326+2192*]. something in common, sharing, participation:– fellowship [1]

3353 μέτοχος, *metochos*, a. GK: *3581* [→ *3326+2192*]. sharing in, partners with:– partakers [4], fellows [1], partners [1]

3354 μετρέω, *metreō*, v. GK: *3582* [→ *3358*]. to measure:– measured [3], measure [3], mete [3], measuring [1]

3355 μετρητής, *metrētēs*, n. GK: *3583* [→ *3358*]. measure (about nine or ten gallons):– firkins [1]

3356 μετριοπαθέω, *metriopatheō*, v. GK: *3584* [→ *3358+3958*]. to deal gently:– have compassion [1]

3357 μετρίως, *metriōs*, adv. GK: *3585* [→ *3358*]. not greatly, moderately:– little [1]

3358 μέτρον, *metron*, n. GK: *3586* [→ *280, 488, 3354, 3355, 3356, 3357, 4620*]. measure, limit, what is apportioned:– measure [13]

3359 μέτωπον, *metōpon*, n. GK: *3587* [→ *3326+3708*]. forehead:– foreheads [6], forehead [2]

3360 μέχρι, *mechri*; or μέχρις, *mechris*, c.&pp.*. GK: *3588 & 3589*. until, to the point of:– until [7], unto [7], at [1], till (+*3739*) [1], till [1], to [1]

3361 μή, *mē*, pt.neg. GK: *3590* [→ *3365, 3366, 3367, 3368, 3369, 3371, 3379, 3380, 3381, 3383, 3385, 3387, 3386*]. no, not, absolutely not; a marker that negates a statement. At the beginning of a Greek question, it anticipates a negative response:– not [575], no [56], God forbid (+*1096*) [15], lest [14], never (+*165+1519+3588+3756*) [5], neither (+*2532*) [4], neither [3], none [3], but [2], cannot (+*1410*) [2], cannot [2], no (+*3956*) [2], none (+*5100*) [2], nor [2], not

(+*3756*) [2], nothing (+*5100*) [2], any [1], but (+*1437*) [1], but (+*1487+1622*) [1], but (+*1487*) [1], but that [1], except (+*1437*) [1], except (+*1487+1622*) [1], forbear [1], in no wise (+*1519+3588+3838*) [1], lacked (+*2192*) [1], lacketh (+*3918*) [1], lest (+*1519+3588*) [1], never (+*3756+4218*) [1], never (+*3756+4455*) [1], never [1], no (+*5100*) [1], no more at all (+*3756+3765*) [1], not withal [1], nothing (+*5101*) [1], nothing (+*846+1537*) [1], nothing [1], unless (+*1487+1622*) [1], untaken away (+*343*) [1], without [1]

3362 **ἐὰν μή, *ean mē***, c.+pt.neg. GK: *1569 + 3590* [→ *1437+3361*]. if not, except, unless:– except [32], but [2], if not [1], not [1]

3363 **ἵνα μή, *hina mē***, c.+pt.neg. GK: *2671 + 3590* [→ *2443+3361*]. that not, lest:– lest [42]

3364 **οὐ μή, *ou mē***, pt.neg. GK: *4024 + 3590* [→ *3756+3361*]. intense negative: by no means, not at all, never:– not [58], no [7], in no wise [6], no at all [5], never [2], by any means [1], by no means [1], in no case [1], neither (+*2532*) [1], neither [1], nor ever [1], not at all [1], not in any wise [1], not one [1]

3365 **μηδαμῶς, *mēdamōs***, adv. GK: *3592 & 3598* [→ *3361+1161+1473*]. surely not, by no means, certainly not:– not so [1], so [1]

3366 **μηδέ, *mēde***, pt.neg.disj. GK: *3593* [→ *3361+1161*]. nor, or not, and not, but not:– neither [32], nor [17], not [4], nor yet [2], no not [1], not once [1], not so much as [1], or [1]

3367 **μηδείς, *mēdeis***, a. GK: *3594 & 3599* [→ *3361+1161+1520*]. no one, not anyone, nobody, nothing:– no [46], nothing [27], none [6], any [4], not any [2], no man [1], no more (+*2089*) [1], not a whit [1], not at all [1], not [1], without any [1]

3368 **μηδέποτε, *mēdepote***, adv. GK: *3595* [→ *3361+1161+4226*]. never:– never [1]

3369 **μηδέπω, *mēdepō***, adv. GK: *3596* [→ *3361+1161*]. not yet:– not as yet [1]

3370 **Μῆδος, *Mēdos***, n.pr.g. GK: *3597*. Mede:– Medes [1]

3371 **μηκέτι, *mēketi***, adv. GK: *3600* [→ *3361+2089*]. no longer, never again:– no more [8], no longer [4], henceforth not [2], any longer [1], henceforth [1], hereafter [1], no henceforward [1], not any more [1], not henceforth [1], no [1]

3372 **μῆκος, *mēkos***, n. GK: *3601* [→ *3112, 3113, 3114, 3115, 3116, 3117, 3118, 3373*]. length:– length [3]

3373 **μηκύνω, *mēkynō***, v. GK: *3602* [→ *3372*]. (pass.) to grow (long), become long:– grow up [1]

3374 **μηλωτή, *mēlōtē***, n. GK: *3603*. sheepskin:– sheepskins [1]

3375 **μήν[1], *mēn*[1]**, pt. GK: *3605* [cf. *3303*]. surely:– surely (+*2229*) [1]

3376 **μήν[2], *mēn*[2]**, n. GK: *3604* [→ *3561, 5072, 5150*]. month:– months [14], month [4]

3377 **μηνύω, *mēnyō***, v. GK: *3606*. to inform, report, tell:– shewed [2], shew [1], told [1]

3378 **μὴ οὐκ, *mē ouk***, pt.neg. GK: *3590 + 4024* [→ *3361+3756*]. intense negative: by no means, not at all, never:– not [4]

3379 **μήποτε, *mēpote***, pt.&c. GK: *3607* [→ *3361+4226*]. never, otherwise, that…not:– lest [12], lest at any time [7], lest haply [2], if peradventure [1], no at all [1], whether or not [1]

3380 **μήπω, *mēpō***, adv. GK: *3609* [→ *3361*]. not yet:– not yet [2]

3381 **μήπως, *mēpōs***, adv. GK: *3610* [→ *3361+4226*]. so that…somehow, lest:– lest [5], lest by any means [3], lest by some means [1], lest haply [1], lest perhaps [1], lest that by any means [1]

3382 **μηρός, *mēros***, n. GK: *3611*. thigh:– thigh [1]

3383 **μήτε, *mēte***, c.neg. GK: *3612* [→ *3361+5037*]. and not, neither, nor:– neither [20], nor [15], so much as [1]

3384 **μήτηρ, *mētēr***, n. GK: *3613* [→ *282, 3388, 3389, 3390*]. mother:– mother [76], mother's [7], mothers [2]

3385 **μήτι, *mēti***, pt.inter.neut. of *3387*. GK: *3614* [→ *3361+5100*]. often not translated; expects a no answer to a question: surely not, unless:– any [3], doth [1], is [1], not [1]

3386 **μήτιγε, *mētige***, pt.inter. GK: *3615* [→ *3361+5100+1065*]. how much more, not to speak of:– how much more [1]

3387 **μήτις, *mētis***, pt.inter. GK: *3614* [→ *3361+5100*]. often not translated; expects a no answer to a question: surely not, unless:–

3388 **μήτρα, *mētra***, n. GK: *3616* [→ *3384*]. womb:– womb [2]

3389 **μητραλῴας, *mētralōas***; or **μητρολῴας, *mētrolōas***, n. GK: *3617 & 3618* [→ *3384+248*]. one who kills a mother:– murderers of mothers [1]

3390 **μητρόπολις, *mētropolis***, n. GK: *3619* [→ *3384+4172*]. capital city:– chiefest city [1]

3391 **μία, *mia***, n.num.f. of *1520*. GK: *1651* [→ *1520*]. one, single; see *1520*:–

3392 **μιαίνω, *miainō***, v. GK: *3620* [→ *283, 3393, 3394*]. to pollute, stain, defile; (pass.) to be defiled, corrupted, become ceremonially unclean; this refers to both ceremonial and moral uncleanness:– defiled [4], defile [1]

3393 **μίασμα, *miasma***, n. GK: *3621* [→ *3392*]. corruption, defilement:– pollutions [1]

3394 **μιασμός, *miasmos***, n. GK: *3622* [→ *3392*]. corruption, pollution, defilement:– uncleanness [1]

3395 **μίγμα, *migma***, n. GK: *3623* [→ *3396*]. mixture, compound:– mixture [1]

3396 **μίγνυμι, *mignymi***, v. GK: *3502 & 3503 & 3624* [→ *3395, 4874*]. to mix, mingle:– mingled [4]

3397 **μικρόν, *mikron***, a.neut. of *3398*. GK: *3625* [→ *3398*]. little, small, short, lesser:–

3398 **μικρός, *mikros***, a. GK: *3625* [→ *3397*]. little, small, short, lesser:– little [16], little while [8], least [6], little ones [6], small [6], less than [1], less [1], little while (+*3745+3745*) [1], while [1]

3399 **Μίλητος, *Milētos***, n.pr. GK: *3626*. Miletus:– Miletus [2], Miletum [1]

3400 **μίλιον, *milion***, n. GK: *3627*. (Roman) mile (about 4,854 feet):– mile [1]

3401 **μιμέομαι, *mimeomai***, v. GK: *3628* [→ *3402, 4831*]. to imitate, follow an example, use as a model:– follow [4]

3402 **μιμητής, *mimētēs***, n. GK: *3629* [→ *3401*]. imitator, an example:– followers [7]

3403 **μιμνήσκομαι, *mimnēskomai***, v. GK: *3630* [→ *3421*]. to remember, recall, bring to remembrance, often with an implication that a response or action of some kind will occur:– mindful [1], remember [1]

3404 **μισέω, *miseō***, v. GK: *3631*. to hate; (pass.) to be hated, detestable:– hate [16], hated [12], hateth [10], hating [2], hateful [1], hatest [1]

3405 **μισθαποδοσία, *misthapodosia***, n. GK: *3632* [→ *3408+575+1325*]. reward; punishment:– recompence of reward [2], reward [1]

3406 **μισθαποδότης, *misthapodotēs***, n. GK: *3633* [→ *3408+575+1325*]. rewarder:– rewarder [1]

3407 **μίσθιος, *misthios***, n. GK: *3634* [→ *3408*]. hired worker:– hired [2]

3408 **μισθός, *misthos***, n. GK: *3635* [→ *489, 3405, 3406, 3407, 3409, 3410, 3411*]. wage; reward; what is paid back:– reward [24], hire [3], wages [2]

3409 **μισθόω, *misthoō***, v. GK: *3636* [→ *3408*]. to hire:– hired [1], hire [1]

3410 **μίσθωμα, *misthōma***, n. GK: *3637* [→ *3408*]. rented house, rented lodging:– hired house [1]

3411 **μισθωτός, *misthōtos***, n. GK: *3638* [→ *3408*]. hired worker:– hireling [3], hired servants [1]

3412 **Μιτυλήνη, *Mitylēnē***, n.pr. GK: *3639*. Mitylene:– Mitylene [1]

3413 **Μιχαήλ, *Michaēl***, n.pr. GK: *3640*. Michael, "*Who is like God [El]?*":– Michael [2]

3414 **μνᾶ, *mna***, n. GK: *3641*. mina (100 drachmas or denarii, about 100 days' wages):– pounds [5], pound [4]

3415 **μνάομαι, *mnaomai***, v. GK: *3642* [→ *3423*]. be engaged, betrothed:– remember [9], remembered [6], mindful [2], remembrance [2], came in remembrance [1], rememberest [1]

3416 **Μνάσων, *Mnasōn***, n.pr. GK: *3643*. Mnason:– Mnason [1]

3417 **μνεία, *mneia***, n. GK: *3644* [→ *3421*]. remembrance, mention:– mention [4], remembrance [3]

3418 **μνῆμα, *mnēma***, n. GK: *3645* [→ *3421*]. (burial) tomb:– sepulchre [4], tombs [2], graves [1]

3419 **μνημεῖον, *mnēmeion***, n. GK: *3646* [→ *3421*]. tomb, grave:– sepulchre [26], graves [4], grave [4], sepulchres [3], tombs [3], tomb [2]

3420 **μνήμη, *mnēmē***, n. GK: *3647* [→ *3421*]. remembrance, recalling, memory:– remembrance [1]

3421 **μνημονεύω, *mnēmoneuō***, v. GK: *3648* [→ *363, 364, 1878, 3403, 3417, 3418, 3419, 3420, 3422, 5279, 5280*]. to remember; to think of:– remember [16], made mention [1], mindful [1], remembered [1], remembereth [1], remembering [1]

3422 **μνημόσυνον, *mnēmosynon***, n. GK: *3649* [→ *3421*]. memory, remembrance; memorial offering:– memorial [3]

3423 **μνηστεύω, *mnēsteuō***, v. GK: *3650* [→ *3415*]. (pass.) to be pledged to marriage, betrothed, become engaged:– espoused [3]

3424 μογιλάλος, ***mogilalos***, a. GK: *3651 & 3652* [→ *3425+2980*]. hardly able to talk, speaking with difficulty; speaking in a hoarse or weak voice:– impediment in speech [1]

3425 μόγις, ***mogis***, adv. GK: *3653* [→ *3424, 3433, 3449*]. scarcely ever:– hardly [1]

3426 μόδιος, ***modios***, n. GK: *3654*. large bowl (holds about eight dry quarts):– bushel [3]

3427 μοί, ***moi***, pers.p.dat. of *1473*. GK: *1609* [→ *1473*]. me, for me, to me; see *1473*:–

3428 μοιχαλίς, ***moichalis***, n. GK: *3655* [→ *3432*]. adulteress; (a.) adulterous:– adulterous [3], adulteress [2], adulteresses [1], adultery [1]

3429 μοιχάω, ***moichaō***, v. GK: *3656* [→ *3432*]. to commit adultery:– committeth adultery [4], commit adultery [2]

3430 μοιχεία, ***moicheia***, n. GK: *3657* [→ *3432*]. (the state or condition of) adultery:– adulteries [2], adultery [2]

3431 μοιχεύω, ***moicheuō***, v. GK: *3658* [→ *3432*]. (act.) to commit adultery; (pass.) to become an adulterer:– commit adultery [10], committeth adultery [2], adultery [1], committed adultery [1]

3432 μοιχός, ***moichos***, n. GK: *3659* [→ *3428, 3429, 3430, 3431*]. adulterer:– adulterers [4]

3433 μόλις, ***molis***, adv. GK: *3660* [→ *3425*]. with difficulty, hardly; very rarely:– scarcely [2], scarce [2], had much work (*+2480*) [1], hardly [1]

3434 Μολόχ, ***Moloch***, n.pr. GK: *3661*. Molech, "*"shameful" king*":– Moloch [1]

3435 μολύνω, ***molynō***, v. GK: *3662* [→ *3436*]. to defile, soil, stain, make impure:– defiled [3]

3436 μολυσμός, ***molysmos***, n. GK: *3663* [→ *3435*]. contamination, defilement:– filthiness [1]

3437 μομφή, ***momphē***, n. GK: *3664* [→ *3201*]. grievance, cause for complaint:– quarrel [1]

3438 μονή, ***monē***, n. GK: *3665* [→ *3306*]. room; dwelling place, abode:– abode [1], mansions [1]

3439 μονογενής, ***monogenēs***, a. GK: *3666* [→ *3441+1096*]. one and only, unique:– only begotten [6], one only [1], only child [1], only [1]

3440 μόνον, ***monon***, adv. GK: *3667* [→ *3441*]. only, alone; just, even, simply:– only [62], alone [3], but [1]

3441 μόνος, ***monos***, a. GK: *3668* [→ *2651, 3439, 3440, 3442, 3443*]. only, alone, by oneself:– only [24], alone [21], by themselves [2], alone (*+2596*) [1]

3442 μονόφθαλμος, ***monophthalmos***, a. GK: *3669* [→ *3441+3788*]. one-eyed:– one eye [2]

3443 μονόω, ***monoō***, v. GK: *3670* [→ *3441*]. (pass.) to be left alone:– desolate [1]

3444 μορφή, ***morphē***, n. GK: *3671* [→ *3339, 3445, 3446, 4832, 4833*]. form, outward appearance; nature, character:– form [3]

3445 μορφόω, ***morphoō***, v. GK: *3672* [→ *3444*]. (pass.) to be formed, take on a form:– formed [1]

3446 μόρφωσις, ***morphōsis***, n. GK: *3673* [→ *3444*]. embodiment, formulation; (outward) form, appearance:– form [2]

3447 μοσχοποιέω, ***moschopoieō***, v. GK: *3674* [→ *3448+4160*]. to make an idol in the shape of a calf:– made a calf [1]

3448 μόσχος, ***moschos***, n. GK: *3675* [→ *3447*]. calf, ox, young bull:– calf [4], calves [2]

3449 μόχθος, ***mochthos***, n. GK: *3677* [→ *3425*]. toil, hardship, exertion:– travail [2], painfulness [1]

3450 μοῦ, ***mou***, pers.p.gen. of *1473*. GK: *1609* [→ *1473*]. my, mine; see *1473*:–

3451 μουσικός, ***mousikos***, a. GK: *3676*. (n.) musician:– musicians [1]

3452 μυελός, ***myelos***, n. GK: *3678*. marrow:– marrow [1]

3453 μυέω, ***myeō***, v. GK: *3679* [→ *3466*]. (pass.) to learn a secret:– instructed [1]

3454 μῦθος, ***mythos***, n. GK: *3680* [→ *3888, 3889, 3890*]. myth, story, tale:– fables [5]

3455 μυκάομαι, ***mykaomai***, v. GK: *3681*. to roar:– roareth [1]

3456 μυκτηρίζω, ***myktērizō***, v. GK: *3682* [→ *1592*]. (pass.) to be mocked, treated with contempt:– mocked [1]

3457 μυλικός, ***mylikos***, a. GK: *3683* [→ *3458*]. pertaining to a grinding mill:– millstone (*+3037*) [1]

3458 μύλος, ***mylos***, n. GK: *3685* [→ *3457, 3459*]. hand mill or millstone for grinding:– millstone (*+3684*) [2], millstone [2]

3459 μυλών, ***mylōn***, n. GK: *3686* [→ *3458*]. millhouse:– mill [1]

3460 Μύρα, ***Myra***, n.pr. GK: *3688 & 3694*. Myra:– Myra [1]

3461 μυριάς, ***myrias***, n. GK: *3689* [→ *3463*]. myriad, ten thousand; thousands upon thousands, a practically uncountable number:– ten thousand [2], fifty thousand (*+4002*) [1], innumerable company [1], innumerable multitude [1], ten thousands [1], thousands [1], two hundred thousand thousand (*+1417*) [1]

3462 μυρίζω, ***myrizō***, v. GK: *3690* [→ *3464*]. to pour perfume, anoint:– anoint [1]

3463 μύριοι, ***myrioi***, a.num. GK: *3691 & 3692* [→ *3461*]. ten thousand; a practically uncountable number:– ten thousand [3]

3464 μύρον, ***myron***, n. GK: *3693* [→ *3462*]. perfume, myrrh, ointment:– ointment [12], ointments [2]

3465 Μυσία, ***Mysia***, n.pr. GK: *3695*. Mysia:– Mysia [2]

3466 μυστήριον, ***mystērion***, n. GK: *3696* [→ *3453*]. mystery, secret; often refers to a misunderstood part of the OT that, with Christ's coming, is now unveiled:– mystery [22], mysteries [5]

3467 μυωπάζω, ***myōpazō***, v. GK: *3697*. to be nearsighted:– cannot see far off [1]

3468 μώλωψ, ***mōlōps***, n. GK: *3698*. wound, welt, bruise:– stripes [1]

3469 μωμάομαι, ***mōmaomai***, v. GK: *3699* [→ *3201*]. (mid.) to criticize, find fault, blame; (pass.) to be discredited, have fault found with:– blamed [1], blame [1]

3470 μῶμος, ***mōmos***, n. GK: *3700* [→ *3201*]. blemish:– blemishes [1]

3471 μωραίνω, ***mōrainō***, v. GK: *3701* [→ *3474*]. (act.) to make foolish, show one foolish; (pass.) to become a fool, be made a fool; (pass.) to become saltless, tasteless, inert:– lost savour [2], fools [1], made foolish [1]

3472 μωρία, ***mōria***, n. GK: *3702* [→ *3474*]. foolishness:– foolishness [5]

3473 μωρολογία, ***mōrologia***, n. GK: *3703* [→ *3474+3004*]. foolish talk:– foolish talking [1]

3474 μωρός, ***mōros***, a. GK: *3704* [→ *3471, 3472, 3473*]. foolish:– foolish [7], fools [3], fool [2], foolishness [1]

3475 Μωσεύς, ***Mōseus***; or Μωσῆς, ***Mōsēs***; or Μωϋσῆς, ***Mōysēs***, n.pr. GK: *3705 & 3706 & 3707*. Moses, "*drawn out* [Ex. 2:10]; [Egyptian] *son*":– Moses [77], Moses' [3]

3476 Ναασσών, ***Naassōn***, n.pr. GK: *3709*. Nahshon, "*small viper*":– Naasson [3]

3477 Ναγγαί, ***Nangai***, n.pr. GK: *3710*. Naggai:– Nagge [1]

3478 Ναζαρέθ, ***Nazareth***; or Ναζαρέτ, ***Nazaret***, n.pr. GK: *3711 & 3712 & 3713 & 3714 & 3715* [→ *3479, 3480*]. Nazareth, "[poss.] *sprout, branch or watchtower*":– Nazareth [12]

3479 Ναζαρηνός, ***Nazarēnos***, a.pr.g. GK: *3716* [→ *3478*]. of Nazareth; (n.) Nazarene (in no way connected to the OT Nazirite):– Nazareth [2], of Nazareth [2]

3480 Ναζωραῖος, ***Nazōraios***, n.pr.g. GK: *3717* [→ *3478*]. Nazarene, of Nazareth:– of Nazareth [13], Nazarenes [1], Nazarene [1]

3481 Ναθάν, ***Nathan***; or Ναθάμ, ***Natham***, n.pr. GK: *3718 & 3719*. Nathan, Natham, "*gift*":– Nathan [1]

3482 Ναθαναήλ, ***Nathanaēl***, n.pr. GK: *3720*. Nathanael, "*gift of God [El]*":– Nathanael [6]

3483 ναί, ***nai***, pt.aff. or emph. GK: *3721*. yes, indeed, a marker of strong agreement, affirmation, or emphasis:– yea [23], even so [5], yes [3], surely [1], truth [1], verily [1]

3484 Ναΐν, ***Nain***, n.pr. GK: *3723*. Nain, "*pleasant, delightful*":– Nain [1]

3485 ναός, ***naos***, n. GK: *3724* [→ *3511*]. temple; of the temple in Jerusalem, it generally denotes the temple building. Also used figuratively for the church as the dwelling place of the Holy Spirit:– temple [43], temples [2], shrines [1]

3486 Ναούμ, ***Naoum***, n.pr. GK: *3725*. Nahum, "*comfort*":– Naum [1]

3487 νάρδος, ***nardos***, n. GK: *3726*. nard, the oil of (spike)nard, extracted from the root:– spikenard (*+4101*) [2]

3488 Νάρκισσος, ***Narkissos***, n.pr. GK: *3727*. Narcissus:– Narcissus [1]

3489 ναυαγέω, ***nauageō***, v. GK: *3728* [→ *3491+2608*]. to be shipwrecked, have a shipwreck:– made shipwrack [1], suffered shipwrack [1]

3490 ναύκληρος, ***nauklēros***, n. GK: *3729* [→ *3491+2819*]. ship owner or captain:– owner of the ship [1]

3491 ναῦς, ***naus***, n. GK: *3730* [→ *3489, 3490, 3492*]. ship:– ship [1]

3492 ναύτης, ***nautēs***, n. GK: *3731* [→ *3491*]. sailor:– shipmen [2], sailers [1]

3493 Ναχώρ, ***Nachōr***, n.pr. GK: *3732*. Nahor:– Nachor [1]

3494 **νεανίας**, ***neanias***, n. GK: *3733* [→ *3501*]. young man:– young man [4], young man's [1]

3495 **νεανίσκος**, ***neaniskos***, n. GK: *3734* [→ *3501*]. young man:– young man [5], young men [5]

3496 **Νεάπολις**, ***Neapolis***, n.pr. GK: *3735 & 3736* [→ *3501+4172*]. Neapolis, "*new city*":– Neapolis [1]

3497 **Νεεμάν**, ***Neeman***; or **Ναιμάν**, ***Naiman***, n.pr. GK: *3722 & 3737*. Naaman, "*pleasantness*":– Naaman [1]

3498 **νεκρός**, ***nekros***, a. GK: *3738* [→ *3499, 3500*]. dead (can be used physically or fig., of both persons and things); (n.) dead person, corpse:– dead [131], one dead [1]

3499 **νεκρόω**, ***nekroō***, v. GK: *3739* [→ *3498*]. (act.) to put to death; (pass.) to be as good as dead:– as good as dead [1], dead [1], mortify [1]

3500 **νέκρωσις**, ***nekrōsis***, n. GK: *3740* [→ *3498*]. death, deadness:– deadness [1], dying [1]

3501 **νέος**, ***neos***, a. GK: *3742* [→ *365, 3494, 3495, 3496, 3502, 3503, 3504, 3512, 3555, 3556, 3561*]. new, fresh, young, younger:– new [12], younger [8], young [3], young men [1]

3502 **νεοσσός**, ***neossos***, n. GK: *3743 & 3801* [→ *3501*]. the young (of a bird):– young [1]

3503 **νεότης**, ***neotēs***, n. GK: *3744* [→ *3501*]. youth, childhood:– youth [5]

3504 **νεόφυτος**, ***neophytos***, a. GK: *3745* [→ *3501+5453*]. newly converted, a fig. extension of a new plant, not found in the NT:– novice [1]

3505 **Νέρων**, ***Nerōn***, n.pr. GK: *3746*. Nero, "*[family name]*":– Nero [1]

3506 **νεύω**, ***neuō***, v. GK: *3748* [→ *1269, 1593, 1770, 1962, 2656*]. to motion, nod (as a signal):– beckoned [2]

3507 **νεφέλη**, ***nephelē***, n. GK: *3749* [→ *3509*]. cloud:– cloud [18], clouds [8]

3508 **Νεφθαλίμ**, ***Nephthalim***, n.pr. GK: *3750*. Naphtali:– Nephthalim [3]

3509 **νέφος**, ***nephos***, n. GK: *3751* [→ *3507*]. cloud:– cloud [1]

3510 **νεφρός**, ***nephros***, n. GK: *3752*. mind, the part of the inner person that feels, desires, and gives intent; a fig. extension of the kidney (not found in the NT):– reins [1]

3511 **νεωκόρος**, ***neōkoros***, n. GK: *3753* [→ *3485*]. guardian of the temple:– worshipper [1]

3512 **νεωτερικός**, ***neōterikos***, a. GK: *3754* [→ *3501*]. pertaining to youth, youthful:– youthful [1]

νεώτερος, ***neōteros***. See ***3501***.

3513 **νή**, ***nē***, pt.aff. GK: *3755*. as surely as:– I protest [1]

3514 **νήθω**, ***nēthō***, v. GK: *3756*. to spin (yarn):– spin [2]

3515 **νηπιάζω**, ***nēpiazō***, v. GK: *3757* [→ *3516*]. to be (like) a child:– children [1]

3516 **νήπιος**, ***nēpios***, a. GK: *3758* [→ *3515*]. (n.) child, infant; (a.) childlike, childish, infantile, with a negative implication of immaturity or positive implication of innocence, depending on the context:– babes [5], child [5], children [2], babe [1], childish [1]

3517 **Νηρεύς**, ***Nēreus***, n.pr. GK: *3759*. Nereus:– Nereus [1]

3518 **Νηρί**, ***Nēri***, n.pr. GK: *3760*. Neri, "*lamp of Yahweh*":– Neri [1]

3519 **νησίον**, ***nēsion***, n. GK: *3761* [→ *3520*]. small island:– island [1]

3520 **νῆσος**, ***nēsos***, n. GK: *3762* [→ *3519*]. island:– island [6], isle [3]

3521 **νηστεία**, ***nēsteia***, n. GK: *3763* [→ *3522, 3523; cf. 2068*]. fasting, going without food:– fasting [4], fastings [3], fast [1]

3522 **νηστεύω**, ***nēsteuō***, v. GK: *3764* [→ *3521*]. to fast, go without food:– fast [16], fasted [3], fastest [1], fasting [1]

3523 **νῆστις**, ***nēstis***, n. GK: *3765* [→ *3521*]. hungry, without food:– fasting [2]

3524 **νηφαλέος**, ***nēphaleos***; or **νηφάλιος**, ***nēphalios***, a. GK: *3766 & 3767* [→ *3525*]. temperate (in the use of alcohol):– sober [2], vigilant [1]

3525 **νήφω**, ***nēphō***, v. GK: *3768* [→ *366, 1594, 3524*]. to be self-controlled, clear-headed:– sober [4], watch [2]

3526 **Νίγερ**, ***Niger***, n.pr. GK: *3769*. Niger, "*black*":– Niger [1]

3527 **Νικάνωρ**, ***Nikanōr***, n.pr. GK: *3770* [→ *3529+435*]. Nicanor, "*victor*":– Nicanor [1]

3528 **νικάω**, ***nikaō***, v. GK: *3771* [→ *3529*]. to overcome, overpower; to conquer, triumph:– overcometh [11], overcome [11], overcame [2], conquering [1], conquer [1], gotten the victory [1], prevailed [1]

3529 **νίκη**, ***nikē***, n. GK: *3772* [→ *408, 959, 2131, 3527, 3528, 3530, 3531, 3532, 3533, 3534, 5245*]. victory:– victory [1]

3530 **Νικόδημος**, ***Nikodēmos***, n.pr. GK: *3773* [→ *3529+1218*]. Nicodemus, "*victor over people*":– Nicodemus [5]

3531 **Νικολαΐτης**, ***Nikolaitēs***, n.pr.g. GK: *3774* [→ *3529+2992*]. Nicolaitan, "*follower of Nicolas*":– Nicolaitans [2]

3532 **Νικόλαος**, ***Nikolaos***, n.pr. GK: *3775* [→ *3529+2992*]. Nicolas, "*victor over people*":– Nicolas [1]

3533 **Νικόπολις**, ***Nikopolis***, n.pr. GK: *3776* [→ *3529+4172*]. Nicopolis, "*victory city*":– Nicopolis [2]

3534 **νῖκος**, ***nikos***, n. GK: *3777* [→ *3529*]. victory:– victory [4]

3535 **Νινευΐ**, ***Nineui***, n.pr. GK: *3778 & 3779* [→ *3536*]. Nineveh:– Nineveh [1]

3536 **Νινευίτης**, ***Nineuitēs***, n.pr.g. GK: *3780* [→ *3535*]. Ninevite:– Ninevites [1], of Nineveh [1]

3537 **νιπτήρ**, ***niptēr***, n. GK: *3781* [→ *3538*]. basin for washing:– bason [1]

3538 **νίπτω**, ***niptō***, v. GK: *3782* [→ *449, 633, 3537*]. to wash; bathe:– wash [11], washed [6]

3539 **νοέω**, ***noeō***, v. GK: *3783* [→ *3563*]. to understand, see with insight, reflect:– understand [8], perceive [2], consider [1], think [1], understanding [1], understood [1]

3540 **νόημα**, ***noēma***, n. GK: *3784* [→ *3563*]. thought, mind; scheme, design, plot:– minds [4], devices [1], thought [1]

3541 **νόθος**, ***nothos***, a. GK: *3785*. illegitimate, born out of wedlock:– bastards [1]

3542 **νομή**, ***nomē***, n. GK: *3786* [→ *3551*]. pasture:– eat (+*2192*) [1], pasture [1]

3543 **νομίζω**, ***nomizō***, v. GK: *3787* [→ *3551*]. to think, suppose, expect, consider:– supposed [4], supposing [4], think [4], suppose [1], thought [1], wont [1]

3544 **νομικός**, ***nomikos***, a. GK: *3788* [→ *3551*]. pertaining to the law; (n.) expert in the law, lawyer:– lawyers [5], lawyer [3], about law [1]

3545 **νομίμως**, ***nomimōs***, adv. GK: *3789* [→ *3551*]. properly, in accordance to the rules:– lawfully [2]

3546 **νόμισμα**, ***nomisma***, n. GK: *3790* [→ *3551*]. coin:– money [1]

3547 **νομοδιδάσκαλος**, ***nomodidaskalos***, n. GK: *3791* [→ *3551+1321*]. teacher of the law:– doctor of law [1], doctors of the law [1], teachers of the law [1]

3548 **νομοθεσία**, ***nomothesia***, n. GK: *3792* [→ *3551+5087*]. law, legislation:– giving of the law [1]

3549 **νομοθετέω**, ***nomotheteō***, v. GK: *3793* [→ *3551+5087*]. (pass.) to be given law; to be founded, enacted:– established [1], received law [1]

3550 **νομοθέτης**, ***nomothetēs***, n. GK: *3794* [→ *3551+5087*]. lawgiver:– lawgiver [1]

3551 **νόμος**, ***nomos***, n. GK: *3795* [→ *458, 459, 460, 632, 1268, 1772, 2624, 2816, 2817, 2818, 3542, 3543, 3544, 3545, 3546, 3547, 3548, 3549, 3550, 3621, 3622, 3623, 3891, 3892, 4789*]. law, regulation, principle; this has a broad range of meanings and referents, ranging from law as a principle revealed in nature or reason, to the OT Scriptures as a body, the first five books of the Scriptures, or any single command of the Scriptures:– law [195], laws [2]

3552 **νοσέω**, ***noseō***, v. GK: *3796* [→ *3554*]. to be unhealthy, ill:– doting [1]

3553 **νόσημα**, ***nosēma***, n. GK: *3797* [→ *3554*]. disease:– disease [1]

3554 **νόσος**, ***nosos***, n. GK: *3798* [→ *3552, 3553*]. disease, illness:– diseases [6], sickness [3], sicknesses [2], infirmities [1]

3555 **νοσσιά**, ***nossia***, n. GK: *3799* [→ *3501*]. chick, young (of a bird):– brood [1]

3556 **νοσσίον**, ***nossion***, n. GK: *3800* [→ *3501*]. young (of a bird):– chickens [1]

3557 **νοσφίζω**, ***nosphizō***, v. GK: *3802*. (mid.) to hold back for oneself, steal by misappropriating:– keep back [1], kept back [1], purloining [1]

3558 **νότος**, ***notos***, n. GK: *3803*. south, south wind:– south [4], south wind [3]

3559 **νουθεσία**, ***nouthesia***, n. GK: *3804* [→ *3563+5087*]. warning, admonition; instruction:– admonition [3]

3560 **νουθετέω**, ***noutheteō***, v. GK: *3805* [→ *3563+5087*]. to warn, admonish; instruct:– admonish [3], warn [3], admonishing [1], warning [1]

3561 **νουμηνία**, ***noumēnia***, n. GK: *3741 & 3806* [→ *3501+3375*]. New Moon Celebration:– new moon [1]

3562 **νουνεχῶς**, ***nounechōs***, adv. GK: *3807* [→ *3563+2192*]. wisely, thoughtfully:– discreetly [1]

3563 **νοῦς**, ***nous***, n. GK: *3808* [→ *279, 453, 454, 1270, 1271, 1425, 1771, 1963, 2132,*

2133, 2657, 3340, 3341, 3539, 3540, 3559, 3560, 3562, 4306, 4307, 5282, 5283]. mind, thinking; understanding, insight; "to open the mind" means "to understand something":– mind [15], understanding [7], minds [2]

3564 Νυμφᾶς, ***Nymphas***, n.pr. GK: *3809 & 3810* [→ *3565*]. Nymphas:– Nymphas [1]

3565 *νύμφη*, ***nymphē***, n. GK: *3811* [→ *3564, 3566, 3567*]. bride; daughter-in-law:– bride [5], daughter in law [3]

3566 *νυμφίος*, ***nymphios***, n. GK: *3812* [→ *3565*]. bridegroom:– bridegroom [15], bridegroom's [1]

3567 *νυμφών*, ***nymphōn***, n. GK: *3813* [→ *3565*]. bridegroom:– bridechamber [3]

3568 *νῦν*, ***nyn***, adv. GK: *3814* [→ *3570, 3569, 5106*]. now, as it is; (with the art.) the present (time):– now [119], present [4], henceforth (+*3588*) [3], this time (+*3588*) [2], at this time [1], henceforth (+*575*+*3588*) [1], henceforth [1], hereafter (+*575*+*3588*) [1], now (+*2089*) [1], now henceforth [1], of late [1], this (+*3588*) [1], this [1], time [1]

3569 *ταννῦν*, ***tanyn***, contr. [art.+adv.]. GK: *5422* [→ *3588*+*3568*]. concerning the present, now:– now [5]

3570 *νυνί*, ***nyni***, adv. GK: *3815* [→ *3568*]. now, as it is; indeed, in fact:– now [21]

3571 *νύξ*, ***nyx***, n. GK: *3816* [→ *1273, 1773, 3317, 3574*]. night, evening:– night [60], nights [3], at midnight (+*3319*) [1], midnight (+*3319*+*3588*) [1]

3572 *νύσσω*, ***nyssō***, v. GK: *3817* [→ *2659, 2660*]. to pierce, stab:– pierced [1]

3573 *νυστάζω*, ***nystazō***, v. GK: *3818*. to become drowsy; to sleep, be idle:– slumbered [1], slumbereth [1]

3574 *νυχθήμερον*, ***nychthēmeron***, n. GK: *3819* [→ *3571*+*2250*]. a night and a day, about 24 hours:– a night and a day [1]

3575 Νῶε, ***Nōe***, n.pr. GK: *3820*. Noah, "*rest, comfort*":– Noe [5], Noah [3]

3576 *νωθρός*, ***nōthros***, a. GK: *3821*. slow to learn; lazy, sluggish:– dull [1], slothful [1]

3577 *νῶτος*, ***nōtos***, n. GK: *3822*. back (of a human body); to have a "bent back" means to be "in trouble or oppression":– back [1]

3578 *ξενία*, ***xenia***, n. GK: *3825* [→ *3581*]. place to stay, guest room:– lodging [2]

3579 *ξενίζω*, ***xenizō***, v. GK: *3826* [→ *3581*]. to receive a guest, entertain; (pass.) to stay as a guest; to think of something as strange, be surprised, astonished:– lodged [4], think it strange [2], entertained [1], lodgeth [1], lodge [1], strange [1]

3580 *ξενοδοχέω*, ***xenodocheō***, v. GK: *3827* [→ *3581*+*1209*]. to show hospitality:– lodged strangers [1]

3581 *ξένος*, ***xenos***, a. GK: *3828* [→ *3578, 3579, 3580, 5381, 5382*]. strange, foreign, alien; (n.) foreigner, stranger, alien; host, one who shows hospitality:– strangers [6], stranger [4], strange [3], host [1]

3582 *ξέστης*, ***xestēs***, n. GK: *3829*. pitcher, jug:– pots [2]

3583 *ξηραίνω*, ***xērainō***, v. GK: *3830* [→ *3584*]. to wither, shrivel; become rigid:– withered away [6], dried up [3], withered [3], withereth [2], pineth away [1], ripe [1]

3584 *ξηρός*, ***xēros***, a. GK: *3831* [→ *3583*]. dried up, (n.) dry land; shriveled, by extension: withered, paralyzed, of an atrophied limb of the body:– withered [4], dry [2], land [1]

3585 *ξύλινος*, ***xylinos***, a. GK: *3832* [→ *3586, 3587*]. made of wood, wooden:– of wood [2]

3586 *ξύλον*, ***xylon***, n. GK: *3833* [→ *3585*]. wood; tree; wooden club, stocks:– tree [10], staves [5], wood [3], stocks [1]

3587 *ξυράω*, ***xyraō***, v. GK: *3834* [→ *3585*]. to have one's hair shaved:– shaven [2], shave [1]

3588 *ὁ*, ***ho***, art. GK: *3836* [→ *2006, 3592, 3634, 3569, 5024, 5107, 5108, 5120, 5121, 5122, 5602*]. (often not translated) the, this, that, who:– *usually untranslated* [9495], the [7887], he [450], which [392], that [353], them [267], they [259], a [179], him [134], who [93], those [41], that (+*1519*) [27], to (+*1519*) [24], because (+*1223*) [21], she [18], what [18], as (+*1722*) [15], after (+*3326*) [12], an [12], their [12], when (+*1722*) [12], his [11], some [10]*

ὅ, ***ho***. See ***3739***.

3589 *ὀγδοήκοντα*, ***ogdoēkonta***, n.num. GK: *3837* [→ *3638*]. eighty:– fourscore [2]

3590 *ὄγδοος*, ***ogdoos***, a. GK: *3838* [→ *3638*]. eighth:– eighth [5]

3591 *ὄγκος*, ***onkos***, n. GK: *3839* [→ *5246*]. hinderance, impediment:– weight [1]

3592 *ὅδε*, ***hode***, p.demo. GK: *3840* [→ *3588*]. this (one); thus:– these [7], after this manner [1], he [1], she [1], such [1], thus [1]

3593 *ὁδεύω*, ***hodeuō***, v. GK: *3841* [→ *3598*]. to travel:– journeyed [1]

3594 *ὁδηγέω*, ***hodēgeō***, v. GK: *3842* [→ *3598*+*71*]. to lead, guide; explain, instruct:– lead [3], guide [2]

3595 *ὁδηγός*, ***hodēgos***, n. GK: *3843* [→ *3598*+*71*]. guide, leader:– guides [2], guide [2], leaders [1]

3596 *ὁδοιπορέω*, ***hodoiporeō***, v. GK: *3844* [→ *3598*+*4198*]. to be on a journey, travel:– went on journey [1]

3597 *ὁδοιπορία*, ***hodoiporia***, n. GK: *3845* [→ *3598*+*4198*]. journey:– journeyings [1], journey [1]

3598 *ὁδός*, ***hodos***, n. GK: *3847* [→ *296, 1327, 1353, 1529, 1841, 2136, 2137, 3180, 3593, 3594, 3595, 3596, 3597, 3938, 4922, 4923*]. road, path, a general term for a thoroughfare to get from one place to another; by extension: way, manner of life; "the Way" is a term for the Christian lifestyle (Ac 9:2; 19:9):– way [75], ways [11], journey [5], way side [5], highways [2], as went (+*4160*) [1], highway side [1], highways (+*1327*+*3588*) [1], sabbath day's journey (+*2192*+*4521*) [1]

3599 *ὀδούς*, ***odous***, n. GK: *3848*. tooth:– teeth [10], tooth [2]

3600 *ὀδυνάω*, ***odynaō***, v. GK: *3849* [→ *3601*]. to grieve, be anxious, in agony:– sorrowing [2], tormented [2]

3601 *ὀδύνη*, ***odynē***, n. GK: *3850* [→ *3600*]. anguish, grief, pain:– sorrows [1], sorrow [1]

3602 *ὀδυρμός*, ***odyrmos***, n. GK: *3851*. deep sorrow, mourning, lamentation:– mourning [2]

3603 *ὅ ἐστι*, ***hō esti***; or *ὅ ἐστιν*, ***hō estin***, p.rel.+v. GK: *4005* + *1639* [→ *3739*+*1510*]. that is, which is; see *1510* and *3739*:–

3604 Ὀζίας, ***Ozias***, n.pr. GK: *3852*. Uzziah, "*Yahweh is [my] strength*":– Ozias [2]

3605 *ὄζω*, ***ozō***, v. GK: *3853* [→ *2175, 2238, 3744, 3750*]. to give off a bad odor, stink, smell:– stinketh [1]

3606 *ὅθεν*, ***hothen***, adv. GK: *3854* [→ *3739*]. from where, from there; therefore, this is why:– wherefore [4], whereupon [3], from whence [2], whence [2], where [2], from thence [1], whereby [1]

3607 *ὀθόνη*, ***othonē***, n. GK: *3855* [→ *3608*]. linen sheet:– sheet [2]

3608 *ὀθόνιον*, ***othonion***, n. GK: *3856* [→ *3607*]. (pl.) strips of linen, bandages:– linen clothes [5]

3609 *οἰκεῖος*, ***oikeios***, a. GK: *3858* [→ *3624*]. belonging to the household, of the immediate family:– household [1], house [1], of household [1]

3610 *οἰκέτης*, ***oiketēs***, n. GK: *3860* [→ *3624*]. house servant, domestic slave:– servant [3], household servants [1], servants [1]

3611 *οἰκέω*, ***oikeō***, v. GK: *3861* [→ *3624*]. to live, dwell:– dwelleth [4], dwell [4], dwelling [1]

3612 *οἴκημα*, ***oikēma***, n. GK: *3862* [→ *3624*]. cell, room in a prison:– prison [1]

3613 *οἰκητήριον*, ***oikētērion***, n. GK: *3863* [→ *3624*]. dwelling, home:– habitation [1], house [1]

3614 *οἰκία*, ***oikia***, n. GK: *3864* [→ *3624*]. house, home; family:– house [84], houses [8], from house to house (+*3588*) [1], home [1], household [1]

3615 *οἰκιακός*, ***oikiakos***, n. GK: *3865* [→ *3624*]. member of a household:– of household [2]

3616 *οἰκοδεσποτέω*, ***oikodespoteō***, v. GK: *3866* [→ *3624*+*1203*]. to manage one's home:– guide the house [1]

3617 *οἰκοδεσπότης*, ***oikodespotēs***, n. GK: *3867* [→ *3624*+*1203*]. head or owner of the house, landowner:– goodman of the house [4], householder [3], master of the house [3], goodman [1], householder (+*444*) [1]

3618 *οἰκοδομέω*, ***oikodomeō***, v. GK: *3868* [→ *3624*+*1430*]. to build, build up, rebuild, a physical edifice; by extension: to edify, strengthen, develop another person's life through acts and words of love and encouragement:– build [12], built [10], builders [5], edifieth [3], buildest [2], edified [2], edify [2], builded [1], building [1], emboldened [1]

3619 *οἰκοδομή*, ***oikodomē***, n. GK: *3869* [→ *3624*+*1430*]. building, construction, a physical edifice; by extension: building up, edification, strengthening, developing another person's life through acts and words of love and encouragement:– edifying [7], edification [4], buildings [3], building [3], edify [1]

3620 *οἰκοδομία*, ***oikodomia***, n. GK: *3870* [→ *3624*+*1430*]. edification:–

3621 *οἰκονομέω*, ***oikonomeō***, v. GK: *3872* [→ *3624*+*3551*]. to manage:– steward [1]

3622 *οἰκονομία*, ***oikonomia***, n. GK: *3873* [→ *3624*+*3551*]. management, administration, job of administration; what is put into effect, plan:– dispensation [4], stewardship [3], edifying [1]

3623 οἰκονόμος, ***oikonomos***, n. GK: *3874* [→ *3624+3551*]. manager, administrator, director, trustee:– steward [5], stewards [3], chamberlain [1], governors [1]

3624 οἶκος, ***oikos***, n. GK: *3875* [→ *456, 1460, 1774, 2026, 2730, 2731, 2732, 2733, 3350, 3351, 3609, 3610, 3611, 3612, 3613, 3614, 3615, 3616, 3617, 3618, 3619, 3620, 3621, 3622, 3623, 3625, 3626, 3832, 3939, 3940, 3941, 4039, 4040, 4924, 4925*]. house, home, a physical edifice; of royalty: palace; of deity: temple; by extension: family, lineage, people who live in or originated in a particular house:– house [96], home [5], houses [5], household [3], from house to house (*+2596*) [2], every house (*+2596*) [1], in every house (*+2596*) [1], temple [1]

3625 οἰκουμένη, ***oikoumenē***, n. GK: *3876* [→ *3624*]. the (inhabited) world, (Roman) world; humankind:– world [14], earth [1]

3626 οἰκουρός, ***oikouros***; or οἰκουργός, ***oikourgos***, a. GK: *3877 & 3878* [→ *3624*]. staying at home, domestic:– keepers at home [1]

3627 οἰκτείρω, ***oikteirō***, v. GK: *3879 & 3882* [→ *3628, 3629*]. to have compassion on:– have compassion [2]

3628 οἰκτιρμός, ***oiktirmos***, n. GK: *3880* [→ *3627*]. compassion, mercy, pity:– mercies [4], mercy [1]

3629 οἰκτίρμων, ***oiktirmōn***, a. GK: *3881* [→ *3627*]. merciful, compassionate:– merciful [2], tender mercy [1]

οἶμαι, ***oimai***. See ***3633***.

3630 οἰνοπότης, ***oinopotēs***, n. GK: *3884* [→ *3631+4095*]. drunkard, wine-drinker:– winebibber [2]

3631 οἶνος, ***oinos***, n. GK: *3885* [→ *3630, 3632, 3943*]. wine:– wine [32], winepress (*+3025*) [1]

3632 οἰνοφλυγία, ***oinophlygia***, n. GK: *3886* [→ *3631+5397*]. drunkenness:– excess of wine [1]

3633 οἴομαι, ***oiomai***; or οἶμαι, ***oimai***, v. GK: *3883 & 3887*. to suppose, think, expect:– suppose [1], supposing [1], think [1]

3634 οἷος, ***hoios***, p.rel. GK: *3888* [→ *4169*]. what sort of, what kind of:– such as [5], as [4], what manner [2], which [2], so as [1], what [1]

οἴω, ***oiō***. See ***5342***.

3635 ὀκνέω, ***okneō***, v. GK: *3890* [→ *3636*]. to delay, hesitate:– delay [1]

3636 ὀκνηρός, ***oknēros***, a. GK: *3891* [→ *3635*]. lazy, idle, not active; troublesome:– slothful [2], grievous [1]

3637 ὀκταήμερος, ***oktaēmeros***, a. GK: *3892* [→ *3638+2250*]. eighth day:– eighth day [1]

3638 ὀκτώ, ***oktō***, n.num. GK: *3893* [→ *3589, 3590, 3637*]. eight:– eight [6], eighteen (*+1176+2532*) [3]

3639 ὄλεθρος, ***olethros***, n. GK: *3897* [→ *622, 623, 684, 1842, 3644, 3645, 4881*]. destruction, ruin:– destruction [4]

3640 ὀλιγόπιστος, ***oligopistos***, a. GK: *3899* [→ *3641+4103*]. of little faith:– of little faith [5]

3641 ὀλίγος, ***oligos***, a. GK: *3900* [→ *3640, 3642, 3643*]. little, small, short; (pl.) few:– few [20], little [9], small [5], almost (*+1722*) [2], short [2], while [2], briefly (*+1223*) [1], long (*+3756*) [1], season [1]

3642 ὀλιγόψυχος, ***oligopsychos***, a. GK: *3901* [→ *3641+5594*]. timid, fainthearted, discouraged:– feebleminded [1]

3643 ὀλιγωρέω, ***oligōreō***, v. GK: *3902* [→ *3641*]. to make light of, despise:– despise [1]

3644 ὀλοθρευτής, ***olothreutēs***, n. GK: *3894 & 3904* [→ *3639*]. destroyer:– destroyer [1]

3645 ὀλοθρεύω, ***olothreuō***, v. GK: *3895 & 3905* [→ *3639*]. to destroy:– destroyed [1]

3646 ὁλοκαύτωμα, ***holokautōma***, n. GK: *3906* [→ *3650+2545*]. burnt offering, wholly consumed on the altar as dedicated to God:– burnt offerings [2], whole burnt offerings [1]

3647 ὁλοκληρία, ***holoklēria***, n. GK: *3907* [→ *3650+2819*]. completeness, wholeness (in healing):– perfect soundness [1]

3648 ὁλόκληρος, ***holoklēros***, a. GK: *3908* [→ *3650+2819*]. whole, complete:– entire [1], whole [1]

3649 ὀλολύζω, ***ololyzō***, v. GK: *3909*. to wail, cry out:– howl [1]

3650 ὅλος, ***holos***, a. GK: *3910* [→ *2526', 2527, 3646, 3647, 3648, 3651, 3654*]. all, whole, entire; throughout:– all [63], whole [43], every whit [2], all (*+1722*) [1], all long [1], altogether [1], throughout (*+1223*) [1]

3651 ὁλοτελής, ***holotelēs***, a. GK: *3911* [→ *3650+5056*]. through and through, wholly, completely:– wholly [1]

3652 Ὀλυμπᾶς, ***Olympas***, n.pr. GK: *3912*. Olympas:– Olympas [1]

3653 ὄλυνθος, ***olynthos***, n. GK: *3913*. late fig:– untimely figs [1]

3654 ὅλως, ***holōs***, adv. GK: *3914* [→ *3650*]. completely, (not) at all; actually:– at all [2], commonly [1], utterly [1]

3655 ὄμβρος, ***ombros***, n. GK: *3915*. rainstorm (that may include thunder and lightning):– shower [1]

3656 ὁμιλέω, ***homileō***, v. GK: *3917* [→ *3657, 3658, 4926; cf. 3664*]. to talk, converse:– communed [2], talked [2]

3657 ὁμιλία, ***homilia***, n. GK: *3918* [→ *3656*]. company, associations:– communications [1]

3658 ὅμιλος, ***homilos***, n. GK: *3919* [→ *3656*]. crowd, throng:– company [1]

3659 ὄμμα, ***omma***, n. GK: *3921* [→ *3708*]. eye:– eyes [1]

3660 ὀμνύω, ***omnyō***, v. GK: *3922 & 3923* [→ *3728, 4945*]. to declare an oath, swear an oath, promise with an oath:– swear [13], sware [7], sweareth [4], sworn [3]

3661 ὁμοθυμαδόν, ***homothymadon***, adv. GK: *3924* [→ *3664+2372*]. united, in togetherness, as one:– with one accord [11], one mind [1]

3662 ὁμοιάζω, ***homoiazō***, v. GK: *3925* [→ *3664*]. to be like, resemble:– agreeth [1]

3663 ὁμοιοπαθής, ***homoiopathēs***, a. GK: *3926* [→ *3664+3958*]. like, of the same quality or kind of desires:– of like passions with [1], subject to like passions [1]

3664 ὅμοιος, ***homoios***, a. GK: *3927* [→ *871, 3661, 3662, 3663, 3665, 3666, 3667, 3668, 3669, 3670, 3673, 3674, 3675, 3676, 3945, 3946, 4927; cf. 3656, 3670*]. like, similar, of a same or similar nature or quality:– like [41], like unto [4], unto [2]

3665 ὁμοιότης, ***homoiotēs***, n. GK: *3928* [→ *3664*]. similarity, likeness:– like as (*+2596*) [1], similitude [1]

3666 ὁμοιόω, ***homoioō***, v. GK: *3929* [→ *3664*]. to make like, compare; (pass.) to be like, become like:– liken [5], likened [4], like [2], made like [2], likeness [1], resemble [1]

3667 ὁμοίωμα, ***homoiōma***, n. GK: *3930* [→ *3664*]. likeness; looking like, image; form, appearance:– likeness [2], in likeness [1], like to [1], shapes [1], similitude [1]

3668 ὁμοίως, ***homoiōs***, adv. GK: *3931* [→ *3664*]. likewise, in the same way, similarly:– likewise [27], likewise (*+3305*) [1], moreover [1], so [1]

3669 ὁμοίωσις, ***homoiōsis***, n. GK: *3932* [→ *3664*]. likeness:– similitude [1]

3670 ὁμολογέω, ***homologeō***, v. GK: *3933* [→ *437, 1843, 3671, 3672*]. to confess, acknowledge, agree, admit, declare; this can be a profession of allegiance, an admission of bad behavior, or an emphatic declaration of a truth:– confess [12], confessed [3], confesseth [2], profess [2], confession made [1], giving thanks [1], professed [1], promised [1]

3671 ὁμολογία, ***homologia***, n. GK: *3934* [→ *3670*]. confession, profession, acknowledgment, to openly express commitment and allegiance:– profession [4], confession [1], professed [1]

3672 ὁμολογουμένως, ***homologoumenōs***, adv. GK: *3935* [→ *3670*]. beyond all question, most certainly:– without controversy [1]

3673 ὁμότεχνος, ***homotechnos***, a. GK: *3937* [→ *3664+5078*]. of the same trade:– same craft [1]

3674 ὁμοῦ, ***homou***, adv. GK: *3938* [→ *3664*]. together:– together [3]

3675 ὁμόφρων, ***homophrōn***, a. GK: *3939* [→ *3664+5424*]. living in harmony with, like-minded:– one mind [1]

ὀμόω, ***omoō***. See ***3660***.

3676 ὅμως, ***homōs***, adv. GK: *3940* [→ *3664*]. just as; at the same time:– even [1], nevertheless (*+3305*) [1], though but [1]

3677 ὄναρ, ***onar***, n. GK: *3941*. dream:– dream [6]

3678 ὀνάριον, ***onarion***, n. GK: *3942* [→ *3688*]. young donkey:– young ass [1]

ὀνάω, ***onaō***. See ***3685***.

3679 ὀνειδίζω, ***oneidizō***, v. GK: *3943* [→ *3681*]. to heap insults on, denounce, find fault, rebuke:– reproached [2], cast in teeth [1], reproach [1], reviled [1], revile [1], suffer reproach [1], upbraided [1], upbraideth [1], upbraid [1]

3680 ὀνειδισμός, ***oneidismos***, n. GK: *3944* [→ *3681*]. disgrace, insult:– reproach [3], reproaches [2]

3681 ὄνειδος, ***oneidos***, n. GK: *3945* [→ *3679, 3680*]. disgrace:– reproach [1]

3682 Ὀνήσιμος, ***Onēsimos***, n.pr. GK: *3946* [→ *3685*]. Onesimus, "*useful*":– Onesimus [4]

3683 Ὀνησίφορος, ***Onēsiphoros,*** n.pr. GK: *3947* [→ *3685+5342*]. Onesiphorus, "*one bringing usefulness*":– Onesiphorus [2]

3684 ὀνικός, ***onikos,*** a. GK: *3948* [→ *3688*]. pertaining to a donkey, millstone worked by a donkey:– millstone (*+3458*) [2]

3685 ὀνίνημι, ***oninēmi,*** v. GK: *3949* [→ *3682, 3683*]. to have benefit or joy:– joy [1]

3686 ὄνομα, ***onoma,*** n. GK: *3950* [→ *2028, 2176, 3687, 5122, 5581*]. name; title; reputation:– name [172], named [28], name's [11], names [11], called [4], men (*+444*) [1], surnamed (*+2007*) [1]

3687 ὀνομάζω, ***onomazō,*** v. GK: *3951* [→ *3686*]. to give a name, designate a name; to confess; (mid.) to call oneself; (pass.) to be named; be known:– named [7], called [1], call [1], nameth [1]

3688 ὄνος, ***onos,*** n. GK: *3952* [→ *3678, 3684*]. donkey (female or male):– ass [5], ass's [1]

3689 ὄντως, ***ontōs,*** adv. GK: *3953* [→ *1510*]. really, certainly, surely:– indeed [6], certainly [1], clean [1], of a truth [1], verily [1]

3690 ὄξος, ***oxos,*** n. GK: *3954* [→ *3691*]. wine vinegar:– vinegar [7]

3691 ὀξύς, ***oxys,*** a. GK: *3955* [→ *3690, 3947, 3948*]. sharp; swift, quick:– sharp [7], swift [1]

3692 ὀπή, ***opē,*** n. GK: *3956*. hole, opening:– caves [1], place [1]

3693 ὄπισθεν, ***opisthen,*** adv. GK: *3957* [→ *3694*]. from behind; after:– behind [4], after [2], on the backside [1]

3694 ὀπίσω, ***opisō,*** adv. GK: *3958* [→ *3693*]. behind, after, following:– after [22], behind [6], back (*+1519+3588*) [3], again (*+1519+3588*) [1], backward (*+1519+3588*) [1], back [1], follow (*+1205*) [1], went back (*+565+1519+3588*) [1]

3695 ὁπλίζω, ***hoplizō,*** v. GK: *3959* [→ *3696*]. (mid.) to arm oneself with:– arm [1]

3696 ὅπλον, ***hoplon,*** n. GK: *3960* [→ *2528, 3695, 3833*]. instrument, weapon, armor:– armour [2], instruments [2], weapons [2]

3697 ὁποῖος, ***hopoios,*** a. GK: *3961* [→ *4226*]. what kind of, what sort of:– what manner of [2], of what sort [1], such as (*+5108*) [1], whatsoever [1]

3698 ὁπότε, ***hopote,*** pt.temp. GK: *3962* [→ *4226*]. when:– when [1]

3699 ὅπου, ***hopou,*** pt.pl. GK: *3963* [→ *4226*]. where, wherever; whenever:– where [58], whither [9], whithersoever (*+302*) [4], wheresoever (*+1437*) [3], whereas [2], wheresoever (*+302*) [2], in what place soever (*+1437*) [1], wheresoever [1], whithersoever (*+1437*) [1]

3700 ὀπτάνομαι, ***optanomai,*** v. GK: *3964* [→ *3708*]. (mid.) to appear:– see [29], appeared [15], seen [8], appear [2], look [2], shewed [1]

3701 ὀπτασία, ***optasia,*** n. GK: *3965* [→ *3708*]. (supernatural) vision:– vision [3], visions [1]

ὄπτομαι, ***optomai.*** See ***3700.***

3702 ὀπτός, ***optos,*** a. GK: *3966*. broiled, roasted:– broiled [1]

3703 ὀπώρα, ***opōra,*** n. GK: *3967* [→ *5352*]. fruit:– fruits [1]

3704 ὅπως, ***hopōs,*** c.&adv. GK: *3968* [→ *4226*]. that, so that, (in order) to:– that [41], how [4], to [4], that (*+302*) [3], because [1], might [1], so that [1], when (*+302*) [1]

3705 ὅραμα, ***horama,*** n. GK: *3969* [→ *3708*]. (supernatural) vision; sight (from God):– vision [11], sight [1]

3706 ὅρασις, ***horasis,*** n. GK: *3970* [→ *3708*]. appearance; vision:– in sight [1], look [1], visions [1], vision [1]

3707 ὁρατός, ***horatos,*** a. GK: *3971* [→ *3708*]. pertaining to things visible, things seen:– visible [1]

3708 ὁράω, ***horaō,*** v. GK: *1625 & 3972* [→ *517, 542, 845, 872, 1799, 1896, 2029, 2030, 2072, 2529, 2714, 2734, 3359, 3659, 3700, 3701, 3705, 3706, 3707, 3799, 4275, 4308, 4383, 4659, 4893?, 4894?, 5299, 5432; cf. 3788, 4383*]. to see, notice; perceive; (pass.) to appear, be seen:– seen [33], see [12], saw [5], take heed [5], beholding [1], perceive [1], seeing [1], seeth [1]

3709 ὀργή, ***orgē,*** n. GK: *3973* [→ *3710, 3711, 3949, 3950; cf. 3713*]. wrath, anger, the feeling and expression of strong displeasure and hostility; this can range from petty human anger to the righteous anger of God toward sinful disobedience:– wrath [31], anger [3], indignation [1], vengeance [1]

3710 ὀργίζω, ***orgizō,*** v. GK: *3974* [→ *3709*]. (mid./pass.) to be angry, enraged, to feel and express strong displeasure and hostility; this can range from petty human anger to the righteous anger of God toward sinful disobedience:– angry [5], wroth [3]

3711 ὀργίλος, ***orgilos,*** a. GK: *3975* [→ *3709*]. quick-tempered, inclined to anger:– soon angry [1]

3712 ὀργυιά, ***orgyia,*** n. GK: *3976* [→ *3713*]. fathom (about six feet):– fathoms [2]

3713 ὀρέγω, ***oregō,*** v. GK: *3977* [→ *3712, 3715; cf. 3709*]. (mid.) to set one's heart on, strive for, aspire to, desire:– desire [2], coveted after [1]

3714 ὀρεινός, ***oreinos,*** a. GK: *3978* [→ *3735*]. hilly, (n.) hill country:– hill country [2]

3715 ὄρεξις, ***orexis,*** n. GK: *3979* [→ *3713*]. lust, desire:– lust [1]

3716 ὀρθοποδέω, ***orthopodeō,*** v. GK: *3980* [→ *3717+4228*]. to act in line with (the truth), act rightly:– walked uprightly [1]

3717 ὀρθός, ***orthos,*** a. GK: *3981* [→ *461, 1357, 1882, 1930, 2735, 3716, 3718, 3723*]. straight, level:– straight [1], upright [1]

3718 ὀρθοτομέω, ***orthotomeō,*** v. GK: *3982* [→ *3717+5114*]. to handle correctly, guide on a straight path:– rightly dividing [1]

3719 ὀρθρίζω, ***orthrizō,*** v. GK: *3983* [→ *3722*]. to get up early in the morning:– came early in the morning [1]

3720 ὀρθρινός, ***orthrinos,*** a. GK: *3984* [→ *3722*]. early in the morning:– morning [1]

3721 ὄρθριος, ***orthrios,*** a. GK: *3985* [→ *3722*]. early in the morning:– early [1]

3722 ὄρθρος, ***orthros,*** n. GK: *3986* [→ *3719, 3720, 3721*]. dawn, daybreak, early in the morning:– early in the morning (*+3588+5259*) [1], early in the morning [1], very early in the morning (*+901*) [1]

3723 ὀρθῶς, ***orthōs,*** adv. GK: *3987* [→ *3717*]. correctly, rightly, plainly:– rightly [2], plain [1], right [1]

3724 ὁρίζω, ***horizō,*** v. GK: *3988* [→ *592, 873, 3181, 3725, 3734, 4309, 4927*]. to determine, set, appoint, decree:– determined [3], ordained [2], declared [1], determinate [1], limiteth [1]

3725 ὅριον, ***horion,*** n. GK: *3990* [→ *3724*]. region, area, vicinity:– coasts [10], borders [1]

3726 ὁρκίζω, ***horkizō,*** v. GK: *1941 & 3991* [→ *3727*]. to command; implore, adjure:– adjure [2], charge [1]

3727 ὅρκος, ***horkos,*** n. GK: *3992* [→ *1844, 1845, 1964, 1965, 3726, 3728*]. oath:– oath [7], oaths' [2], oaths [1]

3728 ὁρκωμοσία, ***horkōmosia,*** n. GK: *3993* [→ *3727+3660*]. oath, taking of an oath:– oath [4]

3729 ὁρμάω, ***hormaō,*** v. GK: *3994* [→ *3730*]. to rush (as in a stampede):– ran violently [3], ran [1], rushed [1]

3730 ὁρμή, ***hormē,*** n. GK: *3995* [→ *874, 2868, 3729, 3731*]. plot, decision; impulse, desire:– assault [1], governor [1]

3731 ὅρμημα, ***hormēma,*** n. GK: *3996* [→ *3730*]. sudden violence:– violence [1]

3732 ὄρνεον, ***orneon,*** n. GK: *3997* [→ *3733*]. bird:– fowls [2], bird [1]

3733 ὄρνις, ***ornis,*** n. GK: *3989 & 3998* [→ *3732*]. hen, bird:– hen [2]

3734 ὁροθεσία, ***horothesia,*** n. GK: *3999* [→ *3724+5087*]. exact place, fixed boundary:– bounds [1]

3735 ὄρος, ***oros,*** n. GK: *4001* [→ *3714*]. hill, hillside, mountain, mountainside; this can refer to any elevated place from mounds to high mountains:– mountain [28], mount [21], mountains [13], hill [3]

3736 ὀρύσσω, ***oryssō,*** v. GK: *4002* [→ *1358, 1846*]. to dig up, dig out:– digged [3]

3737 ὀρφανός, ***orphanos,*** a. GK: *4003* [→ *642*]. (n.) an orphan:– comfortless [1], fatherless [1]

3738 ὀρχέομαι, ***orcheomai,*** v. GK: *4004*. to dance:– danced [4]

3739 ὅς, ***hos,*** p.rel. GK: *4005* [→ *1352, 1355, 1360, 1539, 2505, 2509, 2526, 2530, 3606, 3634, 3746, 3748, 3755, 3752, 3753, 3754, 3757, 3842, 4212, 5119*]. who, which, what, that; anyone, someone, a certain one:– which [452], whom [267], that [144], who [85], whose [53], what [45], whosoever (*+302*) [32], wherein (*+1722*) [23], whosoever (*+1437*) [19], whatsoever (*+1437*) [15], whereof [15], some [14], he [10], one [9], till (*+2193*) [9], wherewith [9], another [8], whatsoever (*+302*) [7], whereby (*+1722*) [6], whereunto (*+1519*) [6], until (*+2193*) [5], whereunto [5], because (*+473*) [4], since (*+575*) [4], the [4], till (*+891*) [4], until (*+891*) [4], whatsoever [4], when [4], where (*+1722*) [4], whereon (*+1909*) [4], whomsoever (*+1437*) [4], whomsoever (*+302*) [4], as (*+5158*) [3], such [3], whatsoever (*+302+5100*) [3], whereby (*+1223*) [3], wherefore (*+156+1223*) [3], wherein (*+1519*) [3], wherein (*+1909*) [3], wherein [3], while (*+1722*) [3], whom (*+302*) [3], whoso (*+302*) [3], whosoever

(+302+3956) [3], other [2], that (+1437) [2], when (+1722) [2], whereas (+1722) [2], wherefore (+1223) [2], whereof (+4012) [2], whereupon (+1722) [2], wherewith (+1722) [2], while (+2193) [2], while (+891) [2], whom (+1437) [2], another (+3303) [1], as (+2596+5158) [1], as (+302+5100) [1], as many as (+3956) [1], as [1], because (+1752) [1], called [1], even as (+2596+3779+5158) [1], even as (+5158) [1], he that (+302) [1], him [1], howbeit whereinsoever (+302+1161+1722) [1], in the mean time (+1722) [1], like [1], moreover (+1161+3062) [1], nothing (+3756) [1], once (+302+575) [1], one (+3303) [1], one man [1], others [1], since the time (+575) [1], soever (+302) [1], some (+3303) [1], that (+1722) [1], that (+302) [1], that (+575) [1], therefore (+473) [1], they [1], this [1], those [1], till (+302+891) [1], till (+3360) [1], what (+1437) [1], what (+5101) [1], whatsoever (+1437+5100) [1], whatsoever (+302+302+5100) [1], whatsoever (+3956) [1], whence [1], whereby (+4012) [1], whereby (+4314) [1], wherefore (+1519) [1], wherefore (+1909) [1], wherefore (+5484) [1], wherein (+1223) [1], wherein (+1722+3778) [1], wherein (+4012) [1], whereinto (+1519) [1], whereof (+1537) [1], whereon [1], whereto (+1519) [1], whereunto (+3825) [1], where [1], whether (+1520) [1], whither (+1519) [1], whomsoever (+3956) [1], whoso (+1437) [1], whosoever (+3956) [1]

3740 ὁσάκις, hosakis, adv. GK: 4006 [→ 3745]. as often as, whenever:– as oft as (+302) [1], as often as (+1437) [1], as often as (+302) [1]

3741 ὅσιος, hosios, a. GK: 4008 [→ 462, 3742, 3743]. holy, pious, devout; (n.) Holy One; divine decree (Ac 13:34):– holy [4], holy one [2], mercies [1]

3742 ὁσιότης, hosiotēs, n. GK: 4009 [→ 3741]. holiness:– holiness [2]

3743 ὁσίως, hosiōs, adv. GK: 4010 [→ 3741]. holy, in a devout manner:– holily [1]

3744 ὀσμή, osmē, n. GK: 4011 [→ 3605]. fragrance, odor:– savour [4], odour [2]

3745 ὅσος, hosos, a. GK: 4012 [→ 3740, 4214]. how great, how much, how far; as, just as:– as many as [25], whatsoever [17], that [9], whatsoever (+302) [6], how great [5], what [5], all that [4], as long as (+1909+5550) [3], as many as (+302) [3], as [3], how much [3], which [3], all [2], as long as (+1909) [2], inasmuch as (+1909) [2], inasmuch as (+2596) [2], little while (+3398+3745) [2], that ever [2], whatsoever (+1437) [2], whosoever (+302) [2], as (+2596) [1], as long as (+5550) [1], as many as (+1437) [1], as much as [1], ever [1], how many [1], inasmuch as (+1909+3303+3767) [1], more [1], so many as [1], what great [1], what soever [1], wherewith soever (+302) [1], who [1]

3746 ὅσπερ, hosper, p.rel.&pt. GK: 4013 [→ 3739+4007]. whosoever:– whomsoever [1]

3747 ὀστέον, osteon; or **ὀστοῦν, ostoun,** n. GK: 4014 & 4016. bone:– bones [4], bone [1]

3748 ὅστις, hostis, p.rel.&indef. GK: 4015 [→ 3739+5100]. who, whoever, whatever; someone, anyone, everyone; a marker of time relationships: until, while:– which [82], who [30], whosoever [10], that [7], they [3], whosoever (+302) [3], till (+2193) [2], until (+2193) [2], whosoever (+3956) [2], as [1], a [1], he that [1], in that [1], such as [1], whatsoever (+1437+3956+5100) [1], whatsoever (+302) [1], what [1], whereas [1], which (+302) [1], whiles (+2193) [1]

3749 ὀστράκινος, ostrakinos, a. GK: 4017. made of clay:– earthen [1], of earth [1]

3750 ὄσφρησις, osphrēsis, n. GK: 4018 [→ 3605]. sense of smell:– smelling [1]

3751 ὀσφῦς, osphys, n. GK: 4019. waist, loins, body; belt:– loins [8]

3752 ὅταν, hotan, pt.temp. GK: 4020 [→ 3739+5037+302]. when, whenever; at once; as soon as:– when [115], as soon as [2], as long as [1], that [1], till (+1508) [1], whensoever [1], while [1]

3753 ὅτε, hote, pt.temp. GK: 4021 [→ 3739+5037]. when, while, after; as, as soon as:– when [99], after [3], as soon as [2], that [1], while [1], whilst [1]

3754 ὅτι, hoti, c. GK: 4022 [→ 3739+5101]. that; because, since; for:– that [622], for [265], *usually untranslated* [206], because [177], how that [20], how [11], because that [4], though [3], in that [1], seeing that [1], seeing [1], to [1], why [1]

3755 ὅτου, hotou, p.rel.&indef.gen. of 3748. GK: 4015 [→ 3739+5100]. a marker of time relationships: until, while; see 3748:–

3756 οὐ, ou, adv.neg. GK: 4024 [→ 1847, 1848, 3760, 3761, 3762, 3763, 3764, 3765, 3766, 3768, 3777, 3780]. no, not, not at all, in no way, absolutely not. At the beginning of a Greek question, it anticipates a positive response:– not [1209], no [140], cannot (+1410) [45], none [20], neither (+2532) [16], neither [12], nay [11], cannot [10], no (+3956) [7], never (+165+1519+3361+3588) [5], nothing [4], never [3], nothing (+5101) [3], neither (+1161) [2], nor (+2532) [2], nor [2], not (+3361) [2], but (+2228+4183) [1], cannot (+1510) [1], cannot (+1735) [1], cannot (+2192) [1], cannot (+2480) [1], long (+3641) [1], neither any (+3762) [1], never (+165+1487+1519+3588) [1], never (+165+1519+3588) [1], never (+3361+4218) [1], never (+3361+4455) [1], never before (+3764) [1], no more at all (+3361+3765) [1], no not one (+1520+2193) [1], none (+3762) [1], nothing (+3739) [1], nothing (+3956+4487) [1], nothing (+5100) [1], nothing at all (+3762) [1], special (+3588+5177) [1], unworthy (+514) [1], without (+3326) [1]

3757 οὗ, hou, adv.pl. GK: 4023 [→ 3739]. where; to which:– where [22], whither [2], whence [1], when [1], wherein [1], whithersoever (+1437) [1]

3758 οὐά, oua, pt.interj. GK: 4025. so!, aha!:– ah [1]

3759 οὐαί, ouai, pt.interj. GK: 4026. woe!, how dreadful!, alas!:– woe [40], alas [6], woes [1]

3760 οὐδαμῶς, oudamōs, adv. GK: 4027 [→ 3756+1161]. by no means:– not [1]

3761 οὐδέ, oude, c.neg. GK: 4028 [→ 3756+1161]. and not, nor, neither, not either, not even:– neither [68], nor [30], not [17], no [3], nor yet [2], not so much as [2], then not [2], also not [1], and no so much as (+2532) [1], and not [1], even not [1], neither (+2532) [1], never [1], no more [1], no not so much [1], not even [1], not so much as (+235) [1], nothing (+5100) [1], yet not [1]

3762 οὐδείς, oudeis, a. GK: 4029 & 4032 [→ 3756+1161+1520]. no one, not anyone, nothing:– no [116], nothing [68], none [26], any [7], man [2], not any [2], all [1], despised (+1519+3049) [1], neither any (+1161) [1], neither any (+2532) [1], neither any (+3756) [1], never (+3768) [1], none (+3056) [1], none (+3756) [1], not at all [1], nothing at all (+3756) [1], not [1], nought [1], ought [1], yet never (+4455) [1]

3763 οὐδέποτε, oudepote, adv. GK: 4030 [→ 3756+1161+4226+5037]. never:– never [14], neither at any time (+2532) [1], nothing at any time (+3956) [1]

3764 οὐδέπω, oudepō, adv. GK: 4031 [→ 3756+1161]. not yet, not ever:– as yet not [1], never before (+3756) [1], never yet [1], not yet [1], yet [1]

3765 οὐκέτι, ouketi, adv. GK: 4033 [→ 3756+2089]. no longer, not again, not any more, no further:– no more [29], any more [3], after that [2], not [2], now not [2], any moe [1], henceforth not [1], hereafter not [1], more [1], no longer [1], no more at all (+3361+3756) [1], not now [1], not yet [1], yet [1]

3766 οὐκοῦν, oukoun, adv. GK: 4034 [→ 3756+3767]. so, then (to introduce a question):– then [1]

3767 οὖν, oun, pt.infer.&trans. GK: 4036 [→ 3304, 3766, 5105]. therefore, then, so then:– therefore [257], then [195], so [16], and [9], now [9], wherefore [8], therefore (+686) [7], but [4], seeing then [3], then (+5119) [2], when [2], and so [1], forasmuch then as [1], forasmuch then [1], inasmuch as (+1909+3303+3745) [1], therefore seeing [1]

3768 οὔπω, oupō, adv. GK: 4037 [→ 3756]. not yet, still not; not ever:– not yet [20], hitherto not [1], never (+3762) [1], no as yet [1], yet [1]

3769 οὐρά, oura, n. GK: 4038. tail:– tails [4], tail [1]

3770 οὐράνιος, ouranios, a. GK: 4039 [→ 3772]. heavenly, in heaven, from heaven:– heavenly [6]

3771 οὐρανόθεν, ouranothen, adv. GK: 4040 [→ 3772]. from heaven:– from heaven [2]

3772 οὐρανός, ouranos, n. GK: 4041 [→ 2032, 3321, 3770, 3771]. sky, air, firmament, any area above the earth; heaven(s), the place of sun, moon, and stars; heaven, in which God dwells. "The third heaven" may be a Jewish technical term for God's dwelling place; "heaven" in some contexts is a euphemism for "God" (Lk 15:18):– heaven [248], heavens [19], air [10], sky [5], heaven's [1], heavenly (+1537) [1]

3773 Οὐρβανός, Ourbanos, n.pr. GK: 4042. Urbanus, *"refined, elegant"*:– Urban [1]

3774 Οὐρίας, Ourias, n.pr. GK: 4043. Uriah, *"Yahweh is [my] flame, light"*:– Urias [1]

3775 οὖς, ous, n. GK: 4044 [→ 1801, 5621]. ear; listening, responding:– ears [24], ear [13]

3776 οὐσία, ousia, n. GK: 4045 [→ 1510]. wealth; estate, property:– goods [1], substance [1]

3777 **οὔτε**, ***oute***, adv. [used as neg.]. GK: *4046* [→ *3756+5037*]. and not, neither, nor:– neither [45], nor [42], not [3], nor yet [2], none [1], nothing [1]

3778 **οὗτος**, ***houtos***, p.demo. GK: *4047* [→ *3779, 5023, 5025, 5026, 5082, 5108, 5118, 5123, 5124, 5125, 5126, 5127, 5128, 5129, 5130*]. this, this one, these; (as object) him, her, it, them:– this [666], these [358], that [58], therefore (+*1223*) [43], the same [36], he [33], him [30], thus [21], for this cause (+*1223*) [14], they [13], those [13], she [12], them [11], it [9], such [9], hereby (+*1722*) [8], herein (+*1722*) [7], wherefore (+*1223*) [7], same [6], so [6], the [6], afterward (+*3326*) [4], hereafter (+*3326*) [4], therefore (+*1519*) [3], for this cause (+*1519*) [2], for this cause (+*1752*) [2], therefore (+*3844*) [2], therein (+*1722*) [2], thereunto (+*1519*) [2], to this end (+*1519*) [2], and partly (+*1161*) [1], by reason hereof (+*1223*) [1], from thenceforth (+*1537*) [1], hence (+*3326*) [1], hereby (+*1537*) [1], hereof [1], hereunto (+*1519*) [1], her [1], one [1], partly (+*3303*) [1], that same [1], that should follow (+*3326*) [1], the same (+*846*) [1], their [1], themselves [1], thereabout (+*4012*) [1], therein [1], thereunto (+*846+1519*) [1], therewith (+*1909*) [1], therewith [1], thus far (+*2193*) [1], wherein (+*1722+3739*) [1], which [1], who [1]

3779 **οὕτως**, ***houtōs***, adv. GK: *4048* [→ *3778*]. in this manner, thus, in the same way, likewise:– so [171], thus [17], likewise [6], on this wise [6], after this manner [3], after that [1], as [1], can [1], even as (+*2596+3739+5158*) [1], for all that [1], in this manner [1], on this fashion [1], so in like manner (+*2532*) [1], what [1]

3780 **οὐχί**, ***ouchi***, adv.neg. GK: *4049* [→ *3756*]. not, no!:– not [51], nay [5]

3781 **ὀφειλέτης**, ***opheiletēs***, n. GK: *4050* [→ *3784*]. debtor, one who owes, is obligated, guilty:– debtors [3], debtor [2], ought [1], sinners [1]

3782 **ὀφειλή**, ***opheilē***, n. GK: *4051* [→ *3784*]. debt; marital duty; (pl.) taxes:– debt [1], dues [1]

3783 **ὀφείλημα**, ***opheilēma***, n. GK: *4052* [→ *3784*]. debt, obligation, what is owed:– debts [1], debt [1]

3784 **ὀφείλω**, ***opheilō***, v. GK: *4053* [→ *3781, 3782, 3783, 3785, 4359, 5533*]. to owe, be in debt; be bound by oath; be obligated, ought, must:– ought [17], owest [3], bound [2], due [2], duty [2], behoved [1], debtor [1], debt [1], guilty [1], indebted [1], must needs [1], need [1], oweth [1], owe [1], should [1]

3785 **ὄφελον**, ***ophelon***, pt. GK: *4054* [→ *3784*]. How I wish! How I hope!:– would [4]

3786 **ὄφελος**, ***ophelos***, n. GK: *4055* [→ *5623*]. good, gain, benefit:– profit [2], advantageth [1]

3787 **ὀφθαλμοδουλία**, ***ophthalmodoulia***, n. GK: *4056* [→ *3788+1401*]. eye-service, service performed to attract attention:– eyeservice [2]

3788 **ὀφθαλμός**, ***ophthalmos***, n. GK: *4057* [→ *503, 3442, 3787; cf. 3708*]. eye, the organ of sight; by extension: the faculty of mental perception and understanding:– eyes [71], eye [30], sight [1]

3789 **ὄφις**, ***ophis***, n. GK: *4058*. snake, serpent:– serpent [8], serpents [6]

3790 **ὀφρῦς**, ***ophrys***, n. GK: *4059*. eyebrow, brow (of a hill):– brow [1]

3791 **ὀχλέω**, ***ochleō***, v. GK: *4061* [→ *3793*]. (pass.) to be tormented, disturbed:– vexed [2]

3792 **ὀχλοποιέω**, ***ochlopoieō***, v. GK: *4062* [→ *3793+4160*]. to form a mob:– gathered a company [1]

3793 **ὄχλος**, ***ochlos***, n. GK: *4063* [→ *1776, 3791, 3792, 3926*]. crowd, people, multitude, mob, a gathering of any size, sometimes with the implication that these are common folk and not leaders or nobility:– people [83], multitude [59], multitudes [20], company [7], press [5], number [1]

3794 **ὀχύρωμα**, ***ochyrōma***, n. GK: *4065* [→ *2192*]. stronghold, fortress; some translate as "prison":– strong holds [1]

3795 **ὀψάριον**, ***opsarion***, n. GK: *4066* [→ *3800, 3953*]. (small) fish:– fish [3], fishes [1], small fishes [1]

3796 **ὀψέ**, ***opse***, adv. GK: *4067* [→ *3797, 3798*]. in the evening, late in the day; (pp.) after:– at even [1], even [1], in the end [1]

3797 **ὄψιμος**, ***opsimos***, a. GK: *4069* [→ *3796*]. late (in the season, April-May in the modern calendar), spring:– latter [1]

3798 **ὄψιος**, ***opsios***, a. GK: *4070* [→ *3796*]. late; (n.) evening:– even [8], evening [5], at even (+*1096*) [1], eventide (+*3588+5610*) [1]

3799 **ὄψις**, ***opsis***, n. GK: *4071* [→ *3708*]. face; appearance:– appearance [1], countenance [1], face [1]

3800 **ὀψώνιον**, ***opsōnion***, n. GK: *4072* [→ *3795+5608*]. pay, wage; support, compensation:– wages [3], charges [1]

3801 **ὁ ὢν καί ὁ ἦν καί ὁ ἐρχόμενος**, ***hō ōn kai hō én kai hō ērchōmēnōs***, rel.p.+v.+c. GK: *3836 + 1639 + 2779 + 2262* [→ *3588+1510+2064+2532*]. who is and who was and who is to come, a title of Christ:–

3802 **παγιδεύω**, ***pagideuō***, v. GK: *4074* [→ *4078*]. to trap, entrap:– entangle [1]

3803 **παγίς**, ***pagis***, n. GK: *4075* [→ *4078*]. trap, snare:– snare [5]

Πάγος, ***Pagos***. See *697*.

3804 **πάθημα**, ***pathēma***, n. GK: *4077* [→ *3958*]. suffering, misfortune; passion:– sufferings [10], afflictions [3], affections [1], motions [1], suffering [1]

3805 **παθητός**, ***pathētos***, a. GK: *4078* [→ *3958*]. subject to suffering:– suffer [1]

3806 **πάθος**, ***pathos***, n. GK: *4079* [→ *3958*]. lust, sexual passion:– affections [1], inordinate affection [1], lust [1]

πάθω, ***pathō***. See ***3958***.

3807 **παιδαγωγός**, ***paidagōgos***, n. GK: *4080* [→ *3816+71*]. guardian, custodian, supervisor:– schoolmaster [2], instructors [1]

3808 **παιδάριον**, ***paidarion***, n. GK: *4081* [→ *3816*]. little boy, child:– children [1], lad [1]

3809 **παιδεία**, ***paideia***, n. GK: *4082* [→ *3816*]. discipline, training:– chastening [3], chastisement [1], instruction [1], nurture [1]

3810 **παιδευτής**, ***paideutēs***, n. GK: *4083* [→ *3816*]. instructor, teacher; discipliner, corrector:– corrected [1], instructor [1]

3811 **παιδεύω**, ***paideuō***, v. GK: *4084* [→ *3816*]. instruct, train, educate, as an on-going matter, in accord with rules and proper conduct; discipline, punish, for the purpose of better behavior:– chastened [3], chasteneth [2], chastise [2], chasten [1], instructing [1], learned [1], learn [1], taught [1], teaching [1]

3812 **παιδιόθεν**, ***paidiothen***, adv. GK: *4085 & 4088* [→ *3816*]. from childhood:– of a child [1]

3813 **παιδίον**, ***paidion***, n. GK: *4086* [→ *3816*]. child:– child [15], children [9], young child [8], little children [7], little child [5], damsel [4], children's [1], young child's [1], young children [1]

3814 **παιδίσκη**, ***paidiskē***, n. GK: *4087* [→ *3816*]. female servant, female slave, maidservant:– bondwoman [4], damsel [4], maid [2], bondmaid [1], maidens [1], maids [1]

3815 **παίζω**, ***paizō***, v. GK: *4089* [→ *1701, 1702, 1703; cf. 3816*]. to indulge in revelry, play, amuse oneself, dance, sometimes a euphemism for sexual immorality:– play [1]

3816 **παῖς**, ***pais***, n. GK: *4090* [→ *521, 3807, 3808, 3809, 3810, 3811, 3812, 3813, 3814; cf. 3815*]. boy, child, youth, usually below the age of puberty and not necessarily male; a personal servant, slave, attendant, with a possible implication of kind regard or close relationship; the word used in the Greek version of Isaiah, quoted in NT, for "servant" of the Lord:– servant [8], child [5], son [3], children [2], servants [2], maiden [1], maid [1], menservants [1], young man [1]

3817 **παίω**, ***paiō***, v. GK: *4091*. to strike, hit (and so wound):– smote [4], striketh [1]

3818 **Πακατιανός**, ***Pakatianos***, a.pr.g. GK: *4092*. Pacatian, "*in Pacatia*":– Pacatiana [1]

3819 **πάλαι**, ***palai***, adv. GK: *4093* [→ *1597, 3820, 3821, 3822*]. long ago, in the past, already:– any while [1], great while ago [1], long ago [1], of old [1], old [1], past [1]

3820 **παλαιός**, ***palaios***, a. GK: *4094* [→ *3819*]. old:– old [19]

3821 **παλαιότης**, ***palaiotēs***, n. GK: *4095* [→ *3819*]. the old way, obsoleteness, age:– oldness [1]

3822 **παλαιόω**, ***palaioō***, v. GK: *4096* [→ *3819*]. (act.) to make obsolete; (pass.) to wear out, become obsolete, become old:– wax old [2], decayeth [1], made old [1]

3823 **πάλη**, ***palē***, n. GK: *4097*. struggle:– wrestle (+*1510*) [1]

3824 **παλιγγενεσία**, ***palingenesia***, n. GK: *4098 & 4100* [→ *3825+1096*]. renewal; rebirth, regeneration:– regeneration [2]

3825 **πάλιν**, ***palin***, adv. GK: *4099* [→ *3824*]. again, once more; furthermore; on the other hand:– again [141], whereunto (+*3739*) [1]

3826 **παμπληθεί**, ***pamplēthei***, adv. GK: *4101 & 4113* [→ *3956+4130*]. with one voice, all together:– all at once [1]

3827 **πάμπολυς**, ***pampolys***, a. GK: *4102* [→ *3956+4183*]. very great:– very great [1]

3828 **Παμφυλία**, ***Pamphylia***, n.pr. GK: *4103* [→ *3956+5453*]. Pamphylia:– Pamphylia [5]

3829 **πανδοχεῖον**, ***pandocheion***, n. GK: *4104 & 4106* [→ *3956+1209*]. inn:– inn [1]

3830 **πανδοχεύς**, ***pandocheus***, n. GK: *4105 & 4107* [→ *3956+1209*]. innkeeper:– host [1]

3831 πανήγυρις, **panēgyris**, n. GK: 4108 [→ 3956+71]. joyful assembly, festal gathering:– general assembly [1]

3832 πανοικεί, **panoikei**, adv. GK: 4109 [→ 3956+3624]. with one's whole family:– all house [1]

3833 πανοπλία, **panoplia**, n. GK: 4110 [→ 3956+3696]. full armor, worn by a heavily armed soldier:– whole armour [2], all armour [1]

3834 πανουργία, **panourgia**, n. GK: 4111 [→ 3956+2041]. cunning, craftiness, deception, duplicity:– craftiness [3], cunning craftiness [1], subtilty [1]

3835 πανοῦργος, **panourgos**, a. GK: 4112 [→ 3956+2041]. crafty, clever, sly:– crafty [1]

3836 πανταχόθεν, **pantachothen**, adv. GK: 4115 [→ 3956]. from every direction:– from every quarter [1]

3837 πανταχοῦ, **pantachou**, adv. GK: 4114 & 4116 [→ 3956]. everywhere; in all directions:– every where [6], in all places [1], throughout (+1519) [1]

3838 παντελής, **pantelēs**, a. GK: 4117 [→ 3956+5056]. complete, perfect, absolute; at all:– in no wise (+1519+3361+3588) [1], uttermost [1]

3839 πάντῃ, **pantē**, adv. GK: 4118 [→ 3956]. in every way:– always [1]

3840 πάντοθεν, **pantothen**, adv. GK: 4119 [→ 3956]. from all directions; completely, entirely:– on every side [1], round about [1]

3841 παντοκράτωρ, **pantokratōr**, n. GK: 4120 [→ 3956+2904]. Almighty; this title for God translates the Hebrew 7372, [Lord] "of Hosts" (the heavenly armies), and Hebrew 8724, "Shaddai," (probably) God the Mountain, powerful and immovable:– Almighty [9], Omnipotent [1]

3842 πάντοτε, **pantote**, adv. GK: 4121 [→ 3956+3739+5037]. always, at all times, forever:– always [29], ever [6], alway [5], evermore [2]

3843 πάντως, **pantōs**, adv. GK: 4122 [→ 3956]. surely, certainly, by all possible means, quite:– altogether [2], by all means [2], at all [1], in no wise [1], must needs (+1163) [1], no doubt [1], surely [1]

3844 παρά, **para**, pp. GK: 4123 [→ 492, 531, 532, 3845, 3846, 3847, 3848, 3849, 3850, 3851, 3852, 3853, 3854, 3855, 3856, 3858, 3859, 3860, 3861, 3862, 3863, 3864, 3865, 3866, 3867, 3868, 3869, 3870, 3871, 3872, 3873, 3874, 3875, 3876, 3877, 3878, 3879, 3880, 3881, 3882, 3883, 3884, 3885, 3886, 3887, 3888, 3889, 3890, 3891, 3892, 3893, 3894, 3895, 3896, 3897, 3898, 3899, 3900, 3901, 3902, 3903, 3904, 3905, 3906, 3907, 3908, 3909, 3910, 3911, 3912, 3914, 3915, 3916, 3918, 3919, 3920, 3921, 3922, 3923, 3924, 3925, 3926, 3927, 3928, 3929, 3930, 3931, 3935, 3936, 3938, 3939, 3940, 3941, 3943, 3944, 3945, 3946, 3947, 3948, 3949, 3950, 3951, 3952, 3953, 3970, 4836, 4837, 4838, 4839, 4840]. (gen.) from; (dat.) with, before, among, in the sight of; (acc.) beside, along side, by, at:– of [53], with [42], from [24], by [14], at [12], by side [9], than [9], above [4], before [3], contrary to [3], against [2], among [2], any other than [2], in [2], more than [2], nigh unto [2], therefore (+3778) [2], amongst [1], friends (+3588) [1], had (+3588) [1], in the sight [1], past [1], save [1], such as give (+3588) [1]

3845 παραβαίνω, **parabainō**, v. GK: 4124 [→ 3844+305]. to break, transgress; to leave, turn aside:– transgress [2], by transgression fell [1], transgresseth [1]

3846 παραβάλλω, **paraballō**, v. GK: 4125 [→ 3844+906]. to come near (by ship); compare:– arrived [1], compare [1]

3847 παράβασις, **parabasis**, n. GK: 4126 [→ 3844+305]. transgression, breaking, violation:– transgression [4], transgressions [2], breaking [1]

3848 παραβάτης, **parabatēs**, n. GK: 4127 [→ 3844+305]. lawbreaker, transgressor:– transgressor [2], breaker [1], transgressors [1], transgress [1]

3849 παραβιάζομαι, **parabiazomai**, v. GK: 4128 [→ 3844+970]. to urge strongly, persuade:– constrained [2]

3850 παραβολή, **parabolē**, n. GK: 4130 [→ 3844+906]. parable, an illustration that teaches in a story or extended figure of speech; proverb, a short pithy saying:– parable [31], parables [15], figure [2], comparison [1], proverb [1]

3851 παραβουλεύομαι, **parabouleuomai**; or παραβολεύομαι, **paraboleuomai**, v. GK: 4131 [→ 3844+1014]. to be careless, have no concern:– not regarding [1]

3852 παραγγελία, **parangelia**, n. GK: 4132 [→ 3844+32]. order, command; instruction:– charge [2], commandments [1], commandment [1], straitly command (+3853) [1]

3853 παραγγέλλω, **parangellō**, v. GK: 4133 [→ 3844+32]. to order, command, direct; to give instruction:– commanded [11], command [7], charged [3], charge [2], charging [1], commandeth [1], declare [1], gave commandment [1], give charge [1], give in charge [1], straitly command (+3852) [1]

3854 παραγίνομαι, **paraginomai**, v. GK: 4134 [→ 3844+1096]. to come, arrive, be present; to appear:– came [16], come [15], cometh [3], coming [1], present [1], went [1]

3855 παράγω, **paragō**, v. GK: 4135 [→ 3844+71]. to pass by, go on, walk beside; to pass away:– passed by [5], passeth away [2], departed [1], passed forth [1], past [1]

3856 παραδειγματίζω, **paradeigmatizō**, v. GK: 4136 [→ 3844+1164]. to subject to public disgrace, hold up to contempt:– make a publick example [1], put to open shame [1]

3857 παράδεισος, **paradeisos**, n. GK: 4137. paradise, a place of blessedness, from the base meaning of "garden":– paradise [3]

3858 παραδέχομαι, **paradechomai**, v. GK: 4138 [→ 3844+1209]. to accept, welcome, receive:– receive [4], receiveth [1]

3859 παραδιατριβή, **paradiatribē**, n. GK: 4139 [→ 3844+1223+5147]. useless occupation:– perverse disputings [1]

3860 παραδίδωμι, **paradidōmi**, v. GK: 4140 [→ 3844+1325]. to hand over, betray, deliver to prison; to entrust, commit:– delivered [39], betrayed [19], betray [17], deliver [9], deliver up [6], delivered up [4], gave up [4], betrayeth [3], committed [2], deliveredst [2], gave [2], recommended [2], betrayest [1], brought forth [1], cast into prison [1], delivered into [1], delivering up [1], delivering [1], gave over [1], given over [1], given [1], give [1], hazarded [1], put in prison [1]

3861 παράδοξος, **paradoxos**, a. GK: 4141 [→ 3844+1391]. remarkable, wonderful:– strange [1]

3862 παράδοσις, **paradosis**, n. GK: 4142 [→ 3844+1325]. tradition; teachings:– tradition [10], traditions [2], ordinances [1]

3863 παραζηλόω, **parazēloō**, v. GK: 4143 [→ 3844+2205]. to make envious, arouse jealousy:– provoke to jealousy [3], provoke to emulation [1]

3864 παραθαλάσσιος, **parathalassios**, a. GK: 4144 [→ 3844+2281]. by the lake, by the sea:– upon the sea coast [1]

3865 παραθεωρέω, **paratheōreō**, v. GK: 4145 [→ 3844+2334]. (pass.) to be overlooked, neglected:– neglected [1]

3866 παραθήκη, **parathēkē**, n. GK: 4146 [→ 3844+5087]. deposit, thing entrusted to:– committed unto [1]

3867 παραινέω, **paraineō**, v. GK: 4147 [→ 3844+136]. to warn, urge:– admonished [1], exhort [1]

3868 παραιτέομαι, **paraiteomai**, v. GK: 4148 [→ 3844+154]. to request, beg; to make excuses; to refuse, reject:– refuse [4], excused [2], avoid [1], intreated [1], make excuse [1], refused [1], reject [1]

3869 παρακαθίζω, **parakathizō**, v. GK: 4149 & 4150 [→ 3844+2523]. to sit down beside:– sat [1]

3870 παρακαλέω, **parakaleō**, v. GK: 4151 [→ 3844+2564]. to ask, beg, plead; to comfort, encourage, exhort, urge; to call, invite:– besought [21], beseech [20], exhort [14], comforted [13], comfort [8], desired [5], pray [4], exhorted [3], exhorting [3], beseeching [2], comforteth [2], desiring [2], intreat [2], prayed [2], called for [1], desiredst [1], exhortation [1], exhorteth [1], given exhortation (+3056) [1], intreated [1], of good comfort [1]

3871 παρακαλύπτω, **parakalyptō**, v. GK: 4152 [→ 3844+2572]. (pass.) to be hidden:– hid [1]

3872 παρακαταθήκη, **parakatathēkē**, n. GK: 4153 [→ 3844+2596+5087]. deposit:– committed to trust [1], committed unto [1]

3873 παράκειμαι, **parakeimai**, v. GK: 4154 [→ 3844+2749]. to be present, ready:– present [2]

3874 παράκλησις, **paraklēsis**, n. GK: 4155 [→ 3844+2564]. encouragement, comfort, consolation, appeal:– consolation [14], exhortation [8], comfort [6], intreaty [1]

3875 παράκλητος, **paraklētos**, n. GK: 4156 [→ 3844+2564]. counselor, intercessor, helper, one who encourages and comforts; in the NT it refers exclusively to the Holy Spirit and to Jesus Christ:– comforter [4], advocate [1]

3876 παρακοή, **parakoē**, n. GK: 4157 [→ 3844+191]. disobedience, unwillingness to hear:– disobedience [3]

3877 παρακολουθέω, **parakoloutheō**, v. GK: 4158 [→ 3844+190; cf. 1.3]. to follow, accompany; to know all about; to investigate:– attained [1], follow [1], fully known [1], understanding [1]

3878 παρακούω, **parakouō**, v. GK: 4159 [→ 3844+191]. to refuse to listen, ignore:– neglect to hear [2]

3879 **παρακύπτω**, ***parakyptō***, v. GK: *4160* [→ *3844+2955*]. to bend over; to look (intently):– looketh [1], look [1], stooped down and looked [1], stooping down and looking [1], stooping down [1]

3880 **παραλαμβάνω**, ***paralambanō***, v. GK: *4161* [→ *3844+2983*]. to take with; take charge of; to receive, accept:– took [14], received [13], taketh [6], taken [5], take [4], took unto [2], receive [1], receiving [1], take unto [1], taketh to [1], taketh with [1], took with [1]

3881 **παραλέγομαι**, ***paralegomai***, v. GK: *4162* [→ *3844+3004*]. to sail past, move along:– passing [1], sailed [1]

3882 **παράλιος**, ***paralios***, a. GK: *4163* [→ *3844+217*]. (located) by the sea; (n.) seacoast:– sea coast [1]

3883 **παραλλαγή**, ***parallagē***, n. GK: *4164* [→ *3844+236*]. change, variation:– variableness [1]

3884 **παραλογίζομαι**, ***paralogizomai***, v. GK: *4165* [→ *3844+3004*]. to deceive, delude:– beguile [1], deceiving [1]

3885 **παραλυτικός**, ***paralytikos***, a. GK: *4166 & 4167* [→ *3844+3089*]. (n.) paralytic, lame person:– sick of the palsy [7], had the palsy [1], man sick of the palsy [1], one sick of the palsy [1]

3886 **παραλύω**, ***paralyō***, v. GK: *4168* [→ *3844+3089*]. (pass.) to be paralyzed, disabled; (n.) paralytic:– sick of the palsy [2], feeble [1], taken with a palsy [1], taken with palsies [1]

3887 **παραμένω**, ***paramenō***, v. GK: *4169* [→ *3844+3306*]. to continue; to remain with:– abide [1], continueth [1], continue [1]

3888 **παραμυθέομαι**, ***paramytheomai***, v. GK: *4170* [→ *3844+3454*]. to comfort, encourage, console:– comforted [2], comfort [2]

3889 **παραμυθία**, ***paramythia***, n. GK: *4171* [→ *3844+3454*]. comfort, consolation:– comfort [1]

3890 **παραμύθιον**, ***paramythion***, n. GK: *4172* [→ *3844+3454*]. comfort, consolation, encouragement:– comfort [1]

3891 **παρανομέω**, ***paranomeō***, v. GK: *4174* [→ *3844+3551*]. to violate the law, act contrary to the law:– contrary to law [1]

3892 **παρανομία**, ***paranomia***, n. GK: *4175* [→ *3844+3551*]. wrongdoing, lawlessness:– iniquity [1]

3893 **παραπικραίνω**, ***parapikrainō***, v. GK: *4176* [→ *3844+4089*]. to rebel, disobey:– provoke [1]

3894 **παραπικρασμός**, ***parapikrasmos***, n. GK: *4177* [→ *3844+4089*]. rebellion, revolt:– provocation [2]

3895 **παραπίπτω**, ***parapiptō***, v. GK: *4178* [→ *3844+4098*]. to fall away, commit apostasy:– fall away [1]

3896 **παραπλέω**, ***parapleō***, v. GK: *4179* [→ *3844+4126*]. to sail past:– sail by [1]

3897 **παραπλήσιος**, ***paraplēsios***, a. GK: *4180* [→ *3844+4139*]. (adv.) almost, nearly:– nigh unto [1]

3898 **παραπλησίως**, ***paraplēsiōs***, adv. GK: *4181* [→ *3844+4139*]. in just the same way:– likewise [1]

3899 **παραπορεύομαι**, ***paraporeuomai***, v. GK: *4182* [→ *3844+4198*]. to pass by, go through:– passed by [3], passed [1], went [1]

3900 **παράπτωμα**, ***paraptōma***, n. GK: *4183* [→ *3844+4098*]. trespass, transgression, sin against, to sin as a moral failure to keep a command, fig., stepping out of the bounds of God's law:– trespasses [9], offence [5], sins [3], fall [2], offences [2], faults [1], fault [1]

3901 **παραρρέω**, ***pararreō***, v. GK: *4184* [→ *3844+4482*]. to drift away, flow past, slip away:– slip [1]

3902 **παράσημος**, ***parasēmos***, a. GK: *4185* [→ *3844+4592*]. distinguished, marked; (n.) figurehead, emblem (on a ship):– sign [1]

3903 **παρασκευάζω**, ***paraskeuazō***, v. GK: *4186* [→ *3844+4632*]. (act.) to prepare; (mid.) to get ready; (mid./pass.) to be ready:– ready [2], made ready [1], prepare [1]

3904 **παρασκευή**, ***paraskeuē***, n. GK: *4187* [→ *3844+4632*]. Preparation Day:– preparation [6]

3905 **παρατείνω**, ***parateinō***, v. GK: *4189* [→ *1614; cf. 3844*]. to keep on, prolong, extend:– continued [1]

3906 **παρατηρέω**, ***paratēreō***, v. GK: *4190* [→ *3844+5083*]. to watch closely, observe:– watched [5], observe [1]

3907 **παρατήρησις**, ***paratērēsis***, n. GK: *4191* [→ *3844+5083*]. careful observation:– observation [1]

3908 **παρατίθημι**, ***paratithēmi***, v. GK: *4192* [→ *3844+5087*]. (act.) to set before; (mid.) to entrust, commit:– set before [8], commend [2], commit [2], put forth [2], alleging [1], commended [1], commit the keeping [1], committed [1], set meat before (*+5132*) [1]

3909 **παρατυγχάνω**, ***paratynchanō***, v. GK: *4193* [→ *3844+5177*]. to happen to be there:– met with [1]

3910 **παραυτίκα**, ***parautika***, adv. GK: *4194* [→ *3844+846*]. (a.) momentary:– for a moment [1]

3911 **παραφέρω**, ***parapherō***, v. GK: *4195* [→ *3844+5342*]. to take away, remove; (pass.) to be carried away:– remove [1], take away [1]

3912 **παραφρονέω**, ***paraphroneō***, v. GK: *4196* [→ *3913*]. to be out of one's mind, insane:– fool [1]

3913 **παραφρονία**, ***paraphronia***, n. GK: *4197* [→ *3912*]. madness, insanity:– madness [1]

3914 **παραχειμάζω**, ***paracheimazō***, v. GK: *4199* [→ *3844+5510*]. to spend the winter:– winter [3], wintered [1]

3915 **παραχειμασία**, ***paracheimasia***, n. GK: *4200* [→ *3844+5510*]. spending the winter:– winter in [1]

3916 **παραχρῆμα**, ***parachrēma***, adv. GK: *4202* [→ *3844+5530*]. immediately, instantly, at once:– immediately [13], straightway [3], forthwith [1], presently [1], soon [1]

3917 **πάρδαλις**, ***pardalis***, n. GK: *4203*. leopard:– leopard [1]

3918 **πάρειμι**, ***pareimi***, v. GK: *4205* [→ *3844+1510*]. to be present, here; to have come:– present [12], come [6], came [1], have [1], here present [1], here [1], lacketh (*+3361*) [1]

3919 **παρεισάγω**, ***pareisagō***, v. GK: *4206* [→ *3844+1519+71*]. to bring in secretly:– privily bring in [1]

3920 **παρείσακτος**, ***pareisaktos***, a. GK: *4207* [→ *3844+1519+71*]. brought in secretly, infiltrated:– unawares brought in [1]

3921 **παρεισδύω**, ***pareisdyō***, v. GK: *4208* [→ *3844+1519+1416*]. to slip in secretly:– crept in unawares [1]

3922 **παρεισέρχομαι**, ***pareiserchomai***, v. GK: *4209* [→ *3844+1519+2064*]. to come in, sneak in; to add to:– came in privily [1], entered [1]

3923 **παρεισφέρω**, ***pareispherō***, v. GK: *4210* [→ *3844+1519+5342*]. to do one's best:– giving [1]

3924 **παρεκτός**, ***parektos***, adv.&pp.*. GK: *4211* [→ *3844+1537*]. (adv.) besides; (pp.) except for, apart from:– except [1], saving for [1], without [1]

3925 **παρεμβολή**, ***parembolē***, n. GK: *4213* [→ *3844+1722+906*]. camp, barracks; army:– castle [6], camp [3], armies [1]

3926 **παρενοχλέω**, ***parenochleō***, v. GK: *4214* [→ *3844+1722+3793*]. to make difficult, trouble:– trouble [1]

3927 **παρεπίδημος**, ***parepidēmos***, a. GK: *4215* [→ *3844+1909+1218*]. (n.) stranger:– pilgrims [2], strangers [1]

3928 **παρέρχομαι**, ***parerchomai***, v. GK: *4216* [→ *3844+2064*]. to go by, pass by; (pass.) to pass away, come to an end, disappear; be taken away:– pass away [10], pass [8], past [3], came [1], come forth [1], go [1], pass over [1], passed away [1], passed by [1], passeth by [1], passing by [1], past away [1], transgressed [1]

3929 **πάρεσις**, ***paresis***, n. GK: *4217* [→ *863; cf. 3844*]. leaving unpunished, passing over:– remission [1]

3930 **παρέχω**, ***parechō***, v. GK: *4218* [→ *3844+2192*]. to present, give; to show, give proof; to cause, bring about, promote; (mid.) to set (an example); to provide; to get for oneself:– trouble (*+2873*) [4], brought [2], do [1], give unto [1], given [1], giveth [1], kept [1], minister [1], offer [1], shewed [1], shewing [1], troubleth (*+2873*) [1]

3931 **παρηγορία**, ***parēgoria***, n. GK: *4219* [→ *3844+71*]. comfort:– comfort [1]

3932 **παρθενία**, ***parthenia***, n. GK: *4220* [→ *3933*]. virginity:– virginity [1]

3933 **παρθένος**, ***parthenos***, n. GK: *4221* [→ *3932*]. virgin (male and female), one who has never engaged in sexual relations:– virgin [7], virgins [6], virgin's [1]

3934 **Πάρθοι**, ***Parthoi***, n.pr.g. GK: *4222*. Parthian:– Parthians [1]

3935 **παρίημι**, ***pariēmi***, v. GK: *4223* [→ *863; cf. 3844*]. to leave undone, neglect; (pass.) to be feeble, weakened, listless:– hang down [1]

3936 **παρίστημι**, ***paristēmi***; or **παριστάνω**, ***paristanō***, v. GK: *4225* [→ *3844+2476*]. to place beside, put at disposal; to present, make an offering; (intr.) to stand before, provide, come to aid:– stood by [11], present [7], yield [4], brought before [2], stand [2], assist [1], come [1], commendeth [1], give [1], presented before [1], presented [1], prove [1], provide [1], shewed [1], shew [1], stand before [1], standing by [1], stood up [1], stood with [1], stood [1], yielded [1]

3937 **Παρμενᾶς**, ***Parmenas***, n.pr. GK: *4226*. Parmenas, *"steady, reliable"*:– Parmenas [1]

3938 **πάροδος**, ***parodos***, n. GK: *4227* [→ *3844+3598*]. passing by:– way [1]

3939 **παροικέω**, ***paroikeō***, v. GK: *4228* [→ *3844+3624*]. to live as a stranger, visit; to migrate:– sojourned [1], stranger [1]

3940 **παροικία**, ***paroikia***, n. GK: *4229* [→ *3844+3624*]. residence as a stranger:– dwelt as strangers [1], sojourning [1]

3941 **πάροικος**, ***paroikos***, a. GK: *4230* [→ *3844+3624*]. strange; (n.) alien, foreigner, stranger:– foreigners [1], sojourn (+*1510*) [1], strangers [1], stranger [1]

3942 **παροιμία**, ***paroimia***, n. GK: *4231*. figure of speech, proverb, maxim:– proverbs [2], proverb [2], parable [1]

3943 **πάροινος**, ***paroinos***, a. GK: *4232* [→ *3844+3631*]. drunken, given to drunkenness:– given to wine [2]

3944 **παροίχομαι**, ***paroichomai***, v. GK: *4233* [→ *3844*]. to pass by:– past [1]

3945 **παρομοιάζω**, ***paromoiazō***, v. GK: *4234* [→ *3844+3664*]. to be like:– like [1]

3946 **παρόμοιος**, ***paromoios***, a. GK: *4235* [→ *3844+3664*]. like, similar:– like [2]

3947 **παροξύνω**, ***paroxynō***, v. GK: *4236* [→ *3844+3691*]. (intr.) to be greatly distressed; to be angered, irritated:– easily provoked [1], stirred [1]

3948 **παροξυσμός**, ***paroxysmos***, n. GK: *4237* [→ *3844+3691*]. sharp disagreement; spurring on, encouraging:– contention sharp [1], provoke unto [1]

3949 **παροργίζω**, ***parorgizō***, v. GK: *4239* [→ *3844+3709*]. to anger, exasperate:– anger [1], provoke to wrath [1]

3950 **παροργισμός**, ***parorgismos***, n. GK: *4240* [→ *3844+3709*]. anger:– wrath [1]

3951 **παροτρύνω**, ***parotrynō***, v. GK: *4241* [→ *3844*]. to incite, arouse:– stirred up [1]

3952 **παρουσία**, ***parousia***, n. GK: *4242* [→ *3844+1510*]. presence; coming, advent; in the NT usually of the second coming of the Son of Man, arriving as a conquering king:– coming [22], presence [2]

3953 **παροψίς**, ***paropsis***, n. GK: *4243* [→ *3844+3795*]. dish:– platter [2]

3954 **παρρησία**, ***parrēsia***, n. GK: *4244* [→ *3956+4487*]. boldness, confidence, frankness; public, openness (of speech):– boldness [8], confidence [6], openly [4], plainly [3], boldly (+*1722*) [1], boldly (+*3326*) [1], boldly [1], boldness of speech [1], bold [1], freely (+*3326*) [1], known openly (+*1722*) [1], openly (+*1722*) [1], plainly (+*1722*) [1], plainness of speech [1]

3955 **παρρησιάζομαι**, ***parrēsiazomai***, v. GK: *4245* [→ *3956+4487*]. to speak boldly, preach fearlessly:– speak boldly [2], boldly [1], bold [1], freely [1], preached boldly [1], spake boldly [1], speaking boldly [1], waxed bold [1]

3956 **πᾶς**, ***pas***, a. GK: *4246* [→ *537, 1275, 3826, 3827, 3828, 3829, 3830, 3831, 3832, 3833, 3834, 3835, 3836, 3837, 3838, 3839, 3840, 3841, 3842, 3843, 3954, 3955*]. all, every (thing, one), whole; always:– all [976], every [133], whosoever [31], every one [28], whole [12], any [9], no (+*3756*) [7], whatsoever [7], always (+*1223*) [3], every (+*2596*) [3], whosoever (+*302+3739*) [3], always (+*1722+2540*) [2], no (+*3361*) [2], whosoever (+*3748*) [2], all manner [1], alway (+*2250+3588*) [1], any one [1], as many as (+*3739*) [1], as many as [1], continually (+*1223*) [1], daily (+*2250+2596*) [1], daily (+*2250*) [1], ever (+*165+1519+3588*) [1], every man [1], every one's [1], every thing [1], every where [1], nothing (+*3756+4487*) [1], nothing at any time (+*3763*) [1], throughly (+*1722*) [1], whatsoever (+*1437+3748+5100*) [1], whatsoever (+*3739*) [1], whomsoever (+*3739*) [1], whosoever (+*3739*) [1]

3957 **πάσχα**, ***pascha***, n. GK: *4247*. Passover, Passover week; Passover meal; Passover lamb:– passover [28], Easter [1]

3958 **πάσχω**, ***paschō***, v. GK: *4248* [→ *2552, 2553, 3356, 3663, 3804, 3805, 3806, 4310, 4777, 4834, 4835, 4841*]. to experience, suffer, endure (almost always in NT with reference to unpleasant experiences):– suffer [21], suffered [17], felt [1], passion [1], suffering [1], vexed [1]

3959 **Πάταρα**, ***Patara***, n.pr. GK: *4249*. Patara:– Patara [1]

3960 **πατάσσω**, ***patassō***, v. GK: *4250*. to hit, strike; kill:– smite [5], smote [4], stroke [1]

3961 **πατέω**, ***pateō***, v. GK: *4251* [→ *1704, 2662, 4043*]. to trample on, tread on:– tread under foot [1], treadeth [1], tread [1], trodden down [1], trodden [1]

3962 **πατήρ**, ***patēr***, n. GK: *4252* [→ *493, 494, 540, 2810, 3964, 3965, 3966, 3967, 3968, 3969, 3970, 3971, 4986, 4989*]. father, a male parent or ancestor; by extension: an honorific title, leader, archetype; (pl.) parents, ancestors (of both genders):– father [347], fathers [52], father's [17], fathers' [1], parents [1]

3963 **Πάτμος**, ***Patmos***, n.pr. GK: *4253*. Patmos:– Patmos [1]

3964 **πατραλῴας**, ***patralōas***, n. GK: *4254 & 4260* [→ *3962+248*]. one who kills one's father:– murderers of fathers [1]

3965 **πατριά**, ***patria***, n. GK: *4255* [→ *3962*]. family, family line, clan; people, nation:– family [1], kindreds [1], lineage [1]

3966 **πατριάρχης**, ***patriarchēs***, n. GK: *4256* [→ *3962+757*]. patriarch, father of a nation:– patriarchs [2], patriarch [2]

3967 **πατρικός**, ***patrikos***, a. GK: *4257* [→ *3962*]. paternal, from one's ancestors:– fathers [1]

3968 **πατρίς**, ***patris***, n. GK: *4258* [→ *3962*]. hometown, homeland, land of one's ancestors:– country [8]

3969 **Πατροβᾶς**, ***Patrobas***, n.pr. GK: *4259* [→ *3962+979*]. Patrobas, *"father of existence"*:– Patrobas [1]

3970 **πατροπαράδοτος**, ***patroparadotos***, a. GK: *4261* [→ *3962+3844+1325*]. handed down from forefathers:– received by tradition from fathers [1]

3971 **πατρῷος**, ***patrōos***, a. GK: *4262* [→ *3962*]. ancestral, from forefathers:– fathers [3]

3972 **Παῦλος**, ***Paulos***, n.pr. GK: *4263*. Paul, Paulus, *"little"*:– Paul [157], Paul's [6], Paulus [1]

3973 **παύω**, ***pauō***, v. GK: *4264* [→ *180, 372, 373, 1879, 2663, 2664, 4875*]. (act.) to cause to stop; (mid.) to stop, cease, finish:– ceased [7], cease [4], left [2], ceaseth [1], refrain [1]

3974 **Πάφος**, ***Paphos***, n.pr. GK: *4265*. Paphos:– Paphos [2]

3975 **παχύνω**, ***pachynō***, v. GK: *4266*. to become calloused of heart, make fat, and so unable to understand:– waxed gross [2]

3976 **πέδη**, ***pedē***, n. GK: *4267* [→ *3978*]. foot shackle, fetter:– fetters [3]

3977 **πεδινός**, ***pedinos***, a. GK: *4268* [→ *3978*]. level, flat:– plain (+*5117*) [1]

3978 **πεζεύω**, ***pezeuō***, v. GK: *4269* [→ *3976, 3977, 3979, 4759, 4760, 5132, 5133*]. to go on foot, travel by walking:– go afoot [1]

3979 **πεζῇ**, ***pezē***, adv. GK: *4270 & 4271* [→ *3978*]. on foot:– afoot [1], on foot [1]

3980 **πειθαρχέω**, ***peitharcheō***, v. GK: *4272* [→ *3982+757*]. to obey; to take advice:– obey [2], hearkened [1], obey magistrates [1]

3981 **πειθός**, ***peithos***, a. GK: *4273* [→ *3982*]. persuasive:– enticing [1]

3982 **πείθω**, ***peithō***, v. GK: *4275* [→ *374, 543, 544, 545, 2138, 3980, 3981, 3988, 4006, 4086; cf. 4103*]. to convince, persuade; to trust in, have confidence in, be persuaded:– persuaded [16], trust [6], obey [5], believed [3], confidence [3], persuade [3], trusted [3], confident [2], having confidence [2], obeyed [2], persuading [2], agreed [1], assure [1], have confidence [1], made friend [1], persuadest [1], put trust [1], waxing confident [1], yield unto [1]

3983 **πεινάω**, ***peinaō***, v. GK: *4277* [→ *4361*]. to be hungry:– hungred [9], hunger [8], hungry [4], hungered [2]

3984 **πεῖρα**, ***peira***, n. GK: *4278* [→ *551, 552, 1598, 3985, 3986, 3987*]. to try to do, attempt; to face, experience:– assaying [1], trial [1]

3985 **πειράζω**, ***peirazō***, v. GK: *4279* [→ *3984*]. to test, tempt; to try to trap; to examine (oneself). The difference between a test and a temptation is found in the tester's motivations and expectations; the devil tempts that the believer might fail God's standards of faith and so sin; God tests that he might determine and sharpen true character, with no focus on making the believer fail:– tempted [15], tempting [7], tempt [6], tried [3], tempter [2], assayed [1], examine [1], gone about [1], prove [1], tempteth [1], try [1]

3986 **πειρασμός**, ***peirasmos***, n. GK: *4280* [→ *3984*]. test; trial; temptation:– temptation [15], temptations [5], try [1]

3987 **πειράω**, ***peiraō***, v. GK: *4281* [→ *3984*]. to try, attempt:– assayed [1], went about [1]

3988 **πεισμονή**, ***peismonē***, n. GK: *4282* [→ *3982*]. persuasion:– persuasion [1]

3989 **πέλαγος**, ***pelagos***, n. GK: *4283*. open sea; depths:– depth [1], sea [1]

3990 **πελεκίζω**, ***pelekizō***, v. GK: *4284*. to behead, a derivative of the Greek noun "ax," not found in the NT:– beheaded [1]

3991 **πέμπτος**, ***pemptos***, a. GK: *4286* [→ *4002*]. fifth:– fifth [4]

3992 **πέμπω**, ***pempō***, v. GK: *4287* [→ *375, 1599, 3343, 4311, 4842*]. to send:– sent [52], send [25], thrust in [2], sending [1], sent forth [1]

3993 **πένης**, ***penēs***, a. GK: *4288* [→ *3998; cf. 4192*]. poor:– poor [1]

3994 πενθερά, ***penthera***, n. GK: *4289* [→ *3995*]. mother-in-law:– mother in law [3], wife's mother [3]

3995 πενθερός, ***pentheros***, n. GK: *4290* [→ *3994*]. father-in-law:– father in law [1]

3996 πενθέω, ***pentheō***, v. GK: *4291* [→ *3997*]. to mourn, grieve (over):– mourn [5], mourned [2], wailing [2], bewail [1]

3997 πένθος, ***penthos***, n. GK: *4292* [→ *3996*]. mourning, grief, sadness:– sorrow [3], mourning [2]

3998 πενιχρός, ***penichros***, a. GK: *4293* [→ *3993*]. poor, needy:– poor [1]

3999 πεντάκις, ***pentakis***, adv. GK: *4294* [→ *4002*]. five times:– five times [1]

4000 πεντακισχίλιοι, ***pentakischilioi***, a.num. GK: *4295* [→ *4002+5507*]. five thousand:– five thousand [6]

4001 πεντακόσιοι, ***pentakosioi***, a.num. GK: *4296* [→ *4002*]. five hundred:– five hundred [2]

4002 πέντε, ***pente***, n.num. GK: *4297* [→ *1178, 3991, 3999, 4000, 4001, 4003, 4004, 4005*]. five:– five [36], fifty thousand (+*3461*) [1], threescore and fifteen (+*1440*) [1]

4003 πεντεκαιδέκατος, ***pentekaidekatos***, a. GK: *4298* [→ *4002+2532+1176*]. fifteenth:– fifteenth [1]

4004 πεντήκοντα, ***pentēkonta***, n.num. GK: *4299* [→ *4002*]. fifty:– fifty [5], fifties [2]

4005 πεντηκοστή, ***pentēkostē***, n. GK: *4300* [→ *4002*]. Pentecost, fiftieth (day after Passover):– Pentecost [3]

4006 πεποίθησις, ***pepoithēsis***, n. GK: *4301* [→ *3982*]. confidence, trust:– confidence [5], trust [1]

4007 -περ, ***-per***, pt.emph. GK: *4302* [→ *1355, 1512, 1895, 1897, 2260, 2509, 2539, 3746, 5618, 5619*]. an affix for various kinds of emphasis:– if (+*1437*) [3]

4008 πέραν, ***peran***, adv. GK: *4305* [→ *495, 562, 1276, 4009, 4070, 4097; cf. 4198*]. on the other side; (n.) opposite side, region across:– other side [10], beyond [7], over [3], on the other side [2], farther side [1]

4009 πέρας, ***peras***, n. GK: *4306* [→ *4008*]. end, limit:– ends [1], end [1], utmost parts [1], uttermost parts [1]

4010 Πέργαμος, ***Pergamos***, n.pr. GK: *4307*. Pergamum:– Pergamos [2]

4011 Πέργη, ***Pergē***, n.pr. GK: *4308*. Perga:– Perga [3]

4012 περί, ***peri***, pp. GK: *4309* [→ *563, 564, 1704, 2139, 4013, 4014, 681, 4015, 4016, 4017, 4018, 4019, 4020, 4021, 4022, 4023, 4024, 4025, 4026, 4027, 4028, 4029, 4030, 4031, 4032, 4033, 4034, 4035, 4036, 4037, 4038, 4039, 4040, 4041, 4042, 4043, 4044, 4045, 4046, 4047, 4048, 4049, 4059, 4060, 4061, 4062, 4063, 4064, 4065, 4066, 4067, 4843; cf. 4053*]. (gen.) about, concerning, in regard to; (acc.) around, about, nearby:– of [148], for [62], concerning [41], about [29], as touching [7], touching [4], at [3], against [2], as concerning [2], on [2], over [2], state (+*3588*) [2], whereof (+*3739*) [2], with [2], above [1], affairs (+*3588*) [1], affairs [1], among [1], company (+*3588*) [1], concern [1], estate [1], for sake [1], how it will go with (+*3588*) [1], in [1], of company [1], on behalf [1], pertaining [1], round about [1], same (+*1565*) [1], thereabout (+*3778*) [1], thereof [1], whereby (+*3739*) [1], wherein (+*3739*) [1], whereof (+*5101*) [1]

4013 περιάγω, ***periagō***, v. GK: *4310* [→ *4012+71*]. (tr.) to take (a wife); (intr.) to go about, travel about:– went about [3], compass [1], lead about [1], went [1]

4014 περιαιρέω, ***periaireō***, v. GK: *4311* [→ *4012+138*]. to take away; (pass.) to be taken away; to cut loose, set sail; to be given up, abandoned:– taken away [2], take away [1], taken up [1]

4015 περιαστράπτω, ***periastraptō***, v. GK: *4313* [→ *4012+796*]. to flash around, shine around:– shined round about [1], shone [1]

4016 περιβάλλω, ***periballō***, v. GK: *4314* [→ *4012+906*]. to dress, clothe, wrap around:– clothed [8], arrayed in [4], clothed in [3], clothed with [3], arrayed [2], cast about [2], cast [1], put on [1]

4017 περιβλέπω, ***periblepō***, v. GK: *4315* [→ *4012+991*]. to look around at:– looked round about [5], looked [1], looking round about [1]

4018 περιβόλαιον, ***peribolaion***, n. GK: *4316* [→ *4012+906*]. covering, robe:– covering [1], vesture [1]

4019 περιδέω, ***perideō***, v. GK: *4317* [→ *4012+1210*]. to wrap around:– bound about [1]

περιδρέμω, ***peridremō***. See ***4063***.

περιέλλω, ***periellō***. See ***4014***.

περιέλθω, ***perielthō***. See ***4022***.

4020 περιεργάζομαι, ***periergazomai***, v. GK: *4318* [→ *4012+2041*]. to be a busybody:– busybodies [1]

4021 περίεργος, ***periergos***, a. GK: *4319* [→ *4012+2041*]. meddlesome, curious; (n.) busybody; (pl.) sorcery, magical arts:– busybodies [1], curious arts [1]

4022 περιέρχομαι, ***perierchomai***, v. GK: *4320* [→ *4012+2064*]. to go around:– fet a compass [1], vagabond [1], wandered about [1], wandering about [1]

4023 περιέχω, ***periechō***, v. GK: *4321* [→ *4012+2192*]. to seize, encircle; to contain, to say:– after [1], astonished (+*2285*) [1], contained [1]

4024 περιζώννυμι, ***perizōnnymi***, v. GK: *4322 & 4323* [→ *4012+2224*]. to buckle a belt around, gird, dress for service:– gird [3], girded about [1], girded [1], girt about [1], girt [1]

4025 περίθεσις, ***perithesis***, n. GK: *4324* [→ *4012+5087*]. wearing, putting on:– wearing [1]

4026 περιΐστημι, ***periistēmi***, v. GK: *4325* [→ *4012+2476*]. to stand around; avoid, shun:– avoid [1], shun [1], stand by [1], stood round about [1]

4027 περικάθαρμα, ***perikatharma***, n. GK: *4326* [→ *4012+2513*]. scum, refuse:– filth [1]

4028 περικαλύπτω, ***perikalyptō***, v. GK: *4328* [→ *4012+2572*]. to blindfold, cover the face or eyes; to cover (with gold):– blindfolded [1], cover [1], overlaid [1]

4029 περίκειμαι, ***perikeimai***, v. GK: *4329* [→ *4012+2749*]. to surround, place or tie around; to be subject to:– bound with [1], compassed about [1], compassed with [1], hanged about [1], hanged [1]

4030 περικεφαλαία, ***perikephalaia***, n. GK: *4330* [→ *4012+2776*]. helmet:– helmet [2]

4031 περικρατής, ***perikratēs***, a. GK: *4331* [→ *4012+2904*]. secure, having power, being in command of, getting under control:– come by (+*1096*) [1]

4032 περικρύπτω, ***perikryptō***, v. GK: *4332* [→ *4012+2928*]. to seclude oneself, hide, conceal oneself:– hid [1]

4033 περικυκλόω, ***perikykloō***, v. GK: *4333* [→ *4012+2945*]. to encircle, surround:– compass round [1]

4034 περιλάμπω, ***perilampō***, v. GK: *4334* [→ *4012+2989*]. to shine around, blaze around:– shining round about [1], shone round about [1]

4035 περιλείπομαι, ***perileipomai***, v. GK: *4335* [→ *4012+3007*]. to be left, remain:– remain [2]

4036 περίλυπος, ***perilypos***, a. GK: *4337* [→ *4012+3077*]. overwhelmingly sorrowful; greatly distressing:– exceeding sorrowful [2], very sorrowful [2], exceeding sorry [1]

4037 περιμένω, ***perimenō***, v. GK: *4338* [→ *4012+3306*]. to wait for:– wait for [1]

4038 πέριξ, ***perix***, adv. GK: *4339* [→ *4012*]. around:– round about [1]

4039 περιοικέω, ***perioikeō***, v. GK: *4340* [→ *4012+3624*]. to live in a neighborhood; (n.) neighbor:– dwelt round about [1]

4040 περίοικος, ***perioikos***, a. GK: *4341* [→ *4012+3624*]. neighboring; (n.) neighbor:– neighbours [1]

4041 περιούσιος, ***periousios***, a. GK: *4342* [→ *4012+1510*]. one's very own, special:– peculiar [1]

4042 περιοχή, ***periochē***, n. GK: *4343* [→ *4012+2192*]. passage (of Scripture), portion:– place [1]

4043 περιπατέω, ***peripateō***, v. GK: *4344* [→ *4012+3961*]. to walk (around); to live, conduct one's life:– walk [56], walked [18], walking [12], walketh [4], walkest [2], go [1], occupied therein [1], walkedst [1], walketh about [1]

4044 περιπείρω, ***peripeirō***, v. GK: *4345* [→ *4012*]. to pierce:– pierced through [1]

4045 περιπίπτω, ***peripiptō***, v. GK: *4346* [→ *4012+4098*]. to fall into the hands of; to strike; to face, be involved in:– fall into [1], falling [1], fell among [1]

4046 περιποιέω, ***peripoieō***, v. GK: *4347* [→ *4012+4160*]. (mid.) to keep, save; to gain for oneself; to buy, acquire:– purchased [1], purchase [1]

4047 περιποίησις, ***peripoiēsis***, n. GK: *4348* [→ *4012+4160*]. possession, property; sharing in, gaining; saving:– obtaining [1], obtain [1], peculiar (+*1519*) [1], purchased possession [1], saving [1]

4048 περιρήγνυμι, ***perirēgnymi***, v. GK: *4351* [→ *4012+4486*]. to strip off, tear off:– rent off [1]

4049 περισπάω, ***perispaō***, v. GK: *4352* [→ *4012+4685*]. (pass.) to be distracted:– cumbered [1]

4050 περισσεία, ***perisseia***, n. GK: *4353* [→ *4053*]. abundance, prevalence:– abundance [2], abundantly (+*1519*) [1], superfluity [1]

4051 περίσσευμα, ***perisseuma***, n. GK: *4354* [→ *4053*]. overflow, plenty; what is left over, scraps:– abundance [4], left [1]

***4052* περισσεύω, *perisseuō*,** v. GK: *4355* [→ *4053*]. to have abundance, more than enough, overflow, to have an excessive amount of something, ranging from moderate excess to a very great degree of excess:– abound [11], abounded [4], abundance [3], abounding [2], abundant [2], have abundance [2], remained [2], aboundeth [1], better [1], exceed (+*4183*) [1], exceed [1], excel [1], have enough and to spare [1], increased [1], increase [1], left [1], make abound [1], redound [1], remained over and above [1], remain [1]

***4053* περισσός, *perissos*,** a. GK: *4356* [→ *4050, 4051, 4052, 4054, 4055, 4056, 4057, 5248, 5249; cf. 4012*]. exceeding, going beyond; full, abundant; (compar.) more than; (n.) advantage:– greater [2], more than [2], abundantly (+*1537*) [1], abundantly [1], advantage [1], exceedingly (+*1537*+*5228*) [1], highly (+*1537*) [1], measure [1], more [1], superfluous [1], vehemently (+*1537*) [1]

***4054* περισσότερον, *perissoteron*,** adv. GK: *4357* [→ *4053*]. even more, so much more:– more [2], far more [1], great deal [1], greater [1], more abundantly than [1], more abundantly [1], much more than [1]

***4055* περισσότερος, *perissoteros*,** a. GK: *4358* [→ *4053*]. more than, even more; greater than; with special honor:– more abundant [3], more (+*5100*) [1], overmuch [1]

***4056* περισσοτέρως, *perissoterōs*,** adv. GK: *4359* [→ *4053*]. to a much greater degree; especially, frequently, extremely:– more abundantly [4], more abundant [2], more exceedingly [2], exceedingly [1], more earnest [1], more frequent [1], much more [1], rather [1]

***4057* περισσῶς, *perissōs*,** adv. GK: *4360* [→ *4053*]. even more, all the more:– exceedingly [1], more [1], out of measure [1]

***4058* περιστερά, *peristera*,** n. GK: *4361*. dove, pigeon:– doves [5], dove [4], pigeons [1]

***4059* περιτέμνω, *peritemnō*,** v. GK: *4362* [→ *4012*+*5114*]. to circumcise:– circumcised [13], circumcise [4], circumcising [1]

***4060* περιτίθημι, *peritithēmi*,** v. GK: *4363* [→ *4012*+*5087*]. to put on, set on; to treat with:– put on [3], bestow [1], put about [1], put upon [1], round about [1], set about [1]

***4061* περιτομή, *peritomē*,** n. GK: *4364* [→ *4012*+*5114*]. circumcision; fig., the Jews (as a group of people who adhered to the ritual of circumcision):– circumcision [35], circumcised [1]

***4062* περιτρέπω, *peritrepō*,** v. GK: *4365* [→ *4012*+*5157*]. to drive (to insanity):– make mad (+*1519*+*3130*) [1]

***4063* περιτρέχω, *peritrechō*,** v. GK: *4366* [→ *4012*+*5143*]. to run throughout, run about:– ran through [1]

***4064* περιφέρω, *peripherō*,** v. GK: *4367* [→ *4012*+*5342*]. to carry, carry around; (pass.) to be blown about, carried here and there:– carried about [3], bearing about [1], carry about [1]

***4065* περιφρονέω, *periphroneō*,** v. GK: *4368* [→ *4012*+*5424*]. to despise, look down on:– despise [1]

***4066* περίχωρος, *perichōros*,** a. GK: *4369* [→ *4012*+*5562*]. neighboring; (n.) surrounding country:– region round about [5], country round about [3], country about [1], region that lieth round about [1]

***4067* περίψημα, *peripsēma*,** n. GK: *4370* [→ *4012*+*5597*]. refuse, garbage, that which is removed in the process of cleaning:– offscouring [1]

***4068* περπερεύομαι, *perpereuomai*,** v. GK: *4371*. to boast, brag:– vaunteth [1]

***4069* Περσίς, *Persis*,** n.pr. GK: *4372*. Persis, "*female Persian*":– Persis [1]

***4070* πέρυσι, *perysi*,** adv. GK: *4373* [→ *4008*]. from last year, since last year:– a year ago (+*575*) [2]

πετάομαι, *petaomai*. See ***4072***.

***4071* πετεινόν, *peteinon*,** n. GK: *4374* [→ *4072*]. bird:– fowls [9], birds [5]

***4072* πέτομαι, *petomai*,** v. GK: *4375* [→ *1600, 2665, 4071, 4419, 4420, 4421*]. to fly:– fly [3], flying [2]

***4073* πέτρα, *petra*,** n. GK: *4376* [→ *4074, 4075*]. rock, bedrock, rocky crag, or other large rock formation, in contrast to individual stones (cf. *4074*), with a focus that this is a suitable, solid foundation:– rock [13], rocks [3]

***4074* Πέτρος, *Petros*,** n.pr. GK: *4377* [→ *4073*]. Peter; this has the designative meaning "rock" or "individual stone", "*rock, stone*":– Peter [157], Peter's [4], stone [1]

***4075* πετρώδης, *petrōdēs*,** a. GK: *4378* [→ *4073*+*1491*]. rocky, stony; (n.) rocky place, thin soil with larger rocks or bedrock underneath:– stony ground [2], stony [2]

***4076* πήγανον, *pēganon*,** n. GK: *4379*. rue (a garden herb):– rue [1]

***4077* πηγή, *pēgē*,** n. GK: *4380*. spring, well (of water); flow (of blood):– fountains [4], fountain [4], well [3], wells [1]

***4078* πήγνυμι, *pēgnymi*,** v. GK: *4381* [→ *3802, 3803, 4362, 4634*]. to set up:– pitched [1]

***4079* πηδάλιον, *pēdalion*,** n. GK: *4382*. rudder, steering paddle:– helm [1], rudder [1]

***4080* πηλίκος, *pēlikos*,** a. GK: *4383* [→ *2245*]. how great, how large:– how great [1], how large [1]

***4081* πηλός, *pēlos*,** n. GK: *4384*. mud, lump of clay:– clay [6]

***4082* πήρα, *pēra*,** n. GK: *4385*. traveler's bag:– scrip [6]

***4083* πῆχυς, *pēchys*,** n. GK: *4388*. measure of length: cubit, or time: hour:– cubits [2], cubit [2]

***4084* πιάζω, *piazō*,** v. GK: *4389* [→ *4085*]. to seize, to grasp an object, usually with the hand; by extension: to arrest, capture, place in confinement:– take [4], caught [2], taken [2], apprehended [1], apprehend [1], laid hands on [1], took [1]

***4085* πιέζω, *piezō*,** v. GK: *4390* [→ *4084*]. (pass.) to be pressed down:– pressed down [1]

***4086* πιθανολογία, *pithanologia*,** n. GK: *4391* [→ *3982*+*3004*]. fine-sounding arguments, persuasive speech, a plausible yet false argument:– enticing words [1]

***4087* πικραίνω, *pikrainō*,** v. GK: *4393* [→ *4089*]. to turn sour, make bitter; to become sour, embittered:– bitter [2], made bitter [1], make bitter [1]

***4088* πικρία, *pikria*,** n. GK: *4394* [→ *4089*]. bitterness:– bitterness [4]

***4089* πικρός, *pikros*,** a. GK: *4395* [→ *3893, 3894, 4087, 4088, 4090*]. bitter, salty:– bitter [2]

***4090* πικρῶς, *pikrōs*,** adv. GK: *4396* [→ *4089*]. bitterly:– bitterly [2]

***4091* Πιλᾶτος, *Pilatos*,** n.pr. GK: *4276* & *4397*. Pilate, "*[family name]*":– Pilate [55]

πίμπλημι, *pimplēmi*. See ***4130***.

***4092* πίμπρημι, *pimprēmi*,** v. GK: *4399* [→ *1714*]. to swell:– swollen [1]

***4093* πινακίδιον, *pinakidion*,** n. GK: *4400* & *4401* [→ *4094*]. (small) writing tablet:– writing table [1]

***4094* πίναξ, *pinax*,** n. GK: *4402* [→ *4093*]. platter, dish:– charger [4], platter [1]

***4095* πίνω, *pinō*,** v. GK: *4403* [→ *2666, 3630, 4188, 4213, 4221, 4222, 4224, 4844, 4849, 5202; cf. 4215*]. to drink:– drink [52], drinketh [8], drinking [6], drank [5], drunk [3], drunken [1]

***4096* πιότης, *piotēs*,** n. GK: *4404*. richness, nourishing sap:– fatness [1]

***4097* πιπράσκω, *pipraskō*,** v. GK: *4405* [→ *4008*]. to sell:– sold [9]

***4098* πίπτω, *piptō*,** v. GK: *4406* [→ *377, 496, 634, 1120, 1356, 1601, 1706, 1968, 2667, 3895, 3900, 4045, 4312, 4363, 4430, 4431*]. to fall, collapse; to bow down; to die:– fell [42], fall [20], fell down [14], fallen [5], falleth [3], fall down [2], fail [1], fallen down [1], falling down [1], light [1]

***4099* Πισιδία, *Pisidia*,** n.pr. GK: *4407* & *4408*. Pisidia:– Pisidia [2]

***4100* πιστεύω, *pisteuō*,** v. GK: *4409* [→ *4103*]. to believe, put one's faith in, trust, with an implication that actions based on that trust may follow; (pass.) entrust:– believe [115], believed [77], believeth [33], believest [8], believing [6], committed [3], believers [1], commit to trust [1], committed to trust [1], committed unto [1], commit [1], put in trust [1]

***4101* πιστικός, *pistikos*,** a. GK: *4410* [→ *4103*]. pure:– spikenard (+*3487*) [2]

***4102* πίστις, *pistis*,** n. GK: *4411* [→ *4103*]. faith, faithfulness, belief, trust, with an implication that actions based on that trust may follow; "the faith" often refers to the Christian system of belief and lifestyle:– faith [239], assurance [1], belief [1], believeth [1], believe [1], fidelity [1]

***4103* πιστός, *pistos*,** a. GK: *4412* [→ *569, 570, 571, 3640, 4100, 4101, 4102, 4104; cf. 3982*]. faithful, trustworthy, reliable, believing:– faithful [53], believed [2], believe [2], believing [2], true [2], believers [1], believeth [1], faithfully [1], man[s] [1], sure [1], woman that believeth [1]

***4104* πιστόω, *pistoō*,** v. GK: *4413* [→ *4103*]. (pass.) to be convinced of:– assured [1]

***4105* πλανάω, *planaō*,** v. GK: *4414* [→ *4106*]. to lead astray, cause to wander, deceive; (mid./pass.) to be deceived, deluded:– deceived [10], deceive [10], err [6], deceiveth [3], gone astray [3], seduce [2], deceiving [1], going astray [1], out of the way [1], wandered [1], went astray [1]

***4106* πλάνη, *planē*,** n. GK: *4415* [→ *635, 4105, 4107, 4108*]. error, delusion, deception:– error [7], deceit [1], deceive [1], delusion [1]

4107 πλανήτης, **planētēs**, n. GK: *4417* [→ *4106*]. wanderer; (a.) wandering:– wandering [1]

4108 πλάνος, **planos**, a. GK: *4418* [→ *4106*]. deceiving, leading astray; (n.) deceiver, imposter; fig. extensions of the base meaning "to wander off a path," not found in the NT:– deceivers [2], deceiver [2], seducing [1]

4109 πλάξ, **plax**, n. GK: *4419*. stone tablet:– tables [3]

4110 πλάσμα, **plasma**, n. GK: *4420* [→ *4111*]. what is formed, molded:– formed [1]

4111 πλάσσω, **plassō**, v. GK: *4421* [→ *4110, 4112*]. to form, mold:– formed [2]

4112 πλαστός, **plastos**, a. GK: *4422* [→ *4111*]. made up, fabricated, false:– feigned [1]

4113 πλατεῖα, **plateia**, n. GK: *4423* [→ *4116*]. (main) street, wide road:– streets [6], street [3]

4114 πλάτος, **platos**, n. GK: *4424* [→ *4116*]. width, breadth:– breadth [4]

4115 πλατύνω, **platynō**, v. GK: *4425* [→ *4116*]. to open wide, make wide:– enlarged [2], make broad [1]

4116 πλατύς, **platys**, a. GK: *4426* [→ *4113, 4114, 4115*]. wide, broad:– wide [1]

4117 πλέγμα, **plegma**, n. GK: *4427* [→ *4120*]. something braided or woven:– broided hair [1]

πλεῖον, **pleion**. See **4119**.

4118 πλεῖστος, **pleistos**, a.super. of *4183*. GK: *4498* [→ *4183*]. the most; very large:–

4119 πλείων, **pleiōn**, a.compar. of *4183* GK: *4498* [→ *4183*]. more than, greater than:–

4120 πλέκω, **plekō**, v. GK: *4428* [→ *1707, 1708, 4117*]. to twist together, weave, braid:– platted [3]

πλέον, **pleon**. See **4119**.

4121 πλεονάζω, **pleonazō**, v. GK: *4429* [→ *4137*]. to make increase; (intr.) to grow, increase, have abundance:– abound [4], abounded [1], aboundeth [1], abundant [1], had over [1], make to increase [1]

4122 πλεονεκτέω, **pleonekteō**, v. GK: *4430* [→ *4137+2192*]. to exploit, take advantage of, outwit:– make a gain [2], defrauded [1], defraud [1], get an advantage [1]

4123 πλεονέκτης, **pleonektēs**, n. GK: *4431* [→ *4137+2192*]. greedy person:– covetous [3], covetous man [1]

4124 πλεονεξία, **pleonexia**, n. GK: *4432* [→ *4137+2192*]. greediness, avarice:– covetousness [8], covetous practices [1], greediness [1]

4125 πλευρά, **pleura**, n. GK: *4433*. side (of the body):– side [5]

4126 πλέω, **pleō**, v. GK: *4434* [→ *636, 1020, 1277, 1602, 2668, 3896, 4142, 4143, 4144, 5284*]. to travel by ship, sail:– sailed [2], sail [2], sailing [1]

4127 πληγή, **plēgē**, n. GK: *4435* [→ *4141*]. plague; punishment: beating, flogging, wounding:– plagues [10], stripes [5], wound [3], plague [2], wounded (+*2007*) [1]

4128 πλῆθος, **plēthos**, n. GK: *4436* [→ *4130*]. large number, crowd, multitude, assembly:– multitude [29], bundle [1], company [1], multitudes [1]

4129 πληθύνω, **plēthynō**, v. GK: *4437* [→ *4130*]. to increase, grow in numbers, abound:– multiplied [8], multiply [2], abound [1], multiplying [1]

4130 πίμπλημι, **pimplēmi**, v. GK: *4398* [→ *1705, 3826, 4128, 4129, 4132, 4140*]. to fill; (pass.) to be filled, completed:– filled [18], accomplished [4], full came [1], furnished [1]

4131 πλήκτης, **plēktēs**, n. GK: *4438* [→ *4141*]. violent man, bully:– striker [2]

4132 πλήμμυρα, **plēmmyra**, n. GK: *4439* [→ *4130*]. flood, high water; in context likely a flash flood in a narrow valley (wadi):– flood [1]

4133 πλήν, **plēn**, c.&pp.*. GK: *4440* [→ *4137*]. but, however, only, yet:– but [14], nevertheless [7], notwithstanding [4], but rather [2], except [1], nevertheless (+*2532*) [1], save [1], than [1]

4134 πλήρης, **plērēs**, a. GK: *4441* [→ *4137*]. full:– full [17]

4135 πληροφορέω, **plērophoreō**, v. GK: *4442* [→ *4137+5342*]. to fulfill (completely); (pass.) to be fully assured, convinced, persuaded:– fully persuaded [2], fully known [1], make full proof [1], most surely believed [1]

4136 πληροφορία, **plērophoria**, n. GK: *4443* [→ *4137+5342*]. full assurance, certainty, conviction:– full assurance [3], assurance [1]

4137 πληρόω, **plēroō**, v. GK: *4444* [→ *378, 466, 1603, 1604, 4121, 4122, 4123, 4124, 4133, 4134, 4135, 4136, 4138, 4322, 4845, 5250*]. to fulfill, make full; (pass.) to be filled, full, complete (often used with reference to the fulfillment of the OT Scriptures):– fulfilled [45], filled [15], full [7], fulfil [6], complete [2], ended [2], accomplish [1], after [1], expired [1], fill up [1], fill with [1], filled with [1], filleth [1], fill [1], full come [1], fully [1], make full [1], perfect [1], supply [1]

4138 πλήρωμα, **plērōma**, n. GK: *4445* [→ *4137*]. fullness, fulfillment:– fulness [13], fulfilling [1], full [1], piece that filled up [1], put in to fill up [1]

4139 πλησίον, **plēsion**, adv.&pp.*&n. GK: *4446* [→ *3897, 3898*]. near, close by; (n.) neighbor; (pp.) near:– neighbour [16], near [1]

4140 πλησμονή, **plēsmonē**, n. GK: *4447* [→ *4130*]. indulgence, gratification:– satisfying [1]

4141 πλήσσω, **plēssō**, v. GK: *4448* [→ *1605, 1969, 4127, 4131*]. (pass.) to be struck:– smitten [1]

4142 πλοιάριον, **ploiarion**, n. GK: *4449* [→ *4126*]. (small) boat:– boat [2], boats [1], little ships [1], little ship [1], small ship [1]

4143 πλοῖον, **ploion**, n. GK: *4450* [→ *4126*]. boat, ship:– ship [58], ships [8], took shipping (+*1519+1684+3588*) [1]

4144 πλόος, **ploos**, n. GK: *4452 & 4453* [→ *4126*]. voyage, navigation:– course [1], sailing [1], voyage [1]

4145 πλούσιος, **plousios**, a. GK: *4454* [→ *4149*]. rich, wealthy; (n.) rich person:– rich [28]

4146 πλουσίως, **plousiōs**, adv. GK: *4455* [→ *4149*]. richly, generously, abundantly:– abundantly [2], richly [2]

4147 πλουτέω, **plouteō**, v. GK: *4456* [→ *4149*]. to be rich; (pf.) to have acquired wealth:– rich [8], made rich [2], increased with goods [1], waxed rich [1]

4148 πλουτίζω, **ploutizō**, v. GK: *4457* [→ *4149*]. to make rich; (pass.) to be enriched:– enriched [2], making rich [1]

4149 πλοῦτος, **ploutos**, n. GK: *4458* [→ *4145, 4146, 4147, 4148*]. riches, wealth:– riches [22]

4150 πλύνω, **plynō**, v. GK: *4459* [→ *637*]. to wash (things):– washed [1]

4151 πνεῦμα, **pneuma**, n. GK: *4460* [→ *4154*]. wind, breath, things which are commonly perceived as having no material substance; by extension: spirit, heart, mind, the immaterial part of the inner person that can respond to God; spirit being: (evil) spirit, ghost, God the Holy Spirit:– spirit [257], ghost [92], spirits [32], life [1], spiritually [1], spiritual [1], wind [1]

4152 πνευματικός, **pneumatikos**, a. GK: *4461* [→ *4154*]. spiritual, pertaining to the Spirit; (n.) spiritual person:– spiritual [26]

4153 πνευματικῶς, **pneumatikōs**, adv. GK: *4462* [→ *4154*]. spiritually; figuratively:– spiritually [2]

4154 πνέω, **pneō**, v. GK: *4463* [→ *1606, 1709, 2315, 4151, 4152, 4153, 4157, 5285*]. to blow (of wind):– blew [3], blow [2], bloweth [1], wind [1]

4155 πνίγω, **pnigō**, v. GK: *4464* [→ *638, 1970, 4156, 4846*]. to choke or strangle; drown:– choked [1], took by the throat [1]

4156 πνικτός, **pniktos**, a. GK: *4465* [→ *4155*]. strangled, choked; (n.) meat of strangled animals:– strangled [2], things strangled [1]

4157 πνοή, **pnoē**, n. GK: *4466* [→ *4154*]. wind, breath:– breath [1], wind [1]

4158 ποδήρης, **podērēs**, a. GK: *4468* [→ *4228*]. reaching to the feet; (n.) robe reaching to the feet:– down to the foot [1]

4159 πόθεν, **pothen**, adv. GK: *4470*. from where, from which:– whence [20], from whence [8]

4160 ποιέω, **poieō**, v. GK: *4472* [→ *15, 16, 17, 886, 1517, 1518, 2140, 2227, 2554, 2555, 2569, 3447, 3792, 4046, 4047, 4161, 4162, 4163, 4364, 4635, 4806, 5499*]. to do, make, practice, produce, a generic term of action or performance: note the many contextual translations in the NIV:– do [196], did [54], done [52], made [50], make [47], doeth [34], doest [13], doing [8], bringeth forth [7], maketh [6], making [6], bring forth [5], wrought [5], cause [4], committed [4], makest [4], shewed [4], causeth [3], committeth [3], bare [2], bear [2], caused [2], commit [2], continue [2], dealt [2], execute [2], fulfil [2], gave [2], keep [2], perform [2], put [2], working [2], able [1], abode [1], agree (+*1106+1520*) [1], appointed [1], as went (+*3598*) [1], avenge (+*1557+3588*) [1], avenged (+*1557*) [1], banded together (+*4963*) [1], been [1], bewrayeth (+*1212*) [1], bringing forth [1], bring [1], brought forth [1], cast out (+*1570*) [1], content (+*2425*) [1], delay (+*311*) [1], exerciseth [1], fulfilling [1], gained [1], held [1], journeying (+*4197*) [1], keepeth [1], kept [1], laying wait (+*1747*) [1], lightened the ship (+*1546*) [1], move [1], observe [1], ordained [1], provide [1], purged (+*2512*) [1], purposed [1], raising up

(+*1999*) [1], redeemed (+*3085*) [1], secure (+*275*) [1], shewest [1], shooteth out [1], spent [1], tarried a space (+*5550*) [1], took [1], transgresseth law (+*458*) [1], weep (+*2799*) [1], will [1], worketh [1], yield [1]

4161 ποίημα, ***poiēma***, n. GK: *4473* [→ *4160*]. what is made, workmanship, creation:– things that are made [1], workmanship [1]

4162 ποίησις, ***poiēsis***, n. GK: *4474* [→ *4160*]. doing, working:– deed [1]

4163 ποιητής, ***poiētēs***, n. GK: *4475* [→ *4160*]. doer, keeper, obeyer; poet:– doer [3], doers [2], poets [1]

4164 ποικίλος, ***poikilos***, a. GK: *4476* [→ *4182*]. of various kinds, of all kinds:– divers [8], manifold [2]

4165 ποιμαίνω, ***poimainō***, v. GK: *4477* [→ *4166*]. to shepherd, take care of sheep; to rule, lead:– feed [4], rule [4], feedeth [1], feeding cattle [1], feeding [1]

4166 ποιμήν, ***poimēn***, n. GK: *4478* [→ *750, 4165, 4167, 4168*]. shepherd; pastor:– shepherd [13], shepherds [4], pastors [1]

4167 ποίμνη, ***poimnē***, n. GK: *4479* [→ *4166*]. flock:– flock [4], fold [1]

4168 ποίμνιον, ***poimnion***, n. GK: *4480* [→ *4166*]. flock:– flock [5]

4169 ποῖος, ***poios***, a. GK: *4481* [→ *3634*]. what?, which?, of what kind?:– what [29], which [4], what manner [1]

4170 πολεμέω, ***polemeō***, v. GK: *4482* [→ *4171*]. to fight, make war:– make war [3], fought [2], fight [1], war [1]

4171 πόλεμος, ***polemos***, n. GK: *4483* [→ *4170*]. war, battle, fight:– wars [6], battle [5], war [5], fight [1], make war against (+*1519+4820*) [1]

4172 πόλις, ***polis***, n. GK: *4484* [→ *295, 1179, 2404, 2969, 3390, 3496, 3533, 4173, 4174, 4175, 4176, 4177, 4847*]. city, town, village:– city [145], cities [19]

4173 πολιτάρχης, ***politarchēs***, n. GK: *4485* [→ *4172+757*]. city official, formally, "politarch":– rulers of the city [2]

4174 πολιτεία, ***politeia***, n. GK: *4486* [→ *4172*]. citizenship:– commonwealth [1], freedom [1]

4175 πολίτευμα, ***politeuma***, n. GK: *4487* [→ *4172*]. citizenship:– conversation [1]

4176 πολιτεύομαι, ***politeuomai***, v. GK: *4488* [→ *4172*]. to fulfill one's duty; to conduct oneself, lead one's life:– conversation [1], lived [1]

4177 πολίτης, ***politēs***, n. GK: *4489* [→ *4172*]. citizen, subjects of a kingdom; neighbor:– citizen [2], citizens [1]

4178 πολλάκις, ***pollakis***, adv. GK: *4490* [→ *4183*]. many times, again and again, often, constantly:– often [7], oft [5], oftentimes [3], ofttimes [3]

4179 πολλαπλασίων, ***pollaplasiōn***, a. GK: *4491* [→ *4183*]. many times as much:– manifold more [1]

4180 πολυλογία, ***polylogia***, n. GK: *4494* [→ *4183+3004*]. speaking many words, wordiness:– much speaking [1]

4181 πολυμερῶς, ***polymerōs***, adv. GK: *4495* [→ *4183+3313*]. at many times, in many ways:– times [1]

4182 πολυποίκιλος, ***polypoikilos***, a. GK: *4497* [→ *4183+4164*]. manifold, (very) many sided:– manifold [1]

4183 πολύς, ***polys***, a. GK: *4498* [→ *3827, 4118, 4119, 4178, 4179, 4180, 4181, 4182, 4184, 4185, 4186, 4187*]. many, great, large; (compar.) more than, greater than; (super.) the most; very large:– many [221], much [74], great [59], more [11], more than [7], greater than [4], greatly [4], long [4], moe [4], most [4], further (+*1909*) [3], more part [2], straitly [2], a great while (+*1909*) [1], above [1], abundant [1], altogether (+*1722*) [1], but (+*2228+3756*) [1], common [1], exceed (+*4052*) [1], far (+*3123*) [1], far passed [1], far [1], great deal [1], greater part [1], greater [1], long (+*1909*) [1], longer (+*1909*) [1], many moe [1], many things [1], moe than [1], more excellent [1], oftentimes (+*5550*) [1], oft [1], plenteous [1], sore [1], very great [1], very many [1]

4184 πολύσπλαγχνος, ***polysplanchnos***, a. GK: *4492 & 4499* [→ *4183+4698*]. full of compassion, full of mercy:– very pitiful [1]

4185 πολυτελής, ***polytelēs***, a. GK: *4500* [→ *4183+5056*]. expensive, of great worth, costly:– costly [1], great price [1], very precious [1]

4186 πολύτιμος, ***polytimos***, a. GK: *4501* [→ *4183+5092*]. expensive, of great worth, valuable:– great price [1], very costly [1]

4187 πολυτρόπως, ***polytropōs***, adv. GK: *4502* [→ *4183+5157*]. in various ways:– manners [1]

4188 πόμα, ***poma***, n. GK: *4503* [→ *4095*]. drink:– drinks [1], drink [1]

4189 πονηρία, ***ponēria***, n. GK: *4504* [→ *4190*]. evil, wickedness, malice, in the NT always a negative moral quality opposed to God and his goodness:– wickedness [6], iniquities [1]

4190 πονηρός, ***ponēros***, a. GK: *4505* [→ *4189, 4191; cf. 4192*]. bad, the negative quality of an object; evil, wicked, crime, the negative moral quality of a person or action opposed to God and his goodness; (n.) wicked deed, wicked thing; the Evil One, a title of Satan:– evil [52], wicked [11], wicked one [6], bad [1], evils [1], grievous [1], harm [1], lewd [1], malicious [1], wickedness [1]

4191 πονηρότερος, ***ponēroteros***, a.compar. of *4190* GK: *4505* [→ *4190*]. more evil, more wicked; see *4190*:– more wicked than [2]

4192 πόνος, ***ponos***, n. GK: *4506* [→ *1278, 2669; cf. 3993, 4190*]. pain, agony; hard work, toil:– pain [2], pains [1]

4193 Ποντικός, ***Pontikos***, a.pr.g. GK: *4507*. from Pontus:– Pontus [1]

4194 Πόντιος, ***Pontios***, n.pr. GK: *4508*. Pontius, "*[tribal name]*":– Pontius [4]

4195 Πόντος, ***Pontos***, n.pr. GK: *4510*. Pontus, "*sea*":– Pontus [2]

4196 Πόπλιος, ***Poplios***, n.pr. GK: *4511*. Publius, "*first*":– Publius [2]

4197 πορεία, ***poreia***, n. GK: *4512 & 4515* [→ *4198*]. journey, trip; going about one's business, way of life, conduct:– journeying (+*4160*) [1], ways [1]

4198 πορεύομαι, ***poreuomai***, v. GK: *4513* [→ *639, 640, 1279, 1280, 1531, 1607, 1710, 1711, 1712, 1713, 1820, 1975, 2141, 2142, 3596, 3597, 3899, 4197, 4200, 4313, 4365, 4848; cf. 4008*]. to come, go, travel:– go [74], went [44], goeth [7], departed [6], depart [5], walking [4], walk [4], gone [3], going [2], journeyed [2], made journey [1], take journey [1], walked [1]

4199 πορθέω, ***portheō***, v. GK: *4514*. to destroy, annihilate; to raise havoc, pillage:– destroyed [2], wasted [1]

4200 πορισμός, ***porismos***, n. GK: *4516* [→ *4198*]. means of gain:– gain [2]

4201 Πόρκιος, ***Porkios***, n.pr. GK: *4517*. Porcius, "*[tribal name]*":– Porcius [1]

4202 πορνεία, ***porneia***, n. GK: *4518* [→ *4204*]. sexual immorality, fornication, marital unfaithfulness, prostitution, adultery, a generic term for sexual sin of any kind:– fornication [24], fornications [2]

4203 πορνεύω, ***porneuō***, v. GK: *4519* [→ *4204*]. to commit sexual immorality of any kind, adultery:– commit fornication [3], committed fornication [3], committed [1], committeth fornication [1]

4204 πόρνη, ***pornē***, n. GK: *4520* [→ *1608, 4202, 4203, 4205*]. prostitute, a woman who practices sexual immorality for payment; this can refer to religious unfaithfulness:– harlots [4], harlot [4], whore [4]

4205 πόρνος, ***pornos***, n. GK: *4521* [→ *4204*]. one who is sexually immoral (male or female), in some contexts distinguished from an adulterer (1Co 6:9):– whoremongers [4], fornicators [3], fornicator [2], whoremonger [1]

4206 πόρρω, ***porrō***, adv. GK: *4522* [→ *4253*]. far, a long way off; (compar.) farther:– far [2], great way off [1]

4207 πόρρωθεν, ***porrōthen***, adv. GK: *4523* [→ *4253*]. from a distance, at a distance:– afar off [2]

4208 πορρωτέρω, ***porrōterō***, adv. GK: *4524* [→ *4253*]. farther:– further [1]

4209 πορφύρα, ***porphyra***, n. GK: *4525* [→ *4210, 4211*]. purple (cloth or robe):– purple [5]

4210 πορφυροῦς, ***porphyrous***, a. GK: *4526 & 4528* [→ *4209*]. purple, purple cloth, in some contexts implying royalty:– purple [3]

4211 πορφυρόπωλις, ***porphyropōlis***, n. GK: *4527* [→ *4209+4453*]. dealer in purple cloth:– seller of purple [1]

4212 ποσάκις, ***posakis***, adv. GK: *4529* [→ *3739*]. how many times?, how often!:– how often [2], how oft [1]

4213 πόσις, ***posis***, n. GK: *4530* [→ *4095*]. drinking; a drink:– drink [3]

4214 πόσος, ***posos***, a. GK: *4531* [→ *3745*]. how great?, how much?, how many?; how great!, how many!, how much!:– how much [13], how many [11], how great [1], how [1], what [1]

4215 ποταμός, ***potamos***, n. GK: *4532* [→ *3318, 4216; cf. 4095*]. river, stream, torrent:– river [6], rivers [3], floods [2], flood [2], stream [2], waters [1]

4216 ποταμοφόρητος, ***potamophorētos***, a. GK: *4533* [→ *4215+5342*]. swept away by a torrential flow of a river:– carried away of the flood [1]

4217 ποταπός, ***potapos***, a. GK: *4467 & 4534* [→ *575+4226*]. of what kind?; how great!:– what manner [4], what manner of man [1], what manner of [1], what [1]

4218 ποτέ, ***pote***, pt. GK: *4537* [→ *4226*]. once, at one time, formerly; now, now at last:– in time past [4], at any time [3], in times past [3], sometimes [3], sometime [3], in old time [2], once [2], aforetime [1], any time [1], at last [1], at length [1], ever yet [1], in time passed [1], never (*+3361+3756*) [1], were (*+1510*) [1], when [1]

4219 πότε, ***pote***, adv.inter. GK: *4536* [→ *4226*]. when? how long?:– when [12], how long (*+2193*) [7]

4220 πότερον, ***poteron***, a. or pt. GK: *4538* [→ *4226+2087*]. whether:– whether [1]

4221 ποτήριον, ***potērion***, n. GK: *4539* [→ *4095*]. cup:– cup [31], cups [2]

4222 ποτίζω, ***potizō***, v. GK: *4540* [→ *4095*]. to give or offer a drink; to water:– gave drink [3], gave to drink [2], give to drink [2], watereth [2], fed [1], give drink [1], made drink [1], made to drink [1], watered [1], watering [1]

4223 Ποτίολοι, ***Potioloi***, n.pr. GK: *4541*. Puteoli, *"rotten [sulphur] smell* or *well, spring"*:– Puteoli [1]

4224 πότος, ***potos***, n. GK: *4542* [→ *4095*]. carousing, drinking party, orgy:– banquetings [1]

4225 πού, ***pou***, adv. GK: *4543* [→ *4226*]. somewhere, a place where; about, approximately:– a certain place [2], about [1]

4226 ποῦ, ***pou***, adv.inter.pl. GK: *4544* [→ *1221, 1222, 1513, 3368, 3379, 3381, 3697, 3698, 3699, 3704, 3763, 4217, 4219, 4218, 4220, 4225*]. where?, at what place?:– where [37], whither [10]

4227 Πούδης, ***Poudēs***, n.pr. GK: *4545*. Pudens, *"modest"*:– Pudens [1]

4228 πούς, ***pous***, n. GK: *4546* [→ *405, 3716, 4158, 5074, 5286*]. foot; leg:– feet [76], foot [9]

4229 πρᾶγμα, ***pragma***, n. GK: *4547* [→ *4238*]. thing, matter, practice:– things [4], matter [3], thing [2], business [1], work [1]

4230 πραγματεία, ***pragmateia***, n. GK: *4548* [→ *4238*]. (pl.) affairs, concerns:– affairs [1]

4231 πραγματεύομαι, ***pragmateuomai***, v. GK: *4549* [→ *4238*]. to put capital to work, do business:– occupy [1]

4232 πραιτώριον, ***praitōrion***, n. GK: *4550*. Praetorium; palace (of the governor); palace guard:– judgment hall [4], Pretorium [1], common hall [1], hall of judgment [1], palace [1]

4233 πράκτωρ, ***praktōr***, n. GK: *4551* [→ *4238*]. officer, a bailiff or constable in charge of a debtor's prison:– officer [2]

4234 πρᾶξις, ***praxis***, n. GK: *4552* [→ *4238*]. deed, action, practice; function:– deeds [3], deed [1], office [1], works [1]

4235 πρᾶος, ***praos***, a. GK: *4553* [→ *4239*]. gentle, humble, considerate:– meek [1]

4236 πραότης, ***praotēs***, n. GK: *4554* [→ *4239*]. gentleness, humility, courtesy, considerateness:– meekness [9]

4237 πρασιά, ***prasia***, n. GK: *4555* [→ *5556*]. group; in context this word is doubled: group by group:– in ranks (*+4237*) [2]

4238 πράσσω, ***prassō***, v. GK: *4556* [→ *1281, 4229, 4230, 4231, 4233, 4234*]. to do, act, practice:– do [17], done [6], committed [3], doeth [3], commit [2], deeds [1], did [1], doest [1], exact [1], keep [1], required [1], used [1]

4239 πραΰς, ***praus***, a. GK: *4558* [→ *4235, 4236, 4240*]. gentle, meek, the positive moral quality of dealing with people in a kind manner, with humility and consideration:– meek [3]

4240 πραΰτης, ***prautēs***, n. GK: *4559* [→ *4239*]. gentleness, meekness, humility:– meekness [3]

4241 πρέπω, ***prepō***, v. GK: *4560* [→ *2143, 2412, 3169*]. to be proper, appropriate, fitting:– becometh [3], became [2], become [1], comely [1]

4242 πρεσβεία, ***presbeia***, n. GK: *4561* [→ *4245*]. delegation, ambassador:– ambassage [1], message [1]

4243 πρεσβεύω, ***presbeuō***, v. GK: *4563* [→ *4245*]. to be an ambassador:– ambassadors [1], ambassador [1]

4244 πρεσβυτέριον, ***presbyterion***, n. GK: *4564* [→ *4245*]. body or council of the elders, Sanhedrin:– elders [1], estate of the elders [1], presbytery [1]

4245 πρεσβύτερος, ***presbyteros***, a. GK: *4565* [→ *4242, 4243, 4244, 4246, 4247, 4850*]. older; ancestral; (n.) in the Gospels and Acts, "elder," usually as an official leader of the Jewish community, in the epistles, "older man" and "older woman," who may or may not be official leaders of the church, depending on the context:– elders [58], elder [7], eldest [1], old men [1]

4246 πρεσβύτης, ***presbytēs***, n. GK: *4562 & 4566* [→ *4245*]. older man, possibly an official of the church in some contexts:– aged men [1], aged [1], old man [1]

4247 πρεσβῦτις, ***presbytis***, n. GK: *4567* [→ *4245*]. older woman, possibly an official of the church in context:– aged women [1]

πρήθω, ***prēthō***. See **4092**.

4248 πρηνής, ***prēnēs***, a. GK: *4568*. headlong, headfirst in prone position; some translate as "swollen, distended":– falling headlong (*+1096*) [1]

4249 πρίζω, ***prizō***, v. GK: *4569 & 4573* [→ *1282*]. (pass.) to be sawn in two:– sawn asunder [1]

4250 πρίν, ***prin***, adv. GK: *4570* [→ *4253*]. before:– before [7], before (*+2228*) [6], ere [1]

4251 Πρίσκα, ***Priska***, n.pr. GK: *4571* [→ *4252*]. Prisca, Priscilla:– Prisca [1]

4252 Πρίσκιλλα, ***Priskilla***, n.pr. GK: *4572* [→ *4251*]. Priscilla, Prisca:– Priscilla [5]

4253 πρό, ***pro***, pp. GK: *4574* [→ *4206, 4207, 4208, 4250, 4254, 4255, 4256, 4257, 4258, 4259, 4260, 4261, 4262, 4263, 4264, 4265, 4266, 4267, 4268, 4269, 4270, 4271, 4272, 4273, 4274, 4275, 4276, 4277, 4278, 4279, 4280, 4281, 4282, 4283, 4284, 4285, 4286, 4287, 4288, 4289, 4290, 4291, 4292, 4293, 4294, 4295, 4296, 4297, 4298, 4299, 4300, 4301, 4302, 4303, 4304, 4305, 4306, 4307, 4308, 4309, 4310, 4311, 4312, 4313, 4315, 4368, 4372, 4373, 4384, 4385, 4386, 4387, 4388, 4389, 4390, 4391, 4392, 4393, 4394, 4399, 4400, 4401, 4402, 4408, 5432; cf. 4404, 4413*]. (of place) before, at; (of time) before, some time ago:– before [37], before (*+3588*) [5], above [3], before (*+4383*) [1], before that (*+3588*) [1], ever (*+3588*) [1]

4254 προάγω, ***proagō***, v. GK: *4575* [→ *4253+71*]. to go on ahead, lead the way; to bring out, bring to trial:– went before [6], go before [5], brought forth [2], goeth before [2], going before [2], brought [1]

4255 προαιρέω, ***proaireō***, v. GK: *4576* [→ *4253+138*]. (mid.) to decide, determine:– purposeth [1]

4256 προαιτιάομαι, ***proaitiaomai***, v. GK: *4577* [→ *4253+156*]. to make a charge beforehand:– before proved [1]

4257 προακούω, ***proakouō***, v. GK: *4578* [→ *4253+191*]. to hear about beforehand:– heard before [1]

4258 προαμαρτάνω, ***proamartanō***, v. GK: *4579* [→ *4253+264*]. to sin earlier, to have sinned beforehand:– heretofore sinned [1], sinned already [1]

4259 προαύλιον, ***proaulion***, n. GK: *4580* [→ *4253+833*]. entryway, gateway:– porch [1]

4260 προβαίνω, ***probainō***, v. GK: *4581* [→ *4253+305*]. (spacial) to go on, go on farther; (temporal) to be well along (in years), advanced (in age):– well stricken [2], age (*+1722+2250*) [1], going on [1], gone further [1]

4261 προβάλλω, ***proballō***, v. GK: *4582* [→ *4253+906*]. to push to the front, cause to come to the front; to sprout, put forth:– putting forward [1], shoot forth [1]

4262 προβατικός, ***probatikos***, a. GK: *4583* [→ *4253+305*]. pertaining to sheep; (pr.n.) the Sheep (Gate):– sheep [1]

4263 πρόβατον, ***probaton***, n. GK: *4585* [→ *4253+305*]. sheep:– sheep [39], sheep's [1], sheepfold (*+833+3588*) [1]

4264 προβιβάζω, ***probibazō***, v. GK: *4586* [→ *4253+305*]. (pass.) to be prompted, caused to come forward:– before instructed [1], drew [1]

4265 προβλέπω, ***problepō***, v. GK: *4587* [→ *4253+991*]. (mid.) to plan, select, provide:– provided [1]

4266 προγίνομαι, ***proginomai***, v. GK: *4588* [→ *4253+1096*]. to commit beforehand, happen previously:– past [1]

4267 προγινώσκω, ***proginōskō***, v. GK: *4589* [→ *4253+1097*]. to know beforehand, foreknow; (mid.) to choose beforehand:– foreknew [1], foreknow [1], foreordained [1], knew [1], know before [1]

4268 πρόγνωσις, ***prognōsis***, n. GK: *4590* [→ *4253+1097*]. foreknowledge:– foreknowledge [2]

4269 πρόγονος, ***progonos***, a. GK: *4591* [→ *4253+1096*]. (pl.) parents, forefathers, ancestors:– forefathers [1], parents [1]

4270 προγράφω, ***prographō***, v. GK: *4592* [→ *4253+1125*]. to write beforehand; to show clearly, advertise, proclaim:– before ordained [1], evidently set forth [1], written aforetime [1], written [1], wrote afore [1]

4271 πρόδηλος, ***prodēlos***, a. GK: *4593* [→ *4253+1212*]. obvious, clear, evident:– evident [1], manifest beforehand [1], open beforehand [1]

4272 προδίδωμι, ***prodidōmi***, v. GK: *4594* [→ *4253+1325*]. to give beforehand:– first given [1]

4273 προδότης, ***prodotēs***, n. GK: *4595* [→ *4253+1325*]. traitor, betrayer, treacherous one:– betrayers [1], traitors [1], traitor [1]

προδρέμω, *prodremō*. See ***4390***.

4274 πρόδρομος, ***prodromos***, a. GK: *4596* [→ *4253+5143*]. going before, forerunner:– forerunner [1]

4275 προείδω, ***proeidō***, v. GK: *4632* [→ *4253+3708*]. to see previously; to see ahead, foresee:– foreseeing [1], seeing before [1]

προειρέω, *proeireō*. See ***4280***.

4276 προελπίζω, ***proelpizō***, v. GK: *4598* [→ *4253+1680*]. to be the first to hope, hope beforehand:– first trusted [1]

4277 προέπω, ***proepō***, v. GK: *4625* [→ *4253+3004*]. to tell beforehand; to speak in the past:–

4278 προενάρχομαι, ***proenarchomai***, v. GK: *4599* [→ *4253+1722+757*]. to begin beforehand, begin previously:– begun before [1], begun [1]

4279 προεπαγγέλλω, ***proepangellō***, v. GK: *4600* [→ *4253+1909+32*]. (mid.) to promise beforehand; (pass.) to be promised previously:– promised afore [1]

4280 προερέω, ***proereō***, v. GK: *4625* [→ *4253+3004*]. to tell beforehand; to speak in the past:–

4281 προέρχομαι, ***proerchomai***, v. GK: *4601* [→ *4253+2064*]. to go on ahead; to lead; to visit in advance:– went before [2], go before [1], going before [1], go [1], outwent [1], passed on [1], went forward [1], went further [1]

4282 προετοιμάζω, ***proetoimazō***, v. GK: *4602* [→ *4253+2092*]. to prepare in advance:– afore prepared [1], before ordained [1]

4283 προευαγγελίζομαι, ***proeuangelizomai***, v. GK: *4603* [→ *4253+2095+32*]. to announce the gospel in advance:– preached before the gospel [1]

4284 προέχω, ***proechō***, v. GK: *4604* [→ *4253+2192*]. (mid.) to be better off, have an advantage:– better [1]

4285 προηγέομαι, ***proēgeomai***, v. GK: *4605* [→ *4253+71*]. to put above, go before:– preferring [1]

4286 πρόθεσις, ***prothesis***, n. GK: *4606 & 4671* [→ *4253+5087*]. setting forth: plan, purpose, will; (a.) consecrated (bread):– purpose [8], shewbread (*+740+3588*) [3], shewbread (*+740*) [1]

4287 προθεσμία, ***prothesmia***, n. GK: *4607* [→ *4253+5087*]. set time, fixed or limited time:– time appointed [1]

4288 προθυμία, ***prothymia***, n. GK: *4608* [→ *4253+2372*]. eagerness, willingness, readiness:– forwardness of mind [1], readiness of mind [1], readiness [1], ready mind [1], willing mind [1]

4289 πρόθυμος, ***prothymos***, a. GK: *4609* [→ *4253+2372*]. willing, eager:– ready [2], willing [1]

4290 προθύμως, ***prothymōs***, adv. GK: *4610* [→ *4253+2372*]. eagerly, willingly:– of a ready mind [1]

4291 προΐστημι, ***proistēmi***, v. GK: *4613* [→ *4253+2476*]. (act/mid) to manage, direct, lead; (mid.) to devote oneself, busy oneself to:– maintain [2], ruleth [2], rule [2], over [1], ruling [1]

4292 προκαλέω, ***prokaleō***, v. GK: *4614* [→ *4253+2564*]. (mid.) to provoke, challenge:– provoking [1]

4293 προκαταγγέλλω, ***prokatangellō***, v. GK: *4615* [→ *4253+2596+32*]. to foretell, predict, announce beforehand:– before shewed [1], foretold [1], had notice before [1], shewed before [1]

4294 προκαταρτίζω, ***prokatartizō***, v. GK: *4616* [→ *4253+2596+737*]. to arrange for in advance, get ready beforehand:– make up beforehand [1]

4295 πρόκειμαι, ***prokeimai***, v. GK: *4618* [→ *4253+2749*]. (pass.) to be set before, present:– set before [3], first [1], set forth for [1]

4296 προκηρύσσω, ***prokēryssō***, v. GK: *4619* [→ *4253+2783*]. to preach beforehand:– before preached [1], first preached [1]

4297 προκοπή, ***prokopē***, n. GK: *4620* [→ *4253+2875*]. progress, advancement:– furtherance [2], profiting [1]

4298 προκόπτω, ***prokoptō***, v. GK: *4621* [→ *4253+2875*]. to go ahead, go forward, advance:– far spent [1], increased [1], increase [1], proceed [1], profited [1], wax [1]

4299 πρόκριμα, ***prokrima***, n. GK: *4622* [→ *4253+2919*]. partiality, discrimination, prejudice:– preferring [1]

4300 προκυρόω, ***prokyroō***, v. GK: *4623* [→ *4253+2964*]. to establish previously, ratify beforehand:– confirmed before [1]

4301 προλαμβάνω, ***prolambanō***, v. GK: *4624* [→ *4253+2983*]. to take beforehand; to go on ahead; (pass.) to be caught, detected:– come aforehand [1], overtaken [1], taketh before [1]

4302 προλέγω, ***prolegō***, v. GK: *4625* [→ *4253+3004*]. to tell beforehand; to speak in the past:– said before [4], told before [3], spoken before [2], foretell [1], foretold [1], forewarned [1], spake before [1], tell before [1], told in time past [1]

4303 προμαρτύρομαι, ***promartyromai***, v. GK: *4626* [→ *4253+3144*]. to predict, bear witness to beforehand:– testified beforehand [1]

4304 προμελετάω, ***promeletaō***, v. GK: *4627* [→ *4253+3199*]. to worry beforehand; some translate "to plan ahead":– meditate before [1]

4305 προμεριμνάω, ***promerimnaō***, v. GK: *4628* [→ *4253+3308*]. to worry or be anxious beforehand:– take thought beforehand [1]

4306 προνοέω, ***pronoeō***, v. GK: *4629* [→ *4253+3563*]. to provide for, care for; to consider, have regard for:– provide for [1], provide [1], providing [1]

4307 πρόνοια, ***pronoia***, n. GK: *4630* [→ *4253+3563*]. foresight, provision, care:– providence [1], provision for [1]

4308 προοράω, ***prooraō***, v. GK: *4632* [→ *4253+3708*]. to see previously; to see ahead, foresee; (mid.) to see in front of:– foresaw [1], seen before [1]

4309 προορίζω, ***proorizō***, v. GK: *4633* [→ *4253+3724*]. to predestine, decide beforehand:– predestinated [2], predestinate [2], determined before [1], ordained [1]

4310 προπάσχω, ***propaschō***, v. GK: *4634* [→ *4253+3958*]. to suffer previously:– suffered before [1]

4311 προπέμπω, ***propempō***, v. GK: *4636* [→ *4253+3992*]. to accompany, escort; to send on one's way, help on one's journey:– brought on way [3], bring on journey [2], accompanied [1], bring forward on journey [1], brought on [1], conduct forth [1]

4312 προπετής, ***propetēs***, a. GK: *4637* [→ *4253+4098*]. rash, reckless, thoughtless:– heady [1], rashly [1]

4313 προπορεύομαι, ***proporeuomai***, v. GK: *4638* [→ *4253+4198*]. to go before:– go before [1], go [1]

4314 πρός, ***pros***, pp. GK: *4639* [→ *676, 677, 1715, 2144, 2145, 4316, 4317, 4318, 4319, 4320, 4321, 4322, 4323, 4324, 4325, 4326, 4327, 4328, 4329, 4330, 4331, 4332, 4333, 4334, 4335, 4336, 4337, 4338, 4339, 4340, 4341, 4342, 4343, 4344, 4345, 4346, 4347, 4348, 4349, 4350, 4351, 4354, 4355, 4356, 4357, 4358, 4359, 4360, 4361, 4362, 4363, 4364, 4365, 4366, 4367, 4369, 4370, 4371, 4374, 4375, 4376, 4377, 4378, 4379, 4383; cf. 4352*]. (gen.) to, for; (dat.) on, at, near, by; (acc.) to, toward; with; in order to; against:– unto [344], to [200], with [43], for [26], against [24], among [18], at [15], toward [8], by [4], according to [3], in [3], of [3], that (*+3588*) [3], about [2], amongst [2], before [2], between [2], pertaining to [2], that [2], to (*+3588*) [2], towards [2], as [1], because (*+3588*) [1], because of [1], belong unto [1], compared with [1], for (*+3588*) [1], nigh unto [1], pertain to [1], to do [1], together (*+240*) [1], whereby (*+3739*) [1], whereby [1], within [1]

4315 προσάββατον, ***prosabbaton***, n. GK: *4640* [→ *4253+4521*]. day before the Sabbath (Friday):– day before the sabbath [1]

4316 προσαγορεύω, ***prosagoreuō***, v. GK: *4641* [→ *4314+71*]. to designate:– called [1]

4317 προσάγω, ***prosagō***, v. GK: *4642* [→ *4314+71*]. to bring to; to approach, come near:– bring [2], brought to [1], drew near [1]

4318 προσαγωγή, ***prosagōgē***, n. GK: *4643* [→ *4314+71*]. access; approach:– access [3]

4319 προσαιτέω, ***prosaiteō***, v. GK: *4644* [→ *4314+154*]. to beg:– begging [2], begged [1]

4320 προσαναβαίνω, ***prosanabainō***, v. GK: *4646* [→ *4314+303+305*]. to move up, go up:– go up [1]

4321 προσαναλίσκω, ***prosanaliskō***, v. GK: *4648 & 4649* [→ *4314+303+259*]. to spend lavishly or in addition:– spent [1]

4322 προσαναπληρόω, ***prosanaplēroō***, v. GK: *4650* [→ *4314+303+4137*]. to supply, fill up:– supplied [1], supplieth [1]

4323 προσανατίθημι, ***prosanatithēmi***, v. GK: *4651* [→ *4314+303+5087*]. to add; to consult, ask advice:– conferred [1], in conference added [1]

4324 προσαπειλέω, ***prosapeileō***, v. GK: *4653* [→ *4314+547*]. to threaten further:– further threatened [1]

4325 προσδαπανάω, ***prosdapanaō***, v. GK: *4655* [→ *4314+1160*]. to spend extra:– spendest more [1]

4326 προσδέομαι, ***prosdeomai***, v. GK: *4656* [→ *4314+1189*]. to need:– needed [1]

4327 προσδέχομαι, ***prosdechomai***, v. GK: *4657* [*→ 4314+1209*]. to receive, welcome, accept; to wait for, anticipate:– looking for [3], receive [2], accepting [1], allow [1], looked for [1], receiveth [1], took [1], wait for [1], waited for [1], waited [1], waiting for [1]

4328 προσδοκάω, ***prosdokaō***, v. GK: *4659* [*→ 4314+1380*]. to look forward to, expect, wait for:– look for [5], looked [2], waited for [2], expecting to [1], in expectation [1], looketh for [1], looketh [1], looking for [1], tarried [1], waiting for [1]

4329 προσδοκία, ***prosdokia***, n. GK: *4660* [*→ 4314+1380*]. anticipation, expectation; apprehension:– expectation [1], looking after [1]

προσδρέμω, ***prosdremō***. See ***4370***.

4330 προσεάω, ***proseaō***, v. GK: *4661* [*→ 4314+1439*]. to allow to go farther:– suffering [1]

4331 προσεγγίζω, ***prosengizō***, v. GK: *4662* [*→ 4314+1451*]. to approach, come near:– come nigh [1]

4332 προσεδρεύω, ***prosedreuō***, v. GK: *4663* [*→ 4314+1476*]. to serve, wait upon:– wait at [1]

4333 προσεργάζομαι, ***prosergazomai***, v. GK: *4664* [*→ 4314+2041*]. to earn more:– gained [1]

4334 προσέρχομαι, ***proserchomai***, v. GK: *4665* [*→ 4314+2064*]. to come to, approach, draw near; to agree to:– came [35], came to [22], came unto [8], come unto [4], come [2], coming [2], went to [2], went unto [2], comers [1], cometh [1], coming to [1], consent to [1], draw near [1], drew near [1], go near [1], goeth [1], went [1]

4335 προσευχή, ***proseuchē***, n. GK: *4666* [*→ 4314+2172*]. prayer; place of prayer:– prayer [21], prayers [15], prayed earnestly (*+4336*) [1]

4336 προσεύχομαι, ***proseuchomai***, v. GK: *4667* [*→ 4314+2172*]. to pray:– pray [42], prayed [24], praying [12], prayeth [3], make prayers [2], prayest [2], make prayer [1], prayed earnestly (*+4335*) [1]

4337 προσέχω, ***prosechō***, v. GK: *4668* [*→ 4314+2192*]. to watch out, be on guard, beware; to pay attention, devote, apply oneself:– beware [7], take heed [6], gave heed [2], giving heed [2], attended unto [1], gave attendance at [1], give attendance [1], give heed to [1], give heed [1], given to [1], had regard [1]

4338 προσηλόω, ***prosēloō***, v. GK: *4669* [*→ 4314+2247*]. to nail to:– nailing [1]

4339 προσήλυτος, ***prosēlytos***, n. GK: *4670* [*→ 4314+2064*]. Gentile convert (to Judaism), transliterated as "proselyte":– proselytes [2], proselyte [2]

4340 πρόσκαιρος, ***proskairos***, a. GK: *4672* [*→ 4314+2540*]. lasting only for a short time, temporary:– for a time [1], for a while [1], season [1], temporal [1]

4341 προσκαλέω, ***proskaleō***, v. GK: *4673* [*→ 4314+2564*]. (mid.) to call, summon, send for; gather together:– called unto [16], called [6], calleth unto [2], calling unto [2], call for [1], called for [1], called to [1], call [1]

4342 προσκαρτερέω, ***proskartereō***, v. GK: *4674* [*→ 4314+2594*]. to join, adhere to; to be ready; to give attention, be faithful; to spend much time together:– continued [2], attending continually [1], continue in [1], continued stedfastly [1], continuing instant [1], continuing [1], give continually to [1], wait on [1], waited on continually [1]

4343 προσκαρτέρησις, ***proskarterēsis***, n. GK: *4675* [*→ 4314+2594*]. perseverance, patience:– perseverance [1]

4344 προσκεφάλαιον, ***proskephalaion***, n. GK: *4676* [*→ 4314+2776*]. cushion, pillow:– pillow [1]

4345 προσκληρόω, ***prosklēroō***, v. GK: *4677* [*→ 4314+2819*]. (pass.) to be joined with, associated with:– consorted with [1]

4346 πρόσκλισις, ***prosklisis***, n. GK: *4680* [*→ 4314+2827*]. favoritism, partiality:– partiality [1]

4347 προσκολλάω, ***proskollaō***, v. GK: *4681* [*→ 4314+2853*]. (pass.) to be united to:– joined [2], cleave to [1], cleave [1]

4348 πρόσκομμα, ***proskomma***, n. GK: *4682* [*→ 4314+2875*]. stumbling block, something that causes one to stumble:– stumblingblock [2], stumblingstone (*+3037*) [2], offence [1], stumbling [1]

4349 προσκοπή, ***proskopē***, n. GK: *4683* [*→ 4314+2875*]. stumbling block, occasion for stumbling; fig. of sinning:– offence [1]

4350 προσκόπτω, ***proskoptō***, v. GK: *4684* [*→ 4314+2875*]. to strike, beat; (intr.) to stumble, fall:– stumbleth [3], dash [2], beat upon [1], stumbled [1], stumble [1]

4351 προσκυλίω, ***proskyliō***, v. GK: *4685* [*→ 4314+2947*]. to roll in front of, roll up to:– rolled [2]

4352 προσκυνέω, ***proskyneō***, v. GK: *4686* [*→ 4353; cf. 4314*]. to worship, pay homage, show reverence; to kneel down (before):– worship [35], worshipped [24], worshipping [1]

4353 προσκυνητής, ***proskynētēs***, n. GK: *4687* [*→ 4352*]. worshiper:– worshippers [1]

4354 προσλαλέω, ***proslaleō***, v. GK: *4688* [*→ 4314+2980*]. to talk with:– speak with [1], speaking to [1]

4355 προσλαμβάνω, ***proslambanō***, v. GK: *4689* [*→ 4314+2983*]. to take aside, take along; to partake; to welcome, accept:– receive [4], took [4], received [3], taken [1], take [1], took unto [1]

4356 πρόσληψις, ***proslēpsis***, n. GK: *4691 & 4692* [*→ 4314+2983*]. acceptance:– receiving [1]

4357 προσμένω, ***prosmenō***, v. GK: *4693* [*→ 4314+3306*]. to be with, continue in, remain, stay:– abide [1], been [1], cleave unto [1], continueth [1], continue [1], tarried [1]

4358 προσορμίζω, ***prosormizō***, v. GK: *4694* [*→ 4314*]. (pass.) to be anchored, come into harbor:– drew to shore [1]

4359 προσοφείλω, ***prosopheilō***, v. GK: *4695* [*→ 4314+3784*]. to owe (in addition):– owest besides [1]

4360 προσοχθίζω, ***prosochthizō***, v. GK: *4696* [*→ 4314*]. to be angry, provoked:– grieved [2]

4361 πρόσπεινος, ***prospeinos***, a. GK: *4698* [*→ 4314+3983*]. hungry:– hungry [1]

4362 προσπήγνυμι, ***prospēgnymi***, v. GK: *4699* [*→ 4314+4078*]. to nail to (the cross):– crucified [1]

4363 προσπίπτω, ***prospiptō***, v. GK: *4700* [*→ 4314+4098*]. to fall down before; to beat against, strike against:– fell down before [4], beat upon [1], falling down before [1], fell down at [1], fell [1]

4364 προσποιέω, ***prospoieō***, v. GK: *4701* [*→ 4314+4160*]. to act as if, pretend:– made as though [1]

4365 προσπορεύομαι, ***prosporeuomai***, v. GK: *4702* [*→ 4314+4198*]. to come to, approach:– come unto [1]

4366 προσρήγνυμι, ***prosrēgnymi***, v. GK: *4703 & 4704* [*→ 4314+4486*]. to strike upon:– against beat vehemently [1], beat vehemently upon [1]

4367 προστάσσω, ***prostassō***, v. GK: *4705* [*→ 4314+5021*]. (act./mid.) to command, order; (pass.) to be set, prescribed:– commanded [6], bidden [1]

4368 προστάτις, ***prostatis***, n. GK: *4706* [*→ 4253+2476*]. helper:– succourer [1]

4369 προστίθημι, ***prostithēmi***, v. GK: *4707* [*→ 4314+5087*]. to add to, increase ; (pass.) to be brought to, given:– added [7], add [2], again [2], added to [1], added unto [1], any more [1], increase [1], laid [1], more given [1], proceeded further [1]

4370 προστρέχω, ***prostrechō***, v. GK: *4708* [*→ 4314+5143*]. to run up to:– came running [1], ran to [1], running to [1]

4371 προσφάγιον, ***prosphagion***, n. GK: *4709* [*→ 4314+5314*]. (little) fish:– meat [1]

4372 πρόσφατος, ***prosphatos***, a. GK: *4710* [*→ 4253+5348 or* 5408]. new:– new [1]

4373 προσφάτως, ***prosphatōs***, adv. GK: *4711* [*→ 4253+5348 or* 5408]. recently:– lately [1]

4374 προσφέρω, ***prospherō***, v. GK: *4712* [*→ 4314+5342*]. to bring to, present, offer; to treat as, deal with:– brought [12], offered [12], offer [10], offered up [3], bring [2], brought unto [2], offering [2], brought to [1], dealeth [1], doeth [1], presented [1], put [1]

4375 προσφιλής, ***prosphilēs***, a. GK: *4713* [*→ 4314+5384*]. lovely, pleasing:– lovely [1]

4376 προσφορά, ***prosphora***, n. GK: *4714* [*→ 4314+5342*]. offering, presentation:– offering [7], offering up [1], offerings [1]

4377 προσφωνέω, ***prosphōneō***, v. GK: *4715* [*→ 4314+5456*]. to call out; speak to, address:– spake [2], called to [1], called unto [1], calling to [1], calling unto [1], spake unto [1]

4378 πρόσχυσις, ***proschysis***, n. GK: *4717* [*→ 1632; cf. 4314*]. sprinkling:– sprinkling [1]

4379 προσψαύω, ***prospsauō***, v. GK: *4718* [*→ 4314+5597*]. to touch:– touch [1]

4380 προσωποληπτέω, ***prosōpolēpteō***, v. GK: *4719 & 4722* [*→ 4383+2983*]. to show favoritism, partiality:– have respect to persons [1]

4381 προσωπολήπτης, ***prosōpolēptēs***, n. GK: *4720 & 4723* [*→ 4383+2983*]. one who shows favoritism, partiality:– respecter of persons [1]

4382 προσωποληψία, ***prosōpolēpsia***, n. GK: *4721 & 4724* [*→ 4383+2983*]. favoritism, partiality:– respect of persons [4]

4383 πρόσωπον, ***prosōpon***, n. GK: *4725* [→ *678, 2146, 4380, 4381, 4382*]. face, a part of the body; by extension: in someone's presence, sight; (with various pp.) before, in front of, on the surface of:– face [49], faces [6], person [5], presence [5], countenance [3], appearance [1], before (+*1519*) [1], before (+*4253*) [1], face to face (+*2596*) [1], fashion [1], having in admiration (+*2296*) [1], in presence [1], in the presence (+*2596*) [1], outward appearance [1], persons [1]

4384 προτάσσω, ***protassō***, v. GK: *4726* [→ *4253+5021*]. to determine beforehand, allot beforehand:– before appointed [1]

4385 προτείνω, ***proteinō***, v. GK: *4727* [→ *1614; cf. 4253*]. to stretch out:– bound [1]

4386 πρότερον, ***prōterōn***, a.neut. of *4387*. GK: *4728* [→ *4253*]. before; (adv.) before, formerly, an earlier time:–

4387 πρότερος, ***proteros***, a. GK: *4728* [→ *4253*]. before; (adv.) before, formerly, an earlier time:– before [5], former [3], first [2], at first [1]

4388 προτίθημι, ***protithēmi***, v. GK: *4729* [→ *4253+5087*]. (mid.) to plan, purpose; to present, bring forth:– purposed [2], set forth [1]

4389 προτρέπω, ***protrepō***, v. GK: *4730* [→ *4253+5157*]. to encourage, urge on:– exhorting [1]

4390 προτρέχω, ***protrechō***, v. GK: *4731* [→ *4253+5143*]. to run ahead:– outrun (+*5030*) [1], ran before [1]

4391 προϋπάρχω, ***prouparchō***, v. GK: *4732* [→ *4253+5259+757*]. to exist formerly:– beforetime [1], before [1]

4392 πρόφασις, ***prophasis***, n. GK: *4733* [→ *4253+5316*]. excuse; pretense, show, cover:– pretence [3], cloke [2], shew [1], under colour [1]

4393 προφέρω, ***propherō***, v. GK: *4734* [→ *4253+5342*]. to bring out:– bringeth forth [2]

4394 προφητεία, ***prophēteia***, n. GK: *4735* [→ *4395, 4396, 4397, 4398, 5578*]. prophecy, an inspired message, sometimes encouraging obedience to God, sometimes proclaiming the future as a warning to preparedness and continued obedience:– prophecy [14], prophecies [2], prophesying [2], prophesyings [1]

4395 προφητεύω, ***prophēteuō***, v. GK: *4736* [→ *4394*]. to prophesy, to speak an inspired message, sometimes encouraging obedience to God, sometimes proclaiming the future as a warning to preparedness and continued obedience:– prophesy [14], prophesied [9], prophesieth [4], prophesying [1]

4396 προφήτης, ***prophētēs***, n. GK: *4737* [→ *4394*]. prophet, one who speaks inspired utterances; the writings of the OT prophets; see also *4394*:– prophets [81], prophet [67], prophet's [1]

4397 προφητικός, ***prophētikos***, a. GK: *4738* [→ *4394*]. prophetic, prophesy; see also *4394*:– of prophecy [1], prophets [1]

4398 προφῆτις, ***prophētis***, n. GK: *4739* [→ *4394*]. prophetess, a woman who speaks inspired utterances; see also *4394*:– prophetess [2]

4399 προφθάνω, ***prophthanō***, v. GK: *4740* [→ *4253+5348*]. to anticipate, come before:– prevented [1]

4400 προχειρίζω, ***procheirizō***, v. GK: *4741* [→ *4253+5495*]. (mid.) to choose, appoint:– chosen [1], make [1]

4401 προχειροτονέω, ***procheirotoneō***, v. GK: *4742* [→ *1614*]. to choose beforehand, appoint beforehand:– chosen before [1]

4402 Πρόχορος, ***Prochoros***, n.pr. GK: *4743* [→ *4253+5525*]. Procorus:– Prochorus [1]

4403 πρύμνα, ***prymna***, n. GK: *4744*. stern (of a vessel):– hinder part of ship [1], hinder part [1], stern [1]

4404 πρωΐ, ***prōi***, adv. GK: *4745* [→ *4405, 4406, 4407; cf. 4253*]. early in the morning:– in the morning [4], early [2], morning [2], early in the morning (+*260*) [1], early in the morning [1]

4405 πρωΐα, ***prōia***, n. GK: *4746* [→ *4404*]. early morning:– morning [2], early [1], in the morning [1]

4406 πρώϊμος, ***prōimos***, a. GK: *4611 & 4747* [→ *4404*]. early; (n.) autumn rains (in October of the modern calendar):– early [1]

4407 πρωϊνός, ***prōinos***, a. GK: *4612 & 4748* [→ *4404*]. early, pertaining to the morning:– morning [1]

4408 πρῷρα, ***prōra***, n. GK: *4749* [→ *4253*]. bow (of a vessel):– forepart [1], foreship [1]

4409 πρωτεύω, ***prōteuō***, v. GK: *4750* [→ *4413*]. to be supreme, first, have first place:– preeminence [1]

4410 πρωτοκαθεδρία, ***prōtokathedria***, n. GK: *4751* [→ *4413+2516*]. most important seat, seat of honor:– chief seats [2], highest seats [1], uppermost seats [1]

4411 πρωτοκλισία, ***prōtoklisia***, n. GK: *4752* [→ *4413+2827*]. place of honor:– chief rooms [2], uppermost rooms [2], highest room [1]

4412 πρῶτον, ***prōton***, adv. GK: *4754* [→ *4413*]. first; earlier; above all:– first [55], at first [2], at the beginning [1], before [1], chiefly [1], first of all [1]

4413 πρῶτος, ***prōtos***, a. GK: *4755* [→ *1207, 4409, 4410, 4411, 4412, 4414, 4415, 4416, 5383; cf. 4253*]. first (chronologically or in order of importance):– first [86], chief [10], before [2], former [2], beginning [1], best [1], chiefest [1], first (+*1722*) [1]

4414 πρωτοστάτης, ***prōtostatēs***, n. GK: *4756* [→ *4413+2476*]. ringleader, leader:– ringleader [1]

4415 πρωτοτόκια, ***prōtotokia***, n. GK: *4757* [→ *4413+5088*]. inheritance rights (of the firstborn):– birthright [1]

4416 πρωτότοκος, ***prōtotokos***, a. GK: *4758* [→ *4413+5088*]. firstborn (human or animal). In biblical culture, the firstborn had higher status and received a greater share of the inheritance. Jesus Christ, as the firstborn of God, is of supreme status and inherits all things:– firstborn [7], first begotten [1], firstbegotten [1]

4417 πταίω, ***ptaiō***, v. GK: *4760* [→ *679*]. to stumble, fall, trip:– offend [3], fall [1], stumbled [1]

4418 πτέρνα, ***pterna***, n. GK: *4761*. heel:– heel [1]

4419 πτερύγιον, ***pterygion***, n. GK: *4762* [→ *4072*]. highest point:– pinnacle [2]

4420 πτέρυξ, ***pteryx***, n. GK: *4763* [→ *4072*]. wing:– wings [5]

4421 πτηνός, ***ptēnos***, a. GK: *4764* [→ *4072*]. what is winged or feathered; (n.) bird:– birds [1]

4422 πτοέω, ***ptoeō***, v. GK: *4765* [→ *4423*]. (pass.) to be startled, frightened:– terrified [2]

4423 πτόησις, ***ptoēsis***, n. GK: *4766* [→ *4422*]. something alarming:– amazement [1]

4424 Πτολεμαΐς, ***Ptolemais***, n.pr. GK: *4767*. Ptolemais:– Ptolemais [1]

4425 πτύον, ***ptyon***, n. GK: *4768* [→ *4429*]. winnowing fork or shovel:– fan [2]

4426 πτύρω, ***ptyrō***, v. GK: *4769*. (pass.) to be frightened:– terrified [1]

4427 πτύσμα, ***ptysma***, n. GK: *4770* [→ *4429*]. saliva, spit:– spittle [1]

4428 πτύσσω, ***ptyssō***, v. GK: *4771* [→ *380*]. to roll up:– closed [1]

4429 πτύω, ***ptyō***, v. GK: *4772* [→ *1609, 1716, 4425, 4427*]. to spit (saliva):– spit [2], spat [1]

4430 πτῶμα, ***ptōma***, n. GK: *4773* [→ *4098*]. dead body, carcass, corpse:– dead bodies [3], carcase [1], corpse [1]

4431 πτῶσις, ***ptōsis***, n. GK: *4774* [→ *4098*]. falling, crash:– fall [2]

4432 πτωχεία, ***ptōcheia***, n. GK: *4775* [→ *4434*]. poverty:– poverty [3]

4433 πτωχεύω, ***ptōcheuō***, v. GK: *4776* [→ *4434*]. to be or become poor:– poor [1]

4434 πτωχός, ***ptōchos***, a. GK: *4777* [→ *4432, 4433*]. poor; (n.) poor, beggar, a person of few resources, culturally considered oppressed, despised, and miserable. "The poor in spirit" are not lacking in spirit, but have the positive moral quality of humility, realizing they have nothing to offer God but are in need of his free gifts:– poor [31], beggar [2], beggarly [1]

4435 πυγμή, ***pygmē***, n. GK: *4778* [→ *4437, 4438*]. fist; with a fist = NIV "ceremonial":– oft [1]

4436 πύθων, ***pythōn***, n. GK: *4780*. spirit of divination:– of divination [1]

4437 πυκνός, ***pyknos***, a. GK: *4781* [→ *4435*]. (a.) often, frequent, numerous; (adv.) often, as a comparative: quite often, as often as possible:– often [2], oftener [1]

4438 πυκτεύω, ***pykteuō***, v. GK: *4782* [→ *4435*]. to fight with the fist, box:– fight [1]

4439 πύλη, ***pylē***, n. GK: *4783* [→ *4440*]. (city) gate:– gate [8], gates [2]

4440 πυλών, ***pylōn***, n. GK: *4784* [→ *4439*]. gate, door, entryway:– gates [11], gate [6], porch [1]

4441 πυνθάνομαι, ***pynthanomai***, v. GK: *4785*. to ask, inquire, question:– asked [5], ask [2], demanded [2], inquired [1], inquire [1], understood [1]

4442 πῦρ, ***pyr***, n. GK: *4786* [→ *329, 4443, 4445, 4446, 4447, 4448, 4449, 4450, 4451*]. fire, flames:– fire [73], fiery [1]

4443 πυρά, ***pyra***, n. GK: *4787* [→ *4442*]. fire:– fire [2]

4444 πύργος, ***pyrgos***, n. GK: *4788*. tower, watchtower:– tower [4]

4445 πυρέσσω, ***pyressō***, v. GK: *4789* [→ *4442*]. to burn with a fever:– sick of a fever [2]

4446* πυρετός, *pyretos, n. GK: *4790* [→ *4442*]. fever:– fever [6]

4447* πύρινος, *pyrinos, a. GK: *4791* [→ *4442*]. fiery red, the color of fire:– fire [1]

4448* πυρόω, *pyroō, v. GK: *4792* [→ *4442*]. to burn; to burn inwardly:– burn [2], burned [1], fiery [1], on fire [1], tried [1]

4449* πυρράζω, *pyrrazō, v. GK: *4793* [→ *4442*]. to be red, the color of fire:– red [2]

4450* πυρρός, *pyrros, a. GK: *4794* [→ *4442*]. fiery red, the color of fire:– red [2]

4451* πύρωσις, *pyrōsis, n. GK: *4796* [→ *4442*]. burning, painful:– burning [2], fiery trial [1]

4452* -πω, *-pō, pt. GK: * [→ *4458*]. an enclitic particle of indefiniteness; yet, even; used only in composition. See *3369, 3380, 3764, 3768, 4455*.:–

4453* πωλέω, *pōleō, v. GK: *4797* [→ *4211*]. to sell:– sold [14], sell [7], selleth [1]

4454* πῶλος, *pōlos, n. GK: *4798*. colt:– colt [12]

4455* πώποτε, *pōpote, adv. GK: *4799*. ever, at any time:– at any time [3], never (*+3361+3756*) [1], never [1], yet never (*+3762*) [1]

4456* πωρόω, *pōroō, v. GK: *4800* [→ *4457*]. to harden, deaden, make dull:– hardened [3], blinded [2]

4457* πώρωσις, *pōrōsis, n. GK: *4801* [→ *4456*]. hardening, stubbornness:– blindness [2], hardness [1]

4458* πώς, *pōs, pt. GK: *4803* [→ *4452*]. somehow, in some way:–

4459* πῶς, *pōs, pt.inter. GK: *4802*. how? in what way?; how!:– how [97], by what means [2], after what manner [1], how (*+302+1063*) [1], how can [1], that [1]

4460* Ῥαάβ, *Rhaab, n.pr. GK: *4805*. Rahab, "*spacious, broad*":– Rahab [2]

4461* ῥαββί, *rhabbi, l.[n.]. GK: *4806* [→ *4462*]. Rabbi, a title of a teacher:– master [9], Rabbi [8]

4462* ῥαββονί, *rhabboni; or **ῥαββουνί, *rhabbouni***, l.[n.]. GK: *4807 & 4808 & 4809* [→ *4461*]. Rabboni, a title of a teacher:– Lord [1], Rabboni [1]

4463* ῥαβδίζω, *rhabdizō, v. GK: *4810* [→ *4464*]. to beat with a rod:– beaten with rods [1], beat [1]

4464* ῥάβδος, *rhabdos, n. GK: *4811* [→ *4463, 4465, 4474, 4475*]. rod, staff, stick; measuring rod; scepter:– rod [6], sceptre [2], staff [2], staves [2]

4465* ῥαβδοῦχος, *rhabdouchos, n. GK: *4812* [→ *4464+2192*]. officer, the Roman *lictor,* a policeman:– sergeants [2]

4466* Ῥαγαύ, *Rhagau, n.pr. GK: *4814*. Reu, "*friend [of God]*":– Ragau [1]

4467* ῥᾳδιούργημα, *rhadiourgēma, n. GK: *4815* [→ *4468*]. crime, legal infraction:– lewdness [1]

4468* ῥᾳδιουργία, *rhadiourgia, n. GK: *4816* [→ *4467; cf. 2041*]. trickery:– mischief [1]

4469* ῥακά, *rhaka, l.[a.]. GK: *4819 & 4828*. Raca (a term of abuse, derived from Aramaic *rêqa'*, meaning "empty[-headed] one"), "*empty-headed [?]*":– Raca [1]

4470* ῥάκος, *rhakos, n. GK: *4820*. piece of cloth:– cloth [2]

4471* Ῥαμά, *Rhama, n.pr. GK: *4821*. Ramah, "*elevated spot*":– Rama [1]

4472* ῥαντίζω, *rhantizō, v. GK: *4822* [→ *4473*]. to sprinkle:– sprinkled [3], sprinkling [1]

4473* ῥαντισμός, *rhantismos, n. GK: *4823* [→ *4472*]. sprinkling:– sprinkling [2]

4474* ῥαπίζω, *rhapizō, v. GK: *4824* [→ *4464*]. to strike, slap:– smite [1], smote with the palms of hands [1]

4475* ῥάπισμα, *rhapisma, n. GK: *4825* [→ *4464*]. slap, strike:– smote with hands (*+1325*) [1], strike with the palms of hands (*+906*) [1], stroke with the palm of hand (*+1325*) [1]

4476* ῥαφίς, *rhaphis, n. GK: *4827* [→ *729, 1976*]. needle:– needle [2], needle's [1]

4477* Ῥαχάβ, *Rhachab, n.pr. GK: *4829*. Rahab, "*spacious, broad*":– Rachab [1]

4478* Ῥαχήλ, *Rachēl, n.pr. GK: *4830*. Rachel, "*ewe*":– Rachel [1]

4479* Ῥεβέκκα, *Rhebekka, n.pr. GK: *4831*. Rebekah, "[poss.] *choice calf*":– Rebecca [1]

4480* ῥέδη, *rhedē, n. GK: *4832*. carriage:– chariots [1]

4481* Ῥεμφάν, *Rhemphan; or **Ῥαιφάν, *Rhaiphan***, n.pr. GK: *4818 & 4833 & 4834 & 4854* [→ *4481, 4481, 4481*]. Rephan, Remphan:– Remphan [1]

4482* ῥέω, *rheō, v. GK: *4835* [→ *131, 3901, 4511, 5493*]. to flow:– flow [1]

4483* ῥέω, *rheō; and **ἐρέω, *ereō***, v. GK: *3306* [→ *3004*]. to utter, speak, say:–

4484* Ῥήγιον, *Rhēgion, n.pr. GK: *4836*. Rhegium:– Rhegium [1]

4485* ῥῆγμα, *rhēgma, n. GK: *4837* [→ *4486*]. destruction, ruin:– ruin [1]

4486* ῥήγνυμι, *rhēgnymi; or **ῥήσσω, *rhēssō***, v. GK: *4838* [→ *1284, 4048, 4366, 4485*]. to burst, break forth; to tear to pieces; to throw violently:– burst [2], break forth [1], break [1], rent [1], teareth [1], threw down [1]

4487* ῥῆμα, *rhēma, n. GK: *4839* [→ *368, 369, 731, 3954, 3955, 4489, 4490*]. word, saying; matter; thing:– words [31], word [25], saying [6], sayings [3], things [2], nothing (*+3756+3956*) [1], thing [1]

4488* Ῥησά, *Rhēsa, n.pr. GK: *4840*. Rhesa:– Rhesa [1]

4489* ῥήτωρ, *rhētōr, n. GK: *4842* [→ *4487*]. lawyer:– orator [1]

4490* ῥητῶς, *rhētōs, adv. GK: *4843* [→ *4487*]. clearly, exactly:– expressly [1]

4491* ῥίζα, *rhiza, n. GK: *4844* [→ *1610, 4492*]. root, rootstock:– root [16], roots [1]

4492* ῥιζόω, *rhizoō, v. GK: *4845* [→ *4491*]. (pass.) to be rooted, with the associative meaning that a rooted object is strong and healthy:– rooted [2]

4493* ῥιπή, *rhipē, n. GK: *4846 & 4856* [→ *4496*]. twinkling, rapid movement (of the eye); some translate as "the blink (of an eye)":– twinkling [1]

4494* ῥιπίζω, *rhipizō, v. GK: *4847* [→ *4496*]. (pass.) to be tossed about:– tossed [1]

4495* ῥιπτέω, *rhipteō, v. GK: *4848* [→ *4496*]. to throw off:– cast [1]

4496* ῥίπτω, *rhiptō, v. GK: *4849* [→ *641, 1977, 4493, 4494, 4495*]. to throw, drop; to lay; (pass.) to be helpless, laid out:– cast [4], cast down [1], scattered abroad [1], thrown [1]

4497* Ῥοβοάμ, *Rhoboam, n.pr. GK: *4850*. Rehoboam, "*[my] people will enlarge, expand*":– Roboam [2]

4498* Ῥόδη, *Rhodē, n.pr. GK: *4851*. Rhoda, "*rose*":– Rhoda [1]

4499* Ῥόδος, *Rhodos, n.pr. GK: *4852*. Rhodes, "*rose*":– Rhodes [1]

4500* ῥοιζηδόν, *rhoizēdon, adv. GK: *4853*. with a roar; a derivative of a Greek noun meaning, "the noise made by a passing arrow," not found in the NT:– great noise [1]

4501* ῥομφαία, *rhomphaia, n. GK: *4855*. (long) sword:– sword [7]

4502* Ῥουβήν, *Rhoubēn, n.pr. GK: *4857*. Reuben, "*See, a son! [Ge. 29:32]; substitute a son*":– Reuben [1]

4503* Ῥούθ, *Rhouth, n.pr. GK: *4858*. Ruth, "*friendship,* poss. *comrade, companion; refreshed*":– Ruth [1]

4504* Ῥοῦφος, *Rhouphos, n.pr. GK: *4859*. Rufus, "*red-haired*":– Rufus [2]

4505* ῥύμη, *rhymē, n. GK: *4860*. street, alley, lane:– street [2], lanes [1], streets [1]

4506* ῥύομαι, *rhyomai, v. GK: *4861*. to rescue, deliver:– delivered [9], deliver [8], deliverer [1]

4507* ῥυπαρία, *rhyparia, n. GK: *4864* [→ *4509*]. (moral) filth:– filthiness [1]

4508* ῥυπαρός, *rhyparos, a. GK: *4865* [→ *4509*]. shabby, dirty; moral vileness, filthiness:– vile [1]

4509* ῥύπος, *rhypos, n. GK: *4866* [→ *4507, 4508, 4510*]. dirt:– filth [1]

4510* ῥυπόω, *rhypoō, v. GK: *4867* [→ *4509*]. to defile, pollute:– filthy [2]

4511* ῥύσις, *rhysis, n. GK: *4868* [→ *4482*]. flow (of blood), bleeding:– issue [3]

4512* ῥυτίς, *rhytis, n. GK: *4869*. wrinkle:– wrinkle [1]

4513* Ῥωμαϊκός, *Rhōmaikos, a.pr. GK: *4870* [→ *4516*]. Roman, Latin:– Latin [1]

4514* Ῥωμαῖος, *Rhōmaios, a.pr.g. GK: *4871* [→ *4516*]. Roman, from Rome; (n.) Roman citizen:– Romans [6], Roman [5], Romans (*+444*) [1], of Rome [1]

4515* Ῥωμαϊστί, *Rhōmaisti, adv.pr. GK: *4872* [→ *4516*]. in Latin (language):– Latin [1]

4516* Ῥώμη, *Rhōmē, n.pr. GK: *4873* [→ *4513, 4514, 4515*]. Rome:– Rome [14]

4517* ῥώννυμι, *rhōnnymi, v. GK: *4874* [→ *732*]. to be strong; (pass.) farewell, goodbye, as the closing of a letter:– fare well [1], farewell [1]

4518* σαβαχθάνι, *sabachthani, l.[v.+p.]. GK: *2407 & 4876*. sabachthani (Aramaic: "you have forsaken me"):– sabachthani [2]

4519* Σαβαώθ, *Sabaōth, l.[pr.n.]. GK: *4877*. Almighty ["of Hosts"], a Greek transliteration of the Hebrew word 7372, "armies, hosts." This title has the associative meanings of power and potent authority, and pictures the Lord as a great, powerful, supreme general:– sabaoth [2]

4520* σαββατισμός, *sabbatismos, n. GK: *4878* [→ *4521*]. Sabbath-rest, Sabbath observance; "a sabbath's day journey" reckoned at 800 to 900 yards (2,000 cubits):– rest [1]

4521 **σάββατον**, ***sabbaton***, n. GK: *4879* [→ *4315, 4520*]. Sabbath:– sabbath [57], week [9], sabbath day's journey (+*2192+3598*) [1], sabbath days [1]

4522 **σαγήνη**, ***sagēnē***, n. GK: *4880*. (large) dragnet, a net with weights on the bottom and dragged through the water:– net [1]

4523 **Σαδδουκαῖος**, ***Saddoukaios***, n.pr. GK: *4881* [cf. *4524*]. Sadducee, "[poss.] *followers of Zadok; righteous*":– Sadducees [14]

4524 **Σαδώκ**, ***Sadōk***, n.pr. GK: *4882* [cf. *4523*]. Zadok, "*righteous one*":– Sadoc [2]

4525 **σαίνω**, ***sainō***, v. GK: *4883*. (pass.) to be unsettled, disturbed:– moved [1]

4526 **σάκκος**, ***sakkos***, n. GK: *4884*. sackcloth, a heavy coarse cloth used for making sacks, but worn by the penitent or mournful as a sign of contrition and sorrow:– sackcloth [4]

4527 **Σαλά**, ***Sala***, n.pr. GK: *4885*. Sala, "*missile [a weapon], sprout*":– Sala [1]

4528 **Σαλαθιήλ**, ***Salathiēl***, n.pr. GK: *4886*. Shealtiel, "*I have asked [him] of God [El]*; poss. *God [El] is a shield*":– Salathiel [3]

4529 **Σαλαμίς**, ***Salamis***, n.pr. GK: *4887*. Salamis, "*peace*":– Salamis [1]

4530 **Σαλίμ**, ***Salim***, n.pr. GK: *4890*. Salim:– Salim [1]

4531 **σαλεύω**, ***saleuō***, v. GK: *4888* [→ *761, 4535; cf. 242*]. to shake up; agitate; (pass.) to be shaken, swayed, unsettled:– shaken [11], moved [1], shake [1], shook [1], stirred up [1]

4532 **Σαλήμ**, ***Salēm***, n.pr. GK: *4889*. Salem, "*peace*":– Salem [2]

4533 **Σαλμών**, ***Salmōn***, n.pr. GK: *4891*. Salmon, "*little spark*":– Salmon [3]

4534 **Σαλμώνη**, ***Salmōnē***, n.pr. GK: *4892*. Salmone:– Salmone [1]

4535 **σάλος**, ***salos***, n. GK: *4893* [→ *4531*]. tossing motion, rolling motion (of the surging waves):– waves [1]

4536 **σάλπιγξ**, ***salpinx***, n. GK: *4894* [→ *4537*]. trumpet:– trumpet [7], trumpets [2], trump [2]

4537 **σαλπίζω**, ***salpizō***, v. GK: *4895* [→ *4536, 4538*]. to sound a trumpet, announce with a trumpet:– sounded [7], sound [3], sound a trumpet [1], trumpet sound [1]

4538 **σαλπιστής**, ***salpistēs***, n. GK: *4896* [→ *4537*]. trumpeter:– trumpeters [1]

4539 **Σαλώμη**, ***Salōmē***, n.pr. GK: *4897*. Salome, "*peaceful, prosperous one*":– Salome [2]

4540 **Σαμάρεια**, ***Samareia***, n.pr. GK: *4899 & 4900* [→ *4541, 4542*]. Samaria, "*belonging to the clan of Shemer [1Ki 16:24]*":– Samaria [11]

4541 **Σαμαρίτης**, ***Samaritēs***, n.pr.g. GK: *4901* [→ *4540*]. Samaritan:– Samaritans [6], Samaritan [3]

4542 **Σαμαρῖτις**, ***Samaritis***, n.pr.g.&a. GK: *4902* [→ *4540*]. Samaritan:– Samaria [2]

4543 **Σαμοθράκη**, ***Samothrakē***, n.pr. GK: *4903*. Samothrace, "*Thracian Samos*":– Samothracia [1]

4544 **Σάμος**, ***Samos***, n.pr. GK: *4904*. Samos, "*heights, lofty place*":– Samos [1]

4545 **Σαμουήλ**, ***Samouēl***, n.pr. GK: *4905*. Samuel, "*his name is God [El]; heard of God [El]; the unnamed god is El*":– Samuel [3]

4546 **Σαμψών**, ***Sampsōn***, n.pr. GK: *4907*. Samson, "*little one of Shemesh [pagan sun god]* or *sunny*":– Samson [1]

4547 **σανδάλιον**, ***sandalion***, n. GK: *4908*. sandal:– sandals [2]

4548 **σανίς**, ***sanis***, n. GK: *4909*. plank, board:– boards [1]

4549 **Σαούλ**, ***Saoul***, n.pr. GK: *4910*. Saul, "*asked of God* or poss. *dedicated to God*":– Saul [9]

4550 **σαπρός**, ***sapros***, a. GK: *4911* [→ *4595*]. bad, rotten, decayed; unwholesome:– corrupt [7], bad [1]

4551 **Σάπφιρα**, ***Sapphira***, n.pr. GK: *4912* [→ *4552*]. Sapphira, "*beautiful*":– Sapphira [1]

4552 **σάπφιρος**, ***sapphiros***, n. GK: *4913* [→ *4551*]. sapphire stone:– sapphire [1]

4553 **σαργάνη**, ***sarganē***, n. GK: *4914*. (large flexible) basket, possibly made of ropes:– basket [1]

4554 **Σάρδεις**, ***Sardeis***, n.pr. GK: *4915*. Sardis:– Sardis [3]

4555 **σάρδινος**, ***sardinos***, n. GK: *4916* [→ *4556*]. carnelian, sard:– sardine [1]

4556 **σάρδιον**, ***sardion***, n. GK: *4917* [→ *4555, 4557*]. carnelian (a reddish precious stone):– sardius [1]

4557 **σαρδόνυξ**, ***sardonyx***, n. GK: *4918* [→ *4556*]. sardonyx (a variety of agate):– sardonyx [1]

4558 **Σάρεπτα**, ***Sarepta***, n.pr. GK: *4919*. Zarephath, "[poss.] *smelting place; place of pigmenting, staining*":– Sarepta [1]

4559 **σαρκικός**, ***sarkikos***, a. GK: *4920* [→ *4561*]. material; worldly, sinful; pertaining to the flesh; see also *4561*:– carnal [9], fleshly [2]

4560 **σάρκινος**, ***sarkinos***, a. GK: *4921* [→ *4561*]. fleshly, made of flesh; human; worldly, unspiritual; see also *4561*:– fleshy [1]

4561 **σάρξ**, ***sarx***, n. GK: *4922* [→ *4559, 4560*]. flesh, body, the soft tissue of a creature, often in contrast to bone, ligament, or sinew; by extension human, humankind, with a focus on the fallen human nature, which is frail and corrupt in contrast to immaterial (spiritual) things, thus the NIV translation "sinful nature":– flesh [147], carnal [2], carnally [1], fleshly [1]

4562 **Σαρούχ**, ***Sarouch***; or **Σερούχ**, ***Serouch***, n.pr. GK: *4923 & 4951 & 4952*. Serug, "*descendant, i.e., younger branch*":– Saruch [1]

4563 **σαρόω**, ***saroō***, v. GK: *4924*. to sweep, sweep clean:– swept [2], sweep [1]

4564 **Σάρρα**, ***Sarra***, n.pr. GK: *4925*. Sarah, "*princess*":– Sara [3], Sara's [1]

4565 **Σαρών**, ***Sarōn***, n.pr. GK: *4926*. Sharon, "*plain, level country*":– Saron [1]

4566 **Σατάν**, ***Satan***, n.pr. GK: *4927* [→ *4567*]. Satan, "*hostile opponent*":– Satan [1]

4567 **Σατανᾶς**, ***Satanas***, n.pr. GK: *4928* [→ *4566*]. Satan, "*hostile opponent*":– Satan [35], Satan's [1]

4568 **σάτον**, ***saton***, n. GK: *4929*. seah (dry measure of about 12 quarts):– measures [2]

4569 **Σαῦλος**, ***Saulos***, n.pr. GK: *4930*. Saul, "*asked for* poss. *dedicated to God*":– Saul [17]

σαυτοῦ, ***sautou***. See ***4572***.

4570 **σβέννυμι**, ***sbennymi***, v. GK: *4931* [→ *762*]. to extinguish, quench, snuff out:– quenched [4], quench [3], gone out [1]

4571 **σέ**, ***sē***, p.pers.a. of *4771*. GK: *5148* [→ *4771*]. you, thee; see *4771*:–

4572 **σεαυτοῦ**, ***seautou***, p.reflex. GK: *4932* [→ *4771+846*]. yourself:– thyself [38], thine own self [2], thee [1], thy [1]

4573 **σεβάζομαι**, ***sebazomai***, v. GK: *4933* [→ *4576*]. to worship:– worshipped [1]

4574 **σέβασμα**, ***sebasma***, n. GK: *4934* [→ *4576*]. object of worship; some translate as a place of worship: sanctuary:– devotions [1], worshipped [1]

4575 **σεβαστός**, ***sebastos***, a. GK: *4935* [→ *4576*]. (a.) revered, worthy of reverence, imperial (not found in the NT); (n.) Emperor, a title of reverence or veneration:– Augustus [2], Augustus' [1]

4576 **σέβω**, ***sebō***, v. GK: *4936* [→ *763, 764, 765, 2150, 2151, 2152, 2153, 2317, 2318, 4573, 4574, 4575, 4586, 4587*]. (mid.) to worship, be devout, God-fearing:– devout [3], worship [3], worshipped [2], religious [1], worshippeth [1]

4577 **σειρά**, ***seira***, n. GK: *4937*. chain:– chains [1]

4578 **σεισμός**, ***seismos***, n. GK: *4939* [→ *4579*]. earthquake; storm:– earthquake [10], earthquakes [3], tempest [1]

4579 **σείω**, ***seiō***, v. GK: *4940* [→ *383, 1286, 2678, 4578*]. to cause to shake; (pass.) to be shaken, stirred up:– shake [2], moved [1], quake [1], shaken [1]

4580 **Σεκοῦνδος**, ***Sekoundos***, n.pr. GK: *4941*. Secundus, "*second*":– Secundus [1]

4581 **Σελεύκεια**, ***Seleukeia***, n.pr. GK: *4942*. Seleucia:– Seleucia [1]

4582 **σελήνη**, ***selēnē***, n. GK: *4943* [→ *4583*]. moon:– moon [9]

4583 **σεληνιάζομαι**, ***selēniazomai***, v. GK: *4944* [→ *4582*]. (pass.) to have a seizure:– lunatick [2]

4584 **Σεμεΐ**, ***Semei***; or **Σεμεΐν**, ***Semein***, n.pr. GK: *4945 & 4946*. Semei, "*Yahweh has heard*":– Semei [1]

4585 **σεμίδαλις**, ***semidalis***, n. GK: *4947*. finely ground flour:– fine flour [1]

4586 **σεμνός**, ***semnos***, a. GK: *4948* [→ *4576*]. worthy of respect, noble:– grave [3], honest [1]

4587 **σεμνότης**, ***semnotēs***, n. GK: *4949* [→ *4576*]. holiness, seriousness, respect:– gravity [2], honesty [1]

4588 **Σέργιος**, ***Sergios***, n.pr. GK: *4950*. Sergius:– Sergius [1]

4589 **Σήθ**, ***Sēth***, n.pr. GK: *4953*. Seth, "*determined, granted [Ge 4:25]; restitution*":– Seth [1]

4590 **Σήμ**, ***Sēm***, n.pr. GK: *4954*. Shem, "*name, fame*":– Sem [1]

4591 **σημαίνω**, ***sēmainō***, v. GK: *4955* [→ *4592*]. to make known; to indicate (beforehand), predict, foretell:– signifying [3], signified [2], signify [1]

4592 **σημεῖον**, ***sēmeion***, n. GK: *4956* [→ *767, 1978, 2154, 3902, 4591, 4593, 4953*]. (miraculous) sign, signal, mark:– sign [29], signs [22], miracles [15], miracle [7], wonder [2], token [1], wonders [1]

4593 σημειόω, ***sēmeioō***, v. GK: *4957* [→ *4592*]. (mid.) to take special note of:– note [1]

4594 σήμερον, ***sēmeron***, adv. GK: *4958* [→ *2250*]. today, this day:– this day [19], to day [18], this day (+*2250*) [3], this day's [1]

4595 σήπω, ***sēpō***, v. GK: *4960* [→ *4550*]. to rot, decay:– corrupted [1]

4596 σηρικός, ***sērikos***; σιρικός, ***sirikos***, a. GK: *4961 & 4986*. silken; (n.) silk (cloth):– silk [1]

4597 σής, ***sēs***, n. GK: *4962* [→ *4598*]. moth:– moth [3]

4598 σητόβρωτος, ***sētobrōtos***, a. GK: *4963* [→ *4597+977*]. moth-eaten:– motheaten [1]

4599 σθενόω, ***sthenoō***, v. GK: *4964* [→ *769, 770, 771, 772*]. to strengthen, make strong:– strengthen [1]

4600 σιαγών, ***siagōn***, n. GK: *4965*. cheek:– cheek [2]

4601 σιγάω, ***sigaō***, v. GK: *4967* [→ *4602*]. to be or become silent; (pass.) to be hidden, concealed:– held peace [2], hold peace [2], keep silence [2], kept close [1], kept secret [1], kept silence [1]

4602 σιγή, ***sigē***, n. GK: *4968* [→ *4601*]. silence:– silence [2]

4603 σιδήρεος, ***sidēreos***, a. GK: *4969 & 4971* [→ *4604*]. made of iron:– of iron [4], iron [1]

4604 σίδηρος, ***sidēros***, n. GK: *4970* [→ *4603*]. iron:– iron [1]

4605 Σιδών, ***Sidōn***, n.pr. GK: *4972* [→ *4606*]. Sidon, "*fishery*":– Sidon [11]

4606 Σιδώνιος, ***Sidōnios***, a.pr.g. GK: *4973* [→ *4605*]. Sidonian, a person of Sidon:– Sidon [1]

4607 σικάριος, ***sikarios***, n. GK: *4974*. terrorist, assassin:– murderers [1]

4608 σίκερα, ***sikera***, l.[n.]. GK: *4975*. fermented drink, beer:– strong drink [1]

4609 Σίλας, ***Silas***, n.pr. GK: *4976* [→ *4610*]. Silas, "*asked for* poss. *dedicated to God*":– Silas [13]

4610 Σιλουανός, ***Silouanos***, n.pr. GK: *4977* [→ *4609*]. Silas, Silvanus, "*asked for* poss. *dedicated to God*":– Silvanus [4]

4611 Σιλωάμ, ***Silōam***, n.pr. GK: *4978*. Siloam, "*sent*":– Siloam [3]

4612 σιμικίνθιον, ***simikinthion***, n. GK: *4959 & 4980*. apron:– aprons [1]

4613 Σίμων, ***Simōn***, n.pr. GK: *4981* [→ *4826*]. Simon, "*he has heard* or *obedient one*":– Simon [68], Simon's [7]

4614 Σινᾶ, ***Sina***, n.pr. GK: *4982*. Sinai, "*Sin [pagan moon god]; glare [from white chalk]*":– Sinai [2], Sina [2]

4615 σίναπι, ***sinapi***, n. GK: *4983*. mustard plant:– mustard [5]

4616 σινδών, ***sindōn***, n. GK: *4984*. linen (cloth or garment):– linen cloth [3], linen [2], fine linen [1]

4617 σινιάζω, ***siniazō***, v. GK: *4985*. to sift, shake in a sieve:– sift [1]

σῖτα, ***sita***. See ***4621***.

4618 σιτευτός, ***siteutos***, a. GK: *4988* [→ *4621*]. fattened:– fatted [3]

4619 σιτιστός, ***sitistos***, a. GK: *4990* [→ *4621*]. fattened; (n.) fattened cattle:– fatlings [1]

4620 σιτομέτριον, ***sitometrion***, n. GK: *4991* [→ *4621+3358*]. measured allowance of food, ration of grain:– portion of meat [1]

4621 σῖτος, ***sitos***, n. GK: *4992* [→ *776, 777, 1979, 4618, 4619, 4620*]. wheat, grain:– wheat [12], corn [2]

4622 Σιών, ***Siōn***, n.pr. GK: *4994*. Zion, "*citadel*":– Sion [7]

4623 σιωπάω, ***siōpaō***, v. GK: *4995*. to be quiet, remain silent; to be calm, not agitated:– hold peace [5], held peace [4], dumb [1], peace [1]

4624 σκανδαλίζω, ***skandalizō***, v. GK: *4997* [→ *4625*]. to cause to sin, cause to fall (into sin), offend; to fall away (from the faith), go astray; to take offense:– offended [16], offend [12], make to offend [2]

4625 σκάνδαλον, ***skandalon***, n. GK: *4998* [→ *4624*]. stumbling block, obstacle, offense; something that causes sin:– offence [5], offences [4], stumblingblock [3], occasion of stumbling [1], occasion to fall [1], things that offend [1]

4626 σκάπτω, ***skaptō***, v. GK: *4999* [→ *2679, 4627*]. to dig:– dig [2], digged [1]

4627 σκάφη, ***skaphē***, n. GK: *5002* [→ *4626*]. lifeboat, (small) boat:– boat [3]

4628 σκέλος, ***skelos***, n. GK: *5003*. leg:– legs [3]

4629 σκέπασμα, ***skepasma***, n. GK: *5004*. clothing, covering; this can refer to shelter or personal covering:– raiment [1]

4630 Σκευᾶς, ***Skeuas***, n.pr. GK: *5005*. Sceva:– Sceva [1]

4631 σκευή, ***skeuē***, n. GK: *5006* [→ *4632*]. (ship's) tackle, gear:– tackling [1]

4632 σκεῦος, ***skeuos***, n. GK: *5007* [→ *384, 532, 643, 2680, 3903, 3904, 4631*]. possession, merchandise, object, thing; jar, vessel, dish; a general term that can refer to a human being:– vessel [11], vessels [8], goods [2], sail [1], stuff [1]

4633 σκηνή, ***skēnē***, n. GK: *5008* [→ *1981, 2681, 2682, 4634, 4635, 4636, 4637, 4638*]. tabernacle; tent, shelter, dwelling:– tabernacle [15], tabernacles [4], habitations [1]

4634 σκηνοπηγία, ***skēnopēgia***, n. GK: *5009* [→ *4633+4078*]. (Feast of) Tabernacles:– tabernacles [1]

4635 σκηνοποιός, ***skēnopoios***, n. GK: *5010* [→ *4633+4160*]. tentmaker; some translate more generally: leather worker:– tentmakers [1]

4636 σκῆνος, ***skēnos***, n. GK: *5011* [→ *4633*]. tent:– tabernacle [2]

4637 σκηνόω, ***skēnoō***, v. GK: *5012* [→ *4633*]. to live, dwell; to spread a tent:– dwell [4], dwelt [1]

4638 σκήνωμα, ***skēnōma***, n. GK: *5013* [→ *4633*]. tent, dwelling place, lodging place:– tabernacle [3]

4639 σκιά, ***skia***, n. GK: *5014* [→ *644, 1982, 2683*]. shadow, shade:– shadow [7]

4640 σκιρτάω, ***skirtaō***, v. GK: *5015*. to leap, with an implication that the one leaping is joyful:– leaped [2], leap [1]

4641 σκληροκαρδία, ***sklērokardia***, n. GK: *5016* [→ *4645+2588*]. hardness of heart, stubbornness, obstinacy:– hardness of heart [2], hardness of hearts [1]

4642 σκληρός, ***sklēros***, a. GK: *5017* [→ *4645*]. hard, harsh:– hard [5], fierce [1]

4643 σκληρότης, ***sklērotēs***, n. GK: *5018* [→ *4645*]. hardness, stubbornness:– hardness [1]

4644 σκληροτράχηλος, ***sklērotrachēlos***, a. GK: *5019* [→ *4645+5137*]. stiff-necked, stubborn:– stiffnecked [1]

4645 σκληρύνω, ***sklērynō***, v. GK: *5020* [→ *4641, 4642, 4643, 4644*]. to harden (the heart), make obstinate, make stubborn; (pass.) to be hardened, become obstinate:– harden [3], hardened [2], hardeneth [1]

4646 σκολιός, ***skolios***, a. GK: *5021*. crooked; corrupt:– crooked [2], froward [1], untoward [1]

4647 σκόλοψ, ***skolops***, n. GK: *5022*. thorn; some translate this as a "splinter":– thorn [1]

4648 σκοπέω, ***skopeō***, v. GK: *5023* [→ *244, 1980, 1983, 1984, 1985, 2684, 2685, 4649*]. to watch out for, take notice of, look to:– mark [2], considering [1], look at [1], look [1], take heed [1]

4649 σκοπός, ***skopos***, n. GK: *5024* [→ *4648*]. goal:– mark [1]

4650 σκορπίζω, ***skorpizō***, v. GK: *5025* [→ *1287, 4651*]. to scatter, disperse:– scattereth [2], dispersed abroad [1], scattered [1], scattereth abroad [1]

4651 σκορπίος, ***skorpios***, n. GK: *5026* [→ *4650*]. scorpion:– scorpions [3], scorpion [2]

4652 σκοτεινός, ***skoteinos***, a. GK: *5027* [→ *4655*]. dark:– full of darkness [2], dark [1]

4653 σκοτία, ***skotia***, n. GK: *5028* [→ *4655*]. darkness, the dark:– darkness [14], dark [2]

4654 σκοτίζομαι, ***skotizomai***, v. GK: *5029* [→ *4655*]. (pass.) to be or become dark, be darkened:– darkened [8]

4655 σκότος, ***skotos***, n. GK: *5030* [→ *4652, 4653, 4654, 4656*]. darkness, the dark:– darkness [32]

4656 σκοτόω, ***skotoō***, v. GK: *5031* [→ *4655*]. (pass.) to be or become darkened:– full of darkness [1]

4657 σκύβαλον, ***skybalon***, n. GK: *5032*. rubbish, refuse, dung; this can refer to any of a number of rotten, decaying things, all that is worth getting rid of:– dung [1]

4658 Σκύθης, ***Skythēs***, n.pr.g. GK: *5033*. Scythian:– Scythian [1]

4659 σκυθρωπός, ***skythrōpos***, a. GK: *5034* [→ *3708*]. to look somber, appear downcast, implying a sad or sullen attitude:– sad countenance [1], sad [1]

4660 σκύλλω, ***skyllō***, v. GK: *5035* [→ *4661*]. to bother, annoy; (pass.) to be harassed; (mid.) to trouble oneself:– trouble [2], troublest [1]

4661 σκῦλον, ***skylon***, n. GK: *5036* [→ *4660*]. (pl.) spoils, booty:– spoils [1]

4662 σκωληκόβρωτος, ***skōlēkobrōtos***, a. GK: *5037* [→ *4663+977*]. eaten by worms:– eaten of worms [1]

4663 σκώληξ, ***skōlēx***, n. GK: *5038* [→ *4662*]. worm:– worm [3]

4664 σμαράγδινος, ***smaragdinos***, a. GK: *5039* [→ *4665*]. (of) emerald:– emerald [1]

4665 σμάραγδος, ***smaragdos***, n. GK: *5040* [→ *4664*]. emerald:– emerald [1]

4666 σμύρνα[1], ***smyrna1***, n. GK: *5043* [→ *4667, 4668, 4669*]. myrrh, an aromatic resinous gum:– myrrh [2]

4667 Σμύρνα[2], Smyrna2, n.pr. GK: *5044* [→ *4666*]. Smyrna:– Smyrna [1]

4668 Σμυρναῖος, Smyrnaios, a.pr.g. GK: *5045* [→ *4666*]. Smyrnaean:– Smyrna [1]

4669 σμυρνίζω, smyrnizō, v. GK: *5046* [→ *4666*]. to mix with myrrh, referring to wine mixed with myrrh as a drug to deaden the senses and mind:– mingled with myrrh [1]

4670 Σόδομα, Sodoma, n.pr. GK: *5047*. Sodom:– Sodom [9], Sodoma [1]

4671 σοί, soi, p.pers.dat. of *4771*. GK: *5148* [→ *4771*]. to you, for you, your; see *4771*:–

4672 Σολομών, Solomōn, n.pr. GK: *4898 & 5048*. Solomon, *"peace, well being"*:– Solomon [9], Solomon's [3]

4673 σορός, soros, n. GK: *5049*. coffin, bier:– bier [1]

4674 σός, sos, a.poss. GK: *5050* [→ *4771*]. (s.) your, yours:– thy [15], thine [9], thine own [3]

4675 σοῦ, sou, p.pers.gen. of *4771*. GK: *5148* [→ *4771*]. of you, your; see *4771*:–

4676 σουδάριον, soudarion, n. GK: *5051*. piece of cloth, burial cloth, handkerchief:– napkin [3], handkerchiefs [1]

4677 Σουσάννα, Sousanna, n.pr. GK: *5052*. Susanna, *"lily"*:– Susanna [1]

4678 σοφία, sophia, n. GK: *5053* [→ *4680*]. wisdom (either secular or divine). Christ is called "the wisdom of God" in 1Co 1:24, 30. On the basis of the OT, wisdom can be personified:– wisdom [51]

4679 σοφίζω, sophizō, v. GK: *5054* [→ *4680*]. to make wise; (pass.) to be cleverly invented:– cunningly devised [1], make wise [1]

4680 σοφός, sophos, a. GK: *5055* [→ *781, 2686, 4678, 4679, 5385, 5386*]. wise; expert, skilled; (n.) a person who is skilled or expert, often as a class or kind, a wise man or woman:– wise [21], wiser than [1]

4681 Σπανία, Spania, n.pr. GK: *5056*. Spain:– Spain [2]

4682 σπαράσσω, sparassō, v. GK: *5057* [→ *4685*]. to convulse, shake violently:– rent [1], tare [1], teareth [1], torn [1]

4683 σπαργανόω, sparganoō, v. GK: *5058*. to wrap (in cloth), to bind a newborn infant in strips of long cloth, a normal act of child care for warmth, security, etc:– wrapped in swaddling clothes [2]

4684 σπαταλάω, spatalaō, v. GK: *5059*. to live in pleasure, in self-indulgence:– liveth in pleasure [1], wanton [1]

4685 σπάω, spaō, v. GK: *5060* [→ *385, 563, 645, 1288, 1986, 4049, 4682, 4952*]. (mid.) to draw (a sword):– drew out [1], drew [1]

4686 σπεῖρα, speira, n. GK: *5061*. company of soldiers, cohort; technically one tenth of a Roman legion: 600 fighting men:– band [7]

4687 σπείρω, speirō, v. GK: *5062* [→ *1289, 1290, 4690, 4691, 4701, 4702, 4703*]. to sow seed, scatter seed:– sown [15], soweth [9], sowed [8], sow [8], sower [6], received seed [4], sowest [3]

4688 σπεκουλάτωρ, spekoulatōr, n. GK: *5063*. executioner:– executioner [1]

4689 σπένδω, spendō, v. GK: *5064* [→ *786*]. (pass.) to be poured out like a drink offering:– offered [2]

4690 σπέρμα, sperma, n. GK: *5065* [→ *4687*]. seed, the part of a plant or animal that can propagate the species (cf. "sperm"); by extension: children, offspring, descendants:– seed [40], seeds [3], issue [1]

4691 σπερμολόγος, spermologos, a. GK: *5066* [→ *4687+3004*]. babbler, chatterer, implying the person has low status, living by picking up scraps:– babbler [1]

4692 σπεύδω, speudō, v. GK: *5067* [→ *4704, 4705, 4706, 4707, 4708, 4709, 4710*]. to hurry, hasten:– make haste [2], hasted [1], hasting [1], made haste [1], with haste [1]

4693 σπήλαιον, spēlaion, n. GK: *5068*. den, cave, hideout:– den [3], dens [2], cave [1]

4694 σπιλάς, spilas, n. GK: *5069* [→ *4696*]. blemish, spot:– spots [1]

4695 σπιλόω, spiloō, v. GK: *5071* [→ *4696*]. to corrupt; (pass.) to be stained, defiled:– defileth [1], spotted [1]

4696 σπίλος, spilos, n. GK: *5070* [→ *784, 4694, 4695*]. stain, blot:– spots [1], spot [1]

4697 σπλαγχνίζομαι, splanchnizomai, v. GK: *5072* [→ *4698*]. to have compassion on, have pity on:– moved with compassion [5], had compassion [4], have compassion [3]

4698 σπλάγχνον, splanchnon, n. GK: *5073* [→ *2155, 4184, 4697*]. inward parts of body: intestines; of emotion: *heart, affection, tenderness, compassion*:– bowels [9], inward affection [1], tender mercy (*+1656*) [1]

4699 σπόγγος, spongos, n. GK: *5074*. sponge:– spunge [3]

4700 σποδός, spodos, n. GK: *5075*. ashes:– ashes [3]

4701 σπορά, spora, n. GK: *5076* [→ *4687*]. seed:– seed [1]

4702 σπόριμος, sporimos, a. GK: *5077* [→ *4687*]. what is sown; (pl.n.) grainfield:– corn fields [2], corn [1]

4703 σπόρος, sporos, n. GK: *5078* [→ *4687*]. seed:– seed [4], seed sown [1]

4704 σπουδάζω, spoudazō, v. GK: *5079* [→ *4692*]. to be eager, make every effort, do one's best:– diligent [2], do diligence [2], endeavoured [1], endeavouring [1], endeavour [1], forward [1], give diligence [1], labour [1], study [1]

4705 σπουδαῖος, spoudaios, a. GK: *5080* [→ *4692*]. zealous, eager, earnest; (compar.) more enthusiastic, very earnest:– diligent [1]

4706 σπουδαιότερον, spoudaioteron, a.compar.neut. of *4705*. GK: *5080* [→ *4692*]. (compar.) more enthusiastic, very earnest:– very diligently [1]

4707 σπουδαιότερος, spoudaioteros, a.compar. of *4705*. GK: *5080* [→ *4692*]. (compar.) more enthusiastic, very earnest:– diligent [1], more forward [1]

4708 σπουδαιοτέρως, spoudaioterōs, adv.compar. of *4709*. GK: *5081* [→ *4692*]. (compar.) all the more eager, with special urgency:– more carefully [1]

4709 σπουδαίως, spoudaiōs, adv. GK: *5081* [→ *4692*]. earnestly, zealously, with vigor; (compar.) all the more eager, with special urgency:– diligently [1], instantly [1]

4710 σπουδή, spoudē, n. GK: *5082* [→ *4692*]. hurry, haste; earnestness, diligence, zeal, eagerness:– diligence [5], haste [2], business [1], carefulness [1], care [1], earnest care [1], forwardness [1]

4711 σπυρίς, spyris, n. GK: *5083*. basket:– baskets [4], basket [1]

4712 στάδιον, stadion, n. GK: *5084* [→ *2476*]. arena, stadium, race course; a unit of length: stade (about 200 yards):– furlongs [5], race [1]

4713 στάμνος, stamnos, n. GK: *5085* [→ *2476*]. jar:– pot [1]

4714 στάσις, stasis, n. GK: *5087* [→ *2476*]. continuance, state of existence; uprising, insurrection, riot; dispute, discord:– dissension [3], sedition [3], insurrection [1], standing [1], uproar [1]

4715 στατήρ, statēr, n. GK: *5088* [→ *2476*]. four-drachma coin, stater (four days' wages):– piece of money [1]

4716 σταυρός, stauros, n. GK: *5089* [→ *388, 4717, 4957; cf. 2476*]. cross:– cross [28]

4717 σταυρόω, stauroō, v. GK: *5090* [→ *4716*]. to crucify:– crucified [31], crucify [15]

4718 σταφυλή, staphylē, n. GK: *5091*. (bunch of) grapes:– grapes [3]

4719 στάχυς[1], stachys[1], n. GK: *5092* [→ *4720*]. head of grain:– ears of corn [3], ear [2]

4720 Στάχυς[2], Stachys[2], n.pr. GK: *5093* [→ *4719*]. Stachys, *"head of grain"*:– Stachys [1]

4721 στέγη, stegē, n. GK: *5094* [→ *4722*]. roof:– roof [3]

4722 στέγω, stegō, v. GK: *5095* [→ *648, 4721, 5152*]. to put up with, stand, endure; to protect, cover:– forbear [2], beareth [1], suffer [1]

4723 στεῖρα, steira, n. GK: *5096* [→ *4731*]. (state of) barrenness, infertility:– barren [4]

4724 στέλλω, stellō, v. GK: *5097* [→ *649, 1291, 1293, 1992, 2687, 2689, 4749, 4958, 5288, 5289*]. (mid.) to avoid, keep away from:– avoiding [1], withdraw [1]

4725 στέμμα, stemma, n. GK: *5098* [→ *4737*]. wreath, garland:– garlands [1]

4726 στεναγμός, stenagmos, n. GK: *5099* [→ *4728*]. groan, sigh:– groanings [1], groaning [1]

4727 στενάζω, stenazō, v. GK: *5100* [→ *4728*]. to groan, sigh; to grumble:– groan [3], grief [1], grudge [1], sighed [1]

4728 στενός, stenos, a. GK: *5101* [→ *389, 4726, 4727, 4729, 4730, 4959*]. narrow:– strait [3]

4729 στενοχωρέω, stenochōreō, v. GK: *5102* [→ *4728+5562*]. (pass.) to be crushed; to withhold, be restricted:– straitened [2], distressed [1]

4730 στενοχωρία, stenochōria, n. GK: *5103* [→ *4728+5562*]. distress, hardship, difficulty:– distresses [2], anguish [1], distress [1]

4731 στερεός, stereos, a. GK: *5104* [→ *4723, 4732, 4733*]. solid, strong; standing firm, steadfast:– strong [2], stedfast [1], sure [1]

4732 στερεόω, stereoō, v. GK: *5105* [→ *4731*]. to make strong; (pass.) to become strong, be strengthened:– established [1], made strong [1], received strength [1]

4733 στερέωμα, stereōma, n. GK: *5106* [→ *4731*]. firmness, steadfastness:– stedfastness [1]

4734 Στεφανᾶς, Stephanas, n.pr. GK: *5107* [→ *4737*]. Stephanas, "*victor's wreath*":– Stephanas [4]

4735 στέφανος², stephanos², n. GK: *5109* [→ *4737*]. woven crown, wreath, victory garland; of various shapes and various materials, leaves, twigs, flowers, even metal, as a sign of victory, honor, and in some contexts, authority:– crown [15], crowns [3]

4736 Στέφανος¹, Stephanos¹, n.pr. GK: *5108* [→ *4737*]. Stephen, "*victor's wreath*":– Stephen [7]

4737 στεφανόω, stephanoō, v. GK: *5110* [→ *4725, 4734, 4736, 4735*]. to crown, present a wreath:– crowned [2], crownedst [1]

4738 στῆθος, stēthos, n. GK: *5111*. chest, breast:– breast [3], breasts [2]

4739 στήκω, stēkō, v. GK: *5112* [→ *2476*]. to stand, stand firm, be steadfast:– stand fast [6], standeth [1], stand [1]

4740 στηριγμός, stērigmos, n. GK: *5113* [→ *4741*]. security, firmness:– stedfastness [1]

4741 στηρίζω, stērizō, v. GK: *5114* [→ *793, 1991, 4740*]. to strengthen, establish, stand firm; to be resolute:– stablish [6], strengthen [2], established [1], establish [1], fixed [1], stablished [1], stedfastly set [1]

4742 στίγμα, stigma, n. GK: *5116* [→ *4743*]. mark, scar; in context Paul is likely referring to the scars he received in service to Jesus as marks of ownership by his master:– marks [1]

4743 στιγμή, stigmē, n. GK: *5117* [→ *4742*]. instant, moment:– moment [1]

4744 στίλβω, stilbō, v. GK: *5118*. to dazzle, be radiant:– shining [1]

4745 στοά, stoa, n. GK: *5119* [→ *4770; cf. 2476*]. covered colonnade, portico:– porch [3], porches [1]

4746 στοιβάς, stoibas; or **στιβάς, stibas**, n. GK: *5115 & 5120*. leafy branch:– branches [1]

4747 στοιχεῖον, stoicheion, n. GK: *5122* [→ *4748*]. principle, basic principle; element (of nature); elementary truths:– elements [4], rudiments [2], principles [1]

4748 στοιχέω, stoicheō, v. GK: *5123* [→ *4747, 4960*]. to follow, walk in, adhere to:– walk [4], walkest orderly [1]

4749 στολή, stolē, n. GK: *5124* [→ *4724*]. (flowing) robe:– robes [4], long clothing [1], long garment [1], long robes [1], robe [1]

4750 στόμα, stoma, n. GK: *5125* [→ *653, 1366, 1993, 4751*]. mouth; by extension: edge (of a sword):– mouth [69], face [4], mouths [4], edge [2]

4751 στόμαχος, stomachos, n. GK: *5126* [→ *4750*]. stomach:– stomach's [1]

4752 στρατεία, strateia, n. GK: *5127* [→ *4756*]. warfare; fight:– warfare [2]

4753 στράτευμα, strateuma, n. GK: *5128* [→ *4756*]. army, troops, soldiers:– armies [3], army [3], men of war [1], soldiers [1]

4754 στρατεύομαι, strateuomai, v. GK: *5129* [→ *4756*]. (mid.) to serve as a soldier; to wage war, fight, battle:– war [4], goeth a warfare [1], soldiers [1], warreth [1]

4755 στρατηγός, stratēgos, n. GK: *5130* [→ *4756+71*]. magistrate, praetor; captain, officer:– magistrates [5], captain [3], captains [2]

4756 στρατιά, stratia, n. GK: *5131* [→ *497, 4752, 4753, 4754, 4755, 4757, 4758, 4759, 4760, 4961*]. host, army (of heaven), (celestial) bodies:– host [2]

4757 στρατιώτης, stratiōtēs, n. GK: *5132* [→ *4756*]. soldier:– soldiers [21], soldier [4], soldiers' [1]

4758 στρατολογέω, stratologeō, v. GK: *5133* [→ *4756+3004*]. to gather an army; (ptcp.) commanding officer, with a focus on enlisting soldiers:– chosen to be a soldier [1]

4759 στρατοπεδάρχης, stratopedarchēs, n. GK: *5134 & 5135* [→ *4756+3978+757*]. military commander, commander of a camp:– captain of the guard [1]

4760 στρατόπεδον, stratopedon, n. GK: *5136* [→ *4756+3978*]. army:– armies [1]

4761 στρεβλόω, strebloō, v. GK: *5137* [→ *4762*]. to distort, twist:– wrest [1]

4762 στρέφω, strephō, v. GK: *5138* [→ *390, 391, 654, 1294, 1612, 1994, 1995, 2690, 2692, 3344, 4761, 4962, 4963, 5290*]. to turn, turn away, return; to change, repent, turn one's life:– turned [12], turn [4], converted [1], turning [1]

4763 στρηνιάω, strēniaō, v. GK: *5139* [→ *4764*]. to live in luxury, with an implication that this luxury contributes to improper sensuality and immorality:– lived deliciously [2]

4764 στρῆνος, strēnos, n. GK: *5140* [→ *2691, 4763*]. luxury:– delicacies [1]

4765 στρουθίον, strouthion, n. GK: *5141*. sparrow:– sparrows [4]

4766 στρώννυμι, strōnnymi; or **στρωννύω, strōnnyō**, v. GK: *5142 & 5143* [→ *2693, 3038, 5291*]. to spread out; (pass.) to be furnished:– furnished [2], spread [2], strawed [2], make bed [1]

4767 στυγητός, stygētos, a. GK: *5144* [→ *655, 2319, 4768*]. hated:– hateful [1]

4768 στυγνάζω, stygnazō, v. GK: *5145* [→ *4767*]. to be gloomy, sad, others translate "shocked, appalled"; (of weather) to be overcast, gloomy:– lowring [1], sad [1]

4769 στῦλος, stylos, n. GK: *5146*. pillar, column; (fig.) leader:– pillars [2], pillar [2]

4770 Στωϊκός, Stōikos, a.pr. GK: *5121 & 5147* [→ *4745*]. Stoic:– Stoicks [1]

4771 σύ, sy, p.pers. GK: *5148* [→ *4571, 4671, 4572, 4674, 4675, 5209, 5210, 5212, 5213, 5216*]. you, your:– you [1194], thee [453], your [375], thy [363], ye [282], thou [213], thine [49], yourselves [9], thine own [8], your own [4], yours [4], youward [2], on your part [1], you (*+3588+5590*) [1], your (*+1537*) [1], your (*+2596*) [1], your own (*+2596*) [1], yours (*+3588*) [1], youwards [1]

4772 συγγένεια, syngeneia, n. GK: *5149* [→ *4862+1096*]. family, relative, one's own people:– kindred [3]

4773 συγγενής, syngenēs, a. GK: *5150 & 5151* [→ *4862+1096*]. family, relative, one's own race or people:– kinsmen [5], kinsman [2], cousins [1], cousin [1], kinsfolks [1], kinsfolk [1], kin [1]

4774 συγγνώμη, syngnōmē, n. GK: *5152* [→ *4862+1097*]. concession:– permission [1]

4775 συγκάθημαι, synkathēmai, v. GK: *5153* [→ *4862+2516*]. to sit with:– sat with [1], sat [1]

4776 συγκαθίζω, synkathizō, v. GK: *5154* [→ *4862+2523*]. to sit down together; to be seated together:– made sit together [1], set down together [1]

4777 συγκακοπαθέω, synkakopatheō, v. GK: *5155* [→ *4862+2556+3958*]. to suffer together with, endure hardship with:– partaker of afflictions [1]

4778 συγκακουχέομαι, synkakoucheomai, v. GK: *5156* [→ *4862+2556+2192*]. (pass.) to be mistreated with:– suffer affliction with [1]

4779 συγκαλέω, synkaleō, v. GK: *5157* [→ *4862+2564*]. (act.) to call together; (mid.) to call to one's side, summon:– called together [5], calleth together [2], call together [1]

4780 συγκαλύπτω, synkalyptō, v. GK: *5158* [→ *4862+2572*]. to conceal:– covered [1]

4781 συγκάμπτω, synkamptō, v. GK: *5159* [→ *4862+2578*]. (pass.) to be bent over:– bow down [1]

4782 συγκαταβαίνω, synkatabainō, v. GK: *5160* [→ *4862+2596+305*]. to come, go down with:– go down with [1]

4783 συγκατάθεσις, synkatathesis, n. GK: *5161* [→ *4862+2596+5087*]. agreement:– agreement [1]

4784 συγκατατίθημι, synkatatithēmi, v. GK: *5163* [→ *4862+2596+5087*]. (mid.) to consent, agree with:– consented [1]

4785 συγκαταψηφίζομαι, synkatapsēphizomai, v. GK: *5164* [→ *4862+2596+5586*]. (pass.) to be added, chosen together with:– numbered [1]

4786 συγκεράννυμι, synkerannymi, v. GK: *5166* [→ *4862+2767*]. to combine, unite:– mixed [1], tempered together [1]

4787 συγκινέω, synkineō, v. GK: *5167* [→ *4862+2795*]. to stir up, arouse:– stirred up [1]

4788 συγκλείω, synkleiō, v. GK: *5168* [→ *4862+2808*]. to catch (fish hemmed up in a net); to confine, imprison, lock up:– concluded [2], inclosed [1], shut up [1]

4789 συγκληρονόμος, synklēronomos, a. GK: *5169* [→ *4862+2819+3551*]. inheriting together; (n.) co-heir:– fellowheirs [1], heirs together [1], heirs with [1], jointheirs with [1]

4790 συγκοινωνέω, synkoinōneō, v. GK: *5170* [→ *4862+2839*]. to share with, be connected with:– communicate with [1], have fellowship with [1], partakers [1]

4791 συγκοινωνός, synkoinōnos, n. GK: *5171* [→ *4862+2839*]. sharer, companion, participant, partner:– companion [1], partaker with [1], partakers [1], partakest (*+1096*) [1]

4792 συγκομίζω, synkomizō, v. GK: *5172* [→ *4862+2889*]. to bury, entomb:– carried [1]

4793 συγκρίνω, synkrinō, v. GK: *5173* [→ *4862+2919*]. to express, explain; to compare:– compare with [1], comparing amongst [1], comparing [1]

4794 συγκύπτω, synkyptō, v. GK: *5174* [→ *4862+2955*]. to bend over, be crippled:– bowed together [1]

4795 **συγκυρία, *synkyria*,** n. GK: *5175* [→ *4862*]. event that just happens, coincidence:– chance [1]

4796 **συγχαίρω, *synchairō*,** v. GK: *5176* [→ *4862+5463*]. to rejoice with:– rejoice with [5], rejoiced with [1], rejoiceth in [1]

4797 **συγχέω, *syncheō*;** or **συγχύνω, *synchynō*,** v. GK: *5177 & 5179* [→ *1632; cf. 4862*]. to baffle, confuse; to stir up, cause trouble; (pass.) to be bewildered, confused; to be in an uproar, stirred up:– confounded [2], confused [1], in an uproar [1], stirred up [1]

4798 **συγχράομαι, *synchraomai*,** v. GK: *5178* [→ *4862+5530*]. to associate with, have (friendly) dealings with:– have dealings with [1]

4799 **σύγχυσις, *synchysis*,** n. GK: *5180* [→ *1632; cf. 4862*]. uproar, confusion:– confusion [1]

4800 **συζάω, *syzaō*,** v. GK: *5182* [→ *4862+2198*]. to live with:– live with [3]

4801 **συζεύγνυμι, *syzeugnymi*,** v. GK: *5183* [→ *4862+2218*]. to join together:– joined together [2]

4802 **συζητέω, *syzēteō*,** v. GK: *5184* [→ *4862+2212*]. to discuss; to debate, argue:– disputed [1], disputing [1], inquire [1], question with [1], questioned [1], questioning with [1], questioning [1], question [1], reasoned [1], reasoning together [1]

4803 **συζήτησις, *syzētēsis*,** n. GK: *5185* [→ *4862+2212*]. dispute, discussion:– disputation [1], disputing [1], reasoning [1]

4804 **συζητητής, *syzētētēs*,** n. GK: *5186* [→ *4862+2212*]. philosopher, debater:– disputer [1]

4805 **σύζυγος, *syzygos*,** a. GK: *5187* [→ *4862+2218*]. yokefellow, comrade:– yokefellow [1]

4806 **συζωοποιέω, *syzōopoieō*,** v. GK: *5188* [→ *4862+2198+4160*]. to make alive with (someone):– quickened together with [1], quickened together [1]

4807 **συκάμινος, *sykaminos*,** n. GK: *5189*. mulberry tree:– sycamine tree [1]

4808 **συκῆ, *sykē*,** n. GK: *5190* [→ *4810*]. fig tree:– fig tree [16]

4809 **συκομορέα, *sykomorea*,** n. GK: *5191* [→ *4810*]. sycamore-fig tree:– sycomore tree [1]

4810 **σῦκον, *sykon*,** n. GK: *5192* [→ *4808, 4809, 4811*]. fig:– figs [4]

4811 **συκοφαντέω, *sykophanteō*,** v. GK: *5193* [→ *4810+5316*]. to accuse falsely, oppress; to cheat, extort:– accuse falsely [1], taken by false accusation [1]

4812 **συλαγωγέω, *sylagōgeō*,** v. GK: *5194* [→ *4813+71*]. to take captive:– spoil [1]

4813 **συλάω, *sylaō*,** v. GK: *5195* [→ *2416, 2417, 4812*]. to rob:– robbed [1]

4814 **συλλαλέω, *syllaleō*,** v. GK: *5196* [→ *4862+2980*]. to talk with, discuss with, confer with:– communed with [1], conferred [1], spake [1], talked with [1], talking with [1], talking [1]

4815 **συλλαμβάνω, *syllambanō*,** v. GK: *5197* [→ *4862+2983*]. to seize, arrest, capture; to become pregnant, conceive; to help, come to the aid of:– conceived [4], take [3], took [3], help [2], taken [2], caught [1], conceive [1]

4816 **συλλέγω, *syllegō*,** v. GK: *5198* [→ *4862+3004*]. to pick, pull up, collect:– gather [3], gather up [2], gathered [2], gather together [1]

4817 **συλλογίζομαι, *syllogizomai*,** v. GK: *5199* [→ *4862+3004*]. to discuss together:– reasoned [1]

4818 **συλλυπέω, *syllypeō*,** v. GK: *5200* [→ *4862+3077*]. (pass.) to be deeply distressed, grieved with:– grieved [1]

4819 **συμβαίνω, *symbainō*,** v. GK: *5201* [→ *4862+305*]. to happen; to come about:– happened [5], befell [1], happen [1], so [1]

4820 **συμβάλλω, *symballō*,** v. GK: *5202* [→ *4862+906*]. to dispute with; to confer with, meet with; to ponder; to engage in (war); (mid.) to help, assist:– conferred [1], encountered [1], helped [1], make war against (+*1519+4171*) [1], met with [1], pondered [1]

4821 **συμβασιλεύω, *symbasileuō*,** v. GK: *5203* [→ *4862+935*]. to reign with, be king with:– reign with [2]

4822 **συμβιβάζω, *symbibazō*,** v. GK: *5204* [→ *4862+305*]. (pass.) to be held together; to be united; (act.) to conclude; to prove; to instruct, teach, advise:– knit together [2], assuredly gathering [1], compacted [1], instruct [1], proving [1]

4823 **συμβουλεύω, *symbouleuō*,** v. GK: *5205* [→ *4862+1014*]. to advise, counsel; (mid.) to plot, conspire, consult:– consulted [1], counsel [1], gave counsel [1], took counsel together [1], took counsel [1]

4824 **συμβούλιον, *symboulion*,** n. GK: *5206* [→ *4862+1014*]. plan, plot; decision; council:– counsel [5], council [2], consultation [1]

4825 **σύμβουλος, *symboulos*,** n. GK: *5207* [→ *4862+1014*]. counselor, advisor:– counseller [1]

4826 **Συμεών, *Symeōn*,** n.pr. GK: *5208* [→ *4613*]. Simeon, Simon, *"he has heard* or *obedient one"*:– Simeon [6], Simon [1]

4827 **συμμαθητής, *symmathētēs*,** n. GK: *5209* [→ *4862+3129*]. fellow disciple:– fellowdisciples [1]

4828 **συμμαρτυρέω, *symmartyreō*,** v. GK: *5210* [→ *4862+3144*]. to testify with; to confirm:– also bearing witness [2], beareth witness with [1], testify [1]

4829 **συμμερίζομαι, *symmerizomai*,** v. GK: *5211* [→ *4862+3313*]. to share with:– partakers with [1]

4830 **συμμέτοχος, *symmetochos*,** a. GK: *5212* [→ *4862+3326+2192*]. sharing with, being partner with, derived from the Greek verb "to share in the possession of something," not found in the NT:– partakers with [1], partakers [1]

4831 **συμμιμητής, *symmimētēs*,** n. GK: *5213* [→ *4862+3401*]. fellow imitator:– followers together [1]

4832 **σύμμορφος, *symmorphos*,** a. GK: *5215* [→ *4862+3444*]. conformed, being like:– conformed to [1], fashioned like unto [1]

4833 **συμμορφόω, *symmorphoō*,** v. GK: *5214 & 5216* [→ *4862+3444*]. to give the same form:– made conformable [1]

4834 **συμπαθέω, *sympatheō*,** v. GK: *5217* [→ *4862+3958*]. to sympathize with:– had compassion [1], touched with the feeling [1]

4835 **συμπαθής, *sympathēs*,** a. GK: *5218* [→ *4862+3958*]. sympathetic:– compassion one of another [1]

4836 **συμπαραγίνομαι, *symparaginomai*,** v. GK: *5219* [→ *4862+3844+1096*]. (mid.) to come together:– came together [1], stood with [1]

4837 **συμπαρακαλέω, *symparakaleō*,** v. GK: *5220* [→ *4862+3844+2564*]. (pass.) to be mutually encouraged:– comforted together [1]

4838 **συμπαραλαμβάνω, *symparalambanō*,** v. GK: *5221* [→ *4862+3844+2983*]. to take along with:– take with [2], took with [2]

4839 **συμπαραμένω, *symparamenō*,** v. GK: *5222* [→ *4862+3844+3306*]. to stay with (someone) to help:– continue with [1]

4840 **συμπάρειμι, *sympareimi*,** v. GK: *5223* [→ *4862+3844+1510*]. to be present with:– here present with [1]

4841 **συμπάσχω, *sympaschō*,** v. GK: *5224* [→ *4862+3958*]. to suffer with, share in suffering:– suffer with [2]

4842 **συμπέμπω, *sympempō*,** v. GK: *5225* [→ *4862+3992*]. to send with:– sent with [1], sent [1]

4843 **συμπεριλαμβάνω, *symperilambanō*,** v. GK: *5227* [→ *4862+4012+2983*]. to put one's arms around, embrace:– embracing [1]

4844 **συμπίνω, *sympinō*,** v. GK: *5228* [→ *4862+4095*]. to drink with:– drink with [1]

4845 **συμπληρόω, *symplēroō*,** v. GK: *5230* [→ *4862+4137*]. (pass.) to be swamped, become full; to be fulfilled, come to an end:– come [1], filled [1], fully come [1]

4846 **συμπνίγω, *sympnigō*,** v. GK: *5231* [→ *4862+4155*]. to choke; to crush:– choked [2], choke [2], thronged [1]

4847 **συμπολίτης, *sympolitēs*,** n. GK: *5232* [→ *4862+4172*]. fellow citizen:– fellowcitizens with [1]

4848 **συμπορεύομαι, *symporeuomai*,** v. GK: *5233* [→ *4862+4198*]. to go with, come together:– went with [3], resort [1]

4849 **συμπόσιον, *symposion*,** n. GK: *5235* [→ *4862+4095*]. group:– by companies (+*4849*) [2]

4850 **συμπρεσβύτερος, *sympresbyteros*,** n. GK: *5236* [→ *4862+4245*]. fellow elder:– also an elder [1]

συμφάγω, *sumphagō*. See ***4906***.

4851 **συμφέρω, *sympherō*,** v. GK: *5237* [→ *4862+5342*]. to bring together; to be helpful, be gained; (n.) common good; (imper. verb) it is good, better, beneficial:– expedient [7], profitable [3], profit [3], better [1], brought together [1], good [1], profit withal [1]

4852 **σύμφημι, *symphēmi*,** v. GK: *5238* [→ *4862+5346*]. to agree with:– consent [1]

4853 **συμφυλέτης, *symphyletēs*,** n. GK: *5241* [→ *4862+5443*]. (pl.) one's own countrymen, people:– countrymen [1]

4854 **σύμφυτος, *symphytos*,** a. GK: *5242* [→ *4862+5453*]. united, being one with:– planted together [1]

4855 **συμφύω, *symphyō*,** v. GK: *5243* [→ *4862+5453*]. to grow up with:– sprang up with [1]

4856 συμφωνέω, ***symphōneō***, v. GK: *5244* [→ *4862+5456*]. to agree with; to match, fit in with:– agree [2], agree with [1], agreed together [1], agreed [1], agreeth [1]

4857 συμφώνησις, ***symphōnēsis***, n. GK: *5245* [→ *4862+5456*]. harmony, agreement:– concord [1]

4858 συμφωνία, ***symphōnia***, n. GK: *5246* [→ *4862+5456*]. music:– musick [1]

4859 σύμφωνος, ***symphōnos***, a. GK: *5247* [→ *4862+5456*]. mutually consenting, agreeing; (n.) mutual agreement:– consent [1]

4860 συμψηφίζω, ***sympsēphizō***, v. GK: *5248* [→ *4862+5586*]. to calculate, compute:– counted [1]

4861 σύμψυχος, ***sympsychos***, a. GK: *5249* [→ *4862+5594*]. united in spirit, harmonious:– one accord [1]

4862 σύν, ***syn***, pp. GK: *5250* [→ *799, 800, 801, 802, 1996, 1998, 1999, 3342, 4772, 4773, 4774, 4775, 4776, 4777, 4778, 4779, 4780, 4781, 4782, 4783, 4784, 4785, 4786, 4787, 4788, 4789, 4790, 4791, 4792, 4793, 4794, 4795, 4796, 4797, 4798, 4799, 4800, 4801, 4802, 4803, 4804, 4805, 4806, 4814, 4815, 4816, 4817, 4818, 4819, 4820, 4821, 4822, 4823, 4824, 4825, 4827, 4828, 4829, 4830, 4831, 4832, 4833, 4834, 4835, 4836, 4837, 4838, 4839, 4840, 4841, 4842, 4843, 4844, 4845, 4846, 4847, 4848, 4849, 4850, 4851, 4852, 4853, 4854, 4855, 4856, 4857, 4858, 4859, 4860, 4861, 4863, 4864, 4865, 4866, 4867, 4868, 4869, 4870, 4872, 4873, 4874, 4875, 4876, 4877, 4878, 4879, 4880, 4881, 4882, 4883, 4884, 4885, 4886, 4887, 4888, 4889, 4890, 4891, 4892, 4893, 4894, 4895, 4896, 4897, 4898, 4899, 4900, 4901, 4902, 4903, 4904, 4905, 4906, 4907, 4908, 4909, 4910, 4911, 4912, 4913, 4914, 4915, 4916, 4917, 4918, 4919, 4920, 4921, 4922, 4923, 4924, 4925, 4926, 4927, 4928, 4929, 4930, 4931, 4932, 4933, 4934, 4935, 4936, 4937, 4938, 4939, 4940, 4941, 4942, 4943, 4944, 4945, 4952, 4953, 4954, 4955, 4956, 4957, 4958, 4959, 4960, 4961, 4962, 4963, 4964*]. with; as, besides, a marker which shows association with another thing or person:– with [121], accompanied (*+2064*) [1], and [1], beside [1], with also [1]

4863 συνάγω, ***synagō***, v. GK: *5251* [→ *4862+71*]. to gather together, assemble; invite, call together:– gathered together [20], gathered [8], gather [7], came together [6], assembled [4], gather together [3], gathereth [3], took in [3], assembled together [2], bestow [2], gather up [1], gathering [1], leadeth [1], resorted [1]

4864 συναγωγή, ***synagōgē***, n. GK: *5252* [→ *656, 752, 1997*]. synagogue, congregation, meeting, a gathering of worshipers, usually a Jewish congregation, though in some contexts it may refer to a Christian assembly; a synagogue building:– synagogue [33], synagogues [22], assembly [1], congregation [1]

4865 συναγωνίζομαι, ***synagōnizomai***, v. GK: *5253* [→ *4862+73*]. to join in a struggle, help, assist:– strive together with [1]

4866 συναθλέω, ***synathleō***, v. GK: *5254* [→ *4862+118*]. to contend at one's side, together:– laboured with [1], striving together [1]

4867 συναθροίζω, ***synathroizō***, v. GK: *5255* [→ *4862; cf. 1865*]. to bring together; (pass.) to be gathered:– gathered together [2], called together [1]

4868 συναίρω, ***synairō***, v. GK: *5256* [→ *4862+142*]. to settle (monetary accounts):– reckoneth (*+3056*) [1], reckon [1], take [1]

4869 συναιχμάλωτος, ***synaichmalōtos***, n. GK: *5257* [→ *4862+164*]. fellow prisoner:– fellowprisoner [2], fellowprisoners [1]

4870 συνακολουθέω, ***synakoloutheō***, v. GK: *5258* [→ *4862+190; cf. 1.3*]. to follow, accompany:– followed [1], follow [1]

4871 συναλίζω, ***synalizō***, v. GK: *5259*. to eat with:– assembled together with [1]

4872 συναναβαίνω, ***synanabainō***, v. GK: *5262* [→ *4862+303+305*]. to come with, travel with:– came up with [2]

4873 συνανάκειμαι, ***synanakeimai***, v. GK: *5263* [→ *4862+303+2749*]. to eat with, have dinner with:– sat at meat with [2], sat with [2], sat also together with [1], sat at the table with [1], sat down with [1], sat with at meat [1], sit at meat with [1]

4874 συναναμείγνυμι, ***synanameignymi***, v. GK: *5264* [→ *4862+303+3396*]. to associate with:– company with [1], have company with [1], keep company [1]

4875 συναναπαύομαι, ***synanapauomai***, v. GK: *5265* [→ *4862+303+3973*]. to find rest together, be refreshed together:– with refreshed [1]

4876 συναντάω, ***synantaō***, v. GK: *5267* [→ *4862+473*]. to meet; to happen to:– met [4], befall [1], meet [1]

4877 συνάντησις, ***synantēsis***, n. GK: *5268* [→ *4862+473*]. meeting:– meet [1]

4878 συναντιλαμβάνομαι, ***synantilambanomai***, v. GK: *5269* [→ *4862+473+2983*]. to help, come to the aid of:– helpeth [1], help [1]

4879 συναπάγω, ***synapagō***, v. GK: *5270* [→ *4862+575+71*]. (pass.) to be led away, carried off; to associate with (the lowly):– carried away with [1], condescend to [1], led away with [1]

4880 συναποθνήσκω, ***synapothnēskō***, v. GK: *5271* [→ *4862+575+2348*]. to die with:– dead with [1], die with [1], die [1]

4881 συναπόλλυμι, ***synapollymi***, v. GK: *5272* [→ *4862+575+3639*]. (mid.) to die with, perish with:– perished with [1]

4882 συναποστέλλω, ***synapostellō***, v. GK: *5273* [→ *4862+649*]. to send with:– sent [1]

4883 συναρμολογέω, ***synarmologeō***, v. GK: *5274* [→ *4862+718+3004*]. (pass.) to be joined together, fit together:– fitly framed together [1], fitly joined together [1]

4884 συναρπάζω, ***synarpazō***, v. GK: *5275* [→ *4862+726*]. to seize; (pass.) to be caught, seized:– caught [4]

4885 συναυξάνω, ***synauxanō***, v. GK: *5277* [→ *4862+837*]. to grow together:– grow together [1]

4886 σύνδεσμος, ***syndesmos***, n. GK: *5278* [→ *4862+1210*]. bond; sinew; captive:– bond [3], bands [1]

4887 συνδέω, ***syndeō***, v. GK: *5279* [→ *4862+1210*]. (pass.) to be imprisoned with, bound with:– bound with [1]

4888 συνδοξάζω, ***syndoxazō***, v. GK: *5280* [→ *4862+1391*]. (pass.) to be glorified with, share glory with:– glorified together [1]

4889 σύνδουλος, ***syndoulos***, n. GK: *5281* [→ *4862+1401*]. fellow servant, fellow slave:– fellowservant [6], fellowservants [4]

συνδρέμω, ***sundremō***. See **4936**.

4890 συνδρομή, ***syndromē***, n. GK: *5282* [→ *4862+5143*]. running together:– ran together (*+1096*) [1]

4891 συνεγείρω, ***synegeirō***, v. GK: *5283* [→ *4862+1453*]. to raise up with:– risen with [2], raised up together [1]

4892 συνέδριον, ***synedrion***, n. GK: *5284* [→ *4862+1476*]. Sanhedrin; (local) council:– council [20], councils [2]

4893 συνείδησις, ***syneidēsis***, n. GK: *5287* [→ *4862+1492 or* 3708]. conscience:– conscience [31], consciences [1]

4894 συνείδω, ***syneidō***, v. GK: *5288* [→ *4862+1492 or* 3708]. to consider, know:– considered [1], know [1], privy [1], ware [1]

4895 σύνειμι[1], ***syneimi***[1], v. GK: *5289* [→ *4862+1510*]. to be with; (n.) companion:– with [2]

4896 σύνειμι[2], ***syneimi***[2], v. GK: *5290* [→ *4862*]. to gather together, come together:– gathered together [1]

4897 συνεισέρχομαι, ***syneiserchomai***, v. GK: *5291* [→ *4862+1519+2064*]. to enter together with:– went in with [1], went with [1]

4898 συνέκδημος, ***synekdēmos***, n. GK: *5292* [→ *4862+1537+1218*]. traveling companion:– companions in travel [1], travel with [1]

4899 συνεκλεκτός, ***syneklektos***, a. GK: *5293* [→ *4862+1537+3004*]. chosen together with:– elected together with [1]

4900 συνελαύνω, ***synelaunō***, v. GK: *5295* [→ *4862+1643*]. to drive, force, bring:– set at one (*+1515+1519*) [1]

4901 συνεπιμαρτυρέω, ***synepimartyreō***, v. GK: *5296* [→ *4862+1909+3144*]. to testify at the same time:– also bearing witness [1]

4902 συνέπομαι, ***synepomai***, v. GK: *5299* [→ *4862*]. to accompany:– accompanied [1]

4903 συνεργέω, ***synergeō***, v. GK: *5300* [→ *4862+2041*]. to work together, work with; (n.) fellow worker:– helpeth with [1], work together [1], workers together [1], working with [1], wrought with [1]

4904 συνεργός, ***synergos***, a. GK: *5301* [→ *4862+2041*]. fellow worker:– fellowlabourers [2], fellowlabourer [2], helpers [2], companion in labour [1], fellowhelpers [1], fellowhelper [1], fellowworkers [1], helper [1], labourers together with [1], workfellow [1]

4905 συνέρχομαι, ***synerchomai***, v. GK: *5302* [→ *4862+2064*]. to come together, gather, assemble; to go along with, accompany:– come together [12], came together [4], came with [3], went with [3], come [2], accompanied [1], came [1], cometh together [1], companied with [1], go with [1], resorted [1], resort [1], with assembled [1]

4906 συνεσθίω, ***synesthiō***, v. GK: *5303* [→ *4862+2068*]. to eat with:– eat [2], eat with [1], eateth with [1], with to eat [1]

4907 συνεσις, *synesis*, n. GK: *5304* [→ *863; cf. 4862*]. understanding, insight; intelligence, the faculty of comprehension, often referring to wisdom and insight in spiritual matters:– understanding [6], knowledge [1]

4908 συνετός, *synetos*, a. GK: *5305* [→ *863; cf. 4862*]. intelligent, learned, with good sense:– prudent [4]

4909 συνευδοκέω, *syneudokeō*, v. GK: *5306* [→ *4862+2095+1380*]. to approve of, give approval; to be willing:– consenting [2], pleased [2], allow [1], pleasure [1]

4910 συνευωχέομαι, *syneuōcheomai*, v. GK: *5307* [→ *4862+2095+2192*]. to partake in a feast together:– feast with [2]

4911 συνεφίστημι, *synephistēmi*, v. GK: *5308* [→ *4862+1909+2476*]. to join in an attack:– rose up together [1]

4912 συνέχω, *synechō*, v. GK: *5309* [→ *4862+2192*]. to cover (ears); to crowd (against); to guard, hold in custody; to compel, urge on; (pass.) to suffer, be distressed; to be devoted to:– taken with [2], constraineth [1], held [1], in a strait [1], keep in [1], pressed [1], sick of [1], stopped [1], straitened [1], taken [1], throng [1]

4913 συνήδομαι, *synēdomai*, v. GK: *5310* [→ *4862+2237*]. to delight in agreement:– delight in [1]

4914 συνήθεια, *synētheia*, n. GK: *5311* [→ *4862+1485*]. custom, practice:– custom [2]

4915 συνηλικιώτης, *synēlikiōtēs*, n. GK: *5312* [→ *4862+2245*]. person of one's own age, contemporary:– equals [1]

4916 συνθάπτω, *synthaptō*, v. GK: *5313* [→ *4862+2290*]. (pass.) to be buried with:– buried with [2]

4917 συνθλάω, *synthlaō*, v. GK: *5314* [→ *4862*]. (pass.) to be broken to pieces:– broken [2]

4918 συνθλίβω, *synthlibō*, v. GK: *5315* [→ *4862+2346*]. to press around, crowd against:– thronged [1], thronging [1]

4919 συνθρύπτω, *synthryptō*, v. GK: *5316* [→ *4862*]. to break:– break [1]

4920 συνίημι, *syniēmi*, v. GK: *5317 & 5320* [→ *863; cf. 4862*]. to understand, realize:– understand [13], understood [7], understandeth [3], considered [1], understanding [1], wise [1]

4921 συνιστάω, *synistaō*; or συνίστημι, *synistēmi*, v. GK: *5318 & 5319* [→ *4862+2476*]. to commend, recommend; to demonstrate, bring out, prove to be; (intr.) to stand with; to hold together; to be formed:– commend [5], commendeth [3], approved [1], approving [1], commended [1], commending [1], consist [1], make [1], standing [1], stood with [1]

4922 συνοδεύω, *synodeuō*, v. GK: *5321* [→ *4862+3598*]. to travel with:– journeyed with [1]

4923 συνοδία, *synodia*, n. GK: *5322* [→ *4862+3598*]. company of travelers, caravan:– company [1]

4924 συνοικέω, *synoikeō*, v. GK: *5324* [→ *4862+3624*]. to live with:– dwell with [1]

4925 συνοικοδομέω, *synoikodomeō*, v. GK: *5325* [→ *4862+3624+1430*]. (pass.) to be built up together:– builded together [1]

4926 συνομιλέω, *synomileō*, v. GK: *5326* [→ *4862+3656*]. to talk with, converse with:– talked with [1]

4927 συνομορέω, *synomoreō*, v. GK: *5327* [→ *4862+3664+3724*]. to be next door to:– joined hard to [1]

4928 συνοχή, *synochē*, n. GK: *5330* [→ *4862+2192*]. anguish, distress:– anguish [1], distress [1]

4929 συντάσσω, *syntassō*, v. GK: *5332* [→ *4862+5021*]. to command, direct, instruct:– appointed [2]

4930 συντέλεια, *synteleia*, n. GK: *5333* [→ *4862+5056*]. end, close, completion:– end [6]

4931 συντελέω, *synteleō*, v. GK: *5334* [→ *4862+5056*]. to finish, accomplish; (pass.) to be fulfilled, be over, accomplished:– ended [4], finish [1], fulfilled [1], make [1]

4932 συντέμνω, *syntemnō*, v. GK: *5335* [→ *4862+5114*]. to cut short, speed up:– cut short [1], short [1]

4933 συντηρέω, *syntēreō*, v. GK: *5337* [→ *4862+5083*]. to protect, defend; to treasure, preserve in memory; (pass.) to be preserved:– preserved [2], kept [1], observed [1]

4934 συντίθημι, *syntithēmi*, v. GK: *5338* [→ *4862+5087*]. (mid.) to agree, decide:– agreed [2], assented [1], covenanted [1]

4935 συντόμως, *syntomōs*, adv. GK: *5339* [→ *4862+5114*]. briefly:– few words [1]

4936 συντρέχω, *syntrechō*, v. GK: *5340* [→ *4862+5143*]. to run together, go together; by extension, to be closely associated in a particular behavior or undertaking:– ran together [1], ran [1], run with [1]

4937 συντρίβω, *syntribō*, v. GK: *5341* [→ *4862+5147*]. to break, destroy; (pass.) to be broken, bruised, dashed to pieces:– brake [1], broken in pieces [1], broken to shivers [1], brokenhearted [1], broken [1], bruised [1], bruise [1], bruising [1]

4938 σύντριμμα, *syntrimma*, n. GK: *5342* [→ *4862+5147*]. ruin, destruction:– destruction [1]

4939 σύντροφος, *syntrophos*, a. GK: *5343* [→ *4862+5142*]. brought up with (in a family); this can refer to a foster sibling or an intimate friend:– brought up with [1]

4940 συντυγχάνω, *syntynchanō*, v. GK: *5344* [→ *4862+5177*]. to come together with, meet:– come at [1]

4941 Συντύχη, *Syntychē*, n.pr. GK: *5345* [→ *4862+5177*]. Syntyche, "*coincidence, success*":– Syntyche [1]

4942 συνυποκρίνομαι, *synypokrinomai*, v. GK: *5347* [→ *4862+5259+2919*]. to join in one's hypocrisy:– dissembled with [1]

4943 συνυπουργέω, *synypourgeō*, v. GK: *5348* [→ *4862+5259+2041*]. to join to help:– helping together [1]

4944 συνωδίνω, *synōdinō*, v. GK: *5349* [→ *4862+5604*]. to join in the pains of childbirth, suffer agony together:– travaileth in pain together [1]

4945 συνωμοσία, *synōmosia*, n. GK: *5350* [→ *4862+3660*]. plot, conspiracy:– conspiracy [1]

4946 Συράκουσαι, *Syrakousai*, n.pr. GK: *5352*. Syracuse:– Syracuse [1]

4947 Συρία, *Syria*, n.pr. GK: *5353* [→ *4948*]. Syria:– Syria [8]

4948 Σύρος, *Syros*, n.pr.g. GK: *5354* [→ *4947, 4949*]. Syrian:– Syrian [1]

4949 Συροφοίνισσα, *Syrophoinissa*, n.pr.g. GK: *5356* [→ *4948+5404*]. Syrophoenician:– Syrophenician [1]

4950 Σύρτις, *Syrtis*, n.pr. GK: *5358* [→ *4951*]. Syrtis, feared for its shifting sandbars and unpredictable currents:– quicksands [1]

4951 σύρω, *syrō*, v. GK: *5359* [→ *2694, 4950*]. to drag, tow; to sweep:– drew [3], dragging [1], haling [1]

4952 συσπαράσσω, *sysparassō*, v. GK: *5360* [→ *4862+4685*]. to cause to convulse:– tare [1]

4953 σύσσημον, *syssēmon*, n. GK: *5361* [→ *4862+4592*]. signal:– token [1]

4954 σύσσωμος, *syssōmos*, a. GK: *5362* [→ *4862+4983*]. co-member of a body:– of same body [1]

4955 συστασιαστής, *systasiastēs*, n. GK: *5363* [→ *4862+2476*]. fellow insurrectionist:– made insurrection with [1]

4956 συστατικός, *systatikos*, a. GK: *5364* [→ *4862+2476*]. commendatory, recommended:– commendation [2]

4957 συσταυρόω, *systauroō*, v. GK: *5365* [→ *4862+4716*]. (pass.) to be crucified with:– crucified with [5]

4958 συστέλλω, *systellō*, v. GK: *5366* [→ *4862+4724*]. to wrap up, cover up; (pass.) to be shortened, limited:– short [1], wound up [1]

4959 συστενάζω, *systenazō*, v. GK: *5367* [→ *4862+4728*]. to join in groaning, groan together:– groaneth [1]

4960 συστοιχέω, *systoicheō*, v. GK: *5368* [→ *4862+4748*]. to correspond:– answereth to [1]

4961 συστρατιώτης, *systratiōtēs*, n. GK: *5369* [→ *4862+4756*]. fellow soldier:– fellowsoldier [2]

4962 συστρέφω, *systrephō*, v. GK: *5370* [→ *4862+4762*]. to gather up, bring together:– gathered [1]

4963 συστροφή, *systrophē*, n. GK: *5371* [→ *4862+4762*]. commotion, disorderly gathering, mob; conspiracy, plot:– banded together (*+4160*) [1], concourse [1]

4964 συσχηματίζω, *syschēmatizō*, v. GK: *5372* [→ *4862+4976*]. (mid.) to conform to a pattern or mold; (pass.) to be conformed to a pattern or mold:– conformed to [1], fashioning according to [1]

4965 Συχάρ, *Sychar*, n.pr. GK: *4993 & 5373*. Sychar:– Sychar [1]

4966 Συχέμ, *Sychem*, n.pr. GK: *5374*. Shechem, "[poss.] *shoulder [saddle of a hill]; shoulders [and upper back]*":– Sychem [2]

4967 σφαγή, *sphagē*, n. GK: *5375* [→ *4969*]. slaughter:– slaughter [3]

4968 σφάγιον, *sphagion*, n. GK: *5376* [→ *4969*]. offering for slaughter:– slain beasts [1]

4969 σφάζω, *sphazō*, v. GK: *5377* [→ *2695, 4967, 4968*]. to kill, slay, murder:– slain [6], slew [2], kill [1], wounded [1]

4970 **σφόδρα, *sphodra***, adv. GK: *5379* [→ *4971*]. very, greatly, exceedingly:– exceeding [4], very [3], greatly [2], exceedingly [1], sore [1]

4971 **σφοδρῶς, *sphodrōs***, adv. GK: *5380* [→ *4970*]. violently:– exceedingly [1]

4972 **σφραγίζω, *sphragizō***, v. GK: *5381* [→ *4973*]. to seal, to put a mark on an object to show possession, authority, identity, or security:– sealed [20], seal [2], sealing [1], set a seal [1], set to seal [1]

4973 **σφραγίς, *sphragis***, n. GK: *5382* [→ *2696, 4972*]. seal:– seal [11], seals [5]

4974 **σφυρόν, *sphyron***, n. GK: *5383 & 5384*. ankle or heel:– ankle [1]

4975 **σχεδόν, *schedon***, adv. GK: *5385* [→ *2192*]. nearly, almost:– almost [3]

σχέω, *scheō*. See ***2192***.

4976 **σχῆμα, *schēma***, n. GK: *5386* [→ *807, 808, 809, 2156, 2157, 2158, 3345, 4964; cf. 2192*]. form, outward appearance:– fashion [1], in fashion [1]

4977 **σχίζω, *schizō***, v. GK: *5387* [→ *4978*]. to tear, divide; (pass.) to be torn, divided, split (in opinion):– rent [5], divided [2], broken [1], maketh a rent [1], opened [1]

4978 **σχίσμα, *schisma***, n. GK: *5388* [→ *4977*]. tear, split, divide an object into parts, with an implication that the object is now damaged; by extension: division, dissension, implying discord and damage to the unity of the original group:– division [3], divisions [2], rent [2], schism [1]

4979 **σχοινίον, *schoinion***, n. GK: *5389*. (pl.) cords, ropes:– ropes [1], small cords [1]

4980 **σχολάζω, *scholazō***, v. GK: *5390* [→ *4981*]. to devote oneself to; to be unoccupied, stand empty:– empty [1], give [1]

4981 **σχολή, *scholē***, n. GK: *5391* [→ *4980*]. lecture hall, a building in which students meet for discussion and study, school:– school [1]

4982 **σῴζω, *sōzō***, v. GK: *5392* [→ *810, 811, 1295, 4986, 4989, 4990, 4991, 4992*]. to save, rescue, deliver; to heal; by extension: to be in right relationship with God, with the implication that the condition before salvation was one of grave danger or distress:– saved [53], save [41], made whole [9], healed [3], whole [2], do well [1], preserve [1]

4983 **σῶμα, *sōma***, n. GK: *5393* [→ *4954, 4984, 4985*]. body, the mass of anything, usually a corporeal tissue, human, animal, or plant, though it can also refer to a heavenly body; the church is said to be like a (human) body, emphasizing its essential unity with very important diversities of function within the unity:– body [132], bodies [11], bodily [1], body's [1], slaves [1]

4984 **σωματικός, *sōmatikos***, a. GK: *5394* [→ *4983*]. bodily, physical:– bodily [2]

4985 **σωματικῶς, *sōmatikōs***, adv. GK: *5395* [→ *4983*]. in bodily form, corporeally:– bodily [1]

4986 **Σώπατρος, *Sōpatros***, n.pr. GK: *5396* [→ *4982+3962*]. Sopater, *"saving one's father"*:– Sopater [1]

4987 **σωρεύω, *sōreuō***, v. GK: *5397* [→ *2002*]. to heap up, pile up; (pass.) to be loaded down:– heap [1], laden [1]

4988 **Σωσθένης, *Sōsthenēs***, n.pr. GK: *5398*. Sosthenes:– Sosthenes [2]

4989 **Σωσίπατρος, *Sōsipatros***, n.pr. GK: *5399* [→ *4982+3962*]. Sosipater, *"saving one's father"*:– Sosipater [1]

4990 **σωτήρ, *sōtēr***, n. GK: *5400* [→ *4982*]. Savior, one who delivers from grave danger; note that in the NT this always refers to God the Father and Jesus Christ as Savior of believers from righteous wrath to a proper relationship with God:– saviour [24]

4991 **σωτηρία, *sōtēria***, n. GK: *5401* [→ *4982*]. salvation, rescue, deliverance, the state of not being in grave danger and so being safe; this can refer to ordinary dangers and conditions on earth, but it usually refers to the state of believers being safe from righteous wrath in a proper relationship with God:– salvation [40], saved [2], deliver (+*1325*) [1], health [1], saving [1]

4992 **σωτήριον, *sōtērion***, n. GK: *5402* [→ *4982*]. salvation; this word can focus on the message or means of salvation:– salvation [5]

4993 **σωφρονέω, *sōphroneō***, v. GK: *5404* [→ *4994, 4995, 4996, 4997, 4998; cf. 5424*]. to be in a right state of mind, have sober judgment; to be self-controlled:– in right mind [2], sober [2], sober minded [1], soberly [1]

4994 **σωφρονίζω, *sōphronizō***, v. GK: *5405* [→ *4993*]. to train, encourage, advise, urge:– teach to be sober [1]

4995 **σωφρονισμός, *sōphronismos***, n. GK: *5406* [→ *4993*]. self-discipline, with an implication that this discipline demonstrates prudence and wisdom:– sound mind [1]

4996 **σωφρόνως, *sōphronōs***, adv. GK: *5407* [→ *4993*]. in self-control:– soberly [1]

4997 **σωφροσύνη, *sōphrosynē***, n. GK: *5408* [→ *4993*]. propriety, appropriateness; reasonableness, mental soundness:– sobriety [2], soberness [1]

4998 **σώφρων, *sōphrōn***, a. GK: *5409* [→ *4993*]. self-controlled, implied to be wise and prudent in nature:– sober [2], discreet [1], temperate [1]

τά, *ta*. See ***3588***.

4999 **ταβέρναι, *tabernai***, n. GK: *5411* [→ *5140+4999*]. tavern, shop, store:– taverns [1]

5000 **Ταβιθά, *Tabitha***, n.pr. GK: *5412*. Tabitha, *"gazelle"*:– Tabitha [2]

5001 **τάγμα, *tagma***, n. GK: *5413* [→ *5021*]. turn, order, arrangement:– order [1]

5002 **τακτός, *taktos***, a. GK: *5414* [→ *5021*]. appointed, fixed:– set [1]

5003 **ταλαιπωρέω, *talaipōreō***, v. GK: *5415* [→ *5005*]. to grieve, lament:– afflicted [1]

5004 **ταλαιπωρία, *talaipōria***, n. GK: *5416* [→ *5005*]. misery, distress:– miseries [1], misery [1]

5005 **ταλαίπωρος, *talaipōros***, a. GK: *5417* [→ *5003, 5004*]. wretched, miserable:– wretched [2]

5006 **ταλαντιαῖος, *talantiaios***, a. GK: *5418* [→ *5007*]. weighing a talent (about 57 to 80 lbs.):– weight of a talent [1]

5007 **τάλαντον, *talanton***, n. GK: *5419* [→ *5006*]. talent (weight and monetary unit; about 57 to 80 lbs.); a talent of silver was about 6,000 days' wages (denarii) of a common laborer and a talent of gold was about 180,000 day's wages, often implying a vast, unattainable amount:– talents [12], talent [3]

5008 **ταλιθά, *talitha***, l.[n.]. GK: *5420*. talitha (Aramaic: "little girl"):– talitha [1]

5009 **ταμεῖον, *tameion***, n. GK: *5421* [→ *5114*]. room, inner room, storeroom:– closets [1], closet [1], secret chambers [1], storehouse [1]

τανῦν, *tanun*. See ***3568, 3569***.

5010 **τάξις, *taxis***, n. GK: *5423* [→ *5021*]. order, succession; kind, nature:– order [10]

5011 **ταπεινός, *tapeinos***, a. GK: *5424* [→ *5012, 5013, 5014*]. humble, lowly, downcast, timid:– humble [2], low degree [2], base [1], cast down [1], lowly [1], of low estate [1]

5012 **ταπεινοφροσύνη, *tapeinophrosynē***, n. GK: *5425* [→ *5011+5424*]. humility, humbleness, modesty:– humility [3], humbleness of mind [1], humility of mind [1], lowliness of mind [1], lowliness [1]

5013 **ταπεινόω, *tapeinoō***, v. GK: *5427* [→ *5011*]. (act.) to humble (oneself), lower (oneself); (pass.) to be humbled, brought low, in need:– humble [5], abased [4], humbleth [2], abasing [1], brought low [1], humbled [1]

5014 **ταπείνωσις, *tapeinōsis***, n. GK: *5428* [→ *5011*]. humbleness, lowliness, humiliation:– humiliation [1], low estate [1], made low [1], vile [1]

5015 **ταράσσω, *tarassō***, v. GK: *5429* [→ *1298, 1613, 5016, 5017*]. to trouble, disturb, throw into confusion; (pass.) to be disturbed, terrified, confused; to be stirred up:– troubled [15], troubleth [1], trouble [1]

5016 **ταραχή, *tarachē***, n. GK: *5430* [→ *5015*]. disturbance:– troubles [1], troubling [1]

5017 **τάραχος, *tarachos***, n. GK: *5431* [→ *5015*]. commotion; disturbance:– stir [2]

5018 **Ταρσεύς, *Tarseus***, n.pr.g. GK: *5432* [→ *5019*]. Tarsus:– Tarsus [2]

5019 **Ταρσός, *Tarsos***, n.pr. GK: *5433* [→ *5018*]. Tarsus:– Tarsus [3]

5020 **ταρταρόω, *tartaroō***, v. GK: *5434*. to send to hell, hold captive in Tartarus; a derivative of the Greek noun "Tartarus," a place of torture and torment lower than Hades in Greek and Jewish apocalyptic literature, not found in the NT:– cast down to hell [1]

5021 **τάσσω, *tassō***, v. GK: *5435* [→ *392, 498, 506, 657, 812, 813, 814, 1296, 1297, 1299, 1928, 2003, 2004, 4367, 4384, 4929, 5001, 5002, 5010, 5292, 5293*]. (act./mid.) to appoint, determine, arrange; devote; (pass.) to be established, appointed, assigned:– appointed [3], ordained [2], addicted [1], determined [1], set [1]

5022 **ταῦρος, *tauros***, n. GK: *5436*. bull, ox:– bulls [2], oxen [2]

5023 **ταῦτα, *tauta***, p.demo.neut.pl. of *3778*. GK: *4047* [→ *3778*]. these; see *3778*:–

5024 **ταὐτά, *tauta***, contr. [art.+p.]. GK: *5437* [→ *3588+846*]. the same things:– even thus (+*2596*) [1], like [1]

5025 **ταύταις, *tautais***, p.demo.fem.pl. of *3778*. GK: *4047* [→ *3778*]. to, for, by these; see *3778*:–

5026 **ταύτῃ, *tautē***, p.demo.fem.s. of *3778*. GK: *4047* [→ *3778*]. to, for, by this; see *3778*:–

5027 **ταφή, *taphē*,** n. GK: *5438* [→ *5028*]. burial place:– bury [1]

5028 **τάφος, *taphos*,** n. GK: *5439* [→ *1779, 1780, 5027; cf. 2290*]. tomb, grave:– sepulchre [5], sepulchres [1], tombs [1]

5029 **τάχα, *tacha*,** adv. GK: *5440* [→ *5036*]. perhaps, possibly:– peradventure [1], perhaps [1]

5030 **ταχέως, *tacheōs*,** adv. GK: *5441* [→ *5036*]. quickly, in haste; very soon:– shortly [6], quickly [3], soon [2], hastily [1], outrun (+*4390*) [1], sooner [1], suddenly [1], with all speed (+*5613*) [1]

5031 **ταχινός, *tachinos*,** a. GK: *5442* [→ *5036*]. swift; soon, imminent:– shortly [1], swift [1]

5032 **τάχιον, *tachion*,** adv.compar.neut. of *5030*. GK: *5441* [→ *5036*]. very quickly, in haste; very soon:–

5033 **τάχιστα, *tachista*,** adv.super. of *5030*. GK: *5441* [→ *5036*]. most quickly, hastily; as soon as possible:–

5034 **τάχος, *tachos*,** n. GK: *5443* [→ *5036*]. quickness, immediateness; (in pp. phrase) quickly, immediately, soon:– shortly (+*1722*) [4], quickly (+*1722*) [2], quickly [1], speedily (+*1722*) [1]

5035 **ταχύ, *tachu*,** a.neut.s. of *5036*. GK: *5444* [→ *5036*]. (adv.) quickly, momentarily, soon:–

5036 **ταχύς, *tachys*,** a. GK: *5444* [→ *5029, 5030, 5031, 5032, 5033, 5034, 5035*]. quick, swift; (adv.) quickly, momentarily, soon:– quickly [11], lightly [1], swift [1]

5037 **τέ, *te*,** pt. GK: *5445* [→ *1535, 1539, 3383, 3752, 3753, 3763, 3777, 3842, 5119, 5620*]. and, but (often not translated):– and [127], both [36], also [2], then [2], whether (+*1437*) [2], and whether (+*1437*) [1], between [1], even [1], inasmuch as both [1], or (+*1437*) [1], whether [1], yea (+*2089*) [1]

5038 **τεῖχος, *teichos*,** n. GK: *5446* [→ *3320, 5109*]. wall:– wall [8], walls [1]

5039 **τεκμήριον, *tekmērion*,** n. GK: *5447*. convincing proof:– infallible proofs [1]

5040 **τεκνίον, *teknion*,** n. GK: *5448* [→ *5088*]. dear children, little children:– little children [9]

5041 **τεκνογονέω, *teknogoneō*,** v. GK: *5449* [→ *5088+1096*]. to have children, bear a child:– bear children [1]

5042 **τεκνογονία, *teknogonia*,** n. GK: *5450* [→ *5088+1096*]. childbearing:– childbearing [1]

5043 **τέκνον, *teknon*,** n. GK: *5451* [→ *5088*]. child, son, daughter, offspring, descendant:– children [70], son [15], sons [6], child [5], children's [2], daughters [1]

5044 **τεκνοτροφέω, *teknotropheō*,** v. GK: *5452* [→ *5088+5142*]. to bring up children:– brought up children [1]

5045 **τέκτων, *tektōn*,** n. GK: *5454* [→ *5078*]. carpenter, woodworker; more generally: construction worker, including stonemason and metalworker:– carpenter's [1], carpenter [1]

5046 **τέλειος, *teleios*,** a. GK: *5455* [→ *5056*]. perfect, mature, finished:– perfect [16], full age [1], men [1], more perfect [1]

5047 **τελειότης, *teleiotēs*,** n. GK: *5456* [→ *5056*]. perfection, maturity, completeness:– perfection [1], perfectness [1]

5048 **τελειόω, *teleioō*,** v. GK: *5457* [→ *5056*]. to perfect, complete, finish; (pass.) to reach a goal, be fulfilled, completed, made perfect:– made perfect [9], perfected [4], finish [3], make perfect [3], fulfilled [2], consecrated [1], finished [1], perfect [1]

5049 **τελείως, *teleiōs*,** adv. GK: *5458* [→ *5056*]. fully, completely, perfectly:– end [1]

5050 **τελείωσις, *teleiōsis*,** n. GK: *5459* [→ *5056*]. perfection, accomplishment, fulfillment:– perfection [1], performance [1]

5051 **τελειωτής, *teleiōtēs*,** n. GK: *5460* [→ *5056*]. perfecter:– finisher [1]

5052 **τελεσφορέω, *telesphoreō*,** v. GK: *5461* [→ *5056+5342*]. to mature (to fruitfulness):– bring to perfection [1]

5053 **τελευτάω, *teleutaō*,** v. GK: *5462* [→ *5054; cf. 5056*]. to die:– dead [3], dieth [3], die [3], died [2], deceased [1]

5054 **τελευτή, *teleutē*,** n. GK: *5463* [→ *5053*]. death:– death [1]

5055 **τελέω, *teleō*,** v. GK: *5464* [→ *5056*]. to finish, complete, fulfill; (pass.) to be finished, be completed, fulfilled, perfected:– finished [8], accomplished [4], fulfilled [4], fulfil [3], pay [2], expired [1], filled up [1], gone over [1], made an end [1], performed [1]

5056 **τέλος, *telos*,** n. GK: *5465* [→ *255, 658, 1300, 1615, 2005, 3081, 3651, 3838, 4185, 4930, 4931, 5046, 5047, 5048, 5049, 5050, 5051, 5052, 5055; cf. 5053, 5057*]. end, result, outcome, finish, goal; revenue, tax, duty:– end [34], custom [3], by continual (+*1519*) [1], ending [1], ends [1], finally (+*3588*) [1], uttermost [1]

5057 **τελώνης, *telōnēs*,** n. GK: *5467* [→ *754, 5057, 5058*]. tax collector:– publicans [16], publican [6]

5058 **τελώνιον, *telōnion*,** n. GK: *5466 & 5468* [→ *5057*]. tax collector's booth:– receipt of custom [3]

5059 **τέρας, *teras*,** n. GK: *5469*. wonder, miracle, which is by implication a sign or portent:– wonders [16]

5060 **Τέρτιος, *Tertios*,** n.pr. GK: *5470*. Tertius, "*third*":– Tertius [1]

5061 **Τέρτυλλος, *Tertyllos*,** n.pr. GK: *5472*. Tertullus, "*third*":– Tertullus [2]

τέσσαρα, *tessara*. See ***5064***.

5062 **τεσσαράκοντα, *tessarakonta*,** n.num. GK: *5473 & 5477* [→ *5064*]. forty:– forty [22]

5063 **τεσσαρακονταετής, *tessarakontaetēs*,** a.num. GK: *5474 & 5478* [→ *5064+2094*]. (of) forty years:– forty years [2]

5064 **τέσσαρες, *tessares*,** n.num. GK: *5475* [→ *1180, 5062, 5063, 5065, 5066, 5067, 5068, 5069, 5070, 5071, 5072, 5073, 5074, 5075, 5076, 5132, 5133*]. four:– four [42]

5065 **τεσσαρεσκαιδέκατος, *tessareskaidekatos*,** a.num. GK: *5476* [→ *5064+2532+1176*]. fourteenth:– fourteenth [2]

5066 **τεταρταῖος, *tetartaios*,** a. GK: *5479* [→ *5064*]. fourth (day):– four days [1]

5067 **τέταρτος, *tetartos*,** a. GK: *5480* [→ *5064*]. fourth in a series or collection; (n.) the fourth (fractional) part of something:– fourth [9], four [1]

5068 **τετράγωνος, *tetragōnos*,** a. GK: *5481* [→ *5064+1137*]. square, cubical:– foursquare [1]

5069 **τετράδιον, *tetradion*,** n. GK: *5482* [→ *5064*]. squad of four soldiers:– quaternions [1]

5070 **τετρακισχίλιοι, *tetrakischilioi*,** a.num. GK: *5483* [→ *5064+5507*]. four thousand:– four thousand [5]

5071 **τετρακόσιοι, *tetrakosioi*,** a.num. GK: *5484* [→ *5064*]. four hundred:– four hundred [4]

5072 **τετράμηνος, *tetramēnos*,** a. GK: *5485* [→ *5064+3375*]. (for) four months:– four months [1]

5073 **τετραπλόος, *tetraploos*,** a. [used as adv.]. GK: *5486 & 5487* [→ *5064*]. four times (as much):– fourfold [1]

5074 **τετράπους, *tetrapous*,** a. GK: *5488* [→ *5064+4228*]. four-footed; (n.) four-footed animal of any kind:– fourfooted beasts [3]

5075 **τετραρχέω, *tetrarcheō*,** v. GK: *5489* [→ *5064+757*]. to be a tetrarch:– tetrarch [3]

5076 **τετράρχης, *tetrarchēs*,** n. GK: *5490* [→ *5064+757*]. tetrarch, a ruler of less rank and authority than a king:– tetrarch [4]

τεύχω, *teuchō*. See ***5177***.

5077 **τεφρόω, *tephroō*,** v. GK: *5491* [→ *5188*]. to reduce to ashes by fire:– turning into ashes [1]

5078 **τέχνη, *technē*,** n. GK: *5492* [→ *753, 3673, 5045, 5079; cf. 5088*]. skill, trade, craft:– art [1], craft [1], occupation [1]

5079 **τεχνίτης, *technitēs*,** n. GK: *5493* [→ *5078*]. craftsman, skilled worker, architect, designer, one who engages in a craft or trade, in some contexts with a focus or the design and planning of what is crafted:– craftsmen [2], builder [1], craftsman [1]

5080 **τήκομαι, *tēkomai*,** v. GK: *5494*. (pass.) to be melted:– melt [1]

5081 **τηλαυγῶς, *tēlaugōs*,** adv. GK: *5495* [→ *827*]. clearly, plainly:– clearly [1]

5082 **τηλικοῦτος, *tēlikoutos*,** p.demo. GK: *5496* [→ *2245+3778*]. so great, so large:– so great [2], great [1], mighty [1]

5083 **τηρέω, *tēreō*,** v. GK: *5498* [→ *1301, 3906, 3907, 4933, 5084*]. to keep, guard, obey, observe:– keep [32], kept [15], keepeth [10], reserved [7], observe [4], preserved [2], hold fast [1], keepers [1], reserve [1], watched [1], watching [1]

5084 **τήρησις, *tērēsis*,** n. GK: *5499* [→ *5083*]. jail, prison, custody; keeping, observance:– hold [1], keeping [1], prison [1]

τῇ, *tēi*, τήν, *tēn*, τῆς, *tēs*. See ***3588***.

5085 **Τιβεριάς, *Tiberias*,** n.pr. GK: *5500* [→ *5086*]. Tiberias:– Tiberias [3]

5086 **Τιβέριος, *Tiberios*,** n.pr. GK: *5501* [→ *5085*]. Tiberius:– Tiberius [1]

5087 **τίθημι, *tithēmi*,** v. GK: *5502* [→ *113, 114, 115, 121, 276, 394, 428, 475, 477, 595, 659, 802, 1242, 1303, 1570, 1620, 1936, 2007, 2111, 2336, 2653, 2698, 3331, 3346, 3548, 3549, 3550, 3559, 3560, 3734, 3866, 3872, 3908, 4025, 4060, 4286, 4287, 4323, 4369, 4388, 4783, 4784, 4934, 5206, 5294; cf. 331, 2310, 2344, 2653*]. (act.) to place, put; (pass.) to be placed or put; (mid.) to set, appoint, decide, arrange:– laid [24], put [14], lay down [8], make [6], kneeled down (+*1119+3588*) [5], lay [5], appointed [4], set [4], made [3], appoint [2], laid down [2], ordained [2], putteth [2], advised (+*1012*) [1], bowing [1], committed [1], conceived [1], giveth [1], laid aside [1], laid up [1], layedst down [1], making [1], purposed [1], put in way [1], putting [1], set forth [1], settle [1], sink down [1]

5088 **τίκτω, *tiktō***, v. GK: *5503* [→ *815, 4415, 4416, 5040, 5041, 5042, 5043, 5044, 5110, 5388; cf. 5078*]. to give birth to; bear, produce:– brought forth [4], delivered [4], born [3], bring forth [3], bringeth forth [2], bearest [1], delivered of a child [1], in travail [1]

5089 **τίλλω, *tillō***, v. GK: *5504*. to pick (heads of grain):– pluck [2], plucked [1]

5090 **Τιμαῖος, *Timaios***, n.pr. GK: *5505* [→ *5092*]. Timaeus, "*precious, valuable*":– Timeus [1]

5091 **τιμάω, *timaō***, v. GK: *5506* [→ *5092*]. to honor, show respect, give recognition:– honour [14], honoureth [4], honoured [1], valued [1], value [1]

5092 **τιμή, *timē***, n. GK: *5507* [→ *818, 819, 820, 821, 927, 1784, 2008, 2009, 2472, 4186, 5090, 5091, 5093, 5094, 5095, 5096, 5097, 5098, 5389*]. honor, value, respect; nobility, specialness; money, cost:– honour [32], price [7], honours [1], precious [1], prices [1], sum [1]

5093 **τίμιος, *timios***, a. GK: *5508* [→ *5092*]. precious, valuable, honored; costly:– precious [8], most precious [2], dear [1], honourable [1], more precious [1], reputation [1]

5094 **τιμιότης, *timiotēs***, n. GK: *5509* [→ *5092*]. wealth:– costliness [1]

5095 **Τιμόθεος, *Timotheos***, n.pr. GK: *5510* [→ *5092+2316*]. Timothy, "*precious one of God*":– Timotheus [19], Timothy [9]

5096 **Τίμων, *Timōn***, n.pr. GK: *5511* [→ *5092*]. Timon, "*precious, valuable*":– Timon [1]

5097 **τιμωρέω, *timōreō***, v. GK: *5512* [→ *5092+142*]. to punish:– punished [2]

5098 **τιμωρία, *timōria***, n. GK: *5513* [→ *5092+142*]. punishment:– punishment [1]

5099 **τίνω, *tinō***, v. GK: *5514* [→ *661*]. to pay (a price or penalty), in context the penalty is suffering:– punished (+*1349*) [1]

5100 **τὶς, *tis***, p.indef. GK: *5516* [→ *3385, 3387, 3386, 3748, 3755*]. one, anyone, anything; some, someone, something:– any [131], certain [114], some [79], one [36], man [25], a [14], ought [7], somewhat [6], something [5], whatsoever (+*302+3739*) [3], divers [2], he [2], none (+*3361*) [2], nothing (+*3361*) [2], one (+*1520*) [2], somebody [2], what [2], whose [2], another (+*243*) [1], as (+*302+3739*) [1], broken[s] pieces [1], every [1], kind [1], man's [1], matter [1], more (+*4055*) [1], no (+*3361*) [1], nothing (+*3756*) [1], nothing (+*3761*) [1], partly (+*3313*) [1], same [1], that [1], whatsoever (+*1437+3739*) [1], whatsoever (+*1437+3748+3956*) [1], whatsoever (+*302+302+3739*) [1], whatsoever [1], whomsoever (+*1437*) [1]

5101 **τίς, *tis***, p.inter. GK: *5515* [→ *1302, 1360, 2444, 2530, 3754*]. who?, what?, which?, why?:– what [258], who [101], why [66], whom [25], which [16], how [10], whose [9], whether [8], whereunto [5], nothing (+*3756*) [3], what (+*302*) [3], wherefore [3], wherewith (+*1722*) [3], every [2], what (+*687*) [2], why (+*1519*) [2], any [1], how much [1], nothing (+*3361*) [1], one [1], that [1], what (+*3739*) [1], what have I to do (+*1473*) [1], what man (+*687*) [1], what mean [1], what purpose [1], whereby (+*2596*) [1], wherefore (+*1519*) [1], wherefore (+*1752*) [1], wherefore (+*5484*) [1], whereof (+*4012*) [1], whereunto (+*302*) [1], wherewithal [1], wherewith [1], where [1], which (+*302*) [1], who (+*302*) [1]

5102 **τίτλος, *titlos***, n. GK: *5518*. sign, prepared notice, inscription:– title [2]

5103 **Τίτος, *Titos***, n.pr. GK: *5519*. Titus:– Titus [15]

τίω, *tiō*. See **5099**.

τό, *to*. See **3588**.

5104 **τοί, *toi***, pt. GK: *5520* [→ *2273, 2543, 2544, 3305, 5105, 5106*]. surely (emphasizing reliability):–

5105 **τοιγαροῦν, *toigaroun***, pt. GK: *5521* [→ *5104+1063+3767*]. therefore, then:– therefore [1], wherefore seeing [1]

τοίγε, *toige*. See **2544**.

5106 **τοίνυν, *toinyn***, pt.infer. GK: *5523* [→ *5104+3568*]. then, therefore:– therefore [3], then [1]

5107 **τοιόσδε, *toiosde***, a. GK: *5524* [→ *3588*]. such as this, of this kind:– such [1]

5108 **τοιοῦτος, *toioutos***, a. GK: *5525* [→ *3588+3778*]. such, such as this, of such a kind:– such [51], such a one [8], like occupation [1], such as (+*3697*) [1]

5109 **τοῖχος, *toichos***, n. GK: *5526* [→ *5038*]. wall:– wall [1]

5110 **τόκος, *tokos***, n. GK: *5527* [→ *5088*]. interest (on a monetary loan):– usury [2]

5111 **τολμάω, *tolmaō***, v. GK: *5528* [→ *662, 5112, 5113*]. to dare, be bold, courageous:– durst [7], bold [4], dare [4], boldly [1]

5112 **τολμηρότερον, *tolmēroteron***, adv.comp. GK: *5530* [→ *5111*]. rather boldly:– more boldly [1]

5113 **τολμητής, *tolmētēs***, n. GK: *5532* [→ *5111*]. bold man, daring man:– presumptuous [1]

5114 **τομός, *tomos***, a. GK: *5533* [→ *564, 663, 664, 823, 1371, 2699, 3718, 4059, 4061, 4932, 4935, 5009*]. cutting, sharp; (compar.) sharper:– sharper [1]

5115 **τόξον, *toxon***, n. GK: *5534* [→ *2700*]. bow (weapon):– bow [1]

5116 **τοπάζιον, *topazion***, n. GK: *5535*. topaz (a bright yellow precious stone):– topaz [1]

5117 **τόπος, *topos***, n. GK: *5536* [→ *824, 1786*]. place, location; passage (in a book); position; possibility, opportunity:– place [73], places [7], room [5], quarters [2], coasts [1], licence [1], plain (+*3977*) [1], rocks (+*5138*) [1], where [1]

5118 **τοσοῦτος, *tosoutos***, a. GK: *5537* [→ *3778*]. so great, so many, so large, so long:– so much [7], so great [5], so many [4], so long [2], all so many [1], large [1], these many [1]

5119 **τότε, *tote***, adv. GK: *5538* [→ *3739+5037*]. then, when, at that time:– then [147], that time [2], then (+*3767*) [2], after (+*5225*) [1], and (+*2532*) [1], that time forth [1], time [1], when [1]

5120 **τοῦ, *tou***, art.gen.s. of *3588*. GK: *3836* [→ *3588*]. (often not translated) his, her, its; see *3588*:–

5121 **τοὐναντίον, *tounantion***, contr. [art.+pp.*]. GK: *5539* [→ *3588+1725*]. but, on the contrary:– contrariwise [3]

5122 **τοὔνομα, *tounoma***, contr. [art.+n.]. GK: *5540* [→ *3588+3686*]. named, by name:– named [1]

5123 **τουτέστιν, *toutestin***, contr. [art.+v.]. GK: *5542* [→ *3778+1510*]. that is to say, by this we mean:–

5124 **τοῦτο, *touto***, p.demo.neut.s. of *3778*. GK: *4047* [→ *3778*]. this; see *3778*:–

5125 **τούτοις, *toutois***, p.demo.dat.pl. of *3778*. GK: *4047* [→ *3778*]. to, for, by these; see *3778*:–

5126 **τοῦτον, *touton***, p.demo.acc.s. of *3778*. GK: *4047* [→ *3778*]. this; see *3778*:–

5127 **τούτου, *toutou***, p.demo.gen.s. of *3778*. GK: *4047* [→ *3778*]. from, of this; see *3778*:–

5128 **τούτους, *toutous***, p.demo.acc.pl. of *3778*. GK: *4047* [→ *3778*]. these; see *3778*:–

5129 **τούτῳ, *toutō***, p.demo.dat.s. of *3778*. GK: *4047* [→ *3778*]. to, for, by this; see *3778*:–

5130 **τούτων, *toutōn***, p.demo.gen.pl. of *3778*. GK: *4047* [→ *3778*]. from, of these; see *3778*:–

5131 **τράγος, *tragos***, n. GK: *5543* [→ *5176*]. male goat:– goats [4]

5132 **τράπεζα, *trapeza***, n. GK: *5544* [→ *5064+3978*]. table:– table [9], tables [4], bank [1], set meat before (+*3908*) [1]

5133 **τραπεζίτης, *trapezitēs***, n. GK: *5545* [→ *5064+3978*]. banker:– exchangers [1]

5134 **τραῦμα, *trauma***, n. GK: *5546* [→ *1626, 5135*]. (pl.) wounds:– wounds [1]

5135 **τραυματίζω, *traumatizō***, v. GK: *5547* [→ *5134*]. to wound:– wounded [2]

5136 **τραχηλίζω, *trachēlizō***, v. GK: *5548* [→ *5137*]. (pass.) to be laid bare:– opened [1]

5137 **τράχηλος, *trachēlos***, n. GK: *5549* [→ *4644, 5136*]. neck, throat:– neck [6], necks [1]

5138 **τραχύς, *trachys***, a. GK: *5550* [→ *5139*]. rough, uneven:– rocks (+*5117*) [1], rough [1]

5139 **Τραχωνῖτις, *Trachōnitis***, n.pr. GK: *5551* [→ *5138*]. Traconitis, "*rough, stony district*":– Trachonitis [1]

5140 **τρεῖς, *treis***, n.num. GK: *5552* [→ *755, 5144, 5145, 5146, 5148, 5150, 5151, 5152, 5153, 5154*]. three:– three [69]

5141 **τρέμω, *tremō***, v. GK: *5554* [→ *1790, 5156*]. to tremble, fear:– trembling [3], afraid [1]

5142 **τρέφω, *trephō***, v. GK: *5555* [→ *397, 1305, 1361, 1625, 1789, 2353, 4939, 5044, 5160, 5161, 5162*]. to care for, feed, nurse; (pass.) to be nurtured, cared for:– nourished [3], feedeth [2], brought up [1], fed [1], feed [1]

5143 **τρέχω, *trechō***, v. GK: *5556* [→ *1408, 1532, 1998, 2113, 2701, 4063, 4274, 4370, 4390, 4890, 4936, 5163, 5164, 5295*]. to run; to strive, give effort:– run [10], ran [6], runneth [2], course [1], running [1]

5144 τριάκοντα, *triakonta*, n.num. GK: *5558* [→ *5140*]. thirty:– thirty [9], thirtyfold [2]

5145 τριακόσιοι, *triakosioi*, a.num. GK: *5559* [→ *5140*]. three hundred:– three hundred [2]

5146 τρίβολος, *tribolos*, n. GK: *5560* [→ *5140+906*]. thistle:– briers [1], thistles [1]

5147 τρίβος, *tribos*, n. GK: *5561* [→ *1304, 3859, 4937, 4938, 5551*]. path:– paths [3]

5148 τριετία, *trietia*, n. GK: *5562* [→ *5140+2094*]. (for) three years:– three years [1]

5149 τρίζω, *trizō*, v. GK: *5563*. to gnash, grind:– gnasheth [1]

5150 τρίμηνος, *trimēnos*, a. GK: *5564* [→ *5140+3375*]. a period of three months:– three months [1]

5151 τρίς, *tris*, adv. GK: *5565* [→ *5140*]. three times:– thrice [10], three times (*+1909*) [1], thrice (*+1909*) [1]

5152 τρίστεγον, *tristegon*, n. GK: *5566* [→ *5140+4722*]. third story (of a building):– third loft [1]

5153 τρισχίλιοι, *trischilioi*, a.num. GK: *5567* [→ *5140+5507*]. three thousand:– three thousand [1]

5154 τρίτος, *tritos*, a. GK: *5568 & 5569* [→ *5140*]. third:– third [50], third time [5], third time (*+1537*) [1], thirdly [1]

τρίχες, *triches*. See **2359**.

5155 τρίχινος, *trichinos*, a. GK: *5570* [→ *2359*]. made of hair, hairy:– of hair [1]

5156 τρόμος, *tromos*, n. GK: *5571* [→ *5141*]. trembling, fear:– trembling [4], trembled (*+2192*) [1]

5157 τροπή, *tropē*, n. GK: *5572* [→ *396, 665, 1624, 1788, 1791, 2010, 2011, 2012, 2160, 4062, 4187, 4389, 5158, 5159*]. shifting, turning, variation, change:– turning [1]

5158 τρόπος, *tropos*, n. GK: *5573* [→ *5157*]. manner, way, kind; way of life:– as (*+3739*) [3], manner [2], means [2], way [2], as (*+2596+3739*) [1], conversation [1], even as (*+2596+3739+3779*) [1], even as (*+3739*) [1]

5159 τροποφορέω, *tropophoreō*, v. GK: *5574* [→ *5157+5342*]. to endure, put up with:– suffered manners [1]

5160 τροφή, *trophē*, n. GK: *5575* [→ *5142*]. food, nourishment:– meat [13], food [2], eaten enough (*+2880*) [1]

5161 Τρόφιμος, *Trophimos*, n.pr. GK: *5576* [→ *5142*]. Trophimus, "*nourished [child]*":– Trophimus [3]

5162 τροφός, *trophos*, n. GK: *5577* [→ *5142*]. mother, nurse:– nurse [1]

5163 τροχιά, *trochia*, n. GK: *5579* [→ *5143*]. path, course:– paths [1]

5164 τροχός, *trochos*, n. GK: *5580* [→ *5143*]. wheel; (fig.) whole course (of life):– course [1]

5165 τρύβλιον, *tryblion*, n. GK: *5581*. bowl:– dish [2]

5166 τρυγάω, *trygaō*, v. GK: *5582*. to gather or pick (grapes):– gather [2], gathered [1]

5167 τρυγών, *trygōn*, n. GK: *5583*. (pl.) doves, turtledoves:– turtledoves [1]

5168 τρυμαλιά, *trymalia*, n. GK: *5584* [→ *5169*]. eye (the tear-drop shaped hole of a needle through which thread is passed):– eye [2]

5169 τρύπημα, *trypēma*, n. GK: *5585* [→ *5168*]. eye (of a needle):– eye [1]

5170 Τρύφαινα, *Tryphaina*, n.pr. GK: *5586* [→ *5172*]. Tryphena, "*dainty*":– Tryphena [1]

5171 τρυφάω, *tryphaō*, v. GK: *5587* [→ *5172*]. to live in luxury, lead a life of self-indulgence:– lived in pleasure [1]

5172 τρυφή, *tryphē*, n. GK: *5588* [→ *1792, 5170, 5171, 5173*]. luxury, splendor; carousal, indulgence, reveling:– delicately [1], riot [1]

5173 Τρυφῶσα, *Tryphōsa*, n.pr. GK: *5589* [→ *5172*]. Tryphosa, "*delicate*":– Tryphosa [1]

5174 Τρῳάς, *Trōas*, n.pr. GK: *5590*. Troas:– Troas [6]

5175 Τρωγύλλιον, *Trōgyllion*, n.pr. GK: *5591*. Trogyllium:– Trogyllium [1]

5176 τρώγω, *trōgō*, v. GK: *5592* [→ *5131*]. to eat, feed on:– eateth [5], eating [1]

5177 τυγχάνω, *tynchanō*, v. GK: *5593* [→ *1783, 1793, 2013, 2161, 3909, 4940, 4941, 5190, 5241*]. to take part in; to obtain, provide; (intr.) to happen a certain way, to be extraordinary; perhaps:– obtain [3], obtained [2], enjoy [1], it may be (*+1487*) [1], it may be [1], it may chance (*+1487*) [1], little [1], refresh (*+1958*) [1], special (*+3588+3756*) [1]

5178 τυμπανίζω, *tympanizō*, v. GK: *5594* [→ *5180*]. (pass.) to be tortured, tormented:– tortured [1]

5179 τύπος, *typos*, n. GK: *5596* [→ *5180*]. pattern, model, example, type, a visual form to be copied, such as in crafting an idol; by extension: a pattern of behavior to be emulated:– ensamples [3], ensample [2], pattern [2], print [2], examples [1], example [1], fashion [1], figures [1], figure [1], form [1], manner [1]

5180 τύπτω, *typtō*, v. GK: *5597* [→ *499, 1795, 5178, 5179, 5296*]. to strike, beat, wound:– smote [4], smite [3], beat [2], beating [1], smiteth [1], smitten [1], stroke [1], wound [1]

5181 Τύραννος[1], *Tyrannos[1]*, n.pr. GK: *5598*. Tyrannus, "*ruler*":– Tyrannus [1]

5182 τυρβάζω, *tyrbazō*, v. GK: *5600*. (mid.) trouble oneself; (pass.) to be troubled:– troubled [1]

5183 Τύριος, *Tyrios*, n.pr.g. GK: *5601* [→ *5184*]. Tyrian:– of Tyre [1]

5184 Τύρος, *Tyros*, n.pr. GK: *5602* [→ *5183*]. Tyre, "*rocky place*":– Tyre [11]

5185 τυφλός, *typhlos*, a. GK: *5603* [→ *5186*]. blind; (n.) blind person:– blind [43], blind man [7], blind men [3]

5186 τυφλόω, *typhloō*, v. GK: *5604* [→ *5185*]. to cause blindness, deprive of sight:– blinded [3]

5187 τυφόομαι, *typhoomai*, v. GK: *5605* [→ *5188*]. (pass.) to be or become conceited, implying foolishness:– highminded [1], lifted up with pride [1], proud [1]

5188 τύφω, *typhō*, v. GK: *5606* [→ *5077, 5187*]. (pass.) to smolder, smoke:– smoking [1]

5189 τυφωνικός, *typhōnikos*, a. GK: *5607*. of hurricane force:– tempestuous [1]

5190 Τυχικός, *Tychikos*, n.pr. GK: *5608* [→ *5177*]. Tychicus, "*good fortune*":– Tychicus [7]

5191 ὑακίνθινος, *hyakinthinos*, a. GK: *5610* [→ *5192*]. dark blue, *poss.* dark red:– jacinth [1]

5192 ὑάκινθος, *hyakinthos*, n. GK: *5611* [→ *5191*]. jacinth:– jacinth [1]

5193 ὑάλινος, *hyalinos*, a. GK: *5612* [→ *5194*]. of glass:– of glass [3]

5194 ὕαλος, *hyalos*, n. GK: *5613* [→ *5193*]. glass, some translate "crystal":– glass [2]

5195 ὑβρίζω, *hybrizō*, v. GK: *5614* [→ *5196*]. to insult, mistreat:– entreated spitefully [1], reproachest [1], shamefully entreated [1], spitefully entreated [1], use despitefully [1]

5196 ὕβρις, *hybris*, n. GK: *5615* [→ *1796, 5195, 5197*]. insult, mistreatment; disaster, damage:– harm [1], hurt [1], reproaches [1]

5197 ὑβριστής, *hybristēs*, n. GK: *5616* [→ *5196*]. insolent man, violent man:– despiteful [1], injurious [1]

5198 ὑγιαίνω, *hygiainō*, v. GK: *5617* [→ *5199*]. to be healthy, sound:– sound [8], whole [2], health [1], wholesome [1]

5199 ὑγιής, *hygiēs*, a. GK: *5618* [→ *5198*]. healthy, sound, well:– whole [13], sound [1]

5200 ὑγρός, *hygros*, a. GK: *5619* [→ *5205*]. moist, green:– green [1]

5201 ὑδρία, *hydria*, n. GK: *5620* [→ *5204*]. water jar:– waterpots [2], waterpot [1]

5202 ὑδροποτέω, *hydropoteō*, v. GK: *5621* [→ *5204+4095*]. to drink water (exclusively):– drink water [1]

5203 ὑδρωπικός, *hydrōpikos*, a. GK: *5622* [→ *5204*]. suffering from dropsy (edema, abnormal swelling from accumulated fluids):– had the dropsy [1]

5204 ὕδωρ, *hydōr*, n. GK: *5623* [→ *504, 5201, 5202, 5203; cf. 5205*]. water:– water [64], waters [15]

5205 ὑετός, *hyetos*, n. GK: *5624* [→ *5200; cf. 5204*]. rain:– rain [5], rain (*+1026*) [1]

5206 υἱοθεσία, *huiothesia*, n. GK: *5625* [→ *5207+5087*]. adoption as sons, sonship; in NT culture a son received greater inheritance and honor, but in Christ men and women inherit equally:– adoption [3], adoption of children [1], adoption of sons [1]

5207 υἱός, *huios*, n. GK: *5626* [→ *5206*]. son, child (of either gender), descendant (in any generation); by extension: a term of endearment; one of a class or kind, for example, a "son of the resurrection" is one who participates in the resurrection. "The Son of Man" is an OT phrase usually meaning "human being," that in the NT is used almost exclusively as a messianic title (see Da 7:13), emphasizing Jesus' humanity:– son [306], children [47], sons [24], child [3], foal [1]

5208 ὕλη, *hylē*, n. GK: *5627* [→ *1368*]. forest, wood:– matter [1]

5209 ὑμᾶς, *humas*, p.pers.acc.pl. of *4771*. GK: *5148* [→ *4771*]. you, your; see *4771*:–

5210 ὑμεῖς, *humeis*, p.pers.nom.pl. of *4771*. GK: *5148* [→ *4771*]. you, your; see *4771*:–

5211 Ὑμέναιος, ***Hymenaios***, n.pr. GK: *5628*. Hymenaeus, "*of [pagan god] Hymen*":– Hymeneus [2]

5212 ὑμέτερος, ***hymeteros***, a. GK: *5629* [→ *4771*]. (pl.) your, your own:– your [7], yours [2], your own [1]

5213 ὑμῖν, ***humin***, p.pers.dat.pl. of *4771*. GK: *5148* [→ *4771*]. you, your; see *4771*:–

5214 ὑμνέω, ***hymneō***, v. GK: *5630* [→ *5215*]. to sing hymns, sing praises:– sung a hymn [2], sang praises [1], sing praise [1]

5215 ὕμνος, ***hymnos***, n. GK: *5631* [→ *5214*]. hymn, song of praise:– hymns [2]

5216 ὑμῶν, ***humōn***, p.pers.gen.pl. of *4771*. GK: *5148* [→ *4771*]. you, your; see *4771*:–

5217 ὑπάγω, ***hypagō***, v. GK: *5632* [→ *5259+71*]. to go (away):– go [53], goeth [9], goest [5], went [4], get [3], go away [2], departing [1], depart [1], get hence [1], going [1], went away [1]

5218 ὑπακοή, ***hypakoē***, n. GK: *5633* [→ *5259+191*]. obedience:– obedience [11], obedient [2], obeying [1], obey [1]

5219 ὑπακούω, ***hypakouō***, v. GK: *5634* [→ *5259+191*]. to obey, be obedient; to answer (the door):– obey [13], obeyed [5], obedient [2], hearken [1]

5220 ὕπανδρος, ***hypandros***, a. GK: *5635* [→ *5259+435*]. married, legally bound to a man in marriage:– husband [1]

5221 ὑπαντάω, ***hypantaō***, v. GK: *5636* [→ *5259+473*]. to go out to meet; to oppose:– met [4], went and met [1]

5222 ὑπάντησις, ***hypantēsis***, n. GK: *5637* [→ *5259+473*]. meeting:– meet [1]

5223 ὕπαρξις, ***hyparxis***, n. GK: *5638* [→ *5259+757*]. property, goods, possessions:– goods [1], substance [1]

5224 ὑπάρχοντα, ***huparchonta***, v.ptcp. of *5225*. GK: *5639* [→ *5259+757*]. possessions, property:–

5225 ὑπάρχω, ***hyparchō***, v. GK: *5639* [→ *5259+757*]. to have, possess; (n.) possessions; to be, exist:– being [13], was [8], be [7], goods [7], is [6], were [5], are [3], hath [2], have [2], after (*+5119*) [1], hast [1], live [1], possessed [1], possesseth [1], substance [1]

5226 ὑπείκω, ***hypeikō***, v. GK: *5640* [→ *5259+1502*]. to submit, yield:– submit [1]

5227 ὑπεναντίος, ***hypenantios***, a. GK: *5641* [→ *5259+1725*]. opposing, being against; (n.) enemy:– adversaries [1], contrary [1]

5228 ὑπέρ, ***hyper***, pp. GK: *5642* [→ *5229, 5230, 5231, 5232, 5233, 5234, 5235, 5236, 5237, 5238, 5239, 5240, 5241, 5242, 5243, 5244, 5245, 5246, 5247, 5248, 5249, 5250, 5251, 5252, 5253*]. (acc.) above, beyond, more than; (gen.) for, in behalf of, for the sake of; in place of:– for [104], above [12], of [12], for sake [7], more than [3], on behalf [3], very [3], than [2], beyond [1], by [1], concerning [1], exceedingly (*+1537+4053*) [1], exceeding [1], for sakes [1], in behalf of [1], in stead [1], more [1], on part [1], over [1], stead [1], toward [1], to [1]

5229 ὑπεραίρομαι, ***hyperairomai***, v. GK: *5643* [→ *5228+142*]. to become conceited, exalt oneself:– exalted above measure [2], exalteth [1]

5230 ὑπέρακμος, ***hyperakmos***, a. GK: *5644* [→ *5228+206*]. past one's prime, getting along in years:– pass the flower of age (*+1510*) [1]

5231 ὑπεράνω, ***hyperanō***, adv. GK: *5645* [→ *5228+507*]. far above, high above:– far above [2], over [1]

5232 ὑπεραυξάνω, ***hyperauxanō***, v. GK: *5647* [→ *5228+837*]. to grow more and more, increase abundantly:– groweth exceedingly [1]

5233 ὑπερβαίνω, ***hyperbainō***, v. GK: *5648* [→ *5228+305*]. to wrong, transgress against, sin against:– go beyond [1]

5234 ὑπερβαλλόντως, ***hyperballontōs***, adv. GK: *5649* [→ *5228+906*]. more severely, to a much greater degree:– above measure [1]

5235 ὑπερβάλλω, ***hyperballō***, v. GK: *5650* [→ *5228+906*]. to go beyond, surpass, be incomparable:– exceeding [3], excelleth [1], passeth [1]

5236 ὑπερβολή, ***hyperbolē***, n. GK: *5651* [→ *5228+906*]. all-surpassing, surpassingly great, most excellent, beyond measure:– far more exceeding (*+1519+2596+5236*) [2], abundance [1], beyond measure (*+2596*) [1], exceeding (*+2596*) [1], excellency [1], more excellent (*+2596*) [1], out of measure (*+2596*) [1]

5237 ὑπερείδω, ***hypereidō***, v. GK: *5653* [→ *5228+1491*]. to overlook, not punish:– winked at [1]

5238 ὑπερέκεινα, ***hyperekeina***, adv. GK: *5654* [→ *5228+1563*]. beyond; (n.) regions beyond:– beyond [1]

5239 ὑπερεκτείνω, ***hyperekteinō***, v. GK: *5657* [→ *1614; cf. 5228*]. to go too far, overextend, stretch out beyond:– stretch beyond [1]

5240 ὑπερεκχύννω, ***hyperekchynnō***, v. GK: *5658* [→ *1632*]. (pass.) to be running over, overflowing:– running over [1]

ὑπερεκπερισσοῦ, ***huperekperissou***. See ***5228*** and ***1537*** and ***4053***.

5241 ὑπερεντυγχάνω, ***hyperentynchanō***, v. GK: *5659* [→ *5228+1722+5177*]. to intercede:– maketh intercession [1]

5242 ὑπερέχω, ***hyperechō***, v. GK: *5660* [→ *5228+2192*]. to govern, have authority; to be better than, transcend; (n.) surpassing greatness:– better than [1], excellency [1], higher [1], passeth [1], supreme [1]

5243 ὑπερηφανία, ***hyperēphania***, n. GK: *5661* [→ *5228+5316*]. arrogance, pride:– pride [1]

5244 ὑπερήφανος, ***hyperēphanos***, a. GK: *5662* [→ *5228+5316*]. proud, arrogant:– proud [5]

ὑπερλίαν, ***huperlian***. See ***5228*** and ***3029***.

5245 ὑπερνικάω, ***hypernikaō***, v. GK: *5664* [→ *5228+3529*]. to thoroughly conquer, go beyond conquest:– more than conquerors [1]

5246 ὑπέρογκος, ***hyperonkos***, a. GK: *5665* [→ *5228+3591*]. boastful, bombastic:– great swelling [2]

5247 ὑπεροχή, ***hyperochē***, n. GK: *5667* [→ *5228+2192*]. authority, superiority:– authority [1], excellency [1]

5248 ὑπερπερισσεύω, ***hyperperisseuō***, v. GK: *5668* [→ *5228+4053*]. to increase all the more, exceed bounds, overflow:– exceeding [1], much more abound [1]

5249 ὑπερπερισσῶς, ***hyperperissōs***, adv. GK: *5669* [→ *5228+4053*]. beyond all measure, exceedingly:– beyond measure [1]

5250 ὑπερπλεονάζω, ***hyperpleonazō***, v. GK: *5670* [→ *5228+4137*]. to be (greatly) abundant:– exceeding abundant [1]

5251 ὑπερυψόω, ***hyperypsoō***, v. GK: *5671* [→ *5228+5311*]. to exalt to the highest place:– highly exalted [1]

5252 ὑπερφρονέω, ***hyperphroneō***, v. GK: *5672* [→ *5228+5424*]. to think too highly of oneself:– think highly [1]

5253 ὑπερῷον, ***hyperōon***, n. GK: *5673* [→ *5228*]. upstairs room, upper story:– upper chamber [3], upper room [1]

5254 ὑπέχω, ***hypechō***, v. GK: *5674* [→ *5259+2192*]. to experience:– suffering [1]

5255 ὑπήκοος, ***hypēkoos***, a. GK: *5675* [→ *5259+191*]. obedient:– obedient [2], obey (*+1096*) [1]

5256 ὑπηρετέω, ***hypēreteō***, v. GK: *5676* [→ *5257*]. to serve, care for needs:– ministered [1], minister [1], served [1]

5257 ὑπηρέτης, ***hypēretēs***, n. GK: *5677* [→ *5256; cf. 5259*]. servant, attendant, helper, one who serves or attends, not distinguished in status from other words for servant:– officers [10], servants [4], minister [3], ministers [2], officer [1]

5258 ὕπνος, ***hypnos***, n. GK: *5678* [→ *69, 70, 879, 1797, 1798, 1852, 1853*]. sleep, slumber:– sleep [6]

5259 ὑπό, ***hypo***, pp. GK: *5679* [→ *505, 506, 4391, 4942, 4943, 5217, 5218, 5219, 5220, 5221, 5222, 5223, 5224, 5225, 5226, 5227, 5254, 5255, 5260, 5261, 5262, 5263, 5264, 5265, 5266, 5267, 5268, 5269, 5270, 5271, 5272, 5273, 5274, 5275, 5276, 5277, 5278, 5279, 5280, 5281, 5282, 5283, 5284, 5285, 5286, 5287, 5288, 5289, 5290, 5291, 5292, 5293, 5294, 5295, 5296, 5297, 5298, 5299; cf. 5257*]. (gen.) by, by means of; (acc.) under (in space as well as in status or authority); at (a time of day):– of [117], under [48], by [42], with [14], from [2], among [1], early in the morning (*+3588+3722*) [1], into [1], unto [1], whereof [1]

5260 ὑποβάλλω, ***hypoballō***, v. GK: *5680* [→ *5259+906*]. to secretly persuade, instigate secretly:– suborned [1]

5261 ὑπογραμμός, ***hypogrammos***, n. GK: *5681* [→ *5259+1125*]. example, model:– example [1]

5262 ὑπόδειγμα, ***hypodeigma***, n. GK: *5682* [→ *5259+1164*]. example, model, pattern, copy:– example [4], ensample [1], patterns [1]

5263 ὑποδείκνυμι, ***hypodeiknymi***, v. GK: *5683 & 5684* [→ *5259+1166*]. to show; to warn:– shew [2], warned [2], forewarn [1], shewed [1]

5264 ὑποδέχομαι, ***hypodechomai***, v. GK: *5685* [→ *5259+1209*]. to welcome, receive as a guest:– received [4]

5265 ὑποδέω, ***hypodeō***, v. GK: *5686* [→ *5259+1210*]. (mid.) to put on (sandals):– shod [2], bind on [1]

5266 ὑπόδημα, ***hypodēma***, n. GK: *5687* [→ *5259+1210*]. sandal:– shoes [9], shoe's [1]

5267 ὑπόδικος, ***hypodikos***, a. GK: *5688* [→ *5259+1349*]. accountable, answerable:– guilty before [1]

5268 ὑποζύγιον, ***hypozygion***, n. GK: *5689* [→ *5259+2218*]. donkey:– ass [2]

5269 ὑποζώννυμι, hypozōnnymi, v. GK: *5690* [→ *5259+2224*]. to undergird, brace:– undergirding [1]

5270 ὑποκάτω, hypokatō, adv. GK: *5691* [→ *5259+2596*]. (pp.*) under:– under [9]

5271 ὑποκρίνομαι, hypokrinomai, v. GK: *5693* [→ *5259+2919*]. to pretend, make believe; see also *5273*:– feign [1]

5272 ὑπόκρισις, hypokrisis, n. GK: *5694* [→ *5259+2919*]. hypocrisy (an extension of an actor in a play, not found in the NT), implying arrogance and hardness of heart, utterly devoid of sincerity and genuineness:– hypocrisy [4], dissimulation [1], hypocrisies [1]

5273 ὑποκριτής, hypokritēs, n. GK: *5695* [→ *5259+2919*]. hypocrite (an extension of an actor in a play, not found in the NT), implying arrogance and hardness of heart, utterly devoid of sincerity and genuineness:– hypocrites [17], hypocrite [3]

5274 ὑπολαμβάνω, hypolambanō, v. GK: *5696* [→ *5259+2983*]. to take up; to show hospitality; to reply; to suppose, think, believe:– suppose [2], answering [1], received [1]

5275 ὑπολείπω, hypoleipō, v. GK: *5699* [→ *5259+3007*]. (pass.) to be left, remaining:– left [1]

5276 ὑπολήνιον, hypolēnion, n. GK: *5700* [→ *5259+3025*]. pit for a winepress:– winefat [1]

5277 ὑπολιμπάνω, hypolimpanō, v. GK: *5701* [→ *5259+3007*]. to leave behind:– leaving [1]

5278 ὑπομένω, hypomenō, v. GK: *5702* [→ *5259+3306*]. to stay behind; to stand firm, endure, persevere:– endure [5], endured [3], endureth [3], take it patiently [2], abode still [1], patient [1], suffer [1], tarried behind [1]

5279 ὑπομιμνήσκω, hypomimnēskō, v. GK: *5703* [→ *5259+3421*]. to remind, call to mind; (pass.) to remember:– put in remembrance [3], bring to remembrance [1], put in mind [1], remembered [1], remember [1]

5280 ὑπόμνησις, hypomnēsis, n. GK: *5704* [→ *5259+3421*]. reminder, memory, remembrance:– remembrance [2], putting in remembrance [1]

5281 ὑπομονή, hypomonē, n. GK: *5705* [→ *5259+3306*]. perseverance, endurance, patience:– patience [29], enduring [1], patient continuance [1], patient waiting [1]

5282 ὑπονοέω, hyponoeō, v. GK: *5706* [→ *5259+3563*]. to think, suppose; expect; to sense, suspect:– deemed [1], supposed [1], think [1]

5283 ὑπόνοια, hyponoia, n. GK: *5707* [→ *5259+3563*]. suspicion:– surmisings [1]

5284 ὑποπλέω, hypopleō, v. GK: *5709* [→ *5259+4126*]. to sail to the lee of, to move to the side that offers protection or shelter:– sailed under [2]

5285 ὑποπνέω, hypopneō, v. GK: *5710* [→ *5259+4154*]. to blow gently (of wind):– blew softly [1]

5286 ὑποπόδιον, hypopodion, n. GK: *5711* [→ *5259+4228*]. footstool:– footstool [9]

5287 ὑπόστασις, hypostasis, n. GK: *5712* [→ *5259+2476*]. confidence, trust, being sure; being, essence:– confidence [2], confident [1], person [1], substance [1]

5288 ὑποστέλλω, hypostellō, v. GK: *5713* [→ *5259+4724*]. (act.) to draw back, withdraw; (mid.) to hesitate, shrink back:– draw back [1], kept back [1], shunned [1], withdrew [1]

5289 ὑποστολή, hypostolē, n. GK: *5714* [→ *5259+4724*]. shrinking back:– draw back [1]

5290 ὑποστρέφω, hypostrephō, v. GK: *5715* [→ *5259+4762*]. to turn back toward, return; to turn one's back on, turn away:– returned [24], return [5], returning [3], come again [1], turned back again [1], turned back [1]

5291 ὑποστρωννύω, hypostrōnnyō, v. GK: *5716* [→ *5259+4766*]. to spread out:– spread [1]

5292 ὑποταγή, hypotagē, n. GK: *5717* [→ *5259+5021*]. obedience, submission:– subjection [4]

5293 ὑποτάσσω, hypotassō, v. GK: *5718* [→ *5259+5021*]. to put in subjection, subject, subordinate; (pass.) to submit, be subject to:– subject [10], submit [6], put under [4], made subject [2], obedient [2], put in subjection [2], put [2], subject to [2], subjection [2], in subjection [1], put in subjection under [1], subdued [1], subdue [1], subjected [1], submitted [1], submitting [1], under obedience [1]

5294 ὑποτίθημι, hypotithēmi, v. GK: *5719* [→ *5259+5087*]. (act.) to risk, lay down (a life); (mid.) to point out, teach:– laid down [1], put in remembrance [1]

5295 ὑποτρέχω, hypotrechō, v. GK: *5720* [→ *5259+5143*]. to sail to the lee of, to move to the side that offers protection or shelter:– running under [1]

5296 ὑποτύπωσις, hypotypōsis, n. GK: *5721* [→ *5259+5180*]. example, pattern:– form [1], pattern [1]

5297 ὑποφέρω, hypopherō, v. GK: *5722* [→ *5259+5342*]. to endure, bear up under, stand up under:– bear [1], endured [1], endure [1]

5298 ὑποχωρέω, hypochōreō, v. GK: *5723* [→ *5259+5562*]. to withdraw, retreat:– went aside [1], withdrew [1]

5299 ὑπωπιάζω, hypōpiazō, v. GK: *5708 & 5724* [→ *5259+3708*]. to wear out, weaken; to beat up, treat roughly:– keep under [1], weary [1]

5300 ὗς, hys, n. GK: *5725*. female pig, sow:– sow [1]

5301 ὕσσωπος, hyssōpos, n. GK: *5727*. hyssop, highly aromatic leaves used in purification rites and at Passover:– hyssop [2]

5302 ὑστερέω, hystereō, v. GK: *5728* [→ *5306*]. to lack, be in need, destitute; to be inferior; to fall short:– behind [2], come short [2], lacked [2], wanted [2], come behind [1], destitute [1], fail [1], in want [1], lackest [1], lack [1], suffer need [1], worse [1]

5303 ὑστέρημα, hysterēma, n. GK: *5729* [→ *5306*]. what is lacking; poverty; what is needed:– lacking [3], want [3], behind [1], lack [1], penury [1]

5304 ὑστέρησις, hysterēsis, n. GK: *5730* [→ *5306*]. need, poverty, lack:– want [2]

5305 ὕστερον, husteron, a.neut. of *5306*. GK: *5731* [→ *5306*]. finally, last of all:–

5306 ὕστερος, hysteros, a. GK: *5731* [→ *5302, 5303, 5304, 5305*]. (comp.) later, second; (neu.) finally, last of all:– afterward [7], last [3], afterwards [1], at the last [1], latter [1]

5307 ὑφαντός, hyphantos, a. GK: *5733*. woven:– woven [1]

5308 ὑψηλός, hypsēlos, a. GK: *5734* [→ *5311*]. high, mighty; proud, arrogant; highly valued; (compar.) more exalted:– high [9], higher than [1], highly esteemed [1]

5309 ὑψηλοφρονέω, hypsēlophroneō, v. GK: *5735* [→ *5311+5424*]. to be arrogant, proud:– highminded [2]

5310 ὕψιστος, hypsistos, a. GK: *5736* [→ *5311*]. highest, most exalted; (as a title of God) the Most High:– highest [8], most high [5]

5311 ὕψος, hypsos, n. GK: *5737* [→ *5251, 5308, 5309, 5310, 5312, 5313*]. height, high position, heaven:– height [2], on high [2], exalted [1], high [1]

5312 ὑψόω, hypsoō, v. GK: *5738* [→ *5311*]. to lift up, elevate, exalt:– exalted [10], lift up [3], lifted up [3], exalteth [2], exalt [2]

5313 ὕψωμα, hypsōma, n. GK: *5739* [→ *5311*]. height; pretension:– height [1], high [1]

5314 φάγος, phagos, n. GK: *5741* [→ *4371; cf. 2068*]. glutton:– gluttonous [2]

5315 φάγω, phagō, v. GK: *2266* [→ *2068*]. to eat, consume, devour:– eat [88], eaten [5], meat [3], eating [1]

φαιλόνης, **phailonēs**. Alternate spelling of **5341**.

5316 φαίνω, phainō, v. GK: *5743* [→ *398, 852, 853, 854, 855, 1307, 1717, 1718, 2014, 2015, 2016, 2017, 2020, 2726, 4392, 4811, 5243, 5244, 5318, 5319, 5320, 5321, 5322, 5324, 5325, 5326, 5334?, 5335?, 5402, 5457, 5458, 5459, 5460, 5461, 5462*]. (act.) to shine, give light; (mid./pass.) to appear, be visible;:– appear [9], appeared [5], shineth [5], appeareth [3], shine [3], seen [2], seemed [1], shining [1], shone [1], think [1]

5317 Φάλεκ, Phalek, n.pr. GK: *5744*. Peleg, "*water canal*":– Phalec [1]

5318 φανερός, phaneros, a. GK: *5745* [→ *5316*]. visible, clear, plain, known:– manifest [9], known [3], openly (*+1722*) [3], abroad (*+1519*) [2], appear [1], outward (*+1722+3588*) [1], outwardly (*+1722+3588*) [1], spread abroad [1]

5319 φανερόω, phaneroō, v. GK: *5746* [→ *5316*]. (act.) to reveal, make known, show; (pass.) to appear, be disclosed, displayed, revealed:– made manifest [15], appear [9], manifested [9], shewed [4], appeared [3], make manifest [3], manifest [2], maketh manifest [1], manifested forth [1], manifestly declared [1], shew [1]

5320 φανερῶς, phanerōs, adv. GK: *5747* [→ *5316*]. openly, publicly:– openly [2], evidently [1]

5321 φανέρωσις, phanerōsis, n. GK: *5748* [→ *5316*]. manifestation, disclosure, revelation:– manifestation [2]

5322 φανός, phanos, n. GK: *5749* [→ *5316*]. torch, lantern:– lanterns [1]

5323 Φανουήλ, Phanouēl, n.pr. GK: *5750*. Phanuel, "*face of God [El]*":– Phanuel [1]

5324 **φαντάζω, *phantazō***, v. GK: *5751* [→ *5316*]. (pass.) to become visible; (n.) a sight:– sight [1]

5325 **φαντασία, *phantasia***, n. GK: *5752* [→ *5316*]. pomp, pageantry:– pomp [1]

5326 **φάντασμα, *phantasma***, n. GK: *5753* [→ *5316*]. ghost, apparition, transliterated as "phantasm":– spirit [2]

5327 **φάραγξ, *pharanx***, n. GK: *5754*. valley, ravine:– valley [1]

5328 **Φαραώ, *Pharaō***, n.pr. GK: *5755*. Pharaoh, "*the great house*":– Pharaoh [3], Pharaoh's [2]

5329 **Φαρές, *Phares***, n.pr. GK: *5756*. Perez, "*breaking out*":– Phares [3]

5330 **Φαρισαῖος, *Pharisaios***, n.pr. GK: *5757*. Pharisee, "*separate ones*":– Pharisees [86], Pharisee [11], Pharisee's [2], Pharisees' [1]

5331 **φαρμακεία, *pharmakeia***, n. GK: *5758* [→ *5332, 5333*]. witchcraft, magic, the use of spells and potions of magic, often involving drugs:– sorceries [2], witchcraft [1]

5332 **φαρμακεύς, *pharmakeus***, n. GK: *5759* [→ *5331*]. magician, sorcerer:– sorcerers [1]

5333 **φάρμακος, *pharmakos***, n. GK: *5761* [→ *5331*]. one who practices magical arts, magician:– sorcerers [1]

5334 **φάσις, *phasis***, n. GK: *5762* [→ *5346 or* 5316]. news, report:– tidings [1]

5335 **φάσκω, *phaskō***, v. GK: *5763* [→ *5346 or* 5316]. to claim, assert:– affirmed [1], professing [1], saying [1], say [1]

5336 **φάτνη, *phatnē***, n. GK: *5764*. manger, stall:– manger [3], stall [1]

5337 **φαῦλος, *phaulos***, a. GK: *5765*. evil, bad:– evil [4]

5338 **φέγγος, *phengos***, n. GK: *5766*. light, radiance:– light [3]

5339 **φείδομαι, *pheidomai***, v. GK: *5767* [→ *857, 5340*]. to spare, refrain from:– spared [4], spare [4], forbear [1], sparing [1]

5340 **φειδομένως, *pheidomenōs***, adv. GK: *5768* [→ *5339*]. sparingly:– sparingly [2]

5341 **φελόνης, *phelonēs***; or **φαιλόνης, *phailonēs***, n. GK: *5742 & 5769*. cloak:– cloke [1]

5342 **φέρω, *pherō***, v. GK: *5770* [→ *399, 667, 670, 959, 1308, 1313, 1336, 1533, 1627, 2018, 2164, 2287, 2592, 2593, 2702, 3683, 3911, 3923, 4064, 4135, 4136, 4216, 4374, 4376, 4393, 4851, 5052, 5159, 5297, 5409, 5411, 5412, 5413, 5414, 5459*]. to bring, bear, carry; lead:– brought [16], bring [14], bear [4], bringing [3], came [3], beareth [2], bring forth [2], bringeth forth [2], reach [2], bare [1], bearing [1], be [1], bring hither [1], brought forth [1], carry [1], driven [1], endured [1], endure [1], go on [1], laid [1], leadeth [1], let drive (+*1929*) [1], moved [1], rushing [1], upholding [1]

5343 **φεύγω, *pheugō***, v. GK: *5771* [→ *668, 1309, 1628, 2703, 5437*]. flee, escape, elude:– flee [15], fled [11], escaped [2], fleeth [2], escape [1]

5344 **Φῆλιξ, *Phēlix***, n.pr. GK: *5772*. Felix, "*fortunate, lucky*":– Felix [8], Felix' [1]

5345 **φήμη, *phēmē***, n. GK: *5773* [→ *5346*]. news, report:– fame [2]

5346 **φημί, *phēmi***, v. GK: *5774* [→ *1310, 2162, 2163, 4394, 4852, 5334?, 5335?, 5345; cf. 987, 1426, 4394*]. to say, declare, affirm:– said [47], saith [5], say [5], affirm [1]

5347 **Φῆστος, *Phēstos***, n.pr. GK: *5776*. Festus, "*festal, joyful*":– Festus [12], Festus' [1]

5348 **φθάνω, *phthanō***, v. GK: *5777* [→ *4372?, 4373?, 4399*]. to precede; to arrive, attain, come:– come [4], attained [2], prevent [1]

5349 **φθαρτός, *phthartos***, a. GK: *5778* [→ *5351*]. perishable, not lasting, mortal:– corruptible [6]

5350 **φθέγγομαι, *phthengomai***, v. GK: *5779* [→ *669, 5353*]. to speak, proclaim:– speak [2], speaking [1]

5351 **φθείρω, *phtheirō***, v. GK: *5780* [→ *90, 861, 862, 1311, 1312, 2704, 5349, 5352, 5356*]. to destroy, corrupt; (pass.) to be corrupted, destroyed, perish; to be led astray:– corrupt [4], corrupted [2], defile [1], destroy [1]

5352 **φθινοπωρινός, *phthinopōrinos***, a. GK: *5781* [→ *5351+3703*]. pertaining to the (late) autumn:– fruit withereth [1]

5353 **φθόγγος, *phthongos***, n. GK: *5782* [→ *5350*]. voice, sound; note, musical tone:– sounds [1], sound [1]

5354 **φθονέω, *phthoneō***, v. GK: *5783* [→ *5355*]. to envy, be jealous of:– envying [1]

5355 **φθόνος, *phthonos***, n. GK: *5784* [→ *5354*]. envy:– envy [7], envies [1], envyings [1]

5356 **φθορά, *phthora***, n. GK: *5785* [→ *5351*]. perishableness, destruction, corruption; depravity:– corruption [7], destroyed [1], perish [1]

5357 **φιάλη, *phialē***, n. GK: *5786*. bowl:– vial [7], vials [5]

5358 **φιλάγαθος, *philagathos***, a. GK: *5787* [→ *5384+18*]. loving what is good:– lover of good [1]

5359 **Φιλαδέλφεια, *Philadelpheia***, n.pr. GK: *5788* [→ *5384+80; cf. 1.3*]. Philadelphia, "*love of brother/sister*":– Philadelphia [2]

5360 **φιλαδελφία, *philadelphia***, n. GK: *5789* [→ *5384+80; cf. 1.3*]. brotherly love; brotherly kindness:– brotherly love [3], brotherly kindness [2], love of brethren [1]

5361 **φιλάδελφος, *philadelphos***, a. GK: *5790* [→ *5384+80; cf. 1.3*]. loving as brothers:– love as brethren [1]

5362 **φίλανδρος, *philandros***, a. GK: *5791* [→ *5384+435*]. loving one's husband:– love husbands (+*1510*) [1]

5363 **φιλανθρωπία, *philanthrōpia***, n. GK: *5792* [→ *5384+444*]. love, kindness:– kindness [1], love toward man [1]

5364 **φιλανθρώπως, *philanthrōpōs***, adv. GK: *5793* [→ *5384+444*]. in kindness, kindly:– courteously [1]

5365 **φιλαργυρία, *philargyria***, n. GK: *5794* [→ *5384+696*]. love of money, avarice, greed:– love of money [1]

5366 **φιλάργυρος, *philargyros***, a. GK: *5795* [→ *5384+696*]. money-loving, avaricious, greedy:– covetous [2]

5367 **φίλαυτος, *philautos***, a. GK: *5796* [→ *5384+846*]. loving oneself, selfish:– lovers of own selves [1]

5368 **φιλέω, *phileō***, v. GK: *5797* [→ *5384*]. to love, to have affection and regard of a very high order, not unlike *26*, and overlapping in meaning in some contexts:– love [10], loveth [6], kiss [3], loved [3], lovest [3]

5369 **φιλήδονος, *philēdonos***, a. GK: *5798* [→ *5384+2237*]. loving pleasure:– lovers of pleasures [1]

5370 **φίλημα, *philēma***, n. GK: *5799* [→ *5384*]. kiss:– kiss [7]

5371 **Φιλήμων, *Philēmōn***, n.pr. GK: *5800* [→ *5384*]. Philemon, "*beloved*":– Philemon [2]

5372 **Φίλητος, *Philētos***, n.pr. GK: *5801* [→ *5384*]. Philetus, "*beloved*":– Philetus [1]

5373 **φιλία, *philia***, n. GK: *5802* [→ *5384*]. friendship, love:– friendship [1]

5374 **Φιλιππήσιος, *Philippēsios***, n.pr.g. GK: *5803* [→ *5384+2462*]. Philippian:– Philippians [2]

5375 **Φίλιπποι, *Philippoi***, n.pr. GK: *5804* [→ *5384+2462*]. Philippi:– Philippi [6]

5376 **Φίλιππος, *Philippos***, n.pr. GK: *5805* [→ *5384+2462*]. Philip, "*horse lover*":– Philip [33], Philip's [3], Philippi [2]

5377 **φιλόθεος, *philotheos***, a. GK: *5806* [→ *5384+2316*]. loving God:– lovers of God [1]

5378 **Φιλόλογος, *Philologos***, n.pr. GK: *5807* [→ *5384+3004*]. Philologus, "*lover of words [education]*":– Philologus [1]

5379 **φιλονεικία, *philoneikia***, n. GK: *5808* [→ *5380; cf. 5384*]. dispute, strife:– strife [1]

5380 **φιλόνεικος, *philoneikos***, a. GK: *5809* [→ *5379*]. contentious, quarrelsome:– contentious [1]

5381 **φιλοξενία, *philoxenia***, n. GK: *5810* [→ *5384+3581*]. hospitality, entertainment of strangers:– entertain strangers [1], hospitality [1]

5382 **φιλόξενος, *philoxenos***, a. GK: *5811* [→ *5384+3581*]. hospitable:– given to hospitality [1], hospitality [1], lover of hospitality [1]

5383 **φιλοπρωτεύω, *philoprōteuō***, v. GK: *5812* [→ *5384+4413*]. to love to be first:– loveth to have preeminence among [1]

5384 **φίλος, *philos***, a. GK: *5813* [→ *865, 866, 2321, 2705, 4375, 5358, 5359, 5360, 5361, 5362, 5363, 5364, 5365, 5366, 5367, 5368, 5369, 5370, 5371, 5372, 5373, 5374, 5375, 5376, 5377, 5378, 5381, 5382, 5383, 5385, 5386, 5387, 5388, 5389, 5390, 5391; cf. 5379*]. (a.) friendly; (n.) friend (male or female):– friends [17], friend [12]

5385 **φιλοσοφία, *philosophia***, n. GK: *5814* [→ *5384+4680*]. philosophy, human wisdom:– philosophy [1]

5386 **φιλόσοφος, *philosophos***, n. GK: *5815* [→ *5384+4680*]. philosopher:– philosophers [1]

5387 **φιλόστοργος, *philostorgos***, a. GK: *5816* [→ *5384*]. devoted, loving dearly:– kindly affectioned [1]

5388 **φιλότεκνος, *philoteknos***, a. GK: *5817* [→ *5384+5088*]. loving one's children:– love children [1]

5389 **φιλοτιμέομαι, *philotimeomai***, v. GK: *5818* [→ *5384+5092*]. to have an ambition, aspire to a goal:– labour [1], strived [1], study [1]

5390 φιλοφρόνως, *philophronōs*, adv. GK: *5819* [→ *5384+5424*]. hospitably, in a friendly manner:– courteously [1]

5391 φιλόφρων, *philophrōn*, a. GK: *5820* [→ *5384+5424*]. well disposed, friendly, kind:– courteous [1]

5392 φιμόω, *phimoō*, v. GK: *5821*. to muzzle; to silence; (pass.) to be quiet:– hold peace [2], muzzle [2], put to silence [2], speechless [1], still [1]

5393 Φλέγων, *Phlegōn*, n.pr. GK: *5823* [→ *5395*]. Phlegon, "*burning*":– Phlegon [1]

5394 φλογίζω, *phlogizō*, v. GK: *5824* [→ *5395*]. to set on fire:– set on fire [1], setteth on fire [1]

5395 φλόξ, *phlox*, n. GK: *5825* [→ *5393, 5394*]. flame, blaze:– flame [6], flaming [1]

5396 φλυαρέω, *phlyareō*, v. GK: *5826* [→ *5397*]. to gossip, talk nonsense:– prating against [1]

5397 φλύαρος, *phlyaros*, a. GK: *5827* [→ *3632, 5396*]. gossipy:– tattlers [1]

5398 φοβερός, *phoberos*, a. GK: *5829* [→ *5401*]. fearful, dreadful, terrible:– fearful [2], terrible [1]

5399 φοβέω, *phobeō*, v. GK: *5828 & 5830* [→ *5401*]. to fear, be afraid, alarmed, in some contexts improper and an impediment to faith and love; to reverence, respect, worship, in other contexts a proper fear for God, a deep reverence and awe:– fear [35], afraid [28], feared [17], fearing [6], feareth [4], afraid (+*5401*) [1], feared (+*5401*) [1], reverence [1]

5400 φόβητρον, *phobētron*, n. GK: *5831* [→ *5401*]. fearful event:– fearful sights [1]

5401 φόβος, *phobos*, n. GK: *5832* [→ *870, 1629, 1630, 1719, 5398, 5399, 5400*]. fear, terror; respect, reverence:– fear [40], terror [3], afraid (+*5399*) [1], fear (+*2192*) [1], feared (+*5399*) [1], fears [1]

5402 Φοίβη, *Phoibē*, n.pr. GK: *5833* [→ *5316*]. Phoebe, "*radiant*":– Phebe [2]

5403 Φοινίκη, *Phoinikē*, n.pr. GK: *5834* [→ *5404*]. Phoenicia, "*land of purple [dye]; poss. land of date palms*":– Phenice [2], Phenicia [1]

5404 φοῖνιξ^{1}, *phoinix^{1}*, n. GK: *5836* [→ *4949, 5403, 5405*]. palm tree, palm branch:– palm trees [1], palms [1]

5405 Φοῖνιξ^{2}, *Phoinix^{2}*, n.pr. GK: *5837* [→ *5404*]. Phoenix:– Phenice [1]

5406 φονεύς, *phoneus*, n. GK: *5838* [→ *5408*]. murderer:– murderers [4], murderer [2], murderer (+*435*) [1]

5407 φονεύω, *phoneuō*, v. GK: *5839* [→ *5408*]. to commit murder, kill:– kill [8], killed [2], murder [1], slew [1]

5408 φόνος, *phonos*, n. GK: *5840* [→ *409, 4372?, 4373?, 5406, 5407*]. murder, killing:– murders [4], murder [4], slain (+*599*) [1], slaughter [1]

5409 φορέω, *phoreō*, v. GK: *5841* [→ *5342*]. to wear, bear:– beareth [1], bear [1], borne [1], weareth [1], wearing [1], wear [1]

5410 φόρον, *phoron*, n. GK: *5842*. forum, used only as a compound proper name "Forum of Appius," a market town south of Rome:– forum [1]

5411 φόρος, *phoros*, n. GK: *5843* [→ *5342*]. tax:– tribute [5]

5412 φορτίζω, *phortizō*, v. GK: *5844* [→ *5342*]. to load down (with a burden); (pass.) to be burdened:– heavy laden [1], lade [1]

5413 φορτίον, *phortion*, n. GK: *5845* [→ *5342*]. burden, load, cargo:– burdens [3], burden [2]

5414 φόρτος, *phortos*, n. GK: *5846* [→ *5342*]. cargo:– lading [1]

5415 Φορτουνᾶτος, *Phortounatos*, n.pr. GK: *5847*. Fortunatus, "*fortunate*":– Fortunatus [2]

5416 φραγέλλιον, *phragellion*, n. GK: *5848* [→ *5417*]. whip:– scourge [1]

5417 φραγελλόω, *phragelloō*, v. GK: *5849* [→ *5416*]. to flog:– scourged [2]

5418 φραγμός, *phragmos*, n. GK: *5850* [→ *5420*]. barrier, wall, country lane:– hedged [1], hedges [1], hedge [1], partition [1]

5419 φράζω, *phrazō*, v. GK: *5851*. to explain, interpret:– declare [2]

5420 φράσσω, *phrassō*, v. GK: *5852* [→ *5418*]. to shut; (pass.) to be stopped, silenced:– stopped [2], stop [1]

5421 φρέαρ, *phrear*, n. GK: *5853*. well, shaft, Abyss:– pit [5], well [2]

5422 φρεναπατάω, *phrenapataō*, v. GK: *5854* [→ *5424+539*]. to deceive:– deceiveth [1]

5423 φρεναπάτης, *phrenapatēs*, n. GK: *5855* [→ *5424+539*]. deceiver:– deceivers [1]

5424 φρήν, *phrēn*, n. GK: *5856* [→ *877, 878, 3675, 4065, 5012, 5252, 5309, 5390, 5391, 5422, 5423, 5426, 5427, 5428, 5429, 5430, 5431; cf. 2165, 2706, 3912, 4993*]. (pl.) thinking, understanding:– understanding [2]

5425 φρίσσω, *phrissō*, v. GK: *5857*. to shudder:– tremble [1]

5426 φρονέω, *phroneō*, v. GK: *5858* [→ *5424*]. to think, regard, hold an opinion; to set one's mind on; to have a (certain) attitude:– mind [9], think [4], minded [3], regardeth [3], likeminded (+*846+3588*) [2], savourest [2], careful [1], care [1], regard [1], set affection on [1], thinkest [1], understood [1]

5427 φρόνημα, *phronēma*, n. GK: *5859* [→ *5424*]. mind:– minded [2], mind [2]

5428 φρόνησις, *phronēsis*, n. GK: *5860* [→ *5424*]. wisdom, understanding:– prudence [1], wisdom [1]

5429 φρόνιμος, *phronimos*, a. GK: *5861* [→ *5424*]. wise, sensible, shrewd; conceited:– wise [13], wiser [1]

5430 φρονίμως, *phronimōs*, adv. GK: *5862* [→ *5424*]. shrewdly, wisely:– wisely [1]

5431 φροντίζω, *phrontizō*, v. GK: *5863* [→ *5424*]. to be careful, concerned:– careful [1]

5432 φρουρέω, *phroureō*, v. GK: *5864* [→ *4253+3708*]. to guard; (pass.) to be held prisoner; to be shielded:– kept [3], keep [1]

5433 φρυάσσω, *phryassō*, v. GK: *5865*. to rage, rave:– rage [1]

5434 φρύγανον, *phryganon*, n. GK: *5866*. brushwood, firewood:– sticks [1]

5435 Φρυγία, *Phrygia*, n.pr. GK: *5867*. Phrygia:– Phrygia [4]

5436 Φύγελος, *Phygelos*, n.pr. GK: *5869*. Phygelus, "*fugitive*":– Phygellus [1]

5437 φυγή, *phygē*, n. GK: *5870* [→ *5343*]. flight, fleeing:– flight [2]

5438 φυλακή, *phylakē*, n. GK: *5871* [→ *5442*]. prison, jail, haunt; guard; watch (of the night):– prison [33], watch [5], prisons [3], cage [1], hold [1], imprisonments [1], imprisonment [1], keeping watch (+*5442*) [1], ward [1]

5439 φυλακίζω, *phylakizō*, v. GK: *5872* [→ *5442*]. to imprison:– imprisoned [1]

5440 φυλακτήριον, *phylaktērion*, n. GK: *5873* [→ *5442*]. phylactery, a small box containing Scripture verses, traditionally bound on the forehead and arm by the Jews during prayer:– phylacteries [1]

5441 φύλαξ, *phylax*, n. GK: *5874* [→ *5442*]. guard, sentry:– keepers [3]

5442 φυλάσσω, *phylassō*, v. GK: *5875* [→ *1049, 1200, 1314, 5438, 5439, 5440, 5441*]. to obey, keep; to guard, watch; to keep away from, abstain:– keep [11], kept [8], beware [2], keep from [2], be ware [1], keepest [1], keepeth [1], keeping watch (+*5438*) [1], observed [1], observe [1], saved [1]

5443 φυλή, *phylē*, n. GK: *5876* [→ *246, 1429, 4853; cf. 5453*]. tribe; people, nation:– tribe [19], tribes [6], kindreds [4], kindred [2]

5444 φύλλον, *phyllon*, n. GK: *5877*. leaf:– leaves [6]

5445 φύραμα, *phyrama*, n. GK: *5878*. lump (of clay), batch (of dough); derived from a Greek verb, "to mix (wet or dry) substances," not found in the NT:– lump [5]

5446 φυσικός, *physikos*, a. GK: *5879* [→ *5453*]. pertaining to things of nature: natural, instinctive; (n.) creatures of instinct:– natural [3]

5447 φυσικῶς, *physikōs*, adv. GK: *5880* [→ *5453*]. by instinct, naturally:– naturally [1]

5448 φυσιόω, *physioō*, v. GK: *5881* [→ *5453*]. to puff up, inflate; (pass.) to be proud, arrogant:– puffed up [5], puffeth up [1], puft up [1]

5449 φύσις, *physis*, n. GK: *5882* [→ *5453*]. nature; natural state of being or characteristics:– nature [10], natural (+*2596*) [2], kind [1]

5450 φυσίωσις, *physiōsis*, n. GK: *5883* [→ *5453*]. arrogance, pride:– swellings [1]

5451 φυτεία, *phyteia*, n. GK: *5884* [→ *5453*]. plant:– plant [1]

5452 φυτεύω, *phyteuō*, v. GK: *5885* [→ *5453*]. to plant:– planted [8], planteth [3]

5453 φύω, *phyō*, v. GK: *5886* [→ *1631, 1720, 1721, 3504, 3828, 4854, 4855, 5446, 5447, 5448, 5449, 5450, 5451, 5452; cf. 5443*]. to grow up, come up, referring to plant growth:– sprang up [1], springing [1], sprung up [1]

5454 φωλεός, *phōleos*, n. GK: *5887*. hole (in the ground), den:– holes [2]

5455 φωνέω, *phōneō*, v. GK: *5888* [→ *5456*]. to call (out), summon:– called [16], crow [7], crew [5], cried [5], call [4], calleth [3], calleth for [1], calling [1]

5456 φωνή, *phōnē*, n. GK: *5889* [→ *219, 400, 800, 880, 2019, 2757, 4377, 4856, 4857, 4858, 4859, 5455*]. voice, sound, tone, noise of any kind; by extension: speaking, language:– voice [116], voices [15], sound [8], noise [1], was noised abroad (+*1096*+*3588*) [1]

5457 **φῶς**, ***phōs***, n. GK: *5890* [→ *5316*]. light; daylight; firelight:– light [67], fire [2], lights [1]

5458 **φωστήρ**, ***phōstēr***, n. GK: *5891* [→ *5316*]. star; brilliance, splendor:– lights [1], light [1]

5459 **φωσφόρος**, ***phōsphoros***, a. GK: *5892* [→ *5316*+*5342*]. light-bearing; (n.) morning star, likely referring to the planet Venus:– day star [1]

5460 **φωτεινός**, ***phōteinos***, a. GK: *5893* [→ *5316*]. full of light; bright:– full of light [4], bright [1]

5461 **φωτίζω**, ***phōtizō***, v. GK: *5894* [→ *5316*]. to give light, shine; (pass.) to be enlightened, illuminated:– enlightened [2], bring to light [1], brought to light [1], give light [1], giveth light [1], illuminated [1], lightened [1], lighten [1], lighteth [1], make see [1]

5462 **φωτισμός**, ***phōtismos***, n. GK: *5895* [→ *5316*]. light, illumination:– light [2]

5463 **χαίρω**, ***chairō***, v. GK: *5897* [→ *884*, *2168*, *2169*, *2170*, *4796*, *5479*, *5483*, *5484*, *5485*, *5486*, *5487*]. to rejoice, be glad, delighted; (as a greeting) Hail!, Greetings!:– rejoice [26], glad [14], rejoiced [8], hail [6], rejoicing [5], greeting [3], joy [3], God speed [2], rejoiceth [2], farewell [1], joyed [1], joyfully [1], joying [1], rejoiceth greatly (+*5479*) [1]

5464 **χάλαζα**, ***chalaza***, n. GK: *5898*. hail, hailstorm, hailstone:– hail [4]

5465 **χαλάω**, ***chalaō***, v. GK: *5899* [→ *5468*, *5469*]. to lower, let down:– let down [5], let down (+*2524*) [1], strake [1]

5466 **Χαλδαῖος**, ***Chaldaios***, n.pr.g. GK: *5900*. Chaldean:– Chaldeans [1]

5467 **χαλεπός**, ***chalepos***, a. GK: *5901*. difficult, harsh; violent:– fierce [1], perilous [1]

5468 **χαλιναγωγέω**, ***chalinagōgeō***, v. GK: *5902* [→ *5465*+*71*]. to keep in check, keep a rein on one's mouth:– bridleth [1], bridle [1]

5469 **χαλινός**, ***chalinos***, n. GK: *5903* [→ *5465*]. bit, bridle:– bits [1], bridles [1]

5470 **χάλκεος**, ***chalkeos***, a. GK: *5905* & *5911* [→ *5475*]. made of bronze:– brass [1]

5471 **χαλκεύς**, ***chalkeus***, n. GK: *5906* [→ *5475*]. metalworker:– coppersmith [1]

5472 **χαλκηδών**, ***chalkēdōn***, n. GK: *5907* [→ *5475*]. chalcedony:– chalcedony [1]

5473 **χαλκίον**, ***chalkion***, n. GK: *5908* [→ *5475*]. (copper or bronze) kettle:– brasen vessels [1]

5474 **χαλκολίβανον**, ***chalkolibanon***, n. GK: *5909* [→ *5475*]. burnished bronze, fine bronze:– fine brass [2]

5475 **χαλκός**, ***chalkos***, n. GK: *5910* [→ *5470*, *5471*, *5472*, *5473*, *5474*]. copper, bronze; objects of copper:– brass [3], money [2]

5476 **χαμαί**, ***chamai***, adv. GK: *5912*. to the ground, on the ground:– on the ground [1], to the ground [1]

5477 **Χανάαν**, ***Chanaan***, n.pr. GK: *5913* [→ *5478*]. Canaan, "*land of purple* hence *merchant trader*":– Canaan [2]

5478 **Χαναναῖος**, ***Chananaios***, a.pr.g. GK: *5914* [→ *5477*]. Canaanite:– of Canaan [1]

5479 **χαρά**, ***chara***, n. GK: *5915* [→ *5463*]. joy, rejoicing, happiness, gladness:– joy [52], gladness [3], joyfully (+*3326*) [1], joyfulness [1], joyful [1], joyous [1], rejoiceth greatly (+*5463*) [1]

5480 **χάραγμα**, ***charagma***, n. GK: *5916* [→ *5481*, *5482*, *5489*]. mark, stamp; image, idol:– mark [8], graven [1]

5481 **χαρακτήρ**, ***charaktēr***, n. GK: *5917* [→ *5480*]. exact representation, reproduction:– express image [1]

5482 **χάραξ**, ***charax***, n. GK: *5918* [→ *5480*]. barricade, palisade (a defensive line or fence):– trench [1]

5483 **χαρίζομαι**, ***charizomai***, v. GK: *5919* [→ *5463*]. to give grace; to forgive, cancel (a debt); to grant; to hand over into custody:– forgave [4], given [4], forgive [3], deliver [2], forgiven [2], forgiving [2], gave [2], frankly forgave [1], freely given [1], freely give [1], granted [1]

5484 **χάριν**, ***charin***, c. or pp.*. GK: *5920* [→ *5463*]. therefore, because of this, for this reason:– for cause [3], because of [2], for sake [1], to [1], wherefore (+*3739*) [1], wherefore (+*5101*) [1]

5485 **χάρις**, ***charis***, n. GK: *5921* [→ *5463*]. grace, the state of kindness and favor toward someone, often with a focus on a benefit given to the object; by extension: gift, benefit; credit; words of kindness and benefit: thanks, blessing:– grace [130], favour [6], thanks [4], thank (+*2192*) [3], thank [3], pleasure [2], acceptable [1], benefit [1], gift [1], gracious [1], liberality [1], thanked [1], thankworthy [1]

5486 **χάρισμα**, ***charisma***, n. GK: *5922* [→ *5463*]. gracious gift; see also *5485*:– gift [8], gifts [7], free gift [2]

5487 **χαριτόω**, ***charitoō***, v. GK: *5923* [→ *5463*]. to give graciously, to show acts of kindness by freely giving; (n.) one highly favored; see also *5485*:– highly favoured [1], made accepted [1]

5488 **Χαρράν**, ***Charran***, n.pr. GK: *5924*. Haran, "[earlier] *mountaineer; perhaps sanctuary*":– Charran [2]

5489 **χάρτης**, ***chartēs***, n. GK: *5925* [→ *5480*]. (papyrus) paper:– paper [1]

5490 **χάσμα**, ***chasma***, n. GK: *5926*. chasm:– gulf [1]

5491 **χεῖλος**, ***cheilos***, n. GK: *5927*. lip; edge (of a shoreline):– lips [6], shore [1]

5492 **χειμάζω**, ***cheimazō***, v. GK: *5928* [→ *5494*]. (pass.) to be battered in a storm:– tossed with a tempest [1]

5493 **χείμαρρος**, ***cheimarros***, n. GK: *5929* [→ *5494*+*4482*]. valley, ravine, wadi:– brook [1]

5494 **χειμών**, ***cheimōn***, n. GK: *5930* [→ *5492*, *5493*]. winter; stormy weather:– winter [4], foul weather [1], tempest [1]

5495 **χείρ**, ***cheir***, n. GK: *5931* [→ *849*, *886*, *1315*, *2021*, *4400*, *5496*, *5497*, *5498*, *5499*; *cf.* *4401*, *5500*]. hand, area or portion of the hand; power, control:– hands [90], hand [88], by (+*1223*) [1]

5496 **χειραγωγέω**, ***cheiragōgeō***, v. GK: *5932* [→ *5495*+*71*]. to lead by the hand:– led by the hand [2]

5497 **χειραγωγός**, ***cheiragōgos***, n. GK: *5933* [→ *5495*+*71*]. someone who leads by the hand, leader:– lead by the hand [1]

5498 **χειρόγραφον**, ***cheirographon***, n. GK: *5934* [→ *5495*+*1125*]. written code, record of debt:– handwriting [1]

5499 **χειροποίητος**, ***cheiropoiētos***, a. GK: *5935* [→ *5495*+*4160*]. hand-made, man-made:– made with hands [5], made by hands [1]

5500 **χειροτονέω**, ***cheirotoneō***, v. GK: *5936* [→ *1614*; *cf.* *5495*]. to appoint, choose:– ordained [3], chosen [1]

5501 **χείρων**, ***cheirōn***, a. GK: *5937*. worse (than); more severe than:– worse than [5], worse [4], sorer [1], worse and worse (+*1909*+*3588*) [1]

5502 **Χερούβ**, ***Cheroub***, n.pr. GK: *5938*. (pl.) cherubim:– cherubims [1]

5503 **χήρα**, ***chēra***, n. GK: *5939*. widow:– widow [13], widows [11], widows' [3]

5504 **χθές**, ***chthes***, adv. GK: *5940*. yesterday:– yesterday [3]

5505 **χιλιάς**, ***chilias***, n. GK: *5942* [→ *5507*]. thousand:– thousand [21], thousands [2]

5506 **χιλίαρχος**, ***chiliarchos***, n. GK: *5941* [→ *5507*+*757*]. military officer, commander; technically an officer of 1,000 soldiers; in the ancient Roman military an officer of a cohort, one tenth of a legion, about 600 soldiers:– chief captain [17], chief captains [2], captains [1], captain [1], high captains [1]

5507 **χίλιοι**, ***chilioi***, a.num. GK: *5943* [→ *1367*, *2035*, *4000*, *5070*, *5153*, *5506*, *5505*]. thousand:– thousand [11]

5508 **Χίος**, ***Chios***, n.pr. GK: *5944*. Kios:– Chios [1]

5509 **χιτών**, ***chitōn***, n. GK: *5945*. tunic, robe, clothing, undergarment:– coats [5], coat [4], clothes [1], garment [1]

5510 **χιών**, ***chiōn***, n. GK: *5946* [→ *3914*, *3915*]. snow:– snow [3]

5511 **χλαμύς**, ***chlamys***, n. GK: *5948*. robe, cloak, a heavy outer garment used by soldiers and travelers:– robe [2]

5512 **χλευάζω**, ***chleuazō***, v. GK: *5949*. to sneer, mock, scoff:– mocked [1], mocking [1]

5513 **χλιαρός**, ***chliaros***, a. GK: *5950*. lukewarm:– lukewarm [1]

5514 **Χλόη**, ***Chloē***, n.pr. GK: *5951* [→ *5515*]. Chloe, "*tender shoot*":– Chloe [1]

5515 **χλωρός**, ***chlōros***, a. GK: *5952* [→ *5514*]. light green; pale; (n.) green plant:– green [3], pale [1]

5516 **χξϛʹ**, ***chi xi stigma***, n.num. GK: *5953*. 666:– six hundred threescore six [1]

5517 **χοϊκός**, ***choikos***, a. GK: *5954* [→ *1632*]. made of dust, of the earth:– earthy [4]

5518 **χοῖνιξ**, ***choinix***, n. GK: *5955*. (almost one liter or) quart:– measures [1], measure [1]

5519 **χοῖρος**, ***choiros***, n. GK: *5956*. pig:– swine [14]

5520 **χολάω**, ***cholaō***, v. GK: *5957* [→ *5521*]. to be angry:– angry [1]

5521 **χολή**, ***cholē***, n. GK: *5958* [→ *5520*]. gall, bile:– gall [2]

5522 **χόος**, ***choos***, n. GK: *5959* [→ *1632*]. dust:– dust [2]

5523 **Χοραζίν**, ***Chorazin***, n.pr. GK: *5960* & *6002*. Korazin:– Chorazin [2]

5524 χορηγέω, ***chorēgeō***, v. GK: *5961* [→ *5525+71*]. to supply, provide:– giveth [1], minister [1]

5525 χορός, ***choros***, n. GK: *5962* [→ *2023, 2024, 4402, 5524*]. dance; (pl.) dancing:– dancing [1]

5526 χορτάζω, ***chortazō***, v. GK: *5963* [→ *5528*]. to feed; (pass.) to be filled to satisfaction, eat one's fill:– filled [11], fed [1], fill [1], full [1], satisfy [1]

5527 χόρτασμα, ***chortasma***, n. GK: *5964* [→ *5528*]. food:– sustenance [1]

5528 χόρτος, ***chortos***, n. GK: *5965* [→ *5526, 5527*]. grass, plant; this can refer to plants in various forms and stages: hay, stalk, field, etc:– grass [12], blade [2], hay [1]

5529 Χουζᾶς, ***Chouzas***, n.pr. GK: *5966*. Cuza, "*little judge*":– Chuza [1]

5530 χράομαι, ***chraomai***, v. GK: *5968* [→ *671, 888, 889, 890, 2173, 2710, 3916, 4798, 5532, 5533, 5534, 5535, 5536, 5539, 5540, 5541, 5542, 5543, 5544; cf. 5531*]. to make use of, use; to do, act, proceed:– use [7], used [3], entreated [1]

5531 χράω, ***chraō***, v. GK: *5969* [→ *5537, 5538; cf. 5530*]. to lend:– lend [1]

5532 χρεία, ***chreia***, n. GK: *5970* [→ *5530*]. need, necessity:– need [25], need (+*2192*) [10], necessity [2], needeth (+*2192*) [2], business [1], lack [1], necessary [1], necessities [1], needed (+*2192*) [1], needest (+*2192*) [1], needful [1], uses [1], use [1], wants [1]

5533 χρεωφειλέτης, ***chreōpheiletēs***, n. GK: *5971 & 5972* [→ *5530+3784*]. debtor:– debtors [2]

5534 χρή, ***chrē***, pt. or v.imper. GK: *5973* [→ *5530*]. it should, it is necessary:– ought [1]

5535 χρῄζω, ***chrēzō***, v. GK: *5974* [→ *5530*]. to need, have need of:– have need [2], need [2], needeth [1]

5536 χρῆμα, ***chrēma***, n. GK: *5975* [→ *5530*]. money, wealth, possessions:– money [4], riches [3]

5537 χρηματίζω, ***chrēmatizō***, v. GK: *5976* [→ *5531*]. to warn; (pass.) to bear a name; to be warned, told about, revealed to:– warned of God [3], called [2], admonished of God [1], revealed [1], spake [1], warned from God [1]

5538 χρηματισμός, ***chrēmatismos***, n. GK: *5977* [→ *5531*]. proclamation or answer from God:– answer of God [1]

5539 χρήσιμος, ***chrēsimos***, n. GK: *5978* [→ *5530*]. pertaining to value, usefulness, advantage:– profit [1]

5540 χρῆσις, ***chrēsis***, n. GK: *5979* [→ *5530*]. relations, functions:– use [2]

5541 χρηστεύομαι, ***chrēsteuomai***, v. GK: *5980* [→ *5530*]. to be kind:– kind [1]

5542 χρηστολογία, ***chrēstologia***, n. GK: *5981* [→ *5530+3004*]. smooth talk, attractive speech:– good words [1]

5543 χρηστός, ***chrēstos***, a. GK: *5982* [→ *5530*]. easy, good; kind, loving, benevolent:– kind [2], better [1], easy [1], goodness [1], good [1], gracious [1]

5544 χρηστότης, ***chrēstotēs***, n. GK: *5983* [→ *5530*]. kindness, goodness:– goodness [4], kindness [4], gentleness [1], good [1]

5545 χρῖσμα, ***chrisma***, n. GK: *5984* [→ *5548*]. anointing:– anointing [2], unction [1]

5546 Χριστιανός, ***Christianos***, n.pr.g. GK: *5985* [→ *5547*]. Christian:– Christian [2], Christians [1]

5547 Χριστός, ***Christos***, n.pr. GK: *5986* [→ *500, 5546, 5580; cf. 5548*]. Christ, Anointed One, Messiah, the Greek translation of the Hebrew 4899 (cf. Greek *3323*). The Messiah is the Son of David, an anointed leader expected to bring in an age of peace and liberty from all oppression. In the NT, the Messiah is Jesus, who came first to bring liberty from sin and peace with God and who will come again to bring all things under his control:– Christ [553], Christ's [16]

5548 χρίω, ***chriō***, v. GK: *5987* [→ *1472, 2025, 5545; cf. 5547*]. to anoint (physically, with oil; spiritually, with the Holy Spirit), to assign a person to a special task, implying a giving of power by God to accomplish the task:– anointed [5]

5549 χρονίζω, ***chronizō***, v. GK: *5988* [→ *5550*]. to take a long time, delay; to stay a long time:– delayeth [2], tarried long [1], tarried [1], tarry [1]

5550 χρόνος, ***chronos***, n. GK: *5989* [→ *3118, 5549, 5551*]. time, period of time:– time [28], times [5], while [4], as long as (+*1909+3745*) [3], season [3], world began (+*166*) [2], as long as (+*3745*) [1], long ago [1], oftentimes (+*4183*) [1], old [1], seasons [1], since world began (+*166*) [1], space [1], tarried a space (+*4160*) [1]

5551 χρονοτριβέω, ***chronotribeō***, v. GK: *5990* [→ *5550+5147*]. to spend time:– spend time [1]

5552 χρύσεος, ***chryseos***, a. GK: *5991 & 5997* [→ *5557*]. made of gold:– golden [15], gold [2], of gold [1]

5553 χρυσίον, ***chrysion***, n. GK: *5992* [→ *5557*]. gold; gold jewelry or coins:– gold [9]

5554 χρυσοδακτύλιος, ***chrysodaktylios***, a. GK: *5993* [→ *5557+1147*]. having or wearing a gold ring:– with a gold ring [1]

5555 χρυσόλιθος, ***chrysolithos***, n. GK: *5994* [→ *5557+3037*]. chrysolite:– chrysolite [1]

5556 χρυσόπρασος, ***chrysoprasos***, n. GK: *5995* [→ *5557+4237*]. chrysoprase (an apple-green quartz):– chrysoprasus [1]

5557 χρυσός, ***chrysos***, n. GK: *5996* [→ *5552, 5553, 5554, 5555, 5556, 5558*]. gold:– gold [12], decked with gold (+*5558*) [1]

5558 χρυσόω, ***chrysoō***, v. GK: *5998* [→ *5557*]. (pass.) to be adorned with gold:– decked with gold (+*5557*) [1], decked [1]

5559 χρώς, ***chrōs***, n. GK: *5999*. skin, surface of the body:– body [1]

5560 χωλός, ***chōlos***, a. GK: *6000*. lame, crippled:– lame [10], halt [4], cripple [1]

5561 χώρα, ***chōra***, n. GK: *6001* [→ *5562*]. country, land, region; countryside, field:– country [13], region [4], land [3], fields [2], coasts [1], countries [1], field [1], ground [1], regions [1]

5562 χωρέω, ***chōreō***, v. GK: *6003* [→ *402, 672, 1633, 2149, 4066, 4729, 4730, 5298, 5561, 5564*]. to go, come; to accept; to make room, have room:– receive [4], come [1], containing [1], contain [1], goeth [1], hath place [1], room [1]

5563 χωρίζω, ***chōrizō***, v. GK: *6004* [→ *5565*]. to divide, separate, leave; (pass.) to be separated from, set apart:– depart [6], separate [3], departed [2], put asunder [2]

5564 χωρίον, ***chōrion***, n. GK: *6005* [→ *5562*]. place, parcel of land, field:– field [3], land [2], place [2], lands [1], parcel of ground [1], possessions [1]

5565 χωρίς, ***chōris***, adv. GK: *6006* [→ *673, 1316, 5563*]. (adv.) by itself, separately; (pp.*) without, besides, apart from, independent from:– without [36], beside [2], besides [1], by itself [1]

5566 χῶρος, ***chōros***, n. GK: *6008*. northwest:– north west [1]

5567 ψάλλω, ***psallō***, v. GK: *6010* [→ *5568*]. to sing hymns, sing songs of praise:– sing [3], making melody [1], sing psalms [1]

5568 ψαλμός, ***psalmos***, n. GK: *6011* [→ *5567*]. Psalms (book of or section of OT); psalm, hymn of praise:– psalms [5], psalm [2]

5569 ψευδάδελφος, ***pseudadelphos***, n. GK: *6012* [→ *5574+80; cf. 1.3*]. false brother:– false brethren [2]

5570 ψευδαπόστολος, ***pseudapostolos***, n. GK: *6013* [→ *5574+649*]. false apostle:– false apostles [1]

5571 ψευδής, ***pseudēs***, a. GK: *6014* [→ *5574*]. false, lying; (n.) liar:– liars [2], false [1]

5572 ψευδοδιδάσκαλος, ***pseudodidaskalos***, n. GK: *6015* [→ *5574+1321*]. false teacher:– false teachers [1]

5573 ψευδολόγος, ***pseudologos***, a. GK: *6016* [→ *5574+3004*]. false of speech; (n.) liar:– speaking lies [1]

5574 ψεύδομαι, ***pseudomai***, v. GK: *6017* [→ *893, 5569, 5570, 5571, 5572, 5573, 5576, 5577, 5575, 5578, 5579, 5580, 5581, 5582, 5583*]. to lie, speak untruths:– lie [10], falsely [1], lied [1]

5575 ψευδόμαρτυς, ***pseudomartys***, n. GK: *6020* [→ *5574+3144*]. false witness, one who gives false testimony:– false witnesses [3]

5576 ψευδομαρτυρέω, ***pseudomartyreō***, v. GK: *6018* [→ *5574+3144*]. to give false testimony:– bear false witness [4], bare false witness [2]

5577 ψευδομαρτυρία, ***pseudomartyria***, n. GK: *6019* [→ *5574+3144*]. false testimony:– false witness [2]

5578 ψευδοπροφήτης, ***pseudoprophētēs***, n. GK: *6021* [→ *5574+4394*]. false prophet:– false prophets [7], false prophet [4]

5579 ψεῦδος, ***pseudos***, n. GK: *6022* [→ *5574*]. lie, falsehood, deception:– lie [7], lying [2]

5580 ψευδόχριστος, ***pseudochristos***, n. GK: *6023* [→ *5574+5547*]. (pl.) false Christs:– false Christs [2]

5581 ψευδώνυμος, ***pseudōnymos***, a. GK: *6024* [→ *5574+3686*]. falsely called or identified:– falsely called [1]

5582 ψεῦσμα, ***pseusma***, n. GK: *6025* [→ *5574*]. falsehood, untruth:– lie [1]

5583 ψεύστης, ***pseustēs***, n. GK: *6026* [→ *5574*]. liar:– liar [8], liars [2]

5584 ψηλαφάω, ***psēlaphaō***, v. GK: *6027* [→ *5597*]. to touch, handle:– feel after [1], handled [1], handle [1], touched [1]

5585 ψηφίζω, ***psēphizō***, v. GK: *6028* [→ *5586*]. to calculate; to estimate:– counteth [1], count [1]

5586 ψῆφος, ***psēphos***, n. GK: *6029* [→ *4785, 4860, 5585; cf. 5597*]. stone, vote (cast by stones); in NT times a white stone usually meant a vote for innocence, a black stone a vote for guilt; the white stone of Rev 2:17 may picture the innocence of its owner:– stone [2], voice against [1]

5587 ψιθυρισμός, ***psithyrismos***, n. GK: *6030* [→ *5588*]. whispering gossip:– whisperings [1]

5588 ψιθυριστής, ***psithyristēs***, n. GK: *6031* [→ *5587*]. gossip, whisperer:– whisperers [1]

5589 ψιχίον, ***psichion***, n. GK: *6033*. crumb, very small piece:– crumbs [3]

5590 ψυχή, ***psychē***, n. GK: *6034* [→ *5594*]. life, soul; heart, mind; a person; the immaterial (and eternal) part of inner person, often meaning the animate self, which can be translated by pronouns: "my soul" = "I, myself":– soul [39], life [35], souls [19], lives [5], minds [2], heartily (*+1537*) [1], heart [1], make to doubt (*+142+3588*) [1], mind [1], you (*+3588+4771*) [1]

5591 ψυχικός, ***psychikos***, a. GK: *6035* [→ *5594*]. pertaining to the natural state: physical, unspiritual, without the Spirit:– natural [4], sensual [2]

5592 ψῦχος, ***psychos***, n. GK: *6036* [→ *5594*]. cold:– cold [3]

5593 ψυχρός, ***psychros***, a. GK: *6037* [→ *5594*]. cold:– cold [4]

5594 ψύχω, ***psychō***, v. GK: *6038* [→ *403, 404, 674, 895, 1374, 1634, 2174, 2473, 2711, 3642, 4861, 5590, 5591, 5592, 5593*]. (pass.) to grow cold:– wax cold [1]

5595 ψωμίζω, ***psōmizō***, v. GK: *6039* [→ *5596*]. to feed; to give to the poor:– bestow to feed [1], feed [1]

5596 ψωμίον, ***psōmion***, n. GK: *6040* [→ *5595; cf. 5597*]. piece of bread:– sop [4]

5597 ψώχω, ***psōchō***, v. GK: *6041* [→ *4067, 4379, 5584; cf. 5586, 5596*]. to rub:– rubbing [1]

5598 Ὦ[1], ***Ō[1]***, letter; n.pr. GK: *6042*. letter of the Greek alphabet; Omega:– Omega [4]

5599 ὦ[2], ***ō[2]***, pt.interj. GK: *6043*. O!, Oh!:– O [16]

5600 ὦ, ***ō***, v.subj. of *1510*. GK: *1639* [→ *1510*]. it may, might, could be; see *1510*:–

5601 Ὠβήδ, ***Ōbēd***, n.pr. GK: *6044*. Obed, "*servant* or *worshiper*":– Obed [3]

5602 ὧδε, ***hōde***, adv. GK: *6045* [→ *3588*]. here:– here [43], hither [13], here in a place [1], in this place [1], there [1], this place [1]

5603 ᾠδή, ***ōdē***, n. GK: *6046* [→ *103, 2790*]. song:– song [5], songs [2]

5604 ὠδίν, ***ōdin***, n. GK: *6047* [→ *4944, 5605*]. labor, birth pain; agony (of death):– sorrows [2], pains [1], travail [1]

5605 ὠδίνω, ***ōdinō***, v. GK: *6048* [→ *5604*]. to suffer the pains of childbirth:– travail in birth [1], travailest [1], travailing in birth [1]

5606 ὦμος, ***ōmos***, n. GK: *6049*. (pl.) shoulders:– shoulders [2]

5607 ὤν, ***ōn***, v.ptcp. of *1510*. GK: *1639* [→ *1510*]. to be, exist, be present; all forms of this verb are indexed under *1510*:–

5608 ὠνέομαι, ***ōneomai***, v. GK: *6050* [→ *3800; cf. 5057*]. to buy:– bought [1]

5609 ᾠόν, ***ōon***, n. GK: *6051*. egg:– egg [1]

5610 ὥρα, ***hōra***, n. GK: *6052* [→ *2256, 2256, 5611*]. hour, portion of time, while, moment:– hour [86], time [11], hours [3], season [3], day [1], eventide (*+3588+3798*) [1], instant [1], now high time (*+2235*) [1], short [1]

5611 ὡραῖος, ***hōraios***, a. GK: *6053* [→ *5610*]. beautiful:– beautiful [4]

5612 ὠρύομαι, ***ōryomai***, v. GK: *6054*. to roar:– roaring [1]

5613 ὡς, ***hōs***, pt.&c. GK: *6055* [→ *2531, 5615, 5616, 5618, 5619, 5620*]. as, that, how, about, when; like, as:– as [352], when [39], how [18], as though [16], about [14], like [9], as soon as [7], that [6], while [4], according as [3], like unto [3], after [2], as (*+302*) [2], as it were [2], for [2], after that [1], and [1], are [1], as if [1], even as [1], how that [1], since [1], so soon as (*+302*) [1], so that [1], so [1], to wit [1], unto [1], when (*+1063*) [1], when (*+1161*) [1], when (*+302*) [1], whensoever (*+1437*) [1], with all speed (*+5030*) [1]

5614 ὡσαννά, ***hōsanna***, l.[v.+pt.]. GK: *6057*. Hosanna! (exclamation of praise, originally "Save [us]!"):– hosanna [6]

5615 ὡσαύτως, ***hōsautōs***, adv. GK: *6058* [→ *5613+846*]. in the same way, so also, likewise, similarly:– likewise [13], in like manner [2], after the same manner [1], even so [1]

5616 ὡσεί, ***hōsei***, pt.comp. GK: *6059* [→ *5613+1487*]. like, as; about (an approximation):– about [18], as [8], like [5], as it had been [1], as it were [1], like as [1]

5617 Ὡσηέ, ***Hōsēe***, n.pr. GK: *6060*. Hosea, "*salvation*":– Osee [1]

5618 ὥσπερ, ***hōsper***, pt.comp. GK: *6061* [→ *5613+4007*]. as, just as; like:– as [39], even as [2], like as [1]

5619 ὡσπερεί, ***hōsperei***, pt.comp. GK: *6062* [→ *5613+4007+1487*]. like, as though, as it were:– as [1]

5620 ὥστε, ***hōste***, pt. GK: *6063* [→ *5613+5037*]. a marker for introducing clauses: for this reason, therefore, so; so that, resulting in; to, for the purpose of:– so that [24], wherefore [16], insomuch that [15], therefore [9], that [7], so then [5], to [3], as [1], because [1], insomuch as [1], so that (*+2532*) [1], wherefore (*+2532*) [1]

5621 ὠτίον, ***ōtion***, n. GK: *6065* [→ *3775*]. ear:– ear [5]

5622 ὠφέλεια, ***ōpheleia***, n. GK: *6066* [→ *5623*]. value, advantage:– advantage [1], profit [1]

5623 ὠφελέω, ***ōpheleō***, v. GK: *6067* [→ *512, 3786, 5622, 5624*]. to be of good use; to have value; to help; to devote (as a gift) to God:– profited [4], profit [4], profiteth [3], prevail [2], advantaged [1], bettered [1]

5624 ὠφέλιμος, ***ōphelimos***, a. GK: *6068* [→ *5623*]. valuable, useful, profitable:– profitable [3], profiteth (*+1510*) [1]